Southern Sky

The Macmillan Encyclopedia

Southern Sky

The Macmillan Encyclopedia

The Macmillan Encyclopedia

GUILD PUBLISHING
LONDON

This edition published 1988 by
Guild Publishing
By arrangement with
Macmillan London Limited
London and Basingstoke
CN 8968
Reprinted 1989
Compiled and prepared for automatic typesetting by
Market House Books Ltd, Aylesbury (formerly Laurence Urdang Associates Ltd)

Printed in Great Britain at The Bath Press, Avon

Picture Credits

Foreword

In 1877 my great-uncle Alexander Macmillan published Autenrieth's *Homeric Dictionary*. This standard work of reference is still available (though no longer, alas, at its original price of six shillings). In the course of a hundred years many dictionaries and encyclopedias have appeared over the imprint of Macmillan. They have dealt, for instance, with Quotations, with Music and Musicians, and with many more specialised subjects such as Educational Media, Labour Biography and even Diseased English. But the present work is our first attempt to produce a comprehensive general encyclopedia covering the whole field of human knowledge within the compass of a single volume. This is indeed a formidable task, for in these hundred years progress in science and technology has been vast and all too often bewildering. It is my hope and belief – and I speak as one whose Fellowship of the Royal Society is more a mark of his respect for the Sciences than of any personal proficiency in them – that the articles in these pages upon such matters, clearly written in precise and reasonably simple terms, will serve to alleviate that bewilderment. Nor is it only upon scientific questions that this work should provide instant answers. The team of editors has drawn upon a wide range of authoritative skills in compiling succinct entries upon many other aspects of the physical world, upon men and women, upon the arts, upon the ideas which we need to understand in order to appreciate the intellectual currents of our time. More than usual care has been taken to ensure that the hundreds of illustrations, many of them in colour, should enlighten the mind as well as please the eye. Moreover this encyclopedia, taking advantage of the technology which it is one of its functions to elucidate, has been compiled with the aid of a computer, which vastly simplifies the task of revising subsequent editions and keeping them up to date. Accordingly, I have every hope that this new encyclopedia will have a fair chance of following Autenrieth's precedent and being on sale in a hundred years' time. Be that as it may, there is no doubt in my mind that it will help to provide thousands of readers with those many rudiments of knowledge without which even the greatest wisdom is powerless to act.

Harold Macmillan

Preface

Following Bacon, we have tried in this entirely new encyclopedia to cover, in some 25 000 articles and almost 1.5 million words, the whole range of human activity – arts, sciences, ideas, beliefs, history, biography, and geography, as well as sports, hobbies, and pastimes. To accomplish this somewhat daunting undertaking we have made extensive use of our own computerized system, designed to assist in the compilation and typesetting of large reference books. This system has enabled us to create an easily and quickly updatable data base with automatic checking of cross references. It has also enabled us to compile the book by subject, rather than alphabetically, thus ensuring an even and consistent treatment within each subject. Automatic alphabetization meant that the rules of alphabetization could be laid down and followed without fear of human error.

To cover such a wide range of subjects in a relatively compact volume we have also been obliged to discipline our contributors and editors to provide the maximum amount of information in the space allotted to them and to confine themselves to facts rather than opinions. We were also faced with the problem of making complex and sometimes sophisticated concepts intelligible in a limited space to readers with no specialized knowledge of a subject. Our solution to this problem has been guided by three principles. The first is not to distort the facts by oversimplification; the second is to avoid all forms of jargon and to write in simple nontechnical language comprehensible to the general reader; and the last is to ensure that the articles are sufficiently informative to be of value to students. It should, however, be said that a one-volume general encyclopedia containing 25 000 articles cannot provide the depth of knowledge possible in a multivolume set. Each kind of encyclopedia fulfils its own purpose. This book is essentially for quick, easy, and accurate reference. Who was *Gurdjieff* and what did he believe? What is a *capybara* and what does it look like? When did *Martin Luther King* die and who killed him? Where is *Samarkand* and how many people live there? What is the theory of *relativity* about and what are its practical applications? How does Australian Rules *football* differ from Rugby football and what size ball is used in each? What is the *theatre of the absurd* and who are its chief exponents? It is to this kind of question that we have sought to provide precise and intelligible answers.

Finally, I would like to take this opportunity of thanking all the editors, contributors, and advisers whose industry enables me to claim the accuracy, wide scope, and comprehensibility essential to a reference book of this kind.

A. I.

Notes

1. *Cross references*

The extensive use of cross references has made the book virtually self-indexing. Few abbreviations have been used in the text and only two symbols occur: an asterisk (*) preceding a word tells the reader that further information on the entry he is reading will be found at the article on the word asterisked; a raised square (□) tells the reader that an illustration relevant to the article he is reading will be found at or near the word so marked; the article itself at that word may also contain pertinent information. The colour plates, to which the reader may also be directed (e.g. *see* Plate I), are collected at the centre of the book.

2. *Chinese transliterations*

This encyclopedia follows official Chinese practice in using the pinyin system of transliterating Chinese names. Thus, almost all articles appear under the pinyin transliteration of the subject's name. However, the transliteration of the name in the Wade-Giles system (formerly the system most commonly used in the English-speaking world) will also be found in its alphabetical place, where the reader will be cross referred to the pinyin name under which the article appears. The Wade-Giles equivalent (unless the Wade-Giles and pinyin transliterations are almost identical) and, when it exists, the conventional western name is given in brackets following the pinyin name. A small number of names are so well known in their Wade-Giles or conventional western forms that it has become usual to retain these very familiar spellings. They are Canton, Chiang Kai-shek, China, Chou En-lai, Inner Mongolia, Mao Tse-tung, Peking, Sun Yat-sen, Tibet, Yangtze River, Yellow River.

3. *Population figures*

For towns and cities the population figures given refer, wherever possible, to the town or city proper rather than the urban agglomeration of which it forms part.

KINGS AND QUEENS OF ENGLAND

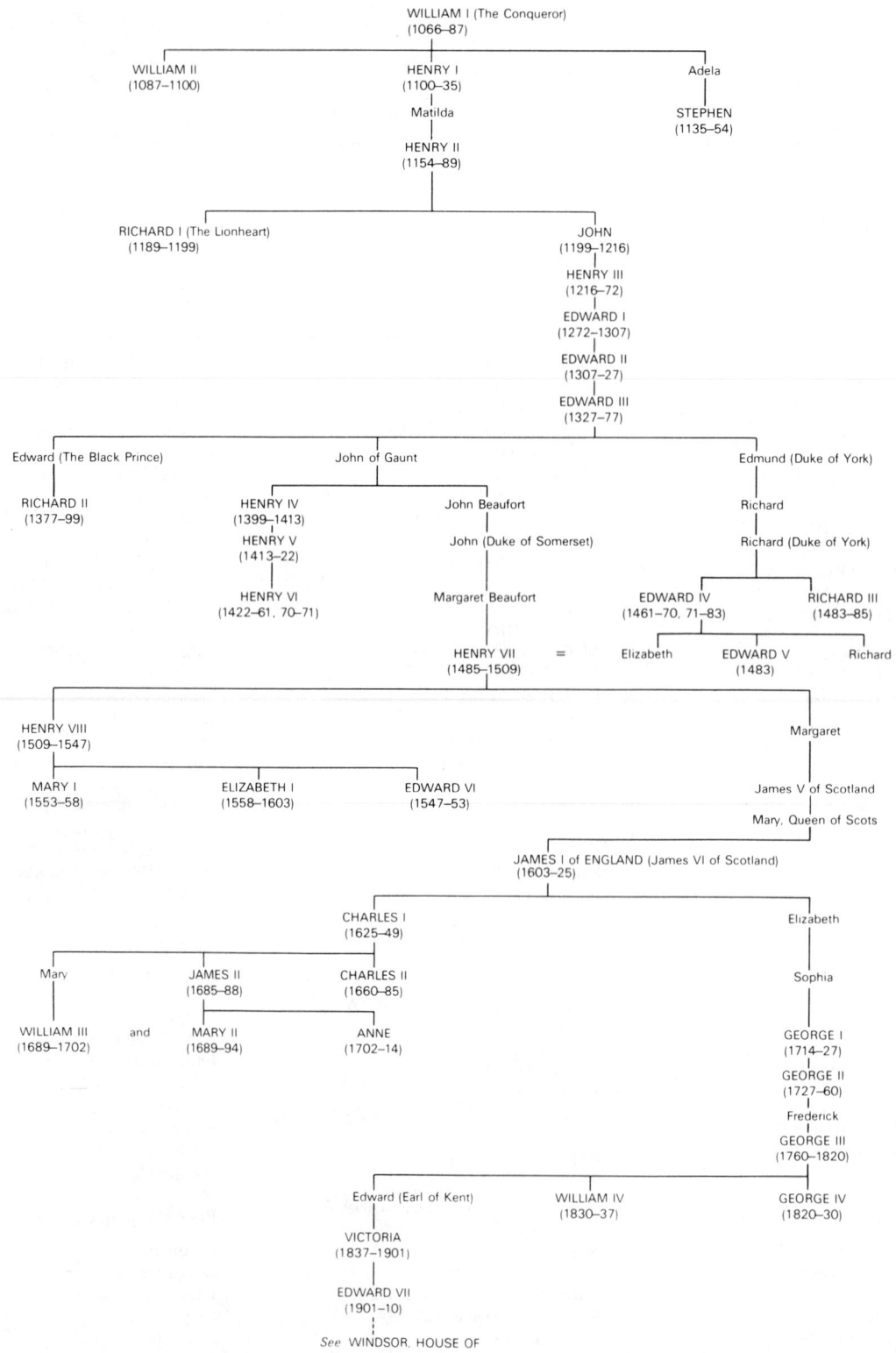

A

Aachen (French name: Aix-la-Chapelle) 50 46N 06 06E A spa city in W West Germany, in North Rhine-Westphalia near the Belgian and Dutch borders. It is an important industrial centre with iron and steel and textile industries. Its technical university was established in 1870. *History*: it was the N capital of Charlemagne's empire and many Holy Roman Emperors were crowned in the cathedral (founded in 796 AD). It was annexed by France in 1801 and passed to Prussia (1815). Extensively damaged during World War II, it was the first major German city captured by the Allies (1944). Population (1980 est): 242 700.

Aalborg. *See* Ålborg.

Aalst (French name: Alost) 50 47N 05 12E A town in N central Belgium, on the River Dender. It possesses the country's oldest town hall (begun 1200). Industries include textiles and brewing. Population (1981 est): 78 860.

Aalto, Alvar (1898–1976) Finnish architect and furniture designer. Aalto established a distinctive "Finnish" style, with his use of timber and high pitched roofs. After World War II he became increasingly individualistic and his hall of residence at the Massachusetts Institute of Technology (USA) and the Helsinki Hall of Culture (1958) are among his best work.

Aaltonen, Wäinö (1894–1966) Finnish sculptor. He is known for the portrait sculptures of the Finnish Olympic runner Paavo Nurmi (1924) and of Sibelius (1928).

AARDVARK *This strange animal feeds entirely on termites and ants. It has very few teeth, which are weak and peg-shaped and specialized to cope with its diet.*

aardvark (Afrikaans: earth pig) A nocturnal African mammal, *Orycteropus afer*, also called ant bear. It is about 1.5 m long, lives in grassland, and has a long snout, large ears, and a thick tail. Its strong claws are used to dig burrows and tear open the mounds of termites, which are picked up with its long sticky tongue. The aardvark is the only member of its order (*Tubulidentata*).

aardwolf A nocturnal mammal, *Proteles cristatus*, that lives in open and bushy regions of southern and eastern Africa. It resembles a small striped hyena, about 50 cm high at the shoulder, but has small simple teeth suitable for feeding on termites (which form the main part of its diet). It spends the day in burrows, often those deserted by other animals. Family: *Hyaenidae* (hyenas); order: *Carnivora*.

Aarhus. *See* Århus.

Aaron In the Old Testament, the elder brother of Moses, whom he assisted as leader of the Israelites in their journey from Egypt to the Promised Land (Canaan). Although he yielded to the people's demand to build the *golden calf as an idol, he and his descendants were confirmed by Jehovah as priests of the Hebrew nation.

abaca (*or* Manila hemp) A fibre obtained from the leafstalks of a palmlike plant, *Musa textilis* of the Philippines, related to the banana. It is used for ships' ropes and similar objects as it is buoyant and resistant to the action of sea water.

abacus A calculating device consisting of balls strung on wires or rods set in a frame. It is probably of Babylonian origin but its use declined in Europe with the introduction of *Arabic numerals in about the 10th century AD. Until recently it was still in use in the Middle East and Japan.

Abadan 30 20N 48 15E A city in SW Iran, on an island in the Shatt (river) al-Arab. Much of Iran's oil is brought here by pipeline for refining or exporting. Population (1976): 296 081.

Abakan 53 43N 91 25E A city in the Soviet Union, the capital of the Khakass autonomous region (*oblast*) in the RSFSR at the confluence of the Rivers Abakan and Yenisei. It is the centre of a coalmining district. Population (1980 est): 123 000.

abalone A marine *gastropod mollusc belonging to the widely distributed family *Haliotidae*, of rocky coasts, also called ear shell or ormer. Up to 30 cm long, their dishlike ⬜shells have a row of holes along the outer edge through which deoxygenated water and waste products are expelled from the body. The large foot is considered a delicacy and the shells are used as mother-of-pearl for ornaments.

abandonment In law, the voluntary relinquishment of property or rights without passing them on to another. For example, when a ship is left crewless and adrift, notice of abandonment can be issued to the insurers and a claim made for a constructive total loss (as opposed to an actual total loss if it sinks).

Abbadids A Muslim dynasty in Andalusia (1023–91). Abbad I (reigned 1023–42) declared Seville's independence from Córdoba (1023) and by war and intrigue enlarged his territory. Abbad II (reigned 1042–69) continued this expansion, but failed to capture Córdoba. He is remembered for his delight in a flower garden planted over his enemies' skulls. Abbad III (d. 1095; reigned 1069–91), poet and king, made Seville an important cultural centre. The hostility of Spanish Christians forced him into an alliance with the *Almoravids, who later deposed him (1091) and exiled him to N Africa, where he died.

Abbas, Ferhat (1899–) Algerian nationalist leader. He joined the *Front de Libération nationale (FLN) in 1956 and was the first president of the provisional government of the Algerian republic (1958–61). In 1962 he became president of the Constituent Assembly of newly independent Algeria but resigned (1963) when the FLN excluded the Assembly from participation in the drafting of the constitution.

'Abbasids A powerful dynasty of *caliphs, which ruled Islam from 750 AD to 1258. They were descended from Mohammed's uncle al-Abbas (566–652). In 750 they seized power from the Umayyads in Damascus and moved their capital to Baghdad. The 'Abbasids were known for their imposition of strict religious orthodoxy and their patronage of scholarship. Under *Harun ar-Rashid (786–809) the dynasty was at its peak. By the 10th century its powers were declining as provincial governors asserted their independence of Baghdad, which was still, however, an important commercial, cultural, and intellectual centre. Baghdad fell to the Mongols in 1258 and a branch of the 'Abbasids was installed in Cairo until that city fell to the *Ottomans in 1517. The last of the line died in 1538.

Abbas (I) the Great (1557–1628) Shah of Persia (1588–1628) of the Safavid dynasty, who greatly extended Persian territory by defeating the Uzbeks (near Herat, 1598) and the Ottomans (1605, 1618). He created a standing army, established the Persian capital of Isfahan, and was an effective patron of the arts.

Abbas II (1874–1944) The last Khedive of Egypt (1892–1914), who supported nationalist opposition to British influence and was deposed when Britain declared a protectorate over Egypt in 1914.

Abbeville 50 06N 1 57E A town in N France, in the Somme department situated near the mouth of the River Somme. It was here that Louis XII married Mary, sister of Henry VIII of England. Notable buildings include a gothic church (15th–17th centuries) and there are brewing, sugar-refining, and carpet industries. Population (1982 est): 25 998.

Abbevillian A culture of the Lower *Palaeolithic in Europe. It is characterized by crude stone hand axes made by hammering flakes off a flint with another stone. Named after *Abbeville in France, the Abbevillian also appears in Britain but in Africa similar early hand axes are designated *Acheulian.

Abbey Theatre A Dublin theatre opened in 1904 and closely associated with the *Irish Literary Renaissance. Annie Horniman (1860–1937), a friend of W. B. Yeats, initiated the building of the theatre as a home for the Irish National Dramatic Society, a company founded by the actors Frank Fay (1870–1931) and his brother W. G. Fay (1872–1947). The Abbey Theatre produced plays by Yeats, Lady Gregory, Synge, George Russell (pseudonym AE; 1867–1935), Shaw, and (somewhat later) O'Casey and gained an international reputation as a repertory theatre dedicated to performing mainly plays by Irish playwrights on Irish subjects. The original playhouse burnt down in 1951, but a new theatre was built and opened in 1966.

Abd Allah (1846–99) Sudanese leader, known as the Khalifa (caliph). In 1885 he succeeded Muhammad Ahmad (see Mahdi, al-) as leader of the uprising against the Egyptian government of the Sudan. He was defeated by *Kitchener in 1898 and was killed in subsequent mopping-up operations.

'Abd al-Malik ibn Marwan (c. 646–705 AD) Fifth *caliph (685–705) of the Umayyad dynasty, who subdued opposition to Umayyad rule of Islam. He defeated the northern Arab tribes in 691 and, with the help of his general al-Hajjaj, overcame resistance in Iraq (692). In 697 he captured Carthage. During his reign, Arabic became the administrative language of the empire and a new Muslim currency was coined.

'Abd ar-Rahman III an-Nasir (891–961 AD) Emir (912–29) and first caliph (929–61) of the Umayyad Arab dynasty of Córdoba. He conquered Muslim Spain and also campaigned against the Christian north: in 924 he took Pampalona, the capital of Navarre, but was defeated by the King of León in 939. Under his rule, Córdoba became a noted centre of learning and the arts.

Abdelkader (c. 1807–83) Algerian nationalist, who resisted the French invasion. He became Emir of Mascara in 1832 and gained control of the Oran region. Victories against the French (1835–37) facilitated a further extension of his territories. Defeated in 1841, he withdrew to Morocco and finally surrendered to the French in 1847.

abdomen In mammals (including man), the region of the body extending from the lower surface of the diaphragm to the pelvis. The abdomen contains the intestines, liver, pancreas, kidneys, gall bladder, and—in females—the ovaries and womb. In arthropods, the abdomen is the posterior section of the body, which is usually segmented.

Abdulhamid II (1842–1918) Sultan of the Ottoman Empire (1876–1909), notorious for the Armenian massacres (1894–96). Following defeat by Russia (1877), he dismissed parliament and suspended the constitution. Thereafter he ruled autocratically, instituting many administrative reforms, especially in education, and opposing western interference in Ottoman affairs. The revolt of the *Young Turks in 1908 brought about his deposition.

Abdullah (1882–1951) Emir of Transjordan (1921–46) and first King of Jordan (1946–51). He fought with T. E. *Lawrence in the Arab revolt against Turkish rule during World War I. He was assassinated in 1951.

Abdul Rahman, Tunku (1903–73) Malaysian statesman. He was the first prime minister of independent Malaya (1957–63) and of Malaysia (1963–70). He led the Alliance Party to electoral victory in 1955, becoming chief minister and negotiating Malayan independence from Britain (1957) and the formation of Malaysia (1963).

Abel. See Cain.

Abel, Sir Frederick Augustus (1827–1902) British chemist. He improved guncotton manufacture and helped Sir James Dewar (1842–1923) to invent cordite. Abel also invented an apparatus to determine the flashpoint of petroleum. He received the Bessemer medal (1897) for research into steel manufacture.

Abel, Niels Henrik (1802–29) Norwegian mathematician. One of the great mathematical problems of Abel's day was to find a general solution for a class of equations called quintics. Abel solved the problem by proving that such a solution was impossible, but died before his achievement could be recognized.

Abelard, Peter (1079–1142) French philosopher. His ill-fated marriage with Heloïse, niece of a canon of Paris, ended when Abelard was castrated by thugs hired by the canon (1118). He retired to a monastery and she became a nun. Abelard turned his formidable powers as a logician to establishing a coherent relationship between faith and reason (see scholasticism). A quarrelsome disputant, Abelard was perpetually in trouble with the church authorities; his Sic et Non (For and Against), for example, outraged opponents by listing points on which acknowledged authorities differed.

abelmosk A flowering plant, Hibiscus moschatus (H. abelmoschus), native to India. It has large flowers with yellow petals and red centres and grows to a height of 60–180 cm. Abelmosk is cultivated for its seeds, which yield musk used in perfumes, and for its young fruits, which are used as vegetables. Family: Malvaceae (mallow family).

Abeokuta 7 10N 3 26E A city in SW Nigeria. It is an important quarrying and agricultural centre but manufacturing is limited. Population (1983): 308 800.

Abercrombie, Sir (Leslie) Patrick (1879–1957) British town planner and architect. His first venture was the replanning of Dublin (1913) but he is best known for his detailed schemes for London, The County of London Plan (1943) and The Greater London Plan (1944). Later plans include those for Edinburgh, Hull, and the West Midlands. He was professor at Liverpool University (1915–35) and London University (1935–46).

Abercromby, Sir Ralph (1734–1801) British general, whose successes against the French in the Netherlands and the West Indies during the French Revolutionary Wars helped to restore the morale of the British army. He brilliantly organized the landing at Aboukir of the Anglo-Turkish force that drove the French out of Egypt but was killed in battle a few days later.

Aberdare 51 43N 3 27W A town in South Wales, in Mid Glamorgan. Light industries, including the manufacture of electrical cables, have replaced coalmining as the principal economic activities. Population (1981): 36 621.

Aberdeen 57 10N 2 04W A city, port, and former county of NE Scotland, the administrative centre of Grampian Region situated on the North Sea coast between the mouths of the Rivers Don and Dee. Aberdeen is an old cathedral city with a university dating from 1494 (King's College). Fishing has always been important, as has the working of local granite; the "Granite City" provided stone for London's cobbled streets in the 18th century. Other industries include shipbuilding, paper making, textiles, chemicals, and engineering. Aberdeen's proximity to North Sea oil has transformed it into an important service centre for the oil industry. Aberdeen has well-known research institutes for fisheries, soils, and animal nutrition. Population (1981): 190 200.

Aberdeen (or Aberdeenshire) A former county of NE Scotland. Under local government reorganization in 1975 it became part of Grampian Region.

Aberdeen, George Hamilton-Gordon, 4th Earl of (1784–1860) British statesman; prime minister (1852–55). He was foreign secretary in Sir Robert *Peel's Conservative government (1841–46) and supported the repeal of the *Corn Laws (1846), which led Peel's supporters to break away from the Conservative Party. Aberdeen succeeded Peel as leader of the "Peelites" (1850) and became prime minister of a coalition government of Whigs and Peelites. He was forced to resign because of his mismanagement of the *Crimean War.

Aberdeen Angus A breed of polled (naturally hornless) beef cattle, originating from NE Scotland. Short, stocky, and usually black (some have red coats), they are hardy and adapt well to different climates. Angus bulls are commonly mated with dairy breeds to produce a polled beef cross.

Aberdeen terrier. See Scottish terrier.

Aberfan 51 42N 3 21W A coalmining village in South Wales, in Mid Glamorgan. In 1966 mining waste from a giant slag heap engulfed part of the village (including the school), with the loss of 144 lives, including 116 children.

aberration 1. A defect in a lens or mirror that causes blurring or distortion of the image. The three most important types are spherical aberration, chromatic aberration, and *astigmatism. Spherical aberration is caused by rays from the outside of the lens or mirror being brought to a focus at a different point from those nearer to the centre. In chromatic aberration, different colours are focused at different points, since the refractive index of glass varies with the wavelength (see achromatic lens). 2. An apparent displacement in the position of a star or other heavenly body due to the motion of the observer with the earth in its orbit round the sun.

Aberystwyth 52 25N 4 05W A town and resort in Wales, in Dyfed on Cardigan Bay. A college of the University of Wales was established in 1872 and the National Library of Wales, in 1911. Population (1981): 8666.

Abidjan 5 19N 4 00W The capital of the Ivory Coast, off the Gulf of Guinea. A small village until developed by the French in the 1920s, it became the capital in 1934. It is now an important port, linked to the sea by the Vridi Canal. The National University was founded in 1964. Population (1981 est): 1 686 100.

Abilene 32 27N 99 45W A city in the USA, in central Texas. It has two universities and an air force base. A major trading centre for agricultural products and livestock, it has electronic and food-processing industries. Population (1980): 98 315.

Abingdon 51 41N 1 17W A market town in S England, in Oxfordshire on the River Thames. Its many historical buildings include the remains of a Benedictine abbey dissolved by Henry VIII. Among its varied industries are brewing and the manufacture of leather goods. Population (1981): 22 686.

Abjuration, Act of (1581) The declaration of independence by the United Provinces. The Dutch thus renounced their allegiance to *Philip II of Spain. See also Revolt of the Netherlands.

Abkhaz Autonomous Soviet Socialist Republic (or Abkhazia) An administrative division in the S Soviet Union, in the Georgian SSR between the Black Sea and the Caucasus Mountains. Most of the population is Abkhazian or Georgian and lives along the narrow subtropical coastal lowland. The region is predominantly agricultural, producing tobacco, tea, and citrus fruits, and the chief mineral is coal. There are several health resorts. History: invaded by the Romans, it later gained independence before coming under the Ottoman Turks in the 16th century. It became a Russian protectorate in 1810 and an autonomous republic in 1921. Area: 8600 sq km (3320 sq mi). Population (1981 est): 509 000. Capital: Sukhumi.

Abo. See Turku.

Abolition Movement The campaign to abolish *slavery in the USA. Opponents of slavery formed an antislavery society in 1833. They helped runaway slaves escape to Canada via their secret *Underground Railroad route; such publications as Uncle Tom's Cabin by Harriet Beecher *Stowe unveiled the slavery issue, which was ultimately settled by the *Civil War.

Abomey 7 14N 2 00E A town in S Benin. It was the capital of the Yoruba kingdom of Dahomey until captured by the French (1893). Population (1982): 54 418.

Abominable Snowman A creature, also called Yeti (Tibetan: Snowman), that is believed to live at high altitudes in the Himalayas. There have been no authenticated sightings, but gigantic footprints in the snow have been photographed (which may have other natural causes).

ABORIGINES *This piece of aboriginal art painted on a rock wall in the Kimberley area of northwest Australia represents a Dream-Time person created at the primordial dawn.*

Aborigines 1. The dark-skinned hunters and gatherers who inhabited Australia before European settlement. There were about 500 Aboriginal tribes, which were linguistic groups having no social or political unity. The main social units were seminomadic bands. They were a diverse people culturally but, in general, material culture was rudimentary, while kinship organization and terminology were complex.

Political affairs were conducted by older men. Male initiation and circumcision were commonly practised. Aboriginal mythology was generally rich and elaborate and included accounts of creation during the primordial dawn, which they call "Dream Time." There are roughly 136 000 people of Aboriginal descent in Australia. The small proportion who maintain a nomadic way of life are threatened by encroachments upon their lands as these are opened up for mineral exploitation. A movement to protect Aborigines' rights has gathered momentum and in 1971 the first Aborigine MP was elected. **2.** Any indigenous people inhabiting a country, especially as contrasted with invaders or colonizers.

abortion The expulsion or removal of a fetus from the womb before it is capable of independent survival. In the UK a fetus is not legally viable until 28 weeks old, but there are moves to reduce this to 24 weeks. (Expulsion of a dead fetus at any later time is called a stillbirth.) Abortion may be natural, i.e. spontaneous (a miscarriage), or induced for therapeutic or social reasons. In the UK it is illegal to induce an abortion unless it is carried out under the terms of the Abortion Act (1968): two doctors must agree that termination of the pregnancy is necessary (e.g. to prevent the birth of a severely deformed or abnormal child or to preserve the health of the mother) and the operation must be performed in approved premises. Methods used include *dilatation and curettage, suction of the products of conception using a vacuum aspirator, and the administration of certain drugs.

Aboukir, Battle of (25 July, 1799) The land battle in which Napoleon defeated the Ottoman Turks during his occupation of Egypt. The 7000-strong French army defeated the unruly Turkish force of 18 000.

Abraham In the Old Testament, patriarch and founder of the Hebrew nation, whose story as given in Genesis (11-25) appears to refer to events before 2000 BC. Born at Ur in Chaldaea, he followed a divine command and went first to Haran in N Mesopotamia and then to Canaan, accompanied by Sarah, his wife, and his nephew Lot. After being forced to withdraw to Egypt because of a famine, he returned to Canaan, where God promised him that the land would belong to his descendants. He had eight sons. God tested his obedience by commanding him to sacrifice his son Isaac; when he was about to obey, a ram was substituted and God reaffirmed the promises regarding Abraham's posterity.

Abraham, Plains of A plateau in E Canada, on the W edge of Quebec citadel. Here Gen James Wolfe defeated the French under Gen Montcalm (13 September, 1759), leading to British control over Canada.

abrasives Hard rough substances used to wear down the surfaces of less resistant materials. They are widely used in both industry and the home for polishing, grinding, cleaning, and shaping. Abrasives are either natural, such as sandpaper, emery, and pumice, or synthetic, such as silicon carbide and carborundum.

abraxas A mystic word, the Greek letters of which make 365 when read as numbers. Such words are found engraved and sometimes personified as a half-animal half-human deity on gemstones used as charms until the 13th century AD. It is particularly associated with *Gnosticism.

Abruzzi (or Abruzzo) A region in E central Italy. It consists of the Apennines in the W and a coastal region in the E. Agriculture is limited, producing mainly cereals. Manufacturing industry is primarily for local needs but there is a large fishing fleet. Area: 10 794 sq km (4167 sq mi). Population (1980 est): 1 245 112. Capital: L'Aquila.

Absalon (or Axel; c. 1128-1201) Danish ecclesiastic and statesman, who was chief adviser to Valdemar I and Canute VI (1163-1202; reigned 1182-1202) successively and the founder of Copenhagen. His campaign against the Wends in 1169 and on the S Baltic coast extended Danish territories.

As Archbishop of Lund from 1177, he contributed to the systematization of Danish ecclesiastical law.

abscess A pus-filled cavity surrounded by inflamed tissue, usually caused by bacterial infection. Abscesses may form anywhere in the body, including the skin, gums, and internal organs. They may heal without treatment, but usually they require draining and sometimes also antibiotics.

abscission The separation of a plant organ, such as a fruit or a leaf, from its stem. Individual cells at the base of the organ weaken by losing calcium from their cell walls and a sealant layer of cells protects the newly exposed surface. Abscission is controlled by plant hormones (see auxin).

absinthe A highly alcoholic drink made from spirits infused with herbs, including aniseed and wormwood. Absinthe has been banned in many countries because of the harmful effects of wormwood, and substitutes, known by different names (e.g. anis, pastis), are drunk instead. Absinthe is pale green and becomes cloudy when diluted with water.

absolute magnitude. See magnitude.

absolute zero The lowest temperature that can theoretically be attained. It is equal to -273.15°C or 0 K. In practice, absolute zero can never be reached, although temperatures of a few thousandths of a degree above absolute zero have been achieved. See cryogenics.

absolutism A political system, characteristic of European monarchies between the 16th and 18th centuries, in which the sovereign attempted (with limited practical success) to centralize power in his own person. *Louis XIV of France is often regarded as the typical absolute monarch. Justified by the theory of the *divine right of kings, absolutism was associated in the 18th century with enlightened despotism (see Enlightenment) but was challenged by the ideals of the *American and *French Revolutions.

absorption The assimilation of a substance by a solid or liquid, with or without chemical reaction. Moisture, for instance, can be absorbed from air by dehydrating agents, such as sulphuric acid. Certain porous solids, such as charcoal and zeolites, are able to absorb large quantities of gas. The process is distinguished from *adsorption in that the absorbed substance is held in the bulk of the solid rather than on a surface.

abstract art A nonobjective and nonrepresentational form of art. Tendencies to abstraction can be found in almost any age or school of art, particularly oriental and decorative art. However, the widespread use of *photography in the 20th century to create a permanent visual record of people, places, events, etc., made the strictly representational function of painting much less important. This shift of emphasis released artists from the confines of realism, enabling them to explore the wider fields of abstraction. In about 1910 *Kandinsky produced the first abstract watercolour, heralding the free expression of such artists as Jackson *Pollock; in contrast, *cubism led to the geometric abstract style of such painters as Piet *Mondrian and Kasimir *Malevich. A particular characteristic of abstract sculpture is the use of new materials, such as plastic, glass, and steel. See also action painting; constructivism; minimal art; op art; orphism; Stijl, de; suprematism.

abstract expressionism. See action painting.

Abstraction-Création An international group of abstract geometric artists, active from 1931 to 1936 and based in France under Georges Vantongerloo (1886-1965) and Auguste Herbin (1882-1960). It was also the name of their annual journal and exhibition.

Abu al-Wafa (940-98 AD) Persian mathematician and astronomer, who made notable contributions to *trigonometry. He invented the secant and cosecant functions (the inverse of the sine and cosine), drawing up accurate tables for them and for the sine and tangent functions.

Abu Bakar (c. 1843-95) Sultan of Johore (now in Malaysia) from 1885 to 1895. He became ruler of Johore in 1862, a year after Britain gained control of the state's foreign affairs, and contributed greatly to the maintenance of internal stability, fostering trade and agricultural development.

Abu Bakr (c. 573–634 AD) The first *caliph (632–34), known as as-Siddiq (the righteous). One of the earliest Muslims, Abu Bakr accompanied Mohammed to Medina and became caliph on his death. As caliph he defeated the rebellious tribes and began the invasion of Syria and Iraq.

Abu Dhabi. *See* United Arab Emirates.

Abu Hanifah (700–67 AD) Influential Muslim theologian and teacher of jurisprudence. Of Persian origin, he lived in Kufa (now in Iraq), where he died, perhaps in prison, after refusing to accept a post under the ruling dynasty. He left virtually no writings, but was known as a champion of the use of reason and analogy in law. His teachings form the basis of one of the two orthodox schools of the *Sunnites.

Abuja 9 10N 7 06E The federal capital of Nigeria since 1982. Agriculture is the most important activity with some local manufacturing. Population (1972 est): 14 476.

Abu Nuwas (c. 762–c. 813 AD) Arab poet. Although he learned his craft from older poets and from the Bedouins, he abandoned traditional poetic forms for sophisticated lyrics celebrating the pleasures of wine and erotic affairs with women and boys. A favourite at the Abbasid court of *Harun ar-Rashid at Baghdad, he is portrayed in the *Arabian Nights* as a free-thinking pleasure-seeker.

Abu Simbel A monumental rock-cut temple complex constructed about 1250 BC by Pharaoh Ramses II in *Nubia. Four colossal statues of Ramses, each 20 m (66 ft) high, at the entrance were raised to escape inundation by Lake Nasser (1968).

Abutilon A genus of tropical and subtropical perennial herbs and shrubs (over 100 species). The plants reach a height of 30–150 cm and have drooping stems with bell-shaped flowers. Some species are grown as ornamental plants. *A. avicennae* is cultivated in China for fibre (China jute). Family: *Malvaceae* (mallow family).

Abydos An ancient city in Upper Egypt, founded before 3000 BC and continuously occupied until Roman times. It was a principal centre of *Osiris worship. The most impressive remaining structure is Seti I's Great Temple (c. 1300 BC), with shrines for six deities and the god pharaoh. The Table of Abydos, a king list carved on its walls, provides information about earlier pharaohs.

abyssal zone The ocean depths lying below 1000 m. It is the zone of greatest ocean depth, lying seawards of the continental slope (*see* continental shelf). Since no light penetrates to these depths, they contain relatively little marine life and the temperature never rises above 4°C. The ocean depths below 6000 m, the deep-sea trenches, are sometimes classified separately as the **hadal zone.**

Abyssinian cat A breed of short-haired cat, many individuals of which are descendants of one exported to the UK from Abyssinia in the 19th century. They have slender bodies and wedge-shaped heads with large ears. The reddish-brown coat has black or brown markings and the eyes are green, yellow, or hazel. The Red Abyssinian is a rich copper-red.

Acacia A genus of tropical and subtropical trees and shrubs (over 700 species), particularly abundant in Australia (*see* wattle). Acacias have clusters of yellow or white flowers, produce long flattened pods, and usually have compound leaves consisting of many small leaflets. In some species the leaflets do not develop and the leafstalks assume their function, being broad and flattened. These species are often very spiny. Acacias yield a number of useful products: gums (including *gum arabic), tannins, dyes, and woods suitable for furniture. Many are grown as ornamental plants. Family: *Leguminosae*.

Académie Française The French literary academy founded

by Cardinal de Richelieu in 1634 (incorporated 1635) to preserve the French literary heritage. Its membership is limited at any one time to 40 "immortals," who have included Corneille, Racine, and Voltaire. It is continuously engaged in the revision of the official French dictionary.

Academy, Greek The college founded (c. 385 BC) near Athens by Plato, which continued in various guises until its dissolution by Justinian in 529 AD. It is famed mainly for contributions to philosophy and science. At first metaphysics and mathematics predominated but in the mid-3rd century BC philosophical scepticism took precedence.

Academy of Motion Picture Arts and Sciences An organization founded in Hollywood in 1927 to raise the artistic and technical standards of the film industry. It is responsible for the annual presentation of the Academy Awards, popularly known as Oscars, for excellence in acting, writing, directing, and other aspects of film production.

Acadia A former French colony in E Canada centred on present-day Novia Scotia. The original French settlement was destroyed by the British in 1613. Conflict over Acadia between French and British continued until 1763, when it fell finally to the British. Many Acadians were deported by the British and resettled in Louisiana, where their descendants, called Cajuns, still live. Longfellow's poem *Evangeline* tells their story.

Acanthus A genus of perennial herbaceous plants (about 50 species), mostly native to the Mediterranean region: *A. mollis* and *A. spinosus* are the species most commonly planted in temperate gardens. Growing to a height of 1–1.5 m, they have tough leaves, often spiny and with deeply cut margins, and spikes of purple and white flowers. The fruit—a capsule—explodes to disperse the seeds. Family: *Acanthaceae*.

ACANTHUS *The spiky leaf of* Acanthus spinosus *inspired the decorative architectural motif used on Corinthian and Composite columns.*

acanthus A decorative element of classical architecture. It is mainly found on the capitals of Corinthian and Composite columns, comprising heavy carvings of stylized leaves.

a cappella (Italian: in the church style) A marking on a piece of music for several voices, indicating that it is to be sung unaccompanied.

Acapulco 16 51N 99 56W A seaside resort in S Mexico, on the Pacific Ocean. Known as the Riviera of Mexico, it has fine sandy beaches and many hotels. Population (1980): 409 335.

ACAS (*a*dvisory, *c*onciliation and *a*rbitration *s*ervice) A public body set up by parliament in 1975 to work with trade unions and employers to settle disputes and promote methods of collective bargaining.

Accademia The principal art gallery in Venice, opened in 1756 to display work by Venetian artists. Formerly a monastery, it houses masterpieces by such painters as Bellini, Titian, and Canaletto in a collection with items dating from the 13th century.

acceleration The rate of change of a body's velocity. Linear acceleration is the rate of change of linear velocity. It is measured in such units as metres per second per second. Angular acceleration is the rate of change of angular velocity and is measured in such units as radians per second per second.

acceleration of free fall (g) Formerly called acceleration due to gravity; the acceleration of a falling body when air resistance is neglected. Caused by gravitational attraction between the body and the earth, it varies slightly at different points on the earth's surface. Its standard value is 9.806 metres per second per second.

accelerator principle The economic principle that investment will accentuate economic booms and *depressions. As income rises, businesses gain confidence in the expected future level of demand and increase their investment in plant and equipment; this pushes up employment in the capital-goods industries and heightens the boom. The converse applies to a slump.

accelerators Large machines that are used for accelerating beams of charged particles (electrons, protons, etc.) to very high speeds primarily for research in *particle physics. The particles are accelerated by electric fields either in a straight line, as in the *linear accelerator, or in a circle, as in the *cyclotron, *synchrotron, and *synchrocyclotron. The beam is confined to its path by magnetic fields. The energies of the particles are measured in millions of electronvolts (MeV) or giga-electronvolts (1000 MeV = 1 GeV), some modern accelerators attaining several hundred GeV. Particle accelerators are used by directing a beam of particles at a stationary target or, for greater energy, by colliding two beams of particles together. Accelerators are also used to create artificial isotopes and in *radiotherapy. The first accelerator was a linear accelerator, produced in 1932 by *Cockcroft and *Walton.

accentor A small sparrow-like songbird belonging to an Old World family (*Prunellidae*; 12 species), usually restricted to northern and mountain regions. It has a red or brownish-grey plumage with grey underparts, often streaked or striped. Accentors feed on insects or—in winter—seeds and berries. The family includes the *dunnock (hedge sparrow).

acceptance house A financial institution (usually a merchant bank) that deals in *bills of exchange. It buys them at a discount, the value of which depends on the standing of the drawer, and either holds them to maturity or endorses them and resells them at a smaller discount. An **acceptance credit** is a bill of exchange made payable to an exporter by his foreign customer and drawn on an acceptance house. The exporter can discount the bill to receive payment before the bill falls due.

accessory In law, a person who incites another to commit a crime but is not present when the crime is committed is an accessory before the fact. (An abettor is distinguished from an accessory before the fact by being present at the commission of a crime.) A person who assists another whom he knows has committed a crime is an accessory after the fact.

Accius, Lucius (170–c. 85 BC) Roman tragic dramatist, admired for his melodramatic plots and lively rhetorical style. About 700 lines survive from over 40 of his plays, mainly on Greek mythological themes. He also wrote treatises on poetry and grammar.

accomplice In law, a person concerned with one or more other persons in committing a crime, either as its actual perpetrator or as an abettor or *accessory.

Accoramboni, Vittoria (1557–85) Italian woman, whose life story was portrayed by John *Webster in *The White Devil* (1612) and by Ludwig Tieck in his novel *Vittoria Accoramboni* (1840). She married the Duke of Bracchiano (d. 1585) after the murder of her first husband by her brother in 1581. She was killed by Ludovico Orsini, a relative of Bracchiano.

accordion A portable musical instrument invented in Berlin in 1822. A member of the reed-organ family, the accordion is a boxlike instrument in which bellows operated by the left arm force air through reeds mounted in end panels. In the modern **piano accordion** a small piano-like keyboard played by the right hand supplies the melody, while buttons operated by the left hand produce chords. The instrument is supported in front of the player's body by straps.

accountancy The profession of preparing, verifying, and interpreting the accounts of a business. The main branches are bookkeeping, auditing, financial accounting, and cost accounting. Bookkeeping is concerned with the preparation of records of all the financial transactions undertaken by a firm or a self-employed person, usually on a day-to-day basis. The books of account kept by a firm usually include a cash book to record all payments and receipts, a nominal ledger in which all transactions with named clients, suppliers, etc., are recorded, a purchase and a sales ledger, and sometimes purchase and sales day books. Auditing is the process of verifying that the bookkeeping and the preparation of accounts have been carried out accurately and truthfully. In most countries, including the UK and the USA, auditing is carried out by an independent firm of accountants, which is required to certify that a company's accounts are a true record of its transactions during the past year. Financial accounting consists of analysing a firm's transactions and summarizing them in the firm's annual accounts. These will normally consist of a profit and loss account and a balance sheet. The former lists the total sales, total purchases, opening and closing value of the stock (or work in progress), and the expenses, enabling the profit or loss in the period to be calculated. The balance sheet lists the firm's assets and liabilities. Cost accounting identifies the costs of production at all stages of a manufacturing process. Unlike financial accounting it can be used to measure economic performance and the relative efficiency of the constituent parts of a business.

In the UK, members of the Institute of Chartered Accountants (founded 1880) specialize in financial accounting and auditing and have been trained with a professional partnership. Members of the Association of Certified Accountants (1904), who train in commerce, industry, or the public services, are also empowered to audit accounts. Members of the Institute of Cost and Management Accountants (1919) specialize in cost accounting and are not authorized auditors.

Accra 5 32N 0 12W The capital of Ghana, a port on the Gulf of Guinea. It is built on the site of three 17th-century trading fortresses founded by the English, Dutch, and Danish. It became the capital of the Gold Coast in 1877. Following the opening of a railway to the agricultural hinterland (1923) it developed rapidly into the commercial centre of Ghana. The University of Ghana was founded in 1948 at Legon, just outside Accra. Population (1980 est): 998 800.

Accrington 53 46N 2 21W An industrial town in NW England, in Lancashire. It specializes in textiles, textile and general engineering, and brick manufacturing. Population (1981): 35 891.

accumulator A cell or battery that can be recharged by passing a current through it in the direction opposite to that of the discharge current, thus reversing the chemical changes occurring during discharge at the electrodes. The most common example is the lead-acid accumulator used in motor vehicles. This consists, when charged, of a positive lead dioxide electrode and a negative spongy lead electrode, both immersed in sulphuric acid with a relative density of 1.20–1.28. During discharge lead sulphate forms on the electrodes and the acid density falls.

ACCUMULATOR *A single cell of a lead (Pb) sulphuric acid (H_2SO_4) accumulator. The reactions shown are those taking place during discharge. During charging the lead sulphate ($PbSO_4$) is converted back to lead dioxide (PbO_2) and sulphuric acid, the density of which rises.*

Nickel-iron (NiFe) accumulators with an electrolyte of 20% potassium hydroxide are also used. Interest in *electric cars has stimulated accumulator development in recent years. While lead accumulators will deliver up 8×10^4 joules per kilogram, the newer zinc-air accumulator can produce five times this energy density.

acetaldehyde (CH_3CHO) A colourless liquid *aldehyde with a pungent smell, formed by the oxidation of *ethanol. On further oxidation it becomes acetic acid.

acetic acid (*or* ethanoic acid; CH_3COOH) The *acid contained (3% to 6%) in vinegar. It can be made from alcohol but for industrial purposes is commonly made from *acetaldehyde and is used in the manufacture of plastics.

acetone (*or* propanone; CH_3COCH_3) A colourless inflammable liquid used as a solvent, for example in nail-polish remover and in the manufacture of rayon.

acetylcholine A chemical that transmits impulses between the ends of two adjacent nerves and is confined largely to the parasympathetic nervous system. Acetylcholine is released on stimulation of the nerve and diffuses across the gap of the *synapse to stimulate the adjacent nerve. It is rapidly converted to an inactive form by the enzyme cholinesterase, permitting the passage of a further impulse.

acetylene (*or* ethyne; C_2H_2) A colourless toxic inflammable gas. The two carbon atoms are joined by a triple bond and it forms the basis of a series of compounds called *alkynes. Acetylene is made by the action of water on calcium carbide and is widely used as a starting material for many organic compounds. Because of its high flame temperature (about 3300°C) it is used in oxy-acetylene welding.

Achaea A region of ancient Greece occupying the N coast of the Peloponnesus and SE Thessaly. The 12 towns of the region formed the **Achaean League** in the 4th century BC. Dissolved in the late 4th century, it was revived by the ten surviving cities in 280 BC and included non-Achaean cities, such as Sicyon. The League finally disintegrated when Achaea was annexed by Rome in 146 BC. Its NW part approximates the modern department of Achaea.

Achaeans An ancient Greek people mentioned by Homer as being among the besiegers of *Troy. They were probably related to the *Dorian Greeks but also seem to have had associations with *Mycenaean culture.

Achaemenians An ancient Persian dynasty founded by Achaemenes in the 7th century BC. Cyrus I (reigned c. 645-

602 BC), Cambyses I (c. 602-559 BC), *Cyrus the Great (559-530 BC), who founded the Achaemenian (or Persian) Empire, and *Cambyses II (529-521 BC) belonged to the senior branch of the family. *Darius I (522-486 BC) headed the junior line, which included *Xerxes I (486-465 BC). The Achaemenian dynasty ended in 330 BC, when Alexander the Great defeated Darius III (336-330 BC).

Achard, Franz Karl (1753-1821) German chemist, who became professor at the Berlin Academy of Sciences. He pioneered the extraction of the sugar from beetroot, his imperfect process producing considerable amounts of sugar on an estate granted to him in about 1800.

Achebe, Chinua (1930-) Nigerian novelist of the Ibo tribe. His first novel, *Things Fall Apart* (1958), deals with the arrival of missionaries and colonial government in the Ibo homeland. The conflict between traditional African society and western values is a central theme in all his work. His other works include the novels *A Man of the People* (1966) and *Anthills of the Savannah* (1987), a collection of short stories, and a book of poems, *Beware Soul Brother* (1971).

achene A small dry *fruit having a single seed that is attached to the fruit wall at one point only. The fruit does not open at maturity (i.e. the fruit is indehiscent) and the seed is thus retained until germination. Lettuce fruits are examples of achenes.

Achernar A conspicuous blue star, apparent magnitude 0.5 and 114 light years distant, that is the brightest star in the constellation Eridanus.

Acheron A river in N Greece, in Greek mythology the chief river of the underworld. In Dante, it is the river across which the souls of the dead are ferried to hell by *Charon.

Acheson, Dean (Gooderham) (1893-1971) US lawyer and statesman. As secretary of state in *Truman's cabinet (1949-53), his foreign policy aimed at the containment of Soviet communism. This led him to play a leading role in developing the Truman Doctrine, the *Marshall Plan, and the *North Atlantic Treaty Organization. After 1953 he continued advising American presidents.

Acheulian A culture of the Lower *Palaeolithic. It is characterized by hand axes made by hammering flakes off a flint with a hammer of wood, antler, or bone, thus producing a more regular and effective tool than the *Abbevillian hand axe. Named after St Acheul near Amiens (N France) the Acheulian occurs widely in Eurasia and also in Africa where it apparently originated and survived longest (until about 58 000 years ago). Acheulian sites provide the earliest evidence of man's use of fire and are often associated with *Homo erectus* remains (*see* Homo).

Achilles In Greek mythology, the greatest Greek warrior in the Trojan War. The son of Peleus, King of Thessaly, and Thetis, a sea nymph, he was dipped by his mother in the River Styx as a child, which made his whole body invulnerable except for the heel by which she had held him. After a quarrel with *Agamemnon he ceased fighting until the death of his friend *Patroclus at the hand of *Hector. Achilles then slew Hector and was himself later killed by Paris, who shot a poisoned arrow into his heel.

Achill Island 54 00N 10 00W A mountainous island in the Republic of Ireland, off the W coast of Co Mayo. The chief occupations are farming and fishing. Area: 148 sq km (57 sq mi). Population (1981): 3107.

achromatic lens A combination of lenses used to eliminate chromatic *aberration in an optical system. The simplest type has two lenses of different powers made from different kinds of glass. The chromatic aberration of one lens is cancelled by the chromatic aberration of the other lens.

acid rain Rain that contains sulphuric and nitric acids as a result of the absorption of sulphur dioxide and nitrogen oxides in the atmosphere. It is contended that the effects can include destruction of fish, crops, and trees, as well as damage to buildings. Attempts to control the

ACID RAIN   *Sulphur deposits in Europe.*

presence of these oxides, especially from industrial and vehicle emissions, have been hampered by absence of international agreement.

acids and bases   Acids are chemical compounds containing hydrogen that can be replaced by a metal atom to produce a *salt. They have a sour taste and turn litmus red. When dissolved in water they dissociate into ions. Hydrochloric acid (HCl), for instance, gives chloride ions and hydrogen ions: $HCl + H_2O \rightarrow Cl^- + H^+ + H_2O$. The hydrogen ion is associated with a water molecule, a combination referred to as a hydroxonium ion (H_3O^+).

Strong acids dissociate completely in water; hydrochloric acid, sulphuric acid, and nitric acid are common examples. Such compounds are extremely corrosive, sulphuric and nitric acids being particularly so because they are also powerful oxidizing agents. **Weak acids** do not dissociate completely. Many are organic compounds, usually carboxylic acids, containing the carboxylate group –CO.OH, and occur naturally: for example, acetic acid in vinegar, citric acid in citrus fruits, and lactic acid in milk.

Bases are compounds that react with acids to form salts and water. Bases that dissolve in water, known as **alkalis**, produce hydroxide ions (OH^-). Many are metal hydroxides, such as sodium hydroxide (NaOH) and potassium hydroxide (KOH). Ammonia is also a base, reacting with water molecules to form ammonium ions and hydroxide ions: $NH_3 + H_2O \rightarrow NH_4^+ + OH^-$. The neutralization of an acid by a base in solution is a reaction in which hydrogen and hydroxide ions combine to give water. In chemistry the simple concept of acids and bases has been extended to include the concept of an acid as any compound that can donate a proton and a base as a proton acceptor. This (the Brönsted-Lowry theory) can be applied to reactions in nonaqueous solvents. A further extension of the terms (Lewis theory) defines an acid as an acceptor of an unshared electron pair and a base as a pair donor. *See also* pH.

acmeism   A movement in Russian poetry in the 1910s and 1920s that asserted the value of precision against what was seen as the abstract vagueness of the symbolist movement. Because it was apolitical it met with official hostility, and several of its members, including *Akhmatova and *Mandelstam, were persecuted.

acne   A skin condition, common in adolescence, affecting the face, chest, and back. Acne is caused by overactivity and inflammation of the sebaceous glands: oily sebum accumulates in the hair follicles, producing pustules and blackheads. Severe cases can be treated with antibiotics.

Aconcagua, Mount (Spanish name: Cerro Aconcagua) 32 40S 70 02W A mountain in W Argentina, in the Andes, regarded as being the highest point in the W hemisphere. It is of volcanic origin. Height: 6960 m (22 835 ft).

aconite   A European herbaceous plant, *Aconitum napellus*, also known as monkshood. Growing to a height of 1 m, its flowers are usually purplish-blue and hood-shaped; the bulbous roots yield poisonous *alkaloids, including aconitine, which have been used in medicine as *narcotics and analgesics. The genus, which is restricted to N temperate regions, also includes wolfsbane (*A. lycotonum*). Family: *Ranunculaceae* (buttercup family).

acornworm   A wormlike marine invertebrate animal, 5–180 cm long, that burrows in soft sand or mud. Its front end is acorn-shaped, with the mouth at the base. It filters food particles from sea water, which enters the mouth and passes out through gill slits along the length of the body. Chief genera: *Balanoglossus*, *Saccoglossus*; phylum: *Hemichordata*.

acouchi (*or* acushi)   A small long-legged *rodent belonging to the genus *Myoprocta* (about 5 species). Acouchis have the same habits and lifestyle as the closely related agoutis but are smaller, measuring up to 45 cm long. They have a thin white-tipped tail and lack the coloured rump hairs of agoutis.

acoustics   The branch of physics concerned with the production, propagation, reception, properties, and uses of sound. It has several subdivisions. The most important, architectural acoustics, is concerned with the design of public auditoriums so that sounds can be heard in all parts of them with the maximum clarity and the minimum distortion. *Ultrasonics is the study of very high frequency sound. The structure and function of sound sources, such as loudspeakers, and sound receptors, such as microphones, also form part of acoustics. Other fields include speech communication and the design of machines that can understand spoken instructions.

acquired character.   *See* Lamarckism.

acquittal   In law, the clearing of an accused person of the charge against him, usually by court verdict. In England there must be a verdict of "not guilty"; in Scotland the verdict may be either "not guilty" or "not proven." Acquittal prevents a person from being prosecuted for the same offence again. Anyone charged as an *accessory to a crime is automatically acquitted if the principal is acquitted.

Acre (Arabic name: 'Akko) 32 58N 35 06E A town in N Israel, on the Mediterranean coast. Acre was held by the Crusaders for many years and was in Turkish hands for several centuries. Allocated to the Arabs under the UN plan for *Palestine, it fell to the Jews in May, 1948, and became part of Israel. It contains walls and a mosque from the 18th century, and caravanserais. It is a fishing port and a centre for light industry. Population (1982): 39 100.

acrolith   A statue made, especially in ancient Greece, of marble for the flesh and gilded wood for the clothing. This method was a cheaper substitute for chryselephantine (gold and ivory) statuary.

acromegaly   A rare disease in which a noncancerous tumour of the pituitary gland secretes abnormally large amounts of *growth hormone. This causes enlargement of the face, hands, feet, and heart. The tumour can be destroyed by X-rays or surgically removed.

acropolis (Greek: high town)   In ancient Greek towns, the isolated rocky plateau on which stood the religious and administrative nucleus of the town and which served as a citadel in time of war. The most famous is the Acropolis of Athens, which is still adorned by remains of buildings erected by *Cimon, *Themistocles, and *Pericles after the sack of Athens by the Persians (480 BC). These buildings include the *Propylaea, *Parthenon, and the reconstructed Erectheum (completed 1987) and temple of Athena Nike.

acrylic painting   A method of painting using acrylic paint. An opaque bright smooth easily applied mixture, it has been used by many pop artists, notably David *Hockney.

acrylics   Synthetic materials produced by *polymerization of acrylonitrile (vinyl cyanide; CH_2:CHCN). Acrylic resins are used in paints and plastics, the most common being *Perspex. Acrylic fibre is widely used in textiles, mainly for knitwear, furnishing fabrics, and carpets. The fibres are strong, absorb little water, and resist most substances encountered in use, although they become plastic in hot water or steam. Modacrylic is acrylic fabric or yarn with more than 15% of other fibres added.

Acta The ancient Roman *Acta Senatus* (*Senate Business*) were official records of *Senate proceedings compiled by a senator chosen by the emperor. The *Acta Diurna* (*Daily News*) constituted a popular gazette of political and social news, instituted by Julius Caesar in 59 BC and continuing until 300 AD. The emperor's official enactments were also known as *Acta*.

Actaeon A mythological Greek hunter, son of the god Aristaeus and Autonoe, daughter of Cadmus, King of Thebes. Ovid, in his *Metamorphoses*, relates how Actaeon accidentally caught sight of the goddess Artemis bathing naked and was turned by her into a stag and killed by his own hounds.

ACTH (adrenocorticotrophic hormone) A peptide hormone, secreted by the anterior lobe of the pituitary gland, that stimulates the cortex of the adrenal glands to produce three types of *corticosteroid hormones. Secretion of ACTH is stimulated by physical stress and is regulated by secretions of the *hypothalamus of the brain.

actinides A group of related chemical elements in the periodic table ranging from actinium (atomic number 89) to lawrencium (atomic number 103). They are all radioactive and include a number of *transuranic elements. Chemically, they resemble the *lanthanides, having unfilled inner electron shells.

actinium (Ac) A highly radioactive metal that occurs naturally in uranium minerals. It is the first of the actinide series of elements and is chemically similar to the lanthanide elements. It was discovered in 1899 by A. L. Debierne (1874-1949). At no 89; at wt (227); mp 1050°C; half-life of ^{227}Ac 21.6 yrs.

actinium series One of three naturally occurring series of radioactive decays. The actinium series is headed by uranium-235 (known as actino-uranium), which undergoes a series of alpha and beta decays ending with the stable isotope lead-207. *See also* thorium series; uranium series.

actinomycetes Bacteria belonging to the order *Actinomycetales*. They have rigid cell walls and often form branching filamentous mouldlike colonies. Some may cause diseases in plants and animals, particularly *Mycobacterium tuberculosis*, which causes tuberculosis, and *M. leprae*, which causes leprosy; others are relatively harmless parasites inhabiting the gastrointestinal tract. Many are found in soil, where they decompose organic matter. Certain species produce valuable *antibiotics.

action painting A modern style, also called abstract expressionism, in which paint is sprayed, splashed, or dribbled over a large canvas to form an unpremeditated and usually abstract design. Jackson *Pollock invented it in 1947 to give free rein to his own emotions. It was later also used by Willem *de Kooning to produce figurative pictures. Together with colour-field painting (*see* Rothko, Mark), action painting was the dominant style in the USA in the 1950s and made New York, for the first time, the most advanced centre of modern art.

action potential The change in electric potential on the surface of a nerve cell that occurs when the cell is stimulated. It results from sodium and potassium ions moving across the cell membrane. The electrochemical impulse travels along the nerve fibre, and in this way information is transmitted through the *nervous system. *See also* neurone; synapse.

Actium, Battle of (31 BC) The decisive land and sea battle that ended the civil war in ancient Rome. Octavian, later

*Augustus (the first Roman emperor), defeated the forces of *Mark Antony and *Cleopatra.

activated charcoal Charcoal that has been processed to increase its power of absorption by heating it to drive off absorbed gas. It then has a high capacity for further absorption of gas in its pores. Uses of activated charcoal include removing impurities from gases and liquids and as filters in gas masks.

active galaxy A galaxy that emits an unusually large amount of energy from a very compact central source. *Quasars, *Seyfert galaxies, and *radio galaxies are examples. The energy is thought to arise as a result of gas spiralling into a supermassive *black hole at the centre of the galaxy.

act of God In law, an occurrence due to a sudden violent natural cause, such as a storm, which could not reasonably have been guarded against and loss from which could not have been avoided or predicted.

Act of Parliament. *See* parliament.

Acton, John Emerich Edward Dalberg-Acton, 1st Baron (1834-1902) British historian, born in Naples. As a Whig MP (1859-66) he formed a close friendship with Gladstone. Acton mobilized liberal Roman Catholic opinion against the doctrine of papal infallibility promulgated in 1870. Appointed professor of modern history at Cambridge (1895) he planned the *Cambridge Modern History*.

Actors' Studio An actors' workshop founded in New York in 1947 by Elia *Kazan and others. Under its director Lee Strasberg (1901-82), who joined it in 1950, it became famous for its emphasis on "method" acting, which was developed from the theories of *Stanislavsky. Film actors influenced by it include Marlon *Brando, Rod Steiger (1925-), and James *Dean.

Acts of the Apostles The fifth book of the New Testament, written by Luke about 63 AD as a sequel to his Gospel. Starting with the ascension of Christ, it deals with the rise and spread of the Christian Church from a single Jewish congregation at Jerusalem, where Peter is prominent, to Paul's first missionary journey and his eventual imprisonment at Rome.

actuary A mathematician employed by an *insurance company to calculate the premiums payable on policies. The calculations are based on statistically determined risks and eventualities (e.g. sickness, life expectancy). In the UK qualifications are awarded by the Institute of Actuaries through examination.

acupuncture A traditional Chinese system of healing in which thin metal needles are inserted into selected points in the body. The needles are stimulated either by manual rotation or electrically. Acupuncture is used in the Far East to relieve pain and in China as an anaesthetic for surgical operations. The traditional explanation of its effectiveness, dating back to 2500 BC, relates to balancing the opposing life forces *yin and yang. Recent research in the West suggests that the needles may activate deep sensory nerves, which cause the pituitary and midbrain to release endorphins (natural pain killers; *see* encephalins).

Adad A Babylonian and Assyrian weather god. He was worshipped as both creator and destroyer of life: his summer rains ensured a good harvest but his storms and floods brought terror and death. His father was Anu, god of the heavens.

Adalbert (c. 1000-72) German churchman, Archbishop of Bremen. From a noble Saxon family, he became a trusted and powerful adviser to Emperor Henry III. He was active in the evangelization of Scandinavia, the Orkneys, Iceland, and Greenland until his exile from Henry IV's court in 1066.

Adam, Adolphe-Charles (1803-56) French composer. He composed over 60 operas but is primarily remembered for his romantic ballet *Giselle* (1841), the earliest full-length ballet in the traditional repertoire.

Adam, Robert (1728-92) British architect and interior

designer, born in Kirkcaldy, Fifeshire, the son of the Palladian architect **William Adam** (1689-1748). He evolved a unique style that blended the *rococo and *neoclassicism, although he occasionally used *gothic forms. After visiting Italy (1755-58), Robert, often in collaboration with his brother **James Adam** (1732-94), built many country houses, notably Kenwood House (1768), the interior of Syon House (1769), and Osterley Park (1780). His building of town houses in London, such as Apsley House (1775), led him into severe financial difficulties. In his last years in Edinburgh he produced much of his finest work, for instance Charlotte Square (1791).

Adam and Eve In the Old Testament, the first human beings. According to Genesis (2.7-3.24), Jehovah (or Yahweh) created Adam from dust in his own image and put him in the Garden of Eden. His wife Eve was created from one of his ribs. Tempted by the serpent (the devil) to eat the forbidden fruit of the Tree of Knowledge of Good and Evil, Eve succumbed to the temptation and induced Adam to eat the fruit also. They became aware of their guilt and were expelled from Eden. Their sons included *Cain and Abel.

Adam de la Halle (c. 1240-1290) French poet and musician. He travelled with his patron Robert II of Artois and became famous at the court of Charles of Anjou in Naples, where he died. His *Jeu de la feuillée* and *Jeu de Robin et Marion*, the first comic opera, combined popular songs with a sequence of realistic narrative scenes.

adamellite A variety of *granite consisting of roughly equal proportions of potassium feldspar and sodic plagioclase feldspar, with one or more ferromagnesian minerals.

Adamnan, St (c. 625-704 AD) Abbot of *Iona, born in Co Donegal, Ireland. He is chiefly remembered for championing the Roman system of dating Easter, which differed from the system used by the Celtic Churches, and for his biography of his predecessor, St *Columba. Feast day: 23 Sept.

Adamov, Arthur (1908-70) French dramatist of the *Theatre of the Absurd. Born in Russia, Adamov went to Paris in 1924 and edited a surrealist journal, *Discontinuité*. The experimental forms of his plays owe much to the images and logic of dreams: *La Parodie* (1947) features a handless clock and in *Le Ping Pong* (1955) men are dominated by the futile relentless action of a pinball machine. His later, more political, work included anti-Gaullist sketches. He committed suicide in Paris.

Adams, Charles Francis (1807-86) US diplomat; ambassador to Britain (1861-68). He was influential in keeping Britain neutral during the US Civil War and attempted to prevent British-built ships from joining the Confederate fleet, protesting against the dispatch of the *Alabama* (1862). He represented the USA in the subsequent *Alabama* claims for compensation against Britain (1871).

Adams, Henry (1838-1918) US historian. After working as a radical political journalist, he became disillusioned with active politics and turned to fiction and history, writing a long history of early democracy in America (1889-91). His most influential works were *Mont Saint Michel and Chartres* (1913), a study of the unity of art and religion in the middle ages, and his autobiography, *The Education of Henry Adams* (1918).

Adams, John (1735-1826) US statesman; first vice president (1789-97) and second president of the USA (1797-1801). Adams was prominent in the development of North American revolutionary thought. During the American Revolution he successfully mobilized European support for the North American cause, which he represented in the peace negotiations. His term as president was troubled by disputes with his vice president, Thomas *Jefferson, over US policy towards Revolutionary France. Adams was defeated by Jefferson in the election of 1800. His son **John Quincy Adams** (1767-1848) was sixth president of the USA (1825-

29). As a young man Adams practised law, wrote political articles and pamphlets, and began his successful career as a diplomat. From 1803 to 1808 he was a member of the Senate and from 1809 to 1817 he was US minister to several European countries, including Russia and Great Britain. As secretary of state (1817-25) he was largely responsible for the *Monroe Doctrine (1823). His term as president was made difficult by the opposition of Andrew *Jackson, who defeated Adams in the presidential election in 1828. From 1831 Adams served in the House of Representatives, where he campaigned vigorously against slavery.

Adams, John Couch (1819-92) English astronomer, who became professor at Cambridge University (1858). He predicted (1845) to within 2° the position of the then undiscovered planet Neptune, which was confirmed in 1846 following *Leverrier's independent prediction. Adams later worked on lunar parallax, the earth's magnetism, and the Leonid meteors.

Adams, Richard (1920-) British novelist. He worked in the civil service from 1948 to 1974, latterly in the Department of the Environment. His children's book *Watership Down* (1972), an epic treatment of the adventures of a community of rabbits, became an international bestseller. His later novels include *Shardik* (1974), *The Plague Dogs* (1977), and *The Girl in a Swing* (1980).

Adams, Samuel (1722-1803) US politician. A propagandist of revolution against Britain, he led the *Stamp Act agitation of 1765. His protests against British troops in Boston led to the Boston Massacre (1770) and he helped to plan the *Boston Tea Party (1773). He signed the Declaration of Independence (1776), served in the *Continental Congress until 1781, and was then governor of Massachusetts (1794-97).

Adamson, Robert. *See* Hill, David Octavius.

Adana 37 00N 35 19E A city in S Turkey, the fourth largest in the country. The prosperity of this important agricultural and industrial centre comes from the surrounding fertile valleys, where much cotton is grown, and its position on the Anatolian-Arabian trade routes. It has a university (1973). Population (1980): 574 515.

adaptive radiation The process by which a uniform population of animals or plants evolves into a number of different forms over a period of time. The original population increases in size and spreads to occupy different habitats. It forms several subpopulations, each adapted to the particular conditions of its habitat. In time—and if the subpopulations differ sufficiently—a number of new species will be formed from the original stock. The Australian marsupials evolved in this way into burrowers, fliers, carnivores, herbivores, and many other different forms.

addax A rare African antelope, *Addax nasomaculatus*, about 1 m high at the shoulder, that lives in small herds in the Sahara Desert. It has a greyish hide with a white patch on the face, long spirally twisted horns, and broad hooves suitable for running over loose sand. ⬜mammal.

adder A widely distributed European *viper, *Vipera berus*, about 80 cm long, common in heathland areas. It is usually greyish with a broad black zigzag line along its back and black spots on its sides. Although venomous, its bite is rarely fatal. It is one of the three species of snakes found in Britain. The name adder is also given to a highly venomous Australian snake (death adder) of the cobra family and to some harmless North American snakes. ⬜reptile. *See also* puff adder.

addiction. *See* drug dependence.

Addington, Henry, 1st Viscount Sidmouth (1757-1844) British statesman; prime minister (1801-04), replacing Pitt the Younger. Addington was attacked for his management of the Napoleonic Wars and resigned. As home secretary (1812-21) he introduced stern measures against radical and working-class movements and he has been held responsible for the *Peterloo Massacre.

Addinsell, Richard (1904-77) British composer. He read law at Oxford, but went on to study music in London, Berlin, and Vienna. His compositions include scores for many plays, revues, and films; the *Warsaw Concerto* for piano and orchestra from the film *Dangerous Moonlight* (1941) earned him great popularity.

Addis Ababa 9 02N 38 43E The capital of Ethiopia, on a central plateau 2440 m (8000 ft) above sea level. It became the new capital of Ethiopia in 1889 and was capital of Italian East Africa (1936-41). Growth in the 20th century has been rapid. It is the country's administrative centre and chief market place. Its major industries produce cement, tobacco, textiles, and shoes. A railway line links the city with the port of Djibouti on the Gulf of Aden. It is also an important pan-African centre with the headquarters of the Organization of African Unity and the UN Economic Commission for Africa. The National University was established in 1961. Population (1981 est): 1 200 000.

Addison, Joseph (1672-1719) British essayist, poet, and Whig statesman. He studied and taught at Oxford until 1699. On his return from a European tour in 1703 he published "The Campaign" (1705), a poem commissioned by the government to celebrate Marlborough's victory at Blenheim, and in 1706 became an undersecretary in the Whig administration. He was elected to parliament in 1708. He began to contribute to Richard *Steele's journal, the *Tatler*, and in 1711 Addison and Steele founded the *Spectator*, for which Addison wrote essays famous for their clarity, wit, and elegance. He is also remembered for the tragedy *Cato* (1713).

Addison, Thomas (1793-1860) British physician, who was the first person to ascribe correctly the symptoms of what is now called *Addison's disease to a functional deficiency of the adrenal glands. He also described pernicious (Addison's) *anaemia and made a study of poisons.

Addison's disease A rare disease of the adrenal glands, first described by Thomas *Addison, characterized by a reduced secretion of corticosteroid hormones. This leads to weakness, intestinal upsets, darkening of the skin, low blood pressure, and collapse. Formerly fatal, Addison's disease can now be readily treated with synthetic steroids.

addition reaction A chemical reaction in which atoms or molecules combine to form a single molecule. It is frequently encountered in organic *chemistry, since many substances readily add to the double or triple bonds in alkenes, alkynes, aldehydes, etc. *Aromatic compounds are less susceptible, while *alkanes do not undergo addition. *See also* polymerization; substitution reaction.

additive process. *See* colour.

Adelaide 34 56S 138 36E The capital of South Australia, on the Torrens River. Founded in 1837, the city was laid out in wide straight streets according to plans by Col William Light (South Australia's first surveyor general). Extensive parklands remain, separating the city from its suburbs. The University of Adelaide was founded in 1874; other notable buildings include the Anglican cathedral of St Peter and the Roman Catholic cathedral. It is an important commercial and industrial centre with harbour facilities at *Port Adelaide. Industries include the manufacture of cars and textiles, oil refining, and electronics. Population (1983): 969 200.

Adélie Land. *See* Terre Adélie.

Aden 12 50N 45 03E The capital of South Yemen, on the **Gulf of Aden,** an arm of the Indian Ocean connecting the main body with the Red Sea. Taken by the British in 1839, Aden was an important coaling station on the route to India through the Suez Canal (opened 1869). It became part of the Federation of Saudi Arabia in 1963 and was the scene of fighting between rival nationalist groups until 1968, when it became the capital of the independent republic of South Yemen. Economic activity centres on the port, which suffered from the closure of the Suez Canal (1967-75), and an oil refinery. Population (1980 est): 264 326.

Adenauer, Konrad (1876-1967) German statesman. He was a successful Rhineland politician until the Nazi government forced him out of public life (1934) and imprisoned him (1934, 1944). In 1946 Adenauer re-emerged as chairman of the Christian Democratic Union (CDU) and became the first chancellor (1949-63) of the Federal Republic of Germany. He presided over the German economic miracle but was personally more concerned with foreign policy. He established that West Germany was part of W Europe, did much to restore its international prestige, and built up Franco-German friendship.

adenoids Two masses of tissue situated at the back of the nose. They consist of lymphatic tissue, which destroys disease-causing microbes in the throat. In children they are normally large, and when associated with recurrent throat infections or persistent breathing through the mouth are usually removed surgically. This operation is often combined with tonsillectomy (removal of the tonsils) as the tonsils tend to be infected at the same time.

adenosine triphosphate. *See* ATP.

Ader, Clément (1841-1926) French engineer, inventor, and an early enthusiast of air travel. In 1890 he constructed a steam-powered aircraft with bat-shaped wings. The craft, which could not be steered, made the first heavier-than-air flight.

adhesives Substances used for bonding materials together. Adhesives are usually colloidal solutions that set to a hard film adhering to the surfaces of the materials. There are many different types. Animal glues are forms of collagen (a protein) produced by boiling bones, hides, horns, etc., and drying the resulting jelly. They are water soluble and usually contain additives to preserve them. Vegetable glues (mucilages) are also water-soluble substances, such as starch, or gums, such as gum arabic or tragacanth. Other natural adhesives include waterglass, pitch, and rubber latex. In addition many synthetic resins are used as adhesives. **Thermoplastic adhesives** (polymers, such as polystyrene, asphalt, and polyvinyl compounds) remain soluble after setting and melt when heated; these are used where flexible bonding is needed, for example in attaching the soles of shoes, safety glass, sticky tape, etc. **Thermosetting adhesives** (condensation polymers, such as *epoxy resins) are insoluble, chemically inert, and will not melt. They are set by heat or by an added catalyst (hardener). They are used for bonding wood, paper, textiles, plastics, etc.

adiabatic process Any process in which heat neither enters nor leaves a system. Usually, such a process changes the temperature of the system. An example is the sudden compression of a gas, causing its temperature to rise. The compression is assumed to take place so quickly that the gas loses none of its acquired heat.

Adige, River A river in Italy, rising in the N and flowing mainly SE, entering the Adriatic Sea near the Po. Navigation is difficult because of its rapid current. Length: 354 km (220 mi).

Ádi Granth The sacred canonical scriptures of *Sikhism, compiled in 1604 by Arjun Mal (1581-1606). It consists of about 6000 hymns, mostly the work of the first five *gurus, together with the writings of some Bhakta saints and Muslim Sufis (*see* Sufism). The Sikhs do not venerate images but the *Ádi Granth* has itself become the object of worship.

Adirondack Mountains A mountain range in the USA, in N New York state. It consists of a glaciated plateau rising to 1629 m (5344 ft) at Mount Marcy. Its scenic gorges, waterfalls, and many lakes make it a popular tourist area.

adjutant stork A large carrion-eating *stork, *Leptotilos dubius*, occurring in Asia and similar to the related

ADJUTANT STORK *Standing about 1.5 m tall, this grotesque bird builds its nest in tall trees; both parents incubate the eggs and care for the young.*

*marabou. It has a white plumage with dark-grey back, wings, and tail, a short neck, and a heavy pointed bill. Its head and neck are naked and a bald pouch hangs from the throat. Order: *Ciconiiformes*.

Adler, Alfred (1870–1937) Austrian psychiatrist, whose theories concerning the psychology of the individual introduced the concept of the inferiority complex. Initially an associate of Sigmund *Freud, Adler's views diverged from Freud's and by 1911 he had founded his own school of thought. Adler viewed each individual as a unique entity striving to compensate for feelings of inferiority resulting from physical or social disabilities (*The Neurotic Constitution*, 1912) and regarded sex as simply an opportunity to express dominance. Adler emphasized the importance of education and, in 1921, opened the first of his child-guidance clinics in Vienna.

Adler, Felix (1851–1933) German-born US educationalist, who founded the Society for Ethical Culture (1876). Through the resulting ethical movement and in books, such as *An Ethical Philosophy of Life* (1918), he proclaimed the importance of morality in human affairs and advanced the view that moral considerations arose independently of any religious creeds. He instigated many educational and social reforms.

Adler, Larry (1914–) US harmonica player and entertainer, now resident in the UK. His virtuosity inspired Vaughan Williams, Darius Milhaud, Malcolm Arnold, and others to write serious music for the harmonica.

administrative law The law regulating the organization, responsibilities, and powers of a country's administrative bodies, such as the civil service, customs and excise, and social services. Many countries enforce this law through special courts, but in *common law countries, such as England, it is dealt with in the ordinary courts.

Admiral's Cup A biennial sailing competition (instituted in 1957) held by the Royal Ocean Racing Club in the English Channel. Three yachts represent each nation and the competition comprises five races (the fifth race was added in 1977), including the Fastnet Cup.

Admiralty, Board of The government department that from 1832 to 1964 administered the British navy. It succeeded the Navy Board, which was first established in 1546 and developed out of the office of the Keeper of the King's Ships, which evolved in the 13th century. In 1964 the Board was absorbed by the Ministry of Defence. The office of Lord High Admiral was held by an individual or in commission until being invested in the person of the monarch in 1964.

Admiralty Court. *See* maritime law.

Admiralty Islands A group of about 40 islands in the SW Pacific Ocean, in Papua New Guinea in the Bismarck Archipelago. Copra and pearls are exported. The main island is Manus with the chief town, Lorengau. Area: about 2000 sq km (800 sq mi). Population (1980): 25 844.

Adonis In Greek mythology, a youth from Cyprus, loved by *Aphrodite for his great beauty. *Zeus decreed that his time should be divided between Aphrodite on earth, Persephone, queen of the underworld, and himself. He was celebrated in many festivals as a vegetation god, his death and resurrection representing the seasonal decay and regeneration of nature.

adoption In law, the process whereby the natural parent's legal rights and obligations towards an unmarried *minor are transferred to another adult. The need for a male heir has traditionally been one of the prime motives for adoption and the welfare of the adopted child was not the main consideration. This was reflected in Roman Civil law, which subsequently influenced the adoption laws of a number of European and Latin-American countries. Adoption had no place in English law until 1926, much later than some Commonwealth countries (e.g. New Zealand; 1895). Later legislation, now consolidated in the Adoption Act (1976), controls the work of adoption societies, rights of the natural parents, and the adopted child's right to know his original name. The increased effectiveness of birth control, the legalization of abortion, and the social acceptance of one-parent families has decreased the number of children available for adoption in recent years. However, greater emphasis, including publicity on television, has been given to finding adoptive homes for children with special needs, e.g. older children, children of mixed race, and the physically or mentally handicapped.

Adowa (Adwa *or* Aduwa) 14 02N 38 58E A town in N Ethiopia. Emperor Menelik II defeated the Italians nearby in 1896, halting their expansion into Ethiopia until 1935. It is a market centre for agricultural produce including grains, honey, and coffee. Population (1982): 26 782.

adrenal glands Two small pyramid-shaped *endocrine glands in man and other mammals, one at the upper end of each of the kidneys. Each gland has an outer cortex, controlled by hormones secreted by the pituitary gland, and an inner medulla, controlled directly by the nervous system. The cortex secretes three classes of steroid hormones that regulate the balance of salts and water, the use of carbohydrates, and the activity of the sex glands (*see* corticosteroid). The medulla produces the hormones *adrenaline and *noradrenaline. *See also* Addison's disease; Cushing's syndrome.

adrenaline (*or* epinephrine) A hormone secreted by the central core (medulla) of the adrenal glands. A *catecholamine derived from the amino acid tyrosine, adrenaline increases heart rate, raises blood pressure, and increases the level of blood glucose. Its release is triggered by stress in preparation by the body for "fight or flight." Adrenaline is also secreted by nerve endings of the sympathetic nervous system. *See also* noradrenaline.

adrenocorticotrophic hormone. *See* ACTH.

Adrian, Edgar Douglas, 1st Baron (1889–1977) British physiologist, whose work was largely concerned with the electrical properties of the nervous system. He developed techniques for recording nerve impulses from single nerve fibres and later studied the electrical activity of the brain. He shared a Nobel Prize (1932) with Sir Charles *Sherrington and was awarded the OM (1942).

Adrian IV (Nicholas Breakspear; c. 1100–59) Pope (1154–59). The only English pope, also known as Hadrian IV, he was unanimously elected after a career of papal service, leading the mission to the Scandinavian churches (1152). His claim that the Holy Roman Empire was held by papal grant occasioned a major quarrel with Emperor *Frederick Barbarossa, whom he refused to crown until Frederick had done homage for his office. Adrian also intervened in the internal politics of France and Sicily.

Adrianople, Battle of (378 AD) The battle in which the Eastern Roman emperor *Valens was defeated and killed defending Adrianople (now Edirne, Turkey) against the Visigoths. The Huns had driven the Visigoths across the Danube in 376 AD, prompting them to attack the Romans at Adrianople.

Adriatic Sea A northern arm of the Mediterranean Sea, extending between Italy and Yugoslavia for about 750 km (466 mi). Its principal ports are Brindisi, Bari, Venice, Trieste, and Rijeka. The Italian and Yugoslav coasts are strikingly different: the one flat and sandy, the other rocky and irregular with many offshore islands.

adsorption The production of a layer of atoms or molecules of a substance on a solid or liquid surface. The adsorbed atoms or molecules may be strongly held by chemical bonds (**chemisorption**), in which case the adsorbed layer is usually only one molecule thick. Adsorption may also occur through weaker physical forces (**physisorption**), often giving rise to several molecular layers.

Adullamites A group of disaffected Liberal MPs, led by Robert Lowe (1811–92), who opposed parliamentary reform and defeated the Liberal reform bill of 1866 (*see* Reform Acts). The group's name comes from Adullam's cave of the discontented (I Samuel 22.1–2).

adult education Education of all kinds for adults, but usually the various forms of education provided for adults once their formal education has ceased. Adult education may be specifically vocational or assist in general cultural development. Its origins in the UK date from the 19th century, when such establishments as the London Mechanics' Institute and the London Working Men's College were founded (1823, 1854). The modern university-extension provision evolved from work in Cambridge in 1873 and closely associated with this movement were Ruskin College (1899) and the Workers' Educational Association (WEA). The latter was founded in 1903 by Albert Mansbridge (1876–1952), who sought to involve the university-extension service with the cooperative and trades-union movements. Some 150 000 students now follow classes organized by more than 800 WEA branches. The Education Act (1944) made Local Education Authorities (LEAs) responsible for the provision of full-time and part-time education for adults. However, the provision of a system of recurrent access to part-time education in industrialized societies throughout people's working lives remains largely underdeveloped. *See also* Open University.

ADULT EDUCATION *An evening class at Birkbeck Institute (1877).*

adultery Voluntary sexual intercourse between a married person and someone who is not that person's husband or wife. In many countries, including some US states, adultery is a crime; under some systems, such as Islamic law, it may carry the death penalty. Generally, however, it is only a ground for *divorce or judicial separation, as in English law, where it is considered proof of the "irretrievable breakdown" of a marriage.

Aduwa. *See* Adowa.

advaita (Sanskrit: nondualism) The Hindu philosophical view, derived from the *Upanishads, that the individual soul and ultimate reality are indivisibly one; the apparent separation of subject and object, or spirit and matter, is only illusion. Realization of this truth leads to liberation. Some thinkers see all phenomena, including the self, as altogether unreal; others maintain that the existence of the soul is qualified by, or dependent upon, *Brahman, who alone is fully real. Chief among the proponents of *advaita* is the 8th-century philosopher *Shankara.

Advent (from Latin: *adventus*, coming) The first season of the *church year, leading up to *Christmas. It begins on the Sunday nearest St Andrew's Day (30 Nov). From the 6th century it has been observed as a solemn preparation for celebrating Christ's birth and for his Second Coming.

adventists Several Protestant Christian denominations that stress a belief in the imminent Second Coming of Christ. In the USA adventism began in 1831 with the millenarian preaching of William Miller (1782–1849), who predicted the Second Coming for 1843–44, but postponed the date when his prediction proved false. In the UK a similar movement was founded in 1832 as the Catholic Apostolic Church. There have been many adventist movements, the Seventh-Day Adventists being the main church today.

advertising The publicizing of a product or service, usually in order to increase sales. In some cases it is used to discourage sales (e.g. of cigarettes) or to promote noncommercial activities (e.g. road safety). Although some 2% of the *gross national product in the UK and some 3% in the USA is spent on advertising, there is no evidence to show that advertising actually persuades people to buy things they do not want. Consumer advertising seeks to sell one branded product at the expense of others (e.g. toothpaste), to publicize a manufacturer's name when his product is the same as everyone else's (e.g. petrol), or to persuade people that a category of products (e.g. wool) should be bought in preference to some other category (e.g. man-made fibres). Trade advertising is restricted to specific sections of the public (e.g. doctors or caterers). Advertisements may be informative, assisting purchasers to make a choice between products, or persuasive, in which case it may exaggerate some aspect of a product by appealing to the purchaser's image of himself, often in relation to his sexual fantasies. Advertising is carried by the press (about 70–75% of advertising expenditure in the UK), by television and radio (20–25%), and on hoardings and buses, in cinemas, and at the point of sale (making up the balance). Advertising in the UK is controlled by the industry's own Advertising Standards Authority (which issues its own code of practice), by the Trade Descriptions Act (1968), and by the Independent Broadcasting Authority (which vets all broadcast advertisements). The industry in the UK and the USA is largely in the hands of advertising agencies, which work closely with their clients researching, copywriting, and producing the advertisements as well as booking space in the press and time for broadcasting.

advocaat A liqueur, originally Dutch, made from brandy and egg yolks flavoured with vanilla.

advocate In Scotland and in some countries, such as France, having a legal system based on Roman law, a person whose profession is to plead the cases of others in a court of justice. The English equivalent is a *barrister. In Scotland, the **Lord Advocate** is the chief law officer of the Crown, generally equivalent to the *attorney general in England.

Adwa. *See* Adowa.

Adygei An autonomous region (*oblast*) in the SW Soviet Union, in the RSFSR. It was formed in 1922 for the Muslim Adyghian people. It has valuable forests and oil and natural-gas deposits. Area: 7600 sq km (2934 sq mi). Population (1980 est): 405 300. Capital: Maikop.

Adzhar Autonomous Soviet Socialist Republic (*or* Adzharia) An administrative division in the S Soviet Union, in the Georgian SSR on the Black Sea. It is mainly mountainous with a subtropical coastal plain. A popular holiday region, it is also the country's main producer of tea and citrus fruits. Industries include shipyards and oil refining. Area: 3000 sq km (1160 sq mi). Population (1981 est): 362 000. Capital: Batumi.

Aechmea A genus of herbaceous plants (over 140 species), native to South America, where they grow upon the branches of trees (but are not parasitic). From the centre of a rosette of spiny-toothed leaves, 30–60 cm long, grow showy red or yellow flowers, often with blue tips. Some species, for example *A. fulgens* and *A. fasciata*, are grown as greenhouse ornamentals. Family: *Bromeliaceae* (pineapples, etc.).

Aedes A genus of mosquitoes, widespread in the tropics and subtropics, that transmit diseases of man and livestock including yellow fever and dengue (transmitted by *A. aegypti*) and Rift Valley fever (transmitted by *A. cabalus*).

Aegae (modern name: Vergina) The capital, with *Pella, of ancient Macedon (*see* Macedonia). During the 1970s archaeological work on a nearby mound revealed tombs believed to be those of *Philip II of Macedon and his immediate family. Treasures found here include magnificent wall paintings, golden jewellery, and silver vases.

Aegean civilizations The prehistoric settlements on the islands of the Aegean Sea (between mainland Greece and Asia Minor). At the beginning of the Bronze Age (c. 3000 BC) an influx of immigrants to the *Cyclades islands (S Aegean) brought a high level of sophistication and prosperity, which can be seen from the excavations on Thera (*or* Santorini). The subsequent civilization of *Minoan Crete was at its greatest between the 17th and 15th centuries BC. At the end of the 15th century the related *Mycenaean civilization of mainland Greece began to assert its supremacy, lasting until about 1200.

Aegean Sea A section of the NE Mediterranean Sea, lying between Greece and Turkey and containing many islands, including the Cyclades, Dodecanese, and N Sporades.

Aegina (Modern Greek name: Aiyina) A Greek island in the Aegean Sea, one of the largest in the Saronic group lying SSW of Piraeus. It achieved its greatest prosperity in the 5th century BC but fell to Athens (458), which later expelled all its inhabitants. Today it serves as a holiday resort for Athenians. Area: 85 sq km (33 sq mi).

Aegina, Gulf of. *See* Saronic Gulf.

Aegis In Greek mythology, a breastplate worn by Zeus and his daughter Athena. At its centre was an image of *Medusa, which petrified enemies.

Aelfric (c. 955–c. 1020) Anglo-Saxon prose writer and Abbot of Eynsham from 1005. His *Catholic Homilies* (990–92), collections of sermons, and his *Lives of the Saints* (996–97) were important contributions to the spread of learning in the 10th century, directed at a wider audience than the monks at the monastery of Cernel (now Cerne Abbas, Dorset) where he was novice master. He also wrote a Latin grammar, thus acquiring his nickname, Grammaticus.

Aeneas A legendary Trojan leader, son of *Anchises and *Aphrodite, and hero of Virgil's *Aeneid*. After the Greek victory in the Trojan War, he sailed away from burning Troy with his family and other survivors and was shipwrecked near Carthage. He fell in love with *Dido but abandoned her to continue his divinely ordained voyage to Italy, where he founded what was to become Rome.

Aeneas Silvius. *See* Pius II.

aeolian harp A musical instrument named after the Greek wind god *Aeolus, consisting of a wooden resonating box strung with gut strings of varying thicknesses. When hung in the open air it produces chordal sounds that vary according to the wind pressure.

Aeolus The Greek god of the winds and ruler of Aeolia. In Homer's *Odyssey* he gave Odysseus a bag containing contrary winds; Odysseus' companions untied it, causing his ship to be blown back to Aeolia.

Aepyornis A genus of extinct flightless birds, also called elephant birds because of their huge size. They are known only from fossil bones and eggs found in Madagascar.

aerial (*or* antenna) An electrical conductor that transmits and receives ▢ radio or other electromagnetic waves. An oscillating *electromagnetic field, caused by waves from a distant source, induces an oscillating current in the receiving aerial. A transmitting aerial works by the same process in reverse, creating waves from an electrical signal. A modern aerial for UHF (ultra-high frequency) and VHF (very high frequency) consists of a dipole formed from two metal rods, each approximately one-quarter of the operating wavelength. In the Yagi aerial named after H. Yagi (1886–1976), a reflector rod is set behind the dipole and several director rods are placed in front of it. This provides a more directional array than the simple dipole and is widely used as a receiving and transmitting aerial for television.

aerobe An organism that requires free oxygen for oxidation of foodstuffs to release chemical energy in the process of *respiration. Most living organisms are aerobes; exceptions include certain yeasts and bacteria. These organisms, called **anaerobes**, produce chemical energy by a series of reactions in which free oxygen is not required. **Obligate anaerobes** never use oxygen for respiration, while **facultative anaerobes** normally use oxygen but are able to switch to anaerobic respiration when free oxygen is deficient.

aerobics A method of keeping fit by exercising to stimulate the heart and lungs to work faster, thereby increasing the volume of oxygen available to the body. It involves repetitive and sustained use of the muscles and claims to reduce the resting pulse rate and increase the efficiency of the heart. The system was started in the USA by Dr Ken Cooper for the US forces in the 1970s and subsequently adapted by Jackie Sorensen as a dance and exercise form.

aerodynamics The study of the behaviour and flow of air around objects. As air is a viscous fluid any object moving through it experiences a drag. Aerodynamics is important in the design of vehicles travelling at more than 50 km per hour (31 mph), buildings and bridges, engines, furnaces, as well as aircraft (*see* aeronautics) and missiles. Proposed cross-sections of models of such objects are often tested in wind tunnels or in water, smoke or coloured dyes being used to trace the flow of the fluid around the surface and to measure the lift and drag forces. This enables the best streamlined shapes to be found in order to avoid *turbulence.

aerofoil. *See* aeronautics.

aeronautics The science and history (*see also* aircraft) of flight. An object flying through air is subject to four basic forces: its own weight (vertically downwards as a result of gravity), lift (to counterbalance weight and keep it in the air), thrust (to force it through the air), and drag (resulting from friction between the body and the air). Birds and insects use their wings to provide both lift and thrust; man, in his heavier-than-air fixed-wing craft, uses an aerofoil to provide the lift and an *internal-combustion engine (propeller or jet) to provide the thrust (*see also* gliders). *Helicopters use rotating aerofoils to provide lift, while *rockets use no lift surfaces, the jet of expanding gas providing both lift and thrust. Man's lighter-than-air craft (*see* airships; balloons) use helium or hydrogen to reduce the craft's weight in relation to the volume of air it displaces to such an

forces acting on aircraft

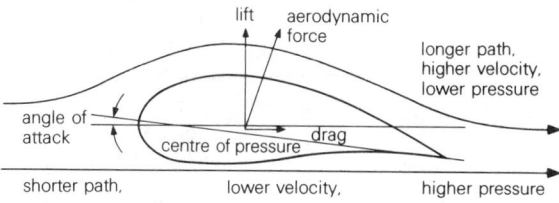

cross-section of aerofoil

AERONAUTICS   *The forces acting on an aircraft. The aerofoil cross-section shows how the lift, which keeps it in the air, results from the passage of the aerofoil through the air, causing a lower pressure above it and a higher pressure below it.*

extent that the lift is provided by buoyancy. The use of aerofoils as lift surfaces depends on *Bernoulli's theorem, according to which the total energy of a flowing fluid remains constant; thus, if the velocity of the fluid increases, its pressure decreases in proportion. An aerofoil is a wing so shaped that (at subsonic speeds) air is accelerated over its rounded leading edge and curved upper surface, causing a reduced pressure above it. A smaller reduction in air velocity on its underside causes a slightly increased pressure below it. The combination of these pressure differences provides the lift. The design of practical aircraft wings has to take into account a number of complex factors, including suitable streamlining to avoid *turbulence in the airflow, stability over different angles of attack, the provision of suitable control surfaces (flaps, ailerons, etc.), and adequate strength and rigidity. At supersonic speeds these forces are somewhat altered (*see* sound barrier) and the aerofoil has to be more sweptback and more streamlined. At hypersonic speeds (i.e. in excess of five times the speed of sound) the *aerodynamics changes again and blunter noses and even smaller wings are needed.

aerosol   A colloidal suspension of particles of liquid or solid in a gaseous medium. Fog, mist, and smoke are common natural examples. By means of pressurized packages, aerosols can be produced from a huge range of substances, including insecticides, paints, hairsprays, etc. In these, the substance is mixed with an easily liquefied gas (often a fluorinated or chlorinated hydrocarbon), which acts as a propellant when the pressure is released. Fears have been expressed that fluorinated hydrocarbons, being lighter than air, could cause chain reactions in the upper atmosphere, which could destroy the *ozone layer. As this layer protects life on earth from the sun's ultraviolet radiation, measures have been encouraged to ban the use of fluorinated hydrocarbons in aerosols. *See* colloids.

Aeschines   (c. 397–c. 322 BC) Athenian orator, who was an opponent of *Demosthenes. He was part of the Greek embassy

to Philip of Macedon that in 350 negotiated peace, for which Demosthenes tried unsuccessfully in 343 to convict him of treason. In 330 Aeschines was defeated in his attempt to prevent Demosthenes being awarded a crown for his services to Athens and he retired to Rhodes.

Aeschylus   (c. 525–456 BC) Greek tragic dramatist, the first of the great trio of Athenian tragedians that included Sophocles and Euripides. He wrote over 80 plays, of which only 7 survive: *The Persians* (472), *Seven against Thebes* (467), the *Oresteia* trilogy (*Agamemnon, Libation Bearers*, and *Eumenides*; 458), *Suppliant Women* and *Prometheus Bound*. His introduction of a second actor, allowing dialogue and action independent of the chorus, and his innovations in costume and scenery, transformed the conventions of drama. His deeply religious plays dramatize the perpetual conflict between human passions and divine will.

Aesculapius.   *See* Asclepius.

Aesop   The supposed author of a collection of Greek fables, said by Herodotus to be a slave from Samos who lived in the 6th century BC. Originating in popular folklore, the fables are anecdotal stories whose animal characters are used to illustrate a moral point. The Roman poet Phaedrus popularized them in the 1st century AD, and the French poet La Fontaine wrote more sophisticated versions in the 17th century.

Aesthetic movement   A British literary and artistic movement of the late 19th century, summarized in the slogan "art for art's sake." Reacting against the ugliness of industrialism and against contemporary utilitarian social philosophies, its followers sought to create beauty for its own sake, self-consciously divorcing art from life. Their artistic precursors were the *Pre-Raphaelite Brotherhood, formed in 1848, whose emphasis on pure aesthetics was continued by Swinburne, William Morris, and others, culminating in the work of Oscar Wilde, Aubrey Beardsley, and the other contributors to the periodical *The Yellow Book* (1894–97).

aesthetics   The philosophical study of art and critical judgments about art. It includes questions concerning the nature of beauty and general questions about ascribing value—what we mean when we say that a work of art is good and how we arrive at standards of judgment. Objective views hold that beauty or value is in the object and that aesthetic judgments are true or false. Subjective views see value as something an observer brings to the work of art—it may be purely a matter of personal preference or, as *Kant held, something that can be universally agreed on. There are also various approaches to evaluation, including analytical views that discuss the standards and logic of evaluation, and those that consider the social or moral significance of art.

Aeth–.   For names beginning Aeth *see* Eth–.

Aetius, Flavius   (d. 454 AD) Roman general. After a chequered early career, he became virtual ruler of the western Empire, dominating the emperor, Valentian III (reigned 425–55). Aetius defeated the Huns under Attila at the *Catalaunian Plains (451) but was powerless to halt their invasion of Italy. He was subsequently murdered by Valentian.

Aetolia   A region of ancient Greece N of the Gulf of Corinth. In 326 BC the tribes of Aetolia formed the **Aetolian League**, a federation that became a leading military power in Greece. In 27 BC Aetolia was included in the Roman province of Achaea. It forms part of the modern department of Aetolia and Acarnania.

Afars   A Cushitic-speaking people of the Horn of Africa, also known as Danakils. They are mainly nomads, herding goats and camels. Their social organization is complicated, with patrilineal kinship groups, age sets each under the authority of a chief, and a class division between the Asaimara (red men) nobles and the Adoimara (white men) lower class. Afars are nominally Muslim but the influence of earlier Cushitic beliefs persists.

Afars and the Issas, French territory of the. *See* Djibouti, Republic of.

Affenpinscher A breed of toy dog, also called monkey terrier. Small but sturdy, it has small erect ears, a short tail, and a short usually black coat with long hair on the legs and face. Height: 23.5–28 cm.

Afghan hound A breed of large dog having long legs, large drooping ears, and a very long silky coat, which may be of any colour. The Afghan probably originated in ancient Egypt and was later used in Afghanistan to hunt leopards and gazelles. Height: 68–73 cm (dogs); 61–66 cm (bitches).

Afghani, Jamal ad-Din al- (1838–97) Muslim religious and political reformer. Of obscure origins, al-Afghani lived at various times in Istanbul, Egypt, Paris, India, and Persia. He argued for the unity of all Muslims and resistance to European interference in the Muslim countries. He has been seen as a forerunner of Arab nationalists.

Afghanistan, Republic of A state in central Asia. The country is mountainous, the Hindu Kush range rising over 6000 m (20 000 ft). The only lower-lying areas are along the River Amu Darya (ancient name: Oxus) in the N and the delta of the River Helmand in the SW. The population consists of mixed ethnic groups, the largest being the *Pathans and the Tadzhiks. *Economy*: largely agricultural, primarily stock raising (especially of fat-tailed sheep). There has been industrial development in recent years, especially since the discovery of natural gas in the N. The first natural-gas power station was opened in 1972. Textiles are important, especially carpet making, and attempts are being made to develop mineral resources and improve communications. Building of asphalt roads has been carried out with US and Soviet help. There is still no substantial railway system in Afghanistan. Main exports include Persian lambskins, fruit, cotton, wool, carpets, and natural gas (to the Soviet Union). *History*: before the opening up of international sea routes in the 15th century Afghanistan was an important centre on the overland routes across central Asia. For centuries under the rule of different powers, including the Mongol Genghis Khan in the 13th century, it became an independent kingdom in 1747. During the 19th century Afghanistan became involved in the struggle between Britain and Russia for influence in central Asia. After two wars with Britain (1839–42 and 1878–80) it became a buffer state between British India and Russia, with Britain controlling its foreign policy. In 1919, under the leadership of *Amanollah Khan, Afghanistan attempted to free itself of British influence, which led to further fighting between the two countries. This third Afghan War led to independence in 1921. In 1926 Amanollah declared himself king. He was deposed in 1929 by a brigand chief, Habibullah, who was in turn defeated by Nader Khan. When the latter was assassinated in 1933 he was succeeded by his son, King Zahir. Since World War II there has been friction with Pakistan over the question of an independent Pathan state in Pakistan. In 1973 the monarchy was overthrown by Mohammed Daud, a cousin of King Zahir, and a republic established. A new constitution was adopted in 1977, with Daud as president. In 1978 he was killed in a military coup and a new government under Nur Mohammed Taraki (1917–79) was set up by the Marxist People's Democratic Party. Two further coups occurred in 1979; in the second Babrak Karmal came to power with Soviet aid. Soviet military occupation of Afghanistan provoked worldwide condemnation and prejudiced the 1980 Olympic Games in Moscow. Since then Afghan rebels have waged a guerrilla war against the government despite a shortage of weapons and Soviet bombing of rural areas. In 1986 several units of the occupying Soviet forces were withdrawn from Afghanistan as a gesture of goodwill. In 1986 Karmal resigned and Mohammad Najibullah (1947–) became head of a collective leadership. Complete evacuation of Soviet troops is planned for 1988. Joint official languages: Pushtu and Dari Persian. Official currency: afghani of 100 puls. Area: 657 500 sq km (250 000 sq mi). Population (1981 est): 16 400 000. Capital:

Kabul.

aflatoxin. *See* Aspergillus.

AFRICA *In the scramble for Africa the European powers annexed most of the continent. The map shows the positions in 1914.*

Africa The second largest continent in the world. Linked to SW Asia by the Isthmus of Suez, it is of irregular triangular shape with more than two-thirds of its area lying to the N of the equator, which runs across the centre of the continent. Except for Australia, its relief is the most uniform of all the continents, consisting principally of two well-defined physical regions: a S tableland and a lower but still elevated plain in the N. A notable feature of the NE is the *Great Rift Valley, which contains the most extensive system of freshwater lakes in the world after North America, as well as the continent's highest point, Mount *Kilimanjaro. Madagascar, the fourth largest island in the world, lies off the SE coast but there are few island groups. The principal rivers are the Nile, Niger, Zaïre, and Zambezi. Africa's climate and vegetation vary considerably from the arid desert of the Sahara to the tropical rainforest of the Congo basin. The inhabitants of Africa are principally of Negroid origin, although the originators of the Berber language group remain dominant in N Africa and the Sahara and there are a few Cushite-speaking peoples in the NE. *History*: Africa's long history has been substantiated by Louis *Leakey's finds of hominoid man at Olduvai Gorge. The earliest African civilization was established in Egypt in about 3400 BC. Also in N Africa the Phoenicians founded Carthage (9th century BC), later conquered by the Romans (146 BC). From the 7th century AD Arab influence was strong and Islam spread with the trans-Saharan and East African coastal trade. Several African kingdoms and empires emerged during this period, notably the Sudanese empires of Ghana, Mali, and Songhai. From the 15th century European exploration and exploitation began, initiated by the Portuguese. Slaves, ivory, and gold were exported from Africa from the 17th to the late 19th centuries, during which time the Atlantic slave trade was active, over 10 million slaves being shipped to the plantations of America and the West Indies. This enforced migration considerably changed the composition of the American and West Indian populations. From 1880 to 1912 most of Africa was partitioned by the European powers, which imposed political boundaries upon the continent that bore no relationship to former political and social organizations; this resulted in long-standing problems. In the 1950s there was movement towards independence and Africa now consists of independent nations. Area: about 30 300 000 sq km (11 700 000 sq mi). Population (1981 est): 486 000 000.

African art The traditional art of the peoples of sub-Saharan or Black Africa. Among these peoples the visual or plastic arts were not distinguished one from another or from the religious and cultural life of the community. Artists, however, were professionals who enjoyed a respected and sometimes priestly and hereditary status, working on commission or with royal patronage. They produced ceremonial masks, figures for use in the ancestor cults, weapons, furnishings, and everyday utensils. Carving and sculpture in wood, ivory, copper alloys, terracotta, and clay were the dominant forms, but artistic skills extended to textiles, basketry, leatherwork, and wall and body painting; they also included the mastery of sophisticated techniques, such as the *cire perdue process of bronze-casting. Most of the extant examples of traditional art are less than 200 years old, but these are often representative of much earlier developments. Art flourished in the area of W Africa roughly extending from Senegal and Mali in the N, through the countries bordering the Atlantic, to N Angola and Zambia and E to the chain of great lakes. Within this area a large number of styles are evident. The Dogon of Mali are noted for their stylized rectangular wooden masks. The Yoruba of Nigeria and Dahomey (now Benin) made naturalistic human heads and figures, and similar figures in brass and terracotta were produced at the Yoruba centre, Ife, in Nigeria, as early as the 12th century. The skill in casting metal passed from Ife to Dahomey, where the Edo people produced brass reliefs and sculpture. The Baule of the Ivory Coast made finely polished masks and figures; they and the Ashanti of Ghana are the only African people to have used gold leaf to cover sculptures and other carved wooden objects. In the Congo region, ancestral figures, masks, fetishes, and other decorated objects were made in great profusion, chiefly in human and animal forms that were rendered not naturalistically but symbolically, as part of a magical or religious view of reality. It was this quality in African art that perhaps most appealed to many 20th-century western artists, including Picasso, Modigliani, and Epstein, upon whom it has had a profound effect.

African languages A geographical classification of the heterogeneous languages spoken in the African continent. The *Hamito-Semitic group extends across N Africa from Mauritania to Somalia. The *Nilo-Saharan group is spoken in many dialects in central Africa, and the *Niger-Congo languages, many of them *Bantu languages, cover most of the area S of the Sahara. In S Africa the *Khoisan languages survive. There are up to a thousand indigenous languages of the continent as well as the European languages (*English, *Afrikaans, *French, *Portuguese) imported by colonizers. *Malagasy, a language of *Austronesian origin, is spoken in Madagascar. *Swahili is an important lingua franca in East Africa. Certain African languages are unique in using click sounds in their phonology; predominance of certain consonantal groups (kp, gb, mb, nd) is also common in Africa.

African National Congress (ANC) A Black nationalist movement in S Africa. Founded in 1912 as the South African Native National Congress to promote Black interests, the ANC is now fighting apartheid in South Africa and has been criticized for its failure to condemn violence. Although Oliver

Tambo (1917–) is its official leader, Nelson *Mandela is its symbolic head.

African violet A flowering plant, *Saintpaulia ionantha*, native to tropical E Africa. The plants have rosettes of hairy, often deeply ridged, leaves, bear clusters of pink, blue, purple, or white flowers, and grow to a height of 10–15 cm. Many varieties and hybrids have been developed as ornamentals. Family: *Gesneriaceae*.

Afrikaans. *See* Afrikaner.

Afrikaner A South African of Dutch or *Huguenot descent. The Afrikaners comprise about 60% of the Republic's White population. Formerly called "Boers" (farmers), they have undergone considerable urbanization since the 1930s. In the 18th and 19th centuries they led a seminomadic life, resisting governmental control from Cape Town. Their two independent states, the South African Republic and the Orange Free State, came under British rule after the second *Boer War. Their language, Afrikaans, derives, but is distinct, from Dutch and together with English has been an official language of South Africa since 1925. *See also* Great Trek.

Afro-Asiatic languages. *See* Hamito-Semitic languages.

Agade. *See* Akkad.

Agadir 30 30N 9 40W A port in SW Morocco, on the Atlantic coast. Its growth has followed the development of the port and inland resources. An earthquake in 1960 destroyed much of the town and killed about 12 000 people. Population (1982): 110 479.

Aga Khan III (1877–1957) Imam (leader) of the *Ismaili sect of Muslims (1885–1957). He was an early president of the All-India Muslim League and represented India at the League of Nations in 1932 and from 1934 to 1937.

Aga Khan IV (1936–) Imam (leader) of the *Ismaili sect of Muslims (1957–), succeeding his grandfather *Aga Khan III. He married (1969) an Englishwoman, Sarah Croker Poole.

agama A common African broad-headed lizard belonging to the family *Agamidae* (50 species). 30–45 cm long, agamas have a thick body and a tapering tail and feed on insects. The common agama (*Agama agama*) is variously coloured: dominant males have a brick-red head, blue body and legs, and banded tail; other males are duller coloured, like the females.

Agamemnon King of Mycenae and commander of the Greek army in the Trojan War. His quarrel with Achilles is the main theme of Homer's *Iliad*. After his return from Troy with Cassandra, the captured daughter of King Priam, he was murdered by his wife Clytemnestra and her lover Aegisthus. The subsequent vengeance of his son Orestes is the central theme of *Aeschylus' *Oresteia* trilogy.

Agaña 13 28N 144 45E The capital of Guam in the W Pacific Ocean, in the Mariana Islands. The city was largely destroyed in World War II. The University of Guam was established here in 1952. Population (1980): 881.

Agapanthus A genus of herbaceous plants native to South Africa and cultivated for ornament in greenhouses and tropical gardens. *A. africanus* (African lily) has long strap-shaped leaves and large clusters of blue funnel-shaped flowers borne on a tall stalk. There are many cultivated varieties and hybrids. Family: *Amaryllidaceae*.

agar-agar A gelatinous substance obtained from seaweed. A solution in water sets to a firm jelly, which is used for growing bacteria.

agaric A fungus belonging to a large family (*Agaricaceae*) found throughout the world. The group includes many edible mushrooms, such as the white mushroom (*Agaricus bisporus*) and field mushroom (*A. campestris*), as well as the poisonous death cap (*see* Amanita). The visible part of the fungus consists of a stipe (stalk) bearing a cap with gills on the undersurface. Class: *Basidiomycetes*. *See also* fly agaric; mushroom.

Agartala 23 49N 91 15E A city in NE India, the capital of Tripura. It is a commercial centre. Population (1981 est): 132 186.

Agassiz, Jean Louis Rodolphe (1807-73) Swiss natural historian. Agassiz's early work centred on the study of extinct species, fossilization, and glaciation. His later theories on animal species were contrary to those of Charles Darwin. In his *Essay on Classification* (1859) he argued that organisms were immutable and independent of each other and that there was no possibility of evolution from one source. As professor of zoology at Harvard University, his innovative teaching methods revolutionized the study of natural science in the USA. His son **Alexander Agassiz** (1835-1910) was a marine zoologist and mining engineer. His copper mine became noted for its modern and enlightened management. He was a benefactor to various biological institutions and founded his own research station, from which he mounted expeditions to study marine fauna and the sea bed.

agate A banded or concentrically patterned form of *chalcedony. The banding is due to intermittent deposition in rock cavities and the colours, ranging from white, milky blue, yellow, and brown to red, are due to traces of mineral or organic colouring matter. Being hard, it is used for mortars for grinding. It is also used for ornamental purposes, for which the stone may be artificially dyed.

Agathocles (361-289 BC) Tyrant (317-304) and King (304-289) of Syracuse. After seizing power he gained control of E Sicily but fled to Africa after his defeat (311) by the Carthaginians. By 304 he had brutally pacified the Sicilian opposition and took the title of king. He died without establishing a dynasty.

AGAVE *The leaves of this plant are coated with wax. Only 2-3 grow per year and they store large reserves of food materials.*

Agave A genus of plants (about 300 species) of the S USA and tropical America, many of which are widely grown for ornament. Agaves have a basal tuft of thick fleshy, sometimes toothed, leaves and a cluster of flowers that—in some species—grows on a tall stalk (up to 12 m high). Growth is slow—it may be 60 or more years before flowers are produced; after flowering the plant dies. Several species are commercially important as a source of fibre, especially *sisal; the fermented juice of others is used as an alcoholic drink (pulque) or distilled to produce spirits (*see* tequila). Family: *Agavaceae* (or *Amaryllidaceae*). *See also* century plant.

Agee, James (1909-55) US poet, novelist, and film critic.

After graduating from Harvard he published a book of poems, *Permit Me Voyage* (1934), and wrote influential film reviews for various magazines. *Let Us Now Praise Famous Men* (1941), in collaboration with the photographer Walker Evans, is a bitter account of the lives of Alabama sharecroppers. He also produced two autobiographical novels, *The Morning Watch* (1951) and *A Death in the Family* (1957, Pulitzer Prize), and several filmscripts.

ageing (*or* senescence) The degenerative process in an organism that precedes death. In man ageing is characterized by a gradual decline in the efficiency of the repair mechanisms of the body tissues, leading to increased susceptibility to disease; it is also associated with a reduction and then loss of fertility. In some elderly people there is marked physical and mental deterioration (senility). There are several theories to account for the ageing process. Some maintain that it is due to the accumulation of errors in metabolism brought about by faulty protein synthesis in the cells; others that ageing—particularly in plants after flowering and some animals after reproduction—is a genetically programmed event.

Agence France-Presse. *See* news agency.

Age of Reason. *See* Enlightenment.

age set A recognized group of persons, usually males initiated at the same time, that is an important feature of the organization of many primitive societies. Each age set may pass through a series of stages (age grades) to which are assigned various functions requiring abilities dependent upon age, such as physical strength, experience, and wisdom. Typically there will be one or more grades of warriors and of elders who exercise political and often ritual authority. *See also* initiation rites.

Agesilaus II (444-360 BC) King of Sparta (c. 399-360). A noted general, he achieved some success against the Persians in Asia Minor (396-395) and against the Boeotians at Coronea (394). His subsequent diplomatic activities contributed to Sparta's disastrous defeat by the Thebans at Leuctra (371). Xenophon wrote a memoir of Agesilaus.

agglomerate A rock composed of a mixture of coarse angular fragments and finer-grained material formed by volcanic explosions; it is usually found in or near the volcanic vent.

Agha Mohammad Khan (1742-97) Shah of Persia (1796-97), who founded the Qajar dynasty (1796-1925). The chief (1758) of one of the clans of the Qajar tribe, he made himself ruler of the whole of Persia and was crowned in 1796. He was the first ruler to make Tehran his capital.

Agincourt, Battle of (25 October, 1415) The battle that took place during the *Hundred Years' War at Agincourt (now in the Pas-de-Calais), in which the French were defeated by an English army led by Henry V. The decisive English victory, which owed much to their outstanding archers, was achieved with not more than 1600 dead; the French may have lost as many as 6000 men.

Agnes, St (4th century AD) Roman virgin and martyr. Nothing certain is known about her life, but according to legend she was martyred under Diocletian for refusing to marry and subsequently resisting plans to make her a prostitute. Feast day: 21 Jan. Emblem: a lamb.

Agnesi, Maria Gaetana (1718-99) Italian mathematician and philosopher. A child prodigy, Agnesi became the first woman to occupy a chair of mathematics when she was appointed to that at Bologna University in 1750. On the death of her father in 1752, she devoted herself to religion and charitable work. The curve $x^2y = a^2(a - y)$ is known as the "Witch of Agnesi" because she called it a *versiera* (Latin: turning), a word also meaning witch in colloquial Italian.

Agnew, Spiro T(heodore) (1918-) US Republican politician; vice president (1969-73), who gained notoriety for his attacks on the critics of President Nixon. In 1973 a federal tax case forced him to resign his office. He was given a suspended prison sentence and fined $10,000.

Agnon, Shmuel Yosef (Samuel Josef Czaczkes; 1888–1970) Jewish novelist, born in Galicia, who settled in Palestine in 1907. His treatment of contemporary Jewish themes in *The Day Before Yesterday* (1945) and other works was influenced by folklore and traditional religious literature. In 1966 he shared the Nobel Prize.

agnosticism The philosophical view that doubts the existence of God and other spiritual phenomena and claims that even if they do exist it is impossible to know anything about them. Although this position occurs sporadically throughout history, the term was apparently coined by T. H. *Huxley in 1869. Agnosticism was subsequently enthusiastically embraced by rationalists, who hesitated on philosophical or social grounds to adopt outright *atheism. Agnosticism is now frequently loosely used to mean neither knowing nor caring about the supernatural world.

agora A central feature of ancient Greek town planning. Similar to the Roman *forum, the primary function of the agora was as the town market. In addition, however, it also became the main social and political meeting place. Together with the acropolis, it normally contained the most important buildings of the town.

agoraphobia. *See* phobia.

Agostini, Giacomo (1944–   ) Italian racing motorcyclist, winner of a record 15 world championship titles: 350 cc in 1968–74 and 500 cc in 1966–72 and 1975. He is the only man to have won two world championships in five consecutive years.

agouti A rabbit-sized rodent belonging to a genus (*Dasyprocta*; 13 species) of Central and South American forests. Agoutis have long legs, small ears, and a very short hairless tail. The hair on the rump is often long and brightly coloured and can be erected when the animal is alarmed. Agoutis feed on leaves, roots, and berries and are commonly eaten by the Indians. Family: *Dasyproctidae* (agoutis and pacas); suborder: *Hystricomorpha*.

Agra 27 09N 78 00E A city in India, in Uttar Pradesh on the River Jumna. Former capital of the Mogul Empire (1566–69 and 1601–58), it fell to the British in 1803 and from 1835 until 1862 was capital of the North-West Provinces. Notable buildings include the celebrated *Taj Mahal and a fine 16th-century fort. Its university was established in 1927. A major commercial, industrial, and communications centre, it produces carpets. Population (1981 est): 747 318.

agranulocytosis The condition resulting from a deficiency or absence of certain white blood cells (called granulocytes). Agranulocytosis may be caused by an allergic reaction to drugs, cytotoxic drugs (which damage the bone marrow), and severe infection. Symptoms include weakness, fever, and a sore throat; treatment includes withdrawal of the suspect drug, fresh-blood transfusions, and antibiotics.

Agricola, Georgius (George Bauer; 1494–1555) German physician and mineralogist. Working as a physician in several mining towns, he carried out a systematic study of mining and minerals; this study consistently discounted the traditional "magical" attributes of minerals, describing instead their observable physical properties. His publications concerning these properties culminated in his *De re metallica* (1556), which for two centuries was the standard text on mining and metallurgy.

Agricola, Gnaeus Julius (40–93 AD) Roman governor of Britain and father-in-law of his biographer Tacitus. Sent to govern Britain in 78, after holding previous legionary posts there, he followed a policy of romanization, exploration, and expansion. He circumnavigated the mainland and advanced the Roman frontiers in annual campaigns, reaching the Scottish Highlands before his recall in 84.

Agricola, Johann (Johannes Schnitter; c. 1494–1566) German Protestant reformer. A pupil of *Luther at Wittenberg,

he later worked as a reformer in Frankfurt and Eisleben. From 1536 he taught at Wittenberg but quarrelled with Luther over doctrine and in 1540 moved to Berlin, where he became court preacher to the Elector of Brandenburg.

agricultural revolution The name given to the changes in agriculture in Britain that took place mainly in the 18th century. The open-field system of strip farming was replaced by larger enclosed fields, hedged and ditched, in which improved agricultural methods and new implements could be used (*see* Tull, Jethro; Townshend, Charles, 2nd Viscount); the quality of cattle and sheep was improved by scientific stock breeding (*see* Bakewell, Robert). This resulted in a greater production of food for the growing industrial population (*see* industrial revolution), although it meant hardship for those farmers who were displaced by *enclosure.

agriculture The study of farming. Settled farming probably dates back to the 10th millennium BC, when in many regions of the world it began to replace man's activities as a hunter and gatherer of food. The domestication of cattle, goats, sheep, and pigs together with the cropping of wheat, barley, rice, etc., enabled settled communities to evolve and primitive civilizations to flourish in such regions as the fertile river basins of the Tigris, Euphrates, and Nile.

Farming has developed in various ways in different parts of the world, depending largely on climatic conditions, the type of land, and the local system of land tenure. Many areas are suitable only for *livestock farming whereas in many others large-scale *arable farming is possible. In some cases the most economically successful farms are mixed arable and livestock.

Until the end of the 19th century farming was based on energy derived from man and his draught animals. Some parts of the world still use such traditional methods; however, during the 20th century, especially in developed countries, the *tractor has become the primary energy source. In this century, too, there has been great success in improving breeds of plants and animals, improving soil fertility (*see* fertilizers), increasing mechanization, and control of plant and animal pests, measures that have enormously increased the quantity and quality of food produced. These measures are now being applied in the developing world, where they are bringing about the Green Revolution that is needed to feed the world's growing population.

However, misuse of modern intensive farming methods can cause such problems as soil erosion, while pollution by excessive use of fertilizers, weedkillers, insecticides, etc., can seriously damage the environment. The reconciliation of optimum food production with conservation of the environment is one of the principal tasks of the UN *Food and Agriculture Organization.

Agrigento 37 19N 13 35E A seaport in Italy, in S Sicily. Founded about 580 BC, it has famous ancient temples and is the birthplace of the philosopher Empedocles. Sulphur mining is the main occupation. Population (1981): 51 931.

agrimony A herbaceous perennial plant of the genus *Agrimonia* (especially *A. eupatoria*), native to Europe but grown in most temperate regions. Up to 1 m tall, it has a spike of small yellow flowers and toothed oval leaves that yield a yellow dye. Family: *Rosaceae*.

Agrippa, Marcus Vipsanius (?63–12 BC) Roman general and close associate of Emperor *Augustus, whose daughter Julia was his third wife. After military successes in Gaul (38 BC) Agrippa became consul (37 BC). He played an important part in the defeat of Mark Antony at *Actium (31 BC) and greatly contributed to the military successes of Augustus.

Agrippina the Elder (?13 BC–33 AD) The daughter of *Agrippa, wife of *Germanicus Caesar, and mother of Emperor *Caligula. A courageous and high-minded woman, she accompanied her husband on his campaigns. After his death she incurred the hostility of Tiberius, who exiled her to Pandataria, where she died in suspicious circumstances. Her daughter, **Agrippina the Younger** (15–59 AD), was notorious for her political intrigues. She probably murdered her uncle, Emperor Claudius, who was also her third husband, to make way for the succession of her son, Nero. She exerted considerable political influence early in Nero's reign, but after they had quarrelled he had her murdered.

agronomy   The management of land, especially for the production of arable crops. Agronomy involves the determination of the nature of a soil and how its fertility may be improved by such processes as drainage, irrigation, the application of natural and artificial fertilizers, and husbandry techniques (e.g. *crop rotation). Equally important is the breeding of crop plants that are suited to a particular soil.

Aguascalientes   21 51N 102 18W A city in central Mexico. The commercial centre for a region producing fruit and vegetables, its industries include ceramics production, tanning, and railway engineering. There are medicinal hot springs nearby. Population (1980): 359 454.

Agulhas, Cape   34 50S 20 00E A cape in South Africa, in W Cape Province. It is the most southerly point of the African continent and has a lighthouse (1849).

Ahad Ha'am   (Asher Ginsberg; 1856–1927) Hebrew essayist and an influential Zionist thinker. Born in Russia, he moved to London in 1908 and participated in negotiations leading to the *Balfour Declaration. In 1922 he settled in Palestine. Critical of political *Zionism, he looked to nationalism to achieve a Jewish moral and cultural regeneration. His adopted name means "One of the People."

Ahaggar Mountains (*or* Hoggar Mts)   A plateau area in S Algeria, in the central Sahara. It averages about 900 m (2950 ft) but reaches 2918 m (9573 ft) at Mount Tahat.

ahimsa (Sanskrit: noninjury)   The ethical practice, strictly observed in *Jainism but also of fundamental importance in *Hinduism and *Buddhism, of not causing harm to any living thing. Because of the belief in reincarnation, these religions respect all forms of life as being parts of the cycle of rebirth. Vegetarianism is consequently widespread in Asia. *Gandhi's doctrine of nonviolent resistance (*satyagraha*) was derived from the principle of ahimsa.

Ahmadabad (*or* Ahmedabad)   23 03N 72 40E An industrial city in central India, in Gujarat. Founded in 1411, it is a major rail centre and its textile industry (established 1859–61) is one of the largest in the country. Its university was established in 1949. Population (1981 est): 2 548 057.

Ahmadiya   A religious sect founded in the Punjab by Mirza Ghulam Ahmad of Qadiyan (1839–1908), who was of Muslim background. His teaching combined elements of Islam, Christianity, and Hinduism. He taught that Jesus was buried in Srinigar and that he himself was the messiah and *Mahdi. In 1918 the Ahmadiya split into two groups, the larger regarding Mirza Ahmad as a prophet, the smaller regarding him only as a reformer. Both groups are based in Pakistan, but have communities elsewhere.

Ahmad Khan, Sir Sayyid   (1817–'98) Indian educationalist and scholar, who led a major revival in Indian Islamic society and culture. He wrote books on religion and history, encouraged translation of English works into Urdu, and founded several schools; the one at Aligarh in Uttar Pradesh (1875) became the Aligarh Muslim University.

Ahmadnagar (*or* Ahmednagar)   19 08N 74 48E A town in W India, in Maharashtra. It was conquered in 1490 by Ahmad Nizam Shah, founder of the Ahmadnagar dynasty. A commercial centre, its industries include cotton and leather processing. Population (1981 est): 181 210.

Ahmad Shah Durrani   (c. 1723–73) Afghan ruler (1747–73), who founded the Durrani dynasty. Ahmad was commander in India for the Persian *Nader Shah. When Nader died (1747), Ahmad became shah and built an empire that was bordered by the River Oxus, Tibet, the River Indus, and Persia. After his death, the empire collapsed.

Ahmed III   (1673–1736) Sultan of the Ottoman Empire (1703–30). After a successful war against Russia (1711–13) Ahmed was defeated by Austria; by the Peace of Passarowitz (1718) the Ottomans lost their last possessions in Hungary and parts of Serbia. He was deposed and died in captivity. His reign is known as the Tulip Age because of the flower's contemporary popularity.

Ahmose I   King of Egypt (c. 1570–1546 BC), who founded the 18th dynasty. He liberated Egypt from the *Hyksos, retaking Memphis, and reasserted Egyptian power in Nubia and Palestine. After more than a century of alien domination, he reorganized his reunited country and encouraged trade.

Ahmose II   King of Egypt (570–526 BC) of the 26th dynasty. He came to power in a military coup but ruled for 44 years in peace and prosperity.

Ahriman.   *See* Ahura Mazda.

Ahura Mazda   The supreme deity of *Zoroastrianism, creator of all things good and just. He represents the creative principle, living in eternal light, and is opposed to Ahriman, the destructive principle of greed, anger, etc., living in darkness.

Ahvaz   31 17N 48 43E A town in SW Iran, the capital of Khuzestan province. On the site of an ancient city it is a centre for the nearby oilfields. Population (1985 est): 508 500.

Ahvenanmaa Islands.   *See* Åland Islands.

ai.   *See* sloth.

Aidan, St   (c. 600–51 AD) Irish monk at *Iona until his consecration as bishop of Northumbria in 635. He founded the monastery at Lindisfarne (*see* Holy Island), the centre of his missionary activity in N England. His life is described by *Bede in his *Ecclesiastical History*. Feast day: 31 Aug.

AIDS (*acquired immune deficiency syndrome*)   A viral disease characterized by a decrease of certain T-lymphocytes, resulting in a breakdown of the immune system and increased susceptibility to other diseases. First described in 1981, it originated in central Africa, possibly by the mutation of a virus carried by green monkeys. The three currently known causative agents, the viruses HIV, LAV 2, and SBL 6669 V 2, are transmitted in blood, semen, or vaginal fluid. It is possible that a very high proportion of virus carriers will develop the disease but the exact percentage is uncertain. AIDS occurs most frequently in homosexual and bisexual males and intravenous drug users who share needles, but it can also be transmitted to heterosexuals by any penetrative intercourse with an AIDS carrier and to those who receive transfusions of infected blood (all of which is now tested). By the end of 1987 about 100 000 cases of the disease had been reported worldwide; in Britain 1227 recorded cases had resulted in 697 deaths. Until a vaccine or cure has been found (the drug azidothymidine (AZT) merely alleviates symptoms), western governments are attempting to limit its spread, especially into the heterosexual community. The British government began a campaign in 1986 to discourage casual sexual relationships and encourage the use of condoms.

Aiken, Howard Hathaway   (1900–73) US mathematician, who pioneered the construction of electronic computers. His Mark I, built in 1944 and later used by the US navy, anticipated the modern digital computer.

aikido   A Japanese form of unarmed combat, primarily for self-defence by means of dodging an attacker and leading him in the direction in which his momentum takes him before subduing him without injury. Like other *martial arts it emphasizes the need for a calm frame of mind and total physical control. In sporting competitions two people fight in one or two one-minute rounds. *See also* judo; jujitsu.

Ailanthus.   *See* tree of heaven.

Ailred of Rievaulx, St   (1109–67) Abbot (from 1147) of the Cistercian monastery of Rievaulx in Yorkshire, known as the English St Bernard. Part of his youth was spent at the court of David I of Scotland. His influential theological writings contain an element of mysticism and include *De spirituali amicitia*, a treatise on friendship considered in spiritual terms and based on Cicero's *De amicitia*. He also wrote a life of Edward the Confessor. Feast day: 12 Jan or 3 March.

Ailsa Craig 55 16N 5 07W A granite cone-shaped island in Scotland, rising abruptly out of the sea at the mouth of the Firth of Clyde. Its rock is quarried to produce *curling stones. Area: about 2.6 sq km (1 sq mi).

Ain, River A river in E France, flowing SSW from the Jura Mountains to join the River Rhône 29 km (18 mi) above Lyons. Length: 190 km (118 mi).

Ainsworth, W(illiam) Harrison (1805–82) British historical novelist. He followed the success of his first novel, *Rookwood* (1834), about the highwayman Dick Turpin, with 38 others, the best known of which are *The Tower of London* (1840), *Old St Paul's* (1841), *Windsor Castle* (1843), and *The Lancashire Witches* (1848). He also edited three popular magazines.

Aintree 53 29N 2 57W A suburb of Liverpool, NW England, with a famous racecourse where the Grand National steeplechase has been held annually since 1839. It also has a motor-racing circuit.

Ainu A Caucasoid people living on certain islands of Japan and the Soviet Union (Hokkaido, Sakhalin, Kurile Islands). Traditionally a hunting and food-gathering people, distinct from the surrounding Mongoloid peoples, they are now few in number and much changed in both appearance and culture. They were once noted for their profusion of body hair, but intermixture has made them resemble the Japanese and their traditional culture has largely disappeared. They speak a language that is not related to any other known language.

air. *See* atmosphere.

aircraft Any machine capable of flying. Man's attempts to fly fall into two categories: those using lighter-than-air machines (*see* airships; balloons) and those using heavier-than-air machines. The latter include wing-flapping birdlike devices, rotating wing machines (*see* helicopters), and fixed-wing aircraft, first *gliders and then powered aeroplanes. By the end of the 19th century it was clear to all but the most eccentric that man was both too weak and too heavy to emulate birds. Flapping wings combine both thrust and lift (*see* aeronautics) in one device; man needs to separate these two components, obtaining lift from a fixed wing and thrust from an engine. 19th-century experience of gliding, especially by Otto *Lilienthal, provided the Wright Brothers with the information they needed to build their first powered aircraft. The power source was provided by the Otto-Daimler *internal-combustion engine. By 1907 the Wrights were able to remain airborne for 45 minutes; in 1909 the Frenchman Louis *Blériot flew across the English Channel, and in the same year the French rotary Gnome engine revolutionized aircraft-engine design (this engine and its derivatives powered many early aircraft, including several used in World War I). By the beginning of the war aircraft were sufficiently advanced to be used for reconnaissance and their usefulness as bombers soon became evident. Fast manoeuvrable fighters to shoot down the slower heavily laden bombers were an obvious subsequent development. By the end of the war aerial combat was established as an integral part of modern warfare, both sides being equipped with a range of fighters, bombers, and reconnaissance aircraft.

After the war and during the 1920s, air circuses and flying clubs run by ex-wartime pilots using World War I aircraft sprang up all over the world, popularizing the concept of flying and heralding the age of civil aviation. In 1924 Imperial Airways was formed in the UK, using Handley

*Page airliners, and during the 1930s a worldwide network of commercial routes developed. The Atlantic was first flown nonstop from New York to Paris in 1927 by Charles *Lindberg and by 1939 there was a transatlantic service using Class C Short flying boats with in-flight refuelling.

Between the wars all the main countries of the world were also building up their air forces. By the outbreak of World War II aircraft of all kinds were poised for aerial combat. The first RAF bombing raid of the war was carried out by Vickers Wellingtons and Bristol Blenheims (of which some 3500 were built). During the course of the war these bombers were augmented by some 6000 Handley Page Halifaxes (which entered service in 1940) and 7400 Avro Lancasters (1942). The USA's main bombing force consisted of 12 700 Boeing B17s, 18 000 Consolidated B24 Liberators, and towards the end of the war, a fleet of Boeing B29 Superfortresses. Germany entered the war with 370 Dornier Do 17s and the Heinkel He 111, some 7300 of which had been made by the end of the war. The Junkers 88 entered service in 1940 and at the end of the war (1945) the Arado Ar 234 jet bomber was used for the first time. Dominant British fighters were the Supermarine Spitfire and the Hawker Hurricane, the latter being slightly slower than the main German fighter, the Messerschmitt Me Bf109. Later British fighters included the Bristol Beaufighter and the De Havilland Mosquito. The US fighter pilots had some 10 000 Lockheed P38 Lightnings and 15 000 P51 Mustangs. The British jet-powered Gloster Meteor entered service in 1944, as did the German Messerschmitt Me 262 jet.

By the end of war the practicality of the *jet engine had been established and it has dominated aircraft design ever since. However, the first postwar generation of civil aircraft used the jet engine to drive propellers (e.g. the Vickers Viscount), the first true jet to enter passenger service being the ill-fated British Comet. The highly successful Boeing 707 (with its four engines in pods suspended below the wings) followed in 1954 and the French Caravelle (with two rear-mounted engines) in 1959.

The first aircraft to break the *sound barrier were military and nearly all modern warplanes are supersonic and armed with missiles. Examples include the British Hawker Hunter and Avro Vulcan; the US McDonnell Douglas Phantom, Convair Hustler, and General Dynamics Swingwing F111; the French Mirage; and the Soviet MiGs. The first propeller-driven fighter plane to be developed since the advent of the supersonic jet fighter was the 'heliplane' P1233-1 (1987), which is designed for manoeuvrability in low-level dogfights. The first supersonic passenger aircraft (SST) to fly was the Soviet Tupolev Tu-144 in 1968. This was followed a year later by the Anglo-French Concorde, which despite opposition from conservationists, is now in service. However, long- and medium-range passenger services are likely to be dominated for most of the remainder of this century by the wide-bodied (jumbo) jets, such as the Boeing 747 and the European Airbus.

aircraft carrier A naval vessel with a large flat deck for launching and landing warplanes. The first flight from the deck of a ship was made in 1910, and the first true aircraft carrier, HMS *Argus*, was completed for the Royal Navy in 1918, too late for action in World War I. Carriers played a dominant role in World War II, despite early predictions that *battleships would be the most important warships. Carriers were especially effective in the war against the Japanese, where they were employed in combined UK and US operations and were instrumental in destroying the Japanese fleet. After World War II carriers came to be regarded chiefly as tactical units, although they saw considerable action in the Korean and Vietnam Wars. The USS *Enterprise*, the first nuclear-powered carrier (1961), displaced 76 000 tonnes and steamed more than 432 000 km (270 000 mi) before requiring refuelling. The introduction of larger and heavier aircraft required the refitting of carriers. Because of the increased range of aircraft, the enormous cost

Wright Brothers' Flyer *The first powered flight at Kitty Hawk, North Carolina, USA, on 17 December, 1903 lasted 12 seconds.*

Blériot XI *Louis Bleriot's 30-minute flight from Calais to Dover on 25 July, 1909 was the first cross-channel flight.*

Handley Page 42E Hannibal *In 1928 the British airline, Imperial Airways, bought eight HP42 aircraft. The 24-seater Hannibal had a top speed of 100 mph (160 km/hr).*

Douglas DC3 *Introduced in 1936, it was widely used in World War II as the Dakota transport. Its Pratt and Whitney 1200 hp engines gave it a maximum speed of 200 mph (320 km/hr).*

Vickers Viscount *Introduced into service in 1950, it was the first successful turboprop airliner. Powered by four Rolls-Royce Dart engines, it carried 60 passengers.*

De Havilland Comet I *The first jet airliner, it went into service in 1952. Crashes due to metal fatigue caused its withdrawal and in 1958 it was replaced by the Comet IV.*

Boeing 747 *Nicknamed the "jumbo jet" this wide-bodied jetliner, which can carry up to 500 passengers, has been in service with many airlines since 1970.*

Concorde *The first supersonic airliner, it was built by the French and British in cooperation. Powered by four Rolls-Royce Olympus engines, it came into service in 1976.*

Sopwith Camel   *A highly manoeuvrable fighter, first delivered to the RFC in 1917. Its 130 hp Clerget engine gave it a top speed of 113 mph (181 km/hr).*

Fokker Eindecker EIII   *German fighter, in service from 1915. It had a top speed of 83 mph (133 km/hr) and the first machine gun synchronized to fire through the propeller.*

Handley Page 0/400   *The largest World War I bomber. Its twin 360 hp Rolls-Royce engines enabled it to carry 2000 lbs (907 kg) of bombs.*

Supermarine Spitfire   *British fighter designed by R.J. Mitchell. Originally powered by a Rolls-Royce Merlin engine, it later had the Griffon engine, giving it a top speed of 450 mph (724 km/hr).*

Boeing B–29 Superfortress   *This enormous US bomber entered the war in 1943 and was used to drop the atom bombs on Japan.*

Messerschmitt 109   *German fighter, designed in 1935. The latest version (the 109G) had an 1800 hp engine enabling it to fly at 430 mph (692 km/hr).*

General Dynamics FIII   *US fighter and fighter-bomber, the first warplane to have swing wings (1967). It is powered by a Pratt and Whitney TF30 turbo fan.*

Hawker Siddeley Harrier   *British VTOL aircraft developed in 1969. Two movable nozzles direct the thrust of its Bristol Pegasus engine downwards for vertical take-off.*

of carriers, and the development of sophisticated missiles, there have been few aircraft carriers built in the 1970s, and indications are that their size, cost, low speed, and vulnerability will preclude their extensive use in the future. HMS *Ark Royal*, the UK's last aircraft carrier, was withdrawn from service in 1979, but a new *Ark Royal* was commissioned in 1985.

air-cushion vehicle. *See* Hovercraft.

Airdrie 55 52N 3 59W A town in Scotland, in Strathclyde Region. Industries include the manufacture of metal goods and drugs, engineering, electronics, and whisky distilling. Population (1981): 45 643.

Airedale terrier The largest breed of terrier, originating in Yorkshire. It has a long squarish muzzle, a short tail, and a tan-coloured wiry coat with a black saddle region. A powerful and intelligent dog, the Airedale has been used as a guard dog, for hunting, and as a police dog. Height: 58-61 cm (dogs); 56-58 cm (bitches). □dog.

air sac In zoology, a thin-walled air-filled sac that functions in the breathing mechanism of birds, some insects, and some lizards. In birds there are five pairs in the spaces between the internal organs and around or in some bones. They are connected with the air passages and enable a constant supply of air to the lungs during flight.

airships Dirigible *balloons that obtain their thrust from a propeller. The first airship to fly was a French steam-powered machine, designed in 1852 by H. Giffard; however, the first practical airship was the electrically powered *La France* (1884), built by Renard and Krebs. By 1900 the initiative in airships had passed to Germany, with the machines of Count Ferdinand von Zeppelin (1838-1917) leading the field. Between 1910 and 1914 Zeppelins were in extensive passenger service, carrying some 35 000 passengers, without mishap. In World War I these machines were used by the Germans to bomb England—the first effective use of aerial bombardment. From then onwards the history of airships is one of disaster followed by disaster. The British *R101* caught fire at Beauvais in 1930, the US *Shenandoah* and the *Akron* were lost in 1933, and the German *Hindenburg* was destroyed in 1937. These disasters with hydrogen-filled airships cost many lives and gave them a reputation from which they have never recovered. However, the availability of the nonflammable gas helium has created a mild revival of interest in the 1970s, especially in the Soviet Union.

air space In international law, the space above a country over which that country is sovereign. Under the Outer Space Treaty (1967), outer space is not subject to national appropriation.

Airy, Sir George Biddell (1801-92) British astronomer, who was astronomer royal from 1835 to 1881. He uncovered errors in current planetary theory, showing that the motions of the earth and Venus are not in simple ratio. He is noted for his estimate (1826) of the earth's density from gravity measurements in mines.

Aisne, River A river in N France. Rising in the Argonne Forest, it flows mainly NW joining the River Oise near Compiègne. It was a major battleground of *World War I. Length: 282 km (175 mi).

Aistulf (d. 756) King of the Lombards (749-56). Aistulf captured Ravenna (751) and then threatened Rome. The pope sought the aid of *Pepin, King of the Franks, who twice defeated Aistulf at Pavia (755, 756).

Aix-en-Provence (Latin name: Aquae Sextiae) 43 31N 5 27E A city in S France, in the Bouches-du-Rhône department. The capital of Provence in the middle ages, it has a gothic cathedral and a university (1409). The artist Cézanne was born here. An agricultural centre, it trades in olive oil and fruit. Population (1982 est): 124 550.

Aix-la-Chapelle. *See* Aachen.

Aix-la-Chapelle, Congress of (1818) Meeting of the Quadruple Alliance (Great Britain, Austria, Prussia, and Russia) and France at Aix-la-Chapelle (now Aachen). The Alliance reaffirmed the political reorganization of Europe established by the Congress of *Vienna (1814-15) and restored France's status as an independent power: it withdrew its occupying forces and admitted France into what thus became the Quintuple Alliance.

Aix-les-Bains (Latin name: Aquae Gratianae) 45 41N 5 55E A spa and resort in E France, in the Savoie department. Situated in a picturesque valley, it is noted for its hot sulphurous springs. Population (1982 est): 22 534.

Ajaccio 41 51N 8 43E The capital of Corsica, a port on the Gulf of Ajaccio. Napoleon I was born here and his home is now preserved as a museum. Tourism is the principal industry. Population (1982 est): 55 279.

Ajanta 20 30N 75 48E A village in W India, in Maharashtra. It is renowned for its Buddhist caves hewn out of the granite cliffs. Dating from the 1st century BC to the 7th century AD, they consist of monasteries and temples, some of which contain remarkable paintings illustrating the life of the times.

Ajax A legendary Greek hero, son of Telamon, King of Salamis. Described in Homer's *Iliad* as great in stature and in courage, he fought *Hector in single combat. He became insane with rage after being defeated by Odysseus in the contest for the armour of the dead *Achilles. *Sophocles' play *Ajax* depicts the hero recovering his sanity, only to be driven by shame to suicide.

Ajmer (Ajmere *or* Ajmir) 26 29N 74 40E A city in India, in Rajasthan. It contains the white marble tomb of a Muslim saint and a Mogul palace. A focal point of road and rail routes, it is a commercial and industrial centre. Population (1981 est): 375 593.

Akashic records The "pictures" of all past events, emotions, and thoughts, believed by occultists to be retained in supersensory fluid called Akasha. Clairvoyants and mediums claim to have access to these records.

Akbar (I) the Great (1542-1605) The third Mogul emperor (1556-1605). After establishing his authority, Akbar embarked on the extension of his rule over all N India by a series of military campaigns in Punjab, Rajput, Gujarat, Bengal, Kashmir, and Sind. Late in his reign he conquered the Deccan, further to the south. As ruler he was noted for his able administration, the development of trade, reforms of taxation, the abolition of extortion, and his tolerance towards non-Muslims. *See also* Mogul art.

Akhenaton (*or* Ikhnaton) King of Egypt (1379-1362 BC) of the 18th dynasty, one of whose wives was *Nefertiti. He replaced the traditional *Amon cult with the monotheistic worship of the sun god, *Aton, and built a new capital Akhetaton (*see* Tell el-Amarna). Internal disorder during his reign enabled the Hittite king, *Suppiluliumas, to remove N Syria from Egyptian control.

Akhmatova, Anna (Anna Andreevna Gorenko; 1889-1966) Russian poet. Her first books, *Evening* (1912) and *Beads* (1914), consisting chiefly of short, intensely lyrical, love poems, were immediately successful. She was married to Nikolai Gumiliov (1886-1921), founder of *acmeism, from 1910 until 1918. After the Revolution she wrote on public as well as personal themes, but her essential style remained unchanged. Her works were banned from 1922 until 1940, and she was again denounced in 1946. In the 1960s, however, her work was restored to favour.

Akiba ben Joseph (died c. 135 AD) One of the outstanding teachers of early rabbinic Judaism. He came to scholarship late in life, but became a master of biblical interpretation and law. He supported the revolt of *Bar Kokhba and was martyred by the Romans.

Akkad The capital city and dynastic name of a S Mesopotamian kingdom established about 2300 BC, N of *Sumer. Akkad, the site of which is still unidentified, was founded by *Sargon, who extended his rule over most of Mesopotamia. The Semitic language of Akkad, Old

Akkadian, spread to much of the Middle East, developing later into the languages of both *Babylonia and *Assyria. About 2150 BC, barbarian invasions brought about Akkad's decline and the short-lived reascendancy of *Ur.

Akola 20 40N 77 05E A town in W India, in Maharashtra. It is an educational and commercial centre. Population (1981 est): 176 385.

Akron 41 04N 81 31W A city in the USA, in Ohio. It is the main centre of the US rubber industry, specializing in tyres; other industries include plastics and chemicals. Its university was established in 1870. Population (1980): 231 177.

aksak A type of musical metre, found in the vigorous asymmetrical dance rhythms of the E Mediterranean, deriving from Turkish sources. *Bartók recorded examples of these rhythms in Bulgaria and named them Bulgarian rhythms.

Aksum (or Axum) 14 05N 38 40E An ancient town in N Ethiopia. It was capital of the Christian Aksumite Empire (1st–6th centuries AD). According to tradition, the *Ark of the Covenant was brought here from Jerusalem. The old town is now a popular tourist attraction.

Aktyubinsk 53 43N 91 25E A city in the S Soviet Union, in the Kazakh SSR on the River Ilek. Founded (1869) as a Russian fort, it is now an important industrial centre. Population (1981 est): 205 000.

Akureyri 65 41N 18 04W A town in N central Iceland, on Eyja Fjord. It is an important trading and cultural centre; industries include fishing and textiles. Population (1980 est): 13 420.

Alabama A state in the SE USA, on the Gulf of Mexico. Except for the forested uplands in the NE it consists of an undulating plain, drained by the Alabama and Tombigbee Rivers. The iron and steel industry, based on deposits of iron ore, coal, and limestone around the state's largest city, Birmingham, is the most important industry. Other industries include the production of oil, metal goods, chemicals, plastics, and defence and space projects. Mobile on the coast is an important seaport. Cotton production in the central Black Belt has decreased since the boll weevil blight (1915) but remains a principal crop along with peanuts, soya beans, wheat, and maize; the raising of cattle and poultry is also important. Although one of the poorest states because of its depressed agriculture, it has a rich rural culture particularly among its large Black community. *History*: first explored by the Spanish in the 16th century, it passed to the British (1763) following disputes with the Spanish and French. In 1783 it came under US control and with an area to the S added in the Louisiana Purchase (1803) became a state in 1819. New settlers established large cotton plantations based on slave labour and following secession from the Union (1861), the state sent most of its White male population to fight againt the N. The period since its readmittance (1868) has been marked by troubled race relations between the White and Black communities. During the last three decades there have been many civil-rights protests, including the *Montgomery bus boycott (1955–56). Area: 133 677 sq km (51 609 sq mi). Population (1980): 3 893 888. Capital: Montgomery.

Alabama claims Compensation claimed by the US Government from Britain for damage caused by the *Alabama* and other warships of the *Confederate states in the Civil War (1861–65). Britain was accused of violating its neutrality by allowing these ships to be built or equipped in its shipyards. In 1871 the dispute was referred to arbitration by Italy, Switzerland, and Brazil. Britain was found liable and ordered to pay £3 million. This was the first major settlement of an international dispute by arbitration.

alabaster A pure fine-grained form of *gypsum. It is white or delicately shaded and often translucent and attractively veined. It has long been worked ornamentally, for carvings, etc., but weathers too easily for external use. The alabaster of Volterra,

Tuscany, is well known.

Alain-Fournier (Henri-Alban Fournier; 1886–1914) French novelist. The son of a country schoolmaster, he became a literary journalist in Paris and was killed in World War I. The mood of his one completed novel, *Le Grand Meaulnes* (1913), is nostalgic and almost mystical; set in the French countryside of his childhood, it describes a young man's search for a girl he has glimpsed only briefly.

Alamo, the A mission in the USA, in San Antonio, Texas. During the Texas revolution it was defended from 24 Feb until 6 March, 1836, by less than 200 Texan volunteers (including the legendary Davy Crockett), who were all massacred during the onslaught of 4000 Mexican troops led by Santa Anna. Six weeks later a victory at San Jacinto secured Texan independence.

Alamogordo 32 54N 105 57W A town in the USA, in S New Mexico. The first atom bomb was exploded in a test near here on 16 July, 1945. Population (1980): 24 024.

Alanbrooke, Alan Francis Brooke, 1st Viscount (1883–1963) British field marshal. He joined the Royal Field Artillery in 1902, serving as a staff officer in World War I. In World War II, after service in France, he became commander in chief of the home forces. Appointed Chief of the Imperial General Staff in 1941, he advised Churchill at all his conferences with Roosevelt and Stalin.

Åland Islands (Finnish name: Ahvenanmaa Islands) A group of over 6000 islands and islets under Finnish administration, at the entrance to the Gulf of Bothnia. Population (1982): 23 196. Capital: Mariehamn.

Alarcón, Pedro Antonio de (1833–91) Spanish novelist. He began his career as a poet and journalist, but his literary reputation is based on his later novels, especially *The Three-Cornered Hat* (1874), which was used by Manuel de *Falla as the basis for a ballet.

Alarcón y Mendoza, Juan Ruiz de (1581–1639) Spanish dramatist. Born in Mexico, he became one of the leading dramatists of the Golden Age of Spanish drama. His best-known play is *La verdad sospechosa* (?1619), a satirical comedy. He apparently ceased to write after being appointed to the Council for the Indies in 1626.

Alaric I (c. 370–410 AD) King of the *Visigoths. Alaric served in the Roman army as the commander of the Gothic auxiliary forces before his election as King of the Visigoths. After failing to reach a peaceful agreement with the Roman imperial administration, he invaded Greece and Italy. Alaric died shortly after his forces sacked Rome (410).

Alaska The largest state in the USA, occupying the extreme NW corner of the North American continent. It is a mountainous volcanic area, rising over 6000 m (20 000 ft) to Mount McKinley, the highest peak in North America. There are numerous rivers, chief of which is the Yukon flowing W into the Bering Sea. It has an indented coastline with many islands. One third of state lies within the Arctic Circle. The economy is based principally on the state's rich mineral wealth. The discovery of oil (1950) and subsequent finds (1968) have made oil production the major industry and there are rich supplies of natural gas. Coal, gold, and copper are mined. Fishing, especially salmon, and forestry are also major industries. Agricultural development is hindered by the short growing season and severe climate. Fur trapping has declined in importance although sealskins (from the offshore Pribilof Islands) remain an important export. Conflict between further development and the preservation of the natural landscape has become a major problem. *History*: first settled by Russians following voyages by the Dane, Vitus Bering (1728, 1741), it was under the trade control of the Russian American company until 1867 when it was purchased by the USA (it became known as Seward's Folly after the secretary of state who had led the negotiations). A number of gold rushes in the late 19th century helped to swell the sparse population. It became the 49th state in 1959. Area: 1 518 800 sq km (586 412 sq mi). Population (1980): 401 851. Capital: Juneau.

Alaska Highway A road from Dawson Creek, Canada to Fairbanks, Alaska, built for defence against Japan (1942). Open throughout the year, it now serves tourism and economic development. Length: 2437 km (1523 mi).

Alaskan malamute. See husky.

Alastor In Greek legend, the son of Neleus and brother of Nestor, killed by Heracles on the island of Pylos. The name was also applied to the personified spirit of vengeance that could possess a man.

Alba, Fernando Alvarez de Toledo, Duke of (or Alva; 1507–83) Spanish general, who successfully commanded Habsburg forces against Protestants in Germany and the French in Italy. Philip II of Spain placed him in command of the Netherlands (1567–73), where his ruthless attempts to subdue the Dutch Protestants made him very unpopular, both in Spain and the Netherlands, and led to his recall. He led the successful expedition against Portugal (1580–81). See also Revolt of the Netherlands.

Albacete 39 00N 1 52W A city in SE central Spain, in Murcia. A market centre, it is famous for the manufacture of cutlery and daggers. Its notable buildings include the 16th-century cathedral. Population (1981): 117 126.

albacore A fast-swimming *tuna fish, Thunnus alalunga, found in warm seas. Up to 1 m long, it has very long pectoral fins. It is the chief source of tuna for canning.

Alba-Iulia (German name: Karlsburg) 46 04N 23 33E A town in W central Romania, on the River Mureş. A former capital of Transylvania, its manufactures include leather goods and wine. Population (1983): 56 625.

Alban, St (3rd century AD) The first English martyr. A pagan soldier, he protected a Christian priest and was converted by him. On admitting this to the Roman authorities, he was scourged and beheaded on a site subsequently dedicated to him as the Abbey of St Albans. Feast day: 22 or 17 June. Emblem: a stag.

Albania, Socialist People's Republic of (Albanian name: Shqiperia) A country in SE Europe, occupying part of the Balkan Peninsula on the Adriatic Sea. It consists of a mountainous interior, rising to over 2700 m (9000 ft), with extensive forests and fertile coastal lowlands. The people, of whose origins little is known, belong to two main groups, the *Ghegs (N of the River Shkumbi) and the *Tosks (S). Economy: mainly agricultural, organized into state farms and collectives, although industrial development is increasing (the principal industries being agricultural processing, textiles, oil products, and cement). There have been recent attempts to develop the rich mineral resources, especially oil, lignite, copper, chromium, limestone, salt, and bauxite, as well as the rich natural-gas deposits. Main exports include crude oil, bitumen, chrome ore, copper wire, tobacco, fruit, and vegetables. History: became independent in 1912 after more than four centuries of Turkish rule. Following a civil war, in which Italy intervened, Albania became a republic in 1925 and a monarchy in 1928, when its president, Ahmed Beg Zogu (1895–1961), was proclaimed as King Zog. After occupation by Italy and Germany during World War II, another republic was set up in 1946, with a communist-controlled assembly. It aligned itself with the Soviet Union but after the death of Stalin relations between the two countries weakened and in 1961 diplomatic relations were broken off. Meanwhile Albania, alone of the East European communist states, maintained close relations with China. Enver *Hoxha, as first party secretary, was executive leader from 1946 to 1985. Head of state: Ramiz Alia (1925–). Official language: Albanian. Currency: lek of 100 qintars. Area: 28 748 sq km (11 101 sq mi). Population (1981 est): 2 800 000. Capital: Tirana. Main port: Durrës.

Albanian An Indo-European language, the only modern representative of a distinct branch of this linguistic group, spoken by two million Albanians and known by them as Shqiptar. It is divided into two main dialects, *Gheg and *Tosk.

Albany 42 40N 73 49W A city in the USA, the capital of New York state on the Hudson River. Founded in 1614 by the Dutch, it is one of North America's oldest cities and has several notable public buildings, including the state capitol (1879). Economic growth accelerated with the building of the Erie Canal (1825) and today its main manufactures are electrical goods, textiles, dental goods, chemicals, and building materials. Population (1980): 101 727.

Albany 34 57S 117 54E A port in SW Western Australia, on King George Sound. Industries include fish and meat canning. Population (1983 est): 13 940.

ALBATROSS The waved albatross (Diomedea irrorata) breeds on the Galápagos Islands.

albatross A large seabird belonging to a family (Diomedeidae; 14 species) that occurs mainly in southern oceans. It has a stout hooked bill; usually a white or brown plumage, often with darker markings on the back, wings, or tail; and very long narrow wings (the wandering albatross, Diomedea exulans, has the largest wingspan of any bird, reaching up to 3.5 m). Albatrosses can glide for hours over the open sea, feeding on squids and cuttlefish; they come ashore only to breed. Order: Procellariiformes (see petrels).

albedo A measure of the reflecting power of a nonluminous object, such as a planet or natural satellite or a surface feature on such a body. It is the ratio of the amount of light reflected in all directions from the object to the amount of incident light. Clouds, snow, and ice have high albedos while volcanic rocks have very low albedos.

Albee, Edward (1928–) US dramatist. His early one-act plays, notably Zoo Story (1958) and The Death of Bessie Smith (1960), analyse contemporary social tensions using techniques of the *Theatre of the Absurd. His first three-act play, Who's Afraid of Virginia Woolf? (1962), which dramatizes the love-hate relationship of an academic couple, was very successful. Later plays include A Delicate Balance (1967, Pulitzer Prize) and Seascape (1975).

Albéniz, Isaac Manuel Francisco (1860–1909) Spanish composer and pianist. A child prodigy, he frequently ran away from home, giving recitals in North and South America and Europe. He began serious composition after studying with d'Indy and Dukas in Paris. His works include operas, songs, and *Iberia* (1906–09), a collection of 12 piano pieces.

Alberoni, Giulio (1664–1752) Spanish-Italian cardinal and statesman, who rose to prominence during the War of the Spanish succession. In 1713 he was appointed consular agent for Parma at the court of Philip V of Spain and in 1715 became prime minister of Spain and a cardinal. An ambitious foreign policy, which angered England, France, and Holland, resulted in his banishment to Italy (1719).

Albers, Josef (1888–1976) German abstract painter, designer, and poet. His successful career as an influential art teacher and theoretician began at the *Bauhaus school of design and after 1933 continued in the USA, where he painted a famous series of abstract paintings entitled *Homage to the Square*.

Albert I (1875–1934) King of the Belgians (1909–34). As commander in chief of the Belgian army, Albert led his country's heroic but unsuccessful resistance to the German invasion (1914) and contributed to the Allied victory in World War I. After the war he did much to encourage industrial reconstruction and currency reform.

Albert (I) the Bear (?1100–70) The first Margrave of Brandenburg (1150–70), who took the title following conquests that brought him Havelland in E Europe. Further campaigns extended his territories, in which he sponsored land-reclamation schemes and missionary work.

Albert II Alcibiades (1522–57) Margrave of Brandenburg, prominent in the conflict between Emperor Charles V and the German Protestants. A Protestant, he nevertheless supported Charles until 1551, when he turned his coat and joined Maurice of Saxony and the French. Defeated by Charles' brother Ferdinand, in 1553, he was outlawed and fled to France.

Albert III (1443–1500) Duke of Saxony jointly with his brother Ernest (1441–86) from 1464 until 1485, when the Saxon lands were divided between them. He campaigned for the Holy Roman Emperor and in 1488–89 restored imperial authority in Holland, Flanders, and Brabant. He died while repressing a rebellion in Friesland, where he was governor (1498–1500).

Albert, Lake. *See* Mobutu, Lake.

Albert, Prince (1819–61) Prince Consort of the United Kingdom and younger son of Ernest I, Duke of Saxe-Coburg-Gotha. In 1840 he married his cousin Queen Victoria and became her chief adviser. Although he was initially unpopular, his devotion to duty and his active patronage of the arts, science, and industry eventually won him respect. He is perhaps best remembered for his organization of the *Great Exhibition (1851). He died of typhoid.

Alberta A province of W Canada, mostly on the Great Plains. It consists mainly of a plateau, rising to the foothills of the *Rocky Mountains in the SW. The undulating S prairie and parkland further N support profitable ranches and grain farms. Alberta is Canada's largest oil and gas producer, possesses vast coalfields, and includes the Athabasca tar sands, one of the world's largest oil reserves (at present untapped). Manufacturing is based on agriculture and mineral resources. Lumbering, construction, and tourism are also important. *History*: first explored in the 18th century, Alberta became Canadian territory in 1869. The arrival of the railway from E Canada (1883) facilitated agricultural settlement, and Alberta grew rapidly (especially 1900–14), becoming a province in 1905. Alberta's government tends to be controlled by one party for long periods, notably by the Social Credit Party (1935–71). Area: 644 389 sq km (248 799 sq mi). Population (1981 est): 2 237 724. Capital: Edmonton.

Albert Canal A canal in Belgium, completed in 1939. It links the River Meuse at Liège with the River Scheldt at Antwerp. Length: 130 km (80 mi).

LEON BATTISTA ALBERTI *The west front of Sta Maria Novella (Florence).*

Alberti, Leon Battista (1404–72) Italian Renaissance architect. Alberti, who was also a painter, writer, musician, and scientist, is known mainly for being among the first Renaissance architects fully to grasp the principles of classical architecture. As his innovative façade of Sta Maria Novella in Florence demonstrates, he adapted these rules to 15th-century requirements. He built relatively little, his most significant buildings being the churches of S Sebastiano and S Andrea in Mantua and the incomplete Tempio Malatestiano in Rimini. His abiding influence upon architecture was through his treatise *De re aedificatoria* (*On Architecture*; 1452), which was translated into several European languages in the 16th century.

Alberti, Raphael (1902–) Spanish poet. Born into a poor branch of a respectable Catholic family, he rebelled against his family and his Jesuit education. His first collection of poems, *Marineo en tierra* (1924), won the National Prize for Literature. In 1927 he suffered a mental breakdown, an experience analysed in *Sobre los ángeles* (1929). In 1931 he became a communist and after the Civil War exiled himself to Argentina.

Albert of Brandenburg (1490–1545) German churchman, Cardinal Archbishop and Elector of Mainz. Although a religious liberal, a patron of the arts, and a friend of *Erasmus, he is chiefly remembered as the object of Luther's attacks for his sale of indulgences. In later life he supported the *Counter-Reformation.

Albertsville. *See* Kalemie.

Albertus Magnus, St (c. 1200–80) German bishop, philosopher, and Doctor of the Church. Provincial of the German Dominicans (1254–57) and for a short time Bishop of Regensburg, he taught constantly throughout his life. His best-known pupil was *Aquinas. An outstanding scholar, he wrote extensively on logic, natural and moral sciences, scripture, and theology. Feast day: 15 Nov.

Albi 43 56N 2 08E A town in S France, the capital of the Tarn department on the River Tarn. A centre of Catharism, it gave its name to the Albigensian heresy (*see* Albigenses). Notable buildings include the gothic cathedral and the 13th-century archbishop's palace, which is now a museum housing works by Toulouse-Lautrec (a native of Albi). An agricultural market, it has textile, glass, and cement industries. Population (1982 est): 48 341.

Albigenses Followers of the Christian heresy of Catharism (*see* Cathari), who flourished in southern France in the 12th and 13th centuries. The Albigenses, named after the town of Albi in Languedoc, were the object of the Albigensian Crusade, launched in 1208 and led by the father of Simon de *Montfort. They were finally suppressed by the Inquisition, which operated in the area from 1233.

albinism An inherited disorder in which tyrosinase, one of the enzymes required for the formation of the pigment *melanin, is absent. Albinos have abnormally pale skin, fair hair, and pink or light-blue irises. The condition can be eased by the use of spectacles to treat the lens abnormalities common in albinos and by protection of the skin and eyes from direct sunlight. Albinism, which can affect all human races, is also seen in wild and domestic animals.

Albino horse A horse exhibiting the characteristics of albinism and bred to maintain the colour type. Albinos have pinkish sensitive skin, pure-white hair, and blue eyes. Defective eyesight is common, lessening its usefulness as a riding horse.

Albinoni, Tomaso (1671-1750) Italian composer and court musician to the Duke of Mantua. His works, which influenced J. S. Bach, include 50 operas, a violin concerto, and two oboe concertos. The *Adagio* for organ and strings often attributed to Albinoni was in fact composed by his Italian biographer Remo Giazotto (1910-   ) and incorporates a fragment of a bass part by Albinoni.

Alboin (died c. 573) King of the Lombards (c. 565-c. 573). He succeeded to lands in central Europe and then conquered N Italy, establishing the kingdom of Lombardy (572), with his capital at Pavia.

Ålborg (*or* Aalborg) 57 03N 09 56E A city and seaport in Denmark, in N Jutland. Founded in 1342 AD, it has a gothic cathedral and a 16th-century castle. A university was established in 1974. Its industries include shipbuilding and textiles. Population (1981 est): 154 385.

albumins A class of proteins that are soluble in both water and dilute aqueous salt solutions. Serum albumins are constituents of blood; ß-lactalbumin is found in milk; and ovalbumin is part of egg white. Preparations of albumins are used in therapeutic transfusions.

Albuquerque 35 05N 106 38W A city in the USA, in New Mexico on the Rio Grande. The state's largest city, it is situated in a rich agricultural area and food canning and the manufacture of livestock products are its principal industries. It is the home of the University of New Mexico (1892). Population (1980): 331 767.

Albuquerque, Alfonso de (1453-1515) Portuguese governor in India (1509-15). He was already a veteran soldier when he led his first expedition to India (1503). By a series of conquests he established Portuguese influence in the Indian Ocean based on three strongholds—Goa, Ceylon, and Malacca. He led the first European fleet to sail into the Red Sea and took Hormuz in 1515. Private enemies at the Portuguese court sought to discredit him and he was recalled, dying at sea.

Albury 36 03S 146 53E A city in Australia, in New South Wales on the Murray River. Designated a growth area as part of the state's decentralization plans, Albury is an important trading centre with engineering, clothing, and food-processing industries. Population (1983): 38 650.

Al Bu Sa'id The ruling dynasty of Oman since 1749 and of Zanzibar from 1749 to 1964. In 1749 Ahmad ibn Sa'id, the dynasty's founder, seized power over Oman and Zanzibar. In 1856 Oman and Zanzibar were divided. Zanzibar continued under Bu Sa'idi rule under the British protectorate (1890-1963) but the dynasty was overthrown when Zanzibar

was incorporated into Tanzania (1964). The present ruler of Oman is Qaboos ibn Sa'id.

Alcaeus (6th century BC) Greek lyric poet. A member of the aristocracy of the island of Lesbos and a friend of *Sappho, he went into exile when the tyrant Pittacus gained power and wandered for many years in Thrace and Egypt. His work, only fragments of which survive, was greatly admired by *Horace.

Alcántara 39 44N 6 53W A town in W Spain in Estremadura. A magnificent Roman bridge (105 AD) spans the River Tagus here. Population (1981): 2317.

Alcatraz An island in the USA, in W California in San Francisco Bay. It was the site of a notorious maximum security prison from 1934 until 1962.

alcázar (Arabic *al-qasr*: castle, palace) A Spanish fortress built during the conflicts between Moors and Christians in the 14th and 15th centuries. The most renowned is the Alcázar of *Seville, built by King *Pedro the Cruel. The word remains an element in certain placenames, e.g. Alcázar de San Juan.

Alcázar de San Juan 39 42N 3 12W A town in S central Spain, in New Castile on La Mancha plain. It is associated with Cervantes' *Don Quixote.* Population (1981): 25 185.

alchemy A pseudoscience combining practical *chemistry with magical or mystical views of man and his relationship to the universe. Originating independently in China and Egypt, probably before the 3rd century BC, alchemy remained a legitimate branch of science and philosophy in Asia, Europe, and the Islamic lands for over 1500 years and is the ancestor of modern chemistry. It had three principal goals, the emphasis on which varied from place to place: the elixir of life (to ensure immortality), the panacea (or universal medicine), and the means of transmuting base metals into gold (*see* philosopher's stone). In China, *Taoism, which highly esteemed long life, fostered alchemical experimentation in search of the elixir. In Europe, concentration upon gold-making brought alchemy into disrepute.

Alcibiades (c. 450-404 BC) Athenian general and politician. Brought up by *Pericles, he was the pupil and lover of *Socrates. Alcibiades encouraged Athenian imperialism during the *Peloponnesian War (431-404) until, accused of desecrating monuments in Athens, he defected to Sparta (415). He regained Athenian favour (410) and was a successful commander until defeat, the fault of a subordinate, forced him into exile (406). He was murdered in Phrygia.

Alcmaeon (c. 500 BC) Greek pioneer in medical science, from Croton (S Italy). Following *Pythagoras' experimental tradition, Alcmaeon used dissection and vivisection to investigate human sense organs. He discovered the optic nerve and located the centre of sensation in the brain.

Alcmaeon In Greek mythology, the son of Amphiarus, one of the *Seven Against Thebes, and Eriphyle. He killed his mother to avenge the death of Amphiarus, and was pursued by the Furies. His first wife was Arsinoë, daughter of King Pegeus of Psophis, but on his wanderings he married the daughter of the river god Achelous, and was pursued and killed by Pegeus and his sons. His own sons later avenged his death by killing Pegeus.

Alcmaeonids An aristocratic family prominent in virtually all ancient Athenian political crises, usually on the radical side. In 632 BC Megacles (an Alcmaeonid) violated the sanctuary of Athena by having a political opponent treacherously murdered there. The oracle of Delphi placed a hereditary curse on the family, banishing it from Athens. The Alcmaeonids returned under Solon, withdrew under Pisistratus, and returned again after the expulsion of Hippias (511/510 BC). *Cleisthenes was an Alcmaeonid; *Pericles and *Alcibiades had Alcmaeonid mothers.

Alcock, Sir John (William) (1892-1919) British aviator. He served with the Royal Naval Air Service in World War I and in 1919, accompanied by **(Sir) Arthur Brown** (1886-1948), was the first to fly the Atlantic Ocean. They flew a Vickers-Vimy from St John's, Newfoundland, to Clifden, Co Galway, in 16 hours 27 minutes. A few months later Alcock was killed in a flying accident.

Alcock Convention (1869) A treaty between Britain and China, drawn up by Sir Rutherford Alcock (1809-1907) but not ratified owing largely to the objections of British merchants. It intended that Britain would lose its most-favoured-nation relationship with China, gained after the second *Opium War, in return for tax concessions and freedom to navigate China's waterways.

Alcoforado, Marianna (1640-1723) Portuguese nun. She was long mistakenly believed to be the author of a famous series of five love letters written to a French officer who had deserted the author and who was also wrongly identified as Noël Bouton (1636-1715), Comte de Chamilly and Marshal of France. The letters, published as *Lettres portugaises* (1669), were in fact the work of the Vicomte de Guilleragues (d. 1685), who until recently was believed to have been only the translator. The title of the book was referred to in that of the feminist *New Portuguese Letters* (1972) by the so-called Three Marias (Maria Isabel Barreno, Maria Teresa Horta, and Maria Velho da Costa), who were then imprisoned until the revolution of 1974.

Alcoholics Anonymous A voluntary organization started in the USA in 1934 to help alcoholics to help themselves. Members, who must have an honest desire to stop drinking, help one another on the basis of group therapy by sharing their experiences of alcoholism. There are local autonomous groups in over 90 countries, including the UK, which has more than 950 groups. An associated organization, AL-ANON, provides support for the close relatives of alcoholics.

alcoholism An illness caused by physical and psychological dependence on alcohol (*see also* drug dependence). The incidence of alcoholism varies between different societies: it is most common in countries where alcohol is readily available and where heavy drinking is socially acceptable. Alcoholism causes mood changes, deterioration in personal standards and habits, and periods of memory loss. Continued heavy consumption will eventually lead to cirrhosis of the liver, heart disease, and damage to the nerves. Sudden withdrawal may produce specific symptoms: tremor, delusions, and hallucinations. Treatment, which is lengthy and difficult, includes initial alcohol withdrawal (with appropriate sedation) accompanied and followed by adequate psychological support. Drugs such as disulfiram (Antabuse), which cause vomiting after drinking alcohol, may assist the treatment. Nonmedical solutions to problems of alcoholism include group therapy in the company of other alcoholics (*see* Alcoholics Anonymous).

alcohols The class of organic compounds that includes *ethanol (ethyl alcohol; C_2H_5OH) and *methanol (methyl alcohol; CH_3OH). Ethanol is the common alcohol found in intoxicating drinks and is often called simply "alcohol." Alcohols contain at least one hydroxyl group and have the general formula ROH, where R is a *hydrocarbon group. They react with *acids to give *esters and water. Primary alcohols oxidize to form *aldehydes and secondary alcohols to form *ketones.

alcohol strength The measurement of the percentage volume of *ethanol (ethyl alcohol) in alcoholic drinks in order to calculate government duty on them. In the USA, 100° proof is 50% alcohol by volume. Until January, 1980, the UK used a similar system for spirits, but with 57.06%, measured at 15°C, as the standard (100° proof), pure alcohol being 175° proof. France and Italy formerly used the Gay-Lussac scale, which simply states the percentage volume of alcohol, measured at 15°C. The **OMIL** (International Organization of Legal Metrology) system, now used throughout the EEC, is based on percentage volume of alcohol at 20°C. Thus a bottle of spirits labelled in the EEC "35% vol" is approximately equivalent to 61° proof in the former UK system or 70° proof in the US system.

In most taxation systems distilled spirits and fermented liquors containing more than 23% alcohol are taxed on the volume of alcohol present. Beers and wines, on the other hand, are taxed on the volume of drink, the rate of duty depending on the alcohol content—progressively higher strength bands commanding a higher rate.

Alcott, Louisa May (1832-88) US novelist. Daughter of the social theorist Bronson Alcott, her education was supplemented by instruction from *Thoreau, *Emerson, and her neighbour Nathaniel *Hawthorne. Her first book, *Flower Fables* (1854), was written when she was 16 to raise money for her family. *Hospital Sketches* (1863) recounted her experiences as a nurse in the Civil War. *Little Women* (1868-69), her most famous book, was largely autobiographical. Other works include *An Old-Fashioned Girl* (1870), *Little Men* (1871), and *Jo's Boys* (1886).

Alcuin (c. 735-804 AD) English theologian and educator, who inspired the Carolingian renaissance. Born at York and educated at the cathedral school, he became the religious and educational adviser to Charlemagne after meeting him in 781. He established important libraries and developed a method of teaching based on *Boethius, St *Augustine, and the study of grammar. Among his pupils was Rabanus Maurus (c. 780-856). He compiled numerous educational manuals and was also a poet. His letters are important sources for the study of Carolingian society.

Aldabra Islands 9 45S 46 22E An atoll in the W Indian Ocean. Formerly administered from the Seychelles, they were part of the British Indian Ocean Territory from 1965 to 1976. There are no permanent inhabitants and the wildlife, notably the giant tortoise, is protected.

Aldanov, Mark (M. Aleksandrovich Landau; 1886-1957) Russian novelist. He emigrated to France in 1919 and to the USA in 1941. His best-known work is a trilogy about Revolutionary France, comprising *Saint Helena* (1924), *The Ninth Thermidor* (1926), and *The Devil's Bridge* (1928). *The Fifth Seal* (1936) was an anti-Soviet satire and *The Tenth Symphony* (1931), a portrait of Beethoven's Vienna.

Aldebaran A conspicuous *red giant, apparent magnitude 0.9 and 68 light years distant, that is the brightest star in the constellation Taurus. It is both a visual *binary star and an irregular *variable star.

Aldeburgh 52 9N 1 35E A small resort in SE England in Suffolk. Once an important port, it is now famous for its annual music festival established in 1948 by Benjamin *Britten, who lived here. It is the birthplace of the poet, George *Crabbe, and Dr Elizabeth Garrett *Anderson was elected the first woman mayor in England here in 1908. Population (1981): 2911.

aldehydes A class of organic chemicals that contain the -CHO group. They are prepared by the oxidation of alcohols and are themselves oxidized to form carboxylic acids. Common aldehydes are *formaldehyde and *acetaldehyde.

alder A tree or shrub belonging to a genus (*Alnus*; about 30 species) of the N hemisphere. The leaves are roundish and toothed; the flowers grow as separate male and female catkins on the same tree. The fruit is a woody cone containing small winged nuts. The black alder (*A. glutinosa*), about 20 m high, is found in wet places throughout Europe and Asia and in N Africa. Its timber is used in general turnery. Family: *Betulaceae* (birch family).

alderfly An insect, also known as a fish fly, having two pairs of delicate finely veined wings and long antennae. Up to 50 mm long (including the wings), alderflies live near fresh water, feeding on smaller insects and laying their eggs on reeds. The larvae, which are also carnivorous, live in the water and crawl out to pupate in burrows in the soil. Family: *Sialidae*; order: *Neuroptera* (lacewings, etc.).

alderman In the UK, senior members of the major local authorities, normally elected by the directly elected members, until the Local Government Act (1972) abolished the office as an active rank except in the *City of London. The term derives from the Anglo-Saxon local official—the ealdorman. In the USA, many cities call their local-government officers aldermen but their powers vary from city to city.

Aldermaston 51 23N 1 09W A village in S England, in Berkshire. It is associated with protest marches (1958–63) organized by the *Campaign for Nuclear Disarmament and is the site of the Atomic Weapons Research Establishment. Population (1987 est): 2157.

Alderney (French name: Aurigny) 49 43N 2 12W The third largest of the Channel Islands, separated from France by the dangerous Race of Alderney channel. Its economy is based on dairy farming and tourism. Area: 8 sq km (3 sq mi). Population (1980 est): 2000. Chief town: St Anne.

Aldershot 51 15N 0 47W A town in S England, in Hampshire. It is the chief garrison town and army training centre in the UK. Population (1981): 32 654.

Aldhelm, St (c. 640–709 AD) English abbot and bishop. Abbot of Malmesbury from about 675, he became Bishop of Sherborne about 705. He founded several churches and monasteries. His Latin writings include various treatises, a work on saints, and religious poems. Feast day: 25 May.

Aldington, Richard (1892–1962) British poet, novelist, and biographer. In 1913 he married his fellow Imagist poet Hilda *Doolittle. He suffered shell shock in World War I; *Death of a Hero* (1929), *The Colonel's Daughter* (1931), and other novels mirrored postwar anger and disillusion. Among his frequently controversial biographies are studies of D. H. Lawrence (1950) and T. E. Lawrence (1955).

Aldiss, Brian W(ilson) (1925–) British novelist, best known for his science fiction. He was president of the British Science Fiction Association (1960–64) and has written a history of the genre, *Trillion Year Spree* (1986). Editor of many science-fiction anthologies, his individual collections include *The Saliva Tree* (1966) and *Last Orders* (1977).

aldol An organic compound that contains a *hydroxyl group (OH) and an *aldehyde group (CHO) bound to adjacent carbon atoms. **Acetaldol** ($CH_3CHOHCH_2CHO$) is used as a sedative and hypnotic drug.

aldosterone A steroid hormone that acts on the kidney tubules to regulate the content of salts and water in the body. Derived from cholesterol, aldosterone is produced by the cortex of the adrenal glands in response to changing blood volume, changing levels of sodium and potassium, and the presence of the pituitary hormone *ACTH.

Aldrich, Thomas Bailey (1836–1907) US short story writer and poet. He left school at 13 and began writing for magazines while working in New York as a clerk. He is also known for his autobiography, *The Story of a Bad Boy* (1870).

Aldridge, Ira Frederick (1804–67) US actor. The first great Black tragedian, he made his debut as Othello in London in 1826 and toured Europe in Shakespearian roles. He became a naturalized British citizen in 1863.

Aldridge-Brownhills A town in Central England, in the metropolitan county of West Midlands. Formed by the amalgamation of neighbouring towns in 1966, it is a developing industrial centre. Population (1981): 87 219.

Aldrin, Jr, Edwin Eugene (1930–) US astronaut, the second man to walk on the moon. Known as "Buzz", he was an air force pilot during the Korean War before becoming an astronaut in 1963. He undertook a 5½-hour spacewalk in 1966 and was lunar module pilot (under Neil *Armstrong) in Apollo 11 when it made the first moon landing in 1969.

ale. *See* beer.

aleatoric music Music that incorporates elements of chance in its structure. The term from Latin *alea*, a game of dice, was first used in the 1950s to describe John *Cage's experiments in determining compositional procedures of pitch, rhythm, structure, and dynamics by the use of the *I Ching.

Alegría, Ciro (1909–61) Peruvian novelist, imprisoned and finally exiled to Chile and the USA from 1934 until 1948 for his political activities. His works embody his deep knowledge of, and sympathy for, the Peruvian Indians: his best-known novel, *Broad and Alien Is the World* (1941), deals with the resistance of an Indian tribe to the usurping White man.

Alekhine, Alexander (1892–1946) French chess player, born in Russia. He became world champion by defeating *Capablanca (1927), losing the championship in 1935, but holding it again from 1937 until his death. He regarded chess as an art, the aesthetic merits of which were more important to him than winning.

Alemán, Mateo (1547–?1614) Spanish writer, famous for his picaresque novel *Guzman de Alfarache* (1599–1604), the scurrilous adventures of a youth who runs away from home and is finally condemned to the galleys, where he repents. The book became popular throughout Europe. Alemán himself was often imprisoned for debt and emigrated to Mexico in 1607.

Alençon 48 25N 0 05E A town in NW France, the capital of the Orne department situated at the confluence of the Rivers Sarthe and Briant. The former capital of the duchy of Alençon, it is famed for its lace (especially point d'Alençon). It serves an agricultural area. Population (1982 est): 32 526.

Aleppo (Arabic name: Halab) 36 14N 37 10E A town in NW Syria. The Crusaders tried in vain to capture it, and from 1516 to 1919 Aleppo was part of the Ottoman Empire. After World War II, it was incorporated into independent Syria. It is now an industrial centre and the terminus of a pipeline from Iraq; its university was founded in 1960. Population (1982 est): 985 413.

Alessandria 44 55N 8 37E A town in N Italy, in Piedmont on the River Tanaro. It is a railway centre and has an important engineering industry. The surrounding district is agricultural. Population (1980 est): 101 075.

Ålesund (or Aalesund) 62 28N 6 11E A seaport in W Norway. Founded in the 9th century AD, it is an important trading centre, especially for fishing in northern waters. Population (1981 est): 34 630.

Aletsch Glacier The largest glacier in Europe, in Switzerland in the Bernese Oberland lying SE of the Aletschhorn mountain. Length: 26 km (16 mi).

Aleut A native of the Aleutian Islands and W Alaska, similar to the *Eskimo in culture. Aleuts hunted seals, whales, and walrus, using skin-covered boats called bidarkas, which were like *kayaks but often two-manned. They also fished for salmon and in some areas hunted caribou and bear. They produced fine basketry and worked stone, bone, and ivory. Their population was considerably reduced during the Russian administration of the area and today their culture has been much changed by the impact of the modern world. Their language is closely related to Eskimo. It has three dialects, the two principal ones being Attuan and Unalaskan.

Aleutian Islands A chain of volcanic Alaskan islands lying between the Bering Sea and the Pacific Ocean, divided politically between the Soviet Union and the USA. The chief settlements are on Unalaska. Russian exploitation of supplies after 1741 greatly reduced the population, but fishing and seal, otter, and fox hunting are now regulated. There are strategic US military stations on the islands and underground nuclear tests have been made (since 1971).

alewife A small silvery fish, *Pandopus pseudoharengus*, up to 30 cm long. It occurs chiefly in the Atlantic coastal waters of North America but has recently become established in the

Great Lakes. It is an important food fish and is also used in the manufacture of fertilizers. Family: *Clupeidae* (herrings).

Alexander (1876-1903) King of Serbia (1889-1903); the last of the *Obrenović dynasty. Alexander's arbitrary rule, including the abolition of the liberal constitution in 1894, and his unpopular marriage in 1900 led to his assassination, and that of his wife, by a group of army officers.

Alexander I (c. 1077-1124) King of the Scots (1107-24), who ruled the highlands while his brother and successor David ruled the lowlands. He was noted for his reform of the Scottish church and his foundation of the monastery of Scone (1114). He aided Henry I of England's campaign against Wales (1114).

Alexander I (1777-1825) Emperor of Russia (1801-25), succeeding his unstable father Paul I. Alexander made some educational and administrative reforms but was more concerned with foreign policy. France's defeat of Russia at *Friedland in 1807 forced Alexander to agree to the Treaty of *Tilsit, which lasted until Napoleon's unsuccessful invasion of Russia in 1812. After Napoleon's defeat, Russia controlled the *Congress Kingdom of Poland. Alexander turned to religious mysticism, hoping to establish a new Christian order in Europe by means of the Holy Alliance (1815) with Austria and Prussia. Towards the end of his life he withdrew into seclusion.

Alexander II (1198-1249) King of the Scots (1214-49). Hoping to regain the northern counties of England, he supported the unsuccessful *Barons' War (1215-17) against King John. In 1221 he married Joan, the sister of Henry III of England, and gave up his claims to English territory in 1237, when the present border between England and Scotland was fixed.

Alexander II (1818-81) Emperor of Russia (1855-81). After the conclusion of the *Crimean War (1856) Alexander embarked upon a programme of modernization. He emancipated the serfs (1861) and reorganized administration, the army, the judicial system, local government, and education. These reforms were not wholly successful because Alexander lacked personnel able to implement them. He presided over Russian expansion into Central Asia and the victorious war against Turkey (1877-78). The end of his reign saw the growth of radical opposition and he was killed by a bomb thrown into his coach.

ALEXANDER (III) THE GREAT *A detail of a mosaic at Pompeii, which shows Alexander on his horse Bucephalus pursuing the fleeing Darius III (d. 330) of Persia. Alexander's decisive victory was fought at Gaugamela in 331.*

Alexander (III) the Great (356-323 BC) King of Macedon (336-323), who between 334 and his death conquered most of the world known to antiquity. Alexander, who was a pupil of Aristotle, inherited a plan to invade Persia from his father Philip II; having secured his position in Macedon and Greece, he put this plan into action. In 333 he defeated the Persian king Darius III at Issus; in 332 he reduced Tyre in his greatest victory. Alexander then proceeded to conquer Egypt and Babylon (331). Moving on to Media and then east into central Asia, he finally embarked on the Indian expedition (327-325). He crossed the River Indus and conquered the Punjab. Forced to turn back by his reluctant army, he died at Babylon shortly after the marathon return journey. In the administration of his empire Alexander adopted a novel policy of appointing subject races to posts of responsibility, which some historians have called idealism and others, opportunism. His outstanding gifts as a general, however, are indisputable.

Alexander III (Rolando Bandinelli; c. 1105-81) Italian pope. Elected in 1159, he was immediately challenged by the antipope Victor IV, who was supported by *Frederick Barbarossa. He eventually forced Frederick to reconcile himself with the Church at the Peace of Venice in 1177. He imposed penance on *Henry II of England for the murder of Thomas *Becket. He called and presided at the third *Lateran Council, which conferred the exclusive right of papal elections on the cardinals.

Alexander III (1241-86) King of the Scots (1249-86). He married (1251) Margaret, daughter of Henry III of England. Under his leadership, the Scots defeated the Norwegians at the battle of Largs (1263) and by the Treaty of Perth (1266) gained the Isle of Man and the Hebrides from Norway.

Alexander III (1845-94) Emperor of Russia (1881-94). Owing to the assassination of his father Alexander II and the influence of the lawyer K. P. Pobedonostsev (1827-1907), Alexander's reign showed extreme conservatism. He increased police powers, persecuted revolutionaries, permitted education to decline, and encouraged the russification of subject races. Under him, Russia made its last conquests in Central Asia.

Alexander VI (Rodrigo Borgia; c. 1431-1503) Pope (1492-1503), notorious for his immorality, nepotism, and extravagance. Father of four illegitimate children, he used papal wealth to further the career of his son, Cesare *Borgia, who pursued Alexander's territorial ambitions in Italy. He was a generous patron of artists and was responsible for demarcating the respective areas of influence of Spain and Portugal in the New World.

Alexander, Sir William, 1st Earl of Stirling (c. 1576-1640) Scottish poet and colonist, who founded Nova Scotia (New Scotland). In 1604 he published a collection of sonnets, *Aurora*, and, in 1614, *Doomesday, or the Great Day of the Lord's Judgement*. In 1621 he was granted territory in NW Newfoundland but subsequently settled in Nova Scotia. He was forced by war with the French to relinquish the province in 1629.

Alexander Archipelago A chain of islands in the USA, off the SE coast of Alaska. They consist of the summits of a submerged mountain chain and their rugged densely forested terrain supports an abundance of wildlife.

Alexander Nevsky (c. 1220-63) Prince of Novgorod (1236-63) and Grand Prince of Vladimir (1252-63). Alexander's fame rests on his defeat of the Swedes (1240) near the Neva River (thus acquiring his name Nevsky) and of the Teutonic Knights (1242) on Lake Peipus. Despite the opposition of many Russians, he accepted the overlordship of the invading Mongols, thereby saving N Russia from certain devastation.

Alexander of Hales (c. 1170-1245) English scholastic philosopher, born at Hales (Gloucestershire). He became professor of theology in Paris and in 1236 a Franciscan. He is renowned for his efforts to combine the newly redis-covered *Aristotelianism, as mediated by the Arabic thinkers, such as *Averroes, with the Platonist tradition mediated by St *Augustine of Hippo.

Alexander of Tunis, Harold, 1st Earl (1891-1969) British field marshal. After distinguished service in World War I, Alexander held command in India. In World War II he commanded the evacuation of British forces from Dunkirk and was the last man to leave France. He became commander in chief in the Middle East (1942) and then, as Eisenhower's deputy, directed the offensive that defeated the Germans in N Africa (1943). He ended the war as Allied supreme commander in the Mediterranean and was subsequently governor general of Canada (1946-52) and Conservative minister of defence (1952-54). ⌐Tito.

Alexander Severus. *See* Severus Alexander.

Alexandra (1844-1925) A Danish princess who married (1863) Edward VII of the United Kingdom, when he was the Prince of Wales. In 1902 she founded Queen Alexandra's Imperial (now Royal) Army Nursing Corps and in 1912 she instituted the Alexandra Rose Day in aid of hospitals.

Alexandra (1872-1918) The wife from 1894 of *Nicholas II of Russia. A German princess and granddaughter of Queen Victoria, Alexandra fell under the evil influence of *Rasputin. His disastrous domination of her government while Nicholas was supreme commander of the Russian forces in World War I precipitated the Russian Revolution and the execution of Alexandra and her family by the Bolsheviks.

Alexandria (Arabic name: al-Iskandariyah) 31 13N 22 55E The chief seaport and second largest city in Egypt, between Lake Mareotis and the Mediterranean Sea: It handles most of Egypt's trade and the chief export is cotton; industries include oil refining and cotton ginning. The University of Alexandria was established in 1942. *History:* founded in 332 BC by Alexander the Great, partly on the island of Pharos, which was linked to the mainland by a mole, it remained the Egyptian capital for over a thousand years. It was a Greek and Jewish cultural centre with a famous library (*see* Alexandria, Library of) and in 30 BC fell to the Romans, becoming their most important regional capital. It declined following the discovery of the Cape of Good Hope passage and the removal of the capital to Cairo. It was bombarded by the British in 1882, Pompey's Pillar being one of the few ancient monuments to escape destruction. Two obelisks that also survived, *Cleopatra's Needles, were removed and one is now in London, the other in New York. During World War II the city suffered many air raids but since then has seen rapid expansion. Population (1979): 2 462 000.

Alexandria, Catechetical School of A Christian theological school at Alexandria from the late 2nd to the 4th century AD. Its early teachers, *Clement and *Origen, dominated the School's approach, which was a Platonic mystical philosophy that stressed divine transcendence, the deity of Christ, and a Trinitarianism that was almost tritheism. Athanasius was typically Alexandrian in opposing the Arian and related heresies.

Alexandria, Library of The greatest library of the ancient world, which in its heyday may have contained more than 700 000 items. A composite library, museum, and school, it was founded in the 3rd century BC by Ptolemy I Soter and his son, Ptolemy II Philadelphus. Large parts were destroyed in fires, notably in 97 BC, and it was finally destroyed by the Arabs in 696 AD. The survival of much of classical Greek literature is due to the work of its scholars.

alexandrine A verse metre consisting of a line of 12 syllables usually with major stresses on the sixth and final syllables. The name is derived from 12th-century French poems about Alexander the Great. It was the dominant verse form in 17th-century French poetry and was used by *Racine and *Corneille.

Alexis (1690-1718) The son and heir of *Peter the Great of Russia. Alexis' unhappy relations with his father pro-

gressively worsened and in 1716 Alexis fled to Vienna. Peter lured him back and condemned him to death for treason. He died before his execution.

Alexius I Comnenus (1048-1118) Byzantine emperor (1081-1118), who founded the Comnenian dynasty. Seizing the throne in a coup, Alexius revived the weakened Byzantine state, defeating the Normans and Seljuq Turks, who were encroaching on Byzantine territory, and introducing administrative reforms. However, in the second half of his reign, the Empire was threatened by the advance of the Crusaders. His achievements were celebrated in the *Alexiad* of his daughter *Anna Comnena.

alfalfa A perennial flowering plant, *Medicago sativa*, also called lucerne. Growing to a height of 1 m, it resembles clover, having clusters of small purple flowers. Native to Europe, it is widely grown as forage for cattle and because of its ability to fix nitrogen. Family: *Leguminosae*.

al-Farabi, Mohammed ibn Tarkhan (d. 950) Muslim philosopher, physician, mathematician, and musician, of Central Asian origin. He is acknowledged to be one of the greatest Muslim thinkers and his works on medicine and music became standard treatises. But it was his contribution to Arabic philosophy that earned him renown. A staunch believer in the truth of Islam, Al-Farabi strove to bring the whole of Greek philosophy into conformity with its doctrines.

Alfieri, Vittorio, Count (1749-1803) Italian poet and dramatist. He abandoned a military career in order to travel widely throughout Europe (1767-72). After the success of his first play, *Cleopatra* (1775), he devoted himself entirely to literature. He wrote 28 plays, of which his 19 tragedies, among them *Saul* and *Mirra*, depict romantic heroes struggling against tyranny and oppression. He also wrote poetry and an autobiography, *La vita* (1804).

Alfonso (V) the Magnanimous (1385-1458) King of Aragon (1416-58) and, as Alfonso I, of Sicily (1416-58) and Naples (1443-58). During the 1420s he helped Queen Joanna II of Naples (1371-1435; reigned 1414-35) to resist the claims of Louis III of Anjou (1403-34) to the Neapolitan throne. After her death he seized the throne himself and his court at Naples became a brilliant centre of Renaissance culture.

Alfonso VI (d. 1109) King of León (1065-1109) and of Castile (1072-1109). In 1085 Alfonso took Toledo from the Muslims but in the following year suffered defeat by the Almoravids of N Africa, with whom conflict continued until 1108. Alfonso's marriage to Constance of Burgundy brought cultural ties with France and he supported the introduction of Cluniac monasticism to León. His reign is also notable for the exploits of El Cid.

Alfonso VIII (d. 1214) King of Castile (1158-1214), famous for his defeat of the Moors at Navas de Tolosa (1212). He married Eleanor, a daughter of Henry II of England; their daughter was *Blanche of Castile.

Alfonso (X) the Wise (c. 1221-84) King of Castile and León (1252-84). He made his court at Toledo a centre of learning and a haven for Arab and Jewish, as well as Christian, scholars. He compiled a legal code, the Seven Divisions of the Law, but it never came into effective use. He also failed in an attempt (1257) to become the first Spanish Holy Roman Emperor.

Alfonso XIII (1886-1941) King of Spain from birth until 1931. Alfonso, who came of age in 1902, ruled during a turbulent period of social unrest and political instability and several attempts were made on his life. The dictatorship (1923-30) of Miguel *Primo de Rivera undermined his reign and he abdicated in 1931 following Republican victories in municipal elections.

Alfred the Great (849-99) King of Wessex (871-99). He prevented the Danish conquest of England, defeating them at Edington (878) after a campaign of guerrilla warfare based at *Athelney. The legend of the king, travelling incognito, burning the peasant housewife's cakes, and being severely reprimanded by her, possibly refers to this unsettled period of his life. After his victory he allowed the Danes to keep their conquests in Mercia and East Anglia provided that Guthrum, their king, was converted to Christianity. Alfred built a navy of warships to defend the south coast against further Danish invasions (885–86; 892–96) and protected Wessex with a chain of fortifications. He took London (886), thus gaining control of all England save the Danish areas. Alfred did much to revive learning, translating important Latin works into English. He also devised a legal code.

Alfvén, Hannes Olof Gösta (1908–) Swedish astrophysicist. A specialist in *plasma physics, his original work includes studies of sunspots, cosmic rays, and the aurora. His work on the interaction of plasma with magnetic fields (magnetohydrodynamics) forms the basis of several proposed systems for harnessing nuclear fusion power; he shared the 1970 Nobel Prize for this work.

algae A vast group of simple plants (about 25 000 species) that contain the green pigment chlorophyll (and can therefore carry out photosynthesis) but have no true stems, roots, or leaves (see Thallophyta). They range from single-celled organisms to the giant seaweeds. Most algae are aquatic, although some live in damp places on land—on rocks, trees, or in soils. A few are parasitic or associate with other organisms (see lichen). Reproduction is extremely variable and may involve asexual means, such as cell division, fragmentation, or spore production, and/or sexual means by gamete production. The more advanced algae often alternate between sexual and asexual phases. Algae provide a valuable food source for aquatic herbivorous animals and many are used as fertilizers and in industry. There are generally considered to be seven divisions of algae, including the *green, *blue-green, *yellow-green, *brown, and *red algae. Some of the unicellular forms are alternatively classed as *Protozoa.

Algarve The most southerly province of Portugal, bordering on Spain and the Atlantic Ocean. It became a Moorish kingdom in 1140 and was the last stronghold of the Moors in Portugal, being reconquered in 1249. Sparsely populated inland, its fertile coastal belt is densely populated and produces chiefly maize, figs, almonds, and olives; fishing is also important. Tourism is a flourishing industry. Area: 5071 sq km (1957 sq mi). Population (1979 est): 308 800. Chief town: Faro.

algebra The branch of mathematics that uses symbols to represent unknown quantities. The first treatise on the subject was written by Diophantus of Alexandria in the 3rd century AD and the name derives from the Arabic al-jabr, a term used by the mathematician al-Khwarizmi to denote the addition of equal quantities to both sides of an equation and later adopted as the name for the whole subject. Algebra was used in ancient Babylon, Egypt, and India and brought to Europe by the Arabs. In classical algebra symbols, such as x and y, represent ordinary numbers and the central part of the subject is the study of algebraic equations. Modern, or abstract, algebra is concerned with any system of quantities that obey a particular set of general rules and relationships. Such systems may or may not obey the *commutative laws or even the *associative laws that hold in arithmetic.

Algeciras 36 08N 5 27W A port in S Spain, in Andalusia on the Bay of Gibraltar. Founded in 713 AD, it was destroyed by Alfonso XI of Castile (1311–50; reigned 1312–50) in 1344. The present town was rebuilt in 1760. In 1906 it was the site of the Algeciras Conference, a meeting of European powers to solve their dispute over Morocco. Its exports include oranges and cork. Population (1981): 86 042.

Algeria, Democratic and Popular Republic of A country in N Africa, on the Mediterranean Sea. It consists chiefly of the

N Sahara Desert, with the Atlas Mountains in the N and small fertile areas near the coast. The inhabitants, who live almost entirely in the N, are mainly Arabs and Berbers. *Economy*: mainly agricultural although industrialization has proceeded rapidly since independence, financed by the discovery of oil (the main export) and natural gas in the desert areas. *History*: a former province of the Roman Empire, Algeria was subjugated in the 7th century by the Arabs, who introduced Islam. Overrun by Turks in the 16th century, it became a pirate state in the 18th century under the domination of *deys*, independent rulers who preyed on Mediterranean shipping. Algeria was annexed by the French in the 19th century and in 1881 the N section became part of Metropolitan France. A war of independence, waged by the *Front de Libération nationale (FLN), lasted from 1954 to 1962 when independence was granted by de Gaulle, following referenda held in both Algeria and France. A republic was set up under Ahmed *Ben Bella but was overthrown in 1965 by a Council of Revolution. Col Houari *Boumédienne became president and in 1976 was elected for a further six years in office. In the same year a new constitution was adopted in which the one-party principle was reaffirmed, the FLN being the only political party permitted in Algeria. Following Boumédienne's death in December, 1978, Col Benjedid Chadli (1929–) became the new president. Official language: Arabic; French is also widely spoken. Official religion: Islam. Currency: dinar of 100 centimes. Area: 2 381 745 sq km (919 595 sq mi). Population (1981 est): 19 300 000. Capital and main port: Algiers.

Algiers (Arabic name: al-Jaza'ir; French name: Alger) 36 45N 3 05E The capital of Algeria, an important port in the N of the Mediterranean Sea. Its main exports include wine, citrus fruits, and iron ore. The University of Algiers was founded in 1879 and the University of Science and Technology in 1974. *History*: originally founded by the Phoenicians, it was re-established by the Arabs in the 10th century. Overrun by Turks in the 16th century, it became a base for Barbary pirates until taken by the French in 1830. During World War II it was the headquarters of the Allied forces in N Africa and for a time the seat of the French government-in-exile. It was the scene of several uprisings during the Algerian struggle for independence from France (1954–62). Population (1980 est): 2 200 000.

algin (sodium alginate) A slimy substance extracted from seaweed. It is used as a thickener in such foods as ice cream and in industrial compounds.

Algirdas (or Olgierd; d. 1377) Grand Duke of Lithuania (1345–77). A pagan ruler, Algirdas was nevertheless tolerant of the Orthodox Church. He fought the Poles, Mongols, and Teutonic Knights and extended Lithuania eastwards.

Algol (or Winking Demon) A white 2nd-magnitude star in the constellation Perseus. Its regular variations in brightness have been long known. The prototype of the **Algol variables**, a class of eclipsing *binary stars, Algol and its fainter companion revolve around one another in 2.87 days.

ALGOL (*algo*rithmic *l*anguage) A computer-programming language. It is used to express mathematical and scientific problems in a way that can be processed by computer. ALGOL is a high-level language, i.e. statements made in it resemble English and algebraic formulae rather than a computer notation. See program.

Algonkian A group of North American Indian languages, including *Cree, *Cheyenne, *Blackfoot, and others, spoken by tribes living to the S and E of Hudson Bay and in the eastern woodland zone. The Algonkian tribes lived by hunting and fishing and roamed widely in small family groups and bands. They moved possessions by means of toboggans and dressed in clothes made from the skins of animals, such as caribou and moose, decorated with bright quillwork and beadwork. Religion was little developed, involving belief in a single creator god, fear of spirits and witches, and reliance on the protective and curative powers of medicine men, the only persons with authority.

Algonkin The language and name of a North American Indian people of Quebec and Ottawa in Canada. The *Algonkian language group was named after it. Algonkin culture was similar to that of other Algonkian-speaking tribes of the area.

Algren, Nelson (1909–81) US novelist. He trained as a journalist in Chicago, where most of his fiction is set, and briefly became a migrant worker during the Depression. In his novels, such as *Never Come Morning* (1942), he portrayed the underworld of American city life in an intense naturalistic style. *The Man with the Golden Arm* (1949), about drug addiction, brought him international fame.

ALHAMBRA *The arcade round the Court of the Lions features the horseshoe arches characteristic of Moorish architecture.*

Alhambra A castle on a hilly terrace outside *Granada (Spain), built between 1238 and 1358. It was the last stronghold of the Muslim kings of Granada. Combining citadel and palace, it is an outstanding example of Moorish architecture, with magnificent courts and gardens. The name derives from Arabic *al-hamra*, the red, an allusion to the red stucco used on the walls.

Al Hudaydah. *See* Hodeida.

Ali (c. 600–67) The cousin of *Mohammed and his son-in-law by marriage to *Fatimah. Born at Mecca, he was the second, or perhaps the first, person to embrace Islam. He became the fourth caliph in 656, but faced much opposition and was murdered in 661 at Kufa, Iraq. His tomb is venerated at Najaf. According to *Shiite Muslims, Ali was the only legitimate successor of Mohammed and only his descendants are recognized as *imams.

Ali, Muhammad (Cassius Marcellus Clay; 1942–) US boxer. A gold medallist in the 1960 Olympic Games, he became professional world heavyweight champion (1964). On becoming a Black Muslim he changed his name and was soon afterwards stripped of his title for three years because of his refusal to join the US army. Defeated (1971) by Joe *Frazier, he again became champion in 1974 by defeating George Foreman (1949–), losing the title briefly in 1978 to Leon Spinks. His defeat of Spinks later that year made him the only boxer to become world champion three times. In 1980 he was defeated by Larry Holmes in his bid to regain the world title. He is renowned for his extrovert personality.

Alicante 38 21N 0 29W A port in SE Spain, in Valencia on the Mediterranean Sea. Exports include wine, olive oil, and fruits and it serves as an outlet for Madrid. Industries include oil refining, textiles, chemicals, soap, and tobacco. It is a popular tourist resort. Population (1981): 251 387.

Alice Springs 23 42S 133 52E A town in central Australia, in S Northern Territory. It is a major centre for beef cattle and mineral transportation, linked by air, road, and rail with Adelaide and by air and the Stuart Highway with Darwin. It is also a base for tourism. Population (1982): 19 610.

alien A person who, according to the law of a state, is not a citizen of that state. According to the British Nationality Act (1981), an alien is someone who is neither a commonwealth citizen (*see* British citizenship), nor a British-protected person, nor a citizen of the Republic of Ireland. Aliens may own property in the UK (but not a British ship) but may not vote or hold public office. *See also* migration, human; naturalization.

Alien and Sedition Acts (1798) Four laws enacted in the USA ostensibly to prevent domestic subversion but actually to check the threat posed to the *Federalist Party by Thomas Jefferson's Republican Party. The Naturalization Act delayed voting rights for the immigrants upon whom the Republicans depended for support. The Alien Act and Alien Enemies Act authorized deportation of aliens suspected of threatening the government and the Sedition Act prohibited criticism of the government, thereby nullifying the First Amendment. When Jefferson became president (1800) three of the laws were allowed to lapse; the Naturalization Act was repealed in 1802.

alienation A pathological feeling of self-estrangement and loss of moral purpose. Hegel used the term to refer to a condition in which an individual's freedom of choice and action appears to him to have become an independent force constraining him. Marx made special use of the concept of alienated labour, believing that when men are forced to sell their labour to employers they are alienated from their own productive abilities. In contemporary common usage the term is applied loosely to situations in which people feel alienated from society, considering themselves to be "outsiders" with no sense of belonging to a community. In this meaning it overlaps the concept of *anomie.

Aligarh 27 42N 78 25E A city in N India, in Uttar Pradesh. An agricultural trading centre, it is the site of the notable Aligarh Muslim University (founded as a college in 1875). Population (1981 est): 320 861.

Ali Pasa, Mehmed Emin (1815–71) Grand Vizier (chief

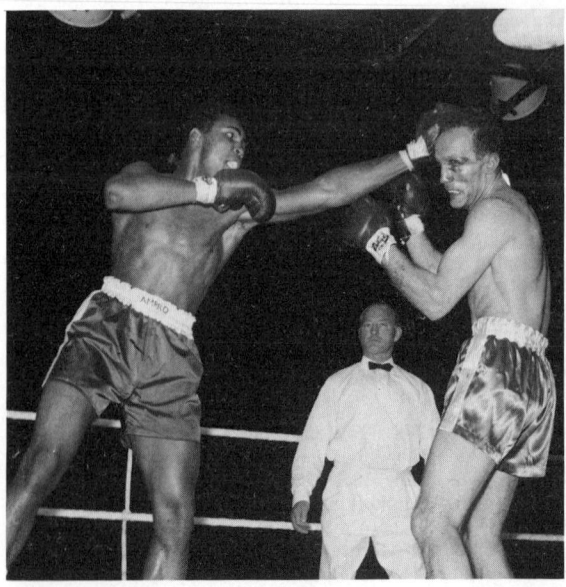

MUHAMMED ALI *Cassius Clay, as he then was, fighting Henry Cooper at Wembley Stadium in June, 1963.*

minister) of the Ottoman Empire five times between 1852 and 1871. He represented the Ottomans at the Congress of Paris (1856) following the Crimean War and was an advocate of Ottoman friendship with France and Britain. He was one of the architects of the period (1839-76) of Ottoman reform known as the Tanzimat (Reorganization).

aliphatic compounds Organic chemical compounds that are not *aromatic. They include the *alkanes, *alkenes, and *alkynes as well as some cyclic compounds (cycloalkanes).

Aliutor. *See* Palaeo-Siberian languages.

alizarin (1,2 dihydroxy-anthraquinone; $C_{14}H_6O_2(OH)_2$) An orange-red crystalline solid, formerly extracted from madder root and used in dyeing. It is almost insoluble in water but dissolves in alcohol. Alizarin is now made from *anthracene and yields a wide variety of dyes.

alkali. *See* acids and bases.

alkali metals The elements forming group I of the *periodic table: lithium, sodium, potassium, rubidium, caesium, and francium. All are soft, silvery-white *metals with low densities, melting points, and boiling points. In chemical reactions they tend to form positive ions and have a valence of 1. They are highly reactive, form soluble salts with nonmetals, generally release hydrogen on contact with water, and react with air to form oxides. The oxides and hydroxides are alkalis.

alkaline-earth metals The elements forming group II of the *periodic table: beryllium, magnesium, calcium, strontium, barium, and radium. They are similar to the *alkali metals in appearance and chemistry, but are harder, have higher melting and boiling points, and are somewhat less reactive. They have a valence of 2. The **alkaline earths** are the oxides of these metals.

alkaloids A group of nitrogen-containing basic compounds that are produced by plants and have diverse effects on the body. Many alkaloids are used as medicinal drugs, including quinine, reserpine, morphine, scopolamine, and atropine. Others, such as strychnine and coniine (from hemlock) are poisons. Caffeine, nicotine, and LSD are also alkaloids.

Alkan, Charles Henri Valentin (C. H. V. Morhange; 1813-88) French pianist and composer. By his teens he was a brilliant performer but became a recluse early in life. His many compositions, chiefly for the piano, are always original and difficult, and frequently very large scale. He was killed by a falling bookcase.

alkanes (*or* paraffins) A series of hydrocarbons, which contain only single bonds between the carbon atoms. They have the general formula C_nH_{2n+2}. The first four members of the series methane (CH_4), ethane (C_2H_6), propane (C_3H_8), and butane (C_4H_{10}) are gases, higher members are liquids or waxes. They are obtained from natural gas or oil and they and their substitution products have many uses.

alkanet A herbaceous plant of the genus *Anchusa*, native to Eurasia but widely grown for ornament (*A. azurea* is a common garden plant). It may reach a height of 50-120 cm, with clusters of small blue or white flowers and narrow or oval leaves. Family: *Boraginaceae*.
A similar and related plant, *Pentaglottis sempervirens*, is also called alkanet.

alkenes (*or* olefins) Hydrocarbons that contain at least one carbon-carbon double bond in their molecules. The simplest types, with one double bond, have the general formula C_nH_{2n}; ethylene (*or* ethene, C_2H_4) is the first member of this series. The alkenes are more reactive than the *alkanes, undergoing addition and polymerization reactions. They are obtained by cracking petroleum and their main use is as starting materials in industrial chemistry.

Al Khalil. *See* Hebron.

al-Khwarizmi, Muhammed ibn Musa (c. 780-c. 850 AD) Arabic mathematician, who introduced the Hindu decimal system and the use of zero into Arabic mathematics. He also extended the work of Diophantus on algebraic equations in a

book the title of which included the word *al-jabr* ("transposition"), from which the modern word "algebra" is derived.

Al-Kindi, Abu Yusuf Ya'qub ibn Ishaq (died c. 870) Muslim Arab philosopher, born in al-Kufa (now in Iraq). He was dubbed "philosopher of the Arabs" as he was the only Arabic philosopher of pure Arab stock. He made the whole field of Greek science his own and was among the first Arabic scholars to interest himself in philosophy from a scientific rather than a theological viewpoint.

Alkmaar 52 38W 4 44E A town in the NW Netherlands, in North Holland province. A commercial centre, it holds a famous cheese market between May and Oct. Population (1983): 80 992.

Al Kut 32 30N 45 51E A town in E Iraq, on the River Tigris to the SE of Baghdad. It was the scene of heavy fighting between the British and the Turks in World War I. The Kut barrage (completed 1939) diverts water into irrigation channels.

alkynes (*or* acetylenes) Hydrocarbons that contain at least one carbon-carbon triple bond in their molecules. The simplest types, with one triple bond, have the general formula C_nH_{2n-2}; acetylene (*or* ethyne, C_2H_2) is the first member of this series. The alkynes, like the *alkenes, undergo addition and polymerization reactions. They are extremely reactive, tending to explode under pressure, and are difficult to use in large quantities.

Allah (Arabic, probably from *al-ilah*: the god) The Islamic name of God. Allah was worshipped in pre-Islamic Arabia as early as the 3rd century BC. In Mecca he was given special rank as "the god," but lesser tribal gods continued to be worshipped alongside him until *Mohammed proclaimed the rigorous monotheism of Islam. As formulated by Mohammed, Allah is the one omnipotent and omniscient God, the same God as worshipped by Jews and Christians. He is eternal, the creator of the universe, the judge of men, merciful and compassionate. His word is embodied in the *Koran.

Allahabad 25 57N 81 50E A city in N India, in Uttar Pradesh at the confluence of the Rivers Ganges and Jumna. It is principally an administrative and educational centre; its university was established in 1887. There is an annual religious festival and a much larger one every 12 years. A former centre of the independence movement, it was the home of the Nehru family. Population (1981 est): 650 070.

Allbutt, Sir Thomas Clifford (1836-1925) British physician, who (in 1866) introduced the modern clinical thermometer. Allbutt also made valuable contributions to the study of syphilis and heart disease, most notably angina pectoris.

Allegheny Mountains A mountain range in the USA, extending from North Carolina to Pennsylvania. Part of the Appalachian Mountains, it consists of well-rounded uplands rising to 1480 m (4860 ft) at Spruce Knob. It forms the watershed between the Atlantic Ocean and the Mississippi River and was for many years a frontier zone between French settlers in the Mississippi Basin and English colonists along the coast.

allegory A verse or prose narrative in which characters and events in the plot refer to a deeper, usually moral, meaning. It is an ancient and universal form, similar to but usually longer than the *fable and the parable. Examples of allegory include the French *Roman de la rose* (13th century), Bunyan's *The Pilgrim's Progress* (1678), Swift's *Gulliver's Travels* (1726), and Orwell's *Animal Farm* (1945).

Allegri, Gregorio (1582-1652) Italian composer. He was appointed a singer in Pope *Urban VIII's chapel in 1629. An important composer of church music, his works include a *Miserere* for nine voices, two volumes of concertinos, and two volumes of motets.

allele Any one of the various alternative forms of a *gene that can occur at the same site on a *chromosome. In *Drosophila* fruit flies, for example, several alternative eye colours are possible depending on which of the various alleles of the gene for eye colour is present in the individual.

allemande A 16th-century processional dance in 4/4 time originating in Germany. Popular in France and in England under the name almand or almain, it reappeared in the 18th century as an elaborate figure dance for couples, in 2/4 time. A stylized version of the early dance was frequently used by Bach, Couperin, and other contemporary composers to open a suite. The name is also applied to a lively German-Swiss folk dance resembling the *Ländler*.

Allen, Bog of (Irish name: Moin Almkaine) An area of peat bogs in the Republic of Ireland, covering much of the central plain. The peat is used for fuelling power stations and for domestic use. Area: 958 sq km (370 sq mi).

Allen, Ethan (1739–89) American soldier, who pursued the independence from New York and New Hampshire of the Green Mountain region (now Vermont). Between 1770 and 1775 he commanded the *Green Mountain Boys, which with Benedict *Arnold's forces captured Fort Ticonderoga (1775), the first American victory in the American Revolution. He was imprisoned by the British (1775–78) and died shortly before Vermont achieved statehood in 1789.

Allen, William, Cardinal (1532–94) English churchman. He was principal of St Mary's Hall, Oxford. With the accession of Elizabeth I, he went into exile rather than take the oath of supremacy. He founded the Roman Catholic seminary at Douai (1568), where priests were trained for mission work in England and where the *Douai Bible was begun with his encouragement. He was made cardinal in 1587 and supported the Spanish Armada in 1588, a decision that adversely affected his influence among many English Roman Catholics. He spent his last years at the English college at Rome, which he had founded.

WOODY ALLEN *He is an enthusiastic amateur jazz clarinetist.*

Allen, Woody (Allen Stewart Konigsberg; 1935–   ) US film actor and director. His performances are witty portrayals of social inadequacy and embarrassment. His films include *Play*

It Again, Sam (1972), *Annie Hall* (1977), and, as director, *Interiors* (1978), *Manhattan* (1979), *Broadway Danny Rose* (1984), and the Oscar-winning *Hannah and Her Sisters* (1986).

Allenby, Edmund Henry Hynman, 1st Viscount (1861–1936) British field marshal. After experience in the Boer War, he commanded the Third Army in France in World War I. In 1917, appointed commander in chief of the Egyptian Expeditionary Force against the Turks in Palestine, he captured (9 Dec) Jerusalem (as a "Christmas present" for the British people) and then went on to devastate the Turks at Megiddo (1918). He ended his career as high commissioner in Egypt (1919–25).

Allende (Gossens), Salvador (1908–73) Chilean statesman; president of Chile (1970–73), the first Marxist to come to power through free elections. A founder of the Chilean Socialist Party, Allende governed a coalition of left-wing parties. His nationalization policies created much opposition and he was overthrown and killed by a military coup.

Allentown 40 37N 75 30W A town in the USA, in Pennsylvania. It has important steel and machinery industries. Population (1980): 106 500.

allergy An abnormal reaction by the body that is provoked by certain substances, including pollen, dust, certain foods and drugs, fur, moulds, etc. Normally all foreign substances (antigens) entering the body are destroyed by *antibodies without further trouble. Allergic people, however, become hypersensitive to certain antigens (called allergens), so that whenever they are subsequently encountered they stimulate not only the normal antibody reaction but also the specific symptoms of the allergy. Allergic conditions include *hay fever, some forms of *asthma and *dermatitis, and *urticaria. Treatment includes the use of *antihistamines, corticosteroids, and *desensitization.

Alleyn, Edward (1566–1626) English actor. He acted in many of the plays of Christopher Marlowe and was the main rival of Richard *Burbage in the Elizabethan theatre. He became a prosperous theatre owner and founded Dulwich College in 1619.

Allied Powers The nations united in opposition to the *Central Powers in World War I and to the *Axis Powers in World War II. In World War I the Allies were initially the UK, France, and Russia, bound by the Treaty of London (1914), and later included Italy, Japan, and Portugal; the USA was an associated power from 1917. In World War II the chief Allies were the UK, France (1939–40, 1944–45), the Soviet Union (from June, 1941), the USA (from December, 1941), and China.

Allier, River A river in central France. Rising in the Cévennes, it flows NNW through the fertile Limagne area, joining the River Loire near Nevers. Length: 403 km (250 mi).

alligator A large broad-snouted □reptile belonging to the genus *Alligator* (2 species). Each side of the jaw contains 17–22 teeth, which are all covered when the mouth is closed. The American alligator (*A. mississippiensis*) is mainly black and lives in rivers of the SE USA, reaching a length of 5–6 m; the rare Chinese alligator (*A. sinensis*) of the Yangtze River is smaller. They dig burrows in which they hibernate during cold weather. Order: *Crocodilia* (see crocodile).

Allingham, Margery (1904–66) British detective-story writer. Her mild-mannered likeable detective Albert Campion appeared in a popular series of novels begun in the 1920s and ending with *Cargo of Eagles* (1968). *Tiger in the Smoke* (1952), *The China Governess* (1963), and *The Mind Readers* (1965) are among her most acclaimed books.

Allium A genus of herbaceous plants (about 450 species), including the *onion, *shallot, *garlic, *leek, *chive, etc. They have bulbs, those of several species being widely used in temperate regions for food and flavouring, and in many the flowers are replaced by small bulbs (bulbils), by means of which the plants can be propagated. Family: *Liliaceae* (or *Alliaceae* according to some authorities).

Alloa 56 07N 3 49W A town in Scotland, in the Central Region at the head of the Forth estuary. Industries include brewing, engineering, textiles, and agricultural implements. Population (1981): 26 390.

allopathy Literally, the use of drugs or other means to induce a reaction in the body that will counteract—and therefore relieve—the symptoms of a disease. The term is used by practitioners of *homeopathy to describe the orthodox system of medicine.

Allosaurus A large bipedal dinosaur of the Jurassic and Cretaceous periods (200-65 million years ago). Up to 11 m long, it had large strong hind limbs, a well-developed tail, small forelegs, and thick protective knobs of bone over the eyes. Although fairly slow, it hunted prey, possibly in groups, and was equipped with sharp claws, powerful jaws, and sharp pointed teeth. Order: *Saurischia.

allotropes Two or more different physical forms of the same element or compound. Allotropes have different arrangements of atoms in their crystals or molecules and occasionally quite different chemical behaviour. Diamond and graphite, for example, are allotropes of carbon.

Alloway 55 26N 4 38W A village in SW Scotland, in Strathclyde Region on the River Doon. The birthplace of Robert Burns, it has many associations with his poems.

alloy A blend of a metal with other metals or nonmetals, formed by mixing the molten substances and allowing the mixture to cool and solidify. An alloy is usually harder than any of its constituents. The first alloy was probably *bronze, which was used in Europe in about 2000 BC. *Steel and *brass are the most widely used alloys. Alloys of aluminium are also widely used, especially in the aircraft industry. Some metals, such as lead and aluminium, will not mix when they are melted together because their different densities make them separate into two layers. However, many metals do combine to form alloys, which may consist of inter-metallic compounds, solid solutions, heterogenous mixtures, or any combination of these forms. In general, intermetallic compounds tend to be hard and brittle: iron carbide, which strengthens iron to form *steel is an example. Solid solutions, on the other hand, are usually soft and ductile: cartridge-case *brass is a typical example.

Most alloys melt over a range of temperatures unlike a pure metal, which has a specific melting point. **Eutectic alloys** are an exception to this rule, they consist of solid solutions having the lowest melting point of all the possible mixtures of the components. They are used in fuses and other safety mechanisms.

All Saints' Day A Christian feast commemorating all saints, whether known or unknown. In the Eastern Churches it has always been observed on the first Sunday after Pentecost. In the West its date varied until fixed as 1 Nov by Gregory III. *See also* Hallowe'en.

All Souls' Day A Christian feast in the Western Church commemorating all Christians who have died (the "faithful departed"). It is observed on 2 Nov. Requiem masses, containing the *Dies Irae*, are celebrated.

allspice (*or* pimento) A widely used aromatic spice, so named because it combines the flavours of several different spices. It is derived from the powdered dried unripe berries of an evergreen tree, *Pimenta dioca*, which is native to Central America and the West Indies and grows to a height of 9 m. Family: *Myrtaceae*.

Allston, Washington (1779-1843) The earliest US Romantic painter. He studied at Harvard University before training at the Royal Academy (1801-03) in England. He finally settled in Boston in 1818. The drama of his early landscapes and biblical subjects was replaced by a quieter mood in such later works as *Moonlight Landscape* (Boston). He also wrote poetry and one novel.

Alma Ata 43 19N 76 55E (name until 1921: Verny) A city in the S Soviet Union, the capital of the Kazakh SSR. Situated in the foothills of the Trans-Alay Alatau (mountains), it is one of the Soviet Union's most beautiful cities. Industries include food and tobacco processing, and it has a thriving film industry. Its museum is housed in the former Russian Orthodox cathedral, the world's second highest wooden building. It has many educational institutions. *History*: founded in 1854 as a fort, it soon became a trade centre. The completion of the Turkistan-Siberian railway in 1930, on which it is situated, resulted in its rapid growth. Population (1981 est): 975 000.

Almada 38 40N 9 09W A town in S central Portugal, on the Tagus estuary opposite Lisbon. A statue of Christ, 110 m (360 ft) high, was erected here in 1959. Population (1981): 41 468.

Almadén 38 47N 4 50W A town in W central Spain in New Castile. It possesses rich mercury mines, which have been worked since Roman times. Population (1981): 9521.

Almagest. *See* Ptolemy.

almanac A calendar of the months and days of the year containing astronomical and other miscellaneous data. It usually includes information about eclipses, phases of the moon, positions of the planets, times of sunset and sunrise and of high and low tides, as well as religious and secular holidays. A well-known example is *Old Moore's Almanac*, founded in 1699 by Francis Moore (1675-1715) to promote sales of his medicines. Modern almanacs include official government publications listing national statistics.

al-Mansurah. *See* Mansura, El.

Alma-Tadema, Sir Lawrence (1836-1912) Painter of Dutch birth, whose successful career began in Antwerp and continued from about 1870 in England, where he took British nationality. A visit to Italy (1863) developed his interest in Egyptian and classical antiquity, which thereafter became almost his sole subject matter. His first Royal Academy success was *Pyrrhic Dance* (1869; Guildhall, London).

Almeida, Francisco de (c. 1450-1510) Portuguese colonialist. The first viceroy of Portuguese India (1505-09), Almeida consolidated Portuguese rule there and expanded its power in the Indian Ocean. He organized further voyages of discovery that reached Madagascar and fought the Arabs on the African coast.

Almelo 52 21N 6 40E A town in the E Netherlands, in Overijssel province on the Overijssel Canal. An industrial centre, it produces furniture and textiles. Population (1981 est): 73 766.

Almería 36 50N 2 26W A port in S Spain, in Andalusia on the Gulf of Almería. It was a thriving town under the Moors (8th-15th centuries) and has a fine 16th-century cathedral. Its exports include grapes and oranges. Population (1982): 124 925.

Almohads A fundamentalist reforming Muslim movement that ruled much of N Africa and Spain (1130-1269). Comprising the Masmudah Berber tribe, the Almohads recognized Ibn Tumart (d. 1130) as their leader in 1121 and he directed them against the ruling *Almoravids, taking the title of mahdi. On his death he was succeeded by Abd al-Mu'min (d. 1163), who completed the conquest of N Africa and Spain from the Almoravids. The Almohads regarded Muslims who did not follow them as unbelievers and Abd al-Mu'min became their *caliph. His descendants ruled the state until the fall of Marrakech to the Marinid Berber dynasty in 1269.

almond A tree, *Prunus amygdalus*, native to SW Asia but widely grown in warm regions for its nuts. The edible nuts are produced by a variety called sweet almond; the nuts of the bitter almond yield aromatic almond oil, used as a flavouring. Almond trees grow to a height of 7 m; they have attractive pink flowers and are grown for ornament in cooler regions. Family: *Rosaceae*. *See also* Prunus.

Almoravids A military Muslim missionary movement that ruled much of N Africa and Spain in the 11th and 12th centuries. The Almoravids were founded by Ibn Yasin (d. 1059) and after his death Yusuf ibn Tashufin (d. 1107) conquered NW Africa and invaded Spain. At the battle of Zallaqah (1086) he defeated the rising Christian power of León and Castile and Muslim Spain now came under Almoravid control. After Yusuf's death in Marrakech, the Almoravid capital that he had founded, his state was ruled by his descendants until 1147, when it fell to the *Almohads.

Alnico An *alloy of aluminium, nickel, and cobalt. It is a ferromagnetic material and is used to make permanent magnets.

Aloe A genus of succulent herbaceous plants (about 200 species), all native to Africa. A stem is usually absent, the toothed fleshy leaves forming a basal rosette, up to 40 cm in diameter. The flowers are red or yellow and some species are ornamental (e.g. *A. variegata*); the juice of some species, especially *A. vera*, is used as a purgative (bitter aloes). Family: *Liliaceae*.

Aloysius, St (Luigi Gonzaga; 1568-91) Italian patron of youth. A noble, he entered the Society of Jesus against his father's wishes in 1585 and studied philosophy and theology. Famous for his simple piety and charity, he died while tending plague victims in Rome. Feast day: 21 June.

alpaca A shaggy-coated hoofed mammal, *Lama pacos*, traditionally domesticated and bred in the South American Andes. Its dark fine high-quality fleece reaches nearly to the ground from its shoulder height of 90 cm and is shorn every two years, each animal yielding about 3 kg. Alpacas thrive at high altitudes, keeping to damp grassy plateaus. Family: *Camelidae* (camels).

Alp Arslan (c. 1029-1072) Sultan of Turkey (1063-72) of the Seljuq dynasty. He succeeded his uncle *Toghril Beg. His victory over the Byzantines at Manzikert in 1071 opened Asia Minor to Muslim penetration for the first time.

alphabets Writing systems in which each symbol represents a speech sound (*see* phonetics). Many *pictographic writing systems developed as far as ideography and even *syllabaries, but the breakthrough to true alphabetic phonetic writing took place, it seems, only on the E shores of the Mediterranean around 2000 BC. From this *Semitic alphabet all the major alphabets in use today—Roman, Greek, *Cyrillic, Hebrew, Arabic, and *Devanagari—are ultimately derived.

It is hard now to appreciate the achievement of identifying speech sounds separately from meaning and of analysing syllables into vowels and consonants. It meant that the number of symbols required to record a language was reduced from many thousands to between 20 and 40. Moreover, it became possible to write down unfamiliar or foreign words without reference to their sense.

Correspondence between conventional *spelling and speech sounds is rarely exact. Speech sounds change continually over the centuries, while spelling forms tend to become conventionalized and static. In Greek, for example, where the alphabet has been used to represent the language for almost 3000 years, the letters ι, η, υ, ει, and οι, which originally represented different sounds, now all represent the sound /i:/; by contrast, γ, which used to represent a single sound, now represents four quite distinct sounds, depending on the letters adjoining it. On the other hand, Czech and Turkish, both of which have adopted or revised a modified version of the Roman alphabet within the last hundred years, display great regularity between sound and spelling. These two and many other languages that have taken over the Roman alphabet use accents and other diacritics to indicate sounds for which there is no standard Roman alphabet symbol. With the passage of time,

Phoenician	Early Hebrew	Early Aramaic	Early Greek	Classical Greek	Etruscan	Early Latin	Classical Latin	Russian-Cyrillic	Modern Roman
⟨	⟨	⟨	A	A	A	A	A	А	A
⅃	⅃	⅃	ᗷ	B	⅃	B	B	Б	B
⅂	⅄	⅂	Ꮜ	Γ	⅂	<	C	Г	C
⫝̸	⫝̸	⫝̸	ᐃ	Δ	⫝̸	D	D	Д	D
⅃	⅃	⅄	ᗱ	E	⅃	E	E	Е	E
Y	Y	⅄	⅂		⅄	F	F	Ф	F
⅃	⅃	⅄	⅃	Γ	⅃	<	G	Г	G
ᗷ	ᗷ	⊞	ᗷ	H	ᗷ	H	H	И	H
⅀	⅀	⅄	⅄	I	I	I	I	I	I
⅀	⅀	⅄	⅄	I	I	I	I		J
⅄	⅃	⅄	⅄	K	K	K	K	К	K
⅃	⅃	⅃	⅃	Λ	⅃	⅃	L	Л	L
⅍	⅍	M	M	M	M	M	M	М	M
⅄	⅄	⅄	⅄	N	И	N	N	Н	N
O	⅂	O	O	O	O	O	O	О	O
⅂	⅂	⅂	⅂	Π	⅂	Γ	P	П	P
Φ	⅄	Φ	Φ		Φ	Q	Q		Q
⅄	⅄	⅄	⅃	P	⅃	P	R	Р	R
W	W	W	⅀	Σ	⅀	⅄	S	С	S
+	X	X	X	T	T	⅄	T	Т	T
Y	Y	⅄	Y	Y	Y	⅄	V	У	U
Y	Y	⅄	Y	Y	⅄	V	V		V
									W
⅄	⅄	⅄	⅄	Ξ	X	X	X	X	X
⅄	⅄	⅄	⅄			Y	Y	Y	Y
⅄	⅄	⅄	I	Z	⅄	Z	Z	³	Z

ALPHABETS *The letters of the modern Roman alphabet have developed from the ancient Phoenician syllabary. This script in its Aramaic form was also the ultimate source of the Arabic alphabet and probably of the Brahmi alphabet, from which the many scripts of modern India are derived. The Cyrillic alphabet was derived directly from the Greek, whereas the Roman came through Etruscan and Latin.*

however, the use of diacritics itself becomes conventionalized and unsystematic.

From time to time, attempts have been made to develop alphabets that record speech sounds absolutely regularly and systematically. The most important of these is the *International Phonetic Alphabet.

Alpha Centauri A conspicuous nearby *multiple star in the constellation Centaurus. The two brightest components form a yellow visual *binary star that is seen as the third brightest star in the sky, magnitude -0.27. The much fainter third component, **Proxima Centauri**, is the nearest known star, lying 4.3 light years away.

alpha decay A spontaneous radioactive disintegration in which a nucleus ejects an *alpha particle. This process reduces the mass number of the nucleus by four and its atomic number by two. An example is the decay of uranium-238 into thorium-234.

alpha particle The nucleus of a helium-4 atom, consisting of two protons and two neutrons. It is extremely stable and is emitted by some radioactive nuclei in the process known as *alpha decay.

Alphege, St (954-1012) Archbishop of Canterbury and

martyr. He became Bishop of Winchester in 984 and was appointed Archbishop of Canterbury in 1006. He was captured by the Danes in 1011 and murdered because he refused to save himself at the expense of his tenants. Feast day: 19 April.

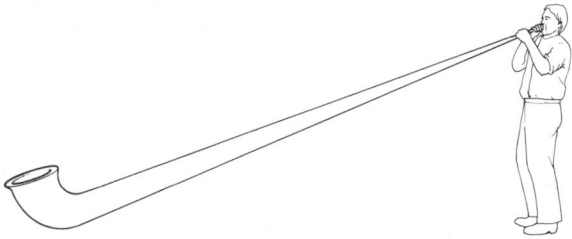

ALPHORN *The instrument is constructed from long wooden staves bound together with birch bark. Instruments similar to the alphorn are used in Poland and Scandinavia as well as in Switzerland.*

alphorn A musical instrument used in Switzerland for calling cattle. Made of wood, it is commonly 2 m long or more. Its mouthpiece is similar to that of a cornet. Being valveless, it plays only harmonics.

Alpine orogeny The period of mountain building that occurred mainly during the Tertiary period, beginning about 65 million years ago. The regions most affected extend from S Europe and N Africa across S Asia to Indonesia, resulting in the formation of the Alps, Atlas Mountains, and Himalayas, and across a belt bordering on the Pacific Ocean. It is the most recent *orogeny and is probably still continuing in some parts of the world.

Alps The highest mountain range in Europe. It extends some 800 km (497 mi) in an arc roughly E-W through France, Switzerland, Italy, and Austria, and rises to 4807 m (15 771 ft) at Mont Blanc near the W end. Several major rivers rise here, including the Rhône, Rhine, Drava, and Po. The snowline varies between 2400 m and 3000 m (7874 ft and 9843 ft) and many of the lower slopes are used as pasture in summer, while in winter the Alps are Europe's major skiing area. There are several road and rail routes across the chain, including a number of tunnels. *See also* Maritime Alps.

Alsace (German name: Elsass) A planning region and former province in NE France, separated from West Germany by the River Rhine. It is a fertile agricultural area and has important potassium deposits. *History*: it was often a scene of conflict between France and Germany. Under Roman occupation from the 1st century AD, it became a Frankish duchy in the 5th century and was part of the Holy Roman Empire from the 10th to the 17th centuries. Its cities, which became effectively independent in the middle ages, were important centres of the Reformation in the 16th century. The French gained control of Alsace in 1648, after the Thirty Years' War, but it was lost to Germany in 1871, after the Franco-Prussian War, and linked with *Lorraine to form the German imperial territory of **Alsace-Lorraine**. This existed until it reverted to France in 1919. It came under German control again in World War II and was restored to France in 1945. Area: 8310 sq km (3208 sq mi). Population (1981 est): 1 570 500.

Alsatian dog. *See* German shepherd dog.

alsike A perennial Eurasian *clover, *Trifolium hybridum*, also called Swedish or Alsatian clover, with typically three-lobed leaves and a pink flower head about 1 cm in diameter. Capable of fixing atmospheric nitrogen, it is often used to improve the nitrate level in soil. Family: *Leguminosae*.

Altaic languages A family of languages comprising languages of the *Turkic, *Mongolian, and *Manchu-

Tungus groups. Named after the Central Asian Altai Mountains, languages of this family are spoken in N China, the Mongolian People's Republic, the Soviet Union, Afghanistan, Iran, and Turkey. The genetic relationship between the various Altaic languages is debatable, but certain common features are discernible, notably sound harmony. The connection of *Japanese and *Korean with this family is questionable.

Altai Mountains A mountain system in Asia, extending from Siberia, Soviet Union, into China and Mongolia. It rises to 4506 m (14 783 ft) at Belukha in the Soviet Union and has important lead, silver, and zinc reserves.

Altair A conspicuous white star, apparent magnitude 0.77 and 16.5 light years distant, that is the brightest star in the constellation Aquila.

Altamira Upper *Palaeolithic cave site in N Spain, recognized in 1879. Doubts as to the authenticity of the 150 magnificent polychrome paintings of animals on the cave's ceiling were eventually settled by Henri *Breuil in 1901. Bison, painted in red ochre with black manganese manes, tails, and hooves, are the chief species depicted. *See also* Magdalenian.

Altdorf 46 53N 8 38E The town in central Switzerland where William Tell engaged in his legendary exploits. Population (1980): 8230.

Altdorfer, Albrecht (c. 1480-1538) German artist, who was one of the first European painters to paint landscapes for their own sake. His masterpieces, few of which survive, show his love of forested mountains, depicted in minute detail, and include *The Battle of Issus* and *St George* (both Alte Pinakothek, Munich). He worked in Regensburg, where he became city architect and a member of the council.

$$\text{voltage} = 340 \sin (2\pi \times 50)t$$

$$\text{power} = 340\, I_0 \sin^2 (2\pi \times 50)$$

ALTERNATING CURRENT *The voltage and power waveforms in a 240-volt, 50-hertz domestic mains supply. The current (I = $I_0 \sin (2\pi \times 50)$ t) has a similar waveform to the voltage.*

alternating current (ac) Electrical current that periodically reverses its direction. It is the form of current that is produced when a coil of wire rotates in a magnetic field and, as this is the way in which current is produced in *power stations by *electric generators, it is the form of current most widely used. The electromotive force (emf), E, produced by a generator is equal to $E^1 \sin \omega t$, where E^1 is the maximum emf, ω is the angular velocity of rotation, and t is the time. Thus the current has the form of a sine wave, with a frequency $\omega/2\pi$.

The chief advantage of ac is that the voltage can be stepped up with a transformer before transmission to minimize energy losses in the lines and then reduced to a safer level by another transformer for domestic use. In the UK the ac supply has a frequency of 50 hertz, is transmitted at several hundreds of kilovolts, and is used at 240 volts. In the USA the supply frequency is 60 hertz.

alternation of generations   A phenomenon occurring in the *life cycles of many plants and some animals (particularly *coelenterates) in which there is an alternation between two distinct forms (generations), which differ from each other in structure, reproduction, and also often in habit. In plants the generation reproducing sexually is the gametophyte and the asexual generation is the sporophyte. Either phase may be predominant in a particular species; for example, the gametophyte is dominant in mosses and the sporophyte in flowering plants. In coelenterates sedentary asexual polyps alternate with free-living sexual medusae.

alternative energy   The investigation and use of new sources of power, based on natural energy flows in the environment. Most countries now rely heavily on *fossil fuels (oil, coal, and natural gas) and nuclear power for their energy needs. However, reserves of fossil fuels are declining and, although dates for their total exhaustion vary, their price must rise as they become increasingly scarce. The estimates of reserves of recoverable uranium are also uncertain and there is opposition to the development of nuclear breeder reactors, mainly on the grounds of safety and environmental hazard from waste disposal. Fusion reactors are still very much in the experimental stage. Although nuclear power is still regarded as the main option, it is also necessary to explore the alternatives. Renewable energy sources are those that do not use up finite mineral resources. Of these *solar power, *wind power, and *wave power are being most seriously investigated in the UK. *Hydroelectric power is already in use and has limited potential for further expansion. Tidal power is the use of water raised by the tide and collected behind a barrage to generate electricity in a similar way to hydroelectric generation. The Severn estuary, which has an average tidal rise of 8.8 m, is said to form the best site in Europe. Geothermal power comes from the heat beneath the earth's crust. In Iceland naturally heated water is taken from rocks near the surface, but in most places geothermal power is not feasible. Biomass energy, or biogas, methane generated from sewage, refuse, or specially cultivated organisms, is also being utilized, especially on a small scale in third world countries.

alternative medicine   Systems of treatment of physical and mental illness used as alternatives to those of orthodox *medicine. Known also as fringe, natural, and unorthodox medicine, its recent growth is undoubtedly due to the fact that many diseases, such as allergies, arthritis, cancer, and depression, often fail to respond to conventional treatment. It includes such specialties as *osteopathy, *homeopathy, *acupuncture, and *hypnosis, which are recognized and practised by some qualified doctors, as well as many others, including *chiropractic, naturopathy, herbalism, dietary treatments, the laying on of hands, and self-healing (e.g. by yoga, biofeedback, etc.). See also holistic medicine.

Althing   The parliament of Iceland, the oldest in the world, founded in about 930 AD. Since independence in 1944 it has been the country's sovereign legislature. It has 60 members in two houses of equal power.

Althusius, Johannes   (1557–1638) German political philosopher. He became professor of law at Herborn Calvinist college (1594), where he wrote his most famous work, *Politics Methodically Arranged and Illustrated by Holy and Profane Examples* (1603). Althusius attempted a systematic approach to political science, based on the concept of contracts between different groupings in society.

Altichiero   (c. 1330–c. 1390) Italian painter. Influenced by *Giotto, Altichiero is credited with founding the Veronese school. His only surviving works in Verona are frescoes in S Anastasia but there are also cycles in the Basilica of S Antonio and the Oratorio di S Giorgio in Padua.

altimeter   A device for measuring altitude in one of two ways.

A **pressure altimeter** consists of an aneroid *barometer calibrated in metres (or feet) above sea level. A **radio altimeter** consists of a device that measures the time taken for a radio or radar signal to reach the ground and return.

altitude   The angular distance of an astronomical body above or below an observer's horizon. It reaches a maximum of 90° when the body is directly overhead. It is used with the angular distance **azimuth**, measured eastwards along the horizon from the direction of N, to specify the position of an astronomical body on the *celestial sphere.

alto   A high adult male singing voice produced by falsetto. Range: that of the *countertenor and *contralto.

altocumulus cloud (Ac)   A medium type of *cloud appearing as globular masses in bands across the sky.

altostratus cloud (As)   A medium type of *cloud appearing as a greyish sheet, sometimes thin enough for the sun to be seen through it. It usually heralds rain.

Altrincham   53 24N 2 21W   A town in NW England, in Greater Manchester. Originally a market town, it is now a suburb of Manchester. Population (1981): 39 641.

altruism.   *See* egoism.

aluminium (Al)   A light silvery-white metal first isolated by Wöhler in 1827. It is the most abundant metal in the earth's crust and the main source is *bauxite, an impure hydrated oxide. The metal is extracted by electrolysis of the oxide dissolved in a flux of low melting point with the mineral cryolite. Its most important uses depend on its lightness (relative density 2.70), ductility, and good electrical conductivity. It is used in electrical power cables, kitchen utensils, and many industrial applications. Pure aluminium is soft, but its alloys with copper, magnesium, and other elements have considerable strength. This combined with their low densities makes such alloys important in aircraft construction. Compounds include alum ($K_2SO_4Al_2(SO_4)_3.24H_2O$) and the oxide ($Al_2O_3$), which occurs naturally as corundum and *ruby and is used as an abrasive, a gem, and in *lasers. The hydroxide ($Al(OH)_3$) is used in glass manufacture and as an antacid in medicine. At no 13; at wt 26.9815; mp 660.4°C; bp 1800°C.

alums   Crystalline hydrated double sulphates of monovalent and trivalent metals. The typical example is potash alum (often called simply alum; $K_2SO_4.Al_2(SO_4)_3.24H_2O$), which is used as a mordant, size for paper, styptic, and astringent. In other alums the potassium and aluminium ions are replaced by other monovalent or trivalent ions respectively. For example, **chrome alum** ($K_2SO_4.Cr_2(SO_4)_3$) is a dark-purple substance used in dyes, printing, and tanning.

alunite (*or* alumstone)   A mineral consisting of potassium and aluminium sulphate and aluminium hydroxide, $K_2SO_4.Al_2(SO_4)_3.4Al(OH)_3$. A source of alum, it is usually found associated with volcanic rocks altered by sulphurous gases.

Alvarado, Pedro de   (c. 1485–1541) Spanish conquistador, who accompanied Hernán Cortés in his conquest of Mexico, becoming governor of Tenochtitlán (Mexico City). He conquered parts of Guatemala (1523–24) and El Salvador (1524). In 1534 he embarked on an expedition to take Ecuador but was bought off by a rival.

Alvarez, Luis Walter   (1911–   ) US physicist, who works at the University of California. Working with F. *Bloch he made the first measurement of the neutron's magnetic moment and won the Nobel Prize (1968) for research on short-lived fundamental particles. During World War II, he worked on the development of the atom bomb.

Alvárez Quintero brothers   Spanish dramatists, Serafin (1871–1938) and Joaquin (1873–1944) Alvárez Quintero. In collaboration, they wrote nearly 200 popular plays, set mainly in their native Andalusia. *El Amor que pasa* (1904) and *Malvaloca* (1912) were more serious works.

Alvars   A group of wandering poets and mystics, fervently devoted to Vishnu, which flourished in S India in the 7th–10th centuries AD. Almost exclusively male, they worshipped ecstatically, with song and dance. Their 4000 hymns in the Tamil language, collected in the 10th century, sing the praises of Vishnu and his various incarnations.

alveolus. *See* lung.

Alyattes (d. 560 BC) Fourth King of Lydia (c. 617–560), which he made a major power. Alyattes extended his kingdom as far as the River Halys (585) following a war against Media that was ended by the combatants' fear at the sight of the sun's eclipse. Alyattes, who was buried in a huge round tomb near Sardis, was succeeded by his son Croesus.

Alypius (4th century AD) Greek writer, from Alexandria in Egypt. His *Introduction to Music* is the chief surviving guide to classical Greek music, preserving its notation and complex scale system.

Alyssum A genus of low-growing herbaceous plants (about 150 species), mostly native to S Europe but widely grown in gardens. Alyssums have small flowers grouped in terminal clusters. Varieties of sweet alyssum (*A. maritimum*), 10–15 cm high, have white or pink flowers and are grown as annuals. Perennial alyssums include *A. saxatile*, which grows to 30 cm high and has yellow flowers. Family: *Cruciferae*.

Alzheimer's disease (*or* presenile dementia) A degenerative disease that affects nerve cells of the brain. It causes speech disturbances, progressive loss of mental faculties, and other symptoms of senility though it may occur in middle age. Its cause is uncertain but it is thought that a virus may be responsible. Named after the German neurologist Alois Alzheimer (1864–1915).

Amadeus String Quartet An internationally famous string quartet that gave its first concert in January, 1948, at the Wigmore Hall in London, and was dissolved in 1987. The members of the quartet were: Norbert Brainin (first violin; 1923–), Siegmund Nissel (second violin; 1922–), Peter Schidlof (viola; 1922–87), and Martin Lovett (cello; 1927–).

Amadeus (VIII) the Peaceful (1383–1451) Count of Savoy (1391–1434). Amadeus became duke in 1416, when Savoy was made a duchy by Emperor Sigismund. Amadeus abdicated in 1434 and in 1439 was elected antipope as Felix V by the schismatic Council of *Basle. He resigned in 1449.

Amagasaki 34 42N 135 23E A port in Japan, in S Honshu on Osaka Bay. An industrial centre, it has metal, chemical, and textile industries. Population (1980): 524 000.

Amalasuntha (*or* Amalasuentha; 498–535 AD) The daughter of Theodoric, King of the Ostrogoths, and regent (526–34) for her son Athalaric (516–34). After Athalaric's death she shared the throne with her cousin and second husband, Theodahad (d. 536), who, having banished her, was party to her murder.

Amalekites In the Old Testament, a nomadic tribe living in SW Palestine and the Sinai, who were descended from Esau. They attacked the Israelites on their journey out of Egypt and remained their enemies until finally suppressed during the reign of Hezekiah.

Amalfi 40 37N 14 36E A seaport and resort in Italy in Campania on the Gulf of Salerno. A major port in the 10th century, its maritime code of law was recognized in the Mediterranean area until the latter half of the 18th century.

Amalia, Anna (1739–1807) Duchess of Saxe-Weimar after her marriage (1756) to Ernst August, Duke of Saxe-Weimar; (ruled 1748–58). After her husband's death, she was regent (1758–75) for her son Carl August (1757–1828; ruled 1758–1828). She is remembered for her patronage of such writers as *Goethe and *Herder.

Amanita A genus of widely distributed mushroom fungi (about 100 species). Several species are extremely poisonous, including the deadly destroying angels (*A. vena* and *A. virosa*), the *death cap, and the *fly agaric. Some species are harmless

and sometimes eaten, for example panther cap (*A. pantherina*). Family: *Agaricaceae* (*see* agaric).

Amanollah Khan (1892–1960) Emir (1919–26) and King (1926–29) of Afghanistan. Amanollah obtained Afghan independence from Britain in 1919. He introduced a policy of westernization and declared Afghanistan a kingdom in 1926. In 1929 a revolt forced him into exile in Switzerland.

Amaranthus A genus of herbaceous plants (50–60 species) native to tropical and subtropical regions but now widely distributed (*see* pigweed). The small petal-less flowers grow in long drooping spikes. Several species are grown for ornament, including *A. caudatus* (love-lies-bleeding), 60–100 cm tall with dark-red flowers, *A. tricolor* (Joseph's coat), with purple flowers and red, yellow, and green leaves. Family: *Amaranthaceae*.

Amaravati school A style of Indian religious sculpture that originated in Amaravati in S India in the 2nd century BC and flourished until the 3rd century AD. A series of bas-reliefs of the life of Buddha have survived from Amaravati, showing the school's fusion of naturalism with elegance. The style spread through Ceylon to SE Asia.

Amarillo 35 14N 101 50W A city in the USA, in N Texas. Expansion followed the arrival of the railway (1887) and the discovery of gas (1918) and oil (1921). Today Amarillo has meat-packing, metal-refining, clothing, and fibreglass industries. Population (1980): 149 230.

Amarna Tablets *Cuneiform inscriptions found at Tell el-Amarna (Middle Egypt) in 1887. Most of the tablets were written about 1350 BC. They record administrative correspondence between the pharaoh and his vassal kings in Palestine and Syria.

Amaryllis A perennial herbaceous plant, *Amaryllis belladonna*, also called belladonna lily, native to South Africa but widely cultivated for ornament. Growing from bulbs, it has strap-shaped leaves and a 45 cm long stem bearing a cluster of 5–12 funnel-shaped sweet-scented flowers, usually rose-pink and often veined. Family: *Amaryllidaceae*.

Amaterasu In Japanese mythology, the sun goddess, supreme among the *kami* (spirits). She was the daughter of *Izanagi, born either from his eye or from a mirror held by him. She was symbolized by a mirror, which she gave to her grandson Ninigi, forerunner of the Japanese emperors, as part of the imperial regalia. It is still preserved at the Shinto shrine at Ise (S Honshu).

Amateur Athletic Association The governing body for men's athletics in England and Wales, founded in Oxford (1880). It holds annual championships, which are given the status of unofficial British championships.

Amati A family of violin makers in Cremona, Italy. **Andrea Amati** (c. 1520–c. 1578) developed the design that became the standard modern violin. His sons **Antonio Amati** (?1550–1638) and **Girolamo Amati** (1551–1635) worked as a team. Girolamo's son **Nicolò Amati** (1596–1684) was the family's greatest craftsman and taught Andrea *Guarneri and *Stradivari. They also made violas and cellos.

Amazon, River (Portuguese name: Rio Amazônas) The largest river system and the second longest river in the world, it is the chief river of South America. Rising as the Río Marañón in the Andes, in Peru, it flows generally W–E to enter the Atlantic Ocean in NE Brazil. Its drainage basin extends over much of Brazil, and parts of Venezuela, Colombia, Ecuador, Peru, and Bolivia. It is covered by a mantle of tropical rain forest (selva) and provides valuable forest products including rubber, quinine, and nuts. Navigable to oceangoing vessels as far as Iquitos, 3700 km (2300 mi) upstream, the river and its tributaries provide an essential communications system. New roads, including the Trans-Amazonian Highway, are now opening up the hinterland. Length: 6440 km (4000 mi). Drainage basin area: about 5 827 500 sq km (2 250 000 sq mi).

Amazon ant A *slave-making ant of the genus *Polyergus* (especially *P. rufescens* or *P. lucidus*). Amazon ants, which have long sharp sickle-shaped mandibles, raid nests of *Formica* ants to steal eggs and larvae that hatch to become workers in their own colony. Amazon ants cannot feed or brood without slave workers.

Amazons (Greek: breastless ones) A mythical nation of female warriors who were believed by the ancient Greeks to live in Pontus, near the Black Sea. Trained for war and hunting, the Amazons got their name from their habit of removing the right breast to facilitate the drawing of bows. They intervened in the *Trojan War against the Greeks, but Achilles killed their queen, Penthesilea. The Athenians said that at one time they invaded Attica but were defeated by *Theseus, who took their queen Hippolyte captive.

Ambartsumian, Viktor A(mazaspovich) (1908-) Soviet astrophysicist, who taught at the University of Leningrad before becoming director of the Byurakan Observatory. He wrote the first classic Russian textbook of theoretical astrophysics. His most notable work was the description of radio sources as explosions in the core of galaxies.

amber A translucent or opaque yellow fossil resin exuded by coniferous trees; insects and leaves are often preserved in the mineral, having been trapped on the sticky surface prior to hardening. It is found predominantly in Tertiary deposits around the S Baltic coast. It is used for beads, ornaments, and amber varnish.

ambergris A waxy substance found in the intestines of sperm whales. Mainly cholesterol, with fatty oils and steroids, it has a musky scent. It is used in making perfumes.

Ambler, Eric (1909-) British novelist. He began writing suspense novels in the 1930s, skilfully creating an atmosphere of fear and tension appropriate to the times. These novels, which include *The Dark Frontier* (1936), *The Mark of Dmitrios* (1939), and *Journey into Fear* (1940), were set mostly in W Europe; in later novels, such as *A Passage of Arms* (1959), he used more exotic settings. Other works are *The Nightcomers* (1956), *The Light of the Day* (1965), and *In Case of Time* (1981).

Ambleside 54 26N 2 58W A small town in the English Lake District, in Cumbria at the N end of Lake Windermere. It is a centre for tourism and outdoor pursuits. Population (1981): 3130.

ambo A raised platform in early churches with a reading stand for the reading of the Bible during services. It was most popular in Italy, although even there it began to be replaced by the pulpit during the 14th century.

Amboise 47 25N 1 00E A town in France, in the Indre-et-Loire department on the River Loire. Its fine gothic chateau was damaged during World War II but has since been restored. Population (1982): 11 415.

Ambon (*or* Amboina) 03 41S 128 10E An Indonesian island off SW Ceram. Produce includes cloves, nutmegs, and copra. Area: 1000 sq km (386 sq mi). Chief town: Ambon.

amboyna A tropical Asian tree, *Pterocarpus indicus*, that reaches a height of about 9 m and yields reddish beautifully grained wood used for furniture. Family: *Leguminosae*.

Ambrose, St (c. 339-97 AD) Italian bishop of Milan and Doctor of the Church. Born at Trier, he was appointed a provincial governor in 370 with his headquarters at Milan. After becoming a priest, he was made Bishop of Milan in 374 and was famous as a preacher and for his breadth of scholarship. He championed orthodoxy and the rights of the church against the civil power. Feast day: 7 Dec.

ambrosia beetle A wood-boring beetle, *Trypodendron lineatum*, that tunnels into the wood of dying and fallen trees. It carries its food supply—a type of fungus—with it and this produces black spores that colour infected wood distinctively. Family: *Scolytidae* (bark beetles).

Amenemhet III King of Egypt (c. 1842-1797 BC) of the 12th dynasty. He regulated the lake of El *Faiyum to irrigate S Egypt, and built the Labyrinth (later described by

the Greek historian Herodotus) nearby as an administrative centre.

Amenhotep III King of Egypt (c. 1417-1379 BC) of the 18th dynasty. He controlled Palestine and Syria through vassal kings and maintained good relations with *Babylon. Many of the monumental buildings at *Karnak, *Luxor, and elsewhere in Egypt were erected by him. He was the father of *Akhenaton.

America. *See* United States of America.

American eagle. *See* bald eagle.

American Federation of Labor-Congress of Industrial Organizations (AFL-CIO) A federation of US trade unions formed by the amalgamation in 1955 of the two major US unions—the AFL and CIO. It is currently composed of about 110 national and international unions giving a US membership of about 13.5 million and an affiliated membership of 55 000. Delegates from the member unions attend a biennial convention to decide policy. Committees contribute recommendations on subjects ranging from civil rights to safety and occupational health. Affiliated members must conform to requirements laid down by the AFL-CIO but remain autonomous within these limits.

American football. *See* football.

American Import Duties Act. *See* Townshend Acts.

AMERICAN INDIANS *A Bolivian-Indian woman and her child, direct descendants of the Incas.*

American Indians A diverse group of peoples of North, Central, and South America and the Caribbean Islands. In many respects they resemble the Mongoloid peoples of Asia, which has led to their classification as a subtype of the *Mongoloid race. However, their physical diversity, and the possession of certain features not common among Mongoloids, suggests other origins. Their ancestors probably migrated to the Americas from Asia via Alaska between 10 000 and 20 000 years ago (or earlier). They have coarse dark and usually straight hair, a skin coloration ranging from copper-brown to a yellowish-brown, dark eyes, and sparse body hair. They speak a great variety of languages and their traditional cultures range from that of primitive hunters and gatherers to the elaborate and complex civilizations of the *Aztecs, *Mayas, and *Incas.

American literature The literature in English of the British colonies of North America and, after 1776, of the United States. The earliest colonial literature consisted mainly of religious and political tracts. The first notable poets were Anne Bradstreet (1612-72) and Edward Taylor (1642-1729), both of Massachusetts. The intellectual dominance of New England was continued into the early 18th century by the theologian and metaphysician Jonathan Edwards (1703–58). The period of the American Revolution was dominated by political writers, such as Benjamin Franklin and Thomas Paine. Influential writers of the early 19th century included Washington Irving, James Fenimore Cooper, and Edgar Allan Poe and American literature came to its full maturity in the works of the New England writers Nathaniel Hawthorne, Ralph Waldo Emerson, and Herman Melville, the poets Walt Whitman and Emily Dickinson, and the humorist Mark Twain. The influence of English literature on the early development of American literature was now reciprocated, notably in the works of the novelist Henry James and the poets T. S. Eliot and Ezra Pound, all of whom went to live in Europe. They were followed in the 1920s by Ernest Hemingway and F. Scott Fitzgerald. Other writers who achieved a transatlantic reputation include the dramatists Eugene O'Neill, Tennessee Williams, and Arthur Miller and the poets Robert Frost, Robert Lowell, and John Berryman. The vitality of 20th-century American literature is most evident in the novel, practitioners of which include such writers as William Faulkner, John Steinbeck, Henry Miller, Thomas Wolfe, Norman Mailer, Saul Bellow, John Updike, and Thomas Pynchon.

American Revolution (or American War of Independence; 1775–83) The conflict in which the 13 colonies of North America gained independence from Britain. American resentment at Britain's authoritative rule focused in the mid-18th century on taxation. Protests against such legislation as the *Stamp Act (1765) and *Townshend Acts (1767) culminated in the *Boston Tea Party (1773), to which Britain responded with the punitive *Intolerable Acts (1774). The first *Continental Congress was summoned at Philadelphia and, after attempts by both sides at negotiation had failed, the first shots of the war were fired at *Lexington and Concord (April, 1775). In the autumn the Americans invaded Canada, taking Montreal and besieging Quebec until forced to withdraw to Ticonderoga in Spring, 1776. On 4 July the second Continental Congress issued the *Declaration of Independence. Gen Howe landed on Long Island in August and defeated the newly appointed American commander in chief, Washington, near White Plains. At the beginning of January, 1777, however, Washington dealt a counterblow at Princeton before settling in winter quarters. Britain's strategy in 1777 was based on a plan for Burgoyne to march S from Canada and join forces with Howe at the Hudson River. Burgoyne duly arrived at the Hudson (Aug) but Howe had left New York by sea, landed at Chesapeake Bay, and defeated Washington at the Brandywine, taking Philadelphia (Sept). Burgoyne, meanwhile, was forced to surrender his army at *Saratoga, a defeat that proved a turning point by bringing France into the war on the American side. In 1778 the British began an offensive in the S. Howe's successor, Clinton, took Charleston, South Carolina, and Cornwallis defeated Gates at Camden (1780). In early 1781 the British lost badly at Cowpens (17 Jan) but won, with heavy casualties, the battle of Guilford Court House (15 March). Cornwallis now moved into Virginia, establishing a base at Yorktown. There besieged by a Franco-American force under the Comte de Rochambeau (1725–1807) and Washington, on 19 October Cornwallis surrendered. Ultimate American victory was now assured although conflict continued, chiefly at sea. The British navy had been threatened throughout by American privateers and the activities of such commanders as John Paul *Jones, but the main threat at sea came from America's European allies—the French, Spanish (from 1779), and Dutch (from 1780), who gained control of the English Channel and threatened invasion. Rodney's success (1782) in the West Indies was not sufficient to reverse the effect of Yorktown but enabled Britain to regain control of the Atlantic. In 1783 Britain acknowledged American independence in the Treaty of *Paris.

The American Revolution was a major issue in British politics and the administration of Lord *North, dominated by George III, came under violent attack. However, the loss of the colonies can only in part be attributed to the incompetence of British direction; the leadership of Washington and French aid were also significant factors.

America's Cup A cup offered in a yacht race at Cowes in 1851 and won by the US schooner *America*. Since 1857 it has been the prize in a periodic sailing competition. The New York Yacht Club retained it until 1983, when it was won by an Australian syndicate. The USA regained it in 1987.

americium (Am) The fourth transuranic element, synthesized (1944) by G. T. Seaborg and others by addition of neutrons to plutonium followed by β-decay. It forms the oxide (AmO_2) and such trihalides as $AmCl_3$; it is strongly radioactive. At no 95; at wt (243); mp 994°C.

Amersfoort 52 09N 5 23E A town in the central Netherlands, in Utrecht province. Its medieval buildings include a 14th-century watergate. Industries include chemicals, machinery, and carpets. Population (1981 est): 88 365.

amethyst A gemstone comprising a purple variety of *quartz. Its colour is due to impurities, particularly iron oxide. The best crystals are found in Brazil and the Urals. It is used for jewellery. Birthstone for February.

Amhara A descendant of the invading Semitic conquerors of the Cushitic peoples of Ethiopia. They occupy the southern area of the central highlands of Ethiopia over which, with the Tigré, they have exercised political dominance until the present day. Their society is hierarchical and largely feudal. The emperors were believed to be descended from the biblical king *Solomon. They are a Christian people, who belong to the Coptic Church. Amharic is the language of the Amharas and the principal and official language of Ethiopia. It is derived from a language related to Ethiopic or Ge'ez, the liturgical language of the Ethiopian Church, and is written in Ge'ez characters. It is similar to *Semitic languages in grammar but its vocabulary is largely *Cushitic.

Amherst, Jeffrey, Baron (1717–97) British soldier prominent in the *Seven Years' War against the French in North America. In 1758 he took the fortress of Louisburg and became commander in chief in America. By 1760 he had conquered Montreal. He was governor general of British North America from 1760 to 1763.

Amici, Giovanni Battista (1786–1863) Italian astronomer, microscopist, and optical instrument maker. He is best known as the inventor of the *achromatic lens. With his own microscopes he discovered many details of orchid pollination and seed development; in astronomy, he studied double stars and Jupiter's moons, as well as designing improved mirrors for reflecting telescopes.

Amiel, Henri Frédéric (1821–81) Swiss philosopher and writer. Amiel's principal work is his diary (kept 1847–81), *Fragments d'un journal intime* (1883), which contains some fine descriptive writing and penetrating observations.

Amiens 49 54N 2 18E A city in NE France, the capital of the Somme department situated on the River Somme. Known as Samarobriva in pre-Roman times, it was the ancient capital of Picardy. The Peace of Amiens (1802), which marked a respite in the Revolutionary and Napoleonic Wars, was signed here. Its fine gothic cathedral survived the damage of both World Wars. An important railway junction, Amiens' industries include textiles, tyres, and chemicals. Population (1982 est): 136 358.

Amin Dada, Idi (c. 1925–) Ugandan politician; president (1971–79). He rose rapidly in the army, becoming commander in 1966. He overthrew Milton *Obote to become president and in 1972 ordered the expulsion of 80 000 non-Ugandan Asians. In 1975 he became president of the

Organization of African Unity. A flamboyant and unpredictable personality, he and his government were notorious for their brutality; Amin was overthrown in a Tanzanian-backed coup after which he went into exile.

Amindivi Islands. *See* Lakshadweep.

amines A class of basic organic compounds derived from ammonia (NH_3), in which one (primary amines), two (secondary amines), or three (tertiary amines) of the hydrogen atoms are replaced by organic radicals or groups. *See also* amino acids.

amino acids A group of organic acids characterized by having at least one carboxyl group ($-COOH$) and at least one amino group ($-NH_2$). About 20 different amino acids comprise the basic constituents of *proteins, the arrangement and types of amino acids determining the structure and hence the function of the protein molecule. Certain essential amino acids cannot be manufactured by the body and must be supplied in the diet. In man these are: arginine, histidine, isoleucine, leucine, lysine, methionine, phenylalanine, threonine, tryptophan, and valine.

Amirante Islands An archipelago of sparsely populated coral islands in the W Indian Ocean, belonging to the Seychelles. They are leased to private companies, usually for coconut plantations.

Amis, Kingsley (1922–) British novelist and poet, one of the *Angry Young Men of the 1950s. Educated at Oxford, he taught at Swansea and Cambridge universities and in the USA. His first novel, *Lucky Jim* (1954), a comic satire on middle-class academic life, was a popular success. In later novels, such as *I Want It Now* (1968), *Ending Up* (1974), *Jake's Thing* (1978), and *Stanley and the Women* (1984), his humour became progressively darker; in 1986 he won the Booker Prize for *The Old Devils*. He has published poetry, contributed to the important verse anthology *New Lines* (1956), and edited the *Oxford Book of Light Verse* (1978). He was married (1965–83) to the novelist Elizabeth Jane Howard (1923–). His son **Martin Amis** (1949–) is the author of such books as *The Rachel Papers* (1974), *Money* (1984), and *The Moronic Inferno* (1986).

Amman 31 57N 35 56E The capital of Jordan. Amman was the capital of the biblical Ammonites, and there are some Greek and Roman remains. Under the British mandate in Palestine, the town grew from a small village, and in 1946 it became the capital of independent Jordan. The city has had large influxes of refugees following fighting in the Arab-Israeli Wars (1948, 1967, and 1973); in 1970 tension resulting from the refugee presence led to fighting on the streets of Amman between Jordanian forces and Palestinians. The university was founded in 1962. Amman is now an important communications centre, with some manufacturing industry. Population (1980 est): 1 232 600.

Ammanati, Bartolommeo (1511–92) Florentine mannerist architect and sculptor. Beginning as an assistant of *Sansovino in Venice, Ammanati later worked with *Vasari in Rome on the Villa Giulia. In Florence he was responsible for the Ponte Sta Trinità and the garden façade of the Palazzo Pitti; as a sculptor he is best known for the Neptune fountain in the Piazza della Signoria.

ammeter An instrument for measuring electric current. The two most common types are the moving-coil and the moving-iron ammeters. The moving-coil ammeter is more sensitive but will only measure alternating current. The moving-iron ammeter will measure both alternating and direct current but is less sensitive and its scale is nonlinear. Some instruments are electronic and have a digital display.

ammonia (NH_3) A colourless toxic gas used for the manufacture of fertilizers, nitric acid, explosives, and synthetic fibres. When dissolved in water, ammonia produces an alkaline solution of ammonium hydroxide (NH_4OH), an unstable compound that cannot be isolated from solution.

ammonite A *cephalopod mollusc belonging to the subclass *Ammonoidea* (over 600 genera), abundant during the late Palaeozoic and Mesozoic eras, becoming extinct 100 million years ago. Their fossilized remains have either straight or coiled shells, some up to 200 cm in diameter, containing many chambers, which provided buoyancy for the free-swimming animal. □fossil.

Ammonites An ancient Semitic tribe who were descended from Ben-ammi, the son of Lot, and lived E of Jordan. They worshipped the god Moloch and often warred against the Israelites.

amnesia Loss of memory resulting from such causes as head injuries, drugs, hysteria, senility, or psychological illness. The memory loss may be for events before the injury or disease (retrograde amnesia) or for events after it (anterograde amnesia). In some cases specific areas of the brain show pathological changes. Treatment is related to the cause.

Amnesty International An organization, founded by Peter Benenson in the UK in 1961, aiming to defend freedom of speech, opinion, and religion in all parts of the world. Its work consists of campaigns for the release of "prisoners of conscience," against torture, and for human rights and it is concerned for the welfare of refugees. It has some 100 000 members in 75 countries and is funded by voluntary contributions.

amniocentesis The removal for examination of a small quantity of the fluid (amniotic fluid) that surrounds an unborn baby in the mother's womb. The specimen may be taken by needle through the abdominal wall or, later in pregnancy, the opening of the womb. Tests on the amniotic fluid may reveal the presence of certain diseases or congenital disorders in the baby (e.g. Down's syndrome or spina bifida). If serious abnormality is detected, the possibility of abortion at an early and safe stage can be considered. Amniocentesis is particularly useful when there is a family history of serious congenital disease. *See also* prenatal diagnosis.

Amoeba A genus of free-living microscopic animals (□*Protozoa*). They occur widely in soil, fresh water, and salt water and their flexible cells assume various shapes. The common amoeba (*A. proteus*) may be up to 0.5 mm long. Amoebas move by extending their cytoplasm into broad lobes (pseudopodia), which are also used to engulf food particles (e.g. bacteria and other protozoans) and liquids. They reproduce by binary *fission and under adverse conditions form cysts with a thick protective wall surrounding the cell. Some related forms are parasitic, including *Entamoeba histolytica*, which causes amoebic dysentery in man. Class: *Sarcodina*.

Amon The supreme Egyptian deity. Originally a local god of Thebes, he acquired major status in the ascendancy of the 18th (Theban) dynasty in about 1570 BC. He became associated with the rival god *Ra and as Amon-Ra became the national god. Great temples were built to him at Luxor and Karnak (c. 1400 BC). Except during the brief reign of *Akhenaton, Amon-Ra remained supreme god until the Assyrians captured Thebes in 663 BC.

Amorites Semitic nomads of Palestine and Syria, who invaded the centres of civilization of Mesopotamia during the late 3rd millennium and 2nd millennium BC. They occupied *Babylonia, assimilated its culture and established numerous small kingdoms. Many Babylonian kings, including *Hammurabi, were of Amorite stock. *Mari and *Aleppo were important centres under Amorite control.

amortization 1. The discharging of a debt (e.g. a mortgage) through (usually equal) periodic payments of principal and interest. 2. The depreciation of an asset through wear or obsolescence. The value of a fixed asset purchased by a company is not charged in full to its profit and loss account in the year in which it is purchased. Instead it is amortized over its useful life in the accounts, i.e. only a certain portion of its cost is charged to the profit and loss account each year.

Amos (early 8th century BC) An Old Testament prophet of Judah. **The Book of Amos** contains his prophecies delivered in Israel. He denounces the luxury and injustice of the privileged nation and predicts God's judgment by means of an Assyrian invasion and natural calamities.

amount of substance A quantity proportional to the number of particles, such as atoms or ions, in a substance. The constant of proportionality is *Avogadro's number. Amount of substance is measured in *moles.

Amoy. *See* Xiamen.

ampere (A) The *SI unit of electric current equal to the current that when passed through two parallel infinitely long conductors placed 1 metre apart in a vacuum produces a force between them of 2×10^{-7} newton per metre of length. This 1948 definition replaced all former definitions including that of the international ampere based on the rate of deposition of silver from a solution of silver nitrate. Named after A. M. *Ampère.

Ampère, André Marie (1775-1836) French physicist, who was a professor at Bourg and later in Paris. He is remembered for his fundamental work on the physics and mathematics of electricity and electromagnetism. He introduced the important distinctions between electrostatics and electric currents and between current and voltage, demonstrated that current-carrying wires exert a force on each other, and gave an explanation of magnetism in terms of electric currents. The unit of electric current is named after him.

Ampère's law The strength of the magnetic field at any point produced by a current (I) flowing through a conductor of length l is proportional to Il/d^2 where d is the distance between the point and the conductor. Named after A. M. *Ampère.

amphetamine A stimulant drug that produces a feeling of alertness and wellbeing, increases muscular activity, and reduces fatigue and appetite. Because of the risk of addiction, particularly when combined with barbiturates ("purple hearts"), amphetamine is now rarely prescribed. It is occasionally used to treat obesity and narcolepsy (a tendency to fall asleep at any time). Trade name: Benzedrine. *See also* drug dependence.

amphibian An animal belonging to the class *Amphibia*, which contains over 2500 species of frogs, toads, newts, salamanders, and caecilians. Adult amphibians breathe through lungs and have adapted to a wide range of habitats; however they require damp surroundings in order to minimize loss of body fluids through their thin, moist and usually scaleless skin. Generally amphibians lay their eggs in ponds or rivers, often migrating long distances to do so. The eggs hatch into aquatic tadpole larvae that breathe using gills and develop into adults by a complete bodily transformation known as *metamorphosis.

amphiboles A group of rock-forming minerals, mostly complex hydrous ferromagnesian silicates. The anthophyllite-cummingtonite subgroup contains anthophyllite, gedrite, cummingtonite, and grunerite; the hornblende subgroup contains tremolite, actinolite, hornblende, edenite, hastingsite, and kaersutite; the alkali amphibole subgroup contains glaucophane, nebeckite, richterite, and katophorite. Amphiboles are common in igneous and metamorphic rocks and often occur in fibrous or acicular forms, including some forms of *asbestos.

amphioxus A small slender fishlike animal, also called lancelet, belonging to the subphylum *Cephalochordata* (about 30 species). Up to 5 cm long, they occur in shallow coastal waters, living mostly in burrows with the front end protruding. Food particles are filtered from the water, which enters the mouth and leaves through gill slits, there is a supportive rodlike *notochord and a nerve cord running the

length of the body. Amphioxus is thought to resemble the primitive ancestors of other chordate animals, including vertebrates. Genera: *Branchiostoma*; *Asymmetron*. *See also* Chordata.

amphisbaena A wormlike lizard, also called worm lizard, belonging to the family *Amphisbaenidae* (120 species) occurring in tropical and subtropical America and Africa and the Mediterranean region. Up to 60 cm long, amphisbaenas are specialized for burrowing having reduced eyes, a small head with thick skull bones, and, except for one genus (*Bipes*), no legs. They feed on insects and larvae.

amphitheatre An elliptical or circular building with tiers of seats surrounding an arena, designed by the Romans as a setting for gladiatorial and wild-beast shows, mock sea battles, etc. Small wooden amphitheatres were built throughout the Roman world. The earliest stone amphitheatre is that at Pompeii (c. 70 BC). The largest is the *Colosseum in Rome but there are also impressive remains of amphitheatres in Arles, Nîmes, Capua, Verona, and in Sicily and N Africa.

Amphitrite The Greek goddess of the sea. Poseidon chose her to be his wife when he saw her dancing with her sister Nereids. She rejected him and fled to the island of Naxos, but he sent a dolphin to reclaim her. She bore him three sons, Triton, Rhodos, and Benthesicyma.

Amphitryon In Greek mythology, a grandson of Perseus who was betrothed to Alcmene, daughter of the King of Mycenae. While he was away at war, Zeus assumed his appearance and seduced Alcmene, who conceived *Heracles from the union.

AMPHORA *A Greek form of the 6th century BC.*

amphora An ancient Greek two-handled vase used as a container for liquids and fruit, and sometimes as an urn for holding ashes of the dead or for prize awards. The most important are the Black Figure vases (600-480 BC) of black-painted red earthenware, depicting mythological scenes. Other undecorated types, sometimes tapering to a pointed base, were in general use for transporting oil and wine until Roman times.

amplifier A device for increasing the magnitude of some quantity by using power from an external source. The term usually refers to an electronic device for intensifying an electrical signal in an alternating-current circuit, with an external steady voltage supply. Originally built with *thermionic valves, but now almost exclusively with *transistors, amplifiers are designed to multiply the input (current, voltage, or power) by a specific factor, known as the gain. Often an amplifier consists of several stages, the output from one stage becoming the input to the next stage. This method is used in the more complex and specialized type of amplifier used in sound-reproduction systems.

amplitude modulation. *See* modulation.

Amr ibn al-As (d. 663 AD) Arab soldier, who led the Muslim conquest of Egypt. Following the conquest of Syria he led the invasion of Egypt; Alexandria fell in 642. Having helped *Muʻawiyah I secure the caliphate (661), he governed Egypt until his death.

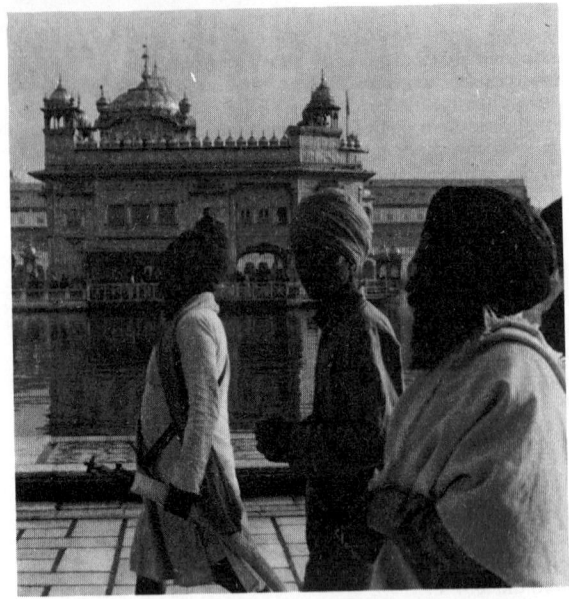

AMRITSAR *The Golden Temple, centre of the Sikh religion; it is built on an island on a small lake called the "Pool of Immortality".*

Amritsar 31 35N 74 56E A city in NW India, in Punjab. Founded in 1577 by the fourth guru of the Sikhs, Ram Das, it has become the centre of the Sikh faith. It was the scene of a massacre (1919), in which hundreds of Indian nationalists were killed when fired upon by troops under British control. In 1984 about 1000 people died when the Sikh shrine, the Golden Temple, was fortified by Sikh extremists and stormed by the Indian army. The assassination of Mrs *Gandhi later in the year was a reprisal for this event. A commercial, cultural, and communications centre, it manufactures textiles and silk. Population (1981 est): 594 844.

Amsterdam 52 21N 4 54E The official capital of the Netherlands, in North Holland province on the Rivers Amstel and IJ. The government seat is at The Hague. Linked to the North Sea by canal (1876), it is a major seaport. It is also an important financial and industrial centre, possessing a renowned diamond cutting and polishing trade. Industries include shipbuilding, dairy produce, tobacco, and brewing. The city is mostly built on piles and linked with a radial system of canals and approximately 1000 bridges. Notable buildings include the 13th-century Oude Kerk (Old Church), the 15th-century Nieuwe Kerk (New Church), and a royal palace (1665). It possesses two universities, the Rijksmuseum, containing a superb collection of Dutch and Flemish paintings, and the Stedelijk Museum with its leading modern-art collection. *History*: chartered in 1300, it joined the Hanseatic League in 1369. During the 17th century it prospered as a seaport; it gained significantly through Antwerp's loss of trade following the closure of the River Scheldt under the Treaty of Westphalia (1648). It became the capital in 1808. Population (1981 est): 712 294.

Amu Darya, River A river in central Asia. Rising in the Pamirs, it flows mainly NW through the Hindu Kush and the Turkmen and Uzbek SSRs to join the Aral Sea through a large delta. It forms part of the border between Afghanistan and the Soviet Union and it is important for irrigation. It is navigable for over 1450 km (800 mi). Length: 2400 km (1500 mi).

Amundsen, Roald (1872–1928) Norwegian explorer, the first person to reach the South Pole. In 1897 he became first mate on the *Belgica*, which was engaged in Antarctic exploration. After sailing the *Northwest Passage in the *Gjöa* (1903–06) he abandoned his plan to reach the North Pole on hearing of *Peary's success (1909). He himself beat *Scott to the South Pole in 1911. In 1926 he flew a dirigible over the North Pole with Umberto *Nobile. Amundsen died while searching for Nobile following the latter's dirigible crash in the Arctic Ocean.

Amundsen Sea A small section of the S Pacific Ocean, bordering on Ellsworth Land in Antarctica.

Amur, River (Chinese name: Heilong Jiang *or* Hei-Lung Chiang) A river in NE Asia. Rising in N Mongolia, it flows generally SE and NE through Mongolia, the Soviet Union, and China, to the Sea of Okhotsk. The border betweeen the Soviet Union and Manchuria, it has been the scene of much Sino-Soviet friction since the 1960s. Length: 4350 km (2700 mi).

amyl alcohol ($C_5H_{11}OH$) A colourless oily liquid *alcohol that has eight *isomers: pentan-1-ol, pentan-2-ol, etc. It is obtained from *fusel oil and is used as a solvent.

amylase A digestive enzyme that breaks down starch and glycogen into maltose. It is present in saliva (as ptyalin) and in pancreatic juice.

Amyot, Jacques (1513–93) French bishop and scholar. He was in turn tutor to *Henry II's sons, grand chaplain of France, and Bishop of Auxerre. His writings are mainly translations of classical works, the most famous being his version of Plutarch's *Lives*, *Les Vies des hommes illustres Grecs et Romains* (1559), which greatly influenced Renaissance humanism in France and England.

Anabaptists (from Greek: rebaptizers) Any of various radical religious groups originating in several continental countries during the *Reformation. They were called Anabaptists because they rejected infant baptism in favour of baptizing adults when they professed their faith. Persecuted by Roman Catholics and Protestants, they were accused of fanaticism, heresy, and immorality. They believed in pacifism, common ownership of goods, millenarianism, and held radical political views. Prominent leaders were the German Thomas Münzer (c. 1490–1525), killed after the Peasants' Revolt, and *John of Leiden. Their modern descendants, such as the *Mennonites, number more than 500 000.

anabolic steroids. *See* androgens.

anabolism. *See* metabolism.

anaconda A nonvenomous South American *constrictor snake, *Eunectes murinus*. Up to 10 m long, it is typically dark green with oval black spots and lives in swamps and rivers, feeding on fish and small caymans and also hunting deer, peccaries, and birds along the water's edge.

Anacreon (6th century BC) Greek lyric poet. He fled from his native island of Teos before the Persian invasion, and lived at Samos and then Athens, under the patronage of Hipparchus. His work, only fragments of which survive, consisted chiefly of love lyrics and drinking songs, written in a formal and restrained style.

anaemia A reduction in the number of red cells or the quantity of red pigment (*see* haemoglobin) in the blood. It may be due to loss of blood, for example after an accident or operation or from chronic bleeding of a peptic ulcer, or lack of iron, which is necessary for the production of haemoglobin. **Haemolytic anaemias** are caused by increased destruction of the red blood cells, as may occur in certain blood diseases (e.g. *sickle-cell disease and *thalassaemia) and malaria or because of the presence of toxic chemicals. Anaemia can also result from the defective production of red cells, such as occurs in **pernicious anaemia** (when it is due to deficiency of *vitamin B_{12}).

The main symptoms of anaemia are extreme tiredness and fatiguability, breathlessness, pallor, palpitations, and poor resistance to infection. The treatment depends on the cause.

anaerobe. *See* aerobe.

anaesthesia A state of insensitivity to pain. Anaesthesia occurs in certain diseases of the nervous system, but the term usually refers to the state induced artificially for surgical operations. It may be produced by anaesthetic drugs or other means, including *hypnosis and *acupuncture. Alcohol and opium derivatives have been used as anaesthetics for centuries, but it was not until the 1840s that the first anaesthetic gases—ether, nitrous oxide, and chloroform—were used to induce **general anaesthesia** (total unconsciousness). This procedure now involves premedication (including administration of sedatives) to prepare the patient for surgery, followed by induction of anaesthesia by injecting a short-acting barbiturate (usually sodium thiopentone). Anaesthesia is maintained by inhalation of an anaesthetic gas (e.g. *halothane). **Local anaesthesia** is usually used for dental surgery and also for other operations when the medical state of the patient makes general anaesthesia unadvisable. Procaine and lignocaine are widely used local anaesthetics. **Spinal anaesthesia** (epidural or subarachnoid) produces loss of sensation in a particular part of the body by injecting a local anaesthetic into the space round the spinal cord. It may be used, for example, during a difficult childbirth.

anagnoresis (Greek: recognition) A literary term referring to the moment of recognition of a previously unsuspected truth. The concept was defined in Aristotle's *Poetics*. It is considered an essential part of the plot of tragedy, in which the protagonist's recognition of his tragic flaw occurs at the climax and leads to his downfall. The best-known example occurs in Sophocles' *Oedipus Rex* when Oedipus discovers that he has unknowingly killed his father and married his mother.

Anaheim 33 50N 117 56W A city in the USA, in S California near Los Angeles. It is a major tourist centre, containing the famous Disneyland opened in 1955. Population (1985): 236 000.

analgesics A class of drugs that relieve pain. **Narcotic analgesics**, such as *morphine, are powerful pain killers that act directly on the brain. Some anaesthetics also have analgesic properties. *Aspirin and paracetemol are examples of **antipyretic analgesics**, which also reduce fever. These drugs are not addictive but are less potent than the narcotics. *See also* drug dependence; narcotics.

analog computer. *See* computer.

analytic geometry The study of geometrical relations by algebraic methods. Geometrical figures are placed in a *coordinate system, each point in the figure being represented by its coordinates, which satisfy an algebraic equation. Also known as coordinate geometry or Cartesian geometry, after its inventor René *Descartes.

anamorphosis A perspective technique used in painting and drawing to distort an image or object seen from a normal viewpoint. The image's true form is only recreated when viewed from an angle or through a special device, such as a peephole. A famous example is the elongated skull in Hans Holbein's *Ambassadors* (1533; National Gallery, London).

Ananda (5th century BC) The first cousin, favourite disciple, and personal attendant of the Buddha. At his insistence a Buddhist order was founded to admit women.

anaphylaxis A form of *allergy that follows the interaction of the foreign substance (allergen) with antibody that is bound to the surface of certain cells (mast cells). This leads to the release of bradykinin, *histamine, and other chemicals, which cause the symptoms. Symptoms are either local (such as asthma) or general (shock and collapse). The latter usually follows injection of the allergen (such as penicillin) and is a medical emergency; it is treated with injections of corticosteroids and adrenaline.

anarchism A political theory advocating abolition of the state and all governmental authority. Most anarchists believe that voluntary cooperation between individuals and groups is not only a fairer and more moral way of organizing society but is also more effective and orderly. Anarchism aims at maximizing personal freedom and holds that societies in which freedom is limited by coercion and authority are inherently unstable. *Proudhon thought that anarchism could be achieved by peaceful change, but *Bakunin believed that violent means were necessary. As an influential political force, anarchism was defeated in Russia by communism but persisted in Europe, especially in Spain until the end of the Civil War (1939).

Anastasia (1901–?1918) The youngest daughter of *Nicholas II of Russia. Although she was believed to have been executed after the Russian Revolution, a Mrs Anna Anderson (d. 1984) claimed from 1920 that she was Anastasia. In 1961 her claim was officially rejected.

Anastasius I (c. 430–518 AD) Byzantine emperor (491–518). Anastasius instituted thorough financial and administrative reforms and built a defensive wall to protect Constantinople. His adherence to the heretical *Monophysite doctrine was unpopular.

Anatolia. *See* Asia Minor.

Anatolian languages An extinct subgroup of the *Indo-European language family, which included Palaic, Luwian, Lydian, and Lycian. Originally spoken in Asia Minor, some date back to 2000 BC. The classification is sometimes used in a geographical sense to include all the languages of ancient Asia Minor, some of non-Indo-European origin. There is some confusion about the relation of the Anatolian languages to *Hittite and a precise classification of the relations between these and Indo-European has not been achieved. *See also* Indo-Hittite languages.

anatomy The study of the structure of living organisms. Early studies of human anatomy were made by the Greek physician Galen, in the 2nd century AD, but it was not until the 16th century that the prejudice against dissecting human cadavers was overcome and anatomists—notably *Vesalius—made valuable contributions to the science. In the 17th century William *Harvey discovered the circulation of blood and the development of the microscope enabled advances in the detailed structure of the body to be made by such microscopists as *Malpighi, *Leeuwenhoek, and *Swammerdam. In the 20th century anatomy received a valuable tool with the development of the electron microscope, which greatly extended the investigation of microscopic structure. Today anatomy explores structure within the context of function (*see* physiology). Specialized branches of anatomy include embryology (the study of development), *histology (tissues), and *cytology (cells).

Anaxagoras (c. 500–428 BC) Greek philosopher, born at Clazomenae (Asia Minor). In about 480 he moved to Athens, but because of his influence on *Pericles, he was eventually (450) banished on a trumped-up charge of impiety. He diverged from some other early Greek philosophers by stating that the physical universe was made up of an infinite number of substances and that matter was infinitely divisible. He was also the first to explain solar eclipses.

Anaximander (c. 610–c. 546 BC) Greek philosopher, born in Miletus (Asia Minor). He was one of the earliest thinkers to develop a systematic philosophical view of the physical universe. He held that it came from something unlimited, not just one particular kind of matter, and maintained that the earth lay unsupported at the centre of the universe. He also had an evolutionary view of the origin of life, holding that it arose in the sea, and that man evolved from some more primitive species.

Anaximenes (died c. 528 BC) Greek philosopher, who lived in Miletus (Asia Minor). He believed that the universe fundamentally consisted of air or vapour; different degrees of condensation corresponded to different degrees of density in matter. He held that air, being constantly in motion, possessed life and that its motion accounted for changes in physical objects.

ancestor worship In many primitive societies, the propitiation of the spirits of dead forebears, usually with the object of persuading them to exert their powers on behalf of their descendants in hunting, warfare, etc. Ancestor cults can also be socially important in reinforcing the authority of living elders, who, as guardians of the ancestral shrines, are the spirits' mouthpieces. Festivals for the dead involving visits to the tombs, food offerings, and sacrifices were features of ancient Greek and Roman religion. An ancestor cult formed an important part of traditional Chinese religion and also survives in the Buddhist family altar (*butsudan*) in Japanese households.

Anchieta, José de (1534–97) Portuguese poet and scholar. He became a Jesuit in 1551, and in 1553 joined a mission in Brazil. He helped protect the Indians from slavery and was one of the founders of the city of São Paulo. As well as his chiefly religious poetry and historical works he wrote a grammar of the Indian language, Tupí, and descriptions of the Indian culture.

Anchises In Greek mythology, a Trojan nobleman, father of *Aeneas by *Aphrodite. He was blinded for boasting of his relationship with the goddess. Carried from burning *Troy on Aeneas' back, he died in Sicily.

Admiralty pattern

CQR

stockless

ANCHOR *Three common forms of anchor.*

anchor Any device used for mooring a vessel to the bottom of a body of water. In ancient times a heavy stone was used, attached to the vessel by a rope. Today various patent anchors are in use. They are designed for different kinds of bottom—sandy, rocky, muddy, etc.—and usually dig into the bottom with their bladelike flukes. Depending on the size of the vessel, the anchor rode, or attachment to the vessel, may be entirely of heavy chain, as in the case of larger boats and ships, or of a short length of chain to which a rope, usually of nylon, is attached.

Anchorage 61 10N 150 00E A city and major port in the USA, in S Alaska at the head of Cook Inlet. Founded in 1914 as the terminus of the Alaska Railroad, its main industries are defence projects and the development of natural resources, especially coal and gold. Population (1984): 244 030.

anchovy A small herring-like fish belonging to the tropical and warm-temperate family *Engraulidae* (100 species). 10–25 cm long, anchovies have a large mouth extending behind the eye, a small lower jaw, and a pointed snout. They live in large shoals, chiefly in coastal waters, and are widely fished for food, bait, and animal feeds. ◻oceans.

Anchusa. *See* alkanet.

ancien régime The social and political system of France prior to the *French Revolution.

ancient lights In English law, the right of an owner of a building to have uninterrupted light through a window. The passage of light through a window is protected against obstruction if it has been enjoyed without interruption for at least 20 years.

Ancona 43 37N 13 31E A seaport in central Italy, the capital of Marche on the Adriatic Sea. It dates from 1500 BC, when it was founded by the Dorians. Its industries are connected with shipbuilding, engineering, and sugar refining. Population (1981): 106 498.

Andalusia (Spanish name: Andalucía) The southernmost region of Spain, bordering on the Atlantic Ocean and Mediterranean Sea. It occupies chiefly the river basin of the Guadalquivir and is one of Spain's most fertile regions producing citrus fruit, olives, and wine. Under Roman control after the 2nd century BC, the region was named Andalusia (after its 5th-century Vandal settlers) by the Muslims, who invaded the region in the early 8th century; much evidence of the Muslim occupation remains. In the 15th century Castile finally recovered Andalusia from the Muslims. After the *Moriscos (Christians of Moorish descent) were expelled in 1609 the region's prosperity diminished. It is now popular with tourists, who are attracted by the great Moorish buildings found especially in Córdoba, Seville, and Granada.

Andalusian horse A breed of large strong horse developed in Spain in the 15th century. Andalusian horses are usually grey (but sometimes bay or black), with a long silky mane and tail and a high stepping movement. Docile and attractive, they are often used in parades and bullfighting. Height: 1.60–1.70 m (15¾–16¾ hands).

Andaman and Nicobar Islands A Union Territory of India, comprising two island groups in the E Bay of Bengal. The Andaman forests support plywood and match industries. Coconuts, rubber, and coffee are also important. The Nicobar Islands 120 km (75 mi) S of the Andaman Islands, produce coconuts, arecanuts, and fish. *History*: the Andaman Islands were an Indian penal colony until 1945. Both groups were occupied by Japan (1942–45) and transferred to India (1947). Area: 8293 sq km (3215 sq mi). Population (1981): 188 254. Capital: Port Blair.

Andamanese The indigenous inhabitants of the Andaman and Nicobar Islands in the Bay of Bengal. They are of negrito racial type. Their traditional culture, surviving only in southern areas among the Jarawa and Onge tribes, was based upon gathering shellfish, fishing, and hunting, using single outrigger canoes, nets, lines, and bows and arrows. Tools and weapons were often made from large shells. There was no method known to them of making fire. Social organization was simple. Tribes were divided into hunting bands, several of which might acknowledge a common chief. Trading between coastal and inland bands was extensive. Ritual initiation was important and various taboos were a prominent feature of their ritual life. Their language Andamanese, is almost extinct and has no known relations.

Andersen, Hans Christian (1805–75) Danish author, famous for his fairy tales. The son of a shoemaker, he attempted to become an actor in Copenhagen. A benefactor enabled him to attend the university there in 1828; he subsequently travelled widely in Europe and wrote novels, plays, and travel books. His international reputation, however, was earned by the 168 fairy tales that he wrote between 1835 and 1872. These include such classics as "The Snow Queen," "The Little Mermaid," and "The Ugly Duckling."

HANS CHRISTIAN ANDERSEN

Anderson, Carl David (1905–) US physicist, who works at the California Institute of Technology. He shared the 1936 Nobel Prize for showing (1932) that cloud-chamber tracks were made by *positrons, whose existence had been predicted by Dirac. In 1935 Anderson discovered the first *meson, thinking it was the particle predicted by *Yukawa. In fact Anderson's meson is now known as the muon, whereas Yukawa's particle is known as the pion (discovered by *Powell).

Anderson, Elizabeth Garrett (1836–1917) British physician, who pioneered the admission of women into the medical profession. Refused admission to medical schools, she studied privately and in 1865 was granted a licence to practise. She helped establish a hospital for women in London, now named after her.

Anderson, John, 1st Viscount Waverley (1882–1958) British civil servant and politician. In World War II he was home secretary and minister of home security (1939–40), when the Anderson air raid shelter was named after him; he was chancellor of the exchequer (1943–45).

Anderson, Sherwood (1876–1941) US author. Born in a small town in Ohio, he held a variety of jobs before abandoning job and family in 1906 to become a writer. He was encouraged by Theodore *Dreiser, Carl *Sandburg, and other Chicago writers and by Gertrude *Stein in Paris. He finally settled in Virginia as a newspaper owner; there he in turn encouraged *Faulkner and *Hemingway. *Winesburg, Ohio* (1919), his best-known book, is a series of tales about the stunted lives of a small-town community. His novels included *Poor White* (1920) and *Dark Laughter* (1925).

Andes (Spanish name: Cordillera de los Andes) A mountain system in W South America. It extends N for about 7250 km (4500 mi) from Cape Horn to the Isthmus of Panama, reaching 6960 m (22 835 ft) at Mount Aconcagua and separating a narrow coastal belt from the rest of the continent. Comprising a series of parallel mountain ranges, it is chiefly of volcanic origin and contains several active volcanoes, including *Cotopaxi; earthquakes are common phenomena. It is rich in mineral wealth; the chief metals

extracted include gold, silver, platinum, mercury, copper, and lead.

andesite A group of volcanic rocks comprising the fine-grained equivalent of *diorite. They consist mainly of plagioclase-feldspar and one or more ferromagnesian minerals, and many andesites are porphyritic. They are found associated with basalts and rhyolites in island arcs and orogenic regions. The Andesite Line is the geographic boundary between continental andesitic rocks and oceanic basalts, traced through the Pacific.

Andhra Pradesh A state in E central India, on the Bay of Bengal. The coastal plain rises westwards over the Eastern *Ghats into the *Deccan plateau. Rice, sugar cane, cotton, tobacco, and pulses are farmed. Large forests provide teak, bamboo, and fruit trees. Manganese, iron ore, mica, and coal are mined. A few industries exist, such as textile, machinery, and shipbuilding, which has been developed with cheap hydroelectricity. *History*: the Andhra people and culture have flourished since the 1st century BC. From 1700 local rulers gradually lost control to France and Britain. A centre of 20th-century Indian nationalism, the Telegu-speaking area of *Madras became Andhra Pradesh state in 1953. Further boundary adjustments were made in 1956 and 1960. Area: 275 281 sq km (106 258 sq mi). Population (1981): 53 403 619. Capital: Hyderabad. Chief seaport: Vishakhapatnam.

Andizhan 40 40N 72 12E A city in the SW Soviet Union, in the Uzbek SSR on the River Andizhan-Say. Situated in the fertile *Fergana Valley, Andizhan has always been the region's main trade centre. Its industries include engineering. Population (1981 est): 238 000.

Andong (*or* An-tung) 40 06N 124 25E A port in NE China, in Liaoning province on the Yalu estuary and on the border with North Korea. It was opened to foreign trade in 1907. Its industries, developed under the Japanese occupation (1931–45), include paper, silk, cotton, and chemicals. Population (1980): 102 024.

Andorra, Coprincipality of (Catalan name: Valls d'Andorra; French name: Les Vallées d'Andorre) A small principality in the E Pyrenees, between France and Spain. It is mountainous with peaks reaching heights of almost 3000 m (about 9500 ft). *Economy*: tourism is an important source of revenue supplementing the primarily agrarian economy (wheat, potatoes, livestock raising, and tobacco). *History*: records of Andorra's existence as a state date from 1278, when it was placed under the joint overlordship of the Bishop of Urgel in Spain and the Comte de Foix in France. The latter's rights passed in the 16th century to the French Crown and are now held by the president. Andorra pays dues in alternate years of 960 francs to France and 460 pesetas to the bishopric respectively. Executive and legislative powers lie with the coprinces' permanent delegates in Andorra while a Council General of the Valleys holds responsiblity for administration. Andorra is a tax haven and immigration has been substantial in recent years. Official language: Catalan; French and Spanish are also spoken. Official currencies: French and Spanish currencies are both in use. Area: 465 sq km (179 sq mi). Population (1981): 35 460. Capital: Andorra la Vella.

Andrássy, Gyula, Count (1823–90) Hungarian revolutionary and statesman. In the *Revolution of 1848 Andrássy supported Lajos *Kossuth. With Ferenc *Deák he negotiated the Dual Monarchy of *Austria-Hungary (1867) and was Hungary's first constitutional prime minister (1867–71). From 1871 to 1879 he was the Austro-Hungarian foreign minister and strove to halt Russian expansion into the Balkans.

André, John (1751–80) British soldier. While serving as adjutant to the commander in chief of British troops in the American Revolution, he negotiated with the treacherous Benedict *Arnold, the commander of West Point, for its

Andrea del Sarto surrender. He was captured by Washington's army and tried and executed as a spy.

Andrea del Sarto (Andrea d'Agnolo; 1486–1530) A leading Florentine Renaissance painter, whose work, through its influence on his pupils *Pontormo, Giovanni Battista Rosso (1494–1540), and *Vasari, became a starting point for Tuscan *mannerism. He was able to combine Florentine draughtsmanship with a Venetian feeling for colour and atmosphere and his compositions resemble relief sculpture. Andrea spent most of his life in Florence, producing a series of frescoes in the cloister of the Scalzi and the SS Annunziata. Among his most important paintings are several representing the Holy Family, some portraits, and the *Madonna of the Harpies* (1517; Uffizi).

Andrew, St In the New Testament, one of the 12 Apostles. Originally a fisherman in partnership with his brother Simon Peter, he was a disciple of John the Baptist before following Jesus. Apparently crucified, he is the patron saint of Scotland and Russia. Feast day: 30 Nov.

Andrewes, Lancelot (1555–1626) Anglican bishop and writer. A fellow of Pembroke College, Cambridge, he became Bishop of Winchester in 1619 and acted as adviser to James I. He was renowned as a preacher and liturgist but is best remembered for his *Private Prayers* (written in Greek for his personal use and published posthumously).

Andrew II (1175–1235) King of Hungary (1205–35). Andrew was forced by his recalcitrant barons to accept the *Golden Bull in 1222, which limited royal powers. He participated in the fifth Crusade (1218).

Andrić, Ivo (1892–1975) Serbian writer. He wrote his first major book, *Ex Ponto* (1918), while imprisoned by the Austrians as a Yugoslav nationalist. He later served abroad in the Yugoslav diplomatic service, but his native Bosnia provided the settings and themes for his novels, notably *Bosnian Story* (1945) and *The Bridge on the Drina* (1945). He was awarded the Nobel Prize in 1961.

Androcles The hero of a story by Aulus Gellius (?125–?165 AD). Androcles was an escaped slave who removed a thorn from the paw of a lion. The lion later recognized the recaptured slave in the arena and spared him; both were freed. The story was satirized in the play, *Androcles and the Lion*, by G. B. *Shaw.

androgens A group of steroid hormones that influence the development and function of the male reproductive system and determine male secondary sexual characteristics, such as the growth of body hair and deepening of the voice at puberty. The major androgens are *testosterone and androsterone, produced by the testes in higher animals and man and also in small amounts by the adrenal glands and ovaries in mammals. Natural and synthetic androgens are used in medicine to treat conditions caused by androgen deficiency. Some androgens promote the growth of muscle and bone. These—the anabolic steroids —have been used for body-building in debilitated patients and athletes.

Andromache In Greek mythology, the wife of Hector, the chief Trojan warrior. She appears in Homer's *Iliad*. After the fall of Troy she became the slave of Neoptolemus, son of Achilles, and bore him three sons. After his death she married Helenus, brother of Hector.

Andromeda A constellation in the N sky near Cassiopeia. The brightest star is the 2nd-magnitude Alpheratz. The constellation contains the spiral **Andromeda galaxy**, which is the largest of the nearby galaxies in the *Local Group.

Andropov, Yuri Vladimirovich (1914–84) Soviet statesman; general secretary of the Soviet Communist Party (1982–84) and president of the Soviet Union (1983–84). He was ambassador to Hungary (1953–57) during the 1956 uprising and headed the KGB (1967–82). In 1984 the city of Rybinsk was renamed Andropov in his honour.

androsterone. *See* androgens.

anechoic chamber A room used in acoustical experiments that is designed to absorb nearly all the sounds produced in it. Its walls, floor, and ceiling are constructed from insulating and absorbent materials.

Aneirin (6th century AD) Welsh poet. His poem "Y Gododdin," preserved in the manuscript *Book of Aneirin* (c. 1250), celebrates the heroes of an expedition sent from Edinburgh to recapture Catterick from the Saxons. Out of 300 warriors only one survived.

anemometer An instrument for measuring the velocity of a fluid, often the velocity of the wind. In one type, the fluid drives a small windmill or set of cups, the rate of rotation of which is a measure of the velocity of the fluid. Two other common types of anemometer are the *Pitot tube and the *Venturi tube.

Anemone A genus of herbaceous perennial plants (about 150 species) mostly native to N temperate regions. The leaves are segmented and the flowers lack true petals (the sepals function as petals). The Eurasian wood anemone (*A. nemorosa*), 10–15 cm high, has white flowers. Many species are cultivated as ornamentals for their brightly coloured flowers, including the poppy and Japanese anemones (*A. coronaria* and *A. japonica*). Family: *Ranunculaceae*.

aneroid barometer. *See* barometer.

aneurysm A swelling in the wall of an artery, due to a weakness in the wall. The most common cause in the western world is now *atherosclerosis. Aneurysms may rupture, causing fatal haemorrhage. Treatment consists of surgical removal of the aneurysm and its replacement with a graft.

Angara, River A river in the Soviet Union, in SE Siberia. It flows mainly NNW from Lake Baikal to the River Yenisei. Length: 1840 km (1150 mi).

Angarsk 52 31N 103 55E A city in the Soviet Union, in the SE central RSFSR on the Trans-Siberian Railway. An oil-refining centre, it is connected by pipeline to the Volga-Urals field. Population (1981 est): 245 000.

Angel Falls (Spanish name: Salto Angel) The highest cataract in the world, in SE Venezuela on a tributary of the Río Caroní. Height: 979 m (3211 ft).

FRA ANGELICO *Detail from* The Annunciation (*St Mark's Convent, Florence*).

angelfish 1. A fish of the tropical marine family *Chaetodontidae*, having a narrow oval laterally compressed body, a small mouth, and often an elongated snout. Up to 70 cm long, angelfish are solitary, living around coral reefs and feeding on small invertebrates. They are usually patterned in a variety of brilliant colours. **2.** A South American *cichlid fish of the genus *Pterophyllum*, especially *P. scalare*, which is valued as an aquarium fish.

Angelica A genus of tall perennial herbs (about 70 species) distributed in the N hemisphere and New Zealand. They grow up to 2 m tall and have umbrella-like clusters of white or greenish flowers. The Eurasian species *A. archangelica* yields an oil used in liqueur and perfume making, and its stems are candied to make the confectionary angelica. *A. sylvestris* (wild angelica) is native to Europe and Asia and introduced in Canada. Family: *Umbelliferae*.

Angelico, Fra (Guido di Pietro; c. 1400–55) Italian painter of the early *Renaissance, born in Vicchio (Tuscany). In the early 1420s he became a Dominican monk in Fiesole. His order transferred in 1436 to St Mark's Convent, Florence, where he painted several frescoes, including a famous *Annunciation*. From 1445 to about 1450 he painted fresco cycles in the Vatican but only the *Scenes from the Lives of SS Stephen and Lawrence* has survived. His other major work is *The Coronation of the Virgin* (Uffizi). He was an exclusively religious painter, whose spiritual serenity is reflected both in his art and his "angelic" nature (hence his popular name).

Angell, Sir Norman (1874–1967) British author, economist, and Labour politician. He received the Nobel Peace Prize in 1933 for his opposition to totalitarianism and his influential antiwar book *The Great Illusion* (1910).

angels (Greek: messengers) In Christianity, Judaism, and Islam, supernatural beings who were created at the same time as the material universe and whose primary role was to praise and serve God. Many, however, followed *Lucifer in his rebellion, becoming devils in *hell. In both Old and New Testaments angels appear as emissaries from God to man. *Dionysius the Areopagite systematized angelology into nine orders in the celestial hierarchy, the rank of angel being the lowest of these. Later medieval theologians debated such questions as the nature of angels' bodies, but since the 17th century angelology has been generally ignored. In art, angels are usually depicted as winged human figures. *See also* archangels.

Angers 47 29N 0 32W A city in W France, the capital of the Maine-et-Loire department on the River Maine. The former capital of Anjou, it has many fine buildings, including a 13th-century moated chateau, a cathedral (12th–13th centuries), and the 15th-century Logis Barrault (Barrault House). Its varied manufactures include wine, textiles, and agricultural machinery. Population (1982 est): 141 143.

Angevins Two dynasties descended from the rulers of the medieval French duchy of *Anjou. Founded by Fulk I (d. 938), his successors as Counts of Anjou, notably Fulk III Nerra (972–1040) and *Geoffrey Martel, expanded the county in France during the 10th and 11th centuries. The marriage in 1128 of Geoffrey Plantagenet, Count of Anjou, to *Matilda, daughter of Henry I of England, gave rise to the accession to the English throne in 1154 of their son as Henry II, the first *Plantagenet King of England. The so-called Angevin empire, which stretched from the River Tweed to the Pyrenees, was broken up by *Philip II Augustus of France in the early 13th century and in 1246 Louis VIII's brother Charles became Count of Anjou. Charles conquered Naples and Sicily, where as *Charles I he founded a second Angevin dynasty. The Angevin claim to Naples and Sicily passed to the French Crown in 1486.

angina pectoris Chest pain caused by a reduction in the supply of blood to the heart due to narrowing of the coronary blood vessels supplying the heart. It is usually associated with *atherosclerosis, is brought on by exercise, and can herald a heart attack. Treatment includes rest and administration of glyceryl trinitrate and drugs to reduce blood pressure.

angiosperm Any flowering plant. Angiosperms comprise a vast group of diverse leafy green plants (about 250 000 species) in which the seeds are formed within an ovary, which becomes the *fruit. They are thought to have evolved from the cone-bearing *gymnosperms in the Jurassic period (about 180 million years ago), rapidly radiating and becoming the dominant plants in the mid-Cretaceous (about 100 million years ago).They include many trees and shrubs but most are herbaceous. The 300 families are grouped into two classes: the *monocotyledons and *dicotyledons.

Angkor A ruined city in Kampuchea, founded about 880 AD as capital of the *Khmer empire. It was rediscovered, covered by jungle, in 1860. Angkor was the centre of a sophisticated irrigation system, with huge reservoirs (barays) for controlling water supplies to the surrounding rice fields. Its temples, decorated with extensive relief sculpture, were intended to emulate mountains in dressed stone; chief of these are the Angkor Wat (early 12th century) and Bayon (c. 1200).

anglerfish A marine fish, also called goosefish, belonging to the order *Lophiiformes*. Anglerfish are generally small and have flat bodies, large heads, and wide mouths. The first ray of the spiny dorsal fin is modified to form a "fishing line" ending with a fleshy flap of skin—the "bait," which is often luminous in deepsea species. Fish, invertebrates, and even seabirds are lured and snapped up by the huge mouth. In some deepsea species, the male is parasitic on the female, becoming permanently anchored by the mouth and dependent upon her for nourishment. □oceans.

Angles A Germanic tribe originating from the Angeln district of Schleswig, which together with the *Saxons and *Jutes invaded and conquered most of England during the 5th century AD. They settled in *Northumbria, *Mercia, and *East Anglia. England is named after them.

Anglesey (Welsh name: Ynys Môn; Latin name: Mona) A low-lying island off the NW coast of Wales, linked to the mainland by road and rail bridges over the Menai Strait. Now part of Gwynedd, it formed a separate county until local government reorganization in 1974. The chief agricultural activity is sheep rearing. Tourism, especially along the coast, is developing in importance. The terminus of the Irish ferry from Dublin is at Holyhead on an adjoining island in the NW. Recent industrial developments include the building of an aluminium smelter. Area: 705 sq km (272 sq mi). Population (1981 est): 67 340. Chief town: Beaumaris.

Anglesey, Henry William Paget, 1st Marquess of (1768–1854) British field marshal. He served with distinion in command of the cavalry at Waterloo, where he lost a leg. He later became lord lieutenant of Ireland, where he became an advocate of *Catholic emancipation.

Anglican Communion The fellowship of episcopal Churches in communion with the see of Canterbury. Until 1786, when the consecration of bishops for foreign sees was legalized, it consisted of the Churches of England, Ireland, and Wales and the Episcopal Church of Scotland. In 1787 the Protestant Episcopal Church of the USA was founded and thereafter Anglican dioceses were formed in all parts of the British Empire and elsewhere. The member churches are fully autonomous, comprising about 350 dioceses; they meet for consultation at the *Lambeth Conferences. Total membership is estimated at 65 million.

angling Fishing with a baited hook, line, and usually a rod. There are four main categories. Game fishing, for salmon and trout, takes place in fast streams and rivers. Coarse fishing for members of the carp family, such as roach and bream, is a sport in which the fish are returned to the water. Sea fishing for mackerel, flatfish, etc., is popular in shallow waters round the UK. Big-game fishing for shark, tuna, and swordfish requires specially equipped motorboats. Competitions were common in Britain by the 18th century. The National Angling Championship was instituted in 1906 and in 1957 the first world championship was staged.

Anglo-Burmese Wars The wars that resulted in the British annexation of Burma. In the first Anglo-Burmese War (1824–26) Burmese forces provoked the British-Indian forces into war by crossing into Bengal to attack Arakanese refugees and Britain captured, and kept, Rangoon. The aggressive action of a British naval officer provoked the second war (1852), which resulted in the annexation of Lower Burma. In the third war (1885), which occurred when the French, encouraged by the Burmese king, threatened British interests in Burma, Britain gained Upper Burma.

Anglo-Catholicism A movement within the Anglican Communion that stresses the continuity of the Church of England with Catholic Christianity. The main impetus of modern Anglo-Catholicism was provided by the *Oxford Movement, which sought to revive the High Church ideals of earlier, especially 17th-century, Anglican churchmen. Anglo-Catholics emphasize the historic episcopate, the sacramental life of the Church, and traditional Catholic practices with regard to the celebration of the Eucharist, vestments, etc. At present Anglo-Catholicism is a major influence in most Churches of the Anglican Communion.

Anglo-Egyptian Treaty (1936) The treaty between Britain and Egypt whereby Egypt gained independence after 50 years of British occupation. Britain maintained a military alliance with Egypt and a naval base at Alexandria.

Anglo-Japanese Alliance (1902–23) The alliance between Britain and Japan contracted to maintain their interests in China and Korea respectively against Russian encroachment. The alliance brought Japan into World War I but subsequently lapsed as Britain sought friendship with the USA, Japan's rival in the Pacific.

Anglo-Saxons The Germanic conquerors of Britain during the 5th century AD (see Angles; Saxons; Jutes). They first established a number of separate kingdoms, principally *Northumbria, *Mercia, and *Wessex, but eventually England was unified under an Anglo-Saxon dynasty. Kings ruled with the assistance of a *witan or council of wise men. Popular government and justice at the local level took the form of *hundred courts. They were converted to Christianity as a result of the mission of St *Augustine of Canterbury. The Anglo-Saxons developed a rich art and literature. Their language is also known as Old English. *See also* English.

Angola, People's Republic of A country in SW Africa, on the Atlantic Ocean situated mainly to the S of the River Congo. The Cabinda district, however, lies to the N of the Congo and is separated from the rest of the country by a section of Zaïre. The country consists of a narrow coastal plain and a broad dissected plateau that reaches heights of over 2000 m (6500 ft). The inhabitants are almost all Negroes (mainly of Bantu origin) with small numbers of mixed race and a rapidly decreasing White population. *Economy*: agriculture is now being reorganized on a state-run and cooperative basis and the main crops are sugar cane and coffee. Ango a is rich in mineral resources and diamonds have long been an important source of revenue. There is considerable oil production, especially offshore from Cabinda, and this has opened up new possibilities for industrial development. Hydroelectricity is being harnessed from the short steep river systems descending to the coastal plains and these schemes will provide irrigation as well as power. Main exports include oil, coffee, diamonds, and iron ore. The economy was severely disturbed by the civil wars (1974–76) and one effect was the withdrawal of Portuguese technicians, but these are being replaced to some extent by Cubans. *History*: discovered and settled by the Portuguese in the late 15th century, the area remained a Portuguese colony (apart from a brief period of Dutch occupation from 1641 to 1648) until 1951 when it became an overseas province of Portugal. During the 1950s and 1960s there was a rise in nationalism and three main independence movements emerged: the MPLA (Popular Movement for the Liberation of

Angola), the FNLA (National Front for the Liberation of Angola), and UNITA (National Union for the Total Independence of Angola). After its own change of government in 1974 Portugal agreed in principle to independence for Angola but, owing to lack of internal unity and opposition from the remaining White population, civil war broke out. The various groups took over different parts of the country and in November, 1975, Portugal granted independence to the "Angolan people" rather than to any one group. The People's Republic of Angola was declared by the MPLA, with its capital in Luanda, and a coalition of the FNLA and UNITA formed a People's Democratic Republic of Angola, based on Huambo. The MPLA was supported by the Soviet Union and Cuba and the FNLA by the USA and certain W European countries. Eventually, with further help from Cuba, the MPLA gained control in 1976 but opposition continued with increased South African involvement during the 1980s. President: Dr José Eduardo dos Santos. Official language: Portuguese. Official currency: kwanza of 100 lwei. Area: 1 246 700 sq km (481 351 sq mi). Population (1981 est): 6 920 000. Capital and main port: Luanda.

Angora goat A breed of goat, originating in Turkey, whose long silky hair is regularly sheared and used commercially to make *mohair. Mohair is now also obtained from several other goat breeds derived from the Angora.

Angora rabbit A breed of domesticated rabbit, originating in France in the 17th century, of which there are now both English and French varieties. The long wool, which is usually white but can be black or blue, is periodically shorn and spun for use in clothing manufacture (**Angora wool**).

angostura A bitters made from distilled herbs and plants. Angostura bitters originated in Ciudad Bolívar (formerly Angostura) in Venezuela as a tonic and febrifuge but its manufacture was transferred to Trinidad in 1975. A few drops are added to gin to make a pink gin.

Angoulême 45 40N 0 10E A town in SW France, the capital of the Charente department on the River Charente. The site of a 12th-century cathedral, its varied manufactures include paper, refrigerators, felt, and iron. Population (1982 est): 50 151.

Angoulême, Charles de Valois, Duc d' (1573–1650) French soldier. An illegitimate son of Charles IX, he was imprisoned (1605–16) for conspiring against Henry IV. He subsequently rose through the influence of Richelieu and then Mazarin to several important military commands, including that of the siege of Huguenot-held La Rochelle (1627).

Angry Young Men A group of British novelists and dramatists in the 1950s whose attitudes included dissatisfaction with postwar British society and disrespect for the so-called "Establishment" and its traditional institutions. Many of them came from working-class or lower-middle-class backgrounds. The phrase "angry young man" was first applied to the dramatist John *Osborne. Among other writers associated with this group were the novelists Kingsley *Amis, John *Wain, and John *Braine, the dramatist Arnold *Wesker, and the critic Colin *Wilson.

Ångström, Anders Jonas (1814–74) Swedish physicist and astronomer. He was a founder of spectroscopy, his work on solar spectra leading to the discovery (1862) of hydrogen in the sun. He also studied geomagnetism. The **angstrom**, a unit of wavelength equal to 10^{-10} m (one tenth of a nanometre), is named after him.

Anguilla 18 14N 63 05W A West Indian island in the E Caribbean Sea, in the Leeward Islands. Formerly part of the UK Associated State of St Kitts-Nevis-Anguilla, it became a separate British dependency in December, 1980. Its economy is based chiefly on stock raising, salt production, boatbuilding, and fishing. Area: 90 sq km (35 sq mi). Population (1980 est): 6500. *See also* St Kitts-Nevis.

angular momentum The product of the *moment of inertia of a body and its angular velocity about an axis. It is an important quantity in physics since the total angular momentum of a closed system is conserved.

angular velocity. See velocity.

Angus A former county (once called Forfarshire) of Scotland. Under local government reorganization in 1975 its boundaries were adjusted to form a district of the same name, in Tayside Region.

angwantibo A small rare nocturnal arboreal prosimian primate, *Arctocebus calabarensis*, also called golden potto, found in West African forests. 23–30 cm long, it has pale-brown fur and large eyes and feeds chiefly on insects. Family: *Lorisidae*.

Anhui (or Anhwei) A province in E China. The Yangtze River in the S and the Huai River in the N are linked by ancient waterways, which provide transport and irrigation. Main products are tea, rice, soya beans, silk, and steel. Area: 13 986 sq km (54 000 sq mi). Population (1980 est): 48 030 000. Capital: Hefei.

Anhwei. See Anhui.

anil A small shrub, *Indigofera anil*, native to India and the original source of the blue dye *indigo, which is now produced synthetically. Family: *Leguminosae*.

aniline (or phenylamine; $C_6H_5NH_2$) A colourless oily nonflammable liquid *amine. It is used to make dyes, plastics, and drugs and is made by the reduction of nitrobenzene obtained from *coal tar.

animal A living organism belonging to the kingdom *Animalia*. Animals are typically mobile and feed on *plants, other animals, or their remains. Their body *cells lack the rigid cellulose wall of plant cells and they require specialized tissues, such as bone, for protection and support. Because of their activity, animals have specialized organs for sensing the nature of their environment; information from the sense organs is transmitted and coordinated by means of a nervous system. Individuals of the same species have a consistent body form; growth occurs in all regions of the body and ceases at a certain stage of development, usually when sexual maturity has been attained. There are over one million species of animals, grouped into about 30 phyla. See also life; taxonomy.

animal behaviour. See ethology.

animal rights movement A campaign conducted by several organizations in protest against cruelty to and exploitation of animals. Targets of the movement, which developed in the 1970s, include zoos, animal research centres, foxhunts, and retailers of animal products. Some groups, such as the League Against Cruel Sports, favour parliamentary action, while others, such as the Animal Liberation Front, condone criminal acts, including the release of research animals and damage to property.

animal worship. See totemism.

animism 1. The belief that the physical world is permeated by a spirit sometimes called the *anima mundi*. Georg Ernst *Stahl was its leading proponent. 2. In anthropology, all forms of belief in spiritual agencies. *Tylor, who coined this use of the word, distinguished two classes of such beings: the souls of the dead (see ancestor worship) and other personalized supernatural entities.

anise An annual Egyptian herb, *Pimpinella anisum*, growing to a height of up to 75 cm and having umbrella-like clusters of small yellow-white flowers. It is cultivated in subtropical areas for the liquorice-flavoured oil (principally anthole) extracted from its small seeds, which is used in certain foods, beverages, and liqueurs. Family: *Umbelliferae*.

Anjou A former province in W central France, approximating to the present-day Maine-et-Loire department. Anjou was inherited by the future Henry II of England in 1151 and remained under the same ruler as England until the early 13th century. Permanently annexed to the French Crown in 1480, it ceased to exist as a province in 1790. See also Angevins.

Ankara 39 55N 32 50E The capital of Turkey, in the W central region of the country. There is evidence of human settlement from very early times, and it has long been an important trading town. Conquered by Alexander the Great in the 4th century BC, it later came within the Roman and Byzantine Empires. It was attacked by Persians and Arabs, and in the 11th century it was defeated by the Turks. It

phylum (approx. no. species)	important classes	representative members	phylum (approx. no. species)	important classes	representative members
Protozoa (30 000)	Sarcodina Ciliata Flagellata Sporozoa	*Amoeba* *Stentor* *Trypanosoma* *Plasmodium*	Annelida (9000)	Oligochaeta Polychaeta Hirudinea	earthworms lugworms leeches
Porifera (5000)		sponges	Arthropoda (>1 000 000)	Arachnida Crustacea Insecta	spiders, scorpions lobsters, crabs, woodlice beetles, wasps, ants, flies, bugs
Coelenterata (9000)	Hydrozoa Scyphozoa Anthozoa	*Hydra*, Portuguese man-of-war jellyfish sea anemones, corals	Myriapoda Echinodermata (6000)	Asteroidea Echinoidea Holothuroidea	centipedes, millipedes starfish sea urchins sea cucumbers
Platyhelminthes (9000)	Turbellaria Trematoda Cestoda	planarians flukes tapeworms	Chordata (55 000)	Chondrichthyes Osteichthyes	sharks, rays bony fish (salmon, carp, eels, perch, etc.)
Nematoda (10 000)		roundworms		Amphibia	frogs, toads, newts, salamanders
Mollusca (100 000)	Gastropoda Bivalvia Cephalopoda	snails, slugs mussels, oysters, cockles squids, octopus		Reptilia Aves Mammalia	lizards, snakes, crocodiles, turtles birds mammals, including man

ANIMAL *A simplified classification of the animal kingdom (major phyla only are listed).*

became the capital of modern Turkey in 1923 and since then has expanded considerably; it has three universities including the Middle East Technical University (1956). Population (1980): 1 877 755.

Ankhesenamen (born c. 1373 BC) The wife of *Tutankhamen, portrayed on several of the objects discovered in his tomb. After his death she offered to marry a son of *Suppiluliumas I, thus making him King of Egypt, but the Hittite prince was murdered en route to Egypt. She became instead the consort of Tutankhamen's adviser Ay, who thus became king.

ankylosaur A heavily armoured dinosaur of the late Cretaceous period, which ended 65 million years ago. Ankylosaurs were low and flat and their backs were covered with hard protective bony plates. *Euoplocephalus* (or *Ankylosaurus*) reached a length of 5 m, weighed 3 tonnes, and its plated tail ended in a large bony knob. Order: *Ornithischia*.

An Lu Shan (703-57 AD) Chinese military governor, who in 756 declared himself emperor of a new Yan dynasty. Tang imperial troops opposed him but An Lu Shan seized the capital Chang An and the emperor was forced to flee. An Lu Shan was murdered shortly afterwards but only in 763 did the imperial army succeed in putting down the rebellion.

Annaba (former name: Bône) 36 57N 7 39E A large port in E Algeria, on the Mediterranean Sea. An early centre of Christianity, it held the bishopric of St Augustine (396-430 AD). In 1832 it was captured by the French. Mineral exports are important, particularly phosphates and iron ore. Industries include flour milling and iron and steel processing. Population (1980 est): 284 000.

Anna Comnena (1083-?1148 AD) Byzantine historian. The daughter of Emperor *Alexius I Comnenus, Anna married (1097) Nicephorus Bryennius (?1062-1137) and conspired (1118) to depose her brother John II (1088-1143; reigned 1118-43) in favour of her husband. She was banished to a convent, where she wrote the *Alexiad*, an account of her father's achievements and of the early Crusades from a Byzantine point of view.

Anna Ivanovna (1693-1740) Empress of Russia (1730-40). A niece of *Peter the Great, Anna married (1710) Frederick William, Duke of Courland (d. 1710). She was elected by the Supreme Privy Council to become empress on the condition that she accept a number of provisions curtailing her powers. In practice, however, she became an autocrat, whose administration was run by her German advisers. In the Russo-Turkish War (1736-39) she regained Azov.

Annam A region in central Vietnam, long ruled from Hue. The Chinese, who had occupied it in 111 BC, were driven out in 939 AD, and it was a powerful independent state until becoming a French protectorate in 1884. In 1949 it became part of independent Vietnam.

Annapolis 38 59N 76 30W A city in the USA, the capital of Maryland on the Severn River. Founded in 1648, it was here that Congress received George Washington's resignation as commander in chief of the Continental Army and ratified the peace treaty ending the American Revolution (1783). The US Naval Academy was established here in 1845 and many historic buildings and riverside setting make it a popular tourist resort. It is also a minor seaport and has seafood industries. Population (1980 est): 31 740.

Annapolis Royal 44 44N 65 32W A town and port in E Canada, in Nova Scotia. One of the first settlements in Canada (1632), it was Nova Scotia's capital until 1749. A market town, it attracts many tourists. Population (1984 est): 600.

Annapurna, Mount 28 34N 83 50E A massif in NW central Nepal, in the Himalayas. Its highest peak **Annapurna I**, at 8078 m (26 504 ft), was first climbed in 1950 by a French team.

Ann Arbor 42 18N 83 43W A city in the USA, in Michigan. A research and educational centre, it is the site of the University of Michigan (1817) and its manufactures include chemicals and precision instruments. Population (1980): 107 316.

Anne (1665-1714) Queen of England and Scotland (Great Britain from 1707) and Ireland (1702-14). Anne, the last Stuart monarch, was the daughter of the Roman Catholic James II but was herself brought up as a Protestant. Following the overthrow (1688) of James, she supported the accession of her Protestant brother-in-law, William III, whose heiress she became. She married (1683) Prince George of Denmark (1653-1708) and was pregnant 18 times by him; none of her five children born alive survived childhood. Anne therefore agreed to the Act of *Settlement (1701), which provided for the Hanoverian succession after her death. Anne was greatly influenced by the Duke and Duchess of *Marlborough. This friendship led her to abandon her Tory and Anglican loyalties and follow the Marlboroughs in supporting the rival Whigs (see Whigs; Tories), especially in their aggressive stategy in the War of the *Spanish Succession. In 1710, however, having quarrelled with the Marlboroughs and being faced with a country dissatisfied with the Whig leadership, Anne appointed a Tory ministry.

Anne (Elizabeth Alice Louise) (1950–) Princess of the United Kingdom, sixth in line of succession to the throne, the only daughter of *Elizabeth II and Prince Philip. An accomplished horsewoman, in 1973 she married Lieut Mark Phillips (1948–), a gold medallist in the equestrian events in the 1972 Olympic Games. Their son Peter was born in 1977 and daughter Zara in 1981. As president of the Save the Children Fund she has attracted considerable acclaim. She was granted the title Princess Royal in 1987.

annealing. See heat treatment.

Annecy 45 54N 6 07E A town in SE France, the capital of the Haute-Savoie department. Its situation on Lake Annecy and pleasant climate have made it a popular tourist centre. Population (1982 est): 51 593.

annelid worm An invertebrate animal belonging to a phylum (*Annelida*) of about 9000 species, widely distributed in salt water, fresh water, and on land. The body is characteristically a muscular cylinder divided into many fluid-filled segments. Annelids vary greatly in form and habit and are divided into three classes: the Polychaeta, or bristleworms (see ragworm; lugworm; fanworm); the Oligochaeta (see earthworm; tubifex), and the Hirudinea (see leech).

Anne of Austria (1601-66) The wife (1615-43) of Louis XIII of France, whose antipathy towards her was aggravated by that of his chief minister Cardinal de Richelieu. After her husband's death she was regent (1643-51) for her son Louis XIV and chose her lover *Mazarin to succeed Richelieu.

Anne of Bohemia (1366-94) The first wife (from 1382) of Richard II of England and daughter of Emperor Charles IV. Her household extravagance was a cause of dissension between Richard and parliament. She died of the plague.

Anne of Brittany (1477-1514) Duchess of Brittany (1488-1514), succeeding her father Francis I (1435-88; ruled 1458-88). Her marriages to Charles VIII of France (1491) and to his successor Louis XII (1499) initiated the union of Brittany with France, in spite of Anne's desire to preserve Breton autonomy.

Anne of Cleves (1515-57) The fourth wife of Henry VIII of England. The marriage (January, 1540) was arranged to effect an alliance with German Protestant rulers but Henry found Anne unattractive and quickly divorced her (July, 1540).

Anne of Denmark (1574-1619) The wife (from 1589) of James I of England and VI of Scotland. She spent heavily on building and court entertainments (appearing herself in Ben

Jonson's masques) and was suspected of Roman Catholic sympathies.

Annigoni, Pietro (1910-) Italian painter. One of the most famous 20th-century artists to use the techniques of the Old Masters, Annigoni has worked chiefly in *tempera and *fresco. He is best known for his portraits of President Kennedy (1961) and Queen Elizabeth II (1955 and 1970). In recent years he has devoted himself to a fresco cycle of the life of Christ in the Church of S Michele Arcangelo, in Ponte Buggianese, near Florence.

annihilation The conversion of a particle and its antiparticle into electromagnetic radiation (annihilation radiation) as a result of a collision. The energy of the radiation is equivalent to the combined mass of the two particles. *See also* antimatter.

annual rings (*or* growth rings) A pattern of rings visible in a cross section of a tree trunk, produced by different rates of wood growth corresponding to the seasonal fluctuations in climate in temperate regions. Each year the wood produced in spring consists of large cells corresponding to vigorous growth; autumn wood has small cells as growth slows down, and in winter growth ceases. The number of rings gives an estimate of the age of the tree. *See also* dendrochronology.

annuals Plants that complete their life cycle—from germination, flowering, and seed production to death—within one year. Many annuals are used for bedding plants (e.g. marigolds) and flower extensively in the summer months. *Compare* perennials.

annuity A form of pension in which an *insurance company makes a series of periodic payments to a person (annuitant) or his or her dependents over a number of years (term), in return for money paid to the insurance company either in a lump sum or in instalments. An immediate annuity begins at once and a deferred annuity after a fixed period. An annuity certain is for a specific number of years. A life annuity is paid from a certain age until death. A perpetuity continues indefinitely.

annulment The process establishing that a marriage is not legally valid, as opposed to *divorce, which ends a valid marriage. An invalid marriage is considered void, never to have existed. A marriage is void from the beginning if there is a serious defect, for example if the husband or wife is insane, too young, or already married. In less serious cases, for example when the husband or wife is unable or unwilling to consummate the marriage, the marriage may be declared void if either partner wishes it.

Annunciation In the Bible, the announcement by the angel Gabriel to the Virgin Mary of her conception of Christ (Luke 1.26-38). The feast, in full called the Annunciation of the Blessed Virgin Mary, or Lady Day, is celebrated on 25 March.

anoa A rare black hoofed mammal, *Anoa depressicornis*, standing 1 m high at the shoulder. Anoas occur in thick tropical forests of Sulawesi (Indonesia) and nearby islands and are hunted for their hides, horns, and meat. Family: *Bovidae*.

anode The positive electrode of an electrolytic cell, valve, etc. It is the electrode by which the electrons leave the system. *Compare* cathode.

anodizing A process in which a light metal or alloy, usually aluminium, is covered with a protective layer by oxidation in an electrolytic cell. Usually the cell contains chromic acid; the metal treated is the anode of the cell. A porous layer of oxide is formed, which can be dyed to give a coloured finish.

anole A small arboreal New World lizard belonging to the genus *Anolis* (165 species). 12-45 cm long, anoles have a triangular head and pads on their fingers and toes covered with minute hooks for grip. Their skin changes colour from brown to green in response to changes in temperature, light,

or danger. Males have an expansible red or yellow throat fan (dewlap). Family: *Iguanidae*.

anomie A condition of a society or of individuals in which social standards or goals are unclear, in conflict, or absent. Anomic individuals reject or are unable to find meaningful social norms by which to interpret or organize their lives. Losing their sense of social belonging, they may turn to crime, the selfish pursuit of power, or even suicide. The term was first introduced into sociology in a systematic form by *Durkheim in his *Suicide* (1897).

Anopheles A widespread genus of *mosquitoes (about 350 species), the females of which are important as vectors of the malarial parasite *Plasmodium*. The best-known malaria carrier is *A. maculipennis*. Some species transmit filariasis and encephalitis. Unlike other mosquitoes the larvae lack a siphon and lie flat on the surface of the water.

anorexia nervosa A psychological illness in which the patient, usually an adolescent girl, refuses food over a long period. It often starts with dieting to lose weight, which becomes obsessional: the patient becomes emaciated and may—without treatment—starve to death. The psychological causes are complex, often involving disturbances in family relationships. Hospitalization may be required for the treatment, which involves intensive nursing, sedation, and *psychotherapy.

Anouilh, Jean (1910-87) French dramatist. His commitment to the theatre was early and total; his first play, *The Ermine*, was performed in 1932. He achieved his first success in 1937 with *Traveller without Luggage*. His plays include reworkings of Greek myths (*Antigone*, 1944), social comedies (*Ring Round the Moon*, 1950), and historical dramas (*Becket*, 1962). A skilled craftsman, he exploited the most basic dramatic conventions, such as coincidences and flashbacks. His work, although often considered old-fashioned, remains popular both in France and abroad.

Anschluss (German: union; 1938) The union of Austria with Germany. Following the forced resignation of the Austrian chancellor *Schuschnigg, Nazi forces entered Austria and Schuschnigg was imprisoned. *Anschluss* was declared and ratified by a plebiscite.

Anselm of Canterbury, St (c. 1033-1109) Italian theologian and philosopher, Archbishop of Canterbury, and Doctor of the Church. Appointed to the see of Canterbury in 1093, Anselm defended church rights against William II Rufus until he went into exile to Rome in 1097. Recalled by *Henry I in 1100, he eventually reached an uneasy compromise with him. He is the leading early scholastic philosopher and is perhaps best known for his formulation of the ontological argument for the existence of God, which states that if God is "that than which nothing greater can be conceived," then the existence of God is necessary, for to argue that God does not exist involves one in a contradiction since it is possible to conceive of a greater entity than a nonexistent God. Feast day: 21 April. Emblem: a ship.

Ansermet, Ernest (1883-1969) Swiss conductor. Briefly a mathematics teacher, he studied composition with *Bloch and conducting with *Nikisch. After touring with *Diaghilev's ballet company he founded the Suisse Romande Orchestra in 1918, remaining its director until 1967. He was famous for his interpretations of *Stravinsky and other 20th-century composers.

Ansgar, St (*or* Anskar; c. 801-65) A native of Picardy; missionary to and patron saint of Scandinavia. Appointed in 832 as papal legate to the Scandinavians, Ansgar preached in Denmark and Sweden, building the first church in Sweden. Despite his extensive activity, Scandinavia lapsed into paganism after his death. Feast day: 3 Feb.

Anshan (*or* An-shan) 41 05N 122 58E A city in NE China, in Liaoning province. Its steel complex, the largest in China, was developed under Japanese occupation (1931-45), when its population grew rapidly. It also has engineering, chemical, and cement industries. Population (1983 est): 1 210 000.

Anson, George Anson, Baron (1697–1762) British admiral. During the War of the Austrian Succession, he commanded six ships in attacks on Spanish possessions in South America (1740). He went on to circumnavigate the world in a voyage lasting four years, returning to Britain with only one surviving vessel but with Spanish treasure worth £500,000. He related his adventures in *A Voyage round the World* (1748).

ant An insect belonging to the family *Formicidae* (over 10 000 species). Ants occur in almost all terrestrial habitats, are 0.05–25 cm long, and show a high degree of social organization. A colony consists of wingless sterile female workers and a smaller number of fertile males and females that are generally the progeny of a single queen. The young males and females fly from the nest to mate, after which the males die and the young queens found new colonies. Ant societies range from simple groups of a few individuals to large complex nests comprising millions of ants and sometimes involving a second species taken as slaves to work in the colony (*see* slave-making ant).

Some ants have stings; others secrete burning acids (such as formic acid) as a defence. Feeding habits vary from rapacious predators (*see* army ant) to harmless scavengers; others milk honeydew from aphids and certain species cultivate fungi as a food supply within the nest. Order: **Hymenoptera.* □insect.

Antakya. *See* Antioch.

Antalya 36 53N 30 42E A city in SW Turkey, on the Gulf of Antalya. Founded in the 2nd century BC, it flourished particularly under the Seljuqs in the 13th century, and it is now an important coastal resort. Nearby are two Roman amphitheatres and the ruins of Perga. Population (1980): 173 501.

Antananarivo (former name: Tananarive) 18 52S 47 30E The capital of Madagascar. It was occupied by the French in 1895. A cultural centre, it has a university (1961) and two cathedrals. Industries include tobacco and leather goods. Population (1982 est): 600 000.

Antar (6th century AD) Arab poet and warrior, celebrated in the 10th-century *Romance of Antar* as the model of desert chivalry. The son of a Bedouin chieftain and a slave girl, Antar was said to have proved his courage in numerous battles and adventures before being allowed to marry his beloved Abla.

Antarctica The most southerly continent, surrounding the South Pole. Almost circular in shape, it is indented by the Weddell and Ross Seas. It consists chiefly of a vast ice-covered plateau and contains about 90% of the world's ice. Calculations suggest that should this ice melt sea levels would rise by about 60 m (200 ft). The continent's climate is the severest in the world; in 1960 the world's lowest recorded temperature–of −87.8°C (−126°F)–was made at the Soviet station of Vostok. Although lacking in vegetation it has abundant wildlife including whales, seals, and penguins. Scientific stations were established during the International Geophysical Year (1957–58). Some nations (*see* Australian Antarctic Territory; British Antarctic Territory; Norwegian Antarctic Territory; Ross Dependency; Terre Adélie) have political claims to territory in Antarctica. Argentina and Chile have also laid claims, as yet unrecognized, to portions of British Antarctic Territory (*see also* Antarctic Treaty). *History*: in his voyage of 1772–75 Capt James Cook reached 71°10'S. Many discoveries and explorations took place during the 19th century culminating in the famous race for the South Pole. This was reached first by Roald *Amundsen of the Norwegian Antarctic Expedition on 14 December, 1911, and a month later by *Scott of the British Antarctic Terra Nova Expedition. Scott and his team perished on the return journey. Area: about 14 200 000 sq km (5 500 000 sq mi).

Antarctic Ocean The sections of the S Atlantic, Pacific, and Indian Oceans around Antarctica. Except in the height of summer (late Feb to early March), it is covered by drifting pack ice.

Antarctic Peninsula A peninsula extending 1930 km (1200 mi) N from Antarctica towards South America, claimed by

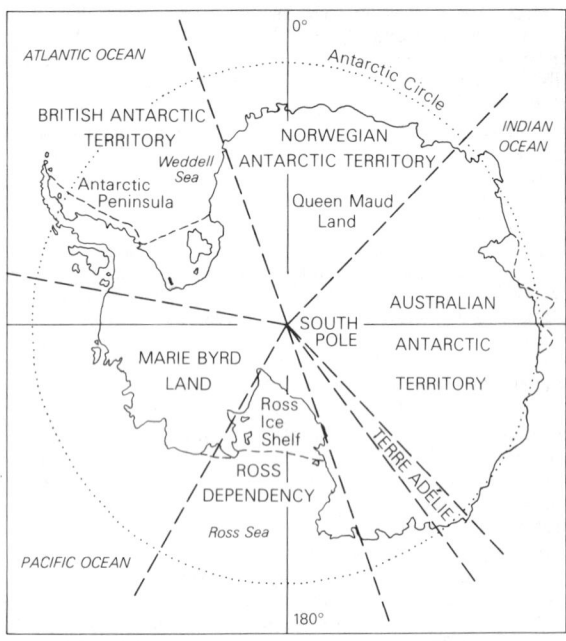

ANTARCTICA *Under the Antarctic Treaty (1959) all political claims were halted and freedom of scientific research in the continent was ensured.*

the UK. The first part of Antarctica to be sighted (1820), it has volcanic mountains in the S.

Antarctic Treaty (1959) An agreement, signed by Argentina, Australia, Belgium, Chile, France, Japan, New Zealand, Norway, South Africa, the Soviet Union, the UK, and the USA, to maintain the Antarctic as a demilitarized zone for 30 years.

Antares An immense remote yet conspicuous red *supergiant, apparent magnitude 0.94 and about 400 light years distant, that is the brightest star in the constellation Scorpius. It is a visual *binary star.

ant bear. *See* aardvark.

antbird A passerine bird belonging to a large family (*Formicariidae*; 223 species) occurring in the forest undergrowth of Central and South America. About 8–35 cm long, antbirds have shrill voices and hooked bills and feed chiefly on insects (although the larger species may eat small lizards, snakes, and young birds). The female is dull brown but the male usually has a brightly patterned plumage.

anteater A long-tailed animal belonging to a family (*Myrmecophagidae*; 3 species) occurring in tropical South America. It is toothless and has a narrow snout with a long sticky tongue used to pick up ants and termites after tearing open their nests with its powerful claws. The giant anteater (*Myrmecophaga tridactyla*) reaches 1.8 m in length and has grey and black fur and a bushy tail (□mammal). The other species are smaller arboreal animals with prehensile tails (*see* tamandua). Order: *Edentata*.

The name anteater is given to several other unrelated animals that feed on ants or termites: the *pangolins (scaly anteaters), *echidnas (spiny anteaters), and *aardvark.

Antelami, Benedetto (active 1177–1233) Italian sculptor. The most famous Italian sculptor of the medieval period, Antelami developed a style that marked the transition between the *romanesque and the *gothic. His best-known works are the reliefs on the doors of the baptistry at Parma, of which he was probably also the architect.

antelope A hoofed mammal belonging to the family *Bovidae* and occurring chiefly in Africa but occasionally in Asia. Antelopes are typically fast-running and graceful, grazing or browsing in large herds on open grasslands, although some are more solitary and live in bush and woodland. The shoulder height varies from 25 cm in the *royal antelope to 180 cm in the *eland. All male antelopes and some females have horns. *See also* dik-dik; duiker; gazelle; gnu; kudu; waterbuck.

antenna (radio). *See* aerial.

antenna (zoology) The sensory feeler of insects, crustaceans, and many other arthropods, one or two pairs of which are attached to the head. They are usually jointed threadlike structures containing receptors of sound, smell, touch, and temperature.

Antenor (late 6th century BC) Athenian sculptor. His signature appears on the base of a marble *kore on the Athenian Acropolis. He sculpted the Harmodios and Aristogeiton group, looted by Xerxes (480 BC) and restored after Alexander the Great's Persian expedition.

Antheil, George (1900–59) US composer. He studied with Ernest *Bloch and in 1922 moved to Europe, where his avantgarde work *Le Ballet mécanique* (1924) for bells, motor horns, aeroplane propellers, etc., caused a furore. His later works are more traditional in style and include several film scores.

anthelminthics Drugs used to treat infections of the intestines caused by parasitic worms. Piperazine is commonly used to expel roundworms and threadworms. Tapeworm infections are treated with niclosamide or dichlorophen.

anthem A piece of music for church choir, authorized for use in the Anglican service but not a part of the liturgy; it developed from the Latin *motet. In Tudor and early Stuart times "full anthems," by composers, such as *Tallis and *Byrd, were written for unaccompanied choir, although in practice the vocal parts were often strengthened instrumentally. After the Restoration *Purcell, *Blow, and others inserted solos between the choral sections, accompanying these "verse anthems" with independent organ or orchestral parts.

anther. *See* stamen.

antheridium The reproductive organ producing the male cells (gametes) in ferns, mosses, algae, and fungi. It is usually a club-shaped structure, the rounded head containing the gametes.

Anthony of Egypt, St (c. 251–356 AD) Egyptian hermit and founder of Christian monasticism. An ascetic from the age of 20, he withdrew until 305 into complete isolation, emerging to organize followers into a monastic community living according to a rule. When he was about a hundred years old, he preached against *Arianism. His combat with temptation in the desert is described in Athanasius' *Life of Saint Anthony*; it became a frequent subject in Christian art. Feast day: 17 Jan. Emblem: a piganda bell.

Anthony of Padua, St (1195–1231) Portuguese friar and Doctor of the Church. Famous for his preaching, he devoted his efforts to converting heretics in N Italy and the Albigenses in S France until his appointment as professor of theology to the Franciscan Order in 1223. He is often invoked as a finder of lost property. Feast day: 13 June.

anthracene ($C_{14}H_{10}$) A colourless crystalline *aromatic compound. It is obtained from coal tar and is used in making dyes.

anthracite. *See* coal.

anthrax A contagious disease of many animals, including farm livestock, that can be transmitted to man. Caused by the bacterium *Bacillus anthracis*, it is usually contracted by eating contaminated food. Onset is often sudden with a rise in body temperature, staggering, respiratory distress, convulsions, and death. In horses and pigs a subacute form may occur, with progressive swelling of the throat and neck resulting in laboured breathing and choking. In many countries the authorities must be notified of any outbreaks. Treatment is with antibiotics and prevention is by vaccination of herds in areas where the disease is endemic. Man may develop localized swellings after handling infected carcasses or acquire a pneumonia from inhaling the bacterial spores (woolsorters' disease).

anthropoid ape A tailless *primate belonging to the family *Pongidae*, includes the gibbons, chimpanzees, orang-utans, and gorillas. *See* ape.

anthropology The scientific study of man in his physical and social aspects. In the widest meaning of the term it includes *archaeology, *linguistics, cultural or social anthropology, and physical anthropology. It is particularly concerned with the systematic and comparative study of human diversity. Physical anthropology is concerned with the origins and evolution of man through the examination of his fossil remains, and the study and classification of the races of man through comparison of anatomical and physiological characteristics (*see also* anthropometry). Cultural anthropology is concerned with the evolution of human society and culture, including language, and with the systematic comparison of social, linguistic, technical, and behavioural diversity. Social anthropology has a more restricted meaning and is the comparative study of social behaviour, social organization, social forms and institutions, custom, culture, and belief, and has traditionally confined itself to the study of "primitive" societies.

anthropometry The science concerned with the measurement of the human body, particularly with respect to the variation that exists between different populations and races. Anthropometry ranges from the measurement of structural characteristics, such as height, cranial capacity, etc., to the analysis of chemical constituents of the body, such as blood groups. By comparing fossil and present-day measurements anthropometry has also helped to reveal the sequence of events that has occurred during the evolution of man.

anthropomorphism Mankind's tendency to ascribe to nonhuman creatures the motives, feelings, etc., of human beings. This is particularly evident in the concept of God. The anthropomorphism of ancient Greek religion was ridiculed by *Xenophanes of Colophon (6th century BC) but Christian discussions of the divine personality, will, etc., have still not escaped from an implicit anthropomorphism. Religious art can scarcely avoid being anthropomorphic.

anthroposophy A philosophy propounded by Rudolf *Steiner, which holds that the key to an understanding of the cosmos exists in man himself and that man should therefore find means to develop his latent spiritual powers.

Anthurium A genus of tropical American plants (550 species), some of which are cultivated as greenhouse or pot plants for their ornamental flowers or foliage. The flower heads consist of a cylindrical cluster (spadix) of tiny flowers surrounded by a large petal-like part (spathe), which is often brightly coloured (e.g. in *A. scherzerianum* it is red). Family: *Araceae* (arum family).

anti-aircraft gun Any gun capable of rapid fire, high elevation, and speedy adjustment. Calibres are 20 mm to 140 mm (0.8–5.5 in) but most common pieces are 87 mm to 100 mm. Upper range limit is about 12 000 m (40 000 ft) and targets may be engaged at a few hundred feet. Guns are aimed visually or electronically so that the aircraft flies into the round or shellburst. The role of anti-aircraft guns has largely been replaced by ground-to-air guided missiles.

antiballistic missiles High-speed nuclear weapons used to attack hostile *ballistic missiles. Operated by ground-based radar and computers, they rely for their final attack on their own guidance systems, destroying the target by radiation from their warheads. Short-range versions with low-yield warheads (e.g. US *Sprint*) are designed to seek and destroy targets within the earth's atmosphere; long-range missiles with high-yield warheads operate in space (e.g. US *Spartan*, Soviet *Galosh*).

Antibes 43 35N 7 07E A town in France, in the Alpes-Maritimes department. A tourist resort and a port for pleasure craft on the Côte d'Azur, it produces flowers, perfumes, and chocolates. Population (1982 est): 63 248.

antibiotics Drugs derived from microorganisms and used to treat infections caused by bacteria or fungi. Synthetic drugs with similar properties are also known as antibiotics. Bacteriocidal antibiotics, such as *penicillin, actually kill bacteria, whereas bacteriostatic antibiotics, such as *tetracycline and *chloramphenicol, simply halt their growth. Examples of antifungal antibiotics are nystatin and griseofulvin. Possible adverse effects of antibiotic treatment include allergic reactions, and the indiscriminate use of antibiotics has resulted in the appearance of some new life-threatening infections that do not respond to existing drugs; efforts are under way to develop new antibiotics to combat these resistant strains of bacteria.

antibody A protein produced by certain white blood cells (lymphocytes) that reacts specifically with and neutralizes a foreign protein (e.g. a bacterium), which is known as the **antigen**. Antibody production is stimulated by contact with the antigen: subsequent exposure to the antigen produces a greater antibody response, which provides the basis of *immunity. Antibodies contribute to the body's resistance to infection and are responsible for the rejection of foreign tissue or organ transplants.

Antichrist In the New Testament, a person or institution opposed to Christ, whose appearance will precede His second coming (John 2.18–22). Some Christians believed *Nero to be the Antichrist; many reformers, for example Wycliffe and Luther, saw the pope or the papacy in this role.

anticline An arch-shaped *fold or upfold in folded rock strata, the oldest rocks occurring at the core. In areas of complex folding an upfold may have its youngest rocks at the core, the resulting structure being termed an antiform. *Compare* syncline.

anticoagulants Drugs, such as heparin and warfarin, that interfere with blood clotting. They are used when there has been, or there is a risk of, clots forming in the blood vessels, as after *thrombosis of the leg veins.

Anti-Comintern Pact An agreement among the Axis powers in opposition to the Comintern (*or* Third *International). Germany and Japan signed the Pact in 1936 to protect themselves against communism and they were later joined by Italy (1937) and Spain (1939).

Anti-Corn Law League An organization formed in 1839 to work for the repeal of the *Corn Laws. Under the able leadership of Richard *Cobden and John *Bright, the League gained widespread support from manufacturers as well as workers and achieved its objective in 1846.

anticyclone (*or* high) An area of atmospheric pressure higher than the surrounding air with one or more isobars of approximately circular form around its centre. Winds, generally light, circulate around the high pressure centre in a clockwise direction in the N hemisphere and anticlockwise in the S hemisphere. Calm settled weather is usually synonymous with anticyclones in temperate latitudes.

antidepressants A class of drugs used to relieve depression. The most widely used are the tricyclic antidepressants, which include amitriptyline and imipramine, and the tetracyclic antidepressants. They provide a wide range of drugs to treat a variety of depressive symptoms. The MAO inhibitors prevent the action of the enzyme monoamine oxidase in breaking down adrenaline and related compounds that affect mood. These antidepressants may have serious side effects and are therefore restricted to the treatment of severe psychological disorders.

Antietam, Battle of (17 September, 1862) A decisive engagement in the US ▢Civil War, which prevented the Confederate capture of Washington, DC. In the last of a series of battles, the advance of the Confederate general Robert E. *Lee, was checked at Antietam by the Federal general George B. *McClellan. The South lost about 10 000 men but McClellan allowed Lee to withdraw into Virginia.

antiferromagnetism The magnetic property of a material that has its microscopic magnetic *moments lined up in domains, as in *ferromagnetism, except that in these materials the antiparallel arrays oppose each other. The lower the temperature, the greater this alignment; up to a certain temperature, known as the Néel temperature, the relative magnetic *permeability is slightly greater than one and increases with temperature. Above this temperature the material is paramagnetic (*see* paramagnetism).

antifreeze A substance added to water in cooling systems to lower the freezing point and thus prevent damage in cold weather from freezing. Glycols and methanol, together with a corrosion inhibitor, are commonly used.

antigen. *See* antibody.

Antigone In Greek mythology, the daughter of *Oedipus and Jocasta, whose story forms the basis of Sophocles' tragedy *Antigone*. When her father was banished from Thebes she accompanied him into exile in Colonus. Her brothers Eteocles and *Polyneices had agreed to reign alternately in Thebes, but Eteocles' refusal to yield the crown led to their killing each other in single combat. Despite the Theban senate's decree prohibiting the burial of Polyneices, Antigone performed the funeral rites for her brother. She was consequently ordered to be buried alive by Creon, ruler of Thebes, and hanged herself.

Antigonus I (c. 382–301 BC) Macedonian general, nicknamed Monophthalmus or Cyclops (One-eye). After the death of his patron *Antipater, Antigonus became ruler of Asia Minor. He declared himself king in 306 but his ambition to rule a reunited Macedonian empire was opposed. His rivals combined forces, after Antigonus' successes against them individually, and defeated and killed him in battle at Ipsus.

Antigonus II Gonatas (c. 320–239 BC) King of Macedon (276–239), who re-established Macedonian hegemony in Greece. He defeated Athens and Sparta in the Chremonidean War (c. 267–c. 262) and Ptolemy II of Egypt in the naval battle of Cos. During his reign the Macedonian court became a centre of culture.

Antigua and Barbuda A West Indian country in the E Caribbean Sea, comprising the islands of Antigua, Barbuda, and Redonda. Tourism is the chief source of revenue; sugar and cotton production are also important. *History*: Antigua was discovered by Columbus (1493) and colonized by British settlers in 1632. It formed an associated state within the British Commonwealth from 1967 until gaining independence in 1981. It is a member of CARICOM. Prime minister: Vere C. Bird. Area: 440 sq km (170 sq mi). Population (1983 est): 78 000. Capital: St John's.

antihistamines Drugs that interfere with the action of *histamine, a chemical produced by the body that is responsible for the symptoms of an allergic reaction. Antihistamines are therefore used to treat hay fever, nettle rash, and other allergies. Some antihistamines (e.g. dramamine) are used to prevent travel sickness and others are effective sedatives (drowsiness is a common side effect of many antihistamines).

Anti-Lebanon Mountains A mountain range running NE-SW for 150 km (93 mi) along the Lebanese-Syrian border and rising to 2814 m (9232 ft) at Mount Hermon.

Antilles The islands of the West Indies, excluding the Bahamas. The group is divided into the *Greater Antilles and the *Lesser Antilles.

Anti-Masonic Party A minority US political party that arose after the disappearance of a former freemason in 1826. The widely held belief that the man had been murdered by freemasons for revealing their secrets led to the formation of the party to oppose Masonic candidates for office in the New York Assembly. Effective on the state level, the party held the first national nominating convention in US politics (1831), a system later adopted by the major parties. The Anti-Masons merged with the Whigs (who opposed the policies of Andrew Jackson) in 1838.

antimatter Hypothetical matter in which the constituent atoms consist of antiparticles. For every elementary particle (*see* particle physics) there exists an antiparticle that is identical except for certain of its properties, such as electric charge and isospin number, which are of equal magnitude but opposite in sign. The photon and the neutral pion are their own antiparticles. An atom of antimatter would contain a nucleus of antiprotons and antineutrons surrounded by positrons (antielectrons). If matter were to meet antimatter, they would annihilate each other in a burst of radiation. *See also* annihilation.

antimony (Sb) A metallic element, probably known in antiquity. It occurs in nature as the element and more commonly in the sulphide *stibnite (Sb_2S_3). The element exists in two forms: the normal metallic form, which is brittle bluish-white and flaky, and an amorphous grey form. Antimony is a poor conductor of heat and electricity. It forms the oxide (Sb_2O_3) by burning in air and the volatile hydride, stibine (SbH_3), which like many antimony compounds is toxic. Pure antimony is used in making *semiconductors; other uses include addition to lead to increase its hardness in battery plates, in type metal, and as oxides or sulphides in paints, glasses, and ceramics. At no 51; at wt 121.75; mp 630.7°C; bp 1750°C.

anti-novel. *See* nouveau roman.

Antioch (modern Turkish name: Antakya) 36 12N 36 10E A town in central S Turkey, near the coast and the Syrian border. Founded in 301 BC, it had a large early Christian community, and there are notable Roman mosaics in the Archaeological Museum. Population (1980): 94 942.

Antiochus I Soter (324-261 BC) King of Syria (281-261) of the Seleucid dynasty. Antiochus lost some Seleucid territory to Egypt but achieved peace with Macedon (278) and repulsed a Gallic invasion, which earned him the title Soter (Saviour). He founded many cities.

Antiochus II (c. 287-246 BC) King of Syria (261-246) of the Seleucid dynasty. Little is known of his reign apart from his reconquest (260-253) of some of the territory in Asia Minor lost by his father *Antiochus I Soter and his political marriage (252) to the Egyptian princess Berenice.

Antiochus (III) the Great (c. 242-187 BC) King of Syria (223-187) of the Seleucid dynasty. After crushing separatist revolts at home, Antiochus initiated a policy of expansion. His incursions on Egyptian territory were temporarily halted by his defeat at Raphia (217) but his great campaign (212-206) through Armenia, Parthia, and Bactria to the River Indus paralleled that of Alexander the Great. He finally defeated the Egyptians in 198. Antiochus then became involved in hostile diplomacy with Rome and in 192 invaded Greece. Driven out by the Romans (190), his defeat destroyed Seleucid power in the Mediterranean.

Antiochus IV Epiphanes (c. 215-163 BC) King of Syria (175-163) of the Seleucid dynasty. Antiochus maintained the empire, campaigning successfully against the Egyptians until forced by the Romans to withdraw (168). He pro-

moted Greek culture throughout the empire but met with resistance from the *Maccabees (167-160) when he ruthlessly imposed Greek religion on the Jews.

Antiochus VII Sidetes (c. 159-129 BC) The last Seleucid King of Syria (139-129). Following early military successes, including the reconquest of Jerusalem (134), he attempted to postpone the Parthian conquest of the Seleucid empire and died in battle.

anti-oxidants Substances that inhibit oxidation of such products as foods, paints, plastics, fuels, etc. Natural anti-oxidants include ascorbic acid (vitamin C). Additives are usually phenol derivatives.

antiparticle. *See* antimatter.

Antipater (397-319 BC) Macedonian general. Antipater was chief military and diplomatic aide to Philip of Macedon and then to Alexander the Great, becoming regent after Alexander's departure for the East. To maintain this position after Alexander's death, he suppressed internal rebellions and crushed the imperial ambitions of Alexander's second-in-command Perdiccas (d. 321). After Antipater's death Alexander's empire began to disintegrate.

Antipater (d. 4 BC) The son of *Herod the Great. Disowned in infancy, but restored to favour in about 17 BC, he struggled ruthlessly to succeed his father. He had his half-brothers executed in about 7 BC but was himself executed shortly before Herod's own death.

Antipater the Idumaean (d. 43 BC) Procurator (governor) of Judaea (47-43). His adroit manipulation of successive Roman backers, including *Caesar, who appointed him procurator, brought privileges for Judaea and financial advantages for himself. He was assassinated and his son *Herod the Great subsequently succeeded to his position.

Antiphon (c. 480-411 BC) Athenian orator, important in the development of a vigorous and precise Greek prose style. Antiphon conspired to establish oligarchic rule at Athens (411) but a more moderate democratic government prevailed and he was tried and executed despite a brilliant self-defence.

Antipodes Islands 49 42S 178 50E A small group of rocky uninhabited islands in the S Pacific Ocean, belonging to New Zealand. Their fur seal population has been greatly reduced by hunting. Area: 62 sq km (24 sq mi).

antipope Those raised to the papacy in opposition to a lawfully elected pope. There have been about 40 antipopes. The first, Hippolitus, was created in the early 3rd century. During the later Roman Empire and during the middle ages most antipopes represented rival factions supporting different political or doctrinal claims. In the 11th and 12th centuries some 14 antipopes were chosen by the Holy Roman Emperors, who had had until 1059 a considerable voice in papal elections and who resented the Church's growing independence from lay control. From 1378 another group of antipopes was elected following the *Great Schism, when a group of cardinals left Avignon (*see* Avignon papacy) to return to Rome; the popes remaining at Avignon and under French control were styled antipopes thereafter. The Council of Pisa (1409) elected a new pope to end the Schism, but he too was regarded as an antipope until unity was restored at the Council of *Constance (1415). There have been no antipopes since the mid-15th century.

antique An artefact of aesthetic and historical or sociological significance, now not in general use or manufacture. The term does not include painting and sculpture. Until recently an antique was required to predate about 1830, when factory production increased, but today import and export laws of most countries require an age of a hundred years for antiques. Antique collecting was a pastime of the wealthy aristocracy until the 20th century, when its increasing popularity has widened the scope of collectable items to include all kinds of domestic ephemera.

Antirrhinum A genus of chiefly Mediterranean and W

North American herbaceous plants (about 40 species). The most widely cultivated species is the ornamental snapdragon (*A. majus*), 30–80 cm high with brightly coloured two-lipped tubular flowers adapted to pollination by large bees. It grows naturally as a perennial but is usually treated as an annual and grown from seed. Family: *Scrophulariaceae*.

antisemitism Hostility towards the *Jews, which has characterized their existence since the *Diaspora (6th century BC). Its origins perhaps go back to the distrust invariably felt for a coherent minority held together by strong religious and cultural ties, which are themselves strengthened as the hostility intensifies. The early history of the Jews did nothing to dispel this inherent mistrust: represented as God's chosen people in the Old Testament and the betrayers of Christ in the New Testament, their unpopularity in medieval Europe was reflected in totally unfounded beliefs that they used Christian children as human sacrifices. Encouraged and, in some cases, forced to become moneylenders (an activity forbidden to Christians by canon law; *see* usury), they were by the 13th century persecuted throughout Europe. Expulsion (England, 1290; France, 1306; Spain, 1492), massacre (Germany, 1348; Spain, 1391), the Inquisition (1478), and papal bull (1555) deprived medieval Europe of large numbers of its Jews, many of whom enriched the Muslim countries of N Africa and Turkey. It was not until the 18th-century *Enlightenment had introduced a degree of religious freedom that they came back in any numbers. However, in the 19th century antisemitism gained new impetus from nationalist sentiments, especially in Germany. In France, it became public in the *Dreyfus affair. In Russia, government-tolerated (and sometimes government-inspired) *pogroms were common in the late 19th and early 20th centuries but antisemitism reached its peak in Hitler's final solution, which cost the Jews between five and six million lives (*see* holocaust). In the postwar years, since the establishment of the state of Israel, antisemitism has to some extent been replaced by Arab anti-Zionism, but it continues to be active in E Europe, especially the Soviet Union. Social discrimination, such as the exclusion of Jews from private clubs, still exists in even apparently tolerant western countries that have legislation against racial discrimination.

antiseptic A substance that kills bacteria and other dangerous microorganisms and can be applied to the skin (to cleanse wounds, before surgery, etc.) or taken internally. Antiseptics are generally distinguished from *disinfectants, which are too toxic to be used on or within the body.

Antisthenes (c. 445–c. 360 BC) Greek philosopher and disciple of *Socrates. Antisthenes was a critic of society and is regarded as a formative influence on cynicism (*see* Cynics). Principally a moral philosopher, he argued for a simple and virtuous way of life that would lead to happiness.

antitank gun Any flat-trajectory *gun using ammunition suitable for destroying *tanks. Guns in tanks themselves are the most common examples. Artillery weapons are light low-silhouette easily deployed pieces. Short-range specialized missiles are replacing the lighter antitank guns.

antitoxin An *antibody produced against a toxin. Antitoxins can be isolated from inoculated healthy animals and used to treat or prevent specific infections; for example, an antitoxin against tetanus is obtained from the plasma of animals inoculated against tetanus.

antitrust acts US legislation to control *monopolies and preserve a freely competitive market. In the 19th century some businessmen fixed prices and destroyed rival businesses by manipulating raw materials and access to transport. The Sherman Antitrust Act (1890), the first of several measures, prohibited contracts "in restraint of trade." Interpreted narrowly at first, these laws were strengthened by successive legislation (including the Clayton Act 1914 and the Antimerger Act 1950) prohibiting or restricting interlocking directorships, price fixing, and takeovers. In the UK, the less

stringent Fair Trading Act (1973) performs similar functions.

antlers The paired bony structures growing from the heads of deer, generally confined to males. In temperate regions the antlers begin to grow in early summer: they are at first covered with velvety skin, which is later shed. Used for fighting and display, the antlers are shed each year at the end of the mating season. Deer grow their first set of antlers, which are usually straight spikes, at the age of 1–2 years. The number of points is increased in successive years.

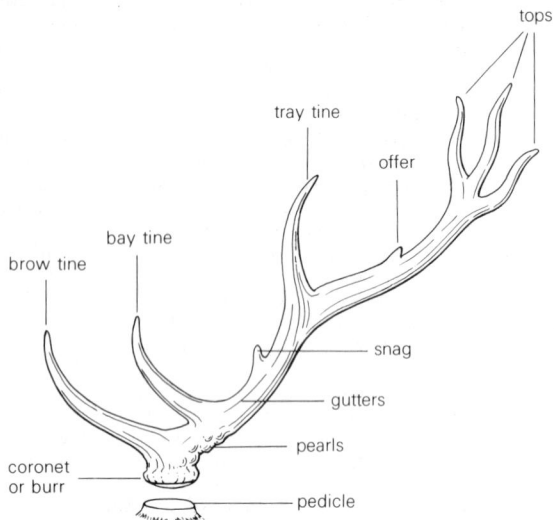

ANTLERS *The number of branches increases with the age of the stag. This antler has 6 branches; a stag with a head of 12 branches is called a royal.*

antlion An insect belonging to a family (*Myrmeleontidae*) in which the adults resemble dragonflies and live only long enough to mate and lay eggs. The predatory larva lives 1–3 years, generally at the bottom of a conical pit in loose sand: any insect that falls into the pit is snapped up with its large jaws, which protrude from the sand. Order: *Neuroptera*.

Antofagasta 21 51S 102 18W A city in NW Chile, a port on the Pacific Ocean. It is a commercial and industrial centre. The chief industries are metal refining and founding; exports include nitrates and copper. The University of the North was established here in 1956. Population (1980 est): 161 226.

Antonello da Messina (c. 1430–c. 1479) Italian painter, born in Messina (Sicily). He trained in Naples, where he probably learned the Flemish technique of oil painting; this he introduced to Venice during a visit in 1475. The realism of Flemish art also deeply influenced his style, particularly in *St Jerome in His Study* and *Portrait of a Man* (both National Gallery, London).

Antonescu, Ion (1882–1946) Romanian general and politician. A pro-Nazi, he became prime minister (1940), replacing *Carol II's government with a totalitarian regime. In 1941 he commanded the army in Bessarabia. He was executed for war crimes.

Antonine Wall A Roman frontier defence work 58.5 km (36.5 mi) long, linking the Firths of Forth and Clyde in S Scotland and still surviving in places. It was built about 142 AD by Lollius Urbicus, governor of Britain, for the emperor *Antoninus Pius, and abandoned in 196 AD. A military road linked 29 small forts along a turf wall 3 m (10 ft) high and 4.3 m (14 ft) wide, behind a substantial ditch. See also Hadrian's Wall.

Antoninus Pius (86–161 AD) Roman emperor (138–61).

Antoninus was admitted by Emperor Hadrian to his advisory council and adopted as his successor in 138. His reign was peaceful and generally prosperous. Only minor campaigns were fought abroad and noted legal reforms were introduced; the *Antonine Wall was built during his reign. He was deified after his death.

Antonioni, Michelangelo (1912–) Italian film maker. Born into a bourgeois provincial family and interested in film making as a student, in 1939 he moved to Rome to work for the magazine *Cinema*. His first films were *Gente del Po* (1943–47) and *Cronaca di un amore* (1950). Later films include *L'avventura* (1959), *La notte* (1961), *Blow-Up* (1966), *Zabriskie Point* (1970), and *The Passenger* (1975).

Antrim A former county in NE Northern Ireland, bordering on the Atlantic Ocean and the Irish Sea. It consists mainly of a basalt plateau sloping inland to Lough Neagh in the SW. There are many peat bogs in the interior. On the N coast is the famous *Giant's Causeway. The county is predominantly agricultural producing oats, potatoes, flax, and livestock. Industry includes the manufacture of man-made fibres, which has largely replaced traditional linen production. Area: 3100 sq km (1200 sq mi). County town: Belfast.

An-tung. *See* Andong.

Antwerp (Flemish name: Antwerpen; French name: Anvers) 51 13N 4 25E A city in Belgium, on the River Scheldt. Antwerp is one of the largest seaports in the world and has important shipbuilding and ship-repairing industries. Other industries include oil refining, diamond cutting, textiles, and electronics. It possesses many fine buildings, including the 14th-century gothic cathedral, the printer Christopher Plantin's house (now a museum), and the 16th-century Butchers' Hall. It is the birthplace of Rubens and Van Dyck and some of their paintings form part of a fine collection housed in the Royal Gallery of Fine Arts. There is a large Flemish-speaking population. *History*: it was the leading commercial centre of western Europe in the 16th century but religious strife and its sacking by Spaniards (1576) led to its decline, further hastened by the closure of the River Scheldt (1648). The revival of its economy began when Belgium purchased the shipping rights of the river from the Netherlands. Antwerp was occupied and damaged in both World Wars. Population (1981 est): 190 652.

Anu The Mesopotamian god of the heavens and father of all the gods. He represented the infinite and all-embracing sky and was worshipped as the source of all order and rule.

Anubis Egyptian god of the dead, usually represented as a crouching jackal or a jackal-headed man. He supervised the weighing of the souls of the dead, and also the embalming of the body. He was reputed to have invented this process to preserve the body of *Osiris.

Anura An order of amphibians (over 2000 species) comprising the *frogs and *toads. Anurans are specialized for jumping, having a short backbone, no tail, and large muscular hind legs. The eggs hatch into tadpoles, which undergo *metamorphosis. This order is also called the *Salientia*.

Anuradhapura 8 20N 80 25E A town in Sri Lanka. The ancient capital of the island (5th century BC to 8th century AD), it is the site of the sacred bo tree descended from the original at *Buddh Gaya and the first Buddhist temple in Ceylon. Population (1981): 36 248.

anus. *See* intestine.

Anvers. *See* Antwerp.

Anville, Jean-Baptiste Bourguignon d' (1697–1782) French geographer and cartographer, specializing chiefly in ancient and medieval geography. As geographer to the French king from 1719, he greatly improved the accuracy of maps of Italy, Asia, and Africa.

anxiety Generalized pervasive fear. Anxiety is partly the feeling of apprehension, partly the behaviour of avoiding frightening situations, and partly the associated bodily changes, such as sweating, a fast pulse, and tense muscles. It is normal to feel anxiety when some danger is present or expected. Severe anxiety out of all proportion to any real threats can be treated by tranquillizing drugs, *psychotherapy, *behaviour therapy, and *autosuggestion. *See also* neurosis; phobia.

Anyang 36 04N 114 20E A city in E China, in Henan province. The last capital (1384–1111 BC) of the Shang dynasty, it has many archaeological remains. Industries include cotton and steel. Population (1980): 253 541.

ANZAC The *A*ustralian and *N*ew *Z*ealand *A*rmy *C*orps, which served in World War I in Europe and the Middle East. On ANZAC Day, 25 April (the day of the ANZAC landing in Gallipoli in 1915), in Australia and New Zealand the dead of both World Wars are remembered.

Anzengruber, Ludwig (1839–89) Austrian dramatist and novelist. Originally an actor, he wrote a successful series of realistic plays about rural life. They include the tragedy *Der Meineidbauer* (1871) and the comedy *Die Kreuzelschreiber* (1872). He also wrote short stories and two novels.

Anzio 41 27N 12 38E A seaport and resort in Italy, in Lazio on the Tyrrhenian Sea. The birthplace of Nero, it was the scene of Allied landings in World War II. Population (1981): 27 094.

ANZUS A security treaty concluded in 1951 by *A*ustralia, *N*ew *Z*ealand, and the *US*A, requiring members to provide mutual aid in the event of aggression by foreign powers.

Aomori 40 50N 140 43E A city in Japan, in N Honshu on Mutsu Bay. One of Japan's major ports, it exports rice, fish, and timber. Population (1980): 288 000.

aorta. *See* artery; heart.

Aosta 45 43N 7 19E A town in Italy, capital of Valle d'Aosta on the River Dora Baltea. Situated amidst impressive mountain scenery, it has important Roman remains and a cathedral (12th–19th centuries). Population (1981): 37 682.

aoudad A tawny-coloured sheep, *Ammotragus lervia*, also called Barbary sheep, that is the only wild sheep in Africa. Aoudads live in dry rocky northern regions. They stand 102 cm at the shoulder and have outward-curving horns and a long fringe of hair hanging from the neck and chest.

Aouita, Saïd (1960–) Moroccan middle-distance runner. In 1987 he demonstrated his versatility by becoming the holder of world records in the 2000 m, 5000 m, and 15 000 m events.

Apache A North American Indian people with six major divisions: the Jicarillos, Mescaleros, Chiricahuas, and Western Apache of the S Plains and SW region of the USA; and the Lipan and Kiowa-Apache living further to the east. Their language is of *Athabascan type. They frequently raided the villages of Pueblo Indians and Spanish settlements to steal cattle and horses. In addition to hunting, some groups practised farming. Normally tribal unity was slight but occasionally independent local groups of matrilineal kin would form alliances under the leadership of chiefs, such as Cochise, Geronimo, and Victorio, who led guerrilla campaigns against the Americans during the late 19th century. There are today about 10 000 Apaches on reservations.

apartheid (Afrikaans: apartness) The policy of separate development of the White and non-White populations in South Africa. Apartheid, which was introduced by the Afrikaner National Party in 1948, aims to divide South Africa into separate regions for Whites and Blacks. The White minority that governs South Africa has been criticized for this policy and in 1961 South Africa was forced to withdraw from the British Commonwealth. In 1985 non-Whites won limited constitutional rights and interracial marriage was allowed. Increased internal unrest, combined with pressure from outside, led to the declaration of a state of emergency in 1986, sanctioning restrictions on press coverage and detention of Black activists.

apatite The commonest phosphorous mineral, of composition $Ca_5(PO_4)_3(OH,F,Cl)$. It is found as an accessory mineral in many igneous rocks, especially pegmatites, as well as metamorphosed limestones. It is used in the production of fertilizers. The enamel of teeth is composed almost entirely of apatite (*see also* fluoridation) and the chief inorganic constituent of bone is hydroxyapatite, $Ca_{10}(PO_4)_6(OH)_2$. *See* Plate III.

Apatosaurus A huge herbivorous dinosaur, formerly called *Brontosaurus*, of the late Jurassic period, which ended about 135 million years ago. Up to 21 m long and weighing up to 30 tonnes, it had massive pillar-like legs, a long neck and tail, and spent most of its time in swamps, coming ashore to lay eggs. With its nostrils placed high on its head, it was able to stand almost fully submerged. Order: *Saurischia.* ▢fossil.

ape A highly intelligent tailless *primate belonging to the family *Pongidae* (11 species), found in central Africa and S Asia. There are two subfamilies: the arboreal *Hylobatinae* (*see* gibbons; siamang) and the ground-dwelling *Ponginae* (*see* chimpanzees; orang-utans; gorillas), also called great apes. Forest apes are often solitary but ground-dwelling apes live in complex societies and all have highly developed means of communication.
Some tailless primates of other families are also called apes.

Apeldoorn 52 13N 5 57E A city in the E central Netherlands, in Gelderland province. The 17th-century Castle Loo, a royal summer residence, is nearby. Its industries include blanket, cloth, and paper production. Population (1981 est): 140 769.

Apelles (4th century BC) The court painter of Alexander the Great. He seems to have specialized in portraits and allegories aiming, like many contemporary artists, at *trompe l'oeil* realism. His most famous pictures included *Aphrodite Rising from the Waves* and *Alexander as Zeus*. His style of portraiture influenced fashions in painting for more than two centuries.

Apennines (Italian name: Appennini) A mountain range in Italy. It extends about 1050 km (652 mi) down the Italian peninsula from the Maritime Alps in the NW to the Strait of Messina in the S. The range is not generally very high but it affords few easy crossing points; the highest peak is Monte Corno at 2914 m (9560 ft). The Apennines are volcanic in the S (*see* Vesuvius).

aphelion The point in the orbit of a body around the sun at which the body is furthest from the sun. The earth is at aphelion on 3 July. *Compare* perihelion.

aphid An ▢insect, also called a plant louse, belonging to a family (*Aphidae*) of important plant pests. Small, soft, and often wingless, aphids have long thin antennae and weak legs and are usually green (greenfly), red, or brown. There are two thin tubes projecting from the abdomen from which honeydew is secreted. Aphids feed on plant sap, piercing plant tissues with sharp beaklike mouthparts, causing leaf curl, retardation of growth, and often forming galls. The aphid's great fecundity and the ability of the female to reproduce by *parthenogenesis results in frequent outbreaks of the pest. Order: *Hemiptera.*

Aphraates (4th century AD) The first Father of the Syrian Church. He lived a monastic life and may also have been a bishop. He wrote numerous tractates summarizing the Christian faith.

aphrodisiac A drug that increases sexual desire or sexual performance. No true aphrodiasic has yet been discovered and most preparations act (if at all) by suggestion. Some drugs (such as *alcohol and *morphine) produce a general euphoria and reduce inhibitions but usually have an adverse effect on sexual performance. Local irritants, such as cantharides (Spanish fly), can prolong an erection at the cost of considerable discomfort.

Aphrodite In Greek mythology, the goddess of love, called *Venus by the Romans. According to Homer she was the daughter of Dione and Zeus; Hesiod says that she was born from the foam after *Uranus had been castrated and his genitals thrown into the sea. She was said to have emerged from the sea at Paphos in Cyprus or at the island of Cythera. She was the wife of Hephaestus but was unfaithful to him and had an affair with Ares. She is portrayed by later writers as the mother of Eros. Paris' choice of her as the most beautiful of the three goddesses at the wedding feast of Peleus and Thetis (the others were Hera and Athena) caused the *Trojan War. She was revered throughout Greece as the personification of spiritual love but she also embodied sensual lust.

Apia 13 48S 171 45W The capital and chief port of Western Samoa, in N Upolu on the S Pacific Ocean. The head of state's residence was formerly the home of Robert Louis Stevenson. Copra, bananas, and cocoa are exported. Population (1981 est): 36 000.

APIS *The sacred bull of Memphis was associated with the solar cult and was often depicted with its emblem, the sun disc, between its horns.*

Apis The Egyptian bull god. Originally a minor fertility god, he became associated with *Ptah and later *Osiris, at which point he became known as Serapis. A bull sacred to him was kept until another with appropriate markings was found; it was then ritually drowned in the Nile and its body mummified in the Serapeum vault at Saqqarah.

apocalypse (Greek: revelation) In the New Testament, the Revelation of St John the Divine. The term is also used of various noncanonical writings, such as the *Book of Enoch*, and of parts of the Old Testament books of *Isaiah*, *Ezekiel*, and *Daniel*. These are all examples of "apocalyptic literature." Full of symbolism and imagery, they describe visions of a great new era that will suddenly supersede the present age of suffering.

Apocrypha (Greek: hidden things) Twelve books taken over by the early Christian Church from the Greek version of the Old Testament but not forming part of the Hebrew Bible. They originated in the Hellenistic Judaism of Alexandria but were not accepted as canonical by orthodox Jews and were treated in various ways in Christian Bibles. In the

*Vulgate, most of them are printed with the Old Testament but they are omitted or printed as a separate section in Protestant versions of the Bible. They are: I Esdras, Tobit, Judith, the Rest of Esther, the Wisdom of Solomon, Ecclesiasticus, Baruch with the Epistle of Jeremy, the Song of the Three Holy Children, the History of Susanna, Bel and the Dragon, the Prayer of Manasses, and I and II Maccabees.

apogee The point in the orbit of the moon or of an artificial satellite around the earth at which the body is furthest from the earth. *Compare* perigee.

Apollinaire, Guillaume (Wilhelm de Kostrowitzky; 1880–1918) French poet. Born in Italy, he settled in Paris in 1900. A champion of *cubism and other avantgarde movements, he blended lyricism with experiment in his poetry, first collected in *Alcools* (1913). While recovering from a head wound sustained in World War I, he wrote a surrealist play, *Les Mamelles de Tirésias* (1917), and a modernist manifesto, *L'Esprit nouveau et les poètes*. The poems in *Calligrammes* (1918) included daring typographical experiments. He died in the 1918 flu epidemic.

Apollo A Greek god of many aspects, symbol of light, of reason, and of male beauty. He is also associated with medicine, prophecy, music and poetry, the care of animals and crops, morality, and the maintenance of society. He and his sister *Artemis were the children of *Zeus by *Leda. He established his oracle at Delphi after killing Python, its dragon guardian.

Apollo moon programme The US programme to land men on the moon by 1970, announced by President Kennedy in 1961. The programme was directed by *NASA. The preliminary manned Mercury (1961–63) and Gemini (1965–66) projects provided valuable information and experience. The method selected for the landing was for a Saturn V rocket to launch the Apollo spacecraft towards the moon and, once the craft was in lunar orbit, for a capsule—the lunar module—to descend to the moon's surface carrying two astronauts. The third astronaut remained in the orbiting craft. At the end of the surface mission the lunar module's descent stage was left on the moon while its ascent stage was shot into lunar orbit and docked with the orbiting craft. Following the transfer of the two astronauts, the ascent stage was jettisoned and the spacecraft put in a flight path towards earth. The astronauts travelled to and from the moon in the command module, the rocket engines for in-flight manoeuvres, fuel cells, etc., being carried in the separate service module. The latter was jettisoned prior to re-entering the earth's atmosphere; the command module finally splashed down in the ocean.

The first six Apollo missions were unmanned test flights, the next four being manned. Apollo 11 made the first manned lunar landing in July, 1969. Of the six ensuing missions, all, except Apollo 13, were highly successful, the scientific content of the information obtained increasing with each lunar landing.

Apollonius (2nd century AD) Greek grammarian, nicknamed Dyskolos (Bad-tempered). Of his 29 works on grammar, 4 survive. He introduced critical methods into grammar, seeking explanations rather than descriptions of sentence structure.

Apollonius of Perga (c. 261–c. 190 BC) Greek mathematician, who studied under *Archimedes. In a series of eight books, he described a family of curves known as *conic sections, comprising the circle, ellipse, parabola, and hyperbola.

Apollonius of Rhodes (3rd century BC) Greek epic poet. He was sometime head of the Library of Alexandria and was the chief rival of the poet *Callimachus. His four-volume *Argonautica*, in the style of *Homer, tells the story of the quest for the *Golden Fleece and is notable for its treatment of Medea's love for Jason, showing a sympathy to the

woman's viewpoint unusual at this time. He also wrote epigrams, and commentaries on other Greek poets.

Apollonius of Tyana (1st century AD) Pythagorean philosopher and reputed miracle worker, from Tyana in Cappadocia. He was the subject of a biography by the Roman Flavius Philostratus in about 200 AD, possibly commissioned as anti-Christian propaganda by the empress Julia Domna.

apologetics In Christianity, the defence of the faith by theologians using intellectual and philosophical arguments. The name apologists refers especially to 2nd-century writers, such as *Justin Martyr and *Tertullian, who argued for Christianity against paganism. Later apologists defended orthodox Christian doctrines against heretical ones. In the 20th century one of the main apologetic tasks has been to explain how orthodox Christian belief is still reasonable in a scientific age.

apomixis The formation and development of an embryo without the fusion of male and female sex cells. This can occur in both plants and animals. The embryo is usually formed from the unfertilized egg (*see* parthenogenesis). In certain cases apomixis is triggered by a male sex cell that enters the egg but does not fuse with it.

apoplexy. *See* stroke.

Apostles In the New Testament, the 12 men chosen by Jesus as his disciples who, after his death, were to spread his teaching throughout the Roman world. Originally they were: Andrew, Bartholomew (*or* Nathaniel), James son of Alphaeus, James son of Zebedee, John, Jude (*or* Thaddeus), Judas Iscariot, Matthew (*or* Levi), Philip, Simon Peter, Simon the Zealot, and Thomas. After his suicide Judas Iscariot was replaced by Matthias. St Paul was also included among the Apostles because of his claim to having seen Jesus after the resurrection. *See also* Acts of the Apostles.

Apostles' Creed A Christian profession of faith in three sections concerning God the Father, Jesus Christ, and the Holy Spirit. Widely used in the Western Churches, it is of uncertain date but its present title first occurs in a letter of St Ambrose of about 390 AD.

Apostolic Constitutions A collection of Christian ecclesiastical administrative regulations and instructions for worship. Although its full title is "Ordinances of the Holy Apostles through Clement," and it ends with the 85 "Apostolic Canons," it probably originated in late 4th-century Syria and not from the Apostles. Its eight books contain much that is derived from the 3rd-century *Didascalia Apostolorum* and the 2nd-century *Didache*, which are significant sources of information about the early Church.

apostolic succession A Christian doctrine held by the Roman Catholic and Orthodox Churches and by some Anglicans. Its upholders claim that the Apostles appointed the first bishops and that there is thus a continuous line of succession from the Apostles to the present ministries of these Churches along which the power and authority given by Christ to the former have passed to the latter.

Appalachian Mountains A mountain range in the USA. It extends NE–SW from the Mohawk River to Alabama, separating the Mississippi-Missouri lowlands from the Atlantic coastal plain. It consists of a series of mountain ranges and plateaus, including the *Allegheny Mountains, the *Catskill Mountains, and the White Mountains of New Hampshire. Its highest point is Mount Mitchell, at 2038 m (6684 ft). Coalmining is important, providing anthracite and bitumen; iron ore is also extracted. Poor communications and lack of employment have contributed to the establishment of a regional assistance programme within the area. It also contains the **Appalachian Trail**, the longest continuous footpath in the world.

Appaloosa An American breed of spotted riding horse with a wispy mane and tail. The white Appaloosa is completely white with dark spots over the whole body but other

craft	astronauts	launch date	comments
Apollo 7	W. Schirra W. Cunningham D. Eisele	11 October, 1968	first manned flight of Apollo spacecraft
Apollo 8	F. Borman J. Lovell W. Anders	21 December, 1968	first manned flight around moon
Apollo 9	J. McDivitt D. Scott R. Schweickart	3 March, 1969	complete Apollo craft tested in earth orbit
Apollo 10	T. Stafford J. Young E. Cernan	18 May, 1969	rehearsal of moon landing
Apollo 11	N. Armstrong E. Aldrin M. Collins	16 July, 1969	first manned moon landing, 20 July
Apollo 12	C. Conrad A. Bean R. Gordon	14 November, 1969	second moon landing
Apollo 13	J. Lovell F. Haise J. Swigert	11 April, 1970	mission aborted after in-flight explosion in service module
Apollo 14	A. Shepard E. Mitchell S. Roosa	31 January, 1971	third moon landing
Apollo 15	D. Scott J. Irwin A. Worden	26 July, 1971	fourth moon landing
Apollo 16	J. Young C. Duke T. Mattingly	16 April, 1972	fifth moon landing
Apollo 17	E. Cernan H. Schmitt R. Evans	7 December, 1972	last moon landing

APOLLO MOON PROGRAMME

types may be of any colour as long as the hindquarters are white with spots of the colour of the rest of the coat. Height: 1.47–1.60 m (14½–15¾ hands).

apparent magnitude. *See* magnitude.

appeal   In law, the review of a court decision by a higher court, usually at the request of one of the parties to the case. The decisions of some administrative or professional bodies may also be appealed against in the courts. Appeals in *common law systems are usually based on alleged errors of law in the original trial, but may sometimes also be based on errors of fact. *See also* courts of law.

appeasement   The policy implemented by the British prime minister, Neville *Chamberlain, of giving way to the demands of Hitler and Mussolini in the hope of maintaining peace. It culminated in the *Munich Agreement (1938) and was finally shown to be futile in March, 1939, when Hitler seized Czechoslovakia.

appendicitis   Inflammation of the *appendix. Appendicitis is most common in childhood and adolescence. It usually starts with a vague pain around the navel that becomes localized in the right lower region of the abdomen. Diarrhoea may also occur. Surgical removal to prevent rupture of the appendix and subsequent *peritonitis is usually required.

appendix (*or* vermiform appendix)   A thin blind-ended tube, 7–10 cm long, that opens from the end of the large intestine. It has no known function in man and is prone to infection (*see* appendicitis). In herbivorous animals (e.g. rabbits and cows) the appendix is large and functions in the digestion of vegetable matter. *See* Plate IV.

Appert, Nicolas   (1750–1841) French inventor, who discovered that food can be preserved by boiling it in sealed containers. In 1812 he opened the world's first commercial canning factory.

Appian Way   The road, built about 312 BC by the statesman Appius Claudius, between Rome and Capua. It was the first in the strategic network of Roman roads. A short stretch is still visible near Rome.

apple   A deciduous tree or shrub of the genus *Malus* (about 35 species), native to N temperate regions and widely cultivated for their rounded fleshy □ fruits (pomes). Several species have been cultivated, especially *M. pumila* of W Asia, with the development of numerous varieties of dessert, cooking, and *cider apples. Shoots of the required variety are grafted onto selected rootstocks. Some varieties are ornamental. Apples are also used for soft drinks and as a source of pectin. Family: *Rosaceae*. *See also* crab apple.

Appleby   54 36N 2 29W An ancient market town in NW England, in Cumbria on the River Eden. Appleby has a castle, a bullring, and holds an annual horse fair. Population (1981): 2384.

Appleton layer.   *See* ionosphere.

Appomattox   37 21N 78 51W A town in the USA, in central Virginia. The Confederate leader, Robert E. Lee, surrendered here to Ulysses Grant on 9 April, 1865, effectively ending the US Civil War.

apricot   A tree, *Prunus armenica*, native to China and widely grown in warm temperate countries, especially Spain, for its fruits. It is 6–9 m tall and has white five-petalled flowers and toothed heart-shaped leaves. The hairy-skinned orange-yellow fruits have sweet flesh and smooth stones. Family: *Rosaceae*.

April Theses   The *Bolshevik party programme devised by *Lenin during the *Russian Revolution (1917). Its demands included the cessation of Bolshevik support for the Provisional Government, Russia's withdrawal from World War I, and the redistribution of land among the peasants.

a priori knowledge   Any kind of knowledge that is in no way derived from sense exerience, observation, or experiment. Many philosophers therefore hold that a priori knowledge is impossible. However, those attracted to *intuitionism have defended its possibility, especially with regard to theological problems. Kant insisted on the reality of a priori knowledge in the form of the necessary conditions of our having any experience at all, e.g. the notions of causality, space, and time.

apse   A semicircular or polygonal eastern end of a church, characteristic of the *basilica and *romanesque and *Norman architecture. Seats for the clergy ran round the apse walls behind the centrally placed altar.

Apuleius, Lucius   (2nd century AD) Roman writer and rhetorician. Educated at Carthage and Athens, he travelled in the East before returning to Africa to marry Pudentilla, a rich widow. His *Apologia* is his defence against a charge that he had won her by magic. *The Golden Ass*, the only surviving complete Latin novel, describes the misadventures of one Lucius, who is accidentally turned into an ass; he is finally restored to human form by Isis.

Apulia (*or* Puglia)   A region in SE Italy, on the Adriatic Sea. It consists of lowlands in the N and S (the "heel" of Italy) and a hilly central area. Wheat is the main agricultural crop; tobacco, vegetables, olives, figs, vines, and almonds are also produced. Manufacturing industry is mainly related to agriculture although modern industries are being developed, particularly at Taranto. Area: 19 347 sq km (7470 sq mi). Population (1982 est): 3 908 484. Capital: Bari.

Aqaba   29 32N 35 00E A port in Jordan, on the **Gulf of Aqaba**, a narrow inlet at the NE end of the Red Sea. Aqaba was the Roman stronghold of Aelana. Being Jordan's only port, it has been considerably expanded, despite difficult navigation and an exposed site, to handle the export of phosphates. Population (1979 est): 26 999.

aquamarine   A pale blue or green variety of *beryl. Many fine specimens of this gemstone come from Brazil, Madagascar, and California.

aqua regia   A fuming yellow corrosive mixture of one part *nitric acid to three or four parts *hydrochloric acid. It dissolves all metals, even gold, and is used in *metallurgy.

aquarium   A receptacle containing fresh or salt water for maintaining aquatic plants or animals (particularly fish) or a building in which such receptacles are kept or displayed. To duplicate natural conditions, modifications including the use of a water heater (for tropical species), aerator, and filter may be necessary. The first public aquarium was opened at the London Zoo in Regent's Park, London, in 1853.

Aquarius (Latin: Water Bearer)   A large constellation in the S sky, lying on the *zodiac between Pisces and Capricornus.

aquatint   An etching technique that produces a tonal effect similar to that of wash drawing. A satisfactory method was invented in the 1760s by a Frenchman, Jean Baptiste Le Prince (1733–81). Sharply defined areas of tone are employed, usually in conjunction with etched lines. A printing plate is sprinkled with powdered asphaltum or resin, which is then fixed to the plate by heating. Stopping-out varnish is used to mask different areas as the plate is immersed for varying lengths of time in an acid bath. *Goya, *Picasso, and *Miró have used the technique with outstanding effect.

aquavit   A *spirit distilled from grains and flavoured with caraway seeds. It is best served ice cold. Aquavit is drunk predominantly in Scandinavia.

Aquaviva, Claudio   (1543–1615) Italian churchman, the fifth general of the Society of Jesus, elected in 1581. The son of a nobleman, he saw Jesuit numbers increase from 5000 to 13 000 during his office and laid down definitive educational guidelines for the order in *Ratio studiorum* (1599).

AQUEDUCT *The* Pont du Gard *built by the Romans in 19* BC *across the River Gard in Provence (France).*

aqueduct   A narrow bridge, channel, or conduit designed to enable water to flow at a steady rate over an irregular natural terrain, such as a valley. Aqueducts were built by the Greeks, but the technique was developed to its highest level of sophistication by the Romans. Impressive Roman examples still survive at Nîmes, Segovia, and Rome. Much the same principles are still used in modern irrigation systems throughout the world.

Aquila (Latin: Eagle)   An equatorial constellation lying in the Milky Way near Cygnus. The brightest star is *Altair.

Aquilegia   A genus of perennial herbaceous plants (100 species) of temperate regions, commonly known as columbines. Their showy flowers have petals with long honey-secreting spurs. A favourite garden flower, aquilegias have been cultivated since the 16th century. Many modern garden hybrids, which have large long-spurred flowers, are derived from the European columbine (*A. vulgaris*), 40–100 cm high with purple to white flowers. Family: *Ranunculaceae*.

Aquilèia 45 47N 13 22E A town in N Italy, at the head of the Adriatic Sea. Founded by the Romans in 181 BC, it was of great strategic and military importance but failed to regain its former prominence following its destruction by Attila in 452 AD. Population (1981): 3281.

Aquinas, St Thomas (c. 1225–74) Italian Dominican theologian, scholastic philosopher, and Doctor of the Church, known as *Doctor Angelicus*. Born near Naples, the son of Count Landulf of Aquino, he was educated at the Benedictine school at Monte Cassino and at the University of Naples. Joining the Dominican Order in 1244 in spite of parental opposition, he became a pupil of *Albertus Magnus in Paris (1245) and followed him to Cologne in 1248. He returned to Paris as a lecturer in 1252, becoming a leading defender of the Dominicans against their critics at the University of Paris. He was a lecturer and theological adviser to the papal Curia between 1259 and 1269 and then taught at Paris until 1272, when he was appointed a professor at Naples. He died at Fossanova on his way to the Council of Lyons and was canonized in 1323. His prolific writings include commentaries on the Scriptures, on Aristotle and other philosophers, and academic disputations. His two most influential works are the *Summa contra gentiles* (1259–64), written for the use of missionaries, and the uncompleted *Summa theologica* (1266–73), the first systematic work on Latin theology. In opposition to the Averroists (*see* Averroes) and Augustinians he attempted to reconcile Christian faith and human reason. His arguments to prove the existence of God have been very influential and the Roman Catholic Church recognizes him as one of its most important theologians. Feast day: 7 March.

Aquino, Cory (Corazón Aquino; 1933–) Philippine stateswoman; president (1986–). She became a popular political leader after the assassination of her husband **Benigno S. Aquino** (1933–83) and head of state when the corrupt Marcos regime came to an end; since then her government has survived a number of attempted coups.

Aquitaine (Latin name: Aquitania) A planning region in SW France, bordering on the Bay of Biscay. Formerly an administrative region in Roman Gaul, it extended from the Pyrenees N to the River Loire. It became an independent duchy under the Merovingians (7th century). The marriages of Eleanor of Aquitaine to Louis VII of France and then to Henry II of England resulted in rival French-English claims to the territory (*see* Hundred Years' War). Area: 41 408 sq km (15 984 sq mi). Population (1981 est): 2 584 400.

arabesque A type of decorative design employing intricate geometrical patterns on a flat surface. The term (meaning "Arabian") was first used in England in the mid-17th century to describe panels of scrollwork ornamentation that were thought to resemble the Arab style. Historically, however, arabesque decoration is Greco-Roman in origin.

Arab horse An ancient breed of horse originally bred by the Bedouins in Arabia. It is usually grey, chestnut, or bay with a long silky mane and tail and an arched neck. The Arab is prized as a riding horse because of its speed, hardiness, and docility. Height: 1.42–1.52 m (14–15 hands).

Arabia A peninsula in the Middle East, forming the SW tip of Asia and bordered by the Red Sea, the Gulf of Aden, the Gulf of Oman, and the Persian Gulf. It consists of Saudi Arabia, North and South Yemen, Oman, the United Arab Emirates, Qatar, Bahrain, and Kuwait. Mountains in the W (most fertile in the S) slope downwards to steppe and desert in the E. Agriculture is still the main occupation, despite flourishing modern oil industries. *History*: as remains of irrigation systems show, S Arabia was the site of technologically advanced ancient civilizations. Arabia was often conquered in part, but its total conquest was long prevented by its deserts. It was conquered briefly by the Persians in 575 AD and later unified from Mecca by Islam in the 7th century. Arabia quickly became disunited again, how-

ever. From the 16th century until World War I the Ottoman Turks held nominal control over much of the peninsula, challenged chiefly by the *Wahhabiyah, a Muslim sect that was led by the Saud family, which conquered Arabia (except for the SW) and finally established Saudi Arabia (1932). From the mid-19th century until the late 1960s the UK was the chief foreign presence.

Arabian Desert 1. A desert chiefly in Saudi Arabia, covering most of *Arabia. Area: about 2 300 000 sq km (887 844 sq mi). 2. A desert in E Egypt between the River Nile and the Red Sea.

Arabian Sea A section of the NW Indian Ocean between Arabia and India. Connected to the Mediterranean Sea by the Red Sea and the Suez Canal, it forms a major shipping route.

Arabic A member of the *Semitic group of languages. It is written from right to left. Arabic is the mother-tongue of some 110 million people inhabiting SW Asia (the Middle East) and the countries of N Africa. Arabic can be roughly classified into three parts: (a) Classical Arabic, the language of the *Koran and the great Arab writers and poets; (b) Modern Literary, or Standard, Arabic, the language of the press and broadcasting; and (c) the colloquial dialects (vernaculars), which differ from country to country. Categories (a) and (b) are known as "Written Arabic," the vernaculars are almost entirely spoken forms.

Arabic literature The literature of the Arabic-speaking peoples, the majority of whom live in N Africa and the Middle East. Most Arabic writing is scholarly, consisting of works on religion, philosophy, grammar, history, translations from the Greek, etc. Literature strictly speaking may be divided into two periods, the classical (6th–16th centuries) and the modern literary revival in the Middle East, which started in the 19th century and reflected a heavy indebtedness to the West. The earliest example of classical literature was a pre-Islamic poetic form, the *qasidah* (6th century), which continued to dominate Arabic verse for generations. An ode of 60 to 100 lines, it was written in praise of the poet himself, his tribe, or his patron. Its main interest for modern readers lies in the dramatic descriptions of early Bedouin desert life; the most important collection is the *Mu'allaqat* (8th century). During the Umayyad period (661–750) there arose a second important poetic genre, the *ghazal*, a short love poem. The golden age of classical Arabic literature developed during the 'Abbasid period (750–1055) with the assimilation of many Greek and Roman authors and the growth of a cosmopolitan urban culture, of which *Abu Nuwas was the outstanding poet. The traditional verse continued to flourish, however, its most famous practitioner being al-*Mutanabbi, who brought a new rhetorical sophistication to the *qasidah*. Literary prose also developed during the 'Abbasid period; among the most influential writers were the essayist al-Jahiz (d. 869) and the critic and philologist Ibn Qutaybah (d. 899). Because of the authority of the Koran, Arabic was maintained as the language of religion and scholarship, but declined as a literary medium under the *Mamelukes (1250–1517) and in the Ottoman Empire (16th–19th centuries). Nationalist movements especially in Egypt and Syria beginning in the late 19th century largely account for the modern literary renaissance in these countries, where writers have adopted such western forms as the novel and drama.

Arabic numerals The number symbols 0, 1, 2, 3, 4, 5, 6, 7, 8, 9. They are believed to have originated in India and were introduced into Europe by the Arabs in about the 10th century AD. *Compare* Roman numerals.

Arab-Israeli Wars. *See* Israel, State of.

Arab League An organization formed to promote Arab unity and cooperation. Formed in Cairo in 1945, it consisted of those Arab countries that were then independent; others joined on attaining independence. A secretariat was established in Cairo. The League has had some success in the scientific and cultural field but in politics has been split between its conservative and progressive members. In 1979, following the Egyptian-Israeli peace treaty, Egypt was expelled from the League.

arable farming The cultivation of plants for food, fibres, vegetable oils, etc., especially on a field scale. Fruit and vegetable production is usually considered as a specialized farming activity (see horticulture). The methods employed in arable farming depend on the crop being grown, the climate and soil type of the region, farming traditions, and the economic state of the farmer and his market. Arable farming is often carried out in conjunction with livestock farming, enabling the farmer to grow his own animal feeds and to make use of animal manures as *fertilizers. Grass is the chief feed for *ruminant livestock and a major arable crop. Special seed mixtures are sown to produce either permanent pasture or a temporary grass ley lasting only a few years, often as part of a system of *crop rotation. Apart from grazing, grass is cut and conserved for winter food as either hay (dried grass) or *silage.

Cereal crops are a principal source of food for man and are important animal feedstuffs. The major cereals are wheat, barley, rice, and maize with oats, millet, sorghum, and rye cultivated to a lesser extent. Wheat may be sown either in autumn or spring, according to the variety, and is harvested in late summer when the grain is hard, yielding between 1.5 and 4 tonnes of grain per hectare. Cereals are harvested using a *combine harvester and the grain is often dried to ensure safe storage.

Beans are grown as a major source of vegetable protein, the most important being *soyabean, produced chiefly in China and the USA. They are harvested mechanically using a specially adapted combine harvester that separates the beans from the rest of the crop. Harvesting root crops, such as potatoes and sugar beet, requires specialized machines that excavate the crop and remove soil. Turnips and swedes are root crops grown mainly for animal fodder. Crops grown for their oil content include sunflower, groundnut, linseed, cottonseed, and rape; cotton, flax, and jute are important sources of textile fibres. Many other crops, including tea, coffee, and tobacco, are of major economic importance and each requires specialized husbandry techniques to give maximum yields. Modern scientific investigation of arable crops (see agronomy) and their requirements together with innovations in mechanization, fertilizers, pesticides, *irrigation, and plant breeding have resulted in dramatic increases in crop yields and productivity, bringing about a Green Revolution in western countries and, more recently, in developing countries.

Arabs A Semitic people originally inhabiting the Arabian peninsula. They are roughly divided into two cultural groups: the nomadic *Bedouin tribes and the settled communities of the towns and oases. Wealth from oil has recently led to industrialization and westernization in the towns, but Islam remains a strong conservative force in social customs, particularly in the restrictions it places upon women's role in society. The Arabs were known in antiquity to the Greeks, Romans, and Jews and are mentioned by name in the later Old Testament books. They appeared as a power in world history early in the 7th century AD, with the rise of Islam, and they carried their language (see Arabic), religion, and culture as far as Spain in the W and Indonesia in the E. In modern usage "Arab" designates Arabic-speaking peoples of SW Asia, Egypt, N Africa, and parts of sub-Saharan Africa, whether or not they are of Arab descent.

Aracajú 10 54S 37 07W A city and port in NE Brazil, the capital of Sergipe state near the mouth of the Rio Continguiba. It is a commercial and industrial centre; the chief industries are sugar refining, cotton milling, and tanning. Its university was founded in 1967. Population (1980): 273 100.

Arachne In Greek mythology, a girl from Lydia who defeated Athena in a tapestry-weaving contest. The jealous goddess destroyed all Arachne's work; she attempted to hang herself, but Athena changed her into a spider.

arachnid An invertebrate animal belonging to an order (Arachnida; 65 000 species) of chiefly terrestrial *arthropods, including the *spiders, *scorpions, *harvestmen, *ticks, and *mites. An arachnid's body is divided into two parts: a combined head and thorax (cephalothorax) and an abdomen. The cephalothorax bears four pairs of legs and two pairs of head appendages, one of which consists of strong pincer-like claws. Arachnids are mostly carnivorous, feeding on the body juices of insects and other small animals; many secrete poison from specialized glands to kill prey or enemies. Others are parasites, some of which are carriers of disease. Arachnids usually lay eggs, which hatch into immature adults.

Arad 46 10N 21 19E An industrial city in W Romania, on the River Mureş. It was Austro-Hungarian until 1919 and has a large Hungarian community. Population (1983): 171 198.

Arafat, Yassir (1929–) Palestinian leader. In the 1950s he was one of the founders of al-*Fatah and in 1968 became president of the *Palestine Liberation Organization.

Arafura Sea A shallow section of the W Pacific Ocean between Australia and New Guinea. It contains uncharted rocks, which make navigation dangerous.

Arago, (Dominique) François (Jean) (1786–1853) French astronomer and physicist, who was professor of physics at the École Polytechnique in Paris. He did important work in astronomy, electricity, magnetism, meteorology, and optics (particularly polarized light). He was an advocate of the wave theory of light and worked with *Fresnel to obtain experimental evidence to support it.

Aragon A region and medieval kingdom in NE Spain, of which Ramoir I (d. 1063) was the first king (1035–63). A series of conquests during the 11th and 12th centuries brought the Aragonese rule over much of N Spain. Union with Catalonia was secured by marriage in 1140. Later expansion gave the Aragonese Sicily (1282) and Sardinia (1320) and culminated in the conquest by *Alfonso the Magnanimous of the kingdom of Naples (1442). In 1469 *Ferdinand the Catholic, heir to the Aragonese throne, married *Isabella the Catholic of Castile and on his accession in 1479 the two kingdoms were united.

Aragon, Louis (1897–1982) French poet, novelist, and journalist. In 1919 he and André *Breton founded the surrealist journal Littérature; his first books of poetry, Feu de joie (1920) and Le Mouvement perpétuel (1925), and his novel, Le Paysan de Paris (1926), are vigorously surrealist. He committed himself to communism after a visit to the Soviet Union in 1930, and began his lifelong relationship with Elsa Triolet, sister-in-law of the poet Mayakovsky. He then turned to Marxist-oriented social realism, especially in novels, such as Holy Week (1958) and the series entitled Le Monde reél (1933–51). He was editor of the left-wing weekly Les Lettres françaises.

aragonite A white or greyish mineral consisting of calcium carbonate, usually with sharp orthorhombic crystals that are often twinned. With age, heat, or pressure aragonite changes into calcite and is therefore generally found in relatively young rocks. Many shells consist of aragonite.

Araguaia, Rio A river in central Brazil, rising in the Brazilian Highlands and flowing generally NE to join the Rio Tocantins. Length: over 1771 km (1100 mi).

Arakan A state in W Burma, extending along the Bay of Bengal and flanked by the Arakan Yoma, a mountain range rising over 3000 m (1000 ft). The principal economic activity is the cultivation of rice. The majority of the inhabitants are of Burmese descent but there is a large minority of Bengali Muslims in the N. History: a powerful kingdom in the 15th century, it was absorbed into Burma

Arakcheev, Aleksei Andreevich, Count (1783) before passing to Britain (1826–1948). The activities of secessionist movements led to its change of status (from a division to a state) in 1975. Area: 36 762 sq km (14 191 sq mi). Population (1973): 1 710 506. Capital: Sittwe.

Arakcheev, Aleksei Andreevich, Count (1769–1834) Russian soldier and statesman. From 1796 to 1798 Arakcheev reorganized the Russian army but his brutality led to his dismissal. He was recalled by Alexander I in 1808 and became war minister. After Napoleon's defeat (1815) he served as minister of internal affairs, establishing many military-agricultural communities, in which Russia's army lived in times of peace. He resigned in 1826, after the accession of Nicholas I (1825).

Aral Sea The fourth largest lake in the world, in the SW Soviet Union in the Kazakh and Uzbek SSRs. It receives the Rivers Amu Darya and Syr Darya and has no outlets. Its maximum depth varies by 10%. Area: about 66 000 sq km (25 477 sq mi).

Aram, Eugene (1704–59) British philologist. Aram's extensive knowledge of etymology led him to compile a *Comparative Lexicon of the English, Latin, Greek, Hebrew, and Celtic Languages*. His career was curtailed when he was hanged for murdering (1745) a former friend, Daniel Clark.

Aramaic A western branch of the Semitic group of languages. Its 22-character alphabet is the ancestor of both Hebrew and Arabic alphabets. Aramaic became extensively used during the late Babylonian empire and was the official language of the Persian Empire under *Darius I. It replaced Hebrew as the language of the Jews from about the time of the Exile in 605 BC until after the rise of Islam.

Aran Islands (Irish name: Arainn) A group of islands in Galway Bay, off the W coast of the Republic of Ireland, comprising Inishmore (the largest), Inishmaan, and Inisheer. Their harsh environment was portrayed in J. M. Synge's *Riders to the Sea*. Area: 46 sq km (18 sq mi). Chief town: Kilronan.

Aranjuez 40 02N 3 37W A town in central Spain, in New Castile on the River Tagus. Its fine palace (1778) was used by the Spanish court until 1890. It is a tourist resort and market town. Population (1981): 35 936.

Arany, János (1817–82) Hungarian poet. Born into a poor peasant family, he became a teacher, editor, and notary. His poem *Toldi* (1847), the adventures of a peasant youth at the 14th-century Hungarian court, was acclaimed as a national epic; he added two sequels, the romantic *Toldi szerelme* (1848) and the comic *Toldi estége* (1854). He took part in the Revolution of 1848, and in 1858 became a member of the Hungarian Academy of Sciences. His powerful but melancholy ballads are perhaps his finest works.

Ararat, Mount (Turkish name: Ağrı Dağı) 39 44N 44 15E A mountain in E Turkey, near the Soviet and Iranian borders. It is volcanic in origin and isolated but for a secondary peak 12 km (7 mi) away. Traditionally, Noah's ark came to rest here after the flood (Genesis 8.4). Height: 5165 m (16 946 ft).

Araucanians Indians of central Chile, divided into three major groups, the Picunche, Mapuche, and Huilliche. They were farmers and herders of llamas, living in small autonomous hamlets of patrilineal kin. They could build in stone but lacked the elaborate culture of other Andean peoples, such as the *Inca. The Mapuche resisted Chilean rule until late in the 19th century. There are now about 200 000 living on reservations. The Araucanian language has been comparatively resistant to Spanish influence.

Araucaria A genus of coniferous trees (about 15 species), native to Australasia and South America (it is named after a district of Chile). They have whorled horizontal branches covered with scale leaves, and male and female flowers usually grow on separate trees. The genus includes the ornamental *monkey puzzle and several trees yielding useful timber, including the Norfolk Island pine (*A. heterophylla*); the hoop pine (*A. cunninghamii*) and the bunya bunya (*A. bidwillii*), both from E Australia; and the parana pine (*A. angustifolia*), of Brazil. Family: *Araucariaceae*.

Arawak Indians of the Greater Antilles and northern and western areas of the Amazon basin. Their languages are the most widespread of the South American Indian languages and include Goajiro in Colombia, Campa and Machiguenga in Peru, and Mojo and Bauré in Bolivia. They are sedentary farmers growing manioc and maize. Prior to the Spanish conquests they were divided into numerous hereditary chiefdoms. They were never a warlike people and in the Caribbean area *Carib tribes frequently raided Arawak groups and enslaved Arawak women. Their religion involved belief in personal guardian spirits. The tribal gods were the spirits of chiefs represented by a hierarchy of idols called zemis, which were housed in temples.

Arbil. *See* Irbil.

arbitration 1. A method of settling a commercial dispute in which each party presents his case to one or more disinterested parties (arbitrators), who are often appointed by a trade association. Arbitration awards can be appealed against in the courts on questions of law. This method of settling disputes is widely used in commerce because it is quicker and cheaper than litigation. In the UK, arbitrations are governed by the Arbitration Act (1979). 2. An attempt to settle an industrial dispute by submitting the case to an arbitrator, such as a government conciliation service (*see* ACAS). In this case the award is usually accepted as binding on both sides, but usually it is an issue, such as wage rates, that cannot be settled by law.

arbor vitae A coniferous tree of the genus *Thuja* (6 species), native to North America and E Asia. They have scalelike leaves, which densely cover the flattened stems, and small scaly cones, 1–1.8 cm long. The Chinese arbor vitae or cedar (*T. orientalis*), which grows to a height of 30 m, is a popular ornamental tree; the giant arbor vitae, or western red cedar (*T. plicata*), of W North America, grows to a height of 40 m and yields a valuable timber. Family: *Cupressaceae*.

Arbroath 56 34N 2 35W A town and fishing port in E Scotland, in Tayside Region. It has a ruined abbey, where Scotland declared its independence in 1320. Population (1981): 24 093.

Arbuthnot, John (1667–1735) Scottish writer and physician. He became one of Queen Anne's physicians in 1705 and a Fellow of the College of Physicians in 1710. He wrote about many scientific subjects but is best known as a friend of *Pope and *Swift and a leading member of the *Scriblerus Club. His *History of John Bull* (1712), a political satire, was the first appearance of that famous character.

Arbutus A genus of evergreen trees and shrubs (about 20 species) distributed in Central and North America and W Europe. The small white or pinkish flowers are borne in terminal clusters and the berries are fleshy and reddish. The leaves are tough, dark green, toothed, and shiny above. The strawberry tree (*A. unedo*) of SW Europe is widely grown as an ornamental, reaching a height of 9 m. Family: *Ericaceae*.

Arcadia A mountainous region of ancient Greece, in the central Peloponnesus, that was identified in the literature of Greece, Rome, and the Renaissance (e.g. in Sidney's *Arcadia*) as an earthly paradise. It is a modern department.

Arc de Triomphe A ceremonial arch standing at the centre of the Étoile at the top of the Champs Elysées in Paris. It was commissioned to celebrate the victories of *Napoleon I and built between 1806 and 1836 to the designs of Jean Chalgrin (1739–1811).

arch In architecture, a structure spanning a horizontal space. The development of the arch was one of the greatest Roman contributions to building technology. By using interlocking and mutually supporting pieces of stone it is possible to span greater distances than can be achieved with

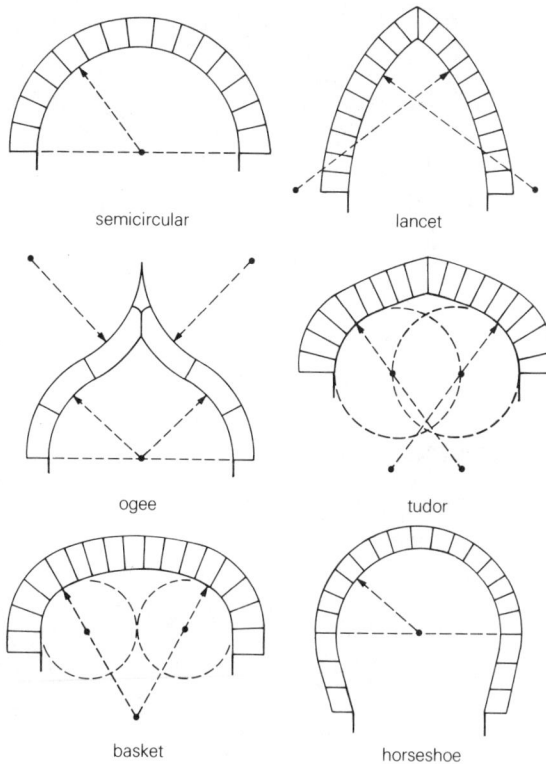

semicircular   lancet

ogee   tudor

basket   horseshoe

ARCH   *The semicircular arch characterized Roman, Romanesque, and Norman architecture; the lancet, ogee, Tudor, and basket arches were gothic and later medieval developments; the horseshoe arch is typical of Islamic architecture.*

single megaliths; also arches can be employed to provide a more even distribution of pressure throughout the building. The basic forms of arch are the pointed, or gothic, arch, and the rounded, or classical, arch.

archaeology   The scientific study that is concerned with the recovery and interpretation of the material remains of man's past. Archaeology may be supplemented by written records, where they exist, but its techniques are principally concerned with nonliterary evidence for man's social and cultural development. Modern archaeology has numerous specialized branches—classical, industrial, underwater, etc. Before the 19th century, digging was carried out to plunder precious objects from ruins. Scientific excavation followed the realization that often more could be learnt from the surroundings in which objects are discovered than from the objects themselves. Essential techniques include stratigraphy, based on the principle that in any sequence of deposits the uppermost is latest and the lowest earliest, and typology, the study of changes in forms (e.g. of pottery). New methods of dating constantly evolve: *radiometric dating, *palaeomagnetism, *thermoluminescence, *varve dating, and *dendrochronology are all valuable with different types of material.

Archaeopteryx   A genus of extinct primitive birds, fossils of which date from the Jurassic period (160-120 million years ago). It had many reptilian features, such as numerous teeth, a long bony tail, and claws on the hand, but was fully feathered and is believed to be the ancestor of modern birds. *Archaeopteryx* lived in dense forests, climbing trees using its claws and gliding down in search of food.

Archangel (Russian name: Arkhangelsk)   64 32N 40 40E A port in the NW Soviet Union, in the RSFSR on the River

Dvina, 50 km (30 mi) from the White Sea. Founded in 1584, it was Russia's leading port until the early 18th century. The Soviet Union's largest timber-exporting port, it has timber-processing and shipbuilding industries and also supports a fishing fleet. Population (1983): 399 000.

archangels   In Christian belief, supernatural beings ranked immediately above *angels in the celestial hierarchy. Michael is the only archangel mentioned in the New Testament (Jude); in Revelation 12 he is the leader of the angels who cast out the dragon from heaven. Gabriel, as the angel of the annunciation, is traditionally included among the archangels, as is Raphael, the helper of Tobias in the apocryphal Book of Tobit. Another archangel, Uriel, is named in II Esdras.

archbishop   A chief bishop who has some jurisdiction over the other bishops in an ecclesiastical province, i.e. a group of dioceses, as well as having authority in his own diocese. Until the 8th or 9th century such men were called "metropolitans," a title still used by Orthodox Christians whose archbishops are of lower rank. Some Roman Catholic archbishops have no provincial authority, their titles being merely honorary. The Church of England has only the Archbishops of Canterbury and of York.

archegonium   The reproductive organ producing the female cells (gametes) in ferns, mosses, algae, fungi, and some gymnosperms. It is flask-shaped, the swollen base containing the egg cell and the neck providing an entrance for the male gametes.

Archer, Frederick Scott   (1813-57) British inventor and sculptor. In 1851 he developed the wet collodion photographic process, enabling multiple copies of pictures to be made. This system was used for several decades.

Archer, Thomas   (1668-1743) English baroque architect. Having studied abroad, Archer had a considerable knowledge of the work of *Bernini and *Borromini, whose influence is apparent in his own buildings, for example at Heythrop House (1710). He is mainly known for his two London churches, St John's, Smith Square (1714), and St Paul's, Deptford (1712), as well as for his work at Chatsworth (Derbyshire).

Archer, William   (1856-1924) British drama critic. He worked as a theatre critic in London from 1879. *Pillars of Society* (1880) was the first of his pioneering translations of Ibsen's plays, culminating in the *Collected Works* (12 vols, 1906-12). He advocated a British national theatre company and encouraged G. B. Shaw during his early career.

archer fish   A small fish of the genus *Toxotes*, especially *T. jaculatrix*, which occurs in coastal and estuarine waters of SE Asia and Australia. Up to 18 cm long, archer fish capture flying insects by firing a stream of water droplets through the mouth and are able to shoot down prey over distances of more than 1 m. Family: *Toxotidae*.

archery   A sport in which generally a specified number of arrows are shot at a target over a prescribed distance. The modern bow developed from the medieval longbow, but the skill of shooting arrows from a bow dates back 30 millenniums. **Target archery** consists of shooting at a target of standard size marked with five or ten scoring zones. Different competitions require different permutations of distances and numbers of arrows. **Field archery** consists of shooting at large animal figures with superimposed scoring rings. In **clout shooting** arrows are shot into the air to fall on a target marked on the ground, while in **flight shooting** the purpose is to achieve the maximum distance. Archery is an amateur sport, governed internationally by the Fédération internationale de Tir à l'Arc (founded 1931).

Archilochus   (c. 680-c. 640 BC) Greek poet. Probably the bastard son of an aristocrat of Paros and a slave woman, he was forbidden to marry Neobule by her father Lycambes, who became the target of viciously satirical poems. Archilochus became a mercenary soldier and probably died

Mesopotamia and the Levant *Kingdoms and towns* (c. 2000–700 BC).

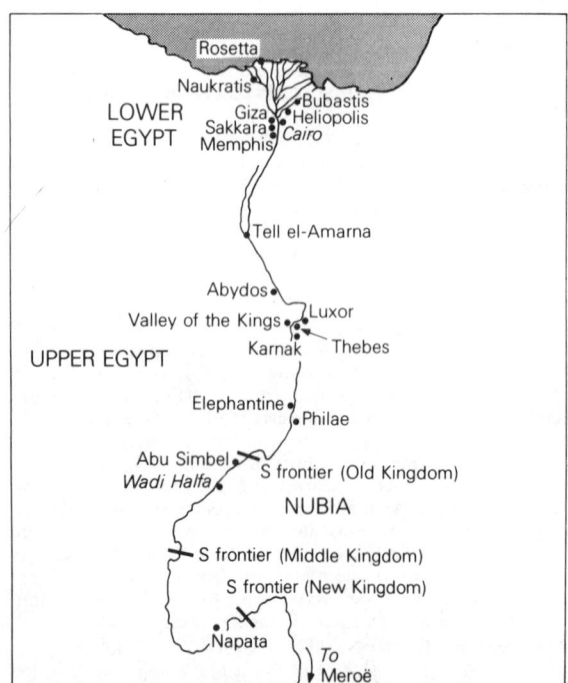

Ancient Egypt *Civilization grew up in the narrow fertile strip along the banks of the Nile* (c.4500

Pre-Columban Mesoamerica *The homelands of the principal ancient Mesoamerican peoples and the sites of their towns* (c.1000 BC–1500 AD).

(a)

A plan of an ancient Greek burial mound showing the relative positions of the original mortuary chamber and other burials in the mound.

Roman well

slab-lined cist

stream bed in the Greek period

mortuary chamber

Roman grave

X

X

modern stream

N

0   1   2   3   4 m

modern ground level   Roman ground level   Roman grave   Greek ground level

(b)

A stratigraphic section (through XX) of the same mound showing the comparative levels of the ground at various periods.

Achaean ground level   slab-lined cist   woman   mortuary chamber   man   stream bed

The discovery and subsequent restoration of an Early Bronze Age jar, which was excavated at Myrtos (Crete) in 1968 (see below).

in battle. His poems, only fragments of which survive, range from the lyrical to the biting, and are frequently colloquial in style.

Archimedes (c. 287–c. 212 BC) Greek mathematician and inventor, regarded as the greatest scientist of classical times. Archimedes was born in Syracuse, Sicily, and studied in Alexandria, afterwards returning to Syracuse, where he remained for the rest of his life. He is best known for his discovery of *Archimedes' principle, supposedly in response to the King of Syracuse asking him to determine whether a gold crown had been adulterated with silver. Legend has it that he made his discovery while taking a bath and ran through the streets of Syracuse shouting "Eureka!" He is also credited with the invention of *Archimedes' screw, although the device was probably already known to the Egyptians. He was killed by a soldier during the Roman invasion of Syracuse.

Archimedes' principle The principle that when a body is partly or wholly immersed in a fluid its apparent loss of weight is equal to the weight of the liquid displaced. Named after *Archimedes.

Archimedes' screw A device for raising water, reputed to have been invented by *Archimedes. It consists of an inclined helical screw rotated about a central axis in a trough of water.

archipelago A group of islands within close proximity to each other. The term was formerly used for the sea in which the islands are scattered, originally being applied to the Aegean Sea.

Archipenko, Alexander (1887–1964) Russian-born sculptor and painter. From 1908 he worked in Paris, where he was associated with *cubism. He introduced the use of the hole as an elemental part of sculpture and created the first works of art combining sculpture and painting. His sculptures of moving figures, which were abstracted into geometrical shapes, declined in quality after his move to New York (1923).

architecture The art of designing and constructing buildings that are both functionally and aesthetically satisfying. Factors principally influencing an architect are: the use to which the building will be put; the materials obtainable; the resources available in money and labour; and contemporary artistic taste. The earliest civilizations built on a monumental scale for their gods or the deified dead (*see* pyramids; ziggurat). Secular architecture reflected the needs of local rulers for security, comfort, and—very important—display. The Greeks were the first to develop the concepts of proportion and harmony that still influence western architectural theory. Roman engineers greatly extended flexibility of design by their use of arches and domes. Medieval European architecture reached its zenith in the gothic *cathedral but the Renaissance brought a resurgence of interest in all types of building; the rediscovered principles of classical architecture dominated theory and practice until the *gothic revival at the beginning of the 19th century. In the 20th century technical advances in the use of prestressed concrete opened the way to modern architecture; while the necessities of engineering increasingly determine a building's appearance, the best modern architects demonstrate that architecture can still survive as an art form.

archons The supreme magistrates in most ancient Greek city states. At Athens there were nine archons, including an eponymous archon, who was the chief archon and gave his name to the year, a king-archon (responsible for religion), and a polemarch (responsible for military affairs). In origin the Athenian archons were a ruling aristocracy, which had replaced the earlier monarchy. After 487 BC they were chosen by lot and their authority declined, their role becoming chiefly judicial.

Archytas (early 4th century BC) Greek mathematician,

from Tarentum (S Italy). Famous in antiquity as an innovator in many fields of mathematics, he distinguished between geometrical, arithmetical, and harmonic progressions, worked out the numerical relations between notes of different musical scales, and found a geometrical construction to double the cube.

Arcimboldo, Giuseppe (1527–93) Mannerist painter, born in Milan. He moved to Prague in 1562, becoming painter and designer of court pageants to successive Habsburg emperors. Contemporaries praised his ingenious symbolism and he is remembered for his grotesque portraits, such as the head of a cook composed of pots and pans, fish and meat.

Arctic Circle The area around the North Pole enclosed by the parallel of latitude 66°32′N. It includes parts of Greenland, the Soviet Union, the USA, Canada, and Scandinavia and extensive areas of ice-covered ocean, notably the Arctic Ocean. Within the Arctic Circle the sun remains below the level of the horizon for a period of time in winter and remains above it in summer; the length of time for which this occurs increases polewards. The population consists mainly of Eskimos, who live by hunting. *History*: during the 16th century exploration of the Arctic by the Dutch and English began in the search for a Northeast or Northwest Passage to the Far East. In 1725–42 the Russian Imperial Navy carried out exploration following the ideas of Peter the Great and Russia became the most active of the Arctic explorers. In 1879 a US expedition under G. W. De Long (1844–81) became trapped in the ice while attempting to reach the North Pole and its ship was crushed. Wreckage found off the coast of Greenland having drifted across the Arctic Ocean suggested that a sea route through the ice was possible. The Norwegian Fridtjof *Nansen in the *Fram* drifted for nearly two years (1893–95) through the ice and proved that the North Pole was within an ice-covered sea. Robert E. *Peary was the first to reach the North Pole (1909). Since then extensive exploration has been carried out with mapping and geological and meteorological studies; the Soviet Union has been particularly active and, like the USA, has established several drifting scientific stations.

Arctic fox A small fox, *Alopex lagopus*, found throughout tundra regions. It feeds on birds and small mammals, especially lemmings and Arctic hares, and grows a dense woolly coat of fur in winter. There are two colour varieties: the white fox, which has a white winter coat and a brown summer coat; and the blue fox, which is dark grey in summer and pale grey in winter. Arctic foxes have been farmed commercially for their fur.

Arctic Ocean The world's smallest ocean, almost completely enclosed by North America, Eurasia, and Greenland. Explored since the 17th century, it is covered by ice.

Arctic tern A slender red-billed *tern, *Sterna paradisaea*, up to 38 cm long and having a white plumage with grey wings and a black crown. It breeds in coastal regions from N Britain to the Arctic and migrates to Antarctic seas in winter.

Arcturus A conspicuous *red giant in the constellation Boötes that is the brightest star in the N sky. It has an apparent magnitude of –0.05 and is 36 light years distant. The three stars in the handle of the *Plough curve in its direction.

Ardashir I Shah of Persia (224–41 AD), who founded the Sasanian dynasty. In 224 Ardashir defeated and killed the last Parthian ruler at the battle of Hormizdagan. He made *Zoroastrianism the state religion and is honoured in Zoroastrian tradition.

Ardebil 38 15N 48 18E A town in NW Iran, close to the border with the Soviet Union and to the Caspian Sea. It has a carpet- and rug-making industry. Population (1985 est): 258 100.

Arden, Forest of An area in the Midlands of England, in Warwickshire. Formerly part of an extensive forest, it is the setting for Shakespeare's *As You Like It*.

the orders of classical architecture

Doric Tuscan Ionic Corinthian Composite

some terms in classical architecture

some terms in gothic architecture

Sagrada Familia (1903-26; Barcelona) *By Antonio Gaudi y Cornet.*

The Seagram Building (1956-58; New York) *By Mies van der Rohe and Philip Johnson (1906-).*

Guggenheim Museum (1956-59; New York) *By Frank Lloyd Wright.*

Chapel Notre-Dame-du-Haut (1950-55; Ronchamp) *By Le Corbusier.*

Georges Pompidou Centre (1972-77; Paris) *By Richard Rogers (1933-) and Renzo Piano (1937-).*

Sydney Opera House (1957-73) *By Jøern Utzon (1918-).*

ARCHITECTURE *The early 20th century, just before World War I, saw the birth of the modern movement in architecture. The use of steel and the introduction of reinforced concrete (first used in France), together with the extensive use of glass, enabled new architectural concepts, such as the skyscraper, to be developed. Modern architecture has been characterized by a functional approach and a greater freedom in design.*

Ardennes A chain of hills in W Europe. It extends through N Luxembourg, S Belgium, and NE France at an average height of about 500 m (1640 ft), forming the watershed between the Rivers Meuse and Moselle. Chiefly wooded, agriculture is limited to pastoralism. There was heavy fighting here in both World Wars.

Arduin (or Ardoin; d. 1015) Marquess of Ivrea, who seized the Italian throne (1002). Forced by Emperor Henry II to withdraw (1004), Arduin continued to harass Henry's authority in N Italy until defeated in 1014. He retired to a monastery.

are (a) A unit of area in the *metric system equal to 100 square metres. The *hectare is more frequently used than the are.

Areca. See betel.

Areopagus A hill NW of the Acropolis and the name of the ancient Athenian court that met there. Originally an aristocratic council, the Areopagus became primarily a homicide court after about 462 BC, when its political authority was transferred to the democratic assembly.

Arequipa 16 25S 71 32W A city in S Peru. Originally an Inca city, it was refounded by the Spanish (1540). Notable buildings include the cathedral (1612) and two universities. It is an important commercial centre and the wool-processing centre of Peru. Population (1980 est): 455 200.

Ares The Greek god of war, identified by the Romans with *Mars. Son of Zeus and Hera, his popularity never rivalled that of the other Olympian gods. He loved *Aphrodite, by whom he had three offspring, Deimos, Phobos, and Harmonia.

Aretino, Pietro (1492–1556) Italian satirist. Son of a shoemaker, he claimed to be the bastard son of a nobleman. He lived in Rome (1517–27), patronized by Pope Leo X and becoming famous for his vicious satires and bawdy lyrics. He then settled in Venice, where he made a fortune by writing scurrilous satires on people or by being bribed not to do so. His letters, published in six volumes (1537–57), provide a vivid portrait both of Aretino and of his times. The earthy *Ragionamenti* (1534–36) portrayed the underworld of prostitutes. He also wrote five comedies.

Arezzo 43 28N 11 53E A city in central Italy, in Tuscany. Originally an Etruscan settlement, it has many fine medieval buildings. Petrarch was born here. A market town, it has various industries. Population (1981): 91 535.

argali A race of mountain-dwelling sheep, *Ovis ammon ammon*, of central Asia. Argalis are the largest Eurasian wild sheep, reaching a weight of 170 kg and having massive deeply ridged curved horns. They live in herds and graze at very high altitudes during the summer.

Argenteuil 48 52N 2 20E A town in France, a NW suburb of Paris on the River Seine. An industrial centre, it developed around the 7th-century convent of which Héloïse was abbess. Population (1982 est): 96,045.

Argentina, Republic of The second largest country in South America, occupying almost all the land S of the Tropic of Capricorn and E of the Andes. It includes the E part of the island of Tierra del Fuego and has claims to the *Falkland Islands and their dependencies in the Antarctic. It consists chiefly of subtropical plains and forests (the Gran Chaco) in the N, the fertile temperate pampas in the centre, the Andes in the W, and the semidesert Patagonian plateau in the S. The inhabitants are almost entirely European in origin, mainly Italian and Spanish, with a very small and dwindling Indian population. *Economy*: chiefly agricultural with stock rearing, especially cattle, having overwhelming importance. The main industries have traditionally been meat processing and packing but there has been recent growth in a variety of areas, including oil refining, plastics, textiles, and chemicals. Natural-gas deposits have been intensively explored and developed and Argentina is practically self-sufficient in oil, the most notable oilfields being

around Comodoro Rivadavia. Nuclear energy is also being developed. Main exports include meat and meat products (badly affected by the EEC ban on meat imports in 1974), wool, cereals, minerals, and metals. *History*: colonized by the Spanish from 1515 onwards. During this period the native Indian inhabitants, who had previously had to defend themselves against the Incas, put up a fierce resistance but, by the 19th century they had almost been wiped out. The country gained its independence in 1816, under José de San Martin, and a new constitution in 1853 marked the end of a period of civil war and unrest. Since the late 19th century Argentina has been ruled for most of the time by a series of military dictatorships. Most prominent among the rulers since World War II has been Lt Gen Juán *Perón, who came to power in 1946. Following the death (1952) of his very popular wife, Eva, his power was weakened and in 1955 he was overthrown in a military revolution. The Perónist movement, however, continued to attract strong popular support and in 1973, following the election of one of his supporters, Dr Hector Campóra, he returned to power but died the following year. He was succeeded by his second wife, Isabel, but as the economic situation continued to deteriorate and political violence and industrial unrest increased, many allegations of corruption were made against her government. In 1976 Lt Gen Jorge Rafael Videla (1925–) came to power at the head of a three-man junta and strong measures were introduced to combat the violence and unrest and to steady the economy. Lt Gen Roberta Viola succeeded Videla as president in 1981 but was later removed from office by the military junta, led by Gen Leopoldo Galtieri, who subsequently became president in December, 1981. On 2 April, 1982, Argentina launched an invasion of the Falkland Islands (which it calls the Islas Malvinas) but following armed conflict with a task force sent by the UK was forced to surrender on 14 June, 1982; a defeat that forced Galtieri's resignation. Gen Reynaldo Bignone replaced him until Raúl Alfonsín (1926–) was elected president in October, 1983, ending seven years of military rule. Official language: Spanish. Official religion: Roman Catholic. Official currency: Argentine peso of 100 centavos. Area: 2 777 815 sq km (1 072 515 sq mi). Population (1980 est): 27 862 771. Capital and main port: Buenos Aires.

argentite An important ore of silver, sometimes called silver glance. It is a sulphide of silver, found in association with other sulphide ores, such as lead, zinc, and copper.

argon (Ar) A noble gas that occurs in the atmosphere (0.94%). Although previously observed in the solar spectrum, it was first isolated in 1894 by Rayleigh and Ramsay, by the distillation of liquid air. Because it is chemically inert, it is used to fill fluorescent lamps and as an inert gas blanket for welding reactive metals. At no 18; at wt 39.948; mp −189.2°C; bp −185.7°C.

Argonauts In Greek mythology, the 50-man crew of *Jason's ship *Argo*, on the quest of the *Golden Fleece. Accounts of its composition vary, but all agree that it included the shipbuilder Argo, the tireless helmsman Tiphys, the keen-sighted Lynceus, *Heracles and his follower Hylas, and even *Orpheus and the Dioscuri, *Castor and Pollux. During the voyage the Argonauts encountered such perils as the *Sirens, the *Harpies, the Symplegades (moving rocks that crushed ships) and the bronze giant Talos.

Argonne A hilly forested area in NE France. It was the scene of heavy fighting during both World Wars.

Argos 37 38N 22 43E A town in the NE Peloponnese (S Greece). Belonging in Homeric times to a follower of *Agamemnon, Argos gave its name to the surrounding district (the Argolid). Eclipsed by nearby Sparta after the 6th century BC, Argos remained neutral or the ineffective ally of Athens during the 5th-century struggles between Sparta and Athens. Considerable remains of the city survive.

Argyll (or Argyllshire) A former county of W Scotland.

Under local government reorganization in 1975 it became part of Argyll and Bute District, in Strathclyde Region.

Argyll, Archibald Campbell, 1st Marquess of (1607–61) Scottish statesman. He became a member of Charles I's privy council in 1626 but relinquished his post after becoming a *Covenanter in support of Presbyterianism. In the English Civil War he defeated the royalist *Montrose (1645) and became ruler of Scotland until the Scots' defeat by Cromwell in 1651. He was executed after the Restoration of Charles II.

Århus (or Aarhus) 56 10N 10 13E A seaport in Denmark, in E Jutland. One of the oldest cities in Denmark, it has a gothic cathedral and a university (1928). Its industries include oil refining, machinery, and textiles. Population (1981 est): 245 565.

aria (Italian: air) A solo song with instrumental accompaniment, usually in an opera or oratorio. The name was originally also used of separate instrumental pieces but its meaning became restricted with the development of the three part *aria da capo* in the works of Monteverdi, Scarlatti, and Handel. Attacked as undramatic by reformers, such as Gluck and Wagner, the aria form is little used in modern opera.

Ariadne In Greek legend, the daughter of *Minos, King of Crete, and Pasiphaë. She helped *Theseus to kill the Minotaur and escape from its labyrinth. He abandoned her on the island of Naxos, where she was found by *Dionysus, who married her.

Ariane. See European Space Agency.

Arianism A Christian heresy started by *Arius, which held that the Son of God, Jesus Christ, was not truly divine. In 325 AD the Council of Nicaea banished the Arians, who included some influential bishops, and affirmed that the Father and the Son were coequal, coeternal, and "of one substance." Although the Arians were soon restored and a version of the heresy was officially accepted for a time, Arianism was finally defeated at the Council of Constantinople in 381 AD.

Arica 18 30S 70 20W An oasis town and port in N Chile, on the Pacific Ocean. A railway line connects it with La Paz in Bolivia and it handles about half Bolivia's trade. Population (1983 est): 123 211.

Ariel A computerized system used by institutional investors (e.g. pension funds) in the UK to buy and sell equity shares by negotiating directly with each other through a television network. The *acceptance houses set it up in 1974 to enable subscribers to save on *stock-exchange commission. It is based on *Instinct*, a similar system used in the USA.

Aries (Latin: Ram) A constellation in the N sky, lying on the *zodiac between Taurus and Pisces. The brightest star, Hamal, is of 2nd magnitude.

Arikara An Indian people of North America who lived along the Missouri River in what are now North and South Dakota. They were related to the *Pawnee in their language, which belongs to the Caddoan group, and in culture, which was of Plains Indian type. They were expert corn growers and their farming villages were often trade centres visited by the nomadic hunting tribes. They practised the sun-dance cult involving self-torture. There are today approximately 700 living on the Fort Berthold Reservation.

Ariosto, Ludovico (1474–1533) Italian poet. He spent most of his life in the active service of the Este, the ducal family of Ferrara. He wrote several plays and much lyric verse but is best known for his long epic poem, *Orlando furioso* (1516). One of the greatest works of the Italian Renaissance, it recounts the adventures of the paladin Roland (see Charlemagne) and the wars between the Franks and Saracens. It was published in its final revised form in 1532. Its precursor was the *Orlando innamorato* (1483) of *Boiardo.

Aristaeus In Greek legend, the son of *Apollo and the nymph Cyrene. He was the patron of bee keepers, and was credited with the introduction of the vine and the olive. According to Virgil, he caused the death of *Eurydice.

Aristagoras (5th century BC) Tyrant of *Miletus (Asia Minor). Aristagoras persuaded the Greek cities of *Ionia to rebel against Persian rule (499) but despite Athenian assistance the rebellion failed (494). He died fighting in Thrace.

Aristarchus of Samos (c. 310–230 BC) Greek astronomer, who maintained that the earth rotates upon its axis and orbits the sun. He made the first attempts to estimate trigonometrically the size and distance from the earth of the sun and the moon.

Aristarchus of Samothrace (c. 217–145 BC) Greek critic and grammarian. He was head of the great Library of Alexandria from about 180 to 145, and later retired to Cyprus. He edited important editions of *Homer and wrote commentaries on *Aeschylus, *Sophocles, *Herodotus, and many other writers.

Aristides the Just (c. 520–c. 468 BC) Athenian statesman and noted commander in the *Greek-Persian Wars. Ostracized (c. 485) because of his opposition to Themistocles' naval policy, Aristides returned in 480 and offered his services against the Persians, commanding land forces at Salamis. In 477 he was chosen to assess the tribute required from each member of the *Delian League.

Aristippus (c. 435–c. 356 BC) Greek philosopher and a pupil of *Socrates. Aristippus founded the Cyrenaic school of *hedonism and was exclusively concerned with practical morality (see Cyrenaics). He equated the highest good with pleasure, virtue he equated with the rationally controlled pursuit of enjoyment.

Aristophanes (c. 450–c. 385 BC) Greek comic dramatist. He wrote about 40 plays, of which 11 survive: *The Acharnians* (425), *The Knights* (424), *The Clouds* (423), *The Wasps* (422), *The Peace* (421), *The Birds* (414), *Lysistrata* (411), *Thesmophoriazusae* (410), *The Frogs* (405), *Women in Parliament* (393), and *Plutus* (388). His plots were satirical fantasies on contemporary topics, such as literature, *Socrates, social manners, and militaristic Athenian foreign policy; this led to his unsuccessful prosecution by the politician *Cleon.

Aristotelianism Tendencies in philosophical thought that originated with *Aristotle. Interpretations of his work appeared until the eclipse of ancient philosophy in the 6th century AD. Texts were preserved by Arab scholars, their work culminating in the 12th-century commentaries of *Averroes. *Aquinas in the 13th century made Aristotle the metaphysical basis of Christian theology but the Latin Averroists produced their own conflicting theories, holding, for instance, that a proposition can be philosophically true although theologically false. In the Renaissance the term Aristotelianism became synonymous with obscurantist opposition to new learning and science.

Aristotle (384–322 BC) Greek philosopher and scientist. His father was court physician in Macedonia. Aristotle joined *Plato's Academy at Athens (367–347) but, failing to become head of the Academy at Plato's death, he accepted the protection of Hermeias, ruler of Atarneus in Asia Minor, and married his patron's niece. About 343 *Philip of Macedon appointed Aristotle tutor to his son *Alexander, then aged 13. After Alexander's accession in 336, Aristotle founded, with generous assistance from Alexander, a research community complete with library and museum at Athens (the *Lyceum). There *Theophrastus studied botany and Aristoxenus (born c. 370) music, and Aristotle, among other projects, organized a comparative study of 158 constitutions of Greek states. When Alexander died in 323 BC, anti-Macedonian reaction at Athens forced Aristotle to withdraw to *Chalcis, where he died. Aristotle wrote over 400 books on every branch of learning, including logic, ethics, politics, metaphysics, biology, physics, psychology, poetry, and rhetoric. Ironically, those that survive (about one-quarter), edited by Andronicus of Rhodes about 40 BC, are apparently memoranda for his students' use, not intended for general publication. *See also* Aristotelianism.

arithmetic The branch of mathematics that deals with elementary theories of numbers, measurement, and computation. The fundamental operations of arithmetic are addition, subtraction, multiplication, and division. Addition and multiplication are assumed to obey the *associative law, the *commutative law, and the *distributive law. Other operations in arithmetic include extracting roots, raising a number to a power, and taking *logarithms. Arithmetic is also concerned with fractions and the various number systems, such as the *decimal system and the *binary system.

arithmetic progression (*or* arithmetic sequence) A sequence of numbers in which successive terms have a constant difference, for example, 1, 4, 7, 10, 13....

Arius (c. 250–336) Libyan theologian, who initiated the heresy *Arianism. He was a priest at Alexandria until excommunicated for his views in 321. However, by enlisting the support of such prominent churchmen as *Eusebius, Arius developed his cause into a major controversy. At the first Council of *Nicaea (325) he was condemned through the influence of *Athanasius. Recalled from exile (c. 334), he died a few days before he was to be received back into the Church.

Arizona A state in the SW USA. It falls into two natural regions: in the NE lies part of the Colorado Plateau, an area of dry plains and escarpments, and in the S and W is an area of desert basins and gentle valleys, drained by the Gila and Salt Rivers. The Colorado River flows through the Grand Canyon in the NW of the state. In such an arid region inadequate water supplies have long been a problem and a number of major irrigation projects have been built since the beginning of 20th century. Most of the population lives in urban settlements in the S and W. Manufacturing (electrical, communications, aeronautical, and aluminium products) is the major industry. The state produces over half of the USA's copper as well as gold, silver, oil, and timber. Tourism is an important source of revenue. The main crops are cotton, vegetables, and citrus fruits; livestock is also important. It is traditionally a centre for Indian folk arts and crafts, having the largest Indian population in the USA; the main tribes are the Navajo, Hopi, and Apache. *History*: inhabited by Indians as early as 25 000 BC, the area was explored by the Spanish in the 16th century. Following the Mexican War, Arizona, then part of New Mexico, was ceded to the USA (1848). It was swept by Apache wars until 1877 and became a state in 1912. Area: 295 023 sq km (113 909 sq mi). Population (1980): 2 717 866. Capital: Phoenix.

Arkansas A state in the S central USA, lying W of the Mississippi River. It consists chiefly of the largely forested uplands of the N and W, descending to the Mississippi alluvial plain in the E and the West Gulf coastal plain in the S. The Arkansas River bisects the state from W to E. The state is no longer primarily agricultural although the Mississippi Plain provides rich fertile agricultural land; soya beans and rice have replaced cotton as the major crop. Oil production began in 1921; there are major lumbering, petroleum, and gas developments around Smackover and El Dorado and coal deposits in the Arkansas River Valley. The state produces 90% of US bauxite from an area to the S and SW of Little Rock. Manufactures include electronic equipment and wood products. Arkansas remains, however, one of the poorest US states. *History*: explored by the Spanish and French in the 16th and 17th centuries, it formed part of the *Louisiana Purchase by the USA in 1803. It became a state in 1836, seceded from the Union in 1861, and was readmitted in 1868. Area: 137 539 sq km (53 104 sq mi). Population (1980 est): 2 286 435. Capital: Little Rock.

Arkansas River A river in the S central USA, rising in central Colorado and flowing E and SE to join the Mississippi in Arkansas. Length: 2335 km (1450 mi).

Arkhangelsk. See Archangel.

Ark of the Covenant In the Old Testament, the sacred chest of the Israelites that contained the tablets of the law (*see* Ten Commandments) and was symbolic of God's presence and the *covenant made between God and Israel. Made of acacia wood, inlaid, and covered with gold, it was eventually placed in the Temple of Jerusalem. It probably disappeared during the *Babylonian exile. The shrine in a synagogue where the encased scrolls of the *Torah are kept is also called an ark or "holy ark" (*aron kodesh*).

ark shell A *bivalve mollusc belonging to a chiefly tropical family (*Arcidae*). Ark shells are boat-shaped and are attached to rocks by means of strong threads. The Noah's ark shell (*Arca tetragona*) occurs in rock crevices along the S coast of Britain and is about 4.5 cm long.

Arkwright, Sir Richard (1732–92) British inventor and industrialist, who invented a spinning frame powered by water, the so-called water frame (patented in 1769). Arkwright subsequently mechanized other spinning processes and his mills were vandalized by spinners put out of work by the incipient factory system.

Arlberg Pass A mountain pass in W Austria, in the Alps, linking Vorarlberg with the Tirol by road. A railway tunnel (completed 1884) cuts through the mountain for a distance of over 10 km (6 mi). Height: 1802 m (5910 ft).

Arles 43 41N 4 38E A town in SE France, in the Bouches-du-Rhône department on the Rhône delta. An important Roman settlement, it became the capital of Gaul in the 4th century AD and the capital of the kingdom of Arles (formed from the kingdoms of Burgundy and Provence) in the 10th century. It has many Roman remains, including an amphitheatre. Other notable buildings include the 11th-century cathedral and the museum of arts and crafts founded by the poet Mistral. Several painters have lived and worked here, including Van Gogh and Gauguin. An agricultural market, it manufactures chemicals, machinery, and food products. Population (1982 est): 50 772.

Arlington, Henry Bennet, 1st Earl of (1618–85) English statesman, who was a leading member of the faction called the *Cabal. As secretary of state (1662–74) he negotiated (1668) the Triple Alliance of England, the Netherlands, and Sweden against France but was involved in Charles II's secret Treaty of Dover (1670) with the French king, Louis XIV. In 1674 Arlington was impeached for embezzlement and, although cleared, resigned and became Lord Chamberlain.

Arlington National Cemetery The largest cemetery in the USA, comprising 170 hectares (420 acres). Since 1864 it has been the burial ground of Americans killed in action and of eminent public servants.

arm In human anatomy, the upper limb, which extends from the shoulder to the wrist. The bone of the upper arm (the humerus) is connected by a ball-and-socket joint to the shoulder bone, permitting a wide range of movements. It forms a hinge joint at the elbow with the bones of the forearm (the ulna and radius), permitting movement in one plane only. The radius can be twisted across the ulna, enabling the palm of the hand to be turned upwards. *See* Plate IV.

Armada, Spanish The fleet of 130 ships sent by Philip II of Spain in 1588 to invade England. After indecisive encounters with the English fleet led by Howard of Effingham, under whom Sir John Hawkins held command, the Armada anchored off Calais only to be dispersed by English fireships during the night of 28 July. A major engagement off Gravelines followed, in which the Armada was defeated. It suffered further losses in storms as it escaped round Scotland and Ireland, arriving in Spain with 86 ships. The defeat was

armadillo

a major psychological blow to Spain, which had claimed divine authority for its crusade against Protestant England. *See also* Drake, Sir Francis.

armadillo A mammal belonging to the family *Dasypodidae* (12 species), widespread in open country in the southern USA and South America. Armadillos have a covering of jointed bands or horny plates that enables them to roll themselves into a ball for protection. They have long-clawed toes for burrowing, simple peglike teeth, and feed on insects and other invertebrates. Armadillos range in size from the giant armadillo (*Priodontes giganteus*), about 120 cm long, to the rare pink fairy armadillo (*Chlamyphorus truncatus*), 12 cm long. Order: *Edentata*.

Armageddon. *See* Megiddo.

Armagh A former inland county in S Northern Ireland, bordering on the Republic of Ireland. It consists of lowlands with extensive bogs in the N, adjoining Lough Neagh, and low hills in the S. Armagh is predominantly agricultural; produce includes potatoes, flax, and apples. There are few industries. Area: 1326 sq km (512 sq mi). County town: Armagh.

Armenian Church The Church founded by St Gregory the Illuminator (c. 240–332) about 300 AD. Armenia was the first nation to adopt Christianity as a state religion. Its Church is the second largest of the Eastern Christian Churches and has much in common with the others, although it has also absorbed some Western influences. The head of the Church is the Patriarch of Etchmiadzin, called the Catholicos. There are Armenian churches in several parts of the world, including London and Manchester.

Armenians A people of NE Turkey and SW Russia speaking an Indo-European language. Approximately 1.5 million live in Turkey, Europe, and America and 4 million in the Armenian Soviet Socialist Republic, with smaller numbers in the Georgian and Azerbaidzhan SSRs. Their culture is ancient and highly developed, with a literature written in an alphabet derived from Greek and Syriac script. Their language is the only representative of a distinct branch of the Indo-European family. Herodotus claimed they were related to the ancient Phrygians. They call themselves Hay and their land Hayastan. They are mainly Monophysite Christians and belong to the *Armenian Church. During the 19th and 20th centuries they suffered massacres by the Ottoman Turks, their rulers since the 16th century, who feared growing nationalism among them.

Armenian Soviet Socialist Republic A constituent republic in the S Soviet Union. It is a densely populated and mountainous region, with no navigable rivers. Industry is developing rapidly and includes food processing, metallurgy, and chemicals. The rich mineral deposits include copper, lead, and zinc. The raising of livestock is the chief agricultural activity. *History*: the region formed the E part of the historic area inhabited by the *Armenians. It was acquired by Russia in 1828. The Russian province declared its independence in 1918 but it subsequently formed part of the Transcaucasian Soviet Federated Republic (*see* Transcaucasia). It became a separate republic in 1936. Area: 29 800 sq km (11 490 sq mi). Population (1983): 3 219 000. Capital: Yerevan.

Armentières 50 41N 2 53E A town in N France, in the Nord department on the River Lys. Its complete destruction in World War I was commemorated in the song "Mademoiselle from Armentières." Its manufactures include linen and hosiery. Population (1982 est): 25 992.

Armero 4 59N 74 55W A town in Colombia, completely destroyed during the eruption of the Nevado del Ruiz volcano in November 1985. An estimated 25 000 people died; it was decided that the town would never be rebuilt.

Armidale 30 42S 151 40E A town in Australia, in NE New South Wales. Often regarded as *New England's "capital," it is a tourist resort. It is the site of the University of New England (1954). Population (1980 est): 21 400.

Arminius (c. 18 BC–17 AD) Leader of the Germanic tribe of the Cherusci, famous as a master of the surprise attack. He organized a revolt against the Romans (9 AD), destroying three Roman legions. Defeated (16 AD) by Germanicus, Arminius nevertheless thwarted the Roman conquest of Germany. He was killed by a pro-Roman German tribesman.

Arminius, Jacobus (1560-1609) Dutch Protestant theologian and reformer. A pupil of *Beza, he was a professor of theology at Leiden. Current Calvinist theology taught that God preordained some men to salvation and others to destruction. Arminius, however, emphasized God's grace and man's freedom to accept or reject salvation. This controversial doctrine later came to be known as Arminianism.

Armory show The first exhibition of European avantgarde art organized in the USA. It was held by a group of New York artists in the 69th regiment armory in New York in 1913. *Picasso, *Braque, *Matisse, and the entire cubist school were given great prominence.

ARMOUR *The skill of the European armourer reached its height in the late 15th and early 16th centuries, when suits of plate armour were made to cover the entire body.*

armour Defensive equipment used as a protection in warfare. Body armour (helmet, breastplate, greaves) was used in Bronze Age Greece. The Romans evolved heavier armour for both men and horses. In the early Middle Ages *chainmail was widely used but after about 1300 plate armour, often sumptuously decorated and encasing the whole body, was worn by knights on horseback. Gunpowder gradually rendered body armour obsolete, although in World War I metal helmets were revived as a protection from shrapnel.

Armour is also used to protect modern war vehicles and their occupants against projectiles or fragments. Armour plate includes hardened metal alloys cast in varying thicknesses and designed to be mounted with sloping surfaces to give protection against armour-piercing projectiles. Its considerable weight has prompted experiments in light alloys and plastics, using multiple skins to inhibit projectile penetration. Most recent is the "Chobham" armour, produced by the Military Vehicle and Engineering Establishment at Chobham, Surrey.

armoured car A wheeled armoured patrol vehicle, first used in combat in Libya (1912). Early types included converted lorries with poor protection, armament, and cross-country performance. They now have independent suspension, all-wheel drive, better armour, carry machine guns or a light gun, and may be amphibious.

arms control. *See* disarmament.

Armstrong, Edwin Howard (1890–1954) US electrical engineer, who in 1939 introduced frequency *modulation as a method of broadcasting radio signals to reduce the static associated with amplitude modulation. He had earlier invented the *superheterodyne receiver, which improved radio reception and greatly increased the popularity of radio sets. A contentious and litigious man, he committed suicide.

LOUIS ARMSTRONG

Armstrong, Louis (1900–71) US Black jazz trumpeter and singer, known as "Satchmo." Born in New Orleans, he learned to play the cornet in his youth. His career took him to Chicago, where he made many recordings (some of them with Earl Hines), which earned him a worldwide reputation. He played with several large orchestras as a soloist and toured Europe in 1932. His gravelly singing voice and superb trumpet playing were featured in many films.

Armstrong, Neil Alden (1930–) US astronaut, the first man to walk on the moon. A navy pilot during the Korean War, he worked for the National Aeronautics and Space Administration (NASA) (1955–71) and became an astronaut in 1962. He flew Gemini 7 (1966) and was commander of Apollo 11 (1969). As he stepped onto the moon he said "That's one small step for a man, one giant leap for mankind."

Armstrong, William George, Baron (1810–1900) British engineer and industrialist, who pioneered the design and construction of hydraulic machinery. His hydroelectric generator utilized high-pressure steam issuing through nozzles from a boiler. He also invented a breech-loading gun, a landmark in the development of artillery.

army An organized force of soldiers, which may be composed of full-time professionals, *militia reserves, conscripts, or mercenaries or of a combination of these. Armies exist for combat and to enhance a nation's prestige; they may also exert domestic political power and provide manpower for such activities as roadbuilding and land development.

Armies were raised throughout the ancient world, where merce-

naries were usually relied upon to supplement a militia (as in the Greek city states) or a standing army (as in Rome). The medieval armies of Europe depended upon the mounted feudal knight, who was obliged to undertake short-term military service for his lord. As campaigns became longer, mercenaries were increasingly relied upon and with the introduction of firearms in the 15th century the foot soldier became important. Early modern standing armies reached their zenith with those of the 17th- and 18th-century absolute monarchs, especially Louis XIV of France and Frederick the Great of Prussia. By comparison the standing army maintained since 1661 in England was small, Cromwell's *New Model Army having left a lasting distrust of militarism. The 19th century saw a growing emphasis on the mass armies that resulted from *conscription—a measure widely adopted in Continental Europe. The British army, which had declined from the brilliance attained under *Wellington, was reorganized between 1871 and 1907, especially by *Cardwell and *Haldane, and a highly trained reserve (see Territorial Army) replaced the volunteer militia. With the adoption of conscription in World War I Britain was able to field 5 585 000 imperial troops by 1918. Its numbers declined between the wars and again after World War II. Postwar trends have included the combination of national armies into allied forces, such as those of NATO and the Warsaw Pact states, and the growing specialization of armies in response to technological advances.

army ant A New World *ant of the genus *Eciton* or related genera that does not build a permanent nest but has alternating nomadic and static phases synchronized to the egg-laying of the wingless queen. The wasplike males are large and winged and the soldier ants have large hooked jaws and hunt in vast "armies," killing other insects and small animals. Subfamily: *Dorylinae*. *See also* driver ant.

army worm The *caterpillar of a widely distributed moth, *Leucania unipunctata*. Army worms periodically swarm in large numbers, eating crops in their path and causing severe damage, especially in North America.

Arnauld, Antoine (1612–94) French theologian, philosopher, and logician; member of a prominent Jansenist family connected with the Abbey of Port-Royal. His attacks on the Jesuits, especially *De la fréquente communion* (1643), forced him into exile in Brussels. He raised important objections to *Descartes' *Meditations* and, with *Pascal and Pierre Nicole (1625–95), wrote the influential *La Logique ou l'art de penser* (1662), known as the *Port-Royal Logic*.

Arne, Thomas Augustine (1710–78) British composer of great popularity in his lifetime. His most famous work is probably the song "Rule Britannia!" from the masque *Alfred* (1740). He wrote at least 30 operas and stage works, including music for Shakespeare's plays and Milton's *Comus*.

Arnhem 52 00N 5 53E A city in the E Netherlands, the capital of Gelderland province. In World War II a large airborne landing of British troops attempted to secure a bridgehead over the River Rhine here to facilitate an Allied invasion of Germany. The attempt failed with heavy casualties in the ensuing battle (17–27 September, 1944). A railway junction, its industries include engineering and pharmaceuticals. Population (1981 est): 128 717.

Arnhem Land A plateau in Australia, in N Northern Territory. It is primarily an Aboriginal reserve. Bauxite deposits are worked at Gove. Area: about 150 000 sq km (60 000 sq mi).

Arno, River A river in central Italy. Rising in the Apennines, it flows mainly W through Florence and Pisa to the Ligurian Sea. It burst its banks in 1966 causing disastrous floods in Florence. Length: 240 km (150 mi).

Arnold, Benedict (1741–1801) American general in the American Revolution. Brilliant but erratic, he served with distinction at Fort Ticonderoga and Quebec (1775), commanded a fleet on Lake Champlain (1776), and fought in Connecticut, the Mohawk Valley, and Saratoga (1777). In 1780 he treacherously planned to surrender the vital West Point position. The plot miscarried and he fled to the British for whom he led raids in Virginia and Connecticut. From 1781 he lived in England.

Arnold, Malcolm (1921–) British composer. He began his career as trumpeter with the London Philharmonic Orchestra. His compositions include eight symphonies, concertos for guitar, harmonica, and trumpet, overtures, and ballet and film music.

Arnold, Thomas (1795–1842) British educator. Appointed headmaster of Rugby (1828), Arnold reformed the school and instituted the form and prefectorial systems, which came to characterize English public schools. Arnold's piety was infectious, and Rugby became noted for "muscular Christianity." *Tom Brown's Schooldays* (*see* Hughes, Thomas) provides a eulogistic record of Arnold's achievement. His son **Matthew Arnold** (1822–88) was a poet and critic. He worked as a government inspector of schools from 1851 to 1886. His critical works include *Essays in Criticism* (1865; 1888) and *Culture and Anarchy* (1869), in which he advocated literary and cultural values as an antidote to the progressive materialism of Victorian society. His moral beliefs and doubts were given more personal expression in his poetry, which included "Dover Beach" (1867) and the narrative poems "The Scholar Gypsy" (1853) and "Sohrab and Rustum" (1853).

Arnold of Brescia (d. 1155) Italian religious reformer. He studied at Paris, perhaps under *Abelard, and became an Augustinian canon after returning to Italy, where he immediately condemned the worldliness prevalent in the Church. He argued, among other things, that the papacy should not have secular power. He was excommunicated in 1148 and was eventually captured by Emperor Frederick Barbarossa, condemned, and hanged at Rome.

aromatic compound A type of cyclic organic chemical compound that includes *benzene and its derivatives. On conventional theories of valence these compounds appear to be unsaturated (i.e. contain double bonds). However, benzene and similar compounds are much less reactive than the *alkenes, tending to undergo substitution reactions rather than addition reactions. The explanation for the stability of the benzene ring lies in a model in which the carbon atoms are joined by single bonds and the extra six valence electrons are free to move around the ring in a delocalized orbital. The phenomenon also occurs in some other compounds having an unsaturated ring, for example ferrocene (Fe-$(C_5H_5)_2$). Aromatic compounds were originally distinguished from *aliphatic compounds because of the distinctive properties of benzene compounds, many of which have a fragrant odour.

Arp, Jean (Hans) (1887–1966) French sculptor and poet. He was one of the founders of the *dada movement (1916) and later associated with the surrealist movement in Paris. Arp experimented with collages of torn coloured papers, designed according to chance, and produced numerous painted wood reliefs. In about 1930 he began his abstract sculptures suggesting organic rather than geometric forms. His wife and occasional collaborator was the artist Sophie Tauber (1889–1943).

Árpád (died c. 907 AD) Magyar chieftain. In 875 Árpád led the Magyars from the Caucasus region into present-day Hungary in search of a new homeland after their defeat by the Pechenegs. He founded the first Hungarian royal dynasty, the Árpád, which ruled Hungary until 1301.

arquebus. *See* musket.

Arrabal, Fernando (1932–) Spanish playwright and novelist, who writes in French and lives in France. His plays, which have some of the characteristics of the *Theatre of the Absurd, deal chiefly with themes of terror and violence; they include *Le Cimitière des voitures* (1958), *Le Grand Cérémonial* (1966), and *And They Put Handcuffs on the Flowers* (1973).

Arran 55 35N 5 15W A Scottish island in the Firth of Clyde, off the Mull of Kintyre. Chiefly mountainous, its picturesque scenery contributes to its popularity as a tourist centre. Area: 427 sq km (165 sq mi). Population (1981): 4726.

Arras 50 17N 2 46E A town in N France, the capital of the Pas-de-Calais department on the River Scarpe. The former capital of Artois, it passed to France in 1640. It had a famous medieval tapestry trade and the tapestry called "arras" is named after it. Robespierre was born here. The 18th-century cathedral and fine 16th-century town hall were badly damaged during World War I. An agricultural market, its industries include agricultural machinery and hosiery. Population (1982 est): 45 364.

*The conventional formula of benzene devised by F. A. Kekulé von Stradonitz (1829–96). With alternating double bonds it would be unsaturated and have properties similar to the *alkenes.*

In the benzene molecule the bonds are actually intermediate between single and double bonds. This is often represented as a resonance hybrid between the two conventional structures.

often represented as

The modern explanation of the bonding involves a delocalized orbital above and below the ring. The six valence electrons (one from each carbon atom) are free to move in this orbital. This explains the properties of benzene and the fact that all C-C bonds are equal.

AROMATIC COMPOUND

Arrau, Claudio (1903–) Chilean pianist. He gave his first recital at the age of five and studied in Berlin under Martin Krause (1853–1918), a pupil of Liszt. He returned to Chile in 1940 to found a piano school. He is famous particularly for his interpretations of Beethoven and Brahms.

arrest The forcible detention of a person to compel obedience to the law. In England, a person may be arrested on a magistrate's warrant to answer to a criminal charge, or for a civil offence, such as contempt of court. He may also be arrested if he commits, or is clearly about to commit, a crime. In theory any citizen can make an arrest and is bound to do so if a felony or breach of the peace is committed in his presence, but in practice most valid arrests are made by the police or other law-enforcement officers, who are empowered to make arrests without warrants.

Arrhenius, Svante August (1859-1927) Swedish physicist and chemist, who became professor of the University of Stockholm in 1895. He won the 1903 Nobel Prize for Chemistry for his theory of electrolytic dissociation. He later worked on the application of physical chemistry to living processes. His theory of universal life-diffusion involved "spores" emitted by habitable worlds and driven by light-pressure across space.

arrhythmia An abnormal rhythm of the heart beat. Sometimes this may produce symptoms, such as palpitation, breathlessness, and chest pain. Arrhythmias may be associated with heart disease but may occur without any obvious cause.

Arrian (Flavius Arrianus; 2nd century AD) Roman historian. As governor of *Cappadocia, he defeated a barbarian invasion (134 AD). He wrote several works on Asian history; his *Anabasis* is our most important source of information about *Alexander the Great.

Arromanches-les-Bains 49 20N 0 38W A village in NW France, in the Calvados department. The main supply centre for the Allied Normandy invasion of 1944, it is the site of one of the two prefabricated Mulberry harbours.

arrow-poison frog A small generally brightly coloured terrestrial frog belonging to a family (*Dendrobatidae*) occurring in Central and South American forests. Poisons produced by skin glands protect the frogs from predators and were used by Indians to poison arrow tips. In many species the young are incubated on the back of the male. Chief genera: *Dendrobates, Phyllobates*.

arrowroot A herbaceous perennial plant, *Maranta arundinacea*, native to Guyana but widely cultivated in the West Indies for the edible and very pure fine starch that is extracted from its underground fleshy tubers and used in cooking. The plant is about 1.5 m high and has short-stalked white flowers and broad-bladed leaves with long narrow sheaths. Several other species yield a similar starch. Family: *Marantaceae*.

Arrowsmith, Aaron (1750-1823) British cartographer, who founded a map-making firm (1790) that produced maps of exceptional quality. The business was carried on by his sons and by his nephew **John Arrowsmith** (1790-1873), who produced the *London Atlas* (1834) and was a founder of the Royal Geographical Society.

Arrow War. *See* Opium Wars.

arrow worm A small planktonic invertebrate animal belonging to a phylum (*Chaetognatha*; 50 species) occurring chiefly in tropical seas. Arrow worms have an elongated arrow-shaped body divided into a head, trunk, and tail, with fins on the sides and tail. They feed on crustaceans, larvae, etc.

ars antiqua (Latin: old art) A style of European music of the 13th century. It was particularly associated with composers of the Parisian school, such as *Pérotin and Léonin (late 12th century), and characterized by the use of complex forms of *organum. It was succeeded by *ars nova.

arsenic (As) A brittle semimetal that occurs in nature in a variety of forms: native, as the sulphides realgar (As_2S_2) and orpiment (As_2S_3), as sulpharsenides, such as arsenopyrite ($FeSAs$), and as arsenates. The element occurs in several forms and was known to the ancients. Pure arsenic has important uses as a dopant in the semiconductor industry. Arsenic and its common compounds are extremely poisonous; tests for its presence need to be accurate and reliable. Compounds include the white oxide (As_2O_3), the gaseous hydride arsine (AsH_3) and arsenates, some of which are used as insecticides. At no 33; at wt 74.9216; mp 817°C (28 atm); sublimes 613°C.

arsine (*or* hydrogen arsenide; AsH_3) A colourless poisonous gas that smells like garlic. It is an unstable compound and decomposes into *arsenic and hydrogen.

Arsinoe II (c. 316-270 BC) The daughter of *Ptolemy I

Soter of Egypt. After two dynastic marriages she became the wife of and coruler with her brother *Ptolemy II Philadelphus (c. 276). Ambitious, forceful, and capable, she was an active participant in war, politics, and administration.

Arsinoe III (c. 235-c. 204 BC) The sister and wife of Ptolemy IV Philopator (reigned 221-203 BC) of Egypt. She participated energetically in the power politics surrounding her lethargic husband. News of her murder, suppressed until Ptolemy's death, caused rioting, which overthrew her former rivals.

ars nova (Latin: new art) A style of European music of the 14th century, which succeeded *ars antiqua. The name was taken from the title of a treatise by Philippe de Vitry (1291-1361), which set out new principles for the composition of *motets and for the notation of complex rhythms. Its greatest French exponents were *Machaut and *Dufay.

arson At common law, maliciously setting fire to something, originally someone else's house or building, but later including other substantial objects, such as bridges and vehicles. As a distinct offence, arson was abolished in English law by the Criminal Damage Act (1971), which is the statute covering all types of criminal damage (the destruction or damage of property belonging to another). Criminal damage committed by fire is still, however, charged as arson.

Artaud, Antonin (1896-1948) French actor, poet, producer, and theoretician of the theatre. In the 1920s he was involved with *surrealism and cofounded, with the poet and playwright Roger Vitrac (1899-1952), the Théâtre Alfred Jarry, where surrealist-inspired plays were produced that were forerunners of the *Theatre of the Absurd. Impressed by the symbolism, gesture, and other nonlinguistic elements of oriental theatre, he developed the theory of a *Theatre of Cruelty in essays later collected in *Le Théâtre et son double* (1938).

Artaxerxes II (c. 436-358 BC) King of Persia (404-358). He defended his position against his brother *Cyrus the Younger, who was defeated and killed at *Cunaxa (401), and against a revolt of the provincial governors, the Satraps (366-358). Persia nevertheless declined under his rule.

Art Deco The style of design predominant in the decorative arts of the 1920s and 1930s. The name derives from the 1925 Exposition Internationale des Arts Décoratifs et Industriels Modernes in Paris. In deliberate contrast to *Art Nouveau, Art Deco was characterized by emphatic geometrical lines and shapes, vibrant colour schemes, and the use of modern man-made substances, such as plastic. Influenced by the *Bauhaus, Art Deco included among its practitioners *Lalique and *Erté. It was debased by shoddy mass production, but interest in it rekindled late in the 1960s. □cinema.

Artemis In Greek mythology, the daughter of Zeus and Leto and twin sister of Apollo. Settled in *Arcadia, she and her band of Oceanids and nymphs spent their time hunting. Love was banned, and Artemis rigorously punished all transgressors. *Actaeon was killed for watching her bathe and *Orion for touching her. Despite this severity, her help was invoked during childbirth, and she was protectress of both animal and human young. Ephesus was the most famous centre of her worship. She was associated with the moon and identified by the Romans with *Diana. *Compare* Hecate.

Artemis, Temple of One of the Seven Wonders of the World, built at *Ephesus in 356 BC. The deity worshipped here was the many-breasted fertility goddess called Diana of the Ephesians in Acts 19.28, rather than the classical *Artemis.

Artemisia (5th century BC) Queen of Halicarnassus. She accompanied Xerxes I on his invasion of Greece, despite her prophecy that the mission would fail, and fought bravely at Salamis (480).

Artemisia (died c. 350 BC) Queen of Caria (c. 353–c. 350), who succeeded her brother and husband Mausolus. Artemisia initiated the construction of his famous tomb, the *Mausoleum. In 350 she subjugated Rhodes.

arteriosclerosis The loss of elasticity in the walls of arteries. It covers various conditions of the arteries and arterioles (small arteries) associated with the ageing process. It is also used as a synonym for *atherosclerosis.

artery A thick-walled blood vessel that carries oxygen-rich blood away from the *heart to supply all the tissues and organs of the body. The largest is the aorta, which leads directly from the heart and descends into the abdomen, giving rise to all the other arteries (*see* Plate IV). In middle age the lining of the arteries commonly becomes thickened by *atherosclerosis, which may lead to various diseases caused by obstruction of blood flow (e.g. strokes, heart attacks). *See also* blood pressure.

artesian well A well sunk into an aquifer (a water-saturated rock stratum) that is confined between two layers of impermeable rock and through which water flows upwards under pressure. The aquifer reaches the surface and receives rainfall where the water table is higher than the site of the well, resulting in a head of pressure.

Artevelde, Jacob van (c. 1290–1345) Flemish statesman. In the 1330s he established the alliance of Flemish towns with those of Brabant, Hainault, and Holland to protect the Low Countries from the economic repercussions of the war between France and England. His dictatorial policies in Ghent, his home town, led to his assassination in 1345.

arthritis Inflammation of one or more joints, causing pain, swelling, and restriction of movement. Many different diseases can cause arthritis, the most important of which are *osteoarthritis, rheumatoid arthritis, and *gout. **Rheumatoid arthritis**, which is more common in women, usually affects the hands and feet and often also the hips, knees, and shoulders. The synovial membrane lining the joint becomes inflamed, resulting in damage to the cartilage over the joint with consequent pain and deformity. An autoimmune disease (*see* autoimmunity), it is diagnosed by a blood test (the blood contains the rheumatoid factor) and X-rays. Treatment is usually based on analgesic and anti-inflammatory drugs; some patients benefit from gold salts and steroids, while severe cases may require surgical replacement of the affected joint(s).

arthropod An invertebrate animal belonging to the largest and most diverse phylum (*Arthropoda*) of the animal kingdom, containing about a million species (i.e. 75% of all known species). There are about 12 classes, the most important of which are the *arachnids, *crustaceans, *insects, *centipedes, and *millipedes. An arthropod has a segmented body with a hard outer skeleton (cuticle) made of *chitin, which is shed periodically to allow the body to grow. Jointed appendages are modified for swimming, walking, feeding, respiration, reproduction, etc. Young arthropods often go through *metamorphosis to reach the adult form. Arthropods are found in fresh and salt water, air, and land and have exploited every food source. Many are harmful—as pests, parasites, or vectors of disease—but others are beneficial to man, as pollinators, food sources, predators of pests, and decomposers of organic wastes.

Arthur, Chester A(lan) (1830–86) US statesman; Republican president (1881–84). Arthur came to power through the New York City Republican patronage system. As president he ran a surprisingly honest administration, which tried to reform the spoils system of appointments based on party service.

Arthur I (1187–1203) Duke of Brittany, who claimed the English throne after the death (1199) of his uncle Richard I. Captured by Richard's successor John, Arthur was murdered, perhaps at John's command.

Arthurian legend The body of medieval *romances concern-ing the legendary British king Arthur and his knights. Arthur first emerges as a figure of romance in the *Historia Regum Britanniae* of *Geoffrey of Monmouth, although a 6th-century military leader of the Welsh may have been a historical model. In the legend, he is the son of Uther Pendragon, was born at Tintagel in Cornwall, became king of Britain at 15, and won a number of famous victories. He married Guinevere and held court at Caerleon in Wales (or, in some versions, at □Camelot, which may have been near South Cadbury, Somerset). Involved in a war at Rome, he left his kingdom in the charge of his nephew Modred, who betrayed him and abducted Guinevere. Arthur returned to Britain and defeated Modred but was himself mortally wounded. He was taken away to the Isle of Avalon (the Celtic paradise, associated with Glastonbury) to be healed. Succeeding writers added new characters, themes, and episodes. *Wace introduced the knightly fellowship of the Round Table and also mentioned the ancient tradition that one day Arthur would return from Avalon to rule Britain again. *Layamon added magical elements to the story, and French and other writers from the 12th century onwards, starting with *Chrétien de Troyes, took up the exploits of individual knights, such as Lancelot, Perceval, Gawain, and Galahad, and focused on the quest of the *Holy Grail, the adulterous affair of Guinevere and Lancelot, and other episodes. Other well-known characters were the magician Merlin and the sorceress Morgan le Fay (Arthur's sister). Sir Thomas *Malory's *Morte d'Arthur* (c. 1470) was the culmination of the medieval tradition, although the material has continued to inspire such versions as Tennyson's *Idylls of the King* (from 1842) and T. H. White's *The Once and Future King* (1958).

Arthur's Pass 42 55S 171 34E A pass in the Southern Alps, New Zealand, linking the W coast by road and rail with Christchurch in the E. Height: 926 m (3038 ft).

artichoke A perennial thistle-like herbaceous plant, *Cynara scolemus*, also known as globe artichoke, native to central and W Mediterranean regions and widely grown in warm temperate areas for its nutty-tasting immature flower heads, which are considered a great delicacy. The hairy indented straplike leaves, 1 m long, arise each year from the base of the short annual stems, which carry branched flower stalks bearing purplish flowers. Family: *Compositae. *See also* Jerusalem artichoke.

Articles of Confederation The first constitution of the USA (written 1776–77, adopted 1781), which was replaced by the Constitution of 1789. The leaders of the American Revolution feared the abuses of a centralized government and adopted a federal system that guaranteed each state its "sovereignty, freedom, and independence." The *Continental Congress could not levy taxes but could wage war and borrow and issue money.

artificial insemination The artificial introduction of semen into the vagina of a female at a stage in the menstrual or oestrous cycle when the chances of conception are high (i.e. at ovulation). Although practised as early as the 14th century by Arab horse breeders, the techniques of artificial insemination used in the livestock industry were developed largely in the Soviet Union during the early 20th century. Semen collected from a single well-bred male can be stored at low temperatures for months before being used to fertilize many females. This has resulted in dramatic breed improvements and the control of venereal disease. Artificial insemination is occasionally used in human medicine; stores of human semen are kept frozen in sperm banks. In cases when the husband is infertile semen is obtained from an anonymous donor (artificial insemination donor—AID). Semen may be provided by the husband in cases of impotence (artificial insemination husband—AIH). When the wife is infertile the husband's semen may be used to artificially inseminate a surrogate mother. This woman gives birth to the child, usually for money, and must then be prepared to relinquish all claims on it to the natural father and his wife. Commercial surrogacy is growing in the USA, but in the UK legislation is being introduced to ban it. *See also* test-tube baby.

artificial intelligence (AI) The design of computer programs to perform tasks that involve intelligence when carried out by human beings. Tasks performed by AI include playing games, learning, understanding natural language and speech, formulating plans, proving theorems, and visual perception. Perceptual tasks involve unconscious computation in humans, which is hard to simulate. AI programs sometimes simulate human behaviour by building computer models of cognitive processes, but in most cases they adopt any technique that will do the task set or do it better than it has been done before.

artificial kidney. *See* dialysis.

artificial respiration The restoration of the flow of air into and out of the lungs when the patient's own breathing movements have ceased, for example after drowning, poisoning, etc. Mouth-to-mouth respiration—the "kiss of life"—involves a person breathing out into the patient's mouth: carbon dioxide in this exhaled air acts as a stimulus for the natural breathing reflexes. In hospitals artificial respiration by a *respirator is sometimes provided during surgery, severe pneumonias, and after head injuries.

Artigas, José Gervasio (1764–1850) The national hero of Uruguay. He fought for his country's independence from Argentina until he was driven into exile in Paraguay in 1820.

artillery *Firearms with a calibre in excess of 20 mm, used to bombard enemy positions, disrupt communications, destroy enemy artillery, and provide cover and support for friendly troop deployments. Early guns were classed by projectile weight, e.g. 12-pounder. Modern weapons are identified by calibre: light (below 120 mm), medium (121–160 mm), heavy (161–210 mm), and super or very heavy (above 211 mm). *Gun projectiles have flat trajectories, while *mortars and *howitzers have high trajectories, with correspondingly short ranges. Artillery rockets (excluding antitank missiles) deliver more explosive further, without needing heavy launchers. Some artillery projectiles have nuclear warheads, but most are high explosive. Modern electronic equipment enables artillery fire to score a direct hit with near certainty on any visible target; as this also applies to the guns themselves (as targets) the tendency is now for artillery to be fired by remote control.

Artiodactyla An order of hoofed mammals (150 species), distributed worldwide except for Australasia and Antarctica. Artiodactyls are terrestrial herbivores having two or four toes on each foot and often bearing horns. The group is divided into three suborders: *Suiformes* (pigs, peccaries, and hippopotamuses); *Tylopoda* (camels and llamas); and *Ruminantia* (*see* ruminant), which comprises deer, cattle, antelopes, giraffes, pronghorns, and chevrotains. *Compare* Perissodactyla.

Art Nouveau A decorative style pervading all visual art forms in Britain, France, Germany (*see* Jugendstil), Austria (Sezessionstil), Belgium, Spain, and the USA in the 1890s and early 1900s. It is characterized by designs of naturalistic foliage and biomorphic shapes linked by undulating lines. In Britain it is associated with the *Arts and Crafts movement of William *Morris, the designs of C. R. *Mackintosh, and the graphic work of Aubrey *Beardsley. On the Continent leading examples of Art Nouveau are the Parisian metro designs of Hector Guimard (1867–1942), the extravagant Barcelona flats and hotels of Antonio *Gaudí, and the Belgian stores and houses of Victor *Horta. A parallel effect in glassware of tinted glass and lead solder was achieved by René *Lalique and Emile *Gallé.

Artois A former province of NW France approximating to the present-day Pas-de-Calais. It belonged until 1180 to the Counts of *Flanders, after which it passed to *Philip II Augustus of France. Acquired by the Counts of *Burgundy in 1329, it passed to the *Habsburgs in 1500 until regained by France during the *Thirty Years' War (1618–48).

Arts and Crafts movement An English 19th-century aesthetic movement derived from William *Morris and his Pre-Raphaelite associates, whose firm was founded (1861) to produce handmade furnishings. The movement revived the principles of medieval craftsmanship and respect for materials; it also promoted the ideal of the artist as craftsman-designer. It culminated in the establishment of the Century Guild for Craftsmen (1882) and the Arts and Crafts Exhibition Society (1888). The preference for curvilinear patterns helped to create the emerging *Art Nouveau style.

Arts Council of Great Britain An organization established by royal charter in 1946 to make the arts more accessible to the public and to encourage higher standards of artistic performance. The Council has not more than 19 members, who serve for five years and are appointed by the minister for the arts. Four specialist panels deal respectively with music, drama, the visual arts, and literature. There are separate committees for Scotland and Wales. The Council is funded largely by the Department of Education and Science. Chairman: Sir William Rees-Mogg.

Aruba 12 30N 70 00W A West Indian island, formerly (until 1986) part of the Netherlands Antilles. Oil refining is important. Area: 193 sq km (75 sq mi). Population (1983): 67 014. Chief town: Oranjestad.

arum (*or* arum lily) A plant of the tropical African genus *Zantedeschia* (8 species), especially *Z. aethiopica*, widely grown as an ornamental. It has arrow-shaped leaves and a flower head of tiny yellow flowers surrounded by a white funnel-shaped spathe. Family: *Araceae*. The European genus *Arum*, of the same family, contains the *cuckoopint. The related bog arum, or wild calla (*Calla palustris*), grows in swamps of N temperate and subarctic regions. It has heart-shaped leaves and small flowers enveloped in a white spathe.

Arunachal Pradesh (name until 1972: North-East Frontier Agency) A state in NE India, stretching N from the Brahmaputra Valley to the Himalayas. There it shares a disputed border with Tibet, from which Chinese troops have twice invaded since 1945. For security reasons it was a union territory until 1975. Mostly rainforest, Arunachal Pradesh is inhabited by hill tribes. Area: 81 426 sq km (31 430 sq mi). Population (1981 est): 631 839. Capital: Ziro.

Arundel 50 51N 0 34W A market town in SE England, in West Sussex on the River Arun. Its 11th-century castle (mainly rebuilt in the 19th century) is the seat of the Dukes of Norfolk. Other notable buildings include the 19th-century Roman Catholic cathedral. Population (1981): 2235.

Arundel, Thomas (1353–1414) English churchman, Archbishop of Canterbury (1396–97, 1399–1414). Impeached for opposing Richard II in 1397, he returned from banishment with Bolingbroke in 1399 and crowned him Henry IV. He actively suppressed the *Lollards.

Arval Brethren (Latin: *Fratres Arvales*, Brothers of the Field) In ancient Rome, a college of 12 priests, who organized a festival every May dedicated to the corn goddess Dea Dia. The priests were chosen from high-ranking officials and included the emperor.

Aryans Peoples speaking *Indo-European, *Indo-Iranian, or *Indo-Aryan languages. It has been claimed that all the Indo-European peoples originated from an Aryan people who dispersed from a common homeland into Europe and N India. Indo-Aryan-speaking peoples certainly invaded and settled in N India in the second millennium BC. They were tribal herdsmen who later became farmers. The earliest literature of India, the Vedas, written in *Sanskrit, contains hymns, spells, and details of Aryan ritual practices.

Arya Samaj A controversial Hindu theosophical movement, founded in 1875 at Bombay by Swami Dayananda

Saraswali (1824–83). It denounced popular idolatry and advocated a return to the oldest Vedic authorities. It also supported the emancipation of women and untouchables, because the old authorities neither justified nor assumed their lower status. Unlike many contemporary movements, Arya Samaj made no attempt to convert non-Indians.

ASA rating The American Standards Association measure of the sensitivity or speed of photographic *film. A film rated at 200 is twice as fast (i.e. needs half the exposure time) as 100 ASA film. General-purpose films have speeds between 50 and 160 ASA. High-speed films for indoor photography and poor light are rated between 200 and 500 ASA.

asbestos A fibrous form of certain silicate minerals, particularly the *amphiboles anthophyllite, tremolite, riebeckite, and actinolite, or a fibrous form of *serpentine, called chrysotile. Blue asbestos is crocidolite, a fibrous riebeckite. Asbestos is heat-resistant, chemically inert, and has a high electrical resistance; it has therefore a wide industrial application. The fibres are spun and woven or made into blocks. The main producers are Canada, the Soviet Union, and Brazil. *See also* asbestosis.

asbestosis A lung disease caused by the inhalation of asbestos fibres. It is an occupational disease to which those exposed to large amounts of the mineral are particularly prone: tighter factory health controls have greatly reduced its incidence. It affects the air sacs of the lungs, which become thickened and scarred, causing breathlessness: patients are liable to develop lung cancer.

Ascaris A genus of *nematode worms with a worldwide distribution, important as parasites of livestocks and man. Adult worms are smooth and cylindrical, 15-30 cm in length, and can live in the intestines of their hosts for up to a year. After mating, eggs pass out in the host's faeces and infection occurs when food contaminated with eggs is eaten.

Ascension 7 57S 14 22W A rocky island in the S Atlantic Ocean, a dependency of St Helena. It has little vegetation and was uninhabited until 1815. A British telecommunications centre, it is also a US air base and space research station. Area: 88 sq km (35 sq mi). Population (1981): 971. Chief settlement: Georgetown.

Ascension In the Christian calendar, the day on which it is believed Christ ascended into Heaven (*see* Acts 1.4–11). Since the 4th century it has been celebrated 40 days after Easter.

asceticism Systematic self-discipline for spiritual ends, usually involving fasting, vigils, sexual abstinence, and renunciation of worldly goods and pleasures. *Stoicism advocated ascetic practices in order to subdue unruly passions. Christian asceticism is based on the theory of identifying with Christ's sufferings and is viewed not as an end in itself but as a means to contemplation of and spiritual union with the divine. It became an important element in certain monastic orders and in Christian *mysticism. In Islam, asceticism is particularly associated with *sufism and there is also a strong tradition of asceticism in Buddhism and Hinduism (*see* fakir).

Asch, Sholem (1880–1957) Jewish novelist, born in Poland, who wrote chiefly in Yiddish. He travelled in Europe, Israel, and the USA, becoming a US citizen in 1920. In his controversial later novels, which include *The Nazarene* (1929) and *The Apostle* (1943), he expressed his belief in the essential unity of Judaism and Christianity.

Aschaffenburg 49 58N 9 10E A town in S central West Germany, in Bavaria on the River Main. It contains the 17th-century Johannisburg Castle, a former residence of the Archbishops of Mainz. Its varied manufactures include clothing and precision instruments. Population (1982): 59 643.

Ascham, Roger (1515–68) English scholar and writer. His humanist scholarship was founded on his classical studies at Cambridge University. He served as Latin secretary to Edward VI, Mary, and Elizabeth I. His major works were *Toxophilus* (1545), a treatise on archery, and *The Scholemaster* (1570), a practical treatise on education written in a distinctively plain but elegant prose.

Asclepius (*or* Aesculapius) In Greek mythology, a son of *Apollo and the god of medicine. He was instructed by the centaur *Chiron in hunting and medicine and learned to effect many miraculous cures. When he restored *Hippolytus to life as a favour to Artemis, Zeus became angry and struck him dead with a thunderbolt. The sick, believing in Asclepius' power to cure them through dreams, came to sleep in his temples, the chief of which were at Epidaurus and on the island of Cos.

Ascoli Piceno 42 52N 13 35E A town in central Italy, in Marche. An ancient settlement, it has many Roman and medieval remains. Its manufactures include glass, chemicals, and textiles. Population (1981): 54 193.

Ascomycetes A large class of fungi (about 15 000 species), known as sac fungi because their spores are formed in a saclike structure (called an ascus). The nonreproductive part of these fungi is often a microscopical meshwork of cells. The group includes the *truffles, *yeasts, *Penicillium*, and *Aspergillus*.

ascorbic acid. *See* vitamin C.

Ascot 51 25N 0 41W A village in S England, in Berkshire. The construction of its famous racecourse was ordered by Queen Anne in 1711. Traditionally the sovereign opens the Royal Ascot meeting in June, driving in an open carriage round the course from nearby Windsor Castle. Population (1983 est): 13 234, with Sunningdale.

ASDIC. *See* echo sounding.

ASEAN. *See* Association of South-East Asian Nations.

asepsis The condition in which material is uncontaminated by bacteria, fungi, and other disease-causing microorganisms. Surgical operations, the packaging of surgical supplies, and the preparation of intravenous drugs are carried out under aseptic conditions, which are produced by using *antiseptics, heat, or radiation.

Asgard In Norse mythology, the home of the gods and of heroes killed in battle, comprising over 12 kingdoms and palaces, as well as *Valhalla. From earth it was reached by the bridge Bifrost (the rainbow).

ash A tree of the genus *Fraxinus* (about 50 species), native to the N hemisphere. Many species yield a pale-yellow wood of commercial importance and others are widely grown as ornamentals. Reaching a height of 30 m, ashes have compound leaves made up of pairs of oval or lance-shaped leaflets, small inconspicuous flowers, and winged fruits ("ash keys"). Most species are deciduous, including the European ash (*F. excelsior*). Family: *Oleaceae* (olive family). *See also* mountain ash.

Ashanti A people of the S part of Ghana, who speak the Twi language. They are an agricultural people producing crops for local markets and cocoa for export. Their social organization is based upon matrilineal kin groups living in villages governed by headmen. The Ashanti established an empire in S Ghana during the 18th and 19th centuries, ruled by a paramount chief with military and religious functions. They worship a pantheon of gods and practise an ancestor cult.

Ashanti A former kingdom in W Africa, now comprising S Ghana. During the 18th century it was active in the slave trade, supplying slaves to British and Dutch traders. Following several wars it became a British colony in 1902. The modern region of Ashanti occupies part of its area.

Ashby-de-la-Zouch 52 46N 1 28W A market town in central England, in Leicestershire. Mary, Queen of Scots, was imprisoned in its castle in 1569. Population (1981): 11 518.

Ashcroft, Dame Peggy (1907–) British actress. She

made her debut at the Birmingham Repertory Theatre in 1926. Her most notable performances include Juliet in 1935, Hedda Gabler in 1954, and more recent roles in plays by Pinter and Beckett. She won an Oscar for her performance in the film *A Passage to India* (1984).

Ashdod 31 48N 34 38S A town in central Israel, on the Mediterranean coast. It was an important city in the ancient Philistine Empire, and an artificial harbour (started 1961) has now made it into one of Israel's major ports. There is also textile manufacturing. Population (1982 est): 66 000.

Ashe, Arthur (Robert) (1943–) US tennis player, the first Black player to win the US singles title (1968) and winner of the 1975 singles title at Wimbledon. South Africa's refusal to allow him to play there in 1970 led to its exclusion from the *Davis Cup.

Asher, tribe of One of the 12 *tribes of Israel. It claimed descent from Asher, the son of Jacob and Jacob's concubine Zilpah. Its original territory was to the W and NW of the Sea of Galilee, adjoining Phoenicia.

In Affectionate Remembrance
OF

ENGLISH CRICKET,
WHICH DIED AT THE OVAL
ON

29th AUGUST, 1882,
Deeply lamented by a large circle of sorrowing friends and acquaintances.

R. I. P.

N.B.—The body will be cremated and the ashes taken to Australia.

ASHES *The original advertisement that appeared as a joke in the* Sporting Times *in August, 1882.*

Ashes A mock trophy awarded to the winning team in cricket Test matches between England and Australia. It originated with the first Australian victory (1882), when an obituary for English cricket in the *Sporting Times* ended with words: "The body will be cremated and the ashes taken to Australia." In 1883 the victorious English captain was presented with an urn (now kept in the pavilion at *Lord's cricket ground) containing the ashes of the stumps used in the match.

Ashford 51 09N 0 53E A market town in SE England, in Kent. It has railway workshops, light engineering, and brewing industries. Population (1981): 39 974.

Ashkelon (*or* Ashqelon) 31 40N 34 35E A seaport 19 km (12 mi) N of Gaza (Israel), known from the biblical story of Samson as a *Philistine stronghold. In Hellenistic times it was a cultural centre. The Arabs captured it in 636 AD. During the Crusades it changed hands several times before being destroyed by Sultan *Baybars (1270). The modern Israeli settlement was established in 1948.

Ashkenazim Jews of German or Eastern European origin, as opposed to *Sephardim. They have a distinct tradition of pronouncing Hebrew, as well as other customs, and until this century they mostly spoke *Yiddish. The first Ashkenazy synagogue in London was founded in 1690. Ashkenazim now form some 85% of world Jewry.

Ashkenazy, Vladimir (1937–) Russian pianist and conductor, famous for his interpretations of Mozart and Chopin, among others. He won the 1955 Warsaw Chopin Competition and was joint winner of the 1962 Tchaikovsky Competition. In 1973 he settled in Iceland.

Ashkhabad 37 58N 58 24E A city in the SW Soviet Union, the capital of the Turkmen SSR. It is near the Iranian border in an oasis in the *Kara Kum desert. Although virtually destroyed in 1948 by an earthquake, it has been rebuilt and is now an administrative, industrial, and transportation centre, producing food, carpets, glass, and machinery. Population (1984): 346 000.

Ashley Cooper, Anthony. *See* Shaftesbury, Anthony Ashley Cooper, 1st Earl of.

Ashmolean Museum A museum in Oxford, housing paintings and archaeological collections. The collection was donated to Oxford University in 1675 by Elias Ashmole (1617–92) and put on public display in 1683. Now in C. R. *Cockerell's neoclassical building (1845), its highlights include Italian Renaissance paintings and English 19th-century works.

ashrama In *Brahmanism, the *ashramas* are the four ideal stages of life through which Hindus of the upper three castes should pass. First comes the celibate student of religion, then the married householder, the forest hermit, and finally the wandering ascetic. Only in later life, therefore, can spiritual release be sought.

Ashton, Sir Frederick (William Mallandaine) (1904–) British ballet dancer and choreographer, born in Ecuador. He joined the Sadler's Wells Ballet in 1935, became an associate director in 1952, and was director of the Royal Ballet from 1963 to 1970. His works include *Cinderella* (1948), *Ondine* (1958), *La Fille mal gardée* (1960), and many ballets choreographed for Margot Fonteyn.

Ashton-under-Lyne 53 29N 2 06W A town in N England, in Greater Manchester. It has plastics, engineering, and leather-goods industries. Population (1981): 44 671.

Ashur The oldest Assyrian capital (modern Qalat Sharqat) on the River Tigris 96 km (60 mi) S of Mosul in Iraq. Ashur was already an important trading city in the heyday of *Sumer and *Akkad. Named after its guardian sun-god, Ashur became capital of the rising *Assyrian empire (14th century BC) to which it gave its name. With its later cocapitals *Nimrud and *Nineveh it was destroyed in 612 BC. First excavated in 1903, Ashur's ruins include major temples and a *ziggurat.

Ashurbanipal King of Assyria (668–?627 BC), son of Esarhaddon. He suppressed two serious revolts during his reign and conquered the city of Tyre, but is best known as the founder of a remarkable library at Nineveh, some of the items in which are now in the British Museum.

Ashurnasirpal II King of Assyria (883–859 BC), who continued the restoration of the *Assyrian Empire by efficient administration, an invincible army, and brutality in punishing rebellion. He used deported captives to rebuild Kalhu (now *Nimrud, Iraq).

Ash Wednesday In the Christian calendar, the first day of *Lent, which is so named from the custom, probably dating from the 8th century, of marking the foreheads of the congregation with ashes as a sign of penitence.

Asia The largest continent in the world, it occupies about one-third of the dry land in the world. Asia is generally accepted as extending W to the Ural Mountains in the Soviet Union, although physically Europe is a peninsula of Asia. It is separated from the continent of Africa by the Red Sea and bounded on the N by the Arctic Ocean. Its S and E limits are less distinct and it includes the islands of Indonesia, Japan, the Philippines, and Taiwan. Asia is a continent of great diversity. Topographically it is the highest of the continents and has the greatest relief. It contains the world's highest point (Mount *Everest) and also its lowest (the *Dead Sea). Its great central mass of mountains and plateaus, which include the Himalayas, has historically formed a major barrier between N and S Asia. Vast alluvial plains border the major rivers, including the Rivers Ganges, Mekong, and Ob and the Yangtze and Yellow Rivers. Containing about half of the world's total population, it is the most populous continent, the highest concentrations being in the SE (China, India, and Japan). There are three main population groups: Negroid (in the Philippines), Mongoloid (including the Chinese, Japanese, and Koreans), and Caucasoid (including the Arabs, Afghans, and Pakistanis). Other groups, including the Malays, are a mixture of these main races. All the world's major religions originated in Asia, only Christianity spreading W to any great extent. Others include Hinduism (with the largest following), Buddhism, Islam, Confucianism (in China), and Shintoism (in Japan). Agriculture is the chief occupation, employing about two-thirds of the total population. Asia also has important mineral resources, notably the oil and natural-gas deposits of the Arab states. Area: 44 391 162 sq km (17 139 445 sq mi). Population (1981 est): 2 608 000 000.

Asia Minor (or Anatolia) The westernmost part of Asia between the Black Sea in the N, the Mediterranean Sea in the S, and the Aegean Sea in the W; it approximates present-day Turkey in Asia. For much of the second millennium BC, Asia Minor was the centre of the *Hittite empire. After the Hittites' collapse (12th century BC) central and W Asia Minor were dominated by *Phrygia, which reached its zenith in the 8th century, when the Assyrian Empire conquered SE Asia Minor. Phrygia fell to *Lydia in the 6th century but in 546 Cyrus the Great established Achaemenian control over Asia Minor. In 333 it was conquered by Alexander the Great of Macedon and after his death, during the *Hellenistic age, the S was contested by the *Seleucids and the *Ptolemies, while small kingdoms, such as *Pergamum, *Cappadocia, *Bithynia, and *Pontus, established themselves elsewhere. Asia Minor came under Roman control in the 2nd and 1st centuries BC, forming part of the *Roman Empire and then the *Eastern Roman (subsequently Byzantine) Empire. Conquered by the Seljuq Turks in the 11th century AD and overrun by the Mongols in the 13th, Asia Minor was incorporated in the Ottoman Empire during the 14th and 15th centuries.

Asian Games An athletics meeting for all Asian countries affiliated to the International Amateur Athletic Federation. Quadrennial from 1954, they began in New Delhi in 1951.

asiento de negros A contract between the Spanish Crown and a private contractor, in which the Crown sold the exclusive rights to import slaves into its American colonies. The *asiento* began in 1595 and was held successively by Portuguese, Genoese, French, English, and Spanish contractors before it was suppressed in 1778.

Asimov, Isaac (1920–) US science fiction writer and biochemist, born in Russia. He began writing science fiction in 1939. His many books include the *Foundation Trilogy* (1951–53; sequel 1982) and collections of short stories, notably *I, Robot* (1950), *Nightfall* (1969), and *The Edge of Tomorrow* (1986). His books popularizing scientific topics include *Inside the Atom* (1956), *The Human Brain* (1964), and *The Stars in their Courses* (1971).

Aske, Robert. *See* Pilgrimage of Grace.

Asmara (or Asmera) 15 20N 38 49E A city in N Ethiopia, the capital of Eritrea province. The population still includes many Italians, Eritrea having been an Italian colony from 1890 until Allied occupation (1941). Notable buildings include the cathedral (1922) and Grand Mosque (1937); it has a university (1958). Industries include meat processing, distilling, and clothes manufacture. Population (1981 est): 240 000.

Aso, Mount 32 55N 131 02E A volcano in Japan, on central Kyushu. It has five cones, one with the longest active crater in the world, 114 km (71 mi) in circumference. Height: 1592 m (5223 ft).

Asoka (died c. 232 BC) Emperor of India (c. 270–c. 232 BC) of the Maurya dynasty (c. 321–c. 185 BC). His dominion extended over the whole of N India and most of the S. After his conquests he adopted the Buddhist faith and had his edicts carved on rock and stone pillars throughout the empire, telling the story of his conversion and issuing orders to comply with the morality of the new faith.

asp An aggressive European *viper, *Vipera aspis*, that lives in dry habitats. About 60 cm long, it is grey-brown to coppery brown with dark bars or zigzags, grey, yellowish, or blackish underparts, and a yellow patch under the tail tip. The snout is upturned into a small spike.

The asp that killed Cleopatra was probably the Egyptian cobra (*Naja haje*).

Asparagus A genus of herbaceous plants (about 300 species), with creeping underground stems (rhizomes), found throughout the Old World. *A. officinalis* is widely cultivated in temperate and subtropical regions for its young edible shoots, which are considered a delicacy. Several African species are ornamental: *A. plumosus*, known as **asparagus fern**, produces attractive feathery sprays of branchlets. Family: *Liliaceae*.

aspen One of several *poplar trees having slender flattened leafstalks, so that the leaves tremble in the faintest breeze. The European aspen (*Populus tremula*), which grows to a height of 25 m has rounded toothed leaves. Its soft white wood is used for matches and paper pulp.

Aspergillus A genus of fungi that includes many common moulds, often found on rotting food. Some species, especially *A. fumigatus*, can cause disease in man (aspergillosis), the most severe form of which affects the lungs producing tuberculosis-like symptoms. *A. flavus*, a mould that infects peanuts, produces the poison aflatoxin, which may be responsible for certain cancers. Class: *Ascomycetes*.

asphalt A black highly viscous or solid hydrocarbon compound, used in road construction and the manufacture of roofing materials. It is obtained from the distillation of certain crude oils and from surface deposits (asphalt lakes), which occur naturally after the lighter fractions of a crude oil reservoir have evaporated.

asphodel A white- or yellow-flowered lily-like plant of the mostly Mediterranean genera *Asphodelus* and *Asphodeline*. In Greek mythology, the asphodel associated with the dead and said to grow in the Elysian fields was *Asphodeline lutea*, which has yellow flowers. The asphodel of the early English and French poets was probably the daffodil. The bog asphodel (*Narthecium ossifragum*), of NW Europe, grows in swampy regions. It grows to a height of 30 cm and has a head of small yellow flowers. Family: *Liliaceae*.

asphyxia Suffocation: obstruction to the supply of oxygen to the tissues. This is a life-threatening condition since the brain cannot survive for longer than about four minutes without oxygen. It can result from any condition that prevents air from reaching the lungs, including drowning and choking. Breathing poisonous gas (e.g. carbon monoxide) also causes asphyxia..

Aspidistra A genus of herbaceous plants (8 species) native to E Asia. *A. elatior* is commonly grown as a hardy pot plant in western countries for its ornamental leaves, which are long, stiff, dark green (sometimes striped), and grow in sheaves from the reduced stem. It may occasionally produce small purple bell-shaped flowers. Family: *Liliaceae*.

aspirin Acetylsalicylic acid: a drug widely used in the form of tablets to treat mild pain, such as headache and toothache. It also relieves inflammation and is therefore helpful in the treatment of rheumatoid arthritis, and it reduces fever. In some people aspirin may cause bleeding from the stomach. *See also* analgesics.

Asquith, Herbert Henry, 1st Earl of Oxford and (1852–1928) British statesman and Liberal prime minister (1908–16). Asquith's government introduced important social reforms, including noncontributory old-age pensions (1908 budget) and the National Insurance Act (1911); it ended the veto power of the House of Lords with the 1911 Parliament Act. After the outbreak of World War I Asquith headed a Liberal-Conservative coalition government (1915–16). He remained leader of the Liberal Party until 1926. His second wife **Margot Asquith** (1865–1945) wrote an outspoken *Autobiography* (1922). His children by his first marriage included **Lady Violet Bonham-Carter, Baroness Asquith** (1887–1969), who was president of the Liberal Party Organization (1944–45). His children by his second marriage included **Anthony Asquith** (1902–68), director of such films as *Shooting Stars* (1928), *The Winslow Boy* (1948), and *The Millionairess* (1961).

ass A small fast-running mammal belonging to the genus *Equus* (horses), native to Africa and Asia. Asses are about 200 cm long, weighing up to 250 kg, and have characteristically long ears. The Asiatic wild ass (*E. hemionus*) has a grey or tan hide, a dark bristly mane, and a dark stripe along the back. The African wild ass (*E. asinus*) is the ancestor of the domestic donkey. Asses have long been used as pack animals. *See also* mule.

Assad, Hafiz al- (1928–) Syrian statesman; president (1971–). In 1966, following the coup in Syria by the radical Ba'athists, he became minister of defence. In 1970 he led a coup by the military wing of the *Ba'ath party and was elected president the following year.

Assam A state in NE India, mostly in the Brahmaputra Valley beyond Bangladesh. High rainfall supports tea, Assam's economic mainstay. Rice, jute, sugar cane, and cotton are also grown. Other than forest products and crafts there is little manufacturing. Assam produces half of India's oil, as well as coal. *History*: a flourishing region by 1000 BC, Assam received later migrants from China and Burma. Burmese invasions led Britain to assume control (1826). In World War II Assam played a strategic role in the Allied advance into Burma. Area: 78 523 sq km (30 310 sq mi). Population (1981): 19 902 826. Capital: Dispur.

assassin bug An insect belonging to a widely distributed family (*Reduviidae*; 4000 species), usually black or brown with a long beak used to pierce the skin and suck blood or body fluids from its prey. Assassin bugs generally prey on other insects but some attack mammals, including man. As well as inflicting a painful bite, they may transmit diseases, such as kala-azar and Chagas' disease. Suborder: *Heteroptera*; order: *Hemiptera*.

Assassins (Arabic: hashish eaters) A sect of the Ismaili. In Persia and Syria in the 12th and 13th centuries they were notorious for their practice of stabbing opponents to further their political and religious aims. It was commonly believed that the stabbings were carried out while they were under the influence of hashish, hence their name. They killed mainly Muslims, but also some Crusaders.

assault and battery In law, battery is the unlawful use of any physical force on someone else. Assault is an attempt to commit a battery or any other unlawful act that makes someone reasonably fear battery, whether or not there is any real intention to harm him. The offender is likely to face criminal charges and may also be sued for damages by his victim. Some "aggravated" assaults, as for example with a deadly weapon, carry higher penalties.

assemblage A work of art in which random objects and materials are integrated on a panel or in a free-standing construction, often to produce a satirical or surrealist effect. Early examples, from around 1915, include the *ready-mades of *Duchamp and the collages of Picasso. More recent assemblages are those of the *pop art movement, using everyday objects, such as clothing, furniture, and household utensils.

assembler A computer *program that makes up part of the *software of a computer. It converts instructions in a programming language into a form that the machine can follow directly.

Asser (died c. 909) Welsh monk and Bishop of Sherborne. Known for his learning, he was invited to the court of Alfred the Great and today is remembered chiefly as Alfred's biographer. The biography, *De rebus gestis Alfredi Magni*, ends in 887 and is the chief source of historical information about Alfred's reign.

assignats Paper money issued (1789–96) during the *French Revolution in order to pay off the government's debts. Initially they stimulated the economy and solved the problem of money shortage but ultimately they caused inflation, which reached a peak in 1795, when assignats with a face value of 45,500 million francs but virtually no real value were in circulation.

Assiniboine River A river in W Canada, rising in SE Saskatchewan and flowing generally SE through wheat-growing country to join the Red River at Winnipeg. Length: 950 km (590 mi).

Assisi 43 04N 12 37E A town in central Italy, in Umbria. It is the birthplace of St *Francis of Assisi, who founded the Franciscan Order in 1209, and is the site of a Franciscan convent, which has two gothic churches containing frescoes by Giotto. Population (1981 est): 24 440.

Associated Press. *See* news agency.

association In psychology, the linking of one idea to another. Similarity of meaning, physical similarity, and contrast can all cause an idea to call forth several others. When two mental events occur together an association forms between them: this is the basis of one kind of learning. According to the associationist school of psychology, the association of ideas is the basic process underlying human behaviour. **Free association** is the chief method of *psychoanalysis: a patient speaks aloud his stream of consciousness, from which the analyst obtains clues to the underlying unconscious thought processes.

Association football. *See* football.

Association of South-East Asian Nations (ASEAN) An international organization, founded in 1967, to assist the cultural, economic, and social development of its member states (Indonesia, Malaysia, the Philippines, Singapore, and Thailand). It aims to eliminate trade barriers, promote cultural exchanges, facilitate communications between members, and improve technology, commerce, and industry.

associative law The mathematical rule, obeyed by addition and multiplication in ordinary *arithmetic, that the order in which successive identical operations are performed does not affect the result: for addition $a + (b + c) = (a + b) + c$; for multiplication $a(bc) = (ab)c$

assurance A form of *insurance against an event, such as death, that must occur. There are four main types: term assurance, whole-life assurance, endowment assurance, and an *annuity. Term assurance is a form of life assurance that only pays out if the assured dies within a stipulated period (e.g. while a businessman is on a specific journey). Whole-life assurance pays out on the death of the assured whenever it occurs. Premiums may continue to be paid throughout the assured's life or may cease at a stipulated age (e.g. 65). Endowment assurance pays out either on the death of the assured, whenever it occurs, or after a fixed number of years (e.g. when the assured reaches the age of 60). Most assurers require the assured to submit to a medical examination before granting whole-life or endowment assurance. Policies may be "with profits," entitling the assured to a share in the assurer's profits (which is added to the sum assured when it is paid out), or, for a lower premium, "without profits," in which case only the sum assured is paid out (which in times of inflation may have considerably less purchasing power than the assurer intended).

Assyrian Empire   An ancient kingdom on the Upper Tigris (now N Iraq), where the Assyrians (named after their god Ashur) settled in about 2500 BC, forming a dependency of Babylon. Ashur-uballit I (c. 1365-c. 1330) laid the foundations of the Empire, which after a period of decline was extended by *Tiglath-pileser I (1120-1074), who conquered the city of Babylon. A new era of aggressive expansion was initiated by *Ashurnasirpal II (883-859). The Assyrian domain was extended to Syria and Palestine under Shalmaneser III (858-824) and Assyrian ascendancy reached its zenith under *Tiglath-pileser III (745-727). *Sargon II (722-705), *Sennacherib (704-681), and *Esarhaddon (680-669) maintained the Empire but *Nineveh, the capital, fell to Media and Babylon in 612. The Assyrians built magnificent palaces with friezes that reflected their warlike character.

Astaire, Fred   (Frederick Austerlitz; 1899-1987) US dancer and film star. He began his career as a music-hall dancer. His best-known films are the 1930s musicals in which he partnered Ginger Rogers. These include *Top Hat* (1935), *Follow the Fleet* (1936), and *Shall We Dance* (1937). His later co-stars included Judy Garland, Leslie Caron, and Audrey Hepburn.

Astarte   The Phoenician goddess of love and fertility, equivalent to the Babylonian *Ishtar and sometimes regarded as the counterpart of *Aphrodite. She was associated with the moon and often represented by a crescent.

astatine (At)   A short-lived radioactive *halogen. Its longest-lived isotope, ^{210}At, has a half-life of 8.3 hours. Small amounts exist in nature as a result of uranium and thorium decay. At no 85; at wt (210); mp 302°C; bp 337°C.

Astbury, John   (1688-1743) English potter, to whom are attributed some of the earliest Staffordshire figures in red clay decorated with white. He also made tableware and it is possible that he originated the groups of figures known as pew groups. Astburyware, produced also by his son Thomas Astbury (1719-60), is of a very fine quality and is now extremely valuable.

Aster   A genus of perennial herbaceous plants (about 500 species), many species of which are commonly known as Michaelmas daisies. Native to N temperate regions, they are widely grown as garden plants. Usually 60-100 cm tall, they have flowers with blue, red, or white rays and a central yellow disc. *A. amellus* and *A. aeris* are common ornamental species. Family: *Compositae.

asteroid.   *See* minor planet.

asthma   A disorder in which breathlessness and wheezing are aggravated by certain stimuli, which cause the bronchi (which conduct air to the lungs) to become constricted. Bronchial asthma may be stimulated by a wide range of conditions and substances: it may be an allergic reaction (*see* allergy), it may occur secondarily to respiratory infection, or it may be brought on by exertion, certain drugs, or strong emotion. The most common treatment is by means of bronchodilator drugs (which dilate the bronchi), which are usually administered in the form of aerosol inhalers; severe asthmatic attacks require corticosteroid inhalers. Cardiac asthma is associated with some forms of heart disease and requires a different treatment.

Asti   44 54N 8 13E A town in NW Italy, in Piedmont. It is famous for its sparkling wine (Asti Spumante). Population (1981): 76 950.

astigmatism   A form of *aberration that can occur in mirrors and lenses (including the eye). It results when the curvature is different in two mutually perpendicular planes; rays in one plane may then be in focus while rays in the other are out of focus. It is corrected in the eye by the use of cylindrical lenses.

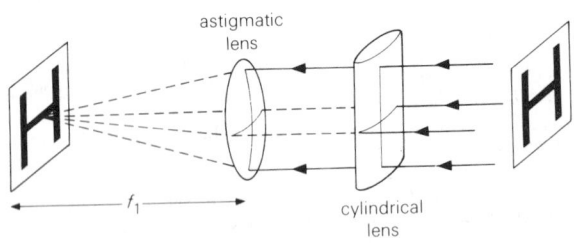

ASTIGMATISM *An astigmatic lens cannot focus vertical and horizontal lines at the same time. Here the vertical focal length f_1 is shorter than the horizontal focal length f_2. In the human eye this would be corrected by spectacles with cylindrical lenses, reducing the overall focal length in the horizontal plane only, so that both vertical and horizontal lines are in sharp focus at distance f_1.*

Astilbe   A genus of perennial herbaceous flowering plants (about 25 species), native to E Asia and North America and commonly cultivated for ornament in temperate regions. The flowers (usually pink or red) grow in branching plumelike clusters; the plants may reach a height of 1.5 m. Family: *Saxifragaceae.*

Aston, Francis William   (1877-1945) British chemist, who worked in the Cavendish Laboratory, Cambridge. He developed the mass spectrometer for separating ions according to their atomic weight. His discovery of the isotopes of many nonradioactive elements, and of the whole-number rule governing their masses, won him the 1922 Nobel Prize for Chemistry.

Astor, John Jacob   (1763-1848) US businessman; founder of the well-known family of financiers. A German emigrant, he made a fortune with his monopolistic American Fur Company. He then invested so extensively in New York property that the Astor family became known as the landlords of New York. He died reputedly the richest man in the USA.

Astor, Nancy Witcher, Viscountess   (1879-1964) British politician, who was the first woman MP to sit in the House of Commons (1919-45). An American by birth, she championed the causes of women's rights and education, representing the constituency that was formerly that of her husband Waldorf, 2nd Viscount Astor (1879-1952). An MP from 1910 to 1919, Astor (the great-great-grandson of John Jacob *Astor) was proprietor (1919-45) of the *Observer* newspaper.

Astrakhan   46 22N 48 04E A port in the Soviet Union, in the SE RSFSR on the River Volga. The city was an important trading centre with the East until the Russian Revolution, after which its importance declined. Astrakhan fur, from the Karakul lamb of central Asia, was first brought to Russia by Astrakhan traders. More than half the population is employed in fishing or allied occupations. Population (1981 est): 470 000.

astrobiology (*or* exobiology)   The branch of biology that investigates the possibility of life on other planets. Astrobiologists monitor the electromagnetic spectrum, including light and radio waves, emitted by the stars for evidence of the organic molecules that are a prerequisite of life on earth. They are also involved in designing life-detecting experiments carried to planets in our own solar system by space probes, such as the US Viking series.

astrology The study of the movements and positions of the heavenly bodies in relation to their presumed influence upon human affairs. Astrology originated in *Babylonia and then passed to Greece, India, China, and the Islamic lands. In medieval Europe astrologers had a respected role in public and personal life. Astrology is based upon an elaborate system of putative correspondences between celestial and mundane phenomena: each "house" (*see* zodiac), for instance, imparts a particular character to those born under its influence and the sun, moon, and principal planets in various positions relative to the houses and to each other predispose people to good or ill. The two branches of astrology are "natural" (concerned mainly with observations and theory) and "judicial" (foretelling events in individual lives by means of a *horoscope).

astrometry The measurement of the positions of stars and other celestial objects using optical or radio astronomy techniques.

astronomer royal An eminent British astronomer appointed by the sovereign on the advice of the prime minister. Until 1971 the astronomer royal was also head of the Royal Observatory (formerly at Greenwich, now at Herstmonceaux). The first holder was John Flamsteed appointed in 1675, when the Observatory was founded. The present holder is Prof. F. Graham Smith.

astronomical unit (AU) A unit of length equal to the mean distance between the earth and the sun (1.495×10^{11} metres, 92.9×10^{6} miles).

astronomy The study of celestial bodies and the universe of which they form part. One of the most ancient of the sciences, naked-eye astronomy flourished in China, Babylonia, Egypt, and classical Greece (*see* Aristarchus of Samos; Hipparchus; Ptolemaic system). After the decline of ancient Greek culture, interest in astronomy was the preserve of the Arabs for many centuries. European interest in the heavens, transmitted from the Arabs through Spain, reawakened in the 16th century with the work of *Copernicus and Tycho *Brahe, who were able to separate the science of astronomy from *astrology. But it was not until 1609 that Galileo's refracting *telescope (invented in Holland in 1608) enabled the sky to be investigated in any detail; in 1671 Newton devised the more effective reflecting telescope. These devices provided the means for the development of *astrometry and *celestial mechanics. In the 19th century, the use of spectroscopy (*see* spectrum) to study the physical and chemical composition of celestial bodies provided the basis for the new sciences of *astrophysics and astrochemistry.

Until the 1930s all observations of the heavens were made by observing the light that passed through the "optical window" in the earth's atmosphere: light, near-ultraviolet, and near-infrared radiation, spanning wavelengths from about 300–900 nanometres, can pass through the atmosphere without significant absorption by atoms and molecules. There is also a "radio window" allowing radio waves with wavelengths of about 30 metres to less than a millimetre to be transmitted to the earth's surface. Jansky's discovery (1932) of the first cosmic radio source marked the beginnings of *radio astronomy. The optical and radio windows, together with several narrow-band infrared windows are the only wavelength ranges at which ground-based astronomical observations are possible.

The advent of high-altitude balloons and rockets and then artificial satellites orbiting above the atmosphere has revolutionized astronomy: the radiation from space that is absorbed by the atmosphere—gamma rays, X-rays, ultraviolet, and most wavelengths of infrared radiation—can now be studied in ever-increasing detail by equipment carried on these platforms. Investigations of cosmic sources of X-rays, gamma rays, and ultraviolet radiation are providing information on the more violent phenomena occurring in the universe. Observations of infrared sources, by satellite-based and high-altitude ground-based telescopes, are yielding information on, for example, the birth of stars. In addition planetary probes, such as the two Voyager craft, have greatly increased our knowledge of many members of the solar system.

Highly sensitive electronic devices are now available to detect the various forms of radiation from celestial bodies, while computer systems are used to control the major telescopes and their anciliary instruments and to process the information they gather. The advances in observational astronomy produce results that in turn develop the theoretical branches of astronomy, such as *cosmology.

astrophysics The study of the physical and chemical processes and characteristics associated with celestial objects. It is based on theories developed in astronomy, physics, and chemistry and on observations of the radiation emitted by the objects. Originally only studies at optical and then at radio and infrared wavelengths were made, but with the recent advent of rockets and artificial satellites, sources of X-rays, gamma rays, and ultraviolet radiation can also be observed. *See also* cosmology.

Asturias A coastal region in NW Spain corresponding to the present-day province of Oviedo. When the Muslims invaded Spain in 718, the Visigoths withdrew to Asturias, where, protected by the Cantabrian Mountains in the S, they established a new kingdom, preserving Visigothic and Christian traditions. During the next two centuries, Asturias, the sole surviving Christian Spanish kingdom and the centre of resistance to the Muslim advance, expanded into León and Galicia, especially under Alfonso III (reigned 866–c. 910). After his death the kingdom was divided between León, Castile, and Navarre.

Asturias, Miguel Ángel (1899–1974) Guatemalan novelist and poet. His novel *El Señor Presidente* (1946) is a study of political dictatorship; many of his other works, such as *Hombres de Maíz* (1949) and *Mulata de tal* (1960), reflect his interest in Mayan mythology and culture. He was awarded the Nobel Prize in 1967.

Asunción 25 15S 57 40W The capital of Paraguay, an important port in the S on the River Paraguay. Founded in 1536, it was for a time the centre of the Spanish settlements in the area. The National University was founded in 1890 and the Catholic University in 1960. Industries include flour milling, food processing, and textiles. Population (1983): 708 000.

Aswan (*or* Assuan; Greek name: Syene) 24 05N 32 56E A city in S Egypt, on the River Nile. Some ruins of the ancient city of Syene remain. The city is a popular tourist centre and winter resort. Nearby quarries supplied granite for many Egyptian monuments. The *Aswan High Dam and earlier Aswan Dam are also nearby and have stimulated growth within the city. Population (1983 est): 174 000.

Aswan High Dam A major dam in Egypt, on the River Nile near Aswan. Begun in 1960 and financed by the Soviet Union, it was completed in 1970. It is about 5 km (3 mi) long and 100 m (328 ft) high; its reservoir, **Lake Nasser**, extends for about 560 km (350 mi) behind the dam. Since its construction the famous annual Nile floods have been controlled and water is available for irrigation, for domestic and industrial purposes, and for hydroelectric power. Ancient Nubian monuments (notably the *Abu Simbel and Philae temples) that were threatened with permanent flooding were moved to new sites. About 7 km (4 mi) downstream is the earlier **Aswan Dam** (completed 1902); 2 km (1.2 mi) long and 54 m (177 ft) high, this provides irrigation water.

asymptote A straight line that a two-dimensional curve approaches but never meets as the curve is extended infinitely.

Asyut (*or* Assiut; ancient name: Lycopolis) 27 14N 31 07S The largest city in Upper Egypt, on the River Nile. It is an important commercial centre and is renowned for its handicrafts, such as ivory carvings and tulle shawls, and its textile industries. Below the city the Asyut barrage provides water for irrigation. It has a university (1957). Population (1983): 259 300.

Atacama Desert (Spanish name: Desierto de Atacama) A cool arid area in N central Chile, extending for about 1100 km (700 mi) S from the Peruvian border. It consists chiefly of a series of salt basins and is one of the driest areas in the world; in some parts no rain has ever been recorded. There are valuable deposits of copper and it is a major source of nitrates. Area: about 80 290 sq km (31 000 sq mi).

Atahuallpa (or Atahualpa; d. 1533) The last King of the Inca Empire (1532–33). On the death of his father Huayna Capac (1525) the Empire was divided between Atahuallpa and his brother Huascar. Atahuallpa overthrew his brother and declared himself king but was then captured by the Spanish conquistador Pizarro and, in spite of agreeing to the payment of a ransom, was executed.

Atalanta A swift-footed huntress of Greek mythology. Hippomenes (or Meilanion), on his promise to marry any man who could outrun her, raced with her. Furnished with three of the Hesperides' golden apples by *Aphrodite, which he dropped to distract her, he won the race and married her.

KEMAL ATATÜRK *In the centre, photographed in 1922.*

Atatürk, Kemal (Mustafa Kemal; 1881–1938) Turkish statesman, who was the chief founder of modern Turkey; president (1923–38). Born in Salonika, he entered the army and distinguished himself in World War I. After the war he opposed the humiliating Treaty of Sèvres and as president of the provisional government organized the defeat of the Greek invasion of Asia Minor (1920). In 1922 the Ottoman sultan was deposed and Mustafa Kemal became the first president of Turkey. From then until his death he worked to make Turkey a modern secular state. He took the surname Atatürk (Father of the Turks) in 1934.

ataxia Loss of muscular coordination, often caused by disease of the part of the brain (the cerebellum) that controls movement. Ataxia may accompany severe vitamin B_{12} and folic acid deficiencies or follow a brain haemorrhage.

Atget, (Jean) Eugène (Auguste) (1856–1927) French photographer. He turned to photography in 1898 after a career first at sea and later on the stage. He specialized in scenes of Parisian life, including a notable series on brothels (commissioned 1921). Apart from Man *Ray's interest in the surrealist effect of his shop-window series, he received recognition only after his death.

Athabasca, Lake A lake in W Canada, in NW Saskatchewan and NE Alberta, drained by the Slave River. Uranium ores were discovered on the N shore (1950s). Area: 8080 sq km (3120 sq mi).

Athabascan A group of North American Indian languages spoken by tribes living to the west of Hudson Bay in Alaska and Canada, and by some tribes of the SW USA. The northern group includes Koyukon, Tanana, *Chippewa, Slave, and Yellowknife, and the southern group includes *Apache and *Navajo.

Athabasca River A river in W Canada, in N Alberta flowing from the Rocky Mountains to Lake Athabasca through tar sands estimated to contain half the world's known oil reserves. Length: 1230 km (765 mi).

Athanasian Creed A Christian profession of faith traditionally attributed to St *Athanasius but probably dating from the 5th century. Its central statements concern the doctrines of the *Trinity and of the *Incarnation. Once popular in the Western Churches, it is now little used.

Athanasius, St (296–373 AD) Egyptian churchman, Bishop of Alexandria. After attending the Council of *Nicaea in 325, he was appointed Bishop of Alexandria in 328 and remained primate of Egypt for 43 years. During this time he led the opposition to the powerful *Arianism that flourished in the East under the emperors Constantine and Constantius. He was expelled from his see four times, but his orthodox teaching regarding the divinity of Jesus Christ was ultimately affirmed by the Council of Constantinople (381). Feast day: 2 May.

atheism The denial of the existence of God (or gods). Historically atheism has taken many different forms. In theocratic societies charges of atheism were frequently made against individuals or groups suspected of antisocial behaviour or of dissent from the prevailing orthodoxy. Philosophical materialists, such as *Hobbes, were also attacked as atheists but the spread of *rationalism in the 18th century created a climate sympathetic to atheism. In the 19th century, scientific advances challenged the old arguments for the existence of God, making atheism respectable philosophically, if not socially. Today rigorous atheists hold either that the concept of God, being untestable, is simply meaningless (*see* logical positivism) or that all we know by scientific means about the universe suggests that God is a false notion (*see* humanism). *Compare* agnosticism.

Athelney, Isle of A small area in Somerset, near the confluence of the Rivers Tone and Parrett. It was formerly an island, isolated by marshes. Alfred the Great built a small fortification here in 878 as a base for his campaign against the Danes.

Athelstan (d. 939) King of England (925–39), succeeding his father Edward the Elder; he was crowned King of Mercia in 924. He defeated a Scottish invasion force in 937 and is also known for six extant legal codes.

Athena (or Pallas Athena) The Greek goddess of war and of wisdom, the protectress of Athens. Born from the head of Zeus, fully armed with a javelin, she was his favourite child. In the Trojan War she constantly aided the Greeks. She also helped Heracles in his labours and guided Perseus on his expedition against the Gorgons. Odysseus voyaged home from Troy under her protection. A virgin goddess, in peacetime she was a patroness of the arts and industry. Athens is named after her, and the Parthenon was the centre of her worship. She is identified with the Roman *Minerva.

Athenagoras (2nd century AD) Greek Christian apologist, who taught in Athens and Alexandria. His *Apology* or

Legatio pro Christianis (177) addressed to *Marcus Aurelius, defended Christianity against charges of cannibalism and licentiousness arising from misunderstandings of the doctrines of the Eucharist and universal love.

ATHENS *The Parthenon.*

Athens (Modern Greek name: Athínai) 37 59N 23 42E The capital of Greece, situated on a plain in the SE of the country near the Saronic Gulf. It is the administrative, cultural, and economic centre of the country and is administratively joined to its port and main industrial sector, *Piraeus. Tourism is an important source of revenue. Athens is a city that combines the ancient and the modern, with only one or two small Byzantine and neo-Byzantine churches surviving to testify to the period between Roman times and the early 19th century. The many remains of ancient Athens are focused on the Acropolis. Crowned by the *Parthenon, it contains the Ionic Erechtheum, the Propylaea (a gateway), and the tiny temple of Athena Nike. To the NW, the recently restored Agora (market), contains the Theseum (5th century BC), probably the best-preserved ancient temple. To the N and E lies modern Athens, which includes the university, founded in 1837. *History*: there is evidence of settlements dating back to the 3rd millennium BC. Athens probably enjoyed its first rise to fame under Pisistratus and his sons in the 6th century BC. Around the year 506 Cleisthenes established a democracy for the free men of Athens. During the following century it became the leading Greek city state, defeating the Persians with the aid of its powerful navy (*see* Greek-Persian Wars). The Long Walls, connecting the city to Piraeus, and the Parthenon date from this period. Under Pericles, it reached a peak of intellectual brilliance with the philosophy of Socrates and the drama of Aeschylus, Sophocles, and Euripides. Defeated by Sparta in the *Peloponnesian War (431–404), it recovered slowly, regaining its intellectual supremacy with such figures as Plato, Aristotle, and Aristophanes. Its role as a major political power, however, was finally lost when defeated by Philip of Macedon in 338 BC, and in the 2nd century BC it came under the rule of Rome. Owing to the influence of Hellenic culture on the Romans it continued to prosper and, despite being overrun by Germanic tribes in the 4th century AD, maintained its academic standing until the closure of the schools of philosophy by Justinian in 529. The city fell to the Crusaders in 1204 and was under Turkish occupation from 1456 until 1833, when it became the capital of the newly independent kingdom of Greece. It has been the scene of frequent revolts and civil wars and was occupied by the Germans in World War II. Population (1981): 885 136.

atherosclerosis (*or* atheroma) Patchy thickening of the lining of arteries caused by the deposition of fatty material and fibrous tissue. This tends to obstruct the blood flow and predisposes to *thrombosis, which may lead to a heart attack or a stroke. In the western world atherosclerosis is common in adults: its cause is believed to be associated with a diet high in animal fats (*see* cholesterol) and refined sugar, cigarette smok-

ing, and obesity. Its incidence increases with age and it is exacerbated by high blood pressure. Its extent can be reduced by treatment of any underlying illness.

athlete's foot. *See* ringworm.

athletics Sports that involve running, walking, throwing, and jumping competitions. They are divided into track and field events. At international level the track events include races over 100 m, 200 m, 400 m, 800 m, 1500 m, 5000 m, and 10 000 m; the 110 m and 400 m hurdles (*see* hurdling); the 4 × 100 and 4 × 400 m relay races; the 3000 m steeplechase; the *marathon; and the 20 km walk (*see* walking). The standard field events are *high jump, *long jump, *triple jump, *pole vault, *shot put, *discus throw, *hammer throw, and *javelin throw. In addition there are the *decathlon (for men), the modern pentathlon, and the *pentathlon (for women). The governing body is the International Amateur Athletic Federation.

Athlone, Alexander Cambridge, 1st Earl of (1874–1957) British soldier and administrator, who was the brother of George V's consort Queen Mary and married Princess Alice (1883–1981), a granddaughter of Queen Victoria. After service in the Boer War and World War I, he was governor general of South Africa (1925–31) and of Canada (1940–45).

Athos, Mount 1. 40 10N 24 19E A mountain in NE Greece, at the end of Aktí, the easternmost promontory of Chalcidice. Height: 2033 m (6670 ft). 2. An autonomous Greek Orthodox monastic republic occupying the mountain. Area: 80 sq km (31 sq mi). Population (1981): 1472.

Atlanta 33 45N 84 23W A city in the USA, the capital of Georgia, situated at the foot of the Appalachian Mountains. Founded in 1837 and partly destroyed by Gen Sherman in 1864, it is now the industrial, administrative, transportation, and cultural centre of the SE USA. Its major industries include aircraft, machinery, cottonseed oil, textiles, clothing, and chemicals. Population (1980): 425 022.

Atlantic, Battle of the. *See* World War II.

Atlantic Charter (1941) A declaration made by Franklin D. Roosevelt and Winston Churchill that stated common national policies. These included freedom of choice of government, improved economic and social conditions, freedom of the seas, and the abolition of Nazism.

Atlantic City 39 23N 74 27W A city in the USA, in New Jersey on Absecon Beach (an island on the Atlantic coast). A major pleasure resort, it has five piers and a multitude of amusements, shops, hotels, and parks; gambling casinos were introduced in the late 1970s. A popular conference centre, it is the site of the annual Miss America Pageant (first held in 1921). Its industries include glassware, china, and confectionery. Population (1980): 40 199.

Atlantic Intracoastal Waterway A shipping route along the Atlantic coast of the USA. It serves the ports between Cape Cod and Florida Bay. Length: 2495 km (1550 mi).

Atlantic Ocean The world's second largest ocean, extending between Antarctica, America, Europe, and Africa. It is the world's most heavily travelled seaway, although floating ice is a hazard. Its major currents include the *Gulf Stream crossing it W–E. Its floor is rich in minerals, oil and gas now being exploited. The Mid-Atlantic Ridge rises above sea level as islands, such as the Azores. The youngest ocean, the Atlantic was formed when the continents now surrounding it split apart 200 million years ago.

Atlantic Wall The extensive fortifications built by the Germans in *World War II along the Atlantic coast. They failed to prevent *D-day Normandy landings by US and British troops (6 June, 1944).

Atlantis In Greek legend, a large island civilization in the Atlantic beyond the Pillars of Hercules (Straits of Gibraltar), which, according to Plato's dialogues the *Timaeus* and *Critias*, was destroyed by earthquake. The story, transmitted to the Greeks by the Egyptians, may refer to a cataclysmic volcanic eruption (c. 1450 BC) on the island of *Thera in the Cyclades N of Crete.

Atlas In Greek mythology, the brother of Prometheus and son of the Titan Iapetus and the nymph Clymene. As a punishment for his part in the revolt of the Titans against the Olympians he was forced to hold up the pillars separating heaven from earth. From the 16th century this was commonly depicted in the frontispieces of books of maps, which thus came to be called atlases.

Atlas Mountains A mountain system in NW Africa, extending generally NE from the Atlantic coast of Morocco to Tunisia. It consists of several mountain chains and plateaus and rises to 4165 m (13 664 ft) at Mount Toubkal in the Moroccan Great Atlas range.

atman (Sanskrit: breath, soul) A fundamental concept of Hinduism, signifying the individual soul or the eternal essential self. When the body dies the *atman* is continuously reincarnated until final spiritual release is achieved. In the later *Upanishads, and in the Hindu philosophical schools of Samkhya and orthodox Vedanta, the function of *atman* and its relation to *Brahman is the central issue. Some thinkers regard these two as analogous principles only; for others they are essentially identical.

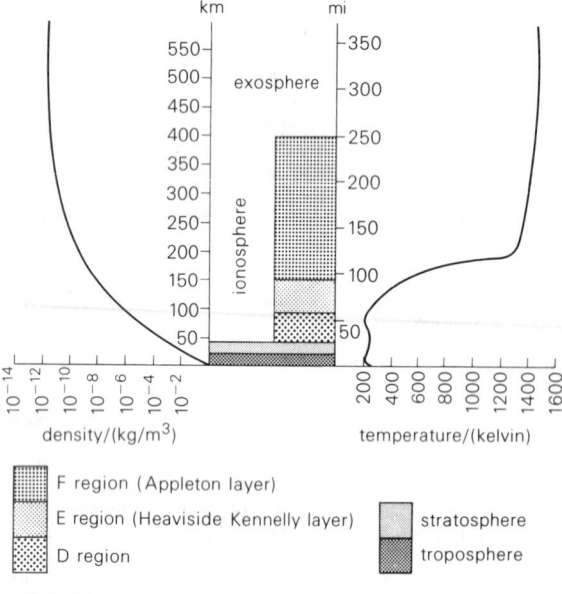

ATMOSPHERE *The density of the atmosphere falls off sharply with height above the earth's surface. The more complicated temperature variation is shown in the graph, which also illustrates the regions of the ionosphere.*

atmosphere (meteorology) The gaseous envelope surrounding the earth or any other celestial body. The earth's atmosphere is composed of nitrogen (78.08%), oxygen (20.95%), argon (0.93%), and carbon dioxide (0.03%), together with small proportions of other gases and variable amounts of water vapour. In the lowest layer of the earth's atmosphere, the **troposphere**, air temperature decreases as height increases. The thickness of this layer varies from about 7 km (4.5 mi) to about 16 km (10 mi) at the equator. It is here that most meteorological phenomena occur. In the **stratosphere**, which goes up to about 50 km (31 mi), temperature is fairly constant because the sun's radiation counteracts the effect of decreasing density. Above the stratosphere lie the **mesosphere**, extending up to about 80 km (50 mi), in which temperatures decrease with height, and the **thermosphere**, in which temperatures increase with height; these fall within the *ionosphere. The outermost

layer, from about 400 km (248 mi), is called the **exosphere**. From 100 km (62 mi) upwards the oxygen dissociates into atoms. There is little nitrogen above 150 km (93 mi). The atmosphere protects the earth from excessive radiation and cosmic particles and is important in maintaining the heat balance of the earth. *See also* ozone.

atmosphere (unit) A unit of pressure equal to 101 325 pascals or 760 millimetres of mercury.

atmospheric pressure The pressure exerted by the atmosphere. It decreases with altitude and, at ground level, varies around 760 millimetres of mercury, 101 325 pascals, or 1013.25 millibars.

atom. *See* atomic theory.

atomic bomb. *See* nuclear weapons.

atomic clock A highly accurate clock based on the frequency at which certain atoms or molecules vibrate between two states. For example, the nitrogen atom in the ammonia molecule vibrates through the plane of the three hydrogen atoms and back again with a frequency of 23 870 hertz. In the ammonia clock, a quartz-crystal oscillator feeds energy into ammonia gas at this frequency. The ammonia only absorbs energy at this frequency, enabling a feedback circuit to control the frequency of the oscillator. *See also* caesium clock.

atomic energy. *See* nuclear energy.

Atomic Energy Authority A UK body established in 1954 to research into and develop nuclear energy. Its principal research establishments are situated at Harwell and Culham, both in Oxfordshire.

Atomic Energy Commission A US agency established in 1946 to control the production of nuclear weapons and atomic energy.

atomic mass unit (amu) A unit of mass equal to one-twelfth of the mass of an atom of carbon-12 (1.660 33 × 10^{-27} kg). Atomic weights (relative atomic masses) are based on this unit. The unit is also called the dalton (after John *Dalton).

atomic number (Z) The number of protons in a nucleus of an atom. It determines the position of the element in the *periodic table and, in a neutral atom, is equal to the number of electrons surrounding the nucleus. It is also known as proton number.

atomic theory The theory that an atom is the smallest particle of an element that can take part in a chemical reaction. *Democritus is credited with first conceiving the idea, which was, however, vigorously attacked by *Aristotle since Democritus's atoms existed in a vacuum, an idea repugnant to Aristotle. The atomic concept fell from favour until the early 19th century, when John *Dalton used the idea to explain the fact that elements combined together in simple proportions. The structure of the atom was first investigated by Lord *Rutherford, who discovered that it consisted of a heavy positively charged core (the *nucleus) surrounded by *electrons. Niels Bohr elaborated on this model (*see* Bohr atom) but the modern concept of the atom was not finally elucidated until the advent of Schrödinger's *wave mechanics.

Almost all of the atom's mass is concentrated in the nucleus, which consists of positively charged *protons and neutral *neutrons of almost equal mass (the mass of the electron is only 1/1836 that of the proton). The number of electrons in a neutral atom is equal to the number of protons in the nucleus, as the charge on the proton is equal but opposite to that of the electron. The electrons can be thought of as existing in a series of shells around the nucleus, each shell corresponding to a particular energy level. According to the *Pauli exclusion principle each shell may only hold a certain number of electrons. The chemical behaviour of an atom is largely determined by the number of electrons in its outermost shell, as atoms are most stable when they have no partly filled shells, a state often achieved by chemical

There is no simple way to illustrate an atom:

by the 19th century it was regarded as a minute solid billiard ball;

with the work of Rutherford between 1906 and 1914 and Bohr in 1913 it was depicted as a miniature solar system with a central nucleus and orbiting electron;

Sommerfeld's refinements of quantum theory in 1916 led to a model with precessing elliptical orbits and spinning electrons;

by 1926 Schrödinger's wave mechanics had been published, based on de Broglie's dual wave – particle concept of electrons. The atom is now regarded as a nucleus surrounded by a "haze" of probabilities that electrons will occur in certain positions.

The main characteristic of an atom, as the smallest particle of matter, is not what our models of it look like but the way it absorbs and emits energy.

When an atom absorbs energy (e.g. when light of the right wavelength falls on it) its electrons jump to a higher energy level.

When these electrons fall back to their original (ground) state they emit energy (as light, ultraviolet, etc.).

All matter and therefore all atoms, according to modern physics, consists of two kinds of particles: leptons and quarks. Electrons are leptons; the particles of the nucleus (protons and neutrons) are each made up of different arrangements of three quarks.

The simplest atomic nucleus is the hydrogen nucleus consisting of one proton.

An isotope of hydrogen, deuterium, has a nucleus consisting of one proton and one neutron.

All other nuclei consist of arrangements of protons and neutrons. The carbon nucleus consists of six protons and six neutrons.

ATOMIC THEORY

combination. In combining, atoms may either share electrons to form covalent bonds or gain (or lose) electrons to form electrovalent (ionic) bonds (*see* chemical bond).
All the nuclei of an element contain the same number of protons (p) but not always the same number of neutrons (n). Atoms with the same value of p but a different value of n are called istopes of that element. The value of ($n + p$) is called the mass number. Isotopes are referred to in several ways, e.g. uranium-235, U-235, ^{235}U, $^{235}_{92}$U (the subscript in this case being the *atomic number, the value 235 being the mass number of a particular uranium isotope). *See also* particle physics.

atomic weight The ratio of the average mass of the atoms in a given sample to one-twelfth the mass of a carbon-12 atom. The modern, more correct, name is relative atomic mass.

atomism The philosophical attitude that seeks irreducible elements, whether of matter or thought, to account for the

(compound) phenomena that we actually experience. The Greek *Democritus believed that the world is composed of qualitatively similar atoms of different shapes. In this view, atoms may be either completely independent of one another or related in contingent or necessary ways. *Lucretius was an influential proponent of atomism, and *Gassendi, *Boyle, and *Locke revived it in the 17th century. Logical atomism, held temporarily by both *Russell and *Wittgenstein, assumed that there were unanalysable specks of meaning that could be articulated in atomic propositions, from which no subordinate proposition could be derived.

Aton In Egyptian religion, the one supreme god proclaimed by *Akhenaton and symbolized by a solar disc with arms.

atonality The use in music of all 12 notes of the scale in such a way as to avoid *tonality. Atonality arose from the increasing *chromaticism of the music of the late 19th century. Schoenberg's second string quartet (1907-08), for example, begins in the key of F sharp minor but has an atonal final movement. *See also* serialism.

atonement In religious belief, the idea of reconciliation between God and man or, literally, at-one-ment with God. The idea implies that the relationship between God and mankind has been interrupted or damaged by human failing or sin. In Judaism, *Yom Kippur or the Day of Atonement is the holiest day of the year. In Christianity, the crucifixion of Christ is traditionally interpreted as a sacrifice for men's sins that effects a reconciliation with God and brings to an end the estrangement started by Adam's sin.

ATP (adenosine triphosphate) An energy-rich compound (a nucleotide) with an important role in the metabolism of living organisms. On its formation from ADP (adenosine diphosphate) in the mitochondria of cells, ATP incorporates a large amount of energy that, on release, is used by cells to manufacture proteins, carbohydrates, etc., and to provide energy for muscle contraction and other dynamic processes.

Atreus In Greek mythology, King of Mycenae, the son of Pelops and father of Agamemnon and Menelaus. His house was cursed as a result of a feud between him and his brother Thyestes over the throne of Mycenae. After Thyestes had seduced his wife, Atreus killed Thyestes' sons and served them at a feast. Another son of Thyestes, Aegisthus, later killed Atreus.

atrium (architecture) **1.** Originally an important part of a Roman house, a central, partly covered court, frequently colonnaded, which often contained the shrine to the household god. Around it were the entrances to the main rooms. Later it became the main reception room of the house. **2.** An open area or courtyard in front of early Christian churches.

atropine An alkaloid, extracted from deadly nightshade, that acts on certain nerves of the autonomic nervous system. It is used during anaesthesia to decrease lung secretions, which lowers the risk of postoperative chest infections. It also dilates the pupil and speeds up the heart rate.

Atropos. *See* Fates.

Attalus I Soter (269–197 BC) Ruler of *Pergamum (241–197), who took the title of king after a victory over the Galatians (before 230). By his conquests in Asia Minor and his support of Rome against Philip V of Macedon (237–179; reigned 220–179), he made Pergamum a significant power.

attar of roses (otto of rose *or* essence of rose) A fragrant colourless or pale-yellow oil distilled from fresh rose petals. It is produced in Bulgaria, S France, Morocco, and Turkey. About 1 gram of attar is extracted from 4 kilograms of roses. Rosewater is a by-product of the distillation. It is used to make perfumes and in flavourings.

Attenborough, Sir Richard (1923–) British film actor, director, and producer. After numerous appearances in British war films and comedies he developed into a versatile character actor in such films as *Loot* (1969) and *10 Rillington Place* (1971). As director, his films include *Young Winston* (1974), *A Bridge Too Far* (1977), *Gandhi* (1982), *A Chorus Line* (1985), and *Cry Freedom* (1987). His brother **Sir David Attenborough** (1926–) is a naturalist and broadcaster, whose television series include *Zoo Quest* (1954), *Life on Earth* (1978), and *The Living Planet* (1983).

attenuation The reduction in amplitude of an electromagnetic wave or an electric current during transmission. In electric circuits attenuation is often introduced to reduce unwanted components of a signal. Broadcast electromagnetic radiation is attenuated as it passes through buildings, etc., and to a lesser extent by its passage through the atmosphere. In space, however, the attenuation is negligible.

Attica A region of ancient E central Greece. According to Greek legend the 12 towns of Attica were united by Theseus into a single state, which was dominated by Athens by the 5th century BC.

Attila (c. 406–53) King of the Huns (434–53), known as the Scourge of God. After murdering his brother and coruler, Bleda, he extended his possessions in central Europe and attacked (441–43) the eastern frontier of the Roman Empire. In 451 he invaded Gaul and suffered his only defeat, at the battle of the *Catalaunian Plains. His campaigns in Italy (452) caused much destruction. The pope paid him to spare Rome and Attila died shortly afterwards.

Attlee, Clement (Richard), 1st Earl (1883–1967) British statesman; Labour prime minister (1945–51). A barrister by profession, Attlee taught at the London School of Economics (1913–23) and became mayor of Stepney (1919). He was elected MP for Limehouse in 1922 and was leader of the Labour Party (1935–55) and deputy prime minister of the wartime coalition government (1942–45). As the first postwar prime minister he presided over the establishment of the welfare state, nationalizing major industries and introducing the *National Health Service. His government also granted independence within the Commonwealth to India.

attorney general The chief law officer of the Crown in England and Wales and its representative in the courts. He is legal adviser to the government and the House of Commons, of which he is always a member and to which he is answerable, and is head of the English bar. He advises on the drafting of Acts of Parliament. With his subordinate, the director of public prosecutions, he prosecutes crimes in the sovereign's name.

Aube, River A river in N central France, rising on the Plateau de Langres and flowing NW to the River Seine. Length: 225 km (140 mi).

Auber, Daniel François Esprit (1782–1871) French composer. He is remembered for his 48 operas, chiefly light works to librettos by the playwright A. E. Scribe (1791–1861), written for the Paris Opéra-Comique. Of these only *La Muette de Portici* (1828) and *Fra Diavolo* (1830) are performed with any frequency.

aubergine A spiny herbaceous plant, *Solanum melongena*, native to S Asia and also known as eggplant. It is commonly grown in warmer regions for its fruit, a large white, yellow, or purple berry that is eaten as a vegetable. The plant grows to a height of 60–100 cm. Family: *Solanaceae*.

Aubrey, John (1626–97) English antiquary. *Miscellanies* (1696), a collection of folklore, was his only work published during his lifetime, but he is best known for the biographical material he collected, which was published during the 19th century as *Lives of Eminent Men* (1813) and *Brief Lives* (1898). A successful one-man play based on his *Brief Lives* was produced in 1967.

Aubrietia (*or* Aubrieta) A genus of trailing herbaceous perennial flowering plants (about 15 species), native to mountainous areas of E Europe and W Asia. *A. deltoidea* is commonly grown in rock gardens, bearing small purple, red, or pink flowers. Family: *Cruciferae*.

Aubusson 45 58N 2 10E A town in central France, in the Creuse department on the River Creuse. It has been renowned for its carpets and tapestries since the 16th century. Population (1982 est): 6153.

Aubusson, Pierre d' (1423–1503) French cardinal and grand master of the Knights *Hospitallers. Remembered chiefly for his defence of Rhodes against the Turks in 1480, he secured a long-term truce in 1481 by agreeing to imprison the Ottoman sultan's enemy and brother.

Auch 43 40N 0 36E A market town in SW France, the capital of the Gers department on the River Gers. The former capital of Armagnac and Gascony, it has a gothic cathedral with a magnificent 17th-century organ. Population (1982 est): 25 543.

Auchinleck, Sir Claude (1884–1981) British field marshal. He served his apprenticeship in the Middle East in World War I. In World War II, after a brief period in Norway and then as commander in chief in India, he succeeded Wavell in

N Africa (1941). He reached Cyrenaica, only to be pushed back by Rommel. Blamed, probably unjustly, for the retreat, he was replaced by Alexander and returned to his previous post in India.

Auckland 36 55S 174 47E The largest city and port in New Zealand, on North Island occupying an isthmus between Waitemata Harbour and Manukau Harbour. Founded in 1840, it was the capital of New Zealand until 1865. The University of Auckland was established in 1882 and there are two cathedrals (Roman Catholic and Anglican). The city is connected with the mainly residential North Shore by Auckland Harbour Bridge (1959). Auckland is a major industrial centre with engineering, food processing, ship-building, and chemical industries. The chief exports are iron and steel, dairy products, and meat. Population (1985 est): 894 000.

Auckland, George Eden, Earl of (1784–1849) British statesman; governor general of India (1836–42). He attempted to control Afghanistan against Russian and Persian expansion in central Asia. Following Afghan attacks on British forces, he was recalled.

Auckland Islands 50 35S 166 00E A group of six uninhabited islands in the S Pacific Ocean, belonging to New Zealand. An attempt to introduce cattle and sheep was unsuccessful (1852). Area: 611 sq km (234 sq mi).

auction A method of selling goods publicly, in which many prospective buyers compete with each other, the sale being made to the highest bidder. If bidding does not reach a reserve price specified by the vendor, then the auctioneer withdraws the goods. Rules vary from trade to trade, but the auctioneer usually acts as the seller's agent, charging him a commission on goods sold. Antiques, works of art, houses, and some commercial commodities are sold by auction. In a **Dutch auction**, the sale is offered first at an unrealistically high price, which is lowered gradually until a bid is made.

Auden, W(ystan) H(ugh) (1907–73) British poet. His early volumes, beginning with *Poems* (1930) and *Look, Stranger!* (1936), established him as the leading figure of a group of left-wing poets of the 1930s, the other members of which were Stephen *Spender, Louis *MacNeice, and C. *Day Lewis. He also wrote verse dramas in collaboration with Christopher *Isherwood, with whom he went to the USA in 1939. He became a US citizen in 1946, returning to England while he was professor of poetry at Oxford (1956–61). He wrote several opera libretti, notably for Stravinsky's *The Rake's Progress* (1951), and his later poetry was characterized by a form of Christian existentialism that replaced his earlier Marxism.

Audenarde. See Oudenaarde.

audio frequency A frequency in the range 20 to 20 000 hertz, i.e. the range of frequencies to which the human ear is sensitive.

audiovisual education Education carried out with the help of audio (sound) or visual techniques. There are a whole range of audiovisual aids, including television, tape and video recorders, teaching machines, overhead projectors, and the long-established wallcharts and blackboards. Although audiovisual education has been used throughout history, its systematic application developed in the 20th century. Research has shown that, when properly used, it increases both the student's interest and his recall of the material presented. Since 1958 the US Congress has provided aid for educational broadcasting. In the UK, the BBC and the independent television companies run an extensive educational service. *See also* Open University.

auditing. See accountancy.

Audubon, John James (1785–1851) US naturalist and artist noted for his lifelike drawings and paintings of birds. Educated in France, Audubon emigrated to the USA, where he developed an interest in bird migration and began painting birds and other animals. *The Birds of America* (4 vols,

1827–38) established his reputation as an illustrator. The National Audubon Society, founded in his honour in 1886, is dedicated to the conservation of birds throughout the USA.

Augereau, Pierre François Charles, Duc de Castiglione (1757–1816) French marshal. He rose rapidly in the French army, serving under Napoleon in Italy. In 1797 he directed the coup d'état against the royalists who threatened the government of the *Directory. He subsequently opposed Napoleon but his uncertain loyalties forced his retirement after the restoration of the monarchy.

Auger effect The spontaneous ejection of an electron from an excited, singly charged, positive ion to form a doubly charged ion. The ion may be excited by a gamma ray from its nucleus or by bombarding it with particles, such as photons or electrons. It is named after the French physicist Pierre Auger (1899–).

Aughrim, Battle of (12 July, 1691) The final defeat of the main army of the former King James II of England by the army of William III in Ireland. It was the most disastrous battle in Irish history, with 7000 Jacobite dead. It is still celebrated, together with the battle of the *Boyne, by Ulster Unionists on its anniversary (*see also* Orange Order).

Augsburg 48 21N 10 54E A city in S West Germany, in Bavaria at the confluence of the Rivers Wertach and Lech. It is a major industrial centre; its manufactures include textiles, chemicals, cars, aircraft, and printing machinery. Many of its historic buildings, including the 10th-century cathedral, survived the bombardment of World War II. *History*: founded by the Romans in 15 BC, it became an important banking and commercial centre in the 15th and 16th centuries mainly with the aid of the Fugger and Welsen merchant families. An imperial free city from 1276, it was the seat of the notable diets of 1530 (*see* Augsburg Confession) and 1555 (*see* Augsburg, Peace of). It is the birthplace of Holbein and Brecht. Population (1980 est): 246 600.

Augsburg, League of (1686) An alliance originally consisting of the Holy Roman Empire, Spain, Sweden, and several German states. In 1689 they were joined by England, Holland, and Savoy, thus forming the *Grand Alliance, which waged war on Louis XIV of France from 1689 to 1697.

Augsburg, Peace of (1555) A religious compromise issued by an imperial diet at Augsburg, over which the future Emperor *Ferdinand I presided, which established the coexistence of Roman Catholicism and Lutheranism in Germany. Each prince was to determine the denomination of his territory, which was to be either Catholicism or Lutheranism. In order to safeguard Catholic property, any prince who became a Protestant was to renounce his land and revenues. The settlement gave Germany 50 years of peace.

Augsburg Confession The main and distinctive confession of faith of the Lutheran Churches. Drawn up in its original form by Melancthon and approved by Luther, it was presented to the imperial diet that Emperor Charles V had summoned at Augsburg in 1530 to judge Luther's controversial preaching.

augury Ritual divination practised in ancient Rome by augurs, priests skilled in the auspices, or interpretation of certain natural occurrences. The word "auspice" derives from the Latin for "bird" + "observation"; the commonest means of augury were the flight and song of birds, but thunder, lightning, movements of animals, and the appetites of tame chickens were also studied. Signs on the augur's left were propitious, those on his right unpropitious. Augury accompanied every major undertaking, to ascertain through the auspices whether the gods were favourably inclined.

Augusta 33 29N 82 00W A town in the USA, in Georgia on the Savannah River. It is a medical and service centre for the many government installations nearby. Population (1980): 47 532.

Augusta 44 17N 69 50W A city in the USA, the capital of Maine on the Kennebec River. Established as a trading post in 1628, it has a large timber industry. Population (1980): 21 819.

Augustine of Canterbury, St (died c. 604) Italian churchman, the first Archbishop of Canterbury. Chosen by Pope *Gregory I to evangelize England in 596, he converted Ethelbert I of Kent and successfully established Canterbury as the primatial see. He was less successful in persuading the already existing Welsh Celtic Church to acknowledge him as primate. Feast day: 26 or 27 May.

Augustine of Hippo, St (354-430 AD) North African theologian; Father and Doctor of the Church, born at Tagaste. His mother was a Christian but, after studying at Carthage, he became a Manichaean. He taught rhetoric in Rome and in Milan, where he was attracted to *Neoplatonism. However, under the influence of St *Ambrose, Bishop of Milan, he was finally converted to Christianity in 386. On his return to Africa, he lived as a monk until he was ordained at Hippo in 391. He became Bishop of Hippo in 396 and died there during a Vandal siege. His works are the most important and influential of those written by the early Fathers, especially *The City of God*, a defence of Christianity in 22 books, and his spiritual autobiography, *The Confessions*. His other writings include commentaries on the scriptures, sermons, letters, and treatises against the heresies *Manichaeism, Donatism (*see* Donatists), and Pelagianism (*see* Pelagius). He was most actively involved in the Pelagian controversy, in which he upheld the doctrines of original sin and divine grace. Feast day: 28 Aug.

Augustinians A term sometimes used generally to refer to all the Roman Catholic religious orders that follow the Rule of St Augustine, a programme for the religious life drawn up by *Augustine of Hippo. More specifically it refers to the orders of the Augustinian (*or* Austin) Canons, founded in the 11th century, and the Augustinian Hermits (*or* Austin Friars), founded in the 13th century, both of which have corresponding orders for women.

AUGUSTUS *During his reign the coinage was restored to the control of the Senate and coins were marked S.C. (senatus consulto, by decree of the Senate); the emperor's head is shown on the obverse (British Museum, London).*

Augustus (*or* Octavian; 63 BC-14 AD) The first Roman emperor, who restored the greatness of the Roman world following the disintegration of the Republic. Augustus, who was born Gaius Octavius, was the great-nephew and adopted son of Julius Caesar. After Caesar's assassination in 44, Augustus (now Gaius Julius Caesar Octavianus; *or* Octavian) came to an agreement with *Mark Antony and in 43 they formed the second *Triumvirate with *Lepidus. Lepidus was forced to retire in 36 and Augustus' relations with Mark Antony failed to withstand Antony's abandonment of his wife Octavia (Augustus' sister) for *Cleopatra. Antony's defeat at Actium in 31 allowed Augustus to establish his personal supremacy at the head of an autocratic

government known as the principate. In 27 he was proclaimed Augustus (sacred).

Augustus was an outstanding administrator and consolidated the so-called Pax Romana (Roman Peace) that he had established with a durable administrative and financial system. The patronage of his close adviser *Maecenas fostered a literary renaissance and with the military assistance of *Agrippa, and later of his own stepson *Tiberius, he secured and then expanded the Empire. In 4 AD he named Tiberius, the son of his third wife *Livia Drusilla, his heir. Augustus was deified after his death.

Augustus I (1526-86) Elector of Saxony (1553-86). A moderate Protestant, he was a follower of Lutheranism and a harsh opponent of Calvinism. His economic, administrative, and social reforms made Saxony one of the most prosperous German states.

Augustus (II) the Strong (1670-1733) King of Poland (1697-1706, 1710-33). Augustus' invasion of Livonia (1700) began the Great *Northern War, in which he was defeated by Charles XII of Sweden (1702). Augustus was deposed by the Polish diet (1704), formally abdicating in 1706, but was restored by Russia in 1710. His malgovernment precipitated Poland's decline.

auk A stout-bodied seabird belonging to a family (*Alcidae*; 22 species) occurring in the N hemisphere and having a black and white plumage and short pointed wings. The family includes *puffins, *razorbills, *guillemots, the little auk (*Plautus alle*), and the extinct flightless great auk (*Pinguinus impennis*). Order: *Charadriiformes* (gulls, plovers, etc.).

Aung San (c. 1914-47) Burmese statesman; leader of the independence movement. Committed to radical politics from his student days at Rangoon University, Aung San founded the Anti-Fascist People's Freedom League in 1944. He played a crucial role in the negotiations that led to Burmese independence from Britain but was assassinated before it was fully attained.

Aurangzeb (1618-1707) The last Mogul emperor of India (1658-1707); the youngest son of *Shah Jahan. When Shah Jahan fell ill in 1657 Aurangzeb fought a war of succession against his older brother Dara Shikoh. Easily winning, he ascended the throne of Delhi with the title Alamgir ("world-seizer"). A ruthless ruler, he augmented the empire to its greatest extent but in his fervent Muslim orthodoxy he made enemies of his Hindu subjects and in effect weakened Mogul power.

Aurelian(us), Lucius Domitius (c. 215-275 AD) Roman emperor (270-75). Aurelian was of humble birth and owed his accession to the army. He restored imperial unity by his victories over the Vandals, *Zenobia of Palmyra, and the Gallic Empire at Châlons. He was murdered near Byzantium.

Auric, Georges (1899-1983) French composer. Initially influenced by *Ravel and *Debussy, he later became a member of the avantgarde group Les *Six. He is best known for his scores for films, such as *À nous la liberté* (1932), *The Lavender Hill Mob* (1951), and *Moulin Rouge* (1952).

auricula A *primula, *P. auricula*, or any of the hybrids derived from it. Native to the Alps, it is widely grown as a garden plant, having showy yellow flowers.

Auriga (Latin: Charioteer) A conspicuous constellation in the N sky near Orion, lying in the Milky Way. The brightest star is *Capella.

Aurignacian A culture of the Upper *Palaeolithic marked by the use of thick scrapers and heavy blades of stone and flint, flat bone points, and polished bone or antler pins. First recognized at Aurignac (SW France) in 1860 the industry dates back to about 34 000 BC. Since it differs, especially in bonework, from earlier and later (*Gravettian) toolkits, Aurignacian culture may have come from outside Europe.

These people hunted mammoth and horse; they also engraved symbols and pictures on rocks (*see* Lascaux).

auroch An extinct European wild ox, *Bos primigenius*, that survived in Poland until the early 17th century. Standing 1.8 m at the shoulder, aurochs were black with long curved horns and are believed to be ancestors of modern domestic cattle.

aurora A display of diffuse changing coloured light seen high in the earth's atmosphere, often taking the form of streamers or drapery and usually green or red. Aurorae occur predominantly in polar regions when energetic charged particles from the sun become trapped in the earth's magnetic field. The rapidly moving particles interact with atoms and molecules in the upper atmosphere and cause them to emit light.

Aurora In Roman mythology, the goddess of the dawn. She was called Eos by the Greeks.

Auschwitz. *See* Oświęcim.

auscultation The use of a *stethoscope to listen to sounds produced within the body, which forms an essential part of a medical examination. Auscultation of lungs, heart, and intestines are the most useful for reaching a diagnosis.

Ausgleich (German: compromise; 1867) The constitutional settlement that established the Dual Monarchy of *Austria–Hungary (1867–1918).

Ausonius, Decimus Magnus (died c. 395 AD) Roman poet, born at Burdigala (Bordeaux). The tutor of *Gratian, Emperor Valentinian's son, Ausonius became governor of Gaul. *Mosella*, his most famous poem, was written in hexameters and described the River Moselle and its surrounding countryside.

JANE AUSTEN *The only portrait of her from life, which was done by her sister Cassandra.*

Austen, Jane (1775–1817) British novelist. She was the daughter of a clergyman and lived an outwardly uneventful life with her family in the south of England, settling in Chawton in Hampshire in 1809. Her six major novels are *Sense and Sensibility* (1811), *Pride and Prejudice* (1813), *Mansfield Park* (1814), *Emma* (1815–16), *Northanger Abbey* (1818), and *Persuasion* (1818). Their heroines are drawn from the rural landed gentry, and their plots trace the development of relationships that generally culminate in marriage. Her novels are distinguished by her delicate and often ironic wit and her sensitive insight into personal and social tensions.

austenite A form of *steel that exists when the metal is heated to about 1000°C, in which the carbon exists as a solid solution in the iron. Austenitic steels retain this structure at room temperature because of the presence of an alloying element, such as manganese. Austenite is nonmagnetic and has a high ductility. Named after Sir William C. Roberts-Austen (1843–1902).

Austerlitz, Battle of (2 December, 1805) The battle in which Napoleon's 68 000-strong army outmanoeuvred and defeated almost 90 000 Russians and Austrians led by *Kutuzov. It took place near Austerlitz (now Slavkov u Brna, Czechoslovakia). Napoleon's great victory forced the Austrians to make peace with France by the Treaty of Pressburg and the Russian army to return to Russia.

Austin 30 18N 97 47W A city in the USA, the capital of Texas on the Colorado River. The site of the University of Texas (1883), its industries include tourism and some manufacturing. Population (1980): 345 496.

Austin, Herbert, 1st Baron (1866–1941) British engineer, who founded the Austin Motor Company. He designed his first car, a three-wheeler named the Wolseley, in 1895. Production of Austin motor cars began in 1906 and the famous Austin Seven was first produced in 1921.

Austin, John (1790–1859) British jurist, famous for his work in jurisprudence. He was called to the Bar in 1818 and was later a professor at London University (1826–32), his lectures there providing the basis for his best-known book, *The Province of Jurisprudence Determined* (1832). In this he clarified the distinctions between the laws of the sovereign authority and the moral laws of God and man. Although unsupported in his own lifetime, Austin's ideas later became very influential in legal education.

Austin, John Langshaw (1911–60) British philosopher, who lived and worked in Oxford. Austin was an influential proponent of linguistic philosophy, holding that philosophical and conceptual difficulties can be elucidated and often dissolved by examining the language ordinarily used to talk about such concepts. He used this approach in his lectures, published posthumously in 1962 as *Sense and Sensibilia* and *How to Do Things with Words*. In the former he criticized certain philosophical views on perception and in the latter analysed the effects of meaningful utterances, which he called "speech acts."

Australasia A term applied loosely to encompass the islands of the S Pacific: Australia, New Zealand, New Guinea, and their associated islands. The Malay Archipelago and the Philippines are also sometimes included. *See also* Oceania.

Australia, Commonwealth of A country in the S Pacific, comprising the whole of the smallest continent and the island of Tasmania to the SE. External territories include *Norfolk Island, *Christmas Island, the *Cocos (Keeling) Islands, and the *Australian Antarctic Territory. Much of the country has a hot dry climate and a large part of the vast central plains are desert or semidesert. The most fertile areas are in the E, along the coastal plains, and in the extreme SW. The Great Barrier Reef lies off the tropical NE coast and the highest mountains, rising over 2000 m (7000 ft), are in the Great Dividing Range, which runs parallel to the E coast. The Murray River and its tributaries in the SE form the main river system. The inhabitants are very largely of European, especially British, origin but there are about 100 000 Aborigines and people of mixed race living in the interior. Since World War II the population has increased dramatically, largely as a result of immigration. *Economy*: agriculture continues to make a substantial contribution to the economy, the main crops being wheat and other cereals, sugar cane, and fruit. Livestock, particularly sheep and cattle, is also important. Since the 1960s, however, growth in the industrial sector has been especially marked, the leading manufactures being iron and steel products, transportation equipment, and machinery. Mining is now of vital importance, especially the extraction of coal, iron, bauxite, uranium, copper, lead, and zinc. There have been significant discoveries of oil and natural gas and about 70% of oil for home consumption is now produced in Australia. The main exports are wool, meat, cereals, sugar, iron ore, and nonferrous ores. *History*: the country was inhabited by the Aborigines, immigrants from SE Asia, for approximately 20 000 years before the arrival of the Europeans, beginning with the Portuguese in the 16th century and the Dutch in the early 17th century. In 1770 Captain Cook claimed the fertile E coast for Britain and the area, known as New South Wales, was at first used mainly as a penal colony, the American colonies no longer being available for this purpose. After the introduction of the merino sheep, however, civilian settlements were established further to the N and W towards the interior, eventually reaching the far side of the Blue Mountains in 1813. Colonies were developed in Tasmania, Western Australia, Victoria, South Australia, and Queensland. By 1829 the whole continent was a British dependency. Notable among the explorations carried out were those of Hamilton *Hume, Charles *Sturt, John McDouall *Stuart, and Robert *Burke and William John Wills (1834–61). The discovery of gold in Victoria in 1851 attracted large numbers of immigrants and from this period the colonies struggled for greater independence, developing broadly similar structures and policies. In 1901 the six colonies were federated to form the Commonwealth, becoming an independent dominion of the British Empire. In 1911 the site for the federal capital, under the title of the Australian Capital Territory, and the Northern Territory were added to the Commonwealth. Strong measures were introduced in the late 19th century to prevent immigration by non-Whites and these had a continuing influence on immigration policy. In 1974, however, Gough *Whitlam abolished the "white Australia" policy and a new immigration scheme was introduced in 1979, which was aimed at extending the country's nondiscriminatory image. Australia played a significant part in both World Wars, taking an important role in the Gallipoli campaign in World War I and cooperating closely with the USA in World War II. Since the war closer ties have been developed with Asia, especially with Japan, which now takes a third of Australia's exports. New Zealand and the USA also provide important export markets. In 1978 the Northern Territory achieved self-government although the federal government retained control over uranium. Australia is a member of the British Commonwealth. In 1986 Elizabeth II signed legislation formally ending constitutional links between Australia and the UK. Prime minister: Robert Hawke. Official language: English. Official currency: Australian dollar of 100 cents. Area: 7 686 884 sq km (2 967 283 sq mi). Population (1983 est): 15 451 900. Capital: Canberra. Main port: Sydney.

Australian Alps A mountain range in SE Australia. Part of the *Great Dividing Range, it extends from E Victoria into SE New South Wales and contains the *Snowy Mountains and Mount *Kosciusko, Australia's highest mountain. It is a popular winter-sports area.

Australian Antarctic Territory The area of Antarctica claimed by Australia. It includes all the land lying S of latitude 60°S and between longitudes 45°E and 160°E, excluding *Terre Adélie. Several research stations are sited here.

Australian Capital Territory An administrative division of SE Australia. It was created in 1911 from the Limestone Plains region of New South Wales as a site for *Canberra, the capital of Australia. Jervis Bay was transferred to the territory in 1915 for development as a seaport. It is the site of several important institutions, including the Australian Academy of Science, the Royal Military College, and the Royal Australian Naval College (at Jervis Bay). Area: 2432 sq km (939 sq mi). Population (1980 est): 226 600.

Australian Rules. *See* football.

Austral Islands. *See* Tubuai Islands.

Australopithecus A genus of fossil manlike higher primates of the late Pliocene and Pleistocene eras of S and E Africa. Although small in brain size, their cranial and skeletal structures were more like those of modern man than of apes. They walked erect and probably hunted and used primitive tools. They may have been the direct ancestors of modern man, but opinion differs on this. The question is complicated by the fact that there were two basic types of australopithecine, a more robust apelike form called *Paranthropus* and the more manlike form of *Australopithecus*. One branch of the latter may have evolved into *Homo erectus* (□*Homo*). The creature discovered by Louis *Leakey at *Olduvai in 1959 and given by him the generic name of *Zinjanthropus* has now been included with the other australopithecines as *Australopithecus boisei*.

Austrasia The eastern Frankish kingdom created together with *Neustria by the partition in 511 of the Merovingian kingdom by *Clovis. Occupying an area that is now NE France and West Germany, its capital from 629 was at Metz. Austrasia was increasingly dominated by the mayors of the palace (viceroys), the last of which, *Pepin the Short, deposed the Merovingians in 751 and reunited the Frankish territories into what became the Carolingian empire. *See also* Franks.

Austria, Republic of (German name: Österreich) A country in central Europe, on the N side of the Alps. A large part of the country is mountainous but the E area consists of lower hills and plains, with the River Danube flowing through the NE. Most of the inhabitants are German but there are minorities of Croats, Slovenes, and others. *Economy*: although agriculture and forestry are important, there is considerable heavy industry, based particularly on iron and steel. Hydroelectric power is a valuable source of energy. Tourism has grown in recent years, both summer and winter. Main exports include iron and steel, machinery, paper and paper products, wood, and textiles. *History*: Austria has a long history of human habitation, going back to the Celtic settlements of the early Iron Age. The area was part of the Roman Empire from 15 BC until the 5th century AD when it was overrun by Germanic tribes. In succeeding centuries it was occupied in turn by Slavs and Magyars from whom it was taken in 955 by the Holy Roman Emperor *Otto I. He conferred it upon Leopold of Babenberg, who founded the first Austrian dynasty. In 1282 the *Habsburgs acquired Austria, which was to become the core of their vast empire. In 1526 Bohemia and Hungary were united under the Austrian Crown. The Austrian Empire continued to hold a predominant position in Europe until the middle of the 19th century when its power was lessened by successive defeats, especially in the *Austro-Prussian War. In 1867 the Habsburgs were forced to acknowledge the nationalist aspirations of Hungary and formed the Dual Monarchy of *Austria-Hungary, under the Emperor *Francis Joseph. During his reign there was considerable unrest, especially among the Slav peoples of the very diverse Empire; the assassination of the Archduke Francis Ferdinand by Serbian nationalists in 1914 was the immediate cause of World War I. In 1918 Austria became a republic. In spite of efforts on the part of the chancellor *Schuschnigg to maintain independence, it was annexed by Nazi Germany in 1938 (*see* Anschluss). After World War II it was occupied jointly by the Allies, regaining its independence as a republic in

1955. Chancellor Bruno *Kreisky who came to power in 1970 as head of Austria's first all-socialist government, resigned in 1983 and was succeeded by Dr Fred Sinowatz. President: Kurt *Waldheim. Official language: German. Currency: schilling of 100 groschen. Area: 85 853 sq km (32 375 sq mi). Population (1981 est): 7 559 440. Capital: Vienna.

Austria-Hungary, Dual Monarchy of The Habsburg monarchy from 1867 to 1918. It was established by the *Ausgleich* (compromise) in response to the militant demands of Hungarian nationalism. The empire of Austria and the kingdom of Hungary each had its own laws, parliament, and ministries but were united by the monarch (Emperors *Francis Joseph and then *Charles), minister for foreign affairs and minister for war, and by the biannual meetings of delegations of representatives of each parliament. The Dual Monarchy was weakened by resurgent nationalism in the early 20th century and disappeared in 1918 with the proclamation of an Austrian republic.

Austrian Succession, War of the (1740–48) The war between Austria and Prussia, in which Britain supported Austria and France and Spain were allied to Prussia. It was brought about by the disputed succession of *Maria Theresa to the Austrian lands. Hostilities were begun by *Frederick the Great of Prussia, who annexed the Austrian province of Silesia in 1740. Unstable alliances were formed between European powers on the Continent and hostilities overseas, especially between France and Britain, were exacerbated. The war was ended by the Treaty of *Aix-la-Chapelle, at which Prussia obtained the greater share of Silesia.

Austro-Asiatic languages A family of about 150 languages and dialects spoken in SE Asia. They include Vietnamese, *Khmer, Nicobarese in the Nicobar Islands, and the *Munda languages of India. In fact there is little superficial resemblance among languages of the family, and their common ancestors and date of separation are difficult to establish. There have, accordingly, been attempts to link them to other language families, as was done in the Austro-Tai hypothesis (first proposed in 1906), which postulated a super-family to include the Austro-Asiatic languages, the *Austronesian languages, and certain languages of Indochina.

Austronesian languages A large language family, also called Malayo-Polynesian, spoken in the Malay peninsula, Taiwan, Madagascar, and the islands of the Pacific Ocean. There are two subgroups: the Western branch, which has up to 200 member languages and includes Malay, Indonesian, Malagasy, Javanese, and Tagalog; and the Eastern or Oceanic branch, which has up to 300 members and includes the languages of the islands in the S and central Pacific, such as Samoa, Tahiti, Tonga, Fiji, New Guinea, and Hawaii. There is some doubt as to whether the languages of Taiwan form a separate group or are to be included in the Western branch.

Austro-Prussian War (*or* Seven Weeks' War; 1866) A war between German states led respectively by Austria and Prussia. The Prussian victory was an important landmark in Bismarck's strategy for uniting Germany under Prussian leadership.

auteur theory In film criticism, emphasis on the dominant role of the director. It was developed in the 1950s by several writers for the French magazine *Cahiers du Cinéma* who later became directors themselves, notably Truffaut, Godard, Rohmer, and Chabrol. Their method of evaluation, which was based on a consideration of the director's technique, intentions, and personal style, influenced several British and US film critics during the 1960s.

Authorized Version. *See* King James Version.

autism A rare and severe mental illness that starts in early childhood. Autistic children are aloof and do not form normal personal relationships but they can become emotionally attached to things. They do not communicate normally, often cannot form abstract concepts, and are very upset by tiny changes in their familiar surroundings. Most, but not all, are mentally retarded. Autism can be caused by brain damage and can also be inherited. Lengthy specialized education is usually necessary for autistic children.

auto-da-fé (Portuguese: act of faith) The public ceremony at which persons convicted of crimes by the *Inquisition in Portugal, Spain, and their colonies were sentenced. Punishment of victims, including the burning of heretics, was the responsibility of the secular authorities. The first *auto-da-fé* was held in Seville in 1481 and the last, in Mexico in 1815.

autogiro An aircraft with large horizontal freely rotating blades to obtain lift. It differs from the *helicopter in that a propeller provides forward motion, which in turn causes the rotation of the unmotorized horizontal blades.

autoimmunity A condition in which the body produces antibodies (called autoantibodies) that damage or destroy its own tissues. This produces symptoms of various **autoimmune diseases**, the majority of which are poorly understood. Rheumatoid *arthritis is caused by the production of autoantibodies against joint tissue; the disease can be diagnosed by the detection of these antibodies in the serum. A more general production of autoantibodies causes systemic *lupus erythematosis, which can affect most tissues in the body.

automatic pilot A device utilizing a gyroscope for keeping an aircraft on a given course. When the aircraft goes off course, the gyro axis rotates, operating electrical contacts, which make the necessary adjustments to the control surfaces.

automation The use of electronic devices controlled by a computer in mechanical processes that would otherwise be controlled by human operators. It has made considerable impact on production engineering in such fields as steel and chemical manufacture. Telecommunications (automatic telephone exchanges), transport (navigation, railway signals), and mining also employ automated systems.

autopsy (necropsy *or* postmortem) The dissection and examination of a dead body. An autopsy is performed when the cause of death is uncertain: it may provide further information on a poorly understood disease or evidence of criminal involvement. Except for sudden death or death due to obscure causes, permission for autopsy must be granted by the relatives.

autoradiography The use of photography to examine the distribution of a *radioisotope in a thin specimen. The specimen is placed on a photographic plate, which after development shows the distribution of the radioisotope.

autosuggestion A way of changing one's behaviour by firmly repeating ideas to oneself. It can be used to control undesirable habits or to cope with anxiety and is sometimes taught to psychiatric patients. *See also* hypnosis.

autumnal equinox. *See* equinox.

autumn crocus A herbaceous perennial European plant, *Colchicum autumnale*, also called meadow saffron. It has narrow strap-shaped leaves, up to 30 cm long, and a single purple-blue crocus-like flower, which appears in autumn after the leaves have died. The drug colchicine, extracted from the corms, is used in the treatment of gout and in genetic research. Some plants of the genus are cultivated for ornament. Family: *Liliaceae. Compare* Crocus.

Autun 46 58N 4 18E A town in central France, in the Saône-et-Loire department on the River Arroux. Famous for its school of rhetoric during Roman times, it has several Roman remains. Its manufactures include furniture and leather. Population (1975): 22 949.

Auvergne A planning region and former province in S central France. Its name derives from the Averni, who strongly resisted Roman control of the area. Crossed by the volcanic Auvergne Mountains that rise to over 1800 m (6000 ft), it has many mineral springs and some level fertile districts. It is predominantly agricultural and is noted for the growing of wheat and grapes and the rearing of cattle; cheese and wine are also produced. Area: 25 988 sq km (10 032 sq mi). Population (1981 est): 1 320 000.

Auxerre 47 48N 3 35W A town in central France, the capital of the Yonne department on the River Yonne. Its gothic cathedral has exceptional 13th-century stained glass windows. Wine and metal goods are produced here. Population (1982 est): 40 698.

auxin An organic substance, produced within a plant, that stimulates, inhibits, or modifies growth of the plant. Auxins are sometimes known as plant hormones. The main auxin is indoleacetic acid (IAA). Auxins are responsible for a variety of effects, for example shoot curvature, leaf fall, and fruit growth. Synthetic auxins, such as 2,4-dichlorophenoxyacetic acid (2,4-D), are used as weedkillers for broad-leaved weeds (*see* herbicide).

Ava The former Burmese capital (1364–1783, 1823–37), 9.5 km (6 mi) S of *Mandalay, formerly famous for its Buddhist temples.

avadavat A small plump songbird, *Estrilda amandava*, also called red munia. Occurring in meadows and marshes of Asia, it is the only *waxbill found outside Africa. In the breeding season the male plumage is bright red with mottled brown patches and white speckling.

avalanche A rapid movement of snow and ice, and sometimes rock debris, down steep slopes. They may occur in winter, when fresh snow slides off an older compacted snow surface, and in spring, when thaws cause the mass to slip. Avalanches can cause severe damage with loss of life and property and in populous mountain areas steel avalanche-sheds are used to protect roads and railways.

Avalon The paradise of Celtic mythology to which King Arthur (*see* Arthurian legend) was taken after his final battle. It was ruled by *Morgan le Fay, famous for her magical powers, and has been identified with Glastonbury in Somerset.

Avebury 51 27N 1 51W A village in S England, in Wiltshire, on the site of a large complex of Neolithic and early Bronze Age stone circles, banks, and ditches. The principal circle, with its ditch and outer bank, encloses over 12 hectares (30 acres); within it are two smaller ones. Nearby is *Silbury Hill.

Aveiro 40 38N 8 40W A port in NW Portugal, on an inlet of the Atlantic Ocean. Its museum contains medieval art treasures. It has agricultural industries. Population (1981 est): 28 625.

Avellaneda 34 40S 58 20W A city in Argentina, a suburb of Buenos Aires on the Río de la Plata. It is highly industrialized with meat processing, oil refining, and tanning. Population (1980): 334 145.

avens A perennial herbaceous plant of the genus *Geum* (about 40 species), native to temperate and Arctic regions. Most species rarely exceed 60 cm in height. Their flowers, 2–3 cm long, are white, yellow, orange, or red, either solitary or in clusters. *G. coccineum* is a common ornamental. Family: *Rosaceae*.

average 1. (mathematics) A representative or middle value of a set of quantities. The arithmetical average (*or* arithmetical mean) is found by adding the quantities in a set and dividing the total by the number of quantities: the arithmetical average of 7, 8, 13, and 20 is 12 (48 divided by 4). The geometric average (*or* geometric mean) is found by multiplying together the numbers in a set and extracting a root equal to the number of quantities: the geometric average of 2, 9, and 12 is 6 ($\sqrt[3]{216}$). 2. (insurance) Loss or damage to property. In *marine insurance it refers to a partial loss. A **particular average** affects only one interest, whereas a **general average** is shared among all the parties concerned (e.g. if a deck cargo has to be jettisoned to save a ship in a storm, all the cargo owners have to contribute to the loss). In fire insurance, average is used to combat underin-surance. For example, if an insurer has only insured his goods for a proportion of their total value, he will only be paid that proportion of any claim for a partial loss.

Avernus, Lake A small crater lake near Naples and Cumae (the earliest Greek colony in Italy). In ancient times it was believed to be the entrance to the infernal regions, and *Avernus* was often used by writers as a synonym for the underworld. In Virgil's *Aeneid*, Aeneas descends to the underworld through a cave near the lake.

Averroes (Ibn Rushd; 1126–98) Muslim philosopher and a judge in Córdoba and Seville. Averroes' main works were his commentaries on Aristotle, which greatly influenced the philosophy of medieval Christianity. He defended philosophy as the highest form of enquiry, holding that faith and reason are not necessarily in conflict but are separate ways of arriving at the truth.

aversion therapy A form of *conditioning used to treat some kinds of undesirable behaviour, such as sexual deviation, alcoholism, and drug addiction. An unpleasant stimulus (e.g. an electric shock) is associated with a stimulus related to the problem behaviour (e.g. the taste of alcohol). *See also* behaviour therapy.

AVALANCHE   *An avalanche sliding down Mt Nast in Colorado, USA, at 50 km/hr (32 mph).*

Avery, Oswald Theodore (1877–1955) Canadian bacteriologist, whose work demonstrated the importance of *DNA and led Watson and Crick to investigate its structure and method of replication. It was known that an extract (nonliving) of smooth-coated (S) bacteria contained a substance capable of converting living rough-coated bacteria into the S strain. In 1944, Avery identified this substance as DNA.

Avesta The sacred scriptures of *Zoroastrianism. Written in Old Iranian, the five books of the *Avesta* contain prayers (probably by Zoroaster himself) hymns, ritual and liturgical instruction, and the main body of Zoroastrian law. Its surviving form dates from about the 6th century AD.

Avicenna (980–1037) Persian philosopher and physician. Avicenna received extensive education in science and philosophy and served various rulers during his life, as government official and physician. His encyclopedia of philosophy, *Ash-Shifa* (*The Recovery*), encompasses logic, psychology, metaphysics, and natural sciences and parts were subsequently translated into Latin. Avicenna's *Canon of Medicine*, based on Roman and Arabic medicine and his own medical knowledge, became a popular text throughout the Middle East and Europe.

Aviemore 57 12N 3 50W A winter sports resort in Scotland, in the Highland Region on the River Spey, between the Monadhliath and Cairngorm Mountains.

Avignon 43 56N 4 48E A town in SE France, the capital of the Vaucluse department on the River Rhône. The papacy, under French control, was removed to Avignon (1309–77; *see* Avignon papacy) and there were subsequently rival popes at Rome and Avignon until 1417 (*see* Great Schism). Famous landmarks include the 14th-century papal palace and the 12th-century bridge, of which only four arches remain. A popular tourist centre, Avignon trades in wine and has chemical, soap, and cement industries. Population (1982 est): 91 474.

Avignon papacy (1309–77) The period during which the popes resided in Avignon (France) rather than Rome. It is sometimes called the Babylonian Capitivity (in reference to the *Babylonian exile in Jewish history). The papal court was established in Avignon, a papal fief, by *Clement V, who, like his six successors in Avignon, was French. English and German criticism of French dominance over the papacy eventually forced its return to Rome under Gregory XI. Shortly afterwards the division in the Church known as the *Great Schism occurred, largely in response to the increased power acquired by the cardinals during the Avignon papacy.

Avignon school A school of painting established when Clement V moved the papal court from Rome to Avignon in 1309 and imported Italian 14th-century masters, notably Simone *Martini, to decorate the papal palace. After the pope's return to Rome (1377) painters remaining in Avignon developed a unique style, fusing Italian and Flemish influences. The artists of the school include Nicholas Froment (active 1450–90) and its most celebrated work is the anonymous *Villeneuve Pietà* (c. 1460; Louvre).

Avila 40 39N 4 42W A town in central Spain, in Old Castile on the River Adaja. A popular tourist centre, the old part of the town is enclosed by 12th-century walls and has a notable gothic cathedral (11th–15th centuries). St Teresa was born here. Population (1981): 86 584.

avocado A tree, *Persia americana*, up to 18 m tall, native to Mexico and Central America but now extensively cultivated in Florida, California, and South Africa for its fruit. These fruits—avocado pears—may reach a weight of 2 kg: they have a green to dark-purple skin, a fatty flesh rich in fat, protein, and vitamins A and B, and a single hard seed.

avocet A wading bird of the genus *Recurvirostra*, having long slender legs and a long thin upcurved bill used to skim the surface of mud or water in search of small invertebrates. The Eurasian avocet (*R. avosetta*), 50 cm long, has a black-and-white plumage and grey-blue legs and is protected in Britain. Family: *Recurvirostridae*; order: *Charadriiformes* (gulls, plovers, etc.). See Plate V.

Avogadro, Amedeo, Conte di Quaregna e Ceretto (1776–1856) Italian physicist, who became professor of physics at the University of Turin. He developed *Gay-Lussac's hypothesis that equal volumes of gases contain equal numbers of particles, establishing the difference between atoms and molecules. Because he made this vital distinction the theory is now known as Avogadro's hypothesis. His name is also commemorated in **Avogadro's number** (*or* the Avogadro constant), the number of molecules in one mole of substance (it has the value $6.022\,52 \times 10^{23}$). Avogadro's work was largely neglected during his life and was not acknowledged until *Cannizzaro brought it to public notice in 1854.

Avon A county of SW England, bordering on the Severn estuary. It was formed in 1974 from parts of NE Somerset and SW Gloucestershire. It consists mainly of a low-lying basin, rising to the Cotswold Hills in the NE and the Mendip Hills in the S. The River Avon flows W into the Severn estuary. Dairy farming is the chief agricultural activity. Industry, including engineering, printing, chemicals, tobacco processing, and aircraft manufacture, is concentrated in the Bristol area. Avonmouth is a major port. There is a thriving tourist industry, notably at Weston-super-Mare and Bath. Area: 1337 sq km (516 sq mi). Population (1981): 909 408. Administrative centre: Bristol.

Avon, (Robert) Anthony Eden, 1st Earl of (1897–1977) British statesman; Conservative prime minister (1955–57). Foreign secretary from 1935 to 1938, he resigned in opposition to Neville Chamberlain's policy of *appeasement. During World War II he was secretary for war and then (1940–45) foreign secretary. From 1951 to 1955 he was again foreign secretary, playing an important part in the 1954 *Geneva Conference and in the establishment of the *European Defence Community. He succeeded Churchill as prime minister and in 1956, following Nasser's nationalization of the *Suez Canal and an Israeli attack on Egypt, joined France in an offensive against Egypt, while claiming to separate the contestants. Egypt retained control of Suez and, despite Eden's claim that the Anglo-French initiative had ended the war between Egypt and Israel, he was much criticized and resigned shortly afterwards. He became Earl of Avon in 1961.

Avon, River The name of several rivers in the UK, including: **1.** A river in central England, flowing SW from Northamptonshire to the River Severn at Tewkesbury. Length: 154 km (96 mi). **2.** A river in SW England, flowing S and W from Gloucestershire to the Severn estuary at Avonmouth. Length: 120 km (75 mi). **3.** A river in S England, flowing S from Wiltshire to the English Channel. Length: 96 km (60 mi).

Awolowo, Obafemi (1909–) Nigerian politician. He qualified as a lawyer in Britain and returned home to form the Action Group (1950), becoming premier of the Western Region of Nigeria (1954–59). On independence (1960) he led the opposition to the government in the Federal House of Representatives until 1963, when he was imprisoned for treason until 1966.

Axholme, Isle of A low-lying area in England, in NW Lincolnshire between the Rivers Don, Idle, and Trent. Once waterlogged, it was drained in the early 17th century as part of the *Fens.

axiology The theory of values in ethics and aesthetics, particularly the search for the good and its nature. Axiology investigates basic principles governing moral judgment, types of value, and the place of values (or norms) within the frameworks of philosophical systems. *Plato, for instance, held to an absolute theory of the Idea of the Good, while *Hume and others believed that values were relative, depending on degrees of approval felt by persons making value judgments. *Kant found the source of value in practical reason, while in *utilitarianism it lay in the principle of the greatest happiness for the greatest number.

axiom An assumption or principle, used to prove a theorem, that is itself accepted as true without proof. Some mathematicians reserve the term for an assumption in logic, using postulate for an assumption made in other fields.

axis deer A slender deer, *Axis axis*, also called chital, that usually lives in small herds near rivers in India and Sri Lanka. Axis deer measure up to 100 cm at the shoulder and are reddish with white spots and pale underparts.

Axis Powers The coalition of Germany, Italy, and Japan that opposed the *Allied Powers in *World War II. It originated in agreements going back to 1936 and it culminated in the Tripartite Pact (1940).

Axminster carpet A type of carpet developed at a factory in Axminster, England (1755–1835). It was handmade in Axminster and elsewhere until the 19th-century mechan-

axolotl

ization of the carpet industry. Although the industry was only revived in Axminster in 1937, Axminster carpets had been in continuous production in other towns, a special loom having been invented in 1876. Their distinguishing features were a long soft pile and tufts individually coloured to produce patterns of unlimited complexity.

axolotl A salamander, *Ambystoma mexicanum*, occurring in Mexican lakes. It reaches a length of 25 cm, has a long tail and weak limbs, and is typically dark brown. Axolotls retain their larval characteristics permanently, reproducing in this state, although under certain conditions they may develop into adults. Family: *Ambystomatidae*.

axon. *See* neurone.

Axum. *See* Aksum.

Ayacucho 13 10S 74 15W A city in S central Peru. The battle of Ayacucho (1824) was fought nearby, resulting in Peru gaining independence from Spain. An agricultural centre, tourism is also important. It has a university (founded 1677 and reopened 1957). Population (1981): 69 533.

Ayatollah Ruholla Khomeini. *See* Khomeini, Ayatollah Ruholla.

Ayckbourn, Alan (1939-) British dramatist. After working in provincial repertory theatre, he gained his first London success with *Relatively Speaking* (1967). His later comedies include *Absurd Person Singular* (1973), the trilogy *The Norman Conquests* (1974), *Bedroom Farce* (1976), *Season's Greetings* (1984), and *A Chorus of Disapproval* (1985), all characterized by ingenious construction and detailed observation of middle-class life. He directs a repertory theatre in Scarborough.

aye-aye A rare arboreal *prosimian primate, *Daubentonia madagascariensis*, occurring only in the coastal forests of N Madagascar. It is 86–104 cm long including the tail (50–60 cm) and has dark shaggy fur and large ears used to detect wood-boring insects, extracting them with its incisor teeth and narrow elongated third finger. Family: *Daubentoniidae*.

Ayer, Sir Alfred (Jules) (1910-) British philosopher; Wykeham Professor of Logic at Oxford (1959-78). Ayer's major contribution to British philosophy was his bringing to England the teachings of the *Vienna Circle, in particular the doctrine of *logical positivism. This he expounded in *Language, Truth and Logic* (1936), which taught that if a proposition is neither verifiable by sense experience, nor a tautology, then it can contain no meaning. His later books include *The Foundations of Empirical Knowledge* (1940), *The Problem of Knowledge* (1956), and an autobiography *Part of My Life* (1977).

AYERS ROCK

Ayers Rock The largest monolith in the world, in Australia, in SW Northern Territory. It consists of a vast red rock rising 335 m (1099 ft) above the surrounding plain with a circumference of 10 km (6.25 mi). Its colour varies according to atmospheric changes and the position of the sun.

Ayesha (c. 613-78) The third and favourite wife of *Mohammed and daughter of *Abu Bakr. She married at the age of nine. She led a revolt against *Ali but was defeated (656) and ended her life in exile in Medina. She is known as "the mother of believers."

Aylesbury 51 50N 0 50W A market town in S central England, the administrative centre for Buckinghamshire. Lying in an agricultural area it has food-processing industries as well as printing, engineering, and various light industries. Population (1981): 48 159.

Aylward, Gladys (1903-70) British missionary. From 1930 she worked as an independent missionary in China. Her life story was the subject of a popular film, *The Inn of the Sixth Happiness* (1958), in which she was played by Ingrid Bergman.

Aymara A people of the Peruvian and Bolivian highlands. They grow potatoes and other crops and herd llamas and alpacas. Their costume is characterized by the woollen poncho and conical headwear with earflaps. They live in small extended-family settlements in which elders, who are also ritual shamans (*see* shamanism), have authority. In the 15th century the Aymara were incorporated into the Inca empire under Viracocha. Later Spanish influence made them nominally Catholic but earlier beliefs persist. Today there are approximately 1 360 000 Aymaras and their language, Aymaran, is one of the strongest surviving native Indian languages.

Ayr 55 28N 4 38W A port and resort in SW Scotland, in Strathclyde Region where the River Ayr enters the Firth of Clyde. Many of its historic buildings are associated with Robert Burns. It exports coal, iron, and agricultural produce. Population (1981): 49 481.

Ayr (*or* Ayrshire) A former county of SW Scotland. Under local government reorganization in 1975 it became part of Strathclyde Region.

ayre A type of song of the Elizabethan period, consisting of a principal voice part accompanied by instruments or other voices, each verse being sung to the same music. In 1597 John Dowland published his *First Book of Songs and Ayres of Four Parts*; other composers of ayres include Morley and Campion.

Ayrshire cattle A breed of red or brown and white cattle originating in Ayrshire, SW Scotland. A hardy breed, Ayrshires are primarily producers of good quality milk, used especially in cheese making. Many herds have been replaced by the higher yielding *Friesians.

Ayub Khan, Mohammad (1907-74) Pakistani statesman; president (1958-69). After a distinguished military career he became defence minister in 1954. Following President Iskander Mirza's coup d'état in 1958 Ayub Khan became chief martial law administrator and then ousted Mirza to become president. He negotiated (1966) the ceasefire agreement with *Shastri following the India-Pakistan war of 1965. He was forced to resign following civil unrest in East Pakistan.

Ayutthaya (*or* Ayuthi) 14 20N 100 35E A city in central Thailand. The former capital of the country (1350-1767), it is noted for its exceptional architecture, which survived a sacking by the Burmese. Population (1980): 47 189.

azalea A deciduous shrub of the genus *Rhododendron*. (Most horticulturalists prefer to restrict the term rhododendron to the large evergreen species.) Growing to a height of up to 2 m, azaleas are all native to the uplands of North America and S Asia but are now widely cultivated as ornamentals. The attractive flowers are large, fragrant, and funnel-shaped (about 6 cm in diameter) and of various colours. Family: *Ericaceae*.

Azaña, Manuel (1880-1940) Spanish statesman, who was prominent in the Second Republic (1931-39). His premiership (1931-33) introduced internal reforms but was unpopular for its repression of opposition. He was president (1936-39) during the Spanish Civil War and fled to France after Gen Franco's Nationalist victory.

Azande An African people speaking a Sudanic language who live in areas of the Sudan, Zaïre, and the Central African Republic. They are an ethnically mixed people, who practise agriculture, hunting, and various crafts, including ironwork. They were traditionally divided into a number of warring kingdoms. They live in scattered homesteads and are organized into a number of dispersed patrilineal clans. Their religion takes the form of an ancestor cult. Belief in witchcraft is a central aspect of their lives, most misfortunes being attributed to it.

Azerbaidzhan Soviet Socialist Republic A constituent republic in the S Soviet Union, on the Caspian Sea. It consists mainly of the hot dry plain of the Rivers Kura and Araks, surrounded by the Caucasus Mountains. The Azerbaidzhani, who comprise most of the population, are a Turkic-speaking Shiite Muslim people renowned for their carpet weaving. The region was acquired by Russia from Persia in the early 19th century, proclaimed its independence in 1918, but subsequently formed part of the Transcaucasian Soviet Federated Socialist Republic (*see* Transcaucasia), becoming a separate republic in 1936. Azerbaidzhan is one of the oldest oil-producing areas of the world and its most important industries are oil and gas, with a developing chemical industry. Agriculture is diversified and expansion is planned. The main crops are cotton, tobacco, and fruit, including grapes for wine. Area: 86 600 sq km (33 430 sq mi). Population (1981 est): 6 200 000. Capital: Baku.

Azhar, al- A mosque and centre of traditional Muslim studies in Cairo. Inaugurated in 972 AD following the Fatimid conquest of Egypt, al-Azhar was originally controlled by the *Ismaili. It became a *Sunnite institution under Saladin but it was not until after the Ottoman conquest (1517) that it gained its present pre-eminence. It is now regarded as the most authoritative centre of Islam and receives students from the whole Muslim world. In Egypt it has university status.

Azikiwe, (Benjamin) Nnamdi (1904-) A prominent figure in the struggle for independence in Nigeria. Popularly known as Zik, in 1944 he founded the National Council of Nigeria and the Cameroons to fight colonial rule. At independence (1960) he was appointed governor general and when Nigeria became a republic became its first president (1963-66).

azimuth. *See* altitude.

Aznavour, Charles (Varenagh Aznavourian; 1924-) French singer, actor, and songwriter. Aznavour has appeared in many films and written many songs in both French and English.

azo dyes A class of synthetic dyes containing the **azo group** (-N=N-). First produced in 1858, they now outsell all other dyes combined. This success is due to exceptional colour-fastness and versatility in application, including the ability to dye natural and synthetic fibres direct, i.e. without a mordant. Virtually any colour may be obtained; examples are methyl orange, Bismarck brown, and Congo red.

Azores (Portuguese name: Açôres) 38 30N 28 00W Three groups of volcanic islands in the N Atlantic Ocean, in Portugal. The chief islands include São Miguel, Terceira, Faial, and Flores. Settled by the Portuguese in the 15th century, they were previously uninhabited. Naval fighting between the English and Spanish took place here in the 16th and 17th centuries. The site of US air bases, they produce fruit, tobacco, and wine. Area: 2300 sq km (888 sq mi).

Population (1981): 243 410. Capital: Ponta Delgada, on São Miguel.

Azorín (José Martinéz Ruíz; 1874-1967) Spanish novelist, essayist, and critic. His works include the autobiographical novels *La voluntad* (1902) and *Antonio Azorín* (1903), as well as the collection of essays *Los pueblos* (1905), inspired by the history and landscape of Castile.

Azov, Sea of A NE arm of the Black Sea, to the main body of which it is connected by the narrow Kerch Strait. Area: 38 000 sq km (14 668 sq mi).

AZTECS *The calendar stone in the National Museum of Anthropology, Mexico City. The inner circle contains the 20 day signs of the Aztec calendar, while the central panel depicts the day on which the Aztecs believed the world would be destroyed by earthquake.*

Aztecs A *Nahuatl-speaking people who ruled an empire in central and S Mexico before their defeat by Hernán Cortés in the 16th century. They had an advanced, elaborate, and rich civilization centred on their capital Tenochtitlán and other cities. They were expert builders and constructed large palaces and temples in which they worshipped many gods, especially Huitzilopochtli to whom they sacrificed human victims, captives of warfare, by ripping out their hearts while they still lived. Their social organization was hierarchical with authority and influence vested in a class of chiefs and priests and in the kings, the last of whom was *Montezuma.

Aztec-Tanoan languages An American Indian language group, spoken in the SW USA and central America. It has two branches: Uto-Aztecan and Kiowa-Tanoan. Uto-Aztecan is the larger; its most widely used language, Nahua, is spoken by the *Nahuatl people of central and W Mexico. Other Uto-Aztecan languages include those of the Paiute Indians in California and Utah, the *Hopi in Arizona, and the *Comanche in Texas. The Kiowa-Tanoan branch has only four members and is spoken in New Mexico and by the *Kiowa of Oklahoma.

Azuela, Mariano (1873-1952) Mexican novelist. He practised medicine in Mexico City before joining Pancho Villa's forces during the Mexican revolution. *The Underdogs* (1916) described the suffering it caused. Later novels, such as *Los caciques* (1917) and the posthumous *Esa sangre*, express disgust with Mexican society both before and after the revolution.

B

Baader-Meinhof Gang A group of West German terrorists, calling themselves the Rote Armee Fraktion (Red Army Faction), who are dedicated to the violent overthrow of capitalist society. The gang is named after two of its leading members, Andreas Baader (1943–77) and Ulrike Meinhof (1934–76), both of whom died in prison. By mid-1984 most of the gang had been arrested, although further violent attacks occur sporadically.

Baal An ancient fertility god worshipped throughout the Near East, especially in Canaan. As champion of the divine order against chaos he defeated the sea god Yamm. The myth of his conflict with Mot, god of death and sterility, is closely linked to the natural processes of vegetation: his defeat and descent into the underworld represents famine and drought, and his resurrection and victory over Mot symbolizes rain and fertility.

Baalbek 34 00N 36 12E A town in E Lebanon, originally commanding Phoenician trade routes. The Roman colony here, called Heliopolis, has left extensive and imposing remains, including temples dedicated to Jupiter and Venus (1st–3rd centuries AD).

Ba'al Shem Tov (Israel ben Eliezer; c. 1700–60) Charismatic Jewish leader and mystic, the founder of *Hasidism. He lived in Podolia (then part of Poland) and attracted an enormous following by his powerful personality and his teaching, a blend of popular pietism and mystical Judaism. He is the subject of many colourful legends. His name means "Master of the Good Name."

Ba'ath Party An Arab political party, influential in many Middle Eastern countries, notably Syria and Iraq, that urges the creation of a united socialist Arab nation. The Ba'athists supported the formation of the *United Arab Republic (1958–61) and rose to power in Iraq and Syria in 1963.

Babbage, Charles (1792–1871) British mathematician and inventor. In an attempt to produce more accurate mathematical tables, Babbage conceived the idea of a mechanical computer that could store information. Although he never completed the machine, it was the forerunner of the modern computer. He was an outspoken critic of the Royal Society for its complacency and of British mathematics in general for languishing in the shadow of Newton.

Babbitt, Irving (1865–1933) US scholar and critic. While professor of French at Harvard (1894–1935), he wrote extensive works on literature and social questions, including *Rousseau and Romanticism* (1919) and *Democracy and Leadership* (1924). He was a leader of the "neohumanist" thinkers, who opposed Romanticism and advocated the classical values of restraint and moderation.

Babbitt, Milton (1916–) US composer. He taught music and mathematics at Princeton University. His compositions employ *serialism and include music for synthesizers; they include *Philomel* (1963–64) and *A Solo Requiem* (1976–77).

babbler A small songbird belonging to a family (*Timaliidae*; 280 species) occurring in Old World regions, particularly in SE Asia. Babblers have short rounded wings, a long tail, strong legs and bill, and a noisy babbling cry. The plumage is often brightly coloured, although some species are plain brown. Babblers live in wooded regions, searching the undergrowth in groups for insects and berries.

Babel, Isaac Emmanuilovich (1894–1941) Russian short-story writer. Of Jewish descent, he served in the imperial army, but fought for the Bolsheviks in 1917. His *Odessa Tales* were published in 1916 in a journal edited by *Gorki. *Red Cavalry* (1926) was a series of sketches based on his experience in the war against Poland. He died in a Siberian prison camp, a victim of Stalin's purges, but was posthumously rehabilitated in the 1950s.

Babel, Tower of In the Bible (Genesis 2.1–9), a tower intended to reach heaven. Angered by the presumption of the building, Jehovah caused the builders to speak different languages, so that they were incomprehensible to each other and were forced to abandon the work. The legend attempts to account for the diversification of languages. It also probably alludes to the Babylonian ziggurats, which for the Israelites were examples of Gentile pride.

Bab el-Mandeb A strait between Africa and the SW Arabian Peninsula, connecting the Red Sea with the Gulf of Aden. It is 32 km (20 mi) wide and at one point is divided by Perim Island.

Babeuf, François-Noël (1760–97) French revolutionary. Propagator of extreme egalitarian ideas, he plotted to overthrow the *Directory. His "conspiracy of equals" was exposed and Babeuf was executed. Secret societies perpetuated his doctrines, known as Babouvism.

Babi faith A religion founded in 1844 by Mirza 'Ali Mohammed (1819–50), who became known as the Bab (the Gate). He proclaimed himself the 12th and last imam of certain *Shiite sects, which had prophesied his reappearance. He was imprisoned and later shot on government orders, and his followers were subsequently persecuted. Babism centred on the belief that God reveals himself to man through prophets who would continue to appear until the end of the world. It was the immediate precursor of the *Baha'i faith.

Babington, Anthony (1561–86) English conspirator, who with John Ballard plotted to kill Elizabeth I and place Mary, Queen of Scots, on the throne. The conspiracy failed: Babington, Ballard, and subsequently Mary were executed.

babirusa A hairless wild pig, *Babyrousa babyrussa*, of Sulawesi (Indonesia). About 100 cm long, babirusas live in damp forests and are good swimmers, feeding on water plants, fruit, and tubers. Males have two pairs of curved tusks; the tuskless females have only one pair of teats.

baboon A large *Old World monkey belonging to the genus *Papio* (5 species), of African and Asian grassland. Baboons are 95–185 cm long including the tail (45–70 cm) and have a shaggy mane and a long doglike face with large teeth. They feed on insects, small vertebrates, and vegetable matter. They live in well-organized troops containing 40–150 individuals arranged in a social hierarchy according to age and sex. *See also* hamadryas. □mammal.

Babur (Zahir-ud-din Muhammad; 1483–1530) Emperor of India (1526–30), who founded the *Mogul dynasty. Descended from Genghis Khan and Timur, Babur became ruler of Fergana (1495) in Uzbekistan but failed to reconquer his ancestors' kingdom of Samarkand. Capturing Kabul, he invaded India from Afghanistan in 1525. In 1526 he defeated and killed Ibrahim Lodhi, Sultan of Delhi (1517–26), and rapidly subjugated all of N India. His story is told in his memoirs, the *Babur-Nameh*.

Babylon The capital of ancient Babylonia, strategically positioned on the River *Euphrates S of modern Baghdad. Its first period of prominence was about 2150 to 1740 BC, under a dynasty of which *Hammurabi was the most illustrious member. Subsequently, rising *Assyrian power threatened Babylonian independence, though some Babylonians, such as Nebuchadnezzar I (reigned c. 1146–1123), temporarily reversed the trend. Sacked by *Sennacherib (689 BC), Babylon was rebuilt from 625 BC onwards, especially during the reign (c. 605–562) of *Nebuchadnezzar II. It was the remains of this city that were excavated by

*Koldewey and from which the famous Ishtar Gate was recovered. In 539 BC Babylon surrendered to *Cyrus the Great of Persia. By 275 BC it was virtually depopulated. *See also* Hanging Gardens; Babel, Tower of; ziggurat.

Babylonia The area of *Mesopotamia on the alluvial plain along the lower reaches of the River Euphrates, which was controlled by ancient *Babylon. Before about 2000 BC approximately the same area was known as *Sumer. The Babylonians were a blend of Semitic peoples, like their rivals, the *Assyrians, to the NW. Apart from Babylon, the former Sumerian capital of *Ur and the port of *Eridu were major cities.

Babylonian exile The period from the destruction of the Jerusalem *Temple by *Nebuchadnezzar (586 BC) to the Jews' return under *Cyrus the Great (538 BC), during which time most of the Jews lived in exile in *Babylonia. It was here that parts of the Hebrew Bible were written, and that certain characteristic Jewish attitudes and institutions (e.g. the *synagogue) developed. This exile established the beginnings of the *diaspora; many Jews remained in Babylonia, and in late antiquity and the middle ages it had one of the largest and most important Jewish communities in the world.

Bacău 46 32N 26 59E A city in E Romania, on the River Bistriła. An important road and rail junction, its industries include oil refining, textiles, and paper manufacture. Population (1983): 156 891.

baccarat games Various related card games, the object of which is to hold cards totalling nine, counting only the final digit of a total of ten or over (thus 10 equals 0). **Chemin de fer** was formerly popular in casinos. In this game the punters take turns to be banker, against whom the other punters make their bets. The banker then deals two cards to another punter and two to himself. If the cards of either total nine, or failing that eight, this total wins and bets are settled accordingly. Otherwise a third card is taken or refused as necessary (taken if the total is four or under, refused if six or over). The highest total wins. **Punto banco,** the form now most widely played in UK casinos, is identical to chemin de fer except that bets are placed against the casino on either the banker or his opponent.

Bacchanalia The Roman form of the Hellenistic mystery rites in honour of Bacchus (*see* Dionysus). The cult reached Rome from S Italy in the 2nd century BC. Originally involving only women, Bacchic worship included ecstatic rituals and secret orgies. In 186 BC a decree of the Senate prohibited Bacchanalia in Rome.

Bacchus. *See* Dionysus.

Bacchylides (c. 516–c. 450 BC) Greek lyric poet, nephew of Simonides and a rival of Pindar. Born on the island of Ceos, he lived at the court of Syracuse until the death of his patron Hiero in 467. Egyptian papyrus fragments discovered in 1896 contain parts of 14 odes and 6 dithyrambs (choral songs).

Bach, Johann Sebastian (1685–1750) German composer and keyboard player, the greatest member of a large musical family. An orphan from the age of nine, he was brought up and taught by his brother Johann Christoph Bach (1671–1721). He subsequently became a chorister in Lüneburg and in 1703 a violinist at the Weimar court. In 1707 he married his cousin Maria Barbara Bach (1684–1720); after her death he married Anna Magdalena Wilcken (1701–60). In 1708 he rejoined the Weimar court as organist, remaining there for nine years. He became kapellmeister at the court of Prince Leopold of Anhalt at Köthen in 1717 and finally cantor of St Thomas's Church, Leipzig, in 1723. During his lifetime Bach achieved greater recognition as an organist than as a composer; he composed much organ music and was a skilled improviser on keyboard instruments. Among his greatest works are the *St John Passion* (1723), the *St Matthew Passion* (1729), and the *Mass in B minor* (1733–38), as well as over

JOHANN SEBASTIAN BACH

200 cantatas. His compositions for orchestra include violin and harpsichord concertos and the *Brandenburg Concertos* (1721). For the harpsichord and clavichord he composed a collection of 48 preludes and fugues entitled the *Well-Tempered Clavier* (Part I, 1722; Part II, 1744) and the *Goldberg Variations* (1742); he also wrote music for the violin, cello, and lute. Bach's music did not become widely known until Mendelssohn revived it, giving the first performance of the *St Matthew Passion* since Bach's time in 1829.

Of Bach's 20 children, 3 sons became famous musicians. His eldest son **Wilhelm Friedemann Bach** (1710–84) studied in Leipzig and became church organist in Dresden (1733–46) and subsequently in Halle (1746–64). He ended his life in poverty, leaving cantatas, concertos, and symphonies.

His third son **Karl Philipp Emanuel Bach** (1714–88) studied law and philosophy but later turned to music, becoming musician to Frederick the Great in Berlin and subsequently becoming director of the principal church in Hamburg in succession to Telemann. In his works, which were highly regarded by Haydn and Mozart, he developed a new monophonic style of composition that became the basis of the classical style. His works include symphonies, concertos, and much keyboard music.

J. S. Bach's 11th son **Johann Christian Bach** (1735–82), called the English (or London) Bach, studied in Berlin and after holding posts in Italy became music master to the British royal family. He composed 13 operas, as well as concertos, church music, and piano pieces.

bacillus Any rod-shaped bacterium. The term is used specifically for bacteria of the genus *Bacillus*: spore-forming species including parasites of plants and animals. *B. anthracis* was first shown to cause anthrax in livestock by Robert *Koch.

backcross The mating of an organism with one of its parents. Backcrosses are used in animal and plant breeding to select individuals that will be pure-breeding for a particular desirable characteristic.

backgammon A board game for two players that was known in ancient Mesopotamia, Greece, and Rome and in medieval England (as "the tables"). Each player has 15 pieces, which are moved round the 24 chevrons (points) marked on the board, the number of points moved being indicated by the throws of two dice. From their prescribed starting positions the players move in opposite directions. Each tries to bring all his pieces into the last quarter (his home board or inner table), after which he can remove them from the board (bear them off). Simultaneously he must block his opponent's moves. A chevron is occupied (point is made) when a player has two or more pieces on it, i.e. his opponent cannot land on it. A single piece on a point is a blot, i.e. vulnerable to the opponent's taking it and forcing it to travel round the board again.

background radiation Low-intensity radiation naturally present on the earth. It results either from the bombardment of the earth by *cosmic rays or from naturally occurring radioactive substances in the earth's crust.

backswimmer A *water bug, belonging to the worldwide family *Notonectidae* (nearly 200 species), that swims on its back, using a pair of oarlike legs for propulsion. Backswimmers can fly but are normally found in fresh water, preying voraciously on insects, tadpoles, and small fish. They must return to the surface periodically to replenish their air store.

Bacolod 10 38N 122 58E A port in the central Philippines, in NW Negros. It is a sugar-refining centre serving the Philippines' most important sugar-growing area. Population (1980): 266 604.

Bacon, Francis (1909–) British painter, born in Dublin of English parentage. He was self-taught and began painting in the 1930s; his characteristic mature style is evident in 1945, when his *Three Studies* (of figures for the base of a *Crucifixion*) ensured him an undeniable place in modern British art. Another of his well-known paintings is *Study after Velázquez* (1951), a version of Velázquez's portrait of pope Innocent X. His paintings are characterized by strong rich colours, a sinister blurring or erasure of human features, and an often violent dramatic quality.

Bacon, Francis, 1st Baron Verulam, Viscount St Albans (1561–1626) English lawyer and philosopher. He was called to the Bar in 1582 and became an MP in 1584. During the 1590s, in the hope of political advancement, he cultivated the friendship of the 2nd Earl of *Essex but in 1601 assisted the prosecution for treason of his former patron. Under James I (reigned 1603–25) Bacon's career advanced more smoothly: he became a commissioner for the union of Scotland and England (1604), attorney general (1613), and Lord Chancellor (1618). In 1621, however, he was found guilty of bribery and corruption; he was fined £40,000 and banished from office and parliament.

Bacon's fame rests more securely on his philosophical and literary output and his influence on scientific thought in the later 17th century was considerable. In 1597 he published his first group of *Essays* on truth, death, friendship, etc.; further such discourses appeared in 1625. *The Advancement of Learning* (1605) presented a new classification of sciences and was expanded in the *De augmentis scientiarum* of 1623. In *Novum organum scientiarum* (1620) he argued that knowledge can be derived only from experience, advocating the scientific method of *induction. His other works include a *History of Henry VII* (1622) and the *New Atlantis* (1626), which describes his ideal state.

Bacon, John (1740–99) British neoclassical sculptor. He trained as a porcelain modeller, but is noted for tombs, such as the Chatham monument in Westminster Abbey (1779). He also improved the pointing machine, a device for reproducing a plaster cast in stone or marble.

Bacon, Roger (c. 1214–c. 1292) English monk, scholar, and scientist, called Doctor Mirabilis for his diverse skills and learning. In three books written for Pope Clement IV he attempted to systematize the current state of knowledge; other works prophesied aeroplanes, microscopes, round-the-world voyages, steam engines, and telescopes. His astronomical knowledge enabled him to detect errors in the Julian *calendar. He has also been credited with the invention of *gunpowder and of the magnifying glass.

bacteria Microscopic single-celled organisms found wherever life is possible. Generally 0.0001–0.005 mm long, they may be spherical (*see* coccus), rodlike (*see* bacillus), or spiral-shaped

(spirillum) and often occur in chains or clusters of cells. The so-called true bacteria have a rigid cell wall, which may be surrounded by a slimy capsule, and they often have long whiplike flagella for locomotion and short hairlike pili used in a form of sexual reproduction. A few bacteria are autotrophic, i.e. they can grow on simple inorganic substrates using carbon dioxide gas from the atmosphere to manufacture their own nutrients, but the majority are heterotrophic, requiring a source of organic carbon and a variety of other nutrients for growth. A single bacterium reproduces by dividing into two new cells; some species can do so every 15 minutes leading to rapid population growth. Some form resistant spores, which can survive for several years in adverse conditions.

The most important role of bacteria is in decomposing dead plant and animal tissues and releasing their constituents to the soil (*see* carbon cycle). Nitrogen-fixing bacteria in the soil or sea convert atmospheric nitrogen gas to nitrites and nitrates, which can then be used by plants (*see* nitrogen cycle). Many industrial processes are dependent on bacteria, including cheese making and *fermentation reactions. Bacteria inhabit the digestive systems of animals and play an important part in digestion, especially in *ruminants. However, certain (pathogenic) species may infect body tissues and cause disease while others, such as *Salmonella*, can cause *food poisoning.

bacteriophage (*or* phage) A *virus that infects a bacterium. 25–800 nanometres in size, phages may be spherical, filamentous, or tadpole-shaped with a head and tail. They consist of a protein coat surrounding a core of nucleic acid (either DNA or RNA) that is inserted into the bacterium. The viral genes then use the protein-synthesis apparatus of the bacterium to produce new phages, which are released from the cell, usually causing its destruction.

Bactria An ancient region of central Asia, SE of the Aral Sea. An Achaemenian province from about 600 BC, it was conquered, despite fierce resistance, by Alexander the Great and subsequently passed to the Seleucids. In the mid-3rd century BC Diodotus I (died c. 239) established an independent Bactrian-Greek kingdom that later encompassed present-day Soviet Central Asia, Afghanistan, and Pakistan. From the 1st century AD the nomadic Kushan tribe occupied Bactria, introducing Buddhism and artistic styles influenced by Buddhist, Iranian, and Greek-Roman sources. Until about 600 AD Bactria was the hub of overland trade between east and west and a centre for the interchange of religious and artistic ideas.

Badajoz 38 53N 6 58W A city in SW Spain, in Estremadura on the River Guadiana. Attacked on numerous occasions, it was pillaged by Wellington's troops (1812) during the Peninsular War. It has a 13th-century cathedral. Population (1981): 114 361.

Badalona 41 27N 2 15E A port in NE Spain, in Catalonia, forming an industrial suburb of Barcelona. Industries include glass, shipbuilding, and textiles. Population (1981): 227 744.

Baden 47 28N 8 19E A spa town in N Switzerland. The diet (assembly) of the Swiss Confederation met here (1424–1712). Its hot sulphur springs have been visited since Roman times. Population (1981): 23 140.

Baden-Baden 48 45N 8 15E A spa in SW West Germany, in Baden-Württemberg in the Black Forest. The hot springs have been used since Roman times. Population (1983): 48 886.

Baden-Powell, Robert Stephenson Smyth, 1st Baron (1857–1941) British general and founder of the Boy Scouts. After service in India and various parts of Africa, he achieved fame through his defence of Mafeking in the *Boer War (1899–1900). Utilizing the experience of character training he had gained overseas, he founded the Boy Scouts in 1908 and, with his sister Agnes, the *Girl Guides in 1910. *See also* Scout Association.

Baden-Württemberg A *Land* in SW West Germany, bordering on France and Switzerland, formed by an amalgamation of three former *Länder* (1952). It contains the Black Forest, several spas, and fertile agricultural land. Its population and economy have expanded greatly since World War II, when many refugees from further E settled here. A large proportion of Germany's watches, jewellery, and musical and medical instruments are made in Baden-Württemberg and there are also textile, chemical, and car industries. Area: 35 751 sq km (13 800 sq mi). Population (1980 est): 9 235 600. Capital: Stuttgart.

Bader, Sir Douglas (1910–82) British fighter pilot. After losing his legs in a flying accident (1931), Bader argued himself back into the RAF at the start of World War II. Becoming a national hero, he was finally shot down and imprisoned by the Germans, who only prevented his escape by depriving him of his artificial legs. In 1976 he was knighted for his work for the disabled.

badger A nocturnal burrowing mammal of the *weasel family (*Mustelidae*). The largest of the eight species is the gregarious Eurasian badger (*Meles meles*), about 90 cm long, with short strong legs, long coarse greyish hair on the body, and a black and white striped head. It lives in a complex of burrows (a set) and feeds on insects, rodents, worms, berries, etc. The American badger (*Taxidea taxus*) is smaller and lives alone when not breeding. The remaining badgers are found in S and SE Asia and include the smallest species–the ferret badgers (genus *Melogale*), about 60 cm long.

Bad Godesberg. *See* Godesberg.

badlands An elevated area dissected by gullies and deep valleys. This type of landscape is typical of arid and semiarid areas, where rainfall is intermittent and an adequate vegetation cover is prevented from forming or is destroyed through, for example, overgrazing; severe soil erosion may occur. The name was originally applied to the Bad lands of S Dakota (USA).

BADMINTON *The dimensions of the court. The top of the net at the centre is 5 ft (1.5 m) above the floor.*

badminton An indoor court game for two or four players, played with rackets and a shuttlecock of nylon or cork and feathers. It originated in about 1870, probably from battledore and shuttlecock and may have first been played in the park of *Badminton House. It is a volleying game (the shuttles do not bounce) and points are scored only by the serving side. If the serving side fails to make a good return the service changes (in doubles games both partners serve before their opponents). A game is usually played to 15 points (women's singles go to 11 points).

Badminton 51 33N 2 17W A village in England, in Avon. In the park of Badminton House (1682), the home of the Duke of Beaufort, annual horse trials are held. The game of *badminton probably originated here.

Badoglio, Pietro (1871–1956) Italian general, who rose to prominence during World War I. He directed Mussolini's conquest of Ethiopia (1935–36) but in 1940 resigned during the disastrous Italian campaign in Greece. After Mussolini's fall (1943), he became prime minister and negotiated the armistice with the Allies. He resigned in 1944.

Baeck, Leo (1873–1956) German Jewish theologian. Under the *Nazis, he became the spiritual leader of German Jewry, continuing to teach in Theresienstadt concentration camp (1943–45). After the war he settled in London. In his major work, *The Essence of Judaism* (1905), Baeck argued for the superiority of Judaism to Christianity.

Baedeker, Karl (1801–59) German publisher of guidebooks. His first guide, to Coblenz (1829), was followed by a series that became internationally famous.

Baekeland, Leo Hendrik (1863–1944) US industrial chemist, born in Belgium. He invented Bakelite (*see* urea-formaldehyde resins), the first synthetic thermosetting plastic. The discovery was made while Baekeland was searching for a synthetic substitute for *shellac.

Baer, Karl Ernest von (1792–1876) Russian embryologist. He showed that mammalian eggs were not the follicles of the ovary but microscopic particles inside the follicles. He described the development of the embryo from layers of tissue, which he called *germ layers*, and demonstrated similarities in the embryos of different species of vertebrates.

Baeyer, (Johann Friedrich Wilhelm) Adolf von (1835–1917) German chemist, who became professor at the University of Strassburg and then at Munich. He discovered barbituric acid (1865), synthesized indigo (1878), and developed several organic dyes. Baeyer also calculated the angles between the carbon atoms in organic compounds, showing (1885) how strained bonds affect chemical reactivity in closed carbon chains. He was awarded the 1905 Nobel Prize for his synthesis of indigo.

Baez, Joan (1941–) US folksinger, whose performance at the 1959 Newport Festival led to a series of successful recordings of folksongs and later of contemporary protest songs. An active pacifist, she opposed the Vietnam War.

Baffin, William (c. 1584–1622) English navigator. In two voyages (1615, 1616) with Capt Robert Bylot he attempted in the *Discovery* to find the *Northwest Passage. He eventually despaired of its existence but explored the Hudson Strait, giving his name to Baffin Bay and Baffin Island.

Baffin Island The largest island of the Canadian Arctic, in Franklin district lying N of Hudson Strait. It is separated from Greenland by a Strait forming **Baffin Bay** (in the N) and Davis Strait. Mountainous with many glaciers and snowfields, its sparse population is concentrated in Frobisher Bay. Area: 476 068 sq km (183 810 sq mi).

Bagehot, Walter (1826–77) British economist, political theorist, literary critic, and journalist. He first worked as a banker, his interest in banking theories being reflected in his *Lombard Street* (1873). While editor of the *Economist* magazine (1860–77), he wrote his major political works, *The English Constitution* (1867), which analyses the comparative powers of the British organs of government, and *Physics and Politics* (1872), applying Darwin's principles of natural selection to political society.

Baghdad 33 20N 44 26E The capital of Iraq, on the River Tigris near the centre of the country. Built by the caliph (Islamic leader) Mansur in the 8th century, it was a centre of commerce, learning, and religion until sacked by the Mongols in 1258. Modern Baghdad grew after becoming the capital of independent Iraq (1927) and is now an important administrative, communications, and manufacturing centre with three universities (1947, 1957, and 1963). Population (1982 est): 4 038 430.

Baghdad Pact A treaty between Turkey, Iraq, Iran, Pakistan, and the UK. Signed in 1955, its goals were military, economic, and social cooperation in the Middle East. When Iraq withdrew from it in 1959, its headquarters moved to

Ankara from Baghdad and it was renamed the *Central Treaty Organization.

Baghdad Railway A rail link between Europe and Asia Minor, running from Turkey to Iraq. Its construction, begun in the late 19th century with German finance, was seen by the British as a threat to their position in India and it was a point of contention in World War I.

Baglioni A family that dominated Perugia (Italy) from 1425 until 1534. Its leading members were **Malatesta Baglioni** (1389–1437), who established the family's position in Perugia; **Giampaolo Baglioni** (c. 1470–1520), who came to power in 1500 following a family feud that resulted in the assassination of many of his relatives; and **Malatesta Baglioni** (1491–1531), a *condottiere who served both Venice and Florence, betraying the latter to the pope in 1530. The Baglioni were banished from Perugia in 1534.

bagpipes A reed-pipe instrument of ancient origin, found in many countries. Air is forced into a windbag either by the mouth (Scottish bagpipes) or by a bellows (Northumbrian pipes). By pressing the bag under his arm the player pushes air into the sounding pipes, which consist of one to three drones and a single chanter pipe. Drone pipes each sound one continuous note. The chanter pipe is fitted with holes, which are covered by the player's fingers. Bagpipes are regarded as the national instrument of Scotland, having been introduced to the British Isles in the 13th century.

Baguio 16 25N 120 37E A city in the N Philippines, in W Luzon. It is a popular summer resort and the site of the national military academy. Gold and copper are mined. Population (1980): 119 009.

bagworm moth A moth belonging to the widely distributed family *Psychidae* (800 species). The larvae live in cases made of silk covered with leaves, twigs, grass, etc., with only the head and forelegs projecting. Males emerge after pupation, flying in search of the wingless females, which remain in their cases.

Baha'i faith A religion founded in Persia in 1863 by Mirza Husain 'Ali (1817–92), who was known as Baha' Allah (Glory of God). He proclaimed himself to be the Promised One whose coming was foretold by the Bab (*see* Babi faith). His eldest son and then his great-grandson led the Baha'is after his death until 1957. Since 1963 the faith has been governed by the Universal House of Justice, a council at Haifa, Israel, elected by national spiritual assemblies. The basic tenet of the faith is that God reveals himself to man through prophets who appear at various stages in history and the most recent of these is Baha' Allah. Baha'is advocate a universal faith, world peace, an international language, the equality of men and women, and the abolition of all prejudices. The faith has now spread to the West despite persecution in Iran and prohibition in Indonesia.

Bahamas, Commonwealth of the A state consisting of about 700 islands and innumerable cays in the West Indies, off the SE coast of Florida. The principal islands, which are mainly low lying, include New Providence (with the capital Nassau), Grand Bahama, Abaco, Eleuthera, Andros, and Watling Island (San Salvador). The majority of the population is of African descent. *Economy*: with its mild subtropical climate and beautiful beaches, the main industry of the Bahamas is tourism, which accounts for over 50% of revenue and employment. Efforts are now being made to develop agriculture and fisheries, finance, and industry (especially oil refining). Foreign investment is encouraged by the tax position, 90% of companies being foreign-owned. Main exports include cement, petroleum and petroleum products, chemicals, and fish. *History*: in 1492 Columbus made his first landing in the W hemisphere on the island of San Salvador. The first European occupation comprised an English religious settlement in the mid-17th century, and the islands became a British crown colony in 1717. From 1964 the country had increasing control over its own affairs and in

1973 it attained full independence within the Commonwealth. Prime minister: Lynden Oscar Pindling (1930–). Official language: English. Official currency: Bahamian dollar of 100 cents. Area: 13 864 sq km (5353 sq mi). Population (1980): 209 505. Capital and main port: Nassau.

Bahawalpur 29 24N 71 47E A city in Pakistan, situated on the railway between Karachi and Lahore. It is an expanding industrial centre producing cotton and soap. Population (1981): 178 000.

Bahia. *See* Salvador.

Bahía Blanca 38 45S 62 15W A port in Argentina. It is a major distribution centre; exports include grain, meat, and wool. The National University of the South was founded here in 1956. Population (1980): 233 126.

Bahrain, State of An independent sheikdom in the Arabian Gulf, occupying a low-lying archipelago between Saudi Arabia and the Qatar Peninsula. The two main islands, Bahrain and Al-Muharraq, are connected by a causeway and there are also plans for a causeway to Saudi Arabia. The inhabitants are mainly Arabs. *Economy*: almost totally dependent upon oil. A large refinery on Bahrain Island processes not only the relatively small amounts of local oil, first discovered in 1931, but also much larger amounts coming from Saudi Arabia by pipeline. Efforts are being made to develop other industry with some success. An aluminium smelter on Bahrain is the largest non-oil industrial plant in the Gulf. The formerly important pearl-fishing industry is now in decline. Bahrain is important as a transport centre in the Gulf and the modern harbour of Mina Salman has extensive shipping facilities and a free transport area. In 1975 the government licensed the setting up of Offshore Banking Units, a move that could give Bahrain increased commercial importance in the Gulf. *History*: the islands were under Portuguese rule from 1521 until 1602, and during parts of the 17th century Iran had control, eventually being expelled by the Khalifa family, who have ruled the area for most of the time since. It was a British protected state from 1861 until 1971 when full independence was declared by the emir, Sheik Isa ibn Sulman al-Khalifa (1933–). In 1975 political unrest led to the dissolution of the National Assembly. Bahrain became a member of OPEC in 1970. Official language: Arabic; English is also widely spoken. Official religion: Islam. Official currency: Bahrain dinar of 1000 fils. Area: 660 sq km (255 sq mi). Population (1983): 383 000. Capital and main port: Manama.

Baikal, Lake A lake in the SE central Soviet Union, in the Buryat ASSR. It is the largest freshwater lake in Asia and at 1620 m (5316 ft) the deepest in the world. It is fed by over 300 streams but drained by only one, the River Angara. Area: 31 500 sq km (12 160 sq mi).

bail The release by a court of an imprisoned person, usually while awaiting trial, into the keeping of people who agree to ensure his reappearance at a particular date and time. If these people, called "sureties," then fail to produce him, they forfeit whatever sum of money the court has set for bail. The person bailed must also stand as surety for himself; if thought trustworthy, he may be bailed without other sureties, "in his own recognizance." Judges have wide discretion as to whether bail should be granted and for what amount.

Bailey bridge A type of military bridge invented by Sir Donald Bailey (1901–85) during World War II. Consisting of light strong standardized interlocking truss sections, it can be easily assembled in the field. Pontoons can be provided for longer spans, the longest of which was that of the 1200 m (4000 ft) bridge built across the River Maas in Holland.

Baily, Francis (1774–1844) British amateur astronomer, who gave his name to "Baily's beads," the broken line of sunlight shining through lunar valleys close to total eclipse.

He revised current star catalogues and calculated accurate values for the earth's density and ellipticity.

Bain, Alexander (1818–1903) Scottish psychologist and scholar, who was professor of logic at Aberdeen University (1860–80). His psychological work sought to relate mental to physiological functions (*see also* behaviourism). He founded the philosophical journal *Mind* (1876) and published treatises on logic, English grammar, and philosophy.

Bainbridge, Beryl (1934–) British novelist and playwright. She worked as an actress before writing such novels as *The Dressmaker* (1973), *The Bottle Factory Outing* (1974), and *Injury Time* (1977). Her plays include *It's a Lovely Day Tomorrow* (1977) and *Somewhere More Central* (1981).

Baird, John Logie (1888–1946) British electrical engineer, who invented an early television system. In 1924 he succeeded in transmitting the outline of shapes; in 1925 he could transmit features and by 1926, moving objects; he produced colour-television pictures in 1928. However, his 240-line television system was not adopted by the BBC. Baird also pioneered the use of radar and fibre optics.

Bairnsfather, (Charles) Bruce (1888–1959) British cartoonist and author. He became famous in World War I for his war cartoons featuring the character Old Bill and during World War II he was an official war cartoonist.

Baja California. *See* Lower California.

Bakelite. *See* urea-formaldehyde resins.

Baker, Sir Benjamin (1840–1907) British civil engineer, who worked with Sir John Fowler (1817–1918) on the construction of the first underground railway, the London District line from Westminster to the City (1869), and on the Forth railway bridge. Baker also designed Avonmouth docks.

Baker, Dame Janet (Abbott) (1933–) British mezzo-soprano. After studying at the Royal College of Music, she made a brilliant career singing lieder and in oratorio. Her appearances in Mozart's *Così fan tutte* and Berlioz's *The Trojans* launched her successful operatic career. She was awarded the DBE in 1976 and retired from opera in 1982.

Baker, Kenneth (1935–) British Conservative politician; secretary of state for the environment (1985–87). In 1987 he succeeded Sir Keith Joseph as secretary of state for education and science.

Baker, Sir Samuel White (1821–93) British explorer. In 1861, accompanied by his wife, he set off from Cairo to discover the source of the Nile. Informed by *Speke and J. A. Grant (1827–92) of an unexplored great lake, he found (1864) and named Lake Albert (now Lake Mobutu). He led an Egyptian expedition to annex the S Nile basin, where as Egypt's governor general (1869–74) he abolished slavery.

Bakewell 53 13N 1 40W A market town in N England, in Derbyshire in the Peak District National Park. A tart filled with almond-flavoured sponge on a layer of jam (Bakewell tart) originated here. Nearby are two stately homes (Chatsworth House and Haddon Hall). Population (1985): 4000.

Bakewell, Robert (1725–95) British agriculturalist, whose breeding techniques transformed livestock farming. By rigorous selection and culling he improved several breeds of cattle and sheep as meat producers.

Bakhtaran (name until 1987: Kermanshar) 34 19N 47 04E A town in W Iran, with a largely Kurdish population. It has a university (1974) and an oil refinery that is connected by pipeline to oilfields near the Iraqi border. Population (1985 est): 536 500.

Bakhtyari A major tribe of W Iran of some 400 000 Muslims speaking the Luri dialect of Persian. About one-third are still nomadic herdsman living in tents. They make a gruelling annual migration of 150 miles from their winter pastures on the plains to the summer pastures in the mountains. Authority is vested in hereditary chiefs, who have often played an influential role in Iranian politics. Their women have a greater degree of freedom than is usual among Muslims.

baking powder A mixture, usually of *sodium bicarbonate and *tartaric acid or *cream of tartar, used in baking. It generates carbon dioxide on heating or wetting, thus making the dough rise.

Bakst, Léon (Lev Samoilovich Rosenberg; 1866–1924) Russian artist, who modernized theatre design. He was born in St Petersburg, where he trained in the Imperial Academy of Arts and became court painter, before turning to scenery design in 1900. His greatest achievements were for ballets produced by Sergei *Diaghilev in Paris, where he later settled.

Baku 40 22N 49 53E A port in the S Soviet Union, the capital of Azerbaidzhan SSR on the Caspian Sea. The old town is a maze of narrow streets and ancient buildings, including mosques and a 17th-century palace. It is the oldest centre of Soviet oil production, and oil is still the basis of its economy. Population (1981 est): 1 046 000.

Bakunin, Mikhail Aleksandrovich (1814–76) Russian anarchist. An interest in dialectics led Bakunin to study German philosophy at Berlin University, where he became exposed to socialist philosophy. He participated in the Revolutions of 1848 and in 1849 he was arrested in Dresden, handed over to Russian officials, and exiled to Siberia. In 1861 he escaped to London. He participated in the First *International but came into conflict with Marx and was expelled.

Bakwanga. *See* Mbuji-Mayi.

Bala, Lake (Welsh name: Llyn Tegid) The largest natural lake in Wales, in E Gwynedd. It is used for angling and sailing. The town of Bala lies at its N end. Length: 6 km (4 mi).

Balaclava, Battle of (25 October, 1854) An indecisive battle between Russian and British-Turkish forces in the *Crimean War. It is notorious for the heavy British casualties caused by misunderstanding between Lord *Raglan, the British commander in chief, and Lord Lucan (1800–88), the cavalry commander. The courageous Light Brigade charged Russian artillery at the end of a narrow valley and of its 673 men, 113 were killed and 134 wounded. The battle was made famous by Tennyson's poem "Charge of the Light Brigade".

Balakirev, Mili Alekseevich (1837–1910) Russian composer, one of the *Five and founder of the Free School of Music in St Petersburg (1862). His works, such as the tone poem *Tamara* (1867–82) and the piano fantasy *Islamey* (1869), reflect his romanticism and Russian nationalism.

balalaika A Russian plucked instrument of the guitar family, played singly or in a balalaika orchestra. It has a long fretted fingerboard, a triangular body, and three wire strings that are plucked with a plectrum. The smaller size is held like a guitar and the larger balanced on the floor like a double bass.

balance A sensitive device for comparing two masses, consisting of a beam pivoted at its centre (usually on an agate knife edge) with pans hanging from each of its ends. The material of unknown mass is placed in one pan and standard weights are placed in the other. A pointer indicates when the beam is horizontal and the whole device is enclosed in a glass case to avoid draughts and temperature changes. The accuracy of a balance is increased by using a rider—a small weight hung on a calibrated scale on the balance arm itself. A standard balance will weigh to the nearest 0.0001 g, while extremely sensitive **microbalances** can be used to weigh objects with a mass of only 1 microgram. *See also* spring balance.

balance of payments The difference between a country's income and its expenditure abroad. It is usually divided into a current account and a capital account. The current account records the country's *balance-of-trade earnings or deficit on visible goods and its invisible earnings or deficit on such items as insurance, transport, tourism, and some kinds of government spending. The capital account records all long-and short-term capital flows, both in the public and private sectors. If the sum of the current and capital accounts shows a deficit there will be a net loss of foreign exchange, which the government must take steps to remedy. Measures include deflation by *monetary or *fiscal policy to reduce imports, the imposition of *tariffs or import *quotas, incentives to increase exports, the introduction of stringent *exchange control regulations, and ultimately *devaluation of the currency. If the balance of payments shows a persistent surplus a revaluation of the currency may be required.

balance of power   The principle seeking to ensure that no nation or group of nations becomes too dominant. Practised by Greek city states, which formed intercity alliances, the principle was adopted in Europe in the alliance system of 15th-century Italy. In 1815 at the Congress of *Vienna, Prussia, Russia, Britain, France, and Austria realigned European frontiers to establish themselves as equal powers and to ensure peace. Tensions remained, however, and rival alliances led to further wars to prevent or restore national dominance. In the 20th century the League of Nations and the UN have both tried to establish international harmony, but the development of nuclear weapons acts as the greatest deterrent to any state sufficiently ambitious to threaten international equilibrium.

balance of trade   The difference in money between the value of a country's imports and its exports. The balance of trade is sometimes known as the visibles account because it refers only to actual goods. Together with the invisibles account and capital transfers it makes up the *balance of payments. The invisibles account includes such earnings as selling insurance abroad and spending by foreign tourists. Thus the balance of trade can be in deficit without necessarily meaning that the balance of payments will also be in deficit.

Balanchine, George   (Georgy Melitonovich Balanchivadze; 1904–83) US ballet dancer and choreographer, born in Russia. He worked for Diaghilev's Ballets Russes in Europe from 1924 and went to the USA in 1933. In 1948 he became first artistic director of the New York City Ballet. His ballets include *Firebird* (1950) and *Don Quixote* (1965), and he also choreographed for films and stage musicals.

Balaton, Lake   A lake in W Hungary, the largest in central Europe. There are vineyards and holiday resorts on its shore and its outlet is a canal leading to a tributary of the River Danube. Area: 598 sq km (231 sq mi).

Balboa   8 57N 79 33W A port in the Panama Canal Zone, at the Pacific end of the Panama Canal. It was named after the explorer, Vasco Núñez de *Balboa. It has extensive harbour facilities. Population (1980): 1952.

Balboa, Vasco Núñez de   (c. 1475–1517) Spanish explorer. Having settled in Hispaniola, he became a stowaway on an expedition to present-day Colombia (1510), moved on to Panama, and founded a settlement at Darién (1511). In 1513 he set off across the Isthmus in search of gold. Sighting the Pacific, which he called the South Sea, after 25 gruelling days, he claimed it for Spain. He was subsequently accused, unjustly, of treason and beheaded by the governor of Darién, Pedrarias (d. 1531).

Balchin, Nigel   (1908–70) British novelist. He studied natural science at Cambridge and later worked as an industrial psychologist. *The Small Back Room* (1943) is based on his experience as a scientific adviser to the Army Council during World War II. *Mine Own Executioner* (1945) and *The Fall of the Sparrow* (1955) are brilliant psychological character studies.

Balcon, Sir Michael   (1896–1977) British film producer. As executive producer of Ealing Studios from 1938 to 1959 he was responsible for many successful comedies such as *Kind Hearts and Coronets* (1949) and *The Lavender Hill Mob* (1951).

bald eagle   A large sea *eagle, *Haliaetus leucocephalus*, also called the American eagle; it is the national emblem of the USA and an endangered species. It is dark brown with a white head and tail and has a prominent curved beak and unfeathered legs. It feeds on carrion and fish and has rough skin on the toes for

grasping slippery prey.

Baldwin, James Arthur   (1924–87) US Black novelist, essayist, and dramatist. His first novel, *Go Tell It on the Mountain* (1953), is based on his experience of poverty and religion in Harlem, New York City, where he was born. He lived in Paris from 1948 to 1957, when he returned to the USA as an active civil-rights campaigner. His works include novels, such as *Giovanni's Room* (1956), *Tell Me How Long the Train's Been Gone* (1968), and *Just Above My Head* (1979), two plays, and essays, notably *The Fire Next Time* (1963) and *Evidence of Things not Seen* (1986).

Baldwin of Bewdley, Stanley, 1st Earl   (1867–1947) British statesman and Conservative politician, who was prime minister (1923–24, 1924–29, 1935–37). As chancellor of the exchequer (1922–23), Baldwin negotiated the British World War I debt to the USA. He dealt as prime minister with the *General Strike (1926), to which his government responded with the anti-union Trade Disputes Act (1927). Baldwin was much criticized for condoning Italy's conquest of Ethiopia and his apparent reluctance to rearm in the face of Germany's military build-up. His management of the events leading to Edward VIII's abdication reflected public opinion.

Baldwin I   (c. 1058–1118) King of Jerusalem (1100– 18). Baldwin succeeded his brother Godfrey of Bouillon, whom he had accompanied on the first Crusade, taking Edessa in 1098. Baldwin considerably expanded the territory of Jerusalem.

Balearic Islands   An archipelago in the W Mediterranean Sea comprising a Spanish province. It includes the chief islands of *Majorca, *Minorca, *Ibiza, and Formentera, together with several islets. The islands were conquered by Aragon from the Moors in the 14th century. Area: 5014 sq km (1936 sq mi). Population (1982): 669 101. Capital: Palma, on Majorca.

baleen (*or* whalebone)   The horny material that forms the food-sieving plates in whalebone *whales. Baleen was formerly used to manufacture stays in corsets, but has now largely been replaced by synthetic materials.

Balenciaga, Cristóbal   (1895–1972) Spanish fashion designer, who moved to Paris in 1937. He built up an elite clientele, which was attracted by his starkly elegant styles, especially his tailored suits.

Balfour, Arthur James, 1st Earl of   (1848–1930) British statesman and Conservative prime minister (1902–05). As secretary for Ireland (1887–92) he incurred the nickname Bloody Balfour, failing in his policy of "killing Home Rule by kindness." His government passed an *Education Act (1902), the Irish Land Purchase Act (1903; *see* Land Acts, Irish), and concluded the Anglo-French entente (1904). In World War I Balfour was foreign secretary (1916–19), issuing his famous *Balfour Declaration.

Balfour Declaration   (1917) The decision of the British Government, made known in a letter of 2 Nov from the British foreign secretary, Arthur *Balfour, to Lionel Walter, 2nd Baron Rothschild (1868–1937), the chairman of the British Zionist Federation, to support the establishment of a national Jewish home in Palestine. The letter promised British aid to Zionist efforts to establish such a home, providing that the interests of existing non-Jewish communities in Palestine be maintained as well as the rights and political status of Jews in any other country. Arab aspirations in Palestine, however, prevented the British Government from fulfilling the promise of the Declaration, which was abandoned in 1939.

Bali   An Indonesian island off E Java. Mountainous and volcanic, it has southern fertile plains that produce chiefly rice. The Balinese are famed for their arts and handicrafts, and it is a popular tourist resort. *History*: Hindu since the 7th century AD, Bali resisted the 16th–17th century spread of Islam through Indonesia and became an enclave of Hindu culture. Dutch rule became complete only in 1908, although trade began in the 17th century. In the 1965–67 Indonesian purge of communists 40 000 people were killed. Area: 5558 sq km (2146 sq mi). Population (1980): 2 469 930. Chief town: Denpasar.

Balikpapan 1 15S 116 50E A port in Indonesia, in SE Kalimantan on the Makassar Strait. Its refinery processes local and imported oil. Population (1980): 280 875.

Balkan Mountains (Bulgarian name: Stara Planina) A mountain range extending 500 km (311 mi) E–W for the entire width of central Bulgaria. It rises to 2376 m (7795 ft) at Botev Peak.

Balkans An area in SE Europe consisting of present-day Greece, Albania, Yugoslavia, Bulgaria, part of Romania, and the European part of Turkey. Part of the Roman empire from the 2nd century BC and of the Eastern Roman (Byzantine) Empire from the 5th century AD, the Balkans were ruled by the Ottoman Turks from the 15th to the 19th and 20th centuries, when independence was granted to Greece (1829), Serbia (1878), Romania (1878), Bulgaria (1908), and Albania (1912). The competition between European powers for control of the Balkans contributed to the outbreak of World War I, after which Yugoslavia was created out of Serbia. All the Balkan states, except Greece, became communist after *World War II.

Balkan Wars (1912–13) Two military confrontations that preceded World War I. In the first (1912–13) the Balkan League (Bulgaria, Serbia, Greece, and Montenegro) defeated Turkey. In the concluding Treaty of London, Turkey lost all its European possessions except E Thrace. In the second Balkan War (1913) the victors fought over their acquisitions in Macedonia, from most of which Bulgaria was excluded by the Treaty of *Bucharest; Turkey regained Thrace.

Balkhash, Lake A lake in the S central Soviet Union, in the E Kazakh SSR. Since it has no outlet, it fluctuates in size, and it is generally shrinking. Area: about 20 000 sq km (7720 sq mi).

Ball, John (d. 1381) English rebel, one of the leaders of the *Peasants' Revolt (1381). An unbeneficed priest, he was noted for his inflammatory sermons and became the ideological spokesman for the peasants. He was executed after the rising's failure.

Balla, Giacomo (1871–1958) Italian futurist painter. He was influenced by *pointillism before he became associated with *futurism (1910) and painted many dynamic studies of light and movement, notably birds in flight, and the humorous *Dog on a Leash* (1912; Buffalo, USA).

ballad A form of popular narrative poetry. Originally intended for singing or recitation, ballads have a simple basic stanza form (four lines rhyming *abcb*); repetition and direct speech are characteristic devices. Subject matter includes love, family feuds, war, magic, biblical tales, and the deeds of Robin Hood and the knights of the Round Table (see Arthurian legend). Many fine ballads were composed in the 15th century in N England and Scotland; debased versions were later printed on single sheets of paper (broadside ballads) for sale by pedlars. Later still a tradition of literary ballads grew up (e.g. Kipling's "Danny Deever"). Notable ballad collections are Bishop *Percy's *Reliques* (1765) and F. J. Child's *English and Scottish Popular Ballads* (1883–98).

ballade A form of medieval French lyric poetry or song. It consists of three stanzas and a final *envoi* (address); each stanza has the same rhyme scheme and final line, which serves as a refrain. It was used for formal and commemorative songs. Guillaume de *Machaut pioneered this form in the 14th century, and in the 15th century it was used by Charles d'*Orléans and François *Villon, among others.

Ballesteros, Severiano (1957–) Spanish golfer. His first major win was the Dutch Open Championship (1976). Subsequent victories included two British Open Championships (1979, 1984) and the Barcelona Open Championship (1985).

ballet A dramatic art in which dancing and mime, accompanied by music, combine to tell a story or evoke a mood. Ballet originated in the formal dances of French court entertainments, notably under Louis XIV (see Lully). In the 18th century ballet established itself in the public theatre but still as an adjunct to *opera or other forms of drama. Idolized ballerinas such as Sallé (1707–56) and Carmargo (1710–70) introduced less constricting dress and Jean-Georges Noverre (1727–1810) extended ballet's dramatic range. Dancing on the tips of the toes (*sur les pointes*) was introduced early in the 19th century, possibly by Taglioni (1804–84). This period saw the heyday of romantic ballet, epitomized in Coralli's *Giselle* (1841). Modern ballet arose in the early 20th century when *Fokine and *Diaghilev (see also Ballets Russes) combined the polished technique of the imperial Russian dancers with the naturalism advocated by the American Isadora *Duncan. This gave scope to the talents of such dancers as *Nijinsky and *Pavlova, the composers *Stravinsky and *Ravel, the choreographers *Massine and *Balanchine, and the designer *Bakst. Independent ballet companies grew up all over Europe and the USA during the 1930s. England had two such groups, one led by Marie *Rambert (now the Ballet Rambert) and the other by Ninette de *Valois and Frederick *Ashton (now the *Royal Ballet). Other notable companies are the *Bolshoi and *Kirov from the Soviet Union and the American New York City Ballet. Since World War II innovative choreographers such as *Cranko, *Béjart, and Twyla Tharpe have created new ballets inspired by folk dance, jazz, and even gymnastics. □ p. 112.

Ballets Russes A Russian ballet company (1909–29) founded in Paris by *Diaghilev. It gave the West its first opportunity to see Russian imperial dancers. In attempting to fuse dance, mime, music, and scenery into a harmonious unity, it fostered the most avantgarde talents of the period and greatly influenced the subsequent development of ballet. Its choreographers included *Fokine, *Massine, *Balanchine, and *Nijinsky, who was also one of its principal dancers. *Ravel and *Stravinsky composed music for several of its ballets. Among its scene designers were *Bakst and the painters *Picasso, *Matisse, and *Miró.

Balliol, John de (c. 1250–1314) King of the Scots (1292–96), chosen by Edward I of England, arbitrator in the contest for the throne. In 1295 he rebelled against English domination and was defeated by Edward at Dunbar (1296) and deposed. He ended his life in exile in France. His son **Edward de Balliol** (d. 1364) became King of the Scots in 1332, after invading Scotland, supported by Edward III of England. An uprising against Balliol was put down by Edward (1333), who retained the Scottish lowlands, but internal opposition forced Balliol's abdication in 1356.

ballistic missiles Rocket-powered nuclear missiles without wings or other lift surfaces that are propelled to desired altitudes and velocities and then follow an unpowered trajectory similar to that of a projectile fired from a gun. Their accuracy requires careful thrust calculations and on-board preset or inertial guidance systems and is calculated as a probability (e.g. 45–60%) of landing within a stated radius about their target (Circular Error of Probability). Intercontinental ballistic missiles (ICBMs) are capable of reaching any point on the surface of the earth. Both the USA and the Soviet Union possess large numbers of these, some of which (MIRVs—multiple independently targeted re-entry vehicles) have up to ten separate warheads. See also antiballistic missiles; V-2 rocket.

ballistics The study of projectiles and the extent to which their trajectories are affected by shape, propulsion systems, gravity, temperature, wind, etc. There are three branches: interior, dealing with all aspects of propulsion within a gun barrel or at launch; exterior, concerned with the trajectory of the projectile in flight; and terminal, relating to the effects of the missile on the target.

BALLET

first   second   third   fourth   fifth

the five ballet positions

left side   right side

5   4   3   2   1

arm   foot   foot   arm   1   2   3   4   5

Labanotation *Since Rudolph Laban (1879–1958) published his system for recording dance movements in 1928 it has gained widespread acceptance. In this simple example, the initial positions of the legs and arms are indicated at (1). Subsequent positions (2–5) are seen by reading upwards from the bottom. The dancer, starting with feet together and arms at her sides, takes four even steps forward, beginning with the right foot, and moves her arms upwards and outwards (the different shadings representing low, middle, and high positions).*

ball lightning A luminous moving sphere, several centimetres in diameter, occurring just above the ground on rare occasions during thunderstorms. It hisses, has a distinct odour, and may be either red, orange, or yellow. It lasts for only a few seconds and then either dies away or explodes. The phenomenon is not fully understood but one theory suggests that it consists of *plasma.

balloons Lighter-than-air craft, consisting of a bag of gas that displaces a volume of air of greater mass than the total mass of the balloon and its contents. The first successful balloon flight, indeed man's first aerial voyage, was made in 1783 by the *Montgolfier brothers' hot-air balloon; it flew 9 km across Paris. Two years later a *Charlière* hydrogen balloon (designed by J. A. C. Charles, the formulator of *Charles's Law) flew across the English Channel. In 1821 coal gas was used for the first time as a cheap alternative to hydrogen. This opened the way for many exploits by showmen, scientists, and explorers. Balloons must be tethered (for parachuting, scientific experiments, etc.) or they will fly where the wind blows them; dirigible balloons (*see* airships) first appeared in the middle of

the 19th century. However, by the end of the century interest in flying was centred on heavier-than-air machines (*see* aircraft). The use of balloons in war began with Napoleon's observation balloons in 1794, after which they continued to play a sporadic but largely ineffectual part, until their extensive use in both World Wars in the form of barrage balloons.

The sport of **ballooning** has enjoyed a revival in recent years, the preferred vehicle being a hot-air balloon carrying its own propane air heater. The height record for a manned balloon is 30 480 m (D. Simons, US Air Force, 1957). The first Atlantic crossing by a helium balloon was achieved in 1978. In 1987 Richard Branson made the first crossing by hot-air balloon.

balm A fragrant-leaved herbaceous plant of, or related to, the genus *Melissa*, native to the Old World. Lemon balm, or balm gentle (*M. officinalis*), is widely grown in temperate regions and used for flavouring foods or beverages and scenting perfumes. The European bastard balm (*Melittis melissophylum*) is more strongly scented. Others species include bee balm (*Monarda didyma*) and horse balm (*Collinsonia canadensis*). Family: *Labiatae.

Balmoral Castle The principal country residence of the

British monarch in Scotland, situated in SW Aberdeenshire by the River Dee. It was bought by the royal family in 1848 and rebuilt in the 1850s in the revived Scottish baronial style. It is also noted for its extensive and carefully landscaped gardens.

balsa An evergreen tree, *Ochroma pyramidale*, native to Central and South America, also called corkwood. About 12 m tall, it is the source of an extremely light pale-coloured wood, which is widely used for corks, canoes, floats, etc. Although easily crushed, it is technically a hardwood. Family: *Bombacaceae*.

balsam An aromatic resinous substance of plant origin, used in medicine for its soothing and healing properties and in perfumery. Balsam of Peru is derived from the Central American leguminous tree *Myroxylon peneirae*, grown in El Salvador.

The name is also given to many plants of the family *Balsaminaceae*. The garden balsam (*Impatiens balsamina*), native to India, is widely cultivated for its showy red flowers, which have a tubular spur and five unequal petals. The balsam apple (*Momardica balsamina*) is an ornamental vine.

Baltic Exchange A market in the City of London where cargo space on ships and aircraft is bought and sold by members on behalf of clients. The exchange also contains a grain market. It originated in the Baltic coffee house in the 18th century.

Baltic languages A group of Indo-European languages closely related to the Slavonic languages and spoken on the E shores of the Baltic Sea. *Lithuanian and *Latvian (Lettish) are still extant: Old Prussian has been extinct since the 17th century. Deriving from northern Proto-Indo-European, the Baltic, Slavonic, and Germanic languages share important morphological and word-formation features.

Baltic Sea A section of the Atlantic Ocean in N Europe, bounded by Denmark, Sweden, Finland, the Soviet Union, Poland, and East and West Germany. To the W, it leads into the Little Belt, the Great Belt, and the Sound, and to the E, the Gulfs of Bothnia, Finland, and Riga. Receiving rivers draining almost one-fifth of Europe, it has low salinity, and can freeze sufficiently to hinder navigation.

Baltic Shield. *See* shield.

Baltic states The territories on the SE coast of the Baltic Sea that comprise the present-day Latvian, Lithuanian, and Estonian SSRs of the Soviet Union. The Danes conquered N Estonia in the 13th century while S Estonia with Latvia (then comprising Livonia) fell to the Teutonic Knights. Lithuania formed an independent state united with Poland in 1569 in the Union of *Lublin. The region came under Russian rule in the 18th century but briefly, between World Wars I and II, formed the independent states of Latvia, Lithuania, and Estonia.

Baltimore 39 25N 76 40W A city in the USA, the largest in Maryland at the mouth of the Patapsco River. Established in 1729, it was named after the Barons Baltimore, the first of whom, George Calvert (c. 1580–1632), founded Maryland. It was the starting point of the USA's first railway (1827). It is the site of many historical buildings, including the USA's first Roman Catholic cathedral (1806–21) and the Edgar Allan Poe House (1830). Baltimore is a major educational and cultural centre and contains a number of universities; in the 1980s considerable rebuilding in the port area has revitalized the city. It has been a busy seaport and shipbuilding centre since the late 18th century (Baltimore clippers were renowned throughout the world); other important industries include the manufacture of steel, sugar and food processing, oil refining, and chemicals. Population (1980): 786 775.

Baltimore oriole An American *oriole, *Icterus galbula*, of North America, so named because the black and orange plumage of the male resembles the colours of the Barons Baltimore (*see* Baltimore). It feeds on insects, has an attractive song, and builds a woven pouchlike nest.

Baluchistan A province in W Pakistan, on the Arabian Sea and the Iranian and Afghani borders. Mostly rough arid highlands, it is inhabited by pastoral Pathans, Baluchs, and other peoples. The NW deserts are practically uninhabited but the coastal plain and E lowlands support cereals and herbs. There is little industry other than crafts, textiles, and food processing. It has extensive mineral resources. *History*: on trade routes from India to the Middle East, Baluchistan has flourished since ancient times. Nominally part of larger empires, it usually enjoyed autonomy until Britain won control (19th century). In 1947 it became part of Pakistan. Area: 347 190 sq km (134 050 sq mi). Population (1981): 4 332 000. Capital: Quetta.

Baluchitherium An extinct hornless rhinoceros that lived in the Oligocene epoch (between 30 million and 20 million years ago). Fossilized remains found in central Asia show that it was over 5 m high, with a heavy giraffe-like body, and was probably the largest terrestrial mammal ever.

Balzac, Honoré de (1799–1850) French novelist. Educated at Vendôme, he became a lawyer's clerk in Paris. He wrote popular novels under pseudonyms, and then attempted to become a businessman; in 1828, however, bankruptcy forced him to turn to writing again. *Les Chouans* (1829), a historical novel about Breton peasants, was his first successful novel, and in the next 20 years he added over 40 novels to his life's work, the cycle *La Comédie humaine*. In these novels, which included *Eugénie Grandet* (1833), *Le Père Goriot* (1834), and *La Cousine Bette* (1846), he developed new techniques of realism to explore human behaviour. Balzac lived extravagantly in Parisian society, constantly in debt and in love, and married his last mistress, Eveline Hanska, during his fatal illness in 1850.

Bamako 12 40N 7 59W The capital of Mali, a port in the S on the River Niger. A centre of Muslim learning under the medieval Mali Empire, it had dwindled to a small village by the end of the 19th century when it was occupied by the French. It became the capital of the French Sudan in 1905. Population (1981): 620 000.

Bamberg 49 54N 10 54E A town in SE West Germany, in Bavaria on the River Regnitz. The romanesque cathedral was founded in 1004 and its bishops were princes of the Holy Roman Empire until 1803. Its varied industries include engineering and textiles. Population (1982): 72 500.

bamboo A treelike plant of the tribe *Bambuseae*, native to tropical and subtropical regions, particularly SE Asia. From an underground stem (rhizome) arise hollow woody jointed stems, which may reach a height of 40 m in some species. These are used for building and a variety of other purposes, while the young shoots are eaten as a vegetable. Some bamboos are cultivated in temperate gardens for their graceful foliage. Family: *Gramineae* (grasses).

Bana (7th century AD) Sanskrit writer. He travelled widely in India before becoming court poet of the Buddhist emperor *Harsa. The *Harsacarita* is a prose chronicle written to celebrate his patron's accession to the throne. The prose romance *Kadambari* exploits sophisticated narrative techniques to describe a complex love intrigue.

Banaba. *See* Ocean Island.

banana A palmlike plant of the Old World tropical genus *Musa*, especially *M. paradisiaca sapientum*, cultivated throughout the tropics from prehistoric times for its edible fruit. The "trunk," up to 9 m high, is composed of the overlapping bases of the leaves, which are often 3 m or more long. The tip of the flowering stem bears male flowers and hangs down; clusters of female flowers, further up the stem, develop into seedless fruits, up to 30 cm long, without being fertilized. (All cultivated bananas are sterile hybrids: the plants are propagated from suckers arising from the underground rhizome.) Most bananas are eaten fresh, but varieties called plantains are cooked and eaten when still green, forming a staple food in East and West Africa and the Caribbean. Family: *Musaceae*.

Banbury 52 04N 1 20W A market town in central England, in Oxfordshire on the River Cherwell. The original Banbury Cross of the nursery rhyme was destroyed in 1602 by Puritans but replaced in the 19th century. As well as being an important livestock centre, it has various light industries. Population (1981): 35 796.

Banda, Hastings Kamuzu (c. 1906-) Malawi statesman; president (1964-). A physician, he worked in the UK and the USA before returning home (then Nyasaland) in 1958 to lead the fight against federation with Rhodesia and for independence. On independence (1964) he became president, becoming life president of the republic of Malawi in 1971.

Bandar Abbas 27 12N 56 15E A town in S Iran, on the Strait of Hormuz. It is a naval base important to the security of the Persian Gulf.

Bandaranaike, S(olomon) W(est) R(idgeway) D(ias) (1899-1959) Sri Lankan statesman; prime minister (1956-59). In 1951 he founded the Sri Lanka Freedom Party (SLFP) and became prime minister as head of an alliance of socialist and nationalist parties—the People's United Front, which pursued a neutral foreign policy and nationalist domestic policies (including the substitution of English with Sinhalese as the official language). He was assassinated by a Buddhist monk and was succeeded as head of the SLFP by his wife **Sirimavo Ratwatte Dias Bandaranaike** (1916-), the world's first woman prime minister (1960-65, 1970-77). Her socialist coalition with the Marxist party was defeated in 1965 but returned to power in 1970.

Bandar-e Bushehr. *See* Bushire.

Bandar Seri Begawan (former name: Brunei Town) 4 56N 114 58E The capital of Brunei, a port in the NE near the mouth of the Brunei River. Population (1981): 49 902.

Bandeira, Manuel Carneiró de Sousa (1886-1968) Brazilian poet. He was forced by tuberculosis to give up his architectural studies in São Paulo. After meeting the French poet Paul *Eluard while in a Swiss sanatorium, he decided to try a literary career. The originality of his first book, *A cinza das horas* (1917), was immediately recognized; his modernist style developed more fully in *Libertinagem* (1930) and *Estrêla da Manhã* (1936). He was also an influential critic, translator, and university professor.

BANGLADESH *Jute being retted in flood waters. Bangladesh grows half the world's raw jute.*

bandicoot A ratlike *marsupial mammal of a family (*Peramelidae*; 20 species) occurring in Australia (including Tasmania) and New Guinea. About the size of rabbits,

bandicoots are mainly carnivorous, eating insects, worms, and grubs. They are shy creatures and build nests of grass and leaves among thick vegetation.

Bandjermasin. *See* Banjarmasin.

Bandung 6 57S 107 34E A city in Indonesia, in W Java. A cultural and industrial centre and tourist resort, it was formerly the administrative centre of the Netherlands East Indies. Its chief industries are chemicals, quinine, plastics, metal processing, and textiles. It has two universities, established in 1957 and 1959, and a nuclear research centre (1964). At the **Bandung Conference** of 1955 representatives of 29 African and Asian countries met to oppose colonialism. Population (1981): 1 400 000.

Banff 57 40N 2 31W A town in NE Scotland, in Grampian Region on the Moray Firth, at the mouth of the River Deveron. It is a resort with fishing and distilling industries, and was the county town of the former county of Banff, covering 1632 sq km (630 sq mi) from the Moray Firth to the Cairngorm Mountains. Population (1984 est): 4246.

Banff 51 10N 115 34W A town in W Canada, in Alberta in the Rocky Mountains. The headquarters of Banff National Park, it is a mountain resort and conference centre and has a School of Fine Arts. Population (1981): 4208.

Bangalore 12 58N 77 35E A city in S India, the capital of Karnataka. Founded in the 16th century, it fell to the British in 1791. The Institute of Science was established in 1909 and Bangalore University in 1964. An expanding industrial centre, Bangalore's many modern industries include aircraft assembly, machine tools, and electronics. Population (1983): 2 914 000.

Bangka (*or* Banka) An Indonesian island in the Java Sea, off SE Sumatra. Its government-owned tinmines are among the world's most productive; other mineral deposits include gold, manganese, and iron. The population is largely Chinese. Area: 11 914 sq km (4600 sq mi). Chief town: Pangkalpinang.

Bangkok (Thai name: Krung Threp) 13 44N 100 30E The capital and main port of Thailand, in the SW near the mouth of the River Chao Phraya. It became a royal city and the capital in 1782. Distinctive features of the city are its canal system and the many Buddhist temples. There has been considerable expansion since World War II. Most of the country's industry and commerce is centred on Bangkok and it has eight universities. Population (1983 est): 4 300 000.

Bangladesh, People's Republic of A country in the Indian subcontinent, lying between the Himalayas and the Bay of Bengal, in the delta of the Rivers Ganges and Brahmaputra. The land, which is generally low lying, is on the whole fertile but it has to support a very large population, most of whom are Bengalis. *Economy*: about three-quarters of the inhabitants are occupied in agriculture, rice being by far the most important food crop. Bangladesh produces 50% of the world's raw jute, its main export. Fishing, both freshwater and saltwater, is important not only as a valuable food source, but also for oil and other fish products. Traditional industries include jute milling and textile manufacture but plans for further industrial development are hindered by the comparative lack of mineral resources. Most industry is now nationalized. Communications are greatly aided by the many natural shipping channels that the country's rivers provide. *History*: the area formed part of the kingdom of Bengal, and its conquest by the Afghans in the 12th century led to the growth of the Islamic religion. It was part of British India from 1857 until 1947 when it became independent as a province of Pakistan (East Pakistan). Discontentment under a government centred in West Pakistan, aggravated by the disparity in allocation of development funds to each province, led to the outbreak of civil war in 1971, Indian forces coming to the aid of the Bengalis. In 1972 East Pakistan achieved independence as Bangladesh and Sheikh *Mujibur Rahman became prime minster. In 1974 floods and famine led to political unrest and terrorism and in 1975 Mujib assumed absolute power on a one-party basis but shortly afterwards he and his family were assassinated in a military coup. After several more coups and countercoups, Gen *Ziaur Rahman assumed power in 1976. In 1977 amendments to the constitution established Bangladesh as an Islamic state. Gen Ziaur was elected president in 1978 in the first presidential election on a basis of adult suffrage; he was assassinated in 1981. The military, led by Lt Gen Hussain Mohammed Ershad, took power in March, 1982, and in 1983 Ershad became president. Martial law was lifted in 1986, but political demonstrations continue. Bangladesh became a member of the Commonwealth in 1972. Official language: Bengali. Official religion: Islam. Official currency: taka of 100 paisa. Area: 142 797 sq km (55 126 sq mi). Population (1984 est): 96 000 000. Capital: Dhaka. Main port: Chittagong.

Bangor   54 40N 5 40W A resort in Northern Ireland, in Co Down lying on Belfast Lough. Its abbey was founded by St Comgall in 558 AD. Population (1981): 38 282.

Bangor   53 13N 4 08W A city in North Wales, in Gwynedd on the mainland shore of the Menai Strait. A college of the University of Wales was established in 1884. Bangor cathedral, founded in the 6th century by St Deiniol, contains the tombs of Welsh princes. Population (1981): 12 174.

Bangui   4 23N 19 20E The capital of the Central African Republic, a port in the SW on the Ubangi River. Founded in 1889, the port handles goods for both the Central African Republic and Chad; its main exports are cotton and coffee. The Jean Bédel Bokassa University was established in 1969. Population (1981 est): 367 100.

Bangweulu, Lake   11 15S 29 45E A lake in E Zambia. Discovered by Livingstone (1868), it is shallow and bordered by swamps. During the rainy season its waters cover an area of up to 9800 sq km (3783 sq mi).

Banja Luka   44 47N 17 11E A town in W Yugoslavia, in Bosnia and Hercegovina on the River Vrbas. It has several mosques, a university (1975), and diverse industries. Population (1981): 183 618.

Banjarmasin (*or* Bandjermasin)   3 22S 114 33E A port in Indonesia, in S Kalimantan on the Barito delta. Its exports include rubber and timber. Its university was established in 1960. Population (1980): 381 286.

banjo   A plucked string instrument of US origin, originally played by plantation slaves. The banjo became popular in minstrel shows, vaudeville, jazz, and folk music. The body of the banjo is a round metal hoop covered with parchment on one side; the fretted fingerboard has five or six strings, which are plucked with the fingers or with a plectrum.

Banjul (name until 1973: Bathurst)   13 20N 16 38W The capital of The Gambia, a port in the W at the mouth of the River Gambia, founded by the British in 1816. Population (1982 est): 40 000.

Banka.   *See* Bangka.

Bank for International Settlements (BIS)   A bank in Basle, Switzerland, which acts as a bank for *central banks (mostly European and American) and is governed by representatives of several of them. It was set up in 1930 to coordinate reparations after World War I. Although most of its functions are now performed by the *International Monetary Fund, it has important duties as a trustee.

Bankhead, Tallulah   (1903–68) US actress. She won critical acclaim as a stage actress in such plays as Lillian Hellman's *Little Foxes* (1939) and Thornton Wilder's *The Skin of Our Teeth* (1942), but her popularity as a film star owed more to her extravagant lifestyle than to the quality of her performances.

bank holidays   The days designated as holidays in the UK, so called because they were originally the days on which the Bank of England was closed. The bank holidays common to England,

Scotland, and Northern Ireland are New Year holiday, Good Friday, May Day, Spring holiday, Late Summer holiday, and Christmas Day. England and Northern Ireland also enjoy Easter Monday and Boxing Day, and Northern Ireland alone enjoys St Patrick's Day (17 March).

Bank of England   The British *central bank, which was nationalized in 1946. It was originally incorporated in 1694, being set up by a group of London merchants to lend money to William III. Since the mid-19th century it has been the only bank authorized to issue banknotes. The Bank conducts *monetary policy through *open-market operations (acting as lender-of-the-last-resort to the *discount houses), and through regulation of the supply of credit by way of the high interest rate it charges on special deposits called from the *commercial banks. The Bank is also responsible for financing the national debt and for holding the country's gold reserves.

Bank of the United States   One of two consecutive US banks set up to act as banker to the Federal Government. The first, based in Philadelphia, was established by Alexander Hamilton in 1791 and closed down in 1811. The second was established in 1816 with a 20-year charter to reorganize government finances after the War of 1812 with Britain. President Andrew Jackson would not renew the charter and in 1833 put the government's money into state banks. *See also* Federal Reserve System.

bank rate.   *See* minimum lending rate.

bankruptcy   The legal process by which the property of a person who cannot pay his debts is distributed among his creditors. In England bankruptcy was originally a branch of the criminal law aimed at preventing fraudulent traders evading their creditors, but since the reign of Queen Anne the law has also sought to protect the bankrupt by ending his obligation to repay most of his past debts. Modern bankruptcy law, almost entirely contained in the Bankruptcy Act (1914) and the Insolvency Acts (1976, 1985), stipulates the circumstances in which a person may be made bankrupt, what portion of his property is to be distributed, and the creditors who are to be paid in priority to others. Liquidation is the equivalent process applicable to a company.

banks.   *See* Bank for International Settlements; Bank of England; Bank of the United States; central bank; commercial bank; International Bank for Reconstruction and Development; merchant bank.

Banks, Sir Joseph   (1743–1820) British botanist and explorer. During his most famous expedition, around the world with James *Cook (1768–71), he showed that the marsupial mammals of Australia were more primitive than the placental mammals of other continents and he also discovered many new species of plants. Banks promoted the introduction of economic plants from their native regions to other countries and he was known as a patron of young scientists. He was president of the Royal Society from 1778 until his death.

Banksia   A genus of shrubs and trees (about 50 species) all native to dry areas of Australia; some are known as Australian honeysuckles. The flowers are borne in dense spikes and give rise to hard winged seeds. Family: *Proteaceae*.

Banks Island   The westernmost island of Canada's Arctic Archipelago, in Franklin district. Mostly hilly plateau, it supports numerous Arctic animals. Area: 60 166 sq km (23 230 sq mi).

Banner System   A system of military organization adopted by the Manchu tribes and used by the *Qing dynasty to rule China. It was initiated in 1601 by *Nurhachi, who enrolled his warriors under yellow, white, blue, or red banners. Later four bordered banners were added and all tribesmen were enrolled. Each banner formed an administrative unit, which contributed a quota of men when it became necessary to raise an army and also facilitated taxation. In return banner-men were allocated land. After the Manchu conquest of China and the establishment of the Qing, eight Chinese and eight Mongol banners were added.

Bannister, Sir Roger (Gilbert) (1929–) British doctor and middle-distance runner, who on 6 May, 1954, was the first man to run a mile in under 4 minutes (3 minutes 59.4 seconds).

Bannockburn 56 06N 3 55W A village in Scotland, in the Central Region near Stirling on the Bannock Burn (a tributary of the River Forth). 1.5 km (1 mi) NW is Scotland's most famous battlefield, where in 1314 Robert the Bruce, King of the Scots, routed the English under Edward II, who had come to relieve the besieged Stirling Castle. Population (1981): 6068.

banshee (Irish *bean-sidhe*: woman of the fairies) In Irish folklore, a female spectre whose weeping announced the imminent death of a person.

bantam One of many breeds of dwarf fowl, possibly named after the district of Bantam in Indonesia, from where they were formerly exported to the West. Bantams generally weigh about 500 g or less.

Banten A region in W Java (Indonesia), which was the centre of a Muslim sultanate until 1683 when it became part of the Dutch East Indies. The town of Banten was a flourishing port for the European spice trade from the 16th to the 18th centuries, after which the harbour silted up.

banteng A wild ox, *Bos banteng*, of forests in SE Asia. About 150 cm high at the shoulder, bantengs are brown with white socks and a white rump patch and have relatively small horns. They feed on young grass and bamboo shoots.

Banting, Sir Frederick Grant (1891-1941) Canadian physiologist, who, with C. H. *Best, discovered a technique for the successful isolation of the hormone *insulin from pancreatic tissue in 1921. This enabled the successful treatment of patients suffering from *diabetes (caused by lack of insulin). Banting was awarded a Nobel Prize (1923) with J. J. R.*Macleod but he divided his share with Best in recognition of his colleague's achievement.

Bantu A large subgroup of African languages of the *Niger-Congo group spoken over the whole of the S half of Africa by about 60 million people. It includes Zulu, Xhosa, and Kongo; perhaps the most widely known representative is *Swahili, the language of Tanzania and lingua franca of E Africa. The Bantu languages are tonal, with the exception of Swahili, and make extensive use of suffixes and prefixes. Many use a number of click sounds. The Bantu people are very diverse in culture and social organization and include herdsmen, farmers, hunter-gatherers, and fishers. They probably migrated southwards from an area near the Cameroon-Nigeria border, displacing small pygmy and Bushmen tribes, approximately 2000 years ago.

Bantu Homelands (*or* Bantustans) The areas of South Africa designated for the Black populations, comprising just over 13% of the land area. Acts of parliament in 1913 and 1936 controlled the extent of African lands and prohibited Blacks from holding land in White areas. The Bantu Authorities Act (1951) gave limited administrative and legislative powers to the Bantu authorities, and the Bantu Self-Government Act (1959) divided the Black populations into national units, most of them with homelands in several separate areas. Limited self-government was to be granted to these areas; the *Transkei was the first to receive this (1963). The Bantu Homelands Constitution Act (1971) aimed at similar self-government for other areas. Full independence has been granted to Transkei (1976), *Bophutha Tswana (1977), *Venda (1979), and Ciskei (1981). Other Bantu Homelands include Gazankulu, KaNgwane, KwaZulu, Lebowa, and Qwaqwa. The Bantustan policy has been constantly opposed by African leaders (in particular Chief Gatsha Buthelezi of KwaZulu), and many of the territories have resisted moves towards self-government and

BANTU HOMELANDS *The areas designated as Black African territories in South Africa are dispersed over the E and N parts of the Republic.*

independence, regarding it as a poor substitute for majority rule in South Africa as a whole.

Banville, Théodore Faullain de (1823–89) French poet. He wrote a technical treatise on French poetry and revived old forms, such as the *ballade and the *rondeau. His best-known collection is *Odes funambulesques* (1857). He helped many younger writers, including *Rimbaud.

banyan A tropical Asian tree, *Ficus benghalensis*, related to the fig and reaching a height of 30 m. Individual trees commonly grow into impenetrable thickets as the branches produce supporting aerial roots, which grow down to penetrate the soil and subsequently give rise to thorny branches of their own. Family: *Moraceae*.

baobab A tropical African tree, *Adansonia digitata*, with a tapering conical trunk (the base of which may exceed 10 m in diameter) reaching a height of 18 m and bearing branches at its apex. The drab bat-pollinated flowers give rise to fruits that contain a succulent edible pulp surrounded by a tough woody capsule. The bark yields a fibre of local importance, and the trees are grown as ornamentals in some subtropical areas. Family: *Bombacaceae*.

Baotou (*or* Pao-t'ou) 40 38N 109 59E A city in N China, in the Inner Mongolia AR on the Yellow River. It is a major industrial centre, with a nuclear power station. Industries include iron and steel, aluminium, sugar, and textiles. Population (1983): 1 042 000.

baptism A ceremony of initiation, occurring in many religions, involving the use of water as a symbol of purification from sin. In the Christian Church, where it is a *sacrament and is done in the name of the Father, the Son, and the Holy Spirit, it involves the candidate's total or partial immersion in water or the mere wetting of his head. Both the *Baptists and the modern descendants of the *Anabaptists practise adult baptism, but most other Churches prefer infant baptism.

Baptists Protestant Christians who baptize, by immersion, only those old enough consciously to accept the Christian faith. Each Baptist Church is autonomous, but in the UK there used to be two main types, "General Baptist" Churches, owing their origin in 1612 to John Smyth (c. 1554–1612) and Thomas Helwys (c. 1550–c. 1616), and "Particular Baptist" Churches, founded in 1633 by Calvinists who' believed that salvation was only for a particular few. The latter had modified its doctrines by 1891, when both movements merged into the Baptist Union. The first Baptist Church in America was established at Providence, Rhode Island, by Roger Williams in 1639. The majority of Baptists, of whom there are over 30 million worldwide, live in the USA and most of them are associated with the Baptist World Alliance.

Baqqarah A cattle-herding Arab people of Chad and the Sudan. As a result of contact and intermixture with other local peoples they have dark skins and speak a distinct dialect of Arabic. They migrate seasonally between northern wet-season grazing lands and southern dry-season river areas.

bar A unit of pressure equal to 10^5 pascals (0.987 atmosphere). The commonly used unit is the millibar (one-thousandth of a bar).

BANYAN *In India it is regarded as a sacred tree and is carefully tended.*

Baranof Island An island in the USA, off the coast of SE Alaska in the Alexander Archipelago. Area: 4162 sq km (1607 sq mi). Chief town: Sitka.

Barbados, State of An island state in the West Indies, E of the Windward Islands. It is generally low lying except for a district in the NE and is subject to hurricanes. Most of the population is of African descent. *Economy*: high-density agriculture, with sugar cane as the main crop, and tourism are important. The policy of encouraging some small industries has been helped by the discovery of offshore oil and natural gas. Main exports include sugar and sugar products (including rum), petroleum and petroleum products, clothing, and electrical goods. *History*: occupied by the British in 1627, it remained a British colony until 1966, when it became a fully independent state within the Commonwealth. Prime minister: Erskine Sandiford (1937–   ). Official language: English. Official currency: Barbados dollar

of 100 cents. Area: 430 sq km (166 sq mi). Population (1983 est): 251 000. Capital and main port: Bridgetown.

Barbarossa (Khayr ad-Din; d. 1546) Turkish pirate. Barbarossa (Italian: Redbeard) entered the service of the Ottoman Sultan of Turkey to protect his possessions on the Barbary coast of N Africa against Spanish and Portuguese attack. He captured Algiers in 1529 and Tunisia in 1534 and his defeat of Emperor Charles V's fleet in 1538 gave the Turks control of the E Mediterranean.

Barbary A region in N Africa stretching from Egypt to the Atlantic Ocean and from the Mediterranean Sea to the Sahara. It is named after its oldest inhabitants, the *Berbers. In antiquity it consisted of Mauritania, Numidia, Africa, Propria, and Cyrenaica. It was successively conquered by the Romans, Vandals, Arabs, Turks, Spaniards (parts of Morocco), French (Algeria, Tunisia, and Morocco), and Italians (Tripoli). Between the 16th and 18th centuries, Barbary was notorious for its pirates, who caused havoc in the Mediterranean.

Barbary ape A large monkey, *Macaca sylvana*, also called magot, the only *macaque found in N Africa. Barbary apes are tailless and roam in bands over the forest floor, feeding on seeds, leaves, insects, and small animals. The colony of Barbary apes in Gibraltar was probably introduced by man.

barbastelle A large-eared insect-eating bat, *Barbastella barbastella*, of Europe, S Asia, and NE Africa. About 5 cm long, slender, and long-legged, barbastelles fly early in the evening. Family: *Vespertilionidae*.

barbel A long slender freshwater fish, belonging to the genus *Barbus*, that is related to *carp and occurs in clear fresh waters of Asia, Africa, and Europe. It has four fleshy threadlike appendages (barbels) near its mouth, which detect prey, mainly invertebrates, while exploring the river bed. *B. barbus* of Europe is usually 30–50 cm long.

Barber, Samuel (1910–81) US composer. Two of his works, the opera *Vanessa* (1958) and the piano concerto (1963), won Pulitzer Prizes. His style, although basically lyrical, became increasingly dissonant in his later works. His output included chamber music, choral works, symphonies, and concertos. His best-known work is the *Adagio for Strings*, an arrangement of the slow movement of his string quartet (1936).

barberry. *See* Berberis.

barbet A small brightly coloured forest bird belonging to a tropical family (*Capitonidae*; 76 species) most commonly found in Africa. 8–30 cm long, barbets have large heavy bills with bristles around the chin and beak and a monotonously repeated call. They feed mainly on fruit but also take insects, lizards, and birds' eggs. Order: *Piciformes* (woodpeckers, etc.).

Barbirolli, Sir John (1899–1970) British conductor of Franco-Italian parents. Originally a cellist, he organized his own string orchestra, and subsequently became conductor of several major opera companies and orchestras in Britain and the USA. From 1949 until his death he was principal conductor of the Hallé Orchestra, Manchester.

barbiturates A class of drugs that act by depressing the activity of the brain. Short-acting barbiturates, such as thiopentone, are used for inducing *anaesthesia. Medium-acting barbiturates, such as pentobarbitone, are used as sleeping tablets. Small doses of long-acting barbiturates, such as phenobarbitone, are used for day-time sedation and to control epilepsy. As barbiturates are habit-forming and may cause true addiction, with serious effects on the mind and body, their use is now severely limited. They have been shown to be associated with the increased incidence of falls and fractures in elderly patients. Overdosage is a medical emergency and can cause death by inhibiting the breathing centre in the brain.

Barbizon school A group of French landscape painters who worked in the village of Barbizon, near the Forest of

Fontainebleau, in the 1840s. Truth to nature combined with romantic settings typify the works of the school's founder Theodore *Rousseau, *Daubigny, Narcisse-Virgile Diaz de la Pena (c. 1807–76), and others. Dark trees and ponds betray their debt to Dutch landscape painting but their constant practice of open-air oil sketching to capture light effects inspired the impressionists to paint finished works outside. Fringe members of the school included *Corot and *Millet.

Barbour, John (1316–95) Scottish poet. He became archdeacon of Aberdeen in 1357, studied at Oxford and Paris, and received a royal pension in 1388. In *The Bruce*, a Scottish national epic, he celebrated Scotland's fight for independence under *Robert (I) the Bruce and James Douglas.

Barbusse, Henri (1873–1935) French novelist. His novel *Under Fire* (1916), based on his experiences in World War I, expresses the disillusion that led him first to pacifism and later to communism. *Clarté* (1919) lent its name to a short-lived international movement. Barbusse died in the Soviet Union.

barcarolle A piece of music in imitation of the songs of Venetian gondoliers. It is usually in 6/8 or 12/8 time and has a gentle rocking movement. Examples include Offenbach's *Barcarolle* from *The Tales of Hoffman* and Chopin's *Barcarolle* for the piano.

Barcelona 41 25N 2 10E A city in NE Spain, in Catalonia on the Mediterranean Sea. It is Spain's second largest city, its largest port and leading commercial and industrial centre. Manufactures include locomotives, aircraft, textiles, and electrical equipment. The country's cultural centre and the focus of Catalan art and literature, it has many educational establishments, libraries, and museums; the University of Barcelona was founded in 1430. The city's numerous fine buildings include the palace of the Aragón kings, a cathedral (14th–15th centuries), and a 14th-century monastery. It has several Art Nouveau buildings designed by Antonio Gaudí, notably the Sagrada Familia church (1903–26). *History*: founded by the Carthaginians, it was taken by the Moors in 713 AD and by Charlemagne in 801 AD. In 1137 Catalonia and Aragón united and Barcelona became the capital, rivalling Genoa and Venice as a leading European port. During the 19th century it became important industrially through its cotton industry. The centre of the Catalan separatist government, it was the seat of the Catalan autonomous government · and later of the Republican government, during the Spanish Civil War (1936–39). In 1939 Barcelona fell to Gen Franco and the Republican government finally surrendered. The 1992 Olympics will be held here. Population (1981): 1 754 900.

Barclay de Tolly, Mikhail Bogdanovich, Prince (1761–1818) Russian field marshal. In 1810, after brilliant campaigns against Napoleon, he became minister of war. Promoted field marshal (1814), he commanded the army that invaded France in 1815.

Barcoo River. *See* Cooper Creek.

bard In ancient Celtic societies, a poet whose duty was to eulogize heroes and to celebrate notable events, such as victories, and the laws and traditions of the community. Bards constituted a distinct social class with hereditary rights and privileges. The class was at one time subdivided according to functions. In 10th-century Wales the three bardic ranks were *pencerdd* (chief of song), *bardd teulu* (household bard), and *cerddor* (minstrel); an earlier Irish classification was *druid*, *filid*, and *baird*. Bards ceased to exist in Gaul at an early date, but they survived in Scotland and Ireland to the 18th century and, in a somewhat artificial and diminished role, continue to exist in Wales to the present. *See also* eisteddfod; Welsh literature.

Bardeen, John (1908–) US physicist, who became professor at the University of Illinois in 1951. He shared the 1956 Nobel Prize for his part in the invention of the transistor (with W. B. *Shockley and W. H. *Brattain) while working at the Bell Telephone Laboratories in 1948. He also shared the 1972 Nobel Prize for his work on the theory of superconductivity (with L. N. Cooper and J. R. Schrieffer). This theory is known as the BCS theory after the initials of its authors.

Bardot, Brigitte (1934–) French film actress. Her films include *And God Created Woman* (1956), *Vie privée* (1961), *Viva Maria* (1965), and *Shalako* (1968). She became probably the best-known sex symbol of the 1960s.

Bardsey 52 46N 4 48W A Welsh island in St Georges Channel, off the SW coast of the Lleyn Peninsula. It contains the ruins of a 6th-century abbey and was a place of pilgrimage in the middle ages.

Barebones Parliament The assembly, also known as the parliament of saints, called by Oliver *Cromwell in July, 1653. It consisted mainly of merchants and lesser gentry, "godly men" nominated by the congregations, and was named after one of them, Praisegod Barebone (c. 1596–1679). In Dec the moderates among them resigned their power to Cromwell.

Bareilly 28 20N 79 24E A city in India, in Uttar Pradesh. Founded in 1537, it was a centre of the Indian Mutiny. The Indian Veterinary Research Institute was established nearby in 1889. Manufactures include sugar, rope, and furniture. Population (1981): 438 000.

DANIEL BARENBOIM *Conducting the Orchestre de Paris.*

Barenboim, Daniel (1942–) Israeli pianist and conductor who studied in Salzburg, Paris, and Rome. He made his debut in London in 1955. In 1967 he married the cellist Jacqueline *du Pré, with whom he gave recitals. Increasingly active as a conductor in the 1970s, Barenboim has conducted the Orchestre de Paris since 1975.

Barents, Willem (c. 1550–97) Dutch navigator. He led three expeditions (1594, 1595, 1596) to discover a *Northeast Passage, reaching the Novaya Zemlya islands and discovering Spitsbergen (1596). On his last voyage he was forced to winter at Icehaven, where his camp was found in 1871. He died at sea on his return journey. The Barents Sea is named after him.

Barents Sea A section of the Arctic Ocean between Eurasia and Svalbard, Franz Josef Land, and Novaya Zemlya. It covers part of the Eurasian continental shelf, which before the Pleistocene Ice Age was land. It is rich in fish.

Barère, Bertrand (1755–1841) French revolutionary. Initially a moderate in the National Convention, he subsequently became a member of the Committee of *Public Safety during the *Reign of Terror. Imprisoned after the fall of Robespierre (July, 1794), he escaped into exile, returning to France in 1830.

Barghest (*or* Barguest) In English superstition, a terrifying enormous dog whose appearance varied in different parts of the country. In Manchester it was headless and in E Anglia one-eyed. Those who saw it were supposed to die.

Barham, Richard Harris (1788–1845) British humorous writer. He became a clergyman in 1813 after studying at Oxford and began writing while recovering from serious illness. He is best known for the verse narratives of *The Ingoldsby Legends*, comic treatments of largely supernatural themes. Written for magazines, they were collected in three volumes (1840, 1842, 1847).

Bar Hebraeus (1226–86) Syrian bishop and scholar. Bar Hebraeus studied medicine at Antioch and Tripoli. He was consecrated bishop in 1246 and became Primate of the East in 1264. His writings, in Syriac and Arabic, include the *Granary of Mysteries* and the *Chronicle*.

Bari 41 07N 16 52E A seaport in Italy, the capital of Apulia on the Adriatic Sea. It has a cathedral (12th–15th centuries) and a university (1924). Industries include chemicals, textiles, and oil refining. Population (1980 est): 387 710.

Baring, Evelyn. *See* Cromer, Evelyn Baring, 1st Earl of.

barite (*or* barytes) A barium ore consisting of barium sulphate, sometimes called heavy spar. It is colourless when pure, but often white, yellow, or brown, due to impurities. It is used in the manufacture of paint and heavy paper, as a mineral filler in rubber and linoleum manufacture, and in concrete and glassmaking. The chief producers are the USA, West Germany, and Ireland.

baritone A deep adult male singing voice, lower than tenor and higher than bass. Range: G at the bottom of the bass stave to G two octaves above.

barium (Ba) A silvery reactive metal that resembles calcium in its behaviour. It was discovered in 1808 by Sir Humphry Davy and occurs naturally as barytes ($BaSO_4$) and witherite ($BaCO_3$). The sulphate is used as a white pigment in paint and, because of its opacity to X-rays, is used in X-ray diagnosis. All soluble barium compounds are toxic, the carbonate being used as rat poison. At no 56; at wt 137.34; mp 725°C.

bark The dead outer layer of the stems and roots of woody plants, which protects the inner tissues from desiccation, extremes of temperature, pests and diseases, and physical damage. Antiseptic deposits, such as tannins, give the colour. Bark may include layers of insulating *cork, which is responsible for the characteristic ridges and patterns on some tree trunks. Small breathing pores (called lenticels) in the bark are conspicuous in many of the smooth-barked trees (such as *Prunus* species) but are hidden in the cracks of rough-barked species. The bark of some trees is of commercial importance, being a source of cinnamon, quinine, and various other products.

bark beetle A hard cylindrical beetle, also called an engraver beetle, belonging to a family (Scolytidae; 7000 species) of wood borers. It is usually less than 6 mm long, coloured red-brown or black, and causes considerable damage to trees. It burrows underneath the bark to lay eggs that develop into burrowing larvae: the elaborate patterns of tunnels produced are generally characteristic of the species. Certain species also transmit diseases (*see* elm bark beetle) and can be serious economic pests.

Barker, George (1913–) British poet. He left school at 14 but taught in universities in England, Japan, America, and Italy. His poetry is noted for its passionate vigorous lyricism; it first achieved wide popularity in the 1940s. His many books include *Collected Poems* (1957), *The True Confession of George*

Barker (1950), and *Dialogues, Etc.* (1976).

Barker, Harley Granville. See Granville-Barker, Harley.

Barkhausen, Heinrich (1881–1956) German physicist, who became professor of electrical engineering at the University of Dresden. He discovered (1919) the effect in which ferromagnetic materials placed in an increasing magnetic field become magnetized in small jumps (Barkhausen effect).

Barking and Dagenham A borough of E Greater London, created in 1965 from most of the former boroughs of Barking and Dagenham. Industries include a large power station and the manufacture of motor vehicles. Population (1981): 150 175.

barking deer. *See* muntjac.

Barkly Tableland An area of Australia, extending SE of the Gulf of Carpentaria, in Northern Territory, into Queensland. It consists of undulating uplands on which beef cattle are raised. Area: about 130 000 sq km (50 000 sq mi).

Bar Kokhba (Simeon bar Kosiba; d. 135 AD) Jewish freedom fighter. In 132 he launched a revolt against Roman rule and attempted to set up an independent Jewish state. He was hailed as Messiah by *Akiba, but did not enjoy widespread support and was killed when his last stronghold, Betar, fell. Some of his correspondence has been recovered from caves in the Judaean desert.

Barlach, Ernst (1870–1938) German expressionist sculptor and playwright. First influenced by *Jugendstil*, he only found his mature style after visiting Russia (1906). His bulky figures, usually in wood, with their expressive faces and angular and rigid outlines were inspired both by his studies of Russian peasants and by *gothic sculpture. The Nazis destroyed much of his work.

Bar-le-Duc 48 46N 5 10E A town in NE France, the capital of the Meuse department on the River Ornain. Its manufactures include metal goods, textiles, and jams. Population (1982 est): 20 029.

Barletta 41 20N 16 17E A seaport in Italy, in Apulia on the Adriatic coast. It possesses a romanesque cathedral and a castle. An agricultural centre, it has an important wine trade; chemicals and cement are also manufactured. Population (1981): 83 719.

barley A *cereal grass of the genus *Hordeum*, especially *H. vulgare*, which produces its grain in four rows and can be grown as far north as N Norway; *H. distichon* (two-rowed barley); and *H. hexadistichon* (six-rowed barley). Over 165 million tonnes of grain are harvested annually in temperate, subtropical, and subarctic regions from the various strains of barley. It is malted and used in the brewing industry, made into food for cattle and pigs, milled to produce pearl and pot barley (used in soups and stews), and used in breadmaking.

Bar Mitzvah (Hebrew: son of the commandment) The ceremony marking the initiation of a Jewish boy into the adult community at the age of 13. At this age he assumes his full religious responsibilities and it is customary for him to read publicly from the *Torah in the synagogue for the first time. In some communities a parallel ceremony (Bat Mitzvah) exists for girls.

Barnabas, St In the New Testament (Acts), a Christian Apostle of the 1st century. After going with St Paul to evangelize Cyprus (his birthplace) and the European mainland, he clashed with him and they parted company. He is traditionally regarded as the founder of the Cypriot Church. Feast day: 11 June.

barnacle A marine *crustacean belonging to the subclass Cirripedia (1000 species). Some members of the group are parasites, but the typical (nonparasitic) barnacles live attached—head downwards—to rocks, ships' hulls, etc., and filter food particles from the water with long feathery pendages, which protrude from the calcareous sh.

Goose barnacles (e.g. *Lepas anatifera*)—so called because they were believed in the middle ages to be an immature form of the barnacle goose—are attached by means of a stalk; others, including the acorn barnacle (*Balanus*), are unstalked. Barnacles are hermaphrodite; their larvae are free-swimming, but later settle and become fixed to a surface by means of a cement-like substance secreted by their antennae.

barnacle goose A European *goose, *Branta leucopsis*, which is a regular winter visitor to Britain. It has a distinctive cream face, dark crown and breast, and a white chevron on the tail and grazes on coastal meadows and salt marshes. They were once believed to hatch from barnacles!

Barnard, Christiaan Neethling (1922–) South African surgeon, who (in 1967 at the Groote Schuur Hospital in Cape Town) performed the world's first successful heart transplant operation. His patient, Louis Washkansky, received the heart of a road-accident victim but died 18 days later from pneumonia. Barnard retired in 1983.

Barnard, Edward Emerson (1857–1923) US astronomer, who became professor at the University of Chicago (1895). He discovered Jupiter's fifth satellite (1892), a total of 16 comets, and **Barnard's Star** (1916) in the constellation Ophiuchus, the star with the most rapid proper motion.

Barnardo, Thomas John (1845–1905) British doctor and philanthropist. In 1867 Barnardo founded the first of his famous homes at Stepney, London, to care for destitute children by taking them from a damaging environment and providing a home, education, and training. Over a hundred homes exist in the UK, with others in Australia and New Zealand.

Barnaul 53 21N 83 45E A city in the S Soviet Union, in the RSFSR on the River Ob. The centre of an industrial and mining area, its industries include engineering, textiles, chemicals, and timber. Population (1981 est): 549 000.

Barnave, Antoine Pierre (1761–93) French revolutionary. A chief spokesman of the *Jacobins, he developed royalist sympathies in 1791 through personal contact with Louis XVI. Advocating a constitutional monarchy, he became leader of the *Feuillants and was executed.

Barnes, William (1801–86) British poet. His *Poems of Rural Life in the Dorset Dialect* (1879) expressed his deep feeling for the landscape and traditional customs of Dorset, where he worked as a schoolteacher and clergyman. He also wrote philological works.

Barnet A residential borough of NW Greater London, created in 1965 from parts of Hertfordshire and Middlesex, including *Finchley and *Hendon. It was the site of a Yorkist victory (1471) in the Wars of the Roses, when the Earl of Warwick was killed. Population (1981): 292 331.

barn owl An *owl belonging to a family (*Tytonidae*; 9 species) with a worldwide distribution. Barn owls have heart-shaped faces, long feathered legs, and usually a reddish plumage with pale underparts. The common barn owl (*Tyto alba*), 30–45 cm long, nests in old barns and belfries and hunts for small rodents.

Barnsley 53 34N 1 28W A town in N England, in South Yorkshire on the River Dearne. Principally a coalmining centre, Barnsley's other industries include glass manufacture, engineering, textiles, clothing, furniture, carpets, and boxes. It is the site of a large mining and technical college. Population (1985 est): 225 890.

Barnstaple 51 5N 4 04W A town and resort in SW England, in N Devon on the estuary of the River Taw. Formerly a port, it is now the regional administrative and agricultural centre for N Devon. Population (1981): 19 025.

Barnum, Phineas Taylor (1810–91) US showman. His presentation of such novel exhibits as human freaks and natural curiosities at the American Museum from 1842 attracted unprecedented crowds. In 1850 he organized the successful US tour of the Swedish singer Jenny Lind. His circus, established in

1871, merged with that of his rival, J. A. Bailey (1847–1906), to become the Barnum and Bailey Circus in 1881.

Baroda (Name from 1976: Vadodara) 22 19N 73 14E A city in India, in Gujarat. The siting of an oil refinery at nearby Kouali has helped to promote Baroda's industrial growth and its chief products include petrochemicals, cotton textiles, wood, and tobacco. Population (1981): 744 881.

Baroja, Pío (1872–1956) Spanish novelist. He abandoned a career as a doctor to manage a family bakery in Madrid. His first book of short stories, *Vida sombrías* (1900), was followed by nearly a hundred novels. His early heroes were rebels or reformers embodying his own desire to inspire political action, but the tone of later books—especially *Laura, o la soledad sin remedio* (1939)—was more sceptical and pessimistic.

Torricellian vacuum

760 mm

air pressure

mercury

levers transmit pressure change

evacuated metal box

air pressure

mercury barometer

aneroid barometer

BAROMETER *In the mercury barometer the height of the mercury column is directly proportional to the air pressure and is independent of the diameter of the tube. In the aneroid barometer movements of the lid of the evacuated metal box are transmitted to the pointer by the levers.*

barometer An instrument for measuring atmospheric pressure. There are two main types: the mercury barometer and the aneroid barometer. In the mercury barometer, atmospheric pressure forces mercury from a reservoir into a vertical evacuated glass tube marked with a scale. The height of the mercury column is directly proportional to the atmospheric pressure. In the aneroid barometer, variations in the atmospheric pressure on the lid of an evacuated metal box cause a pointer to move round a dial. The aneroid barometer is less sensitive than the mercury barometer but it is smaller, more portable, and more convenient to use.

Barons' Wars 1. (1215–17) The civil war between King John of England and his barons. John's failure to honour the *Magna Carta led the barons to offer the English Crown to the future Louis VIII of France, who invaded England. John's death and the reissue of Magna Carta (1216) removed many baronial grievances but war continued until the barons' defeat at Lincoln and Sandwich (1217). Peace was established and the Magna Carta again reissued. 2. (1264–67) The civil war between Henry III of England and his barons led by Simon de *Montfort. War broke out following Henry's repudiation of the Provisions of *Oxford. He was captured at the battle of *Lewes (1264) and England was controlled by de Montfort until his death at Evesham

(1265). Hostilities continued until the royalist capture of the Isle of Ely in 1267.

baroque In architecture, a style dominant in European Roman Catholic countries during the 17th and early 18th centuries. The name probably derives from the Spanish *barrueco*, an irregularly shaped pearl. The baroque began in Italy as a reaction against *classicism. It was characterized by curved and broken lines, ornate decoration (which led to the *rococo), and elaborate spatial effects. English architects, such as *Wren and *Vanbrugh, were influenced by it.

In art, the baroque was a style that developed from Italian *mannerism, complementing baroque architecture. Both art and architecture were used to popularize Catholic beliefs during the *Counter-Reformation. Baroque art was characterized by the vivid presentation of stories of saints, miracles, and the crucifixion. Leading exponents of the baroque were the sculptor and architect *Bernini, the architect *Borromini, and the painters *Caravaggio and *Rubens.

In music, the compositions of the 17th and early 18th centuries, from Monteverdi to Bach, are frequently called baroque music. A variety of styles and forms flourished during this period, the use of the term referring to the period rather than a particular style. This period saw the development of *opera, *oratorio, the concerto grosso (*see* Corelli, Arcangelo), and the trio sonata.

Barossa Valley. *See* South Australia.

Barotse. *See* Lozi.

Barotseland A former kingdom in central Africa, now comprising Western Province in Zambia. Inhabited by the *Lozi people, it was put under British protection through two treaties (1890, 1900) by the Lozi chief, Lewanika (d. 1916). The area attempted to break away as a separate kingdom on Zambian independence (1964).

barque A sailing vessel with three or more masts. Square sails are set on all masts except the aftermast, which carries fore-and-aft sails. In a **barquentine** only the foremast has square-rigged sails.

Barquisimeto 10 03N 69 18W A city in NW Venezuela. It is the commercial centre of a coffee-growing area and has a university (1963). Population (1981 est): 459 000.

Barra An island in NW Scotland, in the Outer Hebrides separated from South Uist by the Sound of Barra. Its economy is based on fishing, crofting, and tourism. Area: 91 sq km (35 sq mi). Population (1981): 1339. Chief settlement: Castlebay.

barracuda A shoaling fish of the family *Sphyraenidae* (about 20 species), found in all tropical seas and caught for food and sport. Its body is up to 1.8 m long and bears two dorsal fins. Barracudas feed voraciously on other fish and the larger species are considered dangerous to man. Order: *Perciformes*.

Barranquilla 11 00N 74 50W An important port in NW Colombia, on the Río Magdalena near its mouth on the Caribbean Sea. Its manufactures include textiles, vegetable oils, and chemicals. It has two universities (1941, 1967). Population (1981 est): 690 471.

Barras, Paul François Jean Nicolas, Vicomte de (1755–1829) French revolutionary. Although he joined the National Convention as a Jacobin, Barras turned against Robespierre and helped to secure his downfall in 1794. As commander of Paris, Barras suppressed a royalist uprising in 1795 by allowing Napoleon Bonaparte to turn his guns on the agitators. A member of the Directory from 1795 to 1799, Barras resigned during Napoleon's coup d'état (1799).

Barrault, Jean-Louis (1910–) French actor and director. He has directed influential productions of both classical and avantgarde plays and was director of the Théâtre de France from 1959 to 1968. He is also renowned for his mime, especially in the film *Les Enfants du paradis* (1944).

barrel organ 1. A musical instrument popular in the 18th and 19th centuries, much used in churches. It consists of a simple organ mechanism operated by a wooden cylinder (or barrel) set with brass pins and turned by a handle, which also works a bellows. 2. A musical instrument of the 19th century more properly called **barrel piano** and often confused with the barrel organ. A popular street instrument, its barrel and pin mechanism causes leather-covered hammers to strike strings.

Barren Grounds (*or* Lands) The largely uninhabited permafrost plain of N Canada, stretching from about 59°N to the Arctic Ocean and from Hudson Bay to the Mackenzie Valley. Caribou and other animals live on the short grasses and other flowering plants.

Barrès, Maurice (1862–1923) French writer and politician. In the trilogy *La Culte de moi* (1888–91) he described a searching period of self-analysis resulting in his entry into politics. His rigid nationalism was expounded in another trilogy, *Le Roman de l'énergie nationale* (1897–1902), and linked with Catholicism in *La Colline inspirée* (1913). His memoirs, *Mes cahiers* (14 vols, 1929–57), were published posthumously.

Barrie, Sir James (Matthew) (1860–1937) British dramatist and novelist. The son of a Scots weaver, he came to London as a freelance writer in 1885. After two successful novels about Scottish rural life he wrote mostly for the theatre. His best-known plays are *The Admirable Crichton* (1902), *Peter Pan* (1904), which has also remained a popular children's book, and *Dear Brutus* (1917).

barrier reef. *See* reef.

barrister A member of the legal profession in England and Wales or Northern Ireland who has the exclusive right to present and argue cases in the Court of Appeal and the High Court and a nonexclusive right in other courts. Barristers also act as specialist advisers to clients through their solicitors. The term barrister is not used in Scotland or in other countries in which the legal profession is divided into two classes. In Scotland they are known as advocates, and elsewhere as advocates or attorneys. The right to confer the title of barrister-at-law is restricted to the *Inns of Court. In order to qualify, a student must "keep" 12 terms by dining a set number of times per term at his Inn and must pass the examinations set by the Council of Legal Education. On the payment of fees, he is then "called to the Bar." At this time, or earlier, he must spend one year as a pupil in the chambers of a practising barrister. A barrister is instructed by a *solicitor before he conducts a case in court. He cannot be sued for negligence in presenting a case nor can he sue a client for unpaid fees. *See also* Queen's Counsel.

barrow A prehistoric burial mound, also called a tumulus or cairn. From about 2000 BC earth barrows, concealing stone or timber passages and burial chambers, were built all over Europe for the interment of warrior chiefs. Long (i.e. rectangular or trapezoidal) barrows, such as at West Kennet (S England), were used for Neolithic multiple burials. Round barrows were more usual in Bronze Age cultures. Barrows continued in use in Iron Age Europe, for example the *Hallstatt barrow cemetery at Hohmichele (Germany) on the Upper Danube (6th century BC), and as late as the 7th century AD, for example the *Sutton Hoo ship burial.

Barrow-in-Furness 54 07N 3 14W A town in NW England, on the S coast of Cumbria. Rich local iron ore (now exhausted) gave rise to iron and steel industries, and shipbuilding followed. The first British nuclear submarine was built here. Population (1981): 61 704.

Barry 51 24N 3 18W A port in South Wales, in South Glamorgan on the Bristol Channel. It exports coal, steel products, and cement. Barry Island, to the SW, is a holiday resort. Population (1981): 43 828.

Barry, Sir Charles (1795–1860) British architect. Barry worked in both classical and gothic styles. In 1836 he won the competition to rebuild the Houses of Parliament (*see*

Palace of Westminster), which, assisted by *Pugin, he designed in the gothic manner. He also designed the Travellers' Club (1829–31) and Reform Club (1837) in London.

Barrymore, Lionel (1878–1954) US actor. After studying art in Paris and achieving success as a stage actor he became known primarily as a film actor. He is remembered for his performances in the first series of *Dr Kildare* films. His sister **Ethel Barrymore** (1879–1959) acted with Sir Henry Irving in London, and later became a leading stage actress in the USA. A theatre in New York was named after her in 1928. Their brother **John Barrymore** (1882–1942) was also an actor. His greatest stage success was his performance of Hamlet in 1922. As a film star during his later career he was famous for such films as *Grand Hotel* (1932) and *Moby Dick* (1930). He was also renowned for his tempestuous private life.

Bart, Jean (1650–1702) French admiral, whose early successes against pirates earned him swift promotion under Louis XIV. He fought in the Dutch War of 1672–78 and in the War of the *Grand Alliance (1689–97), when he was captured by the English; escaping from Plymouth, he was received as a hero by Louis at Versailles.

Bart, Lionel (1930–   ) British composer and playwright, who wrote the music and lyrics for *Fings Ain't Wot They Used T'Be* (1959) and *Oliver* (1960).

Barth, Heinrich (1821–65) German explorer and geographer. He travelled widely in the Mediterranean (1845–47) and in 1850 joined, as scientific observer, an expedition to West Africa sponsored by the British Government. Setting out from Tripoli he crossed the Sahara and, in spite of the death of his two companions, covered 19 200 km (12 000 mi). He recorded this expedition in *Travels and Discoveries in North and Central Africa* (5 vols, 1857–58).

Barth, John (1930–   ) US novelist and academic. His novels, which combine philosophical seriousness with bawdy humour, include *The Sotweed Factor* (1960), *Giles Goat-Boy* (1966), *Chimera* (1974), *Letters* (1979), and *Sabbatical*, (1982). He often emphasizes the artificiality of fiction by parodying literary conventions.

Barth, Karl (1886–1968) Swiss Protestant theologian. As a pastor during World War I, he became disillusioned with modern liberal theology in the face of extreme suffering. In such influential works as *Epistle to the Romans* (1919) and the four-volume *Church Dogmatics* (1932–67) he returned to the principles of the Reformation and the teachings of the Bible, emphasizing God's sovereignty and man's sinfulness, which necessitates grace. He held professorships at several German universities (1921–35) and at Basle (1935–62).

Bartholdi, Frédéric August (1834–1904) French sculptor, famous for his patriotic monuments. Best known are the Lion of Belfort, commemorating the gallant defence of Belfort during the Franco-Prussian War (1870–71), and the *Statue of Liberty.

Bartholomew, St Christian Apostle. Although mentioned in lists of the Apostles, his name is never connected with any incident from the New Testament. He is sometimes identified with the Nathanael mentioned by John (1.45–51; 21.2). The historian Eusebius tells of his taking the Gospel to India. Feast day: 24 Aug.

Bartók, Béla (1881–1945) Hungarian composer. Bartók studied and taught at the Budapest Academy of Music, where he and *Kodály undertook research into Hungarian folksong. In 1940 he went to live in the USA, where he died in poverty. His music blends elements of E European folk music with dissonant harmonies into an astringent and often percussive style. A virtuoso pianist, he composed three piano concertos, a set of progressive pieces for students, entitled *Mikrokosmos* (1926–37), and other piano works. His stage works include the opera *Duke Bluebeard's Castle* (1911) and the ballet *The Miraculous Mandarin* (1919). In his six string quartets and *Music for Strings, Percussion, and Celesta* (1936) he explored unusual sonorities. His most popular work is the *Concerto for Orchestra*

(1943).

Bartolommeo, Fra (Baccio della Porta; c. 1472–1517) Florentine Renaissance painter. After training under Cosimo Rosselli (1439–1507), he became a supporter of *Savonarola, whose death moved him to join the Dominican monastery of S Marco (1500) and abandon painting until 1504. His exclusively religious works were close to *Raphael and *Leonardo in style; they include *St Mark* and the *Pietà* (both Palazzo Pitti, Florence).

Barton, Clara (1821–1912) US schoolteacher, who founded the American Red Cross. During the American Civil War (1861–65) she helped obtain supplies for wounded soldiers. She later worked for the International Red Cross in the Franco-Prussian War (1870–71) and then established its American branch, serving as its first president (1881–1904).

Barton, Sir Edmund (1849–1920) Australian statesman; Australia's first prime minister (1901–03). He was leader of the Federal Convention in 1897 that drafted the bill to unite the separate states of Australia. He resigned in 1903 to become a High Court judge.

Barton, Elizabeth (c. 1506–34) English nun, known as the Maid of Kent. A servant girl, she was subject to trances and claimed to foretell the future. After she became a nun, her pronouncements criticized Henry VIII's intention to divorce Catherine of Aragon. Examined by Cranmer, she confessed that her trances were false and was executed.

Baruch, Bernard (1870–1965) US economist and adviser to Presidents Wilson, F. D. Roosevelt, and Truman. He helped to coordinate US industries during World War I and to draft the economic items of the Treaty of Versailles. He served on the UN *Atomic Energy Commission.

baryon A collective term for *nucleons and other elementary particles that have a proton or neutron in their decay products. All baryons have a *quantum number called the baryon number of $+1$ (or -1 for antiparticles), which is conserved in interactions. *See* particle physics.

Baryshnikov, Mikhail (Nikolayevich) (1948–   ) Soviet-born ballet dancer. A leading dancer with the Kirov Ballet (1967–74), he defected to the West in 1974, while on tour in Canada. He then danced with the American Ballet Theatre (ABT) (1974–78) and the New York City Ballet (1978–79) before becoming artistic director of the ABT (1980–   ). In 1986 he appeared in the film *White Nights*.

barytes. *See* barite.

baryton A musical instrument of the *viol family popular in the 18th century. Held between the knees, it had six gut strings and a number of sympathetic wire strings, which could be plucked. Haydn, whose patron Prince Esterhazy was a keen player, wrote many pieces for it.

basalt A volcanic rock of basic composition, typically dark, heavy, and fine textured. It consists essentially of calcic plagioclase feldspar and pyroxene, with magnetite, apatite, and often olivine as accessory minerals. Three broad groups of basalt are recognized: alkali basalt, high-alumina basalt, and tholeiite. The basalts constituting the ocean floor, generated at midocean ridges, are tholeiites. Many volcanoes and huge lava plateaus consist of basalt, which constitutes over 90% of volcanic rocks.

baseball A nine-a-side bat-and-ball game that evolved from *rounders, played mainly in the USA, Japan, and Latin America. The object for each team while batting is to score as many runs as possible and while fielding to prevent the other team from doing so; the team with the highest score wins. A team bats until three players are out; one turn at bat for both teams constitutes an inning, of which there are usually nine in a game. The pitcher, standing at the pitcher's mound, throws the ball to the batter, standing at home plate, who tries to strike it into fair territory and run. He scores a home run by making a complete circuit of the bases (first, second, third, and home). A player may be struck out (if he misses the ball or hits it into foul territory in each of three

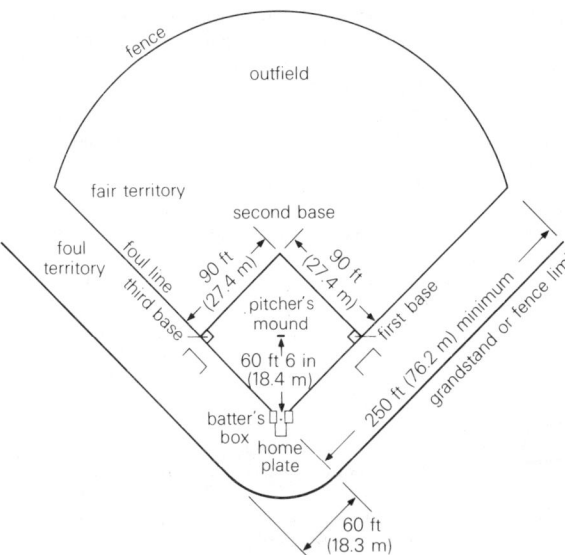

BASEBALL *The dimensions of the field.*

attempts), caught out, tagged out (if he or the base he is running towards is touched by a player with the ball), or put out by being hit by a batted ball while running.

Basel. *See* Basle.

basenji A breed of dog originating in central Africa. It is lightly built, has a wrinkled forehead, pricked ears, and tightly curled tail, and does not bark. The short glossy coat is usually chestnut with white markings but can be black and white. Height: 40–43 cm.

bases. *See* acids and bases.

Bashkir A Turkic language and people of the Bashkir ASSR in the Soviet Union. The language is related to Tatar and Kazakh. The Bashkirs, originally nomads herding mainly horses and sheep, settled in their present territory under Mongol rule (13th–15th centuries). Russian domination of the area after 1551 led to the encouragement of agriculture and village life. Collectivization has obliterated the traditional tribal and clan organization. The Bashkirs are either Muslims or Eastern Orthodox Christians by faith.

Bashkir Autonomous Soviet Socialist Republic (*or* Bashkiria) An administrative division in the E central Soviet Union, in the RSFSR. The Turkic-speaking Bashkirs comprise some 25% of the population. Bashkiria has large oil and natural-gas deposits, as well as coal, iron ore, and copper and has expanding chemical, coal, steel, and timber industries. Grains are the chief agricultural product. It was the first autonomous Soviet republic (1919). Area: 143 600 sq km (55 430 sq mi). Population (1981 est): 3 860 000. Capital: Ufa.

Basic A computer language developed in the USA in the 1960s. Designed principally for use by inexperienced programmers, it is one of the easiest languages to learn and is widely used, in more recent versions, in personal *computers.

Basic English A simplified form of the English language, which uses a vocabulary of 850 common English words. It was developed in the late 1920s by the linguist C. K. *Ogden, who intended it to be a simply learnt method of international communication and a rival to *Esperanto. The vocabulary divides into 600 nouns, 150 adjectives, and 100 operations, which include verbs. These building blocks are used to form complex ideas without the necessity of complex vocabulary items; for instance the concept "prepare" would be expressed as "get ready," and such combinations can replace 4000 standard English verbs.

Basidiomycetes A large class of fungi (about 13 000 species) that includes many *mushrooms, the *bracket fungi, *puffballs, etc., as well as important microscopic forms, such as the parasitic *rusts and *smuts of crops. They reproduce by basidia, which are typically club-shaped and produce spores at the tips of stalklike projections.

Basie, Count (William B.; 1904–84) US Black jazz pianist and band leader. He was influenced by Harlem ragtime pianists, played in vaudeville shows, and formed his own band in 1935. He became famous for his distinctive "big band" style and his piano playing. He recorded many albums, including *Atomic Mr Basie* and *Straight Ahead.*

basil An annual herbaceous plant of the Indian genus *Ocimum*, cultivated as a pot herb. Sweet basil (*O. basilicum*), up to 30 cm high, has toothed leaves and small white or bluish flowers. The dried clove-scented leaves are used to flavour various dishes. Family: *Labiatae.*

Basil (I) the Macedonian (d. 886 AD) Byzantine emperor (876–86), who founded the Macedonian dynasty. Of humble origin, Basil became coemperor (867) with Michael III (reigned 842–68) but murdered him in 868. He strengthened Byzantine power in Asia Minor and in S Italy and revived Roman law in a legal text known as the Basilica.

Basil II Buigaroctonus (c. 958–1025 AD) Byzantine emperor (976–1025). He secured Byzantine conquests in Syria and conquered territory in Georgia and Armenia. He was named Bulgaroctonus (slayer of the Bulgars) after defeating the Bulgarians at Ochrida (1014): he blinded their entire army except for every 100th man, who was left with one eye with which to lead his comrades back to their ruler; the Bulgarian khan died of shock.

Basildon 51 34N 0 25E A town in SE England, in Essex. Created as a new town in 1949 from several townships, its industries include engineering, printing, tobacco, and other light industry. Population (1981): 152 301.

basilica 1. A Roman public meeting hall. In imperial times, many had a layout similar to the Basilica of Maxentius in Rome: rectangular ground plan, colonnaded aisles, entrance porch (narthex), and windows in the upper storey (clerestory). **2.** A Christian church based on a similar plan (e.g. S Giovanni in Laterano in Rome). The influence of the plan can still be seen in western church architecture.

Basilicata A mountainous region in S Italy. A poor region economically, it is almost entirely dependent upon agriculture producing wheat, olives, vines, potatoes, sheep, and goats. Area: 9987 sq km (3856 sq mi). Population (1976 est): 617 257. Capital: Potenza.

basilisk 1. An arboreal lizard belonging to the tropical American genus *Basiliscus*. Up to 60 cm long, it has a narrow body, a long whiplike tail, and a flat lobe protruding from the back of its head. It has long hind legs with lobed toes fringed with scales, enabling it to run over the surface of water. Family: *Iguanidae.* **2.** A legendary snakelike serpent of ancient Greece and Rome whose glance was believed to be fatal to all living things except the weasel, and later the cock, which both had the power to destroy it.

Basil the Great, St (c. 330–79 AD) Bishop of Caesarea in Cappadocia. His name is usually linked with St *Gregory of Nazianzus and St *Gregory of Nyssa (his brother). Known as the Cappadocian Fathers, they were the chief defenders of orthodox Christian philosophy against *Arianism in the 4th century. Thoroughly educated in both classical pagan and Christian culture, he adopted a monastic life and then lived as a hermit before becoming Bishop of Caesarea in 370. He developed a rule that formed the basis of monasticism in the Eastern Church. He is traditionally considered the author of the liturgy of St Basil, still used on certain days in the Orthodox Church. He wrote many theological works. Feast day: 14 June.

Basingstoke 51 16N 1 05W A town in S England, in Hampshire. Considerable industrial and residential development has been carried out in recent years. It is the headquarters of the Civil Service Commission and the Automobile Association. Its manufactures include agricultural machinery, scientific instruments, and leather goods. It is also developing as a warehousing and distribution centre for southern England. Population (1984 est): 80 000.

Baskerville, John (1706–75) British printer, who designed the typeface that bears his name. His first work, a Virgil, was printed in 1757 and, while printer to Cambridge University (1758–68), he produced a masterly edition of the Bible (1763). His work was distinguished by the use of original high-gloss paper and black ink.

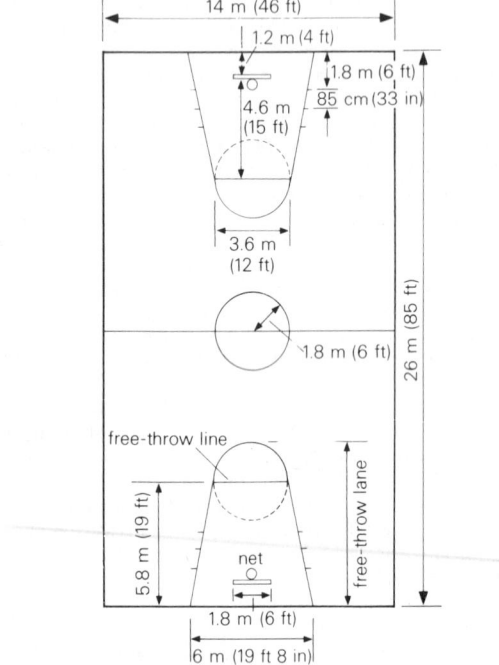

BASKETBALL *The dimensions of the court.*

basketball A five-a-side court game invented in the USA (1891) by James Naismith (1861–1939). The object is to toss or put an inflated ball into the opponents' basket, a net mounted 3.05 m (10 ft) above the floor on a backboard. Players use only their hands, passing the ball or dribbling it by bouncing, and they may not run with it. A professional game has 4 12-minute quarters. Five substitutes are allowed to each side. The Americans have won all Olympic tournaments (except in 1972) between 1936 and 1976. The premier professional basketball league is the National Basketball Association in the USA (founded in 1949). *See also* Harlem Globetrotters.

basking shark A large *shark belonging to the family *Cetorhinidae*. Up to 15 m long, they are grey-brown or blackish and inhabit cold and temperate regions of the Atlantic, Pacific, and Indian Oceans. Basking sharks usually occur in shoals near the surface and float or swim slowly, feeding on plankton.

Basle (French name: Bâle; German name: Basel) 47 33N 7 36E The second largest city in Switzerland, on the River Rhine where the French, German, and Swiss borders meet. A Roman fort originally occupied the site. During the Reformation it became a major literary centre and the scholar Erasmus taught at the university (founded 1460). Its notable features include the medieval city gates and the cathedral. Basle is a major commercial and industrial centre, strategically positioned in the

European railway system and the chief riverport in Switzerland. Industries include chemicals, pharmaceuticals, and engineering. The Bank for International Settlements was established here in 1929. Population (1980 est): 182 143.

Basle, Council of A general council of the Roman Catholic Church summoned by Pope Martin V in 1431 to consider the heretical *Hussites and the nature of papal power. The council, having reaffirmed the principle that general councils are answerable only to God, grew increasingly antipapal and in 1437 Eugenius IV, Martin's successor, moved it to Ferrara. However, a minority of councillors remained at Basle, electing the antipope, Felix V, in 1439. He resigned in 1449 and the council was brought to an end.

Basque A non-Indo-European language spoken by the Basque people of the W Pyrenean areas of Spain and France. Basque is a very ancient language, apparently unrelated to any other and called Euskara by the Basques themselves. It is still spoken by about 500 000 people. The Basques, predominantly farmers and seafarers, are descended from a people known to the Romans as the Vascones. Today there are about 750 000 Basques in Spain and 170 000 in France. They are strongly Roman Catholic and traditionally enjoyed a degree of regional autonomy, forming an independent government (1936–37) at the time of the Spanish Civil War. Nationalism remains a significant force among them in many areas today.

Basra 30 30N 47 50E A town in SE Iraq, on the Shatt (river) al-Arab. It is linked by rail and river steamer to Baghdad; the modern port (Al Ma'qil) was built by the British during World War I. Population (1970 est): 333 684.

bass (fish) One of several perchlike *bony fish of the order *Perciformes*, often valued as food and game fish. The majority belong to the family *Serranidae* (*see* sea bass), which includes the common European bass (*Dicentrarchus labrax*). This can grow up to 1 m long and has a grey or blue back with a white or yellowish belly and silvery flanks. North American freshwater bass belong to the family *Centrarchidae*.

bass (music) **1.** The deepest adult male singing voice. Range: E below the bass stave to E two octaves above. **2.** The lowest voice or instrumental part of a piece of music.

Bassano, Jacopo (Jacopo *or* Giacomo da Ponte; c. 1517–92) Italian painter of the Venetian school, born in Bassano, the son of a painter. In Venice he was influenced by Titian before adopting the elongated figure style of *Parmigianino. He was one of the earliest painters of rustic life, in both secular, e.g. *Pastoral* (Lugano), and religious scenes, e.g. *Adoration of the Kings* (National Gallery, Edinburgh).

Bassein 16 46N 94 45E A port in Lower Burma, on the River Bassein. Situated at the terminus of a railway to Rangoon, it is the country's second port exporting chiefly rice, coal, and salt. Population (1983): 144 092.

basset horn A woodwind instrument, the tenor member of the *clarinet family. It has a rich velvety tone but lacks the brilliance of the upper range of the A or B flat clarinet. Mozart wrote for it.

basset hound A breed of □dog originating in France. It has a long body with very short legs and a narrow face with drooping ears and a mournful expression. The short smooth coat ranges from black to light brown in colour with white patches. Basset hounds have a keen sense of smell and were formerly popular hunting dogs. Height: 33–38 cm.

bassoon A musical instrument of the woodwind family. Its conically bored tube is about 2.5 m (8 ft) long and is bent back on itself. It has a metal crook into which a double reed is inserted. Its extensive compass (about three and a half octaves above B flat below the bass stave) allows it a melodic as well as a bass role. Composers have made much use of its humorous staccato quality.

Bass Rock 56 05N 2 38W A Scottish islet at the mouth of

the Firth of Forth. It consists of a circular volcanic plug 1.6 km (1 mi) in circumference and is noted for its colonies of seabirds.

Bass Strait A channel separating the mainland of Australia from Tasmania. It has valuable oil and natural-gas deposits. Length: 290 km (180 mi). Maximum width: 240 km (150 mi).

basswood A *lime tree, *Tilia americana*, also called American lime or linden, sometimes exceeding 25 m in height. It yields commercially important timber that is especially prized for carving, and a tough fibre derived from the bark is of local importance.

bast fibres Fibres, such as *flax, *hemp, and *jute, that are obtained from the stems of certain plants. The fibres are freed from the stalk by retting (soaking) or mechanical peeling and are used for textiles, sacking, twines, and ropes.

Bastia 42 41N 9 26E A port in Corsica, on the NE coast. Founded by the Genoese in the 14th century, it was the former capital of Corsica and is the island's largest city. Fishing and the manufacture of tobacco and wine are the principal economic activities. Population (1982 est): 45 081.

Bastille A fortress in Paris, which was a state prison in the 17th and 18th centuries and a symbol of the corrupt and despotic Bourbon monarchy. It was built in about 1370 to protect the wall around Paris against English attack and became a state prison under Cardinal de *Richelieu. The storming of the Bastille on 14 July, 1789, is regarded as the beginning of the *French Revolution.

Basutoland. *See* Lesotho, Kingdom of.

bat A flying mammal belonging to the order *Chiroptera* (981 species), distributed in most temperate and tropical regions. There are two suborders: the *fruit bats (*Megachiroptera*; 150 species) and the insect-eating bats (*Microchiroptera*; 831 species). Bats may also feed on pollen, nectar, blood, and small animals. The wings are extensions of skin that are supported between the forelimb, with its very long fingers, the hind limbs, and the tail. Insectivorous bats use *echolocation for navigation and catching prey on the wing whereas fruit bats have large eyes adapted for night vision. Bats roost in caves and buildings during daytime.

Bataan A mountainous forested peninsula in the Philippines, in W Luzon W of Manila Bay. In a famous action during World War II, US-Filipino forces resisted the Japanese invasion for almost three months here (1942); after their capture, thousands died on a forced Death March. Length: about 48 km (30 mi).

bateleur An African snake *eagle, *Terathopius ecaudatus*, having very long wings and a short tail. It is highly manoeuvrable and flies vast distances, preying on snakes, other reptiles, mammals, and carrion, which it seizes with its short rough powerful toes.

Bates, H(erbert) E(rnest) (1905–74) British writer. After working as a solicitor's clerk and provincial journalist he began to write novels about English rural life. His service in the Royal Air Force in World War II yielded many short stories—as "Flying Officer X"—and three novels under his own name, of which the best known is *Fair Stood the Wind for France* (1944). In *The Darling Buds of May* (1958) he created his famous Larkin family characters.

Bates, Henry Walter (1825–92) British naturalist and explorer, who demonstrated the phenomenon of *mimicry in animals. In the Amazon valley he observed that many animals resembled their natural backgrounds and that certain species of butterfly mimicked the coloration of others, distasteful to predators. This latter phenomenon is now called Batesian mimicry.

Bateson, William (1861–1926) British biologist, whose experiments on inheritance helped found the science of genetics, a term that he first proposed. Bateson investigated the way in which certain traits, such as comb shape in fowl, are transmitted from one generation to the next. His results (1905–08) corrobo-

rated the findings of Gregor *Mendel published in 1865. He also found that certain characteristics were inherited together (a phenomenon now known as linkage, due to the occurrence of the controlling genes on the same chromosome), but he refused to accept the chromosome theory proposed by T. H. *Morgan to account for this.

batfish A carnivorous fish, belonging to a family (*Ogcocephalidae*; about 60 species) of *anglerfish, found in tropical and temperate seas. It has a slender lumpy-skinned body up to 36 cm long and a broad flat head with an elongated upturned snout. Using thickened limblike pectoral and pelvic fins, it crawls on the bottom searching for prey.

Bath 51 23N 2 22W A city in SW England, in Avon on the River Avon. A spa town of great architectural interest, it was an early Roman centre known as Aquae Sulis because of its hot natural springs, at a temperature of around 49°C (120°F). The Roman baths have survived and are considered the best Roman remains in the UK. Bath became fashionable as a spa town in the 18th century when many of the finest buildings were built, including the Royal Crescent and the Assembly Rooms. Bath Abbey, mainly 16th-century, lies in the town centre. Bath University dates from 1966. Population (1981): 79 965. □Georgian style.

BASTILLE *The murder, during the storming of the fortress, of Bernard de Launay (1740–89), its last commander.*

Bath, Order of the A British order of knighthood, formed by George I in 1725 as a successor to the Knights of the Bath, traditionally founded by Henry IV in 1399. It comprises the sovereign and three classes of knights companions: knights and dames grand cross (GCB), knights and dames commanders (KCB), and companions (CB). Women have been admitted since 1971. Its name is derived from the bathing ceremony that formed the principal rite of admission to the original order.

batholith A large mass of intrusive igneous rock of unknown depth and often occupying many thousands of square kilometres. They are composed mainly of granite and occur in association with mountain belts. They are often surrounded by a zone of mineralized rocks (metamorphic aureole).

Bathurst 33 27S 149 35E A city in Australia, in E central New South Wales, on the Macquarie River. Founded in 1815, it is Australia's oldest inland city. Population (1983): 24 500.

Bathurst. *See* Banjul.

batik Cloth, traditionally cotton, dyed by a special method. An ancient Indonesian craft, developed especially in Java, batik work involves the application of melted wax, later removed, to protect parts of the material from the dye; repeating the process using different wax patterns and several dyeings produces intricate multicoloured geometric patterns, symbolic motifs, or stylized pictures of birds, animals, or flowers. Some designs have been passed on in families for a thousand years.

Batista y Zaldívar, Fulgencio (1901–73) Cuban statesman, who was president from 1940 to 1944 and, after returning to power in 1952 by means of a military coup, from 1954 to 1958. His authoritarian government generated opposition, notably from Castro's guerrilla movement, by which Batista was ousted.

Batley 53 44N 1 37W A town in N England, in West Yorkshire. It has long been associated with wool textiles; shoddy (woollen material made from reclaimed fibres) was invented here and Batley now specializes in finished cloths. Population (1981): 42 572.

Baton Rouge 30 30N 91 10W A city in the USA, the capital of Louisiana situated on the Mississippi River at the head of oceangoing navigation. It is a major deepwater port with oil and sugar refineries. It has several state institutions, including the Louisiana State University (1860). Population (1980): 241 483.

Battani, al- (Latin name: Albatenius; c. 858–929) Islamic astronomer, born in Haran (Turkey) and noted for his book on stellar motions. Using trigonometric methods, he improved the accuracy of many astronomical measurements, including the length of the year, the precession of the equinoxes, and the inclination of the ecliptic.

Batten, Jean (1909–) New Zealand aviator. In 1935 she became the first woman to fly solo from Australia to Britain. She later established records for the fastest flights between these countries.

Battenberg. *See* Mountbatten of Burma, Louis, 1st Earl.

battered baby syndrome Injuries inflicted on babies or young children by their parents. Battering usually occurs in the first six months of life and commonly takes the form of facial bruises, cigarette burns, head injuries (often with brain damage), and fractured bones. The parents are often emotionally disturbed or have themselves suffered from physical abuse in infancy or early childhood. Two-thirds of battered children suffer from further injury if discharged from hospital without the support of a social worker and surveillance of family doctor and health visitor; a care order is often necessary to safeguard a child from further abuse.

Battersea A district in the Greater London borough of Wandsworth, on the River Thames. It is noted for its power station (to be developed into a leisure centre) and dogs' home.

Battle 50 55N 0 29E A town in S England, in East Sussex. It was the scene of the battle of Hastings (1066) in which Harold II was defeated by William the Conqueror, who built Battle Abbey to commemorate his victory. Population (1981): 5141.

battleship A heavily armoured naval vessel designed to combine large size, manoeuvrability, and extensive cruising range with the most powerful armament. Larger than a *cruiser and smaller than an *aircraft carrier, the battleship was the flagship vessel of a fleet. No new battleships have been built since World War II, as they have been largely replaced by more versatile less expensive vessels.

Batumi 41 37N 41 36E A port in the S Soviet Union, in the Georgian SSR on the Black Sea. It has an oil refinery, shipping

oil piped from Baku, a range of light industries, and there are tea plantations on the city's outskirts. Population (1981 est): 124 000.

Baudelaire, Charles (1821–67) French poet. He inherited his father's fortune in 1842 and lived extravagantly until what was left of the capital was placed in trust by his family (1844). Forced to earn a living, he began to publish art criticism and poetry and wrote the autobiographical novel *La Fanfarlo* (1847). In 1852 he discovered Edgar Allan *Poe, publishing several translations of his works (1856–65). His only volume of poetry, *Les Fleurs du mal* (1857, revised 1861), contained several erotic poems, which led to his being convicted for obscenity. He became increasingly disillusioned; while in Belgium in 1866 he became paralysed as a result of venereal disease and died in Paris soon after.

Baudouin I (1930–) King of the Belgians (1951–), succeeding his father Leopold III. He was interned by the Nazis in World War II. In 1960 he married Fabiola de Mora y Aragón (1928–).

Bauhaus A German school of design. One of the most important influences on 20th-century art, the Bauhaus enjoyed a short life. Founded in 1919 at Weimar it was closed by the Nazis in 1933. From 1925 to 1932 it was housed at Dessau in a building designed by *Gropius (its director until 1928), itself a work of great influence. Connected with some of the best designers of the age, the Bauhaus sought to produce a practical synthesis of all the arts, from furniture design to architecture, and to develop a coherent style appropriate for the industrial 20th century. The functional style the Bauhaus helped to evolve still has considerable influence in the arts, from the international style of architecture to tubular steel furniture. *See also* Kandinsky; Klee; Mies van der Rohe; Moholy-Nagy.

Baum, L(yman) Frank (1856–1919) US novelist. After working as a journalist, he created in *The Wonderful Wizard of Oz* (1900) a classic children's fantasy land that provided material for 13 sequels; in all, he wrote about 60 books, mostly for children.

Baumgarten, Alexander Gottlieb (1714–62) German philosopher, a follower of Christian Wolff (1679–1754) and *Leibniz. In 1740, he became professor of philosophy at Frankfurt-am-Oder. He invented the term *aesthetics and his *Aesthetica* (1750) is a pioneering work on that subject.

Baur, Ferdinand Christian (1792–1860) German Protestant theologian. Baur's early work was concerned with the gnostic background of Christianity. He was much influenced by *Hegel. In 1826, he became professor of theology at Tübingen University, and his later work on St Paul led him to question the authenticity of the New Testament and marked the beginnings of radical biblical criticism.

Bautzen 51 14N 14 23E A town in SE East Germany, on the River Spree. A battle was fought here in 1813, in which Napoleon's army defeated an allied army of Russians and Prussians. Its industries include the manufacture of vehicles and machinery. Population (1983): 49 767.

bauxite The chief ore of aluminium. It is a residual deposit formed by the weathering of aluminium-rich rocks (mainly syenites) under tropical conditions and consists mainly of hydrated aluminium oxide. The main producers are Australia, Jamaica, Surinam, Guyana, Guinea, Sierra Leone, and Yugoslavia.

Bavaria (German name: Bayern) The largest *Land* of West Germany, bordering on Austria, Czechoslovakia, and East Germany. A third is forested, providing valuable timber resources. Predominantly agricultural, the main crops are rye, wheat, and barley; hops are grown around Munich. Bavaria is a popular tourist area. *History*: a duchy and later a kingdom ruled by the Wittelsbachs from 1180 to 1918, it then became a republic. From the ensuing political unrest Hitler drew much of his early support. Area: 70 547 sq km (29 232 sq mi). Population (1980 est): 10 896 900. Capital: Munich.

Bax, Sir Arnold Edward Trevor (1883-1953) British composer. Of his large output his tone poems, such as *Tintagel* (1917) and *The Garden of Fand* (1916), and his seven symphonies remain his most popular works. Knighted in 1937, he was Master of the King's Music from 1941 until his death.

Baxter, Richard (1615-91) English Puritan minister and author. A noted clergyman during the Commonwealth period, after the Restoration he was offered a bishopric, but was forced to leave the Church because of the Act of Uniformity (1662). In about 1673 he took out a licence as a Nonconformist minister. His best-remembered work, *The Saints' Everlasting Rest* (1650), is devotional.

bay A Mediterranean evergreen tree, *Laurus nobilis*, also known as sweet bay and bay laurel, widely grown as an ornamental shrub or pot plant. It can reach a height of 20 m, has aromatic dark-green lance-shaped leaves, small yellowish flowers, and blackish berries. The leaves are used to season food. Family: *Lauraceae* (*see* laurel).

Bayar, Mahmud Celal (1884-1986) Turkish statesman; president (1950-60). He became involved in politics after an early career in banking. As minister of the economy (1932-37) under *Atatürk, he encouraged state direction of the economy (etatism), a policy he abandoned as president. He was a founder (1946) of the Democratic Party. In 1960 an army coup deposed him and he was sentenced to death but later reprieved.

Bayard, Pierre Terrail, Seigneur de (c. 1473-1524) French soldier, known as "le bon chevalier sans peur et sans reproche" (the good knight without fear and without reproach). He served in the Italian wars of Charles VIII, Louis XII, and Francis I, gaining particular distinction at Fornovo (1495) and Marignano (1515). Pope Julius II sought unsuccessfully to hire him.

Baybars I (1223-77) Sultan of Egypt and Syria (1260-77) of the *Mameluke dynasty. Brought to Egypt as a slave, he rose in the army and in 1260 he was prominent at the decisive victory over the Mongols at Ayn Jalut. Between 1263 and 1271 he severely reduced the power of the Crusaders in Syria. He became the subject of a popular folk biography.

bayberry A deciduous shrub, *Myrica pensilvanica*, rarely exceeding 3 m in height, bearing flowers in catkins and oblong 10-cm-long leaves. It is native to E North America and sometimes cultivated in other temperate areas. Family: *Myricaceae*.The name is also given to the purple-blue berries of the *bay tree.

Bayeux 49 16N 0 42W A town in NW France, in the Calvados department on the River Aure. Its museum houses the famous *Bayeux tapestry and there is a fine 13th-century cathedral. It was the first French town to be liberated by the Allies in World War II (7 June, 1944). Industries include dairy foods and plastics. Population (1982 est): 15 237.

Bayeux tapestry An 11th-century embroidered linen strip, 69 m (231 ft) long, which depicts the Norman conquest of England (1066). The tapestry, which starts with King Harold's visit to Normandy and ends with the battle of Hastings, is of great historical value. It was reputedly commissioned for Bayeux cathedral by its bishop, Odo, the half-brother of William the Conqueror, whose wife Matilda is traditionally credited with its making. Experts have concluded, however, that it was made in England. The tapestry now hangs in the museum at Bayeux (France).

Bayezid II (c. 1447-1512) Ottoman Sultan of Turkey (1481-1512). During his reign Turkish dominions in the Balkans and the Crimea were extended; war with Venice (1499-1503) brought territory in Greece and the Adriatic.

Warfare with Egypt and the Safavid dynasty of Persia occupied the last decade of his reign. In 1512 Bayezid abdicated, dying soon afterwards.

Bayle, Pierre (1647-1706) French Protestant critic and controversialist. He taught philosophy at Sedan from 1675 until forced into exile in Rotterdam. There he was professor of philosophy from 1781 to 1793, when his contentious religious tracts and determined opponents lost him the chair. Undeterred, he began publication of his masterwork, the *Dictionnaire historique et critique* (1796), a model of scholarship, style, and philosophical scepticism, which was both influential and successful.

Baylis, Lilian (1874-1937) British theatre manager. She founded the first *Old Vic company at the Victoria Theatre, a music hall, in 1912, and supervised the production of all of Shakespeare's plays between 1914 and 1923. In 1931 she founded the Sadler's Wells company for opera and ballet.

Bayliss, Sir William Maddock (1860-1924) British physiologist, who, with Ernest Starling (1866-1927), made the first discovery of a hormone. Working with dogs they showed how food stimulated the secretion of a messenger chemical by the duodenum. This chemical—secretin, which they called a hormone—circulated in the blood to activate the secretion of digestive juice by the pancreas.

Bay of Pigs (Spanish name: Bahia de los Cochinos) A bay on the SW coast of Cuba where on 17 April, 1961, about 1200 Cuban exiles attempted to invade the country. Hoping to overthrow the Marxist regime of Fidel *Castro, and supported by the US *Central Intelligence Agency, the invasion was unsuccessful largely because it lacked sufficient US military backing.

bayonet A blade that may be attached to the muzzle of a firearm. The bayonet, which is thought to have originated in the early 17th century in Bayonne (France), replaced the pike. Early bayonets were inserted into the gun, which could not then be fired, a drawback resolved in the 1680s by the development of the socket bayonet. This was attached to a tube that was placed over the muzzle. Bayonets were used in both World Wars.

Bayonne 43 30N 1 28W A town in SW France, in the Pyrénées-Atlantiques department at the confluence of the Rivers Adour and Nive. The chief port of the Basque country, it was formerly famous for its swords and knives; the bayonet was developed here in the early 17th century. Its varied industries include aircraft, distilling, and leather. Population (1982 est): 42 970.

Bay Psalm Book Probably the first book printed in America, which contained the Psalms in metrical form. It was published in 1640 in Cambridge, Massachusetts, by a group of Congregationalists.

Bayreuth 49 27N 11 35E A town in SE West Germany, in Bavaria. It is famous as the home and burial place of Richard Wagner, who designed its Festival Theatre (1872-76), where his operas are performed annually. Its industries include the manufacture of textiles and machinery. Population (1983): 70 957.

Bazaine, Achille François (1811-88) French marshal, who served in the Crimean War (1854-56), in Italy against Austria (1859), and in Mexico (1863). He was commander in chief in the Franco-Prussian War (1870-71), when he surrendered after being besieged at Metz. For this he was condemned for treason but escaped to exile in Spain.

bazooka Originally a 2.36 inch (60 mm) antitank rocket launcher fired from the shoulder and used by the US army in World War II. It consisted of a 54 inch (1.4 m) breech-loaded tube, open at both ends, firing a 3½ lb (1.6 kg) rocket to an effective range of about 135 m (150 yd). The term was later applied to all similar weapons. The name came from a tubular wind instrument made famous by Bob Burns, an American comedian.

BBC. *See* British Broadcasting Corporation.

BCG (*bacille Calmette Guérin*) A vaccine consisting of a weakened form of the tuberculosis bacterium, which is injected to give partial protection against tuberculosis. It acts by stimulating the body's defence system without causing the disease. A successful vaccination produces a lump at the injection site.

Beachy Head 50 44N 0 16E A headland in SE England, on the East Sussex coast. It consists of vertical chalk cliffs 171 m (570 ft) high and forms the E end of the South Downs.

Beaconsfield 51 37N 0 39W A town in SE England, in Buckinghamshire. It has associations with the statesmen Edmund *Burke and Benjamin *Disraeli (Earl of Beaconsfield). Its elaborate model village, Bekonscot, is famous. Population (1981): 10 909.

Beaconsfield, Benjamin Disraeli, 1st Earl of. *See* Disraeli, Benjamin.

Beadle, George Wells (1903–) US geneticist, who provided fundamental evidence for the nature of gene function. Working with moulds, he proposed the theory that each gene was responsible for the production of a single enzyme, which itself controlled a particular chemical reaction in the cell. He shared a Nobel Prize (1958) with *Tatum and *Lederberg.

beagle A long-established breed of dog originating in the UK. It has a deep chest, strong shoulders, and drooping ears. The short smooth coat is usually dark brown to light tan with white patches. With their keen sense of smell, beagles have long been used as hunting hounds; more recently, they have become popular household pets. Height: 33–40 cm.

Beale, Dorothea (1831–1906) British schoolmistress. A pioneer of women's education and suffrage, Dorothea Beale became principal of Cheltenham Ladies' College in 1858. Her introduction of a curriculum similar to that followed in the male public schools revolutionized women's education.

bean The seed or fruit of certain herbs, shrubs, or trees of the family *Leguminosae*. They are widely cultivated and not only form a good source of protein for man and livestock but also provide raw material for a wide range of derived products. *See* broad bean; carob bean; French bean; haricot bean; Lima bean; mung bean; runner bean; soya bean; tonka bean.

bear A large heavy mammal belonging to a family (*Ursidae*; 7 species) found in Europe, Asia, and America. Bears have a shaggy coat and a short tail and walk flat on the soles of their broad feet. They can stand erect and make good use of their powerful limbs and long curved claws. Eyesight and hearing are poor but bears have an excellent sense of smell; they can exist on any kind of food but most of them are vegetarian. Newly born bears are very small (about the size of rats), blind, and toothless. The female stays in the den suckling her young until they can accompany her outside. Order: *Carnivora*. *See* black bear; brown bear; polar bear; sloth bear; spectacled bear; sun bear.

bearbaiting A *blood sport formerly popular in Britain and Europe. A bear, sometimes blinded, was chained to a stake in a bear pit or bear garden and dogs were let loose to attack it, many being killed. As dogs were expendable but bears were valuable the bears were not generally allowed to die. **Bullbaiting** used bulls in a similar way. Both bearbaiting and bullbaiting were made illegal in the UK in 1835.

bearberry A prostrate evergreen shrub of the genus *Arctostaphylos*, native to North and Central America, especially *A. uva-ursi*, which is also widespread in Europe and Asia. The woody stems may reach 2 m in length, sending out roots at intervals. The flowers are white to pink and bell-shaped, and the berries are red. The plant is an important colonist. Family: *Ericaceae*.

bearded lizard An Australian lizard, *Amphibolurus barbatus*, occurring in scrub and desert regions. Up to 60 cm long, it has a long head, a whiplike tail, a grey to yellowish spiny skin, and a bright-yellow mouth; a throat pouch swells to resemble a spiny beard during aggressive or courtship displays. It feeds on insects, small lizards, and snakes.

bearded tit. *See* reedling.

bearded vulture. *See* lammergeier.

Beardsley, Aubrey Vincent (1872–98) British illustrator. Virtually self-taught, he was encouraged by *Burne Jones. As illustrator of the periodicals *The Yellow Book* and *The Savoy* and of several books, including Wilde's *Salome* and Pope's *Rape of the Lock*, he achieved notoriety with his grotesque and erotic imagery. His designs are composed of curved lines, characteristic of *Art Nouveau, which contrast with dense areas of black ink. He died of tuberculosis in France.

beardworm A deep-sea wormlike animal, up to 30 cm long, belonging to the invertebrate phylum *Pogonophora* (20 species). Beardworms live in tubes built in the mud of the ocean floor. Their head ends are crowned with tentacles, which protrude from the tubes and are believed to function in respiration and feeding (beardworms lack a digestive system).

deep groove ball bearing   taper roller bearing

BEARINGS   *Common examples of ball bearings and roller bearings.*

bearings A support for a rotating shaft or the interface between a crank and a reciprocating part. Bearings are designed to reduce friction and wear to a minimum and to dissipate the heat generated. In plain bearings, lubrication is achieved by maintaining a film of lubricant between the faces either as a result of their relative motion or by pumping it through channels into the interface. Some small bearings, made of powdered copper or bronze impregnated with oil or graphite, are self-lubricating, while some low-friction plastics (e.g. polytetrafluoroethylene) do not require lubrication. Bearing surfaces or shells are usually made of softer materials (e.g. brass or white metal) than is the shaft.

In **ball and roller bearings** friction between the faces is reduced by replacing the sliding action of a plain bearing by a rolling action. The balls or rollers are usually made from chromium (0.5–2.0%) steels.

bear market A stock and share market or commodity market in which there is a continuing downward movement in prices. An initial fall in prices, caused by adverse economic factors, is often magnified by consequent selling by investors. *Compare* bull market.

Beas, River A river in NW India, flowing mainly W from the Himalayas to the River Sutlej. It forms part of the Punjab irrigation scheme. Length: 470 km (290 mi).

beating the bounds A traditional ceremony that takes place in several English towns and villages on Ascension Day. Primarily a religious event, it evolved during the reign of Elizabeth I, and is derived from the earlier ceremonies of Rogationtide. A priest leads those present round the parish boundaries offering prayers for the harvest while young boys beat the boundary stones with sticks. An equivalent Scottish ceremony is called riding the marches.

BEATLES   *(From left) Paul McCartney, George Harrison, John Lennon, and Ringo Starr.*

Beatitudes   In the New Testament, the eight blessings with which Jesus opened the Sermon on the Mount (Matthew 5.3–12). They describe such Christian virtues as meekness, mercy, and purity of heart (e.g. "Blessed are the meek: for they shall inherit the earth."). The word derives from the Latin of the *Vulgate, beati sunt* (blessed are).

Beatles   A British rock group, which achieved worldwide popularity during the 1960s. The Beatles appeared at the Cavern Club in Liverpool in 1962 and subsequently recorded "Love Me Do" and "She Loves You," which became top of the Hit Parade in 1963. By this time the group consisted of George *Harrison, John *Lennon, Paul *McCartney, and Ringo *Starr; they toured the USA successfully, made two films, and were awarded MBEs in 1965. The most original of the group's subsequent albums were *Sergeant Pepper's Lonely Hearts Club Band* (1967), which reflected the Beatles' experience of drugs and eastern mysticism, and the double *White Album* (1968). In 1970 they disbanded to pursue separate careers.

Beat movement   US literary and social movement of the 1950s that opposed conventional society by seeking personal liberation through art, drugs, sex, and any other "consciousness-expanding" means. The movement centred on the artistic communities of Greenwich Village in New York and of San Francisco and Los Angeles. Among its prominent writers were William *Burroughs, Allen *Ginsberg, and Jack *Kerouac, and later the poets Lawrence *Ferlinghetti and Gregory Corso (1930–).

Beaton, Sir Cecil (Walter Hardy)   (1904–80) British photographer. From the 1920s onwards he became famous for his society portraits, many taken for *Vanity Fair* and *Vogue* magazines. After World War II he turned also to scenery and costume designs for ballet, theatre, and films, notably *My Fair Lady*. His photographic books include *The Book of Beauty* (1930). □ Garbo, Greta; Picasso, Pablo.

Beaton, David   (1494–1546) Scottish cardinal, who led the pro-French anti-Protestant faction at the Scottish court under *James V and *Mary, Queen of Scots. He became Archbishop of St Andrews in 1539. A vigorous persecutor of the Protes-

tants, he was murdered by Protestant nobles at St Andrews.

Beatrix   (1938–) Queen of the Netherlands since the abdication (1980) of her mother Queen Juliana. Her marriage (1966) to the West German Claus von Amsberg (1926–) caused some controversy.

beats   Variations in the intensity of sound when two tones of nearly equal frequency are heard. The effect is similar to that of *interference. At certain times, the amplitudes of the waves reinforce each other and, at intermediate times, they tend to cancel each other out. The frequency of the beats is equal to the difference in the frequencies of the two notes.

Beatty, David, 1st Earl   (1871–1936) British admiral. As commander of a cruiser squadron in World War I, Beatty took part in the destruction of three German cruisers in Heligoland Bight (1914) and the sinking of the *Blücher* near Dogger Bank (1915). He also fought in the battle of Jutland (1916). As commander of the Grand Fleet, he received the German naval surrender in 1918. He was first sea lord from 1919 to 1927.

Beauce   An area in central France, in the Paris Basin. Consisting of a fertile plain, it is an important wheat-growing area and is known as the "granary of France."

Beaufort, Henry   (c. 1374–1447) English cardinal; half-brother of Henry IV. He became Bishop of Winchester in 1404 and was chancellor three times (1403–04, 1413–17, 1424–26). In 1427 he was appointed papal legate to oppose the Hussites. One of the most influential figures in the minority and early government of Henry VI, he successfully resisted the attempts of his nephew Humphrey, Duke of *Gloucester, to demote him.

Beaufort, Margaret   (1443–1509) Countess of Richmond. In 1455 she married Edmund Tudor (d. 1456). Their son Henry VII traced his Lancastrian claim to the English throne through Margaret to *John of Gaunt. During the Wars of the *Roses, she was imprisoned (1461) by the Yorkists. She was a patron of *Caxton and supported foundations at Oxford and Cambridge.

Beaufort scale   A scale of wind speed. It is based on easily observable indicators, such as smoke, tree movement, and damage incurred, and was devised in 1805 by Admiral Sir Francis Beaufort (1774–1857). □ p. 130.

Beaufort Sea   The section of the Arctic Ocean N of North America, between the Chukchi Sea and the Canadian archipelago. It is often covered by floating ice.

Beauharnais, Alexandre, Vicomte de   (1760–94) French general, who served in the American Revolution and then became involved in French Revolutionary politics. He commanded in the Rhine (1793) but was guillotined (1794) for failing to relieve Metz. His widow *Joséphine married Napoleon, whom his son **Eugène de Beauharnais** (1781–1824) served in Italy and Egypt. In 1805 he became viceroy of Italy and in 1812 commanded in Napoleon's Russian campaign. He lived in exile after Napoleon's fall. His sister **Hortense de Beauharnais** (1783–1837) married (1802) Napoleon's brother Louis *Bonaparte, King of Holland. Their son was the future Napoleon III.

Beaulieu   50 49N 1 27W A village in S England, in Hampshire. The parish church was formerly the refectory of a Cistercian abbey founded here in 1204 by King John. In the grounds of the Palace House, home of Lord Montague, is the National Motor Museum. Population (1981): 877.

Beaumarchais, Pierre-Augustin Caron de   (1732–99) French dramatist. Son of a watchmaker, he became rich and famous with *The Barber of Seville* (1775) and *The Marriage of Figaro* (1778), his comedies about the busybodying intrigues of a cunning valet; they inspired operas by *Rossini and *Mozart. He undertook secret missions abroad for Louis XV and Louis XVI, supplied arms to the American revolutionaries, and sponsored the first complete edition of *Voltaire's works. Constantly involved in lawsuits, he wrote *Mémoires* (1773–75) in self-defence.

Beaumaris   53 16N 4 05W A resort in North Wales, in

Beaufort number	description of wind	wind speed	
		knots	metres per second
0	calm	< 1	0.0– 0.2
1	light air	1– 3	0.3– 1.5
2	light breeze	4– 6	1.6– 3.3
3	gentle breeze	7–10	3.4– 5.4
4	moderate breeze	11–16	5.5– 7.9
5	fresh breeze	17–21	8.0–10.7
6	strong breeze	22–27	10.8–13.8
7	near gale	28–33	13.9–17.1
8	gale	34–40	17.2–20.7
9	strong gale	41–47	20.8–24.4
10	storm	48–55	24.5–28.4
11	violent storm	56–63	28.5–32.6
12	hurricane	≥64	≥32.7

BEAUFORT SCALE

Gwynedd, situated on the island of Anglesey at the N end of the Menai Strait. It is a yachting centre with a moated castle (1295). Population (1981): 2046.

Beaumont 30 04N 94 06W A city and port in the USA, in Texas on the canal from Port Arthur. Following the first Texan oil strike (1901) at nearby Spindletop, Beaumont developed into a major oil city. Population (1980): 118 102.

Beaumont, Francis (1584–1616) British dramatist. He studied law at Oxford and at the Inner Temple in London. From about 1607, he collaborated with John *Fletcher in writing about 12 plays, including *Philaster* (1610) and *The Maides Tragedy* (1611). He was probably sole author of *The Knight of the Burning Pestle* (1607). In 1613 he married and retired from the theatre.

Beaumont, William (1785–1853) US physician, who investigated digestion in the human stomach. As an army surgeon in 1822, he treated a trapper named Alexis St Martin for shotgun injuries. These left a permanent opening in his patient's stomach wall and abdomen through which Beaumont sampled the stomach contents. He recognized the chemical nature of digestion, including the importance of hydrochloric acid. His patient lived to the age of 82.

Beaune 47 02N 4 50E A town in E central France, in the Côte-d'Or department. The centre for the wine trade of Burgundy, it has a wine museum and its manufactures include casks, oil, and mustard. Population (1982 est): 21 127.

Beauvais 49 26N 2 05E A town in N France, in the Oise department. Its fine cathedral (begun 1227) was damaged during World War II and the factory in which the famous Gobelin tapestries had been made since the 17th century was completely destroyed (the industry was subsequently moved to Paris). Beauvais is a market town, trading in dairy produce, fruit, and cereals. Population (1982 est): 54 147.

Beauvais tapestry Tapestry produced by the state-subsidized Beauvais factory, in France, established in 1664. The court painter François *Boucher designed pastoral, Italian, and Chinese scenes for the workshops, which specialized in furniture and screen tapestries. Production declined in the 19th century.

Beauvoir, Simone de (1908–86) French novelist and essayist. The constant companion of Jean-Paul *Sartre, whom she met at the Sorbonne in 1929, her writings explored the implications of *existentialism. Her novels include *The Blood of Others* (1948), *The Mandarins* (1956), *The Coming of Age* (1973), and *All Said and Done* (1975). *The Second Sex* (1953) argued for the liberation of women from their traditional roles in a male-dominated society.

beaver A large aquatic *rodent, *Castor fiber*, of Europe, Asia, and North America. Over 1 m long and weighing up to 40 kg, beavers have a dark sleek waterproof coat and a broad flat tail used for balance and swimming. They live in family groups, building a "lodge" of sticks and mud with underwater entrances and dams above and below. They use their large incisor teeth to cut wood for building and bark for a winter food. During the summer they feed on vegetation. Family: *Castoridae*. □mammal.

Beaverbrook, Max(well) Aitken, 1st Baron (1879–1964) British newspaper proprietor and politician, born in Canada. In 1919 he bought a majority interest in the *Daily Express*, which became the most widely read daily in Britain. In 1921 he founded the *Sunday Express* and in 1929 bought the *Evening Standard* (London). In World War I he served in Lloyd George's War Cabinet as minister of information (1918). His posts in Churchill's World War II Cabinet included that of minister of aircraft production (1940–41).

Bebel, August (1840–1913) German socialist leader. Bebel became interested in the labour movement while living in Leipzig, where in 1865 he came under the influence of Wilhelm *Liebknecht. In 1869 he helped to found the German Social Democratic Party, for which he became a leading spokesman in the Reichstag.

Bebington 53 25N 3 01W A town in NW England, in Merseyside on the Wirral Peninsula. It contains Port Sunlight, a model village built in 1888 for workers at the Lever Brothers (now Unilever) factory. Other industries include oil and chemicals. Population (1981 est): 64 174.

bebop. *See* bop.

Beccaria, Cesare Bonesana, Marchese de (1738–94) Italian legal theorist and political economist. He achieved international fame with the publication of his *Crimes and Punishments* (1764), the first comprehensive account of the principles behind criminal law. In attacking legal corruption, torture, capital punishment, etc., it was responsible for the reform of penal codes in many countries. Beccaria became a professor of political philosophy at Milan in 1768 and held several important public offices in Austria.

bêche-de-mer. *See* trepang.

Bechet, Sidney (1897–1959) US Black jazz clarinetist and soprano saxophone player. He achieved wide recognition after a tour of Europe in 1919, subsequently worked with Duke Ellington, and after World War II lived in Paris.

Bechuanaland. *See* Botswana, Republic of.

Becker, Boris (1967–) West German tennis player. In 1985, aged 17, he became the youngest player ever to win the men's singles at Wimbledon. He was also the first unseeded player to win the event. He won the title again in 1986.

Becket, St Thomas (c. 1118–70) English churchman. The son of a London merchant, Becket entered the household of Theobald (d. 1161), Archbishop of Canterbury, and in 1154

THOMAS BECKET   *This drawing from a 13th-century manuscript shows the archbishop arguing with Henry II of England (above) and Louis VII of France (below).*

became *Henry II's chancellor. Succeeding Theobald as archbishop in 1162, Becket resigned the chancellorship and quarrelled with Henry on the issues of criminous clerks (*see* benefit of clergy), freedom of ecclesiastical elections, and the right of appeals to Rome. Becket's refusal to swear allegiance to the Constitutions of *Clarendon forced his exile in France (1164–70). Subsequent attempts to resolve the quarrel failed and on 29 December, 1170, he was murdered in Canterbury Cathedral by four courtiers at Henry's instigation. Canonized in 1173, his shrine at Canterbury became one of the most important centres of pilgrimage in medieval Europe.

Beckett, Samuel   (1906–) Irish novelist, dramatist, and poet. After studying at Trinity College, Dublin, and travelling for several years in Europe, he settled finally in Paris in 1937. He writes in both French and English. His plays, which include *Waiting for Godot* (1954), and his prose works, such as *Malone Dies* (1956) and *How It Is* (1964), treat human existence with a nihilism tempered by desperate humour. His later works, such as *Breath* (1972) and *Not I* (1973), are notably brief and concentrated. He won the Nobel Prize in 1969.

Beckford, William   (?1760–1844) British writer. He inherited his father's vast fortune at the age of 11 and used the rest of his life to spend it. He commissioned James *Wyatt to build *Fonthill Abbey (a short-lived masterpiece of the gothic architectural revival), collected art, travelled in Europe, and became an MP. He wrote the classic gothic novel *Vathek* (1782), two travel books, and a journal.

Beckmann, Max   (1884–1950) German expressionist painter, born in Leipzig. His experiences of World War I inspired his grotesque paintings of distorted sometimes mutilated bodies, often indicting German social evils, as in *Night* (1919; Düsseldorf). In later years in Amsterdam and the USA he painted a series of triptychs influenced partly by *Bosch.

becquerel   (Bq) The *SI unit of activity (radioactivity) equal to the number of atoms of a radioactive substance that disintegrate in one second. Named after Antoine Henri *Becquerel.

Becquerel, (Antoine) Henri   (1852–1908) French phy-

sicist, who was professor at the Conservatoire des Arts et Métiers in Paris. He discovered radioactivity (1896) by chance, on finding that invisible rays from uranium salts could affect a photographic plate even through a light-proof wrapper. For his fundamental research on these radiations, Becquerel shared the Nobel Prize (1903) with his associates Pierre and Marie *Curie. He also performed research in magnetism and in optics, particularly polarization and absorption in crystals. His grandfather **Antoine César Becquerel** (1788–1878) left the army to join *Ampère in his study of electricity, becoming one of the founders of electrochemistry.

bedbug   A flat wingless insect, about 5 mm long, belonging to a family (*Cimicidae*; 30 species) of blood-sucking parasites. In temperate regions *Cimex lectularius* is the species that most commonly attacks man, hiding by day in bedding, furniture, etc., and becoming active at night. It inflicts a painful bite but does not transmit disease. Bedbugs can be easily eradicated by insecticide sprays or fumigation. Order: *Hemiptera* (bugs).

Bedchamber Crisis   (1839) The issue in British politics over Queen Victoria's ladies of the bedchamber. After the resignation of Lord Melbourne, a Whig, Peel attempted to form a Tory ministry and requested that Victoria dismiss her Whig ladies. She refused and Melbourne remained in office until his government fell in 1841, when Victoria, influenced by Prince *Albert, consented to the dismissal of three ladies.

Beddoes, Thomas Lovell   (1803–49) British poet. After 1825 he lived mostly in Europe, where he studied medicine and became involved in revolutionary politics. His obsessive interest in death dominates all his works, especially *Death's Jest-Book, or the Fool's Tragedy* (1850). He visited England for the last time in 1846–47, and committed suicide two years later in Basle, Switzerland.

Bede, St   (c. 673–735 AD) English historian, known as the Venerable Bede. After 682 he lived at the monastery of Jarrow in Northumberland. His *Ecclesiastical History of the English People* (c. 731), written in Latin and later translated into English under King Alfred, is a great historical work and remains an important source for British history, especially the early Anglo-Saxon period (5th–8th centuries). He also wrote poems in English, but only one is extant, his "Death Song." He was the author of many grammatical, scientific, and historical works. Feast day: 27 May.

Bedford   52 08N 0 29W A town in S England, the administrative centre of Bedfordshire on the River Ouse. John *Bunyan was born nearby and spent 12 years in Bedford gaol. Manufactures include Diesel engines, transistors, and metal tubes. Population (1983 est): 89 200.

Bedford, John, Duke of   (1389–1435) The third son of Henry IV; known as John of Lancaster. He was protector of England and regent of France (1422–35) during the minority of his nephew Henry VI. He pursued the *Hundred Years' War and procured the execution of Joan of Arc (1431).

Bedford Level.   See Fens, the.

Bedfordshire   A county in the South Midlands of England. It is chiefly low lying, rising to the Chiltern Hills in the SW, and is drained by the Great Ouse River. Agricultural products include wheat and vegetables. The chief industries, centred on Luton, Dunstable, and Bedford, are motor vehicles, agricultural engineering, and electrical manufactures. Area: 1235 sq km (477 sq mi). Population (1981): 504 986. Administrative centre: Bedford.

Bedlam   The popular name for the Bethlehem Royal Hospital, a mental hospital located from 1815 until 1931 at what is now the Imperial War Museum in Lambeth, S London. Founded in Bishopsgate as a priory (1247), it moved to Moorfields in 1676 and then to Lambeth; in 1931 it was transferred to Beckenham, in Kent. Bethlehem Hospital now forms part of the Kings College Hospital group.

"Bedlam" has passed into the English language as a synonym for "madhouse."

Bedlington terrier   A breed of dog originating in Bedlington, N England, in the early 19th century. It has long legs and a long narrow face and is a popular sporting dog locally. The thick coat may be blue, blue and tan, liver, or sandy. Height: about 40 cm.

Bedouin   The nomadic *Arab tribes of the Syrian and Arabian deserts and other desert regions of the Arab world. Their economy is based on camels, sheep, and goats. At present they are found within the political boundaries of Saudi Arabia, Yemen, the United Arab Emirates, Kuwait, Iraq, Jordan, Israel, Egypt, and the *Maghrib states. The policies of these countries are to restrict the movements of the nomadic population and induce them to take up a settled existence. Courageous fighters, the Bedouin played an active role in the early Arab conquests.

bedsore   An ulcer that develops in areas of skin subject to continuous pressure, such as may occur in elderly or other bedridden patients who are unable to change their position frequently. The pressure reduces the blood supply to the affected part. Patients at risk require careful nursing, with frequent changes of position and massage to prevent bedsores from developing.

bedstraw   A weak, often climbing, plant of the widely distributed genus *Galium* (300 species), common in damp places. Lady's bedstraw (*G. verum*), native to Europe, is a weedy perennial, up to 75 cm tall, with small yellow flowers. Its name derives from the legend that Mary rested on a bed of these plants while giving birth to Christ. Family: *Rubiaceae* (madder family). *See also* cleavers.

Bedworth   52 28N 1 29W A market town in central England, in Warwickshire. It has coalmining, brick-making, and light engineering industries. Population (1981): 41 991.

bee   A four-winged insect (10–30 mm long) belonging to the superfamily *Apoidea* (about 12 000 species), of worldwide distribution. Bees feed on pollen and nectar from flowering plants using well-developed tongues and are important pollinators, transferring pollen on their hairy bodies and broad back legs. The ovipositor is used to sting attackers and in some species is barbed, remaining in the wound.

Most solitary bees nest in soil, hollow trees, or wall cavities. Some, however, tunnel into wood (*see* carpenter bee) or construct nests using earth (*see* mason bee) or leaves (*see* leafcutter bee). The female lays one or more eggs in a nest that is then sealed, leaving the larvae to develop. The social bees (families *Apidae* and *Halictidae*) live in communities organized into castes—workers (infertile females), drones (males, developed from unfertilized eggs), and a queen (a fertile female). Colonies are established in trees, walls, or cliffs (*see also* honeybee). Order: *Hymenoptera*.

Beebe, Charles William   (1877–1962) US explorer and naturalist. He led many expeditions and, in 1934, made a record undersea descent of 923 m (3028 ft) in a bathysphere. He wrote many books describing his observations and adventures.

beech   A tree of the genus *Fagus* (10 species), native to N temperate regions. Beeches have smooth grey bark and a broad dense crown, occasionally reaching a height of 40 m. The leaves are oval, pointed, and toothed, the flowers are unisexual and inconspicuous, and the fruits are nutlike seeds enclosed in husks (beechnuts or mast). The common beech of Europe and Asia is *Fagus sylvatica*, the timber of which is used for furniture and flooring, while that of North America is *F. grandiflora*. Family: *Fagaceae*.

In the S hemisphere beeches are represented by a related genus (*Notofagus*; 14 species) and differ in being evergreen and having separate trees bearing male or female flowers. Some are of importance for their durable timber, edible nuts, or ornamental

value.

Beecham, Sir Thomas   (1879–1961) British conductor. He used his inherited fortune for the advancement of English musical life. He was a memorable interpreter of Haydn and Mozart and championed the works of Richard Strauss, Sibelius, and particularly Delius, whose friend and biographer he became. He founded the London Philharmonic Orchestra (1932) and the Royal Philharmonic Orchestra (1947).

Beecher, Henry Ward   (1813–87) US Congregational preacher and author. He was the son of a distinguished preacher, and brother of Harriet Beecher *Stowe. He was a pastor first in Indianapolis and then for 40 years in Brooklyn, New York, where his sermons and his antislavery writings were widely influential.

bee-eater   A brightly coloured bird belonging to a family (*Meropidae*; 24 species) occurring mainly in tropical Old World regions. Bee-eaters have pointed wings, long central tail feathers, a slender curved bill, and, commonly, a black eye stripe. They nest in burrows and feed in flight, chiefly on bees and wasps. Order: *Coraciiformes* (hornbills, kingfishers, etc.).

beefwood.   *See* Casuarina.

beekeeping (*or* apiculture)   The rearing of colonies of *honeybees in hives either for their *honey or *beeswax or for pollinating flowers. Sheets of wax in wooden frames (starter combs) are hung vertically inside the hive. Onto these the bees build wax cells that they fill with honey and seal. When a frame is full it is removed, the honey is extracted, and the comb is reused. A colony makes about 32 kg of honey in a summer, but 14 kg of this is needed by the bees for food during the winter; following a bad summer they must be fed sugar syrup. About 10 000–20 000 bees survive the winter; during the spring, when a colony has increased to over 50 000, a large group is likely to leave the hive (i.e. it swarms). The beekeeper collects the swarm and puts it into an empty hive.

beer and brewing   Beer is an alcoholic drink made from fermented malt flavoured with hops. Brewing is the process of making beer. Barley, or other grain, is first malted by being allowed to germinate, the resulting malt being dried (kilned), ground, and heated with water (mashed). Starch in the grain is converted into soluble carbohydrates by enzymes in the malt. The resulting liquid wort is boiled with hops to concentrate the wort and utilize the bitter flavour of the hops. The wort is then filtered and cooled ready for fermentation. Yeast is added and the carbohydrates in the wort are converted into alchohol. The liquid is drained and stored. Different brewing methods and types of ingredients produce different varieties of beer. Beer was drunk in ancient Egypt and has been enjoyed in a great many countries ever since. **Ale** was originally a stronger drink than beer, brewed without hops. The terms are now interchangeable, although ale is sometimes reserved for stronger brews fermented at higher temperatures. **Mild** beer is made with fewer hops than **bitter** and a darker malt is used to impart colour. **Lager** is traditionally a light beer matured over a long period at low temperature. **Stout** is made from a blend of roasted barley and malts.

Beerbohm, Sir Max   (1872–1956) British caricaturist and writer. He published several collections of essays, caricatures, and brillant parodies during the 1890s. His only novel, *Zuleika Dobson* (1911), is an ironic romance set at Oxford University. From 1911 to his death he lived in Rapallo (Italy), returning to England only during World War II.

Beersheba   31 15N 34 47E A town in S Israel, the largest in the Negev. In World War I it was the scene of a British victory over the Turks. Beersheba has a university (1965) and manufactures chemicals and glass. Population (1983): 110 800.

beeswax   A substance produced by bees to build honey-combs. It is collected by heating the honeycomb in water (after removing the honey) so that the floating wax can be separated after solidification on cooling. Beeswax (melting point 61-69°C) is used in high-quality polishes, etc.

beet A herbaceous plant, *Beta vulgaris*, native to Europe and the Mediterranean region, stemless but sometimes exceeding 1 m in height. Several varieties are widely cultivated in temperate areas, the most important of which is the *sugar beet. The taproot of the red or garden beet yields beetroot, while the mangel-wurzel (*B. vulgaris vulgaris*) is an important fodder variety. The spinach beet is grown for its leaves, used as a vegetable. Family: *Chenopodiaceae*.

LUDWIG VAN BEETHOVEN *This portrait of Beethoven as a young man is considered to be one of the best likenesses of him.*

Beethoven, Ludwig van (1770-1827) German composer, born in Bonn. His father, a court musician, attempted to exploit him as a child prodigy. Often boorish and temperamental, he nevertheless won a considerable following for his piano playing and compositions in Vienna, where he settled in 1792 after studying there with Haydn. At the age of 30 he began to go deaf, an experience that increased his loneliness and eccentricity, but did not stop him composing. His later years were plagued by illness and by his adoption of his troublesome nephew Karl. About 200 of Beethoven's works survive, among them 9 symphonies, 5 piano concertos, 1 violin concerto, 16 string quartets, 10 violin and piano sonatas, 32 piano sonatas, 2 ballets, 2 masses, 1 opera, and about 200 song settings. His early masterpieces, influenced by Mozart and Haydn, include much chamber music, piano works, and the first and second symphonies. During his middle years he produced the *Emperor* piano concerto (1809), the *Kreutzer* sonata (1803), the opera *Fidelio* (1805-14), and the rest of the symphonies, up to the eighth. His last most intense works include the *Missa Solemnis* (1818-23), the ninth symphony (1817-23), and the innovative late string quartets.

beetle An insect belonging to the largest order (*Coleoptera*; about 278 000 species) of the animal kingdom. The forewings are specialized as hard structures (called elytra), which cover the functional hindwings when these are not in use. The elytra and the thick cuticle provide protection against predation and desiccation and enable aquatic species to trap a store of air. Beetles occupy a wide range of habitats and have exploited all possible food sources—many feed on plants or animals or scavenge their remains and a few are parasitic.

Many beetles are of great economic importance: some species are serious pests of crops, timber, textiles, and stored grains and cereals; others are useful by preying on insect pests or by speeding up the process of *decomposition. *See also* weevil.

Beeton, Isabella Mary (1836-65) British writer, author of one of the most famous English cookery books, *The Book of Household Management* (1861), first published in a women's magazine founded by her husband.

beetroot. *See* beet.

Begin, Menachem (1913-) Israeli statesman; prime minister (1977-83). Born in Russia, he led the Zionist Youth Movement in Poland at the outset of World War II and from 1942 commanded Jewish forces in Palestine. In 1948 he founded the Freedom (Herut) Movement and in 1973 became joint chairman of the Unity Party. In 1979, under the instigation of the US president Jimmy Carter, he negotiated a peace treaty with President *Sadat of Egypt, for which Begin and Sadat were jointly awarded the Nobel Peace Prize.

Begonia A genus of generally succulent herbaceous plants (about 1000 species) native to the tropics. They are widely grown as ornamental pot or garden plants for their attractive, often brightly coloured, flowers with pink, yellow, or white "petals" in two unequal pairs (as in *B. semperflorens*) or for their variegated leaves (as in *B. rex*). The underground parts are long lived and may be tuberous, fibrous, or rhizomatous. Family: *Begoniaceae*.

Behan, Brendan (1923-64) Irish playwright. His first play, *The Quare Fellow* (1954), and his autobiography, *Borstal Boy* (1958), were based on his years of detention and imprisonment for Irish Republican Army (IRA) activities. His best-known play, *The Hostage* (1956), treated a basically tragic situation with characteristic liveliness and boisterous comedy.

behaviourism A school of psychology, founded in the USA by J. B. *Watson in the early 20th century, in which the emphasis is on describing and predicting observable behaviour: unconscious ideas, feelings, and the process of thinking are regarded as unimportant. The behaviourist concentrates on understanding the laws relating a stimulus to a response, how responses are built up into complex behaviours, and how *conditioning affects behaviour. The approach was successful in describing how animals learnt tasks in the laboratory but has been limited in its ability to account for such complex processes as emotion, language, and interpersonal relationships. *Behaviour therapy was developed from behaviourism.

behaviour therapy A method of treating mental disorders that is based on the view that psychological problems are the result of faulty learning. It was developed mainly by H. *Eysenck. Sometimes *conditioning is used to teach new behaviour, such as better ways of relating to other people, or to eliminate undesirable behaviour, such as excessive drinking (*see* aversion therapy). It includes treatment for *phobias, in which repeated exposure to the feared object or situation gradually reduces the subject's fear of it. *See also* behaviourism.

Behn, Aphra (1640-89) British novelist and dramatist. She attracted much attention (and scandal) in London but the details of her life are uncertain. She wrote many popular plays, notably *The Rover* (1678), but is chiefly remembered for her exotic novel, *Oroonoko* (1688), about an enslaved Negro prince.

Behrens, Peter (1868-1940) German architect. Coming

to architecture from the *Arts and Crafts movement, he erected his most influential buildings before World War I. He occupies a transitional period in architectural development, evolving a modernistic style that echoed a functional classicism and was notable for its complete lack of ornamentation in design. His most important building was the AEG turbine works in Berlin (1909–11), which was one of the first industrial buildings to be evaluated as a work of architecture.

Behring, Emil Adolf von (1854–1917) German bacteriologist, who produced an antitoxin that conferred passive immunity against tetanus. By 1882 Behring and Paul *Ehrlich had developed a serum that provided effective immunity against diphtheria and also aided its treatment in established cases. He was awarded a Nobel Prize in 1901.

Behzad (c. 1455–c. 1536) Persian painter, regarded as one of the greatest of Islamic miniaturists. As director of the academy at Herat he was an influential teacher and the many imitators of his richly coloured and dramatic style have made his works —few of which are signed—difficult to identify.

Beibu Gulf. *See* Tonkin, Gulf of.

Beida. *See* Zawiyat al-Bayda'.

Beiderbecke, Bix (Leon Bismarck B.; 1903–31) US jazz cornetist and pianist. Towards the end of his short life he played with Louis Armstrong and in the band of Paul Whiteman (1891–1967). The originality of his own compositions is evident in "In a Mist" (1927) for piano.

Beijing. *See* Peking.

Beira 19 49S 34 52E A port in E Mozambique, on the Mozambique Channel. Founded in 1891 by the Portuguese, it became a major port serving central S Africa. It was the main export outlet of Rhodesia (now Zimbabwe) until Mozambique's independence (1975). Exports include ores, cotton, and food products. Population (1982): 113 770.

Beirut 33 52N 35 30E The capital of the Lebanon, situated on the E Mediterranean Sea. After centuries of Turkish domination, it was held by the French from World War I until 1941, when it became the capital of the newly independent Lebanon. It was badly damaged in the civil war (1975–76) and in 1982 when Israeli forces besieged the city and forced the Palestine Liberation Organization to leave. Inter-factional conflict motivated a series of car bomb explosions in 1986. It has four universities. Population (1982 est): 1 100 000.

Béjart, Maurice (Maurice-Jean de Berger; 1928–) French ballet dancer and choreographer. His works were influenced by jazz and Indian mysticism. In 1954 he founded his own company, renamed Le Ballet du XXme Siècle when based in Brussels in 1960; it transferred to Lausanne in 1987.

bel. *See* decibel.

Belau, Republic of (name until 1981: Palau *or* Pelew) A group of islands in the W Pacific Ocean, within the UN Trust Territory of the *Pacific Islands. Self-government was achieved in 1981. In 1986 the Republic of Belau voted in favour of an increased level of independence from the USA, although defence matters would be left in US hands. President: Lazarus Salii. Area: 476 sq km (184 sq mi). Population (1980): 12 116.

bel canto (Italian: fine singing) A delicate and lyrical style of singing that was developed in Italian opera during the 17th and 18th centuries and reached its peak in the 19th century. Notable singers included Farinelli (1705–82) and Jenny *Lind.

Belém 1 27S 48 29W A port in N Brazil, the capital of Pará state on the Rio do Pará. It exports products from the Amazon basin including nuts, jute, and rubber. Its university was founded in 1957. Population (1980 est): 758 117.

belemnite The fossilized shell of an extinct *cuttlefish, sometimes called a thunderbolt. Cylindrical and pointed at one end, they are most commonly found in deposits of the Jurassic and Cretaceous periods (150–65 million years ago).

Belfast 54 40N 5 50W The capital of Northern Ireland, a seaport situated where the River Lagan enters Belfast Lough on the border between Co Antrim and Co Down. It is the province's commercial and administrative centre and its industries include shipbuilding, electronics, and engineering. The principal buildings, including the City Hall (1906) and Parliament Buildings (1932) at Stormont, were built in the late 19th and early 20th centuries. Queen's University received a royal charter in 1909. *History*: large-scale growth of Belfast came with the expansion of the linen-making and shipbuilding industries in the 19th century; it became a city in 1888. The Parliament of Northern Ireland sat in the city from 1921 to 1972. Its recent history has been marked by the conflict between Protestant and Roman Catholic communities; each has become increasingly concentrated in ghettoes. This has led to an exacerbation of the housing problem, which is now one of the worst in Europe. The British army has maintained a presence on the streets of Belfast since August, 1969. Population (1981): 297 983.

Belfort 44 17N 1 32E A town in E France, the capital of the Territoire de Belfort. Strategically situated between the Vosges and Jura mountains, it has been besieged many times. Industries include wine. Population (1982 est): 52 739.

Belgae The Germanic tribes occupying NE *Gaul in ancient Roman times. Julius Caesar named them and considered them the most warlike of the Gauls. He defeated them in 57 BC but they continued their opposition to the Romans from SE Britain, to which area they had been migrating from about 100 BC.

Belgaum 15 54N 74 36E A city in India, in Karnataka. Manufactures include cotton, furniture, and leather. Population (1981): 300 000.

Belgian Congo. *See* Zaïre, Republic of.

Belgium, Kingdom of (French name: Belgique; Flemish name: België) A country in NW Europe, on the North Sea. It is generally low lying except for the Ardennes in the SE. The main rivers are the Scheldt and the Meuse and these and others are linked by canals to form an extensive network of inland waterways. The population is divided between the French and the Flemish, with small minorities of Germans and others. *Economy*: highly industrialized, with coal and iron resources supporting considerable heavy industry. Food processing and textiles are also important. Agriculture is highly intensive, the main cash crop being sugar beet. Belgium is an important centre for trade and has been since the middle ages. It still has one of the highest proportions of export revenue to total income in the world. In 1921 a customs union was formed with Luxembourg and in 1948 both joined with the Netherlands to form the *Benelux Economic Union. Belgium is also a member of the EEC and almost two-thirds of its trade is with other members. Main exports include iron and steel, chemicals, machinery, and motor vehicles. *History*: the name Belgium comes from the *Belgae, a Celtic tribe named by Caesar, and the area was part of the Roman Empire until about the end of the 2nd century AD, when it was invaded by Germanic tribes. In medieval times it was divided into several counties, duchies, and the bishopric of Liège, during which time the cities of Ghent, Bruges, and Ypres rose to virtual independence and economic prosperity through the wool industry. Particularly in view of its strategic position, Belgium had considerable importance in the balance of power in Europe over the centuries and from the middle ages onwards it was ruled by several European nations in turn, including Austria, Spain, and France. After being occupied by France during the Napoleonic Wars, it was joined to the Netherlands in 1815. Following an uprising, it became independent in 1830, and the National Congress elected Prince Leopold of Saxe-Coburg as King of the Belgians (*see* Leopold I) in 1831. The country was eventually recognized by all of Europe in 1839. In spite of efforts to remain neutral it was attacked and occupied by Germany in both World Wars. When the

Germans invaded in 1940, King *Leopold III surrendered immediately but the government struggled on in exile in London. In 1950, after a political crisis, the king was persuaded to abdicate in favour of his son, *Baudouin. The main political problem since World War II has been tension between the French-speaking Walloons in the S and the Flemish-speaking community in the N. Efforts are being made to create a federal structure of government under which the Flemish, French-speaking, and bilingual Brussels regions would obtain a large measure of regional autonomy. The loss in 1960 of the Belgian Congo, now Zaïre, had an adverse effect on Belgium's economy. Dr Wilfried Martens (1936–   ), who led a series of coalition governments (1979–81; 1981–87), resigned in October 1987 over the French–Flemish problem but agreed to carry on as caretaker prime minister after an indecisive election. Official languages: French, Flemish, Dutch, and German. Official currency: Belgian franc of 100 centimes. Area: 30 513 sq km (11 778 sq mi). Population (1980 est): 9 863 374. Capital: Brussels. Main port: Antwerp.

Belgorod-Dnestrovski (Romanian name: Cetatea Alba)   46 10N 30 19E A port in the Soviet Union, in the SW Ukrainian SSR on the Dnestr estuary. A commercial centre, it has fishing, fish-processing, and winemaking industries. *History*: founded by Greek colonists in the 6th century BC, it subsequently passed to the Romans and then the Byzantines. Turkish from 1484, it was acquired by Russia in the 19th century. It was under Romanian rule from 1918 to 1940. Population (1981 est): 255 000.

Belgrade (Serbo-Croat name: Beograd)   44 50N 20 30E The capital of Yugoslavia and of Serbia, situated in the NE at the confluence of the Rivers Danube and Sava. A settlement and route centre from very early times, it became the Serbian capital in the early 15th century. It later suffered Turkish and Austrian occupations but again became capital of Serbia in the late 19th century and of Yugoslavia after World War I. It was occupied by the Germans in World War II and has expanded considerably in the years since then. The University of Belgrade was founded in 1863 and the Arts University in 1973. Population (1981): 1 407 073.

Belgravia A district, mainly in the Greater London borough of the City of Westminster. It contains residential squares, including Belgrave and Eaton Squares, planned by Thomas Cubitt and built on reclaimed marshland (1825–30).

Belinsky, Vissarion (1811–48) Russian literary critic, an influential advocate of social realism and naturalism. He championed *Pushkin, *Lermontov, and *Gogol, whom he later denounced as a betrayer of naturalism.

Belisarius (c. 505–65 AD) Byzantine general of *Justinian I's reign. After successfully checking Persian invasions on the empire's eastern frontier and overthrowing the African Vandal kingdom (534), Belisarius began his conquest of the Ostrogoths of Italy, and captured Rome, Naples, and Ravenna (540) before being recalled to Constantinople. In 546 he returned to Italy to quell the resurgent Ostrogoths but was again recalled, his command being given to *Narses.

Belitung (or Billiton) An Indonesian island in the Java Sea. Its tinmines, now government owned, have attracted a large Chinese community. Area: 4833 sq km (1866 sq mi). Chief town: Tanjungpandan.

Belize, Colony of (name until 1973: British Honduras) A country in Central America, on the Caribbean Sea between Mexico and Guatemala. The country is generally low lying, rising to the Maya Mountains in the SW. It is subject to hurricanes, one of which severely damaged the former capital, Belize City, in 1961. The population is of African, Spanish-American, and Mayan Indian descent, with small minorities of E Indians, Syrians, and Chinese. *Economy*: mainly agricultural; although almost half the country is forested, the combined value of sugar and citrus exports have exceeded that of timber since the early 1960s. *History*:

archaeological evidence suggests that the area was once an important Mayan settlement. The coast was discovered by Columbus in 1502 but the first European occupation was an independent settlement of British woodcutters, which held out against the Spanish throughout the 17th century. From the late 18th century more control was exercised by the British Government and in 1862 it became a colony under Jamaica. It became an independent colony in 1884 and attained internal self-government in 1964. Claims, based on early Spanish treaties, were made to it by Guatemala but despite disputes Belize gained its independence in 1981. Prime minister: Manuel Esquivel. Official language: English; Spanish is also widely spoken. Official currency: Belize dollar of 100 cents. Area: 22 963 sq km (8867 sq mi). Population (1980 est): 144 857. Capital: Belmopan.

Belize City   17 29N 88 10W The chief port of Belize, on the Caribbean coast. It was formerly capital of Belize but following a severe hurricane (1961), Belmopan, which became capital in 1970, was constructed inland. The main exports are timber, coconuts, and maize. Population (1980): 39 887.

ALEXANDER GRAHAM BELL *Inaugurating the New York – Chicago telephone line in 1892.*

Bell, Alexander Graham (1847–1922) Scottish scientist and inventor. He went to Canada in 1870 and to the USA in 1873, where he became professor of vocal physiology at Boston University. Bell's work in telegraphy and telephony led to the invention of the telephone, which he patented in 1876, demonstrated at American exhibitions, and had in commercial use by 1877. He also performed basic work in sound recording, electro-optical communication, and aerodynamics.

Bell, Gertrude (Margaret Lowthian; 1868–1926) British traveller and scholar. She travelled widely in the Middle East and in World War I was political secretary in Baghdad (1917). She translated the Persian poet *Hafiz and wrote several travel books.

belladonna. *See* deadly nightshade.

belladonna lily. *See* Amaryllis.

Bellarmine, St Robert (1542–1621) Italian Jesuit theologian, cardinal (from 1549), and archbishop of Capua (1602–05): canonized in 1930. An influential counter-Reformation theologian, he held Galileo in high esteem and privately advised him to regard the Copernican system as hypothetical, although he formally pronounced the system "false and erroneous". His writings include *Disputationes de controversiis Christianae fidei* (1586–93), a statement of Catholic doctrine, and he played an important part in the revised edition of the Vulgate published in 1592. Stoneware wine jugs with a bearded face made in the Rhineland between about 1550 and 1700 became known as Bellarmines, on the grounds that they were Protestant caricatures of the cardinal.

Bellay, Joachim de (1522–60) French poet. In 1549 he published *Défense et illustration de la langue française*, the manifesto of the *Pléiade, and *Olive*, the first book of love sonnets in French. While accompanying his cousin Cardinal Jean du Bellay on a mission to Rome, he wrote *Antiquités de Rome* (1558) and *Regrets* (1558).

Bell Bay 41 8S 146 53E A port in Australia, in N Tasmania on the River Tamar estuary. It is the site of a large aluminium plant using bauxite from Queensland.

Bellerophon In Greek mythology, the grandson of Sisyphus and son of Glaucus, King of Corinth. Sent by Iobates, King of Lycia, to kill the *Chimera, he was able to carry out his task by flying above the dragon on Pegasus, a winged horse he had previously captured and tamed with the aid of Athena.

Bellingshausen, Fabian Gottlieb, Baron von (1778–1852) Russian explorer. In 1819 he led an expedition to the Antarctic, surveying the South Georgia and South Sandwich Islands and discovering the islands Peter I and Alexander I. The Bellingshausen Sea was named after him.

Bellingshausen Sea A section of the S Pacific Ocean bordering on Antarctica, extending between the Antarctic Peninsula and Ellsworth Land. It always contains pack ice.

Bellini, Jacopo (c. 1400–c. 1470) Venetian painter, who was a pupil of *Gentile da Fabriano. In the early 1420s he probably visited Florence, where he became familiar with the artistic developments of the Renaissance. Although his few surviving paintings retain the decorative conventions of Byzantine and Gothic art, his two sketchbooks (British Museum and Louvre) reveal a remarkable understanding of perspective. They influenced his son-in-law Andrea *Mantegna and his two sons, who both trained under him. The eldest, **Gentile Bellini** (c. 1429–1507), is best known for his portraits and procession scenes. *The Procession in St Mark's Square* (Accademia, Venice) depicts his native city with a realism that anticipates Canaletto. In 1479 he accompanied the Doge to Constantinople, where he painted Sultan Mehmed II (National Gallery, London). Gentile's brother **Giovanni Bellini** (c. 1430–1516) was an important influence on Venetian art, especially through his pupils *Titian and *Giorgione. His early work is indebted to Mantegna. From about 1475 his use of the Flemish technique of oil painting, introduced to him by *Antonello da Messina, led to his richer use of colour and softer treatment of form. His paintings included several altarpieces, such as *Madonna and Saints* (S Zaccaria, Venice) in which he gave great importance to the landscape, and portraits, such as *Doge Loredano* (National Gallery, London).

Bellini, Vincenzo (1801–35) Italian opera composer. Of his 11 operas, *La somnambula* and *Norma* (both 1831) and *I Puritani* (1835) remain popular, although they require singers of outstanding ability to meet the demands of the *coloratura style.

Bellinzona 46 12N 9 02E A town in S Switzerland, on the River Ticino. It is dominated by three 15th-century castles. A tourist centre, it also has small industries. Population (1983):

16 793.

Bello, Andrés (1781–1865) Venezuelan scholar and poet. He accompanied Simón Bolívar on a revolutionary mission to London in 1810 and stayed there until 1829. The pastoral poems of *Silvas americanas* (1826–27) are influenced by Virgil. He founded the University of Chile (1843), drafted the country's legal code, and wrote books on many subjects, including a definitive Spanish grammar (1847).

Belloc, (Joseph-Pierre) Hilaire (1870–1953) British poet and essayist. Born in France, he was educated at Oxford and served as a Liberal MP from 1906 to 1910. His works include essays, historical biographies, and satirical novels, often illustrated by his friend G. K. *Chesterton. An energetic Roman Catholic apologist, he vigorously opposed the socialism of G. B. *Shaw and H. G. *Wells. His most popular works are light verse, such as *Cautionary Tales* (1907).

Bellow, Saul (1915–) Canadian-born US novelist, the son of poor Russian Jewish immigrants. His first novel, *Dangling Man* (1944), was influenced by *existentialism. His later novels, such as *Mr Sammler's Planet* (1970), *Humboldt's Gift* (1975), and *The Dean's December* (1982), are ironic studies of urban Jewish intellectuals. Other publications include *Him with his Foot in his Mouth* (1986) and *More Die of Heartbreak* (1987); in 1976 he won the Nobel Prize.

bell ringing. *See* change ringing.

Bell Rock (*or* Inchcape Rock) 56 26N 2 24W A reef off the NE coast of Scotland, in the North Sea. A lighthouse designed by Robert Stevenson, grandfather of Robert Louis Stevenson, was built here (1807–11).

Belmonte y García, Juan (1892–1962) Spanish matador, who was active from 1913 until 1934. His technique of working very close to bulls, using his cape to induce them to move round him, revolutionized bullfighting.

Belmopan 17 12N 88 00W The capital of Belize, on the River Belize about 80 km (50 mi) inland from Belize City, which it succeeded as capital in 1970 after the latter was damaged by a hurricane in 1961. Population (1980): 2932.

Belo Horizonte 19 54S 43 54W A city in SE Brazil, in Minas Gerais state. Founded in 1897, it was Brazil's first planned city. Distinctive architecture includes Oscar Niemayer's Chapel of São Francisco. The chief industries include cotton textiles, meat processing, and iron and steel. It is the site of two universities. Population (1980 est): 1 442 483.

Belorussian Soviet Socialist Republic (Belorussia *or* White Russia) A constituent republic in the W Soviet Union. The majority of its inhabitants are Belorussians, an Eastern *Slav people. Belorussia has an important engineering industry and the largest petrochemical complex in Europe. Cereals are the basis of agriculture, and dairy farming and pig breeding are expanding. Belorussia (formed in 1919) was badly devastated in World War II. It has a separate seat in the UN. Area: 207 600 sq km (80 134 sq mi). Population (1981 est): 9 700 000. Capital: Minsk.

Belshazzar In the Old Testament, the son of *Nebuchadnezzar and the last King of Babylon. At a feast given by him, the prophet Daniel interpreted the supernatural handwriting that appeared on the wall—*Mene, Mene, Tekel, Upharsin*—as foretelling the destruction of Babylon and Belshazzar's downfall (Daniel 5.25).

beluga 1. A giant *sturgeon, *Huso huso*, up to 8.4 m long, that occurs in the Caspian and Black Seas and the River Volga of E Europe. It is a highly prolific egg producer and the source of the best caviar. 2. *See* white whale.

Belyi, Andrei (Boris Nikolaevich Bugaev; 1880–1934) Russian symbolist poet and critic. He studied mathematics and philosophy at Moscow University, but his interest in mysticism led him into symbolism. In 1901 he published

Simfoniya, an attempted synthesis of all the arts around a prose poem, and several volumes of poetry and criticism. Disillusioned with the aftermath of the Revolution, he lived abroad from 1921 to 1923.

Bemba A Central *Bantu people of NE Zambia and neighbouring areas of Zaïre and Rhodesia whose language has become widely spoken in Zambia. They were traditionally ruled by members of the matrilineal royal clan from which the supreme chief, or Chitimukulu, came.

Bembo, Pietro (1470–1547) Italian scholar. He was secretary to Pope Leo X from 1513 to 1521 and was made cardinal in 1539. His most important work, *Prose della volgar lingua* (1525), set out to develop Italian into a literary language equal to Latin. *Rime* (1530) is a collection of his Italian poetry.

Benares. *See* Varanasi.

Ben Bella, Ahmed (1916–) Algerian statesman; president (1963–65). A leading figure in the struggle for the independence of Algeria, after service in the French army during World War II he helped to form the *Front de Libération nationale (FLN) in 1954. Imprisoned by the French for six years, he was released at independence in 1962 and elected prime minister (1962–63) and then president. He was overthrown in 1965 by *Boumédienne and imprisoned until 1979.

Benbow, John (1653–1702) English naval officer. During the War of the Spanish Succession, Benbow fought a superior French force off Santa Marta for four days, unsupported by his fellow captains, who disobeyed his orders. Although he was wounded, he continued to direct the battle from the deck, but was compelled to withdraw and died in Jamaica.

Benchley, Robert Charles (1889–1945) US humorist. He edited *Vanity Fair* and worked as drama critic for *Life* and the *New Yorker*. He published 15 volumes of his collected humorous essays, including *My Ten Years in a Quandary* (1936). He acted in several films and himself made 46 short comic films.

Benda, Julien (1867–1956) French novelist and philosopher. An advocate of the classical ideals of reason and order, he wrote several books attacking the philosophy of *Bergson. His most famous work, *La Trahison des clercs* (1927), demanded that the intellectual's commitment to truth should not be compromised by political or emotional involvements.

Bendigo 36 48S 144 21E A city in Australia, in central Victoria. It grew rapidly following a gold discovery in 1851 and is now a commercial centre with the third largest livestock market in Australia. Population (1985 est): 62 000.

bends. *See* decompression sickness.

Benedict XV (Giacomo della Chiesa; 1854–1922) Pope (1914–22). A papal diplomat, he was elected shortly after the outbreak of World War I, in which he maintained a strict neutrality while attempting to negotiate peace and to curb atrocities. Thereafter he reformed papal administration and diplomacy and was a notable supporter of missionary activity.

Benedictines The monks and nuns belonging to the Roman Catholic Order of St Benedict (OSB), a union of independent abbeys all of which follow the Rule of St *Benedict of Nursia. They have always acted as scholars and educators and were important in preserving the learning of antiquity after the fall of the Roman Empire. They have also exercised a great influence in maintaining high standards for the sacred art and music used in the liturgy. The liqueur Bénédictine is named after the order and is made at Fécamp, France.

Benedict of Nursia, St (c. 480–c. 550) Italian saint, the father of western monasticism. Educated at Rome, he withdrew from society about 500 and lived for a time as a hermit near Rome. He eventually established 12 monasteries with 12 monks each. About 525 he and a few monks established themselves at Monte Cassino, where he drew up his monastic rule, which pro-

vided for government by an elected abbot, residence in one place, obedience, observance of prayers at fixed hours (the Divine Office), common ownership of property, and a life of work, prayer, and study. The Rule was originally intended for laymen, and Benedict himself was apparently not ordained. He was buried at Monte Cassino. Feast day: 21 March. Emblems: a broken cup and a raven.

benefit of clergy The development in England of the 12th-century canon law that criminous clerks (criminal clerics) should not be tried by both ecclesiastical and secular courts. Henry II's acceptance of this principle gave all clerics the right to be tried solely in ecclesiastical courts. These could not inflict capital punishment, from which clergy were thus immune. Much abused in the later middle ages, the privilege was increasingly limited during and after the Reformation although it was not finally abolished until the early 19th century.

Bene Israel (Hebrew: Children of Israel) Indian Jewish community of uncertain origin, now concentrated mainly in Bombay.

Benelux The customs union formed by *Be*lgium, the *Ne*therlands, and *Lux*embourg in 1948. It was the first free-trade market in Europe. The three countries standardized prices, welfare benefits, wages, and taxes and allowed free immigration and movement of labour and capital between them. All three countries are now members of the *EEC, which has similar aims.

Beneš, Edvard (1884–1948) Czechoslovak statesman. In 1918 Beneš helped Tomáš *Masaryk to found Czechoslovakia and became foreign minister, playing an important role in the League of Nations. In 1935 he became president but went into exile when he was forced to cede the *Sudetenland to Germany (1938). He spent World War II as president of a provisional government in London, returning to Czechoslovakia in 1945. He resigned the presidency in 1948, when Czechoslovakia became a communist state.

Benét, Stephen Vincent (1898–1943) US poet and novelist. Son of an army officer, he wrote chiefly on themes of American history and myth. His best-known work is *John Brown's Body* (1928), an epic poem about the Civil War.

Benevento 41 08N 14 46E A town in S Italy, in Campania. It has Roman remains, including Trajan's Arch (114–17 AD), and a 9th-century cathedral. Its manufactures include leather goods, agricultural machinery, confectionery, and Strega liqueur. Population (1981): 61 443.

Bengal A region of the Indian subcontinent, in the NE on the Bay of Bengal around the vast Ganges and Brahmaputra deltas. Divided between India and Bangladesh, it has a flourishing culture. *History*: on the fringe of early Indian civilization, Bengal became the centre of Buddhist (8th–12th centuries), Hindu (11th–13th centuries), and finally Islamic dynasties. The base for British expansion through India, it was partitioned between India and Pakistan at independence (1947). *See also* West Bengal.

Bengal, Bay of The shallow NE limb of the Indian Ocean, between the Indian subcontinent on the W and Burma and the Andaman and Nicobar Islands on the E. Shipping and coastal life are dominated by the NE winter monsoon and the SW summer monsoon.

Bengali An Indo-Aryan language spoken by 80 million people in Bangladesh and West Bengal (India). The literary form of the language uses many *Sanskrit words. It was the first Indian language to imitate western literary modes in fiction, drama, and poetry. There is a distinct colloquial form.

Benghazi (*or* Banghazi; Italian name: Bengasi) 32 07N 20 05E The second largest city in Libya, on the Gulf of Sidra. Severely damaged during World War II, it has experienced recent growth with the development of local oilfields; other industries include light engineering. Population (1979 est): 267 700.

Benguela (*or* Benguella) 12 34S 13 24E A town in W Angola, on the Atlantic Ocean. It is overshadowed as a port by Lobito; industries include fish drying and soap production. Population (1975): 41 000.

DAVID BEN-GURION *The father of the Israeli nation, noted for his informality, had a magnetic personality that caused him to be revered throughout the world.*

Ben-Gurion, David (1886–1973) Israeli statesman, known as the Father of the Nation. He was Israel's first prime minister (1948–53, 1955–63). Born David Gruen in Poland, he adopted the Hebrew name Ben-Gurion after arriving in Palestine in 1906. In 1917 he joined the British Army's Jewish Legion to free Palestine from Ottoman control (achieved in 1918) and after the establishment of British rule worked to establish a Jewish home in Palestine, promised in the *Balfour Declaration. In 1920 he founded the General Federation of Labour (the Histadrut) and in 1930, the Israeli Workers' Party (Mapai). Becoming chairman of the Zionist Executive in 1935, he led the Zionist effort to establish a Jewish state, finally achieved in 1948. As prime minister he formed an Israeli army from the varous guerrilla groups and adopted a tough line against Arab attack. After resigning the prime ministership in 1963, he was leader of the opposition party, the Rafi, until his retirement in 1970.

Beni, Río A river in Bolivia. Rising near La Paz, it flows generally NE to join the Río Mamoré. Length: over 1600 km (1000 mi).

Benin, People's Republic of (name until 1975: Dahomey) A country in West Africa, on the Gulf of Guinea. Flat forests and swamps in the S rise to plateaus in the centre and to mountains in the N. The population is mainly Fon and Yoruba in the N and Somba and Bariba in the S. *Economy*: chiefly agricultural, the main crops being maize, cassava, rice, and vegetables. Cotton has been introduced in the N and coffee in the S, and these provide the main exports. Forests produce palm oil and kernels, and there is some freshwater fishing. Offshore oil has

been found and hydroelectric schemes are being planned in conjunction with Togo. Most industry has been nationalized. *History*: the powerful Aja kingdom of Dahomey was a centre of the slave trade in the 17th century but was conquered by the French in 1893 and became part of French West Africa. Dahomey attained self-government in 1958 and became an independent republic within the French Community in 1960. Since then the country has been shaken by a series of military coups; in the last (1972) Brig Gen Mathieu Kerékou (1933–) seized power. In 1974 he established a Marxist-Leninist state and in 1984 was re-elected as president. Official language: French. Official currency: CFA (Communauté financière africaine) franc of 100 centimes. Area: 112 600 sq km (43 464 sq mi). Population (1981): 3 800 000. Capital: Porto Novo. Main port: Cotonou.

Benin City 6 19N 5 41E A city in Nigeria. It is an important centre for the rubber industry and also exports palm oil. Population (1984): 231 976.

Benjamin In the Old Testament, the youngest son of Jacob by Rachel, who died during childbirth. He was named Ben-oni (son of ill luck) by Rachel before she died but called Benjamin (son of good luck) by Jacob. He became his father's favourite after Joseph was sold into slavery in Egypt. Figuratively he represents the especially loved younger son. His descendants formed one of the 12 *tribes of Israel and later, with the tribe of Judah, formed the southern kingdom of Judah.

Benn, Anthony (Neil) Wedgwood (1925–) British Labour politician, a leader of the party's left wing. The 2nd Viscount Stansgate from 1960, he renounced his peerage in 1963, the first person to do so under the Peerage Act (1963). He was minister of technology (1966–70), for industry (1974–75), and for energy (1975–79). He lost his seat in the 1983 general election but won a by-election at Chesterfield in 1984.

Benn, Gottfried (1886–1956) German poet. He worked as a doctor in Berlin and, during both World Wars, in the army. His early expressionist style, evident in *Morgue* (1912) and *Fleisch* (1917), gave way to the more precise intellectual style evident in *Statische Gedichte* (1948). His theories of poetry, contained in *Probleme der Lyrik* (1951), attracted T. S. *Eliot.

Bennett, (Enoch) Arnold (1837–1931) British novelist. The son of a solicitor in Newcastle-under-Lyme, he became a magazine editor in London. He published his first novel, *A Man from the North*, in 1898 and lived in Paris from 1902 to 1912. His best-known novels are about life in the Potteries area of Staffordshire, where he grew up. They include *Anna of the Five Towns* (1902), *The Old Wives' Tale* (1908), and *Clayhanger* (1910).

Bennett, James Gordon (1795–1872) US newspaper editor, born in Scotland. He founded the *New York Herald* (1835), in which he pioneered many of the techniques of modern journalism. His son **James Gordon Bennett** (1841–1918) became editor of the *Herald* in 1867. He financed several explorers, including Stanley in his quest for Livingstone.

Bennett, Richard Bedford, Viscount (1870–1947) Canadian statesman; Conservative prime minister (1930–35). A lawyer and businessman, he was a champion of protective tariffs. In 1932 he presided over the Imperial Economic Conference in Ottawa, which established bilateral trade agreements between countries in the British Commonwealth.

Bennett, Richard Rodney (1936–) British composer known primarily for his atmospheric scores for such films as *Far from the Madding Crowd* (1967) and *Murder on the Orient Express* (1974) and for his five major operas, including *The Mines of Sulphur* (1963) and *Victory* (1970). Also active as a pianist in jazz and classical music, he has written an opera for children, *All the King's Men* (1969), and many varied instrumental works.

Bennett, Sir William Sterndale (1816–75) British pianist, conductor, and composer. A child prodigy, his first piano concerto (1832) impressed Mendelssohn, who introduced him to Schumann. Bennett was a prolific composer of opera and instrumental works; his works are little known today.

Ben Nevis 56 48N 5 00W The highest mountain in the British Isles, in the Highland Region of Scotland, in the Grampians. Height: 1343 m (4406 ft).

Benny, Jack (Benjamin Kubelsky; 1894–1974) US comedian. In vaudeville from an early age, he began making films in 1929. His act featured meanness, joke playing of the violin, and, from 1933, always being 39 years old. His film *To Be or Not To Be* (1942) was outstanding and he had his own radio (1932–55) and television (1950–65) shows.

Benoit de Sainte-Maure (12th century AD) French poet. His long epic poem, *Roman de Troie*, is loosely based on the legends of *Troy. He is possibly also the author of a verse history of the Dukes of Normandy, commissioned by Henry II in 1174.

Benoni 26 12S 28 18E A city in South Africa, in the S Transvaal on the Witwatersrand. Founded in 1903 as a gold-mining centre, it is an important industrial city, especially for engineering. Population (1980 est): 206 810.

Benson, Sir Frank (1858–1939) British actor-manager. In 1883 he founded his own company, which toured Britain with productions of Shakespeare. He trained many actors and was knighted on stage in 1916.

Bentham, Jeremy (1748–1832) British philosopher, pioneer of *utilitarianism. From a wealthy middle-class background, he went to Oxford and then, aged only 15, to Lincoln's Inn. He preferred legal theory to practice and in 1776 published *A Fragment on Government*. In 1789 *Principles of Morals and Legislation* presented utilitarianism to the world. He travelled widely, championing prison reform and the French Revolution. He retired to the country in 1814, a republican hero, and wrote copiously on politics and ethics until his death. He founded the *Westminster Review* (1823) to promote philosophical radicalism.

Bentinck, Lord William (Henry Cavendish). *See* Portland, William Henry Cavendish Bentinck, 3rd Duke of.

Bentivoglio An aristocratic family that ruled Bologna (Italy) from 1447 until 1506. **Sante Bentivoglio** (1424–63) established his family's supremacy in Bologna. He and his son **Giovanni Bentivoglio** (1443–1508) were notable patrons of the arts. Increasingly autocratic and unpopular, Giovanni and his family were expelled from Bologna in 1506 with the support of Pope *Julius II. Subsequent members of the family, notably **Guido Bentivoglio** (1579–1644), were famous diplomats and authors.

Bentley, Edmund Clerihew (1875–1956) British writer. A close friend of G. K. *Chesterton, he wrote a classic detective novel, *Trent's Last Case* (1913). He invented the clerihew, a humorous verse form consisting of two rhyming couplets, the first rhyme being provided by the subject's name: Sir Christopher Wren Said, "I am going to dine with some men. If anybody calls Say I am designing St Paul's."

Bentley, Richard (1662–1742) English scholar. Bentley was appointed Keeper of the Royal Libraries in 1694 and in 1700 Master of Trinity College, Cambridge. His critical works on the scriptures and the classics, in particular his famous *Dissertation on the Letters of Phalaris* (1699), combined the philological and historical approaches, paving the way for modern textual criticism.

Benton, Thomas Hart (1889–1975) US painter of rural life. As the leader and spokesman of the American Regionalist painters of the 1930s, Benton advocated the need to free US painting from the overwhelming influence of French abstract art and to create an indigenous artistic tradition. He is also known for his murals for such public institutions as the New School of Social Research, New York, and the Missouri State Capitol in Jefferson City.

bentwood furniture Furniture constructed by a mass-production process invented by a Viennese designer Michael Thonet (1796–1871). It involved steaming beechwood rods and laminated board until they could be bent into the desired shapes. The shaped sections were transported unassembled and screwed together at the destination. Typical chairs, coat stands, etc., are curved in rococo style. The technique has been exploited by modern designers, such as Marcel *Breuer and many Scandinavian designers.

Benue, River A river in West Africa. Rising in N Cameroon, it flows W across Nigeria to join the River Niger at Lokoja. Length: 1400 km (870 mi).

Benxi (*or* Pen-ki) 41 21N 123 45E A city in NE China, in Liaoning province. It is a centre of iron and steel production. Population (1982): 669 000.

Benz, Karl (Friedrich) (1844–1929) German engineer and car manufacturer. In 1885 he built the first car to be driven by an internal-combustion engine. The Benz Company merged with Daimler in 1926 to form Daimler-Benz, the makers of Mercedes-Benz cars.

Benzedrine. *See* amphetamine.

benzene (*or* benzol; C_6H_6) A colourless highly flammable liquid. It is the simplest aromatic compound, its molecules consisting of a ring of six carbon atoms each with a hydrogen atom attached. Benzene is obtained from *oil and from *coal tar. It is widely used in the chemical industry, for example in making *detergents, *nylon, and *insecticides.

benzodiazepines A class of tranquillizing drugs that act by depressing specific areas of the brain. Despite this, overdosage of these drugs is rarely dangerous. Benzodiazepines, such as diazepam (Valium) and chlordiazepoxide (Librium), are used as *sedatives. Diazepam is also used to control epileptic fits and chlordiazepoxide is helpful in the treatment of alcohol-withdrawal symptoms. Nitrazepam (Mogadon) is used as a sleeping pill (*see* hypnotics). Both nitrazepam and diazepam are habit forming.

benzoic acid (C_6H_5COOH) A white crystalline powder, the simplest of the aromatic *fatty acids. It occurs naturally in many plants and is used in preserving food.

benzoin 1. ($C_6H_5CHOHCOC_6H_5$) A white or yellowish crystalline substance used to make other organic compounds. 2. (*or* gum benjamin) A fragrant gum resin obtained from the trunk of a SE Asian tree, *Styrax benzoin*. It is used in medicine (as a constituent of friar's balsam), in cosmetics, and in perfumery.

Ben-Zvi, Itzhak (1884–1963) Israeli statesman; president (1952–63). Born in Russia, where he was an active Zionist, he went to Palestine in 1907. With David *Ben-Gurion, Ben-Zvi helped to found the state of Israel (1947). He was also a noted archaeologist.

Beowulf An Anglo-Saxon epic poem preserved in a late 10th-century manuscript. Probably composed or at least reworked in the 8th century by a Christian poet sympathetic to pagan ideals of honour and courage, it alludes to historical events of early 6th-century Scandinavia. In the first part the hero, Beowulf, kills the marauding monster, Grendel; when Grendel's mother retaliates he kills her in her underwater cave. In the second part, Beowulf, now king of the Swedish tribe of Geats, slays a dragon and seizes its hoard of treasure, but is mortally wounded.

Bérain the Elder, Jean (1637–1711) French designer, engraver, and painter; royal designer to Louis XIV of France. He designed festival decorations, furniture, tapestries, and opera costumes for the court, often decorated with immense detail, which influenced the later rococo style. He used many Chinese motifs in his designs to satisfy the king's fondness for oriental art.

Beranger, Pierre Jean de (1780–1857) French poet and songwriter. His satirical verse and republican sentiments led to his imprisonment under the Bourbon monarchy.

Berbera 10 30N 45 25E A port in N Somalia, on the Gulf of Aden. It has a deepwater harbour and exports sheep, leather, ghee, frankincense, and myrrh. Population (1980 est): 65 000.

Berberis A genus of deciduous or evergreen spiny shrubs (over 400 species), commonly known as barberry, mostly native to Central and E Asia and South America but also occurring in parts of Europe, Africa, and North America. The small yellow or orange flowers usually grow in clusters and the fruits are bright-red berries. Several species are widely grown as ornamentals for their flowers, fruits, or attractive autumn foliage. Berberis is implicated in a rust disease of wheat and is therefore outlawed in some areas. Family: *Berberidaceae*.

Berbers A Muslim people occupying parts of N Africa (Morocco, Algeria, Tunisia, and adjacent regions) and speaking a non-Semitic language. Prior to the Arab conquests of the 7th century AD and the establishment of Arabic speech, Berber languages were spoken over the whole of the area from Egypt to the Atlantic. Though Arabic has long been the dominant language it has not entirely ousted Berber, which is spoken by an estimated ten million people, and Morocco is still predominantly Berber in population. The Berbers played an important role in the Islamic conquest of the Iberian peninsula in the 8th century and in the subsequent occupation of Spain. The Berbers are largely agriculturalists, although some still follow a nomadic way of life.

Berchtesgaden 47 38N 13 00E A resort in SE West Germany, in the Bavarian Alps. It is the site of Hitler's fortified mountain retreat, the Berghof. Salt has been mined here since the 12th century. Population (1983): 8186.

Berdyaev, Nikolai (1874–1948) Russian mystical philosopher. He was expelled from Russia (1922) for teaching religion and until World War II his academy near Paris and his journal *The Path* spread his ideas in Europe. He saw communism as an ungodly manifestation of Russia's messianic destiny. *Dreams and Reality* (1950) summarizes his ideas.

Berdyansk (name from 1939 until 1958: Osipenko) 46·45N 36 47E A port in the SW Soviet Union, in the Ukrainian SSR on the Sea of Azov. It is a seaside resort and its most important economic activities relate to fishing. Flour milling and oil refining are also carried out. Population (1980 est): 124 000.

Berenson, Bernard (1865–1959) US art historian, whose works set new standards of criticism. Inspired by the beauty of Italy, where he spent much time, he wrote the definitive *Italian Painters of the Renaissance* (1894–1907). His aesthetic delight is captured in *Drawings of the Florentine Painters* (1903).

Berezniki 59 26N 56 49E A port in the E Soviet Union, in the RSFSR on the River Kama. Founded in 1883, it is now one of the largest centres for the chemical industry in the Soviet Union. Population (1981 est): 188 000.

Berg, Alban (1885–1935) Austrian composer. A friend and pupil of *Schoenberg, he adopted *atonality and used *serialism, though in a highly personal and original fashion. His greatest works are the operas *Wozzeck* (1915–21) from the play by *Büchner and *Lulu* (1928–35) from plays by *Wedekind, the intensely personal *Lyric Suite* (for string quartet; 1925–26), and a violin concerto (1935).

Bergamo 45 42N 9 40E A city in Italy, in Lombardy in the foothills of the Alps. It has a 12th-century romanesque cathedral. Machinery, textiles, and cement are manufactured. Population (1980 est): 124 150.

bergamot A tree, *Citrus bergamia*, closely related to the orange. An essence (oil of bergamot) extracted from the rind of its fruit is used in perfumery, for which the tree is cultivated in S Italy and Sicily. *See* Citrus.

The name is also given to two plants of the mint family (*Labiatae*): *Mentha citrata*, which yields an extract similar to oil of bergamot, and *Monarda citriodora* (lemon bergamot) sometimes used in a tealike beverage.

Bergen 60 23N 5 20E A seaport and second largest city in Norway, situated in the SW. Founded about 1070 AD, it became the chief commercial city and the country's capital (12th–13th centuries). It had important connections with Hanseatic merchants (14th–18th centuries). It was rebuilt after damage by fire in 1702, 1855, and 1916 and by bombing during World War II. It is a cultural centre with a university (1948), several museums, and an art gallery. Other notable buildings include the 12th-century Mariakirke (a stone-built church) and the 13th-century Håkonshall (a royal palace). Its industries include shipbuilding and oil refining. It exports fish products and base metals. Population (1984): 207 506.

Bergenia A genus of herbaceous perennial plants (6 species), native to central and E Asia but often cultivated as ornamentals for their attractive foliage and early-blooming pink or white flowers. Family: *Saxifragaceae*.

Bergen op Zoom 51 30N 4 17E A port in the SW Netherlands, in North Brabant province. An important 15th-century cloth and fishing centre, its industries now include oyster fisheries and iron and steel processing. Population (1981 est): 44 422.

Bergius, Friedrich (1884–1949) German chemist, who shared the 1931 Nobel Prize with C. Bosch for research in high-pressure chemical techniques. He manufactured light motor fuels from either coal or heavy petroleum residues by treating them with hydrogen under high pressure and temperature (1913). This process was used extensively by Germany in World War II. After Germany's defeat he emigrated to Spain and then to Argentina.

Bergman, Hjalmar (Fredrik Elgérus) (1883–1931) Swedish novelist and dramatist. His two novels of provincial life, *Markurells i Wadköping* (*God's Orchid*; 1919) and *Farmor och vår Herre* (*Thy Rod and Thy Staff*; 1921), drew upon his early life in the town of Örebro. He wrote a number of film and radio scripts as well as such plays as *Swedenhielms* (1925).

Bergman, Ingmar (1918–) Swedish film and stage director. His films, which express his austere human vision with great intensity, include *The Seventh Seal* (1956), *Wild Strawberries* (1957), *Persona* (1966), *Scenes from a Marriage* (1974), *Autumn Sonata* (1978), and *Fanny and Alexander* (1982). He was director of the Royal Dramatic Theatre, Stockholm, from 1963 to 1966.

Bergman, Ingrid (1915–82) Swedish actress. She went to Hollywood in 1939 and became an international film star, appearing in such films as *Casablanca* (1942), *Gaslight* (1944), and numerous other major films, her last being *Autumn Sonata* (1978). She also played in several notable stage productions.

Bergson, Henri (1859–1941) French philosopher and psychologist, one of the greatest thinkers of his time. To reconcile free will and *determinism, Bergson distinguishes between consciousness, an indivisible flow of cumulative states in which (free) will operates, and the external physical world where causality reigns and objects and events are fixed and discrete. He championed creative against analytic thinking in stylish and penetrating works that include *Matière et mémoire* (1896) and *L'Évolution créatrice* (1907). He won the Nobel Prize for Literature in 1927.

Beria, Lavrenti Pavlovich (1899–1953) Soviet politician. Head of the Soviet secret police from 1938, Beria became a member of the politburo (now the presidium) in 1946. After Stalin's death in March, 1953, he was involved in a power struggle with Malenkov and Khrushchev. He was accused of conspiracy in July, tried secretly, and executed in December.

beriberi A disease caused by deficiency of *vitamin B_1 (thiamine), common in areas where the staple diet is polished rice (thiamine occurs mainly in the rice husks). Dry beriberi affects the peripheral nerves, causing muscular weakness and pain. Wet beriberi is probably the result of combined protein malnutrition and thiamine deficiency: it causes accumulation of fluid and swelling of the limbs, leading eventually to heart failure. Treatment consists of providing a diet with adequate thiamine and vitamin supplements.

Bering, Vitus Jonassen (or V. J. Behring; 1681–1741) Danish navigator. In 1724 he was commissioned by the Russians to explore the area between Siberia and America. He made several voyages from Kamchatka on the last of which (1741) he sighted Alaska from the strait named after him. On his way back, suffering from scurvy, he was wrecked off Bering Island, where he died. The Bering Sea is also named after him.

Bering Sea A section of the N Pacific Ocean between the Soviet Union, Alaska, and the Aleutian Islands. Navigation is difficult, with storms and a partial ice covering in winter. The NE continental shelf contains oil and gas, as yet unexploited.

Bering Strait A narrow shallow channel between Asia and North America, connecting the Bering Sea with the Arctic Ocean. During the Ice Age it bridged the continents when the sea level fell.

Berio, Luciano (1925–) Italian composer, a pupil of Dallapiccola. He has lived in the USA since 1962 and was married (1950–65) to the soprano Cathy Berberian (1925–83). A leading composer of the avantgarde, Berio has used serialism, electronic effects, taped sounds, and unusual instrumental techniques in his works. These include a number of *Sequenzas*, each for a different solo instrument, *Omaggio a Joyce* (for taped voice; 1958), and *Sinfonia* (1968), partly based on fragments of music by Debussy and Mahler.

Beriosova, Svetlana (1932–) Russian ballet dancer. In 1952 she joined the British Sadler's Wells company, becoming prima ballerina in 1955. She danced both classical and modern roles, and was especially noted for her *Giselle* (1956). She officially retired in 1975.

Berkeley 37 53N 122 17W A city in the USA, in California on San Francisco Bay. It is the headquarters of the University of California, where *berkelium was discovered. Its manufactures include soap, paint, and chemicals. Population (1980): 103 328.

Berkeley, Busby (William Berkeley Enos; 1895–1976) US dance director. He is best known for his elaborate choreography for Hollywood film musicals in the 1930s and 1940s. These include *42nd Street* (1933), the *Gold Diggers* series (1933–37), and *Babes in Arms* (1939).

Berkeley, George (1685–1753) Irish bishop and idealist philosopher. In *A New Theory of Vision* (1709), *Principles of Human Knowledge* (1710), and *Three Dialogues between Hylas and Philonous* (1713), he argued that the material world exists only in being perceived by the mind, a view that influenced *Hume and, indirectly, *Kant. Berkeley's later works, such as *Siris* (1744) are interesting but increasingly eccentric.

Berkeley, Sir Lennox Randal Francis (1903–) British composer. He studied under Nadia Boulanger and taught at the Royal Academy of Music from 1946 to 1968. Berkeley's compositions include the *Serenade for Strings* (1939), *Four Poems of St Teresa* for contralto and strings (1947), and the fourth symphony (1978).

Berkeley, Sir William (1606–77) English colonist; governor of Virginia (1641–49, 1660–77). His attempts to foster trade relations with the Indians were thwarted by Nathaniel Bacon (1647–76), who led a force against the Indians that was defeated by Berkeley's troops (Bacon's Rebellion). Berkeley is also noted as the author of a play, *The Lost Lady* (1638).

berkelium (Bk) A synthetic transuranic element synthesized by Seaborg and others in 1949 by bombarding americium with helium ions. The longest-lived isotope (^{249}Bk) has a half-life of 314 days; visible amounts of the chloride (BkCl$_3$) have been produced. At no 97; at wt (247).

Berkshire A county of S England. Under local government reorganization in 1974 it lost a substantial part of the NW to Oxfordshire, while gaining part of SW Buckinghamshire, including Slough. It consists mainly of lowlands rising to the Berkshire Downs in the N. It is bordered by the River Thames in the NE and crossed by the River Kennet. It is predominantly agricultural; chief products are barley, dairy produce, pigs, and poultry. Industries include paints, plastics, and pharmaceutical goods at Slough and light engineering and horticulture at Reading; the Atomic Research Establishment is at Aldermaston. Area: 1256 sq km (485 sq mi). Population (1981): 675 153. Administrative centre: Reading.

Berlichingen, Götz von (1480–1562) German knight and mercenary. A professional adventurer, he was already famous for his exploits, in which he lost his right hand, when he became a rebel leader in the *Peasants' War (1525). After a period of imprisonment he continued his career, serving Emperor Charles V against the Turks in the 1540s. His exploits inspired Goethe's *Götz von Berlichingen* (1773).

Berlin 52 31N 13 20E A city in N Germany, on the River Spree, divided since 1948 into East Berlin, now capital of the German Democratic Republic (East Germany), and West Berlin, part of the Federal Republic of Germany (West Germany). *History*: founded in the 13th century, it was an important strategic and commercial centre and a member of the Hanseatic League. Its independence was reduced by the *Hohenzollern Electors of Brandenburg from the 15th century, but it became their capital and grew in importance with their increasing power, becoming the capital of Prussia in the 18th century and of the German Empire in 1871. Badly damaged in World War II, it was occupied by the four major powers after the defeat of Germany. In 1948 Berlin became two separate administrative units: Soviet-controlled East Berlin and West Berlin, formed from the US, UK, and French zones. The Soviet Union blockaded the city for almost a year but it failed to extend its influence to West Berlin (*see* Berlin airlift). In 1961 a dividing wall was built to curb the flow of refugees from E to W.

East Berlin The capital of East Germany. Postwar recovery has been slower than in West Berlin. Industrial products include electrical goods, chemicals, machinery, and clothing. At the border with West Berlin stands the *Brandenburg Gate, E of which runs the Unter den Linden (the famous tree-lined avenue), carefully restored in the 1960s. But the Wilhelmstrasse, where Hitler had his chancellery, has failed to regain its former importance. East Berlin is the site of Humboldt University, formerly Frederick William University (1810), where famous scholars such as Humboldt, Fichte, Hegel, and Ranke worked. Area: 403 sq km (156 sq mi). Population (1980 est): 1 145 743.

West Berlin The largest city and a *Land* of West Germany, forming an enclave within East Germany. Despite difficulties in communications it is an active industrial and commercial centre, subsidized by West Germany. Its numerous industries include the manufacture of electrical equipment, clothing, and chemicals as well as publishing and printing. A major landmark is the Kaiser Wilhelm Church, the ruins of which have been preserved as a reminder of the World Wars. The Free University of Berlin was established in 1948. Area: 480 sq km (188 sq mi). Population (1980 est): 1 898 900. □ p. 142.

Berlin, Congress of (1878) A meeting of European powers, which revised the Treaty of *San Stefano that had ended the 1877–78 Russo-Turkish War. The Congress, which was dominated by the German chancellor, *Bismarck, limited Russian naval expansion, permitted Austria-Hungary to occupy Bosnia-Herzegovina, and gained Turkish recognition of the independence of Serbia, Romania, and Montenegro and of Bulgarian autonomy under Turkish suzerainty.

Berlin, Irving (Israel Baline; 1888–) US composer of musical comedies and film scores, born in Russia. He emigrated with his family to the USA in 1893. He wrote "Alexander's Ragtime Band" while working as a singing waiter and subsequently composed the music for many musicals, including *Annie Get Your Gun* (1946) and *Mr President* (1962).

Berlin, Sir Isaiah (1909–) British philosopher and historian. Although based mostly in Oxford, he was also a diplomat in Washington and Moscow. His works include *The Inevitability of History* (1954), *The Age of Enlightenment* (1956), and *Two Concepts of Liberty* (1959).

Berlin airlift (1948–49) An operation by the Allies after World War II to supply isolated West Berlin with the necessities of life. In 1948 the Soviet Union cut off all rail, road, and water links with the city in an attempt to force the Allies to abandon their rights there. The airlift continued until the blockade was lifted as a result of an embargo on exports from the E European states.

Berliner Ensemble A theatre company founded by Bertolt *Brecht in East Berlin in 1949. It became fully independent after its move to the Theatre am Schiffbauerdamm in 1945 and was directed after Brecht's death in 1956 by his widow, Helene Weigel (1900–71). The company devoted itself exclusively to works written or adapted by Brecht, and its several European tours won international acclaim for his work.

Berlinguer, Enrico (1922–84) Italian politician; leader of the Italian Communist Party (1958–84). He was noted for his willingness to work through parliamentary channels and was instrumental in March, 1978, in establishing Communist support for the coalition government of Giulio *Andreotti.

Berlin West Africa Conference (1884–85) A series of meetings held at Berlin under the chairmanship of *Bismarck to settle the dispute over possession of the Congo Basin (Central Africa). Among the powers that attended were France, Germany, the UK, Belgium, and Portugal. The Conference declared that the Congo Basin should be neutral with free trade and shipping and that an independent Congo Free State be established; it forbade slave trading.

Berlioz, (Louis) Hector (1803–69) French Romantic composer and conductor. Against family opposition he abandoned medicine for music. His first successful work, the *Symphonie Fantastique* (1830–31), was influenced by his love for an Irish actress, Harriet Smithson (1800–54). As winner of the Prix de Rome he went to Italy to study; on his return in 1833 he married Harriet. His dramatic symphony *Harold in Italy* (1834) and choral symphony *Romeo and Juliet* (1839) were popular successes, but the cantata *The Damnation of Faust* (1846) and the opera *Benvenuto Cellini* (1834–38) failed. The oratorio *The Childhood of Christ* (1850–54) was his last major success, for his two-part opera *The Trojans* (1856–59) was not performed complete in his lifetime. Other orchestral works include the overture *Le Corsaire* (1851–52) and *Le Carnaval romain* (1844). He was the author of a famous treatise on orchestration and a volume of memoirs.

Bermejo, Río A river of S central South America. Rising in S Bolivia, it flows SE into Argentina to join the River Paraguay. Length: 1046 km (650 mi).

Bermuda A British crown colony, comprising some 300 coral islands (of which 20 are inhabited), in the W Atlantic Ocean. The largest island is Bermuda (or Great Bermuda), while smaller ones include Somerset, Ireland, and St George. Approximately three-quarters of the population is Black. *Economy*: the subtropical climate with its mild winters has contributed to tourism, which forms the basis of the islands' economy. Agricultural products include vegetables and bananas; onions, potatoes, and lily bulbs are exported to the USA. *History*: visited by the Spanish navigator Juan de Bermudez in 1515, the islands were first settled in 1609 by English colonists shipwrecked there on the way to Virginia. They became the responsibility of the English Crown in 1684 and became self-governing in 1968 but demands for independence have grown; the governor was assassinated in 1973 and there was serious rioting in 1977. Governor: Viscount Dunrossil (1926–). Official language: English. Official currency: Bermuda dollar of 100 cents. Area: 53 sq km (20 sq mi). Population (1980): 54 670. Capital: Hamilton.

BERLIN *King Edward VII and Queen Alexandra of Great Britain entering Berlin through the Brandenburg Gate on a state visit to the Emperor William II in 1906.*

Bermuda Triangle The most notorious of several geographic regions, all lying roughly between 30° and 40° of latitude, in which numerous ships and aircraft have vanished without trace. The Triangle covers about 3 900 000 sq km (1 500 000 sq mi) between Bermuda, Florida, and Puerto Rico. No generally satisfactory explanation of these disappearances has been advanced, but the great depth of the sea and powerful currents may explain the lack of wreckage.

Bern (French name: Berne) 46 57N 95 58W The capital of Switzerland, on the River Aare. Founded as a military post in the 12th century, it joined the Swiss Confederation in 1353 and became the capital in 1848. Its many notable buildings include the gothic cathedral (15th century). Since the 16th century it has had a bear pit, now maintained as a tourist attraction. The university was founded in 1834. It has considerable industry and contains the headquarters of several international organizations. Population (1984 est): 140 000.

Bernadette of Lourdes, St (1844–79) French peasant girl, who in 1858 claimed to have had 18 visions of the Virgin Mary at a grotto near Lourdes. At 20 she became a nun. She was canonized in 1933. The shrine built at the spot is a place of international pilgrimage where miraculous cures are claimed to have occurred. Feast day: 18 Feb or 16 April.

Bernadotte, Folke, Count (1895–1948) The nephew of Gustavus V of Sweden (1858–1950; reigned 1907–50). He became president of the Swedish Red Cross in 1946. In 1948 he was appointed mediator in Palestine but was assassinated by Jewish terrorists.

Bernadotte, Jean Baptiste Jules (c. 1763–1844) French marshal, who was King of Sweden (1818–44) as Charles XIV John, founding the present Swedish royal house. Rising from the ranks, he became famous under Napoleon with whose support in 1810 Bernadotte was adopted as heir by the dying Charles XIII of Sweden. Turning against Napoleon, Bernadotte contributed to his defeat at Leipzig (1813). In 1814 he forced Denmark to cede Norway to the Swedish monarchy.

Bernanos, Georges (1888–1948) French novelist and Catholic polemicist. His constant theme was the war between good and evil, characteristically portrayed in his best-known book, *The Diary of a Country Priest* (1936). Disturbed by European political trends, he lived in exile in Brazil from 1938 to 1945.

Bernard, Claude (1813–78) French physiologist, who helped establish the experimental principles used in modern research. A student of François *Magendie, Bernard discovered that a secretion of the pancreas breaks down fat into its constituents and that the liver is able to synthesize glucose from glycogen. He also showed how blood flow through capillaries is regulated by contraction of their walls, controlled by vasoconstrictor nerves. Bernard developed the concept of the internal environment (*milieu intérieur*) of the body, the regulation of which is a basic physiological function.

Bernardin de Saint-Pierre, Jacques Henri (1737–1814) French naturalist and writer. He was a disciple of Rousseau, whose ideas influenced the didactic romance for which he is chiefly remembered, *Paul et Virginie* (1787), which is set on the island of Mauritius.

Bernard of Chartres (died c. 1130) French scholastic philosopher, who taught at Chartres (1114–24). A Platonist, he held a realist theory of universals (*see* realism) but tried to reconcile Platonic and Aristotelian metaphysics. His only extant work is a treatise on Neoplatonism.

Bernard of Clairvaux, St (1090–1153) French theologian and Doctor of the Church. A Cistercian, he established in 1115 a monastery at Clairvaux that became a model of reform and influenced other monasteries in France and elsewhere. He was chosen by Pope Eugenius III to preach the second Crusade in 1146. His faith was based on an exalted mysticism, which is the subject of many of his Latin writings. Feast day: 20 Aug. Emblem: a beehive.

Bernard of Menthon, St (923–1008) Italian churchman and vicar general of the diocese of Aosta. A native of Savoy, he established hospices on two Alpine passes, which are named after him, as are the dogs that were kept by the monks and trained to aid travellers. Feast day: 28 May.

Berne Convention An international *copyright agreement of 1866. Its main provision guarantees copyright in all signatory countries of any work copyrighted in any one of them. The USA is still not a signatory.

Bernese Oberland (*or* Bernese Alps) A section of the Alps in SW Switzerland, 105 km (65 mi) long, between the Rivers Rhône and Aare. Its mountain peaks include the Eiger and the Finsteraarhorn and it is a popular area for mountain climbing.

Bernhard of Saxe-Weimar, Duke (1604–39) German general, who fought for the Protestants in the *Thirty Years' War. He took command of the forces of Gustavus Adolphus on Gustavus' death in 1632 and campaigned successfully in S Germany. After losing at Nördlingen (1634) he held command for the French in SW Germany.

SARAH BERNHARDT *In the role of Hamlet at the Adelphi Theatre, London (1889).*

Bernhardt, Sarah (Sarah Henriette Rosine Bernard; 1844–1923) French actress. Her voice and emotional power were especially suited to tragic roles. Plays in which she gave notable performances include *Phèdre* (1879), *La Dame aux camélias*, and *L'Aiglon* by Edmond Rostand. Her worldwide tours gained her international acclaim. She was also manager of several theatres in Paris and opened the old Théâtre des Nations as the Théâtre Sarah Bernhardt.

Bernina, Piz 46 23N 9 54E A mountain in SE Switzerland, in the Alps near St Moritz. Height: 4049 m (13 284 ft).

Bernini, Gian Lorenzo (1598–1680) Italian *baroque sculptor and architect, born in Naples, the son of a sculptor. Precociously talented, he worked chiefly in □Rome under papal patronage. His first major sculptures were for Cardinal Scipione Borghese and included *Apollo and Daphne* (1622–24; Borghese Gallery, Rome). Encouraged by Urban VIII, he extended his talents into the fields of painting and, more successfully, architecture, major works being the baldachin over the tomb of St Peter (1624–33) and the piazza and colonnade (1656–67) of St Peter's, Rome. Later sculptures included fountains for Roman piazzas, *The Ecstasy of St Teresa* (1645–52; Cornaro Chapel, Sta Maria della Vittoria, Rome), and such portrait busts as *Louis XIV* (1665; Versailles).

Bernoulli A family of notable Swiss mathematicians and physicists, who, as Flemish Protestants, were driven out of the Netherlands in the 1580s. The most famous was **Daniel Bernoulli** (1700–82), who made important contributions to fluid dynamics, especially his discovery in 1738 of *Bernoulli's principle concerning the speed and pressure of fluid flow. He also attempted to explain the properties of gases at varying temperatures and pressures by regarding the gas as consisting of many tiny particles. His father **Jean Bernoulli** (1667–1748) and uncle **Jacques Bernoulli** (1654–1705) were both eminent mathematicians, who often worked together and jointly developed the calculus of variations. Jean also made discoveries in *probability theory and Jacques in *complex numbers. Daniel's brother **Nicolas Bernoulli** (1695–1726) also contributed to the theory of probability.

Bernoulli's principle The principle of conservation of energy applied to fluid flow. If the effects of friction are neglected the total energy of the flow at any point in a pipe is equal to the sum of the kinetic energy due to the flow velocity, the gravitational potential energy due to height, and the energy of pressure in the fluid itself. Bernoulli's theorem states that the sum of these three components is constant throughout a flow system. Named after Daniel *Bernoulli.

Bernstein, Eduard (1850–1932) German politician. A journalist, Bernstein joined the Socialist Democratic Party in 1872. In 1878 he was exiled from Germany on account of his political beliefs. He returned to Berlin in 1901, becoming the leader of the revisionist movement. He was elected to the Reichstag in 1902. As a protest against his party's support of World War I, he joined the Independent Social Democrats. His most important book, *Evolutionary Socialism* (1898), contains his criticisms of Marxist theory.

Bernstein, Leonard (1918–) US conductor, composer, and pianist. From 1958 to 1969 he was musical director and conductor of the New York Philharmonic Orchestra and became famous for his concerts and recordings. His compositions, including symphonies, choral works, and songs, often contain jazz and folk elements. His musicals, such as *On the Town* (1944) and *West Side Story* (1957), have been widely popular.

Berre, Étang de 43 27N 5 05E A saltwater lagoon in S France, in the Bouches-du-Rhône department. Connected by canal to the Mediterranean Sea (through the Rove tunnel) and the Gulf of Fos, it has important oil refineries and saltworks situated around its shores. Area: 155 sq km (60 sq mi).

Berruguete, Pedro (c. 1450–c. 1504) Castillian Renaissance painter. In the 1470s he worked in Italy at the court of Urbino, where he painted *Federigo da Montefeltro and his Son* (Urbino). On returning to Spain (1482), he painted frescoes for Toledo cathedral and altarpieces for the Dominican order, in Avila. His son **Alonso Berruguete** (c. 1489–1561) was a mannerist painter and sculptor, who worked in Italy (c. 1504–c. 1517) and became court painter to Emperor Charles V (1518). He combined his talents in his masterpiece the San Benito altar-

piece (now dismantled) in Valladolid.

berry Loosely, any small succulent *fruit. Botanically, a berry is a simple fruit with a thin skin and pulpy flesh containing many loose seeds: the tomato and grape are examples. Blackberries and raspberries are not strictly berries, but collections of small *drupes.

Berry A French province that was sold to the Crown by the Viscount of Bourges in 1101 and was absorbed by the departments of Cher and Indre in 1790.

Berry, Chuck (Charles Edward B.; 1926–) US singer and songwriter, who was one of the first musicians to popularize rock and roll. His songs, such as "Maybellene," "Johnny B. Goode," and "Roll Over, Beethoven" influenced the Beatles, the Rolling Stones, and others.

Berry, Jean de France, Duc de (1340–1416) The third son of John II of France, who was appointed (1358) governor of Auvergne, Languedoc, Périgord, and Poitou, where his repressive policies caused a peasants' revolt (1381–84). He was coregent during the minority (1380–88) of his nephew Charles VI.

Berry, Marie-Caroline de Bourbon-Sicile, Duchesse de (1798–1870) The wife of Charles, Duc de Berry (1778–1820), the son of Charles X of France. After Charles X's death, she conspired to obtain the French throne for her son Henri, Comte de Chambord (1820–83), instigating an unsuccessful revolt in the Vendée (1832).

Bersaglieri A corps of light infantry sharpshooters raised in 1836 by Charles Albert of Sardinia-Piedmont as part of his reorganization of the Sardinian army. They served with distinction in the Crimean War and in both World Wars.

berserkers (Old Norse: bear-shirts) In Scandinavian mythology, savage warriors whose frenzy in battle transformed them from men into wolves or bears and made them immune from being harmed by the sword or fire. In the frenzy of battle they would howl and foam at the mouth—hence the phrase "to go berserk." They were devotees of *Odin and, in early Scandinavian history, warriors called berserkers were often employed as bodyguards to nobles.

Berthelot, (Pierre Eugène) Marcelin (1827–1907) French chemist and politician, who became professor at the Collège de France (1865). A pioneer of organic chemical synthesis, he demolished the theory that organic compounds contained a "vital force." As a student of chemical thermodynamics he distinguished between endothermic and exothermic reactions, but wrongly concluded that the heat of a reaction was its driving force. He became a senator in 1881 and foreign secretary in 1895.

Berthollet, Claude Louis, Comte (1748–1822) French chemist and physician. He discovered potassium chlorate and introduced bleaching by chlorine; he also showed that ammonia consists of hydrogen and nitrogen. Berthollet helped to clarify the concept of chemical affinity and, working with *Lavoisier, developed a new chemical nomenclature. He travelled to Egypt as scientific adviser to Napoleon, who made him a senator and a count.

Bertillon, Alphonse (1853–1914) French criminal investigator, who developed a system for identifying criminals based on the description and measurement of physical characteristics. The system, also known as anthropometry, was eventually superseded by fingerprinting techniques. His brother **Jacques Bertillon** (1851–1922) was a statistician. As head of the Paris bureau of social statistics, he developed new systems of data analysis. He was particularly interested in the high incidence of alcoholism in France and the decline of the French population in comparison with rates in other countries.

Bertolucci, Bernardo (1940–) Italian film director. Many of his films are strongly influenced by Marxist ideology, notably *Before the Revolution* (1965) and the epic *1900* (1977). He achieved his greatest commercial success with the controversial *Last Tango in Paris* (1972).

Bertrand, Henri Gratien, Comte (1773-1844) French marshal, who in 1804 became an aide de camp to Napoleon, whose complete trust he won. He accompanied Napoleon into exile, both to Elba and St Helena, where he kept a diary that is an important historical source.

Bertran de Born (?1140-?1215) French knight and troubadour poet. He composed lyrics glorifying love, ambition, and especially war. His castle at Hautefort was besieged and captured by Richard Lionheart, whose loyal officer he became.

Berwick, James Fitzjames, Duke of (1670-1734) Marshal of France, who was the illegitimate son of James II of England. He was educated in France and gained military experience in Europe. On the deposition of James (1688), Berwick supported his attempts to regain the throne and played a prominent part in the battle of the *Boyne. His victory in the employ of France at Almansa (1707) established Philip V on the Spanish throne. He was killed besieging Philippsburg in the War of the Polish Succession.

Berwickshire A former county of SE Scotland. Under local government reorganization in 1975 its boundaries were adjusted to form a district of the same name, in the Borders Region.

Berwick-upon-Tweed 55 46N 2 00W A town in NE England, in Northumberland at the mouth of the River Tweed. A border town long disputed between England and Scotland, Berwick changed hands 14 times. Industries include engineering, fertilizers, food processing, and salmon fishing. Population (1981): 12 169.

beryl A mineral consisting of beryllium alumino-silicate, found principally in granites and granite pegmatites. It occurs as crystals up to one metre in length and is white, pale blue, or green. It is the chief source of beryllium. *Aquamarine and *emerald are gem varieties. *See* Plate III.

beryllium (Be) A light (relative density 2.34) alkaline-earth metal that was discovered in 1828 by F. Wöhler and A. Bussy (1794-1882) independently. Its salts are highly toxic and require careful handling. It occurs in nature in such minerals as *beryl and phenacite (Be_2SiO_4). It is transparent to X-rays and is used as windows on X-ray tubes. Alloys with copper are extensively used and the oxide (BeO), having a high melting point (2530°C), is used as a ceramic. At no 4; at wt 9.0122; mp 1278°C; bp 2450°C.

Berzelius, Jöns Jakob, Baron (1779-1848) Swedish chemist, whose main work was the discovery of atomic compositions of chemical compounds. He discovered the elements selenium (1817), silicon (1824), and thorium (1828) and determined the atomic and molecular weights of more than 2000 elements and compounds. He introduced the current notation for chemical formulae and the use of oxygen as a reference standard for atomic weights. Following the invention of electric cells, Berzelius experimented on electrolysis and developed a theory of electrostatic bonding in compounds. He published a standard textbook of chemistry in 1830.

Bes The Egyptian god of recreation, also associated with children and childbirth. Images of the god, represented as a grotesque dwarf with a tail, were kept in homes as protection against evil.

Besançon 47 14N 6 02E A town in E France, the capital of the Doubs department on the River Doubs. It has a cathedral (11th-13th centuries) and a university (1691). Victor Hugo was born here. It is the French watchmaking centre and produces cars and textiles. Population (1982 est): 119 687.

Besant, Annie (1847-1933) British theosophist and political campaigner. A friend of Charles *Bradlaugh, Annie Besant promoted the causes of atheism, birth control, and trades unionism until her conversion (1889) to theosophy by Madame *Blavatsky. In 1893, Mrs Besant went to India, where she founded a Hindu university and worked for Indian home rule.

Besant, Sir Walter (1836-1901) British novelist and social reformer. His best-known novels, *All Sorts and Conditions of Men* (1882) and *Children of Gibeon* (1886), describe life in the slums of E London, where (in 1887) he helped to found the People's Palace for popular recreation. He was a founder member of the Society of Authors (1884).

Bessarabia A region in the SW Soviet Union, largely in the Moldavian and Ukrainian SSRs and with a predominantly Moldavian population. Bessarabia is very fertile, the main crops being wine grapes, fruit, wheat, and tobacco; cattle and sheep are raised. The chief industry is agricultural processing. *History*: the region was colonized by the Greeks and later fell successively to the Romans, Huns, Magyars, Mongols, and Turks, passing to Russia in 1812. In 1918 Bessarabia declared its independence, later voting for union with Romania. In 1940 Romania ceded Bessarabia to the Soviet Union. Area: about 44 300 sq km (17 100 sq mi).

Bessarion, John (c. 1400-72) Greek scholar and cardinal. As Archbishop of Nicaea, he attempted to unite the Byzantine and Western Churches, eventually joining the latter and settling in Italy, where he became a cardinal in 1439. He was an outstanding scholar and exercised an important influence in introducing the study of Greek in the Renaissance. His large library of Greek manuscripts is preserved in Venice.

Bessemer, Sir Henry (1813-98) British engineer and inventor, who patented (1855) a process for manufacturing cheap steel (*see* Bessemer process). His Sheffield steelworks, built in 1859, are still producing steel. Bessemer was a prolific inventor, patenting some 114 inventions.

Bessemer process A steelmaking process invented by Sir Henry *Bessemer in 1855. A long cylindrical vessel (Bessemer converter) is charged with molten pig iron; air, introduced through holes in the bottom of the converter, is blown through the iron to oxidize the carbon, silicon, and manganese impurities. Phosphorus is removed by reaction with the converter's basic refractory lining. Carbon, in the form of spiegel, is then added to give steel of the required carbon content. In the modern VLN (very low nitrogen) process, a mixture of oxygen and steam is blown through the iron instead of air, to avoid absorption of nitrogen by the steel.

Best, Charles Herbert (1899-1978) US physiologist, who, as an undergraduate research assistant to *Banting, helped discover the technique for isolating the hormone insulin from pancreatic tissue in 1921. Best also discovered choline, a B vitamin. The Banting and Best department of medical research was created at Toronto University in 1923.

bestiary A medieval treatise containing short accounts of different species of animal, both real and imaginary. Based on ancient Greek and Latin sources, bestiaries were very popular and were often fancifully illustrated. They were generally wildly inaccurate in their natural history, as their compilers were more interested in the morals to be drawn from each beast's real or supposed attributes than in scientific fact.

Bestuzhev-Riumin, Aleksei Petrovich, Count (1693-1766) Russian statesman. Bestuzhev served as a diplomat abroad until 1740. In the reign of the empress *Elizabeth he directed foreign policy and was Russia's chancellor from 1744 to 1758. He allied Russia with Austria and Britain against France and Prussia, a policy made obsolete by the realignment of European alliances on the eve of the *Seven Years' War. He was dismissed in 1758 and banished to his estate.

Beta Centauri A remote yet conspicuous blue *giant star, apparent magnitude 0.63 and about 390 light years distant, that is the second brightest star in the constellation Centaurus.

beta decay   A radioactive process in which a neutron within a nucleus decays by the *weak interaction into a proton, an electron (beta particle), and an antineutrino; alternatively, a proton may decay into a neutron, a positron, and a neutrino. Since the nuclear charge changes by one in both cases, the nucleus is converted into the nucleus of another element.

betatron   A type of particle *accelerator used for producing very high energy electrons. The electrons are accelerated round a circular path in an evacuated torus-shaped chamber, by means of a large pulsed magnetic field. Electron energies up to 300 MeV have been produced.

betel   A mixture of the boiled dried seeds (**betel nuts**) of the areca, or betel palm (*Areca catechu*), and the leaves of the betel pepper (*Piper betle*), which produces copious salivation when chewed with lime–a practice common among the populations of S Asia and the East Indies. Betel nuts contain an alkaloid of some value in expelling intestinal worms, and the mild stimulation resulting from chewing the mixture has led to its use in some religious ceremonies.

Betelgeuse   An immense remote yet conspicuous red *supergiant, over 500 light years distant, that is the second brightest star in the constellation *Orion. It is a *variable star with its magnitude ranging, usually, from 0.3 to 0.9 over a period of about 5.8 years.

Bethany (present-day name: Al-'Ayzariyah)   31 46N 35 15E A village on the *West Bank of the River Jordan, near Jerusalem. It is now named after Lazarus, whom Christ resurrected here (John 11.1–44).

Bethe, Hans Albrecht   (1906–   ) US physicist, born in Germany. After studying under *Rutherford he returned to Germany but left when Hitler came to power. After two years in England he finally settled in the USA, working on the atom bomb during World War II. His earlier researches in quantum electrodynamics proved valuable in working out the details of the nuclear fusion process that occurs in stars. For this work he received the 1967 Nobel Prize.

Bethlehem   31 42N 35 12E A town on the *West Bank of the River Jordan, near Jerusalem. The Church of the Nativity was built in 326 over the grotto that is the presumed birthplace of Jesus Christ. A university was founded here in 1973. Population (1984): 20 000.

Bethlehem   40 36N 75 22W A city in the USA, in Pennsylvania. A major steel centre, it also has cement, textile, and electrical-equipment industries. Population (1980): 70 419.

Bethlen, Gábor   (1580–1629) Prince of Transylvania (1613–29), a Protestant, who opposed Emperor Ferdinand II during the Thirty Years' War. Bethlen, after seizing northern Hungary, was elected King in 1620 but renounced the Crown (1621) in exchange for Ferdinand's agreement to allow Hungarian Protestants to worship freely. Bethlen again took up arms against Ferdinand in 1623 and 1626 but then withdrew from the war.

Bethmann-Hollweg, Theobald von   (1856–1921) German statesman. As minister of the interior, secretary of state, and chancellor (1909–17) successively, he instituted a number of electoral and legal reforms. In 1914, attempting to justify aggressive German foreign policy, he described the treaty guaranteeing Belgian neutrality as a "scrap of paper." In 1917 his efforts to secure a negotiated peace led to his overthrow by *Ludendorff and *Hindenburg.

Béthune   50 32N 2 38E A town in France, in the Pas-de-Calais department. An important coalmining centre, it also produces beet sugar and textiles. Population (1982 est): 26 105.

Betjeman, Sir John   (1906–84) British poet. Educated at Marlborough and Oxford, he published his first book of poetry in 1933. His verse autobiography, *Summoned by Bells* (1960), reflected the nostalgia and gentle social satire characteristic of his other poems. He also revived and fostered interest in Victo-

rian and Edwardian architecture. He was poet laureate from 1972.

betony   A perennial herb, *Stachys officinalis* (or *Betonica officinalis*), up to 30 cm high. It has round-toothed leaves and a dense head of reddish-purple tubular flowers. Betony is found on open grassland, heaths, and hedgerows from Eurasia to N Africa. The leaves may be used for tea and for herbal tobacco. Family: *Labiatae*.

Betterton, Thomas   (?1635–1710) English actor. He acted in many Restoration and Shakespearian plays. He became a theatre manager and adapted several Elizabethan and Jacobean plays to suit contemporary taste.

Betti, Ugo   (1892–1953) Italian dramatist. He studied law and became a magistrate and, after 1944, librarian at the Ministry of Justice. The themes of many of his 26 plays, notably *Corruption in the Palace of Justice* (1944) and *The Fugitive* (1953), concern justice and social responsibility.

Betty Trask Award   An annual prize of £12,500 for authors under 35 awarded for a first novel "of a romantic or traditional, rather than experimental, nature." Set up in 1984 by a legacy of the writer Betty Trask and administered by the Society of Authors, it was at its inception Britain's largest literary prize.

Betws-y-Coed   53 05N 3 48W A village and resort in North Wales, in Gwynedd in Snowdonia at the confluence of the Rivers Llugwy and Conway. It is renowned for its scenery, especially its waterfalls. Population (1981): 658.

Beust, Friedrich Ferdinand, Count von   (1809–86) German statesman; the chief opponent of *Bismarck. As prime minister of Saxony (1853–66) he allied Saxony with Austria in the Austro-Prussian War of 1866. He became chancellor of the Austrian Empire in 1867 and negotiated the *Augsleich* that established the Dual Monarchy of *Austria-Hungary.

Bevan, Aneurin   (1897–1960) British Labour politician, A brilliant orator, Nye Bevan clashed with the Labour Party in 1939 over what he considered to be its ambivalence towards Hitler. He edited the socialist *Tribune* from 1940 to 1945. As minister of health (1945–51), he was the architect of the *National Health Service. He was also minister of labour in 1951. His wife **Jenny, Baroness Lee** (1904–   ), a Labour MP (1929–31, 1945–70), was minister for the arts (1967–70).

bevatron   A type of *synchrotron used for accelerating protons at Berkeley, California (USA). It can produce protons with energies up to 6 GeV.

Beveridge, William Henry Beveridge, 1st Baron   (1879–1963) British economist, writer, and academic. Beveridge joined the Board of Trade in 1908 and became an authority on unemployment. His best-known work was the *Report on Social Insurance and Allied Services* (1942), the so-called **Beveridge Report**, which created the welfare state.

Beverley   53 51N 0 26W A market town in NE England, in Humberside. Beverley Minster dates from the 13th century. The principal industries are tanning, car accessories, and industrial plastics. Population (1981): 16 433.

Beverly Hills   A city in the USA, in California. A residential suburb of Los Angeles, it is the home of many film and television celebrities. Population (1980): 32 367.

Bevin, Ernest   (1881–1951) British politician and trade-union leader. Bevin formed, and was general secretary (1921–40) of, the Transport and General Workers' Union and in 1937 became chairman of the TUC. In 1940 he became minister of labour, serving in Churchill's war cabinet. He was foreign secretary (1945–51) in the postwar Labour Government, when he helped to form NATO.

Bewick, Thomas   (1753–1828) British wood engraver, born near Newcastle upon Tyne, where he spent most of his life. Although trained under a local metal engraver, whose partner he later became, he specialized in *wood engraving, which he revived as an art form and raised to a new level of technical virtuosity.   He   was   an   amateur   naturalist   and   his

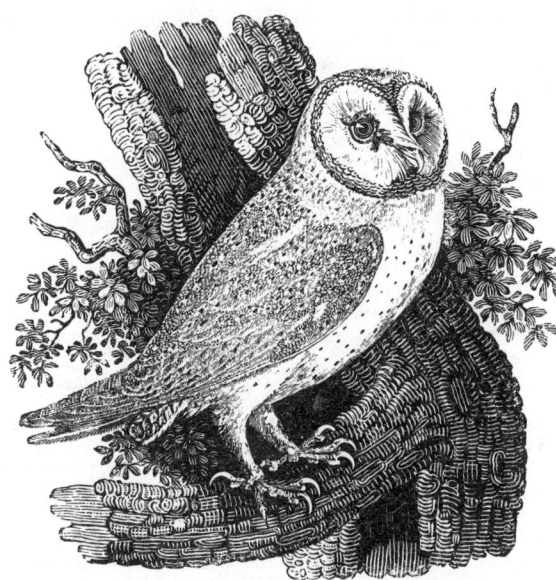

THOMAS BEWICK   *"The Yellow Owl", a wood engraving from his* History of British Birds, *1797-1804 (vol. 1, 1847 edit.).*

best works are his animal studies, particularly in *The History of British Birds* (*Land Birds*, 1797; *Water Birds*, 1804).

Bexhill-on-Sea   50 50N 0 29E A resort in SE England, on the East Sussex coast near Hastings. Population (1981): 35 529.

Bexley   A borough of SE Greater London, bordering on the River Thames in the N. Created in 1965 from part of Kent, it is an industrial as well as a residential area. Population (1981): 214 818.

Beza, Theodore   (1519–1605) French Calvinist theologian. Trained as a lawyer, he went to Geneva in 1548, having formally renounced the Roman Catholic faith. He became professor of Greek at Lausanne University and first rector of the Geneva Academy (1559), which Calvin had just founded for the education of Protestant theologians. He is remembered both as a Bible translator and a defender of Protestantism. After Calvin's death (1564) Beza succeeded to his leadership of the Swiss Calvinists.

Béziers   43 21N 3 13E A town in S France, in the Hérault department. In 1209 many of the inhabitants were massacred by Simon de Montfort during the crusade against the Albigenses. It is a commercial centre for wines and spirits and its manufactures include chemicals and textiles. Population (1982 est): 78 447.

bezique   A card game, usually for two players, that became popular in France about 1860. Two packs of 32 cards are used (standard packs with the cards from two to six removed). Each player is dealt eight cards; the next card indicates the trump suit and the rest from the stockpile. The object is to score points by collecting melds (certain combinations of cards) and to take tricks containing brisques (aces and tens). Play continues until one player's score reaches 1000 or 1500.

Bhagalpur   25 14N 86 59E A city in India, in Bihar. An agricultural trading centre, its manufactures include textiles (especially silk). Its university was established in 1960. Population (1981): 225 062.

Bhagavadgita   (Sanskrit: Song of the Lord)   Hindu poem probably composed about 300 BC, forming part of the epic *Mahabharata*. It blends and reconciles a number of Hindu philosophies. Arjuna, one of the five Pandava brothers, is compelled to battle with his kinsmen, the Kauravas; he is persuaded

by *Krishna, acting as his charioteer, of the virtue of selflessly performing the duties of caste. Krishna enumerates the ways by which one can attain liberation from the limitations of matter: by virtuous actions, by devotion to God, by philosophical speculation, by asceticism, or by meditation.

Bhamo   24 15N 97 15E A town in Burma, on the Irrawaddy River near the border with China. Principally a trading centre, it has a government sugar factory.

Bharat.   *See* India, Republic of.

Bharhut   A Buddhist stupa (shrine) complex in Nagod state (N India), excavated in 1874. It provided evidence for the earliest phases of Buddhist architecture; carvings on the stone railings are the earliest representational reliefs from India (2nd century BC). Nothing now remains at the site.

Bhatpara   22 51N 88 31E A city in India, in West Bengal. It is an ancient seat of Sanskrit learning. Jute processing is the principal industry. Population (1981): 260 761.

Bhavachakra   (Sanskrit: wheel of becoming)   In Buddhism, an image of the cyclical nature of earthly existence, in the form of a wheel held by the demon of impermanence. Its segments represent the six possible states into which beings are reborn: the realms of gods, titans, hungry ghosts, humans, animals, and demons. At the centre, turning the wheel, are greed, hatred, and delusion, depicted as a cockerel, snake, and pig, biting each other's tails. Around the rim, the 12 stages in the cycle of life are symbolically expressed.

Bhavnagar   21 59N 72 19E A port in India, in Gujarat on the Gulf of Cambay. An important industrial and commercial centre, its manufactures include textiles, bricks, and tiles. Population (1981): 308 000.

Bhopal   23 17N 77 28E A city in India, the capital of Madhya Pradesh. Notable buildings include the unfinished Taj-ul-Masjid, the largest mosque in India. Its university was established in 1970. Bhopal's varied manufactures include vehicle parts and cotton textiles. In 1984 over 2000 people died after poisonous isocyanate gas escaped from the US-owned Union Carbide factory in the city. Population (1981): 672 000.

Bhoskhara II   (1114–c. 1185) Indian mathematician, who was the first to use the decimal system in a written work, invented the + and – convention, and used letters to represent unknown quantities as in modern algebra.

Bhubaneswar   20 13N 85 50E A city in India, the capital of Orissa. An ancient city dating back to 500 AD, it is famous for its many temples. Utkal University (founded in 1943) was moved here in 1962. Population (1981): 219 211.

Bhutan, Kingdom of   (Bhutanese name: Druk-yul)   A small country in the E Himalayas, strategically positioned between India and Tibet. It is entirely mountainous, rising over 7300 m (21 900 ft) in the N. Over half the population are of Tibetan origin, known as Bhutias, with minorities of Nepalese in the S and Indians in the E. *Economy*: mainly agricultural; forests cover almost 70% of the land and there are plans for further planting. As well as traditional industries, such as bamboo and lacquer woodwork, other small industries are being encouraged and hydroelectricity is being developed. A new postal system was inaugurated in 1972 and since then postage stamps have been a valuable source of foreign currency, together with tourism, which has only recently been developed. *History*: although the early history of Bhutan is obscure it does appear to have existed as a political entity for many centuries. In 1865 part of S Bhutan was annexed by the British, following various border disputes, and a treaty was concluded in which Britain agreed to pay an annual subsidy. By a further treaty in 1910 Britain agreed not to interfere in Bhutan's internal affairs and in 1949 this was replaced by a similar treaty concluded with India. In 1910 Sir Ugyen Wangchuk was elected the first hereditary maharaja (now referred to as king). In 1969 the absolute monarchy was replaced by a "democratic monarchy" and power is now divided between the king, the Council of Ministers, the National Assembly, and the monastic head of Bhutan's lamas. Head of state: King Jigme Singye Wangchuk (1955-). Official language: Dzongkha Bhutanese. Official currency: ngultrum of 100 chetrums. Area: 46 600 sq km (18 000 sq mi). Population (1981 est): 1 300 000. Capital: Thimphu.

Bhutto, Zulfikar Ali (1928-79) Pakistani statesman; president (1971-73) and then prime minister (1973-77). He formed the Pakistan People's Party in 1967 and became president after the secession of East Pakistan (Bangladesh). Ousted by a military coup, he was defeated in the subsequent election and executed (1979) for conspiring to murder an opponent. His daughter **Benazir Bhutto** (1953-) is acting president of her father's party.

Biafra The Ibo secessionist eastern region of the Federal Republic of Nigeria (1967-70). In an attempt to protect the interests of the *Ibo people against the dominant *Hausa, a unilateral declaration of independence was made under the leadership of Lieut Col Odumegwu Ojukwu (1933-). The federal government under Gen *Gowon refused to recognize the new state and took up arms against it. The decimated Ibo surrendered on 15 January, 1970.

Biafra, Bight of. *See* Bonny, Bight of.

Bialik, Chaim Nachman (1873-1934) Jewish poet and translator, born in the Ukraine. The success of his major poem *The Talmud Student* (1894) established his reputation as the leading Hebrew poet of his time. His poetry is often lyrical and visionary but also condemns Jewish passivity in the face of oppression. He left the Soviet Union in 1921 and settled in Palestine in 1924.

Białystok 53 09N 23 10E A city in NE Poland. It grew mainly under the Branicki family in the 18th century. In World War II the Germans killed half the population and destroyed the industry but cloth manufacture has been revived. Population (1981): 230 000.

Biarritz 43 29N 1 33W A town in SW France, in the Pyrénées-Atlantiques department on the Bay of Biscay. It became a fashionable resort under the patronage of the Empress Eugénie in the mid-19th century. Population (1982 est): 26 647.

biathlon **1.** An athletic event consisting of combined shooting and cross-country *skiing, first included in the Winter Olympic Games in 1960; competitors ski 20 km (12.5 mi) with rifles and ammunition and at each of four points along the course take five shots at 150 m (164 yd). **2.** An athletic event consisting of running 4000 m (2.5 mi) and swimming 300 m (328 yd), introduced in 1968 by the Modern Pentathlon Association of Great Britain as a preparation for the full modern *pentathlon.

Bible (Greek *biblia*, books) The collected books of the *Old Testament, the *New Testament, and the *Apocrypha. *Canon*: the canon of the Hebrew Old Testament was definitively established by the rabbinical council of Jamnia (90-100 AD), although most of the books had acquired authority much earlier. The council rejected a number of books that formed part of the Greek version of the Old Testament, the *Septuagint, and these constitute most of the Apocrypha, accepted in varying degrees as sacred scripture by some Christian Churches and rejected by others. The New Testament canon was also established gradually but had essentially its present form by the 3rd century AD. To Christians it represented the complete fulfilment of the prophecies of the Old Testament. *Divine inspiration and biblical criticism*: both Jews and Christians originally regarded their scriptures as divinely inspired, hence correct in every particular. Although Roman Catholics and Protestants differed as to whether the Bible was the sole source of revealed truth, all Christians agreed, until relatively recently, on the literal truth of the contents, a belief slowly eroded by the development of science from the 17th century

onwards. Despite the attempts to condemn scientific findings when these appeared to conflict with scripture, as in the case of *Galileo, scientific method was soon applied to the study of the Bible itself and the procedures of historical scholarship, textual criticism, archaeology, etc., were brought to bear on all aspects of the text. *Texts*: the oldest extant complete manuscript of the Old Testament dates from the 11th century AD, but there are much earlier versions of parts of the text, for example the Pentateuch (*see also* Dead Sea Scrolls). The fact that there is almost no variation among the many manuscripts of the Old Testament attests to the care with which the Jewish scribes, known as the Masoretes, preserved the text from the 6th century AD onwards. The earliest fragments of the New Testament date from the 2nd century AD; thereafter there are an extremely large number of manuscripts of quite early date. *Translations*: the first translation of the Bible is the Latin *Vulgate of St Jerome. In England translations were made in Old English and Norman French. Major English versions are: the version prefaced by *Wycliffe (1382-88), the last manuscript Bible written before the introduction of printing; the New Testament (1525) and other sections by *Tyndale; the Bible of Miles *Coverdale; the Great Bible (1539), supervised by Coverdale under the patronage of Thomas Cromwell; the *Geneva (*or* Breeches) Bible; the Bishops' Bible (1568); the *Douai Bible; the *King James (*or* Authorized) Version; the *Revised Version* (1881-95); the *Revised Standard Version* (1946-57), a modernization of the King James Version; and *The New English Bible* (1961-70).

Bible Societies Various Protestant organizations formed to promote and distribute Bibles to all peoples. One of the first societies, the Society for Promoting Christian Knowledge, was founded in England in 1698. The large interdenominational British and Foreign Bible Society was founded in 1804. The American Bible Society distributes several million Bibles annually. In 1946 some 20 international societies combined to form the United Bible Societies.

Bibliothèque Nationale The national *library of France in Paris, containing around seven million volumes. It is based on the royal libraries of Charles the Wise (1364-80) and his successors, notably those of Louis XI, Charles VIII, and Francis I. From 1537 it received a copy of every book published in France. It was given its present name in 1795.

bicycles Light two-wheeled vehicles, the wheels of which are moved by cranks attached to pedals operated by the rider. Bicycles developed in the 19th century from a two-wheeled hobby-horse type of conveyance known as the dandy-horse or celeripede. Around 1840 a Scotsman, Kirkpatrick Macmillan, applied the dandy-horse principle to models with pedals. The first true bicycles, with rotary cranks on their front wheels, went into production in Paris in 1865. Known as velocipedes, these heavy-framed wooden-wheeled devices were nicknamed "boneshakers," but nevertheless popularized cycling as a pastime. To increase efficiency the front wheel was gradually made larger, resulting in the 20-year vogue of the ordinary (*or* pennyfarthing) bicycle. This was superseded by the so-called safety bicycle, which had a chain and sprocket drive to the rear wheel and was essentially the same as the modern bicycle. Invented by 1876, it went into production in 1885. Pneumatic rubber tyres (1889), a freewheeling mechanism (1894), and variable gears (1899) were later refinements.

An inexpensive means of transport and recreation, bicycles have enjoyed a revival in developed countries since the fuel crises of the 1970s. Cycling is also a form of competitive sport. Racing first became popular in France, where the earliest race was held (1868) and now has a wide following throughout Europe (*see* Tour de France). Road races take place on public roads, sometimes through normal traffic, using lightweight bicycles with sophisticated gears. Track races are run on special steeply banked tracks and cyclo-cross races are held across country.

Bidault, Georges (1899–1983) French statesman; prime minister (1946, 1949–50). A leader of the French resistance during World War II, Bidault served as president of the Resistance Council in 1944 and foreign minister and president in de Gaulle's first (provisional) government. He broke with the Gaullists over their policy towards Algerian independence, becoming head of the Organisation de l'Armée secrète, and from 1962 to 1968 lived in exile.

Biddle, John (1615–62) English religious leader, founder of Unitarianism (*see* Unitarians). While a schoolmaster he wrote his *Twelve Arguments* against the deity of the Holy Ghost, for which he was imprisoned in 1645. Although his adherents began to meet openly from 1652, he was arrested and banished under Cromwell and finally died in prison in London.

Bideford 51 01N 4 13W A town in SW England, in N Devon on the Torridge estuary. Once a busy port (used by *Drake, *Raleigh, and *Grenville), it is now mainly a resort and market town. Population (1981): 12 211.

Biedermeier style A style of furniture and painting that flourished under bourgeois patronage in Austria, Germany, and Scandinavia from about 1816 to about 1848. It was satirically named after the fictional character Gottlieb Biedermeier, who was created by the poet Ludwig Eichrocht (1827–92) to characterize bourgeois bad taste. Biedermeier furniture, which was the first to be mass produced, utilized French *Empire style design for modern functional purposes. Biedermeier paintings aimed at extreme naturalism in outdoor scenes and intimacy in interiors and portraits.

Biel (French name: Bienne) 47 09N 7 16E A town in NW Switzerland, on Lake Biel. It is the only official bilingual Swiss town (French and German). A watchmaking centre, it also manufactures machinery. Population (1980 est): 53 793.

Biela's comet A comet, period 6.6 years, that was discovered in 1826 and was observed on its 1846 return to split in two. Although seen in 1852 the portions subsequently disintegrated. The resulting stream of meteoroids (*see* meteor) produced spectacular meteor storms in November, 1872 and 1885. It was named after the Austrian astronomer Wilhelm von Biela (1782–1856).

Bielefeld 52 02N 8 32E A city in N West Germany, in North Rhine-Westphalia. Its linen mills were the first in Germany to be mechanized (1851). Silks, clothing, and machinery are also manufactured here. Population (1985): 306 000.

Bielsko-Biała 49 50N 19 00E A town in S Poland. It was formed in 1951 from two separate towns on the River Biała. It has an important textile industry. Population (1981 est): 170 000.

Bien Hoa 10 58N 106 50E An ancient city in S Vietnam, on the River Dong Nai. Known for its pottery, it also has paper, steel, and chemical industries, supplied by hydroelectric power. Population (1979): 190 086.

Bienne. *See* Biel.

Bierce, Ambrose Gwinnett (1842–?1914) US writer. After service in the Civil War, he became a journalist in California and London (1872–75). His story collections, *In the Midst of Life* (1891) and *Can Such Things Be?* (1893), and *The Devil's Dictionary* (1906), reflect his preoccupation with death and its aftermath. He disappeared in Mexico during *Villa's revolt.

bigamy The offence of marrying a person while being married to another. Defences to a charge of bigamy include an honest and reasonable belief in the death of the original marriage partner, especially if absent for seven years or more, and an honest and reasonable belief that the first marriage was invalid or has been dissolved. Although a person would not be guilty of bigamy if he can prove these defences, the second marriage will still be invalid in such cases.

big-bang theory A cosmological theory (*see* cosmology),

first proposed in the 1920s, that all the matter and radiation in the universe originated in an immense explosion that began the expansion of the universe, which still continues. The explosion occurred about 10 to 20 thousand million years ago. As the initially high temperature of the early constituents decreased, hydrogen and helium were able to form: the observed cosmic abundance of helium agrees very well with the predicted value. This matter eventually interacted to form galaxies. The theory also predicts that the radiation formed shortly after the explosion should by now have cooled to about three kelvin. This is indeed the temperature of the isotropic microwave background radiation, detected in 1965 and now considered strong evidence for the big-bang theory.

Big Ben The 14-ton bell in the clock tower of the *Palace of Westminster (London), named after Sir Benjamin Hall (1802–67), commissioner of works when the clock was installed (1859). The sound of Big Ben striking the hour, first broadcast in 1923, has become a British national institution. Both the clock and the tower itself are also known by this name.

bighorn A mountain sheep, *Ovis canadensis*, of North America. There is considerable variation within the species, ranging from the small Nelson's bighorn to the largest Rocky Mountain bighorns, which stand 100 cm at the shoulder. Bighorns have transversely ribbed horns that grow in a spiral up to 100 cm long.

Bihar A state in N India, bordering on Nepal. The densely populated rural Ganges plain in the N produces rice, other grains, sugar cane, pulses, and vegetables. The S Chota Nagpur plateau yields minerals, including much of the world's mica, and supports iron and steel and engineering works. *History*: the centre of N Indian civilization from 1500 BC, Bihar was part of numerous empires and witnessed the early development of Buddhism and Jainism. It was a centre of 19th-century Indian nationalism. Area: 173 876 sq km (67 116 sq mi). Population (1981): 69 823 154. Capital: Patna.

Bihari An Indo-Aryan language spoken in Bihar (India) and in Nepal by about 40 million people. It is related to *Bengali and less closely to *Hindi. There are three main dialects; only one, Maithili, has any significant literature.

Bijapur 16 52N 75 47E A city in India, in Karnataka. The ancient capital of a powerful Islamic kingdom (1489–1686), it has many fine Islamic buildings. Population (1981): 147 313.

Bikaner 28 01N 73 22E A city in India, in Rajasthan. The former centre of a princely state, its fort (1571–1611) houses a fine collection of Sanskrit and Persian manuscripts. Bikaner is famous for the manufacture of carpets, shawls, and blankets. Population (1981): 280 000.

Bikini Atoll 11 35N 165 20E An atoll in the central Pacific Ocean in the *Marshall Islands. It was the site of US atomic and hydrogen bomb tests (some underwater) from 1946 to 1958.

Biko, Steven. *See* Black Consciousness.

Bilbao 43 15N 2 56W A port in N Spain, the largest city in the Basque Provinces on the River Nervión. One of Spain's chief ports, its exports include iron ore, lead, and wine. Metallurgical industries are especially important; others include chemicals, fishing, and shipbuilding. Its university was founded in 1968. Population (1981): 433 030.

bilberry A deciduous shrub, *Vaccinium myrtillus*, 30–60 cm high, also known as blaeberry, huckleberry, and whortleberry. It is found on acid moors and mountains in N Europe and N Asia. The green angular stems bear small pointed leaves that turn red in autumn. The globular pink flowers, which droop like tiny bells, develop into blue berries. These may be eaten raw or cooked, used in preserves, or used to make wine and spirits. Family: *Ericaceae* (heath family).

Bilderdijk, Willem (1756–1831) Dutch poet and dramatist.

He was a precursor of Romanticism in Dutch literature. Of his many poetic works, the most memorable is an unfinished epic poem on biblical themes entitled *De ondergang der eerste wareld* (*The Destruction of the First World*; 1810).

bile A yellow, green, or brown alkaline fluid secreted by the liver and stored in the *gall bladder. Contraction of the gall bladder, which is triggered by a hormone that is released from the duodenum in the presence of food, causes the bile to be expelled through the common bile duct into the intestine. Bile is composed of a mixture of bile salts (which emulsifies fatty foods for digestion) and bilirubin (a breakdown product of the blood pigment *haemoglobin).

bilharziasis. *See* schistosomiasis.

bill, parliamentary. *See* parliament.

billiards A game for two players or pairs of players, using cues and balls on a table. There are various forms but in **English billiards** the table measures 12×6 ft (3.6×1.8 m) and has six pockets (holes round the edges of the table); points are scored using three balls 2 in (5.2 cm) in diameter, which are white, white with a spot, and red. The white and the white-with-a-spot balls are cue balls, one for each player. A cannon, in which the cue ball strikes both the other balls, scores two points; a winning hazard, in which the cue ball pockets another ball, scores two points (white) or three (red); a losing hazard, in which the cue ball is pocketed after striking another ball, scores two points (off white) or three (off red). A turn (*or* break) lasts until the player fails to score. **Carom billiards** is played on a smaller table with no pockets and scoring is by cannons (*or* caroms). **Bar billiards** is played on a small table with a timing device and holes in the surface, into which balls are potted off each other until the time runs out. *See also* pool; snooker.

Billingsgate The oldest market in London. It was originally situated on the N bank of the River Thames by London Bridge but in 1982 was moved to its present location on the Isle of Dogs. A fish market since the 16th century, royal tolls were collected at the spot from the 10th century. The market porters are known for their heavy leather hats on which they balance boxes of fish.

Billiton. *See* Belitung.

bill of exchange (*or* monetary draft) A written order signed by one person (drawer) requiring a second person (drawee) to pay on demand or at a stated date an amount of money to, or to the order of, a specified person or the bearer (payee). A cheque is a bill of exchange payable on demand and drawn on a banker. Bills of exchange are used in foreign trade and can be discounted (sold for cash before their maturity date at less than their face value) with an *acceptance house, bank, etc.

Bill of Rights **1.** An act of parliament that incorporated the Declaration of Rights, the conditions on which the English throne was offered to William and Mary in 1689 (*see* Glorious Revolution). It curtailed the royal prerogative to ensure that the monarch ruled according to law. MPs were to be freely elected and guaranteed freedom of speech. Roman Catholics were barred from the throne. **2.** (1791) The first ten amendments to the US Constitution, described by Jefferson as "what the people are entitled to against every government on earth." They are (1) freedom of press, speech, and religion; (2) the right to bear arms; (3) prohibition of quartering of troops; (4) protection against unlawful search and seizure; (5) the right of due process of law; (6) the right to a fair and public trial; (7) the right to a trial by jury; (8) prohibition of cruel punishments; (9) protection of nonenumerated rights; and (10) reservation of powers, i.e. powers not reserved for the federal government reside in the states.

Billroth, Christian Albert Theodor (1829–94) Prussian-born surgeon. At Vienna University from 1867, he pioneered —with the aid of antiseptic techniques— several important operations on the stomach and intestine.

bimetallism A monetary system in which currency was convertible into either of two metals (usually gold and silver) in a fixed ratio. Widely adopted in the early 19th century, it proved unstable, as one metal was always undervalued and one overvalued. *Compare* gold standard.

binary star Two stars moving around each other under mutual gravitational attraction. Possibly 50% of stars are members of binary or other multiple systems. The components of a **visual binary** can be distinguished by telescope whereas a **spectroscopic binary** can only be detected by spectroscope measurements, the components usually being very close. In an **eclipsing binary** the orbital plane is so orientated that one component passes alternately in front of and then behind the other, causing the combined brightness to fluctuate. In a **close binary** the two components are close enough to exchange gaseous matter and can even share gas. This greatly affects their evolution and can lead to violent phenomena, such as *nova explosions or intense X-ray emission, if one component is a *white dwarf, a *neutron star, or a *black hole.

binary system A number system that uses only two digits 0 and 1. Numbers are expressed in powers of 2 instead of powers of 10, as in the decimal system. In binary notation, 2 is written as 10, 3 as 11, 4 as 100, 5 as 101, and so on. *Computers calculate in binary notation, the two digits corresponding to two switching positions (e.g. on or off) in the individual electronic devices in the logic circuits.

binding energy The energy released when protons and neutrons bind together to form an atomic nucleus. The mass of a nucleus is always less than the sum of the masses of the constituent protons and neutrons. The missing mass is converted into the binding energy according to *Einstein's law $E = mc^2$.

bindweed A widely distributed climbing plant of the temperate and subtropical genera *Convolvulus* and *Calystegia*. Bindweeds twine their stems around other plants for support and can be persistent weeds. The leaves are large and arrow-shaped and the conspicuous white, pink, or yellow flowers are funnel-shaped. Family: *Convolvulaceae*.

Black bindweed and copse bindweed (genus *Bilderdykia*; 3 species) lack the conspicuous flowers of the other bindweeds. Family: *Polygonaceae* (dock family).

Binet, Alfred (1857–1911) French psychologist, who pioneered the principles used in intelligence tests. Binet observed how his two young daughters responded to his tests using simple objects and pictures to assess their character and intelligence (*Experimental Study of Intelligence*, 1903). He later applied his techniques to measure the educational achievements of schoolchildren.

Bing, Sir Rudolf (1902–) British opera administrator, born in Austria. General manager of the Glyndebourne Festival Opera (1934–39; 1946–49), he helped found the Edinburgh Festival and was its artistic manager (1947–49). He managed the Metropolitan Opera, New York, from 1950 until 1972.

Bingen 49 58N 7 55E A town in W West Germany, in Rhineland-Palatinate at the confluence of the Rivers Rhine and Nahe. According to legend Archbishop Hatto II was devoured (c. 970) by mice on a nearby rock in the Rhine for maltreating his subjects. It is a centre of the wine and tourist trades. Population (1983): 23 110.

bingo (former names: tombola; housy-housy) A gambling game that developed in the 1880s from the children's game of lotto. Each player buys a card containing lines of random numbers (from 1 to 75 in the USA and usually from 1 to 90 in the UK). As numbers are called out, the players cover corresponding squares on their cards with counters; the first person to complete a line or the card wins. The stake money is pooled. It has been particularly popular in the UK following a relaxation of the gaming laws during the 1960s, many local cinemas having been converted into bingo halls.

binoculars A portable optical instrument used for magnifying distant objects. It consists of two telescopes fixed side by side, one for each eye, inside which there are a number of lenses for magnifying and focusing the image and usually prisms for altering the direction of the light and thus increasing the effective length of the telescope.

binomial nomenclature A system devised by *Linnaeus in the 18th century for the scientific naming of plants and animals, each species being identified by two internationally recognized Latin names—the name of the genus (written with an initial capital letter) followed by the name of the species. The names are usually written in italics and the specific name may be followed by the author's name, usually abbreviated. Thus the wolf is *Canis lupus* L (for Linnaeus).

binomial theorem The theorem, discovered by *Newton in 1676, that the quantity $(a + n)^n$, where n is an integer, can be expanded in a series: $(a + b)^n = a^n + na^{n-1}b + [n(n-1) a^{n-2}b^2] / 2! + [n(n-1)(n-2) a^{n-3}b^3] / 3! + \ldots + b^n$ where, for example, 3! (called factorial three) is $3 \times 2 \times 1$.

binturong A mammal, *Arctictis binturong*, of SE Asia, closely related to the *palm civets. It has a dark-grey shaggy coat, tufted ears, short legs, and a bushy prehensile tail (60 cm long). the animal measures up to 1.5 m long from head to tail. Binturongs live in trees and feed mainly on fruit and other vegetation; they are more vocal than civets, often growling or hissing.

Binyon, Laurence (1869–1943) British poet, also known for his influential studies of Far Eastern art, as Keeper of the Department of Oriental Prints and Drawings in the British Museum (1913–32). Among his more memorable works are the World War I elegy, "For the Fallen" (1914), and a translation of Dante's *Divine Comedy* (1933–43).

bioassay A test of the strength or quantity of a biologically active substance by a comparison of its effect upon animals, isolated tissues, or microorganisms with that of a standard preparation.

Bío-Bío, River A river in Chile. Rising in the Andes, it flows generally NW to enter the Pacific Ocean and forms the S boundary of middle Chile. Length: about 390 km (240 mi).

biochemistry The scientific study of the chemical composition and reactions of living organisms. Development of the appropriate analytical techniques has enabled great advances in modern biochemistry, which dates from the 1900s. Central to biochemistry is *metabolism and the determination of the complex sequence of reactions involved in the digestion of food, the utilization of energy, the manufacture of new tissues, the breakdown of old tissues, and the formation of excretory products. Biochemists are also concerned with the role of *genes, *hormones, and *enzymes in initiating and controlling metabolic reactions. This understanding is necessary to determine the requirements of a balanced diet as well as the causes and possible treatment of many diseases.

biodegradable substances Materials that can be broken down by biological processes—such as decomposition by fungi and bacteria—and can therefore be reused by living organisms (*see* recycling). Substances that are **nonbiodegradable**, such as plastics, can persist in the environment, causing pollution.

bioengineering (*or* biomechanics) The application of biological and engineering principles to the design and manufacture of equipment for use in conjunction with biological systems. Examples include artificial limbs, heart pacemakers, heart-lung machines, life-support systems for astronauts, etc.

biogas. *See* alternative energy.

biogenetic law (*or* recapitulation theory) A theory postulated by Ernst *Haeckel in 1866 stating that the development of an animal in its lifetime (*see* ontogeny) tends to recapitulate the evolutionary development of its ancestors (*see* phylogeny).

Bioko. *See* Equatorial Guinea.

biological control The control of pests by the use of living organisms. The controlling agent is usually a predator, parasite, or disease of the pest organism. For example, the virus disease myxomatosis was introduced to Australia and Britain to control the rabbit population. Recent methods of controlling insect

pests include the release of sterile males to mate among the population, so reducing the numbers of eggs laid. Biological control avoids the indiscriminate action and environmental pollution of chemical pesticides.

biological sciences The scientific disciplines concerned with the study of life. The earliest recorded biological observations come from ancient Egypt but it was Greek and Roman scholars, such as *Aristotle, *Hippocrates, and *Galen, who made the first detailed anatomical descriptions of living things. Not until the 16th and 17th centuries were further advances made by such anatomists as *Vesalius and William *Harvey. The introduction of the microscope in the 17th century enabled microorganisms, tissues, and individual cells (*see* cytology) to be observed for the first time.

By the 18th century a wealth of descriptions of individual organisms had been produced and attempts were made to arrange them into related groups (*see* taxonomy), notably by *Linnaeus, whose system is still in use today, and Georges *Cuvier, whose studies of fossilized animal remains founded the science of palaeontology. Various theories of *evolution culminated in the publication of Charles *Darwin's theory of the origin of species in 1858. Six years later, Gregor *Mendel reported his findings on the principles of inheritance, which are fundamental to *genetics, although it was not until 1953 that James *Watson and Francis *Crick determined the molecular structure of *DNA—the genetic material.

During the 20th century progress in *biochemistry, *physiology, *cell biology, and *biophysics has been made possible by innovations in microscopical and analytical techniques, such as electron microscopy, chromatography, and the use of *radioactive tracers. Biological discoveries have revolutionized both medicine and agriculture. *See also* botany; ecology; ethology; zoology.

biological warfare The use of disease-causing microorganisms as weapons. In World War I, the Germans infected Allied cavalry horses with bacteria causing *glanders. Although biological warfare is now officially banned by the major powers, research continues in developing new strains of such organisms as the plague bacterium (*Pasteurella pestis*) and the smallpox virus. The organisms are required to be highly virulent (but not necessarily lethal) and would be deployed probably in an aerosol package dropped by bombers or delivered in the warhead of a missile. Alternatively,

BIOLOGICAL WARFARE *Nuclear, bacteriological, and chemical warfare suits (NBC suits) as issued to the military.*

they could be added to water or food supplies in a covert operation.

bioluminescence The production of light by living organisms, including certain bacteria, fungi, and various animals (e.g. fireflies and glowworms, protozoans, and bony fishes). In some the *luminescence is due to symbiotic light-producing bacteria. The light is emitted by the compound luciferin when it is oxidized: the reaction is catalysed by an enzyme, luciferase. The emission of light may be continuous, as in bacteria, or intermittent, as in the flash of fireflies. The significance of bioluminescence is unknown in most species, but in some it attracts mates or lures prey.

biomass The total weight (mass) of all living organisms (or of all members of a particular species) found in a given area. Biomass is expressed as mass per unit area.

biomass energy. *See* alternative energy.

biome A geographical region that is characterized by a predominant type of vegetation and associated fauna. Examples include grassland, desert, tropical forest, etc.

bionics The study of living systems in order to design manmade systems based on similar principles. It assumes that most living creatures have adapted in the best possible way to their environments. The applications of bionics include the design of a ship's propellor modelled on a fish's tail and the use of knowledge of nerve physiology in data-processing systems.

bionomics. *See* ecology.

biophysics The scientific discipline concerned with the explanation of biological phenomena in terms of the laws of physics. Biophysics emerged in the 1940s with the work of such scientists as Max *Perutz and John *Kendrew, who applied the phenomenon of *X-ray diffraction to determine the structure of biological molecules; this was followed by Maurice *Wilkins' work on DNA. More recent topics include the nature of the nervous impulse, the properties of biological membranes, the mechanism of muscle contraction, and the operation of sense organs, showing how aspects of chemistry, physiology, and other biological disciplines are necessarily involved in biophysics.

biopsy The removal of a sample of living tissue from the body for microscopic examination. Biopsies are used to assist in the diagnosis of diseases, including cancer (from biopsies of tumours), jaundice (from a liver biopsy), and anaemia (from a bone-marrow biopsy).

biosphere The zone of the earth and its atmosphere that is occupied by living organisms. The most heavily populated regions of the biosphere are the surfaces of land and sea.

biotechnology Technology based on biological processes. This traditionally includes such processes as the manufacture of beer, cheese, yogurt, etc., involving fermentation, and the production of antibiotics from moulds. Since the advent of *genetic engineering, which enables the isolation of a desired gene sequence and the large-scale growth of its product, the scope of biotechnology has widened to include the manufacture of hormones (e.g. insulin), vaccines, *monoclonal antibodies, and other medically useful products.

biotin. *See* vitamin B complex.

birch A deciduous tree or shrub of the genus *Betula* (40 species), of the N hemisphere. Birches grow to a height of up to 25 m and have thin smooth bark, pale grey or yellowish-white, that peels off in strips. The glossy leaves are usually triangular, with toothed edges. The flowers are male and female catkins producing tiny winged nuts. Birch wood, especially that of the Eurasian silver birch (*B. pendula*), is used for turned articles. Birch bark is used for tanning and roofing, and the bark of the paper birch (*B. papyrifera*) was used by American Indians to make birch-bark canoes. Family: *Betulaceae*.

bird A warm-blooded animal belonging to the class *Aves* (about 8600 species), adapted for flight by having fore limbs modified as wings and a body covering of *feathers. Other adaptations include a light skeleton with hollow bones and a large keel-shaped breastbone providing attachment for the powerful flight muscles. The jaws are elongated into a horny bill (teeth are absent or reduced). Birds have good eyesight and colour vision and most are active by day. Through flight, they have managed to colonize almost every available terrestrial, freshwater, and marine habitat.

Social behaviour plays an important part in the life of birds, which show complex patterns of behaviour in territorial and courtship displays, *nest building, egg incubation, and care of the young. Many communicate by means of song (*see* songbird) and some undergo long seasonal *migrations.

Birds are of great economic importance to man. The eggs and flesh of many provide food, several species being domesticated and bred for this purpose (*see* poultry), and wildfowl and game birds are hunted for sport. Other species are pests, damaging crops (particularly cereals) or fouling buildings in cities. Certain diseases, notably psittacosis, are transmitted to man by birds. Modern birds include both flying and flightless species (*see* ratite); they are grouped into 28 orders, the largest of which is the *Passeriformes* (*see* passerine bird). *See also* ornithology.

bird cherry A small tree, *Prunus padus*, of upland Europe, up to 15 m high with dark bark and pale-green oval leaves, finely serrated around the margins. The sweet-scented white flowers are grouped in loose clusters. The small black bitter-tasting fruits are fermented to make alcoholic drinks. Family: *Rosaceae*. *See also* cherry.

bird of paradise A bird, 30–65 cm long, belonging to a family (*Paradisaeidae*; 40 species) occurring in New Guinea and neighbouring islands. The male is usually brightly coloured, with long tail feathers and ornamental plumes, and performs an acrobatic display to attract the dull-coloured female. Their feathers are much prized and were formerly exported for use in ladies' hats. *See* Plate V.

bird-of-paradise flower A herbaceous perennial plant, *Strelitzia reginae*, native to South Africa and cultivated for ornament. The flower cluster, 20 cm long, is orange, scarlet, and blue and resembles a bird's head. The oblong leaves rise to a height of 90 cm from the rootstock. Family: *Musaceae* (banana family).

bird of prey A bird that hunts other animals for food, also called raptor. Birds of prey are divided into the nocturnal hunters, comprising the owls (order *Strigiformes*), and those that hunt by day, comprising the eagles, falcons, hawks, secretary bird, and the vultures (order *Falconiformes*). Live prey is normally taken but the vultures specialize in feeding on carrion. Birds of prey are characterized by their strong hooked bills for tearing flesh, clawed talons, and powerful flight with a high-speed dive onto prey.

bird's nest fern An Old World tropical *fern, *Asplenium nidus*, that has a dense rosette of leaves, 60–120 cm long, with a central hollow forming a nest in which humus collects. The roots branch into this to obtain water and nutrients. The plant is grown for ornament. Family: *Aspleniaceae*.

bird's nest orchid A widely distributed saprophytic *orchid, *Neottia nidus-avis*, most commonly growing in beech woodlands. Named from the dense round cluster of roots at the stem base, it reaches a height of 25–40 cm and produces spikes of brown flowers in early summer.

bird spider Any of the large *tarantula spiders that may catch and eat small birds.

Birdum 15 38S 133 12E A small town in Australia, in N Northern Territory. The last station on the North Australia Railway, it is the centre of a large cattle-raising region.

bireme. *See* ships.

Birendra Bir Bikram Shah Dev (1945–) King of Nepal (1972–), following the death of his father Mahendra, whose policies he undertook to follow. He married (1970) Aishwarya Rajya Laxmi Devi Rana.

Birkbeck, George (1776–1841) British educationalist. As professor of natural philosophy at the Andersonian Institute, Glasgow, Birkbeck lectured unpaid to working men. With Brougham, *Bentham, *Cobbett, and others, he founded the London Mechanics' Institute (1824). This became affiliated to London University and is now Birkbeck College.

Birkenhead 53 24N 3 02W A port in NW England, in Merseyside on the Wirral Peninsula, linked with Liverpool across the River Mersey by road and rail tunnels and ferry. An important industrial centre, it has shipbuilding, engineering, and flour-milling industries. Population (1981): 123 907.

Birkenhead, F(rederick) E(dwin) Smith, 1st Earl of (1872–1930) British Conservative politician. A barrister, Birkenhead entered parliament in 1906. As attorney general (1915–19) he was famous for his prosecution of Sir Roger *Casement and while lord chancellor (1919–22) he introduced major land-law reforms. He was secretary for India (1924–28).

Birkhoff, George David (1864–1944) US mathematician, who gave the Maxwell-Boltzmann theory of gases a rigorous mathematical basis. He also produced a mathematical theory of aesthetics and a theory of gravitation. *See also* statistical mechanics.

Birmingham 52 30N 1 50W A city in central England, in the West Midlands. Britain's second largest city, it is a centre of the motor-vehicles industry and besides general engineering and metalworking also produces bicycles, firearms, chemicals, plastics, tyres, chocolate, and jewellery. A cultural centre, it possesses two universities, Aston University (1966) and Birmingham University (1900), an art gallery (1874–81), a symphony orchestra, a repertory theatre founded in 1913 by Sir Barry Jackson (1879–1961), and several museums. It has an 18th-century cathedral and a Roman Catholic cathedral (1839–41) designed by Pugin. Among postwar developments are a modern shopping complex centred on the Bull Ring, where a market has been held since ancient times, The National Exhibition Centre (1976) at Bickenhill, and Spaghetti Junction, where several motorways meet. *History*: originally an Anglo-Saxon settlement, its development dates largely from the industrial revolution although its metalworking tradition is much older. Lying on the edge of the *Black Country Birmingham had easy access to the necessary raw materials and produced every kind of hardware. It was severely damaged by bombing during World War II. In 1985 tension between ethnic groups and the authorities resulted in rioting in the Handsworth area. Population (1981): 920 389.

Birmingham 33 30N 86 55W A city in the USA, in Alabama. Settled in 1813, it is the state's largest city and the main industrial centre of the South. It has an important iron and steel industry, which uses local iron ore deposits; other industries include engineering, construction, and paint. Population (1980): 284 413.

Biró, Laszlo (1900–85) Hungarian inventor, who in 1938 patented the ballpoint pen containing quick-drying ink. Such pens are now commonly known as biros.

Birobidzhan. *See* Jewish autonomous region.

birthmark A blemish that is present on the skin at birth. Known medically as a naevus, it is usually harmless and may disappear with age. Birthmarks are caused by a defect in the skin cells or underlying blood vessels.

birthstone In *astrology, a gemstone associated with a particular date of birth. The wearing of one's birthstone as a lucky charm originated in the ancient belief that certain gems had supernatural powers. The modern list of birthstones is usually as follows: January–garnet; February–amethyst; March –bloodstone; April–diamond; May–emerald; June–pearl; July–ruby; August–sardonyx; September–sapphire; October –opal; November–topaz; December–turquoise.

Birtwistle, Harrison (1934–) British avantgarde composer. His compositions include the opera *Punch and Judy* (1966–67), the chamber ensemble *Medusa* (1969–70), and *An Imaginary Landscape* (for orchestra; 1971).

Biscay, Bay of (French name: Golfe de Gascogne; Spanish name: Golfo de Vizcaya) An inlet of the Atlantic Ocean, off the coast of W France and N Spain. It is comparatively deep and subject to gales and rough seas. The fish caught here include anchovies, cod, sardines, and tuna. Width: about 320 km (199 mi).

bisexuality. *See* homosexuality.

Bishop, Sir Henry Rowley (1786–1855) British composer and conductor. He is remembered for "Home, Sweet Home" and other ballads.

Bishop Auckland 54 40N 1 40W A town in NE England, in Durham on the River Wear. Its palace is the traditional seat of the bishops of Durham. It has engineering, electrical, and various light industries. Population (1981 est): 32 572.

Bishops' Wars (1639, 1640) The wars fought between the Scots and Charles I of Great Britain following his attempts to enforce the Anglican Prayer Book and government of the Church by bishops on the Presbyterian Scots.

Biskra 34 50N 5 45E An oasis town in N Algeria, on the N edge of the Sahara. It is an important centre for the date trade. Population (1977): 90 471.

Bisley 51 20N 0 39W A village in SE England, in Surrey. Rifle ranges were constructed on Bisley Common in 1890 by the National Rifle Association, which still meets here annually.

Bismarck 46 50N 100 48W A city in the USA, the capital of North Dakota on the Missouri River. Named after Otto von Bismarck (1873) to entice German investment, it is an agricultural market centre. Population (1980): 44 485.

DROPPING THE PILOT.

BISMARCK *A Punch* cartoon (1890) satirizes the chancellor's resignation following disagreements with the emperor.

Bismarck, Otto Eduard Leopold, Prince von (1815–98) Prussian statesman; first chancellor of the German Empire (1871–90). A conservative, known as the Iron Chancellor, Bismarck came to prominence after the collapse of the *Revolution of 1848. As Prussian prime minister (1862–90) he was determined to establish Prussian hegemony in Germany and to undermine Austrian dominance there. He embroiled Austria in war over Schleswig-Holstein and following its defeat in the Austro-Prussian War of 1866 *William I of Prussia became president of the North German Confederation. After victory in the *Franco-Prussian War (1870–71) William accepted the imperial crown and Bismarck became chancellor of the new German Empire. Bismarck's domestic policy in succeeding years was concerned chiefly with keeping liberalism at bay. He also came into conflict with the Roman Catholic Church (*see* Kulturkampf) and, abroad, presided over the Congress of *Berlin (1878) and formed the *Triple Alliance with Austria and Italy. Losing the support of William II, Bismarck resigned in 1890 over the abolition of anti-socialist laws. □ p. 153.

Bismarck Archipelago A group of volcanic islands in the SW Pacific Ocean, in Papua New Guinea. It includes New Britain, New Ireland, and the Admiralty Islands. Area: 49 658 sq km (19 173 sq mi). Population (1980 est): 314 308.

bismuth (Bi) A dense white brittle metal, similar in properties to tin and lead. It was first distinguished by C. Geoffroy in 1753. It is obtained as a by-product of lead, copper, tin, silver, and gold refining and also occurs naturally as the pure metal, the sulphide (Bi_2S_3), and the oxide (Bi_2O_3). It has unusual properties for a metal, having low thermal and electrical conductivity, and decreasing in volume on melting. With tin and cadmium it is used to make low-melting alloys in *fire prevention systems. At no 83; at wt 208.9808; mp 271.3°C; bp 1560°C.

bison A massive hoofed □mammal belonging to the genus *Bison* (2 species). The North American bison (*B. bison*) was once abundant on the plains but is now found only on reserves. Over 150 cm at the shoulder and weighing up to 1000 kg, it has a shaggy mane and low-slung head with incurved horns. The smaller European bison (*B. bonasus*), also called wisent, is now found only in zoos. Family: *Bovidae*.

Bissau 11 50N 15 37N The capital and chief port of Guinea-Bissau, on the Geba estuary. Founded by the Portuguese in 1687, it became capital of Portuguese Guinea in 1941. In 1974 Madina do Boe was chosen as the site of a planned new capital. Population (1979): 109 486.

bistort A perennial herb, *Polygonum bistorta*, of temperate Europe, also called snake-root or Easter-ledges. The upper leaves are triangular, with sheathing bases, and there is a dense terminal spike of tiny pink flowers. Family: *Polygonaceae* (dock family).

bit A *binary digit*. The basic unit of information in information theory and computer memory stores. It is the amount of information needed to specify one of two alternatives, i.e. to distinguish between 1 and 0 in the *binary notation.

Bithynia An ancient region of Asia Minor, S of the Black Sea. Of Thracian origin, the Bithynians long remained independent, resisting the aggression of the Achaemenians, Alexander the Great, and the Seleucids. By the 3rd century BC it had become a kingdom and expanded territorially and commercially. Conflict with Pergamum and later Pontus brought Roman involvement. Bequeathed by Nicomedes IV (reigned 91–74 BC) to Rome, Bithynia became an increasingly important province as Rome's frontiers expanded E.

Bitola (Turkish name: Monastir) 41 01N 21 21E A town in S Yugoslavia, in Macedonia. After five centuries of Turkish rule, it was taken by the Serbs in 1912. Its products include sugar, carpets, and textiles. Population (1981): 137 835.

bittern A bird belonging to the subfamily *Botaurinae*, occurring throughout the world in swamps and reedbeds. The European bittern (*Botaurus stellaris*) is a solitary bird, about 70 cm long, with a yellow-brown dark-streaked plumage that provides excellent camouflage. The male produces a "booming" call. The little bittern (*Ixobrychus minutus*) is only 34 cm long with buffish-white wing patches. Family: *Ardeidae* (herons, etc.).

bittersweet A perennial plant, the woody *nightshade.

bitumen The tarry residue left after *distillation of oil, lignite, or coal, consisting almost entirely of a mixture of carbon with large *hydrocarbon molecules. Its principal uses are in roadmaking, waterproofing buildings, and binding cement. Bitumen sometimes occurs naturally in asphalt lakes.

bivalve A *mollusc belonging to the class *Bivalvia* (also called *Lamellibranchia* and *Pelecypoda*; about 10 000 species). Bivalves are characterized by having two hinged shell plates (valves) and include *clams, *mussels, *oysters, and *scallops. Bivalves inhabit both salt and fresh water: some are free swimming; others burrow in sand, mud, or rock. They draw water between the shell valves using their ciliated gills and inner surfaces (mantle) to extract oxygen and food particles from it. Most bivalves are of separate sexes but some are hermaphrodite. Some hermaphrodite bivalves, including *Ostrea* oysters, incubate the fertilized eggs.

Bizerte (*or* Bizerta) 37 18N 9 52E A port in N Tunisia, on the Mediterranean Sea. It dates back to Phoenician times as a port and was known as Hippo Zarytus or Diarrhytus. Retained by the French as a naval base following Tunisian independence (1956), fighting broke out before France surrendered the base in 1963. Population (1984): 94 509.

Bizet, Georges (Alexandre César Léopold B.; 1838–75) French composer. He studied under *Gounod and *Halévy and in 1855 produced his first major work, the symphony in C major. He won the Prix de Rome in 1857. Among his best-known works are the incidental music to *Daudet's play *L'Arlésienne* (1872) and the opera *Carmen* (1873–74), which was at first disliked by the public and attacked by the critics. The strain of this hastened Bizet's death three months after the premiere; it is now one of the world's most popular operas.

Bjerknes, Vilhelm Friman Koren (1862–1951) Norwegian meteorologist and physicist. A pioneer of weather forecasting, his 1897 mathematical models of atmospheric and oceanic motions led to his full-scale meteorological predictions (1904). His son **Jakob Bjerknes** (1897–), also a meteorologist, initiated the use of high-altitude photography in weather surveys and forecasting (1952).

Björling, Jussi (Johann Jonaton B.; 1911–60) Swedish tenor. Trained at the Royal Opera School, Stockholm, he made his debut there in 1930. He sang in all the world's major opera houses.

Bjørnson, Bjørnstjerne (Martinius) (1832–1910) Norwegian novelist, poet, and playwright, who was also active in politics and worked as a theatre director and newspaper editor. His works, based on the sagas and his knowledge of rural life, include the novel *På Guds veje* (*In God's Way*; 1889) and the plays *En fallit* (*The Bankrupt*; 1875) and *Det ny system* (*The New System*; 1879). He is also remembered as the author of the Norwegian national anthem. He was awarded the Nobel Prize in 1903.

Black, Joseph (1728–99) Scottish physician and chemist, born in Bordeaux, who became professor at Glasgow University and later at Edinburgh University. He independently discovered carbon dioxide, deduced its presence in air, and discovered the bicarbonate compounds. His work on heat led him to introduce the concepts caloric, heat of fusion, latent heat, specific heat, and thermal capacity. He was also the first to distinguish between heat and temperature.

Black and Tans The soldiers recruited by the British Government to fight the IRA in Ireland in 1920–21. Their name derives from their uniform, khaki with black caps and belts. They acted with great severity and were hated by the Irish.

black bear The native bear of North American forests, *Ursus* (or *Euarctos*) *americanus*. American black bears grow to a weight of 150 kg; they climb well and eat berries, pine cones, and grass as well as small animals.

The name is also used for the Himalayan black, or moon, bear, *Selenarctos thibetanus*, which inhabits forests of central and E Asia and has a white V-shaped mark on its chest.

Blackbeard. *See* Teach, Edward.

black beetle. *See* cockroach.

blackberry (*or* bramble) A prickly scrambling shrub, *Rubus fruticosus* (an aggregate species), occurring throughout Europe. The stems, up to 5 m long, root wherever they touch the ground. The dark-green leaves usually consist of five oval toothed leaflets and the pinkish-white flowers are borne in terminal clusters. The fruits, each of which consists of an aggregate of several small berries, are eaten raw or made into pies, jellies, preserves, etc. Family: *Rosaceae*.

blackbird A songbird, *Turdus merula*, that is one of the commonest European birds, particularly in urban areas. The male, about 25 cm long, is black with a bright-yellow bill and eye ring; the larger female is dark brown with a dark bill. Blackbirds feed chiefly on worms and other invertebrates but will also eat scraps. Family: *Turdidae* (thrushes).

blackbirding The kidnapping of Polynesians to provide slave labour for the sugar and cotton plantations of Australia and the South Pacific islands. Legislation against it was passed in Australia (1868) but was not effective, although blackbirding among British subjects was reduced by British government legislation, and it was not until the beginning of the 20th century that the practice died out.

black body A theoretical body that absorbs all the electromagnetic radiation falling upon it. When heated it emits radiation (black-body radiation) having a continuous distribution of wavelengths with a maximum at a particular wavelength, which depends only on the temperature of the body.

blackbuck A common antelope, *Antilope cervicapra*, of Indian grasslands. Blackbucks are about 80 cm high; females are yellowish brown and males darker, both with white underparts. Males have ridged spiral horns up to 65 cm long. They live in herds of 10–30 animals, grazing at dawn and dusk.

Blackburn 53 45N 2 29W A town in NW England, in Lancashire on the Leeds-Liverpool Canal. Traditionally a cotton-weaving town, its chief industry now is engineering (including carpet machinery); textiles, electronics, paper, and paint are also important. Population (1981): 88 236.

blackcap A European *warbler, *Sylvia atricapillus*. About 14 cm long, it has an olive-brown plumage with paler underparts and a darker cap (black in the male and reddish-brown in the female). Blackcaps feed chiefly on insects but—before migrating—they eat fruit to build up energy reserves.

Black Consciousness The recognition by minority Black communities throughout the world of their identity, history, and culture, as distinct from that of Whites. Political and social movements contributing to the development of Black Consciousness in the USA have included the Universal Negro Improvement Association in the 1920s, the National Association for the Advancement of Coloured People, and the later *Black Muslims. In South Africa the Black Consciousness Movement was led by **Steven Biko** (d. 1977), whose death from extensive injuries while in police detention provoked worldwide concern.

Black Country, the An industrial area of central England. Situated N of Birmingham, it corresponds roughly to the S Staffordshire coalfield. It gained its name from the grime produced by intense industrialization in the 19th century. Although mining is no longer practiced there are numerous metal-processing and manufacturing industries in the area.

blackcurrant A shrub, *Ribes nigrum*, native to most of Europe and N Asia and widely cultivated. The stems and three-lobed leaves emit a characteristic smell. The drooping clusters of greenish bell-shaped flowers develop into edible black berries, used in preserves, wine, beverages, and as a source of vitamin C. Family: *Grossulariaceae* (gooseberry family).

Black Death The worst outbreak of *plague, principally bubonic but also pneumonic and septicaemic, of the medieval period. Orginating in the Far East, it spread through Europe and England in May, 1348. Estimates of mortality rates vary from 20% to more than 50%. The outbreak had a profound effect not only on demographic trends but also upon rural society and the economy as a whole. Further outbreaks followed in the 1350s and 1370s.

black earth. *See* chernozem.

Blackett, Patrick Maynard Stuart, Baron (1897–1974) British physicist, who was professor at Birkbeck College, London (1933–37), Manchester University (1937–63), and Imperial College, London (1963–74). Working at the Cavendish Laboratory in Cambridge he made the first cloud-chamber photographs showing nuclear disintegrations as a result of bombardment (1925) and identified the disintegration products. He improved the Wilson cloud-chamber detector and used it in the study of cosmic radiation, for which work he received the Nobel Prize (1948). He was awarded the OM in 1967 and made a life peer in 1969.

black-eyed Susan A North American perennial herb of the genus *Rudbeckia* (19 species) with showy flower heads, the rays generally yellow, darker at the base and disc flowers blackish and prominent. The plants grow to a height of 60 cm and have rough narrow leaves. Also called coneflowers, many species (e.g. *R. fulgida* var *speciosa*) are cultivated in gardens. Family: *Compositae*.

blackfly Any black *aphid, especially the bean aphid (*Aphis fabae*). Bean aphids occur in masses on beans, spinach, dock, etc., in summer months. They overwinter as fertilized eggs in *Euonymus*, *Viburnum*, and *Philadelphus* trees.

black fly A small humpbacked fly, also called buffalo gnat and turkey gnat, belonging to a family (*Simuliidae*; about 300 species) of worldwide distribution. The bloodsucking females attack man and domestic animals and some are vectors of disease. In Africa, for example, *Simulium damnosum* and *S. neavei* transmit a filarial worm that causes "river blindness."

Blackfoot An Algonkian language and confederacy of three North American Indian peoples of the Plains: the Siksikas, Piegans, and Bloods. They were nomadic buffalo hunters and fierce warriors, who resisted the white man's encroachments in Alberta and Montana for many years.

Black Forest (German name: Schwarzwald) An extensively forested mountainous area in SW West Germany, in Baden-Württemberg E of the Rhine Valley. Covered chiefly with coniferous forests, the timber industry is important with associated cuckoo-clock making and woodcrafts; it is also a popular tourist area.

black grouse A Eurasian *grouse, *Lyrurus tetrix*, of moorlands. The male (also called blackcock), 50 cm long, has a glossy black plumage and a lyre-shaped tail; the female is reddish brown. Both have conspicuous red wattles above the eyes. In the breeding season the males perform an elaborate courtship display (lek) on a communal display ground.

Black Hand A Serbian secret society pledged to the liberation of Serbs from Habsburg and Ottoman rule. On 28 June, 1914, they were responsible for the assassination of the Austrian archduke, Francis Ferdinand, an event contributing to the outbreak of World War I.

Black Hawk War (1832) A conflict between the USA and

the Sauk and Fox Indians. The Indian chief Black Hawk (1767–1838) resisted attempts to force his people W of the Mississippi River and near La Crosse, Wisconsin, nearly a thousand Indians were massacred by the US army despite a flag of surrender.

Blackheath 51 28N 0 01E A residential district mainly in the Greater London boroughs of Lewisham and Greenwich. Originally an extensive heath, it was the rallying point of two rebellions led by Wat Tyler (1381) and Jack Cade (1450) and was notorious as a haunt of highwaymen.

black hole A celestial "object" that has undergone such total *gravitational collapse that no light can escape from it: its *escape velocity exceeds the speed of light (see velocity of light). Once a collapsing object's radius has shrunk below a critical value (the Schwarzschild radius) it becomes a black hole; for a star, this radius is about 10 km or less. The surface having this radius is called the event horizon of the black hole. The object will continue to contract until compressed to an infinite density at a single central point—a singularity. A black hole is thus a region of greatly distorted space (and time) the size of which increases with the mass of the contracting material.

No black hole has as yet been unambiguously detected. The collapsed core remaining from the *supernova explosions of massive stars are, however, promising candidates, especially if they are components of a *binary star and thus more easy to detect. The X-ray binary Cygnus X-1 has a probable black-hole component. Black holes of immense mass (10^6 to 10^9 solar masses) are now thought to exist at the centres of certain galaxies, possibly including our own, and to be the powerful sources of energy in *active galaxies such as *quasars.

Black Hole of Calcutta A small cell (5.5 m × 4.5 m) in which over one hundred British soldiers were allegedly confined overnight in 1756. According to their commander John Holwell less than 25 men survived. The outrage was perpetrated by the Nawab of Bengal, who, objecting to the fortification of Calcutta by the East India Company, attacked and defeated the British garrison.

blackjack A card game based on *pontoon (or vingt-et-un) played by a croupier and six punters in casinos. Using four standard packs, the objective is for the punters to score exactly 21, counting court cards as 10 and the ace as 1 or 11. The croupier deals two cards face up to each punter and 1 to himself; blackjack consists of a 10 and an ace, and pays 3 to 2, unless the dealer also makes blackjack on his second card (a "standoff" in which no money changes hands).

blackmail In law, the criminal offence of making any unwarranted demand with a view to gain, backed up by a threat of violence or injury to the person involved or to his property or by a threat of exposing his immorality or misconduct.

black mass An obscene and blasphemous parody of the Roman Catholic mass, celebrated by satanists in honour of the devil. A naked woman is usually present at or on the altar and participants take hallucinatory drugs or other potions. See satanism.

Blackmore, R(ichard) D(oddridge) (1825–1900) British historical novelist, famous chiefly for Lorna Doone (1869), a romance set on Exmoor during the Restoration.

Black Mountain A ridge in South Wales, in E Dyfed and W Powys, rising to 802 m (2632 ft) at Carmarthen Van.

Black Mountains A mountain range in SE Wales, in Powys, mainly in the Brecon Beacons National Park. It rises to 811 m (2660 ft) at Wann Fach.

Black Muslims Members of the Nation of Islam movement founded in Detroit (USA) in 1930 by W. D. Fard, known variously as Walli Farrad, Wallace Fard Muhammad, etc., and believed by Black Muslims to be the Mahdi or Saviour. After the disappearance of Fard in 1933, the movement was led by Elijah Muhammad (1897–1975) and won support among Blacks in northern industrial cities. *Malcolm X was a leading member

until 1964. Restricted to Blacks, it aims to establish a new Islamic state and follows many Muslim practices, although some of its beliefs are unorthodox.

Blackpool 53 50N 3 03W A resort in NW England, on the Lancashire coast. It is an entertainments centre famous for its Tower (modelled on the Eiffel Tower), Pleasure Beach, and illuminations; it is also a conference centre. Population (1983): 147 000.

Black Prince, Edward the. See Edward, the Black Prince.

Black Rod In the UK, an official of the House of Lords, appointed in 1522, having been usher of the Order of the *Garter since 1350. He maintains order in the House, and when the monarch delivers a speech there, summons members of the Commons by knocking on their door with his staff of office (the black rod).

Black Sea An inland sea bounded by Bulgaria, Romania, the Soviet Union, and Turkey; it is connected to the Mediterranean Sea via the Bosporus in the SW and to the sea of Azov in the N. The principal towns on its coast are Burgas and Varna in Bulgaria, Constanţa in Romania, Odessa and Sevastopol in the Soviet Union, and Trabzon in Turkey. Its salinity is kept low principally by the influx of fresh water from the Rivers Danube and Dnepr.

Blackshirts The colloquial name for the Fasci di Combattimento, founded by Mussolini in 1919 and forming the backbone of Italian *fascism. They wore distinctive black shirts; their name is also used in reference to the *SS.

black snake A small-headed venomous snake, Pseudeschis porphyriacus, of Australian wetlands. About 1.5 m long, it is blue-black with a red belly. Family: Elapidae (cobras, mambas, coral snakes). In North America the name is given to a nonvenomous snake, Zamenis constrictor.

Blackstone, Sir William (1723–80) British jurist. His fame rests largely on his Commentaries on the Laws of England (1765–69), a series of lectures that he had earlier delivered to his students at Oxford. Highly influential in legal education, they presented the first comprehensive account of English law. Blackstone became an MP in 1791 and a judge of the Court of Common Pleas in 1770.

black swan The only Australian *swan, Cygnus atratus. Almost 1 m in length, both sexes have a pure black plumage, red bill, and a trumpeting call.

blackthorn (or sloe) A thorny shrub, Prunus spinos, forming dense thickets, up to 4 m high, in many parts of Europe and Asia. The clusters of white flowers usually appear before the leaves, which are oval and toothed. The bitter-tasting blue-black stone fruits are used to flavour sloe gin; the hard wood is used for walking sticks and tool handles. Family: Rosaceae.

blackwater fever A serious complication of malaria in which the malarial parasite causes widespread destruction of red blood cells, leading to the excretion of blood pigments in the urine (which becomes dark brown—hence the name). The patient has a high fever and jaundice and requires careful nursing, with blood transfusions if necessary.

black widow A venomous *spider, also called button or redback spider, that belongs to a genus (Latrodectus; about 6 species) found in tropical and subtropical regions. The female of L. mactans, the most common North American species, has a shiny black body, 25 mm long, with red markings on the abdomen. (The male is about 6 mm long and usually killed and eaten by the female after mating.) The bite of this spider—although serious—is rarely fatal. Family: Theridiidae.

Blackwood, Algernon Henry (1869–1951) British novelist and short-story writer. He worked in Canada and the USA before returning to England in 1899. The Empty House (1906), a collection of ghost stories, was followed by many works concerning the supernatural, including Tales of the Uncanny and Supernatural (1949).

bladder In anatomy, any hollow organ containing fluid, especially the urinary bladder situated in the pelvis, into which urine drains from the *kidneys (via the ureters). Urine is stored in the bladder and released at intervals by relaxation of a circular (sphincter) muscle at its opening into the urethra (which leads to the exterior; *see* Plate IV). Bladder emptying is normally under voluntary control.

bladderwort A plant of the widely distributed genus *Utricularia* (about 200 species, many tropical). Most bladderworts are submerged aquatic plants with finely divided leaves bearing small bladders, which trap tiny aquatic animals by a trapdoor mechanism triggered by sensitive hairs. The two-lipped tubular flowers protrude above the water. Some bladderworts are troublesome weeds of ricefields. Family: *Lentibulariaceae*.

Blake, Peter (1932–) British painter, born in Dartford. In the 1960s he became one of the leading British exponents of *pop art with his half-painted half-collage pinup girls, pop singers, wrestlers, and advertisements.

Blake, Robert (1599–1657) English admiral. A Parliamentarian in the Civil War, Blake became one of *Cromwell's most successful commanders and in 1650 destroyed Prince Rupert's Royalist fleet. In the first *Dutch War, Blake was largely responsible for the English victory and decisively defeated *Tromp at the battle of Portland (1653). He destroyed a pirate fleet off Tunis (1655) and sank 16 Spanish ships at Santa Cruz off Tenerife (1657). He died while returning to Plymouth.

Blake, William (1757–1827) British visionary poet, painter, and engraver. Born in London, he trained under the engraver James Basire (1730–1802) between about 1772 and 1779, when he entered the Royal Academy schools. His books of poems, the texts of which he engraved and illustrated, include *Songs of Innocence* (1789), *Songs of Experience* (1794), various "Prophetic Books," *Milton* (1808), and *Jerusalem* (1820). All were influenced by his unorthodox Christian and political beliefs and by such mystics as *Böhme. As an artist his imaginative watercolours for *The Book of Job* (1826) and Dante's *Divine Comedy* (1827) were inspired by his visions, gothic sculpture, and engravings after Michelangelo. Although unrecognized by his generation, except by his patron John Linnell (1792–1882) and other artist friends, such as *Fuseli and *Palmer, he was a precursor of Romanticism.

Blanc, Louis (1811–82) French socialist. A utopian and revolutionary, from 1839 Blanc propagated his doctrines of economic equality in his journal *Revue du progrès*; the axiom "from each according to his ability, to each according to his needs" formed the basis of his thought. Although a member of the provisional government in the *Revolution of 1848, he found little support for his views among his colleagues and fled to England. Returning to Paris in 1870, he remained active in left-wing causes until his death. His books include *Organisation du travail* (1840).

Blanchard, Jean Pierre François (1753–1809) French balloonist. With **John Jeffries** (1744–1819), an American, he made the first Channel crossing in a balloon, from Dover to Calais (1785). He invented a parachute and was killed using it to jump from a balloon.

Blanche of Castile (c. 1188–1252) The daughter of Alfonso VIII of Castile, she married (1200) *Louis VIII of France. She was Queen of France (1223–26) and regent for her son *Louis IX during his minority (1226–36) and during his Crusade (1248–52). She ruled firmly, suppressing a revolt of the nobility and effecting peace with England.

blank verse Unrhymed iambic pentameter lines, the distinctive form of English narrative and dramatic verse since its introduction from Italy in the early 16th century by Henry Howard, Earl of *Surrey. It was used in the plays of *Marlowe and *Shakespeare. The form allows considerable variation and has been used by most major English poets to suit their different ends: in *Milton's *Paradise Lost* (1667) it is formal and grand,

in *Wordsworth's *Prelude* (1805) it is intimate and casual.

Blanqui, Louis Auguste (1805–81) French revolutionary. Interested in the practice of revolution rather than in abstract ideas, Blanqui introduced the notion, later taken up by Marx, that revolutions must begin with the temporary dictatorship of a revolutionary elite devoted to the socialist cause. From 1830 he built up a network of secret societies committed to violent insurrection. In 1871, although in prison, he was elected president of the *Commune of Paris. His followers, the Blanquists, joined with the Marxists in 1881.

WILLIAM BLAKE *An engraving (plate 14) from* The Book of Job. *These biblical illustrations, of which Blake produced 22, were commissioned by Linnell in 1821 and engraved 1823-25.*

Blantyre (or Blantyre-Limbe) 15 46S 35 00E The largest city in Malawi, in the Shire Highlands. In 1956 it was linked with the nearby town of Limbe, a major railway centre, and is Malawi's chief commercial and industrial centre. Industries include distilling, textiles, and cigarette production. Population (1982 est): 250 000.

Blantyre 55 47N 4 06W A town in Scotland, in Strathclyde Region near Glasgow. It is the birthplace of David Livingstone, whose home is now a national memorial. Formerly the centre of a coalmining area, it now has engineering industries. Population (1981 est): 19 875.

Blarney 51 56N 8 34W A village in the Republic of Ireland, in Co Cork. Blarney Castle contains the famous

Blarney Stone, which is kissed in order to receive the gift of "blarney" or smooth talk. Population (1981): 3186.

Blasco Ibáñez, Vicente (1867-1928) Spanish novelist. He wrote many novels set in Valencia but is best known for his World War I novels, especially *The Four Horsemen of the Apocalypse* (1916), three times filmed. He was frequently penalized for his political activities and in 1923 exiled himself to France.

Blasis, Carlo (1803-78) Italian dance teacher. In 1837 he became director of the dance academy at La Scala, Milan. His books on the theory of classical ballet, especially *Treatise on the Dance* (1820) and *The Code of Terpsichore* (1828), had an international influence.

BLAST FURNACE

blast furnace A furnace heated by solid fuel, usually coke, through which a blast of air is blown to aid combustion. Blast furnaces are used in the *smelting of ore. In steel making, iron ore, coke, and limestone are poured in at the top of a vertical furnace and hot air is blown in at the bottom to burn the coke. Molten iron is drawn off at the bottom. A glassy waste, called slag, is also produced.

blastula A hollow sphere of cells (blastomeres) produced by repeated *cleavage of a fertilized egg cell (zygote). It is an early stage in embryonic development, before differentiation into tissues and organs has begun. A blastula consists of an outer layer (the blastoderm) surrounding a cavity (the blastocoel).

Blaue Reiter, Der (German: The Blue Rider) A group of artists formed in Munich in 1911 by *Marc and *Kandinsky when the latter's work was rejected by the exhibition committee of *Neue Künstlervereinigung. Their manifesto *Der Blaue Reiter Almanac* (1911) and their exhibitions illustrated their diverse influences: primitive and naive art, children's pictures, religious paintings on glass, and their modern favourites *Cézanne and *Delaunay. Their aim was to unite in an expressionist style (*see* expressionism) the symbolic and spiritual elements manifest in the art of all ages. The group, which also included Paul *Klee and August *Macke, disbanded during World War I.

Blavatsky, Helen Petrovna (1831-91) Russian theosophist, who founded the Theosophical Society in New York in 1875. She later established a following in India, but her claims to supernatural powers were discredited by scientific investigations during the 1880s and 1890s. Her best-known book is *Isis Unveiled* (1877). *See also* theosophy.

Blaydon 54 58N 1 42W A town in NE England, in Tyne

and Wear on the River Tyne. It is concerned chiefly with the manufacture of coal by-products, chemicals, and engineering. Population (1981):*10 563.

bleaching The whitening, lightening, or removing of colour by chemical treatment, exposure to sunlight, air, or moisture. Most bleaching agents are oxidizing agents, which convert a pigment into an oxidized colourless form. Examples are hydrogen peroxide, *bleaching powder, and hypochlorites. In some processes reducing agents, such as sulphur dioxide, are used. Bleaching is an important part of textile and paper manufacture.

bleaching powder (*or* chloride of lime) A whitish powder containing calcium hypochlorite $(Ca(OCl)_2)$, calcium chloride $(CaCl_2)$, calcium hydroxide $(Ca(OH)_2)$, and water. It reacts with dilute acids to produce chlorine, which acts as a bleaching agent.

bleak A fish, *Alburnus alburnus*, related to the *carp, with a slender silvery-green body, about 20 cm long. It lives in schools near the surface of fresh waters in N Europe and feeds on invertebrates. The scales are used in the manufacture of artificial pearls.

bleeding. *See* haemorrhage.

bleeding heart An ornamental plant of the genus *Dicentra*, especially *D. spectabilis* from Siberia and Japan and *D. eximia* from North America. They are perennials with arching stems, up to 90 cm long, bearing strings of large rose-red heart-shaped flowers with whitish tips, which glisten when the blooms are fresh. Some species have attractive fernlike foliage. Family: *Fumariaceae*.

Blenheim, Battle of (13 August, 1704) The battle won by the Duke of *Marlborough and *Eugene of Savoy against the French army in the War of the *Spanish Succession. It was fought at Blenheim (now Blindheim) on the Danube River and *Blenheim Palace was built for Marlborough by a grateful parliament.

CHARLES BLONDIN *Crossing the Niagara Falls on a tightrope in 1859.*

Blenheim Palace The baroque palace built between 1705 and 1725 at Woodstock, Oxfordshire (England). Designed by *Vanbrugh, it was a gift from Queen Anne to the Duke of *Marlborough as a monument to his victories over the French. The gardens were laid out by Capability *Brown. Sir Winston *Churchill was born at Blenheim.

Blenkinsop, John (1783-1831) British engineer, who built the first practical steam locomotive (1812), a twin-cylinder engine driving cogs that engaged with rack rails. It was used for transporting coal from Middleton to Leeds.

blenny A small fish belonging to a family (*Blenniidae*; about 300 species) found among rocks in shallow waters of tropical and temperate seas. Blennies have an elongated scaleless body with a blunt nose, a long dorsal fin, and one- to three-rayed pelvic fins located in front of the larger pectoral fins. Many have small tentacles on their heads. The name is also used for several other fish of the order *Perciformes*.

Blériot, Louis (1872-1936) French aviator. Beginning his career as a motorcar engineer he was the first to fly the English Channel (1909), from Calais to Dover, in a monoplane. He later became a manufacturer of ▢aircraft.

blesbok A small fast-running South African antelope, *Damaliscus dorcas*. About 110 cm high at the shoulder, blesboks are red with a white muzzle, rump, and shanks and have lyre-shaped ridged horns. Bonteboks (*D. dorcas dorcas*) are a subspecies with a larger rump patch and more white on the legs.

Blessington, Marguerite, Countess of (1789-1849) Irish author. A London society hostess, from 1822 she and her husband travelled in France and Italy, where they befriended Byron. Widowed in 1829, she began writing to pay off her debts. Her best-known work is *Conversations of Lord Byron* (1834).

blewits An edible *mushroom, *Tricholoma* (or *Lepista*) *saevum*, occurring mainly in open pastures. It has a bluish-grey stalk and a flat clay-coloured cap, 6-12 cm in diameter, producing pale-pink spores. The wood blewits (*T. nudum*) has a lilac or purple cap and is usually found beneath trees. It also is edible. Family: *Tricholomataceae*.

Bligh, William (1754-1817) British admiral. He accompanied *Cook on his second voyage round the world and in 1787 was sent to Tahiti on the *Bounty* to collect specimens of the breadfruit tree. Setting sail for home, his crew mutinied and deserted, leaving Bligh and 18 officers aboard a small boat without maps. He eventually reached safety. In 1805 he was made governor of New South Wales but again fell foul of his subordinates (*see* Rum Rebellion). He returned to Britain in 1811.

blight A severe disease of plants caused by pests, fungi, or other agents or by a mineral deficiency. Symptoms commonly include spotting followed by wilting, and the plant eventually withers and dies. The notorious potato blight that devastated Ireland in the mid-19th century was caused by the fungus *Phytophthora infestans*. Control measures against blights vary according to the cause of the disease.

blindness Partial or complete loss of sight (degrees of visual impairment less severe than total loss of sight are classified as blindness for administrative purposes). Sudden blindness may be caused by direct injury to the eye or to the part of the brain that receives the visual signals. Blindness that develops gradually is caused by a wide variety of diseases, including *trachoma, *glaucoma, *cataracts, diabetes mellitus, and tumours (especially of the pituitary gland), that compress the optic nerve. There are various aids available for the visually handicapped, including books in *Braille or on tape or records and specially trained *guide dogs. In many countries the blind are entitled to special education and financial benefits. *See also* colour blindness.

blindworm. *See* slowworm.

Bliss, Sir Arthur Edward Drummond (1891-1975) British composer. He studied under Stanford and Vaughan Williams. Director of music at the BBC (1942-44), Bliss was knighted in 1950 and was Master of the Queen's Music from 1953 until his death. His works include *A Colour Symphony* (1922), music for the film *The Shape of Things to Come* (1935), the opera *The Olympians* (1948-49), and a cello concerto (1970).

blister An accumulation of fluid (usually colourless serum) within the skin. Blisters can be caused by continuous friction, sensitivity to chemicals, and *burns. They may also develop in certain diseases, including chickenpox. Blisters usually heal spontaneously, but some (especially severe burns or those on the feet, in contact with shoes) require

dressings. They should not be burst intentionally as this provides an entrance for infection.

blister beetle A brightly coloured beetle, about 10-15 mm long, belonging to a widely distributed family (*Meloidae*; about 2000 species), which also includes the *oil beetles. The larvae are parasitic upon other insects, while the adults generally feed on plants—often causing severe damage. Their secretion of cantharidin, a powerful blistering agent, has led to the medicinal use of various European and Asian species, especially *Spanish fly.

Blitzkrieg (German: lightning war) A military tactic aiming to shock and disorganize enemy forces by swift suprise attacks using tanks and aerial bombardment. It was extensively used by the Germans in *World War II in Poland, Belgium, the Netherlands, France, and Africa. It was also used by the US general, Patton, in Europe in 1944. The **Blitz** refers to the intensive German air raids on London during the battle of Britain in *World War II. Between July and December, 1940, 23 000 civilians died.

Blixen, Karen. *See* Dinesen, Isak.

Bloch, Ernest (1880-1959) Swiss-born composer of Jewish descent. He lived in various countries before taking up residence in the USA in 1916. His opera *Macbeth* (1903-09), a rhapsody for cello and orchestra entitled *Schelomo* (1916), *Concerto Grosso* (1925), and *Sacred Service* (1930-33) incorporate Jewish musical elements into a cosmopolitan 20th-century style.

Bloch, Felix (1905-83) US physicist, born in Zurich. After working in Germany he left Europe when Hitler came to power and emigrated to the USA, becoming a US citizen in 1939. He developed the *nuclear magnetic resonance technique for magnetic field measurements in atomic nuclei, for which he shared the Nobel Prize (1952) with the independent discoverer, E. M. *Purcell. Bloch's concept of magnetic neutron polarization (1934) enabled him, in conjunction with L. *Alvarez, to measure the neutron's magnetic moment. During World War II he worked on the development of the atomic bomb. In 1954 he became the first director of CERN.

Bloemfontein 29 07S 26 14E The judicial capital of South Africa and the capital of the Orange Free State. Founded in 1846, it is an important transportation and agricultural centre. Industrial development is being encouraged with the opening of new gold mines nearby. It has the University of the Orange Free State (1855) and the US universities of Harvard and Michigan have observatories here to take advantage of the dry clear atmosphere. Population (1980 est): 230 688.

Bloemfontein Convention. *See* Sand River Convention.

Blois 47 36N 1 20E A town in France, the capital of the Loir-et-Cher department on the River Loire. It has a famous chateau, begun in the 13th century, and trades in wine, brandy, and grain. Population (1982 est): 49 422.

Blok, Aleksandr Aleksandrovich (1880-1921) The leading Russian symbolist poet. His early poetry, notable *Verses about the Beautiful Lady* (1901-02), celebrated the spiritual fulfilment of his love for Liubov Mendeleyeva, whom he married in 1903. But his love for Russia was the deeper theme, and in *Scythians* (1918) and *The Twelve* (1918) he expressed a revolutionary optimism that soon turned to deep disillusion.

Blondel, Maurice (1861-1949) French philosopher. He invented a philosophy of action, seeking a compromise between intellectualism and pragmatism. His chief works are *Action* (1893), *The Process of Intelligence* (1922), and *Being and Beings* (1935).

Blondin, Charles (Jean-François Gravelet; 1824-97) French acrobat and tightrope walker. In 1859 he walked across a tightrope suspended over Niagara Falls and later repeated the feat several times with various acrobatic variations.

BLOOD   *Blood cells and platelets, showing surface and side views of a red cell and five types of white cell (above). Human blood, magnified about 1500 times (below) containing a single white cell, a mass of red cells, and two clusters of platelets.*

blood   The red fluid contained within the arteries and veins and pumped around the body by the *heart. Blood consists of a watery fluid (*see* plasma) in which are suspended various blood cells—the red cells (*see* erythrocyte), containing the red oxygen-carrying pigment haemoglobin, and several kinds of white cells (*see* leucocyte), concerned with the body's defence mechanisms. The *platelets are small particles involved in blood clotting. Blood acts as a medium for transporting oxygen, carbon dioxide, digested food, hormones, waste materials, salts, and many other substances to and from the tissues. An average adult has about 70 millilitres of blood per kilogram of body weight (i.e. about 5 litres in an average man). Blood is present in all animals with a circulatory system: its functions are similar to that of human blood although its composition varies. *See also* blood clotting; blood groups; circulation of the blood.

Blood, Colonel Thomas   (c. 1618-80) Irish adventurer, best known for his attempt in 1671 to steal the crown jewels. Visited in prison by Charles II, Blood ingratiated himself with the king and was released.

Blood, Council of   (*or* Council of Troubles; 1567-74) A court established in the Low Countries during the *Revolt of the Netherlands by the Spanish governor, the Duke of *Alba, to suppress Protestantism and particularism. Thousands were imprisoned or executed without proper trial and, following the arrest of two prominent magnates, *Egmont and *Horn, many others fled abroad. Alba used the threat of the council to impose the tenth penny, an unpopular tax that united Catholics and Calvinists against Spain. After Alba's departure (1573), the council was abolished.

blood clotting   The mechanism by which blood is converted from a liquid to a solid state, which normally occurs after injury to blood vessels and prevents loss of blood. The process involves a number of chemical reactions between certain soluble proteins (clotting factors) in the blood, resulting in the formation of a fibrous protein (fibrin), which forms the basis of the blood clot. *Platelets accumulate at the site of the injury, their presence being essential for the reactions to occur. *See also* thrombosis.

blood fluke   A parasitic flatworm of the genus *Schistosoma* (3 species), which causes the disease *schistosomiasis among human populations in many parts of the world. The flukes are carried by freshwater snails and enter their human hosts to inhabit blood vessels, feeding on blood and causing severe debilitation. *See also* fluke.

blood groups   The different types into which blood can be classified on the basis of the presence or absence of certain proteins (*see* antibody) on the surface of the red cells, which is genetically determined. The major grouping is the ABO system, which was the first human blood system to be discovered—in 1900, by Karl Landsteiner (1868-1943). It consists of four groups: A, B, AB, and O. Group A cells carry the A antigen and the plasma contains *antibodies against B antigen (anti-B antibodies); the converse applies to group B blood. Transfusion of blood between these groups will cause destruction of the donor blood cells (*see* blood transfusion). Group O blood contains neither antigen and can therefore be used in transfusions to people of groups A and B. Group AB blood contains neither anti-A nor anti-B antibody: people of this blood group can accept both A and B blood during transfusion. There are numerous other minor blood-group systems of which the rhesus system is the most important (*see* rhesus factor).

bloodhound   An ancient breed of dog with a keen sense of smell, widely used for tracking purposes. It has a sturdy frame and a large dome-shaped head with long drooping ears and wrinkled skin around the eyes. Bloodhounds are black and tan, liver and tan, or red in colour. Height: 63-69 cm (dogs); 58-64 cm (bitches).

blood poisoning   (*or* septicaemia)   The presence of bacteria or bacterial toxins in the blood. The symptoms include fever, rigors, and various aches and pains. The bacteria may come from any infected region (such as an abscess) and they may be carried to other parts of the body, including the brain and kidneys. Treatment consists of the injection of large doses of antibiotics.

blood pressure   The pressure that blood exerts on the walls of the arteries, due to the pumping action of the heart. Blood pressure is at its lowest between heartbeats (i.e. at diastole) and at its highest when the ventricles of the heart are contracting (i.e. systole). It is recorded, using an instrument called a *sphygmomanometer, as the height in millimetres of a column of mercury (mmHg). Blood pressure varies with age and individual variations are common within each age group depending on such external factors as stress, but a healthy adult might have a systolic pressure of about 120 mmHg and a diastolic pressure of 80 mmHg. This is normally expressed as 120/80. Abnormally high blood pressure (*see* hypertension) may be associated with various diseases or it may arise without any obvious cause. Abnormally low blood pressure occurs in *shock.

blood sports   Sports in which a quarry is hunted and killed or a spectacle is made of an animal being killed. In the UK most of the blood sports in the latter category have been made illegal—bullbaiting and *bearbaiting since 1835, *cockfighting since 1849, and badger baiting since 1973. *Bullfighting, however, continues in Spain and several other countries. In the former category, *foxhunting, staghunting, beagling, and *coursing still continue in the UK and elsewhere, although the League against Cruel Sports has been fighting to make them illegal.

bloodstone   A mineral of a green colour speckled with red. It is a variety of *chalcedony. Birthstone for March.

blood test   An analysis of a blood sample. Such tests may be useful in the diagnosis of disease. A common test is the measurement of the erythrocyte sedimentation rate (ESR)—the rate at which red blood cells settle out of plasma, which increases in rheumatic disease, cancer, and some infections. Other tests include plasma viscosity, red-cell counts (in the diagnosis of anaemia), blood-sugar estimation (when diabetes mellitus is suspected), and the determination of alcohol, drugs, or bacteria in the blood or the individual's blood group. The blood is usually taken from a vein using a hypodermic needle.

blood transfusion The transfer of blood from one individual (the donor) to another (the recipient). As blood of a different *blood group from that of the recipient may cause a serious reaction, the blood groups of both the donor and the recipient must be determined beforehand. Direct person-to-person transfusion is now rarely performed; the donor blood is usually stored, at a temperature of 4°C, in a **blood bank** and should be used within 3–4 weeks of collection. Blood transfusion is performed when there has been extensive loss of blood; for example, during surgery or following an accident. Some people (e.g. Jehovah's Witnesses) object to transfusion on religious grounds.

bloodworm The larva of nonbiting *midges of the genus *Chironomus*. It lives in stagnant water and is red owing to the pigment *haemoglobin, which it uses to help increase its supply of oxygen.

Bloody Assizes. *See* Jeffreys of Wem, George, 1st Baron.

Bloomfield, Leonard (1887–1949) US linguist, whose book *Language* (1933) outlines a strictly scientific behaviourist framework for the description of language, on which modern American structural *linguistics is based. He also did pioneer descriptive fieldwork in both Malayo-Polynesian and American Indian languages.

Bloomsbury group A group of English writers and artists active in the 1910s and 1920s who met in private houses in Bloomsbury, London, for aesthetic and philosophic discussions. The group included the writers Virginia *Woolf (and her sister Vanessa Bell; 1879–1961), E. M. *Forster, and Lytton *Strachey, the art critics Clive Bell (1881–1964) and Roger *Fry, and the economist J. M. *Keynes. Most of them had studied at Cambridge University and were influenced by G. E. *Moore's *Principia Ethica* (1903) in their belief in the overriding importance of personal relationships and aesthetic experience.

Blow, John (1649–1708) English composer. Blow was organist of the Chapel Royal and Westminister Abbey, where he taught Henry Purcell. The first Composer for the Chapel Royal (1699), he is remembered today for his Church services, anthems, and organ pieces, and for the masque *Venus and Adonis* (1680–85).

blowfly A large buzzing fly belonging to the family *Calliphoridae*. Some blowflies lay their eggs in human food, but more commonly the larvae develop in dung or decaying organic material. The larvae of certain species (e.g. of the American genus *Cochliomyia*)—known as screwworms—are serious pests of sheep and cattle. Chief genera: *Calliphora* (bluebottles), *Lucilia* (greenbottles).

Blücher, Gebhard Leberecht von, Prince of Wahlstatt (1742–1819) Prussian general, known as Marshal Forward. He fought against Revolutionary France and subsequently held command in the War of Liberation against Napoleon, whom he helped to defeat at Leipzig (1813). In 1814 he crossed the Rhine and marched to Paris. His pursuit of Napoleon's forces at Waterloo contributed to the allied victory.

Bluebeard A European folktale character who murders successive wives and locks their bodies in a forbidden room. His new wife discovers the bodies and is rescued by her brothers. The story may have been based on the crimes of Gilles de Retz or of an ancient Breton chieftain.

bluebell One of several plants having bell-shaped blue flowers. In England the bluebell is *Endymion non-scriptus*, a peren-

nial herb, up to 50 cm high, very common in woods and shady places. It overwinters as a bulb and produces blue (sometimes white or pink) flowers in spring. Family: *Liliaceae*. In Scotland the name is applied to the *harebell.

bluebird A songbird of the New World genus *Sialia* (3 species). The eastern bluebird (*S. sialis*) of E North America is about 17 cm long and has a blue back and red-brown breast. Family: *Turdidae* (thrushes). *Compare* fairy bluebird.

bluebottle. *See* blowfly.

Bluefields 12 00N 83 49W The chief Caribbean port of Nicaragua, in the SE near the River Escondido. A 17th-century base (as Blewfeldt) of Dutch pirates, it was the capital of the British Mosquito Coast until 1850. Population (1980): 20 800.

bluefish A food fish, *Pomatomus saltator* (or *P. saltatrix*), also called tailor or snapper. The only member of the family *Pomatomidae*, it is found in all warm seas. It has a blue-green elongated body, up to 1.2 m long, with a whitish belly, a large mouth, and two dorsal fins. It lives in large schools and preys voraciously on other fish. Order: *Perciformes*.

blue fox. *See* Arctic fox.

bluegrass A perennial grass, *Poa pratensis*, also called meadow grass, native to Europe, Asia, and North America. It has erect stems, 30–90 cm high, smooth leaves (which may be blue-tinged or green), and flower clusters 5–20 cm long.

blue-green algae Microscopic *algae of the division *Cyanophyta* (1500 species), which contain a blue pigment (phycocyanin), in addition to the green chlorophyll. They are single cells or filaments and resemble bacteria in their primitive structure (e.g. the genetic material is not organized into a distinct nucleus). Reproduction is asexual. They occur on moist surfaces of rocks and trees, and in the soil, where they contribute to *nitrogen fixation. Aquatic blue-green algae are a constituent of plankton, sometimes forming colourful dense concentrations (blooms).

blue gum A fast-growing evergreen Australian □tree, *Eucalyptus globulus*, up to 40 m high with patchy grey and fawn bark. It has sickle-shaped blue-green leaves up to 25 cm long. The timber is used for construction work and pulp, and eucalyptus oil is distilled from the leaves. Family: *Myrtaceae*. *See also* Eucalyptus.

Blue Mountains A mountain range in Australia, in New South Wales. Part of the *Great Dividing Range, it reaches 1180 m (3871 ft) at Bird Rock and contains the Blue Mountains National Park. It is a popular tourist area.

Blue Riband of the Atlantic An award given for the fastest seaborne crossing of the Atlantic. First awarded in 1838, the title has been held by many famous passenger liners, notably the *Queen Mary* (1938–52) and the *United States* (1952–), which won it with a time of 3 days, 10 hours, and 40 minutes. In 1986 Richard Branson's *Virgin Atlantic Challenger II* powerboat reduced this to 3 days, 8 hours, and 31 minutes.

blues A type of US folk music that evolved from the Negro spirituals and work songs of the 1860s and became a song form used in jazz, rhythm and blues, and rock. The blues is a slow bitter-sweet song the syncopated melodic line and harmonies of which contain "blue" notes, which are flattened versions of certain notes in the major or minor scale. In origin it always consisted of three sets of four bars, in which the second set is a repetition of the first. The final line is improvised. The first published blues were "Memphis Blues" (1912) by W. C. Handy (1873–1958) and Jelly Roll Morton's "Jelly Roll Blues" (1915). The blues influenced the development of jazz and rock music and stimulated classical composers such as George Gershwin, who wrote the orchestral *Rhapsody in Blue* (1924).

blue shark A *shark, *Prionace glauca*, that is abundant in warm-temperate and tropical seas. It has a slender dark-blue body, up to 4 m long, with a white belly and long sickle-shaped pectoral fins. It is found usually near the surface and feeds voraciously on shoaling fish, squid, and other sharks. Family: *Carcharhinidae*.

Bluestockings A group of intellectual society hostesses in 18th-century England. They included Lady Mary Wortley *Montagu and the novelist Fanny *Burney; their guests were Samuel *Johnson, Horace *Walpole, David *Garrick, and others, some of whom were accustomed to wearing ordinary blue, rather than formal dress, stockings to the meetings. The term is still used to describe intellectual women.

bluetit A European tit, *Parus caeruleus*, formerly a woodland species but now common in towns and gardens. It has a blue crown and wings, a yellow breast, white face and wing bars, and a black collar and eyestripe. Bluetits are acrobatic birds and feed chiefly on insect larvae.

bluets A tufted herb of the genus *Houstonia* (about 25 species), native to North America and widely grown in rock gardens. The small white, blue, or purple funnel-shaped flowers are borne singly or in clusters. Some species form mats, providing a close ground cover in shade. Family: *Rubiaceae* (madder family).

blue whale The largest living *whale, *Balaenoptera musculus*, probably the largest animal ever. It grows to over 30 m and weighs over 150 tonnes. Widely distributed, blue whales are nearing extinction due to overhunting. Family: *Balaenopteridae* (*see* rorqual). □mammal.

Blum, Léon (1872–1950) French socialist, statesman, and writer; prime minister (1936–37, 1938, 1946–47). His *popular front government of 1936–37 brought about radical reforms in labour organizations and nationalized the Bank of France. After the fall of France to the Germans in 1940 Blum was arrested by the Vichy government and spent the remainder of the war in prison. From 1946 until his death he led the moderate socialist wing in France. His books include *L'Exercice du pouvoir* (1937) and *À l'échelle humaine* (1945).

Blunden, Edmund Charles (1896–1974) British poet and critic. Educated at Oxford, he lived and taught in Japan in the 1920s and late 1940s and at Hong Kong University from 1953 to 1964. *Undertones of War* (1928) is an account of his experiences in World War I. His love of nature and the English countryside is a constant theme of his work.

blunderbuss A short-range smoothbore gun with a bell-shaped muzzle, firing many balls. In use from the 17th to 19th centuries, its name is derived from the Dutch word *donderbus*, thunder gun. It ranged in size from the pistol to the small artillery piece.

Blunt, Anthony. *See* Maclean, Donald.

Blyth 55 07N 1 30W A port in NE England, in Northumberland at the mouth of the River Blyth. It exports local coal and imports timber. Fishing is important and there are dry docks. Population (1981): 36 466.

Blyth, Chay (Charles Blyth; 1940–) British yachtsman. After service in the armed forces (1958–67), he embarked on a series of voyages, circumnavigating the world: westwards in 1970–71 (solo) and eastwards in 1973–74 (with a crew). He has also won a number of races, including the Observer double-handed transatlantic race (1981). In 1984 he was rescued off Chile when his yacht sank.

Blyton, Enid (1897–1968) British writer of children's books. She trained as a kindergarten teacher and worked in educational journalism. She published her first book in 1923 and introduced her famous character Noddy in 1949. She wrote over 600 books for children of all ages.

boa A snake belonging to the subfamily *Boinae* (40–60 species) of the *constrictor family and occurring in Old and New World regions. 20–760 cm long, boas may be terrestrial, semi-aquatic, or arboreal and are usually green, brown, or yellowish with a camouflaging pattern of blotches and diamonds. They kill their prey by biting and then constricting. The boa constrictor (*Boa constrictor*), occurring from Mexico to Argentina, is about 3.5 m long, hunts birds and small mammals at night,

and bears live young.

Boadicea (Latin name: Boudicca; d. 60 AD) Queen of the *Iceni. Her husband Prasutagus ruled in what is now Norfolk (England). At his death in 60, Roman officials attempted to seize his wealth and maltreated Boadicea and her daughters. She led the Iceni into open rebellion, sacking Colchester, London, and St Albans. The Roman governor Suetonius Paulinus defeated the rebels at or near Fenny Stratford on Watling Street. Boadicea committed suicide.

boar, wild A Eurasian wild *pig, *Sus scrofa*, once common in forests throughout Europe. Up to 1.5 m long and 1 m high at the shoulder, wild boars have a rough bristly coat coloured greyish brown. The ancestors of domestic pigs, they are still hunted for sport in some regions. Males have four tusks.

Boas, Franz (1858–1942) German-born US anthropologist. In 1886 Boas left his post of assistant curator of the Berlin Royal Ethnological Museum and embarked upon extensive research among the Indians of the NW American coast. In 1899 he became the first professor of anthropology at Columbia University. His most famous books are *The Mind of Primitive Man* (1911), *Primitive Art* (1927), and *Race, Language and Culture* (1940). Boas was concerned not only with the physical features of ethnic groups, but also with cultural and psychological aspects. He strongly opposed the racial theories propounded by the Nazis.

boatbill A nocturnal heron, *Cochlearius cochlearius*, occurring in tropical American swamps. It is about 50 cm tall and has a grey plumage with black markings on the head and neck. It closely resembles the *night heron but has a characteristic broad flattened hook-tipped bill. *See* Plate V.

Boat Race An annual *rowing race on the River Thames between Oxford and Cambridge Universities, first held in 1829 at Henley. The present course of 6.8 km (4.25 mi) from Putney to Mortlake was established in 1845. By 1987 Cambridge had won 69 races and Oxford 63, with one dead heat (1877). The first woman to participate in the race was Susan Brown, the Oxford cox, in 1981. Record: 16 minutes 45 seconds by Oxford (1984).

Boa Vista 2 51N 60 43W A town in N Brazil, the capital of Roraima territory on the Rio Branco. Important mineral resources include diamonds, gold, bauxite, and cassiterite. Population (1980): 43 131.

bobcat A short-tailed cat *Felis rufa*, resembling a lynx, found in North America from S Canada to Mexico. About 90 cm long, it is brown with grey or white markings and has large ears tipped with a tuft of hairs. Bobcats feed at night on a wide variety of small birds, rodents, and deer.

Bobo-Dioulasso 11 11N 1 18W A city in SW Upper Volta. It is the country's main trade, industrial, and communications centre. Industries include food processing and handicrafts. Population (1981 est): 150 000.

bobolink An American *oriole, *Dolichonyx oryzivorus*, that nests in Canada and the northern USA and migrates to South America in winter. It is black below and white above and nests on the ground, foraging for insects and seeds.

Bobruisk (*or* Bobruysk) 53 08N 29 10E A port in the W central Soviet Union, in the Belorussian SSR on the River Berezina. It has an 18th-century fortress and its industries include engineering, timber, and tyre manufacturing. Population (1981 est): 203 000.

bobsledding The sport of racing bobsleds (also called bobsleighs or bobs), which was developed by British sportsmen at St Moritz (Switzerland) in the late 19th century. A bobsled is a steel-bodied toboggan with two pairs of runners, the front pair steerable, and a rear brake, holding two or four people. In a race, the bobsleds slide one at a time down a narrow icy chute some 1500 m (1640 yd) long with high walls and banked turns, reaching speeds of over 130 km per hour (81 mph).

Boccaccio, Giovanni (1313–75) Italian writer and poet. Son of a merchant of Florence, he was sent to Naples about

BOER WAR On Cronjè's Heels *(1900), by the British war artist H. Seppings Wright. The tactics of the Boers and the unfamiliar terrain caused problems for the conventionally trained British troops.*

1328 to learn business. Literature interested him more, however; between then and 1341, when he returned to Florence, he wrote *Filocolo*, a prose romance, *Filostrato*, which supplied the plot of Chaucer's *Troilus and Criseyde*, and *Teseida*, the source of Chaucer's *Knight's Tale*. Between 1348 and 1353 he composed the *Decameron*, a collection of a hundred stories told by a party of young people escaping from plague-stricken Florence in 1348. He met *Petrarch in 1350 and was much influenced by him. In later life he chiefly wrote scholarly works in Latin and lectured on Dante's *Divine Comedy*. He also founded the first chair of Greek in W Europe, at the University of Florence.

Boccherini, Luigi (1743–1805) Italian violoncellist and composer. He became famous in Rome while still a boy. Boccherini produced his first opera *La confederazione* (1765) in Lucca. His large output includes cello concertos and sonatas, symphonies, choral works, and string quintets and quartets.

Boccioni, Umberto (1882–1916) Italian futurist painter and sculptor. He trained under *Balla before settling in Milan (1907), where, influenced by the poet *Marinetti, he aimed to express the violence and speed of modern life in such paintings as *The City Rises* (1910; New York). His manifesto of futurist sculpture (1912) advocated the use of materials such as glass, cement, lightbulbs, etc.

Bochum 51 28N 7 11E A city in NW West Germany, in North Rhine-Westphalia. It is the site of the Ruhr University (1965). The manufacture of cars, textiles, and chemicals has replaced coalmining and iron and steel production. Population (1980 est): 402 000.

Bodawpaya (d. 1819) King of Burma (1789–1819). His aggressive policies ensured considerable expansion of Burmese territory during his reign. He annexed Arakan (1785), Manipur (1813), and Assam (1816) and almost precipitated an Anglo-Burmese war by demanding the surrender of Chittagong, Dacca, and Murshidabad from the British Indian government. His sudden death averted a confrontation. The *Burmese Domesday Book* (1784), a survey of Burma, was compiled during his reign.

Bodensee. *See* Constance, Lake.

Bode's law (*or* Titius-Bode law) A relationship between the distances of the planets from the sun. Take the number sequence 0, 3, 6, 12, 24, . . . , add 4 to each number, and divide each sum by 10. The resulting sequence is in good agreement with observed planetary distances (in astronomical units) out to Uranus, provided the belt of *minor planets is considered a single entity. Formulated by Johann Titius (1729–96) and popularized in 1772 by Johann Bode (1747–1826), it is still unexplained by theory.

Bodhidharma (6th century AD) Indian Buddhist patriarch from Conjeeveram, near Madras. He entered China about 520. Teaching a form of meditation called *dhyana* (Chinese *ch'an*, Japanese *zen*), he is credited with founding *Zen Buddhism.

Bodhisattva In Mahayana Buddhism, the title of a person who is to become a Buddha. The term is also used to describe the Buddha (Gautama) before his enlightenment. The Bodhisattva ideal is that of the individual who seeks enlightenment not for himself alone but for all beings. In Indian art the Bodhisattvas are depicted as youthful and represent various aspects of the nature of Buddha.

Bodin, Jean (1530–96) French philosopher and jurist. Although a Protestant, he was a successful lawyer and became parliamentary representative of Vermandois (1576). He visited Britain in 1581 where his belief in witchcraft, propounded in *Démonomanie des sorciers* (1580), later influenced James I. His greatest work, *La République* (1576), is a comprehensive political philosophy.

Bodleian Library The major *library of Oxford University, first established in 1409 and restored and enlarged by Sir Thomas Bodley from 1598 to 1602. Since 1610 it has been entitled to receive a free copy of every book published in Britain; it contains well over 2.5 million volumes.

Bodmin 50 29N 4 43W A market town in SW England, the administrative centre of Cornwall. Nearby is **Bodmin Moor**, a granite upland reaching 420 m (1375 ft) at Brown Willy. Population (1981): 12 148.

Bodoni, Giambattista (1740–1813) Italian printer. In 1768 he became the Duke of Parma's printer and, influenced by François-Ambroise Didot (1730–1804), began to design his own typefaces. The best known, designed in 1790 and named after him, is still in use.

Boehm, Theobald (1794–1881) German flautist. He invented the **Boehm System**, a keyed mechanism for the flute that is still in use today and has been applied successfully to the clarinet and the oboe.

Boehme, Jakob. *See* Böhme.

Boeotia A region of central Greece, N and W of *Attica. Its main geographical features are rich central plains, surrounded by hills and mountains, and Lake Copaïs (now drained). The dozen or so city states that shared the territory formed a federal state dominated by *Thebes in 446 BC. The Boeotians had a reputation for good living and stupidity, belied by the military success of Thebes and the poetry of *Hesiod and *Pindar, among others. Boeotians took no part in Greek colonization overseas.

Boer. *See* Afrikaner.

Boer Wars (*or* South African Wars) The wars fought against the British by the Boers or *Afrikaners of South Africa. In the first (1880–81) the Boers of the Transvaal under *Kruger rebelled against British rule. After inflicting a massive defeat on the British garrison at *Majuba Hill, the Transvaal regained its independence under the *Pretoria Convention. In the second Boer War (1899–1902) the Boer forces of the South African Republic (previously the Transvaal) and Orange Free State were initially successful, besieging Ladysmith, Mafeking (held courageously by *Baden-Powell from October, 1899, until his relief in February, 1900), and Kimberley. They suffered reverses during 1900 but, using guerrilla tactics, were able to hold off the British under *Kitchener and F. S. *Roberts. The British devastated the countryside, rounded up Boer women and children, of whom some 20 000 died in concentration camps, and finally defeated the Boers, who lost their independence in the Peace of Vereeniging (1902). □p. 163.

Boethius, Anicius Manlius Severinus (c. 480–524 AD) Roman statesman and philosopher. A patrician by birth, Boethius was consul in 510 during the Gothic occupation of Rome under *Theodoric, to whom he became chief minister. His championing of Roman traditions and institutions earned Theoderic's displeasure, and Boethius was imprisoned, tortured, and eventually executed. His translations of Aristotle and treatises on music and mathematics were standard texts in medieval Europe but his most famous work is *The Consolation of Philosophy*, written while he was in prison. A dialogue between the author and the personification of philosophy, the *Consolation* seeks to prove that virtue alone remains constant and the knowledge of God is the only true wisdom.

Bogarde, Dirk (Derek van den Bogaerde; 1921–) British film actor of Dutch descent. He acted in many British films in the 1950s and 1960s, including *Doctor in the House* (1953) and *The Servant* (1963), but his major performances were in later films of international stature, such as *The Damned* (1969), *Death in Venice* (1970), and *Providence* (1978). Also a writer, he is the author of the autobiographical *A Postilion Struck by Lightning* (1977), *Snakes and Ladders* (1978), and *An Orderly Man* (1983) as well as the novels *Gentle Occupation* (1980) and *Voices in the Garden* (1981).

Bogart, Humphrey (1899–1957) US film actor. He achieved international success in the 1940s with his portrayals of tough heroes whose cynicism masked a romantic idealism. His films include *Casablanca* (1942), *To Have and Have Not* (1944), in which Lauren Bacall (1924–), whom he subsequently married, made her screen debut, *The Big Sleep* (1946), and *The African Queen* (1951).

Boğazköy (*or* Boğazkale). *See* Hattusas.

Bognor Regis 50 47N 0 41W A resort on the S coast of England, in West Sussex. George V convalesced here in 1929 and granted Bognor its title. Population (1981): 39 536

Bogomils. *See* Cathari.

Bogor (former name: Buitenzorg) 6 34S 106 45E A city in Indonesia, on W Java. It is famed for its botanical garden (1817) and former Dutch governor general's residence (1745). It is an agricultural centre with an agricultural university (founded 1963) and an important research institute. Population (1980): 247 409.

Bogotá, Santa Fé de 4 38N 74 15W The capital of Colombia, on a fertile central plateau of the E Andes at an altitude of 2640 m (8600 ft). Founded by the Spanish in the early 16th century on the site of the conquered Indian settlement of Bacatá, it became capital of the viceroyalty of New Grenada and an important cultural centre. Today it possesses a university (1867), a number of colleges, and several notable technical schools. Regular airlines have helped to improve its rather isolated position from the rest of the country. Population (1981 est): 4 486 200.

Bohai. *See* Chihli, Gulf of.

Bohemia (Czech name: Čechy; German name: Böhmen) An area and former province (1918–49) of W Czechoslovakia. It consists chiefly of a plateau enclosed by mountains. The most industrialized part of Czechoslovakia, Bohemia possesses important mineral resources, including uranium, coal, and iron ore. Agriculture is well developed. It is renowned for its many mineral springs. *History*: Bohemia derives its name from the Boii (the first known inhabitants), who were displaced by the Czechs (1st-5th centuries AD). Bohemia became part of the greater Moravian empire in the 9th century, during which period Christianity was introduced. St Wenceslas was the first great Bohemian ruler but his brother, Boleslav I (d. 967; reigned 929-67), was forced to acknowledge the rule of Emperor Otto I and for many centuries thereafter Bohemia was linked with the Holy Roman Empire. During the 11th century there was a successful expedition into Moravia, which was linked from then on with Bohemia. It achieved the height of its power following the acquisitions of the Přemyslid Otakar II (1230-78; reigned 1253-78). The Přemyslid dynasty came to an end with the assassination of Wencelas III (1289-1306; reigned 1305-06) and John of Luxembourg was subsequently elected king (1310). The golden age of Bohemia was established by his son Charles I (Emperor *Charles IV), who founded the university at Prague in 1348. The reigns of his successors were marked by religious upheavals inspired

HUMPHREY BOGART *With Rod Steiger (right) in* The Harder They Fall *(1956).*

by Jan Hus (see Hussites). The accession (1526) of Archduke Ferdinand began the long Habsburg domination of Bohemia. It was laid waste during the Thirty Years' War and after the Peace of Westphalia (1648) forcible Germanization and oppressive taxation reduced most Czechs to misery. There was a rebirth of Czech nationalism during the 19th century but full independence was only attained at the end of World War I, when Bohemia became part of the Republic of Czechoslovakia.

Bohemond I (or Bohemund; c. 1056-1111) Prince of Antioch (1099-1111). He fought (1080-85) with his father Robert Guiscard against Alexius I Comnenus and was a leader of the first Crusade, during which he took Antioch (1098). He was captured by the Turks (1100-03) and after renewed warfare with Alexius became his vassal (1108).

Böhm, Karl (1894-1981) Austrian conductor, who was noted particularly for his performances of operas by Mozart and Richard Strauss. He was conductor of the Dresden State Opera (1934-43) and the Vienna State Opera (1943-45).

Böhme, Jakob (or Boehme; 1575-1624) German Lutheran theosophist, who lived most of his life as a shoemaker in Silesia. His first work, the *Aurora* (1612), was condemned by the local authorities. Although forbidden to write, he later published such works as *Der Weg zu Christo* and *Mysterium magnum* (both 1623). He was influenced by *Paracelsus, alchemy, and astrology but also claimed divine inspiration for his writings. His central belief was that God was the source of everything, including evil, since he had two wills, one good and the other evil. He has influenced many thinkers, notably *Hegel and *Schelling.

Bohr, Niels Henrik David (1885-1962) Danish physicist, who worked with J. J. *Thomson at Cambridge and *Rutherford at Manchester. He made an immense contribution to atomic theory by combining Rutherford's nuclear model with Planck's quantum theory. The model of the atom he proposed (the *Bohr atom) was modified by *Sommerfeld but is essentially the basis for modern atomic theory. Bohr also invented the concept of complementarity to combine the particle and wave aspects of subatomic particles. In 1916 he returned to Copenhagen as professor of physics and was awarded a Nobel Prize in 1922. During the 1930s his Institute of Theoretical Physics in Copenhagen became a haven for many Jewish and other physicists expelled by Hitler. In 1939 he took news of *Meitner's and *Hahn's uranium fission work to the USA and started the process that culminated in the manufacture of the atomic bomb. Bohr himself later worked at Los Alamos on the bomb, after escaping from German-occupied Denmark. A fervent advocate of atomic energy for peaceful uses, he organized the first Atoms for Peace Conference in 1955. His son **Aage Bohr** (1922-) shared the 1975 Nobel Prize for Physics for his work on atomic theory.

Bohr atom A model of the atom, put forward by Niels *Bohr in 1913. His model assumes that electrons move around a central nucleus in circular orbits. The electrons are confined to fixed orbits at fixed distances from the nucleus, each orbit corresponding to a specific energy level. If the electron gains or loses the right amount of energy, in the form of a photon of electromagnetic radiation, it jumps or falls into another orbit. The jumps are quantized (see quantum theory), the energy associated with each jump being equal to hf, where h is the Planck constant and f is the frequency of . the radiation. The model gives a good explanation of the spectral emission of the hydrogen atom and was later modified by *Sommerfeld to explain the fine structure of the hydrogen lines, by assuming that the electrons move in precessing elliptical orbits.

Boiardo, Matteo Maria, Conte di Scandiano (1441-94) Italian poet. He served the Dukes of Ferrara as governor of Modena (1480-82) and Reggio (1487-94). His chief work was the unfinished *Orlando innamorato* (1483), a chivalrous

epic about Roland (see Charlemagne) and the precursor of the more famous *Orlando furioso* by *Ariosto.

boil An inflamed pus-filled swelling on the skin, usually caused by infection of a hair follicle with the bacterium *Staphylococcus aureus*. Boils are more likely to develop when constitutional resistance is low or when the diet is inadequate. The application of a warm poultice will bring the boil to a head and allow the pus to drain. A **carbuncle** is a collection of boils situated close together; it is slightly more difficult to treat and may require the use of antibiotics.

Boileau(-Despréaux), Nicolas (1636-1711) French poet and critic. After the publication of his satires in 1666 he became friendly with *Molière, *Racine, and other leading writers. *L'Art poétique* (1674) was received as a definitive guide to the classical principles in literature and had a powerful contemporary influence in France and England. He also wrote a mock epic, *Le Lutrin* (1674), and translated *Longinus' treatise *On the Sublime*.

boiling point The temperature at which the *vapour pressure of a liquid is equal to the atmospheric pressure. The boiling point of a liquid is usually given at standard atmospheric pressure (101 325 pascals).

Bois de Boulogne A park in W Paris, France, bordering on the River Seine. It was presented to the city in 1852 by Napoleon III and contains the Auteuil and Longchamp racecourses. Area: 860 ha (2125 acres).

Boise 43 38N 116 12W A city in the USA, the capital and largest city of Idaho. The centre of a gold rush in 1862, it has timber, food-processing, and agricultural industries. Population (1980): 102 451.

Boito, Arrigo (1842-1918) Italian composer, librettist, and poet. He wrote the librettos for Verdi's operas *Otello* (1887) and *Falstaff* (1893) and adapted the libretto of his own opera *Mefistofele* (1868) and from *Goethe's *Faust*.

Bokassa I (Jean Bedel B.; 1921-) Emperor of the Central African Empire from 1977 until his overthrow in 1979. He seized power in the Central African Republic in 1966, becoming president and later proclaiming himself emperor. After returning from exile (1986), he was sentenced to death for atrocities committed during his reign.

Bokhara. *See* Bukhara.

Bolden, Buddy (Charles B.; 1868-1931) US Black jazz cornettist, originally a barber. He frequently worked with several bands in the course of one evening. He became insane in 1907 and died in hospital.

Bolesław (I) the Brave (c. 966-1025) The first King of Poland, who extended the territory of the Polish principality, which he inherited in 992, and was crowned king (1000) by Emperor Otto III. He reorganized the Polish church, making it responsible directly to the pope and independent of the German church.

Bolesław (II) the Generous (1039-81) King of Poland (1058-79), recognized by the pope in 1076. Bolesław successfully pursued Polish interests at the expense of German influence until a revolt of the clergy and nobility led to his excommunication and deposition.

Bolesław (III) the Wry-Mouthed (1086-1138) Ruler of Poland (1102-38). Bolesław never took the title of king. Between 1113 and 1135 he reconquered and christianized Pomerania.

Boletus A genus of mushrooms (about 50 species). The undersurface of the cap bears a series of vertical tubes (instead of gills), in which the spores are formed. Most grow near trees and they are generally edible or harmless (see cèpe). An exception is Satan's boletus (*B. satanas*), which is poisonous but not deadly. It has a short stalk and a grey or greyish-green cap 10-20 cm in diameter. Family: *Boletaceae*; class: *Basidiomycetes*.

Boleyn, Anne (c. 1507-36) The second wife (from 1533) of Henry VIII of England and the mother of Elizabeth

I. Henry soon tired of Anne, who was accused of treason by committing adultery and executed.

Bolingbroke, Henry St John, 1st Viscount (1678–1751) English statesman and philosopher. A Tory, he became an MP in 1701 and was secretary of war (1704–08) before becoming secretary of state for the north in 1710. A supporter of the *Jacobites, he fled to France on the accession of George I (1714), where he helped to organize the Fifteen Rebellion. In France he encountered the major thinkers of the *Enlightenment and wrote *Reflections upon Exile* and *Reflections Concerning Innate Moral Principles*. Returning to England in 1725, he became the bitter opponent of *Walpole and in contributions to the journal, *The Craftsman*, outlined his aim, which he never achieved, to create a Country Party of Whigs and Tories united by their opposition to Walpole. In 1735 he returned to France. He also wrote *The Idea of a Patriot King* (1749).

Bolívar, Simón (1783–1830) South American soldier and statesman, known as the Liberator. The son of a wealthy Venezuelan creole family, his childhood tutor and subsequent travels in Europe instilled in Bolívar an admiration for the ideas of the Enlightenment. He returned to Latin America in 1807 and devoted the rest of his life to its liberation from Spain. In 1813 he seized Caracas but after defeat in 1814 went into exile until 1817. His victory at the battle of *Boyacá (1819) achieved the liberation of New Granada, which was renamed Colombia. Bolívar became its president and, after liberating Venezuela and Quito (Ecuador) in 1821, organized a federation of the three newly independent states. Latin America was finally freed of the Spanish by campaigns in Peru, and Upper Peru took the name Bolivia in honour of Bolívar. His dream of a united Andean republic was never realized and he died disillusioned by the political bickering that thwarted this goal.

Bolivia, Republic of An inland country in central South America consisting of low plains in the N and E, crossed by the Madre de Dios, Bené, and Mamoré river systems; in the W, ranges of the Andes rise to over 6400 m (21 000 ft) and the Altiplano, a plateau averaging about 3900 m (13 000 ft), contains Lakes Titicaca and Poopó. Bolivia has some of the world's highest inhabited regions, most of the population, which is of mixed Indian and Spanish descent, living at altitudes of over 3000 m (10 000 ft). *Economy*: tinmining has long been of the first importance to Bolivia's economy and remains the principal industry. The main tin producers have been nationalized in recent years. Other minerals include zinc, lead, antimony, and copper. Silver is much less important than previously. Agriculture is being improved in the E part and the main crops are sugar cane, potatoes, maize, rice, and wheat. Livestock, including llamas, is raised and forestry is being developed. Main exports include tin and other minerals, oil (through a pipeline to Arica on the Chilean coast), natural gas (to Argentina), hides and skins, and vicuña wool. *History*: ruins near Tiahuanaco indicate the existence of a pre-Inca civilization (the Aymaras) going back to the 10th century. The area later became part of the Inca Empire and was conquered by the Spanish in the 16th century, when it became known as Alto Peru. The discovery of tin and silver at Potosí soon after the Spanish conquest led to great prosperity. In 1776 it became part of the viceroyalty of Buenos Aires. After a long war it gained its independence with the help of Simón Bolívar in 1825 and became a republic with Antonio José de *Sucre as first president. During the remainder of the century as a result of civil wars and struggles with neighbouring countries Bolivia lost much territory, including access to the Pacific coast. Political unrest and violent changes of government have continued into the 20th century and in 1971 a military coup brought Gen Hugo Banzer Suárez to power. He achieved a measure of political stability, remaining in office until overthrown in a coup in 1978. Since then frequent political upheavals have resumed; Victor Paz Estenssoro was re-elected president in 1985 for a fourth term. Disputes with Peru and Chile continue over the question of access to the Pacific coast. Official languages: Spanish, Quechua, and Aymara. Official currency: peso boliviano of 100 centavos. Area: 1 098 580 sq km (424 160 sq mi). Population (1983 est): 5 883 000. Capital: La Paz (legal capital: Sucre).

Böll, Heinrich (1917–85) German novelist. After infantry service in World War II, he eventually settled down as a full-time writer in 1951. His novels and stories include *The Train Was on Time* (1949), *The Clown* (1963), *The Lost Honour of Katharina Blum* (1975), and *The Safety Net* (1982). He frequently depicted ironically the moral degeneration of postwar German society. He won the Nobel Prize in 1972.

Bollandists The *Jesuit scholars who continued the work on the *Acta Sanctorum*, an authoritative edition of the lives of the saints, begun by the founder and first editor of the project, John van Bolland (1596–1665). The first two volumes of the work were published in Antwerp in 1643, and the most recent one appeared in 1940.

boll weevil A stout brownish *weevil, *Anthonomus grandis*, also called cotton boll weevil. Originally a native of the New World tropics, it is now a major insect pest of cotton crops in the W hemisphere. The female lays a single egg within each cotton boll, which thus fails to develop.

Bologna 44 30N 11 20E A city in N Italy, the capital of Emilia-Romagna. The history of the site of Bologna dates from Etruscan times. It became a free city in the middle ages and the Emperor Charles V was crowned here in 1530. It has an ancient university (1088) and a 14th-century gothic church. Its industries include engineering and food processing. Population (1980 est): 466 593.

Bologna, Giovanni da. *See* Giambologna.

Bolsheviks One of the two factions into which the Russian Social Democratic Workers' Party split in 1903 in London (the other was the *Mensheviks). The Bolsheviks, which means those in the majority, were led by *Lenin, who believed that the revolution must be guided by a single centralized party of professional revolutionaries (*see also* Leninism). The Bolsheviks came to power in the *Russian Revolution (1917) and from 1918 until 1952 the Soviet Communist Party was termed Communist Party (Bolsheviks).

Bolshoi Ballet The principal Russian ballet company, based at the Bolshoi Theatre in Moscow. It originated from a dancing class established by the Moscow orphanage in the late 18th century and moved into its present premises in 1856 after fire had destroyed the first Bolshoi Theatre. Known for its dramatic style and its realistic and elaborate scenery, it first appeared in the West in 1956 in London and has since become one of the world's leading ballet companies.

Bolt, Robert Oxton (1924–   ) British dramatist, famous for the play and film *A Man for All Seasons* (1960), a study of Sir Thomas *More. He has written screenplays for *Lawrence of Arabia* and other films directed by David *Lean.

Bolton 53 35W 2 26W A town in NW England, in Greater Manchester. Traditionally a cotton-spinning town (Samuel Crompton, inventor of the spinning mule, was born here), Bolton also manufactures textile machinery and chemicals and is involved in engineering. Population (1981): 146 722.

Boltzmann, Ludwig Eduard (1844–1906) Austrian physicist, who developed statistical mechanics with J. C. *Maxwell and J. W. *Gibbs, notably the Maxwell–Boltzmann statistics of particle systems obeying classical laws. He also linked thermodynamics with molecular physics by showing that increasing entropy is related to increasing disorder among particles. Working with his teacher Josef Stefan (1835–93), he showed that Stefan's law could be derived thermodynamically and it is now usually known as the *Stefan–Boltzmann law.

Boltzmann constant (k) A constant, obtained by dividing the *gas constant by *Avogadro's number, equal to 1.3806×10^{-23} joule per kelvin. Named after Ludwig *Boltzmann.

Bolyai, János (1802-60) Hungarian mathematician, who (with *Lobachevski) was the first to study the properties of spaces with *non-Euclidean geometry.

Bolzano 46 30N 11 22E A city in Italy, in Trentino-Alto Adige. It has a 14th-century gothic cathedral. Bolzano is a centre for tourism and trades in fruit and wine. There are steel and textile industries. Population (1980 est): 105 854.

Boma 5 50S 13 03E A port in SW Zaïre, on the Zaïre River. It was formerly the capital of the Congo Free State, later the Belgian Congo (1886-1926). Forest products, such as palm oil, are exported. Population (1976): 93 965.

bombardier beetle A blue-grey and orange beetle, about 9 mm long, belonging to a widely distributed genus (*Brachinus*) of *ground beetles. It has an efficient means of chemical defence, emitting puffs of an irritant secretion from the anal glands. Similar beetles of the genus *Pherosophus* occur in Africa, Asia, and the East Indies.

Bombay 18 56N 72 51E A city in India, the capital of Maharashtra and the country's main seaport on the W coast. The city proper occupies a group of islands that are united by a system of causeways and breakwaters; the site, known as Bombay Island, is linked with Salsette Island in the N. Its natural harbour, 11 km (7 mi) wide, is the focus of most of India's international trade. Bombay is also the financial and commercial centre of the country. The Tata hydroelectric system powers much of Bombay's industry, which includes cotton textiles, food processing, and oil refining. The city is also the site of the country's first nuclear reactor. The harbour is dominated by the Gateway of India, a monumental arch that was built to commemorate the visit of George V of the UK in 1911. The University of Bombay (1857) and numerous government buildings are situated in the centre of the city and the many temples (dating from the 8th century AD and earlier) reflect the cultural and religious diversity to be found in the city. The population is mainly Hindu but there are large Muslim, Christian, and Jewish minorities. The city's island location has led to problems of overcrowding and a twin city on the mainland is planned. *History:* ceded to the Portuguese in 1534, it passed to Charles II of England in 1661 and to the British East India Company in 1668. The arrival of the railways, the opening of the Suez Canal, and land reclamation led to considerable expansion in the 19th century. Population (1981): 8 227 000.

Bombay duck A fish, *Harpodon nehereus*, found in the estuaries of N India, where it is widely used for food. It has a grey or brown body, about 40 cm long, with small dark speckles and large pectoral and pelvic fins. Order: *Myctophiformes*.

Bon The pre-Buddhist religion of Tibet, characterized by the belief in a supreme sky god and a hierarchy of good and evil spirits, gods, demons, and ghosts. Elaborate ritual, including animal or even human sacrifice, abounded; religious practice was presided over by a class of shamans (*see* shamanism), priest-magicians who could influence the spirits by means of white or black magic, even being able to open the gate between earth and heaven. It was absorbed into Tibetan Buddhism, to which it lent a very individual character.

Bon, Cape 37 05N 11 02E A peninsula in NE Tunisia, extending into the Mediterranean Sea. Its fertile plains produce oranges, olives, and market-garden produce. Length: about 75 km (46 mi). Width: 35 km (22 mi).

Bonaparte (*or* Buonaparte) A Corsican family that included the French emperors, *Napoleon I and *Napoleon III, and the nominal emperor, *Napoleon II. **Carlo Bonaparte** (1746-85), a lawyer, had four sons. **Joseph Bonaparte** (1768-1844) was a diplomat of indifferent qualities who rose to high office by virtue of the position of his brother Napoleon I, from whom he received the thrones of Naples (1806) and Spain (1808). After Napoleon's defeat at Waterloo (1815) Joseph lived in exile. **Lucien Bonaparte** (1775-1840) was president of the Council of Five Hundred under the Directory and became a critic of Napoleon's policies. The brothers were reconciled, however, on the eve of Waterloo and after Napoleon's defeat Lucien lived in exile in Italy. **Louis Bonaparte** (1778-1846) was created King of Holland by Napoleon in 1806 but, exasperated by Louis' inability to enforce the *Continental System, Napoleon obliged him to relinquish the Crown in 1810. He too died in exile. His son by Hortense de *Beauharnais became Napoleon III. **Jérôme Bonaparte** (1784-1860) was created King of Westphalia in 1807 and was a commander in Napoleon's Russian invasion and at Waterloo. He survived to become a dignitary in the Second Empire (1852-70), established by his nephew Napoleon III.

The exploits of these and other members of the Bonaparte family formed the iconography of **Bonapartism**, a movement that sought to recreate the Napoleonic empire and to establish the dynasty in France. Louis Napoleon's *Des idées napoléoniennes* (1839) typified the romantic and conservative nature of Bonapartism.

Bonaventure, St (Giovanni di Fidanza; c. 1221-74) Italian Franciscan theologian, known as Doctor Seraphicus. He studied and lectured at Paris, in 1257 receiving the degree of doctor and becoming minister general of the Franciscan Order. He wrote the official biography of St Francis. As a theologian, he supported the traditional teachings of St Augustine, as opposed to the new Aristotelian thought that influenced his contemporary St Thomas *Aquinas. Feast day: 14 July. Emblem: a cardinal's hat.

bond A security issued by a government, local authority, or public company as a means of raising capital. Most bonds pay a fixed rate of interest and are redeemable on a stated day. *See also* gilt-edged securities.

Bond, Edward (1934-) British dramatist. He uses techniques of both realism and epic theatre to express his bleak vision of the cruelty of human society. His direct portrayal of violence in *Saved* (1965) aroused much controversy. His other plays include *Narrow Road to the Deep North* (1968) and *The Women* (1978).

Bondi, Sir Hermann (1919-) British cosmologist and mathematician, born in Vienna. With Fred *Hoyle and T. *Gold he developed the steady-state theory of the universe. Formerly director of ESRO, he became (1980) chairman of the Natural Environment Research Council.

bone A rigid tissue that forms most of the skeleton of higher animals and man. The shape of individual bones is governed by their function (*see* skeleton). Most bones have a central cavity filled with *marrow. Bone is composed of a matrix of fibres of the protein collagen, responsible for the strength of bones, and bone salts, chiefly calcium salts (*see* apatite). This tissue is formed by activity of bone cells (osteoblasts), which become enclosed in the matrix when they have ceased to function. Bone formation starts during embryonic life. Most bones (including the long bones) develop from cartilage and the process is complete at birth. Membrane bones (e.g. the skull bones) are formed directly in connective tissue, the process being completed after birth (hence the gap (called a fontanelle) in a newborn baby's skull). The branch of medicine concerned with the diagnosis and treatment of diseases of bones is called **osteology**. *See* Plate IV.

Bône. *See* Annaba.

bone-black (*or* animal charcoal) *Charcoal obtained by heating bones. It is about one-tenth carbon, the rest being calcium and magnesium phosphates and other salts. Bone-black is used as an absorbent, for example in removing colouring, refining sugar, and removing *fusel oil from whisky.

boneset A plant of the genus *Eupatorium*, also called thoroughwort, found in tropical South America, Mexico, and the West Indies but grown elsewhere as greenhouse or border plants. Boneset is a perennial herb, shrub, or small tree. The flat-topped flower heads consist of disc florets, usually rose or white, with protruding styles. Family: *Compositae. See also* comfrey.

bongo An antelope, *Boocerus euryceros*, of dense tropical central African forests. About 120 cm high at the shoulder, bongos are red-brown with vertical white body stripes and white markings on the head and legs. The male has spiralled horns up to 100 cm long. Bulls are solitary; cows and calves live in small herds. They feed on leaves and shoots. □mammals.

Bonhoeffer, Dietrich (1906–45) German pastor and theologian. As a young theological lecturer and pastor, Bonhoeffer identified himself with the German *Confessing Church, which opposed the pro-Nazi part of the Lutheran church, and during the war became involved with anti-Hitler conspirators. He was arrested in 1943, sent to Buchenwald concentration camp, and finally hanged. His posthumous *Letters and Papers from Prison* (1953) and radical theological writings continue to be influential.

Boniface, St (or St Wynfrith; c. 680–754 AD) English missionary, known as the Apostle of Germany. He was born in Crediton, Devon, and entered the Benedictine Order. He visited Frisia in 716 and in 718 was granted papal authority to evangelize the Germans. He successfully established Christianity in several German states and instituted church reforms elsewhere, culminating in his appointment as Archbishop of Mainz in 751. He was martyred with 53 companions in Frisia. Feast day: 5 June.

Boniface VIII (Benedict Caetani; c. 1234–1303) Pope (1294–1303). He was elected after a long career in papal administration. An expert in canon law, he repeatedly clashed with *Philip IV of France over the royal claim to judge and tax the clergy (which he also disputed with *Edward I of England). The bull *Unam Sanctam* (*One Holy*; 1302) proclaimed papal supremacy over temporal powers. In 1303 he was captured in Italy by Philip's forces and although soon released died shortly after.

Bonington, Chris (Christian John Storey B.; 1934–) British mountaineer, author, and photographer. He is famous especially for the first British ascent of the N face of the Eiger (1962) as well as his leadership of the 1970 Annapurna I and the 1975 Everest expeditions. He finally reached the summit of Everest in 1985.

Bonington, Richard Parkes (1801–28) British landscape watercolourist and oil painter. He was born near Nottingham but lived in France after 1817. In Paris he studied under Baron *Gros and became friendly with *Delacroix. Together they studied Rubens and Constable and their visit to England (1825) inspired Bonington to devote more time to history painting.

Bonin Islands A Japanese group of about 30 forested volcanic islands in the central Pacific Ocean, the most important being Chichi-jima. Strategically important during World War II, they were captured by the USA in 1945 (returned 1968). Sugar cane, cocoa, and bananas are produced, timber is exported, and there is offshore whaling. Area: 103 sq km (40 sq mi). Population (1980): 2010. Chief settlement: Omura.

bonito A swift marine food and game fish, belonging to the worldwide genus *Sarda*, which is related to *mackerel and *tuna. About 75 cm long, bonitos are greenish blue above, with dark longitudinal stripes, and silvery below. Other related fish called bonito include the leaping bonito (*Cybiosarda elegans*), plain bonito (*Orcynopsis unicolor*), and *skipjack tuna. □oceans.

Bonn 50 43N 7 07E The capital of the Federal Republic of Germany (West Germany), in North Rhine-Westphalia on the River Rhine. The old part of the town contains the cathedral (12th–13th centuries) and Beethoven's birthplace (now a museum). The university was founded in 1786. *History*: originally settled by the Romans, it was destroyed by the Normans in the 9th century AD, and was the seat of the Electors of Cologne from the 13th to the 16th centuries. It passed from France to Prussia in 1815 and was made the federal capital in 1949. Population (1985 est): 289 900.

Bonnard, Pierre (1867–1947) French painter. He took up art in Paris in the 1880s, after studying law, and as a member of the *Nabis, he painted decorative domestic scenes, influenced by Japanese prints. More original works of this period were his lithographs, *Aspects of the Life of Paris* (1895), and illustrations for Verlaine's book *Parallèlement* (1900). After 1900 his paintings of interiors, landscapes, and bathing women were treated increasingly with dazzling colour and light.

Bonnet, Charles (1720–93) Swiss naturalist, noted for his speculations about evolution. He demonstrated that aphid eggs could develop without fertilization (*see* parthenogenesis). This led him to propose that every organism contained a sequence of preformed individuals corresponding to successive generations. His catastrophe theory of evolution argued that periodic destruction of most life forms was followed by evolutionary advancement of the survivors.

Bonneville Salt Flats (or Bonneville Flats) A barren salt plain in the USA, in NW Utah. The flats form part of the Great Salt Lake Desert and are a relict feature of an ancient lake. Several world land speed records have been established here since 1935.

Bonnie Prince Charlie. *See* Charles Edward Stuart, the Young Pretender.

Bonny, Bight of (name until 1975: Bight of Biafra) An inlet of the Atlantic Ocean, bordering on Nigeria and Cameroon. It is the innermost bay of the Gulf of Guinea.

bonsai An ordinary shrub or tree, such as a conifer or flowering cherry, that is developed as a miniature (up to about 60 cm high). The technique was first practised as an art form in China over 700 years ago, probably using weather-beaten trees, which were considered aesthetically pleasing. It was later perfected by the Japanese (who treat good specimens as heirlooms) and has now spread to the W hemisphere. Bonsais grow from seeds or cuttings planted usually in earthenware pots with one or more drainage holes and containing a compost with a limited nutrient and water supply. Both branches and roots are trained and pruned. The trees may take ten years or more to acquire an aged appearance, and some live 300–400 years. Good hardy species may be kept outdoors for most of the year.

bontebok. *See* blesbok.

bony fish Any fish belonging to the class *Osteichthyes* (or *Pisces*), which includes the majority of food and game fishes (*see* teleost). They have bony skeletons and their gills are covered by a structure called an operculum. Many species use a swim bladder for buoyancy control and even for breathing air (*see* lungfish). Fertilization of the eggs occurs outside the body. Subclasses: *Actinopterygii*; *Sarcopterygii*.

booby A large tropical seabird belonging to the family *Sulidae* (gannets, etc.; 9 species) characterized by a large head, a long stout tapering bill, large webbed feet, and a wedge-shaped tail. Boobies are 65–85 cm long and typically have a white plumage with brown markings. Boobies soar high over the sea, diving to catch fish and squids.

boogie-woogie A piano blues in which the left hand establishes a driving repetitive pattern with eight beats to the bar, while the right provides a variety of syncopation. Originating in the SW USA, it was popular in the 1930s.

book A set of sheets of paper or similar material, usually bearing printed or handwritten words, folded and bound together between protective covers. The handwritten book (the codex), combining compactness, strength, and ease of use, began to oust its predecessor, the cumbersome papyrus scroll, during the 2nd century AD. Vellum (or parchment), being more durable than papyrus, became the preferred writing surface until the use of *paper spread slowly across Europe from 11th-century Byzantium. Printing at first brought no radical changes in book production, the sheets still being folded and bound by hand. Development of more efficient presses and cheaper paper production in the late 18th and early 19th centuries gradually brought the price of books within reach of the general public. During the 20th century paper binding (paperbacks), pioneered in the UK by Penguin Books Ltd, brought about a revolution in publishing so that in the UK alone over 35 000 new titles are published each year. In response to this deluge libraries have evolved new methods of data storage, using microfiche and microfilm (see microcopy).

bookbinding   The practice of sewing or gluing together the pages of a *book along one edge and securing them between protective covers (boards) joined across the back (spine) by a flexible hinge. Utilitarian in purpose, bookbinding has none the less long been practised as a decorative art. In the middle ages wooden boards were common and elaborate examples were encrusted with precious metals and gems. The advent of printing encouraged diversification in the types of material used for binding, with leather and vellum becoming paramount. Gold tooling, the commonest form of decoration, reached a peak of elaboration in the 17th and 18th centuries. The spread of literacy caused a demand for still cheaper binding materials; cloth bindings (1822), and in the 20th century paper and plastics, have catered for this need.

Nowadays books are bound by machinery, first invented in the late 19th century. The bindings are similar to hand bindings except in paperbacks, which are simply glued together. Hand binding remains a specialist craft employed in the production of luxury books.

Booker Prize   An annual prize of £15,000 for a work of British fiction. It was set up in 1968 by the British engineering and trading company Booker McConnell, in conjunction with the Publishers' Association, on the lines of the French Prix Goncourt (see Goncourt, Edmond de). Since 1971 it has been administered by the National Book League. Recent winners include Anita *Brookner (1984), Keri Hulme (1985), Kingsley *Amis (1986), and Penelope Lively (1987).

bookkeeping.   See accountancy.

booklouse   A soft-bodied wingless insect (1–7 mm long), also called dustlouse, belonging to the order *Psocoptera* (about 1600 species). Booklice inhabit buildings, often feeding on old books, papers, and entomological collections. See also bookworm.

Book of Changes. See I Ching.

Book of the Dead   A collection of ancient Egyptian texts dating from the 16th century BC. They consist of charms, formulas, and spells written on papyrus and placed inside mummy cases for use by the dead in the afterlife.

bookworm   Any insect that damages books by gnawing the bindings and boring holes in the paper. Bookworms therefore include *silverfish, booklice, moth and beetle larvae, etc.

Boole, George   (1815–64) British mathematician, who applied the methods of algebra to logic. By replacing logical operations by symbols, Boole showed that the operations could be manipulated to give logically consistent results. His method, known as Boolean algebra or symbolic logic, led to mathematics being given a logically consistent foundation. The subject was further developed by G. *Frege, B. A. W. *Russell, and A. N. *Whitehead.

boom   The phase in the *trade cycle in which output reaches a peak. Booms are characterized by full employment, rising prices, high profits, and high investment that goes with business confidence. Compare depression; recession.

boomerang   A curved hand-thrown wooden missile used by Australian Aborigines to kill game, as a weapon of war, or in play. The angled shape and the spin given to the missile when thrown enables the light types to return to the thrower if they miss their target. Up to 75 cm (30 in) long, they can be effective to a distance of 45 m (50 yd).

boomslang   A venomous green snake, *Dispholidus typus*, occurring in African savanna and reaching 1.8 m in length. It feeds on birds and chameleons, lying in wait and often holding its body erect and motionless before striking. Small amounts of its venom can cause fatal haemorrhaging in man. Family: *Colubridae*.

Boone, Daniel   (1734–1820) American pioneer. Between 1767 and 1773 he explored Kentucky and in 1775 led an expedition to establish a colony there for the Transylvania Company. He formed the first settlement in Kentucky at Boonesborough, which he courageously defended against Indian attack. He died in Missouri, where he was driven by land disputes. Boonville was named after him.

Boötes   (Latin: herdsman)   A large constellation in the N sky near Ursa Major. The brightest star is *Arcturus.

Booth, Charles   (1840–1916) British sociologist. Booth's *Life and Labour of the People in London* (1891–1903) was the first accurate sociological analysis of poverty to be published in England. His later work on the aged poor led him to devise the old-age pension.

Booth, Edwin   (1833–93) US actor. He was best known for his performances in Shakespearian tragic roles, especially Hamlet, which he performed for a hundred consecutive nights in 1864. He toured Europe several times. His brother **John Wilkes Booth** (1839–65), also an actor, shot President Abraham □Lincoln on 14 April, 1865. The president died next morning and Wilkes was killed two weeks later, while attempting to evade capture.

Booth, William   (1829–1912) British preacher and founder of the *Salvation Army. He was born in Nottingham and became an itinerant Methodist preacher, but left the Methodists in order to do evangelistic work among the poor. He established a mission in Whitechapel in 1865. The reluctance of established churches to accept his slum converts led to the foundation of the Salvation Army, with Booth as General (1877). His eldest son **William Bramwell Booth** (1856–1929) was chief of staff of the Salvation Army from 1880 and later General (1912–29). His daughter **Evangeline Booth** (1865–1950) was also a leading officer and then General (1934–39).

Boothia Peninsula   A peninsula of N Canada projecting

BOOK OF THE DEAD   *Detail from a papyrus of the Book of the Dead of Ani (c. 1250 BC) showing the scribe's heart being weighed in the afterlife by the gods Anubis and Thoth.*

into the Arctic Ocean, in Franklin district. The northernmost part of the North American mainland, it is sparsely populated, with a police post and trading post. Area: 32 375 sq km (12 500 sq mi).

Bootle 53 28N 3 00W A town in NW England, on the River Mersey adjacent to N Liverpool. Bootle's docks are extensive and modern and its industries include engineering, tanning, tin smelting, and flour milling. Population (1981): 62 463.

bootlegging The illegal distribution or production of highly taxed goods, especially liquor or cigarettes. During *Prohibition (1920–33) in the USA, when the manufacture, sale, and transportation of alcohol was banned, a well-organized illegal industry developed. Gangsters, such as Al *Capone, controlled both speakeasies (illegal bars) and private distribution systems. Other illegal activities (graft, extortion, protection rackets, prostitution) accompanied bootlegging and became the basis of the organized crime empires active in the USA today. Bootlegging, including the use of illegal stills, continues in certain areas of the USA, especially "dry" areas (where alcoholic spirits are not sold).

bootstrap theory The theory in which no elementary particle is regarded as being more fundamental than any other. Each particle exists by virtue of the existence of all the others. Its name derives from the phrase "to pull oneself up by the bootstraps." The theory avoids the problem of a series of classes of particles, each more fundamental than the last. *See also* particle physics.

bop (*or* bebop) A type of *jazz that originated in the USA in the 1940s as a reaction against swing. Bop emphasized the art of melodic improvisation neglected during the swing era, but was also characterized by harmonic and rhythmic experimentation. In New York City, Dizzy Gillespie and Charlie "Bird" Parker established small bop bands that required the audience to listen rather than dance.

Bophutha Tswana, Republic of A small country in South Africa, consisting of several separate landlocked areas. The majority of the population is Tswana. *Economy*: chiefly subsistence agriculture, especially livestock; much is being done to improve production by means of irrigation schemes. Large numbers of people still work and live in South Africa. Rich mineral resources include chrome, platinum, asbestos, and iron. *History*: in 1972 it became the first *Bantu Homeland to receive self-government under the Bantu Homelands Constitution Act (1971). It was granted independence in 1977, but this is recognized only by South Africa. President and prime minister: Chief L. L. M. Mangope (1923–). Official currency: South African rand. Area: 38 261 sq km (14 769 sq mi). Population (1984 est): 1 420 000, of whom 65% lived in South Africa. Capital: Montshiwa.

borage A widely grown annual Mediterranean herb, *Borago officinalis*. Borage is a stiff hairy plant, up to 60 cm high, with terminal clusters of small blue flowers with backward-pointing petals. It is used in herbal remedies, pot-pourri, beverages, and salads and the flowers may be candied. Family: *Boraginaceae*.

boranes Compounds of boron and hydrogen. The simplest is diborane B_2H_6, which is made by reacting sodium borohydride ($NaBH_4$) with *sulphuric acid. The formulas of boranes are not accounted for by classical theories of valence and their molecules contain electron-deficient bonds.

Borås 57 44N 12 55E A town in S Sweden. It is an important centre of the textile industry. Population (1983): 100 184.

borax (*or* sodium tetraborate; $Na_2B_4O_7$) A natural substance, usually occurring in hydrated crystalline form. It is found in some salt lakes and in alkaline soils and is used in the manufacture of glass and enamel.

Bordeaux (Latin name: Burdigala) 44 50N 0 34W A city in SW France, the capital of the Gironde department on the River Garonne. It is a major seaport and wine centre. Industries include shipbuilding, engineering, oil and sugar refining, and chemicals. There are many fine 18th-century buildings and squares, a cathedral (12th-15th centuries), and a university (1441). *History*: an important commercial centre under the Romans, it became the capital of Aquitania (*see* Aquitaine) but declined following the collapse of the Roman Empire. It flourished once again under English rule (1154–1453). It became a centre of the Fronde in the 17th century and of the Girondins during the French Revolution. It was the seat of the French government for a brief period in 1914 and again in 1940. Population (1982 est): 211 197.

Borden, Sir Robert Laird (1854–1937) Canadian statesman; Conservative prime minister (1911–20). An advocate of economic independence, he opposed a reciprocal trade agreement with the USA and came to power after defeating the Liberals on this issue. He formed a coalition government to introduce conscription in 1917 and gave women the vote in 1918. Borden supported British policies but claimed more independence for Canada in world affairs, winning separate Canadian representation at the League of Nations.

Borders Region An administrative region in SE Scotland, bordering on England. It was created under local government reorganization in 1975 from the counties of Berwick, Roxburgh, Peebles, Selkirk, and the SW part of Midlothian. The region consists chiefly of uplands descending E to the Merse lowlands. It is predominantly agricultural; sheep farming and associated industries, such as the manufacture of tweed and knitwear, are the principal activities. Area: 4672 sq km (1804 sq mi). Population (1981): 99 248. Administrative centre: Newtown St Boswells.

border terrier A breed of working dog originating in the border region of England and Scotland. It has a deep narrow body, triangular forward-falling ears, and a short strong muzzle. The coat is red, yellowish-brown, grey and tan, or blue and tan. Weight: 6–7 kg (dogs); 5–6 kg (bitches).

Bordet, Jules Jean Baptiste Vincent (1870–1961) Belgian bacteriologist, who discovered (1895) the two factors (antibody and complement) in blood serum responsible for the rupture of bacterial cells. This fundamental discovery paved the way for diagnostic tests for many bacterial diseases, including syphilis. Bordet founded the Pasteur Institute, Brussels (1901), and was awarded the 1919 Nobel Prize for Medicine.

bore In oceanography, a tidal flood wave with a steep front occurring in certain estuaries and travelling upstream at great speed, sometimes to a distance of several kilometres. It occurs when the spring flood tide brings sea water into an estuary more quickly than it can travel up the river, so that a ridge of water builds up.

Borelli, Giovanni Alfonso (1608–79) Italian physicist and physiologist, who attempted to explain the workings of the body in purely mechanical terms (*De Motu Animalium*, 1680–81). A friend of *Galileo, Borelli made contributions to astronomy, including ideas concerning the attractive forces between planets, their orbits, and the path taken by comets through space.

Borg, Bjorn (1956–) Swedish tennis player, the world's leading player in the late 1970s. In 1980 he won the men's singles at Wimbledon for the fifth consecutive year, having beaten Fred *Perry's record of three consecutive wins in 1979. He retired from world-class tennis in 1983.

Borgå. *See* Porvoo.

Borges, Jorge Luis (1899–1986) Argentinian writer and scholar. Educated in Europe, he joined the Spanish avantgarde Ultraist movement in 1920. In 1921 he returned to Argentina, where he founded three literary journals and published a book of poems in 1923. His best-known works are collections of intricate, fantastic, and paradoxical stories, especially *Fictions* (1944, 1966) and *The Aleph* (1949, 1970).

His last book (with Maria Kodama) was *Atlas* (1986). He became director of the National Library (1955) after losing his sight.

Borghese An Italian family that originated in Siena and rose to fame following its move to Rome in the 16th century and the election in 1605 of **Camillo Borghese** (1552–1621) as Pope Paul V. He advanced his family's fortunes, particularly those of his adopted nephew **Scipione Caffarelli** (1576–1633), a church politician and art patron, who sponsored *Bernini and built the Villa Borghese (now an art gallery) in Rome. In 1803 **Camillo Filippo Ludovico Borghese** (1775–1832) married Napoleon's sister, Marie Pauline (1780–1825). The family split into two branches later in the 19th century.

Borgia, Cesare (c. 1475–1507) Duke of the Romagna and captain general of the armies of the Church. The illegitimate son of Pope *Alexander VI, Borgia became Archbishop of Valencia and a cardinal following his father's election to the papacy (1492). He surrendered his cardinalship to marry the sister of the King of Navarre and to become captain general of the Church. He won the Romagna, with French help, in three campaigns (1499–1502), for which Machiavelli regarded him as the saviour of Italy. Borgia was forced to relinquish the Romagna after Alexander's death (1502) and was imprisoned. He escaped and died in the employ of the Navarrese king. His sister **Lucrezia Borgia**, unfairly notorious for immorality, was married three times by her father Alexander VI to further his political aims. Her third husband Alfonso (1486–1534) became Duke of Este and she presided over a culturally distinguished court at Ferrara.

Borglum, Gutzon (1867–1941) US sculptor, famous for his gigantic sculptured heads of US presidents, inspired by similar ancient Egyptian monuments. Best known are those carved on rocks of the *Mount Rushmore National Memorial, the head of Lincoln in the US Capitol Rotunda, and the 12 apostles in the Church of St John the Divine, New York.

Boris (I) of Bulgaria (d. 907 AD) Khan of Bulgaria (852–89). Boris was converted to Orthodox Christianity in 865 and encouraged the spread of Christianity among the Bulgars. His reign gave birth to Slavonic-Bulgarian literature and civilization. In 889 he abdicated and entered a monastery.

Boris III (1894–1943) King of Bulgaria (1918–1943). Boris ruled as a dictator from 1938 and supported the Axis Powers in World War II. He apparently died of a heart attack but may have been assassinated.

Borlaug, Norman (1914–) US plant breeder, who developed new strains of wheat and rice for underdeveloped countries. Working in Mexico since 1944, he received the Nobel Peace Prize (1970) for his role in the "green revolution."

Bormann, Martin (1900–45) German Nazi leader. Prominent in the Nazi Party from 1925, he became Hitler's personal secretary in 1942. He was sentenced to death in absentia at Nuremberg. In 1973 it was established that he had committed suicide in May, 1945.

Born, Max (1882–1970) British physicist, born in Germany. He shared the 1954 Nobel Prize with W. Bothe for his work in statistical mechanics. Born and *Heisenberg developed matrix mechanics, which *Schrödinger was able to show was equivalent to his own wave mechanics. Born was professor of natural philosophy at Edinburgh University from 1936 to 1953.

Borneo An island SE of Peninsular Malaysia, in the Greater Sunda Islands, the third largest island in the world. During the 19th century Borneo was settled and virtually partitioned by the Dutch and British to protect their East India companies from piracy. It now consists politically of the Indonesian territory of *Kalimantan, the Malaysian states of *Sabah and *Sarawak, and the British-protected sultanate of *Brunei. It is mountainous with coastal swamps and dense jungle. The chief population groups are the coastal Malays and indigenous Dyaks. It possesses valuable resources of oil, coal, and gold. Area:

750 000 sq km (290 000 sq mi).

Bornholm 55 02N 15 00E A Danish island in the Baltic Sea, SE of Sweden. Dairy farming is practised and industries include pottery, using locally worked clay, and watchmaking; tourism is important during summer. Area: 588 sq km (227 sq mi). Population (1984): 47 243. Chief town: Ronne.

Bornu A former Muslim Negro kingdom in West Africa. It existed from the 11th century until the late 19th century, when it was divided between Britain, France, and Germany. Most of the area was incorporated into the protectorate of Northern Nigeria in 1900 and the modern Nigerian state of Bornu encompasses part of the former kingdom.

BOROBUDUR *The walls of the temple are inset with statues depicting the life of Buddha. During the restoration of the buildings they all had to be removed.*

Borobudur A huge Buddhist stupa (shrine) complex in central Java, built about 800 AD and abandoned, unfinished, about 1000. It has five square terraces of diminishing size, one on top of the other, on the vertical surfaces of which is carved a continuous relief depicting the Buddha's life and doctrine. On top, three circular terraces support 72 stupas around a crowning central stupa, all with a Buddha icon. Restored (1973–83) at a cost of £20 million, it was badly damaged in a terrorist attack in 1985.

Borodin, Aleksandr Porfirevich (1833–87) Russian composer, one of the *Five. A professor of chemistry and medicine, he had little formal training and lacked time to compose. Nevertheless, he produced two symphonies (1867 and 1876), the tone poem *In the Steppes of Central Asia* (1880), three string quartets, and the opera *Prince Igor* (completed by *Rimsky-Korsakov and Glazunov in 1890), which contains the famous *Polovtsian Dances*.

boron (B) A nonmetallic element isolated (1808) by Sir Humphry Davy. It has two forms: an impure brownish amorphous powder and pure brown crystals. The main source, kernite ($Na_2B_4O_7.4H_2O$), is mined in California. Boron is used in semiconductors and in hardened steel. Boron fibres are used in lightweight composite materials. The isotope boron-10 absorbs neutrons: boron carbide

(B_4C) and boron alloys are used in the control rods and shielding of nuclear reactors. Other compounds include borax ($Na_2B_4O_7.10H_2O$), used in glass manufacture, and boric acid (H_3BO_3), used in ceramics and fireproofing. At no 5; at wt 10.81; mp 2300°C.

borough A unit of local government originating in Anglo-Saxon England. In the UK, county boroughs were set up by the Local Government Act (1888) but were wound up by the Local Government Act (1972). Boroughs remain the units of local government in *London (outside the City); a district council may now be granted the title borough (and the council chairman entitled *mayor) by royal charter but this is purely of ceremonial significance.

Borromeo, St Charles (1538–84) Italian churchman, Cardinal and Archbishop of Milan. He was appointed to his offices in 1560 by his uncle, Pope Pius IV. He played a leading part in the third convocation of the Council of Trent (1562–63) and actively supported the evangelization of Switzerland. These activities and the capable reforms he carried out in his archdiocese made him an important Counter-Reformation figure. Feast day: 4 Nov.

Borromini, Francesco (1599–1667) Italian baroque architect. Born in N Italy, he settled in □Rome, where all his work was executed. With his rival *Bernini, he brought the baroque style in Rome to its peak. His highly individual approach expressed the classical architectural style in forms never before achieved. Although much less successful than Bernini he was in many ways a greater genius as an architect. His main buildings, S Carlo (1641), S Ivo (1660), and the oratorio of S Filippo Neri (1650), showed a virtuosity of decoration and a command of complex spatial effects that Bernini never approached.

Borrow, George Henry (1803–81) British writer. Son of an army officer, he spent most of his life wandering round rural England and on the Continent. These travels provided the material for his many books, such as *Lavengro* (1851) and *The Romany Rye* (1857), in which he gave a romantic account of gipsy life.

Borrowdale A scenic valley in NW England, in Cumbria extending southwards from Derwentwater towards Scafell. Borrowdale gives its name to a series of volcanic rocks that cover the central Lake District.

Borstal system An English penal system established by the Prevention of Crime Act (1908) for the rehabilitation of offenders aged between 15 and 21. They could be detained in an institution called a Borstal for up to two years. Following release, the offender remained under supervision for two years and could be recalled if he committed an offence. The name derives from the prison at Borstal near Rochester, Kent, where the system was introduced. Borstal sentences were abolished by the Criminal Justice Act (1982).

borzoi A breed of large □dog originating in Russia, also called Russian wolfhound and used originally for hunting wolves and for hare coursing. The borzoi is a lightly built swift runner with a long silky coat, which is usually white with black to light-brown patches. Height: about 70 cm.

Bosanquet, Bernard (1848–1923) British philosopher. His early neo-Hegelian philosophy saw the individuality of persons, institutions, and works of art as a combination of abstract general concepts (universals). His *Philosophical Theory of the State* (1899) presents a solution to the problem of communal will and individual liberty. *Bradley influenced his later work.

Bosch, Carl (1874–1940) German chemist, who developed the *Haber process for the conversion of atmospheric nitrogen into ammonia, so that it could be used industrially. This Haber-Bosch process has been used to manufacture enormous quantities of nitrates for both explosives and fertilizers. He shared the 1931 Nobel Prize for Chemistry for his work on high-pressure reactions.

Bosch, Hieronymus (Jerome van Aeken; c. 1450–c. 1516) Dutch painter. He was born in 's-Hertogenbosch (hence his name), where from 1486 he belonged to the Roman Catholic Brotherhood of Our Lady. His allegories have been interpreted variously as forerunners of *surrealism or as expressions of heretical beliefs but as his patrons, including Philip II of Spain, were devout Catholics, they were probably intended as sermons on evil and its consequences. The often inexplicable symbolism and fantastic imagery of half-animal half-human creatures and devils was inspired by contemporary proverbs and writings. Among his major works are *The Haywain* (El Escorial) and *Garden of Earthly Delights* (Prado).

Bose, Sir Jagadis Chandra (1858–1937) Indian plant physiologist and physicist. His research into plant behaviour, in which he showed how plants responded to external stimuli (such as injury), revealed parallels between plant and animal tissues. He also invented the crescograph (a device for measuring plant growth) and founded the Bose Research Institute, Calcutta.

Bose, Subhas Chandra (c. 1897–c. 1945) Indian nationalist leader. He was a civil servant before joining Gandhi's movement of noncooperation with the British. He became president of the *Indian National Congress in 1938 but resigned in 1939 because of disagreement with Gandhi over policy. Arrested and imprisoned in Calcutta (1940), he left India in 1941. With Japanese help he organized in Singapore the Indian National Army to free India from British rule (1943). He was said to have been killed in an air crash in 1945.

Bose-Einstein statistics One of two statistical approaches to quantum mechanical problems: it assumes that any number of identical particles may occupy the same energy level. The other statistical method is called *Fermi-Dirac statistics. Particles that obey Bose-Einstein statistics are called *bosons. Named after S. N. Bose (1894–1974) and A. *Einstein.

Bosnia and Hercegovina (Serbo-Croat name: Bosna i Hercegovina) A constituent republic of Yugoslavia. It consists of a chiefly mountainous triangular-shaped area with karst topography in the SW. It is primarily agricultural, producing mainly cereals, vegetables, fruit, and tobacco; sheep are also raised. *History*: part of ancient Illyria, the region was inhabited by Slavs from the 7th century AD onwards. Bosnia became a separate political entity in the 10th century but later came under the control of Hungary. It became an independent kingdom in the late 14th century and annexed Hercegovina but fell to the Turks in 1463, remaining under their control for four centuries. In 1908 it was annexed to Austria-Hungary; Serbian opposition to this led to the assassination of Archduke Francis Ferdinand, precipitating World War I. Area: 51 129 sq km (19 737 sq mi). Population (1981): 4 124 008. Capital: Sarajevo.

boson A class of elementary particles with integral spin. Bosons always obey *Bose-Einstein statistics and include all the *mesons and the *photon. *See* particle physics.

Bosporus (Turkish name: Karadeniz Boğazi) A strait separating Europe and Asia and connecting the Black Sea with the Sea of Marmara. It has Istanbul at its S end and it is spanned by one of the world's longest suspension bridges. Length: about 30 km (19 mi). Width: about 0.6–4 km (0.4–2.5 mi).

boss In architecture, a small projection in a roof vault, covering the crossing of the supporting ribs. Although sometimes plain, medieval bosses were frequently carved into decorative shapes. *See also* gothic architecture.

Bossuet, Jacques Bénigne (1627–1704) French Roman Catholic bishop and preacher. He became famous for several funeral orations on prominent persons, such as that on *Henrietta Maria delivered in 1669. He became Bishop of Meaux in 1681, having first been tutor to the dauphin, and later attempted to bring about a compromise between Louis XIV and the pope on the issue of *Gallicanism. He wrote a number of devotional and apologetic works.

Boston 42 20N 71 05W A city in the USA, the capital of Massachusetts on Massachusetts Bay. It is an important port and market for fish and a major financial centre. Its industries include publishing, food processing, and the manufacture of machinery. An architecturally exceptional city, its most notable buildings are the old State House (1748), Faneuil Hall (1762), and the State Capitol (1798). Boston is a major cultural and educational centre. It is the site of Boston University (1869), Northeastern University (1898), and Boston Latin School (established in 1635 and one of the country's first free secondary schools). Harvard Medical School is also situated here. Notable residents have included Nathaniel Hawthorne, Henry Thoreau, Ralph Emerson, and Longfellow. *History*: founded in 1630 by Puritan Englishmen, it prospered as the main colony of the Massachusetts Bay Company. It became a centre of opposition to the British prior to the American Revolution (*see* Boston Tea Party). Often dubbed the "Hub of the Universe," Boston flourished as the commercial, industrial, and financial centre of the New England states during the early 19th century. It was a leading force in the antislavery movement during the 1830s. Population (1980): 562 994.

Boston 52 59N 0 01W A market town and small port in E England, in Lincolnshire on the River Witham. Industries include canning. Population (1981): 26 425.

Boston Tea Party (1773) An expression of colonial hostility towards Britain before the *American Revolution. A group of American radicals objecting to the import of cheap tea, enforced by the Tea Act to rid the East India Company of its surplus stocks, threw a cargo of tea into Boston harbour. Britain retaliated with the *Intolerable Acts. *See also* Stamp Act.

Boston terrier A breed of □dog originating in the USA from crosses between bulldogs and terriers. It is compactly built with a short square muzzle and a short tail. The short smooth coat is brown to brownish-yellow with white markings. Height: about 38 cm.

Boswell, James (1740–95) Scottish writer, the biographer of Samuel *Johnson. Son of an Edinburgh advocate, he came to London in 1760 and first met Johnson in 1763. He travelled widely on the Continent from 1764 to 1766, meeting other famous men, such as Voltaire and Rousseau. Although he practised law in Edinburgh from 1766 to 1788 he maintained a close relationship with Johnson. The biography, published in 1791, was widely acclaimed but in later years he suffered from severe depression and alcoholism.

Bosworth Field, Battle of (22 August, 1485) The battle fought near Market Bosworth, Leicestershire, in which Henry Tudor defeated Richard III, thereby ending the Wars of the *Roses. Richard was killed in the battle and Henry became the first *Tudor monarch, as Henry VII.

botanic gardens Collections of growing plants designed to display both familiar native plants and more unusual alien species, particularly ornamentals. Often the plants are grouped to demonstrate their evolutionary and geographical relationships or their similar ecological requirements. Some gardens concentrate on certain types of plants: an arboretum is one specializing in trees and shrubs. Botanic gardens originated in ancient China, as collections of fruit, vegetables, and medicinal plants, but it was not until the 16th and 17th centuries that they became popular in Europe, the first being established in Italy, at Pisa (1543) and Padua (1545). Today the larger botanic gardens have extensive herbaria, where dried labelled specimens are kept for reference. Many have their own laboratories and libraries, providing facilities for research scientists, and often hold courses in horticultural techniques for trainee gardeners. Most gardens preserve and propagate rare species, with elaborate greenhouses and culture techniques for those with special-

ized needs. *See also* Kew Gardens.

botany The scientific study of plants. From ancient times plants have figured prominently in human cultures as man is dependent on them for food, shelter, drugs, and many other purposes. Scientific botany dates from the 4th century BC, with the studies of the ancient Greeks—notably *Theophrastus, who is said to have founded the science, and *Dioscorides, who published one of the first herbals. Until the 17th century botany was almost entirely restricted to the description and properties of medicinal plants. The basic principles of modern plant classification were laid down by John *Ray at the end of the 17th century, and by the middle of the 18th century *Linnaeus had published his works on the naming and classification of plants, which established the principles of *taxonomy still used today for both plants and animals. The invention of the microscope in the 16th century enabled detailed studies of plant structure, culminating in *Schleiden's theory of the cellular nature of plants in the 1830s. The 18th century saw important advances in plant physiology with the discovery of *photosynthesis, the food-manufacturing process of green plants. During the 19th century the origin of plant species was elucidated in Charles *Darwin's theory of evolution and Gregor *Mendel—working with plants—established the mechanisms of inheritance.

Botany in the 20th century has been revolutionized by advances in physiology, biochemistry, and breeding techniques, which have greatly increased the economic importance of plants and enabled a scientific approach to the related disciplines of *horticulture, *agriculture, and forestry. *See also* biological sciences.

Botany Bay An inlet of the Tasman Sea, in SE Australia. It was the site of Capt Cook's first landing in Australia (1770). A convict settlement that Capt Arthur Phillip planned to establish here (1788) was moved to *Port Jackson 9 km (5 mi) to the N. The bay is now surrounded by the suburbs of Sydney. Industries, located chiefly on the N shore, include chemicals, plastics, and fibreglass, with an oil refinery on the SE shore. Area: about 42 sq km (16 sq mi).

bot fly A hairy beelike fly belonging to the families *Gasterophilidae* (horsebot flies), *Calliphoridae* (e.g. the deer bot fly), or *Oestridae* (e.g. the sheep bot fly). The larvae are parasitic in mammals, often living within nasal and sinus cavities or in the digestive tract to cause irritation, weakening, and vertigo. When mature the larvae pass out with the faeces. *Compare* warble fly.

Botha, Louis (1862–1919) South African statesman; the first prime minister of the Union of South Africa (1910–19). In 1897 he became a member of the Transvaal Volksraad (parliament) and commanded the Transvaal's forces during the second *Boer War. He became prime minister of the Transvaal in 1907. In World War I he suppressed a revolt of Afrikaner nationalists led by *de Wet and conquered German South West Africa.

Botha, Pieter Willem (1916–) South African statesman; prime minister (1978–84) and president (1984–). As defence minister (1966–78) he involved South Africa in the Angolan civil war (1975). Although a supporter of *apartheid, he presided over the new constitution of 1984, which allowed some non-Whites limited political power.

Botham, Ian Terence (1955–) British cricketer. A brilliant all-rounder, he played for Somerset (1973–86), Worcestershire (1987–), Queensland (1987–), and England (1977–), captaining the side (1980–81). In 1986 he was suspended for part of the season after admitting he had formerly taken drugs.

Bothe, Walther Wilhelm Georg Franz (1891–1957) German experimental physicist, who (with H. *Geiger) developed the coincidence method for particle counting. The use of this technique in cosmic radiation research brought him a share (with Max *Born) in the Nobel Prize for 1954. During World War II he built Germany's first cyclotron. He was responsible for discovering the particle later identified by *Chadwick as the neutron.

Bothnia, Gulf of A shallow section of the Baltic Sea, between Sweden and Finland. It remains frozen for about five months of the year because of its low salinity. Its many small islands restrict navigation. Area: about 117 000 sq km (45 200 sq mi).

Bothwell, James Hepburn, 4th Earl of (c. 1535–78) The third husband of Mary, Queen of Scots. He was almost certainly responsible for the murder of her second husband *Darnley in 1567, after which he allegedly abducted Mary and married her; they may already have been lovers. Following their defeat at Carberry Hill, Bothwell escaped to Denmark, where he died, insane, in captivity.

bo tree An Indian tree, *Ficus religiosa*, up to 30 m high, also called the peepul or pipal. It has heart-shaped leaves, the tips of which are drawn out into a long narrow tail, and globular fleshy purple fruits. Related to the fig, the bo tree is sacred to Buddhists, as it was the tree under which Buddha sat when he attained enlightenment. Family: *Moraceae* (mulberry family).

Botswana, Republic of (former name until 1966: Bechuanaland) A country in the centre of S Africa, lying between the Rivers Zambezi and Molopo. It is largely an arid plateau, with the Kalahari Desert in the S and W and some hills in the E. The River Okavango in the N, with its marshy basin, is important for irrigation. The majority of the population, consisting mainly of the Bantu-speaking Tswana group, lives along the E border. The original inhabitants, the Bushmen, now comprise only a small minority. *Economy*: formerly chiefly agricultural, with beef cattle predominating; traditional agriculture is still the most important occupation. Large quantities of minerals, including diamonds, nickel, copper, and coal, were discovered in the 1960s, and by the mid-1980s diamonds provided two-thirds of export revenue. These developments, together with foreign aid, have financed a policy of government-directed economic and structural development, and Botswana's economy is currently one of the fastest growing in Africa. *History*: the area became the British Protectorate of Bechuanaland in 1885 and was annexed to the Cape Colony in 1895. It later became a British High Commission Territory, gaining internal self-government in 1965 and full independence in 1966 as the Republic of Botswana within the Commonwealth. Until 1980 it was under the democratic rule of Sir Seretse *Khama, who maintained a delicate balance in his opposition to the policies of neighbouring countries, in spite of being dependent on them for communications and trade. Head of state: Dr Quett Masire. Official language: English; the main African language is Tswana. Official currency: pula of 100 thebe. Area: 575 000 sq km (222 000 sq mi). Population (1986 est): 1 131 700. Capital: Gaborone.

Botticelli, Sandro (Alessandro di Mariano Filipepi; c. 1445–1510) Florentine *Renaissance painter, named after his brother's nickname, meaning "little barrel." He trained under Filippo *Lippi. His chief patrons were the Medici, for whom he produced illustrations for Dante's *Divine Comedy* and allegorical paintings, influenced by humanist writers, such as *Primavera*, *Birth of Venus* (both Uffizi), and *Mars and Venus* (National Gallery, London). They are notable for their graceful draughtsmanship. In 1481–82 he worked on frescoes for the Sistine Chapel, in the Vatican. Probably under the influence of the religious leader *Savonarola, his later works, e.g. *Mystic Nativity* (1501; National Gallery, London), became more religious and emotional.

bottlebrush An evergreen Australian shrub or tree of the genus *Callistemon* (25 species). Growing to a height of about 6 m, it has stiff narrow leaves, 5 cm long. The flower heads consist mainly of bunches of fluffy red or yellow stamens, resembling bottle brushes. The fruits are woody. Bottlebrushes may be grown as ornamental hedges and shrubs. Family: *Myrtaceae*.

bottlenose A *dolphin, *Tursiops truncatus*, with a short beak. Grey-blue and growing to 4 m, bottlenose dolphins are a shallow-water species and have become popular in dolphinariums. They have been the subject of research into the social behaviour and language of whales. ▯mammal.

Bottrop 51 31N 6 55E A city in NW West Germany, in North Rhine-Westphalia in the *Ruhr. Its main industries are coalmining and the manufacture of by-products. Population (1980 est): 114 600.

botulism A rare and serious form of *food poisoning from foods containing the toxin produced by the bacterium *Clostridium botulinum*. The toxin can affect the cardiac and respiratory centres of the brain and may result in death by heart or lung failure. The bacterium thrives in improperly preserved foods, such as tinned raw meats. The toxin is invariably destroyed in cooking.

Botvinnik, Mikhail Moiseivich (1911–) Soviet chess player, who was world champion (1948–57, 1958–60, 1961–63), losing the title to *Petrosian (1963). He was also a successful electrical engineer.

Bouaké 7 42N 5 00W A city in the central Ivory Coast. It is an important trade centre, linked by rail and road to Abidjan, with a trade in coffee, cocoa, and rice. Population (1982 est): 640 000.

Boucher, François (1703–70) French *rococo painter, born in Paris, the son of a lacemaker. He studied in Italy (1727–31) but was chiefly influenced by *Watteau, many of whose drawings he engraved. He worked for Louis XV, and Madame de Pompadour, whom he painted (National Gallery of Scotland), and to whom he gave art lessons. He became director of both the Gobelins tapestry factory (1755), for which he produced designs, and of the French Academy (1765). His paintings are mainly mythological and pastoral scenes and nudes.

Boucher de Perthes, Jacques (1788–1868) French antiquary. In the Somme valley he discovered stone implements together with extinct animal remains; these made him challenge contemporary theories about human origins. His *De la création* (1838–41) and *Antiquités celtiques et antédiluviennes* (1847) argue for the human race's great antiquity.

Boudicca. *See* Boadicea.

Boudin, Eugène (1824–98) French painter and forerunner of *impressionism, born in Honfleur. He painted his coastal scenes in the open air instead of the studio and encouraged *Monet in this practice.

Bougainville A volcanic forested island in the SW Pacific Ocean, the largest in the *Solomon Islands archipelago and a province of Papua New Guinea. Copra, cocoa, timber, and tortoise shell are exported. Area: about 10 360 sq km (4000 sq mi). Population (1980): 109 000. Chief town: Kieta.

Bougainville, Louis Antoine de (1729–1811) French navigator. After service in the Seven Years' War in Canada he joined the navy. Between 1766 and 1769 he circumnavigated the world and wrote an account of the journey in *A Voyage round the World* (1771). He was later a successful commander in the American Revolution. Several geographical features, including the island Bougainville, and the plant genus *Bougainvillea* are named after him.

Bougainvillea A genus of tropical South American shrubs (18 species) climbing by means of hooked thorns. The shrubs bear numerous showy "flowers," usually reddish-purple, for most of the year. The coloured parts are actually large bracts, which surround the small inconspicuous flowers. *Bougainvillea* is grown as an ornamental throughout the tropics and subtropics. Family: *Nyctaginaceae*.

Boulanger, Nadia (Juliette) (1887–1979) French composer, teacher, and conductor. Lennox *Berkeley and Aaron *Copland were among her pupils. Her works include the cantata *La Sirène* (1908; awarded the Prix de Rome), the opera *La Ville morte* (1911), choral works, and instrumental pieces.

Boulder.   *See* Kalgoorlie-Boulder.

FRANÇOIS BOUCHER *Portrait of Madame de Pompadour* (*National Gallery of Scotland*).

boulder clay.   *See* till.

boules   A French game similar to *bowls, often played on rough ground. The players aim small metal bowls at a target ball (*cochonnet*).

Boulez, Pierre   (1925–   ) French composer and conductor, a pupil of Messiaen. Boulez has been active as a conductor of contemporary music and his own work reflects the influence of Schoenberg, Webern, and Cage. He has used total *serialism in such works as *Structures I and II* (for two pianos; 1951–52 and 1956–61) and has set poems by René Char in *Le Marteau sans maître* (for contralto and 6 instruments; 1953–55) as well as poems by Mallarmé in *Pli selon pli* (for soprano and orchestra; 1957–60).

Boulle, André Charles   (*or* Buhl; 1642–1732) French cabinetmaker in the service of Louis XIV. He gave his name to the technique of boullework (*or* buhlwork), a style of marquetry using brass, tortoiseshell, mother of pearl, etc., inlaid on ebony.

Boulogne-sur-Mer   50 43N 1 37E A port and resort in N France, in the Pas-de-Calais department on the English Channel. It was severely damaged in World War II. It is the country's main fishing port and has a ferry service to England. Industries include boatbuilding, textiles, and steel. Population (1982 est): 48 349.

Boult, Sir Adrian (Cedric)   (1889–1983) British conductor. A pupil of Arthur Nikisch (1855–1922), he was conductor of the BBC Symphony Orchestra (1930–49) and the London Philharmonic Orchestra (1949–57). He was knighted in 1937. He was associated particularly with the works of Elgar, Holst, and Vaughan Williams.

Boulter, Hugh   (1672–1742) English churchman; Anglican Archbishop of Armagh (1724–42). Lord Justice as well as head of the Church of Ireland, he intensified the penal laws against Roman Catholics (1728).

Boulton, Matthew.   *See* Watt, James.

Boumédienne, Houari (Mohammed Boukharouba; 1925–78) Algerian statesman; president (1965–78). In 1960 he became chief of staff of the nationalist forces fighting the French. After independence in 1962 he became minister of defence and then vice president under *Ben Bella. In 1965 he overthrew Ben Bella to become president.

Bounty, HMS.   *See* Bligh, William.

Bourbaki, Nicolas   A pseudonym for a group of French mathematicians who, since 1939, have been producing, from a few basic premisses, a rigorous development of mathematics, often at variance with conventional mathematics.

bourbon (whiskey).   *See* whisky.

Bourbons   A European ruling dynasty that originated in Bourbonnais (now Allier, central France). It acquired ducal status in 1272, when Agnès Bourbon married the sixth son of Louis IX. The first Bourbon king of France was *Henry IV (reigned 1589–1610) after whom the house continued to rule until the *French Revolution (1792). The Bourbons were restored after the defeat of Napoleon (1814), but were again expelled (1830) in favour of a cadet branch, which ruled until the *Revolution of 1848 (*see* Louis Philippe). The present pretender to the French throne is Henry, Count of Paris (1908–   ).

The Bourbon Louis XIV's grandson became (1700) *Philip V of Spain, where the Bourbons ruled almost continuously until the abdication of *Alfonso XIII in 1931. His grandson *Juan Carlos was restored to the Spanish throne in 1975. In Naples and Sicily Bourbons ruled between 1734 and 1860.

Bourdelle, Émile   (1861–1929) French sculptor. Influenced by his teacher *Rodin, Bourdelle initially relied on vigorous surface carving but after 1910 his work, inspired by classical Greek sculpture, became more popular.

Bourgeois, Léon   (1851–1925) French statesman; prime minister (1895–96). He was the chief theorist of solidarism, the concept that an individual's rights in society must be balanced by his responsibility to it. Prominent in the League of Nations, he won the Nobel Peace Prize in 1920.

bourgeoisie   Originally, the urban merchants who developed trade at the end of the middle ages and who led the struggle against the feudal aristocracy for the rights of citizenship. The meaning was later extended to include the whole middle class. In the 19th century, *Marx used the concept within his theory of class struggle to describe the propertied entrepreneurs who created industrial capitalism and liberal democracy; conflict between the bourgeoisie and the *proletariat would ultimately lead to revolution. *See* Marxism.

Bourges (Latin name: Avaricum)   47 05N 2 23E A city in central France, the capital of the Cher department. An important town of Aquitaine, it became the capital of Berry in the 12th century and the French centre of power following the battle of Agincourt (1415). It has a fine gothic cathedral. Industries include textiles and armaments. Population (1982 est): 79 408.

Bourguiba, Habib   (1902–   ) Tunisian statesman; president (1956–87). A leading figure in the struggle for Tunisian independence, he formed the Neo-Destour Party in 1934. He spent ten years between 1934 and 1955 in French prisons. On independence in 1956 he became president, being re-elected three times (1959, 1964, 1969), and in 1975 became life president; he was deposed in a bloodless coup.

Bourmont, Louis Auguste Victor de Ghaisnes, Comte de (1773–1846) French marshal, who lived in exile (1793–99) during the French Revolution but subsequently served Napoleon. He deserted Napoleon for the allies shortly before Waterloo. In 1829 he became minister of war but went into exile after the July Revolution (1830).

Bournemouth   50 43N 1 54W A resort in S England, in Dorset on Poole Bay. It is a large all-year-round resort with many tourist attractions, including 10 km (6 mi) of sands. It has a famous symphony orchestra. Population (1981 est): 144 803.

Bournville   A suburb of Birmingham, in the Midlands of England. It was founded as a model factory (1879) and village (1894) by George Cadbury and was a forerunner of the garden cities.

Bouts, Dierick   (c. 1400–75) Netherlandish painter, born in Haarlem, who lived and worked in Louvain. His paintings, strongly influenced by van der *Weyden, are notable for their treatment of landscape. *The Last Supper* (S Pierre, Louvain) and *The Justice of Emperor Otto* (Brussels) are his major works.

Bouvet 54 26S 3 24E An uninhabited Norwegian island in the S Atlantic Ocean. It is rocky with ice cliffs. Area: 48 sq km (19 sq mi).

Bouvines, Battle of (27 July, 1214) The battle in which *Philip II Augustus of France defeated the Holy Roman Emperor *Otto IV. The failure of the planned diversionary attack by King John of England facilitated Philip's victory, which increased the baronial opposition to John in England (*see* Barons' Wars).

Boveri, Theodor Heinrich (1862-1915) German cell biologist, noted for his studies of chromosomes. Boveri showed that the egg nucleus and the sperm nucleus both contribute hereditary material during the formation of a new cell (zygote) and that irregular distribution of chromosomes leads to abnormal development. These findings led *Sutton to propose his chromosome theory of inheritance in 1903.

Bovet, Daniel (1907-) Swiss pharmacologist, who discovered pyrilamine, the first of the allergy-relieving antihistamine drugs (1944). He also made various synthetic substitutes for the muscle-relaxing drug curare (1947). He received the Nobel Prize for Physiology in 1957.

Bovidae A family of hoofed *ruminant mammals (about 128 species), comprising antelopes, cattle, sheep, and goats. Most live in herds and graze on the plains, although some inhabit mountainous regions. Several species have been domesticated by man for meat, milk, hides, and wool. Order: *Artiodactyla*.

Bow, Clara (1905–65) US film actress. She personified the vivacious spirit of the 1920s in such films as *Mantrap* (1926) and *It* (1927), after which she became known as the "It" girl. She retired from acting in the 1930s, after being unsuccessful in sound films.

Bowdler, Thomas (1754-1825) British doctor and editor. His *Family Shakespeare* (1818) expurgated all words, expressions (and even plots) "which cannot with propriety be read aloud in a family." He similarly "bowdlerized" Gibbon's *History of the Decline and Fall of the Roman Empire* (1826).

Bowen, Elizabeth (1899-1973) British novelist. Born in Dublin, daughter of an Anglo-Irish landowner, she was brought to England as a child. Her novels, in which themes of loneliness and personal relationships are delicately explored, include *The Death of the Heart* (1938) and *The Heat of the Day* (1949).

Bowen, Norman Levi (1887-1956) Canadian experimental petrologist, who was professor at Queens University, Kingston (1919-21), and Chicago University (1937-47) and worked at various times at the Geophysical Laboratory, Washington. His important work on the role of silicates in igneous rocks is summarized in *The Evolution of Igneous Rocks* (1928).

Bower, Frederick Orpen (1855-1948) British botanist, who elucidated the origin and evolution of primitive land plants. Many years studying liverworts, mosses, and ferns led him to conclude that they had evolved from algal ancestors.

bowerbird A songbird belonging to a family (*Ptilonorhynchidae*; 18 species) found in Australasian forests. 22-35 cm long, it is closely related to the bird of paradise but has a duller plumage, often grey or black. Male bowerbirds court females by building typically dome-shaped bowers with twigs, moss, and stones, often decorating them with feathers, flowers, and shells.

bowfin A *bony fish, *Amia calva*, also called grundle or mudfish, found in fresh waters of E North America. It has a mottled green body, up to 60 cm long, a long dorsal fin, and feeds on fish and invertebrates. Family: *Amiidae*; order: *Amiiformes*.

BOXER RISING *A cartoon by a Chinese artist in a Shanghai newspaper of August 1900 showing Europeans fleeing from members of the Chinese secret society, the Fists of Righteous Harmony.*

Bowie, David (David Jones; 1947-) British pop singer. Both his style of singing and his theatrical public image have undergone several changes during the course of his career in progressive pop music. His albums include *Ziggy Stardust* (1972) and *Stage* (1978). He has also acted in films, notably *The Man Who Fell to Earth* (1976).

bowling (*or* tenpin bowling) A game in which two players or teams compete by attempting to knock down standing pins with rolling balls. The ten pins, 38.1 cm (15 in) high and each weighing about 1.5 kg (3.5 lb), are placed in a triangle 18.29 m (20 yd) distant at the end of a wooden lane. The balls, which have a thumb hole and two finger holes, have a maximum circumference of 68.5 cm (27 in) and a maximum weight of 7.26 kg (16 lb). Each player has two tries to knock the pins down, points being awarded accordingly. The pins are then reset for the next frame. Ten frames comprise a game.

bowls A game in which biased bowls ("woods") are rolled towards a smaller one (the "jack"). **Flat green bowls** is played on a level grass surface 40-44 yd (36.6-40.2 m) square (for championship greens). Matches are usually played between two sides of four, each player using two bowls; a contest consists of three to six simultaneous matches. The jack is rolled onto the green by the first player and is followed by the other bowls in turn, the object being to position them as near the jack as possible. Playing all the bowls constitutes one "end." A score is agreed and the bowls are then delivered in the other direction for the next end. Matches between fours are played to 21 ends. **Crown green bowls** is played, mainly in N England, on a green 30-60 yd (27.4-54.9 m) square and sloping up to a central area raised 6-12 in (15-30 cm). Matches are usually singles, each player using two bowls; they last until one player reaches a score of 21. Bowls are also played indoors. *See also* boules.

Bow porcelain A mid-18th-century English soft-paste *porcelain made at or near Bow (London). The makers were two London merchants using a patent of Thomas Frye, first registered in 1744. The factory closed about 1776. Wares included portrait and fictional figures, copies of Chinese porcelains (particularly blue and white), and *Meissen derivatives.

box A small evergreen tree, *Buxus sempervirens*, up to 9 m high, native to S Europe, Africa, and S England. The leaves are small and glossy and the flowers and seedpods inconspicuous. Being slow growing, box is widely grown as hedges for topiary or screening. The hard wood is used for decorative inlay work and engravings. Family: *Buxaceae*.

box elder   A *maple tree, *Acer negundo*, up to 20 m high, native to North America but widely planted in Europe as a street ornamental. Also called ash-leafed maple, it has compound pale-green leaves with five toothed leaflets.

boxer   A breed of working dog originating in Germany. It has a powerful frame with long straight legs and a broad muzzle. The short glossy coat is fawn to yellowish-brown or brindle, sometimes with white markings, and the mask is black. Height: 56–61 cm (dogs); 53–58 cm (bitches).

Boxer Rising   (1900) A rebellion in China so called because the rebels belonged to a secret society named the Fists of Righteous Harmony. They opposed the western presence in China and engaged in violence against foreign missionaries and Chinese Christians. Wearing yellow sashes and believing themselves invulnerable to foreign weapons, they marched on Peking, killing and pillaging as they went. The rebellion was eventually suppressed by an international force of troops from seven nations and a crippling indemnity was imposed on China.

boxing   Fist-fighting between men wearing gloves in a roped-off ring. Organized boxing in modern times began in 18th-century England, where it became an aristocratic pastime. The basis of modern boxing rules are the **Queensberry Rules**, drawn up under the patronage of the Marquess of Queensberry (1844–1900), published in 1867, and first used in 1892. They established the use of gloves as opposed to fighting with bare fists, which was the custom in the prize fights of the time. In professional boxing the ring is 14 × 20 ft (4 × 6 m) square. The weight limits for professional boxers are: flyweight, 112 lb (50.8 kg); bantamweight, 118 lb (53.5 kg); featherweight, 126 lb (57.2 kg); lightweight, 135 lb (61.2 kg); light welterweight, 140 lb (63.5 kg); welterweight, 147 lb (66.7 kg); light middleweight, 154 lb (69.8 kg); middleweight, 160 lb (72.6 kg); light heavyweight, 175 lb (79.4 kg); heavyweight, unlimited. A bout consists of up to 15 3-minute rounds, separated by 1-minute intervals, and is presided over by a referee. A boxer is assisted by two or four seconds. A fight may be decided on points (marks awarded by the referee or judges after each round), by disqualification, or by knockout (inability to rise within ten seconds). Concern has been expressed regarding the danger to health of this sport. World titles are currently offered by the World Boxing Council, the World Boxing Association, and the International Boxing Federation.

box turtle   A terrestrial turtle belonging to the North American genus *Terrapene* (6 species). Up to 18 cm long, box turtles have a high-domed rounded carapace patterned with brown and yellow and a hinged plastron, which allows tight closure of the shell, forming a protective box. They feed on worms, insects, and berries. Family: *Emydidae*.

Boyacá, Battle of   (7 August, 1819) The victory, after a heroic crossing of the Andes, of Simón *Bolívar's army of 3000 men over a Spanish force. It assured the liberation of Venezuela and Colombia.

Boyce, William   (c. 1710–79) British composer. Boyce was composer to the Chapel Royal, director of the Three Choirs Festival, and Master of the King's Music. He wrote choral anthems, sonatas, overtures, songs, and symphonies; he also collected and edited *Cathedral Music* (1760–78).

Boycott, Charles Cunningham   (1832–97) British estate manager in Ireland. Boycott clashed with the *Land League over its request for rent reductions and as a result the local community refused to associate with, or "boycotted," him.

Boycott, Geoffrey   (1940–   ) British cricketer who played for Yorkshire (1962–86; captain 1970–78) and England (1964–74, 1977–81). An outstanding opening batsman, he made 150 centuries in first-class cricket.

Boyd-Orr of Brechin Mearns, John, 1st Baron (1880–1971) Scottish scientist and expert on nutrition. In the 1930s he identified nutritional problems among the British population and helped formulate adequate nutritional standards. First director general of the United Nations Food and Agriculture Organization (1945–48), he was awarded the Nobel Peace Prize (1949).

Boyer, Charles   (1899–1978) French film actor. He went to Hollywood in 1929 and specialized in the roles of romantic lovers in such films as *Mayerling* (1937) and *Love Affair* (1939).

Boyle, Robert   (1627–91) British physicist and chemist, born in Ireland. Boyle showed that air possesses weight, that it is necessary for sound propagation, and that its pressure affects the boiling point of water. His chemical work, summarized in *The Skeptical Chymist* (1661), distinguished between elements, compounds, and mixtures and dismissed the Aristotelian concept of the four elements. His work on gases and vacuums, with Robert *Hooke, led to the law that bears his name. Boyle published his law in 1663, but in France the law is known as Marriotte's law, after Edmé Marriotte (1620–84), who did not publish it until 1676.

Boyle's law   At constant temperature, the pressure of unit mass of a gas is inversely proportional to its volume. This law is only approximately true for real gases. A gas that obeys Boyle's law exactly is called an *ideal gas. Named after Robert *Boyle.

Boyne, Battle of the   (1 July, 1690) The victory of William III of England over the former King James II in Ireland. The battle was fought at the River Boyne, N of Dublin, where James hoped to halt the Williamites' advance southwards. It was not an overwhelming victory, losses being comparatively slight on both sides, but the sensation of two kings fighting in Ireland for an English throne ensured its fame. The battles of the Boyne and of *Aughrim are still celebrated by Ulster Unionists on the latter's anniversary, 12 July.

Boyoma Falls (former name: Stanley Falls)   A series of seven cataracts in NE central Zaïre, on a 100-km (62-mi) stretch of the River Lualuba, where it becomes the Zaïre River, close to Kisangani.

Boy Scouts.   *See* Scout Association.

Bo Zhu Yi   (*or* Po Chü-i; 772–846) Chinese poet and imperial official, he became a governor in the provinces and eventually president of the imperial board of war (841). His many poems and ballads deal with the social problems of his age. Their lasting popularity rests on their lucid language, which, according to tradition, he achieved by reading his work to a peasant woman and deleting anything she did not understand.

Brabant   1. A former duchy in the Low Countries, between the Rivers Meuse and Scheldt. On Belgian independence (1830) it was divided, forming the Belgian provinces of Antwerp and Brabant and the Dutch province of *North Brabant. 2. A province in central Belgium. It is densely populated with large industrial areas, including Brussels. Agriculture is highly developed, with dairy farming and the production of cereals, fruit, and vegetables. Area: 3284 sq km (1268 sq mi). Population (1980 est): 2 221 782. Capital: Brussels.

Brabham, Jack   (John Arthur B.; 1926–   ) Australian motor-racing driver, who won 14 Grand Prix races between 1955 and 1970 and was world champion in 1959, 1960, and 1966. From 1961 he built his own cars, which were highly successful.

Bracegirdle, Anne   (c. 1673–1748) English actress. She was trained by Thomas *Betterton and achieved her greatest successes in the plays of Congreve, whose mistress she was for some years. She retired in 1707.

Brachiopoda   A phylum of primitive marine invertebrate animals (about 250 species) called lamp shells because of their resemblance to ancient Roman oil lamps. The body is

bracken

178

protected by two shell valves, usually attached to the sea bed by a fleshy stalk (peduncle). Ciliated tentacles filter food particles from the water and propel them into the mouth. Eggs and sperm are discharged into the sea and produce free-swimming ciliated larvae.

bracken (*or* brake) A *fern, *Pteridium aquilinum*, that is abundant almost throughout the world. Its black underground rhizome creeps extensively, producing aerial fronds, up to 5 m high, with stout erect stalks bearing triangular blades made up of branches of paired leaflets. Spore capsules occur in brownish clusters (sori) around the margins on the underside of the leaflets. Bracken is sometimes considered a pest by farmers; the roots have been used in tanning and the fronds in thatching and as fodder. Family: *Dennstaedtiaceae*.

bracket fungus A fungus that forms a fruiting body resembling a shelf or bracket, usually on trees or timber. The spores are produced in fine tubes that open at pores on the surface. A common species is *Coriolus versicolor*, the semicircular brackets of which, 3–5 cm across, are found on stumps and branches of deciduous trees. The brackets are marked with concentric coloured zones of brown, yellow, grey, or green. Family: *Polyporaceae*; class: *Basidiomycetes*.

Bracknell 51 26N 0 46W A town in SE England, in Berkshire. Developed as a new town since 1949, industries include engineering, electronics, clothing, and furniture manufacture. The Meteorological Office has its headquarters here. Population (1981): 48 752

bract A modified leaf, often small and scalelike, found at the base of a flower or inflorescence (flower cluster). Occasionally bracts are large and brightly coloured, resembling petals, as in the poinsettias. Smaller bracts (bracteoles) may be found on the flower stalk.

Bracton, Henry de (*or* Bratton; d. 1268) English jurist. He was a justice of assize in SW England from 1248 until his death and a judge in the king's court until 1257. He is best known for his treatise, *De legibus et consuetudinibus*, which is the most comprehensive work on English medieval law.

Bradbury, Ray (1920–) US science-fiction writer. Many of his works of fantasy and science fiction deal essentially with the themes of conventional fiction, and his literary style has been much admired. His novels include *The Illustrated Man* (1951), *Fahrenheit 451* (1953), and *Death is a Lonely Business* (1986), and his many collections of stories include *I Sing the Body Electric* (1969).

Bradford 53 48N 1 45W A city in N England, in West Yorkshire near Leeds. It is the foremost wool textile town in the UK and a world centre for the raw-wool market. Besides woollens and worsteds, many other fabrics are manufactured and engineering is important. Bradford has a university (1966). In 1985 56 people died when a timber grandstand at Bradford City's football ground caught fire. Population (1984 est): 467 000.

Bradford, William (1663–1752) British printer, who emigrated to Pennsylvania in 1682. In 1725 he founded the *New York Gazette*, the first New York newspaper.

Bradlaugh, Charles (1833–91) British radical reformer. An atheist, Bradlaugh pressed for greater freedom for the individual and in 1877 he was unsuccessfully prosecuted with Annie *Besant for republishing *Fruits of Philosophy*, which advocated birth control. He became an MP in 1880 but refused to take the parliamentary oath and was not permitted to take his seat until 1886.

Bradley, Andrew Cecil (1851–1935) British literary critic. Educated at Oxford, he held professorships at the Universities of Liverpool (1882–89), Glasgow (1889–1900), and Oxford (1901–06). His *Shakespearian Tragedy* (1904) has had a lasting influence on Shakespeare criticism.

Bradley, Francis Herbert (1846–1924) British philosopher. He lived as a semi-invalid, holding a sinecural fellowship at Oxford. Indebted to *Hegel, his idealist metaphysics are often brilliant in detail and grandiose in conception, but unwieldy in

overall effect. In his greatest work, *Appearance and Reality* (1893), he argues against the acceptance of any general categories as absolutely real. Truth is relative and reality is unknowable and transcendent.

Bradley, Omar Nelson (1893–1981) US general. In World War II, he commanded in North Africa and Sicily (1945) and the First US Army in the invasion of France (1944). In 1948 he became army chief of staff and was then the first chairman of the joint chiefs of staff (1949–53).

SIR DONALD BRADMAN

Bradman, Sir Donald George (1908–) Australian cricketer, who played for New South Wales, South Australia, and Australia (1928–48) and was the most successful batsman of his era. He scored 117 centuries in 338 first-class innings and in Test matches averaged 99.94 runs. His best score was 452 not out (1929–30). As Australian captain (1936–48) he never lost a series and on retirement (1949) he became an administrator of the game.

Braemar 57 01N 2 34W A village in NE Scotland, in Grampian Region on Clunie Water (a tributary of the River

Dee). It is a resort and the scene of the annual Highland games.

Braga 41 32N 8 26W A city in N Portugal. It has a cathedral (12th–17th centuries) and is the seat of the primate of Portugal. A nearby holy sanctuary is visited by many pilgrims. Industries include jewellery and cutlery. Population (1981): 63 771.

Bragança (or Braganza) The ruling dynasty of Portugal from 1640 to 1910 and of Brazil from 1822 to 1889. The family was descended from Alfonso, illegitimate son of *John I and 1st Duke of Bragança. The first Bragança king was *John IV (1640–56) and the last was Manuel II (1889–1932; reigned 1908–10), after whose deposition Portugal became a republic. When Brazil became independent (1822), it was ruled by two members of the family, *Pedro I (1822–31) and *Pedro II (1831–89), before becoming a republic (1889).

Bragg, Sir William Henry (1862–1942) British physicist, who worked in Australia from 1886 to 1908. His early research, described in *Studies in Radioactivity* (1912), concerned the passage of alpha and beta particle and gamma rays through matter. He invented the Bragg diffractometer for measurement of X-ray wavelengths (1912) and with his son **Sir (William) Lawrence Bragg** (1890–1971) discovered the law of X-ray diffraction that bears their name. Together they wrote *X-rays and Crystal Structure* (1915) and were jointly awarded the Nobel Prize for 1915.

Bragg's law A law stating that, if two parallel X-rays of wavelength λ are reflected by adjacent planes, distance d apart, in a crystal lattice and the rays then constructively interfere, then $2d\sin\theta = n\lambda$, where n is an integer and θ the angle between the X-rays and the planes. θ is called the Bragg angle. If n is half-integral, then destructive *interference is observed. Named after Sir William and Sir Lawrence *Bragg.

Brahe, Tycho (1546–1601) Danish astronomer, who made accurate astronomical instruments and used them to make observations enabling him to revise the existing, often inaccurate, astronomical tables. He first attracted attention by observing a nova in 1572. As a result King Frederick II had two observatories built for him on the island of Hveen, where he worked from 1580 to 1597. During this period he made extensive observations, which led him to support *Copernicus' theory that the planets revolve round the sun. However, he believed the earth to be immovable, with the sun and planets revolving round it. After Frederick's death, he quarrelled with his successor and moved to Prague: there he met *Kepler, who became his student. After Tycho's death, Kepler used his teacher's observations to test his laws of planetary motion.

Brahma The creator god of later Vedic religion. Arising from the cosmic Golden Egg, he brings into existence the cyclical process of the creation and destruction of the world. His four heads and arms represent the four *Vedas, castes, and yugas (ages of the world). Brahma represents the creative aspect of supreme deity in the *trimurti triad but since the 7th century his worship has been superseded by that of *Siva and *Vishnu, the other members of the triad.

Brahman (Hinduism) In the *Upanishads, the absolute unmanifest changeless source of the phenomenal universe, seen as self-existent, extra-temporal Being, all-pervading and infinite. Brahman is both the basis of existence and the state of one who has achieved release (see atman). Brahman originally meant "the sacred Word," and as such was the exclusive domain of the literate priestly caste. In its extended significance it therefore came to be considered the proper spiritual object of that class alone. See Brahmanism.

Brahman (cattle). See zebu.

Brahmanas Commentaries on the *Vedas, written in Sanskrit between about 1000 and 600 BC. They systematically explore Aryan legends and folklore in order to account for

traditional rituals and are major sources of Indian philosophy, theology, and myth.

Brahmanism An early speculative rather than devotional form of *Hinduism, derived from the *Vedas and characterized by the veneration of an elite priestly caste, who, as the privileged keepers of religious knowledge, were seen as actually embodying the sacred word. See also Brahman.

Brahmaputra River A river in S Asia. Rising in SW Tibet as the Tsangpo, it flows generally E across the Himalayas before turning S into the Assam Valley of NE India as the Dihang. From here, as the Brahmaputra, it flows WSW across NE India to join the River *Ganges N of Gaolundo Ghat. Together they enter the Bay of Bengal in a large delta. The floodplains are highly cultivated. Length: 2900 km (1800 mi).

brahmin (or brahman) The first of the four major Hindu castes, that of the priests. Observing many social taboos and being innately more ritually pure than the warrior, merchant, or peasant classes, brahmins alone are able to perform the most important religious tasks, to study and recite the scriptures. Since in India spiritual and secular knowledge are virtually inseparable, brahmins frequently hold considerable intellectual and political power. After India achieved independence in 1947, opposition to brahminical elitism strengthened, but this has not yet significantly weakened their sacerdotal role.

Brahmo Samaj A Hindu revivalist movement, arising in response to contact with Christianity. Founded by Rammohan Ray (1772–1833), it intended to restore monotheistic Hinduism and the authority of the *Upanishads. Unlike the *Arya Samaj, it set out to be a universal religion. Disagreements between advocates of devotion or asceticism, rather than rational theism, led to schisms and the incorporation of Christian elements and in some cases to wholly new philosophical formulations.

Brahms, Johannes (1833–97) German composer, born in Hamburg. Brahms' precociousness was demonstrated by his youthful piano compositions; as a young man he became a friend of the violinist Joseph Joachim (1831–1907), Liszt, and the Schumanns. Brahms moved to Vienna in 1863 and later became musical director of the Gesellschaft der Musikfreunde (Society of Friends of Music; 1872–75). Musically conservative, Brahms composed in traditional forms and was unsympathetic to the progressive ideas espoused by Wagner and Liszt, although his compositions abound in lyrical melodies and rich harmonies. His main orchestral works comprise four symphonies, two piano concertos, a violin concerto, and a concerto for violin and cello. His choral works include *A German Requiem* (1868) and the *Alto Rhapsody* (1869). He wrote a large quantity of chamber music, including a piano quintet, three piano quartets, and three piano trios; string sextets, quintets, and quartets; a clarinet quintet and trio; and sonatas for violin, cello, and clarinet. He also composed much piano music and many songs.

Brăila 46 82N 27 58E A port in E Romania, situated at the limit for oceangoing ships on the River Danube. Following the Turkish occupation of the city (1544–1828), it was rebuilt with radiating and concentric streets. It is a major grain centre. Population (1983): 214 561.

Braille, Louis (1809–52) French teacher, who, blinded by an accident at the age of three, published a system of writing that allows the blind to read by touch. He later applied the Braille system to the reading of music. Modern Braille consists of 63 characters, each of which is made up of one to six embossed dots. □ p.180.

brain The mass of nervous tissue that lies within the skull and is ensheathed by three membranes (meninges). It is the organ of the mind and it controls many bodily activities. The hindmost part of the brain, joining the *spinal cord, is the medulla oblongata: this ascends to the pons, which joins the striped bass   grass snake   pigeon   cat

chimpanzee

man

BRAIN *The brains of these representative vertebrates (drawn to the same scale) show a progressive increase in the size and complexity of the cerebrum. In man this development is such that the cerebrum covers or encloses all the other parts of the brain.*

midbrain. These parts are together called the brainstem, which contains the vital centres controlling breathing and heartbeat and also regulates the level of consciousness and conveys information to and from the cerebrum. The cerebellum is connected to the brainstem and is important in the coordination of movements. The upper end of the brainstem is connected to the largest and most highly developed part of the brain—the cerebrum. This consists of two cerebral hemispheres connected to each other by a tract of nerve fibres. Its surface is intricately folded and is made up of an outer layer of nerve cell bodies (grey matter) and an inner mass of nerve fibres (white matter). The cerebrum is largely responsible for understanding the environment, language, rational thought, and the voluntary control of movements. The hemispheres differ in function: one hemisphere controls the dominant side of the body (normally the left hemisphere in right-handed people) and that hemisphere controls speech. The nondominant hemisphere specializes in analysing how things are arranged in space. Deep within the cerebrum and brainstem lie cavities (ventricles) filled with *cerebrospinal fluid. The brain of vertebrate animals is similar but less highly developed than the human brain; in lower animals a collection of ganglia (nerve cell bodies) functions as the brain. *See also* electroencephalography; hypothalamus; nervous system; neurone.

Braine, John (1922–86) British novelist, born in Bradford. The radical views expressed in *Room at the Top* (1957) established him as one of the *Angry Young Men. Later works include *Life at the Top* (1962).

brake 1. A device used to slow down or stop the rotation of a shaft. An essential component of all vehicles, modern braking systems depend either on the friction between a pair of expanding shoes and the inside of a drum attached to the wheel (**drum brakes**) or between two caliper-operated pads and the two sides of a disc (**disc brakes**). 2. A device that absorbs and measures the power developed by an engine or motor. Brake horsepower is the power so measured. 1 brake HP = 746 watts.

Bramah, Joseph (1748–1814) British engineer and inventor, who in 1784 designed a lock that remained pick-proof until 1851. Bramah went into partnership with Henry *Maudslay and their innovations in manufacturing the parts of the lock to the required accuracy greatly advanced the precision of machine tools. Bramah also invented (1795) a hydraulic press.

Bramante, Donato (1444–1514) Italian Renaissance architect. Bramante started his career as a painter and later

a b c d e f g h i j

k l m n o p q r s t

u v w x y z

and for of the with numeral sign

BRAILLE *The alphabet.*

executed his first building projects in Milan. However, he spent his last 16 years in Rome, where most of the buildings for which he is remembered were erected, showing as they do a much more sophisticated handling of classical forms. His earlier buildings, such as S Maria delle Grazie (1480s) in Milan, do not show the same assurance that he exhibited in, for example, the Tempietto di S Pietro in Montorio (1502). The Palazzo Caprini (1514) influenced secular architects and Bramante's designs for St Peter's are reflected in the later designs of *Michelangelo.

bramble.   *See* blackberry.

brambling   A finch, *Fringilla montifringilla*, 14.5 cm long, that breeds in Asia and N Europe and migrates south in winter. It has a brown-speckled plumage with white wing bars and orange underparts but in winter the male has a black head and back.

Bran   A legendary Celtic god-king of Britain, whose story is told in the *Mabinogion*. Of giant stature, he once waded across the sea between Britain and Ireland. His severed head lived on for some 80 years, renowned for the good advice and entertainment it gave his followers. In accordance with his wish, Bran's head was buried in London to protect Britain from invasion. It was dug up by King Arthur, who believed that the country was better protected by the valour of individuals.

Branchiopoda   A subclass of small *crustaceans (over 800 species) that, except for the brine shrimp, occur in fresh water. They include the *fairy shrimps, *tadpole shrimps, *water fleas, and clam shrimps, all bearing flat fringed appendages used for locomotion, respiration, and filter feeding. *Parthenogenesis is common.

Brancusi, Constantin   (1876–1957) Romanian sculptor. At first locally trained, he moved to Paris in 1904, where he developed a highly individual style. His stone and metal sculptures show a search for abstract simplicity and surface polish, such as the *Sleeping Muse* series beginning in 1906 and the *Birds* variations (1912–40). His wood sculptures, such as the *Prodigal Son* (1915), are often mythological or religious in theme.

Brandenburg   52 24N 12 31E A city in central East Germany, on the River Havel. It was the former capital of the Prussian province of Brandenburg. The city was severely damaged during World War II and has been largely rebuilt. Its industries include steelworks and machinery and textile manufacturing. Population (1983): 95 052.

Brandenburg   A former state corresponding to the present-day districts of Magdeburg, Potsdam, Neubrandenburg, and Frankfurt of East Germany and to part of W Poland. The region was conquered by the Germans between the 10th and 12th centuries and in 1157 *Albert (I) the Bear became margrave, and then *elector, of Brandenburg. Under *Frederick William, the Great Elector (1640–88), Brandenburg gained suzerainty of Prussia and became a leading German power. In 1701 the Elector of Brandenburg became *Frederick I of Prussia.

Brandenburg Gate   A ceremonial gateway now in East □Berlin. The Brandenburg Gate was built (1789) in the neoclassical style by the architect C. G. Langhans (1732–1808). Situated at the W end of Unter den Linden, it became the symbol of the modernized city.

Brandes, Georg Morris Cohen   (1842–1927) Danish literary critic. Brandes opposed all that was staid and reactionary in literature, and because of radical and atheistic tendencies he was denied a professorship at Copenhagen University until 1902. *Mainstreams in the Literature of the Nineteenth Century* (1872–75) established his reputation. There followed monographs on *Kierkegaard* (1871), *Ibsen* (1899), and *Anatole France* (1905), and a study of Shakespeare (1897–98).

Brando, Marlon   (1924–   ) US film actor. His acting was influenced by the "method" style developed by the New York Actors' Studio in the 1950s from the theories of *Stanislavsky. His films include *A Streetcar Named Desire* (1951), *On the Wa-* terfront (1954), *The Godfather* (1972), and *Apocalypse Now* (1979).

MARLON BRANDO   *In the title role of* The Godfather.

Brandt, Bill   (1905–83) British photographer. He is best known for his photographs of British life in the 1930s, particularly the working classes, and for photographic books, such as *The English at Home* (1936) and *Perspective of Nudes* (1961).

Brandt, Willy   (1913–   ) West German statesman; chancellor (1969–74). In Norway from 1933, he was a leader of the resistance movement against the Nazis throughout World War II, after which he was Norwegian press attaché in Berlin (1945–48). A member of the Social Democratic Party from 1931, he was its chairman from 1964 to 1987. As chancellor he negotiated treaties with Russia, Poland, and East Germany and in 1971 was awarded the Nobel Peace Prize. He resigned the chancellorship when it was revealed that one of his aides was an East German spy. He subsequently chaired an international commission on the state of the world economy (the Brandt Commission), which published its report in 1980.

brandy   A *spirit distilled from fermented grape juice (wine); the term also denotes drinks distilled from the fermented juices of other fruits. The best types of wine brandy are matured in oak casks and named after the Cognac and Armagnac districts of France where they are made. Marc (French) or grappa (Italian) brandy is made from the refermented grape pips, skins, and stems left after pressing for wine. VSOP—very superior old pale —brandy is usually 20–25 years old.

Brandywine, Battle of the   (11 September, 1777) A battle fought in SE Pennsylvania during the *American Revolution. Sir William *Howe, advancing on Philadelphia, encircled *Washington's troops in an attempt to cut off the city. Howe crossed the Brandywine Creek, defeated Washington's troops, and subsequently occupied Philadelphia.

Branson, Richard   (1950–   ) British entrepreneur, who in 1969 founded the Virgin record company; his later diversifications included an airline. His nationwide clean-up campaign attracted considerable publicity as did his fastest Atlantic crossing in *Virgin Atlantic Challenger II* (1986) and his hot-air balloon crossing in 1987.

Brant, Joseph   (1742–1807) Mohawk Indian chief. He went to a mission school, where he became an Anglican, and commanded the Mohawks on the British side in the American Revolution. He subsequently settled them in Canada and in 1785 he visited England to claim compensation for war losses. He later resisted the taking of Mohawk lands by speculators.

Brant, Sebastian (?1458–1521) German poet. He studied and taught law at Basle, and was made an imperial councillor by Maximilian I. His most important work was *The Ship of Fools* (1494); a series of satires on contemporary vices (with illustrations ascribed to Dürer). It became popular throughout Europe.

Branting, Karl Hjalmar (1860–1925) Swedish statesman; prime minister (1920, 1921–23, 1924–25). His domestic policy pioneered welfare state legislation in Sweden. An enthusiastic supporter of the League of Nations, he was awarded, with the Norwegian pacifist, Christian Lange (1869–1938), the Nobel Peace Prize in 1921.

Brantôme, Pierre, Abbé and Seigneur de Bourdeille (c. 1540–1614) French chronicler. Only nominally a priest, he was a courtier under Marguerite de Valois and Henry II and travelled throughout Europe as a soldier. He began writing when crippled in a riding accident. His *Mémoires* (1665–66) chronicle the lives of illustrious men and women of his time.

Braque, Georges (1882–1963) French painter, who with *Picasso developed *cubism. He was initially influenced by impressionism and later fauvism before painting his earliest cubist landscapes (1908–09) at L'Estaque and Guyon, inspired by *Cézanne. His favourite subjects were still lifes, which during their period of close collaboration, sometimes looked identical to those of Picasso. Notable among Braque's innovations were the use of lettering in compositions, e.g. *The Portuguese* (1911; Basle), mixing paint with sand to produce interesting textures, and papiers collés (paper pasted on canvases). After World War II he painted independently in large flat planes instead of small fragmented cubes. In his later years he produced sculpture and eight paintings of studio interiors (1948–55).

Brasília 16 0S 48 10W The capital and a federal district of Brazil, situated on the central plateau. The idea of a capital in the interior was first suggested in 1789, but it was not until 1956 that the present site was chosen. It was inaugurated in 1960, the chief designer being Lúcio Costa and the principal architect, Oscar *Niemeyer. Its fine modern buildings include the National Congress Building and the cathedral. The university was founded in 1962. Population (1980): 411 305.

Braşov (German name: Kronstadt) 45 39N 25 35E A city in E central Romania, surrounded by the Transylvanian Alps. It has many historic buildings and the first book printed in Romanian appeared here in the 16th century. Its varied industries include motor vehicles, chemicals, and textiles. Population (1983): 290 772.

brass An *alloy of copper and zinc. Brasses containing less than 36% zinc are ductile when cold and can be easily worked into complex shapes. Those with more than 36% zinc are harder and stronger. Brass is easy to machine and stamp into shape and is used for screws, hinges, and a wide variety of articles. It does not rust but exposure to sea water causes dezincification (leaching out of the zinc). This is partially prevented by the addition of tin (1%) in Naval Brass, sometimes with about 0.05% of arsenic. *See also* Muntz metal.

Brassica A genus of mainly annual or biennial herbs (about 40 species, especially in the Mediterranean region), with erect clusters of four-petalled yellow flowers. Many species have basal rosettes of large simple leaves, but in others the leaves are spaced out up the main stem. The genus includes many important vegetables, mostly cultivated varieties of native species; the leaves, buds, stems, or roots may be eaten. *See also* broccoli; Brussels sprout; cabbage; cauliflower; kale; rape; swede; turnip.

brass instruments Wind instruments made of brass. The *French horn, *trumpet, *trombone, and *tuba are commonly used in the symphony orchestra; brass bands use a greater variety, including *bugles and *cornets. Brass instruments have either a cup-shaped or cone-shaped mouthpiece, the shape of which influences the tone quality, as does the type of bore, which may be conical (horn) or cylindrical (trumpet). A brass instrument plays the harmonic series natural to its length; additional series are made available by the use of crooks, slides, or valves.

Bratby, John (1928–) British painter and writer. He studied at the Royal College of Art and from 1955 exhibited annually at the Royal Academy. He became known for his domestic interiors and more recently for his representation of his bohemian life. His paintings for the film (1958) of Joyce Carey's novel *The Horse's Mouth* (1944) became widely known.

Bratislava (German name: Pressburg; Hungarian name: Pozsony) 48 10N 17 10E The third largest city in Czechoslovakia, the capital of the Slovak Republic on the River Danube. It was the capital of Hungary (1526–1784). Notable buildings include the gothic cathedral (13th century), where many of the kings of Hungary were crowned, and its castle. The university was founded in 1919. It is an important industrial centre; oil, piped from the Soviet Union via the Friendship Oil Pipeline, is refined here. Population (1980 est): 375 000.

Brattain, Walter Houser (1902–) US physicist, who shared the 1956 Nobel Prize for his part in the invention of the transistor (with W. B. *Shockley and John *Bardeen) while working at the Bell Telephone Laboratories in 1948.

Brauchitsch, Walther von (1881–1948) German general. He became commander in chief of the German army in 1938 but was dismissed (1941) by Hitler after the failure of the Moscow campaign. He died awaiting trial for alleged war crimes.

Braun, Eva (1910–45) The mistress and finally the wife of Adolf Hitler. Their relationship probably began in 1933 and they were married shortly before their suicides on 30 April, 1945.

Braunau am Inn 48 16N 13 03E A city in N Austria, in Upper Austria. It has numerous 16th–17th-century houses and several notable gothic churches. Adolf Hitler was born here. It has Austria's largest aluminium plant. Population (1981): 16 185.

Braunschweig. *See* Brunswick.

Brazil, Federal Republic of (Portuguese name: Brasil) A country comprising almost half the area of South America, situated in the NE. The N of the country is dominated by the Amazon basin with its tropical rain forests. The land rises to the Guiana Highlands in the N and the Brazilian Highlands in the S, with large tracts of grassland in between. The Mato Grosso Plateau in the SW is arid savanna. The population is largely of European descent, with some African and Asian minorities and a very small and dwindling Indian minority. Most of the inhabitants live along the coast, especially in the S and SE, although the government has launched ambitious road and regional plans in an attempt to open up and develop the interior. The building of *Brasília was the most impressive single attempt to draw the population away from the overcrowded coastal areas. *Economy*: despite a remarkably high annual growth rate (especially in the period 1960 to 1970) and recent industrialization, Brazil is still mainly an agricultural country, the chief crops being sugar cane, manioc, maize, rice, and beans. Brazil was formerly the world's largest producer of coffee but overproduction has led to a decline in its position. Severe frosts in 1975 caused a 60% loss in the coffee crop. Cocoa, bananas, and oranges are also important. Numbers of livestock have increased and Brazil is now ahead of Argentina as a cattle producer. The fishing industry has been nationalized and in 1971 territorial waters were extended to 320 km (200 mi). Brazil is exceptionally rich in mineral resources, many of them as yet untapped, although more mines are now being opened up in the interior. The iron-ore reserves are estimated to be the largest in the world. There are gold deposits in most parts of the country and the large mine at Minas Gerais was discovered in the late 17th century. Recently large deposits of phosphates have been discovered there, as well as uranium, manganese, and copper. The country's many other minerals include high-grade quartz crystal. Efforts to encourage industrial development since the 1960s have included an increase in steel production, which in turn is designed to encourage shipbuilding. The most important manufacturing industry, however, is textiles, although motor-vehicle production is on the increase. 90% of power comes from hydroelectric sources. There is now an agreement with West Germany, based on Brazil's rich uranium deposits, to build eight nuclear power stations. Oil production only provides a fraction of Brazil's domestic needs although new offshore fields have been found near Campos. Main exports include sugar, coffee, cotton, and minerals, especially iron ore. *History*: claimed by the Portuguese in 1500, it became a Portuguese settlement. During the Napoleonic Wars the Portuguese court was transferred to Brazil and in 1815 it was made a kingdom. In 1822 independence was declared by *Pedro I, son of John VI of Portugal, with a constitution that proclaimed him emperor. In 1889 his son *Pedro II was deposed and Brazil became a republic. From 1930 to 1945 it was ruled under the benevolent dictatorship of Getúlio *Vargas. Less stable governments followed, including a further period under Vargas (1950–54). In 1964 Gen Humberto Castelo Branco (1900–67) came to power in a military coup. In 1967 Marshal Artur da Costa e Silva (1902–69) was elected president and in 1968 he assumed absolute powers. He resigned in 1969 and was replaced by a junta comprising the three heads of the armed forces. Elections were held in 1985; when president elect Tancredo Neves (1910–85) died before taking office, vice-president José Sarney assumed power. Official language: Portuguese. Official currency: cruzado (equal to 1000 former cruzeiros). Area: 8 511 965 sq km (3 286 000 sq mi). Population (1980): 119 098 992. Capital: Brasília. Main port: Rio de Janeiro.

Brazil nut The seed of a tall forest tree, *Bertholletia excelsa*, up to 45 m high, native to tropical South America. The tree produces showy fluffy flowers that develop into hard woody fruits, up to 15 cm in diameter, each containing 12–24 seeds (the nuts). Commercial supplies come entirely from wild trees. Family: *Lecythidaceae*.

brazilwood An evergreen tree, *Caesalpinia brasiliensis*, of tropical South America. The leaves are bipinnate—each leaflet is divided into smaller leaflets—and the irregular orange flowers develop into seed pods. The tree yields a very hard wood from which a red dye is extracted; the wood is also used for cabinet-work. Family: *Leguminosae*.

brazing. *See* solder.

Brazza, Pierre Paul François Camille Savorgnan de (1852–1905) French explorer of Italian descent. In 1878 he explored, claimed, and colonized French Equatorial Africa, founding Brazzaville. He was the first governor of the French Congo (1886–97).

Brazzaville 4 07W 15 15E The capital of the People's Republic of Congo, situated in the S on the Zaïre River opposite Kinshasa (Zaïre). Founded in the 1880s, it developed as a European centre and an important riverport, and became capital of French Equatorial Africa in 1910. During World War II it was the centre of the Free French forces in Africa. It became capital of the newly independent Republic of Congo in 1960. The Marien-Ngouabi University was founded in 1972. Population (1980 est): 310 500.

bread A staple food made basically by baking a mixture of *flour and water. Ordinary leavened bread is made by mixing a dough of flour, water, yeast, sugar, salt, and sometimes other ingredients. The dough is kneaded and left to rise twice, a process that can take several hours, before being baked. White loaves, rolls, French sticks, and brown bread are made from different types of wheat flour. Rye bread is another variety, which has a stronger more bitter flavour and can be black, brown, or white.

Bread has been baked since the earliest times, evidence of barley cakes having been found in Neolithic dwellings.

breadfruit The starchy fruit of a tropical tree *Artocarpus communis*. When roasted it forms a staple part of the diet in the Pacific islands, to which it is native, and it is widely cultivated elsewhere. The tree grows to a height of 30 m and has thick shiny divided leaves. The large round fruits, as much as 30 cm across, have a thick warty rind and develop from long female catkins. Family: *Moraceae*.

bread mould A fungus that grows on bread, especially one of the genera *Rhizopus* or *Mucor*. Black bread mould (*R. stolonifer*) forms a filamentous branching structure from which arise erect stalks bearing black spore cases resembling pinheads. It also grows on fruit, manure, and other decaying organic matter. Class: *Phycomycetes*.

bream One of several *teleost fishes, especially *Abramis brama*, a food and game fish related to *carp that occurs in European lakes and slow-moving rivers. Its deep body, 30–70 cm long, is bluish grey or brown above and silvery below. It lives in schools in deep water and feeds on invertebrates or small fish. *See also* sea bream.

Bream, Julian Alexander (1933–) British guitarist and lutenist. Taught by his father, Bream gave his first public performance at the age of 12. His outstanding talent attracted Andrés Segovia's attention. His repertoire includes arrangements of baroque and Renaissance pieces as well as works written for him by Britten and Henze.

BRAZIL *The capital from 1763 to 1960, Rio de Janeiro is dominated by the giant Christ overlooking the Sugar Loaf Mountain.*

breast The milk-producing (mammary) gland of women. Each of the two breasts consists of a mass of fatty tissue in which are embedded milk-secreting lobes, which drain through a series of ducts to the nipple. Breast cancer is the commonest form of cancer in women. Treatment usually involves surgical removal of the breast (*see* mastectomy), sometimes with radiotherapy or *cytotoxic drugs. The activity of the gland is controlled by the hormone prolactin, secreted by the pituitary gland (*see* lactation).

breathalyzer A roadside test used by the police to estimate the amount of alcohol in the breath, which reflects the level of alcohol in the blood. In the UK a suspected driver blows through a tube containing potassium dichromate crystals into a balloon. When the ballon is inflated (i.e. sufficient breath has been examined) the crystals are observed for colour change. If the colour change extends beyond a line marked on the tube the driver is considered to have a blood alcohol level in excess of the legal limit (80 mg per litre of blood). He is then taken to a police station to have a blood or urine test in the presence of a doctor.

breathing. *See* respiration.

Brébeuf, St Jean de (1593–1649) French Jesuit missionary and patron saint of Canada. Ordained in 1623, he evangelized the Huron Indians in New France in several expeditions, until he was captured and tortured to death by the Hurons' enemies, the Iroquois. Feast day: 26 Sept.

breccia A sedimentary rock consisting of relatively large (over 2 mm in diameter) angular fragments of pre-existing rocks. These fragments have usually undergone little transport from their source and are poorly sorted. Scree material cemented together forms one kind of breccia.

Brecht, Bertolt (1898–1956) German dramatist and poet. He first studied medicine, serving briefly as a medical orderly in 1918. He abandoned the exuberant expressionism of his early plays after his conversion to Marxism in 1928, producing his best-known work the next year, *Die Dreigroschenoper*, an adaptation of John Gay's *The Beggar's Opera* with music by Kurt Weil. In 1933 he left Germany and lived in Scandinavia and the USA (1941–47). During these years he wrote his most powerful plays, notably *Galileo* (1938), *Mother Courage* (1939) and *The Caucasian Chalk Circle* (1949). These exploit his "distancing" technique, in which by emphasizing the unreality of the play he increases its didactic impact. In 1949 he returned to East Berlin and founded his famous Berliner Ensemble Company.

Breconshire A former county of SE Wales. Under local government reorganization in 1974 it became part of *Powys, *Mid Glamorgan, and *Gwent.

Breda 51 35N 4 46E A town in the SW Netherlands, in North Brabant province. Occupied several times, its capture by the Spanish in 1625 is depicted in Velázquez' famous painting, *The Surrender of Breda*. Its industries include engineering and chemicals. Population (1985): 120 000.

Breeches Bible. *See* Geneva Bible.

breeder reactor. *See* fast reactor.

breeding The controlled mating of selected animals or plants, usually in order to produce offspring with improved performance, such as a higher milk yield in dairy cattle, or certain desirable characteristics, such as a particular flower colour in garden plants. Based on careful selection of parents (often over many generations) and a knowledge of genetics, modern plant and animal breeding is aimed at improving yield, resistance to disease, hardiness to climate, consumer appeal of the product, etc., and has helped meet increased world demand for food.

Bregenz 47 31N 9 46E A town in W Austria, the capital of Vorarlberg on Lake Constance. A tourist resort, it manufactures textiles and machinery. Population (1981): 24 624.

Brehon Laws A collection of ancient Irish laws, dating back to the 8th century, which constitute one of the most important sources for the history of contemporary Irish society. The Brehon was an official who pronounced upon the law. The Laws describe conditions of tenure and transfer of land and the legal status and responsibilities of clan members, besides fixing pen-

alties and fines for criminal acts.

Breitenfeld, Battles of Two battles fought in Germany during the *Thirty Years' War and won by Sweden. *Gustavus II Adolphus led the Swedish-Saxon army to victory against the Catholic and imperial forces under *Tilly in 1631. The second battle (1642) was a Swedish victory against the imperial army in a campaign to win Saxony.

Bremen 53 05N 8 48E The second largest port in West Germany, capital of the *Land* of Bremen on the River Weser. Its cathedral (founded 1043) was restored following damage during World War II. Its industries include shipbuilding, oil refining, and food processing. Population (1980 est): 555 700.

Bremen The smallest *Land* of West Germany, comprising the cities of *Bremen and *Bremerhaven enclosed by the *Land* of Lower Saxony. Area: 404 sq km (156 sq mi). Population (1980 est): 694 600.

Bremerhaven 53 33N 8 35E A city in N West Germany, in Bremen on the Weser estuary. A major fishing, freight, and passenger port, its industries include fish processing and shipbuilding. Population (1985 est): 134 500.

bremmstrahlung Electromagnetic radiation emitted by a charged particle when it is decelerated on passing close to a nucleus. The effect is most often observed with electrons since they are light and therefore easily decelerated. The radiation from one particle is emitted as a single photon. It is an important method by which *cosmic rays dissipate their energy on entering the earth's atmosphere.

Brendan, St (484–c. 578 AD) Irish abbot. He is traditionally credited with founding the monastery at Clonfert (Cluain Fearta), Co Galway. The Latin *Navigation of St Brendan* (c. 1050) recounts his legendary voyage to "northern and western islands," which may refer to the Orkneys and Hebrides. Feast day: 16 May.

Brendel, Alfred (1931–) Austrian pianist. He has toured worldwide and is famous as an interpreter of Beethoven, Mozart, and Schubert.

Bren gun A gas-operated light machine gun with interchangeable barrels first built at *Br*no, Czechoslovakia (1933), and later manufactured at *En*field, UK (1935). Widely used in World War II, it was accurate, reliable, easily maintained, and used 0.303 calibre ammunition.

Brenner Pass (German name: Brenner Sattel; Italian name: Passo del Brennero) 47 02N 11 32E The lowest of the chief passes in the Alps, on the Austrian-Italian border. Important since Roman times, it links Innsbruck (Austria) with Verona (Italy) by road and rail.

Brent A borough of NW Greater London, created in 1965 from the former municipal boroughs of *Wembley and Willesden. Population (1981): 251 257.

Brentano, Clemens (1778–1842) German writer, a member of the Heidelberg School of Romantic writers. With Achim von Arnim he published the influential folksong collection, *Des Knaben Wunderhorn* (1805–08). Emotionally unstable in early life, he became a Roman Catholic in 1817, and for six years was a monk.

Brentano, Franz (1838–1916) German psychologist and philosopher. He trained as a priest but resigned over the doctrine of papal infallibility. Thinking psychology a necessary foundation for philosophy, he suggested distinguishing marks for psychic phenomena, chief among which was intentionality ("directedness-to-an-object") adopted by *Russell and *Moore. His main works are *Psychology from an Empirical Standpoint* (1874) and *The Origin of Ethical Knowledge* (1889).

brent goose A dark-coloured *goose, *Branta bernicla*. 53–58 cm long, it breeds in the Arctic and winters in temperate N Atlantic coastal regions, feeding chiefly on eelgrass on mudflats. The pale-bellied form occurring in Canada and the eastern USA and the dark-bellied form of Arctic Russia and European coasts are both geographic races.

Brescia 45 33N 10 13E A city in Italy, in Lombardy. It has Roman remains, 9th-century and 17th-century cathedrals, and a 12th-century palace. A railway junction, its manufactures include metal goods, firearms, machinery, and textiles. Population (1980 est): 210 027.

Breslau. *See* Wrocław.

Bresson, Robert (1907–) French film director. In most of his austere films concerning moral and religious dilemmas he uses unknown actors. His films include *Le Journal d'un curé de campagne* (1950), *Mouchette* (1967), and *Lancelot du lac* (1974).

Brest (name until 1921: Brest-Litovsk; Polish name: Brześć nad Bu-giem) 52 08N 23 40E A port in the W Soviet Union, in the Belorussian SSR on the Rivers Bug and Mukhavets near the Polish border. The Treaties of *Brest-Litovsk were negotiated here in World War I. It is a major industrial, commercial, and transportation centre. Population (1981 est): 194 000.

Brest 48 23N 4 30W A port and naval base in NW France, in the Finistère department on the Atlantic Ocean. A German U-boat base in World War II, it was almost entirely destroyed by Allied bombing. It is the site of the University of Brittany. Industries include fishing, chemicals, and clothing. Population (1982 est): 160 355.

Brest-Litovsk, Treaties of (1918) The peace treaties between the Central Powers and, respectively, the Ukraine and Soviet Russia towards the end of World War I. An independent Ukraine was recognized by the first treaty. By the second, Russia acknowledged Ukrainian independence and also lost its Polish and Baltic possessions. The treaties were annulled following the ultimate defeat of the Central Powers.

Brethren Members of the Protestant Brethren Churches. The largest, called the Church of the Brethren, was founded in Germany in the early 18th century. Persecution forced its members to emigrate to America, where they became known as "Tunkers," "Dunkers," or "German Baptists." They believe in temperance and pacifism and practise adult baptism by triple immersion.

Brétigny, Treaty of (1360) The treaty that concluded the first phase of the *Hundred Years' War. Never fully effective, it promised a ransom of £500,000 for *John II of France (captured at Poitiers in 1356) and granted territories, including Aquitaine, to Edward III of England. In return, Edward was to renounce his claim to the French throne.

Breton A Celtic language with four distinct dialects spoken in Brittany by about one million people. It was originally introduced to this area by immigrants from SW England, who had been displaced by invading Anglo-Saxon tribes. It is related to *Cornish and *Welsh but has been strongly influenced by French. It has a literature that dates from the 15th century. Official encouragement of French has tended to decrease the number of Breton speakers.

Breton, André (1896–1966) French poet. After involvement with *dada, he became the leader of French *surrealism in 1922 and wrote three manifestos (1924, 1930, 1942) defining its aims. His many essays explore surrealist themes, such as the relationship between dreams and reality. His novel *Nadja* (1928) freely blends real and surreal; *Poèmes* (1948) seeks to express the unconscious mind. Briefly a Communist Party member, he lived in the USA from 1938 to 1946.

Bretton Woods Conference (1944) A conference held at Bretton Woods, New Hampshire (USA), at which the USA, UK, and Canada established a system of international financial rules, which led to the setting up of the *International Monetary Fund (IMF) and the *International Bank for Reconstruction and Development (World Bank). The chief features of the system were, first, an obligation for each country to maintain the exchange value of its currency within 1% of a value fixed in terms of gold; and, secondly, the provision by the IMF of finance to bridge temporary payments imbalances. The system eventually collapsed in 1971, following the US Government's suspension of convertibility from dollars to gold.

Breuer, Josef (1842–1925) Austrian physiologist and pioneer of psychoanalysis. After successfully treating hysteria in one of his patients, Breuer collaborated with Sigmund *Freud in writing *Studies in Hysteria* (1895). Earlier, working with Ewald Hering (1834–1918), Breuer described the Hering-Breuer reflex involved in the nervous control of breathing movements.

Breuer, Marcel Lajos (1902–81) US architect, furniture designer, and teacher, born in Hungary. In the 1920s he taught at the *Bauhaus, designing the first tubular steel chair (1925). After 1937 he practised in the USA as an architect. One of the best-known buildings on which he worked is the UNESCO headquarters in Paris (1958).

Breuil, Henri (1877–1961) French archaeologist, famous for his work on *Palaeolithic art. Although ordained an abbé (1900), Breuil devoted his outstanding talents as a draughtsman to copying cave paintings all over Europe (*see also* Altamira) and in N Africa, China, and S Africa. He was professor at the Collège de France (1929–47) and published over 600 books and articles.

brewing. *See* beer and brewing.

Brewster, Sir David (1781–1868) Scottish physicist, who studied the polarization of light, double refraction in crystals, and relations between crystalline forms and optical properties (*see* Brewster's law). He also invented and patented the kaleidoscope. In 1831 he helped to found the British Association for the Advancement of Science.

Brewster's law Light reflected from a solid surface is plane polarized, with maximum polarization occurring when the tangent of the angle of incidence is equal to the refractive index. Named after Sir David *Brewster.

Brezhnev, Leonid Ilich (1906–82) Soviet statesman; secretary of the Soviet Communist Party (1964–82) and president of the Soviet Union (1977–82). Brezhnev, a metallurgist, was a political leader in the Red Army during World War II. He became a member of the presidium in 1957 and its chairman in 1960. He and *Kosygin forced Khrushchev to resign in 1964 and Brezhnev became first secretary of the Communist Party. By the late 1960s he had became the most powerful Soviet leader and in 1977 became president. Soviet denunciation of his leadership began in 1987 during the more liberal administration of Gorbachov.

Brian, Havergal (1876–1972) British composer. He was self-taught and his work was largely neglected until shortly before his death. His 32 symphonies form the core of a large output of music of all kinds; the *Gothic Symphony* (1919–22) is one of the longest symphonies in existence and requires a huge number of performers.

Brian Boru (926–1014) High King of Ireland (1001–14) after victories over the Danes and the other Irish. He was murdered after his victory at the battle of Clontarf. Brian was the last high king with effective jurisdiction over most of Ireland.

Briand, Aristide (1862–1932) French socialist statesman; prime minister (1909–11, 1913, 1915–17, 1921–22, 1925–26, 1929) and foreign minister (1925–32). The crisis of Verdun in *World War I precipitated the fall of his government in March, 1917, when Clemenceau's attacks upon Briand for his attempt to negotiate peace forced him to retire. From 1919 he was a leading advocate of international cooperation and was instrumental in securing the *Locarno Pact (1925) and *Kellog-Briand Pact (1928). With Gustav *Stresemann, he shared the Noble Peace Prize in 1926.

briar A shrubby rambling *rose with arching prickly stems, found in hedgerows and scrub in many parts of Europe. The

bribery and corruption

principal species are *Rosa rubiginosa*, *R. micrantha*, *R. agrestis*, and *R. elliptica*. *See also* sweet briar.

Briar is also the name of a shrubby white *heath (*Erica arborea*), the roots and knotted stems of which are used for making briar pipes.

bribery and corruption The giving of a gift to a person in a position of trust, to induce him to act contrary to his duty. If such a gift is secretly given and received it is presumed to be corrupt. If an agent acting on behalf of another (his principal) accepts a bribe from the other side of the negotiations (third party), the principal is not bound by any *contract that may result. Both the agent and the third party may be punished by a fine or imprisonment according to the Prevention of Corruption Acts (1906, 1916). Bribery of public servants is illegal according to the Public Bodies Corrupt Practices Act (1889). Obtaining a title or similar honour by bribery is a crime according to the Honours (Prevention of Abuses) Act (1925). Bribery in connection with parliamentary and other elections is a corrupt practice forbidden by the Parliamentary Elections Act (1868) and the Representation of the People Act (1949).

stretcher bond

stretcher   header

English bond

closer

Flemish bond

BRICKS *The factors of cost, strength, and decorative effect influence a bricklayer's choice of bond for a particular task.*

bricks A traditional building material in the form of a rectangular block usually measuring 225 × 112 × 75 mm. They are normally made from clay and baked or fired in a kiln at about 900°C. Water is driven off, organic matter becomes oxidized, and some of the clay minerals fuse and fill the gaps between the clay particles. Iron oxide gives the brick its reddish colour. London stock bricks are yellowish on account of the sand and alumina they contain. Bricks are laid in various patterns, known as bonds. Refractory bricks made from fireclay are used to line furnaces.

Bride, St. *See* Bridget, St.

bridge A card game deriving from *whist. **Straight bridge** was first played in Britain about 1880; having overtaken whist in popularity, about 1911 it was displaced by its descendant, **auction bridge**, in which the opposing pairs of partners competed to decide the trump suit. By 1929 **contract bridge**, which had developed in the USA, was popularized by Ely *Culbertson, and put greater emphasis on skill, supplanted other forms of bridge. Two pairs of partners (referred to as North-South and East-West in bridge notation) bid to name the trump suit (or to play without a trump suit, i.e. in "no trumps") and "contract" to win a specified number of tricks (e.g. "four spades") above the six tricks of the "book." A game consists of 100 points, with each spade or heart trick counting 30, each diamond or club 20, and for a bid in no trumps 40 for the first trick and 30 for subsequent tricks. Only the tricks contracted for in the bidding are counted towards game; extra points are awarded separately for "honours" (ace to ten of trumps), overtricks, and for slams (when the partners have bid for and won all the tricks or all but one trick in a hand). Penalty points are awarded to the opponents for undertricks (when the partners who have declared trumps fail to win the number of tricks they contracted for in the bidding). The side winning two games consecutively or two games out of three wins the rubber, which counts as either 500 or 700 extra points. The playing of the hand after the bidding is similar to whist, except that the declarer's partner, called the dummy, puts his entire hand face upwards on the table to be played by the declarer.

Bridge, Frank (1879-1941) British composer. Bridge studied composition with Stanford and played the viola in the English String Quartet. The orchestral suite *The Sea* (1910-11) earned him early popularity. His later works, such as the third string quartet (1926) and *Oration* (for cello and orchestra; 1930), are in a highly individual modern idiom. He was the teacher of Benjamin *Britten.

Bridge of Sighs (Italian name: Ponte dei Sospiri) A covered bridge in Venice (Italy) linking the Doge's Palace with the state prison. Its name derives from the sighs of the prisoners who were conducted over it.

Bridgeport 41 12N 73 12W A city in the USA, in SW Connecticut on Long Island Sound. The showman P. T. Barnum lived here and the main attraction of his circus, the midget *Tom Thumb, was born here. An industrial city, its manufactures include electrical equipment and aircraft. Population (1980 est): 143 000.

bridges Structures that provide a means of crossing a river, valley, road, or railway. There are three basic designs, which differ in the way they bear the weight of the bridge and its load; some bridges consist of composite structures. **Beam** (*or* girder) **bridges** are supported at their ends by the ground, with the weight thrusting downwards. The cantilever is a more complex form of girder. **Arch bridges** thrust outwards as well as downwards at their ends and are in compression. **Suspension bridges** use cables under tension to pull inwards against anchorages in the ground. The roadway, or a truss supporting it, hangs from the main cables by a network of vertical cables. In certain bridges, there is insufficient room to allow traffic to pass underneath them. In these cases the bridges are designed with movable parts. Swing bridges can rotate horizontally. Bascule bridges are cantilever-type bridges with a counterweight and hinge to rotate the bridge vertically. Lift bridges have towers that lift the whole of one section of the bridge upwards. *See also* Bailey bridge; pontoon bridge.

Bridges, Robert Seymour (1844-1930) British poet. Educated at Oxford, he worked as a doctor until 1882. He published several volumes of lyrics and a long philosophical poem, *The Testament of Beauty* (1929), but an even greater contribution to literature was his edition of the poems of his friend Gerard Manley *Hopkins. He was made poet laureate in 1913.

Bridget, St (St Bride or St Brigit; died c. 523 AD) Irish abbess and second patron saint of Ireland. The traditions regarding her life are various, but she is believed to have founded the first Irish convent, at Kildare. Feast day: 1 Feb.

Bridgetown 14 05N 59 35W The capital of Barbados, a port in the SW on Carlisle Bay, founded in 1628. The main industries are sugar, rum, and tourism. The University of the West Indies was founded in 1963. Population (1980): 7517.

Bridgewater Canal A waterway constructed in 1761–76 by James *Brindley (1716–72) from Worsley to Manchester (later extended to Liverpool) for transporting coal. It is a gravity-flow canal constructed on an aqueduct across the Irwell Valley and is a masterpiece of 18th-century engineering. It was the first British canal.

simple girder

arch

cantilever

suspension

BRIDGES *The arrows show how forces are exerted onto or away from the foundations in each of the basic structural types.*

Bridgman, Percy Williams (1882–1961) US physicist, whose experiments with high pressures led to the invention of a seal the efficiency of which increased with pressure, enabling him to attain pressures of up to 20 000 atmospheres. Bridgman studied the effects of such pressures on solids and, in 1955, his methods were used by the General Electric Company to synthesize diamonds. For this work he was awarded the Nobel Prize in 1946. In *The Logic of Modern Physics* (1927) he made an important contribution to the (operational) concept of scientific meaning.

Bridgwater 51 08N 3 00W A market town in SW England,

in Somerset on the River Parrett. The battle of Sedgemoor (1685) was fought nearby. Its varied industries include the manufacture of bricks, furniture, and plastics. Population (1981): 26 132.

Bridie, James (Osborne Henry Mavor; 1888–1951) British dramatist. For many of his popular comedies of the 1930s and 1940s he drew on his Glaswegian background and his interest in medicine. His plays, which were never popular outside the UK, include *Tobias and the Angel* (1930) and *The Anatomist* (1931). He was the founder of the Glasgow Citizens' Theatre.

Brie An area in N France, between the Rivers Seine and Marne. Predominantly agricultural, it produces wheat and sugar beet and is noted for its cheese. Area: 6500 sq km (2510 sq mi).

brig A sailing vessel with two masts, both carrying square sails.

brigantine A sailing vessel with two masts, square-rigged on the foremast, with a fore-and-aft topsail.

Briggs, Henry (1561–1630) English mathematician. On hearing of *Napier's use of *logarithms, which have a base of e, Briggs realized that logarithms to the base ten, known as common or Briggsian logarithms, would make calculations simpler. Common logarithms are now widely used although Naperian logarithms are used for some purposes.

Bright, John (1811–89) British radical politician. Bright, a Quaker, was a leader with *Cobden of the *Anti-Corn Law League, which successfully achieved the repeal of the Corn Laws in 1846. One of the Manchester School of middle-class liberal reformers, and an outstanding orator, he became an MP in 1843. He bitterly opposed the *Crimean War and led the campaign for an extension of the franchise, achieved in the 1867 Reform Act.

Bright, Richard (1789–1858) British physician, who described many disorders, particularly the group of symptoms, including oedema (retention of body fluid), that he showed to be due to kidney disease. This is sometimes called **Bright's disease** (*see* nephritis).

Brighton 50 50N 0 10W A resort in S England, on the East Sussex coast. Originally a fishing village, its growth began with the development of sea bathing in the 1750s and the patronage of the Prince Regent (later George IV), who had the Royal Pavilion redesigned by John *Nash in oriental style. Other notable features include the Lanes (famous for their antique shops) and the boating marina (completed in 1979). Brighton is also a conference centre and site of the University of Sussex (1961). Population (1981): 146 134.

Brigit A Celtic goddess of fire, fertility, learning, culture, and crafts. Elements of her cult were passed into the traditions surrounding St *Bridget, notably the burning of a sacred fire by her shrine.

brill An edible *flatfish, *Scophthalmus rhombus*, related to *turbot, that occurs in European coastal waters, down to depths of 70 m. Its smooth body, up to 70 cm long, is sandy to grey or dark-brown with light and dark spots above and white with darker blotches below.

Brillat-Savarin, Anthelme (1755–1826) French lawyer and writer. His *Physiologie du goût* (1825) is a collection of gastronomical anecdotes and aphorisms. After the Revolution he became a judge of the French supreme court.

brilliant cut A method of cutting diamonds and other gems to impart maximum brilliance. The upper and lower halves of the stone are cut into 33 and 25 polished facets respectively. These facets meet around the girdle or perimeter of the circular stone.

brimstone A lemon-yellow butterfly, *Gonopteryx rhamni*, found in Europe, N Africa, and parts of Asia. Adults hibernate, flying early in spring. The next generation emerges in June or later, the caterpillars feeding on buckthorn. Family: *Pieridae*.

Brindisi (Latin name: Brundisium) 40 37N 17 57E A seaport in SE Italy, in Apulia. It was an important Roman naval base and a centre of the Crusades in the middle ages. It has a 12th-century cathedral and a castle. Population (1981): 88 947.

Brindley, James (1716–72) British canal builder. He built his first canal (*see* Bridgewater Canal) for the Duke of Bridgewater in 1759. Altogether he designed and built some 588 km of canals, without ever using diagrams or calculations.

brine shrimp A crustacean belonging to a genus (*Artemia*) of *fairy shrimps that lives in salty pools and lakes. The widely distributed species *A. salina*, 10 mm long, is often cultivated for fish food.

briquette A block of compressed coal dust bound with pitch or a similar substance. Briquetting converts fuel that would otherwise be of little use into one of higher quality that can be sold for domestic heating.

Brisbane 27 30S 153 00E The third largest city in Australia, the capital and chief port of Queensland on the Brisbane River. The chief industries are engineering, shipbuilding, oil refining, food processing, and wool scouring. Exports include wool, meat, mineral sands, and wheat. The University of Queensland was established in 1910 and Griffith University in 1975; other notable buildings include Parliament House (1869), two cathedrals, the Observatory (1829) built by convicts, and the Queen Elizabeth II Stadium built for the 1982 Commonwealth Games. *History*: originally a penal settlement, it was opened to colonists in 1842. Population (1983 est): 1 138 400.

brisling. *See* sprat.

Brissot, Jacques-Pierre (1754–93) French journalist and revolutionary. A legal reformer and humanitarian before the French Revolution, he became leader of the Brissotins, later called the *Girondins, in 1789. A proponent of revolutionary war, his policies led to the French declaration of war on Austria in 1792. Internal rivalries and disputes over the war produced a power struggle with the *Jacobins. After the defeat of the Girondins, Brissot was executed.

bristlecone pine A *pine tree, *Pinus aristata*, native to mountainous regions of Colorado, Arizona, and New Mexico. Up to 15 m tall, it has cones about 7.5 cm long with bristles on each scale. Bristlecone pines are among the longest-lived trees: some trees have reached an age of 5000 years and have been used in *dendrochronology.

bristletail A slender wingless insect, 5–20 mm long, that has two or three long tail bristles and belongs to the orders *Thysanura* (three-pronged bristletails) or *Diplura* (two-pronged bristletails). Most bristletails live in damp sheltered places, e.g. under stones and logs, and feed on plant detritus. However, a few species feed on books and papers or anything containing starch (*see* silverfish; firebrat).

bristle worm. *See* annelid worm.

Bristol 51 27N 2 35W A port and industrial city in SW England, the administrative centre of Avon on the River Avon, 11 km (7 mi) from the Bristol Channel. A major port in the 17th and 18th centuries, trading mostly with the Americas (and prospering greatly from the slave trade), its docks at Avonmouth and Portishead (including the modern Portbury dock) on the Bristol Channel now handle much import and export trade. Notable buildings include the 12th-century cathedral, the 14th-century Church of St Mary Redcliffe, and the circular Roman Catholic cathedral (1973). Nearby is the Avon Gorge, spanned by Brunel's Clifton Suspension Bridge (1832–64). Bristol University dates from 1909. Bristol's industries include engineering (particularly aircraft manufacture), chemicals, tobacco, soap, paper manufacture, chocolate, printing, and nonferrous metal refining. Population (1981): 387 977.

Bristol Channel An inlet of the Atlantic Ocean in the UK, between South Wales and SW England. It forms an extension of the Severn Estuary and has the greatest tidal range in England. Length: about 137 km (85 mi).

Bristow, Eric (1957–) British darts player, known as "The Crafty Cockney." He won the World Masters Championship a record five times (1977, 1979, 1981, 1983–84) and the World Professional Championship a record five times (1980–81, 1984–86).

britannia A British gold coin, introduced in 1987 for investment purposes in response to growing unpopularity of the South African *krugerrand. Although subject to VAT it is expected to become the main European bullion coin.

Britannia metal An *alloy of tin (80–90%) with variable amounts of antimony and copper. It resembles silver and was formerly used for tableware instead of *pewter.

British Academy A learned society formed in 1901 to provide British representation of the humanities at the International Association of Academies. Incorporated in 1902, it promotes the study of languages and literatures, history, archaeology, philosophy, religion, law, economics, and the visual arts, from which fields its Fellows are elected.

British Antarctic Territory A British colony established in 1962 that consists of the South Orkney and South Shetland islands and a part of the Antarctic. It is used as a base for the British Antarctic Survey stations.

British Broadcasting Corporation (BBC) A broadcasting authority in the UK. The BBC was first set up as a private company in 1922 and was incorporated as a public body under royal charter in 1927; it is responsible to parliament and is politically neutral and independent. It runs two national television stations, four national radio stations, and a number of local radio stations. It relies on revenue from television licences as it is not permitted to carry advertising. The BBC provides external services in 38 languages, for which it receives a subsidy from the government.

British citizenship A new form of citizenship introduced on 1 January 1983 by the British Nationality Act (1981). It is acquired by birth in the UK to a parent who is either a British citizen or a settled resident there, by descent, by registration, or by *naturalization. With two other new forms, British Dependent Territories citizenship and British Overseas citizenship, it replaced the composite citizenship of the UK and Colonies created by the British Nationality Act (1948). The expression commonwealth citizen is used to cover all who have one of the new citizenships, or citizenship of one of the independent countries of the Commonwealth.

British Columbia The westernmost province of Canada, on the Pacific Ocean. Mostly in the mountainous Cordilleran region, it is bounded by the *Rocky Mountains in the E and the *Coast Range, including islands, in the W. The main rivers (the Fraser, Kootenay, Thompson, and Columbia) and their tributaries are swift flowing and there are many lakes and waterfalls. Forests cover over 55% of the surface and provide the basis for most manufacturing. Fishing, hydroelectricity, and tourism are also economically important. There are rich mineral resources; gold, silver, lead, zinc, copper, coal, and oil are all produced. Although only a small area is farmed, dairy produce, mixed farming, and fruit are valuable. Prosperous and urbanized, British Columbia is Canada's fastest-growing province; half the population lives in the Lower Mainland. *History*: visited by Captain Cook (1778), British Columbia also attracted Russians, Spaniards, and Canadians. A British colony established on Vancouver Island (1849) spread to the mainland when gold was discovered (1858). Entry into Canada (1871) and the transcontinental railway (1885) provided the basis for economic development. Area: 930 528 sq km (359 277 sq mi). Population (1981): 2 744 467. Capital: Victoria.

British Council An institution set up in 1934 and incorporated by royal charter in 1940. The Council's chief aims are to promote a knowledge of the UK abroad, to promote the teaching of English, and to foster educational cooperation between the developing countries and the UK.

British Council of Churches A body, set up in 1947, of

representatives of the major Churches in Britain and Ireland except the Roman Catholic Church (although this sends observers to meetings). The recommendations it makes to member Churches are designed to effect unity and joint action. It founded Christian Aid and is an Associate Council of the *World Council of Churches.

British Dependent Territories Overseas territories for which constitutional responsibility rests with the Foreign and Commonwealth Office. There are currently 15 such territories: Anguilla, Bermuda, British Antarctic Territory, British Indian Ocean Territory, British Virgin Islands, Cayman Islands, Falkland Islands, Falkland Islands Dependencies, Gibraltar, Hong Kong, Montserrat, Pitcairn Group of Islands, St Helena, St Helena Dependencies, and Turks and Caicos Islands.

British Expeditionary Force (BEF) Army formations that helped France counter German invasions in World Wars I and II. In World War I, its 6 divisions had increased to 65 by 1918 and it suffered almost 3 million casualties, of which 900 000 were fatal. In World War II it consisted of 10 divisions until its evacuation from Dunkirk (1940).

British Guiana. *See* Guyana, Cooperative Republic of.

British Honduras. *See* Belize, Colony of.

British Indian Ocean Territory A British colony established in 1965 consisting of the Chagos Archipelago, largest island of which is Diego Garcia, claimed by Mauritius. Aldabra, Farquhar, and Desroches were returned to the Seychelles in 1976. Although the islands are at present leased to companies that run copra plantations, they were acquired as a base for military activities. Population (1982 est): 3000.

British Isles An archipelago separated from the mainland of NW Europe by the North Sea and the English Channel. It consists of Great Britain, Ireland, the Isle of Man, and the Channel Islands. Area: about 314 950 sq km (121 577 sq mi).

British Legion. *See* Royal British Legion.

British Library The national *library, founded in 1753 and housed in the *British Museum, to which George II presented the royal library in 1757. It receives a copy of every book published in Britain and contains over 8.5 million volumes. A move to a new building complex is planned for the year 2000.

British Museum The national museum containing probably the finest collection of antiquities in the world. Founded in 1753 to house the private collection of Sir Hans *Sloane, it now occupies Sir Robert Smirke's neoclassical building (1847) in Bloomsbury, London. Its Egyptian, Assyrian, Greek, Roman, Chinese, and Cambodian collections are unique and include a number of Egyptian mummies, the Elgin Marbles, and the Rosetta Stone. Its reading room (*see also* British Library) is available only to ticket holders. The natural history exhibits were transferred to the Natural History Museum (designed by *Waterhouse and built 1873–80) in South Kensington.

British North America Act (1867) An act passed by the British parliament uniting the colonies of Novia Scotia, New Brunswick, Canada West (now Ontario), and Canada East (now Quebec) as the Dominion of Canada.

British Open Championship An annual golf tournament inaugurated at Prestwick in 1860 and held successively on different British courses. It is one of the major championship tournaments for both amateurs and professionals.

British Standards Institution (BSI) An institution founded in 1901 (renamed in 1931). Its function is to approve standards for various products, especially in the fields of engineering, building, textiles, and chemicals, with a view to establishing minimum standards of quality and avoiding duplication of design, sizes, and patterns. Products that conform to BSI standards bear the Kite mark as a symbol of quality. *See also* International Organization for Standardization.

British thermal unit (btu) A unit of energy equal to the amount of heat required to raise the temperature of 1 lb of water through 1°F. It equals 1055.06 joules (251.997 calories).

Britons The indigenous inhabitants of Britain before the Anglo-Saxon settlements. They spoke languages of the Brythonic branch of the *Celtic language family. At the Roman conquest (1st century AD) Britain was divided into tribal kingdoms with a common Celtic culture (*see* La Tène). Religious affairs were conducted by *Druids. *See also* Belgae.

Brittany (Breton name: Breiz; French name: Bretagne) A planning region and former province in NW France. It consists of a peninsula between the Bay of Biscay and English Channel. It was part of ancient Armorica and in 56 BC was conquered by Julius Caesar. During the 5th–6th centuries AD Celts from Britain migrated here to escape the Anglo-Saxon invasion. Finally incorporated into France in 1532, it has retained its own distinctive culture. An important area for tourism, Brittany suffered from oil pollution on many beaches following the *Amoco Cadiz* oil tanker disaster in March, 1978. Area: 27 184 sq km (10 494 sq mi). Population (1981 est): 2 665 200.

BENJAMIN BRITTEN *His opera* Gloriana *(1953), on the story of Queen Elizabeth I and Essex, was written for the coronation of Queen Elizabeth II.*

Britten, (Edward) Benjamin, Baron (1913–76) British composer and pianist, a pupil of Frank *Bridge. He spent the years 1939–42 in the USA and subsequently founded the English Opera Group (1947) and the Aldeburgh Festival (1948). He wrote many works, as well as leading roles in his operas, for his lifelong friend, the tenor Peter *Pears. Among Britten's best-known compositions are the operas *Peter Grimes* (1945), *Billy Budd* (1951), and *Death in Venice* (1973); the orchestral works *Variations on a Theme by Frank Bridge* (1937) and the *Cello Symphony* (1964); choral works, such as the *Spring Symphony* (1949) and *A War Requiem* (1962); and many chamber and instrumental works.

brittle star A marine invertebrate animal, also called sand star or serpent star, belonging to a class (*Ophiuroidea*) of *echinoderms. It has a small dislike body bearing five long fragile arms, used for locomotion. Brittle stars sometimes occur in large numbers on soft muddy sea beds and are active at night, feeding on small crustaceans, molluscs, and bottom debris.
oceans.

Brixham 50 02N 3 30W A small resort and fishing port in

SW England, in S Devon. It was the landing place of William of Orange (1688) and there are several notable palaeolithic remains nearby. Population (1981 est):15 171.

Brno (German name: Brünn) 49 12N 16 40E The second largest city in Czechoslovakia, in S Moravia, formerly the capital of the province of Moravia. A fortified town in the middle ages, it contains the Spilberk fortress, an Austrian political prison (1621–1857). Other notable buildings include the 15th-century cathedral; its university was founded in 1919. The botanist Gregor Mendel devised his fundamental principles of heredity here (1865). Brno is now an important industrial centre specializing in engineering and textiles; the *Bren gun was originally developed here. Population (1980 est): 373 000.

broad bean A stiff upright annual plant, *Vicia faba*, 60–150 cm tall, with a ribbed stem and compound grey-green leaves composed of a few large leaflets. The flowers have white petals and dark-purple blotches on the wings. The large pod has a woolly lining surrounding large flat edible beans, for which the plant is cultivated throughout Europe, both as a vegetable and as an animal feed. *See also* bean.

broadbill A brightly coloured passerine bird belonging to a family (*Eurylaimidae*; 14 species) of tropical African and Asian forests. It is about 12 cm long with a large head, partly joined toes, and a very broad short bill. Most species are insectivorous, feeding in trees or on the wing.

Broadmoor A high-security hospital for mentally ill criminals in S England, at Crowthorne in Berkshire, capable of housing 775 patients. It was opened in 1863.

Broads, the A low-lying area in E England, mainly in Norfolk but extending into Suffolk. It consists of a system of shallow lakes, believed to have originated as medieval peat diggings, linked to the Rivers Bure and Yare and their tributaries. They are now of major recreational importance providing boating and fishing facilities. Its profusion of vegetation and wildlife also make it an area of interest to naturalists.

Broadway A major street in New York City along and near which are sited most of the leading commercial theatres. The word is used to refer to commercial theatre in the USA in general. *See also* Off-Broadway theatres.

Broadwood, John (1732–1812) Scottish manufacturer of pianos and harpsichords. Broadwood worked for Burkhard Tschudi (1702–73), the Swiss-born harpsichord maker, became his partner (1770), and took sole control of the company in 1782. He produced his first piano in 1773 and made a number of innovations.

broccoli A cultivated variety of wild *cabbage (*Brassica oleracea*) with a stout upright stem and a loose cluster of flower heads at the top. The leaves are narrow and curly; the lower ones are shed as the plant grows, leaving a scarred stem. Sprouting broccoli has purple or white flowers. Calabrese or green sprouting broccoli is an Italian variety, often with fused parallel stems. Both are eaten as vegetables while the flowers are in bud. *See also* Brassica.

broch A circular dry-stone defensive structure built in N Scotland and adjacent islands, probably in the period 100 BC to 100 AD. The six-storey-high broch at Mousa (Shetland) is a famous example.

Broch, Hermann (1886–1951) Austrian novelist. In 1927 he sold the family textile business to return to the University of Vienna. His trilogy *The Sleepwalkers* (1931–32) is a historical study of Europe in a variety of literary forms. Briefly imprisoned by the Nazis, he emigrated to the USA in 1940. There he continued to experiment with innovative literary techniques, most notably in *The Death of Virgil* (1945).

Brocken 51 48N 10 37E A mountain in W East Germany, the highest of the Harz Mountains. According to legend, this bare granite peak is the scene of the witches' sabbath (*see* witchcraft) on Walpurgis Night (1 May). The **Brocken spectre** (or

Brocken bow), first observed here, is a magnified shadow of the observer cast against mist or cloud below the level of the summit and surrounded by coloured fringes resulting from the diffraction of light.

Broglie, Louis Victor, 7th Duc de. *See* de Broglie, Louis Victor, 7th Duc de.

Broken Hill 31 57S 141 30E A mining city in Australia, in W central New South Wales. The rich silver, lead, and zinc deposits were discovered in 1883. The city helped to establish the trades union movement and the Barrier Industrial Council (representing the unions) plays an important role in the city's affairs. Population (1983): 27 400.

Broken Hill (Zambia). *See* Kabwe.

bromine (Br) A dense reddish-brown liquid element, discovered by A. J. Balard (1802–76) in 1826. It is extracted from sea water and other natural brines by electrolysis or by displacement with chlorine. The liquid element is volatile and its vapour has a pungent smell reminiscent of chlorine with severe irritating effects on the eyes and throat. Compounds include silver bromide (AgBr), used in photography, and ethylene dibromide ($C_2H_4Br_2$), used to scavenge lead in making additives for motor fuel. Other compounds are used as fumigants, dyes, flameproofing agents, and in medicine. At no 35; at wt 79.904; mp −7.2°C; bp 58.78°C.

Bromley The largest borough of Greater London, situated in the SE. A mainly residential area, it was created in 1965 from land that was formerly part of Kent, including Orpington and Penge, and parts of Chislehurst and Sidcup. Population: (1981): 294 451.

bronchial tubes. *See* lung.

bronchitis Inflammation of the bronchi—the tubes conducting air to the lungs. Acute bronchitis is often due to a virus infection, particularly a cold or influenza. Chronic bronchitis is common in middle-aged and elderly men in the UK, being aggravated by cigarette smoking and air pollution. Irritation of the mucus-secreting glands in the bronchi results in a persistent cough, with the production of large amounts of sputum. The patient is breathless and liable to chest infections. Treatment consists of stopping smoking (and reducing exposure to other irritants) and the prompt management of any chest infection.

Bronowski, Jacob (1908–74) British mathematician, science writer, and broadcaster, born in Poland. He became widely known for his highly successful television series *The Ascent of Man* (1973), a history of the development of science and technology. His writings include commentaries on poetry, particularly that of William *Blake, and the importance of the scientific method, especially in *The Commonsense of Science* (1951).

Brontë sisters Three British novelists, daughters of the rector of Haworth, an isolated village in Yorkshire. After briefly attending a local boarding school, **Charlotte Brontë** (1816–55) and **Emily Brontë** (1818–48) rejoined their sister **Anne Brontë** (1820–49) at home. Their early writings chronicled the imaginary kingdoms of Angria and Gondal. All the sisters worked for brief periods as governesses and teachers to help pay off the debts of their artist brother, **Patrick Branwell Brontë** (1817–48), an alcoholic and opium addict who died of tuberculosis. In 1846 the sisters published *Poems by Currer, Ellis, and Acton Bell* and in 1847, under the same pseudonyms, the novels *Jane Eyre* (by Charlotte), *Wuthering Heights* (by Emily), and *Agnes Gray* (by Anne). In 1848 Emily died of tuberculosis, as did Anne in 1849. Charlotte published *Shirley* (1849) and *Villette* (1853). She married her father's curate in 1854 and died in pregnancy a year later. □ p. 191.

Brontosaurus. *See* Apatosaurus.

Brontotherium A genus of extinct North American hoofed mammals—*titanotheres—that lived during the Oligocene epoch (between 38 and 26 million years ago). Standing

2.5 m at the shoulder, *Brontotherium* had a large skull with a pair of bony horns.

Bronx, the   40 50N 73 52W One of the five boroughs of New York City, USA, situated NE of the Harlem River. It is mainly residential but has an industrialized waterfront. Overcrowding and poor housing conditions have made it the object of local and federal urbanization programmes. Area: 107 sq km (41 sq mi). Population (1980): 1 169 115.

bronze   An *alloy of copper and (4–11%) tin. Because it melts between 900°C and 1000°C, about the temperature of an ordinary wood fire, it was one of the first metals to be used for making weapons and utensils, being known around 2000 BC in Britain. It is harder than pure copper and "copper" coins are usually made of bronze containing 95% copper, 4% tin, 1% zinc, and occasionally other metals. Phosphor bronze contains 0.5% phosphorus. *See also* gun metal.

BRONTË SISTERS   *Detail from a portrait (c. 1834) by Branwell Brontë of (from left) Anne, Emily, and Charlotte.*

Bronze Age   The cultural phase during which metallurgical technology, based first on copper (in the Chalcolithic period) and then on bronze (copper alloyed with tin), replaced the stone technology (*see* Stone Age) of the *Neolithic period. In Eurasia the development of international trade, literacy, the plough, and the wheel took place during this phase, which began at varying dates according to locality (the earliest being about 6500 BC in Anatolia); it gave way to the *Iron Age in about 1000 BC. In Africa, iron, discovered about 800 BC, replaced stone without an intervening Bronze Age. In the Americas, copper, discovered about 100 AD, was followed rapidly by iron, while in Australasia, the introduction of metallurgy occurred in the colonial period.

Bronzino, Il   (Agnolo di Cosimo; 1503–72) Florentine mannerist painter (*see* mannerism). His religious and allegorical works, such as *Venus, Cupid, and Folly* (National Gallery, London), were influenced by *Michelangelo and Bronzino's teacher *Pontormo. As court painter to Cosimo I de' Medici he painted many portraits, including *Eleanor of Toledo and Her Son Giovanni* (Uffizi), a characteristic work having a cold detached dignity and a marble-like finish.

Brook, Peter   (1925–) British theatre director. His work for the Royal Shakespeare Company, of which he became a director in 1962, included experimental productions of Shake-

speare and of such modern plays as Peter Weiss' *The Marat/Sade* (1962). Since 1970 he has worked with the International Centre for Theatre Research in Paris, where he has developed acting techniques evolved during a tour of Africa and Asia. He has also directed films, including *Lord of the Flies* (1962) and *King Lear* (1969).

Brooke, Sir James   (1803–68) British explorer. Born in India, he bought an armed yacht—the *Royalist*—in England and departed on a voyage of exploration. He helped to suppress a rebellion in Sarawak for which service he was made raja by the Sultan of Brunei (Borneo). He formed a native council and strove to abolish head hunting, piracy, and opium smuggling. In 1847 he became British consul general for Borneo.

Brooke, Rupert (Chawner)   (1887–1915) British poet and critic. His scholarship, charm, and good looks gained him influential friends in literary and political circles. He received a naval commission in 1914 but died of blood poisoning on a hospital ship in the Aegean, without having seen action. His romantic image and the patriotism of his wartime poetry, *1914 and Other Poems* (1915), made him a national hero.

Brookeborough, Basil Stanlake Brooke, 1st Viscount (1888–1973) Northern Irish statesman; prime minister of Northern Ireland (1943–63). He became a Unionist MP in 1929 and was minister of agriculture (1933–41) and then minister of commerce (1941–43). He was firmly committed to union with Great Britain.

Brooklyn   40 40N 73 58W One of the five boroughs of New York City, USA, situated at the SW end of Long Island. Settled by Dutch farmers in 1636, it has many colonial buildings and is the site of Pratt Institute (1887), Brooklyn Institute of Arts and Sciences (1823; comprising Brooklyn Museum, Brooklyn Children's Museum, and Brooklyn Botanic Garden and Arboretum), and branches of four New York universities. The New York Naval Shipyard, which was established here in 1801, was converted to civilian use in the 1960s. Three bridges, including the famous Brooklyn Bridge (1869–83), span the East River connecting Brooklyn with Manhattan. A major port, it handles a vast amount of shipping and its waterfront is 53 km (33 mi) long. Area: 210 sq km (81 sq mi). Population (1980): 2 230 936.

Brookner, Anita   (1938–) British writer and art historian. A teacher at the Courtauld Institute of Art, London, she has written several books on art but is better known for her novels, including *Hotel du Lac* (1984) for which she won the Booker Prize, *Family and Friends* (1985), and *Friends from England* (1987).

Brooks, Mel   (Melvyn Kaminsky; 1926–) US comedy writer, actor, and film director. Initially a television scriptwriter, he is known for his offbeat slapstick humour. His films include *The Producers* (1968), *Blazing Saddles* (1974), *Young Frankenstein* (1974), and *High Anxiety* (1977).

broom   A bushy deciduous shrub, *Sarothamnus scoparius* (or *Cytisus scoparius*), 60–200 cm high, with shiny green stems, small pointed compound leaves, and yellow flowers. Broom is found in heaths and woodland glades in Europe and is often grown as an ornamental. The branches are used for brooms and thatching. Family: *Leguminosae*.

Broome, David   (1940–) British show jumper. He won the European championships in 1961, 1967, and 1969, Olympic bronze medals in 1960 and 1968, and the world championship in 1970. Professional from 1973, he continued as a leading British rider during the 1980s.

broomrape   A parasitic plant of the worldwide genus *Orobanche* (about 100 species), lacking chlorophyll but having underground tubers attached to the roots of the host plant. The flowering shoots rise 5–70 cm above ground on scaly stems topped by spikes of tubular two-lipped flowers, which may be white, yellow, or purple. Family: *Orobanchaceae*.

brotulid   A fish, also called brotula, belonging to the family *Brotulidae* (it is sometimes placed with the cusk eels in the family *Ophidiidae*). Brotulids have an eel-like body, up to about 90 cm in length, and most live in deep marine waters. Order: *Perciformes*.

Brough, Louise (1923–) US tennis player, who in 1948 and 1950 won all three titles at Wimbledon (singles, doubles, and mixed doubles). She also won all 22 of her *Wightman Cup rubbers (1946–57).

brougham A compact four-wheeled carriage light enough to be drawn by one horse. The original brougham was designed by Lord Brougham (1778–1868) in 1838.

Brouwer, Adriaen (c. 1605–38) Flemish painter, who worked in Holland, initially as a pupil of *Hals, and later in Antwerp. He excelled in small paintings of brawling and drunken peasants, the sombre colouring of which was increasingly influenced by Dutch art.

Brouwer, L(uitzen) E(gbertus) J(an) (1881–1966) Dutch mathematician, who made important contributions to the development of *topology. He is often regarded as the founder of the subject in its modern form. He is also the founder of a school of mathematics known as intuitional mathematics, which holds that mathematics is a mental construction in which laws should be self-evident and derived by intuition.

Brown, Sir Arthur. *See* Alcock, Sir John.

Brown, Capability (Lancelot B.; 1716–83) British landscape gardener. Brown, carrying on the work of William *Kent, established a purely English style of garden layout. Abandoning the formal continental style, Brown's gardens, as for example at □Blenheim Palace (1765), sought to create a stylized imitation of nature. He was also an architect, designing houses and garden buildings. His nickname arose because he frequently told his patrons that their grounds had "capabilities" for landscaping.

Brown, Ford Madox (1821–93) British painter, born in Calais. After studying in Belgium, Paris, and Rome, he returned to England, where he was influenced by the Pre-Raphaelites. He painted chiefly historical themes, although his most famous paintings, *Work* (Manchester) and *The Last of England* (Birmingham), are contemporary subjects. He also decorated Manchester town hall.

Brown, George. *See* George-Brown, Baron.

Brown, John (1800–59) US abolitionist, who believed slaves must be freed by force. He raided the Federal Arsenal at Harpers Ferry, Virginia, in an attempt to establish a slave refuge and a base for promoting slave uprisings. He was captured and executed for treason, becoming an abolitionist martyr; he is the hero of the song "John Brown's Body."

Brown, Robert (1773–1858) Scottish botanist, who in 1831 first recognized the *nucleus as a fundamental constituent of cells. Four years earlier, while observing a solution of pollen grains in water under a microscope, he discovered, but was unable to explain, the effect now known as the *Brownian movement.

brown algae *Algae of the division *Phaeophyta* (1500 species), which contain a brown pigment (fucoxanthin) in addition to and sometimes masking the green chlorophyll. Brown algae include all the larger *seaweeds, such as wracks and kelps. They are mainly marine and are abundant along coasts in colder regions. Many show an *alternation of generations.

brown bear A large bear, *Ursus arctos*, of the N hemisphere. Brown bears have a thick shaggy coat, humped on the shoulders and varying in colour from blackish-brown to grey, and they take a wide variety of food including fish, fruit, and cattle. There are many local races and subspecies, including the North American grizzly and Kodiac bears. The reputedly ferocious grizzly bear (*U. arctos horribilis*), mostly restricted to N Canada and Alaska, reaches a length of 2.5 m and a weight of 550 kg; the Alaskan Kodiac bear—a giant race of grizzly—is the largest living land carnivore, reaching a length of 2.8 m and a weight of 760 kg.

Browne, Hablot Knight (1815–82) British artist, better

HABLOT BROWNE   *"Nicholas starts for Yorkshire", one of the illustrations to* Nicholas Nickleby *(1839) by Charles Dickens.*

known as Phiz. He is renowned mainly for his illustrations of books by Charles Dickens, notably *The Pickwick Papers*. He also produced cartoons for *Punch* and watercolours.

Browne, Robert (c. 1550–1633) Puritan separatist, whose followers, known as Brownists, were the spiritual ancestors of Congregationalists. After founding self-governing congregations in Norwich and preaching against the discipline of the Established Church, he was imprisoned and forced into exile in Holland (1581–84). He was later reconciled with the Church of England, becoming rector of Aldchurch, Northamptonshire, in 1591.

Browne, Sir Thomas (1605–82) English physician and writer. He studied medicine at Oxford and in Europe and settled in Norwich in 1637. *Religio Medici* (1643) is a book of personal philosophic and religious reflections, written in elaborate rhythmical prose. In *Pseudodoxia Epidemica* (1646, also known as *Vulgar Errors*) he critically surveyed many popular superstitions. He also wrote two antiquarian treatises, *Hydriotaphia: Urn Burial* (1658) and *The Garden of Cyrus* (1658).

Brownian movement The continuous random movement of very small particles (less than about one-thousandth of a millimetre in diameter) when suspended in a fluid. It is caused by collisions between the particles and the atoms or molecules of the fluid. Brownian movement can be observed in smoke suspended in air and in a suspension of pollen grains in a liquid. Named after Robert *Brown.

Browning, Robert (1812–89) British poet. The son of a bank clerk, his early education consisted chiefly of wide reading in his father's library. After the failure of his autobiographical poem *Pauline* (1833) he wrote several verse dramas and dramatic monologues, including the famous "My Last Duchess" (1842). The epic but uneven poem cycle *The*

Ring and the Book was his last major work. His wife **Elizabeth Barrett Browning** (1806-61) was also a poet. A spinal injury when she was 15 made her a lifelong semi-invalid. She met Robert Browning in 1845 and in 1846 she defied her domineering father and eloped with Browning to Italy. Here she wrote her most famous work, *Sonnets from the Portuguese* (1850). In later years she became involved in Italian politics, the abolition of slavery, and spiritualism.

Browning Automatic Rifle (BAR) A gas-operated shoulder-fired automatic *rifle designed in 1917 by John Moses Browning (1855-1926). The standard automatic weapon in the US army until the Korean War, it weighed over 8.6 kg (19 lbs), including its 20-round magazine.

Brownshirts The colloquial name for the Nazi Sturmabteilung (SA; stormtroopers). Their name refers to their brown uniforms. They were founded in 1921 and reorganized by Ernst *Röhm in 1930. Squads of thugs, who molested and murdered the Nazis' opponents, they numbered two million by 1933. In 1934 Hitler eliminated Röhm and greatly reduced the power of the Brownshirts. *See also* SS.

Brubeck, Dave (1920-) US jazz pianist and composer, who studied composition with Darius Milhaud and Arnold Schoenberg. Brubeck introduced complex rhythms into jazz and formed a quartet in 1951. Among his most famous pieces are "Take Five," and "Blue Rondo à la Turque."

Bruce, James (1730-94) British explorer, who in the course of an arduous expedition that set out from Cairo in 1768 reached Lake Tana, source of the Blue Nile (1770). He described his experiences in *Travels to Discover the Source of the Nile* (1790).

Bruce, Robert. *See* Robert (I) the Bruce.

brucellosis (*or* undulant fever) An infectious disease of cattle and other farm animals that is caused by the bacterium *Brucella abortus* and can be contracted by man through drinking unpasteurized contaminated milk. Symptoms include fever (which may be intermittent), sweating, weakness, cough, joint pain, and sometimes swelling of the lymph nodes. Tetracycline usually cures the disease. The slaughter of infected animals has reduced the incidence of brucellosis in Europe.

Bruce of Melbourne, Stanley Melbourne, 1st Viscount (1883-1967) Australian statesman; prime minister (1923-29). He fought with the British Army in World War I and entered politics as a member of the National Party in 1918. His coalition government of National and Country Parties implemented social and welfare legislation in the areas of public health and devised a scheme of national insurance against unemployment. From 1933 to 1945 he was high commissioner in London and represented Australia in the British war cabinet (1942-45).

Bruch, Max (1838-1920) German composer. He wrote in a romantic but conservative style. He is best known for his first violin concerto (1868) and *Kol Nidrei* (1880) for cello and orchestra, based on a Jewish hymn.

Brücke, Die (German: The Bridge) An organization of German artists founded in 1905 to promote modern art. Its members, notably *Kirchner, were influenced, like their French contemporaries, the fauves (*see* fauvism), by *Van Gogh, *Gauguin, *Munch, and primitive art. However, unlike the fauves, their crudely painted and vibrantly coloured figure studies and landscapes expressed an underlying anxiety more typical of such early German artists as *Grünewald. Although the group broke up in 1913, it has had a lasting influence on the graphic arts, particularly the *woodcut. *See also* expressionism.

Bruckner, Anton (1824-96) Austrian composer and organist. He was a professor at the Vienna conservatoire (1871-91). In 1891 he was granted a pension and apartments in the Belvedere palace in Vienna, where he revised his compositions and worked on his ninth symphony (1887-96),

which remained unfinished at his death. His symphonies, which exhibit the influence of Wagner and Schubert, had a mixed reception during his lifetime and were frequently performed in shortened versions. Bruckner also composed choral music in a polyphonic style, chamber music, organ music, and a *Te Deum* (1881-84) for orchestra, soloists, and chorus.

Brueghel the Elder, Pieter (*or* Bruegel; 1525-69) Flemish painter, noted for his often satirical scenes of peasant life and his landscapes. Although popularly called Peasant Brueghel, he was a learned man, whose patrons included Cardinal de Granvelle (1517-86). He studied under Pieter Coecke van Aelst (1502-50), whose daughter he later married, but was chiefly influenced by *Bosch in such works as the macabre *Triumph of Death* (Prado). He visited Italy (c. 1551-53) but Italian art influenced his style only in his last years. In 1563 he settled in Brussels, where he executed his best-known works, e.g. *Peasant Wedding* (Kunsthistorisches Museum, Vienna), and a landscape series entitled the *Labours of the Months*. Many of his paintings were copied by his eldest son **Pieter Brueghel the Younger** (?1564-?1638). His younger son **Jan Brueghel the Elder** (1568-1625), popularly called Velvet Brueghel, is noted for his flower and landscape paintings. He was a friend and sometimes assistant of Rubens.

Bruges (Flemish name: Brugge) 51 13N 3 14E A town in NW Belgium. It was the capital of Flanders in the 12th century and during the 13th and 14th centuries it became the centre of the Hanseatic League in N Europe. It has many fine gothic buildings, including the 14th-century cathedral, the Church of Notre Dame (containing Michelangelo's marble statue, the Virgin and Child) and the Market Hall (13th-15th centuries) with its famous belfry and 47-bell carillon. It is linked by canal to many European ports. The traditional industry is lace; newer industrial developments include the manufacture of ships and electronic equipment. Population (1981 est): 118 212.

bruise An area of discoloured skin caused by the leakage of blood from damaged blood vessels beneath the skin. Bruises are usually caused by a blow to the skin and are always more pronounced where the blood vessels are loosely suspended in the tissue (e.g. around the eye). They change from bluish to greenish yellow, as the blood pigment is chemically broken down and absorbed.

Brummell, George Bryan (1778-1840) British dandy, known as Beau Brummell. He was a prominent member of fashionable society and a close friend of the Prince Regent, later George IV. He fled to France to evade his creditors in 1816 and died in an asylum.

Brunei, State of A small sultanate in NW Borneo, on the South China Sea. It consists of two separate areas, entirely bounded (except for its coast) by the Malaysian state of Sarawak. It is mainly low lying with some hills in the S; the interior is largely dense forest. The people are mainly Malays, while about a quarter of the population are Chinese or other small minorities. *Economy*: dominated by oil (the main export) since the discovery of the Seria oilfield in 1929, production is being maintained by the addition of offshore oilfields. Recent efforts to diversify the economy include the construction of a deepwater port and a natural-gas liquefaction plant. Agriculture is also being encouraged in an attempt to make Brunei more self-sufficient in food production. *History*: a powerful state in the 16th century controlling the whole of Borneo, as well as parts of the Philippines, it became a British protected state in 1888. In 1962 there was a revolt, mainly in protest against the proposal to join the Federation of Malaysia, and since then the sultan has ruled by decree. In 1967 Hassanal Bolkia Mu'izuddin Waddaulah (1946-) succeeded his father as sultan. Internal self-government was achieved in 1971, and full independence in 1983. Official language: Malay; Chinese and English are also widely spoken. Official religion:

Islam. Official currency: Brunei dollar of 100 cents. Area: 5800 sq km (2226 sq mi). Population (1983 est): 209 000. Capital and main port: Bandar Seri Begawan.

Brunel, Isambard Kingdom (1806–59) British engineer, who was one of the most original inventors of the 19th century. His most famous works were the Clifton suspension bridge, which spanned the Avon Gorge, completed in 1864, and his ships the *Great Western* (1837), the *Great Britain* (1843; □ship), the first large ship to be driven by screw propellers and now preserved in Bristol, and the *Great Eastern* (1858). Much of his work was done for the Great Western Railway, for which he built over 1600 km of track, using the broad (7 ft) gauge rather than the standard (4 ft 8½ in) gauge. His father **Sir Marc Isambard Brunel** (1769–1849) was also an engineer. Born in France, he worked in New York after fleeing the French Revolution in 1793. He moved to England in 1799, where he became famous for his work on tunnelling. In 1818 he patented the tunnelling shield, which allowed tunnels to be dug below water. In 1825 he began tunnelling beneath the River Thames from Rotherhithe to Wapping, a project fraught with difficulties that was not completed until 1842 and not used for transportation until 1865. The tunnel, which was 460 metres long, 11 metres wide, and 7 metres high, was viewed by over a million people after its opening in 1843.

Brunelleschi, Filippo (1377–1446) Italian architect. The founder of Renaissance architecture, Brunelleschi began his career as a goldsmith, only taking up architecture in his thirties, after spending some time studying Roman remains. His taste for classical architecture probably arose from a desire to understand Roman building techniques. This is demonstrated by his most famous construction, the dome of Florence cathedral (1430s), which used classical methods of construction. The Ospedale degli Innocenti (1419–26) is often regarded as the first architectural expression of the Renaissance.

Brunhild (*or* Brynhild) A heroine of Norse and Germanic legend. In the *Volsungasaga* she is the daughter of Odin, doomed to sleep on a fire-encircled rock until wakened by a mortal (*see* Siegfried). In the *Nibelungenlied* she is the queen of Issland.

Brüning, Heinrich (1885–1970) German statesman. As chancellor without a majority in the Reichstag, he governed by decree from 1930 to 1932. His deflationary policies brought him unpopularity and he resigned. In 1934 he left Germany, holding academic posts at Harvard (1937–52) and then at Cologne Universities.

Brünn. *See* Brno.

Brunner, Emil (1889–1965) Swiss Protestant theologian. A professor at the University of Zurich from 1924 to 1953, he became a supporter of the theological views of *Barth. However, he differed from Barth in allowing that God's image in mankind survived the Fall, despite man's fundamental sinfulness.

Bruno, Giordano (1548–1600) Italian philosopher. He became a Dominican (1563) but in 1576 his heretical opinions forced him to flee, first to Geneva, then to France, England, and Germany. Returning to Italy (1592) he was tried by the Inquisition, refused to recant, and was burned. His pantheistic philosophy, viewing all creation as one life, animated by God as "world-soul," influenced *Spinoza, *Descartes, and *Leibniz among others.

Bruno of Cologne, St (c. 1032–1101) German founder of the Carthusian order. He was educated at Cologne and Rheims, where he later taught at the cathedral school. He eventually withdrew with six companions to the mountainous region near Grenoble and built a monastery on the site of the present Grande Chartreuse, which became the mother house of the Carthusians. Called to Italy by Pope Urban II, his former pupil, he founded the monastery of La Torre in Calabria, where he died. Feast day: 6 Oct.

Brunswick (German name: Braunschweig) 52 15N 10 30E A city in NE West Germany, in Lower Saxony on the River Oker. It was the capital of the former duchy of Brunswick. Notable buildings include the castle and the romanesque cathedral (both 12th-century), the old town hall (14th-15th centuries), and the ducal palace (1768–69). It also has the oldest technical university in Germany (1745). Its industries include metal working and the manufacture of motor vehicles and pianos. Population (1980 est): 261 500.

brush turkey A *megapode bird, *Alectura lathami*, occurring in dense rain forests of New Guinea and E Australia. It is 65–70 cm long with a black plumage and builds a huge mound of fermenting plant material in which the eggs are incubated.

BRUNELLESCHI *Florence Cathedral showing Brunelleschi's spectacular dome (1430s).*

Brussels (Flemish name: Brussel; French name: Bruxelles) 50 51N 4 22E The capital of Belgium, situated in the centre of the country on the River Senne. As headquarters of the EEC and NATO, it is an important international centre. Its varied industries include the manufacture of machinery, chemicals, and lace. Fine buildings include the 15th-century gothic town hall, the 13th-century Maison du Roi, the church of St Gudule, the 18th-century Palais de la Nation (parliament building), and the Royal Palace. The Free University was founded in 1834 and a Flemish-speaking counterpart became independent in 1970. *History*: settled by the French in the 7th century AD, it developed into a centre of the wool industry in the 13th century. It became the capital of the Spanish Netherlands in the 15th century and later of the Austrian S Netherlands. In 1830 it was chosen as capital of the new kingdom of Belgium. It was occupied by the Germans in both World Wars. Population (1981 est): 1 000 221.

Brussels sprout A variety of wild cabbage, *Brassica oleracea* var. *gemmifera*, cultivated for its large edible buds. The stout erect shoots, up to 80 cm high, have long-stalked curly leaves arranged spirally up the stem; in the angle between the leaf bases and the stem are large buds, like miniature cabbages up to 5 cm in diameter. The lower leaves gradually fall, leaving the stem densely covered in buds. *See also* Brassica.

Brutus, Marcus Junius (?85–42 BC) Roman soldier and one of the assassins of Julius Caesar. Brutus, who supported Pompey against Caesar in the civil war, was pardoned by Caesar and made governor of Cisalpine Gaul (46) but subsequently joined the conspiracy to murder Caesar (44). He committed suicide after his defeat by Antony and Octavian at Philippi (42).

Bryansk 53 15N 34 09E A city in the W Soviet Union, in the RSFSR. It dates from at least the 12th century and is a communications centre with varied industries. Population (1981 est): 407 000.

Bryant, William Cullen (1794–1878) US poet, journalist, and critic. He wrote his most famous poem, "Thanatopsis," when he was 17. The success of his *Poems* (1821) enabled him to abandon his law practice and move to New York. From 1829 he was editor of the liberal newspaper *Evening Post*.

Bryce, James, 1st Viscount (1838–1922) British Liberal politician, historian, and ambassador to the USA (1907-13). An MP (1880-1907), Bryce headed the Bryce Commission (1894-95), which recommended the establishment of a ministry of education. He founded the *English Historical Review* with Lord *Acton (1885) and wrote *The American Commonwealth* (1888).

bryony Either of two unrelated Eurasian plants. **Black bryony** (*Tamus communis*) is a herbaceous climber with heart-shaped leaves that turn yellow in autumn. The bell-shaped yellow flowers are borne in separate male and female spikes. The fruits are scarlet berries, and the plant overwinters as a tuber. Family: *Dioscoreaceae* (yam family).
White bryony (*Bryonia dioica*) is a perennial herb climbing by means of tendrils. The hairy stem arises from a large rootstock and the leaves are palmately lobed. Greenish male and female flowers occur on separate plants and produce poisonous scarlet berries. Family: *Cucurbitaceae* (gourd family).

bryophyte A small flowerless green plant of the division *Bryophyta* (about 25 000 species), comprising the *liverworts and *mosses. The plant body is either differentiated into stems and leaves or is a flat branching structure (thallus). Bryophytes range in size from microscopic to over 1 m long; they lack true vascular (conducting) tissues and roots (the rootlike rhizoids serve mainly for anchorage). Bryophytes show *alternation of generations: the plant itself is the sexual (gametophyte) phase, which bears male and female sex organs (antheridia and archegonia, respectively). Fertilization of an egg cell results in the development of a spore capsule—the asexual (sporophyte) phase—which remains attached to the gametophyte and largely dependent on it. The spores are dispersed by wind, insects, or water and germinate to form new plants.

Bryozoa (*or* Ectoprocta) A phylum of aquatic colonial invertebrate animals (about 6000 species), called moss animals, found chiefly in seas as matlike encrustations on rocks. A colony consists of individuals, each up to 3 mm long and with a chitinous or gelatinous case and a ring of ciliated tentacles around the mouth. These are extended, creating a feeding current that brings food particles into the U-shaped digestive tract. Ciliated larvae establish new colonies by budding off more individuals.

Brythonic languages. *See* Celtic languages.

Brześć nad Bu-giem. *See* Brest.

Bubastis (modern name: Tall Bastah) A ruined temple city in Lower Egypt. Bubastis was the capital of the 18th nome (province) and attained importance when the pharaohs of the 19th dynasty (1320-1200 BC) moved their capital to the Nile Delta. It became a royal residence when Sheshonk I was pharaoh (952 BC). After the Persian conquest (525 BC) the city declined. Bubastis was sacred to the cat goddess Bast.

bubble chamber An instrument that makes visible the tracks of ionizing particles, used for observing particle decays and interactions. It contains a liquid, usually hydrogen, helium, or deuterium, under pressure and at a temperature slightly above its normal boiling point. The particle induces boiling along its path and the bubbles are photographed to record the particle's track. and those of any charged decay or reaction products.

Buber, Martin (1878-1965) Austrian-born Jewish religious philosopher. He wrote on *Hasidism, to which he was deeply sympathetic, and from 1925 produced, with F. *Ro-

senzweig, a remarkable German translation of the Bible. However, his best-known and most influential work was *I and Thou* (1923), which sets out his philosophy of religious faith in the form of a dialogue between man and God. Buber was a committed Zionist (he settled in Palestine in 1938), and advocated a joint Arab-Jewish state.

bubonic plague. *See* plague.

Bucaramanga 7 08N 73 10W A city in N Colombia. Situated in mountainous country, it is the commercial centre for an area producing coffee and tobacco; manufactures include cigarettes and textiles. The Industrial University of Santander was founded here in 1947. Population (1980): 459 000.

buccaneers Bands of pirates who lived by plunder in the Caribbean in the second half of the 17th century. Most were English or French and they preyed primarily on Spanish shipping and settlements. They were often hired by the French governors of Tortuga and the English of Jamaica. By 1670 they had become, under the leadership of Henry *Morgan, a major problem for all countries and a number of treaties promised to bring them under control. In 1685 the English navy began to hunt buccaneers and after 1697 no European country employed them.

Bucer, Martin (1491-1551) German Protestant reformer. A Dominican friar, Bucer abandoned his vows and married in 1522, settling in Strasbourg. He advised Henry VIII on his divorce from Catherine of Aragon and tried to mediate between *Luther and *Zwingli in their debate concerning the Eucharist. In 1549 he went to England and became Regius Professor of Divinity at Cambridge. His views on the Eucharist had some influence on the Prayer Book of 1552.

Buchan, John, 1st Baron Tweedsmuir (1875-1940) British novelist. *Prester John* (1910) was the first of a series of vigorous adventure novels that included *The Thirty-Nine Steps* (1915), in which his character Richard Hannay first appeared, and *The Three Hostages* (1924). Director of Information during World War 1, he was made governor general of Canada in 1935.

Buchanan, George (1506-82) Scottish historian and scholar. He held academic posts in France, Portugal, and Scotland besides tutoring Mary, Queen of Scots, and James VI. As well as political works and his *History of Scotland* (1582) he wrote powerful satires and plays, all in Latin.

Buchanan, James (1791-1868) US statesman; Democratic president (1857-61). A moderate abolitionist, Buchanan tried to avert civil war by compromise, dividing his cabinet between representatives of slave-holding and free states. However, he split the Democrats by recommending a proslavery constitution for Kansas and lost the 1860 election to Abraham Lincoln.

Bucharest (Romanian name: Bucureşti) 44 25N 26 07E The capital of Romania, in the SE on a tributary of the Danube. As well as being the administrative and cultural centre of the country, Bucharest has many industries, including flour milling, textiles, chemicals, and oil refining. *History*: there is evidence of human settlement from prehistoric times. A fortress was built against Turkish invasion in the 15th century and it became capital of Wallachia in 1659. During the 19th century Bucharest played an important role in revolutionary movements, becoming capital of Romania in 1862. The university was founded in 1864. It was badly damaged by German bombing in World War II and since then has developed considerably. Population (1980 est): 1 861 007.

Bucharest, Treaties of 1. (1812) The treaty ending the Russo-Turkish war of 1806-12. It assigned Bessarabia to Russia and Walachia and Moldavia to Turkey; the Serbs were to receive autonomy. **2.** (1886) The treaty ending the Serbian-Bulgarian war (1885-86) over Eastern *Rumelia, which was kept by Bulgaria. **3.** (1913) The treaty ending the second *Balkan War, which partitioned Macedonia between

Serbia, Greece, Romania, and the defeated Bulgaria. **4.** (1918) The treaty in which Romania acknowledged its defeat by the Central Powers in World War I. It was annulled after their defeat by the Allies.

Büchner, Georg (1813-37) German dramatist. A medical student, he fled to Zürich after publishing a revolutionary pamphlet in 1834. He wrote three plays, the tragedies *Danton's Death* (1835) and *Woyzeck* (1836) and the comedy *Leonce und Lena* (1836), and a fragment of a novel, *Lenz* (1836). His innovatory techniques influenced later expressionist writers.

Buck, Pearl S(ydenstricker) (1892-1973) US novelist. The daughter of Presbyterian missionaries, she grew up in China and later returned there as a teacher. Her novels about China include *The Good Earth* (1931) and *The Three Daughters of Madame Liang* (1969). She won the Nobel Prize in 1938.

Buckingham 52 00N 1 00W A market town in S central England, in N Buckinghamshire on the River Ouse. Nearby is Stowe House, a public school since 1923 but formerly the seat of the dukes of Buckingham. The University College at Buckingham, the only independent university in the UK, was established here in 1975. Industries include light engineering. Population (1981): 6627.

Buckingham, George Villiers, 1st Duke of (1592-1628) A favourite of James I of England. He replaced Robert Carr, Earl of *Somerset, in the king's favour (1615), becoming Earl of Buckingham (1617), Lord High Admiral (1619), and Duke of Buckingham (1623). His attempt to negotiate the marriage of Prince Charles to the daughter of the Spanish king failed (1623), as did his planned expedition to Cádiz (1625) in the subsequent hostilities. Charles I resisted parliament's attempts to impeach Buckingham, who was assassinated after his unsuccessful expedition to relieve the Huguenots at La Rochelle (1627). His son **George Villiers, 2nd Duke of Buckingham** (1628-87) was a member of the powerful political group, the *Cabal, under Charles II. After his father's death he was brought up in the royal family, with whom he went into exile after the final royalist defeat in the Civil War (1651). Becoming a privy councillor at the Restoration, he helped oust *Clarendon (1667) but was overshadowed by *Arlington when the Cabal came to power. Also a playwright, he wrote the satirical *The Rehearsal* (1671); he is portrayed by Zimri in Dryden's *Absalom and Achitophel*.

Buckingham Palace The London residence of the British monarch. It was built about 1705 for the Duke of Buckingham, becoming a royal residence in 1761. It was completely redesigned by Nash for George IV, although its main façade was not added until 1913.

Buckinghamshire A county in the South Midlands of England, bordering on Greater London. Under local government reorganization in 1974 it lost part of the S, including Slough, to Berkshire. Known appropriately as Leafy Bucks because of the many trees throughout the county, the land rises gently N from the River Thames to the Chiltern Hills before descending to the fertile Vale of Aylesbury in the N. It is mainly agricultural, the chief crops being barley, wheat, and oats; sheep, cattle, poultry, and pig farming is also significant. Industry includes the manufacture of furniture at High Wycombe, based on the extensive beech woods. Area: 1878 sq km (725 sq mi). Population (1981): 565 992. Administrative centre: Aylesbury.

buckthorn A small thorny deciduous tree or shrub of the genus *Rhamnus* (about 13 species), widespread in the N hemisphere. The leaves are oval, with attractive autumn colours. The small green flowers produce blue-black berries. The wood is used for charcoal and slow fuses, and the bark for dyes. The alder buckthorn (*Frangula alnus*) is a similar and related shrub that lacks thorns. Family: *Rhamnaceae*.

buckwheat A herbaceous plant of the genus *Fagopyrum*,

especially *F. esculentum*. Up to 60 cm tall, they have arrow-shaped leaves and clusters of densely packed small pink or white flowers. Buckwheats are native to Asia but widely cultivated for their seed, used as a cereal substitute, or as green fodder. Family: *Polygonaceae* (dock family).

Budapest 47 33N 19 03E The capital of Hungary, situated in the N of the country on the River Danube. Most of Hungary's industry is sited here and includes machinery, iron and steel, and chemicals. The university was founded in 1635. *History*: from the 14th century the fortress of Buda, on the W bank of the Danube, was the seat of the Magyar kings. After occupation by the Turks, it came under Habsburg rule in the 17th century. In 1872 it united with Pest to form the city that became the capital of Hungary in 1918. In 1956 it was the scene of a popular rising, suppressed by Soviet troops. Population (1980 est): 2 060 000.

Budd, Zola (1966–) South African athlete, who received British nationality in 1984 and competed for Britain in the 1984 Olympic Games. She has set world records for the 5000 metres (1985; 14 mins 48.07 secs) and 3000 metres (1986; 8 mins 39.66 secs), but was barred from the 1986 Commonwealth Games on residency grounds.

BUDDHA *A 13th-century bronze statue at Kamakura in Japan. 13 metres (48 ft) high, it weighs 94 tons.*

Buddha, title of **Gautama Siddhartha** (c. 563–c. 483 BC) Indian prince, whose teachings formed the basis of Buddhism. The son of Suddhodana and his queen, Maya, in Kapilavastu (Nepal), Gautama was reputed to have been a child of exceptional intelligence and beauty about whom many stories and legends have been told. At the age of 16 he married his cousin Princess Yasodhara, who some 13 years later bore him a son, Rahula. Soon after this event Gautama, renouncing his life of indolence and luxury, abandoned his family and set out to seek solutions to the problems of the transcience and suffering of human existence. He was then about 29. After six years of emaciating asceticism he reluctantly concluded that austerity was as unlikely as triviality to provide the solution he sought. Abandoned now by his five companions for his rejection of mortification, he determined to seek enlightenment, alone, within himself. According to tradition, this he achieved while seated beneath a banyan tree, in what is now called Buddh Gaya, in Bihar (his title, *Buddha*, is Sanskrit for the Awakened One). Probably 35 years old at this time, he devoted the rest of his life to teaching the principles (*see* dharma) of this enlightenment, first moving to Benares, where he founded the Buddhist order of monks, and thereafter teaching in various places in N India. He died at Kusinagara in Uttar Pradesh. *See also* Buddhism.

Buddhaghosa (5th century BC) Buddhist scholar. A Brahman convert from Buddh Gaya, he wrote the *Visuddhi-magga* (*Path of Purity*), a collation of Sinhalese Buddhist commentaries that he collected in Ceylon and translated into Pali.

Buddh Gaya (*or* Bodh Gaya) 24 42N 85 00E A village in India, in Bihar. It was here that Gautama Buddha attained enlightenment under the sacred bo (*or* bodhi) tree. Population (1981): 15 724.

Buddhism The nontheistic religion and philosophical system founded in NE India in the 6th century BC by Gautama Siddhartha (the *Buddha). His followers seek to emulate his example of perfect morality, wisdom, and compassion, culminating in a transformation of consciousness known as enlightenment. Buddhism teaches that greed, hatred, and delusion separate the individual from the true preception of the nature of things, causing him to remain tied to the *bhavachakra. The apparent substantiality of all objects, including the self, is illusion; everything mundane is impermanent and ultimately unsatisfying. The central beliefs of Buddhism are based on the Buddha's *Four Noble Truths, the last of which is the *Eightfold Path by which enlightenment may be attained and the individual self annihilated in *Nirvana. Buddhism is not dogmatic, but through its long history has developed into many schools (*see* Mahayana; Theravada; Zen Buddhism). With more than 500 million followers in Sri Lanka, Nepal, Japan, and elsewhere in the Far East, Buddhism is currently gaining adherents in the West.

budding In biology, a method of asexual reproduction in lower plants and animals, for example liverworts and coelenterates, in which new individuals develop from outgrowths of cells (buds) on the parent. The process also occurs in single-celled fungi, for example yeasts. In horticulture the term is used for the *grafting of a bud onto a stock.

Buddleia A genus of trees and shrubs (about 100 species), mostly native to tropical or warm temperate regions but widely introduced. The small four-petalled flowers are usually clustered in dense heads; the fruit is a capsule or berry. Many species are grown as ornamentals, especially *D. davidii* (butterfly bush) 4–5 m high, the long purple flower heads of which attract many butterflies; and *B. globosa*, which has round orange flower heads. Family: *Buddleiaceae*.

Budé, Guillaume (1467–1540) French Renaissance scholar. Budé wrote many important Greek commentaries and philological works. He founded the Collège de France (1530) and as royal librarian built the library that formed the nucleus of the Bibliothèque Nationale.

Budge, (James) Don(ald) (1916–) US tennis player, the first to win all four major singles titles (Australian, French, US, and Wimbledon) in one year (1938). He was also an outstanding doubles player.

budgerigar A small *parakeet, *Melopsitticus undulatus*, occurring in large flocks in arid regions of Australia. It is 19 cm long and has a green and yellow plumage with barred upper parts. Since its introduction to Britain in 1840 it has become a popular cagebird; white, violet, yellow, blue, and grey forms have been produced by selective breeding.

budget A prediction of the financial behaviour of a firm, government, etc., over a specified period. Careful budgeting enables any deviation from a plan to be noted early and the appropriate action to be taken.

In the UK, the government's budget is presented to parliament by the chancellor of the exchequer, usually in March or April (in times of crisis supplementary budgets may be introduced at other times of the year). The chief components of the budget are the *taxation rates (which become incorporated in the Finance Act) and the planned public expenditure (incorporated in the Appropriations Act), which together determine the impact the government will have on the economy. In the 19th and early 20th centuries, governments attempted to run balanced budgets (i.e. neither in surplus nor in deficit) by analogy with good individual housekeeping. Since World War II governments have used the budget in attempts to counter the effects of the *trade cycle (*see* deficit financing; fiscal policy), evoking considerable controversy (*see* Keynesianism; monetarism).

Buenaventura 3 54N 77 02W A port in W Colombia, on the Pacific Ocean. Exports include coffee and sugar from the Cauca Valley and gold and platinum from the Chocó district. Population (1973): 115 770.

Bueno, Maria (Esther) (1939–) Brazilian tennis player, who was Wimbledon singles champion in 1959, 1960, and 1964. She also won the US singles title four times, the Wimbledon doubles five times, and the US doubles four times.

BUFFALO *Most buffalo are now confined to game reserves, like this one in the Kruger National Park (South Africa).*

Buenos Aires 34 50S 58 37W The capital of Argentina, the largest city in South America and one of the world's largest ports, situated on the Río de la Plata estuary. It is the financial, commercial, and industrial centre of the country. Its chief exports are beef and wool. A cultural centre, Buenos Aires possesses many universities (including the University of Buenos Aires, 1821), the national library, and a famous opera house (the Teatro Colón). There are several fine avenues, including the Avenida de Mayo and the Avenida de Julio. Notable buildings include the cathedral (completed in 1804). *History*: founded in 1580, after Indian attacks on earlier settlements, it became capital of the newly created viceroyalty of the Río de la Plata in 1776 and of the new Republic of Argentina in 1880. In the late 19th and early 20th centuries its population was greatly swelled by European immigrants, especially Spanish and Italian. Population (1980 est): 2 922 800.

buffalo A large African hoofed mammal, *Syncerus caffer*, also called Cape buffalo. Weighing over 700 kg and measuring 110–150 cm at the shoulder, buffaloes have massive curved horns and a smooth black coat. They live in large herds in grassy areas where both tree cover and water are available. Once numerous, their numbers have been reduced by hunting and disease. Family: *Bovidae*. *Compare* bison; water buffalo.

Buffalo 42 52N 78 55W A city in the USA, in New York state on Lake Erie and the Niagara River. The state's second largest city, it is linked to New York City by the New York State Barge Canal (formerly Erie Canal). A major port, its industries include iron and steel, motor vehicles, and electrical equipment. Population (1980 est): 357 870.

Buffalo Bill. *See* Cody, William F(rederick).

buffalo gnat. *See* black fly.

buffer solution A solution the *pH of which is insensitive to dilution or the addition of moderate amounts of acid or base. Generally it consists of a mixture of a weak acid or base and its salt. If, for example, acid is added to an acetic acid-acetate mixture, the hydrogen ions will combine with acetate ions to form acetic acid molecules, thus lowering the acidity. Buffers are present in many living organisms, as fluctuations in pH would destroy the enzymes, etc.

Buffet, Bernard (1928–) French painter. Precociously talented, he established his reputation by 1948. His realistic paintings are notable for their strong black lines, melancholy colours, and elongated forms.

Buffon, Georges Louis Leclerc, Comte de (1707–88) French naturalist, who formulated a crude theory of evolution and was the first to suggest that the earth might be considerably older than suggested by the Bible. He estimated the age of the earth to be 75 000 years, with life emerging some 40 000 years ago.

bug A common name for any insect-like animal. Specifically, the term refers to insects of the order *Hemiptera (the true bugs), especially the *bedbug and insects of the suborder *Heteroptera* (plant bugs, water bugs, etc.).

Bug, River 1. (*or* Western Bug) A river in E central Europe, rising in the Soviet Union, in the SW Ukrainian SSR, and flowing NW as part of the border between the Soviet Union and Poland to the River Vistula. Length: 724 km (450 mi). 2. (*or* Southern Bug) A river in the SW Soviet Union, rising in the W Ukraine and flowing SE to the Dnieper estuary on the Black Sea. Length: 853 km (530 mi).

Buganda A former kingdom in East Africa, now comprising an administrative region of Uganda bordering on Lake Victoria. The UK Government assumed responsibility for Buganda in 1893. When Uganda became a republic (1963) the kabaka (king) of Buganda became president of Uganda. His arrest (1966) by the former prime minister Dr Milton Obote caused widespread rioting in Buganda.

Bugatti, Ettore (Arco Isidoro) (1881–1947) Italian ⬜car manufacturer. In 1909 he founded a factory in Molsheim, Alsace, to produce cars to race at Le Mans. His finest car was probably the Type 41–the Golden Bugatti.

bugle A high-pitched brass (or copper) instrument with a wide conical tube, a cup-shaped mouthpiece, and a small bell. It lacks valves and so can only play a single harmonic series (usually having the fundamental of C). Formerly much used for military signalling, it is also used on ceremonial occasions and in the brass band.

bugloss A biennial herb of the Eurasian genus *Echium* (about 30 species), e.g. viper's bugloss (*E. vulgare*). Up to 90 cm high, the plants are covered in bristly hairs and produce spikes of funnel-shaped flowers, about 2 cm long, usually bluish with several protruding stamens. Another plant called bugloss is *Lycopsis arvensis*, an annual similar to *Echium* species but with smaller flowers. Family: *Boraginaceae*.

building society An association in the UK that accepts savings from the public, paying a specified rate of interest, and uses these funds to provide *mortgages to home buyers. Over 400 such societies belong to the Building Societies Association, which agrees the rates of *interest to be paid on deposits and the rate to be charged for mortgages. Building-society interest

rates move in line with other interest rates to enable them to attract sufficient funds. Interest earned on building-society savings is not subject to basic income tax (it is subject to higher-rate income tax) and in certain circumstances interest paid can be deducted from taxable income. Recently some societies have provided cheque accounts for investors on which interest is paid, challenging the banks' unwillingness to pay interest on current accounts.

Bujumbura (former name: Usumbura) 3 30S 29 20E The capital of Burundi, a port on the NE shore of Lake Tanganyika. Founded in the 19th century, it became the capital of Ruanda-Urundi after World War I. The university was founded in 1960. Population (1980 est): 200 000.

Bukavu (name until 1966: Costermansville) 2 20S 28 52E A port in E Zaïre, on Lake Kivu. A commercial centre, it has local agricultural and brewing industries. Population (1981): 209 051.

Bukhara (*or* Bokhara) 39 47N 64 26E A city in the SW Soviet Union, in the Uzbek SSR. The Bukhara region (*oblast*) of which it is the capital was the centre of a powerful kingdom, which was ceded to Russia in 1868. It grew rapidly in the 1950s after the discovery of natural gas. It has textile industries, and the traditional crafts of gold embroidery and metalworking are still practised. Population (1981 est): 192 000.

Bukhari, al- (810–70 AD) Muslim scholar and historian. After extensive travels, he collected more than 600 000 traditional records (*see* Hadith) of the words and deeds of the prophet Mohammed. He published a selection of these, arranged by subject, which he considered authentic teachings. The resulting collection is revered by orthodox Muslims as second in authority only to the Koran.

Bukharin, Nikolai Ivanovich (1888–1938) Soviet politician and communist theoretician. In exile after 1911, Bukharin edited the socialist newspaper *Novy Mir*, in New York. He returned to Russia during the Revolution and became editor of the newspaper *Pravda*. He believed that Russia should achieve socialism slowly and therefore supported Lenin's New Economic Policy (1924). He was chairman of the Comintern until dismissed by Stalin in 1929. He helped draft the 1936 constitution but was expelled from the Communist Party shortly afterwards and died in Stalin's purges.

Bukovina (*or* Bucovina) An area in E Europe, in the NE Carpathian Mountains. As part of the principality of Moldavia, it fell to the Turks in 1512 and was ceded to Austria in 1775. Occupied by the Romanians in 1918, the N part was ceded to the Soviet Union (1940), later becoming part of the Ukrainian SSR. S Bukovina remained a Romanian province until it was abolished in 1952.

Bulawayo 20 10S 28 43E The second largest city in Zimbabwe. It was founded on its present site in 1894 by the British, near to its original site of the kraal of Lobengula, the centre of the Ndebele tribe. Nearby are the popular tourist attractions of Rhodes Matapos National Park and the Khami Ruins. The city is the country's chief industrial centre with metal, motor-tyre, and cement industries. Population (1980 est): 373 000.

bulb A modified underground stem of certain perennial herbaceous plants, for example onions, daffodils, and tulips, that serves as an overwintering organ. Food is stored in overlapping fleshy leaves or leaf bases, borne on a very short stem, and is used to produce one or more plants the following season. When a bulb produces two or more plants it acts as an organ of vegetative reproduction. East Anglia (UK) and the Netherlands are centres for the commercial production of spring-flowering bulbs.

bulbul A gregarious forest-dwelling songbird belonging to an Old World family (*Pycnonotidae*; 120 species). 12–22 cm long, bulbuls are yellow, green, or brown, sometimes with bright patches on the head and beneath the tail. They have a

199   **bullfinch**

slender bill surrounded by stiff bristles and feed largely on fruit and berries.

Bulganin, Nikolai Aleksandrovich (1895–1975) Soviet statesman; prime minister (1955–58). Bulganin began his career in 1918, when he joined *CHEKA. In World War II he became (1944) a member of Stalin's war cabinet and in 1947, defence minister. As prime minister, Bulganin participated in the attempt to oust Khrushchev in 1957 and was subsequently dismissed.

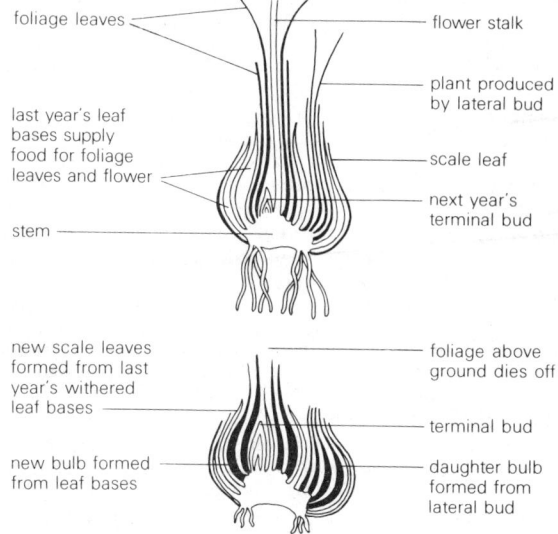

foliage leaves

flower stalk

plant produced by lateral bud

last year's leaf bases supply food for foliage leaves and flower

scale leaf

next year's terminal bud

stem

new scale leaves formed from last year's withered leaf bases

foliage above ground dies off

terminal bud

new bulb formed from leaf bases

daughter bulb formed from lateral bud

BULB *A section through a daffodil bulb in spring (above) and summer (below) to show growth cycle.*

Bulgaria, People's Republic of A country in SE Europe, in the E Balkans on the Black Sea. The low-lying Danube basin in the N rises to the Balkan Mountains in the centre of the country; further S, beyond the valley of the River Maritsa, the Rhodope Mountains reach heights of almost 3000 m (10 000 ft). The inhabitants are mainly Bulgars, with minorities of Macedonians, Turks, and Gipsies. *Economy:* industrialization has proceeded rapidly since World War II, following the introduction of a centrally planned economy. Particular emphasis has been given to heavy manufacturing industries. The industrial sector has recently been reorganized into several large combines. Coal, iron, and other minerals are mined and hydroelectricity and nuclear energy contribute to power supplies. Oil has been found offshore in the Black Sea and natural gas is also being produced. Agricultural production, the traditional mainstay of 'the economy prior to 1945, has been mechanized and organized on a cooperative basis, the main crops being wheat, maize, beet, and barley. Tourism has been considerably developed in recent years. Main exports include machinery, chemicals, food products, textiles, tobacco, and nonferrous metals. Bulgaria is a member of *COMECON. *History:* following the invasion of the Bulgars in the 7th century AD and their gradual adoption of the culture and language of the conquered Slavs, Bulgaria became a significant power in SE Europe. Despite coming under Turkish rule in 1396, the Bulgars succeeded in retaining their national identity over the centuries until they once again became independent in 1908 under the Saxe-Coburg ruler *Ferdinand, who took the title of tsar. Bulgaria aligned itself with Germany in both World Wars. In 1944 it was occupied by the Soviet Union and power was seized by the Fatherland Front, a left-wing alliance, which formed a pro-Soviet government that declared war on Germany. In 1946 a People's Republic was proclaimed and since then Bulgaria has remained one of the most loyal of the Soviet Union's satellite states. Under a new constitution in 1971 Todor *Zhivkov became chairman of the Council of State and first secretary of the Communist Party. Official language: Bulgarian. Official currency: lev of 100 stotinki. Area: 110 912 sq km (42 823 sq mi). Population (1980 est): 8 880 000. Capital: Sofia. Main port: Varna.

Bulgarian A language belonging to the South *Slavonic group spoken by eight million people in Bulgaria, Greece, Romania, and areas of the Soviet Union. It differs from other Slavonic languages in several respects as it lacks case declensions for nouns and shares grammatical features and vocabulary elements with other non-Slavonic Balkan languages. The literature written in Bulgarian dates from the establishment of Christianity (9th century).

Bulge, Battle of the. *See* World War II.

bulk modulus. *See* elastic modulus.

bull (from Latin: *bulla*, seal) Originally, the seal attached to papal edicts. The term was later used for the documents themselves, but now refers only to the most important missives. Named by their opening word or phrase, for example *Pastor Aeternus* (Eternal Father; 1870), they are issued to assert doctrine.

Bull, John (c. 1562–1628) English composer and organist at the Chapel Royal (1591–92). He was appointed music professor at Gresham College (1596), but left England in 1613 and became organist of Antwerp Cathedral (1617). He wrote church music, fantasies for viols, and keyboard music.

Bull, John (caricature). *See* John Bull.

bullace A type of *plum, *Prunus insititia*, cultivated for centuries but probably originating in SW Asia. The young branches are very hairy and have few thorns. The blue-black fruit is similar to that of the blackthorn but larger and sweeter.

bullbaiting. *See* bearbaiting.

bulldog A breed of dog originating in England, where it was used in bull- and bear-baiting. It has a compact rounded body with short sturdy legs and a short tail. The relatively large head has an undershot jaw (i.e. the lower jaw projects in front of the upper) and loose folds of skin. The fine short coat can be of any colour except black. Weight: 25 kg (dogs); 23 kg (bitches).

bulldozer A powerful caterpillar tractor equipped with a blade or shovel for moving or digging earth and often used for preliminary clearing and levelling of building sites, roads, etc. The blade can be raised or lowered hydraulically or set at an angle for sideways shifting of earth.

bullfighting Subduing and killing bulls. The national spectator sport of Spain, it is also popular in parts of France and Latin America, and mounted bullfighting, in which the bulls are not killed, is practised in Portugal. The bulls are specially bred. At a normal Spanish *corrida de toros* (bullfight) three matadors kill two bulls each. Following the initial ceremonial procession the first bull enters the ring. Preliminary passes are made by the *banderilleros* (assistants) with their capes to attract the bull's attention and allow the matador to assess the bull's reactions. The matador then makes his first series of passes with his cape, controlling the direction and extent of the bull's charge. During the next stage, the matadors make the bull charge at a mounted picador, who uses a form of lance to stab the bull's neck, weakening the muscle so that it lowers its head. This procedure is repeated up to three times, each of the three matadors taking turns to draw the bull away from the horse and continue the capework. During the following stage the neck muscle is further weakened by pairs of barbed sticks (*banderillas*) thrust into it by the *banderilleros*. In the final stage the matador performs a series of passes with his *muleta* (a small red cape folded over a stick) to weaken the bull further until he can reach over its head to thrust his sword in at the right angle to sever its aorta.

bullfinch A plump woodland *finch, *Pyrrhula pyrrhula*, of N Eurasia. It is about 14 cm long and has a grey back, a pinkish breast, and black head, wings, and tail. Bullfinches have strong stout bills and strip buds and flowers from trees, for which they are often regarded as pests.

bullfrog A large frog, *Rana catesbiana*, of North America. Dull green with a slightly warty skin, bullfrogs grow to about 20 cm and can jump up to 2 m. Females are larger than males. They are the only common American frogs large enough to be used as food.
Other large frogs—*Pyxicephalus adspersus* in Africa and *Rana tigrina* in India—are also called bullfrogs.

bullhead One of several predatory bottom-dwelling fish, also called sculpin, belonging to the family *Cottidae*, including the Eurasian miller's thumb (*Cottus gobio*). Bullheads have a tapering conical body, up to 30 cm long and often covered with spiny bony plates, a broad spiny head, and two dorsal fins. They are found in fresh water and shallow seas of the N hemisphere. Order: *Perciformes*. *See also* catfish.

bull market A stock and share market or commodity market in which there is a continuing upward movement in prices. An initial rise in prices, caused by favourable economic factors, is often magnified by consequent buying by investors. *Compare* bear market.

bull mastiff A breed of dog resulting from crosses between bulldogs and mastiffs. It is sturdily built with a short broad muzzle and folds of skin surrounding the face. The short coat is red, fawn, or streaked brown. Height: 63-68 cm (dogs); 61-66 cm (bitches).

Bull Run, Battles of (*or* Battles of Manassas) Two battles in the US *Civil War fought in NE Virginia. Both were Confederate victories. In the first (21 July, 1861), Federal forces failed to prevent the unification of Confederate forces under Gen P. G. T. Beauregard (1818-93) and Gen Joseph E. Johnstone (1807-91) at Manassas Junction near a stream named Bull Run. The untried Federal troops were repulsed after an unsuccessful attack. The second battle (29-30 August, 1862) followed an unsuccessful Federal attempt to capture Gordonsville, a rail junction near Richmond, the Confederate capital. The 70 000 Federal troops had withdrawn to await reinforcements when Stonewall *Jackson attacked and forced their retreat to Washington.

bull terrier A breed of ▯dog originating in the UK from crosses between bulldogs and terriers. It is strongly built with a courageous temperament. The coat is either pure white (with darker head markings) or coloured. Height: 48-56 cm. (Miniature bull terriers must not exceed 36 cm in height.)

Bülow, Bernhard Heinrich, Fürst von (1849-1929) German statesman and diplomat; chancellor (1900-09). He pursued aggressive foreign policies that contributed to German isolation in Europe. He alienated France over the Moroccan crisis in 1905 and Russia over the Bosnian crisis in 1908. He resigned after losing the confidence of Emperor William II and of the Reichstag and served from 1914 to 1915 as ambassador to Italy.

Bülow, Hans Guido, Freiherr von (1830-94) German pianist and the outstanding conductor of his time. Bülow championed Wagner until his wife Cosima (Liszt's daughter) eloped with Wagner in 1866. From that time he championed the works of Brahms.

bulrush A widely distributed perennial herbaceous plant, *Scirpus lacustris*, growing in ponds, lakes, and rivers. 1-3 m high, it has cylindrical leafless stems bearing branched clusters of small reddish-brown flowers. Family: *Cyperaceae* (sedges, etc.). The name is also applied to the *reedmace, and the biblical bulrush is the *papyrus.

Bultmann, Rudolf (Karl) (1884-1976) German New Testament scholar. A professor at Marburg University (1921-51), he allied himself with the anti-Nazi *Confessing Church during the Third Reich. In his influential writings he argued that the New Testament message must be

"demythologized" (or stripped of its no longer acceptable mythical concepts) if it was to have any relevance to contemporary man.

Bulwer-Lytton, Edward George Earle. *See* Lytton, Edward George Earle Bulwer-Lytton, 1st Baron.

bumblebee A social *bee, also called humblebee, belonging to a genus (*Bombus*) found mainly in temperate regions. Bumblebees, 15-25 mm long, are usually black with yellow or orange bands. They live in colonies, on or below the ground, containing 100-400 workers in the summer. Their life cycle is like that of the *honeybee, although only young fertilized queens survive the winter. Solitary parasitic bumblebees belong to the genus *Psithyrus*. Family: *Apidae*. ▯insect.

Bunbury 33 20S 115 34E A port in SW Western Australia, at the junction of the Collie and Preston Rivers. It is protected by a breakwater 1.5 km (1 mi) long. The main exports are wheat, timber, and fruit. Population (1981): 21 749.

Bunche, Ralph (1904-71) US political scientist and UN official. As a government official Bunche specialized in colonial areas during World War II and became the first Black American to hold an important position in the State Department. He was a founder of the UN and director of its trusteeship division. Bunche won the Nobel Peace Prize for negotiating the 1949 Arab-Israeli truce and supervised the UN Congo peace force in 1960.

Bundaberg 24 50S 152 21E A port in Australia, in E Queensland on the Burnett River. It is a commercial centre for an important sugar-producing region; associated industries include rum distilling. Population (1980 est): 32 000.

Bundelkhand A region in present-day Madhya Pradesh state, in N central India, taking its name from the Bundela Rajputs, a dynasty that ruled here from the 14th to the 18th centuries. The area is rich in architectural history; in the 10th and 11th centuries the Candella kings built many beautiful temples at Khajuraho and a fine fortress was erected later at Jhansi.

Bunin, Ivan Alekseevich (1879-1953) Russian poet and novelist. He published his first book of poems in 1891, and translated works by *Byron and *Longfellow. His prose works include novels (*The Village*, 1910), short stories (*The Gentleman from San Francisco*, 1916), and autobiographical works (*The Well of Days*, 1910). In 1920 he emigrated to Finland. He won the Nobel Prize in 1933.

bunion A deformity and swelling at the joint at the base of the big toe. It is usually caused by pressure from ill-fitting shoes: the toe becomes bent towards the others and a fibrous fluid-filled sac (bursa) develops over the affected joint. Bunions may require surgical treatment.

Bunker Hill, Battle of (17 June, 1775) A battle of the *American Revolution actually fought on Breed's Hill (next to Bunker Hill) in Charlestown, near Boston. The Americans defended the strategic hill from two British attacks but Sir William *Howe displaced the Americans at the third attempt. The American defence helped raise support for the Revolutionary cause.

Bunsen, Robert Wilhelm (1811-99) German chemist, after whom the Bunsen burner is named. He did not, however, invent the Bunsen burner although he did popularize it. In collaboration with *Kirchhoff, Bunsen developed the technique of *spectroscopy, using a Bunsen burner to heat the substance. In 1860 they used the technique to discover the elements *rubidium and *caesium. He also invented a carbon-zinc electric cell (1841).

Bunsen burner A gas burner for laboratory use, popularized by R. *Bunsen. It consists of a vertical metal tube with a variable air inlet at the bottom. Gas is led into the bottom of the tube and the gas-air mixture burnt at the top. Adjustment of the air inlet allows control of combustion intensity, temperature, sooting, and other flame properties.

bunting A sparrow-like bird belonging to a subfamily (*Emberizinae*) of the *finches. Buntings are 12–20 cm long and usually have a brownish or greyish plumage. They live on the ground or in bushes and thickets and scratch for seeds with their characteristically large feet. The subfamily includes the *yellowhammer and the *snow bunting. *See* Plate V.

Buñuel, Luis (1900–83) Spanish film director. He worked mainly in France and Mexico. His films are characterized by surrealist techniques and by their anticlericalism and satire on social hypocrisy. They include *Un Chien andalou* (1928), *Viridiana* (1961), *The Discreet Charm of the Bourgeoisie* (1972), and *That Obscure Object of Desire* (1977).

bunya bunya. *See* Araucaria.

Bunyan, John (1628–88) British writer. Son of a tinker, he fought in the parliamentary army during the Civil War. From 1650 to 1656 he underwent a spiritual crisis, finally resolved by his conversion to religion. He became the leader of a group of Baptists in Bedford and in 1660 he was imprisoned for preaching without a licence. During his 12 years in prison he wrote his spiritual autobiography, *Grace Abounding* (1666), and began his major work, *The Pilgrim's Progress* (1678). An imaginative allegory written in plain but majestic prose, it has been widely read and admired for centuries.

Burbage, Richard (c. 1567–1619) English actor. He played leading roles in the first productions of many of Shakespeare's plays. He also acted in plays by Kyd, Webster, and Ben Jonson, and was a shareholder in the Blackfriars and the Globe theatres.

Burbank, Luther (1849–1926) US plant breeder, who developed many new varieties of agricultural importance. His first commercial success, the Burbank potato, enabled him to settle in California, where—by skilful selection and breeding techniques—he originated more than 800 new strains and varieties of fruit, vegetables, and flowers.

burbot A food fish, *Lota lota*, that is similar and related to the *ling. Up to 1.1 m long, it lives on the bottom in cold fresh waters of Europe, Asia, and North America and feeds voraciously on other fish.

Burckhardt, Jacob Christoph (1818–97) Swiss art and cultural historian. The son of a Protestant clergyman, he studied at the Universities of Berlin and Bonn. From 1843 he lectured at Basle University, becoming professor of history there in 1858, after three years at Zürich. His most important work, *The Civilization of the Renaissance in Italy* (1860), was a model for later cultural histories, with its thorough and systematic analysis of the period.

burdock A tall stiff biennial plant of the genus *Arctium* (about 5 species), 60–130 cm high, found in Europe and Asia. They have broad heart-shaped leaves and reddish-purple thistle-like flower heads, surrounded by many large stiff hooked bracts, which are retained by the fruits. Family: *Compositae*.

Burgas 42 30N 29 29E A city in E Bulgaria, on the Black Sea. Bulgaria's second largest port (after Varna), its industries include fishing, mining, and oil refining. Population (1982): 178 239.

Bürgi, Joost (1552–1632) Swiss mathematician, who invented *logarithms independently of, and probably before, John *Napier. He also contributed to the exponential notation (i.e. y^x to indicate y multiplied by itself x times).

Burgenland A federal state in E Austria, bordering on Hungary. It was ceded to Austria by Hungary following World War I. Predominantly agricultural, it produces cereals, root crops, and fruit and vegetables; livestock are also extensively raised. Area: 3965 sq km (1531 sq mi). Population (1981): 272 568. Capital: Eisenstadt.

Bürger, Gottfried (1747–94) German poet. At Göttingen University he studied law and eventually became professor of

aesthetics. His ballad *Lenore* (1773) influenced writers of the early Romantic period throughout Europe. He also translated many traditional English and Scots ballads.

Burgess, Anthony (John Burgess Wilson; 1917–) British novelist and critic. A teacher and lecturer in English literature and phonetics, he became a full-time writer in 1959. His novels include the sinister tragicomedy *A Clockwork Orange* (1962), which was filmed by Stanley *Kubrick, *Inside Mr Enderby* (1963), *Nothing like the Sun* (1964), *Napoleon Symphony* (1974), *Earthly Powers* (1980), and *The Kingdom of the Wicked* (1985). His *Flame into Being* (1986) is a study of D. H. Lawrence.

Burgess, Guy. *See* Maclean, Donald.

Burgh, Hubert de (d. 1243) Jucticiar of England (1215–32) under John and then Henry III. He supported John against the baronial rebels (*see* Barons' Wars) and became one of the most important members of the minority council of Henry III. He was created justiciar for life in 1227 but fell from favour in 1232 and was outlawed. Restored to grace in 1234, he never again regained his former ascendancy.

Burghley, William Cecil, Lord (1520–98) English statesman; close adviser to Elizabeth I from her accession (1558). He served both Somerset and Northumberland under Edward VI and outwardly espoused Roman Catholicism under Mary I. A moderating influence on Elizabeth, his pragmatism is evident in her religious settlement (*see* Reformation). He helped to bring about the Treaty of Edinburgh (1660) with Scotland, which undermined French influence there. He influenced Elizabeth's pro-Protestant foreign policy, aiding the Revolt of the Netherlands against Spain, and helped to prepare England for the threatened Spanish invasion (*see* Armada, Spanish). He was instrumental in securing the execution of Mary, Queen of Scots, in 1587. He was succeeded as royal adviser by his son **Robert Cecil, 1st Earl of Salisbury** (c. 1563–1612), who negotiated the accession of James VI of Scotland to the English throne as James I (1603). As lord treasurer (1608–12), he was James' chief adviser.

burglary In law, entering a building, ship, or other inhabited vehicle as a trespasser, intending to commit serious crimes, such as theft, rape, grievous bodily harm, or unlawful damage. The possession of weapons, such as firearms or explosives, in these circumstances is the more serious crime of aggravated burglary.

Burgos 42 21N 3 41W A city in N Spain, in Old Castile. Its cathedral (13th–16th centuries) contains the remains of the legendary hero El Cid. Population (1981): 156 449.

Burgoyne, John (1722–92) British general and dramatist. In the American Revolution he commanded the British force in the N, ordered in conjunction with a column from New York under Sir William *Howe to divide the Americans along the Hudson River. Howe's progress was blocked and Burgoyne was defeated by *Gates at Saratoga (1777). His plays include *The Heiress* (1786).

Burgundian school A group of musicians working at the court of the Dukes of Burgundy in the 15th century. Under Philip the Good, who reigned from 1419 to 1467, there was a great flowering of the arts. Two composers are outstanding: Guillaume *Dufay and Gilles Binchois (c. 1400–60). Their compositions include chansons with French texts, motets, masses, and magnificats. The composers of the Burgundian school were influenced by such English composers as John *Dunstable.

Burgundy A region in France, E of the Rivers Rhône and Saône. The Burgundians were a Scandinavian people who occupied the region in the 4th century AD, establishing a powerful kingdom that was conquered by the Franks in 534. The NW part of the former kingdom became a duchy in the 9th century and passed to the French Crown in the mid-14th century. John the Good transferred it to his fourth son, Philip the Bold, and after the death (1477) of his descendant Charles the Bold it was annexed by the Crown.

Buridan, Jean (c. 1297–c. 1358) French scholastic philosopher. He became professor of philosophy at Paris and famed as a debater. He is associated with "Buridan's ass," an illustration of a position in arguments about free will; the animal starves through being unable to choose between equally attractive piles of hay.

Burke, Edmund (1729–97) British political philosopher and politician. An MP from 1765, he became a Rockingham Whig. He attacked George III's exalted view of the monarch's political role in the pamphlet *Thoughts on the Cause of the Present Discontents* (1770) and in two famous speeches, "On American Taxation" (1774) and "On Moving His Resolutions for Conciliation with the Colonies" (1777), blamed the unrest in the American colonies on British misgovernment. He also campaigned against the corrupt Indian administration of the *East India Company, bringing about the impeachment of Warren *Hastings (1788). An opponent of democracy on the grounds that it brought demagogues to the fore, he believed that the common good was best secured by responsible aristocratic government. He thus condemned the French Revolution (*Reflections on the Revolution in France*, 1790). He has been regarded as the foremost Conservative philosopher. He also wrote a widely read work on aesthetics, *A Philosophical Enquiry into the Origin of Our Ideas of the Sublime and Beautiful* (1757).

Burke, Robert O'Hara (1820–61) Irish explorer of Australia. Educated in Belgium, he served in the Austrian army and later joined the Irish police. In 1853 he emigrated to Australia and organized an expedition (which included W. J. *Wills) to cross Australia from S to N (1860). Burke and Wills, and two others, reached the mouth of the Flinders in 1861 but on the return journey both died of starvation.

Burke, William (1792–1829) Irish criminal. In company with William Hare, his landlord in Edinburgh and a fellow Irishman, he murdered at least 15 people and also dug up corpses to sell them to medical schools. After their arrest, Hare turned king's evidence and Burke was hanged.

Burkina Faso (name until 1984: Upper Volta) A landlocked country in West Africa. It consists mainly of a low-lying plateau, crossed by the headwaters of the River Volta: the Black, Red, and White Voltas. The population is almost entirely African, the largest groups being the Mossi and Fulani. *Economy*: chiefly agricultural, the main food crops being millet and sorghum; livestock is important and is the main export. Production of rice, groundnuts, cotton, and sugar is being increased by means of schemes to improve water supplies, although these advances were hampered by the severe droughts affecting the Sahel region in the early 1970s. Some minerals, including manganese, have been found but lack of communications makes their exploitation difficult. *History*: the area was occupied by powerful Mossi states from the 14th century. It became part of the French protectorate of Soudan in 1898 and in 1919 the separate protectorate of Upper Volta was formed. In 1932 it was divided between Niger, Ivory Coast, and Soudan but was reconstituted in 1947. In 1958 Upper Volta became an autonomous republic, gaining full independence outside the French Community in 1960. A military coup in 1966 brought Lt Col (later Gen) Sangoulé Lamizana (1916–   ) to power; he was elected president in 1978 but was overthrown in 1980. In 1983, after another military coup, Capt Thomas Sankara assumed power; a further coup in 1987, led by Capt Blaise Compaore (1951–   ), resulted in Sankara's death and a promise of a return to democracy. Since 1985 territorial disputes have caused armed conflict with Mali. Official language: French. Official currency: CFA (Communauté financière africaine) franc of 100 centimes. Area: 274 002 sq km (105 764 sq mi). Population (1981 est): 7 094 000. Capital: Ouagadougou.

Burlington 44 28N 73 14W A city in the USA, in Vermont on Lake Champlain. Settled in 1773, the University of Vermont was founded here in 1791. The state's largest city, its chief manufactures are furniture, business machines, textiles, and steel goods. Population (1980): 37 712.

Burlington, Richard Boyle, 3rd Earl of (1694–1753) English connoisseur and architect. Famous for his devotion to ☐Palladianism, Burlington was a notable patron of the arts and launched the career of William *Kent. He was also a competent architect, building his own villa at Chiswick (1725), and the Assembly Rooms at York (1731).

Burma, Socialist Republic of the Union of A country in SE Asia, on the Bay of Bengal and the Andaman Sea. The principal river system, that of the Irrawaddy and its main tributary, the Chindwin, forms a narrow plain running N–S, rising to the Arakan Mountains and the Chin Hills in the W and the Shan Plateau in the E. The Tenasserim Hills lie along the coast in the SE. The majority of the population, concentrated in the Irrawaddy delta, is Burmese, but there are several minorities, including the Shan, Karen, Chachin, and Chin peoples. *Economy*: priority has been given to the development of agriculture, the main crop being rice, and in 1976 plans were introduced by the government to set up cooperative farming, mainly on virgin land. Almost half the land (all of which is nationalized) is under forest and teak is a valuable export. There is some mining, especially of lead and zinc. Other industries are mainly based on food processing and all industry is now nationalized. Inland waterways provide an important means of communication. All foreign trade is carried out through government trading organizations and the main exports include rice and rice products, rubber, jute, and timber. *History*: by the 13th century the Burmese had developed a civilization based on Hinayana Buddhism. In the centuries following defeat by the Mongols in 1287, the area was under the rule of the Shans and the Mons. The rule of the Burmese Alaungpaya in the 18th century began a period of increased prosperity. After successive wars it came totally under British rule in 1885 as part of British India. In 1937 it attained a certain measure of self-government and was separated from India. In World War II it was occupied by Japanese forces, fighting first with the Japanese and later against them in support of the British. In 1948 it became a republic outside the Commonwealth. In 1962 its parliamentary democracy was overthrown in a military coup by Gen U *Ne Win. 1974 saw the end of military rule and the formation of a one-party socialist republic. Following U Ne Win's resignation in 1981 Gen San Yu (1919–   ) was elected president. Fighting on the Chinese border between government troops and communist rebels flared up in the mid-1980s. Official language: Burmese. Official currency: kyat of 100 pyas. Area: 678 000 sq km (261 789 sq mi). Population (1982 est): 35 200 000. Capital and main port: Rangoon.

Burmese A language of the Tibeto-Burman branch of the *Sino-Tibetan language family spoken by 20 million people in Burma, where it is the official language. Written in an alphabet derived from the *Pali script of India, Burmese literature dates from the 11th century AD.

Burmese cat A breed of short-haired cat originating from an Asian hybrid imported into the USA in 1933. The Burmese has a long slender body, large ears, greenish-yellow eyes, and usually a dark-brown coat. Other colours include silvery-grey (the Blue Burmese), red, and cream.

Burne-Jones, Sir Edward Coley (1833–98) Pre-Raphaelite painter and designer. After meeting *Rossetti (1856) he began his art career but only established his reputation in an exhibition in 1877. Typical of his dreamy romantic paintings, inspired by Botticelli's style, is *King Cophetua and the Beggar Maid* (Tate Gallery). More influential for the 20th century were his designs for stained glass and tapestries, often for the firm of William *Morris, for whose Kelmscott Press he also illustrated the works of Chaucer (1896).

burnet A slender perennial herb of the genera *Sanguisorba* (about 3 species) and *Poterium* (about 25 species), of N temperate regions. 500–1000 cm high, they have pinnate toothed leaves and oval heads of crimson or greenish petal-less flowers borne on long stems. The leaves are used to flavour salads and soups. Family: *Rosaceae*.

ROBERT BURNS *A portrait by Alexander Nasmyth (Scottish National Portrait Gallery).*

Burnet, Sir Frank Macfarlane (1899–1985) Australian physician, who advanced understanding of virus diseases and immunology. Burnet discovered the phenomenon of acquired immunological tolerance to foreign tissue transplants, for which he shared a Nobel Prize (1960) with Sir Peter *Medawar. He did important work in the identification of bacteria and in the culture of viruses. He received the OM in 1957.

Burnet, Gilbert (1643–1715) English bishop and historian, born in Edinburgh. He was a minister in the Church of Scotland and a professor at Glasgow University before settling in England in 1674. While abroad during James II's reign, he became a friend of William of Orange, with whom he sailed to England in 1688 and who appointed him Bishop of Salisbury in 1689. His books include *History of My Own Time* (1723–34).

Burnett, Frances Eliza Hodgson (1849–1924) British novelist. The daughter of a Manchester manufacturer, she moved to the USA in 1865. Her best-known works are the children's books *Little Lord Fauntleroy* (1885), *The Little Princess* (1905), and *The Secret Garden* (1909).

Burney, Charles (1726–1814) British musicologist, organist, and composer, best known for his *General History of Music* (1776–89).

Burney, Fanny (Mrs Frances Burney D'Arblay; 1752–1840) British novelist, daughter of the music historian Charles *Burney. After the success of her first novel, *Evelina* (1778), she became a close friend of Dr *Johnson. She held a court position under Queen Charlotte from 1786 until 1791.

In 1793 she married a French emigré, Alexandre D'Arblay. Her letters and journals provide a lively record of her period.

Burnley 53 48N 2 14W A town in N England, in Lancashire in the Calder Valley. Traditionally a cotton-weaving town (with some spinning and dyeing), there has been some diversification of industry in recent years (light engineering, chemicals). Population (1981 est): 93 779.

burns Damage to the skin caused by heat, electricity, chemicals, or radiation. In order of increasing severity, burns may cause reddening of the skin, as in sunburn (first-degree burn), blistering (second-degree burn), and finally damage to the tissues beneath the skin (third-degree burn). The extent rather than the thickness of the burn determines its effect. Both second- and third-degree burns cause fluid loss, which may be extensive enough to lead to *shock. Treatment consists of the application of wet dressings and later the administration of intravenous fluids and transfer of the patient to clean surroundings, where the burns are exposed and allowed to heal. The danger of infection can be prevented by the use of antibiotics. Skin grafting may be necessary to replace the skin destroyed by severe burns.

Burns, John Elliot (1858–1943) British socialist and trade-union leader. A member of the Amalgamated Society of Engineers, Burns was a leader of the dockers' strike in 1889. In 1892 he entered parliament and in 1905 became the first working-class cabinet minister as president of the Local Government Board. He was appointed president of the Board of Trade in 1914 but resigned on the outbreak of World War I.

Burns, Robert (1759–96) Scottish poet. Son of a poor farmer in Ayrshire, in 1783 he began writing poems in traditional styles. *Poems, Chiefly in the Scottish Dialect* (1786), published in Kilmarnock, won him immediate fame; from 1786 until 1788 he was lionized by Edinburgh society, which was little to his taste (he was a lifelong radical) or his profit. His return to farming was a failure and from 1789 he worked for the excise service. His poems range from sentimental love lyrics, often patterned on traditional songs, to broad humour, as in "Tam o'Shanter" (1788), and scathing satire, as in "The Twa Dogs" (1786) and "Holy Willie's Prayer" (1785). He collected and wrote numerous songs for inclusion in *The Scots Musical Museum* (1787–1803) and *Select Scottish Airs* (1793–1818).

Burr, Aaron (1756–1836) US statesman; Republican vice president (1801–05) after tying with Jefferson in the election of 1800. In 1804, after killing his political rival Alexander *Hamilton in a duel, Burr fled to Philadelphia and plotted to establish an empire in the West. Arrested for treason but acquitted, after further intrigues, including a scheme for Napoleon to conquer Florida, Burr gave up politics for law.

Burra, Edward (1905–76) British painter. His early watercolours were chiefly scenes of Mediterranean low life. Later, in response to the horrors of the Spanish Civil War and World War II, he began to paint sinister subjects in a realistic style. His works include *Soldiers* (1942; Tate Gallery).

Burroughs, Edgar Rice (1875–1950) US novelist. After a variety of unsuccessful jobs he gained wealth and international fame from his fantasy fiction. *Tarzan of the Apes* (1914) introduced his most famous character, an English nobleman's child, abandoned in the African jungle and reared by apes.

Burroughs, William (1914–) US novelist. He graduated from Harvard in 1936 and wandered in the USA and Europe. In 1944 he became a drug addict. *Junkie* (1953) and *The Naked Lunch* (1959) were influential novels of the *Beat movement. He lived mostly in Paris, London, and Tangiers, continuing his literary experiments in such novels as *Nova Express* (1964).

burrowing owl A long-legged ground-dwelling *owl, *Speotyto cunicularia*, of grasslands from Florida and the western USA to Argentina. 22 cm long, it nests in colonies, often in disused rodent burrows, and feeds at night on frogs, lizards, mice, and insects.

BUSHBABY *The enormous eyes and large sensitive ears of the common bushbaby make it well suited to a nocturnal existence.*

Bursa 40 12N 29 04E A town in NW Turkey. It was the capital of the Ottoman Turks for most of the 14th century and contains notable mosques and sultans' tombs and a university (1975). Population (1980): 445 113.

Burton, Sir Richard (1821–90) British explorer, diplomat, and translator. After military service in India he travelled in Arabia (entering the sacred city of Mecca in 1853 disguised as a Muslim) and Somaliland. He made two attempts (1855, 1857–58) to discover the source of the Nile and on the second, with *Speke, discovered Lake Tanganyika. The two men later quarrelled over Speke's claim to have discovered the Nile source in Lake Victoria. Burton subsequently served as consul in Fernando Po (1861), Santos (1865), Damascus (1869), and Trieste (1872), where he died. Apart from his many travel books, he published superb translations of oriental erotica, including *Kama Sutra of Vatsyayana* (1883), *The Perfumed Garden of the Cheikh Nefzaoui* (1886), and the *Arabian Nights* (16 vols, 1885–88). After his death his wife burned almost all his diaries.

Burton, Richard (Richard Jenkins; 1925–84) British actor, born in Wales. He first achieved success as a stage actor, especially in Shakespearian roles, but from the 1950s acted almost exclusively in films. These included *Look Back in Anger* (1959), *Becket* (1964), and *Who's Afraid of Virginia Woolf?* (1966). His two marriages to Elizabeth Taylor were highly publicized.

Burton, Robert (1577–1640) British scholar. He was educated at Oxford and spent his life there as a don. *The Anatomy of Melancholy* (1621, revised five times) is a vast, witty, and erudite miscellany of Jacobean knowledge on what is now called depression; it includes folklore, superstitions, and the learning of the ancient Greeks and Arabs.

Burton-upon-Trent 52 49N 1 36W A town in central England, in E Staffordshire on the River Trent. Formerly a cotton-spinning town, its main industries now are brewing, engineering, the manufacture of tyres and rubber products, and food processing. Burton's brewing tradition, aided by the calcium sulphate content of the local water, dates back to brewing by the Benedictine monks of Burton Abbey (founded 1002). Population (1981): 47 930.

Burundi, Republic of A small inland country in central Africa, bordering on Lake Tanganyika in the SW. It consists chiefly of high plateau along the main Nile-Congo dividing range, descending rapidly to the Great Rift Valley in the W. Most of the population belongs to the Hutu, a Bantu tribe, but the rulers are Tutsi and there are other tribal minorities. *Economy*: mainly subsistence agriculture; coffee is the main

export and tea is also being developed. Minerals have been found including gold, cassiterite, and nickel, and there has been considerable development in recent years, although industry still provides only a very small proportion of the revenue. *History*: the area (with present-day Rwanda) became part of German East Africa in 1890 and from 1919, as the S part of Ruanda-Urundi, it was administered by Belgium, first under League of Nations mandate and then as a UN trust territory. It became independent in 1962 and in 1964 a monetary and customs union with Rwanda was dissolved. In 1966 the hereditary Mwami Mwambutsa IV was deposed by his son, who was enthroned as Mwami Ntare V. In the same year, following a military coup, Capt (later Lt Gen) Michel Micombero (1940–83) set up a republic with himself as president. In 1972 he assumed absolute powers and fighting broke out in which thousands were killed, including the deposed king. In 1976 Micombero was overthrown in a coup and Jean-Baptiste Bagaza (1946–) became president; in 1987 Bagaza himself was overthrown in a bloodless coup and a military junta, headed by Maj Pierre Buyoya, assumed power. Official languages: French and Kirundi; Swahili is also used commercially. Official currency: Burundi franc of 100 centimes. Area: 27 834 sq km (10 759 sq mi). Population (1983): 4 561 000. Capital: Bujumbura.

Bury 53 36N 2 17N A town in NW England, in Greater Manchester on the River Irwell. A textile town concentrating on cotton spinning and weaving, the woollen and felt industries are important, as are the bleach, dye, and print works, engineering, and paper making. Population (1981): 67 529.

Buryat Autonomous Soviet Socialist Republic (*or* Buryatia) An administrative division in SE central Soviet Union, in the RSFSR. Over half its area is covered by forest. The Buryats, who comprise about 35% of the population, are traditionally nomads and speak a Mongolian language. The region is one of Siberia's most prosperous, having valuable mineral deposits, including coal, molybdenum, and gold. The main industries are mining, timber, and food processing; spring wheat and fodder crops are grown and stock breeding is also important. Area: 350 300 sq km (135 650 sq mi). Population (1983): 970 000. Capital: Ulan Ude.

burying beetle A strong beetle, also called a sexton beetle, belonging to a genus (*Necrophorus*) occurring chiefly in N temperate regions. Burying beetles are 1.5–35 mm long and many have conspicuous black and orange markings. They feed and lay their eggs on the dead bodies of small animals, which they first bury: the larvae use the same food source. Family: *Silphidae* (carrion beetles).

Bury St Edmunds 52 15N 0 43E A town in E England, in Suffolk. Its ruined abbey, which was built to house the shrine of St Edmund, last King of East Anglia (martyred in 870 AD), became a famous place of pilgrimage. Bury St Edmunds is a market town with brewing, sugar-refining and agricultural machinery industries. Population (1981): 28 914.

Busby, Matt (Sir Matthew B.; 1909–) British Association footballer, who played for Manchester City (1929–36), Liverpool (1936–39), and Scotland. He later managed Manchester United (1946–69), which under his control won the FA Cup twice and the League championship five times. He was largely responsible for rebuilding the team after the deaths of several players in an aircrash at Munich.

Bush, Alan Dudley (1900–) British composer. He studied at the Royal Academy and was appointed professor of composition there in 1925. Bush's adherence to Marxism is reflected in his operas *Wat Tyler* (1950) and *Men of Blackmoor* (1956).

Bush, George (Herbert Walker) (1924–) US statesman; Republican vice president (1981–). Ambassador to the *UN (1971–72) and chairman of the Republican National Committee (1972–73), he was director of the *CIA (1976–77) before bidding unsuccessfully for the Republican presidential nomination in 1980. He became vice president under Ronald *Reagan.

bushbaby A small nocturnal *prosimian primate belonging to the genus *Galago* (4 species), of African forests and bush. They are 27–80 cm long including the tail (15–40 cm). Common bushbabies (*G. senegalensis*) have soft dense greyish fur and a long bushy tail. They live in small groups and climb acrobatically among the trees in search of large insects; they also eat fruit and leaves. Family: *Lorisidae*.

bushbuck A small antelope, *Tragelaphus scriptus*, of tropical African bush and forest, also called harnessed antelope. 66–109 cm high at the shoulder, bushbucks are red with white spots and stripes on the flanks and legs. Males have black-tipped horns with a single spiral turn. They are shy and nocturnal, living in pairs.

bush cricket A *cricket belonging to the family *Tettigoniidae* (over 4000 species), having a green or brown body and short tail appendages (cerci). Bush crickets rarely fly or jump, but crawl among bushes and trees in fields and meadows. The swordlike ovipositor with which the female inserts eggs into plant tissues can cause considerable damage. Many species are carnivorous, usually eating small insects. □insect.

bushel A unit of capacity (dry or liquid) equal to 8 gallons or 2219.36 cubic inches in the UK and 2150.42 cubic inches in the USA.

Bushido The military and ethical code of the Japanese *samurai class. It originated in about the 13th century, although the term was not used until the 17th. Obedience to one's lord and fearlessness were its main virtues, along with austerity, honesty, and kindness. In the 13th–14th centuries it was influenced by Zen Buddhism and in the 17th–19th centuries, by Confucianism. In the mid-19th century it became the basis of Japanese emperor worship and nationalism. *See also* martial arts.

Bushire (*or* Bandar-e Bushehr) 28 59N 50 50E A town in SW Iran, on the N shore of the Persian Gulf. The port serves inland Iran but has lost trade to Abadan. Population (1976): 57 681.

Bushman. *See* Khoisan.

bushmaster A *pit viper, *Lachesis muta*, occurring in scrub and forests of Central and South America. The longest venomous snake of the New World, it reaches a length of 1.8 m and is brownish pink with dark diamond-shaped blotches. Its venom can prove fatal to man.

Bushnell, David (1742–1824) US inventor, who in 1776 built the first submarine, nicknamed the Turtle. It was intended to be a combat vessel, laying mines on the hulls of enemy ships, but it lacked the necessary manoeuvrability.

bushrangers Outlaws in the Australian outback in the late-18th and 19th centuries. They robbed farmsteads and stagecoaches, murdered, and plundered, but while some were ruthless and cruel, others shared their gains with the poor. The most famous of the Australian bushrangers is probably Ned *Kelly.

Busoni, Ferruccio (1866–1924) Italian virtuoso pianist and composer. An admirer of Liszt, he exploited the extreme possibilities of the piano in both his playing and in his transcriptions and compositions for the instrument. Among his works are a piano concerto (1903–04), the *Fantasia contrappuntistica* (for piano; 1910), and the opera *Doktor Faust* (1916–24).

Buss, Frances Mary (1827–94) English educationalist. As teacher and later headmistress at the North London Collegiate School she set new standards for girls' secondary education and campaigned for the admission of women to universities.

Bustamante y Sirvén, Antonio Sánchez de (1865–1951) Cuban lawyer. He is best known for the Bustamante Code, a system of international law regarding the security of people and property. It was ratified by the sixth Pan-American Congress in 1928.

bustard A large omnivorous bird belonging to a family (*Otididae*; 22 species) occurring in grassland regions of the Old World and having long legs adapted for running. Bustards have a long stout neck, broad wings, and a grey or brown mottled plumage, often with ornamental plumes. The great bustard (*Otis tarda*), 120 cm long and weighing 14 kg, is the largest European land bird. Order: *Gruiformes* (cranes, rails, etc.).

butadiene ($H_2C:CHHC:CH_2$) A colourless flammable gas made from *butanes and butenes. It is used in making synthetic rubbers.

butane (C_4H_{10}) A colourless flammable gaseous *alkane found in crude oil. It is used in the manufacture of synthetic rubber and, in its pressurized liquefied form, as a fuel.

butcherbird. *See* shrike.

butcher's broom A small evergreen European shrub, *Ruscus aculeatus*, up to 80 cm high. The leaves are reduced to small brown scales, but the plant has oval flattened branches that function as leaves. There are separate male and female flowers, which are small and greenish and grow on separate plants. The fruit is a red berry. Family: *Liliaceae*.

Bute A Scottish island in the Firth of Clyde, in Strathclyde Region separated from the mainland by the Kyles of Bute. Until 1975 it was within the former county of Buteshire. Agriculture consists of sheep and cattle rearing, dairy farming, and the production of oats. The island serves Glasgow as a popular holiday resort. Area: 121 sq km (47 sq mi). Population (1981): 7733. Chief town: Rothesay.

Bute, John Stuart, 3rd Earl of (1713–92) British statesman; prime minister (1762–63). A close friend of George III and extremely unpopular, he was forced to resign after securing the passage of a cider tax. He continued unofficially to influence the king until 1765.

Butler, Benjamin Franklin (1838–93) US statesman; Republican congressman (1866–75, 1877–79). Butler was hated by southerners for his military governorship of New Orleans during the Civil War. As a Radical Republican congressman, he advocated the impeachment of President Andrew *Jackson and harsh Reconstruction policies. After several attempts he became governor of Massachusetts for one year (1882) and ran unsuccessfully for the presidency on a populist ticket in 1884.

Butler, Joseph (1692–1752) English theologian. He was successively Bishop of Bristol (1738), Dean of St Paul's (1740), and Bishop of Durham (1750). He is best known for his *Analogy of Religion* (1736), defending the reasonableness of the Christian conception of the world against the popular deist teachings of the period (*see* deism).

Butler, R(ichard) A(usten), Baron (1902–82) British Conservative politician. An MP from 1929, he became minister of eduction in 1941 and was responsible for the 1944 *Education Act. He was chancellor of the exchequer from 1951 to 1955 and then Lord Privy Seal and leader of the House of Commons. He was twice defeated in the bid for the Conservative Party leadership—by Macmillan in 1957 and by Douglas-Home in 1963, under whom he was home secretary (1957–62) and then foreign secretary (1963–64). He was Master of Trinity College, Cambridge (1965–78), and was the author of *The Art of the Possible* (1971).

Butler, Reg(inald) Cotterell (1913–81) British sculptor. Butler trained as an architect and practised as an engineer (1939–50) before devoting himself to sculpture. Influenced by Henry *Moore and Alexander *Calder, he produced iron and stainless steel constructions suggestive of plant and insect forms.

Butler, Samuel (1612–80) British satirical poet. The son of a farmer, he was made steward of Ludlow Castle after the Restoration and later became secretary to George Villiers, 2nd Duke of *Buckingham. In the mock romance *Hudibras* (3 parts, 1663, 1664, 1678) he satirized the fanaticism and intellectual hypocrisy of the Puritans. The newly founded Royal Society was among the targets of his other works.

. LORD BYRON   *Portrait by Thomas Phillips (1770-1845).*

Butler, Samuel (1835–1902) British novelist. Son of a village rector and grandson of a bishop, he rejected his family, religion, and prospects, emigrating to New Zealand from 1859 to 1864, when he returned wealthy. After failing as an artist, he turned to literature and engaged in the Darwinian controversy. *Erewhon* (1872), which made him famous, satirizes Victorian utopian ideals. The autobiographical *The Way of All Flesh* (1903) recounts his painful liberation from his claustrophobic family background.

Butor, Michel (1926–) French experimental novelist and critic. He studied philosophy at the Sorbonne and has taught in Egypt, Thessalonika, Geneva, and Manchester. His novels, employing the techniques of the anti-novel (*see* nouveau roman), include *Passing Time* (1956), *Second Thoughts* (1957), *Degrees* (1960), *Mobile* (1962), and *Third Below* (1977).

Butt, Dame Clara (1873–1936) British contralto singer, noted for her deep resonant voice. Elgar wrote his song cycle *Sea Pictures* for her and she frequently sang with her husband, the baritone Kennerley Rumford (1870–1957). She was made a DBE in 1920.

butte A small steep-sided mass of rock left upstanding after the erosion of a *mesa. It usually consists of a resistant rock capping that protects the underlying rock from erosion.

buttercup An annual or perennial herbaceous plant of·the worldwide genus *Ranunculus* (about 300 species), usually with much divided leaves. The flowers are usually yellow, with spirally arranged petals and stamens. The fruit is a head of small nutlets (achenes). A common Eurasian species, widely introduced, is the perennial meadow buttercup (*R. acris*), up to 70 cm high. The genus, which is poisonous to livestock, also includes the *crowfoots. Family: *Ranunculaceae*.

Butterfield, William (1814–1900) British architect of the *gothic revival. Although predominantly a builder of churches, Butterfield is probably best known for his design of Keble College, Oxford (1870). This epitomizes his style, with the use of brick, often multicoloured and arranged in patterns, in an idiosyncratic interpretation of the gothic form.

butterflies and moths Insects belonging to the order *Lepidoptera* (about 100 000 species), distributed worldwide. The adults have two pairs of scale-covered wings, which are often highly coloured and patterned. They range in size from the smallest moths, with a wingspan of only 4 mm, to butterflies with wingspans of up to 300 mm. They all undergo a complete metamorphosis comprising a four-stage life cycle: egg, larva (*see* caterpillar), *pupa (chrysalis), and adult (imago). The caterpillars feed mainly on plants, eating leaves or boring into stems and roots, in some cases becoming serious crop pests (e.g. the cabbage white butterfly and the spruce budworm). Some species pupate by spinning silken cocoons (*see* silkworm moth). The adults are often strong fliers, seeking out a mate and migrating long distances. They feed mainly on nectar and other plant juices using a long tubular proboscis and may aid plant pollination in the process (*see* yucca moth). The forewings and hindwings of moths are locked together by a "bristle-and-catch" device (frenulum). Butterflies generally are active by day and rest with their wings held together vertically; moths, which are mainly nocturnal, generally rest with their wings flat. Another differentiating feature is the antennae, which are smooth and club-shaped in butterflies and plumed or feathery in moths. *See* Plate I.

butterfly bush. *See* Buddleia.

Buttermere, Lake A lake in NW England, in Cumbria in the Lake District. Set amid picturesque scenery, it is popular with tourists. Length: 2 km (1.25 mi).

butterwort A *carnivorous plant of the genus *Pinguicula* (about 30 species), found in the N hemisphere and South America. These perennial herbs, 12–15 cm high, have a rosette of yellow-green leaves covered with sticky glands on which insects are trapped. The single spurred funnel-shaped violet or pink flower arises on a slender stalk. Family: *Lentibulariaceae*.

button quail A small ground-dwelling bird belonging to a family (*Turnicidae*; 15 species) found in warm Old World grassland regions. Button quails are 13–19 cm long with a brown streaked plumage, short wings, and a small slender bill. The female courts the male and leaves him to incubate the eggs and tend the young. Order: *Gruiformes* (cranes, rails, etc.).

buttress A projecting mass of masonry strengthening a wall. The huge vaults of Roman and Byzantine public buildings caused buttresses to be built to counteract the outward thrust of the roof. In *gothic architecture, the graceful but highly functional **flying buttress** developed to support the upper walls of large churches.

butyl rubber A synthetic *rubber made by copolymerization of isobutylene with small amounts of *isoprene. It is less permeable to gas than natural rubbers and is used in tyre inner tubes.

Buxtehude, Dietrich (1637–1707) Danish organist and composer. He settled in Germany in 1668 as organist at the Marienkirche, Lübeck. In 1673 he started his famous *Abendmusiken* ("evening concerts"); J. S. Bach walked 200 miles to Lübeck to hear Buxtehude's music. One of the most influential of the North German school of organists, he composed much organ music and sacred music.

Buxton 53 17N 1 55W A spa and resort in N central England, in the Peak District of Derbyshire on the River Wye. Its famous mineral waters were first used by the Romans. Notable buildings include the Crescent and the Devonshire Royal Hospital. During the 1970s Buxton Opera House, built in 1903 and formerly used only as a theatre and cinema, was restored to its original condition. Population (1981): 20 797.

buzzard A *hawk belonging to a widespread genus (*Buteo*) characterized by broad wings, a large rounded tail, and a brown plumage. Buzzards hunt in open country for small mammals, reptiles, insects, and carrion and soar gracefully at great heights. The common Eurasian buzzard (*B. buteo*), 55 cm long, occurs in a number of races; the migratory rough-legged buzzard (*B. lagopus*) is distinguished by its feathered legs.

buzz bomb. *See* V-1 missile.

Byblos 34 08N 35 38E A *Phoenician city state on the E Mediterranean coast, now Jubeil (Lebanon). Egyptian records from the 14th to the 10th centuries BC attest a thriving trade with Byblos; excavations here have revealed strong cultural links with Egypt. Under Greek and Roman rule Byblos dwindled in relative commercial importance but remained famous as the centre of orgiastic worship of Astarte (*see* Aphrodite) and her lover *Adonis. *See also* Sidon; Tyre.

Bydgoszcz (German name: Bromberg) 53 16N 17 33E A city in N Poland. It is an important inland port on a canal linking the Rivers Vistula and Oder. Industries include engineering, printing, and the processing of forest products. Population (1982): 356 000.

Bylot, Robert. *See* Baffin, William.

Byng, George, Viscount Torrington (1663–1733) English admiral. An ardent supporter of William III he gained rapid promotion and in the War of the Spanish Succession captured Gibraltar (1704). He defeated the fleet of *James Edward Stuart, the Old Pretender, off Scotland (1708) and crowned his career by destroying a Spanish fleet off Messina (1717). His son **John Byng** (1704–57) was also an admiral, owing his rapid promotion to his father's influence. In 1756, however, he failed ignominiously to relieve Minorca, then under attack by the French, and retreated to Gibraltar. He was shot for failing to do his duty—or, in Voltaire's satirical view, as a warning to his colleagues ("pour encourager les autres").

Byng of Vimy, Julian, 1st Viscount (1862–1935) British field marshal. He won distinction in World War I first at *Gallipoli, then as commander of the successful Canadian troops at Vimy Ridge. After the war he was governor general of Canada (1921–26) and then commissioner of the Metropolitan Police (1928–31).

Byrd, Richard E(velyn) (1888–1957) US explorer. A naval pilot, he served in World War I and in 1926 began a series of record-breaking flights over the two Poles and the Atlantic Ocean. In 1928 he set out on the first of several expeditions to explore Antarctica from the air. In 1934–35, he spent five months alone in a hut at Bolling Advance Base, describing his experience in *Alone* (1938).

Byrd, William (?1543–1623) English composer. Despite being a Roman Catholic he retained the regard of Queen Elizabeth and was made organist of Lincoln Cathedral and subsequently of the Chapel Royal (1572). His compositions include Catholic masses and motets, Anglican services, psalm settings and anthems, pieces for the virginals (he is known as the father of keyboard music), solo songs, and music for viols. With *Tallis (his teacher) he held a music printing monopoly.

Byrd Land. *See* Marie Byrd Land.

Byron, George Gordon, Lord (1788–1824) British poet. Born with deformed ankles and a clubfoot, he grew up lacking parental affection. His first book, *Hours of Idleness* (1807), was followed in 1809 by a satire aimed at its ungenerous reviewers. After two years travelling in Europe he published *Childe Harolde's Pilgrimage* (1812) to immediate acclaim and was lionized by London society. He was bisexual and among many love affairs had an incestuous relationship with his half-sister Augusta Leigh. He married Annabella Milbanke in 1815 but she left him the following year. Byron then left England for ever. He stayed near Geneva with *Shelley and then went to Italy. In 1818 he began writing the witty verse satire *Don Juan*. In 1823 he became involved in the Greek struggle for independence and he died while training troops at Missolonghi.

Bytom (German name: Beuthen) 50 21N 18 51E A town in SW Poland. It is a major heavy-industry centre in a coal, zinc, and lead mining area. Population (1982): 238 000.

Byzantine art and architecture The painting, architecture, and decoration that developed in the ancient city of Constantinople (formerly Byzantium; modern Istanbul) after 330 AD, when it became the new Roman imperial capital, until 1453, when Constantinople fell to the Turks. Primarily religious and often symbolic or didactic, Byzantine art suppressed both realistic portrayal and opportunities for individual artistic expression. Owing to Constantinople's position as a meeting point of Asia and Europe, the bright colours and intricacy of oriental design mingle in Byzantine mosaics and *icons with Christian symbolism. Three main phases of Byzantine art succeeded one another between 330 and 1453 AD. The first phase (330–726) came to an end with the Iconoclastic controversy (726–843), which resulted in the destruction of many works of art (*see* iconoclasm). During the second golden age (843–1204) and the final phase (1204–1453) a complicated iconography of religious pictures was evolved, wherein each divine person, prophet, saint, angel, and apostle was allocated their strict position on the wall, apse, or dome of the church. This was possible because of the design of the Byzantine *basilica with its characteristic dome rising from a square base—an innovation that greatly extended the versatility of the Roman dome, which was restricted to circular buildings. The Church of Holy Wisdom (Hagia Sophia) in Constantinople, built between 532 and 537, is the outstanding example of a Byzantine basilica with a central dome (in this case buttressed by semidomes). The characteristic brickwork, pillars, and internal mosaics of Byzantine buildings also had a profound effect on western architecture from the spectacular St Mark's (11th century) in Venice to the somewhat surprising Westminster Cathedral in London in the 20th century.

Byzantium. *See* Istanbul.

C

cab A horse-drawn passenger vehicle introduced into London streets from Paris early in the 19th century. The name is an abbreviation of the French *cabriolet*, a two-wheeled carriage invented in the 17th century as a private vehicle for two people. London cabs, painted yellow, were first licensed for hire in 1823, the fare being fixed at two thirds of the *hackney-coach fare. Their popularity led to the invention in 1834 of the lighter and faster **hansom cab** by the architect Joseph Aloysius Hansom (1803–82). The name cab was extended to include the four-wheeled "growler," a descendant of the hackney coach, and both types were controlled by a series of acts, including the Hackney Carriage Act (1831) and the London Cab Act (1934). By the end of the 19th century, when taximeters were introduced to record the fare automatically, there were over 7000 hansoms and 4000 four wheelers plying the London streets. Motorized cabs, introduced in 1907 and widely known as taxis, had completely replaced the horse-drawn vehicles by 1918. The design of the modern London taxi was influenced by the Model T Ford, many characteristics of which it retains.

CAB *A 19th-century hansom cab with its characteristic elevated driver's seat at the rear.*

Cabal Five ministers of Charles II of England who dominated politics from 1667 to about 1674. They were Sir Thomas Clifford (1630–73), Lord *A*shley (later 1st Earl of *Shaftesbury), the 2nd Duke of *Buckingham, the Earl of *Arlington, and the Earl of *Lauderdale. It was not a united body: the king played one minister off against another to retain control of policy. Clifford and Arlington supported a secret pro-Catholic policy of friendship with France, which cost them their offices in 1673–74.

Caballé, Montserrat (1933–) Spanish soprano. She sang at La Scala, Milan, and in 1965 made her debut in New York. A member of the Metropolitan Opera, she specializes in bel canto roles, such as the title role in Bellini's *Norma*.

cabbage A flowering plant, *Brassica oleracea* var. *capitata*, widely cultivated as a vegetable. The short stem bears a round heart, up to 25 cm in diameter, of tightly compressed leaves. Many varieties have been developed for cooking, salads, and pickling. For example, the Savoy cabbage is a cooking variety with dark-green wrinkled leaves. All cabbages and many other brassicas—including cauliflower, broccoli, kale, and Brussels sprouts—are derived from the wild cabbage (*B. oleracea*), a perennial herb native to coastal regions of W Europe. 30–60 cm high, its straggling stem bears a spike of yellow flowers. Family: *Cruciferae*.

cabbage palm A West Indian palm tree, *Roystonea oleracea*, that may grow to a height of 30 m but is often cut when young

for its cabbage-like head of leaves, which is eaten as a vegetable. An oil and a type of sago is obtained from the fruit. The name is given to several other palms, including *Livistona australis*, of E Australia.

cabbage root fly A plant-eating fly, *Erioischia brassicae*, whose larva is a serious economic pest. The larvae feed on the roots of cabbages, radishes, etc., having developed from eggs laid around the stems. Family: *Muscidae*.

cabbage white butterfly A white butterfly belonging to the genus *Pieris*, whose caterpillars eat cabbages and related vegetables. The species are the large white (*P. brassicae*), the green-veined white (*P. napi*), and the small white (*P. rapae*).

caber tossing An event in Scottish athletics. A competitor carries the caber, a tapering tree trunk 4–5 m (13–17 ft) long, vertically in his cradled hands and then tosses it forwards. As the top end hits the ground, the other end should continue over it so that the tossed caber should lie in the direction in which it was thrown; a toss more than 90° askew is invalid. Each competitor has three tosses, followed by more if there is a tie in the number of perfect tosses. If no competitor achieves a toss, the caber is either shortened or replaced by a lighter one. The Braemar caber, which weighs 54.5 kg (120 lb) and is 5.8 m (19 ft) long, was tossed in 1951 by George Clark, after remaining untossed since 1891.

Cabimas 10 26N 71 27W A city in NW Venezuela, on the NE shore of Lake Maracaibo. It is an important centre within the Ambrosio oilfields. Population (1981 est): 162 300.

Cabinda (*or* Kabinda) A district of Angola, forming an enclave between the Congo and Zaïre on the Atlantic coast. Extensive oil deposits were discovered offshore in 1968 and led to the expansion of the chief town, Cabinda. The area also produces coffee, palm oil, timber, and cocoa. Area: 7270 sq km (2806 sq mi). Population (1970): 80 857.

cabinet A committee of the executive heads of government. In the UK the cabinet originated in the 16th-century cabinet council, a committee of the *Privy Council the growing size of which led to the monarch's reliance on a small inner group of advisers. Cabinet power was enhanced by William III's recognition that his ministers should be selected from the political group prominent in parliament and by the emergence in the 18th century of the *prime minister, who chaired cabinet meetings in the customary absence from them of George I and George II. By the end of the 19th century the principle of collective cabinet responsibility to parliament, and not to the Crown, had been established. Cabinets now consist of some 20 leading ministers, from either house of parliament, whom the prime minister has appointed to head executive departments. Cabinet meetings are secret and minutes may not be made publicly available until 30 years have elapsed. However, the principle of cabinet secrecy was undermined in 1975 by the failure of the attorney general to gain an injunction to prevent publication of the *Crossman diaries.

In the USA the cabinet comprises the heads of the 11 executive departments and the attorney general, who are not members of *Congress and are responsible only to the *president. The extent of its role depends on the extent to which the president chooses to consult it.

cable TV A system of television broadcasting in which signals are transmitted by cables instead of by radio waves. Developed in 1949 to improve reception in areas in which aerials were unsatisfactory, cable TV was first widely adopted in the USA in the 1970s with the easing of government controls and increased access to communications satellites. A commercial cable TV system in the UK was debated in the early 1980s, with limited services being installed in selected areas to test reception and wider programme choice, as well as the possibilities of interactive home banking, shopping, and information.

Cabora Bassa Dam   15 34S 33 00E A dam in Mozambique, on the Zambezi River. It is the largest dam in S Africa.

Cabot, John (Italian name: Giovanni Caboto; c. 1450–c. 1499) Italian explorer. He settled in England in about 1484 and under Henry VII's patronage discovered Cape Breton Island (which he thought to be Asia) in 1497. He set out on a second voyage in 1498 and appears to have died at sea. His son **Sebastian Cabot** (c. 1476–1557) was a cartographer to Henry VIII. In Spanish service he explored the coast of South America (1525–28).

Cabral, Pedro Álvares (?1467–1520) Portuguese navigator. In 1500, on his way to India with 13 ships, he landed in Brazil, which he claimed for Portugal. Resuming his voyage E, he landed at Mozambique, of which he later gave an interesting account, and thence reached Calicut, where he established the first commercial treaty between Portugal and India. He returned to Portugal in 1501 with only four ships.

Cabrini, St Frances Xavier (1850–1917) Italian founder of the Missionary Sisters of the Sacred Heart, known as Mother Cabrini. She sailed in 1889 to the USA and established 67 houses there and in Buenos Aires, Paris, and Madrid. She worked mainly among poor Italian immigrants and was the first US citizen to be canonized. Feast day: 13 Nov.

cacao.   See cocoa and chocolate.

Caccini, Giulio (c. 1545–c. 1618) Italian singer and composer. He developed the monodic style (a single vocal line supported by a chordal bass), which led to the earliest operas; his opera *Euridice* was performed in 1602.

Cáceres   39 29N 6 23W A market town in W Spain, in Estremadura. It produces textiles and cork. The old part of the town is surrounded by Roman and Moorish walls. Population (1981): 71 852.

cachalot.   See sperm whale.

cacomistle   An arboreal nocturnal mammal of the American genus *Bassariscus* (2 species). Cacomistles are greyish brown with small faces, long ears, and pointed snouts; the long bushy tail, patterned with black and white rings, accounts for about half the total body length (60–100 cm). They feed on small animals and fruit. The North American cacomistle, or ringtailed cat (*B. astutus*) occurs from the SW USA to S Mexico; the South American cacomistle extends from Central America to Peru. Family: *Procyonidae* (raccoons, etc.); order: *Carnivora*.

Cactoblastis.   See cactus moth.

cactus   A flowering plant belonging to the family *Cactaceae* (over 2000 species). These perennial herbs and shrubs grow chiefly in the drier regions of tropical America and the West Indies. Plant size and shape varies widely; the larger species may grow to a height of 10 m or more. Cacti show pronounced modifications to prevent water loss—their leaves or shoots are reduced to spines, they have thick waxy outer layers, and many possess succulent water-storing stems. The flowers, borne singly, are large and brightly coloured. Some genera are cultivated for their soft timber or alkaloid content, and the fruits of many species are edible (*see* prickly pear). Cacti are grown as ornamentals over the world.

cactus moth   A South American cactus-boring *pyralid moth, *Cactoblastis cactorum*, that was introduced into Australia in 1925 as a means of biologically controlling the prickly pear cactus, which had ruined large areas.

Cadbury, George (1839–1922) British businessman and Quaker, who in 1861 took over, with his brother **Richard Cadbury** (1835–99), his father's cocoa and chocolate business and established Cadbury Brothers. The Cadburys greatly improved working conditions and George founded (1894) a garden village at Bournville, near Birmingham, which influenced subsequent town planning.

caddis fly   A mothlike insect, also called sedge fly, belonging to the worldwide order *Trichoptera* (about 5000 species). Caddis flies—1.5–40 mm long, with long antennae—are found in cool damp places and feed on nectar. The omnivorous larvae (called caddis worms) live in flowing fresh water, often in portable cases constructed from sand, stones, pieces of leaf, etc.

Caddo   A North American Indian language and people of the SE USA. The Caddoan group of languages is named after the Caddo, a semisedentary agricultural people. Their villages of conical huts were built around a central temple mound. Their kinship organization was matrilineal; political and ritual affairs were conducted by a hereditary elite.

cade   A *juniper tree or shrub, *Juniperus oxycedrus*, native to Mediterranean coastal regions and growing to a height of 8 m. Also called prickly juniper, it has needles and rounded reddish berry-like fruits, 6–10 mm in diameter. Oil of cade is distilled from the wood and used in medicine.

Cade, Jack (d. 1450) English rebel, who led a Kentish rebellion in 1450 against Henry VI. The rebels, who were chiefly opposing high taxes and court corruption, demanded the recall of Richard Plantagenet, Duke of York, from Ireland. In spite of initial successes in Kent and London the rebellion was soon quelled and Cade was killed.

Cader Idris   A mountain ridge in NW Wales, in Gwynedd, in Snowdonia National Park. It rises to 892 m (2927 ft) at Pen-y-Gader.

Cádiz   36 32N 6 18W A city and seaport in SW Spain, in

CACTUS   *The giant tree cactus,* Carnegiea gigantea (*or* Cereus giganteus) *of Arizona, can reach a height of 21 m.*

Andalusia on the Gulf of Cádiz. Founded by Phoenician merchants (c. 1100 BC), it was taken from the Moors by Alfonso the Wise of Castile in 1262. Following the discovery of America it prospered as a base for the Spanish treasure fleet; the harbour was burned by Sir Francis Drake in 1587, destroying many ships. It has two cathedrals and a notable collection of works by the artist Murillo. An important port and naval base, it has tuna fisheries and shipbuilding industries. Population (1981): 157 766.

cadmium (Cd) A soft dense metal, discovered in 1817 by Friedrich Strohmeyer (1776-1835). Cadmium occurs naturally as the mineral greenockite (CdS) and in zinc, copper, and lead sulphide ores. It is chemically similar to lead and is a component of low-melting-point alloys. It is used in the control rods of nuclear reactors, in light meters, television-tube phosphors, batteries, solders, and in special low-friction alloys for bearings. Cadmium and its compounds are poisonous and care should be taken in working with solders (e.g. silver solder) that contain cadmium. Compounds include several salts, the yellow sulphide (CdS) and the oxide (CdO). At no 48; at wt 112.40; mp 320.9°C; bp 765°C.

Cadmus A legendary Greek hero. Obeying the oracle of Delphi, he followed a cow into Boeotia and founded the city of Thebes where it lay down. From the teeth of a dragon he had killed a race of fierce warriors is said to have emerged. He married Harmonia, daughter of Ares and Aphrodite, and is reputed to have introduced the alphabet into Greece from Phoenicia.

caecilian A limbless burrowing *amphibian of the order *Apoda*, or *Gymnophiona* (over 150 species), found in tropical and warm temperate regions of the world. Resembling earthworms, caecilians are 11-140 cm long and feed on termites and earthworms.

Caedmon (died c. 680 AD) English poet, known only from the account given by *Bede in his *Ecclesiastical History*. He was an illiterate herdsman who in his old age was suddenly divinely inspired to compose a hymn on the Creation. The *Hymn* is a typical example of Old English oral verse. Caedmon later entered the monastery of Whitby, where he composed many poems on biblical themes.

Caen 49 11N 0 22W A city and port in NW France, the capital of the Calvados department on the River Orne. Situated at the centre of an agricultural and horse-breeding area, Caen has iron, silk, and leather industries. Stone from nearby quarries was used to build several cathedrals and churches in England. A cultural centre, its university was established in 1432 (reorganized in 1970). It has many fine churches. *History*: captured by the English in 1346 and again in 1417, it became a Huguenot stronghold in the 17th century. Caen was badly damaged during the Normandy campaign (1944) of World War II. Population (1982 est): 117 119.

Caerleon 51 37N 2 57W A town in South Wales, in S Gwent on the River Usk. A Roman legionary fortress (called Isca) was built here (c. 75 AD) to control the British tribe of the Silures. There was accommodation for 5000 troops and an *amphitheatre, the best preserved in Britain. Before 300 the garrison was withdrawn. Caerleon is also associated with *Arthurian legend. Population (1981): 6711.

Caernarfon (English name: Caernarvon) 53 08N 4 16W A town in North Wales, the administrative centre of Gwynedd on the Menai Strait. Caernarfon is a tourist centre, market town, and small port. Its castle (built by Edward I in 1284) is the likely birthplace of Edward II, the first Prince of Wales, and was the scene of the investiture of Prince *Charles as Prince of Wales in 1969. Population (1981): 9506.

Caernarfonshire (*or* Caernarvonshire) A former county of

NW Wales. Under local government reorganization in 1974 it became part of *Gwynedd.

Caerphilly 51 35N 3 14W A market town in South Wales, in Mid Glamorgan. Situated in a coalmining area, it is best known for Caerphilly cheese (originally made here) and its castle, the largest in Wales. Population (1981): 42 736.

Caesar, (Gaius) Julius (100-44 BC) Roman general and statesman, whose career marked the end of the Roman Republic. Caesar, born of a patrician family, allied himself with the popular party by his marriage in 84 to *Cinna's daughter Cornelia. After her death in 68, he married Pompeia, whom he divorced in 62, and in 59 he married Calpurnia.

During the 60s Caesar ascended the political ladder, joining *Pompey and *Crassus in the first *Triumvirate (60) and becoming consul (59) and then governor of Gaul. Caesar's subjugation of Gaul (58-50), and his brief campaigns in Britain (55, 54), confirmed his military reputation and made him a popular hero. Crassus's death (53) and Pompey's developing association with Caesar's opponents in the Senate brought the Triumvirate to an end (50) and the Senate, with Pompey's support, asked Caesar to resign his armies. He refused and, crossing the River Rubicon into Italy (49), initiated the civil war. Caesar defeated Pompey at *Pharsalus (48) and spent the following winter in Alexandria with *Cleopatra, who became his lover. She is reputed to have had a son, Caesarion, by him. Caesar then campaigned in NE Anatolia, defeating Pharnaces II at Zela (47), the victory provoking his comment "veni, vidi, vici" ("I came, I saw, I conquered"). He went on to defeat the remnants of Pompey's party at *Thapsus (46) and Munda (45), after which he returned to Rome as dictator. There, he introduced many reforms, including the sponsorship of a revised (Julian) *calendar, but on the Ides of March (15 March, 44), Caesar was assassinated in the Senate House by republicans, including *Brutus and *Cassius, who feared his monarchical aspirations.

A distinguished prose stylist, Caesar wrote outstanding accounts of his campaigns in Gaul (*De bello gallico*) and the civil war (*De bello civili*).

Caesarea 32 30N 34 54E An ancient town in Israel, on the Mediterranean coast between Tel Aviv-Yafo and Haifa. Built by Herod the Great, it had a large early Christian community and was for a time the capital of Roman Palestine. Caesarea was twice held by the Crusaders and finally destroyed by Muslims in 1265. The Israelis have excavated many Roman remains and are developing a tourist resort here.

Caesarean section A surgical operation in which a baby is delivered through an incision made in the abdominal wall and the womb, so called because Julius Caesar was said to have been born in this way. Caesarean section is employed when a baby cannot be delivered through the vagina; for instance, because it is abnormally positioned in the womb or is too large to pass through the birth canal.

caesium (Cs) The most reactive and electropositive alkali metal. It was discovered by Bunsen and Kirchhoff in 1860 and occurs naturally in the mica lepidolite and as pollucite, $(Cs,K)AlSi_2O_6.nH_2O$. Caesium reacts explosively with water to give the hydroxide (CsOH) and is used in *caesium clocks and in photoelectric cells. Chief compounds are the nitrate ($CsNO_3$) and chloride (CsCl). At no 55; at wt 132.905; mp 28.40°C; bp 690°C.

caesium clock An *atomic clock that depends on the energy difference between two states of the caesium nucleus in a magnetic field. A nonuniform magnetic field is used to split a beam of caesium atoms into two components. Nuclei in the lower energy state are irradiated by radio-frequency radiation at the difference frequency between the two states, so that some are excited to the higher state. By reanalysing the mixture, the radio-frequency oscillator can be locked to the difference frequency of 9 192 631 770 hertz with an accuracy of one part in 10^{13}. This extremely accurate clock is now used in the definition of the *second.

Caffaggiolo maiolica An important category of Italian pottery mainly produced from about 1504 to 1540 under Medici patronage. Its main characteristic is bold bright decoration in orange, yellow, red, and green, on a cobalt-blue background. *See* maiolica.

caffeine (*or* theine; $C_8H_{10}O_2N_4$) The substance in coffee and tea that acts as a stimulant. In its pure form it is white and crystalline.

Cage, John (1912–) Avantgarde US composer, who studied with Schoenberg and Varèse. His works include *Sonatas and Interludes* (1946–48) for prepared piano (with pieces of wood, metal, etc., fixed across its strings); *Imaginary Landscape No 4* (1951) for 12 randomly tuned radio sets; *4 minutes 33 seconds* (1954), silence in three movements for any instrument(s); *Reunion* (1968); and *Apartment Building 1776* (1976). His books, including *Silence* (1961), reflect his philosophy of indeterminism.

Cagliari 39 13N 9 08E A seaport in Italy, in Sardinia. It has Roman remains, a 14th-century cathedral, and a university (1606). There are milling, tanning, and fishing industries. Lead, salt, and zinc are exported. Population (1980 est): 240 366.

Cagliostro, Alessandro, Conte di (Giuseppe Balsamo; 1743–95) Italian adventurer. His pretended skills in alchemy and magic gained him fame throughout Europe, especially in Paris. He was arrested for promoting freemasonry and died in prison in Italy.

Cagney, James (1899–1986) US actor. He began making films in the 1930s, after working as a vaudeville singer and dancer, and became famous for his portrayals of tough gangsters. His films include *Public Enemy* (1931) and *The Roaring Twenties* (1939).

Caicos Islands. *See* Turks and Caicos Islands.

Caillaux, Joseph (1863–1944) French statesman; prime minister (1911–12). He was finance minister three times before World War I and introduced direct income tax into France. In 1914 his wife shot and killed Gaston Calmette (1858–1914), the editor of *Le Figaro*, who had cast aspersions on his financial dealings while in office. An advocate of a negotiated peace during World War I, Caillaux was arrested in 1917 on a charge of dealing with the enemy. His civil rights were restored in 1925.

Cain In the Old Testament, the elder son of Adam and Eve. He became jealous of his younger brother Abel, a shepherd whose burnt offerings were accepted by God in preference to his own. He murdered Abel and was banished, marked as the world's first murderer.

Caine, Michael (Maurice Micklewhite; 1933–) British film actor. Films include *The Ipcress File* (1965), *Alfie* (1966), *Sleuth* (1973), and *Educating Rita* (1983). He won an Oscar for his performance in *Hannah and Her Sisters* (1986).

Cainozoic era. *See* Cenozoic era.

cairn. *See* barrow.

Cairngorm Mountains A mountain range in NE Scotland, in Grampian Region, forming a N extension of the Grampians. Its highest peaks include Ben Macdhui at 1309 m (4296 ft) and Braeriach at 1296 m (4252 ft). The area is popular for winter sports, centred on Aviemore.

Cairns 16 51S 145 43E A port in Australia, in NE Queensland on Trinity Bay. It is the commercial centre for an agricultural, mining, and timber region; sugar is exported. Population (1980 est): 37 100.

cairn terrier A breed of small □dog originating in the Scottish Highlands, where it was used to flush game from cover (such as stone cairns). It has a long outer coat and a short soft undercoat; the colour varies from red, sandy, or mottled grey to almost black. Height: about 25 cm.

CAIRO *The mosque of El Azhar was founded in 970 AD. It is the earliest surviving Fatimid building.*

Cairo (Arabic name: El Qahira) 80 01N 31 14E The capital of Egypt, situated in the N of the country on the E bank of the River Nile. It is the largest city in Africa and the cultural and commercial centre of Egypt. Industry has developed dramatically since the 1920s and in particular since the revolution of 1952, with traditional textile manufacturing and food processing retaining importance alongside newer industries, such as metallurgy and plastics. Its many mosques include the Mosque of Omar (643 AD), Cairo's earliest remaining Arabic building, and the Mohammed Ali Mosque, housed in the 12th-century citadel. The Mosque and University of El Azhar was founded in 970 AD; three other universities were established in the 20th century. *History*: the Arabic city of El Fustat was founded in 641 AD, and from the 9th century, as El Qahira, it was successively the capital of the Fatimid, Ayyubite, and Mameluke dynasties. It was under the Mamelukes that the city enjoyed the period of its greatest prosperity. Following its conquest by the Turks in the 16th century, it declined in power, but in the 19th century its prosperity was restored under Mehemet *Ali and his successors. During World War II it was the seat of the Allied headquarters in the Middle East. Population (1980): 5 650 000. *See also* Giza, El.

caisson A large cylindrical or box-shaped structure sunk into the ground during excavation work. Caissons aid construction of underwater foundations, for example in the construction of piers for bridges, and may become part of the permanent structure.

caisson disease. *See* decompression sickness.

Caithness A former county of NE Scotland. Under local government reorganization in 1975 its boundaries were adjusted to form a district of the same name, in the Highlands Region.

cakewalk A ballroom dance popular in the early 1900s, originally performed by Black slaves satirizing the elegance of plantation society. Couples walked round in a square, being judged for the grace and inventiveness of their movements. The winners were awarded a cake, whence the expression "to take the cake."

Calabar (former name: Old Calabar) 4 56N 8 22E A port in SE Nigeria. It was a centre of the slave trade in the 18th and 19th centuries; exports now include palm oil, rubber, timber, and cocoa. Population (1983 est): 126 000.

calabash A tree, *Crescentia cujete*, 7.5–15 m tall, native to tropical America (particularly Brazil). Funnel-shaped flowers are borne on the old stems and produce gourdlike fruits, up to 50 cm long. These fruits have woody outer layers and, after removal of the inner pulp, are used as pots, cooking utensils, etc. Family: *Bignoniaceae*.

Calabria A mountainous region occupying the southern "toe" of Italy. It is basically a poor agricultural region (producing olives, citrus fruits, vines, and cereals) with the lowest per capita income of any Italian region. Crotone is the main industrial centre. Area: 15 080 sq km (5822 sq mi). Population (1980 est): 2 087 231. Capital: Catanzaro.

Calais 50 57N 1 52E A port in N France, in the Pas-de-Calais department. Its prosperity lies in being on the shortest sea route to England. It produces lace, tulle, and other textiles. *History*: besieged and captured by the English under Edward III in 1346 (commemorated in Rodin's statue *The Burghers of Calais*), Calais remained in English hands until 1558. In World War I it was a British base; in World War II it was the target of savage bombardment and was heroically defended in support of the withdrawal from *Dunkirk. Population (1982 est): 76 935.

calamine An ore of zinc. In English usage it refers to zinc carbonate (smithsonite) and in the USA it refers to zinc silicate (hemimorphite). A skin lotion of the same name contains zinc oxide.

Calamites An extinct genus of treelike pteridophyte plants, prominent during the Carboniferous period, 345–280 million years ago. Their fossilized remains form a major constituent of the Carboniferous coal seams (*see also* Lepidodendron). Class: *Sphenopsida* (*see* horsetails).

Calamity Jane (Martha Canary; c. 1852–1903) US frontierswoman, who featured in many stories and legends of the Wild West. She worked in frontier towns and camps, frequently dressed as a man, and was skilled in riding and shooting. She later appeared in Wild West Shows.

Calas, Jean (1698–1762) French Huguenot, who was accused of the murder of his son in 1761 in order to prevent his becoming a Roman Catholic. He protested his innocence but was tried and executed. His conviction was reversed after *Voltaire, at the request of his widow, led a campaign for religious toleration and legal reform.

Calceolaria A genus of perennial herbs and shrubs (300–400 species) native to temperate South America. The plants grow to a height of 30–70 cm and bear brightly coloured slipper-shaped flowers. Some species and hybrids are grown as ornamentals. Family: *Scrophulariaceae*.

Calchas A legendary Greek prophet who foretold the length of the *Trojan War and advised the Greeks to build the wooden horse by which they gained entry to Troy. He died after being defeated by Mopsus in a trial of prophecy.

calcite A common rock-forming mineral consisting of crystalline calcium carbonate. It is usually colourless or white. It occurs in igneous, metamorphic, and sedimentary rocks. Most *limestones consist largely of calcite, sometimes in the form of fossil shells, and calcite is a common cementing material in coarse-grained sedimentary rocks. Calcite is very soluble in slightly acidic water.

calcitonin A polypeptide hormone, secreted by the thyroid gland in mammals, that reduces the level of calcium in the blood when this rises above normal. A hormone from the *parathyroid gland raises blood calcium levels and therefore acts antagonistically.

calcium (Ca) A reactive metal, first isolated by Sir Humphry Davy in 1808. It occurs in nature as *limestone ($CaCO_3$), *fluorite (CaF_2), and *gypsum ($CaSO_4.2H_2O$) and is an essential constituent of shells, bones, and teeth. The element is extracted by electrolysis of the molten chloride ($CaCl_2$). It forms many compounds. These include quicklime (CaO), which has many industrial uses as a base in addition to its role in *cement, the nitrate ($Ca(NO_3)_2$), chloride ($CaCl_2$), and carbide (CaC_2), from which acetylene is produced by the addition of water. The metal is reactive. It is used to clear residual gases from vacuum systems and as a reducing agent in the production of uranium. At no 20; at wt 40.08; mp $839 \pm 2°C$; bp $1484°C$.

calculator Any device for carrying out mathematical functions ($+, -, \times, \div$). Originally mechanical, they were later electrically operated; purely electronic calculators, based on the digital *computer, have now replaced all others. Electronic calculators use a silicon chip *integrated-circuit package, often smaller than a 2p piece, that contains the equivalent of hundreds of *transistors built into complex logic circuits, which perform the basic functions using binary arithmetic (*see* binary system). Multiplication and division are performed by repeated additions or subtractions. The high speed of a modern calculator enables the solution to a problem to appear on the digital display apparently instantaneously. Many electronic calculators have more complex functions available (percentages, square roots, trigonometric functions, etc.) by pressing a single key and some provide a memory in which the intermediate results of a chain of calculations can be stored. Advanced types enable the user to program a sequence of functions for the calculator to perform automatically.

calculus The mathematical techniques, developed by *Newton and *Leibniz, based on the concept of infinitely small changes in continuously varying quantities. For example, calculus is used to define the velocity of a moving body as the rate of change of its position at any instant. Velocity (v) is said to be the derivative of position (x) with respect to time (t); in calculus it is written $v = dx/dt$. In this notation dt is a vanishingly small time interval and dx is the distance the body travels in this time. If x is a known function of t, values for v at any time can be obtained by calculating the derivative of (differentiating) this function with respect to time. Similarly, the derivative of the velocity (or the second derivative of position) at any instant gives its acceleration (a), i.e. $d^2x/dt^2 = dv/dt = a$. The **differential calculus** is the system of rules for making such calculations. On a graph, the derivative of a function is the gradient of the curve at any point. A maximum or minimum value of the function can be found, as they occur when the gradient is zero. The **integral calculus** is concerned with the same process in reverse. If velocity is a continuously varying function of time, the change in position over a measurable time interval is calculated by summing the products of v and dt for each of the infinitely small intervals of time (dt) that make up the interval. The extraction of integrals follows general rules, each type of function having a corresponding integral. The integral of v between time t_1 and t_2, written

$$\int_{t_1}^{t_2} v.dt,$$

gives the change in position in this interval. On a graph, the area between the curve of a function and the horizontal axis is the integral of the function over the specified interval.

Equations that contain derivatives are called **differential equations**. They are solved by guessing at a general form of solution and trying it in the equation, using the rules of differential calculus.

Calcutta 22 35N 88 21E A city in India, the capital of West Bengal on the River Hooghly. It is a major industrial centre and the most important seaport on the E coast India. Jute manufacturing, engineering, cotton textiles, and chemicals are important. Calcutta is the focal point of rail, road, and air routes and its port is a major outlet for iron, coal, manganese, mica, and jute goods. The city is part of a conurbation that has a combined population of over nine million, many of whom live in appalling conditions; less than one-third of the conurbation is sewered, water supplies are inadequate, and many thousands sleep on the streets. By way of contrast, the city centre contains many imposing buildings, situated around Fort William (a British building dating from 1758). There are three universities, in-

Gregorian calendar	Hebrew calendar	Islamic calendar	Chinese calendar	
solar year of 365.2425 days	lunar year The year 5750 starts on Sept 18 1990	lunar year The year 1410 starts on Jan 1 1990	lunar and solar cycles; 24 fortnightly periods	
January (31 d)	Shevat (30 d) (Jan/Feb)	Muharran (30 d)	Xiao Han Da Han	Jan Jan/Feb.
February (28 d; 29 days in leap year)	Adar (29 d) (Feb/Mar)	Safar (29 d)	Li Chun Yu Shui	Feb Feb/Mar
March (31 d)	Nisan (30 d) (Mar/Apr)	Rabi'I (30 d)	Jing Zhe Chun Fen	Mar Mar/Apr
April (30 d)	Iyar (29 d) (Apr/May)	Rabi'II (29 d)	Qing Ming Gu Yu	Apr Apr/May
May (31 d)	Sivan (30 d) (May/June)	Jumādā I (30 d)	Li Xia Xiao Man	May May/June
June (30 d)	Tammuz (29 d) (June/July)	Jamādā II (29 d)	Mang Zhong Xia Zhi	June June/July
July (31 d)	Av (30 d) (July/Aug)	Rajab (30 d)	Xiao Shu Da Shu	July July/Aug
August (31 d)	Elul (29 d) (Aug/Sept)	Sha'ban (29 d)	Li Qiu Chu Shu	Aug Aug/Sept
September (30 d)	Tishri (30 d) (Sept/Oct)	Ramadān (30 d)	Bai Lu Qui Fen	Sept Sept/Oct
October (31 d)	Heshvan (29 or 30 d) (Oct/Nov)	Shawwāl (29 d)	Han Lu Shuang Jiang	Oct Oct/Nov
November (30 d)	Kislev (29 or 30 d) (Nov/Dec)	Dhūal-Qa'dah (30 d)	Li Dong Xiao Xue	Nov Nov/Dec
December (31 d)	Tevet (29 d) (Dec/Jan)	Dhūal-Hijjah (20 or 30 d)	Da Xue Dong Zhi	Dec Dec/Jan

CALENDAR *Four calendars still in use*

cluding Calcutta University (1857). *History*: founded in 1692 as a trading post for the British East India Company, it was the scene of fighting (1756–57) between the British under Clive and the forces of Siraj-ud-Dawlah, Nawab of Bengal (*see* Black Hole of Calcutta). Population (1981 est): 9 165 650.

Calder, Alexander (1898–) US sculptor, who invented the mobile. Calder trained as an engineer and worked as a commercial artist before producing his first mobiles in Paris (c. 1931). Originally motorized, the abstract shapes of these flat metal discs suspended from wires were chiefly influenced by the painter *Miró. Calder later turned to monumental free-standing constructions.

caldera. *See* volcano.

Calderón de la Barca, Pedro (1600–81) Spanish dramatist. He studied law and theology but rejected a career in the Church; in 1623 he began writing plays at the court of Philip IV. After the death of *Lope de Vega he became the leading Spanish dramatist. His many plays include *The Constant Prince* (1629), *Life Is a Dream* (1635), and *The Mayor of Zalamea* (1640). He was ordained in 1651, after which he wrote mainly masques, operas, and religious dramas.

Caldy (Welsh name: Ynys Byr) 51 38N 4 42W A Welsh island, off the Dyfed coast. Historically a religious retreat, it has been the property of a Cistercian community since 1929.

Caledonia The name given by ancient Roman writers to Scotland. Remote and rugged, Caledonia was scarcely known in antiquity. The Roman governor in Britain, Gnaeus Julius Agricola, in an exploratory expedition defeated the Caledonians in 83 AD near present-day Inverness, as did the emperor Lucius Septimius Severus in 209, but the clans and their chieftains remained independent until united under Kenneth I MacAlpine in the 9th century.

Caledonian Canal A system of lochs and canals in Scotland, linking the North Sea with the Irish Sea, via the Great Glen.

Engineered by Thomas Telford, it was opened to navigation in 1822. Today it is used mainly by small craft. Length: about 100 km (60 mi).

Caledonian orogeny. *See* orogeny.

calendar Any of a variety of systems for the reckoning of time over an extended period. Calendars are usually based on the earth's orbital period around the sun (a year), although in some systems the moon's orbital period around the earth (a month) is taken as the basis. Since the seasons recur after each tropical *year (which contains 365.2422 days), the length of the calendar year, averaged over many years, should correspond as closely as possible to that of the tropical year. This is achieved by using leap years, which contain one more day than the usual calendar year.

In 46 BC, Julius Caesar established the so-called **Julian calendar** in which a period of three years, each of 365 days, was followed by a leap year of 366 days. The average length of the year was therefore 365.25 days. Since this was over 11 minutes longer than the tropical year, an extra day appeared about every 128 years. This discrepancy was amended by the **Gregorian calendar**, which was introduced in Roman Catholic countries in 1582 by Pope Gregory XIII, was made law in Britain and its colonies in 1752, and is now in almost worldwide use. Leap years are restricted to century years divisible by 400 (e.g. 1600 and 2000) and any other year divisible by four. This reduces the average length of the calendar year to a much more acceptable 365.2425 days. *See also* French Republican calendar.

Calgary 51 05N 114 05W A city in W Canada, in Alberta. It developed with the arrival of the railway (1884) and local oil discoveries, becoming the centre of Canada's petroleum industry. Calgary is the distribution and farming centre of S Alberta and is the site of the University of Calgary (1945). The Calgary Stampede, a famous rodeo, is celebrated annually. Population (1984): 619 000.

Calhoun, John C(aldwell) (1782-1850) US statesman; vice president (1824-32), a champion of the southern states and a defender of slavery. His famous Nullification theory claimed the rights of states to nullify congressional laws that they considered unconstitutional. He encouraged the annexation of Texas to provide another slaveholding state and to strengthen the power of the South.

Cali 3 24N 76 30W The third largest city in Colombia. It is the industrial and commercial centre for a rich agricultural area producing coffee, sugar, and cotton. Its university was founded in 1945. Population (1981 est): 967 908.

calico A simple woven cotton fabric that originated as a printed fabric from Calicut, India. Strong and serviceable with a wide range of textures, it is used mainly for dresses and domestic purposes. British calico is now usually bleached or plain white; US calico is generally printed.

Calicut. *See* Kozhikode.

California The third largest state in the USA, on the W coast. It consists of a narrow coastal plain rising to the Coast Range, with the fertile central valleys of the Sacramento and San Joaquin Rivers, deserts in the S, and the Sierra Nevada Mountains in the E. It is the most populous state in the USA and the predominantly urban population is concentrated along the coast. It is the most prosperous state and has a varied economy. Oil is exploited along with natural gas, cement, sand and gravel, and borate. Aircraft and ship construction are important industries, as well as general construction and food processing; wine production is especially important. Employment is also provided by the many military bases and the film industry. Tourism is important in the many national parks throughout the state. California's agriculture is famous and the state produces grapes, tomatoes, cotton, sugar beet, strawberries, citrus fruits, hay, beef cattle, and turkeys. The state has a large number of cultural and educational institutions, many supported by public finance like the University of California. *History*: first discovered by the Spanish (1542) it remained under their control until it was ceded to the USA (1848). In the same year gold was discovered, leading to a rapid increase in the number of immigrants. California became a state in 1850. Area: 411 013 sq km (158 693 sq mi). Population (1980): 23 668 562. Capital: Sacramento.

California, Gulf of An inlet of the Pacific Ocean, in Mexico between the state of Sonora and the peninsula of Lower California. Length: 1223 km (760 mi).

californium (Cf) A synthetic transuranic element first isolated in 1950. Californium-252 is an intense neutron emitter. It is used as a neutron source in instruments for determining moisture contents and discovering precious metals. At no 98; at wt (251).

Caligula (Gaius Caesar; 12-41 AD) Roman emperor (37-41), son of Germanicus Caesar and Agrippina the Elder. Succeeding Tiberius, he initially enjoyed great popularity but his subsequent tyrannical and extravagant behaviour brought allegations of madness, from both contemporaries and historians, and he was assassinated.

caliph The title borne by the leaders of Islam. The first caliph was *Abu Bakr, who succeeded Mohammed in 632. The *Umayyads ruled from 661 to 750 and were overthrown by the *Abbasids, who ruled in Baghdad until 1258 and then in Egypt, until ousted by the Ottomans in 1517. The title was then borne by the Ottoman sultans until 1922 and was abolished in 1924. Rival Muslim dynasties, such as the Egyptian *Fatimids (909-1171), also claimed the title.

calisaya. *See* Cinchona.

calisthenics. *See* gymnastics.

calla. *See* arum.

Callaghan, (Leonard) James, Baron (1912–) British statesman; Labour prime minister (1976-79). Born in Portsmouth, he served in the Royal Navy throughout World War II, entering parliament in 1945. He was chancellor of the ex-chequer (1964-67), resigning in protest against Harold *Wilson's devaluation of the pound, and then home secretary (1967-70) and foreign secretary (1974-76). He became prime minister when Wilson resigned and was defeated in the 1979 election by Margaret *Thatcher, but remained leader of the Labour Party, until 1980.

Callao 12 05S 77 08W A major port in W Peru, on the Pacific Ocean. It was the site of the first railway in South America (1851) connecting Callao with Lima. Chief exports include minerals, metals, and fishmeal. Population (1981): 443 413.

Callas, Maria (Maria Anna Kalageropoulos; 1923-77) US-born soprano of Greek parentage. She possessed a brilliant coloratura voice and fine acting ability. From 1950 she was prima donna of La Scala, Milan, where she was famous for her interpretations of Bellini, Donizetti, Verdi, and Puccini.

Calles, Plutarco Elías (1877-1945) Mexican soldier in the post-1910 revolutionary movement and statesman. As president (1924-28) his anticlerical policies caused the rebellion of the Church's supporters (the *cristeros*) and his attempts to control oil rights brought conflict with the USA. He wielded dictatorial power from 1928 to 1934, when he was succeeded by Lázaro *Cárdenas, who forced Calles into exile in 1936.

Callias (5th century BC) Athenian diplomat. He may have negotiated the so-called peace of Callias with Persia (c. 450), which established Persian and Athenian spheres of influence. He probably also helped negotiate the Thirty Years' Peace with Sparta (c. 446).

Callicrates (5th century BC) Athenian architect, chiefly famous for his collaboration with *Ictinus over the design of the *Parthenon. The temple of Athena Nike (450 BC) on the Athenian Acropolis was also his work.

calligraphy The art of handwriting. The term derives from the Greek words meaning beautiful writing. The aim of the calligrapher is to produce a script of intrinsic beauty appropriate to the subject matter, using the type of paper, ink, and writing instrument most suited to his purpose. In Europe, monks practised calligraphy from the 6th century, at first using Roman capital letters called majuscules, but scripts using *minuscules were soon developed. From these arose the beautiful *italic and 19th-century copperplate scripts suitable for formal and commercial documents. In England calligraphy was revived in the 20th century by Edward Johnston (1872-1944). In China, Japan, and Islamic countries calligraphy has a long history as a pure art form in which the artist combines the medium, the sentiment, and the format into an artistic composition.

Callimachus (c. 305-c. 240 BC) Greek poet and scholar. His many works, of which only fragments remain, include a catalogue of the Library of Alexandria, some fine epigrams, of which 64 survive in the *Greek Anthology* and the *Aetia*.

Callimachus (late 5th century BC) Greek sculptor, reputedly the inventor of the Corinthian *capital and an innovator in the use of the drill in sculpture. Little is known of his work, but ancient critics accused him of overelaboration.

Calliope In Greek legend, goddess of epic poetry and the chief of the nine *Muses. She was loved by Apollo; her children included Hymen, Ialemus, and *Orpheus.

Callisto. *See* Galilean satellites.

Callot, Jacques (c. 1592-1635) French graphic artist, born in Nancy. In Italy (c. 1609-21) he worked for the Medici, principally on etchings of pageants. After returning to Nancy he made many etchings of beggars, hunchbacks, etc., which show his gift for caricature, but his best work is the *Miseries of War* series (1632-33) evoked by the Thirty Years' War.

callus A region of thickened hardened skin produced by constant friction or pressure. Skin calluses occur most commonly on the palms of the hands and soles of the feet. A bone callus is the mass of tissue that forms around the broken ends of a fractured bone, enabling normal healing and union. A similar tissue is produced by plants at the site of an injury.

Calmette, Albert Léon Charles (1863–1933) French bacteriologist. A pupil of Louis *Pasteur, he developed the vaccine Bacillus Calmette-Guérin (see BCG vaccine) in conjunction with Camille Guérin. He founded the Pasteur Institute at Lille, France (1896).

calomel. See laxatives.

calorie A unit of heat now being replaced by the joule. Formerly defined as the amount of heat required to raise the temperature of 1 gram of water through 1°C, the calorie is now defined as 4.1868 joules. The kilocalorie or Calorie (with a capital "C") is equal to 1000 calories and was formerly used to express the energy value of foods.

Caltanissetta 37 29N 14 04E A town in Italy, in Sicily. It has a 17th-century cathedral. It has an important sulphur industry. Population (1981 est): 60 713.

Calvary A hill beyond the walls of Jerusalem where Christ was crucified. The Hebrew name is Golgotha (a skull). Its precise location is unknown. Traditionally it has been taken as the spot, now within the Church of the Holy Sepulchre, where St Helena discovered a supposed relic of the Cross in 327 AD. Some have suggested that it was outside Jerusalem's Damascus Gate.

Calvin, John (1509–64) French Protestant reformer, founder of *Calvinism. He studied law and theology and in the early 1530s openly sided with Protestantism. Settling in Basle in 1536, he published the first edition of his influential Institutes. During a visit to Geneva in 1536 he met the Protestant reformer, Guillaume *Farel, who persuaded him to stay. Their efforts to organize the Reformation in the city resulted in their exile (1538). Calvin then preached in Strasbourg, where he met other reformers, notably *Bucer. He was invited back to Geneva in 1541, remaining there as its virtual dictator until his death. He sought to shape Geneva as a model community where every citizen came under the legal discipline of the Church.

Calvin, Melvin (1911–) US biochemist, who determined the series of reactions by which green plants use carbon dioxide to manufacture starch during *photosynthesis. Calvin was awarded a Nobel Prize in 1961.

Calvinism The Christian teaching of John *Calvin, much of it published in his work The Institutes. On it are based the doctrines of most of the reformed Churches that are not Lutheran, including the state Churches of Holland and Scotland (see Presbyterianism), various Nonconformist Churches, and some Churches in North America and Germany. Calvin's systematic writings stress the transcendent power of God and man's total depravity outside God's redeeming grace. Like Luther, Calvin believed that faith must be based on Scripture alone, that justification (that is, righteousness in God's eyes) could only be achieved through faith, and that men lacked free will. Unlike Luther, he believed that some people, the elect, were predestined for salvation and the rest for damnation and also that the church should control the state.

calx. See phlogiston theory.

calypso A type of popular song that originated in Trinidad. The text, often containing nonsense syllables, is sung rapidly and without regard for natural word stress. Accompanied by guitars and percussion, the calypso usually satirizes local events. Calypso melodies have been popularized by steel bands playing on tuned oil drums.

calypso orchid A rare and highly prized perennial orchid, Calypso bulbosa, also known as the fairy slipper orchid, native to cold N temperate regions. 8–10 cm high, it has a solitary pink flower with brown, purple, and yellow markings and a single crinkled dark-green leaf.

Camagüey 21 25N 77 55W A city in E central Cuba. Founded in the 16th century, it has many old buildings, including the cathedral (1617). It is the centre of an area important for cattle raising and sugar. Population (1981): 480 620.

Camargue, la The Rhône delta area in S France, between the river channels of the Grand Rhône and the Petit Rhône. Once chiefly marshy, much land reclamation has occurred and cattle, especially bulls for the bullring, and horses are reared. Rice is also grown here. Area: about 560 sq km (215 sq mi).

Cambacérès, Jean Jacques Régis, Duc de (1753–1824) French lawyer. During the French Revolution he was a member of the National Convention and then of the Committee of Public Safety. Under Napoleon, he served as arch chancellor of the empire. His chief interest was in the development of principles of revolutionary jurisprudence and he contributed to the *Code Napoléon.

Camberwell beauty A *nymphalid butterfly, Nymphalis antiopa, occurring in temperate Eurasia and in North America, where it is called mourning cloak because of its sombre coloration: purple wings with cream edges. The adults hibernate and the caterpillars feed on various trees.

cambium A layer of cells in woody plants that is responsible for producing additional *xylem and *phloem tissue, bringing about an increase in girth. The cambium also produces bark and protective callus tissue after injury. See also meristem.

Cambodia. See Kampuchea, Democratic.

Camborne-Redruth 50 12N 5 19W A town in SW England in Cornwall. It is a tinmining centre with a School of Metalliferous Mining. Population (1981): 46 482.

Cambrai (ancient name: Camaracum) 50 10N 3 14E A town in NE France, in the Nord department. Industries include textiles (cambric was first made here in the 16th century) and sugar refining. The town suffered damage in both World Wars. Population (1982 est): 36 618.

Cambrian Mountains A mountain system in Wales, extending N–S and including Snowdonia, Plynlimon, and the Black Mountains.

Cambrian period The earliest geological period of the *Palaeozoic era. It began about 590 million years ago and lasted at least 70 million years, lying between the Precambrian and Ordovician periods. Rocks of this period are the first to contain an abundance of fossils, including primitive representatives of most invertebrates living today. Trilobites were very abundant, as well as brachiopods and gastropods. The Cambrian period is divided into Lower, Middle, and Upper.

Cambridge 52 12N 0 07E A city in E England, the administrative centre of Cambridgeshire on the River Cam (or Granta), a tributary of the Great Ouse. The city is dominated by its university (see Cambridge, University of). Cambridge has electronics and printing industries and manufactures scientific instruments. It is also an important market centre for East Anglia. Its many historic university buildings, its famous Backs (lawns sloping down to the river), and Bridge of Sighs make it a popular tourist centre. Population (1981): 90 440.

Cambridge 42 22N 71 06W A city in the USA, in Massachusetts on the Charles River opposite Boston. A famous educational centre, it is the site of Harvard University (1636) and the Massachusetts Institute of Technology (MIT). The first printing press in America was set up here (1639) and at the start of the American Revolution, George Washington established his headquarters (1775–76) in Craigie House, later the home of Longfellow. Industries include printing and publishing. Population (1980): 95 322.

Cambridge, University of One of the oldest universities in Europe. It is organized as a federation of colleges (see Oxford, University of), the oldest of which, Peterhouse, dates from 1284. Kings College was founded in 1441 and its chapel (built 1446-1515 in the perpendicular gothic style) is a distinctive landmark. The largest college, Trinity, was founded by Henry VIII in 1546. Written examinations were first introduced in 1772, and in the 19th century other reforms were made in an attempt to improve academic standards. The first college for women, Girton, opened in 1869 (although it was not initially located at Cambridge); many of the colleges now take students of both sexes. In 1981-82 there were 11 663 men and women students and 1213 staff.

Cambridge Platonists A group of 17th-century English philosophers and theologians under the leadership of Benjamin Whichcote (1609-83). Philosophically they took their ideas from *Platonism and *Neoplatonism and opposed the rationalism of *Hobbes. In religion they favoured mysticism and religious tolerance and attempted to reconcile Christianity with the new ideas being produced by the rapid scientific advances made in their time. They believed in an absolute standard of morality based on reason that is independent of the divine will of God.

Cambridgeshire A county of E England. Since 1974 it has included the former counties of Huntingdon and Peterborough, Cambridgeshire and the *Isle of Ely (combined in 1965), as well as parts of W Suffolk. It consists chiefly of low-lying fenland, crossed by the Rivers Ouse and Nene. It is predominantly agricultural, the main products being cereals, fruit, and vegetables. Area: 3409 sq km (1316 sq mi). Population (1983): 606 000. Administrative centre: Cambridge.

Cambyses II King of Persia (529-522 BC) of the Achaemenian dynasty; the son of *Cyrus the Great. He conquered Egypt (525), where, according to the Greek historian, Herodotus, his tyrannical disrespect for native religion caused resentment. He campaigned unsuccessfully against Carthage and Ethiopia. Cambyses died, perhaps a suicide, during a revolt against his rule.

Camden A borough of NW Greater London, created in 1965 from the former metropolitan boroughs of *Hampstead, Holborn, and St Pancras. Population (1981): 171 563.

Camden 39 52N 75 07W A city in the USA, in New Jersey on the Delaware River. The former home of Walt Whitman, it manufactures textiles and radio and television appliances. Population (1980): 84 910.

Camden, Battle of (16 August, 1780) A battle of the *American Revolution. In an attempt to take the British stronghold at Camden, South Carolina, after the fall of *Charleston, the Americans were surprised and routed by Lord *Cornwallis. The Americans lost almost all their small regular force and their inexperienced militia fled in disarray.

Camden, William (1551-1623) English historian and antiquarian. A dedicated scholar, he wrote *Britannia* (published in Latin 1586; English translation 1610), which was a landmark in the topographical study of Britain. He taught at Westminster School (1575-97) and endowed a chair of ancient history at Oxford (1622). The Camden Society (founded 1838) for the promotion of historical publications is named after him.

Camden Town group An association of London painters founded in 1911 by *Sickert and his circle, including Spencer Gore (1878-1914), Harold Gilman (1876-1919), and Charles Ginner (1879-1952). A breakaway group from the *New English Art Club, its members specialized in contemporary London scenes, particularly theatre and café scenes and dully lit and depressing domestic interiors. They were largely responsible for introducing *postimpressionism into the UK. In 1913 the Camden Town group became part of the London group, an amalgam of several art societies.

camel A hoofed □mammal belonging to the genus *Camelus* (2 species). Camels are now almost entirely domesticated and are used for riding, as pack animals, and as a source of milk, meat, wool, and hides. The one-humped Arabian camel (*C. dromedarius*) is about 2 m high at the shoulder and generally brown in colour. The dromedary is a long-legged breed of Arabian camel, developed for racing and riding. The heavier two-humped Bactrian camel (*C. bactrianus*) is native to central Asian steppes, where wild herds still exist. Adapted to living in sandy deserts, camels can close their nostrils, have heavy protective eyelashes, hairy ear openings, and horny knee pads for kneeling. Although unable to store water, camels can replace rapidly the water that is lost from the body, drinking up to 60 litres of water at a time. Fat is stored in the hump, which shrinks when food is scarce. Family: *Camelidae*; order: *Artiodactyla*.

Camellia A genus of evergreen shrubs and trees (80-100 species) native to India, China, and Japan. Several species are widely grown as ornamentals. The best known, *C. japonica*, grows to a height of 9 m and has attractive glossy oval leaves. The popular double-flowered varieties have overlapping petals ranging from white to pink and red. The genus also includes the *tea plant. Family: *Theaceae*.

CAMELOT *A 19th-century romantic rendering of Arthur's capital by Gustave Doré in his illustrations of Tennyson's* Idylls.

Camelot The legendary capital of King Arthur's kingdom (*see* Arthurian legend). Cadbury Camp, near Yeovil, and Winchester are among the places identified with it.

Camembert 48 52N 0 10E A village in NW France, in the Orme department. Camembert is famous for the creamy cheese named after it.

cameo A semiprecious stone ornamented with a portrait or figures carved in relief. Cameo makers achieved brilliant skills during the Renaissance, when collectors paid high prices for modern gems, as well as for the earliest Hellenistic and Roman examples.

camera, photographic A device for producing a photographic image. Basically, a camera consists of a light-tight box containing a lens and light-sensitive *film or plate. The light image coming through the lens is brought into focus on the film by adjusting the distance between the film and the lens. A picture is taken by opening the shutter over the lens for a certain period to expose the film. The exposure time is determined by the shutter speed. The diameter of the opening (aperture) in front of the lens is measured by its *f-number. Shutter speed and lens aperture determine the light available to record the image on the film. In the simplest cameras they are fixed, but more sophisticated cameras have variable settings. Sometimes the aperture or the shutter speed can be controlled automatically by an *exposure meter. *See also* cinematography.

camera, television A camera for the instantaneous transmission of *television pictures. The scene to be televised is focused onto a screen in the electronic camera tube. This optical image is scanned in horizontal lines, fast enough to appear as a continuous moving picture to the human eye; in most cameras, the image is scanned 25 to 30 times per second. The intensity of light at each point of the image is converted to an electrical signal, which is amplified before being transmitted together with the sound and synchronization signals.

Cameron, (Mark) James (Walter) (1911–85) British journalist, author, and broadcaster. He probably won more awards than any other international reporter. His books included *Witness in Vietnam* (1966) and *Point of Departure* (1967), and his radio play *The Pump* (1973) won the Prix Italia.

Cameron, Julia Margaret (1815–79) British photographer, born in Calcutta. In England, she devoted herself chiefly to spiritually penetrating portrait photographs, notably of her friends Tennyson, Longfellow, Charles Darwin, and Ellen Terry. She died in Ceylon.

Cameroon, United Republic of (French name: République Unie du Cameroun) A country in West Africa, on the Gulf of Guinea. Hot swampy coastal plains rise to forested plateaus in the centre and to the Adamwa Highlands in the N. The main river is the Sanaga. The population consists of over a hundred different ethnic groups, the most numerous being the Bamileke. *Economy*: chiefly subsistence agriculture; the main cash crop is coffee. Aluminium smelting is the chief industry. Oil was discovered in 1973 and provides half the country's revenue. *History*: the area was largely uninhabited when the coast was explored by the Portuguese and others in the 15th and 16th centuries. In 1884 the German protectorate of Kamerun was established and after World War I it was divided into the French and British Cameroons, which were governed from 1922 under League of Nations mandate and from 1946 as UN trust territories. The French Cameroons attained self-government in 1957 and became independent as the Federal Republic of the Cameroon in 1960 with Ahmadou Ahidjo (1924–) as president (1960–82). After a plebiscite in the British Cameroons in 1961, the N joined Nigeria and the S joined Cameroon, declared a united republic in 1972. The country is now governed on a one-party basis by the Cameroon National Union. In 1986 a cloud of toxic gas from a volcanic lake claimed 1534 lives. President: Paul Biya (1933–). Official languages: French and English. Official currency: CFA (Communauté financière africaine) franc of 100 centimes. Area: 475 442 sq km (183 530 sq mi). Population (1986 est): 10 000 000. Capital: Yaoundé. Main port: Doula.

Camisards Protestants in the Bas-Languedoc and Cévennes regions of S France who in 1702 rebelled against persecution by Louis XIV. They sacked and burned churches and killed or expelled priests. The government responded with executions and the burning of villages. By 1705 the revolt was over, although sporadic unrest continued until 1710.

Camões, Luís de (c. 1524–80) Portuguese poet and soldier of fortune. After 1553 he spent 17 years wandering in the Portuguese colonies in India and China, suffering shipwreck and returning destitute to Lisbon. In 1572 he published *The Lusiads*, a national epic celebrating the 1497 voyage of Vasco da Gama and the Portuguese empire. His lyrical poetry, largely ignored in his own lifetime and published posthumously in 1595, is now greatly admired.

camomile (*or* chamomile) A perennial scented European herb, *Anthemis nobilis* (or *Chamaemelum nobile*). The spreading much-branched stems (10–30 cm in length) carry long-stalked daisy-like flowers. An infusion of the flowers (camo-

mile tea) is used as a general tonic. Family: *Compositae.*

Camorra A criminal secret society, at its height in 19th-century Naples. The Bourbon kings used its members in the police, army, and civil service but after Naples became part of a united Italy (1861) the society was suppressed and its members fled to the USA, where they joined the *Mafia.

Campaign for Nuclear Disarmament (CND) An organization formed in 1958 to campaign for Britain's nuclear disarmament. In the late 1950s and early 1960s, led by Canon John Collins (1905–82) and Bertrand *Russell, it organized large demonstrations, including the Aldermaston marches. It revived in the early 1980s amid new fears of nuclear war. General secretary: Meg Beresford.

Campagna di Roma A plain in W central Italy, surrounding Rome. Well populated and fertile during classical times, it subsequently deteriorated into malarial marshes. Recently drained, it now produces fruit and vegetables for Rome. Area: about 2000 sq km (800 sq mi).

Campanella, Tommaso (1568–1639) Italian philosopher and Dominican friar. He opposed *Aristotelianism, believing that the foundations of philosophy should be empirical. From 1599 to 1629 he was imprisoned by the Spaniards ostensibly for political reasons but probably because of his religious heterodoxy. After 1634 he lived under *Richelieu's protection in Paris. His *City of the Sun* (1623) describes a Platonic-Christian utopia (*see* utopianism).

Campania A region in S Italy. It consists of a coastal plain along the Tyrrhenian Sea and mountains in the interior and the Sorrento Peninsula. The region produces fruits, vines, olives, and grains. An industrial belt stretches from Caserta along the Bay of Naples. There are many modern coastal resorts. Area: 13 595 sq km (5249 sq mi). Population (1980 est): 5 491 658. Capital: Naples.

Campanula A genus of annual and perennial herbaceous plants (about 300 species), often known as bellflowers, native to N temperate zones (particularly the Mediterranean region) and tropical mountains. 15–120 cm high, they bear spikes of blue, pink, or white bell-shaped flowers. The fruit is a capsule. Some species (including *Canterbury bell) are grown as ornamentals. Family: *Campanulaceae.*

Campbell, Colin, Baron Clyde (1792–1863) British field marshal. Campbell had a varied career, serving outstandingly in the *Peninsular War against Napoleon, the second Sikh War (1848–49), and the *Crimean War; as commander in chief in India he suppressed the *Indian Mutiny (1858).

Campbell, Sir Malcolm (1885–1949) British motor engineer, who broke the land-speed record nine times between 1924 and 1935 and the water-speed record three times between 1937 and 1939. He was the first man to exceed 483 km per hour (300 mph; 1935). His son **Donald Malcolm Campbell** (1921–67) also set land- and water-speed records, including 648.7 km per hour (403.1 mph) for a wheel-driven car at Lake Eyre (1964). He was killed in an attempt to break his own water-speed record on Coniston Water. The speed at which he crashed, 527.9 km per hour (328 mph), is still the unofficial record. His daughter **Gina Campbell** (1948–) broke the women's water-speed record in 1984. □p. 218.

Campbell, Mrs Patrick (Beatrice Stella Tanner; 1865–1940) British actress. Her stage successes included plays by Shakespeare and Ibsen. Famed for her wit as well as her passionate acting, she created the role of Eliza Doolittle in *Pygmalion* by her friend George Bernard Shaw.

Campbell, Roy (Dunnachie) (1901–57) South African poet. His active life, mostly in France, Spain, and Portugal, is flamboyantly chronicled in *Light on a Dark Horse* (1951). The energetic style of his first book, *The Flaming Terrapin* (1924), is characteristic of all his work, which includes satires, romantic lyrics, and translations.

Campbell, Thomas (1777–1844) British poet, remembered

primarily for "The Pleasures of Hope" (1799), a conventional quasi-philosophic poem in the manner of Alexander *Pope, and patriotic poems, such as "Hohenlinden."

Campbell-Bannerman, Sir Henry (1836–1908) British statesman; Liberal prime minister (1905–08), whose personal popularity held together a cabinet of great talent, including *Lloyd George, *Asquith, *Churchill, and *Haldane. Campbell-Bannerman's government granted the Transvaal and Orange River Colony responsible government and passed the Trades Disputes Act (1906), which gave trades unionists greater freedom to strike. Resigning shortly before his death, he left his successor Asquith a strong and united Liberal Party.

DONALD CAMPBELL   *At Coniston Water (1966) with his sand-bagged boat. Both father and son used the name* Bluebird *for their record-breaking cars and boats.*

Camp David   The retreat in the Appalachian Mountains, Maryland, of the president of the USA. It was here that Anwar Sadat and Menachem Begin agreed in September, 1978, to a framework for establishing peace in the Middle East. This agreement, mediated by President Jimmy Carter, laid the foundations for the peace treaty between Israel and Egypt signed in March, 1979.

Campeche   19 50N 90 30W A port in SE Mexico, on the Gulf of Mexico. Founded in 1540, its importance as a port has declined since Spanish occupation and the shallow waters hinder further development. The chief exports include timber, fish, and sugar cane and it has a university (1954). Population (1980): 151 805.

Camperdown   A village in the NW Netherlands, in North Holland province, on the North Sea. The British defeated the Dutch in a naval battle off the coast here (1797).

camphor ($C_{10}H_{16}O$)   A colourless crystalline *ketone. It is obtained from the wood of the camphor tree and also made synthetically; it is used in the manufacture of celluloid and as an insect repellent.

camphor tree   A tree, *Cinnamomum camphora*, native to China, Japan, and Formosa. It is cultivated for the *camphor that can be distilled from its wood and young shoots. Family: *Lauraceae*.

Campi, Giulio   (1502–72) Italian Renaissance architect and the founder of the Cremonese school of painting, which was influenced by such painters as Titian and Correggio. His followers included his brothers **Vincenzo Campi** (1539–91) and

Antonio Campi (1536–c. 1591).

Campina Grande   7 15S 35 53W A city in NE Brazil, in Paraíba state. It is an important commercial and industrial centre and has a university (1966). Population (1980 est): 265 600.

Campinas   22 54S 47 06W A city in S Brazil, in São Paulo state. It is a trading centre for coffee and serves an extensive agricultural area. Population (1980 est): 566 517.

campion   An annual or perennial flowering plant of the genus *Silene*. Campions are native to N temperate (particularly the Mediterranean) and cold regions, grow to a .height of 30–100 cm, and bear pink, red, or white flowers. The fruit is a capsule. Species include moss campion (*S. acaulis*) and bladder campion (*S. vulgaris*). Family: *Caryophyllaceae*.

Campion, Edmund   (1540–81) English Jesuit martyr. He was educated at St John's College, Oxford, and ordained an Anglican deacon, but was uneasy about his commitment and, leaving England first for Dublin and then Douai, was received into the Roman Catholic Church (1571). He became a Jesuit and returned to England in 1580 as a secret missionary. After distributing copies of an anti-Anglican pamphlet in Oxford in 1581, he was arrested, tortured, convicted of treason, and hanged, refusing to deny his faith. He was beatified in 1886. Feast Day: 1 Dec.

Campion, Thomas   (*or* Campian; 1567–1620) English composer, poet, and physician. He composed songs with lute accompaniment, publishing several collections in conjunction with his friend Philip Rosseter (1568–1623), masques, and theoretical works on composing and on the art of writing poetry.

Campo Formio, Treaty of   (1797) The settlement between France and Austria signed at present-day Campoformido, NE Italy, following Austria's defeat by Napoleon during his first Italian campaign. Austria gained Venice, thus ending Venetian independence, and ceded its Belgian provinces to France.

Campo Grande   20 24S 54 35W A city in SW Brazil, the capital of Mato Grosso do Sul state situated on the São Paulo-Corumbá railway. Its university was founded in 1970. Population (1980 est): 282 844.

Campos   21 40S 41 21W A city in E Brazil, in Rio de Janeiro state. The chief products are cacao, sugar cane, and *aguardiente* (a form of brandy). Population (1980 est): 356 600.

Cam Ranh Bay   11 53N 109 10E An inlet of the South China Sea, on the coast of central S Vietnam. About 20 km (12 mi) wide and almost enclosed by two peninsulas, it makes an excellent harbour: the bay and the northern peninsula were used as a vast US military, naval, and air base during the Vietnam War.

camshaft   A rotating shaft equipped with a series of eccentric circular or pear-shaped discs (cams). These enable irregular or intermittent motion to be transferred to "followers" set perpendicularly to the camshaft, which move up and down as the cams rotate. Camshafts thus convert rotary motion into reciprocating motion and are used to control the valves in a four-stroke *internal-combustion engine. An **overhead camshaft** is set in the cylinder head and operates the valves directly, but in many engines the camshaft is at the base of the engine and operates the valves through pushrods.

Camus, Albert   (1913–60) French novelist, an exponent of *existentialism. Born in poverty in Algiers, he won a school scholarship and studied philosophy at university. During World War II he edited *Combat*, a journal of the French Resistance. He published several collections of essays and plays, and three novels, notably *The Outsider* (1942), *The Plague* (1947), and *The Rebel* (1953); *The Rebel* provoked a fierce intellectual controversy with Jean-Paul *Sartre. In 1957 he won the Nobel Prize. He was killed in a car accident.

Canaan   An area roughly corresponding to modern Israel, W Jordan, and S Syria, known from the Bible as the land promised by God to the Israelites before the Exodus. As early as the 18th century BC Canaan was mentioned in a document from *Mari as a political entity, probably comprising loosely allied city states. Excavations at *Jericho, Hazor, and elsewhere have revealed sophisticated Bronze Age cultures prior to the Hebrew settlement (c. 1200 BC).

Canada, Dominion of A country occupying the entire northern half of the North American continent (except for Alaska). More than half of Canada consists of the Canadian Shield, at the centre of which lies the Hudson Bay lowlands. The Western Cordillera, which is partly made up of the Coast Mountains and the Rocky Mountains, runs parallel to the Pacific coast and contains Mount *Logan, Canada's highest peak. Between the Rocky Mountains and the Canadian Shield lie the Interior Lowlands (consisting of prairies, plains, and the Mackenzie Lowlands). The SE region of Canada is dominated by the St Lawrence River and the *Great Lakes and is the most densely populated area in the country. The N end of the Appalachian Mountains lies in the extreme SE. The N Arctic region of lakes and islands is one of the world's least populated areas. The population is mainly of British and French descent but there are several substantial minorities, including Germans, Italians, Ukrainians, and Dutch as well as the original inhabitants, the Indians and Eskimos. *Economy*: both agriculture and industry are highly developed and the numerous manufacturing industries (concentrated mainly in Ontario and Quebec) include paper, iron and steel, motor vehicles, and food processing. As well as iron ore, the rich mineral resources include asbestos, nickel, zinc, molybdenum, uranium, silver, and gold. Oil production has increased considerably since the discovery of large oilfields in Alberta and an extensive pipeline system includes the Interprovincial Pipeline from Edmonton (Alberta) to Port Credit (Ontario) and the Trans-Mountain pipeline from Edmonton to Vancouver. Natural gas is also produced and the Trans-Canada pipeline from the prairies to Montreal is the longest in the world. Agriculture, most of it highly mechanized, is important, with cereals in the Prairie Provinces and considerable fruit growing in British Columbia and Ontario. There is a valuable fishing industry; salmon, lobster, and cod are the most important catches. Forests cover over a third of the land and forestry has long been important to Canada's economy. The other traditional industry, the fur trade, continues, especially with mink farms and the trapping of beaver in the wild. Tourism is an important source of revenue, the majority of visitors coming from the USA, with whom Canada has very close links. Almost two-thirds of its trade is with the USA. Main exports include motor vehicles, oil, wheat, wood pulp, and paper. *History*: there is evidence of Viking settlement in the NE of Canada around 1000 AD. In 1497 John Cabot reached the coasts of Newfoundland and Nova Scotia, the first of which was claimed for England in 1583. In 1534 Jacques Cartier explored the Gulf of St Lawrence and in 1608 Champlain established the first permanent settlement at Quebec. Known as New France, this settlement became a royal province in 1663. In the course of his explorations Champlain supported the *Huron Indians in their alliance with the northern tribes against the *Iroquois and later in the 17th century, when the Iroquois defeated the Huron, the French colony was almost completely destroyed. The fur trade was of extreme importance to all settlers and in 1670 the English set up the Hudson's Bay Company. By 1696 the French and English were in open conflict: in 1713 the Treaty of Utrecht gave *Acadia, Newfoundland, and Hudson Bay to Britain and after the Seven Years' War, during which Gen Wolfe defeated the French under Gen Montcalm (1759), Canada was ceded to Britain by the Treaty of Paris (1763). In the late 18th century the United Empire Loyalists, fleeing from the American Revolution, settled in Canada. The ensuing racial tension led to the division of Quebec into French-speaking Lower Canada and English-speaking Upper Canada (1791), which were reunited again in 1841. By the British North America Act (1867) a confederation of Lower Canada (Quebec), Upper Canada (Ontario), Nova Scotia, and New Brunswick was established. In 1869 Rupert's Land was bought from the Hudson's Bay Company and the province of Manitoba was created from it in the following year. In 1871 British Columbia and in 1873 Prince Edward Island joined the confederation. Alberta and Saskatchewan were created from the NW Territories in 1905. Canada's position as an independent constitutional monarchy in the British Commonwealth was defined by the Statute of Westminster in 1931. It played an important part in both World Wars. The main political problem in recent years has been French-Canadian separatist agitation, led by the Quebec Liberation Front (Parti québecois).The Liberal Party, which had held office for 36 out of the previous 43 years (the last 11 under the leadership of Pierre *Trudeau), was ousted from power in May, 1979, by the Progressive Conservatives under Joseph Clark. In the elections of February, 1980, the Liberal Party under Trudeau was again returned to power. In 1982 a new constitution for Canada was signed by Elizabeth II. In 1984 Trudeau retired and the Progressive Conservatives under Brian Mulroney won the ensuing general election. Official languages: English and French. Official currency: Canadian dollar of 100 cents. Area: 9 976 169 sq km (3 851 809 sq mi). Population (1981 est): 24 200 000. Capital: Ottawa. Main port: Montreal.

Canada balsam A transparent resin obtained from fir trees. It is used as an adhesive in optical instruments because its refractive index is similar to that of glass.

CANADA GOOSE   *These birds pair for life and both male and female may incubate the eggs and care for the young.*

Canada goose A large *goose, *Branta canadensis*, that breeds in Canada and Alaska, migrating in flocks to the southern USA for the winter. It is 60–100 cm long and has a black head and neck, white throat, dark-brown back, and pale underparts. The Canada goose has been introduced to parts of Europe as a sporting bird.

Canadian railways Canada has two great transcontinental systems: the Canadian Pacific Limited (CP Rail) and the Canadian National Railway (CN). The CP, running from

Halifax on the Atlantic Ocean to Vancouver on the Pacific Ocean was the first to be completed in 1885.

Canadian River A river in the S central USA, flowing generally E from NE New Mexico to the Arkansas River in Oklahoma. Length: 1458 km (906 mi).

Canadian Shield. *See* shield.

Canaletto (Antonio Canal; 1697-1768) Venetian painter, famous for his views of Venice. He trained under his father, a theatrical-scenery painter, before visiting Rome (1719-20), where he designed opera sets. His popularity with English collectors led to a stay in England (1746-55), where he painted views of London. His early work, painted in the open air, was considerably freer than his later much more architectural painting, for which he used mechanical drawing instruments.

canals Man-made open water channels. They are divided into two categories: conveyance canals and navigation canals. The former carry water for irrigation, power, or drainage; the latter, to facilitate transportation, often connect two natural waterways. Canals have been dug from ancient times. The Grand Canal in China, started in 109 BC, was 1000 km (620 mi) long by the 8th century and carried 1.8 million tonnes of freight per annum. Some modern ship canals achieve spectacular reductions in voyage distances, especially the *Suez Canal (completed in 1869) and the *Panama Canal (1914). Others of considerable local importance include the Corinth Canal (1893), the Kiel Canal (1895), and the St Lawrence Seaway (1959) connecting the Great Lakes. In canal construction, the availability of water is the primary concern. Conveyance canals are often narrow, have a high water velocity, and are earth lined and consequently are subject to erosion. Barge or ship canals are often completely lined with concrete or have concrete edges to prevent wave erosion. Variations in land or water level are common and *locks must be installed to conserve water and allow for the passage of vessels.

canary A small songbird, *Serinus canarius*, native to the Canary Islands, Madeira, and the Azores. Wild canaries have an olive-green plumage with yellow to grey underparts streaked with black. Popular as cagebirds since the 15th century, they have been selectively bred both for their musical song and attractive plumage—usually pure yellow but sometimes white or striped and occasionally with ornamental plumes. Subfamily: *Carduelinae*; family: *Fringillidae* (finches).

canary grass An annual grass, *Phalaris canariensis*, 20-60 cm high, native to the Canary Islands and N Africa and cultivated commercially in Europe for birdseed. The related reed canary grass (*P. arundinaceae*), which is widely distributed, is an important forage grass and grows 61-183 cm high.

Canary Islands (Spanish name: Islas Canarias) A group of Spanish islands in the Atlantic Ocean, close to NW Africa. Since 1927 they have constituted two provinces named after their capitals of Las Palmas (including the islands of Fuerteventura, Gran Canaria, and Lanzarote) and Santa Cruz de Tenerife (including the islands of Ferro, Gomera, La Palma, and *Tenerife). The islands became Spanish possessions in the 15th century; the earliest inhabitants, the Guanches, are now extinct. The islands are of volcanic formation and, with the help of irrigation, fruit such as bananas and tomatoes are grown for export. Tourism is also a major source of revenue. Total area: 7270 sq km (2807 sq mi). Population (1981): 1 444 626.

canasta. *See* rummy games.

Canaveral, Cape (name from 1963 until 1973: Cape Kennedy) A barrier island in the USA, in E central Florida separated from the mainland by lagoons. It is the site of operations by NASA at the Kennedy Space Center. The first flight to land on the moon was launched here in 1969. In 1973 Skylab, the first orbiting laboratory, was launched from here.

Canberra 35 15S 149 10E The capital of Australia, in the Australian Capital Territory on the Molonglo River. As a result of a competition in 1911, it was planned by the American architect Walter Burley Griffin, as the new federal capital, being formally inaugurated in 1927. The establishment of the National University in 1946 and the growth of government departments have led to sizeable increases in population. Population (1980 est): 245 500.

cancan A boisterous dance originally performed in Parisian dance halls around 1830 as a solo or by groups of women. Tourists flocked to see its spectacular and indecorous high kicking. Famous cancan music includes the galop from Offenbach's *Orpheus in the Underworld*.

cancer A group of diseases caused by the abnormal and uncontrolled division of cells to form tumours that invade and destroy the tissues in which they arise. Such tumours are described as malignant: their cells spread through the bloodstream or lymphatic system or across body cavities to set up secondary tumours at other sites in the body (this spread is called metastasis). The cause of cancer remains uncertain, although it is known that exposure to certain substances (*see* carcinogen) will produce it. Cancer can arise in almost any tissue: in the western world the breasts, colon, lungs, bronchi, prostate gland, and stomach are common sites. Carcinomas are cancers arising in *epithelium; less common but more malignant are sarcomas—cancers of connective tissue (bone, cartilage, muscle, etc.). *Leukaemia is a form of sarcoma affecting the bone marrow and other blood-forming tissues. Treatment, which varies with the type of cancer, includes *cytotoxic drugs, radiotherapy, and surgery.

Cancer (Latin: Crab) An inconspicuous constellation in the N sky, lying on the *zodiac between Leo and Gemini. It contains the star cluster *Praesepe.

candela (cd) The *SI unit of luminous intensity equal to the intensity of 1/600 000 square metre of the surface of a black body maintained at the freezing point of platinum.

Candela, Felix (1910-) Mexican architect and engineer, born in Spain. Employing a naturalistic modern style, his work is characterized by use of thin, prestressed concrete roofs, often spanning large distances, e.g. the Church of the Miraculous Virgin, Mexico City (1953).

Candia. *See* Iráklion.

Candida A genus of yeastlike fungi. They are typically spherical, ovoid, or elongated cells that reproduce by budding and spore formation; they do not undergo sexual reproduction. Several species, especially *C. albicans*, cause *candidiasis. Family: *Cryptococcaceae*; class: *Blastomycetes*.

candidiasis An infection caused by a species of yeast (*Candida albicans*). Popularly known as thrush, it affects the mouth and vagina most frequently; it may develop after treatment with certain antibiotics and with diseases (e.g. leukaemia) and drugs (e.g. steroids) that reduce the natural immunity of the body. The infection is cleared readily by such fungicides as nystatin.

Candlemas The Christian feast of the Purification of the Virgin Mary and the Presentation of Christ in the Temple (Luke 2.22-38), which is observed on 2 Feb. It is so called because of the distribution of candles, symbolizing Christ's appearance as the "light of the world."

candytuft An annual or perennial flowering plant of the genus *Iberis* (about 30 species), native to S Europe and Asia and growing well in dry chalky soils. The stems (up to 15-50 cm in height) bear white, pink, red, or blue flowers in flat-topped clusters. The fruits are pods containing winged seeds. Some species are grown as garden plants. Family: *Cruciferae*.

cane The stem of certain large grasses and of some palms. In some species it is hollow and jointed, e.g. *reeds (*Phragmites species), *bamboo (*Bambusa* species), and *sugar cane; in others it is solid, e.g. *rattan and Malacca (*Calamus* species) used for making furniture, walking sticks, etc.

Canea (Greek name: Khaniá) 35 31N 24 01E The capital of Crete, on the Gulf of Khaniá. Founded by Venetians in 1252, it is surrounded by massive Venetian walls. The island's main port with an important coastal trade, it exports leather, olives, olive oil, and fruit. Population (1981): 47 804.

cane rat An African *rodent belonging to the genus *Thryonomys* (2 species) common in reed beds. About 40 cm long, cane rats have bright-orange incisor teeth, feeding on reeds, roots, bulbs, grasses, and sugar cane and can become a pest in plantations. Family: *Thryonomyidae*.

Canidae The dog family: a family of mammals belonging to the order *Carnivora*. It includes the dogs, wolves, jackals, coyote, and foxes.

Canis Major (Latin: Great Dog) A conspicuous constellation in the S sky near Orion. The brightest stars are *Sirius, the *giants Adhara and Mirzam, and the *supergiant Wezen.

Canis Minor (Latin: Little Dog) A small constellation in the S sky, lying near Canis Major and Orion. The brightest star is *Procyon.

canker 1. A disease of plants, especially fruit trees, caused by various fungi and bacteria. Cankers can be seen as dead, discoloured, irregular, or cracked areas on the stem and branches; mechanical or climatic injury and attack by insect pests often predispose to infection. Treatment is by removal of the diseased parts. 2. A chronic disease of horses' hooves, caused by continually wet conditions underfoot. The affected hooves become soft and swollen and eventually infected, causing inflammation and discharge. Treatment is by removing affected tissue and dressing with antibiotics. Prevention is by ensuring a dry stable floor. 3. Inflammation of the outer ear affecting dogs, cats, and rabbits and causing irritation and itching. Treatment is by application of an antiseptic lotion or powder.

canna A genus of ornamental herbaceous plants (about 155 species), native to tropical and subtropical America. Up to 3 m high, they have spirally arranged leaves, which may be green, bronze, or purple, and terminal clusters of showy flowers, 15 cm across and ranging from pale yellow to scarlet. Cannas are grown widely as bedding plants. Family: *Cannaceae*.

cannabis The resin (hashish) or crushed leaves and flowers (marihuana, "grass," or "pot") obtained from certain species of *hemp. The drug is eaten or inhaled and produces a variety of effects on the mind. These include euphoria, distortion of time sense, and increased awareness of sight, sound, and memory. Occasionally feelings of anxiety and apprehension are experienced. The long-term effects of cannabis use are obscure but may affect memory. Cannabis can cause dependence, progression to "hard" drugs, and loss of the will to work. *See also* drug dependence; hallucinogen.

Cannae, Battle of (216 BC) The battle, fought at the village of Cannae in Apulia (SE Italy), in which *Hannibal and the Carthaginians killed almost 50 000 Romans. It is the worst Roman defeat on record.

Cannes 43 33N 7 00E A resort in S France, in the Alpes-Maritimes department on the French Riviera. Its development as a fashionable resort dates from 1834, when the British statesman Lord Brougham (1778-1868) built a villa here. It has numerous hotels, sports facilities, boulevards, and casinos; an annual film festival is held here. The Île St Honorat contains the oldest monastery in W Europe. There are aircraft and textile industries and fruit and flowers are grown. Population (1982 est): 72 787.

cannibalism The practice of eating human flesh, either as food or for ritual or magical purposes. Extreme hunger has prompted modern occurrences among concentration-camp prisoners and aircrash survivors. In ritual cannibalism certain parts of a defeated enemy may be eaten in order to absorb his strength and courage or to prevent his spirit taking revenge. In other cases (endocannibalism) it forms part of rituals performed at the death of a kinsman. The word is derived from the *Arawak term for the *Carib Indians among whom it was common. Ritual cannibalism was practised also by the New Zealand Maoris, the Fijian islanders, in Polynesia, in parts of Africa, in New Guinea, and among some North American Indian peoples.

canning The preservation of meat, fish, or fruit in vacuum-sealed airtight metal containers, which have been sterilized by heating followed by rapid cooling. Fruit keeps safely for at least one year, meat and vegetables for two, although in practice they may stay fresh for much longer, especially if kept cool. Canning was introduced in the 18th century and originally used pure *tin cans. Now cans are made of *tinplate. Canned foods may be reheated but do not need further cooking. *See also* food preservation.

Canning, George (1770-1827) British statesman; foreign secretary (1807-09, 1822-27) and Tory prime minister (1827). An MP from 1793, he held office under Pitt and contributed (1797-98) to the weekly *Anti-Jacobin*, which opposed the French Revolution. He became foreign secretary in 1807 but resigned in 1809 in opposition to the management of the Napoleonic Wars by the secretary for war, Castlereagh. Castlereagh challenged Canning to a duel in which Canning was slightly hurt. He again became foreign secretary after Castlereagh's suicide and was responsible, with Huskisson, for the liberalization of Tory policies in the 1820s. He supported the revolt of Spain's American Colonies (1823) and the War of *Greek Independence (1825-27), before briefly becoming prime minister. His son **Charles John, Earl Canning** (1812-62) was governor general of India (1856-62), where he became known as Clemency Canning because of his mild handling of the Indian Mutiny.

Canning Basin (former name: Desert Artesian Basin) An arid and largely unexplored sedimentary basin of NW Western Australia. It forms part of the *Great Sandy Desert and is covered chiefly by active longitudinal sand dunes. Area: about 400 000 sq km (150 000 sq mi).

Cannizzaro, Stanislao (1826-1910) Italian chemist, who resurrected *Avogadro's hypothesis, which had been neglected for 50 years, and used it to clarify the problem of representing compounds by formulas. He also discovered a method, called Cannizzaro's reaction, of converting an aldehyde into an acid and an alcohol.

Cannock 52 42N 2 01W A town in W central England, in Staffordshire. Cannock is a commuter town for the West Midlands conurbation; local industries include coalmining, brick making, and light industries. To the E lies **Cannock Chase**, a wooded plateau that was once a royal hunting ground. It is designated an area of outstanding natural beauty and is a recreational area for the West Midland towns. Population (1981): 59 235.

cannon An early form of *artillery firearm used primarily until 1670 as a siege gun. A 14th-century invention (by the German monk, Berthold Schwarz), early cannon were made of wrought-iron rods welded together, covered in lead, and wrapped with iron bands. Some had a removable breech. Cast guns were made in England after 1500. They fired stones, cast-iron and wrought-iron balls. Modern cannons include *guns, *mortars, and *howitzers.

Cannon, Walter Bradford (1871-1945) US physiologist, who pioneered the use of X-rays in physiological studies. By administering a suspension, or meal, of radio-opaque bismuth, the intestine could be revealed on X-rays. Cannon also investigated the body's reaction to stress, particularly the role of the sympathetic nervous system, and he identified an adrenaline-like chemical transmitter secreted by sympathetic nerve endings, which he termed "sympathin."

Cano, Juan Sebastián del (c. 1460-1526) Spanish navigator. He accompanied Magellan's expedition, taking command after Magellan's death. He successfully completed the voyage—the first round the world—in 1522. He died on a second expedition.

canoe A double-ended vessel designed mainly for propulsion by paddles, although certain kinds are equipped with sails (sailing canoe). The modern canoe is, typically, about 3-7 m (10-20 ft) long, and they are usually single or two seaters although Canadian canoes can accommodate up to four people. It is made of waterproofed canvas stretched over a ribbed frame or of aluminium, wood, or fibreglass. The modern canoe is modelled on native craft that have been in use in the Americas and in the Pacific for thousands of years. Some Pacific native war canoes, equipped with outriggers, could accommodate as many as 40 people. Other large canoes served, until the 20th century, as the chief means of transport among the islands of the Pacific. Depending on their age and provenance, native canoes were made by hollowing out logs or by stretching animal skins or birchbark over a ribbed frame. Canoes are much favoured for sport on lakes and rivers, being easy to manoeuvre and readily portable. *See also* kayak.

canonization In the Christian Church, the conferring of the status of *saint on a dead person. In the Roman Catholic Church this is done by a formal declaration of the pope after a long investigation of the person's suitability. Beatification, by which the Church permits the veneration of a person, with the title "Blessed," within a particular diocese, order, or other limited area, precedes canonization and depends on evidence of the person's exceptional virtue and authentic miracles. The Church then puts the case for the canonization and appoints someone, the *Promotor Fidei* (Latin: promoter of the faith, popularly known as the devil's advocate), to oppose it, and completes the process after proof of further miracles. In the early days of Christianity each area recognized its own saints, who were usually local martyrs. Ulrich of Augsburg (c. 890-973) is the first person known to have been canonized by a pope (in 993 AD). About 1170 Pope Alexander III decreed that only the Roman Catholic Church could add new names to the list of saints.

canon law The laws of Christian Churches, particularly the Roman Catholic, Anglican, and Orthodox Churches. They include regulations governing the clergy, the ecclesiastical courts, matters of worship and doctrine, and so on. The origins of canon law lie in the decrees of the various councils of bishops in the early Church, in authoritative pronouncements of important bishops, and in the Decretals, or letters having the force of law, of the Popes. In the 12th century many laws from these sources were included by Gratian (died c. 1179) in his *Decretum*, a collection of rules that the Roman Catholic Church recognized as authoritative. The *Decretum* in turn formed part of a later collection, the *Corpus Juris Canonici*, which in 1917 was revised to form the Codex Juris Canonici, the present Roman Catholic code of law. The ecclesiastical law of the Church of England was mainly contained in the early-17th-century *Book of Canons*, but new laws were introduced in the 1960s.

Canopic jars Earthenware jars used in ancient Egypt in sets of four as containers for the internal organs removed from mummified bodies. Their lids, originally plain, were later modelled as the human, falcon, dog, and jackal heads of the four sons of the god *Horus.

Canopus A conspicuous luminous white *supergiant, apparent magnitude −0.7 and 200 light years distant, that is the brightest star in the constellation Carina and the second brightest star in the sky.

Canossa A 10th-century castle near Reggio nel Emilia, in Italy. It is famous as the place in which Emperor Henry IV received absolution from Gregory VII in 1077 to end the *investiture controversy.

Canova, Antonio (1757-1822) Italian sculptor. One of the finest interpreters of the style of *neoclassicism, Canova worked first in Venice, in Rome after 1781, in Vienna, and in Paris, where he was employed by Napoleon. He achieved a wide reputation with his idealized marbles, usually of classical subjects. His best-known works are *The Tomb of Clement XIII* (1783-87; SS Apostoli, Rome) and *Pauline Borghese as Venus Victrix* (1805-07; Borghese Gallery, Rome).

Cánovas del Castillo, Antonio (1828-97) Spanish statesman and writer. Following the overthrow of the First Republic in 1874 and the restoration of the monarchy he created a system of government by two parties in rotation, which remained in force until 1923. He led the conservative party and was many times prime minister. He was assassinated by an anarchist.

Cantabrian Mountains (Spanish name: Cordillera Cantábrica) A mountain range in N Spain extending E-W along the Atlantic coast and rising to 2648 m (8868 ft).

Cantacuzino A family prominent in Romania from the 17th century. Descended from an imperial Byzantine family, the Cantacuzino settled in Moldavia and Walachia (present-day Romania) in the 16th century. Its members included Şerban Cantacuzino (d. 1688), who ruled Walachia from 1679 to 1688, and his nephew Ştefan Cantacuzino, who ruled from 1714 until ousted and executed in 1716. Şerban's cousin **Dumitraşcu Cantacuzino** (1648-85) was an unpopular ruler of Moldavia (1673-75, 1684-85). A descendant **Constantin Cantacuzino** (1793-1877) governed Walachia (1848-49, 1854).

Canterbury 51 17N 1 05E A city in SE England, in Kent on the River Stour. The cathedral (11th-15th centuries), where Thomas *Becket was martyred in 1170, is the seat of the Archbishop and Primate of the Anglican Church. Canterbury is a tourist, market, and educational centre; the University of Kent (1960) overlooks the city. Population (1981): 34 404.

Canterbury, Archbishop of The chief bishop of the *Anglican Communion of churches, called Primate of All England. The first of the line was St *Augustine of Canterbury. He takes precedence after the royal princes and before the Lord Chancellor and the other peers and signs himself with his Christian name and the Latin abbreviation of Canterbury, for example "Robert Cantuar." Recent archbishops are: Geoffrey, Baron Fisher (1887-1972; 99th Archbishop 1945-61); Arthur Michael, Baron Ramsey (1904- ; 100th Archbishop 1961-74); (Frederick) Donald Coggan (1909- ; 101st Archbishop 1974-80); Robert Alexander Kennedy Runcie (1921- ; 102nd Archbishop 1980-).

Canterbury bell An annual or biennial flowering plant, *Campanula medium*, native to S Europe and frequently grown as a garden ornamental. The plant grows to a height of 75 cm and bears spikes of pink, rose, lavender, blue, or white bell-shaped flowers, each 5 cm or more long. Family: *Campanulaceae*.

Canterbury Plains A low-lying area of New Zealand, on E central South Island bordering on the Pacific Ocean. It is the most densely populated area of South Island and is important agriculturally, especially for fat-lamb raising and the production of cereals, fodder crops, and vegetables. Area: about 10 000 sq km (4000 sq mi). Chief town: Christchurch.

cantharidin. *See* Spanish fly.

Can Tho 10 03N 105 46E A port in S Vietnam, on the Mekong delta. It is the industrial centre of an important rice-growing area, with a university (1956). Population (1979): 182 856.

Canton (Chinese names: Guangzhou *or* Kuang-chou) 23

08N 113 20E A port in S China, the capital of Guangdong province on the Zhu Jiang (Pearl River) delta. Densely populated, it is the commercial and industrial centre of S China and attracts much of the country's foreign trade through its biannual trade fair. It has a university and various colleges. Its industries include steel, shipbuilding, paper, textiles, and the manufacture of machinery and chemicals. *History*: Chinese since the 3rd century BC, it was the first Chinese city to trade regularly with Europeans (from the 16th century), having long traded with Hindus and Arabs, and was the focus of the first Opium War (1839–42). The birthplace of *Sun Yat-sen, it was the starting point of the revolution against the Qing (1911). His Guomindang (Nationalist) government was based here in the early 1920s. Canton was occupied by Japan (1938–45). Population (1981 est): 5 200 000.

Canton 40 48N 81 23W A city in the USA, in NE Ohio. An important industrial centre, it has a large iron and steel industry. It was the home of President McKinley. Population (1980): 94 632.

Canton and Enderbury Two uninhabited coral atolls in the S Pacific Ocean, in the Phoenix Islands. Claims between the USA and the UK were settled in 1939, when they agreed to exercise joint control over the islands for 50 years. Canton was used as an international airport for transpacific flights until the advent of long-range jets.

Cantonese. *See* Chinese.

Cantor, Georg (1845–1918) Russian mathematician, born in St Petersburg. Cantor's family moved in 1856 to Germany, where he spent the rest of his life. He was the first mathematician to set the concept of infinity on a rigorous mathematical foundation. He defined different types of infinity for the set of integers, the set of real numbers, etc., each type being represented by a number known as a transfinite number. His ideas created great controversy and were viciously attacked, by Leopold Kronecker (1823–91) in particular. Cantor broke down in 1884 under the strain and died in a mental asylum.

Canute II (*or* Cnut; c. 994–1035) Danish King of England after defeating *Edmund Ironside (1016). He became King of Denmark (1019) and of Norway (1028). He defended England from Viking attacks (1017, 1026, 1028) and subjected Malcolm II of Scotland (1028). He went on a pilgrimage to Rome in 1027 to attend the coronation of Emperor *Conrad II. According to legend, he proved to flatterers the limits of his powers by demonstrating his inability to induce the waves to recede.

canyon A deep steep-sided gorge found mainly in arid and semiarid areas, the depth of which considerably exceeds its width. Canyons are often formed by rapidly eroding rivers down-cutting into soft rock in arid areas. The lack of rainfall hinders weathering and maintains the steep slopes; where hard- and soft-rock bands occur, a stepped formation results. The largest and best-known canyon is the *Grand Canyon (USA).

Cao Chan (*or* Zao Zhan; ?1715–63) Chinese novelist, famous for the semiautobiographical *Dream of the Red Chamber*, a novel written in the last years of his life. It combines a tragic love story with a description of the downfall of a great Chinese family. It mirrors the fortunes of Cao Chan's own family, which held the hereditary office of commissioner of imperial textiles in Nanking.

Capablanca y Graupera, José Raúl (1888–1942) Cuban chess player, who was world champion from 1921 to 1927. Extraordinarily gifted, he played at speed and with exceptional insight. He worked as a diplomat and wrote books on chess, including *Chess Fundamentals* (1922).

capacitance The ability of an electrical component to store charge. It is measured in *farads and defined as the ratio of the stored charge in coulombs to the voltage drop across the component. Capacitance is one of the factors that control the frequency response of circuits and components to alternating currents.

capacitor An electrical component (formerly called a condenser), with an appreciable *capacitance. It consists of two conductor or semiconductor plates separated by a *dielectric. The value of the capacitance is a function of the geometry and the electrical properties of the dielectric and often also of the operating voltage and the frequency. Variable capacitors are used for tuning electronic circuits.

Cape Breton Island An island in SE Canada, in Nova Scotia, separated from the mainland by the Strait of Canso. Hilly and forested, it encloses tidal salt lakes. Coal, steel, fishing, and tourism are important. It was ceded to Britain by the French (1763). Area: 10 280 sq km (3975 sq mi). Population (1981): 170 088.

Cape Coast 5 10N 1 13W A town in central Ghana, on the Gulf of Guinea. It was the capital of the British colony of the Gold Coast until 1874. It has a cathedral and a university (1962). Fishing industries are important. Population (1982 est): 72 142.

Cape Cod A sandy peninsula in the USA, in Massachusetts between Cape Cod Bay and the Atlantic Ocean. A popular summer resort area, it also produces cranberries and asparagus. Length: 105 km (65 mi).

Cape Frontier Wars (1779–1878) The wars fought intermittently in S Africa between the White settlers moving E from the Cape and the *Xhosa people who had settled in the E Cape area. Conflict between the two groups arose mainly over land and cattle. The Xhosa had been driven back along the coast by the colonists beyond the Keiskamma River by 1819 and in 1846 the land between the Fish and the Keiskamma Rivers was annexed as British Kaffraria. The final war was in 1877–78 in which the Xhosa were defeated and their lands absorbed into the Cape Colony.

Cape Horn (Spanish name: Cabo de Hornes) The most southerly point in South America, at the S end of Horn Island, Chile. It is notorious for its stormy weather.

Capella A conspicuous yellow *giant star, apparent magnitude 0.1 and 45 light years distant, that is the brightest star in the constellation Auriga. It is a *multiple star, having three components.

Cape of Good Hope A headland in South Africa, in the SW extremity of Cape Province. It was discovered (1488) by Dias, who named it the Cape of Storms.

Cape Province (official name: Cape of Good Hope Province; Afrikaans name: Kaapprovinsie) The largest province in South Africa, in the extreme S of the African continent. It consists chiefly of plateaus separated by mountain ranges. In the diversified economy agriculture is important. The SW produces most of South Africa's fruit and vegetables for export and has many vineyards; sheep and cattle rearing is extensive and wheat and alfalfa are grown. Diamonds and copper are the chief minerals, others being asbestos, manganese, and iron ore. Industries include food processing and canning, textiles, and motor-vehicle production. *History*: first settled by the Dutch (1652), it was ceded to Britain in 1814, becoming known as the Cape Colony. The discovery of diamonds in Griqualand West led to its annexation to the Cape Colony (1871). In 1910 the colony became a province in the Union of South Africa. Area: 646 332 sq km (400 762 sq mi). Population (1980): 4 007 875. Capital: Cape Town.

caper A bramble-like spiny shrub, *Capparis spinosa*, native to drier regions of S Europe. The pickled flower buds are the capers used in flavouring. The fruit is a berry. Family: *Capparidaceae*.

capercaillie The largest European *grouse, *Tetrao urogallus*, of Eurasian coniferous forests, where it feeds on pine buds and needles. The male, almost 100 cm long, is black with a blue-green gloss and red wattles above the eyes. The smaller female is brown with black and white markings.

Capernaum 32 53N 35 34E An ancient town in N Israel, on the N shore of the Sea of Galilee. It is the site of many biblical events, and a synagogue dating from about 200 AD has been excavated.

Capetians The ruling dynasty of France from 987 to 1328. It was founded by *Hugh Capet, who became King of France in 987, replacing the Carolingians. Successive kings, notably *Philip II Augustus and *Louis IX, expanded their own authority and the territory under their control (originally comprising little more than the Île-de-France). The Capetians established a royal bureaucracy, from which the *parlements developed, and were the first kings to summon the *States General.

CAPE TOWN *The city is noted for its scenic beauty set against Table Mountain, 1082 m (3550 ft) high.*

Cape Town (Afrikaans name: Kaapstad) 33 56S 18 28E The legislative capital of South Africa and capital of Cape Province, on the Atlantic Ocean. Founded by Jan van Riebeeck in 1652 as a supply post for the Dutch East India Company, it is the oldest White settlement in South Africa. The famous National Botanical Gardens at Kirstenbosch were part of the Groot Schuur estate, the home of Cecil Rhodes. Cape Town castle (17th century) is the oldest building in South Africa; the university was established in 1918 and has an observatory. Cape Town is a major port, with modern dockyard facilities, and is an important commercial and industrial city besides being a popular holiday centre. Its industries include oil refining, chemicals, motor vehicles, and textiles. Population (1980): 213 830.

Cape Verde, Republic of (Portuguese name: Cabo Verde) A country occupying an archipelago in the N Atlantic Ocean, off the coast of West Africa. It consists of ten islands and five islets, most of which are mountainous. The majority of the population is of mixed African and European descent. *Economy*: mainly subsistence agriculture. Ship refuelling is important and fishing has considerable potential for development; fish and fish products are the main exports. *History*: the Cape Verde Islands were settled by the Portuguese in the mid-15th century, becoming a Portuguese colony in the 19th century and gaining full independence in 1975. Plans for union with Guinea-Bissau on the African coast still meet with opposition in certain quarters, although there is already a considerable amount of cooperation. President: Aristides Maria Pereira (1924–). Official language: Portuguese. Official currency: Cape Verdean escudo of 100 centavos. Area: 4033 sq km (1557 sq mi). Population (1983): 297 000. Capital: Praia. Main port: Mindelo.

Cape York Peninsula The most northerly part of Australia, in Queensland, situated between the Gulf of Carpentaria and the Coral Sea. It is mainly low-lying grass and scrubland in the W, rising to the Great Dividing Range in the E and contains large areas that are uninhabited although bauxite mining is important.

Cap Haïtien (*or* Le Cap) 19 47N 72 17W A port in N Haiti, on the Atlantic Ocean. The chief exports are coffee and sugar and it is the site of one of the world's largest sisal plantations. Population (1982): 64 406.

capillary In anatomy, a minute thin-walled blood vessel (0.005–0.02 mm diameter), networks of which connect the smallest *arteries with the smallest *veins. Nutrients and oxygen diffuse across the capillary walls to nourish the tissues. Waste products and carbon dioxide return from the tissues to the capillary blood.

capital An element of architecture used to join a column to the part of the building it supports. In classical architecture there are five orders of columns with strictly defined types of capital, of varying degrees of ornateness, for each (*see* orders of architecture). In romanesque and gothic architecture, the rules became less strict and the type of capital used depended mainly on the skill and taste of the masons involved. Thus the capital could vary from the plain (called a cushion capital) to the highly ornate, decorated with carvings of foliage, people, and animals (grotesque and historiated types).

capital-gains tax A UK tax, introduced in 1965, on the profit arising from the disposal of an asset by sale or gift (and until 1971 by death). It applies to stocks and shares (except some government stocks), to dwellings that are not the owner's only residence, and to all other saleable assets with some exceptions (e.g. cars, assets sold for less than £2,000). It does not apply to gains from betting, football pools, or life assurance policies. The rate of tax is 30% on the gain, but the first £6,300 of a person's gains in any year are exempt. Similar taxes are levied in other countries, including the USA.

capitalism An economic and political system that developed following the industrial revolution. Essential features of the system are uncontrolled free markets, based on the profit motive, and unrestricted ownership of the means of production (capital). If the system is allowed to develop without restriction it has certain undesirable attributes (*see* laissez-faire). This has led western countries to restrict capitalism by the establishment of mixed economies, characterized by substantial government regulation. Communist countries have followed the doctrines of Karl Marx (*see* Marxism), who maintained that capitalism contains the seeds of its own destruction, and have abolished capitalism and the free-market system, replacing them with central direction of the economy by the government and state ownership of all the means of production.

capital punishment The punishment of a convicted criminal by execution, in Britain formerly by beheading or hanging. In 18th-century Britain over 200 offences carried the death penalty, including such crimes as petty theft and forgery. It was, in fact, imposed for only a few offences. In 1868 public executions were abolished and by the Homicide Act (1957) only certain kinds of murder remained punishable by death (murder committed in the course or furtherance of theft, in resisting arrest, etc.). In 1965 the death penalty was abolished for all forms of murder, leaving treason, violent piracy, and (until 1971) arson in royal dockyards as the only capital crimes. In 1979 and 1983 motions that it be reintroduced for certain murders were defeated in a free vote in the House of Commons.

In many other countries, including some states of the USA, the death penalty has either been abolished or is no longer in use, although there has been a call for its restitution from some quarters as a result of the recent rise of terrorism. Its effectiveness as a deterrent is still an open question, but the macabre and uncivilized procedure of execution, the reluctance of juries to convict, and the inability to repair a miscarriage of justice have made it an unpopular form of punishment in the modern world.

capital-transfer tax. *See* inheritance tax.

Capitol 1. (*or* Capitoline Temple) A temple built on the Capitoline Hill (one of the seven hills of Rome) by Tarquinius Priscus (d. 578 BC) but not dedicated until 509 BC. Destroyed by lightning in 183 BC, burnt during the civil wars in 83 BC, and subsequently burnt and rebuilt several times, it was finally plundered by the Vandals in 455 AD. *Michelangelo's Piazza del Campidoglio now stands on the site. 2. The meeting place of the US Congress in Washington, DC. It was designed by William Thornton, a West Indian doctor with no previous architectural experience. The cornerstone was laid by George Washington in 1793.

capitulary Legal and administrative instruments of the *Carolingian kings, arranged in *capitula* (articles). These documents are concerned with many topics, both secular and ecclesiastical, including law and order, the regulation of trade, and the administration of royal estates. Although originals do not survive, copies amply illustrate the scope and power of early Carolingian administration.

Capodimonte porcelain A valuable soft-paste *porcelain made (1743–59) near Naples at a factory started by Charles IV of Naples. Typical pieces were peasant figures and vessels and services modelled like local sea shells and seaweeds.

Capone, Al (1899–1947) US gangster, born in Italy. He dominated the Chicago underworld of organized crime in the late 1920s. In the St Valentine's Day Massacre of 1929, his men killed seven members of a rival gang. He was imprisoned in 1931 for income-tax evasion.

Caporetto. *See* Kobarid.

Capote, Truman (1924–84) US novelist. In his early novels and stories, such as *Other Voices, Other Rooms* (1948), he explored traditional southern literary themes of loneliness and the macabre. Later he turned to journalism, an interest reflected in *In Cold Blood* (1966), a novel about an actual multiple murder. Other works include *Breakfast at Tiffany's* (1958) and *Music for Chameleons* (1980).

Capp, Al (Alfred Caplin; 1909–79) US cartoonist, born in New Haven, Connecticut. He is famous for his comic strip *Li'l Abner* depicting the hillbillies of Dogpatch, Kentucky, which first appeared in the *New York Mirror* in 1934 and which he continued to produce until 1977.

Cappadocia The eastern region of Asia Minor. After early colonization by Semitic merchants, subjection to the Hittites, and invasions from the east, Cappadocia was conquered by the Persians in 584 BC but became an independent kingdom in the 3rd century BC. Feudal and isolated, Cappadocia resisted the hellenizing efforts of its ruling dynasty, which was largely pro-Roman; as the Roman Empire expanded eastwards Cappadocia became strategically important and was a Roman province by 17 AD.

Capra, Frank (1897–) US film director, born in Italy. His best-known films include several popular sentimental comedies, notably *It Happened One Night* (1934), *Arsenic and Old Lace* (1942), and *It's a Wonderful Life* (1946). During World War II he directed propaganda films for the US War Department.

Capri, Island of (Latin name: Capreae) An Italian island at the SW entrance to the Bay of Naples. Its mild climate, fine scenery, and beaches have made it a popular resort since Roman times. The Blue Grotto, a cavern accessible only by sea, is a notable feature. Area: about 13 sq km (5 sq mi). Population (1981 est): 7489.

capriccio. *See* veduta.

Capricorn (astrology). *See* zodiac.

Capricornus (Latin: Goat) A constellation in the S sky, lying on the *zodiac between Aquarius and Sagittarius.

Caprivi Strip A narrow extension of NE Namibia giving the country access to the Zambezi River. Length: about 450 km (280 mi).

Capsicum A genus of annual and perennial flowering plants (about 50 species), native to Central and South America. The fruits (berries) of some species, particularly the various cultivated varieties of *C. annuum* and *C. frutescens*, are the *chillies and peppers used in cookery. Large fruits (up to about 10 cm long) are the sweet peppers, which have a mild taste and are used in salads or cooked as a vegetable. They are usually green but may be red (the red varieties—paprika—can be ground to produce a spice). Smaller berries (about 2 cm long) are the hot-tasting red peppers (or chillies); when dried and ground these form cayenne pepper. Dwarf varieties are grown for ornament. Family: *Solanaceae*.

capsid A delicate *plant bug belonging to the family *Miridae* (about 8000 species). Capsids are 2.5–6 mm long and usually green or brown. They are found among all types of vegetation, feeding on plant juices, and are often serious crop pests. A few species prey on small arthropods.

capsule In botany, a type of dry *fruit that releases its seeds at maturity through pores, teeth, or slits: an example is the poppy capsule. The term also refers to the spore-producing structures of mosses and liverworts and the slimy envelope surrounding some bacterial cells. In zoology, it is the layer of connective tissue surrounding some organs, for example the kidney.

Capua 41 06N 14 12E A market town in S Italy, in Campania on the River Volturno. It has Roman remains and a 9th-century cathedral. Population (1981 est): 18 053.

capuchin monkey A long-tailed *monkey belonging to the genus *Cebus* (4 species), of South America. Capuchins are 70–90 cm long including the tail (40–50 cm) and live in large troops in the treetops, feeding chiefly on fruit but also eating insects, birds, and eggs. They became familiar as organ-grinders' monkeys. Family: *Cebidae*.

Capuchins A Roman Catholic order of friars founded in 1525. They are reformed *Franciscans, named after the pointed cowl (capuche) they wear in emulation of St Francis. Opposed by the established Franciscans, they were almost suppressed in 1542, but survived to become an important force during the Counter-Reformation, being recognized in 1619 as one of the three independent branches of the Franciscan order. From their foundation they were noted for their works of charity and their asceticism.

capybara The largest living rodent, *Hydrochoerus hydrochaeris*. Resembling giant guinea-pigs, up to 1.25 m long and 50 cm high, capybaras graze on river banks in Central and South America, living in groups of up to 20 individuals. They have short coarse yellowish-brown hair and partially webbed feet (they are expert swimmers). The capybara is the only member of its family (*Hydrochoeridae*).

CAPYBARA *These rodents are semiaquatic; they can swim underwater using their partly webbed feet.*

car A self-propelled road vehicle. The search for a means of replacing the horse as a means of transport began seriously at the beginning of the 18th century, when *Newcomen and *Watt had shown that steam could be harnessed to produce power. Joseph Cugnot (1725–1804) in 1770 used a steam engine to drive a gun tractor and in 1808 Richard *Trevithick built a working steam carriage. But neither these vehicles nor the many other steam carriages of the first half of the 19th century were more than cumbersome novelties. An effective horseless carriage needed a smaller more efficient power source. This was eventually provided by two German engineers, Nikolaus *Otto and Gottlieb *Daimler, who in 1876 patented the Otto-cycle *internal-combustion engine. In 1885, another German, Karl *Benz, used a 3 hp version of this engine to power a tricycle capable of 15 mph (20 km per hour). By 1890 both Daimler and Benz were selling the motorized dog carts that were the forerunners of the modern car. In France, during the closing decade of the 19th century, Panhard, Comte Albert de Dion, Georges Bouton, and Peugeot were all producing and selling cars. In the USA, Henry Ford built his first car in 1896. In the UK, however, the development of the motor car from the early steam carriages was hampered by nervous legislation introduced in 1865, which insisted that they must be preceded on the roads by a man carrying a red flag. This law was not repealed until 1896. Some ten years later Henry *Royce, dissatisfied with the quality of imported cars, decided to build his own. In partnership with C. S. *Rolls, he sold his first Rolls-Royce Silver Ghost in 1907.

By the start of World War I, some 130 000 cars were registered in the UK; by this time they were much the same in basic shape and design as they are today. Propeller shafts had replaced chains and belts, pneumatic tyres had ousted solid tyres, and open carriage bodies had given way to saloons. Although World War I was the last of the "horse" wars, by 1918 more and more motorized vehicles (including *tanks) were in military use. Nevertheless, motoring was still the preserve of the rich. In the early 1920s a family Ford, Austin, Citroën, Morris, or Renault cost about £500. It was not until 1925, when Ford brought the price of his Model T down to $290 in the USA and £185 in the UK, that motoring became more widely accessible. During the 1930s the price of cars steadily declined until at the beginning of World War II a British-made Ford 8 or Austin 7 could be bought for about £100. But the real mass market did not develop until after World War II. Before the war it was rare for a model to sell a million vehicles, now a popular car has to do so to be a commercial success.

Since the 1950s competition throughout the world has been fierce. In the UK, which used to be the most prolific manufacturer of cars, major competitors in world mass markets now include the Rover Group, Jaguar, and Ford. Over half the cars sold in the UK are imported, mostly from France, Germany, Italy, and Japan. The cars themselves are not greatly changed from the prewar vehicles. They are slightly faster (most family saloons are capable of 100 mph, although laws in many countries do not allow them to exceed 70 mph), somewhat more economical (small family cars can do 50 miles per gallon), and considerably more reliable than they used to be. They are also more comfortable and safer.

The future of the private car is uncertain: diminishing world reserves of oil make fuel increasingly expensive, the cost of the cars themselves has risen sharply, and the pollution and noise they create makes them the enemy of conservationists and townplanners. It may be that the petrol supplies will hold out until an economic alternative is found (*see* electric car) or it may be that once again the private car will become the privilege of the rich.

caracal A long-legged short-tailed *cat, *Felis caracal*, of African and Asian deserts, bush, and mountains. Caracals are about 70 cm long with a reddish-brown coat, and feed mainly on birds but also catch small mammals.

Caracalla (Marcus Aurelius Antoninus; 188–217 AD) Roman emperor (211–17). Rivalry between Caracalla and his brother and coemperor Geta (189–212) threatened to divide the Empire until Caracalla procured Geta's murder. Caracalla extended Roman citizenship to all free inhabitants of the Empire–probably for financial reasons (212). In 214 he embarked on war against the Parthians, claiming to be following Alexander the Great's ambition to unite East and West, but was assassinated during the campaign.

caracara A long-legged *falcon belonging to the subfamily *Daptriinae*, of Central and South America. Caracaras can run swiftly and spend much time on the ground. They are omnivorous and frequently feed on carrion.

Caracas 10 35N 66 56W The capital of Venezuela, situated near the N coast and linked by road to its port, La Guaira. Founded by the Spanish as Santiago de León de Caracas in the 16th century, it suffered damage and destruction from the English and the French in the 16th and 18th centuries and later from severe earthquakes. In the 20th century it has grown considerably, especially since the oil boom of the 1950s. The Central University of Venezuela was founded in 1725, and there are three other universities. It is the birthplace of Simón Bolívar. Population (1981 est): 2 700 000.

carat 1. A unit of weight for precious stones, formerly defined as 4 grains (Troy), but now equal to 0.200 grams. 2. A measure of the fineness of gold equal to the number of parts of gold by weight in 24 parts of the alloy. Thus 18-carat gold contains 18/24ths pure gold.

Caratacus (*or* Caractacus; 1st century AD) King of the Catuvellauni; son of *Cunobelinus (Cymbeline). Caratacus organized resistance to the Roman invasion of 43 AD. Defeated, he fled first to Wales then to the north British queen, Cartimandua, who betrayed him. He was pardoned by Emperor Claudius but died in exile.

Caravaggio (Michelangelo Merisi; 1573–1610) An influential Italian *baroque painter, whose nickname derives from his birthplace. In Rome his chief patron was Cardinal Francesco del Monte, for whom he painted scenes of the life of St Matthew in S Luigi dei Francesi. He executed numerous altarpieces, some of which, e.g. *Death of the Virgin* (Louvre), were condemned for depicting sacred personages as coarse peasants. He is also noted for his dramatic contrasts of light and shade in such paintings as *Supper at Emmaus* (National Gallery, London), which were extremely influential, particularly in N Europe. His violent temper led him to kill a man after a disputed tennis match in 1606. He spent his last years in exile in Naples, Malta, and Sicily.

caravel A sailing vessel used by the Spanish and Portuguese from the middle ages onwards. It was usually rigged with a lateen sail on two or more masts.

caraway A perennial flowering plant, *Carum carvi*, native to N temperate regions from Europe to the Himalayas. The much-branched stem grows to a height of 25–60 cm and terminates in clusters of small white flowers. The fruit is an oblong capsule containing the familiar caraway seeds, used in cookery. Family: *Umbelliferae*.

carbohydrate One of a large group of chemical compounds containing the elements carbon, hydrogen, and oxygen and having the general formula $C_x(H_2O)_x$. Green plants manufacture carbohydrates–such as *sugars and *starch–during *photosynthesis and their cell walls consist largely of carbohydrates–predominantly *cellulose. Hence plant carbohydrates are the primary source of food energy for animals. *Glycogen is a carbohydrate energy reserve found in animals, while chitin is a structural carbohydrate occurring in arthropods (and also in fungi). Chemically, carbohydrates can be classified according to the number of

Benz 8hp *1600 of these "horseless carriages" were sold between 1898 and 1900. Described as the first reliable car offered to the public, its twin-cyclinder 1570 cc engine gave it a top speed of 18 mph (29 km/hr).*

Rolls-Royce Silver Ghost *First built in 1907 (and continuing in production until 1927) it quickly established itself as "the best car in the world." Its 7-litre 6-cylinder engine gave it a top speed of 65 mph (105 km/hr).*

Ford Model T *15 million of this first mass-produced car (nicknamed the "Tin Lizzie") were made between 1908 and 1927. Its 4-cylinder, 2898 cc engine gave it a top speed of 40 mph (64 km/hr).*

Bugatti Royale *Made to compete with the Rolls-Royce, this 13-litre 8-cylinder car cost over £5000 in 1927 – too much for even its intended royal customers. Six were sold. In 1987 one survivor was sold for £5.5 M.*

Volkswagen *Nicknamed "the Beetle," this 1937 German design by Ferdinand Porsche was still selling in the 1970s, making it the best selling car ever made. Its air-cooled slow-revving rear engine increased from 1131 to 1600 cc over the years.*

MG TC *This post-war British sports car (1946-55) was little changed from the TA model first built in 1937. The TC had a 1250 cc engine.*

Buick *This 1949 US car represented a release from wartime restrictions and set the trend for a generation of large American cars.*

Mini *The best selling British car ever made. Designed by Alec Issigonis, the Mini was introduced in 1959 and is still selling. Its frontwheel drive, transverse engine, and 10-inch wheels make it an extremely roomy car for its size.*

Citroen BX *This 1987 French 1900 cc diesel-powered model has a top speed of 103 mph (166 km/hr) and claims a fuel consumption of 61.4 mpg at 56 mph (90 km/hr). It also features Citroen's self-levelling hydropneumatic suspension.*

sugar units they contain—one (*see* monosaccharides), several (oligosaccharides), or many (*see* polysaccharides).

carbolic acid. *See* phenol.

carbon (C) A chemical element that is unique in terms of the huge number and variety of its compounds. Carbon is the basis of organic *chemistry and of all living systems. The element occurs naturally in two forms: *graphite, which is a soft greyish-black mineral, and *diamond, the hardest substance known. *Charcoal and *coke are also composed of carbon. Large amounts of carbon are fixed as calcium carbonate ($CaCO_3$) in *limestones. The extensive and varied chemistry of carbon results from its ability to form single, double, and triple bonds with itself and other elements. Simple compounds of carbon may join together to form large polymers; for example polyethylene, $(C_2H_4)_n$, from ethylene. At no 6; at wt 12.011; sublimes at 3367 ± 25°C.

Carbonari Members of a secret society in early 19th-century Italy that advocated constitutional government. The Carbonari emerged as opponents of Joachim *Murat, who ruled Naples for Napoleon. The movement spread to N Italy and was supported by those dissatisfied with the conservative regimes imposed on Italy after the fall of Napoleon. Support for the Carbonari dwindled following the formation of *Young Italy by Mazzini but the society had helped pave the way for the unification of Italy (*see* Risorgimento).

carbon cycle (biology) The process by which carbon (in the form of carbon dioxide) in the atmosphere is taken up by plants during photosynthesis and transferred from one organism to the next in a *food chain, i.e. the plants are eaten by herbivorous animals that are themselves eaten by carnivores. At various stages carbon is returned to the environment with the release of carbon dioxide at *respiration and through decay.

carbon cycle (physics) A cycle of thermonuclear reactions in which a nucleus of carbon-12 acts as a catalyst in converting four hydrogen nuclei into a helium nucleus. The cycle produces energy and is believed to be a major source of energy in some stars. The reactions are:

$$^1_1H + ^{12}_6C \rightarrow ^{13}_7N \rightarrow ^{13}_6C + ^0_1e$$
$$^1_1H + ^{13}_6C \rightarrow ^{14}_7N$$
$$^1_1H + ^{14}_7N \rightarrow ^{15}_8O \rightarrow ^{15}_7N + ^0_1e$$
$$^1_1H + ^{15}_7N \rightarrow ^{12}_6C + ^4_2He.$$

carbon dioxide (CO_2) A colourless odourless noncombustible gas. It is present (about 0.03% by volume) in air, being produced by combustion of carbon compounds and by respiration. Industrially, CO_2 is made from chalk or limestone and is used as a coolant in nuclear reactors, as a refrigerant, in fire extinguishers, and in "fizzy" drinks.

carbon fibres Black silky threads of pure carbon, made by the heat treatment of organic textile fibres (such as Courtelle) so that the side chains of the molecules are removed. They are some eight times stronger than steel and are used to reinforce resinous, ceramic, or metallic substances (with up to 600 000 fibres per square centimetre) to make components for jet engines, rockets, etc.

Carboniferous period A geological period of the *Palaeozoic era occurring about 370-280 million years ago between the Devonian and Permian periods. During the period land plants increased prolifically and led to the formation of the world's major coal deposits. Amphibians became more common and by the end of the period some reptiles had evolved. The Carboniferous is divided into Lower and Upper (Mississippian and Pennsylvanian). Limestone deposits were widespread in the Lower Carboniferous; millstone grits and the Coal Measures (alternating beds of coal, sandstone, shale, and clay), in the Upper.

carbon monoxide (CO) A colourless odourless flammable gas. It is produced by the incomplete combustion of carbon compounds (e.g. coke or natural gas) and is used as a fuel

(*see* water gas). CO is highly toxic, combining with red blood cells and preventing them from carrying oxygen. It is present in the exhaust fumes of internal-combustion engines.

carbon tetrachloride (CCl_4) A colourless nonflammable heavy liquid that gives off toxic fumes. It is used as a solvent but its use in fire extinguishers has been discontinued owing to its toxic products of combustion.

carborundum A dark crystalline compound (silicon carbide) manufactured by heating silica (sand) with carbon (coke). It is used as an abrasive and as a refractory material.

carboxylic acids. *See* fatty acid.

carbuncle. *See* boil.

CARBURETTOR *The level of petrol is kept constant in the float chamber. After atomization by passing through the fine jet it is mixed with air and passed to the engine. The engine speed is controlled by the throttle valve. The mixture strength is varied by the choke, a richer mixture being required for starting from cold.*

carburettor The device in a petrol engine that vaporizes the fuel and mixes it with air in the correct proportions. Vaporization is carried out by sucking the liquid petrol through a fine jet situated in (or near to) the throat of a tube through which the combustion air enters the engine. The carburettor also contains a choke to make the petrol-air mixture richer (i.e. contain more petrol and less air) for cold starting, a throttle valve (which controls the speed of the engine by admitting more or less of the mixture), and an air filter. In some petrol engines the carburettor is replaced by a *fuel-injection system.

Carcassonne 43 13N 2 21E A town in SW France, the capital of the Aude department. It comprises a medieval fortified town, surrounded by towers and ramparts crowning a hill on the right bank of the River Aude, and a largely modern town, where there is a 13th-century cathedral (restored), on the left bank. A tourist centre, Carcassonne is situated in a wine-producing region. Population (1982 est): 42 450.

Carchemish A *Hittite stronghold on the Upper Euphrates

in E Turkey. After the Hittite empire's collapse (12th century BC), Carchemish survived as an independent kingdom until conquered by *Sargon II of Assyria (717 BC). In 605 BC it was the scene of a battle in which the Babylonians defeated an Egyptian army. *Woolley and T. E. *Lawrence excavated fine Hittite reliefs there (1912-14, 1919).

carcinogen An agent that causes cancer. Carcinogens can be chemicals, radiation, and some viruses. Chemical carcinogens include tar (such as that produced by cigarette smoking), aniline, and azo dyes. Large doses of radiation and the polyoma virus are known to cause cancer, particularly leukaemia.

carcinoma. *See* cancer.

cardamon A perennial herb, *Elettaria cardamomum*, native to India. 1.5-3 m tall, it has large leaves, green and purple veined flowers, and small capsules filled with hard angular seeds. The spice cardamon consists of whole or ground dried fruit or seeds. It is cultivated in India, Sri Lanka, and Guatemala. Family: *Zingiberaceae* (ginger family).

Cardano, Girolamo (1501-76) Italian mathematician, who contributed to the development of negative and imaginary *numbers and, being an inveterate gambler, constructed a mathematical theory of chance. He also published a method of solving cubic equations known as Cardano's rule, although it was first derived by Niccolò Tartaglia (1500-57). His main works were *De subtilitate rerum* (1551) and *De varietate rerum* (1557).

Cárdenas, Lázaro (1895-1970) Mexican statesman. As president (1934-40) Cárdenas strove to realize many of the promises of the post-1910 revolutionary movement. He redistributed land, promoted mass education, and supported organized labour. His most famous achievement was the nationalization of the oil industry in 1938.

Cardiff (Welsh name: Caerdydd) 51 30N 3 13W The capital of Wales and the administrative centre of South Glamorgan and Mid Glamorgan, situated in the SE of the country at the mouth of the River Taff. Its port still handles general cargo but employment in the city is now largely dependent on service occupations. At the centre of the city lies the Norman castle, rebuilt by the 3rd Marquess of Bute in the 1870s. University College, Cardiff (founded 1883), the University of Wales Registry (1893), the University of Wales Institute of Science and Technology (UWIST), the Welsh National School of Medicine, and the National Museum of Wales are all located in the city. Cardiff Arms Park is the home of Welsh rugby. The cathedral at *Llandaff and the Welsh Folk Museum at St Fagans are situated on the outskirts of the city. *History*: originally a small Roman fort, the site was reoccupied by the Normans, who built the stone castle keep. It received its first royal charter in 1581, at which time it was a favourite haunt of pirates. It was not until 1881, however, that Cardiff expanded from a small market town to become the largest town in Wales. Its prosperity was based on coal from the valleys to the N of the city and by 1913 it was the largest coal-exporting port in the world. Trade declined rapidly, however, after World War I. The import of iron ore was switched to other ports and in 1978 the East Moors steelworks were closed down. The quayside area, known as Tiger Bay, has subsequently been developed as a suburb. Cardiff was chosen as the capital of Wales in 1955. Population (1981): 273 856.

Cardigan, James Thomas Brudenell, 7th Earl of (1797-1868) British cavalry officer. In 1824 Cardigan bought himself a command in the Hussars, where his arrogant behaviour led to a notorious duel. In 1854, during the Crimean War, he led the fatal charge of the Light Brigade at *Balaclava, made famous by Tennyson. The woollen garment known as a cardigan was named after him.

Cardiganshire A former county of W Wales. Under local government reorganization in 1974 it became part of *Dyfed.

Cardin, Pierre (1922-) French fashion designer, who after opening a fashion house in Paris (1949) made his reputation in the 1950s with his oriental styles and slim coats with huge collars. He was the first couturier to show a collection for men (1960).

cardinal A North American *bunting, *Pyrrhuloxia cardinalis*, having a strong stout bill and a crested head. The male, about 20 cm long, has a bright scarlet plumage with a black bib; the female is yellowish brown with a red crest.

cardinals, college of (or Sacred College) The body of the highest dignitaries next to the pope in the *Roman Catholic Church. Originating in the advisory roles played by the parish priests and deacons of the city of Rome, the body was later extended to include six cardinal bishops responsible for the election of the pope. This function was invested in the college as a whole by the Third *Lateran Council (1179). Since then the number of cardinal bishops, priests, and deacons has increased from a total of 70 under Sixtus V (1586) to the present membership of 125 established under John XXIII and Paul VI. Cardinals from all over the world are nominated and elected by the pope, who invests them with the flat broad-brimmed red hat symbolic of their rank. They assist the pope as a privy council, conducting the temporal affairs of the Church, advising on questions of doctrine, etc.; they elect the pope from among their own number.

Carducci, Giosuè (1835-1907) Italian poet and critic. The son of a country doctor, he became professor of Italian literature at Bologna University in 1860 and won the Nobel Prize in 1906. He was elected senator in 1890. He wrote vigorous, patriotic, and anticlerical poetry but *Rime nuove* (1861-87) and *Odi Barbare* (1877-89) also contain more lyrical verse with classical influences.

Cardwell, Edward, Viscount (1813-86) British politician best known for his work in reforming the army. As secretary of state for war (1868-74), Cardwell, in spite of bitter opposition, abolished peacetime flogging in the army, shortened the period of service, abolished the purchase of commissions, and reorganized the war office.

Carew, Thomas (c. 1595-1640) British poet. He served in the diplomatic service in Venice, The Hague, and Paris before receiving a court appointment in 1628. His love lyrics and his elegy on John Donne were widely circulated in manuscript. He wrote a masque, *Coelum Britannicum* (1634), for performance at court.

Carey, William (1761-1834) British Baptist missionary. A dissenting pastor who supported himself as a shoemaker, Carey helped to found the Baptist Missionary Society in 1792. In 1793 he sailed for Bengal, where he lived until his death, translating the Bible into various Indian dialects and compiling Indian grammars and dictionaries.

cargo cults Religious cults found chiefly in Melanesia since the late 19th century. Their adherents believe that a new paradise will be heralded mainly by the arrival of a supernatural cargo of goods brought by spirits, who are variously viewed as gods, ancestors, or White foreigners. The cults probably evolved from Christian millennial teachings and native jealousy of the colonial European's material wealth.

Caria A mountainous area in SW Asia Minor under the rule of *Lydia until 546 BC, when it passed to the Persians. The Carians joined the Ionian Greeks' unsuccessful revolt against the Persians (499-493 BC). Under the Hecatomnid dynasty (395-334 BC), Caria was absorbed into the Greek world.

Carib An American Indian people of the Lesser Antilles and northern South America, after whom the Caribbean was named. The maritime island Caribs were warriors and cannibals, who before the advent of the Spaniards expelled the *Arawak Indians from the Lesser Antilles, enslaving the women and killing and eating the men. As a consequence, in these islands men spoke Carib and women, Arawak. The mainland Caribs were less aggressive and their culture was adapted to the tropical forest region. They cultivated manioc and hunted with the blowpipe.

Caribbean Community (CARICOM) An association of 13 states in the Caribbean region (Antigua and Barbuda, Bahamas, Barbados, Belize, Dominica, Grenada, Guyana, Jamaica, Montserrat, St Kitts-Nevis, St Lucia, St Vincent and the Grenadines, and Trinidad and Tobago). It was established in 1973 and aims to coordinate the economic policies of member states through the Caribbean Common Market (which replaced the Caribbean Free Trade Area (CARITA) formed in 1968); to coordinate foreign policies; and to foster cooperation. Its headquarters are in Georgetown (Guyana).

Caribbean Sea A section of the Atlantic Ocean, between the West Indies, E Central America, and N South America. With the opening of the Panama Canal (1914) it became an important shipping route. Its tropical climate and warm waters have led to the increasing importance of tourism throughout the Caribbean islands. Area: 2 718 200 sq km (1 049 500 sq mi). Maximum depth: 7686 m (25 216 ft).

caribou. See reindeer.

CARICOM. See Caribbean Community.

caries Cavities in the teeth caused by bacterial erosion of the enamel and dentine. The bacteria feed on sugar from the diet: the sugar and bacteria become attached to the teeth to form a layer called plaque, and acid formed by bacterial breakdown of the sugar causes the damage of caries. Caries is particularly common in children and adolescents; a high-sugar diet is a major contributory factor. Treatment consists of drilling away the damaged part of the tooth and replacing it with filling. The absorption of fluoride by growing teeth strengthens them against bacterial attack; *fluoridation of the public water supply is an aspect of preventive dentistry.

carillon A set of bells hung in a tower, activated from a manual and pedal console similar to that of an organ. It is a popular instrument in Belgium and Holland. Carillons vary in size from two to four octaves. The wooden keys are depressed with the closed hand. The name is also applied to an organ stop that produces a bell-like sound.

Carina (Latin: Keel) A constellation in the S sky near Crux. The brightest star is *Canopus.

Carinthia (German name: Kärnten) A federal state in S Austria. It first came into Austrian possession in 1335; following World War I parts were ceded to neighbouring Italy and Yugoslavia. Chiefly mountainous, it has picturesque alpine scenery and many lakes. The main occupations are livestock rearing, forestry, mining, and tourism. Area: 9537 sq km (3681 sq mi). Population (1981): 537 212. Capital: Klagenfurt.

Carisbrooke 51 41N 1 19W A village in S England, near Newport on the Isle of Wight. Charles I was imprisoned in its 11th-century castle.

Carl August (1757–1828) Duke (1758–1815) and Grand Duke (1815–28) of Saxe-Weimar-Eisenach, who was the first German ruler to grant his state a liberal constitution. Carl August participated in the wars against Napoleon and made territorial gains at the Congress of Vienna (1815). He was a friend and patron of *Goethe and other German writers.

Carl XVI Gustaf (1946–) King of Sweden (1973–), succeeding his grandfather Gustaf VI (1882–1973). The Swedish monarch became little more than a figurehead under a new constitution effective from Carl's succession. In 1976 he married Silvia Sommerlath (1943–). They have three children.

Carlisle 54 54N 2 55W A city in NW England, the administrative centre of Cumbria on the River Eden. Once a Roman military centre (Luguvallum) and important fortress in the border wars with the Scots, it has a 12th-century cathedral and a castle (11th-13th centuries). Industries include flour milling,

biscuit making, textiles, and agricultural engineering. Population (1981 est): 71 503.

Carlism A Spanish conservative movement, initiated by those who supported as *Ferdinand VII's successor in 1833 his brother Don *Carlos, rather than Ferdinand's daughter *Isabella II. The Carlists wanted a more severe repression of liberals, the restoration of the Spanish Inquisition, and the maintenance of traditional regional liberties (*fueros*). In the first Carlist War (1833–39), they were supported by the small landowners in the northeast but were eventually defeated. Carlism survived in its strongholds of Navarre and Aragon but in the second Carlist War (1872–76) was again defeated. During the Spanish Civil War Carlist regiments fought with Franco's armies but many Carlists became critical of Franco's government. The present Carlist pretender is Carlos Hugo de Bourbon-Parma (1930–), who married (1964) Princess Irene of the Netherlands.

Carlos, Don (1788–1855) Spanish pretender. The brother of *Ferdinand VII and an ultra-Catholic reactionary, he contested the succession of his niece *Isabella II in 1833. His followers, who became known as Carlists, opposed Isabella's government in a series of Carlist wars (see Carlism).

Carlow (Irish name: Ceatharlach) A county in the E Republic of Ireland, in Leinster. Chiefly low lying, it rises to mountains in the E. Agriculture is intensive producing barley, wheat, and sugar beet. Area: 896 sq km (346 sq mi). Population (1981): 39 820. County town: Carlow.

Carlsbad 32 25N 104 14W A city in the USA, in SE New Mexico on the Pecos River. Founded in 1887, the nearby Carlsbad Caverns National Park (containing large limestone caves) makes it a popular tourist centre. Potash, discovered in 1931, is extensively mined and it is a shipping point for cotton, alfalfa, oil, and livestock. Population (1980): 31 351.

Carlyle, Thomas (1795–1881) Scottish historian and essayist. He worked unhappily as a teacher until 1819. In 1826 he married Jane Baillie Welsh and moved to London in 1834. *Sartor Resartus* (1836), a blend of fiction, philosophy, and autobiography, was published in 1836 and was followed by his major work, *The French Revolution*, in 1837. This and later works express his view of history as shaped by the "Hero," or inspired individual. After his wife's death in 1866 he became grief-stricken at his neglect of her and retired from public life.

Carmarthenshire A former county of SW Wales. Under local government reorganization in 1974 it became part of *Dyfed.

Carmel, Mount 32 45N 35 02E A mountain in N Israel, extending in a ridge for 25 km (16 mi) SE from the coast at Haifa. The Carmelite religious order was founded here. Height: 546 m (1791 ft).

Carmelites A Roman Catholic religious order founded around the mid-12th century by St Berthold (died c. 1195), who claimed direct inspiration from Elijah and established a monastery at Mount Carmel. With the collapse of the Crusader kingdoms, the order moved to Europe. The original strict rule was relaxed in some respects. In 1452 an order of Carmelite nuns was instituted. In the 16th century the order was reformed by St *Teresa of Àvila and emphasized the cultivation of the contemplative life, which became a distinctive feature of the order.

Carmina Burana A miscellany of lyrics, mainly in Latin, preserved together with six religious dramas in a 13th-century manuscript from Benediktbeuern, Bavaria. The work of earlier medieval wandering scholars, they encompass religious, pastoral, and erotic themes and range from satires on the Church to drinking songs. See also Orff, Carl.

Carnac 47 35N 3 05W A village in Brittany (NW France). It is famous for the megalithic monuments in its vicinity (see megalith). Chief of these, and unique of their kind, are the avenues (alignments) of monoliths, set upright in parallel

CARNAC *Nearly 3000 menhirs still stand in the Carnac alignments.*

rows that run continuously for hundreds of metres. The three main groups, called Ménec, Kermario, and Kerlescan, may have had both ritual and astronomical significance.

Carnap, Rudolf (1891-1970) German-born logical positivist philosopher. A founder of the *Vienna Circle, he was professor of philosophy successively at Vienna, Prague, Chicago, and California Universities. He worked on formal logic and its applications to science and *epistemology, believing that the analysis and clarification of knowledge should be the purpose of philosophy. By developing logical syntax and *semantics, he tried to construct a formal language for the empirical sciences to eliminate confusion, ambiguity, and similar obstacles to knowledge.

Carnarvon Range A plateau in Australia, in SE Queensland. Part of the Great Dividing Range, it lies within a nature reserve and is being developed as a tourist area.

Carnatic music The music of S India as opposed to that of N India. Not having been subjected to the influences of invading cultures, the S has kept an unbroken tradition that lays stress on complex rhythmic patterns. The scale is subdivided into 12 sections similar to those of the European chromatic scale. Primarily vocal, it also employs instruments, especially drums.

carnation A large-flowered cultivated form of the clove pink (*Dianthus caryophyllus*). These perennials grow to heights of 40-60 cm, have tufts of dense grasslike foliage, and double flowers in white, yellow, orange, pink, red, or lavender. Hardy border carnations are suitable for outdoor cultivation, while the perpetual flowering varieties should be grown under glass. Flowers of carnations (and pinks) are noted for their clovelike fragrance. Family: *Caryophyllaceae*. *See also* Dianthus.

carnauba wax A hard high-quality wax gathered from the leaves of the Brazilian carnauba palm (*Copernica cerifera*) and used for making high-gloss polishes. The tree secretes the wax to prevent excess evaporation from its leaves.

Carné, Marcel (1903-) French film director. He collaborated with the scriptwriter Jacques *Prévert on several films noted for their fatalistic treatment of social themes and their powerful evocation of atmosphere. These include *Le Jour se lève* (1939) and *Les Portes de la nuit* (1946).

Carnegie, Andrew (1835-1919) US industrialist, born in Scotland. He founded the Keystone Bridge Company (1865) to manufacture iron and, increasingly, steel. By 1888 he owned auxiliary coal- and iron-fields, railways, and steamships and in 1901 his companies merged with the US Steel Corporation. A noted philanthropist, he believed that a rich man should distribute his wealth for the benefit of society and donated over £70 million to causes in the USA and the UK. He founded the Carnegie Institute of Technology in Pittsburgh in 1900, the Carnegie Institution in Washington in 1902, and many libraries. He also contributed substantially to the building of Carnegie Hall.

Carnera, Primo (1906-67) Italian boxer, who was idolized during the 1930s although he was heavyweight champion only briefly (1933-34). 6.5 ft (1.98 m) tall, he was known for his knockout victories. He later took up wrestling and acted in the film *On the Waterfront* (1954).

Carnivora An order of mammals adapted for hunting and eating flesh. Carnivores have strong jaws, with sharp incisor teeth and pointed canine teeth; some of the cheek (molar) teeth, called carnassials, act as shears to chop up meat. They are the major predators and most species are terrestrial, stalking or pouncing on their prey. The 252 species are divided into seven families: *Canidae (dogs); Ursidae (see bears); Procyonidae (see raccoons; pandas); *Mustelidae (weasels, skunks, etc.); *Viverridae (genets, mongooses, etc.); and *Felidae (cats).

carnivorous plant A plant that obtains at least some of its nutrients by the digestion of insects and other small animals. Carnivorous, or insectivorous, plants show remarkable structural adaptations for their mode of life. *Butterworts and *sundews trap and digest insects by means of the sticky secretions produced by glands in the leaves. The *Venus flytrap traps its prey between bilobed hinged leaves with marginal teeth. Another common method of capture and digestion is by means of liquid-filled "pitchers" into which the insects fall (*see* pitcher plant).

Carnot, (Nicolas Léonard) Sadi (1796-1832) French scientist and soldier, whose investigations of the efficiency of steam engines led him to the concept of ideal reversible cycles, a fundamental idea in the study of *thermodynamics. His *Réflexions sur la puissance motrice du feu* (1824) describes what are now known as the *Carnot cycle and Carnot's theorem (no engine can be more efficient than a reversible engine working between the same temperatures). His father **Lazare Nicolas Marguerite Carnot** (1753-1823) was a statesman and military engineer, known as the "organizer of victory" in the French Revolutionary Wars. He was a member of the Legislative Assembly (1791), the National Convention (1792), and the Committee of *Public Safety. Carnot was exiled in 1815 and settled in Magdeburg. His *De la défense de places fortes* (1810) became a classic work on fortifications.

Carnot cycle A reversible thermodynamic cycle of changes of pressure and temperature in the gas in an ideal heat engine. The gas is compressed adiabatically (at constant heat content), thus raising its temperature, say from T_1 to T_2. It is then expanded isothermally (at constant temperature). The gas is then expanded adiabatically, lowering its temperature from T_2 back to T_1, and finally compressed isothermally at T_1, thus completing the cycle. The efficiency of this cycle depends not on the nature of the gas but only on the temperature range, i.e. it is equal to $(T_1-T_2)/T_1$, where T_1 and T_2 are absolute temperatures. Named after Sadi *Carnot.

Caro, Joseph (1488-1575) Jewish legal scholar and mystic. A refugee from Spain (1492), he settled in Safed (Galilee), an important centre of the *kabbalah. His most enduring work is the legal code *Shulhan Arukh* (*The Prepared Table*; 1564-65), which is still regarded as authoritative by orthodox Jews.

carob The horn-shaped edible fruit pod of the carob tree,

Ceratonia siliqua, an evergreen native to the Mediterranean region. The pods, sometimes known as algaroba or St John's bread, contain a sugary pulp and are used for fodder. The seeds are believed to have been the original carats of jewellers. Carob is also widely used as a substitute for chocolate. Family: *Leguminosae*.

carol A song of a joyful nature, originally accompanied by dancing. During the middle ages the word was applied to a variety of different types of song. Generally written in a simple verse-plus-refrain form, carols became associated with Christmas or Easter, but often had roots in pre-Christian beliefs. The first printed carol was the *Boar's Head Carol* (1521), one of many associated with the feast of the winter solstice. Others derive from miracle and mystery plays; the few that survive in manuscripts of the 15th century celebrate the events of the first Christmas; carols continued to be written on this theme until the 19th century.

Carol I (1839–1914) The first King of Romania (1881–1914). A German prince, elected to the Romanian princedom in 1866, he became king when Romania gained independence from the Ottoman Empire. He introduced reforms and exploited Romania's oilfields but his economic programme did not help the peasants, who rebelled in 1907.

Carol II (1893–1953) King of Romania (1930–40). In 1925 Carol renounced his right of succession to the throne to live in Paris with his mistress Magda Lupescu and his son *Michael succeeded in 1927. Carol returned to Romania in 1930 and was proclaimed king but was forced to abdicate in 1940 by the pro-German *Antonescu. He settled finally in Mexico, where in 1947 he married Mme Lupescu.

Carolina. *See* North Carolina; South Carolina.

Caroline Islands An archipelago in the W Pacific Ocean, part of the UN trust territory of the *Pacific Islands, administered by the USA. It includes the Truk, Yap, and Palau island groups and the large volcanic islands of Kusaie and Ponape. Copra is the main export. Area: 1183 sq km (457 sq mi). Population (1980 est): 86 000.

Caroline of Ansbach (1683–1737) The wife of George II of Great Britain and a strong supporter of Sir Robert *Walpole. She was appointed regent during George's absences abroad.

Caroline of Brunswick (1768–1821) The wife of George IV of the United Kingdom. After their separation (1796), he forbade her to see their child Charlotte. When George became king (1820), his attempt to divorce Caroline failed owing to popular support for her but she was excluded from the coronation (1821).

Carolingians The second Frankish ruling dynasty. It was founded by *Pepin the Short, who deposed the last *Merovingian king in 751, and it was named after Pepin's son *Charlemagne, who greatly expanded the Frankish territories. Crowned Emperor of the West in 800 by Pope Leo III, Charlemagne and his son *Louis the Pious were great patrons of learning, fostering the Carolingian renaissance (*see* Alcuin; Einhard). After the death of Louis the Carolingian empire was split into three kingdoms (843). The middle Frankish kingdom was divided into Italy, Lotharingia (Lorraine), and Provence; in the eastern Frankish kingdom (Germany) the dynasty survived until 911; and the western Frankish kingdom (France) was ruled by Carolingians until the failure of the line in 987.

Carossa, Hans (1878–1956) German novelist. A practising doctor, he was influenced by Goethe's scientific theories as well as his literary works. Among his best-known novels are the autobiographical sequence *Eine Kindheit* (1922), *Rumänisches Tagebuch* (1924), and *Verwandlungen einer Jugend* (1928) and the anti-Nazi *Ungleiche Welten* (1951).

carotenoids A group of yellow, orange, or red pigments manufactured by bacteria, fungi, and plants and essential in the diet of animals. There are two groups—carotenes (including beta-carotene, a precursor of *vitamin A) and xanthophylls.

Carotenoid pigments are important for display and camouflage colouring in both plants and animals and also as eye pigments.

carp An omnivorous freshwater fish, *Cyprinus carpio*, native to Asia but widely introduced elsewhere and raised for food. It has an elongated body, usually about 35 cm long, with large scales, greenish or brownish above and paler below, four barbels on the upper lip, and a long dorsal fin. During the winter it hibernates in the bottom mud. Related fish include the Crucian carp and golden carp (*see* goldfish). Family: *Cyprinidae* (about 2000 species); order: *Cypriniformes*.

Carpaccio, Vittore (c. 1460–c. 1525) Venetian painter, noted for his paintings of his native city and his narrative cycles. His works, influenced by Gentile and Giovanni *Bellini, include a cycle of *Scenes from the Life of St Ursula* and *The Miracle of the Cross* (Accademia, Venice).

Carpathian Mountains A mountain range in Czechoslovakia, Poland, Hungary, the Soviet Union, and Romania. They form a rough semicircle about 1450 km (90 mi) long (including the Transylvanian Alps, which are also known as the **Southern Carpathians**) between Bratislava and the Iron Gate, both on the River Danube. The highest peak is Mount Gerlachovka, at 2663 m (8737 ft), in NE Czechoslovakia.

carpel The female organ of a flower, consisting of the stigma, style, and ovary (□plant). After fertilization, each carpel may ripen to produce a fruit containing one or more seeds. *See also* pistil.

Carpentaria, Gulf of A shallow inlet of the Arafura Sea, in N Australia situated between Arnhem Land and Cape York Peninsula. It contains many islands, the most important being *Groote Eylandt and Wellesley. There are important bauxite and manganese deposits. Area: about 287 500 sq km (11 000 sq mi).

carpenter bee A large black solitary *bee belonging to the European genus *Xylocopa*. *X. violacea* (25 mm long) excavates galleries in wood or large plant stems to make its nest. The lesser carpenter bees (genus *Ceratina*) are found mainly in Africa. Family: *Apidae*.

Carpentier, Georges (1894–1975) French boxer, who was world light-heavyweight champion from 1920 to 1922. His unsuccessful fight against Jack *Dempsey (1921) drew the first million-dollar gate. He also fought at several other weights.

Ghiordes   Senneh

CARPET *The two varieties of knot used in oriental hand-knotted carpets are the Ghiordes (Turkish) and Senneh (Persian) knots.*

carpet A floor covering of fabric. Although tapestries were sometimes used as floor coverings in the middle ages, knotted carpets originated in Asia and date back to about the 3rd century BC. They are woven with tufts of wool, or sometimes silk, knotted round the warp threads as the carpet is woven or round a jute or hessian backing to form a pile. Oriental carpets traditionally have symbolic designs and colours, which distinguish them as Persian, Turkish, Indian, etc. From the 12th century onwards, these designs have been used and adapted by European carpet manufacturers, the Savonnier carpets of 17th-century France being a typical example. Modern machine-made carpets, such as Wilton, have the pile formed by cut loops instead of knots, while Brussels carpet has uncut loops. In the type of carpet now called "tufted" the tufts are held in place by a foam-rubber backing. Synthetic fibre is replacing wool, especially for fitted carpet, which is made in rolls instead of the traditional squares or rectangles and cut to meet individual requirements.

Carpetbaggers Northern profiteers during the *Reconstruction of the South (1865–77) after the US Civil War, who often carried their possessions in a heavy cloth satchel (carpetbag). By manipulating the uneducated newly enfranchised Black voters, the carpetbaggers helped the Republicans gain local and state control. A few carpetbaggers, however, were sincere advocates of equal rights for Blacks.

carpet beetle A small oval beetle, up to 10 mm long, belonging to a genus (*Anthrenus*) of worldwide pests. It is the hairy red-brown or golden-brown larvae that cause the damage, by feeding on virtually all materials of animal origin, especially furs and fabrics. *A. musaeorum* is a major pest of museum collections. Family: *Dermestidae*.

Carpini, Giovanni da Pian del (c. 1180–c. 1252) Italian traveller in Mongolia. A Franciscan friar, at Pope Innocent IV's behest he led a remarkable mission to the Mongols, whose incursions into Christian lands were causing alarm. He departed from Lyon in 1245, reached Karakoram, where he was presented to the khan, in 1246, and then made the return trip largely in winter (1246–47).

Carr, Robert. *See* Somerset, Robert Carr, Earl of.

Carracci A family of Bolognese painters, who were instrumental in reviving the Renaissance art of Raphael, Titian, and Correggio after the heyday of *mannerism. They founded an influential teaching academy (1582) and collaborated on decorations for Bolognese palaces. **Ludovico Carracci** (1555–1619) devoted his life to art instruction and painting altarpieces. His cousin **Agostino Carracci** (1557–1602) was a noted engraver and assisted his brother **Annibale Carracci** (1560–1609), the most famous of the three, on decorations in the gallery of the Farnese Palace, Rome.

carrageen (or caraceen) An edible brownish-red *seaweed, *Chondrus crispus*, also called Irish or sea moss, that grows abundantly on rocky coasts of W Britain and Ireland, N Europe, and North America. A red alga, it has thin, usually flat branching fronds, about 5–30 cm long, and contains a gelatinous substance (carrageenin) used in jellies, lotions, cosmetics, food products, shoe polishes, etc.

Carrantuohill 52 00N 9 45W The highest mountain in Ireland, in Co Kerry, in Macgillicuddy's Reeks. Height: 1041 m (3414 ft).

Carranza, Venustiano (1859–1920) Mexican statesman and soldier in the post-1910 revolutionary movement. He was the first president (1917–20) under the 1917 constitution and his nationalist policies brought him into conflict with the USA. He was deposed and killed in a coup in 1920.

Carrara 44 04N 10 06E A town in central Italy, in Tuscany. It is famous for its white marble, which was used by the sculptor Michelangelo. Population (1981 est): 68 460.

Carrel, Alexis (1873–1944) French surgeon, who pioneered the technique for sewing (suturing) blood vessels together. He perfected this after moving to the USA, where he also worked on techniques for keeping organs alive outside the body. He was awarded a Nobel Prize (1912).

Carrhae, Battle of (53 BC) The battle near Carrhae (now Haran, Turkey) in which the Roman forces under Marcus Licinius *Crassus were defeated by the Parthians.

Carrickfergus 54 43N 5 49N A town in Northern Ireland, in Co Antrim on Belfast Lough. It is a fishing port with a textile industry. Population (1985 est): 30 000.

Carrington, Peter Alexander Rupert Carrington, 6th Baron (1919–   ) British Conservative politician. He was UK high commissioner in Australia (1956–59), first lord of the admiralty (1959–63), secretary of state for defence (1970–74), and leader of the opposition in the House of Lords (1964–70, 1974–79). As foreign secretary (1979–82), he was instrumental in establishing Zimbabwe's independence (1980); he resigned following the Argentinian invasion of the *Falkland Islands (April, 1982). Carrington was appointed secretary general of NATO in 1984.

carrion crow An omnivorous Eurasian crow, *Corvus corone corone*, about 46 cm long with a pure-black plumage and a harsh croaking call. It is a notorious egg thief, unpopular with gamekeepers. *See also* hooded crow.

carrion flower A cactus-like succulent plant belonging to the genus *Stapelia* (60 species), native to arid parts of Africa. Several are grown for their showy purplish flowers, although they have a foetid odour. *S. gigantea* has a leafless square stem, 5–30 cm high, bearing a flower with a diameter of 30 cm. Family: *Asclepiadaceae*.
The name is also given to a species of *greenbrier, *Smilax herbacea*, which has small green evil-smelling flowers.

Carroll, Lewis (Charles Lutwidge Dodgson; 1832–98) British writer and mathematician. He lectured in mathematics at Oxford University from 1855 to 1881, and took holy orders in 1861 but never held a benefice. The children's classic, *Alice's Adventures in Wonderland* (1865), was written for the young Alice Liddell, the daughter of the head of his Oxford College. It and the sequel, *Through the Looking-Glass* (1872), are sophisticated books that combine elements of fantasy, logic, and nonsense and have had a lasting appeal to adults as well as children. He also wrote nonsense verse, notably *The Hunting of the Snark* (1876), and was a pioneer of portrait photography.

carrot A biennial flowering plant, *Daucus carota*, found in grassy places in temperate regions from Europe to India. The stem grows to a height of 30–100 cm and bears a head of small white flowers. *Daucus carota sativus* is the cultivated carrot. This is grown as an annual, and produces an orange thick fleshy edible root. Many varieties of the cultivated carrot have been developed. Family: *Umbelliferae*.

Carson, Edward Henry, Baron (1854–1935) Irish politician and barrister at both the Irish and English bars; solicitor general for Ireland (1892) and England (1900–06). In 1895 Carson successfully defended Lord Queensberry in the Oscar *Wilde libel case. As an MP in the English parliament (1892–1921), he led the Ulster opposition to the Irish *Home Rule bill (1912) and raised the Ulster Volunteers to oppose its enactment. In World War I he served in Asquith's and Lloyd George's cabinets.

Carson, Kit (Christopher C.; 1809–68) US frontiersman. A saddler in Missouri, stationed on the Santa Fe trail, he joined a wagon train in 1826 and made Taos, New Mexico, his headquarters for a career as a guide. Well-versed in Indian ways, he was a guide in *Frémont's expeditions to the West in the 1840s and after distinguished service in the Mexican War became US Indian agent at Taos (1853). He subsequently fought for the Federals in the Civil War. Illiterate, Carson dictated his memoirs (1856), published as *Dear Old Kit* (1968).

Carson, Rachel Louise (1907–64) US science writer, who worked as a genetic biologist (1936–52) and later as editor for the US Fish and Wildlife Service. Her books, notably *The Sea around Us* (1951) and *Silent Spring* (1962), greatly increased public awareness of the natural environment and warned of the dangers of pollution.

Carson City 39 10N 119 46W A city in the USA, the capital of Nevada. It is named after the famous frontiersman Kit Carson. Although silver and copper are mined, the main industry is gambling. Population (1985): 35 000.

Cartagena 10 24N 75 33W A port in N Colombia, on the Caribbean Sea. It is important industrially, producing textiles, petrochemicals, and pharmaceuticals. It receives oil by pipeline from Berrancabermeja; exports include coffee and oil. The University of Cartagena was founded in 1827. Population (1980): 368 000.

Cartagena (*or* Carthagena) 37 36N 0 59W A port in SE Spain, in Murcia on the Mediterranean Sea. Founded by the Carthaginian general, Hasdrubal, in the 3rd century BC, it was destroyed by Ferdinand II of Castile in 1243. In the 16th century, under Philip II of Spain, it became a great naval port and remains the country's chief Mediterranean naval base. It exports minerals, olive oil, and fruits and has boatbuilding industries. Population (1981): 172 751.

Cartago 9 50N 83 52W A town in central Costa Rica, at the foot of the volcano Irazú. It serves an agricultural area. Population (1981 est): 26 341.

Carte, Richard D'Oyly. *See* D'Oyly Carte, Richard.

cartel An association of producers who join together to secure a higher price for their products by restricting the supply. However, a cartel is inherently unstable; all the members have an interest in producing as much as they can at the new price, in defiance of the cartel agreement. The need to enrol all producers and to maintain strict discipline explains why the highly successful oil cartel OPEC has not been followed by other primary-product cartels.

Carter, Elliott (Cook) (1908–) US composer. He studied with Walter Piston (1894–1976) at Harvard and Nadia Boulanger in Paris. Since 1950 he has evolved a contrapuntal style of great rhythmical complexity. His works include a *Double Concerto* (for piano, harpsichord, and two chamber orchestras; 1961) and *Symphony for Three Orchestras* (1978).

Carter, Howard (1874–1939) British archaeologist. Carter worked in Egypt from 1892 and collaborated with Lord Carnarvon (1866–1923) after 1907. In 1922 they discovered the tomb of *Tutankhamen, work on which occupied Carter for the next ten years.

JIMMY CARTER *The president brings together Sadat of Egypt (left) and Begin of Israel (right) at Camp David (1979).*

Carter, Jimmy (James Earl C.; 1924–) US statesman; Democratic president (1977–81). Carter left his family peanut farming and warehousing business in Georgia for politics. He was governor of Georgia from 1970 to 1974 and in his presidential campaign promised ambitious social and economic reforms. He signed a treaty giving up US control of the Panama Canal by 2000 AD, attempted to limit US energy consumption,

but is best known for bringing about the peace treaty between Egypt and Israel (1979).

Carteret, John. *See* Granville, John Carteret, 1st Earl.

Cartesian coordinates. *See* coordinate systems.

Carthage (Punic name: *Kart-Hadasht*, New City) An ancient city of N Africa, near modern Tunis. Traditionally founded 814 BC by *Dido and exiles from *Tyre, Carthage rapidly became leader of the *Phoenician trading cities of N Africa, waging intermittent war with the Greeks of Marseilles and Sicily. From 264 BC Carthage fought the three *Punic Wars with *Rome, her former ally, and was totally destroyed (146 BC). Refounded by Julius *Caesar (45 BC), Carthage became, in turn, the commercial, cultural, and administrative capital of Roman Africa, the capital of the *Vandal kingdom (439–533 AD), and a Byzantine outpost, until destroyed by the Muslims in 697 AD.

Carthusians A contemplative Roman Catholic religious order founded in 1084 by St Bruno and taking its name from the location of the first community, La Grande Chartreuse, near Grenoble. Although originally without a written rule, the Carthusians observed a rigorous life of fasting and solitude and were vowed to silence. The order remained fairly small but disciplined. At the time of the dissolution of the monasteries there were nine Carthusian monasteries, or *Charterhouses, in England. At present the order's English headquarters is the Charterhouse, Parkminster, Sussex. The French monks are noted for the liqueur Chartreuse, which they make.

Cartier, Jacques (1491–1557) French navigator. In 1534, under the patronage of Francis I, he sailed in search of the *Northwest Passage and explored the coast of N Canada and Newfoundland. The next year he sailed up the St Lawrence as far as what became Montreal but failed to found a colony there (1536). His discoveries were important to French claims in Canada in the 17th century.

Cartier-Bresson, Henri (1908–) French photographer and pioneer of photojournalism. He studied painting before taking up photography in 1932. Although also providing a record of events on his worldwide travels, his often poignant photographs, collected in such books as *The Decisive Moment* (1952) and *Europeans* (1955), concentrate on ordinary people and their fleeting expressions and gestures. As a film maker, he collaborated with Jean *Renoir in the late 1930s and returned to this medium in the 1960s.

cartilage A flexible supportive tissue consisting chiefly of a *polysaccharide—chondroitin sulphate—in which elastic or collagen fibres may be embedded. Cartilage lines the bone ends at joints and also provides the skeleton of the nose, external ear, and parts of the throat (larynx) and airways of the respiratory tract. A tough cartilage forms the intervertebral discs between the bones of the spine. During development a large amount of *bone is formed from pre-existing cartilage.

cartilaginous fish Any *fish belonging to the class *Chondrichthyes*, comprising the *sharks, *rays, and *chimaeras. They have a cartilaginous skeleton, usually a ventrally situated mouth, and exposed gill slits. The males have pelvic fins modified to form copulatory organs (claspers) and fertilization occurs inside the female's body. Some species deposit their eggs on the sea bed while in others the eggs are retained and develop internally resulting in the birth of live young.

cartography The science of map and chart making. Belief in the flatness of the world, the centrality of the Mediterranean lands (or Jerusalem in Christian maps), and an all-encircling Ocean dominated classical and medieval cartography. Maps and charts were individually hand drawn at first, but 15th- and 16th-century maps were printed by woodblock and coloured by hand. More elaborate maps and charts, richly decorated with lettering and illustrations were introduced by the Italians in the mid-16th century. The difficulty of accurately representing the curved surface of the earth on the plane surface of a map is dealt with by using

235

Caspian Sea

different □map projections for different purposes. Modern map making is assisted by aerial surveying and satellite photography. *See also* digital maps.

cartoon 1. A full-sized preparatory drawing or painting for a mural, easel painting, tapestry, or mosaic. Among the most famous are Raphael's cartoons (Victoria and Albert Museum) for tapestries for the Sistine Chapel, in the Vatican. 2. A nonrealistic portrait or figure drawing transferring a person's most readily recognizable features into a comic likeness. Beginning in Italy as a branch of high art with *Leonardo da Vinci's grotesque heads and *Bernini's political drawings, caricatures became a favourite genre in British popular and broadsheet art with the political satires of *Rowlandson and *Gillray. This tradition was carried into middle-class journalism in the Victorian period by such artists as Phiz (*see* Browne, Hablot) and *Cruikshank and has now become the widely used cartoon strip of modern newspapers.

Cartwright, Edmund (1743–1823) British inventor and industrialist, who contributed to the mechanization of weaving and spinning. In 1785 he invented a power loom and then set up a factory in Doncaster for weaving and spinning yarn. Four years later he invented a machine for combing wool. In 1793 his business failed but parliament recognized his achievements in 1809 with an award of £10,000.

Caruso, Enrico (1873–1921) Italian tenor, born in Naples. The greatest lyric tenor of his time, he excelled in Verdi and Puccini and was acclaimed in Europe and the USA, where he sang at the Metropolitan Opera, New York.

Carver, George Washington (1864–1943) US agriculturalist, born into a Black slave family. Carver demonstrated to southern farmers how fertility could be restored to their land by diversification, especially by planting peanuts and sweet potatoes. He also discovered a wide range of by-products that could be obtained from these crops.

Cary, (Arthur) Joyce (Lunel) (1888–1957) British novelist. His early novels, notably *Mister Johnson* (1939), are mostly set in West Africa, where he worked before settling in Oxford in 1920. His best-known book, *The Horse's Mouth* (1944), is part of a trilogy about art; he also wrote a second trilogy, about politics.

caryatid A carved column in the shape of a draped female figure that first appeared in Greek architecture around 500 BC. The most notable caryatids to have survived are on the Erechtheum on the *Acropolis of Athens. Caryatids were infrequent in Roman architecture but enjoyed a limited revival in 19th-century classicism.

caryopsis A grain: the small dry *fruit of grasses and cereals. It resembles an achene, being single-seeded and indehiscent, but differs in having the seed completely fused to the fruit wall.

Casablanca (Arabic name: Dar-el-Beida) 33 39N 7 35W A port in Morocco, on the Atlantic coast. First established by the Portuguese (1515), it was taken by the French in 1907. During World War II it was the scene of the Casablanca Conference (1943), a summit meeting between Franklin D. Roosevelt and Sir Winston Churchill. The largest and most important city in Morocco, its port handles most of the country's trade, the chief export being phosphates. Its major industries include textiles, electronics, chemicals, cement, and food processing. Fishing and tourism are also important. Population (1982): 2 139 204.

Casals, Pablo (Pau C.; 1876–1973) Spanish cellist, conductor, and composer. He performed and conducted in every European country and in the USA. Casals revolutionized the style and technique of cello playing and excelled as an interpreter of Bach's six suites for unaccompanied cello and of the cello concertos of Dvořák, Elgar, and Schumann. An opponent of the Franco regime in Spain, Casals settled in

Prades in France, near the Spanish border; he established a chamber-music festival there in 1950.

Casanova, Giovanni Giacomo, Chevalier de Seingalt (1725–98) Italian adventurer. He lived in many European cities, working at different times as a violinist, a spy, and a librarian. His adventures, which included a dramatic escape from prison in Venice in 1756 and many romantic liaisons, are recorded in his memoirs, of which the first complete edition was published in 1960.

Cascade Range A volcanic mountain range in North America. It extends N–S, nearly parallel to the Pacific coast, between the Fraser River in British Columbia (Canada) and N California (USA), where it becomes continuous with the *Sierra Nevada. It reaches 4392 m (14 408 ft) at Mount Rainier.

case hardening A surface-hardening process in *steel manufacture, in which the metal is heated to over 900°C for several hours in the presence of carbon. The carbon is absorbed on the surface to a depth depending on the temperature and duration of the treatment. The steel is then cooled quickly (quenched) to complete the process. *See also* heat treatment.

casein The major protein present in milk. Casein is easily digested and contains a good balance of essential *amino acids, making it—in dietary terms—a high-quality protein. Cheese consists largely of insoluble para-casein, formed from casein by the action of enzymes. Casein is also used industrially to make thermoplastics (e.g. knife handles), paints, and adhesives.

Casement, Sir Roger (David) (1864–1916) British consular official and Irish nationalist, who was executed by the British for treason. Casement spent his consular career in Africa, where he disclosed the atrocities suffered by native labour in the Congo. He retired to his birthplace, Ireland, in 1912. In World War I he tried unsuccessfully to raise German help for the Irish nationalists. Returning to Ireland in a German submarine, he was arrested, tried, and hanged. His controversial diaries, which describe his homosexuality, were not released by the government until 1959.

Caserta 41 04N 14 20E A market town in S Italy, in Campania. The centre of Garibaldi's campaigns for the unification of Italy in the 19th century, it has a 12th-century cathedral and a palace. Population (1981 est): 66 754.

Cash, Pat (1965–) Australian tennis player. Despite setbacks due to injury during his early career he became Wimbledon singles champion in 1987, beating Ivan Lendl.

cashew A tree, *Anacardium occidentale*, native to tropical America and cultivated widely in the tropics. It grows to 12 m and has sweet-scented red flowers. The fruit is a kidney-shaped nut that develops at the end of a hanging pear-shaped receptacle. The edible kernel—the cashew nut—is extracted after the fruit is roasted. Family: *Anacardiaceae*.

cashmere A warm soft wool-like fabric made from the undercoat of the *Kashmir goat, produced mainly in China, Mongolia, and Iran. Originally used in shawls from Kashmir, it is an expensive fabric as each goat produces only small quantities of fine soft hair and processing is costly. Imitations are common.

Casimir (III) the Great (1310–70) King of Poland (1333–70). Casimir extended Polish territory, codified laws, and founded Cracow University (1364). He encouraged the development of Polish culture and bettered the lot of the peasants.

Casimir IV (1427–92) Grand Duke of Lithuania (1440–92) and King of Poland (1447–92), whose reign saw a flowering of Polish culture. Casimir greatly enhanced the prestige of the Jagiellon dynasty by his own and his children's political marriages. After a 13-year war with the *Teutonic Knights he won control of W Prussia (1466).

Caspian Sea The largest inland sea in the world, bounded by Iran and the Soviet Union and fed chiefly by the River Volga. Its surface is 28.5 m (93.5 ft) below sea level and is generally becoming lower due to irrigation and increased evaporation from the Volga. The chief ports are Astrakhan and Baku, both in the Soviet Union. Sturgeon and seals are caught here and oil and gas extracted. Area: about 370 000 sq km (142 827 sq mi).

Cassander (c. 358-297 BC) King of Macedon (305-297). In the wars of succession that followed the death of Alexander the Great in 323, Cassander fought for control of parts of Alexander's empire and won most of Macedon and Greece. He murdered Alexander's mother, widow, and son to secure his position.

Cassandra A legendary Greek prophetess, daughter of King Priam of Troy. After she had refused to submit to Apollo's advances, he condemned her prophecies to eternal disbelief. When Troy fell she was taken by Agamemnon, with whom she was later murdered.

MARY CASSATT   Morning Toilet, *painted in 1886.*

Cassatt, Mary (1844-1926) US painter. She worked chiefly in Paris, where she exhibited with the impressionists (1879-81, 1886) and was influenced by her friend *Degas. Typical of her work are mother-and-child scenes.

cassava A shrubby flowering plant, *Manihot esculentus* (or *M. utilissimus*), also known as manioc, native to tropical America. Many varieties of this species—divided into two groups, sweet and bitter cassavas—are cultivated in the tropics for their edible starchy tuberous roots. These can be processed into tapioca, ground to produce manioc or cassava meal (Brazilian arrowroot), used as animal fodder, or cooked and eaten as a vegetable. Family: *Euphorbiaceae* (spurge family).

cassette A plastic case containing a length of magnetic recording tape wound onto two spools. Cassettes are easy to use but can hold only relatively short tapes, their length being limited by the minimum thickness of tape that can be used without breakage. Commercial cassettes are two-track, i.e. can be used to record in both directions, and are available with 30, 60, 90, or 120 minutes playing time.

cassia The aromatic bark of a Chinese tree, *Cinnamomum cassia*, used as a substitute for cinnamon. The dried unripe fruits (cassia buds) are also used as a spice. Family: *Lauraceae*.

Cassia A genus of trees, shrubs, and herbs (500-600 species) of tropical and warm regions of Asia, Africa, and America. The laxative drug senna is extracted from the dried leaves and pods (fruits) of many cultivated species. The fruit of *C. fistula* (cassia pods or purging cassia) is also used as a laxative. Some species are grown as ornamentals. Family: *Leguminosae.*

Cassino 41 29N 13 50E A town in central Italy, in Lazio. It was a key position during World War II and the town and Benedictine monastery (Monte Cassino) were destroyed in the fighting of 1944. Population (1981 est): 31 139.

Cassiodorus, Flavius Magnus Aurelius (c. 490-c. 583 AD) Christian writer, born in S Italy, who helped to preserve classical learning. After serving in the government of the Ostrogothic king, Theodoric I, Cassiodorus retired to found a monastery at Vivarium in Calabria (550); his most famous work, the *Institutiones*, was a guide to the education of monks.

Cassiopeia A conspicuous constellation in the northern sky, lying partly in the Milky Way. The five brightest stars form a W-shape. It contains the remnants of two recent *supernovae—Tycho's star and the intense radio source Cassiopeia A.

cassiopeium. *See* lutetium.

Cassirer, Ernst (1874-1945) German philosopher and historian. He taught in Hamburg (1919-34) until Nazism forced him into exile in the USA. Interested in people's formation of concepts, he added mythical, historical, and practical categories, based on analysis of language, to *Kant's scientific ones, seeing these as complementary views of one reality. His works include *Substance and Function* (1910) and *Philosophy of Symbolic Forms* (1923).

cassiterite The only commercial ore of tin, consisting of stannic oxide. It is found in association with acid igneous rocks and as alluvial deposits. It is brown or black.

Cassius Longinus, Gaius (d. 42 BC) Roman general. Having shown competence in eastern campaigns, Cassius supported *Pompey until Pompey's defeat by Julius Caesar at *Pharsalus. He was then pardoned by Caesar but joined the conspiracy to assassinate him in 44. Outlawed, Cassius committed suicide after defeat in the battle of *Philippi.

Cassivelaunus King of the Catuvellauni, who organized, with some success, resistance to Caesar's invasion of SE Britain in 54 BC. Only after his stronghold was captured did Cassivelaunus agree peace terms.

Casson, Sir Hugh (Maxwell) (1910-) British architect. A planning adviser to many war-damaged areas in England after World War II, he became director of architecture for the Festival of Britain in 1948. His books on architecture include *Victorian Architecture* (1948). He was professor at the Royal College of Art (1953-75) and president of the Royal Academy of Arts (1976-84).

cassowary A large flightless bird belonging to a family (*Casuariidae*; 3 species) occurring in rain forests of Australia and New Guinea. The largest cassowary (*Casuarius casuarius*) is 150 cm tall and has a black plumage, two red throat wattles, and a blue head with a protective bony helmet. Cassowaries have long powerful legs, each having a long sharp claw, and feed on seeds and berries. Order: *Casuariiformes.*

Castagno, Andrea del (Andrea di Bartolo de Simone; c. 1421-57) Italian *Renaissance painter, who was born near Castagno but settled in Florence. His major frescoes depict the *Last Supper* and the *Passion* (Sta Apollonia, Florence). Later works, showing the influence of *Donatello, include the equestrian portrait of *Niccolò da Tolentino* (Duomo, Florence).

castanets A percussion instrument used in Spain and Italy, consisting of two small cup-shaped pieces of wood (usually chestnut) attached to the finger and thumb of each hand. These are clapped together and dancers often accompany themselves with them. In the symphony orchestra the characteristic sound is produced by two wooden cups attached to a handle and shaken. □musical instruments.

Castel Gandolfo (Latin name: Alba Longa) 41 45N 12 39E A village in central Italy, in Lazio on the shore of Lake Albano. The summer residence of the pope is situated here.

Castellammare di Stabia 38 01N 12 52E A seaport and resort in Campania in Italy, on the Bay of Naples. It was the site of the Roman resort of Stabiae, which was destroyed by the eruption of Vesuvius in 79 AD. Industries include marine engineering and textiles. Population (1981 est): 70 317.

Castellón de la Plana 39 59N 0 03W A city in E Spain. Its industries include textiles and paper and it exports oranges and almonds through its port, El Gráo. Population (1981 est): 126 464.

Castelo Branco, Camilo (1825–95) Portuguese novelist. An illegitimate child with little formal education, he led an adventurous life that is reflected in his many popular novels and stories. His best-known work, *Amor de Perdição* (1862), was written while he was in prison for adultery. Suffering from blindness, he committed suicide.

castes The elements of a system of social stratification in which social boundaries are very definite. A pure caste system consists of a hierarchy of hereditary endogamous occupational groups, in which positions are fixed and mobility from one caste to another is prevented by ritual systems. The classical Hindu caste system (Sanskrit word: varna) of India provides the cardinal example. Traditionally there are four main caste divisions: brahmins (priests), ksatriyas (warriors), vaisyas (merchants), and sundras (serfs). Outside these groups are the "outcastes" or "untouchables." Each stratum is elaborately subdivided; the 1901 census identified 2378 main castes, some of which had several hundred subcastes. Vigorous attempts have been made to abolish the system, especially by Mahatma Gandhi, but despite legislation (1947) abolishing "untouchability" and prohibiting discrimination on the basis of caste, prejudice remains strong.

Castiglione, Baldassare (1478–1529) Italian courtier and writer. A member of an aristocratic family, he was born near Mantua and in 1503 entered the service of the Duke of Urbino, whose court was one of the most distinguished in Renaissance Italy. He performed important diplomatic missions for the Duke; he was later Mantuan ambassador in Rome and after 1524 in the service of Pope Clement VII as papal nuncio in Spain. His literary reputation rests on *Il Cortegiano* (1528), prose dialogues, set in the court of Urbino, which describe the qualities of the ideal courtier. The work was translated into English as *The Courtier* by Sir Thomas Hoby (1530–66) in 1561 and exercised a great influence on such writers as Surrey, Wyatt, and Sidney.

Castile A former kingdom in central Spain. Originally a district at the foot of the Cantabrian Mountains, Castile expanded to the River Duero in the 9th and 10th centuries, becoming a united county. In 1035 it became a kingdom and in 1230 was united with the kingdom of *León, a union dominated by Castile. In 1479 Spain was virtually united following the marriage of *Isabella of Castile to *Ferdinand the Catholic and Castile became the political, administrative, cultural, and linguistic centre of Spain. Today, opposition to Castilian dominance persists.

Castilho, Antonio Feliciano de (1800–75) Portuguese poet. Blind from childhood, he achieved literary distinction after publishing several volumes of romantic poetry, notably *A Noite de Castelo* (1836). After 1840 he worked mainly on translations, and his advocacy of neoclassical doctrines provoked fierce controversy.

casting metals The process of shaping molten metals in a mould. In casting individual items a sand mould is often used. A solid pattern of the shape, made of wood, plastic, or metal, is placed in a moulding box packed tightly with sand bonded with oil or clay. The pattern is then carefully removed leaving a shaped cavity into which the molten metal is poured and allowed to solidify. If the casting is to be repeated, permanent metal moulds called dies are used. **Die casting** is faster and can make more complex shapes than foundry sand casting. **Centrifugal casting**, spinning the molten material at a high speed so that the centrifugal force flings it outwards into a surrounding mould, is used for pipes and similar shapes.

cast iron A form of impure iron containing between 2.5% and 4.5% of carbon by weight. The high carbon content makes it relatively hard and brittle and it tends to crack under tension. Cast iron is made by casting *pig iron and adjusting its composition to improve the strength. It is used for complicated shapes.

castle A fortified defensive building. Its name deriving from Latin *castellum*, a small fortified place, the castle underwent many changes in its history to counteract the development of increasingly powerful weapons. In the early middle ages a castle consisted of a simple building on a mound of earth surrounded by a wooden fence (the motte and bailey castle), a design later copied in stone. The simplest stone castle, such as the White Tower in London, is called a keep or donjon. Later designs became more complicated, involving extensive outworks of battlemented towers and walls (curtain walls), for example Caernarfon Castle in Wales. As they could not be built to withstand cannon fire castles lost their military usefulness; some, such as Windsor Castle, were converted into large houses.

shell keep

concentric castle

artillery fort

CASTLE *The early medieval shell keep gave way to the massive fortifications of the 14th and 15th centuries, which were in turn superseded by the artillery fort with its low walls and sweeping lines of fire.*

Castleford 43 44N 1 21W A town in N England, in West Yorkshire on the River Aire. Traditionally a coalmining town, it also produces glass, chemicals, and earthenware. Population (1981): 36 032.

Castle Hill Rising (1804) A rising in New South Wales (Australia) led by Irish convicts against the government. The rebels seized the convict station at Parramatta but were defeated by government troops, who killed 15 convicts. Nine rebels were tried and hanged.

Castlemaine 37 05S 144 19E A town in Australia, in central Victoria. It is the site of one of the oldest gold diggings in the country. Population (1981): 7583.

Castlereagh, Robert Stewart, Viscount (1769–1822) British statesman, born in Ulster; foreign secretary (1812–22). An MP in the Irish parliament (1790), he became Viscount Castlereagh in 1796, when his father Robert Stewart (1739–1821) became 1st Marquess of Londonderry. Appointed chief secretary for Ireland in 1798, he resigned in 1801, when George III rejected Catholic Emancipation. His policies as secretary for war (1807–09) were attacked by Canning, with whom Castlereagh fought a duel. As foreign secretary he played an important role at the Congress of *Vienna (1814–15) and at subsequent congresses of European powers. He later opposed Metternich's interference in the internal affairs of other states. He was unfairly blamed for the reactionary policies of Lord Liverpool's government and his unpopularity was exacerbated by his austere personality. There was rejoicing in the streets of London after he committed suicide, believing himself to be being blackmailed for homosexual acts.

Castner process The production of sodium cyanide from molten sodium, charcoal, and ammonia. Sodamide and sodium cyanamide are by-products. The extremely poisonous sodium cyanide finds use in the extraction of gold and silver, in hardening steel, and in dye manufacture. Named after Hamilton Young Castner (1859–99).

Castor A white star, apparent magnitude 1.56 and 46 light years distant, that is the second brightest star in the constellation Gemini. It is a *multiple star. Castor and *Pollux are named after the twins of classical mythology.

Castor and Pollux Twin heroes of classical mythology, also known as the Dioscuri. Pollux was immortal, the son of *Zeus and *Leda; Castor was mortal, the son of Tyndareus and Leda. When Castor died, Pollux asked Zeus to allow them to remain unseparated. Transformed into the Gemini constellation, they were the patrons of mariners.

castor oil A pale yellow viscous oil extracted from the seeds of the *castor-oil plant. It is used as a laxative and is also a raw material for the manufacture of resins, plastics, and lubricants.

castor-oil plant A flowering plant, *Ricinus communis*, up to 12 m high, native to tropical Africa and Asia. It is cultivated widely, in the tropics for its seeds, from which castor oil is extracted, and in temperate regions as an ornamental shrub with attractive fanlike leaves (ornamental forms are seldom taller than 2 m). Family: *Euphorbiaceae* (spurge family).

castration Removal of the testes (orchidectomy) or ovaries (oophorectomy). In medicine, castration may be performed in cases of cancer of the testes: it always produces sterility but –unless done before puberty–need not cause impotence. Testicular castration is widely used in livestock management to increase meat production or docility.

castrato A eunuch singer, fashionable in Italian opera and in church choirs during the 17th and 18th centuries. Castration before puberty ensured that the soprano (or sometimes alto) voice quality remained in adulthood. Among the most technically brilliant of the castrati was Giuseppe Farinelli (1705–1782). Composers of Italian opera, such as Handel, frequently wrote the leading male role in the soprano range for a eunuch.

Castres 43 36N 2 14E A town in S France, in the Tarn department. A Huguenot stronghold in the 16th century, it has a major machine-tool industry. Population (1982 est): 46 877.

Castries 14 01N 60 59W The chief town and main port of St Lucia, in the Windward Islands. Founded by the French in 1650, it has a fine harbour. Population (1981 est): 45 000.

Castro (Ruz), Fidel (1926–) Cuban statesman. The son of a wealthy sugar planter, Castro became an opponent of the dictator Fulgencio *Batista. On 26 July, 1953, he led an unsuccessful attack on the Moncada barracks and was imprisoned until 1955. In 1956 he invaded Cuba from Mexico with a small armed band and after a long guerrilla war he defeated government troops. He entered Havana on 1 January, 1959. Castro established a socialist government, which the USA attempted to subvert. As a result, Cuba became heavily dependent on the Soviet Union. *See also* Bay of Pigs.

FIDEL CASTRO

Castrop-Rauxel 51 33N 07 18E A town in NW West Germany, in North Rhine-Westphalia in the *Ruhr. Its industries include coalmining and chemicals. Population (1983 est): 77 659.

Casuarina A genus of shrubs and trees (about 45 species) native to Australia, tropical SE Asia, Malaysia, Polynesia, the Mascarene Islands, and Pacific islands. The young branches, which are slender, green, and drooping, function as leaves (the true leaves are reduced to scales). The she oak (*C. equisetifolia*), up to 45 m tall, is widely cultivated in warm regions for its very hard reddish-brown wood (beefwood or ironwood) and as an ornamental. Family: *Casuarinaceae*.

cat A carnivorous mammal belonging to the family *Felidae* (36 species). Most cats have sheathed claws and sharp canine teeth to kill their prey, which consists of mammals, birds, and fish. Their acute vision (especially in poor light), sense of smell, and hearing are adaptations for hunting stealthily, often at night. With no natural enemies, the kittens (or cubs) are born blind and toothless and learn hunting techniques through play. The wide range of different breeds of domestic cat (*Felis catus*), including *Persian, *Siamese, and *Abyssinian, are thought to have been developed from the African wildcat, or cafer cat (*F. lybica*) and possibly the European *wildcat. Wild species range in size from the *tiger to the tiny South

African black-footed cat (*F. nigripes*), which is smaller than the average domestic cat.

catabolism. *See* metabolism.

catacombs Subterranean cemeteries, especially those containing early Christian graves. The earliest and biggest catacombs are in Rome, particularly those of St Calixtus and St Sebastian along the *Appian Way. Most catacombs consist of narrow passages into the walls of which the burial niches were cut. With the acceptance of Christianity they fell into disuse, although some remained as centres of pilgrimage.

Catalan A *Romance language spoken by about five million people in Catalonia and the Balearic Islands in Spain, Andorra, and the Roussillon region of France. It is closely related to Spanish and to the Occitan language of France. It was the official language of Aragon in the 12th century and has a literature dating from this period.

Catalaunian Plains, Battle of the (451 AD) The battle on the Catalaunian Plains, probably near modern Châlons-sur-Marne in Champagne (E France), in which the Huns under *Attila were defeated by a combined force of Romans and Visigoths under *Aetius and Theodoric I.

catalepsy A condition associated with certain abnormal mental states, including schizophrenia and hysteria, in which the patient, usually female, remains motionless, often with the limbs in fixed positions, for a variable length of time.

Catalhüyük A Neolithic site SE of Konya (S Turkey), discovered in 1958. It was a settlement of cattle breeders and agriculturalists, dating from the late 7th and early 6th millenniums BC. Houses built to a standard pattern and luxury goods, such as obsidian mirrors, suggest advanced social organization. Notable finds include numerous shrines with frescoes or plasterwork decorations depicting animals.

Catalonia (Spanish name: Cataluña; Catalan name: Catalunya) A mainly mountainous region of NE Spain, on the Mediterranean Sea. Agriculture is important, the main crops being cereals, olives, and grapes. It is the most highly industrialized region in Spain, being well provided with hydroelectric power from the River Ebro (and its tributaries). Tourism is important, especially on the coast. *History*: united with Aragon in 1137 and Castile in 1497, Catalonia has nevertheless maintained a strong separatist tradition. In 1932 an autonomous government was established and this lasted throughout the Civil War (1936–39), in which Catalonia played a prominent role on the Republican side. A centre of opposition throughout the Franco regime, the Catalan government was restored provisionally in 1977. Area: 31 932 sq km (12 329 sq mi). Population (1981): 5 958 208. Capital: Barcelona.

Catalpa A genus of trees (11 species) native to E Asia, North America, and the West Indies. They were widely grown as ornamentals for their attractive heart-shaped leaves, 12–30 cm long, and trumpet-shaped flowers, which are white with yellow and purple markings. The fruit is a long pod. The genus includes the Indian bean tree (*C. bignonioides*), up to 15 m high, which yields a durable timber. Family: *Bignoniaceae*.

catalysis The acceleration of a *chemical reaction by a substance (catalyst) that is not itself consumed in the reaction. Virtually every reaction must overcome an energy barrier as the molecules of the reactants rearrange to form the products. The catalyst allows the reaction to proceed via a different lower-energy pathway. Since the reverse reaction is also accelerated, catalysis does not shift the chemical equilibrium, merely speeds its attainment. Catalysis may be homogeneous (all substances in the same phase), as the catalysis of carbon-monoxide combustion by steam; or heterogeneous (at an interface) as in the *Haber-Bosch process. Catalysis by a reaction product is called auto-catalysis. Catalysis is used extensively in industrial chemical

processes. In living organisms *enzymes are catalysts for biochemical reactions.

catalytic cracking A chemical process used in *oil refining. Crude oil, which contains large molecules, is decomposed by heat and pressure in the presence of a catalyst, usually a clay-type substance containing alumina and silica. Without a catalyst the same process, known as thermal cracking, needs a pressure of between 20 and 40 atmospheres and a temperature of 540°C. Catalytic cracking is carried out at between two and three atmospheres at a slightly lower temperature.

catamaran A modern sailing vessel with two identical hulls, rigidly fastened parallel to one another, and, usually, a single mast with a triangular mainsail and jib. Because of their buoyancy, the hulls of a catamaran offer very little resistance to the water, making it extremely fast. The modern catamaran is modelled on a native canoe-like vessel of the SW Pacific, which in some forms was basically a raft with a sail. *See also* trimaran.

Catania 37 31N 15 06E A port in Italy, in E Sicily near Mount Etna. Destroyed by an earthquake in 1693, it was rebuilt in a baroque style. The university was founded in 1434. Its industries include sulphur refining. Population (1980 est): 398 168.

Catanzaro 38 54N 16 36E A market town in S Italy, the capital of Calabria. Citrus fruit is grown in the area. Population (1983 est): 101 662.

cataract (geography). *See* waterfall.

cataract (ophthalmology) Opacities in the lens of the eye resulting in blurred vision and caused by the deposition of small crystals or changes in the composition of the lens substance. The former condition increases with age; such cataracts are a common cause of blindness in the elderly. Certain diseases, such as poorly controlled diabetes mellitus, can also lead to cataracts. Cataracts are usually treated by surgical removal of the lens and the use of appropriate spectacles. In some cases a plastic lens may be implanted to replace the one removed.

catarrh Inflammation of the mucous membranes lining the nose, nasal sinuses, throat, or air passages, causing the production of thick phlegm. Catarrh is commonly due to viral infections, particularly the common cold, and hay fever.

catastrophe theory A theory of dynamic systems using methods of *topology. Originally, catastrophe theory was developed by the French mathematician René Thom (1923–), in 1972, as a theory of biological differentiation, in which gradual growth stimulates and is stimulated by "catastrophic" large-scale changes. It has since been applied to other fields, including optics, engineering, sociology, economics, and linguistics. The theory is based on analogy with topological form. For instance, if a system depends on three factors, a particular state of the system can be represented by a point in three-dimensional space and possible states are represented by a region (or shape). The behaviour of the system is investigated by considering the topological classification of these representations, in particular the theory shows how discontinuous catastrophic changes can occur. In engineering, a structure may be stable under a certain range of conditions and collapse if other conditions are applied.

catastrophism A formerly held theory according to which geological changes have occurred as a result of sudden short-lived catastrophes. Such events do occur (e.g. floods), but they have temporary and local effects. *Compare* uniformitarianism.

catchment area The area from which a river is fed with water; it is usually bounded by a *watershed or divide.

catechism A form of instruction in the essentials of Christian doctrine. Catechisms were originally for the instruction of converts preparing for *baptism, frequently taking the form of a set of responses. With the spread of infant baptism, from the 6th century their function became the basic education of children in the faith, often as preparation for *confirmation. After the Reformation, printed forms of catechisms were also used as an expression of particular Churches' beliefs, as, for example, that printed in the Book of *Common Prayer.

catechol (pyrocatechol *or* 1,2 dihydroxy-benzene; $C_6H_4(OH)_2$) A colourless crystalline *aromatic compound used as a developer in photography. *See also* catecholamines.

catecholamines Amine derivatives of *catechol. They include *adrenaline, *noradrenaline, and dopamine, which act as neurotransmitters and hormones. Depletion of dopamine in the basal ganglia of the brain is associated with *parkinsonism.

catechu A vegetable extract containing *tannin and used in tanning and dying. Black catechu is obtained mainly from wood. Pale catechu (gambier; terra japonica) is produced from leaves and is used in medicine as an astringent. Extract from betel or areca nuts is also called catechu.

categorical imperative The fundamental moral law in *Kant's ethical theory: an act is moral only if the principle on which it is justified is universally applicable.

catenary The curve obtained by suspending a string between two points. If the middle of the string, the lowest point, is at height a above a reference level, then the height, y, at distance x along the string from the middle is given by: $y = \frac{1}{2}a(e^{x/a} + e^{-x/a})$.

caterpillar The larva of *butterflies and moths. Soft-bodied and wingless, all caterpillars have a head and 13 body segments with 3 pairs of true thoracic legs and 5 pairs of abdominal prolegs, which aid in locomotion. The mouthparts are adapted for chewing leaves or feeding on sap. Some species are serious crop pests. Caterpillars exhibit a wide variety of camouflaging colours and shapes. Some produce irritating or poisonous secretions.

Catesby, Robert. *See* Fawkes, Guy.

catfish A *bony fish of the order *Siluriformes* (about 2500 species), with a stout scaleless body, 4–450 cm long, a broad flat head, and long whisker-like barbels. Freshwater catfish (family *Ictaluridae*), sometimes called bullheads, occur worldwide; marine catfish (family *Ariidae*) inhabit tropical and coastal waters and are generally bottom-dwelling scavengers used as food, game, and aquarium fish. *See also* candiru; wels. The name is also used for marine fish of the family *Anarhichadidae* (order *Perciformes*).

catgut The tough cord made from the intestines of the sheep or sometimes the ox and the horse (but not the cat). It is used for stringing tennis rackets, violin strings, and for surgical stitching.

Cathari (*or* Cathars) A heretical sect in medieval Europe. It spread from Bulgaria, where its adherents were called Bogomils, to W Europe in the 11th century. From the mid-12th century the Cathari flourished in S France (*see* Albigenses) and in Italy until they were wiped out in the 14th century by the Inquisition. Their doctrine, influenced by *Gnosticism and *Manichaeism, taught that the material world was irredeemably evil but that man's soul was good and could secure its reunion with God. They were sceptical about much biblical doctrine, holding, for instance, that Christ was only an angel. They were divided into two classes, the perfect and the believers. The perfect lived in celibacy, marriage being regarded, with all other fleshly indulgences, as evil. The believers could join the perfect immediately before death by receiving the Cathari's chief rite, a laying on of hands, called the *consolamentum*.

Cathay The medieval European name for China, derived from Khitan, the name of a Mongol people who invaded N China in the 10th century. It was introduced to Europe by such early travellers as Marco Polo. China is still called Khitan by the Russians.

cathedral The principal church of an ecclesiastical area (diocese), governed by a bishop or an archbishop. The name comes from Latin *cathedra*, bishop's seat. Generally larger and more magnificent than other churches, cathedrals, such as *St Peter's Basilica, Rome, *St Paul's Cathedral, London, and *Notre-Dame de Paris, contain some of their country's finest works of art. Of the 45 Anglican cathedrals in England, less than half are medieval. Only three have been built in the 20th century: Liverpool (begun 1904), Guildford (built between 1936 and 1965), and the rebuilt Coventry cathedral (consecrated 1962). The Roman Catholic cathedrals of Westminster (1895–1903) and Liverpool (opened 1967) are buildings of architectural interest.

Catherine I (1684–1727) The second wife from 1712 of Peter the Great and Empress of Russia (1725–27). Of Lithuanian peasant origin, Catherine was captured in 1702 in the Great Northern War and became Peter's mistress. After Peter's death in 1725, his adviser Prince A. D. Menshikov (1672–1729), supported by the palace guards, secured the throne for Catherine.

Catherine (II) the Great (1729–96) Empress of Russia (1762–96), who gained the throne in a coup in which her unpopular husband, Emperor Peter III (1728–62; reigned 1762), was murdered. Catherine's reign marked the expansion of Russian territory as a result of her successful wars against the Turks (1768–74, 1787–92) and the partition of Poland (1772, 1793, 1795). Influenced by the ideas of the Enlightenment, she had to abandon her scheme to emancipate the serfs in the face of opposition from their masters. Of her many lovers, only *Potemkin exerted a durable influence on government.

Catherine de' Medici (1519–89) Regent of France (1560–63) during the minority of her second son, Charles IX, and virtual ruler until his death (1574). The daughter of Lorenzo de' Medici, Duke of Urbino, she married Henry II of France in 1533. Intent on upholding royal authority during the *Wars of Religion, she advocated tolerance for the *Huguenots but later supported the Catholics. She was largely responsible for the *St Bartholomew's Day Massacre. Her influence waned during the reign of her third son *Henry III.

Catherine of Alexandria, St Legendary 4th-century Christian martyr, who protested to the emperor Maxentius at the persecution of Christians. The wheel on which she was being broken (after which the firework known as the Catherine wheel is named) was reputedly shattered by an angel and she was instead beheaded. Her feast day (25 Nov) was removed from the church calendar in 1969.

Catherine of Aragon (1485–1536) The first wife (1509–33) of Henry VIII of England and the mother of Mary I. Failing to bear him a son, she was divorced by Henry, who argued that their marriage was invalid because Catherine was the widow of his brother Arthur. The pope's refusal to accept their divorce provoked the English *Reformation.

Catherine of Braganza (1638–1705) The wife (from 1662) of Charles II of England. A Portuguese princess and a devout Roman Catholic, her unpopularity was intensified by her failure to produce an heir to the throne.

Catherine of Genoa, St (1447–1510) Italian mystic. From a noble family, she married at the age of 16 but underwent a religious conversion 10 years later and devoted herself to caring for the sick. She had a number of mystical experiences, which are recounted in *Vita e dottrina* (1551). Feast day: 15 Sept.

Catherine of Siena, St (Caterina Benincasa; 1347–80) Italian nun and mystic. She joined the Dominican Tertiary Order at 16 and devoted herself to caring for the sick and poor and to contemplation. In 1376 she went to Avignon to persuade Pope Gregory IX to return to Rome. She was reported to have received the stigmata on her body in 1375. Her letters and a work on mysticism, the *Dialogue*, are extant. Feast day: 30 April.

catheter A tube inserted into a hollow organ of the body in order to drain or introduce fluids. A urinary catheter is inserted into the bladder through the urethra to relieve obstruction (commonly caused by enlargement of the prostate gland in elderly men) to the flow of urine. Cardiac catheters are used to measure blood pressure in the heart; similar catheters are used to inject radio-opaque substances into blood vessels for X-ray examination.

cathode The negative electrode of an electrolytic cell, valve, etc. It is the electrode by which the electrons enter the system. *Compare* anode.

cathode-ray oscilloscope (CRO) An instrument that displays electrical quantities on the screen of a *cathode-ray tube. It can be used to show the variation of a signal strength with time or with another electrical quantity. The CRO is used extensively in electronics laboratories and in other scientific work.

cathode rays A stream of electrons emitted by a *cathode, when a voltage is applied between a cathode and an *anode either in an evacuated glass tube or one containing gas at low pressure. The electron beam can be focused onto a fluorescent screen to produce a visual display. This effect is used in the *cathode-ray tube used in television receivers, radar screens, and oscilloscopes.

cathode-ray tube (CRT) A vacuum tube that converts electrical signals into visible form by projecting a beam of electrons onto a fluorescent screen. It is an essential component of the television receiver and the *cathode-ray oscilloscope (CRO). The electron beam is produced by an electron gun, and deflected horizontally and vertically by an arrangement of plates and magnets, which move it back and forth across the screen and focus it by creating an *electromagnetic field, the strength of which varies according to input signals. In a television tube the beam intensity varies to form the light and dark regions of the picture.

Catholic emancipation A campaign in Britain and Ireland to secure full civil and political rights for Roman Catholics. Since the Reformation, Catholics had been subject to a number of restrictions concerning property ownership, inheritance, and government employment and could not sit in parliament. In the late 18th century several relief acts were passed but parliamentary representation was still denied. The opposition of the Tory establishment and the monarchy continued until *O'Connell's efforts achieved the Catholic Emancipation Act of 1829.

Catiline (Lucius Sergius Catilina; d. 62 BC) Roman politician, who plotted to seize power in 62. Thwarted by Cicero, Catiline fled to a rebel force in Etruria and his fellow conspirators were executed. He was defeated and killed in battle.

Catlin, George (1796-1872) Pennsylvanian artist and author. He is famous for his painted and written studies of the American Indians, among whom he lived (1832-40). His best-known book is *Manners, Customs, and Conditions of North American Indians* (1841).

catmint A perennial flowering plant, *Nepeta cataria*, native to chalky regions of temperate Europe. The branching stem grows to a height of 40-100 cm and bears toothed heart-shaped leaves and small white flowers spotted with purple. The plant has a strong minty scent, attractive to cats. Family: *Labiatae*.

Cato Street Conspiracy (1820) A conspiracy against the British government led by Arthur Thistlewood (1770-1820). A fanatical idealist, Thistlewood and four others planned to murder all the ministers of the cabinet as a prelude to insurrection. Their attempt was foiled and the leaders, arrested in Cato Street, NW London, were hanged.

Cato the Elder (Marcus Porcius C.; 234-149 BC) Roman statesman, who wrote the first history of Rome. A moral and political conservative, Cato as censor (184) legislated against luxury and sponsored improvements in public works.

GEORGE CATLIN   *A painting by the artist depicting himself (left) in the tent of a Mandan Indian chief. Catlin made a number of drawings and paintings of this people in 1832.*

His embassy to Carthage (153) led him to fear the resurgence of Rome's old enemy; "Carthage must be destroyed" was his repeated cry until the third *Punic War was declared (149). His simple writing style was influential and he is the first important Latin prose author.

Cato the Younger (Marcus Porcius C.; 95-46 BC) Roman politician; the great-grandson of Cato the Elder and an opponent of Julius Caesar. Caesar, with *Pompey and *Crassus, created the first *Triumvirate (60) partly to neutralize Cato's opposition to their political ambitions. Forced to support Pompey in the civil war in an attempt to save the Republic, Cato escaped after Pompey's death to Utica, in Africa. On hearing of Caesar's victory at *Thapsus, he committed suicide after ensuring the evacuation of his supporters.

Catskill Mountains A mountain range in the USA, in the N Appalachian Mountains. Consisting of forested steep-sided mountains, it rises to 1261 m (4204 ft) at Slide Mountain. The area supplies water to New York City and is a popular recreation area for New Yorkers. The mountains are associated with the fictional character Rip Van Winkle, created by Washington Irving.

cat's-tail. *See* reedmace.

Catterick 54 22N 1 38W A village in N England, in North Yorkshire on the River Swale. Nearby is an important army garrison; there is also a famous racecourse.

cattle *Ruminant mammals belonging to the genus *Bos* (7 species), also called oxen, native to Eurasia and Africa. Modern domestic cattle (*B. taurus*), which are probably descended from such ancestors as the *auroch, vary in body shape, size, and colour according to breed but are generally 90-110 cm high at the shoulder and weigh 400-900 kg. *Zebus and *gayals are similarly now found only in the domestic state. Cattle are used for milk and meat production and for draught purposes (*see* livestock farming). Family: *Bovidae*. *See also* banteng; gaur; yak.

Cattleya A genus of tropical American epiphytic *orchids (about 65 species), grown commercially for ornament and the florist trade. They have large pseudobulbs, one or two leaves, and clusters of 1-30 large brightly coloured flowers. *C. labiata* has been crossed with other orchid genera to produce many showy hybrids.

Catullus, Valerius (c. 84-c. 54 BC) Roman poet. Born in Verona, he became the leading member of a group of young innovatory poets in Rome. 116 poems survive, of which the most famous are the 25 lyrics addressed to a married woman named Lesbia, recording in passionate language the shifting moods of love from ecstasy to despair. The other poems include elegies and vicious satirical attacks on Julius Caesar and other politicians.

Caucasian languages. *See* Northeast Caucasian; Northwest Caucasian; South Caucasian.

Caucasoid A race or group of races and peoples originally inhabiting Europe, North Africa, and the Near East. In modern times Caucasoids have spread to North and South America, Australia, New Zealand, parts of Africa, and elsewhere. They are characterized by skin pigmentation ranging from very pale to dark brown, straight to curly hair, narrow high-bridged noses, plentiful body hair, and a high frequency of Rh-negative blood type.

Caucasus Mountains (Russian name: Kavkaz) Two mountain ranges in the SW Soviet Union extending NW–SE between the Black Sea and the Caspian Sea and separated by the River Kura: the **Great Caucasus**, some 1000 km (621 mi) long, to the N and the **Little Caucasus**, about half that length, along the Turkish border. Their highest point is Mount *Elbrus. *See also* Ciscaucasia; Transcaucasia.

Cauchy, Augustin Louis, Baron (1789–1857) French mathematician, who pioneered the study of functions of *complex numbers. He also derived a mathematical basis for the luminiferous ether. An outspoken and extreme conservative, Cauchy went into exile in Italy in 1830 on the accession of King Louis Philippe.

cauliflower A variety of wild *cabbage, *Brassica oleracea* var. *botrytis*, cultivated as a vegetable. The short stem bears a round white heart, up to 25 cm in diameter, of tightly compressed flower buds surrounded by green leaves. *See also* Brassica.

Cauvery, River (*or* R. Kaveri) A river in S India. Rising in the Western Ghats, it flows mainly ENE to the Bay of Bengal. It has a wide delta, the principal channel being the Coleroon, and it irrigates the area by way of a system of canals. It is sacred to the Hindus. Length: 756 km (470 mi).

Cavafy, Constantine (C. Kavafis; 1863–1933) Greek poet. He lived nearly all his life in Alexandria, where he worked as a civil servant. Many of his poems are ironic treatments of subjects from the ancient Hellenistic world; he also wrote erotic homosexual love poems. He spoke and read English and had a strong influence on E. M. *Forster and Lawrence *Durrell.

Cavalcanti, Guido (c. 1255–1300) Italian poet. A friend of Dante, he wrote about 50 poems on themes of love and emotional suffering. He died of a disease contracted while exiled from Florence for his political activities.

Cavalier poets A group of English poets connected with the court of Charles I (1625–49). They included Richard *Lovelace, Robert *Herrick, Thomas *Carew, Edmund *Waller, and Sir John *Suckling. Their love lyrics and poems about war and honour were characterized by a sophisticated elegance appropriate to their positions as courtiers and gentlemen.

Cavaliers The royalist party during the English *Civil War. After the *Restoration of the monarchy (1660) the name was kept by the court party and was given to the parliament that sat from 1661 to 1679. The cavaliers were distinguished by their elaborate dress, with lace ruffles, feathers, and velvet, in contrast to the sober attire of the *Roundheads.

Cavalli, Francesco (1602–76) Italian composer of opera and church music. A pupil of Monteverdi in Venice, he wrote over 40 dramatic works based on legends of gods and heroes. *Calisto* (1651), in an edition prepared by Raymond Leppard (1927–), was revived at Glyndebourne in 1970.

Cavallini, Pietro (c. 1250–c. 1330) Roman fresco painter and mosaicist. He was the first to abandon the stylizations of *Byzantine art and his chief works are the mosaics of the *Life of the Virgin* for Sta Maria in Trastevere and the frescoes in Sta Cecilia.

cavalry A force of mounted soldiers. Employed throughout the ancient world for its speed and mobility, the invention of stirrups (c. 400 AD) increased its usefulness by enabling

heavily armoured lancers and swordsmen to fight on horseback. The introduction of *small arms in the 15th century shifted the emphasis in warfare to infantry and the use of *machine guns from the late 19th century rendered the role of cavalry in battle suicidal. Modern armoured units have adopted the name and role of cavalry.

Cavan (Irish name: Cabhán) A county in the NE Republic of Ireland, in Ulster. It is generally hilly, drained chiefly by the River Erne, with lakes and *drumlins. Although largely infertile, agriculture is the mainstay of the economy producing oats, potatoes, and dairy products. Some small industries exist in the towns. Area: 1890 sq km (730 sq mi). Population (1981): 53 855. County town: Cavan.

cave fish One of several cave-dwelling *teleost fishes, especially members of the family *Amblyopsidae*, found in fresh water in dark limestone caves of North America. They have translucent colourless elongated bodies, about 10 cm long, reduced nonfunctional eyes, and numerous sensory papillae covering the body to compensate for blindness.

Cavell, Edith (1865–1915) British nurse. From 1907 she worked at a training institute for nurses in Brussels. She was executed by the Germans in 1915 for helping Allied soldiers to escape from German-occupied Belgium. Before she died she is reputed to have said "I realize that patriotism is not enough. I must have no hatred or bitterness towards anyone."

Cavendish (Henry Jones; 1831–99) British authority on card games. He is known particularly for his treatise *The Principles of Whist, Stated and Explained by "Cavendish"* (1862).

Cavendish, Lord Frederick Charles. *See* Phoenix Park Murders.

Cavendish, Henry (1731–1810) British physicist; grandson of the Duke of Devonshire, from whom he inherited a fortune. He discovered hydrogen and investigated its properties. He also identified the gases in the atmosphere and showed that water is a compound. The first to measure accurately the universal gravitational constant, he used it to calculate the mass of the earth. The Cavendish Laboratory at Cambridge University is named after him.

caves Underground hollows, usually opening directly onto the ground surface or connected with it by a passage. In limestone regions, where most caves occur, many constitute part of a system of natural underground drainage and are connected by subterranean streams. These caves are excavated by the slow solution of limestone by slightly acidic rain water percolating through its joints. The other main type of cave is that eroded from the base of a cliff by the sea. Such caves are located at some point of weakness in an otherwise resistant rock, such as a fault plane or bed of softer material. *Fingal's Cave in the Scottish Hebrides is a spectacular cavern in columnar basalt, the sea forming its floor.

caviare A delicacy, eaten as an hors d'oeuvre, which consists of sturgeon's roe, salted and freed from all fat. It is a Russian speciality. The roe of the beluga is considered the best, although caviare is also obtained from other types of sturgeon. Real caviare is extremely expensive, but a substitute made from lumpfish roe is relatively inexpensive.

Cavite 14 30N 120 54E A town in the N Philippines, in SW Luzon on Manila Bay. Formerly a centre of opposition to Spanish and US rule, it is the site of a major US naval base. Population (1980): 87 666.

Cavour, Camillo Benso di, Count (1810–61) Italian statesman; the architect of Italian unification (*see* Risorgimento). Committed to liberal politics from boyhood, he helped to found the organ *Il risorgimento* in 1847. In 1852 he formed his first government under *Victor Emmanuel II of Sardinia-Piedmont. Cavour accepted an alliance with France and Britain during the Crimean War and negotiated a further alliance with France at Plombières in 1859 to oust

243 Cecilia, St

Austria from Italy. He resigned when France came to terms with Austria but became prime minister again in 1860, negotiating the union of Sardinia-Piedmont with Parma, Modena, Tuscany, and the Romagna, and by 1861 had achieved the establishment of a united Italy.

cavy A small South American *rodent belonging to the genus *Cavia* (6 species); the ancestor of the domestic guinea pig. Cavies are mainly nocturnal and live in groups in scrub and grassland, digging burrows and feeding on vegetation and seeds. The adults generally breed twice a year and the young cavies are independent at three weeks. Family: *Caviidae*.

Cawdor 57 32N 3 55W A village in Scotland, in the E Highland Region. Cawdor Castle is the traditional site of Macbeth's murder of Duncan (1040).

WILLIAM CAXTON Aesop's Fables, *translated into English and printed by William Caxton in Westminster in 1483.*

Cawley, Evonne (*born* E. Goolagong; 1951–) Australian tennis player, who twice became Wimbledon singles champion (1971, 1980) and won the doubles in 1974. She was Australian singles champion (1974–76) and Australian doubles champion in 1971, 1974, and 1975.

Cawnpore. *See* Kanpur.

Caxton, William (c. 1422–91) The first English printer. A cloth merchant, Caxton lived in Bruges from 1446 until 1470, when he moved to Cologne. There he learned the technique of printing and in 1474 set up a press that produced the first printed book in English, *Recuyell of the Historyes of Troye* (1475). On returning to England (1476), he set up a press at Westminster, where he printed a long and varied list, including Chaucer's *Canterbury Tales* (1478) and an encyclopedia that was the first illustrated English book, *The Myrrour of the Worlde* (1481).

Cayenne 4 55N 52 18W The capital and main Atlantic port of French Guiana, in the NW of the Île de Cayenne. Founded by the French in 1643, it served as a French penal settlement (1854–1938). Cayenne pepper derives its name from a plant grown in the area. Population (1980): 36 215.

Cayley, Arthur (1821–95) British mathematician, who invented *matrices, a branch of mathematics that remained a cu-

riosity until Werner *Heisenberg used it in his theory of quantum mechanics. He also worked on analytical and *non-Euclidean geometry and was largely responsible for the resurgence of mathematics in Britain during his lifetime.

Cayley, Sir George (1773–1857) British engineer and pioneer designer of flying machines. He studied the effects of streamlining, the properties of different shapes of wings, and the basic shape of heavier-than-air aircraft. He tested his theories with models and in 1853 built the first successful manned glider. He also invented the caterpillar tractor.

cayman (*or* caiman) An amphibious reptile occurring in rivers of Central and South America. 1.2–4.5 m long, it feeds on fish, birds, and insects. Genera: *Caiman* (2 species), *Melanosuchus* (1 species), *Paleosuchus* (2 species); subfamily: *Alligatorinae* (alligators and caimans); order: *Crodilia* (*see* crocodile).

Cayman Islands A British colony in the Caribbean Sea, consisting of three low-lying coral islands (Grand Cayman, Little Cayman, and Cayman Brac) lying about 320 km (200 mi) NW of Jamaica. The population is mainly of mixed African and European descent. *Economy*: depends mainly on tourism, although there have been developments in recent years in areas such as banking, encouraged by the favourable tax position. The main exports are turtle shell, dried turtle meat, and tropical fish. *History*: discovered in 1503 by Columbus, who named them Las Tortugas because of the abundance of turtles. Formerly attached to Jamaica, they gained a certain measure of self-government in 1959 and became a separate British colony in 1962. Official language: English. Official currency: Jamaican dollar of 100 cents. Area: 260 sq km (100 sq mi). Population (1981 est): 17 035. Capital and main port: Georgetown.

CBE. *See* Order of the British Empire.

CBI. *See* Confederation of British Industry.

CD-ROM. *See* compact disc.

Ceanannus Mór. *See* Kells.

Ceará. *See* Fortaleza.

Ceauşescu, Nicolae (1918–) Romanian statesman; president (1974–). Noted for his opposition to Soviet interference in Romanian affairs. Ceauşescu's rise in the Party hierarchy began in 1948. In 1965 he became the Party's general secretary and in 1967 president of the state council.

Cebu 10 17N 123 56E A port in the central Philippines, in E Cebu. The first Spanish settlement in the Philippines (founded 1565), it has a Roman Catholic cathedral and bishop's palace. Its four universities include the University of San Carlos (1595). An important commercial centre, its industries include textiles and food processing. Population (1980): 489 208.

Cebu An island in the central Philippines, in the Visayan Islands. Its populous coastal plains are cultivated chiefly with coconuts, maize, sugar cane, and hemp. Coal and copper are mined. Area: 5086 sq km (1964 sq mi). Population (1980): 2 091 602. Chief town: Cebu.

Cecil, Lord David (Lord Edward Christian David Gascoyne C.; 1902–86) British literary critic, professor of English literature at Oxford University from 1948 to 1970. His books include a study of William Cowper entitled *The Stricken Deer* (1929) and biographies of Jane Austen (1935), Hardy (1943), and Max Beerbohm (1964). His later work includes *A Portrait of Jane Austen* (1978).

Cecil, Robert Gascoyne-Cecil, 1st Viscount (1864–1958) British statesman. Cecil was minister of blockade and then deputy foreign secretary in World War I. He took part in the Paris Peace Conference (1919) and helped draft the charter of the League of Nations; he was awarded the Nobel Peace Prize in 1937.

Cecilia, St (2nd or 3rd century AD) Roman Christian martyr. According to legend, she converted her pagan husband Valerian and his brother Tiburtius, who were martyred

before her. Although there is doubt concerning her authenticity, she remains the patron saint of sacred music. Feast
day: 22 Nov. Emblem: an organ.

cecropia moth   A large brown and reddish *Saturniid
moth, *Platysamia cecropia*. With a wingspan of 155 mm, it is
the largest North American moth. The caterpillars are green
and feed on a variety of trees.

cedar   A conifer of the genus *Cedrus* (4 species), native to
the Mediterranean region and the Himalayas and widely
planted for ornament and timber. Cedars usually grow to a
height of 40 m. Their stiff needle-like leaves grow in tufts of
10–40 on short spurs and their cones are erect and barrel-
shaped, 5–14 cm long. The best-known species are the *deodar; the Atlas cedar (*C. atlantica*), from the Atlas mountains;
and the cedar of Lebanon (*C. libani*), of the E
Mediterranean. Family: *Pinaceae*.
A number of unrelated trees are also known as cedars (*see*
incense cedar; Japanese cedar; pencil cedar), and conifers of
the genus *Thuja* (*see* arbor vitae) are sometimes called
cedars.

Cedar Rapids   41 59N 91 39W A city in the USA, in E
central Iowa. Its industries include cereals and agricultural
machinery. Population (1980): 110 243.

Ceefax.   *See* teletext.

celandine   Either of two unrelated perennial herbaceous
plants. **Greater celandine** (*Chelidonium majus*) is found in
cool temperate and subarctic regions throughout Europe and
Asia. The brittle branching stems, 30–90 cm long, bear
deeply lobed leaves and bright-yellow flowers. The fruit is a
narrow capsule, 3–5 cm long. Family: *Papaveraceae*.
Lesser celandine (*Ranunculus ficaria*), sometimes known as
pilewort, is native to Europe. The branching stems, 5–25 cm
long, bear long-stalked leaves and bright-yellow flowers,
which fade to white. The roots form numerous tubers.
Family: *Ranunculaceae*.

Celaya   20 32N 100 48W A city in central Mexico. An
agricultural trading centre, it contains several churches by
the noted Mexican architect, Francisco Eduardo de
Tresguerras (1763–1833). Population (1980): 219 010.

Celebes.   *See* Sulawesi.

celeriac   A variety of cultivated *celery, *Apium graveolens*
var. *rapaceum*, also known as turnip-rooted or knob celery,
grown for its globular edible root. The root, up to 15 cm in
diameter, has a celery-like flavour.

celery   The cultivated form of wild celery, or smallage
(*Apium graveolens*), a biennial herb native to grassy coastal
areas from Europe to India and Africa. Many varieties of
cultivated celery have been developed for their edible
leafstalks (up to 30 cm in length), which may be pink,
yellow, or green. Traditionally, the green varieties are
blanched to tenderize the tissues. The wild plant has an erect
grooved stem, 30–60 cm long, bearing whorls of clusters of
small greenish-white flowers. Family: *Umbelliferae*.

celesta   A small keyboard instrument the quiet bell-like
tone of which is produced by hammers striking steel plates
hung over wooden resonators. Invented about 1880, it was
used by Tchaikovsky in his ballet *Casse-Noisette*.

celestial mechanics   The study of the motions of celestial
bodies subject to mutual gravitational interaction through
the application of the laws of *gravitation and of
*mechanics.

celestial sphere   The imaginary sphere, of immense size, at
the centre of which lies the earth and on the inner surface of
which can be projected the stars and other celestial bodies.
The directions of these bodies, as seen from earth, are
measured in terms of their angular distances from certain
points and circles on the celestial sphere. These circles
include the *ecliptic, the observer's horizon, and the **celestial
equator**, where the earth's equatorial plane meets the
celestial sphere. The reference points include the *equinoxes,
the *zenith, and the **celestial poles**, where the earth's axis

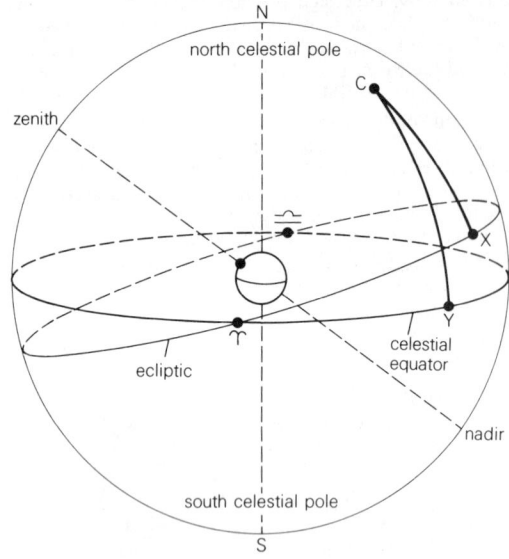

♈	first point of Aries; vernal equinox
♎	first point of Libra; autumnal equinox
C	celestial object
♈Y	right ascension of C (in hours anticlockwise from ♈)
♈X	celestial longitude of C (in degrees anticlockwise from ♈)
YC	declination of C
XC	celestial latitude of C

CELESTIAL SPHERE

meets the celestial sphere. The earth's daily rotation causes
an apparent and opposite rotation of the celestial sphere.

Céline, Louis Ferdinand   (L. F. Destouches; 1884–1961)
French novelist. The unrelieved cynicism of his controversial first book, *Journey to the End of the Night* (1932), was
characteristic of all his novels, including *Death on the
Instalment Plan* (1936) and *North* (1960). He suffered
imprisonment and exile in Denmark for his outspoken
antisemitic opinions.

cell   The basic unit of living matter, which performs the
vital processes of producing energy, synthesizing new
molecules from raw materials, division, and self-replication.
All plants and animals are composed of cells, the average
size of which ranges from 0.01 to 0.1 mm; the simplest
organisms (bacteria, protozoa, etc.) consist only of a single
cell. The fundamental importance of cells was first
recognized by *Schleiden and Schwann in 1838–39. A cell
consists essentially of a mass of protoplasm bounded by a
membrane. All cells except those of bacteria and blue-green
algae and mammalian red blood cells possess a *nucleus,
containing the genetic material, and cytoplasm, within which
are structures (organelles) specialized for different metabolic
functions (*see* Golgi apparatus; lysosome; mitochondria;
ribosome). The cells of the body that are not involved in
reproduction (called the somatic cells) divide by *mitosis to
produce daughter cells identical to themselves. The reproductive cells divide by *meiosis to produce gametes, each
containing half the number of chromosomes of the somatic
cells. The basic difference between plant and animal cells is
the presence in the former of a rigid cellulose cell wall and
chlorophyll for use in photosynthesis (*see* chloroplast).

Celle   52 37N 10 05E A town in NE West Germany, in
Lower Saxony. Its former ducal palace (1292) is famed for
its theatre, used since 1674. Wax and dyes are long
established manufactures. The concentration camp of Belsen
was nearby. Population (1983 est): 71 919.

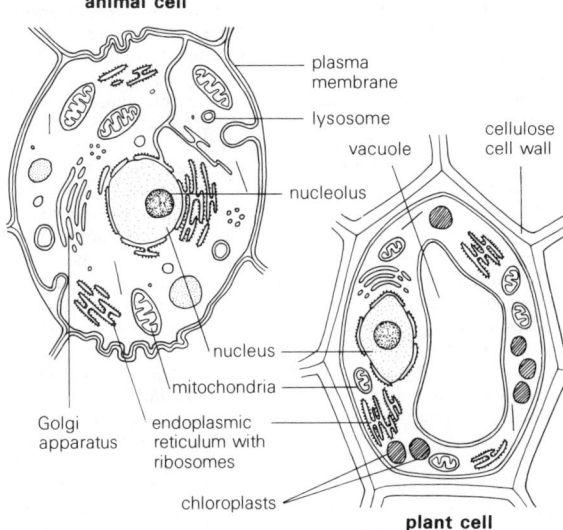

animal cell

plasma membrane

lysosome

cellulose cell wall

vacuole

nucleolus

nucleus

mitochondria

Golgi apparatus

endoplasmic reticulum with ribosomes

chloroplasts

plant cell

CELL *Plant and animal cells are basically similar but plant cells are supported by cellulose cell walls and contain the green pigment chlorophyll within chloroplasts. Plant cells often also have large fluid-filled vacuoles, which help to control turgidity of the cell.*

Cellini, Benvenuto (1500–71) Florentine goldsmith and sculptor, famous for his autobiography (1558–62). First published in 1728, it provides a valuable account of his life and times. Cellini worked chiefly as a medallist and craftsman for the papacy in Rome, the Medici in Florence, and Francis I in France. The famous gold saltcellar (Kunsthistorisches Museum, Vienna) was made for Francis. As a sculptor he was largely unfulfilled, although his *Perseus* (Loggia dei Lanzi, Florence) attests to his skills in this medium.

cello (full name: violoncello) A musical instrument of the *violin family, held between the knees and supported at its lower end by an adjustable pin. It has an extensive range above its lowest note (C two octaves below middle C). Its four strings are tuned C, G, D, A. Used to strengthen the bass line in baroque music, it emerged as a solo instrument in the 18th and 19th centuries. In the 20th century its greatest exponent has been Pablo Casals.

celluloid A highly flammable thermoplastic material made from cellulose nitrate and *camphor. It was the first commercially made plastic, introduced over a hundred years ago. Although superseded for many applications by less flammable plastics, there are many specialist uses for which it is still the most suitable material because of its resistance to water, oils, and dilute acids. These include table-tennis balls, mortar-bomb capsules, and film.

cellulose ($C_6H_{10}O_5)_n$ A *carbohydrate that is an important constituent of the cell walls of plants and consists of linked glucose units. Industrially, it is made from wood pulp and is used to manufacture rayon and cellulose-acetate plastics. Cellulose has an important role in the human diet since it—together with other indigestible plant products—constitutes dietary *fibre.

cellulose nitrate (*or* nitrocellulose) A range of compounds made by treating cellulose with a mixture of nitric acid and sulphuric acid. As it is a nitric acid ester the correct name is cellulose nitrate. It is used as an explosive (gun cotton) and rocket propellant.

Celsius scale The official name of the *centigrade temperature scale. It was devised by the Swedish astronomer

Anders Celsius (1701–44), who originally designated zero as the boiling point of water and 100° as the freezing point. The scale was later reversed.

Celsus, Aulus Cornelius (1st century AD) Roman scholar, who wrote an encyclopedic work embracing agriculture, law, philosophy, and medicine, of which only the medical section has survived (*De medicina*). Popular during the Renaissance, this work is today of great historical interest, dealing with hygiene, heart attacks, the surgical removal of gallstones, and many other topics common to contemporary medicine.

Celtiberia A region of NE Spain, S of the River Ebro. From the 3rd century BC the area was inhabited by the warlike Celtiberians, who were descendants of the Celtic invaders of Spain and the Iberian natives. The Celtiberians were defeated by the Romans in 195 BC but their capital, Numantia, was not taken until Scipio Aemilianus forced its capitulation in 133 BC.

Celtic art The style of ornamentation developed by ancient tribes in central Europe (*see* Celts). Primitive examples, found in the middle Rhine and Champagne districts, date from around 450 BC: masks and brooches in bronzework with increasingly sophisticated geometric patterns, animal and floral motifs, and, eventually, realistic human-head designs. The most elaborate jewellery, decorated swords, scabbards, and helmets belong to the *La Tène period (c. 350 BC). In Britain, Celtic craftsmanship flourished throughout the Roman occupation, producing work in gold and silver, shields inlaid with enamel, and bronze mirrors. Subsequently, Christian monks adapted traditional designs to adorn religious manuscripts, as in the 9th-century Book of *Kells.

Celtic languages A branch of the Indo-European language family formerly widespread in W Europe. It is divided into two subgroups: Gaulish and Insular Celtic. The Gaulish languages are now extinct, being superseded in early medieval times by *Romance, *Germanic, and other languages. Insular Celtic can be further divided into a Goidelic branch (including *Manx and *Gaelic) and a Brythonic branch (including *Welsh, *Cornish, and *Breton).

Celtic League An Irish-based organization, founded in 1975, that aims to maintain links between the Celtic peoples of Scotland, Brittany, Wales, Ireland, Cornwall, and the Isle of Man. The League strongly favours independence for all the Celtic peoples and works to preserve their cultural as well as their political consciousness.

CELTIC ART *An Iron Age hand mirror made of bronze and decorated with Celtic patterns. It dates to the 1st century BC.*

Celtic Sea

Celtic Sea The part of the Atlantic Ocean between Ireland, Wales, and SW England that was explored for oil and gas during the 1970s.

Celts A people who occupied a large part of Iron Age Europe. They were known to the Greeks as Keltoi and to the Romans as Gauls. There were numerous Celtic tribes and chiefdoms sharing a culture that can be traced back to the Bronze Age of central Europe (c. 1200 BC). Distinct stages in its development are represented by the *Urnfield and *Hallstatt cultures and it reached its highest level around the 5th century BC, a period represented by the *La Tène culture. The Celtic warrior aristocracy commanded considerable wealth and power. Burials (e.g. at Vix, France) were often rich and elaborate, containing objects of excellent craftsmanship and aesthetic quality. The Druidic priesthood conducted sacrifices and was responsible for the education of young nobles.

cement A powdered mixture of calcium silicates and aluminates. On mixing with water it undergoes complex hydration processes and sets into a hard solid mass. **Portland cement** and similar materials are made by heating limestone with clay and grinding the product. Portland cement was invented by a British stonemason, Joseph Aspdin (1799–1855), and named after the stone quarried at Portland, Dorset, which it resembles. It is used extensively in *mortars and in *concrete.

cementation The heating of *wrought iron with charcoal powder to form steel. The process was used to make swords and cutting tools before modern methods were developed. It is similar to *case hardening but the iron was often heated for days before quenching.

cementite Iron carbide (Fe_3C), a constituent of *steel and *cast iron. It is a hard brittle white material that combines with ferrite (pure iron) in different ways depending on the type of steel. See also pearlite.

Cennini, Cennino (di Drea) (c. 1370–c. 1440) Florentine painter. His paintings have disappeared but he is famous for his *Il libro dell' arte*. Translated as *The Craftsman's Handbook* (1933), it is a valuable source of information about early artistic techniques, particularly *tempera painting.

cenotaph Any memorial to the dead that does not contain a body. The term is increasingly identified with war memorials. One of the most famous is that designed (1919–20) by *Lutyens in Whitehall, London, to commemorate the dead of World War I. See also Remembrance Sunday.

Cenozoic era (or Cainozoic era) The geological era beginning about 65 million years ago and following the *Mesozoic era. It is usually taken to include both the Tertiary and Quaternary periods. During this era the mammals flourished, after the extinction of most of the reptiles dominant in the Mesozoic; the Cenozoic is sometimes known as the age of mammals. Birds and flowering plants also flourished. The *Alpine orogeny took place in the earlier part of this era.

censors Civil magistrates of ancient Rome responsible for the census, public morality, revision of the senatorial roll, and property investment. Two censors were elected every five years. They generally held office for 18 months. The censorship was instituted in about 443 BC and became the most prestigious magistracy until Sulla curtailed its authority in 81. It lasted until 22 BC.

censorship The examination of printed matter, plays, films, broadcasts, etc., and the suppression of any material considered irreligious, obscene, or seditious. Censorship is thus the instrument by which religious, political, and moral freedom can be curtailed. It was practised throughout the ancient world and in the middle ages, but controlling the dissemination of texts and doctrines considered undesirable by the authorities only really became a problem when *printing enabled material to be widely distributed. The most notorious instance of religious censorship was the Roman Catholic Church's *Index Librorum Prohibitorum*. Instituted in 1564 in reaction to the spread of Protestantism and scientific inquiry, it only ceased publication in 1966.

Censorship on political grounds in the UK was at first operated through the Stationers' Company (incorporated 1557) and certain secular or spiritual dignitaries. Licensing was introduced in 1538 and legislation to enforce state control continued throughout the Tudor and Stuart periods. It was finally dropped in 1695. Licensing of plays for performance was subject to similar restrictions, being carried out by the monarch's Master of the Revels from about 1574; the Lord Chamberlain took over the function in the early 18th century. Freedom from political censorship characterizes western democracies but strict censorship is prevalent in the Soviet bloc, the People's Republic of China, and most of South America and Africa.

Legislation in the area of moral censorship is notoriously difficult to draft. In the UK the Obscene Publications Act (1857) prevented publication of unexpurgated editions of such works as D. H. Lawrence's *Lady Chatterley's Lover*. By the Obscene Publications Act (1959) the opinion of experts was allowed to be consulted as to the literary or artistic merits of a work, a relaxation tested in the celebrated *Lady Chatterley* trial (1960). The modified Act of 1964 further liberalized the law respecting material hitherto regarded as pornographic. In 1968 licensing of plays by the Lord Chamberlain was abolished.

In the UK films are censored by the British Board of Film Censors (BBFC), an unofficial body founded in 1912. Local authorities generally demand that films shown in their areas have been certified by the BBFC. Films are classed as 18 (for viewing only by adults over 18), 15 (filmgoers over 15), PG (filmgoers under 15 accompanied by an adult), or U (all filmgoers).

census A survey ordered by a government to discover certain characteristics of the population, such as its size, occupations, distribution, and trends in fertility, emigration, and immigration. Censuses were taken in ancient China and ancient Rome but the earliest regular census was initiated in America in 1770. In the UK the first census of England and Scotland was taken by parish officials in 1801, since when a census has been taken every ten years. The census is now the responsibility of the Office of Population Censuses and Surveys. Questions in the 1971 census form about country of origin aroused fears in the immigrant community of possible consequential anti-immigrant policies.

centaur In Greek legend, one of a race of wild creatures, half-human and half-horse, living in the mountains of Thessaly and descended from Ixion, King of the Lapiths. They were defeated by the Lapiths in a battle resulting from their characteristically unruly behaviour at the wedding of Ixion's son. See also Chiron.

Centaurus (Latin: Centaur) A large conspicuous constellation in the S sky near Crux. The brightest stars are *Alpha and *Beta Centauri. The constellation contains the huge intense radio source **Centaurus A** and the X-ray binary star **Centaurus X-3**.

centaury An annual or perennial flowering plant belonging to the genus *Centaurium* (or *Erythraea*) (40–50 species), found in most regions except for tropical and S Africa. The common centaury (*C. erythraea*) is widely distributed in temperate regions. Growing to a height of up to 50 cm, the branching stems bear clusters of small pink flowers. Family: *Gentianaceae*.

Certain plants closely related to *Centaurium* species are also called centaury, e.g. yellow centaury (*Cicendia filiformis*) and Guernsey centaury (*Exaculum pusillum*).

centigrade scale A temperature scale using the freezing point of water as zero and the boiling point of water as 100 degrees. The scale is now officially called the *Celsius scale. Each centigrade (or Celsius) degree is equal to one *kelvin.

centipede An *arthropod belonging to the worldwide class *Chilopoda* (about 2800 species). It has long antennae and a slender flattened body of 15-181 segments. The first segment bears a pair of poison claws and nearly all the remaining segments bear a single pair of legs (*compare* millipede). The tropical order *Scolopendrida* contain the largest species, up to 280 mm long. Centipedes are found under stones, logs, and leaf litter during the day and at night prey on earthworms, insects, and sometimes small vertebrates. They lay eggs or produce live young.

CENTO. *See* Central Treaty Organization.

Central African Federation. *See* Rhodesia and Nyasaland, Federation of.

Central African Republic (name from 1976 until 1979: Central African Empire) A country in central Africa, consisting mainly of a plateau lying at about 900 m (3000 ft). The dense forests in the S are drained by the River Ubangi, an important channel of communication. Most of the population belongs to the Banda and Baya tribes. *Economy*: chiefly subsistence agriculture, although diamonds have been successfully mined in recent years and there is now a state uranium mine. The main exports are cotton and coffee. *History*: as Ubangi-Shari it was one of the four territories of French Equatorial Africa and from 1958 had internal self-government as a member of the French Community. It became independent in 1960 as the Central African Republic under the presidency of David Dacko (1930-   ). In a military coup in 1965, Jean Bédel *Bokassa came to power. A new constitution was adopted in 1976 in which the country became a parliamentary monarchy known as the Central African Empire, with Bokassa as Emperor Bokassa I. He was ousted following allegations of massacres and forced to flee the country in 1979. Dacko then returned to power but was overthrown in 1981 by Gen André Kolingba. Official language: French; Sango is the national language. Official currency: CFA (Communauté financière africaine) franc of 100 centimes. Area: 625 000 sq km (241 250 sq mi). Population (1981 est): 2 420 000. Capital: Bangui.

Central America An isthmus of S North America, extending from the Isthmus of Tehuantepec to the NW border of Colombia and comprising an area of 596 000 sq km (230 000 sq mi). It consists of Belize, Costa Rica, El Salvador, Guatemala, Honduras, Nicaragua, and Panama, together with four Mexican states. It is chiefly mountainous with many volcanoes, including Tajumulco, which rises to 4210 m (13 846 ft), and its fertile volcanic regions yield many crops (especially bananas, coffee, and cocoa). The people are mainly of mixed European and Indian origin. Following the overthrow of Spanish colonial rule Costa Rica, El Salvador, Guatemala, Honduras, and Nicaragua formed (1823-38) the **Central American Federation** (*or* United Provinces of Central America). In 1960 Costa Rica, El Salvador, Nicaragua, and Honduras (which withdrew in 1970) formed the **Central American Common Market** to coordinate their economic policies.

central bank A bank that implements a government's *monetary policy, acting as banker to the government and to the commercial banks. Central banks are responsible for holding a country's gold reserves, conducting monetary relations with other countries, and financing the government debt. These objectives sometimes conflict: for example, the bank may wish to depress interest rates to stimulate investment at home, while wishing to raise interest rates to attract money into the country to aid the balance of payments. Most countries have a central bank; in the UK it is the *Bank of England.

Central Criminal Court The *Crown Court having jurisdiction to try all offences committed in the City of London and Greater London. The recorder of London and common serjeant are permanent judges of the court and all judges of

the Queen's Bench Division also officiate on a rota system. The court is known as the *Old Bailey.

Central Intelligence Agency (CIA) A US government department established in 1947 to coordinate US intelligence operations. It is not permitted to operate within the USA and its involvement in the *Watergate affair raised considerable concern. There have also been criticisms about its interference in the internal affairs of foreign countries and it has been subjected in recent years to official inquiry.

Central Powers The coalition, including Germany, Austria-Hungary, Turkey, and Bulgaria, that opposed the *Allied Powers during *World War I.

Central Region An administrative region in central Scotland, created under local government reorganization in 1975 from the counties of Clackmannan, most of Stirling, S Perth, and part of West Lothian. It consists of the lowland plain of the Rivers Forth and Teith rising to uplands in the N and S. Agriculture includes cattle and dairy farming in the W and arable and livestock farming in the E. Industry is important with coalmining around Fallin and oil refining. Tourism is a thriving industry, especially around the Trossachs in the N of the region. Area: 2518 sq km (971 sq mi). Population (1981): 273 078. Administrative centre: Stirling.

Central Treaty Organization (CENTO) A mutual defence alliance between the UK, Iran, Pakistan, and Turkey. It succeeded the *Baghdad Pact. Its objective was military cooperation and the economic development of its Middle Eastern members. Because the UK and the USA, which was an associate member, saw CENTO primarily as an anti-Soviet military alliance and neglected the economic development of the organization's Middle Eastern members, Iran, Turkey, and Pakistan withdrew from the organization in 1979.

centre of gravity A fixed point through which the resultant gravitational force on a body always passes no matter what its orientation.

centrifugal force. *See* centripetal force.

centrifuge A device for rotating mixtures of substances at high speed so that the heavier components can be separated from the lighter; the heavier components experience a greater centrifugal force, thus enabling components of different densities (e.g. milk and cream) to separate. The ultracentrifuge is a high-speed device used in the determination of molecular weights and in biochemistry. Large centrifuges are used in physiological research and in training programmes to obtain a high *acceleration of free fall (g).

centripetal force A force that acts on a moving body causing it to move in a curved path. An object is constrained to move in a circle by a centripetal force directed towards the centre. It has an acceleration towards the centre of v^2/r, where v is the object's velocity and r the radius of the circle. The centripetal force is necessary to overcome the object's tendency to move in a straight line and appears to be balanced by an equal **centrifugal force** directed radially outwards.

century The ancient Roman unit of a hundred. In the Roman army centuries were the 60 subdivisions, composed of about a hundred infantrymen, of a legion and were commanded by centurions. Centuries were also political divisions of Roman citizens, each of which had a group vote in the assembly of centuries (*see* comitia).

century plant A perennial herbaceous plant, *Agave americana*, native to SW North America. It is stemless but has spiny leaves, 1.5-1.8 m long, and after 10-15 years it produces a branched spike of yellow flowers, 7.5-12 m tall. After flowering it dies, leaving small plants growing around its base. Century plant is cultivated indoors and outdoors as an ornamental. Family: *Agavaceae*.

ceorl The free peasant (as distinct from the slave) of Anglo-Saxon England. The economic pressures of the Danish invasions and the Norman conquest contributed to the ceorl's declining status and eventual absorption amongst the unfree *villeins. Thus "churl" has come to mean an uncouth person.

cèpe An edible mushroom, *Boletus edulis*. Common in temperate woodlands from August to November, it has a stout whitish or brown stalk and a hemispherical cap, brown to white in colour and 6–20 cm in diameter.

Cephalonia (Modern Greek name: Kefallinía) A Greek island in the E Ionian Sea, the largest of the Ionian group. It is mountainous, rising to 1628 m (5341 ft), but produces crops that include olives and grapes. Area: 935 sq km (360 sq mi). Population (1981): 31 297.

cephalopod A *mollusc belonging to the class *Cephalopoda* (about 600 species), which includes *octopuses, *squids, and *cuttlefishes. The most advanced of the molluscs, cephalopods are carnivorous and mostly free swimming, with a ring of tentacles around the mouth, well-developed eyes, and shells that are reduced and often absent. They are found in both shallow and deepwater marine habitats. In cephalopods the sexes are usually separate and fertilization is internal, often preceded by courtship behaviour.

cephalosporins A group of *antibiotics with a similar action and chemical structure to penicillin. They may be used to treat penicillin-resistant bacterial infections and infections of the urinary tract.

Cepheid variable A highly luminous supergiant star the brightness of which varies very regularly in a period (1–70 days) that depends on the *luminosity of the star. By measuring the period and the average apparent *magnitude of a Cepheid, its distance can be determined. *See also* variable stars. Cepheids occur in ours and other galaxies and are a major means of measuring distances of galaxies up to about 20 million light years away.

Cepheus (Latin: Whale) A constellation in the N sky near Cassiopeia. The brightest star is the 2nd-magnitude Alderamin. *See also* Cepheid variable.

Ceram (*or* Serang) An Indonesian island in the Moluccas. Mountainous and forested, its exports include copra, dried fish, and birds of paradise. Area: 17 150 sq km (6622 sq mi). Chief town: Wahai.

ceramics Any nonmetallic inorganic material that is made by heat treatment into useful articles. The main categories are heavy articles made of baked clay, such as bricks and tiles, refractories to withstand high temperatures, such as furnace linings, sintered articles, such as abrasives, and domestic products made from earthenware, stoneware, or *porcelain (*see also* pottery). Earthenware is made from clay, which when strongly heated fuses into a hard porous substance. The defect of porosity is overcome by glazing with a vitreous coating of silicate. Chinese examples date from about 3000 BC. Stoneware is made from a more siliceous clay and fired at a higher temperature than earthenware. It is vitrified, resonant, and almost impervious. Porcelain, developed by the Chinese from stoneware, is vitrified, impervious, resonant, translucent, and white. It need not be glazed but usually is.

Cerberus In Greek legend, the monstrous dog who guarded the entrance to the underworld, usually portrayed as having three heads and a dragon's neck and tail. The final task of *Heracles was to overpower this monster.

cereals Cultivated *grasses selected for their high yields of grain, which constitutes a major item in the diet of man and livestock. *Wheat, *rice, and *maize are the most important cereals, but *barley, *oats, *rye, and *millet are also widely cultivated. Cereals are usually sown annually and, under certain conditions (especially with rice), two or more harvests may be possible in one year. *See also* arable farming.

cerebellum. *See* brain.

cerebral palsy Damage to the developing brain resulting in

uncoordinated movements and muscular weakness and paralysis (the affected child is called a spastic). The brain damage may be caused by injury during birth, insufficient oxygen before birth, or a viral infection of the brain. In some cases intelligence is affected. Treatment includes appropriate physiotherapy to improve movement and special education; speech therapy may also be needed.

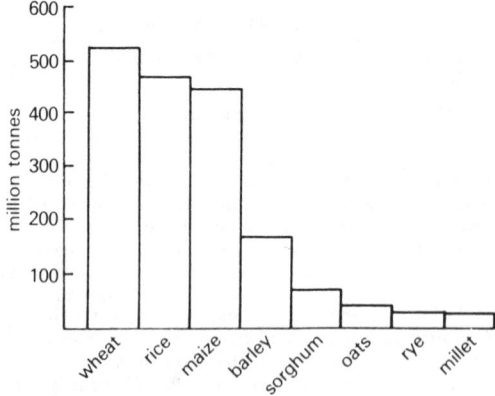

CEREALS *World production of cereals (1984).*

cerebrospinal fluid The fluid that surrounds the *brain and *spinal cord. It is produced by special blood vessels inside the cerebrum and is reabsorbed by special bunches of veins. It acts as a shock absorber and support for the central nervous system. A normal adult has 130 ml of clear fluid; samples of it are taken for diagnostic tests for diseases of the nervous system.

cerebrum. *See* brain.

Ceres (astronomy) The largest *minor planet, 1003 km in diameter, and the first to be discovered (in 1801 by Piazzi). It orbits at between 2.55 and 2.98 astronomical units from the sun, with a period of 4.6 years.

Ceres (mythology). *See* Demeter.

cerium (Ce) The most abundant lanthanide element, discovered in 1803 by Berzelius and others. It occurs naturally in several minerals including monazite, $(Ce,La,Th)PO_4$, and allanite, a complex aluminosilicate. It is used as a catalyst in self-cleaning ovens, in gas mantles, as a polishing agent, and as an oxidant for volumetric analysis. At no 58; at wt 140.12; mp 799°C; bp 3426°C.

CERN (Organisation (previously Conseil) européenne pour la Recherche nucléaire) A W European organization founded in 1954 to carry out nuclear research. Its headquarters are in Geneva and its staff are recruited from CERN's 12 member countries. It built and runs a 28GeV proton synchrotron *accelerator, with an intersecting storage ring system, which is 300 m (328 yd) in diameter.

Cernauti. *See* Chernovtsy.

Cerro de Pasco 10 43S 76 15W A mining town in central Peru, in the central Andes 4400 m (14 436 ft) above sea level. Minerals extracted include copper, zinc, and lead. Population (1981): 71 558.

Cervantes, Miguel de (1547–1616) Spanish novelist. Son of an unsuccessful surgeon, he was largely self-educated. In 1569 he went to Italy and fought at the battle of Lepanto in 1571. Returning to Spain in 1575, he was captured by pirates and imprisoned in Algiers for five years. After 1580 he held several minor jobs in the civil service while writing a pastoral novel, *La Galatea* (1585), and several plays. *Don*

249   **Chad, Lake**

Quixote (Part I, 1605; Part II, 1615), his revolutionary picaresque novel about a self-deluding knight errant and his simple but cunning squire, Sancho Panza, won him fame throughout Europe but little financial reward.

cervix The lower part (neck) of the womb, leading into the vagina (the term is also used for any necklike part). Childbirth is dependent on the effective dilation of the cervix.

Cesenà 44 09N 12 15E A town in N Italy, in Emilia-Romagna on the River Savio. It is the site of the Malatesta library (15th century), which contains many valuable manuscripts. Pope Pius VI and Pope Pius VII were born here. Pasta, wine, and beet sugar are produced. Population (1981): 89 620.

České Budějovice (German name: Budweis) 49 00N 14 30E An industrial town in W Czechoslovakia. Founded in 1265, it has an arcaded square. Manufactures include chemicals, machinery, and pencils. Population (1980 est): 89 000. .

Cessnock 32 51S 151 21E A town in Australia, in E New South Wales in the Hunter Valley. The chief industries are tourism, aluminium, and wine production. Population (1981): 16 916.

Cestoda. *See* tapeworm.

Cetacea An order of carnivorous marine mammals comprising *whales and *dolphins.

cetane number A quality rating for Diesel fuel, similar to the *octane number for petrol. Two reference fuel compounds, cetane and alpha-methylnaphthalene, are given the numbers 100 and 0 respectively. Mixtures of these two have intermediate numbers and other Diesel fuels are compared with them in a standard engine. Most Diesel engines can run on fuel that has a cetane number of 40 or 50.

Cetatea Alba. *See* Belgorod-Dnestrovski.

Cetinje 42 23N 18 55E A town in S central Yugoslavia, in Montenegro. The former capital of the principality of Montenegro, it has a fortified monastery, which was the seat of the Montenegrin prince bishops. Population (1981): 20 213.

Cetshwayo (c. 1826-84) King of the Zulus (1873-79), whose kingdom was conquered by the British. Although Cetshwayo inflicted a severe defeat on the British at Isandhlwana (1879) he could not hold out against them and was overwhelmed at Ulundi (1879). Captured, he was allowed to present his case in London and in 1883 was restored to central Zululand.

Ceuta 35 53N 5 19W A Spanish military post and port, forming an enclave in NW Morocco on the Mediterranean coast. It has a fine 15th-century cathedral. Population (1981): 70 864.

Cévennes A mountain range in SE France, constituting the SE edge of the Massif Central and rising to 1754 m (5755 ft).

Ceylon. *See* Sri Lanka, Democratic Socialist Republic of.

Cézanne, Paul (1839-1906) French postimpressionist painter, born in Aix-en-Provence, the son of a banker. After studying law for two years, he was encouraged by his childhood friend Emile *Zola to settle in Paris (1861). His crude and often erotic early paintings failed, however, to find favour. In 1872, while working with *Pissarro in Pontoise, he turned to *impressionism, a period represented by *The Suicide's House* (Louvre) but he soon rejected its flickering effects of light and movement in favour of more stability and solidity. His view that nature should be painted in the forms of the cone, cube, and cylinder and his distortion of perspective strongly influenced the development of *cubism. Living mainly in Provence, he painted portraits, e.g. *The Card Players* (Louvre), still lifes, landscapes, especially of Mont St Victoire and L'Éstaque, and a series of *Bathers*.

c.g.s. system A metric system of units based on the centimetre, gram, and second. It includes dynes, ergs, and both electrostatic and electromagnetic units. It has been replaced for scientiffc purposes by *SI units.

Chablis 47 49N 3 48E A village in central France, in the Yonne department. Chablis is famous for the white wine named after it.

Chabrier, Emmanuel (1841-94) French composer. Prevented by his father from becoming a professional musician, he graduated in law and composed in his spare time. A performance of Wagner's *Tristan and Isolde* in 1880 made him decide to devote his whole life to music. His most famous composition is the colourful orchestral rhapsody *España* (1883).

Chabrol, Claude (1930-) French film director. He was a leading member of the *New Wave group of French directors in the late 1950s. His films, many of which are influenced by Alfred Hitchcock and use murder plots to illuminate bourgeois social relationships, include *Les Biches* (1968), *Le Boucher* (1969), and *Inspecteur Lavardin* (1986).

CETSHWAYO *Portrait by Carl Sohn (1845-1908), artist to Queen Victoria, which was painted during Cetshwayo's visit to England in 1882.*

Chaco. *See* Gran Chaco.

Chaco War (1932-35) The war between Bolivia and Paraguay resulting from a long-standing dispute over the vast Gran Chaco region. The dispute, which had arisen in the 19th century, flared up again in the 1920s when new Paraguayan settlements and word of oil deposits in Chaco upset the uneasy truce. Over 100 000 men died in this bloody war. The League of Nations failed to arbitrate a settlement but mediation by Argentina, Brazil, Chile, Peru, and the USA led to an armistice. The treaty, signed in 1938, favoured the military victor, Paraguay, which received most of the Chaco.

Chad, Lake A lake in West Africa, between Chad, Niger, Nigeria, and Cameroon. It is shallow and has no outlet; its area varies between about 10 000 and 25 000 sq km (3860–9650 sq mi).

Chad, Republic of (French name: Tchad) A country covering an extensive area in N central Africa, consisting mainly of poor semidesert. The land rises from Lake Chad in the SW to the Tibesti Mountains in the N, reaching heights of about 3400 m (11 000 ft). The majority of the rather sparse population (concentrated in the S) is Sara, a Bantu people; most of the nomadic peoples of the N are Muslims. *Economy*: mainly subsistence agriculture with livestock and fishing. Some oil and other minerals have been found but there is very little industry. The main exports are cotton and meat. *History*: one of the four territories of French Equatorial Africa, it had internal self-government as a member of the French Community from 1958, gaining independence in 1960. Since 1963 there has been considerable rebellion and unrest in the N where the Muslim inhabitants have traditionally opposed the Black population of the S. In 1975 President Nagarta Tombalbaye was assassinated in a military coup and succeeded by Gen Félix Malloum. In 1979 a transitional government under President Goukouni Oueddei was formed. In 1982 the capital N'djamena was taken by rebel forces led by Hissene Habré, who subsequently became president. Renewed fighting broke out in mid-1983 between Libyan-backed rebel forces led by Oueddei and the French-backed government forces; in 1987 Libyan forces were successfully expelled but subsequently counterattacked. Official language: French. Official currency: CFA (Communauté financière africaine) franc of 100 centimes. Area: 1 284 000 sq km (495 624 sq mi). Population (1983 est): 4 990 000. Capital: N'djamena.

Chadwick, Sir Edwin (1800–90) British social reformer, who was a disciple of Jeremy *Bentham. Chadwick was secretary to the poor-law commissioners (1834–46) and his famous *Report on the Sanitary Condition of the Labouring Population of Great Britain* (1842) prompted such reforming legislation as the Public Health Act of 1848. He was a member of the Board of Health from 1848 to 1854, when it was abolished largely because of the unpopularity that his tactlessness brought it.

Chadwick, Sir James (1891–1974) British physicist, who worked at Cambridge with *Rutherford and went on to discover the *neutron in 1932. Physicists had previously suspected the existence of neutrons but had been unable to detect them: by analysing the radiation emitted by beryllium when bombarded with alpha particles, Chadwick was able to show that it consisted of neutrons. He was awarded the 1935 Nobel Prize.

Chadwick, Lynn (1914–) British sculptor and designer. His first sculptures in the 1940s were chiefly mobiles in iron, bronze, glass, etc., influenced by Alexander *Calder, but he subsequently specialized in stable constructions in iron.

Chaeronea, Battles of 1. (338 BC) The battle in which *Philip II of Macedon, and his crack army, defeated Athenian and Theban forces at Chaeronea (on the River Cephisus in N Boeotia). It forced the Greek city states to acknowledge Philip's hegemony over Greece and the end of their autonomy. 2. (86 BC) The battle won by the Roman general *Sulla over *Mithridates VI Eupator of Pontus at the same spot.

chafer A herbivorous beetle belonging to the family *Scarabaeidae* (*see* scarab beetle). Chafers cause much damage to trees and crops by eating the foliage and flowers; the larvae, which live in the soil, attack the roots. Chief genera: *Melolontha* (*see* cockchafer), *Cetonia* (rose chafers), and *Phyllopertha* (garden chafers).

chaffinch A *finch, *Fringilla coelebs*, about 15 cm long, that is common in woods and parks in Europe, W Asia, and N Africa. The male chaffinch has a chestnut back, pinkish breast, greyish-blue crown and nape, and two conspicuous white wing bars. The female has a duller plumage with an olive-green back. Chaffinches are often migratory and have a lively song.

MARC CHAGALL

Chagall, Marc (1887–1985) Russian-born painter and printmaker of Jewish parentage. After studying in St Petersburg (1907–10) under *Bakst, he visited Paris (1910). There he painted some of his best-known works, recalling Russian village life, such as *Me and the Village* (1911; New York). His childlike figures and objects, distorted in scale and often floating upside down in space, influenced the surrealists. Moving to France (1922), he illustrated Gogol's *Dead Souls* and La Fontaine's *Fables*. During World War II he lived in the USA, where he designed ballet sets and costumes and subsequently worked on mosaics and tapestries for the Israeli Knesset building (1966). With *Picasso, he was the only painter to have an exhibition at the Louvre during his lifetime.

Chagas' disease A South American disease caused by infection with a protozoan of the genus *Trypanosoma*. Named after a Brazilian physician, Carlos Chagas (1879–1934), it is a form of *trypanosomiasis transmitted by bugs. It may result in serious damage to the heart and brain; there is no effective treatment.

Chagos Islands. *See* British Indian Ocean Territory.

chain 1. A measure of length equal to 66 feet. 2. A measuring device used in surveying. A Gunter's chain is 66 feet long (consisting of 100 links), whereas an Engineer's chain is 100 feet long (also 100 links).

Chain, Sir Ernst Boris (1906–79) British biochemist, born in Germany, who—with Lord *Florey—isolated and purified penicillin and performed the first clinical trials. Coming to England in 1933, Chain worked first at Cambridge under Sir Frederick *Hopkins and then at Oxford with Florey. For their work, Chain, Florey, and Sir Alexander *Fleming (the discoverer of penicillin) were awarded a Nobel Prize (1945).

chainmail Body armour made by welding or rivetting interlaced iron rings. Light and providing adequate protection, it was popular from about 1100 to about 1400, when plate, first worn under and then over chainmail, began to replace it. Chainmail garments include coifs, mittens, and stockings and ultimately covered the entire body. Worn over felt or leather coats, examples from about 1200 weigh between 14 kg (30 lb) and 23 kg (50 lb).

chain reaction A series of reactions in which the product of each reaction sets off further reactions. In a nuclear chain reaction each nuclear fission is induced by a neutron ejected by a previous fission. For example, the fission of a uranium-235 nucleus produces either two or three neutrons each of which can induce the fission of another uranium-235 nucleus. Chain reactions are used as a source of energy in *nuclear reactors and *nuclear weapons. *See also* critical mass.

chaise A light two- or four-wheeled carriage drawn by one, two, or four horses. A chaise usually had a collapsible hood (calash). "Chaise" could also apply to a *curricle or *phaeton. *Compare* postchaise.

Chaitanya movement A Hindu *Bhakti school, named after its founder, the Bengali brahmin mystic Chaitanya (1485-1533). Through the ecstatic singing of hymns and mantras, devotees express their blissful surrender to *Krishna and Radha, who epitomize the quasi-erotic mutual love of God and the human soul; Chaitanya himself came to be worshipped as an incarnation of these divine lovers. The Sanskrit scriptures of the movement were subsequently evolved by a group of disciples, known as the six *gosvamins*. Most of the present sect leaders are their descendants and bear the same title.

Chakkri The ruling dynasty of Thailand (formerly Siam). Its first king, Phraya Chakkri (1737-1809), styled himself Rama I after his accession in 1782. A capable military commander, he had put an end to the hostilities of the neighbouring Burmese by 1792 and then established the new capital of Bangkok. During the reigns of Rama II (1768-1824; reigned 1809-24) and Rama III (d. 1851; reigned 1824-51) Siam's relations with the West improved. Mongkut (posthumously styled Rama IV; 1804-68; reigned 1851-68) and *Chulalongkon (Rama V; reigned 1868-1910) introduced various social and administrative reforms. A revolt against Prajadhipok (Rama VII; 1893-1941; reigned 1925-35) led to the establishment of a constitutional monarchy in 1932; he abdicated in 1935. The present king, Bhumibol Adulyadej (1927-   ), ascended the throne in 1946.

Chalcedon (modern name: Kadiköy) A Megarian colony founded in the 7th century BC on the Asian side of the Bosporus. It was known as the city of the blind because it occupied a less strategic site than the opposite side of the Bosporus on which Byzantium (*see* Istanbul) was built. Absorbed first by Pergamum and later forming part of the Roman province of Asia, Chalcedon eventually became a suburb of Byzantium. It was the site in 451 AD of the Council of Chalcedon, the fourth ecumenical council of the Church. It condemned heresies relating to the dual (human and divine) nature of Christ and reaffirmed the doctrines of the Council of *Nicaea and the first Council of *Constantinople.

chalcedony A cryptocrystalline (submicroscopically grained) sometimes fibrous *silica mineral. The numerous varieties include carnelian (red); agate, onyx, and sardonyx (banded); jasper (red or brown); and chert and flint (opaque grey or black). The last two occur in limestones; others occur mainly in veins and amygdales.

Chalcidice (Modern Greek name: Khalkidhiki) A peninsula in NE Greece. It ends in three promontories, the northernmost of which contains Mount *Athos. There are fertile low-lying areas but it is mostly wooded and mountainous. Area: 2945 sq km (1149 sq mi).

Chalcis (modern name: Khalkís) 38 28N 23 36E The capital of the Greek island of *Euboea, famous as a trading and metalworking centre from the 8th to the 1st centuries BC; Aristotle died here in 322 BC. Chalcis established colonies in Italy, Sicily, and the peninsular region named after it, *Chalcidice. It joined Athens against the Persians in 480 BC but the two cities' traditional rivalry was successfully exploited by Philip of Macedon in the 4th century BC. It was partly destroyed in 146 BC by the Romans but was subsequently developed by the Venetians from the 13th century AD and was incorporated in the kingdom of Greece in 1830. Population (1981): 44 774.

chalcopyrite The principal ore of copper, sometimes called copper pyrites, of composition $CuFeS_2$. It is brassy yellow with a greenish black streak and contains 34.5% copper. It occurs mainly in veins associated with the upper part of an acid igneous intrusion.

Chaldea (*or* Chaldaea) The region of S Babylonia where the new Babylonian empire was established by Nabopolassar (d. 605 BC) in 625 in the last years of the Assyrian empire. At its height under *Nebuchadnezzar II (reigned 604-562), the Chaldean empire, centred on the rebuilt city of Babylon, dominated the Middle East for about 70 years until overthrown by the Achaemenians in 539. The Chaldeans' reputation as astronomers survived undiminished until Roman times.

Chaliapin, Feodor Ivanovich (1873-1938) Russian bass. After a penurious youth, he was discovered as a singer and made his debut at La Scala, Milan, in 1901. He became world famous in the title role of Mussorgski's *Boris Godunov*.

chalk A sedimentary rock that is a pure-white fine-grained variety of *limestone (calcium carbonate). Coccoliths (the calcareous remains of extinct unicellular organisms) are the main constituents of chalk although other invertebrate remains are included. Chalk is very characteristic of the Upper Cretaceous period in W Europe and the Chalk is sometimes used synonymously with the Upper Cretaceous. Nodules of flint are often found in chalk; these are formed from the remains of siliceous organisms, dissolved and redeposited.

Challoner, Richard (1691-1781) English Roman Catholic churchman and writer. Educated and ordained at Douai, from 1730 he led the Roman Catholic community in London, being consecrated a bishop in Hammersmith in 1741. He published a new translation of the Bible, and his prayer book for laymen, *Garden of the Soul* (1740), has remained very popular.

Chalmers, Thomas (1780-1847) Scottish preacher and theologian. Ordained in the Church of Scotland in 1803, Chalmers was an influential minister in Glasgow, where he introduced important changes in parish structures. From 1823 he was a university professor at St Andrew's and then in Edinburgh. He was a leader in the Disruption of 1843, which led to the founding of the Free Church of Scotland.

chalones A group of substances, found in mammalian tissues, that can inhibit cell division. They are thought to be important in ageing processes and in cancer.

Châlons-sur-Marne 48 58N 4 22E A town in NE France, the capital of the Marne department. In 451 AD Attila and the Huns were defeated by the Romans on a nearby plain. The 13th-century cathedral suffered damage in World War II. It is the centre of the wine trade of Champagne. Population (1982 est): 54 359.

Chalon-sur-Saône 46 47N 4 51E A town in E central France, in the Saône-et-Loire department on the River Saône. An important commercial centre, it has an engineering industry and a wine market. Population (1982 est): 57 967.

chamberlain An officer appointed by a monarch, nobleman, or corporation to carry out ceremonial duties. The chamberlains of medieval England were financial officers and were figures of great political importance in the 12th century. The chamberlain was succeeded by the Lord Chamberlain, who is responsible for the administration of the royal household. Until 1968 he also licensed plays for public performance.

Chamberlain, Joseph (1836-1914) British politician. As mayor of Birmingham (1873-76), Chamberlain effected a considerable improvement programme. He became a Liberal MP in 1876 and in 1885 presented the so-called unauthorized programme, which advocated such radical policies as free education and, with the phrase "three acres and a cow," the creation of smallholdings. In 1886 he split the Liberal Party because of Gladstone's support of Irish Home Rule. As leader of the anti-Gladstonian Liberal-Unionists, he supported the Conservatives and in 1895 became colonial secretary in the Conservative Government. His reputation was enhanced by his policies in the *Boer War but his commitment to *imperial preference in tariff rates caused a rift in the Conservative ranks, which led to his resignation (1903). His eldest son **Sir (Joseph) Austen Chamberlain** (1863–1937) became a Liberal-Unionist MP in 1892. He was chancellor of the exchequer (1919–21) and then foreign secretary (1924–29), when he negotiated the *Locarno Pact and was awarded the Nobel Peace Prize (1925). Joseph's son by his second marriage **(Arthur) Neville Chamberlain** (1869–1940) was a Conservative MP and prime minister (1937–40) of the National Government, when he advocated a policy of appeasement towards the fascist powers. He recognized Italy's conquest of Ethiopia and kept out of the Spanish Civil War. To avoid a European war he visited Hitler three times in 1938, coming to the *Munich Agreement, which recognized Germany's possession of the Sudetenland. He returned to Britain claiming to have brought "peace for our time" but was forced by Hitler's invasion of Czechoslovakia to abandon appeasement. He declared war after Hitler's attack on Poland but his ineffective direction of the war led to his resignation in May, 1940, when he joined Churchill's war cabinet.

Chamberlain, Owen (1920-) US physicist, who shared the 1959 Nobel Prize with Emilio *Segrè for their discovery of the antiproton (*see* antimatter) in 1955. They created the particle by bombarding a copper target with high-energy protons in the Berkeley *bevatron. During World War II he worked on the development of the atom bomb.

chamber music Music written to be played in the intimacy of a room rather than in a large hall, church, or theatre. In the baroque period chamber sonatas were distinguished from church sonatas and in the late 18th century Haydn, Mozart, and Beethoven established the piano trio (violin, cello, and piano), the duo sonata (one instrument and piano), and the string quartet (two violins, viola, and cello) as the main chamber music forms. Chamber music has been written for other combinations of players, including the woodwind quintet (oboe, flute, clarinet, horn, and bassoon), the clarinet quintet (clarinet and string quartet), and the piano quintet (piano and string quartet). Haydn, Mozart, Beethoven, Schubert, Brahms, Dvořák, and Britten all wrote important chamber music compositions.

chamber of commerce An organization that protects and promotes the interests of a town's manufacturers and merchants. Chambers of commerce occur in many countries, sometimes government sponsored and sometimes, as in the UK, as voluntary organizations. Many are authorized to issue certificates of origin and to certify commercial documents, some provide an *arbitration service for their members, and some (such as the London Chamber of Commerce) act as an examining board in commercial subjects. The Association of British Chambers of Commerce has some 90 members and is a member of the EEC Permanent Conference of Chambers of Commerce and the International Chamber of Commerce.

Chambers, Sir William (1723-96) British architect and interior designer. Trained in Paris and Rome, Chambers became the most reputable architect of his period, holding assorted official posts and practising a precise, sometimes dull, classicism. His major work was *Somerset House, London (1776). His *Treatise on Civil Architecture* (1759) became an influential text.

Chambéry 45 34N 5 55E A town in E France, the capital of the Savoie department. It was the capital of Savoy (1232-1562) and has a 16th-century cathedral. Industries include tourism, aluminium, and vermouth production. Population (1982 est): 54 896.

Chambord A chateau in the Loire Valley (France). Chambord was begun by Francis I in 1519 and was one of his most extravagant building projects. Elaborately decorated and much imitated, Chambord was never completed after work stopped in 1540.

chameleon An arboreal lizard belonging to the Old World family *Chamaeleontidae* (84 species) and characterized by its ability to change its skin colour. 17-25 cm long, chameleons have a narrow body, an extensile tongue for capturing insects, and bulging eyes that can move independently. Some species have a helmet-shaped head or conspicuous horns. They may be green, yellow, cream, or dark brown, often with spots, and change colour by concentration or dispersion of pigment in skin cells. Genera: *Brookesia*, *Chamaeleo*. ⌑reptile.

CHAMOIS *The hide of this increasingly rare animal was formerly used for chamois (or shammy) leather, which is now made from the skins of sheep and goats.*

chamois An agile hoofed *mammal, *Rupicapra rupicapra*, of mountainous regions in Europe and SW Asia. Chamois grow to about 75 cm high at the shoulder and have distinctive narrow upright horns with backward-pointing hooked tips. Their tawny coat becomes darker and longer in winter, when they descend from the high slopes to the forests below. Family: *Bovidae*.

chamomile. *See* camomile.

Chamonix 45 55N 6 52E A town in E France, in the Haute-Savoie department near the Swiss and Italian borders. Close to Mont Blanc, it is a mountaineering and winter-sports centre. Population (1982 est): 9255.

Champa An ancient Indochinese kingdom. The Chams were Indonesian in origin but when they established their kingdom on the coastal region of South Vietnam in 192 AD following the collapse of the Chinese Han dynasty their culture became predominantly Indian. Champa's prosperity was greatest between the 6th and 10th centuries, after the demise of Chinese domination and before the Vietnamese kingdom threatened its autonomy. Champa was finally absorbed by Vietnam in the 17th century.

champagne A wine, usually sparkling, produced in the districts around Reims and Épernay, NE France. Champagne is usually made from black (*pinot noir*) and white (*pinot chardonnay*) grapes. After fermentation sugar and yeast are added to the still wine, which, when bottled, undergoes a secondary fermentation, which produces the sparkle. A dosage of sugar syrup determines whether it will be sweet (*sec*) or dry (*brut*) champagne.

Champagne A former province in NE France, now incorporated in the planning region of **Champagne-Ardenne**. Ruled by counts during the middle ages, it became important for its trade fairs and at the end of the 17th century began to produce the sparkling *champagne for which it is famous.

Champaigne, Philippe de (1602–74) Painter of portraits and historical and religious scenes, born in Brussels. In 1621 he moved to Paris, where he worked for Marie de' Medici and Richelieu. His association with the Jansenists at Port Royal influenced his later portraits, notably *Ex Voto de 1662* (Louvre), which shows his daughter, a nun, after her recovery from paralysis.

champignon One of several edible mushrooms of the family *Agaricaceae* (*see* agaric). The fairy-ring champignon (*Marasmius oreades*), common on meadows and lawns, has a light-brown cap, 2–5 cm in diameter, and a slender stalk. They occur in rings of mushrooms marking the perimeter of the underground body of the fungus.

Champlain, Lake A long narrow lake in North America. It extends S from the Richelieu River in Canada, forming the boundary between Vermont and New York state in the USA for much of its length. It is named after Samuel de Champlain. Length: 172 km (107 mi).

Champlain, Samuel de (1567–1635) French explorer. In 1603 he followed in *Cartier's footsteps, exploring the St Lawrence and the coast from a base in Acadia. In 1608 he founded a colony at Quebec—New France—of which he became commandant (1612). When Quebec was captured by the English in 1629 he was taken prisoner. Lake Champlain, which he visited in 1609, is named after him.

champlevé (French: raised field) A technique of decorating metal surfaces with polychrome *enamelwork. The enamel is held in depressions incised in the metal. Fine examples survive from Celtic England, medieval Europe, and India.

Champollion, Jean-François (1790–1832) French Egyptologist. After studying *Coptic, he started deciphering Egyptian *hieroglyphics, building on the intuitions of Thomas *Young about royal names on the *Rosetta Stone. His *Lettre à M. Dacier* (1822) identified and assigned phonetic values to about 40 symbols. These results were confirmed and expanded in the *Précis du système hiéroglyphique* (1824).

chancellor In the UK, the name of various state officials. The chancellor, dating from the 10th century, was the head of the Chancery, the secretariat department of the *Curia Regis (King's Court). The name derives from the screen (Latin *cancelli*) behind which the secretaries worked within call of the King. By the 12th century he was the monarch's chief minister but his political prominence subsequently declined as his judicial activities in the Court of *Chancery developed and since the 17th century the **Lord (High) Chancellor**, as he came to be called, has always been a lawyer. He is appointed by the Crown on the advice of the prime minister, is a member of the cabinet, and speaker of the House of Lords (where he sits on the *woolsack) as well as being head of the judiciary. His rank follows that of the royal family and the Archbishop of Canterbury. Current Lord Chancellor: Baron Mackay of Clashfern. The **chancellor of the exchequer** is the name given in the 13th century to the clerk of the Exchequer. He is now the minister responsible for the national economy and the presentation of

the annual *budget. Current chancellor: Nigel *Lawson. *See also* Lancaster, Duchy of.

Chancery, Court of In English law, the court in which the system of *equity developed. It developed in the 15th century as the personal court of the king's chief law officer, the Lord Chancellor (*see* chancellor), in which he dealt with cases for which the *common law could not provide a remedy. It dealt with such matters as partnerships, the administration of estates, and the execution of *trusts. In 1875 it was merged with the Supreme Court of Judicature; it survives as the Chancery Division of the High Court.

Chan Chan The capital city of the pre-Inca *Chimú Kingdom, near Trujillo (Peru). Its adobe (mud brick) ruins of temples, residential buildings, cemeteries, and storerooms are divided into nine compounds, covering 36 sq km (14 sq mi). The multiplicity of reservoirs and aqueducts indicate the importance of irrigation in this arid region.

Chandernagore 22 52N 88 22E A port in India, in West Bengal on the River Hooghly. A former French settlement (1673–1950), its industries include jute and cotton. Population (1981 est): 101 925.

Chandigarh 30 43N 76 47E A Union Territory and modern (1953) city in NW India, on the Haryana-Punjab border. The joint capital of both states, it was planned by *Le Corbusier in 30 rectangular sectors for housing, government, and industry. Punjab University was established here in 1947. Area: 114 sq km (44 sq mi). Population (1981 est): 451 610.

Chandler, Raymond (1888–1959) US novelist. Educated at Dulwich College, England, he returned to the USA and worked in business before starting to write detective stories in the 1930s. The detective Philip Marlowe features in all his nine novels, which include *The Big Sleep* (1939), *Farewell My Lovely* (1940), and *The Long Goodbye* (1954).

Chandra Gupta I Emperor of India (320–c. 330 AD), who founded the Gupta dynasty. Crowned at Pataliputra, he married the daughter of the king of the neighbouring Lichavi clan and established the beginnings of a large empire.

Chandra Gupta II (c. 375–415 AD) Emperor of India (c. 380–c. 415) of the Gupta dynasty; the grandson of *Chandra Gupta I. He extended the imperial boundaries to the Arabian Sea and was a patron of the arts.

Chandragupta Maurya Emperor of India (c. 321–c. 297 BC), who founded the Maurya dynasty (c. 321–185 BC). He ousted the previous Nanda dynasty. According to tradition, he destroyed the garrison left behind by Alexander the Great. He extended his empire over the whole of India. The Greek ambassador and historian, Megasthenes, left accounts of the splendour of his reign.

Chandrasekhar, Subrahmanyan (1910–) US astronomer, born in Lahore, India (now in Pakistan), whose theoretical work has led to a greater understanding of the evolution of stars, especially white dwarfs.

Chanel, Coco (Gabrielle C.; 1883–1971) French fashion designer, who revolutionized women's clothes, introducing a note of simplicity and comfort. She opened a fashion house in Paris in 1924, becoming known particularly for her jersey dresses and suits and for her perfumes, including Chanel No 5. She retired in 1939 but began designing again in 1954.

Chang-chia-k'ou. *See* Zhangjiakou.

Chang-chou. *See* Changzhou.

Changchun 43 50N 125 20E A city in NE China, the capital of Jilin province. Jilin University was established here in 1958. Its chief industry is the manufacture of motor vehicles. Population (1983 est): 1 740 000.

Chang E In Chinese mythology, the moon goddess. She stole the drug of immortality from her consort and fled to the moon, where she lives in the form of a toad.

change ringing The sounding of a peal of church bells (which contains from 5 to 12 bells) in a fixed order. Each bell is rung by a single individual. The changes are prescribed by numerical order, e.g. 12345, 21345, 23145, etc. Traditional variations have such names as "Bob Major" or "Grandsire Triple." Change ringing is practised in English-speaking countries; one of its early protagonists was the Englishman Fabian Stedman, the author of *Tintinnalogia* (1688). A peal of bells operated by a keyboard is called a carillon.

Chang Jiang. *See* Yangtze River.

Changsha 28 10N 113 00E A port in S China, the capital of Hunan province on the Xiang (*or* Siang) River. It has long been a commercial and cultural centre, Hunan University being established here in 1959. Population (1983): 1 072 000.

Changzhou (*or* Chang-chou) 31 45N 119 57E A city in E China, in Jiangsu province on the *Grand Canal. A long-established commercial centre for agricultural produce, it has textile and engineering industries. Population (1982): 425 000.

Channel Country An area of Australia, in SW Queensland. It consists of flat alluvial land dissected by numerous river channels cut during annual floods. Following these it provides excellent pasture for cattle grazing.

Channel Islands (French name: Îles Normandes) A group of islands in the English Channel, off the coast of NW France. The chief islands comprise *Jersey (the largest), *Guernsey, *Alderney, and *Sark. Since the Norman conquest (1066) they have been a dependency of the British Crown. During World War II they were the only British territory to come under German occupation. Tourism is of major economic importance but the islands are also noted for their early agricultural and horticultural produce, most of which is exported to the UK. This includes flowers, fruit, potatoes, and tomatoes; the Jersey and Guernsey breeds of cattle are world famous. Area: 194 sq km (75 sq mi). Population (1981): 133 000.

Channel tunnel (*or* Chunnel) A proposed tunnel linking Britain with France. First suggested to Napoleon in 1802, digging was actually started by two private companies in each country in 1882 at Folkestone in England (about 1.8 km of tunnel) and Sangatte in France. A press outcry in Britain forced the government to intervene on security grounds and the scheme was abandoned in 1883. In 1964 the two governments revived the project, simultaneously considering plans for a Channel bridge. The tunnel was agreed upon and in the early 1970s work again started, to be abandoned on economic grounds in 1974. In 1987 Britain and France began work on a rail tunnel, to be opened in 1993, at a cost of £2.3 billion.

cha-no-yu The Japanese tea ceremony. The ceremony originated in China but was practised by Zen priests in Japan from the 14th century and later by other members of society. Taking place in a room of simple perfection, it is presided over by a tea master. Its object is to achieve a contemplative calm, in which attention is exclusively fixed on the ritual and utensils used. The kettle, tea bowls, bamboo whisk, and serving ladle are chosen for their artistic merit.

chanson de geste A type of epic poem composed in Old French. Versions survive from the early 12th century but the genre is probably at least a century older. Loyalty and valour are typical themes in the *chanson*, many of which relate the real or imaginary deeds of Charlemagne's knights. The most famous is the *Chanson de Roland* about the heroic last stand of some of these knights at Roncesvalles in the Pyrenees (778).

chant The short melodies to which psalms and canticles are sung in the Anglican Church. They may be single (one tune adapted for each verse) or double (alternating tunes for alternating verses). "Triple" or "quadruple" chants are less common. Many are adaptations from Latin plainsong made

by John Marbeck (died c. 1585) in his *Booke of Common Praier Noted* (1550).

chanterelle An edible *mushroom, *Cantharellus cibarius*, occurring in temperate woodlands. It is funnel-shaped and yellow with the gills clearly visible and measures 3–10 cm across the cap. The flesh is regarded as a delicacy if cooked slowly. Family: *Cantharellaceae*; class: *Basidiomycetes*.

Chantilly 49 12N 2 28E A town in France, in the Oise department near the Forest of Chantilly. Once renowned for its lace making, Chantilly is famous for its racecourse and the Grand Château's art collection. Population (1982 est): 10 208.

Chao K'uang Yin. *See* Song.

Chao Phraya, River The chief river in Thailand, rising in the N and flowing S through Bangkok to a delta on the Gulf of Thailand. Length: 1200 km (750 mi).

Chaos In earliest Greek mythology, the goddess representing the primeval emptiness from which evolved Night, Erebus (darkness), Tartarus (the underworld), and Eros (desire). The concept of a confused and formless mass, out of which the ordered universe was created, dates from the time of Ovid.

chaparral A scrub form of vegetation occurring in S California (USA) and NW Mexico. It consists chiefly of sclerophyllous broad-leaved evergreen shrubs and bushes and is closely related to the maquis of lands bordering the Mediterranean. The climate with which this form of vegetation is associated, with mild wet winters and hot dry summers, is sometimes described as the Mediterranean type.

chapbook A small cheap booklet or tract of a few stitched pages in multiples of four. Catering to popular tastes, they related heroic tales, legends, lessons, etc., and were often illustrated with woodcuts. From the 16th century chapmen sold them throughout Europe and subsequently in North America, until they were superseded by magazines in the 19th century.

CHA-NO-YU *The Japanese tea ceremony requires humility from its participants, who enter the tearoom on their knees.*

Chapel Royal A chapel for the private use of a royal household. The most famous English example is St George's Chapel, Windsor Castle. In Paris, the Sainte Chapelle originally served the French court.

Chaplin, Charlie (Sir Charles C.; 1889–1977) US film actor, born in Britain and recruited by the Keystone Studio while touring the USA with Fred Karno's pantomine company in 1913. He gained immediate popular success with his portrayals of the tramp, a sensitive but pathetic

CHARLIE CHAPLIN

figure dressed in baggy trousers and a bowler hat, and from 1918 he wrote and directed his own films. These included *The Gold Rush* (1924), *City Lights* (1931), and, following the introduction of sound, *Modern Times* (1936) and *The Great Dictator* (1940). Accused of having communist sympathies, he left the USA in 1952 to live in Switzerland. Chaplin was married four times; Paulette Goddard was his third wife and Oona O'Neill (daughter of Eugene O'Neill) his fourth. He was awarded an Oscar in 1973 and was knighted in 1976.

Chapman, George (c. 1560–1634) British poet and dramatist, famous for his translations of Homer's *Iliad* (1598–1611) and *Odyssey* (1616). His epic poem *Euthymiae Raptus* (1609) expresses his complex philosophy. His plays include the comedy *Eastward Ho* (1605), for which he and his collaborators John *Marston and Ben *Jonson were imprisoned, and the tragedy *Bussy d'Ambois* (1604).

Chappell, Greg (Gregory Stephen C.; 1948–) Australian cricketer, who played for South Australia, Queensland, Somerset, and Australia (1970–84; captain 1975–77, 1979–81, 1981–83). He was the first Australian to score over 7000 test runs. His brother **Ian Chappell** (1943–) also captained Australia (1971–75).

char A food and game fish belonging to the genus *Salvelinus*, related to *trout, especially *S. alpinus*, found in Arctic coastal waters and fresh waters of Europe and North America. Its torpedo-shaped body, about 30 cm long, is olive-green to moss-green with yellow spots above and silvery or bright red below.

charabanc 1. A large horsedrawn wagon with rows of bench seats, used to carry large groups of people. 2. A motor coach, used for similar purposes.

characin A predatory freshwater fish of the family *Characidae* (about 1000 species), found in tropical Africa and America. Characins have toothed jaws and two dorsal fins. Although they range from 2.5 to 152 cm long, most species are small and make colourful lively aquarium fish. Order: *Cypriniformes*. *See also* piranha; tetra; tigerfish.

charcoal The form of *carbon that is produced as a black porous residue from the partial burning of wood, bones,

etc. It is a very clean smokeless fuel useful, for example, in barbecues and saunas. It is also extensively used in gas filters. *See also* activated charcoal.

Charcot, Jean-Martin (1825–93) French physiologist, noted for his studies of the nervous system. He described various diseases, including **Charcot's joint**—degeneration of the joints associated with disease of the nervous system. He was a famous teacher—Sigmund *Freud was one of his students—and interested in hypnosis.

chard 1. The blanched leaves of a sucker growth of the globe *artichoke, used as a vegetable. 2. The edible leaves of a variety of beet, *Beta vulgaris cicla*, also called Swiss chard.

Chardin, Jean-Baptiste-Siméon (1699–1779) French painter of still lifes and domestic interiors in the Dutch tradition of *Vermeer. The writer *Diderot admired the simplicity of his paintings, e.g. *The Housewife* (Louvre) and *The Young Schoolmistress* (National Gallery, London), and his skill at rendering textures. Working in pastel in his later years because of failing eyesight, he produced his celebrated portraits of himself and his wife (both Louvre).

Charente, River A river in W central France. Rising in the Haute-Vienne department, it flows mainly W through Angoulême and Cognac to the Bay of Biscay. Length: 362 km (225 mi).

Chari, River (*or* R. Shari) A river in N central Africa. Rising in the N Central African Republic, it flows N to Lake Chad, forming part of the Chad–Cameroon border. Length: 2250 km (1400 mi).

Charing Cross A district in the Greater London borough of the city of Westminster. Located at the W end of the Strand, it is regarded as being the heart of London. The last of 12 crosses, marking the resting places of Queen Eleanor's coffin on its journey to Westminster Abbey, was erected here (1290) by Edward I.

chariot 1. A two-wheeled horsedrawn vehicle used for warfare in ancient Asian and European civilizations. Commonly drawn by two horses, a war chariot generally carried two men: the driver and an archer or spearman. 2. A fashionable small travelling carriage of the 18th and early 19th centuries, drawn by two or four horses.

Charlemagne (c. 742–814) King of the Franks (771–814) and the first postclassical western emperor (800–14). The son of Pepin the Short, he conquered the Saxon tribes (772–81) and became King of Lombardy (773). In 778 he campaigned in NE Spain, where at Roncesvalles his paladin Roland, later to be immortalized as the hero of the *Chanson de Roland*, was killed. In 800, having conquered most of western Christendom, he was crowned emperor of the West by Pope Leo III.

Charlemagne did much to centralize the administration of the empire while maintaining the traditional customs of his conquered territories. His court at Aix-la-Chapelle became a great European centre, where Charlemagne, the patron of such scholars as *Alcuin and *Einhard, fostered the cultural revival known as the Carolingian renaissance.

Charlemagne Prize Award made annually since 1950 by the city of Aachen, West Germany, to a person who has contributed outstandingly to European cooperation. Recipients include Konrad Adenauer, Sir Winston Churchill, and Edward Heath.

Charleroi 50 25N 4 27E A town in S central Belgium, on the River Sambre. The centre of a major coal-producing area, its industries include iron foundries and cutlery. Population (1981 est): 218 944.

Charles (1887–1922) The last emperor of the Dual Monarchy of *Austria-Hungary (1916–18). Charles failed in his attempts to withdraw Austria-Hungary from World War I and following its defeat was exiled. He was formally deposed in 1919.

Charles (**Philip Arthur George**) (1948–) Prince of Wales and heir-apparent to the throne of the United King-

PRINCE CHARLES   *The Prince and Princess of Wales in a photograph by Lord Snowdon.*

dom as the eldest son of Elizabeth II. After studying at Trinity College, Cambridge (1967–70), he served in the RAF and the Royal Navy before undertaking more public duties. In 1981 he married Lady Diana Spencer (1961–   ), the daughter of Edward John, 8th Earl Spencer (1924–   ) and his first wife, Frances Roche (1936–   ), now Mrs Shand Kydd. Their first child, Prince William Arthur Philip Louis of Wales, was born in 1982 and their second, Prince Henry Charles Albert David, in 1984.

Charles I   (1226–85) The first Angevin King of Naples and Sicily, after defeating Manfred (c. 1232–66; reigned 1258–66) at Benevento (1266) and Conradin (1252–68; reigned 1266–68) at Tagliacozzo (1268). Charles' rule gave rise (1282) to the revolt known as the *Sicilian Vespers and he was driven from his kingdom in 1284.

Charles I   (1600–49) King of England, Scotland, and Ireland (1625–49), succeeding his father James I. Charles' disputes with parliament led ultimately to the *Civil War and his execution. His first three parliaments (1625; 1626; 1628–29) were dominated by Puritan members, who distrusted Charles' Roman Catholic queen *Henrietta Maria, and his own High Church loyalties. Parliament also disliked Charles' reliance on his favourite adviser, the Duke of *Buckingham, and attempted to make its award of financial grants to the king dependent on his agreement to its demands. Charles resorted to levying taxes without parliamentary consent and ruled without parliament from 1629 to 1640. His government, largely in the hands of *Strafford and *Laud, became increasingly unpopular and his attempt to impose Laud's Anglican prayer book on Presbyterian Scotland led to the *Bishops' Wars (1639–40). The financial demands of the Wars forced Charles to summon parliament again but the so-called Short Parliament (April–May 1640) proved so critical that he soon dissolved it. The *Long Parliament, summoned in November following Charles' defeat by the Scots, impeached Strafford and Laud, beheaded Strafford, and demanded far-reaching reforms. Charles attempted to arrest five members of the House of Commons and in April 1642 the Civil War broke out. After his defeat at Naseby (1645), Charles' cause was lost and he surrendered to the Scots at Newark in 1646. He was handed to parliament (January, 1647), seized by the army (June, 1647), and escaped to the Isle of Wight, where he was held at Carisbrooke Castle. Charles negotiated secretly with the Scots but, after their defeat by Parliament at Preston (1648) brought the Civil War to an end, Charles was tried at Westminster Hall, found guilty of treason, and beheaded (30 January, 1649).

Charles I   (King of France). *See* Charles II (Holy Roman Emperor).

Charles (II) the Bald   (823–77) Holy Roman Emperor (875–77) and, as Charles I, King of France (843–77). After the death of his father Louis I, civil war broke out between Charles and his three older brothers. By 843 Charles had procured by the Treaty of Verdun the western Frankish territories, the nucleus of what was to become France.

Charles II   (1630–85) King of England, Scotland, and Ireland (1660–85). He fought with his father, Charles I, in the Civil War and, after his father's execution (1649), was crowned by the Scots. Defeated by Cromwell (1651), he was forced into exile. After the fall of the Protectorate (1659), George *Monck negotiated the *Restoration of the monarchy and Charles became king after promising a general pardon and liberty of conscience in the Declaration of Breda. In 1662 he married *Catherine of Braganza. At first dependent on the Earl of *Clarendon, Charles was forced to dismiss his adviser (1667) after the failure of the *Dutch War of 1665–67 and replaced him with a group of ministers known as the *Cabal. In 1670 he negotiated the Treaty of Dover with Louis XIV, promising to aid France against Holland and, in a secret clause, to declare himself a Roman Catholic, in return for annual French subsidies. His Roman Catholic sympathies became clear with his Declaration of Indulgence (1672), which annulled the penal laws against Dissenters and Roman Catholics. Parliament responded with the Test Act (1673) excluding Dissenters and Roman Catholics from office, which together with the unpopular Dutch War of 1672–74 served to destroy the Cabal. Fear of Roman Catholicism exacerbated by Catherine's childlessness, came to head with the *Popish Plot (1678), which fabricated a Catholic plot to murder Charles and place his Roman Catholic brother and heir, later James II, on the throne. Charles resisted subsequent parliamentary attempts to exclude James from the succession and from 1681 ruled without parliament. On his deathbed he acknowledged his Roman Catholicism.

Charles II   (1661–1700) The last Habsburg King of Spain (1665–1700). Charles became effective ruler in 1675. His reign saw the recognition of Portuguese independence (1668) and the final eclipse of Spanish power in Europe. Charles' childlessness gave rise on his death to the War of the *Spanish Succession.

Charles II (King of France).   *See* Charles III (Holy Roman Emperor).

Charles (III) the Fat   (839–88) Holy Roman Emperor (881–87) and, as Charles II, King of France (884–87). Charles was the great-grandson of Charlemagne, whose empire he reunited after becoming King of Swabia (876), of Italy (879), and of the eastern Franks (882) and western Franks (France; 884). He was deposed in 887.

Charles III   (1716–88) King of Spain (1759–88). Charles ascended the Spanish throne after ruling (1734–59) Naples and Sicily. An enlightened despot (*see* Enlightenment), he encouraged efforts to modernize Spain, to develop its economy, and restore its international position. He sided with France in the Seven Years' War, losing Florida until 1783, when he regained it after the American Revolution.

CHARLES I   Charles I in Three Positions *by Van Dyck (c. 1637), the king's painter.*

Charles (IV) the Fair (1294-1328) King of France (1322-28). Charles was the brother of *Isabella of France, with whom he conspired against her husband Edward II of England.

Charles IV (1316-78) King of Bohemia (1346-78) and Holy Roman Emperor (1355-78). He made Prague his capital, where he founded (1348) Charles University. In 1356 he issued the Golden Bull, an imperial constitution, which confirmed the status of the seven imperial *electors.

Charles IV (1748-1819) King of Spain (1788-1808), who was dominated by his wife María Luisa (1751-1819) and her favourite Manuel de *Godoy. Military defeat and Godoy's unpopularity led to aristocratic and popular opposition, which caused Charles to abdicate.

Charles (V) the Wise (1337-80) King of France (1364-80) during the Hundred Years' War with England. As regent (1356-60) for his father John II, Charles suppressed the peasants' revolt known as the Jacquerie (1358). Between 1369 and 1375 he regained with the help of Bertrand du *Guesclin most of the territory lost to England by the disastrous Treaty of Brétigny (1360).

Charles V (1500-58) Holy Roman Emperor (1519-56). Charles inherited Burgundy and the Netherlands (1506) from his father Philip of Burgundy (1478-1506); he became King of Spain and Naples (1516) on the death of his maternal grandfather Ferdinand II of Aragon and Holy Roman Emperor on the death of his paternal grandfather Maximilian I. Charles' vast possessions provoked intermittent warfare with *Francis I of France: in 1525, having defeated Francis at Pavia, Charles briefly took the French king prisoner and in 1527, in response to an alliance between France, the papacy, Venice, and Milan, Charles' troops sacked Rome. Their contest for European hegemony ended inconclusively with the Treaty of Crépy (1544). Charles also faced the aggression of the Ottoman Turks, who twice besieged Vienna (1529, 1532), but his commitments elsewhere in the Empire prevented a decisive confrontation and the Turks continued to threaten Christendom. Charles' reign saw the emergence of the *Reformation and in 1521 he presided over the Diet of Worms, which condemned *Luther. His subsequent attempts to conciliate the Protestants failed and in 1546 Charles took up arms against the Protestant Schmalkaldic League, defeating it at Mühlberg (1547). In 1551, however, two German Protestant rulers allied with Henry II of France and Charles was forced to

accept Protestant demands (*see* Augsburg, Peace of). Exhausted by the great and complex problems of his Empire, Charles retired to a Spanish monastery, dividing his possessions between his son, who became *Philip II of Spain, and his brother, Emperor *Ferdinand I.

Charles (VI) the Well-Beloved (1368-1422) King of France (1380-1422). Charles suffered attacks of insanity from 1392 and the ensuing conflict for the regency led to civil war between the Armagnacs and the Burgundians. In 1415 Henry V of England invaded France and defeated the French at *Agincourt. After further campaigns, Henry married (1420) Charles' daughter Catherine of Valois (1401-37) and was named as regent of France and Charles' heir.

Charles VI (1685-1740) Holy Roman Emperor (1711-40), who issued the Pragmatic Sanction (1713) to secure the succession of his daughter *Maria Theresa to his Austrian possessions. His claim (1700) to the Spanish throne gave rise to the War of the *Spanish Succession (1701-14), in which he was unsuccessful. In 1716-18 and 1736-39 he fought the Turks; he lost the War of the Polish Succession (1733-38).

Charles VII (1403-61) King of France (1422-61). He suffered losses to the invading English and their Burgundian allies until 1429 when, with *Joan of Arc, he liberated Orleans. By 1453, he had driven the English from all of France, except Calais. He instituted reforms to strengthen the monarchy but his last years were troubled by the intrigues of the dauphin. *See also* Hundred Years' War.

Charles VII (1697-1745) Holy Roman Emperor (1742-45) during the War of the *Austrian Succession. The Elector of Bavaria (1726-45), Charles joined the alliance against Maria Theresa when she claimed the Austrian inheritance. He was elected emperor in opposition to Maria Theresa's husband Francis (subsequently Emperor Francis I).

Charles VIII (1470-98) King of France (1483-98), who unsuccessfully claimed the throne of Naples. He entered Naples in 1495 but was forced to withdraw in the face of an alliance between Austria, Milan, Venice, and the papacy.

Charles IX (1550-74) King of France (1560-74) during the *Wars of Religion. His mother *Catherine de' Medici dominated his reign and was largely responsible for the *Saint Bartholomew's Day Massacre of Huguenots that Charles ordered in 1572.

Charles IX (1550-1611) King of Sweden (1607-11). During the absence of his nephew King Sigismund (1566-1632; reigned 1592-1604), who was also King of Poland (1587-1632), Charles virtually ruled Sweden, restoring Lutheranism (1593-99). He defeated Sigismund (1598) to become king.

Charles X Gustavus (1622-60) King of Sweden (1654-60), who attempted to establish a united northern state. He invaded Poland in 1655 and declared war on Denmark in 1657, from which he regained lands in S Sweden by the Treaty of Roskilde (1658). He died during a second campaign against Denmark.

Charles X (1757-1836) King of France (1824-30). Charles lived abroad after the French revolution, returning at the Bourbon restoration (1815), when he became leader of the ultraroyalist party. His reactionary rule led to his overthrow (1830) and he fled to England.

Charles XI (1655-97) King of Sweden (1660-97), who reduced the power of the nobles to establish absolute rule. He was defeated (1675) by the Dutch alliance in the Dutch War of 1672-78 but was victorious (1678) against Denmark, marrying (1680) the sister of the Danish king. Thereafter he maintained Swedish neutrality.

Charles XII (1682-1718) King of Sweden (1697-1718) during the Great *Northern War. In the face of an alliance between Denmark, Poland, and Russia, Charles invaded Denmark (1699) and attacked Russia, winning a victory on the Narva (1700). He dethroned the hostile Polish king

(1704) and again invaded Russia (1707), where he suffered defeat and fled to Turkey. He died while invading Norway.

CHARLESTON *Dancing in the 1920s, from a cartoon in* Punch.

Charles XIV John (King of Sweden). *See* Bernadotte, Jean Baptiste Jules.

Charles, Ray (1930–   ) US Black pianist, singer, and composer. His style was influenced by gospel music and rhythm and blues; he recorded a number of songs, such as "Georgia On My Mind," in a modern jazz style.

Charles Albert (1798–1849) King of Sardinia-Piedmont (1831–49) during the Risorgimento (the movement for Italian Unification). He introduced many administrative and economic reforms but reluctantly granted representative government to Sardinia in 1848. He joined Milan's revolt against its Austrian government but was defeated at Custoza (1848) and Novara (1849) and abdicated.

Charles Edward Stuart, the Young Pretender (1720–88) The son of the Old Pretender, *James Edward Stuart. Romantically known as Bonnie Prince Charlie, in 1745 he landed in Scotland, rallied his *Jacobite supporters and marched S to claim the English throne. Lack of support forced his withdrawal again to Scotland. Defeated in battle at Culloden (1746), he escaped to exile in Europe.

Charles Martel (c. 689–741) Mayor of the palace of Austrasia (the eastern Frankish empire). After the death (714) of his father Pepin of Herstal, Charles, an illegitimate son, competed for the succession with Pepin's widow, Plectrude, who was regent for her grandsons. Successful by 719, Charles extended his rule over all the Franks. In 732 near Poitiers, he defeated the invading Muslims.

Charles's law For a gas at constant pressure, its volume is directly proportional to its absolute temperature. The law is not strictly obeyed but is closely approximated in gases above their *critical state. An alternative statement of the law is that gases expand by 1/273 of their volume at 0°C for every 1°C rise in temperature. Named after Jacques Charles (1746–1823).

Charles the Bold (1433–77) The last Duke of Burgundy (1467–77), who attempted to create a Burgundian kingdom. In 1465 Charles joined a revolt against Louis XI of France, with whom he was repeatedly in conflict until 1477. He extended his territory to the Rhine, conquering Lorraine in 1475. He then invaded Switzerland (1476) but was defeated near Granson and at Morat and died in battle while laying siege to Nancy.

Charleston 38 23N 81 40W A city in the USA, the capital of West Virginia. It was the home (1788–95) of Daniel Boone. Industries include chemicals, glass, and paints. Population (1980): 63 968.

Charleston 32 48N 79 58W A city in the USA, in South Car-

olina near the Atlantic coast. Founded in 1670, the first military action of the US Civil War took place here with the bombardment of Fort Sumter by Confederate troops in 1861. Despite earthquake damage in 1866, many of its colonial buildings remain, making it a popular tourist centre, with famous gardens. A major port, its manufactures include fertilizer, paper, and steel. Population (1980): 69 510.

Charleston A ballroom dance of the 1920s named after Charleston, South Carolina, where it had been a popular Black dance in the early 1900s. It became a national craze following the Black musical *Runnin' Wild* (1923) with its 4/4 time, syncopated rhythms, and twisting toe-in steps.

Charleston, Battles of Two battles of the *American Revolution fought at Charleston, South Carolina. In the first (1776) the Americans repulsed the British, whose invasion of the South was thus delayed. In the second the Americans surrendered (12 May, 1780) Charleston after a 45-day siege.

charlock An annual herb, *Sinapis arvensis*, also called wild mustard. 30–80 cm high, with bright-yellow flowers and hairy toothed leaves, it is found throughout Eurasia and N Africa and has been introduced elsewhere. It is a serious weed of spring-sown crops. Family: *Cruciferae*.

Charlotte 35 03N 80 50W A city in the USA, in North Carolina. The commercial and industrial centre of the Carolina manufacturing belt, its products include textiles, machinery, and chemicals. Population (1980): 314 447.

Charlotte Amalie (name from 1921 until 1936: St Thomas) 18 21N 64 56W The capital of the US Virgin Islands, a port on St Thomas Island. Established by the Danes in 1672, it is now a tourist resort. Population (1980): 11 756.

Charlottenburg 52 31N 13 15E A district of West Berlin, West Germany, on the River Spree. The 1936 Olympic Games were held here. Population (1983): 150 000.

Charlottesville 38 02N 78 29W A city in the USA, in central Virginia. It was the home of Thomas Jefferson, who established the University of Virginia here in 1819. Population (1980 est): 39 916.

Charlottetown 46 14N 63 09W A city and port in E Canada, the capital of Prince Edward Island. Founded in 1790, it is the province's commercial, industrial, and educational centre. Population (1981): 15 282.

Charlton, Bobby (Robert C.; 1937–   ) British Association footballer, who played for Manchester United (1956–73). He also played for England 106 times and scored a record 49 goals; he was a member of the England team that won the 1966 World Cup. His brother **Jackie Charlton** (John C.; 1935–   ) was also an Association footballer, who played for Leeds United and England.

charm A property of matter, expressed as a *quantum number, postulated to account for the unusually long lifetime of the psi particle (discovered in 1974). According to this hypothesis a quark (*see* particle physics) exists having the property called charm. The psi particle itself is a meson having zero charm as it consists of a charmed quark and its antiquark. However, there is evidence that some charmed *hadrons exist. Charm is believed to be conserved in *strong interactions and in electromagnetic interactions.

Charnley, Sir John (1911–82) British orthopaedic surgeon, whose invention of an artificial hip joint has enabled thousands of arthritic patients to benefit from hip replacement surgery. He became a fellow of the Royal Society (1975) and was knighted in 1977.

Charon In Greek legend, the ferryman who carried the souls of the dead over the Rivers Styx and Acheron to the underworld. Only the correctly buried dead were taken. A coin placed in the mouth of the corpse was his payment.

Charpentier, Gustave (1860–1956) French composer and pupil of Massenet. He wrote one successful opera, *Louise*

(1900), a naturalistic treatment of the life of a Parisian working girl.

Charron, Pierre (1541–1603) French theologian and philosopher. An intimate of *Montaigne, Charron studied law but entered the Church, becoming a fashionable preacher with a court appointment. *Les Trois Vérités* (1594) is a defence of Roman Catholicism. *De la sagesse* (1601), contrastingly sceptical and rationalistic, foreshadows *deism, and offers a moral philosophy divorced from Christian sanctions.

Charterhouse The English part-translation of the French *maison chartreuse*, *Carthusian house or monastery. The term was especially applied to the most famous monastery of the order, which was founded in 1371 near Aldersgate in the City of London. The monastery was dissolved in 1535, and in 1611 Thomas Sutton (1532–1611), a rich businessman, endowed a chapel, hospital, and school on the site. The school was removed to its present location near Godalming, Surrey, in 1871.

chartering The hiring of a tramp steamer to carry a specific cargo for a particular voyage (voyage charter) or for a particular period (time charter). Most of the world's chartering is arranged on the London *Baltic Exchange. Although tramp steamers used to be smaller than liners, they now include large ships with *containerization facilities and some are tankers.

Charteris, Leslie (L. Charles Bowyer Yin; 1907–) British novelist, born in Singapore. In *Enter the Saint* (1930) he created the character of Simon Templar, better known as The Saint, who featured in many subsequent popular adventure novels. He became a US citizen in 1941.

Chartier, Alain (c. 1385–c. 1440) French poet and prose writer. He served as secretary to Charles VI and as foreign emissary for Charles VII. His works include the *Quadrilogue invectif* (1422), a debate on the state of France and a call for national unity, and the poem, *La Belle Dame sans merci* (1424).

Chartism A British working–class movement for political reform, centring on William *Lovett's London Working Men's Association (LWMA). Founded in June, 1836, the LWMA drew up a People's Charter (1838) of six points: universal male suffrage, the secret ballot, equal electoral districts, abolition of the property qualifications for MPs, payment of MPs, and annual general elections. The Chartists quickly gained support throughout the country and presented their Charter with 1.2 million signatures to parliament (1839). It was rejected, as were their two later petitions (1842, 1848). Chartism lost support in the 1840s because of lack of organization, rivalry between its leaders, Lovett and Feargus *O'Connor, and reviving trade and greater prosperity. The movement was spent by the end of the decade.

Chartres 48 27N 1 30E A town in N central France, the capital of the Eure-et-Loire department on the River Eure. The gothic cathedral (begun c. 1194) is famous, especially for its 13th-century stained glass, and there are several other noteworthy churches (particularly St Pierre). Chartres is the principal market town of the Beauce region. Population (1982 est): 39 243.

Chartreuse, La Grande A *Carthusian monastery in a remote valley in SE France, in the Isère department. The buildings date mainly from the 17th century. The liqueur Chartreuse is made by the monks, the income from it being devoted to maintaining Carthusian monasteries and to several charities.

Charybdis. *See* Scylla and Charybdis.

chat A songbird belonging to the *thrush family. True chats include *stonechats, *whinchats, *wheatears, and *redstarts although the name is also given to certain Australian wrens (family *Muscicapidae*) and to American wood warblers (family *Parulidae*).

chateau A French castle or large country house. In the middle ages it was the fortified stronghold of the local seigneur. By the 16th century, however, defence needs had decreased and chateaux became the lightly fortified country residences of the nobility. Among the most famous are the chateaux of *Blois (1498–1524), *Chambord (1519–40), and d'Azay-le-Rideau (1520) in the Loire Valley. Under Louis XIV chateau building declined with the aristocracy's increasing dependence on the Crown for its income and the resultant need to live in Paris.

An estate or plantation in Bordeaux that produces wine is also called a chateau, whether a large house is attached to the estate or not. These Bordeaux chateau wines are known as claret if they are red.

Chateaubriand, Vicomte de (1768–1848) French writer and diplomat. Son of a minor nobleman, he sailed to America in 1791 but soon returned to fight in the royalist army. He lived in England from 1793 to 1800. On returning to France, he published *Atala* (1801), an unfinished epic based on his experiences with the American Indians, and *Le Génie du Christianisme* (1802). After the restoration of the monarchy in 1814 he served as ambassador and as minister for foreign affairs. He is best known for his *Mémoires d'outre-tombe* (1849–50).

Chateauroux 46 49N 1 41E A town in central France, the capital of the Indre department on the River Indre. Named after its 10th-century chateau, it has textile, machinery, and tobacco industries. Population (1982 est): 53 967.

Château-Thierry 49 03N 3 24E A town in N France, in the Aisne department on the River Marne on the slopes of a hill surmounted by the ruins of an 8th-century castle. The site of many battles throughout the centuries, it was badly damaged in both world wars. Population (1982 est): 14 920.

Chatham 51 23N 0 32E A town in SE England, in Kent on the Medway estuary. It is a naval base dating from Tudor times, with extensive dockyards. Population (1981): 61 909.

Chatham, 1st Earl of. *See* Pitt the Elder, William.

Chatham Islands 44 00S 176 30W A group of islands in the S Pacific Ocean, comprising part of New Zealand. The main occupation is sheep farming. Area: 963 sq km (372 sq mi). Population (1983): 770. Chief settlement: Waitangi.

Chatsworth An impressive country house in Derbyshire (England) belonging to the Dukes of Devonshire. Originally a Tudor house, Chatsworth was extensively remodelled (1686–96) by William Talman (1650–1719). Building continued fitfully until completed (1820–30) by Sir Jeffrey Wyatville (1766–1840).

Chattanooga 35 02N 85 18W A city in the USA, in SE Tennessee on the Tennessee River. It was settled in 1815 and was the site of a decisive battle in the US Civil War (1863). It grew rapidly following the provision of cheap hydroelectric power by the Tennessee Valley Authority in the 1930s. Its varied industries include the manufacture of textiles, boilers, nuclear reactors, furniture, and chemicals. Population (1980): 169 565.

Chatterjee, Bankim Chandra (1838–94) Indian novelist. A pioneer of the novel in India, he wrote romances, such as *Anandamath* (1882), the heroes of which are usually champions of Hindu nationalism. Many of his books were first published serially in *Banga Darshan*, the journal he founded in 1872.

Chatterton, Thomas (1752–70) British poet. A solitary and precocious boy, he wrote and published poems purporting to be the work of a 15th-century Bristol monk, Thomas Rowley. Despite the genuine talent he displayed, he was ostracized when his deception was uncovered and subsequently committed suicide. His tragic life made him a hero of Romanticism.

Chaucer, Geoffrey (c. 1342–1400) English poet, whose works established the Southern English dialect as the literary language of England. Chaucer made various journeys to

GEOFFREY CHAUCER   *An engraving based on an illumination in a manuscript of Chaucer's works.*

Europe as a soldier and diplomat, held positions in the customs service, and received pensions from Richard II and Henry IV. He translated part of the French poem *Le Roman de la rose* into English and his own poems *The Book of the Duchess* and *The Parliament of Fowls* derive from the French tradition of the allegorical dream poem. Chaucer was also influenced by Dante, Petrarch, and Boccaccio: he parodied Dante's *Divine Comedy* in *The House of Fame* and used Boccaccio's poem *Il filostrato* as the basis for *Troilus and Criseyde*, a long poem dealing with the transitoriness of earthly love, human free will, and divine foreknowledge. Chaucer's best-known work is *The Canterbury Tales*, a collection of stories told by a group of pilgrims travelling from London to Canterbury. The tales range from the tragedy of *The Knight's Tale* to the bawdiness of *The Miller's Tale*. Colourful portraits of each pilgrim are contained in the famous Prologue.

chaulmoogra   Either of two trees, *Hydnocarpus wightiana* of SW Asia or *Taraktogenos kurzii* of Burma, both of which yield a medicinal oil used in treating leprosy. Family: *Flacourtiaceae*.

Chausson, Ernest   (1855–99) French composer. His compositions were influenced by his teacher Franck and by Wagner. His small output includes *Poème de l'amour et de la mer* (for voice and orchestra; 1882–92), *Poème* (for violin and orchestra; 1896), and a symphony (1890). He was killed in a cycling accident.

Cheapside   A street in the City of London, between St Paul's Cathedral and Poultry. Once an important market place it became a centre for goldsmiths and silversmiths. It was badly damaged by bombing during World War II, but Sir Christopher Wren's church of St Mary-le-Bow (1680), famous for its Bow Bells, still stands here.

Cheb (German name: Eger)   50 04N 12 20E A town in W Czechoslovakia. It was a major border fortress, with a 12th-century castle, guarding the NW approach to Bohemia. Wallenstein was murdered here (1634). Following World War I it was a centre of the Sudeten-German movement. Population (1983): 31 239.

Chebishev, Pafnuti Lvovich   (1821–94) Russian mathematician, who made many discoveries in the field of *prime numbers, the most important of which was a method of determining the number of primes below a given number. He also contributed to probability theory and mechanics.

Cheboksary   56 08N 47 12E A port in the central Soviet Union, the capital of Chuvash ASSR in the RSFSR on the River Volga. Its manufactures include electrical equipment and it has a large hydroelectric station. Population (1981 est): 340 000.

Checheno-Ingush Autonomous Soviet Socialist Republic   An administrative division in the S Soviet Union, in the RSFSR in the N Caucasus. The population is 50% Chechen and 10% Ingushe (both Muslim) and 35% Russian. Checheno-Ingush has one of the major Soviet oilfields as well as sizable deposits of natural gas and minerals. Its main industries are engineering, chemicals, manufacture of building materials, food canning, and wine and cognac making. The presence of mineral waters has resulted in the development of health resorts. *History*: the Chechens and Ingushes were conquered by Russia in the late 1850s. Each nationality became (1922 and 1924 respectively) a separate autonomous *oblast* (region) before uniting in 1936 to become one autonomous republic. Following collaboration with the Germans in World War II, many Chechens and Ingushes were deported to Central Asia, being returned in 1956. The republic was re-established in 1957. Area: 19 300 sq km (7350 sq mi). Population (1981 est): 1 170 000. Capital: Grozny.

Cheddar   51 17N 2 46W A village in SW England, in Somerset, famous for its cheese, soft fruit (especially strawberries), and the caverns (containing stalagmites and stalactites) and rare limestone flora of the **Cheddar Gorge**, a pass through the Mendip Hills. Population (1983): 3994.

cheese   A dairy product made from separated milk solids (curd). Curd is made by coagulating milk with rennet or some other enzyme and removing the liquid (whey). It is then salted, pressed into blocks, and left to mature. Cheese is a rich source of protein and calcium. It contains fat but little carbohydrate since most of it is left in the whey. **Hard cheeses**, such as Emmental and Cheddar, are left to mature for some time—years in the case of Italian Parmesan. Cheshire, Port Salut, Edam, and Gouda are **semihard cheeses**. **Soft cheeses** may be eaten relatively fresh, after one day in the case of fresh cream cheese. Brie, Camembert, and Limburg are surface-ripened soft cheeses. Blue cheese, Stilton, Gorgonzola, and Roquefort are ripened by moulds inside the cheese.

cheetah   A large *cat, *Acinonyx jubatus*, of Africa and SW Asia, also called hunting leopard. It has a reddish-yellow coat with black spots and grows to about 2 m in length. Cheetahs have nonretractable claws and rough pads and they hunt by running down prey, such as antelope. They are the fastest mammals, sprinting at up to 110 km per hour (70 mph).

Chefoo.   *See* Yantai.

CHEKA   The first Soviet secret police agency. Founded in 1917, its full name was the Extraordinary Commission to Combat Counterrevolution, Sabotage, and Speculation. It was headed by Feliks Dzerzhinskii (1877–1926) and fought all anti-Bolshevik groups. Owing to its extreme brutality, it came under severe criticism and was reorganized in 1922.

Chekhov, Anton Pavlovich   (1860–1904) Russian dramatist and short-story writer. He began writing comic sketches while studying medicine at Moscow University and developed as a more serious writer after graduating in

1884. Suffering from tuberculosis, he bought a farm at Melikhovo in 1892 and, after a haemorrhage in 1897, lived at Yalta in the Crimea. His first play, *The Seagull* (1896), failed at first but succeeded triumphantly when revived in 1898 by Stanislavsky's Moscow Art Theatre. His major plays—*Uncle Vanya* (1897), *The Three Sisters* (1901), and *The Cherry Orchard* (1904)—were written for this company, and in 1901 he married one of the actresses, Olga Knipper.

Chekiang. *See* Zhejiang.

chelate An inorganic chemical complex in which a closed ring of atoms is formed including a metallic ion. For example, two molecules of ethylenediamine form two chelate rings with a cupric ion. Chlorophyll (with a central magnesium ion) and haemoglobin (with a central iron ion) are chelates. Chelating agents are used for sequestering unwanted metal ions. For example, they are added to shampoos in order to soften the water used with them by "locking up" calcium and magnesium ions.

Chelmsford 51 44N 0 28E A city in SE England, the administrative centre of Essex. It is a market town and manufactures electronic communications equipment, electronic equipment, and bearings. Population (1981): 58 159.

Chelonia An order of reptiles (600 species) comprising the aquatic *turtles and *terrapins and the terrestrial *tortoises, widely distributed in warm and temperate regions. They have a protective shell consisting of an upper carapace and a lower plastron joined together at the sides with openings for the head, tail, and limbs. The neck is long and mobile and can be withdrawn into the shell.

Chelsea A residential district in the Greater London borough of Kensington and Chelsea, on the N bank of the River Thames. It is noted for the Chelsea Royal Hospital for old soldiers (Chelsea Pensioners), designed by *Wren and completed in 1692. It has a long history of literary and artistic associations, particularly in the 18th and 19th centuries.

Chelsea porcelain A pioneer soft-paste *porcelain made at Chelsea (London) between 1743 and 1785. From early sparsely decorated figures and small dishes the factory improved to become one of the most important in contemporary Europe. Products included octagonal table wares from Japanese models, copies of Chinese vases and figures, scent bottles and toilet articles in *Meissen style, and splendid *rococo vases and figures with sumptuous gilding on rich claret, green, and blue grounds in the Sèvres style. *See also* Derby ware.

Cheltenham 51 54N 2 04W A town in SW England, in Gloucestershire. A fashionable spa town in the 18th century, it is famous for its schools (Cheltenham College, a boys' public school, and Cheltenham Ladies' College) and racecourse. Population (1981): 73 229.

Chelyabinsk 55 12N 61 25E A city in the W Soviet Union, in the RSFSR. It is one of the country's major industrial centres, whose products include steel and chemicals. Population (1981 est): 1 055 000.

Chelyuskin, Cape 77 44N 103 55E A headland in the central N Soviet Union, the most northerly point of any continent.

chemical bond The force that holds the atoms together in a molecule or the ions together in a crystalline solid. In general, atoms combine to form molecules and ions combine to form crystals in order to increase their stability by sharing or transferring outer electrons in such a way that the stable noble-gas configuration results (*see* atomic theory). In **covalent bonds**, atoms are held together by sharing pairs of electrons in their outer shells. In methane (CH_4), for example, each hydrogen atom forms a bond by sharing its only electron with one of the four electrons in the outer shell of the carbon atom. Each hydrogen atom then has a pair of electrons, giving it the stable two-electron outer shell of helium. The carbon atom, with four pairs of electrons in its

outer shell, has the stable eight-electron outer shell of argon. In the **electrovalent** (*or* ionic) **bond** an outer electron is transferred from one atom to another so that ions are formed. The electrostatic force between the ions holds the molecule or crystal together. For example, a molecule of sodium chloride (NaCl) is formed when the single electron in the outer shell of the sodium atom is transferred to the chlorine atom. As the chlorine atom has seven electrons, the additional electron gives it the eight-electron argon stability. **Coordinate** (*or* dative) **bonds** are covalent bonds in which both electrons are donated by the same atom. They thus combine the concepts of sharing and transferring. *See also* hydrogen bonds.

chemical energy Energy released in a usable form by a chemical reaction. In molecules, energy is stored as the potential energy of the electrons. During a reaction, rearrangement of the electrons takes place and excess energy is converted to other forms. The energy is usually transformed into heat, as in combustion, acid-base neutralization, etc., but it can be made available as electrical energy in cells. Occasionally, it gives rise to *luminescence.

chemical engineering The design, maintenance, and operation of equipment used in industrial chemical processes. Chemical engineers study both chemistry and engineering subjects. In the UK the profession is controlled by the Institution of Chemical Engineers.

chemical reaction A process in which one or more chemical substances change to other substances, either spontaneously or as a result of heat, irradiation, etc. Chemical reaction involves partial or complete transfer of one or more electrons between reacting species and a rearrangement of atoms to form different molecules. For a reaction to occur, reactant atoms (or molecules, ions, etc.) must collide. Most reactions are thus bimolecular (involving collision between two molecules); a few are termolecular (three molecules). Many apparently complicated reactions proceed in a sequence of simple steps. *See also* catalysis.

chemical warfare The use of toxic substances to kill or disable personnel, pollute food or water supplies, or make any other military use of chemicals, for example smoke screens, etc. (explosives are excluded). Toxic substances are generally fired in shells as liquids or solids that form aerosols on explosion. Chlorine, phosgene, and mustard gas were used in World War I but are ineffective against modern protection. They were not used in World War II. Poisons have now been developed to penetrate the skin, circumventing gas masks. Chemical warfare permits great flexibility in the amount and type of injuries inflicted, ranging from the relatively humane *tear gas to the lethal *nerve gases.

chemiluminescence The emission of light without heat in the course of a chemical reaction; often known as cold light. It occurs when the reaction yields product molecules in an excited energy state; light is emitted as the molecules revert to their ground state. Under certain conditions, the oxidation of many organic compounds, including glucose and formaldehyde, results in chemiluminescence. *See also* bioluminescence.

chemin de fer. *See* baccarat.

chemisorption. *See* adsorption.

chemistry The scientific study of matter, especially the changes and interactions it can undergo. Chemistry can be said to have originated with *Aristotle's four-element (earth, air, fire, water) analysis of matter. This totally incorrect view of the substance of the world persisted unchallenged, untested, and unrefuted from the 4th century BC, through some 2000 years of *alchemy, until it was finally demolished by Robert *Boyle in his *Skeptical Chymist* (1661). The modern concept of an element, as a substance incapable of further decomposition, was provided by Boyle, who also correctly distinguished between elements, compounds, and mixtures. The elucidation of the structure of compounds in terms of the elements they contain was developed by such 18th-century chemists as *Cavendish, *Priestley, and *Lavoisier. *Berzelius' law of constant proportions and *Dalton's atomic theory, produced at the beginning of the 19th century, established chemistry on a quantitative basis. However, it was not until the beginning of the 20th century that the work of J. J. Thomson and Rutherford (*see* atomic theory) had established the structure of the atom, enabling the electronic theory of *valence to emerge. This theory made sense of the work of Newlands and *Mendeleyev in ordering the elements into the structure of the *periodic table. **Inorganic chemistry** is concerned with the study of all these elements (except carbon) and their compounds and interactions. **Organic chemistry** is the study of the enormous number of compounds of carbon. It originated with *Wöhler's synthesis of urea in 1828 and developed throughout the 19th century. Organic chemicals fall broadly into two classes: *aliphatic compounds (*see also* alkanes; alkenes; alkynes) and *aromatic compounds. Many industries, including dyeing, explosives, plastics, and pharmaceuticals, depend very largely on organic chemistry. **Physical chemistry** is concerned with the application of physics to a quantitative assessment of the structures and properties of compounds and the laws that control chemical reactions. Electrochemistry and *electrolysis, reaction kinetics, photochemistry, chemical *thermodynamics, and colloid chemistry are some of its main branches.

Chemnitz. *See* Karl-Marx-Stadt.

chemoreception The reception by an organism of chemical stimuli. In man and other air-breathing vertebrates, chemicals ingested in food, etc., are sensed by taste buds on the tongue and walls of the mouth, while airborne chemicals are detected by smell (olfactory) receptors in the lining of the nasal passages (*see also* pheromones). Both smell and taste organs are present in fish but worms and other lower animals have only a general sensitivity to chemicals over the body surface. Chemoreception is used by animals for locating and identifying other organisms, food sources, and scent marks and trails.

chemotherapy The treatment of disease by means of drugs. The term was originally coined by Paul *Ehrlich, for the synthetic chemicals used to treat infectious diseases (e.g. salvarsan for syphilis), but it was later expanded to include antibiotics. Today chemotherapy commonly refers to the chemical treatment of cancer—by means of *cytotoxic and other drugs, which inhibit the action of cancer cells—as distinct from treatment with X-rays (*see* radiotherapy).

Chenab, River A river in NW India and Pakistan, one of the five rivers of the Punjab. Rising in the Himalayas, it flows SW to join the River Sutlej in Pakistan. Length: 1087 km (675 mi).

Chen-chiang. *See* Jinjiang.

Cheng Ch'eng-kung. *See* Zheng Cheng Gong.

Cheng-chou. *See* Zhengzhou.

Chengde (*or* Ch'eng-te; English name: Jehol) 40 48N 118 06E A city in NE China, in Hebei province. During the 18th and 19th centuries the Qing emperors spent the summers here. It was the capital of the former province of Jehol (1928–56). Population (1982): 150 000.

Chengdu (*or* Ch'eng-tu) 30 37N 104 06E A city in central China, the capital of Sichuan province and the site of its university. An ancient cultural, and now also an industrial, centre, it produces textiles, chemicals, and machinery. Population (1983): 2 470 000.

Cheng Ho. *See* Zheng He.

Ch'eng-te. *See* Chengde.

Ch'eng-tu. *See* Chengdu.

Chénier, André de (1762–94) French poet, born in Istanbul of Greek-French parentage. He studied in Paris and worked in London before returning to Revolutionary France in 1789. An outspoken political journalist, he was arrested and guillotined.

His posthumously published poems, notably the *Iambes* and *Odes*, had a strong influence on later Romantic poets.

Cheops. *See* Khufu.

Chephren. *See* Khafre.

Chepstow 51 39N 2 41W A town in South Wales, in Gwent on the River Wye. It is a tourist centre with light industry; the remains of Tintern Abbey are nearby. Population (1981): 9309.

cheque card A card issued by a bank to approved customers that guarantees payment by the bank to the payees of that customer's cheques regardless of the state of his bank balance. A cheque that has been supported by a cheque card cannot be stopped.

Chequers (*or* Chequers Court) A country house in S England, in Buckinghamshire near Princes Risborough. Dating from 1565, it was given to the nation by Arthur Hamilton, 1st Viscount Lee of Fareham (1868–1947), and has been the official country residence of British prime ministers since 1921, when it was occupied by David Lloyd George.

Cher, River A river in central France, rising in the Massif Central near Aubusson and flowing NW to join the River Loire near Tours. Length: 354 km (220 mi).

Cherbourg 49 38N 1 37W A seaport in NW France, in the Manche department on the Cotentin Peninsula. Cherbourg has civil and military docks and large shipbuilding yards. In the heyday of ocean liners Cherbourg was an important transatlantic port; the cross-channel service to Southampton remains important. Population (1982 est): 30 112.

Cheremkhovo 53 08N 103 01E A city in the Soviet Union, in the SE RSFSR. A coalmining centre, it also refines oil and produces chemicals. Population (1983 est): 74 000.

Cherenkov, Pavel Alekseievich (1904–) Soviet physicist, who discovered **Cherenkov radiation** in 1934. This radiation consists of blue-white light emitted by the atoms of a medium through which a high-energy charged particle is passing at a velocity in excess of the velocity of light in that medium. Three years later the effect was explained by *Franck and Igor Tamm (1895–1971). The three physicists shared the 1958 Nobel Prize for their work.

Cheribon. *See* Tjirebon.

Chernenko, Konstantin Ustinovich (1911–85) Soviet statesman; secretary of the Soviet Communist Party and president of the Soviet Union (1984–85). A protégé of Brezhnev, he made few reforms in his short period in office.

Chernigov 51 30N 31 18E A city in the SW Soviet Union, in the Ukrainian SSR on the River Desna. Chernigov was heavily bombed during World War II although several medieval buildings remain. It is an important railway junction and its manufactures include tyres, pianos, and consumer goods. Population (1981 est): 252 000.

Chernobyl 51 17N 30 15E A town in the SW Soviet Union, in the Ukrainian SSR. In 1986 the nuclear reactor exploded, causing the deaths of 27 people and increased levels of radioactivity in many parts of the world. Mass evacuation of those near the reactor followed and several countries placed restrictions upon food imports from E Europe; the reactor itself was subsequently entombed in concrete. The accident led to widespread reviews of safety in the nuclear industry.

Chernovtsy (Romanian name: Cernauti) 48 19N 25 52E A city in the SW Soviet Union, in the Ukrainian SSR on the River Prut. It was held by Romania between 1918 and 1940. It is an important rail junction, industrial, cultural, and scientific centre. Population (1981 est): 224 000.

chernozem (*or* black earth) A type of soil that is characteristic of the grasslands of the continental interiors. There is a dark surface layer rich in alkaline humus, underlain by calcium carbonate concretions. Chernozems are agriculturally among the richest soils in the world.

Cherokee A North American Indian people of the hill country of E Tennessee and North Carolina, speaking an Iroquoian language. They lived in farming towns of 30 to 60 log cabins. There were about 60 such towns organized into two groups, the red (or war) towns and the white (or peace) towns, each under the authority of a separate chief and each separately responsible for the performance of ceremonies associated with war or peace.

Cherrapunji 25 16N 91 42E A village in India, in Meghalaya. It has the world's second highest mean annual rainfall: 11 430 mm (450 in).

cherry A tree or shrub of the genus *Prunus*, of N temperate regions, having small rounded juicy fruits surrounding a hard stone containing a seed. Cherry trees produce clusters of white or pinkish flowers in spring, and some varieties are grown only for ornament. Cherries cultivated for their fruits are of two main types—sour and sweet. Sour cherries have been developed from *P. cerasus*, a widespread shrubby tree growing to 7 m. Morello—the best variety—has dark-red fruits used in jams and liqueurs. Sweet dessert cherries arose from the gean (*P. avium*), native to Eurasia and N Africa. Found in woods and hedges, it grows to 25 m. Fruits of cultivated forms vary from pale yellow to dark red. Hybrids between *P. cerasus* and *P. avium* are used for cooking. *See also* bird cherry.

cherry laurel An evergreen shrub, *Prunus laurocerasus*, 2–6 m high, producing spikes of fragrant whitish flowers in spring. A native of SE Europe and SW Asia, it has been introduced and locally naturalized elsewhere in hedges and woodlands. Family: *Rosaceae*.

chert A variety of chalcedony, occurring in a stratified form. It consists of minute crystals of silica, of either organic or inorganic origin, found in sedimentary rocks.

cherubim and seraphim Supernatural beings who, according to *Dionysius the Areopagite, are the two highest orders of *angels in the celestial hierarchy. The seraphim are described by Isaiah (Isaiah 6.2–7) as six-winged attendants upon God's throne. The cherubim, who are traditionally depicted as winged heads, appear in the Bible as guardians of the divine presence; for instance, they bar the approaches to the Garden of Eden after the Fall (Genesis 3.24).

Cherubini, Maria Luigi (1760–1842) Italian composer. He spent much of his life in France, becoming director of the Paris Conservatoire in 1822. He was primarily an operatic composer; his *Deux Journées* (1800; English title: *The Watercarrier*) influenced Beethoven. He also wrote two settings of the requiem mass and six string quartets in an original style.

chervil An annual herb, *Anthriscus cerefolium*, 30–50 cm high, grown for its leaves, used for salads and seasonings. Its white flowers grow in umbrella-like clusters. A native of central, E, and S Europe, it now grows on hedgebanks and waste ground throughout Europe, the Americas, N Africa, and New Zealand. Family: *Umbelliferae*.

Cherwell, Viscount. *See* Lindemann, Frederick Alexander, 1st Viscount Cherwell.

Chesapeake Bay The largest inlet on the USA's Atlantic coast, bordering on Virginia and Maryland. Length: approximately 320 km (200 mi).

Cheshire A county in NW England, bordering on Wales. It consists chiefly of the low-lying Cheshire Plain rising to the Pennines in the E. It is predominatly agricultural, dairy farming being especially important. In the local government reorganization in 1974 the northern industrial part of the Wirral Peninsula, including Birkenhead, became part of Merseyside and the areas in the NE, including Stockport, passed to Greater Manchester. Remaining industries include chemicals, based on the Cheshire salt fields, and textiles. Area: 2322 sq km (897 sq mi). Population (1981): 926 293. Administrative centre: Chester.

Cheshire, (Geoffrey) Leonard, Group Capt (1917–)

British philanthropist. In the RAF during World War II, he won the Victoria Cross. His horror at the atomic bombing of Nagasaki, at which he was a British observer, led him to devote himself to the relief of suffering. He founded the Cheshire Foundation Homes for the incurably sick, of which there are 222 in 44 countries. He married (1959) **Sue, Baroness Ryder** (1923–), who founded the Sue Ryder Foundation for the Sick and Disabled of All Age Groups. A chain of charity shops fund her philanthropic activities, which began with refugee relief work after World War II.

Chesil Beach (*or* Chesil Bank) 50 36N 2 32W A shingle spit in S England, on the Dorset coast, extending 14 km (9 mi) from Portland to Abbotsbury.

chess A board game for two players, each of whom controls 16 pieces. The pieces are moved according to strict rules, the object of the game being to force the opponent's king into a position from which it cannot escape. A player attempts to weaken his opponent's position by capturing his pieces. This he does by moving his own pieces onto the squares occupied by his opponent's pieces. Only the kings cannot be captured in this way. After an initial lottery to choose the player who makes the first move, the game becomes one of pure skill with a vast literature devoted to its tactics and strategy. Chess has been variously described as a game, sport, art, science, vocation, and (with advertising) the greatest waste of human ingenuity. To the extent that it simulates war it has been regarded as a psychological sublimation of human aggression, although more lyrical writers have seen it as a source of Indian symbolism and allegory. Chess pieces dating back to the 2nd century demonstrate the game's antiquity. Well known to 5th-century Hindus, it seems to have reached Europe, via Persia and Arabia, in the 10th century. The rules of the game have hardly changed since the 16th century, although the identities of some of the pieces have. Since 1922 the rules have been controlled by the Fédération internationale des Échecs (FIDE), which has also organized world championships since 1946. In 1985, because of the prolonged indecisive 1984 championship contest, it stipulated a maximum of 24 matches to decide the title. Famous world champions include Emanuel *Lasker (1894–1921), José *Capablanca (1921–27), Alexander *Alekhine, (1927–35; 1937–46), Boris *Spassky (1969–72), Bobby *Fischer (1972–75), and Anatoly *Karpov (1975–). □ p. 264.

chest A large domestic storage box. Chests from ancient Egypt are among the earliest surviving furniture. In Europe they were essential pieces of portable furniture doubling as a bed, table, or seat. The simplest consist of six boards nailed together with one forming a lid, but between the 15th and the 18th centuries they were elaborated into fine decorative furniture. In Europe specimens were panelled and carved but 16th-century Italian chests (cassoni) might be carved and gilded.

Chester 53 12N 2 54W A city in NW England, the administrative centre of Cheshire on the River Dee. It was a Roman fortress (Deva) and a medieval walled city and port (the walls remain intact and there are many half-timbered buildings). The Rows are two-tiered arcades of shops with covered balustrades. Its cathedral dates from the 11th century. Chester is a commercial and railway centre, with clothing and metallurgical industries. Population (1981): 58 436.

chesterfield A kind of settee introduced in 19th-century England. It has a low back curving to form upright armrests and is comfortably upholstered with coil springs.

Chesterfield 53 15N 1 25W A town in N central England, in Derbyshire. Its 14th-century parish church has a famous crooked spire. Chesterfield's industries include engineering, iron founding, chemicals, glass, and pottery. Population (1981): 70 546.

Chesterfield, Philip Dormer Stanhope, 4th Earl of (1694–1773) British statesman, diplomat, and writer. He served as ambassador to The Hague (1728–36), lord

rook bishop king knight
knight queen bishop rook

black pawns

white pawns

rook bishop king knight
knight queen bishop rook

The chessboard ready for play. A white square is always on the player's right. The queen always starts on a square of her own colour.

BLACK

	a	b	c	d	e	f	g	h	
8	QR1 QR8	QN1 QN8	QB1 QB8	Q1 Q8	K1 K8	KB1 KB8	KN1 KN8	KR1 KR8	8
7	QR2 QR7	QN2 QN7	QB2 QB7	Q2 Q7	K2 K7	KB2 KB7	KN2 KN7	KR2 KR7	7
6	QR3 QR6	QN3 QN6	QB3 QB6	Q3 Q6	K3 K6	KB3 KB6	KN3 KN6	KR3 KR6	6
5	QR4 QR5	QN4 QN5	QB4 QB5	Q4 Q5	K4 K5	KB4 KB5	KN4 KN5	KR4 KR5	5
4	QR5 QR4	QN5 QN4	QB5 QB4	Q5 Q4	K5 K4	KB5 KB4	KN5 KN4	KR5 KR4	4
3	QR6 QR3	QN6 QN3	QB6 QB3	Q6 Q3	K6 K3	KB6 KB3	KN6 KN3	KR6 KR3	3
2	QR7 QR2	QN7 QN2	QB7 QB2	Q7 Q2	K7 K2	KB7 KB2	KN7 KN2	KR7 KR2	2
1	QR8 QR1	QN8 QN1	QB8 QB1	Q8 Q1	K8 K1	KB8 KB1	KN8 KN1	KR8 KR1	1
	a	b	c	d	e	f	g	h	

WHITE

Chess notations. In the algebraic notation each square is referred to by a file letter a–h and a rank number 1–8. In the descriptive notation the files bear the names of the piece on the first rank. The ranks are counted 1–8 away from the player.

The king, weak and vulnerable, moves only one square at a time (in any direction). The name of the game is a corruption of the Persian word for king–shah.

The queen, the most powerful piece, moves any distance in any direction. Originally known as the counsellor, its present name and moves were adopted in the 15th century.

The rook or castle moves any distance vertically or horizontally. Originally represented as a chariot (Arabic: rukh), it is known in many languages as a castle or tower (French: tour).

The knight, the only piece to jump over other pieces, moves one square horizontally and two vertically or two horizontally and one vertically. Usually represented by a horse's head, it is sometimes known as the horse (as it was in the Arabic version).

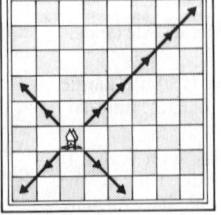

The bishop moves any direction diagonally. In the Hindu and Arabic games the piece was called an elephant. In the European games the piece has aquired a variety of identities: a bishop in English, a jester (fou) in French, a runner (Laufer) in German, but still an elephant (slon) in Russian.

The pawn moves forward one square (or two on its first move). In Arabic it was called a foot-soldier, the English word deriving from the Latin pes, pedis. In some European languages the piece is called a peasant (e.g. German: Bauer).

lieutenant of Ireland (1745–46), and secretary of state (1746–48). A patron of many authors, he is best remembered for his worldly and sophisticated *Letters to His Son* (1774).

Chesterton, G(ilbert) K(eith) (1874–1936) British essayist, novelist, and poet. His best work was done as literary journalism, although the detective stories featuring a Roman Catholic priest and beginning with *The Innocence of Father Brown* (1911) were also highly successful. He met Hilaire *Belloc in 1900. Their names were often linked as romantic opponents of the socialism of G. B. Shaw and H. G. Wells. Chesterton was converted to Roman Catholicism in 1922, and thereafter most of his work was devoted to religious subjects, for example *St Francis of Assisi* (1923). His published work amounts to more than 100 volumes, among which are the critical studies *Dickens* (1906) and *The Victorian Age in Literature* (1913) and the fictional works *The Napoleon of Notting Hill* (1904), *The Club of Queer Trades*, (1905), and *The Man Who Was Thursday* (1908).

chestnut A tree, *Castanea sativa*, also called sweet or Spanish chestnut, bearing large brown edible nuts inside prickly burs. Native to Europe and N Africa and widely introduced, it grows to a height of 30 m. The leaves—10–25 cm long—are toothed and pointed and the flowers grow in yellow catkins, 10–12 cm long. The North American chestnut (*C. dentata*)—once one of the largest common trees of eastern areas—has been largely destroyed by the chestnut blight fungus. Family: *Fagaceae* (beech family). *Compare* horse chestnut.

Chetniks Members of a Yugoslav resistance movement in World War II. They were organized in groups by General Draža *Mihajlović in March, 1941, against the German invasion but were chiefly in conflict with the communist Partisans under *Tito. In 1944 the Allies transferred their support from the Chetniks to Tito. After the war the Chetniks were proscribed.

Chevalier, Maurice (1888–1972) French singer and actor. Starting as an entertainer in Parisian revues, he went to Hollywood in the 1930s and starred in many successful musical films. These included *Love Me Tonight* (1932), *Love in the Afternoon* (1957), and *Gigi* (1958).

cheviot A woollen fabric manufactured from the soft fine easily spun fleece of Cheviot sheep found in the English-Scottish border country. The cloth is much used as heavy suiting material; *worsted is sometimes added for greater firmness of texture.

Cheviot Hills A range of hills in the UK. They extend along the border between Scotland and England, mainly in Northumberland, reaching 816 m (2677 ft) at The Cheviot.

chevrotain A small hoofed mammal of the family *Tragulidae*. Asiatic chevrotains (genus *Tragulus*; 3–6 species), also called mouse deer, of SE Asia, measure 20–33 cm at the shoulder and resemble small deer. Their brownish coats have white underparts; some species have white stripes or spots on the body. They are not true deer, lacking antlers and having a three-chambered stomach; males have enlarged upper canine teeth that form tusks. The African water chevrotain (*Hyemoschus aquaticus*) is very similar.

chewing gum A sweetened flavoured gum made from *chicle or a synthetic substitute, the milky juice of the sapodilla tree, which is chewed to extract its flavour but not swallowed. It was first patented (1871) in the USA.

Cheyenne An Algonkian-speaking North American Indian people of the Plains region. They orginally lived in what is now Minnesota but intertribal wars forced the abandonment of their agriculturalist life in favour of the nomadic buffalo-hunting culture of the Plains. After a period of wandering they eventually divided into a northern branch and a southern branch. They had an elaborate religious ritual, including the sun dance. They were governed by a council of 44 chiefs; an important feature of their social organization was the military or warrior societies.

They frequently fought with white settlers and the northern branch was present at the battle of the Little Bighorn (1876).

Cheyenne 41 08N 104 50W A city in the USA, the capital and largest city of Wyoming. It is an agricultural trading centre. Population (1980): 47 207.

Chiang Ch'ing. *See* Jiang Qing.

Chiang Ching-kuo. *See* Chiang Kai-shek.

CHIANG KAI-SHEK *At the Cairo Conference (1943) with Roosevelt (centre) and Churchill (right). The Allies discussed a joint operation in N Burma.*

Chiang Kai-shek (or Jiang Jie Shi; 1887–1975) Nationalist Chinese soldier and statesman. He took part in the overthrow of the *Qing dynasty in 1911, joined *Sun Yat-sen's *Guomindang (Nationalist People's Party) in 1918, and became commandant of the Whampoa military academy in 1923. After Sun's death (1925), Chiang became leader of the Guomindang and in 1926, in alliance with the communists (*see* United Fronts), launched the Northern Expedition to regain China from the *warlords. The Communist-Guomindang coalition ended in 1927 and Chiang, with his capital at Nanjing, fought the communists until Japan invaded China in 1931. Chiang's own army (*see* Xi An incident) forced him to join forces with the communists against their common enemy, Japan (*see* Sino-Japanese Wars), but following Japan's defeat in World War II civil war again broke out in China (1946), ending with Guomindang defeat (1949). Chiang was forced to flee to *Taiwan, where he established the Republic of China. His son **Jiang Jing Guo** (*or* Chiang Ching-kuo; 1910–), prime minister (1971–78) and president (1978–) studied in the Soviet Union and married a Russian. On returning to China in 1937, he joined the Guomindang, fleeing with his father to Taiwan in 1949.

Chianti A region of hills in N central Italy, in the Apennines between Florence and Siena. Chianti wine is produced here.

chiaroscuro (Italian: light-dark) The overall pattern of light and shade in a picture. Controlled chiaroscuro was an important element of *Renaissance composition, while strong contrasts of light and shade were a main feature of *baroque painting. Chiaroscuro is displayed to supreme effect in the etchings of *Rembrandt and *Whistler.

Chiba 35 38N 140 07E A city and seaport in Japan, in central Honshu on Tokyo Bay. It is the site of an 8th-century Buddhist temple and a university (1949). Industries include steel, paper, and textiles. Population (1980): 746 000.

Chibcha A South American Indian people of the central highlands of Colombia. At the time of the Spanish conquest they were more advanced socially and politically than any people in the area, except the *Inca. Chiefs, treated with great respect, inherited their position matrilineally. Their accession ceremonies, at which the new chief coated his body with gold dust before immersion in a sacred lake, are the probable origin of the *Eldorado legend.

Chicago 41 50N 87 45N A city and major port in the USA, in Illinois on Lake Michigan. The second largest city in the country, it is the focal point of air, rail, and road routes and the commercial, financial, and industrial centre for a large region. Its manufactures include iron and steel, textiles, and chemicals and there are large grain mills and meat-packing plants, although many of the stockyards are now closing as this industry moves further W. The first of its towering skyscrapers was built in 1887 and the Sears Tower (1974) is the world's tallest building, 443 m (1454 ft) high. It has several universities, including the University of Chicago (1892) and Northwestern University (1851); the Chicago Symphony Orchestra enjoys worldwide fame. *History*: founded in 1803 near the site of Fort Dearborn, it became a city in 1837 and expanded rapidly with the construction of the railways. In 1871 it was almost completely destroyed by a disastrous fire, in which several hundred people were killed. Chicago was subsequently rebuilt in stone and steel. During the Prohibition years (1919-33), Chicago was notorious for its gangster activities, especially those of Al *Capone. Population (1980): 3 005 072.

Chichén Itzá A Maya city in N Yucatán (Mexico) that was the political and religious centre of a wide area under Toltec influence from the late 10th to the 13th centuries. Remains include El Castillo (a pyramidal temple mound), an astronomical observatory, and a cenote (natural well), from which gold, jade, and other sacrificial objects have been recovered.

Chicherin, Georgi Vasilievich (1872-1936) Soviet statesman. Chicherin began his career in the Tsarist ministry of foreign affairs but in 1904, having become a revolutionary, he left Russia and lived in W Europe. In 1918, after the Revolution, he returned to Russia and was entrusted by Lenin with Soviet diplomacy. Chicherin lost his position in 1928, following Stalin's rise to power.

Chichester 50 50N 0 48W A market town in SW England, the administrative centre of West Sussex. Chichester has Roman remains, including its street plan. Its cathedral dates from the 11th century. Other notable buildings include a 16th-century octagonal market cross and the Festival Theatre (1962). Population (1981): 24 189.

SIR FRANCIS CHICHESTER *With his wife and son aboard* Gipsy Moth IV *after his voyage round the world (1966-67)*.

Chichester, Sir Francis (Charles) (1901-72) British yachtsman. He won the first solo transatlantic race (in 40 days) in *Gipsy Moth III* (1960) and in 1966-67, in *Gipsy Moth IV*, was the first to sail round the world singlehanded making only one stop: he sailed from Plymouth, reaching Sydney in

107 days, and then back to Plymouth, in 119 days, going on to Greenwich, where he was knighted with Sir Francis Drake's sword.

chicken. *See* fowl, domestic.

chickenpox A common very infectious virus disease. It is usually contracted in childhood and one attack normally gives an immunity that lasts for life. At the end of the incubation period (about a fortnight) the patient develops a fever and an irritating rash. Small raised spots appear on the chest and spread—in the next few days—over the body, face, and limbs. The spots become sore reddened blisters, which then dry and flake off, usually in less than a week. The patient is infectious until the last blister has flaked off. *See also* shingles.

chick pea An annual plant, *Cicer arietinum*, up to 40 cm high, with whitish flowers and edible pealike seeds. It is the chief pulse crop of India, where the cooked seeds are called dhal. Probably native to W Asia, it has long been cultivated in S Europe and is widely introduced, though of little commercial importance, elsewhere. Family: *Leguminosae*.

chickweed A widely distributed annual or overwintering herb, *Stellaria media*, 5-40 cm high with small star-shaped white flowers. The plant is a common weed and is readily eaten by birds. It was formerly used as a poultice for ulcers and carbuncles. Family: *Caryophyllaceae*.

Chiclayo 6 47S 79 47W A city in N Peru, in the Lambayeque Valley. It is the commercial centre for an area producing sugar cane, cotton, and rice. Population (1980 est): 292 000.

chicle A gum formed from the coagulated milky substance obtained from the *sapodilla tree found in Central America. Chicle was formerly used in the manufacture of chewing gum, but it has now been replaced by synthetic substances.

chicory A perennial herb, *Cichorium intybus*, 30-120 cm high, with bright-blue flowers. The dried ground roots yield chicory, a coffee additive, while the blanched leaves are used in salads. A native of Eurasia and N Africa, it is widely cultivated elsewhere. Family: *Compositae*. *See also* endive.

Chiemsee (*or* Bayrisches Meer) 47 53N 12 25E A lake in SE West Germany. On one of its islands Louis II of Bavaria built a palace imitating that of Versailles. Area: 85 sq km (33 sq mi).

Chiengmai (*or* Chiang Mai) 18 48N 98 59E A town in NW Thailand, near the Burmese border. The northern commercial and cultural centre, it has teak, silver, and silk industries. The university was established in 1964. Population (1980): 101 594.

Ch'ien-lung. *See* Qian Long.

chiffchaff A woodland *warbler, *Phylloscopus collybita*, about 10 cm long, with a grey-green plumage and whitish underparts. It occurs in Europe and W Asia during the summer and winters in S Europe and Africa. It resembles the willow warbler but can usually be distinguished by its "chiff-chaff" call.

Chifley, Joseph Benedict (1885-1951) Australian statesman; Labor prime minister (1945-49). Famous for seeing the "light on the hill" of socialism, he introduced welfare reforms and nationalization policies.

chigger. *See* harvest mite.

chigoe A *flea, *Tunga penetrans*, 1 mm long, also called jigger or sand flea, that spread to Africa and Asia from South America to become a pest of man. The female burrows beneath the skin, especially on the feet, to form ulcer-like sores that cause intense itching and can become gangrenous. Family: *Pulicidae*.

Chihli, Gulf of (Chinese name: Bohai *or* Po Hai) A large inlet of the Yellow Sea on the coast of NE China.

Chihuahua 28 40N 106 06W A city in N Mexico. Miguel Hidalgo y Costillo, a leader in the Mexican independence movement, was executed here (1811). Its varied industries include smelting, timber, and meat packing and it has a university (1954). Population (1980): 406 830.

Chihuahua A breed of ▯dog originating from an ancient Mexican breed and developed in the USA. Its coat is variable in colour and either smooth and glossy or long and soft. Height: about 13 cm.

Chikamatsu Monzaemon (Sugimori Nobumori; 1653–1724) Japanese dramatist. His psychological insight and realistic techniques revolutionized the previously unsophisticated tradition of puppet theatre. *The Battles of Coxingo* (1715) and *The Love Suicide at Amijima* (1720) are the best-known examples of his two main types of plays, historical romances and domestic tragedies.

chilblain An itchy red swelling, usually on the fingers or toes, that develops in cold weather. A chilblain may lead to scaling and blistering of the affected part. Prevention, by wearing warm clothing, is the best form of treatment, but drugs that dilate the blood vessels may also be used.

childbirth (*or* labour) The series of events that lead to the birth of a baby. It usually starts spontaneously about 280 days (plus or minus 14 days) after conception but it may be induced by artificial means. The first stage of childbirth may last several hours: it is marked by rupture of the membranes surrounding the fetus and by regular contractions of the womb (uterus). This stage ends when the cervical canal is fully dilated. In the second stage continuing uterine contractions—assisted by conscious pushing by the mother—eases the baby through the cervix and out through the vagina. The *placenta (afterbirth) is delivered in the third stage of labour. The baby is normally born headfirst, although childbirth can occur with the baby in a variety of positions. *See also* Caesarean section; infant mortality.

Childers, Robert Erskine (1870–1922) Irish nationalist executed by the Irish Free State for his support of the republican cause. In 1921 he became a Sinn Féin member of the Irish Assembly (Dáil Éireann) and minister of propaganda. He opposed the treaty that established the Irish Free State, joined the IRA, and was captured and shot. Also a writer, his books include the thriller *The Riddle of the Sands* (1903), which was made into a film in 1979. His son **Erskine Childers** (1905–74) was president of Ireland (1973–74).

Children's Crusade (1212) A bizarre episode of the *Crusades, in which some 50 000 children set out from France and Germany to capture Jerusalem. None reached their destination and few returned home, most being sold into slavery. The enthusiasm aroused by the Children's Crusade encouraged Pope *Innocent III to summon the fifth Crusade.

Chile, Republic of A country in South America, extending in a narrow strip along the W coast of the S half of the continent. There are many islands off the coast, some of which (including *Easter Island) are well out into the Pacific Ocean. Chile also includes half of the island of Tierra del Fuego and has claims to part of Antarctica. The country is dominated by the Andes, which are separated from a lower coastal range by a central valley. The majority of the population is of mixed Spanish and Indian descent. *Economy*: based chiefly on the export of minerals, found principally in the N. Chile is one of the world's largest producers and exporters of copper, while the production of iron ore now exceeds that of nitrates. Coal is also mined in quantity and oil was found in the S in 1945. Production of natural gas is more than enough for domestic needs. The enormous agricultural potential of the country, however, is far from developed, a situation that has been made worse by recent political events. Major land reforms were introduced (1970–73) but much of the land has been returned to its original owners since the fall of the Allende government. The main crops are wheat, sugar beet, potatoes, and maize and there is an expanding wine industry. Fruit and forest production is growing

in importance and there are government attempts to promote the dairy industry. *History*: when Magellan, the first European to set eyes on what became Chile, sailed through (1520) the strait named after him, S Chile was occupied by the Araucanian Indians, who continued to control the region until the 19th century. In the N the Atacama Indians had been subjugated in the 15th century by the Incas, who were themselves conquered by the Spaniards in 1532. A Spanish colony was founded at Santiago in 1541 and Chile was attached to the viceroyalty of Peru. It maintained, however, a certain independence and individuality throughout the colonial period, partly because of its inaccessibility. The revolt against Spain began in 1810, when a provisional republic was declared, but victory over the Spaniards was achieved only in 1817 with the military help of the Argentine liberator José de *San Martín. In 1818 the Republic of Chile was established under Bernardo *O'Higgins. Following the ratification of a constitution in 1833 Chile enjoyed political stability and prosperity, becoming the world's leading copper producer. Frontier disputes with Bolivia and Peru culminated in the War of the *Pacific (1879–83), in which Chile, with its superior navy, was victorious, gaining the provinces of Antofagasta from Bolivia and Tarapacá and Arica from Peru. The early 20th century witnessed economic decline, exacerbated by considerable European immigration and resistance from landlords to reform. The enlightened first presidency (1920–25) of Arturo Alessandri Palma (1868–1952) was followed by a military dictatorship and his increasingly right-wing second term (1932–38) led to the election of a socialist Popular Front government. The postwar period saw a return to conservatism and in 1964 Eduardo *Frei, the first Christian Democratic president, was elected. In 1970 Salvador *Allende became the first democratically elected Marxist head of state but was overthrown in 1973 by a military coup led by Gen *Pinochet. In 1978 Pinochet announced civilian appointments to his cabinet as a step towards the reintroduction of democracy but faced strong opposition to the regime both at home and abroad, narrowly escaping assassination in 1986. Chile is a member of the OAS and LAFTA. Official language: Spanish. Official currency: Chilean peso of 100 centavos. Area: 741 767 sq km (286 397 sq mi). Population (1983 est): 11 486 000. Capital: Santiago. Main port: Valparaiso.

Chillán 36 37S 72 10W A city in central Chile, in the Central Valley. Prone to earthquake damage, Chillán serves an agricultural region producing chiefly grapes, fruit, cereals, and livestock. Population (1983 est): 123 571.

chilli A tropical American shrubby plant, *Capsicum frutescens*, also called red pepper, bearing elongated hot-tasting red fruits, 2–3 cm long. Sun-dried for storage, they are used in cooking and are also an essential ingredient of curry powder and tabasco sauce. Family: *Solanaceae*.

Chillon A mainly 13th-century fortress at the E end of Lake Geneva (Switzerland). It was the prison (1530–36) of François Bonward (?1494–1570), the Genevan patriot made famous by Byron's poem *The Prisoner of Chillon* (1816).

Chiloé Island An island administered by Chile, off the W coast of South America in the Pacific Ocean. The chief export is timber. Area: 8394 sq km (3241 sq mi). Chief town: Ancud.

Chiltern Hills A chalk escarpment in S central England. It extends NE from the Goring Gap in the Thames Valley, reaching 255 m (852 ft) at Coombe Hill. Many of its hills are covered with beech woods.

Chiltern Hundreds In the UK, a nominal office of profit under the Crown, the holder of which is disqualified from membership of the House of Commons. It is one of the stewardships (the other is the Manor of Northstead, Yorks) for which an MP who wishes to resign (which he may not do directly) has been able to apply since the mid-18th century.

Chi-lung. *See* Jilong.

chimaera **1.** A *cartilaginous fish, also called ghost shark, ratfish, or rabbit fish, belonging to the order *Chimaeriformes* (about 28 species). It has a dark or silvery body, 60–200 cm long, a slender whiplike tail, a sharp spine in front of the first dorsal fin, and a variously shaped snout. It lives in cold ocean waters, down to 2500 m, and feeds on fish and invertebrates. Subclass: *Holocephali.* □fish. **2.** (*or* chimera) An organism that is composed of cells of two genetically different types. Plants with variegated leaves are chimaeras resulting from a mutation in a cell in the growing region (apical meristem). Plant chimaeras can also be produced by *grafting, being known as graft hybrids.

Chimborazo, Mount 1 29S 78 52W An extinct volcano in the Andes, the highest point in Ecuador. Height: 6267 m (20 681 ft).

Chimbote 9 04S 78 34W A port in NW Peru, on the Pacific Ocean. Steel processing and fishmeal production are the chief industries. Population (1980 est): 264 000.

Chimera A legendary Greek fire-breathing monster with a lion's head, a goat's body, and a serpent's tail. After ravaging Lycia she was killed by Bellerophon. The name now applies to any fantastic imaginary creation.

Chimkent 42 16N 69 05E A city in the Soviet Union, in the S Kazakh SSR. It is an important railway junction and has chemical and textile industries. Population (1981 est): 334 000.

CHINA *Concerned with its population problem, the Chinese government has been at great lengths to advertise the merits of the one-child family.*

chimpanzee An ape, *Pan troglodytes*, of West African forests. Chimpanzees are 100–170 cm tall when standing erect and live in small groups, mostly on the ground, feeding chiefly on fruit and leaves but occasionally eating meat. They communicate by facial expressions and a repertoire of calls and possess considerable intelligence, often using tools (such as branches). Bonobos are a race of smaller chimpanzees with black faces.

Chimú A South American Indian people who established a large kingdom in Peru during the 14th century AD. Its capital was at *Chan Chan. They were conquered (c. 1470) by the *Incas, whose civilization was based on Chimú achievements in building, road construction, irrigation, and political organization. The Chimú produced elaborate pottery with moulded reliefs, fine textiles, and precious metalwork,

Ch'in *See* Qin.

China, People's Republic of A country in E Asia, covering vast areas of land ranging from the low-lying and densely populated plains of the NE to the high peaks of the Tibetan Plateau in the W, rising well over 5000 m (16 500 ft). In the far NW much of the land is desert or semidesert. China proper falls into three natural regions, formed around the three main rivers: the Yellow River in the N, the Yangtze in the centre, and the Xi Jiang in the S. Over 90% of the inhabitants are Han Chinese. *Economy*: mainly dependent upon agriculture, which is constantly threatened by drought and flood. There are however schemes to safeguard and increase production by means of irrigation, soil conservation, and fertilization. Agriculture is now socialized through a system of communes, although there are still some very small private holdings. The emphasis is on foodcrops, rice in the S, wheat and millet in the N, as well as livestock, especially pigs. Cotton is grown in the N and tea in the S. The once vast forests have been largely cleared over the centuries but considerable reafforestation is now taking place. Coal is extensively mined in all parts of the country and is the major source of power. China has been self-sufficient in oil since 1973 and small amounts of natural gas are also produced. The potential for hydroelectric energy is extensive and there are several projects throughout the country. Iron ore is the most important mineral deposit and China is the main world producer of tungsten ore. Other minerals include antimony, lead, bauxite, and manganese. Traditional small industries continue but there has been considerable development of more modern industries, especially textiles, steel, flour mills, and chemicals. Exports include farm produce, textiles, and minerals. *History*: China is one of the world's oldest civilizations, with a history of organized society going back over nearly four millenniums. The first important recorded dynasty was the Shang in the valley of the Yellow River (18th–12th centuries BC). From the 12th to the 3rd centuries BC the *Zhou spread S and E. Under the *Qin, in the 3rd century BC, a unified empire came into being and the first Great Wall was built. The rule of the *Han dynasty, from the 3rd century BC to the early 3rd century AD, saw spectacular advances in technology and manufacturing but its decline was followed by centuries of struggle between different parts of the empire. With the *Tang dynasty (7th–10th centuries) China was once more reunited and reached the high point of its civilization. It was followed by the *Song (10th–13th centuries), the *Mongol (13th–14th centuries), the *Ming (14th–17th centuries), and the *Qing, which lasted until 1912. From the 16th century Europeans came to China and set up trading posts despite opposition from the Qing. British efforts to open up the country to free trade led to the Opium War in 1839 and to the opening of treaty ports (and also to the cession of Hong Kong). Later other trade concessions were made to several European countries and Chinese opposition to these moves included the Taiping Rebellion (1851–64) and the anti-foreign Boxer Rebellion (1899–1900). In 1911 a revolution under the leadership of Sun Yat-sen ousted the Qing and a republic was set up. The 1920s saw the rise of the Guomindang (Nationalist People's Party) under Gen Chiang Kai-shek and the foundation of the Chinese Communist Party in 1921. In 1926 relations between them broke down and a struggle began that, in effect, continued until after World War II. In the 1930s threats from Japan culminated in open attack and the occupation of parts of the country, which lasted until the end of World War II. This put a temporary halt to internal party struggles, but in 1949 the Guomindang was defeated by the communists and a People's Republic was set up by *Mao Tse-tung. Chiang Kai-shek retreated to Taiwan, where he set up the Republic of China. During the early years of the communist regime relations with the Soviet Union were close but they later deteriorated. In 1966 Mao Tse-tung launched the Great Proletarian Cultural Revolution, designed to eradicate "revisionism" and to prevent the rise of a ruling class. From the late 1960s the question of a successor to Mao Tse-tung became an important issue and first *Lin Biao and later *Deng Xiao Ping rose and fell, the latter being dismissed by a "radical" faction of the Politburo. Both Mao Tse-tung and the prime minister, Chou En-lai, died in 1976 and were succeeded by the moderate *Hua Guo Feng. Attempts by the "radical" faction (known as the Gang of Four and including Mao's widow Jiang Qing) to gain power were thwarted by the arrest of its members. Deng Xiao Ping was reinstated in 1977 and remained the dominant force in government for the next 10 years; in 1982 the post of chairman was abolished. Following a period of liberalization and a series of student protests against the government, Zhao Ziyang replaced Hu Yaobang as general secretary of the Communist Party in 1987. Since 1971 China has had a seat at the UN. Prime minister: Li Peng. Official language: Mandarin Chinese. Official currency: yuan of 10 chiao and 100 fen. Area: 9 597 000 sq km (3 704 400 sq mi). Population (1985): 1 050 000 000. Capital: Peking. Main port: Shanghai.

china clay A mineral deposit consisting mainly of kaolin, a hydrous aluminium silicate. Kaolin is produced by weathering or by hydrothermal processes acting on the feldspars in granite. It is used for making high-grade ceramic products and in many industrial processes, including paper making.

chinch bug A *ground bug, *Blissus leucopteris*, that has a black body (up to 5 mm long), red legs, and white wings. Native to tropical America, it has spread to North America to become a serious pest of cereal crops. The female lays eggs on the roots and stems and the larvae suck the sap.

chinchilla A *rodent belonging to the genus *Chinchilla* (2 species), widely bred for its valuable long soft blue-grey fur. Measuring 30–50 cm long, wild chinchillas are found high in the Andes, living among rocks and feeding at night on vegetation. They faced extermination before the Chilean government banned hunting and established breeding farms. South American captive chinchillas are mostly short-tailed (*C. brevicaudata*) while in North America the long-tailed species (*C. laniger*) is bred. Family: *Chinchillidae*.

Chinchilla cat A breed of long-haired cat. Chinchillas have a compact body with short legs and a broad head with a snub nose and small tufted ears. The white fur is tipped with black on the back, flanks, head, ears, and tail, giving it a silvery lustre. The eyes are emerald or blue-green.

Chinchilla rabbit A breed of domesticated rabbit originating in France in the early 20th century. Although its thick bluish coat does not resemble that of the South American *chinchilla, it has been bred for its pelts.

Chindits The 77th Indian Brigade, organized by Orde *Wingate in 1943 in Burma as a "long-range penetration" infantry division. A guerrilla force, the Chindits were so called after the mythological Burmese temple guardian, the *chinthe*, and because they operated beyond the River Chindwin. Initially successful in severing Japanese lines of communication they were later in danger of being encircled and were forced to return to India in small groups.

Chindwin, River A river in N Burma, flowing S to join the Irrawaddy River near Myingyan. Length: 1046 km (650 mi).

Chinese A language or group of languages of the Sino-Tibetan family spoken widely in E Asia. The many distinct forms or dialects of Chinese, which include Mandarin, Min, Kan, Hakka, Hsiang, Wu, and Cantonese (or Yüeh), are mutually unintelligible. In China there have been attempts recently to standardize the language, using Mandarin as a basis. Chinese is a tonal language, many words, otherwise identical, having quite distinct meanings according to intonation. Words are usually monosyllabic and do not change their form to indicate part of speech. The language is written in logographic characters or symbols of pictorial origin (*see* ideographic writing systems), which enables them to be understood by speakers of any Chinese dialect. There are as many as 40 000 of these of which 10 000 are in common use. Literacy requires knowledge of about 2000 of them. For transliteration purposes, Pinyin (phonetic spelling) is superseding the older Wade-Giles system, which does not attempt as close a phonetic description of the language. Pinyin is used in this book.

Chinese art Early Chinese art (c. 1550–480 BC) consisted of magical, symbolic, and ritualistic objects of jade and bronze. These combine a few symbols to produce evocative nonrepresentational forms. During the Han dynasty (206 BC–220 AD) these forms were succeeded by sculptural art and painting, both influenced by the rise of Buddhism. Funerary ceramic art flourished and produced animal and human forms and copies of everyday artefacts. The Tang dynasty (618–906 AD) continued to make funerary objects, particularly realistic horsemen, warriors, and tomb guardians, but sculptures of Buddhist figures are dominant. The realistic outlook of the period was also reflected in landscape and figure painting.

The ensuing Song dynasty (960–1279 AD) was a golden age, when dreamlike landscape, animal, and bird painting flourished alongside *calligraphy, one of the most ancient and important Chinese arts. Monochrome ceramics of very refined form were made as objects of contemplation. This period saw the end of real creativity, the following Yuan dynasty being one of Mongol-inspired taste with a few exceptions, notably the four masters of the Yuan Dynasty. During the following Ming and Qing periods (14th–20th centuries) ceramic art excelled, the most famous example being the blue and white porcelain. At first it was restorative and of native origin and later innovatory, responding to European influence.

Chinese lantern plant A hardy ornamental, *Physalis alkekengi*, also called bladder cherry or winter cherry. A native of S and central Europe, it grows to a height of 20–60 cm. The edible fruit is enclosed in a reddish inflated calyx resembling a lantern. Family: *Solanaceae*.

Chinese literature The oldest written records in Chinese date from about 1400 BC. The earliest major literary productions, however, were written mainly between about 200 BC and 200 AD. These were the Confucian classics, nine texts for instruction and discussion by *Confucius and his disciples. They are devoted to poetry, philosophy, history, ceremonies, and codes of protocol and have had a profound effect on Chinese thought and literary style to the present. The earliest is probably the manual of divination, the *I Ching. The *Shu Jing* (or *Shu Ching*; *Book of Documents*) covers political aspects of Confucian thought; the *Shih Jing* (or *Shih Ching*; *Book of Songs*) contains lyrics some of which are perhaps as early as the 10th century BC. Of the remaining classics, the best known are two books belonging to the historical work *Zuo Zhuan* (or *Tso Chuan*): the *Analects*, a collection of Confucius' sayings and discussions with his disciples, and *The Book of Mencius*. The work of China's first known poet, *Chu Yuan, is a long poem occupying the most prominent place in the *Chuchi* (or *Ch'u Tz'u*), an anthology that, together with the *Book of Songs*, had an enduring effect on verse forms. During the Qin and Han dynasties (221 BC–220 AD), the development of poetry was fostered by the creation in 133 BC of the Yuefu (Music Bureau) for the collection of folksongs. Under Buddhist influences poetry became increasingly individualistic and enjoyed a golden age during the Tang dynasty (618-906 AD). *Li Bo, *Du Fu, and the Buddhist Wang Wei (699-759) were the leading poets, while Han Yu (768-824) pioneered new genres of prose. Musical drama was the major literary genre during the Yuan (Mongol) dynasty (1279-1368), and the novel, originating in printed versions of the tales of professional storytellers, flourished during the Ming dynasty (1368-1644). The two major novels of this period are the *Romance of the Three Kingdoms* and *The Water Margin*, both attributed to Luo Guan-zhong (*or* Luo Kuan-chung; 14th century). These works, dealing with heroic adventures, are skilfully shaped from episodic material and contrast with *The Dream of the Red Chamber* by *Cao Chan (*or* Zao Zhan), which is more realistic and partly autobiographical. The Qing (Manchu) dynasty (1644-1911) was unremarkable for literary work, but western influences were introduced through translations during the 19th century, and in the 20th century there arose a number of writers indebted to western ideas, for example to Romanticism and Symbolism. After the establishment of the republic in 1911, the outstanding poet was Hu Shi (1891-1962) and the leading writer was the satirist Lu Xun. Since the late 1930s literature has been generally subservient to political orthodoxy; although recent official patronage of the arts has encouraged a large number of new writers, no single reputation has become well established outside China.

Chinese water deer A very small *deer, *Hydropotes inermis*, most common along the banks of the Yangtze River in China. Only 50 cm high at the shoulder, with a pale-brown coat and short tail, it has no antlers; the male's upper canine teeth are elongated into tusks.

Ch'ing. *See* Qing.

Ch'ing-hai. *See* Qinghai.

Ching-te-chen. *See* Fuliang.

Chinkiang. *See* Jinjiang.

chinoiserie Decorative art and architecture that incorporated Chinese motifs into European fantasy designs and was popular in the late 17th and 18th centuries. The fashion was inspired by importation into Europe of Chinese porcelain, lacquer, etc., in the 17th century. French *rococo artists and architects enthusiastically adopted the style for interiors, furniture, silver, wallpaper, textiles, etc., as did *Meissen designers. Instances of chinoiserie in England include the *willow pattern, combining Chinese elements into a new design; the interior of the Brighton Royal Pavilion is an architectural example.

Chinook A North American Indian people of the NW Pacific coast of the USA. The Chinook language forms part of a division of the *Penutian language family. The Chinook were salmon fishers and traders, their location along the lower Columbia River being ideally suited for exchanging goods with peoples to the N and S and in the interior. Chinook Jargon, a combination of Chinook, *Nootka, and other Indian languages mixed with English and French words, became the trading language of the entire W coast of America. The Chinook practised the *potlatch and their religion emphasized the quest for a personal guiding spirit by undergoing ordeals of various kinds.

Chioggia 45 13N 12 17E A fishing port in Italy, on an island in the Venetian lagoon. Population (1981 est): 53 566.

chipmunk A *ground squirrel belonging to the genus *Tamias* (18 species), of North America and Asian forests. Chipmunks are 15-30 cm long and have a black and white striped back and strong feet and claws for digging. They live in burrows and, in the winter, do not hibernate but feed on a store of nuts and dried fruit carried under ground in their large cheek pouches.

Chippendale, Thomas (1718-79) British cabinetmaker, famous for his elegant furniture designs, especially his chairs. His illustrated collection of rococo furniture designs, *The Gentleman and Cabinet Maker's Director* (1754), was the

CHINOISERIE   *A bedstead in the Chinese style, probably made (c. 1750-55) by Thomas Chippendale.*

first comprehensive furniture catalogue and was widely influential in England and America, although his later neoclassical styles are considered the finest. His son, also **Thomas Chippendale** (died c. 1822), continued the business.

Chippewa. *See* Ojibwa.

Chirac, Jacques (1932-) French statesman; prime minister (1974–76; 1986–). After resigning in 1976 over policy differences with *Giscard d'Estaing, he reorganized the Gaullist movement and, in 1986, became prime minister under the presidency of François *Mitterrand. He has been mayor of Paris since 1977.

Chirico, Giorgio de (1888-1978) Italian painter and forerunner of *surrealism, born in Greece. He trained in Munich and was influenced by Nietzsche's philosophy. In Paris (1911-15) he worked on scenes of eerie and deserted Italian squares. At Ferrara (1917) he established with Carlo Carrà (1881-1966) the school of *metaphysical painting, but reverted to a traditional style after 1919.

chiromancy. *See* palmistry.

Chiron In Greek legend, a *centaur, son of Cronos and the sea nymph Philyra. Unlike his fellow centaurs, he was revered for his wisdom and knowledge of medicine. After being accidentally wounded by Heracles he bequeathed his immortality to Prometheus and was transformed into the constellation *Sagittarius.

chiropody The paramedical specialty that deals with the care of feet and the treatment of minor ailments of the feet, such as corns, calluses, and ingrowing toenails. In the UK the governing body is the Society of Chiropodists, which has its headquarters in London.

chiropractic A fringe medical specialty based on the assumption that most diseases originate from disorders of the nervous system, particularly as a result of compression of the nerve roots as they emerge from the spine. A chiropractor attempts to relieve symptoms by manipulating the spine with his hands.

Chiroptera. *See* bat.

chiru An antelope, *Pantholops hodgsoni*, of Tibetan plateaus. About 80 cm high at the shoulder, chirus have a dense woolly pinkish-brown coat with white underparts; males have slender black horns up to 70 cm long. They live singly or in small groups and excavate shallow depressions for shelter.

Chita 52 03N 113 35E A city in the SE central Soviet Union, in the RSFSR. Founded by the *Cossacks (1653), it is a prosperous city with machine-building, textiles, and food-processing industries. Population (1981 est): 315 000.

chital. *See* axis deer.

chitarrone (Italian: big guitar) A large fretted instrument of the lute family, able to accommodate bass strings of over 1.5 metres (5 ft) in length. It was popular for accompanying singing in the early 17th century.

chitin A complex carbohydrate that, in association with proteins, is the principal component of the outer cuticle of insects and other arthropods. Chitin occurs in several other animal groups and is a constituent of the cell walls of fungi.

CHIVALRY *This 15th-century manuscript illustrates a joust between a French knight and a Spanish knight.*

chiton A primitive *mollusc of the class *Amphineura* (about 600 species), also called sea cradle. Elliptical and measuring up to 30 × 15 cm, chitons live on rocky shores, clinging tightly and grazing on encrusted algae. They have eight shell plates with a fleshy girdle and curl up when detached.

Chittagong 22 20N 91 48E A city and major port in Bangladesh, on the Indian Ocean. The focal point of road, rail, and air routes, it is the second most important industrial centre in the country. Its university was established in 1966. Population (1984 est): 1 600 000.

chivalry The ideology and code of conduct of the knightly class of medieval Europe. Chivalric behaviour depended on the concepts of honour and courtesy and received a notable impetus during the 12th century from the *Crusades and the development of the ideals of *courtly love in such literature as the Arthurian romances. All ties between the chivalric code and military conduct ended with the decline of cavalry and the invention of gunpowder, although elaborate jousts and tourna-

ments kept its memory alive until the 16th century.

chive A small hardy perennial plant, *Allium schoenoprasum*, native to Europe. It has small white elongated bulbs and produces clumps of thin tubular leaves and dense attractive spherical heads of bluish or lilac flowers on long stalks. The leaves are used for seasoning and garnishing foods. Family: *Liliaceae*.

chloral (*or* trichlorethanal; CCl_3CHO) A colourless oily liquid made by treating acetaldehyde with chlorine. It is used in the manufacture of DDT.

chloramphenicol An *antibiotic usually reserved for severe bacterial infections. It is particularly useful in the treatment of typhoid fever and some forms of pneumonia and meningitis. In rare cases chloramphenicol causes serious blood disorders.

chlordiazepoxide. *See* benzodiazepines.

Chlorella A genus of unicellular *green algae found in fresh water or damp soil, some forming symbiotic relationships with fungi to give *lichens. Because they are rich in proteins, carbohydrates, and fats and reproduce rapidly by cell division, their use as a food source for man is now under study.

chlorine (Cl) A greenish poisonous *halogen gas, discovered in 1774 by C. W. Scheele. It is found in nature only in compounds, especially common salt (NaCl), sylvite (KCl), and carnallite ($KMgCl_3.6H_2O$). Chlorine is liberated by the electrolysis of brine. It irritates the respiratory system and was used as a poisonous gas in World War I. Chlorine gas is reactive and combines directly with most elements. Its oxidizing properties make it a useful disinfectant for drinking-water supplies and swimming pools. It is used in the manufacture of *bromine, in bleach (NaOCl), hydrochloric acid (HCl), and carbon tetrachloride (CCl_4). Chlorinated organic chemicals are used in dyes, antiseptics, and insecticides. At no 17; at wt 35.453; mp $-100.98°C$; bp $-34.6°C$.

chloroform (*or* trichloromethane; $CHCl_3$) A colourless volatile liquid. It is made by reacting *bleaching powder with acetone, acetaldehyde, or ethanol. Its main use is now in the manufacture of *fluorocarbons but it is also used as a solvent and as an anaesthetic.

chlorophyll A green pigment present in organisms capable of *photosynthesis. Higher plants possess chlorophylls *a* and *b*, located in *chloroplasts; chlorophyll *c* is found in some primitive marine plants, and bacteriochlorophyll occurs in photosynthetic bacteria. The chlorophylls absorb red and blue light, trapping light energy for photosynthesis.

chloroplast A structure within a plant cell in which the process of *photosynthesis takes place. It is bounded by a membrane and contains the green pigment *chlorophyll. Chloroplasts vary greatly in shape and number within a cell. The greatest concentration occurs in the palisade mesophyll tissue of the leaves—the main photosynthesizing region.

chloroquine A drug used to prevent and treat malaria. It acts by preventing the digestion of haemoglobin (the red pigment of blood) by the malaria parasite. Chloroquine is also used in the treatment of rheumatoid arthritis and related diseases.

chlorpromazine. *See* phenothiazines.

chocolate. *See* cocoa and chocolate.

Choctaw A North American Indian people and language of the Muskogean group originally of SE Mississippi. They were skilled farmers, growing corn, maize, and beans. They practised the green corn (first-fruits) ceremony. They wore their hair long and practised head flattening through deformation during infancy. After supporting the French against the English during the 18th century, they were forced to move west, settling in Oklahoma during the 1830s.

Chodowiecki, Daniel Nikolaus (1726–1801) German painter and engraver, who specialized in scenes of middle-class life. A noted book illustrator, he engraved editions of Cervantes' *Don Quixote* and Goldsmith's *Vicar of Wakefield*.

His best-known painting is *The Parting of Jean Calas from his Family* (1767; Berlin-Dahlem Museum).

choir 1. A group of trained singers. In the Christian Church the use of a choir was derived from Judaism and traditionally consisted of men and boys only. The choir leads the singing of the congregation as well as singing anthems. The most usual division of parts in a choir is into four: soprano, alto, tenor, and bass (SATB). In secular music the choir is often called a chorus. 2. The part of the chancel of a church, where the choir sits.

Choiseul, Étienne François, Duc de (1719-85) French statesman; foreign minister (1758-70). As ambassador to Vienna in 1757 he began negotiations for the marriage of Marie Antoinette to the future Louis XVI. He secured good terms for France in the Treaty of *Paris at the close of the Seven Years' War (1763). The influence of Louis XV's mistress, Mme *Du Barry, undermined his position at court and he was exiled in 1770.

cholera An acute infection of the intestine caused by the bacterium *Vibrio cholerae*, which is transmitted in drinking water contaminated by faeces of a patient. Epidemics of cholera occur in regions where sanitation is poor. After an incubation period of 1-5 days, cholera causes severe vomiting and diarrhoea, which—untreated—leads to dehydration that can be fatal. Treatment consists of replacement of fluid and salts by intravenous injections. Vaccinations against cholera provide only temporary immunity.

cholesterol A compound derived from steroids and found in many animal tissues. Cholesterol is manufactured by the liver and other tissues and its derivatives form constituents of cell membranes, bile, blood, and gallstones. High levels of cholesterol in the blood have been associated with an increased risk of heart disease, as a result of fatty deposits in the walls of arteries. *See also* atherosclerosis.

Cholon 10 45N 106 39E A port in S Vietnam, a part since 1932 of present-day *Ho Chi Minh City. It is the city's Chinese quarter (founded c. 1778). A trading centre for rice and fish, it has rice-milling, timber, and pottery industries. It suffered badly during the Vietnam War.

Cholula (or Cholula de Rivadabia) 19 05N 98 20W A town in central Mexico. A major religious centre dedicated to the god Quetzalcoatl before the Spanish conquest, it is the site of a pyramid 53 m (177 ft) high, which was begun in the Teotihuacán period and subsequently enlarged. Population (1970): 15 399.

Chomsky, Noam (1928-) US linguist, under whose influence the aims and methods of general linguistic theory and especially of *grammar were radically revised. *Syntactic Structures* (1957) and *Aspects of the Theory of Syntax* (1965) work out implications of the observation that, although the number of grammatically well-formed sentences in a language is infinite, the rules according to which they are generated form a finite set. Chomsky's work draws on and develops that of his teacher Zellig *Harris on the transformations by which a sentence may be generated from an underlying "deep structure." Chomsky has also undertaken controversial studies of the theory of speech sounds and of semantic structures. He was a vociferous opponent of US involvement in the Vietnam War.

Ch'ŏngjin 41 50N 129 55E A city and seaport in North Korea, on the NE coast. Originally a small fishing village, it developed rapidly under Japanese occupation (1910-45). It is an important centre for the manufacture of iron and steel; other industries include shipbuilding, chemicals, and textiles. Population (1980): 490 000.

Chongqing (Ch'ung ch'ing or Chungking) 29 32N 106 45E A port in central China, in Sichuan province at the confluence of the Yangtze and Jialing (or Chia-ling) Rivers. A major commercial and industrial centre, it is a former capital of China (1937-46). Population (1982): 1 990 000.

Chopin, Frédéric (François) (1810-49) Polish composer and pianist of French descent. He studied in Warsaw but later settled in Paris and never returned to Poland. He lived with the novelist George *Sand from 1838 to 1847, but never married her. A fervent nationalist, he was a student of Polish culture and much of his music was influenced by Polish folk music. He developed a highly characteristic style of writing for the piano, for which he composed 2 concertos, 3 sonatas, 24 preludes, and many waltzes, nocturnes, polonaises, and studies. He also wrote a cello sonata, a piano trio, and songs.

Chordata A phylum of animals that comprises the primitive *protochordates and the vertebrates (*see* Vertebrata). They are distinguished from other animals by three features: a hollow dorsal nerve cord; a rodlike *notochord that forms the basis of the internal skeleton; and paired gill slits in the wall of the pharynx behind the head, although in higher chordates these are apparent only in early embryonic stages.

chorea Involuntary jerky movements, particularly of the hips, shoulders, and face, caused by disease of the part of the brain controlling voluntary movement. Sydenham's chorea—formerly known as *St Vitus's dance—is often associated with rheumatic fever in children. It causes no permanent damage and responds to sedatives.

choreography The art of composing *ballet and other theatrical dances. Choreography originally referred only to a dance notation, the lack of which has made precise reconstruction of many ballets difficult. The most comprehensive system for recording dance steps is that devised by the Hungarian dancer Rudolph Laban (1829-1958), known as Labanotation. The choreographer is usually a professional dancer, who selects, arranges into sequences, and teaches the dancers each step of the ballet. Often he works in close collaboration with composers, notable partnerships being between *Tchaikovsky and *Petipa and *Stravinsky and *Fokine. Famous contemporary choreographers include *Cranko, *Robbins, *Béjart, *Ashton, and *Balanchine.

chorus 1. In Greek drama, a group of actors who described and commented on the dramatic action through dance, song, and chanting. Greek tragedy originated in songs and dances performed by a chorus in honour of Dionysus. The dramas of Aeschylus were performed by a chorus and only two actors, but its dramatic role declined in the plays of Sophocles (who introduced a third actor) and Euripides. The chorus, not directly involved in the actions of the main protagonists, represented the responses and judgments of average humanity. Its role has been revived in certain plays by *Brecht, Eugene *O'Neill, and T. S. *Eliot. 2. A body of singers or dancers who perform together (in contrast to soloists) as in opera or ballet.

Chorzów 50 19N 18 56E A town in SW Poland. One of Silesia's first coalmining centres (1790), it remains a major mining and metallurgical town. Population (1982): 158 000.

Chota Nagpur. *See* Bihar.

Chou. *See* Zhou.

Chouans Peasants in W France, including dealers in contraband salt, who revolted in 1793 against the government established by the French Revolution. They were provoked by such measures as the abolition of the salt tax (which ruined the contraband trade) and the enforcement of conscription. The revolt, which was led by Jean Cottereau (1757-94), was ultimately unsuccessful. It is the subject of Balzac's *Les Chouans* (1829).

Chou En-lai (or Zhou En Lai; 1898-1976) Chinese communist statesman; prime minister (1949-76) and foreign minister (1949-58). Chou studied in Japan, France, and Germany. In 1924 he became a political instructor at the Whampoa Military Academy and secretary of the Canton provincial Communist Party. He led workers in the 1927 general strike in Shanghai, after which he escaped *Guomindang (Nationalist) assassins and fled to Nanchang, where he helped to organize an uprising. In 1932 he became political commissar to the Red Army and during the *Sino-Japanese War (1937-45) his reputation as a negotiator grew. After the establishment in 1949 of the People's Republic of China, he gained worldwide prominence as a diplomat and at home was largely responsible for establishing communist China's bureaucracy. Regarded as a moderate he exercised a stabilizing influence on his extremist colleagues.

CHOLERA   *Open sewers, like this one in Calcutta, carry disease microorganisms, which can contaminate drinking water.*

chough   A large black songbird, *Pyrrhocorax pyrrhocorax*, about 37 cm long, with red legs and a long red down-curved bill. It occurs in the Alps, Spain, and a few sea cliffs around Britain where it can be seen giving displays of aerial acrobatics. The yellow-billed Alpine chough (*P. graculus*) occurs at high altitudes in European mountains. Family: *Corvidae* (crows).

chow chow   A breed of □dog originating in China more than 200 years ago. The chow has a compact body and—unusually—a blue-black tongue. The thick coat forms a mane around the neck and shoulders and the tail is held well over the back. Height: 46-51 cm.

Chrétien de Troyes   (12th century AD) French poet, author of the earliest romances dealing with the *Arthurian legend. He was a native of Champagne and a member of the court of Marie, countess of Champagne, to whom his romance *Lancelot* was dedicated. Little else is known of his life. His octosyllabic verse introduced a psychological subtlety in the treatment of *courtly love and chivalry that contrasts strongly with the heroic themes of the *chansons de geste*. His romances include *Erec*, *Cligès*, *Yvain*, and *Perceval* (or *Conte del Graal*), in which the *Holy Grail appears in a literary work for the first time.

Christadelphians   A religious movement founded in Brooklyn, New York, in 1848 by John Thomas (1805-71), an English immigrant. The sect rejects much orthodox Christian teaching, including the Trinity, the existence of Christ prior to the Incarnation, and the immortality of the soul. They are organized into autonomous democratic ecclesias (congregations). The sect is strongest in Britain and the USA.

Christchurch   43 33S 172 40E A city in New Zealand, on E South Island. Founded in 1850, it has a gothic-style

cathedral (completed in 1901) and many fine parks. The University of Canterbury was established in 1873. Industries, primarily associated with the rich agriculture of the Canterbury Plains, include meat processing, tanning, chemicals, and flour milling. Population (1983 est): 322 200.

Christchurch   50 44N 1 54W A resort in S England, in Dorset on Christchurch Harbour. It has a famous priory church. Population (1981): 32 789.

Christian I   (1426-81) King of Denmark and Norway (1450-81) and Sweden (1457-64), who founded the Oldenburg ruling dynasty of Denmark (1450-1863). His claim to the Swedish Crown, which was disputed by Charles VIII of Sweden (d. 1470; reigned 1448-57, 1464-65, 1467-70), was finally ended by Christian's defeat at Brunkeberg (1471). In 1460 he gained Schleswig and Holstein but in 1469 the Norwegian islands of Orkney and Shetland were mortgaged to Scotland as part of his daughter Margaret's dowry on her marriage to the Scottish king James III.

Christian (II) the Cruel   (1481-1559) King of Denmark and Norway (1513-23) and of Sweden (1520-23). He acquired his nickname for his massacre of Swedish nobles in his conquest of Sweden. He was subsequently deposed and, following an attempt to regain Norway, imprisoned (1532-59).

Christian III   (1503-59) King of Denmark and Norway (1534-59), who established the state Lutheran Church in Denmark (1536) after the *Count's War (1533-36). His administrative reforms laid the foundation for 17th-century Danish absolutism.

Christian IV   (1577-1648) King of Denmark and Norway (1588-1648). He entered the *Thirty Years' War in 1624 to defend the Protestant cause and Danish interests in the Baltic but was defeated by the Catholic League and withdrew (1629). At war with Sweden (1643-45), he suffered a crushing defeat (1645) with considerable loss of territory and domestic authority. He founded many new towns, including Christiania (now Oslo).

Christian IX   (1818-1906) King of Denmark (1863-1906), who fought unsuccessfully with Germany over *Schleswig-Holstein. He succeeded to the throne through his marriage to the cousin of the childless Frederick VII of Denmark (1808-63; reigned 1848-63). He supported minority conservative governments until 1901, when he was forced to accept a liberal ministry.

Christian X   (1870-1947) King of Denmark (1912-47), whose courage and dignity during the German occupation of his country (1940-45) won him international respect; rejecting Nazi antisemitic legislation in 1942, he was imprisoned from 1943 to 1945.

Christian Aid   A British organization founded in 1949 by the *British Council of Churches to direct the use of donations made to assist the Third World. Christian Aid, which makes no distinctions as to race, religion, or politics, supports development programmes in agriculture, health, and education, giving relief aid in emergencies.

Christian Democrats   Political parties having programmes based on Christian principles and generally of a conservative nature. In West Germany the **Christlich-Demokratische Union** (Christian Democratic Union; CDU), founded in 1945 held power, in alliance with the Christlich-Soziale Union (*see* Christian Social Union; CSU), from 1948 to 1969 under Konrad *Adenauer. The CDU/CSU alliance is now led by Franz Josef Strauss (1915-   ). In Italy the **Democrazia Cristiana** (Christian Democratic Party; DC), founded in 1943 as the successor to the Partito Popolare Italiano (Italian Popular Party), has dominated government since 1945. In 1963 Aldo *Moro brought the Italian Socialist Party into a coalition government with the DC, which has in the mid-1970s depended on the support of the Communist

Party. Other Christian Democratic parties are found in Austria, Belgium, France, Norway, and Spain.

Christianity The religious faith based on the teachings of *Jesus Christ, which had its origin in *Judaism. Its believers hold that Jesus is the Messiah prophesied in the Old Testament. It began as a movement within Judaism, and one of the first disputes among the early Christians was the right of the Gentiles to be admitted to the faith. Chiefly through the missionary activities of St Paul, the Apostle of the Gentiles, Christianity spread rapidly through the Roman Empire, despite persecutions under Nero and later emperors. Christian belief was at first taught by the Apostles by word of mouth; however, the need for a written record of Jesus' life and teaching was soon fulfilled by the *Gospels. The definition of Christian belief and the authority of bishops and scriptures was well developed when Constantine became emperor (312). A series of general councils, the first held in 325 at *Nicaea, defined orthodox Christian belief. Constantine's establishment of his new capital, Constantinople, led to a growing polarization between the Eastern *Orthodox Church and the Western *Roman Catholic Church. Despite the collapse of the Western Empire, Western Christianity, under the Bishop of Rome who claimed authority as St Peter's successor, spread vigorously. The Orthodox Church, not so rigorously centralized, became increasingly isolated, and with the development of doctrinal differences the two Churches drifted apart. The date of the formal separation is generally regarded as 1054. The Orthodox Church, under pressure from Islam to the east and often hostile Christians to the west, nevertheless established itself among the Slavs. The Western Church by the end of the first millennium was rapidly gaining power, the papacy reaching the zenith of its influence in the 13th century under Pope *Innocent III. In the later middle ages increasing nationalism and the assertion of power by temporal rulers weakened the united structure of the papacy and *Holy Roman Empire. With the attack on central authority came a greater boldness in dissident criticism of the Church, such as that of John *Wycliffe in England.

By the 16th century the Church no longer had the power to override national interests; in this weakened state it was unable to resist the inevitable fragmentation caused by the *Reformation. Some reformers, such as the followers of Martin *Luther and the English Church, were comparatively conservative, while the *Calvinists, centred in Geneva, were considerably more radical. Coinciding with the exploration of the globe, the Reformation and the Roman Catholic response to it, the *Counter-Reformation, in fact stimulated the spread of Christianity throughout the world, giving rise to the many different Christian denominations and communions of the modern world.

Challenged in the 19th and 20th centuries by materialism, atheism, and agnosticism, the Christian Churches have come under severe pressure in many parts of the world. The ecumenical movement of the 20th century has sought to unite Christendom and after centuries of hostility has had some success in healing its various schisms. The belief of Christianity is based on the New Testament and for most Christians is summarized in the traditional *creeds of the Church. The doctrines of the *Trinity, the *Incarnation of Christ, and the Resurrection are central, as is Christ's role as the redeemer of mankind. The total number of Christians has been estimated at more than 944 million, or approximately 24% of the world population.

Christian Science A religious movement founded by Mary Baker *Eddy. After being healed of various illnesses in 1862 by P. P. Quimby (d. 1866), a mesmerist, she formulated a set of principles of faith healing based on Christ's healing powers, which she claimed to have discovered and which she expounded in *Science and Health* (1875). The First Church of Christ, Scientist, opened in Boston, Massachusetts, in 1879. The movement

spread to Europe with the establishment of 3500 branches by 1980. The principles of the movement are based on denial of the reality of the material world and healing through spiritual control. The form of service is simple, including hymns, Bible readings, and relevant commentary from Mrs Eddy's works.

Christian Social Union (German name: Christlich-Soziale Union; CSU) A West German political party, the affiliate of the Christian Democratic Union (see Christian Democrats). The two parties held power from 1948 to 1969. In 1976, while in opposition, the CSU, led by Franz Josef Strauss (1915–), staged a walkout on the Christian Democrats. Both parties stood to lose from a split, and after a month the coalition had reformed and is now led by Strauss. Despite its name, the CSU forms the conservative wing in German politics.

Christians of St Thomas The Christians of the Malabar Coast, in SW India. According to tradition, St Thomas the Apostle brought Christianity to the area. Their Church used a Syriac liturgy and originally held *Nestorian beliefs, but since the 16th century the Roman Catholic Church has played a prominent role in its development.

Christie, Dame Agatha (1891–1976) British author of detective fiction and playwright. She introduced her most famous character, the Belgian detective Hercule Poirot, in *The Mysterious Affair at Styles* (1920); he met his end in *Curtain* (1975). Later detective novels include *The Murder of Roger Ackroyd* (1926), *Murder on the Orient Express* (1934), and *Death on the Nile* (1937); a number of these had locales with which she had become familiar after accompanying her second husband, the archaeologist Sir Max Mallowan (1904–78), on his expeditions. She wrote over 50 popular detective stories, creating other well-known fictional detectives, including Miss Jane Marple. Several stories have been filmed, and her play *The Mousetrap* has had an unparalleled long run in London since its opening in 1952.

Christina (1626–89) Queen of Sweden (1632–54). After reaching her majority (1644), she clashed repeatedly with her former regent *Oxenstierna. Her secret conversion to Roman Catholicism (then illegal in Sweden) led to her abdication, after which she lived in Rome. There, she became an outstanding patron of the arts, sponsoring the composers Scarlatti and Corelli and the architect and sculptor Bernini.

Christmas The Feast of the Nativity of Christ. In the West it has been celebrated on 25 Dec since 336 AD, partly in order to replace the pagan sun worship on the same date. In the East, both the Nativity and Epiphany were originally celebrated on 6 Jan, but by the end of the 4th century 25 Dec was almost universally accepted, although the Armenian Church still celebrates Christmas on 6 Jan. Many of the popular customs associated with Christmas can be traced back to pagan origins.

Christmas Island An island in the Indian Ocean, SW of Java. It became a territory of the Commonwealth of Australia in 1958. The only commercial activity is phosphate mining. Area: 135 sq km (52 sq mi). Population (1980 est): 3184.

Christmas Island A large coral atoll in the W central Pacific Ocean, in Kiribati in the Line Islands. British and US nuclear tests were held here between 1957 and 1962. It has coconut plantations. Area: 359 sq km (139 sq mi). Population (1980 est): 1265.

Christmas rose A perennial herbaceous plant, *Helleborus niger*, about 35 cm tall, native to central and S Europe and Asia Minor. Grown in gardens for its attractive white or pink winter-flowering blossoms, it prefers rich moist shady sites. The poisonous rhizomes are irritant to the skin when fresh. Dried, they have been used medicinally. Family: *Ranunculaceae*.

Christoff, Boris (1919–) Bulgarian singer. His powerful bass voice and skilful characterization have made him a world-famous opera singer. He is particularly well known in the title role of Mussorgsky's opera *Boris Godunov*.

Christophe, Henri (1767–1820) Haitian ruler. An ex-slave, Christophe served with *Toussaint L'Ouverture against the French and then joined *Dessalines' revolt. After Dessalines' assassination, in which Christophe took part, he ruled N Haiti (1808–20; as king from 1811). His cruelty caused a revolt and he shot himself.

Christopher, St (3rd century AD) Christian martyr of Syria. According to legend, he carried a child across a river where he was working as a ferryman. The child grew heavier and he learned that it was in fact Christ and he was thus carrying the weight of the world. He is the patron saint of travellers. Feast day: 25 July.

chromaticism The use in music of notes that are not part of the normal diatonic *scale: the word comes from the Greek *chroma*, colour. Under the system of equal *temperament the octave is split into 12 equal parts, containing 7 diatonic and 5 chromatic notes. The practice of "colouring" music by the use of these chromatic notes dates from the 16th century and was widely used by Liszt and Wagner to effect frequent modulations from one key to another. In the early music of Schoenberg chromaticism became so heavy that the concept of key became meaningless and *atonality resulted.

chromatid. *See* chromosome.

chromatography A method of chemical analysis in which a mixture to be analysed constitutes a mobile phase, which moves in contact with an absorbent stationary phase. In **gas chromatography** (*or* gas-liquid chromatography) the mobile phase is a mixture of volatile substances diluted with an inert gas (e.g. argon). The stationary phase consists of a non-volatile liquid supported on an inert material of uniform particles (e.g. diatomaceous earth) in a tall column. The components of the mobile phase are selectively absorbed by the stationary phase. A detector measures the conductivity (or some other property) of the gas leaving the column, the resulting peaks on a strip chart of the detector output indicating the presence and concentration of the various components of the mixture. When the mobile phase is a liquid it can be introduced into a column of the solid stationary phase. The components of the mixture are selectively absorbed and form coloured bands down the length of the column. This method is known as **column chromatography**. In column chromatography, the stationary phase is an absorbent material such as alumina. **Thin-layer chromatography** is a similar technique used for analysis. The stationary phase is a thin layer of alumina on a glass plate, and a spot of sample is separated into spots of the constituents. More commonly, **paper chromatography** is used, in which the stationary phase is a sheet of absorbent paper. The solvent soaks along the paper carrying the constituents with it at different rates. Colourless compounds can be made visible by ultraviolet light or chemical developers. The rate at which a constituent moves relative to movement of the solvent can be used to identify it.

chromatophore A granular cell containing pigment, found in great numbers in the skin of many animals. The distribution of the chromatophores accounts for the distinctive colours of these animals. Some animals (e.g. chameleons) have the ability to change the concentration and dispersion of pigment within the chromatophore very rapidly, effecting a change of skin colour that is of value in camouflage.

chrome dyes Pigments consisting of chromium salts. **Chrome yellow** and **chrome orange** contain lead chromate ($PbCrO_4$), lead sulphate ($PbSO_4$), and lead monoxide (PbO). They display a range of shades, depending on the composition, and are used in paints. **Chrome green** contains chromic oxide (Cr_2O_3) and, unlike chrome yellow, is resistant to light and heat.

chromium (Cr) A hard grey transition metal, discovered in 1798 by Louis Nicolas Vauquelin (1763–1829). It occurs in nature principally as chromite ($FeCr_2O_4$), which is mined in the Soviet Union, Zimbabwe, and elsewhere. The metal is extracted by reducing the oxide (Cr_2O_3) with aluminium. The principal uses of chromium are in electroplating steel and in making alloys with iron. All chromium compounds are coloured and the most widely used, other than the oxide, are chromates (for example K_2CrO_4) and dichromates ($K_2Cr_2O_7$), which are used as oxidizing agents and in the dyeing industry. Lead chromate ($PbCrO_4$) is bright yellow and is used as a pigment. At no 24; at wt 51.996; mp $1857 \pm 20°C$; bp $2482°C$.

chromophore A group of atoms, generally in an organic compound, that absorbs light of characteristic wavelengths, thus imparting colour to the compound. Typical examples are the *azo ($-N=N-$) and nitroso ($-N=O$) groups. In dyes, groups called auxochromes (colour enhancers) help to modify the colour conferred by the chromophore, as well as the solubility and related properties of the dye molecule. A group derived from sulphonic acid ($-SO_3H$) is a typical auxochrome.

chromosome One of the threadlike structures that carry the genetic information (*see* gene) of living organisms and are found in the nuclei of their cells. Chromosomes consist of a central axis of *DNA with associated *RNA and proteins. Before cell division, the long filamentous threads contract and thicken and each chromosome can be seen as two identical threads (chromatids) joined at the centromere. The chromatids later separate to become the daughter chromosomes (*see* mitosis). Chromosome number is characteristic of a species. For example, a normal human body cell has 46 chromosomes comprising 22 matched pairs (called autosomes) and two *sex chromosomes. A human sperm or egg cell has half this number (*see* meiosis). Abnormal numbers or parts of chromosomes often lead to abnormalities in the individual concerned. *Down's syndrome (mongolism) in man is caused by the presence of an extra number 21 chromosome.

chromosphere The layer of a star's atmosphere that lies between the *photosphere and the *corona. It is very much less dense than the photosphere. The sun's chromosphere is a few thousand kilometres thick; the temperature increases rapidly from about 4000°C near the photosphere to about 500 000°C at the base of the corona, with the atmosphere becoming increasingly rarified with height. The solar chromosphere cannot be seen without special equipment, except at a total solar *eclipse.

chronicle plays Plays that dramatize historical events in order to convey general moral lessons. The successors to the medieval *morality plays, they were popular in England during the Elizabethan era. Examples are Marlowe's *Edward II* (first produced in 1592) and Shakespeare's *King John* (c. 1596). Many of the plots were taken from Holinshed's *Chronicles* (1578).

Chronicles, Books of Two Old Testament books covering the history of Judah from the Creation to the end of the *Babylonian exile (538 BC). They were probably written in the 4th century BC and originally formed a continuous history with the books of Ezra and Nehemiah. After opening with genealogies from Adam, they describe the reigns of David and Solomon and the succeeding Kings of Judah. Special emphasis is given to the building of the Temple at Jerusalem.

chronometer. *See* clock.

chrysalis The *pupa of most insects of the order Lepidoptera. *See also* butterflies and moths.

Chrysanthemum A genus of herbaceous plants and shrubs (about 200 species) native to Eurasia, Africa, and North America. The wild ancestors of the horticultural chrysanthemums are not known, but probably more than one species—almost certainly of Japanese and Chinese origin—was involved. The showy forms are widely and easily cultivated, having colourful single or double long-lasting flower heads. The different varieties may bloom at any time from early spring to autumn. Family: *Compositae. See also* pyrethrum.

Chrysoloras, Manuel (c. 1365–1415) Greek scholar and envoy. Chrysoloras was sent on several diplomatic missions by the Byzantine Emperor Manuel Palaeologus. In Florence, Chrysoloras taught the humanists Bruni, Poggio, and Guarino. His work on grammar, *Erotemata*, introduced Greek to the West.

chrysoprase An apple-green variety of *chalcedony, used as a gem.

Chrysostom, St John (c. 347–407 AD) Bishop of Constantinople and Doctor of the Church. After a period as a hermit, he was ordained in 386 in Antioch and preached extensively there, soon gaining the epithet Chrysostom (Greek: golden-mouthed). As Patriarch of Constantinople from 398, he was a zealous reformer but alienated the Empress Eudoxia (d. 404) and other powerful persons. In 403 he was unjustifiably condemned on a number of charges, deposed from his see, and banished. He died while journeying to the Black Sea. His *Homilies* are important expositions of various biblical books. The liturgy in general use in the Orthodox Churches is attributed to him, although in its present form it dates from a much later period. Feast day: 27 Jan.

Chuang-tzu. *See* Zhuangzi.

chub One of several freshwater fish related to *carp, found in Europe and North America and used as food, game, or bait fish. The European chub (*Leucixus cephalus*) has a plump elongated body, usually 30–40 cm long, and is dark blue or green above and silvery below. Certain unrelated freshwater fish of the genus *Leucichthys* (order: *Salmoniformes*) are also called chub.

Chu Chiang. *See* Zhu Jiang.

Ch'ü Ch'iu-pai. *See* Qu Qiu Bai.

chuckwalla A North American lizard, *Sauromalus obesus*, occurring in SW arid and rocky regions. 50 cm long, it is dark-grey with a red-banded and blotched tail. It feeds on vegetation, storing water in sacs beneath the skin, and shelters in rock crevices; if molested it inflates its lungs to increase its body size making it difficult to dislodge. Family: *Iguanidae.*

Chukchi A people of the Chukchi peninsula in extreme NE Siberia. One branch consists of nomadic reindeer herders; the other is a maritime fishing people whose members also hunt whale, walrus, and seal, and live in fixed villages. Their language is of Palaeo-Siberian type.

Chulalongkorn (1853–1910) King of Siam (now Thailand) from 1868 to 1910. He built roads and railways, improved education, abolished slavery, and remodelled Siam's administration on western lines. His diplomatic handling of France and Britain ensured Siam's continued independence.

Chungking. *See* Chongqing.

Chur (French name: Coire; Romansh name: Cuera) 46 52N 9 32E A town in E Switzerland. A tourist centre, it also trades in Valtelline wines. Population (1983 est): 31 758.

Churchill 58 45N 94 00W A town and port in central Canada, in Manitoba on Hudson Bay. Originally a trading post (1685), it exports prairie grain. Rocketry and weather research are conducted here. Population (1985 est): 1304.

Churchill, Charles (1731–64) British poet. The success of his satire on actors, *The Rosciad* (1761), allowed him to abandon a career in the church and engage wholeheartedly in London society and politics. A friend of John *Wilkes, he wrote several caustic attacks on the government, including *The Prophecy of Famine* (1763) and *The Candidate* (1764).

Churchill, Lord Randolph Henry Spencer (1849–95)

British Conservative politician; third son of the 7th Duke of Marlborough and the father of Sir Winston *Churchill. He entered parliament in 1874 and led the group of Tory Democrats known as the Fourth Party. After serving as secretary for India (1885–86), he was briefly chancellor of the exchequer, when his budget was not accepted by the prime minister, Lord *Salisbury, because Churchill wished to reduce funds allocated to the armed forces. He married (1874) Jeanette (Jennie) Jerome (1854–1921), an American.

SIR WINSTON CHURCHILL *Touring Berlin during a visit in July 1945.*

Churchill, Sir Winston (Leonard Spencer) (1874–1965) British statesman and author. The son of Lord Randolph *Churchill, he was a direct descendant of the 1st Duke of Marlborough. Churchill served in the army and as a war correspondent in the second Boer War before becoming a Conservative MP in 1900. In 1904 he joined the Liberals and subsequently served as president of the Board of Trade (1908–10), home secretary (1910–11), and first lord of the admiralty (1911–15). In 1915, during World War I, he rejoined the army and served in France. In 1917 he became minister of munitions, supporting the development of the *tank. Churchill lost his parliamentary seat in 1922 but was re-elected as a constitutionalist in 1924, becoming chancellor of the exchequer in Baldwin's government. From 1929 he was out of office until the outbreak of World War II, when he became first lord of the admiralty and then, in 1940, prime minister of a coalition government. During *World War II, his remarkable oratory and outstanding qualities as a leader made him a symbol of British resistance to tyranny throughout the free world. He was largely responsible for Britain's victorious alliance with the Soviet Union and the USA (1941) but came to view Soviet communism as a future threat, speaking later of an "iron curtain" drawn across Europe. Churchill's coalition government was defeated in 1945 but he returned as Conservative prime minister in 1951, serving until his resignation in 1955.

His writings include *The Second World War* (1948–54) and *A History of the English-Speaking Peoples* (1956–58); he won the 1953 Nobel Prize for Literature.

Churchill Falls A waterfall in E Canada in W Labrador on the Churchill River. In 1967 work began on a huge hydroelectricity project expected to generate 5 222 000 kW. Height: 75 m (245 ft); 316 m (1038 ft) including rapids.

Churchill River A river in W Canada, flowing from NW Saskatchewan E and NE through Manitoba to Hudson Bay. Length: 1610 km (1000 mi).

Church of England The established church in England, which embodies Protestant elements but also claims continuity with the English Church as established by St *Augustine, the first Archbishop of Canterbury. Christianity was probably introduced in Britain during the Roman occupation in the 2nd century AD. Prior to the mission of St

Augustine (597), the native Church was dominated by Celtic missionaries from Ireland and Scotland. Conflicts between the indigenous Celtic Church and Rome were resolved in favour of Roman usage at the Synod of *Whitby (664), and thereafter the English Church remained under papal authority until the *Reformation. Under *Henry VIII, papal supremacy was rejected and the king was acknowledged Supreme Head of the Church. The two bases of Anglican doctrine and worship were formulated in the succeeding reigns: the Book of *Common Prayer, introduced in the reign of *Edward VI, and the *Thirty-Nine Articles, published under Elizabeth I, whose excommunication (1570) by the pope completed the break with Rome. The Church was disestablished during the Commonwealth but re-established by Charles II. By the 19th century three parties had developed within the Church and these continue to the present: the Low Church or Evangelical group, which emphasizes the Protestant tradition; the High Church group (see Anglo-Catholicism); and a Liberal group stressing adaptation to modern ideas. The two provinces of the Church are the archbishoprics of Canterbury (see Canterbury, Archbishop of) and York (see York, Archbishop of), each of which is further divided into bishoprics. Ecclesiastical affairs are supervised by the General Synod (established 1970 to replace the Church Assembly), composed of bishops, clergy, and laity; its decisions are subject to parliamentary approval. In 1987 the Synod agreed in principle to the ordination of women and discussed union with the Catholic church. Church property and endowments are administered by the Church Commissioners for England (established 1948). See also Anglican Communion; Lambeth Conferences; Latitudinarianism.

Church of Scotland   The Established Church in Scotland. The Scottish Church's secession from Rome was effected in 1560, largely under the influence of John *Knox. The argument over Church government between Episcopalians and Presbyterians continued until the reign of William of Orange, who established the Presbyterian Church in 1690. During the 18th century, disputes arose between traditional Evangelicals and Moderates, and this, together with the question of patronage, led to secessions. During the 19th and 20th centuries many of these divisions were healed, especially following abolition of patronage in 1874.

church year   The organization of the Christian churches' calendar around the great festivals of Christianity. In the Western Churches, the beginning of Advent (the Sunday nearest to the Feast of St Andrew, 30 Nov) marks the opening of the year. The Sundays of Advent are numbered one to four, leading to Christmas (25 Dec). Epiphany (6 Jan) follows after one or two intervening Sundays. The other major festivals are linked to the date of Easter, itself associated with the Jewish Passover. There are six Sundays in Lent and eight from Easter to Pentecost. The dates of Ash Wednesday, Good Friday and Ascension Day are dependent on Easter. The Eastern Churches' year begins with Easter and ends with Lent.

Churriguera   A Spanish family of architects consisting of three brothers, José (1665–1725), Joaquín (1674–1724), and Alberto (1676–1750). The Churrigueras evolved a distinctive, highly decorative form of the *baroque later dubbed "Churrigueresque." This can be seen in all their work, notably in José's church of S Estéban, Salamanca (1693).

Chu Teh.   See Zhu De.

Chuvash Autonomous Soviet Socialist Republic   An administrative division in the W central Soviet Union, in the RSFSR. The region is a wooded steppe with peat bogs and mineral deposits. The Chuvash, who comprise about 70% of the population, are a Turkic-speaking people. Industries include engineering, oil and natural-gas refining, chemicals, and food processing, but the economy is predominantly agricultural, producing chiefly cereals and fodder crops;

livestock is also important. Area: 18 300 sq km (7064 sq mi). Population (1981 est): 1 311 000. Capital: Cheboksary.

Chu Xi   (or Chu Hsi; 1130–1200) Chinese philosopher, born in Fujian province, the son of a government official. He was a precocious student and entered the government service, holding various important public posts for most of his life. His major work consists of four commentaries known as the Ssu shu or Four Books. These contain the formulation of *Confucianism that was adopted as the official philosophy of China until the communist revolution in the 20th century.

Chu Yuan   (c. 343 BC–c. 289 BC) Chinese poet, the earliest known by name. A nobleman of the state of Ch'u, he was banished to the S after court intrigues and drowned himself in the River Mi-lo. His contribution to the anthology Ch'u tz'u greatly influenced the development of early Chinese poetry.

CIA.   See Central Intelligence Agency.

Ciano, Galeazzo   (1903–44) Italian fascist leader. *Mussolini's son-in-law, Ciano was foreign minister from 1936 to 1943 and helped to form the military pact with Germany. In 1943 he voted against Mussolini in the Fascist Supreme Council and was shot by Mussolini's supporters in N Italy.

Cibber, Colley   (1671–1757) British actor, dramatist, and theatre manager. Son of a Danish sculptor, he wrote the sentimental comedy Love's Last Shift (1696) to supplement his earnings as an actor. His adaptation of Shakespeare's Richard III was the preferred acting version until the 19th century. His appointment as poet laureate in 1730 made him the target for satirical attacks by *Pope.

cicada   An insect belonging to the mainly tropical family Cicadidae (over 2000 species). Cicadas are 20-50 mm long and have large membranous wings. Males produce a variety of loud noises by vibrating two membranes at the base of the abdomen (this is called stridulation). Cicadas usually inhabit trees and the females lay eggs in the wood. The *nymphs (immature cicadas) drop to the ground and burrow underground to feed on plant juices from roots. After 1-17 years they emerge as adults. Order: *Hemiptera.

cicely   A perennial herbaceous plant, Myrrhis odorata, also called sweet cicely. 60-100 cm high, it has umbrella-like clusters of white flowers and a strong aromatic smell. Cicely is native to Europe and also occurs in Chile (where it was probably introduced). Formerly widely used as a vegetable, it is still used for seasoning. Family: *Umbelliferae.

Cicero   (Elyesa Bazna; 1904–70) German secret agent. He gained access to secret documents while working as valet to the British ambassador in Turkey in 1943–44, but the German authorities did not completely trust the information he supplied. He ended his working life as a nightwatchman in Munich.

Cicero, Marcus Tullius   (106–43 BC) Roman orator and statesman. Established as a prominent lawyer by 70 BC, he was elected consul in 63 BC. His execution of the Catiline conspirators without trial lost him support and he was exiled in 58 BC for 18 months. During the civil war he supported Pompey against Caesar and lived privately in Rome during the latter's dictatorship. After the assassination of Caesar in 44 BC he made a series of attacks on Antony, the Philippics, for which he was later arrested and killed. The greatest of Roman orators, he also wrote treatises on rhetoric and philosophical works influenced by Greek political theory.

cichlid   A freshwater fish of the family Cichlidae (over 6000 species), found in tropical regions, especially Africa. Cichlids have a brightly coloured deep body, up to 30 cm long, and a single long dorsal fin; they feed on plants or animals. Most build nests for their eggs and guard the young but some species carry the eggs in their mouths (see mouthbrooder). Many are popular aquarium fish. Order: Perciformes.

CID.   See Criminal Investigation Department.

cider An alcoholic drink made from fermented apple juice. In England cider is made predominantly in the West Country, from apples grown specifically for cider making. They are crushed to press out the juice, which ferments spontaneously. Fermentation lasts weeks or months, varying according to the apples used. The cider is then drawn off from the yeast deposit and stored in a cool place. Sweet cider has a large amount of unfermented sugar, dry cider little sugar, and rough cider is dry cider with some acetic acid. Cider is also made in France, especially in Normandy and Brittany, Spain, and the USA, where cider denotes unfermented apple juice and hard cider denotes cider.

Cienfuegos 22 10N 80 27W A port in S Cuba, on the Caribbean Sea. A picturesque city with many fine buildings, it trades in tobacco, cattle products, and molasses and is the site of a naval base. Population (1981): 235 293.

cigar A cylindrical roll of tobacco leaf, smoked originally by the Indians of the Americas and copied by sailors from Portugal and Spain; by the 19th century they became common in N Europe. The most expensive cigars are still made by hand in Cuba and Jamaica, machine-made cigars being made extensively in the USA, Europe, and the Far East. The cigar was replaced to some extent by the cigarette from the end of the 19th century, but small cigars have enjoyed some popularity in recent years.

cigarette A small cigar consisting of a cylindrical roll of fine-cut tobacco, rolled in thin paper. Cigarettes became popular in the late 19th century and is now the form in which most tobacco is smoked. The tobacco most commonly used for cigarettes is Virginia-cut, a type that originated in the USA; this has now been successfully grown in other countries, such as Canada. Since the 1960s there has been widespread concern over the effects that smoking has on health; it is associated with lung *cancer, *bronchitis, and *heart disease. In the UK this has led the government to impose a ban on cigarette advertising on television and to take other steps to cut down smoking, especially of high-tar brands.

Ciliata A class of microscopic single-celled animals (*see* Protozoa) having two nuclei and tracts of hairlike cilia over the cell surface, used for feeding and swimming. Most are free-swimming (*see* Paramecium) but some are attached to the substrate by a stalk (*see* Stentor; Vorticella). Most ciliates feed on organic detritus, other protozoans, etc., but some are parasitic, especially on fish and other aquatic animals.

Cilicia The SE coastal region of Asia Minor. It was subject consecutively to the Hittites, the Assyrians, the Achaemenians, the Macedonians, and the Seleucids. From the 2nd century BC pirates based on Cilicia seriously threatened Mediterranean trade until suppressed by Pompey in 67, after which the region was incorporated into a series of Roman provinces.

Cilician Gates (Turkish name: Külek Boğazi) 37 17N 34 46E A mountain pass in central S Turkey, in the Taurus Mountains. It lies on the route from Ankara to Adana and has been used for centuries.

Cimabue, Giovanni (Cenni de Peppi; c. 1240–c. 1302) Florentine painter, who introduced a degree of naturalism into the stylized *Byzantine art of his period. His only certain work is a mosaic of St John (Duomo, Pisa) but the fresco cycle in the upper Church of St Francis, Assisi, and the *Santa Trinità Madonna* (Uffizi) are attributed to him. *Giotto was probably his pupil.

Cimarosa, Domenico (1749–1801) Italian composer. He became court musician in St Petersburg and Vienna and was famous for his many operas. His best-known work is the *opera buffa *The Secret Marriage* (1792), which shows his flair for vocal ensemble writing and fine comic talent. He also wrote church music and chamber music.

cimbalom The traditional musical instrument of Hungary; a type of dulcimer. The cimbalom has ten pairs of wire strings

stretched over a shallow three-sided soundbox. The strings are struck with a small hammer. The Hungarian composer Kodály used it in the suite *Háry János* (1927).

Cimbri A Germanic tribe from N Jutland. At the end of the 2nd century BC the Cimbri migrated southwards, defeating Roman armies in 113 BC (Noricum), 110 BC (Rhône valley), and 105 BC (Arausio, now Orange, France). In 101 BC Marius destroyed them; a remnant survived in Jutland.

Cimon (died c. 450 BC) Athenian general and politician. The son of *Miltiades, Cimon opposed *Themistocles' policy of enmity towards the Spartans, believing Persia was the common Greek enemy, and in about 466 he scored a great victory against the Persians. His opponents, including *Pericles, caused him to be ostracized (461) but after his return to Athens, Cimon negotiated a truce with Sparta (c. 450) and died fighting the Persians in Cyprus.

Cinchona A genus of trees (40 species) of the South American Andes, now cultivated elsewhere in the tropics, especially India. One of the most important species is calisaya (*C. calisaya*). The bark yields powerful medicinal drugs, including cinchonidine and *quinine, used in the treatment and prevention of malaria, and cinchona, useful for coughs and sore throats. Cultivation, which is generally by coppicing, has lost importance since the development of similar synthetic drugs lacking side-effects. Family: *Rubiaceae*.

Cincinnati 39 10N 84 30W A city in the USA, in SW Ohio on the Ohio River. Founded in 1788, it developed as a meat-packing centre in the 19th century. Today it is an important inland port and major manufacturing centre best known as a producer of machine tools. The University of Cincinnati was established here in 1819. Population (1980): 385 457.

Cincinnatus, Lucius Quinctius (5th century BC) Roman statesman. He was made dictator to rescue a Roman legion that was besieged by an Italian tribe. After his victory he returned to his farm, despite pleas that he remain dictator. His rejection of autocratic rule made him a symbol of traditional Roman values.

Cinderella The heroine of a folktale, of which the first recorded version dates from 9th-century China. The story is of a girl treated cruelly by her stepfamily who receives help from a supernatural agent, in most versions an animal or her fairy godmother, and finally marries a prince. The story was introduced to England through Charles Perrault's *Tales of Mother Goose* (1697).

cinema The art form and industry of films. The first

CINEMA *The director David Lean on location while making* A Passage to India *(1984).*

motion picture exhibited to a public audience was made in 1895 by the French brothers Louis and Auguste *Lumière, whose equipment was developed from the inventions of Thomas *Edison, and the first commercial success was the American film *The Great Train Robbery* (1903). Influential pioneers of the silent cinema in the USA were D. W. *Griffith, Mack *Sennett, and Charlie *Chaplin. In Europe, technological developments were creatively exploited by such directors as F. W. Murnau (1889-1931) in Germany and *Eisenstein in Russia. The end of the era of silent films was signalled by the success of Al *Jolson's *The Jazz Singer* (1927), which had a synchronized musical score; colour film, introduced in the 1930s, added further popular appeal. The French directors René *Clair and Jean *Renoir made notable contributions to the early development of sound cinema. Between 1930 and 1945 the cinema industry in the USA became essentially an entertainment factory, controlled by the giant Hollywood studios MGM and Paramount. The decline in cinema audiences from the late 1940s because of the rival attraction of television caused the break-up of the Hollywood system, and since World War II the most significant developments in the cinema have been achieved by directors elsewhere. There was a postwar resurgence of the British film industry, which had developed in the 1930s as a result of the influence of the producer J. Arthur Rank. Prominent directors included Carol Reed, David Lean, and Alfred Hitchcock; Michael Balcon's Ealing comedies and the Boulting brothers' social satires also added considerable prestige to British films. Prominent continental directors include *Fellini, *Antonioni, *Bergman, and *Buñuel, and, more recently, directors from Japan and India have come to the fore.

cinematography The recording of moving pictures. Essentially a motion film records a rapid sequence of still pictures (each slightly different from the previous one) fast enough to appear continuous to the human eye. The film moves through the camera in a series of jumps. There are usually 18 pictures (frames) per second in silent film and 24 per second in sound film. The sequence of transparencies produced by developing the film is passed through a *projector in the same way. Sound can be carried as a magnetic or optical signal on a narrow strip at the side of the film, to synchronize with the picture. Various widths of film are used: 8 mm for educational and laboratory applications; 16 mm for portable equipment for amateur filming and many other uses; 35 mm for the professional cinema.

cineraria A herbaceous perennial pot plant developed from *Senecio cruentus* of the Canary Islands. There are numerous horticultural varieties, noted for their handsome, sometimes brilliantly coloured, daisy-like flowers. Useful for spring and winter flowering, they require a cool moist draught- and frost-free atmosphere. Family: *Compositae*.

Cinna, Lucius Cornelius (d. 84 BC) Roman politician. Expelled from Rome by his opponent Sulla (87), Cinna with *Marius returned and captured Rome. He tried to restrain Marius' brutal revenge on their opponents and as consul (86-84) restored order. He was killed in a mutiny shortly before Sulla's return to Italy.

cinnabar (moth) A moth, *Callimorpha jacobaeae*, of Europe and Asia. Both the adults—scarlet and black—and the caterpillars—striped black and yellow—taste bad: their warning coloration discourages predators. The caterpillars feed on ragwort and have been used to control this weed. Superfamily: *Caradrinoidea* (noctuids, tiger moths, etc.).

cinnabar (ore) A mineral consisting of mercury sulphide, the chief ore of mercury. It is bright red and occurs in veins and impregnations associated with volcanic rocks. Spain, the Soviet Union, Italy, and Mexico are the main producers.

cinnamon An evergreen tree, *Cinnámomum zeylanicum*, 7-10 m high, native to Sri Lanka and cultivated widely in the tropics. Before 1776 only wild plants were used, owing to

the belief that cultivation would destroy its flavour. It is coppiced, the bark of the twigs being peeled off and rolled up to form the spice. Family: *Lauraceae*.

cinquefoil A shrub or herbaceous plant of the genus *Potentilla*, having leaves with five divisions each. Creeping cinquefoil (*P. reptans*) has been used medicinally, and shrubby cinquefoil (*P. fruticosa*) is often grown in gardens. Family: *Rosaceae*.

Cinque Ports An association of five English ports (Sandwich, Dover, Hythe, New Romney, Hastings) in Kent and Sussex formed during the 11th century to defend the Channel coast. After the Norman conquest they were granted considerable privileges in return for providing the nucleus of the navy. Winchelsea and Rye were added to their number and many other towns in the southeast became associate members. In the later middle ages their power declined both because of competition from other ports and the silting-up of their harbours. The Lord Warden of the Cinque Ports survives as an honorary office. Held by Sir Winston Churchill (1941-65) and Sir Robert Menzies (1965-78), the present holder is Elizabeth the Queen Mother.

Ciompi, Revolt of the (1378) A rising of the poorer wage-earners of Florence against the oligarchic rule of the major guilds. The Ciompi (wool workers) seized power together with the minor guilds, but a split in this alliance allowed the major guilds to destroy the revolt and to abolish the Ciompi's newly formed guild.

Circassia An area in the Soviet Union, NW of the Great Caucasus. It is inhabited by the Circassian (*or* Cherkess) people, who, although Christian since the 6th century, adopted Islam under the influence of the Ottoman Empire in the 17th century and subsequently strongly resisted Russian rule until the Ottoman Turks ceded Circassia to Russia in 1829.

Circe Legendary Greek sorceress, who had the power to transform men into beasts. Odysseus, who visited her island of Aeaea on his voyage from Troy, was protected by the herb moly, and forced her to restore his men to human form.

circle A curve defined as the locus of all the points lying in a plane at a certain distance, called the radius, from a fixed point, called the centre. Its diameter is any straight line joining two points on the circle and passing through the centre. The ratio of the distance around any circle (the circumference) to its diameter is equal to the number π (*see* pi). The area of a circle, radius r, is πr^2.

circuit breaker A mechanism for breaking an electrical power circuit under load. Similar in function to a fuse, it has the advantage of being able to be reset immediately. It is used extensively in power stations and high-voltage distribution lines and now often replaces fuses in low-voltage circuits.

circulation of the blood The passage of blood through the heart and the network of arteries and veins associated with it. By supplying the tissues with blood, the circulatory system effects the transport of oxygen, nutrients, etc., and the removal of waste products. Oxygen-rich blood is pumped out of the *heart into the aorta and then, via the arteries, to all the tissues of the body. Here oxygen is removed, and deoxygenated blood returns, through the veins, to the heart. This blood is then pumped to the lungs, where it is reoxygenated, and returned to the heart to repeat the circuit. The circulation of the blood was first discovered by William *Harvey in 1628. *See* Plate IV.

circumcision The removal of all or part of the foreskin. In many primitive societies circumcision usually forms part of a ceremony initiating youths into adulthood. Among some Islamic peoples it is performed just before marriage; Jewish babies are circumcised in a religious ceremony when they are eight days old. Its origin is unknown but it has hygienic advantages, especially in hot climates, and cancer of the penis occurs infrequently among circumcised men. It is also carried out for medical reasons in certain circumstances. Female circumcision (the removal of the clitoris) is also practised among some primitive peoples.

Cirencester 51 44N 1 59W A market town in SW England, in Gloucestershire. In Roman times it was the second largest town in Britain (Corinium) and it was an important wool centre in the middle ages. The Royal Agricultural College is situated here. Population (1981): 15 622.

cire perdue (French: lost wax) A technique of metal casting used for small detailed castings, particularly statuary. A wax original model is encased in a mould. When molten metal is poured into the mould the wax melts and is replaced by metal. The process was already known in *Ur (c. 3000 BC) and was perfected in China about 500 BC.

cirque (*or* corrie) A rounded rock basin with steep sides, often containing a lake or cirque glacier. Common in glaciated mountain ranges, cirques form through freeze-thaw action on the headwall and basin floor together with abrasion by slipping ice and debris.

cirrhosis Destruction of the cells of the liver followed by their replacement with fibrous tissue, which eventually produces symptoms of liver failure (e.g. jaundice, swelling of the legs and abdomen, and vomiting of blood). Cirrhosis may be caused by *alcoholism, *hepatitis, obstruction of the bile duct, and heart failure, but often the cause is not known. Treatment is determined by the underlying condition.

cirrocumulus cloud (Cc) A high *cloud with a mottled appearance composed of ice crystals; it is sometimes known as "mackerel sky."

cirrostratus cloud (Cs) A high thin veil of *cloud composed of ice crystals, visible as a halo around the sun or moon.

cirrus cloud (Ci) A high detached *cloud occurring in the troposphere above 6000 m (20 000 ft), composed of ice crystals and appearing wispy and fibrous. It is usually associated with fair weather.

Ciscaucasia (*or* North Caucasia) A region in the SE Soviet Union. Mainly steppe, it rises in the S to the Great *Caucasus range. Its main product is oil.

Ciskei. *See* Bantu Homelands.

Cis-Sutlej states Sikh principalities in India, so called by the British because they were on the British side (Latin *cis,* on this side of) of the River Sutlej. They were first united in 1785 under the Maratha, whose rule was broken by the rise of *Ranjit Singh and British power in the subcontinent. The majority of the Cis-Sutlej states came under British government in 1809, the remainder passing to Ranjit Singh. They continued to exist until Indian independence in 1947.

Cistercians An order of Roman Catholic monks founded by St Robert of Molesme (c. 1027–1111) as a stricter offshoot of the *Benedictine order. The mother house at Cîteaux, France, from whence the order took its name, was founded in 1098. St *Bernard of Clairvaux contributed considerably to the order's prestige, and communities were established throughout W Europe in the 12th century. In the 17th century the order underwent a reform resulting in two groups: the monks of the Strict Observance, as opposed to the Common Observance, are known as *Trappists.

Citizens' Advice Bureaux, National Association of (CAB) A British organization with some 900 branches throughout the UK that provides free and confidential advice to anyone on any subject. Their trained staff is equipped to advise on such matters as the social and health services, housing, and legal-aid schemes, as well as on personal matters. Director: Jeremy Leighton.

citizens band radio (CB) A short-distance two-way radio link, commonly installed in motor vehicles. These systems became popular in Britain in the 1970s although they were illegal and interfered with the radio network of the emergency services. Many CB clubs were formed and a special CB language

evolved. After a CB channel was authorized in 1981, interest in this activity declined sharply.

Citlaltépetl (Spanish name: Volcan Citlaltépetl) 19 00N 97 18W A dormant volcano in S central Mexico, the highest point in the country. Height: 5699 m (18 697 ft).

citric acid An organic compound that occurs in plant and animal tissues and is involved in the series of metabolic reactions called the *Krebs cycle. A commercial preparation of citric acid is used as a flavouring agent in foods.

citron A *citrus tree, *Citrus medica,* 2–3 m high. Originally from the Far East, it was introduced into the Mediterranean region in about 300 BC; this remains the main centre of commercial cultivation. The rough yellowish sour fruits are used to make candied peel, produced by soaking in brine and preserving in sugar.

citronella A *grass, *Cymbopogon nardus,* cultivated in tropical regions of Africa and Asia and introduced into tropical America. It forms dense tufts and contains geraniol or citronella oil, used in cosmetics and insect repellents.

Citrus The largest and most important genus of tropical and subtropical fruits (10 species), originating in SE Asia. All the species are small evergreen trees or shrubs with simple glossy leaves and five-petalled, usually white, flowers. The juicy fruits are rich in vitamin C, citric acid, and pectin (used in jam making). The most important are the *orange, *lemon, *lime, *grapefruit, *citron, and *tangerine. All contain essential oils used in perfumery and soap making (*bergamot is grown especially for this). Family: *Rutaceae.*

cittern An instrument of the guitar family with a pear-shaped body, a fretted fingerboard, a flat back, and four pairs of wire strings. Being small and easy to play, it was popular between the early 16th and mid-18th centuries.

City of London, Corporation of the The governing body of the City of London. It comprises three courts: the Court of Aldermen (*see* alderman), which elects the Lord Mayor (*see* mayor); the Court of Common Hall, which elects the *sheriffs and comprises the Lord Mayor, the 25 other aldermen, and the freemen and liverymen of the 84 City *livery companies; and the Court of Common Council, which is responsible for local government and comprises the Lord Mayor, the 25 other aldermen, and 155 councilmen. The aldermen and the councilmen are elected by the City's ratepayers.

city states Independent municipalities, each comprising a town and its surrounding countryside, characteristic of ancient Greece. There were several hundreds of city states, of which Athens was the largest. Each enjoyed autonomy, its own laws and constitution (democratic, as at Athens, or oligarchic, as at Sparta), and its own presiding deity. The Greeks were so proud of their allegiance to the city state that Greek unity was somewhat precarious.

Ciudad Bolívar 8 06N 63 36W A port in E Venezuela, on the River Orinoco. Accessible to oceangoing vessels, its chief exports include gold, diamonds, and chicle. Population (1981 est): 153 900.

Ciudad Guayana (former name: Santo Tomé de Guayana) 8 22N 62 37W An industrial complex in E Venezuela, on the River Orinoco. Founded in 1961, it amalgamated several existing industrial centres into one; industries include iron and steel processing and gold mining. Population (1981 est): 212 000.

Ciudad Juárez 31 42N 106 29W A city in N Mexico, on the Rio Grande. Its importance is due to its location on the US border and as a marketing centre for cotton. Its university was founded in 1973. Population (1980): 567 365.

Ciudad Real 38 59N 3 55W A town in S central Spain, in New Castile. It has a 13th-century gothic cathedral. An agricultural centre, it produces flour and brandy. Population (1982): 48 656.

civet A solitary nocturnal mammal belonging to the family

Viverridae. The African civet (*Viverra civetta*) is cat-like, about 1.2 m long with coarse greyish spotted fur. Mainly carnivorous, civets also eat fruit and roots. The secretion of their anal glands is used in perfumes as a fixative, making other scents last longer. *See also* palm civet.

Civic Trust A charity, founded in 1957 and supported by voluntary contributions, aiming to improve the quality of the environment in the UK. It supports local amenity groups, advises on town planning, and encourages the construction and preservation of fine buildings.

ENGLISH CIVIL WAR   *Charles I at the Battle of Naseby – a major defeat for the royalists.*

civil defence Arrangements for the defence of a civilian population, especially against air raids. In the UK, during World War II, the Air Raid Precautions (ARP), planned by the ministry of home security, included the training of air-raid wardens and firewatchers, gasmask distribution, the building of shelters, and the organization of rescue services in conjunction with the police, fire services, and ambulance brigade. Since World War II the UK has reduced its civil defence commitment on the grounds of economy and the difficulty of providing protection against nuclear attack. This view is not shared by the USA, where there is an extensive system of *fallout shelters capable of protecting 160 million people.

civil engineering The branch of *engineering that deals with the design and construction of buildings and public structures, such as roads, railways, dams, canals, etc. The term was first used in 1750 by John Smeaton (1724–92) to distinguish himself from military engineers, although the practice went back to ancient times. It has diversified into numerous branches calling on specialized scientific knowledge and developing such new materials as prestressed concrete. The professional body in the UK is the Institution of Civil Engineers (granted a royal charter in 1828).

civil law The body of law governing the rights of private individuals and their relationships with each other rather than with the state. It is also called private law, as distinguished from public law and *criminal law. The term is also used of the European legal systems derived from *Roman law, which are different from *common law systems in important respects. For example, in civil law court decisions have no legal force in the decision of similar cases. Roman law was revived in Europe from the 11th and 12th centuries and formed the basis of the *Code Napoléon* (1804), on which other European, Latin American, and some Asian states modelled their legal systems. English-speaking countries generally use common law, although the law of Scotland is more closely related to civil law.

civil list In the UK, the sum given annually from the Consoli-

dated Fund to the monarch and his or her consort and children (except the Prince of Wales, who receives the revenues of the Duchy of Cornwall) to meet their expenses. The list was introduced in 1689, became law in 1697, and in 1830 all government expenses were removed from it. Originally parliament voted at the monarch's accession the sum to be paid annually but because of inflation Parliament increased the amount fixed in 1952 both in 1972 and 1975 and it may now be increased by Treasury order. **Civil list pensions**, charged to the Consolidated Fund but not forming part of the civil list, are awarded by the monarch on the advice of the prime minister to distinguished persons.

civil rights The individual's rights to liberty, equality of treatment, education, etc., under the law and safeguarded by the state. In countries with a written constitution, such as the USA, they form part of the constitution. In England there have been a number of unsuccessful attempts to codify these rights, which are still only protected by the general law. *See also* Bill of Rights; human rights.

civil-rights movement In the USA, the political struggle for racial equality in the 1950s and 1960s led chiefly by Martin Luther *King, Jr. The movement's goals were equal rights for US Blacks in voting, housing, and education. Its first success was in the campaign (1955–56) in Montgomery, Alabama, to desegregate the city's buses and the Civil Rights Acts of 1957, 1960, and 1964 prohibited racial discrimination in every important aspect of life.

civil service The bureaucracy that implements government policies. In the UK, civil servants were recruited by patronage until 1855, when the Civil Service Commission was established and initiated the recruitment of candidates by examination. As a result of the report of the Fulton Committee (1968), the Civil Service Commission came under a new Civil Service Department headed by the prime minister. This was subsequently disbanded but the prime minister remains minister for the Civil Service. The civil service is organized into such ministries as the *Home Office and the *Foreign and Commonwealth Office and has been criticized for the power of its permanent civil servants in comparison to that of relatively short-term ministers. The secretariats of such organizations as the UN are regarded as forming an international civil service.

Civil War, English (1642–51) The war between Charles I and parliament, which led to the execution of the king (1649) and the establishment of Oliver Cromwell's *Protectorate (1653). The Civil War was the outcome of a conflict between king and parliament that had steadily worsened during the reigns of James I (1603–25) and Charles. The struggle for power culminated in the events of the *Long Parliament (summoned in 1640). War was precipitated by Charles' rejection of parliament's Nineteen Propositions in June, 1642, and on 22 Aug he raised his standard at Nottingham. The first battle, at Edgehill, ended indecisively but during 1643 the royalists (*or* *Cavaliers) gained ground in the N and W. The parliamentarian (*see* Roundheads) negotiation of the *Solemn League and Covenant with the Scots led to its victory at *Marston Moor (1644); the formation of the *New Model Army brought about the decisive defeat of Charles at *Naseby (1645). In 1646 Charles surrendered to the Scots at Newark and the first Civil War was brought to an end. He was handed over to parliament in January, 1647, but was seized by the army in June. He escaped to the Isle of Wight and in December reopened negotiations with the Scots. The second Civil War ensued (1648), with royalist uprisings in Wales and Kent, ending with Cromwell's defeat of the Scots at Preston in August. In the following year, Charles was tried and executed and the *Commonwealth was established by the Rump Parliament. The Civil War was concluded by Cromwell's subjection of Ireland (1649–50), his defeat of Charles' heir (later Charles II) at Dunbar (1650), and his victory against the Scots at Worcester in 1651. In 1653 he dismissed the Rump and established the *Protectorate, which governed England until preparations for the *Restoration of the monarchy were initiated in 1659.

Civil War, US (1861-65) The conflict between the Federal government of the USA and the 11 *Confederate States in the South. The war arose from the conflict of interest between the predominantly agricultural slave-owning South and the industrialized North. The election of a president, Abraham Lincoln, opposed to slavery precipitated the secession of the southern states under Jefferson Davis, and war broke out when the Confederates opened fire on Fort Sumter, South Carolina, which the Federal government had refused to evacuate. The opening campaigns in Virginia culminated in the Confederate victory at the first battle of *Bull Run (July). Early in 1862 the Confederate Stonewall Jackson conducted a brilliant campaign in the Shenandoah Valley but on 4 May the Federal Army of the Potomac under George B. McClellan captured Yorktown and defeated Robert E. Lee's force in the Seven Days' battles (25 June-1 July). The Confederates retaliated in August by scoring a victory at the second battle of Bull Run and Lee pushed N into Maryland. Defeated at *Antietam (Sept), the Confederates were then victorious at Fredericksburg (Dec). In Tennessee, meanwhile, the Confederate success at Shiloh (6-7 April) was followed by a reverse at Stones River (31 Dec-2 Jan). In 1863, following his victory at Chancellorsville, Virginia (1-5 May), Lee began his second invasion of the N, only to be defeated at *Gettysburg (July). In the W, Federal troops under Ulysses S. Grant besieged Vicksburg, Mississippi, which fell on 4 July, and, after defeat at Chickamauga (19-20 Sept), won the victory of Chatanooga (23-25 Nov). In 1864 Grant, by now the Federal general in chief, advanced against Lee, whom he encountered inconclusively at *Cold Harbor (June). Sherman, who held the Federal command in the W, took Atlanta (Sept) before making his historic March to the Sea. After capturing Savannah in September, Sherman moved N through the Carolinas and on 9 April, 1865, Lee surrendered at Appomatox Court House. By 2 June the Federal victory was complete and the task of *Reconstruction lay ahead.

civitas Citizenship in ancient Rome acquired either by birth or by grant from the people or emperor. It was a much coveted privilege, entailing voting rights and facilitating an administrative or military career. As Rome expanded *civitas* was gradually extended to its Italian allies (89 BC) and to subjects of some Roman provinces (from 43 BC). In 212 AD all free inhabitants of the Empire were made citizens. An autonomous provincial city was also known as a *civitas*.

Civitavecchia 42 05N 11 47E A seaport in central Italy, in Lazio. It has Etruscan and Roman remains and a citadel designed by Michelangelo. There is a fishing industry. Population (1981 est): 45 836.

Clackmannan (*or* Clackmannanshire) A former county of central Scotland. Under local government reorganization in 1975 its boundaries were adjusted to form Clackmannan District, in the Central Region.

Clacton-on-Sea 51 48N 1 9E A resort in SE England, on the Essex coast. Population (1981): 43 571.

Clair, René (René Chomette; 1898-1981) French film director. Both his early silent comedies and his pioneering sound films, such as *Sous les toits de Paris* (1930), were distinguished by his gifts for humour and fantasy. During World War II he worked in Hollywood, and his later films included *Les Belles de nuit* (1952).

Clairvaux (Latin: *clara vallis*, beautiful valley) The *Cistercian monastery founded (1115) by St *Bernard of Clairvaux in the Aube Valley (NE France), which remained the most influential Cistercian house until its suppression (1790) during the French Revolution.

clairvoyance. *See* extrasensory perception.

US CIVIL WAR *Bodies at Antietam (1862). Taken by Mathew Brady (1823–96), this was one of the earliest war photographs.*

clam A *bivalve mollusc with two equal shells and a muscular burrowing foot. Burrowing clams live buried in sand and mud, mainly in shallow coastal waters; they feed by taking in water through a tube (siphon) extended into the water. The largest burrowing clam is the geoduck (*Panopea generosa*), weighing up to 5 kg, while the giant clam (*Tridacna gigas*) can exceed 250 kg.

clan A group tracing actual or putative descent in either the male or female line from a common ancestor. Clans are frequently important divisions in primitive societies, as in the pre-18th-century Scottish Highlands. They are often exogamous (prohibiting marriage between members). Many have a totemic emblem taking the form of an animal or plant, from which members are believed to descend, and perform collective ceremonies.
The Scottish clans, until their suppression following the *Jacobite rebellions of 1715 and 1745, controlled distinctive territories and were frequently rivals. The members of a clan wore characteristic clothing (*see* Highland dress) and often bore the name of its founder preceded by Mac (son of), e.g. MacDonald. The clan chiefs are still officially recognized, both in Scotland and Ireland.

Clapham Sect (c. 1790-1830) A group of well-to-do Evangelicals, who supported the missionary movement, the abolition of the slave trade, and domestic social reform. Members included William *Wilberforce, Henry Thornton (1760-1815), James Stephen (1758-1832), and John Venn (1759-1813), the rector of Clapham.

Clare (Irish name: Chláir) A county in the W Republic of Ireland, in Munster situated between Galway Bay and the Shannon estuary. It consists of a low-lying central plain rising E to mountains and W to the limestone area of the Burren. Agriculture is the chief occupation with cattle rearing and dairy farming. The salmon fisheries are important. Area: 3188 sq km (1231 sq mi). Population (1981): 87 567. County town: Ennis.

Clare, John (1793-1864) British poet, the self-educated son of a farm labourer in Northamptonshire. His first book, *Poems Descriptive of Rural Life and Scenery* (1820), brought him fame and patronage in London. Three further volumes, including his best-known work, *The Shepherd's Calendar* (1827), were less successful, and he lived in great poverty. In 1837 he became insane and in 1841 was confined to a lunatic asylum in Northampton, where he wrote some of his best poems.

Clarendon, Constitutions of (1164) Regulations concerning the relations between church and state issued by Henry II of England. They aimed to limit the power of the church, especially of the ecclesiastical courts, and to bring the church more firmly under royal authority. Thomas *Becket, Archbishop of Canterbury, repudiated his allegiance to the Constitutions, which action eventually led to his murder.

Clarendon, Edward Hyde, 1st Earl of (1609-74) English statesman and historian. In the events that led up to the English *Civil War he tried to influence Charles I towards moderation. He served as the king's chancellor of the exchequer during the war and went into exile in 1646, settling eventually with the future Charles II in France. At the Restoration (1660) he became Lord Chancellor and gave his name to the *Clarendon Code of anti-Nonconformist legislation. His daughter Anne married the future James II. Criticized for the sale of Dunkirk to France (1662) and for his handling of the second *Dutch War (1664-67), the *Cabal brought about his fall. Forced again into exile, he completed his monumental *History of the Rebellion and Civil Wars in England* (1702-04). He died at Rouen.

Clarendon Code (1661-65) A series of Acts, passed by Charles II's government, that were directed against *Nonconformists (or Dissenters). The Corporation Act (1661) excluded Nonconformists from municipal office, the Act of Uniformity (1662) enforced the use of the Church of England's Book of Common Prayer, the Conventicle Act (1664) prohibited Nonconformist services, and the Five Mile Act (1665) outlawed former Nonconformist ministers from the towns. The Code is named after the king's first minister, the Earl of *Clarendon.

Clare of Assisi, St (1194-1253) Italian nun, founder of the "Poor Clares." Influenced by the teaching of St *Francis of Assisi, she gave up all her possessions and followed him. St Francis established a community of women with Clare as abbess in 1215. They lived in absolute poverty without even communal property. She was canonized in 1255. Because of an incident in which she saw mass celebrated at a distance, she was proclaimed patron saint of television in 1958. Feast day: 12 Aug.

clarinet A woodwind instrument with a single reed and a cylindrical bore. It is a transposing instrument existing in several sizes and generally has a fundamental of A or B flat; it has a range of three and a half octaves. The clarinet did not become a regular member of the orchestra until the late 18th century. Mozart popularized it, using it in several symphonies and writing a concerto and quintet for the instrument. The **bass clarinet** is pitched an octave lower than the B flat clarinet. ⬚musical instruments.

Clark, Jim (James C.; 1937-68) British motor-racing driver, who won a total of 25 Grand Prix races between 1959 and 1968, when he was killed in a crash. He was world champion in 1963 and 1965.

Clark, (Charles) Joseph (1939-) Canadian statesman; Progressive Conservative prime minister (1979-80). He became his party's leader in 1976 and defeated Trudeau's Liberal government to become Canada's youngest ever prime minister. He was defeated by Trudeau in the 1980 election and lost the party leadership to Brian Mulroney in 1983.

Clark, Kenneth (Mackenzie), Baron (1903–83) British art historian. As a young man, Clark worked with *Berenson in Florence. He was director of the National Gallery (1934–45), Slade Professor of Fine Art at Oxford (1946–50, 1961–62), and professor of art history at the Royal Academy (1977–83). His books and particularly his television series *Civilization* (1969) stimulated public appreciation of art. He became a life peer (1969) and a member of the OM (1976).

Clarke, Jeremiah (?1673-1707) English composer and organist, a pupil of John Blow. He shot himself as the result of an unhappy love affair. The "Trumpet Voluntary" often attributed to Purcell is an arrangement of "The Prince of Denmark's March," one of Clarke's harpsichord pieces.

Clarke, Marcus (Andrew Hislop) (1846-81) Australian novelist. Born in London, he emigrated to Australia in 1863

and became a journalist. His best-known work, *For the Term of His Natural Life* (1874), is a melodramatic novel about a penal settlement.

Clarkia A genus of herbaceous plants (36 species) found naturally in semiarid environments in California and Chile. Horticultural varieties are grown as summer annuals. About 30 cm tall, they are slender, showy, and mostly pink-flowered. Family: *Onagraceae* (willowherb family).

Clarkson, Thomas (1760-1846) British campaigner for the abolition of slavery. With *Wilberforce and Granville Sharp (1735-1813) he formed an antislavery society in 1787, when he also wrote *A Summary View of the Slave Trade and of the Probable Consequences of Its Abolition*. British abolition of the slave trade was achieved in 1807 and Clarkson then devoted his energies to abolition by other states.

classical art and architecture. *See* Greek art and architecture; Roman art and architecture.

classical literature. *See* Greek literature; Latin literature.

classicism The aesthetic qualities that were embodied in the visual arts and literature of ancient Greece and Rome and served as ideals for various later European artistic movements. Qualities associated with the concept include harmony and balance of form, clarity of expression, and emotional restraint.
The Italian Renaissance of the 15th and 16th centuries was the first and most general attempt to revive these qualities in the arts. Major productions of this period included the sculpture of *Michelangelo, the paintings of *Raphael and *Titian, and the architecture of *Palladio. These achievements provided standards the emulation of which was the goal of artists throughout Europe during the next two centuries. The art of the French 17th-century painters *Poussin and *Claude was greatly influenced by their study of Renaissance and classical models. Examples of the various neoclassical movements in the 18th century include the paintings of *David and *Ingres in France and the sculpture of *Canova in Italy, while in England the lectures of Sir Joshua *Reynolds at the Royal Academy were based on classical and Renaissance doctrines.
In literature, Renaissance interpretations of Aristotle's *Poetics* influenced writers throughout Europe in the 17th and 18th centuries, notably in the reigns of Louis XIV (1643-1715) in France and Anne (1702-14) in England. The tragic dramas of *Racine and *Corneille represent classicism in literature at its height.
Towards the end of the 18th century there was a general reaction against the rigid neoclassicist doctrines, but the influences of classicism can still be seen in, for example, the art of *Picasso, the sculpture of *Rodin, and the poetry of T. S. *Eliot.

Classics In *flat racing in England, five annual races (*see* Derby; Oaks; One Thousand Guineas; St Leger; Two Thousand Guineas) for three-year-old horses only.

clathrate A compound formed by the physical trapping of the molecules of one substance in the crystal lattice of another. No chemical bonds are formed between the host compound and the trapped molecule. Zeolites form clathrates with many simple compounds by virtue of their cagelike crystal structure. Ice can also form clathrate compounds with some of the *noble gases.

Claudel, Paul (1868-1955) French dramatist and poet. He served as a diplomat in Europe, North and South America, and the Far East. Converted to Roman Catholicism at the age of 18, he wrote plays dominated by religious themes, especially the relationship between human and divine love, a theme explored both in the autobiographical *Partage de midi* (1906) and his best-known play, *The Satin Slipper* (1924). In *Cinq grandes odes* (1910) and other books he developed an expansively lyrical free-verse style.

Claude Lorraine (Claude Gellée; 1600-82) French landscape painter. He was born in Lorraine but settled permanently in Rome (1626), where he had earlier received his training. His idealized paintings of the Roman countryside sometimes include small biblical or classical figures and his seascapes and harbour scenes are remarkable for their glowing sunlight. Both were highly esteemed by such patrons as Pope Urban VIII. His *Liber veritatis* (British Museum), dating from 1635, documents his career through drawings and notes and was intended to prevent later forgeries.

Claudian (c. 370-404 AD) Roman poet. Born in Alexandria, he went to Rome in 395. His praise for Stilicho, elected consul in 400, gained him high civil status. His works include panegyrics, satires, epigrams, and the epic poem *The Rape of Proserpine.*

Claudius I (10 BC-54 AD) Roman emperor (41-54). Claudius owed his accession to the chaos that followed the murder of his nephew Emperor *Caligula. His rule was generally efficient: he extended the Empire, taking part in the invasion of Britain (43), but his susceptibility to the influence of freed men and of his third wife Valeria *Messalina alienated the Senate. *Agrippina the Younger, his niece and fourth wife, was suspected of his murder. Claudius had been taught by Livy and he himself wrote histories.

Clausewitz, Karl von (1780-1831) Prussian general and military theorist. In 1812 Clausewitz negotiated the Treaty of Tauroggen, which set in motion the joint Prussian, Russian, and British war effort against Napoleon. In 1818 Clausewitz became director of the German War Academy. Of his many military works the posthumously published *Vom Kriege* is the most famous. Rejecting old ideas of strategy and systems of war in favour of total warfare backed by the will of the people, *Vom Kriege* became a military classic and had a profound influence up to World War I.

Clausius, Rudolf Julius Emanuel (1822-88) German physicist, who in 1854 formulated the concept of *entropy and used it in a statement of the second law of thermodynamics. He also contributed to the development of the *kinetic theory of gases and suggested that electrolysis involved the dissociation of molecules into charged particles.

clavichord A keyboard instrument, popular from the 15th to the 18th centuries and revived in the mid-20th century. Its delicate tone is produced by small brass plates (called tangents) fixed to the end of each key, which strike the strings. Its body consists of a rectangular wooden box, usually without legs, which is portable and able to be placed on a table. It is strung lengthways and has a range of about four octaves. It is said to have been J. S. Bach's favourite instrument.

clavicle The collar bone. There are two clavicles, each running from the upper end of the breastbone to form a joint with the shoulder blade. They brace the shoulders and help to support the arms. Fractures of the clavicle are fairly common, caused by any fall involving the upper arm. *See* Plate IV.

clawed frog A South African aquatic frog, *Xenopus laevis*, also called platanna. Up to 12 cm long, with a flattened head and body, it has three short black claws on its hind feet, probably used for stirring up mud to confuse enemies. It is well known as the frog originally used in pregnancy tests.

clay A sedimentary deposit that has plastic properties when wet and hardens and cracks when dry. It consists of fine rock particles (less than 0.004 mm in diameter), formed from the decomposition of other rocks. The principal minerals present in clays (the clay minerals) are hydrous silicates, mainly of aluminium and magnesium, which occur as crystals with a layered structure, capable of absorbing and losing water. The main groups of clay minerals are kaolinite, montmorillonite-smectite, illite, and vermiculite.

Clay, Cassius. *See* Ali, Muhammad.

Clay, Henry (1777-1852) US politician; secretary of state

(1825-29). He was a leader of the War Hawks, who advocated the expansionist *War of 1812 with Britain. As secretary of state he helped to establish Pan-Americanism. Called "The Great Compromiser," he is best known for his various attempts at compromise (e.g. the Missouri Compromise of 1820) to hold the Union together on the issue of slavery.

clay-pigeon shooting. *See* shooting.

Cleanthes (c. 310-230 BC) Greek philosopher and follower of *Zeno of Citium. Cleanthes taught that reason is inherent in the nature of living things and virtue is voluntary assent to natural reason. *See also* Stoicism.

clearing house 1. An association of UK banks through which all the cheques from their branches are exchanged and the net amount owed by each bank to any other is calculated. The City of London clearing house exchanges cheques for £5,000 or more drawn on banks less than half a mile away in the "town clearing"; all others are dealt with in the "general clearing." The resulting debts and credits are entered as book transactions at the *Bank of England. Nonmember banks make arrangements with members. 2. Any institution that settles debts between members. For example, *commodity markets often use a clearing house to avoid passing cheques between strings of brokers, dealers, etc., all debts being settled by difference accounts through the clearing house on an appointed account day.

clearwing moth A moth of the widely distributed family *Sesiidae* (about 700 species), also called wasp moth. Many have clear wings and dark slender bodies with red or yellow markings, resembling bees and wasps. The larvae bore into roots and stems and are often serious pests.

cleavage The repeated division of a fertilized egg cell (zygote) to produce a ball of cells that forms the *blastula. In egg cells with little yolk, such as those of frogs and mammals, the entire cell divides: this is termed holoblastic cleavage. Meroblastic cleavage occurs in yolky egg cells, such as those of birds, when only the yolk-free region divides.

cleavers An annual herb, *Galium aparine*, also called goosegrass, native to Eurasia and widely introduced elsewhere. 15-120 cm high, this pernicious weed is named because of its habit of clinging by means of tiny hooks on its stems and leaves. Its hooked fruits enable efficient seed dispersal via humans and animals. Family: *Rubiaceae* (madder family).

Cleethorpes 53 34N 0 02W A resort in E England, on the S Humberside coast, at the mouth of the River Humber. Population (1981): 35 544.

clef (French: key) The symbol placed at the beginning of a musical stave to indicate the pitch of the notes. The treble clef, a decorative G, indicates that the second line up of the stave is the G above middle C; the bass clef, an archaic F, indicates that the fourth line up is the F below middle C. The C clef can be set on any of the lines of the stave to establish it as middle C; the alto clef (used for viola music) has the C on the middle line; the tenor clef (used for cello music) has the C on the fourth line up.

cleft palate An abnormality caused by failure of the left and right halves of the palate to fuse during embryonic development. It leaves the nasal and oral cavities in continuity and it may be associated with a *harelip. The cleft can be repaired surgically at 16 to 18 months of age.

Cleisthenes (d. 508 BC) Athenian politician, regarded as the architect of Athenian democracy. Cleisthenes, a member of the *Alcmaeonid family, achieved political power by appealing to the people for support and his democratic reforms (508) broadened the basis of political power in Athens. He is reputed to have introduced *ostracism.

Cleland, John (1709-89) English novelist. He served as consul in Turkey and as an agent for the East India Company, but was later several times imprisoned for debt. His best-known book is the pornographic novel *Fanny Hill* (1748-49).

Clematis A genus of herbaceous or woody plants (about 250 species), mainly climbing perennials, widely distributed in temperate regions. The fruits are often covered with persistent silky hairs, conspicuous and attractive in winter, as in traveller's joy, or old man's beard (*C. vitalba*) of Europe. There are many horticultural varieties, grown for their showy flowers, usually purple, pink, or white. Some species from which popular garden varieties have been developed are *C. alpina*, *C. montana*, and *C. patens*. Family: *Ranunculaceae*.

Clemenceau, Georges (1841-1929) French statesman; prime minister (1906-09, 1917-20). A member of the chamber of deputies from 1876 to 1893, when he became known as the Tiger for his attacks on other politicians, he subsequently devoted much of his energies to polemical journalism. During his first premiership he strengthened ties with Britain and broke irrevocably with the socialists at home. During the prewar years he urged military preparation against Germany and then attacked the World War I government for defeatism until again becoming prime minister, when he led France to victory. He condemned the failure of the Treaty of Versailles to provide for French security.

Clement I, St (late 1st century AD) The fourth bishop of Rome. He was the supposed author of several patristic texts, including a letter to the church of Corinth and the *Apostolic Constitutions*, which suggest that he was highly esteemed by the Church as a mediator and legislator. He probably suffered martyrdom. Feast day: 23 Nov.

Clement V (Bertrand de Got; 1264-1314) Pope (1305-14), first of the Avignon popes (*see* Avignon papacy). Clement was appointed by the influence of *Philip IV of France. Although he was a patron of learning, his pontificate was marked by venality, nepotism, and high taxation.

Clement VII (Giulio de' Medici; 1478-1534) Pope (1523-34). A cousin of *Leo X, as pope he attempted to follow a middle course between the conflicting policies of Emperor *Charles V and *Francis I of France. This affected his ability to deal effectively with *Henry VIII's divorce from Catherine of Aragon and explains his failure to curb Protestantism. Like other early Renaissance popes, he was a patron of the arts and learning.

Clement IX (Giulio Rospigliosi; 1600-69) Pope (1667-69). His pontificate was marked by disputes with Louis XIV concerning control of the French Church and Louis' harsh policy towards the Jansenists, whose persecution was stopped by the Peace of Clement IX (1669). Clement wrote both sacred and comic opera libretti besides sacred poetry and drama.

Clement XI (Giovanni Albani; 1649-1721) Pope (1700-21). Although austere and pious, he largely failed in the exercise of papal diplomacy, especially in the War of the *Spanish Succession, in the latter stages of which he reluctantly supported the Habsburg candidate. He also met with little success in attempts to defeat *Jansenism.

Clementi, Muzio (1752-1832) Italian pianist and composer. After settling in England in 1766, he became famous as a virtuoso, a composer of piano music, a teacher, a music publisher, and a piano manufacturer.

clementine A small *citrus tree bearing edible fruits, regarded by some as a hybrid between the tangerine and sweet orange; by others as a variety of tangerine. It is grown mainly in N Africa.

Clement of Alexandria (c. 150-c. 215 AD) Greek Christian theologian. He was probably born in Athens and is known to have studied Christianity at the school at Alexandria, of which he became head in 190. He was succeeded by his pupil *Origen after he had been forced to flee from Alexandria in 202 because of persecutions. Clement's writings are much influenced by *Gnosticism and his importance lies in

bringing Greek philosophical ideas in to supplement Christian belief.

Cleon (c. 422 BC) Athenian politician and demagogue. An artisan by birth, Cleon opposed the moderate imperialism of the aristocrats in the Peloponnesian War. He persuaded the Athenians to execute the rebellious citizens of Mytilene (427) but the decision was eventually reversed. Cleon opposed peace with Sparta (425) and was killed fighting at Amphipolis.

CLEOPATRA *A relief at the temple of Horus at Edfu shows Cleopatra (second from the right) as the goddess of love.*

Cleopatra VII (69-30 BC) Queen of Egypt (51-48, 47-30), famous as the mistress of Julius Caesar and then of Mark Antony. Cleopatra was coruler with her brother Ptolemy XIII (61-48), who ousted her in 48. Restored by Caesar, she accompanied him to Rome and gave birth to (allegedly) his son Caesarion. After Caesar's murder, Cleopatra returned to Egypt and in 41 she met Antony. In 37 he abandoned his wife Octavia and lived with Cleopatra, who bore him three sons. In 31 Antony's brother-in-law Octavian defeated Antony and Cleopatra at *Actium and in 30 they both committed suicide. Shakespeare's reconstruction of their story follows Plutarch's romantic account.

Cleopatra's Needles A pair of ancient Egyptian *obelisks carved in the reign of Thutmose III (c. 1475 BC) at Heliopolis. They were moved by *Augustus Caesar to Alexandria in 12 BC. They were moved again in 1878, one being set up on the Victoria Embankment, London, the other in Central Park, New York.

Clermont-Ferrand 45 47N 3 05E A city in central France, the capital of the Puy-de-Dôme department. Founded by the Romans, it was the ancient capital of Auvergne in the 16th century. It has a fine gothic cathedral and its university was established in 1810. Clermont-Ferrand has France's largest rubber industry and manufactures textiles, chemicals, food products, and metal goods. Population (1982 est): 151 092.

Cleveland 41 30N 81 41W A city in the USA, in Ohio on Lake Erie. It is a major Great Lakes port and the largest city in Ohio. One of the country's leading iron and steel centres, its other industries include oil refining, food processing, and the manufacture of motor vehicles. Population (1981): 565 775.

Cleveland A county in NE England, bordering on the North Sea. It was created in 1974 from parts of SE Durham and NE Yorkshire. It consists chiefly of lowlands rising to the Cleveland Hills in the S. The main river, the Tees, flows NE. Industry is important and includes chemicals, iron and steel, and engineering. Area: 583 sq km (255 sq mi). Population (1980): 573 822. Administrative centre: Middlesbrough.

Cleveland, Stephen Grover (1837-1908) US statesman; Democratic president (1885-89, 1893-97). His independence and honesty made the powerful Democrats of *Tammany Hall his enemies. In his first term as president he tried to stamp out graft and excessive tariff protection. His second term was troubled by a financial crisis and labour strife. He was repudiated by the Democrats and the Republicans won the election of 1896.

Cleveland Bay A breed of horse developed in the Cleveland region of N Yorkshire, England (now a separate county), and always reddish brown (bay) with black mane, tail, and legs. It has a deep muscular body with relatively short legs and was used as a pack and coach horse. Today Clevelands are used mainly for crossing with Thoroughbreds to produce showjumpers. Height: 1.57-1.68 m (15½-16½ hands).

Clianthus A genus of shrubs (4 species) found in Australia, New Zealand, Indochina, and the Philippines. Several are cultivated for their attractive flowers. The glory pea (*C. formosis*) is an evergreen semiprocumbent shrub, 100 cm high, with red and purple flowers. Family: *Leguminosae*.

click beetle A long narrow flat beetle, also called skipjack beetle, belonging to a large and worldwide family (*Elateridae*; 8000 species). If upturned it is able to right itself by springing into the air, making a clicking sound in the process. The larvae, known as wireworms, are serious pests of root crops. Species of the genus *Pyrophorus* are luminous, resembling *firefly beetles.

cliffbrake A *fern of the genus *Pellaea* (about 80 species), found worldwide on rocks, mainly limestone. It has small elongated blue-green branched fronds, which overlap at the leaf margins to protect the spore capsules. Family: *Sinopteridaceae*.

climate The long-term weather conditions prevalent in an area. Climate is determined by three main factors. The first is latitude and the tilt of the earth's axis, which determines the amount of solar radiation received by an area. Second, the distribution of land and sea will affect climate as the land heats and cools far more rapidly than the sea. Ocean currents will also modify a region's climate, for example, the warm Gulf Stream is responsible for keeping the NW coast of Europe ice free. The third factor is the altitude and topography of an area; temperature will fall with increased altitude and hills and mountain barriers force clouds to rise and produce rainfall. Over long periods major changes in climate may occur, as in the *Ice Age. The study of the climate is called **climatology**.

climax In ecology, the final stage in the process of ecological *succession, in which a stable community of plants and animals becomes established. In Europe, a typical climax community would be a deciduous woodland.

climbing perch A *labyrinth fish, *Anabas testudineus*, also called climbing or walking fish, that occurs in ponds and ditches of Asia. Its brownish-grey or greenish-grey body is about 25 cm long. It can travel overland for short periods using its tail, pectoral fins, and gill covers and during the dry season it lies dormant in mud.

clingfish A *bony fish, also called sucker, belonging to the family *Gobiesocidae* (about 100 species), found mainly in salt water. Clingfish have an elongated scaleless body, up to 7.5 cm long, a wide flattened head, and a suction disc formed from the pelvic fins with which it attaches itself to the bottom. Order: *Gobiesociformes*.

Clinton, De Witt (1769-1828) US statesman; governor of New York (1817-23, 1825-28). He became famous for his scheme to build the Erie Canal—"Clinton's Ditch," which was finished in 1825. It opened up the West by linking the Hudson River with the Great Lakes and made New York the most important US port.

Clio In Greek legend, goddess of history and one of the nine *Muses. She loved Pierus, King of Macedonia, and bore him a son, Hyacinthus.

clipper ship A fast sailing vessel developed in the 19th century for international commerce, so called because it clipped short the time required for a given passage. Clipper ships were designed more for speed than for their cargo capacity, which was relatively limited.

clitellum An external glandular beltlike swelling around the bodies of earthworms and leeches. It secretes the cocoon that contains the fertilized eggs.

clitoris. *See* penis.

Clive of Plassey, Robert, Baron (1725-74) British soldier and colonial administrator, who established British supremacy in India. He joined the East India Company in 1743, went to Madras, and made his name by capturing Arcot (1751) and holding it against a French-Indian force for 53 days. In 1757 he recaptured Calcutta from the Nawab of Bengal, Siraj-ud-Dawlah, whom he then defeated at *Plassey. This victory assured the East India Company control of Bengal, of which Clive was virtual ruler until 1760, when he returned to England. He was appointed governor and commander in chief of Bengal in 1764, remaining in office until 1767. He instituted many reforms but was subsequently named in an inquiry into the East India Company's affairs. He defended himself in parliament and was vindicated (1773) but committed suicide shortly afterwards.

cloaca The posterior chamber of the body in all vertebrate animals except the placental mammals, into which the digestive, urinary, and genital tracts open. Faeces, urine, and eggs or sperm are discharged through its vent.

carriage clock

grandfather (long case) clock   bracket clock

CLOCK *Three traditional forms of domestic clock.*

clock A mechanical device for measuring the passage of time. Clockwork has two essential components: an energy store (a raised weight or a coiled spring) and an escapement that regulates the release of energy from the store. The earliest recorded escapement was in a giant Chinese astronomical clock (c. 1090 AD). Early European clocks (called turret clocks from their usual position in church towers) were crude ironwork with verge escapements, driven by falling weights and recording time by striking on the hour, but the 14th-century Italian family of Dondi introduced dials on their sophisticated astronomical mechanisms. Late medieval clocks, such as the one (1392) in Wells Cathedral, England, were often embellished with ingenious automata. The innovation of mainsprings about 1500 enabled portable clocks (see also watch) to be made. Refinements in the 17th century were the anchor escapement (1671) and the application of pendulums to clockwork (see Huygens). Both resulted in greatly increased accuracy and during the next 150 years clocks successfully challenged *sundials as the principal domestic timekeepers. Long-case (grandfather) and bracket clocks assumed their modern forms. Carriage clocks were introduced in 1810 by the French firm of Breguet. An important advance in the 18th century was the development of an accurate marine chronometer, used by navigators to determine position. Scientific advances in the 20th century have led to the development of clocks powered by the natural vibrations of atoms (see atomic clocks). The *caesium clock, first made in 1955, is so accurate that one specific line in the spectrum of caesium is now the standard by which time is defined (see second), replacing the period of the earth's rotation.

Clodion (Claude Michel; 1738–1814) French *rococo sculptor. Working in Rome (1762–71) and Paris, he enjoyed a wide reputation until the French Revolution, when the rococo style was superseded by *neoclassicism. Although he specialized in small terracotta sculptures of nymphs, satyrs, etc., he also produced more sober works, notably the lifesize marble sculpture of Montesquieu (1783; Versailles).

cloisonné (French: partitioned) A technique of decorating metal surfaces with polychrome *enamelwork. Thin metal strips are soldered edgewise to the surface following the outlines of the design and the resulting compartments filled with coloured enamels. The work is then fired, fusion of the colours being prevented by the strips, and the surface ground smooth and polished. Beautiful cloisonné vases, brooches, etc., were produced in medieval Europe, while China and Japan perfected the technique in the 17th, 18th, and 19th centuries.

clone A population of organisms produced from a single parent cell by asexual division–for example by vegetative reproduction in plants or parthenogenesis in animals. The individuals of a clone are genetically identical. Thus cloning, if it could be achieved in humans, would provide the means of producing a whole generation of identical siblings–a concept that still remains in the realms of science fiction. However, some lower animals have been successfully cloned by inserting the nucleus of a somatic (body) cell of the animal to be cloned into an egg cell from which its own nucleus has been removed.

Clonmel 52 21N 7 42W A market town in the Republic of Ireland, the county town of Co Tipperary. Population (1981): 12 407.

closed shop A place of work in which all employees are required to be members of one or more specified trade unions. Closed shops are usually sanctioned by the employer, whose *collective bargaining position may be made simpler if the union (or unions) can speak for the whole workforce. The disadvantage of closed shops is that they exclude from employment those who object to belonging to a trade union.

Clostridium A genus of rod-shaped spore-forming bacteria that occur widely in soil and the gastrointestinal tract of animals and man. Some produce powerful toxins (poisons), particularly C. tetani, which causes *tetanus, and C. botulinum, which causes *botulism.

clothes moth A small *tineid moth whose larvae feed on clothes, carpets, blankets, etc. There are a number of species of widespread distribution. Adults generally have a wingspan of 12–25 mm and are pale grey-brown in colour. They prefer dark places. Pesticides, dry cleaning, and man-made fibres have reduced their damaging effects.

Clotho. See Fates.

Clotilda. See Clovis.

cloud A mass of minute water droplets or ice crystals, or a combination of both, produced by the condensation of water vapour in the atmosphere. When conditions are favourable the droplets grow and precipitation may occur. Various classifications of clouds exist but the one internationally agreed upon and most extensively used by meteorologists is based on cloud appearance and height and comprises ten principal forms. The high clouds, normally above 5000 m (16 000 ft) are *cirrus (Ci), *cirrostratus (Cs), and *cirrocumulus (Cc). The medium clouds at 2000–5000 m (6500–16 000 ft) comprise *altocumulus (Ac) and *altostratus (As). Below this level the low clouds are *stratus (St), *stratocumulus (Sc), and *nimbostratus (Ns). Some clouds grow vertically and cannot be classified solely by height; these are chiefly *cumulus (Cu) and cumulonimbus.

cloud chamber A device, invented by C. T. R. *Wilson, used to study the properties of ionizing particles. It contains a chamber filled with a saturated vapour. The vapour is expanded adiabatically (usually using a piston) to cool it and so make it supersaturated. When an ionizing particle passes through the chamber drops of liquid condense along its trail, thus making the trail visible.

clouded leopard A large nocturnal forest *cat, Neofelis nebulosa, of SE Asia, Borneo, Sumatra, and Java. It is 120–190 cm long including its tail (60–90 cm) and has a greyish or yellowish coat with black markings. It is an expert climber, using its heavy tail for balance, and feeds on birds and small mammals. □mammal.

Clouet, Jean (c. 1485–1540) Portrait painter, probably of Flemish origin. He worked in France as court painter to Francis I. The influence of Italian *Renaissance portraiture was stronger on his son **François Clouet** (c. 1515–72), who succeeded to his father's post in about 1540. François introduced informal poses, as in his portrait of *Diane de Poitiers (Washington), which shows her in her bath.

clove An evergreen Indonesian tree, Eugenia caryophyllata, growing to a height of 12 m. The dried flower buds are used as spice. The whole tree is aromatic, clove oil being distilled from the buds, stalks, and leaves for use in medicine and as artificial vanilla. Clove production was once a Dutch Indonesian monopoly but the trees are now grown in many regions. Family: Myrtaceae.

Clovelly 51 0N 4 24W A small resort and fishing village in SW England, in Devon, famous for its narrow stepped streets. Population (1981): 422.

clover An annual or perennial plant of the genus Trifolium (about 290 species), which also includes the *trefoils. Clovers, which occur mainly in N temperate regions, have leaves divided into three leaflets and dense heads of flowers. They are valuable as fodder plants and for their nitrogen-fixing ability. *Alsike, red clover (T. pratense), and crimson clover (T. incarnatum) are three widely grown and naturalized species. Family: *Leguminosae.

Clovis (c. 466–511) King of the Salian *Franks (481–511), of the Merovingian dynasty, who conquered N Gaul (494), founding a kingdom that dominated western Europe. He married (c. 493) Clotilda, (c. 475–c. 545), a fervent Christian, whose efforts to convert him succeeded after an important victory over the Alamanni (496), when he was baptized with some 3000 warriors. He was regarded as defender of the faith against *Arianism. After defeating the Visigoths near Poitiers (507), he established his capital at Paris. Clovis sponsored the promulgation of the *Salic Law.

Clovis point A fluted stone weapon point found in sites in many parts of North America after about 10 000 BC. They vary in length from 2.5 cm (1 in) to 19 cm (7½ in). *Compare* Folsom point.

clubfoot A deformity in which the foot is abnormally twisted at the ankle joint, so that the sole cannot rest flat on the ground when the person is standing. Its medical name is talipes. When the defect is present at birth it can often be corrected by strapping the foot in the correct position. Surgical correction may be necessary for severe deformities.

clubmoss A perennial mosslike plant, also called ground pine, belonging to a genus (*Lycopodium*; about 200 species) of *pteridophytes, found mainly in tropical and subtropical forests and mountainous regions. It has a creeping stem with wiry branches, densely covered with green, yellowish, or greyish needle-like leaves. The spore capsules occur at the base of special leaves (sporophylls), which are often arranged in conelike clusters (strobili). Family: *Lycopodiaceae*; class: *Lycopsida*. *See also* Selaginella.

clubroot A disease, caused by the fungus *Plasmodiophora brassicae*, that affects the roots of plants of the family *Cruciferae*, especially brassicas (cabbages, etc.). The infected cells become greatly enlarged, resulting in the deformed nodular roots characteristic of the disease. Control measures include liming, growing in clean soil, and using fungicides.

clubs. *See* London clubs; Working Men's Club and Institute Union.

Cluj (German name: Klausenburg, Hungarian name: Koloszvár) 46 47N 23 37E A city in NW Romania, on the River Someşul. A former capital of Transylvania, it possesses several educational institutions, including a university (1872). Its manufactures include metal products, chemicals, and textiles. Population (1983): 270 820.

Cluny 46 25N 4 39E A town in E France, in the Saône-et-Loire department. Its famous Benedictine abbey (founded 910 AD) became the centre of the Cluniac order, a reformed Benedictine order that was widely influential in Europe (c. 950–c. 1130). Population (1982 est): 47 000.

cluster of galaxies A group of *galaxies that are physically associated by mutual gravitational effects. Most galaxies are members of a cluster: our own Galaxy belongs to the *Local Group. The densest clusters contain a thousand or more galaxies. Adjacent clusters are loosely grouped into **superclusters**. Almost all the matter in the universe is concentrated in clusters and superclusters, which occupy only a few percent of the volume of space. *See also* star cluster.

clutch A device enabling two rotating shafts to be coupled and uncoupled. Positive clutches have square or spiral jaws to transmit torque without slipping. They can be used where slow speeds and light loads are involved, but normally both shafts have to be at rest for engagement. Friction clutches provide a period of slipping while the shafts are being engaged, and they do not have to be stopped for engagement. The torque is transmitted by friction between attachments to each shaft: in a plate clutch the attachments are flat discs, which press against each other; in a hydraulic clutch they are radial vanes immersed in a fluid. In a motor vehicle a clutch is used between the engine and the gearbox, usually a plate clutch for manual gearboxes and a hydraulic clutch for automatic transmissions.

Clutha River A river in New Zealand, the longest river in South Island. It flows generally S from Lake Wanaka, in the Southern Alps, to enter the Pacific Ocean near Kaitangata. Length: 340 km (210 mi).

Clwyd A county of NE Wales, bordering on the Irish Sea and the Dee estuary. It was created under local government reorganization in 1974 from Flintshire, most of Denbighshire, and E Merionethshire. It is mainly hilly with fertile valleys. Its many medieval castles reflect its turbulent past as a battle-

ground between the Welsh and English. Tourism is important. Industry has diversified since World War II to include steel, clothing, plastics, chemicals, and light engineering. Area: 2425 sq km (936 sq mi). Population (1983 est): 395 300. Administrative centre: Mold.

Clyde, Baron. *See* Campbell, Colin, Baron Clyde.

Clyde, River A river in W Scotland. Rising in SE Strathclyde Region, it flows NW through Glasgow and the *Clydebank to enter the Atlantic Ocean at the Firth of Clyde. Length: 170 km (106 mi).

Clydebank 55 54N 4 24W A town in W central Scotland, in Strathclyde Region on the River Clyde. Shipbuilding and the manufacture of sewing machines are the main industries. Population (1981): 51 656.

Clydesdale A breed of draught horse developed in the Clydesdale region of Scotland in the 18th century. It has a compact body with strong legs and feet and may be bay, brown, black, or chestnut. Height: about 1.75 m (17 hands).

Clytemnestra In Greek legend, the daughter of Tyndareus, King of Sparta, and Leda, and wife of *Agamemnon. She and her lover Aegisthus killed Agamemnon after the Trojan War and she herself was killed by her son *Orestes.

CND. *See* Campaign for Nuclear Disarmament.

Cnidos An ancient Greek city at the SW extremity of Asia Minor. Never politically important, Cnidos was known for its wine, *Praxiteles' statue of Aphrodite, and its medical school. The rebuilt city's rectangular street plan (c. 350 BC) is an outstanding example of Greek town planning.

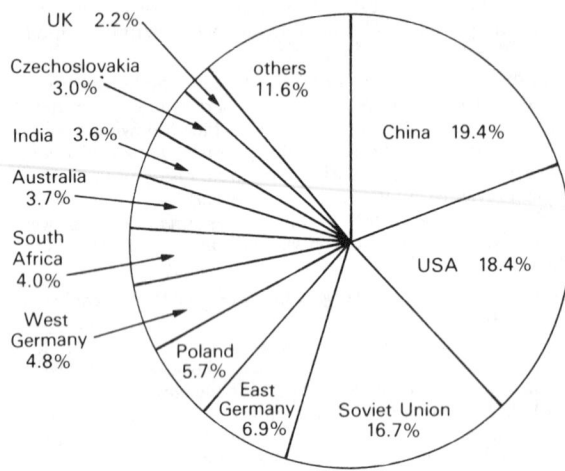

COAL *World production (1985).*

coal A carbonaceous mineral deposit used as a fuel and raw material for the plastics and chemical industries. Coal results from the compaction and heating of partially decomposed fossil vegetable matter. During the coalification process the plant remains are changed progressively from a peatlike material into lignite (brown coal), sub-bituminous and bituminous coal, semianthracite, and anthracite. During this process the percentage of carbon present increases and the moisture and volatile content decreases; anthracite is about 90% carbon. These coals are known as the humic coals. The sapropelic coals (cannel coal and boghead coal) are derived from finely divided vegetable matter (algae, spores, and fungal material). Most coal was formed in the Carboniferous period, although some of the younger coals, for example lignite, date from Mesozoic and Tertiary times.

Coal has been mined (*see* coalmining) in Britain since

Roman times but on a small scale until the industrial revolution. In about 1800 coal was being carbonized on a commercial scale for the first time, the resulting *coal gas being used for gas lighting and the coke for smelting iron ore. By the middle of the 19th century, interest in the by-products (coal tar, ammonia, and pitch) was awakening. The chemistry of the constituents of coal tar developed into the study of organic chemistry, and the use of aromatic compounds from coal tar led to the development of the dyestuffs and explosives industries. In the 20th century these products also became the foundation of the plastics industry. During the 1920s and 1930s processes were also developed (mainly in Germany) for converting coal into oil—providing Germany with valuable quantities of oil during World War II. Subsequently, *natural gas has largely replaced coal gas and petrochemicals (see oil) have to a considerable extent replaced coal tar as sources of organic raw materials. However, the rising price of oil products in the 1970s, reflecting their diminishing reserves, has reawakened a worldwide interest in coal. Recent world consumption is slightly in excess of 3000 million tonnes per annum and known reserves are capable of supplying this quantity for several centuries.

coal gas A gas consisting mainly of hydrogen (50%) and methane (30%), with some carbon monoxide (8%) and other gases. It is made by destructive distillation of coal, a process that involves heating it to 1000°C. Coal gas was formerly supplied to homes for heating and cooking, but it has now been largely replaced, in the UK, by *natural gas from the North Sea.

Coal Measures. *See* Carboniferous period.

coalmining The extraction of coal from below the ground. First, economically viable deposits of coal have to be located, and the necessary shafts sunk. Most mining in the UK is carried out by the **longwall advancing** method, in which a long straight wall of coal is exposed and gradually cut away, advancing from the shaft to the boundary of the mine. The **longwall retreating** method, in which roadways are cut through the coal and then worked back from the boundary to the shaft, is used to a lesser extent. Belt conveyors or railways are used to convey the coal from the face to the shaft; it is then wound mechanically to the surface in cages or skips. To provide for the safe and efficient conduct of coalmining, strict attention has to be paid to mine supports, explosive gases in the mine atmosphere, as well as ventilation, lighting, and drainage of the mine. The actual coalface activity was originally carried out with pick and shovel but in modern mines is now largely mechanized, some mining machinery being operated by remote control. The coal as mined from the coalface contains considerable quantities of dirt (stone and shale), which has to be removed, and the coal has to be graded and sized in preparation plants before it is marketed.

coal tit A Eurasian *tit, *Parus ater*. It is about 11 cm long with a grey back, buff underparts, a black crown and bib, and distinctive white cheeks and nape. It occurs in coniferous woodland, using its slender bill to extract insects from cones and beneath bark.

coastguard A paranaval force formed by some countries during the 19th century to hinder smuggling. In Britain it now deals principally with lifesaving and maritime safety through a network of coast-watching stations and provides a meteorological service. The US Coast Guard provides, in addition, navigational aids, including lighthouses, ice patrols, and ice breaking and is responsible for customs, immigration, oil-pollution control, and the enforcement of maritime law; it can also serve in war.

Coast Mountains A mountain range of W Canada, extending from the US border 1600 km (1000 mi) N into Alaska. Very rugged, it rises steeply from the Pacific coast. It includes Canada's largest mountain mass and a long glacier belt. Mount Waddington at 3978 m (13 260 ft) is the highest point.

Coastwatchers Civilian volunteers working for Australian naval intelligence. First enlisted in 1919 to observe potential attacks off the Australian coast, in World War II they worked in the Japanese-occupied Pacific Islands (1942-44).

Coatbridge 55 52N 4 01W A town in central Scotland, in Strathclyde Region. It has important metallurgical industries. Population (1981): 50 866.

Coates, Joseph Gordon (1878-1943) New Zealand statesman; Reform Party prime minister (1925-28) after W. F. Massey's death. He is best known for his stringent policies while minister of public works (1931-33) and of finance (1931-35) under G. Forbes, when he devalued the New Zealand pound, lowered interest rates, and encouraged trade within the British Commonwealth.

coati A carnivorous mammal, belonging to the genus *Nasua* (3 species), related to the *raccoons and occurring in Central and South American forests. About 1 m long including a 50-cm tapering tail, coatis have long snouts and greyish, reddish, or brown fur; they are good climbers, foraging in groups in trees or on the forest floor for seeds, eggs, and small mammals.

cob A type of horse common in the UK. It has a deep short body with relatively short strong legs, a small well-shaped head, and a powerful neck. Usually calm and steady, cobs are particularly useful for elderly or inexperienced riders. Height: usually under 1.6 m (15¾ hands).

cobalt (Co) A transition metal similar to iron and noted for its deep-blue colour when reacted in ceramics. It was discovered by G. Brandt (1694-1768) in 1735 and occurs naturally as cobaltite ($CoAsS$) and in copper, nickel, iron, silver, and lead ores. Cobalt is mined chiefly in Zaïre and Canada. It is used as an alloy in the manufacture of cutting steels and magnets. The chloride ($CoCl_2$) and oxides (CoO and Co_3O_4) are used in the glass and ceramics industry. The isotope ^{60}Co is a strong gamma-emitter produced in nuclear reactors and used in radiotherapy (the **cobalt bomb**) and in industry. At no 27; at wt 58.9332; mp 1495°C; bp 2870°C.

Cobbett, William (1763-1835) British journalist, who championed the cause of the underprivileged. After army service in Canada he accused his officers of corruption and was forced to flee Britain (1792), returning in 1800. In 1802 he began to publish his weekly *Political Register*. He was imprisoned (1810-12) for attacking the flogging of militiamen and in 1817 was again forced to flee to the USA. Returning to Britain in 1819, he began in 1821 the country tours described in his *Rural Rides* (1830). In 1831 he was prosecuted for encouraging a riot of agricultural labourers but escaped conviction.

Cobden, Richard (1804-65) British politician and economist, who was a leading advocate of free trade. A Manchester manufacturer, with John *Bright he formed the *Anti-Corn Law League (1839), which successfully fought for the repeal of the *Corn Laws (1846). An MP from 1843, he opposed Palmerston's "glory and gunpowder" foreign policy, negotiated an Anglo-French commercial treaty for the reduction of tariffs (1860), and campaigned for the 1867 Reform Act. In common with Bright, he was a leading member of the Manchester school of reformers and an outstanding orator.

Cóbh (name from 1849 until 1922: Queenstown) 51 51N 8 17W A port in the Republic of Ireland, in Co Cork on Cork Harbour. A port of call for Atlantic liners, it is also a resort and yachting centre. Population (1981): 6587.

Coblenz. *See* Koblenz.

cob nut. *See* hazel.

COBOL (*c*ommon *b*usiness *o*riented *l*anguage) An international computer-programming language, developed in the USA and used to express problems in commerce. A high-level language, it can describe business procedures in the form of readable English statements that are sufficiently standardized for use in a computer. *See also* program.

cobra A highly venomous snake occurring in warm regions of Africa and Asia and able to expand its neck ribs to form a hood. The king cobra (*Ophiophagus hannah*) of S Asia is over 3.6 m long, making it the largest venomous snake; it preys chiefly on other snakes. The common Indian cobra (*Naja naja*), used by snake charmers, is 1.7 m long and frequently enters houses at night in search of rats. The spitting cobra, or ringhals (*Hemachatus hemachatus*) and the black-necked cobra (*Naja nigricollis*), spit their venom into the eyes of attackers, causing blindness. Family: *Elapidae* (cobras, mambas, coral snakes). □reptile.

coca A Peruvian tree, *Erythroxylon coca*, cultivated in Java, South America, and Sri Lanka for its leaves, which—when dried —yield cocaine. Coca leaves have been chewed for centuries in South America for their effect in relieving fatigue and hunger; prolonged use can cause addiction and mental and physical damage. Family: *Erythroxylaceae*.

cocaine An alkaloid ($C_{17}H_{21}O_4N$) derived from *coca leaves and also made synthetically. The first drug to be used as a local anaesthetic, it has largely been replaced by safer drugs for this purpose (e.g. procaine) although it is still used in pain-killing mixtures for treating people with terminal illnesses (e.g. cancer). Cocaine is an addictive stimulant: it is taken for the euphoria produced by its action on the brain. *See* anaesthesia; drug dependence.

coccus Any spherical bacterium. Cocci may occur singly, in clusters, or in chains. Examples are *Neisseria gonorrhoeae* (the gonococcus, which causes gonorrhoea), *Staphylococcus*, and *Streptococcus*.

coccyx. *See* spine.

Cochabamba 17 26S 66 10W A city in Bolivia, situated in the E Andes. It is an important agricultural trading centre (especially for grain). Industries include oil refining and it is the site of a university (1832). Population (1982 est): 216 000.

Cochin 9 56N 76 15E A major port in India, in Kerala on the Malabar Coast. Founded by the Portuguese in the 16th century, it achieved its greatest prosperity under Dutch rule (1663–1795). It is the Indian Navy's major training centre. Population (1981 est): 513 249.

Cochinchina A region in S Vietnam, long ruled from Saigon (now Ho Chi Minh City). It was divided for centuries before being annexed by *Annam in the 18th century. Following the dissolution of the Vietnamese empire it was a French colony (1867–1945) and then an overseas territory before becoming part of independent Vietnam (1949).

cochineal A natural red dye obtained from the dried bodies of certain female scale insects, especially *Dactylopius coccus* of Mexico. It has now been largely replaced by aniline dyes, but continues to be used for colouring foodstuffs and cosmetics.

Cochise (d. 1874) Apache Indian chief, who terrorized the SW USA during the 1860s trying to prevent White settlement on his homeland. He surrendered in 1871 and White lines of communication were established. His people were given a reservation on their own land but after his death were ordered to more distant country.

cochlea. *See* ear.

Cochrane, Thomas, 10th Earl of Dundonald (1775–1860) British admiral. Cochrane was knighted after his flamboyant exploits in the Napoleonic Wars. As an MP (from 1806) he attacked naval corruption but in 1814 he was accused of fraud, and lost his knighthood, his parliamentary seat, and his commission. He was reinstated in 1832.

Cockaigne An imaginary land of wealth and luxury, celebrated in medieval folklore. There are houses of barley sugar, roast pigs running in the streets with knives and forks in their backs, and a mountain of cheese. It features in some of the fairytales of the brothers Grimm.

cockatiel A small Australian *cockatoo, *Nymphicus hol-

landicus, of interior grasslands. It is 32 cm long and has a grey plumage with white wing patches, a yellow head and crest, and reddish ear patches.

cockatoo A *parrot belonging to a genus (*Cacatua*; 17 species) ranging throughout Australia, Malaysia, and the Philippines. Cockatoos are usually white, often with a pink or yellow blush, although some species are black; all have a long erectile crest and a large hooked bill used to crack open nuts and extract grubs from wood.

cockchafer A European beetle, *Melolontha melolontha*, also called maybug, that is very destructive to plants (*see* chafer). Up to 35 mm long, it is black with reddish-brown legs and wing cases and has a loud buzzing flight. The larvae—which cause the most damage, particularly to cereals and grasses—are also called white grubs or rookworms.

Cockcroft, Sir John Douglas (1897–1967) British physicist, who shared the 1951 Nobel Prize with Ernest *Walton for their development of the first particle *accelerator. Their machine, built in 1932, was used for accelerating protons to split an atomic nucleus (of lithium) for the first time. In World War II he worked on the atom bomb and in 1946 became director of the Atomic Energy Research Establishment at Harwell. He was awarded the OM in 1957.

Cockerell, Charles Robert (1788–1863) British architect. Son of the architect Samuel Pepys Cockerell (1754–1827), he spent seven years abroad, developing a passion for Greek architecture that strongly influenced his work. His most notable buildings were Cambridge University Library (1836–42) and the Ashmolean Museum, Oxford (1841–45).

Cockerell, Sir Christopher Sydney (1910–   ) British engineer and inventor of the *hovercraft. After working on radar in World War II, he concentrated upon hydrodynamics. He filed his first patent for an air-cushion vehicle in 1955. The first practical hovercraft, the SR.NI, was launched in 1959, since when hovercraft have been built and used in many countries.

cocker spaniel A breed of gundog, thought to be of Spanish origin. It is compact with short legs, a short tail, and a square muzzle. The long flat silky coat is usually black, red, or cream, either plain or in mottled combinations. Height: 39–41 cm (dogs); 38 cm (bitches). □dog.

cockfighting A *blood sport in which two or more game-cocks fight against each other, often to the death. Illegal in Britain since 1849, it is still widespread in certain parts of the world. The cocks are carefully bred and trained, equipped with steel or bone spurs on their legs and set against each other in a cockpit. Being naturally fearless and very aggressive the cocks peck and gouge each other with intense fury. Heavy wagering is a feature of the sport.

cockle A *bivalve mollusc of the family *Cardiidae* (about 250 species). The ribbed shell valves, 1–23 cm in diameter, are rounded, producing a relatively globular bivalve. Cockles burrow in sand or mud, straining food particles from water drawn in through their protruding siphons. The European cockle (*Cardium* (or *Cerastoderma*) *edule*) is edible.

cocklebur An annual plant, *Xanthium strumarium*, 20–75 cm high, the fruiting heads of which are densely covered with hooked spines, which catch onto fur and clothing. It has been so widely and unintentionally dispersed by man and animals in warm and temperate regions that its place of origin is uncertain. Family: *Compositae*.

cockroach A nocturnal □insect belonging to the mainly tropical family *Blattidae* (3500 species). It has a black or brown flat body, 12–50 mm long, with long antennae and leathery forewings. Cockroaches seldom fly; they feed on plant and animal materials and can be household pests. A widely distributed species is the common cockroach, or black beetle (*Blatta orientalis*). Order: *Dictyoptera*.

cocksfoot A perennial *grass, *Dactylis glomerata*, also known as orchard grass, cultivated throughout North

America, Eurasia, and Africa as a pasture grass. It grows in dense tussocks, up to 1 m tall.

cocoa and chocolate Foods derived from the seeds of the cacao □tree (*Theobroma cacao*), native to tropical America and cultivated mainly in West Africa. The tree is pruned to a height of 5–6 m and woody pods, 23–30 cm long, grow directly from its trunk. The pods contain 25–50 seeds (cocoa, or cacao, beans) embedded in a whitish pulp, which are scraped out, fermented, and dried before export. Manufacturing is carried out mainly in the importing countries, where the beans are shelled, roasted, and ground. From them cocoa powder and chocolate are made. Cocoa butter, a fat retained in chocolate but removed from cocoa powder, is a rich source of food energy. Moulded chocolate is run into moulds, which sometimes contain dried fruit, nuts, etc., to make blocks and bars of chocolate. Couverture (or confectionery) chocolate is used for covering biscuits, preserves, etc. Family: *Sterculiaceae*.

cocodemer A *palm tree, *Lodoicea maldivica*, also known as double coconut, native to the Seychelles Islands. It grows 30 m tall and bears fleshy male and female flower spikes on separate plants. The female flowers produce the largest known fruit, up to 9 kg in weight, which takes ten years to ripen. It consists of a fleshy fibrous envelope surrounding a hard two-lobed nutlike portion, containing edible flesh.

coconut The fruit of the coconut *palm, *Cocos nucifera*; one of the most important tropical crops. The tree has a slender trunk, up to 25 m high, which bears a crown of giant feather-like leaves. The coconuts, 30–45 cm long and 15–20 cm in diameter, take a year to ripen and have a thick fibrous husk surrounding a single-seeded nut. The hollow core contains coconut milk; the white kernel is eaten raw or dried to yield copra, from which coconut oil is extracted for use in soaps, synthetic rubbers, and edible oils. The residual coconut cake is used as a livestock feed and the coarse husk fibre (coir) is used for matting, etc.

coconut crab. *See* robber crab.

Cocos Islands (*or* Keeling Islands) Two Australian coral atolls in the E Indian Ocean. They were visited by Charles Darwin (1836). First settled in 1826, they were controlled by the family of a Scottish settler, John Clunies-Ross, from 1827 to 1972, although under Australian administration after 1955. Following a referendum, they became part of Northern Territory in 1984. Copra is produced and there is an important meteorological station. Area: 13 sq km (5 sq mi). Population (1980): 487.

Cocteau, Jean (1889–1963) Immensely versatile French poet and artist. He made his name with the novel *Les Enfants terribles* (1929) and sketches written for *Diaghilev's ballet company, such as *Parade* (1917). In World War I he served as an ambulance driver and became acquainted with *Picasso, *Modigliani, *Apollinaire, and other leading painters and writers. His creative work includes poetry (*L'Ange Heurtebise*, 1925), plays (*Orphée*, 1926), novels, films (*Le Sang d'un poète*, 1929; and his own *Les Enfants terribles*, 1950), and graphic work in various media.

cod A carnivorous fish, *Gadus morhua*, that lives near the bottom in temperate N Atlantic waters and is commercially fished for food and liver oil (*see* Cod Wars). Its elongated body, up to 1.8 m long, is generally dark grey with spots and has three dorsal fins, two anal fins, and a whisker-like barbel on its lower jaw. *G. macrocephalus* is a similar N Pacific species. Family: *Gadidae* (haddock, ling, pollack, whiting, etc.); order: *Gadiformes*.

codeine An *analgesic drug used to relieve mild pain. It is a derivative of morphine but less toxic and less likely to become addictive. The combination of aspirin and codeine is a stronger pain killer than either of the two drugs used separately. Codeine combined with a chalky substance, such as kaolin, is an effective treatment for diarrhoea. It depresses the cough centre of the brain and is therefore often added to cough mixtures.

Code Napoléon The systematic collection of the *civil law of France. Drafted by a commission set up by *Napoleon I when he was first consul, the code—properly called the *Code Civil*—was brought into force in 1804. Representing the progressive legal thought of the time, it set out to be as clear and easily accessible as possible. It and the other codes subsequently produced under Napoleon's administration remain the basis of present French law and served as a model for civil law codes throughout Europe and the rest of the world.

codling moth A small European moth, *Cydia pomonella* (wingspan about 18 mm), whose caterpillars eat apples and similar fruit. A serious economic pest, it has spread worldwide wherever apples are cultivated.

cod-liver oil A pale yellow fatty oil obtained from the liver of the cod. It is a rich source of vitamins A and D and is used in medicine to correct the effects of such diseases as rickets.

JEAN COCTEAU *With Sergei Diaghilev (right), about 1924. Cocteau's memoirs are one of the best sources of information on Diaghilev's circle and the Ballets Russes.*

Cod Wars An intermittent dispute between Iceland and, chiefly, the UK over Iceland's extension of its fishing limits in response to depleted stocks of fish (notably *cod). In 1953 Iceland extended its fishing limit from 5 km (3 mi) to 6 km (4 mi) and in 1958, to 19 km (12 mi), thus seriously undermining the UK fishing industry. In retaliation the UK, on both occasions, temporarily closed its ports to Icelandic fish imports, and the dispute was only settled in 1961, when the UK agreed to the new limit in return for certain concessions. In 1973, however, Iceland extended the limit to 80.5 km (50 mi) but a temporary settlement was soon agreed with the UK. When this ran out in 1975, Iceland again extended the fishing limit, to 322 km (200 mi), which was not recognized by the International Court of Justice. British trawlers continued to fish within the 80.5-km limit and, coming into conflict with Icelandic coastguard vessels, were given the protection of British frigates. In February, 1976, the Icelandic Government broke diplomatic relations with the UK until a temporary settlement was agreed in June.

Cody, William F(rederick) (1846–1917) US showman, known as Buffalo Bill. An army scout and Pony Express rider, he gained his nickname from his success in supplying the men working on the Union (later Kansas) Pacific Railway with buffalo–killing 4280 in eight months (1867–68). In 1883 he began touring the USA and Europe with his Wild West Show.

Coe, Sebastian (1956–) British middle-distance runner. A gold medallist in the 1500 m race at the 1980 and 1984 Olympics, he has held the 1000 m world record (2 mins 12.18 secs) since 1981 and the 800 m record (1 min 41.73 secs) since 1985.

coeducation The education of both sexes together. Although support for the idea dates back to Plato, it has only recently been practised to any extent. Coeducation could be found in some elementary schools in the USA in the 17th century but it did not become widespread at all levels until the 20th century. Coeducation is also the norm in Scandinavia and in communist countries, and following World War II all Japanese schools became in principle coeducational. National attitudes still vary enormously, however, and many Muslim and Roman Catholic countries still favour the separate education of the sexes, especially during adolescence. In the UK mixed schools were slow to gain in popularity; coeducational primary schools are now the rule but until recently girls and boys frequently sat on different sides of the classroom and had separate playgrounds. The move towards comprehensive education has led to the establishment of mixed secondary schools and girls are now admitted to several boys' public schools. There has been a move towards mixed colleges since World War II; most universities are now coeducational.

coelacanth A *bony fish of the suborder *Coelacanthini*. Once thought to have been extinct for 60 million years, several living representatives have been found since the discovery, in 1938, of *Latimeria chalumnae* off the coast of SE Africa. It has a heavy body, up to 1.5 m long, with a short head and limblike fins, and crawls on the bottom, feeding on other fish. Order: *Crossopterygii*.

coelenterate An aquatic invertebrate animal of the phylum *Coelenterata* (or *Cnidaria*; about 9000 species), including *Hydra, *jellyfish, *sea anemones, *corals, etc. There are two different generations of the life cycle (*see* polyp; medusa) and either or both may occur. The body cavity has a single opening (mouth) and stinging cells (nematocysts) are used for defence or catching prey.

coeliac disease A disease in which the small intestine is abnormally sensitive to gliadin (a component of the protein *gluten, found in wheat). It results in abnormalities in the cells of the intestine, which cannot digest or absorb food. The symptoms include diarrhoea, stunted growth, and general malaise; the condition is treated by a gluten-free diet.

coelom The body cavity of many animals. In mammals (including man) the embryonic coelom is divided into three cavities, which become occupied by the lung, heart, and intestines. In the fully developed mammal the coelom is reduced to the virtually nonexistent spaces between the membranes lining the heart (the pericardium), the lungs (the pleura), and the intestines (the peritoneum).

Coen, Jan Pieterszoon (1587–1629) Dutch colonial administrator; governor general of the Dutch East Indies (1618–23, 1627–29). He first visited the East Indies in 1607, in the employ of the Dutch East India Company, which in 1614 appointed him to direct the Company's commerce in Asia. He instigated the conquest of the Banda Islands and the first Dutch settlement in Formosa (now Taiwan).

coenzyme A nonprotein substance that forms a complex with certain enzymes and is essential for the proper functioning of these enzymes. Coenzymes include nucleotide derivatives, such as *ATP and NAD, coenzyme A (important in the *Krebs cycle), and *vitamins of the B complex.

Coeur, Jacques (c. 1395–1456) French merchant, who became *argentier* (court banker) to Charles VII of France around 1440. He helped to finance Charles' recapture of Normandy from the English (1450) but, disliked and envied for his wealth and power, he was arrested (1451) on a false charge. He escaped from prison and fled to Rome.

coffee The seeds (called beans) of certain tropical evergreen trees of the genus *Coffea*, which–when roasted, ground, and brewed in hot water–yield a stimulating drink. *C. arabica* is the most widely grown coffee tree, producing the best quality beans. It is pruned to a height of 3–5 m for easy harvesting. *C. canephora* is more disease resistant, longer living, and can be grown at lower altitudes. *C. liberica*, of still lower quality, is grown in Malaysia and Guyana. The coffee beans are usually fermented, then sun dried before export. The main coffee-producing areas are South and Central America, Jamaica, East Africa, and Mysore in India. Family: *Rubiaceae*.

cofferdam A temporary walled structure to hold back water or earth while excavation or construction work is carried out. Thus they may be used to protect workers during the construction of a permanent *dam or *bridge piers across a river. They are made by driving sheets of sectional steel vertically into the ground and bolting or welding the sheets together. Occasionally concrete is used.

Cognac 45 42N 0 19W A town in W France, in the Charente department. Under French law, the name Cognac may only be applied to brandy produced in a certain area around Cognac. Associated manufactures include bottles, corks, and barrels. Population (1982 est): 20 995.

coherent radiation Electromagnetic radiation in which different waves have a constant *phase difference. Light from most sources is not coherent because it is emitted in random bursts. However, light from a *laser is coherent.

Cohn, Ferdinand Julius (1839–1884) German botanist, considered to be one of the founders of modern bacteriology. Following his early studies of algae and fungi, Cohn became interested in the identification of bacteria and established the basic elements of modern classifications. He also encouraged *Koch to publish his findings on anthrax.

Coimbatore 11 00N 76 57E A city in India, in Tamil Nadu. It is an agricultural processing centre for hides, cotton, and oilseeds and has an expanding manufacturing sector. Population (1981 est): 704 514.

Coimbra 40 12N 8 25W A city in central Portugal. It was formerly the capital of Portugal (1139–1260). It has two cathedrals and Portugal's oldest university, founded in Lisbon (1290) and transferred in 1537. Industries include the production of beer, wine, and pottery. Population (1981): 71 782.

coke A fuel consisting mainly of carbon. It is made by heating coal in the absence of air and is produced as a by-product of *coal gas. Coke is used in *blast furnaces and other industrial processes as well as for domestic heating.

Coke, Sir Edward (1552–1634) English lawyer and politician. Initially a staunch supporter of the Crown, Coke became speaker of the House of Commons in 1593 and attorney general in 1594. Under James I he was appointed chief justice of the King's Bench (1613) but was dismissed in 1616 because of his defence of the common law against the royal prerogative. Reviving his political career in 1620, he became a leading spokesman for the protection of parliament's liberties and was largely responsible for the Petition of Right.

Coke, Thomas William, Earl of Leicester of Holkham

(1752-1842) British agriculturalist, who introduced new farming systems. By using new crops and replacing cattle with sheep, he was able to improve the productivity of his estates at Holkham in Norfolk.

cola. See kola.

Cola A dynasty that ruled S India from the 10th to the 14th centuries. The empire of the Cola kings centred on Kanci and Tanjore and was marked by cultural and artistic distinction and social stability. In the early 11th century Cola power spread to Ceylon and Indonesia.

Colbert, Claudette (Lily Claudette Chauchoin; 1905-) US film actress, born in France. She is best known for her performances in Hollywood light comedies during the 1930s and 1940s. These include *Three-Cornered Moon* (1933), *It Happened One Night* (1934), and *Midnight* (1939).

Colbert, Jean-Baptiste (1619-83) French statesman; an outstanding financial reformer. Rising to power through the influence of Cardinal Mazarin, Colbert became comptroller general of finance in 1665 and strove to make France under *Louis XIV the dominant power in Europe. An advocate of *mercantilism, he reformed taxation, tariffs, and financial administration, built roads and canals, and largely created a French navy. He was a lavish patron of the arts and sciences but his cold personality won him the nickname *le Nord* ("the North").

Colchester 51 54N 0 54E A market town in SE England, in Essex on the River Colne. Founded by Cymbeline (Cunobelinus) in about 10 AD, Colchester was an important Roman town (Camulodunum); the Roman walls remain in part and there is a Norman castle. Essex University (1961) is nearby. Colchester's industries include engineering and printing. Population (1981): 81 945.

colchicine. See autumn crocus.

cold (or common cold) A mild but widespread viral disease affecting the mucous membranes of the nose and throat. Symptoms include a sore throat, running nose, sneezing, headache, a slight fever, and general aches and pains. The disease, which is transmitted by coughing and sneezing, usually lasts about a week: rest and mild *analgesics (such as aspirin) provide the only treatment required.

cold-bloodedness. See poikilothermy.

Cold Harbor, Battles of Two battles in the US *Civil War fought near Richmond, Virginia, the Confederate capital. In the first (27 June, 1862) the Confederate general, Robert E. *Lee defeated the Federal forces under George B. *McClellan, both sides suffering heavy losses. In the second (3-12 June, 1864), the Federal advance on Richmond under Ulysses S. *Grant was temporarily halted when he encountered Lee's entrenched forces. Despite his losses (7000 of his 100 000 men), Grant resumed his advance.

Colditz 51 08N 12 49E A town in East Germany, on the River Mulde. It is famous for its castle, built by *Augustus II on a cliff above the town, which was used as a top-security prisoner-of-war camp during World War II. Many escapes were attempted, some of which were successful.

cold storage A method of storing food or other perishables, such as photographic film, at a low temperature to prevent deterioration. *Refrigeration is used on a domestic scale in *freezing and also on an industrial scale in refrigerated warehouses, lorries, railway wagons, and ships' holds.

Coldstream 55 39N 2 15W A town in SE Scotland, on the English border. The Coldstream Guards were formed here in 1660. Like Gretna Green, it was a refuge for eloping couples. Population (1984): 1677.

Cold War The hostility between the USA and the Soviet Union, and their respective allies, following World War II. The term was first used in 1947 by the US politician Bernard *Baruch. Fear of nuclear war prevented a military confrontation, and the Cold War was fought on economic, political, and ideological fronts. At its most virulent in the

1950s, it had given way by the 1970s to the movement towards detente.

Coleoptera. See beetle.

Coleridge, Samuel Taylor (1772-1834) British poet and critic. His involvement in the 1790s in Robert *Southey's plan to start a utopian community in America resulted only in his unhappy marriage to Sara Fricker. In 1795 he met William *Wordsworth and their joint publication of *Lyrical Ballads* (first edition 1798) marked a decisive break with 18th-century poetry. His finest poems, such as *Kubla Khan* (1797) and *The Rime of the Ancient Mariner* (1797-98), were written at this time, but his personal life was troubled by his marriage, his poverty, and his increasing opium addiction. His subsequent creative energies were committed to journalism, lectures, and the writing of the critical and metaphysical *Biographia Literaria* (1817).

Coleridge-Taylor, Samuel (1875-1912) British composer, the son of a doctor from Sierra Leone and a British mother. Educated at the Royal College of Music, he is best known for the trilogy *Song of Hiawatha* (for solo voices, chorus, and orchestra; 1898-1900).

Colet, John (c. 1466-1519) English theologian and humanist. After his ordination, he lectured at Oxford, collaborating with Thomas More and Erasmus, prior to his appointment as dean of St Paul's Cathedral. He founded St Paul's School in 1509. He was a fierce opponent of Church corruption and published numerous theological works.

Colette (Sidonie-Gabrielle C.; 1873-1954) French novelist. After her divorce from her first husband, who had published her early novels (the *Claudine* series) under his own name, she became a music-hall performer in Paris. With *Chéri* (1920) and *La Fin de Chéri* (1926) she became an established writer, celebrated especially for her treatments of childhood and of the natural world, especially animals. Her long writing career was crowned with many official honours and awards.

Coleus A genus of herbaceous or shrubby plants (150 species) originating in the Old World tropics. Many cultivated varieties of the species *C. blumei* are grown for their variegated leaves of a diversity of colours, including red, purple, yellow, and green. They can easily be grown from cuttings at almost any time of year if kept at a temperature of 16°C. Family: *Labiatae.

colic A severe fluctuating abdominal pain, usually due to contraction of the wall of the intestines and caused by such conditions as constipation or obstruction. Colic in babies is quite common and usually due to air in the intestines.

Coligny, Gaspard II de, Seigneur de Châtillon (1519-72) French *Huguenot leader. He became an admiral of France in 1552 and was converted to Protestantism seven years later. He was chief commander of the Huguenots during the second and third *Wars of Religion but Catherine de' Medici, the mother of Charles IX, determined to end his influence over her son, arranged Coligny's murder in the *Saint Bartholomew's Day Massacre.

colitis Inflammation of the large intestine (the colon), causing abdominal pain and diarrhoea (sometimes with the passage of blood). Colitis can be caused by bacterial infection (e.g. dysentery) or by *Crohn's disease. In 'ulcerative colitis the colon becomes ulcerated. The latter condition, which fluctuates in severity, is treated with corticosteroids or sulphasalazine (a sulphonamide drug). Surgery may be required for severe cases.

collage A picture composed of a variety of glued-on scraps of materials, such as newspaper, wallpaper, cloth, string, wood veneer, etc. The first collage was made by *Picasso in 1912 with a piece of oilcloth. It was later followed by the collages of the *dada painters *Arp, *Ernst, and *Schwitters.

collagen A structural protein that is the main component of the white fibres of connective tissue. Inelastic but with great tensile strength, it is found in tendons and ligaments and also in skin, bone, and cartilage.

collar bone. *See* clavicle.

collards A variety of white cabbage, also called colewort, that is cut for use before the hearts become solid. They are grown from July-sown seed, thinned, but not transplanted. In the USA collards are leaves of *kale.

collateral security Property (e.g. shares, insurance policies, jewellery) pledged by a borrower, in addition to his promise to repay, as a safeguard for the repayment of a loan. On default the lender sells the collateral, deducts his debt and costs from the proceeds, and pays any balance to the borrower.

collective bargaining Bargaining between trade unions and employers on all matters relating to conditions of employment, rates of pay, etc. If agreement cannot be reached by bargaining, the dispute may be referred to *arbitration, or either side may take action against the other (*see* strikes; lockouts).

collective farms Agricultural cooperatives found especially in communist countries. Collectivization was instituted in the Soviet Union, with considerable ruthlessness, by Stalin in the late 1920s; widespread resistance necessitated some modifications in the mid-1930s. The farms and farm equipment belong to the state, which decides what is to be grown and in what quantities, but farmworkers, who live in surrounding villages, pay rent for their homes and are permitted to have their own garden plots and livestock; profits are shared in collective farms while in state farms workers receive wages. Collectivization was introduced into China in 1955. There, communes correspond to the Soviet collective farms. *See also* kibbutz.

collective unconscious In Jungian psychology, a body of images and ideas that are inherited and shared by all humans, rather than acquired by the individual. These ideas are called archetypes and *Jung believed them to be detected in the myths, dreams, and mental disturbances of mankind.

College of Arms (*or* Heralds' College) An English heraldic society, comprising three kings of arms, six heralds, and four pursuivants of arms. Its origins lie in the royal officers of arms, who received a charter from Richard III in 1484. The College was reincorporated in 1555. Its functions include the settling of rights to bear arms, which the kings may grant by letters patent.

colleges of education Institutions for the training of teachers in the UK. Until 1979 three-year nongraduate courses leading to a certificate of education were the norm, but this qualification is now being phased out as part of a move towards an all-graduate profession with direct entry to four-year Bachelor of Education degree courses. Colleges of education are also being gradually incorporated into other institutes of higher education, such as *universities and *polytechnics, or being combined with technical colleges to form colleges of higher education, which provide a full range of courses from A-level to postgraduate. There has been a marked reduction in the number of teachers in training from 100 000 in 1976-77 to 47 000 in 1981.

collie A breed of □dog originating in Scotland and widely used as a sheepdog. It has a streamlined body and a pointed muzzle. The rough-coated collie has a long dense coat and bushy tail; the smooth-coated variety has a shorter smooth coat and the bearded collie has a long coat with a shaggy beard. Collies are grey, fawn, or sandy, with or without white markings. Height: 56-61 cm (dogs); 51-56 cm (bitches).

Collier, Jeremy (1650-1726) English *Nonjuror. Imprisoned for refusing to take the oath of loyalty to William and Mary, Collier was later outlawed for giving absolution to two men who made an attempt on William's life. He became bishop of the Nonjurors in 1713. He is also known

for his *Short View of the Immorality and Profaneness of the English Stage* (1698).

collimator 1. A device used in conjunction with certain optical instruments for producing a beam of parallel light. A simple collimator consists of a slit placed at the focal point of a convex lens. 2. A device used to produce a beam of radiation of the required dimensions in *radiotherapy.

Collingwood, Cuthbert, 1st Baron (1750-1810) British admiral. He joined the navy at the age of 11 and fought outstandingly at the battles of the Glorious First of June (1794) and Cape St Vincent (1797) during the *Revolutionary and Napoleonic Wars. After Nelson's death at *Trafalgar (1805) he succeeded to his command and was eventually buried alongside him in St Paul's Cathedral.

Collingwood, Robin George (1889-1943) British philosopher, archaeologist, and historian, who taught philosophy at Oxford. His *New Leviathan* (1946) defends free institutions. *Essay on Philosophical Method* (1933), *Idea of Nature* (1945), and *Idea of History* (1946) present his own *idealism in relation to that of *Plato, *Hegel, and *Croce.

Collins, Michael (1890-1922) Irish nationalist; leading member of Sinn Féin. He was imprisoned for his part in the *Easter Rising (1916) and subsequently became finance minister in the republican government (1919). He played a major part in the negotiations that led to the establishment of the Irish Free State (1921) but was shot by republicans who opposed the Anglo-Irish treaty.

Collins, William (1721-59) British poet. He published *Persian Eclogues* (1742), influenced by Pope, while still studying at Oxford. His *Odes* (1747) were classical in form but foreshadowed Romanticism. After a breakdown in 1751 he was confined to an asylum in 1759.

Collins, William Wilkie (1824-89) British novelist. He worked in commerce and practised law before publishing *Memoirs* (1848) of his father, a landscape painter. During the 1850s he enjoyed a mutually beneficial association with Dickens and in 1860 published his pioneering mystery novel, *The Woman in White*. His other novels include *No Name* (1862) and *The Moonstone* (1868).

colloid A solution in which the solute (*or* disperse phase) is present in the solvent (dispersion medium) in the form of particles 10^{-9} to 10^{-6} m in length, rather than as single molecules or ions. If the disperse phase is solid and the dispersion medium is liquid the colloid is known as a **sol** (examples include milk, glue, and some drug preparations). If both are liquid the colloid is known as an **emulsion** (e.g. mayonnaise and most ointments). A colloidal suspension in which the particles of the disperse phase link together, with the dispersion medium circulating through the meshwork, is called a **gel** (e.g. a photographic emulsion). *See also* aerosols.

Colloids consist of charged particles. In lyophilic (solvent-loving) colloids, stability is achieved by attraction between the particles and the molecules of the dispersion medium. Lyophilic colloids are reversible in the sense that when the particles are removed from the solution, they will re-form a solution by simply mixing with the dispersion medium. Lyophobic (solvent-hating) colloids usually consist of large inorganic particles (e.g. clays, metals, etc.). They maintain stability by repulsion between similarly charged aggregates. They often precipitate on the addition of a salt and are irreversible.

Colman, George (1732-94) British dramatist and theatre manager. After studying law he became involved in the theatre through his friendship with the actor David *Garrick, with whom he collaborated on his best-known comedy, *The Clandestine Marriage* (1766). His son **George Colman, the Younger** (1762-1836) was a well-known writer of melodramas.

Colman, Ronald (1891-1958) British actor. He went to the USA in 1920 after military service during World War I and played leading romantic roles in such films as *Lost Horizon* (1937) and *Random Harvest* (1943).

Colmar 48 05N 7 21E A town in E France, the capital of the Haut-Rhin department. It was held by Germany from 1871 to 1919, and from 1940 until 1945. It has many notable buildings, including a Dominican monastery (13th–14th centuries). A trading centre for Alsatian wines, it has an important cotton industry. Population (1982 est): 63 764.

colobus A leaf-eating *Old World monkey belonging to the genus *Colobus* (3 species), of African forests, also called guereza. 50–70 cm long, colobus monkeys have long hands with small thumbs and their long silky fur is brightly marked. They have been widely hunted for their skins. □mammal.

colocynth The dried fruit of *Citrullus colocynthus*, a prostrate herbaceous perennial found in N Africa, the Middle East, and India and cultivated in Spain and Cyprus. It is a powerful laxative, used medicinally in very small amounts. It can cause poisoning. Family: *Cucurbitaceae*.

Cologne (German name: Köln) 50 56N 06 57E A city in W West Germany on the River Rhine, the largest in North Rhine-Westphalia. A port and major commercial centre, it is famed for its toilet water. Other industries include textiles, iron and steel, chemicals, and motor manufacture. It is the site of a university (1388) and the largest gothic cathedral in N Europe (founded 1248). The cathedral and the old gothic town hall were among the buildings reconstructed after World War II during which most of the city centre was destroyed. *History*: founded by the Romans, it became the capital of the northern empire in 258 AD and later the seat of Frankish kings. During the middle ages its archbishops were powerful princes and it flourished as a mercantile and cultural centre, where Albertus Magnus, Thomas Aquinas, and John Duns Scotus taught. In 1798 it was annexed by France, passing to Prussia in 1815. Population (1980 est): 976 800.

Colombey-les-Deux-Eglises 48 13N 4 54E A village in E central France, in the Haut-Marne department. It contained the former residence of Gen de Gaulle, who is buried here.

Colombia, Republic of A country in NW South America, on the Pacific Ocean and the Caribbean Sea. It consists chiefly of a hot swampy coastal plain, separated by ranges of the Andes from the pampas and the equatorial forests of the upper Amazon basin. The majority of the population is of mixed Spanish and Indian descent. *Economy*: mainly agricultural, the chief product is coffee, which accounts for over half the total exports. There is also widespread trafficking in and processing of cocaine. Although industry is largely undeveloped, the manufacturing section has expanded rapidly in recent decades and the export of such products as textiles and chemicals has risen sharply. The country is rich in mineral resources; gold production is the highest in South America and silver, copper, lead, and mercury are also mined. Colombia is one of the world's richest sources of platinum and emeralds. The most valuable natural resource, however, is oil. There are also large reserves of coal and natural gas. *History*: inhabited by Chibchas and other Indians before the Spanish colonization of the 16th century. In 1819 Simón Bolívar secured the independence of Greater Colombia, which included what are now Panama, Venezuela, and Ecuador as well as Colombia. This lasted until 1830 when Venezuela and Ecuador broke away; Panama became independent in 1903. In the 1950s civil war, caused by struggles between the Liberal and Conservative Parties, led to the dictatorship of Gen Gustavo Rojas Pinilla (1900–). He was overthrown in a military coup in 1957 and a more democratic government was re-established the following year. Since 1975 there has been considerable unrest, including strikes, student rioting, and guerrilla activity, notably that involving the left-wing organization M-19, which has staged numerous outbreaks of violence. In the 1986 presidential elections Virgilio

Barco Vargas (1921–) was elected to succeed Belisario Betancur, who had been in office since 1982. Official language: Spanish. Official religion: Roman Catholic. Official currency: Colombian peso of 100 centavos. Area: 1 138 914 sq km (456 535 sq mi). Population (1981 est): 27 800 000. Capital: Bogotá. Main port: Barranquilla.

Colombo 6 55N 79 52E The capital and main port of Sri Lanka, on the W coast at the mouth of the River Kelani. Founded by the Arabs in the 8th century AD, it was later developed by the Portuguese, the Dutch, and the British. Colombo has one of the largest artificial harbours in the world, from which tea, spices, and rubber are exported. The University of Sri Lanka was established here in 1972. Population (1981): 585 776.

Colombo, Matteo Realdo (?1516–59) Italian physician, who first described the circulation of blood between the heart and lungs. From his dissections of human cadavers he also described the membrane surrounding the lungs (pleura) and the membrane enclosing the abdominal organs (peritoneum).

Colombo Plan An agreement, signed in Colombo (Ceylon) in 1951, designed to foster economic development in the countries of S and SE Asia. It now has 27 members—21 countries within the region and Australia, Canada, Japan, New Zealand, the UK, and the USA. There is an annual meeting of the Consultative Committee, and financial arrangements are made between individual governments rather than from a central fund.

colon. *See* intestine.

Colón (former name: Aspinwall) 9 21N 79 54W A port in central Panama, at the Caribbean end of the Panama Canal. It is a major commercial centre; industries include oil refining. Population (1981 est): 117 000.

colophony. *See* rosin.

Colorado One of the Mountain States in the W central USA. The flat grass-covered Great Plains of the E are cut by the South Platte and Arkansas Rivers flowing E from the Rocky Mountains which cover the W half of the state and contain the valley of the Colorado River. Most of the population lives and works in a transition zone, the Colorado Piedmont, which divides the two regions. Manufacturing is the most important sector of Colorado's economy, especially the production of machinery, chemicals, military equipment, and food products. Mining is declining, although Colorado produces molybdenum, coal, oil, and sand and gravel. Tourism, especially winter sports, is of growing importance. The state's farmers are major producers of cattle along with pigs and lambs. As well as cultural and educational institutions the state has three important observatories. *History*: explored by the Spanish, part of Colorado was acquired by the USA in the Louisiana Purchase (1803) and part from Mexico in 1848. Following the discovery of gold (1859), it became a territory in 1861 and a state in 1876. Area: 269 998 sq km (104 247 sq mi). Population (1983): 3 139 000. Capital: Denver.

Colorado potato beetle A brown and yellow striped *leaf beetle, *Leptinotarsa decemlineata*, about 10 mm long. Both the adults and larvae eat potato leaves: the larvae also attack the tubers. It is native to W North America but has spread eastwards, throughout Europe, to become a serious pest of potato crops everywhere. □p. 296.

Colorado River A river in the W USA, rising in the Rocky Mountains and flowing SW through Colorado, Utah, and Arizona (where it passes through the *Grand Canyon) to the Gulf of California in Mexico. Its extensive use for irrigation and as a source of power (the many canyons providing ideal sites for dams, of which the Hoover Dam is one) is seen by conservationists as a serious threat to the natural landscape. Length: 2320 km (1440 mi).

COLORADO POTATO BEETLE   *A specimen on potato leaves. A heavy infestation of this pest can completely strip a plant of its leaves, so that the tubers do not develop.*

Colorado Springs 38 50N 104 50W A health resort in the USA, in Colorado situated at the foot of the Rocky Mountains. It is the site of the US Air Force Academy and the US Air Defence Command. Population (1980 est): 215 150.

coloratura (Italian: colouring) A style of vocal music characterized by elaborate and florid decorative passages. A **coloratura soprano** is a soprano whose voice is suited to such music. Donizetti and Verdi made effective use of the coloratura style in many of their operas; the Russian composer Reinhold Glière (1876–1956) wrote a concerto for wordless coloratura soprano voice and orchestra.

Colosseum An *amphitheatre in □Rome. Now one of the most impressive of all Roman remains, the Colosseum was begun (c. 70 AD) by the emperor *Vespasian. It is an elliptical building, four storeys high, 188 m (617 ft) long, and 156 m (512 ft) wide. It could seat 47 000 people and was used mainly for gladiatorial and wild-beast fights, but could be flooded for mock naval battles.

Colossians, Epistle of Paul to the A New Testament book written by the Apostle Paul about 60 AD to the church in Colossae in W Asia Minor. Its theme is that the Christian faith is sufficient and that speculative philosophy, specifically ideas that appear to be derived from *Gnosticism, diverts attention from this truth.

Colossus of Rhodes A gigantic statue of the sun god *Helios by the harbour of Rhodes. Cast in bronze by Chares of Lindos about 280 BC and standing about 31 m (100 ft) tall, it was counted among the *Seven Wonders of the World. An earthquake destroyed it 50 years after its completion.

colour The sensation produced when light of different wavelengths falls on the human eye. Although it is actually continuous, the visible spectrum is usually split into seven major colours: red, orange, yellow, green, blue, indigo, and violet, in order of decreasing wavelength (from about 6.5×10^{-7} m for red light to 4.2×10^{-7} m for violet). A mixture of all these colours in equal proportions gives white light; other colours are produced by varying the proportions or omitting components. Coloured pigments, dyes, and filters selectively absorb certain wavelengths, transmitting or reflecting the rest. Thus a red book illuminated by white light absorbs all the components of white light except red, which is reflected. This is a subtractive process, since the final colour is that remaining after absorption of the others. Combining coloured lights, on the other hand, is an additive process. A mixture of the whole spectrum gives white light, as will a mixture of lights of three *primary colours.

colour blindness The inability to distinguish certain colours. There are various forms of colour blindness, the most common of which is red-green colour blindness (the

inability to distinguish red and green). Colour blindness is an inherited condition: because it is a recessive trait carried on the X chromosome it is far more common in men than women (about 8% of males of Caucasian origin are colour blind). Very occasionally colour blindness may be due to disease of the retina (the light-sensitive layer of the eye). Diagnosis depends on the use of charts in which symbols made of colour dots are buried in a background of other dots. Inherited colour blindness cannot be cured, and sufferers must avoid activities in which the distinction of colour may be of importance.

colour photography The recording of *colour images on photographic *film that has three layers of light-sensitive emulsion, one for each of three *primary colours. Most colour film uses a subtractive reversal process. Coloured light entering the camera first falls on an emulsion sensitive only to blue light. On development of this layer, a black image is formed by deposition of silver where blue light has fallen. The unblackened areas are dyed yellow, the complementary colour of blue, and the silver deposit is removed. Since silver halide emulsions cannot be made insensitive to blue light, there is a yellow filter (to remove blue light) between the blue emulsion and the next layer, which is green-sensitive. This is developed to form a magenta image of the parts where no green light has fallen. The bottom layer is red-sensitive and gives a cyan (blue-green) negative image. When white light shines through the three superimposed images, the cyan dye subtracts red where it does not occur in the picture; the magenta subtracts green; and the yellow subtracts blue. The light emerging therefore reconstructs the original picture on a screen, in the case of a transparency, or onto printing paper. Positive colour paper prints directly from negatives that are not to be used for transparencies. These negatives incorporate dyes to correct for varying sensitivity in the printing-paper emulsion. For printing from transparencies, reversal colour paper is used and good colour reproduction is more difficult.

colour television. *See* television.

colour vision The ability of the human eye (and that of some other animals) to detect differences in the wavelength of light. The ability is due to the presence in the retina of the eye of cells known as cones (*see* retina), of which three types are believed to exist; one type being sensitive to red light, one to blue, and one to green. Light stimulates one or more of these types of cones in varying amounts depending on its colour. *See also* colour blindness.

Colt revolver A *revolver with a five-shot cylinder rotated and locked in line with the single barrel by cocking the weapon. Invented by the US engineer Samuel Colt (1814–62) in 1835, it became the .45 calibre Frontier Peacemaker (1873) and the standard .45 US army and navy revolver, remaining in service until 1945.

coltsfoot A perennial early-flowering herb, *Tussilago farfara*, 5–15 cm high, bearing yellow single flower heads on scaly stems before the leaves appear. Found in Eurasia, N Africa, and North America (introduced), it can be a persistent weed. The dried leaves were previously smoked to cure coughs and asthma. Family: *Compositae*.

colugo An arboreal mammal belonging to the genus *Cyanocephalus* and order *Dermoptera* (2 species), also called flying lemur, found in Asia, Borneo, and the Philippines. About 60 cm long, colugos have a membrane of skin, extending from the chin via the fore and hind limbs to the tail, with which they can glide up to 70 m. Colugos feed on leaves and fruit.

Colum, Padraic (Patrick Colm; 1881–1972) Irish poet and folklorist. Associated with *Yeats, *Synge, and other members of the Celtic literary revival, he founded *The Irish Review* in 1911. From 1914 he lived in the USA. His works include several volumes of lyrical poetry, plays, folklore anthologies, and a reminiscence of James *Joyce.

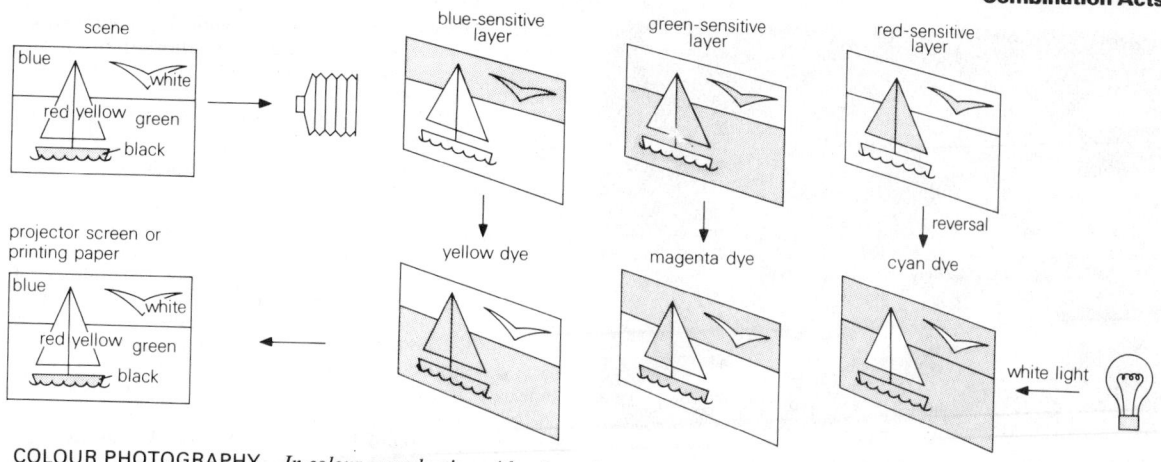

COLOUR PHOTOGRAPHY *In colour reproduction with subtractive reversal film, light from the different coloured areas of the scene forms negatives for each primary colour. These are dyed to form filters that subtract colours from white light to reconstruct the original picture.*

Columba, St (c. 521–597 AD) Irish missionary and abbot. Ordained in 551, he founded churches and monasteries in Ireland before setting up a monastery on Iona. From here, Scotland was evangelized. Feast day: 9 June.

Columban, St (*or St Columbanus; c. 543–615 AD*) Irish missionary and abbot. Establishing himself with 12 companions in Gaul in 590, he founded monasteries in the Vosges. Because of a conflict with the king, his monks went first to Switzerland and then to Italy in 612, where they founded a monastery at Bobbio in N Italy, which became an important centre of learning. Feast day: 23 Nov. Emblem: a bear.

Columbia 34 00N 81 00W A city in the USA, the capital of South Carolina. An important commercial centre, its industries include textiles, plastics, and machinery. Fort Jackson (a major US Army post) is adjacent to the city. The University of Carolina was established here in 1801. Population (1980 est): 101 208.

Columbia River A river in North America, flowing SW from British Columbia, through Washington State, to the Pacific Ocean at Oregon. It is an important source of hydroelectric power and forms the only deepwater harbour N of San Francisco. Length: 1930 km (1200 mi).

columbine. *See* Aquilegia.

columbium. *See* niobium.

Columbus 39 59N 83 03W A city in the USA, the capital of Ohio on the Scioto River. A major industrial and commercial centre of a rich agricultural area, its manufactures include aircraft, machinery, and footwear. It is the site of the Ohio State University (1872). Population ·(1980): 564 871.

Columbus 32 28N 84 59W A city in the USA, in W Georgia on the Chattahoochee River. The state's second largest city, its industries include textiles, food processing, and chemicals. Population (1980): 168 598.

Columbus, Christopher (1451–1506) Italian navigator, who discovered America. He was born in Genoa, became a pirate, and in 1476 was shipwrecked off the coast of Portugal, where he settled. He conceived the idea of reaching the East by sailing westwards but his plan was rejected by the Portuguese king (John the Perfect) and Columbus approached (1486) the Spanish monarchs Ferdinand and Isabella. He eventually won their patronage and on 3 August, 1492, set sail in the *Santa Maria*, accompanied by the *Pinta* and the *Niña*. On 12 Oct he landed on Watling Island (now San Salvador Island, in the Bahamas) and in Nov visited Hispaniola. On his return to Spain he was greatly honoured: Ferdinand and Isabella stood to receive him at court and offered him a seat. On his second voyage (1493–96) he discovered Guadeloupe, Puerto Rico, and Jamaica and founded the first town in the New World—named Isabella, after his patroness, it is now a ruin in the Dominican Republic. His third voyage (1498–1500) achieved the discovery of Trinidad and the mainland of South America but ended in disaster: in 1499, following a revolt against his command, a Spanish governor was dispatched to relieve Columbus, who was sent back in chains to Spain. On his arrival, however, he was released and compensated and shortly afterwards set off on his last voyage (1502–04). From this he returned ill and disheartened, dying not long afterwards in Valladolid. In 1542 his remains were taken to Hispaniola.

column. *See* orders of architecture.

Colwyn Bay 53 18N 3 43W A resort in North Wales, on the coast of Clwyd. Population (1981): 26 278.

coly A small grey or brown bird belonging to a family (*Coliidae*; 6 species) of Central and South Africa, also called mousebird because it creeps mouselike along branches. Colies are 30–35 cm long, including the long stiff tail feathers, and have a short crest, a short curved bill, and red legs with long claws. Order: *Coliiformes*.

coma In medicine, a state of deep unconsciousness in which the subject is unrousable and does not respond to pain. Coma can be caused by a *stroke, drug overdosage, meningitis, or head injuries. Treatment is that of the underlying condition, with the maintenance of respiration.

Comanche A North American Indian people of the southern Plains. They speak a language of the Uto-Aztecan group, closely related to *Shoshone. They migrated to this area from Wyoming in the 18th century. Horse breeders and fierce warriors, they often attacked white settlers in Texas until they agreed to settle in Oklahoma in 1867.

Comaneci, Nadia (1961–) Romanian gymnast, who in the 1976 Olympic Games won gold medals on the beam, the asymmetrical bars, and also in the individual all-round competition for women. She retired from competitive gymnastics in 1984.

Combination Acts (1799, 1800) The British laws that made illegal any combination of working men for the purpose of improving their working conditions. Provoked by the government's fear of revolutionary ideas spreading from France to England, they were unsuccessful in preventing the formation of trade unions and were repealed in 1824. An outbreak of strikes followed the repeal and another Act was passed (1825) allowing trade unions to exist but limiting their right to strike.

combine harvester   298

COMET *Halley's comet, as photographed in 1910, reappears every 76 years. The planet in the top right of the picture is Venus.*

combine harvester A machine for harvesting grain crops that combines the operations of cutting the crop (reaping) and separating the grain (threshing) from the rest of the plant. Horse-drawn models originated in the USA in the 1830s; in the 1940s, the predecessors of the modern self-propelled machines were introduced, replacing the earlier labour-intensive methods.

comb jelly. *See* ctenophere.

combustion A chemical reaction in which a substance combines with oxygen, producing heat and light. For a liquid or a solid to burn, the temperature must initially be high enough to release flammable vapour. To maintain combustion, the heat evolved must maintain this temperature to provide a constant supply of vapour. The oxidation reactions in combustion are generally chain reactions involving free radicals, the principal overall reactions being the oxidation of carbon to carbon dioxide and the oxidation of hydrogen to water (C + $2H_2$ + $2O_2 \rightarrow$ CO_2 + $2H_2O$).

COMECON. *See* Council for Mutual Economic Assistance.

Comédie-Française The French national theatre, founded in 1680 and reconstituted in 1803 by Napoleon. It is organized as a cooperative society, owned by its members. Probationary members are called *pensionnaires* and full members *sociétaires*; a pension is awarded on retirement after 20 years of service. Despite its strong emphasis on tradition, it has produced many of France's most original actors.

comedy A type of drama that evokes amusement and laughter. Traditionally, it deals with ordinary characters in everyday situations and ends happily, usually with a marriage. In *Shakespeare these elements blend with a more romantic narrative vein.
The earliest surviving comedies are those of the Greek dramatist *Aristophanes and the Romans *Plautus and *Terence (*see* Old Comedy; Middle Comedy; New Comedy; Roman Comedy). During the early 17th century the English dramatist Ben *Jonson pioneered the comedy of humours with characters who are gross caricatures of ruling passions. Examples of the satirical comedy of manners, in which more emphasis is placed on sophisticated witty dialogue, are the plays of *Congreve and *Wycherley in the late 17th century. The plays of Oscar *Wilde and Noel *Coward continued the tradition of the witty comedy of manners in England; otherwise comedy in the 20th century often reflects man's changed awareness of his own identity: the plays of *Ionesco and Samuel *Beckett, which often provoke laughter as a response to the meaninglessness of existence, are examples of what is sometimes labelled black comedy.

Comenius, John Amos (1592–1671) Czech theologian and educationalist. Comenius wrote widely on education, advocating a broad curriculum incorporating science, handicrafts, economics, and languages. He was commissioned by *Oxenstierna to reform Swedish schools (1641–48). A virulent opponent of the papacy, he was drawn to the mysticism of Jacob *Böhme.

comet A small body that moves, usually in a very elongated orbit, around the sun. A typical comet consists of a small nucleus of ice and dust surrounded by an immense tenuous luminous cloud of gas and dust, the coma. Tails of gas and of dust only appear when a comet is near the sun; they point away from the sun and may be millions of kilometres long. **Short-period comets** (such as *Halley's comet) have orbital periods of less than 150 years. The remainder have much longer periods, some exceeding 10 000 years, and move in approximately parabolic orbits. A comet eventually decays to produce a stream of meteoroids around its orbit. *See also* Oort cloud.

comfrey A perennial herbaceous plant, *Symphytum officinale*, also called boneset. Up to 100 cm high, it has drooping creamy or purplish flowers. Native to Europe and temperate Asia and formerly used medicinally, it is now grown as a garden flower, as are the related plants *S. grandiflorum* (yellow flowers) and *S. peregrinum* (blue and pink flowers). Family: *Boraginaceae*.

comic opera An opera with a humorous or farcical plot. It is characterized by spoken dialogue and a comic or satirical libretto. Among the most famous comic operas are the Savoy Operas of *Gilbert and *Sullivan. *Compare* opéra comique; opera buffa.

Cominform (Communist Information Bureau) An international communist organization. Founded in 1947, it united the Communist Parties of the Soviet Union, Bulgaria, Czechoslovakia, Hungary, Poland, Romania, Yugoslavia, France, and Italy. In 1948 Yugoslavia was expelled because of its refusal to follow the Soviet line. In 1956, partly in order to improve relations with Yugoslavia, the Soviet Union dissolved the Cominform. *See also* International.

COMMEDIA DELL'ARTE *The clown, Harlequin, and the cuckold, Pantaloon, in typical 16th-century Italian dress.*

Comintern. *See* International.

comitia Assemblies of the Roman people summoned by magistrates and held at an official meeting place (*comitium*) on an appointed day (*comitialis*). The three *comitia* corresponded to the three divisions of the people into curiae (*see* curia), *centuries, and tribes. The Comitia Curiata was the earliest assembly but its legislative functions became largely formal. The Comitia Centuriata elected the chief

299

magistrates and had some judicial powers. The Comitia Tributa was the assembly of the *plebeians; its enactments had authority after 287 BC.

commedia dell'arte An Italian form of popular theatre that flourished throughout Europe from the 16th to the 18th centuries. It was performed by professional actors whose comic and often vulgar improvisations were based on a set of stock situations, usually concerning romantic intrigues, and stereotyped characters. These included the clown *Harlequin, the cuckold Pantaloon, and the lover Inamorato. Its influence can be seen in the works of such contemporary dramatists as Molière and in the dramatic forms of *pantomime and *farce. Its characters were popular subjects for 18th-century porcelain figures. *See also* Punch and Judy.

commensalism A relationship between two individuals of different species in which one (the commensal) lives in, on, or with the other (the host), from which it derives food, shelter, support, or transport. The association neither harms nor benefits the host. An example is provided by certain barnacles, which live attached to whales. *See also* symbiosis.

commercial banks Institutions that safeguard (in current and deposit accounts) and lend money to companies and private individuals. In the UK, the commercial banks (or high-street banks) are public limited companies (joint-stock banks), most of which amalgamated during the 19th century to emerge after World War I as the big five: Barclays Bank, Lloyds Bank, Midland Bank, National Provincial Bank, and Westminster Bank (in 1968 the last two merged to form the National Westminster Bank). The commercial banks make a profit by lending at a higher rate of interest than their borrowing rate. The *Bank of England controls the amount that the commercial banks lend through *open market operations. Many commercial banks own subsidiary *merchant banks, which deal in the profitable secondary markets.

commesso (*or* Florentine mosaic) A method of making mosaic pictures of flowers, landscapes, religious scenes, etc., with polished semiprecious hard stones, such as lapis lazuli, agate, and jasper. Commesso pictures, which were used chiefly as tabletops and small wall panels, have been made since 1588 at a special Florentine workshop, which is now state supported.

Committees of Correspondence Liaison committees originally appointed by the American colonies for communication with England. As the American Revolution neared, the committees encouraged colonial cooperation against the Crown and provided leadership for the coming struggle. These intercolonial committees, first formed in Virginia, organized the first *Continental Congress (1774).

commode A low-level decorative chest of drawers or cupboard. As invented by André-Charles Boulle (1642–1732), the commode was an architectural piece of furniture, sarcophagus-shaped with heavy feet and fitted with drawers. It developed during the 18th century into an elegantly curved chest of drawers with *marquetry and *ormolu decoration. *Chippendale made important English examples.

commodity trading The buying and selling of natural products, such as metals, coffee, rubber, and cocoa, conducted in commodity exchanges or markets (e.g. the London Metal Exchange) by brokers on behalf of clients, who consist of producers, users, and speculators. The majority of dealings are in "futures" (goods for delivery at a stipulated date in the future) although "actuals" (goods for immediate delivery) are also traded in some exchanges. Trading in futures rarely involves the exchange of goods, most transactions being closed out by equal sales or purchases on the same market. Commodity exchanges enable producers and users to hedge their transactions in goods and help to stabilize prices by regulating supply and demand. *See also* international commodity agreements.

Commodus, Lucius Aelius Aurelius (161–93 AD) Roman emperor (180–92). The son of Marcus Aurelius, Commodus showed increasing signs of mental imbalance, believing he was the incarnation of the demigod Hercules. He became increasingly unpopular and was finally assassinated.

Common Agricultural Policy (CAP) The agricultural policy adopted by members of the EEC. The aims of the policy are to ensure reasonable living standards for farmers and to secure regular supplies and reasonable prices for consumers. CAP involves the distribution of grants and a price-support system. Grants for such farm improvements as land drainage account for about one-third of CAP's cost and are uncontroversial. The price-support policy, however, has many critics. Target prices are agreed that make production in the EEC profitable for farmers, but if market prices fall below these targets the EEC engages in support buying to keep the price up to an intervention price level (a proportion of the target price). The system is criticized because it tends to produce embarrassing surpluses (the butter, beef, and wine "mountains" have been notorious) and because there is in principle no limit to the support that may be given. In the 1980s the imposition of production quotas on certain items, such as milk, and attempts by member governments to restrict the import of some foodstuffs caused widespread protest.

Another contentious factor of CAP is **green money**. The green pound is the exchange rate used by the UK when trading with EEC partners in agricultural produce. Green money is criticized because there is no system for the automatic adjustment of green exchange rates. During the 1970s, as the pound devalued in response to market forces (*see* exchange rates), the stationary green pound became overvalued and support at the intervention price was therefore not worth as much to British as to other EEC farmers.

common law The part of the law of England and of most English-speaking countries that was originally unwritten and based on the common customs of the country. It developed with the rise of centralized government in England from the Norman Conquest (1066) to the 13th century, as the body of law common to all areas of the country. Its growth was the result of the principle of judicial precedent, by which an earlier judgment or decision was binding in deciding a similar case. Such decisions can only be overruled by statute or by a higher court. It is not the result of legislation and is therefore distinguished from the statute law established by Acts of Parliament. It is also distinguished from *equity, administered by the Court of *Chancery, and from the *civil law of most European countries.

Common Market. *See* European Economic Community.

Common Prayer, Book of The official liturgy of the Church of England. After the Reformation, Thomas *Cranmer and others began to formulate an order of worship in English. The first Prayer Book was published under Edward VI in 1549, with parliament's approval. Criticism by reformers led to a more Protestant revision in 1552. The Roman Catholic Queen Mary abolished the Prayer Book, and from the accession of Elizabeth I to the end of the Civil War, it was reinstated, further revised, and again abolished, this time by the Puritans. The version of 1662, established by the Act of Uniformity, is still in use; a revised version was authorized in 1928. An alternative service was introduced in 1980.

commons Unenclosed land for the common use of the inhabitants of a particular district. Originally, in every manor there was a tract of uncultivated land over which the inhabitants had **rights of common**, principally the rights to pasture animals, to fish (piscary), to cut wood, furze, etc. (estovers), and to dig turves (turbary). The Commons Registration Act (1965) provides for the maintenance of registers of all common land, village greens, and the rights of common and of ownership.

Commons, House of. *See* parliament.

common sense, philosophy of A philosophical movement

particularly associated with certain Scottish followers of Thomas *Reid and promoted in the 20th century by G. E. *Moore. It rejected the traditional philosphical *scepticism that had raised doubts about such questions as to whether material objects exist unperceived or whether other people exist. Common-sense philosophers base their case on the universal nonphilosophical consent on such subjects; while particular beliefs may be mistaken, there remains a broad base of common-sense views that must be certain.

Commonwealth (1649–53) The period in English history between the execution of Charles I and the establishment of the *Protectorate; the term is sometimes used synonymously with Interregnum to refer to the entire period between the execution of Charles I and the *Restoration in 1660.

Commonwealth (British) A loose association of 49 independent nations once subject to the imperial government of the UK (see Empire, British). The Commonwealth of Nations was established by the Statute of Westminster (1931), which was based on the principles, enunciated at the 1926 *Imperial Conference, of member states' autonomy, equality, and common allegiance to the Crown; its name was modified to the Commonwealth after World War II. Its member states, the populations of which comprise nearly a quarter of the world's population, are Antigua and Barbuda, Australia, the Bahamas, Bangladesh, Barbados, Belize, Botswana, Brunei, Canada, Cyprus, Dominica, Fiji, The Gambia, Ghana, Grenada, Guyana, India, Jamaica, Kenya, Kiribati, Lesotho, Malawi, Malaysia, Malta, Mauritius, New Zealand, Nigeria, Papua New Guinea, St Kitts-Nevis, St Lucia, Seychelles, Sierra Leone, Singapore, Solomon Islands, Sri Lanka, Swaziland, Tanzania, Tonga, Trinidad and Tobago, Uganda, the UK, Vanuatu, Western Samoa, Zambia, and Zimbabwe; Nauru, Tuvalu, Maldives, and St Vincent and the Grenadines are special members and are not represented at the meetings of Commonwealth heads of government; there are in addition a number of associated states and dependent territories. Ireland withdrew from the Commonwealth in 1949, South Africa in 1961, and Pakistan in 1971. Commonwealth heads of government meet every two years but finance ministers meet annually. These meetings are supplemented by other ministerial consultants as well as such permanent organizations as the Agricultural Bureaux, the Education Liaison Committee, and the Science Council. The Commonwealth Secretariat headquarters are at Marlborough House, Pall Mall, London, and its secretary general is the Guyanese, Shridath Ramphal (1928–).

Commonwealth Institute A centre of information about the British *Commonwealth. It moved from the Imperial Institute (founded in 1887) building in South Kensington, London, to a new building in Holland Park in 1962. It organizes exhibitions, conferences, and lectures.

commune An experimental community based on religious, social, political, or technological ideas, which are often incompatible with established social institutions. In the 19th century communes based upon the ideas of such men as Robert *Owen, Charles *Fourier, and William *Morris were established in Europe, the USA, and South America. They sought new physical environments, egalitarian principles of social organization, and the desire to achieve a harmonious integration of family, work, and learning. During the 1960s and 1970s many communes, based on collective living and often influenced by Eastern mysticism, were established by groups dissatisfied with modern technological society.

Commune of Paris (1871) A revolt in Paris against the conservative provisional government established at Versailles following French defeat in the Franco-Prussian War and the collapse of the Second Empire. Fearing a restoration of the monarchy, republican Parisians formed a revolutionary government (March) that was reminiscent of the French Revolutionary Commune (1793). Defeated by government troops in May, the Communards lost some 20 000 supporters, 38 000 were arrested, and 7000 deported.

communications satellite An unmanned artificial satellite by which long-distance television broadcasting, telephone communications, and computer data links are achieved. Radio signals, suitably modulated (see modulation), are sent from one transmitting station to the satellite, where they are amplified and retransmitted (at a different frequency) to one or more receiving stations. The orbits of communications satellites lie above the earth's atmosphere so that high-frequency radio waves (microwaves), which can penetrate the *ionosphere, must be used. The electronic equipment on board is powered primarily by solar cells (see solar power).

The first active satellite was the US Telstar 1, launched in 1962. Telstar and other early satellites were in relatively low elliptical orbits and were only visible for a short portion of their orbit. A communications satellite is now usually placed in a geostationary orbit. This is a circular orbit lying about 36 000 km above the earth's equator. The satellite completes such an orbit in the same time (24 hours) as the earth rotates on its axis and thus to a ground-based radio station appears to remain nearly stationary in the sky. Three or more satellites, suitably placed around the equatorial orbit, can provide worldwide communications links.

Various organizations, serving commercial, private, or government interests, have been set up to provide worldwide communications; notably **Intelsat** (International Telecommunications Satellite Organization), which was founded in 1964 and now has over 100 member countries. Communications satellites fall into four categories: domestic satellites of a country; international satellites in the fixed satellite service (FSS); satellites capable of direct broadcasting services (DBS); communications satellites not otherwise classified.

communism A movement based on the principle of communal ownership of all property. More specifically, it is associated with The Communist Manifesto (1848) of Marx and Engels according to which the capitalist profit-based system of private ownership is replaced by a communist society in which the means of production are communally owned. This process, initiated by the revolutionary overthrow of the bourgeoisie (see Marxism), passes through a transitional period marked by the dictatorship of the proletariat (see Leninism) and the preparatory stage of *socialism.

In the second half of the 19th century Marxist theories motivated several social democratic parties in Europe, although their policies later developed along the lines of reforming capitalism (hence the epithet "reformist") rather than overthrowing it. The exception was the Russian Social Democratic Labour Party, which finally demolished the Tsar's regime in the Revolution of November, 1917. In 1918 this party changed its name to the Communist Party of the Soviet Union, thus establishing the modern distinction between communism and socialism.

After the success of the Russian Revolution many socialist parties in other countries became communist parties, owing allegiance of varying degrees to the Soviet Communist Party (see International). In 1944–46 communist regimes were set up with the aid of the Soviet army in several E European countries, including Poland, Hungary, and Czechoslovakia. In 1949 the communists in China, again with Soviet support, overthrew the Nationalists and inaugurated the People's Republic of China. The subsequent Sino-Soviet split, made public in 1961, has since been an important factor in world politics. Apart from the Soviet Union and China there are now 12 communist states in the world–8 in Eastern Europe and those of North Korea, Vietnam, Mongolia, and Cuba (see also Kampuchea).

Since the early 1970s the term **Eurocommunism** has been used to refer to the policies of communist parties in W Europe, which have sought to break with the tradition of uncritical and unconditional support of the Soviet Union. Such parties are politically active and electorally significant in France and Italy. In the UK, the Communist Party of

Great Britain (founded in 1920) claims some 33 000 members but at present has no MPs.

Communism Peak (Russian name: Pik Kommunizma) 38 59N 72 01E The highest mountain in the Soviet Union, in the Pamirs in the S near the Afghan and Chinese borders. Height: 7495 m (24 589 ft).

community In ecology, an interdependent group of living organisms that occupies a particular habitat. The plants and animals of a community are closely associated with each other in various ecological relationships: for example, they depend on one another for food (*see* food chain). The size and composition of the community depend on the nature of the habitat and its climate; it may show seasonal changes. During ecological *succession, the structure of a community constantly changes until the stable climax community is established. *See also* ecology; ecosystem.

community service A form of sentence originating in Scandinavia and introduced in the UK by the Criminal Justice Act (1972). It requires an offender to work for a prescribed number of hours on behalf of the community instead of being imprisoned or fined. In the UK the offender must be aged 17 or over, have given his consent, and have committed no violence.

commutative law The mathematical rule, obeyed by addition and multiplication but not division, that the result of an operation combining two quantities is independent of the order in which they are taken: for addition, $a + b = b + a$, and for multiplication, $ab = ba$.

Commynes, Philippe de (c. 1445–1511) French statesman and chronicler. He served Charles the Bold, Duke of Burgundy, from 1464 and Louis XI from 1472. On the accession of Charles VIII in 1483 he was imprisoned but later returned to favour. His *Mémoires* (1524) are important historical records of the reign of Louis XI and the Italian expedition of Charles VIII, and embody his advanced political theories.

Como 45 48N 09 05E A city and resort in N Italy, in Lombardy on Lake Como. Known as Comum in Roman times, it is the birthplace of the elder and younger Pliny. It fell to the Visconti in 1335 and in 1859 was liberated from Austrian occupation by Garibaldi. It has a 15th-century marble cathedral and a gothic town hall. Como is an important tourist centre and has several industries, including the famous silk factories. Population (1981 est): 95 183.

Como, Lake A lake in central N Italy, lying in a narrow forked valley at the S foot of the Alps. It is about 50 km (31 mi) long, dividing into two arms about halfway along, with a maximum depth of 410 m (1345 ft). There are many fashionable resorts on its shore such as Bellagio, Como, and Lecco. Area: 145 sq km (55 sq mi).

Comodoro Rivadavia 45 50S 67 30W A port in SE Argentina, on the Atlantic Ocean. It is Argentina's main oil-producing centre; a natural gas pipeline extends for 1770 km (1100 mi) to Buenos Aires. Population (1980 est): 96 865.

Comorin, Cape 08 04N 77 35E A headland in India, the most southerly point of the subcontinent.

Comoros, Federal and Islamic Republic of the A country consisting of a group of islands in the Indian Ocean, between the NW coast of Madagascar and the African mainland. The main islands are Grand Comoro, Anjouan, and Mohéli and exclude the island of Mayotte, which has remained French. The population is of mixed African and Arab descent. *Economy*: almost entirely agricultural. The soils are fertile but the relatively undeveloped farming has suffered since French aid was withdrawn in 1975. Sugar cane was formerly the main crop but others, such as vanilla and perfume plants, are now increasing in importance. Exports include vanilla, sisal, and essential oils such as ylang-ylang. *History*: there were successive African, Malay, Malagasy, Arab, and other immigrations to the islands before they became a French colony in the 19th century. At first joined to Madagascar, the Comoros became a separate French

overseas territory in 1947. Moves towards independence in the early 1970s culminated in a referendum in 1974 in which the majority voted in favour of independence, except for the island of Mayotte, which voted to remain French. Mayotte has since been made an overseas department of France. Ahmed Abdallah became the first president in 1975 but later that year was overthrown in a military coup led by Ali Soilih. The government was taken over by a National Revolutionary Council. In 1976 the independence of the three islands was recognized by France and Soilih was elected president. He was overthrown (and later killed) in a military coup in 1978 and a Political-Military Directorate took over. The exiled Ahmed Abdallah and Mohammed Ahmed were invited to return and appointed copresidents. In October Ahmed Abdallah was elected as the first president of the Federal Islamic Comoro Republic for a six-year term, following the approval of a new federal style constitution, with provision for the inclusion of Mayotte. Official languages: French and Arabic; Swahili is also used commercially. Official currency: CFA franc of 100 centimes. Area: 1862 sq km (719 sq mi). Population (1980 est): 300 200. Capital and main port: Moroni.

compact disc (CD) A 120 mm metal disc covered in clear plastic, used for recording digital information. Data is represented by tracks cut in the disc and is read by a laser beam. The most common application is the high fidelity *recording of sound using digital recording, but compact discs are also used as high capacity read-only memory (**CD-ROM**) for computers.

Companies Act A series of UK Acts of Parliament, for the most part consolidated in the Companies Act (1985), regulating the formation, management, and winding up of companies. The Act enables businesses to be incorporated by registration with the Registrar of Companies. Incorporated companies have a legal identity and *limited liability. The Act prescribes the duties of directors, who manage the company and are responsible for protecting the interests of members (shareholders) and employees. Every company must have two or more members. Shares in a public company are freely transferable, but those in a private company cannot be sold to the public.

Companions of Honour, Order of the (CH) British order of chivalry, instituted in 1917. It comprises the sovereign and not more than 65 men and women who have made conspicuous contributions to the nation.

compass A device for determining the direction of magnetic north. The magnetic compass, which has been in use as an aid to navigation probably since the 2nd century BC, consists of a magnetic needle balanced on a point, allowing it to pivot freely. The S end of the magnet indicates magnetic N, as shown on a card (called a compass card) marked with the points of the compass and fixed below it. In some magnetic compasses, the entire card pivots, indicating direction against a mark on the fixed housing. Such compasses are often filled with a fluid (usually alcohol) for damping. A more sophisticated kind of compass, used on larger vessels and in aircraft, is the **gyrocompass**, which employs the effect of the earth's rotation on the orientation of a spinning object's axis of rotation. Magnetic compasses are subject to interference from nearby ferrous metal objects and fittings, and compasses must be adjusted to compensate for distortion. Compensation must also be made, in the reading of a compass, for magnetic N not being in the same direction as geographic N in most longitudes. Up-to-date navigation charts mark on a compass rose the annual correction for position that must be allowed in various longitudes. □ p. 302.

Compiègne 49 25N 2 50E A town and resort in N France, in the Oise department on the River Oise. Joan of Arc was captured here by the English in 1430. A railway coach in the forest of Compiègne was the scene of the signing of the Armistice (1918) ending World War I and of the agreement made between the Pétain government and Hitler in 1940.

Industries include machinery, printing, and rubber. Population (1982 est): 43 311.

complementarity principle The principle, proposed by Niels *Bohr, that an elementary particle may be regarded as either corpuscular or wavelike. Thus an experiment designed to detect a corpuscular property cannot, at the same time, detect a wave property, and vice versa. *See also* de Broglie wave.

complex In psychoanalysis, a group of associated ideas that are unacceptable to the conscious mind and have therefore been repressed into the *unconscious. Although the individual is no longer aware of these ideas they continue to influence his (or her) behaviour. *See* inferiority complex; Oedipus complex.

magnetic compass

gyro compass

COMPASS *In the magnetic compass, the magnetized needle lines up with the earth's magnetic field. In the gyrocompass a spinning gyroscope is suspended on three mutually perpendicular frames. The axis of spin of a free gyroscope shifts round as the earth rotates: as the axis of the gyrocompass moves from the horizontal at position A to position B, a weight pulls it downwards. As a result of the gyroscopic effect, the axis shifts round at right angles to the gravitational force (precesses) and describes a circle around the N-S direction. When the precession is damped, the gyroscope axis settles down pointing N.*

complex numbers Quantities that consist of a real number and an imaginary number. They may be written in the form $a + ib$, where a and b are real numbers and $i = \sqrt{-1}$. Two complex numbers can be added and subtracted: for example $(a + ib) + (c + id) = (a + c) + i(b + d)$. They may also be multiplied and divided into each other. A complex number $a + ib$ may be thought of as a pair of ordered numbers (a,b) similar

to a pair of *Cartesian coordinates (x,y). Then (a,b) can be regarded as a point on a plane called the complex plane or Argand diagram in which the real axis is taken as horizontal and the imaginary axis as vertical. Complex numbers are widely used in the physical sciences, particularly in electrical engineering in calculations concerning alternating current.

Compositae The largest family of flowering plants (about 900 genera and 14 000 species). They vary from small herbs to trees and are found worldwide. The tiny flowers are grouped into heads that resemble a single large flower. The individual florets may be similar, as in thistles, or of two types (disc and ray flowers), as in daisies. Many composites are cultivated as ornamentals (e.g. chrysanthemums and dahlias); others are agricultural weeds (daisies, dandelions, etc.) and some are edible (such as lettuce).

Composite order. *See* orders of architecture.

comprehensive schools Secondary schools attended by children of all abilities, known in the USA as a "one-track" school system. The extent to which comprehensives select internally for aptitude and ability varies considerably, some schools retaining mixed-ability classes at all levels. In the USA attempts to achieve a balanced "social mix" led to the controversial "bussing" of children from one area to another. In the UK the widespread introduction of comprehensive schools was initiated in 1965 by the Labour Government and by 1977 some 70% of the secondary-school population attended comprehensives. Opposition to comprehensive education remains, however, and since the return of a Conservative Government in 1979 Local Education Authorities (LEAs) are no longer required to abolish selective schools (*see* grammar schools).

compressor A machine for delivering high-pressure gas. They have a wide variety of uses, from small garage machines for inflating tyres to large industrial machines for supplying compressed-air lines. The piston compressor resembles an internal-combustion engine in reverse and is driven by an electric motor or a diesel engine. The centrifugal compressor uses radial vanes to increase the momentum of the gas; they are extensively used in *gas turbines (driven by the turbine shaft) to supply pressurized air to the combustion chambers.

Compton, Arthur Holly (1892–1962) US physicist, who discovered the *Compton effect (1923) while analysing the scattering of X-rays by matter. He could only explain the effect by assuming that the X-rays consisted of photons, then still a novel idea. He shared the 1927 Nobel Prize with C. T. R. *Wilson.

Compton, Denis (Charles Scott) (1918–   ) British cricketer, who played for Middlesex and England (1937–57). In 1947 he broke two records: scoring 18 centuries and a total of 3816 runs in one season. He also played Association football for Arsenal and England.

Compton-Burnett, Dame Ivy (1892–1969) British novelist. *Pastors and Masters* (1925) was the first of a series of 17 novels set in a stylized Victorian-Edwardian upper-class world. The series includes *Brothers and Sisters* (1929), *A House and Its Head* (1935), *A Family and a Fortune* (1939), and *Manservant and Maidservant* (1947).

Compton effect The increase in the wavelength of electromagnetic radiation when it is scattered by free electrons. The effect can only be explained by regarding the radiation as consisting of particles called photons. Part of the photon's energy is transferred to the electron, the velocity of which is thereby increased. Named after Arthur *Compton.

computer A device for processing information at high speeds, by electronic methods. The principles behind the modern computer were conceived by Charles *Babbage in the 19th century. The first practical machines were built in Britain and the USA during World War II. Postwar developments in *information theory and the invention of the *transistor made possible the computer revolution of the next 20 years. Since the 1970s, advances in integrated circuits using silicon chips have led to the development of *minicomputers and then *microcomputers, which have become sufficiently cheap to be bought by private citizens.

A **digital computer** processes information in the form of groups of binary numbers (see bit), which are represented by the on and off positions of electronic switches. The sequence of operations it performs on this information is controlled by a *program, and the suite of programs that enables a computer to perform useful functions is called its *software. The physical equipment, or **hardware**, of a computer generally has three main components: the central processing unit (CPU), main memory, and peripheral devices that enable information to be fed into the machine, display it in a readable form, or act as auxiliary memory. Input, formerly by punched tape or cards, is now by keyboard at a visual display unit (VDU) or by methods of automatic data capture, such as optical character recognition (**OCR**). Output is by printout on paper, VDU, or magnetic disc or tape. New developments, such as the use of *compact discs as large permanent memories and the development of CPUs that work much faster by using optical rather than electrical impulses, promise to increase the power of computers. The **transputer**, which harnesses several microprocessors in parallel, seems to offer microcomputer users the computing speed that is currently only available on large mainframe computers.

An **analog computer** is a device that deals with continuously varying physical quantities, such as current or voltage. They are used mainly for simulation or monitoring and controlling continuous processes in industry or scientific research. Sometimes they act as peripheral devices for a digital computer (a combination known as a **hybrid computer**).

Comte, Auguste (1798–1857) French philosopher. Often said to be the founder of sociology, he coined and defined the term, although work of a sociological nature had been done long before his time. He is best remembered for his positivism (the view that society could be studied scientifically by natural-science methods and was subject to general laws); his Law of the Three Stages of intellectual development (theological, metaphysical, and positive); and his view that the theoretical sciences formed a hierarchy, with sociology at the peak providing a basis for social planning and reorganization. His principal work is *Cours de philosophie positive* (6 vols, 1830–42).

Conakry (or Konakry) 9 25N 13 56W The capital of Guinea, a port in the SW on Tombo Island, which is linked to the mainland by a causeway. It was founded by the French in 1884 and became capital of French Guinea in 1893. Population (1980 est): 575 000.

concentration camps Prisons in which people are held without trial, usually on account of their politics or race. From 1900 to 1902, during the second *Boer War, the British detained civilian Afrikaners in concentration camps, with the loss of some 20 000 lives.

In Germany, camps were first established by the Nazis in 1933 to detain communists and Social Democrats; they were later used to imprison minority groups, such as Gipsies, homosexuals, and, above all, Jews. In 1940 the Nazis established extermination centres, the most notorious being Auschwitz and Treblinka in Poland and Belsen and Buchenwald in Germany. An estimated 20 million people were gassed or died of disease or starvation in Nazi camps, of which some 6 million were Jews –two-thirds of European Jewry. Notorious for their torture, medical experiments on living people, and the cruelty of their gaolers, the Nazi camps and the *holocaust that took place within them have raised doubts as to the validity of western civilization.

In the Soviet Union forced labour camps were first established in 1917 and expanded greatly during Stalin's purges in the 1930s. Although many camps were closed following his death in 1953, they continue to be used for the detention of political dissidents.

Concepción 36 50S 73 03W A city in S Chile, on the River Bío-Bío. It suffered damage (1939 and 1960) from earthquakes. It is an important industrial centre situated near Chile's chief coalfield; industries include steel processing and oil refining. Its university was founded in 1919. Population (1983 est): 209 925.

concertina A hexagonal musical instrument of the reed-organ family, invented in 1829 by Sir Charles Wheatstone. Similar to the *accordion in construction, the concertina is hand held and notes are produced by pressing buttons on panels at either end of the bellows.

concerto A musical composition for one or more solo instruments and orchestra, usually in three movements (a *sonata form movement, a slow movement, and a rondo finale). In the late 18th century Mozart perfected the form in his piano concertos; 19th-century composers treated it more freely and in the 20th century concertos have been written in a number of different styles and forms. In the baroque period and in the 20th century the word concerto has been applied to a variety of other compositions.

concerto grosso. See Corelli, Arcangelo.

conch A heavy-shelled marine *snail of the family *Strombidae* (about 80 species). Conch □shells have a roughly triangular outer whorl with a broad lip and can be 2–35 cm long. Indo-Pacific spider conchs (genus *Lambis*) have long horns around the aperture of their shell.

conciliarism The view of those Roman Catholics who regarded a general council of the Church as a superior authority to the pope. First proposed in the early 13th century, the theory gained support especially in the 15th century. Pius II refuted the doctrine in his bull *Execrabilis* (1460).

Concord 43 13N 71 34W A city in the USA, the capital of New Hampshire. Founded in 1725, it was the home of Mary Baker Eddy (the founder of Christian Science). Industries include printing and publishing. Population (1980): 30 400.

Concord 42 28N 71 17W A city in the USA, in Massachusetts on the Concord River. The first battle of the American Revolution occurred here on 19 April, 1775. Ralph Emerson, Nathaniel Hawthorne, Louisa May Alcott, and Henry Thoreau all lived in Concord. Population (1980): 16 293.

concordance An index of words used in a single book or all the works of an author, with accompanying citations. Originally used for study of the Bible, concordances are now used as a method of textual analysis of major literary authors.

Concorde. See aircraft.

concrete A building material that was used by the Romans but in its modern form came into use after the invention of Portland *cement in 1824. Concrete consists of a mixture of a cement, usually Portland cement, and an aggregate of sand, gravel, and broken stones. The strength of the concrete depends on the proportion of cement to the quantity and type of aggregate. Water is added to this mixture and complex hydration reactions cause the cement to dry out and harden around the aggregate. The material can be reinforced with steel bars (usually up to 50 mm in diameter) to increase its tensile strength. **Reinforced concrete** was invented in France in about 1850. In **prestressed concrete** the concrete is maintained in a state of compression by stretching the steel reinforcing wires (usually 6 mm in diameter) and keeping them in a state of tension after the concrete has set around them. Prestressed concrete is now widely used as a structural material as it has a reduced tendency to bend under load. Concrete parts may be precast in a factory or poured wet on site to harden, usually inside wooden shuttering, into any desired shape.

concussion The sudden and temporary loss of consciousness that may follow a head injury. On recovering consciousness the patient may be disorientated and confused, possibly with some loss of memory. Headache and blurred vision are other possible consequences.

Condé A French princely family, a branch of the *Bourbon royal house. Its first prince **Louis I** (1530-60) was a Huguenot leader during the French *Wars of Religion and was shot after being taken prisoner in battle. He was succeeded as Huguenot leader by his son **Henri I** (1552-88), who fled to Germany followiong the *St Bartholomew's Day Massacre of Huguenots (1572). Henri's grandson was the general **Condé the Great** (Louis II; 1621-86). During the Thirty Years' War he won victories against Spain at Rocroi (1643) and Lens (1648), subsequently being recalled to suppress the first *Fronde (civil war). In the second Fronde he joined the rebels and fled to Spain. After being defeated by *Turenne at the battle of the Dunes Condé was pardoned and became one of Louis XIV's outstanding generals.

condensation 1. A change of physical state from a gas or vapour to a liquid. Thus as a gas is cooled below a certain temperature it may (depending on the pressure) condense to the liquid. Condensation occurs in buildings when warm moist air comes in contact with cold surfaces, such as windows and uninsulated walls. 2. A type of organic chemical reaction in which two molecules combine to form a larger molecule with elimination of a smaller molecule, such as water or methanol. Condensation reactions are the basis of a type of *polymerization process.

Condillac, Étienne Bonnot de (1715-80) French philosopher and psychologist. His ideas in *L'origine des connaissances humaines* (1746), *Traité des systèmes* (1749), and *Traité des animaux* (1755) resemble *Locke's; all knowledge springs from the senses and association of ideas. After 1800 his high reputation waned, but modern psychology largely vindicates his work.

condition A statement in logic that determines the truth of another statement. A **sufficient condition** always ensures the truth of the second statement. A **necessary condition** must be true if the second statement is true.

conditioned reflex A *reflex response that is evoked by a stimulus other than that which normally produces it. A classic example is provided by *Pavlov's experiments with dogs. The normal stimulus causing salivation (i.e. food) was paired with a different stimulus (a ringing bell) so often that eventually the bell by itself caused the dogs to salivate. A conditioned reflex gradually disappears if the stimulus is presented repeatedly; this process is called extinction. *See also* conditioning.

conditioning The process of modifying behaviour by changing the stimuli (and therefore responses) associated with it. Classical conditioning occurs when a response is associated with a stimulus by pairing the stimulus with an event that causes the response by reflex (*see* conditioned reflex). Operant conditioning is brought about by either rewarding or punishing an action by the subject, which thus either encourages or discourages the behaviour (*see also* aversion therapy). *Behaviourism uses both forms of conditioning to explain how people learn.

condominium The joint exercise of sovereignty over a territory by two or more sovereign states, usually brought about by treaty to resolve a territorial dispute. The New Hebrides (now the Vanuatu Republic) was until 1980 the subject of a condominium created by Britain and France in 1906. In some countries, such as the USA, the term applies to multiple ownership of a building by the residents.

condor A huge South American *vulture, *Vultur gryphus*, found high in the Andes. It is black with a white ruff, bare pink head and neck, and has a wingspan of 3 m. It feeds chiefly on carrion but also takes lambs and young deer. The very rare Californian condor (*Gymnogyps californianus*) is smaller with a bare yellow head and red neck.

Condorcet, Marie Jean Antoine de Caritat, Marquis de (1743-94) French philosopher and politician. Distinguished as a mathematician and progressive man of letters in the 1770s and 1780s, after the outbreak of the French Revolution he was elected to the Legislative Assembly (1791). As a moderate *Girondin he was arrested when the *Jacobins became dominant in 1793 and died, perhaps by his own hand, in prison. His most famous work, *Esquisse d'un tableau historique des progrès de l'esprit humain*, was published posthumously (1795).

condottiere A leader of a mercenary army employed by an Italian city or lord between the 14th and 16th centuries. The earliest condottieri (from Italian *condotta*, contract) were foreign, one of the most famous being Sir John Hawkwood (d. 1394), the English adventurer, but by the end of the 14th century the Italians began to raise their own mercenary armies. Condottieri, among them Francesco *Sforza of Milan and Cesare *Borgia, began to conquer territories for themselves. The system disappeared with the foreign invasions and new methods of warfare in the late 15th century.

conductance. *See* resistance.

conduction 1. (thermal) The transfer of heat from a region of high temperature to one of lower temperature, without the transfer of matter. It occurs as a result of the transfer of kinetic *energy by collisions between atoms and molecules in gases, liquids, and nonmetallic solids. In metals, which are the best thermal and electrical conductors, the energy is transferred by collisions between the free electrons that move through the crystal lattice and the ions of the lattice. 2. (electrical) The passage of an electric current through a substance. In metals, the best conductors, it results from the passage of free electrons moving in one direction under the influence of an electric field. In a liquid conductor it is due to the passage of positive ions in one direction and negative ions in the other. In gases it is due to positive ions flowing in one direction and electrons in the other. In *semiconductors it results from the passage of electrons in one direction and positive holes in the other.

cone (botany) The structure, also called a strobilus, that bears the reproductive organs (sporophylls) in some pteridophytes (club mosses, horsetails, etc.) and the gymnosperms (conifers and related plants). In conifers both male and female cones are produced: the familiar woody cones of pines, larches, etc., are female strobili, made up of overlapping woody structures called bract scales, which bear the sporophylls in their axils.

coneflower. *See* black-eyed Susan.

cone shell A carnivorous marine *gastropod mollusc of the family Conidae (about 400 species), occurring in warm seas. 1-30 cm long and cone-shaped, the highly coloured and patterned shells are prized by collectors. The molluscs have a venomous sting and some can be dangerous to man.

Coney Island 40 35N 73 59W A resort in the USA, in New York City on the S shore of Long Island. With its amusement parks, fine beach, and the New York Aquarium it attracts many tourists.

Confederate States The 11 southern states of the USA that seceded from the Union (1860-61), precipitating the US *Civil War. A provisional government was established in February, 1861, before the outbreak of war (April, 1861) and was signed by South Carolina, Georgia, Texas, Virginia, Arkansas, Tennessee, North Carolina, Mississippi, Florida, Alabama, and Louisiana. Jefferson *Davis (Mississippi) was elected president and Alexander H. Stephens (1812-83; Georgia), vice president The Confederate States' decentralized government reflected the southern concern with *states' rights but its loose organization made efficient conduct of the war difficult. Unable to levy taxes, the government instead issued unguaranteed currency and created massive inflation. No foreign government ever recognized the legitimacy of the Confederacy.

Confederation of British Industry (CBI) The employers' federation in the UK. The CBI represents the employers in tripartite talks with the government and the Trades Union Congress on *prices and incomes policies and formulates industry's views on economic and fiscal matters. It was formed in 1965 from the Federation of British Industry, the National Association of British Manufacturers, and the Union of British Employers Confederation.

Confederation of the Rhine (1806-13) The union of the German states (except Austria and Prussia) under *Napoleon I. It facilitated the subsequent movement for German unification, which was achieved in 1871.

Confessing Church A movement among German Evangelicals opposed to the rise of Nazism in the 1930s and to the pro-Nazi German Christian Church. Developing from the Pastors' Emergency League of 1933, it was led by Martin *Niemöller and was openly active until the start of World War II, but lost influence as it was forced underground by the Nazis during the war. It continued as a movement within the Evangelical Church after 1945.

confession The admission of sins made by a penitent seeking forgiveness of them. As a religious practice it originated in Judaism and was taken over by the early Christian Church, in which public confession was customary. The fourth *Lateran Council (1215) made auricular confession (private confession to a priest, who is empowered to grant absolution) incumbent on all Christians once a year. In the Roman Catholic and Orthodox Churches auricular confession is part of the *sacrament of penance. Many Protestant Churches use a form of general confession, made by the whole congregation in public worship, although auricular confession is also practised in some Anglican and Lutheran Churches.

confirmation A Christian rite generally held to complete the initiation of a member into the Church. Originally associated with *baptism, it became separated with the spread of infant baptism and in the middle ages came to be regarded as one of the seven *sacraments. In the Eastern Orthodox Church, it is administered by a priest immediately after baptism and followed by Holy Communion; in the West, it is conferred by a bishop—in the Roman Catholic Church not before the seventh birthday and customarily at the age of 11 or 12, and in the Anglican Churches after the child has been able to learn the catechism.

Confucianism The traditional philosophy and, until recently, the state religion of China. It was founded in the 5th century BC by *Confucius, whose teaching is contained in five classical works or canonical books (not all of which were actually written by Confucius). While retaining the idea of a divine will (*ming*), Confuciansim emphasizes the moral duty of man to his fellows. Man is born good; the superior man follows his true nature and develops sincerity, fearlessness, compassion, and wisdom. Precise rules of conduct are recorded, regulating social intercourse and establishing the forms of ritual sacrifice to one's ancestors. The canonical books also include works on divination, poetry, and history. Although not sanctioned in China since the Cultural Revolution of 1966-68, Confucianism is still practised by expatriate Chinese and, as a fundamental ethical attitude, continues to influence Chinese culture.

Confucius (Kong Zi *or* K'ung-fu-tzu; c. 551-479 BC) Chinese philosopher, the founder of *Confucianism. As a minor official in his native Lu, a small state situated in modern Shandong province, he gathered numerous disciples, mainly young gentlemen who wished to enter government service. Promoted to ministerial rank, he became famous for his just and effective policies, but on the ruler's refusing to heed his advice, he left Lu (c. 496) and spent many years wandering from court to court, seeking a prince receptive to his ideas. Most of the works attributed to him are later compilations but the *Analects* (*Lun Yu*) is probably an authentic collection of his sayings and conversations.

conga A modern Cuban dance in march time in which the second beat in alternating measures is accompanied by a 16th note. Originally a parade dance performed by a line of people, it was popularized by the Spanish bandleader Xavier Cugat (c. 1900-).

conger eel A voracious *eel belonging to a family (*Congridae*; about 100 species) found in all oceans. 1-3 m long, conger eels have a greyish or blackish body with a paler belly, a large head, and a wide mouth with strong teeth.

conglomerates Sedimentary rocks consisting of rounded fragments of former rocks cemented together, usually in sand. These fragments are over 2 mm in diameter and generally consist of hard material, such as quartzite or granite. Some conglomerates are used for crushed stone for road making and other purposes.

Congo, People's Republic of (name until 1960: Middle Congo) A country in W central Africa, bordering on the Zaïre River. The narrow coastal plain rises to hills inland and lower valleys in the E provide fertile grasslands. The uplands give way to plains in the NE. The population is composed chiefly of Bantu tribes. *Economy*: largely agricultural, the main cash crops being sugar cane, palm oil, cocoa, and tobacco. Minerals include lead, zinc, and gold, and oil was discovered in 1969. Forests cover about half the country and timber is one of the main exports; others include sugar. *History*: in the 15th century the Portuguese established trading relations with the Congo kingdom. In the 19th century the exploration of the Frenchman de *Brazza led to the establishment of the colony of Middle Congo, which in 1910 became one of the four territories of French Equatorial Africa. In 1958 it attained internal self-government as a member of the French Community and in 1960 became independent as the Republic of Congo. In 1968 Maj Marien Ngouabi came to power in a military coup and in 1970, under a new Marxist constitution, the country's present name was adopted. Ngouabi was assassinated in 1977 and the government was taken over by a military committee under Col Joachim Yhombi Opango (1939-) until his resignation in 1979. President: Col Denis Sassou-Nguesso. Prime minister: Col Louis-Sylvain Goma (1941-). Official language: French. Official currency: CFA (Communauté financière africaine) franc of 100 centimes. Area: 342 000 sq km (132 018 sq mi). Population (1983 est): 1 694 000. Capital: Brazzaville. Main port: Pointe-Noire.

Congo, Republic of. See Zaïre, Republic of.

congo eel A large eel-like North American nocturnal *salamander of the genus *Amphiuma* and family *Amphiumidae* (2 species). The two-toed *A. means* grows to 85 cm and the three-toed *A. tridactylum* up to 115 cm. Both are light grey-brown, darker above, and feed on snails, crayfish, etc., in their swamp habitats.

Congo River. See Zaïre River.

Congregationalism In Christianity, a form of church government in which centralized authority is rejected and each congregation is democratically autonomous. Congregationalist groups were active at the time of the Reformation, and in England the Independents, as they were known, were prominent during the Commonwealth, having played an important part in the opposition to Charles I. Congregationalism spread to America, where it flourished. In England, the United Reformed Church was founded in 1972 by the union of the Congregationalists with the Presbyterians.

Congress The legislature of the USA instituted by the constitution (1789) and comprising the Senate, the upper house, and the House of Representatives, the lower house. The Senate serves as a check on the larger House of Representatives, with which it has equal legislative responsibility as well as further powers to ratify treaties and confirm appointments. Each state in the Union is equally represented by two senators, who must be at least 30 years old. There are 435 seats in the House of Representatives, which are allocated among the states according to population. Representatives, who must be at least 25 years old, are subject to re-election every two years. Only the House may originate revenue bills and initiate the impeachment of the *president.

Congress Kingdom of Poland (1815-32) A Polish state, formed at the Congress of *Vienna, having administrative autonomy under the Russian Crown. Polish nationalists twice attempted to overthrow Russian dominance but were unsuccessful: after the November Insurrection (1830), Congress Poland lost its autonomy and following the January Insurrection (1863-64), it became a Russian province.

Congreve, William (1670-1729) British dramatist. Born in Yorkshire and educated in Ireland, he returned to England in 1688 to study law but under the patronage of *Dryden entered the literary world instead. The comedies *Love for Love* (1695) and *The Way of the World* (1700) are his best-known plays, although his contemporaries most admired his tragedy *The Mourning Bride* (1697). He wrote little after 1700 and lived off various civil service sinecures.

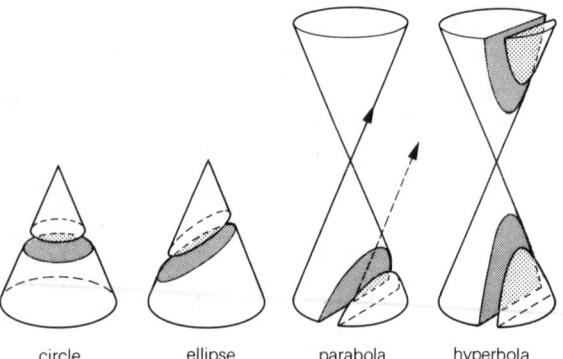

circle   ellipse   parabola   hyperbola

CONIC SECTION *The circle, ellipse, parabola, and hyperbola are produced by slicing through the cone as shown.*

conic section Geometrical figures produced by the intersection of a plane and a cone. If the plane cuts the cone at right angles to its axis the figure is a *circle. If the plane is tilted slightly an *ellipse is formed. If the plane is tilted further, until it lies parallel to the side of the cone, the figure is a *parabola. Tilted more, the figure becomes a *hyperbola. In the case of a hyperbola, the plane also intersects another cone the vertex of which touches the vertex of the first cone, the axes of the two cones being parallel. In this case two conic sections are produced. Therefore a hyperbola has two branches.

conifer A *gymnosperm tree of the widely distributed order *Coniferales* (400-500 species), most abundant in the colder temperate zones, especially in the north; elsewhere they are usually found at high altitudes. Conifers are typically pyramidal in form, with a straight continuously growing stem that can reach great heights (*see* Sequoia). Nearly all conifers are *evergreen (larches are exceptions), with simple needle-like or scalelike leaves. The reproductive organs are typically borne in separate male and female *cones, usually on the same tree, and produce winged seeds that are dispersed by wind (the yew and juniper are exceptions). The wood of conifers—called softwood—is economically important, being used for construction and as a source of paper pulp, etc. (*see* timber).

The principal families are the *Pinaceae* (pines, cedars, spruces, firs, larches, hemlocks, etc.); *Cupressaceae* (cy-

presses, junipers, arbor vitae, etc.); *Taxodiaceae* (sequoias, swamp cypress, etc.); *Taxaceae* (yews); and *Araucariaceae* (monkey puzzle, etc.).

Coniston Water A lake in NW England, in Cumbria in the Lake District. World water-speed records were established here by Sir Malcolm Campbell (1939) and his son Donald Campbell (1959). Length: 8 km (5 mi).

conjugation The process by which exchange of genetic material occurs in certain lower organisms by means of a connection between the cytoplasm of the two "mating" individuals. In ciliate protozoa and certain algae it is a type of sexual reproduction, the gametes (or gametic nuclei) passing through a cytoplasmic bridge (protozoa) or a conjugation tube (algae). In bacteria the connection between "male" and "female" cells is by means of special hairs (pili) or cell-to-cell bridges.

conjunction An alignment of two celestial bodies in the solar system, usually the sun and a planet, that occurs when the angular distance between them as seen from earth (i.e. the angle planet-earth-sun) becomes zero.

conjunctivitis Inflammation of the conjunctiva—the membrane that covers the surface of the eye and lines the eyelids. Popularly known as pinkeye, it is marked by itching, redness, and watering of the eye. It may be caused by allergy to drugs or pollen; bacterial infection (in which case it usually spreads to the other eye); or mechanical irritation.

Conn (2nd century AD) King of Leinster and High King of Ireland. A tireless warrior, known as Conn of the hundred battles, he gained control over the northern half of Ireland and then, shortly before his death, the whole island.

Connacht (*or* Connaught) A province and ancient kingdom of the NW Republic of Ireland. It consists of the counties of Galway, Leitrim, Mayo, Roscommon, and Sligo. Area: 17 122 sq km (6611 sq mi). Population (1981): 424 410.

Connaught. *See* Connacht.

Connecticut A state in the NE USA, in New England. Uplands in the E and W are separated by the central lowlands, which are drained by the Connecticut River. It is one of the most densely populated states in the USA, its large population being fairly evenly distributed throughout the region. Manufacturing is important and traditionally produced goods are clocks, silverware, and brass products, as well as military equipment. Hartford is one of the principal insurance centres in the USA. Farming is only a minor activity producing dairy products, eggs, poultry, and vegetables for local markets with some tobacco for export. The state has a long tradition and culture; Yale University at New Haven is the most famous of its large number of universities and colleges. *History*: one of the original 13 colonies in the USA, it was first explored by the Dutch in the early 17th century. The first settlement was by English colonists from the Massachusetts Bay Colony (1633-35). Area: 12 973 sq km (5009 sq mi). Population (1980): 3 107 576. Capital: Hartford.

connective tissue The tissue that supports, binds, or separates the specialized tissues and organs of the body. Connective tissue consists of a semifluid ground substance of polysaccharide and protein in which are embedded white collagen fibres, yellow elastic fibres, and various cells (including fibroblasts, which produce the ground substance and the fibres). The amount of collagen determines the toughness of the tissue. Specialized connective tissue includes fatty tissue, blood, bone, and cartilage.

Connemara An area in the W Republic of Ireland, in Co Galway bordering on the Atlantic Ocean. It contains many lakes, peat bogs, and the Twelve Bens, a group of quartzite mountains.

Connors, Jimmy (1952–) US tennis player, who was Wimbledon singles champion in 1974 and 1982 and doubles champion in 1973. He also won the US singles title in 1974, 1976, 1978, 1982, and 1983 and the doubles title in 1975.

conquistador (Spanish: conqueror) One of the men who conquered the Indians of Central and South America for Spain in the first half of the 16th century. Few in number, the conquistadores were driven by a fanatical desire to find fame and gold and to serve the Roman Catholic Church. The most famous were Hernán *Cortés and Francisco *Pizarro.

Conrad II (c. 990–1039) German king (1024–39), who founded the Salian dynasty (1024–1125), and Holy Roman Emperor (1027–39). He conquered part of Poland (1028) and Burgundy (1033–34). While attempting to suppress a rebellion in N Italy (1036–38), he lost most of his army in an epidemic.

Conrad III (1093–1152) The first Hohenstaufen German king (1138–52). He was proclaimed antiking (1127) in opposition to Lothair, after whose death (1137) he became king. His election was opposed by the Welf family and although peace was made in 1142 the conflict between the two families was renewed, giving rise to the *Guelf and Ghibelline struggle. In 1147 Conrad joined the second Crusade.

Conrad, Joseph (Teodor Josef Konrad Watęcz Korzeniowski; 1857–1924) Polish-born British novelist, who knew no English before he was 20. Orphaned at the age of 11, he went to Marseilles in 1874, where he became a sailor, serving for 16 years in the British Merchant Navy. He became a naturalized British subject in 1886, and published his first novel, *Almayer's Folly*, in 1895. His seagoing experiences influenced both the themes of his fiction and his own moral outlook. His major novels include *Lord Jim* (1900), *Nostromo* (1904), *The Secret Agent* (1907), and *Under Western Eyes* (1911).

consanguinity Relationship by blood, either real or putative. However, many societies do not consider everyone to whom they are genetically related to be blood kin. For example, some societies do not consider a father to be genetically related to his children and therefore they are not his consanguines. Consanguinity affects laws regarding property inheritance and prohibits marriage between close blood relatives.

Conscience, Hendrik (1812–83) Flemish novelist. The author of over a hundred novels, he began writing sketches in Flemish in the late 1830s, and his historical romance *The Lion of Flanders* (1838) was the first major Flemish novel.

conscientious objection. *See* pacifism.

conscription The compulsory enlistment of recruits for military service. Conscription occurred in the ancient world and during the middle ages, when short-term *militia service was enforced for local defence. Universal male conscription was introduced in Revolutionary France in 1793 and in the early 1800s was adopted by Prussia. During the 19th century conscription was practised by most European powers and during the Civil War (1861–65) by the USA. Britain did not adopt conscription in modern times until World War I, when in 1916 the compulsory recruitment of unmarried men, and shortly afterwards of married men, aged 18–41 was introduced. The first peacetime conscription was enforced in Britain in 1939 and after the outbreak of World War II women were compulsorily recruited for the first time (1941). The National Service Act of 1947 provided for a maximum annual conscription of 150 000 men. Conscription was abolished in Britain in 1962. In the USA, where it had also been adopted in both World Wars, conscription continued until 1973. *See also* pacifism.

Consejo Real (Spanish: Royal Council) The central organ of government in Spain, created in 1386 in *Castille by Juan I. It was dominated by the clergy and nobility until the reforms of Isabella I in 1480 replaced them with lawyers

loyal to the Crown. It survived, with diminishing power, until the 19th century.

Consentes Dii The 12 major Roman and Etruscan gods, six male and six female. They are Jupiter and Juno, Neptune and Minerva, Mars and Venus, Apollo and Diana, Vulcan and Vesta, Mercury and Ceres. They were first collectively mentioned in 217 BC.

conservation The rational use of the earth's resources so that life can be sustained indefinitely. Pressure on both mineral and natural resources, resulting from increased agricultural and industrial activity, has required urgent examination of the consequent effects on the world ecosystem. The prudent use of fossil fuels and minerals and the search for alternatives are becoming both political and economic necessities. The destruction of many natural habitats has led to the creation of nature reserves and national parks where wildlife can be protected. Such areas are also often of aesthetic value and serve as recreational areas for urban populations. Legislation can protect some rare species of animals and plants from extinction but international cooperation is needed to protect economically important species (including whales), to conserve fish stocks, and to prevent pollution of the atmosphere and the oceans. In most cases the technological means to solve these problems are available but their high costs, or conflict with sectional interests, prevent their implementation.

conservation of energy supplies The more efficient use of increasingly scarce fuel supplies. In the 1970s the UK Government, for example, began to subsidize home-insulation improvements and research into the reduction or utilization of waste heat from industrial processes. Similar interest developed in other industrialized countries in parallel with an interest in *alternative energy sources. Thus, most new buildings are now designed to minimize heat losses. In electricity-generating stations the warm water produced from condensed steam may be used for local domestic heating in combined heat and power (CHP) schemes. More efficient burners and boilers have been developed for coal-fired power stations. The introduction of transport systems that are less wasteful than the private petrol-driven car is also likely to become a necessity. *See also* solar power; wave power; wind power.

conservation of mass and energy The principle that, in any closed system, the total of the mass and energy remains constant. It replaced the older laws in which mass and energy were held to be separately conserved, since the special theory of *relativity demonstrates that mass and energy may, in certain circumstances, be interconvertible. The energy (E) equivalent to a mass (m) is given by Einstein's equation: $E = mc^2$, where c is the speed of light in a vacuum.

Conservative Party A UK political party that grew out of the *Tory party in the 1830s under the leadership of Sir Robert *Peel. His repeal of the *Corn Laws (1846) caused a split in the party, with the Peelites later joining the Liberal Party. Under the leadership of *Disraeli the Conservatives acquired a distinct philosophy that combined identification with the monarchy, the British Empire, and the Church of England with social reform. Under *Salisbury and then *Balfour the party was almost continuously in power from 1886 to 1905 and again, under Bonar *Law, *Baldwin, Neville *Chamberlain, and *Churchill, from 1922 to 1945, being the dominant party in the coalitions of 1931–35 and 1940–45. It was again in office from 1951 to 1964, led successively by Churchill, Eden (see Avon, Anthony Eden, Earl of), *Macmillan, and *Home, from 1970 to 1974 under *Heath, and from 1979 under *Thatcher. The party is now firmly committed to the furtherance of private enterprise and individualism rather than *nationalization.

consols. *See* gilt-edged securities.

Constable, John (1776–1837) British landscape painter,

CONSTABLE *Self-portrait in pencil and watercolour.*

born in East Bergholt, Suffolk, the son of a miller. After working for his father, he trained in London at the Royal Academy schools, where he studied *Ruisdael and Claude. He painted the Suffolk countryside, Hampstead Heath, and Salisbury Cathedral with a particular concern for changing weather conditions, exemplified in *The Leaping Horse* (1825; Royal Academy) and *Dedham Vale* (1828; National Gallery, Edinburgh). Although he exhibited regularly at the Royal Academy, he was only elected a member in 1829. He achieved greater recognition in France, where his *Haywain* (National Gallery, London) won a gold medal and influenced *Delacroix. In his last years he assisted in the publication of mezzotints of his landscapes and painted in a gloomier more restless style after the death of his wife (1828).

Constance (German name: Konstanz) 47 40N 09 10E A town in SW West Germany, in Baden-Württemberg on Lake Constance. Its 11th-century church was formerly a cathedral. Manufactures include textiles, computers, and chemicals. Population (1983 est): 69 510.

Constance, Council of (1414-18) The 16th ecumenical council of the Roman Catholic Church, which ended the *Great Schism by electing Pope *Martin V (1417). It decreed that the authority of a general council was superior to that of the pope. The heretics *Wycliffe and *Hus were condemned, and Hus was burned at the stake.

Constance, Lake (German name: Bodensee) A lake on the River Rhine in West Germany, Switzerland, and Austria. Area: 531 sq km (205 sq mi).

Constant, Benjamin (1767-1830) French novelist, born in Switzerland and educated in Germany and Britain. He supported the French Revolution but opposed Napoleon and went into exile. After the restoration of the monarchy he returned to France in 1818 as a leading liberal politician

and journalist. His novel *Adolphe* (1816) was based on his passionate affair with Mme de *Staël. Several volumes of his private journals have also been published.

Constanța 44 10N 28 40E The chief seaport of Romania, situated on the Black Sea. Founded by the Greeks in the 7th century BC, it was rebuilt by Constantine the Great in the 4th century AD. Oil is pumped here from the Ploieşti fields to be refined and exported. Population (1983): 284 801.

constantan An alloy of 55% copper and 45% nickel. It is used in electrical equipment, such as resistors and *thermocouples, because it has a high electrical resistance that does not change with temperature.

Constantine (ancient name: Cirta) 36 23N 6 29E A town in N Algeria. It was destroyed in 311 AD but rebuilt by Constantine the Great in 313 and renamed after him. The old town is popular with tourists and noted for its handicrafts. Population (1980 est): 384 000.

Constantine I (1868-1923) King of Greece (1913-17, 1920-22). Constantine led Greece to victory in the *Balkan War (1912-13) but unpopularly maintained neutrality in World War I and was forced to abdicate (1917). Recalled in 1920, he again abdicated following a military revolt against his war with Turkey.

Constantine II (1940-) King of Greece (1964-67). In 1967, following a military coup, Constantine went into exile, eventually moving to Britain. In 1973 he was officially deposed and Greece became a republic. He married (1964) Princess Anne-Marie of Denmark (1946-).

Constantine VII Porphyrogenitus (905-59 AD) Byzantine emperor (913-59). Constantine reigned (919-45) with his father-in-law and coemperor, Romanus I Lecapenus (d. 948), and while Romanus ruled Constantine devoted himself to studying and writing. His works *On Imperial Administration* and *Ceremonies of the Byzantine Court* are invaluable sources for Byzantine social and economic history.

Constantine, Learie Nicholas, Baron (1902-71) West Indian cricketer, who also played for Lancashire. A brilliant all-round cricketer renowned for his fast bowling, he was also a distinguished public figure. A barrister, he was high commissioner in London for Trinidad and Tobago (1962-64), a member of the British Race Relations Board (1966), and rector of the University of St Andrews (1968).

Constantine the Great (?285-337 AD) Roman emperor in the West (312-24) and sole emperor (324-37). The son of Constantius (c. 250-306), Roman emperor in the West (305-06), Constantine was acclaimed as his father's successor by his troops at York but did not secure his position until he had defeated his rival Maxentius (d. 312). He became sole emperor after defeating the Eastern emperor Licinius (c. 270-325; reigned 311-24). Constantine was the first Roman emperor to adopt Christianity. During his campaign against Maxentius he was reputed to have had a vision of the Christian cross with the words "In this sign, conquer." In 313 Constantine issued the Edict of Milan, which established toleration of Christians, and in 325 summoned the Council of *Nicaea, the first general council of the Church. He was baptized on his deathbed. Constantine introduced administrative and military reforms and founded Constantinople (*see* Istanbul).

Constantinople. *See* Istanbul.

Constantinople, Councils of Three general councils of the Christian Church. 1. (381) The council that was summoned to end the Arian dispute (*see* Arianism) and assert the doctrine of the Council of *Nicaea. 2. (553) The council that attempted to resolve the conflict between the *Nestorians and *Monophysites. 3. (680) The council that condemned the *Monothelite heresy and asserted the doctrines of the Council of *Chalcedon concerning the dual nature of Christ's will.

constellations The 88 areas into which the N and S

hemispheres of the sky are now divided, using established boundaries. Each star, galaxy, or other celestial body lies within, or sometimes overlaps, the boundaries of one of the constellations and is often named in terms of this constellation. The constellations all have Latin names. They originally had no fixed limits but were groups of stars forming a distinctive pattern outlining a mythological hero, animal, etc. The constellations that can be observed at night depend on the latitude of the observer and change with the time of night and the time of year.

constipation The condition in which emptying of the bowels occurs infrequently: faeces are often hard and dry and there may be pain in passing them. Constipation is often associated with advancing age and a diet deficient in vegetable fibre (probably the commonest cause in the western world). It is also caused by some drugs (e.g. codeine) and by obstruction of the bowel. Long-standing constipation not due to disease of the bowel is treated by increasing the amount of vegetable fibre (e.g. bran) in the diet. *Laxatives may also be used.

constitution The principles according to which a country is governed. Constitutions may be written or unwritten. The UK has an unwritten constitution comprising some statutes, much *common law, and a good deal of custom. In the USA and many other countries, the constitution is a single document. The **US constitution** was drawn up in 1787, ratified in 1788, and came into effect in 1789. It contains 7 articles and 27 amendments of which 10 constitute the *Bill of Rights (1791). It defines the separation of powers, designed as a system of checks and balances, between the legislature (*see* Congress), the executive (*see* president), and the judiciary (*see* Supreme Court). Amendments subsequent to the Bill of Rights include the abolition of slavery (13), universal suffrage (15), and *prohibition of liquor (18).

Constitutional Convention (1787) An assembly of the delegates of 12 US states (Rhode Island alone abstained) that met in Philadelphia to draft the US constitution, which replaced the *Articles of Confederation. The Convention adopted a more centralized government and its "Great Compromise" was a bicameral congress with both proportional and equal representation. This allayed the fears of small states that large states would dominate a single-house legislature with proportional representation.

constrictor A snake belonging to the family *Boidae* (70 species) occurring chiefly in tropical regions. Constrictors are nonvenomous and kill their prey by coiling their thick muscular body around it and squeezing until it suffocates. They often have claws, which are vestigial limbs. The family comprises two subfamilies, *Boinae* (*see* boa) and *Pythoninae* (*see* python).

constructivism A movement in abstract sculpture, architecture, and design, which was launched in Russia by the *Realist Manifesto* (1920) of the brothers Naum *Gabo and Antoine *Pevsner with the aim of freeing contemporary art from political and social overtones. The chief principles of constructivism were functionalism, the articulation of space, and the use of modern materials, such as plastic and steel. Many Russian constructivists left their country for Germany or France in 1922 because of state opposition to the movement. The architect, painter, and designer El *Lissitzky was influential at the *Bauhaus school in Germany, while Gabo spread the style to the UK and the USA.

consubstantiation In Christian theology, a doctrine concerning the presence of Christ in the *Eucharist, especially associated with the teaching of Martin *Luther. Traditionally, the consecrated bread and wine were held to become, substantially, the body and blood of Christ (*see* transubstantiation). According to the doctrine of consubstantiation, the substances of the body and blood of Christ and of the bread and wine were held to coexist together in the consecrated Host.

consuls The two magistrates who held supreme civil and military authority under the *Roman Republic. They were elected annually by the Comitia Centuriata (*see* comitia) and presided over the Senate. Under the Empire they were nominated by the emperor and held office for only two to four months, the posts becoming honorary.

consumerism The idea that consumers should influence the design, quality, service, and prices of goods and services provided by commercial enterprises. Movements based on this idea have developed in the USA (*see* Nader, Ralph) and in Europe as a response to the concentration of economic power in modern corporations and to the increased technical complexity of many contemporary consumer goods. Such organizations as the Consumers' Association in the UK, an independent nonprofit-making body, established in 1957, which publishes its findings in its magazine *Which?*, carry out comparative tests on consumer goods and services and use their authority on consumers' behalf.

consumption (economics) Expenditure on goods and services, excluding expenditure on capital goods (*see* investment). A country's national income is spent either on consumption or on investment. Public consumption consists of government spending on services, such as education, health, defence, etc. Private consumption is money spent by individuals on nondurables, such as food and drink, durables, such as cars and washing machines, and services, such as entertainment. There is some controversy as to whether private consumption is determined by an individual's lifetime prospects or his current income. This controversy has important consequences in economic planning: for example, whether or not tax cuts would reduce unemployment by increasing consumption.

contact lenses A removable form of lens worn directly against the eye to replace spectacles for long or short sight or to protect the eye in some disorders of the outer transparent layer (cornea). Originally made of glass, modern contact lenses are made of plastic and become moulded to the shape of the individual's eye. At first the lenses may irritate the eyes, but most people can adapt to them with time.

containerization The use of large cuboid containers built to internationally accepted dimensions (usually 8 × 8 × 20, 30, or 40 ft or 2.4 × 2.4 × 6.1, 9.1 or 12.2 m) for the transport of goods. These containers are transported from the producing factory to the user, distributor, or export dock without being unpacked: thus they cut down on the cost and time involved in handling and reduce the chances of loss through pilferage or damage. Containerization has revolutionized international shipping, as specialized ships are needed to transport the containers efficiently; this has led to the decline of the many docks that are only equipped to handle conventionally packed goods.

conté crayon A stick of soft crayon, named after its inventor, the French scientist Nicholas Jacques Conté (1755–1805). Unlike pastel, its colour is durable and nonsmudging, while its size makes it suitable both for line drawing and shading large areas.

contempt of court An act or omission that tends to undermine the authority of a court or that is likely to prejudice the fair trial of an accused person. Examples are insulting a presiding judge or failing to comply with a court order; magistrates are not empowered to commit for contempt. The publication of matters *sub judice*, that is matters on which the court is to decide, is also a contempt. Contempt can be committed both inside and outside the court and in both civil and criminal proceedings. A person found in contempt is liable to a fine or imprisonment.

continent One of the following major land masses of the earth: Asia, Africa, North America, South America, Europe, Australia, and Antarctica. (These divisions do not correspond to the rigid plates into which the whole of the earth's crust is divided.) The continents occupy about 30% of the earth's surface area. The crust of which they are formed (mainly granitic) is less dense than the oceanic crust (basaltic). The constituents of the continental crust are called sial and those of the oceanic crust, sima. The continents have not always occupied their present positions (*see* continental drift).

Continental Congress (1774–89) The body of representatives of the American colonies, which met in Philadelphia. The first Continental Congress (1774–75) was summoned to protest the *Intolerable Acts of the British parliament. With the outbreak of the *American Revolution, the second Continental Congress (1775–76) became the provisional government and proclaimed the *Declaration of Independence. In 1789 a permanent bicameral congress replaced the Continental Congress.

continental divide A major *watershed separating the drainage basins of a continent. In North America a continental divide extends N–S along the Rocky Mountains dividing the rivers flowing E from those flowing W.

continental drift The theory, first set out in 1912 by Alfred *Wegener and now widely accepted, that the continents are not fixed in position but drift slowly over the earth's surface (*see also* plate tectonics). Wegener's work was based on similarities in rock types, geological structures, flora and fauna, and the coastal outlines of the continents; in recent years geophysical data, particularly from geomagnetic studies, have provided firmer evidence for continental drift. It is believed that about 200 million years ago a supercontinent (termed Pangaea) began to break up and the fragments drifted apart until the continents reached their present positions. It is probable that continents have been joining together and breaking up throughout the earth's history. *See* Plate II.

continental shelf The area of sea floor adjacent to the continents, dipping gently from the shoreline to a depth of about 200 m. At this depth, the shelf edge, the continental slope begins, dipping more steeply to the ocean bottom. Shelves tend to be wider off low-lying regions than mountainous regions; the average width is about 70 km.

Continental System The trade blockade of Britain introduced by Napoleon in 1806 to ruin Britain's commerce and thus force peace on his own terms. Napoleon used his control of the coast from the Baltic to the Adriatic to forbid French allies or neutrals to trade with Britain or its colonies. Britain subjected all countries in alliance with France to counterblockade. The system failed because of the contraband trade and the new British markets in South America.

contraception The prevention of unwanted pregnancy, also known as birth control and family planning. Of the numerous methods available for preventing conception, the rhythm method and coitus interruptus are the most simple but least reliable. In the former sexual intercourse is avoided around the middle of the menstrual cycle, when ovulation is most likely to occur; in the latter the penis is withdrawn from the vagina before ejaculation. Both the condom (or sheath), which is worn over the penis, and the diaphragm, which is fitted over the cervix of the womb and should be used with a spermicidal jelly, are more effective since they prevent the sperm from entering the womb. A far more reliable contraceptive is the intra-uterine device (IUD)—a loop or coil, often impregnated with copper, that is inserted by a doctor into the womb. Its method of action is not known. Some women, however, are unable to use an IUD as it causes unacceptable side effects (such as heavy menstrual bleeding or recurrent infection). Since the 1960s, the most efficient means of preventing pregnancy has been by taking hormonal pills (*see* oral contraceptive), but this, too, may produce side effects and is unsuitable for some women. A long-term contraceptive method is the injection, at three-monthly intervals, of a synthetic hormone (progestogen), but this has recently been linked with the subsequent birth of disabled children and its use is controversial. Permanent contraception is achieved by *sterilization, which includes vasectomy for men

and cutting or blocking the Fallopian tubes for women. Recently developed methods include the use of a soft polythene sponge impregnated with spermicide, which is inserted into the vagina and gives 24-hour protection, and a morning-after pill for women.

Family planning has had a long history, with early methods ranging from infanticide and abortion to the use of such preventive devices as sheep's bladders as condoms. The need for it, however, was not formally discussed until the beginning of the 19th century, when the writings of *Malthus drew attention to the problems of overpopulation. Moral objections and the absence of an appropriate technology delayed the advent of the first family-planning clinics until the 1920s. In the UK they were largely pioneered by Marie *Stopes and in the USA by Margaret Sanger (1883–1966). Contraception is now an accepted means of controlling family size and population growth on an individual basis in most Western countries, even some that are predominantly Roman Catholic, in which their use is forbidden by the church. However, in most third-world countries, where overpopulation, poverty and food shortages cause widespread distress, contraception has to be provided by governments and outside agencies, in the face of Catholic opposition.

contract In law, an enforceable promise or bargain, usually written but sometimes oral. A simple promise for which nothing is given in exchange is not a contract and is only enforceable at law as a *deed. Something of value, called "consideration," must be exchanged in return for the promise; the value must be real but need not be equivalent. Breach of contract, meaning failure to fulfil its conditions, may result in the offender being sued for damages by the other party.

contralto The deepest female singing voice. Range: F below middle C to D an octave and a sixth above.

contrapposto A technique in sculpture for resting a figure's weight on one leg to tilt the body in a realistic pose. Practised by *Polyclitus of Argos (5th century BC), it was revived during the Renaissance, notably in *Michelangelo's statue of David (Accademia, Florence).

Contreras, Battle of (19–20 August, 1847) A battle of the *Mexican War fought near Mexico City. US forces under Gen Winfield Scott (1786–1866) put the Mexican forces to flight and gained control of the road to the Mexican capital.

convection The transfer of heat within a fluid by means of motion of the fluid. Convection may be natural or forced. In natural convection, the fluid flows by virtue of the warmer part being less dense than the cooler part. Thus the warmer fluid rises and the colder fluid sinks under the influence of gravity. In forced convection, some external cause, such as a fan, drives colder fluid into a warmer one, or vice versa.

convergence (*or* convergent evolution) The development in unrelated animals of similarities resulting from adaption to the same way of life. Thus whales (mammals) and fish, both aquatic, have evolved similar features independently.

conversos (Spanish: converts) The Spanish Jews who were forced to become Roman Catholics during the persecution of Jews in the late 14th and 15th centuries. The Spanish Inquisition was created to prevent the apostasy of *conversos* and the Muslim *Moriscos.

Convocations of Canterbury and York The assemblies of the clergy of the two provinces of the Church of England. Dating from at least the 8th century, they were originally assemblies of bishops only. They later divided into two houses, an upper house composed of diocesan bishops and a lower house composed of certain lower clergy. The extent of their powers fluctuated, but essentially they exercised the right to tax themselves and managed to keep this prerogative until after the Restoration. From 1717 to 1852, however, they were prevented from dealing with questions of business and held only formal meetings. In 1969 many of their powers were assumed by the General Synod of the Church of England.

Convolvulus A widely distributed genus of annual or perennial twining plants (about 250 species). The flowers are funnel or bell-shaped and attractive. The Eurasian *bindweed (*C. arvensis*) is a noxious weed with deep persistent roots and rapidly growing stems. Some species, such as *C. althaeoides*, are cultivated in gardens. Some have medicinal (purgative) properties. Family: *Convolvulaceae*.

Conway (Welsh name: Aberconwy) 53 18N 3 52W A market town and resort in North Wales, in Gwynedd on the estuary of the River Conway. One of the few surviving examples of a completely walled medieval town, it has a famous 13th-century castle. Population (1981): 12 969.

cony. *See* hyrax; pika.

Coober Pedy 28 56S 134 45E A town in central South Australia. It is an opal-mining centre producing over half the world's total output of opals. Many of the miners live underground to avoid the high temperatures, which often reach over 50°C (125°F). Population (1976): 1903.

Cooch Behar (*or* Kuch Bihar) 26 18N 89 32E A city in India, in West Bengal. It was the capital of the former state of Cooch Behar, which became part of West Bengal in 1950. Population (1971): 53 684.

Cook, Captain James (1728–79) British navigator and cartographer. After working in ships engaged in the North Sea trade, he joined the Royal Navy (1755) and served in the Seven Years' War (1756–63), during which he surveyed the St Lawrence River. His observations on the eclipse of the sun in 1766 were presented to the Royal Society, which gave him command of an expedition to Tahiti to observe the transit of the planet Venus across the sun and to discover Terra Australis, a presumed southern continent. The expedition set sail in the *Endeavour* in 1768 and, Venus observed, Cook went on to discover and chart New Zealand and the E coast of Australia, returning to England in 1771. The voyage was remarkable not least for the absence of scurvy among his crew–the result of a diet, devised by Cook, that was high in vitamin C. His second voyage (1772–75), in the *Resolution*, accompanied by the *Adventure*, achieved the circumnavigation of the Antarctic. He charted Easter Island and discovered New Caledonia, the South Sandwich Islands, and South Georgia Island. On his return he was made a captain and received the Royal Society's Copley Medal for his dietary work. On his third voyage (1776–79) he was killed in a quarrel with Hawaiians.

Cook, Sir Joseph (1860–1947) Australian statesman, born in England; Liberal prime minister (1913–14). He was hampered by a majority of only one in the House of Representatives and a minority in the Senate.

Cook, Mount (Maori name: Aorangi) 43 37S 170 08E The highest mountain in New Zealand, in South Island in the Southern Alps. It is permanently snow capped and flanked by glaciers. Height: 3764 m (12 349 ft).

Cook, Thomas (1808–92) British travel agent, who introduced conducted excursions and founded the travel agents Thomas Cook and Son. He organized his first excursion in 1841, a railway journey from Leicester to Loughborough for a temperance meeting.

Cookham-on-Thames 51 34N 0 43W A village in SE England, in Berkshire. A picturesque place with boating on the River Thames, it was made famous by the paintings of Stanley *Spencer, who lived here for many years.

Cook Islands A group of scattered islands in the SE Pacific Ocean, a New Zealand dependency. The chief islands are Rarotonga, Atiu, and Aitutaki. Fruit, copra, and mother-of-pearl are exported. Area: 241 sq km (93 sq mi). Population (1981): 17 754. Capital: Avarua.

coolabar A tree, *Eucalyptus microtheca*, growing to 25 m, common inland in W Australia. The wood is grey near the outside, deep red within. Also called jinbul, moolar, blackbox, and dwarf box, it is used for building. Family: *Myrtaceae*. *See also* Eucalyptus.

Coolidge, John Calvin (1872–1933) US statesman; Republican president (1923–29). His presidency followed the scandals of administration (1921–23) of Warren Harding (1865–1923) but Coolidge's own honesty was never questioned. He supported US business at home and abroad believing that "the business of America is business." However, he did little to curb the speculation on the stock market that ended in the 1929 financial crash.

cool jazz (*or* progressive jazz) A style of US *jazz developed on the W coast in the early 1950s. Cool jazz was characterized by subtle rhythms as well as by instruments and harmonies borrowed from European classical music. Less frenetic than *bop, cool jazz was also quieter and more economical. Important cool-jazz musicians include Stan Getz (1927–), Miles Davis, and Dave Brubeck.

Cooper, Gary (Frank James C.; 1901–61) US film actor. He is best known for his portrayals of tough but sensitive heroes in Hollywood westerns. These include *The Virginian* (1929), *The Westerner* (1940), and *High Noon* (1952).

Cooper, Henry (1934–) British boxer, European heavyweight champion (1964; 1968–71). Famous for his left, known as "Henry's Hammer," he is best remembered for knocking down Muhammed □Ali in the fifth round of a non-title fight at Wembley.

Cooper, James Fenimore (1789–1851) US novelist. Expelled from Yale, he served briefly in the navy before his marriage in 1811. Financial need prompted him to start writing, and in *The Pioneers* (1823), his third novel, he portrayed for the first time the realities of frontier life. Sequels included *The Last of the Mohicans* (1826) and *The Pathfinder* (1840). A parallel series of novels about the sea included *The Red Rover* (1827) and *The Sea Lions* (1849). His democratic sympathies were strengthened during his stay in Europe from 1826 to 1833 but his political writings met with little success.

Cooper, Samuel (1609–72) British miniaturist whose sitters included Cromwell, Charles II, and Cosimo III de' Medici. His bold sense of design and use of shadow, qualities usually associated with large-scale painting, are in marked contrast to Nicholas *Hilliard's miniature style. After his death he was often called "the Van Dyck in little."

cooperative societies Societies set up to manufacture, buy, or sell produce, either without profit or with profits distributed to members or shareholders as dividends (i.e. a refund is made for every pound's worth of goods purchased from the cooperative). The cooperative movement was inspired by the British philanthropist Robert *Owen in the early 19th century and was seen as an alternative to the hardship that seemed to be caused by competition. Cooperative societies in agriculture, in which machinery is shared and produce is marketed jointly, are common in both the advanced and developing countries. In the UK the largest cooperative is the Cooperative Wholesale Society (CWS). The CWS distributes dividends to customers by way of stamps, issued in proportion to the value of purchases made, which are redeemable at a higher rate for shareholders than for ordinary customers.

Cooper Creek (*or* Barcoo River) An intermittent river in E central Australia, in the *Channel Country. Rising in central Queensland it flows generally SW into Lake Eyre. Actual water flow in its lower reaches is irregular, occurring only in times of flood. The explorers Burke and Wills died here in 1861. Length: 1420 km (880 mi).

coordinate systems Geometrical systems that locate points in space by a set of numbers.

cartesian coordinates

two-dimensional   three-dimensional

polar coordinates

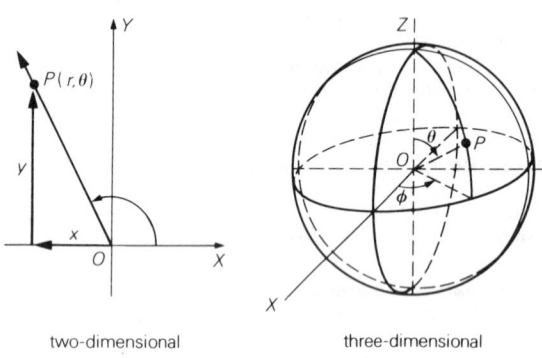

two-dimensional   three-dimensional

COORDINATE SYSTEMS   *In two-dimensional Cartesian co-ordinates a point* P *is located by giving its x- and y-coordinates, in this case 4 and −3 (always given in this order, as shown). In three-dimensional Cartesian coordinates* P *is located in terms of three axes. In polar coordinates* P *is located by a radius* r *and an angle* θ. *In three dimensions a second angle,* φ, *is required. In the diagrams Cartesian coordinates are superimposed on the polar coordinates.*

In **Cartesian coordinates**, devised by René *Descartes, a point is located by its distance from intersecting lines called axes. In a plane (two dimensions) there are two axes and in space (three dimensions) there are three. Usually the axes are at right angles to each other and are known as rectangular axes, but oblique axes are also used in exceptional circumstances.

Polar coordinates denote position by distance and direction. A fixed point, called the origin, and a fixed line, called the polar axis, are taken as the references. For any point, the polar coordinates are the length, r, of the radius of the circle centred at the origin and passing through the point, and the angle, θ, between this radius and the polar axis. In three dimensions, spherical polar coordinates are used. The radius of a sphere centred at the origin and the two angles it makes with the polar axis define the point.

coot   An aquatic *rail of the genus *Fulica* (9 species). Coots have broadly lobed toes, diving deeply to feed on invertebrates and aquatic plants. The European coot (*F. atra*) occurs throughout the Old World and is 37 cm long with black plumage and a white bill and frontal shield.

copal   Any one of the many resins collected from living or fossilized tropical trees and used in the manufacture of varnishes and inks. Copals can vary from brownish-yellow to colourless.

Copán   14 52N 89 10W   A town in Honduras. Extensive ruins with temples, pyramids, astronomical stelae, and a ceremonial stairway remain from its heyday as a *Maya city (c. 300–900 AD). Population (1980 est): 26 100.

Copenhagen (Danish name: Kø̈benhavn)   55 40N 12 35E   The capital and chief port of Denmark, on the E coast of Sjælland. It is an industrial as well as a commercial and shipping centre, with engineering, food processing, and brewing. Notable buildings include the 17th-century Charlottenborg Palace (now the Royal Academy of Arts) and Christiansborg Palace (now the parliamentary and government buildings). An important centre of Scandinavian culture, Copenhagen possesses a university (1479) and several museums. *History*: already a human settlement in the year 900 AD, it became capital of Denmark in 1443. Over the centuries it has been involved in many wars; it was attacked by the Hanseatic League in the middle ages and by Sweden in the 17th century. In 1801 the Danish fleet was destroyed by Nelson at the battle of Copenhagen. In 1728, and again in 1795, it was badly destroyed by fire. Occupied by the Germans in World War II, it became the centre of a strong resistance movement. Population (1981 est): 648 720.

Copepoda   A subclass of *crustaceans (7500 species), mostly 0.5–2 mm long, that have long antennae, a single median eye, and no carapace. There are 11 pairs of appendages on the head and thorax and forked tail filaments (furca). Copepods occur in abundance in fresh and salt water, forming a constituent of plankton. Most feed on microscopic plants or animals but some are parasitic on fish, other crustaceans, etc.

Copernicus, Nicolaus   (1473–1543) Polish astronomer, formulator of the modern heliocentric theory of the solar system. After studying mathematics and music at Cracow and Bologna, Copernicus became interested in the problem of calculating planetary positions, since existing tables were out of date. He noticed that by using a system in which the earth revolved round the sun, instead of *Ptolemy's geocentric system, these calculations would be much easier to make. He then realized that such a system could actually describe the solar system, rather than providing a simple working model of it, since it explained the occasional backward motion of the planets. Copernicus, realizing that these ideas were at variance with the Church's view that the earth was at the centre of the universe, only circulated them to a few friends. The full text of his book *De revolutionibus orbium coelestium* was not published until 1543: legend has it that Copernicus was presented with the first copy on his deathbed.

Copland, Aaron   (1900–) US composer, a pupil of Nadia Boulanger. He has been active as a teacher, pianist, and champion of contemporary music. He is best known for his compositions in a popular style, such as the ballets *Billy the Kid* (1938) and *Rodeo* (1942). His other works employ a variety of styles and include a piano concerto (1927) in a jazz idiom and a *Piano Fantasy* (1950) using *serialism.

copper (Cu)   A reddish-brown metal, known from prehistoric times and named after the island of Cyprus, which was the principal source in Roman times. It occurs naturally as the native element, the sulphide chalcopyrite ($CuFeS_2$), the carbonate malachite ($CuCO_3.Cu(OH)_2$), and other minerals. It is mined in Zambia, Zaïre, Chile, Australia, New Guinea, and elsewhere. Copper is extracted by smelting and electrolysis. It is malleable, ductile, and is important because of its good electrical (second only to silver) and thermal conductivity. Copper is widely used in the electrical industry and in the form of copper pipes in plumbing. It is contained in coins, and in the alloys *brass and *bronze. Common compounds are the oxides (Cu_2O, CuO) and copper sulphate ($CuSO_4$). At no 29; at wt 63.546; mp 1083°C; bp 2595°C.

Copperbelt   An area in central Africa, on the Zaïre-Zambia border. Rich in copper-ore deposits, it has the largest known deposits in the world, after the USA.

copperhead A North American *pit viper, *Agkistrodon contortrix*, occurring in swampy or wooded regions. Up to 1 m long, it is reddish with a coppery head and brown bands on its back. The name is also given to a S Australian snake, *Denisonia superba*, which is about 1.5 m long and usually coppery-brown.

Copperhead A Northerner sympathetic to the South during the US *Civil War, especially one who opposed Lincoln's military or civil policies. Mostly midwestern Democrats, the Copperheads were accused of disloyalty to the northern cause and the Democratic Party suffered by association with them. The name derives from a newspaper reference comparing antiwar Democrats to snakes (a copperhead is a poisonous snake).

Coppermine River A river in N Canada, in Mackenzie district. Rising in Lac de Gras, it flows NW past copper deposits into Coronation Gulf (an arm of the Arctic Ocean). Length: 845 km (525 mi).

copra. *See* coconut.

Coptic A *Hamito-Semitic language spoken in Egypt from the early Christian period until the 8th century AD. It was the last stage of ancient Egyptian and was written in Greek characters with seven additional *demotic letters. There were six dialects of which Sahidic became the standard form in Upper Egypt after the 5th century. Bohairic of Lower Egypt was used for religious purposes by the Coptic Christians and has a literature of scriptural translations from Greek and original writings that reflect Gnostic and Manichaean tendencies within early Christianity.

Coptic Church The largest Christian Church in Egypt. The Copts trace the history of their Church to St *Mark. As a result of its *Monophysite beliefs, which were condemned at the Council of Chalcedon (451), the Coptic Church became somewhat isolated from other Christian bodies. The Muslim conquest of Egypt in 642, together with language and cultural differences, widened the division. The Church suffered some persecution under Arab dominion. In 1741 a number of Copts entered the Roman Catholic communion, becoming the Uniat Coptic Church. Alexandria held an eminent position in the early Church and remains the seat of the Coptic patriarch, who presides over the Church with 12 diocesan bishops. The Copts are in communion with the Armenian and Syrian (Orthodox) Churches.

copyright law The law contained mainly in the Copyright Act (1956), protecting the exclusive right of authors, composers, artists, publishers, and others who create or publish original literary, dramatic, and artistic works to reproduce them (in whole or in part) and to exploit them. Infringement of copyright is known as piracy. The protection in England lasts for 50 years after the death of the owner of the copyright. In contrast to a *patent, copyright cannot exist in an idea, method, or scheme, but only in its expression. Many nations adopted the Universal Copyright Convention in 1952, whereby each signatory undertook to give the same protection to the authors of the other signatories as it gave its own authors.

coracle An ancient boat, usually round, made of wickerwork or laths over which a waterproofed animal skin has been stretched and fitted. Coracles were used in Ireland and in Wales and other parts of W Britain.

coral A sedentary marine animal belonging to a class (*Anthozoa*) of *coelenterates. Individual corals—*polyps—produce a protective skeleton that may be soft and jelly-like, horny, or stony. They usually occur in colonies and are found in all oceans, particularly warm shallow waters, feeding mainly on small animals. Reproduction can be asexual (by budding) or sexual, the eggs being fertilized in the water.
The stony (*or* true) corals (order *Madreporaria*; about 1000 species) secrete a rigid external skeleton made of almost pure calcium carbonate. **Coral reefs** (*see* reef) are produced by

succeeding generations of stony corals, occurring in dense colonies. The principal reef building occurs at depths of less than 50 m and at temperatures above 20°C. Within this zone symbiotic algae (zooxanthellae) are present in coral tissues and stimulate the secretion of calcium carbonate, accelerating the growth of coral skeletons. The Great Barrier Reef off NE Australia is the best-known example.

Coralli, Jean (J. C. Peracini; 1779-1854) Italian ballet dancer and choreographer. He trained in Paris and was choreographer at the Paris Academy from 1831 to 1845. He choreographed many of the most celebrated Romantic ballets, including *Giselle* (1841) and *La Peri* (1843).

Coral Sea A section of the SW Pacific Ocean between NE Australia, New Guinea, and the New Hebrides. It contains many coral reefs, including the *Great Barrier Reef. During World War II it was the scene of a US victory over the Japanese (1942).

coral snake A New World burrowing venomous snake having a boldly patterned skin. They occur chiefly in the tropics and are generally secretive, preying on other snakes. The main genus, *Micrurus* (40 species), ranges from the S USA to Argentina; most species are ringed with red, black, and yellow or white. Old World coral snakes are similar and found in SE Asia (genus *Calliophis*) and Africa (genus *Elaps*). Family: *Elapidae* (cobras, mambas, coral snakes). The rear-fanged false coral snakes have similar patterning but belong to the family *Colubridae* (grass snakes, etc.).

coral tree A Brazilian tree, *Erythrina crista-galli*, 2–3 m high, with clusters of deep-scarlet flowers, for which it is often grown as an ornamental. Family: *Leguminosae*.

cor anglais A double-reeded musical instrument, the alto member of the oboe family. It is a transposing instrument, the notes sounding a fifth lower than written. It has a range of two and a half octaves from the E below middle C. Sibelius used its rich tone in the symphonic poem *The Swan of Tuonela*.

Corbusier, Le. *See* Le Corbusier.

Corby 52 29N 0 40W A town in central England, in Northamptonshire. It was designated a new town in 1950 with plans for an eventual population of 80 000. Closure of Corby's large iron and steel works (1979) resulted in high unemployment. Population (1981): 47 773.

Cordaitales An order of extinct *gymnosperm trees that—with *Calamites—formed vast forests during the Carboniferous and Permian periods (370-240 million years ago); coal was formed from their fossilized remains. The trees probably grew up to 30 m high, with a tall columnar trunk and strap-shaped leaves, up to 1 m long.

Corday, Charlotte (1768-93) French noblewoman, who assassinated Jean-Paul *Marat in his bath on 13 July, 1793. She was guillotined on 17 July. She sympathized with the Girondins, the revolutionary party that opposed the more radical Jacobins.

Cordeliers, Club of the A French Revolutionary club founded in Paris in 1790 to defend the rights of man. It was temporarily disbanded following a demonstration against Louis XVI in 1791. After it was restored, it became more radical and was finally disbanded in 1794 following an unsuccessful insurrection.

cordgrass. *See* Spartina.

Córdoba 31 25S 64 11W A city in central Argentina. Founded in 1573, it has many notable old buildings, including the cathedral (1758) and the university (1613). A commercial and industrial centre, its manufactures include cars, tractors, and textiles. Population (1980 est): 781 565.

Córdoba 37 53N 4 46W A city in S Spain, in Andalusia on the River Guadalquivir. It became the capital of Moorish Spain in 756 AD and by the 10th century was Europe's largest city and a major cultural centre. Its immense Moorish cathedral (8th-10th centuries) was originally a mosque.

Cordon Bleu

Industries include silverware and textiles. Population (1981): 284 737.

Cordon Bleu Originally, the blue ribbon of the knight's grand cross of the Order of the Holy Spirit, the first order of the Bourbon kings. The term is now used to describe food, or a chef, that achieves an (unspecified) degree of excellence.

Corelli, Arcangelo (1653-1713) Italian violinist and composer. He rationalized contemporary violin technique and wrote sonatas for the instrument. He also established the concerto grosso, in which a small group of soloists (typically two violins and cello) is contrasted with the full orchestra, a form much used by baroque composers. His most famous work is the *Christmas Concerto* for strings and continuo.

Corelli, Marie (1854-1924) British novelist. Of Scots-Italian parentage, she was educated in France as a musician. Her first book, the semiautobiographical *A Romance of Two Worlds* (1886), was followed by a series of popular romantic novels that included *Barabbas* (1893), *The Murder of Delicia* (1896), and *The Secret Power* (1921).

Coreopsis A genus of North American, tropical African, and Hawaiian plants (120 species) commonly known as tickseeds (because of the shape of their seedlike fruits). Annual or perennial herbs, they are often grown in gardens for their daisy-like flowers, which are usually yellow with a darker centre. Family: *Compositae*.

Corfu (Latin name: Corcyra; Modern Greek name: Kérkira *or* Kérkyra) A Greek island in the NE Ionian Sea, in the Ionian Islands. It has belonged to many powers, including Venice (1386-1797) and Britain (1815-64). The local produce includes olives, figs, and citrus fruit, and tourism is important. Area: 641 sq km (250 sq mi). Population (1981): 97 102. Chief town: Corfu.

corgi One of two breeds of working □dog originating in SW Wales. Both are low-set: the Cardigan Welsh corgi has a long tail, rounded ears, and a shortish coat, which may be reddish brown, streaked brown, or black and tan; the Pembroke Welsh corgi has a short tail, pointed ears, and a finer coat of red, sable, fawn, or black and tan. Both breeds can have white markings. Height: 30 cm (Cardigan); 25-30 cm (Pembroke).

coriander An annual plant, *Coriander sativum*, 20-70 cm high, with umbrella-like clusters of small pink or white flowers. Probably native to the Mediterranean, it is widespread in waste places and is also cultivated for its fruits, used in curries, alcoholic beverages, as a condiment, and medicinally for flatulence. Family: *Umbelliferae*.

Corineus A legendary Trojan hero after whom Cornwall is named. According to the medieval chronicler *Geoffrey of Monmouth he was a companion of Brutus, the grandson of Aeneas and legendary founder of Britain, and the killer of the giant Gogmagog (*see* Gog and Magog).

Corinth (Greek name: Kórinthos) 37 56N 22 55E A port in S Greece, in the Peloponnese on the Isthmus of Corinth. The modern port was founded in 1858 near the site of the ancient city; its trade includes wine. *History*: a settlement before 3000 BC, the ancient city of Corinth developed in commercial importance during the 8th century BC. It became the second largest and richest of the Greek city states after Athens, rivalry between the two culminating in the *Peloponnesian War. Corinth resisted Roman pressures but was destroyed by them in 146 BC, later to be revived as a Roman colony (44 BC). The city declined during the middle ages. Extensive excavations have taken place since 1896. Population (1981): 22 495.

Corinth, League of (*or* Hellenic League) An alliance of Greek states formed in 338 BC at Corinth under the leadership of *Philip II of Macedon. The League was formed for a joint Greek and Macedonian campaign against Persia and contributed to the Asian campaign of *Alexander the Great, who succeeded Philip in 336. The League was disbanded after Alexander's death (323), being briefly revived in 303.

Corinthian order. *See* orders of architecture.

Corinthians, Epistles of Paul to the Two New Testament books written by the apostle Paul to the Christian Church at Corinth in about 57 AD. In the first he deals with problems that had arisen in the Church and answers questions on a number of practical and doctrinal issues, for example marriage and celibacy, the resurrection of the dead, and the Eucharist. In the second he explains the nature of his own apostolic ministry and defends himself against his opponents at Corinth.

Coriolanus, Gnaeus Marcius Roman general, who defeated the Volsci and captured the town of Corioli. Exiled in 491 BC for his contempt for the common people during a famine, he led the Volsci against Rome but was dissuaded from sacking the city by his wife Virgilia and mother Volumnia. The story is the subject of Shakespeare's *Coriolanus* (1607).

Coriolis force A *force required to account for the motion of a body as seen by an observer in a rotating frame of reference. It is often referred to as a fictitious force as it disappears on changing to a nonrotating frame. For example, a shell shot from a gun at the centre of a rotating table appears to an outside observer to travel in a straight line. To an observer on the table it appears to have a curved path. The Coriolis force is required to account for this apparent tangential acceleration. The Coriolis force is responsible for the formation and direction of rotation of anticyclones and whirlpools. Named after the French physicist Gaspard de Coriolis (1792-1843).

cork Tissue that forms the outer layer of *bark in woody plants. Cork provides extra insulation and physical protection to the internal cells of the plant. The cork oak (*Quercus suber*), an evergreen oak tree of S Europe and N Africa, is cultivated in Portugal and SW Spain as the source of commercial cork. The cork is stripped from the tree every 8-10 years and is used for shock absorbers, bungs, fishing floats, floor and wall coverings, shoe soles, etc.

Cork (Irish name: Corcaigh) The largest county in the Republic of Ireland, in Munster bordering on the Atlantic Ocean. Mountains in the W extend eastwards intersected by valleys, notably that of the River Blackwater. Its many coastal inlets include Bantry Bay and Cork Harbour. Fishing is important; Ballycotton is noted for its game fishing. Agriculture is varied with dairy and arable farming. Its many castles include Blarney Castle, famous for the Blarney Stone. Area: 7459 sq km (2880 sq mi). Population (1981): 266 121. County town: Cork.

Cork (Irish name: Corcaigh) 51 54N 8 28W The second largest city in the Republic of Ireland and county town of Co Cork, on Cork Harbour. The settlement grew up around a monastery (founded in about the 6th century AD) and it has remained important as a centre of learning with the presence of University College (founded 1845), part of the National University of Ireland. It has many notable buildings, especially its cathedrals and St Ann's Shaldon Church, famous for its bells. It is an important industrial and trading centre with a fine harbour. Exports include bacon, dairy produce, and livestock and it has bacon-curing, car assembly, and brewing and distilling industries. Population (1981): 149 792.

corkwood. *See* balsa.

corm A fleshy underground stem base of certain perennial herbaceous plants, such as the crocus and gladiolus, that acts as an overwintering structure. Growth the following season occurs by one or more buds: if two or more plants are produced the corm is acting as an organ of vegetative reproduction.

cormorant A slender long-necked waterbird belonging to a family (*Phalacrocoracidae*; 30 species) and found on most coasts and some inland waters. 50-100 cm in length, cormorants are typically glossy black with white throat markings and have short legs, webbed feet, a long stiff tail, and a long slender hook-tipped bill; they feed mainly on fish caught underwater. Order: *Pelecaniformes* (gannets, pelicans, etc.).

corn 1. *See* maize. 2. The main cereal crop of a particular region; for example wheat in England.

Corn Belt An area in the central USA, S and W of the Great Lakes, extending mainly through Indiana, Illinois, Iowa, and Nebraska. It possesses a distinctive agriculture with intensive maize and soya-bean production used in the raising of fat cattle and pigs.

corn borer A small European *pyralid moth, *Pyrausta nubilalis,* accidentally introduced to North America. It is a serious economic pest, attacking over 200 plant species, including beans, celery, maize, and potatoes. The larvae burrow into plant stems near ground level, sometimes causing them to break off.

corncockle An annual purple-flowered weed of arable land in most temperate regions, *Agrostemma githago,* growing to a height of 100 cm. Once abundant, it is now rare due to efficient seed clearing. Family: *Caryophyllaceae.*

corncrake A migratory bird, *Crex crex,* also called landrail, that breeds in Eurasian grasslands, wintering in S Africa and Asia. It is 26 cm long with a streaked brown plumage and chestnut wing patches and is easily identified by its harsh rasping call. Family: *Rallidae* (rails).

cornea The transparent outer layer at the front of the eyeball, through which light enters the □eye. Corneal grafts have been used successfully to replace diseased areas of cornea; since the cornea has no blood supply the graft cannot be rejected by blood-borne antibodies.

Corneille, Pierre (1606–84) French dramatist. After a Jesuit education he worked in government service in his home town of Rouen from 1628 to 1650. His early comedies, beginning with *Mélite* (1629), were much admired by Cardinal Richelieu. *Le Cid* (1636), the seminal play of French classical tragedy, excited much controversy. Here and in *Horace* (1640), *Cinna* (1641), and *Polyeucte* (1643) he pioneered a dramatic genre the main emphasis of which was on moral conflicts expressed in majestic formal verse, a genre later perfected by his younger contemporary *Racine. In 1647 he moved to Paris and continued to write prolifically until his last play, *Suréna,* in 1674.

CORNUCOPIA

Cornelius, Peter von (1783–1867) German painter, born in Düsseldorf. In Rome (1811–19) he was associated with a group of German artists, the Nazarenes, in the revival of fresco painting. He worked subsequently in Munich on frescoes for the museum of classical sculpture and in Berlin.

Corner Brook 48 58N 57 58W A city in E Canada, in Newfoundland. It has one of the world's largest pulp mills. Population (1981 est): 24 339.

cornet A valved brass instrument, with cup-shaped mouthpiece and conical bore. Pitched in B flat, it is similar to the trumpet but less brilliant. It has a range of two and a half octaves from the E below middle C and plays an important role in the brass band.

cornetfish A tropical marine *bony fish, also called flutemouth, belonging to a family (*Fistulariidae*; about 4 species) related to *pipefish and *seahorses. It has a slender body, up to 1.8 m long, a long threadlike filament extending from the tail fin, and a long siphon-like snout. Order: *Gasterosteiformes.*

cornett A woodwind instrument with a cup-shaped mouthpiece and finger holes. The brilliant tone of the treble cornett was much favoured by composers of the 16th and 17th centuries, such as Giovanni Gabrieli.

cornflower An annual, sometimes overwintering, herbaceous plant, *Centaurea cyanus,* growing to about 75 cm high. Flower heads are bright blue with a purplish centre. Probably native in most of Europe and the Near East, it is widely introduced as a cereal crop weed but is now becoming rare due to improved seed clearing. Horticultural garden varieties are popular. Family: *Compositae.*

Cornforth, Sir John Warcup (1917–) Australian chemist, who shared the 1975 Nobel Prize with Vladimir Prelog (1906–) for their work on stereochemistry. Cornforth showed the importance of stereoisomers in biological systems, using *radioactive tracers to follow the course of their reactions.

Cornish A *Celtic language of the Brythonic group, formerly spoken in Cornwall and Devon, that became extinct in about 1800. It was closely related to Breton, which was introduced to Brittany from this area. A number of miracle and morality plays dating from the 15th century were written in Cornish.

Corn Laws The British laws that regulated (1360–1846) the import and export of corn to guarantee farmers' incomes. The 1815 Corn Law prohibited the import of corn until home-grown corn had reached a price of 80 shillings a quarter (of a hundredweight). In 1828 a sliding scale of import duties was fixed and duties were levied on imported corn when the price of British corn was down to 73 shillings a quarter. These laws were bitterly resented by the working classes, because they kept the price of bread high, and by the manufacturers, who argued that little money was left for the purchase of manufactured goods. Opposition to the Corn Laws was led by the *Anti-Corn Law League and in 1846 Sir Robert *Peel's government repealed them. A nominal duty continued to be levied until 1869.

corn poppy An annual, or sometimes biennial, poppy, *Papaver rhoeas,* with scarlet (occasionally pinkish) flowers. Also called field poppy, it grows to a height of 50 cm. It is a weed of arable and waste places, occurring throughout much of Eurasia and N Africa and introduced to North America, New Zealand, and Australia.

corn salad A slender branching annual plant, *Valerianella locusta,* also called lamb's lettuce. 7–40 cm high, with small pale-lilac flowers, it grows in dryish places and is sometimes cultivated for salads. It is native to Europe, N Africa, and W Asia and introduced to North America. Family: *Valerianaceae.*

cornucopia A decorative motif from Greek antiquity denoting abundance and wealth. It consists of a goat's horn filled with fruit and flowers and was reputedly presented to the nymph Amalthaea by Zeus or vice versa.

Cornwall (Celtic name: Kernow) The most southwesterly county of England, bordering on the Atlantic Ocean and the

English Channel and including the Isles of *Scilly. It consists mainly of rugged hills rising to Bodmin Moor in the E. Dairy farming and market gardening are the main agricultural activities, the equable climate encouraging the growth of early fruit and vegetables. Tourism is a chief source of income. Tinmining, important since early times, was revitalized in the 1960s. In 1974 the Cornish nationalist movement led to the revival of the Stannary or Tinners' Parliament and also to attempts to resurrect the Cornish language. Area: 3546 sq km (1369 sq mi). Population (1981): 430 506. Administrative centre: Truro.

Cornwall, Duchy of A private estate of some 130 000 acres, mostly in Cornwall, Devon, and Somerset, belonging to the eldest son of the sovereign, who becomes Duke of Cornwall at birth or from the moment his parent is crowned. It was established in 1337 by Edward III to support his son, the Black Prince. If there is no Duke of Cornwall the revenue, which exceeded £1M in 1985, is paid to the Treasury. The Prince of Wales pays no tax on the revenue, although the present Prince donates one quarter of the income to the Treasury.

Cornwallis, Charles, 1st Marquess (1738–1805) British general in the *American Revolution. Although he opposed the taxation of the American colonies, he took a command when the revolution broke out and defeated Gates at *Camden (1780). In 1781, however, he was disastrously defeated at Yorktown. He then served twice as governor general of India (1786–93, 1805), where he promulgated the **Cornwallis Code** (1793), on which the government of India was based until 1833. The Code gave financial, judicial, and administrative control to the East India Company. Higher offices of state were reserved for Europeans.

Coromandel Coast The SE coast of India between the Krishna Delta and Point Calimere.

Coromandel screens Large 17th-century Chinese screens originally shipped from the *Coromandel Coast to Europe. They have up to 12 panels with brown or red lacquer grounds and incised polychromatic decoration.

corona The outer layer of a star's atmosphere. It is very tenuous and extensive compared with the *chromosphere and has a temperature of over a million degrees Celsius. The sun's corona has two main components. The **inner corona** lies above the chromosphere and consists of rapidly moving electrons. Its temperature reaches about 2 000 000°C some 75 000 km above the visible solar surface (the *photosphere). The **outer corona** extends for millions of kilometres and consists of comparatively slow-moving dust particles. The solar corona cannot be seen without special equipment, except at a total solar *eclipse. It then appears as a pearly usually unsymmetrical halo around the darkened solar disc, the shape depending on the time of the *sunspot cycle. See also solar wind.

coronary heart disease The most common form of *heart disease in the western world. It is caused by *atherosclerosis of the coronary arteries, which reduces the blood flow to the heart. This may precipitate the formation of a blood clot in these arteries—**coronary thrombosis**. The patient experiences sudden pain in the chest (see angina pectoris) and the result may be a heart attack, when the blood flow to the heart is suddenly stopped (see myocardial infarction). Associated with smoking, lack of exercise, high-fat diets, hypertension, and middle age, it is commoner in men.

coroner In England and Wales, an officer of the Crown appointed for life by a county council from among suitably qualified barristers, solicitors, or qualified medical practitioners. The main duty of a coroner (from Latin *corona*, crown) is to inquire into the death of anyone who dies by an act of violence, in suspicious circumstances, or in prison. He is often assisted by a jury of 7 to 11 people. A jury verdict of manslaughter or murder is equivalent to an indictment, and the coroner can commit the accused for trial. A coroner also inquires into cases of *treasure trove. In Scotland, the coroner's duties are carried out by the procurator fiscal.

Corot, Jean Baptiste Camille (1796–1875) French land-scape painter. After training under two minor landscapists (1822–25), he visited Italy (1825–28), the subject of many of his landscapes. Although he exhibited at the Paris Salon from 1827, he did not achieve critical acclaim until the 1850s, with his poetical misty landscapes populated by nymphs. More popular today are his open-air sketches, small landscapes, and figure studies. He was friendly with the *Barbizon school and influenced the impressionists.

corporate state (or corporative state) A society in which the individual is represented in government by the economic group (corporation) to which he belongs rather than according to his geographical location. The ideas of *Guild Socialism in early 20th-century Britain were akin to corporatism, but it has only been adopted as a system of government by fascist dictators, such as Mussolini, Franco, and Salazar, and the term now has pejorative implications.

corporation tax A tax levied on the profits of a company on an annual basis. In the UK, where the tax replaced profits tax in 1966, the rate of tax is announced by the chancellor of the exchequer in his *budget.

Corpus Christi 27 47N 97 26W A city in the USA, in Texas on Corpus Christi Bay. A popular resort, its port exports cotton, petroleum, and sulphur. Industries include cement and chemicals as well as fishing. Population (1980): 231 999.

Corpus Christi, Feast of (Latin: body of Christ) A Christian feast honouring the institution of the Eucharist, observed in the West on the second Thursday after *Whit Sunday. Originally a local festival in Liège, it was extended to the whole Church by Pope Urban IV in 1264. The chief rite of the feast is the procession of the Blessed Sacrament. It is not generally observed by Protestant Churches.

Corpus Juris Canonici A collection of papal and conciliar decrees comprising the main body of the canon law of the Western Church. It is composed of six collections compiled between the 12th and 15th centuries. Pope Gregory XIII revised it in 1582. It was superseded in 1917 by the Codex Juris Canonici, a revision of the whole of canon law.

Corpus Juris Civilis. See Roman law.

corpus luteum. See ovary.

Correggio (Antonio Allegri; c. 1494–1534) Italian Renaissance painter, born at Correggio, near Modena. Initially influenced by *Mantegna, he later studied *Leonardo and *Michelangelo. He worked chiefly in Parma, where he decorated the Camera di S Paolo, the domed vaulting of S Giovanni Evangelista, and the cathedral with frescoes that anticipate the *baroque. Using strong contrasts between light and shade, he painted religious subjects, e.g. Adoration of the Shepherds or Night (Dresden), and sensuous nudes, e.g. Jupiter and Io (Kunsthistorisches Museum, Vienna).

Corregidor An island in the N Philippines, in the mouth of Manila Bay. It has been fortified since Spanish times. During World War II it held Manila harbour against the Japanese for five months although bombed continuously.

Correns, Carl Erich (1864–1933) German botanist and geneticist, whose work on breeding garden peas confirmed the principles of heredity first established by *Mendel. In 1900, simultaneously with *de Vries, he rediscovered Mendel's original paper, which had been ignored since 1865.

Corrientes 27 30S 58 48W A port in NE Argentina, on the Río Paraná. It is an important export centre for agricultural products, including cotton, rice, and tobacco. It has a university (1957). Population (1980): 180 000.

Corsica (French name: Corse) An island in the Mediterranean Sea, separated from Sardinia by the Strait of Bonifacio. Together with 43 islets it comprises a region of France. It is mountainous with a rugged coastline and much of the island is covered with *maquis*, a dense thorny scrub type of vegetation. Agriculture is relatively undeveloped, producing citrus fruits, olives, vegetables, and tobacco; sheep

317

and goats are extensively reared and tourism is a major source of income. *History*: under Genoese control from the 14th century, it was sold to France in 1768. During World War II it came under Italian occupation but was liberated by the French in 1943, weakening the German position in Italy. Area: 8680 sq km (3350 sq mi). Population (1981 est): 230 100. Capital: Ajaccio.

Cort, Henry (1740–1800) British inventor and industrialist, who in 1784 invented the puddling process for producing wrought iron from pig iron. He also invented a method of producing high-quality iron bars by passing iron through grooved rollers.

Cortes The Spanish parliament, which first met in the kingdom of Léon in 1188. This was the first time that representatives of the townsmen attended the king's court together with the clergy and nobility. The regional Cortes lost their influence during the 16th century. The first national Cortes met in 1810.

Cortés, Hernán (1485–1547) Spanish conquistador. In Hispaniola and Cuba from 1504, he led a small expedition to Mexico in 1519 and reached Tenochtitlán, the capital of the Aztec Empire. In Cortés' absence, dealing with an attack from a Spanish force from Cuba, the Aztecs launched an attack on Tenochtitlán, forcing the Spaniards' retreat—the *noche triste* (night of sorrows). Cortés eventually rebuilt his forces and destroyed Tenochtitlán (1521) and the Aztec Empire, founding New Spain. After an expedition to Honduras (1524–26) Cortés returned to Spain (1528) but renewed his Pacific explorations in the 1530s. He died in poverty in Spain.

cortex The outer tissues of an animal or plant organ. In plants the cortex is situated between the *epidermis and vascular (conducting) tissues of stems and roots. Its cell walls may contain corky and woody materials or silica, providing strength, and also stored food, usually starch. Resins, latex, tannins, and essential oils may also be present. In animals the outer tissue of the *adrenal gland, the cerebrum, and the *kidney is called the cortex.

corticosteroids Steroid hormones secreted by the cortex of the adrenal glands (the term also includes synthetic drugs with similar properties). The glucocorticoids (e.g. cortisone, prednisolone, and dexamethasone) affect carbohydrate metabolism. As anti-inflammatory drugs, they are used to treat allergic conditions (e.g. asthma), inflammatory disorders (e.g. ulcerative colitis and rheumatoid arthritis), and autoimmune diseases. They are also used to treat some cancers. The mineralocorticoids (e.g. aldosterone, fludrocortisone) control salt and water balance in the body.

Cortona 43 17N 11 59E A town in Italy, in Tuscany. It is famous for its Etruscan and Roman remains and has a cathedral dating from the 15th century. Population (1981): 22 281.

Cortot, Alfred (1877–1962) French pianist and conductor. He is remembered as an interpreter of Beethoven's piano concertos, as a conductor of Wagner's operas, and as a member of a famous piano trio with Thibaud and Casals.

corundum A mineral consisting mainly of aluminium oxide, the accessory minerals giving rise to a variety of colours. Sapphire is a blue variety containing iron and titanium; ruby contains chromium. It occurs in silica-poor igneous rocks, in metamorphosed shales, and in some metamorphosed limestone veins. The nongem varieties are used as abrasives (corundum is the second hardest mineral to diamond). *See* Plate III.

Corunna. *See* La Coruña.

corvette A small highly manoeuvrable lightly armed warship displacing approximately 1600 tonnes and carrying a complement of a hundred officers and men. They were used mainly for antisubmarine escort duty during World War II by the Royal Navy. In the days of sail, the corvette, smaller than a *frigate, was a sloop rigged as a ship. Those that remained after World War II were renamed antisubmarine frigates in 1959.

Corvo, Baron. *See* Rolfe, Frederick William.

Corybant One of the Corybantes, the eunuch priests or attendants of the goddess *Cybele, whose worship was accompanied by wild dancing and orgies. They castrated themselves in imitation of the self-mutilation of Cybele's lover, the fertility god Attis.

Corydalis A genus of mainly N temperate herbs (320 species), mostly perennials with underground tubers. The flowers, usually yellow, grow in clusters and resemble those of peas. Garden varieties, 15–60 cm high, prefer shady cool positions. Family: *Fumariaceae*.

Cos (Modern Greek name: Kos) A Greek island in the SE Aegean Sea, in the Dodecanese. It was a member of the Delian League and the home of the Greek physician, Hippocrates. It produces chiefly fruit but also silk and tobacco. Cos lettuce originally came from here. Area: 282 sq km (109 sq mi). Population (1981): 20 350.

Cosenza 39 17N 16 16E A market town in Italy, in Calabria. Its manufactures include furniture and it has a 13th-century cathedral. Population (1980 est): 100 981.

Cosgrave, William Thomas (1880–1965) Irish statesman. A member of *Sinn Féin, he took part in the *Easter Rising (1916) and was elected to the first Irish Assembly (1918). He was first president of the Irish Free State (1922–32) and then led the *Fine Gael opposition until 1944. His son **Liam Cosgrave** (1920–) became leader of Fine Gael in 1965 and was prime minister from 1973 until 1977, when he resigned the party leadership.

Cosmas and Damian, SS (early 4th century AD) Christian martyrs. Nothing certain is known of their lives, but according to tradition they were twin brothers who practised as physicians in Asia Minor, refused to accept payment from their patients, and were martyred under Diocletian. They are patron saints of physicians. Feast day: 27 Sept or 27 Oct.

cosmetics Beauty aids and preparations intended to improve the appearance of face, hair, or nails or the texture of the skin. Historically, among the most common cosmetics have been kohl, for shading around the eyes, and henna, for dyeing hair, fingertips, and toes; their use dates back at least to ancient Egypt. Rouge and face powders were used by the ancient Greeks and Romans. Although periodically cosmetics have met with public disapproval, as in Puritan and Victorian times, during the 20th century the manufacture of cosmetics has become an important industry, catering increasingly for men as well as women. Although modern western cosmetics no longer contain such dangerous ingredients as the lead compounds found in ancient Greek face powders, some ingredients can nevertheless irritate sensitive skins. Many modern cosmetics, such as eyebrow pencils, are wax-based; lipsticks also contain nondrying oils. Petroleum jelly, liquid paraffin, and colouring are also widely used. Creams and lotions are emulsions of wax or oil in water, which evaporates on application; the oily film left prevents the skin from drying out. Face powder consists principally of zinc oxide, precipitated chalk, talc, and zinc stearate. Nail varnish consists of a nitrocellulose base, a plasticizer, and a modifying resin, all in a volatile solvent. Astringent lotions (including aftershave), which close the openings of the hair follicles, are based on alcohol solutions; antiperspirants are usually based on an aluminium salt, which prevents sweat from leaving the sweat ducts.

cosmic rays A continuous stream of very high-energy particles that bombard the earth from space. The primary radiation consists of *protons and light nuclei with smaller numbers of neutral particles, such as *photons and *neutrinos. These particles collide with atomic nuclei in the earth's atmosphere producing large numbers of elementary particles, known as secondary radiation. One primary particle may produce a large number of secondary particles on colliding with a nucleus. This effect is called a shower. Some cosmic rays are believed to originate from the sun, others from outside the solar system.

cosmogony   The study of the origin and evolution of the universe and the astronomical objects it contains, or a theory concerning the origin and development of a particular system, especially the solar system.

cosmology   The study of the origin, evolution, and structure of the universe. A great variety of cosmological models have been put forward through the ages. Two simple but incorrect common-sense models are the flat earth draped by a canopy of stars and the earth-centred (geocentric) universe, the *Ptolemaic system. More accurate theories emerged as instruments were developed to study the heavens (*see* astronomy). Current models are highly mathematical but are closely linked with observation. In every model the universe is expanding (*see* expanding universe). Most assume that there are no preferred places in the universe: all directions appear indistinguishable to an observer and this isotropy exists about every point in space (the cosmological principle). The standard cosmological model is the *big-bang theory in which the universe originated in an explosion some 15 thousand million years ago and has since been expanding and cooling from an initial state of extreme density and temperature. *See also* steady state theory.

Cossacks   A people of S and SW Russia descended from independent Tatar groups and escaped serfs from Poland, Lithuania, and Muscovy. They established a number of independent self-governing communities, which were given special privileges by Russian or Polish rulers in return for military service. Known for their horsemanship, each Cossack community provided a separate army. The Cossacks slowly lost their autonomy as Russia expanded in the 17th and 18th centuries and there were occasional rebellions. Many fled Russia after the Revolution (1918–21) and collectivization subsumed remaining Cossack communities.

Costa Brava   A coastal region in NE Spain, bordering on the Mediterranean Sea. It extends from Barcelona to the French border and is a popular tourist area with many resorts.

cost accounting.   *See* accountancy.

Costa Rica, Republic of   A country in the Central American isthmus between Nicaragua and Panama. It includes the island of Cocos, 483 km (186 mi) to the SW. The Caribbean lowlands rise to a central plateau area, with volcanic peaks reaching 3819 m (12 529 ft). The inhabitants are mainly of Spanish and mixed descent, with a dwindling Indian population. *Economy*: chiefly agricultural, the main crops being coffee, bananas, and sugar (the principal export). Livestock is important and crops, such as cocoa, are being introduced as part of a plan to diversify the economy. Almost 75% of the land is forested with valuable woods, such as mahogany, rosewood, and cedar. Mineral resources include gold, haematite ore, and sulphur; many small industries are being encouraged. *History*: discovered by Columbus in 1502, it became a Spanish colony in the 15th century and the native Indian population was practically wiped out. It was part of the captaincy general of Guatemala until gaining independence in 1821. From 1824 until 1838 it formed part of the Central American Federation. In 1948 José Figueres Ferrer (1906–   ), leader of the socialist National Liberation Party, came to power at the head of a junta. A new constitution brought more democratic rule–the army was abolished and banks nationalized. Since then government has been more stable than in most Latin American countries, each election being won by the party in opposition at the time. President: Oscar Arias Sánchez (1941–   ). Official language: Spanish. Official religion: Roman Catholic. Official currency: colon of 100 centimos. Area: 50 900 sq km (19 653 sq mi). Population (1981 est): 2 276 676. Capital: San José. Main ports: Limón (on the Caribbean) and Puntarenas (on the Pacific).

cost-benefit analysis   An investigation to determine whether a certain investment project is of net benefit to the community or to decide between competing projects. This type of analysis is useful because a purely commercial assessment does not always take account of all the costs and benefits involved; for example, it would not show the benefit of reduced road congestion that might be entailed in building an underground railway. The weakness of cost-benefit analysis is that it is not always possible to quantify all the consequences, such as the destruction of the breeding grounds of a rare bird.

Costermansville.   *See* Bukavu.

costmary   A perennial herb, *Chrysanthemum balsamita*, also called alecost. About 100 cm high, it is native to E Mediterranean regions and naturalized in S Europe. The spicy aromatic leaves were formerly used for flavouring ales and salads and to make an antiseptic tea. Family: *Compositae*.

cost of living   A measure of the income required to purchase essential goods. Usually the Retail Price Index (formerly called the cost of living index), based on a standard "basket" of goods, is used as a guide to the cost of living (*see* price index). The cost of living can vary geographically (e.g. depending on whether heating oil is essential) and with time (e.g. as a result of inflation or revised definitions of what is essential). Rates of *taxation also affect the cost of living.

Cosway, Richard   (1742–1821) British portrait miniaturist. After studying with the portraitist Thomas Hudson (1701–79) he exhibited at the Royal Academy, becoming a member in 1771. He was patronized by the Prince of Wales (later George IV) and became extremely fashionable. His wife Maria Hadfield (1759–1838) was also a miniaturist.

cot death   The death of a baby, usually occurring overnight in its cot, from an unidentifiable cause. Some 20% of *infant mortality in the UK is accounted for in this way. The causes may include virus infections or allergic reactions, but evidence is growing that cot deaths are less likely in breast-fed babies and more likely in households with very low income levels.

Côte d'Ivoire.   *See* Ivory Coast.

Cotman, John Sell   (1782–1842) British landscape watercolourist and etcher of the *Norwich school. Although he worked chiefly in Norfolk, he studied and exhibited in London (c. 1798–1806), settling there in 1834. Typical of his sparsely detailed and bold compositions is *Greta Bridge* (British Museum). After 1831 he produced richly textured landscapes by mixing rice paste with watercolours.

Cotoneaster   A genus of shrubs and small trees (about 50 species) of N temperate regions of the Old World. Some species are evergreen. Many are grown in gardens for their attractive foliage and red or black berries. *C. horizontalis* is a popular ground and wall cover; *C. hybrida pendula* is a weeping standard. Family: *Rosaceae*.

Cotonou   6 24N 2 31E The chief city in Benin, on the Gulf of Guinea. A deepwater port, it is the nation's main commercial and financial centre and industries include textiles and brewing. Its university was founded in 1970. Population (1982 est): 487 020.

Cotopaxi   0 40S 78 28W The world's highest active volcano, in N central Ecuador, in the Andes. It is noted for the beauty of its symmetrical snow-capped cone. Height: 5896 m (19 457 ft).

co-trimoxazole   An *antibiotic widely used in the treatment of urinary-tract infections (such as cystitis). It is a combination of two antibiotics–a *sulphonamide and trimethoprim. Trade names: Bactrim; Septrin.

Cotswold Hills   A range of limestone hills in SW central England, mainly in Gloucestershire. It is noted for its picturesque towns and villages, such as Stow-on-the-Wold, built in the local limestone.

Cottbus (or Kottbus) 51 45N 14 24E A town in E East Germany, on the River Spree. Cottbus has several medieval churches and is a railway junction and industrial centre. Population (1980 est): 111 502.

cotton A herbaceous plant of the genus *Gossypium* (20 or 67 species, according to the classification system), native to tropical and subtropical regions. Several species are cultivated for the whitish outer fibres of their seeds. Usually 1–2 m high, cotton plants bear whitish flowers and produce seed pods (bolls), which burst when filled with the soft masses of fibres. The bolls are harvested mechanically and the fibres separated from the seeds (ginning) and cleaned and aligned (carding), ready for spinning into yarn. The longest and most lustrous fibres are obtained from varieties of Sea Island or Egyptian cotton (*G. bardadense*). Cotton forms a light durable cloth used in a wide range of garments, furnishings, and other products. The seeds are crushed to yield cottonseed oil, used in margarines, cooking oils, soaps, etc., and the residual meal is used as a livestock feed. Family: *Malvaceae*.

cottonmouth. *See* water moccasin.

cotton stainer A black and red *plant bug belonging to the genus *Dysdercus*, widely distributed in warm regions. They are serious pests of cotton plants in North America and India, staining the bolls with excrement and rendering them useless. Family: *Pyrrhocoridae*.

cottonwood A North American poplar the seeds of which resemble cotton seeds, especially *Populus deltoides*, which grows in rich woods and river bottoms and reaches a height of 30 m. Its lightweight wood is used commercially.

cotyledon The seed leaf of *seed-bearing plants (gymnosperms and angiosperms): a food store within seeds providing the embryo plant with sufficient energy to germinate. In some plants the cotyledons become the first leaves of the seedling and are often different in form from subsequent leaves. Flowering plants with one cotyledon are classified as *monocotyledons; those with two as *dicotyledons. *See* germination.

couch grass A *grass, *Agropyron repens*, also known as quack grass or twitch, native to Europe and naturalized in other N temperate regions. 30–120 cm high, it spreads by underground rhizomes and is a serious weed of arable crops, being difficult to eradicate.

cougar A red-brown *cat, *Felis concolor*, of North and South America, also called puma, mountain lion, and catamount. It is a slender muscular animal, 1.5–3 m long including its tail (50–80 cm), with long hind legs enabling a powerful leap. It prefers deer, but feeds on a variety of animals.

coulomb (C) The *SI unit of electric charge equal to the quantity of electricity transferred by a current of one ampere in one second. Named after Charles de *Coulomb.

Coulomb, Charles Augustin de (1736–1806) French physicist, who invented the torsion balance and used it to show that the force between charged particles is proportional to the product of their charges and inversely proportional to the square of the distance between them (*see* Coulomb's law). He developed a similar law for magnetic poles. The unit of charge (*see* coulomb) is named after him.

Coulomb's law The force between two electrically charged bodies is proportional to the product of their charges (q_1 and q_2) and inversely proportional to the square of the distance (d) between them. In free space the law is $F = q_1 q_2/4\pi\varepsilon_0 d^2$, where ε_0 is the *electric constant. The law is named after its discoverer Charles de *Coulomb. The force is known as the **Coulomb** (or electrostatic) **force**. **Coulomb scattering** is the scattering of a charged particle by a nucleus due to the Coulomb force between them.

council. *See* local government.

Council for Mutual Economic Assistance (COMECON) An economic association of communist countries founded in 1949. Its members are the Soviet Union, Bulgaria, Czechoslovakia, East Germany, Hungary, Mongolia, Poland, Romania, and Cuba; Albania ceased to participate in 1961. Its objective, to coordinate the economic policies of its members, has been opposed by Romania and by the more developed East Germany and Hungary, which have argued for greater individualization.

Council of Europe An association of European states, founded in 1949, that is pledged to uphold the principles of parliamentary democracy and to promote the economic and social progress of its members (Austria, Belgium, Cyprus, Denmark, France, Greece, Iceland, the Republic of Ireland, Italy, Luxembourg, Malta, the Netherlands, Norway, Portugal, Spain, Sweden, Switzerland, Turkey, the UK, and West Germany). Its seat is in Strasbourg.

counterfeiting The illegal production of false money for gain. Counterfeiting is a form of forgery, distinguished because of the unique position of *money as a general medium of exchange. Most banknotes are produced with exceptionally fine printing on watermarked paper, often with a strip of metal inserted, in an effort to make them difficult to counterfeit. Many countries are signatories to an agreement of 1929 that allows extradition of counterfeiters.

COUNTERPOINT *An example of counterpoint from J. S. Bach's Fantasia in C minor.*

counterpoint The art of combining two or more melodic lines simultaneously in music. The word derives from the Latin *punctus contra punctum*, point against point (i.e. note against note). The use of counterpoint continued beyond the end of the polyphonic period (*see* polyphony). Composers continue to make use of it today; contrapuntal techniques have been used by Stravinsky, Hindemith, Tippett, and others.

Counter-Reformation A movement within the *Roman Catholic Church dedicated to combating the effects of the Protestant *Reformation by reforming abuses within the Church and eradicating heresy by conversion, etc. Extending from the middle of the 16th to about the middle of the 17th century, it witnessed the emergence of the *Jesuits as a leading missionary body throughout the world, the reforms instituted by the Council of *Trent, the extension of the *Inquisition from Spain to other countries, and in general a revival of Catholic spirituality. Although most of N Europe remained Protestant, Poland and S Germany were stabilized as Catholic during this period.

countertenor A natural high male singing voice, higher than tenor, common in England in the 17th and 18th centuries. It is distinguished from the male *alto voice, which is produced by falsetto, but has the same range. The art of countertenor singing has been revived in the 20th century by Alfred Deller (1917–79) and James Bowman (1941–   ).

country and western A type of US popular music that evolved from the hillbilly ballads of the Appalachian Mountains and the cowboy songs of the West. Country and western is predominantly vocal music, relating the everyday experiences of the common man in sentimental texts. The singer is accompanied by the guitar and other stringed instruments. Influenced by other styles of popular music, country and western has its own offshoots, such as bluegrass. Famous country and western hits include "Your Cheatin' Heart" and "Mule Skinner Blues."

country house In England, a large house on a country estate. The great country houses were mainly built between the reigns of Elizabeth I and Victoria; before about 1550 feudal conditions caused the aristocracy to live in *castles or fortified *manor houses and after 1860 political reform and industrialization shifted the major landowners' power base and attention to the towns. Country houses displayed their owners' wealth and status, enabling them to entertain their political allies in impressive style. Some country houses exhibit the architectural opulence of small palaces (e.g. *Castle Howard and *Chatsworth), contain notable art collections, and are set in magnificent grounds (see Blenheim Palace).

Country Party. See National Country Party.

Count's War (1533–36) The last war of succession in Denmark, constituting a revolt led by Count Christopher of Oldenberg (c. 1504–66) against Christian, heir to the throne. Oldenberg finally surrendered Copenhagen in July, 1536, after which Christian became king as *Christian III.

county A geographical unit of local government. In the UK counties are long established: the name was applied by the Normans to the Anglo-Saxon *shire. The Local Government Act (1972; effective 1974) amalgamated some old counties and established new ones, dividing England into 45 (6 metropolitan and 39 nonmetropolitan) counties and Wales into 8. The Act placed a variety of public services, such as transport planning and fire services, in the hands of elected county councils, but the metropolitan county councils were abolished in 1986. The Local Government (Scotland) Act (1973) created nine new regions and three island areas. Northern Ireland has 6 counties but administration is carried out by 26 district councils. The USA does not have a similarly comprehensive county system and the powers of counties differ widely between states. See map section (British Isles – Counties).

Couperin, François (1668–1733) French composer, called le Grand, the most famous member of a family that produced five generations of musicians. He was organist to Louis XIV and at St Gervais and is best known for his harpsichord music, a series of ordres consisting of pieces in dance forms with descriptive titles. He also wrote organ music, church music, and a book on the art of playing the harpsichord.

Courbet, Gustave (1819–77) French painter, born in Ornans. Self-taught, through copying paintings in the Louvre, he became leader of the school of realism. He painted portraits, including one of his friend Baudelaire, nudes, seascapes, hunting scenes, and everyday life, e.g. Burial at Ornans (Louvre) and Bonjour Monsieur Courbet (Montpellier). Reacting against academic criticism of his work, in 1855 he organized his first private exhibition. A political radical, he was imprisoned for his participation in the Commune of Paris (1871) and in 1873 he fled to Switzerland, where he died.

courgette A variety of *marrow, also called zucchini, eaten when small and immature (up to 15 cm long). Mature courgettes resemble ordinary marrows.

Courrèges, André (1923–) French fashion designer, who opened a fashion house in Paris in 1961 after training with *Balenciaga. In 1964 he presented his "space-age" collection, which included close-fitting silver trousers, worn with short-sleeved jackets and calf-length boots. He helped to promote the unisex fashion.

courser A brownish bird of the subfamily Cursoriinae, having long legs and a pointed curved bill. It occurs in arid regions of Africa, India, and Australia. The cream-coloured courser (Cursorius cursor) of Africa is 25 cm long with white underparts and eye stripes and feeds on insects and lizards. Family: Glareolidae (pratincoles and coursers).

coursing A *blood sport dating back to at least 1500 BC, in which game (now usually hare) is pursued by hounds (usually greyhounds) that hunt by sight rather than scent. A meeting takes place on an open field and is presided over by a mounted umpire. Hounds compete in pairs in a knockout competition, chasing hares that have a start of at least 73 m (80 yd). They are

judged on points for their speed up to the quarry, for overtaking each other, and for forcing the quarry to turn. The kill is less important, as most hares escape. The British coursing season is from September to March and its main event is the Waterloo Cup (first held in 1836), staged in February at Altcar, Lancashire. It lasts 3 days and 64 dogs take part. *Greyhound racing developed from coursing.

Court, Margaret (born Smith; 1942–) Australian tennis player, the first Australian to win the women's singles at Wimbledon (1963). Wimbledon champion again in 1965 and 1970, she was US singles champion five times, French champion five times, and Australian champion a record 11 times, winning 90 titles in all.

Courtauld Institute of Art A gallery and college for the study of art history in Portman Square, London. The manufacturer and art collector Samuel Courtauld (1876–1947) donated the building with his collection of impressionist paintings to London University.

court cupboard A set of three shelves supported by corner columns, often with a recessed cupboard between the top two. Popular throughout N Europe during the 16th century for displaying plate, they were usually made of oak.

courtly love Essentially a literary convention describing passionate love, arising in 12th-century Provence in the poems of the *troubadors. (The term itself was coined in the 19th century.) It is not certain to what extent courtly love actually existed as a social phenomenon in feudal courts. In the literary convention both lover and beloved are of aristocratic rank. The lover is abjectly devoted as a vassal to his chosen lady, whose virtues are idealized with quasi-religious fervour and who remains unobtainable because she is married to someone else. The lover is bound by rules of gallantry and *chivalry and is ennobled by his attachment to the beloved. On the other hand, his love-sickness may be devastating and he can only be cured if his lady takes pity on him, that is, consents to an adulterous affair. Although the lover's virtue is supposed to be exalted by his love, he suffers enormously from fear of exposure, from the capricious behaviour of his lady, etc. The convention, which owes much to the influence of *Ovid, spread from Provence to Italy, influencing the *dolce stil nuovo; to N France, where it formed an important theme in the romances of *Chrétien de Troyes and in the 13th-century Roman de la Rose; to Germany in the work of the *Minnesingers; and to England, where it was treated in detail by Chaucer, especially in Troilus and Criseyde. It continued as an important element in the Elizabethan sonnet through the influence of *Petrarch.

court-martial A court, consisting of commissioned officers in the army, navy, or air force, convened to try a member of any of these services for an offence against military discipline or against ordinary law. An appeal court was established in 1951 and is now governed by the Courts-Martial (Appeals) Act (1968). An offender is not immune from trial by ordinary courts, but they must take into account any punishment to which he was sentenced by the court-martial.

Courtrai (Flemish name: Kortrijk) 50 50N 03 17E A town in Belgium, on the River Lys. It was the site of the battle of the Spurs (1297), in which the French army was defeated by the burghers of Bruges and Ghent. It is an important textile centre. Population (1981 est): 76 072.

courts of law Assemblies in which the law is administered. In England and Wales *civil law (see also common law; equity) is administered by the County Courts and the High Court of Justice and *criminal law is administered by the Magistrates' Courts and the Crown Court. Appeals from the civil law courts lie to the civil division of the Court of Appeal and those from the criminal law courts lie from Magistrate's Courts to the Crown Court and from the Crown Court to the criminal division of the Court of Appeal. Two or more judges of the High Court, when sit-

House of Lords

Court of Appeal
civil division | criminal division

—— appeal
--- case stated

High Court of Justice
Divisional Courts of the High Court

Crown Court

County Court | Magistrates' Court

COURTS OF LAW

ting together, may constitute a Divisional Court, which hears appeals on points of law from Magistrates' Courts, Crown Courts, and certain tribunals. Normally, the appeal is by way of case stated (i.e. the lower court, at the request of one of the litigants, sets out in writing the point or points of law to be decided by the Divisional Court). The Divisional Court can either (1) order the lower court to continue its hearing of the case in point while directing how the law should be applied or (2) allow or dismiss the appeal itself, if all the facts of the case have already been heard and decided by the lower court. The House of Lords is the Supreme Court of Appeal in both criminal and civil cases. The High Court of Justice and the Court of Appeal together with the Crown Court form the Supreme Court of Judicature.

The County Courts have jurisdiction over most civil law actions, subject to financial limitations (e.g. £5000 for claims in contract or tort). *See also* small claim. All divorce petitions start in the County Courts but are transferred to the High Court if defended. The High Court of Justice comprises the *Chancery, Queen's Bench (including the Admiralty Court (*see* maritime law) and the Commercial Court), and Family Divisions.

A criminal case comes first before a Magistrates' Court (*see* Justice of the Peace), which has jurisdiction in less serious cases (e.g. traffic offences) but commits more serious cases for trial at the Crown Court. The Crown Court, which was created in 1971 to replace the Courts of Assize and Courts of Quarter Session, is organized in six circuits (Midland and Oxford, North Eastern, Northern, South Eastern, Wales and Chester, and Western). A Crown Court sits in London as the *Central Criminal Court (Old Bailey). *See also* judge.

In Scotland the supreme court for civil cases is the Court of Session, established in 1532, and the supreme court for criminal cases is the High Court of Judiciary. Appeals from the former lie to the House of Lords and from the latter to a tribunal of three judges of the High Court of Justiciary.

Cousin, Victor (1792–1867) French philosopher. He had a brilliant career, despite anti-establishment sympathies, and was a superb lecturer and prolific writer. As a minister under *Thiers (1840) he reformed French education. His talents were eclectic rather than analytic and his only original work is *Du vrai, du beau, et du bien* (1854).

Cousin the Elder, Jean (1490–1560) French artist and craftsman, who designed tapestries and stained-glass windows. The nude study *Eva Prima Pandora* (Louvre) is attributed to him. His son **Jean Cousin the Younger** (c. 1522–c. 1594) was also a painter, engraver, and stained-glass designer, known for *The Last Judgment* (Louvre).

Cousteau, Jacques Yves (1910–) French naval officer and underwater explorer. He shared in the invention of the aqualung (1943) and invented a way of using television under water. In 1945 he founded the Undersea Research Group of the French navy at Marseilles and in 1950 became commander of the oceanographic research vessel *Calypso*. He is famous for such films as *The Silent World* (1953) and *The Living Sea*

(1963). In 1985 he began a 2½-year voyage in a wind-powered vessel to support fuel saving and protest against nuclear weapons.

couvade A custom, common in many parts of the world among primitive peoples, in which the father retires to bed during his wife's confinement and simulates the pain of childbirth. Its intention is presumably to establish a role for the father and, by magical association, to lessen the pain of the mother. In the 20th century it has been reported among Basques and in Brazil.

covenant A binding agreement between two parties whereby each promises to do something for the other (*see also* deed). In the Old Testament, the covenant between God and Israel forms the basis of the Jewish religion. In return for obedience to the Law (the *Ten Commandments) as delivered to Moses, the Israelites were promised a privileged relationship with God as the chosen people. The symbol of this agreement was the *Ark of the Covenant containing the tablets of the Law. In the New Testament, this belief is interpreted in Christian terms as including all men, who are regarded as having been redeemed by Christ.

Covenanters Scottish Presbyterians who in the 16th and 17th centuries covenanted to defend their church. The National Covenant of 1638 was signed by thousands of Scottish Presbyterians after Charles I's attempt to introduce the English Prayer Book, this opposition culminating in the *Bishops' Wars. In the English *Civil War the Covenanters joined the parliamentarians in 1643 in return for the promise of church reform (*see* Solemn League and Covenant). After the Restoration (1660) they were persecuted and suppressed until the re-establishment of Presbyterianism in Scotland after the Glorious Revolution (1688).

Covent Garden The principal English opera house, officially named the Royal Opera House. The first theatre on the site was opened in 1732, and the present building dates from the 1850s; it is currently the home of both the Royal Opera and the Royal Ballet Company. It takes its name from a square (originally a convent garden) onto which it backs, which was laid out in 1631 by Inigo *Jones. For many years London's fruit and vegetable market occupied the square but in 1973 it moved to Nine Elms (Wandsworth) and the square was redeveloped as a shopping precinct.

Coventry 52 25N 1 30W A city in central England, in the West Midlands. Heavily bombed during World War II, the city centre was almost entirely rebuilt. Its famous cathedral, designed by Sir Basil Spence, was opened in 1962 and retains the ruins of the old cathedral, which was bombed in 1940. Formerly a weaving town, Coventry is now an important centre for the motor-car industry and produces machinery, electrical equipment, and synthetic fabrics. It is also the site of Warwick University. Population (1981): 314 124.

Coverdale, Miles (1488–1568) English Protestant reformer. While an Augustinian friar at Cambridge, he was converted to Protestantism. In exile he published an English translation of the Bible (1535) and was largely responsible for the revisions resulting in the Great Bible of 1539. He was Bishop of Exeter from 1551 until exiled again under Queen Mary. After returning in 1559 he became a Puritan leader. ·

Covilhã, Pêro da (c. 1460–c. 1526) Portuguese explorer. Sent by John II to find *Prester John and explore Africa and the East, he left Portugal in 1487 and travelled via Aden to India, visiting Cannanore, Calicut, and Goa. Later he set off from Cairo for Ethiopia. There he ended his days, honoured but forcibly detained.

Coward, Sir Noel (1899–1973) British dramatist, composer, and actor. He first established his reputation with *The Vortex* (1924), an intense domestic drama, but his best-known plays are witty and elegant comedies of manners, such as *Hay Fever* (1925) and *Blithe Spirit* (1941). He also contributed as writer, director, composer, and performer to

SIR NOËL COWARD   *At Montreux, Switzerland (1967).*

revues, musicals, and films, notably *In Which We Serve* (1942) and *Brief Encounter* (1946). His best-known songs include "Mad Dogs and Englishmen" and "Mad about the Boy."

cowboys Mounted cattle herders and folk heroes of the US West, who from about 1820 worked in the open grassland W of the Mississippi River, from Canada to Mexico. Cowboys used horse, spur, rope, and branding iron to "round-up" the herds, i.e. drive them to market. The legendary cowboy of "western" films, drinking and fighting in a saloon, derives from his twice-yearly spree after the round-ups. Rail transport and barbed wire fences rendered the cowboy's jobs of herding and range riding obsolete. *Compare* gaucho.

Cowdrey, (Michael) Colin (1932–) British cricketer, who played for Kent and was captain of England 27 times. He played in a record number of 114 Test matches and hit 107 centuries during his career (1950–76). His total score of 7624 runs in Test cricket stood unequalled by any other British player for many years.

Cowell, Henry (1897–1965) US composer. He developed the technique of playing tone clusters on the piano by depressing adjacent notes with the forearm. He wrote over a thousand works and was active as a pianist, teacher, and writer.

Cowes 50 45N 1 18W A town in S England, situated on the Isle of Wight on the Medina estuary. It is a resort and internationally famous yachting centre. Cowes has boat-building, marine engineering, and radar industries; hovercraft are made here. Population (1981): 19 663.

Cowley, Abraham (1618–67) English poet. During the Civil War he served as Queen Henrietta Maria's secretary in France and as a royalist secret agent in England. His best-known Metaphysical verse is contained in *The Mistress* (1647, 1656) and *Miscellanies* (1656). His *Pindaric Odes* (1656) introduced this poetic form to English.

cow parsley A biennial herb, *Anthriscus sylvestris*, up to 100 cm high, with conspicuous umbrella-like clusters of white or pinkish flowers. It is found in hedgerows, wood edges, and waste places throughout much of Eurasia and N

Africa and has been introduced to North America. Family: *Umbelliferae.*

cowpea An annual African plant, *Vigna unguiculata*, widely grown in tropical areas and the southern USA. Having a high protein content, cowpeas are an important food crop, especially in Africa. There are two forms: a short erect one grown in Africa and America, whose seeds are used dried, and a tall climbing one grown in SE Asia, whose long pods are eaten when young. Family: *Leguminosae.*

Cowpens, Battle of (17 January, 1781) A battle in the American Revolution in which the Americans defeated the British. Led by Gen Daniel Morgan (1736–1802), the Americans inflicted a surprise defeat on the larger British force, slowing down *Cornwallis' invasion of North Carolina.

Cowper, William (1731–1800) British poet. With John Newton, an evangelical curate, he published *Olney Hymns* in 1779. "John Gilpin's Ride" (1783), a comic ballad, and "The Task" (1785), a long discursive poem on rural themes, were both very successful. He was mentally unstable throughout his life, and frequently attempted suicide. After the death in 1796 of Mary Unwin, a widow with whom he had lived for many years, he expressed his despair in "The Castaway."

cowpox A contagious virus disease of cattle that can be contracted by man. Resembling a mild form of smallpox, it appears as blisters on the teats and udder. Animals should be isolated and recovery is usually complete. Edward *Jenner used fluid from cowpox blisters to produce the first effective smallpox vaccine.

cowrie A *gastropod mollusc of the family *Cypraeidae* (about 160 species), mostly found in warm seas. 1–15 cm long, cowries have glossy ⬜shells with inrolled lips that are covered by the mantle, which is withdrawn inside the shell when the animal is disturbed. Cowries feed at night on small animals. The shell of the tropical money cowrie (*Cypraea moneta*), about 3 cm long, is used as a form of currency in Africa and India.

cowslip A perennial spring-flowering Eurasian herb, *Primula veris*, growing to a height of 20 cm. It has a rosette of crinkled leaves and hanging clusters of bright-yellow five-petalled flowers. It is found from lowland meadows to alpine pastures. Family: *Primulaceae* (primrose family).

coyote A wild *dog, *Canis latrans*, of Central and North American grassland, also called prairie wolf. Coyotes are about 120 cm long, including the bushy tail (30 cm), and have yellowish fur. They hunt alone or in packs and take food ranging from insects to small deer.

coypu A South American aquatic *rodent, *Myocaster coypus*. About 60 cm long (excluding a long hairless tail), it has thick brown fur and webbed hind feet. The underfur of the belly is known as nutria, and coypus are farmed for fur. In Britain escaped coypus are becoming a pest, especially in East Anglia, eating vegetation and undermining river banks by burrowing. Family: *Capromyidae.*

crab A *crustacean belonging to the tribes *Brachyura* (true crabs; about 4500 species) or *Anomura* (about 1300 species, including the *hermit crab). True crabs have a wide flat body covered by a hard carapace, with the small abdomen tucked underneath. There is a large pair of pincers and four pairs of legs used for walking (typically in a sideways scuttle) or swimming. They are carnivores or scavengers and most species are marine (the *land crab is an exception). The European species *Cancer pagurus* is edible. Order: *Decapoda.*

crab apple A ⬜tree, *Malus sylvestris*, 2–10 m high: one of the species from which cultivated *apples have been developed. It has pinkish-white five-petalled flowers that bloom in spring and small sour greenish fruits, used to make jelly. A native of Europe and Asia, it is sometimes grown as an ornamental. Family: *Rosaceae.*

Crabbe, George (1754-1832) British poet, born in Aldeburgh, Suffolk, scene of many of his poems. In 1780 he left his doctor's practice there and went to London. Under the patronage of Edmund Burke he took orders, becoming chaplain to the Duke of Rutland and later vicar of Trowbridge, Wiltshire. *The Village* (1783) was a brutally realistic portrayal of rural life, in stark contrast to conventional idealized treatments. This theme he took up again in the verse tales of *The Borough* (1810), source of *Britten's opera *Peter Grimes*, and *Tales of the Hall* (1819).

crabeater seal A common Antarctic seal, *Lobodon carcinophagus*, that feeds entirely on krill. About 2.5 m long, crabeater seals are dark in winter and almost white in summer; they are slender and can travel fast over ice. ⊓oceans.

Crab nebula A turbulent expanding mass of gas, lying about 6000 light years distant in the constellation Taurus. It is the remnant of a *supernova that was observed in 1054. It emits radiation from all spectral regions and is an especially strong source of radio waves and X-rays. Within the nebula, and supplying energy to it, lies the **Crab pulsar**. This optical *pulsar was produced by the supernova and rotates extremely rapidly with a period of only 0.033 seconds.

Cracow. See Kraków.

Craig, Edward Henry Gordon. See Terry, Ellen.

Craik, Dinah Maria Mulock (1826–87) British novelist. Daughter of a Nonconformist clergyman, her best-known novels are *John Halifax: Gentleman* (1856) and *A Life for a Life* (1859).

Craiova 44 18N 23 47E A city in S Romania, on the River Jiu. Industries include heavy engineering and food manufacture. Its university was established in 1966. Population (1983): 243 117.

crake A small shy bird belonging to the *rail family. Crakes have a short conical bill and are commonly found in marshes and swamps. The Eurasian spotted crake (*Porzana porzana*) is 23 cm long and has a streaked olive back, a lightly spotted breast, and a red ring at the base of the bill.

Cram, Steve (1960–) British middle-distance runner. He won the world championship 1500 m title in 1982–83; in 1985 he set new world records for the mile (3 mins 46.31 secs), and the 2000 m (4 mins 51.39 secs).

cramp Painful spasmodic contraction of a muscle. Cramp is often caused by overexercise, often of the legs (in swimmers) or hands (writers' cramp). It may also be due to salt deficiency or poor circulation.

Cranach the Elder, Lucas (Lucas Müller; 1472–1553) German artist. He studied painting under his father before moving to Wittenberg in 1505 to become court painter to Frederick the Wise, Elector of Saxony, and later to his two successors. Because of his portraits of Reformation leaders including his friend Luther, he is sometimes called the Reformation painter. He is also noted for his stylized but sensuous nudes, e.g. *Adam and Eve* (Courtauld Institute, London).

cranberry A low evergreen shrub of the genus *Vaccinium*, bearing red edible berries and growing in acidic boggy areas. *V. oxycoccus* occurs in Europe, N Asia, and North America. *V. macrocarpon* of North America has larger fruits (about 1.5 cm across). The fruits of both are made into cranberry sauce. Family: *Ericaceae* (heath family).

crane (bird) A large long-legged bird belonging to a family (*Gruidae*; 14 species) occurring in Old World regions and North America. Standing up to 140 cm tall with a wingspan of over 200 cm, cranes vary from grey to white with black wingtips; some species are crested. They have heavy bills, feeding in marshes and plains on grain, shoots, and small animals; northern species are migratory. Order: *Gruiformes* (rails, etc.). See also demoiselle; whooping crane.

crane (machinery) A machine for raising, lowering, or moving heavy objects. It is used in construction work, loading cars, goes onto ships, etc. There are many types but most have an engine to wind cables supported by an inclined or horizontal jib or boom, which either has a pulley system at one end or, in the case of a travelling crane, a pulley system that can move along the whole length of the jib. In a gantry crane the jib is fixed on supports at both ends, which themselves travel along rails. Cranes are often mounted on lorries or locomotives.

Crane, Hart (1899–1932) US poet. After an unhappy childhood in Ohio, he settled in New York in 1923 and began writing poems expressive of the personal conflicts caused by his homosexuality and alcoholism. *White Buildings* was published in 1926. *The Bridge* (1930), an epic poem in 15 parts, unites myth, history, and dream in a celebration of contemporary America. He went to Mexico to write another epic and drowned himself on the return voyage.

Crane, Stephen (1871–1900) US novelist. His early work as a journalist in New York provided him with first-hand knowledge of the poverty and destitution portrayed in his novel *Maggie: A Girl of the Streets* (1893). He is best known for the war novel *The Red Badge of Courage* (1895) and his short stories, especially "The Open Boat." He worked as a war correspondent in Cuba and Greece, lived in England, and died in Germany of tuberculosis.

Crane, Walter (1845–1915) British illustrator, painter, and designer of textiles and wallpaper. The son of a painter, he studied under a wood engraver in London, achieving fame for his illustrations to children's books. He was later associated with the *Arts and Crafts movement.

cranefly A harmless fly, also called daddy longlegs, belonging to the family *Tipulidae*. Craneflies are 6–75 mm long with long delicate legs and wings. They are found near water or vegetation and are attracted to light. The larvae generally occur in water or rotting vegetation. However some—the leatherjackets —live in the soil and are plant pests, feeding on the roots of cereals and grasses. ⊓insect.

cranesbill A herbaceous plant of the genus *Geranium* (about 400 species), widely distributed, especially in temperate regions, and usually having pink or purple flowers. They take their name from the long slender beaklike carpels. The meadow cranesbill (*G. pratense*), a perennial up to 60 cm high, has violet-blue flowers, and is widespread throughout Eurasia and North America. Family: *Geraniaceae*.

Cranko, John (1927–73) British choreographer, born in South Africa. He developed the Stuttgart Ballet into one of the leading European companies during the 1960s. His best-known works are full-length dramatic ballets such as *Romeo and Juliet* (1962) and *Onegin* (1965).

Cranmer, Thomas (1489–1556) Anglican reformer and martyr. He was consecrated Archbishop of Canterbury in 1532, following his support of *Henry VIII in the king's divorce dispute with the pope. He is especially remembered for his contributions to the Prayer Books of 1549 and 1552. Under Queen Mary he was tried as a heretic and, after initially recanting, burned at the stake.

crannog An artificial island of stone, timber, and peat, constructed as sites for houses in Ireland from the early Neolithic to the medieval eras. A notable example is the Lough Gara crannog.

Cranwell 53 2N 0 30W A village in E England, in Lincolnshire. The Royal Air Force College (founded in 1919) is situated here.

craps A dice game used for gambling, especially in the USA. It was developed in the 19th century by Black workers from the more complex game of *hazard. Two dice are used. Each player attempts to throw a "natural," a 7 or 11, which wins. 2, 3, or 12 ("craps") are losing combinations. If he throws a 4, 5, 6, 8, 9, or 10 he continues to throw until he wins by throwing the same number again or loses by throwing a 7. Bets are made by the other players against the thrower, among themselves, or (in a casino) against the house.

Crashaw, Richard (c. 1613–49) British poet. He was ordained priest at Cambridge, where he published a collection of Greek and Latin verses. He became a Roman Catholic in France in 1644 and obtained an ecclesiastical post in Italy. The baroque style of his religious poetry is best illustrated in *Steps to the Temple* (1646).

Crassus, Marcus Licinius (c. 115–53 BC) Roman politician and ally of Caesar, nicknamed *Dives* (wealthy). Crassus suppressed Spartacus' revolt (71), although Pompey took the credit. Failing to manipulate political affairs on his own, Crassus joined Pompey and Caesar in the first Triumvirate (60). He was killed during an invasion of Parthia.

Crawford, Joan (Lucille le Sueur; 1908–77) US film actress. She started her film career in musicals but became famous during the 1930s and 1940s for her dramatic portrayals of ambitious women in such films as *Grand Hotel* (1932) and *Mildred Pierce* (1945).

Crawley 51 7N 0 12W A town in SE England, in West Sussex. Designated a new town in 1947, it has light engineering, electronics, plastics, and furniture industries. Population (1981): 72 756.

crayfish A freshwater *crustacean, also called crawfish and crawdad, belonging to the superfamily *Nephropidea*. It has a small lobster-like body, 25–75 mm long, and occurs under rocks or debris or in burrows in mud banks during the day. At night it feeds on plant and animal material. Some species are edible. Order: *Decapoda*.

Crazy Horse (?1849–77) Sioux Indian chief. Attempting to prevent White settlement in Sioux territory, he joined in the massacre of Gen *Custer's forces (1876). He surrendered in 1877 but was killed while resisting imprisonment.

cream of tartar Potassium hydrogen tartrate that occurs in the later stages of the fermentation of grape juice as a deposit on the sides of the cask. After purification and crystallization it is used in baking powder and medicines.

creamware A cream-coloured English earthenware that replaced *Delft and salt-glazed wares from about 1760. The universal adoption of creamware by English manufacturers was made possible by Josiah *Wedgwood, who perfected it and prevented restrictive patent rights being granted.

creationism A pseudoscience developed in the USA by opponents of neo-*Darwinism to explain evolutionary problems unresolved by Darwin's theory. Based on the biblical account of the Creation, it claims that each species is individually created in its present form, rather than evolving gradually from simpler ancestral forms.

Crécy, Battle of (26 August, 1346) The first land battle of the *Hundred Years' War, fought in N France, in which the English, led by *Edward III, defeated the French under *Philip VI. It was a triumph for the English longbowmen over heavily armoured French knights; about 1500 French soldiers were killed. The victory enabled Edward to move N and beseige Calais.

credit and credit ratings The loan of money to an individual or company by a bank, credit-card organization, retailer, etc. Much consumer purchasing, especially of durables (*see* consumption), in industrial countries is on credit terms. The amount of credit that a person or company can command depends on his credit rating at the bank or on that given by an agency that specializes in listing the creditworthiness of companies. Credit ratings will depend on the applicants' known assets and liabilities, income (profitability for a company), and past record for trustworthiness. Influencing credit advances is a central part of a government's monetary policy. In the UK, during a credit squeeze it can limit credit advances by *open-market operations or by direct controls on *commercial banks. Other countries have similar monetary policies.

credit card A card that enables the holder to obtain goods or services on credit. They are issued by retail stores, banks, and

credit-card companies to approved clients. The bank or credit-card company settles the client's bills, invoicing him monthly and charging interest on any outstanding debts. Their profit comes from the high rate of interest charged, the card-holders' subscriptions, and the fees paid by some organizations that accept cards. *See also* cheque card.

credit insurance A form of insurance that provides cover against bad trade debts. In the UK the government's Export Credits Guarantee Department (ECGD), set up in 1930, provides insurance for exporters, covering insolvency of the buyers, war risk, governmental interference, and exchange-control problems. This service for home traders is also provided by private-sector insurance companies, often in conjunction with *factoring.

Cree An Algonkian-speaking North American Indian people of the region S of Hudson Bay, extending westwards to Lake Winnipeg. They lived by hunting and trapping in small wandering bands. One group, known as Plains Cree, moved into the Plains and, acquiring horses and guns, adopted the buffalo-hunting culture of this region. They were more aggressive than the northern groups, often raiding for horses. Among the Cree, belief in witchcraft and observance of taboos relating to animal spirits were common.

Creed, Frederick (1871–1957) Canadian inventor, who moved to Scotland in 1897 and developed the Creed teleprinter (*see* Telex). The first such device was installed in Fleet Street in 1912 and was soon in widespread use.

creeds In Christianity, formal summaries of the principal items of belief, often recited as part of the eucharistic service in many Churches. They originated as professions of faith said at baptism. The two most widely used are the Apostles' Creed (probably 3rd century AD) and the Nicene Creed, probably a revision by the Council of Constantinople (381) of the creed promulgated at the Council of *Nicaea (325) and accepted by both Western and Eastern churches. The Athanasian Creed, probably dating from the 5th century, is used in the Anglican catechism.

Creek A Muskogean-speaking North American Indian people divided into the Muskogee of Georgia and the Hitchiti of Alabama. They were cultivators and hunters, practised the green corn (first-fruits) ceremony, and tattooed their bodies heavily. Their small towns of rectangular huts were built around a central square often containing a temple mound. Towns were grouped into red and white divisions, respectively concerned with matters of war and peace. A confederacy of Creek towns fought the encroaching whites in the 18th and early 19th centuries. On their defeat in the 1830s they were removed to the area of Oklahoma.

Creeley, Robert (1926–) US poet. He travelled widely in India, Burma, and Europe. As editor of the *Black Mountain Review* for seven years from 1955 he published a group of poets known for their linguistic economy and precision. His own collections include *For Love* (1960) and *Pieces* (1969); he also wrote short stories and a novel, *The Island* (1963).

cremation The disposal of the dead by burning. Practised by many ancient European peoples, cremation was forbidden by the Christian Church on account of the doctrine of bodily resurrection of the dead. With 19th-century urban overcrowding in the West, cremation was revived. The first crematorium in England was founded at Woking in 1885 by the Cremation Society (established 1874), after the practice had been legalized. Since then the practice has grown rapidly. The Roman Catholic Church formerly disapproved of cremation but it is now accepted as it is among Jews (except for the most orthodox). In the East it has remained the most general method of corpse disposal.

Cremona 45 08N 10 01E A town in N Italy, in Lombardy on the River Po. It has a 12th-century cathedral and a 13th-century palace. From the 16th to the 18th centuries it was famous for the manufacture of violins, including those of Stradivari. Population (1981 est): 80 758.

creodont An extinct primitive carnivorous mammal of the early Tertiary period (55–45 million years ago). They were mostly short-legged and slow-moving, preying on herbivores.

creole 1. Originally a White person born in Spanish America during the colonial period (16th to 18th centuries). They suffered social and commercial disadvantages in comparison with the Spanish administrative class. 2. A person of mixed blood living in the Caribbean area or in Latin America, extending to encompass a descendant of slaves in Suriname, a French-speaking descendant of French or Spanish settlers in Louisiana, and various other groups. More loosely, the term refers to people of Caribbean culture. 3. A patois based on French, English, or Dutch and spoken especially in the West Indies as a mother tongue (*compare* pidgin English).

creosote A substance produced by distilling tar. The creosote used for preserving wood is obtained from *coal tar and is a brownish mixture of aromatic hydrocarbons and *phenols. Creosote made from wood tar is a mixture of phenols and is used in pharmacy.

creosote bush A shrub of the genus *Larrea* (5 species), of arid and semiarid areas of North and South America, where it is the dominant feature of the landscape. Up to 2 m high, these plants contain resinous phenolic substances that deter grazing animals, although some insects are adapted to living and feeding on them. Family: *Zygophyllaceae*.

cresol (*or* methylphenol; $CH_3C_6H_4OH$) A liquid *aromatic compound obtained from *coal tar. It has three *isomers, a mixture of which is used as a disinfectant.

cress A plant of the mustard family (*Cruciferae*) the sharp-tasting leaves of which are used in salads, especially garden cress, or peppergrass (*Lepidium sativum*), believed to be native to W Asia but widely cultivated and naturalized in Europe. The seedlings are eaten, often with those of white mustard (*Sinapis alba*), with which it may be grown in containers. The European winter, or land, cress (*Barbarea verna*) grows to a height of 100 cm. Its leaves can be picked throughout the winter.

Cressent, Charles (1685–1768) French cabinetmaker. After working with *Boulle he became official cabinetmaker (1715) to the regent, the Duc d'Orléans, and also made furniture for foreign courts. The leading designer of the period, he made popular the use of coloured-wood marquetry and *ormolu mountings.

crested tit A dull-brown and grey *tit, *Parus cristatus*, of European coniferous forests. It is about 11 cm long and has a pointed black-and-white crest and black C-shaped marking bordering its face. It feeds on insects and seeds, often storing them for winter use.

Creswell Crags A gorge near Creswell (Derbyshire, England) containing caves where *Mousterian flint tools and a *Magdalenian bone engraving of a horse's head have been found.

Cretaceous period A geological period of the Mesozoic era, between about 135 and 65 million years ago, following the Jurassic and preceding the Tertiary (when the Cenozoic era began). It is divided into the Lower and Upper Cretaceous. The period saw a widespread gradual marine transgression, the rocks of the Upper Cretaceous culminating in the thick chalk deposits of N Europe and the midwestern USA. The dinosaurs and other giant reptiles, as well as the ammonites and many other invertebrates, became extinct at the end of the Cretaceous.

Crete (Modern Greek name: Kríti) The largest of the Greek islands, in the E Mediterranean Sea approximately 100 km (63 mi) SE of the mainland. It is generally mountainous, rising over 2400 m (7874 ft). The economy is based primarily on agriculture producing olives, wines, and citrus fruits; the raising of sheep and goats is also important. There is a thriving tourist industry, based on Iráklion. *History*: colonized probably in the 6th millennium BC from Asia Minor, Crete achieved extensive maritime power during the Middle Minoan period (c. 2000–c. 1700 BC), from which many artefacts, inscriptions, and buildings have been discovered (*see* Minoan civilization). The most notable are the palace at *Knossos and clay tablets bearing two different scripts known as *Linear A and *Linear B. Politically insignificant in the history of classical Greece, it fell to Rome (67 BC), Byzantium (395 AD), and the Muslims (826). In 1204 it was sold to the Venetians, who gave both the island and Iráklion the name Candia. It fell to Turkey in 1669 and was officially incorporated into Greece in 1913. During World War II it was the scene (1941) of the first ever large-scale airborne invasion, in which the Germans took the island from British and Commonwealth troops, who had been evacuated here from the Greek mainland. Area: 8332 sq km (3217 sq mi). Population (1981): 502 165. Capital: Khaniá.

cretinism The condition resulting from a deficiency of thyroid hormone, which is present from birth. Affected children are mentally retarded dwarfs with coarse skin and facial features. Cretinism is treated with injections of thyroxine, which must be started early and continued throughout life. *See also* hypothyroidism.

Crèvecoeur, Michel-Guillaume-Jean de (*or* J. Hector St John; 1735–1813) French-American writer. After military service in Canada he stayed in America, where he served as French consul between 1784 and 1790. His *Letters from an American Farmer* (1782) and *Sketches of Eighteenth-Century America* (1925) are the thoughtful records of an early immigrant in the New World.

Crewe 53 05N 2 27W A town in NW England, in Cheshire. Crewe developed as an important railway junction with railway engineering and workshops. It also manufactures motor vehicles, clothing, and chemicals. Population (1981): 47 759.

cribbage (*or* crib) A card game attributed to Sir John *Suckling. It is played by 2, 3, or 4 players with a standard pack of 52 cards. The rules vary in detail, but play basically consists of each player alternately playing a card until the total value of the cards played approaches 31. The last player able to play a card without exceeding 31 scores. Points are also scored for having certain combinations of cards in a hand or for playing during certain sequences of cards. The crib (consisting of cards discarded from each hand) scores for the dealer. The score is kept with small pegs on a cribbage board containing rows of holes.

Crichton, James (1560–82) Scottish scholar and adventurer. After graduating from St Andrews University, Crichton toured Europe. Called "the Admirable Crichton," on account of his literary and athletic gifts, he was apparently killed by a jealous pupil in a brawl in Mantua.

Crick, Francis Harry Compton (1916–) British biophysicist, who (with James D. *Watson) proposed a model for the molecular structure of *DNA (1953). Following this breakthrough, Crick continued to work on DNA, helping to determine the mechanism of protein synthesis. He shared a Nobel Prize (1962) with Watson and Maurice *Wilkins.

cricket (sport) An 11-a-side bat-and-ball team game, in which the object is to score the most runs. It originated in England among shepherds using their crooks as bats; its rules were laid down in 1744 and the game is played almost exclusively in the UK and its former empire. Presided over by two umpires, it is played on a large field; the pitch is a strip of grass 22 yd (20.12 m) long having at each end a wicket of three stumps surmounted by two bails. The cork and twine ball, encased in leather, is 8.8–9 in (22.4–22.9 cm) in circumference and weighs 5.5–5.75 oz (155.9–163 g). The members of one team take turns to bat in pairs, one defending each wicket; the batsmen's objective is to score

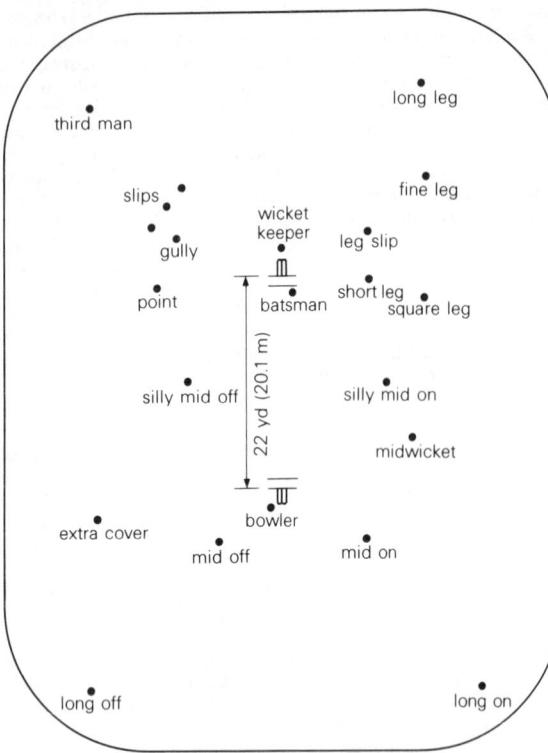

long leg

third man

slips

fine leg

wicket
keeper

gully

leg slip

point

batsman

short leg

square leg

silly mid off

silly mid on

22 yd (20.1 m)

midwicket

extra cover

bowler

mid off

mid on

long off

long on

CRICKET   *The pitch, showing the usual fielding positions (for a right-handed batsman).*

runs by hitting the ball and exchanging ends before the ball is returned to the pitch. Each player bats until he is bowled, caught, stumped, run out, or judged lbw (leg before wicket). The members of the other team field, some taking turns to bowl the ball. After every over of six balls (eight in Australia) the bowler changes, the new bowler bowling from the other wicket. A match consists of one or two innings and may last for a few **hours or up to six days. International cricket, governed by the International Cricket Conference, is played mainly in Test matches between England, Australia, the West Indies, New Zealand, India, Pakistan, and Sri Lanka. The governing body in each country decides which teams are first class; in England first-class cricket chiefly involves the 17 professional first-class county teams. The cricket world was somewhat shaken in 1977 by an Australian businessman, Kerry Packer (1937–), who established an independent series of matches, signing up some of the world's best players for large fees. There has also been controversy over the banning of players who have played in South Africa, which has been excluded from international competitions since 1970 as a protest against *apartheid. See also Ashes; Marylebone Cricket Club.**

cricket (zoology)   An insect, resembling a grasshopper but with longer antennae, belonging to one of several families of the order *Orthoptera. The males stridulate (i.e. make a chirping noise) by rubbing the front wings together. True crickets (family Gryllidae; 2400 species) have black or brown flattened bodies, 3–50 mm long, with long tail appendages (cerci) and short forewings (they do not fly). The females have long needle-like ovipositors for depositing eggs in soil or crevices. True crickets are omnivorous and live in burrows or among vegetation; some, for example the widely distributed house cricket (*Acheta domesticus*), frequent buildings. *See also* bush cricket; mole cricket.

Crimea (Russian name: Krym)   A peninsula and autono-

mous region (*oblast*) in the Ukrainian SSR, in the SW Soviet Union, almost totally surrounded by the Black Sea and the Sea of Azov and connected to the mainland in the N by the Perekop Isthmus. It is mainly flat but rises to 1545 m (5069 ft) in the S. Iron ore is mined here and wheat, tobacco, and wine are produced. The chief towns are Feodosia, Kerch, Sevastopol, Yalta, Yevpatoria, and the capital of the *oblast*, Simferopol. *History*: colonized by Greeks in the 6th century BC, the Crimea was continually invaded by Goths, Huns, and others and in 1239 was made a khanate by Tatars of the *Golden Horde. This was overthrown by Turks in 1475, and the area was annexed by Russia in 1783. Many Tatars emigrated then, and the remainder were deported in 1945 for alleged collaboration with the German forces of occupation between 1941 and 1943. Area: **about 27 000 sq km (10 423 sq mi). Population (1983): 2 277 000.** *See also* Crimean War.

Crimean War   (1853–56) The war between Russia, on one side, and Britain, France, the Ottoman (Turkish) Empire, and (from 1855) Sardinia-Piedmont, on the other. Caused by Russia's expansionist ambitions in the Balkans, the war was precipitated by Russia's desire to establish a protectorate over Orthodox Christians in the Ottoman Empire. In July, 1853, Russia occupied Moldavia and Walachia, in October, Turkey declared war, and in March, 1854, following the destruction of a Turkish fleet at Sinope, Britain and France entered the war. The major battles of the year-long siege of Sevastopol, in the Crimea, were of *Balaclava and *Inkerman, and the Russians eventually evacuated the port in September, 1855. Peace was formally concluded at Paris (1856). Over 250 000 men were lost by each side, many from disease in the appalling hospitals of the Crimea. The British Government dispatched Florence *Nightingale to inspect those at Scutari, where her work had a considerable effect in improving conditions.

Criminal Investigation Department (CID)   The investigative department of *police forces in the UK. A CID was created at *Scotland Yard in 1878, based on the detective branch that had been in existence since 1842. All UK police forces now have their own CIDs, all recruits to which must first have served as uniformed officers.

criminal law   The body of law determining the acts and circumstances that amount to a crime (a wrong against society prohibited by law) and the punishment for crimes. Criminal law, which is distinguished from *civil law, derives in England chiefly from *common law, although statute law has contributed significantly to its development. Most crimes entail both an act (*actus reus*) and a mental element (*mens rea*). However, there is a growing number of crimes in which no mental element is necessary (called crimes of strict liability), such as most motoring offences. *Insanity, infancy (children under the age of ten), or duress (an act committed under threat of death or serious personal injury) may excuse a crime, but ignorance of the law does not if, in cases involving a mental element, the offender intends the result of his acts.

In England all criminal cases appear first before a Magistrates' Court and may then be committed to the Crown Court (*see* courts of law). Punishment of an offender depends on the nature of the crime and the offender's age. A juvenile offender (under 17 years old), who is generally tried in a Juvenile Court, may be made the subject of care proceedings (*see* juvenile delinquency). In criminal proceedings an offender between 14 and 21 may be sent to a detention centre for up to four months, and an offender between 15 and 21 to a youth custody centre for up to one year (or longer if over 17). Detention centres and youth custody centres (the former concentrating on discipline, the latter on training) replace *Borstals. Offenders under 21 may also be required to report periodically to attendance centres. A person under the age of 18 who is convicted of murder may not be sentenced to life imprisonment (mandatory for those of 18 and over) but instead must be ordered to be detained during Her Majesty's pleasure.

An adult (over 21) may be sentenced to death (*see* capital punishment), to life imprisonment, or to a specific term of imprisonment (statutes specify the maximum term that may be imposed for any statutory offence). Alternatively he may receive a suspended sentence of imprisonment of 2 years or less, which he will not serve if he is not convicted of another offence punishable with imprisonment during the period of suspension (1-2 years); or he may be placed in the charge of a probation officer for 1-3 years. Other punishments include community service, fines, and conditional discharges. *See also* prisons.

criminology The study of the cause, nature, and prevention of crime. Crime was generally equated with immorality until the 19th century, when the pioneer Italian criminologist Cesare *Lombroso suggested, in *L'uomo delinquente* (1876), that criminals are born and can be recognized by such physical attributes as a receding forehead. Although this view is no longer accepted, at various times evidence has been produced to suggest that such physiological abnormalities as an extra Y chromosome or an endocrine abnormality do predispose to criminality. Poverty, psychological stress, lack of parental affection in childhood, working mothers, and the decline of the extended family have all been suggested as additional or alternative predisposing factors, and some evidence has been produced to support each of them. But none of this evidence can explain why some people succumb to predisposing factors and become criminals while others, exposed to the same factors, do not.

Deep ethical problems are also involved. To what extent, for example, do predisposing factors affect culpability? To what extent should crime be regarded merely as a deviation from social norms? Should punishment fit the crime or the criminal and to what extent should it attempt to be therapeutic? Criminologists have, as yet, no satisfactory answers to most of these questions. However, research is being actively pursued in such institutions as the Institute of Criminology, Cambridge University.

crinoid A marine invertebrate animal belonging to a class (*Crinoidea*; about 700 species) of *echinoderms, including the sea lilies and feather stars. It has a small cup-shaped body covered with calcareous plates and with five radiating pairs of feathery flexible arms surrounding the mouth at the top. Sea lilies, most of which are now extinct, are fixed to the sea bottom, coral reefs, etc., by a stalk. Feather stars, e.g. *Antedon*, are free-swimming and are usually found on rocky bottoms. Crinoids occur mainly in deep waters and feed on microscopic plankton and detritus caught by the arms and conveyed to the mouth. The larvae are sedentary. □fossil.

Crippen, Hawley Harvey (1862-1910) US murderer. He poisoned his wife in London and then attempted to escape to the USA with his mistress. He was arrested on board ship (following one of the first uses of shore to ship radio) and returned to England, where he was convicted and hanged.

Cripps, Sir (Richard) Stafford (1889-1952) British Labour politician. A barrister, Cripps became solicitor general in 1930, before entering parliament in 1931. In 1939 he was expelled from the Labour Party for campaigning for a Popular Front against Neville *Chamberlain's appeasement policy. He was ambassador to Moscow (1940-42), minister of aircraft production (1942-45), and, once more in the Labour fold, chancellor of the exchequer (1947-50), when his austere economic policy set Britain on the road to recovery after World War II.

Cristofori, Bartolommeo (1655-1731) Italian harpsichord maker and inventor of the *piano. He constructed the escapement system in which the hammer falls away from the string immediately after striking it, leaving it free to vibrate. A damper stops the sound when the key is released.

critical mass The mass of fissile substance that is just capable of sustaining a *chain reaction within it. Below the critical mass, too many of the particles that might have induced a reaction escape and the chain reaction dies away.

critical-path analysis A planning method based on the use of a schematic representation of the network of activities and events involved in a project. Its aim is to aid coordination by identifying the optimum schedule. A critical path is a sequence of activities in which the key parameters, usually time and cost, cannot be increased without endangering the whole project. In large networks, which often need to be analysed by computer, there may be more than one critical path. The method is commonly used in large construction projects.

critical state The state of a gas at its critical temperature, pressure, and volume. The critical temperature is the temperature above which a gas cannot be liquefied by increased pressure alone. The vapour pressure of the gas at this temperature is the critical pressure and its volume, the critical volume. In the critical state the density of the vapour is equal to the density of the liquid.

Crivelli, Carlo (c. 1430-95) Venetian painter, who settled in the Marches of Italy in the late 1460s. He is set apart from the Venetian school by his sharp linear style, influenced by *Mantegna, and the decorative detail that appears in such paintings as *The Annunciation* (National Gallery, London).

croaker. *See* drumfish.

Croatia (Serbo-Croat name: Hrvatska) A constituent republic of NW Yugoslavia, bordering on the Adriatic Sea. It is chiefly mountainous, descending to plains in the NE, where it is drained by the River Drava. It is primarily agricultural, producing cereals, potatoes, tobacco, fruit, and livestock. Industries, centred on the larger towns, include metallurgy and the manufacture of textiles. *History*: settled by the Croats in the 7th century AD, the region was successively controlled by Hungary, Turkey, and Austria until the formation of the kingdom of the Serbs, Croats, and Slovenes (later Yugoslavia) in 1918. Following the occupation of Yugoslavia by the Axis Powers in World War II, Croatia was proclaimed an independent state (1941), ruled over by the fascist dictator Ante Pavelić (1889-1959). In 1945 Croatia once more became part of Yugoslavia as a people's republic. Area: 56 538 sq km (22 050 sq mi). Population (1981): 4 601 469. Capital: Zagreb.

Croatian. *See* Serbo-Croat.

Croce, Benedetto (1866-1952) Italian philosopher. Orphaned at 17 by an earthquake, he attended Rome University, studying art, philosophy, and history. His system is expounded in the four-volume *Philosophy of Mind* (1900-10). The only reality is mental and this reality is divided into theoretical and practical. Theoretical reality comprises intuition (art and aesthetics) and conception (philosophy or history—essentially the same, both being accounts of reality). Practical reality comprises individual will (political and economic activity) and universal will (morality). His aesthetic ideas, aired in numerous other works, are the most influential.

Crockett, Davy (1786-1836) US frontiersman. As a colonel in the Tennessee militia and member of Congress he cultivated the image of a rough frontiersman. He fought for Texas in its struggle for independence from Mexico and was killed at the *Alamo.

Crockford, William (1775-1844) The founder of Crockford's Club in St James's Street, London. Crockford was a fishmonger until his successes as a gambler enabled him to open his sumptuous club in 1827. The principal attraction was the game of hazard, over which Crockford himself presided and at which he won more than £1,200,000. After his death, the original Crockford's declined, but was revived in the 20th century as a bridge club and is now, again, a gambling club. □

crocodile A □reptile belonging to either of two genera, *Crocodylus* or *Osteolaemus*, and distinguished from alligators and caymans by having a more pointed snout and fewer teeth, the fourth tooth of the lower jaw remaining visible when the mouth is closed. Crocodiles occur chiefly in tropical fresh waters although the estuarine crocodile (*C. porosus*), which reaches a length of 6 m, occurs in coastal waters of SE Asia and Australia.

Crocodiles belong to the order *Crocodilia* (about 20 species), along with alligators and caymans. Crocodilians are amphibious mainly nocturnal carnivores living in tropical and subtropical swamps and rivers, where they prey chiefly on fish but also on water birds and land animals. They have long powerful jaws and a covering of thick protective bony plates; the ears and nostrils are placed high on the head and can be closed by valves when under water. The female builds a nest of mud or vegetation in which over a hundred shelled eggs may be laid. She guards the nest until the young, measuring 20–25 cm in length, begin to hatch. Crocodilians may live for over a hundred years. Their skins are used to make leather goods and this has caused a decline in their numbers.

crocodile bird An African riverbank *courser, *Pluvianus aegyptius*, that feeds on parasites picked from crocodiles. It is 23 cm long and is black with white markings on the throat and above the eyes.

Crocus A genus of low-growing plants (75 species), native to Mediterranean regions and widely planted in gardens. They grow from *corms to produce long thin leaves and six-lobed flowers in spring or autumn. Spring-flowering species include *C. vernus*, with white, blue, or purple flowers, and *C. aureus*, with deep-yellow flowers. *C. speciosus* is a purple autumn-flowering species. An Asian species (*C. sativus*) is the source of *saffron. Family: *Iridaceae*. *Compare* autumn crocus.

Croesus (died c. 546 BC) The last king of *Lydia (c. 560–c. 546 BC), famous for his wealth. He conquered the Greek cities on the coast of Asia Minor but was defeated by the Persian king *Cyrus (II) the Great in 546. According to legend, Croesus was saved by Apollo from execution by Cyrus, whose counsellor he then became.

crofting A system of subsistence farming that involves the cultivation of a small parcel of land together with access to common grazing land. Crofting was widely practised in the Scottish Highlands until the introduction of sheep farming together with the eviction of many crofting families in the late 18th century. It is still practised, under the control of the Crofters' Commission, established in 1955.

Crohn's disease An inflammatory disorder that can affect any part of the intestinal tract, most usually the terminal part of the small intestine (ileum). Crohn's disease, named after the US physician B. B. Crohn (1884–1983), occurs most commonly between the ages of 20 and 40 years; symptoms commonly include abdominal pain and diarrhoea. Its cause is not known but it may be a form of *autoimmunity. Patients are treated with drugs, such as prednisolone (a steroid) and sulphasalazine (a sulphonamide); some cases require surgical removal of the affected part of the intestine.

Cro-Magnon A prehistoric race of men believed to be ancestral to modern men. Skeletal remains were found (1868) at Cro-Magnon near Les Eyzies-de-Tayac in the Dordogne (SW France) and similar bones of tall broad-faced individuals have been found at other European sites. They first appeared in Europe about 35 000 years ago and were associated with *Aurignacian and subsequent cultures. They hunted reindeer, bison, and wild horse. They were often cave dwellers but seem also to have constructed huts. They produced the earliest known examples of cave art (*see* Lascaux). *See also* Homo.

Crome, John (1768–1821) British landscape painter and etcher, who founded the *Norwich school and became president of its Society of Artists. He was apprenticed to a sign painter but was otherwise self-taught through the study of Gainsborough and 17th-century Dutch masters. The style of his Norfolk landscapes, such as *Mousehold Heath* (Tate Gallery), was imitated by his son **John Bernay Crome** (1793–1842).

Cromer 52 56N 1 18E A resort in England, on the NE coast of Norfolk. It has a fishing fleet, a lifeboat station, and a lighthouse. Population (1981): 6192.

Cromer, Evelyn Baring, 1st Earl of (1841–1917) British soldier and diplomat. In 1879 Cromer became controller of finance in Egypt. In 1883 he became consul general and was the virtual ruler of Egypt until 1907.

cromlech (Welsh: bent stone) A former name for a megalithic table grave or *dolmen and other prehistoric stone monuments. *See also* megalith.

Crompton, Richmal (Richmal Crompton Lamburn; 1890–1969) British children's author. *Just William*, her first collection of stories about the young ruffian William, was published while she was teaching in 1922. She wrote numerous sequels and a few adult novels.

Crompton, Samuel (1753–1827) British inventor of the spinning mule (1779), so called because it was a cross between *Arkwright's water frame and *Hargreaves' spinning jenny. It was able to produce yarn of a higher quality and at a greater speed than had previously been possible. Unable to afford a patent, Crompton sold his idea for very little money but in 1812 he was awarded a parliamentary grant of £5,000.

OLIVER CROMWELL *Dismissing the Rump of the Long Parliament (1653).*

Cromwell, Oliver (1599–1658) English soldier and statesman; Lord Protector of England (1653–58). Cromwell, a country gentleman, was MP for Huntingdon in the parliament of 1628–29. He emerged as a convinced Puritan and critic of Charles I in the *Long Parliament, summoned in 1640. After the outbreak of the *Civil War he raised a troop of cavalry, the nucleus of his Ironsides (formed 1643), and fought at Edgehill (1642). He held command at *Marston Moor (1644) and was instrumental in the formation of the *New Model Army under Fairfax, which with Cromwell as second in command decisively defeated Charles at *Naseby (1645). Cromwell acted as mediator between the king, parliament, and the New Model Army but his conciliatory attitude hardened after Charles' flight to the Isle of Wight; when the second Civil War ended in Charles' defeat (1648), Cromwell signed the king's death warrant. In the power struggle between parliament and army, he sided with the army and after the establishment of the Commonwealth turned to the final mopping-up campaigns of the Civil War. He ruthlessly subjected Ireland (1649–50) and, after defeating Charles' heir at Dunbar (1650), finally subdued the Scots at Worcester (1651). In 1653 he expelled the Rump of the Long Parliament and following the failure of the *Barebones Parliament accepted the Instrument of Government, which established the *Protectorate. As Lord Protector, Cromwell established Puritanism but permitted religious toleration, allowing the Jews to return to England (1656). His attempt to decentralize government by dividing England into ten districts administered by ten major generals was short lived. His foreign policy was dictated by religious and commercial considerations: he ended the first *Dutch War, allied with France against Spain (gaining Dunkirk), and conquered Jamaica (1655). His relations with parliament were strained. He failed to find a workable constitutional basis for his rule, refusing parliament's offer of the crown in 1657. He was succeeded as Lord Protector by his son **Richard Cromwell** (1626–1712), who was forced by the army to abdicate in 1659 and lived in exile in France until 1680.

Cromwell, Thomas, Earl of Essex (c. 1485–1540) English statesman, who drafted the legislation that made the English Church independent of Rome (see Reformation). Son of a brewer and blacksmith, he entered Wolsey's service in 1514, became an MP in 1529, and by 1532 was Henry VIII's chief adviser; he became chancellor of the exchequer in 1533. He gained Henry's divorce from Catherine of Aragon by a series of Acts that made the king, rather than the pope, head of the English Church. The legalization of the break with Rome by parliamentary statute contributed to parliament's growing influence in government. Between 1536 and 1540 he organized the dissolution of the monasteries, after which his negotiation of Henry's disastrous marriage to the uncomely Anne of Cleves led to his execution for treason.

Cronin, A(rchibald) J(oseph) (1896–1981) British novelist. He practised medicine until he published his successful first novel, *Hatter's Castle* (1931). His later novels include *The Citadel* (1937) and *The Judas Tree* (1961). The radio and television series *Dr Finlay's Casebook* was based on his medical stories.

Cronje, Piet Arnoldus (c. 1840–1911) South African general in the *Boer Wars. He captured Potchefstroom (1881) and the raiders led by *Jameson (1896) and delayed (Magersfontein, 1899) the British advance to relieve Kimberley. He was captured at Paardeburg (1900).

Cronus A Greek deity, the youngest of the Titans. He ruled the universe after castrating his father Uranus. He swallowed all the children he fathered by his sister Rhea except Zeus, for whom a stone was substituted. Zeus was reared secretly in Crete and eventually overthrew Cronus.

Crookes, Sir William (1832–1919) British physicist, whose work on vacuums led him to investigate the newly discovered phenomenon of *cathode rays. Crookes showed that cathode rays consisted of charged particles rather than electromagnetic radiation, since they were deflected by a magnetic field. He invented the Crookes radiometer and Crookes glass, containing cerium, to protect the eyes of the industrial workers. He also discovered the element thalium.

crop rotation The growing on the same land of different crops in sequence. Crop rotation helps maintain soil fertility, prevents the build-up of crop pests, and enables cultivation of the soil to clear weeds. The Norfolk four-course rotation originated in the UK during the 18th century and involved growing turnips, spring barley, clover, and winter wheat in sequence. Nowadays, mechanized farming and the use of artificial fertilizers and pesticides have encouraged monocropping (the repeated growing of the same crop).

croquet A ball-and-mallet game that probably developed from *paille-maille*, a French game played certainly by the 13th century. Croquet was particularly popular in Britain and the USA in the mid- to late-19th century. It is played on a grass court or lawn, ideally 35 × 28 yd (32 × 25.6 m), with an arrangement of six hoops and one peg. Two to four players attempt to follow a prescribed course through the hoops, each using a distinctively coloured ball, the winner being the first to hit the peg with his ball. If a player's ball hits (roquets) another ball, the player may croquet this ball by placing his own ball next to it and striking his own ball so that the opponent's ball is also moved; the object is to advance his own ball towards the peg and to drive his opponent's ball off course. After passing through a hoop or scoring a roquet a player has another turn.

Crosby 53 30N 3 02W A town in NW England, in Merseyside. It is a mainly residential suburb of Liverpool. Population (1981): 53 660.

Crosby, Bing (Harry Lillis C.; 1904–77) US popular singer. He achieved worldwide fame during the 1930s and 1940s as a crooner and is associated with the best-selling recording of all time, Irving Berlin's *White Christmas* (1942). He starred in many films, often with Bob *Hope, and also in his own radio and television shows. □Sinatra, Frank.

crossbill A finch of the genus *Loxia* (3 species), 14.5-17 cm long, whose unique cross-tipped bill is specialized for extracting seeds from unopened cones. The common crossbill (*L. curvirostra*) of Eurasia and North America feeds on spruce seeds. The male is red and the female grey-green; both have dark-brown wings and tail. The parrot crossbill (*L. pytyopsittacus*) feeds exclusively on pine seeds, and the Eurasian two-barred crossbill (*L. leucoptera*) feeds on fir seeds. *See* Plate V.

crossbow A short bow mounted on a stock, used in Europe throughout the middle ages. Crossbows were composite, made of wood, horn, tendons, and by the early 15th century of steel (called an arbalest). They were drawn by hand, a belt hook, or a winch. The bolt or *quarrel* was short, iron-tipped, fletched with wood, leather, or brass, and capable of penetrating armour. Slower and less accurate than the *longbow, it could be fired from behind cover. It is now used for sport.

CROSSES *As a Christian symbol the cross was popularized by Constantine the Great and came into wide use in the 4th century.*

crosses Figures formed by a vertical line or bar intersected by a horizontal. As a symbol, the cross is found in the art of several ancient cultures. One of the earliest Egyptian hieroglyphs is the cruciform ankh (*crux ansata*), the symbol of life. The primary association of the cross is with Christianity, in which it represents the instrument used at Christ's *crucifixion. This had several forms, conventionally distinguished by their Latin names: a simple upright stake (*crux simplex*); a stake with a transverse beam towards the top (*crux immissa*), which is known as the Latin cross and is the common form in the Western Church; a stake topped by a transverse beam (*crux commissa*), also known as the tau cross or cross of St Anthony; and an X-shaped structure (*crux decussata*), known as the cross of St Andrew. In European art, the crucifixion is usually depicted with a Latin cross, and the crucifixes (crosses with the image of the crucified Christ) used on altars, rood screens, etc., are given this form. The Greek cross or cross of St George has vertical and horizontal arms of equal length and is the traditional form in use in Orthodox Churches. The cross has influenced innumerable aspects of religious ritual, dress, and art, including the cruciform plan of churches and cathedrals. It is also one of the earliest of monumental designs (*see* Ruthwell Cross). As a charge in *heraldry, it is given various elaborated forms; a familiar example is the Maltese cross, the insignia of the *Hospitallers and, in Britain, of the St John Ambulance Association.

Crossman, Richard (Howard Stafford) (1907-74) British Labour politician. An MP from 1945, he was minister of housing and local government (1964-66) and then of health and social security (1968-70). The controversial *Crossman Papers* (1975), which revealed details of cabinet discussions, were published in spite of government attempts to suppress them.

Crossopterygii An order of bony fish—the lobe-finned fishes—most of which are now extinct. Their fins were fleshy and contained elements of the internal skeleton, permitting movement both on land and in water. The suborder *Rhipidistia* were predatory freshwater fishes of the Devonian and Carboniferous periods (about 400-280 million years ago), some of which evolved into the amphibians. The suborder *Coelacanthini* contains *Latimeria*, the only surviving member of the order (*see* coelacanth). Subclass: *Sarcopterygii*.

crossword puzzles A word puzzle with a series of clues, the answers to which are written into a diagram divided into squares, some of which are blacked out. (In most puzzles the pattern of the black squares has to be symmetrical.) The first modern crossword was devised by an Englishman, Arthur Wynne (d. 1945), and published in the New York *World* in 1913. They became very popular in the USA during the 1920s, reaching the UK in 1924. They are now a feature of many newspapers, each one having its own style and idiosyncrasies. In the UK the more sophisticated puzzles have clues based on literary references, puns, and cryptic sentences as well as anagrams and synonyms.

Croton A genus of tropical trees and shrubs (750 species) many of which are of economic importance. *C. tiglium* of SE Asia produces croton oil, a powerful laxative now considered unsafe. The bark of *C. cascarilla* and *C. eluteria*, trees of the Bahamas, produces cascarilla, used in tonics. *C. laccifer* from India and Sri Lanka provides a lac used in varnishes. Several Brazilian species produce dragon's-blood resin. Family: *Euphorbiaceae* (spurge family).
The evergreen ornamental plants called crotons are members of the genus *Codiaeum*, grown as pot plants for their variegated foliage.

Crotone (ancient name: Croton) 39 05N 17 08E A town in S Italy, in Calabria on the Gulf of Taranto. It was founded in about 700 BC by the Achaeans. There are chemical and zinc industries. Population (1981 est): 58 281.

crottle A large leafy *lichen belonging to the genus *Parmelia*, which is widely distributed from seashores to mountain tops and resembles crumpled leather. It has a black underside and sometimes reaches 90-120 cm in diameter. It is used as a dye for fabrics.

croup An acute infection of the respiratory tract, usually caused by viruses, resulting in inflammation and obstruction of the larynx (voice box). Croup occurs most commonly in children under five years of age; symptoms include difficulty

in breathing, which is harsh and noisy. Treatment consists of steam inhalations and sedatives; severe cases may require tracheostomy—an operation in which a tube is inserted through a hole in the trachea (windpipe).

crow A large songbird of the widely distributed family *Corvidae* (102 species). 30-65 cm long, crows typically have a black or brightly coloured plumage and a stout bill. They take a variety of food, which often includes carrion, and have a distinctive harsh call. The typical crows are the *carrion, *hooded, and American crows but the family also includes the *rooks, *ravens, *choughs, *jays, and *jackdaws.

Crow A *Siouan-speaking North American Indian people of the Plains originally living in the Yellowstone River region. They moved W in the early 18th century to become traders of horses, guns, and other goods between the village Indians and the *Shoshoni. They hunted buffalo and were a warlike people among whom warriors underwent severe tests of bravery to attain the rank of chief. They used tobacco ritually and their religion emphasized a quest for a spirit guardian experienced through a vision after fasting and other ordeals.

crowberry A dwarf procumbent shrub, *Empetrum nigrum*, of N temperate and arctic heathlands. 15-45 cm high, it has oblong leaves, tiny pinkish flowers, and black edible berries. The name derives from the reputation of the fruit for attracting crows. Family: *Ericaceae* (heath family).

crowfoot A widely distributed herbaceous annual or perennial plant of the genus *Ranunculus*, which also contains the buttercups. They have deeply lobed leaves (hence the name) and white or yellow five-petalled flowers. Some species, such as the European water crowfoot (*R. aquatilis*), are aquatic. Family: *Ranunculaceae*.

Crown Agents for Overseas Governments and Administrations A UK public service, founded in 1833, that acts in a financial, professional, and commercial capacity for overseas governments and public-sector corporations, such as the railways, universities, and central banks. Between 1967 and 1974 they incurred a loss of some £200 million and following a public inquiry were restructured by the Crown Agents Act (1979).

crown colony A territory that is under the direct legislative control of the UK. Most crown colonies have now been granted independence: the most important one remaining is *Hong Kong; most of the others are small islands, chiefly in the Caribbean and the Pacific.

Crown Court. *See* courts of law.

crown jewels Royal insignia and regalia and the personal jewellery inherited or acquired by a sovereign. They are now frequently museum pieces. The British Crown Jewels, now kept in the Tower of London, were mainly amassed after the Restoration, the earlier set having been destroyed under Cromwell. Those used for coronations include a replica of St Edward's crown, the Sword of State, the Orb, and the Sceptre. Those used for other state occasions include the Imperial State Crown and another Sword of State.

Crown land Land that belongs to the UK monarch and is managed by the Crown Estate Commissioners. The profits from the land do not go to the monarch, as all revenues were surrendered by George III in 1760 in exchange for the income provided by the *civil list.

crown of thorns 1. A Madagascan shrub, *Euphorbia splendens*, often cultivated for ornament. Up to 100 cm high, it has spiny stems at the tips of which are a few leaves and clusters of small flowers, each surrounded by rounded scarlet bracts. *See* Euphorbia. 2. A spiny vigorous shrub, *Zizyphus spina-christi*, forming thickets or growing singly as a tree. It is widespread in the Mediterranean region and is said to be the source of Christ's crown of thorns. Family: *Rhamnaceae* (buckthorn family).

crown-of-thorns starfish A reddish starfish, *Acanthaster planci*, that has a spiny body, up to 45 cm across, with 12-19 arms. With the decimation of its chief predator—the Pacific triton (*Charonia tritonis*)—by shell collectors, it has spread throughout the South Pacific since the mid-20th century and now threatens destruction to the coral reefs and islands on which it feeds.

Croydon A mainly residential borough of S Greater London, created in 1965 from the former county borough and adjacent districts, all in Surrey. Population (1981): 316 557.

Cruciferae A family of plants (about 1900 species), mainly annual or perennial herbs, particularly abundant in N temperate regions. The flowers are four-petalled and cross-shaped. Many crucifers are of economic importance as food plants, cattle food, ornamentals, and weeds. Some, such as cabbage and other brassicas, have been grown since ancient times. In some European countries up to 30% of vegetable crop acreage is devoted to crucifers.

crucifixion A form of capital punishment carried out by nailing or binding a person to a *cross by the wrists and feet and leaving him to die from previously inflicted wounds or from exhaustion. It was commonly used in Carthage and adopted in the Roman Empire, where it was regarded as a scandalous form of death and so restricted to slaves and the worst criminals; it could not be inflicted on anyone holding Roman citizenship. Scourging customarily preceded crucifixion and the victim's legs were sometimes broken to hasten death. As a legal punishment it was abolished by the emperor Constantine. The crucifixion of Christ is reported in the four Gospels of the New Testament; the mockery, the crown of thorns, and the piercing of his side with a spear are not typical elements of this form of punishment. According to tradition, St Peter was also crucified, but head downwards, and St Andrew was executed on the X-shaped cross that bears his name. In Christian legend, the cross on which Christ was crucified was discovered in 326 AD by St *Helena.

Cruden, Alexander (1701–70) British scholar and bookseller. Author of the famous biblical concordance (first edition 1737), Cruden was dogged by frequent bouts of insanity. He wrote several pamphlets, one against John *Wilkes, appointing himself "Corrector" of public morals.

Cruft, Charles (1852–1938) British dog breeder. In 1886 he organized a dog show in London, the first of the annual British dog shows known as Cruft's.

Cruikshank, George (1792–1872) British caricaturist, painter, and illustrator. He achieved early success with his satirical political cartoons, superseding *Gillray in popularity. He illustrated such books as Dickens' *Oliver Twist* and Ainsworth's *Tower of London*. His etchings of *The Bottle* and painting of *The Worship of Bacchus* (Tate Gallery) are moralizing sermons on alcoholism.

cruise missile. *See* guided missiles.

cruiser A fast heavily armed warship, smaller than a *battleship but larger than a *destroyer and designed for a larger cruising radius. Cruisers with increased firepower, nuclear power that extends their range almost without limit, and greater versatility have replaced most of the battleships in the world's major navies.

Crusades The military expeditions organized in western Christendom primarily to recover the Holy Places of Palestine from Muslim occupation. The first Crusade (1095–99) was launched under the aegis of the papacy. Jerusalem was captured and the Crusader states of the Kingdom of Jerusalem, the County of Edessa, Antioch, and Tripoli were created. The fall (1144) of Edessa inspired the unsuccessful second Crusade (1147–48) and the capture of Jerusalem by *Saladin in 1187 led to the inconclusive third Crusade (1189–92), led by *Philip II Augustus of France, Emperor *Frederick I Barbarossa, and *Richard (I) the Lionheart of England. The fourth Crusade (1202–04) was diverted from its initial objective, Egypt, and sacked Constantinople (1204). The four Crusades of the 13th century failed to recover lost ground and Acre, the last foothold

of the West in Palestine, was lost in 1291. The Crusades failed in their stated objective, but Europe benefited greatly from the resultant growth of East–West trade and the introduction of eastern concepts into medieval culture. *See also* Children's Crusade.

crustacean An *arthropod of the class *Crustacea* (over 35 000 species), which includes the *barnacles, *woodlouse, *shrimps, *lobsters, *crabs, etc. The head bears two pairs of antennae and three pairs of jaws; the head and thorax together are usually covered by a chitinous carapace. There are numerous pairs of forked appendages, which are modified for different functions. Crustaceans are predominantly aquatic, breathing by means of gills. A few, such as the *fish louse, are parasitic on fish, whales, and other aquatic animals. During reproduction the male transfers sperm to the female, which often carries the fertilized eggs until they hatch. The larvae are mainly free-swimming and pass through several stages (*see* metamorphosis) to reach the adult form.

Crux (Latin: Cross) A small conspicuous constellation, also called the Southern Cross, in the S sky, lying in the Milky Way. The four brightest stars form a cross, the longer arm of which points roughly towards the S celestial pole.

Cruyff, Johann (1947–) Dutch Association footballer, who played for Ajax (1965–73), Barcelona, and the Netherlands. An outstanding centre forward, he captained the Dutch side that reached the final of the 1974 World Cup. He retired from football in 1984.

Cruz, Sor Juana Inéz de la (1651–95) Mexican poet. An infant prodigy, she lived at the Spanish viceroy's court before entering a convent in 1669. She died while nursing nuns during an epidemic. In addition to her metaphysical religious poems she wrote a defence of intellectual freedom and of women's rights to education.

crwth An ancient Welsh musical instrument, consisting of an oblong wooden frame with six strings across a slanting bridge. Four strings could be bowed and stopped against a fingerboard and the other two plucked as a drone bass.

cryogenics The production, effects, and uses of very low temperatures, usually meaning from −150°C down to *absolute zero. The most common method of producing cryogenic temperatures is to use *adiabatic processes. In adiabatic demagnetization, a magnetized paramagnetic substance is thermally isolated and demagnetized, thus cooling it. In adiabatic expansion, a thermally isolated gas is expanded. Cryogenic effects include changes in electrical properties, such as *superconductivity, and changes in mechanical properties, such as superfluidity (*see* superfluid). Cryogenics has been applied to new methods of food preservation, life-support systems in space, and the use of liquid propellants.

cryolite A rare mineral of composition Na_3AlF_6. It is colourless or white and occurs in pegmatite veins. It is only mined in significant quantities in Greenland, although it is known to occur elsewhere. It is used in aluminium refining. Synthetic cryolite is manufactured from hydrofluoric acid, sodium carbonate, and aluminium.

cryptogam Any plant that reproduces by means of spores. The nonvascular cryptogams include the mosses and liverworts (bryophytes), lichens, fungi, and algae; the vascular cryptogams are the ferns, horsetails, and related plants (pteridophytes). *Compare* phanerogam.

Cryptomeria. *See* Japanese cedar.

Cryptozoic time Geological time prior to the *Phanerozoic, i.e. the Precambrian, ending about 590 million years ago. It is the eon of "hidden life"; fossils are rare and obscure.

Crystal Palace A building designed by Joseph *Paxton to house the *Great Exhibition of 1851. The Crystal Palace, which had an area of 69 892 sq m (772 289 sq ft), was built in Hyde Park, London, with the highly advanced use of prefabricated glass and iron. It was later dismantled and reassembled at Sydenham (a suburb in SE London) but burnt down in 1936.

system	edges	angles
cubic	$a = b = c$	$\alpha = \beta = \gamma = 90°$
tetragonal	$a = b \neq c$	$\alpha = \beta = \gamma = 90°$
orthorhombic	$a \neq b \neq c$	$\alpha = \beta = \gamma = 90°$
hexagonal	$a = b \neq c$	$\alpha = \beta = 90°$; $\gamma = 120°$
trigonal	$a = b \neq c$	$\alpha = \beta = \gamma = 90°$
monoclinic	$a \neq b \neq c$	$\alpha = \gamma \neq \beta = 90°$
triclinic	$a \neq b \neq c$	$\alpha \neq \beta \neq \gamma$

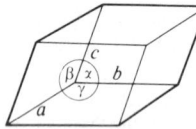

unit cell

CRYSTALS   *The classification of crystals.*

crystals Solids that have a regular geometrical shape because the constituent atoms, ions, or molecules are arranged in an ordered repeating pattern, known as a crystal lattice. Salt grains, for example, are cubic crystals of sodium chloride with sodium and chlorine ions alternating at the corners of a cubic lattice. There are seven crystal systems, into which all crystals are classified. Crystal structures are studied by a variety of techniques, including *X-ray diffraction and electron microscopy. Specialized mathematical notation and stereographic projections are used to describe lattice structure and symmetry. Many crystalline solids are polycrystalline, i.e. they consist of many small crystals. The physical properties of crystals have found many uses, ranging from *piezoelectric transducers to gemstones. **Crystallography** is concerned with the study of the structure and properties of crystals. Noncrystalline solids, such as glass, are said to be amorphous.

Csokonai Vitéz, Mihaly (1773–1805) Hungarian poet. His autobiographical play *Tempefői* (1793) records the struggles and failures of his life as a poet. His work includes a cycle of love poems addressed to "Lilla," a volume of odes, and the highly popular comic epic *Dorottya* (1804).

ctenophore A marine invertebrate animal, also called comb jelly, sea gooseberry, and sea walnut, belonging to the phylum *Ctenophora* (about 80 species). Its transparent gelatinous body is usually rounded and bears eight rows of ciliated comblike plates, used for locomotion. Ctenophores are mainly free-swimming and often occur in swarms in coastal waters, feeding on other planktonic animals captured by long branched tentacles.

Ctesiphon The capital of *Parthian and *Sasanian kings near Baghdad (Iraq). Taken temporarily by the Roman emperors *Trajan (115 AD) and Carus (283), it fell to the Arabs in 637. The remains of the palace of Khosrow I (reigned 531–79) incorporate the largest known brickwork vault, spanning over 25 m (82 ft).

CT scanner. *See* tomography.

Cuba, Republic of A country in the Caribbean Sea, off the S coast of Florida. It consists of two main islands, Cuba (the largest in the Caribbean) and the Isla de Pinos, together with over 1500 small islands and keys. On the island of Cuba fertile plains rise to mountains in the centre and SE and there are some lower hills in the NW. The population is mainly of European origin, with large African and mixed minorities. *Economy*: state controlled, it is primarily agricultural and very much dependent upon its sugar crop (its main source of export revenue); production levels have been generally low and attempts to increase efficiency include the part mechanization of the cane-cutting process. Tobacco (especially for cigars) is another important export crop and meat production is very important in the domestic economy. Fishing has expanded with government help and in 1977 fishing limits were extended to 320 km (200 mi). Important mineral resources include nickel (the second largest export). Largely dependent upon the Soviet Union for its oil supplies, Cuba has undertaken a programme of oil exploration. The fastest growing industries include metallurgy, construction, and textiles. *History*: discovered by Columbus in 1492, it was a Spanish colony (except in 1762–63, when it was occupied by the British) until 1898, when Spain was forced to withdraw following war with the USA. After three years of US occupation Cuba became a republic (1901) but the USA continued to intervene in Cuba's internal affairs and to control its foreign policy until 1934. In 1940 *Batista became president, taking Cuba into World War II on the Allied side. His corrupt dictatorship was threatened by Castro's unsuccessful revolt of 26 July, 1953, but in Castro's second attempt (1959) Batista was overthrown. Relations between Castro's socialist government and the USA were increasingly strained and Cuba moved closer in its international relations to the Soviet Union. In 1961 an invasion of Cuban exiles with US support was defeated at the *Bay of Pigs and in 1962 the Soviet installation of missile bases in Cuba resulted in a US naval blockade. The international crisis was resolved when the Soviet Union agreed to remove the bases. In the early 1970s US economic sanctions were lifted and in 1976 a socialist constitution was approved by a referendum. As a result of serious unemployment in the late 1970s many Cubans emigrated to countries in E Europe and some sought political asylum in South America. In recent years Cuban troops have been involved in revolutionary conflicts in both Africa and the Caribbean. Cuba is a member of COMECON. Head of government and first secretary of the Cuban Communist Party: Fidel Castro Ruz. Official language: Spanish. Official currency: Cuban peso of 100 centavos. Area 148 124 sq km (46 736 sq mi). Population (1983): 9 852 000. Capital and main port: Havana.

cubism A style of painting and sculpture, originating in the works of *Picasso and *Braque in about 1907. It started as an intellectual investigation of how a solid form can be represented in two dimensions without resorting to illusionism. Volume was generally suggested by the fusion of multiple viewpoints of an object in one image, which was presented as a complex of geometrical shapes. The subject matter of early cubism was invariably everyday objects of simple form, such as vases, tables, books, pipes, fruit, and musical instruments, many being suggested by the work of a forerunner of cubism, *Cézanne. Figures, which are rare, often resemble primitive sculpture, the observation of which helped Picasso to break with tradition. After 1911 the development of cubism, in which Juan *Gris now also participated, led to the introduction of *collage and also to a more decorative approach, monochrome tones being replaced by rich colours. Cubism was the principal catalytic influence on the evolution of *abstract art.

cubit An ancient unit of length equal to between 18 and 22 inches; it is based on the distance from the elbow to the tip of the middle finger.

Cubitt, Thomas (1788–1855) London carpenter who became a highly successful builder. With his brother **Lewis Cubitt** (1799–1883), he largely created Bloomsbury, Belgravia, and Pimlico. Thomas also built Osborne House (1845–48) on the Isle of Wight to the specification of the Prince Consort and Lewis built King's Cross Station (1837–39). Another brother, **Sir William Cubitt** (1785–1861), became Lord Mayor of London (1860–61) and it is after him that **Cubitt Town** on the Isle of Dogs is named. He developed the area to house workers in the shipyards and docks (1840–50).

Cuchulain (or **Cú Chulainn**) A legendary Irish hero, resembling *Achilles in his strength and courageous exploits. He was the son of the god Lug (*see* Lugus) but was brought up by his mortal uncle, Conchobar, King of Ulster. Cuchulain is the central subject in a series of ancient Gaelic epics and romances known as the Ulster cycle.

cuckoo A bird belonging to a family (*Cuculidae*; 127 species) occurring worldwide and ranging from 16–70 cm in length. The European cuckoo (*Cuculus canorus*), grey with distinctive white barring and a long tail, belongs to a subfamily of parasitic cuckoos (*Cuculinae*; 47 species); these lay their eggs in the nests of other birds, which rear their young. Parasitic cuckoos' eggs resemble those of the host in order to deceive the host bird. On hatching, the young cuckoo removes the other nestlings from the nest, thus obtaining sufficient food from its adopted parents. Order: *Cuculiformes* (cuckoos and turacos).

cuckoopint A perennial herbaceous European plant, *Arum maculatum*, also called lords-and-ladies. 30–50 cm tall, it has large arrow-shaped shiny green leaves and a cylindrical cluster of tiny flowers, which protrudes from a dull-purple funnel-shaped bract (spathe). The flowers give rise to poisonous red berries. Family: *Araceae*.

cuckoo-shrike A gregarious arboreal songbird of the family *Campephagidae* (70 species), occurring in tropical regions of the Old World. 13–32 cm long, they have a mainly grey plumage, long pointed wings, and a notched bill and feed on insects and fruit.

cuckoo-spit insect. *See* froghopper.

cucumber An annual vine, *Cucumis sativus*, probably originally from Asia but widely cultivated since ancient times. The long green juicy fruits, up to 60 cm long, are eaten raw, cooked, or pickled (*see* gherkin). In northern regions both glasshouse and outdoor (ridge) varieties are grown. Indoor cucumbers produce fruit without fertilization; if pollinated, the fruits taste bitter. Family: *Cucurbitaceae* (gourd family).

cucumber tree A slender North American tree, *Magnolia acuminata*, 16–30 m high. Hardiest of all magnolias, it is found in moist rich woodlands, often on mountain slopes. It has tulip-shaped greenish-white flowers and cucumber-like fruit–greenish at first, ripening to dull crimson. The light yellow satiny textured wood is used for furniture, flooring, etc. Family: *Magnoliaceae*.

Cúcuta (or **San José de Cúcuta**) 7 55N 72 31W A city in N Colombia, on the Pan-American Highway. It is an important commercial centre (especially for coffee). Its university was founded in 1962. Population (1980): 272 000.

Cudworth, Ralph (1617–88) English scholar, a leading member of the *Cambridge Platonists. His *True Intellectual System of the Universe* (1678) defends Christianity as the only genuine source of knowledge against the atheism and materialism of *Hobbes. His work on ethics is embodied in the posthumously published *Treatise concerning Eternal and Immutable Morality* (1731).

Cuenca 40 04N 2 07W A city in central Spain, in New Castile. It has a 13th-century cathedral. Industries include tanning, paper milling, and tourism. Population (1982 est): 39 860.

Cuenca 2 54S 79 00W A city in S central Ecuador. It is the

commercial centre for S Ecuador with a trade in agricultural products, hides, and marble. The university was founded in 1868. Population (1980 est): 139 209.

Cuernavaca 18 57N 99 15W A city and resort in S central Mexico. It is the site of Cortés' palace (now government offices), a Franciscan cathedral (1529), and a university (1939). Many writers, artists, and film stars have resided here. Its varied industries include flour milling, textiles, and sugar refining. Population (1980): 232 355.

Cuiabá 15 32S 56 05W A city in SW Brazil, the capital of Mato Grosso state on the Rio Cuiabá. It is a collecting centre for cattle, rubber, and palm nuts. The Federal University of Mato Grosso was founded here in 1970. Population (1980): 167 894.

cuisine minceur A recently developed style of gourmet cookery in which the traditional generous use of butter, cream, and other rich ingredients is minimized. Cuisine minceur was elaborated by the French chef Michel Guérard (1933–   ) in the 1970s at his restaurant at Eugénie-les-Bains in SW France. This entirely new approach to elegant cooking recommends using concentrated stocks and puréed vegetables to give flavour and texture to sauces and casseroles, eliminating butter, cream, and flour. It emphasizes light delicate food attractively presented, with a liberal use of fresh herbs.

Culbertson, Ely (1891–1955) US bridge authority, born in Romania, who influenced the development of contract bridge and used his wealth flamboyantly to popularize it. Imprisoned in the Caucasus in his youth for anarchist activity, he emigrated after the Russian Revolution. His life after 1938 was devoted to campaigning for world peace. He founded the magazine *The Bridge World* (1929) and wrote many books on bridge, as well as an autobiography *The Strange Lives of One Man* (1940).

Culdees (Old Irish *céle dé*: associate of God) Irish and Scottish monks, originally living in solitude but from about the 8th to 12th centuries existing in small groups. They were probably the last surviving remnant of the Celtic Church and were gradually replaced by Roman monastic orders.

Culham A village in S central England, in Oxfordshire, site of the UK centre for *thermonuclear reactor research (part of the Atomic Energy Authority) and of the JET (Joint European Torus) joint undertaking. This nuclear fusion research takes place as part of a coordinated programme by scientists and engineers from the EEC countries, Sweden, and Switzerland. It is also the site of the first European school in the UK.

Culiacán 24 50N 107 23W A city in W Mexico. It is the commercial centre for an irrigated agricultural area. Population (1980): 560 011.

Cullinan diamond An exceptional diamond weighing 3106 metric carats (c. 621 g) when found in the Premier Mine, South Africa, in 1905. It was cut into 9 major and 96 small stones. The two largest (Star of Africa and Cullinan II) are set in the British royal regalia.

Culloden Moor A moor in N Scotland, in the Highland Region near Inverness. In 1746 it was the scene of the last land battle to be fought in Britain, in which the Young Pretender, Charles Edward Stuart, was defeated by the Duke of Cumberland, thus ending the *Jacobite cause in Britain.

Culpeper, Nicholas (1616–54) English herbalist, physician, and astrologer. In 1649 he published an unauthorized translation of the official London Pharmacopoeia, which was well received (except by the medical profession). This was followed by his famous and equally popular *Complete Herbal* (1653).

Culpeper's Rebellion (1677–79) An American colonial uprising, in which tobacco growers in North Carolina opposed British restrictions on their markets. John Culpeper seized the British deputy governor and governed capably himself until his voluntary surrender for trial in England, at which he was acquitted.

cultivator A farm implement used to till the soil, so destroying weeds and promoting crop growth. Horse-drawn models date from the 19th century but modern tractor-drawn machines consist of a steel frame with curved steel tines to penetrate and disrupt the soil.

Cultural Revolution, Great Proletarian (1966–68) A political rather than cultural movement launched in China by Mao Tse-tung in opposition to bureaucracy and to reinvigorate revolutionary attitudes. Many leading officials were dismissed, the formal educational system was abolished, and reforms to foster correct political views were introduced. Many universities were closed and young people, mobilized as *Red Guards, attacked Party officials and destroyed cultural objects.

culture In microbiology, a colony of micoorganisms grown in a solid or liquid medium for experimental or diagnostic purposes. A widely used medium is agar gel (contained in petri dishes) supplemented with required nutrients, which is inoculated with microorganisms and incubated. Sterile conditions are essential to avoid contamination.

Cumae The first Greek colony in Italy. Founded near Naples about 750 BC by settlers from Chalcis, Cumae expanded rapidly, spreading Greek civilization in S Italy. It repulsed Etruscan influence but was subsequently subject to Rome (from c. 340 BC).

Cumaná 10 29N 64 12W A city in N Venezuela. Exports, through its port of Puerto Sucre on the Caribbean Sea, include sugar, cocoa, and tobacco. Its university was founded in 1958. Population (1981 est): 173 000.

Cumans A nomadic Turkish people, who dominated the W steppes for two centuries until they were driven into Hungary by the Mongol invasions (1237–39). They were absorbed into the Hungarian kingdom in which they had considerable influence.

Cumberland A former county of NW England. Under local government reorganization in 1974 it became part of the new county of *Cumbria.

Cumberland, Richard (1631–1718) English moral philosopher and Bishop of Peterborough from 1691. One of the *Cambridge Platonists, he was renowned for scholarship and virtue. His *De legibus naturae disquisitio philosophica* (1672) opposed *Hobbes' egoism in its principle of universal benevolence and anticipated *utilitarianism.

Cumberland, William Augustus, Duke of (1721–65) British general, who was the son of George II. After serving in the War of the Austrian Succession he crushed the *Jacobite rebellion at Culloden (1746); his subsequent harsh reprisals earned him the nickname Butcher. His career ended in disgrace after his capitulation to the French in the Seven Years' War.

Cumbernauld 55 58N 3 59W A town in central Scotland, in Strathclyde Region. Created a new town in 1956 to relieve overcrowding in Glasgow, it has varied light industries. Population (1981): 61 707.

Cumbria A county in NW England, bordering on the Irish Sea. It was created in 1974 from Westmorland, Cumberland, and parts of NW Lancashire and NW Yorkshire. It consists of the *Lake District, enclosed by coastal lowlands and the Pennine uplands. Agricultural activity includes sheep, dairy, and arable farming. New industries, including chemicals, are replacing the traditional ones of coal, iron, and steel, located chiefly in the coastal towns. Granite and limestone are extracted but coal resources are almost exhausted. Atomic energy establishments exist at Sellafield and Calder Hall. Area: 6809 sq km (2628 sq mi). Population (1983 est): 483 000. Administrative centre: Carlisle.

cumin An annual herb, *Cuminum cyminum*, up to 30 cm high with umbrella-like clusters of small whitish flowers and oblong bristly fruits. Native to the Mediterranean, it has long been cultivated in Europe, India, and China for its bitter fruits, which

resemble caraway seeds and are used in curry powders, to flavour liqueurs, etc. It was once used medicinally as a stimulant and liniment. Family: *Umbelliferae*.

cummings, e(dward) e(stlin) (1894–1962) US poet. His highly experimental lyric verse is characterized by typographical innovations and eccentric punctuation, which he employed to reinforce the verbal element of his poetry. His works include *Tulips and Chimneys* (1923), *Eimi* (1933), *o Thanks* (1935), and *1 × 1* (1944). He also wrote an experimental novel, *The Enormous Room* (1922), a poetic drama *Him* (1927), and a ballet *Tom* (1935).

cumulus cloud (Cu) A low type of *cloud of convective origin having a heaped appearance and developing vertically from a flat base. Fair-weather cumulus clouds are shallow but others are deep and may become **cumulonimbus cloud**. This cloud is heavy and dense, extending vertically to about 6000 m (20 000 ft), and is associated with thunderstorms. Its upper part often spreads out to form an anvil shape.

Cunaxa, Battle of (401 BC) The battle fought between *Cyrus the Younger and his elder brother Arsaces, who had seized the Persian throne as *Artaxerxes II in 404 BC. Cyrus gathered an army of Greek mercenaries (including the historian, Xenophon) and met Artaxerxes at Cunaxa, 70 km N of Babylon. Cyrus was defeated by Artaxerxes' superior cavalry forces and died in the battle.

pictographs		cuneiform	
c. 3500 BC	c. 3000	c. 2800	c. 800
			mountain
			fish
			barley grain

CUNEIFORM *The wedge-shaped strokes of cuneiform writing developed gradually from pictographs.*

cuneiform The oldest *writing system of which records survive, used to represent a number of ancient Near Eastern languages. The name derives from the wedge-shaped marks (Latin *cuneus*, a wedge) made by the imprint of a stylus in soft clay. Originally pictographic, by the 3rd millennium BC cuneiform pictures had become stylized in the form of groups of wedge-shaped imprints, many representing the sounds of syllables. Once hardened the clay tablets were almost indestructible and many are extant today. Probably devised by the Sumerians not later than 3100 BC, cuneiform spread to other language groups in the area. By 100 BC, however, it had largely been superseded by the North Semitic script that was used to represent the increasingly dominant Aramaic language.

Cunningham, Merce (1919–) US dancer and choreographer. He joined the Martha Graham Company in 1945 and founded his own company in 1952. He has frequently collaborated with the composer John *Cage and his many experimental abstract ballets include *Suite for Five* (1956), *Antic Meet* (1958), *Aeon* (1961), *Scramble* (1967), *Landrover* (1972), and *Travelogue* (1977).

Cunobelinus (or Cymbeline; died c. 42 AD) British ruler (c. 10–c. 42) of the Catuvellauni tribe. Their lands embraced much of SE England after they overcame the Trinovantes. He founded Colchester (c. 10).

cup fungus A fungus, belonging to the order *Pezizales*, that produces a cup- or saucer-shaped fruiting body. Cup fungi may or may not have a stalk and the spores are released from the upper surface of the cup. The distinctive scarlet elf cup (*Peziza coccinea*), found on dead branches, is a smooth-rimmed cup, 2–6 cm in diameter, deep red inside and whitish grey or pink outside. Class: *Ascomycetes*.

Cupid The Roman god of love, identified with the Greek Eros, and lover of Psyche. He is usually portrayed as a winged boy shooting arrows of love.

cuprite A red to black mineral of composition Cu_2O, found where deposits of copper have been subject to weathering.

cupronickel A corrosion-resistant alloy of 75% copper and 25% nickel (by weight). In the UK the Coinage Act (1946) substituted cupronickel coinage for silver alloy; the three cupronickel coins now in circulation are the 5p, 10p, and 50p pieces.

Curaçao A West Indian island, the largest in the Netherlands Antilles. Discovered in 1499, it was settled by the Spanish before being colonized by the Dutch in 1634. The refining of oil from Venezuela is of major importance; other industries include the production of Curaçao liqueur and calcium-phosphate mining. Area: 444 sq km (173 sq mi). Population (1983): 165 011. Chief town: Willemstad.

curare A resinous substance obtained from South American trees of the genera *Strychnos* and *Chondodendron*, used as an arrow poison by South American Indians. Curare blocks the action of *acetylcholine, which is released at the junctions of nerve endings and muscles and causes muscular contraction. Curare therefore causes a relaxed paralysis of muscle. Curare-like compounds (e.g. tubocurarine) are injected during general anaesthesia to relax muscles and provide the surgeon with better access to the part of the body on which he is operating.

curassow A long-tailed tropical American gamebird belonging to the family *Cracidae*. Curassows have a long neck and long legs and may reach 100 cm in length. The black males have a crest of curly feathers and a yellow bill ornament; females are smaller and brownish in colour. They are mostly arboreal, feeding on buds, insects, and frogs. Chief genera: *Crax, Pauxi, Mitu*; order: *Galliformes* (pheasants, turkeys, etc.).

curia An ancient division of the Roman people. There were 30 *curiae*, each with a meeting place that was also known as a *curia*. The Senate house of Rome, attributed to Tullus Hostilius, was called the Curia Hostilia and its replacement, built by Julius Caesar, was known as the Curia Julia.

Curia, Roman. *See* Roman Curia.

Curia Regis The King's Court of early medieval Europe. It fulfilled all the functions of royal government—administrative, legislative, and judicial—and from its specialist departments developed the public government offices, such as, in England, the Chancery and the Exchequer, as well as the courts of law and parliament.

curie (Ci) A unit of radioactivity equal to the amount of an isotope that decays at the rate of 3.7×10^{10} disintegrations per second. Named after Marie *Curie.

Curie, Marie (1867–1934) Polish chemist, renowned for her research into *radioactivity. Born Marya Skłodowska, she emigrated to France in 1891, studied at the Sorbonne, and married (1895) **Pierre Curie** (1859–1906), a French physicist. Interested in *Becquerel's discovery of radioactivity, Marie Curie noticed in 1898 that one particular uranium ore emitted an anomalously large amount of radiation. Realizing that the radiation was caused by a new element, she and her husband spent four years isolating one gram of radium salt from eight tons of the ore. The Curies, together with Becquerel, were awarded the 1903 Nobel Prize for Physics and, for her discovery of radium and polonium, she won the 1911 Nobel Prize for Chemistry. Pierre Curie,

MARIE CURIE *The discoverer of radium working with her husband, Pierre, in their laboratory in 1903, the year they were awarded a Nobel Prize.*

before joining his wife's work, had discovered the *piezoelectric effect (1880) and shown that ferromagnetism reverts to paramagnetism (*see* magnetism) above a certain temperature, now known as the Curie point (1895). He was killed in a road accident; she died as a result of the radiation to which she had been exposed. Their daughter **Irène Joliot-Curie** (1896–1956) married the French physicist **Frédéric Joliot** (1900–59) in 1926. Working together in the same field as her parents, they were the first to produce radioactivity artificially. For this work they were awarded the Nobel Prize for Chemistry in 1935.

Curie's law The susceptibility of a paramagnetic substance is inversely proportional to its thermodynamic temperature. The **Curie point** (*or* Curie temperature) is the temperature above which a ferromagnetic substance becomes paramagnetic. Named after Pierre Curie.

Curitiba 25 24S 49 16W A city in SE Brazil, the capital of Paraná state. It has two cathedrals and is the site of the Federal University of Paraná (1894). Curitiba is a commercial and industrial centre producing chiefly furniture, tobacco, and maté. Population (1980): 843 733.

curium (Cm) An artificial transuranic element discovered by Seaborg and others in 1944 and named after Marie and Pierre Curie. All 13 isotopes are radioactive and some intensely so; ^{242}Cm gives out about three watts of heat per gram. Curium is a silvery reactive metal. Its compounds include the oxides (CmO_2, Cm_2O_3) and halides (CmF_3, $CmCl_3$). At no 96; at wt (247); mp 1340 ± 40°C.

curlew A streaked brown or grey bird belonging to the genus *Numenius* (8 species). Curlews have a long neck and long curved bill. They breed in inland subarctic regions and migrate south in winter to marshes and mudflats, feeding on worms and crabs. The common Eurasian curlew (*N. arquata*) is almost 60 cm long and ranges from Britain to central Asia. Family: *Scolopacidae* (snipe, sandpipers, etc.).

curling A target game played on ice with stones fitted with handles, played since at least the early 16th century and strongly associated with Scotland. Two teams of four players take it in turns to slide two curling stones, each up to

36 m (39 yd), along the ice towards the "house," a series of concentric circles at the end of the rink. A team scores one point for each stone finishing nearer the centre of the house than any of its opponents'. Team-mates are allowed to sweep the ice ahead of a moving stone to remove impediments and influence its course.

currant **1.** One of several species of shrubs belonging to the genus *Ribes*. Some are cultivated for their fruit, for example *blackcurrant and *redcurrant, and others, such as the *flowering currant, are grown as ornamentals. Family: *Grossulariaceae*. **2.** The dried berry of a small seedless *grape, grown in the Mediterranean region and used in cooking.

currawong An Australasian songbird of the genus *Strepera* (6 species). About 50 cm long, currawongs are usually black, sometimes with white markings, and have a long hook-tipped bill. They feed on insects, small mammals, and birds and frequently destroy fruit crops. Family: *Cracticidae* (Australian magpies).

currents Flows of water masses moving in a particular direction. The major ocean currents form part of the general circulatory system in the oceans and are permanent, although they may vary with the seasons. They result mainly from the action of the prevailing winds on the sea surface; an example is the North Atlantic Drift. Currents are also induced by the tides, by differences in water density (densities vary with temperature, salinity, and turbidity levels), and by rivers discharging into the sea.

curricle A light two-wheeled carriage usually drawn by two horses harnessed abreast to a pole. Curricles were favoured in the 18th and 19th centuries as rapid and stylish conveyances, equivalents to modern sports cars.

curry A spicy stew of meat, chicken, vegetables, etc., originating in the Indian subcontinent. Long slow cooking over a gentle heat allows the meat to become tender and the different ingredients to intermingle. The essence of curry is the balanced mixture of aromatics: spices (especially yellow turmeric but also cumin, coriander, cardamoms, and ginger), herbs, and seasonings (peppers, chillies, and salt; or sweet seasonings made from sugar or honey; and acid seasonings made from citrus fruit juices). Curries are usually eaten with rice and chutneys. In the West premixed curry powder is often used.

Curry, John (Anthony) (1949-) British ice skater and the only British skater to win the world, Olympic, and European figure-skating titles in the same year (1976). After turning professional, he opened a theatrical ice show in London (1977).

Curtin, John Joseph (1885-1945) Australian statesman; Labor prime minister (1941-45). He implemented many social-welfare policies and developed the military defences of Australia, introducing wide-ranging conscription measures during World War II. He died in office.

Curtiss, Glenn (Hammond) (1878-1930) US aviator and aeronautical engineer. Curtiss made the first one-kilometre flight in the US (1908) and designed and constructed the earliest US seaplanes. He manufactured aircraft for the Allies in World War I.

Curwen, John (1816-80) British Nonconformist minister and teacher. He perfected the Tonic Sol-fa system invented by Sarah Anna Glover (1785-1867). Curwen resigned from the ministry to propagate Tonic Sol-fa and in 1844 founded the music publishing firm that became J. Curwen and Sons Ltd.

Curzon, Sir Clifford (1907-82) British pianist. He studied with Schnabel in Berlin and made his debut at the Queen's Hall, London, at the age of 16. He was particularly well known for his interpretations of Beethoven, Mozart, and Schubert; he also championed the works of Rawsthorne. He was knighted in 1977.

Curzon, George Nathaniel, 1st Marquess (1859-1925) British politician. As viceroy of India (1898-1905) he

established the Northwest Frontier Province and overhauled Indian administration but resigned following disagreements with *Kitchener. In World War I he was Lord Privy Seal (1915-16) and a member of the War Cabinet (1916-19). As foreign secretary (1919-24) he established a short-lived British protectorate over Persia.

Curzon line A line between Poland and the Soviet Union, which they recognized as the border between them in 1945 after World War II. The boundary, named after Lord *Curzon, had initially been suggested during the Russo-Polish War (1919-20).

cuscus A cat-sized *marsupial mammal belonging to the genus *Phalanger*, found in forests of NE Australia, New Guinea, and nearby islands. Cuscuses have a prehensile tail and climb slowly around trees at night, eating mainly leaves and fruit but sometimes catching lizards or roosting birds. Family: *Phalangeridae* (see phalanger).

Cushing, Harvey Williams (1869-1939) US surgeon, noted for his contributions to brain surgery, particularly of the pituitary gland, and his classification of brain tumours. He was the first to describe the hormonal disorder known as *Cushing's disease.

Cushing's disease A disorder resulting from excess *corticosteroid hormones in the body, named after H. W. *Cushing. The symptoms include obesity, loss of minerals from the bones, and reddening of the face and neck; it may be associated with the symptoms of *diabetes mellitus and high blood pressure. It may be caused by a tumour of the pituitary gland or the adrenal gland or by prolonged therapy with high doses of corticosteroids: the treatment is determined by the cause.

Cushitic languages A subgroup of the *Hamito-Semitic languages. They are spoken in the Sudan, Somalia, Ethiopia, and Eritrea, and include Beja and *Somali. This group is the closest in sound to the common ancestor Proto-Hamito-Semitic.

custard apple A small tree of the genus *Annona* of the American tropics, so called because of the custard-like flavour of its fruits. The common custard apple (*A. reticulata*), 5-8 m high and widely grown in the West Indies, produces reddish many-seeded fruits, 8-12 cm in diameter, with a sweetish pulp. See also soursop; sweetsop. Family: *Annonáceae*.

Custer, George A(rmstrong) (1839-76) US cavalry general. After earning distinction in the Civil War, he commanded the Seventh Cavalry during the western campaigns against the Indians. Sent to round up Sioux and Cheyenne forces under Chief *Sitting Bull in S Dakota's Black Hills in 1876, an erroneous reconnaissance report led him to divide his force and he and his force of about 260 were massacred by the main Indian strength at the *Little Bighorn (Custer's Last Stand).

customs and excise duties Indirect taxes (see taxation) applied to goods and services. In the UK these taxes are collected by the Board of Customs and Excise and comprise customs, excise, assessed taxes, and *value-added tax. Customs (or tariffs) are duties payable on import of foreign goods. They may be either specific duties assessed according to the weight or quantity, or ad valorem duties assessed according to the foreign or domestic price of the imported goods. They raise revenue and restrict imports. Excise tax is a duty chargeable on specific goods produced or consumed within a country, e.g. petrol, intoxicating liquors, and tobaccos. Assessed taxes are duties not properly in the nature of excise but classified under that heading because they are levies on particular activities within a country, e.g. motor-vehicle licences.

customs unions Associations of countries that agree to abolish customs duties and tariffs for each other's products and to institute *free trade between themselves. They usually also agree to common external tariffs for nonmembers. The *European Economic Community is an example of a customs union.

Cuthbert, St (c. 635–87 AD) English churchman and missionary. As a monk and later a prior at Melrose, he evangelized among the Northumbrians, earning a reputation as a miracle worker. With his abbot, St Eata, he moved to Lindisfarne in 664 and became its bishop in 685. He died on the island of Farne, where he had earlier lived as a hermit. His body was reburied in Durham Cathedral in the 10th century. Feast day: 20 March.

cutter **1.** A sailing vessel, similar to a *sloop, but with the mast stepped about halfway between the bows and the stern. **2.** A fast armed powerboat used by the US Coast Guard for patrolling coastal waters in the enforcement of customs regulations, to rescue vessels in distress, etc.

cuttlefish A *cephalopod mollusc belonging to the family *Sepiidae* (about 100 species), of temperate coastal waters. 2.5–90 cm long, the body is supported by an internal calcareous leaf-shaped shell–the cuttlebone–which gives buoyancy. When alarmed, the animal emits an inky fluid.

Cutty Sark A clipper ship built at Dumbarton in 1869, preserved as a museum at Greenwich, London.

cutworm The larva of a *noctuid moth belonging to the widely distributed genus *Agrotis*. Cutworms destroy crops, such as cabbage, maize, and pasture grasses, by biting through the stems, often at ground level.

Cuvier, Georges, Baron (1769–1832) French zoologist and father of the sciences of comparative anatomy and palaeontology. His studies at the Museum of Natural History in Paris showed him how the different parts of an animal skeleton were related to each other and to their functions. By extending this to fossils he was able to reconstruct entire skeletons from the incomplete ones in existence. His classification system, described in *Le Règne animal* (1817), grouped animals (including extinct fossil species) into four phyla. This was an advance on the system of Linnaeus although it was later superseded.

Cuxhaven 53 52N 08 42E A seaport in N West Germany, in Lower Saxony on the Elbe estuary. It is the outport for Hamburg, as well as being a major fishing port and fish-processing centre. Population (1983): 57 888.

Cuyp, Aelbert Jacobsz (1620–91) Dutch landscape painter. He was born in Dordrecht, the son and pupil of **Jacob Gerritsz Cuyp** (1594–1651), a portrait and landscape painter. Aelbert's paintings of cattle, river scenes, etc., are distinguished by their glow of golden light, a fine example being *Herdsmen with Cows by a River* (National Gallery, London).

Cuzco 13 32S 71 57W A city in S Peru, in the Andes 3416 m (11 207 ft) above sea level. It was the capital of the Inca Empire prior to the Spanish conquest in 1533; Inca ruins include the Temple of the Sun. It is now a commercial centre serving an agricultural region. It has a university (1962). Population (1981 est): 181 604.

Cwmbran 51 39N 3 00W A town in South Wales, in Gwent. Created a new town in 1949 (local coalmining having ceased) it has engineering, electrical, and food-processing industries. Population (1981): 44 309.

cyanide process The extraction of gold from its ores by chemical treatment with potassium cyanide. The ore is crushed to a fine powder and mixed with a weak solution of cyanide in water. Once the gold is dissolved by the cyanide the resulting compound is precipitated from the solution and the metallic gold separated out by chemically displacing it from the compound with zinc.

cyanocobalamin. *See* vitamin B complex.

cyanogen (C_2N_2) A colourless highly poisonous flammable gas with a smell of bitter almonds. It can be prepared by heating mercury cyanide and has been used as a fumigant, war gas, and rocket fuel.

Cybele An Asiatic earth goddess identified by the Greeks with *Rhea. The centre of her worship was Phrygia, whence her cult spread to Athens and later to Rome. She represented the powers of nature and was a protectress of wild animals. Her priests were eunuchs known as Corybantes.

cybernetics The study of communication and control between men, machines, and organizations. The name was derived from the Greek word meaning "steersman" by Norbert *Wiener, who was largely responsible for pioneering the subject. It is an aspect of *bionics, in which the human ability to adapt to changing circumstances and to make decisions is simulated in the design of computer-controlled systems. Ultimately, the application of cybernetics may extend the process of *automation to the point at which almost every operation in a factory is automatic, with very little human supervision.

Cybernetics has also been used as a link between the physical and life sciences, for instance in using *information theory to explain how messages are transmitted in nervous systems and in genetic processes.

cycad A *gymnosperm plant belonging to the order *Cycadales* (about 100 species), native to warm and tropical regions. They resemble small palms or tree ferns, having short stout stems with a crown of frondlike leaves. Reproductive organs are in the form of separate male and female cones borne on different trees, the female cones often being very large (up to 45 kg). The stems of some species yield a type of *sago.

Cyclades (Modern Greek name: Kikládhes) A group of some 220 Greek islands in the S Aegean Sea, including Andros, Delos, Ios, Míkonos, Melos, Náxos (the largest), Páros, and Syros. Total area: 2578 sq km (995 sq mi). Population (1981): 88 458. Capital: Hermopolis (on Syros).

cyclamate A salt of cyclamic acid ($C_6H_{11}NHSO_3H$). Sodium and calcium cyclamates were formerly extensively used as artificial sweeteners in soft drinks and for diabetics, but their excessive consumption has been shown to have dangerous side effects and their use has been discontinued.

Cyclamen A genus of perennial plants (15 species) native from the European Mediterranean to Iran and widely cultivated as pot and garden plants. The pot varieties are grown from *C. persicum*. The garden cyclamens include attractive dwarf varieties, 5–8 cm high. All cyclamens produce corms but most can be grown from seed. They have marbled heart-shaped leaves and drooping flowers with red, pink, or white reflexed petals. Family: *Primulaceae*.

cycloid The curve traced out by a point on the circumference of a circle as it rolls along a flat surface.

cyclone An area of relatively low atmospheric pressure with a series of closed isobars around its centre. In the N hemisphere wind circulates in an anticlockwise direction around its centre, in the S hemisphere it is clockwise. Except in the tropics, cyclones are now usually referred to as *depressions or lows. Tropical cyclones form over the tropical oceans and are accompanied by strong winds; they include *hurricanes and *typhoons.

Cyclops (Greek mythology) Storm gods who made thunderbolts for Zeus. Homer describes them in the *Odyssey* as one-eyed man-eating giants who lived on an island later identified as Sicily. *See also* Polyphemus.

Cyclops (zoology) A genus (44 species) of very small freshwater crustaceans of the subclass *Copepoda, so named because of their single median eye. In Africa and Asia they transmit the parasitic Guinea worm larvae to man if accidentally swallowed.

cyclostome An eel-like jawless aquatic vertebrate of the class *Cyclostomata*, which includes the *lamprey and *hagfish. Cyclostomes have a long smooth cylindrical body with fins arranged not in pairs but singly (*compare* fish), a cartilaginous skeleton, and a sucking mouth with numerous horny teeth. They occur mainly in temperate fresh waters and salt waters and many are parasitic on fish. Subphylum: *Agnatha*.

cyclotherms

cyclotherms Series of beds of sedimentary rocks deposited in a single cycle (in cyclic sedimentation) or repeated group (in rhythmic sedimentation). Carboniferous strata, particularly the Coal Measures, show such sequences, representing the changes in conditions from terrestrial to marine that repeatedly occurred in the period.

CYCLOTRON *The charged particles are accelerated in the two D-shaped conductors* (D₁ *and* D₂), *which are supported in the magnetic field* B.

cyclotron A type of particle *accelerator in which charged particles are accelerated in an outward spiral path inside two hollow D-shaped conductors (called dees) placed back to back. A magnetic field at right angles to the plane of the dees causes the particles to move in a spiral and, at the same time, they are accelerated by an alternating electric field applied across the gap between the two dees. When the particles reach the edge of the device they are deflected onto the target. The maximum energy of the particles is about 25 MeV. *See also* synchrocyclotron.

Cygnus (Latin: Swan) A large conspicuous constellation in the N sky, lying in the Milky Way. The brightest star, *Deneb, and four other bright stars form the **Northern Cross**. The constellation contains many interesting *variable stars, *binary stars, and dark and emission *nebulae—including the old supernova remnant, the **Cygnus Loop**. **Cygnus A** is an intense double radio source while **Cygnus X-1**, thought to contain a *black hole, is one of several strong X-ray sources.

cymbals Circular metal percussion instruments of indefinite pitch. Orchestral cymbals are clashed together, struck with a drumstick, or suspended and rolled with felt-covered timpani sticks. **Choke cymbals** (*or* hi-hat) are a pair of cymbals on a stick, operated by a foot pedal; they are used in dance bands and pop groups. Small tuned cymbals are known as **ancient cymbals**. □musical instruments.

Cymbeline. *See* Cunobelinus.

Cymbidium A genus of tropical and subtropical *orchids (40–70 species), native to Asia and Australia. Most species have pseudobulbs, straplike leathery leaves, and long-lasting sprays of 6–20 flowers on each flower stalk. Ornamental and very adaptable, cymbidiums are among the most popular orchids in cultivation today. They are popular as ornamentals.

Cynewulf (early 9th century AD) One of the earliest Anglo-Saxon religious poets (*compare* Caedmon). His work shows him to have been a native of Mercia or Northumbria and from a learned background. Four surviving religious poems, preserved in 10th-century manuscripts, carry his runic signature. They are *Elene*, *The Fates of the Apostles*, *The Ascension*, and *Juliana*. All are based on Latin sources and are distinguished by their clear narrative form. Many other Old English poems have been attributed to him.

Cynics The followers of the Greek moral philosopher *Diogenes of Sinope, who were active from the early 3rd century BC. They are notable less as a coherent school with systematic doctrines than as a succession of flamboyant individuals whose characteristic concern was to discount the pursuit of worldly wealth and success and to demonstrate that basic human needs can be very simply satisfied. They were outspoken critics of accepted social values and often lived notably unconventional lives. Positive freedom could be attained by self-realization, but often it was the negative destructive side of the Cynics' beliefs that was emphasized. Their distinction between natural and artificial values strongly influenced other ancient philosophies, such as *Epicureanism.

cypress A conifer of the genus *Cupressus* (true cypresses; 20 species), native to S Europe, E Asia, and North America and widely planted for ornament and timber. Cypresses have tiny scalelike leaves, which densely cover the branches and twigs, and rounded cones, 1–4 cm in diameter, usually ripening from green to brown. The Italian or funeral cypress (*C. sempervirens*), of the Mediterranean region, is 25–45 m high. Cultivated forms, usually narrow and columnar, are planted in gardens and cemeteries. Its strong fragrant long-lasting wood is used for chests, furniture, etc. Family: *Cupressaceae*.

Similar and related trees of the genus *Chamaecyparis* (6 species), of North America and SE Asia, are known as false cypresses. The most important species is Lawson's cypress (*C. lawsoniana*), of W North America, where it grows to a height of 60 m. There are many cultivated varieties, up to 38 m high, widely planted for shelter and ornament. *See also* swamp cypress.

Cypress pine A coniferous tree of the genus *Callitris* (about 16 species), native to Australia and New Caledonia. Their branches are densely covered with small scale leaves and the cones are small and globular. Several species yield a useful timber. Family: *Cupressaceae*.

Cyprian, St (c. 200–58 AD) African churchman; Bishop of Carthage (from c. 248) and Father of the Church, martyred under the Emperor Valerian. In his treatise, *De unitate ecclesiae*, he argues that the bishop's authority provides the basis for the Church's unity. Feast day: 16 Sept.

Cyprus, Republic of (Greek name: Kypros; Turkish name: Kıbrıs) An island state in the E Mediterranean Sea, off the S coast of Turkey. A central plain, the Messaoria, rises to the Kyrenia Range in the N, and in the SW the Troödos Massif rises over 1800 m (6000 ft). Most of the population is Greek or Turkish, the former being in the majority. *Economy*: mainly agricultural. Mineral resources include iron pyrites, asbestos, chromite, and copper ores. Though mining is on the decline, other (mainly light) industries are being rapidly developed. Tourism is important, although, like the rest of the economy, it has been badly affected by the unrest of recent years. There is now an intensive development programme in the Turkish sector, largely based on agriculture and especially citrus fruit for export, with the aim of creating a self-sufficient economy. Exports include wine, citrus fruits, potatoes, and metals. *History*: there was already a Greek colony on Cyprus almost 4000 years ago. It was conquered by Egypt in the 6th century BC and later formed part of the Persian, Macedonian, Roman, Byzantine, and Arab empires. In 1193 it became a Frankish kingdom and in 1489 a Venetian dependency. In 1571 it was conquered by the Turks and this occupation lasted until 1878 when it came under British administration. It became a crown colony in 1925. In the 1930s Greek Cypriots began advocating Enosis (Union with Greece), and in 1955 a Greek Cypriot organization (*see* EOKA), led by Archbishop *Makarios and Gen Grivas, began guerrilla warfare against the British. Cyprus became a republic in 1960 and a member of the Commonwealth in 1961. The UK, however, retained sovereignty over several military bases. There were fierce clashes between the Greek and Turkish communities in the 1960s and in 1964 a UN peacekeeping force was sent to the island. Greek and Turkish talks in 1968 aimed unsuccessfully at better relations between the two sides. In 1971 Gen Grivas began a further terrorist campaign in favour of Enosis; he died in 1974. Following a Greek-supported military coup of the same year, in which Makarios was temporarily overthrown, Turkey invaded the island leading to its virtual partition. The Turks set up their own government in the N as the Turkish Federated State of Cyprus, with Rauf Denktash as president, in 1975. This failed to receive international recognition but was, in 1983, declared to be an independent state as the Turkish Republic of Northern Cyprus. Spyros Kyprianou, elected president on the death of Makarios, was succeeded in 1988 by George Vasiliou (1932–   ). Official languages: Greek and Turkish; English is also widely spoken. Official currency: Cyprus pound of 1000 mils. Area: 9251 sq km (3572 sq mi). Population (1980 est): 633 500. Capital: Nicosia. Main port: Limassol.

Cyrano de Bergerac, Savinien (1619–55) French writer and dramatist. He became famous in his youth as a soldier and fighter of duels. He wrote a comedy, *Le Pédant joué* (1654), some tragedies on classical subjects, and two fantastic satirical romances describing visits to the moon and sun (published posthumously). He was noted for his comically long nose as well as his chivalrous nature; the conflict between his appearance and his noble character is captured in *Rostand's famous play, *Cyrano de Bergerac*.

Cyrenaica A region of E Libya, bordering Egypt on the E, largely desert to the S and inhabited mainly by tribesmen of the Senussi, a puritanical Islamic sect. From early pre-Christian times Cyrenaica was colonized or conquered by Greeks, Egyptians, Romans, Vandals, Arabs, Turks, and Italians successively. The scene of many battles in World War II, it was occupied by the British from 1943 until united with Libya in 1951. It was a province of Libya until 1963.

Cyrenaics A school of Greek philosophers, founded about 400 BC by *Socrates' disciple, Aristippus of Cyrene. The Cyrenaics identified virtue with pleasure and, adopting the *Sophists' view that truth and morality are matters for individual judgment, held that the only purpose of life was immediate gratification of the senses. Among them, Anniceris stressed the pleasures of friendship and family affection, whereas Hegesias, believing that pure pleasure was unattainable, advocated rather the avoidance of pain. Their ethical doctrines foreshadowed *Epicureanism.

Cyrene The chief city of ancient Cyrenaica (now in Libya). Founded by colonists from Thera about 630 BC, Cyrene quickly became prosperous, basing its wealth on trade. Its monopoly in silphium, an important Greek medicinal spice, brought the Cyrenaeans fame as doctors. It fell under the control of the Ptolemies of Egypt in the 4th century BC and was bequeathed by Ptolemy Apion to Rome in 96 BC. Excavations of its extensive remains have provided valuable information about ancient art, architecture, and society.

Cyril, St (c. 827–69 AD) Greek missionary, traditionally the inventor of the *Cyrillic alphabet. With his brother St **Methodius** (c. 825–84) he was sent to Moravia to evangelize the Slavs by the Patriarch of Constantinople in 863. Although highly successful, the brothers initially incurred much hostility from the German rulers and ecclesiastics for their use of the vernacular in the liturgy. After Cyril's death, Methodius translated the Bible into Slavonic. Feast day: 7 July.

Cyrillic alphabet The alphabet used for Russian, Belorus-

sian, Ukrainian, Bulgarian, Serbian, and various other languages of the Soviet Union. It was developed from a Greek alphabet of the 9th century AD in the course of Christian missionary work and is traditionally attributed to the Greek brothers, St *Cyril and St Methodius. It originally consisted of 43 letters, but modern versions have reduced this number to about 30.

Cyril of Alexandria, St (c. 375–444 AD) Christian theologian; Patriarch of Alexandria (from 412) and Doctor of the Church. He became a champion of Christian orthodoxy, expelled the Jews from Alexandria, and opposed Nestorius (*see* Nestorians) on the question of Christ's divinity, eventually succeeding in having him banished as a heretic. He produced numerous works, including biblical commentaries and refutations of paganism. Feast day: 9 Feb.

Cyrus (II) the Great (d. 529 BC) King of Persia (559–529), who founded the Achaemenian Empire. He staged a successful revolt against his overlord Astyages (reigned c. 584–c. 550), gaining control of the empire of the Medes (*see* Media). He then conquered Lydia, Ionia, and Babylonia (539), thereby gaining Syria and Palestine, and territories in Central Asia. He was noted for his humane and tolerant policies towards conquered peoples and permitted the Jews to return to Jerusalem in 537. He was killed fighting in Central Asia: his tomb at *Pasargadae is still to be seen.

Cyrus the Younger (d. 401 BC) The son of Darius II (reigned 423–404) of Persia. Appointed commander of Persian forces in Asia Minor in 407, he helped the Spartan admiral *Lysander defeat Athens in the *Peloponnesian War. When in 404 Cyrus' brother succeeded their father as *Artaxerxes II, Cyrus led a Greek mercenary army, which included the historian *Xenophon, against him. He died leading a cavalry charge at *Cunaxa.

cyst 1. A close fluid-filled sac within the body. Cysts may be caused by blockage of the duct of a gland (e.g. a sebaceous cyst in the skin), dilation of an existing body space (e.g. in the ovary), or by parasitic infection. Some cysts are present from birth. 2. A structure formed during the life cycle of certain lower animals, such as parasitic protozoans and worms. The cysts usually protect the animals when they are most vulnerable.

cystic fibrosis A hereditary disease affecting the mucus-secreting and sweat glands. Symptoms, which appear in early childhood, are due to the production of thick mucus, which obstructs the pancreatic duct, intestinal glands, and bronchi. Patients suffer from malnutrition (because the production of digestive enzymes is blocked) and recurrent chest infections. The sweat contains large quantities of salt, which confirms the diagnosis. Treatment of cystic fibrosis, aimed at relieving its effects, includes antibiotics to combat infections, daily physiotherapy, a low-fat high-protein diet, and the administration of pancreatic enzymes.

cystitis Inflammation of the bladder, usually caused by a bacterial infection. Cystitis is most common in women: symptoms include frequent painful urination and occasionally blood in the urine. It is treated with antibiotics.

cytochromes A group of haem-containing pigments found in the mitochondria of plant and animal cells and involved in cell respiration. Cytochromes b, c_1, c, a, and a_3 form an electron transport chain that captures the energy (in the form of electrons) released by the *Krebs cycle and conserves it for used by the cell through the formation of *ATP molecules. The electrons are transferred ultimately to oxygen with the formation of water.

cytokinins A group of plant growth-stimulating compounds derived from purines. They act in conjunction with *auxins to promote cell division and retard senescence. Synthetic cytokinins, such as kinetin, are used commercially in the storage of vegetables.

cytology The study of the structure and function of cells. It began with the development of techniques for the section-

cytoplasm

ing, fixation, and selective staining of materials for study under the light microscope, which enabled the *nucleus and other organelles to be observed. This led to the identification of chromosomes within the nucleus and of their role in heredity. More recent developments have included the use of phase-contrast and electron microscopy, and the biochemistry and physiology of cells has been studied using such techniques as cell separation and analysis, autoradiography, and tissue culture. Cytology has an important function in medicine. The study of diseased cells can reveal the nature of a disease and how it may be controlled, and cytological tests provide the basis for diagnosis of many diseases, including cancer. *See also* biological sciences.

cytoplasm. *See* cell (biology).

cytotoxic drugs Drugs used to kill cancer cells. These drugs, which include nitrogen mustard and vincristine, have led to major improvements in the treatment of some cancers (e.g. leukaemia). They act by interfering with the multiplication of the malignant cells, but since they may also affect nonmalignant cells they often cause severe side effects, including damage to bone marrow.

Czech A West Slavonic language related to Slovak and Polish and spoken by nine million people in W Czechoslovakia. It is the official language of this area and is written in the Latin alphabet in a standardized form based on the dialect of Prague. Its development as a literary language dates from the 15th and 16th centuries.

Czechoslovakia, Socialist Republic of A landlocked country in central Europe. It is mainly wooded and mountainous, the central lowlands surrounding the River Morava rising to the Bohemian plateau in the W and the Slovakian highlands in the E. The population is about two-thirds Czech and almost a third Slovak, with small minorities of Hungarians, Germans, Poles, and others. *Economy*: industry, already highly developed before the communist era, is now entirely nationalized and since 1961 the emphasis has shifted from heavy to light industry. An important engineering nation, Czechoslovakia produces a large number of motor vehicles; glass, beer, ceramics, footwear, and textiles are also major products. Mineral resources are sparse and Czechoslovakia is dependent upon the Soviet Union for many raw materials. Agriculture is organized mainly in collectives and state farms and the principal crops include sugar beet, wheat, potatoes, and barley. Forestry is important, with rich natural forests as well as much new afforestation. *History*: Czechoslovakia was created, under the leadership of Tomáš *Masaryk and Edvard *Beneš, in 1918 following the collapse of the Austrian Empire. It comprised the former Austrian possessions of *Bohemia, *Moravia, part of *Silesia, and (from 1920) *Ruthenia. The new state encountered threats from the diverse national minorities that peopled it and was unable to withstand the expansionist ambitions of Hitler's Germany. In 1938 he secured the *Munich Agreement to his

CZECHOSLOVAKIA *The Cathedral of St Vitus (left) and Hradčany Castle (centre) in Prague. The statue in the foreground is of the Czech painter Josef Manes (1820-71).*

annexation of the *Sudetenland and in 1939 took control of all Czechoslovakia. During World War II a provisional Czechoslovak government existed in London under Beneš' presidency. Following the war the Allies recognized its former territories, except for Ruthenia, which was ceded to the Soviet Union, and some three million Germans were expelled from Czechoslovakia. By 1948 the Communist Party was in power and Czechoslovakia was closely allied with the Soviet Union. In 1968 a liberalization programme initiated by Dubček provoked a Soviet invasion and Dubček's overthrow. In 1977 Czech dissidents protested against the violation of human rights in Czechoslovakia in a manifesto entitled Charter 77. In 1987 it was announced that Czechoslovakia would adopt similar reforms to those being undertaken in the USSR. President: Milos Jakes (1922–   ). Official languages: Czech and Slovak. Official currency: koruna of 100 haléřů. Area: 127 877 sq km (49 365 sq mi). Population (1983 est): 15 420 000. Capital: Prague.

Czerny, Karl (1791–1857) Austrian pianist, composer, and teacher. A child prodigy, he had lessons with Beethoven and was influenced by Clementi and Hummel. He was a prolific composer but is best known for his piano studies. He was the teacher of Liszt.

Częstochowa 50 49N 19 07E A city in S Poland, on the River Warta. Formed from two separate communities in 1826, it has a monastery that was defended against the Swedes in the Thirty Years' War and to which Roman Catholics make pilgrimages. Its industries include iron and steel production. Population (1982): 238 000.

D

dab One of several *flatfish of the family *Pleuronectidae*, especially the genus *Limanda* found in N Atlantic and N Pacific waters. The European *L. limanda*, up to 30 cm long, is light brown, sometimes with dark spots, and is an important food fish.

dabbling duck A *duck that feeds near the surface of water, rarely diving and frequently feeding on land. With relatively small feet and legs set well forward, dabbling ducks walk efficiently on land; they include the *mallard, *pintail, *shoveler, *teal, and *wigeon. Drakes are usually brightly coloured and generally have a distinctive patch (speculum) on the wing. *Compare* diving duck.

dabchick A small *grebe, *Tachybaptus ruficollis*, common in quiet inland waters of Europe, S Asia, and Africa. It is 23 cm long and has a dark-brown back, pale underparts, and a bright chestnut breast, neck, and cheeks. It feeds on small fish and aquatic invertebrates.

Dacca (Name from 1982: Dhaka) 23 42N 90 22E The capital of Bangladesh, situated in the SE of the country, on the Burhi Ganga River. It is a riverport and commercial and industrial centre producing various textiles and jute. The university was founded in 1921. *History*: with a long history of human settlement, it became the capital of the Bengal province of the Mogul Empire in the 17th century. In the 18th century it came under British rule, and upon independence in 1947 was made capital of East Pakistan. Population (1981): 3 440 147.

dace A slender lively fish, also called dart or dare, belonging to the family *Cyprinidae*, which includes chub, roach, minnow, etc. The European dace (*Leuciscus leuciscus*) is up to 30 cm long, silvery coloured, and lives in fast-flowing streams and rivers, eating plant and animal material.

Dachau 48 15N 11 26E A town in SE West Germany, in Bavaria. It was the site of a Nazi *concentration camp (1933–45). Population (1983 est): 33 171.

dachshund A breed of ⊔dog originating in Germany, where they were developed to pursue badgers to earth. There are two size varieties—standard and miniature—and three coat types—long-haired, smooth-haired, and wire-haired. Dachshunds are usually brownish or black and tan. Height: 18–25 cm (standard); miniatures are smaller, not exceeding 5 kg in weight.

dacoit An armed robber in a gang in India; the term is also applied to members of guerrilla groups in Burma.

dada A European art and literary movement, beginning in Zürich in 1916 and aimed at deflating the status of the art-object. Dada was originally the name of a Zürich literary periodical published by the poet Tristan Tzara (1896–1963) and *Arp. Since it had no coherent style, much of its ideology was more effectively transmitted in poetry periodicals, such as *L'Intransigeant* in France. Manufactured objects were favoured both in graphic art and sculpture. Their violent effect is shown in the collages of Arp, *Ernst, and *Schwitters and the *ready-mades of *Duchamp, who exported dada to the USA. For its most fanatical adherents dada was also a way of life, characterized by calculatedly absurd behaviour. Although dada petered out in the early 1920s, *surrealism absorbed many of its characteristics.

Dadd, Richard (1817–86) British painter of detailed and complex works, mainly biblical scenes, fairy life, and mythology. His best work was produced in an asylum, to which he was committed after killing his father.

daddy longlegs. *See* cranefly.

Dadra and Nagar Haveli A Union Territory of W India, on the Gujarat-Maharashtra border. Formerly a Portuguese colony (1789–1954), it is inhabited largely by tribesmen growing cereals and pulses. Area: 491 sq km (190 sq mi). Population (1981): 103 677. Capital: Silvassa.

Daedalus A legendary Greek craftsman and sculptor, said to have built the labyrinth for King *Minos of Crete. Minos imprisoned him but he created wings for himself and his son Icarus and flew away; Icarus was killed when the sun melted his wings but Daedalus reached Sicily safely.

daffodil A perennial European plant, *Narcissus pseudonarcissus*, widely grown as a garden bulb. It has narrow leaves and yellow flowers, each with a trumpet-shaped central crown surrounded by six segments. The bulbs are poisonous and were once used in medicine as an emetic and cathartic. Family: *Amaryllidaceae*.

Dafydd ap Gwilym (c. 1320–c. 1380) Welsh poet. Born into an aristocratic family in S Wales, he travelled widely and was acquainted with the work of the continental troubadours. He was trained in the bardic tradition but introduced a personal humour and originality into the intricate and obscure conventional forms of his odes.

Dagenham A district in Barking and Dagenham borough. It contains a large Ford motor works; other industries include engineering and chemicals.

Dagestan Autonomous Soviet Socialist Republic An administrative division in the S Soviet Union, in the RSFSR on the Caspian Sea. The Caucasus Mountains lie in the S and much of central and N Dagestan is also mountainous. Over 30 different nationalities inhabit the republic, many of whom are Muslim. Its mineral resources remain largely unexploited, although sizable quantities of oil and natural gas have been extracted in coastal areas. There are large engineering, oil, chemical, and food industries and power stations are under construction. Crops include wheat and fruit; cattle breeding is also important. *History*: conquered by Arabs, Turks, Mongols, and Persians, Dagestan was annexed by Russia in 1813. It became an autonomous republic in 1921. In 1970, the area suffered a severe earthquake. Area: 50 278 sq km (19 416 sq mi). Population (1981 est): 1 700 000. Capital: Makhachkala.

Dagly, Gerhard (c. 1653–?1714) Belgian artist, a master in baroque lacquer work. At the courts of Electors Frederick William and Frederick III in Berlin (1687–1713) he became known for his cabinet cases, making *chinoiserie popular throughout Europe.

dagoba. *See* pagoda.

Daguerre, Louis-Jacques-Mandé (1789–1851) French inventor of the first practicable photographic process (the daguerreotype). Working initially with Joseph Niepce (1765–1833), who had produced the first permanent photographic image (the heliograph), Daguerre succeeded during the 1830s in producing a photograph by focusing light onto a copper plate that had been coated with a silver salt. Daguerreotypes were widely made in the mid-19th century.

Dahl, Roald (1916–) British author, whose work is pervaded by an ironic and frequently very black humour. Of Norwegian parentage, he served in the RAF during World War II. He has published novels, many collections of short stories, including *Kiss Kiss* (1959) and *Switch Bitch* (1974), and several anarchic children's books, including *Charlie and the Chocolate Factory* (1964).

Dahlia A genus of herbaceous perennial tropical American plants (12 species), up to 2 m high, originally cultivated as a food crop for their tubers but now grown mainly for ornament. The brightly coloured flowers, 5–500 cm across, may be single or double and are of two main types. The varieties known as flatheads and pompoms are derived from *D. pinnata*; cactus-type flowers with pointed petals are varieties of *D. juarezii*. Family: *Compositae*. See Plate VI

Dahomey. *See* Benin, People's Republic of.

Daigo II (1287–1339) Emperor of Japan (1318–39), who attempted to restore the power of the throne at the expense of the *shoguns (military overlords). Despite superficial success in 1333, Daigo's plans provoked fierce feudal resistance and led to prolonged civil war and his own exile.

Dáil Éireann The representative assembly of the Republic of Ireland. It is the more important house in the National Parliament, the other house being the Seanad Éireann (the Senate). There are 144 members elected by proportional representation, at least once every 5 years. The president (the nominal head of state) summons and dissolves the Dáil on the advice of the prime minister.

Daimler, Gottlieb (Wilhelm) (1834–1900) German inventor, who contributed to the development of the internal-combustion engine. Daimler started to build his own engines in 1883, which were soon sufficiently light and efficient to power machines; in 1890 he founded a company to manufacture motor *cars. ⌀motorcycles.

daimyo The feudal lords who rose to control one or more provinces of Japan between the 14th and 16th centuries. Their constant warfare was ended by *Tokugawa Ieyasu in 1600 but over 250 *daimyo* ruled their own domains until 1871. They were then given pensions and titles and their lands were incorporated into prefectures.

Dairen. *See* Lüda.

dairy farming The maintenance and management of cattle, goats, and sheep for *milk production. Man has used the milk of his animals as a food for thousands of years and the modern dairy cow is an efficient converter of grass into milk. Herds of 50–200 are milked by machine in milking parlours and the milk passes by pipeline under hygienic conditions to await collection in refrigerated bulk tanks.

Advances in breeding and management of dairy cows have resulted in current annual yields of about 4000 litres per cow in the UK, where the Friesian-Holstein breed is the most popular. Registration of producers and control of marketing is undertaken in the UK by Milk Marketing Boards, established by the government. The EEC coordinates European dairy farming through the *Common Agricultural Policy and the imposition of such measures as milk production quotas. *See also* dairy products.

dairy products Foods and other products derived from the processing of milk. Separation of milk by centrifugation yields skimmed milk and cream. Churning the cream disrupts the fat globules, removes water, and produces butter, containing over 80% fat, and buttermilk. Cream is retailed in various stages of concentration, for example single cream and double cream; other less concentrated forms include evaporated milk (containing about 65% water) and condensed milk (about 26% water). Yogurt (or yoghurt) is produced by inoculating whole milk with bacteria, principally of the genera *Streptococcus* and *Lactobacillus*. The acid they produce during incubation at about 43°C for four to five hours coagulates the milk, to which sweetening and flavouring may be added. Whey is a by-product of *cheese manufacture and, as with skimmed milk, may be dried to a powder form for use in the food industry or fed to farm animals in the fresh liquid state. *See also* dairy farming; milk.

daisy A herbaceous plant of the genus *Bellis* (15 species), native to Eurasia, with flower heads consisting of small central yellow disc florets surrounded by white or purple petal-like ray florets. The entire head is surrounded by bracts (leaflike structures). The flower heads are solitary, arising on long stalks from a basal rosette of simple leaves. Many species are garden orna-

mentals, some with double-flowered varieties. The common wild Eurasian daisy is *B. perennis*, a perennial up to 6 cm high, common in grasslands and lawns. Family: *Compositae*.

Dakar 14 45N 17 08W The capital and main port of Senegal, on Cape Verde peninsula. It was the capital of French West Africa (1904–59). It has a cathedral and a university (1957). The country's main industrial centre and one of Africa's most important cities, its industries include sugar refining and groundnut-oil production. Population (1979 est): 978 553.

Dakota. *See* North Dakota; South Dakota.

Daladier, Édouard (1884–1970) French statesman; prime minister (1933, 1934, 1938–40). He signed the *Munich Agreement in 1938 and resigned in March, 1940, because of the unpopularity aroused by his failure to assist Finland against Russia (*see* Russo-Finnish War). Arrested by the Vichy government (1940) after the fall of France, he was imprisoned by the Germans from 1942 until the end of World War II.

Dalai Lama The title of the spiritual and political ruler of Tibet and head of the Gelukpa Buddhist school. The title, originating in the 14th century, signifies the incarnation of Avalokiteshvara, the *Bodhisattva of compassion. Chosen by oracles after the death of the previous incumbent, the Dalai Lama is regarded as infallible. The 14th Dalai Lama went into exile in India at the beginning of Chinese Communist rule in Tibet in 1959. *See also* Panchen Lama.

Dale, Sir Henry Hallett (1875–1968) British physiologist, who, in 1914, isolated the chemical *acetylcholine from the fungus ergot. His findings of the effects of acetylcholine on living organs corresponded with the discovery by Otto *Loewi, in 1921, that acetylcholine is a chemical transmitter released by the nervous system. Dale shared the 1936 Nobel Prize with Loewi, was president of the Royal Society (1940–45), and was awarded an OM (1944).

d'Alembert, Jean le Rond (1717–83) French mathematician. The illegitimate son of an aristocrat, d'Alembert was raised by a glazier and his wife. His works include the study of vibrating strings, during which he derived the general solution to the wave equation, and a theorem in mechanics known as d'Alembert's principle, which is essentially a form of Newton's second law of motion. He also collaborated with *Diderot in editing the *Encyclopédie* (*see* Encyclopedists).

Dales pony A breed of pony originating in the Dales region of NE England. It is strong and compact with a long flowing tail and hairy heels. Brown, bay, black, or grey, Dales ponies were formerly used for draught work; they are now becoming popular for pony trekking. Height: about 1.45 m (14¼ hands).

Dalhousie, James Ramsay, 1st Marquess of (1812–60) British colonial administrator; governor general of India (1847–56). Elected MP in 1837, he became president of the Board of Trade in 1845 under Peel. The youngest ever governor general, he was criticized for his aggressive annexation of Indian territories. Following the second *Sikh War (1848–49) he annexed the Punjab and after the second Burmese War (1852) he annexed Rangoon. His annexation of Oudh (1856) caused unrest that contributed to the outbreak of the *Indian Mutiny after his departure.

Dali, Salvador (1904–) Spanish surrealist painter. He joined the Paris surrealists (1929) and, inspired by Freudian theories of the unconscious, painted startling dream images with photographic realism during self-induced hallucinatory states. A similar disturbing imagery occurs in *Un Chien Andalou* (1929), a film he made with *Buñuel. While living in New York (1940–55), he turned to religious subjects and became a Roman Catholic. His taste for self-advertisement is evident in his autobiographical writings, such as *Diary of a Genius* (1966).

Dalian. *See* Lüda.

Dallapiccola, Luigi (1904–1975) Italian composer and

pianist. His interest in composition was stimulated by his acquaintance with Alban Berg and he evolved a personal use of *serialism. His compositions include the opera *Ulisse* (1968), as well as many vocal and instrumental works.

Dallas 32 47N 96 48W A city in the USA, in NE Texas on the Trinity River. Founded in 1841, it developed as a cotton market during the late 19th century. The discovery of oil in E Texas during the 1930s accelerated the city's growth, which was further enhanced by the introduction of the aircraft and electronics industries during World War II. Today Dallas is the state's second largest city and the financial and commercial centre of the SW. A notable cultural centre, it is the site of several colleges. President John F. Kennedy was assassinated here on 22 November, 1963. Population (1985): 983 851.

Dalmatia A coastal belt in W Yugoslavia, mainly in Croatia bordering on the Adriatic Sea. It is penetrated by a narrow corridor giving Bosnia and Hercegovina access to the sea. Predominantly mountainous with an indented coastline and many offshore islands, its picturesque scenery forms the basis of a thriving tourist industry. Wine production is especially important. The chief towns are Zadar, Split, and Dubrovnik. *History*: Dalmatia formed part of ancient Illyria. Ceded to Yugoslavia in 1920, it was occupied by Italy during World War II before being returned in 1947.

Dalmatian dog A breed named after the Adriatic coastal region of Dalmatia, from where they were exported to the UK. Dalmatians are strongly built and were formerly used as carriage dogs. The short sleek coat has a pure white background with black or liver (brown) spots. Height: 58–61 cm (dogs); 56–58 cm (bitches). □dog.

dalton. *See* atomic mass unit.

Dalton, John (1766-1844) British chemist and originator of the modern *atomic theory of matter. Dalton's earliest researches into gases led to his discovery of *Dalton's law of partial pressures. He believed that gases consist of particles, extending his theory in 1803 to suggest that all matter is particulate, but he did not distinguish between atoms and molecules. His discovery of the law of multiple proportions in the same year strongly supported his atomic theory.

Dalton's law of partial pressures The total pressure exerted by a certain volume of a gaseous mixture is equal to the sum of the pressures (called partial pressures) exerted by each gas, if it alone occupied the same volume. Named after John *Dalton.

dam A barrier across a river. Dams are used for diverting the flow of water; raising the water level for navigation purposes; storing water for irrigation, industrial use, or water control; and providing a high-pressure source of water for *hydroelectric power. Gravity dams depend on the weight of their bulk to provide strength. Usually made of concrete and having a flat vertical face upstream, they are no longer used for the largest dams. Arch dams consist of curved concrete structures presenting their convex faces upstream, so that pressure is transmitted to the sides of the dams. They can thus be much less massive than gravity dams and are therefore cheaper to build. *See also* Aswan High Dam; Grand Coulee Dam; Grande Dixence Dam; Kariba, Lake; Paraná, Rio.

Dam, Carl Peter Henrik (1895-1976) Danish biochemist, who discovered vitamin K. He showed that certain symptoms in chicks, such as a tendency to bleed, were due to deficiency of a vitamin, which he named *Koagulations-Vitamin*, or vitamin K. Later, both he and Edward A. Doisy (1893–) isolated vitamin K from green leaves. They shared a Nobel Prize (1943).

Daman and Diu A Union Territory in India, on the Gulf of Cambray. It comprised a district of Portuguese India from 1559 until 1961 and was part of Goa, Daman, and Diu until 1987. Area: 456 sq km (176 sq mi). Population (1981): 1 082 117. Chief town: Daman.

Damanhur 31 03N 30 28E A city in N Egypt, on the Nile Delta. It has an important cotton trade with cotton-ginning and textile industries. Population (1983 est): 206 100.

Damaraland An area in N Namibia, named after the Damara people, who, however, now live mainly in the S. It is excellent cattle-grazing country.

Damascus (Arabic name: Esh Sham) 33 30N 36 19E The capital of Syria, in the SE of the country close to the Lebanese border. Under Ottoman rule from 1516 until 1918, Damascus was taken by the French (1920) and became capital of independent Syria in 1941. The Great Mosque and the Gate of God are the most notable buildings in the city. The university was founded in 1923. It is now the commercial centre of the fertile plain to the E. Population (1982 est): 1 112 214.

damask Originally, a woven silk fabric, reversible and elaborately patterned, manufactured in Damascus. Linen damask was later manufactured in France, Flanders, and Ireland but cotton is now usually used. A firm glossy fabric with interwoven designs, damask is chiefly used as table linen.

damask rose An Asian rose, *Rosa damascena*, about 1.5 m high, with spicy-scented pink and white flowers. It is the main source of attar of roses—the rose oil used as the base of many perfumes. Extraction of rose oil is a major industry in Bulgaria and parts of W Asia.

Damien, Father (Joseph de Veuster; 1840-89) Belgian Roman Catholic missionary. He worked in the leper settlement on the Hawaiian Island of Molokai from 1873 until his death from leprosy.

Damietta (Arabic name: Dumyat) 31 26N 31 48E A port in Egypt, on the River Nile. Its industries include the manufacture of cotton and silk. Population (1983 est): 111 900.

dammar A resin used in making varnish, obtained from various trees of SE Asia, especially species of *Shorea* (family *Dipterocarpaceae*) and conifers of the genus *Agathis* (including the New Zealand *Kauri pine).

Damocles Legendary courtier of Dionysius I of Syracuse in the 9th century BC. Dionysius seated him at a banquet beneath a sword suspended by a single hair, thus illustrating the insecurity of human life, irrespective of wealth or power.

Damodar, River A river in NE India. Rising in West Bengal, it flows mainly ESE through Bihar to join the River Hooghly SW of Calcutta. Its valley contains India's most important coalfield, an irrigation works, a hydroelectric project, and important heavy industry. Length: 595 km (370 mi).

Dampier, William (c. 1652-1715) English explorer. As a buccaneer he carried out several raids on Spanish possessions on the W coast of South America and West Africa in the 1680s, reaching Australia (which had disappointingly little booty to offer) in 1686. In 1699 he was employed by the Admiralty to explore Australia and New Guinea, returning to England in 1701. The Dampier Archipelago, off the NW coast of Australia, was named after him. His last voyage (1708-11), with Capt Woodes Rogers (d. 1732), rescued Alexander *Selkirk from the South Seas.

damping-off A disease, usually affecting seedlings, in which the stem base becomes softened and the plant falls over. Fungi of the genus *Pythium* are usually responsible. Soil sterilization may be undertaken as a preventive measure.

damselfish A lively and aggressive deep-bodied fish, also called demoiselle, belonging to the family *Pomacentridae*. Up to 15 cm long, damselfish are often brightly coloured and live mainly among reefs in the tropical regions of the Atlantic, Indian, and Pacific Oceans. They feed on plant and animal material. Order: *Perciformes*.

damselfly A slender delicate insect belonging to the suborder *Zygoptera*, closely related to the *dragonflies. It has similar habits but is smaller and has weaker powers of flight. The wings are held over the body at rest. ⌐insect.

damson The plumlike stone fruit of *Prunus damascena*, a slender twisted tree found across the N hemisphere. It has small white flowers that develop into purple fruits. Damsons may be eaten cooked, used in jam, or pressed into a cake called damson cheese. Family: *Rosaceae*. *See also* plum.

Dan, tribe of One of the 12 *tribes of Israel. It claimed descent from Dan, the son of Jacob by his concubine Bilhah. Its territory lay N of the Sea of Galilee and its city of Dan was situated at the northernmost point of the Hebrew settlement. Some of its people occupied an area NW of Judah, which was gradually absorbed by Judah.

Danae In Greek legend, the daughter of Acrisius, King of Argos. He imprisoned her because an oracle said he would be killed by her child; Zeus visited her, however, and she gave birth to *Perseus. Acrisius cast mother and son out to sea but Polydectes, King of Seriphos, rescued them.

Da Nang (former name: Tourane) 16 04N 108 14E A port in S central Vietnam, on the South China Sea. It was the site of a major US airbase during the Vietnam War. Textiles are the chief industry. Population (1979): 318 655.

Danby, Francis (1793-1861) Irish painter, who lived in England and exhibited his romantic historical paintings and sunrise or sunset landscapes at the Royal Academy. His work was influenced by John *Martin.

Danby, Thomas Osborne, 1st Earl of (1631-1712) English statesman. He became an MP in 1665 and as Lord Treasurer (1673-78) implemented successful economic policies. He was twice impeached by parliament: in 1678 for negotiating a secret treaty with France and in 1694, after becoming the 1st Duke of Leeds, for taking a bribe from the East India Company.

dance A social activity or theatrical art in which the body moves rhythmically, usually to music. In ancient times it was primarily used in religious rituals; such dances still exist today among some primitive tribes. During the middle ages the Church often condemned dancing, particularly when it appeared to be a manifestation of mass hysteria. Dancing as a social activity and as an entertainment largely originated in the European courts. These dances usually developed from peasant dances and among the most popular were the galliard, basse danse, *allemande, and volta. The English country dances, so popular at Elizabeth I's court, eventually spread to the continent in the early 18th century and, together with the minuet, dominated ballrooms until the introduction of the *waltz. From the late 19th century the USA led the way in social dancing with the *cakewalk, *foxtrot, and *tango; it also introduced the tap dance and contributed to the development of *modern dance. Many 20th-century dances were influenced by jazz, notably the *Charleston (1920s) and the jitterbug (1940s); others, such as the rumba, samba, and conga, were of Latin-American origin. Popular dancing from the 1960s, commencing with the twist, has shown a trend towards freer movement, unregulated by a set sequence of steps and without bodily contact between the partners. *See also* ballet; folk dance; choreography.

Dance, George (c. 1700-68) British architect. He became surveyor to the City of London in 1735, building several City churches, the façade of Guy's Hospital (1764), and the Mansion House (1753). His son **George Dance** (1741-1825) was also an architect, who acquired a taste for neoclassicism while studying in Italy. He succeeded his father as City surveyor in 1768, building the austere but impressive Newgate Prison (1778), which was demolished in 1902. His gothic south front to the Guildhall (1789), All Hallows, London Wall (1767), and layout for Finsbury Square can still be seen in London. He was one of the original members of the Royal Academy.

dance of death In late medieval art, literature, and drama, an allegorical dance or procession in which the dead lead the living to the grave; also known as the *danse macabre*. It reflected man's preoccupation with death during an age of plague and warfare and was a popular subject for wall paintings in churches and monasteries in France, Germany, and England during the 14th and 15th centuries. The most famous pictorial version is the series of woodcuts designed by *Holbein the Younger between 1523 and 1526.

dandelion A weedy perennial herbaceous plant of the worldwide genus *Taraxacum*, with a basal rosette of jagged toothed leaves and a solitary flower head of bright-yellow florets, up to 6 cm across, borne on a stalk up to 50 cm high. The seeds have parachutes of fine white hairs and are dispersed by wind. The common dandelion (*T. officinale*) is found throughout the N hemisphere. Its young leaves may be eaten raw in salads or cooked. Family: *Compositae*. ⌐fruit.

Dandie Dinmont terrier A dog breed named after a character in Sir Walter Scott's novel *Guy Mannering* (1812), who owned a pack of them. The Dandie Dinmont has a long body, short legs, and long drooping ears. Its long coat is a mixture of hard and soft hairs and can be either silvery grey to blue-black or fawn to reddish brown. Height: 20-28 cm.

Dandolo, Enrico (c. 1108-1205) Venetian statesman; *doge (1192-1205). He was regarded as the founder of Venice's colonial empire. Dandolo commanded the fleet at the capture of Constantinople during the fourth *Crusade (1204) and secured for Venice a substantial portion of the conquered Greek territories. Defeated near Adrianople in 1205, Dandolo, aged and blind, led the remnants of the Latin army safely back to Constantinople.

dandruff Dry scaling of the scalp, which occurs in everybody to some degree. It is presumed to be due to an infection and may sometimes become more serious, extending to the face. If it is excessive it can be treated with salicylic acid.

Danelaw The area of Anglo-Saxon England E of Watling Street from the River Tees to the River Thames within which Danish laws and customs prevailed from the late 9th to the late 11th centuries.

Dangerfield, Thomas (1650-85) English conspirator. He exploited the anti-Catholic hysteria that followed Titus Oates' allegations of a *Popish Plot to murder Charles II in 1678 by falsely accusing his own Catholic employers. He was convicted of libel in 1685 and died after being pilloried and whipped.

Daniel (6th century BC) An Old Testament prophet and Jewish exile in Babylon. **The Book of Daniel** is credited to him although some believe it to have been been written in the 2nd century BC. The first six chapters tell of various mainly supernatural episodes involving Daniel and his companions under Kings Nebuchadnezzar and Belshazzar. The remaining six chapters are mostly apocalyptic visions concerning the future of the Jews.

Daniel, Samuel (?1562-1619) English poet, dramatist, and critic. He enjoyed the patronage of various noblemen and, from 1604, of James I. His best-known work is the sonnet sequence *Delia* (1592). Among his other works are a verse history of England, *The Civil Wars* (1609), and a more straightforward prose history (1618).

Daniell, John Frederic (1790-1845) British chemist, whose researches into electrochemistry led him to invent the *Daniell cell, the first long-lasting reliable source of electric current. He also invented the hygrometer.

Daniell cell A voltaic cell whose positive pole consists of copper immersed in a solution of copper sulphate and whose negative pole consists of zinc in a solution of sulphuric acid or zinc sulphate. It has an almost constant emf of 1.08 volts. Named after J. F. Daniell.

danio An omnivorous tropical freshwater fish of the genera *Danio* or *Brachydanio*. They have a narrow elongated body,

4–5 cm long, often attractively coloured, and live in shoals. Family: *Cyprinidae*; order: *Cypriniformes*. *See also* zebra fish.

Danish The official language of Denmark, spoken by about five million people. It belongs to the East Scandinavian branch of the North Germanic languages. Separation from the other Scandinavian languages, to which it is closely related, began in about 1000 AD. It is the most altered form of the common ancestral tongue, having lost the case system and incorporated many words from Low German.

Dankworth, John (1927–) British jazz composer, clarinetist, and saxophonist. He formed his own band in 1953 and has often worked with his wife, the jazz singer Cleo Laine (1927–). His works include *Escapade* (1967), *String Quartet* (1971), and scores for various films, including *Saturday Night and Sunday Morning* and *The Servant*.

D'Annunzio, Gabriele (1863–1938) Italian poet, novelist, and dramatist. During the 1890s he wrote several novels strongly influenced by *Nietzsche's philosophy, notably *The Triumph of Death* (1894). The erotic novel *The Flame of Life* (1900) described his stormy relationship with the actress Eleanora *Duse, who inspired some of his best poetry and for whom he wrote *The Daughter of Jorio* (1904) and other plays. A militant nationalist, he fought heroically in the air force in World War I and headed the Italian occupation of the Dalmatian port of Fiume in 1919. He joined the fascist party but spent his later years in peaceful retirement.

Dante Alighieri (1265–1321) Italian poet. Born into a noble Guelf family of Florence (*see* Guelfs and Ghibellines), he became actively involved in the political struggle between the Black Guelfs, supported by the Pope, and the White Guelfs, who favoured a democratic commune. After the Black Guelfs gained control of Florence in 1301, he lived in exile in various Italian cities, finally settling in Ravenna about 1318. His major works include *La vita nuova* (c. 1292), an autobiographical work concerning his youthful love for the mysterious Beatrice (probably the Florentine aristocrat Beatrice Portinari, who was married and who died at the age of 24), and two influential treatises on the value of vernacular Italian as a literary language. *The Divine Comedy*, begun about 1307, is Dante's spiritual testament, narrating his journey, guided by *Virgil, through Hell and Purgatory and finally, guided by Beatrice, to Paradise.

Danton, Georges Jacques (1759–94) French revolutionary. A leader of the *Cordeliers in 1789 and 1790, he became minister of justice in the new republic in 1792. A member of the first Committee of *Public Safety, he was not included in the second and began to lose power as the *Reign of Terror developed. He and his followers were arrested in March, 1794, charged with a conspiracy to overthrow the government, and Danton was guillotined.

Danu In Celtic mythology, the mother of the gods. She was particularly associated with the *Tuatha Dé Danann, but she was also worshipped in other countries under different names.

Danube, River The second longest river in Europe after the River Volga. Rising in the Black Forest in West Germany, it flows mainly ESE across central and SE Europe to enter the Black Sea in Romania. Immensely important commercially, it is linked by the River Altmühl with canals to the Rivers Main and Rhine. Major cities along its course include Vienna, Budapest, and Belgrade. Length: 2850 km (1770 mi).

Danzig. *See* Gdańsk.

Daphne (botany) A genus of evergreen and deciduous shrubs (70 species) of the Old World, including many important ornamentals. The small, often fragrant, flowers occur in clusters near the ends of branches. They have no petals; the calyx (fused sepals) has four spreading lobes. The fruit is a berry. The genus includes the deciduous mezereon (*D. mezereum*), with reddishpurple flowers and red berries, and the evergreen spurge laurel (*D. laureola*), with greenish flowers and black berries. These shrubs are native to Eurasia and grow to a height of 100 cm; their berries are poisonous. Family: *Thymelaeaceae*.

Daphne (Greek mythology) A mountain nymph who rejected Apollo and, to escape him, was transformed by Gaea into a laurel tree. Apollo made the laurel a symbol of honour and victory.

Daphnia. *See* water flea.

Daphnis In Greek legend, a Sicilian shepherd who was punished with blindness for infidelity in love. He consoled himself with songs and was thus revered as the inventor of pastoral poetry and song.

Da Ponte, Lorenzo (1749–1838) Italian author, originally a priest. Banished from Italy in 1779, he settled in Vienna and there wrote the libretti for Mozart's operas *The Marriage of Figaro* (1786), *Don Giovanni* (1787), and *Cosi fan tutte* (1790). In 1805 he went to the USA, where he published four volumes of memoirs (1823–27).

Dardanelles (Turkish name: Çannakale Boğazi; ancient name: Hellespont) A strait separating European and Asian Turkey and connecting the Sea of Marmara with the Aegean Sea. It was the scene of an unsuccessful campaign in *World War I. Length: 60 km (37 mi); width: 1.5–6.5 km (1–4 mi).

Dards A number of peoples of N Pakistan and Kashmir of Aryan origin, who speak Indo-European languages. There are three major subgroups: the Western (*or* Kafir), the Central (*or* Khowar), and the Eastern, including Shina and Kashmiri. The Dards were converted to Islam during the 14th century.

Dar es Salaam 6 48S 39 12E The capital and main port of Tanzania, on the Indian Ocean. Founded in 1862, it was capital of German East Africa (1891–1916) and of Tanganyika (1916–64). The university was established in 1970. It is the terminus of the Tanzam (Tanzania–Zambia) railway and an important commercial and industrial centre. Population (1978): 870 020.

Darién Scheme (1698–99) An attempt by the Company of Scotland to establish a colony in the Darién region, in the E of the Isthmus of Panama. The Scots hoped to control trade between the Atlantic and Pacific Oceans but were forced by the Spanish to abandon their settlement.

Darío, Rubén (Félix García Sarmiento; 1867–1916) Nicaraguan poet. His interest in contemporary French literature greatly influenced his innovatory experiments in both verse and prose. *Azul* (1888) and *Prosas profanas* (1896) were major works of the Spanish-American modernist movement. After 1898 he lived mostly in Europe, working as correspondent for the Argentine paper *La Nación*. His political convictions are expressed in *Cantos de vida y esperanza* (1905).

Darius I (c. 558–486 BC) King of Persia (521–486) of the *Achaemenid dynasty. He obtained the throne after defeating a usurper and on his accession he was forced to deal with revolts throughout the empire. He crushed a revolt of Ionian Greeks (499–94), which precipitated the *Greek-Persian Wars. His invasion of mainland Greece was halted by the Persian defeat at *Marathon (490). Darius was a noted administrator, dividing the empire into provinces known as satrapies. He also encouraged trade and improved communications.

Darjeeling 27 02N 88 20E A town in India, in West Bengal. A popular tourist resort, it has splendid views of the Himalayas, including Mount Kangchenjunga. It is a major tea-growing centre. Population (1981): 57 603.

darkling beetle A black or dark brown flightless beetle, also called nocturnal ground beetle, belonging to a widely distributed family (*Tenebrionidae*; 15 000 species), particularly common in warm regions. Darkling beetles vary from 2 to 35 mm in length. Nearly all are scavengers, feeding on decaying vegetation, dung, fungi, or stored grains and cereals. Mealworms (larvae of *Tenebrio molitor*) are common pests of flour mills, etc., and are also reared commercially as food for birds and fish.

Darlan, Jean (Louis Xavier) François (1881–1942) French admiral. He became commander in chief of the navy in 1939 and served in the Vichy government as navy minister and then as vice premier (1941). He lost his post under Laval (1942) and was sent to command French forces in N Africa, where he brought French resistance to the Allies to an end. His assumption of the post of head of state in French Africa aroused considerable hostility. He was assassinated by a French antifascist.

Darling, Grace (1815–42) British heroine, daughter of a lighthouse keeper on the Northumberland coast. In 1838 she helped her father rescue five people from a ship (*Forfarshire*) that had struck the rocks during a storm.

Darling River A river in E Australia, rising in the Great Dividing Range and flowing generally SW across New South Wales before joining the Murray River at Wentworth. Length: 2740 km (1702 mi).

Darlington 54 31N 1 34W A town in NE England, in Durham. The Stockton–Darlington freight railway (1825) was the world's first railway. Darlington has engineering and construction industries. Population (1985): 96 000.

Darmstadt 49 52N 08 39E A city in central West Germany, in Hessen. It has a 16th-century palace, which survived the bombing in World War II, and a technical university (1836). Its manufactures include machinery and chemicals. Population (1983): 137 800.

darnel A *grass, Lolium temulentum, also known as poison grass, native to temperate Eurasia. It is often infected by a fungus of the genus *Claviceps* (*see* ergot) and is poisonous; it was formerly a serious contaminant of rye bread but modern techniques can separate darnel seeds from rye seeds.

Darnley, Henry Stuart, Lord (1545–67) The second husband of Mary, Queen of Scots, and father of James I of England. He married Mary, his cousin, in 1565 and his unpopularity was intensified by his involvement in the murder of her secretary David *Riccio (1566). Darnley himself was murdered, probably by *Bothwell.

Darrow, Clarence (1857–1938) US lawyer, famous for his defence of union leaders and of people charged with murder. His defence of Eugene Debs in the case arising from the Pullman strike (1894), although unsuccessful, established his reputation. Through his efforts the labour leader William Haywood (1896–1928) was acquitted (1906) from the charge of assassinating the governor of Idaho. He was counsel for the defence in the famous "monkey" trial in Tennessee (1925), in which a science teacher, John Scopes, was tried for teaching Darwin's theory of evolution. He was a passionate opponent of capital punishment.

darter A slender elongated bird belonging to a family (*Anhingidae*; 4 species) occurring in tropical and subtropical inland waters, also called snakebird because of its snakelike neck. Darters are about 88 cm long and black or brown with white markings; males have plumes on the head and neck. They have thin pointed bills for catching fish underwater and are excellent fliers. Order: *Pelecaniformes* (gannets, pelicans, etc.).

Dartford 51 27N 0 14E A town in SE England, in Kent linked with Purfleet (Essex) by the Dartford Tunnel (opened in 1963) under the River Thames. Its industries include paper making, engineering, cement, and pharmaceuticals. Population (1983 est): 77 315.

Dartmoor A moorland area of England, in SW Devon. A national park since 1951, it consists of a rolling granite upland rising to tors, the highest of which is High Willhays at 621 m (2039 ft). Its many historic remains include stone circles and Bronze Age and Iron Age settlements. Used extensively as a military training area, its dramatic scenery, picturesque wooded valleys, and outdoor recreational facilities have also made it a major tourist attraction. Area: 945 sq km (365 sq mi).

Dartmoor pony A breed of pony originating in the Dartmoor region of SW England. It is placid and hardy with a strong body and small head with tiny ears. The coat is usually bay, brown, or black and the mane and tail are profuse. Dartmoors are used in breeding larger riding ponies (including polo ponies). Height: 1.22–1.32 m (12–13 hands).

Dartmouth 50 21N 3 35W A port and resort in SW England, in Devon on the Dart estuary. The Royal Naval College (1905) is situated here. Population (1981): 6298.

Dartmouth 44 40N 63 35W A city and port in E Canada, in Nova Scotia on Halifax Harbour. It is an industrial and naval centre. Population (1985): 62 277.

darts A UK indoor target game, probably deriving from archery, in which players throw flighted metal darts at a round board from a set distance. A standard board is divided into 20 irregularly numbered sectors; outer and inner rings score double and treble respectively and there is a central bull's-eye. Various games are played, but the most common in competitions is 301, in which players score downwards from 301 to 0, beginning and ending on a double. In recent years TV coverage has made darts a popular spectator game.

Darwin 12 23S 130 44E A city in Australia, the capital and chief port of the Northern Territory. The harbour, Port Darwin, adjoins Clarence Strait. It was almost completely destroyed by a cyclone in 1974, but was rebuilt on the same site. It is the focus of a pastoral and mining region; exports include uranium ore. Population (1984): 63 900.

CHARLES DARWIN *In 1860 the Oxford Debate on Darwin's evolutionary theories aroused much controversy and speculation about man's origins, typified by this contemporary cartoon from Punch.*

Darwin, Charles Robert (1809–1882) British naturalist, who originated the concept that living things evolve by means of natural selection. Following attempts to study medicine and theology, Darwin's interest in natural history led him to sail with HMS *Beagle* on an expedition to South America and the Pacific (1831–36). As ship's naturalist, Darwin made exhaustive observations of the geology and natural history of the region, recording these in a journal, which he later published.

Following the voyage, Darwin set about the task of analysing his observations and forming them into a coherent view of nature. In 1858 he presented his findings (jointly with A. R. *Wallace) to the Linnaean Society and in 1859 published his famous *Origin of Species by Means of Natural Selection* (*see* Darwinism). His views aroused bitter controversy because they conflicted with the account of the Creation in the Bible. This culminated in the debate at Oxford in 1860 between Darwin's supporters, led by T. H. *Huxley, and Bishop Samuel Wilberforce. Huxley's arguments won the day. In *The Descent of Man* (1871), Darwin applied his theories to mankind, and—slowly—this fundamental principle of biology gained widespread acceptance. His grandfather **Erasmus Darwin** (1731–1802) was a successful physician noted for his radical views, especially on biology. Among his ideas, which were set to verse (*see* poetry), were speculations about the nature of evolution that anticipated later theories, particularly those of *Lamarck.

Darwinism   The theory of *evolution based on the work of Charles *Darwin. Darwin drew his conclusions from the following observations: (1) in any population the organisms show individual variations; (2) the size of the population remains constant although more offspring are produced than are necessary to maintain it. He concluded that the forces acting on the population—competition, disease, climate, etc.—resulted in the survival of those best fitted to the environment, a process he called **natural selection**. The survivors would breed, thus passing on their inheritable advantageous variations to their offspring. With time—in a gradually changing environment—this process would result in a change in the whole population and ultimately the evolution of new *species.

Darwin's theory has now been reinforced and modified by subsequent discoveries in genetics, which—among other things—have revealed the source of the variation on which it is based (mostly genetic *mutations). The modern version of his theory is known as **neo-Darwinism**.

Darwin's finches   A subfamily of *finches (*Geospizinae*; 13 species) restricted to the Galapagos Islands and also called Galapagos finches. They appear to have evolved from a single species and differ in such features as bill shape, feeding behaviour, and habitat preference in order to avoid competition for available resources. The study of these finches by Charles *Darwin provided evidence for his theory of evolution.

dasyure   A small carnivorous *marsupial mammal belonging to a family (*Dasyuridae*; 45 species) occurring in Australia (including Tasmania) and New Guinea, also called marsupial cat or native cat. Dasyures, which vary from 30 cm to 170 cm in length, are nocturnal and good climbers, hunting prey that ranges from insects to small wallabies. *See also* Tasmanian devil.

data processing   The organization, transmission, and storage of information. **Automatic data processing** usually refers to systems using punch-card machines, paper tape, magnetic tape, etc., as opposed to **electronic data processing**, which is based on electronic computers. In batch processing, data is grouped and coded before processing. The alternative is on-line processing, in which each user feeds data into the system continuously. Many systems incorporate both of these forms of processing for different types of work. Most large organizations now use data-processing techniques extensively. The Data Protection Act (1984) seeks to protect the individual from misuse of data.

date   A *palm tree, *Phoenix dactylifera*, native to N Africa

and SW Asia and cultivated from Morocco to India for its fruits, which are rich in sugar and form a staple food in the producing countries. Male and female flowers grow on separate trees (which reach a height of 25 m); the female flowers develop into clusters of up to 1000 single-seeded berries. The trunk of the tree yields a timber and the leaves are used for basketry, weaving, etc.

dating.   *See* fission-track dating; helium dating; potassium-argon dating; radiocarbon dating; radiometric dating; rubidium-strontium dating; thermoluminescence; uranium-lead dating.

Datini, Francesco   (c. 1335–1410) Italian merchant, whose papers, kept in his birthplace Prato, constitute an important source for contemporary economic and social history. He lived and traded in Avignon, France, from 1350 to 1382 and on his return to Italy expanded into banking and insurance.

Datura   A worldwide genus of shrubs and herbs (about 10 species), with smooth pointed oval leaves and drooping trumpet-shaped flowers, white, pink, orange, or yellow. The commonest species is the *thorn apple. Some species are popular ornamentals: angel's trumpet (*D. suaveolens*), a Mexican shrub up to 5 m high with white musk-scented flowers, is cultivated in greenhouses in temperate regions. Family: *Solanaceae*.

Daubenton, Louis Jean Marie   (1716–1800) French naturalist, who gave anatomical descriptions of many animal species. His other interests included palaeontology, plant physiology, and mineralogy. He was the first director of the Museum of Natural History, Paris (1793).

Daubigny, Charles-François   (1817–78) French landscape painter. He was associated with the *Barbizon school but painted chiefly by the banks of the Seine and Oise, specializing in twilight and moonlight scenes, e.g. *Evening Landscape* (Metropolitan Museum). He strongly influenced the impressionists.

Daudet, Alphonse   (1840–97) French novelist, born at Nîmes. He wrote a number of naturalistic novels on the social and political life of his day but is best remembered for his sketches on Provençal subjects, which were originally written for *Le Figaro* and later collected as *Lettres de mon moulin* (1868). He also wrote plays, notably *L'Arlésienne* (1872), for which Bizet composed incidental music. His son **Léon Daudet** (1867–1942) was a political journalist and novelist. He was violently right-wing in his views and in 1899 helped to found the influential royalist periodical *L'Action française*. His critical essays were published as *Le Stupide XIXᵉ siècle* (1922) and his memoirs, *Souvenirs* (1914–21), cover the years 1890–1905.

Daugavpils   (name from 1893 until 1920: Dvinsk)   55 52N 26 31E A city in the W Soviet Union, in the Latvian SSR. It is an important rail junction and a commercial and industrial centre. Population (1981 est): 117 000.

Daumier, Honoré   (1808–79) French caricaturist, painter, and sculptor. As a cartoonist for *La Caricature* in Paris he was imprisoned (1832) for depicting the king as Rabelais' gluttonous giant Gargantua. He produced numerous documentary lithographs, such as *Rue Transnonain*. After 1835 he worked for *Charivari*, satirizing the legal and medical professions and other social and political targets. Although his paintings were largely ignored in his lifetime, *The Washerwoman* (Louvre) and *The Third Class Railway Carriage* (Ottawa) are admired as forerunners of *impressionism.

dauphin   From 1350 until 1830 the title of the heirs to the French Crown. It was the personal name, and later became the title, of the rulers of the *Dauphiné, which was purchased by the future Charles V in 1350. After becoming king (1364), he granted the Dauphiné and its accompanying title to his son, thus establishing a precedent that was followed until the abdication of Charles X.

Dauphiné   A former province of SE France, corresponding to the present-day departments of Hautes-Alpes, Isère, and Drôme. It formed part of the Holy Roman Empire until 1343, when it was sold to the King of France. From 1350 to 1457, when it was annexed by the Crown, it was governed by the French king's eldest son, who thus acquired the title *dauphin.

Davao City 07 05N 125 38E A port in the SE Philippines, in SE Mindanao. The island's commercial centre, it grew rapidly in the 1960s. It has timber and fishing industries and exports hemp and coffee. Population (1980): 611 311.

Davenant, Sir William (1606–68) English dramatist and poet. Rumoured to be the illegitimate son of Shakespeare, whose works he "revised," he won popular success and the patronage of Charles I with his early plays, notably *The Wits* (1634) and *Love and Honour* (1634). He was appointed poet laureate in 1638. During the Commonwealth he organized secret theatrical performances and after the Restoration he continued to write and stage spectacular plays.

Davenport, Charles Benedict (1866–1944) US zoologist, who introduced the use of statistical techniques into biological research. The need for statistics arose from his studies of population genetics.

Daventry 52 16N 1 09W A town in central England, in Northamptonshire. An overspill area for Birmingham, it has various light industries and is the site of an important radio transmitter. Population (1985 est): 17 000.

David (d. 962 BC) King of Israel (c. 1000–962). Born in Bethlehem, the son of Jesse, David was anointed by Samuel as the successor of Saul, the first King of Israel. He became a close friend of Saul's son, Jonathan, but his successes against the Philistines, including the slaying of Goliath, aroused Saul's jealousy and he became an outlaw. After the death of Saul and Jonathan, David was proclaimed King of Hebron and then of all Israel. He conquered Jerusalem, making it the nation's political and religious centre, finally defeated the Philistines, and united the tribes of Israel. His reign was troubled by the revolt of his son Absalom, who was eventually defeated and killed. David was succeeded by Solomon, his son by Bathsheba. He was the author of some of the psalms. According to the Jewish prophets, the Messiah must be a descendant of David.

David I (1084–1153) King of the Scots (1124–53). The first monarch to recognize Matilda as successor to Henry I of England, he used her cause as an excuse to invade N England (1138) after Stephen had seized the throne. Stephen defeated him in the battle of the Standard (1138), near Northallerton. David founded or refounded over a dozen monasteries.

David II (1324–71) King of the Scots (1329–71), succeeding his father Robert the Bruce. He was forced into exile (1334–41) in France by Edward de *Balliol. He supported France against Edward III of England and was captured and imprisoned (1346–57) by the English.

David, Gerard (c. 1460–1523) Netherlandish painter, who was born in Oudewater (Holland) but settled in Bruges. Apart from his use of Renaissance detail in *Judgment of Cambyses* (Bruges), he was little influenced by the Italianate style current in Antwerp.

David, Jacques Louis (1748–1825) French neoclassical painter, known for his historical paintings and portraits. He trained under Joseph-Marie Vien (1716–1809), before winning the Prix de Rome (1774), which enabled him to study in Italy (1775–80). His mature works depicted heroic scenes from Republican Rome and ancient Greece, e.g. *Oath of the Horatii* (Louvre). During the Revolution he painted some of its martyrs, e.g. *Death of Marat* (Brussels), and actively supported Robespierre; after Robespierre's fall he was imprisoned (1794–95). As court painter to Napoleon I from 1804, his paintings illustrate imperial successes, e.g. *Napoleon Crowning Josephine* (Louvre). After Napoleon's fall David was exiled and died in Brussels.

David, St (*or* St Dewi; c. 520–600 AD) The patron saint of Wales and first abbot of Menevia (now St David's). He was also a missionary and the founder of many churches in Wales. Feast day: 1 March. Emblem: a dove.

David ap Gruffudd (d. 1283) The brother of *Llywelyn ap Gruffudd, after whose death (1282)·David claimed the title Prince of Wales. He was executed by Edward I for leading the Welsh in rebellion against him.

Davies, Sir Peter Maxwell (1934–) British composer and director of the chamber ensemble The Fires of London. Some of his works are based on medieval music but employ modern compositional techniques. He lives on the island of Orkney and has been influenced by the Orcadian landscape and culture. His output includes *Eight Songs for a Mad King* (1969) and three symphonies.

Davies, W(illiam) H(enry) (1871–1940) British poet. He lived for many years as a tramp in England and America before publishing the first of many volumes of simple rural poetry in 1905. G. B. Shaw contributed an introduction to his *Autobiography of a Super-Tramp* (1907).

da Vinci, Leonardo. *See* Leonardo da Vinci.

Davis, Bette (Ruth Elizabeth D.; 1908–) US film actress. From the 1930s to the 1950s she gave intense and dramatic performances in such films as *Jezebel* (1938), *Dark Victory* (1939), and *All About Eve* (1950). In recent years she has played elderly eccentric or neurotic women.

Davis, Sir Colin (1927–) British conductor. During a distinguished career he has conducted the BBC Scottish Symphony Orchestra, the BBC Symphony Orchestra, and the orchestras of the Metropolitan Opera, New York, and the Royal Opera, Covent Garden. He is well known for his performances of Mozart, Berlioz, Stravinsky, and Tippett.

Davis, Jefferson (1808–89) US statesman; president of the Confederate states during the Civil War (1861–65). As senator for Mississippi (1847–51) and then, after serving with distinction in the *Mexican War, secretary of war (1853–57), Davis supported slavery and the rights of states against federal interference. However, his loyalty as Confederate president was to the South as a whole: advocates of *states' rights were hostile to him and his conscription law was unpopular. He was captured in 1865, imprisoned for two years without trial, and released in 1867.

Davis, John (*or* J. Davys; c. 1550–1605) English navigator, who went on three voyages in search of the *Northwest Passage (1585, 1586, 1587), passing through the strait named after him to Baffin Bay. In 1592, seeking the Magellan Strait, he discovered the Falkland Islands. On his last voyage to the East Indies, he was killed by Japanese pirates.

Davis, Miles (1926–) US jazz trumpeter and composer, one of the originators of *cool jazz. He studied music at the Julliard School in New York and formed his own band in 1948. He has made a number of influential albums, including *Miles Ahead* and the innovatory *Kind of Blue*.

Davis, Steve (1957–) British snooker player. He won the world professional championship in 1981, 1983, and 1984.

Davis Cup An international tennis competition that was instituted in 1900 for teams of men. The USA and Australia have won it most often (28 and 26 times respectively).

Davis Strait A section of the Atlantic Ocean, between SW Greenland and Baffin Island (Canada). Length: 640 km (400 mi). Width: 320–640 m (200–400 mi).

Davitt, Michael (1846–1906) Irish nationalist. He joined the *Fenians in 1865 and after seven years' imprisonment founded the *Land League (1879). Davitt urged the reconciliation of extreme and constitutional nationalism. In the 1890s he became an MP.

Davos (Romansh name: Tarau) 46 47N 9 50E A mountain resort in E Switzerland. Comprising two villages at a height of about 1555 m (5100 ft), it is a health resort and winter-sports centre, with the renowned Parsenn ski run. Population (1985 est): 11 500.

Davy, Sir Humphry (1778–1829) British chemist and inventor of the miner's safety lamp (1815), known as the Davy lamp. Davy began his career by discovering the value of nitrous oxide as an anaesthetic. For this work he was invited to join the Royal Institution in London, where his most important work was the discovery of many new metallic elements. By passing electricity through molten metallic compounds, he discovered potassium in 1807 and the following year, sodium, calcium, barium, magnesium and strontium. He also encouraged the young Michael *Faraday, employing him as his assistant at the Royal Institution.

Dawes, Charles G(ates) (1865–1951) US financier; who headed a commission to reconstruct the German economy after World War I and enable it to pay reparations to the Allies. This solution, known as the **Dawes Plan** (1924), saved Europe from economic collapse and earned him, jointly with Austen Chamberlain, the Nobel Peace Prize (1925). He was subsequently Republican vice president (1925–29) under Coolidge and ambassador to the UK (1929–32).

dawn redwood A deciduous conifer, *Metasequoia glyptostroboides*, thought to be extinct until 1941, when the first specimen of modern times was discovered in SW China. Growing to a height of 35 m, dawn redwood has soft needles grouped in two rows and rounded green long-stalked cones. It is quite widely grown for ornament. Family: *Taxodiaceae*.

Dawson 64 04N 139 24W A town in NW Canada, in the Yukon on the *Klondike River. During the gold rush it had over 25 000 inhabitants. Population (1981 est): 1252.

Dawson Creek 55 45N 120 15W A town in W Canada, in British Columbia at the beginning of the *Alaska Highway. Population (1984 est): 12 000.

Dayak (*or* Dyak) A people of Borneo and Sarawak, speaking languages of the Indonesian section of the Malayo-Polynesian family. There are many groups including the Bahau of central and E Borneo, the Land Dayak of SW Borneo and the Iban (*or* Sea Dayak) of Sarawak. They are a riverine people, who live in large communal wooden huts (longhouses). They live by rice cultivation, fishing, and hunting with blowpipes. Formerly head hunting was common.

Dayan, Moshe (1915–81) Israeli general. Born in Palestine, during the 1930s he fought with the Haganah (Jewish irregulars) and in World War II in the British Army, losing an eye in battle in 1941. From 1953 until 1958 he was chief of Israel's general staff. He was defence minister in 1967 and from 1969 to 1974, when he resigned after criticism of Israel's unpreparedness in the Arab-Israeli War of 1973–74. In 1977 he became foreign minister but resigned in 1979 as a result of disagreement with Begin's cabinet on policy towards the Arabs.

Day Lewis, C(ecil) (1904–72) British poet and critic. He was a leading left-wing poet of the 1930s but his later verse, as in *The Whispering Roots* (1970), was more purely lyrical. He published translations of Virgil's *Aeneid* (1952) and other works and was appointed poet laureate in 1968. As "Nicholas Blake" he wrote a series of sophisticated detective stories.

day lily A herbaceous plant of the genus *Hemerocallis*, native to Europe and Asia and cultivated as garden flowers. They have long narrow leaves and long stalks bearing clusters of orange or yellow lily-like flowers, which wither after a short time. *H. lilio-asphodelinus* is grown for its sweet scent, and garden hybrids of *H. flava* bloom for a longer time, producing orange, yellow, pink, and red flowers. Family: *Liliaceae*.

Dayton 39 45N 84 10W A city in the USA, in Ohio on the Great Miami River. It was the home of the Wright brothers; the nearby Wright-Patterson Air Force Base is a centre for military aviation research. Population (1980): 203 588.

Daytona Beach 29 11N 81 01W A resort in the USA, in Florida on the Atlantic coast. Its hard white beach has been used for motor racing since 1902. Population (1980): 54 176.

Dazai Osamu (Tsushima Shuji; 1909–48) Japanese novelist. His fiction exploited the conflict between his wealthy family background and his radical political beliefs. His postwar novels, notably *The Setting Sun* (1947) and *No Longer Human* (1948), expressed the nihilistic mood of a generation bereft of the support of traditional values. He committed suicide in 1948.

DBE. *See* Order of the British Empire.

D-Day (6 June, 1944) The day on which the Allied invasion of Normandy was launched from Britain during *World War II. It led to the liberation of France from German occupation and the final defeat of Germany.

DDT (dichlorophenyltrichloroethane) An organochlorine compound widely used as a contact *insecticide. It is active against many insects, including mosquitoes, flies, fleas, lice, and bedbugs, specifically affecting the central nervous system. However, many insects have become resistant to DDT, which is a very stable compound and accumulates not only in their tissues but also in the tissues of the animals that prey on them, causing toxic effects.

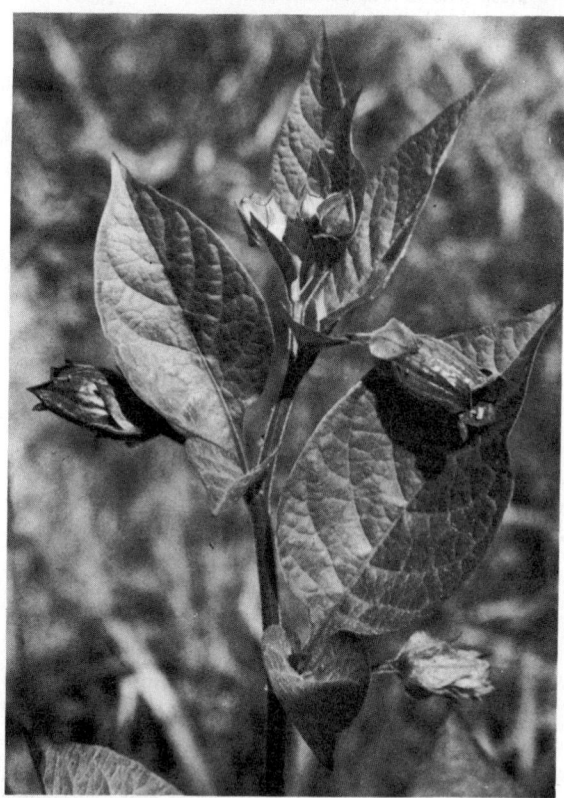

DEADLY NIGHTSHADE *This notorious plant grows in woodlands, thickets, and scrub. It flowers from June to August and produces its deadly black berries from August to November.*

deadly nightshade (*or* belladonna) A branching perennial herb, *Atropa belladonna*, up to 1.5 m tall and native to Eurasia. It has dull green leaves, up to 20 cm long, and solitary purple or greenish bell-shaped flowers. The shiny black berries taste sweet but contain a deadly poison. The plant is a source of a variety of alkaloids, especially hyoscyamine and atropine. Family: *Solanaceae. See also* nightshade.

dead men's fingers A colonial soft *coral, *Alcyonium digitatum*, so called because of its fleshy pink finger-like appearance when out of water. The individual *polyps have an internal skeleton of separate calcareous spicules, which give the tissues a gelatinous consistency. Colonies, which are white, yellow, pink, or orange, are common on rocky coasts of NW Europe.

Dead Sea A lake in E Israel and W Jordan. It is fed by the River Jordan and, having no outlet, is highly saline and supports no life. Area: 1050 sq km (401 sq mi).

Dead Sea Scrolls A group of Hebrew and Aramaic manuscript scrolls, originally stored in jars, found in 11 caves in the area of Khirbat *Qumran, NW of the Dead Sea. The first were accidentally discovered in 1947; the rest were recovered as late as the 1950s. Altogether there are about 500 different documents, dating from 250 BC to 70 AD, which seem to have formed the library of a Jewish, perhaps *Essene, community that existed from about 125 BC to the Jewish revolt in 66–70 AD, when the scrolls were hidden in the caves for safekeeping. They include texts of many Old Testament books, commentaries, prayers, psalms, and material peculiar to the community, including an apocalyptic prophecy. They are valuable as evidence of the accuracy of previously known Old Testament texts, for the information they provide about a Jewish community contemporaneous with early Christianity, and archaeologically as examples of the Hebrew and Aramaic scripts of the period.

deafness A common condition in which hearing is absent or impaired. Deafness is described as either conductive, in which the mechanism for transmitting sound to the inner ear is defective, or sensorineural, when there is damage to the auditory nerve or the part of the brain concerned with hearing. Conductive deafness may be caused by wax in the outer ear, infection in the middle ear, or—as with Beethoven—otosclerosis (a disease of the small bones in the middle ear). Sensorineural deafness occurs commonly in old people but can also be due to infection, head injury, drugs (such as streptomycin), *Ménière's disease, or exposure to continuous loud noise. Some forms of deafness can be treated by removing wax, curing infection, or by microsurgery; untreatable forms can be alleviated with a *hearing aid.

Deák, Ferenc (1803–76) Hungarian statesman. After the *Hungarian Revolution of 1848, Deák became the country's minister of justice and in 1849, after the fall of the revolutionaries, the leader of the opposition to Austrian dominance. Deák believed in the dynastic union of Austria and Hungary but desired separate constitutions and kingdoms and he was largely responsible for the establishment in 1867 of *Austria-Hungary.

Deakin, Alfred (1856–1919) Australian statesman, who was three times prime minister (1903–04, 1905–08, 1909–10). He succeeded Sir Edmund *Barton, and like him was a member of the Federal Convention that drafted the constitution for the new Commonwealth of Australia. He was a considerable influence on the early development of the Commonwealth and introduced the "White Australia" policy restricting non-White immigration.

Deal 51 14N 1 24E A port and resort in SE England, in Kent. It is one of the Cinque Ports and probable landing place of Julius Caesar (55 BC). Population (1981): 25 989.

Dean, Forest of An ancient royal forest in W England, in Gloucestershire between the Rivers Severn and Wye. Private coalmines are operated here.

Dean, James (James Byron; 1931–55) US film actor. He trained at the Actors' Studio, and became a cult hero for his generation. His films were *East of Eden* (1954), *Rebel without a Cause* (1955), and *Giant* (1955), released following his death in a car crash.

Deane, Silas (1737–89) US patriot and diplomat. Active in movements leading to American independence, Deane was sent to Paris by the Continental Congress to buy war supplies and negotiate treaties of commerce and alliance with France (1776–78). Accused of embezzlement he went into exile, settling in London.

Dearborn 42 18N 83 14W A city in the USA, in Michigan near Detroit. The birthplace of Henry Ford, it is the headquarters of the Ford Motor Company. Population (1980): 90 660.

death The permanent cessation of all bodily functions in an organism. Until recently a person was medically pronounced dead when his heartbeat and breathing movements ceased, but since the advent of mechanical ventilators the heart beat may be maintained long after "natural" breathing has stopped as a result of irreversible brain damage. Death is therefore now defined on the basis of brain function: when the parts of the brain that control respiration and other vital reflexes have ceased to function the patient is said to be brain dead, i.e. truly dead, although his heart may continue to beat for some time with the aid of mechanical life-support systems. With recent advances in transplant surgery, it is important to establish brain death in those patients who could be suitable donors of kidneys and other organs.

death cap A highly poisonous mushroom, *Amanita phalloides*, fairly common in and near deciduous woodlands. Its cap, 7–12 cm in diameter, is usually pale greenish yellow but may be olive green or greyish. The stalk is white or greenish white, with a baglike sheath (volva) at its base. Death cap can be fatal, even in small amounts, and symptoms may not appear for up to 24 hours.

death's-head moth A *hawk moth, *Acherontia atropos*, with a wingspan of 125 mm, found in Europe, Africa, and Asia, whose thoracic markings resemble a skull and crossbones. These moths emit squeaks when handled and may enter beehives to steal honey.

Death Valley A desert area in the USA, in SE California. The hottest and driest part of North America, its temperatures exceed 39°C (102°F) during summer. The flora and fauna that survive these harsh conditions are of interest to scientists and many tourists are attracted to the area during winter. In 1933 it was declared a national monument.

deathwatch beetle A widely distributed wood-boring beetle, *Xestobium rufovillosum*, about 7 mm long, that can cause immense damage to old buildings and furniture. It lays its eggs in small crevices in the wood and the larvae tunnel in, eventually reducing it to powder. The pupae often make knocking sounds by repeatedly striking their heads against the walls of their burrows. Family: *Anobiidae*.

Deauville 49 21N 0 04E A seaside resort in NW France, in the Calvados department. It is linked to Trouville by bridge across the River Touques. Population (1982 est): 4769.

de Bary, Heinrich Anton (1831–88) German botanist and founder of mycology (the study of fungi). He determined the life cycles of many fungi, including important disease-causing species. In 1866 he showed that lichens each comprise a fungus and an alga living in a mutually beneficial partnership. For this he coined the word symbiosis.

debenture stock A document setting out the terms of a fixed-interest loan to a company. A **secured debenture** is secured against a specified asset belonging to the company (fixed charge) or against all the company's assets (floating charge). An **unsecured debenture** has no such security, but if it cannot be paid back on the repayment date, debenture holders can force the company into liquidation and they then take priority over other shareholders in having their capital repaid. An **irredeemable debenture** is never repaid, being bought only for the interest it earns.

Debray, (Jules) Régis (1940–) French Marxist writer. Active in Latin-American politics, Debray is known for his writings justifying guerrilla warfare as an instrument of social change. The Bolivians sentenced him to 30 years' imprisonment but he served only three years (1967-70), subsequently involving himself in the Chilean Marxist movement.

Debré, Michel (1912-   ) French statesman; prime minister (1959-62). A Gaullist, Debré became prominent as a member of the Saar Economic Mission in 1947. He became a member of the Rassemblement pour la République upon its formation in 1976 by Jacques *Chirac. Debré is the author of 15 works on politics and economics.

Debrecen 47 30N 21 37E A city in E Hungary. It was a centre of Protestantism in E Europe. Lajos Kossuth proclaimed Hungary independent of the Habsburgs in the Great Church of Debrecen in 1849. There are now various industries and a university (1912). Population (1980): 195 000.

Debrett, John (1752-1822) British publisher. He took over a publishing business with strong Whig connections in 1781; the directory of the peerage, which still bears his name, was first published in 1802.

de Broglie, Louis Victor, 7th Duc (1892-1987) French physicist, who won the 1929 Nobel Prize for his theory that elementary particles have associated waves, known as *de Broglie waves. The theory was confirmed by the subsequent observation of *electron diffraction and forms the basis of the branch of quantum mechanics known as *wave mechanics.

de Broglie wave A wave associated with any moving elementary particle with nonzero mass, since such particles exhibit wave properties under appropriate conditions. For example, they may be diffracted by a crystal lattice. The de Broglie wavelength of a particle mass m and velocity v is h/mv, where h is the *Planck constant. They were first postulated by Louis *de Broglie in 1923.

Debs, Eugene V(ictor) (1855-1926) US labour organizer. Debs formed the American Railway Union (1893). He was imprisoned several times for labour agitation and in 1918, under the Espionage Law, for pacifist speeches. He ran five times for president as candidate for the Social Democratic Party, which he established. His 1920 campaign conducted from prison won almost a million votes. He wrote *Walls and Bars* (1927) on prison conditions.

Deburau, Jean-Gaspard (1796-1846) French pantomimist, born in Bohemia. He joined a troupe of acrobats in Paris in 1811 and created the standard pantomime character of Pierrot, the pale and melancholy lover.

Debussy, Claude (Achille) (1862-1918) French composer. He spent most of his life in Paris and is regarded as the originator of musical impressionism. He married twice and wrote his *Children's Corner Suite* (1906-08) for his daughter Chou-chou. His individual style employed whole-tone, pentatonic, and modal scales as well as unusual harmonies and tone colours. His most famous works include *Prélude à l'après-midi d'un faune* (for orchestra; 1892-94), the opera *Pelléas et Mélisande* (1892-1902), *La Mer* (three symphonic sketches; 1903-05), a string quartet, and a sonata for flute, viola, and harp. He also wrote sonatas for cello and for violin; piano music, including two sets of *Images* (1905, 1907) and 24 preludes (1910-13); and songs.

Debye, Peter Joseph Wilhelm (1884-1966) Dutch physicist and chemist, who was awarded the 1936 Nobel Prize for Chemistry for his theoretical work on *dipole moments and the behaviour of ions in solution. He also extended the technique of *X-ray crystallography so that it could be applied to powders. Most of his work was done in Germany but in 1940 he left Europe for Cornell University (USA), where he remained until his retirement in 1950.

Decadents A group of late-19th-century French symbolist poets and their contemporaries in England. They aimed to create a literature liberated from all moral and social

responsibilities. A journal entitled *Le Décadent* was published in France from 1886 to 1889. Poets linked with the movement included *Rimbaud, *Verlaine, and *Mallarmé in France, and Arthur *Symons, Oscar *Wilde, and Ernest *Dowson in England. *See also* Aesthetic movement.

Decapoda A worldwide order of *crustaceans (over 8500 species), with five pairs of thoracic appendages—anterior pincers and four pairs of walking legs. They include the *shrimps and *prawns (suborder: *Natantia*, "swimming forms") and *lobsters, *crayfish, and *crabs (suborder: *Reptantia*, "walking forms").

decathlon An athletic competition for men, consisting of ten events over two days. On the first are 100 m sprint, long jump, shot put, high jump, and 400 m sprint; on the second are 110 m hurdles, discus throw, pole vault, javelin throw, and 1500 m run. Competitors score for performances in each event, the winner gaining the highest total. World record: 8798 points (1984) by Jurgen Hingsen (West Germany).

Decatur, Stephen (1779-1820) US naval officer. He established his reputation in the war with the Barbary pirates of Tripoli (1800-05), in which he raided Tripoli harbour and burnt the captured US frigate *Philadelphia* (1804). In the *War of 1812 he defeated two British frigates (1812, 1815). He was killed in a duel.

Deccan A region of India, considered either as the entire peninsula or as the arid plateau between the Rivers Narmada and Krishna. Sloping gently from the Western to the Eastern Ghats, it is cut by many rivers flowing E.

Decembrists. *See* Dekabrists.

decibel (dB) A unit used to compare two power levels on a logarithmic scale. It is one-tenth of a bel, but this unit is rarely used. Two power levels P and P_0 differ by n decibels when $n = 10 \log_{10} P/P_0$. The unit is often used to express a sound intensity in which case P_0 is usually taken as the intensity of the lowest audible note of the same frequency as P. *See also* phon.

deciduous plants. *See* evergreen plants.

decimal system The number system in common use, having a base 10 and thus using ten separate numerals. It also involves the use of a decimal point to express numbers less than one, instead of the method of fractions: for example ¼ is expressed as 0.25. The decimal system was invented by the Hindus and adopted by the Arabs in the 9th century (*see also* mathematics). The use of decimal fractions originated in Italy in the 12th century but was first formalized by the mathematician Simon Stévin (1548-1620) in 1585. The use of the decimal point did not occur until the beginning of the 18th century. Decimalization of currency systems was introduced by France after the Revolution and followed by most other European and American countries, except for Britain, which did not decimalize until 1971. *See also* metric system.

Decius, Gaius Messius Quintus Trajanus (c. 201-51 AD) Roman emperor (249-51). Decius attempted to restore Roman traditions, persecuting Christians in the name of Roman state cults. He was defeated and killed by the Goths at Abrittus.

Declaration of Independence (4 July, 1776) The declaration, adopted by the 13 colonies of North America, that announced their independence from Great Britain. Written by Thomas *Jefferson between 11 June and 2 July and revised before adoption, the Declaration is both specific (in its enumeration of grievances) and general (in its statement of principles of governance) and is one of the most influential proclamations in the western political tradition.

Declaratory Act. *See* Stamp Act.

declination. *See* magnetic declination; right ascension.

decomposition The breakdown of the complex organic molecules of dead plants and animals and animal wastes into their simple components by bacteria and fungi. These microorganisms (**decomposers**) serve as the ultimate link in *food chains: the simple nitrogenous compounds released into the soil by decomposition can be used by plants (the producers) to manufacture their own food. *See also* nitrogen cycle.

decompression sickness (*or* caisson disease)   An occupational hazard of pilots and underwater divers caused by too rapid a return to normal atmospheric pressure. At high pressures large amounts of gas can be carried in the blood. A rapid return to normal pressure causes nitrogen (the main component of inhaled air) to form bubbles out in the blood; this interrupts the blood supply to the tissues, producing joint pain (the bends), general discomfort, and respiratory problems (the chokes). Decompression sickness is prevented by a slow return to atmospheric pressure; it is treated by placing the patient in a hyperbaric chamber.

Decorated   The style of gothic architecture predominant in England between 1300 and 1370. In contrast to the geometric restraint of its predecessor, *Early English, Decorated is characterized by complex flowing patterns, especially in window tracery (e.g. the Bishop's Eye *rose window in Lincoln cathedral, c. 1325). Roof vaults were intricately ribbed and the ogee or double curved *arch with elaborate ornamentation became common (e.g. the lady chapel of Ely Cathedral, 1321–49). The early 14th-century nave of Exeter Cathedral demonstrates the style's profusion of ribs and arches. *Compare* Flamboyant.

decorative arts   Arts and crafts the function of which is primarily ornamental. The modern concept of the decorative arts was pioneered by such designers as William *Morris. Despite persistent attempts to demonstrate that mass production need not necessarily compromise design, modern endeavours in the decorative arts tend to centre on small workshops producing individually handmade items in such fields as *bookbinding, *enamelwork, *jewellery, *pottery, and wallpaper.

Dedekind, (Julius Wilhelm) Richard   (1831–1916) German mathematician, who gave the irrational *numbers the same level of respectability as the rational numbers. He achieved this by means of the Dedekind cut, a method of cutting an infinite line representing the real numbers. He became involved in the controversy between Georg *Cantor and Leopold Kronecker (1823–91), taking Cantor's side against Kronecker's attempt to banish all but the integers from mathematics.

deduction   In logic, argument from general principles to particular conclusions. It is thus analytic and certain, in contrast to *induction, the conclusions of which are never more than strong probabilities.

de Duve, Christian   (1917–) Belgian biochemist, noted for his contributions to cell biology. De Duve discovered lysosomes, components of living cells that are responsible for breaking down substances within the cell. He shared a Nobel Prize (1974) with Albert Claude (1899–) and George Emil Palade (1912–).

Dee, John   (1527–1608) English mathematician, astronomer, alchemist, and magician. After studying mathematics and astronomy at Cambridge, Dee lectured at Louvain and Rheims. He was distrusted by Mary I, but favoured and consulted by Elizabeth I. He went into partnership with the conjurer and imposter Edward Kelly (1555–95) and travelled to Bohemia and Poland with him (1583–89). Dee's work and writings reflect Renaissance fascination with magic, but he also wrote an important preface to the first English translation of *Euclid.

Dee, River   The name of three rivers in the UK. **1.** A river in NE Scotland, flowing E to the North Sea at Aberdeen. Length: 140 km (87 mi). **2.** A river in North Wales and NW England, rising in Gwynedd and flowing E and N through Llangollen and Chester to the Irish Sea. Length: 112 km (70 mi). **3.** A river in S Scotland, flowing S to the Solway Firth. Length: 80 km (50 mi).

deed   In law, a document in writing, signed, sealed, and delivered, transferring a right over property (title-deed) or creating an obligation on its maker. To be binding it need not fulfil conditions applicable to a *contract. A deed may be between two parties, to establish mutual obligations, or it may involve one party only (deed poll), as, for example, when a person publishes a change of name.

deer   A *ruminant mammal of the family *Cervidae* (41 species), occurring mainly in the N hemisphere, although a few are found in South America and N Africa and they have been introduced to SE Asia and Australasia. Nearly all deer have bony antlers that are shed and replaced every year (the *Chinese water deer and the *musk deer are exceptions). Deer range in size from the *elk (up to 2 m high) to the South American pudu, which is only about 40 cm high at the shoulder. Most deer live in herds but some, such as the *muntjac, are solitary.

deerhound   A long-established British breed of dog, formerly used for hunting deer. It has a deep-chested long body with long legs and a long tapering head with small ears. The wiry coat is usually blue-grey but may be shades of brown or fawn. Height: 76 cm (dogs); 71 cm (bitches).

deer mouse   A North American rodent belonging to the genus *Peromyscus* (60 species), also called white-footed mouse. 12–37 cm long including the tail (4–20 cm), these climbing and burrowing animals have large eyes and ears; they are omnivorous and are often used as laboratory animals. Family: *Cricetidae*.

defamation   In law, a false and derogatory statement about another person that tends to lower him in the estimation of right-thinking members of the community generally. It is libel if made in a permanent form (e.g. in writing, newspapers, broadcasts, sound films) and slander if made in a transient form, by spoken words or gestures. The remedy for both types of defamation is by civil proceedings, although libel may also be a crime if its publication is calculated to provoke a breach of the peace. Not only the originator of a libel but everyone who has subsequently repeated or published it may be sued by the person libelled. Action for libel cannot be brought against "privileged" proceedings or statements. Judicial and parliamentary proceedings, for example, are "absolutely privileged" and nothing said in them can be the subject of a libel action. A statement judged to be a fair comment on a matter of public interest is also not actionable as defamation.

Defence, Ministry of   The UK government department headed by the secretary of state for defence, that administers the country's armed forces and formulates a coordinated defence policy. It was formed in 1964 from the former Ministry of Defence (established in 1946), the Admiralty, War Office, and Air Ministry. It is the largest user of computers in Europe.

defence mechanisms   In psychoanalysis, the means by which undesirable and antisocial impulses can be unconsciously avoided or controlled by the subject. *Repression, *sublimation, and *projection are important defences. Others include reaction formation, in which an impulse is turned into its opposite, as when one displays excessive concern for a person whom one secretly hates; and displacement, in which an impulse is transferred onto a more acceptable subject (e.g. kicking the dog instead of the boss). Defence mechanisms are a part of normal life, but if they become excessively strong they can distort the development of personality and even give rise to symptoms of *neurosis.

deficit financing   The fiscal policy of stimulating the economy by government spending in excess of revenue by borrowing to finance the resultant deficit. Deficit financing was advocated by the British economist J. M. *Keynes as a method of countering the *Depression of the 1930s; although Keynes' ideas were not assimilated in time to influence that

353

period, deficit financing became normal practice after World War II (*see* multiplier; national debt).

deflation A government action to slow down the economy, with the aim of easing *inflation or cutting down on imports and thus helping the *balance of payments. Both monetary policy (credit "squeeze") and fiscal policy (increasing taxes, cutting government spending) can be used to deflate the economy. *See also* multiplier).

Defoe, Daniel (1660–1731) British novelist, economist, and journalist. His early career as a merchant ended in bankruptcy in 1692. A Nonconformist, he welcomed the arrival of William of Orange in 1688 and wrote *The True-Born Englishman* (1701) in his defence. He worked as a journalist and informer for both Whigs and Tories and suffered imprisonment for his ironic pamphlet, *The Shortest Way with Dissenters*, in 1702. From 1704 to 1713 he wrote most of the thrice-weekly *Review* himself. His famous novels were written late in his career, *Robinson Crusoe* in 1719 and *Moll Flanders* and *Colonel Jack* in 1722.

defoliant A chemical applied to foliage in order to cause premature shedding of leaves; examples are ammonium thiocyanate and cacodylic acid. Defoliants are used to aid mechanical harvesting of cotton and for other peaceful uses. They are also employed in *chemical warfare.

De Forest, Lee (1873–1961) US electrical engineer, who invented the triode valve (1906), which became the basic *amplifier in all electronic circuits until superseded by the transistor. In the early 1920s he developed a method of converting sound waves into light of varying intensity, which was used as the basis of recording film soundtracks.

Degas, (Hilaire Germain) Edgar (1834–1917) French painter and sculptor, born in Paris. He trained in the École des Beaux-Arts, where he was influenced by the draughtsmanship of *Ingres. His early works were portraits, e.g. *The Bellelli Family* (Louvre), recalling the old masters that he had studied in Italy (1856–60), and history paintings, e.g. *Young Spartans Exercising* (National Gallery, London). From the mid-1860s he turned to painting contemporary scenes, particularly of ballet and racecourses. In these works, characterized by informal poses and unusual angles, Degas was indebted both to Japanese prints and to photography. In 1872 he visited his mother's family in New Orleans and painted the *New Orleans Cotton Office* (Pau, France). His pastels of women at their toilet shocked his contemporaries but are now regarded as being among his finest works. He exhibited frequently with the impressionists but was little influenced by their style.

De Gasperi, Alcide (1881–1954) Italian statesman; prime minister (1945–53). After imprisonment (1930–31) as an antifascist, De Gasperi withdrew to the Vatican City, where he worked in the library and organized the moderate Christian Democratic party during World War II. From 1945 to 1953 he headed coalition cabinets, which included communists until 1947, when De Gasperi expelled them. A Christian Democratic electoral victory in 1948 gave popular sanction to this measure.

de Gaulle, Charles André Joseph Marie (1890–1970) French general and statesman who was an outstanding international figure in the mid-20th century; president (1958–69). An advocate of mechanized warfare during the 1930s, when he wrote his best-known book, *Vers l'armée de métier* (1934), he was promoted early in World War II to general (1940). He entered the cabinet of Paul *Reynaud but opposed the Franco-German armistice, becoming leader of the *Free French in London and a symbol of French patriotism. The Free French contributed heroically to the Allied war effort but de Gaulle resented his dependence on Britain and the USA and the antagonism between them was to continue after the war. In 1943 he became head of the newly formed Committee of National Liberation in Algiers and, after the Allied liberation of France (1944), formed a

CHARLES DE GAULLE *Seen here (right) with Field-Marshal Montgomery at Bayeux, after the D-Day landings (1944).*

provisional government of which he was president from 1945 until resigning in 1946. In 1947 he formed the unsuccessful Rassemblement du Peuple Français, dissolving it in 1953. In 1958 he was summoned from retirement to deal with the crisis in Algeria, where French settlers, fearing the establishment of Algerian independence, were in revolt. He became president of the new Fifth Republic in 1959 and moved towards the achievement of Algerian independence. Successful by 1962, he subsequently pursued his vision of a Europe of nationally self-conscious states, free of US influence. He thus opposed the postwar multinational organizations, refusing to sign the *Nuclear Test-Ban Treaty (1963) and withdrawing France from the military structure of NATO (1966). He was also passionately opposed to UK membership of the EEC. At home his position was greatly weakened by the student and industrial unrest of May, 1968, and in the following year he resigned following defeat in a referendum on constitutional reform. His policies, however, have endured in the right-wing Gaullist movement in contemporary French politics.

degree 1. A unit of plane angle equal to 1/360th of a complete revolution. It is subdivided into 60 minutes, each of which consists of 60 seconds. 2. An interval on a temperature scale: 1° on the *Celsius (centigrade) scale is equal to one-hundredth of the difference in temperature between freezing and boiling water. It is also equal in magnitude to 1 *kelvin. 1° on the *Fahrenheit scale is 9/5 times the Celsius degree.

De Havilland, Sir Geoffrey (1882–1965) British □aircraft designer and manufacturer, who produced some of the first jet-propelled aircraft. During both World Wars he designed several military aircraft, including the well-known Mosquito of World War II.

Dehra Dun 30 19N 78 03E A city in India, in Uttar Pradesh. The Indian Military Academy (1932) is situated here. Population (1981): 294 000.

dehydration A potentially serious condition resulting from excessive loss of water from the body. The water that is continuously lost from the body in urine, sweat, expired air, and faeces must be replaced by drinking. Dehydration may result from insufficient intake of water in those shipwrecked or too ill to drink or from excessive loss in fever, vomiting, diarrhoea, or from the skin in hot climates. It may lead, if not treated, to shock and death. It can be avoided by ensuring that patients receive fluid in the form of drinks or intravenous infusions. Intravenous fluids can be given slowly to treat those seriously dehydrated.

Deirdre The tragic heroine of the Irish legend known as *The Fate of the Sons of Usnech*, of which the earliest surviving account appears in the 12th-century *Book of Leinster*. To escape marrying King Conchobar of Ulster, Deirdre eloped with Noíse, son of Usnech. When they returned, Noíse and his brothers were killed by the king and Deirdre died of grief. The legend has been dramatized by J. M. Synge and W. B. Yeats.

deism A system of belief in God that, in contrast to *theism, discounts revealed religion, especially Christianity, and takes God as the philosophical *first cause. More specifically, deism was a rationalistic anti-Christian movement in England in the late 17th and early 18th centuries that criticized and rebutted the Scriptures after the manner of *Locke's *empiricism and regarded dogmatic religions as corruptions of man's natural relation with God. Leading deists were Lord *Herbert of Cherbury, Matthew Tindal (1655-1733), and the 3rd Earl of *Shaftesbury. Deism, often tending towards *atheism, had more influence on German and French thinkers, including *Voltaire, than in England.

Dekabrists (*or* Decembrists) Members of an anti-Tsarist revolt in December, 1825, following the death of Alexander I. They were members of various clandestine organizations formed after the Napoleonic Wars by former military officers, who, after being exposed to western liberalism, had become discontented on their return to Russia with the country's reactionary government. The revolt failed, largely because of poor organization, and five leaders were executed and their followers imprisoned or exiled to Siberia.

Dekker, Thomas (c. 1572-1632) British dramatist and pamphleteer. His best-known play, *The Shoemaker's Holiday* (1600), expresses his exuberant affection for London life. He often collaborated with *Webster, *Middleton, and other dramatists. His pamphlets, such as *The Seven Deadly Sins of London* (1606) and *The Gull's Hornbook* (1609), are racy blends of fact, wit, and homily.

de Kooning, Willem (1904–   ) US painter of Dutch birth, noted for his figurative subject matter. He also painted abstract compositions, some in black and white, influenced by Arshile *Gorky, *Picasso, and *Miró. His famous but controversial series of *Women* (1950–53), portraying females as grotesque and aggressive creatures, established him as a leading exponent of *action painting.

Delacroix, Eugène (1798-1863) French Romantic painter, born near Paris. He studied with Baron Guérin (1774-1883) but was influenced by *Géricault, *Rubens, and *Constable. His richly coloured paintings were often inspired by incidents in Dante, Shakespeare, and Byron, and by contemporary events, e.g. *Massacre at Chios* (1824; Louvre), based on a Turkish atrocity in Greece, and *Liberty Leading the People* (1830; Louvre). The influence of a visit to Morocco (1832) can be seen in some of his exotic later works, e.g. *Women of Algiers* (1834; Louvre). From 1833 he worked on decorations in public buildings, such as the Louvre, Palais-Bourbon, and Saint-Sulpice. He was a friend of *Chopin and George *Sand, both of whom he painted in 1838. His *Journal* contains valuable information on his life and work.

Delagoa Bay (Portuguese name: Baía de Lourenço Marques) An inlet of the Indian Ocean on the coast of S Mozambique. It is about 30 km (19 mi) across and has Maputo at its edge.

De la Mare, Walter (1873-1956) British poet, novelist, and anthologist, whose work is imbued with an atmosphere of mystery and magic. The verse collection *Songs of Childhood* (1902) and the romance *Henry Brocken* (1906) were written while he was working for an oil company, from which he retired on a government pension at 36 to devote

himself to full-time writing. Among his best-known works are the poem "The Listeners" (1912), the fantastic novel *Memoirs of a Midget* (1921), and the anthologies *Come Hither* (1923) and *Love* (1943). In 1953 he received the OM.

De la Roche, Mazo (1885-1961) Canadian novelist. Her romantic saga of the Whiteoak family ran to over 15 books, beginning with *Jalna* (1927), the name of the family estate.

Delaroche, (Hippolyte) Paul (1797-1859) French history and portrait painter. Throughout his life he enjoyed great success with such sentimental history paintings as *The Children of Edward IV in the Tower* (1830; Louvre). He was a professor at the École des Beaux-Arts from 1832, for which he produced the mural of the *Apotheosis of Art* (1837-41).

De La Rue, Warren (1815-89) British astronomer, who pioneered the use of photography in astronomy, discovering solar flares by this process in 1860.

Delaunay, Robert (1885-1941) The earliest French painter of completely abstract compositions. His first major works represented the Eiffel Tower (1910-11) in cubist style but in his series of *Discs* (1912-13) he pioneered *orphism (which he called *simultaneisme*), a style in which colour alone was the subject matter.

Delaware The second smallest state in the USA. It occupies part of the low-lying ground of the Atlantic coastal plain with higher ground in the NW, where most of the state's population and industry is concentrated. It is one of the most industrialized states; Wilmington contains the administrative centres of several large chemical companies and is nicknamed "the chemical capital of the world." Motor vehicles, synthetic rubber, textiles, and food products are also produced. There is limited mining of sand and gravel. The state's farmers produce poultry, soya beans, milk, corn, and vegetables. There is some fishing of coastal and inland waters. *History*: the Dutch established a settlement (1631) but it was the Swedes who founded the first permanent settlement Fort Christiana (now Wilmington) in 1638. Delaware was subsequently captured by the Dutch (1655) and the English (1664). It became part of Pennsylvania in 1682 and shared a governor with that colony until 1776. It was the first of the original 13 states of the USA. Area: 5328 sq km (2057 sq mi). Population (1980): 595 225. Capital: Dover.

Delcassé, Théophile (1852-1923) French politician; foreign minister (1898-1905, 1914-15). His conciliatory policy over the *Fashoda incident (1895) and his negotiations leading to the *Entente Cordiale with Britain (1904) paved the way to the *Triple Entente between Britain, France, and Russia. He urged a strong stand against Germany during the 1905-06 Moroccan crisis but, failing to win support, resigned.

Deledda, Grazia (1871-1936) Italian novelist. Most of her novels, such as *Ashes* (1904) and *The Mother* (1920), are realistic treatments of peasant life in her native Sicily. She won the Nobel Prize in 1926.

Delescluze, Louis Charles (1809-71) French journalist and radical republican. Active in the revolutions of 1830 and 1848, he was deeply opposed to the Second Empire of Napoleon III. A member of the *Commune of Paris, he was shot at the barricades.

Delft 52 01N 4 21E A town in the W Netherlands, in South Holland province. William the Silent was murdered here in 1584. Since the late 16th century it has been famous for its pottery and porcelain known as delftware. Population (1981 est): 84 129.

Delhi 28 40N 77 14E The capital of India, situated midway between the Ganges and Indus Valleys on the W bank of the River Jumna. It consists of the old city (Old Delhi), which was built in 1639 on the site of former cities of Delhi that date from the 15th century BC, and New Delhi, which replaced Calcutta as the capital of British India in 1912. Both the old and new cities together with the surrounding

355   **democracy**

area comprise the Union Territory of Delhi, an administrative unit of some 1418 sq km (553 sq mi). Within the walls of Old Delhi are the massive Red Fort, which contains the Imperial Palace (1638-48) of Shah Jahan, and the Jami Masjid (Principal Mosque). The narrow bustling streets of the old city contrast sharply with the spacious tree-lined streets and imposing government buildings of New Delhi, which was designed chiefly by Sir Edwin Lutyens. The University of Delhi was established in 1922. Population (1981): 5 714 000.

Delian League A confederacy of Greek city states formed in 478 BC during the *Greek-Persian Wars under the leadership of Athens. Members met on the sacred island of Delos, voted on policy, and contributed funds assessed by *Aristides. After the peace between Greece and Persia (c. 450) Athens regarded its allies as subjects. The League treasury was moved to Athens and secession was punished as revolt. The League was disbanded after Athens' defeat (404) in the Peloponnesian War but was revived in defence against Sparta in 378, lasting until the defeat (338) of Athens and Thebes at *Chaeronea.

Delian problem The problem of constructing a cube that has twice the volume of a given cube. Also known as the duplication of the cube, it was first set by the oracle of Delos in the 5th century BC as a condition for ending a plague. The problem cannot be solved by ruler and compass alone, a fact not recognized until the 19th century.

Delibes, Leo (1836-91) French composer, a pupil of Adolphe Adam. Early in his career he wrote a number of operas and operettas. In 1863 he became accompanist at the Paris Opéra and, later, second chorus master. His best-known works are the ballets *Coppélia* (1870) and *Sylvia* (1876).

deliquescence The process in which some crystalline substances, such as calcium chloride ($CaCl_2$), absorb water from the atmosphere to such an extent that they dissolve; this is extreme hygroscopic (water-attracting) behaviour. Deliquescent substances are used in several industries to provide dry atmospheres.

delirium An acute state of mental disturbance in which the patient has hallucinations and delusions and is incoherent, agitated, and restless. It is most commonly associated with a high fever, particularly in children, although it may also be due to a variety of metabolic disorders. It also occurs in association with alcoholic poisoning and with alcohol withdrawal, when it is called **delirium tremens**. It can also be caused by intoxication with other drugs.

Delius, Frederick (1862-1934) British composer of German descent, born in Bradford. After an abortive business career in the family wool business he went to live in Florida and subsequently made his home at Grez-sur-Loing, near Paris. Largely self-taught, he was influenced by Debussy and Grieg. His works include *Paris, the Song of a Great City* (1899), *Appalachia* (for orchestra and chorus; 1902), *On Hearing the First Cuckoo in Spring* (1912), and *North Country Sketches* (1913-14). He also wrote six operas, four concertos, chamber music, choral works, and songs. Delius became blind in 1925 but continued to compose with the help of his amanuensis, Eric Fenby (1906-).

Della Robbia, Luca (1400-82) Florentine Renaissance sculptor. Working first in marble, Luca produced the *Cantoria* (1431-38), his famous relief depicting singers, musicians, and dancers, for the Duomo, Florence. Subsequently he specialized in enamelled terracotta sculptures, the glazing process being his own invention. Their production was carried on by his nephew **Andrea della Robbia** (1435-1525) and Luca's sons **Giovanni della Robbia** (1469-c. 1529) and **Girolamo della Robbia** (1488-1566).

Delorme, Philibert (?1510-70) French architect of the Renaissance. Influenced by classical architecture, which he studied in Rome in the 1530s, his buildings include the Château d'Anet (c. 1552), designed for Diane de Poitiers, and the palace of the Tuileries (1580). He also wrote two treatises on architecture (1561, 1568).

Delos (Modern Greek name: Dhílos) 37 23N 25 15E A Greek island in the S Aegean Sea, one of the Cyclades. It was of great importance in antiquity (*see* Delian League), and many ancient temples and other buildings, an altar built of the horns of sacrificed animals, and nine marble lions have been excavated here. Area: 3 sq km (1 sq mi).

Delphi A village in central Greece. In antiquity, it was the principal sanctuary and oracle of *Apollo. The sacred enclosure, still an imposing sight, is set in spectacular mountain scenery. It contained Apollo's temple, "treasuries" where the Greek states stored their offerings, a theatre, and over 3000 statues. A stadium for the *Pythian Games, a gymnasium, and other shrines stood nearby. The oracle's advice about religion, morality, commerce, and colonial projects, interpreted from the trance utterances of a priestess, was widely sought by individuals and states. As traditional beliefs declined after the 4th century BC the oracle lost influence. It was closed by the Christian emperor, Theodosius (390 AD).

Delphinium A genus of annual or perennial herbs (250 species), also called larkspur, up to 2 m high with tall spikes of deep-blue flowers and divided leaves. Delphiniums, native to the N hemisphere, are popular garden plants. Cultivated varieties usually range from 30 to 180 cm high and have single or double flowers in shades of blue, pink, purple, or white. Family: *Ranunculaceae*.

delta A large fan-shaped accumulation of sediment deposited at the mouth of a river, where it discharges into a sea or lake. It forms when the river's flow is slowed down on meeting the comparatively static sea or lake, resulting in a reduction of the river's load-bearing capacity. Clay particles also coagulate on meeting salt water and are deposited. The river is increasingly divided by the deposition into channels. Being fertile, deltas (such as the Nile Delta) are often extensively cultivated but are also prone to flooding.

Delvaux, Paul (1897-) Belgian painter, who joined the surrealist group in 1935. Influenced by *Magritte and de *Chirico, he specialized in scenes of trancelike nudes and half-clothed women in impressive architectural settings.

demand The quantity of goods or services that consumers wish to buy. Demand can be elastic (when a small change in price causes a large change in the demand), inelastic (a large change in price results in a small change in demand), or of unitary elasticity (a change in price leads to a proportional demand). The elasticity of demand influences government policy in deciding on which goods to levy a *sales tax.

Demerara, River A river in E Guyana, flowing N to enter the Atlantic Ocean at Georgetown. Length: 346 km (215 mi).

Demeter A Greek corn goddess and mother goddess, sister of *Zeus. She was worshipped at Eleusis, whose people helped her in her search for her daughter *Persephone, abducted to the underworld. In gratitude she instructed them in agriculture and religion (*see* Eleusinian Mysteries). She was identified with the Roman goddess Ceres.

de Mille, Cecil B(lount) (1881-1959) US film producer and director. His best-known films were epic productions involving spectacular crowd scenes and special effects. Many of these were based on biblical themes, notably *The Ten Commandments* (1923; remade 1956), *The King of Kings* (1927), and *Samson and Delilah* (1949). His niece **Agnes de Mille** (1909-) is a ballet dancer and choreographer. American themes and traditions were a distinctive feature of her ballets, as in *Rodeo* (1942), choreographed for the Ballets Russes in Monte Carlo. She also choreographed for films and musicals, notably *Oklahoma!* (1943), *Carousel* (1945), and *Paint Your Wagon* (1951).

democracy A form of government in which people either

rule themselves (direct democracy), as in ancient Athens, or elect representatives to rule in their interests (indirect democracy), as in most modern democracies. Elections, to be democratic, must be held regularly, be secret, and provide a choice of candidates; the elected assembly must also be free to legislate and to criticize government policy. Modern democratic ideas stem from 18th-century *utilitarianism and current debate centres on the elitist theory of democracy—that modern democratic government is by a political elite, which although voted into power invites little participation by the electorate.

Democratic Party   One of the two major political parties in the USA (*compare* Republican Party). Originating in Jefferson's Republican Democrats in 1792, it became the Democratic Party during the presidency (1829-37) of Andrew *Jackson. In 1860, just before the Civil War, the Democrats split over the issue of *slavery into northern and southern factions and the party, dominated by southern Democrats, was eclipsed until regaining northern support in the 1880s. With F. D. Roosevelt's *New Deal programme in the 1930s, the Democrats again became identified as a progressive party. Notable Democratic presidents include Woodrow Wilson, F. D. Roosevelt, J. F. Kennedy, and Jimmy Carter.

Democritus   (c. 460-370 BC), Greek philosopher and scientist, born at Abdera (Thrace). He developed the first materialist theory of nature. His *atomism, developed from *Leucippus, considered that all matter consists of minute particles—atoms—the multifarious arrangement of which accounts for different properties of matter apparent to our senses. Democritus wrote also on cosmology, biology, perception, and music. His ethical theory foreshadowed *Epicureanism in valuing spiritual tranquillity most highly. Of his works, many fragments, but nothing complete, survives.

demography   A branch of the social sciences concerned with the statistical study of the sizes, distribution, and composition of human populations. The subject also includes collecting and analysing birth, death, and marriage rates for whole populations or groups within them. Demography is primarily a branch of sociology but it also overlaps with such diverse fields as economics, mathematics, geography, and genetics.

demoiselle   An elegant *crane, *Anthropoides virgo*, of dry grassy regions of central Europe and Asia. It is smoky grey in colour with a black head and neck, long black breast feathers, and long white plumes behind each eye.

De Morgan, Augustus   (1806-71) British mathematician and logician. De Morgan was one of the first to recognize that different *algebras may exist other than the one corresponding to the real numbers, which was then taken to be the only algebra. He also encouraged and collaborated with George *Boole in the development of symbolic logic.

Demosthenes   (384-322 BC) Athenian orator and statesman. Demosthenes attacked Philip of Macedon's imperial ambitions in Greece in a series of orations called the *Philippics* (351, 344, 341) and promoted an Athenian alliance with Thebes against Philip. This was defeated by Philip at *Chaeronea (338), whereby Macedonian supremacy in Greece was assured. After the death of Philip's son, Alexander the Great (323), Demosthenes again encouraged a Greek revolt. Condemned to death by Alexander's successors, Demosthenes fled Athens and committed suicide. His simple yet impassioned oratory was much admired in antiquity but his politics were anachronistic; the military power of Macedon could not be denied by even Demosthenes' oratory.

demotic script   A form of Egyptian hieroglyphic writing. Pictorial hieroglyphics became less realistic and increasingly cursive from about 2500 BC until in the 7th century BC they developed into the cursive script called demotic. This con-

tinued in common use until the 5th century AD. *See also* Rosetta Stone.

Dempsey, Jack   (William Harrison D.; 1895-1983) US boxer, who was world heavyweight champion from 1919 to 1926. Renowned for his persistence and ferocious punching, he attracted enormous audiences and gate money. He lost his title to Gene Tunney (1897-1978).

JACK DEMPSEY

Denbighshire   A former county of North Wales. Under local government reorganization in 1974 it became part of *Clwyd and *Gwynedd.

dendrite.   *See* neurone.

dendrochronology   (*or* tree-ring dating)   An archaeological dating technique based on the *annual rings of trees. Variations in ring widths have been shown to correspond to rainfall and temperature variations and thus very old tree trunks can give a record of past climates. Any construction incorporating timber, for example buildings or ships, can be dated by comparing the timber-ring patterns with a specimen of known age.

dendrology.   *See* tree.

Deneb   An extremely luminous remote white *supergiant star, apparent magnitude 1.25 and about 1600 light years distant, that is the brightest star in the constellation Cygnus.

dengue   A tropical disease caused by a virus and characterized by painful joints, fever, and a rash. The virus is transmitted by the bite of a mosquito, and symptoms begin within a week after the bite. Dengue usually lasts for a week and is rarely fatal. There is no specific treatment.

Deng Xiao Ping   (*or* Teng Hsiao-p'ing; 1904-) Chinese communist statesman; vice premier (1973–76; 1977–80) and vice chairman of the Central Committee of the Chinese Communist Party (1977–82). He held various prominent Party posts after the establishment of the People's Republic of China in 1949 until being dismissed during the *Cultural Revolution. In 1973 he was rehabilitated but was again dismissed three years later. Following his reinstatement in 1977 he has exerted considerable influence on Chinese government and in 1978 made a state visit to the USA. He became the Chairman of the State and Party Military Commissions in 1982, and in 1984 led the negotiations with Britain over the future of Hong Kong. He stepped down as Chairman of the State Commission in 1987.

Denham, Sir John (1615–69) English poet and playwright. A courtier, he established his literary reputation with *The Sophy* (1641), a blank-verse drama, and *Cooper's Hill* (1642), a poem describing the landscape of his home near Windsor. *Cooper's Hill* established a minor genre, the topographical poem; it also helped to make the heroic couplet a standard verse form.

Den Helder 52 58N 4 46E A port in the Netherlands, in North Holland province on the North Sea. It is an important naval and military base. Population (1985 est): 63 528.

denier A unit of weight, used to measure the fineness of woven materials, equal to 1 gram per 9000 metres.

Denikin, Anton Ivanovich (1872–1947) Russian general. After the Russian revolution (1917), he led the *White Russian army against the Bolsheviks. He occupied most of the Ukraine but internal rifts and Bolshevik counterattacks led to eventual defeat (1920). Denikin fled to France.

denim A coarse twill-woven cloth, named after the French fabric *serge de Nîmes*. It is made of cotton, often with an admixture of nylon, and is usually dyed blue. Originally popular for work garments, denim became fashionable for jeans and other casual clothes in the 1970s.

Denis, Maurice (1870–1943) French painter, designer, and art theorist, who was a leading member of the *Nabis. He was responsible for decorating many churches and his religious painting influenced succeeding generations of religious artists. In 1919 he helped to found the Studios of Sacred Art, which also encouraged the revival of religious art.

Denis, St (3rd century) The patron saint of France. Of Italian birth, he was sent to Gaul as a missionary and there became the first Bishop of Paris. He was martyred under the Emperor Valerian. His shrine is in the Benedictine abbey at St Denis near Paris. Feast Day: 9 Oct.

Denmark, Kingdom of (Danish name: Danmark) A country in N Europe, between the Baltic and the North Seas. It consists of the N section of the Jutland peninsula and about a hundred inhabited islands (chiefly Sjælland (Zealand), Fyn, Lolland, Falster, Langeland, and Bornholm). *Greenland and the *Faroe Islands are also part of the Danish kingdom. The country is almost entirely flat with some slightly undulating land in the E of the mainland. *Economy*: agriculture, organized on a cooperative basis, is important both for the home and export markets. Since World War II, however, industry has predominated, with engineering, chemicals, brewing, fishing, and food processing. Furniture, textiles, porcelain, metal goods, and glass are valued for their high-quality design. Its high volume of exports include meat and meat products, dairy produce, cereals, fish, machinery, and metals. *History*: Viking kingdoms occupied the area from the 8th century to the 10th century, when Denmark became a united Christian monarchy under Harald Bluetooth. His grandson, Canute, ruled over Denmark, Norway, and England, forming the Danish Empire, which was dissolved soon after his death. In 1363 Norway again came under the Danish Crown by royal marriage. In 1397 Denmark and Norway joined with Sweden to form the Kalmar Union, which lasted until 1523. The Peace of Copenhagen (1660) concluded a long period of conflict between Denmark and Sweden. At this time it became an absolute monarchy, which continued until 1849, when a more liberal government was formed. Having supported Napoleon in the Napoleonic Wars, Denmark was compelled to cede Norway to Sweden by the Treaty of Kiel (1814). In the middle of the 19th century Denmark lost its S provinces of Schleswig, Holstein, and Lauenburg to Prussia, N

Schleswig being returned (by plebiscite) in 1920. During World War II Denmark was occupied by Germany but a resistance movement grew in strength and aided the Allied victory. Iceland, which had previously been united with Denmark, became independent in 1944. A new constitution was formed in 1953, with a single-chamber parliament (elected by proportional representation) and executive power in the hands of the monarch through his ministers. In 1973 Denmark joined the EEC. Head of state: Queen Margrethe II (1940–). Prime minister: Poul Schlüter (1929–). Official language: Danish. Official religion: Evangelical Lutheran. Official currency: krone of 100 óre. Area: 43 074 sq km (16 631 sq mi). Population (1983 est): 5 115 000. Capital and main port: Copenhagen.

Denning, Alfred Thompson, Baron (1899–) British jurist. A High Court judge from 1944 and Master of the Rolls (1962–82), he headed (1963) the enquiry into the resignation of John *Profumo. His books include *The Changing Law* (1953) and *The Family Story* (1981).

density The mass of unit volume of a substance. In *SI units it is measured in kilograms per cubic metre; in these units water has a density of 1000 kg m^{-3}. **Relative density** (formerly called "specific gravity") is the density of a substance divided by the density of water at 4°C. This value is numerically one thousandth of the density. In the c.g.s. system, density (in grams per cubic centimetre) is numerically equal to relative density. The density of a gas (vapour density) is often expressed as the mass of unit volume of the gas divided by the mass of the same volume of hydrogen at standard temperature and pressure.

dentistry The branch of medical science concerned with the care of the teeth, gums, and mouth. The first dental school was established in the USA, in Philadelphia, in 1840; the first European school was the Royal Dental Hospital, founded in London in 1858. Restorative dentistry is concerned with the repair of teeth damaged by *caries and the replacement of teeth lost through injury or extraction. Orthodontics deals with the correction of badly positioned teeth, usually by means of braces or other appliances but sometimes by surgery on the jaw. Periodontics includes the care of the gums and other structures supporting the teeth and the treatment of ·*periodontal disease. Oral surgery deals with the extraction of teeth and the surgical repair of fractures or abnormalities of the jaws and facial bones. Preventive dentistry is concerned with preventing tooth decay and gum disease by such measures as education in oral hygiene and *fluoridation of the public water supply.

Dent du Midi 46 11N 6 55E A massif in SW Switzerland, in the Alps. It rises to 3259 m (10 692 ft) at Haute Cime.

Denver 39 45N 105 00W A city in the USA, the capital of Colorado on the South Platte River. Founded in 1858 during the Colorado gold rush, Denver is the financial, administrative, and industrial centre for a large agricultural area. A US Mint is sited here and it is within easy reach of 12 national parks. Population (1980): 491 396.

deodar A *cedar, *Cedrus deodara*, native to the Himalayas, where it forms vast forests, and widely planted for ornament in temperate regions and for timber in S Europe. Reaching a height of 75 m in the wild, it has young branches that droop down and large barrel-shaped cones, up to 14 cm long.

d'Éon, Charles de Beaumont, Chevalier (1728–1810) French secret agent in the service of *Louis XV. His fondness for wearing women's clothes, both as a disguise and in normal life, led to wagers in society about his actual sex. He did nothing to prevent such speculation, which continued until the autopsy after his death in London.

deontology A system of *ethics in which duty, rather than rights, virtue, or happiness, is fundamental to morality. It was the title of a book by *Bentham. *Compare* teleology.

deoxyribonucleic acid. *See* DNA.

depreciation The loss in value of capital goods as a result of wear and tear, obsolescence, etc. For example, a machine that costs £10,000 and is expected to last ten years depreciates at the rate of £1,000 a year. To keep its stock of capital goods, therefore, a firm must set aside a certain sum each year to account for depreciation. The calculation of the depreciation provision is sometimes complicated by the difficulty in judging the life of a machine: changes in taste or technological developments may shorten the useful life of a machine. To encourage firms to maintain their capital stock, governments usually allow for depreciation when calculating corporation tax.

depression (economics) A period during the *trade cycle in which demand is low compared to industry's capacity to satisfy it. Profits, and therefore confidence and investment, are also correspondingly low (*see* accelerator principle). A depression is also characterized by high unemployment, as occurred in the 1930s (*see* Depression). The influence of the British economist J. M. *Keynes has led governments since World War II to adopt *deficit financing policies to counter depressions, but the advent in the 1970s of the previously unknown combination of depression and *inflation has led to a revival of interest in the rival doctrine of *monetarism. A depression is also called a slump.

depression (meteorology) A *cyclone in the midlatitudes; also called a low or a disturbance. Frequently accompanied by *fronts, depressions move towards the NE in the N hemisphere and towards the SE in the S hemisphere. They are characterized by unsettled weather and are the main source of rainfall in the lowland areas of the midlatitudes.

depression (psychiatry) Severe and persistent misery. It can be a normal reaction to distressing events, such as bereavement (reactive depression). Sometimes, however, it is out of all proportion to the situation or may have no apparent external cause (endogenous depression): it can then be a sign of mental illness. In *manic-depressive psychosis the depression is severe and leads the sufferer to despairing and guilty beliefs and even to delusions of being evil and worthless; sleep, appetite, and concentration can all be disturbed. In depressive neurosis the symptoms are less extreme but may still lead to *suicide. Treatment with *antidepressant drugs is often effective and psychotherapy is helpful. Severe cases may need *electroconvulsive therapy.

Depression The period, also called the Slump, during the early 1930s, when worldwide economic collapse precipitated commercial failure and mass unemployment. Starting in the USA in 1929, when share prices fell so disastrously that thousands were made bankrupt (☐Wall Street), the Depression caused international repercussions. Overseas trade almost ceased, industrial production dropped, millions in industrialized countries were unemployed, and agricultural countries were impoverished. Roosevelt's *New Deal (1934) brought Americans hope of recovery, but Britain, despite abandoning free trade to protect its industries, never regained its commercial pre-eminence. In Germany the Depression contributed to the rise of Hitler's Nazi movement.

Depretis, Agostino (1813–87) Italian statesman; prime minister (1876–78, 1878–79, 1881–87). At first a supporter of *Mazzini and opponent of *Cavour, Depretis became converted to constitutional monarchism in 1861. He headed several coalitions of moderate Left elements in parliament. His foreign policy contributed to the formation of the 1882 *Triple Alliance of Italy, Austria-Hungary, and Germany.

Deptford A district in the Greater London borough of Lewisham, on the S bank of the River Thames. It was the site of a Royal Naval dockyard (1513–1869).

De Quincey, Thomas (1785–1859) British essayist and critic. In 1802 he ran away from his Manchester business family to Wales and then London, where he lived with a young prostitute called Ann. He then studied at Oxford; there he took opium for toothache and became addicted for life. He lived largely by journalism, writing numerous essays on diverse subjects.

Among his friends were *Wordsworth and *Coleridge. His *Confessions of an English Opium Eater* first appeared in 1822 and was revised in 1856.

Derain, André (1880–1954) French postimpressionist painter. In his bold designs and vibrant colours, particularly in his Thames paintings (1905–06), he was initially a leading exponent of *fauvism, but after 1907 he came under the influence of *Cézanne and painted in a cubist manner. He later reverted to a traditional style after an intensive study of the Old Masters. He produced some notable scenery and costume designs for Diaghilev's *Ballets Russes.

Derby A flat race for three-year-old horses, run over 2.4 km (1.5 mi) at Epsom in early June. The most prestigious of the English Classics, it was instituted (1780) by the 12th Earl of Derby.

Derby 52 55N 1 30W A city in central England, in Derbyshire on the River Derwent. Its growth as a manufacturing centre began in the late 17th century; the first silk mill in England was established here in 1719 and by the 18th century Derby had become a centre of porcelain manufacture. All Saints Church (rebuilt in the 18th century) became the cathedral of the new diocese of Derby in 1927. Today Derby is an important engineering centre (with Rolls-Royce aero engines) and has large railway workshops. Fine porcelain (*see* Derby ware), electrical equipment, paints, and textiles are manufactured. Population (1985 est): 215 000.

Derby, Edward (George Geoffrey Smith) Stanley, 4th Earl of (1799–1869) British statesman; Conservative prime minister (1852, 1858–59 1866–68). A noted orator, he became leader of the Conservative Party after the defection (1846) of the Peelites over the *Corn Laws. His government's achievements included the Jewish Relief Act (1858) and the *Reform Act (1867).

Derbyshire A county in N central England. Under local government reorganization in 1974 it lost part of the NE to South Yorkshire, while gaining part of NE Cheshire. It consists of lowlands in the SE rising to the uplands of the *Peak District in the NW. The main rivers are the Derwent, Trent, Dove, and Rother. Sheep farming is important in the N, while dairy farming predominates in the southern lowlands. The varied industrial activity is centred on the coalfield in the E and SW. Area: 2631 sq km (1016 sq mi). Population (1983): 911 100. Administrative centre: Matlock.

Derby ware Porcelain first produced by William Duesbury (1725–86) at Derby in the 1750s. Early manufactures resemble *Chelsea porcelain and Duesbury later bought the Chelsea works (1770). Utility products were decorated in bold blue, red, and gilt "Japan" patterns, but important portrait and fictional figures were also made in quantity. Leading artists decorated the fine dessert services with landscapes and specimen flora.

dermatitis Inflammation of the skin (the term eczema is often used synonymously with dermatitis). The patient has an itching red rash that may become scaly. Dermatitis may result from contact with irritant or allergy-provoking substances, infections, drugs, or radiation (particularly sunlight) or it may occur without obvious cause. Treatment is aimed at removing the cause and easing the condition with creams.

dermatology. *See* skin.

Dermot MacMurrough (?1110–71) King of Leinster. After being defeated by rival kings and banished (1166) from Ireland, he obtained aid from the English and with their support regained his kingdom in 1169–70. He has been unpopular with Irish nationalists ever since, for introducing the English into Ireland.

dernier A unit of weight, used to measure the fineness of woven materials, equal to 1 gram per 9000 metres.

Derris A genus of tropical woody vines (80 species), especially *D. elliptica* of the East Indies, the roots of which contain rotenone, a useful insecticide. Family: *Leguminosae*.

dervishes Members of Sufi religious brotherhoods (*see* Sufism), which hold various esoteric beliefs and have spread throughout Islam since the 12th century AD. Many of them perform ecstatic rituals, such as hypnotic chanting and whirling dancing, at prayer meetings (called *zikrs*). The dervishes of the Mevlevi order, founded in Anatolia (Turkey) in the 13th century, are famous for their dancing and are commonly called "whirling dervishes."

Derwent, River The name of several rivers in England, including: **1.** A river in N central England, flowing SE from N Derbyshire to the River Trent. Length: 96 km (60 mi). **2.** A river in N England, flowing S from the North York Moors to join the River Ouse between Selby and Goole. Length: 92 km (57 mi). **3.** A river in NW England, flowing N and W from the Borrowdale Fells in Cumbria to the Irish Sea. Length: 54 km (34 mi).

Derwent Water A lake in NW England, in Cumbria in the Lake District. A popular tourist area, it is noted for its picturesque scenery. Area: about 8 sq km (3 sq mi).

Desai, (Shri) Morarji (Ranchhodji) (1896–) Indian statesman; prime minister from 1977 until his resignation in 1979. As a young man he was a follower of Mahatma *Gandhi. Later, in the Congress Party, he came to oppose Indira Gandhi and during the state of emergency declared during her first administration he was imprisoned. In the 1977 elections he defeated her to become prime minister as leader of the new Janata Party.

DESALINATION *The initial and final salinities for various desalination techniques and feed-water sources.*

desalination The removal of salt from brine to produce fresh water. Desalination is used to irrigate arid regions in which sea water is available, especially if solar power can be used as an energy source. Several methods are employed, the most common being evaporation of the sea water by heat or by reducing the pressure on it (flash evaporation). The vapour is condensed to form relatively pure water. Freezing is another technique; pure ice forms from brine as it freezes. The method theoretically requires less energy than evaporation but the process is slower and technically more difficult. Reverse *osmosis is another method used. Pure water and salt water are contained on either side of a permeable membrane. The pressure of the salt water is raised above the osmotic pressure, causing water to pass from the brine to the pure side. Because the osmotic pressure required is about 25 atmospheres there are difficulties with large-scale application. In electrodialysis, the ions are subjected to an electric field instead of increased pressure, the positive and negative ions being filtered off through separate membranes. Another method used for low salinities is ion exchange; in this method the salt ions are chemically removed from the solution.

Descartes, René (1596–1650) French philosopher, one of the most original thinkers of all time. After a Jesuit education he spent nine years in travel and military service before turning to study. After 1628 he settled in Holland, where he lived until 1649, when Queen Christina invited him to Sweden. Here the cold climate and predawn tutorials with the queen caused a fatal attack of pneumonia.

Descartes' *Discourse on Method* (1637) introduced his technique of methodical doubt, which he developed in his greatest work the *Meditations* (1641). Asking "How and what do I know?" he arrived by a process of reduction at his famous statement "Cogito ergo sum" ("I think, therefore I am"). From this core of certainty he proceeded to prove to his own satisfaction God's existence (he was a sincere and lifelong Roman Catholic) and hence the existence of everything else. The importance of this approach lies not in what he proves or discards but in making *epistemology the gateway to knowledge. Equally influential was his dualism: he considered that the world was composed of two different kinds of substance—mind (*res cogitans*), which is the essence of human beings, and matter (*res extensa*). Descartes never satisfactorily answered the problem he thus set of how mind and matter can interact—nor has anyone else.

A distinguished mathematician and scientist, Descartes also contributed to the foundations of geometry (*see* coordinate systems) and optics. He held that mathematics was the supreme science in that the whole phenomenal world could be interpreted in terms of mathematical laws. He avoided confrontation with the Church by hiving off the realm of mathematics from that of theology and by cautiously suppressing his acceptance of the correctness of the Copernican system (*see* Copernicus).

descent The social recognition of biological relationship to a common ancestor. All societies limit the extent to which such relationships are traced but to differing degrees and in different ways. In many primitive societies the descent system is the basis of group membership, property and other rights, and social status. Unilineal systems count descent in one line only and are termed patrilineal or agnatic when this is through males and matrilineal or uxorial when through females. Double unilineal systems count both lines but for distinct purposes. Cognatic systems, usually found in more advanced societies, count descent in either line.

desensitization In immunology, a method of treating some *allergies, such as hay fever. Small amounts of the substance (allergen) that provokes the symptoms of the allergy are injected at intervals. This stimulates the production of *antibodies in the blood that will combine with the allergen during subsequent exposure and prevent it from reacting with a different set of antibodies, attached to certain cells, to cause the allergic symptoms.

desert A virtually barren area of land where precipitation is minimal and sporadic, limiting vegetation growth. The mean annual rainfall is usually taken as being below 250 mm (10 in) for desert conditions to exist. Deserts may occur in areas of high atmospheric pressure, such as the *Sahara, or near the W coast of continents cooled by cold ocean currents (e.g. the *Atacama and *Kalahari Deserts). They are also found in continental interiors where mountain barriers restrict precipitation, such as the *Gobi Desert. Many deserts are characterized by stony scrublands with occasional resistant rock uplands and some areas of shifting sand dunes. The wind is an important agent of erosion and the rain, falling as violent downpours, is capable of moving large amounts of debris.

Desert cultures A group of Stone Age North American cultures in Nevada, Utah, Arizona, and New Mexico dating from the period 8000–2000 BC. Adapted to arid or semiarid conditions, they were based upon hunting small game and gathering wild plant foods in small nomadic groups. Baskets, milling stones, bone tools, and chipped stone weapon points were made.

DESERTIFICATION *Overcutting of firewood is a major cause of desertification. For these people in the Sahel in Africa it is harder to find wood to put under the pot than to find food to cook in it.*

desertification The process by which arid or semiarid areas become deserts through human action or climatic change. Removal of the topsoil, by artificial means or erosion by wind, water, or desiccation, results in a reduction in the ground's water-storage capacity, which can cause crops to fail and famine. Overintensive farming and the cutting of trees for firewood helped to create the *Dust Bowl in the USA and have caused deserts in Africa (recently in areas of Ethiopia) and SW Asia to advance by several kilometres each year. Solutions are now based on effective management of surface cover and climate.

desert rat. *See* jerboa.

De Sica, Vittorio (1901–74) Italian film director. He started his career as an actor and began directing in 1940. His postwar films, in which he treated contemporary social themes with compassion and political awareness, included *Shoeshine* (1946), *Bicycle Thieves* (1948), and *Umberto D* (1952). His later films included several romantic comedies.

Desiderio da Settignano (c. 1430–64) Italian Renaissance sculptor. Working chiefly in Florence, he specialized in marble portrait busts. His tomb for the humanist Carlo Marsuppini (Sta Croce, Florence) is renowned.

desman A small aquatic mammal belonging to the family *Talpidae* (moles). The Russian desman (*Desmana moschata*) is about 20 cm long; the Pyrenean desman (*Galemys pyrenaicus*) is smaller. They have webbed hind feet, live in burrows in river banks, and feed on invertebrates and fish.

Des Moines 41 35N 93 35W A city in the USA, the capital of Iowa. Founded in 1843, it has developed into an important industrial and commercial centre situated in the heart of the Corn Belt. Many insurance companies have their headquarters here. Population (1980): 371 800.

Desmond, Gerald Fitzgerald, 15th Earl of (c.1538–1583) Anglo-Irish magnate, who opposed the imposition of English authority on Ireland. Periodically imprisoned in the 1560s and 1570s, his 1579 rebellion led to his being outlawed. He was captured and killed. His confiscated estates formed the basis of the Munster *Plantation.

Desmoulins, Camille (1760–94) French revolutionary and journalist. His fiery oratory contributed to the storming of the *Bastille (14 July, 1789), and in 1792 he became an unremitting critic of the Girondins. Subsequently counselling moderation, he was arrested with the followers of *Danton in 1794 and guillotined. His best-known work is his *Histoire des Brissotins* (1793).

des Prez, Josquin. *See* Josquin des Prez.

Dessalines, Jean Jacques (c. 1758–1806) Emperor of Haiti (1804–06). He rose to military pre-eminence in the slave revolt led by *Toussaint-L'Ouverture. When Toussaint was captured by the French in 1802 Dessalines assumed the leadership of the Haitians and with British help defeated the French (1803). His habitual cruelty as emperor provoked a palace revolution, during which he was assassinated.

Dessau 51 41N 12 14E A city in W central East Germany, on the River Mulde near its confluence with the River Elbe. Dessau was the former capital of Anhalt state. Many of its historic buildings were destroyed during World War II. Production of armaments, vehicles, and machinery are the main industries. Population (1980 est): 101 969.

destroyer A fast heavily armed naval vessel that is smaller than a *cruiser, has a displacement of about 3000 tonnes, and is 110–150 m (330–450 ft) long. Destroyers are not armoured. Because of their speed, armament, and versatility, they are employed in antisubmarine warfare, in convoy work, and in "hunter-killer" attack groups consisting of one carrier and five or six destroyers.

destroyer escort A smaller lighter somewhat more manoeuvrable version of the *destroyer, developed during World War II mainly as protection for convoys.

Destutt, Antoine Louis Claude, Comte de Tracy (1754–1836) French philosopher and politician. He narrowly escaped the guillotine during the French Revolution. In prison he planned his *Éléments d'idéologie* (1801–15), in which, inspired by *Locke and *Condillac, he derives all thought from sensory "ideas" and their combinations.

detached retina A condition in which the retina–a layer of specialized light-sensitive cells at the back of the eye–becomes separated from the layer beneath it (the choroid). It happens slowly and painlessly and the patient loses part of his vision. It is caused by injury to the eye or inflammation in the eye and is most common in very short-sighted people. Detached retina is treated surgically, sometimes using a laser beam to weld the retina in place.

detective story A genre of popular fiction in which a mystery, often a murder, is solved by logic and intuition, usually by an individual detective. Ancient Chinese literature had a rich detective tradition, but in the modern West the first true detective story is probably *Poe's "Murders in the Rue Morgue" (1841). The form was popularized in England by Wilkie *Collins's *The Moonstone* (1868) and the appearance of Sir Arthur Conan *Doyle's detective Sherlock Holmes. The English tradition is typified by Agatha *Christie and Dorothy L. *Sayers, whose first books appeared in the 1920s. In the 1930s the tersely realistic "thrillers" of the US writers Dashiell *Hammett and Raymond *Chandler began a different trend. Among the best writers of the genre are John Dickson Carr, Ellery Queen, Rex Stout, Josephine Tey, Michael Innes, and R. van Gulik. G. K. *Chesterton, "Nicholas Blake" (C. *Day Lewis), Nicholas Freeling, and Georges *Simenon, among others, have raised it far above a merely popular level.

detergents Chemicals used for cleansing. Although the term includes *soaps it is usually applied in a more restricted sense to synthetic *surfactants. Such detergents have large molecules, typically composed of a hydrocarbon oil-soluble part and a water-soluble part. Alkyl sulphonates are common examples. These compounds are thus able to promote the solution of oil, grease, etc., in water. Household detergents contain other ingredients, including builders, water softeners, bleaches, and fabric brighteners.

determinant. *See* matrix.

determinism The philosophical theory that every event has a cause and that all events are determined by causal physical laws. One view holds that determinism means that every event could be causally explained and could be predicted if the conditions are not too complex for analysis. A stronger view is that a specific event could not have failed to happen, or was predetermined. Applied to human actions, determinism appears to conflict with the concept of *free will. If even desires, intentions, and motives are determined or conditioned (as some psychologists believe) and if actions are, in principle, predictable, this contradicts the idea that actions are freely chosen, and hence the concept of moral responsibility. However, some philosophers believe that determinism and free will are compatible and that a person acts freely if his desires are the cause of his actions. *See also* predestination.

Detmold 51 56N 08 52E A town in NW West Germany, in North Rhine-Westphalia. The capital of the former state of Lippe, it has two palaces. German tribes defeated the Romans here in 9 AD. It has furniture and metallurgical industries. Population (1984 est): 67 850.

detonator A sensitive primary explosive used to ignite a less sensitive high explosive. Detonators may be initiated by percussion, flash, or electrical current. The less sensitive and safer the high explosive is to handle, the stronger the detonator required. Some high explosives require two-stage detonation. A common detonator is mercury fulminate.

Detroit 42 23N 83 05W A city in the USA, in Michigan on the Detroit River. Founded in 1701, it was largely rebuilt following a fire in 1805. The fifth largest city in the USA, it is dominated by the motor-vehicle industry, with General Motors, Ford, and Chrysler factories comprising 7100 industrial plants. A major port (serving the Great Lakes) and rail centre, its other industries include chemicals, steel, and oil refining. It is the home of the University of Detroit (1911) and Wayne State University (1933). Population (1984): 1 100 000.

Dettifoss 65 49N 16 25W A waterfall in NE Iceland, on the River Jökulsa à Fjöllum. It has great hydroelectric-power potential.

Deucalion In Greek legend, the son of Prometheus and father of Hellen, the ancestor of the Greek race. Warned of the flood sent by Zeus to destroy mankind, he and his wife Pyrrha survived on a boat and repopulated the earth.

Deus, João de (1830-96) Portuguese poet. His first book, *Flores do campo* (1868), was praised for its simplicity and directness; after the publication of *Campo de flores* (1893) he was acclaimed as the leading poet of his generation. His advanced method of teaching reading was officially adopted in 1888.

deus ex machina (Latin: god from the machinery) A sudden and improbable resolution of an involved situation. The term refers to the convention in ancient Greek drama in which a god was lowered by a crane to conclude a plot.

deuterium (D; *or* heavy hydrogen ^{2}H) An *isotope of *hydrogen having a nucleus consisting of one proton and one neutron. It occurs naturally in hydrogen to an extent of about 0.0156%. It can be separated from the more common isotope by electrolysis of water. It is used as a radioactive tracer. Heavy water (deuterium oxide; D_2O) is used in *nuclear reactors as a moderator. *See also* thermonuclear reactor. At no 1; at wt 2.014.

Deuteronomy The fifth book of the Old Testament, attributed to Moses, although this is widely disputed; it may have been compiled in the 7th century BC. It is a series of addresses by Moses to the Israelites immediately before the occupation of the Promised Land of Canaan (Palestine). After repeating the *Ten Commandments, he exhorts the people to live differently from the surrounding nations, gives a code of religious and civil laws to be observed in Canaan, blesses those who keep the *covenant and curses those who disobey the Law, appoints Joshua as his successor, and gives custody of the book of the Law to the *Levites. The book closes with the song of Moses, his blessing of the people, and an appendix recording his death.

De Valera, Eamon (1882-1975) Irish statesman; prime minister (1932-48, 1951-54, 1957-59) and president (1959-73). A commandant in the 1916 *Easter Rising, he nevertheless escaped execution and in 1917 was elected to the British parliament and became the president of *Sinn Féin. From 1919 to 1922 he was president of the newly declared Irish Republic but rejected the terms of the Anglo-Irish treaty of 1921 (*see* Home Rule). In 1926 he founded *Fianna Fáil.

de Valois, Dame Ninette (Edris Stannus; 1898-) British ballet dancer and choreographer, born in Ireland. During the 1920s she worked with Diaghilev's Ballets Russes. In 1931 she founded the Sadler's Wells Ballet, the company that became the *Royal Ballet in 1956 and that she directed until she retired in 1963.

devaluation A downward change in the value of one country's currency in terms of other currencies. A country that devalues makes its exports cheaper and its imports more expensive; thus devaluation should help correct a *balance-of-payments deficit by increasing the volume of exports and decreasing the volume of imports. The measure is not always effective, however, because the increased import bill may be larger than the increase in receipts from exports: this is likely if the *demand for the country's exports is elastic, while demand for the imports is inelastic. Under the Bretton Woods fixed-rate system (*see* Bretton Woods Conference) devaluations, such as that undertaken by the UK in 1967, only occurred occasionally but were large and destabilizing. In the floating-rate system that replaced it, the value of a currency in terms of others is determined by supply and demand with a minimum of government interference; as a consequence devaluations are gradual.

Devanagari An alphabetic *writing system used for *Sanskrit, *Hindi, and certain other languages of India. It has 48 letters and is written from left to right. Vowels are frequently omitted in Devanagari, a short *a* being understood after each consonant unless a different vowel is specified. It was developed from the ancient Brahmi script, which was probably derived from Aramaic in the 7th or 8th century BC. It is therefore historically related to the Hebrew, Arabic, Greek, and Roman alphabets.

developing countries Countries that do not have sophisticated industries and consequently have a low per capita income. They include almost all the countries in Africa, Asia, and South America. The economies of these so-called Third World countries are characterized by abundant cheap unskilled labour and a scarcity of capital for investment. Some observers consider the marked difference in incomes between the industrial and the developing nations (the "north-south split") to be politically as important as the division between *communism and *capitalism (the "east-west split"). Some 70% of the world's population lives in developing countries in largely agricultural economies from which poverty, hunger, disease, and illiteracy have not been eliminated, despite the efforts of various UN agencies. Many of these economies rely shakily on one main crop, which in years of crop failure, poor world demand, or low market prices can cause severe hardship.

Deventer 52 16N 6 10E A town in the E central Netherlands, in Overijssel province on the River IJssel. During the middle ages it was a major educational centre; Erasmus and Thomas à Kempis studied here. Population (1981 est): 64 824.

Devil. *See* Lucifer.

devil ray. *See* manta ray.

devil's coach horse A large carnivorous beetle, *Staphylinus olens*, also called a cock-tail. It is about 25 mm long and occurs commonly in gardens of W Europe. If threatened it curls its flexible abdomen upward and forward and releases an offensive odour. Family: *Staphylinidae* (*see* rove beetle).

Devil's Island (French name: Île du Diable) 5 16N 52 34W One of the three Îles du Salut, off the coast of French

Guiana in the S Caribbean Sea. It contained a convict's leper colony before becoming a French penal settlement (1895-1938). Area: less than 2 sq km (1 sq mi).

Devine, George (1910-65) British theatre manager, director, and actor. He taught at the London Theatre Studio from 1936 to 1939, and, after World War II, was director of the Young Vic Company. In 1956 he founded the English Stage Company and he directed and performed in many of its influential productions of plays by new writers at the Royal Court Theatre in London.

Devizes 51 22N 1 59W A market town in S England, in Wiltshire. Its 12th-century castle was destroyed by Cromwell. The main industries are agricultural: bacon and ham curing and dairy products. Population (1982 est): 12 750.

devolution The delegation of political powers from a central government to regional governments. In the UK the establishment of the *Stormont parliament in Northern Ireland was the first important act of devolution. Growing nationalist sentiment in Scotland and Wales led to the introduction of two devolution bills in the House of Commons in November, 1976; in March, 1979, referenda were held in these countries on the bills' final provisions. In Wales there was an absolute majority against the devolution plans; in Scotland a small majority favoured them but the vote in favour of devolution fell short of the 40% of the electorate needed to put the plans into effect.

Devolution, War of (1667-68) The conflict between France and Spain for possession of the Spanish Netherlands, which *Louis XIV of France claimed had devolved (descended) to him through his wife Maria Theresa, daughter of Philip IV of Spain (1605-65; reigned 1621-65). Louis' troops, under *Turenne and *Vauban, invaded the Netherlands but were withdrawn when an alliance between England, the United Provinces of the Netherlands, and Sweden threatened to intervene against the French. Peace was made at Aix-la-Chapelle.

Devon A county of SW England, bordering on the Atlantic Ocean in the N and the English Channel in the S. It consists mainly of the mid-Devon plain, rising to *Dartmoor in the SW and *Exmoor in the NE. The chief rivers are the Dart, Exe, and Tamar. Agricultural activities include dairy farming in the S and E (producing the famous clotted cream), beef cattle in the N and W, and sheep farming in the NE. Some cider is produced on farms but most now comes from factories. Industry is concentrated around Exeter and Plymouth, a major naval base. There is a thriving tourist industry centred on the coastal resorts, especially Torquay, Paignton, and Ilfracombe. Area: 6715 sq km (2591 sq mi). Population (1984 est): 973 000. Administrative centre: Exeter.

Devonian period A geological period of the Upper Palaeozoic era, between the Silurian and Carboniferous periods. It lasted from about 415 to 370 million years ago. It is divided into seven stages, based on invertebrate fossil remains, such as corals, brachiopods, ammonoids, and crinoids. The rocks containing these fossils were marine deposits but the Devonian period also shows extensive continental deposits (Old Red Sandstone). Fossils from these rocks include fish, land plants, and freshwater molluscs.

Devonshire, Spencer Compton Cavendish, 8th Duke of (1833-1908) British Liberal politician, known from 1858 to 1891 as Lord Hartington. Postmaster general in Gladstone's 1868-74 ministry, Hartington led the Liberals during Gladstone's temporary retirement (1874-80). In 1882 he became secretary for war, failing to persuade the cabinet to relieve *Kitchener in Khartoum. He opposed Irish *Home Rule, leaving the Liberal Party to form the Liberal Unionist Party, which defeated Gladstone's Home Rule bills (1886, 1893). He subsequently served in Lord Salisbury's coalition ministry (1895-1902) and under Balfour (1902-05).

de Vries, Hugo Marie (1848-1935) Dutch botanist, who first recognized the importance of *mutation. De Vries observed how, occasionally, a new variety would arise from his plant-breeding experiments. He realized that this sudden variation, which he termed mutation, could play an important part in the evolution of living things. De Vries worked out his own laws of inheritance only to discover, in 1900, *Mendel's original work, which had previously been ignored.

dew The condensation of moisture, which forms on the ground or on objects near the ground, especially at night. It occurs when the cool air near the ground falls to a temperature, called the **dew point**, at which it becomes saturated and the water vapour present condenses into water droplets. The ideal conditions for dew formation are calm weather with a clear sky.

Dewar flask A flask, used to store a substance at constant temperature. It has double glass walls, the space between the walls being evacuated to prevent heat loss by conduction. The inside wall is silvered to prevent heat loss by radiation and the flask is tightly stoppered to prevent heat loss by convection or evaporation. Also known as the Thermos or vacuum flask, it was invented by the Scottish scientist Sir James Dewar (1842-1923).

dewberry A straggling Eurasian shrub, *Rubus caesius*, very similar to the *blackberry but with weaker creeping stems and fewer prickles. The fruit has fewer berries per head and a purplish bloom. The name is also applied to many North American *Rubus* species that trail along the ground. Family: *Rosaceae*.

de Wet, Christian Rudolf (1854-1922) Afrikaner politician and soldier. De Wet commanded the Orange Free State forces in the second *Boer War, organizing the guerrilla tactics that were initially so successful. He was later minister of agriculture in the Orange Free State (1907-10). In 1914 he led a revolt against Botha's plan to conquer German South West Africa and was imprisoned for treason.

Dewey, George (1837-1917) US admiral. He first saw action in the Civil War. During the Spanish-American War (1898) he defeated the Spanish fleet in Manila Bay with few casualties among his own force.

Dewey, John (1859-1952) US philosopher and educationalist. A prominent exponent of *pragmatism, Dewey believed thinking arises where practical problems arise. In works such as *Reconstruction in Philosophy* (1920) he urged the reconstitution of philosophy to confront present experience and produce appropriately new solutions and beliefs. He held that theorizing was, properly, instrumental in problem-solving—hence the term "instrumentalism," applied to his philosophy; education had concentrated on past experience instead of equipping students to deal with present and future.

Dewey Decimal Classification An international system for classifying and arranging the books in a library, originated in 1873 by the US librarian Melvil Dewey (1851-1931) for the Amherst College Library. Books are divided according to subject matter into ten groups, each group having a hundred numbers; principle subdivisions within each group are divided by ten, and with the use of decimal numbers further subdivisions can be generated without limit (e.g. 300: Social Sciences; 370: Education; 372: Elementary Education; 372.3: Elementary Education, Science and Health). The system is being constantly revised and is now in its 18th edition. *See also* Universal Decimal Classification.

De Wint, Peter (1784-1849) British landscape painter of Dutch descent. One of the leading watercolourists of his day, he trained under the London painter and engraver John Raphael Smith (1752-1812) and was influenced by *Girtin. Many of his landscapes are of Lincolnshire.

Dewsbury 53 42N 1 37W A town in N England, in West Yorkshire on the River Calder. It is a centre of the heavy-woollen industry, specializing in processing shoddy. Population (1981): 48 339.

dextrose. *See* glucose.

Dhahran 26 18N 50 05E A new town in E Saudi Arabia, on the Persian Gulf coast opposite Bahrain. It ships out oil brought by pipeline from the Abqaiq area just inland.

Dhaka. *See* Dacca.

dharma A Sanskrit term with various religious and philosophical meanings. In Buddhism it signifies the truth, the teaching of the Buddha in whole or in part. It also denotes the law regarding the ultimate nature of things. In Hinduism, it refers to social law or caste duty.

Dharmashastra Traditional Indian lawbooks, still in force. Written in Sanskrit, they comprise some 5000 works, compilations of maxims, treatises, and commentaries. Their composition extended from the 8th century BC to the 19th century AD and is said to be based on the *Vedas. Their emphasis is on outlining the ethical behaviour proper to one's caste in any given situation, rather than pronouncing definitive legislation; when properly applied, however, they did act as a valid legal system. British influence hardened and regularized the application of the law and introduced the concept of legal precedent. Since 1955 conventional legislation has been introduced to modify the dharmashastra law as applied by the courts and its importance is diminishing.

Dhaulagiri, Mount 28 39N 83 28E A mountain in NW central Nepal, in the Himalayas. It was first climbed in 1960 by a Swiss team. Height: 8172 m (26 810 ft).

dhole A wild *dog, *Cuon alpinus*, of SE Asia, Sumatra, and Java. Dholes are reddish brown, about 1.4 m long including the tail (40 cm); they hunt in packs of 5–40 individuals, attacking mainly deer and antelope but occasionally tigers.

diabetes One of several diseases with a common symptom—the production of large quantities of urine. The term usually refers to **diabetes mellitus** (*or* sugar diabetes), in which the body is unable to utilize sugars to produce energy due to a deficiency of the pancreatic hormone *insulin. Symptoms include thirst, weight loss, and a high level of glucose in the urine and in the blood (hyperglycaemia), which—if untreated—leads to coma. Possible long-term complications of diabetes include damage to the arteries, especially in the eyes (which can affect vision). There appears to be a certain tendency to inherit diabetes, which is often triggered by such factors as physical stress. In children the disease appears more suddenly and is usually more severe than in older people. Treatment is based on a carefully controlled diet, often with insulin injections or pills to reduce the amount of sugar in the blood.

Diabetes insipidus is a rare disease due to a deficiency of the pituitary hormone vasopressin, which regulates water balance in the body. The patient produces large quantities of watery urine and is always thirsty. It is treated with doses of the hormone.

Diaghilev, Sergei (Pavlovich) (1872–1929) Russian ballet impresario. He began his career in the imperial theatres in St Petersburg in 1899 and between 1904 and 1908 organized several art exhibitions there and in Paris. His first theatrical production, the opera *Boris Godunov*, staged at the Paris Opéra (1908), was followed by his season of Russian ballet (1909). Its outstanding success resulted in the organization of a permanent company (1911), known as the *Ballets Russes, which Diaghilev directed until his death. □Cocteau, Jean.

dialect The language of a particular district or group of people. The distinction between language and dialect is not clear cut. As a general rule any two dialects of a language may be expected to be mutually comprehensible. But, for example, the various "dialects" of Chinese are quite separate, being held together only by a common ideographic writing system, while Dutch, Flemish, and Afrikaans are called separate languages for political reasons, although

there is a considerable degree of mutual comprehensibility and they might therefore reasonably be regarded as different dialects of the same language. Dialects develop as a result of geographical separation: slightly differing versions of one original language develop in different places within a generation or so of the time of separation. Social factors also affect dialect development. In English, for example, the medieval dialect of London has developed into a socially prestigious class dialect spoken in most parts of Britain (*see* received pronunciation).

dialectical materialism The official philosophy of *Marxism. Materialism, as opposed to *idealism, Marx and Engels derived from contemporary (1850) science; dialectic, or argument from thesis and antithesis to synthesis, they borrowed from Hegel's idealism. Engels even proposed a dialectical theory of evolution. As philosophy, not surprisingly, dialectical materialism is obscure and apparently unrelated to Marxist political theory. However, **historical materialism**, expounded in the *Communist Manifesto*, is a coherent account of history on an economic basis: for every system of production there is an appropriate organization of class and property. While economic forces continually develop production systems, the class and property structure remains unchanged, causing tension between economic forces and social relations, which continues until the ultimate rational socialist society evolves.

dialysis A process, discovered by Thomas Graham (1804–69), for separating mixtures of fluids by diffusion through a semipermeable membrane. Different substances in a solution diffuse at different rates. The passage of large particles, such as *colloids, is almost completely blocked by a semipermeable membrane, whereas salt solutions pass through easily. The technique of dialysis is used in artificial kidney machines, or dialysers, which take over the function of diseased kidneys by filtering waste material from the blood but leaving behind proteins, blood cells, and other large particles.

diamagnetism A form of magnetism occurring in materials that when placed in a *magnetic field, have an internal field proportional to but less than that outside. Such substances tend to orientate themselves at right angles to the direction of the *flux and tend to move from the stronger part of a field to the weaker part. Diamagnetism is caused by the motion of atomic electrons, which, since they are charged, constitute a current. This current tends to oppose the magnetic field in accordance with *Lenz's law.

diamond The hardest known mineral, comprising a cubic variety of crystalline *carbon, formed under intense heat and pressure. Diamonds are found in ancient volcanic pipes, mainly in S Africa and Siberia, and in deposits off the coast of Namibia. Over 80% of diamonds mined are used industrially, mainly for cutting and grinding tools; the others are used as gems. The largest diamond yet discovered is the *Cullinan diamond (3106 carats), found in 1905 at Pretoria. Many industrial diamonds are produced synthetically from graphite subjected to very high temperatures and pressures (above 3000°C and 100 000 atmospheres). Birthstone for April. *See* Plate III.

diamondback The largest and most dangerous *rattlesnake. The eastern diamondback (*Crotalus adamanteus*) and the western diamondback (*C. atrox*) may reach lengths of 2.5 m.

diamondbird An Australasian *flowerpecker of the genus *Pardalotus* (7–8 species), about 8 cm long with a short tail and a white-spotted plumage. Unlike other flowerpeckers, diamondbirds feed on insects and nest in tree holes and rock crevices.

Diana The Roman goddess identified with the Greek Artemis, associated with women and childbirth and with the moon. She is usually represented as a virgin huntress armed with bow and arrows. The position of priest at her shrine of

Ariccia (Italy) was customarily held by a runaway slave, who murdered his predecessor.

Diane de Poitiers, Duchesse de Valentinois (1499–1566) The mistress of *Henry II of France, who was 20 years her junior. She dominated court life until his death in 1559, when she was forced by Henry's wife *Catherine de' Medici to retire to Chaumont.

Dianthus A genus of annual and perennial herbs (300 species), mainly from Europe and Asia, having flower stems (often branched) with swollen joints and showy white, pink, or red flowers. Common species include *D. barbatus* (*see* sweet william), *D. caryophyllus* (*see* carnation), and *D. plumarius* (*see* pink). Family: *Caryophyllaceae*.

diaphragm 1. In anatomy, a dome-shaped sheet of muscle that separates the thorax (chest cavity) from the abdomen. The diaphragm is attached to the spine, lower ribs, and breastbone and contains a large opening through which the oesophagus (gullet) passes. It plays an important role in producing breathing movements (*see* respiration). 2. *See* contraception.

diarrhoea The frequent passing of liquid stools, usually more than three a day. It is a symptom, not a disease; causes include anxiety, infection or inflammation of the intestines, impaired absorption of food, and side effects of drugs. It can be eased by the use of drugs but proper treatment must aim at eliminating the cause.

Dias, Bartolomeu (c. 1450–c. 1500) Portuguese navigator. In 1486, given command of three ships by John II, he set out to explore the coast of Africa. Blown by a storm round the Cape of Good Hope (which he himself named the Cape of Storms) he reached present-day Algoa Bay on the E coast of Africa but was forced by his unwilling crew to return. He was drowned near the Cape while accompanying *Cabral on the expedition that discovered Brazil.

diaspora (Greek: dispersion) The collective term for Jewish communities outside the land of Israel. Beginning with the *Babylonian exile (6th century BC), Jews spread to most parts of the world, while continuing to regard Israel as their homeland. The resulting tension between Israel and the diaspora has continued to the present day, the dispersion being viewed sometimes negatively, as exile, and sometimes positively. The most important centres of the diaspora were, in antiquity, Babylonia and Egypt; in the middle ages, Spain and France; and in early modern times, E Europe. In the late 19th century there was a massive exodus of Jews from Russia and Poland, and the Nazi *holocaust destroyed many old European communities. The main centre is now the USA, with some six million Jews.

diastole. *See* blood pressure; heart.

diastrophism The large-scale deformation of the earth's crust resulting in the major structural features of the earth's surface, such as the continents, ocean basins, mountain ranges, fault-lines, etc. It is now widely believed that *sea-floor spreading and the consequent movement of the rigid plates that form the earth's crust (*see* plate tectonics) are responsible for diastrophism.

diathermy The production of heat in the body's tissues by means of a high-frequency electric current passing between two electrodes applied to the patient's skin. It has been used to relieve deep-seated pain in rheumatic conditions. The principle has also been utilized in surgery, one electrode, in the form of a knife, snare, or needle, being used to coagulate blood and therefore seal off blood vessels during incisions or to destroy unwanted tissue.

diatoms Microscopic *yellow-green algae of the class *Bacillariophyceae* (about 16 000 species), occurring abundantly as single cells or colonies in fresh water and oceans (forming an important constituent of *plankton) and also in soil. They have silicon-rich cell walls (called frustules), often beautifully sculptured, composed of two halves that fit together like a pill box. Fossilized frustules form a porous

rock called diatomaceous earth (*or* kieselguhr), used in filters, insulators, abrasives, etc.

Díaz, Porfirio (1830–1915) Mexican soldier, who became president (1876–1911) following a coup. He ruled dictatorially, supported by conservative landowners and foreign capitalists. His promotion of economic development benefited only a small elite and no attention was paid to the needs of the Indians. He fled the country in 1911 in the face of a revolution led by Francisco Madero (1873–1913).

diazepam. *See* benzodiazepines.

Dibdin, Charles (1745–1814) British composer, actor, singer, author, publisher, and theatrical promoter. He was self-taught, apart from several years as chorister at Winchester Cathedral, and left a legacy of fine songs, including "Tom Bowling."

Dicentra A genus of annual and perennial herbaceous plants (about 300 species) from North America and E Asia, up to 90 cm high. They have divided compound leaves and sprays of hanging flowers that are flattened sideways, with the outer petals pouched and the inner ones joined at the tips. Many species are ornamentals (*see* bleeding heart; Dutchman's breeches). Family: *Fumariaceae*.

CHARLES DICKENS *The author with his daughters.*

Dickens, Charles (1812–70) British novelist. Son of a naval clerk, he worked in a blacking factory when his father was imprisoned for debt and later as a solicitor's clerk and court reporter. He began his writing career by contributing to popular magazines, achieving sudden fame with *The Pickwick Papers* (1837), which he followed with *Oliver Twist* (1838) and *Nicholas Nickleby* (1839) and the very successful *Old Curiosity Shop* (1840–41); like all his novels, these first appeared in monthly instalments. In the 1840s he travelled abroad, visiting America in 1842, and founded (1846) the liberal *Daily News* and two weekly miscellanies. *David Copperfield* (1849–50) was a strongly autobiographical work, portraying Dickens' father as the feckless Mr Micawber. His later novels, from *Bleak House* (1853) to the incomplete *Edwin Drood* (1870), were increasingly pessimistic in tone;

Great Expectations (1860-61) and *Our Mutual Friend* (1864-65), in their depiction of the destructive powers of money and ambition, develop most fully Dickens' radical view of society. Dickens' marriage was an unhappy one and in 1856 he and his wife agreed to separate. He formed a relationship with Ellen Ternan, a young actress. In 1858 he began his famous public readings from his work, the strain of which hastened his death.

Dickinson, Emily (1830-86) US poet. Daughter of a Calvinist lawyer, she lived a largely secluded life after the age of 30, with her family at Amherst, Massachusetts. She wrote numerous letters and over 1700 poems, mostly brief intense lyrics on themes of love, death, and nature; only seven were published during her lifetime.

dicotyledons The larger of the two main groups of flowering plants, which includes hardwood trees, shrubs, and many herbaceous plants (*compare* monocotyledons). Dicots are characterized by having two seed leaves (cotyledons) in the embryo. Typically the flower parts are arranged in fours or fives (or multiples of these) and the leaves have a netlike pattern of veins. *See also* angiosperms.

dictionaries. *See* lexicography.

Dicynodon A large herbivorous *therapsid (mammal-like) reptile that lived in the late Permian period, which ended 240 million years ago. It occurred worldwide in large numbers and had a long high-domed skull with a horny beaklike jaw and a single upper pair of teeth.

Diderot, Denis (1713-84) French philosopher and writer. With *Voltaire, Diderot helped create the *Enlightenment, mainly through the *Encyclopédie*, which he edited after 1750 (*see* Encyclopedists). Fascinated by science, he developed a form of *pantheism. His writings, notably *Lettre sur les aveugles* (1749), were materialistic and anti-Christian in tenor.

didgeridoo An aboriginal musical instrument, consisting of a wooden tube three to four feet long, sounded by blowing across one of the open ends. The other rests against a hole in the ground to increase resonance. It plays two notes: the fundamental, used to set up a basic rhythm, and a harmonic, used in counterrhythm against it.

Dido In Greek legend, the daughter of a king of Tyre, who fled to Africa when her husband was murdered; there she founded *Carthage. According to legend she burnt herself to death on a funeral pyre to avoid marriage to Iarvas of Numidia; in *Virgil's *Aeneid* she killed herself after being abandoned by her lover *Aeneas.

Diefenbaker, John G(eorge) (1895-1979) Canadian statesman; Progressive Conservative prime minister (1957-63). His party's victory in 1957 broke 22 years of Liberal government and in 1958 the Conservatives gained an overwhelming majority (208 out of 256 seats). He lost the 1963 election following opposition to proposals to build nuclear weapons in Canada and resigned the party leadership in 1967.

dielectric A substance that acts as an electrical *insulator and can sustain an electric field. When a voltage is applied across a perfect dielectric there is no energy loss and the electric field strength changes simultaneously with voltage. In the real dielectrics, such as air, ceramics, or wax, which are used in *capacitors, there is always a small energy loss.

dielectric constant. *See* permittivity.

Diels, Otto Paul Hermann (1876-1954) German chemist, who shared the 1950 Nobel Prize with Kurt Alder (1902-58) for their discovery of the **Diels-Alder reaction**, by which linear organic molecules are converted into cyclic molecules. The reaction is now widely used in the synthesis of alkaloids, polymers, etc.

Dieman, Anthony van (1593-1645) Dutch colonial administrator. As governor general of Batavia from 1636, he was responsible for the conquest of Malacca (1641) and parts of Ceylon (1644) important to the spice trade. He also commissioned *Tasman to explore the S Pacific in the interest of trade (1642, 1644), expeditions that discovered Van Dieman's Land (now Tasmania).

Dien Bien Phu, Battle of (March-May, 1954) The decisive battle of the Indochina war, in NE Vietnam, in which Vietnamese forces defeated the French. The collapse of the French fortress coincided with the Geneva Conference, which ended French control of Indochina.

Dieppe 49 55N 1 05E A port and resort in N France, in the Seine-Maritime department on the English Channel. Occupied by the English (1420-35), it became a Huguenot stronghold but declined in importance after the revocation of the Edict of Nantes. It was the scene of heavy fighting during World War II. Population (1982 est): 35 360.

Diesel engine. *See* internal-combustion engine.

diet, imperial. *See* Reichstag.

dietetics The study of the principles of nutrition and their application to the selection of appropriate diets both to maintain health and as part of the treatment of certain diseases. A balanced diet should contain foods with adequate amounts of all the nutrients—carbohydrates, fats, proteins, minerals, and vitamins—as well as foods with a high content of dietary *fibre. An important aspect of the work of dieticians is to work out the special diets that are required for various diseases. Diabetes mellitus, for instance, requires a diet low in carbohydrate, whereas some liver diseases respond well to a low-protein diet. Obesity can be managed with a low-calorie diet.

MARLENE DIETRICH   *Seen here in* The Blue Angel *(1930), the film that made her an international star.*

Dietrich, Marlene (Maria Magdalene von Losch; 1904-) German film actress and singer. Her image of sultry beauty was developed by Josef von *Sternberg in such films as *The Blue Angel* (1930). In 1930 she went to Hollywood, where she made numerous films of varying quality, including *Shanghai Express* (1932), *Blonde Venus* (1932), *Destry Rides Again* (1939), and *Judgment at Nuremburg* (1961). In her later career she gave many cabaret performances.

diffraction The spreading or bending of light waves as they pass the edge of an object or pass through an aperture. The diffracted waves subsequently interfere with each other producing regions of alternately high and low intensity. This phenomenon, first discovered in 1665 by Francesco Grimaldi (1618-63), can be observed in the irregular boundary of a shadow of an object cast on a screen by a small light source. A similar effect occurs with sound waves. *See also* interference.

diffusion 1. The mixing of different fluids, or the distribution of a substance from a region of high concentration to one of lower concentration, by means of the random thermal motion of its constituents. In gases, according to Graham's law (named after Thomas Graham; 1805–69), the rates at which gases diffuse are inversely proportional to their densities. Mixing of fluids is complete after a certain time unless one set of particles is sufficiently heavy for sedimentation to occur. Diffusion also occurs between certain solids; for example gold will slowly diffuse into lead. 2. The scattering of a beam of radiation on reflection from a rough surface or on transmission through certain media. When diffusion occurs the laws of reflection and refraction are not obeyed.

diffusionism A theory claiming that all civilization and culture were transmitted from certain circumscribed areas of the ancient world and disregarding the possibility of independent invention and discovery. In its most extreme form it held that this original centre was Egypt. Diffusionism dominated *ethnology between 1910 and 1925 but is now largely discredited.

Digby, Sir Kenelm (1603–65) English courtier and scientist. He entered James I's service in 1623 and led a privateering expedition against French ships off Turkey in 1627–28. A Roman Catholic, he supported Charles I against parliament and was forced to leave England during the Civil War. In Paris he wrote *Of the Nature of the Bodies* and *Of the Nature of Man's Soule* (1644). He finally returned to England in 1654. A founder member of the Royal Society (1663), he discovered that plants need oxygen.

digestion The process by which food is converted into substances that can be absorbed by the *intestine. The process begins in the mouth, where the food is chewed and mixed with saliva, and continues with the action of digestive enzymes secreted by the *stomach, duodenum, and *pancreas. Rhythmic contractions of the muscular layer of the intestinal wall (called peristalsis) ensures a constant mixing of enzymes and food and the propulsion of food along the intestine. The products of digestion include amino acids, various sugars (such as lactose, maltose, and glucose), and fat molecules; these are absorbed by the intestine and conveyed to the bloodstream.

Diggers An English sect that flourished under the *Commonwealth, so called because of their attempts to dig common land. Led by Gerrard *Winstanley, the Diggers believed in the economic and social equality of men. In April, 1649, they established a community at St George's Hill, Weybridge, based on agrarian communism. The support they attracted alarmed the government and they were dispersed in March, 1650. *See also* Levellers.

digger wasp A solitary *wasp of the families *Sphercidae* or *Pompilidae* (*see* spider wasp). Digger wasps are black with yellow or orange markings. They burrow into wood, plant stems, or the ground to build nests, which they stock with insects, such as caterpillars and flies; these have been paralysed to provide food for the developing larvae.

digital computer. *See* computer.

digitalis A crude drug prepared from the dried leaves of foxglove plants. Digitalis is purified to digoxin, digitoxin, and lanatoside C. These drugs are used to improve the action of a failing or inefficient heart and to reduce a dangerously fast heart rate. Side effects of digitalis compounds include nausea, vomiting, and pulse irregularities.

digital mapping The production of a map using a system in which the details of the map are stored in computerized form. The points and lines that make up a map are converted, or digitized, into computer data; this information is then stored on magnetic tapes. Subsequent reproduction may be of the whole map or of a selected part; it may be at a different scale and/or on a transformed projection. A print of the map can be pro-

duced or it may be displayed on a visual display unit. Changes can be simply made without the whole map having to be redrawn.

In the UK the *Ordnance Survey began converting its large-scale maps to digital data in 1973; by 1985 25 000 of the 1:1250 and 1:2500 scale maps had been converted.

digital recording. *See* recording of sound.

Dijon 47 20N 5 02E A city in France, the capital of the Côte-d'Or department on the Burgundy Canal. The former capital of Burgundy, it is the site of the palace of the Dukes of Burgundy and has a cathedral (13th–14th centuries). An important railway centre, it has varied industries and is famous for its mustard. Population (1982 est): 145 569.

dik-dik A small African antelope belonging to the genus *Madoqua* (7 species), found in the undergrowth of forested areas. 30–40 cm high at the shoulder, dik-diks are generally solitary and only the males have horns. When disturbed, they take flight in a series of erratic leaps.

dilatation and curettage (D and C) An operation in which the neck (cervix) of the womb is dilatated (widened) and the lining of the womb is scraped out. D and C may be performed for a variety of reasons, including the removal of any residual membranes after a miscarriage, removal of cysts or tumours, removal of a specimen of tissue for examination in the diagnosis of various gynaecological disorders, and for termination of a pregnancy (*see* abortion).

dill A widely cultivated annual or biennial European herb, *Anethum graveolens*, 60 cm high. The smooth stem bears feathery leaves and umbrella-like clusters of small yellow flowers, which produce small hard flat fruits. The young leaves and fruits are used to flavour soups, cakes, salads, fish, and pickled cucumbers. Family: *Umbelliferae*.

Dilthey, Wilhelm (1833–1911) German pioneer of biographical historiography. In contrast to Hegelian reliance on the cosmic spirit and metaphysical enquiry, Dilthey sought to conduct empirical enquiry, using historical facts, biographies, and the surviving records of great personalities.

dimensional analysis A method of testing or deriving a physical equation in which each term is expressed in the dimensions of mass, length, time, and (if electric or magnetic quantities are present) either charge or current. Each term must have the same dimensional formula if the equation is true. Dimensional analysis is also useful in predicting the behaviour of a full-scale system from a model.

diminishing returns, law of The law that as more of a variable factor of production, such as labour, is applied to a fixed quantity of another factor, such as capital (machinery), the returns to each additional unit of the variable factor will eventually decrease. For example, in a small factory, employing one labourer may increase production by freeing machine operators from some tasks, but employing a second labourer will not increase production by as much again.

Dimitrii Donskoi (1350–89) Prince of Moscow (1359–89) and Grand Prince of Vladimir (1362–89). His defeat of Khan Mamai at Kulikovo on the Don River in 1380 began the liberation of Russia from the *Golden Horde.

Dimitrov, Georgi (1882–1949) Bulgarian statesman. Dimitrov became a member of the executive committee of the *Comintern in 1921. Exiled in 1923, he moved in 1929 to Berlin, where in 1933 he was accused with others of setting fire to the Reichstag. Acquitted, he became a citizen of the Soviet Union and secretary general of the Comintern. In 1944 he returned to Bulgaria and became prime minister (1946). He died in Moscow.

Dinan 48 27N 2 02W A town and resort in France, in the Côtes-du-Nord department situated high above the River Rance. Its manufactures include hosiery, cider, and beer. Population (1982 est): 14 157.

Dinant 50 16N 04 55E A town in S Belgium, on the River Meuse. It was famous for its artistic metalwork (*dinanderie*) in the middle ages. A popular tourist centre, it is overlooked by an 11th-century citadel. Population (1982): 12 008.

Dinaric Alps (Serbo-Croat name: Dinara Planina) A mountain range in SW Yugoslavia and N Albania, extending some 700 km (435 mi) NW–SE between the Alps and the Balkan Mountains and rising to 2522 m (8274 ft).

D'Indy, Vincent (1851–1931) French composer, the pupil and biographer of Franck and the cofounder of the Paris Schola Cantorum (1894). He was greatly influenced by Wagner and wrote a number of large-scale orchestral compositions, as well as operas and chamber music. His most famous work is the *Symphony on a French Mountaineer's Song* (for piano and orchestra; 1886).

Dinesen, Isak (Karen Blixen, Baroness Blixen-Finecke; 1885–1962) Danish author, who took up writing after 20 years spent managing a coffee plantation in Kenya. She is best known for two collections of stories in the gothic style: *Seven Gothic Tales* (1934) and *Winter's Tales* (1942).

dingo An Australian wild *dog, *Canis familiaris* (formerly *C. dingo*), introduced about 3000 years ago from Asia. It is about 120 cm long, including the tail (30 cm), and has a tan-coloured coat. It is nocturnal and generally solitary.

Dinka A Nilotic people of the Nile basin region of the Sudan. Warlike and independent, the Dinka move with their cattle from dry-season pastures by the rivers to wet-season settlements, where they grow millet. There are many independent tribes of varying size each with numerous smaller clans and patrilineal kinship units. Age-set organization is important for men, who attain adulthood by undergoing the ordeals of initiation ceremonial. Ritual life emphasizes sacrificing to ancestral spirits and the god Nhial.

dinoflagellates A group of mostly marine unicellular organisms that form part of the *plankton. Usually measuring 0.02–0.1 mm, many have cellulose cell walls. They move by beating two hairlike structures (flagella). Some species contain chlorophyll and can manufacture their own food (by photosynthesis); others engulf food particles. As they have characteristics of both plants and animals, dinoflagellates can be classified as algae or protozoans.

dinosaur An extinct reptile that was the dominant terrestrial animal during the Jurassic and Cretaceous periods (200–65 million years ago). Dinosaurs first appeared about 210 million years ago, ranging in size from about 60 cm to such mighty creatures as *Diplodocus*, which reached 27 m in length. There were two orders: the *Saurischia*, which were mostly carnivores and included the bipedal *Allosaurus* and *Tyrannosaurus*; and the *Ornithischia*, which were all herbivores and included the bipedal *Iguanodon*, the horned *Triceratops*, and *Stegosaurus*. Why both orders died out at the end of the Cretaceous period along with other reptiles, such as *ichthyosaurs, *pterosaurs, and *plesiosaurs, is still not certain. Dinosaurs had large bodies with heavy bones and protective armour and were probably unable to adapt to climatic changes and the effects of a rise in the sea level, which flooded their coastal habitats.

D'Inzeo, Colonel Piero (1923–) Italian show jumper and equestrian, who won four Olympic team medals (1956, 1960, 1964, 1972), two Olympic individual medals (1956, 1960), and was European champion in 1959. His brother **Lieutenant Colonel Raimondo D'Inzeo** (1925–) won the same team medals, a gold medal in the 1960 Olympics, a silver in 1956, and the men's world championships in 1956 and 1960.

Dio Cassius (c. 150–235 AD) Roman historian, who was twice elected consul and was appointed governor of Africa and Dalmatia. In 80 books, written in Greek, he recorded the history of Rome from Aeneas to his own time.

Dio Chrysostom (2nd century AD) Greek philosopher and orator. A friend of the Emperor Trajan, he admired the Roman

state, from his family estates in Bithynia (Asia Minor), and eulogized its compound of monarchy, aristocracy, and democracy.

Diocletian(us), Gaius Aurelius Valerius (245–313 AD) Roman emperor (284–305). He was born in Dalmatia and rose to prominence in the army, to which he owed his accession. In 293 he established the tetrarchy to govern the Empire more effectively in a time of civil strife: the Empire was divided into East and West, with each ruled by an emperor and his associate. Diocletian ruled in the East with *Galerius, who was probably responsible for the persecution of Christians begun in 303. In 305 Diocletian retired to Salona (now Split, Yugoslavia), where his palace can still be seen.

diode. *See* semiconductor diode; thermionic valve.

Diodorus Siculus (1st century BC) Greek historian, born in Sicily. His *Bibliotheca historica* is a history of the Mediterranean countries from their legendary origins up to his own time; of its 40 volumes, only 15 survive.

Diogenes Laertius (3rd century AD) Greek compiler of the opinions and biographical details of classical philosophers, including the *Presocratics. The historical authenticity of his biographical material, for example about the life of *Epicurus, is doubtful.

Diogenes of Sinope (412–322 BC) The founder of the philosophical sect of the *Cynics. Influenced by *Antisthenes, Diogenes claimed, in contrast to almost all Greek thinkers, total freedom and self-sufficiency for the individual. Unlike modern anarchists, he saw no need for violent rebellion to assert his independence, which he thought he already had. His ostentatious disregard for social conventions made him the subject of many stories. He is reported to have lived in a large tub in Athens. According to another story, he went about in daylight with a lamp, saying that he was searching for an honest man.

Diomedes A legendary Greek hero of the Trojan War who commanded 80 ships from Argos. He wounded *Ares and *Aphrodite, took the place of the absent *Achilles in an attack on Troy, and captured the Palladium, the sacred image of *Athena.

Dionysius of Halicarnassus (1st century BC) Greek historian who taught at Rome after 30 BC. He compiled a history of Rome from its origins to the first Punic War in 20 books, of which 10 survive. He also wrote literary criticism and treatises on rhetoric.

Dionysius the Areopagite, St (1st century AD) Greek churchman. He was converted to Christianity by St Paul and was traditionally the first Bishop of Athens. In the middle ages he was thought to be the author of several theological treatises in Greek. These are now attributed to *Pseudo-Dionysius the Areopagite. Feast day: 9 Oct.

Dionysius (I) the Elder (c. 430–367 BC) Tyrant of Syracuse (405–367), who fought the Carthaginians in a series of wars, which were ultimately unsuccessful, for control of Sicily and the Greek cities of S Italy. His son **Dionysius (II) the Younger**, who succeeded him as tyrant (367–356, 347–344), was a patron of writers and philosophers and was taught briefly by Plato.

Dionysus (*or* Bacchus) The Greek god of wine, originally a vegetation god. He was the son of *Semele by Zeus, who saved him at her death; he was reared by the nymphs of Nysa. A common theme of many legends concerning him is a people's refusal to accept his divinity and his subsequent retribution: thus Pentheus, King of Thebes, was torn to death by the god's ecstatic female followers, the maenads. Athens held five festivals in Dionysus' honour.

Diophantus of Alexandria (mid-3rd century AD) Greek mathematician; one of the few Greeks to study algebra rather than geometry. He discovered the method of solving problems by means of algebraic equations. His work was preserved by Arabic mathematicians and, in the 16th century, was translated into Latin after which it inspired many advances in algebra. Diophantine equations are named after him.

dioptre A unit used to measure the power of a lens equal to the reciprocal of its focal length in metres. The power of a converging lens is taken to be positive and that of a diverging lens as negative.

CHRISTIAN DIOR *The French fashion designer in London in 1950 for his first English fashion show. His seven mannequins are all modelling New Look evening dresses.*

Dior, Christian (1905-57) French fashion designer, who first became known with his 1947 collection, which introduced the New Look, characterized by fitted bodices and long full skirts. His later designs, which included the H-line and the A-line, aspired to a similar ideal of femininity.

diorite A coarse-grained plutonic igneous rock of intermediate compostion. It consists mainly of plagioclase feldspar and ferromagnesian minerals (often hornblende, biotite, or pyroxene). It usually occurs in small intrusive masses or in parts of *batholiths.

Dioscorides Pedanius (c. 40-c. 90 AD) Greek physician, who compiled the first pharmacopoeia. He travelled widely as a surgeon in the Roman army and in his work *De materia medica* (c. 77 AD) he described nearly 600 plants and their medicinal properties.

Dioscuri. *See* Castor and Pollux.

dip circle. *See* magnetic dip.

diphtheria An acute bacterial infection primarily affecting the nose, throat, or larynx. It has been virtually eliminated from the UK and most western nations as a result of extensive immunization, although it formerly caused the death of many children. It is still found in Africa and India. Diphtheria produces a membrane across the throat that chokes the child. Alternatively death may be caused by poisons damaging the heart. The disease can be cured using penicillin and antitoxin.

Diplodocus A huge amphibious dinosaur of the Jurassic period (200-136 million years ago) that was the largest terrestrial vertebrate ever to exist, reaching a length of 27 m. It had a narrow body with massive pillar-like legs, a long neck with a tiny head, and a long tail. It fed on soft vegetation found in swamps and shallow lakes and had very few teeth. Order: *Saurischia.

dipole, electric and magnetic A pair of equal and opposite electric charges or *magnetic poles. The dipole moment is defined as the magnitude of one of the charges or poles multiplied by the distance separating them. Some molecules have an electric dipole moment due to the preferential attraction of the bonding electrons for one of the

atoms. In the case of hydrogen chloride, for example, the chlorine atom gains a slight negative charge and the hydrogen atom a slight positive charge. Measurement of dipole moments often provides evidence regarding the shapes of molecules.

dipper An aquatic songbird of the family *Cinclidae* (4 species), also called water ouzel, of Eurasia and America. Dippers are found near fast-flowing mountain streams, diving into the water to search for insects and small fish. The Eurasian white-breasted dipper (*Cinclus cinclus*) is about 17 cm long and has a dense dark-brown plumage with a white breast.

Diprotodon An extinct Australian giant *wombat that was about the size of a rhinoceros. It lived during the Pleistocene epoch, about a million years ago.

Diptera An order of insects comprising the two-winged, or true, flies. *See* fly.

Dirac, Paul Adrien Maurice (1902-84) British physicist, who made two fundamental contributions to the development of the quantum theory. In 1928 he introduced a new notation for handling quantum equations that combined *Schrödinger's use of *differential equations with *Heisenberg's approach using *matrices. Two years later he incorporated *relativity into quantum theory and produced an equation that predicted the existence of antiparticles. For his work he shared the 1933 Nobel Prize with Schrödinger. He was awarded the OM in 1973.

direction finder Equipment for locating the source of a radio signal, such as a ship at sea. It consists of one or more directive *aerials (usually in the form of a loop), designed to detect signals from a specific direction, and a receiver. Frequencies normally used are between 0.1 and 2 megahertz. The process can be automatic, often using a rotating aerial with a *cathode-ray tube to display signal strength and direction. Reflections from mountains or tall buildings can cause errors in a land-based direction-finding system. *Radar is a form of direction finding based on picking up reflections of a transmitted signal.

Directory (1795-99) The government of the First Republic of France, comprising five directors who were elected by a Council of Ancients (men over 40 years old) and a Council of Five Hundred. The Directory, which marked a retreat from the extremity of the early years of the *French Revolution, has been criticized for its corruption and administrative incompetence but it achieved successes in the Revolutionary Wars. It was overthrown by a coup d'état on behalf of *Napoleon.

Dire Dawa 9 40N 41 47E A town in central Ethiopia. It is in a hot dry region with little cultivation. Local industries include manufacturing cotton goods and cement. Population (1980): 82 024.

Dirichlet's theorem A theorem in *number theory stating that there are an infinite number of *prime numbers contained in the set of all numbers of the form $(a \times n) + b$, where a and b are themselves prime and n is a natural number, i.e. 1, 2, 3, ... The theorem was first suggested by *Gauss and proved by the French mathematician Peter Gustav Lejeune Dirichlet (1805-59).

disaccharide A carbohydrate comprising two linked *monosaccharide sugar units. *Lactose, maltose, and *sucrose are important disaccharides.

disarmament The reduction of the fighting capability of a nation. Limited disarmament treaties were made under the auspices of the *League of Nations in the 1930s, in an attempt to avoid a repetition of the disastrous loss of life in World War I. But German rearmament under the Nazis and Japanese expansionism in Asia thwarted these attempts. After World War II the main concern was to contain the spread of nuclear weapons. An attempt was made by the UN to limit both conventional arms and nuclear weapons, especially of the defeated countries, but during the Cold War both the Soviet Union and the western powers assisted in the rearmament of their former enemies. In 1963, however, the Soviet Union, the USA, and the UK signed a *Nuclear Test-Ban Treaty. In 1967 the same countries signed a treaty banning the use of nuclear weapons in outer space; in the same year 59 countries signed a nuclear nonproliferation treaty. By 1986 130 countries had acceded to the treaty but France and China, which have nuclear weapons, had not. Talks between the Soviet Union and USA were started in 1969 to limit and reduce strategic nuclear arms; known as SALT (Strategic Arms Limitation Talks) they reached limited agreements in 1974 (SALT I) and again in 1979 (SALT II), which was never ratified and was repudiated by the USA in 1986. In 1987 the two major powers agreed to reduce medium- and shorter-range nuclear missiles in Europe in an intermediate nuclear forces agreement (INF) and to intensify negotiations on strategic offensive weapons. Since 1983 the proposed US *Strategic Defence Initiative has been an important issue in these talks.

Disciples of Christ (*or* Campbellites) A Christian denomination originating within Presbyterianism in the 19th century but founded as a separate denomination in Philadelphia in 1827 by Alexander Campbell (1788–1866). In Britain they are known as the Churches of Christ. They preach a simple biblical creed, are congregational in organization, and celebrate weekly communion.

discount houses Financial institutions in the UK that discount *bills of exchange and buy and sell *treasury bills, activities that they finance by borrowing short-term funds (money at call) from the *commercial banks and other financial institutions. The discount houses take up the whole of the treasury bill issue each week, and in return the *Bank of England acts as lender of last resort to the discount houses (*see* open-market operations).

discount rate. *See* interest.

discus throw A field event in athletics. The circular discus is made of wood and metal, the men's weighing 2 kg (4.4 lb) and the women's 1 kg (2.2 lb). It is thrown as far as possible with one hand from within a circle 2.5 m (8.2 ft) in diameter. World records: men: 71.86 m (1983) by Y. Dumchev (Soviet Union); women: 73.26 m (1983) by G. Savinkova (Soviet Union).

disinfectant A substance or process that kills germs or prevents them multiplying. Carbolic acid (phenol) was introduced for this purpose in medicine in the 1870s by Joseph *Lister. It is still used, as are many of its derivatives, in cleaning materials and, in weaker solutions, in skin disinfectants. Chlorine and such compounds as sodium hypochlorite kill bacteria and also some viruses. Chlorinated phenols, such as hexachlorophane, are also widely used in pharmaceutical products. Many other chemicals, including hydrogen peroxide (H_2O_2), iodine (I_2), formaldehyde (HCHO), and other aldehydes, are also used as disinfectants. Dry heating to 140°C for about 3 hours will kill all disease-causing germs. Boiling water and ultraviolet light are also effective disinfectants.

dislocation Displacement of a bone at a joint, producing severe pain, difficulty in moving the joint, and usually obvious deformity. Shoulders, elbows, hips, vertebrae, and fingers are all commonly dislocated in injuries. Often one of the bones in the joint will be broken, and for this reason it is unwise to attempt to put the joint back before an X-ray film has been taken.

Disney, Walt (1901–66) US film producer and animator. His most famous cartoon character, Mickey Mouse, was designed in 1928. His films include full-length cartoon features, such as *Snow White and the Seven Dwarfs* (1938), *Pinocchio* (1939), and *Bambi* (1943), nature documentaries, and adventure films, such as *Treasure Island* (1950) and *Mary Poppins* (1964), all made for family audiences. His *Fantasia* (1940) used colourful visual images and cartoons to accompa-ny several pieces of classical music played by an orchestra under *Stokowski. He opened Disneyland, an amusement park, in California in 1955. Walt Disney World was later opened (1971) near Orlando, Florida; similar parks are planned in Paris, Tokyo, and elsewhere.

display In zoology, a specialized means by which animals communicate with each other. Displays can be vocal (such as birdsong), visual (by posture or colourful plumage), chemical (by means of *pheromones), or tactile (for instance bees communicate in a dark hive largely by touch). Displays ensure social integration and cohesion of populations by communicating the whereabouts and identity of individuals. They are used to establish social rank, maintain territory, synchronize breeding, and give warning of danger.

DISRAELI *A contemporary* Punch *cartoon, entitled "A Bad Example," shows the prime minister (right) and Gladstone, his political opponent, throwing mud at one another.*

Disraeli, Benjamin, 1st Earl of Beaconsfield (1804–81) British statesman; Conservative prime minister (1868, 1874–80). Of Italian-Jewish descent, Disraeli was baptized a Christian in 1817. He became an MP in 1837 and led the Young England group of Conservatives. Disraeli was critical of Peel's Conservative Government (1841–46) and opposed the repeal of the *Corn Laws. He was three times chancellor of the exchequer in Derby's governments (1852, 1858–59, 1866–68): in 1858 he introduced an unsuccessful parliamentary reform bill but was largely responsible for the 1867 *Reform Act. He succeeded Derby in February, 1868, but lost office following the autumn election, which was won by the Liberals under Gladstone. His second ministry carried important social legislation, including the Artisans' and Labourers' Dwellings Improvement Act (1874). In 1875 he bought Britain a major stake in the Suez Canal and in 1876 secured passage of a bill that conferred the title Empress of India on Queen Victoria. He successfully pursued British interests at the Congress of *Berlin (1878). Under Disraeli's leadership the Conservative Party came to be clearly identified with policies that upheld the monarchy, Empire, and Church of England, while sponsoring social reform. A flamboyant and witty parliamentarian, he earned the respect and friendship of the queen. Also a writer, Disraeli's novels include *Vivien Grey* (1826), *Coningsby, or the New Generation* (1844), and *Sybil, or the Two Nations* (1845).

dissonance   A combination of two or more musical notes that sounds harsh to the ear. This harshness is caused by the *beats that are produced when two notes (or their overtones) of similar pitch are sounded together. For example C and F sharp are dissonant because the second overtone of C is G, which beats with F sharp. A common type of dissonance in diatonic music consists of chords that sound incomplete in themselves and need to resolve onto a consonance. All diatonic music relies on the contrast between dissonances and consonances, without which such music would sound predictable and uninteresting. The use of *chromaticism in the late 19th century increased the amount of dissonance in music; in the 20th century such composers as Bartok and Stravinsky deliberately cultivated the use of unresolved dissonances.

distemper (veterinary science)   A highly contagious virus disease affecting dogs, foxes, ferrets, badgers, etc. Canine distemper occurs mainly at 3–12 months; symptoms include fever, loss of appetite, and a discharge from the eyes and nose. Complications may include conjunctivitis, bronchitis, pneumonia, and gastroenteritis. The disease can be prevented by vaccination at about 11 weeks with a booster dose at two years.

distemper (*or* whitewash)   An inexpensive water-based paint for interior decoration. It consists of whiting (calcium carbonate), glue, and water. In dry form it is known as calcinine.

distillation   A method of purifying or separating the components of a liquid by boiling or evaporating the liquid and condensing the vapour. It is used for separating either liquids from solids or a mixture of liquids whose components have different boiling points. The latter is known as fractional distillation. Distillation is employed in petroleum refineries to separate the various *hydrocarbons, in the production of alcoholic spirits, and in extracting pure water from sea water.

distribution function   A mathematical function that gives the probability of finding a system in a particular state or within a range of states. For example, the probability of one of the molecules of a gas having a velocity between v and $v + dv$ in a given direction is Fdv, where F is the distribution function.

distributive law   A law concerning the combination of mathematical operations. In arithmetic, for example, multiplication is said to obey the distributive law, or to be distributive, with respect to addition because $a(b + c) = ab + ac$.

District of Columbia   A federal district of the E USA, coextensive with the federal capital, *Washington. Area: 178 sq km (69 sq mi).

dithyramb   An ancient Greek hymn to the god *Dionysus. Originally sung extempore, it developed into a literary form –traditionally originated by the poet Arion–around the 6th and 7th centuries BC. Its best-known authors include *Bacchylides and *Pindar. Aristotle believed that Greek drama developed out of this form.

dittany   A perennial European herbaceous plant, *Dictamnus albus*, also known as the gas plant or burning bush. A strong-scented gland-covered plant, it gives off so much aromatic oil that it is said to burst into flames when ignited. Dittany produces a drooping spike of white or pink flowers. Family: *Rutaceae*. The name is also applied to several other plants. Crete dittany (*Origanum dictamnus*) is a herb closely related to marjoram, with thick woolly leaves and pinkish flower clusters. Family: *Labiatae*.

Diu.   *See* Daman and Diu.

diuretics   A large class of drugs that increase the excretion of urine by the kidneys. Diuretics are used in the treatment of diseases in which fluid accumulates in the tissues. These illnesses include heart failure, kidney failure, and some liver diseases (such as cirrhosis). Some diuretics (e.g. frusemide) cause loss of potassium from the body and are prescribed with a potassium supplement. Diuretics may also be used in the treatment of high blood pressure.

diurnal motion   The apparent daily motion of astronomical bodies from E to W across the sky, in circles parallel to the celestial equator (*see* celestial sphere). It is caused by the earth's W-to-E rotation.

diver   A large aquatic bird belonging to a family (*Gaviidae*; 3 species) occurring in the N hemisphere, also called loon. Divers breed on lakes and ponds and spend the winter in temperate coastal waters. They have small pointed wings and black and white plumage and they dive deeply, feeding on fish, frogs, and aquatic insects. Order: *Gaviiformes*.

divide.   *See* watershed.

dividend   A share in the profits of a company paid to shareholders. The rate of dividend is declared at the company's annual general meeting and will reflect the preceding year's profit. It is usually expressed as a percentage of the par value of the share (e.g. a 5% dividend on a 20p share would pay 1p per share). The dividend **yield** of the share is the income it produces expressed as a percentage of its current value (e.g. a 5% dividend on a 20p share that has a current value of 35p is $20/35 \times 5 = 2.86\%$). Dividends are usually paid twice yearly, an interim dividend and a final dividend.

divine right of kings   A political doctrine claiming that monarchs are responsible only to God and that their subjects owe them unquestioning obedience. The theory originated in the middle ages and was most fully developed in the 16th and 17th centuries, especially in England, where it was associated particularly with the Stuart kings, and in France, where its leading exponent was Louis XIV.

diving beetle   An aquatic beetle–a true *water beetle–belonging to a family (*Dytiscidae*; about 4000 species), occurring worldwide but particularly common in Europe and Asia. Diving beetles have dark streamlined bodies and vary in length from 2 to 38 mm: the largest genera are *Cybister* and *Dytiscus*. The adults and larvae (water tigers) are voracious carnivores.

diving duck   A *duck that dives to the bottom of lakes or rivers to feed, aided by a dense high-domed skull. Diving ducks, which include the *goldeneye, *pochard, and *scaup, usually have a drab plumage, thick neck, narrow wings, and large feet; the legs are set far back and they walk awkwardly on land. *Compare* dabbling duck.

Divisional Court.   *See* courts of law.

division of labour   The separation of tasks in an industrial process, with the allocation of one worker to each specific task in the manufacture of an object. The term was first introduced by Adam *Smith in his *Wealth of Nations* (1776). The object is to increase output; however, extreme division of labour, as in a car factory, can lead to intense boredom condemning a worker to repeating one operation endlessly.

divorce   The legal process by which a marriage is ended. Until the Matrimonial Causes Act (1857), which established a Divorce Court, divorce in England was possible only by special Act of Parliament. Jurisdiction is now vested in the High Court and county courts (*see* courts of law). Since 1971, the only ground for divorce has been that the marriage has irretrievably broken down. The party who applies for the divorce (the petitioner) must show that the other party (the respondent) has (1) committed adultery, (2) behaved in such a way as the petitioner cannot reasonably be expected to live with him or her, (3) deserted the petitioner for two years, (4) lived separate and apart from the petitioner for two years and consents to the divorce, or (5) lived separate and apart from the petitioner for five years. Unless agreed between the parties, the court determines who is to have custody of the children under 16 and what financial arrangements should be made between the parties.

DIWALI *The final day of the five-day festival is dedicated to the tie between brothers and sisters, who exchange special gifts. The bracelet on the boy's wrist, given to him by his sister, symbolizes the bond between them.*

Diwali An important Hindu religious festival. Held over the New Year according to the Vikrama calendar (October–November), it is celebrated especially among the merchant classes and honours *Lakshmi, the goddess of wealth (or in Bengal, Kali). There is feasting, gambling, and lighting of lamps in honour of *Rama. Jains commemorate at this time the death of their saint *Mahavira.

Dixieland A type of jazz played by White musicians in imitation of the traditional *New Orleans style, named after the Original Dixieland Jazz Band (founded 1912). It emerged in the early years of the 20th century but declined during the *swing and bebop eras.

Diyarbakır 37 55N 40 14E A town in SE Turkey, on the River Tigris. It was taken by the Turks in 1515 and has 4th-century walls. Gold and silver filigree work is produced here; wool and grain are traded. It has a university (1966). Population (1980): 235 617.

Djajapura. *See* Jajapura.

Djakarta. *See* Jakarta.

Djambi. *See* Jambi.

Djerba Island 33 45N 11 00E A Tunisian island in the Mediterranean Sea, linked to the mainland by a causeway. Area: 510 sq km (197 sq mi).

Djibouti, Republic of (name until 1977: the French Territory of the Afars and the Issas) A small country in NE Africa, on the Gulf of Aden at its entrance to the Red Sea. It consists chiefly of an arid rocky coastal plain rising to a plateau inland. The main population groups are Somalis (chiefly Issas) and Afars, with Arabic and European minorities. *Economy*: the port of Djibouti (a free port since 1949) is the country's economic focus handling an important transshipment trade but it was adversely affected by the closure of the Suez Canal (1967–75). The port is linked by rail to Ethiopia and handles about half of that country's trade. Exports include hides, skins, sugar, and Ethiopian coffee. Inland the predominantly nomadic population tends goats, sheep, and camels. *History*: French involvement, centred on the port, began in the mid-19th century. It was made a French colony known as French Somaliland in 1896

and proclaimed an overseas territory in 1967. It became independent in 1977 as Djibouti with Hassan Gouled Aptidon (1916–) as its first president. The country suffered from the war between Ethiopia and Somalia through the disruption of trade. Official languages: Hamitic languages of Somali. Official currency: Djibouti franc of 100 centimes. Area: 21 783 sq km (8409 sq mi). Population (1983 est): 316 000. Capital and chief port: Djibouti.

Djilas, Milovan (1911–) Yugoslav politician and writer. A member of *Tito's resistance group in World War II, Djilas became a prominent figure in the postwar communist government. His criticism of the regime led to his demotion (1954) and he was twice imprisoned (1956–61, 1962–66) for publishing critical material abroad. His books include *New Class* (1957), *Land Without Justice* (1958), and *Conversations with Stalin* (1962).

Djokjakarta. *See* Jogjakarta.

Djoser (*or* Zoser) King of Egypt (c. 2980–c. 2950 BC) of the 3rd dynasty, famous for his pyramid at *Saqqarah, near Memphis.

DNA (*or* deoxyribonucleic acid) A nucleic acid that is the chief constituent of the *chromosomes, carrying genetic information, in the form of *genes, necessary for the organization and functioning of living cells.

The molecular structure of DNA was first proposed by J. D. *Watson and F. H. *Crick in 1953. It consists of a double helix of two strands coiled around each other. Each strand is made up of alternating pentose sugar (deoxyribose) and phosphate groups, with an organic base attached to each pentose group. There are four possible bases: adenine (A), guanine (G), cytosine (C), and thymine (T). The bases on each strand are joined by hydrogen bonds and are always paired in the same way: A always binds with T and G with C. During replication, the strands of the helix separate and each provides a template for the synthesis of a new complementary strand, thus producing two identical copies of the original helix. This special property for accurate self-replication enables DNA to duplicate the genes of an organism during the cell divisions of growth (*see* mitosis) and the production of germ cells for the next generation (*see* meiosis).

DNA *The structure of a DNA molecule takes the form of a double helix. The sequence of base pairs constitutes the genetic code, which controls the inheritance of characteristics.*

Dnepr, River (*or* R. Dnieper) A river in the W Soviet Union. Rising in the Valdai Hills, NE of Smolensk, it flows mainly SE through the RSFSR and the Belorussian and Ukrainian SSRs to enter the Black Sea. It is the third longest river in Europe. Length: 2286 km (1420 mi).

Dneprodzerzhinsk (name until 1936: Kamenskoye) 48 30N 34 37E A port in the SW Soviet Union, in the

Ukrainian SSR, on the River Dnepr. A major industrial centre, it produces iron and steel, machine tools, and chemicals. Population (1984): 268 000.

Dnepropetrovsk (name from 1787 until 1796 and from 1802 until 1826: Ekaterinoslav) 48 29N 35 00E A city in the SW Soviet Union, in the Ukrainian SSR on the River Dnepr. It is one of the country's largest industrial cities, producing especially iron and steel, and it is also a transportation centre. Population (1984): 1 140 000.

Dnestr, River (*or* R. Dniester) A river in the SW Soviet Union. It flows mainly SE from the Carpathian Mountains, through the Ukrainian and Moldavian SSRs, to the Black Sea near Odessa. Length: 1411 km (877 mi).

Dobermann pinscher A breed of dog developed by Louis Dobermann in Germany in the late 19th century. It has a powerful streamlined body with a very short tail and a long muzzle. The short smooth coat is black, brown, or blue-grey with tan markings. Dobermanns are widely used as police, guard, and guide dogs. Height: 70 cm (dogs); 64 cm (bitches).

Dobruja (Bulgarian name: Dobrudzha; Romanian name: Dobrogea) An area in E central Europe, in SE Romania and NE Bulgaria. It consists of a low-lying alluvial plain between the River Danube and the Black Sea.

dobsonfly A winged insect belonging to the family *Corydalidae*, occurring in all continents except Europe. Male dobsonflies have enormously exaggerated jaws, sometimes over 25 mm long. Eggs are laid near fresh water and the larvae (hellgrammites) are aquatic, using their biting jaws to feed on insects and small invertebrates. They migrate to the soil to pupate. Order: *Neuroptera*.

Dobzhansky, Theodosius (1900–75) US geneticist, born in Russia. His studies of wild populations of fruit flies revealed the extent of genetic differences between individuals and how, through natural selection, this enabled the populations to adapt rapidly to changing conditions. Dobzhansky also studied the formation of new species and has written influential articles on evolution and philosophy.

dock A plant (usually perennial) of the genus *Rumex*, of temperate regions. 10–200 cm tall, it has a deep stout root and large lance-shaped leaves. The small greenish flowers are borne in small clusters on branched flower stems. They produce small nutlets, often surrounded by the reddish papery remains of the petals. Dock leaves are the traditional antidote to nettle stings. Family: *Polygonaceae. See also* sorrel.

docks Structures designed to enable ships to load and unload cargo or passengers or to undergo repairs. A **wet dock** is situated on a tidal river or on the coast and has gates to maintain the water level irrespective of the tide. Ships can only enter or leave such a dock when the tide brings the water level outside it to the level inside. Where the range of the tide is small (less than 4 m) a **tidal dock** can be used. In this the dock is open to the harbour and ships in dock rise and fall with the tide. In **dry docks** the water enters at one end only and gates enable all the water to be pumped out, so that repairs can be made to a ship's hull. **Floating docks** have the advantage of being movable, but they have a relatively short life. Floating docks also have watertight compartments from which the water can be pumped out and they can be used for repair work. *See also* dredger.

documentary film A film that portrays and interprets factual reality, often for educational purposes. The term was coined by John Grierson, leader of a school of British documentary film directors in the 1930s, to describe one of the most influential early documentaries, Robert *Flaherty's *Nanook of the North* (1920). The propaganda films produced in Nazi Germany, notably Leni Reifenstahl's *Triumph of the Will* (1934), were an exception to the generally left-wing political sympathies of documentary films. Many documentary films have been produced for television.

dodder A twining parasitic plant of the widely distributed genus *Cuscuta* (150 species), which absorbs food by inserting rootlike organs into the stems of other plants. Dodder has no chlorophyll (green pigment): it consists simply of a yellow or pinkish cordlike stem bearing round clusters of tiny yellow or white bell-shaped flowers. The leaves are reduced to scales and there are no roots. Family: *Cuscutaceae*.

Dodecanese (Modern Greek name: Dhodhekánisos) A group of Greek islands in the SE Aegean Sea. Although known as the 12 Islands, it in fact consists of some 20 islands and islets, which include Cos, *Rhodes (the largest), and Pátmos. They were taken from Turkey by Italy in 1912 and passed to Greece in 1947. Total area: 2719 sq km (1050 sq mi). Population (1981): 145 071. Capital: Rhodes.

Dodgson, Charles Lutwidge. *See* Carroll, Lewis.

dodo A large clumsy flightless bird, *Raphus cucullatus*, that lived on Mauritius but was extinct by 1681, due to hunting by man. Weighing about 23 kg, it had a grey-blue wispy plumage, stout yellow legs, tiny wings, a tuft of curly white tail feathers, and a large head with a massive hooked bill; it probably fed on fruit or roots. Family: *Raphidae*; order: *Columbiformes* (pigeons, etc.).

Dodoma 6 10S 35 40E A town in E central Tanzania. It replaced Dar es Salaam as the capital in 1983. Population (1978): 45 703.

Dodsley, Robert (1703–64) British bookseller and writer. Dodsley began to write poetry when he was a footman. Helped by Pope, among others, he set up (1735) as· a bookseller in Pall Mall and published many works including Samuel Johnson's *London* (1738) and Gray's *Elegy* (1751).

dog A carnivorous mammal belonging to the family *Canidae*. Ancestors of the modern domestic dog (*Canis familiaris*), probably derived from wolves or jackals, were first domesticated over 10 000 years ago. Wild dogs generally live and hunt in packs, relying on speed and cooperation to secure their prey. They are specialized hunters with long legs, sharp teeth, strong jaws, and acute hearing and smell.

The intelligence and social nature of dogs have led to their selective breeding by man for a variety of purposes, principally as sporting dogs, working dogs, and ornamental breeds for household pets. There are up to 400 modern breeds and in the UK, standards for over 100 recognized breeds are established by the Kennel Club, founded in 1873. There are many dog shows held annually in the UK, the most prestigious being Crufts, held in London.

dogbane A perennial herb of the genus *Apocynum* (about 7 species), found mostly in the tropics and subtropics, especially the American species *A. androsaemifolium*. Up to 1.5 m high, dogbane has simple leaves and small white or pink bell-shaped flowers clustered at the tips of the shoots. The juice contains alkaloids and has been used in arrow poisons. Family: *Apocynaceae. See also* Indian hemp.

doge The title of the chief magistrate of Venice from about 697 AD to the fall of the Venetian Empire in 1797. The doge was elected for life and wielded considerable power until 1172 when his authority was restricted by the creation of a supreme Great Council of 480 members. Further constitutional checks made the doge little more than a figurehead. The first **Doge's Palace** was built in 814 and destroyed by an uprising in 976. Subsequent structures were destroyed by fire, and the present richly decorated gothic palace originated in the early 14th century, with later additions.

Dogen (1200–53) Japanese Buddhist monk, who introduced the *Soto school of Zen Buddhism to Japan. An orphan of noble birth, he became a monk at 13 and studied the Buddhist scriptures before visiting several Chinese monasteries (1223–27), where he studied Zen. After returning to Japan, he devoted himself to teaching the form

sporting breeds

pointer   cocker spaniel   golden retriever   red setter

hounds

dachshund   borzoi   basset   Rhodesian ridgeback

working breeds

corgi   rough-coated collie   Old English sheepdog   German shepherd

terriers

bull terrier   cairn terrier   Airedale   smooth-haired fox terrier   Sealyham

toy breeds

Chihuahua   Pekingese   toy poodle   pug   Yorkshire terrier

non-sporting breeds

Boston   chow chow   schipperke   Dalmatian

of Zen practice that emphasizes quiet meditation. His teaching is embodied in his chief work, *Shobogenzo* (*Knowledge concerning the Dharma*).

dogfish A small *shark belonging to one of a number of families. *Scyliorhinus stellaris*, up to 1 m long, and *S. canicula*, up to 75 cm long, are brown-spotted dogfish commonly found in Mediterranean and British coastal waters. They are edible and purchased as "rock salmon." Chief families: *Triakidae* (smooth dogfish or smooth hounds); *Squalidae* (spiny dogfish); *Scyliorhinidae* (spotted dogfish).

Dogger Bank A vast sandbank in the central North Sea, 17–36 m (55–120 ft) below water. Several naval battles have taken place on the bank, notably the battle of Dogger Bank (24 January, 1915) between British and German forces. It is a major fishing ground.

doggerel A crude, naive, form of poetry, often irregular in rhythm and metre. Early examples are John *Skelton's *Colin Clout* (1519) and Samuel *Butler's *Hudibras* (1663–78). It is much used in comic verse, as in the work of the US poet Ogden *Nash.

dog rose A shrubby *rose, *Rosa canina*, 1–5 m high. It grows in woods, hedges, and roadsides of Europe, North Africa, and SW Asia. The arching stems have strong curved prickles and bear clusters of scentless white or pink flowers on long stalks.

Dogs, Isle of A district in the Greater London borough of Tower Hamlets, bounded on three sides by the River Thames.

dog's tooth violet A spring-blooming plant of the genus *Erythronium* (20 species), also known as adder's tongue, native to Eurasia and North America. They have white, yellow, or purple nodding flowers with two leaves at the base; the fruit is a pod. Several species are grown as rock-garden ornamentals. A European species is *E. dens-canis*, with purple flowers. Family: *Liliaceae*.

dogwood A shrub or small tree of the genus *Cornus* (about 45 species), mostly of the N hemisphere. It has oval pointed leaves with prominent curved veins and dense clusters of four-petalled flowers. The fruit is a berry. The common European dogwood (*C. sanguinea*) has white flowers, blood-red shoots and autumn leaves, and black berries; Cornelian cherry (*C. mas*), of central and SE Europe, has small yellow flowers and attractive red berries. The American flowering dogwood (*C. florida*) has showy pinkish blossoms and red berries. Family: *Cornaceae*.

Doha 25 15N 51 36E The capital of Qatar, on the E coast. Its modern development (including an international seaport and airport) has been funded by oil revenues. Population (1981 est): 130 000.

Dohnányi, Ernö (Ernst von D.; 1877–1960) Hungarian composer and pianist. He spent his last years in the USA. He was greatly influenced by Brahms, who praised his early works. Unlike his contemporaries, Bartók and Kodály, Dohnányi remained uninfluenced by Hungarian folksong. His best-known composition is the *Variations on a Nursery Theme* (for piano and orchestra; 1913), based on the tune known in England as "Baa Baa Black Sheep."

Dolby system An electronic device for reducing the hiss in sound reproduction, particularly in *tape recorders. It was invented by Ray Dolby (1933–   ), who set up a company to make Dolby noise-reduction units. These are now built into high-quality tape recorders and are increasingly used in film sound tracks and prerecorded cassettes. The Dolby system selectively boosts the higher frequencies in the sound signal before recording it, to drown out the constant hiss produced by the tape, and attenuates them when playing back. Its unique feature is that it operates only when the music is quiet enough for the hiss to be heard. This avoids both distortion that occurs if lower frequencies are boosted to the same level and distortion from boosting already loud higher frequencies.

dolce stil nuovo (Italian: sweet new style) A style of love poetry founded by the Bolognese poet Guido Guinizelli (c. 1240–76) and perfected by the Florentine poets *Cavalcanti and *Dante. It is characterized by a spiritualization of *courtly love, the use of the vernacular, and the sonnet, ballad, and canzone verse forms. Among its best-known examples are Dante's lyrics to Beatrice. The style influenced *Petrarch, *Bembo, Dante Gabriel *Rossetti, and Ezra *Pound.

Dolci, Danilo (1924–   ) Italian social reformer and writer. The author of 13 books, including *To Feed the Hungry* (1959), he has established centres for the study of economic development, unemployment, and poverty. His international standing has brought him a number of awards, including the Lenin Peace Prize of 1958.

doldrums The equatorial belt within which the trade-wind zones converge. Winds are light and variable but the strong upward movement of air caused by the meeting of the trade winds produces frequent thunderstorms, heavy rains, and squalls. Navigation by sailing ships was difficult in these areas; ships often became becalmed for several days.

dolerite A dark-coloured hypabyssal igneous rock, the medium-grained equivalent of gabbros, occurring mainly as dykes, sills, and plugs. It contains calcic plagioclase feldspar and augite, and sometimes olivine, hypersthene, quartz, or feldspathoids. It is called diabase in the USA.

Dolgellau 52 44N 3 53W A market town and tourist centre in North Wales, in Gwynedd. Population (1981): 2321.

D'Oliviera, Basil Lewis (1931–   ) South African-born Coloured cricketer, who played for Worcestershire (from 1965) and England (from 1966). The MCC tours of South Africa were cancelled in 1968 after the South African Government refused to accept him as a team member.

Dollfuss, Engelbert (1892–1934) Austrian statesman; chancellor (1932–34). He became prominent as leader of the Lower Austrian Farmers' League. Ruling by decree from 1933, his chancellorship was increasingly strained by his inability to control the Austrian Nazis or to cooperate with the Social Democrats. He suppressed the Social Democratic revolt in February, 1934, and was assassinated in July during an abortive attempt by the Nazis to seize power.

dolmen (Breton: table stone) A prehistoric tomb made of huge stone slabs set upright and supporting a stone roof. Widely distributed in *Neolithic Europe, dolmens were often covered by a *barrow.

Dolmetsch, Arnold (1858–1940) British musician and instrument maker. He pioneered the rediscovery of early music and its performance on contemporary instruments in its original style. His home at Haslemere became a centre for early music festivals and he made viols, lutes, harpsichords, and recorders there, as well as editing early music. His son **Carl Dolmetsch** (1911–   ) has carried on the tradition and is a virtuoso recorder player.

dolomite A mineral consisting of calcium magnesium carbonate, $CaMg(CO_3)_2$, colourless, white or grey in colour. Rocks containing over 15% magnesium carbonate are called dolomites, those containing less are magnesian limestones, and those containing both dolomite and calcite are dolomitic limestones. Dolomite occurs as a primary sediment, in metalliferous veins and in limestones altered by the process of dolomitization, by which the calcium carbonate is wholly or partly converted to dolomite by magnesium-rich sea water, or by magnesium-rich solutions permeating joints in the rock.

Dolomites (Italian name: Alpi Dolomitiche) A section of the Alps in NE Italy. Composed of dolomitic limestone, they are characterized by their steep-sided rocky peaks, the highest of which is the Marmolada at 3342 m (10 965 ft).

dolphin 1. A toothed *whale of the family *Delphinidae* (about 50 species). Agile and streamlined and up to 4.5 m long, dolphins live in large groups, or schools, and feed mainly on fish; they often accompany ships. They are intelligent creatures with well-developed abilities for social communication and *echolocation. The common dolphin (*Delphinus delphus*), which grows to 2.1 m, is blue-black with a white belly and striped body. *See also* bottlenose; porpoise. **2.** A fast-moving fish of the family Coryphaenidae (2 species). The common dolphin (*Coryphaena hippuras*) has a bluish tapering body, up to 2 m long, with a large blunt head, a forked tail, and a long dorsal fin. It occurs in tropical and temperate seas and feeds on fish and invertebrates. Order: *Perciformes*.

Domagk, Gerhard (1895–1964) German biochemist, who (in 1932) noticed the powerful effects of a dye, Prontosil, in combating bacterial infection. From this dye was isolated the first of the *sulphonamide drugs (sulphanilamide) which paved the way for the treatment of a wide range of bacterial diseases. Domagk received the 1939 Nobel Prize but was prevented from accepting it until 1947, after the fall of Hitler.

dome A roof or ceiling that is hemispherical in section. In classical architecture it was generally supported by a circular drum and topped by a lantern. The Romans developed the technique of building a dome in cast concrete while the Byzantines introduced the use of four pendentives to build a dome over a square section. Another method was invented in the 15th century by *Brunelleschi, using a strong brick cone to bear the weight and a lighter outer shell for visual effect. The Pantheon and St Peter's in Rome, Hagia Sophia, Istanbul, and St Paul's, London, all have famous domes.

Domenichino (Domenico Zampieri; 1581–1641) Italian painter, born in Bologna. He trained under Ludovico *Carracci. In Rome (1602–31) he painted frescoes of the *Life of St Cecilia* (1615–17; S Luigi dei Francesi) and *Last Communion of St Jerome* (Vatican Museum). His landscapes influenced *Poussin and *Claude.

Domenico Veneziano (active c. 1438–1461) Italian painter of the early Renaissance, probably born in Venice. He settled in Florence, where he painted his famous *St Lucy Altarpiece* (central panel; Uffizi).

Dome of the Rock The great mosque in Jerusalem, built in 691 AD by the *Umayyad caliph, 'Abd al-Malik. It is named after the rock (sacred also to the Jews) over which it was built and stands within the enclosure of the destroyed Jewish *Temple of Jerusalem. It is the third most holy place of Islam, after *Mecca and *Medina. The edifice, also erroneously called the mosque of Omar by Europeans, is an impressive example of early Islamic architecture.

Domesday Book (1086) The survey of England ordered by William I to assess the extent of his own possessions and the value for taxation purposes of the estates of his tenants in chief. Parts of N and NW England and some towns, including London and Winchester, were omitted. Royal commissioners collected, shire by shire, details about each *manor, naming its present owner and its owner under Edward the Confessor, changes in its size since Edward's reign, the numbers of its inhabitants and the services or rents they owed, and the numbers of its ploughteams, mills, and fisheries. The survey, in two volumes, is now in the Public Record Office.

dominance In genetics, the condition in which one of the *alleles of a gene predominates in the function of that gene. Gregor *Mendel, in his famous experiments, crossed pea plants from a line producing yellow seeds with plants from a line producing green seeds. The resulting offspring all produced yellow seeds, i.e. the dominant allele of the gene determining seed colour was that of the yellow-seeded plants; the allele of the green-seeded plants was recessive.

Domingo, Placido (1941–) Spanish tenor, educated in Mexico. He made his debut at the Metropolitan Opera, New York, in 1968. A leading tenor, he sings a wide range of roles but specializes in Puccini and Verdi, starring in film versions of *La Traviata* in 1983 and *Otello* in 1986.

Dominic, St (Domingo de Guzmán; c. 1170–1221) Spanish churchman, who founded the *Dominicans. One of the canons regular attached to the cathedral at Osma, Castile, and later its prior, he became one of the first successful missionaries to the heretical *Albigenses in the south of France. In 1216 with papal encouragement he founded a religious order devoted to preaching. From his headquarters in Rome he sent out his preachers to establish houses in many major cities. Feast Day: 4 Aug. Emblems: a star and a dog holding a torch in its mouth.

Dominica, Commonwealth of An island country in the West Indies, the largest of the Windward Islands. It is of volcanic origin and very mountainous. The population is mainly of African descent. *Economy*: chiefly agricultural; exports include bananas, limes, and lime oil. *History*: discovered by Columbus in 1493, it changed hands several times between the French and the British during the 18th century before finally becoming British in 1783. It became internally self-governing in 1967 and an independent republic within the British Commonwealth in November, 1978. President: Clarence A. Seignoret. Prime minister: Mary Eugenia Charles. Official language: English. Official currency: East Caribbean dollar of 100 cents. Area: 728 sq km (289 sq mi). Population (1980): 74 089. Capital: Roseau.

Dominican Republic A country in the Caribbean Sea, occupying the E two-thirds of the island of Hispaniola (Haiti occupies the W third). It is largely mountainous, rising to over 3000 m (10 000 ft). It is subject to hurricanes. The population is mainly of mixed African and European descent. *Economy*: chiefly agricultural, the principal cash crop is sugar. Other cash crops include coffee, cocoa, and bananas. Mining and light industry are being developed in an attempt to diversify the economy. The principal mineral export is ferro-nickel and gold and silver mining began in 1975. Oil and hydroelectricity are being exploited. There is a growing tourist industry. *History*: the island was discovered in 1492 by Columbus, who named it Hispaniola. The E became a Spanish colony, while the French established themselves in the W, in what became Haiti. The Spanish colony was ceded to the French in 1795 and soon fell to the Haitian *Toussaint L'Ouverture, who proclaimed himself ruler of all Hispaniola. The Spanish were restored in the E in 1809 and in 1821 the colony gained independence. It was held by Haiti from 1822 until 1844, when the Dominican Republic was founded. Political and economic instability led to US occupation (1916–22) and the establishment (1930) of Trujillo's 30-year dictatorship. Following his assassination Juan Bosch (1909–) was elected (1962) president only to be deposed (1963) in a military coup. An attempt by constitutionalists to reinstate Bosch was thwarted by the USA in 1965. Joaquín Balaguer, president 1968–78, was re-elected in 1986. Official language: Spanish. Official currency: Dominican Republic peso of 100 centavos. Area: 48 442 sq km (18 700 sq mi). Population (1983 est): 6 248 000. Capital and main port: Santo Domingo.

Dominicans (Latin *Ordo Praedicatorum*: Order of Preachers) A Roman Catholic order of friars, also known as Black Friars, Friar Preachers, or (in France) Jacobins, founded by St *Dominic and formally organized at Bologna in 1220–21. Their purpose was preaching and teaching, the individual friars leading mendicant lives much of the time. Among their great scholars was St Thomas *Aquinas. They were prominent defenders of orthodoxy in the *Inquisition and leading missionaries to the New World, although the Jesuits superseded them in this role during the Counter-Reformation. There are also two orders of Dominican nuns.

Domino, Fats (Antoine D.; 1928–) US Black jazz singer, pianist, and songwriter, who became famous in the rock and roll era. His songs, which contained blues elements, include "Blueberry Hill" and "Jambalaya."

dominoes A game played with rectangular pieces marked at each end with a group of dots or a blank space. In a set of

28 pieces, each group adds up to a number from 1 to 6. Dominoes were used in China in ancient times but not in Europe until the 18th century. There are many games, but in the basic game played in the UK each player first draws seven pieces. The player with the double six places it face up on the table. The next player places next to it a six on the end of another domino; if this domino has, for instance, a two on the other end the third player must match either the two or the remaining six. Doubles are placed crosswise, the others end to end. A player who cannot make a match misses his turn or in some games takes another domino. The first to finish wins.

Domitian(us), Titus Flavius (51–96 AD) Roman emperor (81–96). His frustrating inactivity under his father *Vespasian and his brother *Titus made him a harsh ruler. His government became increasingly absolute and from about 84, as censor for life, he controlled the Senate. His suspicion of treachery culminated in a reign of terror, which precipitated his own murder.

Domrémy-la-Pucelle 48 26N 5 40E A village in NE France, in the Vosges, the birthplace of Joan of Arc.

Don, River A river in the SW Soviet Union, flowing mainly S to the Sea of Azov. A canal links it to the River Volga. Length: 1981 km (1224 mi).

Donatello (Donato de Nicolo di Betti Bardi; c. 1386–1466) Florentine sculptor. A pioneer of the Renaissance style, Donatello first broke with tradition in his marble sculptures of *St Mark* and *St George* (1415) for the exterior of Orsanmichele. These and his prophets for the campanile of the Duomo are modelled as lifelike rather than idealized figures. Simultaneously he developed a new form of relief sculpture, in which he created perspective by incising the surface of the marble rather than modelling it in depth. Working also in bronze from the early 1420s, he produced *David* (c. 1430–35; Bargello, Florence), the influential equestrian monument in Padua known as the *Gattamelata* (1447–53), and the high altar for S Antonio, Padua (1446–50). His late works include the expressive painted wooden sculpture of *Mary Magdalen* (1454–55; Baptistry, Florence).

Donatists Members of a schismatic North African Christian group of the 4th and 5th centuries AD, named after Donatus, one of their bishops. They held that the validity of the sacraments depended on the personal holiness of the minister. St *Augustine's repudiation of their views in the early 5th century crystallized Catholic teaching on these matters. He argued that since the true minister is Christ, the personal worthiness of the priest could not affect the validity of the sacraments.

Donatus, Aelius (4th century AD) Roman grammarian and rhetorician. Donatus was the tutor of St Jerome, and his Latin grammar, *Ars Grammatica*, became a universally accepted textbook in the middle ages.

Donbass. *See* Donets Basin.

Doncaster 53 32N 1 07W An industrial town in N England, in South Yorkshire, with railway workshops and coalmining. Population (1981): 81 610.

Donegal (Irish name: Dún Na Ngall) A county in the N Republic of Ireland, in Ulster bordering on the Atlantic Ocean. Chiefly mountainous, it has a rugged indented coastline. Agricultural products include barley, oats, and potatoes; cattle and sheep are reared. Linen and tweed are manufactured. Area: 4830 sq km (1865 sq mi). Population (1981): 125 112. County town: Lifford.

Donets Basin (or Donbass) An industrial region in the SW Soviet Union, in the Ukrainian SSR. It is the oldest centre of coal production in the country and still its major coal-producing and steel-manufacturing area. Area: about 25 900 sq km (10 000 sq mi).

Donetsk (name until 1924: Yuzovka; name from 1924 until 1961: Stalino) 48 22N 40 02E A city in the SW Soviet Union, in the Ukrainian SSR on the River Kalmius. The major city of the *Donets Basin, it has important coalmining and metallurgical industries. Population (1981 est): 1 040 000.

Dong Hai. *See* East China Sea.

Dongola (or Dunqulah) 19 10N 30 27E A small town in the N Sudan, on the River Nile. It was the capital of the Christian kingdom of Nubia (6th–14th centuries). Population (1973): 5937.

Dongting, Lake (or Lake Tung-t'ing) A lake in SE China. Seasonally fed or drained by the Yangtze River, it regulates the river's flooding. Area: (winter) 3900 sq km (1500 sq mi); (summer) about 10 000 sq km (4000 sq mi).

Dönitz, Karl (1891–1980) German admiral. He made his name as a U-boat commander in World War I and in the first three years of World War II he developed the "pack" system of submarine attack. In 1943 he became grand admiral and then commander in chief of the German navy. He was appointed chancellor after Hitler's death and was imprisoned from 1946 to 1956 for war crimes.

Donizetti, Gaetano (1797–1848) Italian composer of operas. He became paralysed and mentally ill towards the end of his life. He wrote with great facility and his 75 stage works rely more on *coloratura display, the popular characteristic of his age, than on intrinsic dramatic effect. Revivals of such operas as *Lucia di Lammermoor* (1835) and *Daughter of the Regiment* (1840) have been successful with such singers as Joan Sutherland or Maria Callas in the title roles.

Don Juan The great aristocratic libertine of European literature. His probable first appearance was in Tirso de Molina's play *El burlador de Sevilla* (1630), in which he kills the father of his latest victim; he mockingly invites the old man's statue to dinner, and it drags him off to hell. This plot is retained in subsequent versions, most notably *Molière's *Don Juan* (1665) and *Mozart's *Don Giovanni* (1787). In satirical treatments by *Byron (*Don Juan*, 1819–24) and G. B. *Shaw (*Man and Superman*, 1903) Juan is more hunted than hunter.

donkey A domesticated *ass. Donkeys are more commonly used for pack and draught work than for riding: being stronger in the hindquarters than the forequarters, they must bear the load over the pelvis, which is a less comfortable position for a rider. *See also* hinny; mule.

Donleavy, J(ames) P(atrick) (1926–) Irish-American novelist. His successful first novel, *The Ginger Man* (1956), was followed by further comic picaresque novels including *The Onion Eaters* (1971), *The Destinies of Darcy Dancer, Gentleman* (1977), and *Are You Listening Rabbi Löw?* (1987).

Donne, John (1572–1631) English poet, greatest of the Metaphysical school. He received a Roman Catholic education, studied at Oxford and Lincoln's Inn, and took part in naval raids on Spain. In 1601 he secretly married the niece of his patron, Sir Thomas Egerton, and was briefly imprisoned. Failing to gain secular advancement, despite having several influential patrons, he became an Anglican priest in 1615 and was appointed Dean of St Paul's in 1621. His poetry combines passionate feeling for God, woman, and humanity with brilliant intellectual wit. Almost all of it, even religious works, such as *La Corona* (1607) and the Holy Sonnets, was written before 1615.

Doolittle, Hilda (1886–1961) US poet, who wrote under the initials H. D. Born in Pennsylvania, she went to England in 1911 and married Richard *Aldington. A leading exponent of Imagism, her books include *Sea Garden* (1916), *Hymen* (1921), and *Helen in Egypt* (1961).

dopamine. *See* catecholamines.

Doppler, Christian Johann (1803–53) Austrian physicist, who explained and derived, in 1842, an expression for the change in frequency of a wave when the source is moving relative to an observer (*see* Doppler effect). He attempted to apply this principle to the coloration of stars; although the effect is too small to be observed visually, it is now widely used spectroscopically in astronomy.

Doppler effect The apparent change in the frequency of a wave caused by relative motion between the source and the observer. When the source and the observer are approaching each other, the apparent frequency of the wave increases; when one is travelling away from the other, the apparent frequency decreases. An example of the Doppler effect is the change in pitch of a train whistle as the train passes through a station. The effect can also be observed as a shifting of the wavelength of light from a receding star towards the red end of the spectrum. In this case the effect is known as the *redshift. Named after Christian *Doppler.

dor beetle A large shiny black convex beetle, with broad digging legs, belonging to a family (*Geotrupidae*; about 300 species) of dung feeders. Dor beetles burrow into the soil beneath dung and lay their eggs on plugs of dung hauled down for use as a food source.

Dorcas gazelle A small *gazelle, *Gazella dorcas*, of N Africa and S Asia, also called afri. A desert animal, it is light red with a pale flank stripe and distinctive face stripes.

JOHN DONNE *A miniature portrait (1616) by Isaac Oliver.*

Dorchester 50 43N 2 26W A market town in S England, the administrative centre for Dorset on the River Frome. It has several Roman remains and is associated with Thomas Hardy, featuring as Casterbridge in his novels. Population (1981): 14 049.

Dordogne, River A river in SW France. Rising in the Auvergne Mountains, it flows SW and W to enter the Gironde estuary NNE of Bordeaux. It is important for hydroelectric power and has famous vineyards along its lower course. Length: 472 km (293 mi).

Dordrecht (*or* Dort) 51 48N 4 40E A port in the SW Netherlands, in South Holland province. It has a thriving timber trade and metallurgical, shipbuilding, and chemical industries. Population (1985): 107 267.

Doré, (Paul) Gustave (Louis Christophe) (1832–83) French illustrator, painter, and sculptor, born in Strasbourg. He established his wide and lasting popularity in the 1850s

with his illustrations of Rabelais' books and Balzac's *Contes drôlatiques*. These were followed by illustrations to Dante, Cervantes, Tennyson, etc., showing his taste for the grotesque and dramatic. His realistic scenes of poverty in *London* influenced Van Gogh. ⌐Camelot.

Dorgon (1612–50) Prince of Manchuria, who controlled China as regent for a child emperor from 1643 to 1650. Continuing the expansionist policy of his father *Nurhachi, Dorgon helped to lay the foundations of the *Qing dynasty in China, basing its power on centralized government instead of the clan system.

Doria A family that was prominent in Genoa from the 12th to 18th centuries. The most notable member of the family was **Andrea Doria** (1466–1560). An admiral and condottiere, he served the French against Emperor Charles V, ousted imperial troops from Genoa, and then transferred his allegiance to Charles and expelled the French in return for the emperor's recognition of Genoese liberty (1528). He then became the ruler of Genoa, initiating the period of aristocratic rule (1528–1797) during which the Doria family contributed six doges of Genoa.

Dorians Iron Age Greek conquerors of the S Aegean region (c. 1100–1000 BC). Moving southward from Epirus and SW Macedonia, they displaced the *Achaeans and brought about the final collapse of the Bronze Age *Mycenaean civilization. They settled in the S and E Peloponnese, near the isthmus of Corinth, in the S Aegean islands, the Dodecanese, and SW Anatolia. There were three major tribes: the Hylleis, Pamphyloi, and Dymanes. The Doric dialects they spoke belonged to the Western Greek group.

Doric order. *See* orders of architecture.

dormancy A period of reduced metabolic activity during which a plant or animal or a reproductive body (e.g. seeds or spores) can survive unfavourable environmental conditions. The onset of dormancy may be triggered by a number of factors, including changes in temperature, daylength (*see* photoperiodism), and availability of water, oxygen, and carbon dioxide. The dormant phase of a life cycle is represented as spores in bacteria and fungi, cysts in protozoans and some invertebrates, and seeds, buds, and bulbs or similar organs in plants. *See also* hibernation.

dormouse A climbing *rodent belonging to the family *Gliridae* (about 10 species) of Eurasia and Africa. The common dormouse (*Muscardinus avellanarius*) is reddish, about 6 cm long with a 5-cm bushy tail. It sleeps in a nest above ground level during the day, feeding at night on nuts, berries, and seeds. During winter it hibernates beneath debris or tree stumps, occasionally waking to feed on stored food.

Dorneywood A country house in S England, in Buckinghamshire near Burnham Beeches. Administered by the National Trust, it was presented to the nation by Lord Courtauld-Thomson as a residence for ministers of state.

Dornier, Claudius (1884–1969) German aircraft designer and manufacturer, who constructed the first all-metal aircraft (1911). At his works in Friedrichshafen he manufactured both civil and military planes.

Dornoch 57 52N 4 02W A resort in N Scotland, in the Highland Region on Dornoch Firth. It was the site of the last execution for witchcraft (1722) in Scotland and it has a well-known golf course. Population (1985 est): 1100.

Dorpat. *See* Tartu.

Dorset A county of SW England, bordering on the English Channel. Under local government reorganization in 1974 it gained part of SW Hampshire. It consists chiefly of lowlands, crossed by the North Dorset Downs, with Cranborne Chase in the N and the South Dorset Downs near the coast. The chief rivers are the Frome and the Stour. Agriculture is predominant, especially livestock farming. Tourism is important, notably in Bournemouth and Weymouth. Many towns are associated with the writings of Thomas *Hardy, who included Dorset within his fictitious region of Wessex. Area: 2634 sq km (1017 sq mi). Population (1983): 609 100. Administrative centre: Dorchester.

Dort. *See* Dordrecht.

Dortmund 51 32N 07 27E A city in NW West Germany, in North Rhine-Westphalia in the *Ruhr. A port on the Dortmund–Ems Canal and a major industrial centre, it produces steel, furniture, textiles, coal, and beer. Its university was established in 1966. Population (1980 est): 609 400.

Dortmund–Ems Canal A major canal in West Germany. Opened in 1899, it links the Ruhr industrial area with the North Sea near Emden. Length: about 270 km (168 mi).

dory. *See* John Dory.

Dos Passos, John (1896–1970) US novelist. He served as an ambulance driver in World War I and worked as a war correspondent in Spain, Mexico, and the Near East. His major work, the trilogy *U.S.A.*—comprising *The Forty-Second Parallel* (1930), *1919* (1932), and *The Big Money* (1936)—uses experimental techniques in its radical interpretation of American history from 1900 until the Depression.

Dostoievski, Fedor Mikhailovich (1821–81) Russian novelist. Son of a landowner murdered by his serfs, he graduated as a military engineer in 1843, but resigned his commission and began writing. In 1849 he was sentenced to four years hard labour in Siberia, followed by army service, for printing socialist propaganda. In 1864 his wife and brother died, and he incurred heavy gambling debts. He lived in W Europe from 1867 to 1871 with his new wife, his secretary Anna Snitkina, plagued by his epilepsy and compulsive gambling. He returned to Russia in 1871 and became relatively prosperous, stable, and conservative. His major novels, in which he explored moral and political themes with merciless psychological realism, are *Crime and Punishment* (1866), *The Idiot* (1868–69), *The Possessed* (1869–72), and *The Brothers Karamazov* (1879–80).

dotterel A small Eurasian *plover, *Eudromias morinellus*, that nests in tundra regions and migrates to the Mediterranean and SW Asia for the winter. It is 20 cm long and mottled brown above with a broad white eye stripe and a grey breast separated by a narrow white band from its russet belly.

Dou, Gerrit (1613–75) Dutch painter of domestic interiors and portraits, born in Leyden. He studied under *Rembrandt (1628–31), who influenced his early portrait *Rembrandt's Mother* (c. 1630; Rijksmuseum, Amsterdam). *The Poulterer's Shop* (National Gallery, London), showing his interest in still life, is a more typical work.

Douai 50 22N 3 05E A town in N France, in the Nord department. It became a centre for English Roman Catholics following the establishment of a college by William Allen in 1568 and it was here that the *Douai Bible was published. Douai is the coalmining centre of N France and has iron and steel industries. Population (1982): 44 515.

Douai Bible The Roman Catholic version of the Bible in English, translated from the *Vulgate by Roman Catholic scholars from Oxford, who had fled to Europe during the reign of Elizabeth I and who were members of the English College at Douai. The New Testament was published at Reims in 1582 and the Old Testament at Douai in 1609–10. Although it retained a number of difficult technical expressions foreign to colloquial English, its language influenced the translators of the *King James Version.

Douala 4 04N 9 43E The largest city in Cameroon, on the River Wouri estuary. A deepwater port and the chief export point of the country, it is also a major West African industrial centre with brewing, food-processing, textiles, and timber industries. Population (1981 est): 636 980.

double bass The lowest-pitched □musical instrument of the violin family. The flat back and sloping shoulders of some double basses are derived from the *viol family. Unlike the violin,

viola, and cello, its four strings are tuned in fourths (E, A, D, G). It has a range of over three octaves, from the E an octave below the bass stave. The double bass is a member of the symphony orchestra; it is also played in jazz and dance bands, usually by plucking the strings. Music for the double bass is written an octave higher than it sounds.

double vision The condition in which a person sees two images of a single object. Known medically as diplopia, it is caused by lack of coordination between the muscles that move the eyes. Temporary double vision may occur after taking drugs or alcohol; alternatively it may be due to damage or disease of one of the nerves that supply the eye muscles.

Doubs, River A river in E France. Rising in the Jura Mountains and flowing SW to join the River Saône, it forms part of the Swiss–French border. Length: 430 km (267 mi).

Doughty, Charles Montagu (1843–1926) British travel writer and poet. From 1875 to 1877 he travelled in Arabia, observing the life of the Bedouins. *Travels in Arabia Deserta* (1888) is the fruit of his experiences. He also wrote epic poetry.

Douglas 54 09N 4 29W The capital of the Isle of Man, on the E coast. It is a port and resort with legislative buildings, including the House of Keys (parliament house), the Manx Museum, and a casino. Population (1981 est): 64 679.

Douglas, Gavin (?1474–1522) Scots poet. His works include a moral allegory, *The Palice of Honour* (1501), and the first translation of Virgil's *Aeneid* into English (or rather Scots) in 1513. After the death of James III at *Flodden he became involved in political intrigues and died in exile in London.

Douglas, (George) Norman (1868–1952) British novelist. He served in the British diplomatic service in Russia until 1896, when he settled in Italy on the island of Capri, the setting of his novel *South Wind* (1917). *Siren Land* (1911) and *Old Calabria* (1915) are major travel books.

Douglas fir A conifer, *Pseudotsuga menziesii*, native to W North America and cultivated widely both for ornament and for its high-quality timber, used for construction, poles, masts, etc. 60–90 m high, it has flexible blunt-tipped needles and cylindrical cones, about 8 cm long, with three-pronged bracts protruding from the scales. Family: *Pinaceae*.

Douglas-Home, Sir Alec. *See* Home of the Hirsel, Alec Douglas-Home, Baron.

Doukhobors (Russian: fighters against the spirit) Russian nonconformist Christian sect founded in the 18th century. Because of their anarchistic doctrines (denial of the state's right to levy tax, etc.) and heterodox religious views (belief in reincarnation, denial of Christ's divinity), they were for a long time persecuted. With the help of *Tolstoy and English Quakers, they emigrated from Georgia to Canada in 1898, where they subsequently came into conflict with the government over such matters as sending their children to state schools. In 1958 some members of the sect were permitted to return to the Soviet Union.

Doulton English pottery works, originally at Lambeth (London), specializing in salt-glazed stoneware. Brown stoneware vessels with relief moulded portrait and landscape ornament were typical of the period to 1850. From 1856 Sir Henry Doulton (1820–97) encouraged artist potters to produce unique studio pottery in coloured glazes, using wood-fixed kilns. These were exhibited at the 1867 Paris Exhibition.

Dounreay The site in N Scotland, on the N coast of the Highland Region, of the world's first experimental fast-breeder reactor.

Douro, River (Spanish name: Duero) A river in SW Europe. Flowing W from N central Spain, it forms part of the border between Spain and Portugal before entering the Atlantic Ocean at Oporto. Length: 895 km (556 mi).

douroucouli A nocturnal *monkey, *Aotus trivirgatus*, of

Central and South America, also called night monkey or owl monkey. It is 55-75 cm long including the tail (30-40 cm) and moves through trees stalking small animals. It also eats fruit and leaves. Family: *Cebidae*.

dove. *See* pigeon.

Dover 51 08N 1 19E A port in SE England, in Kent on the Strait of Dover. An ancient Cinque Port, it is the UK's chief ferry and Hovercraft port for the Continent. Population (1981): 32 843.

Dover 39 10N 75 32W A city in the USA, the capital of Delaware near Delaware Bay. Founded in 1683, it has many 18th-and 19th-century buildings. Population (1980): 29 006.

Dover, Strait of (French name: Pas de Calais) A channel separating England from NW France comprising the narrowest part of the *English Channel. Minimum width: 34 km (21 mi).

Dowding, Hugh Caswall Tremenheere, 1st Baron (1882-1970) British air chief marshal, who was head of the RAF Fighter Command in 1940. His strategic and tactical genius in coordinating early warning radar, pilots, and equipment played a major role in winning the battle of Britain.

Dow-Jones index A weighted average of the prices on the New York Stock Exchange of 30 industrial shares, computed each working day by Dow Jones and Co. The first index was devised in 1897 using only 12 shares. It is the principal indicator of movements in share prices in the USA.

Dowland, John (1563-1626) English composer and lutenist. He travelled widely and was lutenist at the Danish court (1598-1606). He was one of the first composers to specialize in writing songs with lute accompaniment and also composed the famous "Lachrymae" for lutes, viols, or violins.

Down A former county in E Northern Ireland, bordering on the Irish Sea, with Antrim to the N and Armagh to the W. It consists of lowlands in the E rising to the Mourne Mountains in the SW. Agriculture is the chief occupation; dairy farming is especially important. Area: 2466 sq km (952 sq mi). County town: Downpatrick.

Downing Street A street in the Greater London borough of the City of Westminster, adjoining Whitehall. No 10 is the official residence of the prime minister; the chancellor of the exchequer resides at No 11. It was named after the English statesman Sir George Downing (1623-84).

Downpatrick 54 20N 5 43W A market town in Northern Ireland, the county town of Co Down. It is the reputed burial place of St Patrick. Population (1981): 8245.

Downs, North and South Two roughly parallel ranges of chalk hills in SE England, separated by the *Weald. The North Downs extend W-E between Guildford, in Surrey, and Dover, in Kent. The South Downs extend generally SE from Winchester, in Hampshire, to Beachy Head. The Downs have traditionally been sheep-farming areas.

Down's syndrome A genetic disease in which a baby has one extra chromosome; it is named after J. L. H. Down (1828-96), an English physician who studied the disease. Affected children are mentally retarded and their faces resemble those of orientals, which is why they were formerly called mongols and the disease mongolism. In spite of their handicaps, these children are usually cheerful and with special education can live relatively normal lives in a family. Down's syndrome is more commonly seen in babies of mothers over 40; it can be detected during pregnancy (*see* amniocentesis).

dowsing The use of divining- or dowsing-rods to discover subterranean minerals or water. From the 16th century divining-rods were employed by miners and treasure hunters, a function now largely usurped by metal detectors. Dowsing for water is still of practical value; skilled dowsers can estimate the depth and flow of underground streams. The rod is traditionally a Y-shaped twig which, when its two prongs are grasped, twists in the hands of the dowser as he approaches water. Alternatively metal rods are held parallel a few inches apart and swing across each other. The nature of the stimuli causing these reactions is unexplained.

Dowson, Ernest (Christopher) (1867-1900) British poet, with Yeats a member of the Rhymers' Club. His poetry explored themes of love and worldly renunciation. From 1894 he lived mostly in France, where he died of tuberculosis, aggravated by poverty and addiction to absinthe.

Doyle, Sir Arthur Conan (1859-1930) British author, creator of the archetypal detective Sherlock Holmes. Born in Edinburgh, Conan Doyle graduated in medicine there but soon turned to writing. Holmes, inspired by the diagnostic methods of an Edinburgh lecturer, brought Conan Doyle great success. Holmes first appeared in the novel *A Study in Scarlet* (1887), narrated, as are nearly all the short stories and novels about him, by his dogged but unimaginative friend Dr John H. Watson, almost a self-caricature by the author. Conan Doyle also created the coarsely brilliant Professor Challenger in *The Lost World* (1912) but he valued most highly his historical novels, such as *The White Company* (1890). Knighted in 1902 for his service, and subsequent defence of British involvement, in the second Boer War, Conan Doyle became a champion of *spiritualism after the death of his son in World War I.

D'Oyly Carte, Richard (1844-1901) British theatre impresario and manager. He produced most of the comic operas of Gilbert and Sullivan. The Savoy Theatre, which he opened in 1881 to house these productions, was the first London theatre to have electric lighting.

Drabble, Margaret (1939-) British novelist. Most of her novels concern the moral and emotional problems of women in contemporary society. They include *The Millstone* (1965), *The Needle's Eye* (1972), *The Ice Age* (1977), *The Middle Ground* (1980), and *The Radiant Way* (1987). She has also written a study of Arnold Bennett (1974) and edited the 1985 edition of the *Oxford Companion to Literature*.

Draco (7th century BC) Athenian lawgiver. His legal system is reputedly the first comprehensive code of laws drawn up in Athens. It was so harshly punitive that "draconian" has since been used to describe any rigorous or cruel law. Draco's code prescribed the death penalty by the state for most offences, taking retribution out of the hands of private citizens. *Solon abolished Draco's code in 590 BC, retaining only his homicide laws.

Dracula, Count The central character of Bram *Stoker's gothic novel *Dracula* (1897) and of many horror films, a Transylvanian *vampire. The name, meaning "demon," was applied to Vlad IV the Impaler, a 15th-century Walachian prince who was the prototype of the fictional character.

dragger A motor trawler used in commercial fishing off the NE coast of the USA.

dragonet A small spiny-rayed fish, of the family *Callionymidae*, that has a smooth slender body, 10-20 cm long, flattened anteriorly and often brightly coloured. The pelvic fins are located in front of the pectoral fins. Dragonets live on the bottom in temperate and tropical seas and feed on invertebrates. Order: *Perciformes*.

dragonfish A small *bony fish belonging to an order (*Pegasiformes*; about 5 species) found in warm waters of the Indian and Pacific Oceans. They have an elongated body, up to 16 cm long, with bony armour, a long snout, and large horizontal winglike pectoral fins.

dragonfly A strong agile brightly coloured insect belonging to the widely distributed suborder *Anisoptera* (about 4500 species). It has a long body, large eyes, and transparent veined wings (spanning up to 180 mm), which are held horizontally at rest. Both the adults and freshwater nymphs (naiads) are active carnivores and control many insect pests, such as mosquitoes, flies, and gnats. Order: *Odonata*.

dragonroot A perennial North American herbaceous plant, *Arisaema dracontium*, also called green dragon or dragon arum. The flower comprises a central column of sexual organs surmounted by a long tapering cylindrical structure (the spadix) and surrounded by a much shorter pointed green sheath (the spathe). The tuberous roots were formerly used in medicine. Family: *Araceae*.

dragon's blood A red gum that exudes from the fruit of some palms. It was once used in Europe as a medicine because of its astringent and healing properties. It is used as a varnish for violins and in photoengraving.

DRAGON TREE *This plant is unusual in that — like broadleaved trees — it produces true wood. The most famous of these trees was one in Tenerife, which was said to be 6000 years old.*

dragon tree A treelike plant, *Dracaena draco*, native to the Canary Islands. Growing 18 m tall and 6 m wide, it has large sword-shaped leaves at the tips of the branches and clusters of greenish-white flowers followed by orange berries. The dragon tree is sometimes grown as a pot plant for its foliage. The trunk was formerly used as a source of a red gum resin, *dragon's blood. Family: *Agavaceae*.

dragoon European mounted soldier of the 16th and 17th centuries who could fight as a light cavalryman (*see also* hussars) or as an infantryman. Named after the muzzle-loading carbine called the dragoon that they carried, they were originally used as an arm of the infantry, being organized in companies, and their officers bore infantry titles. By the 18th century most light cavalrymen were called dragoons (or carabiniers).

drag racing 1. A form of *motor racing that originated in the USA. It is held in heats of two cars on a straight strip a quarter of a mile (402 m) long. Using a standing start, races depend heavily on acceleration with the "elapsed time" (from start to finish) and "terminal velocity" of each vehicle measured electronically. Speeds have reached 403 km per hour (250 mph) in specially constructed light powerful vehicles (slingshots *or* rails), although races are also held for modified production models. 2. A form of motorcycle racing organized in the same way.

Drake, Sir Francis (1540–96) English navigator and admiral. Drake's first important voyages were trading expeditions to Guinea and the West Indies and in 1567 he

accompanied Sir John *Hawkins (a relative) to the Gulf of Mexico. In 1572 he embarked on a plundering expedition, destroying towns on the Isthmus of Panama and capturing considerable quantities of booty. In 1578 he became the first Englishman to navigate the Straits of Magellan intending, with Elizabeth I's consent, to raid the Pacific coast. Alone out of five ships, his *Golden Hind* sailed N but unable to find a way back to the Atlantic Ocean crossed the Pacific Ocean, returning home via the Cape of Good Hope. He landed at Plymouth in 1580 and was knighted by Elizabeth on board the *Hind* in 1581. Drake crowned his career by helping to defeat the Spanish *Armada at Gravelines (1588). He died on an expedition to the West Indies.

Drakensberg Mountains (*or* Quathlamba) The chief mountain range in S Africa, extending from Cape Province (South Africa) along the E border of Lesotho to Swaziland, reaching 3482 m (11 425 ft) at Thaba Ntlenyana.

Drammen 59 45N 10 15E A seaport in S Norway, at the mouth of the River Drammen. It exports timber, wood pulp, and paper. Population (1981 est): 49 523.

draughts (US name: checkers) A board game for two players that was developed in 12th-century Europe from an ancient Egyptian game. Each player has 12 disc-shaped pieces (usually black for one and white or red for the other), which are placed on the 12 black squares at the opposite ends of a chessboard. The pieces move only on the black squares and black always starts. One piece per turn is moved diagonally forwards onto a vacant adjacent square. If the next square is occupied by one of the opponent's pieces but the square beyond that is vacant, the playing piece must jump onto the vacant square, removing his opponent's piece from the board. He must make a further jump from there if possible (in the same turn). The 16th-century rule of "huffing" enables a player to remove an opponent's piece that could have jumped but did not. If a piece reaches the opposing back line it becomes a "king" (a second piece is placed on top of it) and it may then move forwards or backwards. The winner is the player who takes or immobilizes all his opponent's pieces.

Drava, River (*or* R. Drave) A river in E central Europe, flowing E from N Italy through Austria, then SE forming part of the Yugoslav-Hungarian border to join the River Danube. Length: 725 km (450 mi).

Dravidian languages A large language family of up to 20 languages spoken mainly in S India. The major languages of the family are *Tamil, which has a literary tradition dating back 2000 years, *Kanarese (*or* Kannada), Telugu, *Malayalam, and Tulu. These are all spoken in a continuous area in India, and Tamil is also spoken in Sri Lanka. There is one Dravidian language, Brahui, that is separated from the main bloc by almost a thousand miles and is spoken in Pakistan. The Dravidian languages are all agglutinative (*see* languages, classification of) and this is strong evidence for separating them from the other major language bloc of the subcontinent, the *Indo-European group.

Drayton, Michael (1563–1631) English poet. A prolific writer, he wrote sonnet sequences, pastoral idylls, and many other conventional poems within traditional Elizabethan genres. His most popular work was *England's Heroical Epistles* (1597), a series of imaginary love letters, and his most ambitious was *Polyolbion* (Part 1, 1612; Part 2, 1622), a patriotic attempt to record the history and splendours of England.

dreams Ideas and images experienced during *sleep. Dreams may take place at any stage of sleep, but they are particularly associated with the paradoxical phase, in which the eyes move rapidly about. Dreams in this stage of sleep are the most vivid in their imagery and the farthest removed from waking thoughts. Everybody has dreams: most people have paradoxical sleep about four or five times a night, for about 20 minutes at a time; whether or not the dream is remembered depends on how quickly after it the sleeper wakes up.

If a person is repeatedly deprived of the chance to dream (by being woken when a dream starts) he becomes irritable, inefficient, and eventually suffers *hallucinations. After such deprivation, he dreams more frequently when he is again allowed to. The new combinations of ideas produced in dreams can be creative and valuable. *Psychoanalysis gives much weight to the content of dreams as an approach to understanding the unconscious mind. Experimental studies indicate that the content of dreams is affected by the dreamer's mood and by stimuli that occur while he sleeps. *See also* nightmares.

dredger   A vessel designed to deepen underwater channels in rivers, docks, canals, etc., by removing material from the bottom. The types used include the suction dredger, which sucks up mud through a rubber pipe from the bottom and either deposits it in barges or in its own tanks; the bucket-ladder dredger, which carriers an endless chain of buckets supported on a frame; and the grab dredger, which operates much like a power shovel.

Dreiser, Theodore   (1871–1945) US novelist. The son of a poor German immigrant, he became a journalist and settled in New York in 1894. *Sister Carrie* (1900), his first novel, was attacked for its raw realism but *An American Tragedy* (1925), based on an actual murder case, brought him critical and financial success. He visited the Soviet Union in 1927 and later joined the Communist Party.

Drenthe   (*or* Drente)   A low-lying province in the E Netherlands, bordering on West Germany. Parts of its extensive bogs and heaths have been reclaimed for agriculture; produce includes potatoes, rye, and dairy products. Oil is extracted around Shoonebeek. Area: 2685 sq km (1037 sq mi). Population (1984 est): 427 336. Capital: Assen.

Dresden   51 5N 13 41E A city in SE East Germany, on the River *Elbe, the former capital of Saxony. One of the world's most beautiful cities prior to its devastation by bombs in 1945, it has since been rebuilt. Dresden is a centre of culture, light industry, and market gardening. The china industry moved to Meissen in 1710. It is the site of a music college and a technical university. Population (1982 est): 522 532.

Dresden, Battle of   (26–27 August, 1813) A battle fought near the capital of Saxony between 120 000 French troops led by Napoleon and an Austrian, Prussian, and Russian force of 170 000. Napoleon inflicted a crushing defeat on the allies, who lost 38 000 men.

Dresden porcelain.   See Meissen porcelain.

dressage   The training of a riding (*or* carriage) horse to make it calm, supple, and responsive to its rider (*or* driver). It was originally a training for military charges; the present, more humane, methods only developed in the 18th century. The most advanced stage is *haute école* equitation in which a horse is taught to perform intricate leaps and movements. This classical art is practised by the *Spanish Riding School in Vienna and the Cadre Noir of the French Cavalry School at Saumur. Dressage competitions consist of a sequence of complex prescribed movements. *See also* equestrianism.

Dreyer, Carl Theodor   (1889–1968) Danish film director. He began his career in films as a scriptwriter in 1912. His major films concern spiritual and supernatural themes and are distinguished by their atmospheric concentration and intensity. They include *La Passion de Jeanne d'Arc* (1928) and *Ordet* (1955).

Dreyer, Johan Ludvig Emil   (1852–1926) Danish astronomer, who compiled the *New General Catalogue of Nebulae and Clusters of Stars* (1888). This work is still a standard reference catalogue for nonstellar objects, which are referred to by their catalogue number, e.g. the galaxy NGC 175.

Dreyfus, Alfred   (1859–1935) French Jewish army officer. Unjustly accused of revealing state secrets to the German military attaché in Paris, in 1894 Dreyfus, the victim of *antisemitism, was deported for life to *Devil's Island. His case was reopened in 1898, largely owing to the championship of Zola and Clemenceau, becoming a cause célèbre and the focus of conflict between royalist, nationalist, and militarist elements on the one hand and socialist, republican, and anticlerical factions on the other. Following a retrial in 1899, Dreyfus was pardoned but not completely cleared until 1906, when he received the Legion of Honour.

Driesch, Hans Adolf Eduard   (1867–1941) German zoologist, whose work gave impetus to modern embryology. His interpretation of studies on developing sea urchin embryos led him to become a lifelong advocate of *vitalism.

drift   **1.** The debris, including boulders, sand, clay, and gravel, deposited by glaciers or by glacial meltwater. **2.** The superficial deposits occurring above the solid underlying rock on the earth's surface. Geological maps are published in both drift and solid editions to distinguish between them.

drill   An *Old World monkey, *Mandrillus eucophaeus*, of central West Africa, smaller than the closely related *mandrill. Drills inhabit inland forests, moving about on the ground in small groups and eating leaves, fruit, and worms.

Drinkwater, John   (1882–1937) British poet, critic, and dramatist. He was a leading contributor to the *Georgian Poetry* anthologies. He helped to found the Birmingham Repertory Theatre in 1913 and wrote several successful historical plays, notably *Abraham Lincoln* (1918) and *Mary Stuart* (1921).

driver ant   An African *ant of the genus *Dorylus* or related genera, which has a lifestyle similar to the New World *army ant. Subfamily: *Dorylinae*.

Drogheda (Irish name: Droichead Atha)   53 43N 6 21W A port in the Republic of Ireland, in Co Louth on the River Boyne. Its garrison was massacred by Cromwell in 1649. Drogheda exports cattle and has brewing, linen and cotton, and engineering industries. Population (1981): 23 247.

dromedary.   See camel.

drone.   See bee.

drongo   A songbird belonging to a family (*Dicruridae*; 20 species) occurring in Old World tropical forests. About 22–35 cm long, drongos are usually black, often with long tail plumes, and have a harsh song. They have stout sharp-hooked bills and feed on large insects, which are often caught in flight. These birds are noted for fiercely defending their territories against intruders.

dropsy.   See oedema.

dropwort   A perennial herb, *Filipendula vulgaris*, of grasslands and clearings in Eurasia and N Africa. Up to 70 cm high, it has compound leaves with 8–20 divided toothed leaflets. The flowers, which occur in flat-topped terminal clusters, have 5–6 red-tinged white petals and long prominent stamens. The tuberous roots may be eaten. Family: *Rosaceae*.

Drosera.   See sundew.

Drosophila   A genus of small *fruit flies (about 1000 species), also called vinegar flies. Most species feed on fermenting materials, such as rotting or damaged fruit, but a few are predatory or parasitic. Some species, especially *D. melanogaster*, have been used extensively in laboratory studies of heredity and evolution because of the large chromosomes in their salivary glands and their short life cycle. Family: *Drosophilidae*.

Droste-Hülshoff, Annette von   (1797–1848) German poet and novelist. She lived in isolation on her aristocratic family's estate. She wrote poems on religious themes and about her native countryside of Westphalia, and a novella, *The Jew's Beech Tree* (1842).

drought   An extended period of dry weather with a virtual absence of precipitation, causing a lack of moisture in the soil. Droughts in densely populated areas reliant on agriculture, such as India and China, can have disastrous effects. In the UK an **absolute drought** is defined as a period of at least 15 consecutive days on none of which is there more than 0.2 mm of rainfall.

drowning Suffocation due to water in the air passages. Death occurs much more rapidly in fresh water than sea water. This is because fresh water flows through the lungs into the blood, causing the red blood cells to burst and release potassium, which causes the heart to stop. Salt water mechanically prevents the oxygen reaching the lungs. It can take up to ten minutes to drown, and anybody rescued should immediately be given *artificial respiration.

drug dependence The condition resulting from regular use of a drug such that its withdrawal causes emotional distress (psychological dependence) or physical illness (physical dependence). Drugs causing psychological dependence include cannabis, LSD, and the nicotine in tobacco. Physical dependence is associated with such drugs as morphine, heroin, barbiturates, and alcohol. Withdrawal of these drugs causes unpleasant symptoms (withdrawal symptoms) that disappear on taking further doses. Overdosage of such drugs is common and can be fatal. Physical dependence is invariably associated with severe psychological dependence and requires specialist treatment. See also alcoholism.

drugs Compounds that alter the physiological state of living organisms (including man). Medicinal drugs are widely used for the treatment, prevention, and diagnosis of disease. The wide range of drugs available for this purpose includes the anaesthetics (see anaesthesia), *analgesics, *antibiotics, *cytotoxic drugs, *diuretics, hormonal drugs, and *tranquillizers.

Some drugs are taken solely for the pleasurable effects they produce. Many such drugs are addictive (see narcotics) and—despite rigorous controls to restrict their use—illegal trade in them continues. In the UK the Misuse of Drugs Act (1971) restricts the use of these dangerous drugs, which include *opium and its derivatives and synthetic substitutes, many stimulants (cocaine, amphetamine, etc.), and some sedatives. See also drug dependence.

Druids Ancient Celtic priests who were also revered as teachers and judges. Information about them is largely derived from Julius Caesar's hostile account in his *Gallic Wars*. They worshipped nature gods, believed in the immortality of the soul and *reincarnation, and also taught astronomy. Their central religious rite involved the sacred oak tree, from which they cut mistletoe with a golden knife. They sacrificed humans, usually criminals, on behalf of those near to death. In Gaul and Britain they were wiped out by the Romans, their last stand being in Anglesey (61 AD), but in Ireland they survived until the arrival of Christian missionaries. They had no proven association with *Stonehenge, despite the use of the site by the revived 20th-century Druidic Order.

drumfish A carnivorous fish, also called croaker, belonging to the family *Sciaenidae* (about 160 species), that occurs mainly along warm seashores. They have two dorsal fins and are usually silvery in colour. Most species produce sounds by amplifying muscle movements through the swim bladder. Order: *Perciformes*.

drumlin A small streamlined hill, formed through glaciation and composed of glacial till or drift, sometimes with a rock core. Drumlins usually occur in groups or swarms (sometimes called basket-of-eggs topography), their long axes parallel to the direction of ice flow. They are common features in Co Down, Northern Ireland.

Drummond of Hawthornden, William (1585-1649) The first major Scots poet to write in deliberately non-Scottish English. His *Poems* (1614, 1616) were strongly influenced by continental models. He also wrote royalist political pamphlets and was a friend of Ben *Jonson and *Drayton.

drums Musical instruments of ancient origin, in which a pitched or unpitched sound is produced by striking a tight skin stretched over a frame or resonating chamber. Drums are played either with sticks of various kinds or with the hands. The family includes the orchestral *timpani, the bass drum, snare drum, and tambourine. *Compare* percussion instruments; stringed instruments; wind instruments.

drupe A stone fruit, such as a cherry, plum, or peach. The fruit wall (pericarp) develops into three layers: an outer skin (epicarp), succulent flesh (mesocarp), and a stone (endocarp) containing the seed.

Drury Lane Theatre The oldest theatre in London, first opened in 1663. The present building dates from 1813. It has housed every form of dramatic production. Its early managers included Colley *Cibber, David *Garrick, and R. B. *Sheridan, and it has strong associations with the actors Edmund *Kean, Charles *Macready, and Sir Henry *Irving.

Druses (or Druzes) Adherents of the Druse religion, a sect probably named after one of its founders, al-Darazi, who preached the divinity of the Fatimid caliph al-Hakim (996-1021 AD). After his death they won some support in S Syria and developed extreme heterodox ideas. Druses are not generally accepted as Muslims. Their scriptures are based on the Bible, the Koran, and on Sufi writings. Today they live mainly in Syria, the Lebanon, and Israel.

dryad In Greek mythology, a type of *nymph inhabiting trees, especially oak trees. A dryad was believed to die when the tree died.

dry cleaning Cleaning fabrics using a solvent other than water. Its main advantage over washing is that it rarely affects the shape or colour of the article. Commercial dry cleaning plant is mainly automatic and the most common solvent is perchloroethylene. Like washing, the solvent, which may contain a detergent, loosens and flushes away dirt particles. Drying is by spinning and warm air. The solvent is recycled.

Dryden, John (1631-1700) British poet and critic. He welcomed the Restoration of the monarchy with two panegyrics to Charles II and was appointed poet laureate in 1668. He wrote several successful plays for the recently reopened theatres, for example *Marriage à la Mode* (1673) and *All for Love* (1677). He also wrote brilliant verse satires, notably *Absalom and Achitophel* (1681) and *MacFlecknoe* (1682). He became a Catholic in 1685 and lost the laureateship on the accession of the Protestant William of Orange in 1688. His last major work was a translation of Virgil (1697).

dry farming Crop production in regions receiving less than 50 cm (20 in) of rainfall per annum. This involves special farming techniques, especially planting quick-growing drought-resistant crops to make the best use of limited rainfall. Traditionally, winter wheat is grown in alternation with a fallow year, in which moisture and nutrient levels are allowed to recover. Appropriate husbandry, such as leaving a protective layer of crop residue, contour ploughing, and the use of fertilizers, all help to maximize yields under difficult conditions.

Dryopithecus A genus of extinct apes, also called oak apes, with teeth and jaws similar to those of chimpanzees and gorillas. Most *Dryopithecus* remains come from India dating from the late Tertiary period (between 19 and 1 million years ago).

Dryopteris A genus of *ferns (about 150 species), known as buckler ferns, found mainly in N temperate regions. They have firm feathery branched fronds, often growing in crowns, 15-150 cm high, from short stout scaly rhizomes. Large clusters of spore capsules (sori) occur in two rows on the underside of the leaflets. A common species is the male fern (*D. filix-mas*). Family: *Aspidiaceae*.

drypoint A technique of engraving. The finished print is characterized by a shadowy effect produced by the ridges thrown up by the incision on the copperplate. Early masters of drypoint include *Durer and *Rembrandt.

dry rot The decay of timber caused by cellulose-digesting fungi, especially *Serpula lacrymans*. Spores are liable to germinate in timber having a moisture content of over 20% and the fungus appears as a whitish mass on the surface. The timber becomes cracked and crumbly and the infection may spread to adjoining dry timbers. Treatment is by removal of infected timbers and application of fungicide to the remaining parts. *Compare* wet rot.

Drysdale, Sir (George) Russell (1912-81) Australian painter, born in England. After training in Melbourne, London, and Paris, he specialized in scenes of the Australian outback.

dualism Any philosophical theory asserting either that the universe is made up of two irreducible and independent substances or that it is based on two fundamental principles (for example, good and evil). It is thus distinguished from monism—the belief in just one substance (or principle)—and pluralism, which holds that there are many. One of the most pervasive dualistic theories in philosophy since *Descartes is the view that the world is constituted of mental substance (mind or consciousness) and physical substance (body or matter).

Dubai. *See* United Arab Emirates.

Du Barry, Marie Jeanne Bécu, Comtesse (?1743-93) The last mistress of *Louis XV of France from 1768 until his death (1774), when she was banished from court. She was guillotined during the French Revolution.

Dubček, Alexander (1921-) Czechoslovak statesman. Dubček participated in the resistance to the Nazi occupation and after World War II rose to become secretary of the Czechoslovak Communist Party in 1968. As leader, he granted Czechoslovakia many liberal reforms, which were opposed by the Soviet Union and led to the Soviet invasion of Czechoslovakia in August, 1968. Dubček was taken to Moscow, where he agreed to cooperate with Soviet demands but in April, 1969, he lost his post and was ousted from the Party in 1970.

DUBLIN *The public viewing the damage in the city centre, following the Easter Rising (1916).*

Dublin (Irish name: Baile Átha Cliath) 53 20N 6 15W The capital of the Republic of Ireland, on Dublin Bay. An important commercial and cultural centre, it is also the largest manufacturing centre and the largest port in the Republic. Its industries include whiskey distilling, brewing (it has the largest brewery in the world), clothing, glass, and food processing. It is noted for its wide streets (notably O'Connell Street) and its 18th-century Georgian squares. It

has the University of Dublin (founded 1592) and the National University of Ireland (founded 1909); Dublin also contains the famous Abbey Theatre. Literary names associated with the city include W. B. Yeats and J. M. Synge. *History*: during the 18th century Dublin prospered as the second largest city of the British Empire but declined during the 19th century. The Easter Rising of 1916 took place here. Population (1981): 525 360.

Dublin (Irish name: Baile Átha Cliath) A county in the E Republic of Ireland, in Leinster bordering on the Irish Sea. Chiefly low lying, it rises in the S to the Wicklow Mountains and is drained by the River Liffey. The county is dominated by the city of Dublin. Agricultural produce includes barley, wheat, and potatoes, and cattle are reared. Area: 922 sq km (356 sq mi). Population (1981): 915 115. County town: Dublin.

Dubna 56 42N 37 09E A town in the Soviet Union, in the RSFSR. Founded in 1956, it is the site of the United Institute of Nuclear Research. Population (1983 est): 59 000.

Dubrovnik (Italian name: Ragusa) 42 40N 18 07E A port in S Yugoslavia, in Croatia on the Adriatic coast. It flourished as a city state until the early 19th century, and now, with its picturesque setting and medieval walls, is popular among tourists. The town was damaged by two earthquakes in April, 1979. Population (1981): 66 131.

Dubuffet, Jean (Phillipe Arthur) (1901-85) French painter and sculptor, who achieved notoriety in 1946 with his "junk" pictures. Using plaster, sand, straw, etc., he produced extremely distorted and flattened images, influenced by graffiti on walls and the art of children and the insane. He showed his own collection of works and those of children and psychiatric patients in a Paris exhibition entitled *l'Art brut* (brutal art) in 1949.

Du Cange, Charles du Fresne, Sieur (1610-88) French historian. An outstandingly prolific writer, Du Cange wrote glossaries of the middle ages that were a significant and original contribution to historical research. He also wrote widely on the Byzantine Empire and edited the works of the medieval chroniclers Villehardouin and Joinville.

Duccio di Buoninsegna (c. 1255-c. 1318) Italian painter, founder of the Sienese school. His major works are the *Rucellai Madonna* (Uffizi) for Sta Maria Novella, Florence, and the *Maestà* (1308-11), an altarpiece for Siena Cathedral, which contemporaries hailed as a masterpiece and carried in procession through the city. A fusion of *Byzantine and *gothic styles, it illustrates his gift for narrative painting.

Duchamp, Marcel (1887-1968) French artist. His first success was *Nude Descending a Staircase* (1912; Philadelphia), influenced by *cubism and *futurism. This was followed by his controversial *ready-made objects, for example a urinal, first exhibited in New York. He lived in New York after 1915 and became leader of its *dada art movement. His best-known work is the glass and wire picture of *The Bride Stripped Bare by Her Bachelors, Even* (1915-23; Philadelphia).

duck A small short-necked waterbird belonging to the family *Anatidae* (ducks, geese, and swans), occurring in salt and fresh waters throughout the world except Antarctica. Ducks are adapted for swimming and diving, having a dense waterproofed outer plumage with a thick underlayer of down. The blunt spatulate bill is covered with a sensitive membrane and has internal horny plates for sifting food from water. The 200 species of duck are mostly gregarious; many are migratory and strong fliers. Ducks feed either at the surface of the water (*see* dabbling duck) or dive to forage in deeper water (*see* diving duck). Order: *Anseriformes* (ducks and geese).

duck-billed platypus An aquatic *monotreme mammal, *Ornithorhynchus anatinus*, of Australia and Tasmania. Platypuses grow to 55 cm long and have webbed feet. They use their broad flat toothless beak for sieving invertebrates from stream bottoms. The female lays two eggs in a grass-lined burrow constructed in a river bank, incubates them for two weeks, then suckles the tiny young (about 17 mm long). Family: *Ornithorhynchidae*.

duckweed A small floating aquatic plant of the genus *Lemna* (about 10 species), forming dense carpets on or just below the surface of ponds, streams, etc. The plants have no distinct stems and leaves, consisting of a group of small round leaflike structures (thalli) that continuously reproduce by budding. Minute petalless flowers are enclosed in a sheath on the margin of the thallus. *L. minor, L. gibba,* and *L. polyrhiza* have roots; *L. triscula* is rootless. Duckweeds are the simplest and smallest of flowering plants. Family: *Lemnaceae*.

Dudley 53 30N 2 06W A town in England, in the West Midlands. An important industrial centre since the middle ages, clothing and light engineering have now replaced coalmining and iron smelting as the principal industries. Population (1981): 187 228.

Duero, River. *See* Douro, River.

Dufay, Guillaume (c. 1400-74) Burgundian composer and priest (*see* Burgundian school), associated with Cambrai Cathedral for much of his life. He travelled in France and Italy and was a member of the papal choir for several years. One of the outstanding composers of the middle ages, he wrote masses, motets, magnificats, and French and Italian chansons. He was also a famous teacher.

Du Fu (*or* Tu Fu; 712-70 AD) Chinese poet of the Tang dynasty. Du Fu's failure to become a high official forced him to lead a life of poverty and travelling to escape famines and rebellions. The major themes of his poetry are thus the social injustices of his time and the effects of civil strife on Chinese life.

Dufy, Raoul (1877-1953) French painter, born in Le Havre. His early influences were *impressionism and then *fauvism. He later developed an individual style in lively and often witty racecourse and regatta scenes, notable for the way forms are drawn sketchily over areas of thinly applied colour. He also designed fabrics, tapestries, and ceramics.

dugong A marine herbivorous mammal, *Dugong dugon*, of the Indo-Pacific region. Up to 3 m long, dugongs—also known as sea cows—have blue-grey rough skin and a bristly snout; the males have short tusks. Their forelimbs are flippers and they lack hind limbs, having a flukelike tail for swimming. Dugongs feed on sea grass on the sea bed and, together with *manatees, are a threatened species. Family: *Dugongidae*; order: *Sirenia*.

Duhamel, Georges (1884-1966) French novelist. Trained as a doctor, he worked as an army surgeon during World War I. His major works are his two novel cycles, *Salavin* (1920-32), exploring the theme of human aspirations in a materialistic age, and *The Pasquier Chronicles* (1933-44).

duiker A small nocturnal African antelope belonging to the subfamily *Cephalophinae* (17 species), inhabiting bush or forest. 35-75 cm high at the shoulder, both sexes usually have smooth backward-pointing horns and often a distinct stripe along the back. They plunge into cover when disturbed, hence their name, which in Afrikaans means "diver."

Duisburg 51 26N 06 45E A city in W West Germany, in North Rhine-Westphalia at the confluence of the Rivers Rhine and Ruhr. Heavily bombed in World War II for its armaments industry, it is the largest European inland port and a steel-producing centre. Its university was established in 1972. Population (1983 est): 553 000.

Dukas, Paul (1865-1935) French composer, teacher, and critic. He is best known for his orchestral scherzo *The Sorcerer's Apprentice* (1897). His works also include the opera *Ariane et Barbe-Bleue* (1907) and the ballet *La Péri* (1912). A perfectionist, he destroyed many of his works shortly before his death.

Duke, Geoffrey E. (1923-   ) British racing motorcyclist,

who was world champion in the 350 cc class in 1951 and 1952 and in the 500 cc class in 1951 and 1953-55.

Dukhobors. *See* Doukhobors.

dulcimer A musical instrument consisting of a shallow resonating box with strings stretched over two moveable bridges. It is played with two small hammers. Descended from the Persian *santir* and much used in European and Asian folk music, it is particularly popular in Hungarian gipsy music under the name *cimbalom.

Dulles, John Foster (1888-1959) US Republican politician and diplomat. He became a senator and secretary of state (1953-59) under Eisenhower and was delegate to the UN, which he helped to establish (1945). Dulles was influential in forming US Cold War foreign policy. He developed a strategy of brinkmanship to confront the People's Republic of China over Quemoy and Matsu, and the Soviet Union during the Berlin crisis.

Dulong and Petit's law The product of the mass of 1 mole of a solid element and its specific heat capacity is constant and equal to 25 joules per kelvin. The law is only true for simple substances and at normal temperatures. Named after the French physicists P. Dulong (1785-1838) and A. Petit (1791-1820).

dulse An edible purplish-red *seaweed, *Rhodymenia palmata*, found growing on rocks, shellfish, and other seaweeds on N Atlantic coasts. A red alga, it has flat leathery lobed fronds, about 12-40 cm long, which are often eaten as a salty confection of the same name.

Duluth 46 45N 92 10W A city in the USA, in Minnesota at the W end of Lake Superior opposite Superior, Wisconsin. It is the commercial and industrial centre of N Minnesota and large quantities of iron ore and grain are shipped from its port. Population (1980): 92 789.

Dulwich 51 27N 0 05W A residential district in the Greater London borough of Southwark. It has a famous public school, Dulwich College (1619), and an art gallery.

Duma The Russian parliament from 1906 to 1917. The Duma, which was established in response to the *Revolution of 1905, transformed Russia into a constitutional monarchy. It was composed of an upper chamber, the state council, and a lower chamber. Half the members of the state council were appointed by the monarch and the remainder of the deputies in both chambers were elected. Owing to their radicalism, the first two Dumas (1906, 1907) were quickly dissolved by Emperor Nicholas II but the third (1907-12) and fourth (1912-17) more conservative Dumas lasted their legal five-year terms. At the beginning of the Russian Revolution the Duma established the provisional government that enforced Nicholas' abdication.

Dumas, Alexandre (1802-70) French novelist and dramatist, often called Dumas *père*. His father was a soldier, son of a marquis and a negress, who became a general in the French Revolutionary armies. Brought up in poverty and largely self-educated, he began writing melodramatic historical plays in 1829. After 1839 he began writing his famous historical romances, including *The Count of Monte Cristo* (1844-45), *The Three Musketeers* (1844), and *The Black Tulip* (1850). His works were hugely successful but the uninhibited extravagance of his private life kept him continually in debt. His illegitimate son **Alexandre Dumas** (1824-95), a dramatist, was often called Dumas *fils*. His best-known work is the novel *La Dame aux camélias* (1848), the basis of a play and Verdi's opera *La Traviata*. His other plays, which include *Le Demi-monde* (1855) and *Le Fils naturel* (1858), were mostly moralistic treatments of such themes as adultery and prostitution.

Du Maurier, George (Louis Palmella Busson) (1834-96) British caricaturist and novelist. Born in Paris, he moved to London in 1860 and contributed caricatures to *Punch* and other magazines. His novel *Trilby* (1894), remembered for its sinister hypnotist Svengali, is based on his life as an art student in Paris. The best-known works of his granddaughter **Dame Daphne Du Maurier** (1907–   ) are romances, usually set in her home county of Cornwall. They include *Rebecca* (1938) and *My Cousin Rachel* (1951).

Dumbarton   55 57N 4 35W A town in W central Scotland, in Strathclyde Region at the confluence of the Rivers Clyde and Leven. Dumbarton has engineering and whisky-distilling industries. Population (1981): 23 430.

Dumfries (*or* Dumfrieshire)   A former county of SW Scotland.   Under local government reorganization in 1975 it became part of Dumfries and Galloway Region.

Dumfries and Galloway Region   An administrative region in SW Scotland, bordering on the Solway Firth. It was formed under local government reorganization in 1975 from the counties of Dumfries, Kirkcudbright, and Wigtown. It consists of uplands and moors in the N descending to coastal lowlands in the S and has an indented coastline. The region is predominantly agricultural with sheep farming and stock raising. There has been considerable reafforestation since World War II and tourism is a growing industry. Industries are generally related to agriculture. Area: 6369 sq km (2460 sq mi). Population (1983): 146 159. Administrative centre: Dumfries.

Du Mont, Allen Balcom   (1901–65) US engineer, who developed the *cathode-ray tube (CRT). He set up a company to manufacture allied electronic devices in 1931 and invented the oscilloscope (*see* cathode-ray oscilloscope), which incorporated his new durable CRTs. He also utilized them in television receivers, which he began manufacturing in 1937.

Dumont d'Urville, Jules Sébastien César   (1790–1842) French navigator. He went on two surveying expeditions to the South Seas (1822–25, 1826–29) and on the second circumnavigated the world in the *Astrolabe*, returning with specimens of plants and rocks. In repeating this exploit (1837–40), he discovered the Adélie (his wife's name) coast of Antarctica.

Dumouriez, Charles François du Périer   (1739–1823) French general. During the French Revolution he became commander of a division in Nantes (1791). In 1792 he became minister of foreign affairs but resigned to command the northern army against Austria and Prussia. He won victories at Valmy and Jemappes (1792) but after defeat in early 1793 conspired to overthrow France's revolutionary government. Deserted by his troops he went over to the Austrians, eventually settling in England.

Dunant, (Jean-)Henri   (1828–1910) Swiss philanthropist, who inspired the foundation (1864) of the International *Red Cross. In 1859 he organized relief for the wounded at the Battle of Solferino, an experience that led him to propose the establishment of an international relief agency. He won the first Nobel Peace Prize in 1901.

Dunbar   56 00N 2 31W A resort and fishing port in E central Scotland, on the Lothian coast, scene of *Cromwell's victory over the Scots (1650). Population (1981): 6015. |

Dunbar, William   (c. 1460–c. 1530) Scots poet, a courtier of James IV, who granted him a pension in 1500. His talent for vigorous satire is evident in *Dance of the Sevin Deidly Sins* and *Flyting of Dunbar and Kennedie*, an exchange of (probably) goodnatured abuse. *Lament for the Makaris* mourns the death of his fellow poets.

Dunbarton (*or* Dunbartonshire)   A former county of W Scotland. Under local government reorganization in 1975 its boundaries were adjusted to form Dunbarton District, in Strathclyde Region.

Duncan I   (d. 1040) King of the Scots (1034–40). His claim to the throne was challenged by Macbeth, by whom he was murdered.

Duncan, Isadora   (1878–1927) US dancer. She lived mostly in Europe, where she gained a reputation for both her innovative modern interpretive dancing and her flamboyant lifestyle. Her accidental death was caused by her scarf being caught in the wheel of the car in which she was travelling.

Dundalk (Irish name: Dún Dealgan)   54 01N 6 25W A port in the Republic of Ireland, the county town of Co Louth. Its chief industries are engineering, brewing, printing, and linen manufacturing, and its main exports are beef and cattle. Population (1981): 25 610.

Dundas (former name: Thule)   76 30N 68 58W A town in NW Greenland. Founded as an Eskimo settlement (1910), it subsequently became a US air and military base, after which the Eskimos founded another Thule further N.

Dundee   56 28N 3 00W A city in E Scotland, the administrative centre of Tayside Region on the Firth of Tay. It is a port and university town, known chiefly for the manufacture of jute goods. Dundee also provides supplies and services for the North Sea oil industry and has engineering and shipbuilding industries. Population (1984 est): 180 000.

Dundee, John Graham of Claverhouse, 1st Viscount (c. 1649–89) Scottish soldier, who led a *Jacobite rebellion (1689) in support of the deposed James VII of Scotland (James II of England). He won an outstanding victory against loyalist forces at Killiecrankie but was mortally wounded.

Dunedin   45 52S 170 30E A port in New Zealand, in SE South Island at the head of Otago Harbour. Founded by Scottish Presbyterians in 1848, it has two cathedrals (Anglican and Roman Catholic) and the University of Otago (the oldest in the country, founded in 1869). Industries include the manufacture of woollen goods, agricultural machinery, and footwear. Population (1983): 112 000.

Dunfermline   56 04N 3 29W A town in E Scotland, in Fife Region on the Firth of Forth. Several Scottish kings, including *Robert the Bruce, are buried in the 11th-century abbey. Dunfermline produces electronic equipment and oil-related products and there are rich coal deposits nearby. It is the birthplace of Andrew *Carnegie. Population (1981): 52 057.

DUNG BEETLE   *Using its head and paddle-like antennae, this beetle constructs balls of dung, which it buries and feeds on. The females lay eggs in dung balls, which provide food for the larvae.*

dung beetle   A *scarab beetle, also called a tumblebug, that has the habit of rolling dung into balls, which serve as a food source for both the adults and larvae. Dung beetles are usually dark and small, varying between 5 and 30 mm in length.
Another group of dung-eating beetles belong to the family *Geotrupidae* (*see* dor beetle).

Dungeness 50 55N 0 58E A shingle headland in SE England, in Kent extending into the English Channel. Two nuclear power stations and an automatic lighthouse are located here.

Dunkirk (French name: Dunkerque) 51 02N 2 23E A port in N France, in the Nord department on the Strait of Dover. Sacked by the English (1388), it was ceded to Cromwell in 1658 but was later sold (1662) by Charles II to Louis XIV. During *World War II British and other Allied troops were successfully evacuated from its beaches (1940) following the fall of France. Dunkirk is a rapidly growing industrial centre and has an oil refinery and naval shipbuilding yards. Population (1982 est): 73 282.

Dun Laoghaire 53 17N 6 08W A port in the E Republic of Ireland, in Co Dublin. It is the terminus of a ferry service from Holyhead, Wales, and a resort and yachting centre. Population (1981): 54 496.

dunlin A common *sandpiper, *Calidris alpina*, that breeds in far northern regions, ranging south to N Britain. 20 cm long, it has a bill with a curved tip and a black and russet plumage that changes to grey in winter.

Dunlop, John Boyd (1840–1921) Scottish inventor, who is credited with inventing the pneumatic tyre (1887). Dunlop began to produce his tyres commercially in 1890. Initially for bicycles, they later contributed greatly to the development of motor cars.

Dunmow Flitch A flitch (side) of bacon awarded on Whit Monday to a married couple of Great Dunmow in Essex, who have not repented their marriage for a year and a day. Originating in the middle ages, the custom was referred to by *Langland and *Chaucer and was revived by the Victorian novelist Harrison Ainsworth.

dunnock A shy inconspicuous songbird, *Prunella modularis*, also called hedge sparrow (although it is an *accentor and not a sparrow). About 14 cm long, the dunnock has a dull-brown plumage with a greyish throat and breast. It has a fine sharp bill and feeds on insects. Cuckoos often lay their eggs in dunnocks' nests.

Dunois, Jean d'Orléans, Comte de (1403–68) French general in the Hundred Years' War. He defeated the English in 1427, then held Orléans until relieved by Joan of Arc (1429). Further victories led to his triumphal entry into Paris (1436). Later he drove the English out of N France.

Dunoon 55 57N 4 56W A resort in W central Scotland, in Strathclyde Region on the Firth of Clyde. Holy Loch, site of the US Navy Polaris submarine base, is nearby. Population (1981): 9372.

Dunsany, Edward John Moreton Drax Plunkett, 18th Baron (1878–1957) Irish author, famous for his richly fantastic and sinister stories and plays, many of them, such as *The Gods of Pegana* (1905) and *The Gods of the Mountain* (1912), set in worlds recalling Eastern mythology. He was also a sportsman, big-game hunter, and chess master.

Dunsinane A hill in E Scotland, in Tayside Region, in the Sidlaw Hills. The ruined fort on its summit is referred to in Shakespeare's play *Macbeth*. Height: 303 m (1012 ft).

Duns Scotus, John (c. 1260–1308) Scottish-born Franciscan philosopher, who, with Roger *Bacon and *William of Ockham, carried on controversy against *Aquinas. Contradicting Aquinas, Duns Scotus held that what makes one thing distinct from another is its form, or essence, that is its essential properties rather than its accidental properties, as the latter may be removed or changed without altering its identity. Although nicknamed the Subtle Doctor by contemporaries, Duns Scotus suffered Renaissance ridicule, his name giving rise to the derisive label "dunce."

Dunstable 51 53N 0 32W A town in SE England, in Bedfordshire. Its industries include engineering, printing, and the manufacture of commercial vehicles, paper, and cement. The headquarters of the London Gliding Club is situated at the foot of the Dunstable Downs. Population (1984): 35 716.

Dunstable, John (d. 1453) English composer, mathematician, and astrologer. His music was known outside England and exists chiefly in continental manuscripts, but little is known of his life. Dunstable wrote motets in which the music accurately reflected the rhythm of the words. He also made a famous setting of the chanson "O Rosa bella."

Dunstan, St (924–88 AD) English churchman and monastic reformer, born near Glastonbury. Of noble birth, he lived as a hermit until appointed Abbot of Glastonbury in 943. He rebuilt its monastery and revived English monasticism. The chief minister under Kings Eadred and Edgar, he became Bishop of Worcester (957), Bishop of London (959), and Archbishop of Canterbury (960). He lost favour under Ethelred II. Feast day: 19 May. Emblem: a pair of tongs.

duodecimal system A system of numbers that has a base of 12 as opposed to the base 10 of the normal *decimal system. For example, the number 31 in the decimal system is 27 in the duodecimal system since $31 = (2 \times 12) + 7$.

duodenal ulcer. *See* peptic ulcer.

duodenum. *See* intestine.

Duparc, Henri (Marie Eugène Henri Foucques D.; 1848–1933) French composer, a pupil of Franck. His reputation rests on the 14 songs he wrote between 1868 and 1884, some of which have orchestral accompaniments. In 1885 he suffered a breakdown in health and spent the rest of his life in seclusion in Switzerland.

du Pré, Jacqueline (1945–87) British cellist. She studied with Paul Tortelier and Mstislav Rostropovich, making her debut in 1961 in Elgar's cello concerto, a work with which she became particularly associated. In 1967 she married the pianist Daniel *Barenboim, with whom she gave recitals. Multiple sclerosis put an end to her performing career in 1973, but she subsequently taught gifted cello students.

Dupré, Marcel (1886–1971) French organist and composer, a pupil of Charles Widor and director of the Paris conservatoire (1954–56). He was well known as a recitalist, improviser, and composer of organ music.

Duralumin An aluminium *alloy containing 3.5% copper and 0.5% magnesium. It becomes harder after heating and quenching and retains this hardness as long as its temperature remains below 150°C. It is used in aircraft manufacture.

Durance, River A River in S France, flowing mainly SSW to the River Rhône near Avignon. It provides Marseilles with water. Length: 304 km (189 mi).

Durango 24 01N 104 40W A city in N Mexico. It lies S of Cerro del Mercado, a hill famous for its iron-ore mines. Industries include iron founding, sugar refining, and textiles. Population (1980): 257 915.

Duras, Marguerite (1914–) French novelist. Born in Indochina, she went to Paris as a student in 1931. Her novels, experimental in technique and often concerned with themes of time and passion, include *The Sea Wall* (1950) and *Destroy, She Said* (1969). She has also written plays and filmscripts, notably for *Hiroshima mon amour* (1960).

Durazzo. *See* Durrës.

Durban 29 53S 31 00E The main seaport in South Africa and the largest city in Natal, on the Indian Ocean. Founded in 1835, its industries include car assembly and sugar refining, and it is an important tourist centre. It contains part of the University of Natal. Population (1980): 505 963.

Dürer, Albrecht (1471-1528) German *Renaissance painter, engraver, draughtsman, and woodcut designer. The son of a goldsmith, he was born in Nuremberg, where he trained under the woodcut designer and altarpiece painter Michael Wohlgemuth (1434-1519). His first Italian visit (1494-95) resulted in a series of watercolours of the Alps. He was influenced by Italian artists, particularly *Mantegna and Antonio *Pollaiuolo, but his woodcuts of the *Apocalypse*

(1498) are still *gothic in style. In about 1500, he became preoccupied with the study of human proportions. Paintings of this period include the *Self-Portrait* as Christ (1500; Alte Pinakothek, Munich) and *Adoration of the Magi* (1504; Uffizi). On his second Italian visit (1505–07) he painted *The Feast of the Rose Garlands* (Prague) for the church of the German community in Venice. He worked for Emperor Maximilian I from 1512 to 1519. In this period he executed his most famous engravings, including *Knight, Death, and the Devil* (British Museum, London). His last important work was *The Four Apostles* (Alte Pinakothek, Munich). He was also a friend of Luther and sympathized with the Reformation.

ALBRECHT DÜRER   *A self-portrait (detail) painted in 1498, when the artist was 26 years old (Prado, Madrid).*

Durham   54 47N 1 34W A city in NE England, the administrative centre of Co Durham on the River Wear. It has a Norman cathedral and an 11th-century castle, now part of Durham University (founded 1832). Durham's industries include carpet making, with coalmining in the vicinity. Population (1981): 26 422.

Durham   A county in NE England, bordering on the North Sea. It consists chiefly of undulating lowlands, rising W to the uplands of the Pennines and is drained by the Rivers Wear and Tees. Agriculture includes sheep and dairy farming. Coalmining, formerly of major importance, is concentrated in the E. Chief industries include iron and steel processing at Consett, light engineering, and clothing manufacture. Under local government reorganization in 1974 it lost the industrial parts of the NE and SE to Tyne and Wear and to Cleveland respectively; it gained part of N Yorkshire. Area: 2436 sq km (964 sq mi). Population (1983): 606 800. Administrative centre: Durham.

Durham, John George Lambton, 1st Earl of   (1792–1840) British colonial administrator; governor general of Canada (1838–39). As Lord Privy Seal he helped to draft the 1832 parliamentary *Reform Act and was sent to Canada after serving (1835–37) as ambassador to Russia. In Canada he was criticized for giving amnesty to rebellious French-Canadians and resigned. His *Report on the Affairs of British North America* (1839), largely written by the chief secretary for Canada, Charles Buller (1806–48), advocated the union of Upper and Lower Canada, which was then implemented, and responsible government; it greatly influenced subsequent British colonial policy (*see* British Empire).

durian   A tree, *Durio zebethinus*, of SE Asia, up to 30 m tall with oblong tapering leaves and large creamy white flowers. The spherical spiny-coated fruit, 15–20 cm in diameter, is notorious for its noxious smell, but the custard-like pulp is eaten in large amounts by local people and animals. The seeds are roasted. Family: *Bombacaceae*.

Durkheim, Emile   (1858–1917) French sociologist and one of the founding fathers of modern *sociology. In opposition to attempts to explain human conduct solely in terms of psychology, he developed an account of stability and change in whole societies in *The Division of Labour in Society* (1893); in *The Rules of Sociological Method* (1895) he set out a methodology for a science of society. His *Suicide* (1897) was a pioneering study in social statistics. Another major work, produced during the latter part of his life, was *The Elementary Forms of Religious Life* (1912), in which he examined the social foundations of religion.

durmast   A Eurasian *oak, *Quercus petraea*, up to 40 m tall. It has long-stalked oval leaves with rounded lobes and hairy undersides and unstalked conical acorns (hence its other name –sessile oak). Its durable wood is used for furniture, construction work, and boat building and the bark for tanning.

durra   An economically important variety of *sorghum, *S. vulgare* var. *durra*, also called millet, native to the Nile valley. Its grain is used chiefly for livestock feed.

Durrell, Lawrence George   (1912–) British novelist and poet. Born in India, he has lived mostly in the Mediterranean countries. His best-known work is *The Alexandria Quartet*, comprising *Justine* (1957), *Balthazar* (1958), *Mountolive* (1958), and *Clea* (1960), an elaborate exploration of the nature of modern love. His later work includes the novels *Tunc* (1968), *Nunquam* (1970), and the first four of a quintet, *Monsieur* (1974), *Livia* (1978), *Constance* (1982), and *Quinx* (1985). In addition he has also written poetry (*Collected Poems*, 1968), humorous sketches (*Esprit de Corps*, 1959), short stories (*Antrobus Complete*, 1985), and travel books on the Greek islands. His brother **Gerald Malcolm Durrell** (1925–) is a naturalist and popular writer, famous for such books as *The Bafut Beagles* (1954), the autobiographical *My Family and Other Animals* (1956), and *The Stationary Ark* (1976), about his zoo and wildlife conservation trust in Jersey.

Dürrenmatt, Friedrich   (1921–) Swiss dramatist and novelist. His plays are often experimental and usually satirical, mocking hypocritically conventional values. The best known are *The Visit* (1956) and *The Physicists* (1962). He has also written short stories and detective novels.

Durrës (Italian name: Durazzo)   41 18N 19 28E A port in W central Albania, on the Adriatic Sea. It was founded by Greeks in the 7th century BC and is now Albania's major commercial town and principal port. Products include flour, salt, and bricks. Population (1982): 72 600.

durum.   *See* wheat.

Duse, Eleonora   (1858–1924) Italian actress. She acted in plays by contemporary French dramatists and is especially associated with plays by Gabriele D'Annunzio, her lover, and by Ibsen. Her international reputation rivalled that of Sarah Bernhardt. She made one film, *Cenere* (1916).

Dushanbe (name until 1929: Dyushambe; name 1929–61: Stalinabad)   38 38N 68 51E A city in the SW Soviet Union, the capital of the Tadzhik SSR on the River Dushanbinka. It has food and textile industries and is a cultural and educational centre. Population (1981 est): 510 000.

Düsseldorf   51 13N 6 47E A city in NW West Germany, capital of North Rhine-Westphalia on the River Rhine. The birthplace of Heinrich Heine, it is noted for its art academy (1767). A port and major commercial and industrial centre of the *Ruhr, its main industry is iron and steel. Population (1985 est): 569 361.

Dust Bowl, the   An area in the USA, extending across W Kansas, Oklahoma, and Texas, and into Colorado and New Mexico. During the 1930s droughts and overfarming caused topsoil erosion. The plight of the farmers was illustrated by the photography of Dorothea Lange (1895–1965) and Steinbeck's novel *The Grapes of Wrath* (1939).

Dutch The national language of the Netherlands, belonging to the West Germanic language group. In Belgium it is one of the two official languages and is known as Flemish (*or* Vlaams). It is derived from Low Franconian, the speech of the Salic Franks, who settled in this area, and has numerous local variants.

Dutch East Indies. *See* Indonesia.

DUTCH ELM DISEASE *The elm bark beetle lays its eggs in burrows beneath the bark of elm trees, where they hatch into larvae (above). The characteristic appearance of affected trees (below) is caused by the burrowing larvae.*

Dutch elm disease A serious disease, first described in the Netherlands in 1919, that reached epidemic proportions in Britain in the 1970s, killing millions of elm trees. The fungus responsible, *Ceratocystis ulmi*, blocks the vessels that carry water to the leaves, which wilt and eventually die. The disease is carried by *bark beetles and was probably introduced into the UK on logs imported from Canada. Protective measures can be taken but are too expensive for widespread use.

Dutch Guiana. *See* Suriname.

Dutchman's breeches An ornamental perennial herb, *Dicentra cucullaria*, from North American woodlands. Its arching stems bear cream or pale-yellow drooping flowers with saclike spurs. The grey-green fernlike leaves arise from underground tubers. Family: *Fumariaceae* (fumitory family). *See also* Dicentra.

Dutchman's pipe An ornamental climbing vine, *Aristolochia durior* (or *A. sipho*), from the American Midwest. Up to 9 m long, it has large kidney-shaped or heart-shaped leaves. The brown-and-black patterned tubular flowers are attached to swollen greenish-yellow tubes, bent to resemble a pipe, and are pollinated by carrion flies. Family: *Aristolochiaceae*.

Dutch metal A highly ductile gold-coloured type of brass that contains between 85% and 88% of copper. It is used for bronzing and imitation gold leaf.

Dutch Republic. *See* United Provinces of the Netherlands.

Dutch Wars 1. (1652-54) The war between England and the Netherlands precipitated by commercial rivalry, which had been aggravated by Oliver Cromwell's *Navigation Act (1651). The English were victorious. 2. (1665-67) The war between England and the Netherlands (supported by France from 1666). Caused by commercial and colonial rivalry, the English defeated the Dutch off Lowestoft (1665) but in 1667 the Dutch entered the Thames and the Medway, bombarding Chatham. The Treaty of Breda concluded the war. 3. (1672-78) The war brought about by the invasion of the Netherlands by Louis XIV of France (supported at sea by England). The English were defeated by the Dutch (1672-73) and concluded the Treaty of *Westminister (1674). By late 1673 France had been forced to withdraw from the Netherlands but entered the Spanish Netherlands and defeated the alliance of Spain, Austria, and the Dutch. The war was concluded by the Treaties of *Nijmegen. 4. (1780-84) The war between Britain and the Netherlands caused by Dutch support for the American colonies during the *American Revolution. The Dutch were defeated.

Duval, Claude (1643-70) French highwayman celebrated for his courtesy to women. He went to England in 1660. He was hanged at Tyburn.

Duvalier, François (1907-71) Haitian politician, known as Papa Doc; president (1957-71). He used his secret police, the Tonton Macoutes, to eliminate all opposition and exploited Negro nationalism and voodoo practices to maintain popular sympathy. His son **Jean-Claude Duvalier** (1951-), known as Baby Doc, succeeded him but had to flee. to France after an uprising in 1986.

Dvina, River 1. (Northern *or* Severnaya) A river in NW Soviet Union, formed by the confluence of the Rivers Sukhona and Yug and flowing generally NW to the White Sea. Length: 750 km (466 mi). 2. (Western *or* Dangava) A river in the W Soviet Union, flowing SW and NW from the Valdai Hills to the Gulf of Riga. Length: 1021 km (634 mi).

Dvinsk. *See* Daugavpils.

Dvořák, Antonín (1841-1904) Czech composer. He was a friend of Brahms and director of the Prague conservatoire (1901-04). His early life was spent playing the violin and viola in orchestras, but after he became famous he made frequent trips to England. From 1892 to 1895 he was director of the National Conservatory in New York, during which time he wrote his famous ninth symphony, entitled "From the New World." Besides the symphonies he wrote concertos for piano, violin, and cello, orchestral tone poems, chamber music, piano music, and songs. His Czech nationalism is particularly evident in his famous *Slavonic Dances* for piano duet (1878-86).

dwarfism Abnormal smallness. The commonest cause is lack of food, and growth can be accelerated if enough food is given. Dwarfism can also occur in children with disease of the pituitary gland, in which insufficient *growth hormone is produced. This can be cured by administration of the growth hormone. Other chronic diseases, such as heart or kidney disease, can cause dwarfism. Children who are emotionally deprived may also fail to grow. The dwarfs seen in circuses are called achondroplastic dwarfs; their small size is due to faulty bone development.

dyarchy A system of government, introduced by the UK Government of India Act (1919), for the provinces of India. Devised by Lionel Curtis (1872-1955), dyarchy divided the provincial executives into Crown-appointed councils and ministers responsible to popular assemblies, permitting greater participation in government by Indians. It lasted until the establishment of provincial autonomy in 1935.

dybbuk (Hebrew: adhesion) In Jewish folklore, an evil spirit, specifically the soul of a sinful person, which, after death, possessed the body of a living person. The dybbuk could be exorcised by invocation of the divine name. Possession by such a spirit is the subject of a famous play, *The Dybbuk*, by the Russian author Solomon Anski (1862–1920).

dyeing The process of permanently changing the colour of a material. Natural dyes, such as *madder and *indigo, have been known since 3000 BC. Mauveine, the first synthetic dye, was discovered in 1856 by W. H. *Perkin. Most modern commercial dyes are made from *aromatic hydrocarbons extracted from coal tar or oil. To dye fibres or textiles, the material is immersed in a solution containing the dye, so that the dye molecules adhere to the surface of the fibres. The solvent is usually water but occasionally other solvents are used. An inorganic chemical (such as a salt of chromium), known as a mordant, may be added to make the dye less soluble once it has adhered to the fibre. Dyes used without a mordant are **direct dyes**. Vat dyes are insoluble in water, but are applied in reduced soluble form and then reoxidized. These are used particularly in cellulosic fibres. *See also* pigments.

dyer's broom A stout biennial or perennial plant, *Isatis tinctoria*, also called dyer's greenweed or dyer's furze. 50–120 cm high, it has arrow-shaped leaves and dense clusters of bright-yellow flowers that produce winged fruits. Native to Eurasia but naturalized elsewhere, its leaves ferment to a distinctive blue dye (*see* woad). Family: *Cruciferae.

dyer's rocket A biennial herb, *Reseda luteola*, also called weld. It is widespread on waste ground throughout most of the N hemisphere. Up to 70 cm high, it has lance-shaped leaves with wavy margins and long slender spikes of pale-yellow flowers, 4–5 mm across, formerly used to make a yellow dye. Family: *Resedaceae*.

Dyfed The largest county of Wales, in the SW bordering on the Irish Sea. It was created under local government reorganization in 1974 from the former counties of Cardiganshire, Carmarthenshire, and Pembrokeshire. It consists mainly of undulating uplands and coastal plains (extensive in the S). Although predominantly agricultural, new industries are being introduced to the long-established coalmining and steel manufacturing areas in the SE and a major oil refining area has developed at Milford Haven. Tourism is also a growing industry. Area: 5765 sq km (2227 sq mi). Population (1983 est): 335 300. Administrative centre: Carmarthen.

dyke A wall-like body of igneous rock that is intruded (usually vertically) into the surrounding rock in such a way that it cuts across the stratification (layering) of this rock. *Compare* sill.

Dylan, Bob (Robert Allen Zimmerman; 1941–) US singer and songwriter. An outstanding lyricist, he spoke for the protest movement of the 1960s with such folk albums as *The Times They Are A-changin'* (1964). In *Highway 61 Revisited* (1965), he introduced electronic instruments and rock rhythms. *John Wesley Harding* (1968), following a two-year retirement, and *Blood on the Tracks* (1975) confirmed his inventiveness. His conversion to Christianity in 1979 resulted in religious albums, including *Saved* (1980) and *Infidels* (1983).

dynamics. *See* mechanics; Newtonian mechanics.

dynamite An explosive plastic solid consisting of 75% nitroglycerine and 25% kieselguhr, a porous form of silicon dioxide (SiO_2). It was invented in 1864 by *Nobel. Nitroglycerine alone is very sensitive to shock. The kieselguhr makes it safe to handle. Dynamite is used for blasting, particularly under water.

dynamo. *See* electric generator.

dyne The unit of force in the *c.g.s. system equal to the force that will impart to a mass of one gram an acceleration of one centimetre per second per second.

dysentery An infection of the large bowel causing painful diarrhoea that often contains blood and mucus. It may be caused either by bacteria of the genus *Shigella* or by amoebae. It can occur wherever there is poor sanitation, but amoebic dysentery is much more common in tropical countries. Treatment for bacillary dysentery is usually by administration of fluids to prevent dehydration, but for amoebic dysentery drugs to kill the amoebae are also given.

dyslexia Difficulty in learning to write, spell, and read. It is commonly discovered at school when a child cannot read as well as would be expected. Dyslexic children are usually of normal intelligence and with special teaching can improve greatly, although some never manage to deal well with the written word. In some cases the cause is genetic.

dysmenorrhoea Painful menstrual periods. In most cases the cause is not known. Treatment is usually with pain killers, but starting a course of oral contraceptive pills will also stop the pain. If the pain starts after years of pain-free periods there may be disease of the reproductive organs.

dyspepsia. *See* indigestion.

dysprosium (Dy) A lanthanide element discovered in 1886. It forms the oxide (Dy_2O_3) and halides (for example DyF_3) and can be separated from the other lanthanides by ion-exchange techniques. At no 66; at wt 162.50; mp 1412°C; bp 2335°C.

Dzerzhinsk (name until 1919: Chernorech; name from 1919 until 1929: Rastyapino) 56 15N 43 30E A port in the central Soviet Union, in the RSFSR on the River Oka. It supports chemical, textiles, and cable industries. Population (1981 est): 263 000.

Dzhambul (name until 1939: Auliye-Ata) 42 50N 71 25E A city in the S central Soviet Union, in the Kazakh SSR on the River Talas. Its industries include phosphates, metal, leather, and food processing. Population (1983 est): 292 000.

Dzungarian Basin. *See* Junggar Pendi.

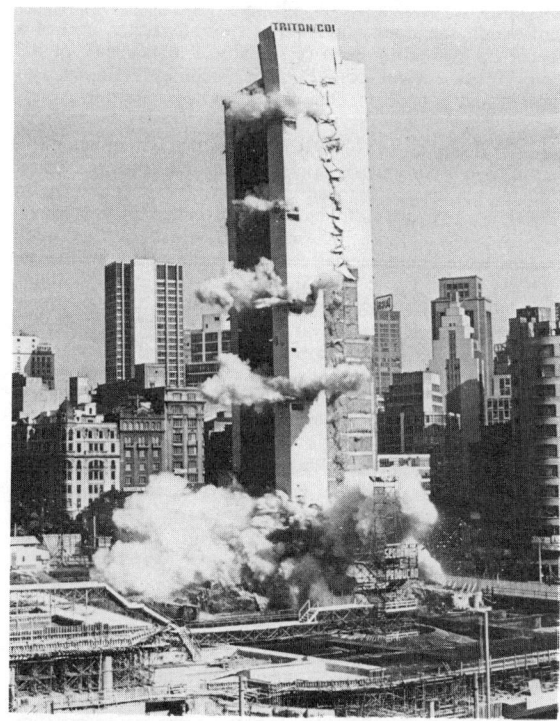

DYNAMITE   *800 lb in 777 charges reduced this 32-storey São Paulo (Brazil) block of flats to rubble in 9 seconds.*

E

Ea (*or* Enki) The ancient Mesopotanian god of water and the sea, with Anu and Enlil one of the supreme triad. He created the Tigris and Euphrates rivers. A guardian against demons and patron of the arts and sciences, including magic, his main attribute was wisdom.

Eadred (d. 955) King of England (946–55), who reconquered Northumbria by expelling Eric Bloodaxe (954), its Norwegian king. Eadred bequeathed a sum of money to relieve the poor in Northumbria and to aid defence against Viking raids.

Eads, John Buchanan (1820–87) US civil engineer, best known for his design and construction of the steel triple-arched Eads Bridge, which spans the Mississippi River at St Louis, Missouri. Opened in 1874, it is now considered a landmark in the history of civil engineering.

Eadwig (*or* Edwy; d. 959) King of England from 955 to 957, when he lost Mercia and Northumbria. He forced St *Dunstan into exile.

eagle A large broad-winged bird of prey occurring throughout the world, mostly in remote mountainous regions. Eagles have a large hooked bill and strong feet with large curved talons and are typically dull brown but may be a combination of black, grey, white, or chestnut; the head is often crested. With a wingspan of 1.3–2.4 m, they can soar for long periods searching for food—generally live prey, such as mammals or reptiles. Family: *Accipitridae* (hawks and eagles). *See also* bald eagle; golden eagle; harpy eagle; Philippine eagle; sea eagle.

eagle owl A large Eurasian *owl of the genus *Bubo*, ranging from cold northern forests to hot southern deserts. It reaches 70 cm in length, is tawny with brown mottling, and has orange eyes and large ear tufts.

eaglewood (*or* aloes wood) The resinous heartwood of a tree of the genus *Aquilaria* (especially *A. agallocha*), of SE Asia. Under certain conditions it becomes resinous and fragrant and is used in religious ceremonies and perfumery. Family: *Thymelaeaceae*.

Eakins, Thomas (1844–1916) US painter of portraits and everyday life, particularly sports scenes. He lived mainly in Philadelphia, except for visits to Paris (1866–69) and Spain (1870), where he was influenced by the realism of Velázquez. His teaching methods, particularly his use of live nude models, were controversial, as were some of his paintings, such as *Gross Clinic* (1875; Jefferson Medical College, Philadelphia), showing a surgeon operating.

ealdorman The chief royal official of the Anglo-Saxon shire. Almost always of noble rank, he presided over the shire court, sharing one-third of its profits, executed royal orders, and raised the shire military levy. Ealdormen later became the hereditary earls, and the sheriffs succeeded to their duties.

Ealing A borough of W Greater London, created in 1965 from the former municipal boroughs of Acton, Ealing, and Southall. Population (1981): 280 042.

Eanes, António dos Santos Ramalho (1935–) Portuguese general and statesman; president (1976–86). Eanes became prominent in the military government established in April, 1974, and helped to suppress the attempted coup of March, 1975.

ear The organ of hearing and balance in vertebrate animals (including man). The human ear is divided into external, middle, and inner parts. Sound waves are transmitted through the auditory meatus and cause the eardrum (tympanic membrane) to vibrate. These vibrations are transmitted through the three small bones (ossicles) of the middle ear to the fenestra ovalis, which leads to the inner ear. A duct (the Eustachian tube) connects the middle ear to the back of the throat (pharynx), enabling the release of pressure that builds up in the middle ear. The cochlea—a spiral organ of the inner ear—contains special cells that convert the sound vibrations into nerve impulses, which are transmitted to the hearing centres of the brain via the cochlear nerve. The inner ear also contains the organs of balance: three semicircular canals, each of which registers movement in a different plane. The semicircular canals and cochlea are filled with fluid and are known together as the labyrinth of the ear.

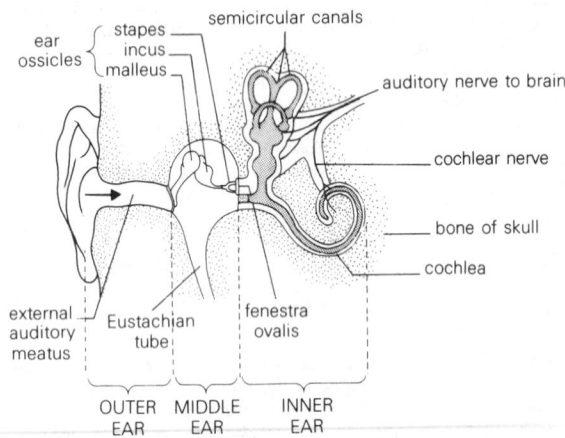

EAR *A vertical section through the human ear shows its internal structure; the middle and inner ears are embedded in the bone of the skull. The arrow indicates the direction of sound waves entering the ear.*

Earhart, Amelia (1898–1937) US aviator, who was the first woman to fly solo across the Atlantic (1932) and Pacific (1935) Oceans. Her plane was lost over the Pacific on an attempted flight around the world with F. J. Noonan.

Early English The style of ▢gothic architecture predominant in England in the 13th century. It is characterized by narrow pointed windows and arches, in contrast to the rounded features of the preceding period (*see* Norman architecture). These lancet windows are often grouped in threes or fives (e.g. the Five Sisters window in York Minster). Dog-tooth carving, heavily undercut crockets (stylized foliage) on capitals, and columns with detached shafts in black Purbeck marble are typical decorative elements. Salisbury Cathedral (begun 1220) and the nave of Lincoln Cathedral (begun 1192) show the style at its best.

earth The third planet from the sun, at an average distance of 149.6 million km (93 million mi) from it. Its diameter at the equator is 12 756 km (7926 mi), slightly less at the Poles; its shape is therefore a flattened sphere (a geoid). It completes an orbit of the sun in 365 days, 6 hours, 8 minutes and makes one rotation on its axis every 23 hours 56 minutes.

The earth is believed to be about 4600 million years old, the oldest rocks so far discovered being 3800 million years old. Geologists divide this time into eras, periods, and epochs (*see* geological time scale). The earth consists of an inner core of solid iron, surrounded by an outer core of molten iron. Surrounding this is the solid mantle, inner and outer, which is separated from the crust by the *Mohorovičić

Discontinuity. The crust consists of basaltic oceanic crust surmounted by less dense granitic continental crust, which forms the continents. The crust varies in thickness from 5 km under the oceans to 60 km under mountain ranges. The composition of the crust is approximately 47% oxygen, 28% silicon, 8% aluminium, 4.5% iron, 3.5% calcium, 2.5% each sodium and potassium, and 2.2% magnesium. All other elements are present to an extent of less than 1% each.

70.8% of the earth's surface is ocean. The greatest ocean depth is over 11 000 m (36 000 ft), in the Marianas Trench; the greatest height of land is 8848 m (29 028 ft), at Mount Everest.

earthnut A slender perennial herb, *Conopodium majus*, of European woods and meadows. Up to 1 m high, it is also called pignut or hognut, as its tubers are eaten by livestock. It has finely divided leaves and clusters of pinkish white flowers. Family: *Umbelliferae*.

The name is also sometimes applied to the *groundnut.

earthquake A series of shocks felt at the earth's surface, ranging from mild tremblings to violent oscillations, resulting from the fracturing of brittle rocks within the earth's crust and upper mantle. The magnitude of an earthquake depends on the amount of energy liberated when the over-strained rocks fracture. The *Richter scale is used for comparing earthquake magnitudes. The point of origin of the *seismic waves produced is the focus and the point on the earth's surface directly above this is the epicentre. The majority of earthquakes occur in certain well-defined seismic zones, corresponding with the junction of lithospheric plates (*see* plate tectonics); these include the circum-Pacific belt, the Alpine-Himalayan belt, and the midocean ridges.

earthstar A fungus of the genus *Geastrum*, with a starlike inedible fruiting body. Initially globular, the outer layer peels back in segments to form the "rays" of the star, surrounding a thin papery inner globe. Spores are released through a pore in the top. The collared earthstar (*G. triplex*), occurring in woodland, is 6–10 cm across, pale brown, and has five or more rays. Class: *Basidiomycetes*.

earthworm A terrestrial *annelid worm belonging to a class (*Oligochaeta*) found all over the world. Earthworms feed on rotting vegetation, pulling the dead leaves down into their burrows and improving the fertility of the soil. The body consists of about 100 segments, each with four pairs of bristles for gripping the surface as the worm moves. The largest earthworm is *Megascolides australis*, which reaches a length of about 3.3 m.

earwig A nocturnal □insect belonging to an order (*Dermaptera*; about 1100 species) found in Europe and warm regions. It has a dark slender body, 5–50 mm long, and a pair of pincers (cerci) at the end of the abdomen. At rest, the membranous semicircular hindwings are covered by short leathery forewings. Most earwigs are herbivorous, sometimes becoming pests in farms and gardens. The females lay eggs in the soil and care for them throughout development.

East Anglia A region in E England, consisting of the counties of Norfolk, Suffolk, and parts of Essex and Cambridgeshire. Originally an Anglo-Saxon kingdom, it became a famous wool centre in the middle ages. The University of East Anglia was established at Norwich in 1962.

Eastbourne 51 00N 0 44W A resort in S England, on the East Sussex coast near Beachy Head, where the South Downs reach the sea. One of the larger English resorts, it developed in the 19th century from a group of hamlets. Population (1981): 77 608.

East Cape 37 42S 178 35E The easternmost point of New Zealand, on North Island.

East China Sea (Chinese name: Dong Hai) A shallow section of the W Pacific Ocean, between China, South Korea, the Ryukyu Islands, and Taiwan. A monsoon area, it is rich in fish.

AMELIA EARHART *A photograph taken in 1932.*

Easter The feast of the resurrection of Christ, the major feast of the Christian calendar. Associated by the early Church with the Jewish *Passover, the date of celebrating Easter was a matter of controversy from earliest times. At the Council of *Nicaea in 325 AD, it was agreed that it would be linked to the full moon on or following the vernal equinox and might thus fall on any Sunday between 22 March and 25 April (*see also* Orthodox Church). The keeping of a vigil on the night of Easter Saturday is a traditional part of the observance. *See also* Good Friday; Lent.

Easter Island (*or* Rapanui) 27 05S 109 20W A Chilean island of volcanic origin in the S Pacific Ocean. It is famed for its stone sculptures 3–12 m (10–40 ft) high, of unknown origin. The population is of Polynesian stock. Fruit and vegetables are grown and wool is exported. Area: 166 sq km (64 sq mi). Population (1982 est): 1867. Chief settlement: Hanga-Roa. □ p. 392.

Eastern Roman Empire (*or* Byzantine Empire) The Roman territories E of the Balkans separated from the western *Roman Empire by *Diocletian in 293 AD. An eastern emperor and magistrates coexisted with their western counterparts at Rome. Under *Constantine the Great the Empire became Christian. Constantinople (previously Byzantium; now *Istanbul) was inaugurated as the "New Rome" in 330 AD. The Eastern Empire survived until the fall of Constantinople to the Ottoman Turks in 1453—almost a millennium after the western Empire.

Eastern Townships A district of E Canada, consisting of approximately 15 Quebec counties lying S of the St Lawrence River and E of Montreal. A prosperous agricultural area, it also has important asbestos mines. Chief town: Sherbrooke.

Easter Rising (1916) An armed insurrection in □Dublin against the British Government. Patrick Pearse, a leader of the Irish Republican Brotherhood, and James Connolly with his Citizen Army, a total of 2000 men, occupied strategic positions in the city and proclaimed the establishment of the Irish Republic. Serious street fighting ensued with the government employing artillery. Hopes of German arms and munitions were frustrated and the insurgents surrendered unconditionally. The rising was largely confined to Dublin

EASTER ISLAND   *The vast stone statues, of which there are over 600 on the island, occupy stone terraces.*

and minor disturbances in Wexford and Galway. Some 15 of the leaders were subsequently executed.

East Germany.   *See* Germany.

East India Company   1. (British) A commercial company that was incorporated in 1600 to trade in East Indian spices and came to wield considerable political power in British India. Its dominance in India was established at the expense of the French *East India Company by Robert *Clive's victories in the Seven Years' War (1756–63). For the next decade the Company controlled government, its powers then being restricted by a series of *Government of India Acts. Supreme political power was vested in a Board of Control, responsible to the British parliament, while the Company retained administrative and commercial powers. In the 19th century these were gradually limited and the Company ceased to exist in 1873. **2.** (Dutch) A commercial company founded in 1602 to foster Dutch trade in the East Indies. By the late 17th century, it concentrated almost exclusively on the administration of *Java. **3.** (French; Compagnie des Indes orientales) A trading company founded by *Colbert in 1664 to administer French commerce and colonialism in India. An unsuccessful rival of the British East India Company, it ceased to exist in 1789.

East Indies   A term now usually referring to the *Malay Archipelago but sometimes to Indonesia (formerly called the Dutch East Indies). It may also include SE Asia and India.

East Kilbride   55 46N 4 10W A town in central Scotland, in Strathclyde Region. Designated for development as a new town in 1947, it has engineering, clothing, and printing industries and manufactures aircraft engines and electrical equipment. Population (1985): 72 000.

East London (former name: Port Rex)   33 00S 27 54E A port in South Africa, in SE Cape Province on the Indian Ocean. It is the gateway to the Transkei and Ciskei Bantu Homelands and an important tourist centre. Population (1980): 160 582.

East Lothian   A former county (once called Haddingtonshire) of SE Scotland. In 1975 its boundaries were adjusted to form a district of the same name, in Lothian Region.

Eastman, George   (1854–1932) US inventor of the Kodak camera (1888). In 1884 he patented a photographic film consisting of a paper base on which the necessary chemicals were fixed rather than being applied to photographic plates when required. The Kodak camera, containing wind-on film, was improved in 1889, when Eastman replaced the paper-based film with celluloid. He founded the Eastman Kodak Company in 1892 and in 1928 developed a process for colour photography.

East Pakistan.   *See* Bangladesh.

East Riding.   *See* Yorkshire.

East River   A river in the E USA, a navigable waterway flowing through New York City and connecting New York Harbour with Long Island Sound. Length: 26 km (16 mi).

East Sussex   A county of SE England, formerly part of *Sussex, bordering on the English Channel. It consists mainly of undulating land with the South Downs, drained by the River Ouse, in the S. It is predominantly agricultural, producing cereals, hops, fruit, and vegetables. Industries include electronics and light engineering. Brighton and Eastbourne are important tourist centres. Area: 1795 sq km (693 sq mi). Population (1983 est): 678 300. Administrative centre: Lewes.

Eastwood, Clint   (1930–   ) US film actor and director, who became popular playing tough taciturn heroes in such films as *The Good The Bad and The Ugly* (1966) and *Dirty Harry* (1971). In 1986 he entered politics as mayor of Carmel, California.

Ebbw Vale   51 47N 3 12W A town in South Wales, in Gwent. It lies in a coalmining district and was formerly known for iron and steel. It now manufactures tinplate and has varied light industry. Population (1981): 24 422.

Ebert, Friedrich   (1871–1925) German statesman; first president of the German *Weimar Republic (1919–25). A trade union leader, he later became a deputy in the Reichstag and from 1913 led the Social Democrats. Although a constitutional monarchist, he accepted the republican presidency when the German Empire collapsed in 1918. As president he suppressed extremists of the Right and Left.

Ebla   An ancient city (modern Tell Mardikh) S of Aleppo (Syria). It was conquered by *Sargon of Akkad and an archive of over 15 000 Akkadian cuneiform tablets containing trade and other records from this period (c. 2300 BC) was discovered here in 1975.

ebony   The valuable heartwood of several tropical evergreen trees of the genus *Diospyros*. Ebony is very hard, heavy, usually deep black, and able to take a high polish. It is used for cabinetwork, inlaying, knife handles, piano keys, and turned articles. The trees have oval leathery leaves, small creamy-white flowers, and round berries. The most important species are *D. ebenum* (up to 15 m high) from India and Sri Lanka and *D. reticulata* from Mauritius. Family: *Ebenaceae*.

Eboracum (*or* Eburacum).   *See* York.

Ebro, River (Latin name: Iberus)   The second longest river in Spain. Rising in the Cantabrian Mountains, it flows SE to the Mediterranean. It is a source of hydroelectricity and irrigation and its delta is canalized. Length: 910 km (565 mi).

Eccles   53 29N 2 21W A town in N England, in Greater Manchester on the Manchester Ship Canal. It manufactures machinery, textiles, and chemicals. Eccles cakes originated here. Population (1981): 37 166.

Eccles, Sir John Carew   (1903–   ) Australian physiologist, who (in the 1950s) showed how the different nerve endings (synapses) could either allow the transmission of nervous impulses to other nerves (excitatory) or could prevent their passage (inhibitory). He was awarded the 1963

Nobel Prize together with A. L. *Hodgkin and A. F. *Huxley.

Ecclesiastes (Greek: the preacher) An Old Testament book, traditionally ascribed to Solomon (10th century BC) but in fact one of the later books to be accepted as part of the Hebrew Bible. It is pessimistic in tone, consisting of poetic reflections on the futility of human life.

Ecclesiasticus A book of the *Apocrypha, also known as the Wisdom of Jesus the son of Sirach. It was written about 180 BC in Palestine by Joshua (or Jesus) ben-Sira. It stresses the need to fear and obey God, gives practical advice for daily living, and underlines the value of having a good name.

Ecevit, Bülent (1925-) Turkish statesman; prime minister (1974, 1977, 1978-79). He represented the Republican People's Party in the Grand National Assembly (1957-60) and was a member of the Constituent Assembly of 1961. From 1961 to 1965 he was minister of labour. In 1974 he ordered the Turkish invasion of Cyprus and in 1978, following violent civil unrest, imposed martial law on Turkey.

Echegaray y Eizaguirre, José (1832-1916) Spanish dramatist. A mathematician and economist, he was appointed minister of finance in 1874. His plays include *Madman or Saint* (1877) and *The Son of Don Juan* (1895), influenced by *Ibsen. He won the Nobel Prize in 1904.

echidna A *monotreme mammal belonging to the family *Tachyglossidae* (5 species), of Australia, Tasmania, and New Guinea. The Australian echidna (*Tachyglossus aculeatus*), or spiny anteater, is about 45 cm long, with very long spines among its fur, and digs for ants, picking them up with its long sticky tongue; it has no teeth. Echidnas lay a single egg, which is incubated in a pouch on the female's belly. The young echidna is suckled at a teat in the pouch.

Echidna In Greek legend, a monster, half woman and half serpent. By the monster *Typhon she gave birth to many other legendary monsters, including Chimera, Cerberus, Orthus, Scylla, the Sphinx, and the dragons of the Hesperides and of Colchis.

echinoderm A marine invertebrate animal of the phylum *Echinodermata* (over 6000 species), including *starfish, *sea urchins, *crinoids, *sea cucumbers, *brittle stars, etc. Echinoderms usually have a skin-covered skeleton of calcareous plates, often bearing spines. They use hydrostatic pressure created by a water vascular system to extend numerous small saclike organs (tube feet) used in locomotion, respiration, feeding, etc. Echinoderms generally occur on the sea floor and are found at all depths, usually feeding on other animals or detritus. The sexes are generally separate and sex cells are fertilized in the sea. The larvae are mostly free-swimming.

Echinoidea A class of marine invertebrate animals (900 species) belonging to the phylum *Echinodermata* (*see* echinoderm), in which the body is covered by a rigid skeleton of calcareous plates bearing movable spines. The class includes the *sea urchins, *heart urchins, and *sand dollars.

Echo In Greek legend, a nymph deprived of speech by Hera and able to repeat only the final words of others. Her hopeless love for *Narcissus caused her to fade away until only her voice remained.

echolocation A method by which certain animals can sense and locate surrounding objects by emitting sounds and detecting the echo. Insectivorous bats emit high-frequency sound pulses (12-150 kHz) and, detecting the echo by means of large ears or folds of the nostril, are able to locate their prey when hunting on the wing. Toothed whales and porpoises emit brief intense clicks, enabling them to discriminate objects as small as fine wires. Some shrews and certain cave-dwelling swiftlets also use echolocation as a means of orientation.

echo sounding The use of sound waves to measure the depth of the sea below a vessel or to detect other vessels or obstacles. The device used consists of a source of ultrasonic pulses (about 30 kHz frequency, usually at 1 pulse per second) and an electronic circuit to measure the time taken for the pulse to reach the sea bed or the other vessel and its echo to return to the transducer. This may be displayed on a *cathode-ray tube, paper chart, or neon light. The device was developed originally by the Allied Submarine Detection Investigation Committee (ASDIC) in 1920 and was formerly known by this acronym. The name was changed to sonar (*sound na*vigation a*nd r*anging) in 1963. Echo-sounding depth-measuring devices are now fitted to most ships.

Eck, Johann Maier von (1486-1543) German Roman Catholic theologian. He was a leading defender of Roman Catholicism during the early years of the Reformation. He publicly disputed with *Luther at Leipzig (1519) and with *Melanchthon at Worms (1541).

Eckermann, Johann Peter (1792-1854) German writer. His early work impressed *Goethe, whose unpaid assistant he became in 1823. His *Conversations with Goethe* (1836-48) is a brilliant literary account of the poet's last years.

Eckert, John Presper (1919-) US electronics engineer, who with **John W. Mauchly** (1907-) built the first electronic computer (1946). Known as ENIAC (*E*lectronic *N*umerical *I*ntegrator *a*nd *C*omputer), it was commissioned by the US Government and used by the army. Eckert and Mauchly also produced Binac (*Bin*ary *A*utomatic *C*omputer) and Univac I (*Univ*ersal *A*utomatic *C*omputer).

Eckhart, Meister (Johannes E.; c. 1260-c. 1327) German Dominican theologian and mystic. Joining the Dominicans in 1275, he studied in Cologne and Paris and became provincial of his order in Saxony in 1303. During his professorship at Cologne University (1320-27) he was charged with heresy and in 1329 his writings were condemned by the pope. They have influenced a number of Protestant theologians and Romantic and existentialist writers.

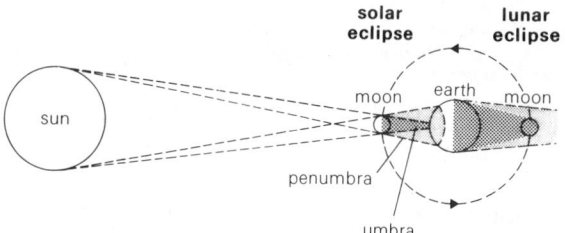

ECLIPSE

eclipse The passage of all or part of an astronomical body into the shadow of another. A **lunar eclipse** occurs when the moon can enter the earth's shadow at full moon. The gradual obscuration of the moon's surface is seen wherever the moon is above the horizon. A **solar eclipse**, which is strictly an *occultation, occurs at new moon, but only when the moon passes directly in front of the sun. The moon's shadow falls on and moves rapidly across the earth. Observers in the outer shadow region (the penumbra) will see a **partial eclipse**, with only part of the sun hidden. Observers in the dark inner (umbral) region of the shadow will see a **total eclipse**, in which the sun's disc is completely but briefly obscured; the *corona can, however, be seen. If the moon is too far away totally to cover the sun, an **annular eclipse** is observed, in which a rim of light is visible around the eclipsed sun.

ecliptic The great circle in which the plane of the earth's orbit around the sun meets the □celestial sphere. As a result of the earth's orbital motion, the ecliptic marks the apparent path of the sun across the celestial sphere, relative to the background stars, over the course of a year.

eclogue A short dramatic poem, originally pastoral in theme and setting. Originated by *Theocritus in the 3rd century BC, the form was used by Virgil and revived during the Renaissance by Dante and other Italian poets. English writers of eclogues include Spenser, Marvell, and Swift. In the 20th century, Louis MacNeice and W. H. Auden have made ironic use of the form.

ecology The scientific study of organisms in their natural environment. Modern ecology, dating from the work of such scientists as Charles *Elton in the 1930s, is concerned with the relationships of different species with each other and with the environment (habitat) in which they live. A *community of organisms and their habitat is called an *ecosystem. Ecologists can calculate the productivity of various ecosystems in terms of energy, with important applications in agriculture. In addition, the effects of man's intervention on natural ecosystems can be predicted, enabling the effective conservation of wildlife and management of game and fish. Ecologists have also introduced biological methods of pest control in certain cases, so avoiding pollution by pesticides.

econometrics The application of statistical techniques to *economics. Econometrics is used in the testing of the validity of economic theories and in forecasting future trends. The usual process is to develop a mathematical model of a specific theory; the model is then tested against observations of the real world and, if the theory is not refuted as a result, the model can then be used to make forecasts.

economic growth An expansion in the output of a nation's economy, measured by an increase in the *gross national product (GNP). Economic growth is generally regarded as desirable because it is the best way of raising the *standard of living; however, it can have drawbacks, such as increased pollution, which do not show up in the GNP. The level of *investment in the economy is an important factor in the rate of growth, but the reasons for faster growth in some countries than in others are not at all certain. It is also necessary to distinguish between growth and growth per capita. In a developing country the rate of growth may be high but the rate of growth per capita may be low because of a large increase in the population.

economics A social science concerned with the production of goods and services, their distribution, exchange, and consumption. **Microeconomics** is concerned with the problems facing individuals and firms, while **macroeconomics** is concerned with the economy of a country and regulation of the economy by governments. The division is useful because what is rational for the individual firm or household is not necessarily rational when considering the whole economy.

Contemporary problems in economics in the western democracies centre upon the control of *inflation, *unemployment, and the *balance of payments, as well as the encouragement of *economic growth. Economics is beset by controversy between the conflicting schools of thought of *monetarism and *Keynesianism as to the extent to which governments can influence economies.

economies of scale An increase in output from a production process that is proportionately larger than the increase in inputs (raw materials, labour, etc.). For instance, a double-decker bus might be able to carry twice as many passengers as a single-decker, using the same number of crew and requiring only 40% more fuel. Such economies of scale are common in the manufacturing industry and are an inducement to use fewer but larger factories.

ecosystem A *community of living organisms together with the nonliving habitat that they occupy. Some ecosystems are clearly defined (for example, a pond or lake); others have no definite boundaries, merging with neighbouring ecosystems. An ecosystem receives inputs of solar energy, nutrients, water, and gases and discharges heat, oxygen, carbon dioxide, and organic compounds. The organisms typically comprise producers (plants, manufacturing organic material from inorganic compounds); consumers (animals, feeding on plants and each other); and decomposers (microorganisms bringing about decay). Together they form an interdependent *food chain or food web.

ectopic pregnancy Pregnancy occurring elsewhere than in the womb. The commonest site of an ectopic pregnancy is in a Fallopian tube but it may also occur in the cervix of the womb or very rarely inside the abdomen. It may lead to abortion or, more seriously, to rupture of the tube, with pain, bleeding, and shock. The usual treatment of an ectopic pregnancy is surgical removal of the fetus and tube. Since the patient has a second tube there is usually no reason why she should not subsequently have a normal pregnancy.

Ecuador, Republic of A country in NW South America, lying on the Equator, from which it takes its name. It includes the *Galápagos Islands 1000 km (600 mi) out in the Pacific. It consists chiefly of a coastal plain in the W, separated from the tropical jungles and rivers of the Amazon basin (Oriente) by ranges and plateaus of the Andes (containing several active volcanoes, including *Cotopaxi). There are frequent earthquakes, which are often disastrous. The population is largely of Indian and mixed race, with minorities of European and African descent. *Economy:* mainly agricultural, with livestock, cereals, and vegetables in the upland valleys and tropical farming in the lower coastal areas, where the main cash crops (bananas, coffee, and cocoa) are grown. Much of the country is forested and valuable hardwoods are produced, although a great deal remains to be exploited. Ecuador is the world's leading producer of balsawood. Fishing is important, especially shrimps, and fishing limits have recently been extended to 320 km (200 mi), in spite of opposition from the USA. There are some mineral resources; the most important is oil, several new oilfields having been discovered in the Oriente in recent years. In 1972 the construction of the Andean pipeline, which brings oil from the E to the coast, was completed and Ecuador is now South America's second largest oil producer (Venezuela being the first). Industry is being developed, especially the petrochemical, pharmaceutical, cement, and steel industries. Main exports include oil, bananas, cocoa, and coffee. *History:* the Andean kingdom of Quito had already been conquered by the Incas when the Spanish established a colony in 1532. It became part of the viceroyalty of Peru and later of New Granada. It gained independence in 1821 after revolts under Marshal Sucre, and in 1822 joined Gran Colombia under Bolívar. In 1830 it became the independent republic of Ecuador. In 1961 the president, Velasco Ibarra (1893–   ), was overthrown in a left-wing military coup and exiled. After several years of unsettled government he was again elected president. In 1970 he assumed dictatorial powers and in 1972 was deposed by a military regime. This regime was replaced by a three-man junta in 1976; a new constitution was introduced in 1979 and in 1984 Léon Febres Cordero was elected president. In recent years Ecuador has been involved in frontier disputes with Peru. It is a member of OPEC. Official language: Spanish; the main Indian language is Quechua. Official currency: sucre of 100 centavos. Area: 270 670 sq km (104 505 sq mi). Population (1983 est): 8 811 000. Capital: Quito. Main port: Guayaquil.

ecumenical movement A movement among Christian Churches to re-establish unity. The first major schism within Christianity was caused by the rupture between the Eastern and Western Churches in the 11th century; the second occurred within the Western Church at the *Reformation. It was only with the growth of missionary activity in the 19th century that the need for reunion became pressing. Historical divisions meant nothing to the new converts in countries outside the traditional sphere of Christianity. In 1910 the

Edinburgh Missionary Conference opened negotiations among the Churches of the Reformation, a process that ultimately led to the foundation of the *World Council of Churches in 1948. The Orthodox Churches gradually came to take a more active role in this body, and further encouragement to the movement came with Pope *John XXIII's invitation to other Churches to send observers to the second *Vatican Council, the results of which clearly indicated Roman Catholic support for ecumenism. Since then the most obvious progress has occurred on the local level, where interdenominational cooperation is now widespread.

eczema. *See* dermatitis.

Edam 52 30N 5 02E A town in the NW Netherlands, in North Holland province on the IJsselmeer. It is famous for its round red-skinned cheeses. Population (1984): 24 019.

Eddas Two Old Norse compilations made in Iceland in the early 13th century. Together they comprise the major store of pagan Scandinavian mythology. The **Poetic** (*or* Elder) **Edda** (c. 1200) contains poems on the gods, heroic legends, and traditional charms and proverbs. The **Prose** (*or* Younger) **Edda** (1223) was the work of Snorri *Sturluson, who planned it as a textbook for writers of *skaldic poetry, prefaced by a section on the Norse cosmogony, pantheon, and myths.

Eddington, Sir Arthur Stanley (1882–1944) British theoretical astronomer, who correctly calculated that the temperature of the sun's interior must be millions of degrees Celsius or it would collapse under gravitational forces. He also showed that the luminosity of a star increases with its mass (the mass-luminosity law). Eddington was a talented popularizer of science: his *Expanding Universe* (1933) contained the novel idea that the galaxies are flying apart. He was awarded the OM in 1938.

Eddy, Mary Baker (1821–1910) US religious leader, founder of *Christian Science. Brought up as a Congregationalist and frequently ill as a young woman, Mrs Eddy was much influenced by the faith healer Phineas Parkhurst Quimby (1802–66). She published her beliefs in *Science and Health* (1875) and in 1879 founded the Church of Christ, Scientist, in Boston.

eddy current An electric current induced in a conductor that experiences a changing magnetic field. In *electric generators, motors, and transformers, energy is lost by unwanted eddy currents, either producing heat or opposing motion. In these devices eddy currents are reduced by laminating the iron cores to increase their resistance. Eddy currents are useful in some applications, such as eddy-current heating, mechanical damping and eddy-current brakes, and electricity meters.

Eddystone Rocks 50 10N 4 16W A dangerous group of rocks off the coast of SW England, in the English Channel. The lighthouse built by John Smeaton (1759) was the first in which dovetail-jointed stones were used; it was replaced in 1882.

Ede 52 03N 5 40E A town in the central Netherlands, in Gelderland province. Its museum contains a fine collection of Van Gogh paintings. Population (1981 est): 83 738.

edelweiss A common perennial alpine plant, *Leontopodium alpinum*, from Europe and South America, often grown in rock gardens. About 15 cm high, it has woolly leaves arranged like a star and clustered heads of tiny yellow flowers surrounded by whitish felted bracts. Family: *Compositae* (daisy family).

Eden, Anthony. *See* Avon, (Robert) Anthony, 1st Earl of.

Eden, Garden of In the Old Testament, the location of Paradise, in which Adam and Eve were created and lived until expelled because of disobedience (Genesis 2–3). Although the narrative may allude to a place in the fertile part of Mesopotamia, the geographical elements are probably mythological.

Edessa (Modern Greek name: Édhessa) 37 08N 38 45E A town in N Greece, in Macedonia. Originally known as Aegea, it was the earliest capital of ancient Macedonia. Today it is a com-mercial and agricultural centre; industries include carpet manufacture. Population (1981): 15 980.

Edgar (c. 943–75) The first king of a united England (959–75). He allowed his Danish subjects to retain Danish laws. Edgar promoted a monastic revival and encouraged trade by reforming the currency. He improved defence by organizing coastal naval patrols and a system for manning warships.

Edgar (c. 1075–1107) King of the Scots (1097–1107); a vassal of William Rufus of England. In 1098 he lost the Hebrides to Norway.

Edgar the Aetheling (c. 1050–c. 1130) The grandson of Edmund II Ironside, his title Aetheling means royal prince. His claim to the English throne was rejected in 1066 owing to his minority and ill health. Although he initially submitted to William I, in 1068 and 1069 he led revolts against the king but came to terms with him in 1074.

Edgehill A ridge in the S Midlands of England, in S Warwickshire. It was the scene of the first battle in the Civil War (1642).

Edgeworth, Maria (1767–1849) Anglo-Irish writer chiefly famous for her novels of Irish regional life, including *Castle Rackrent* (1800), *Patronage* (1814), and *Ormond* (1817), which influenced Sir Walter *Scott. She also wrote imaginative but moralizing children's stories.

Edinburgh 55 57N 3 13W The capital of Scotland and administrative centre of the Lothian Region, situated in the E centre of the country on the S shore of the Firth of Forth. The financial, legal, and cultural centre of Scotland, employment depends largely on service occupations. Food, drink, and printing are the primary manufacturing industries; the city's port is at *Leith. Edinburgh is distinguished by its spacious layout and attractive buildings. In the old town, atop steep basalt cliffs that rise above the city, stands the castle (which includes an 11th-century chapel). The Royal Mile extends E from the castle rock to the Palace of Holyrood House (begun c. 1500). The other famous thoroughfare in the city is Princes Street, flanked by the picturesque Princes Street Gardens. The new town contains fine Georgian architecture situated around a network of broad streets, squares, and circuses, which were originally designed by James Craig (1744–95) and include the work of such men as Robert Adam, who planned Charlotte Square in 1791. The university (1583) is famous for its medical faculty among other notable faculties; Heriot-Watt University (incorporated 1966) also has premises in the city. The Royal Scottish Academy, the Royal Scottish Museum, and other national institutions are situated in Edinburgh. St Giles Cathedral dates from the 12th century. *History*: strategically important in medieval times in the wars between England and Scotland, Edinburgh emerged as the national capital in the 15th century. After James VI of Scotland (James I of England) moved his court to London in 1605 Edinburgh suffered a decline. It entered a golden age in the mid-18th century as a centre of learning: the philosopher David Hume and the diarist James Boswell are associated with Edinburgh in this era. The fame of the city as a cultural centre was revived in 1947 with the foundation of the annual Edinburgh International Festival. Population (1981): 419 187.

Edirne (former name: Adrianople) 41 40N 26 34E A town in European Turkey, at the confluence of the Rivers Tunca and Maritsa. Round the main square are three mosques, one of which, the Selimiye Mosque, has 19 domes. Population (1980): 71 914.

Edison, Thomas Alva (1847–1931) US inventor, perhaps the most prolific of all time. Most of his discoveries were developed in his own large research laboratory in Menlo Park, New Jersey. His most famous invention, the electric light bulb, took over a year to develop but he finally constructed a long-lasting filament bulb in 1879. By 1881

Edison had built a generating station and was supplying electricity to over 80 customers. Among his other 1300 inventions were the gramophone, motion pictures, and improvements to *Bell's telephone. He also discovered thermionic emission (formerly called the Edison effect), enabling J. A. *Fleming to produce the first thermionic valve.

Edmonton 53 34N 113 25W A city in W Canada, the capital of Alberta on the North Saskatchewan River. A 19th-century trading post, it became an agricultural settlement and grew into a city with the arrival of the railway (1891). The discovery of oil (1947) stimulated an economy already prosperous from distribution, transportation, manufacturing, and agricultural industries. Edmonton is the site of the University of Alberta (1906) and numerous cultural institutions. Population (1983): 560 085.

Edmund I (921–46) King of England (939–46), who expelled the Norse king Olaf from Northumbria (944). He supported *Dunstan in the reintroduction of the monastic rule of St Benedict. An outlaw stabbed him to death at Pucklechurch.

Edmund II Ironside (c. 981–1016) The son of Ethelred II of England, his struggle with Canute for the vacant throne ended in Edmund's defeat at Ashingdon (1016). However, Canute agreed on the partition of England with Edmund, but after Edmund's sudden death Canute acquired the whole kingdom.

Edmund, St (Edmund Rich; c.1175–1240) English churchman; Archbishop of Canterbury. After an academic life at Oxford and Paris he was made archbishop in 1234. Supported by the barons he successfully opposed Henry III's policies until his power was diminished by the arrival of the papal legate, Cardinal Otho, in 1237. Feast day: 16 Nov.

Edo A people of S Nigeria living to the W of the Niger River. Their language belongs to the *Kwa subgroup of the Niger-Congo family. They live in villages and grow yams, corn, and the cash crops of rubber and cocoa. Their sacred king (or oba) formerly held political, economic, and ritual authority, but most Edo are now Christians or Muslims.

Edom The mountainous and barren land SW of the Dead Sea, which was traversed in antiquity by important caravan routes. The Edomites, according to the Old Testament, were descendants of Esau and may have been subjected by the Israelites under King David. They were converted to Judaism in the late 2nd century BC after being defeated by the *Maccabees. They later migrated to S Judaea.

education The process of learning. Highly developed systems of learning emerged early in Asia, especially in China. Institutionalized education could also be found in various forms in ancient Greece and Rome, which later influenced the development of formal education in medieval Europe, although the latter owes a great debt to early Arabic and Hebrew scholarship. Medieval European monastic schools originally established for those intending to enter the monasteries gradually admitted other pupils and extended the curriculum to include grammar, logic, rhetoric, geometry, arithmetic, music, and astronomy. A basic education was also provided in some areas for the children of the poor, usually by the local parish priest. Humanist education based upon the classics emerged during the Renaissance; the Gymnasien, which was established at Strasbourg, provided the model for the academic schools of Protestant Europe, although its influence was slow in reaching England. European schools experienced a decline in standards during the 17th and 18th centuries, especially in England, where the old *grammar schools (see also public schools) degenerated to a very low level.

Widespread education could be said to stem from the introduction of compulsory attendance at primary schools (see primary education), first established successfully in Prussia in 1763. It can be argued that the introduction of universal compulsory education and the increasing role of the state in the educational sphere were influenced by the need to supply the skills necessary to the functioning of an industrialized society. The state, however, was slow to intervene in education in England and Wales, since a system of voluntary elementary education provided by the established Church and other religious bodies was already in existence. It was not until the Education Act (1870) that universal elementary education was introduced and the school boards were set up to establish schools where no voluntary schools existed. In 1902 Local Education Authorities (LEAs) took over from the school boards and in 1918 education was made compulsory until the age of 14. However, until the Education Act (1944), only primary education (in elementary schools) was available to those whose parents were unable to afford school fees or those who were not able to obtain scholarships to public or grammar schools. The 1944 Act inaugurated a system of universal *secondary education while maintaining the dual system of grant-assisted independent schools and local-authority schools. During the postwar period many of the ideas of the progressive educationalists, whose theoretical origins date back to *Rousseau (see also Froebel, Friedrich; Montessori system; Neil, A. S.), were incorporated into the state schools, especially at primary level. A further feature of postwar education in England and Wales has been the setting up of Educational Priority Areas (EPAs) to give extra help to children in socially disadvantaged areas, the emphasis being on early intervention. A similar compensatory education programme, known as Head Start, was also established in the USA in the early 1960s. In England and Wales the extent to which children should be selected according to ability remains a controversial issue (see secondary education), as does the extent to which parents should be free to choose their children's schools, with respect to religion, the payment of fees, ethnic minorities, and sex (see coeducation). Scotland's educational tradition has remained quite distinct from that of the rest of the UK, the secretary of state for Scotland being responsible for the central administration of Scottish education.

In West Germany education is administered on a regional basis, most *Länder* (states) retaining a selective system of secondary education with approximately 5% of children entering a *Gymnasium* (grammar school). West Germany is also noted for its well-developed system of vocational education. The educational state system in France is highly centralized. During the 1960s colleges of general education, which provided a more comprehensive system of education for children aged 11 to 15, were introduced although these usually exist alongside the selective *lycées* (academic secondary schools). In the USA education varies from state to state. Secondary education, however, is nonselective and provides both academic and vocational courses. Approximately 80% of children stay on beyond the compulsory school-attendance age of 16 and about 40% enter higher education. The highly centralized system of education in the Soviet Union provides the model for many of the communist countries. Compulsory education from the age of 7 until 17 is carried out in single nonselective coeducational neighbourhood schools. A wide range of vocational courses are provided for the 85% of students who do not proceed to university. See also adult education; special education; tertiary education.

Edward I (1239–1307) King of England (1272–1307), succeeding his father Henry III. He married (1254) *Eleanor of Castile. In the *Barons' War (1264–67) he defeated the barons at Evesham (1265). As king, he is noted for encouraging parliamentary institutions at the expense of feudalism and for subduing Wales, on which he imposed the English system of administration. He later tried to assert his authority over Scotland and died while on his way to fight Robert Bruce (see Robert I).

Edward II (1284-1327) King of England (1307-27), succeeding his father Edward I. He was born in Caernarvon and became the first English Prince of Wales (1301). He married *Isabella of France (1308). His reign was troubled by his extravagance, his military disasters in Scotland, notably at Bannockburn (1314), and the unpopularity of his favourites, Piers Gaveston (d. 1312) and Hugh le Despenser (1262-1326). Isabella and her lover Roger de *Mortimer murdered him.

Edward III (1312-77) King of England (1327-77), succeeding his father Edward II. He married (1328) Philippa of Hainault. Edward assumed effective power in 1330 after imprisoning his mother *Isabella of France and executing her lover Roger de *Mortimer. Thereafter his reign was dominated by military adventures, his victories in Scotland, especially at *Halidon Hill (1333), encouraging him to plan (1363) the union of England and Scotland. Through his mother he claimed the French throne, thus starting (1337) the *Hundred Years' War. His son *John of Gaunt dominated the government during his last years.

Edward IV (1442-83) King of England (1461-70, 1471-83) during the Wars of the *Roses. He married (1464) Elizabeth Woodville. The Yorkist leader, he was crowned after defeating the Lancastrians at Mortimer's Cross and Towton (1461). He was forced from the throne (1470) by the Earl of *Warwick but regained it after defeating the Lancastrians at *Tewkesbury (1471).

Edward V (1470-?1483) King of England (1483), succeeding his father Edward IV. His uncle, the Duke of Gloucester, imprisoned Edward and his brother Richard in the Tower of London, deposed Edward after a reign of only three months, and had himself crowned as Richard III. The two boys, known as the Princes in the Tower, were probably murdered in 1483.

Edward VI (1537-53) King of England (1547-53) and the son of Henry VIII, whom he succeeded, and Jane *Seymour. Effective power was held by the protector, the Duke of *Somerset, until 1550, when the Duke of *Northumberland seized power. Edward became a fervent Protestant and during his reign the *Reformation in England made substantial progress.

Edward VII (1841-1910) King of the United Kingdom (1901-10), succeeding his mother Queen Victoria. He married (1863) *Alexandra of Denmark. As Prince of Wales his indiscretions caused Victoria to exclude him from all affairs of state. A popular king, he ably represented Britain abroad.

Edward VIII (1894-1972) King of the United Kingdom (1936), succeeding his father George V. While both Prince of Wales and king, he expressed sympathy for victims of the Depression. He abdicated on 11 December, 1936, because of objections to his liaison with the twice-divorced Mrs Wallis Simpson (1896-1986), whom he married in France in 1937. He became Duke of Windsor and was appointed governor of the Bahamas during World War II. He subsequently lived in France, where he remained until his death.

Edward, Lake (name from 1976 until 1979: Lake Idi Amin Dada) 0 20S 29 35E A lake in Zaïre and Uganda. Its only outlet, the River Semliki, eventually flows into the River Nile. Area: about 2124 sq km (820 sq mi).

Edward, the Black Prince (1330-76) Prince of Wales and the eldest son of Edward III. His nickname is probably posthumous and may refer to the black armour he was said to have worn at Crécy (1346). He won victories against France in the *Hundred Years' War and ruled Aquitaine from 1360 until ousted (1371) by a revolt, during which he was responsible for the massacre of Limoges (1370).

Edwards, Jonathan (1703-58) American theologian and philosopher. As minister of the Congregational Church at Northampton, Massachusetts (1727-50), his strongly Calvinistic preaching led to the revival movement known as the *Great Awakening. Dismissed because of his overzealous orthodoxy, he continued to preach and in the year of his death became president of the College of Princeton, New Jersey. His best-known theological work, *Freedom of the Will* (1754), is a discussion of determinism.

Edward the Confessor (c. 1003-66) King of England (1042-66), nicknamed for his piety and his foundation of a new Westminster Abbey (consecrated 1065). He lived in Normandy (1016-41) and his early reign was dominated by rivalry between his Norman favourites and his father-in-law Earl *Godwin. After 1053 the Godwins were in the ascendant. Edward's childlessness led ultimately to the Norman conquest. He was canonized in 1161.

Edward the Elder (d. 924) King of England (899-924), succeeding his father Alfred the Great. He defeated the Danes (918), taking East Anglia, and also conquered Mercia (918) and Northumbria (920).

Edward the Martyr (c. 963-78) King of England (975-78), succeeding his father Edgar. He was murdered at Corfe Castle, reputedly by his stepmother Elfthryth. He was canonized in 1001.

Edwin (c. 585-633) King of Northumbria (616-33), who became overlord of all English kingdoms S of the Humber, except for Kent. His marriage to Ethelburh, a Christian, led to his conversion and that of his people to Christianity (627). He was killed in battle against Penda of Mercia.

Edwy. See Eadwig.

EEC. See European Economic Community.

eel A snakelike *bony fish of the worldwide order *Anguilliformes* (or *Apodes*; over 500 species) having, usually, a scaleless body, no pelvic fins, and long dorsal and anal fins continuous with the tail fin. Most species are marine, occurring mainly in shallow waters and feeding on other fish and invertebrates. The freshwater eels (family *Anguillidae*) migrate to the sea to breed—the *Sargasso Sea in the case of European and American species. The transparent leaflike larvae (leptocephali) develop into young eels (elvers) and return to rivers and streams. fish. See also electric eel.

eelgrass A perennial herbaceous marine plant of the genus *Zostera*, especially *Z. marina*, which grows in muddy intertidal flats and estuaries on the coasts of Europe and North America and is one of the few flowering plants to tolerate sea water. It has creeping underground stems (rhizomes), which help to stabilize mudbanks, and broad dark-green grasslike leaves. Family: *Zosteraceae*.

eelpout A thick-lipped eel-like fish of the family *Zoarcidae* (about 60 species) that lives on the bottom in cold oceanic waters and feeds on small fish and invertebrates. Up to 45 cm long, eelpouts have small pelvic fins located near the gills. Many produce live young, for example the European *Zoarces viviparus*. Order: *Perciformes*.

eelworm A very small *nematode worm parasitic on plants, causing damage to agricultural crops. Adult eelworms measure up to 1.5 mm long. The larvae, on hatching, penetrate plant roots, which may react by forming root galls around them. Chief genera: *Anguina, Ditylenchus, Heterodera*.

Efik A people of Calibar province in Nigeria. Their language, Efik-Ibibio, belongs to the *Kwa subgroup of the Niger-Congo family. Their territory became a major trading centre, exporting slaves and, later, palm oil. Most Efik live in forest villages where they farm manioc and yams and there is still a flourishing network of markets. Political and economic power was vested in the Ekpe or Leopard Society, a graded secret society based upon propitiation of forest spirits.

EFTA. See European Free Trade Association.

Egbert (d. 839) King of Wessex (802-39), who laid the foundations for the supremacy of Wessex over a united England. He faced the first Danish raiders from 835.

Eger 47 53N 20 22E A town in NE Hungary. It was

occupied by the Turks from 1596 to 1687 and has a minaret, 35m (115 ft) high. Wine is produced in the surrounding area. Population (1980): 60 000.

Egeria A Roman goddess associated with fountains; she also presided over childbirth. According to legend she gave advice to Numa Pompilius (the successor of Romulus as king of Rome), who met her nightly at her sacred fountain near Rome.

egg (*or* ovum) The female reproductive cell (*see* gamete), which—when fertilized by a male gamete (sperm)—develops into a new individual of the same species. Animal eggs are surrounded by nutritive material (yolk) and—usually—one or more protective membranes, for example a jelly coat in amphibian eggs, the shell and other layers in birds' eggs. The amount of yolk varies, being greater in the eggs of egg-laying animals since the developing embryo depends on the yolk for nourishment: in mammals the egg is nourished from the maternal circulation and thus has little yolk. *See also* ovary.

eggplant. *See* aubergine.

eglantine. *See* sweet briar.

Egmont, Lamoraal, Graaf van (*or* Egmond; 1522–68) Flemish statesman and soldier, who opposed Philip II of Spain's religious policies in the Netherlands. After distinguished service in the victories against the French he was appointed stadholder (chief magistrate) of Flanders. With William the Silent and other magnates Egmont left the state council in 1565 in protest against the continuing persecution of Protestants by Philip II. He subsequently pledged his loyalty to Philip but was executed as a traitor by the Duke of *Alba in 1568. *See also* Revolt of the Netherlands.

Egmont, Mount 39 18S 174 05E A volcanic mountain in New Zealand, in W North Island. It forms an almost perfect cone and is encircled by a fertile ring plain. Height: 2478 m (8260 ft). *See also* Taranaki.

ego In *psychoanalysis, the part of the mind that is closely in touch with the demands of external reality and operates rationally. It includes some motives (such as hunger and ambition), the individual's learned responses, and his (or her) conscious thought. It has to reconcile the conflicting demands of the *id, the *superego, and the outside world.

egoism A philosophical theory of *ethics claiming that morality should be based on the self-interest of the individual. Egoism also claims that self-interest both explains and provides a motivating force for a general adherence to a set of moral principles. The argument is that a system of morality ensures a stable society and that an individual is better off in a stable society. Egoism is the opposite of altruism, which claims that morality has to be based on concern for the welfare of others. Altruists claim that while egoism may provide the motivation for others to obey moral rules, it does not provide such a motivation for the self. This can only arise from a concern for the welfare of others.

egret A white bird belonging to the *heron subfamily. The great white egret (*Egretta alba*) has long silky ornamental plumes in the breeding season that were formerly used for decorating hats. The smaller cattle egret (*Aroleola ibis*) is 50 cm long and follows large grazing animals, feeding on insects disturbed by their hoofs.

Egypt, Arab Republic of (Arabic name: Misr) A country in NE Africa, extending into SW Asia. Most of the country consists of desert—the *Sinai Peninsula, the Eastern Desert (a vast upland area), and the Western Desert (an extensive low plateau), while most of the population is concentrated along the fertile Nile Valley. *Economy*: despite limited resources of water and cultivable land, the introduction of modern irrigation schemes, such as the *Aswan High Dam, has led to an increase in the production of cotton, the chief cash crop, as well as a more diversified agricultural sector (rice, millet, maize, sugar cane, and fruit and vegetables). Nevertheless Egypt is still far from being self-sufficient in

food production. Restriction of land ownership under the Agrarian Reform Law (1952) led to increased private investment in industry but the considerable expansion of the industrial sector since the 1950s, especially heavy industries, such as iron and steel, chemicals, and electricity, has been mainly the result of government planning, utilizing aid from communist countries. More recently, however, there has been an increase in private industrial activity. Oil was discovered in 1909 and in recent years production has greatly increased. Natural gas is also being exploited and other minerals include phosphate, iron ore, and salt. Egypt's many historical and archaeological remains make tourism an important source of revenue. The chief exports are cotton and cotton goods and oil. *History*: ancient Egyptian history is traditionally divided into 30 dynasties, beginning in about 3100 BC with the union of Upper and Lower Egypt by Menes and ending in 343 BC with the death of the last Egyptian king, or *pharaoh, Nectanebo II. The so-called Old Kingdom (3rd–6th dynasties; c. 2686–c. 2160) reached its peak in the reigns of Khufu and his son Khafre, which saw remarkable building achievements, notably the *pyramids at Giza. The 6th dynasty witnessed a decentralization of government and the consequent rise in power of provincial officials, which resulted in the disunity that characterized the First Intermediate Period (7th–11th dynasties; c. 2160–c. 2040). Egypt was reunited by Mentuhotep II (reigned c. 2060–2010), the founder of the Middle Kingdom (12th dynasty; c. 2040–c. 1786), of which the outstanding kings were Sesostris III and Amenemhet III. In the Second Intermediate Period (13th–17th dynasties; c. 1786–c. 1567) Egypt came largely under the control of the invading Asiatic tribes (the Hyksos), which were finally expelled by Ahmose I, founder of the New Kingdom (18th–20th dynasties; c. 1570–1085). During the New Kingdom Thutmose III extended Egypt's frontiers and acquired new territories in Asia and Amenhotep III sponsored buildings at *Karnak and *Luxor. His own son was the heretic king *Akhenaten, but orthodoxy was restored under *Tutankhamen. The reign of Ramses II was troubled by the *Hittites and that of Ramses III, by the Sea Peoples, and the 20th dynasty also saw the priests' power rise at the kings' expense. The outcome of Egypt's decline under the 21st–25th dynasties (1085–664) was the Assyrian invasion under Esarhaddon (671) and the 26th dynasty (664–525) was brought to an end by the Persian Achaemenians. Achaemenian rule was interrupted by the native 28th, 29th, and 30th dynasties (404–343) and was finally ended by Alexander the Great of Macedon, who obtained Egypt in 332.

On Alexander's death Egypt was acquired by the Macedonian Ptolemy I Soter. The Ptolemies ruled until the suicide of *Cleopatra VII in 30 BC, when Egypt passed under Roman rule. In 395 AD, Egypt became part of the Byzantine (Eastern Roman) Empire. The Arabs conquered Egypt in 642 and it was then governed by representatives of the caliphate of Baghdad, under whom Islam was introduced. After 868 it gained virtual autonomy under a series of ruling dynasties. The last of these, the Fatimids, were overthrown by *Saladin, who restored Egypt to the caliphate in 1171. It was ruled by the Mamelukes from 1250 until 1517, when it was conquered by the Ottoman Turks. The Turks governed Egypt through a viceroy but by the early 18th century power was largely in the hands of the Mameluke elite.

In 1798 Napoleon established a French protectorate over Egypt, which in 1801 was overthrown by the British and Ottomans. A mutiny among Albanian soldiers in the Ottoman army in Egypt brought Mehemet 'Ali to power as viceroy (1805) and in 1840 he was recognized by the Ottomans as hereditary ruler. British and French interests in Egypt intensified in the mid-19th century and in 1869 the opening of the Suez Canal enhanced Egypt's international significance. An Arab nationalist revolt was suppressed in 1882 by the British, who thereafter dominated Egyptian government in spite of nominal Ottoman suzerainty. In 1914, on the outbreak of World War I, Egypt became a British protectorate until independence under King Fu'ad I was granted in 1922. In 1936 his son Farouk signed a treaty of alliance with Britain, which retained rights in the Suez Canal zone, and in World War II Egypt joined the Allies. The immediate postwar period saw the first Arab-Israeli War (1948-49) and a military coup (1952) that overthrew the monarchy (1953) and brought *Nasser to power (1954). Nasser's nationalization of the Suez Canal in 1956 precipitated an invasion by Israeli and Anglo-French forces, which were compelled by the UN to withdraw. In 1958 Egypt, Syria, and subsequently North Yemen formed the *United Arab Republic, a name retained by Egypt, in spite of Syria's withdrawal in 1961, until its present designation was adopted in 1971. Conflict with Israel erupted again in 1967, when in the third Arab-Israeli War (the Six Day War) Egypt lost territories that included the Sinai peninsula, partly regained in the fourth war (1973). In 1970 Nasser was succeeded by Sadat, who in 1972 ended Egypt's close relationship with the Soviet Union. In 1979, under US influence, Egypt and Israel signed a momentous peace treaty. Increasing opposition to Sadat's policies culminated in his assassination by Islamic extremists in 1981. He was succeeded by Hosni Mubarak (1929-   ). In the late 1980s Egypt's relations with other Arab states improved. Official language: Arabic. Official religion: Islam. Official currency: Egyptian pound of 100 piastres. Area: 1 000 000 sq km (386 198 sq mi). Population (1986 est): 50 000 000. Capital: Cairo. Main port: Alexandria.

Ehrenberg, Iliya Grigorievich (1891-1967) Soviet author. From 1908 to 1917 he lived in Paris, where he published some poetry; he returned to Russia in 1920 and immediately went back to Paris as a correspondent. He remained in W Europe until 1940. He was a mildly controversial figure under Stalinism but wrote virulent anti-Western propaganda. His novel *The Thaw* (1954) and his memoirs, *Men, Years, Life* (1960-64), were among the earliest open criticisms of Stalin.

Ehrlich, Paul (1854-1915) German bacteriologist. Ehrlich did much to develop the understanding of acquired immunity to disease in animals and, with *Behring, he prepared a serum against diphtheria. In 1910 he announced the discovery of an arsenical compound (Salvarsan) effective in treating syphilis. Ehrlich shared a Nobel Prize (1908) with *Metchnikov.

Eichendorff, Josef, Freiherr von (1788-1857) German Romantic writer. He studied at Heidelberg and Berlin, where he became involved in the Romantic movement, and rose high in the Prussian civil service. His lyrical nature poems were set by many composers. His best-known novel is *Memoirs of a Good-for-Nothing* (1826).

Eichler, August Wilhelm (1839-87) German botanist, who proposed the system on which modern plant classification is based. Eichler divided the plant kingdom into four divisions: Thallophyta (algae and fungi), Bryophyta (liverworts and mosses), Pteridophyta (ferns), and Spermatophyta (seed plants).

Eichmann, Adolf (1906-62) German Nazi politician, prominent in the extermination of Jews during World War II. After the war he went into hiding in Argentina; traced and captured by the Israelis in 1960, he was then tried and hanged for his war crimes.

eider A large sea *duck, *Somateria mollissima*, of far northern sea coasts. About 55 cm long, males are mostly white with a black crown, belly, and tail; females are mottled dark brown. The soft fluffy feathers plucked by the female from her breast to line her nest are the source of eiderdown.

Eiffel Tower A metal tower in □Paris, built for the 1889 Centennial Exposition. The most famous work of the French engineer Alexandre-Gustave Eiffel (1832-1923), the 300 m (984 ft) tower was the highest building in the world

until 1930. Although an outstanding engineering achievement, it was originally much disliked, but has become one of the great Parisian landmarks.

Eiger 46 34N 8 01E A mountain in central S Switzerland, in the Bernese Oberland. Its N face, possibly the most difficult climb in the Alps, was not conquered until 1938. Height: 3970 m (12 697 ft).

Eightfold Path (*or* The Noble Eightfold Path) In Buddhism the fourth of the *Four Noble Truths, which summarizes the eight ways that lead the Buddhist to enlightenment. They are: right understanding, right resolve, right speech, right action, right livelihood, right effort, right mindfulness, and right meditation. The Path, which is not a series of successive steps but an integrated spiritual attitude, was described in the Buddha's first discourse at Benares.

Eijkman, Christiaan (1858-1930) Dutch physician, who originated the concept of dietary deficiency disease. As a doctor in the East Indies, Eijkman noticed that chickens fed on polished rice developed symptoms resembling beriberi. By including rice hulls in their diet, the disease was cured—an effect he attributed to a dietary factor (later shown to be thiamine, or vitamin B_1). Eijkmann received the 1929 Nobel Prize with Sir Frederick *Hopkins.

Eilat (Elat *or* Elath) 29 33N 34 57E A town in extreme S Israel, on the Gulf of Aqaba. Ancient Eilat declined in the 12th century, and the modern city was founded in 1949 as Israel's only port S of the Suez Canal. There is also an oil-refining industry here. Population (1982 est): 19 500.

Eindhoven 51 26N 5 30E A town in the S Netherlands, in North Brabant province. It is a manufacturing centre specializing in electronics and producing light bulbs, radios, and televisions. Population (1984): 192 854.

Einhard (*or* Eginhard; c. 770-840) Frankish historian, a courtier of *Charlemagne. His *Vita Caroli magni*, based on intimate knowledge of the emperor's character and government, is one of the major medieval biographies and a probable source of the 12th-century poem, *Chanson de Roland*.

EINSTEIN   *A photograph taken in 1932.*

Einstein, Albert (1879-1955) German physicist. Born in Ulm, now in West Germany, Einstein was an undistinguished scholar, being interested only in theoretical physics. In 1901 he obtained a post at the Patent Office in Berne, Switzerland, and became a Swiss citizen. While working there, he continued his researches and in 1905 published four highly original papers. One gave a mathematical explanation of the *Brownian movement in molecular terms, the second explained the *photoelectric effect in terms of *photons, the third announced his special theory of *relativity, and the fourth related mass to energy. These papers were so revolutionary that their importance was not immediately recognized and Einstein only secured a university post four years later. In 1915 he extended the theory of relativity to the general case and, when its predictions had been verified in 1917, he became world-famous, receiving the 1921 Nobel Prize for Physics. In 1933, while Einstein was lecturing in California, Hitler came to power; being Jewish, Einstein decided to remain in the USA. He spent the rest of his life at the Institute for Advanced Study in Princeton, unsuccessfully seeking a *unified field theory. He became a US citizen in 1940. Originally a pacifist, Einstein was persuaded in 1939 to write to President Roosevelt warning him that an atom bomb could now be made and that Germany might make one first. Although he took no part in its manufacture, he was an active postwar advocate of nuclear disarmament, aware that without his theory of relativity the nuclear age could not have dawned.

einsteinium (Es) An artificial transuranic element discovered by Ghiorso and others in 1952 in fall-out from the first large hydrogen-bomb explosion. It was named after Albert Einstein. Einsteinium behaves chemically as a trivalent actinide. Its 11 isotopes are all radioactive, the longest-lived having a half-life of 276 days. At no 99; at wt (254).

Einthoven, Willem (1860-1927) Dutch physiologist and pioneer of *electrocardiography. In 1903 Einthoven devised a sensitive galvanometer to detect the electrical rhythms of the heart. He developed his recording technique until he was able to correlate abnormalities in electrical activity with various heart disorders. He was awarded the 1924 Nobel Prize.

Éire. See Ireland, Republic of.

Eisenach 50 59N 10 21E A town and resort in SW East Germany, on the NW slopes of the Thuringian Forest. Among its many notable buildings is Wartburg Castle, where Martin Luther completed his translation of the Bible into German. It is the birthplace of J. S. Bach. Its manufactures include motor vehicles and chemicals. Population (1983 est): 50 796.

Eisenhower, Dwight D(avid) (1890-1969) US general and statesman; Republican president (1953-61). In World War II he was commander of US troops in Europe (1942), of Allied forces in N Africa and Italy (1942-43), and then supreme commander of Allied forces in Europe (1943). He helped to plan and commanded the forces in the D-Day invasion of Normandy. In 1951 he became supreme commander of NATO. A popular president, "Ike" initiated social welfare programmes and used troops to enforce school integration in Arkansas. His administration saw the beginning of space rivalry with the Soviet Union; it spanned the Cold War years and was marred by the anticommunist agitation of Joseph *McCarthy. The **Eisenhower Doctrine** (1957) offered economic and military help to Middle Eastern nations against communist advances.

Eisenstadt 47 51N 16 31E A city in E Austria, the capital of Burgenland. The composer Joseph Haydn lived here (1766-90); his house is now a museum. Population (1981): 10 150.

Eisenstein, Sergei (1898-1948) Russian film director. His films are characterized by their use of montage, an editing technique in which isolated images are used to emphasize intellectual points. His experimental theories, developed during his early work in the theatre, brought him into frequent conflict with the Soviet authorities. His films include *Battleship Potemkin* (1925), *Alexander Nevsky* (1938), and *Ivan the Terrible* (1942-46).

eisteddfod A Welsh assembly in which bards and minstrels compete for prizes in literature, music, and drama. The main literary prizes are a carved oak chair for the best poem in strict Welsh metre and a silver crown for a poem in free metre. Originating in medieval times, the tradition

declined after the 16th century but was revived as the chief national cultural festival during the 19th century.

Ekaterinburg. See Sverdlovsk.

Ekaterinodar. See Krasnodar.

Ekaterinoslav. See Dnepropetrovsk.

El Aaiún 27 00N 13 00W A city in West Africa, the chief city of Western Sahara. Phosphate deposits about 100 km (60 mi) to the SE are exported from here. Population (1982 est): 50 000.

El Alamein, Battle of. See World War II.

Elam An ancient country in SW Iran, roughly corresponding to the present-day province of Khuzistan. The Elamite language, related to no other known tongue, appears in pictographic inscriptions before 3000 BC. Elam's capital was *Susa and it was closely linked culturally and politically with *Sumer and *Babylonia (both of which it temporarily overran in the 2nd millennium BC), before absorption into the Persian *Achaemenian Empire (6th century BC). The Elamites were believed to be descended from Shem, the son of Noah, and were thus related to the Hebrews.

eland An antelope belonging to the genus *Taurotragus* (2 species), of African plains. Up to 180 cm high at the shoulder, both sexes have horns. The common eland (*T. oryx*) is light brown with thin vertical white stripes towards the shoulders. The Derby eland (*T. derbianus*) has a black neck with a white band at the base. Both species have a black-tufted tail and dewlap. Elands live in small herds and have been tamed and used as draught animals.

elasticity In physics, the ability of a body to return to its original shape after being deformed. The deforming force is known as a *stress, the resulting deformation is the *strain (see elastic modulus). A body is elastic only below a certain stress. Above this point, known as the *elastic limit*, the body is permanently deformed. A substance that is permanently deformed by any stress is said to be plastic. See also plasticity.

elastic modulus The ratio of the *stress on a body obeying *Hooke's law to the *strain produced. The strain may be a change in length (Young's Modulus) or a change in volume (bulk modulus).

elastomer A polymer with elastic properties, i.e. one that can be deformed and will revert to its original shape. *Rubber, a natural elastomer, still has many applications, especially for heavy-duty tyres. However, synthetic elastomers of styrene-butadiene, polybutadiene, polyisoprene, *silicones, etc., are now far more widely used, not only in car tyres, but also in belting for machines, sponge rubber, footwear, and many other products.

Elat (or Elath). See Eilat.

Elba An Italian island in the Tyrrhenian Sea. It became famous as the place of exile (1814-15) of Napoleon I of France, following his abdication. Area: 223 sq km (86 sq mi). Population (1981 est): 27 309.

Elbe, River (Czech name: Labe) A river in central Europe, flowing mainly NW from N Czechoslovakia, through East and West Germany to the North Sea at Hamburg. It is connected by various canal systems to the Rivers Weser and Rhine as well as to the River Oder. Length: 1165 km (724 mi).

Elberfeld. See Wuppertal.

Elbert, Mount A mountain in the USA, in Colorado. It is the highest peak in the *Rocky Mountains. Height: 4399 m (14 431 ft).

Elbląg (German name: Elbing) 54 10N 19 25E A port in N Poland, on the River Elbląg. Founded in the 13th century, it became a member of the Hanseatic League and an important port for trade with England. Its chief industries include engineering and shipbuilding. Population (1982 est): 112 915.

Elbrus, Mount (or Mt Elbruz) 43 21N 42 29E A mountain in the SW Soviet Union, the highest in the Caucasus

Mountains. It is an extinct volcano, with two peaks only 38 m (101 ft) vertically apart, and is a tourist and climbing centre. Height: 5633 m (18 481 ft).

Elburz Mountains A mountain range in central N Iran, extending 600 km (373 mi) in an arc parallel with the S shore of the Caspian Sea and rising to 5604 m (18 386 ft) at Mount Demavend.

Elche 38 16N 0 41W A town in SE Spain, in Valencia. Local archaeological finds include a 5th-century Iberian statue, known as *La Dama de Elche*. It produces dates, pomegranates, and figs. Population (1981): 162 873.

El Cid (Rodrigo Díaz de Vivar; c. 1040–99) Spanish warrior, also known as el Campeador (the Champion), who was immortalized in the epic poem *Cantar del mio Cid*. A vassal of Alfonso VI of Castile, he was exiled by the king in 1079 and began a long career as a soldier of fortune, fighting for both Spaniard and Moor. Always loyal to his king, he was returned to favour and became protector and then ruler of Valencia.

elder A shrub or tree (up to 20 m tall) of the genus *Sambucus* (40 species), found in temperate and subtropical areas. The compound leaves have toothed leaflets and the tiny cream-coloured flowers, grouped into flat-topped clusters, can be used in tea or wine. The red or black berries, rich in vitamin C, are used in wine, jams, and jellies. The common European elder is *S. nigra*. Family: *Caprifoliaceae*.

Eldorado (Spanish: the golden one) An Indian ruler in Colombia who, according to legend, ritually coated himself in gold dust before bathing in a lake. The name was later applied to a region of fabulous wealth the existence of which this legend suggested. The conquest of South America in the 16th century was hastened by expeditions seeking Eldorado, notably those of Francisco *Pizarro (1539) and Jiménez de Quesada (1569–72).

Eleanor of Aquitaine (c. 1122–1204) The wife (1137–52) of Louis VII of France and, after the annulment of their marriage, the wife (1154–89) of Henry II of England. Henry imprisoned her (1174–89) for complicity in their sons' rebellion against him. After Henry's death she helped to secure their peaceful accession as Richard I (1189) and John (1199).

Eleanor of Castile (1246–90) The wife (from 1254) of Edward I of England. A devoted wife, she accompanied Edward on a Crusade (1270–73). He erected the **Eleanor Crosses** wherever her body rested on its way from Nottinghamshire, where she died, to her funeral in London.

Eleatics Greek speculative philosophers, active in the 5th century BC, whose leader was *Parmenides of Elea. Their central doctrine was that reality is timeless, motionless, changeless, and indivisible and that any belief to the contrary was illusion occasioned by the frailty of human senses. The early Pythagoreans (*see* Pythagoreanism) were their major opponents. *See also* Zeno of Elea.

electoral college An electoral device laid down by the US constitution for electing the president and vice president. Each state chooses by popular vote a number of electors to send to an electoral college. This number is equal to its number of representatives in the House of Representatives plus its two senators. All the electors chosen by a state pledge themselves to vote in the electoral college for the presidential candidate with the highest popular vote in the state. Thus the elected president usually obtains a greater majority in the College than he would have had on the basis of a popular vote throughout the country. This system of indirect election gives an increased influence to the more populous states.

electors (1257–1806) The German rulers who elected the Holy Roman Emperor. In 1338 the Archbishops of Mainz, Cologne, and Trier and the dynastic princes of the Palatinate, Saxony, and Brandenburg monopolized the right of election, which was confirmed in 1356. Other electors

were the rulers of Bohemia (before 1400 and after 1708), Bavaria (after 1623), and Hanover (after 1708).

Electra In Greek legend, the daughter of Agamemnon and Clytemnestra. She helped her brother Orestes escape after the murder of Agamemnon and later helped him to kill Clytemnestra and her lover Aegisthus. She is the subject of plays by Aeschylus, Sophocles, and Euripides. Electra is also the name of one of the Pleiades, of a daughter of Oceanus, and of the mother of the Harpies.

Electra complex. *See* Oedipus complex.

electrical engineering The branch of engineering concerned with the generation, transmission, distribution, and use of electricity. Its two main branches are power engineering and *electronics (including telecommunications) although the latter is now often regarded as a separate discipline. Electrical engineering emerged in the late 19th century with the mathematical formulation of the basic laws of electricity by James Clerk *Maxwell, followed by the development of such practical applications as the Bell telephone, Edison's incandescent lamp, and the first central generating plants. Electrical power engineers design generators, *power stations, and *electricity supply systems as well as *electric motors and transport and traction systems. Electronics engineers are concerned with all forms of electronic communications and *computers. Electrical engineering is an applied science involving advanced mathematical skills and a profound knowledge of physics, in addition to the basic engineering subjects. In the UK the professional body is the Institution of Electrical Engineers (founded 1871, incorporated 1921).

electric-arc furnace A type of furnace used in making high-grade *steels, usually from scrap steel, in which the heat source is an electric arc. Electric furnaces provide clean working conditions and accurate temperature control. They avoid the contamination that occurs when fuel is burnt in the furnace. Arc furnaces are gradually replacing the *open-hearth process.

electric car A car driven by one or more electric motors, which are powered by batteries. Because of diminishing oil reserves and the pollution problems associated with the *internal-combustion engine, the search for an effective electric car has been intensified in recent years. Electric cars are not new; Queen Alexandra owned an American *Columbia* electric car in 1901 and electric milkfloats and delivery vans have been widely used for short journeys in towns since the 1930s. The basic problem is that some seven tonnes of conventional lead accumulators are required to provide an energy store equivalent to five gallons of petrol. Even allowing that electric motors are several times more efficient than petrol engines, no electric car has yet been produced to compete with a petrol car. Two lines of research are being pursued: improving accumulators and making workable *fuel cells. Several commuter cars using special lead accumulators have been produced, with top speeds around 30 mph (44 km per hour) and a range of 30–50 miles (48–80 km), including the Sinclair C5 introduced in 1985 at under £400. The hybrid electric car carries its own petrol-engine-driven generator for use outside towns.

electric charge A property of certain elementary particles (*see* particle physics) that causes them to undergo *electromagnetic interactions. The magnitude of the charge is always the same and is equal to 1.6021×10^{-19} coulombs (although quarks, if they exist, would have a fractional charge). Charge is of two kinds, arbitrarily called positive and negative. Like charges repel each other and unlike charges attract each other. The force between them can be regarded as being generated by an exchange of virtual photons between the two particles (*see* virtual particles). On a large scale, charge is always due to an excess or deficiency of *electrons compared to the number of protons in the nuclei of a substance.

electric constant (ε_0) A constant that appears in *Coulomb's law when expressed in SI units. Its value is 8.854×10^{-12} farad per metre. It is also known as the absolute *permittivity of free space. *Compare* magnetic constant.

electric eel An eel-like freshwater fish, *Electrophorus electricus*, that occurs in NE South America. Up to 3 m long, it swims by undulating its long anal fin and has *electric organs—modified muscle tissue—in the tail, which produce electric shocks capable of killing fish and other prey and of stunning a man. Family: *Electrophoridae*; order: *Cypriniformes*.

electric field The pattern of the lines of force that surround an electric charge. The field strength at any point is inversely proportional to the square of the distance of that point from the charge (*see* Coulomb's law). Any other charge placed in this field experiences a force proportional to the field strength and to the magnitude of the introduced charge. The force is attractive if the charges are opposite and repulsive if they are alike.

electric generator A device for converting mechanical energy into electricity, usually by *electromagnetic induction. A simple electromagnetic generator, or dynamo, consists of a conducting coil rotated in a magnetic field. Current induced in this coil is fed to an external circuit by slip rings in an alternating-current generator or by a commutator, which rectifies the current, in a direct-current generator.
Most of the electricity from *power stations is produced by generators as three-phase alternating current, i.e. there are three windings on each generator, which can have an output of hundreds of megawatts, producing three separate output voltages. For transmission there are three live conductor wires with a common neutral wire. This three-phase system optimizes generator design and minimizes transmission losses, if the three loads are balanced. Generally, all three phases are supplied to large factories but the supply is split to single phase for homes, shops, and offices.
Small generators driven by Diesel engines are used for emergency supplies in factories, hospitals, etc. In recent years interest has grown in generators using renewable energy sources, such as hydroelectricity and solar, wave, and wind power (*see* alternative energy).

electricity The phenomena that arise as a result of *electric charge. Electricity has two forms: *static electricity, which depends on stationary charges, and current electricity, which consists of a flow of charges, specifically *electrons.
Static electricity, in the form of an attractive force between rubbed amber and pieces of straw, etc., was known to the ancient Greeks but the word electricity was coined in the 16th century by William *Gilbert (from the Greek *elektron*, amber). The distinction between positive and negative electricity was made at the beginning of the 18th century, but did not acquire a theoretical basis until the discovery of the electron in 1897 by J. J. Thomson.
Current electricity was first demonstrated by *Volta in 1800 and investigated by *Ampère during the next 25 years. *Oersted's discovery (1820) that a magnetic needle was deflected by an electric current inspired *Faraday to a deep investigation of the relationship between electricity and magnetism, which led him to the discovery of *electromagnetic induction, the *electric generator, and the *electric motor. The theory of electromagnetism was elucidated by Clerk *Maxwell in the mid 1850s.
The use of electricity as a source of energy, available in homes and factories for heating, lighting, and motive power, is essentially a characteristic of the 20th century. Our dependence upon it is now taken so much for granted that life seems almost unimaginable without it.

electricity supply The system that generates (*see* power station), transmits, and distributes the electric power in an industrialized society. Power stations are interconnected by transmission lines to form a grid. Grid-control centres continuously monitor the load from factories, offices, homes, etc., and match it with the best combination of available generating capacity, maintaining the supply at a constant voltage and frequency. Base-load stations run continuously. These are usually the larger or cheaper-to-run nuclear and coal-fired stations. Less economic or smaller stations that are easier to start up and shut down are brought in to supply the peak demand. The grid voltage is reduced at substations for area distribution and further reduced at local substations to the UK domestic supply voltage of 240 volts. □ p. 404.

electric motor A device that converts electrical energy into mechanical energy usually for driving machinery. Electric motors, which are clean, quiet, and efficient (75–95%), range from tiny models in instrument-control systems using less than a watt to those using several megawatts to drive large pumps.
Electric motors depend on the principle that a current-carrying conductor in a magnetic field experiences a force and that when two electromagnets are placed close together the two magnetic fields force them apart. The simplest type of motor uses this principle to turn a single coil of wire (the armature or rotor) between the poles of a permanent magnet. Practical motors use a stationary winding (stator) in place of a permanent magnet. Most motors work on an alternating-current (ac) supply. In the induction motor, current is fed to the stator, which induces a current in the rotor; interaction between the magnetic field of the stator and the induced rotor current causes the rotor to rotate. In the synchronous ac motor, current is also fed to the rotor (through slip rings) and the rate of rotation is proportional to the supply frequency. In direct-current (dc) motors, current is also fed to both rotor and stator with the two either in series (series wound) or in parallel (shunt wound). In a dc motor current is fed to the rotor through a commutator. *See also* linear motor.

electric organ In zoology, a group of modified muscle cells in certain fish that are capable of generating electric shocks. These can be used to stun prey, as in the *electric eel and *electric ray. Other species, such as the elephant-snout fishes, generate an electric field for the detection of objects (including prey and predators) and for navigation in dark or cloudy waters.

electric ray A fish, also called torpedo ray, numbfish, or crampfish, belonging to a family (*Torpedinidae*) found mainly in shallow waters of warm and temperate regions. 30–200 cm long, rays have *electric organs—modified muscle tissue—on each side of the disclike head to produce electric shocks used in defence and food capture. Order: *Batoidea* (*see* ray).

electrocardiography Examination of the electrical activity of the heart. Impulses generated by the contraction of the heart muscle are transmitted through electrodes attached to the skin to a recording apparatus (electrocardiograph). The recording itself, called an electrocardiogram (ECG), indicates the rhythm of the heart and aids in the diagnosis of heart disease, which may produce characteristic changes in heart rhythm.

electroconvulsive therapy (ECT) A treatment for mental disorders in which an electric current is passed through the brain in order to cause a convulsion. The convulsion is greatly reduced by giving an anaesthetic and drugs to relax the muscles. ECT is used as a treatment for severe cases of endogenous *depression.

electroencephalography The measurement of the electrical activity of the brain and the recording of the brain waves in the form of a tracing—an electroencephalogram (EEG). Brain waves were first recorded from electrodes on the scalp by Hans Berger (1873–1941) in 1926. Electroencephalography is now used widely to diagnose diseases of the brain and to study brain function. The frequency of the electrical

Modern life depends on electricity in so many ways, yet it is not known exactly what it is.

carbon atom

− ve   + ve

electron   proton

Atoms consist of electrons, protons, and neutrons. The electrons cluster round the central nucleus of protons and neutrons.

Electrons have a negative electric charge — protons are positively charged. The charges are equal but opposite.

Similar charges repel each other, opposite charges attract each other. These are the forces harnessed to make electricity.

helium atom

current flow ⟶

An electrical current consists of a flow of electrons in one direction. But in many atoms, such as helium, they are tightly bound to the nucleus. To flow as a current electrons have to be free.

In a metal wire some of the electrons are free to move about between the metal ions (atoms that have lost an electron). Normally they move about at random and no current flows.

When the majority of electrons flow in one direction this is an electric current. 1 ampere is equivalent to a flow of 6×10^{18} electrons per second.

There are two main methods of making electrons flow to generate a current.

coil of wire

N

field

S

current

magnet

rotating slip rings

carbon brush

2e

zinc electrode

copper electrode

H_2SO_4 + 2Zn

2e

SO_4^{2-}

$2Zn^+$

H_2

$2H^+ +$ 2e $2H$

dilute sulphuric acid (H_2SO_4)

One method is to subject them to a changing magnetic field—this is the principle of the dynamo. If a coil of wire is rotated between the poles of a magnet, the electrons are forced round the coil. This is the power-station method; coal or oil is burned to raise steam to drive a turbine, which rotates the coils.

The other way is to make use of a chemical reaction in an electric cell to dissociate the electrons from their atoms and molecules. The separated charges then flow in opposite directions as a result of the forces between them. This is how a battery works. The sulphuric acid dissolves the zinc electrode producing 2 electrons, a sulphate ion (SO_4^{2-}), 2 zinc ions (Zn^+), and 2 hydrogen ions (H^-).

ELECTRICITY

waves and the way they change with stimuli are related to alertness, responsiveness, and expectation.

electroforming A method of manufacturing metallic articles. A metal-coated plastic mould is used as the cathode in *electrolysis and the metal is deposited onto the mould. The method is used for making thin intricately shaped articles.

electroluminescence. See luminescence.

electrolysis The chemical decomposition of a substance by passing an electric current through it. If a voltage is applied across two electrodes placed in a liquid (electrolyte) containing ions, the positive ions will drift towards the negative electrode (cathode) and the negative ions towards the positive electrode (anode). At the electrodes, the ions may give up their charge and form molecules; for example hydrogen gas is released at the cathode when water is electrolysed. Alternatively, the atoms of the electrode may ionize and pass into solution. Electrolysis is used to electroplate metals and in the manufacture of a number of chemicals, such as sodium and chlorine. It is also a way of separating *isotopes. Deuterium (D *or* ^2H), for example, is slower than ordinary hydrogen (^1H) to pick up electrons at the cathode, and so electrolysed water gradually becomes enriched with heavy water (D_2O).

electromagnet. See magnets.

electromagnetic field A concept describing electric and magnetic forces that, like gravitational forces, act without physical contact (action at a distance). Although both electricity and magnetism have been observed separately for thousands of years, it was not until the 19th century that their interaction was investigated experimentally by Oersted, Faraday, and others. Faraday explained the electromagnetic interaction in terms of magnetic lines of force, forming a field of force, which is distorted by the presence of a current-carrying conductor or by another magnet. James Clerk *Maxwell developed the mathematical theory that electricity and magnetism are different manifestations of the same phenomenon (the electromagnetic field), magnetism being the result of relative motion of *electric fields.

electromagnetic induction The production of voltage in an electrical conductor when it is in a changing magnetic field or if it moves in relation to a steady magnetic field. The direction of the induced *electromotive force opposes the generation | transmission (National Grid) | distribution

power station → sub-station → 400 275, or 132 kilovolts → switching sub-station → grid supply point → sub-station

heavy industry 33 kilovolts

light industry 11 kilovolts

step-down transformer

step-up transformer

power stations ← switching sub-station → grid supply points

town sub-station → 240 volts → shops offices houses

local sub-station → 240 volts → houses farms

ELECTRICITY SUPPLY SYSTEM   *A schematic diagram of the UK system.*

change or motion causing it. Since a current-carrying conductor itself induces a magnetic field, if the current changes, **self-inductance** occurs, opposing the current change. **Mutual inductance** occurs between two adjacent conductors that carry changing currents.

electromagnetic interaction An interaction that occurs between those elementary particles that possess an electric charge. The interaction can be visualized as the exchange of virtual photons (*see* virtual particles) between the interacting particles. The electromagnetic interaction is 200 times weaker than the *strong interaction but 10^{10} times stronger than the *weak interaction. *See also* particle physics.

electromagnetic radiation Transverse waves consisting of electric and magnetic fields vibrating perpendicularly to each other and to the direction of propagation. In free space the waves are propagated at a velocity of 2.9979×10^8 metres per second, known as the velocity of light (symbol: c). Their *wavelength, λ, and *frequency, f, are related by the equation $\lambda f = c$. Those with the highest frequencies are known as *gamma radiation; then in descending order of frequency the **electromagnetic spectrum** includes X-rays, *ultraviolet radiation, visible *light, *infrared radiation, *microwaves, and *radio waves. Electromagnetic radiation exhibits typical wave properties, such as *refraction, *diffraction, *interference, and polarization. However, it can

also be regarded as a stream of massless elementary particles called *photons. This dual nature of radiation is analogous to the dual nature of massive elementary particles and *de Broglie waves.

electromagnetic units (emu) A *c.g.s. system of electrical units based on the unit magnet pole, which repels a similar pole one centimetre away with a force of one dyne. Electromagnetic units have the prefix ab- attached to the practical unit (e.g. abvolt).

electromotive force (emf) The electrical potential difference or voltage between two points in an electric circuit. It causes the movement of charge that constitutes an electric current, providing a limited analogy to mechanical force and motion.

electron A stable negatively charged elementary particle with mass $9.109\,56 \times 10^{-31}$ kilogram and spin ½. Electrons are responsible for almost all commonly observed electrical and magnetic effects and, since they orbit the nucleus in atoms, are also responsible for most chemical processes. A **free electron** is one that has become detached from an atom. An electric current passing through a metal or low-pressure gas consists of a flow of free electrons; a current of 1 ampere is equivalent to a flow of 6×10^{18} electrons per second.

electron diffraction The *diffraction of a beam of electrons as it passes through spaces, the widths of which are comparable to the wavelength of the electrons. Electrons can be diffracted, for example, by the spacing between particles in a crystal lattice, an effect governed by *Bragg's law. Electron diffraction demonstrates the wave aspect of electrons (*see* de Broglie wave) since diffraction is specifically a wave effect. The effect is used to investigate the structure of surfaces, films, etc.

electronics The study of devices that control and utilize the movement of *electrons and other charged particles. Originating with the invention of thermionic valves and their use in radios and record players, it expanded rapidly during World War II to include radar, missile guidance systems, and the first electronic *computers. The replacement of bulky *thermionic valves by *semiconductor components, such as *transistors, made possible high-speed digital computers and the miniaturized communications and control systems used in spacecraft. The *integrated circuit was a further step towards more compact and reliable equipment. The latest

electric field

λ

magnetic field

direction of propagation

ELECTROMAGNETIC RADIATION

development is the use of computers to produce tiny wafers of silicon functioning as microprocessors.

The social impact of electronics has been immense, with the development of television, communications satellites, the computerization of office and factory systems, and the widespread use of pocket calculators. The emergence of microprocessors is expected to have even greater impact in replacing human labour by automation.

electronic surveillance The monitoring of events, conversations, or other activities by electronic means from a distance either overtly or covertly. Wiretapping to listen to telephone conversations can now be achieved simply and secretly using electronic equipment; bugging of rooms by minute microphones may not be used as frequently as films and TV serials imply but it is certainly commonplace. Less sinister uses of electronic surveillance include closed circuit TV cameras in banks, stores, and prisons. More sophisticated electro-optical devices have also been developed.

- source of electrons
- condenser lens
- object
- objective lens
- raypath
- intermediate image
- projector lens
- eye
- final image

ELECTRON MICROSCOPE *The beam of electrons in the transmission electron microscope is focused in a similar way to light in an ordinary microscope.*

electron microscope A type of microscope in which a beam of electrons is focused by means of magnetic and electrostatic lenses onto a specimen and scattered by it to produce an image. The *de Broglie wavelength of high-energy electrons is very much less than that of light. Therefore both the *resolving power and the magnification of an electron microscope are much greater than can be obtained with an optical microscope. Typically an electron microscope can resolve two points 10^{-9} metre apart and produce magnifications of up to a million. In the **transmission electron microscope** only very thin specimens can be used: the image appears two-dimensional but a high resolution can be obtained. In the **scanning electron microscope** the specimen, which can be of any thickness, is scanned by the beam producing an apparently three-dimensional image but with lower resolution.

electron probe microanalysis A method of analysing a very small quantity (10^{-16} kg) of a substance by bombarding it with a fine electron beam (about 1 micrometre in diameter) and examining the X-ray spectrum produced for characteristic lines of the elements. The method can also be used quantitatively.

electron spin resonance The resonance of an unpaired electron in a paramagnetic substance when placed in a magnetic field and exposed to microwaves. Since the electron is unpaired it acts as a small magnet and may either align itself with the field or oppose it. If the energy of the microwave *photons is equal to the energy difference between the two states then the electron resonates. The effect is used to study chemical bonding and structure. *See also* nuclear magnetic resonance.

electronvolt (eV) A unit of energy, widely used in nuclear physics, equal to the increase in the energy of an electron when it passes through a rise in potential of one volt. 1 eV = 1.6×10^{-19} joule.

electroplating The process of depositing a layer of one metal on another by making the object to be plated the cathode in an electrolytic bath (*see* electrolysis). Metals used for electroplating include silver (*see* silverplate), gold, chromium, cadmium, copper, zinc, and nickel; they usually form the anode in the bath. The form of the plated layer varies depending on the composition and temperature of the electrolyte, the use of addition agents, and the current density. Some metals do not adhere well to others; for example, chromium does not adhere to steel and it is usual to plate the steel with copper and then nickel before plating with chromium.

electroscope An electrostatic instrument that detects electric charge or radiation. In a gold-leaf electroscope, the deflection of two suspended gold leaves increases with charge. The quartz-fibre electroscope (QFE), which has a quartz fibre instead of gold leaves, is commonly used to detect radiation. The presence of a radioactive source ionizes the air and causes charge to leak away from the initially charged fibre.

electrostatic generators Machines that use mechanical or other energy to separate electric charge, creating an electric potential. They are used to create strong electrostatic fields, particularly in high energy nuclear physics for acclerating charged particles to bombard atomic nuclei. *See also* Van de Graaff generator.

electrostatics. *See* static electricity.

electrostatic separation The use of a strong electric field to separate substances with different electrical properties. The method is used, for example, in separating out iron ores from a mixture of minerals, and to clean air in chimneys by precipitating charged smoke particles.

electrostatic unit (e.s.u.) A *c.g.s. system of electrical units based on the unit of electrical charge, defined as the charge that repels a similar charge one centimetre away with a force of one dyne. Electrostatic units have the prefix stat- attached to the practical unit (e.g. the unit of charged defined above is the statcoulomb).

elementary particles. *See* particle physics.

elements Substances that cannot be broken down into simpler fragments by chemical means. A sample of an element contains atoms that are chemically virtually identical, since they have the same *atomic number and thus the same number of electrons around the nucleus. Samples of a given element may consist of a mixture of *isotopes. Over 100 elements are known, of which about 90 occur naturally, the rest having been synthesized in nuclear reactions. Elements are often classified as *metals, *metalloids, or nonmetals. *See also* periodic table.

elephant A mammal of the order *Proboscidea*: the African elephant (*Loxodonta africana*) or the Indian elephant (*Elephas maximus*). (The extinct *mammoths also belonged to this order.) Elephants have a tough brownish-grey skin and a muscular prehensile proboscis (trunk)—an extension of the nose and upper lip used to convey food (leaves, branches, and other vegetation) and water to the mouth. The upper incisor teeth are continually growing ivory tusks, for which these animals were formerly extensively hunted. Elephants live in herds; they have a gestation period of 21–22 months and a lifespan of 60–70 years.

The African elephant is the largest land mammal, standing 3–4 m high at the shoulder and weighing 5–7.5 tonnes. The smaller Indian elephant—intelligent and readily trained—is used for transport and heavy work in India, Burma, Thailand, and Malaysia. □ p. 406.

elephant birds. *See* Aepyornis.

elephant grass A stout coarse *reedmace, *Typha elephanta*,

elephantiasis

commonly found in marshes and wet habitats from S Europe to the East Indies. It has long tapering leaves, which have been used to make baskets. The name is sometimes also applied to the tropical napier grass (*Pennisetum purpureum*), which resembles sugar cane.

African elephant

Indian elephant

ELEPHANT *The African elephant can be distinguished from the smaller Indian species by its larger ears, flatter forehead, smooth skin, and concave back.*

elephantiasis A condition caused by chronic infection with certain nematode worms, called *filariae. It is therefore a form of filariasis. The worms block the lymphatic channels and cause gross swelling of the legs and scrotum (or vulva). Elephantiasis occurs only in the tropics.

elephant seal A large seal belonging to the genus *Mirounga* (2 species). The male Antarctic elephant seal (*M. leonina*) grows to over 6 m; females are about half that size. The slightly smaller northern elephant seal (*M. angustirostris*) lives off the W coast of North America. Elephant seals feed on fish, crustaceans, octopus, and squid. Family: *Phocidae*.

elephant's ear. See taro.

Eleusinian mysteries An esoteric religious cult (*see* mysteries) in ancient Greece, with its centre at Eleusis. It originated before 600 BC in an agrarian fertility cult, and the main deities worshipped were *Demeter and *Persephone. The myth of Persephone's abduction to the underworld and return was interpreted not only in terms of the dormant seed and the springing corn but also as a symbol of death and resurrection and was probably re-enacted in a darkened room to which only initiates were admitted.

eleven-plus An examination taken in England and Wales by children aged 11 or 12 that was formerly used to select children for *grammar schools. Based on discredited evidence and assumptions, the exam has largely been phased out with the grammar schools, most of which have now been replaced by *comprehensive schools.

Elgar, Sir Edward (1857–1934) British composer. He was taught largely by his father, the organist at a Roman Catholic church in Worcester. A professional violinist, Elgar became involved as a conductor with the Three Choirs Festival, where many of his important choral works received their first performance. He also wrote two symphonies and concertos for violin and cello; at the end of his life he wrote three important chamber-music works. His most famous works are the *Dream of Gerontius* (for soloists, chorus, and orchestra; 1900), the *Enigma Variations* (for orchestra; 1899), and the *Pomp and Circumstance* marches (1901–30).

Elgin 57 39N 3 20W A town in NE Scotland, in Grampian Region on the River Lossie. Elgin has a ruined 13th-century cathedral and nearby is Gordonstoun school (1934). Its industries include distilling and engineering. Population (1983 est): 20 065.

Elgin Marbles Ancient Greek marble sculptures, mostly a frieze from the *Parthenon, sold to the British Museum in 1816 by Lord Elgin for £35,000. He acquired them from the Turks occupying Athens, who were using the Parthenon for target practice. The British government has not yielded to Greek agitation for their return.

Elgon, Mount 1 07N 34 35E An extinct volcano in E Africa, on the Uganda–Kenya border. Its crater is about 8 km (5 mi) in diameter and coffee and bananas are grown on the lower slopes. Height: 4321 m (14 178 ft).

El Greco (Domenikos Theotokopoulos; 1541–1614) Painter of Greek parentage, born in Crete, who worked mainly in Spain. He trained in Venice under Titian in the 1560s and greatly admired the work of Michelangelo, which he saw during a visit to Rome just before he moved to Spain (1577), where he sought the patronage of Philip II. El Greco submitted his *Martyrdom of St Maurice* (1580–82; El Escorial) to Philip but the king rejected it; El Greco then moved to Toledo, where he spent most of the remainder of his life, becoming friendly with leading churchmen and scholars. His early Spanish works, such as the *Assumption of the Virgin* (1577; Chicago), were Venetian in inspiration, but his later paintings of saints and his masterpiece, *The Burial of Count Orgaz* (1586–88; Santo Tomé), are characterized by strident colours and dramatically elongated figures. He also painted three stormy landscapes and a number of portraits.

Elijah An Old Testament prophet, who appears to have lived in the 9th century BC. He attacked the cult of Baal among the Israelites (1 Kings 18) and successfully maintained the monotheistic worship of Jehovah. He was considered the greatest of the Hebrew prophets. He was taken into heaven without dying (2 Kings 2.1–18), and it was believed that he would return before the final restoration of Israel to the people.

Eliot, George (Mary Ann Evans; 1819–80) British woman novelist. Daughter of a Warwickshire estate manager, she was influenced by evangelical Christianity as a girl, but rejected her early religious fervor in 1842. She went to London in 1851, worked on the *Westminster Review*, and lived with the journalist George Henry Lewes, who was married but separated from his wife. After publishing stories based on her childhood she wrote the novels *Adam Bede* (1859), *The Mill on the Floss* (1860), and *Silas Marner* (1861). The pioneering and influential novel *Middlemarch* (1871–72) is a deep and comprehensive depiction of English provincial society. *Daniel Deronda* (1876) contrasts a Jewish family's genuine values with the false ones of society. Lewes died in 1878, and she married a banker, J. W. Cross, six months before her death.

ELGIN MARBLES   *A rider in procession from the west frieze of the Parthenon (c. 440 BC).*

Eliot, Sir John (1592–1632) English parliamentarian; a leading critic of Charles I. He was imprisoned three times for his views: in 1626 after joining the attack on Charles' favourite, the 1st Duke of *Buckingham; in 1627 after refusing to pay *ship money; and in 1628, when he held the speaker of the House of Commons in his chair to prevent his adjournment of parliament before the passing of Eliot's three resolutions against the government. He died, of natural causes, in the Tower of London, becoming a martyr to the parliamentary cause.

Eliot, T(homas) S(tearns) (1888–1965) Anglo-American poet, critic, and dramatist. Born in Missouri, he was educated at Harvard and in Europe, where he met Ezra *Pound. He briefly worked in London as a bank clerk before publication of his first volume of poetry, the innovatory *Prufrock and Other Observations* (1917). *The Waste Land* (1922) is his best-known work, although *Four Quartets* (1935–41) is generally considered to be his major poetic achievement. In 1927 he became an Anglo-Catholic and a British subject. From 1922 to 1939 he edited *The Criterion*, a critical review, and wrote a considerable amount of influential literary criticism. His verse dramas include *Murder in the Cathedral* (1935), *The Cocktail Party* (1949), and *The Elder Statesman* (1958). He was awarded the Nobel Prize in 1948.

Elizabeth 40 40N 74 13W A city and port in the USA, in New Jersey on Newark Bay. Part of the New York conurbation, its industries include electronics, aircraft, and chemicals. Population (1980 est): 106 201.

Elizabeth 34 45S 138 39E A town in South Australia, near Adelaide. Founded in 1955 as part of a decentralization plan, it was named after Elizabeth II of the UK. Population (1976): 33 721.

Elizabeth (1709–62) Empress of Russia (1741–62); the daughter of Peter the Great. Elizabeth came to power in a coup, which ousted the infant Ivan VI (1740–64). She depended on

her advisers, such as *Bestuzhev-Riumin, in government and her reign witnessed no reforms and few territorial acquisitions.

Elizabeth I (1533–1603) Queen of England and Ireland (1558–1603), daughter of Henry VIII and Anne *Boleyn. Her mother's execution and Elizabeth's imprisonment by Mary I made her cautious and suspicious but her devotion to England made her one of its greatest monarchs. Her religious compromise (1559–63) established Protestantism in England (*see* Reformation). Several plots to place her Roman Catholic cousin, *Mary, Queen of Scots, on the throne led to Mary's execution (1587). England won a great naval victory in 1588 by destroying the Spanish *Armada. Elizabeth never married and was called the Virgin Queen, although her relationships with, among others, the Earl of Leicester and the 2nd Earl of Essex caused considerable speculation.

Elizabeth II (1926–) Queen of the United Kingdom (1952–), noted for her scrupulous fulfilment of the roles of constitutional monarch and head of the Commonwealth. She married Prince *Philip in 1947; their four children are Prince *Charles, Princess *Anne, Prince Andrew Albert Christian Edward (1960–), and Prince Edward Antony Richard Louis (1964–).

Elizabeth the Queen Mother (1900–) The widow of George VI of the United Kingdom. Formerly Lady Elizabeth Bowes-Lyon, she married in 1923 and had two children, *Elizabeth II and Princess *Margaret.

Elizabethville. *See* Lubumbashi.

elk The largest deer, *Alces alces*, found in forests of N Eurasia and also in N North America, where it is called a moose. Up to 2 m high at the shoulder, elks have a broad curved muzzle and a short neck with a heavy dewlap. The coat is grey-brown and males grow large palmate antlers spanning up to 180 cm. They feed on leaves and water plants and form herds in winter. □mammal.

elkhound An ancient breed of working dog originating in Norway and used for tracking and hunting game animals, especially elk. It has a short compact body with the tail curled over the back and a broad head with pricked ears. The thick coat is grey tipped with black. Height: 51 cm (dogs); 49 cm (bitches).

QUEEN ELIZABETH   *With Queen Elizabeth the Queen Mother, detail of a photograph by Norman Parkinson.*

Ellenborough, Edward Law, Earl of (1780–1871) British colonial administrator; governor general of India (1742–44). He succeeded *Auckland in India and was recalled after unlawfully annexing the Sind.

Ellesmere Island A Canadian Arctic island W of Greenland, the northernmost part of North America. Mostly rugged plateau with large glaciers, it shelters a few weather stations, police posts, and the remnants of Eskimo settlements. Area: 212 688 sq km (82 119 sq mi).

Ellesmere Port 53 17N 2 54W A port in NW England, in Cheshire on the Mersey estuary and Manchester Ship Canal. Its chief industries are the manufacture of petroleum products, cars, chemicals, paper, and engineering. Population (1981): 63 134.

Ellice Islands. *See* Tuvalu.

Ellington, Duke (Edward Kennedy E.; 1899–1974) US Black jazz composer, band leader, and pianist. After leading bands in Washington, DC, Ellington went to New York, where he established a group of musicians that remained the core of his band for 30 years. The worldwide success of "Mood Indigo" in 1930 led to European tours and annual concerts in Carnegie Hall. Ellington concentrated on composing large-scale works for jazz orchestra, writing the suite *Black, Brown, and Beige* in 1943 and the "religious jazz" work *In the Beginning God* in 1966.

ellipse A closed curve having the shape of an elongated *circle. The sum of the distances from any point on the circumference to each of two fixed points, known as the foci, is a constant. In the Cartesian *coordinate system its equation is $(x - h)^2/a^2 + (y - k)^2/b^2 = 1$, where (h,k) is the centre of the ellipse and a and b are the largest and shortest radii, which are parallel to the coordinate axes. In the case of a and b being equal, the ellipse becomes a *circle of radius a. The ellipse is one of a family of curves known as *conic sections.

Ellis, (Henry) Havelock (1859–1939) British psychologist and essayist, noted for his studies of human sexual behaviour. His major work, *Studies in the Psychology of Sex* (7 vols, 1897–1928), was among the first to deal frankly with sexual problems and met with legal opposition. He was also concerned with women's rights, edited publications in both the arts and sciences, and wrote *Impressions and Comments* (3 vols, 1914–24), a series of essays on art.

Ellis Island 40 42N 74 03W A small island in the USA, in New York Harbor. It served as an entry centre for immigrants to the USA (1892–1943).

Ellora Caves A cluster of rock-cut Hindu, Buddhist, and Jaina temples in Maharashtra state (W India). They were made mainly between the mid-7th and the early 10th centuries AD. The most sumptuous temple is the Kailashanatha, dedicated to Shiva.

Ellsworth Land An area in Antarctica, at the base of the Antarctic Peninsula. It contains the highest peak in Antarctica, *Vinson Massif. UK claims to the area are contested by Argentina and Chile.

elm A □tree of the genus *Ulmus* (about 30 species), widely distributed in N temperate regions. Up to 40 m high, elms have oval pointed toothed leaves, clusters of small reddish flowers, and rounded or heart-shaped winged nuts. Elms are widely planted for shade and ornament and for their strong durable timber. Unfortunately the number of elm trees in Europe and North America has been greatly reduced by *Dutch elm disease. Species include the English elm (*U. procera*), the Eurasian wych elm (*U. glabra*), and the American elm (*U. americana*). Family: *Ulmaceae*. *See also* slippery elm.

elm bark beetle A wood-boring beetle, *Scolytus scolytus*, *S. multistriatus*, or *Hylurgopinus rufipes*, that tunnels under the bark of elm trees and carries the fungus *Ceratostomella ulni*, which causes *Dutch elm disease. Family: *Scolytidae* (*see* bark beetle).

El Obeid 13 15N 30 45E A town in the Sudan. It is a trading centre for gum arabic, cereals, and cattle. Population (1983): 140 024.

Elohim One of the Hebrew names of God. It occurs often in the Old Testament and is strictly the plural of *eloah* (which can

also be a name of God) but it is used with a singular verb when it denotes God rather than gods.

El Paso 31 45N 106 30W A city in the USA, in W Texas on the Rio Grande. Situated on the Mexican border, it is the commercial and industrial centre of a mining and cattle-raising area. It is also a major base for the armed forces. Manufactures include refined oil and food products. Population (1980): 425 259.

Elephanta Island 18 58N 72 54E An islet off the W coast of India, in Bombay Harbour. It is famous for its cave temples and a three-headed bust, 6 m (20 ft) high, of the god Shiva.

El Salvador, Republic of A country in Central America, on the Pacific Ocean. Narrow coastal lowlands rise to a fertile plateau, which is enclosed by volcanic mountains. The country is frequently subject to earthquakes. Most of the population is of mixed European and Indian descent. *Economy*: mainly agricultural, the economy has been dominated by coffee since the late 19th century. Cotton is the second main commercial crop. Forests produce hardwoods, such as mahogany and walnut, but also dye woods and balsam of which El Salvador is the world's principal source. Most of the cultivated land is controlled by a few families, which has led to movement and emigration (especially in the 1960s) of farmers, most of whom rent their land. El Salvador has few mineral resources and the main source of power is hydroelectricity. Traditional industries, such as food processing and textiles, remain important, but tourism is also being developed. *History*: the Aztec population was conquered by the Spaniards in 1526 and after the overthrow of Spanish rule the region formed part of the Central American Federation (1823–38). In 1841 it became an independent republic. Tension arising from the emigration of Salvadoreans to Honduras culminated in war in 1965 and again in 1969, following El Salvador's defeat of Honduras in a World Cup football match. In 1978–79 internal unrest occurred in response to the repressive regime of Gen Carlos Humberto Romero (1924–) with kidnappings of foreigners by left-wing guerillas, occupations of foreign embassies, and assassinations. Romero was deposed in 1979 and a junta took control but the violence continued, including the assassination in 1980 of the archbishop of San Salvador, Oscar Romero. In 1984 José Napoléon Duarte, a US-supported Christian Democrat, was elected president. In 1986 the country suffered a severe earthquake in which 1200 died. El Salvador is a member of the OAS, the Organization of Central American States, and the Central American Common Market. Official language: Spanish. Official religion: Roman Catholic. Official currency: colón of 100 centavos. Area 21 393 sq km (8236 sq mi). Population (1983): 4 685 000. Capital: San Salvador. Main port: Acajutla.

Elsinore. *See* Helsingør.

Elton, Charles (1900–) British zoologist, who pioneered the study of animal ecology. In *Animal Ecology* (1927) Elton laid down many of the basic principles of ecology. His work on animal populations has proved of economic value, for example in enabling more effective control of rodent pests. In 1932 he founded the Bureau of Animal Populations at Oxford.

Éluard, Paul (Eugène Grindel; 1895–1952) French poet, a friend of André *Breton and Louis *Aragon and with them a leader in the early surrealist movement. Their influence is clear in his early poetry collections, such as *Capitale de la douleur* (1926) and *La Rose publique* (1934). He joined the Communist Party in 1942 and adopted a more realistic style in poems circulated secretly among the Resistance. His postwar poetry was more personal and lyrical.

Ely 52 24N 0 16E A city in E England, in Cambridgeshire on the River Ouse. The Isle of Ely, an area of higher ground surrounded by fenland, is famous as the place where Hereward the Wake confronted the Normans. Ely's 12th-century cathedral dominates the fen landscape. Its industries include agricultural engineering, pottery, chemicals, and plastics. Ely is also becoming a waterway cruising centre. Population (1983 est): 11 030.

Elyot, Sir Thomas (c. 1490–1546) English diplomat and scholar, author of *The Boke Named the Governour* (1531), a popular treatise on the education of gentlemen to match their responsibilities. He published many translations and an influential Latin-English dictionary (1538).

Élysée, Palais de l' The official residence of the presidents of France since 1873. The palace, which was built in 1718, was formerly the home of Mme de Pompadour.

Elysium (*or* Elysian Fields) In Greek mythology, the fields on the banks of the River *Oceanus where those favoured by the gods live in eternal happiness. They are also called (by Hesiod) the Isles of the Blessed. In Roman mythology Elysium is part of the underworld.

Emancipation Act (1861) The edict issued by *Alexander II that freed the serfs of Russia (a third of the country's population). The peasants were to receive land from the landlord and pay for it in labour and crops but inequities in land distribution caused considerable discontent.

Emancipation Proclamation (1863) The edict issued by President Abraham *Lincoln that freed slaves in the rebellious southern states of the USA. It was promulgated in part to weaken the Confederate war effort by depriving the South of labourers but Lincoln considered it "the central act" of his administration. The proclamation's provisions were extended and confirmed by the 13th Amendment, which abolished *slavery throughout the nation (1865).

Emancipists Former convicts in New South Wales (Australia) who campaigned in the late 18th and early 19th centuries for equal civil rights with the free settlers of the colony. Barred from a full political and social life, the Emancipists achieved the abolition of such discrimination with the new constitution of 1842. *See also* Exclusionists.

Emba, River A river in the S central Soviet Union, flowing mainly SW from the Mugodzhar Hills, through the Emba oilfield, to the Caspian Sea. Length: 611 km (380 mi).

embalming The techniques for preserving dead bodies from decay. Embalming was frequent in ancient Egypt (*see* mummy). In medieval Europe it was usually carried out by removing the corpse's internal organs, bathing it in spirits of wine, filling cavities made in the flesh with herbs, and finally wrapping it in waxed or tarred sheets. Since the 18th century arterial injections of preservative solutions, now generally a mixture of formaldehyde, alcohols, and salts, have been used.

embargo A resolution by a country or countries not to supply another country with certain goods, or not to import certain goods from another country, for political reasons. In 1979 the Arab countries imposed an oil embargo on Egypt, after Egypt had signed a peace treaty with Israel.

embolism The sudden blocking of an artery by a clot or other material that has come from another part of the body via the bloodstream (the material is called an embolus). The commonest example is when a clot forms in the leg and pieces break away and lodge in the arteries of the lung—a **pulmonary embolism**. A clot may sometimes come from the heart and lodge in the brain, causing a *stroke. Air and fat can also cause embolism. *See also* thrombosis.

embroidery The decoration of fabrics with needlework, usually in silk but occasionally in gold and silver thread. It was practised by the ancient Egyptians but the first important western embroidery was the *Bayeux tapestry. From about the 13th century embroidery was chiefly used for state and church vestments, the Syon Cope (Victoria and Albert Museum) being the most famous English 13th-century example. Gros point and petit point are two common kinds of stitch used to form elaborate overall pictures, and from the 17th century such embroidered fabric was much used for curtains, bed hangings, and seat covers.

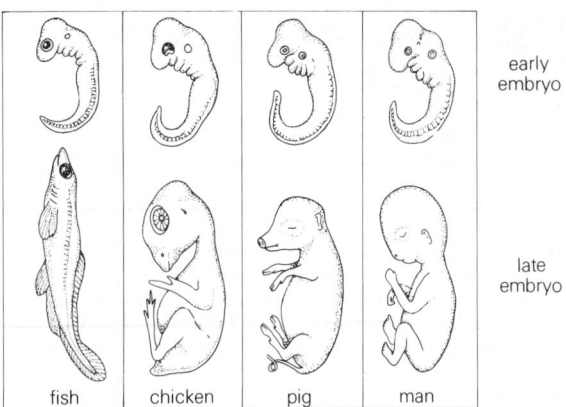

various vertebrate embryos *The different species are hard to distinguish in the early stages of development; later they develop individual characteristics.*

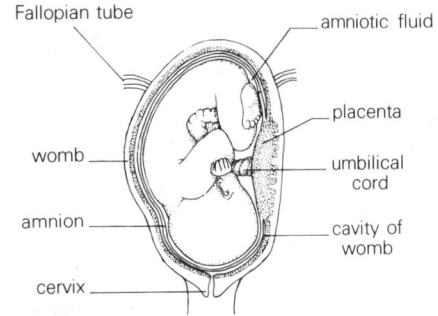

human embryo *A few weeks before birth this fetus is practically fully formed.*
EMBRYO

embryo An animal or plant in the earliest stages of its development. In vertebrate animals the embryonic stage lasts from the first division of the fertilized egg until the young animal either hatches from the egg or is expelled from the womb at birth. A human embryo is called a *fetus from the eighth week of pregnancy. In invertebrate animals the embryo is generally called a *larva. In plants, the embryo lies within the *seed and consists of a root (radicle), shoot (plumule), and cotyledons for nourishment. **Embryology** is the study of the development of embryos. There has been recent controversy in the UK over the experimental use of human embryos formed by *in vitro* fertilization, many of which are produced for implantation as *test-tube babies. The unwanted surplus has been used to investigate genetic and congenital diseases.

Emden 53 23N 07 13E A town in NW West Germany, in Lower Saxony on the Ems estuary. A major seaport for the *Ruhr via the Dortmund-Ems Canal, its industries include shipbuilding and car assembly. Population (1983 est): 50 950.

emerald A green variety of *beryl, the colour being due to the presence of small amounts of chromium. Used as a gemstone, it occurs mainly in metamorphic rocks, particularly mica schists, the finest specimens coming from Muzo, Colombia. It is less resistant to wear than most gemstones. Birthstone for May.

Emerson, Ralph Waldo (1803–82) US essayist and poet, a leading transcendentalist. He was ordained as a Unitarian minister in 1829, but his wife's death in 1831 provoked a radical re-evaluation of his beliefs. After a tour of Europe, during which he met Wordsworth, Coleridge, and Carlyle, he returned to Concord in 1833. There he wrote the confessional *Nature* (1836), his transcendentalist creed. A prolific lecturer, poet, and essayist he expressed his optimistic humanism in *Representative Men* (1850) and *The Conduct of Life* (1860).

emery A granular greyish-black rock composed of *corundum with magnetite, hematite, or spinel. It occurs mainly in metamorphic rocks or sediments, particularly metamorphosed ferruginous bauxite, and altered limestones. It is used as an abrasive, in grinding wheels, emery cloth, and glass polishes, and in the manufacture of certain concrete floors. The principal producers are Turkey and Greece.

emigration. *See* migration, human.

Emilia-Romagna A region in N Italy. It consists of the fertile lowlands of the River Po in the N and E, bounded by the Apennines in the S. It is an important agricultural region producing sugar beet, cereals, vegetables, wine, rice, and fruit. Traditional manufacturing industries associated with agriculture are being replaced by modern chemical and oil-based industries and engineering. Area: 22 122 sq km (8542 sq mi). Population (1980 est): 3 966 649. Capital: Bologna.

Éminence Grise. *See* Joseph, Père.

Emin Paşa, Mehmed (Eduard Schnitzer; 1840–92) German-born physician and naturalist, who became a Muslim and took employment in Egypt. In 1878 *Gordon appointed him chief medical officer in the S Sudan, a post he held until "rescued" (1888) by *Stanley, who thought he was in danger after Gordon's death in Khartoum. He was murdered by Arabs on his way to explore Lake Victoria, but not before making notable contributions to natural history, anthropology, and geography.

Emiscanner. *See* radiology.

Emmen 52 47N 6 55E A town in the NE Netherlands, in Drenthe province. It was formerly a peat-digging centre. Industries include metallurgy, timber processing, and chemicals. Population (1981 est): 90 450.

Emmental (*or* Emmenthal) The valley of the upper River Emme, in W central Switzerland. It is famous for its cheese.

Emmet, Robert (1778–1803) Irish nationalist, who led a rebellion in Dublin for Irish independence in 1803. It amounted to little more than a riot but Emmet's speech before his execution ensured his immortality.

Empedocles (c. 490–430 BC) Sicilian Greek philosopher. He modified the teachings of *Pythagoras and opposed *Parmenides' view of reality as one and unchanging. Empedocles founded the doctrine that earth, air, fire, and water make up the world, and that love and strife (attraction and antipathy) govern their distribution in a cycle of four stages.

emperor moth A large Eurasian *saturniid moth, *Saturnia pavonia*. Males fly by day, attracted by scent to the stationary females. The caterpillars spin a cocoon with an opening that allows easy exit but prevents entrance by predators.

emperor penguin A large *penguin, *Aptenodytes forsteri*. 1.2 m tall and 34 kg in weight, it is the largest seabird and has a blue-grey plumage with a black head and throat, a white belly, and orange patches on the neck. *See* Plate V.

emphysema A disease of the lungs characterized by destruction of lung tissue and distension of the air spaces. It is most commonly caused by cigarette smoking and is often accompanied by chronic *bronchitis. Patients become very breathless on exertion. It is a progressive condition, but the symptoms may be relieved by giving up smoking, breathing exercises, and administration of oxygen.

Empire, British Britain's overseas possessions from the 16th to early 20th centuries. The Empire's origins lay in the discovery by John *Cabot of Cape Breton Island (1497) but permanent settlements in North America were not established until the early 17th century, when colonists, some escaping

religious persecution, were granted charters by the Crown to settle Virginia, Maryland, and New England. The loss of the American colonies in 1783 (*see* American Revolution) was a major blow. In Canada the English came into conflict with the French and only established control in the *Seven Years' War (1756–63) from which they also emerged victorious in India. The East India Company had received its charter in 1600 but its interests in India had remained commercial until the decline of the Mogul Empire provided the chance for territorial expansion. Robert Clive's victory at Plassey (1757) assured British, rather than French, dominance there and the East India Company continued to govern until 1857, when its authority was replaced by the Crown's.

The Napoleonic Wars in the early 19th century brought possessions in the West Indies (Trinidad, Tobago, St Lucia) as well as Mauritius, Ceylon, and, in Africa, the Cape. Britain's first settlement in Africa had been on James Island in the Gambia River (1661) but substantial possessions were not obtained until the late 18th century with the acquisition of what are now Sierra Leone, Ghana, and Nigeria. The 19th-century colonial expansion in Africa was fired by missionary zeal, which motivated such explorers as *Livingstone, as well as the commercial activities of such companies as the Royal Niger, the Imperial British East Africa, and the British South Africa. The late 19th century saw the establishment of British dominance in Egypt and the Sudan but in South Africa it was undermined by *Afrikaner hostility.

Colonies in Australia were initially penal settlements: New South Wales was settled in 1778, Tasmania, in 1803, and Queensland, in 1824. New Zealand was controlled by the British from 1840 and the 19th century also achieved the acquisition of Hong Kong (1841) and Burma (1886).

The colonies were supervised from 1801 by the Colonial Office, which became a separate government department in 1854, and were generally (*compare* crown colonies) self-governing. In the mid-19th century, following the 1839 *Report on the Affairs of British North America* by Lord *Durham, the self-governing colonies in Canada, Australia, New Zealand, and South Africa received responsible government, whereby governors were advised by local ministers. In 1907 Canada, Australia, and New Zealand (and in 1910 South Africa), by now federated, were termed dominions and regular *Imperial Conferences were instituted. In 1931 the *Commonwealth of Nations was established, giving the dominions autonomy, and in the following decades Britain's other colonies gradually achieved full independence.

Empire style The neoclassical style in the decorative arts developing during the Napoleonic empire (1804–14). It was inspired by classical Greek, Roman, and Egyptian models and reflected contemporary interest in archaeology (e.g. *Pompeii). Dark woods, such as rosewood, were favoured, sparsely ornamented with *ormolu. Shapes tended to be plain but caryatids were used as supports. The effect was of restrained but opulent elegance. The **Second Empire style** was the official architectural style of the French Government under Emperor Napoleon III (1852–70). Grandiose and ideally suited to public buildings, it became popular throughout Europe and America.

empiricism The philosophical belief that all knowledge is ultimately based on experience, that is, information received through the senses. It is opposed to *rationalism and denies that we have any *a priori knowledge or innate ideas: we owe all our concepts to experience of the world. Concepts only have meaning if they can be associated with some (actual or possible) experience, and statements asserted to be true can only be justified by appealing to experience. (Mathematical and logical knowledge are often exempted from this requirement by being classified as analytically true—true in virtue of syntax and the meaning of symbols alone.) Since the British empiricists, *Locke, *Berkeley, and

*Hume, empiricism has been an influential force in much of western philosophy.

Empson, Sir William (1906–84) British poet and critic. He established his literary reputation with his first book of criticism, *Seven Types of Ambiguity* (1930). Although slight in volume, his poetry, published in *Poems* (1935) and *The Gathering Storm* (1940), had a great influence on the poets of the 1950s and 60s. He taught in Japan and China, and became professor of English literature at Sheffield University in 1953. He was knighted in 1979.

Ems telegram (13 July, 1870) A communication from *William I of Prussia to his chancellor *Bismarck, the edited and published version of which precipitated the *Franco-Prussian War. The telegram described a disagreement between William and the French ambassador concerning the succession to the Spanish throne. Bismarck altered the telegram to make it read as if each party had insulted the other.

emu A large flightless long-legged Australian bird, *Dromaius novaehollandiae*, found in open plains and forests. Up to 150 cm tall and 45 kg in weight, it has a dark-brown hairlike plumage with a naked blue spot on each side of the neck, and can run at speeds of up to 50 km per hour (30 mph). It is the only member of its family (*Dromaiidae*). *See also* ratite.

emulsion. *See* colloid.

emu wren An Australian *wren of the genus *Stipiturus* (3 species). About 7.5 cm long, it has a brownish plumage and a long (9 cm) cocked tail consisting of six wispy grey feathers.

enamel A glaze that is fused onto the surface of metal. Enamelled gold jewellery dating back to the 13th century BC has been found, and various methods of enamelling have developed since then. Generally, a clear flux made from melted sand, soda potash, and red lead is stained with a metal oxide and left to harden. The resultant enamel cakes are ground and spread on the metal object, which is then placed in a furnace to fuse the enamel with the metal. Painted enamels are applied after the ground enamel has been fired and are not, therefore, true enamels.

enamelwork The art of decorating metal surfaces with coloured glass that is fused by heat onto the metal. There are three main kinds: *cloisonné, *champlevé, and painted enamelwork. The technique of painted enamelwork involves painting powdered wet enamel all over the metal before firing. Painted enamel is particularly associated with Limoges (15th and 16th centuries) and England (18th century).

encaustic painting A method of painting using ground pigments emulsified in hot wax, which are applied thickly with a spatula or brush. Heat is then directed onto the paint to fuse it with the picture surface. Although revived by various artists, it was most successfully employed by ancient Greek and Roman painters.

encephalins (*or* enkephalins) Short peptide molecules, found in parts of the brain and spinal cord, that are thought to relieve pain. These and similar compounds are called **endorphins**. In the spinal cord encephalins are believed to inhibit painful sensations by reacting with specific receptor sites on the sensory nerve endings. In the brain their function is less certain but may be associated with mood. The pain-relieving effects of acupuncture may be due to the release of the body's encephalins.

encephalitis Inflammation of the brain. It usually occurs as a result of a virus infection, but can be caused by malaria, fungi, or parasites (rarely by bacteria). The patient is often drowsy and fevered and has a bad headache. There is no specific treatment for viral encephalitis but the patient usually recovers. *See also* sleepy sickness.

Encke's comet A comet that has a period of only 3.3 years (decreasing by 2.5 hours/revolution) and has been very closely studied during its numerous apparitions. Its period was first established by the German astronomer J. F. Encke (1791–1865).

enclosure The fencing in of open land to make more efficient use of it. Enclosure has occurred in most parts of Europe but is associated particularly with England, where it reached a peak in the 15th-16th and 18th-19th centuries. The enclosing by landlords, without prior agreement, of land to which tenants had enjoyed traditional grazing rights encountered much opposition and in the 16th century a series of Acts against enclosure was passed. The movement again intensified in the 18th century, contributing to the *agricultural revolution. The General Enclosure Acts (1801, 1836, 1845) established procedures to safeguard tenant rights.

encyclical, papal A decree of the pope addressed to the whole Roman Catholic Church. The term referred originally to a letter to all the churches in a particular area, such as a diocese. The most famous example of an encyclical in recent times is *Humanae Vitae* (1968), which was issued by Paul VI and expressed the teaching of the Church on contraception.

encyclopedia A reference book summarizing all human knowledge or comprehensively surveying a particular subject. Greek and Roman encyclopedias, such as *Pliny the Elder's *Historia naturalis* (77 AD), were thematically arranged, as were the medieval Latin compilations, such as Vincent of Beauvais' influential *Speculum maius* (c. 1250). After the Renaissance, alphabetical arrangement with articles written in vernacular languages to facilitate use by the layman became accepted. Ephraim Chambers' *Cyclopaedia* (1728) was the earliest to use cross-references. Diderot's 35-volume *Encyclopédie* (1751-65) used specialist contributors and editors (*see* Encyclopedists), but its ideological bias left gaps that the first *Encyclopaedia Britannica* (1768-71) sought to fill. Major encyclopedias that first appeared in the 19th century and are still published in some form include the German *Brockhaus* (1809), the *Encyclopedia Americana* (1833), *Chamber's Encyclopaedia* (1859), and the French *Grand Dictionnaire Universel* (1865-76) of Larousse. In the 20th century the expansion of scientific knowledge has posed particular problems for compilers, in particular the need to keep pace with technology requires frequent updating of reference works. For this reason some modern encyclopedias, including this one, are compiled on computer-based systems and typeset by computer.

Encyclopedists (French name: Encyclopédistes) The French intellectuals who contributed to *Diderot's monumental *Encyclopédie*, published in 28 volumes between 1751 and 1772. Five more volumes were published in 1776-77. Over 200 scholarly experts, including such leading figures of the *Enlightenment as Voltaire, Rousseau, and d'Alembert, contributed articles that combined scientific facts and radical philosophical thinking. By their appeal to reason rather than faith the Encyclopedists threatened the authority of church and state.

Enderby Land An area in Antarctica, on the Indian Ocean E of Queen Maud Land. The coast is mountainous and the interior consists of an ice-capped plateau. The site of a Soviet research station, it is claimed by Australia.

Enders, John Franklin (1897–) US microbiologist, who shared the 1954 Nobel Prize with Frederick *Robbins and Thomas Weller (1915–) for their work on *viruses. In 1948 they discovered a method of growing virus cultures by adding penicillin to prevent the growth of bacteria, a problem that had plagued previous attempts. Their work paved the way for the development of vaccines to prevent virus diseases.

endive An annual or biennial plant, *Cichorium endivia*, probably native to S Asia and N China and cultivated widely. It has a rosette of shiny leaves, either curled and narrow (var. *crispa*), used for salads, or broad (*latifolia*), used

Endlicher, Stephan Ladislaus

for cooking. The pale-blue daisy-like flowers grow on spikes up to 100 cm high. Family: *Compositae*. *See also* chicory.

Endlicher, Stephan Ladislaus (1804-49) Hungarian botanist, who proposed a system of plant classification based on two groups: thallophytes (algae, fungi, and lichens) and cormophytes (mosses, ferns, and seed plants). Although based on erroneous principles, his system was adopted throughout Europe for a time.

endocrine glands Ductless glands that produce and secrete *hormones into the bloodstream. Most are regulated by hormones from the *pituitary gland, which is itself controlled by neurohormones secreted by the *hypothalamus. Other endocrine glands include the *thyroid, *adrenal, and *parathyroid glands, parts of the *pancreas (the islets of Langerhans), and the ovaries and testes. The wall of the intestine also contains many endocrine cells that release hormones, such as secretin and gastrin, controlling the secretion of digestive enzymes. The study of the endocrine glands in health and disease is called **endocrinology**.

endorphins. *See* encephalins.

endoscopy Examination of the interior of the body by means of a viewing instrument (endoscope) as an aid to diagnosis. There are many types of endoscope, specialized for viewing different organs. The modern endoscope for examining the stomach and intestine is a flexible *fibreoptic instrument, which is swallowed by the patient. It enables all areas to be observed and photographed and often has attachments for removing tissue specimens for *biopsy. Endoscopy of the gastrointestinal tract is particularly useful for identifying sites of intestinal bleeding and for diagnosing peptic ulcers and tumours.

Endymion In Greek legend, a beautiful youth, either a shepherd of Caria or a king of Elis, who was put into an everlasting sleep by Selene, goddess of the moon, so that she could enjoy his beauty forever.

energy A property of a system that enables it to do work, i.e. to move the point of application of a force. The several forms of energy can be converted into each other under appropriate conditions. *Kinetic energy is energy of motion, whereas *potential energy is stored energy, for example the energy stored in a body by virtue of its position in a gravitational or electric field. Other forms of energy include heat (the kinetic energy of the atoms and molecules in a body), chemical energy (the potential energy stored in the chemical bonds between atoms in a substance), nuclear energy (the potential energy stored in the atomic nucleus), and radiant energy (the energy associated with electromagnetic waves).

As a consequence of the special theory of relativity, mass (m) has also to be regarded as a special form of energy (E), in accordance with the equation $E = mc^2$, where c is the velocity of light. Thus the production of nuclear energy involves a loss of mass in the fuel. However, the sum of the mass and the energy is conserved (*see* conservation of mass and energy). Energy is measured in joules (SI units), calories or ergs (c.g.s. units), kilowatt-hours or British thermal units (Imperial units).

Energy sources: man's first use of energy (other than that of his own body or the body of animals) came with the discovery of fire. For combustion is a process in which chemical energy is converted into heat energy. The first fuel was wood; but fossil fuels (asphalt, coal, oil, natural gas) have been in use for about 8000 years. However, it was the *industrial revolution and the later advent of motorized transport that brought explosive increases in the demand for energy and consequently for fossil fuels. These demands have steadily increased during the 20th century, especially with the spread of technology throughout the world. There is now great concern over the remaining reserves of fossil fuels, which some experts believe will be exhausted in less than a hundred years. Nuclear fission reactors (*see* nuclear

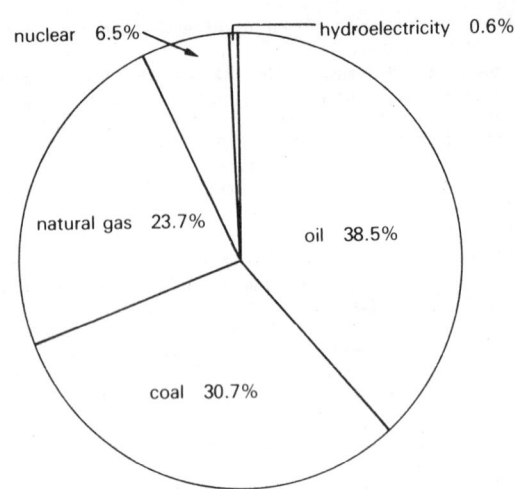

ENERGY *UK primary sources (1985).*

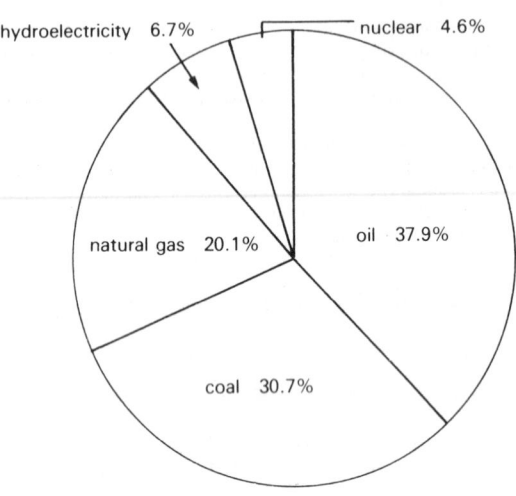

ENERGY *World primary sources (1985).*

energy), a source independent of fossil fuels, now provide some 7% of the world's energy needs and *alternative energy sources are being explored. However, if it can be successfully harnessed, nuclear fusion (*see* thermonuclear reactor) will be the most abundant energy source in the next century. *See* Plate VI.

energy band A concept used to explain the electrical properties of solids, particularly *semiconductors. Electrons need to have a minimum energy, E_v, to free them from the atoms of the solid. Below this energy they are said to be in the valence band. To be able to move through the solid, so that they constitute a current, they need to be above another energy level, E_c, in the so-called conduction band. In an insulator, E_c is significantly greater than E_v and there are effectively no electrons in the conduction band. In a conductor, there are many electrons with energy greater than E_c, and E_c may be less than E_v, i.e. the conduction and valence bands are very close or overlap. A pure semiconductor at *absolute zero behaves like an insulator, but the difference between E_c and E_v is small. With an increase in temperature (a measure of the average energy of the particles in the material), some electrons enter the conduction band. Also, the presence of impurities in a semiconductor crystal brings electrons of an intermediate energy level with it, since E_v and E_c vary from one material to another. Depending on the type of impurity, the number of electrons in either the conduction band or the valence band at a particular temperature, will increase, changing the electrical properties of the solid.

ENERGY BAND *The distribution of electrons over the various energy levels in a conductor, semiconductor, and insulator. There are no electrons in the "forbidden" band between E_c and E_v in semiconductors and insulators.*

Enesco, Georges (G. Enescu; 1881-1955) Romanian violinist and composer. He settled in Paris and had a long and brilliant performing career; he composed symphonies, sonatas, and nationalistic Romanian rhapsodies. A distinguished teacher, his pupils included Menuhin.

Enfield A borough of N Greater London, created in 1965 from the former municipal borough. Its various industries include the arms factory that manufactures the famous Enfield rifles. Population (1983 est): 263 100.

Engadin (French name: Engadine) The Swiss part of the upper Inn Valley, divided into Upper Engadin and Lower Engadin. Tourism is important and it contains several winter-sports centres.

Engels, Friedrich (1820-95) German socialist and chief collaborator of Karl *Marx. For a time he managed a factory in Manchester and was able to introduce Marx to English economic conditions and the British working-class movement. Among other works he wrote the *Condition of the Working Class in England in 1844* (1845). His *Anti-Dühring* (1878) systematizes *dialectical materialism. After Marx's death, he edited the last volume of *Das Kapital* (1885).

engineering The systematic application of scientific knowledge to the design, creation, and use of structures and machines. Engineering has its roots in the constructions in classical times by military engineers of harbours, roads, aqueducts, tunnels, canals, and siege machines. *Civil engineering arose from the study and design of such static structures as bridges, dams, buildings, etc., whereas *mechanical engineering is concerned with dynamical systems, such as machinery and engines. Other important branches of engineering are *electrical engineering, aeronautical engineering, and *chemical engineering.

engineering drawing A systematic method of producing a drawing to scale of machines, their components, or other technical structures to convey the shape, dimensions, and other information to the constructor. They usually consist of a series of orthogonal projections, side elevations, plans, and other views or details depending on the complexity of the object.

England The largest political division in the *United Kingdom. With Wales to the W and Scotland to the N, it is separated from the mainland of Europe by the North Sea and the English Channel and from Ireland by the Irish Sea. It consists of two main zones: the lowlands, which extend across the Midlands, the SE, East Anglia, and the Fens, and the highlands of the Pennines and the Lake District in the N and the granite uplands of Dartmoor and Exmoor in the SW. The chief rivers are the Thames and the Severn. The centre of government and administration of the UK, England is also the wealthiest and most populous of the UK countries. *Economy*: the development of industry has been a major contributor to England's wealth. Mineral extraction has historically been of importance and the recent exploitation of North Sea oil and gas continues to make an important contribution to the economy; seven major fields were in production by 1977. The main English coalfields are situated in the East Midlands, Yorkshire, and Northumberland and Durham. The production of iron ore has declined in recent years and there is an increased reliance on imports. Tin, mined for about 2000 years in Cornwall, has fluctuated in importance. Other minerals include lead ore, china clay, salt, and potash. Manufacturing industries are centred on Greater London, Birmingham, Lancashire, Yorkshire, Tyneside, and Teeside, although there has been a dramatic decline in manufacturing employment in London in recent years. The production of motor vehicles, centred on Dagenham, Luton, Cowley, and the West Midlands, faces strong competition from overseas competitors. Other major industries include heavy engineering, petrochemicals, and pharmaceuticals (Manchester), food processing (Liverpool), and steel processing (Sheffield). Despite the expansion of industries based on advanced technology, together with the reorganization and modernization of older industries, the decline of heavy industry (including shipbuilding), traditionally concentrated in the North and Merseyside, has led to high levels of unemployment in these areas. Agriculture has increased in productivity, although the number of people employed in this sector has decreased. Dairy farming is dominant in the W, while livestock rearing (especially sheep and cattle) is important in the hilly areas of the N and SW. The greatest proportion of crop land is in the E and SE, producing chiefly cereals, potatoes, and sugar beet. Horticulture is important in the E, SE, and West Midlands. Fishing (centred on Hull and Grimsby) and tourism are also important sources of revenue. *History*: there is much archaeological evidence of prehistoric settlement in England but historical records begin with the Roman occupation, from 43 AD until the early 5th century. Christianity was introduced in the 4th century, and conquests between the 3rd and 7th centuries by *Angles, *Saxons, and *Jutes led to the establishment of independent kingdoms (see Mercia; Northumbria; Wessex), which were united in the 9th century under the leadership of Wessex. By the late 800s the Danes had established themselves in the area that came to be known as the *Danelaw and from 1016 to 1042 the English were ruled successively by the Danish kings *Canute and *Hardecanute. The *Norman conquest (1066) ended the *Anglo-Saxon period of English history and established a new dynasty of Norman kings. The Crown was subsequently held by the *Angevins, who also ruled an extensive empire in France that was subsequently lost, except for Calais, in the *Hundred Years' War (1337-1453). In 1455 the rival claims of the Houses of *Lancaster and *York precipitated the Wars of the *Roses, which lasted until Richard III's defeat at Bosworth (1485) by Henry *Tudor. The 16th century saw the establishment of Protestantism in England (see Reformation), the formal union of England and Wales (see Union, Acts of), and, under Elizabeth I, a significant development in overseas exploration and trade. The consequent rivalry with Spain culminated in the English defeat of the *Armada (1588). The Tudors were succeeded by the *Stuarts in 1603, when James VI of Scotland ascended the English throne as *James I. The unpopularity of James and his son Charles I, especially with parliament, brought about the *Civil War, which ended with Charles' execution (1649) and the establishment of republican government. The Stuart

*Restoration (1660) followed the fall of Oliver Cromwell's *Protectorate but the authoritarian and pro-Catholic policies of James II brought about his deposition in 1688 and the succession of William of Orange and his Stuart wife Mary. The crisis of the Glorious Revolution saw the emergence of the rival political groups known as *Whigs (later Liberals) and Tories. The Tories' association with the *Jacobites, who in 1714 threatened the Hanoverian succession (see Settlement, Act of), led to their political isolation until the late 18th century, a century that saw union with Scotland (1707), the development of *cabinet government during the administration of Sir Robert Walpole, and the loss of the American colonies (1783; see American Revolution). Following union with Ireland in 1801, England, Wales, Scotland, and Ireland became the United Kingdom of Great Britain and Ireland. With the *industrial revolution the UK evolved from an agricultural to an industrial economy, a development reflected during the long reign of Victoria in agitation for an extension of the franchise (see Reform Acts) and a shift in political influence from the landowners to the urban middle class. The growing labour movement (especially in the *trade unions) led to the formation in 1900 of the *Labour Party, which was subsequently to replace the Liberals as one of the two chief political parties. The 19th century also saw the heyday of the British *Empire and the beginning of colonial rivalry with Germany, which was a significant factor in the outbreak of *World War I. The interwar years were dominated by the Depression and the growing threat of fascist governments abroad, which culminated in *World War II. The year 1945 saw the return of a Labour government, which began a programme of nationalization. From 1951 to 1964 government was in the hands of the *Conservatives but Labour was then returned (until 1970 and then again from 1974 to 1979). Successive governments have failed to deal effectively with Britain's postwar economic decline and with the prolonged crisis in Northern *Ireland. Area: 130 360 sq km (50 332 sq mi). Population (1982 est): 46 798 600. Capital: London. See also Great Britain.

Engler, Gustav Heinrich Adolf (1844–1930) German botanist, who proposed a system of plant classification that is still widely accepted. Engler adapted *Eichler's system (1883) to encompass the whole plant kingdom. Engler held several important administrative posts in plant science and was an expert on plant geography.

English A West Germanic language spoken originally in Britain but now also in the USA, Canada, New Zealand, Australia, and many other parts of the world. It is the world's most widely known and used language. Its history may be divided into three periods. In the Old English period (c. 450–1100 AD), four dialects were spoken: Northumbrian, Mercian, Kentish, and West Saxon. The last became the standard form at this time as many translations of Latin works were made at Winchester during the reign of Alfred the Great. Middle English refers to the period from 1100 to 1500, when five dialects were spoken: Northern (developed from Northumbrian), West and East Midlands (diverging from Mercian), South Western (from West Saxon) and South Eastern (from Kentish). Each developed in characteristic ways but in general the influence of French after the Norman conquest brought new vocabulary and sound patterns (see also Great Vowel Shift). Modern English covers the period from 1500 and was much influenced by the speech of London. English slowly became a relatively uninflected language with great flexibility in the way words may function. Its vocabulary is about half Germanic and half Romance with many other borrowings.

English art and architecture The styles of art and architecture found in England. Before the Norman conquest the art of the British Isles was identified with *Celtic art, Roman art and architecture, and Anglo-Saxon art. Illuminated manuscripts constituted the outstanding contribution of Anglo-Saxon artists, and manuscripts of a high quality continued to be produced in the later middle ages. The Normans introduced *romanesque art and architecture (of which Durham Cathedral and many smaller churches are examples). In the 12th century, *gothic architecture was introduced, which developed into several distinct styles and became the indigenous church architecture of the middle ages.

The works of the German painter *Holbein were outstanding in 16th-century England but had little influence on native painting, which, however, flourished in the school of miniaturists led by *Hilliard. In the early 17th century the architect Inigo *Jones introduced *Palladianism to England and, among painters, the Flemings *Rubens and *Van Dyck towered above their English contemporaries. Architecture in the late 17th century was dominated by *Wren, *Vanbrugh, and *Hawksmoor, exponents of the *baroque. The 18th and early 19th centuries saw the great era of town architecture, outstandingly expressed in the work of the *Adam brothers and John *Nash; this was followed by the *gothic revival. Notable painters of the 18th century were *Hogarth, *Reynolds, and *Gainsborough. Romanticism found expression in the work of *Turner and *Constable and the 19th century also witnessed the formation of the *Pre-Raphaelite Brotherhood, which, with the work of William *Morris, influenced *Art Nouveau in England. The philosophy of "art for art's sake" was articulated by *Sickert, whose influence led to the formation in 1911 of the *Camden Town Group. The 20th century has produced outstanding sculptors, including *Epstein, *Hepworth, and Henry *Moore, the painters Augustus *John, Graham *Sutherland, Stanley *Spencer, L. S. *Lowry, and Francis *Bacon, and the architects *Spence and *Lasdun.

English Channel (French name: La Manche) An arm of the Atlantic Ocean in NW Europe, between England and France. It is one of the busiest shipping lanes in the world. Many attempts at swimming the Channel (usually across the Strait of *Dover) have been made; the first successful one was by Capt Webb (1875). See also Channel Tunnel.

English literature The earliest works of the Old English period (407–1066 AD) are heroic poems, notably the epic Beowulf, which belong to a Germanic oral tradition of alliterative unrhymed verse and were not put into written form until the 7th century. There are also a number of remarkable shorter poems, such as the elegies The Wanderer and The Seafarer, and many poems on Christian subjects. Major Old English religious writers, such as Bede and Alcuin, wrote in Latin; English prose started with the translations from Latin made by King Alfred and developed in the Anglo-Saxon Chronicle, the compilation of which he initiated.

Norman-French displaced Old English as the dominant written language after the Conquest, but the native language, enriched by French, was firmly re-established in the 14th century in the Middle English poetry of Chaucer, whose works were indebted to Italian Renaissance authors, especially Dante, Petrarch, and Boccaccio. The native alliterative tradition continued in such poems as Piers Plowman, Pearl, and Gawain and the Green Knight. Printing was introduced in 1476 by Caxton, who published the culminating work of the *Arthurian legend, Malory's Morte d'Arthur (1485).

Although Chaucer had introduced Renaissance influences, it was not until the 16th century that the full effects of humanism were felt, especially under Elizabeth I and James I, whose reigns mark the golden age of poetry and drama. The sonnet was introduced by Wyatt and Surrey and polished by Sidney and others. Spenser produced the Elizabethan allegorical epic, The Faerie Queene (1590). The blank-verse plays of Kyd and Marlowe prepared the way for the dramas of Shakespeare (the outstanding figure in this period and in the whole of English literature), Jonson, and their 17th-century successors. Donne and the Metaphysical school are the most important poets of the early 17th century, while Milton dominates the latter part. Among the most influential prose works were the Authorized Version of the Bible and Bunyan's *The Pilgrim's Progress* (1678).

During the Restoration (from 1660), Dryden developed the heroic couplet in his satires and made an important contribution to modern English prose in his criticism. Drama, curbed during the Interregnum, was revived in the comedies of Congreve and Wycherley. The classical ideals of the Augustan Age (c. 1690-1740) were embodied in the satirical verse of Pope and the essays of Addison and Steele and were maintained by later writers, such as Johnson, Goldsmith, and Sheridan. Swift was the outstanding prose satirist of the period.

Various economic and social factors during the early 18th century contributed to the emergence of the novel, pioneered by Richardson, Fielding, Defoe, Smollett, Sterne, and various authors of the "gothic" novel of horror. It reached its full development in the works of Jane Austen, Walter Scott, Thackeray, the Brontës, Dickens, George Eliot, Trollope, Meredith, Hardy, Conrad, Bennett, and the American Henry James.

In the early 19th century the classicism of the previous period was challenged by the Romantic movement. Its precursor was Blake and its leading figures were Wordsworth, Coleridge, Keats, Shelley, and Byron. Their chief successors in the Victorian era were Tennyson, Browning, Matthew Arnold, and Swinburne. Macaulay, John Stuart Mill, Carlyle, Ruskin, and Pater were among the influential prose writers. At the turn of the century the comedies of Wilde and Shaw enlivened the English theatre; prior to World War I Kipling, Hardy, Yeats, Belloc, Chesterton, Wells, Housman, and de la Mare produced a distinguished body of verse as well as fiction and criticism. The poets associated with the war period were Brooke, Owen, Sassoon, and Graves. Postwar poetry was dominated by Eliot, Auden, MacNeice, Day Lewis, Spender, and the later work of Yeats. Among the leading novelists and prose writers were Forster, Joyce, D. H. Lawrence, Woolf, Aldous Huxley, Orwell, Isherwood, Greene, and Evelyn Waugh. Between World War II and the present appeared the poems of Dylan Thomas, Philip Larkin, Ted Hughes, and Thom Gunn; the plays of Osborne, Wesker, Pinter, Beckett, Joe Orton, and Tom Stoppard; and the novels of Angus Wilson, Kingsley Amis, Muriel Spark, Iris Murdoch, Anthony Powell, and Anthony Burgess.

English National Opera (ENO) The name adopted by the Sadler's Wells Opera Company in 1974, five years after the company moved from the *Sadler's Wells Theatre to the London Coliseum. The company continues to present most of its operas in English. Its musical directors have included Sir Charles *Mackerras (1970–78), Sir Charles *Groves (1978–79), and Mark Elder (1947–   ; director 1979–   ). The present managing director is Peter Jonas.

English-Speaking Union An organization, based in London, that promotes friendship and understanding between English-speaking countries. It was founded by Sir Evelyn Wrench (1882-1966) in 1918 and now has 160 branches in the UK, North America, Australasia, India, and the Caribbean.

engraving A method of producing a reproductive plate by chiselling, carving, or biting the design onto a metal or wood plate. Intaglio engraving denotes such methods as *etching, *mezzotint, and soft- or hard-ground engraving, in which the printed impression pulls ink from inside the carved grooves. By contrast, relief engraving denotes methods, such as *woodcut, in which the carved-away areas are not inked. Intaglio engraving allows for extreme delicacy and detail; relief engraving is often exploited for illustrations, where force and clarity are needed.

Enlightenment (*or* Age of Reason) An 18th-century philosophical movement that sought to replace orthodox authoritarian beliefs with rational scientific inquiry. During the 17th century, as scientific knowledge increased, such scholars as Newton, Locke, Pascal, and Descartes questioned accepted beliefs, and criticism of established society and assumptions spread throughout Europe. In France the *Philosophes (e.g. Voltaire) attacked established religion (*see* deism) and the Enlightenment beliefs in individual liberty and equality were embodied in the work of Rousseau and other *Encyclopedists. The movement came to an end with the French Revolution.

Enlightened despots were those European monarchs (e.g. *Joseph II, Frederick the Great of Prussia, and Catherine the Great of Russia) who introduced reforms, based on the ideas of the Enlightenment, by authoritarian means.

Enlil The Sumerian god of the sky and storms. He was the patron deity of *Nippur and with *Anu and *Ea formed the supreme trinity in the Sumerian pantheon.

Ennis (Irish name: Inis) 52 50N 8 59W A market town in the W Republic of Ireland, the county town of Co Clare. It has a cathedral and a ruined 13th-century Franciscan friary. Population (1981): 6223.

Enniskillen (*or* Inniskilling) 54 21N 7 48W A town in Northern Ireland, in Fermanagh between Upper and Lower Lough Erne. A strongly Protestant town, it resisted James II in 1689 and has two regiments named after it. In 1987, IRA bombing at a Remembrance Day parade, resulting in 11 dead and over 60 injured, provoked universal condemnation of the IRA by Catholics and Protestants alike. Population (1981): 10 429.

Ennius, Quintus (238–169 BC) Roman poet. After service in the second Punic War, he was brought to Rome by the elder Cato in 204 and became a Roman citizen in 184. His works include tragic dramas adapted from the Greek, philosophical poems, epigrams, and the *Annals*, a national epic in 18 books narrating the history of Rome from Aeneas to his own time. Only fragments of his works survive.

Enoch An Old Testament patriarch. **The Books of Enoch** are two biblical books ascribed to him; they were in fact written in the 2nd century BC and 1st century AD respectively. The first, a composite work of Jewish origin, is a series of apocalyptic visions. The second is of Hellenistic origin and records revelations supposedly given to Enoch, his journey to heaven, and advice to his children.

enosis. *See* EOKA.

Enragés (French: Madmen) Members of an extremist French Revolutionary group (1793). Led by Jacques Roux (d. 1794), they demanded direct government action to alleviate food shortages and to help the poor. Actively encouraging food riots, their leaders were arrested by the Committee of *Public Safety and their extremist role was adopted by the Hébertists (*see* Hébert).

Enschede 52 13N 06 55E A town in the E Netherlands, in Overijssel province. It is an important centre of the Dutch cotton industry. Population (1981 est): 144 346.

Ensor, James Sydney, Baron (1860–1949) Belgian painter; his father was English but he was born and spent most of his life in Ostend. He was initially condemned for what was thought his crude technique, but the originality of his grotesque imagery of masks and skeletons, as in the symbolic representation of modern social evils in *Entry of Christ into Brussels* (1888), were admired in the 1920s.

Entebbe 0 05N 39 29E A town in Uganda, in Buganda on the NW shore of Lake Victoria. It was the administrative centre of Uganda until 1958 but is now largely residential. It contains Uganda's international airport, where, in 1976, Israeli hostages taken from a hijacked French plane by Palestinian guerrillas were rescued by Israeli troops. Population (1977): 22 000.

entellus. *See* langur.

Entente Cordiale (1904) An agreement between France and Britain. During the 19th century, colonial expansion, especially in Africa, caused tension between France, Britain, and Germany. France feared a German war and Britain and France, partly through Edward VII's efforts to reconcile their traditional enmity, signed the Entente Cordiale. This was not an alliance but a mutual recognition of each other's colonial interests, especially France's in Morocco and Britain's in Egypt. The agreement brought greater diplomatic cooperation against German pressure.

enthalpy (H) A thermodynamic property of a system equal to its internal energy plus the product of its pressure and volume. The change in enthalpy (ΔH) when a chemical reaction takes place is equal to the heat given out or absorbed. By convention ΔH is negative if heat is evolved by he reaction.

entomology The study of insects. Entomology probably has its origins in the observations of *Aristotle. Modern entomology dates from the 17th century, when the introduction of microscopy enabled fine details of insect anatomy to be described; for instance, in the work of the Dutch naturalist Jan *Swammerdam. Today attention is focused especially on insect pests, since knowledge of their physiology and ecology is of prime importance in their control or eradication.

entrepreneur An individual in a capitalist economy who is prepared to commit capital and to initiate a commercial venture. Entrepreneurship is often counted as a fourth factor of production (the others being land, labour, and capital), providing the spark that sets the others off. With the development of large corporations and a large public sector in most economies, the role of the individual entrepreneur has somewhat diminished.

entropy A measure of the disorder of a system, used in *thermodynamics. Thus a solid has less entropy than a liquid since the constituent particles in a solid are in a more ordered state. Originally defined in connection with the second law of thermodynamics, the change in entropy of a reversible system is equal to the energy absorbed by the system divided by the thermodynamic temperature at which the change takes place. The entropy of a closed system never decreases during a thermodynamic process: if it increases the process is irreversible; if it remains unchanged it is reversible. *See also* heat death of the universe.

Enugu 6 20N 7 29E A city in S Nigeria. It developed following the discovery of nearby coal in 1909 and is an important mining, manufacturing, and trade centre. It contains part of the University of Nigeria (1962). Population (1983 est): 228 400.

Enver Pasha (1881-1922) Turkish soldier and politician, who was a leader of the *Young Turk revolution of 1908. During World War I he was one of the three real rulers of the Ottoman Empire. His aim was to unite the Turks of central Asia with those of Turkey in one state. He was killed in a rising in central Asia against the Bolsheviks.

enzymes An important group of proteins that act as biological catalysts, i.e. they speed up (or slow down) the rate of chemical reactions in living organisms. Enzymes are manufactured by cells according to the *genetic code carried by the chromosomes; because each enzyme catalyses a specific reaction, it is the enzymes that determine the function of the cell. The structure of enzymes and the nature of their active sites (where they bind to reacting molecules) can be determined by such techniques as X-ray diffraction. Control of *metabolism is largely exerted through regulation of enzyme production and activity, which are inhibited by such poisons as cyanide. Many enzymes require associated nonprotein *coenzymes to function properly.

Eocene epoch. *See* Tertiary period.

eohippus An extinct ancestor of the *horse, also called *Hyracotherium* or dawn horse, that lived in the Eocene epoch (about 55 million to 40 million years ago). About 28 cm tall, it was a browsing forest dweller with a short neck and had

four toes on the forefoot and three on the hindfoot. *See also* Hipparion.

EOKA (Ethniki Organosis Kipriakou Agonos) The National Organization of Cypriot Struggle formed in about 1955 by Georgios Grivas with the support of Archbishop Makarios. Its aim was to drive the British occupying forces from Cyprus, an end that it pursued by guerrilla action, and to achieve *enosis* ("union") with Greece. It was disbanded in 1959, when Cyprus became independent, but was revived by Grivas in 1971.

Eos. *See* Aurora.

Epaminondas (c. 418-362 BC) Theban general and military strategist, who defeated Sparta at *Leuctra in 371, thereby ending the military supremacy of Sparta in Greece. He was the first to use cavalry to support infantry in a coordinated attack and his military innovations influenced both Philip II and Alexander the Great of Macedon. He died in the battle of Mantinea, in which the Spartans were defeated.

Épernay 49 02N 3 58E A town in NE France, in the Marne department on the River Marne. A centre for the wine industry of Champagne, it has famous underground wine cellars. Population (1982): 28 876.

ephedrine A drug with effects resembling those of *adrenaline. It stimulates the heart, dilates the bronchi (air passages to the lungs), and has marked effects on the nervous system. Ephedrine is used mainly to treat asthma. Side effects include trembling and feelings of anxiety.

ephemeral A plant that completes its life cycle—from germination to seed production—in under a year, enabling more than one generation to be produced within a single year. Many common weeds, such as groundsel and chickweed, are ephemerals.

ephemeris (Greek: diary) A reference manual, usually published annually, that is used in astronomical observation and navigation. It lists the predicted positions of the sun, moon, and planets in the forthcoming year and also gives times of eclipses, stellar positions, and other similar information.

Ephesians, Epistle of Paul to the A New Testament book that originated as a circular letter from the Apostle Paul to churches in Asia Minor. Written about 60 AD, it deals with a number of religious and moral points and stresses the equality of Jewish and Gentile Christians.

Ephesus An ancient Greek city and trading centre on the Ionian coast of *Asia Minor. *Croesus of *Lydia captured it in 550 BC. It maintained its prosperity under the Persians and Alexander the Great. In Roman times Ephesus was rivalled only by *Alexandria as a commercial centre. It was sacked by the *Goths in 262 AD. *See also* Artemis, Temple of.

Ephraim, tribe of One of the 12 *tribes of Israel. It claimed descent from Ephraim, the son of Joseph and grandson of Jacob and Rachel. It occupied mountainous territory NW of the Dead Sea.

epic A long narrative poem concerning a heroic theme and written in an appropriately dignified style. The *Iliad* and the *Odyssey* of Homer (8th century BC) are the earliest epics in western literature and are the models of Virgil's *Aeneid* (c. 29-19 BC), in which the hero Aeneas is seen as representing the national spirit of Rome. The *Aeneid* inspired later national epics, such as Camões' *Os Lusiadas* (1572) and Ronsard's *Franciade* (1572). In English literature, examples include the Old English *Beowulf* (8th century AD), Spenser's *Faerie Queene* (1589-96), a mixture of epic and romance, and Milton's *Paradise Lost* (1667).

epicentre. *See* earthquake.

Epictetus (c. 60-110 AD) Stoic philosopher. A freed slave, Epictetus was banished, with other philosophers, from Rome in 89 AD and settled in Epirus. He taught that loving one's enemies, repudiating pleasure, and understanding that all men are brothers are ways to serenity. Epictetus' teachings were preserved by his pupil *Arrian. *See also* Stoicism.

Epicureanism A school of philosophy founded by *Epicurus around 300 BC in Athens. He taught that the highest good was pleasure and the avoidance of pain, based on tranquillity of mind and conscience. Many seeking a licence for the pursuit of pleasure have styled themselves Epicureans, giving the term its common sense of "unashamed sensualist." True Epicureans, however, seek serenity through detachment from worldly affairs.

Epicurus (341–270 BC) Greek philosopher and founder of the school of *Epicureanism. In 306 BC he began teaching in a garden in Athens. Virtuous and temperate, he was a good friend and citizen but avoided politics, following his maxim "Live unseen and unknown." His surviving works are few and fragmentary but his philosophy, especially his *atomism, was expounded by *Lucretius.

Epidauros A city state of ancient Greece, situated across the Saronic Gulf from *Athens. Its sanctuary of *Asclepius was famous in antiquity. Patients asleep in the temple were visited by the god in their dreams and treated by his priests next morning; grateful inscriptions record numerous cures. The 4th-century BC theatre (part of the temple complex) is sufficiently preserved to be still used for plays.

epidemiology The science that investigates the incidence and causative factors of diseases that are associated with a particular environment or way of life. Epidemiologists have enlarged their studies from the classical epidemics of communicable diseases, such as smallpox and cholera, to include noncommunicable diseases. Thus they have demonstrated the connection between cigarette smoking and lung cancer, diet and coronary heart disease, etc.

epidermis The outermost layer of cells in animals and plants. In lower animals (invertebrates) it often secretes a protective *cuticle. In higher animals (including mammals) it forms the outer layer of the skin. In plants the epidermis usually consists of a single layer of cells, but aerial organs have extra protection in the form of a noncellular waxy cuticle. Both layers prevent dehydration of internal tissues, lessen damage by bacteria and fungi, and reduce attack by such pests as aphids.

epididymis. *See* testis.

epidural. *See* anaesthesia.

epiglottis A leaf-shaped flap of cartilage at the root of the tongue that prevents food and fluid from entering the windpipe during swallowing. As it is swallowed, the food presses the epiglottis down against the opening of the larynx (at the top of the windpipe). This, combined with the reflex upward movement of the larynx that occurs during swallowing, effectively seals off the entrance to the windpipe.

epilepsy A disease characterized by fits or sudden loss of consciousness. Epilepsy is common—Dostoievski, Van Gogh, Julius Caesar, and Byron all suffered from it. There are several different forms. In grand mal epilepsy the patient suddenly becomes stiff, loses consciousness, and has convulsions. The fit last only a few minutes but afterwards he is sleepy and confused. Petit mal is a mild form seen only in children, who suddenly lose consciousness but usually do not fall down. Petit mal attacks last only a few seconds. Temporal lobe epilepsy is characterized by peculiar forms of behaviour and strange sensations. All forms are treated with anticonvulsant drugs.

Épinal 48 10N 6 28E A town in E France, the capital of the Vosges department on the River Moselle. It is the centre for a region manufacturing cotton goods and artificial fibres. Population (1982): 40 954.

epinephrine. *See* adrenaline.

Epiphany (*or* Twelfth Day) A Christian feast celebrated on 6 Jan. In Eastern Orthodox Churches it commemorates the baptism of Jesus. Introduced to the West in the 4th century, it developed as a celebration of the coming of the *Magi to Bethlehem, representing the manifestation (Greek: *epiphaneia*) of Christ to the Gentiles. **Twelfth Night** is the night preceding Epiphany and traditionally devoted to festivities and entertainments. In several countries gifts are exchanged on Epiphany rather than at Christmas.

epiphyte A plant that grows on another plant for support. Epiphytes are not parasites: some obtain nourishment from decaying plant remains and many solve the problem of obtaining water by developing such structures as aerial roots. Some orchids are epiphytic.

Epirus (*or* Ípiros) A coastal region of NW Greece and S Albania, bordering on the Ionian Sea. Its tribes were united in the 4th century BC in a kingdom that reached its peak under *Pyrrhus in the early 3rd century BC. Sacked by the Romans in 167, it became part of the province of Macedonia in 148 BC. In the 13th century AD it briefly formed an independent kingdom before falling to the Serbs and Albanians and then (1430) to the Ottoman Turks. It was divided between Greece and Albania in 1913.

episcopacy In Christian Churches, government by bishops. The biblical basis of episcopacy is equivocal, and many Protestant Churches, for example the Congregational and Presbyterian, have adopted different methods. In the Roman Catholic and Orthodox Churches the episcopal hierarchy is seen as a continuation of the original group of apostles chosen by Christ (*see* Apostolic Succession). Among the Reformed Churches episcopal government is retained in whole or in part by Anglicans, Methodists, and Lutherans.

epistemology The philosophical discipline that considers the nature, basis, and limits of knowledge. Ancient Greek philosophers examined the relations between knowledge, truth, and belief, and the question of whether knowledge exists independently of a knower. *Locke and *Kant, however, first treated epistemology as fundamental to all philosophical and scientific enquiry. It is one of the three main branches of modern *philosophy.

Epistles The 21 books of the *New Testament that were written as letters. These are arranged in two groups, those by Paul (13) and those by others (7), divided by the Epistle to the Hebrews, of which the author is unknown. Of Paul's letters nine are to specific churches and four to individuals. The remainder are attributed to James, Peter (2), John (3), and Jude. In the liturgy of many Christian Churches, the Epistle is the name of the first of two passages of Scripture recited or sung at the celebration of the Eucharist, the second being the Gospel. It is usually a passage from the New Testament Epistles but may be a passage from the Old Testament, Acts, or Revelation.

epithelium A tissue that forms the linings of the mouth, nose, pharynx, intestines, respiratory tract, and the skin. There are different types of epithelia specialized for different functions. For example, the cells of the intestinal epithelium are glandular, secreting digestive enzymes, while the skin epithelium produces a tough protective layer of keratin.

epoch. *See* geological time scale.

epoxy resin A type of synthetic *resin made by polymerizing groups containing a three-membered ring that includes the –O–atom (epoxy group). They are themselves viscous liquids but set to hard clear solids on the addition of such curing agents as amines. Epoxy resins are extensively used as adhesives, the resin and the curing agent being mixed immediately before use.

Epping 51 40N 0 06E A market and residential town in SE England, in Essex on the edge of Epping Forest (one of the country's largest and most popular recreational grounds, formerly part of the ancient forest of Waltham, which once covered the whole of Essex). Population (1981): 11 413.

Epsom 51 20N 0 16W A town in SE England, in Surrey, noted for horse racing on Epsom Downs (the Derby and

Oaks are famous races held here). Population (1985 est): 69 200, with Ewell.

Epstein, Sir Jacob (1880–1959) British sculptor of US birth. Working in London after 1905, he achieved notoriety with his nude figures for the British Medical Association (1907–08; later destroyed) and his memorial tomb to Oscar Wilde (1912) for a Parisian cemetery. After 1912 he briefly experimented with avantgarde sculpture, influenced by primitive art, and continued to provoke public criticism with such sculptures as *Rima*, a memorial to the author William Hudson (1925; Hyde Park), and *Genesis* (1931). However, his bronze portrait busts of such celebrities as Conrad (1924), Einstein (1933), T. S. Eliot, and Vaughan Williams (1950) were more favourably received. His last works included *Christ in Majesty* (1957) for Llandaff Cathedral and *St Michael and the Devil* (1958) for Coventry Cathedral.

equation A mathematical statement in which two expressions, usually containing at least one variable or unknown quantity, are equated. For example, the simple algebraic expression $2x + 4 = 8$ is an equation that can be simplified, or solved, to give a value of 2 for the unknown quantity x: this is known as the root of the equation. Equations are also used to show the general interdependence of several quantities, without necessarily finding their specific values. The degree of an equation is equal to the highest value of the exponent of the variable. A **linear equation** is of the first degree and has the form $y = mx + c$. A *graph of such an equation is a straight line, which (in the Cartesian *coordinate system) has a *gradient equal to m and cuts the y-axis at c. A *quadratic equation is of the second degree, i.e. contains terms in x^2.

Two or more equations in which all the variables must obey all the equations are called **simultaneous equations**. For a complete solution of simultaneous equations there must be as many equations as there are variables.

equation of time. *See* sundial.

equator The great circle around the earth at latitude 0°, lying midway between the poles in a plane at right angles to the earth's axis. It is 40 076 km (24 902 mi) long and divides the N from the S hemisphere.

Equatorial Guinea, Republic of A small country in W central Africa, on the Gulf of Guinea. It consists of two main parts: mainland Río Muni and the island of Bioko (formerly Fernando Po), as well as the island of Pagalu (formerly Annobón) to the SW and several smaller islands. Río Muni is mainly tropical forest, with a coastal plain rising gradually to over 1000 m (3000 ft) in the interior; Bioko is dominated by three extinct volcanoes, the highest of which reaches 3007 m (9865 ft). The inhabitants are mainly *Fang, Fernandinos, and the indigenous Bubi (descendants of slaves from West Africa), who inhabit Bioko. *Economy*: chiefly agricultural, the main crops being cocoa on Bioko, and coffee in Río Muni, where timber is also produced. There is little industry, apart from fish processing on Bioko; the main exports are coffee and cocoa. *History*: formerly a Spanish colony, the area became two Spanish provinces in 1959. The country attained some internal self-government in 1964 and was one of the last of the African colonial territories to become independent (in 1968). In 1975 Nigerian immigrant workers were expelled after 50 years in the country, and this has had an adverse effect on the economy. In 1979 the life president Francisco Macías Nguema (1924–79) was overthrown and executed in a coup led by Lt Col Teodoro Obiang Nguema Mbasogo. Official language: Spanish. Official currency: ekuele of 100 céntimos. Area: 28 051 sq km (10 831 sq mi). Population (1984 est): 321 000. Capital and main port: Malabo (formerly Santa Isabel).

equestrianism The art of horsemanship. As a sport, governed by the Fédération équestre internationale (founded 1921), it involves *showjumping, *dressage, and *horse trials.

equinox Either of the two points at which the *ecliptic intersects the celestial equator (*see* celestial sphere). The ecliptic represents the apparent annual path of the sun around the celestial sphere. The sun crosses the celestial equator from S to N at the **vernal** (*or* spring) **equinox**, usually on 21 March. It crosses from N to S at the **autumnal equinox**, usually on 23 Sept. At the equinoxes the centre of the sun is above and below the horizon for equal lengths of time, and night and day are then of almost equal duration.

Equisetum. *See* horsetail.

equity In law, the body of rules developed by the Court of *Chancery to achieve a fair result in cases in which the application of *common law would fail to do so. The historical distinction between the common law and equity is due to the failure of the common law to provide a remedy in certain cases, bringing about the custom of applying for redress to the king, who referred the question to the Lord Chancellor's court, the Court of Chancery. Here the rules of equity developed separately from but by the same method (judicial precedent) as the common law. The two systems were amalgamated in 1875 with the establishment of the High Court of Justice. Now all courts administer both law and equity, the rules of equity prevailing if in conflict with the common law. *See also* courts of law.

equivalence The relationship between two mathematical or logical statements linked so that one is true if and only if the other is true. For example "a is greater than b" is equivalent to "b is less than a."

era. *See* geological time scale.

Erasistratus of Ceos (3rd century BC) Greek physician, who discovered the difference between sensory and motor nerves and described the heart as part of a system carrying both air and blood to various parts of the body.

Erasmus, Desiderius (1466–1536) Christian humanist and writer, born at Rotterdam. He was perhaps the most influential of Renaissance thinkers and studied and taught all over Europe. His enthusiasm for learning was matched by his zeal for writing, and he produced many original works and compilations, including *Encomium Moriae* (*Praise of Folly*; 1509), written to amuse his host in England, Thomas *More. His translation of the Greek New Testament, the first ever, conclusively exposed the Vulgate as a second-hand document. He opposed dogmatism and priestly power, yet he never rejected Roman Catholic theology and steadfastly remained impartial throughout the Lutheran conflict with the papacy.

Erastianism The subjection of ecclesiastical affairs to secular authority. It is named after Thomas Erastus (1524–83), a Swiss theologian who opposed the strict views of *Calvinists. He argued that the civil authority has complete power in affairs both of church and state. Richard Hooker defended the argument in England in his *Ecclesiastical Polity* (1594). The *Church of England's subjection to the Crown is sometimes described as Erastian.

Eratosthenes of Cyrene (c. 276–c. 194 BC) Greek astronomer; a close friend of *Archimedes. His greatest achievement was his calculation of the earth's circumference. His result, obtained by measuring the sun's position at the summer solstice at two different places, was accurate to within a thousand kilometres.

Erbil. *See* Irbil.

erbium (Er) A lanthanide element, which like *yttrium, *ytterbium, and *terbium is named after Ytterby, a village in Sweden near which lanthanide-rich ores are found. It forms an oxide (Er_2O_3) and halides (e.g. $ErCl_3$). It is added to phosphors, glasses, and alloys. At no 68; at wt 167.26; mp 1529°C; bp 2510°C.

Ercilla, Alonso de (1533–94) Spanish poet. A courtier of *Philip II, he fought the Araucanian Indians in Chile. His epic *La Araucana* (Part I, 1569; Part 2, 1578; Part 3, 1589–

90) is noted for its realistic descriptive passages and its sympathetic treatment of the Indians.

Erebus, Mount 77 40S 167 20E An active volcano on Ross Island, in the Antarctic. Discovered in 1841, it was climbed in 1908. Height: 3794 m (12 520 ft).

Eretria An ancient Greek city in *Euboea. An early leader in commerce and colonization, Eretria was defeated by *Chalcis about 700 BC, after which it declined in importance. The Persians sacked Eretria in 490 BC. It was rebuilt and later joined the *Delian League, but it never regained its former significance.

Erevan. *See* Yerevan.

Erfurt 50 59N 11 00E A city in SW East Germany, on the River Gera. One of the oldest German cities, it became a member of the Hanseatic League in the 15th century and was of great commercial importance in the 16th century. Notable buildings include the cathedral (1154–1476) and the 13th-century Church of St Severus. Its university, established in 1392, was closed in 1816. Martin Luther studied there (1501–05). Industries include the manufacture of machinery, electrical equipment, textiles, and footwear. Population (1982): 214 231.

erg The unit of energy in the *c.g.s. system equal to the work done when a force of one dyne acts through a distance of one centimetre. 1 erg = 10^{-7} joule.

ergonomics The study of the psychological and physical factors that can be used to improve the design of both machines and systems for human use. In the USA the term human-factors engineering is widely used and in other parts of the world ergonomics is known as psychological engineering. The study finds application in many fields, including astronautics, the design of aircraft and cars, and a wide variety of industrial processes. Although it is a young science, having largely grown up since World War II, most university engineering courses now include it.

ergosterol. *See* vitamin D.

ergot A disease caused by the fungus *Claviceps purpurea*, which affects cereals and grasses, especially rye. In affected plants a hard black fungal body develops in place of the grain. Consumption of bread made with diseased grain produces the symptoms of **ergotism**—gangrene of the fingers and toes or convulsions. The gangrenous form of ergotism is accompanied by inflammation and pain in the affected part and in the middle ages it was called St Anthony's fire, since a pilgrimage to St Anthony's tomb was believed to result in a cure. Drugs obtained from ergot include ergometrine, used to induce childbirth, and ergotamine, for relieving migraine.

Erhard, Ludwig (1897–1977) German statesman and economist; Christian Democratic chancellor (1963–66). As minister for economic affairs (1949–63), he was largely responsible for the recovery of German industry after World War II. He succeeded Adenauer as chancellor and subsequently became honorary chairman of the Christian Democratic Party.

Erica. *See* heath.

Ericsson, John (1803–89) US naval engineer, born in Sweden, who in 1836 invented the screw propeller, which replaced paddle wheels in ships. Ericsson also designed the *ironclad *Monitor*, launched in 1862, which was the first warship to have an armoured revolving turret.

Eric the Red (late 10th century) Norwegian explorer. Exiled as a child with his father he was brought up in Iceland. In 982 he set out from Iceland on an exploration westwards and reached Greenland, where he established the first European colony (c. 986). He was the father of *Leif Eriksson.

Eridanus A large constellation in the S sky, named after a river in ancient mythology. The only bright star is *Achernar.

Eridu A city of ancient *Sumer, SW of *Ur (S Iraq),

continuously occupied from around 5000 to 600 BC. Excavations (1946–49) revealed a *ziggurat, probably devoted to the worship of Eridu's patron deity *Ea.

Erie 42 07N 80 05W A city in the USA, in Pennsylvania on Lake Erie. Founded in 1753, it is a Great Lakes port and ships coal, timber, iron, and oil. It is also a major industrial business centre. Population (1980): 119 123.

Erie, Lake The fourth largest of the Great Lakes in North America, between Canada and the USA. Linked with Lake Ontario via the Welland Ship Canal, it forms part of the St Lawrence Seaway system. Its shallow depth causes rapid freezing and it is closed to navigation during winter. Area: 25 718 sq km (9930 sq mi).

Erigena, John Scotus (c. 800–c. 877 AD) Medieval philosopher, probably born in Ireland. He is said to have travelled widely and after about 846 lived under the protection of Charles the Bald in France, where he was appointed head of the court school at Paris. He defied ecclesiastical orthodoxy in his writings on predestination and cosmology, which show leanings towards *Neoplatonism, *Pelagianism, and *pantheism.

Erik XIV (1533–77) King of Sweden (1560–68), whose ambitions in the Baltic led to an inconclusive war with Denmark (1563–70). He unsuccessfully sought marriage with Elizabeth I of England. After becoming insane, he was deposed and imprisoned.

Erinyes (*or* Furies) In Greek legend, spirits of vengeance who lived in the underworld and ruthlessly pursued all evildoers. They were three in number and were named (in later writers) Allecto, Tisiphone, and Megaera. In Roman legend they were known as the Furies (Latin *Furiae* or *Dirae*). *See also* Eumenides.

Eris A Greek goddess personifying strife. She was the sister of *Ares. She threw a golden apple inscribed "To the Fairest" among the gods at the wedding feast of Peleus and Thetis. Aphrodite, Hera, and Athena each claimed the apple. The decision was referred to *Paris, who chose Aphrodite because she offered him in return the most beautiful woman as his wife. This myth, known as the Judgment of Paris, explains the origin of the *Trojan War.

Eritrea A province in Ethiopia, bordering on the Red Sea. It consists of a narrow coastal plain rising inland to the Ethiopian plateau. Locusts and water shortage limit agricultural production, which has also been adversely affected by the recent political upheavals. *History*: made an Italian colony in 1890, it became the base for the Italian invasions of Ethiopia. The area came under British administration in 1941 and was federated as an autonomous unit of Ethiopia in 1952. In 1962 it became an integral part of the Ethiopian empire giving rise to political discontent. During the 1970s this developed into a bloody civil war; many major towns, as well as most of the countryside, fell into the hands of the secessionists but the Ethiopian government, anxious to retain its only two ports (Assab and Massawa), was unwilling to yield to demands for complete independence. In May, 1978, a major government offensive backed by Soviet and Cuban aid was carried out; rebel forces, however, retained control of much of Eritrea throughout the 1980s despite further attacks. Area: 117 600 sq km (45 405 sq mi).

Erlangen 49 36N 11 02E A city in SE West Germany, in Bavaria on the River Regnitz. The university, shared with Nuremburg, was moved here from Bayreuth in 1743. Its manufactures include electrical equipment and textiles. Population (1983 est): 102 400.

Erlanger, Joseph (1874–1965) US physiologist, who, with Herbert *Gasser, developed techniques for recording the electrical impulses in nerve fibres using a cathode-ray oscilloscope. They demonstrated that the conduction rate of impulses depends on the thickness of the fibre and its function and that different fibres transmit different types of impulses, represented by different waveforms. Erlanger and Gasser shared the 1944 Nobel Prize for this work.

ermine A *stoat in its white winter coat. At the onset of winter in northern latitudes, the brown coat is moulted, leaving a pure white coat except for the tip of the tail: excellent camouflage on snow-covered ground.

Ermine Street A Roman road built (43–50 AD) along the route now followed by the A1 between London and the River Humber, as part of the military communications system of Roman Britain.

ERNIE. *See* premium bond.

Ernst, Max (1891–1976) German artist, born in Brühl. At first a philosophy and psychiatric student at Bonn University, he achieved artistic prominence in 1919 as a founder of the Cologne *dada movement. He excelled in collage, particularly of cut-out illustrations, and became a leading practitioner of *surrealism in Paris. He invented the technique of frottage, whereby pencil rubbings of leaves, wood graining, cloth, etc., were used to suggest images of the unconscious mind. In 1941 he moved to the USA.

Eros (astronomy) A small (about 20 km diameter) *minor planet that moves in a highly elliptical orbit bringing it within 170 million km of the sun, and in 1975 passed within 23 million km of earth.

Eros (mythology) The Greek god of love, the son of Aphrodite by Zeus, Hermes, or Ares. He was usually portrayed as a winged youth armed with bow and arrows. He was identified with the Roman Cupid.

Erse. *See* Gaelic.

Erskine, Thomas Erskine, 1st Baron (1750–1823) British jurist. An MP (1783–84, 1790–1806) and briefly Lord Chancellor (1806–07), Erskine is best known for his defence of such English radicals as Tom *Paine, who were charged with sedition and libel during the French Revolution. He also achieved the acquittal of the leader of the *Gordon Riots, Lord George Gordon, in 1781. Another of his famous cases was that of Hadfield (1800), who attempted to kill George III; Erskine defended him on the grounds of insanity.

Erté (Romain de Tirtoff; 1892–) French fashion illustrator and designer, born in Russia. He worked for the US magazine *Harper's Bazaar* (1916–37) and designed extravagant costumes and tableaux for the Folies-Bergère (1919–30) and other theatres. He later produced lithographs and sculpture. Erté comes from the initials of his real name.

erysipelas A skin infection caused by *Streptococcus* bacteria. It starts suddenly and usually on the face, which is red and hot, and the patient has a high fever. Penicillin quickly cures the infection.

erythrocyte (*or* red blood cell) A disc-shaped □blood cell, about 0.007 mm in diameter, that lacks a nucleus and contains *haemoglobin–a complex iron-bearing pigment. Haemoglobin combines reversibly with oxygen and is the means by which blood transports oxygen from the lungs to the tissues. There are normally about 4.5 million erythrocytes per cubic millimetre of blood. A deficiency of red blood cells or haemoglobin is called *anaemia.

Erzgebirge (English name: Ore Mountains; Czech name: Krušné Hory) A range of mountains extending about 130 km (81 mi) along the Czech-East German border between the Fichtelgebirge in the W and the River Elbe in the E. They have been heavily worked for silver, copper, lead, uranium, zinc, iron, and tin ores as well as coal and other minerals. They are also a popular tourist area.

Erzurum 39 57N 41 17E A town in NE Turkey, on the route from Ankara and Trabzon to Iran. Local products include handmade jewellery, and there is a university (1957). Population (1980): 190 241.

Esarhaddon King of Assyria (680–669 BC) in succession to his father *Sennacherib after defeating rivals for the throne. In about 674 he attacked Egypt, conquering it in 671.

Esbjerg 55 28N 8 28E The largest fishing port in Denmark, in the SW on the North Sea coast. Its exports include fish, fish products, meat, and dairy products. Population (1981 est): 79 694.

escalation clause A provision in an industrial contract that allows the contractor to increase his price if his costs exceed a stated limit. Escalation clauses are widely used for long-term projects in a time of inflation.

escalator An automatic moving stairway for transporting passengers from one level to another. Escalators consist of a continuous moving belt of metal stairs, usually driven by an electric motor. The stairs move on tracks between two handrails moving at the same speed. At the top and bottom landings the stairs flatten out and pass through metal combs to dislodge small objects. They are generally about 1.6 m wide and move at 3–3.5 m per second.

escape velocity The initial velocity required by a projectile to enable it, without any further source of power, to escape from the gravitational field of the earth or a celestial body. The escape velocity varies with the mass and diameter of the body but not with the mass of the projectile. It is also independent of the angle of launch. For the earth the escape velocity is 11 200 metres per second and for the moon, 2370 metres per second.

Escaut, River. *See* Scheldt, River.

eschatology (Greek *eschatos*: last) The part of Christian theology concerned with the last things, often summarized as death, judgment, heaven, and hell. It refers to the ultimate fate of both the individual and of human society. Eschatological writing is common to both Old and New Testaments, where it is linked with the expectation of a coming Messiah. The teaching of Christ has also been explained as based on the assumption that the end of the world was imminent and that consequently a concern with the last things was urgent. Recent theological work has attempted to restore the relevance of these concepts in a less mythologically inclined world.

Escoffier, Auguste (1846–1935) French chef. He gained an international reputation while supervising the kitchens at the Savoy and the Carlton hotels in London. He was made a member of the Légion d'Honneur in 1920.

Escorial, El A royal palace, mausoleum, and monastery near Madrid. Built for Philip II beween 1563 and 1584, El Escorial is an austere, square, granite building, measuring 162 m (530 ft) by 204 m (670 ft). Philip himself was probably actively concerned in the design, which was begun by Juan Bautista de Toledo (d. 1567) and completed by Juan de *Herrera. El Escorial houses a magnificent collection of books and paintings.

Esdraelon, Plain of (*or* Valley of Jezreel; Hebrew name: 'Emeq Yizre'el) A lowland area in N Israel, stretching SE from Mount Carmel. In ancient times it was a major commercial route and contains the ancient site of Megiddo. It was swampy until drainage and settlement began in 1921.

Esdras, Books of Two books of the *Apocrypha purporting to be by *Ezra. The first is a compilation of various documents, giving a largely parallel account of events recorded in Chronicles, Ezra, and Nehemiah, but adding a legend explaining how King Darius of Persia was persuaded to permit the rebuilding of the Temple at Jerusalem. The second contains details of several visions consoling the Jews in their suffering and promising them a glorious future.

Esfahan. *See* Isfahan.

Esher 51 23N 0 22W A town in SE England, in Surrey. It is a dormitory town for London with many historical connections (Thomas Wolsey lived at Esher Place) and a famous racecourse (Sandown Park). Population (1981) 61 446.

esker An elongated ridge consisting chiefly of sands and gravels deposited by glaciers. Once the bed of a stream flowing beneath or in a glacier, eskers are left behind once the ice has melted or retreated. They may extend for hundreds of kilometres.

Eskilstuna 59 22N 16 31E A town in SE Sweden. A centre of the iron and steel industries, its manufactures include machinery, precision instruments, electrical equipment, and cutlery. Population (1983): 88 987.

Eskimo A Mongoloid people of the Arctic region of North America and Greenland. The men are traditionally hunters of seals, whales, walrus, and caribou, using harpoons, canoes (*or* kayaks), dogs, and sleds. Fishing is also important. Their clothes, made by the women, are of animal skins. Only some of the many different groups build the familiar snow dwellings (igloos). Others construct semisubterranean sod shelters or use snow-covered skin tents. There is no overall sense of identity among them and the main units are small family bands. Their small ivory or stone carvings are highly prized.

Eskimo-Aleut languages A language group, sometimes included in the classification of American Indian languages. It consists of two distinct languages: Eskimo, spoken in Greenland and in many dialects along the N coast of Canada, and *Aleut, spoken in the Aleutian Islands.

Eskimo dog. *See* husky.

Eskişehir 39 46N 30 30E A town in W Turkey, W of Ankara. Its warm springs are well known, and pipes are made from the local meerschaum deposits. There is a university (1973). Population (1980): 309 431.

ESP. *See* extrasensory perception.

espalier apple

cordon apple   fan-trained peach

ESPALIER *Espalier and cordon apple trees are trained to bring the fruiting stems within arm's reach. Peach trees are particularly suitable for fan training on wires in greenhouses.*

espalier A shrub or tree, especially a fruit tree, that is trained to grow flat against a wall or a framework of wood, iron, or wire to support the fruit-laden branches and facilitate picking the crop. The branches are usually arranged in ladder-like tiers.

Other methods result in a fanlike arrangement of branches or a single stem (cordon).

esparto A perennial *grass, Stipa tenacissima*, also known as alfa or halfa, native to Spain and N Africa, where it is cultivated. It grows in sharp pointed tufts, up to 1 m high, and is used to make paper, cord, and rope.

Esperanto An artificial language invented by a Polish philologist, L. L. Zamenhof (1859–1917), in 1887. It was intended to be a universal medium of communication and is indeed the most successful artificial language, being spoken by over 100 000 people. Grammatically it is entirely regular, its pronunciation is consistent with its spelling, and as well as grammatical rules it has the potential for the formation of new words. The rules of the language are laid down in Zamenhof's *Fundamento de Esperanto* (1905).

Espoo (Swedish name: Esbo) 60 10N 24 42E A town in S Finland, just W of Helsinki. It serves mainly as a dormitory town for the capital. Population (1980): 137 409.

Esquimalt 48 25N 123 29W A town in W Canada, in British Columbia on the SE coast of Vancouver Island. It is a major naval and military base. Population (1981): 15 870.

ESRO. *See* European Space Research Organization.

essay A short literary prose composition in which a subject is discussed in a personal manner. The word *essai* was coined by *Montaigne, whose *Essais* (1580) are informal and intimate discussions of such subjects as vanity and idleness. In contrast, Francis Bacon's *Essays* (1597) were formal treatments of weighty topics. During the 18th and 19th centuries the literary periodicals provided an outlet for the essays of *Addison, *Steele, *Lamb, and *De Quincey. Among well-known later essayists are Max *Beerbohm, Virginia *Woolf, and Aldous *Huxley.

Essen 51 27N 6 57E A city in W West Germany, in North Rhine-Westphalia near the River Ruhr. The 9th-century cathedral survived the bombing of World War II. Formerly the site of the Krupp steelworks, it is now the administrative centre of the *Ruhr. Population (1980 est): 650 200.

Essenes An ancient Jewish sect active between the 2nd century BC and the 2nd century AD in Palestine. Information about them is fragmentary and inconsistent. They seem to have stressed personal purity and asceticism. Many scholars think that the *Dead Sea Scrolls are relics of an Essene community.

essential oils Substances with a characteristic scent produced by the glands of aromatic plants. Essential oils may be extracted by distillation, mechanical pressing, or organic solvents and are used in perfumes, food flavourings, and medicines. Examples include attar of roses, lavender oil, and clove oil.

Essequibo, River A river in Guyana, rising on the Brazilian border and flowing generally N to enter the Atlantic Ocean, draining over half of Guyana. Length: 1014 km (630 mi).

Essex A county of E England, bordering on the North Sea and Greater London, which incorporated the SW of the county in 1965. It is mainly low lying rising gently towards the chalk uplands of the NW. Agriculture is varied; the chief crops are wheat, barley, sugar beet, potatoes, and other vegetables. Oyster beds are important, especially in the Colne estuary. Industry is located mainly in the SW. Southend-on-Sea and Clacton are notable coastal resorts and Harwich is a major ferry port. Area: 3674 sq km (1419 sq mi). Population (1983 est): 1 491 700. Administrative centre: Chelmsford.

Essex, Robert Devereux, 2nd Earl of (?1566–1601) English soldier and courtier to Elizabeth I. He was appointed Master of the Horse (1587) after distinguishing himself against Spain. He commanded an expedition (1591–92) sent to aid Henry IV of France and in 1593 became a privy councillor; he took part in the sack of Cádiz (1596). He was dismissed (1600) after failing to suppress an Irish rebellion and in 1601 raised a riot in London, for which he was executed. His son **Robert Devereux, 3rd Earl of Essex** (1591-1646) was the child of his marriage, unpopular with Elizabeth, to Frances Walsingham, widow of the poet Sir Philip *Sidney. The 3rd earl was an unsuccessful parliamentary general in the Civil War, resigning in 1645.

Esslingen 48 45N 9 19E A town in SW West Germany, in Baden-Württemberg on the River Neckar. It is noted for its gothic church (1321-1516) and its wines. Population (1983 est): 88 782.

estate An interest in land, which in England may be held in one of two ways: (1) freehold tenure (more properly tenure in fee simple), in which the right over land (all of which belongs to the Crown) is for a period that is neither fixed nor liable to determination by another and for the use of which no payment in kind or money is due to another, except for such taxes as rates; (2) leasehold tenure, in which a tenant holds an estate from a landlord for a fixed period (*see* landlord and tenant). Both freeholders and long leaseholders may raise money on their land by *mortgages.

estate duty. *See* capital-transfer tax.

Este An Italian princely family of Lombard origin, which under **Obizzo II** (1264-93) gained control of Ferrara, Modena, and Reggio. His successors maintained control of these three regions in spite of papal opposition and were a dominant force in Italian Renaissance politics and culture until Ferrara was incorporated into the papal states in 1598. The Estensi continued to hold Reggio until the French invasion of 1796 and Modena until the unification of Italy in the mid-19th century.
The **Villa d'Este**, at Tivoli, near Rome, was designed (1550) for Cardinal Ippolito II d'Este (1509-72).

Esterházy A family prominent in Hungarian affairs from the 16th to 19th centuries. **Miklós Esterházy** (1582-1645) became imperial governor of Hungary in 1625. His son **Prince Pál Esterházy** (1635-1713) held command against the Turks and became a prince of the Holy Roman Empire (1687). Pál's grandson **Prince Miklós József Esterházy** (1714-90) rebuilt the family castle, Esterháza, and employed Haydn for 30 years. Miklós Józef's grandson **Prince Miklós Esterházy** (1765-1833) fought against the French in the Napoleonic Wars and accumulated an outstanding art collection. Miklós' son **Prince Pál Antal Esterházy** (1786-1866), a diplomat, was foreign minister in 1848.

esters Organic compounds produced by the reaction of an alcohol with an acid, with the elimination of water. Common organic esters are formed from carboxylic acids and have the general formula R.CO.OR′. The lighter ones often have a pleasant smell and taste and are widely used in perfumes and flavourings. Fats are triesters of long-chain carboxylic acids and glycerol. *See* saponins; soaps.

Esther An Old Testament woman who became the queen of the Persian King Ahasuerus. **The Book of Esther** recounts an event in Persia during the reign of *Xerxes I (called Ahasuerus in the text), when Esther used her influence to frustrate a plot to massacre the Jews. The deliverance leads to the establishment of the Jewish feast of *Purim.

Estienne (*or* Étienne; Latin name: Stephanus) A French family of printers and scholars, who published important classical, lexicographical, and theological works. **Henri Estienne** (c. 1465-1520) established the firm in Paris (c. 1502). His son **Robert Estienne** (1503-59) was printer to Francis I but because of political pressure moved the firm to Geneva (1551). Robert's son **Henri Estienne** (1528-98), a renowned scholar, continued the firm in Geneva.

Estonian A language of the Baltic-Finnic branch of the Finno-Ugric division of the Uralic language family. It is spoken by the Estonians, who number about one million people in the Estonian SSR in the Soviet Union. It is related to Finnish with which it shares the distinctive characteristic

of distinguishing three degrees of consonant and vowel length. The written language is based on a northern dialect, Tallinn, and has a literature dating from the 16th century.

Estonian Soviet Socialist Republic (*or* Estonia) A constituent republic in the NW Soviet Union. Estonia has many lakes and includes numerous islands in the Baltic Sea. Some 70% of the population are Estonians. Fishing is an important occupation, the main catch being herring. Other industries include machine building, radio engineering, and the processing of shale—the most important mineral deposit, from which gas is produced, supplying Leningrad. Pig breeding is the chief agricultural activity and the main crops are barley, oats, and potatoes. *History*: in the 13th century the N was occupied by the Danes and the S by the Livonian Knights (a German order of knighthood). The Danes withdrew in 1346 and the Knights were replaced by the Swedes in the 16th and 17th centuries. Estonia was ceded to Russia in 1721. Rebellions in the 19th century culminated in a declaration of independence (1918), which was recognized by Soviet Russia in 1920. It was assigned to the Soviet Union by the Nazi-Soviet Pact (1939) and became an SSR in 1940. It was occupied by Germany in World War II. Its status is not accepted by the USA. Area: 45 100 sq km (17 410 sq mi). Population (1984 est): 1 500 000. Capital: Tallinn.

Estoril 38 42N 9 23W A seaside resort in W Portugal, on the Atlantic Ocean. It has an outstanding avenue of palm trees between its casino and the seafront. Population (1981 est): 23 940.

Esztergom 47 46N 18 42E A town in N Hungary, on the River Danube opposite the Czechoslovak town of Stúrovo. Stephen I was born and crowned king here. Population (1983 est): 31 000.

etching A method of making prints from a metal plate covered with an acid-resistant ground, on which a design is drawn with a needle. The plate is then placed in acid, the exposed lines being eaten away. These recessed lines retain ink and the design is transferred to the paper by rolling under pressure. Although the first dated etching was made in 1513, it was *Rembrandt who freed the medium from its technical and formal dependence on *engraving. The process continues to be widely used, with *Picasso among the leading 20th-century exponents.

Eteocles. *See* Polyneices.

ethane (C_2H_6) A colourless gas, the second member of the *alkane series. It occurs in *natural gas.

ethanol (*or* ethyl alcohol; C_2H_5OH) A colourless flammable liquid that is the active constituent of alcoholic drinks. It is prepared by fermentation or by the catalytic hydration of *ethylene. It is used as a solvent, a raw material for producing other chemicals, and a fuel. *See also* alcohol strength.

Ethelbert (c. 552-616 AD) King of Kent, who became overlord of all England south of the Humber. Encouraging the conversion of his people to Christianity, he received Augustine's mission from Rome. He wrote the first extant English code of laws.

Etheldreda, St (c. 630-79 AD) The reluctant wife of King Ecgfrith of Northumbria. Greatly influenced by Bishop *Wilfrid, who encouraged her to remain a virgin, Etheldreda became abbess of a double monastery at Ely.

Ethelred I (d. 871 AD) King of England (866-71), in whose reign the Vikings launched a full-scale invasion of England. Ethelred died after his victory at Ashdown, leaving his brother *Alfred the Great to fight on.

Ethelred the Unready (968-1016) King of England (978-1016). In the face of Danish raids, he was forced to pay huge tributes (Danegeld) to the enemy. He was driven into exile by *Sweyn in 1013 but returned after Sweyn's death (1014), dying during *Canute's invasion of England (1015-16).

Ethelwulf (d. 858 AD) King of Wessex (839-58). Renowned for his military prowess, he reputedly defeated

350 Viking ships (851). Ethelwulf reduced taxation, endowed the Church, made lay lands heritable, and provided a system of poor relief.

ether Any member of the group of organic compounds with the general formula R–O–R', which are formed by the condensation of two alcohols. Diethyl ether, $C_2H_5OC_2H_5$, often known simply as ether, is a volatile liquid made by treating *ethanol with concentrated sulphuric acid. It is used as an anaesthetic and solvent.

Etherege, Sir George (c. 1635–c. 1692) English dramatist. A diplomat in Turkey from 1668 to 1671, he fled to Paris after the accession of William III. In his comedies of fashionable London life, *The Comical Revenge* (1664), *She Wou'd If She Cou'd* (1668), and *The Man of Mode* (1674), he introduced the comedy of manners to the British theatre.

Ethical Culture movement A movement originating in New York in the late 19th century to promote the importance of morality in all aspects of life (*see* Adler, Felix). The first English Ethical Society was established at the Chapel in South Place, Finsbury (1888).

ethics The science of morality, also called moral philosophy. It is one of the three main branches of modern *philosophy and seeks to discover a consistent principle by which human actions and character can be judged. Until about a century ago, ethics was prescriptive, aiming to guide men's conduct. Now it is more descriptive, attempting to discover how moral decisions are actually made. In ancient philosophy, *hedonism, which held that the greatest goal was happiness, and rationalism, which held that it was reason, were the rival schools. Plato and Aristotle combined hedonism and *rationalism. Medieval scholasticism took God's will as the sole ethical standard and grafted this onto Aristotelian ethics. After the Renaissance, pragmatists like *Hobbes, *Bentham, and John Stuart Mill (*see* Mill, James) developed *utilitarianism, in which the good of society rather than that of the individual is the criterion. *Kant and other idealists were intuitionists, believing that conscience is to ethics as intelligence is to logic. Today utilitarianism is the implicit basis of commercial, legal, and social ethics, but conscience remains the guide of most individuals.

Ethiopia (former name: Abyssinia) A country in NE Africa, on the Red Sea. It consists of deserts in the SE and NE and a central plateau, crossed by river valleys (including that of the Blue Nile) and by mountain ranges rising over 4300 m (11 500 ft). The population consists of many ethnic groups, including the Galla and *Amhara. *Economy*: Ethiopia remains one of the poorest countries in the world and agriculture is chiefly at subsistence level. The situation has been worsened in recent years by serious crop failures, causing famines. All land was nationalized in 1975 and much of it is now farmed cooperatively, the main emphasis being on the development of the rural areas. Mineral resources are sparse, though there are small amounts of gold and platinum as well as salt in Eritrea. The disrupted *Ogaden region is thought to be a potential source of mineral wealth. Gas and oil are being explored and exploitation of the country's considerable potential for hydroelectricity has already begun. Some industries, such as textiles, cement, and food processing, are being encouraged. The main export is coffee. *History*: Ethiopia has a longer known history than any other country in Africa apart from Egypt and legend claimed the descent of its rulers from Solomon and the Queen of Sheba. From the 2nd to the 9th century AD the Aksumite Empire enjoyed considerable prosperity and expansion, in the 4th century Ethiopia became the first Christian country in Africa. This period was followed by centuries of struggles (especially with the Muslims) and of internal divisions. It was not until the 19th century that the country was once more reunited under Emperor Tewodros II (1818–1868). In 1896 Italian attempts to conquer it were defeated by *Menelik II. However, in 1935 Italy (under Mussolini) invaded Ethiopia. In spite of Anglo-French

ETHIOPIA *Distribution of main ethnic groups.*

attempts (Hoare-Laval Pact) to arrange a settlement and League of Nations sanctions against Italy, in 1936 Addis Ababa fell and the emperor, *Haile Selassie, fled to England. For the next five years Ethiopia formed part of Italian East Africa (with Eritrea and Italian Somaliland). In 1941 the Allies liberated Ethiopia and Haile Selassie returned to the throne. Eritrea again became part of Ethiopia, becoming fully integrated in 1962. Haile Selassie was deposed in 1974 and a provisional military government came to power. After the execution of members of the ruling military council in 1977, the government became known as the Derg (Provisional Military Administrative Council) with Mengistu Haile Mariam (1937–) as president. During this period liberation movements in Eritrea and the Somali-speaking Ogaden area increased their armed struggle against the government. By the end of 1977 Somali troops had occupied most of the Ogaden but with the help of Soviet weapons and Cuban troops, Ethiopia regained control of the area. Encouraged by their victories over Somalia, the government has launched several offensives against Eritrean secessionists since 1978 (*see* Eritrea). Successive droughts (1982, 1984, and 1987) have led to famine throughout the Horn of Africa and forced resettlement from the N to the fertile west. Massive foreign aid has been hampered by internal strife and disorganization. In 1987 Mengistu oversaw the establishment of an elected parliament based on a Marxist-Leninist constitution. *See also* Falashas. Official language: Amharic; English is widely spoken. Official religion: Ethiopian Orthodox (Coptic). Official currency: birr of 100 cents. Area: 1 000 000 sq km (386 000 sq mi). Population (1983 est): 33 008 000. Capital: Addis Ababa. Main port: Massawa.

ethnology The comparative study and theory of contemporary cultures. In most current usages it is synonymous with cultural *anthropology. However, it has also been used to refer to the historical study of cultures, especially preliterate cultures, and sometimes as a synonym for social anthropology. It may be distinguished from ethnography, which is the descriptive study of culture and is less concerned with the development of theory.

ethology The study of animal behaviour. Ethologists are concerned with how animals respond to signals or stimuli (whether from other animals, from their own bodies, or from the environment in which they live), how they sense these signals, and what their response means to other animals and to themselves. They demonstrate the interactions between the inherited (instinctive) aspects of behaviour and those determined by experience (learning).
Ethology was founded in Europe in the 1930s by the work of Konrad *Lorenz and Niko *Tinbergen, who studied animals in their natural states. In the USA the approach was one of comparative psychology, using laboratory animals under strict experimental conditions. The work of ethologists has provided insights into some aspects of human behaviour.

ethyl alcohol. *See* ethanol.

ethylene (*or* ethene; C_2H_4) A colourless flammable gaseous *alkene. It is made by *cracking petroleum and is used to make *polythene (polyethylene). It is also used to ripen fruit artificially.

Etna, Mount 37 45N 15 00E A volcano in E Sicily, having a central crater and over 200 subsidiaries. The first recorded eruption was in 476 BC and significant eruptions this century have occurred in 1928, 1949, and 1971. The coastal town of Catania, 28 km (17 mi) away, has been engulfed twice. Height: 3263 m (10 705 ft).

Eton 51 31N 0 37W A town in SE England, in Berkshire opposite Windsor on the River Thames. Eton College, the famous public school, was founded by Henry VI in 1440. Population (1983): 3473.

Etruria The region of ancient Italy N of Rome, approximating modern Tuscany. Occupied first by *Villanovan peoples, Etruria was inhabited by the *Etruscans from the 8th century BC but by the 3rd century BC had come under Roman control.

Etruscans The ancient inhabitants of Etruria (now Tuscany) in central Italy. From the 8th to the 5th centuries BC their cities, forming a loose political confederacy, dominated their neighbours but after 396 they were rapidly absorbed by the Romans. The Etruscans' origins are mysterious; certain oriental traits in their artefacts and the frescoes decorating their tombs suggest that they were invaders from Asia Minor, but such traits may have arisen through their extensive trading links. Their language was non-Indo-European and although many inscriptions are known and the alphabet is not dissimilar to ancient Greek, it is still untranslated.

Etty, William (1787-1849) British painter, best known for his studies of the nude. His large-scale *The Combat* (1825; National Gallery of Scotland), exhibited at the Royal Academy in 1828, impressed Delacroix.

etymology The study of the history of words, in which words are traced back to their earliest recorded forms and, where sufficient evidence exists, even beyond these to hypothetical reconstructed forms. Most English words are derived either from Proto-Germanic (*see* Germanic languages) or from Latin and French. Many learned English words were taken from Greek or made up from Greek elements, while in the past 200 years English has come to borrow words from languages in every part of the world.

Euboea (Modern Greek name: Évvoia; former English name: Negropont) The second largest Greek island, in the W Aegean Sea. It is separated from the mainland by only a narrow channel and rises to 1743 m (5719 ft) at Mount Delphi. Sheep and cattle are raised and grapes, figs, olives, and cereals, grown. Area: 3908 sq km (1509 sq mi). Population (1981): 188 410. Chief town: Chalcis.

Eucalyptus A genus of tropical and subtropical evergreen trees (about 600 species) native to Australia but widely cultivated elsewhere. Eucalypts—also known as gum trees and stringybarks—are among the tallest trees in the world, 90-100 m high. The blue-grey bark is smooth and often peeling and the mature leaves are long and narrow (young leaves are rounded or oblong). The flowers are showy, with tiny petals and a fluffy mass of red or white stamens. The fruit is a woody pod. Fast-growing and drought-resistant, eucalypts are important sources of timber. The wood is used as fuel and for buildings and fencing; the bark for paper making and tanning. The best known species are the *blue gum and the red gum (*E. ficifolia*). Because they take up much water, eucalypts are used to reclaim marshy land. They are also used for street planting. All parts of the trees contain essential oils (oil of eucalyptus comes from blue gum leaves). Some species are shrubby and are known as *mallees. Family: *Myrtaceae* (myrtle family).

Eucharis A genus of bulb-forming South American plants (10 species), called Amazon lilies. Up to 60 cm tall, they have clusters of large fragrant white flowers, up to 13 cm across, with protruding slender stamens and six backward curling white sepals. The plants are grown for ornament in greenhouses. Family: *Amaryllidaceae*.

Eucharist (Greek *eucharistia*: thanksgiving) The chief *sacrament and central act of worship of the Christian Churches. Also known as Holy Communion, the Lord's Supper, and the Mass, its institution is described in the three Synoptic Gospels. At the last meal of Christ and the apostles, bread and wine were blessed by Christ and shared, representing his death on the cross and the subsequent redemption of mankind. Differing interpretations have been placed on the sense in which Christ is held to be present in the sacrament (*see* consubstantiation; transubstantiation).

Eucken, Rudolf Christoph (1846-1926) German writer. He upheld idealist metaphysics against 19th-century positivism and materialism and sought to isolate the spiritual content of historical movements. He won the Nobel Prize for Literature in 1908.

Euclid (c. 300 BC) Greek mathematician, famous for his book entitled *Elements* in which he derived all that was known of geometry from a few simple axioms. The geometry that obeys Euclid's axioms is known as *Euclidean geometry, all other kinds being called *non-Euclidean.

Euclidean geometry A system of geometry based on the axioms contained in *Euclid's *Elements*. In Euclidean geometry, parallel lines never meet and the angles in a triangle always add up to 180°. The geometry of physical space can be assumed for most purposes to be Euclidean. The surface of a sphere, however, is non-Euclidean. *Compare* non-Euclidean geometry.

Eudoxus of Cnidus (c. 408-c. 355 BC) Greek astronomer and mathematician, who studied under Plato and later founded a school, first on the NW coast of Asia Minor and then in Athens. He studied the motions of the planets and derived many geometric proofs, some of which were later incorporated by *Euclid in his *Elements*.

Eugène of Savoy, Prince (1663-1736) Austrian general. Born in Paris, he was refused a commission by Louis XIV and entered the service of Emperor Leopold I. He fought outstandingly against the Turks, winning victories at Zenta (1697), which freed Hungary of Turkish domination, Peterwardein (1716), and Belgrade (1717). In the War of *Austrian Succession (1701-14), he won, with Marlborough, the victories of *Blenheim (1704), Oudenaarde (1708), and Malplaquet (1709).

eugenics The science that studies the inheritable factors that determine the physical and mental qualities of the human race, with the aim of improving the quality of life for future generations. The term was first coined by Sir Francis *Galton in 1883. Eugenics is now concerned primarily with the detection and—where possible—elimination of such genetic diseases as Down's syndrome with the aid of *prenatal diagnosis.

Eugénie (1826–1920) The influential wife (1853–73) of *Napoleon III of France. She several times acted as his regent and encouraged French intervention in Mexico. After the fall of the Empire (1870) she retired to England.

Euglena A genus of single-celled microorganisms found chiefly in fresh water. They are spindle-shaped, with a flexible cell wall (pellicle) and a gullet from which protrudes a long whiplike flagellum, used for locomotion. Some species contain chlorophyll or other pigments and can manufacture food by photosynthesis; others feed on small organisms, such as bacteria. Euglenas are regarded by some authorities as algae and by others as protozoans of the class *Flagellata*. □Protozoa.

Eulenspiegel, Till A German peasant folk hero, a crafty and often savage joker whose exploits inspired numerous folktales and many literary and musical works, notably the epic poem by Gerhard *Hauptmann (1928) and the tone poem by Richard *Strauss.

Euler, Leonhard (1707–83) Swiss mathematician, widely regarded as the greatest mathematician of the 18th century and certainly the most prolific of all time, writing some 800 papers during his lifetime. Many more were published posthumously. He did much work on the number e, the base of natural *logarithms, which is often known as **Euler's number**. He gave that number its symbol, and introduced the symbol i for the square root of −1 and also the notation $f(x)$ for a function of the variable x.

Eumenides (Greek: the kindly ones) In Greek legend, spirits identical with the *Erinyes. After *Orestes was acquitted by the Areopagus of his mother's murder, the pursuing Erinyes became known as the Eumenides.

Euonymus A genus of widely distributed trees, shrubs, and woody climbers (176 species), often grown as ornamentals for their attractive foliage and fruits, which are surrounded by a bright-pink or orange fleshy coat (aril). The genus includes the *spindle tree. Family: *Celastraceae*.

Eupen-et-Malmédy A region of Belgium, in Liège province. It was ceded by Germany in 1919 by the Treaty of Versailles but was once more occupied by Germany (1940–45). Manufactures include woollen goods, paper, and leather. Population (1983 est): 18 540.

euphonium Brass instrument with a wide conical bore, a cup-shaped mouthpiece, four valves, and a range of about three and a half octaves above the B flat below middle C. Its range is equivalent to that of a tenor *tuba and it is much used in the brass band.

Euphorbia A worldwide genus of herbs and small trees (1600 species), having clusters of small flowers each surrounded by conspicuous petal-like bracts. The genus includes some ornamental shrubs (*see* crown of thorns; poinsettia; snow-on-the-mountain). The herbaceous euphorbias are known as *spurges. Family: *Euphorbiaceae*.

Euphrates, River A river in SW Asia, rising in E Turkey and flowing SE through Syria into Iraq. 190 km (118 mi) from the Persian Gulf, it joins the River Tigris to form the Shatt al-Arab. It flows past the historic sites of Babylon, Ur, Nippur, and Sippara. Length: 2700 km (1678 mi).

Euphronios (late 6th–early 5th centuries BC) Athenian red-figure potter and vase painter. He signed some 15 surviving vases and is mentioned as a rival by another painter. His drawing shows skill in composition and an interest in characterization.

Eupolis (late 5th century BC) Greek dramatist, a rival of *Aristophanes. His comedies satirized contemporary politicians and socialites. Only fragments of his works survive.

Eurasia Europe and Asia considered as one land mass. Geographically, Europe is a peninsula of the Asian continent, divided from it by the Ural Mountains.

EURATOM. *See* European Atomic Energy Community.

Eureka project A European advanced technology cooperation programme. Originally proposed by the French government as an alternative to the US *Special Defence Initiative, the project was launched in 1985: its 18 European member-nations aim to find peaceful applications for joint research.

Eureka Stockade (1854) A miners' rebellion in Victoria (Australia) against oppressive government legislation: prospectors had to pay high licence fees, which were brutally collected, and they were not permitted to vote or to be represented in the Legislative Council. The miners of Ballarat, under Peter *Lalor, stockaded themselves into the Eureka goldfield. They were easily routed by government forces and about 25 miners and 5 troopers were killed.

eurhythmics A system of teaching music by developing the student's physical response to rhythm. Devised by *Jaques-Dalcroze in about 1905, it has since been used in physical education, *ballet and *modern dance training, and even in mental education. The student is taught a series of body movements to express different musical rhythms; he is then encouraged to improvise his movements.

Euripides (c. 480–406 BC) Greek dramatist, the third (after *Aeschylus and *Sophocles) of the three major writers of Attic tragedy. According to tradition he was born in Salamis on the day Xerxes' fleet was defeated in the famous battle. In 408 he went to the court of Archelaus in Macedonia, where he remained for the rest of his life. Of approximately 90 plays, 19 survive, including the tragedies *Medea* (431), *Hippolytus* (428), *Electra* (415), *The Trojan Women* (415), *The Bacchae* (405), and *Iphigenia at Aulis* (405). His technical innovations included naturalistic dialogue and a diminution of the role of the chorus. He also explored feminine psychology. His critical attitude towards traditional religion in some of the plays, which offended his contemporaries, is balanced by incidents portraying real heroism and lyrical passages of great beauty.

Eurodollars An international currency based on US dollar balances held by banks outside the USA. The Eurodollar market developed from 1957 onwards as persistent US *balance-of-payments deficits (largely due to foreign aid and investment programmes) led to a large outflow of dollars, which were put to use in Europe often to finance international trade. Oil-producing countries often have large holdings of Eurodollars, which they may move between investment centres in order to take advantage of the highest interest rates. Eurodollars and other expatriate currencies together make up the Eurocurrency market, which deals in large amounts of short-term funds the volatility and freedom from government control of which may at times pose a threat to the stability of international money markets.

Europa (astronomy). *See* Galilean satellites.

Europa (Greek mythology) The daughter of King Agenor of Tyre. Carried to Crete by Zeus in the form of a bull, she bore him three sons: Minos, Rhadamanthus, and Sarpedon.

Europa Nostra (Italian: Our Europe) An international federation of about 2000 independent organizations devoted to the preservation of Europe's natural and cultural heritage. Established in 1963, with an office in London, it acts in an advisory capacity to the Council of Europe.

Europe A continent bordering on the Arctic Ocean (N), the Atlantic Ocean (W), and the Mediterranean Sea (S); the Ural Mountains, the River Ural, and the Caspian Sea form its E boundary. Europe is the second (after Australasia) smallest continent but owing perhaps to its latitude and geography has exerted a disproportionate influence on the rest of the world. It comprises a peninsula of the land mass of Eurasia and all geological eras have contributed to its formation. Its long coastline is much indented with several peninsulas (e.g. Scandinavia, Italy) and offshore islands (e.g. the British Isles, Iceland). A central plain, extending from the Ural Mountains to the Atlantic Ocean and divided by uplands and the English Channel, comprises two-thirds of the continent. It rises in the S to a series of mountain systems (e.g. the Pyrenees, Alps, Apennines, Carpathian Mountains), and in the N to the mountainous region of Scandinavia and Scotland. The chief rivers flow from the Valdai Hills (e.g Volga, Don, Dnieper) or the Alps (e.g. Danube, Rhine, Rhône, Po). Its four **climatic zones** are characterized by mild winters, cool summers, and rain all the year round (NW); mild winters, hot summers, and chiefly spring and autumn rain (Mediterranean); cold winters, warm summers, and chiefly summer rain (Central Europe); and very cold winters (E Europe). **Vegetation zones** comprise, from N to S: tundra; a coniferous forest belt, predominantly of Scots pine and Norway spruce; a deciduous forest belt, notably of oak and hornbeam in the E and of oak, birch, and holly in the W, with beech in the central lowlands; and the mainly evergreen and scrub vegetation of the Mediterranean. Steppe and semidesert characterize the SE. Forest once covered some 80% of Europe but intense agriculture since the middle ages and industrialization since the 19th century have reduced it to 30% of the land mass. Europe possesses important mineral resources. Coalfields, especially in the UK, Germany, France, Belgium, and the Soviet Union, continue to be an important source of power, and oil and natural-gas reserves are found in the Soviet Union, Romania, Albania, and beneath the North Sea. Iron-ore deposits are found on a large scale only in the Soviet Union, which also has reserves of nickel, tin, and manganese, but nonmetallic minerals, including kaolinite and rock salt, occur widely. Europe's high-density population is concentrated on its industrial regions, which are found chiefly in a central belt extending from England, through N France, the Netherlands, and Germany, to Moscow; N Italy, however, is also densely populated. Most of the unusually large number of national groups in Europe speak an *Indo-European language. The European peoples may be subdivided into racial types (e.g. Nordic, Germanic, Alpine, and Mediterranean) but extensive intermixing has occurred. Christianity, in its various forms, is the dominant religion and has exerted a profound influence on European culture, which also continues to bear the imprint of the civilizations of ancient *Greece and Rome (see Roman Republic; Roman Empire). Nevertheless Europe's medieval and modern history is that of its diverse nations, conflicts between which culminated in the 20th century in the two World Wars. The postwar period has witnessed a split between the communist countries of E Europe, dominated by the Soviet Union, and the countries of W Europe, which have sought to resolve their rivalries by means of economic and, increasingly, political union (see European Economic Community). Area: about 10 400 000 sq km (4 000 000 sq mi). Population (1981): 486 000 000.

European Atomic Energy Community (EURATOM) An international organization founded in 1958 by the Treaty of Rome (1957) to promote and develop the peaceful uses of atomic energy in Europe. In 1967 the merger of EURATOM and the *European Coal and Steel Community with the EEC took place.

European Broadcasting Union An organization founded in 1950 to improve radio and television communications. Its members include Cyprus, Greece, Iceland, Israel, Lebanon, Morocco, Tunisia, Turkey, and Yugoslavia, as well as all the W European nations.

European Coal and Steel Community (ECSC) A body established in 1952 to coordinate the production of coal and steel in France, Italy, West Germany, and the *Benelux countries. In 1967 the merger of the ECSC and the *European Atomic Energy Community with the EEC was begun.

European Defence Community (EDC) An association of European states, established by treaty in 1952, that was pledged to construct a united European army to counterbalance Soviet forces. It was largely unrealized as a result of the serious opposition from some powers, notably France, and a modified association, the *Western European Union, was formed in 1955.

European Economic Community (EEC or Common Market) An organization of W European states created by the Treaty of Rome (1957) to foster economic cooperation and common development with the eventual aim of economic, and a measure of political, unity. Agreements have been reached on the removal of customs tariffs between members, the setting of a Common Customs Tariff for imports from nonmember states, and the abolition of barriers to free movement of labour, services, and capital between member states. The original six signatories were Belgium, France, Italy, Luxembourg, the Netherlands, and West Germany. In 1973 the UK, Denmark, and the Republic of Ireland became members; Greece joined in 1981, and Spain and Portugal joined in 1986. In 1985 Greenland left the EEC, having attained home rule from Denmark. In 1967 the merger of the *European Atomic Energy Community and the *European Coal and Steel Community with the EEC was initiated. The EEC implemented a *Common Agricultural Policy (CAP) in 1962 (modified in 1968) and a Common Fisheries Policy (1983). The European Monetary Union aims to achieve full monetary union (see exchange rates).
The Commission of the European Communities is in Brussels and consists of one member or two appointed by each member country; its president is elected for a four-year term. The Commission acts as an advisory body to, and is responsible for implementing policy decided upon by, the Council of Ministers. The new Commission formed in 1985 is headed by Jacques Delors (1926–). Also in Brussels, the Council comprises ministers from the governments of the member countries. The heads of government meet triannually as the European Council. The European Parliament at Strasbourg or Luxembourg comments on the Commission's legislative proposals; it must be consulted on the annual budgets and may dismiss the Commission. Members are (since 1979) elected by direct vote in the member countries and sit as political groups (e.g. Christian Democrats, Socialists) in the Parliament. The Court of Justice, at Luxembourg, interprets the treaties establishing the Communities, and interprets and applies the laws made by the Council and the Commission.

European Free Trade Association (EFTA) An association of seven states (Austria, Finland, Iceland, Norway, Portugal, Sweden, and Switzerland) founded in 1960 to foster free trade of industrial goods between members. In 1984 free trade was established between the EEC countries and the EFTA countries. Individual countries may negotiate independent trade agreements with nonmember states.

European Southern Observatory A major astronomical observatory near La Serena, Chile, operated by a European intergovernmental organization that includes France, Germany, Belgium, the Netherlands, Denmark, Sweden, Italy, and Switzerland. It houses a 3.6 m (142 in) reflecting telescope.

European Space Agency (ESA) An organization responsible for Europe's space programme, formed in 1975 from the merger of the European Space Research Organization and the European Launcher Development Organization. There are at present 11 full-member nations, including the UK. All ESA *satellites were launched by NASA before completion of the ESA launcher **Ariane**, the first successful launching of which took place in 1979. In 1987 the UK came under pressure for lack of commitment to the programme.

European Space Research Organization (ESRO) An organization founded in 1962 to encourage space research among European states with particular emphasis on its exploitation for peaceful purposes. Activities include the development of scientific, meteorological, and telecommunications programmes.

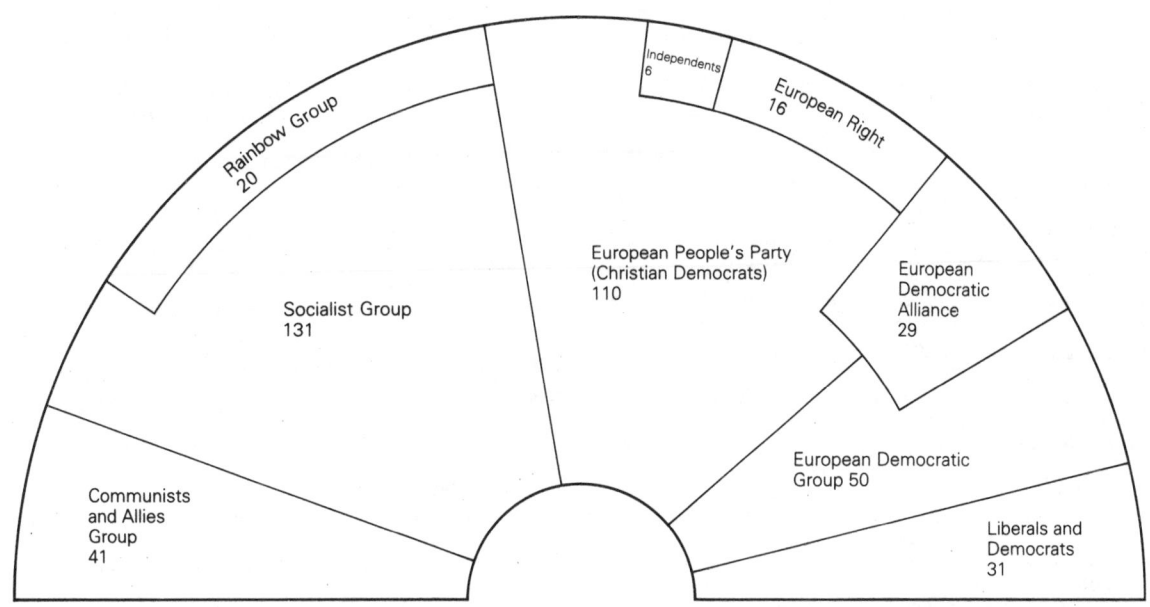

EUROPEAN ECONOMIC COMMUNITY   *The plan of the chamber of the European Parliament, showing political groups and their numerical strength.*

europium (Eu)   A *lanthanide element, used in television-tube phosphors. It forms oxides (EuO, Eu_2O_3), and chlorides ($EuCl_2$, $EuCl_3$). At no 63; at wt 151.96; mp 822°C; bp 1597°C.

Europoort.   *See* Rotterdam.

Eurydice   In Greek legend, a *dryad, the wife of *Orpheus. She died of a snake bite. Orpheus descended to the underworld to recover her but lost her forever when he violated the condition of her release and turned to look at her before emerging.

eurypterid   An extinct *arthropod, also called water scorpion, belonging to a subclass (*Eurypterida*) of the Ordovician and Permian periods, i.e. 500–225 million years ago. Its tapering segmented body, up to 3 m long, bore several pairs of oarlike appendages at the head end. Eurypterids, which lived in salt or brackish waters, were predators of worms and small fish or bottom-dwelling scavengers. ⬚fossil.

Eusebius of Caesarea   (4th century AD) Christian churchman and historian. As Bishop of Caesarea from 313, he took a moderate position with regard to *Arianism and sought a compromise between the conflicting views of Arius and Athanasius; he finally accepted the creed proposed by the Council of *Nicaea. He is famous for his *Ecclesiastical History*, an account of the Church from apostolic times to his own day.

Eustace, St   (2nd century AD) Roman martyr and the patron saint of hunters. According to tradition, he was a general who was converted to Christianity through experiencing a miraculous vision of a stag with a crucifix between its antlers. Feast Day: 20 Sept.

Eustachio, Bartolommeo   (?1520–74) Italian anatomist and physician, who gave his name to the canal connecting the ear and throat (the Eustachian tube) although this had already been discovered by the Greek physician Alcmaeon of Croton (5th century BC). Eustachio's anatomical studies included the ear, kidney, and nervous system but his *Tabulae anatomicae* was not published until 1714.

eustasy   Worldwide changes in sea level, attributed mainly to the accumulation and release of water in the form of ice during the ice ages. Since the last Ice Age sea level has risen gradually.

Euterpe   In Greek legend, one of the *Muses, the patron of tragedy, flute playing, or lyric poetry.

euthanasia (Greek: easy death)   The taking of life to relieve suffering. Euthanasia is a controversial issue concerned with whether or not those with painful and incurable diseases should be provided with a painless means of dying if they ask for it. This is voluntary euthanasia and includes both active steps for taking life (e.g. administration of drugs) and the withholding of life-supporting treatment (passive euthanasia). Even more unacceptable to some people is the concept of compulsory euthanasia, in which the patient—for example, a severely deformed baby—is unable to express his own wishes and the responsibility for deciding to terminate life rests on society or a person acting on authority. Many societies exist to promote the cause of voluntary euthanasia, but in no country has either voluntary or compulsory euthanasia been legalized.

eutrophication   The overfertilization of lakes, due chiefly to pollution by sewage, runoff from the land, and industrial wastes (inorganic nitrates and phosphates). These compounds act as nutrients, stimulating algal growth to produce huge blooms. Their subsequent decomposition reduces the oxygen content in the water, so killing animals with a high oxygen requirement. Much of the nitrate and phosphate settles to the bottom, to promote further growth at a later stage.

Evangelicalism   A movement within Protestant Churches that advocates adherence to traditional concepts of biblical belief. Evangelicals reject the Catholic and Orthodox view of authority residing in the traditions of the Church and the

*Apostolic Succession, while remaining faithful to Trinitarian orthodoxy. They resist the liberalizing trend apparent in nonevangelical Protestant circles, concentrating on the importance of personal salvation and the consequences of accepting the divine inspiration of the Bible.

Evans, Sir Arthur John   (1851–1941) British archaeologist. His interest in Cretan sealstones, while Keeper of the Ashmolean Museum, led him to his life's work, the excavation of *Knossos (1899–1935). In *The Palace of Minos* (1921–36) he firmly established the chronology and main features of *Minoan civilization.

Evans, Dame Edith   (1888–1976) British actress. Her long career included many celebrated performances in Shakespearian roles and in classic comedies such as *The Rivals* and *The Importance of Being Earnest*. She gave some of her most acclaimed stage and film performances during her eighties.

Evans, Sir Geraint   (1922–   ) Welsh baritone, famous as an opera singer. He made his debut at Covent Garden in 1948 in Wagner's *Die Meistersinger*. He is well known for his interpretations of the title roles of Verdi's *Falstaff* and Berg's *Wozzeck*. He retired in 1982.

Evans, Oliver   (1755–1819) American engineer, who conceived the principle of the continuous production line. In 1784 Evans put his ideas into practice in a flour mill: corn entered one end of an automated production line, was processed, and then discharged as flour at the other end. He also patented a high-pressure steam engine in 1790, which was the first major improvement on James *Watt's engine.

Evansville   38 00N 87 33W A city in the USA, in SW Indiana on the Ohio River. Its industries include plastics, meat packing, refrigeration equipment, flour milling, pharmaceuticals, and aluminium. Population (1980): 130 496.

evaporation   The conversion of a liquid into a vapour at temperatures below its boiling point. As it is the most energetic atoms and molecules that escape from the surface in evaporation, the average energy of those that remain is reduced and consequently the liquid is cooled.

Evelyn, John   (1620–1706) English diarist. He travelled in Europe during the Civil War and after the Restoration in 1660 he held several administrative posts and helped to found the Royal Society. He wrote practical works on various subjects but is best known for his *Diary*, a detailed personal record of the years 1641–1706.

evening primrose   A herbaceous plant of the genus *Oenothera* (100 species), 90–100 cm tall, native to the Americas but widespread in Europe. The fragrant yellow flowers, 2–5 cm in diameter, open in the evening. The leaves are spirally arranged and the fruit is a long capsule. Family: *Onagraceae* (willowherb family).

Everest, Mount   27 59N 86 56E The highest mountain in the world, on the Nepal–Tibet border in the Himalayas. It was recognized as the highest in 1852, but the height itself was not established until 1955. Climbing attempts started in 1920 and the 12th expedition, led by Col John *Hunt, was the first to succeed: (Sir) Edmund *Hillary and Sherpa *Tenzing Norgay reached the summit on 29 May, 1953. On 5 May, 1978, two Austrians, Peter Habeler (1942–   ) and Reinhold Messner, became the first to reach the top without the aid of oxygen breathing equipment. Height: 8848 m (29 028 ft).

Everglades   A subtropical swampy area in the USA, in Florida extending S of Lake Okeechobee. The natural vegetation of sawgrass and rushes is preserved in the Everglades National Park but elsewhere large areas have been drained for agriculture.

evergreen plants   Plants the foliage of which is retained throughout the year. The leaves of evergreens, which are tough and waxy, are produced and shed at different times all the year round, individual leaves often remaining on the tree for several years. Most conifers and many tropical broad-leaved trees are evergreen. **Deciduous plants** produce softer leaves, which are all shed before winter, leaving only the woody parts and protected buds exposed. Deciduous trees generally occur in temperate regions in which there are seasonal fluctuations in climate.

everlasting flowers   Any flowers that can be dried without losing their shape or colour and are used in floral arrangements and pictures. They include many members of the *Compositae* (daisy family), such as the true everlastings, or immortelles (*Helichrysum* species), the flower heads of which may be dyed various colours. One of the most popular of these is the strawflower of Australia (*H. bracteatum*). Other plants used include *Anaphalis margaritacea* (the pearly everlasting) and *Gnaphalium* and *Helipterum* species, and striking shapes are supplied by *teasels (*Dipsacus* species). Grasses with showy panicles are often used, especially wild oats and barley.

Evert, Christine.   *See* Lloyd, Christine.

Evesham   52 06N 1 56W A market town in W central England, in Hereford and Worcester on the River Avon. The Vale of Evesham is famous for fruit and vegetables and Evesham has a canning industry. Population (1985 est): 15 300.

evolution   In biology, the gradual and continuous process by which the first and most primitive of living organisms have developed into the diversity of plant and animal life known today. Speculations about the origin of living things go back to the Greek philosophers, notably Aristotle, but until the 18th century it was generally believed that each group of organisms was separately and divinely created. In the 1760s *Linnaeus—in his work on the classification and naming of organisms—recognized the possibility of relationship between similar groups, and his contemporary *Buffon suggested that the differences he observed in fossil organisms were brought about by changes in the environment in which they lived.

The first theory of evolution was published by Lamarck, in 1809 (*see* Lamarckism). His explanation of the process—that changes in form acquired during the lifetime of an animal could be inherited—lacked definite proof, although it

MOUNT EVEREST   *Edmund Hillary and Sherpa Tenzing, with oxygen equipment, on their way to the summit in 1953.*

has had its supporters. A more satisfactory theory was put forward by Charles *Darwin and A. R. *Wallace in 1858: they proposed that new species arose by a process of natural selection acting on individual inheritable variations in a population (*see* Darwinism). Later work has proved that these heritable changes result from spontaneous genetic mutations, and Darwin's theory—with some modifications—is now generally accepted.

Évora (ancient name: Ebora) 38 34N 7 54W A town in Portugal. It contains many Roman ruins including a Roman temple known as the Temple of Diana. Population (1981): 34 072.

Évreux 49 03N 1 11E A town in NW France, the capital of the Eure department. It has a cathedral (11th–18th centuries) and there are Roman remains nearby. Its manufactures include textiles, rubber, and pharmaceuticals. Population (1982): 48 653.

evzones Members of a Greek infantry regiment, originally from Epirus, who fought with distinction in the Balkan Wars and World War II. Evzones wear a distinctive white-skirted uniform; their name derives from the Greek word meaning "dressed for exercise."

Ewald, Johannes (1743–81) Danish Romantic poet and playwright, who ran away at the age of 15 to fight in the Seven Years' War. On returning he began to write; his work was influenced by Klopstock, Shakespeare, and Macpherson's *Ossian*. He was the first Danish writer to use legend and myth as the basis for his works, which include the tragedies *Rolf Krage* (1770) and *Balders Død* (*The Death of Baldur*; 1773). His works have been translated into English by George Borrow, Longfellow, and others.

Ewe A people of SE Ghana and S Togo, numbering approximately one million, who originated from *Oyo in Nigeria. Their language belongs to the *Kwa subgroup of the Niger-Congo family. They practise shifting agriculture and, in coastal areas, seafishing. They are divided into independent groups, which form temporary alliances for war.

Excalibur King Arthur's magic sword. In one legend Arthur succeeds, where others had failed, in drawing it from a stone, thereby proving his claim to the English throne. In another he receives it from the Lady of the Lake, to whom it is thrown back at his death. *See also* Arthurian legend.

excavator A self-propelled vehicle equipped with a hydraulically powered movable boom and shovel used for excavating trenches, loading earth, etc. Larger models are used for mining and quarrying and usually consist of a crawler vehicle on which is mounted a boom with one or several digging buckets controlled by cables from a winch.

exchange control Government regulations to control the extent to which a foreign currency can be purchased to prevent a large outflow of foreign exchange, which might precipitate a *balance-of-payments crisis. The UK has used exchange control extensively in an attempt to influence the market for sterling in the face of the country's chronic tendency to short-term outflows of foreign exchange, but its impact is limited because it does not restrict the activities of nonresident holders of sterling, who tend to be the most active in switching funds between currencies. In 1979 the UK removed nearly all of its exchange-control restrictions.

exchange rates The value of one country's currency in terms of another's. Foreign trade and tourism make it essential for currencies to be convertible at a stable rate of exchange. Until World War I and again briefly between 1925 and 1931 international currencies were backed by, and convertible into, gold (*see* gold standard). Between 1931 and 1947 various systems were in use. In the UK, for instance, the Exchange Equalization Account was set up in 1932 to enable the Bank of England to control the official gold and foreign-exchange reserves. In 1947 the *International Monetary Fund (IMF) came into operation, as a result of the *Bretton Woods Conference

(1944). The IMF fixed par values for members' currencies in terms of gold and these values could not be changed without consulting the IMF. *Special Drawing Rights were introduced in 1970 in an attempt to increase world liquidity, but were unable to maintain the stability of the system: the suspension of convertibility from US dollars to gold in 1971 led to an agreement to allow currencies to float (i.e. to find their own value as a result of market forces). Floating rates avoid the problem of large destabilizing devaluation, which took place under the Bretton Woods fixed-rate system.

The aim of the EEC "snake," and the system that replaces it under the European Monetary Union, is to fix the European currencies in terms of each other. This has the drawback of all fixed-rate systems that weak countries suffer *balance-of-payments problems, which are exacerbated when the price of the weak country's exports are rising faster than those of its competitors.

excise tax. *See* customs and excise duties.

excitation In physics, the raising of a system from its lowest energy level (the ground state) to a higher energy level (the excited state). The term is usually confined to atoms, molecules, ions, and nuclei and is most frequently caused by the absorption of a *photon. In an atom, ion, or nucleus the photon is absorbed by an electron or *nucleon causing it to move to a higher energy level. Molecules can also be excited into higher states of rotational or vibrational energy.

Exclusionists Free settlers in the colony of New South Wales who wished to debar former convicts from equal civil and political rights. The constitution of 1842 ended this inequality. *See also* Emancipists.

excommunication The exclusion of a Christian from the community of the Church for misconduct. There are biblical precedents for various forms of excommunication, especially in the Pauline epistles. In the later Church, exclusion from the sacraments was frequently used as a means of censure, and in the middle ages the papacy used it to apply political pressure against sovereigns. It is still used by the Roman Catholic Church as a form of discipline and is theoretically available in some Protestant Churches.

excretion The elimination of the waste products of metabolism by the body. In higher animals and man this includes the excretion of nitrogenous waste in the form of urine by the *kidneys, the egestion of faeces—the waste products of digestion—from the bowel, and the exhalation of carbon dioxide from the lungs in breathing. A small amount of urea is also excreted in sweat. Lower animals have various simple organs for the excretion of waste products (*see* nephridium).

Exekias (6th century BC) Athenian potter and vase painter, known from his signatures on several vases. One of the last black-figure painters, Exekias painted dignified symmetrical compositions in painstaking but fluent detail.

Exeter 50 43N 3 31W A city in SW England, the administrative centre of Devon on the River Exe. Its 13th-century cathedral, a fine example of gothic architecture, was damaged by bombing in World War II along with many other buildings. Exeter's Guildhall is said to be the oldest municipal building in the country. Exeter University (1955) succeeded the University College of the South West. Industries include tourism, printing, the manufacture of agricultural machinery, and leather goods. Population (1983 est): 101 800.

existentialism A philosophical movement that rejects metaphysics and concentrates on the individual's existence in the world. The forerunner of existentialism, *Kierkegaard, reacting against German *idealism and the complacency of established Christianity, developed a pragmatic psychologically realistic philosophy of existence. This was adapted by French intellectuals, especially Sartre, after World War II. Sartre's existentialism allows individuals freedom in a nihilistic universe: "All human activities are equivalent, all are destined by principle to defeat." But a man is responsible for his effect on others, though only *his* existence is real to him and he is ultimately his own judge. Sartre expounded existentialism chiefly in *Being and Nothingness* (1943), but his plays and novels (and those of *Camus) present existentialist ideas more accessibly.

Exmoor A high moorland and national park of SW England, extending from NE Devon into W Somerset, reaching 520 m (1707 ft) at Dunkery Beacon. Once largely forested, it now supports heather, bracken, and grass and is grazed by Exmoor ponies, wild red deer, and sheep. Parts are now being ploughed for more intensive agriculture. R. D. Blackmore's novel *Lorna Doone* was set here. Area: 686 sq km (265 sq mi).

Exmoor pony A breed of pony originating in the Exmoor region of SW England. It is hardy and sure-footed with a broad deep chest, small hard feet, short ears, and large prominent eyes. The coat is bay, brown, or dun and becomes thick and wiry in winter. Exmoors are used as breeding stock. Height: about 1.27 m (12½ hands). ⌐horse.

Exmouth 50 37N 3 25W A town in SW England, in Devon at the mouth of the River Exe. It is a resort and fishing port, with light industry. Population (1981): 28 787.

exobiology. *See* astrobiology.

Exodus (Greek: going out) The second book of the Bible, traditionally ascribed to Moses. It recounts the events culminating in the departure of the Israelites from Egypt, where they had lived as slaves since the time of Joseph, and their arrival at Mount Sinai, where the *Ten Commandments are given to Moses. The narrative also includes the story of the birth of Moses, the establishment of the *Passover, and the miraculous crossing of the Red Sea. The events themselves perhaps date from the 15th century BC; the book was probably compiled between the 9th and 4th centuries BC.

exorcism The religious practice of driving out evil spirits by means of prayers and other ritual acts. It is a common rite in a number of religions, including ancient Judaism, and was adopted by Christianity on the basis that it was performed by Christ and the apostles in the New Testament. It refers specifically to the prayers, etc., used to expel evil spirits that supposedly possess a person. Although still available in some Churches, the rite may only be performed by a priest with a bishop's permission.

exosphere. *See* atmosphere.

expanding universe The theory that the universe is expanding was first confirmed by Edwin *Hubble in 1929 following observations that the light from distant galaxies is subject to a *redshift, which arises from the recession of the galaxies from us (and from each other). The expansion can be explained by the *big-bang theory. *See also* Hubble constant.

expansion The general increase in dimensions of a substance with increasing temperature. In solids it is caused by the greater vibrational energy of the atoms leading to increased interatomic distances. In liquids and gases the expansion is caused by the greater velocities of the atoms or molecules. The expansion of an ideal gas is described by *Charles's law. The **expansivity** *or* **coefficient of linear expansion** of a substance is its increase in length per unit length caused by a rise in temperature of 1°C.

explosives Substances that can be made to produce a large volume of gas very suddenly. The energy of the expanding gases may be used for a number of industrial or military purposes. There are three main types. **Mechanical explosives** depend on a physical reaction, such as overloading a container of gas until it bursts. They are little used except in specialized mining applications where the release of gas from chemicals is undesirable. In **nuclear explosives**, a nuclear chain reaction (*see* nuclear energy) takes place in a

sudden uncontrolled manner, releasing energy almost instantaneously. This is used for bombs and occasionally for mining. Most explosives used are **chemical explosives**. These include *TNT, *nitroglycerin, *dynamite, and *gelignite. Modern high explosives are often in the form of water gels, which are plastic, water resistant, and easy to handle safely.

exponential function A mathematical function of the general form Ae^{Bx} where A and B are constants and e is the base of natural *logarithms. Bx is called the exponent; if the exponent is a complicated expression, $f(x)$ say, then the function is often written as $\exp[f(x)]$. The function e^x has the important property that its differential is always equal to the function itself. *See also* calculus.

exposure meter A device for measuring the intensity of light falling on a photographic *camera, used to determine the film exposure time and lens *f-number needed to suit the lighting conditions. It often consists of a *photocell that is directed at the subject from the camera, registering light as a reading on an electric current meter. In some cameras this current is used to control the aperture or shutter speed automatically.

expressionism A movement in modern art covering a variety of schools, the common aim of which was to convey the crude force of human emotion. The bright colours and distorted forms of *Van Gogh and *Munch foreshadow expressionism proper. An even earlier forerunner was the German painter *Grünewald. The chief exponents of expressionism were Die *Brücke and Der *Blaue Reiter groups in Germany but independent figures, such as *Rouault, *Soutine, *Schiele, and *Kokoschka also worked in an expressionist style.

extortion In law, a misdemeanour committed by someone holding a public office who, under the guise of his office, wrongfully takes from another money or any valuable thing not due to him. It was abolished in England by the Theft Act (1968) and is now mainly covered by *blackmail.

extrasensory perception (ESP) Acquisition of information not accessible through normal perceptual processes. Three phenomena are usually classified under this heading: clairvoyance (knowledge of distant events and concealed objects), telepathy (thought transference between people), and precognition (knowledge of future events). Evidence for all three tends to be anecdotal, but some experiments in which subjects have been asked to guess symbols on cards of which they can see only the backs or to reproduce, without having seen it, a simple sketch done by another person show a statistically significant success rate. *See also* Rhine, Joseph.

extroversion (*or* extraversion) The tendency to be interested in the outside world more than in oneself. Extroversion is a quality of personality, first described by Carl *Jung and still used in modern theories of personality. Extroverts are gregarious and outgoing. They prefer frequent changes of activity; their interests tend to be practical and scientific rather than philosophical; and they tend to be resistant to permanent *conditioning. *Compare* introversion.

extrusive rock. *See* igneous rock.

eye The organ of sight. The human eyes lie within two bony sockets in the skull and are attached by six muscles, which produce eye movements. At the front of the eye the white fibrous outer layer (sclera) is replaced by a transparent curved layer (*see* cornea). A delicate membrane (the conjunctiva) covers the front of the eye and lines the eyelids: it is liable to become inflamed (*see* conjunctivitis). Light entering the eye is refracted by the cornea and passes through the watery aqueous humour and pupil to the lens. The pigmented *iris controls the amount of light entering the eye. The shape of the lens can be adjusted by means of the ciliary muscles so that an image is focused through the jelly-like vitreous humour onto the *retina. Contraction of the ciliary muscles causes the lens to become

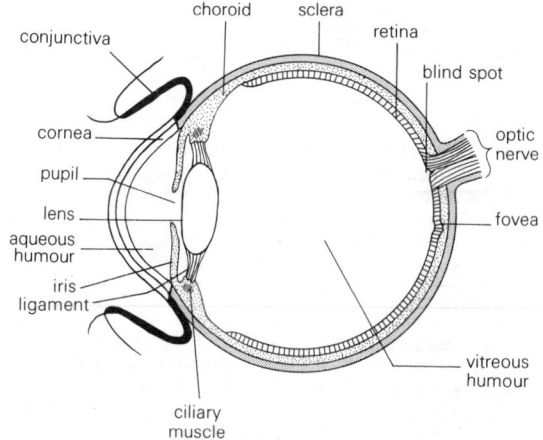

conjunctiva
choroid
sclera
retina
blind spot
cornea
optic nerve
pupil
lens
fovea
aqueous humour
iris
ligament
vitreous humour
ciliary muscle

EYE *The structure of the human eye is revealed in this section. The blind spot, where the optic nerve leaves the eye, contains no visual cells and is therefore insensitive to light. The fovea is the area of acutest vision.*

flattened for focusing distant objects; relaxation of the muscles increases the curvature of the lens for focusing near objects. Light-sensitive cells in the retina send impulses to the brain via the optic nerve. *See also* blindness; longsightedness; ophthalmology; shortsightedness.

eyebright A semiparasitic annual herb of the genus *Euphrasia* (over 130 species), of temperate regions. Eyebrights have small toothed leaves and small unstalked two-lipped flowers, usually white with violet and yellow markings. They grow to a height of 15 cm. Family: *Scrophulariaceae*.

Eyre, Edward John (1815–1901) British explorer and colonial administrator. He led a successful expedition in central Australia (1840–41) and both Lake Eyre and the Eyre Peninsula are named after him. As governor of Jamaica (1864–66) he gained notoriety for his harsh suppression of a revolt (1865), which was followed by over 400 executions. Recalled to England, he was prosecuted by a Jamaican but acquitted.

Eyre, Lake A shallow salt lake of NE South Australia. It is normally dry except during the rainy season when heavy rains from N Queensland and the Northern Territory are fed into the lake by *Cooper Creek and other streams. The last time it was full was in 1950. Lowest point: about 10 m (36 ft) below sea level. Area: about 9100 sq km (3500 sq mi).

Eyre Peninsula A peninsula of South Australia, situated between the Great Australian Bight and Spencer Gulf. Iron ore is mined in the Middleback Range in the NE.

Eysenck, Hans Jürgen (1916–) British psychologist. German-born but educated in France and Britain, Eysenck was appointed professor of psychology at London University in 1955. A critic of conventional psychoanalysis, he developed an alternative treatment—*behaviour therapy—for neurosis and other mental disorders. Eysenck also developed scientifically based methods of evaluating personality and intelligence, partly based on the distinction between introverts and extroverts. His findings on racial differences in intelligence (*Race, Intelligence and Education*, 1971) caused much controversy.

Ezekiel An Old Testament prophet, the successor of *Isaiah and *Jeremiah. **The Book of Ezekiel** records his prophecies probably written during the *Babylonian exile (6th century BC). The prophecies concern the coming destruction of Jerusalem and Israel, denunciations of various foreign states, the renewal of the people, and finally the ideal society and the rebuilding of the Temple at Jerusalem.

Ezra In the Old Testament, a religious reformer, who was sent by the Persian king, possibly *Artaxerxes II (c. 436–358 BC), to regulate Jewish affairs in Jerusalem.

The Book of Ezra in the Old Testament is a sequel to *Chronicles and was compiled by the author of Chronicles and the Book of *Nehemiah. It records the return of the Jews after the *Babylonian exile in about 537 BC, the rebuilding of the Temple, and legal and religious reforms introduced by Ezra.

F

Fabergé, Peter Carl (1846–1920) Russian goldsmith and jeweller. He designed elegant *objets d'art* and was patronized by European royalty. He was especially famous for the jewelled Easter eggs containing surprise gifts given by the tsars to the tsarinas. He died in exile.

Fabian Society A society, named after *Fabius Maximus, formed in London in 1884 for the purpose of peacefully promoting socialist ideas and establishing a socialist state in Britain. Members included George Bernard *Shaw, Sidney and Beatrice *Webb, and Annie *Besant. The Fabians were active in the establishment of the Labour Party and today continue to press the cause of socialism through public lectures, conferences, and publications.

Fabius Maximus, Quintus (d. 203 BC) Roman general of the second *Punic War. Appointed dictator after *Hannibal's defeat of the Romans at Trasimene in 217, Fabius adopted a policy of attrition, harassing Hannibal but avoiding pitched battles. His derogatory title Cunctator (Delayer) became honourable after Hannibal's victory at *Cannae proved the wisdom of Fabius' tactics. It was *Scipio Africanus' aggressive policies, however, that achieved the final triumph over Hannibal, after Fabius' death.

fable A short narrative in prose or verse, often with animal characters, which illustrates a moral truth. The western literary form had its origins in the collection of fables attributed to *Aesop (6th century BC) and later expanded by the Roman poet *Phaedrus (1st century AD). The medieval genre of *beast epic developed from this form, which reached its highest degree of sophistication in the work of *La Fontaine. Authors of children's literature, notably Rudyard *Kipling, Lewis *Carroll, and Beatrix *Potter, have used this form extensively. Modern fables have been written by George *Orwell and James *Thurber.

fabliau A medieval French comic and satiric narrative poem, a type that flourished between 1150 and 1400. About 150 examples survive, mostly simple tales the humour of which is usually broad and obscene. Among known authors is Rutebeuf (*see* trouvères). Chaucer's *Miller's Tale* and *Reeve's Tale* (in the *Canterbury Tales*) are the outstanding examples in English.

Fabre, Jean Henri (1823–1915) French entomologist, noted for his studies of bees, wasps, and other insects. From his observations, Fabre realized the importance of inherited instinct in insect behaviour. He wrote many popular books, including *Souvenirs entomologiques* (1879–1907).

Fabricius ab Aquapendente, Hieronymus (1537–1619) Italian physician. Fabricius was a student of *Fallopius and himself became an eminent teacher, one of his pupils being William *Harvey. Among Fabricius' contributions were studies of embryology and fetal development (*De formata foetu*, 1600) and his discovery of one-way valves in veins.

Fabritius, Carel (1622–54) Dutch painter of portraits and everyday life. In contrast to his teacher Rembrandt, he specialized in daylight scenes, which had some influence on Vermeer. He was killed in an explosion in Delft, which probably also destroyed many of his works; his masterpiece, *The Goldfinch* (The Hague), survives.

Fabry, Charles (1867–1945) French physicist, who while working at the Sorbonne discovered *ozone in the upper atmosphere (1913). This discovery was made with the Fabry-Pérot interferometer, an instrument that he had designed in collaboration with Alfred Pérot (1863–1925) in 1896.

factoring The commercial practice of buying trade debts and collecting them on behalf of clients. If a manufacturer sells his products to a number of customers, some of whom may be slow payers, he can sell these debts to a factor, who will usually pay 80% of the debt immediately and the balance (less a service charge) when the debt has been collected. This service is often combined (for an extra charge) with credit insurance, enabling the debt to be guaranteed even if the debtor fails.

Factory Acts A series of UK parliamentary Acts that regulate conditions of work in factories. A response to the appalling conditions resulting from the *industrial revolution, the early Factory Acts (1802, 1819, 1833) were primarily concerned with the employment of children. Ashley (later Lord *Shaftesbury), leader of the ten-hour movement, was largely responsible for the Acts of 1844 and 1847, the achievements of which were consolidated in subsequent 19th-century legislation. The safety, health, and welfare of factory workers is now regulated by the Factories Act (1961), which is increasingly being replaced by the Health and Safety at Work Act (1974).

Fadden, Sir Arthur William (1895–1973) Australian statesman; prime minister (1941) following Menzies' resignation. He was leader of the Country Party (1941–58).

faeces The material that is expelled from the bowels through the anus. It is a solid or semisolid mass consisting of undigested food (chiefly cellulose and other fibres), mucus, bacteria, and material from the liver, including bile pigments (which are responsible for the colour of faeces). Any persistent change in the appearance of the faeces may be an indication of disease. *See also* constipation; diarrhoea.

Faenza 44 19N 11 54E A town in N Italy, in Emilia-Romagna. During the 15th and 16th centuries it was famous for the manufacture of maiolica earthenware, especially *faience, and a ceramics museum was founded here in 1908. Population (1981 est): 54 904.

Faeroe Islands (*or* Faroe Islands; Danish name: Faerøerne) A Danish group of self-governing islands in the N Atlantic Ocean, between the Shetland Islands and Iceland. 17 of the 22 islands are inhabited, the chief ones being Strømø, Østerø, and Vaagø. Chiefly hilly, the terrain limits agriculture to sheep raising and the production of hay and potatoes. Fishing and fish processing are important. Area: 1400 sq km (540 sq mi). Population (1980): 43 609. Capital: Thorshavn, on Strømø.

Fahd Ibn Abdul Aziz (1922–) King of Saudi Arabia and prime minister (1982–). He succeeded his half-brother, Khalid Ibn Abdul Aziz.

Fahrenheit scale A temperature scale in which the temperature of melting ice is taken as 32 degrees and the temperature of boiling water, as 212 degrees. Named after the German physicist Gabriel Fahrenheit (1686–1736).

Fa-hsien. See Fa Xian.

Faidherbe, Louis (Léon César) (1818–89) French soldier and colonial administrator. He rose to prominence as governor of Senegal (1854–65), where he established French supremacy and founded Dakar. During the Franco-Prussian War (1870–71), as commander in chief of the Army of the North, he temporarily contained the German advance in the NE. He was also a noted archaeologist.

faience Several kinds of tin-glazed earthenware made in France. Strictly, *faience* is French shorthand for *porcellana di Faenza*, a species of *maiolica made in Italy, and the technique of coating fragile porous earthenware with impervious hard white opaque tin glaze derives from maiolica. Italian potters were using the method in France in the 16th century. Centres of production during the 17th and 18th centuries were Lyons, Marseilles, Moustiers, Nevers, and Rouen. Designs drawn from local history (*faience parlante*) and revolutionary events (*faience patriotique*) were popular variations. Richly painted baroque and *rococo styles are common.

Fairbanks 64 50N 147 50W A town in central Alaska. It is the terminus of the Alaska Railroad and the Alaska Highway. The University of Alaska (1935) is situated here. Population (1980): 53 983.

Fairbanks, Douglas (Julius Ullman; 1883-1939) US film actor. With D. W. Griffith, Charlie Chaplin, and his wife Mary Pickford he founded United Artists Corporation in 1919. His films, in which he played the roles of handsome athletic heroes, include *The Mark of Zorro* (1920) and *The Black Pirate* (1926). His son **Douglas Fairbanks Jr** (1909-) was also a film actor. He played roles similar to those of his father, in films such as *The Prisoner of Zenda* (1937) and *Sinbad the Sailor* (1947). He lived for many years in Britain.

Fair Deal The programme of social reform pursued by Harry S. Truman, president of the USA (1945-53). It promised more extensive social security and better labour conditions but only some of its recommendations (notably slum clearance and increased old-age benefits) passed Congress.

Fairfax, Thomas, 3rd Baron (1612-71) English general, who as commander in chief of the *New Model Army defeated Charles I at *Naseby. Fairfax subsequently opposed the king's execution and resigned his command in 1650 in protest against the planned invasion of Scotland. After Cromwell's death he participated in the restoration of Charles II.

fairies Supernatural beings that are half man, half spirit. Folklore depicts them as enigmatic beings skilled in magic and illusion, benevolent or harmful in turn. Some tales tell of their aid to, and even intermarriage with, humans, but others of their abduction of humans, especially children, for whom changelings were substituted. It has been suggested that they represent memories of extinct indigenous peoples, such as the Picts. Modern fairies are usually shown as small, but in folklore they were frequently tall and awesomely beautiful.

Fair Isle 59 32N 1 38W A sparsely inhabited island in the North Sea, off the N coast of Scotland between the Orkney and Shetland Islands. It is famous for its knitted goods with intricate patterns and has an important bird-migration observatory; other occupations include fishing. Area: 16.5 sq km (6 sq mi).

fairy bluebird A songbird of the genus *Irena* (2 species), occurring in tropical evergreen forests and feeding chiefly on fruit and nectar. The blue-backed fairy bluebird (*I. puella*) of Indomalaysia has a glossy black plumage with a bright-blue back and tail and red eyes. Family: *Irenidae* (leafbirds).

fairy penguin The smallest of the *penguins, *Eudyptula minor*, also called little penguin. About 30 cm tall, it is the only penguin commonly occurring on Australian coasts, breeding in dense colonies and nesting in crevices or disused burrows.

fairy shrimp A *crustacean, belonging to the order *Anostraca*, that occurs in mainly freshwater pools and ponds of arid regions (*compare* brine shrimp). It has an elongated body, up to 25 mm long, without a carapace and swims on its back using 11-19 pairs of appendages. Subclass: *Branchiopoda*.

fairy stories Tales for children of a more or less simple kind, involving fantastic or supernatural elements. Most originate in oral tradition, although some are rewritten in sophisticated form, as with *Perrault's *Tales of Mother Goose* (1697); others, like Oscar *Wilde's *The Happy Prince* (1888), are purely literary in origin. The most famous collection of oral tales is *Kinder- und Hausmärchen* (1812-13) by the brothers *Grimm. Probably the most famous writer of

original tales is the Dane Hans Christian *Andersen. Fairy tales often transcend national boundaries; similar tales are found throughout all European countries and sometimes even in the Far East.

Faisal I (1885-1933) King of Iraq (1921-33). He played an important part in the Arab revolt during World War I. After the war he was briefly King of Syria before the French occupation (1920). In 1921 the British installed him as king in mandatory Iraq.

Faisalabad (name until 1979: Lyallpur) 31 25N 73 09E A city in NE Pakistan. It is the centre of an agricultural region specializing in cotton and wheat. Population (1981 est): 1 092 000.

Faisal Ibn Abdul Aziz (1905-75) King of Saudi Arabia (1964-75). A son of *Ibn Saud, Faisal represented Saudi Arabia at the UN. In 1958 he became the real ruler of Saudi Arabia, although his brother *Saud was still nominally king until abdicating in 1964. His reign saw the increased international importance of Saudi Arabia as an oil-producing country. He was assassinated by his nephew.

faith healing (*or* spiritual healing) The curing of illness or disability by supernatural means. The temple of *Asclepius at *Epidaurus was a famous faith-healing centre in antiquity. Christ is credited with several miraculous cures (Matthew 9.2-7, etc.). The need for healing within the framework of the organized churches was recognized by Archbishop William *Temple, who founded the Council for Health and Healing in 1944. Some charismatic healers apparently achieve cures unaccountable to science, particularly at mass rallies where powerful emotional effects operate upon the patients, but the possibilities for deception by callous tricksters are obvious and frauds frequently occur.

Faiyum, El (*or* al-Fayyum) 29 19N 30 50E A city in N Egypt, in the Libyan Desert. Nearby is the ancient site of Crocodilopolis, where the crocodile-god Sobek was worshipped. An agricultural centre, it manufactures cotton textiles. Population (1983 est): 206 100.

Fakhr ad-Din II (c. 1572-1635) Ruler of Lebanon (1593-1633). He took advantage of the weakness of the Ottomans to expand into Syria and Palestine, but in 1635 was captured and executed in Istanbul. He is sometimes seen as a forerunner of Lebanese nationalists.

fakir (Arabic: poor man) A Muslim mendicant who practises ascetic and religious exercises, often a member of a Muslim sect or of a Sufi religious brotherhood (*compare* dervishes). In India the term is applied more generally to any (Muslim or Hindu) ascetic or yogi.

Falabella The smallest breed of pony, developed by the Falabella family in Argentina using Shetland pony stock. It has a fine soft coat of any colour and is popular as a mount for small children. Height: 38-76 cm (3¾-7½ hands).

Falaise 48 54N 0 11W A small town in NW France, in the Calvados department. It is best known as the site of the castle of the Dukes of Normandy, in which William the Conqueror was born. The town was virtually destroyed during the Normandy campaign (*see* World War II).

Falange Española The Spanish Fascist party, created in 1933 by José António *Primo de Rivera. The Falange wanted to regenerate Spain by means of revolution but rejected socialism as atheistic and alien to Spanish traditions. In 1937 Franco merged the Falange with the various Nationalist parties to create the National Movement, which became Spain's only legal party after the Civil War.

Falashas An Ethiopian tribe, who practise an early form of Judaism. They adhere closely to the Bible but do not have the postbiblical Jewish literature or observances. In recent years many Falashas have been introduced to modern Judaism and some emigrated to Israel. In early 1985 the Israelis organized a secret airlift of over 7000 Falashas to Israel from famine-stricken Ethiopia.

falcon A ground-nesting bird of prey belonging to a widely distributed family (*Falconidae*; 58 species). 15–60 cm long, falcons are characterized by long pointed wings and a notched hooked bill. True falcons belong to the genus *Falco;* they kill small birds in flight with their claws or seize small mammals from the ground. The small falconets occur in tropical regions and usually feed on insects. Order: *Falconiformes* (falcons, hawks, etc.). *See also* caracara; gyrfalcon; hobby; kestrel; lanner; merlin; peregrine.

falconry (*or* hawking) The sport of hunting small animals or birds with falcons, other hawks, or sometimes eagles. It was practised in Asia from the 8th century BC and was very popular in Europe from late medieval times to the 17th century. Traditionally the birds are either taken as fledglings (eyasses) or caught as one-year-old birds (passagers) or fully mature birds (haggards), but because many hunting birds are now protected species, they are often bred in captivity. They are then trained to sit hooded on the gloved fist and, by the use of a lure (an imitation bird with meat attached), to hunt and kill (but not retrieve). Large species, such as the peregrine falcon, need open land, while smaller species are used in wooded country.

Falkirk 56 00N 3 48W A town in Scotland, in Central Region on the Forth-Clyde Canal. Here Bonnie Prince Charlie defeated Gen Hawley in 1746. Formerly a prominent market town, Falkirk now has iron founding and aluminium rolling. Population (1981): 37 734.

FALCONRY *Illustration from a treatise on falconry (1248) by Frederick II.*

Falkland Islands (Argentine name: Islas Malvinas) An island group and British crown colony in the S Atlantic Ocean. The main islands of the group of about 100 are East and West Falkland; its dependencies to the SE are *South Georgia and the *South Sandwich group. The population is almost entirely of British origin. Sheep farming is the main occupation on the islands' rough moorland, producing wool for export (chiefly to the UK). *History*: the first landing was by Capt John Strong in 1690. In the early 19th century the islands became a British colony. During World War I the naval battle of the Falkland Islands, in which the Germans were decisively defeated by the British, was fought off Falkland (8 December, 1914). Argentina has long made claims to the group and on 2 April, 1982, invaded the islands. A task force sent by the UK recaptured the Islands on 14 June, after considerable loss of life on both sides. Since then Argentina has refused to declare a cessation of hostilities and the British government has refused to discuss a transfer of sovereignty. A new airport, opened in 1985, improved communications with Britain, and declaration of a fishing zone led to tripling of its income in 1987. Area: 12 173 sq km (4700 sq mi). Population (1980 est): 1813. Capital: Stanley.

Falla, Manuel de (1876–1946) Spanish nationalist composer. He lived in Paris (1907–14), where he met Ravel and De-

bussy, and spent his last years in Argentina. His music was heavily influenced by Spanish folksong and he is best known for his ballet scores *Love the Magician* (1915) and *The Three-Cornered Hat* (1919), *Nights in the Gardens of Spain* (for piano and orchestra; 1909–15), and a concerto for harpsichord and chamber ensemble.

Fallopian tubes. *See* ovary.

Fallopius, Gabriel (1523–62) Italian anatomist, who discovered the tubes leading from the ovaries to the uterus, which were named after him (Fallopian tubes). A pupil of the great anatomist *Vesalius, Fallopius described the semicircular canals of the ear and many features of the reproductive system in his *Observationes anatomicae* (1561).

fallout Radioactive particles deposited from the atmosphere after a nuclear explosion. If large the particles are deposited within a radius of a few hundred kilometres during the first few hours after the explosion. This is known as local fallout. Tropospheric fallout may occur anywhere along the same line of latitude as the explosion during the first week after the explosion. Particles drawn high into the atmosphere can cause stratospheric fallout for several years.

fallow deer A *deer, *Dama dama*, native to Mediterranean forests but widely kept in parks and woodlands. About 90 cm high at the shoulder, fallow deer are fawn with white spots in summer, becoming greyish in winter; males have flattened antlers with numerous points. They feed mainly on grass but also browse on leaves.

Falmouth 50 08N 5 4W A resort in SW England, in Cornwall at the mouth of the Fal estuary. It has a magnificent harbour with repair dockyards and fishing, especially oysters. Population (1981): 18 525.

False Decretals A collection of mostly forged decrees compiled in 9th-century France, but incorporated into *Isidore of Seville's compilation of decrees of Church councils. They were used to establish the authority of the papacy at the time of its ascendancy up to the 11th century and were accepted as genuine throughout the middle ages, being finally discredited only in 1558.

False Dimitrii. *See* Time of Troubles.

Falster A Danish island in the Baltic Sea, linked by bridge to Sjælland and Lolland. Area: 513 sq km (198 sq mi). Population (1981 est): 49 556. Chief town: Nykøbing.

Falun 60 37N 15 40E A town in central Sweden. Copper mining, important since early times, declined in the 17th century. Other industries include engineering and chemical industries. Population (1983): 51 192.

Famagusta 35 07N 33 57E A port in Cyprus, on the E coast. Founded in the 3rd century BC, it did not develop until the 13th century AD, when Christians fled here from Palestine. It has an old walled town and a gothic cathedral (now a mosque). Its port handles most of the island's freight cargo. Population (1982 est): 39 500.

family planning. *See* contraception.

fandango A Spanish dance with three beats to the bar performed by a man and a woman to the accompaniment of guitar and castanets. The dance begins slowly and becomes gradually faster; the dancers freeze when the music stops.

Fang A Bantu people of West Africa comprising a number of tribes in N Gabon, Equatorial Guinea, and S Cameroon. They were originally a warlike hunting people but became ivory traders and craftsmen under colonial rule. Cocoa farming is now important and the Fang have prospered in the post-independence period.

Fangio, Juan Manuel (1911–) Argentinian motor-racing driver, who won 24 Grand Prix races and was world champion a record five times (1951, 1954–57).

Fa Ngum (c. 1316–c. 1373) King of Lan Xang (*or* Lang Chang), which embraced most of present-day Laos, Thailand, and part of Cambodia (1354–73). He proclaimed himself king after forcing the Lao chiefs of the upper Mekong to accept his sovereignty. He then launched further conquests to the S and W. Wearied by constant warfare, his subjects rebelled in 1373, forcing him to abdicate.

Fanning Island (*or* Tabuaeran) 03 52N 159 22W A coral atoll in the W central Pacific Ocean, in Kiribati in the Line Islands. Copra is exported. Area: 33 sq km (13 sq mi). Population (1980): 434.

fantail A *flycatcher of the genus *Rhipidura* (24 species), of S Asia and Australasia, having a long fan-shaped tail. Fantails are 16–22 cm long with a grey, black, or reddish-brown plumage, often with patches of white on the breast, tail, and face.

fantasia (*or* fantasy) In the 16th and 17th centuries, a piece of music (typically for viols or a keyboard instrument) having a polyphonic character. In the early 19th century the name was applied by such composers as Mozart and Beethoven to extended compositions that did not follow the *sonata form. It is also a piece of music constructed from themes from an opera or a number of well-known tunes, such as Liszt's fantasia on Mozart's opera *Don Giovanni*.

Fantin-Latour, (Ignace) Henri (Joseph Théodore) (1836–1904) French painter, born in Grenoble. He is best known for his flower paintings and portrait groups, particularly of his impressionist friends in *Studio in the Batignolles Quarter* and *Homage to Delacroix* (both Louvre).

fanworm A marine *annelid worm belonging to the family *Sabellidae*, also called peacock or feather-duster worm. Fanworms build a parchment-like tube, up to 45 cm long, from which protrudes a feathery crown of tentacles that trap food particles and absorb oxygen. Class: *Polychaeta*.

FAO. *See* Food and Agriculture Organization.

farad (F) The *SI unit of electrical capacitance equal to the capacitance of a parallel-plate capacitor with a potential difference of one volt across its plates when the capacitor is charged with one coulomb. Named after Michael *Faraday.

Faraday, Michael (1791–1867) British chemist and physicist. Born into a poor London family, Faraday was apprenticed to a bookbinder where he found the books to excite his first interest in science. After attending lectures at the Royal Institution he persuaded Sir Humphry *Davy to take him on as his assistant (1813), eventually succeeding Davy there as professor of chemistry (1833). His earliest scientific work was on the liquefaction of gases (1823) and his first major contribution to science was the discovery of benzene (1825). However, it is with electricity and electrochemistry that his name is permanently linked. After discovering the process of electrolysis (1832) he went on to work out the laws that control it (*see* Faraday's laws of electrolysis), no mean feat for a scientist without mathematical training. In electricity, he discovered the connection between electricty and magnetism and, independently of Joseph *Henry, first showed that electromagnetic induction was possible. He used induction to produce the first electrical generator (1831) and also the first transformer. Faraday was a deeply religious man; he had a breakdown in 1839 after which he did little creative work.

Faraday constant The quantity of electricity equivalent to 1 mole of electrons, i.e. the product of *Avogadro's number and the electronic charge. It has the value 96 487 coulombs per mole.

Faraday effect The rotation of the plane of polarization of plane-polarized light when it travels through certain substances in a direction parallel to the lines of force of an applied magnetic field. The effect occurs in quartz and water and is named after Michael *Faraday.

Faraday's laws of electrolysis Two laws formulated by M. Faraday in 1813–14. (1) The mass of a substance produced by an electrolytic reaction varies directly with the amount of electricity passed through the cell. (2) The masses of substances produced by a given amount of electri-city are proportional to the equivalent masses of the substances.

These empirical laws are now understood to hold simply because electricity is composed of uniform discrete particles (electrons). *See also* electrolysis.

farce (from Latin *farcire*: to stuff) A dramatic genre intended only to amuse its audience, a less sophisticated and less intellectual form than pure comedy. Elements common to most farce include peculiar situations, improbable coincidences, and ridiculous exaggerations of character and physical action. The term originally described comic interludes—"stuffing"—in medieval French religious plays. Some of the best farces were written in the late 19th century, notably those of Feydeau and Labiche in France and Pinero and W. S. Gilbert in England.

Far East The countries and areas of E and SE Asia bordering on the Pacific Ocean. It includes Siberia (Soviet Union), China, North and South Korea, and Japan and sometimes Indonesia, Malaysia, and the Philippines. The term is often generally applied to all the countries of E and SE Asia.

Fareham 50 51N 1 10W A town in S England, in Hampshire on Portsmouth Harbour. Its industries include boatbuilding, engineering, and horticulture (particularly strawberry growing). It is also a market town and sailing centre. Population (1981): 88 274.

Farel, Guillaume (1489–1565) French Protestant reformer. Forced to leave France in 1524 because of his beliefs, he settled in Geneva. Although banished from the city, he later returned and succeeded in establishing Protestantism there in 1536. From 1537 he worked with *Calvin, having persuaded him to stay in Geneva.

Farewell, Cape 59 50N 43 40W The S tip of Greenland, on Egger Island. A headland rising to 600 m (2000 ft), it is edged with rocks and is known for its bad weather.

Fargo 46 52N 96 49W A city in the USA, in North Dakota on the Red River. Named after the pioneer expressman W. G. Fargo, it is the trading centre of an agricultural region. The North Dakota State University was established here in 1890. Population (1980): 61 383.

Fargo, William. *See* Wells, Henry.

Farnaby, Giles (c. 1565–1640) English composer. He wrote some fine canzonets in four parts and more than 50 of his pieces for the virginals were included in the Fitzwilliam Virginal Book.

Farnborough 51 17N 0 46W A town in S England, in Hampshire. The Royal Aircraft Establishment, the UK's chief aeronautical research centre, is situated here and there are annual air displays. Napoleon III and the Empress Eugénie, who lived here in exile, are buried at Farnborough Hill. Population (1981): 45 453.

Farne Islands (*or* The Staples) 55 38N 1 36W A group of about 30 islets and rocks in NE England, off the Northumberland coast. St Cuthbert lived on Inner Farne (the largest) and died here in 687 AD. In 1838 a heroic rescue by Grace *Darling took place from Longstone Island lighthouse.

Farnese, Alessandro, Duke of Parma (1545–92) Italian general in the service of *Philip II of Spain (his uncle). In 1571 he fought the Turks at *Lepanto and from 1577 served against the *Revolt of the Netherlands. As governor general of the Netherlands (1578–92), he regained the southern provinces, making peace at *Arras (1579). In 1585 he captured Antwerp following a 13-month siege.

Farnham 51 13N 0 49W A market town in SE England, in Surrey. It has a 12th-century castle, formerly the palace of the Bishops of Winchester, and Waverley Abbey (1128) is nearby. Population (1981): 35 289.

Faro 37 01N 7 56W A port in S Portugal, on the Atlantic Coast. Pillaged by the English in 1596, it was almost destroyed in the earthquakes of 1722 and 1755. It is now a popular tourist town with agricultural industries and sardine fishing. Population (1981 est): 28 622.

Faroe Islands. *See* Faeroe Islands.

Farouk I (1920–65) The last king of Egypt (1936–52). His inability to prevent British intervention in Egyptian affairs, and defeat in the first Arab-Israeli War (1948–49), led to his overthrow and exile in Monaco.

Farquhar, George (1678–1707) Irish dramatist. After studying and acting in Dublin he won immediate success in London with his first play, *Love and a Bottle* (1699). His two best-known plays, *The Recruiting Officer* (1706) and *The Beaux' Stratagem* (1707), replaced the highly mannered and cynical conventions of Restoration drama with a more natural sentimental style.

Fasciola. *See* liver fluke.

fascism A 20th-century political movement. Taking its name from the *fasces*, the bound bundles of rods that symbolized the authority of ancient Roman magistrates, fascism first became an organized movement in Italy in 1919 under *Mussolini. Social and economic backwardness, fear of communist revolution, and frustrated national ambitions following World War I encouraged its growth, and in 1922 Mussolini's *Blackshirts came to power. Fascism became more doctrinaire, rejecting ideas of individual liberty and equality, emphasizing national or racial superiority, and concentrating authority on a dictatorial cult figure. In Germany Hitler, who came to power in 1933 as leader of the *Nazi Party, added antisemitism to fascist militarism and anticommunism. World War II destroyed Mussolini's and Hitler's dictatorships and fascism won little support in other countries, except in Spain, where Franco's regime survived almost 40 years. The term fascist is now often used pejoratively to describe any advocate of extreme right-wing views.

Fashoda incident (1898) A confrontation between Britain and France at Fashoda in the Egyptian Sudan over their rival claims to the area. French forces under Jean-Baptiste Marchand (1863–1914) occupied the fort at Fashoda, which quickly brought *Kitchener and his Anglo-Egyptian force to the spot. After months of diplomatic wrangling, which brought the two countries to the brink of war, France was forced to withdraw and Britain's claims were recognized.

Fassbinder, Rainer Werner (1946–82) German film director. Working with a small group of actors in Munich, he produced a rapid succession of bleak realistic films on contemporary social themes. These include *The Bitter Tears of Petra von Kant* (1972), *Fear Eats the Soul* (1974), *Despair* (1978), and *The Marriage of Maria Braun* (1979).

fast reactor A nuclear reactor (*see* nuclear energy) in which natural uranium enriched with uranium-235 or plutonium-239 is used without a moderator, the chain reaction being sustained by fast neutrons. In these reactors the core is surrounded by a blanket of natural uranium into which neutrons escape. These neutrons collide with U-238 nuclei to form U-239 nuclei, which decay to the fissionable isotope Pu-239. By suitable design, more Pu-239 can be produced in the blanket than is required to enrich the fuel in the core. These reactors are therefore called **breeder reactors** and they are 50 times more economical in uranium usage than *thermal reactors.

Their main disadvantage is that the temperature is so high that a liquid metal (usually sodium) has to be used as coolant: any leakage of sodium could be disastrous. Also, plutonium is both extremely toxic and can be used to make *nuclear weapons. For these reasons fast breeder reactors, although under development in several countries, are somewhat unpopular.

Fatah, al- (Arabic: the victory) A Palestinian organization, also known as the Palestine National Liberation Movement, established in the late 1950s. Led by Yassir *Arafat, al-Fatah began guerrilla warfare against Israel in the mid-1960s. By the early 1980s, the organization had split into factions pro and anti Arafat.

Fatehpur Sikri 27 06N 77 39E A deserted city in Uttar Pradesh (N India). Founded (1569) by *Akbar, it was the Mogul capital until Akbar's move to *Lahore (1585). Its palaces, mosques, and gateways are masterpieces of *Mogul architecture, notably the Buland Darwaza (Victory Gate).

Fateh Singh, Sant (1911–72) Sikh religious leader and civil-rights campaigner. He joined with other Indian leaders in opposing British rule. After independence he agitated for an autonomous Punjabi-speaking Sikh state (established in 1966) and was leader of the rural Sikh population.

Fates In Greek mythology, three goddesses who determine human destinies. The daughters of Zeus and Themis, they are: Lachesis, who assigns a person's position at birth; Clotho, who spins out the thread of his existence; and Atropos, who cuts the thread at death.

Fathers of the Church The title given to certain writers of the early Christian Church whose works were regarded as carrying special weight in matters of doctrine and who were noted for their great learning and holiness. The period in which they lived extends from the 1st to the 7th centuries, and they are classified as ante-Nicene or post-Nicene according as to whether they lived before or after the Council of *Nicaea (325). They include Tertullian, Athanasius, Ambrose, Augustine, Jerome, and Gregory the Great.

fathom A unit used to express depths of water. Originally intended to be the distance between a man's fingertips with his arms outstretched, it is equal to six feet. It has now largely been replaced by the metre.

Fátima 39 37N 8 39W A village in central Portugal. It was here that three children allegedly saw a vision of the Virgin Mary (1917); it is now a place of pilgrimage.

Fatimah (d. 632) The daughter of *Mohammed. She married *Ali and was the mother of his sons, Hasan and Husayn, from whom most of the Shiite *imams were descended. She died shortly after her father. The Fatimid caliphs claimed descent from her.

Fatimids A dynasty of *caliphs ruling in N Africa and Egypt (909–1171). The Fatimids claimed descent from *Fatimah, Mohammed's daughter, and formed a subsect of the *Ismaili. They seized power in Tunisia in 909 and conquered Egypt in 969. In the 11th century their power declined and the caliphs became puppets in the hands of their soldiers. In 1171 they were finally overthrown by *Saladin. □Cairo.

fats and oils *Lipid substances formed by the combination of glycerol with *fatty acids. Fats occur widely in animals and plants as an energy store and as insulating material. Vegetable fats and oils are used in making soaps, margarines, cooking oils, paints, and lubricants. Animal fats are used in foods, soaps, and candles. Oils are distinguished from fats by being liquid at 20°C, whereas fats are solid. Mineral oils are hydrocarbons rather than lipids (*see* oil).

fatty acid (*or* carboxylic acid) An organic acid that comprises one or more carboxyl groups (–COOH) attached to an alkyl group. Fatty acids combine with glycerol to form glycerides, the main constituents of *fats and oils. Animal fats tend to be hard because they contain a high proportion of saturated fatty acids; soft fats, such as vegetable and fish oils, contain greater proportions of unsaturated and polyunsaturated fatty acids (containing one or more double bonds). There is evidence to suggest that the risk of heart disease associated with dietary fat is reduced if the fat consumed is rich in polyunsaturated fatty acids. Certain essential fatty acids are normally required in small amounts in the diet.

Faulkner, William (1897–1962) US novelist. Born in Mississippi, he abandoned his university education to write. He supported himself with various jobs before publishing his first poetry collection, *The Marble Faun*, in 1924. *Sartoris* (1929), the hero of which is based on Faulkner's great-grandfather, also an author, was the first of his stories set in the fictitious Yoknapatawpha County, based on his native northern Mississippi. A tragic decaying society, its characters and their personal tragedies acquire an epic universal grandeur. His major novels, usually experimental in form and technique, include *The Sound and the Fury* (1929), *Absalom, Absalom!* (1936), and *The Reivers* (1962). He was awarded the Nobel Prize in 1949.

fault A fracture plane in the rocks of the earth's crust, the rocks on each side being displaced relative to one another, either vertically, horizontally, or obliquely. Faulting occurs as a result of accumulated strain in the rocks, usually at plate margins (*see* plate tectonics). The extent of vertical displacement of the strata is called the throw; the horizontal displacement is the heave. A horst is an upstanding feature between two parallel faults; conversely a graben or rift valley is downthrown between parallel faults. *See* Plate II.

Fauré, Gabriel (Urbain) (1845-1924) French composer and organist, a pupil of Saint-Saëns. He became organist at the Madeleine (1877) and director or the Paris conservatoire (1905). He was afflicted with deafness in later life. His works include the well-known *Requiem* (1886-87), incidental music for Maeterlincke's play *Pelléas and Mélisande* (1898), the opera *Pénélope* (1913), the orchestral *Pavane* (1887), and much piano music and chamber music. Fauré is probably best known for his songs, such as those in the cycle *La Bonne Chanson* (1891-92).

Faust A legendary medieval German scholar and magician who sold his soul to the Devil in exchange for knowledge and power. Stories of magicians in league with the Devil (often personified by Mephistopheles) combined with the historical Johann Faust (c. 1480-c. 1539), a vagrant scholar and mountebank, to produce a figure who has inspired numerous literary works, notably by *Marlowe (1592), *Lessing (1784), *Goethe (1808, 1832), and Thomas *Mann (1947), as well as musical works, including operas by *Gounod and *Boito. The character of Faust has varied from that of Marlowe's power-seeking magician to that of Goethe's rationalist philosopher.

fauvism A movement in French painting at the turn of the 19th century, characterized by the aggressive use of strong colours. The fauves (French: wild beasts, so called by a critic of their work) included, under the leadership of *Matisse, Raoul *Dufy, Georges *Braque, Georges *Rouault, and Maurice de *Vlaminck. Most of the fauves had become interested in *cubism by 1908.

Fawcett, Dame Millicent Garrett (1847-1929) British campaigner for the vote for women (obtained in Acts of 1918 and 1928); president of the National Union of Women's Suffrage Societies (1897-1919). A sister of Elizabeth Garrett *Anderson, Fawcett opposed the militancy of the Pankhursts. She married **Henry Fawcett** (1833-84), professor of political economy at Cambridge University and an MP (1865-84), who was blind.

Fawkes, Guy (1570-1606) English conspirator. A convert to Roman Catholicism, he served in the Spanish army in the Netherlands during the 1590s and on his return to England became involved in the Gunpowder Plot, led by Robert Catesby (1573-1605), to blow up James I and parliament. The conspirators were informed upon and Fawkes was discovered (5 November, 1605) with the gunpowder in a cellar of the Palace of Westminister. Catesby was killed while resisting arrest and Fawkes was executed. Nov 5 continues to be celebrated with fireworks and the burning on a bonfire of effigies of Fawkes (so-called "guys").

Fa Xian (*or* Fa-hsien; 5th century AD) Chinese Buddhist monk. He travelled to India and Ceylon in about 402 returning to China in about 413 with a large collection of early Sanskrit Buddhist texts. His translation of these and his account of his journey provide important documentation of the beginning of relations between China and India.

FBI. *See* Federal Bureau of Investigation.

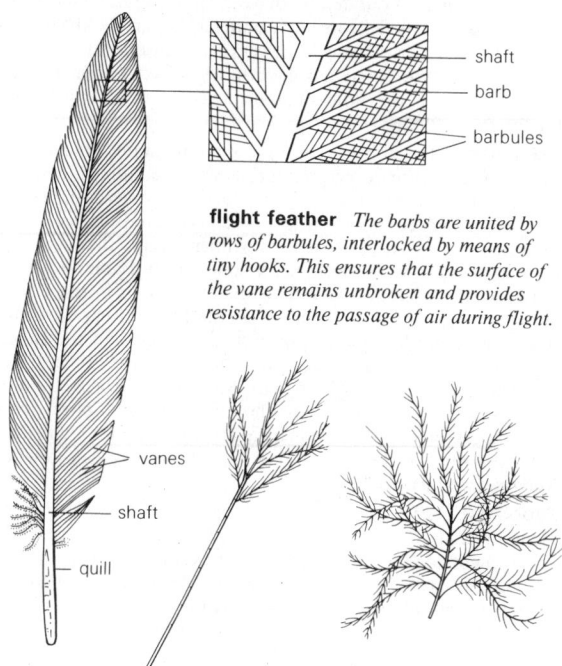

flight feather *The barbs are united by rows of barbules, interlocked by means of tiny hooks. This ensures that the surface of the vane remains unbroken and provides resistance to the passage of air during flight.*

filoplume *This small hairlike feather, which has very few barbs, is found in large numbers between and beneath the quill feathers.*

down feather *This type of feather forms the insulating body covering of nestlings. Its fluffy appearance is due to the lack of interlocking hooks on the barbules.*

FEATHERS

feathers The specialized body covering of birds. Thought to have evolved from the scales of reptilian ancestors, feathers arise from definite tracts over the body surface and are of several types: the down feathers of chicks are short and soft, whereas the quill feathers of adult birds typically have a stiff shaft bearing two vanes with interlocking barbs and are specialized for flight as wing and tail feathers. As well as its role in flight, the plumage has several other functions. Like the hair of mammals, it helps to regulate body temperature and provides protection against the environment. It is also responsible for the bird's distinctive coloration, which is particularly important in courtship or aggressive displays. In order to maintain their function the feathers must be periodically renewed, and most birds undergo at least two moults a year. Moulting is controlled partly by hormones and partly by environmental factors.

feather star. *See* crinoid.

Fécamp 49 45N 0 23E A port in N France, in the Seine-Maritime department on the English Channel. It has an important cod-fishing industry and is famous for its Benedictine liqueur. Population (1982): 21 696.

Fechner, Gustav Theodor (1801-87) German physicist, noted for his work in experimental psychology. Fechner developed techniques for investigating the sensations experienced by human subjects exposed to stimuli of varying strengths. He also proposed a mathematical expression (later shown to be inaccurate) of the theory concerning the just noticeable difference between two stimuli, advanced by E. H. *Weber.

Federal Bureau of Investigation (FBI) The organization within the US Department of Justice that carries out investigations into possible breaches of federal law, especially those related to security. Founded as the Bureau of Investigation in 1908, it became the FBI in 1935; under J. Edgar *Hoover (director 1924–72) it developed considerable autonomy. It was prominent in the campaign against organized crime in the 1930s and also in the anticommunist activities of Joseph *McCarthy in the 1950s.

federalism The political union of separate states, joined together to serve their common interests while retaining a degree of autonomy. A federation usually provides strong central government in such common matters as defence, a national currency system, etc., leaving to state government affairs that depend on local conditions. In most cases states are not able to withdraw from a federation at will, as the *Civil War in the USA demonstrated. In most federations in the 20th century the central government has gained power at the expense of the state government (e.g. in the USA). An exception is the Soviet Union, where republics have been given a greater control over their budgets and in the management of industry. Canada is a federation that is under severe strain owing to the separatist elements in the province of *Quebec. Other federations include those of Malaysia and Australia.

Federalist Party A US political party, led by Alexander *Hamilton and John *Adams, that advocated a strong central government for the infant USA. The Federalists emerged in 1787 as those who wanted to replace the *Articles of Confederation (the nation's first constitution) by the newly written Constitution; they were opposed in this by the Republicans under Thomas *Jefferson, who feared encroachments of individual liberty by a centralized government. The Federalists were in power from 1791 until Jefferson's election as president in 1800 and were responsible for establishing a national administration. After 1800 the Federalist Party declined, their pro-British and aristocratic tendencies being out of touch with America's growing nationalism.

Federal Reserve System The *central bank of the USA, established in 1913, which implements the government's monetary policy. There are 12 Federal Reserve Districts in the USA, each of which has its own Federal Bank, controlled by the Federal Reserve Board in Washington.

Fédération internationale de Football association (FIFA) The world governing body of association football, formed in Paris in 1904. Based in Zurich, it now has over 140 member organizations. It runs the *World Cup competition.

feedback In electronics and communications theory, the process of returning to the input of a device a fraction of the output signal. **Negative feedback**, in which the feedback opposes and therefore reduces the input, is often used in *amplifier circuits. It compensates for noise and distortion in the output signal, although it also reduces the overall amplification. **Positive feedback** reinforces the input signal. If it becomes too high, the circuit oscillates and the output becomes independent of the input. This is the cause of the singing noise heard in a public-address system when the microphone picks up feedback from the loudspeakers.

The principle of negative feedback also operates in biological systems, especially in controlling some biochemical reactions: the product of the reaction inhibits further activity of the enzyme catalysing it.

Feininger, Lyonel (Charles Adrian) (1871–1956) US painter and illustrator, born in New York. He studied painting in Germany and Paris and first worked as an illustrator and cartoonist for various German and French periodicals before concentrating on painting in 1907. His works were exhibited with the *Blaue Reiter group and he taught at the *Bauhaus (1919–33), eventually returning to the USA in 1937. He devel-oped a personal form of *cubism in his oils and watercolours, his favourite subjects being architectural forms, boats, and the sea.

feldspars The most important group of rock-forming minerals and the major constituents of igneous rocks. There are four components of feldspars: anorthite (calcium plagioclase, $CaAl_2Si_2O_8$); albite (sodium plagioclase, $NaAlSi_3O_8$); orthoclase (potassium feldspar, $KAlSi_3O_8$); and celsian (barium feldspar, $BaAl_2Si_2O_8$, which is rare). Feldspars ranging between albite and anorthite in composition are plagioclase feldspars; those ranging between albite and orthoclase are alkali feldspars. Calcic plagioclase includes anorthite, bytownite, and labradorite; sodic plagioclase includes andesine, oligoclase, and albite. Alkali feldspars include sanidine, anorthoclase, orthoclase, microcline, and adularia.

Felidae The *cat family: a family of mammals of the order *Carnivora. It includes the cats, lion, tiger, leopard, and cheetah.

Felix V (antipope). *See* Amadeus VIII.

Felixstowe 51 58N 1 20E A resort in E England, in Suffolk on the North Sea. It has developed rapidly as a container port, with ferry services to Rotterdam and Zeebrugge. Population (1981): 20 858.

Fellini, Federico (1920–   ) Italian film director. He began working in films as an actor and scriptwriter. His films, many of which are characterized by their autobiographical elements and their use of baroque imagery and fantasy, include *La strada* (1954), *8½* (1963), *Roma* (1972), *Amarcord* (1974), *Casanova* (1976), *La città delle donne* (1980), and *Intervista* (1987).

feminism. *See* women's movement.

femur The thigh bone: the longest bone in the human body (*see* Plate IV). It extends from the pelvis, where it forms part of the ball-and-socket hip joint, to the joint of the knee. The head of the femur is commonly fractured in the elderly after falls.

fencing The art of combat with a sword, of which there are three main forms in sport: foil, épée, and sabre. Bouts for all three weapons are fought on a *piste*, or marked-out area 2 × 14 m (6.5 × 46 ft) for foil and épée or 2 × 24 m (6.5 × 78.5 ft) for sabre. A hit is scored against a competitor who crosses the rear limit. The winner is the first to score five hits (for men) or four (for women) in a time limit of six minutes (for men) or five (for women), the form of the hit varying between the three weapons. For major competitions the electric foil and épée are used for automatic judging.

Fénelon, François de Salignac de la Mothe (1651–1715) French Roman Catholic prelate and theologian. As director (from 1678) of an institution for recent Roman Catholic converts, he wrote *Traité de l'éducation des filles* (1687), criticizing the coercive conversion of Huguenots. In 1689 he became tutor to Louis XIV's grandson, the Duke of Burgundy, and in 1695 Archbishop of Cambrai. His famous *Aventures de Télémaque* (1699), written for the duke's instruction, alienated the king and his *Explication des maximes des saints* (1697), containing a defence of *Quietism, was condemned by the pope.

Fenian cycle Irish Gaelic tales and ballads of the Fianna, a legendary band of warrior-poets named after their leader, *Finn MacCool, who was said to have flourished in the 3rd century AD. Many of the tales are collected in *The Colloquy of the Ancient Men* (c. 1200) in which Oisin (*see* Ossian) and Caoilte, members of the Fianna, return to Ireland from the Land of Youth and recount their youthful adventures to St Patrick, and in the manuscripts *The Book of the Dun Cow* (c. 1100) and *The Book of Leinster* (c. 1160).

Fenians Members of a secret Irish-American revolutionary society, the Irish Republican Brotherhood (IRB), formed in 1858 by James Stephens (1825–1901). The Fenians staged an unsuccessful rising in Ireland in 1867 but the IRB's

Parts of a sword

Foil   *The foil weighs a maximum of 500 g. Its blade is quadrangular and very flexible.*

Épée   *The épée weighs a maximum of 770 g. Its blade is triangular and stiffer than that of the foil.*

Sabre   *The sabre weighs a maximum of 500 g. Its blade is a flattened V-shape.*

FENCING

influence continued into the 20th century, when it was superseded by the IRA.

fennec A desert *fox, *Fennecus zerda*, of Africa and the Middle East. It is sandy-coloured and has small pointed ears. Measuring up to 70 cm including the tail (30 cm), it spends the day in a burrow and hunts at night, finding lizards, birds, and insects by ear. □mammal.

fennel A strong-smelling perennial herb, *Foeniculum vulgare*, native to S Europe and cultivated throughout temperate Eurasia. 0.5–1.5 m high, it has feathery dark-green leaves and clusters of small yellow flowers. The leaves are used mostly to flavour foods and sauces. The greenish seeds taste of aniseed and are used to flavour liqueurs, candies, pastries, and sweet pickles. The seed oil is used to scent soaps and perfumes. Florence, or sweet, fennel (*F. dulce*) is cultivated for its bulblike leafstalks, which may be eaten cooked as a vegetable or raw in salads. Family: *Umbelliferae.

Fens, the A low-lying area in E England, W and S of the Wash extending across parts of Cambridgeshire, Lincolnshire, Norfolk, and Suffolk. Once waterlogged, the first drainage attempt was made by the Romans. This was resumed during the 17th century by the Duke of Bedford and his engineer, Cornelius Vermuyden, creating the Bedford Level. Now virtually all drained, the Fens form one of the most fertile areas in the UK, producing cereals, vegetables, potatoes, and bulbs (especially around Spalding).

fenugreek An annual herb, *Trigonella foenum-graecum*, native to the Mediterranean but widely cultivated. About 60 cm high, it has toothed compound leaves and small white flowers that develop into slender curved pods. The brownish seeds are used to flavour curry and chutney. Family: *Leguminosae.

fer-de-lance A common extremely venomous tropical American *pit viper, *Bothrops atrox*. It is much feared by plantation workers and often visits houses in search of rodents. 1.2–2 m long, it has a broad triangular head, is grey or brown with black-edged diamond patterning and a yellowish chin, and generally feeds on small mammals, frogs, and lizards.

Ferdinand (1865–1927) King of Romania (1914–27), who in 1916 joined the Allies in *World War I. In 1918 he annexed Bessarabia from Russia and in 1919 intervened in Hungary to destroy Kun's communist government.

Ferdinand (I) the Great (?1016–65) King of Castile (1037–65). He conquered León (1039) and resumed the offensive against the Moorish border kingdoms, reducing the rulers of Toledo, Saragossa, and Seville to tributaries.

Ferdinand I (1503–64) Holy Roman Emperor (1558–64). His elder brother, Emperor *Charles V, gave him the Habsburg possessions in Germany in 1521 and in 1526 he became King of Bohemia and of Hungary, although his title to the Hungarian crown was challenged by John Zápolya (1487–1540) until 1538. Ferdinand negotiated the religious Peace of *Augsburg (1555).

Ferdinand I (1751–1825) King of Naples and Sicily (Two Sicilies; 1816–25). As Ferdinand IV he was King of Naples (1759–99, 1799–1806), being twice driven into exile in Sicily by the French. He ruled the Two Sicilies despotically.

Ferdinand I (1793–1875) Emperor of Austria (1835–48) and King of Hungary (1830–48). Feeble minded and epileptic, he was dominated by *Metternich. He abdicated during the Revolution of 1848.

Ferdinand I (1861–1948) Prince (1887–1908) and King (1908–18) of Bulgaria. In 1908 Ferdinand declared Bulgaria independent from Turkey but was forced to abdicate in 1918 after supporting the Central Powers.

Ferdinand II (1578–1637) King of Bohemia (1617–37) and Hungary (1618–37) and Holy Roman Emperor (1619–37), who championed the *Counter-Reformation. In 1619 the predominantly Protestant diet (assembly) of Bohemia offered the Bohemian crown to the Protestant, *Frederick V of the Palatinate. The ensuing dispute developed into the *Thirty Years' War. Initially successful, Ferdinand suffered reverses with the intervention into the war of France and Sweden, forcing him to accept the compromise Peace of Prague (1635).

Ferdinand III (1608–57) King of Bohemia and of Hungary (1625–57) and Holy Roman Emperor (1637–57). He created a standing army, reformed the imperial council, and helped conclude the *Thirty Years' War by signing the Peace of *Westphalia (1648).

Ferdinand (V and II) the Catholic (1452–1516) King of Castile as Ferdinand V (1474–1504) and of Aragon as Ferdinand II (1479–1516). He ruled Castile jointly with his wife *Isabella I of Castile and after her death was regent for their daughter Joanna the Mad. Ferdinand's accession to the Aragonese throne effected the union of Castile and Aragon, to which Granada, taken from the Moors in 1492, was added. The introduction of the Inquisition (1480) and the expulsion of the Jews (1492) aimed to strengthen both church and monarchy, to which Ferdinand's reforms in Aragon contributed. His ambitions abroad led to wars with France for hegemony in Italy.

Ferdinand VII (1784–1833) King of Spain (1808, 1814–33). In 1808 Ferdinand was forced by Napoleon to abdicate but returned to the throne in 1814. His repressive policies caused a liberal uprising (1820) and the establishment of a liberal government until 1823, when it was ousted with French help. Alfonso repudiated the Salic Law of succession to enable his daughter *Isabella to succeed him, an act that led to the emergence of *Carlism.

Fergana (*or* Ferghana) 40 23N 71 19E A city in the S Soviet Union, in the Uzbek SSR. It is the industrial and cultural centre of the fertile Fergana Valley, one of the country's main cotton-, silk-, and fruit-growing districts. Population (1984): 191 000.

Feriae The sacred festival days of ancient Rome, which were usually marked by a public holiday, feasts, prayers, and sacrifices to the gods. Feriae were normally held on fixed annual dates.

Ferlinghetti, Lawrence (1919–) US poet. His public readings and his publishing business, the City Lights Bookshop in San Francisco, promoted *Beat movement poetry. His own poetry, published in *Pictures from the Gone World* (1955), *Tyrannus Nix?* (1969), and other collections, is largely political satire. A journal, *Back Roads to Far Places*, was published in 1971.

Fermanagh A former county in SW Northern Ireland, bordering on the Republic of Ireland. It consists of hilly country contained chiefly in the Erne Basin and is divided by the Upper and Lower Lough Erne. It is predominantly agricultural producing livestock and potatoes. Industries include the production of clothing, cotton thread, and tweeds. Area: 1851 sq km (715 sq mi). County town: Enniskillen.

Fermat, Pierre de (1601–65) French mathematician. Professionally a lawyer, Fermat studied mathematics in his spare time. He founded *number theory and, with Blaise *Pascal, *probability theory. He is best known for *Fermat's last theorem and *Fermat's principle.

Fermat's last theorem A theorem, first proposed by Pierre *Fermat, that there are no natural numbers x, y, z, and n such that $x^n + y^n = z^n$ when n is greater than two. The theorem has never been proved for the general case, only for particular examples of n. Fermat himself claimed to have proved it but he never recorded his proof.

Fermat's principle When light travels between two points its path is such that the time taken is a minimum. The principle holds when the light is reflected or refracted between the two points. It is also known as the principle of least time and is named after P. *Fermat.

fermentation The process by which microorganisms and tissues respire in the absence of oxygen (i.e. anaerobically). The fermentation of carbohydrates by yeasts to form alcohol is the basis of making wines and beers (*see* beer and brewing; wine) and the production of industrial alcohol. Other types of fermentation produce lactic acid, as in the souring of milk by bacteria. Fermentation can cause the decomposition of organic materials under anaerobic conditions but the organisms concerned are able to use only a small proportion of the available energy compared to aerobic organisms.

Fermi, Enrico (1901–54) US physicist, born in Italy. His early work in Italy was concerned with the mathematical statistics of nuclear particles; independently of *Dirac he produced the form of statistics known as *Fermi-Dirac statistics. For his work on the bombardment of uranium by thermal neutrons he was awarded the 1938 Nobel Prize. Because of his antifascism and because his wife was Jewish, Fermi and his family sailed direct from the Stockholm Nobel ceremony to the USA, where he remained for the rest of his life. He was the first person to achieve a controlled nuclear chain reaction, in a converted squash court at Chicago University (1942). He later played a central role in the development of the atom bomb at Los Alamos. After his return to Chicago (1946) he bitterly opposed *Teller in the development of the hydrogen bomb.

Fermi-Dirac statistics A quantum-statistical method of analysing a system of indistinguishable particles to determine the probability of the energy distribution. Unlike *Bose-Einstein statistics it assumes that these particles, which are known as fermions, obey the *Pauli exclusion principle. Named after E. *Fermi and P. A. M. *Dirac.

fermion Any elementary particle that obeys *Fermi-Dirac statistic. These particles, which have half-integral spin, include *leptons and *baryons. *Compare* boson.

fermium (Fm) An artificial transuranic element, named after Fermi. Like *einsteinium it was found in debris from the 1952 hydrogen-bomb explosion. The most stable isotope, ^{257}Fm, has a half-life of 80 days. At no 100; at wt (257).

fern A perennial leafy *pteridophyte plant of the class *Pteropsida* (or *Filicinae* according to some classification schemes; about 9000–15 000 species), most abundant in shady damp tropical regions but also widely distributed elsewhere. The life cycle of a fern shows *alternation of generations. The fern plant itself is the asexual (sporophyte) generation, which has a creeping underground stem (rhizome) bearing roots and aerial fronds, which reach a height of 25 m in the *tree ferns. The fronds are feather-like and usually divided one or more times into leaflets. Asexual spores are produced in spore capsules, which usually occur in clusters (sori) protected by a covering (indusium) on the underside of the leaflets. The spores develop into the inconspicuous sexual (gametophyte) generation—a tiny heart-shaped plant (called a prothallus) producing egg and sperm cells. The fertilized egg cell develops into a new sporophyte plant, which grows up from the prothallus. Many tropical and subtropical ferns are cultivated as house plants for their attractive foliage.

FERN *The ancestors of these tree ferns helped to form vast Carboniferous forests, 345–280 million years ago.*

Fernandel (Fernand Joseph Desire Contandin; 1903–71) French comedian. Originally a music-hall singer and comedian, he later acted in numerous films, notably a series in the 1950s in which he played a village priest, Don Camillo, in conflict with the communist mayor.

Fernando Po Former name of Bioko (*see* Equatorial Guinea).

Ferrar, Nicholas (1592–1637) English mystic, who founded an Anglican religious community at Little Gidding, Huntingdonshire (now in Cambridgeshire), in 1625. Much admired by Charles I, the community was dedicated to prayer and hard work, being particularly skilled in bookbinding. It was disbanded by the Puritans in 1647.

Ferrara 44 50N 11 38E A town in N Italy, in Emilia-Romagna. Important in Renaissance times as the seat of the Este family, it has a cathedral, castle, citadel, and university (1391). The religious reformer Savonarola was born here. Ferrara has wine, fruit, and grain trades and its manufactures include plastics, sugar, and chemicals. Population (1980 est): 151 643.

Ferrara-Florence, Council of (1438-45) The Church council at which the last concerted attempt was made to resolve the schism between Eastern and Western Churches. The council endeavoured to reach agreement on doctrinal differences, such as the *Filioque clause, and to provide assistance for Constantinople against the Turks. Agreement was reached in 1439 but was short lived.

ferret A domesticated form of *polecat, Mustela putorius, that is slightly smaller than the European polecat and lighter in colour (sometimes albino). Ferrets were probably bred from an Asian race (sometimes called M. eversmanni) and have been domesticated since at least 400 BC; they are used to drive rats and rabbits from their burrows.

Ferrier, Kathleen (1912-53) British contralto singer of outstanding ability. She sang Lucretia in the first performance of Britten's Rape of · Lucretia (1946) and is especially remembered for her performances of Mahler's Das Lied von der Erde as well as Britten's settings of English folksongs. She died of cancer at the height of her career.

Ferrier, Susan Edmonstone (1782-1854) Scottish novelist. Her three satirical novels about Edinburgh society, all published anonymously, were Marriage (1818), The Inheritance (1824), and Destiny, or the Chief's Daughter (1831). She was encouraged by Sir Walter Scott, whom she visited at Abbotsford during his last illness.

ferrimagnetism A form of magnetism occurring in those *antiferromagnetic materials in which the microscopic *magnetic moments are aligned antiparallel but are not equal. The behaviour is weakly *ferromagnetic below the Néel temperature and *paramagnetic above it.

ferrite 1. A compound of iron with the general chemical formula MFe_2O_4, where M is a metal. Most ferrites are *ferromagnetic or *ferrimagnetic ceramic materials and they are used in transformers and computer memories. 2. Iron in its body-centred cubic crystal structure, either pure or as a constituent of *steel.

Ferrol del Caudillo, El 43 29N 8 14W A city in NW Spain, in Galicia on the Atlantic Ocean. A port and naval base, it has ship-building and ship-repairing industries. Gen Franco was born here. Population (1970): 87 736.

ferromagnetism The property of a material that enables it to become a permanent magnet, i.e. ferromagnetic materials when placed in a *magnetic field develop a very strong internal field and retain some of it when the external field is removed. The most common ferromagnetic substances are iron, cobalt, nickel, and alloys of these metals. Ferromagnetism, like *paramagnetism, is caused by the unbalanced spin of atomic electrons, which creates a magnetic dipole moment having the effect of a tiny magnet. In ferromagnetic substances, the application of an external field causes groups of these tiny magnets, called domains, to become aligned; many of them remain aligned when the field is removed. Above a certain temperature, called the Curie point, thermal agitation destroys the domain structure and the substance becomes paramagnetic. The response of a ferromagnetic material to changes in magnetic field is known as the hysteresis effect; the internal field strength remaining after the external field has been reduced to zero is called the remanence.

Fertile Crescent A strip of land in the Middle East roughly comprising the lower Nile Valley, the E Mediterranean coast, Syria, and *Mesopotamia. Formerly enjoying a wetter climate, it was the cradle of civilization, with sites showing evidence of settled communities from at least 9000 BC.

fertility drugs Drugs given to infertile women to stimulate the release of an egg cell from the ovary. The best known are the *gonadotrophins—hormones normally released by the pituitary gland to control activity of the ovary. Another fertility drug is clomiphene. The dosage of these drugs is carefully controlled in order to prevent multiple pregnancies.

fertilization The union of a male and a female *gamete, involving the fusion of hereditary material: it is the essential process of sexual *reproduction. The resulting cell, called a zygote, undergoes division (see cleavage), growth, and development to form a new individual, in which half the chromosomes (and therefore the genes) are of paternal origin and half of maternal origin. In **self-fertilization** both gametes are produced by the same individual; in **cross-fertilization** they derive from different individuals (these terms are applied particularly to the processes in flowering plants). In most aquatic animals the gametes are expelled into the water and fertilization is external; in most terrestrial animals the sperms are introduced into the body of the female, where fertilization takes place.

fertilizers Substances added to soils to maintain or improve soil fertility. Natural farmyard manures have long been used as a source of plant nutrients and humus, which maintains the physical structure of the soil. Other traditional fertilizers have included bone meal, dried blood, and other animal products. Modern artificial fertilizers, dating from the work of J. B. *Lawes and others in the 19th century, provided the means for dramatic increases in crop yields. The major plant nutrients required are nitrogen (chiefly provided as ammonium nitrate derived from fixation of atmospheric nitrogen), phosphate (derived from naturally occurring rock phosphate), and potassium (from mined potash deposits). These fertilizers are used either individually as "straights" or in combined or "compound" form to provide ratios of plant nutrients matched to the crop requirements.

Artificial fertilizers have been of immense benefit in helping to feed a rapidly expanding human population. The view that they are inferior to natural fertilizers is largely unfounded. Plants take in nitrogen ions, etc., in solution through their roots whether the source is a sack of fertilizer or farmyard manure. However, excessive application of artificial fertilizers can lead to pollution of streams, rivers, and even drinking water.

Fès (or Fez; Arabic name: Fas) 34 05N 5 00W A city in N Morocco. In the 14th century the Islamic city reached its peak as a major centre for commerce and learning. It remains important for Arabic and Islamic teaching and has two mosques; the Qarawiyin Mosque is the oldest in Africa and contains a university (859 AD). The city gave its name to the traditional red felt hat worn by Muslims. It is a trade centre for hides and leather, fruit, and traditional crafts. Population (1982): 448 823.

fescue A *grass of the genus Festuca (about 100 species), native to temperate and cold regions of the N hemisphere. It grows in tufts, 46-152 cm high. Meadow fescue (F. pratensis) is sown as a pasture grass and used for livestock fodder; sheep's fescue (F. ovina) grows on mountains and in dry and exposed soil and the variety F. ovina glauca is used in ornamental borders. Red or creeping fescue (F. rubra) is common in grass mixtures for lawns.

Festival of Britain A celebration organized in 1951 to commemorate the Great Exhibition of 1851 and to demonstrate Britain's postwar development. Exhibitions in science, architecture, agriculture, and the arts were organized throughout the country. The main exhibition site was in London, on the South Bank of the River Thames, where the

Royal Festival Hall was built by the London County Council specially for the occasion.

Festival of Light A campaign started in 1971 as a protest against the "permissive society." It is supported by Lord Longford, Malcolm Muggeridge, and Mary Whitehouse and campaigns for the maintenance of strict moral standards.

fetishism 1. In anthropology, the practice of using charms magically. The term derives from the Portuguese *feitico*, something made. Fetishism is found among W African tribes and, hence, in the West Indies. Auguste *Comte characterized primitive religion as essentially fetishism, by which he meant the attribution of human qualities to nonhuman bodies. Later *Tylor reserved the term for the idea of spirits embodied in or associated with material objects. The term is not very common in modern sociology or anthropology. 2. In psychiatry, the abnormal condition in which sexual satisfaction is obtained by handling or otherwise using nongenital objects (fetishes). The fetish may be an article of clothing (such as shoes or underwear), rubber objects, leather, fur, or hair, and in some cases normal sexual relationships are impossible unless the fetish is present.

fetus (*or* foetus) The developing baby in the womb from the beginning of the ninth week of pregnancy until birth. The fetus is protected by a series of membranes enclosing a fluid (amniotic fluid), which can be extracted and used for diagnostic purposes. The fetus is connected through the *umbilical cord and *placenta to the mother's bloodstream. □embryo. *See also* prenatal diagnosis.

Feuchtwanger, Lion (1884-1958) German novelist and dramatist. Exiled in 1933, he fled to the USA in 1940. His best-known novels are historical romances, notably *Jew Süss* (1925) and *The Pretender* (1936). He collaborated with *Brecht on plays and translations.

feudalism The type of land tenure, characteristic of medieval Europe, in which property was held by a vassal of a lord in return for military service and a pledge of homage. Feudalism originated with the collapse of public order in W Europe during the 8th and 9th centuries. Both kings and great lords distributed life grants of lands and offices in return for promises of loyalty and service. This practice developed into the grant of hereditary fiefs or fees (Latin word: *feoda*, from which the word feudalism is derived) in return for military service. The resulting fragmentation of authority was reflected in the rapid growth of feudal armies, often engaged in private wars, the development of the castle as an administrative and military centre, and the growth of private justice administered by local lords rather than by a central authority. From the 12th century these implications of feudal tenure were challenged by the growing power of western rulers, especially in England, where it was abolished in 1661. Their governments increasingly depended on a royal bureaucracy and an army of mercenaries rather than the feudal bands. The growth of towns, outside the feudal framework, also contributed to the decline of feudalism.

Feuerbach, Ludwig Andreas (1804-72) German philosopher. Critical of Hegelian *idealism, Feuerbach saw the power of history not as a nebulous succession of spirits of the ages but as the total material conditions in any given period that caused people to behave as they did. This view and also his writings on religion, in which he argued that people lost their essential selves by applying their own attributes to imaginary beings, impressed *Marx and *Engels.

Feuillants, Club of the A moderate French Revolutionary political group that met at the former monastery of the Feuillants in Paris. Founded in 1791, the Feuillants opposed extremism, favouring constitutional monarchy. They disbanded in 1792, when the monarchy was abolished.

Feuillère, Edwige (Caroline Cunati; 1907-) French actress. Her performance in *La Dame aux camélias* in 1937 was one of her earliest successes as a stage actress and her

films include *L'Aigle à deux têtes* (1947) and *Le Blé en herbe* (1953).

fever A body temperature greater than 37°C (98.4°F). This is most commonly due to *infection, but other causes include tumours, drugs, a heart attack, and a blood clot in the leg. Sometimes no cause can be found (known as p.u.o.—pyrexia of unknown origin). The patient usually has a headache, shivers, and feels ill.

feverfew A perennial aromatic Eurasian herb, *Tanacetum* (or *Chrysanthemum*) *parthenium*, about 50 cm high, with heads of yellow and white daisy-like flowers. Formerly a popular medicinal herb, it was used to reduce fever. Family: *Compositae.

Feydeau, Georges (1862-1921) French playwright, famous for his many farces, written between 1881 and 1916. They are characterized by fast-moving, intricate, and cheerfully immoral plots, witty dialogue, and complicated stage sets. They include *The Lady from Maxim's* (1889), *Hotel Paradiso* (1894), and *A Flea in Her Ear* (1907).

Feynman, Richard Phillips (1918-88) US physicist, who shared the 1965 Nobel Prize with Julian Schwinger (1918-) and Shinitiro Tomonaga (1906-79) for their development of quantum electrodynamics. He is best known for his invention of Feynman diagrams, which illustrate the interactions between charged particles by the exchange of virtual photons.

Fez. *See* Fès.

Fezzan (*or* Fazzan; Latin name: Phazania) An area in SW Libya, forming part of the Sahara. It was a province until provinces were abolished in 1963.

Ffestiniog 52 58N 3 55W A town in North Wales, in Gwynedd. It is a tourist centre in picturesque surroundings. At nearby **Blaenau Ffestiniog** there are extensive former slate quarries and a pumped-storage hydroelectric power station. Population (1981): 5437.

Fianna Fáil (Irish: Soldiers of Destiny) Irish political party, founded in 1926 by Eamon *De Valera from moderate *Sinn Féin members. The ruling party in the years 1932-48, 1951-54, 1957-73, 1977-81, 1982, and from 1987, its leaders have been De Valera (until 1959), Sean Lemass (until 1966), Jack *Lynch (until 1979), and Charles *Haughey.

Fibonacci, Leonardo (c. 1170-c. 1230) Italian mathematician. He travelled widely, especially in North Africa, where he learnt the *decimal system of numerals and the use of zero, which al-Khwarizmi had, in turn, learnt from the Indians. Fibonacci published the system in Europe, but mathematicians were slow to adopt it. In the **Fibonacci series** (0, 1, 1, 2, 3, 5, 8,...) each number is the sum of the preceding two.

fibre (*or* dietary fibre) The constituent of the human diet that is not digested. It consists of the cell walls of plants, i.e. cellulose, lignin, hemicellulose, and pectic substances. Significant amounts are present in wholewheat cereals and flour, root vegetables, nuts, and fruit: highly refined foods, such as sugar, have a low fibre content. Dietary fibre is considered helpful in preventing constipation, diverticular disease, obesity, diabetes mellitus, and colonic cancer: societies with high-fibre diets rarely suffer from these conditions.

fibreglass (glass fibre *or* spun glass) Material made from glass fibre drawn into fine threads. Glass fibre has excellent heat- and fire-resistant properties and is a good electrical insulator. It is spun and woven into curtain material; made into glass wool for heat, electrical, and sound insulation; woven into coarse mats for filters; and used in reinforcing moulded plastics for boats, car bodies, etc.

fibre optics The use of flexible glass fibres for transmitting light. Each fibre, which may be used singly or in bunches, is usually less than a millimetre thick and has a high refractive index. The light inside the fibre is totally internally reflected and travels through the fibre with little loss of intensity. The fibres are highly polished and coated with a substance of lower refractive index further to reduce dispersion. Glass fibres are used for examining otherwise inaccessible places, for example in medical diagnosis and in specialized industrial processes.

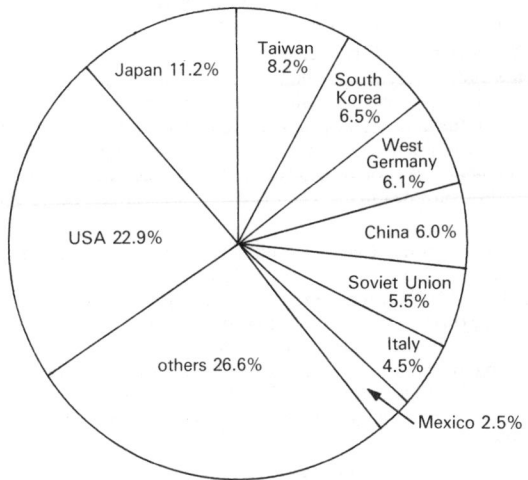

FIBRES   *World production of synthetic fibres (1985).*

fibres   Threadlike substances of animal, vegetable, or man-made origin. *Wool and *silk are the most widely used animal fibres. Vegetable fibres include cotton, flax, hemp, jute, and sisal. Man-made fibres fall into two categories: **modified natural fibres**, including *rayon made from wood cellulose, and **synthetic fibres**, most of which are made by the polymerization of petrochemicals. They include *polyesters, nylon, and *acrylics. Some inorganic substances are also used in the form of fibres: examples include glass (*see* fibreglass; fibre optics), *asbestos, and *carbon fibres.

fibrositis   Inflammation of fibrous tissue, usually of the back muscles and muscle sheaths. This causes sudden pain and stiffness (muscular rheumatism). It is best relieved by rest, but aspirin or similar analgesics may help.

fibula.   *See* leg.

Fichte, Johann Gottlieb   (1762-1814) German philosopher and follower of *Kant. Fichte, however, debunked Kant's world of numinous "things-in-themselves," holding that practical reason and man's autonomously good will originated all that is worthwhile in the world, as well as creating the highest type of human personality. The outer world, a passive place, is the field of action for this human consciousness; by contrast, the Ego, or self, is the only basic reality. The existence of other Egos was, however, essential for the individual's pursuit of moral perfection. Fichte's philosophical works include *Foundation of the Laws of Nature* (1796) and *System of Moral Philosophy* (1798). His popular works strove to kindle German nationalism against Napoleon.

Fichtelgebirge   A mountain range in E West Germany, between Bayreuth and the Czech border. It is mainly wooded (the name means "spruce mountains") and rises to 1051 m (3448 ft) at the Schneeberg. The minerals obtained from it include lead, copper, and marble.

Ficino, Marsilio   (1433-99) Italian Platonist scholar. In 1462, under *Medici patronage, he founded the Platonic Academy to disseminate *Platonism and reconcile it with Christianity. His system was a blend of Neoplatonic metaphysics and Augustinian theology expressed in a hierarchical universe, with strata ranging from body to angels and God. Experience consisted of the ascent of man's immortal soul towards God. Ficino's translations of Plato (1484) remained standard for many years.

fiddler crab   A small burrowing *crab, 25-30 mm long, belonging to the genus *Uca* (about 65 species). The brightly coloured male has an enlarged claw, which it holds somewhat like a violin. Fiddler crabs are found on salt marshes and sandy beaches of tropical and temperate regions, feeding on algae and other organic material. Tribe: *Brachyura.*

field   In physics, a region of space in which a body possessing certain properties can exert a force on similar bodies, when they are not in contact. For example, a body having mass exerts an attractive force on all other massive bodies as a result of its gravitational field. Similarly, an electrically charged body exerts a force (attractive or repulsive, depending on polarity) on other charged bodies and a magnetized body will have a magnetic field around it. A field is often represented by lines of force to indicate the direction in which the force acts at that point. The closeness together of the lines represents the strength of the force, and therefore the field, in that area.

Field, Cyrus West   (1819-92) US businessman, who helped to finance the laying of the first transatlantic telegraph cable, achieved in 1866 after several unsuccessful attempts. He later diversified into railways and newspapers.

Field, John   (1782-1837) Irish pianist and composer. He was taught by Clementi in London and demonstrated Clementi's pianos to buyers. In 1802 they journeyed to Russia and Field settled in St Petersburg as a teacher and composer. After various European tours he returned to Moscow at the end of his life. Field composed much piano music and created the piano "nocturne"; his music influenced Chopin.

field emission   The emission of electrons from the surface of certain materials when they are subjected to a very high electric field. Typically fields of about 10^{10} volts per metre are required. The effect is also known as cold emission or autoemission. It is utilized in the **field-emission microscope**, in which a magnified image of a surface is obtained by subjecting it to a high electric field and observing the distribution of emitted electrons on a cathode-ray screen.

fieldfare   A *thrush, *Turdus pilaris*, of N Europe and Siberia, migrating to S and W Europe. It is about 25 cm long with a speckled brown breast, brown back, white underwings, and blue-grey head.

Fielding, Henry   (1707-54) British novelist and dramatist. He wrote about 25 plays, mostly satirical and topical comedies, between 1728 and 1737, when Walpole's Licensing Act effectively banned his vigorous satire; he then turned to journalism and law studies. *Shamela* (1741), a parody of Samuel Richardson's novel *Pamela* (1740), is almost certainly by Fielding. His major novels include *Joseph Andrews* (1742), the ironical *Jonathan Wild* (1743), and *Tom Jones* (1749). In 1749 he was appointed magistrate for Westminster and Middlesex; in this post he helped develop the Bow Street Runners into an efficient *police force. He died in Lisbon.

fieldmouse   A small nocturnal long-tailed *mouse, *Apodemus sylvaticus*, of Europe, Asia, and N Africa, also called woodmouse. About 9 cm long, with an 8-cm tail, it has a rich brown coat with white underparts. Fieldmice feed on seeds and grain and can become a pest. □ p. 444.

Field of the Cloth of Gold   (1520) The meeting near Calais of Henry VIII of England and Francis I of France. Francis hoped for English support against Emperor Charles V, with whom, however, Henry subsequently formed an alliance.

Fields, Gracie   (Dame Grace Stansfield; 1898-1979) British popular entertainer. She began her career as a music-hall singer and comedian and made several films during the 1930s, notably *Sing as We Go* (1934). During World War II she gave many concerts for the troops; she lived in Capri.

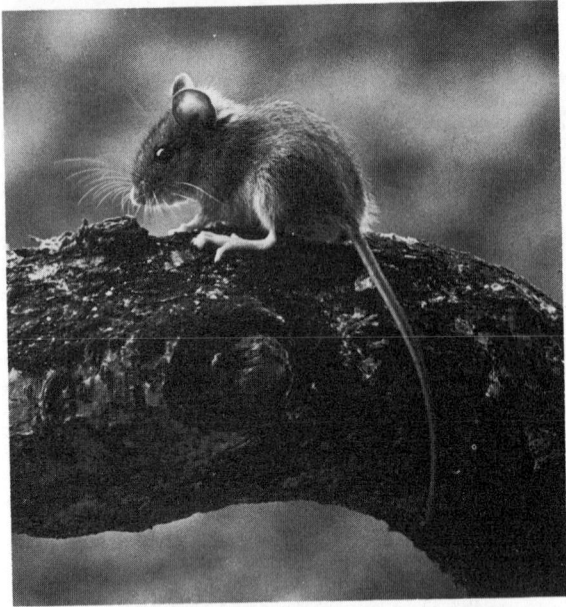

FIELDMOUSE *This mouse tends to prefer succulent food (peas, fruit, leaves, etc.) to dry grain and is sometimes found in houses, as well as gardens.*

Fields, W. C. (William Claude Dukenfield; 1880–1946) US film actor. After working as a vaudeville juggler and comedian he began making films in the 1920s. In *The Bank Dick* (1940), *My Little Chickadee* (1940), and other films, he exploited his genuine eccentricity and intolerance of sentimentality.

Fieschi A leading family of Genoa (Italy) during the 13th, 14th, and 15th centuries. The Fieschi, who were *Guelfs, wielded much political influence as ambassadors, admirals, generals, cardinals, and even popes—*Innocent IV and Adrian V (d. 1276; reigned 1276) were Fieschi.

Fiesole 43 48N 11 17E A town in Italy, in Tuscany situated on a hill near Florence overlooking the River Arno. It has Etruscan and Roman remains and a romanesque cathedral. It is mainly residential. Population (1981 est): 14 486.

FIFA. *See* Fédération internationale de Football association.

fife A small transverse *flute, pitched in B flat and used in military fife-and-drum bands.

Fife, Duncan. *See* Phyfe, Duncan.

Fife Region An administrative region in E Scotland, bordering on the North Sea, coextensive with the former county of Fife. It consists of a lowland peninsula located between the Firths of Forth and Tay. Agriculture is most important in the N, especially on the fertile coastal belt, with the production of cereals, potatoes, and sugar beet. Industry, concentrated in the S, includes iron working, marine engineering, and aluminium refining. Coalmining has declined although the region contains some of Scotland's most modern pits. Area: 1305 sq km (504 sq mi). Population (1981): 326 480. Administrative centre: Glenrothes.

Fifteen Rebellion. *See* Jacobites.

Fifteen Years' War (1591–1606) A struggle between the Austrian Habsburgs and the Ottoman Turks for the possession of Hungary that followed 50 years of intermittent skirmishing. Neither side gained an ascendency but the stalemate was ended when István Bocksay (1557–1606) of Transylvania rebelled against the Habsburgs, made a treaty with the Turks, conquered Habsburg Hungary, and established Transylvania as an effective buffer state between the two belligerents.

fifth column A body of enemy sympathizers working within a country. The term originated in the Spanish Civil War when the Nationalist, Gen Emilio Mola (1887–1937), is supposed to have said "I have four columns operating against Madrid and a fifth inside composed of my sympathizers."

Fifth Monarchy Men An extremist Puritan sect in England in the mid-17th century, which believed in the imminence of the fifth monarchy of Christ that, according to Daniel 2, would succeed the monarchies of Assyria, Persia, Macedonia, and Rome (*see* millenarianism). They supported the *Barebones Parliament but turned against Cromwell when he established the *Protectorate (1653). Their two rebellions (1657, 1661) were suppressed.

fig A spreading tree or shrub, *Ficus carica*, 1–12 m high, probably native to W Asia but widely cultivated in warm temperate and subtropical regions. The dark-green leathery leaves are large (up to 30 × 25 cm) and usually deeply lobed. The tiny flowers are borne inside a fleshy pear-shaped structure, up to 8 cm long, which develops into the edible fig after fertilization of the flowers. Figs—eaten fresh, dried, or preserved—are rich in sugar and iron and have laxative properties. Family: *Moraceae* (mulberry family).

fighting fish One of several *labyrinth fishes, especially of the genus *Betta*, found in SE Asia and the Malay Archipelago. The males are aggressive towards each other and some brood eggs in their mouths. The Siamese fighting fish (*B. splendens*) is about 6.5 cm long and greenish or brown in colour. Long-finned and brightly coloured varieties are bred for use in fighting contests.

fig marigold A plant of the genus *Mesembryanthemum* (about 200 species), found in warm regions, especially South Africa, and cultivated as ornamentals. Fig marigolds are often succulent, with large brilliantly coloured daisy-like flowers and figlike fruits. Family: *Aizoaceae*.

figwort A herbaceous plant of the genus *Scrophularia* (120 species), of N temperate regions. 30–100 cm tall, they have toothed leaves. The brown, yellow, or green flowers are almost spherical, with five small spreading lobes around the opening. A common Eurasian species is *S. nodosa*. Family: *Scrophulariaceae*.

Fiji, State of A country in the S Pacific Ocean. It consists of over 800 islands, only 106 of which are inhabited; the largest are Viti Levu and Vanua Levu. Most of the population are Indians and Fijians with some Europeans, Chinese, and other Pacific islanders. *Economy*: chiefly agricultural, sugar cane being the main cash crop; others include copra and ginger. Some gold is mined on Viti Levu and the chief exports are sugar, copra, coconut oil, and gold. Tourism is important. Fiji is an important staging post on the air routes between North America and Australia and New Zealand. *History*: discovered by the Dutch explorer Tasman in 1643, the islands were visited by Capt Cook in 1774. During the 19th century the search for sandalwood brought many ships and tribal warfare was widespread until Fiji was ceded to Britain in 1874. It became independent within the British Commonwealth in 1970. In 1987 the newly elected Indian-dominated government of Dr Timoci Bavadra was overthrown in a military coup by native Fijian elements under Col Sitiveni Rabuka. A second coup led by Rabuka later the same year resulted in the declaration of a republic and the withdrawal of the Queen as head of state. Official language: English. Official currency: Fiji dollar of 100 cents. Area: 18 272 sq km (7055 sq mi). Population (1987 est): 714 000. Capital and main port: Suva.

Filarete (Antonio Averlino; c. 1400–c. 1469) Italian Renaissance architect. Originally a sculptor, he moved in 1451 to Milan where he designed his masterpiece, the

Ospedale Maggiore. He wrote a treatise on architecture (1461-64) and, although he built little, was influential in promoting Italian classicism.

filaria A parasitic *nematode worm, mainly of central Africa, Asia, and the SW Pacific. The species *Wuchereria bancrofti* and *Brugia malayi* cause the disease **filariasis**. The tiny larval worm, measuring about 1.4 mm, enters the body in the saliva of a biting mosquito or mite. It then grows up to 8 cm long in lymph and blood vessels, causing swelling and pain (*see* elephantiasis).

filbert A Eurasian shrub, *Corylus maxima*, closely related and similar to the *hazel. It is sometimes planted for its nuts, which are larger than hazelnuts and are partly hidden by long bracts.

filefish A *bony fish belonging to a family (*Monacanthidae*) found in warm coastal waters. It has a laterally flattened body, 13-26 cm long, covered with small filelike or velvety scales, two dorsal fin spines, and a very small mouth. Order: *Tetraodontiformes*.

Filioque (Latin: and the Son) An article of Christian faith in the Western Church, added to the *Nicene Creed and referring to the *Holy Spirit, "Who proceedeth from the Father *and the Son*" (rather than from the Father alone). It had appeared in Spain as early as 447 but was not adopted at Rome until the 11th century. The Orthodox Church did not accept it and attacked it as an unwarranted addition made to the Creed by Rome. *Photius denounced it in the 9th century and it was one of the central issues—together with disagreement over the nature of the primacy of the *papacy—that culminated in the schism between East and West in 1054.

Fillmore, Millard (1800-74) US statesman; president (1850-52). A New York lawyer, as vice president (1849-50) he supported the 1850 Missouri Compromise on the extension of slavery, which helped delay civil war for ten years. Succeeding to the presidency when Zachary Taylor died, he lost abolitionist support by introducing the Fugitive Slave Law and was not nominated as presidential candidate in 1852.

film A thin flexible strip of cellulose acetate, or similar transparent plastic, coated with a light-sensitive emulsion. A black-and-white photographic emulsion usually consists of gelatin containing tiny suspended crystals of silver halide (usually bromide or chloride). After exposure to light in a *camera these crystals are easily reduced to metallic silver when treated with the chemicals in the developer. This produces black deposits of fine particles of metallic silver on the parts of the film upon which the light has fallen, giving a reversed (or negative) image. Fixing of the film consists of bathing it in sodium thiosulphate (hypo) or other fixers to render the unchanged silver halides soluble, enabling them to be washed away with water. The sensitivity (speed) of film is usually quoted as an *ASA rating, which determines the amount of light required to form a given amount of metallic silver. *See also* colour photography.

films. *See* cinema.

filter A device that allows one substance to pass through it but not others. For example, a filter is used to remove solid particles from a liquid or gas by passing the mixture through a porous substance, such as paper or *fibreglass, the holes in which are fine enough to prevent the passage of the particles. Such filters are used in some air-conditioning units, for water purification, etc. In optics, coloured glass filters are used to select light with a certain range of wavelengths. In electronics, filters are circuits used to allow alternating currents of a certain frequency range to pass, while currents with frequencies outside the range are stopped.

finch A songbird belonging to a family (*Fringillidae*; 176 species) occurring in most regions of the world except Australia. Finches have hard conical bills used to crack open seeds, although they also feed on buds and fruit. They range in size from 10 to 27 cm and the plumage varies in colour with the species. There are two subfamilies: the *Fringillinae*, including the finer-billed *chaffinch and *brambling of the Old World, and the *Carduelinae*, comprising the heavier-billed species found in both the Old World and North America. *Compare* weaverfinch.

Finchley A district in the Greater London borough of Barnet. Finchley Common, of which little now remains, was once a haunt of highwaymen.

Fine Gael (Irish: Tribe of Gaels) Irish political party, formed in 1933. It was the senior member of ruling coalitions in Ireland (1948–51, 1954–57, 1973–77, 1981–Jan 1982, and Dec 1982–1987), led by John Costello (1891–1976), Liam *Cosgrave, and Dr Garret *FitzGerald. It is more conservative than the rival *Fianna Fáil.

fineness of gold A measure of the purity of gold equal to the number of parts of pure gold in 1000 parts of the alloy. *See also* carat.

finfoot A secretive semiaquatic bird belonging to a family (*Heliornithidae*; 3 species) found in dense vegetation bordering rivers and creeks of tropical and subtropical regions of America, Africa, and Asia. Up to 60 cm long, finfoots have olive-brown plumage and large lobed feet, a long neck, and a stiff rounded tail. Order: *Gruiformes* (cranes, rails, etc.).

Fingal's Cave A spectacular cave on the Scottish island of Staffa, in the Inner Hebrides, composed of basaltic columns. Visited by Felix Mendelssohn (1829), it inspired his overture *Fingal's Cave* (1829, revised 1832). Length: 68 m (227 ft). Height: 35 m (117 ft).

arch   whorl   loop

FINGERPRINT *Loops are the commonest form of pattern (c. 65%), followed by whorls (c. 30%), and then arches (c. 5%).*

fingerprint The impression made by the pattern of ridges on the palmar side of the end joint of the fingers and thumbs. The taking of a person's fingerprints, which are virtually unique, for the purpose of identifying habitual criminals was introduced into the UK in 1901, largely as a result of the work of Sir William Herschel (1833–1917) and Sir Edward Henry (1859-1931). The print is taken by rolling the fingers and thumbs, one by one or simultaneously, in ink and then rolling them on paper. Fingerprints left at the scene of a crime may be taken by photography. The task of classifying and identifying fingerprints is immensely complicated. Scotland Yard has a library of over two million prints of known criminals and the FBI in the USA has more than 70 million. Classification relies on a numerical value given to a print, which identifies the finger and the pattern of ridges (of which there are 1024 primary groups).

Finisterre, Cape 42 52N 9 16W The most westerly point in Spain, on the Atlantic coast.

Finland, Gulf of An arm of the Baltic Sea, extending between Finland and the Soviet Union. The ports of Helsinki and Leningrad lie on the Gulf, which is frozen for 3-5 months of the year. Length: about 400 km (249 mi).

Finland, Republic of (Finnish name: Suomi) A country in N Europe, with S and W coastlines on the Baltic Sea. It includes the *Åland Islands, situated at the mouth of the Gulf of Bothnia. The land is generally low lying apart from some small hills in the NW. Over 10% of the area consists of lakes, which, together with rivers and canals, provide an extensive network of inland waterways. The majority of the population are Finns, with minorities of Swedes, Lapps, and Russians. *Economy*: agriculture is highly mechanized and, together with cereals, dairy produce is of particular importance. Over 70% of the land is under forest, providing ample resources for the timber and pulp and paper industries. Other industries include food processing and textiles. Hydroelectricity provides the main source of power and the principal mineral resources are copper and iron ore. Tourism is an important source of revenue. The main exports are timber, pulp and paper, and machinery. *History*: prehistorically the Finnic peoples migrated into Finland, gradually driving the Lapps northwards. Conquered by Sweden in the 12th century AD, Finland continued to enjoy a considerable degree of independence, becoming a grand duchy in the 16th century. The country suffered considerable hardships, however, in the recurring wars between Sweden and Russia. In the 18th century the SE was occupied by Russia and in 1809 the rest of the country was ceded to Russia, becoming an autonomous grand duchy. During this period Finnish nationalism flourished and in 1863 the Finnish language was officially recognized. It became independent in 1917, following the Russian Revolution, and a republic two years later. In 1939 it was invaded by Soviet forces and in 1940, and again in 1944, was forced to cede certain territories to the Soviet Union. A treaty of friendship between the two countries, first signed in 1948, continues in force. Dr Urho Kaleva Kekkonen (1900-86), who had been president since 1956, resigned in 1981 and was succeeded by Dr Mauno Henrik Koivisto (1923-   ). Official languages: Finnish and Swedish. Official currency: markka of 100 pennia. Area: 305 475 sq km (117 913 sq mi). Population (1983 est): 4 850 000. Capital and main port: Helsinki.

Finlay, Carlos Juan (1833-1915) Cuban physician, who discovered that yellow fever was transmitted by mosquitoes. By 1900, Finlay had persuaded the authorities to control mosquito populations and so eradicate the disease. *See also* Reed, Walter.

Finney, Albert (1936-   ) British actor. Following his early successful performances in plays by modern dramatists he made several films, notably *Saturday Night and Sunday Morning* (1960). He then returned to the theatre to act classic roles, such as Tamburlaine and Hamlet.

Finnic A group of languages of the *Finno-Ugric branch of the Uralic family, which includes Finnish, Estonian, Lapp, Mari, Permic, and a number of other languages, most of which are dwindling in significance. The Finnic peoples, ancestors of the modern Finns and Estonians, migrated in prehistoric times from central Russia to the area of the E Baltic, Finland, and Karelia, bringing grain cultivation with them. Estonia became an important trading area and established a sense of national identity while the Finns inhabited more remote regions and remained fragmented until recent times. The *Lapps in the far north of the region retain their separate identity and language but other groups have mainly lost theirs. All these peoples adopted Christianity during the 11th and 12th centuries.

Finn MacCool A legendary Irish hero, leader of the Fianna (*see* Fenian cycle). The son of Cumhaill (Cool) and the father of the poet Oisin (*see* Ossian), he killed Goll MacMorna, his father's murderer, and became leader of the company.

Finno-Ugric languages A large group of languages of the *Uralic family, spoken by more than 20 million people in dispersed communities in Scandinavia, E Europe, and W Asia. Thought to have diverged about five millennia ago, the Finnic and Ugric languages can be further divided into the following major groups: Ugric (*Hungarian and Ob-Ugric) and *Finnic (Finnish, Estonian, Mari, Permic, and a number of other languages mostly spoken in the Baltic and in the region of the Volga). Periodically and to varying degrees, neighbouring languages have exercised an influence on the vocabularies of the Finno-Ugric languages. Many Turkic forms, for example, have been absorbed into the Hungarian language. Although phonological processes may be shared by the majority of Finno-Ugric languages no single defining characteristic is common to all members.

fins Organs of locomotion and balance in fish and some other aquatic animals. The fins of fish are supported by bony or cartilaginous fin rays and are either median or paired. The median fins include the tail (or caudal) fin, typically used for propulsion (in conjunction with the muscular body) and the dorsal and anal fins, used for balancing. The paired pectoral fins, just behind the gills, and pelvic fins, further back, are used for steering (although in rays the large pectorals provide motive force).

Finsen, Niels Ryberg (1860-1904) Danish physician, who developed the use of light for treating certain bacterial skin diseases. Although now superseded, his work stimulated research into modern radiation therapy. He founded the Medical Light Institute (now the Finsen Institute), Copenhagen, in 1896 and was awarded a Nobel Prize (1903).

Finsteraarhorn 46 32N 8 08E A mountain in S central Switzerland, the highest in the Bernese Oberland. It was first climbed in either 1812 (disputed) or 1829. Height: 4274 m (14 022 ft).

Fiordland The largest national park of New Zealand, in SW South Island. It is a mountainous region with glacial lakes and fjords, including Lakes Manapouri and Te Anau (famous for its glowworm caves), and Milford Sound. Until the construction of the Homer road tunnel (1953), many parts of Fiordland were virtually inaccessible. Area: about 11 400 sq km (4401 sq mi).

fir A coniferous □tree of the genus *Abies* (about 50 species). Mostly native to N temperate regions, these trees are also called silver firs, as many species have leaves with a silvery undersurface. Firs have blunt-tipped needles and erect stout woody cones; they are important softwood trees (*see* timber). The European silver fir (*A. alba*), which forms pure forests in the mountains of central Europe, is widely grown for its timber: it reaches a height of 50 m and its cones are up to 15 cm long. Another widely planted timber tree is the grand, or giant, fir (*A. grandis*), which grows up to 90 m in its native W North America. Family: *Pinaceae*.

Firbank, (Arthur Annesley) Ronald (1886-1926) British novelist. His wealthy family background gave him liberty to write his short witty impressionistic novels, such as *Caprice* (1917), *Valmouth* (1919), and *Prancing Nigger* (1924). His homosexuality and his conversion to Roman Catholicism are major influences on his work.

Firdausi (Abul Qasim Mansur; c. 935-c. 1020) The first major Persian poet, famous as the author of the epic poem *Shah-nama* (*The Book of Kings*; 1010), which recounts the history of Iran and its rulers from legendary beginnings to the conquest of the country by Arabs in 641 AD. It includes the tragic legend of Sohrab and Rustum, familiar to English readers in Matthew *Arnold's version. The *Shah-nama* was written in some 60 000 rhyming couplets (*mathnawi*), which are a distinctive feature of Persian poetry.

fire ant An *ant, *Solenopsis saevissima* (or *S. geminata*), that occurs in South America and S North America. Fire ants are serious pests because of their irritant painful sting. Subfamily: *Myrmicinae*.

firearms Any weapon that uses an explosive to discharge a missile. The two main categories are *artillery, with barrels having an internal diameter of more than 20 mm, and *small arms with calibres below 20 mm (this classification is no longer rigidly adopted).

Although gunpowder was invented in China many centuries before its description by Roger Bacon in the 13th century, a practical *cannon was not invented until the 14th century (by a German monk, Berthold Schwarz). *Guns, *mortars, and *howitzers have all evolved from the early cannon, Small-arms development began in the 15th century with the early form of the *musket, called a harquebus. They have evolved into the *pistol, *rifle, and *machine gun. *Guided missiles constitute a separate class of weapons, but can be considered as firearms in some contexts.

firebrat A primitive wingless insect, *Thermobia domestica*: a three-pronged *bristletail that is abundant in buildings all over the world. It prefers warm moist places, such as around stoves, furnaces, and bakery ovens, where it feeds on starchy or sugary materials.

fireclay A soft unbedded clay often occurring beneath coalseams. It is believed that they are fossil soils or earths in which swamp plants grew. Fireclays consist mainly of aluminium oxide and silica, being deficient in iron and alkalis; kaolin is the principal clay mineral. They are used as refractory materials, and poorer quality fireclay is used in the manufacture of sanitary earthernware.

firecrest A tiny European songbird, *Regulus ignicapillus*. It is about 9 cm long and differs from its close relative, the *goldcrest, only in its black-and-white eyestripe. It uses its fine sharp bill to seek out small insects and larvae.

firefly A nocturnal beetle, also called a lightning beetle, belonging to a family (*Lampyridae*; 2000 species) common in tropical and temperate regions. Fireflies emit a greenish light—often as short rhythmic flashes—from organs on the abdomen (*see* bioluminescence). They are 5–25 mm long and many have conspicuous orange or yellow markings. Most adults never eat (although a few feed on pollen and nectar); the larvae are carnivorous. The wingless females and larvae are called glowworms. *Lampyris noctiluca* is one of the best-known species.
Some *click beetles are also called fireflies.

Firenze. *See* Florence.

Fire of London (2–5 September, 1666) The fire that started in a baker's shop in Pudding Lane and destroyed four-fifths of the City. More than 13 000 buildings, including the medieval St Paul's Cathedral and 87 parish churches, were razed to the ground. Sir Christopher *Wren played a major part in the subsequent rebuilding. The **Monument**, which he designed in 1671, stands close to Pudding Lane to commemorate the Fire.

fire prevention Fire prevention and control depends on: elimination of the causes (about 25% of fires are caused by electrical faults; smoking, overheating of machinery, furnace and flue defects, and burner flames are also important causes); fire-safe design using fire-retardant coatings and compartmentalized structures to reduce the spread of fire; the provision of such protective equipment as portable fire extinguishers and automatic sprinklers; and the existence of an efficient fire-fighting service.
Class A fires (paper, wood, furnishings, and other common solid combustibles) are extinguished by cooling with water, carbon dioxide, foam, etc. A common type of extinguisher, the soda-acid device, uses carbon dioxide produced by the reaction of sulphuric acid on sodium hydrogen carbonate to force water out of a container. Class B fires (flammable liquids, such as oil, petrol, etc.) are extinguished by smothering with chemical foam, dry powder, or carbon dioxide, or by extinguishing with halogenated hydrocarbons (e.g. BCF, bromochlorodifluoromethane). Class C fires involve electrical equipment and require nonconducting extinguishers, such as carbon dioxide, dry chemicals, and halogenated hydrocarbons. Class D fires involve burning metals, such as magnesium, sodium, etc., and require special techniques.
Automatic sprinklers are used in factories and warehouses and are usually controlled by thermostats, which turn on the sprinklers at a specified temperature. Smoke detectors are used where materials are expected to produce smoke before bursting into flame.

fire salamander A mainly terrestrial *salamander, *Salamandra salamandra*, ranging from S Europe to SW Asia. It is 18 cm long and glossy black with yellow or orange stripes and red patches. If molested it secretes a venom (salamandrin), which can be fatal to small mammals, from pores behind its eyes.

firethorn. *See* Pyracantha.

fireworks Combustible devices, used for signals, flares, and displays. Gunpowder rockets and fire crackers were first used in ancient China for military purposes and celebrations and in Europe from the middle ages. The basic explosive, usually gunpowder, is coloured by the addition of metallic salts: sodium salts for yellow, barium for green, strontium for red, and copper for blue. Metal filings are added for sparks and aniline dyes provide coloured smokes. Despite safety precautions by firework manufacturers and restrictions on sales to children, fireworks still cause casualties.

firn (*or* névé) A stage in the transformation of fresh snow to glacier ice. Compaction and recrystallization of the snow increases its density and it becomes firn at a relative density of 0.5. Under further compaction firn may be transformed to glacier ice, this occurring at a relative density of 0.89–0.90.

first aid Procedures that can be carried out by a medically unqualified person on someone immediately after injury in order to save life or facilitate specialist treatment given later. The types of injury requiring first aid include bleeding, burns, choking, drowning, electric shock, fracture, and poisoning. The patient should be removed from the cause of injury unless this would worsen his (or her) condition. The patient's breathing should be checked and constricting clothing loosened. In the absence of breathing *artificial respiration should be attempted. Once the patient is breathing he (or she) is put in the recovery position (lying on the stomach with the head to one side and the leg bent at the hip and the knee). In external bleeding the injury is covered and firm pressure applied. Lifting a wounded limb, provided no fractures are suspected, often reduces bleeding. If severe fractures are suspected the patient should not be moved without specialist supervision.

first cause In the philosophy of Aristotle, and later more generally, the beginning of all the chains of cause and effect that are supposed to explain events in the world on a deterministic basis. The first cause does not itself require a cause. The necessity of a first cause (*or* prime mover) has been used as an argument for God's existence.

First of June, Battle of the Glorious (1 June, 1794) A naval battle during the Revolutionary Wars fought between Britain and France in the Atlantic Ocean 690 km (430 mi) W of Ushant. The British under Richard Howe, in an attempt to prevent a convoy of US grain ships from entering the port of Brest, attacked their French escort ships, capturing six. The grain ships, however, reached their destination.

Firth, J(ohn) R(upert) (1890–1960) British linguist, noted chiefly for his work based on the observation that speech sounds do not have clearcut boundaries (prosodic analysis) and his studies of contextual aspects of meaning and language use.

fiscal policy Government economic policy in which changes in taxation, social-benefit rates, and government expenditure are used to influence the economy. It has been widely used since World War II, following the widespread acceptance of *Keynesianism. According to *monetarism, however, such "fine tuning" of the economy may actually destabilize it.

Fischer, Bobby (Robert James F.; 1943–) US chess player, who became an International Grandmaster at 15 and world champion in 1972. The championship match, against *Spassky at Reykjavik, was greatly publicized and caused a chess boom around the world. He resigned his title in 1975.

Fischer, Emil Hermann (1852–1919) German chemist, who discovered a method of separating different *sugars from each other. He then determined their structure and showed that their *optical activity depended on the three-dimensional arrangement of the atoms in their molecules, thus founding the subject of stereochemistry. For this work he was awarded the Nobel Prize in 1902. In later life, Fischer showed that proteins consist of amino acids; in 1907 he synthesized the first protein molecule from amino acids.

Fischer-Dieskau, Dietrich (1925-) German baritone. He is renowned for his performances of *Lieder* and of a wide range of operatic roles. He has recorded all the songs of Schubert.

Fischer-Tropsch reaction The formation of a variety of organic compounds, chiefly light liquid *hydrocarbons, upon passing a mixture of hydrogen and carbon monoxide over catalysts at around 200°C. The reaction is important in the production of synthetic liquid fuels from coal. It was invented by F. Fischer (d. 1948) and H. Tropsch (d. 1935) in 1925 and was extensively used in Germany during World War II.

Fischer von Erlach, Johann Bernhard (1656-1723) Austrian architect, a genius of German baroque. Fischer trained in Rome under *Bernini. Soon after moving to Vienna he became architect to the Habsburg court (1687). The Karlskirche (1716) and Hofbibliotek (1723) in Vienna are probably his finest achievements. He also built numerous palaces and wrote a wide-ranging history of architecture.

fish A cold-blooded aquatic vertebrate belonging to either of the two classes *Chondrichthyes* (*see* cartilaginous fish) or *Osteichthyes* (*see* bony fish), which together comprise over 30 000 species occurring worldwide in seas and fresh waters. Ranging in size from under 10 mm to over 20 m long, they have streamlined bodies with a covering of bony scales, a fin-bearing tail, an anal fin, one or more dorsal fins, and paired lateral, pectoral (anterior), and pelvic (ventral) fins, which are used in swimming. Oxygen is obtained from water by means of *gills situated in the wall of the mouth cavity, although a few species can also breathe air (*see* lungfish). The majority of fish are carnivorous, feeding mainly on other fish and invertebrates, although some eat plants. Large numbers of small eggs are laid (up to several millions in some cases) and are usually fertilized externally. In some species internal fertilization occurs and live young may be born. Fish are of major importance as a source of food and other products (*see* fishing industry) and for sport (*see* angling). *See also* cyclostomes.

fisher A rare North American mammal, *Martes pennanti* (one of the *martens), also called pekan. Fishers are brown and grow to a length of 1 m. They feed on porcupines, small animals, and fruit and are named after their habit of fishing out the contents of baited traps.

Fisher, Andrew (1862-1928) Australian statesman, born in Scotland; Labor prime minister (1908-09, 1910-13, 1914-15). He pledged Australian support for Britain in World War I.

Fisher, John Arbuthnot, 1st Baron (1841-1920) British admiral. As an active commander, Fisher effected great improvements in naval training and, as first sea lord (1904-10), introduced far-reaching reforms in response to the German threat. He introduced both the Dreadnought battleships and the Invincible battle cruisers. He resigned in 1915 as a protest against the Dardanelles expedition in World War I.

Fisher, St John (c. 1469-1535) English prelate and humanist. The chancellor of Cambridge University and Bishop of Rochester from 1504, he opposed Henry VIII's divorce from Catherine of Aragon. He was made a cardinal a month before his execution for refusing to recognize Henry VIII as head of the Church of England. He was canonized in 1935. Feast day: 9 July.

Fishguard 51 59N 4 59W A port and resort in South

Wales, in SW Dyfed, with ferry crossings to Cork and Rosslare in the Republic of Ireland. It also comprises the original fishing village of Lower Fishguard. Population (1981): 4798.

fish hawk. *See* osprey.

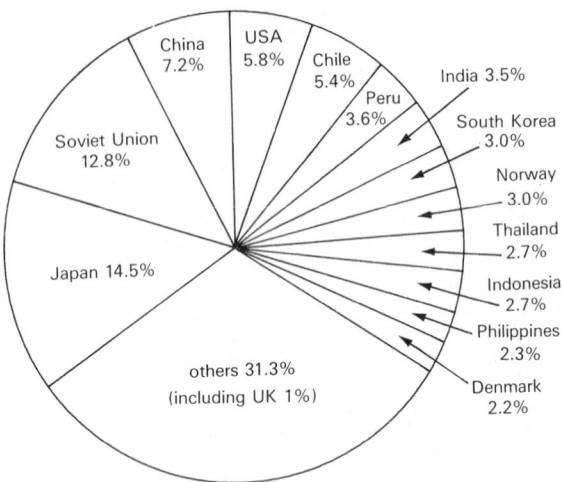

FISHING INDUSTRY *World fish catches (1984).*

fishing industry The recovery and processing of fish, shellfish, etc., for human consumption and other uses. From ancient times man has fished freshwater rivers and lakes and coastal waters using lines and nets. The modern industry uses vessels with refrigerated holds, echo sounding to locate shoals, and efficient nets and recovery gear; the net is often towed behind the vessel (trawling) or left to drift in the ocean. Fish are also dredged up or sucked up, using powerful pumps. The total world catch of about 71 290 000 tonnes (1979 est) comprised many species, including cod, haddock, whiting, herring, lobsters, crabs, shrimps, oysters, mussels, octopus, and squid.

Fish are consumed as human food but provide many other by-products, including fishmeal, fishoils, glues, pharmaceuticals, shells, pearls, etc. Overfishing of natural populations has led to a decline in many species and smaller catches, sometimes causing friction between fishing nations (*see* Cod Wars). International agreement is required to regulate fishing and conserve stocks so that yields can be sustained indefinitely. One alternative is an increased dependence on **fish farming**, the maintenance and management of fish under controlled conditions to provide food. A long-established practice in China and the Far East, fish farming is now of major importance in many other countries, where trout, carp, eels, shrimps, and oysters are commonly reared. Hatching of the eggs and rearing take place under optimum conditions in artificial ponds or enclosures situated in lakes or coastal waters. *See also* whaling.

fish louse A tiny parasitic *crustacean of the subclass Branchiura (75 species) that uses sucking mouthparts to attach itself to fresh- and salt-water fish. Its flattened body has a large disclike carapace covering the head and thorax.

fish owl An *owl specialized for feeding on fish and frogs. Fish owls have naked legs and rough scaly feet to grip their slippery prey. Genera: *Ketupa* (Asia; 4 species), *Scotopelia* (Africa; 3 species).

fission (biology) A form of asexual *reproduction in which an individual splits into two (binary fission) or more (multiple fission) equal parts, each part becoming a new individual. It occurs in a variety of plants, bacteria, protozoa, and some multicellular animals (e.g. corals).

FISH

FISH *There are numerous variations on the structure of a typical bony fish (mackerel: centre). In the flying fish, for instance, the pectoral fins are enlarged as wings; in the lungfish they are fleshy, for moving on land; and in the mangrove ray they are flattened, for swimming. The dorsal and anal fins of the scorpion fish are armed with poisonous spines and the tail of the sea horse is prehensile.*

fission (physics). *See* nuclear energy.

fission-track dating A method of dating based on the spontaneous nuclear fission of uranium-238 in the sample. The fissions are recorded as tracks, which are then compared to the tracks formed by inducing fission in the uranium-235 present. A comparison of the numbers of tracks is used as a measure of the age of the sample.

Fitzgerald, Edward (1809–83) British poet. He lived quietly as a country gentleman with literary tastes. His famous *Rubaiyat of Omar Khayyam* (1859) was a free adaptation of the 12th-century Persian original into his own metre and imagery.

ELLA FITZGERALD

Fitzgerald, Ella (1918–) US Black jazz singer, known as the "First Lady of Song." Discovered in Harlem by Chick Webb (1902–39), she toured with his band. Later she became famous with the song "A-tisket, A-tasket" (1938), performed with such musicians as Duke Ellington and Oscar Peterson, and made many albums, including *Hello Love, Duke Ellington's Song Book*, and the *Gershwin Song Books*.

Fitzgerald, F(rancis) Scott (Key) (1896–1940) US novelist. The success of his autobiographical first novel, *This Side of Paradise* (1920), enabled him to marry Zelda Sayre (1900–47) and to live out his self-created role as representative of the hedonistic Jazz Age. After 1924 Fitzgerald lived chiefly on the French Riviera, where he wrote his masterpiece *The Great Gatsby* (1925). Zelda suffered increasingly from schizophrenia and after 1930 was confined to an asylum. Fitzgerald, plagued by guilt, declined into alcoholism. His other works include *The Beautiful and the Damned* (1922) and *Tender is the Night* (1934). *The Last Tycoon* was unfinished at his death.

Fitzgerald, Garret (1926–) Irish statesman; prime minister of Ireland (1981–82, 1982–87). He was leader of *Fine Gael (1977–87) and foreign minister (1973–77).

Fitzgerald, George Francis (1851–1901) Irish physicist, who (independently of *Lorentz) suggested that objects become shorter as their velocity increases, as an explanation of the negative results of the *Michelson-Morley experiment. Now known as the Lorentz-Fitzgerald contraction, it was later incorporated by Einstein into special *relativity, although Fitzgerald did not live to see it.

Fitzsimmons, Bob (1862–1917) New Zealand boxer, born in England. Of legendary courage and strength, he was world middleweight champion (1891–97), heavyweight champion (1897–99), and light-heavyweight champion (1903–05). He beat many much heavier and bigger men.

Fiume. *See* Rijeka.

Five, the A group of 19th-century Russian composers dedicated to the formation of a nationalist musical tradition based on folk music. Led by *Balakirev, the other members were *Borodin, César Cui (1835–1918), *Mussorgski, and *Rimsky-Korsakov. The original name of the group was *mogutchaya kutchka* (Russian: the mighty handful).

Five Pecks of Rice Band A 2nd-century AD religious cult of the later *Han dynasty, so called because its followers paid an annual tribute of five pecks of rice to the sect leader. Together with a sect called the Yellow Turbans, the Five Pecks of Rice Band took part in two mass Taoist rebellions, which lasted over 30 years and played a significant part in overthrowing the Han dynasty (220 AD).

Five Power Constitution The government constitution drawn up for China by *Sun Yat-sen and put into practice by the *Guomindang (Nationalists) in 1928. The government exercised five powers—executive, legislative, and judicial and those of examination (of candidates for the bureaucracy) and control (of government efficiency). The Constitution is still used by the Guomindang government of the Republic of China (Taiwan).

fives A British court game that originated in *handball and developed in different forms at three public schools, Eton, Rugby, and Winchester. It is played with gloved hands by two or four players on a three- or four-walled court, each side returning the ball in turn to certain areas of wall. It is played largely in schools, although there are associations for the Eton and Rugby versions.

five-year plans Economic plans formulated by *developing countries as part of the process of industrialization; they usually include targets for construction, investment, and output to be achieved in the following five years. They were first adopted in the Soviet Union. Capitalist countries (*see* capitalism) committed to economies based on market forces tend to avoid the direction implied in five-year plans, but in a *mixed economy plans based on exhortation rather than direction are sometimes used (e.g. the plan formulated in the UK by the Department of Economic Affairs in 1965).

fjord (*or* fiord) A long narrow sea inlet lying between steep mountain slopes, especially in Norway. Usually U-shaped, fjords are glaciated valleys that have been flooded by the sea. Many are extremely deep, some in excess of 1000 m (3280 ft), but near their mouths they usually have a considerably shallower bar or threshold.

flag A Eurasian iris, *Iris pseudacorus* (yellow or water flag), growing in marshes and ditches. Up to 1.2 m high, it has yellow flowers and long bladelike leaves. The sweet flag (*Acorus calamus*) is a perennial herbaceous plant native to Asia and North America and naturalized in Britain, growing at the margins of ponds, rivers, etc. About 1 m high, it has wavy-edged leaves, which smell of tangerines when crushed, and the small yellow flowers are tightly packed on a tapering spikelike spadix, 8 cm long. Family: *Araceae*.

flagella Long threadlike structures that project from the surface of a cell and produce lashing or undulating movements, used for locomotion or the production of water currents. Flagella occur in protozoa, motile gametes (usually sperms), lower plants, sponges, and also in bacteria (in a simpler form).

Flagellata (*or* Mastigophora) A class of microscopic single-celled animals (*see* Protozoa) having one or more long *flagella for swimming and collecting bacteria, protozoans, and other food particles. Some species (subclass *Phytomastigophora*) possess chlorophyll and other pigments to make food by photosynthesis (*see* Euglena). They may also be classed as algae. Animal-like flagellates (subclass *Zoomastigophora*) include the parasites causing *trypanosomiasis and *leishmaniasis as well as free-living forms.

flageolet A musical instrument similar to the *recorder but with two thumb holes on the underside and a more complex head fitted with a slender ivory mouthpiece containing a sponge to absorb condensation. The diarist Pepys was a keen player.

flags Emblems of nations, clubs, associations, etc., printed on cloth. The flags of the nations are shown on a coloured plate in the map section.

Flagstad, Kirsten Malfrid (1895–1962) Norwegian soprano, famous for her singing of Wagner roles, such as Brünnhilde in *Der Ring des Nibelungen* and Kundry in *Parsifal*. She also sang the role of Dido in Purcell's *Dido and Aeneas* and championed the songs of Sibelius.

Flaherty, Robert (Joseph) (1884–1951) US film director. His *Nanook of the North* (1922), filmed during a two-year stay with the Canadian Eskimos, and *Moana* (1926), filmed in the Samoan Islands, were the earliest major documentary films. His later films include *Louisiana Story* (1948).

Flamborough Head 54 06N 0 04W A chalk headland in NE England, in Humberside extending into the North Sea. Its cliffs, in parts 120 m (400 ft) high, are the breeding ground for many sea birds.

Flamboyant In French *gothic architecture, the predominant style during the 15th century. Similar to the earlier English *Decorated style, Flamboyant takes its name from its characteristic slender and elaborate curves that wind into flamelike patterns, especially in window tracery. St Maclou, Rouen (begun 1432), is a fine Flamboyant church.

flamboyant tree An attractive tree, *Delonix regia*, also called royal poinciana, flame tree, and peacock flower. It grows to a height of 6–12 m and has showy flame-coloured flowers with long protruding stamens. Native to Madagascar, it is widely planted in the tropics for shade and ornament. Family: *Leguminosae*.

flamenco A type of Spanish music originating in Andalusia, typically consisting of a song (*cante*) accompanied by dancing, in which the men perform intricate toe and heel tapping steps (*zapateados*) and the women rely on graceful hand and body movements. It was developed by gipsies and shows signs of Moorish influence; the predominant styles are *grande* (anguished) and *chico* (gay and amorous), with a variety of intermediate moods. Flamenco guitar playing has become well known outside Spain; it employs a different technique from that of the "classical" guitar, including a percussive effect obtained by tapping the body of the guitar with the fingers.

flame tree One of several unrelated trees with flame-coloured showy flowers. The name is most commonly applied to *Brachychiton acerifolium* (or *Sterculia acerifolia*), a deciduous Australian tree that bears masses of small scarlet bell-like flowers on leafless branches. Family: *Sterculiaceae*. It may also refer to the *flamboyant tree.

flamingo A wading bird belonging to a family (*Phoenicopteridae*; 4 species) occurring in large flocks on saltwater lakes in warm regions of the world. 90–150 cm tall, flamingos have a long neck, a short tail, a broad wingspan, and white plumage, tinged with pink. They separate algae, diatoms, small molluscs, etc., from mud using their bills, which are lined with sievelike filters. Order: *Ciconiiformes* (herons, storks, etc.). See Plate V.

Flaminian Way A Roman road that extended from Rome to Ariminum (now Rimini) on the Adriatic coast. It was named after Gaius *Flaminius, who completed it in 220 BC.

Flamininus, Titus Quinctius (c. 230–c. 174 BC) Roman general, who defeated Philip V (237–179; reigned 220–179) of Macedon at Cynoscephalae (198). In 196, at the Isthmian Games, Flamininus proclaimed the independence of the Greek states from Macedonian hegemony.

Flaminius, Gaius (d. 217 BC) Roman popular leader. An advocate of the plebeians' rights, he often challenged or disregarded senatorial authority. In 220, as consul, he built the *Flaminian Way, Rome's road to N Italy. Popular dissatisfaction with senatorial war policy inspired his election in 217 as leader against *Hannibal, who defeated and killed Flaminius at

Trasimene.

Flamsteed, John (1646–1719) English astronomer, who established, with the permission of Charles II, a national observatory at Greenwich and was appointed the first astronomer royal in 1675. His star catalogue, listing more than 3000 stars, gave their positions with greater precision than ever before. A quarrelsome man, he argued with *Newton and *Halley over their requests for access to his astronomical observations.

Flanders (Flemish name: Vlaanderen; French name: Flandre) A historic region in Europe, in the SW of the Low Countries. It now comprises the provinces of East Flanders and West Flanders in Belgium and parts of N France and the Netherlands. *History*: in the middle ages Flanders formed an autonomous region ruled by the Counts of Flanders and after the 12th century it became a major industrial and commercial centre, its cloth being especially important. The scene of many battles during its history, there was heavy fighting here in both World Wars. During World War II the Battle of Flanders (10 May–2 June, 1940) saw the German attack on Holland, Belgium, and France, which resulted in the Allied withdrawal from *Dunkirk.

flash point The lowest temperature at which an inflammable liquid (generally a hydrocarbon) produces enough vapour to ignite on the application of a small flame under specified conditions. Flash points are useful for setting safety standards, especially for the storage of hydrocarbons and monitoring refinery operations.

flatfish Any carnivorous *bony fish of the order *Pleuronectiformes* (about 600 species), including many important food fishes, such as *halibut, *plaice, *sole, and *turbot. They have a laterally flattened body, 10–200 cm long, fringed with dorsal and anal fins. Both eyes occur on the same side of the head and they lie on their "blind" side, usually on sandy or muddy bottoms of coastal waters; the upper surface is coloured to blend with their surroundings. In the larval stage one eye migrates over the head to lie near the other.

flatfoot Obliteration of the longitudinal arch of the foot, so that the entire sole is in contact with the ground on standing. It is common in young children and they usually grow out of it. Rigid flatfoot is more serious and the result of a congenital abnormality.

flathead A bottom-dwelling carnivorous *bony fish of the family *Platycephalidae*, found in tropical Indian, Pacific, and E Atlantic waters. It has a tapering body, up to 1.3 m long, and a large flat head covered with ridges and spines. It is an important food fish. Order: *Scorpaeniformes* (or *Scleroparei*).

flat racing A form of horse racing in which the horses are not required to jump obstacles. Flat races are usually run over distances between 0.8 km (0.5 mi) and 2.4 km (1.5 mi). *Thoroughbred horses are used, mainly as two- and three-year-olds. Weight handicaps are allotted in most races. The most prestigious races are the English *Classics, the US *Triple Crown, and the French Prix de l'Arc de Triomphe.

flatworm A flat-bodied wormlike animal of the invertebrate phylum *Platyhelminthes* (9000 species). Some flatworms are free-living (*see* planarian) but the majority are parasitic (*see* fluke; tapeworm). They have a simple body, with sense organs and a primitive brain at the front end, and range in size from 1 mm to 15 m. Many are hermaphrodite.

Flaubert, Gustave (1821–80) French novelist. The son of a Rouen surgeon he gave up his law studies in 1843 to dedicate himself wholly to literature. He travelled in the Near East (1849–51) and Tunisia (1857) and was a lover of the poet Louise Colet (1808–76). He worked for five years on his first novel, *Madame Bovary* (1856), a controversially explicit study of an overromantic bourgeois wife. His other major works include the exotic romance *Salammbô* (1862), *L'Éducation sentimentale* (1870), *La Tentation de Saint*

Antoine (1874), and the brilliant short stories in *Trois contes* (1877).

flax A herbaceous plant of the genus *Linum* (230 species), mostly of the N hemisphere. Cultivated flax (*L. usitatissimum*) is an annual, up to 100 cm high, with narrow leaves and blue five-petalled flowers. Its stem fibres are used to make linen, fine writing paper, and cigarette paper. The seeds contain *linseed oil. Flax is cultivated throughout Europe, the main producing countries being the Soviet Union, Belgium, Holland, and Northern Ireland. Family: *Linaceae*.

Flaxman, John Henry (1755–1826) British sculptor and book illustrator. Flaxman chiefly designed and modelled *Wedgwood friezes, portrait medallions, etc., until his visit to Rome (1789–94). There, he won an international reputation as a neoclassical artist with his illustrations to the *Odyssey* and *Iliad* (both 1792), Aeschylus' works, and *The Divine Comedy*. His best-known monuments are those of Lord Mansfield (Westminster Abbey) and Nelson (St Paul's). He became the first professor of sculpture at the Royal Academy (1810).

flea A small wingless ⬜insect belonging to the widely distributed order *Siphonaptera* (about 1600 species). Fleas are bloodsucking parasites of birds and mammals. A flea's body, which is generally brown, is 1–10 mm long and laterally flattened and its legs are modified for jumping. Fleas have irritating bites and change hosts frequently, acting as carriers of some serious diseases. The wormlike larvae use biting mouthparts to feed on dirt, excrement, and dried blood. Two important and widely distributed species are the human flea (*Pulex irritans*) and the oriental rat flea (*Xenopsylla cheopis*), which transmits bubonic plague and typhus to man.

fleabane A perennial herb of the genus *Erigeron* (about 180 species), from America and Europe. 8–40 cm tall, fleabanes have strap-shaped leaves and small daisy-like flower heads with purple or white ray florets and yellow centres. Herbs of the Old World genus *Pulicaria* are also called fleabane. They have daisy-like yellow flowers, 1–3 cm across. Family: *Compositae*.

fleawort One of several herbs of the genus *Senecio*, especially *S. integrifolius*, *S. palustris*, and *S. spathulifolius*, from central and N Europe. The plants are 25–100 cm high, with yellow daisy-like flowers, 2–3 cm across. Family: *Compositae*.

Flecker, (Herman) James Elroy (1884–1915) British poet. A minor diplomat in Turkey and Lebanon, he died of tuberculosis in a Swiss sanatorium. His best-known works are the poem *The Golden Journey to Samarkand* (1913) and the verse drama *Hassan*, posthumously produced in 1922 with music by *Delius; both are lyrical evocations of a richly exotic Orient.

Fleet Street A street in London between the Strand and Ludgate Circus in which most newspapers had offices until the recent move out of central London. It is named after the River Fleet (now a covered sewer).

Fleetwood 53 56N 3 01W A port and resort in NW England, in Lancashire. It is the principal fishing port on the W coast of England. Population (1981): 28 467.

Flémalle, Master of (c. 1378–1444) One of the founders (with the *van Eyck brothers) of the Flemish school of painting (*see* Flemish art). He is usually identified as Robert Campin, an artist active in Tournai from 1406. His name derives from three panels (Frankfurt-am-Main) attributed to him and mistakenly thought to have been commissioned by the abbey of Flémalle near Liège. Other works include the *Mérode Altarpiece* (the Cloisters, New York), the *Annunciation* and *Marriage of the Virgin* (Madrid), and the *Madonna of Humility* (London). His works display the careful realistic rendering of details from everyday life that characterizes the Flemish school as a whole.

Fleming, Sir Alexander (1881–1955) British microbiologist, who discovered the antibiotic *penicillin. In 1928 Fleming noticed that a mould contaminating a bacterial culture had destroyed the bacteria in its vicinity. He identified the mould as *Pencillium notatum* and named the antibacterial substance it produced penicillin. Although he found that penicillin was harmless to human cells, Fleming could not isolate or identify the antibiotic. This was later achieved by Lord *Florey and Sir Ernest *Chain, with whom Fleming shared the 1945 Nobel Prize. Fleming also discovered lysozyme, an antibacterial enzyme found in tears and saliva.

Fleming, Ian (Lancaster) (1908–64) British author and journalist, famous for his creation of the archetypal secret agent, James Bond, in 12 novels and 7 short stories, most of them filmed. Originally a stockbroker, Fleming served as a foreign correspondent in Moscow, and in World War II became a senior naval intelligence officer.

Fleming, Sir John Ambrose (1849–1945) British electrical engineer, who constructed the first rectifying *diode in 1904. His invention greatly stimulated the development of radio and led to the invention of the triode two years later by Lee *De Forest. He also took part in the development of the electric lamp and carried out research into resistance at low temperatures. He was knighted in 1929. *See also* Fleming's rules.

Fleming, Paul (1609–40) German poet. A disciple of Martin *Opitz, his posthumously published love lyrics and religious hymns were distinguished by their sincerity and directness. Many of his poems were inspired by his thwarted love for Elsàbe Niehus, whom he met on a trading journey to Russia and Persia.

Flemings Inhabitants of N and W Belgium who speak Flemish, a dialect of *Dutch known by them as Vlaams. They number approximately 5 500 000. Like the Dutch they are descended from the Salic Franks, a Germanic people, who settled the area during the 3rd and 4th centuries AD. They retain a cultural identity distinct from that of French-speaking Belgians (*see* Walloons).

Fleming's rules A mnemonic, invented by Sir John Ambrose Fleming, for the relationship between the directions of motion, magnetic field, and electric current in *electric motors and generators. The thumb represents motion; the first (index) finger represents the field; and the second finger represents the current. If the right hand is held with the thumb and first two fingers straight and mutually at right angles, the directions in a generator are indicated. The left hand indicates the directions in a motor.

Flemish art A tradition of painting that flourished in Flanders, now Belgium, from the 14th to the 18th centuries. The early dominance of manuscript illuminators was replaced in the 15th century by a major school of painters, which included the Master of *Flémalle, the *van Eycks, van der *Weyden, van der *Goes, *Bouts, *Memling, and Gerard *David. In the 16th century Flemish art was Italianized by such painters as *Gossaert and Frans *Floris, although *Bosch and *Brueghel remained largely within the Flemish tradition. Major 17th-century figures were *Rubens, *Van Dyck, *Jordaens, and *Teniers. Flemish art declined in international importance after the 17th century.

Flensburg 54 47N 9 27E A town in N West Germany, in Schleswig-Holstein on the Baltic Sea. Between 1848 and 1867 it was under Danish rule and in 1945 at the end of World War II the German Government capitulated near here. A port and naval base, its industries include shipbuilding and fishing. Population (1983 est): 86 601.

Fletcher, John (1579–1625) English dramatist. He collaborated with Francis *Beaumont on *Philaster* (1610), *The Maid's Tragedy* (1611), and many other plays, and probably with *Shakespeare on *The Two Noble Kinsmen* and *Henry VIII* (1612).

fleur-de-lys A heraldic device, which has three everted petals, resembling the bearded iris. It was the coat of arms of the French monarchy from the middle ages.

Fleury, André Hercule de, Cardinal (1653–1743) French statesman; chief minister (1726–43) of Louis XV. Fleury carried out important reforms, reorganizing finances, building roads, and encouraging commerce. A successful diplomat, he worked to maintain peace in Europe but involved France in the War of the *Polish Succession (1733–38) on the side of Stanislaw I Leszczyński.

Flinders, Matthew (1774–1814) British navigator and hydrographer. He entered the navy in 1789 and after sailing to the Pacific with Capt *Bligh saw active service in the French Revolutionary War. Having explored (1795–1800) the Bass Strait with George Bass (died c. 1812), he was commissioned to survey the coasts of Australia and Tasmania. Flinders Island, River, and Range are named after him.

Flinders Island. See Furneaux Islands.

Flinders Range A mountain range in E South Australia. It extends N from Gulf St Vincent between Lake Torrens and Lake Frome, reaching 1190 m (3904 ft) at St Mary Peak.

flint A variety of *chalcedony. It is grey to black, is dense and tough, and breaks with a conchoidal (curved) fracture, leaving sharp edges (hence its use by Stone Age man for tools and weapons). It occurs in nodules in chalk along the bedding planes and as pebbles in river gravels and beach material.

Flint 43 03N 83 40W A city in the USA, in Michigan on the Flint River. One of the several cities that surround *Detroit, its main industry is motor vehicles. Population (1981): 159 611.

flint glass A durable, brilliant, and highly refractive glass. It is used in high-quality glassware and also in lenses and prisms since it absorbs very little light. It is also known as lead glass and crystal glass.

Flintshire A former county of NE Wales. Under local government reorganization in 1974 it became part of *Clwyd.

FLN. See Front de Libération nationale.

Flodden, Battle of (9 September, 1513) The battle in which the English under Thomas Howard, Earl of Surrey (1443–1524), defeated the Scots under *James IV at Flodden Edge, Northumberland. The Scots had invaded England after allying with France against Henry VIII.

flood The overflowing of a river onto the surrounding land (**flood plain**) or the surging of sea water at high tide onto the coastal land. Disastrous floods have occurred throughout history. The flood described in Genesis 6.9 (see Noah) is probably apocryphal, although Sir Leonard *Woolley identified at Ur a layer of clay that he believed was deposited during a flood in about 4000 BC. More recent flood disasters include those in Lisbon (1775), Warsaw (1861 and 1964), Paris (1910), the UK's E coast (1953), Florence (1966), and Bangladesh (1974 and 1985). However, floods are not always disastrous; the annual floods of the River *Nile have provided a fertile flood plain, the site of one of the earliest civilizations.

The prevention of disasters by flooding involves the accurate prediction of the behaviour of rivers and tides and the provision of flood-relief channels and barrages.

Flood, Henry (1732–91) Irish politician. An impressive orator, Flood rapidly became the leader of the patriot party in the Irish parliament. In 1775, however, he accepted a government post and the patriots henceforth branded him as an apostate. In 1781 Flood again espoused the patriot cause but quarrelled with its new leader, *Grattan, and declined into political obscurity.

floodgate A movable barrier set up on spillways to control the height of water at *dams. Closure of some of the floodgates at a spillway in times of water shortage may conserve valuable amounts of water, without reducing the full spillway capacity. Vertical-lift gates are raised to permit flow beneath them, while drum gates (solid circular quadrants) rotate downwards to allow water to flow over them.

Flora The Roman goddess of flowers and spring. Her spring festival, the Floralia, instituted in 283 BC, was the occasion for riotous uninhibited behaviour.

Florence (Italian name: Firenze) 43 47N 11 15E A city in Italy, the capital of Tuscany on the River Arno. Florence is a major market town as well as an administrative and educational centre. The manufacture of luxury goods is important but the principal industry is tourism. Its many famous buildings include the 13th-century cathedral of Sta Maria del Fiore (□Brunelleschi, Filippo), the campanile of Giotto, the baptistery, and many churches (including Sta Maria Novella and Sta Croce). The Ponte Vecchio (1345) across the River Arno connects the *Uffizi gallery to the Palazzo Pitti (now an art gallery). Art treasures in Florence include works by Michelangelo, Donatello, Masaccio, Giotto, Fra Angelico, Botticelli, Raphael, Titian, and Rubens. The Italian National Library (Biblioteca Nazionale) is situated here and its university was established in 1321. History: an early Roman colony, it had developed into an important centre of trade and industry by the 12th century. It was torn by the struggles between the *Guelfs and Ghibellines (13th and 14th centuries) but flourished financially and culturally (14th–16th centuries). The rule of the *Medici family began in 1434 and this continued almost uninterrupted (see Savonarola, Girolamo) for three centuries. Following a period of Austrian rule, Florence became part of the new kingdom of Italy in 1861 and was the provisional capital (1865–71). Florence has suffered considerable damage in war (including World War II) and from floods, especially in November, 1966. Population (1983 est): 440 910.

Flores An Indonesian island in the Nusa Tenggara group. Mountainous and volcanic, it is largely unexplored. Agriculture is shifting cultivation producing chiefly maize; sandalwood and copra are exported. Area: 17 150 sq km (6622 sq mi). Chief town: Ende.

Florey, Howard Walter, Baron (1898–1968) Australian pathologist, who, working with Sir Ernst *Chain, isolated and purified the antibiotic *penicillin, first discovered by Sir Alexander *Fleming in 1928. Florey and Chain developed techniques for producing the pure drug in large quantities. In 1941 they conducted the first clinical trials, in which penicillin proved very effective in combating bacterial infections. Florey shared the 1945 Nobel Prize with Chain and Fleming.

Florianópolis (former name: Desterro) 27 35S 48 31W A city and port in Brazil, the capital of Santa Catarina state on Santa Catarina island. It is linked to the mainland by a steel suspension bridge, the longest in Brazil. It exports sugar, tobacco, and fruit and has a university (1960). Population (1980): 153 547.

floribunda. See rose.

Florida A state in the far SE of the USA, between the Atlantic Ocean and the Gulf of Mexico. It is predominantly a low-lying peninsula with many lakes and rivers, Lake Okeechobee being the largest lake. In the diversified economy manufacturing is important, especially food processing and the chemical industry. The state's mines produce phosphate, titanium, zircon, and other heavy minerals. Tourism, based on its subtropical climate, is the most important industry, with many popular resorts, such as Miami Beach and Palm Beach. Most recently the state has become a centre for space exploration with the John F. Kennedy Space Center at Cape Canaveral. Florida produces some 75% of the USA's citrus fruits, as well as large quantities of vegetables. It is also a major region for

FLORIDA *An aerial view of Miami Beach, the state's most famous resort.*

breeding thoroughbred horses. *History*: following its exploration by the Spanish, it was ceded to the British in 1763 but returned to Spain after the American Revolution. It passed to the USA in 1819, becoming a state in 1845. It was a supporter of the Confederate cause during the US Civil War. The arrival of the railways in the 1880s brought access to the agricultural markets of the N and subsequent economic growth. Area: 151 670 sq km (58 560 sq mi). Population (1980): 9 746 324. Capital: Tallahassee.

Florida Keys A chain of small islands in the USA, separated from the S coast of Florida by Florida Bay. It includes the islands of Key West and Key Largo and extends for over 160 km (100 mi). The islands are linked by the Overseas Highway, a complex of roads and 42 bridges.

Florio, John (c. 1553–1625) English writer, of Italian descent. While teaching at Oxford he published his important Italian-English dictionary (1598). He later held appointments at James I's court. His main work was an English translation of Montaigne's *Essays* (1603).

Floris Two Flemish artists. **Cornelis Floris** (1514–75) was an architect and sculptor, best known for designing Antwerp town hall (1561–65). His brother **Frans Floris** (c. 1516–70) was a painter. Both studied in Italy and contributed to the spread of the Italian Renaissance style in the Netherlands.

Flotow, Friedrich von (1812–83) German operatic composer. He had much success in his lifetime but his works, with the exception of the opera *Martha* (1847), have not survived.

flotsam, jetsam, and lagan Goods cast into the sea that respectively remain afloat, sink, or would sink but have attached to them a buoy, which keeps them afloat. Unless claimed by the owner, they belong to the Crown.

flounder A common name for any *flatfish or for certain species. An example is *Platichthys flesus*, which is up to 50 cm long and lives in European coastal and fresh waters. It has a greenish or brownish mottled upper surface and is an important food and game □fish.

flour The powdered grain of wheat or other cereals, used in baking. The chief use of flour is in making bread. When the two proteins in wheat, glutenin and gliadin, are mixed with water they form gluten, which permits the dough to expand and retain the carbon dioxide resulting from fermentation of the yeast in bread dough. Different types of flour are made by varying the percentage of flour separated from the wheat. The principal commercial flours are whole wheat (100%), wholemeal and stoneground (92%), wheatmeal (80–90%), and white flours (70–72%). Many nutritionists consider it important to eat food made from whole wheat and wholemeal flour, rather than white flour. The former retain more of the bran (the outer skin of the wheat grain) and have more iron and calcium than white flour. They are also a good daily source of dietary *fibre. Flour with a high gluten content (strong flour) is best when yeast is called for, as in dough for bread. On the other hand a softer flour with a lower gluten content (fine flour) is used for cakes, shortbread, etc. Plain flour is all-purpose, with a moderate gluten content. Self-raising flour is plain flour with the addition of raising agents.

flower The reproductive organ of flowering □plants (angiosperms), which is essential for the production of seeds and fruits. It is made up of the perianth (petals and sepals) and the sexual organs—the *stamens producing pollen (male gametes) and the *carpels containing the female gametes. The petals and sepals serve to protect the sexual organs and—in flowers pollinated by animals—are brightly coloured, scented, and secrete *nectar to attract insects and birds. Wind-pollinated flowers are typically small and inconspicuous and may lack a perianth.

flowering currant An ornamental garden shrub, *Ribes sanguineum*, native to North America. Up to 2.5 m tall, it has drooping spikes of pink tubular flowers that appear before the maple-shaped leaves. The fruit is a blue-black berry. The shrub has an odour of blackcurrants. Family: *Grossulariaceae* (*see* currant).

flowering quince. *See* japonica.

flowering rush A perennial freshwater plant, *Butomus umbellatus*, native to Eurasia but common throughout N temperate regions: it is a popular garden plant. It has tapering leaves, up to 1 m long, and an umbrella-shaped cluster of pinkish flowers at the tip of a long stalk. Family: *Butomaceae*.

flowerpecker A songbird belonging to a family (*Dicaeidae*; 55 species) occurring in S Asia and Australasia. Ranging in size from 8 cm to 20 cm, they have stumpy tails, short bills, and variable plumage. Flowerpeckers feed on berries and nectar, thereby dispersing seeds and pollinating flowers.

Fludd, Robert (1574–1637) English physician and *Rosicrucian. He studied at Oxford and on the Continent, where he was influenced by the works of the Swiss doctor and philosopher *Paracelsus. His philosophical books were largely a defence of the allegorical interpretation of the Bible, astrology, palmistry, and alchemy against the new science.

fluidics The use of jets of fluid in a circuit to carry out electronic functions. Fluidic circuits can resist much higher temperatures than electronic circuits and are also unaffected by ionizing radiation and magnetic fields. They therefore have uses in nuclear reactors and spacecraft. They are also used as delay lines since they respond much more slowly than electronic circuits.

fluidization The process of supporting very fine solid particles in a stream of gas so that the combination of solid and fluid behaves like a liquid. The process is used in transporting coal dust and in the cleaning of the catalyst in *catalytic cracking in oil refining.

fluid mechanics The study of the mechanical properties of fluids. *Hydrostatics is concerned with the study of fluids at rest and hydrodynamics (*or* fluid dynamics) with fluids that are flowing. Hydraulics deals with the practical applications of these sciences. Two important aspects of hydrodynamics

455

fly

are the conservation of energy in fluid flow (*see* Bernoulli's theorem) and the distinction between streamline and turbulent flow. *See also* aerodynamics; Reynolds number.

fluke A parasitic *flatworm of the class *Trematoda* (over 6000 species). Typically leaf-shaped, some are elongated to fit the body cavities they inhabit. The monogenetic flukes have a single host and are generally external parasites of fishes; the digenetic flukes have life cycles involving up to four different hosts and are mainly internal parasites of vertebrates, passing early larval stages in various invertebrates.

fluorescence. *See* luminescence.

phosphor coating

atoms of mercury vapour

electrons emitted from filament

ultraviolet radiation emitted by mercury atoms

FLUORESCENT LAMP   *Electrons from the filament collide with atoms of mercury vapour in the tube producing ultraviolet radiation. This is converted to visible light by the fluorescent coating on the tube.*

fluorescent lamp A lamp that uses fluorescence (*see* luminescence) as its source of light. It consists of a glass tube containing a low pressure gas, such as mercury vapour. As a current passes through the gas, collisions between the electrons and atoms of the gas excite the atoms, which emit *ultraviolet radiation when they return to the ground state. The radiation strikes a phosphor coating on the inner surface of the tube, causing the phosphor to fluoresce emitting visible light.

fluoridation The addition of fluoride (usually sodium fluoride) to drinking water to reduce dental *caries (tooth decay), especially in children. The fluoride combines with apatite—the chief constituent of tooth enamel—to form fluoroapatite, which has a greater resistance to bacterial decay. The recommended level is one part of fluoride per million and if the natural concentration is below this level it is the policy of some governments to advocate that fluoride is added. In the UK the decision to implement this recommendation rests with local authorities, where controversy sometimes arises on the grounds that "medication" is being forced on people who may not wish to accept it. This measure has been shown to be effective, however, and quite safe in low concentrations (many natural water supplies contain up to four or five parts per million).

fluorine (F) A highly reactive pale-yellow halogen gas, the most electronegative element known. It was first isolated by H. Moissan in 1886 and occurs naturally in volcanic gases and as *fluorite (CaF_2) and *cryolite (Na_2AlF_6). It is prepared by electrolysis of potassium hydrogen fluoride (KHF_2) solution in dry hydrofluoric acid (HF). Fluorine became industrially important with the introduction of

nuclear power. The gas uranium hexafluoride (UF_6) allows separation of the fissile ^{235}U isotope from ^{238}U by gaseous diffusion. Hydrofluoric acid is used to etch glass and can cause very painful burns to the skin. *Fluorocarbons (for example CF_2Cl_2) are chemically unreactive and have many important uses. Trace amounts of fluoride in drinking water are thought to be important in helping to prevent dental decay (*see* fluoridation). At no 9; at wt 18.9984; mp $-219.62°C$; bp $-188.14°C$.

fluorite (*or* fluorspar) A mineral consisting of calcium fluoride, white, green, or yellow in colour. It occurs in hydrothermal veins, often as a gangue material in ore deposits, and in some igneous rocks. Most fluorite is used as a flux in iron and steel making; it is also used as a source of fluorine for manufacturing hydrofluoric acid and in the ceramic- and optical-glass industries. Blue John is a deep blue or purple variety used for ornamental purposes. *See* Plate III.

fluorocarbons Synthetic compounds of carbon and fluorine (sometimes containing also atoms of other halogens). They are extremely resistant to chemical attack, even at very high temperatures, and are nontoxic and nonflammable. They are used as refrigerants, anaesthetics, heat-transfer agents, and high-temperature lubricants. The fluoroanalogue of polythene, polytetrafluoroethylene (Teflon), is a useful plastic in corrosive environments and has a very low coefficient of friction. Its stability at high temperatures enables it to be used for nonstick coatings in cooking utensils. Fluorocarbons have also been used in enormous quantities as propellants for aerosols, although they have been opposed on environmental grounds as photochemical reactions in the upper atmosphere may lead to depletion of the ozone layer, thereby removing protection against harmful ultraviolet radiation.

fluorspar. *See* fluorite.

Flushing (Dutch name: Vlissingen) 51 27N 3 35E A port in the SW Netherlands, in Zeeland province in Walcheren Island. It was the scene of an Allied invasion in 1944. Industries include shipbuilding and oil refining. Population (1983): 46 382.

flute A woodwind instrument of ancient origin, existing in many different cultures. The modern side-blown flute (in which a column of air is made to vibrate by blowing across an elliptical mouth hole) and the *recorder are members of the same family. The flute came into prominence in the 16th century, when it was made of wood; today most flutes are metal. The modern orchestral flute (perfected by Theobald *Boehm) is about 0.6 m (2 ft) long and has a range of three octaves above middle C. ⊓musical instruments.

flux (brazing and soldering) A substance applied to pieces to be soldered to aid the formation of the joint. Soft solder, used in electrical joints, commonly contains a core of flux, often tallow or a similar substance. For hard soldering, at higher temperatures, zinc chloride is often used. The flux lowers the melting point of the solder and also reacts with or removes surface oxides from the metals, thus keeping their surfaces clean and allowing the liquid solder to adhere to the surfaces.

flux (physics) The net amount of a directional quantity passing through a surface area at right angles to the surface. The concept of flux is used to describe phenomena that involve forces or the flow of energy, such as electric flux, magnetic flux, and luminous flux.

fly An insect belonging to the order *Diptera* (over 85 000 species)—the so-called true, or two-winged, flies—of great economic importance in transmitting disease. The adults have only two wings (the front pair), the hind pair being reduced to balancing organs (called halteres). The mouthparts are adapted for piercing or sucking, and most species feed on plant juices or suck the blood of mammals. The larvae—often called maggots—are typically scavengers on plant and animal refuse or parasites of pest status. Blood-sucking species, such as *mosquitoes and *tsetse flies, may transmit such diseases as malaria, sleeping sickness, and yellow fever. The order also includes the *houseflies, *blowflies, *craneflies, and *horse flies.

The name fly is also used for various flying insects of other orders: the alderfly, caddis fly, damselfly, firefly, and mayfly are examples of nondipterous flies.

fly agaric A poisonous mushroom, *Amanita muscaria*, found in woodlands, especially of birch and conifers. Its cap, 6–20 cm in diameter, is scarlet or orange-red with white scales and the white stalk has a membranous collar beneath the cap. Fly agaric is seldom fatal. It was formerly used as a fly killer, hence its name.

flycatcher A small active songbird belonging to an Old World family (*Muscicapidae*; 378 species) and feeding on insects, typically caught in flight. They have small bills surrounded by stiff bristles and delicate legs used only for perching. The typical flycatchers are dull coloured and include the grey-and-brown European spotted flycatcher (*Muscicapa striata*) and the black-and-white pied flycatcher (*Ficedula hypoleuca*). The tropical blue flycatchers and paradise flycatchers are beautifully coloured and ornamented. *Compare* tyrant flycatcher.

Flying Doctor Service of Australia, Royal A scheme begun in 1928 at Cloncurry, Queensland, to transport doctors to patients in remote areas. The development of a Morse radio transmitter-receiver facilitated long-range consultation and emergency treatment. The service, which is free, is financed by state governments, subscriptions from outposts, and charges levied for messages. Similar schemes are run in Canada and East Africa.

Flying Dutchman In sailors' lore, a ghost ship haunting the sea around the Cape of Good Hope. Its captain, driven back from the Cape by a storm, is supposed to have sworn a blasphemous oath to round it or be forever damned. The story became popular in 19th-century literature and inspired Wagner's opera (1843) of the same name.

flying fish A ⬜fish of the family *Exocoetidae* (about 40 species). Up to 45 cm long, flying fish swim just below the surface in warm oceanic waters. If disturbed they launch themselves from the water by rapidly beating the tail and glide through the air using large winglike pectoral fins.

flying fox A fruit *bat belonging to the genus *Pteropus* (51 species), ranging from Africa to Australia. Flying foxes have foxlike heads and a wingspan of up to 1.5 m.

flying lemur. *See* colugo.

flying lizard A lizard belonging to the genus *Draco* (15 species) of SE Asia, having large folds of skin between the legs supported by ribs that are spread out when the lizard jumps from a tree. They have greenish bodies and brightly coloured "wings." Family: *Agamidae* (agamas). ⬜reptile.

flying phalanger A squirrel-like *marsupial mammal, also called marsupial glider. Flying phalangers, found in E Australia and Tasmania, range from 14 to 100 cm in length. They all have soft fur and long bushy tails and a flap of skin between the fore and hind legs enables them to glide from tree to tree. Genera: *Acrobates*, *Petaurus*, *Schoinobates*; family: *Phalangeridae*.

flying saucer. *See* unidentified flying object.

flying snake A slender arboreal snake belonging to the genus *Chrysopelea* (3 species), occurring in S Asia and the East Indies. They are diurnal, feed on small rodents, bats, birds, and lizards, and can glide short distances by launching themselves in the air and flattening their belly scales. Family: *Colubridae*.

flying squirrel A nocturnal *squirrel of the subfamily *Petauristinae* (37 species), occurring in SE Asia, North America, and Eurasia. Flying squirrels have a flap of loose skin from elbow to knee that is stretched tight by extending the legs, enabling them to glide from branch to branch. ⬜mammal.

Flynn, Errol (1909–59) Australian actor, born in Tasmania. After trying a number of odd jobs, he became an actor in Hollywood, playing the handsome adventurous hero in such films as *Captain Blood* (1935), *Gentleman Jim* (1942), and (as John Barrymore) *Too Much Too Soon* (1958). His private life, which was scarcely less eventful than his film roles, was candidly recounted in two autobiographies, *Beam Ends* (1934) and *My Wicked Wicked Ways* (1959).

Fly River A river in New Guinea, rising in W Papua New Guinea and flowing generally S, forming part of the border between Papua New Guinea and West Irian, before entering the Gulf of Papua. Length: 1300 km (800 mi).

flytrap. *See* Venus' flytrap.

flywheel A large heavy wheel attached to the driving shaft of a motor to act as an energy store and to iron out fluctuations in the speed of the machine. The energy stored depends on the speed of rotation and the weight distribution of the wheel. They are used in *internal-combustion engines, power presses, etc.

f-number The ratio of the focal length of a camera lens to the diameter of the shutter opening (aperture). For example, f-8 means that the focal length is eight times the aperture. The smaller the f-number, the greater the illumination of the film. **Relative aperture** is the reciprocal of f-number.

Foch, Ferdinand (1851–1929) French marshal. At the outbreak of World War I he commanded the Ninth Army and was largely responsible for halting the German advance at the Marne and for the Allied victory at Ypres (1915). After the Somme offensive (1916), he became chief of the general staff (1917). He returned to action in 1918 and as Allied commander in chief forced the Germans back to the Rhine, effecting their defeat.

foetus. *See* fetus.

fog A cloud near the ground surface, within which visibility is reduced to less than 1 km (0.6 mi). Fog is the result of the condensation of water vapour in the lower layers of air, usually through the cooling of air to below its *dew point; it is most likely to occur with light wind conditions and a clear sky at night. It often contains dust and smoke particles and in industrial areas the increased supply of these particles causes a greater incidence of fog; in areas in which smoke occurs *smog can develop.

Foggia 41 28N 15 33E A city in Italy, in Apulia. It has a castle dating from the time of the Holy Roman Emperor, Frederick II. Olives, grapes, wheat, and tobacco are grown in the surrounding region and its industries include flour milling, cheese and paper making, and engineering. Population (1980 est): 158 830.

föhn A warm dry wind that descends down the leeward side of mountains. It is a frequent occurrence in the Alps (where the name originated), the Rocky Mountains (where it is known as the **chinook**), and the Andes. In winter it can cause extremely rapid thaws of lying snow, resulting in avalanches.

Fokine, Michel (Mikhail F.; 1880–1942) Russian ballet dancer and choreographer. From 1909 he worked with Diaghilev's Ballets Russes in Paris, for which he choreographed such revolutionary ballets as *The Firebird* (1910) and *Petrushka* (1911). He went to New York in 1923 and became a naturalized US citizen in 1932.

Fokker, Anthony Hermann Gerard (1890–1939) Dutch aircraft manufacturer. Fokker opened an aircraft factory in Germany in 1912. During World War I he supplied Germany with aircraft and invented a method of firing a machine gun through the propeller of an aircraft. He later became a US citizen.

fold A buckling of sedimentary rock strata produced by compressional forces acting on it. Large-scale folding produces mountain ranges; this occurs where two continental plates collide (*see* plate tectonics) and the sediment along their margins is compressed and folded. A simple upfold is called an *anticline and a downfold, a *syncline; however, most folds are much more complex.

Foley, John Henry (1818–74) British sculptor, born in Dublin. One of the leading Victorian sculptors, his works include the bronze equestrian statues of Hardinge and Canning in Calcutta and the statue of Prince Albert on the Albert Memorial in South Kensington.

folic acid. *See* vitamin B complex.

Folies-Bergère A Parisian variety theatre opened in 1869 and celebrated chiefly for its elaborate revues featuring dancing girls and striptease acts. Maurice *Chevalier and many other leading French entertainers have appeared here.

folk dance A form of dance developed by country people, usually for their own amusement. Folk dances derive from ancient ritual dances used in religious worship and to invoke the fertility of the land (the original purpose of the *maypole dance). They have greatly influenced other forms of dances, notably court dancing, 18th- and 19th-century ballroom dances (such as the *waltz and *polka), and *ballet. Many countries have their own traditional dances. In England the most popular types are country dancing and the Morris dance. The revived interest in folk dancing in the 20th century is reflected in the popularity of professional folk-dance companies and folk-dance societies. The English Folk Dance and Song Society was established in 1911 by Cecil *Sharp.

Folkestone 51 5N 1 11E A resort and port in SE England, in Kent, with Channel crossings to Boulogne. Just outside Folkestone is the Warren, an extensive wooded area of geologically important chalk landslips. Population (1981): 43 742.

folklore The social, material, and oral culture of primitive societies. The social culture comprises such forms as festivals, dances, and religious rites; the material culture comprises architecture and arts and crafts; the oral culture includes songs, tales, legends, proverbs, and riddles. The study of folklore, spurred by early collections of folk literature, such as Percy's *Reliques of Ancient English Poetry* (1765) and the *Fairy Tales* (1812–14) of the brothers *Grimm, has played an important role in the work of anthropologists, such as Franz *Boas and J. G. *Frazer.

folk music Song or dance music developed from a communal aural tradition and not composed by an individual, e.g. Irish ballads and cowboy songs. The melody and words of folksongs are often changed by a succession of performances. Folk music is characterized by modal melody and simple forms, such as dances, lullabies, work songs, and love ballads. Traditional English folksongs include "Black Is the Colour of My True Love's Hair" and "Greensleeves." During the revival of folksong in the USA in the 1960s, new music by such composers as Woody Guthrie and Joan Baez was termed folksong or "folk," owing to its similarity to authentic folk music.

follicle-stimulating hormone. *See* gonadotrophin.

Folsom point A fluted lanceolate (leaf-shaped) stone spearhead made between 9000 and 8000 BC in the western grasslands of the USA. The name derives from Folsom, New Mexico, where one was discovered (1926), with the remains of an extinct form of bison. *Compare* Clovis point.

Fomalhaut A conspicuous star, apparent magnitude 1.15 and 23 light years distant, that is the only bright star in the S constellation Piscis Austrinus.

Fon The predominant people of S Benin (formerly Dahomey), who speak a dialect of *Ewe. They grow maize, manioc, and yams and palm oil as a cash crop. Their villages are headed by the oldest male. A hereditary headman has general authority to arbitrate in disputes. During the 18th and 19th centuries the Fon formed the kingdom of Dahomey. The powerful king and his chiefs conducted war ceremonies, received tribute, and presided over courts. An ancestor cult involved the sacrifice of pris-

oners of war in return for supernatural aid.

Fonda, Henry (1905–82) US film actor and director, associated particularly with the portrayal of men of solid integrity, notably in *The Grapes of Wrath* (1940). Other films include *War and Peace* (1956), *Twelve Angry Men* (1957), which he directed, and *On Golden Pond* (1981), which earned him his first Oscar and also starred his daughter **Jane Fonda** (1937–). Her other films include *Barbarella* (1968), an extravaganza of sexual fantasy, and subsequent more serious roles in such films as *Klute* (1971), *Julia* (1977), and *Coming Home* (1978). His son **Peter Fonda** (1939–) made his name as an actor and director with *Easy Rider* (1969).

Fontainebleau 48 24N 2 42E A town in N central France, in the Seine-et-Marne department. The surrounding forest inspired the Barbizon school of painters. The Royal Palace, largely built by Francis I, was the scene of Napoleon I's abdication in 1814. Fontainebleau was the headquarters of NATO from 1954 to 1966. Population (1982): 18 753.

Fontainebleau, school of The painters who decorated the Royal Palace of Fontainebleau (France) between about 1530 and 1560. The Italians Giovanni Battista Rosso (1494–1540), Francesco Primaticcio (c. 1504–70), and Niccolò dell' Abbate (c. 1512–71) were chiefly responsible for developing the particularly sensuous and elegant form of *mannerism that characterizes the school.

FOLSOM POINT *One of the most developed types of Stone Age weapon heads.*

Fontana, Domenico (1543–1607) Italian architect and engineer. In the employ of the pope in Rome, Fontana designed the Sistine Library (1587–90) and helped complete the dome of St Peter's Basilica. He was also responsible for re-erecting the Egyptian obelisk on its present site in front of St Peter's.

Fontane, Theodor (1819–98) German novelist. He began writing novels at the age of 56 after varied experience as a journalist and war correspondent. *Vor dem Sturm* (1878) is a realistic historical novel dealing with the Prussian nobility. Of several novels dealing with the place of women in society the best known is *Effi Briest* (1898).

Fontanne, Lyn. *See* Lunt, Alfred.

Fontenelle, Bernard le Bovier de (1657–1757) French philosopher and writer, who joined his uncle, Pierre *Corneille, in Paris in 1680, becoming a leading light of the contemporary salons. Renowned for his wit and his learning, he popularized the new scientific theories of

Fontenoy, Battle of

Descartes and Newton in such works as *Digressions sur les anciens et les modernes* (1688) and *Éléments de la géométrie de l'infini* (1727). Pouring scorn on ancient myths and beliefs, he was a confirmed "modern," writing his *Théorie des tourbillons cartésiens* when he was 95.

Fontenoy, Battle of (11 May, 1745) The battle in the War of the *Austrian Succession in which France defeated Austria. Fought near Tournai, SE of Brussels, the battle was the French commander de *Saxe's most notable victory, leading to the conquest of Flanders. His artillery and cavalry carried the day against the Austrians, and their Dutch and English allies, who retreated toward Brussels.

Fonteyn, Dame Margot (Margaret Hookham; 1919-) British ballet dancer. She was a member of the Sadler's Wells company and the Royal Ballet from 1934 to 1959 and has also performed with most leading US and European companies, often in partnership with Rudolf *Nureyev. Her most famous performances were in classical ballets such as *Giselle*, *Swan Lake*, and *The Sleeping Beauty*.

Fonthill Abbey An architecturally influential country house near Bath in Wiltshire, designed (1796-1807) in the *gothic revival style by James *Wyatt for William *Beckford. Fonthill was an enormous building, featuring a tower 85 m (278 ft) high. It was quickly and badly built; the tower collapsed in 1827 and the rest was demolished soon after.

Foochow. *See* Fuzhou.

Food and Agriculture Organization (FAO) A specialized agency of the *United Nations constituted in 1945 to coordinate international efforts to raise levels of nutrition and food production and to improve the management of forests. The agency, with headquarters in Rome, conducts research, makes recommendations, organizes educational programmes, and encourages the export of agricultural products.

food chain A series of living organisms associated in a feeding relationship: each animal feeds on the one below it in the series. Most commonly, green plants are at the base of a food chain. They are eaten by herbivores, which in turn may be consumed by carnivores. Any animal or plant parasites are also part of the chain, and different food chains are often interconnected to form a **food web**. Other food chains are based on decomposers—organisms that feed on dead organic remains of plants and animals.

food poisoning An acute illness arising from eating contaminated food. Vomiting and diarrhoea are the usual symptoms. *Salmonella* is the bacterium that most commonly causes food poisoning (salmonellosis), and symptoms begin 12-24 hours after eating the food. Patients usually recover within a few days. Another kind of food poisoning is due to a toxin (poison) produced by staphylococci: symptoms occur within one to three hours of taking the food. *Clostridium* bacteria may also cause food poisoning, the most severe form of which is *botulism.

food preservation The treatment of food to prevent its deterioration and to maintain its eating quality and nutritional value. Breakdown of food tissues is caused by enzymes, either contained within the food or produced by microorganisms—bacteria, yeasts, and fungi—growing in the food. These organisms also produce unpleasant and sometimes harmful substances. Oxidation and dehydration also contribute to spoilage. The principle of food preservation is therefore to alter the condition of food so that the activities of microorganisms are stopped. One of the oldest methods is drying or dehydration—used for meat, vegetables, cereals, milk products, etc. *Freezing is now widely used for both industrial and domestic food preservation. *Freeze drying involves freezing followed by dehydration. Heating kills mircoorganisms and is the principle of *pasteurization, *sterilization, etc. Further growth is prevented if food is sealed in airtight containers, such as cans (*see* canning) or bottles. A wide range of chemicals is added to food to inhibit microbial activity. Boiling with sugar (e.g. in jam) and pickling with salt or vinegar (e.g. onions, cucumbers) are traditional methods. Smoking has also been used to preserve meat and fish. Sodium benzoate, propionates, nitrates, nitrites, sulphur dioxide, and sulphites are all used by the modern food industry as well as many other compounds that enhance colour, flavour, and texture for the consumer.

Fools, Feast of A festival held in medieval Europe (especially in France) on, or near, Holy Innocents' Day (28 Dec). It was organized by lower clergy. A mock pope or bishop (sometimes a boy) was elected and presided over

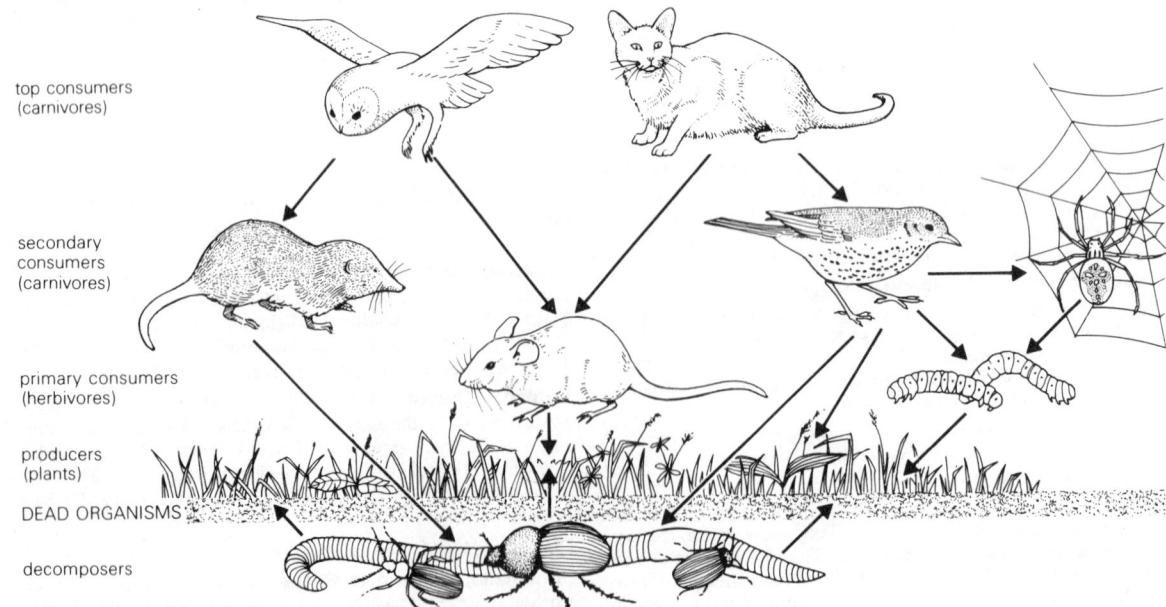

FOOD CHAIN *The feeding relationships between some plants and animals of a meadow habitat are simplified in this food web; in practice many more links and various other organisms are involved.*

top consumers (carnivores)

secondary consumers (carnivores)

primary consumers (herbivores)

producers (plants)

DEAD ORGANISMS

decomposers

burlesque church services. There were also processions and carnival plays as well as festive dancing and drinking.

fool's gold. *See* pyrite.

foot The lowermost part of the leg. The human foot contains 14 bones. There are seven tarsal bones, of which one (the talus) forms a hinge joint with the bones of the lower *leg and another (the calcaneus) forms the projection of the heel. The five metatarsal bones form the body of the foot and articulate with the phalanges, the bones of the toes. The first (big) toe provides a springboard for walking and running. *See* Plate IV.

Foot, Michael (Mackintosh) (1913–) British Labour politician and historian, leader of the Labour Party (1980–83); he was replaced by Neil *Kinnock. A prominent left-wing intellectual, his books include *Loyalists and Loners* (1986).

foot-and-mouth disease An infectious virus disease affecting cattle, sheep, goats, pigs, and many wild animals. Symptoms, which appear 1–15 days after infection, include fever and the development of blisters in the mouth and on the foot with consequent excessive salivation and lameness. Recovery occurs in 95% of cases but production of offspring and milk yield in females is adversely affected. The disease must be notifed to the authorities in many countries. Infected animals and contacts are usually slaughtered and movement of animals restricted. Vaccination is routine where the disease is endemic.

football A field game played throughout the world, the object of which is to score goals with an inflated ball. Team games using a football were played in China around 200 BC, in ancient Greece and Rome, and from the 12th century in England, where the violence and lawlessness of the game resulted in considerable injury. The modern games evolved during the 19th century as rules were formalized; in this the English public schools played a large role.

American football is similar to rugby football and developed in US colleges in the 1870s; it is played with an oval ball on a field marked out as a gridiron. There are 11 players on the field at any one time, but groups of differently specialized players are used in different phases of the game. The teams toss to decide which is to kick off, which gives first possession to the other team. The game progresses in downs, or periods when the offensive team is advancing the ball towards the goal by passing or running with it. A down ends with a successful tackle or missed pass. The team has four downs in which to advance the ball 10 yd (9 m). If it fails, the other team is given possession, having the chance to substitute offensive for defensive players. If the 10 yd is covered, the team maintains possession of the ball. A touchdown, in which the ball is taken across the opponents' goal line, scores six points; a conversion after a touchdown, in which the ball is taken over the goal line again from scrimmage or is kicked between the goalposts scores respectively two points or one point; a field goal (kicked from anywhere on the field) scores three points; a safety, in which a team scores a touchdown against itself, scores two points for its opponents. American football is a violent game requiring protective clothing.

Association football (*or* soccer) dates back to the founding in England of the Football Association (1863). It is an 11-a-side game played with a spherical ball weighing 14–16 oz (396–453 g) and having a circumference of 27–28 in (69–71 cm). The traditional positions of the players are: goalkeeper; right and left back; right, centre, and left halfback; outside right, inside right, centre forward, inside left, and outside left. These positions, established early in the 20th century, have now become very flexible, and a modern line-up consists simply of strikers, midfield players, and defenders. The teams toss for the first kick (the kick-off), following which the teams compete for the ball, trying to kick or head it into the opponents' goal. Only the goalkeeper may use his hands, and then only in his penalty area. Played all over the world, the game is governed internationally by the *Fédération internationale de Football

association.

Australian Rules is an 18-a-side game that originated in the Australian goldfields in the 1850s and is extensively played in some states, especially Victoria. It is a fast open game played with an oval ball measuring 22.75 by 29.5 in (57.2 by 73.6 cm), with which players may run as long as they bounce it every 9 m (10 yd). The ball must be punched instead of thrown (as it is in rugby football). There are four goalposts without crossbars at each end. A goal, kicked between the two inner posts, scores six points; a behind, kicked between an inner and an outer post, scores one point.

Canadian football is similar to American football but is played with 12-a-side teams on a larger field and has slightly different scoring and rules.

Rugby football uses an oval ball that is kicked or passed by hand. The game was first played at Rugby School, England, according to tradition in 1823. In 1871 the Rugby Football Union was formed, but its ban on professionalism led in 1893 to the secession of the Rugby League (then called the Northern Union); there are therefore two types of rugby. Rugby Union football (*or* rugger) is a 15-a-side amateur game played throughout the world. The ball is 11–11.25 in (27.9–28.6 cm) long. A try, in which the ball is touched down behind the opponents' goal line, is worth four points; a goal (a try "converted" by kicking the ball over the crossbar of the goalposts), a further two points; a penalty goal, resulting from a kick awarded as a penalty against the opposing team, three points; and a drop goal, from the field, three points. A scrum, in which the forwards of both teams battle for the ball in a tight mass, is used to restart the game after minor infringements. For more serious infringements a penalty kick is given to the opposing side. Rugby League football is a 13-a-side game with slightly different rules and scoring in which professionalism is allowed; it is played mainly in N England. □ p. 460.

football hooliganism Acts of violence and vandalism by certain elements of crowds attending football matches. Unruly crowd behaviour has long been a feature of football matches: overcrowding and drunkenness exacerbate feelings of hostility towards rival supporters until these flare into overt violence. Some British fans, in particular, seem to regard an outing to a football match as an opportunity for a brawl. This phenomenon reached an unacceptable climax in 1985, when 39 fans (mostly Italians) died at the European Cup Final (Liverpool vs Juventus of Turin) as a result of mob violence led by Liverpool supporters in Brussels. English clubs were subsequently barred from playing abroad and new measures, such as closed circuit TV, segregation of rival fans, and banning of alcohol, were imposed at all grounds.

Football League An English association football competition for professional teams. It was created in the N in 1888 to help finance professional clubs by providing a systematic series of matches, as the Football Association Challenge Cup series did not. The Second Division was added in 1892 with a system of promotion and relegation between the divisions soon after; the Third Division was added in 1920 and the Fourth in 1958. Similar leagues exist in many other countries.

football pools A system of gambling involving postal betting on the results of football matches. First appearing in the UK in 1923, they are now controlled by a few companies registered under the Betting, Gaming and Lotteries Act (1963). The stake money is pooled, some 30% of which is available as prize money (30% goes in running costs and 40% in government duty). Although the Exchequer is the most consistent beneficiary, the weekly opportunity to become rich is the paramount attraction. The most popular pool is now the Treble Chance, in which competitors attempt to predict eight games that will result in a draw. From August to April British matches are used and from May to July the pools rely on Australian matches.

Foraminifera An order of small single-celled animals

FOOTBALL

American football

Association football

Australian Rules

Rugby Union football

FOOTBALL *Dimensions of pitches.*

(□*Protozoa*) found on the sea bed or as part of the *plankton. They form calcareous often multichambered shells, ranging in size from under 0.5 mm to 5 mm, from which they extend fine branching pseudopodia to trap small protozoans and algae. Class: *Sarcodina. See also Globigerina; Nummulites.

Forbes, George William (1869–1947) New Zealand statesman; prime minister (1930–35). Leader of the United (formerly Liberal) Party, he was forced by economic difficulties into a coalition (1931) with the Reform Party but still failed to solve the problems of the Depression.

Forbidden City The central part of *Peking, so called because entry was forbidden to all but the emperor's family and servants. It was surrounded by a wall 4 km (2.5 mi) long and from the 15th century onwards it contained the royal palace and residences and offices of the emperor's servants and ministers. It is now a complex of museums.

force The agency that changes either the speed or the direction of motion of a body (symbol: *F*). It is a *vector quantity defined as the product of the mass of the body and the acceleration produced on it. Force is measured in newtons. *See also* centripetal force; Coriolis force.

Ford, Ford Madox (Ford Hermann Hueffer; 1873–1939) British novelist, grandson of the Pre-Raphaelite artist Ford Madox Brown. Among his 80 or more novels and books of criticism and memoirs are the novels *The Good Soldier* (1915) and *Parade's End* (1924-28), a tetralogy. He founded and edited the *English Review* (1908) and, in Paris, the *Transatlantic Review* (1924), in which he published the early works of *Pound, *Joyce, *Hemingway, and many other writers.

Ford, Gerald R(udolph) (1913–) US statesman; Republican president (1974–77). Born Leslie King, he later took the surname of his eminent Republican stepfather. A lawyer by profession, Ford was appointed as vice president by *Nixon after the resignation of Spiro Agnew in 1973. Following Nixon's resignation, Ford became the first US president to succeed to that office without having been elected. His generous free pardon granted to Nixon and his visits to the Soviet Union and China did not save him from defeat by Carter in the 1976 election.

Ford, Henry (1863–1947) US □car manufacturer, who introduced assembly-line production. The Ford Motor Company was founded in 1903 and in 1912 Ford introduced the assembly line to manufacture the famous Model T, 15 million of which had been mass produced by 1928. The company still produces cars both in the USA and Europe.

Ford, John (1586–c. 1640) English dramatist, the last major figure of Elizabethan and Jacobean drama. He collaborated with *Dekker and others at first, writing his own major plays between 1627 and 1638. Those most frequently performed are the revenge tragedies *The Broken Heart* (c. 1630) and *'Tis Pity She's a Whore* (c. 1632).

Ford, John (Sean O'Feeney; 1895-1973) US film director. He received much critical acclaim for *The Informer* (1935), *The Grapes of Wrath* (1940), and other films on social themes, but is best known as a director of popular westerns. These include *Stagecoach* (1939), *Rio Grande* (1950), and *How the West Was Won* (1962).

foreign aid Help given to poor countries by richer ones. Foreign aid can take several forms, including gratis payments, cheap loans, gifts in kind, etc. Foreign aid is usually given to the *developing countries to relieve natural disasters, to assist them in their efforts to industrialize, or for political reasons, such as to bolster up a friendly regime. One of the most ambitious programmes of foreign aid was the *Marshall Plan in which the USA provided funds to assist the recovery of Europe after World War II.

Foreign and Commonwealth Office The UK government department that deals with foreign and commonwealth affairs and is responsible for presenting and promoting the interests of the UK abroad; it was formed in 1968 by an amalgamation of the Foreign Office and the Commonwealth Office and is headed by the secretary of state for foreign and commonwealth affairs. The Foreign Office emerged from the office of the secretary of state for foreign affairs, a post created in 1782 to replace the secretary of state for the northern department (*compare* Home Office). The Commonwealth Office was itself the product of an amalgamation in 1966 of the Colonial Office (an independent department since 1854) and the Commonwealth Relations Office (formed in 1930 as the Commonwealth Office).

foreign exchange. *See* exchange rates.

Foreign Legion A French military force, the Légion étrangère, formed in 1831 to serve in France's African colonies. Its recruits are international but its officers are usually French. One of its regiments formed the *Organisation de l'Armée secrète (OAS) in Algeria (1961) and was subsequently disbanded. The Legion's headquarters are at Aubagne, near Marseille, with units in Corsica and Djibouti.

Foreland, North and South Two chalk promontories in SE England, in Kent on the Strait of Dover. They mark the E extent of the North Downs.

forensic medicine. *See* medical jurisprudence.

forest An area of land covered largely with trees and undergrowth. Over 20% of world land area is forest, both natural and artificially planted, making forests a vital part of the global ecosystem as major suppliers of oxygen as well as timber. They also provide habitats for wildlife and are widely used for recreation.
The species of trees growing depends mainly on climate. Northern coniferous forests consist largely of pine, spruce, and firs and provide softwood for paper pulp, furniture, construction, etc. In more temperate regions forests consist primarily of mixed deciduous trees, especially oak, ash, elm, beech, sycamore, and other hardwoods, used mainly in furniture. In Mediterranean climates, the trees are adapted to hot dry summers and include the evergreen oaks. Broad-leaved evergreen trees are also found in New Zealand and South America, together with southern conifers. Tropical forests are characterized by a great diversity of species, usually of tall evergreen trees, with many climbing vines and epiphytes. The major tropical rain forests are in the Amazon and Orinoco river basins, with others in Africa and SE Asia. In neighbouring regions of lower and more seasonal rainfall, an open savanna forest predominates, consisting of scattered deciduous trees.

Forestry, the cultivation and management of forests, is of major economic importance. Much research and development has been invested in improving varieties of trees for commercial use and in better methods of planting, pest control, thinning, felling, and extraction and of processing the timber into usable products. In the UK, forestry is controlled by the Forestry Commission (established in 1919), which is now responsible for the production of most home-grown softwoods. It is also involved in nature conservation and the provision of recreational amenities.

Forester, C(ecil) S(cott) (1899-1966) British historical novelist, famous as the creator of Horatio Hornblower, a heroic but self-doubting British naval officer of Napoleonic times whose career he chronicled in a series of novels, beginning with *The Happy Return* (1937). Forester abandoned his medical studies for writing after the success of his first novel, *Payment Deferred* (1926).

Forest Hills A residential district in the USA, in New York City on Long Island. It is noted for its lawn-tennis tournaments at the West Side Tennis Club.

Forfar 56 38N 2 54N A market town in E Scotland, in Tayside Region. Its castle was occupied by early Scottish kings but was destroyed when Robert the Bruce took it from the English in 1308. Forfar manufactures jute, linen, and rayon. Population (1981): 12 742.

Forfarshire. *See* Angus.

forget-me-not An annual or perennial herb of the genus

Myosotis (50 species), of temperate regions. 5–60 cm tall, it has oblong hairy leaves and long spikes of small flowers, usually blue with white centres (young flowers are often pink). The fruits are small nutlets. Several species are grown as garden flowers. Family: *Boraginaceae*.

Forlì 44 13N 12 02E A city in Italy, in Emilia-Romagna. It has some ancient buildings, including a 15th-century citadel. Its various manufactures include furniture, textiles, felt, household appliances, and footwear. Population (1980 est): 110 755.

formaldehyde (*or* methanal; HCHO) A colourless toxic gaseous aldehyde. It dissolves in water to produce a solution known as formalin, which is used as a preservative. Formaldehyde is made by the catalytic oxidation of *methanol or petroleum gases and is used to make synthetic resins.

Forman, Miloš (1932–) Czech film director. His films, which include *The Fireman's Ball* (1967), are noted for their blend of humour and social criticism. In 1968 he went to the USA, where he made *Taking Off* (1970) and *One Flew over the Cuckoo's Nest* (1976).

formic acid (*or* methanoic acid; HCOOH) A colourless corrosive liquid *fatty acid with a pungent smell. It is made industrially by treating sodium formate (HCOONa) with sulphuric acid and is used in textile finishing and chemical manufacture. Formic acid occurs naturally in nettles and insects. Its name comes from the Latin *formica*, ant, whose sting is due to the secretion of formic acid.

Formigny, Battle of (15 April, 1450) The battle during the last period of the *Hundred Years' War in which the French forces routed the English army near Caen. The victory led directly to the fall of Caen, and then of Normandy, to the French.

Formosa. *See* Taiwan.

Forres 57 37N 3 38W A market town in NE Scotland, in Grampian Region. It contains Sueno's Stone, a sculptured monolith believed to date from 900 AD. There are whisky-distilling and engineering industries. Population (1983 est): 7065.

Forster, E(dward) M(organ) (1879–1970) British novelist. Educated at King's College, Cambridge, where he returned as a fellow in 1946, his fiction and social criticism stress the importance of human affection and the need to cultivate both the intellect and the imagination. His novels include *Where Angels Fear to Tread* (1905), *The Longest Journey* (1907), *A Room with a View* (1908), *Howard's End* (1910), and *A Passage to India* (1924). *Maurice*, a novel portraying a homosexual relationship, was published posthumously in 1971.

Forsythia A genus of shrubs (about 7 species), sometimes called golden bell, native to E Europe and Asia and widely grown as garden ornamentals. The masses of four-petalled yellow flowers appear before the leaves, which are toothed and oval. The slender stems make the plants suitable for wall shrubs and hedges. The most common garden forsythia is the hybrid *F. × intermedia*. Family: *Oleaceae* (olive family).

Fortaleza (*or* Ceará) 3 45S 38 35W A city and port in E Brazil, the capital of Ceará state on the Atlantic Ocean. Exports include cotton, rice, coffee, and sugar. Its university was established in 1955. Population (1980): 648 815.

Fort-de-France (former name: Fort Royal) 14 36N 61 05W The capital and main port of Martinique since 1680, on the W coast. It was almost destroyed by an earthquake in 1839 and by fire in 1890. It is an important tourist resort and the site of a French naval base. Exports include sugar, cocoa, and rum. Population (1982): 99 844.

Fortescue, Sir John (c. 1394–1476) English jurist; chief justice of the King's Bench (1442–61). A supporter of the Lancastrian party, Fortescue escaped to France with the royal family in 1463, when the Yorkist Edward IV deposed Henry VI. There he wrote his famous works on English law and government, *De laudibus legum Angliae* and *The Governance of Eng-*

land. Despite his part in the attempted Lancastrian restoration at the battle of Tewkesbury (1471), he was subsequently pardoned by Edward IV.

Forth, River A river in SE Scotland, rising on the NE slopes of Ben Lomond and flowing 104 km (65 mi) E through Stirling to Alloa. The river then expands into the **Firth of Forth** (an inlet of the North Sea) extending 82 km (51 mi) in length and 31 km (19 mi) wide at its mouth. It is spanned by the cantilever iron Forth Rail Bridge (designed in the 1880s by Benjamin Baker) and a road bridge (1964). **The Forth and Clyde Canal**, 60 km (37 mi) long, links the Rivers Forth and Clyde.

Fortin barometer A type of mercury *barometer, invented in 1810 by the French instrument maker, Nicolas Fortin (1750–1831). The reservoir of mercury is contained in a leather bag attached to an evacuated glass tube marked with a fixed scale. The level of the mercury in the reservoir is set at zero by adjusting the leather bag.

Fort Knox 37 54N 85 59W A military base in the USA, in N Kentucky. Established in 1917, it is the site of the US Depository, which contains US gold reserves. Population (1980): 31 055.

Fort Lamy. *See* N'djamena.

Fort Lauderdale 26 08N 80 08W A city and resort in the USA, in SE Florida on the Atlantic Ocean. It has one of the largest marinas in the world. Population (1980): 153 256.

FORTRAN (*fo*rmula *tran*slation) A computer-programming language. It is a high-level language (*see* program) used for representing mathematical formulae in a form that can be processed by a computer. Widely used among scientists and engineers, it has also found applications in the business community.

Fort Stanwix, Treaties of (1768, 1784) Agreements between the British and the Iroquois Indians, in which the British gained present-day W Pennsylvania, West Virginia, New York, and Kentucky for gifts worth $10,000. The fort, located at the site of Rome, New York, was built for defence against the Indians and was renamed Fort Schuyler in 1776.

Fort Sumter. *See* Charleston.

Fortuna The Roman goddess of fortune and good luck. She was usually portrayed standing on a ball or wheel, indicating her mutability, and holding a cornucopia from which she distributes her favours. She is identical with *Tyche.

Fort Wayne 41 05N 85 08W A city in the USA, in NE Indiana on the Maumee River. Founded by the French in 1680, the fort was built in 1794. An important communications centre, its main manufactures are electrical equipment and motor vehicles. Population (1980): 172 196.

Fort William 56 49N 5 07W A town in W Scotland, in the Highland Region at the head of Loch Linnhe. Besides tourism, it has aluminium-smelting, whisky-distilling, and paper-making industries. Population (1981): 11 079.

Fort William (Canada). *See* Thunder Bay.

Fort Worth 32 45N 97 20W A city in the USA, in NE Texas near Dallas. The centre of the N Texas industrial area, its manufactures include aircraft, refined oil, and food products. Population (1980): 385 141.

Forty-five Rebellion. *See* Jacobites.

forty-niners. *See* Gold Rush.

forum A Roman marketplace, similar to the Greek *agora. The forum was the civic centre of the town, containing all the main temples and public buildings. The most famous forum is in Rome; it was laid out in the 1st century BC, but later frequently modified.

Foscolo, Ugo (1778–1827) Italian poet. His early tragedy *Tieste* (1797) and his poem *A Bonaparte liberatore* (1797) reflect the anti-Austrian nationalism that shaped his life. He served in the Napoleonic armies but in 1816 he settled in

England. His best-known works are the patriotic poem *Dei sepolcri* (1807) and the unfinished poem *Le grazie* (1822).

fossa A catlike mammal, *Cryptoprocta ferox*, found only in Madagascar. It is about 150 cm long including the tail (70 cm) and has short legs and short orange-brown fur. It feeds almost entirely on lemurs. Family: *Viverridae; order: Carnivora.

Fosse Way A Roman road from Exeter through Cirencester to Lincoln. It marked the frontier in the first phase of the Roman conquest of Britain (c. 47 AD). Its characteristically straight course is now followed partly by the modern A429.

fossil The remains or traces of a plant or animal that lived in the past, usually preserved in sedimentary rock. It may be the whole or part of the organism itself that is preserved, usually chemically altered; alternatively it may have dissolved away leaving an impression (mould), which preserves its exact shape, or a cast, when it has been replaced exactly by mineral matter. Examples of fossils are whole mammoths preserved in ice, insects preserved in amber, and coal (the carbonized remains of extinct swamp plants). Trace fossils include excrement, burrows, or fossil tracks. A derived fossil is found in a more recent sediment than the one in which it was orginally preserved, because of erosion and redeposition. A zone fossil is used in biostratigraphy to delimit a stratigraphic zone; such fossils must be widely distributed and have a limited vertical range in successive rock strata to be useful for this purpose. The study of fossils is called *palaeontology.   □p. 464.

fossil fuels The mineral fuels *coal, *oil, and *natural gas that occur in rock formations. They were formed by the deposition millions of years ago of the remains of vegetation (coal) and living organisms (oil and gas), which were buried under subsequent deposition and later subjected to heat and pressure.
Fossil fuels supply a large proportion of our current *energy needs, but the reserves are finite. Gas and oil in particular are rapidly being exhausted. *Alternative energy sources are therefore now being investigated and *nuclear energy is being developed to take their place.

Foster, Stephen Collins (1826-64) US composer of such songs as "Swanee River" (1851) and "Beautiful Dreamer" (1864). Foster was self-taught and turned to Black plantation songs for melodic inspiration. Although popular and successful during his lifetime, he died in poverty.

Fothergill, John (1712-80) British physician, who published important descriptions of the symptoms of diphtheria and migraine. A Quaker and philanthropist, Fothergill supported John *Howard in his penal reforms and was an advocate of coffee drinking.

Fotheringhay 52 32N 0 25W A village in England, in Northamptonshire on the River Nene. Fotheringhay Castle (of which little remains) was the scene of Richard III's birth (1452) and the execution of Mary, Queen of Scots (1587).

Foucault, Jean Bernard Léon (1819-68) French physicist, after whom the *Foucault pendulum (1851) is named. He also worked on light, measuring its speed and showing that its speed decreased in water (1850). He also invented the gyroscope (1852).

Foucault pendulum A very long pendulum with a heavy bob, capable of oscillating for a long period. It demonstrates the earth's rotation since, as it swings, its plane of oscillation slowly rotates. At the poles it would rotate through 360° in 24 hours; at a latitude λ, the number of hours for a complete rotation is given by $24/\sin\lambda$. It was invented by Jean *Foucault and first demonstrated in 1851 in Paris using a 28-kg lead ball suspended from a wire 67 m long.

Fouché, Joseph, Duc d'Otrante (1759-1820) French politician. A priest and teacher, he became politically active in the French Revolution, being elected a deputy in the National Convention in 1792. He participated in the overthrow of Robespierre (1794) and became minister of police under Napoleon but was forced into exile in 1816 after the restoration of the monarchy.

Foulness A marshy island in SE England, in Essex, N of the River Thames estuary. Plans to construct London's third airport here and on adjacent Maplin Sands were abandoned in 1973.

Fountains Abbey A ruined *Cistercian abbey 5 km (3 mi) SW of Ripon, Yorkshire. Founded in 1132 it became the leading Cistercian community in England. Its well-preserved ruins, mainly 12th-century, testify to its wealth prior to its dissolution (1539) at the *Reformation.

Fouqué, Friedrich Heinrich Karl, Baron de la Motte (1777-1843) German novelist and dramatist. Of French aristocratic descent, he was a prolific writer of chivalric romances and dramas, many of them adapted from Scandinavian sagas. His best-known work is the romance *Undine* (1811), the story of a watersprite who marries a human.

Fouquet, Jean (c. 1420-81) French painter and manuscript illuminator, born in Tours. After visiting Italy, he worked for Charles VII and later for Louis XI, whose tomb he helped design. For the royal treasurer, Étienne Chevalier, he painted *The Virgin and Child* (Antwerp) and *Chevalier with His Patron St Stephen* (Berlin), which were formerly joined as the *Mehun Diptych*. A manuscript of Josephus' *Jewish Antiquities* (Bibliothèque National, Paris) contains his finest illuminations, noteworthy for their depiction of French towns and countryside.

Fouquet, Nicolas (1615-80) French politician; finance minister (1653-61) under Louis XIV. He amassed a large fortune, partly through fraudulent dealings, which were revealed to the king by *Colbert, and he was arrested and imprisoned for life.

four-eyed fish A freshwater *bony fish of the family Anablepidae (2 species), found in Central and South America. Up to 30 cm long, they have horizontally divided eyes with separate retinas for cruising just below the water surface, the upper halves being modified for aerial vision. Live young are born. Order: *Atheriniformes*.

Fourier, (François Marie) Charles (1772-1837) French socialist. Fourier advocated the organization of society on cooperative principles. He sought the abolition of all constrictions, including marriage, and set out his plan of an ideal society in *Le Nouveau Monde industriel* (1829-30).

Fourier, Jean Baptiste Joseph, Baron (1768-1830) French mathematician and physicist. After a career in the army, during which he served in Egypt under Napoleon, Fourier turned to science, his prime interest. While investigating heat, he discovered a method of expanding a periodic function in terms of sine and cosine waves, now known as **Fourier analysis** (*see* harmonic analysis). The discovery attracted widespread interest and Fourier was subsequently made a baron by Napoleon (1808).

Fourneyron, Benoît (1802-67) French engineer, who invented the modern water *turbine, producing the first large-scale model in 1832. It was quickly adopted by industry but was not used for generating hydroelectric power until 1895.

Four Noble Truths The fundamental doctrine of Buddhism, set forth by Gautama in the first discourse at Benares. The Truths are: existence is characterized by suffering; the cause of suffering is craving; to end craving is to end suffering; the way to achieve this is the *Eightfold Path.

four o'clock plant A bushy perennial herb, *Mirabilis jalapa*, also called marvel of Peru, native to tropical America but widely grown as an ornamental. 40-75 cm high, it bears clusters of red, pink, white, yellow, or streaked flowers, which are tubular with a wide flared mouth and open in the late afternoon. Family: *Nyctaginaceae*.

Fourteen Points (1918) Terms for a peace settlement

FOSSIL

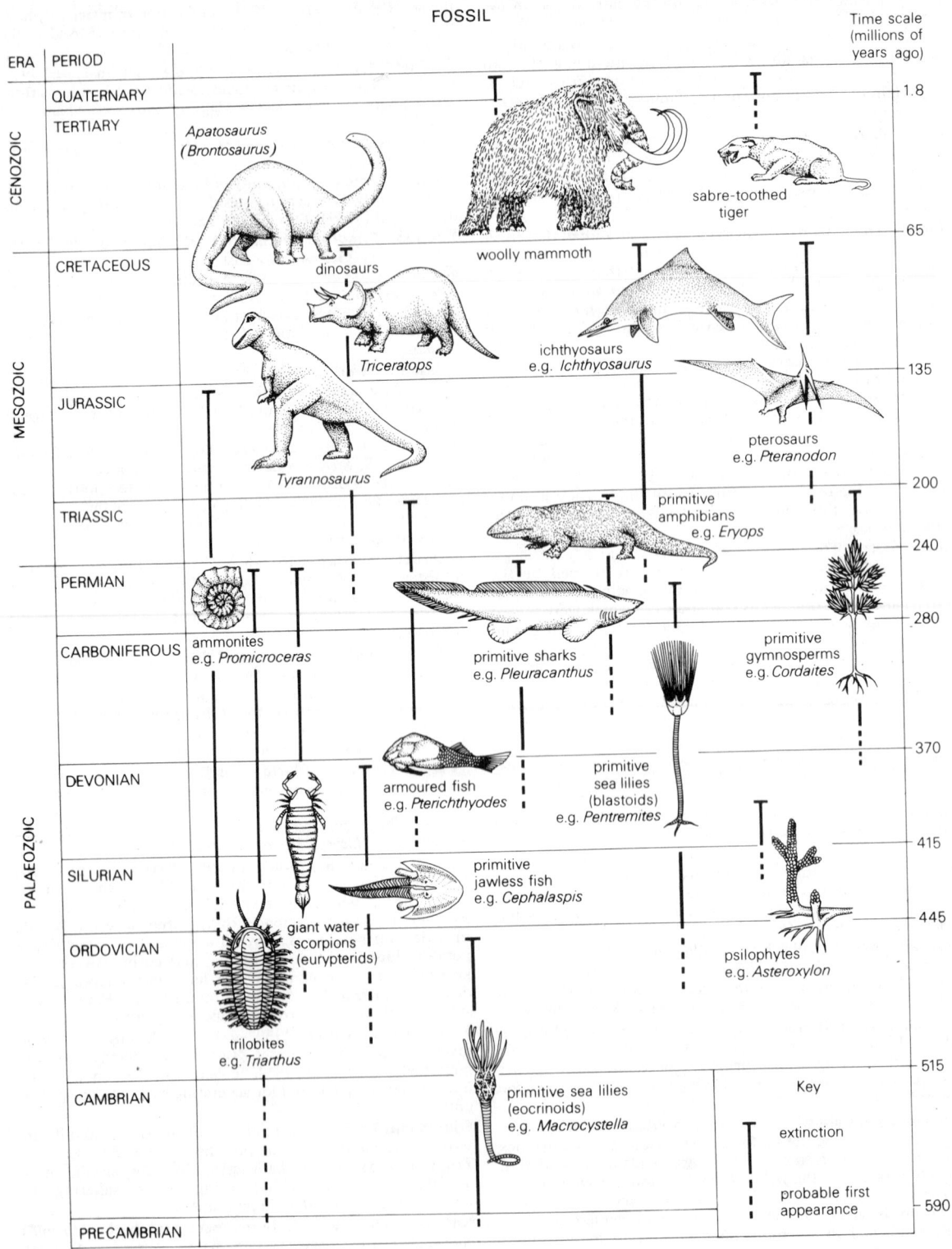

FOSSIL *Some extinct animals and plants from past geological ages.*

proposed by the US president, Woodrow Wilson, in World War I. They called for recognition of national aspirations, free trade, and an international league of nations and inspired the subsequent Treaty of *Versailles.

Fouta Djallon (*or* Futa Jallon) A mountainous plateau area in NW Guinea. The Rivers Niger, Senegal, and Gambia rise in the range. The area is covered chiefly by savanna and cattle raising is the main activity.

Fowey 50 20N 4 38W A resort in SW England, in Cornwall on the estuary of the River Fowey. Once a busy port, Fowey is now concerned principally with exporting china clay and with fishing. Population (1981): 36 639, with St Austell.

fowl, domestic A domesticated form of the red *jungle fowl, *Gallus gallus*, native to Asian forests. It was first domesticated about 4000 years ago as a religious and sacrificial animal and was used by the Romans for food. Since the 19th century, a large number of breeds and varieties have been selected for size, resistance to disease, egg production, shell colour, fertility, and food conversion efficiency. Immature males are castrated and reared for meat as capons. In many countries, males (cockerels) are still used for cockfighting.

Fowler, H(enry) W(atson) (1858-1933) British lexicographer and prescriptive stylist. With his brother **Francis Fowler** (1870-1918) he wrote *The King's English* (1906) and edited the *Concise Oxford Dictionary* (1911). His most famous work, *Modern English Usage* (1926), has been described as "a collection of prejudices erected into a system."

Fowles, John (1926–   ) British novelist, whose works treat philosophical, psychological, and social themes in a rich and often fantastic manner. His novels include *The Collector* (1963), *The Magus* (1966), and *The French Lieutenant's Woman* (1969), which have been filmed, *Daniel Martin* (1977), *Mantissa* (1982), and *A Maggot* (1985). Other books include the short stories in *The Ebony Tower* (1974).

fowl pest An infectious virus disease, also called Newcastle disease, affecting domestic fowl and certain other birds. Symptoms arise 4-11 days after infection and include a fall in egg production (in laying birds), loss of appetite, lethargy, laboured breathing through a gaping beak, and nasal discharge. Mortality may reach 100% and, in the UK, any outbreak must be reported. Vaccination confers immunity after 10-14 days.

fox A carnivorous mammal belonging to the *dog family (*Canidae*). Foxes have pointed ears, short legs with hairy pads on their feet, and large bushy tails. Generally nocturnal, they are solitary stealthy hunters, feeding on small mammals, birds, insects, and some fruit. The most familiar is the *red fox (*Vulpes vulpes*), found in forest and woodland and now venturing into suburban gardens. Some species are specialized for life in difficult habitats, such as the *Arctic fox and the *fennec. The unusual South African bat-eared fox (*Otocyon megalotis*) feeds mainly on termites and has teeth resembling those of an insect-eating mammal. Chief genera: *Vulpes* (9 species), *Dusicyon* (South American foxes; 8 species).

Fox, Charles James (1749-1806) British Whig politician; the first British foreign secretary (1782). He entered parliament (1768) as a supporter of Lord *North but joined the *Rockingham Whigs in opposing North's American policy. Fox resigned following George III's appointment of *Shelburne in succession to Rockingham and joined North in a coalition that briefly took office under the Duke of *Portland in 1783. Fox supported the French Revolution, over which issue many Whigs joined the Tories, and in 1798 he was dismissed from the privy council for opposing war with Revolutionary France. He was briefly foreign secretary again before his death in 1806.

Fox, George (1624-91) English religious leader, founder

of the *Quakers. A Puritan by upbringing and originally a shoemaker's apprentice, Fox became dissatisfied with the formalism of established Christianity and the state's control of the church. In 1646 he had a personal revelation and thereafter preached a gospel of love, stressing the immediate guidance of the Holy Spirit. He was frequently imprisoned for his beliefs and he made several missionary journeys abroad, notably to North America in 1671. His best-known work is his *Journal* (1674).

Foxe, John (1516-87) English religious writer. He fled to the Continent during the reign of Mary I and on his return wrote a history of the English Protestant martyrs from the 14th century to his own time. Usually known as *The Book of Martyrs* (1563), it fed the growing Catholic persecution of the time, to which Foxe himelf was outspokenly opposed.

foxglove A herbaceous plant of the genus *Digitalis*, especially *D. purpurea*, a biennial herb, 45-150 cm tall, native to W Europe but naturalized elsewhere. Foxgloves have large grey-green oblong leaves and tall one-sided spikes of drooping bell-shaped flowers, up to 6.5 cm long, purple, yellow, or white in colour, often with purple spots in the centre. The dried leaves contain *digitalis. Family: *Scrophulariaceae*.

foxhound A dog belonging to one of two breeds used for foxhunting. The English foxhound is strongly built with a deep chest and long neck. The American foxhound is descended from the English breed but is of lighter build. In both, the short coat is a combination of black, tan, and white. Height: 56-63 cm.

foxhunting A sport in which huntsmen on horseback pursue a fox with a pack of 20 to 30 *foxhounds, which hunt their quarry by scent. Fully organized in the UK since the 18th century, hunting achieved the status of a national pastime and has influenced many aspects of rural life.

The hunt officials, who are traditionally dressed in scarlet coats, called pinks, are the master of foxhounds (MFH), who directs the hounds, and one or more whippers-in, who help to control them. Mounted followers (the field) accompany the hunt. The spectacle, described by Oscar Wilde as "the unspeakable in pursuit of the uneatable," has many admirers although its detractors (notably the League against Cruel Sports) are becoming increasingly vociferous. The season runs from November to April. Famous hunts include the Quorn, Pytchley, Belvoir, Cottesmore, and Heythrop. Foxhunting is also popular in the E USA and jackalhunting and draghunting (in which hounds follow a prepared trail) are found as substitutes in other parts of the world.

fox terrier A breed of ▢dog developed in England for hunting foxes and badgers. It is sturdy with a short tail, a broad tapering muzzle, and small ears that are folded forwards over the face. There are two coat varieties—smooth-haired and wire-haired—and colouring is mainly white with black and tan markings. Height: 37-39 cm.

foxtrot A ballroom dance in 4/4 time with a syncopated rhythm in which couples combine slow walking steps with quick running steps. It was developed in the USA about 1914 from the two-step, a dance in 2/4 time with even rhythms.

Foyle, Lough An inlet of the Atlantic Ocean, in N Ireland. Fed by the River Foyle, it lies between NE Co Donegal in the Republic of Ireland and NW Co Londonderry in Northern Ireland.

fracture The breaking of a bone. This usually occurs as a result of injury but it may happen very easily in bones diseased with cancer or *osteoporosis (pathological fracture). In a simple fracture the ends of the broken bone are not displaced; in a compound fracture the broken bone pierces the skin. A stress fracture is a crack arising in a bone exposed to repeated small injuries, for example in soldiers marching long distances. The bones of children are relatively soft and flexible; such bones are more likely to be bent than completely broken—this is called a greenstick fracture. Fractures are treated by aligning the ends of the broken bone and immobilizing them. Healing will result quickly. Sometimes, however, it is necessary to pin fractures surgically.

JEAN HONORÉ FRAGONARD   *The Swing (1768-69) in the Wallace Collection, London. It was commissioned by the Baron de Saint-Julien, who is seen in the bottom left of the painting eyeing his mistress on the swing. The baron had originally specified that the older man pushing the swing should be a bishop.*

Fragonard, Jean Honoré (1732-1806) French *rococo painter, born in Grasse. He trained with *Chardin and *Boucher in Paris and studied in Italy (1756-61), concentrating on the work of *Tiepolo. He established his reputation with a history painting, *Coresus Sacrificing Himself to Save Callirhoë* (1765; Louvre), but soon turned to more light-hearted and delicately erotic subjects, e.g. *The Swing* (Wallace Collection, London) and *The Progress of Love* (Frick Collection, New York). His interest in Dutch painters, whose influence can be seen in a number of his landscapes and portraits, was strengthened by a visit to Holland in the 1770s. He suffered financial ruin during the Revolution. His subject matter and style of painting no longer found popular favour and he died in obscurity.

Frampton, Sir George James (1860-1928) British sculptor known for his *Peter Pan* (Kensington Gardens) and the Edith Cavell memorial near Trafalgar Square, London.

France, Anatole (Jacques Anatole François Thibault; 1844-1924) French novelist, son of a Parisian bookseller. His novels are noted for their erudition, scepticism, and elegance. His intervention in the *Dreyfus case (1897) marked the beginning of his commitment to socialism and, during his final years, communism. In such novels as *L'Île des pingouins* (1909) and *Les Dieux ont soif* (1913) his view of

mankind is deeply pessimistic. He was awarded the Nobel Prize in 1921.

France, Republic of A country in W Europe, bordering on the English Channel in the N, the Atlantic Ocean in the W, and the Mediterranean Sea in the S. It includes the island of Corsica and several overseas regions (Martinique, Guadeloupe, and French Guiana). Overseas territories include French Polynesia, New Caledonia, and St Pierre and Miquelon. Fertile lowlands cover most of the N and W of France, rising to the Pyrenees in the S, the Massif Central in the SE, and the Vosges, Jura, and Alps in the E. The principal rivers are the Seine, the Loire, and the Rhône. *Economy*: compared with other industrial countries in W Europe, agriculture remains important although the number of people employed in this sector has decreased owing to the reorganization of many of the numerous small peasant holdings into larger units. Animal products make up over half the total output and the production of cereals is important; the wine industry is a major source of revenue. There have been large-scale developments in the industrial sector since World War II, especially in iron and steel, motor vehicles, aircraft, mechanical and electrical engineering, textiles, chemicals, and food processing. Its mineral wealth includes iron ore, potash, bauxite, coal, and sulphur. Natural gas is being developed in the foothills of the Pyrenees, but a considerable proportion of power still comes from hydroelectric sources. Exports have risen dramatically in the postwar period, especially textiles, iron and steel, motor vehicles, and machinery, and in 1978 France was the world's third largest exporter of arms. Economic growth has slowed down in recent years, however, and the economic strategies of recent prime ministers have failed to deal with the increasing problems of inflation, trade deficits, and soaring unemployment. *History*: present-day France approximates the ancient region of *Gaul, which was conquered by Julius Caesar in the 1st century BC. It became part of the Roman Empire and in the 1st century AD Christianity was introduced to the provinces into which Gaul was divided. From the 3rd to the 5th centuries, it was overrun by German tribes, including the Goths, Vandals, and *Franks (from whom the name France is derived). The Frankish kingdom reached its peak under Charlemagne (reigned 768-814) and his *Carolingian dynasty continued to rule in France until 987, when Hugh Capet became the first *Capetian king. During the 10th century Norsemen (Vikings) established themselves in what became Normandy and in 1066 invaded England. The claims of English kings to French territory were realized on a large scale by the *Angevins and consequent conflict between France and England culminated in the *Hundred Years' War (1337-1453), as a result of which the English were expelled from all of France, except Calais. The Capetians were succeeded by the *Valois dynasty (1328-1589), a period that saw the beginning of France's long rivalry with Spain for hegemony in Europe. During the *Wars of Religion the last Valois king, Henry III, was succeeded (1589) by the first *Bourbon, Henry IV. The first half of the 17th century was dominated by Cardinal de *Richelieu and his successor as chief minister, Cardinal *Mazarin. They were resonsible for France replacing Spain, after the Thirty Years' War, as the supreme European power (1659). During the reign (1643-1715) of *Louis XIV France reached the zenith of its power and brilliance. Decline, however, began before his death and gathered speed in the following decades. The disastrous *Seven Years' War forced France to recognize British supremacy in North America and India and the political reaction and economic incompetence of the later Bourbon kings precipitated the *French Revolution in 1789. The First Republic was proclaimed (1792) and Louis XVI was guillotined (1793) in spite of the military opposition of the major European powers (*see* Revolutionary and Napoleonic Wars). In 1799 *Napoleon Bonaparte overthrew the

Directory, becoming first consul and, in 1804, emperor. By 1808 he had brought most of continental Europe under his sway but in 1815 he was finally defeated at Waterloo and exiled. The Bourbons were restored until 1830, when the July Revolution raised Louis Philippe to the throne. Overthrown in the *Revolution of 1848, the monarchy was replaced by the Second Republic of which Louis Napoleon became president; in 1852 he proclaimed himself emperor as *Napoleon III. During the Second Empire France underwent the beginnings of industrialization but its prosperity was not sufficient to achieve victory in the *Franco-Prussian War, in which Napoleon's ignominious leadership led to his overthrow (1870). The subsequent Third Republic lasted until 1940, in spite of scandal (e.g. the *Dreyfus and *Stavisky affairs), *World War I, and political dissension (there were 44 successive governments between 1918 and 1940). After the outbreak of World War II France fell to Germany and a pro-German government was established at Vichy, while *de Gaulle led the Free French resistance in London. In 1944 France was liberated by the Allies and de Gaulle established a provisional government that gave way (1946) to the Fourth Republic. The immediate postwar period was overshadowed by war in Indochina and by the crisis in Algeria that precipitated the fall of the Fourth Republic (1958). De Gaulle was recalled from retirement and, as president of the Fifth Republic, instituted a period of firm government. In May, 1968, however, the Republic was shaken by serious revolts among students and a wave of strikes and in 1969 he resigned. Gaullist principles nevertheless continued to influence government under his successors Pompidou and Giscard d'Estaing. Mitterrand's election (1981) made him the first socialist to hold the office of president in 35 years; proportional representation was introduced for subsequent elections. Official language: French. Official currency: franc of 100 centimes. Area: 543 814 sq km (209 912 sq mi). Population (1985 est): 55 166 000. Capital: Paris. Main port: Marseille.

Franche-Comté A planning region and former province in E France, bordering on Switzerland. Part of Burgundy until 843 AD, it was overrun successively by many powers before being finally annexed to France in 1678. The main occupations are farming, especially dairy farming and cattle rearing, and forestry. Area: 15 579 sq km (6014 sq mi). Population (1981 est): 1 090 800.

Francis I (1494–1547) King of France (1515–47). His reign was dominated by rivalry with the Holy Roman Emperor *Charles V. In the course of the conflict, which continued intermittently until 1544, Francis was taken prisoner at *Pavia (1525). At home, he won control over the French church through the Concordat of Bologna (1516), he suppressed French Protestantism, and ordered an attack on the *Waldenses in S France (1545).

Francis I (1708–65) Duke of Lorraine (1729–37), Grand duke of Tuscany (1737–65), and Holy Roman Emperor (1745–65). He married (1736) *Maria Theresa, who succeeded to the Austrian dominions in 1740 in the face of much opposition. He was elected emperor during the consequent War of the *Austrian Succession (1740–48).

Francis I (Emperor of Austria). See Francis II (Holy Roman Emperor).

Francis II (1544–60) King of France (1559–60); the son of *Henry II and *Catherine de' Medici and husband (1558–60) of *Mary, Queen of Scots. He was dominated by the *Guise family, which used him in its struggle against the Protestant *Condé early in the *Wars of Religion.

Francis II (1768–1835) The last Holy Roman Emperor (1792–1806) and, as Francis I, the first Emperor of Austria (1804–35). Following three defeats by the French in the Napoleonic Wars, he allied with *Napoleon until 1813. After the Congress of *Vienna (1815), he was guided by his conservative chief minister *Metternich.

Francis Ferdinand (1863–1914) Archduke of Austria and heir apparent to his uncle, Emperor *Francis Joseph. He was known to favour the development of national cultures within the Empire. His assassination (28 June, 1914) by a Serbian nationalist at Sarajevo precipitated *World War I.

Francis Joseph (1830–1916) Emperor of Austria (1848–1916) and King of Hungary (1867–1916). His long reign saw the rise of national tensions in the Empire, which led to the establishment of the Dual Monarchy of *Austria-Hungary, under which Austria and Hungary coexisted as equal partners under the Austrian Crown. He was defeated by the Prussians in the Austro-Prussian War of 1866 but in 1879 he allied with the recently formed German Empire and in 1882 with Italy, forming the *Triple Alliance. His ultimatum to Serbia, following the assassination by a Serbian nationalist of his nephew, Archduke *Francis Ferdinand (1914), led to *World War I.

Francis of Assisi, St (Giovanni di Bernardone; c. 1182–1226) Italian friar and founder of the *Franciscans, born in Assisi. The son of a merchant, he renounced his worldly life in 1205 to live in poverty and devote himself to prayer and charitable works. By 1209 he had a band of followers with whom he went to Rome (1210), where he obtained papal approval of his new order. He travelled throughout Spain, the Holy Land, and Egypt, later retiring to Assisi and giving up the leadership of his order. A profoundly humble man, in paintings he is often portrayed in the countryside among animals and birds, which he called his sisters and brothers. His love of nature is also reflected in his famous hymn, *Canticle of the Sun*. He received the *stigmata in 1224, was canonized in 1228, and was proclaimed patron saint of ecology in 1980. Feast day: 4 Oct.

Francis of Sales, St (1567–1622) French Roman Catholic prelate and devotional writer, born in Savoy. He played a leading part in the Counter-Reformation by reconverting the people of Chablais from Calvinism to Roman Catholicism. As Bishop of Geneva from 1602 he cofounded the Order of the Visitation, an order of nuns. Feast day: 29 Jan.

Francis Xavier, St (1506–52) Spanish *Jesuit missionary, known as the Apostle of the Indies. While studying in Paris (1523–34) he met St *Ignatius of Loyola and helped him found the Jesuit order. From 1541 he worked in the Indies, India, and Japan, establishing missions and making many converts. Feast day: 3 Dec.

Francis, Sir Philip (1740–1818) British politician, who was probably the author of the Letters of *Junius. He campaigned for the impeachment (1788) of Warren *Hastings, governor general of India, with whom he fought a duel in 1780.

Franciscans An order of friars founded in 1209 by St *Francis of Assisi. His rule was devised to impose both personal and corporate poverty on the order's members. The rule was revised in 1221 and again in 1223, when it was confirmed by the pope. Within Francis' lifetime the expanding order found complete poverty practically difficult, and a schism ensued in the early 14th century regarding how strictly the rule should be followed. Despite a resulting decline, the order survived and has remained an important missionary and charitable branch of the Roman Catholic Church.

francium (Fr) The heaviest alkali metal, a very unstable radioactive element discovered in 1939 by Perey. The longest-lived isotope ^{223}Fr has a half-life of 22 minutes; traces of the element exist in nature, as decay products of ^{227}Ac. At no 87; at wt (223).

Franck, César Auguste (1822–90) Belgian composer, organist, and teacher, who settled in Paris in 1834. He became organist of Ste Clotilde in 1858, a post he held until his death. His pupils included D'Indy and Chausson. Franck was influenced by Bach and evolved a highly chromatic form of harmony. He also developed "cyclic form," the use of the same theme in more than one movement of a work. His compositions include *Symphonic Variations* (for piano and orchestra; 1885), a symphony (1886–88), a violin sonata (1886), and a string quartet (1889).

Franck, James (1882–1964) US physicist, born in Germany, whose experiments in collaboration with Gustav Hertz (1887–1975) on the excitation of gases when bombarded with electrons won them the Nobel Prize in 1925. Their experiments provided evidence that the energy levels inside atoms were quantized. He also made valuable contributions to photochemistry. During World War II Franck worked on the development of the atom bomb but opposed its use on populated areas.

Franco, Francisco (1892–1975) Spanish general and statesman; dictator from 1939 until his death. He entered the Infantry Academy in 1907, aged 14, was posted to Spanish Morocco in 1912, and became the youngest captain in the Spanish army in 1915. By 1935 he was chief of the General Staff and in the following year, on 18 July, joined a military uprising against the Republican Government of *Azaña that precipitated the *Spanish Civil War. In October, 1936, he became head of state in the Nationalist Zone and commander in chief of the rebel forces. By 1939, with help from Hitler and Mussolini, he had defeated the Republican forces and become the absolute leader of Spain. Franco's government, in which the National Movement (*see* Falange Española) was the only political party, remained sympathetic to Hitler but maintained a neutral position throughout World War II. Spain was excluded from the newly formed UN in 1945 but its isolation was broken during the Cold War, when Franco's anticommunism made him a more attractive ally. In 1953 he signed a military-assistance agreement with the USA. Although his government achieved considerable economic advance for Spain, especially in the 1960s, he operated a ruthless dictatorship that tolerated no opposition. However, during his last years he permitted a perceptible liberalization, which foreshadowed the country's move to democracy under his successor, King *Juan Carlos.

francolin A *partridge belonging to a genus (*Francolinus*; 41 species) occurring in Africa and Asia. 27–46 cm long, francolins are usually a dull brownish colour with black, white, or chestnut markings and are popular gamebirds.

Francome, John (1953–) British jockey who retired in 1985 after having ridden 1036 National Hunt winners. He subsequently trained horses on the flat.

Franconia A duchy of early medieval Germany, now in Rhineland-Palatinate, Baden-Württemberg, Hessen, and Bavaria. Its duke, Conrad, was the first elected king of Germany (911–18) but the duchy was subsequently comparatively unimportant and by the 13th century had been fragmented into small principalities.

Franco-Prussian War (1870–71) A war between France and Prussia. Fearing Bismarck's proposals to make a relative of William I of Prussia the king of Spain (*see* Ems telegram), France declared war. Within two months Napoleon III and his army were defeated at the battle of *Sedan but French resistance continued. Napoleon was deposed and the Third Republic was established but the Prussians besieged Paris, which eventually capitulated. The Treaty of Frankfurt imposed a huge indemnity on France, which ceded Alsace and Lorraine to the newly established German Empire; France was left economically weakened and politically divided.

frangipani A tropical American tree, *Plumeria rubra*, cultivated throughout the tropics and known in Asia as pagoda tree or temple flower. Up to 6 m tall, it has tapering long-stalked leaves and round clusters, up to 25 cm across, of fragrant pink, reddish-purple, white, or yellow flowers, used to make perfume. Family: *Apocynaceae*.

Frank, Anne (1929–45) German Jewish girl, who died in a German concentration camp. Her diary became a symbol of Jewish resistance and courage following its publication in 1947. She wrote it while hiding from the Nazis in Amsterdam in 1942–43.

Frankfort 38 11N 84 53W A city in the USA, the capital of Kentucky on the Kentucky River. Its major industry is whiskey distilling. Population (1980): 25 973.

Frankfurt am Main 50 06N 8 41E A city in central West Germany, in Hessen on the River Main. A major banking and commercial centre, it is famed for its trade fairs, especially the annual book fair. Its gothic cathedral is 13th-century and the university was established in 1914. It is the birthplace of Goethe and the original home of the Rothschilds. Its industries include the manufacture of chemicals, pharmaceuticals, and machinery. *History*: it was the seat of the imperial elections (9th to 18th centuries) and coronations (1562–1792) of the Holy Roman emperors. The first German national assembly met here (1848–49). Population (1980 est): 629 200.

Frankfurt an der Oder 52 20N 14 32E A town in E East Germany, on the River Oder. Severely damaged in World War II, the part of the city on the E bank of the river was incorporated into Poland in 1945. A trading centre since medieval times, its manufactures include machinery and furniture. Population (1983): 707 058.

Frankfurter, Felix (1882–1965) US jurist, born in Vienna. He was a professor at Harvard Law School from 1914 until 1939, when he was appointed to the US Supreme Court. During this period he also served as secretary of war (1911–13) and as legal adviser to Woodrow Wilson at the Paris Peace Conference (1919) and to Franklin Roosevelt in the 1930s. Although he helped to found the American Civil Liberties Union (1919), he also supported some measures to limit civil liberties.

frankincense (*or* olibanum) An aromatic gum resin obtained chiefly from trees of the genus *Boswellia*, especially *B. carteri*, which grows in the Middle East. It is usually supplied commercially in yellowish blocks covered with white dust, smells of balsam when heated, and burns brightly giving off a fragrant odour. Frankincense has been known since ancient Egyptian times and is still used as an *incense, in fumigants, and in perfumes.

Franklin The northernmost district of Canada, in the *Northwest Territories, consisting of Canada's Arctic archipelago and some northerly peninsulas. Covered by tundra and ice cap, it has large oil reserves. The inhabitants are mostly Eskimo hunters and fishermen. Area: 1 422 565 sq km (549 253 sq mi). Population (1986): 12 047.

Franklin, Benjamin (1706–90) US diplomat, scientist, and author. He established a printing business in Philadelphia and became well known for his *Poor Richard's Almanac* (1732–57), which contained many maxims on the virtues of thrift and hard work. His experiments with static electricity, especially the famous episode in which he flew a kite during a thunderstorm (and was lucky not to be killed), established the electrical nature of thunderstorms and led him to invent the lightning conductor. His political prominence began in 1737, when he became deputy postmaster of Philadelphia, where he promoted street lighting and the establishment of a city police force. In the disputes that led to the American Revolution he represented Pennsylvania's case to Britain (1757–62, 1766–75) and as a member of the *Continental Congress helped frame the Declaration of Independence (1775). Famous as a diplomat in Paris (1776–85), he enlisted French help for the colonies and later negotiated peace with Britain (1783). Franklin was also the founder of a club that became (1743) the American Philosophical Society. His complete *Autobiography* was first published in 1868.

Franklin, Sir John (1786–1847) British explorer. After service in the Royal Navy, during which he fought at Trafalgar (1805), he was subsequently governor (1836–43) of Van Dieman's Land (now Tasmania). In 1845 he sailed with two ships, never to return, to look for the *Northwest Passage. Successive search expeditions failed to find the men until 1859, when their skeletons and records were found on King William Island. Franklin had virtually discovered the passage but had become ice-bound and he and his companions died of scurvy or starvation.

Franklin, Rosalind Elsie (1920–58) British scientist, whose work in X-ray crystallography contributed to the discovery of the structure of *DNA in conjunction with James *Watson and Francis *Crick. She was working on the structure of tobacco mosaic virus at the time of her premature death from cancer.

Franks A Germanic people, who invaded Roman *Gaul from the Rhineland between the 3rd and 5th centuries AD. One of the Frankish tribes, the Salian Franks, gained control of most of Gaul under their ruler *Clovis (d. 511) and were converted to Christianity. The Frankish state was ruled by the *Merovingian dynasty (named after Clovis' grandfather, Merovech) until its replacement by the *Carolingians (named after *Charlemagne) in 751. The Carolingian empire lasted until its division in 843. The western Frankish kingdom was the nucleus of France.

Franz Josef Land (Russian name: Zemlya Frantsa Iosifa) A Soviet archipelago of about 85 islands in the N Barents Sea, the largest being Aleksandra Land, George Land, Graham Bell Island, Salisbury Island, and Wilczek Land. They were discovered in 1873 by Austrians and annexed by the Soviet Union in 1926. They are 90% icebound and have no permanent population. Total area: about 20 700 sq km (79 905 sq mi).

BENJAMIN FRANKLIN *Flying a kite in June 1752; part of his experiment proving lightning to be an electric discharge.*

Fraser, (John) Malcolm (1930–) Australian statesman; Liberal prime minister (1975–83). Appointed caretaker prime minister on the dismissal of *Whitlam, he remained in office until the Liberals were defeated in the 1983 elections, when he also resigned as leader of the Liberal party.

Fraser, Peter (1884–1950) New Zealand statesman; Labour prime minister (1940–49). Born in Britain, he helped form the Democratic Party (1913; the Labour Party from 1916) and entered parliament in 1918. He influenced Allied strategy in the Pacific during World War II and helped to establish the UN (1945).

Fraser River A river in W Canada, the chief river of British Columbia. Rising near Mount *Robson, it flows rapidly

through mountain gorges until it reaches flat farmland in the SW, where it empties into the Strait of Georgia near Vancouver. Length: 1370 km (850 mi).

fraud In law, making a false representation, by words or conduct or by withholding facts where there is a duty to disclose them, in order to obtain a material advantage. To prove fraud it is necessary to show that a false representation was made (1) knowingly, (2) without belief in its truth, or (3) recklessly, without concern whether it was true or not. To obtain damages it must be shown that the defendant intended the injured party to act on the fraudulent representation and that he did so to his detriment. A contract based on fraud may be declared void.

Fraunhofer, Joseph von (1787–1826) German physicist, who greatly improved the quality of lenses and prisms and made improvements to the design of optical instruments. His superior equipment enabled him to detect numerous dark lines in the sun's spectrum (1814), now known as **Fraunhofer lines**. The eight most prominent lines are still known by the letters he gave them.

Fray Bentos 33 10S 58 20W A port in W Uruguay, on the River Uruguay. It is an important meat-packing centre, especially of corned beef. Population (1975): 19 569.

Frazer, Sir James George (1854–1941) British anthropologist, mythologist, and writer. Frazer's major work *The Golden Bough* (first edition 1890) was a description of "the long evolution by which the thoughts and efforts of man have passed through the successive stages of magic, religion, and science." Although his interpretation of his observations was sometimes unsound, the results of his work were far reaching, influencing people outside the anthropological field, including T. S. Eliot.

Frazier, Joe (1944–) US boxer, who was Olympic heavyweight champion (1964), world heavyweight champion (1971–73), and the first to beat Muhammad *Ali professionally. He was defeated by George Foreman (1948–).

Fredericia 55 34N 9 47E A seaport in Denmark, in SE Jutland at the narrow N end of the Little Belt. It has a large oil refinery. Its exports include frozen fish, silverware, and textiles. Population (1982): 46 085.

Frederick (I) Barbarossa (c. 1123–90) Holy Roman Emperor (1152–90; crowned 1155), who was engaged in a long struggle with the papacy. He made six expeditions to Italy and was ultimately unsuccessful against the Lombard cities, which regained their independence in 1183. Papal opposition to his ambitions was exacerbated when he set up an antipope to *Alexander III, who excommunicated Frederick in 1160. He finally made peace with the pope in 1177. He failed to subdue his powerful cousin, *Henry the Lion, but he established his authority in Poland, Hungary, Bohemia, and Burgundy. In 1189, he set out on the third *Crusade during which he died.

Frederick I (1657–1713) The first King of Prussia (1701–1713) and, as Frederick III, Elector of Brandenburg (1688–1701). Austria conceded him his royal status in return for military aid in the War of the *Spanish Succession (1701–14). He encouraged Prussian industry and agriculture and also fostered the arts and learning; he was a patron of *Leibniz.

Frederick I (King of Sicily). *See* Frederick II (Holy Roman Emperor).

Frederick II (1194–1250) Holy Roman Emperor (1220–50), the last emperor of the *Hohenstaufen dynasty and, as Frederick I, King of Sicily (1198–1250). As leader of the fifth Crusade (1228–29) he captured Jerusalem but remained an opponent of papal policy and was excommunicated three times (1227, 1239, 1245). A man of wide learning, he was a noted patron of the arts and sciences but neglected the government of his possessions, which consequently declined.

Frederick (II) the Great (1712–86) King of Prussia (1740–86), who made Prussia a major European power. He succeeded to the throne after an extraordinarily severe childhood at the hands of his father *Frederick William I. An exponent of enlightened despotism (see Enlightenment), he liberalized the Prussian legal code and introduced economic and social reforms that reinvigorated Prussian society and institutions. His conquest of Silesia (1740) gave rise to the War of the *Austrian Succession (1740-48), after which his possession of the region was confirmed. His victory in the *Seven Years' War (1756-63) confirmed the military supremacy of Prussia, both in Germany and in Europe. At his palace of Sans Souci, near Potsdam, a distinguished circle of artists and writers, including *Voltaire, gathered around Frederick, who was himself a writer and composer.

Frederick III (1415-93) The last Holy Roman Emperor to be crowned by the pope in Rome (1452) and, as Frederick IV, German king (1440-93). As Archduke of Austria from 1424, Frederick unified the major Habsburg domains, but failed to win the Bohemian and Hungarian crowns and to resist the Turks. In 1485 *Matthias Corvinus of Hungary conquered Austria, which was recovered in 1490 by Frederick's son *Maximilian I.

Frederick (III) the Wise (1463-1525) Elector of Saxony (1486-1525), whose possession of silvermines made him Germany's richest ruler. A devout Catholic, he nevertheless protected *Luther at the castle of Wartburg after the papal ban of 1521.

Frederick III (Elector of Brandenburg). See Frederick I (King of Prussia).

Frederick (V) the Winter King (1596-1632) Elector of the Palatinate (1610-23). Frederick, who was the son-in-law of James I of England, accepted the Bohemian Crown in 1619 and led the Protestant revolt against Emperor Ferdinand II (see Thirty Years' War). He was defeated at the battle of White Mountain (1620) and died a throneless exile.

Frederick IX (1899-1972) King of Denmark (1947-72), who as regent (1942-47) had encouraged Danish resistance to the Germans in *World War II.

Frederick Henry (1584-1647) Prince of Orange and Count of Nassau. The younger son of *William the Silent, he became stadholder and captain general of the United Provinces in 1625. He successfully waged war against Spanish rule but his autocratic outlook was unpopular. His attempts to make peace were fulfilled at *Westphalia (1648), shortly after his death.

Frederick William (1620-88) Elector of Brandenburg (1640-88), known as the Great Elector. He inherited Germany's weakest electorate. By furthering dynastic claims in Prussia, Pomerania, and the lower Rhineland, he created for his Hohenzollern family the strongest territorial state in N Germany. His fiscal and administrative reforms established the base upon which the great power of *Prussia was created in the 18th century.

Frederick William I (1688-1740) The second King of Prussia (1713-40), who made his country strong and prosperous. He strengthened the army, passed financial reforms, resettled the east, freed the serfs on his own domain (1719), and instituted compulsory primary education (1717); he also centralized administration and in 1720 acquired most of Swedish Pomerania.

Frederick William II (1744-97) King of Prussia (1786-97), who pursued a policy of territorial aggrandizement. He profited from the second and third partitions of Poland in 1793 and 1795 and from 1792 until 1795 he joined Austria against Revolutionary France. At home his Religious Edict (1788) granted religious toleration, but was limited in effect, and the law code of 1794 included some liberal statutes.

Frederick William III (1770-1840) King of Prussia (1797-1840). His neutral attitude towards Napoleon damaged the prestige of Prussia, which was subjected to France by the Treaty of *Tilsit (1807) following defeat at *Jena and Auerstädt. After Prussia's liberation (1813), Frederick

William introduced some reforms but became more repressive in the face of liberal attacks.

Frederick William IV (1795-1861) King of Prussia (1840-61) in a period of social unrest and nationalism. His conservatism triggered off the *Revolution of 1848, which forced him to grant a constitution (1850). This failed to prevent a resumption of reactionary government, which, owing to Frederick William's insanity, was in the hands of his brother, later *William I, from 1858.

Fredericton 45 57N 66 40W A city in E Canada, the capital of New Brunswick. Its industries include the manufacture of wood and plastic products. Tourism, military administration, and distribution are important. The University of New Brunswick was established here in 1785. Population (1981): 44 500.

Fredrikstad 59 15N 10 55E A port in SE Norway, at the mouth of the River Glomma. Founded in 1567, its industries include saw milling and fishing. Population (1981 est): 27 862.

free enterprise. See capitalism.

free-form jazz A style of US *jazz developed by Ornett Coleman (1930-), John Coltrane (1926-), and others in the 1960s. Free-form jazz is based on a single theme that is subject to any form of melodic, harmonic, or rhythmic improvisation; it espouses highly complex musical relationships that often result in *atonality.

Free French French forces organized in London by Gen *de Gaulle in defiance of Marshal Pétain's surrender to Germany in World War II.

freehold. See estate.

freemasonry A secret society for men, which declares itself to be based on brotherly love, faith, and charity. Its origins are uncertain but it probably developed from the medieval stonemasons' guilds. In its modern form freemasonry dates from the establishment (1717) in England of the Grand Lodge, to which over 8000 private lodges are now affiliated. The Grand Lodge runs a hospital, a benevolent institution, and a school for the orphans of former masons. During the 18th century masonry spread to America and the colonies as well as to continental Europe. Its ceremonies, which are allegorical and illustrated by symbols (many of which are the tools of a working mason), demand a vow of secrecy as well as a belief in God (the great architect of the universe) and are based on Old Testament anecdotes and moralities.

Opposition to masonry orginated with a papal bull (1738) excommunicating masons, since when Roman Catholics have never accepted its principles or its secrecy. In France and some other European countries it assumed a political character and was condemned by governments. Mussolini and Hitler outlawed it and it is banned in E Europe.

free port A port (such as Hong Kong or Singapore) forming a free-trade area, where goods may be landed, handled, processed, and re-exported without incurring *customs duties. Such duties become payable when the goods are moved into adjacent territory. The Hanseatic towns were early examples of free ports. British free ports are Southampton, Liverpool, Prestwick, Cardiff, Belfast, and Birmingham.

Freesia A genus of ornamental South African plants (20 species), cultivated commercially, especially as a source of cut flowers. Growing from corms to a height of 75 cm, they have sword-shaped leaves and funnel-shaped lemon-scented flowers, white, orange, yellow, blue, purple or pink in colour, growing in one-sided clusters. Most cultivated varieties are hybrids derived from *F. refracta* (with yellowish flowers) and *F. armstrongii* (rose-purple flowers). Family: *Iridaceae*.

freestyle wrestling. See wrestling.

Freetown 8 20N 13 05W The capital and main port of Sierra Leone, on the Atlantic coast. It was founded in the late 18th century as a refuge for freed slaves and was capital of British West Africa (1808-74), becoming the capital of

Sierra Leone in 1961. The University of Sierra Leone was founded here in 1967. It has trade in ginger, diamonds, and gold; industries include fish processing. Population (1982): 316 312.

free trade International trade that takes place without tariffs or quotas. World production is maximized by free trade, but the distribution of a particular product may be inequitable and countries may encounter domestic pressures from their own producers to apply *tariffs. Conditions in international trade came closest to free trade in the mid-19th century following the demise of *mercantilism, but since then tariff barriers have been erected again. A group of countries may agree between themselves to lower tariffs and achieve a measure of free trade (see Ottawa Agreements) or they may form a free-trade area (e.g. the *European Economic Community) surrounded by a tariff barrier.

free verse Poetry without regular metre or form and depending on the rhythms and patterns of natural speech. The original French term, *vers libre*, was coined during the 1880s by poets who wished to emphasize rhythm as the essential principle of poetic form. Major exponents of this form include Ezra Pound, D. H. Lawrence, and William Carlos Williams.

free will In philosophy and theology, the ability of man to choose his own destiny, as opposed to the idea that everything that happens to him is inevitable. Philosophers are concerned to discover what the presuppositions and implications of free will are, compared to those of *determinism. They are also concerned to discover to what extent free will and determinism can be compatible. The problem has confronted philosophers since man began to think about abstract matters and is one to which there is no easy solution. In a theistic context, determinism is replaced by *predestination, the view that all events, including human choice, are fixed by the will of God. In the Christian Church, controversy arose in the 5th century between followers of Pelagius, who taught that man is able to choose salvation or damnation, and St *Augustine, who held that man could only be saved by divine grace. The controversy again became a live issue at the Reformation, the Calvinists rejecting free will and claiming that men were consigned from eternity to salvation or damnation, irrespective of merit.

freeze drying A method of drying foods for preservation in which the food is rapidly frozen under very low pressure. Any water present freezes and then sublimes under the low pressure.

freezing The preservation of food by keeping it frozen. The basic principle in all food preservation is to arrest the development of the microorganisms responsible for the decay of the food. Home freezers achieve this by keeping food at a temperature of about -18°C (-0.4°F). On thawing, the deterioration process restarts. Most foods are well preserved by freezing, with little loss in nutritional value, but some with a high water content within the cells of the food, such as strawberries and cucumbers, become soggy after freezing as a result of damage to the cell structure by ice formation. Most vegetables are blanched (boiled for 2-4 minutes) before freezing to arrest the action of enzymes. It is the residual enzymic action that determines the recommended storage time.

Frege, Gottlob (1848-1925) German mathematician and logician, who extended *Boole's work on symbolic logic by using logical symbols not already used in mathematics (symbols for *or, if-then*, etc.). This is now standard practice in logic. Frege published a massive work in which he applied symbolic logic to arithmetic. This, however, was invalidated by a paradox presented by Bertrand *Russell. In Frege's system, some sets, or classes, of things are not members of themselves; for example, the set [all cats] is not itself a cat. Others are; for example, the set [all things that are not animals] is itself not an animal. Russell's paradox is:

is the set [all sets that are not members of themselves] a member of itself?

Frei (Montalva), Eduardo (1911-82) Chilean statesman, who defeated Salvador *Allende in 1964 to become the first Christian Democratic president of Chile. His promises of radical reform were not enough to win him re-election and he was defeated by Allende in 1970.

Freiburg. See Fribourg.

Freiburg im Breisgau 48 00N 7 52E A city in SW West Germany, in Baden-Württemberg in the Black Forest. It has a university (1457) and a notable gothic cathedral, built of red sandstone. A major tourist centre, its manufactures include precision instruments and pharmaceutical products. Population (1980 est): 173 600.

Fréjus 43 26N 6 44E A town in SE France, in the Var department. There are several Roman remains, including an amphitheatre, and it has a 13th-century cathedral. In 1959 several hundred inhabitants lost their lives when the Malpasset Dam collapsed. Its industries include olive oil and wine. Population (1982): 32 698.

Fremantle 32 07S 115 44E A major seaport in Western Australia, SW of Perth at the mouth of the Swan River. Kwinana, an important industrial complex with oil and nickel refineries and bulk-grain facilities, is nearby. Population (1983): 23 460.

Frémont, John C(harles) (1813-90) US explorer, cartographer, and politician. In the 1840s he explored and mapped large areas of the USA W of the Mississippi. He fought in the Mexican War (1846-48) before making a fortune in the Gold Rush (1848-49). In 1856 he became the first Republican Party presidential candidate but was defeated by James Buchanan.

French A Romance language spoken by 45 million people in France, and extensively in Canada, Belgium, Switzerland, and elsewhere. It is the official language of 21 countries. Standard French, based upon the Parisian dialect known as Francien, has been France's official administrative language since 1539. It has replaced most northern dialects, known collectively as *langue d'oïl*, and has superseded the Occitan dialects of S France, known as *langue d'oc* (see Provençal). During the 17th century the *Académie Française and the publication of a standard dictionary (1680) quickly stabilized the language. French grammar has been simplified from Latin and the phonology has greatly altered. There are no noun case declensions and the verb is conjugated for three persons. Pronunciation does not, however, distinguish as many grammatical differences as the written form.

French, John, 1st Earl of Ypres (1852-1925) British field marshal. Before World War I he distinguished himself as a cavalry officer in the Sudan and South Africa and in 1914 was made commander in chief of the *British Expeditionary Force in France. Criticized for indecisiveness, he resigned in 1915 and ended his career as lord lieutenant of Ireland (1918-21).

French and Indian War (1754-63) The conflict for empire in North America between France and Britain that constituted the American front of the *Seven Years' War. France and its Indian allies had the initial advantage of superior land forces but British sea blockades eventually defeated the French. The war's climax was reached in the battle for Quebec in which the commanders of each side, *Montcalm and *Wolfe, were mortally wounded. In the concluding Treaty of *Paris (1763) Britain gained Canada and all lands E of the Mississippi.

French art and architecture The styles of art and architecture in France from the early middle ages. Until the *Renaissance, architecture dominated French artistic expression. Many French cathedrals and churches date from the Merovingian or Carolingian periods, which evolved features that anticipated the *romanesque architecture of the

11th and 12th centuries. The *gothic style is celebrated in the cathedrals of Notre-Dame and at Chartres, Rheims, and Amiens. The 13th century also produced some outstanding miniature painting, especially in Paris, a school that reached its height in the 1320s with the work of Jean *Pucelle. The Renaissance in France found expression chiefly in domestic architecture and decoration, notable examples including the chateaux at Amboise and Chambord. The school of *Fontainebleau, founded by Francis I, was profoundly influenced by Italian *mannerism; the 16th century also saw the work of the *Clouet family, who were portraitists, and of the sculptor Jean *Goujon. The great exponents of classicism—*Poussin, *Claude, and *La Tour—dominated French art in the first half of the 17th century, and the influence of *Versailles was felt throughout Europe. The *rococo style of the 18th century was exemplified by the work of *Watteau, *Fragonard, and *Boucher and contrasted the contemporaneous naturalism of *Chardin. The outstanding exponent of late-18th-century *neoclassicism was *David. The latter's followers, *Géricault and *Delacroix, were notable among the Romantics of the 19th century, which also saw the work of *Ingres, *Courbet, and the *Barbizon school. French art in the late 19th century is associated with *impressionism, but the period also witnessed the work of *Gauguin, *Van Gogh, and *Cézanne, an important influence on the development of *modern art (*see also* cubism). *See also* Louis XIV; Louis XV; Louis XVI.

French bean An annual herb, *Phaseolus vulgaris*, also called kidney bean, probably native to South America but widely cultivated. It has large heart-shaped leaves and white pealike flowers. Both dwarf and twining varieties are grown for their *beans, usually eaten in the pod. Family: *Leguminosae*. *See also* haricot bean.

French Canadians French-speaking citizens of Canada descended from immigrants who settled, mainly in Quebec, as farmers during the 17th and 18th centuries. They comprise approximately 30% of the Canadian population, are mainly Roman Catholic, and have a distinct culture. The desire to preserve their identity has promoted a strong separatist movement.

French Community An association of states, comprising France and its former colonies, established by the new Fifth Republic after a constitutional referendum (1958). It succeeded the French Union, which in turn replaced the empire. In addition to France it includes Guadeloupe, Guiana, Martinique, Mayotte, La Réunion, St Pierre and Miquelon, Southern and Antarctic Territories, French Polynesia, New Caledonia, and Wallis and Futuna.

French Equatorial Africa (French name: Afrique Équatoriale Française) A former federation of French territories in W central Africa comprising (1910-59) the present-day independent states of the Central African Republic, Chad, Congo (People's Republic of), and Gabon.

French Guiana A French overseas region on the NE coast of South America. A narrow fertile coastal belt rises to a mountainous interior, which is covered in dense forest rich in valuable timber. *Economy*: timber is the principal export and sugar is the main commercial crop, although the large reserves of minerals, land, timber, and fish have as yet been little developed. *History*: Europeans in search of *Eldorado explored the region from the early 16th century, but it was not settled until the 17th century, when the French, Dutch, Portuguese, and English competed for possession. In 1817 it was finally obtained by the French, who established penal colonies, including the notorious one on Devil's Island, in the territory. The French Guianese have had full French citizenship since 1848 and have been represented in the National Assembly since 1870. Area: about 91 000 sq km (34 740 sq mi). Population (1981 est): 66 400. Capital: Cayenne.

French horn An orchestral brass instrument, which

evolved from the hunting horn. It consists of a long narrow coiled tube with a wide bell and a cup-shaped mouthpiece. In its original form the horn could only play its own natural harmonic series of notes; in the 18th century crooks of tubing of different length were inserted to enable it to play in a variety of keys. In the 19th century valves were fitted giving the horn in F a complete range of about three octaves above B below the bass stave. It is a transposing instrument, its music being written a fifth higher than it sounds.

French India A former French overseas territory in India, comprising Chandernagor (an enclave in Bengal) and the coastal settlements of Pondicherry, Karikal, Yanam, and Mahé. It was restored to India (1949-54).

French literature Writings in Old French, the *langue d'oïl*, date from the 10th century AD; major works appeared only in the 12th century. The *chansons de geste* celebrated the military exploits of the French nobility in the Crusades and other wars. From classical and Arthurian romances by Chrétien de Troyes and others developed such allegorical romances as *Le Roman de la rose* (c. 1230) of Guillaume de Lorris. The lyric poetry of courtly love of the southern *troubadours and the northern *trouvères was followed in the 15th century by the more personal poetry of Charles d'Orléans and François Villon.

During the 16th century Pierre de Ronsard and the other members of the *Pléiade rivalled the poets of Renaissance Italy, while the major prose works were the comic masterpieces of Rabelais and the *Essais* of Montaigne. The influence of classicism during the 17th century, the golden age of French literature, is seen in the tragic dramas of Corneille and Racine, the comedies of Molière, and the prose of Descartes and Pascal. During the 18th century the greatest writing was that of Rousseau, Voltaire, and Montesquieu, in the field of social philosophy.

Among the leading figures of the Romantic movement during the early 19th century were Chateaubriand and Victor Hugo. Reacting against Romanticism, such novelists as Stendhal, Balzac, Flaubert, and Zola favoured realism and naturalism. Baudelaire, reacting against the Romantic poets de Vigny and de Musset and the Parnassian Gautier, was one of the first Symbolist poets; he was succeeded by Verlaine, Mallarmé, Rimbaud, and, in the 20th century, by Valéry, a contemporary of the surrealist poet Apollinaire.

Major French novelists of the 20th century include Proust, Gide, and Montherlant as well as the existentialists Sartre and Camus. French drama flourished with plays by Anouilh, Jean Cocteau, and the Absurdist writers Ionesco and Beckett. Such novelists as Alain Robbe-Grillet and Nathalie Sarraute pioneered the *nouveau roman*.

French Polynesia (former name: French Settlements in Oceania) A French overseas territory in the S Pacific Ocean consisting of several island groups. The most important of these are the Gambier Islands, the Society Archipelago, the Tuamotu Archipelago, the Tubuai Islands, and the Marquesas Islands. The islands produce copra and phosphates. Area: about 4000 sq km (1500 sq mi). Population (1980): 155 000. Capital: Papeete.

French Republican calendar The calendar adopted (1793) in France during the French Revolution and retained until 1806, when the Gregorian *calendar was reintroduced. The revolutionaries' purpose was to design a calendar without ecclesiastical associations. The year began on 22 Sept (the date in 1792 when the Republic came into being) and had 365 days divided into 12 months of 30 days each. The remaining 5 days (17-22 Sept) were festivals, an extra one being added in a leap year. Each month was divided into 3 periods of 10 days (a *décade*) and was renamed: Vendémiaire (French: vintage; 22 Sept-21 Oct), Brumaire (mist), Frimaire (frost), Nivôse (snow), Pluviôse (rain), Ventôse (wind), Germinal (seedtime), Floréal (blossom), Prairial (meadow), Messidor (harvest), Thermidor (heat), Fructidor (fruits).

French Revolution The overthrow of the French monarchy as a reaction to the corrupt, feudal, and incompetent government of the Bourbon kings. In 1789 Louis XVI was forced to summon the *States General but its Third Estate, opposing aristocratic attempts to dominate proceedings, formed its own National Assembly. Riots followed, the Bastille was stormed, the king was mobbed at Versailles, and the Assembly (from July the Constituent Assembly) promulgated the Declaration of the *Rights of Man. Feudalism was abolished and in September, 1791, a new constitution was accepted by the king following his thwarted attempt to flee France (the flight to Varennes). However, his continuing uncooperativeness fostered the growing republicanism of what became the Legislative Assembly (October, 1791) and then the National Convention (September, 1792). The Convention proclaimed a republic and in January, 1793, Louis was executed. The moderate *Girondins, discredited by France's war reverses (see Revolutionary and Napoleonic Wars), were now ousted by the *Jacobins and power passed to the Committee of *Public Safety. Under *Robespierre the Committee conducted a *Reign of Terror in which thousands of suspected antirevolutionaries were executed but his extremism brought (1794) his downfall on 9 Thermidor (27 July; see French Republican calendar). The so-called Thermidorean reaction led to the establishment of the *Directory (1795), which struggled for four years with economic crises until Napoleon's coup d'état of 18 Brumaire (1799) brought the Revolution to an end.

French Somalia. See Djibouti, Republic of.

French Southern and Antarctic Territories A French territory (since 1955) comprising *Adélie Land in Antarctica with the islands of Amsterdam and St Paul and the Kerguelen and Crozet archipelagos in the Indian Ocean.

French Sudan. See Mali, Republic of.

French West Africa (French name: Afrique Occidentale Française) The former French territories in West Africa comprising (1895–1958) the present-day independent countries of Benin, Guinea, Ivory Coast, Niger, and Senegal.

Freneau, Philip (1752–1832) US poet. He described his experience as a prisoner during the American Revolution in *The British Prison Ship* (1781). After independence he became a sea captain and later edited the popular *National Gazette* (1791–93). He then went back to sea for a period before retiring to his farm, where he wrote philosophical nature poetry.

frequency The number of cycles completed by a vibrating system in unit time, usually one second (symbol: ν or f). The unit of frequency is the *hertz. The angular frequency, ω, is related to the frequency by the equation $\omega = 2\pi f$ and is measured in radians per second.

frequency modulation. See modulation.

fresco A classical and Renaissance method of wall decoration in which pure pigments dissolved in water were applied to the wet lime-plastered surface of a wall, producing a chemical reaction that made the colours a permanent part of the wall. Up to about 1500 the design was sketched freehand onto the rough plaster surface (the *arricciato*). Separate areas of the sketch were then filled in with fine smooth plaster (the *intonaco*) and detailed colour was applied in layers of different pigments. Subsequently the *cartoon, as used by *Michelangelo, *Raphael, *Holbein, and others, allowed for more complicated premeditated design. The composition was drawn on sheets of paper, later applied to the wall, and the design pricked through with a stylus or with charcoal dust forced through the stylus piercings. Fresco painting was revived in the 20th century by the Mexican muralists *Orozco and *Rivera.

Frescobaldi A family of bankers, which dominated the mercantile and political life of Florence until it was divided in the dispute between the *Guelfs and Ghibellines at the end of the 13th century. The Frescobaldi opened a bank in London in the 1270s and financed the wars of Edward I and II. Receiving considerable privileges as reward, they were increasingly unpopular, fleeing the country in 1310 to escape prosecution.

Fresnel, Augustin Jean (1788–1827) French physicist, who (with Thomas *Young) used his work on interference to formulate the wave theory of light. See also Fresnel lens.

Fresnel lens A convex optical lens used principally in spotlights. It is thinner and therefore absorbs less light and heat than a normal convex lens with an equally short focal length. This is achieved by making the surface a series of stepped concentric rings, each with the same curvature as the equivalent normal convex surface at that radius. Named after A. *Fresnel.

SIGMUND FREUD *With his grandson Stephan (child of his youngest son Ernst) in Berlin (1922).*

Freud, Sigmund (1856–1939) Austrian psychiatrist and pioneer of psychoanalysis. Freud studied medicine and, in 1882, joined the staff of a psychiatric clinic in Vienna. An interest in hypnosis developed through his collaboration with Josef *Breuer and his meeting, in 1885, with Jean-Martin *Charcot. Following the publication with Breuer of *Studies in Hysteria* (1895), Freud evolved his theory that neuroses were rooted in suppressed sexual desires and sexual experiences of childhood, either real or imagined. In *The Interpretation of Dreams* (1899), he analysed the content of dreams in terms of unconscious desires and experiences, often dating from childhood. His emphasis on the sexual origin of mental disorders aroused great controversy, particularly his view that the sexual desires of children dated from birth, not puberty. In 1902 Freud established a circle of his colleagues in Vienna, which later (1910) became the International Psycho-Analytical Society. However, many of its members, including Carl *Jung and Alfred *Adler, resigned over disagreements with its founder. Freud left Vienna in 1938, following the Nazi invasion, joining his son in London, where he remained until his death.

Although subsequently modified, Freud's theories shed light on the workings of the unconscious mind and the motives, desires, and conflicts involved in human behaviour. His other books include *The Psychopathology of Everyday Life* (1904), *Totem and Taboo* (1913), *Beyond the Pleasure Principle* (1920), and *Moses and Monotheism* (1939). His daughter **Anna Freud** (1895–1982) was a founder of child psychoanalysis. Coming to London with her father in 1938 she worked at the Hampstead Child Therapy Clinic. Sigmund Freud's grandsons include **Lucian Freud** (1922–), a noted painter, and **Clement Freud** (1924–), a television personality, caterer, and Liberal MP.

Freyja (*or* Freya) The Norse goddess of love and fertility, the sister of Frey, the god of sunshine, rain, and fertility. She is the Norse counterpart of Venus and is the leader of the *Valkyries. In some sources she is identified with *Frigga.

friarbird A noisy chattering *honeyeater of the genus *Philemon* (16 species), also called leatherhead. Friarbirds resemble jackdaws but have naked patches on the head and horny outgrowths on the bill.

Fribourg (German name: Freiburg) 46 50N 7 10E A town in W Switzerland. Its many medieval buildings include the Cathedral of St Nicholas (13th–15th centuries) and it has a university (1889). Industries include the production of beer, chocolate, and machinery. Population (1983 est): 37 100.

friction A force exerted at the boundary between two solids or fluids that retards motion between them. In solid friction a distinction is drawn between sliding friction and rolling friction. Sliding friction is further divided into dynamic friction, defined as the minimum force needed to keep a body sliding, and static friction, defined as the minimum force needed to move a stationary body. The latter is slightly greater than the former. In rolling friction the force of resistance is less than in sliding friction as the rolling body moves up the side of a depression made in the stationary body. This accounts for the effectiveness of wheels and ball bearings. The coefficient of friction is defined as the ratio of the frictional force to the perpendicular reaction between the surfaces. Friction is caused primarily by the two surfaces interlocking at the microscopic level. It is reduced by the use of lubricants, such as grease or graphite (*see* tribology). Where it is sometimes desirable to increase friction between surfaces, as in brake linings, clutch plates, and shoe soles, rough hard-wearing materials are used.

Friedland, Battle of (14 June, 1807) A battle in the Napoleonic Wars fought near Friedland, East Prussia (now Pravdinsk, Soviet Union). The French under Napoleon defeated the Russians, under Gen Levin Bennigsen (1745–1826). The victory enabled the French to occupy Königsberg and led to the Treaty of *Tilsit.

Friedman, Milton (1912–) US economist. A conservative economist, Friedman is known for his theories on monetary supply, which contradict those of *Keynes. His published work, which argues for the free market economy, includes *A Theory of the Consumption Function* (1957) and *Capitalism and Freedom* (1962). With his wife **Rose Friedman** he wrote *Free to Choose* (1980) and *Tyranny of the Status Quo* (1984). He won the 1976 Nobel Prize.

Friedrich, Caspar David (1774–1840) German Romantic landscape painter, who studied at the Copenhagen Academy (1794–98). From 1798 he lived in Dresden, where he became friendly with *Goethe and other writers. His first major painting, an altarpiece painted in 1808, initiated a controversy over the use of landscape in religious subjects; successive works, such as *Wreck of the Hope* (1822; Kunsthalle, Hamburg) are notable for their symbolism of despair and man's insignificance in relation to nature.

Friendly Islands. *See* Tonga, Kingdom of.

friendly societies Voluntary mutual-aid associations the members of which regularly contribute money to central funds that provide financial assistance in times of need caused by illness, old age, or death. First formed in the 17th century, the societies enjoyed their greatest popularity in the 19th century and inspired many other self-help and insurance schemes, including the UK National Insurance Act (1911). There are some 6500 friendly societies in Britain.

Friends of the Earth A British environmental pressure group. Established in 1971, it is organized into 250 local groups in the UK, which campaign on environmental issues through demonstrations, public meetings, and parliamentary legislation. Targets have included motorway projects, commercial

whaling, and industrial pollution (including nuclear power plants). The organization also has branches in 25 countries, directed from the Netherlands.

Friesian cattle A breed of black-and-white cattle originating from the province of Friesland in the Netherlands. They were exported to North America by early settlers and there developed as Holstein-Friesians. They are high-yielding milk producers and crosses, especially with a Charolais or Hereford bull, give good beef.

Friesland A province in the N Netherlands, bordering on the IJsselmeer. Much of the land is below sea level and there are strong dykes and an extensive canal system. Cattle raising and dairy farming are important; the famous Friesian breed of cattle came from here. Area: 3803 sq km (1468 sq mi). Population (1981 est): 589 252. Capital: Leeuwarden.

frigate A naval vessel, smaller than a *destroyer, used mainly for carrying guided missiles and displacing about 2400 tonnes. Revived as the name of a class by the Royal Navy during World War II, earlier sailing frigates included the *Constitution* ("Old Ironsides"), a US vessel that acquired fame in the early history of the USA.

frigate bird A seabird belonging to the genus *Fregata* and family *Fregatidae* (5 species), occurring in tropical and subtropical oceanic regions, also called man-of-war bird because it often steals food from other birds in midair. 80–115 cm long, frigate birds have narrow wings spanning up to 2.3 m, a long hooked bill, and a forked tail. Males are glossy black and develop an inflatable red throat sac in the breeding season; females are brownish black with white underparts. Order: *Pelecaniformes* (gannets, pelicans, etc.).

Frigga (*or* Frigg) The Norse goddess of married love and the hearth, the wife of *Odin. In some legends she is identified with *Freyja; her name is preserved in *Friday*.

frilled lizard A slender pale-brown arboreal lizard, *Chlamydosaurus kingi*, occurring in dry regions of Australia and feeding chiefly on ants. Up to 1 m long, it has a scaly membrane around its neck that forms a large frill, thereby deterring likely enemies. Family: *Agamidae*.

Friml, Rudolph (1879-1972) Czech-born composer and pianist, who settled in the USA in 1906. He is remembered for his operettas, such as *Rose Marie* (1916) and *The Vagabond King* (1925). He also wrote a piano concerto and light pieces for the piano.

Frisch, Karl von (1886–1982) Austrian zoologist, best known for his work on animal behaviour, especially of bees. He found that bees communicate with each other by means of a circling "dance" or by wagging movements to indicate the location of a source of food from the hive. Von Frisch also worked on the sensory abilities of fish. He shared a Nobel Prize (1973) with *Lorenz and Niko *Tinbergen.

Frisch, Max (1911–) Swiss dramatist and novelist. His early literary career was combined with journalism and architectural studies. Many of his plays are Brechtian parables dealing with moral and social themes and attacking complacency. They include the black comedy *The Fire Raisers* (1958) and *Andorra* (1961), a tragedy about antisemitism. His novels include *Stiller* (1954) and *Homo Faber* (1957).

Frisch, Otto Robert (1904–79) Austrian-born physicist, nephew of Lise *Meitner, with whom he worked in Copenhagen on nuclear fission. During World War II he worked at Los Alamos on the atom bomb. In 1947 he became professor of physics at Cambridge University.

Frisch, Ragnar (1895–1973) Norwegian economist. As professor of economics at Oslo University and editor of *Econometrica*, Frisch was concerned with the application of statistics to economics. He received, with Jan *Tinbergen, the first Nobel Prize for Economics (1969).

Frisches Haff. *See* Vistula Lagoon.

Frisian A West Germanic language formerly spoken along the North Sea coastal region of Holland as far as Schleswig in Germany. It is now principally confined to Friesland province in Holland and certain offshore islands including Heligoland. It is the language most closely related to English. The Frisians were a seafaring and commercial people before turning to dairy and beef farming.

Frisian Islands A chain of islands in the North Sea extending along the coast of, and politically divided between, the Netherlands, West Germany, and SW Denmark. The chain comprises three main groups: the West, North, and East Frisian Islands. The chief occupations are fishing, sheep and cattle raising, and tourism.

fritillary (botany) A bulbous perennial plant of the genus *Fritillaria* (80 species), mostly native to N temperate regions. The leaves are narrow and the bell-shaped flowers droop from slender stalks. The European snake's head (*F. meleagris*), also called leopard lily and toad lily, has reddish-purple chequered flowers. The crown imperial (*F. imperialis*), native to N India, has a cluster of pendant red flowers at the top of a tall (120 cm) stem, topped by a tuft of leaves. Both species are popular garden plants. Family: *Liliaceae*.

fritillary (zoology) A *nymphalid butterfly, usually brown or orange marked with black. The caterpillars feed at night—often on violets—but many species hibernate soon after hatching. Chief genera: *Boloria*, *Melitaea*.

Friuli-Venezia Giulia A region in the extreme NE of Italy. It was formed in 1947, incorporating Trieste in 1954, and is semiautonomous. It consists of mountains along the N border with Austria and a coastal plain in the S. The region's farmers produce cereals and maize in the lowlands, fruit and vines in the foothills, and livestock in the mountains. Industries include textiles, food processing, chemicals, and shipbuilding. Area: 7850 sq km (3031 sq mi). Population (1980 est): 1 244 327. Capital: Trieste.

Frobisher, Sir Martin (c. 1535–94) English navigator. He made three attempts (1576, 1577, 1578) to discover the *Northwest Passage, giving his name to a bay on Baffin Island and bringing back "black earth," which was mistakenly thought to contain gold. He later served against the Spanish *Armada and raided Spanish treasure ships.

Frobisher Bay A settlement in N Canada, in the Northwest Territories on Baffin Island. It has police, radio, and weather stations. Population (1982): 2525.

Fröding, Gustaf (1860–1911) One of the most important and popular of Swedish lyric poets. His career was repeatedly interrupted by ill health apparently due to hereditary mental instability. His native Värmland inspired his first highly successful collection, *Guitarr och dragharmonika* (*Guitar and Concertina*; 1891). His later poetry, collected in *Nya Dikter* (*New Poems*; 1894) and *Stänk och flikar* (*Splashes and Rags*; 1896), was influenced by Nietzschean ideas and brought a new level of technical perfection to Swedish verse.

Froebel, Friedrich Wilhelm August (1782–1852) German pioneer of nursery education. Throughout his life, Froebel was fascinated by the underlying unity of all things. His view of man was one of harmonious growth, and he applied this concept to the development of children in *The Education of Man* (1826). Although influenced by *Pestalozzi, Froebel disagreed with his theory that young children should remain only with their mothers. His view that children should spend time together in creative play led him to found the first kindergarten (1837) at Blankenburg.

frog A tail-less amphibian of the family *Ranidae*, which includes bullfrogs, hairy frogs, and leopard frogs. Many other so-called frogs, such as *tree frogs, are actually toads. The European frog (*Rana temporaria*) grows to 10 cm. Greenish-brown with black markings, it spends most of its life on land, feeding on insects, and only returns to water to breed. Other species, such as the edible frog (*R. esculenta*), may spend most of their lives in water. Order: *Anura*.

frog-bit A Eurasian perennial water plant, *Hydrocharis morsus-ranae*, found in ponds, ditches, etc. It has floating stems arising from submerged roots, rounded leaves, and white flowers, 2 cm in diameter. Family: *Hydrocharitaceae*.

frogfish A slow-moving carnivorous fish belonging to a family (*Antennariidae*; about 60 species) occurring on the bottom, usually in shallow tropical waters. Frogfish have a robust body, up to 30 cm long, with camouflaging patterned fleshy flaps and warty skin, limblike pectoral fins, and often a wirelike projection from the snout, which lures prey. Order: *Lophiiformes*.

froghopper A small jumping insect belonging to the family *Cercopidae* (about 2000 species). Froghoppers feed on plant juices, sometimes becoming pests. Eggs are laid on stems or roots and the *nymphs remain stationary until adult. They often protect themselves against predators and desiccation with a cover of white froth ("cuckoo spit"), produced by blowing air mixed with fluid from the anus through a valve in the abdomen. For this reason they are often known as cuckoo-spit insects and spittlebugs. Order: *Hemiptera*.

frogmouth A nocturnal bird belonging to a family (*Podargidae*; 12 species), occurring in forests of SE Asia and Australasia. 25–55 cm long, frogmouths are well camouflaged with a mottled grey and brown plumage. They have a wide-gaping bill and prey chiefly on beetles, frogs, mice, and small birds. Order: *Caprimulgiformes* (nightjars, etc.).

Froissart, Jean (1337–c. 1400) French chronicler and poet. He travelled widely in Europe and served at the court of Edward III of England. His *Chronicles*, covering the years from 1325 to 1400, are a detailed and colourful record of the Hundred Years' War. He also wrote a verse romance, *Méliador*, and many ballades.

Fromm, Erich (1900–80) US psychologist and philosopher, born in Germany. Fromm left Germany for the USA in 1934 and became well known for his controversial analyses of social ills in modern industrial society. In *The Sane Society* (1955), he charged the consumer society with being responsible for isolation, loneliness, and doubt among individuals. His other works include *The Art of Loving* (1956) and *The Revolution of Hope* (1968).

Fronde (French: sling) French uprising between 1648 and 1653 so called because the combatants employed slingshots. The first Fronde, a protest against excessive tax demands and the administration of *Mazarin, was led by the Paris parlement. It was quickly suppressed (1649) by the royal army led by *Condé. In 1650 Condé himself led a second, aristocratic, revolt against Mazarin's authority. Contention among its leaders and an upsurge of support for the monarchy led to its collapse.

front In □meteorology, the interface between two air masses of different thermal characteristics and origins. Where the air masses converge the warm air, being lighter, rises and slopes over the cold air. Distinctive weather phenomena are associated with fronts, particularly the development of depressions, and they are very important in short-term weather forecasting.

Front de Libération nationale (FLN) An Algerian nationalist group that organized the war of independence against France (1954–62). Formed in 1954, the FLN began a campaign of terrorism and sabotage. In 1956 it organized itself like a government, sending diplomatic missions abroad, and in 1958 set up a provisional government in Tunis under Ferhat *Abbas. In 1962 the French under Gen de Gaulle agreed to Algerian independence and when *Ben Bella became president in 1963 the FLN became Algeria's sole political party.

Frontenac, Louis de Buade, Comte de Palluau et de (1620–98) French soldier; governor of New France (1672–82, 1689–98), who promoted French expansion in North America. His fur-trading activities, challenged by the Iroquois Indian confederacy, and his policy of expansion, caused dissension that led to his recall. When war broke out with England in 1689 he was reinstated. He attacked New England settlements with the help of Indian allies, defended Quebec, and eventually subdued the Iroquois.

frost A weather condition that occurs when the temperature falls below 0°C (32°F). It is recognized by the icy deposit that forms but if the air is very dry this will not occur. In weather forecasting grades of severity of frost are distinguished as slight (-0.1 to -3.5°C), moderate (-3.6 to -6.4°C), severe (-6.5 to -11.5°C), and very severe (below -11.5°C). A distinction is made between ground frost, measured at grass level, and air frost, measured at a height of 1.4 m (4 ft).

Frost, Robert Lee (1874–1963) US poet. In 1885 his family moved from San Francisco to New England, where he worked as a teacher and farmer. The poetry collections *A Boy's Will* (1913) and *North of Boston* (1914), published during a stay in England, brought him fame. His work, often pastoral and lyrical, has a dark undercurrent of fear and suffering relieved only by stoical acceptance.

frostbite Damage to part of the body, usually a hand or foot, resulting from exposure to extreme cold. The blood vessels to the affected limb constrict so that little blood (and therefore essential oxygen) reaches the skin, nerves, and muscles. This may lead to loss of sensation, ulcers, and eventually gangrene, necessitating amputation. Initial treatment is gently to warm the affected part.

froth flotation A method of separating mineral ore from waste or one ore from another. The unpurified pulverized ore is agitated with water and a reagent that binds preferentially with the desired ore and alters its surface properties. Air is then passed through the mixture and the ore is carried to the surface by the bubbles to form a froth, which can then be removed.

frottola (Italian: untruth, silly story) A popular Italian song form of the early 16th century. It was a setting of fashionable verse in four parts, the voice being accompanied by three instrumental parts and the music being repeated for each stanza.

Froude, James Anthony (1818-94) British historian. A defector from the *Oxford Movement, Froude was influenced by *Carlyle. Froude's *History of England* (1856-70) established his reputation as a historian, which rested chiefly on his literary talent rather than on his historical understanding.

fructose A simple sugar (monosaccharide) that is sweeter than sucrose and present in green leaves, fruits, and honey. Its phosphate derivatives are important in the carbohydrate metabolism of living organisms.

fruit The fertilized ovary of a flower, which contains the seed (or seeds) and may incorporate other parts of the flower (e.g. the receptacle in strawberries, the bracts in pineapples). The variation in the structure of fruits reflects the different means they have evolved to ensure dispersal of the seeds, which is essential to prevent overcrowding and enable the plant to spread and colonize new habitats. Fleshy fruits, for example, are usually eaten by animals, the seeds passing out with their faeces. Animals can also carry hooked or sticky fruits on their bodies. Seeds dispersed by wind are usually very light: they are either forcibly ejected from their fruits, for example from the *capsule of poppy and the pods of leguminous plants, or they remain attached to the fruit, which can itself remain airborne for considerable distances, for example the winged fruits of sycamores and ash trees. Some fruits are distributed by water: coconut fruits can be transported several hundred miles by sea. The word fruit is popularly restricted to the fleshy edible fruits, many of which are of economic importance to man: **fruit farming** constitutes an important branch of commercial *horticulture. In terms of world production the most important fruit crops are: apples, pears, and cherries (in cool temperate regions);

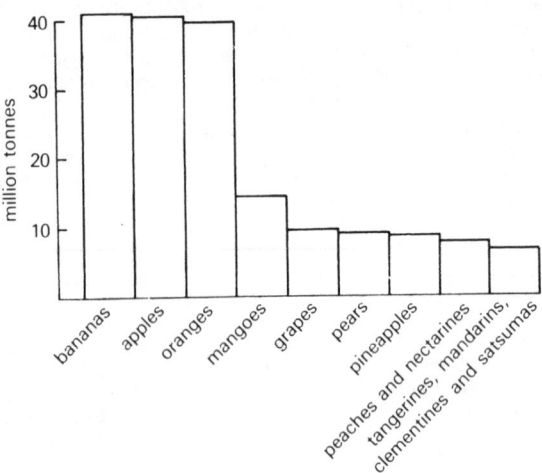

FRUIT *World production of fruit (1984).*

grapes, peaches, and figs (warm temperate); citrus fruits and dates (subtropical); bananas and pineapples (tropical).

fruit bat A vegetarian *bat belonging to the family *Pteropidae* and suborder *Megachiroptera* (150 species). Fruit bats occur in tropical and subtropical regions of the Old World. With a body length of up to 40 cm, they are typically larger than insect-eating bats and have better vision; only one genus (*Rousettus*, 13 species) uses *echolocation. Most eat fruit although some feed on flowers or nectar. Certain tropical trees are adapted for pollination by fruit bats. *See also* flying fox. □mammal.

fruit fly A fly belonging to the family *Trypetidae* (1200 species)—the true fruit flies. (Insects of the family *Drosophilidae* are known as small fruit flies: *see* Drosophila.) True fruit flies have spotted or banded wings and the larvae of many species feed on fruit, often causing serious damage. For example, the Mediterranean fruit fly (*Ceratitis capitata*) is a pest of almost all succulent fruits, while the North American apple maggot (*Rhagoletis pomonella*) tunnels into apples.

Frunze (name until 1925: Pishpek) 42 53N 74 46E A city in the SW Soviet Union, the capital of Kirghiz SSR on the River Chu. Industries developed rapidly after World War II and include the manufacture of agricultural machinery, textiles, food, and tobacco products. Population (1984 est): 590 000.

Fry, Christopher (C. Harris; 1907–) British dramatist. The verbal excitement of his earliest verse plays, *A Phoenix Too Frequent* (1946) and *The Lady's Not for Burning* (1948), seemed to presage a revival of poetic drama, but the popularity of his work declined after the early 1950s. His other plays include *Venus Observed* (1950), *The Light Is Dark Enough* (1954), and *Curtmantle* (1962).

Fry, Elizabeth (1780-1845) British prison reformer. A Quaker, Elizabeth Fry first visited Newgate Prison in 1813. She aimed to improve the conditions under which women prisoners lived by seeing that they were properly fed and clothed, segregated from men, supervised by women, and provided with light work. Later, she travelled throughout Europe, reforming prisons, hospitals, and mental asylums.

Fry, Roger (Eliot) (1866-1934) British painter and art critic. He was educated at Cambridge University, where he later became Slade Professor of Fine Art (1933). He is best known for his influential writings on art, e.g. *Vision and Design* (1920), and artists, e.g. *Bellini* (1899) and *Cézanne*

FRUIT

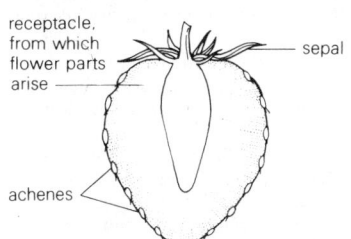

strawberry *The true fruits, which are formed from the ovary and contain the seeds, are the achenes on the surface of the fleshy receptacle.*

poppy *The seeds within the capsule are shaken out through the pores.*

apple *The flesh of the apple is the receptacle; the core develops from the ovary and contains the seeds (pips).*

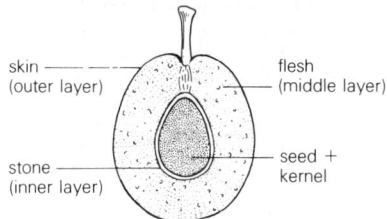

plum *This fruit, like all drupes (stone fruits), is made up of three layers.*

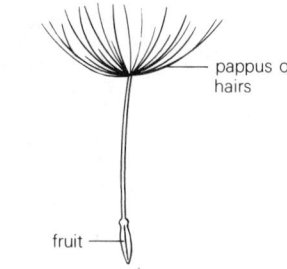

dandelion *The pappus acts as a parachute.*

tomato *The flesh of the tomato (a berry) is formed from the ovary.*

herb bennet *The hooks cling to the fur of animals, which thus disperse the seeds.*

sycamore *The two winged fruits separate and are carried away by the wind.*

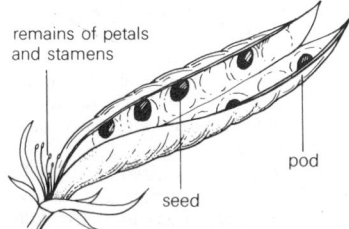

lupin *When ripe, the pod splits open and curls back, ejecting the seeds.*

(1927). Through exhibitions (1910, 1912) he promoted the French postimpressionist painters in Britain.

Fu'ad I (1868–1936) King of Egypt (1922-36). He became sultan in 1917 under the British protectorate and king when Britain granted limited independence in 1922. He tried to curb the nationalist Wafd Party and in 1931 suspended the 1923 constitution. Popular pressure forced him to restore it in 1935.

Fuchs, (Emil Julius) Klaus (1911–88) British physicist and spy, born in Germany. During World War II he worked on atomic bomb research in Britain and the USA and in 1950 was tried and found guilty of having passed secret information to the Soviet Union since 1943. His motives were idealistic. Released from prison in 1959, he lived and worked in East Germany until his death.

Fuchs, Sir Vivian (Ernest) (1908-) British explorer. He was director of the Falkland Islands Dependencies Survey Scientific Bureau (1947-50) and later led the Commonwealth Trans-Antarctic Expedition: with help from Sir Edmund *Hillary he covered and surveyed 3500 km (2173 mi) between 24 November, 1957, and 2 March, 1958. He was again director of the Falkland Islands Survey (British Antarctic Survey from 1962) from 1960 until 1973.

Fuchsia A genus of shrubs and herbs (100 species) mostly native to tropical America and widely cultivated as ornamentals. The plants range from creeping forms, bushes, and small trees to epiphytes. They have deep-pink, red, or purple drooping flowers all along the branches; each flower has four long flaring coloured sepals surrounding the shorter petals, below which the stamens and stigma protrude. Most cultivated forms are varieties of *F. magellanica*, *F. coccinea*, and *F. arborescens* or hybrids between them. Family: *Onagraceae* (willowherb family).

Fucus. *See* wrack.

fuel cell A device that converts the energy of a chemical reaction directly into an electric current. In the simplest type oxygen and hydrogen are fed through two separate porous nickel plates into an electrolytic solution. The gases combine to form water and thus set up a potential difference between the two plates. Fuel cells are distinguished from *accumulators in that the latter need to be recharged and do not consume their reactants. Fuel cells provide a clean source of power but are rather bulky. □ p. 478.

fuel injection The pumping of fuel in the form of a spray directly into the cylinders of an *internal-combustion engine. This is necessary in the case of continuous-combustion engines, such as rocket motors and *gas turbines. In Diesel engines fuel injection is also used and in some petrol engines it replaces the normal *carburettor as it gives a more even fuel distribution in the combustion chamber.

fuels. *See* fossil fuels.

Fugard, Athol (1932-) South African dramatist, educated at Cape Town University. His plays, which include *Blood Knot* (1961) and *Boesma and Lena* (1969), treat the plight of outcast individuals in an uncaring society with humour and humanity.

FUEL CELL *Hydrogen gas (H_2) is passed over a negative electrode containing a catalyst, which ionizes the gas into ions (H^+) and electrons (e). In an acidic electrolyte the ions migrate to the positive electrode over which oxygen is bubbled. The electrons flow through an external circuit as a current. At the positive electrode water is formed according to the equation $2H^+ + \frac{1}{2}O_2 + 2e \rightarrow H_2O$.*

Fugger, Hans (1348-1409) German weaver, who founded a family business that dominated European finance in the 15th and 16th centuries. Through diligence and advantageous marriage the family weaving business expanded under his grandson **Jakob Fugger** (1459-1525) to include mining interests and to handle papal financial business. For a time Fugger financial strength influenced European politics—in 1519 they backed Charles V's election as Holy Roman Emperor—but the family's fortunes subsequently declined and the firm was dissolved after the Thirty Years' War (1618-48).

Fugitives An influential group of US poets and critics associated with Vanderbilt University, Nashville, Tennessee, during the 1920s. They included Allen *Tate, Robert Penn *Warren, and Cleanth Brooks (1906-). The themes of their writing derived from their concern with the history and traditional culture of the American South. They published the poetry magazine *The Fugitive* (1922-25).

fugue A piece of polyphonic music, generally having three or four parts (*or* voices), in which each part enters in turn with a statement of the main theme (*or* subject). After stating the subject each voice continues with the secondary theme (*or* counter-subject). Fugues are not composed to strict patterns; episodes in different tonalities are often interspersed with subsequent groups of entries of the voices. At the climax the voices are overlapped in close succession (*stretto*).

Fujian (Fu-chien *or* Fukien) A province in SE China, on Taiwan Strait, famous for its beauty. Over a hundred dialects have arisen among its mountain population. Since the 17th century food shortages resulting from insufficient agricultural land have prompted much emigration. It is opposite Taiwan and its military strength has been considerably increased since 1950. Chief products are sugar, rice, tea, timber, and fish. There is some light industry. Area: 123 000 sq km (47 970 sq mi). Population (1982 est): 25 931 106. Capital: Fuzhou.

Fujiwara The most illustrious of Japan's noble families. Fujiwara greatness reached a peak between the 9th and 12th centuries. From 858 the office of regent became a Fujiwara monopoly and government was mainly conducted through the Fujiwara family council. Intermarriage with the imperial family became so common that most emperors were partly of Fujiwara blood. The other base of Fujiwara power was their proprietorship of numerous private estates. From the late 11th century, however, their predominance was challenged

by the reinvigorated imperial family and in the 12th century they were forced to yield most of their authority to new provincial warrior leaders.

Fujiwara style A sophisticated and refined sculptural style, also called the Heian style, prevailing in Japan from the 9th to the 12th centuries, when the Fujiwara clan was politically dominant.

Fujiyama (English name: Mount Fuji) 35 23N 138 42E The highest mountain in Japan, it is a dormant volcano in S central Honshu. Long regarded as a symbol of Japan, it has a symmetrical snow-capped (Oct-May) cone and a Shinto shrine. Height: 3776 m (12 388 ft).

Fukien. *See* Fujian.

Fukuoka 33 39N 130 21E A port in Japan in N Kyushu on Hakata Bay. An ancient commercial centre, *Kublai Khan was twice defeated here (1274, 1281). Kyushu University was established in 1910. Industries include textiles and shipbuilding. Population (1983 est): 1 082 000.

Fukushima 37 44N 140 28E A city in Japan, in N Honshu. A major commercial centre, its chief industry is silks. Population (1980): 263 000.

Fukuyama 34 29N 133 21E A city in Japan, in SW Honshu. It developed around a 17th-century castle and is now a commercial and industrial centre. Population (1983 est): 355 000.

Fulani A Muslim people scattered over a large area of W Africa from Lake Chad to the Atlantic coast. They are a mixed Negroid and, probably, Berber racial type. Their language, known as Fulfulde (*or* Fula), belongs to the Atlantic division of the Niger-Congo family. Their social and cultural patterns are varied, reflecting influences from surrounding peoples. They were originally nomadic herdsmen but many have adopted agriculture and a sedentary way of life. The herdsmen remain egalitarian while the latter are organized more hierarchically. They are generally polygynous and favour cousin marriage, which reflects Islamic influence. In N Nigeria many adopted the *Hausa language and culture and, as a result of religious wars (1804-10), established a Muslim empire in which they were the ruling elite.

Fulbright educational program An international exchange scholarship programme, devised by Senator J. W. Fulbright (1905-) of Arkansas (USA) after World War II. The programme is ultimately the responsibility of the US Department of State, which, in association with other governments, has made more than 100 000 awards to students and teachers under the scheme.

Fulham A district in the Greater London borough of Hammersmith, on the N bank of the River Thames. It contains Fulham Palace, residence of the Bishop of London.

Fuliang (former name: Ching-te-chen *or* Jingdezhen) 29 17N 117 12E A town in E China, in Jiangxi province on the Chang River. It has been known for its porcelain since the 6th century AD. Population (1980): 574 000.

Fuller, J(ohn) F(rederick) C(harles) (1878-1966) British soldier and military theorist. He served with the infantry in South Africa and in World War I became staff officer of the tank corps and planned the successful armoured attack at Cambrai (1917). His advocacy of tank warfare and of combined operations by air and land had considerable influence, especially in E Europe. His publications include *Tanks in the Great War* (1920), *Field Service Regulations III* (lectures, 1937), and *A Military History of the Great War* (1954-56).

Fuller, Richard Buckminster (1895-1983) US inventor and architect. One of Fuller's main concerns has been making the best use of energy sources. His Dymaxion house (1928) and car (1933; improved version 1943) were designed to reduce waste and environmental pollution. His chief contribution has been the geodesic dome, a lightweight and cheap structure of mutually supporting interlocking rods that can span large areas. His biggest dome, in Louisiana, has a diameter of 117 m (384 ft). He has also experimented with inexpensive mass-produced housing (the "Wichita House," 1948), which can be dismantled and rebuilt as required. His writings include *Operating Manual for Spaceship Earth* (1969).

Fuller, Roy (Broadbent) (1912–   ) British poet and novelist; also a practising solicitor. His early poetry, beginning with *Poems* (1939), was concerned with social and political themes; his more recent volumes, including *Buff* (1965) and *New Poems* (1968), are more personal and philosophical. He was professor of poetry at Oxford from 1968 to 1973. He has published several novels, notably *Image of a Society* (1956).

Fuller, Thomas (1608–61) British historian. Known chiefly in his own lifetime as a preacher, he wrote many historical works, of which the best known is the *History of the Worthies of England* (1662), a biographical dictionary of famous Englishmen.

fuller's earth A nonplastic *clay rich in montmorillonite, with the property of absorbing and decolorizing oil and grease. It was formerly used for whitening and removing the grease from fleeces (fulling). It is still used in the textile industry and in refining fats and oils. It was probably formed by very fine-grained volcanic ash settling in water.

fulmar A maritime North Atlantic bird, *Fulmarus glacialis*. It is about 46 cm long and dark grey above with white underparts. Its range and numbers have increased, as a result of food in the form of offal from trawlers and whalers. Family: *Procellariidae* (petrels).

Fulton, Robert (1765–1815) American inventor, who built one of the earliest steamships, the *Clermont* (1807), and made steam a practical source of power on the sea. He had earlier constructed a submarine for the French government but its use against the British was not a success.

fumaric acid. *See* maleic acid.

fumitory A branching annual herb of the genus *Fumaria* (about 60 species), native to Eurasia and also found in North America. It has much divided compound leaves (feathery in some species) and dense spikes of pink, white, or reddish-purple flattened tubular flowers. The fruit is a nutlet. A common species is *F. officinalis*. Family: *Fumariaceae*.

Funchal 32 40N 15 55W The capital of the Madeira Islands, on the S coast of Madeira. Its mild climate and picturesque setting make it a popular tourist resort and it has a cathedral (1485–1514). The islands' chief commercial centre, it exports Madeira wines, embroidery, and wickerwork. Population (1981): 48 638.

functionalism (architecture) A doctrine principally associated with the *international style. Its main tenet is that the more fitted to its purpose a building is, the more beautiful it will be. The doctrine was developed under Louis *Sullivan in the 1890s, but found its most vocal advocate in *Le Corbusier, who defined a house as a machine for living in. Functionalism led to a very severe style, lacking in all ornamentation and idiosyncracy. Although still influential, its dominance faded after 1930, and function is no longer accepted as the sole attribute of beauty in architecture.

functionalism (sociology) A perspective, based on an analogy with the workings of a biological organism, which emphasizes the contribution constituent parts of a society (groups and institutions) make to the continuity or change of the whole society. Also known as structural-functionalism, the approach was used by *Durkheim and was a major influence in sociology in the USA and the UK after World War II as a result of the work of Talcott *Parsons.

fundamental constants Any of several constants that frequently appear in physical equations. The term is often reserved for five constants: the velocity of *light (c), *Planck's constant (h), the charge (e) and mass (m_e) of the *electron, and the fine structure constant (α). The latter is defined as $e^2/2hc\varepsilon_0$, where ε_0 is the electric constant; its value is approxi-

mately $1/137$ and it is a measure of the strength of the *electromagnetic interaction. These constants may be regarded as fundamental in that their values determine the magnitude of many physical effects. Other constants sometimes taken as fundamental include the electric constant, the magnetic constant, Avogadro's number, the Boltzmann constant, and the gravitational constant.

fundamental interactions The basic forces that occur in nature. *See* electromagnetic interaction; gravitational interaction; strong interaction; weak interaction.

fundamentalism A religious movement among some US Protestants arising after World War I. It insisted on the completely literal truth of the Bible, of the New Testament miracles, and of such traditional teachings as the Virgin Birth and bodily resurrection of Christ. It rejected any scientific knowledge, such as the theory of evolution, which conflicted with a literal reading of the Bible.

Fundy, Bay of An inlet of the Atlantic Ocean in SE Canada, between Nova Scotia and New Brunswick. Long and narrow, it has tides up to 20 m (66 ft) high, from which electricity is generated.

Fünen. *See* Fyn.

Fünfkirchen. *See* Pécs.

fungi Unicellular or multicellular organisms belonging to the group *Mycota* (about 50 000 known species), usually regarded as plants and including mushrooms, mildews, moulds, yeasts, etc. All fungi lack chlorophyll and therefore (unlike green plants) cannot manufacture their own food by photosynthesis. Some are saprophytes, feeding on dead organic matter by means of digestive enzymes; others are parasites of plants or animals. The body of most fungi consists of a network of branching threadlike structures (hyphae), forming a mycelium. Sexual reproduction results in the formation of spores, which may be produced in a specialized structure called a fruiting body: this is the visible part of mushrooms, puffballs, etc. Other fungi consist of single cells, which can reproduce asexually by simple division into two daughter cells. Fungi are distributed worldwide in terrestrial, freshwater, and marine habitats. Some live in the soil and play a vital role in bringing about *decomposition of dead organic matter. Other fungi (e.g. *Penicillium* and *Streptomyces*) are of great importance as a source of *antibiotics. Many parasitic fungi cause disease in animals and man (*see* infection) or in plants (e.g. the smuts and rusts), while some saprophytes are destructive to timber (*see* dry rot). Some fungi form associations with other plants, most notably with algae to form *lichens.

funnel weaver A *spider, also called funnel web spider, belonging to a worldwide family (*Agelenidae*). It builds funnel-shaped webs in grass, among debris, and under rocks and floorboards. The grass spider (*Agelena naevia*), 18–19 mm long, is a common North American species.

fur The skin of certain mammals including its covering of hair. The hair is usually short and soft next to the skin for insulation with longer guard hairs forming an outer protective layer. The untreated skins (pelts) of such animals as sheep, mink, rabbits, chinchilla, etc., are cleaned and stretched before undergoing tanning to make the skin into *leather. Many wild fur-bearing species are now protected and "furs" made from synthetic fibres have replaced many natural fashion furs.

Furies. *See* Erinyes.

furlong A unit of length traditionally based on the length of a furrow. It is equal to 220 yards (⅛ mile) and is still used in horseracing.

Furneaux Islands 40 0S 148 0E An Australian group of islands, in Bass Strait off the NE coast of Tasmania. The chief islands are Flinders (the largest), Cape Barren, and Clarke. Sheep farming is the principal activity.

Furness A peninsula in NW England, in Cumbria between the Irish Sea and Morecambe Bay. The Cistercian monks of

Ancient Egyptian (c. 1330 BC)   *Furniture found in the tomb of Tutankhamen is made from imported timber, inlaid with semiprecious stones, ebony, and ivory, and opulently gilded to testify to the wealth and status of its owner.*

Elizabethan (16th century AD)   *In England and N Europe gothic detail survived on domestic furniture until the 17th century. Solid oak was the most common wood.*

Louis XV (1723–74)   *The reaction in French taste against Louis XIV's monumental baroque led to the graceful curved lines of Louis XV furniture, the epitome of rococo elegance.*

Modern (20th century)   *Although Mies van der Rohe's Barcelona chair (1929) is the product of a skilled craftsman, new materials (plastic, plate glass, etc.) and mass-production have generally predominated in 20th-century furniture making.*

Furness Abbey (founded 1127) exploited the local iron-ore deposits and during the 19th century Furness became a major industrial centre. Tourism and farming are now important. Chief town: Barrow-in-Furness.

furniture Movable domestic artefacts, which are indispensable for civilized life. Examples exist from as early as 3000 BC in Egypt. In Europe medieval furniture was gothic in style and consisted principally of *chests, beds, seats, and tables, but Renaissance designers and craftsmen, working exclusively for the noble and rich, produced work in which function was subordinated to art, such as cabinets, richly ornamented with jewels and precious metals. During the 17th and 18th centuries architects, such as Robert *Adam, were increasingly concerned with the design of furniture for the interiors of their buildings. Such furniture ranked with paintings and other arts, both socially and economically.

In the 19th century, factory production led to debased design against which a few progressive designers, notably William *Morris, struggled. The 20th century has seen the introduction of simplified design and new materials, such as steel and plastic, reflecting modern functional needs.

Fürstenbund A league of German princes founded in 1785 and led by Frederick the Great of Prussia. Intended as a temporary expedient against Habsburg ambitions in Germany, the league was Prussia's first attempt to unite the other German states under its leadership, finally achieved in 1871.

Fürth 49 28N 11 00E A city in SE West Germany, near Nuremberg in Bavaria on the River Regnitz. The Fürth-Nuremberg railway line (1835) was the first in Germany. Toys and mirrors are manufactured. Population (1983 est): 99 680.

Furtwängler, Wilhelm (1886–1954) German conductor. He took over the Leipzig Gewandhaus concerts from Nikisch in 1922 and conducted the Berlin Philharmonic Orchestra from 1922 to 1954. He conducted opera at Bayreuth and Covent Garden and was also active as a composer. He excelled as a conductor of Beethoven and Wagner.

furze. See gorse.

fuse, electrical A length of wire designed to melt when the electric current passing through it exceeds a specified safe level, thus breaking the circuit. It is used to protect electrical equipment and low-voltage wiring, *circuit breakers being used for higher voltages. Domestic fuses commonly consisted of a length of bare fuse wire (usually tin or copper alloys) connecting two terminals in a porcelain holder, which fitted into a central fuse board. In modern practice, cartridge fuses (wire enclosed in a ceramic or glass cartridge) are fitted into 13-ampere plugs.

Fuseli, Henry (Johann Heinrich Füssli; 1741–1825) British painter of Swiss birth. He first worked as a translator of foreign books in London before studying art in Rome (1770–78). On his return his paintings, notably *Nightmare* (1782) and his illustrations of Shakespeare and Milton, showed his taste for horror and drama. He became professor of painting at the Royal Academy in 1799 and Keeper in 1804.

fusel oil A liquid mixture of organic substances including butanol and iso-amyl alcohol. It has an unpleasant smell and taste and is a by-product of the distillation of alcohol produced by fermentation.

Fushun 41 51N 123 53E A city in NE China, in Liaoning province. Its oil, steel, and chemical industries are based on its oil-shale and vast coal deposits. Aluminium production is also important. Population (1982): 1 190 000.

fusion (physics). See nuclear energy.

Fust, Johann (1400–66) German printer, who financed *Gutenberg's development of the printing press. Fust sued Gutenberg for the repayment of his loan and, when Gutenberg was unable to repay it, took possession of his equipment and set up the first successful printing firm.

Futa Jallon. See Fouta Djallon.

Futuna Islands. See Wallis and Futuna.

futurism 1. In Italy, an early 20th-century movement in the arts. It was founded in 1909, when the poet *Marinetti published a literary manifesto demanding the obliteration of past Italian culture and the establishment of a new society, literature, and art glorifying the speed and mechanization of modern life. A second manifesto (1910) was published by artists led by *Boccioni, *Balla, and *Severini. Using a cubist syle and such subjects as cars, trains, moving animals, etc., they aimed to represent multiple phases of motion in one painting. Italian futurism died during World War I but its influence was sustained in subsequent art movements, notably *vorticism. 2. In Russia, a movement that rejected traditional Russian literature. *Mayakovskii and *Khlebnikov were among the writers and artists who signed a manifesto called "A Slap in the Face for Public Taste" (1912) and adopted an experimental and innovatory attitude towards language. The Russian futurists supported the Revolution but were curbed in the 1930s by the Soviet government.

Fuzhou (Fu-chou or Foochow) 26 10N 119 20E A port in SE China, the capital of Fujian province on the Min delta. An ancient capital, it was the centre of foreign trade from the 10th to the 19th centuries. It is the site of Fujian Medical University. It has varied industries and its exports include timber and sugar cane. Population (1980 est): 800 000.

Fylde An area in NW England, in Lancashire between the estuaries of the River Wyre and Ribble. It is a rich agricultural area and has several resorts, notably Blackpool, along its coast.

Fylingdales The site of an early-warning radar station in NE England, in North Yorkshire, built to give warning of nuclear attack.

Fyns (German name: Fünen) The second largest Danish island, situated between the Little Belt and the Great Belt. Fishing is important and its fertile soil supports cereal growing, dairy farming, and cattle rearing. Area: 3481 sq km (1344 sq mi). Population (1984): 453 921.

G

gabbro A dark-coloured coarse-grained basic igneous rock formed by the crystallization at depth of basalt magma. It is the plutonic equivalent of basalt. Calcic plagioclase feldspar (usually labradorite), clinopyroxene (usually augite), and frequently olivine are the main constituents. Gabbro usually occurs in layered complexes or igneous intrusions.

Gaberones. *See* Gaborone.

Gabin, Jean (Jean-Alexis Moncorgé; 1904–76) French film actor. He is best known for his portrayals of brave but vulnerable heroes in films during the 1930s, notably *La Grande Illusion* (1937) and *Le Jour se lève* (1939). His later films include *L'Affaire Dominici* (1973).

Gable, Clark (1901–60) US film actor. He established his popularity as a leading man during the early 1930s, when he played many tough masculine roles. His films include *A Free Soul* (1931), *It Happened One Night* (1934), *Gone with the Wind* (1939), and *The Misfits* (1961).

Gabo, Naum (Naum Neemia Pevsner; 1890–1977) Russian sculptor. A pioneer of *constructivism, he and his brother Antoine *Pevsner formulated its main ideals in their *Realist Manifesto* published in Russia in 1920. Working later in Berlin (1923–33), England (1936–45), and the USA after 1946, he made numerous constructions of glass, plastic, metals, etc., a favourite device being nylon threads stretched over a plastic framework.

Gabon, Republic of An equatorial country in West Africa, on the Gulf of Guinea. Coastal plains rise to plateaus on either side of the Ogooué basin. The population is mainly Fang. *Economy*: almost three-quarters of the land is forested and timber was formerly the most important resource, especially okoumé, a soft wood used for plywood. Now, however, the exploitation of its vast mineral wealth forms the basis of the economy. Oil and natural gas production are important; other minerals include iron ore, uranium, and manganese. Mining and forestry are both hindered by transport difficulties but the position was improved by the opening (1986) of the trans-Gabon railway. Agriculture consists chiefly of subsistence farming. The main exports are oil, timber, manganese, and uranium. *History*: trading posts were set up by the Portuguese in the late 15th century and the area later became a centre of the slave trade. Settled by the French in the mid-19th century, it became one of the four territories of French Equatorial Africa in 1910. It gained internal self-government as a member of the French Community in 1958 and became independent in 1960. A one-party political system was instituted in 1967; in the 1980s the opposition was led by an underground group known as the *morena*. President: Omar Bongo (Albert Bernard B.; 1935–). Official language: French; Bantu languages are widely spoken. Official currency: CFA (Communauté financière africaine) franc of 100 centimes. Area: 267 000 sq km (103 089 sq mi). Population (1983 est): 921 000. Capital and main port: Libreville.

gaboon viper A highly venomous *puff adder, *Bitis gabonica*, occurring in African rain forests. Up to 2 m long, it has a thick body and a broad head with hornlike projections on its snout and is patterned with buff, brown, and purple rectangles and triangles. It feeds on small vertebrates.

Gabor, Dennis (1900–79) British electrical engineer, born in Hungary. He won the 1971 Nobel Prize for Physics for his invention of *holography.

Gaborone (former name: Gaberones) 24 45S 25 55E The capital of Botswana. The seat of government was transferred here from Mafeking in 1965. It contains part of the University of Botswana and Swaziland. Population (1981 est): 59 700.

Gabriel (c. 1776–1800) The leader of the first significant US slave uprising. He planned to attack Richmond, Virginia, with a thousand slaves, seize the arsenal, and establish an independent Black state. An informer warned the governor and Gabriel was captured and hanged.

Gabrieli, Andrea (c. 1520–86) Italian composer and organist. He became chief organist of St Mark's, Venice, in 1585; he composed madrigals, motets, and instrumental and organ music. His nephew **Giovanni Gabrieli** (c. 1557–1612) became second organist of St Mark's in 1585. He was one of the first composers to incorporate instrumental parts into vocal works and to write antiphonal music for several choirs or orchestras.

Gad, tribe of One of the 12 *tribes of Israel. It claimed descent from Gad, the son of Jacob and his concubine Zilpah. Its territory was in Transjordan, NE of the Dead Sea.

Gaddafi, Moammar al- (or Qaddafi; 1942–) Libyan colonel and statesman. In 1969 he led a revolt that overthrew the Libyan monarchy and in 1970 became chairman of the Revolutionary Command Council. His Arab nationalist and Islamic socialist policies have led to a reorganization of Libyan society and an active foreign policy.

Gaddi, Taddeo (c. 1300–?1366) Florentine painter, who was the pupil and assistant of *Giotto. His independent works include the frescoes of the *Life of the Virgin* (Baroncelli Chapel, Sta Croce, Florence). His son **Agnolo Gaddi** (c. 1350–96), also influenced by Giotto, painted frescoes of the *Story of the True Cross* in the choir of Sta Croce and the *Life of the Virgin* (Duomo, Prato).

gad fly A *bot or *warble fly whose parasitic larvae irritate animals, arousing them to bursts of frantic running.

gadolinium (Gd) A *lanthanide element named after the Finnish chemist J. Gadolin (1760–1852). It is used in television-tube phosphors. At no 64; at wt 157.25; mp 1313°C; bp 3233°C.

Gadsden Purchase (1853) About 77 700 sq km (30 000 sq mi) of land in what are now New Mexico and Arizona, bought by the USA from Mexico for $10 million. The purchase was named after its negotiator, James Gadsden (1788–1858), US minister to Mexico (1854–56).

gadwall A *dabbling duck, *Anas strepera*, that breeds in sheltered inland fresh waters of North America and Eurasia and winters in S Europe, Africa, and the southern United States. It is 48–51 cm long and has a grey barred plumage, a brown head and rump, and white and reddish wing markings.

Gaea (or Gaia) A Greek goddess personifying the earth. The wife and mother of Uranus (Heaven), by whom she bore the *Titans, the *Cyclops, and the *Gigantes, she incited the revolt of the Titans against him. From the blood of the wounded Uranus were born the *Erinyes.

Gaelic A language of the Goidelic group of *Celtic languages. Irish Gaelic is spoken in Ireland as a first language by approximately 100 000 people and as a second language by around 700 000. It is an official language of the Republic of Ireland. Scottish Gaelic (or Erse), which is spoken in the NW coastal region of Scotland and in the Hebrides, is an offshoot of Irish Gaelic that became a distinct dialect around the 13th century.

Gaeta 41 13N 13 36E A fishing port and resort in S central Italy, in Lazio on the Bay of Gaeta. A popular resort in Roman times, it has Roman remains. Industries include an oil refinery and glass making. Population (1981 est): 22 605.

Gafsa (Arabic name: Qafsah) 34 28N 8 43E A town in W central Tunisia, set in an oasis. Its main activities are irrigated fruit growing and the export of phosphates. Population (1984): 60 870.

Gagarin, Yuri Alekseevich (1934–68) Soviet cosmonaut, who on 12 April, 1961, became the first person to orbit the earth. He remained in orbit for 89 minutes, reaching a height of about 301 km (187 mi). He died when a plane he was testing crashed.

Gage, Thomas (1721–87) British soldier; commander in chief of British forces in North America (1763–74). His hostility to the grievances of the colonists contributed to the outbreak of the *American Revolution. He helped to draft the *Intolerable Acts in response to the *Boston Tea Party. He was replaced by William *Howe after military failures at the start of the Revolution.

Gaia. See Gaea.

Gaillardia A genus of herbaceous plants (about 20 species), native to North America. Several species are cultivated in gardens, especially the blanket flowers *G. aristata* and *G. grandiflora* (perennials) and *G. pulchella* (an annual). The single or double daisy-like flowers have purple centres and yellow, orange, or white fringed ray florets. Family: *Compositae*.

GAINSBOROUGH *Detail from* The Painter's Daughters with a Cat *(National Gallery, London). This unfinished picture was painted soon after 1759.*

Gainsborough, Thomas (1727–88) British portrait and landscape painter, born in Sudbury, Suffolk. His London training (1740–46), initially with the French engraver Gravelot, introduced him to *rococo portraiture. In 1759 he moved to Bath, seeking a fashionable clientele. There he studied the art of *Van Dyck, whose elegant style is reflected in Gainsborough's *Countess. Howe* (Kenwood House, London) and the *Blue Boy* (San Marino, California). His landscapes were at first influenced by *Ruisdael and *Hobbema and later by *Rubens, particularly in the *Harvest Wagon* (Barber Institute, Birmingham). On his return to London in 1774 he successfully rivalled *Reynolds for commissions and royal favour. In his later years he painted idyllic rustic scenes, the so-called fancy pictures. He was a founder member of the Royal Academy.

Gaitskell, Hugh (Todd Naylor) (1906–63) British politician; leader of the Labour Party (1955–63). He became an MP in 1945 and was minister of fuel and power (1947–50), minister of economic affairs (1950), and then chancellor of the exchequer (1950–51). He succeeded Attlee as Labour leader, defeating Aneurin Bevan in the leadership bid. After the defeat of the Labour Party in the 1959 general election, Gaitskell unsuccessfully attempted to change the constitution. At the 1960 party conference his opponents voted in favour of unilateral nuclear disarmament, against the policy of the executive. This led to Gaitskell's "Fight, and fight, and fight again" speech, the reversal of the disarmament policy at the 1961 conference, and the reuniting of the party. He opposed British membership of the EEC.

galago. See bushbaby.

Galahad In *Arthurian legend, the son of *Lancelot and Elaine. As the most perfect exemplar of knighthood, he was (in many romances) the only knight to succeed in the quest of the *Holy Grail.

galangal A flavouring obtained from the rhizomes of a Chinese perennial herb, *Alpinia officinarum*, that may be used in place of ginger. The plant grows to a height of 6 m, with long leathery leaves and pink, yellow, or white fragrant flowers in long dense clusters. Family: *Zingiberaceae*.

Galápagos finches. See Darwin's finches.

Galápagos giant tortoise A large rare *tortoise, *Testudo elephantopus*, found on the Galápagos Islands, where they were formerly slaughtered for meat. Up to 1.5 m long and weighing up to 150 kg, there are numerous subspecies, some now extinct, distinguishable by their different shell shapes. The only other surviving species of giant tortoise is *T. gigantica* of the Seychelles.

Galápagos Islands (Spanish name: Archipiélago de Colón) An archipelago in the Pacific Ocean, W of Ecuador. It consists of 12 main islands and several smaller ones, all of volcanic origin. They became well known following Charles *Darwin's visit in 1835, during which he collected evidence that influenced his theories on natural selection. The islands contain a large number of endemic species, including the giant tortoise; many islands now form nature reserves. Area: 7428 sq km (2868 sq mi). Population (1982): 6201.

Galatea 1. In Greek legend, a nymph who loved the shepherd Acis and was loved by Polyphemus. When Acis was killed by his rival she turned him into a river. 2. The name of a statue that came to life in answer to the prayers of *Pygmalion.

Galați 45 27N 28 02E A port in E Romania, on the River Danube. Largely rebuilt after World War II, it has a naval base, the country's largest shipyards, and iron, steel, and textile industries. Population (1983): 254 636.

Galatians, Epistle of Paul to the A New Testament book written by the Apostle Paul to churches in central Asia Minor in the middle of the 1st century AD. In it he defends his claim to be the apostle to the Gentiles, expounds justification by faith, and warns against those who were encouraging the converts to rely on Jewish ceremonial rites for their acceptance by God.

galaxies Huge assemblies of many millions of stars, gas, and dust, bound together by gravitational interactions. The majority are members of *clusters of galaxies. **Spiral galaxies** are large flattened systems with spiral arms winding outwards from a central nucleus. The spiral arms contain much interstellar gas and dust from which stars can form. Spirals have a mass of 10^{10} to 10^{11} solar masses. **Elliptical galaxies** are actually spheroidal with no clear internal structure. There is little interstellar matter so that most of the stars are old. They vary greatly in size and mass, the largest giant ellipticals exceeding 10^{12} solar masses. The third general category, **irregular galaxies**, have no definite shape or structure and are relatively small, with a high content of interstellar matter.

Galaxy (*or* Milky Way system) The spiral *galaxy to which the sun belongs. It contains about a hundred thousand million (10^{11}) stars. Most lie in the flattened galactic disc, comprising two spiral arms that wind out from a bulging central nucleus; the disc is about 120 light years across, the sun lying about 33 000 light years from the centre. The roughly spherical galactic halo surrounds the nucleus and disc; it is only sparsely populated with stars and globular *star clusters, which are considerably older than the stars of the spiral arms. Light cannot penetrate the dust in the innermost regions of the Galaxy but radio, infrared, and X-ray observations have shown complex phenomena to be occurring, possibly arising from the presence of a *black hole at the galactic centre.

Galbraith, John Kenneth (1908–) US economist and diplomat. An economist in the Keynesian tradition, Galbraith became professor of economics at Harvard University in 1949. His works include *American Capitalism: The Concept of Countervailing Power* (1952), *The Affluent Society* (1958), *Economics and the Public Purpose* (1973), and an autobiography *A Life In Our Times* (1981). Galbraith also served in public life as US ambassador to India (1961–63) and adviser to President Kennedy.

Galen (129–c. 199 AD) Greek physician and scholar, whose ideas dominated medicine until the Renaissance. From his studies of such animals as monkeys and dogs, Galen showed the importance of the spinal cord in muscle activity, the role of the ureter in kidney and bladder function, and that arteries carry blood rather than air. However, he held mistaken views on blood circulation, including the idea that blood seeped through minute pores in the wall of the heart separating the two ventricles. Galen also wrote on philosophy, law, and mathematics.

galena The principal ore of lead. It is a lead-grey dense but soft metallic mineral, found as cubic crystals of lead sulphide in hydrothermal veins and as replacement deposits in limestones. Galena ore bodies usually contain silver.

Galerius (Gaius Galerius Valerius Maximianus; c. 250–311 AD) Eastern Roman emperor (305–11) after the abdication of Diocletian. Galerius was probably responsible for continuing the persecution of the Christians begun by Diocletian in 303 but in 311 he proclaimed a limited toleration of Christianity. His authority was challenged by the emperor in the West and the ensuing conflict lasted until 308.

Galicia 1. A medieval kingdom in NW Spain, now in La Coruña, Pontevedra, Lugo, and Orense. Colonized by the *Visigoths from the 6th century, it became a subkingdom of Castile in the late 11th century. It retained its own flourishing language and culture. 2. A province in E Europe, which became an independent principality in 1087 until conquered by the Mongols in the 13th century. Later part of Poland (14th century) and Austria (18th century), Galicia was divided between Poland and Austria after World War I and Poland and the Soviet Union after World War II.

Galilean satellites The four largest *satellites of *Jupiter –Io, Europa, Ganymede, and Callisto–discovered by *Galileo (1610) and studied in detail by the US *Voyager probes (1979). Io, orbiting closest to Jupiter, is the most active volcanic body known in the solar system. Ganymede is the brightest Galilean and the largest satellite in the solar system. Callisto and Ganymede are heavily cratered.

Galilee A district of N Israel, bordering on the River Jordan and the Sea of Galilee. It comprised the northernmost region of ancient Palestine and was the scene of Jesus Christ's early ministry. Under the Romans, Galileans were noted for their religious zeal and nationalism; from the fall of Jerusalem (70 AD) to the middle ages Galilee was a centre for rabbinic scholarship. From 1892, Zionist settlements were established in Galilee, which formed part of the state of Israel (1949). *See also* Zealots.

Galilee, Sea of (Sea of Tiberias; Lake of Gennesaret; Lake Kinneret) A lake in NE Israel. It is fed mainly by and drained by the River Jordan; its surface is 209 m (686 ft) be-

low sea level. It was the scene of many episodes in the life of Christ. Area: 166 sq km (64 sq mi).

Galileo Galilei (1564–1642) Italian mathematician, physicist, and astronomer, whose emphasis on mathematical analysis anticipated the experimental method of scientific inquiry. Born in Pisa, legend has it that he demonstrated that the rate of fall of a body is independent of its mass by dropping weights from the Leaning Tower of Pisa. He is also reputed to have worked out that the period of a pendulum is independent of its amplitude by watching a swinging chandelier in Pisa Cathedral. In 1609 Galileo, on learning of the invention of a simple telescope, designed one himself and used it to study the sky. He soon made a number of discoveries, including sunspots and Jupiter's satellites, which convinced him of the superiority of *Copernicus' heliocentric system over the *Ptolemaic system. He wrote a witty and vigorous book, *Dialogue on Two World Systems* (1632), in which he made Ptolemy's system look foolish. As the Roman Catholic Church had condemned Copernicus' work in 1616, Galileo was forced by the Inquisition to recant his views and placed under house arrest for the rest of his life. Galileo, following his recantation, is said to have murmured "Eppur si muove" ("Still it moves," referring to the earth, which the Church insisted was stationary at the centre of the universe).

gall A swelling or excrescence on plants caused by abnormal proliferation of cells due to mechanical injury or attack by insects, mites, fungi, bacteria, or viruses. Some galls are self-limiting, including the oak apples caused by the *gall wasp, while others are tumorous, such as the crown gall induced by the bacterium *Agrobacterium tumefaciens*.

Gall, Franz Joseph (1758–1828) German physician and founder of the practice of *phrenology. He held the view that the shape of the skull reflected the shape of the underlying brain and hence the character of the individual. Although this idea is now discredited, Gall's work did provide a stimulus for research on the brain itself.

Galla A people of Ethiopia numbering about 10 million and making up about 40% of the Ethiopian population. They were originally nomads who spread from the SE region during the 16th century to many other areas, where they largely adopted a sedentary existence and local customs, losing their own distinctiveness. Their language belongs to the *Hamito-Semitic family.

gall bladder A saclike organ (7–10 cm long), close to the liver, that receives and stores *bile (formerly called gall) formed by the liver. The gall bladder is connected to the liver by the hepatic ducts and to the intestine by the common bile duct. Crystallization of bile components forms *gallstones, which may block the bile duct or cause gall bladder infections (cholecystitis). *See* Plate IV.

Galle (former name: Point de Galle) 6 01N 80 13E A seaport in SW Sri Lanka. The country's chief port under the Portuguese and its capital under the Dutch, it declined with the growth of Colombo. It has a cement factory. Population (1981): 77 183.

Galle, Johann Gottfried (1812–1910) German astronomer, who was the first to observe *Neptune. *Leverrier predicted (1846) the existence of Neptune and asked Galle to search the area in which he expected it to be. Galle discovered it the same day.

galleon A large oceangoing sailing vessel of the 15th–18th centuries, usually having a tall stern and high sides. Galleons were typically square-rigged on the foremast and mainmast and lateen-rigged on one or two after masts. They were widely used by the Spanish as transport between Europe and the New World and were often attacked by pirates. Several sunken galleons, with their treasures still aboard, have been located in the Caribbean Sea.

Gallicanism A movement in France asserting the rights of the French Roman Catholic Church, clergy, and monarchy against papal interference. It was an issue as early as the 13th century but reached its zenith in 1682 with the promulgation by the French bishops, at Louis XIV's instigation, of Four Gallican Articles defending the king's authority in temporal affairs and recognizing the authority of a general council of the Church over that of the pope.

Galli-Curci, Amelita (1882–1963) Italian coloratura soprano. Largely self-taught, she made her debut in Rome in 1909 as Gilda in Verdi's *Rigoletto*. She achieved great success in the same role at her New York debut (1916). She retired, owing to illness, in 1930.

Gallic Wars (58–51 BC) The campaigns in which Julius Caesar annexed Transalpine *Gaul (France). Caesar's intervention in Gallic intertribal warfare was prompted by concern for Italian security; his ambition to conquer Gaul developed later. NE Gaul was pacified by 57 BC and the tribes along the Atlantic coast by 56 BC. In 52 Caesar defeated the tribes of central Gaul, led by *Vercingetorix. Caesar's own account of the Gallic Wars has survived.

gallinule A bird belonging to the family *Rallidae* (rails). Gallinules are widely distributed, occurring on semistagnant water, such as ponds, edged by dense vegetation, and commonly have blue, green, or purple plumage for camouflage. They are 30–45 cm long and have long slender toes enabling them to run over floating vegetation. *See also* moorhen.

Gallipoli (Turkish name: Gelibolu) 40 25N 26 41E A seaport in European Turkey, on the NE coast of the Dardanelles. Taken by Turkey in about 1356, it is strategically important for the defence of Istanbul. The town had to be largely rebuilt after the Gallipoli campaign (*see* World War I). Population (1980): 14 721.

gallium (Ga) A metallic element with a low melting point and high boiling point, discovered in 1875 by Lecoq de Boisbaudran. Gallium is found as a trace element in a number of minerals and is often concentrated in chimney soot. **Gallium arsenide** (GaAs) is a *semiconductor that is widely used in electronic devices, particularly the field-effect *transistor and the Gunn diode (*see* Gunn effect). At no 31; at wt 69.72; mp 29.78°C; bp 2403°C.

Gällivare 67 10N 20 40E A town in N Sweden. The main industry is ironmining, based on the rich deposits discovered in the 18th century. Population (1976): 25 276.

gall midge A small delicate fly with hairy antennae, also called a gallfly and gall gnat, belonging to the family *Cecidomyiidae*. Most species eat plants and lay their eggs in galls. Others are general scavengers or predators and parasites upon other insects. *See also* gall wasp.

gallon An Imperial unit of volume equal to the volume occupied by ten pounds of distilled water under precisely defined conditions. The US gallon is equal to 0.832 68 British gallons.

Galloway An area in SW Scotland, in the Dumfries and Galloway Region. The Mull of Galloway forms the most southerly point in Scotland. Dairy farming is important and the area is noted for its breed of hornless black cattle.

gallstones Stones in the *gall bladder formed from *cholesterol, *bile pigments, or both. In some people they cause no symptoms; in others they may give rise to pain, indigestion, nausea, and vomiting. The usual treatment is surgical removal of the gall bladder (cholecystectomy).

Gallup, George Horace (1901–84) US public-opinion pollster. His techniques for gauging public opinion became a feature of political life following his successful prediction of the result of the US presidential election in 1936.

gall wasp A small *wasp (6–8 mm long), also called gallfly, belonging to the family *Cynipidae*. Gall wasps lay their eggs in plant tissues, particularly oak trees and rose plants, which respond by producing *galls. Thus, *Biorhiza pallida* produces the oak apple gall and *Diplolepis rosae* produces the robin's pincushion gall.

Galois, Évariste (1811–32). French mathematician, who pioneered the branch of modern mathematics known as group theory. His life was dogged by ill luck; three papers that he submitted to the Académie des Sciences were rejected or lost and he was refused admission to the École Polytechnique. He turned to politics, supporting the Republican cause, and was twice arrested. He died following a duel.

Galsworthy, John (1867–1933) British novelist and dramatist. He studied law but embarked on a literary career in 1897 with a volume of short stories, published pseudonymously. *The Man of Property* (1906) began the famous novel series *The Forsyte Saga*, chronicling the decline of a rich English family. His plays, usually rather artificial expositions of moral and social issues, include *The Silver Box* (1906) and *Strife* (1909).

Galt, John (1779–1839) Scottish novelist. As a young businessman he travelled in the Mediterranean countries, where he befriended Byron, and from 1826 to 1829 he worked in Canada. His novels of Scottish rural life include *The Annals of the Parish* (1821) and *The Provost* (1822).

Galton, Sir Francis (1822–1911) British scientist, who studied methods of improving the mental and physical abilities of human populations by selective mating, a science that he called *eugenics. Galton argued that mental as well as physical attributes were inherited, an idea that his cousin Charles *Darwin later endorsed. Galton also made contributions to meteorology and pioneered the use of fingerprinting for personal identification.

Galuppi, Baldassare (1706–85) Venetian opera composer, known as Il Buranello. His comic operas written in collaboration with *Goldoni earned him the appellation "the father of opera buffa." He was also an excellent harpsichordist.

Galvani, Luigi (1737–98) Italian physician, who pioneered research into the electrical properties of living things. He observed how frog muscles twitched when they were touched by metal contacts but he wrongly attributed this to innate "animal electricity" (the current was actually produced by the metal contacts). The *galvanometer was named after him.

galvanized steel Steel coated with zinc to prevent corrosion. The zinc may be deposited by electroplating the steel in molten zinc, spraying with molten zinc, or by coating it with zinc powder and heating it.

galvanometer An instrument for measuring small electric currents. The moving-coil galvanometer consists of a coil of wire suspended in a magnetic field. A current passing through the coil causes it to rotate until balanced by the opposing torsion in the suspending thread. The angle of rotation is used to measure the current. In the moving-magnet instrument the magnet is suspended in the earth's magnetic field and deflection is caused by a current passing through the surrounding coil.

Galveston 29 17N 94 48W A city in the USA, in Texas on the Gulf of Mexico. Subject to hurricanes (one of which killed 8000 people in 1900), it has had to undertake large protective schemes. Its port handles sulphur, cotton, and wheat and industries include chemicals and hardware. Population (1980): 61 601.

Galway (Irish name: Gaillimh) 53 16N 9 03W A port in the Republic of Ireland, the county town of Co Galway. It has the University College (founded 1845), part of the National University of Ireland, and a Roman Catholic cathedral (begun 1957). The Galway Theatre produces Irish-language plays. Salmon and eel fishing are important. Population (1981): 41 861.

Galway (Irish name: Contae Na Gaillimhe) A county in

the W Republic of Ireland, in Connacht bordering on Galway Bay and the Atlantic Ocean. Low lying E of Lough Carrib, it rises to mountains in the W with Connemara (an area of moors and bogs) in the extreme W. Its many offshore islands include the Aran Islands. Agriculture consists chiefly of cattle and sheep rearing. Area: 5939 sq km (2293 sq mi). Population (1981): 172 018. County town: Galway.

Galway, James (1939-) Irish flautist of worldwide reputation. He studied in Paris with Jean-Pierre Rampal (1922-). His silver and gold flutes were made to his own specifications. The composer Rodrigo wrote his *Concierto pastorale* (for flute and orchestra; 1978) for him.

Gama, Vasco da (c. 1469-1524) Portuguese navigator. In 1497, under the patronage of *Manuel I, he departed with three ships to continue *Dias' search for the route to India. He rounded the Cape of Good Hope and reached Mozambique and Malindi (now in Kenya). Aided by an Indian pilot he crossed to Calicut (1498). Received with hostility by the Indians, he withdrew. Following the murder of the Portuguese settlers left by Cabral's expedition to Calicut, da Gama was sent out on a punitive expedition (1502) to establish Portugal's influence in the Indian Ocean. He bombarded Calicut and returned to Portugal with considerable amounts of booty. Some 20 years later he went back to India as Portuguese viceroy and died there.

Gambetta, Léon (1838-82) French statesman. A lawyer, Gambetta, who was an opponent of *Napoleon III (1868), was elected to the Legislative Assembly in 1869. Strongly republican, he took advantage of the capture of Napoleon in 1870 in the *Franco-Prussian War to proclaim a provisional government of national defence. His spectacular escape from besieged Paris in a balloon and his courageous organization of the defences of France from Tours earned him a wide and popular reputation. He was instrumental in founding the *Third Republic but his term as prime minister (1881-82) was unsuccessful because of opposition to his democratic policies and he was forced to resign.

Gambia, Republic of The A country in West Africa, on the Atlantic Ocean, occupying a narrow strip along the River Gambia and surrounded by Senegalese territory. Swamps along the river give way to drier savanna. The majority of the inhabitants are Mandingo. *Economy*: overwhelmingly agricultural, producing groundnuts for export and rice for the home market. Mineral resources are sparse and there is little industry. Attempts to develop the economy include plans for an oil refinery and tourism is being encouraged. *History*: in the 15th century the mouth of the River Gambia was explored by the Portuguese and, in the 16th century, by the English, who established a trading settlement on James Island in 1661. The area was administered from the British colony of Sierra Leone from 1807 until 1843, when it became a crown colony until again coming under Sierra Leone in 1866. Separated again in 1888, it achieved internal self-government in 1963 and independence in 1965 with Sir Dawda Jawara as president, becoming a republic within the British Commonwealth in 1970. An attempted coup in 1981 was subdued with military aid from Senegal; close ties between the two countries were reinforced with the formation of the Senegambia Confederation in 1982. Official language: English. Official currency: dalasi of 100 butut. Area: 10 689 sq km (4125 sq mi). Population (1980 est): 592 000. Capital and main port: Banjul.

Gambia, River A river in West Africa. Rising in the Fouta Djallon plateau in Guinea, it flows mainly NW through Senegal and Gambia to enter the Atlantic Ocean. It is navigable to oceangoing vessels for 320 km (200 mi). Length: 1126 km (700 mi).

Gambier Islands 23 10S 135 00W A group of coral islands in the S Pacific Ocean, in French Polynesia forming an extension of the Tuamotu Archipelago. They have been used for French nuclear tests. Area: 30 sq km (11 sq mi). Population (1977): 556. Chief settlement: Rikitea.

Gamblers' Anonymous An organization founded in the USA in 1957 and in the UK in 1964 to bring compulsive gamblers together so that they may help each other to give up their addiction. **Gam-Anon** is an affiliated organization, founded to provide help and comfort for the families of compulsive gamblers.

gamboge (*or* camboge) A hard brittle gum resin obtained from various SE Asian trees of the genus *Garcinia*. It is orange to brown in colour and turns bright yellow when powdered. Artists use gamboge as a pigment and to colour varnishes. In medicine and veterinary medicine it is used as a strong purgative.

gamebird A bird that is hunted for sport and legally defined as such by game laws, which control the hunting season, etc. Birds that are frequently hunted for sport or food include pheasants, grouse, partridges, turkeys, guinea fowl, ducks, bustards, snipe, and woodcock.

gamelan A type of orchestra common in Indonesia and Thailand, consisting mainly of tuned percussion instruments (particularly gongs and bells). A gamelan was heard at the Great Paris Exhibition of 1889; Debussy was influenced by its sonorities.

gamete A reproductive cell—either male or female—produced in the sex organs of plants or animals and containing half the number of *chromosomes present in a body (somatic) cell. On *fertilization the new individual therefore has a complete set of chromosomes, half from each parent. The female gamete (*see* egg) is large and immotile and contains abundant cytoplasm, while the male gamete (*see* sperm) is motile, with little cytoplasm.

game theory The branch of mathematics that seeks to analyse and solve problems arising in economic, business, or military situations on the assumption that each participant adopts strategies that will maximize gain (payoff) and minimize loss, as in playing a game. Worked out originally by John von *Neumann and Oskar Morganstern (1907-), it was successfully used in World War II in an analysis of submarine warfare.

Distinction is made between games for one player (patience, solitaire) in which no conflict arises, games for two players or teams (chess, football) in which conflict is an essential aspect of strategy, and games in which there are more than two participants (poker, roulette) and one persons's gain is not directly reflected by another person's loss. When chance is important, information is incomplete, or participants' goals are obscure, the theory is more complex.

gametophyte. *See* alternation of generations.

Gamliel The name of several important rabbis. **Gamliel the Elder** (Greek name: Gamaliel; early 1st century AD), a grandson of *Hillel, was president of the Jewish council of Jerusalem and a teacher of St *Paul. His grandson **Gamliel II** succeeded *Johanan ben Zakkai as head of the school at Jabneh (Yavneh) and is regarded as one of the founders of rabbinic Judaism.

gamma globulin. *See* globulin.

gamma radiation Highly energetic electromagnetic radiation emitted by certain radioactive substances as a result of transitions of nucleons from a higher to a lower energy level and when an elementary particle and its antiparticle annihilate each other. The wavelength of gamma radiation is between 10^{-10} and 10^{-14} metre.

Ganda A Bantu people of the region W and N of Lake Victoria. They are agriculturalists, whose staple crop is bananas. The largest tribe in Uganda, they were formerly ruled by a king (Kabaka) in their own kingdom of *Buganda.

Gander 48 58N 54 34W A town in E Canada, in Newfoundland. A major World War II base, it has one of the world's largest airports, responsible for air-traffic control over the North Atlantic. Population (1981): 10 404.

Gandhara An ancient region now in NW Pakistan. It was conquered by the Achaemenians (6th century BC) and by *Alexander the Great (327–325 BC). In the early centuries AD it became a centre for a Buddhist art that combined Greco-Roman and oriental characteristics. *See also* Taxila.

Gandhi, Indira (1917–84) Indian stateswoman; prime minister (1966–77; 1980–84). Daughter of Jawaharlal *Nehru, in 1942 she married Feroz Gandhi (d. 1960), who was not a relation of Mahatma Gandhi. She was a cabinet minister under Lal Bahadur *Shastri, whom she succeeded as prime minister. She won substantial victories in the 1971 and 1972 elections. In 1975 she was accused of electoral malpractices; a state of emergency was subsequently declared and strict authoritarian government imposed. She was defeated in the elections of 1977 by Morarji Desai but returned to power in 1980. In the wake of sectarian violence, she was assassinated in 1984 by Sikh members of her bodyguard. Her elder son **Rajiv Gandhi** (1942–   ) succeeded her as prime minister. His government also came under pressure as a result of conflict between Sikhs and Hindus. Her other son **Sanjay Gandhi** (1946–80) caused controversy over alleged corruption in government office. He died in an air crash.

MOHANDAS (MAHATMA) GANDHI *Leaving the Round Table Conference in London (1931).*

Gandhi, Mohandas Karamchand (1869–1948) Indian nationalist leader. Mahatma ("Great Soul") Gandhi was born in W India and went to England in 1888 to study law. In 1893 he moved to South Africa to practise law and became a champion of the rights of the Indian community, introducing a policy of noncooperation with the civil authorities (*see* satyagraha), which he utilized after his return to India (1914). There he took up the cause of home rule, becoming leader of the *Indian National Congress. His noncooperation policy was inaugurated in 1919 and was then extended to civil disobedience (e.g. nonpayment of taxes). Following imprisonment (1922–24), Gandhi withdrew from national politics to travel around India. He campaigned against the degradation of untouchables and encouraged the development of Indian craft industries. It was in this period that he came to be regarded as a saint by many Indians. Returning to politics in 1927, in 1930 he made his famous walk from Ahmedabad to the sea, where he distilled salt from sea water in protest against the government's salt monopoly, and was again imprisoned. In 1932 he undertook his first "fast unto death," against the government's attitude to untouchables, and in 1933 retired to his ashram at Wardha. Returning to political life in the late 1930s, he became committed to the aim of complete independence for

India. World War II presented Gandhi with his greatest challenge. Recognizing Hitler as an aggressor, he had to reconcile Indian support for Britain with his own policy of nonviolence; moreover, he had to reconcile his belief in an independent India with cooperation with the imperial power. In 1942, when the Japanese were threatening India, the British Government offered India complete independence after the war in exchange for cooperation in winning it. Describing this offer as "a post-dated cheque on a failing bank," Gandhi demanded that the British should withdraw immediately from India. The British responded by gaoling Gandhi and the other Congress leaders until 1944, when they were released to discuss independence and partition.

Gandhi, with ☐Nehru, played a crucial part in the independence talks and although initially opposed to partition he finally accepted the establishment of Pakistan. When violence subsequently broke out in Bengal between Hindus and Muslims, Gandhi undertook a fast in an attempt to halt the conflict. His advocacy of friendship between Hindus and Muslims caused intense resentment among Hindu fanatics, one of whom (Nathuram Godse) assassinated him as he went to a prayer meeting. Gandhi was never a member of the cabinet, but for many years before his death was regarded as the supreme Indian leader. Even the British Government, with which he maintained an ambivalent relationship, respected this remarkable and enigmatic man.

Gandzha. *See* Kirovabad.

Ganesa One of the principle Hindu deities, portrayed as having an elephant's head on a human body. His father *Shiva beheaded him, but then decided to save him and replaced his human head with that of the first creature he found. A popular god, he is the teacher of the gods and is invoked at the start of any undertaking since he is believed to remove obstacles.

Ganga Two related dynasties in medieval India. The **Western Ganga** ruled over much of Mysore in S India (present-day Karnataka) from the 2nd century until the early 11th century, when they were overthrown by the Cola. The **Eastern Ganga** ruled Kalinga from the 11th to the 15th centuries and were responsible for many glorious monuments, perhaps most notably the Jagannath temple at Puri.

Ganges, River (*or* Ganga) The great river of N India. Formed by several headstreams in the Himalayas, one of which emanates from an ice cave, it flows generally E across the broad Ganges plain to join the Brahmaputra River, thereafter continuing as the River Padma, which empties into the Bay of Bengal by way of the largest delta in the world. It is used to irrigate the Ganges plain, which contains several of India's main cities (Delhi, Agra, Varanasi, and Lucknow) and which, after the Yangtze Valley (China), is the world's most populous agricultural area. It is of immense religious importance, being the Hindus' most sacred river. Length: 2507 km (1557 mi).

ganglion (anatomy) A collection of nerve cell bodies, especially one outside the central *nervous system. Sensory ganglia carry out preliminary analysis of the information coming from sense organs. Motor ganglia coordinate the discharges from a number of nerve fibres. *See also* neurone.

ganglion (cyst) A small fluid-filled swelling occurring under the skin and close to a joint, usually the wrist. They are most common in children. Treatment is needed only if the cysts are large or painful, in which case they are surgically removed. A former treatment was to hit them with the family Bible.

Gang of Four. *See* Jiang Qing.

gangrene Death of tissues, most commonly those of a limb. This usually results from narrowing of the blood vessels of the legs by *atherosclerosis or because of diabetes. If the tissues become infected the condition is called wet gangrene. Treatment is aimed at improving the blood flow to the limbs by surgery to the vessels or by reşt; in advanced cases amputation may be necessary.

Gangtok 27 20N 88 39E A city in India, the capital of Sikkim. It is an agricultural trading centre. Population (1981): 36 768.

gannet A seabird belonging to the family *Sulidae*, distributed worldwide. (Tropical members of the family are called *boobies.) The North Atlantic gannet (*Sula bassana*), also called solan goose, reaches 90 cm in length. White with black wingtips, it has a long stout bill and a long wedge-shaped tail. Gannets feed on fish and nest in dense colonies on rocky islands and cliffs. Order: *Pelecaniformes* (cormorants, pelicans, etc.).

Gansu (*or* Kansu) A mountainous province in N China, prone in the E to severe earthquakes. Livestock is kept and cereals, cotton, and tobacco are grown in the river valleys. It has oil, coal, hydroelectric power, and a nuclear plant. *History*: it became a part of China in the 3rd century BC, but after the introduction of Islam in the 13th century its Muslim population was continually rebellious and it only came under full Chinese influence in the 19th century. On the route to China from the Middle East, along which travelled Marco Polo, it is strategically important. Area: 355 100 sq km (137 100 sq mi). Population (1982): 19 569 261. Capital: Lanzhou.

Ganymede (astronomy). *See* Galilean satellites.

Ganymede (mythology) In Greek legend, a Trojan prince of great beauty carried off by Zeus to be his cupbearer in exchange for some immortal horses or a golden vine.

Gao 16 19N 0 09W A town in S central Mali, on the River Niger. It was the centre of a powerful Islamic empire (15–16th centuries) and contains the ruined tomb of a Songhai leader. Population (1976): 30 714.

gaon (Hebrew: eminence) A Jewish scholar and communal leader. The gaonim were the heads of the Jewish Babylonian academies from the 6th to 11th centuries. Much of their surviving work is in the form of *responsa*, discursive replies to questions concerning the Bible, *Talmud, or *Mishnah. The most celebrated gaon was Sa'adya (892–942), Talmudic scholar, philosopher, poet, grammarian, and the translator of the Bible into Arabic.

Gaoxiong (*or* Kao-hsiung; Japanese name: Takao) 22 36N 120 17E A city in SW Taiwan, the second largest on the island and its leading port. Under Japanese occupation (1895–1945) it became an important naval base. It is a major industrial centre, its industries including oil refining, fishing, and food processing. Population (1983 est): 1 248 175.

gar A freshwater *bony fish, also called garpike, belonging to a family (*Lepisosteidae*; 7 species) found in North and Central America. Gars have a slender body, up to 3.5 m long, covered with enamelled scales, and a long alligator-like snout with sharp teeth; they feed mainly on smaller fish. Order: *Semionotiformes*. fish.

Garbo, Greta (Greta Gustafson; 1905–) Swedish actress: Her exceptional beauty and aloofness contributed much to her portrayal of tragic heroines in such films as *Grand Hotel* (1932), *Queen Christina* (1934), *Anna Karenina* (1935), and *Camille* (1936). As a comedienne she excelled in *Ninotchka* (1939). She retired in 1941, her private life remaining as enigmatic as it had been during her years of stardom.

García Lorca, Federico (1898–1936) Spanish poet and dramatist. He began writing poems while a student in Granada and Madrid, winning international fame with *Gipsy Ballads* (1928), noted for their boldly original imagery. His visits to the USA and Cuba (1929–30) inspired the anguished poems of *Poet in New York* (1940). His masterpiece is the trilogy of folk tragedies *Blood Wedding* (1933), *Yerma* (1934), and *The House of Bernarda Alba* (1936). He was shot by Nationalist partisans at the outset of the Spanish Civil War.

Garda, Lake (Latin name: Lacus Benacus) A lake in central N Italy. Sheltered on the N by the Alps, it has a temperate climate that attracts holidaymakers. Area: 370 sq km (143 sq mi).

garden city A town surrounded by countryside and designed to have community land ownership, adequate facilities, and recreational space. The garden city was a reaction to the chronic urban overcrowding produced in England by the industrial revolution. Its main advocate was Ebenezer *Howard, and the earliest examples, notably Letchworth (1903), were imitated throughout Europe. Many English town-planning schemes after World War II were strongly influenced by its example.

garden cress. *See* cress.

Gardenia A genus of ornamental shrubs and trees (60–100 species) native to tropical and subtropical Africa and Asia. Many are richly scented and used in perfumes and tea. The shiny evergreen leaves are oval and pointed. Single flowers have four or five strap-shaped petals, often creamy white, but many cultivated varieties have showy double flowers. The fruits are large and berry-like. *G. jasminoides* is a popular pot plant. Family: *Rubiaceae* (madder family).

Garden of the Gods An area in the USA, in Colorado. It consists of remarkable formations of eroded red sandstone rocks, some of which resemble animals, gargoyles, and cathedral spires.

Gardiner, Stephen (c. 1490–1555) English churchman. Appointed Bishop of Winchester in 1531, he negotiated with Rome over annulling Henry VIII's marriage to Catherine of Aragon. He later opposed the radical Protestant policies of Thomas *Cromwell and was imprisoned (1548) under Edward VI and deprived of his see (1551). He was reinstated by Queen Mary, who made him Lord High Chancellor.

GRETA GARBO *In Ernst Lubitsch's film* Ninotchka *(1939).*

garfish. *See* needlefish.

garganey A small *dabbling duck, *Anas querquedula*, that breeds in shallow fresh waters of N Eurasia and winters along African and Asian coasts. 36–40 cm long, the male is brown with pale underparts, grey wings, green and white wing bars, and a broad white eye stripe; females are mottled brown.

gargoyle A water spout, in the shape of a grotesque person or animal, that appears chiefly in gothic architecture. Gargoyles project from parapet gutters to carry water draining from the roof clear of the walls.

Garibaldi, Giuseppe (1807–82) Italian soldier, a hero of the movement for Italian unification (*see* Risorgimento). Influenced by Mazzini, he joined an attempted republican revolution in Sardinia-Piedmont (1834) and was forced to flee to South America, where he spent ten years fighting in a series of wars of liberation. He returned to Italy to join the *Revolution of 1848, fighting the Austrians and, after the flight of Pope Pius IX, playing a leading part in the heroic but unsuccessful defence of Rome against the French. Following another period of exile, he gave his support to the unification movement led by Cavour and Victor Emmanuel II of Sardinia-Piedmont. In 1860 he set out from Genoa on the Expedition of a *Thousand, which was to achieve the conquest of Sicily and Naples and their incorporation in the new kingdom of Italy. He continued to serve Victor Emmanuel in the 1860s and also fought for the French in the Franco-Prussian War (1870–71).

Garland, Judy (Frances Gumm; 1922–69) US singer and film actress. She began her career at the age of five as a singer in vaudeville. Her films included *The Wizard of Oz* (1939), in which she sang "Over the Rainbow" and established herself as a star, *Meet Me in St Louis* (1944), *A Star is Born* (1954), and *Judgment at Nuremberg* (1961). She married five times; although an unhappy private life interfered with her career, she maintained her reputation as an enormously popular singer. Her daughter **Liza Minnelli** (1946–   ) is also a singer and actress. She is best known for her starring roles in *Cabaret* (1972) and *Arthur* (1981).

garlic A widely cultivated perennial herb, *Allium sativum*, native to Asia and naturalized in S Europe and North America. Its leafless flower stem grows to a height of 60 cm. The garlic bulb has a membraneous skin enclosing up to 20 bulblets, called cloves. The bulb has a pungent aroma and taste and is a classic flavouring agent in cooking.

garlic mustard A biennial or perennial Eurasian herb, *Alliaria petiolata* (*A. officinalis, Sisymbrium alliaria*), up to 100 cm high, also called Jack-by-the-hedge and hedge garlic. The heart-shaped toothed leaves smell of garlic when crushed. Small white four-petalled flowers are borne in a terminal cluster. Family: *Cruciferae*.

garnet A group of minerals with compositions varying within the series pyralspite (pyrope, $Mg_3Al_2Si_3O_{12}$; almandine, $Fe_3^{2+}Al_2Si_3O_{12}$; and spessartite, $Mn_3Al_2Si_3O_{12}$) or ugrandite (grossular, $Ca_3Al_2Si_3O_{12}$; andradite, $Ca_3(Fe^{3+}, Ti)_2Si_3O_{12}$; and uvarovite, $Ca_3Cr_2Si_3O_{12}$). Garnets occur chiefly in metamorphic rocks. They are used as abrasives, almandine being the most important, and flawless crystals are semiprecious stones. Birthstone for January. *See* Plate III.

Garonne, River A river in SW France. Rising in the central Pyrenees, it flows N through Toulouse and joins the River Dordogne near Bordeaux, entering the Atlantic Ocean by the Gironde estuary. It is linked to the Mediterranean Sea by the Canal du Midi. Length: 580 km (360 mi).

garpike. *See* gar.

Garrick, David (1717–79) English actor. He went to London with Samuel *Johnson in 1737 and began his long theatrical career with a highly acclaimed performance as Richard III in 1741. His natural style of acting contrasted with the prevailing formal conventions. As manager of the Drury Lane Theatre from 1747 to 1776, he introduced innovations in production, lighting, and scenery.

Garter, Order of the A British order of knighthood, traditionally founded by Edward III in 1348 and comprising chiefly the sovereign and 25 knights companions. Its motto is *Honi soit qui mal y pense* (The shame be his who thinks badly of it), supposedly the words of Edward III on tying to his leg a garter dropped by a lady at a party. The motto is inscribed on the dark blue garter worn by the knights of the order on the left leg below the knee. The order's chapel is St George's Chapel, Windsor. Since 1987 the order has been open to women.

Gary 41 34N 87 20W A city in the USA, in Indiana on Lake Michigan. Founded by the US Steel Corporation (1905), it is one of the world's major steel producers. Population (1980): 151 953.

gas constant (*R*) The constant that occurs in the ideal *gas law: $pV = RT$. Its value is 8.314 joules per kelvin per mole.

Gascony A former duchy of SW France. After Roman rule Gascony was conquered by the Visigoths and then by the Franks. By the end of the 10th century its dukes had achieved autonomy from the French Crown but in 1052 it fell to Aquitaine and came under English control in the 12th century. It formed the nucleus of English possessions in France until regained by the French at the end of the Hundred Years' War (1453).

gases Substances that distribute themselves evenly throughout a closed container. The behaviour of a gas under variations of temperature, pressure, and volume is fairly accurately described by the *gas laws and the *kinetic theory of gases. When gases are cooled or compressed they become *liquids. However, there is a temperature (the critical temperature) above which a gas cannot be liquefied by pressure alone.

Gaskell, Elizabeth Cleghorn (1810–65) British novelist. In 1832 she married a Unitarian minister and settled in Manchester, the industrial setting of her first novel, *Mary Barton* (1848). Her other novels include *Cranford* (1853), based on her childhood in a rural village, and *North and South* (1855). She also wrote the first biography of her friend Charlotte Brontë (1857).

gas laws Relationships between the absolute temperature (*T*), pressure (*p*), and volume (*V*) of a gas. The simplest laws are *Boyle's law ($p \propto 1/V$) and *Charles's law ($V \propto T$), which are combined in the ideal gas equation: $pV = RT$, where *R* is the *gas constant. However, no real gas obeys this equation exactly. Most later gas laws are modifications of this equation, taking into account the volume occupied by the molecules themselves and the attractive forces between the molecules. The best known of these is *Van der Waals equation.

gas meter A meter for measuring the volume of gas passing through a pipe. The common household gas meter is a positive displacement meter in which two bellows are alternately filled and emptied by means of valves, the motion of the bellows being connected to the valves and a counting mechanism. Larger volumes are measured by a rotary meter, in which the gas flow causes an impeller to rotate.

gas oil A petroleum product used as fuel for *Diesel engines. Diesel buses and lorries use high-quality fuel with a *cetane number of 50. Slower engines, such as those in ships, use lower grade more viscous oil.

Gassendi, Pierre (1592–1655) French physicist and philosopher, an ardent believer in the experimental approach to science. He advocated the atomic theory of matter (*see* atomism) and in this influenced the ideas of Robert *Boyle. His astronomical works supported Galileo's ideas. In philosophy he wrote extensively on *Epicureanism and formulated objections to *Descartes' *Meditations*.

Gasser, Herbert Spencer (1888–1963) US physiologist, who shared a Nobel Prize (1944) with Joseph *Erlanger for their work on the function of nerve fibres.

gastric juice A mixture of hydrochloric acid, protein-digesting enzymes (including the precursor of *pepsin), and mucus secreted by glands in the mucous membrane lining the stomach.

gastric ulcer. *See* peptic ulcer.

gastrin A hormone released by cells of the stomach wall in the presence of food. Gastrin stimulates secretion of gastric juice by the gastric glands.

gastritis Inflammation of the lining of the stomach. Acute gastritis usually results from such irritants as alcohol or aspirin. If the patient stops taking the irritant, the condition usually resolves quickly. Chronic gastritis is common in old people and often symptomless, but it may be associated with pernicious *anaemia.

gastroenteritis Infection of the stomach and intestines. Food poisoning is one cause of gastroenteritis, but usually it cannot be related to a meal and no particular bacteria can be incriminated. Gastroenteritis is characterized by diarrhoea and vomiting and usually occurs in areas where hygiene is poor. It is particularly dangerous in babies.

gastropod A single-shelled *mollusc belonging to the class *Gastropoda* (about 40 000 species), including *snails and *slugs, *limpets, and *sea hares. Measuring 0.1–20 cm in length, gastropods occupy terrestrial, freshwater, and marine habitats. They move by undulating the muscular foot and have two pairs of retractable sensory head tentacles, one pair bearing simple eyes. They feed by scraping plant or animal matter with a rasping tongue (radula). Most gastropods have internal fertilization: the mating individuals may be of separate sexes or hermaphrodite.

Gastrotricha A phylum of minute wormlike animals (1800 species) found in salt and fresh waters. 0.1–1.5 mm long, gastrotrichs have a scaly often spiny cuticle and a ciliated underside; they creep over decaying vegetation, on which they feed. Many are *hermaphrodites and one group exhibits *parthenogenesis, i.e. unfertilized eggs give rise exclusively to females.

gastrula A stage in the embryonic development of an animal in which the cells of the *blastula (the preceding stage) undergo complex movements, resulting in the formation of three distinct germ layers. These layers—the ectoderm, mesoderm, and endoderm—will later differentiate into the tissues and organs of the body. A central cavity (archenteron) is the primitive gut.

gas turbine A form of *internal-combustion engine consisting of a *turbine in which the power to drive the blades is provided by hot gas. The gas turbine is a flexible engine with many applications, the most useful being in aviation (see jet engine). It consists of a *compressor, a combustion chamber, and the turbine. Atmospheric air is fed under pressure from the compressor to the combustion chambers, where a fuel, such as natural gas, paraffin, or oil is burnt; the hot gases then drive the turbine, which in turn drives the compressor. Power is supplied either in the form of thrust from a jet or rotation of the turbine shaft. □heat engine.

Gates, Horatio (?1728–1806) American general. British-born, he saw action in America in the *Seven Years' War and returned to settle there in 1772. During the American Revolution, his army defeated the British under *Burgoyne at *Saratoga (1777). Defeated by Cornwallis at *Camden (1780), he retired until 1782, when he joined Washington's staff.

Gateshead 54 58N 1 35W A town in NE England, in Tyne and Wear, opposite Newcastle across the River Tyne. Gateshead's industries include engineering, clothing, paints, plastics, and glass. The Metro Centre (opened in 1986) is one of the largest shopping complexes in the world. Population (1981): 81 367.

GATT. See General Agreement on Tariffs and Trade.

Gatting, Mike (Michael William G.; 1957–) British cricketer, who has played for Middlesex and England (1978–). A pugnacious batsman, he has captained England since 1986; in 1987 he was involved in a controversy over umpiring in Pakistan.

Gatwick 51 08N 0 11W A village in SE England, 43 km (27 mi) S of London, in Surrey. It is the site of one of London's two subsidiary airports.

gaucho A nomadic cattleherder of the Argentine, Uruguayan, and Paraguayan pampas in the 18th and 19th centuries. Often a mestizo (of mixed European and Indian ancestry), gauchos were at first independent herders but, like the US *cowboys, became employees of ranchers. They disappeared following the ploughing of the pampas and the introduction of pure-breed stock raising. Gauchos were the source of a rich folk tradition.

Gaudier-Brzeska, Henri (1891–1915) French sculptor. Henri Gaudier adopted the name Gaudier-Brzeska from 1911, the year after he met the Polish novelist Sophie Brzeska in Paris. Working in London, Gaudier-Brzeska became a leading member of the vorticist movement (see vorticism). He produced sculptures influenced by cubism and primitive art, the best known being *Red Stone Dancer* (1913; Tate Gallery). He was killed in action in World War I.

Gaudí y Cornet, Antonio (1852–1926) Spanish architect with a highly individual approach. Gaudi's work had strong affiliations to *Art Nouveau, but also drew inspiration from gothic and *Mudéjar sources. He also made use of the style of the *gothic revival in the incomplete Sagrada Familia in Barcelona (1880s). He worked exclusively in Barcelona, beginning with the Casa Vicens (1878) and a house for his patron, Count Güell. In the 1890s his style changed radically, and certain later buildings, for example the Casa Battló (1905), tended to resemble natural growths more than architecture.

gauge theories Mathematical descriptions predicting the behaviour of all the fundamental interactions, except gravitation. Gauge theories are based on the concept of symmetry, i.e. that the solution of a set of equations remain unchanged even when a characteristic of the system they describe is varied. The *quantum theory applied to the *electromagnetic interaction, known as quantum electrodynamics, is a gauge theory in which the electromagnetic force is visualized as a result of the exchange of massless *photons between charged particles, the equations describing the motions of the charged particles remaining unchanged during local symmetry operations. The success of this theory enabled it to be extended to encompass the *weak interaction and to lead to the formulation of the gauge theory applying to *strong interactions, known as quantum chromodynamics (see particle physics).

Gauguin, Paul (1848–1903) French postimpressionist painter, born in Paris. After five years at sea he became a stockbroker (1871), painting only as a hobby. His early works were influenced by the impressionists with whom he exhibited (1881–86). He became a full-time painter in 1883 and moved to Brittany in 1886, where he developed a style called "synthetism in such paintings as *Vision after the Sermon* (National Gallery, Edinburgh). He visited Martinique in 1887 and stayed with Van *Gogh in Arles in 1888. Seeking the inspiration of a primitive civilization, he moved to Tahiti (1891), where the symbolism in such paintings as *Nevermore* (Courtauld Institute, London) was influenced by native superstitions. He is noted also for reviving the art of woodcutting.

Gauhati 26 10N 91 45E A city in India, in Assam. The former centre of British administration in Assam, Gauhati is an important trading centre and has an oil refinery. Its many temple ruins make it a Hindu pilgrimage centre. Its university was established in 1948. Population (1971): 123 783.

Gaul An ancient region of Europe. It was divided by the Romans into Transalpine Gaul (the area bound by the Rhine, Alps, and Pyrenees) and Cisalpine Gaul (N Italy). Transalpine Gaul was settled from about 1500 BC by Celtic tribes, who inhabited Cisalpine Gaul after around 500 BC. Subsequent Gallic expansion southwards brought conflict with Rome, which the Gauls sacked in 390, and the Roman conquest of Cisalpine Gaul was not completed until the mid-2nd century. In 121 the Romans annexed S Transalpine Gaul, which they called Gallia Narbonensis, and between 58 and 50 Caesar subdued the rest of Gaul, finally crushing the Gallic tribal leader *Vercingetorix at Alesia. Augustus organized Transalpine Gaul into four provinces—Narbonensis, Belgica, Lugdunensis, and Aquitania. During the 1st century AD Gaul, especially Narbonensis, was extensively romanized and prospered until the barbarian invasions in the 5th century.

Gaullists The supporters of the policies of Gen *de Gaulle, especially his independent foreign policy and drive towards industrial expansion, which were motivated by a wish to re-establish France as a world power. De Gaulle's Rassemblement du Peuple français (1947–53) was succeeded by the Union de Démocrates pour la' République, which was reorganized by Jacques *Chirac as the Rassemblement pour la République.

gaur The largest of the wild cattle, *Bos gaurus*, of hilly forests in S Asia. Up to 200 cm high at the shoulder, bulls can weigh up to 1 tonne. Gaurs are dark brown with white socks and both sexes have horns, the tips pointing upwards in bulls and inwards in cows.

gauss (G) The unit of magnetic flux density in the *c.g.s. system equal to a flux density of one maxwell per square centimetre. Named after Karl Friedrich *Gauss.

Gauss, Karl Friedrich (1777–1855) German mathematician, regarded (with *Newton and *Archimedes) as one of the greatest mathematicians of all time. He influenced all aspects of mathematics and much of physics. His greatest contributions were in the fields of probability theory, number theory, complex numbers, algebra, and electricity and magnetism.

Gautier, Théophile (1811–72) French Romantic poet and critic. Influenced by Victor *Hugo, his early writings include *Poésies* (1830) and *Les Jeunes-France* (1833). The brief lyrical poems in *Émaux et camées* (1852) embody his belief in the value of art for its own sake. He wrote much influential art, ballet, and dramatic criticism and travelled widely in Europe, the Middle East, and Russia.

Gavaskar, Sunil Manohar (1949–) Indian cricketer, who has played for Bombay, Somerset, and India (1971–) and captained India (1978–83, 1984–85). In 1987 he became the first batsman to score 10 000 runs in Test cricket.

gavial (*or* gharial) A long-snouted □reptile, *Gavialis gangeticus*, occurring in N Indian rivers and sacred to Hindus. 4–5 m long, it has long slender sharp-toothed jaws, which it sweeps from side to side to catch fish. It is the only member of its family (*Gavialidae*). Order: *Crocodilia* (*see* crocodile).

Gävle 60 41N 17 10E A seaport in E Sweden, on an inlet of the Gulf of Bothnia. Ice free for nine months of the year, it exports timber, wood pulp, and paper. Its industries include shipbuilding. Population (1983): 87 671.

Gawain In Arthurian legend, a knight of the Round Table, the nephew of King Arthur and the son of King Lot of Norway and the Orkneys. He was known for his purity and courage.

Gay, John (1685–1732) British poet and dramatist. A friend of Pope, Swift, and other members of the Scriblerus Club, his *Fables* (1727, 1738) were the most successful of his several satirical poems. His best-known work is the ballad opera *The Beggar's Opera* (1728), a comic blend of social satire and parody of fashionable Italian opera, using traditional tunes.

Gaya 24 48N 85 00E A city in NE India, in Bihar. A centre of Hindu pilgrimage, it is situated 10 km (6 mi) S of Buddh Gaya, which is sacred to Buddhists. Population (1981): 344 941.

gayal A species of domestic cattle, *Bos frontalis*, of Burma. Gayals are similar to the wild *gaur, but are smaller, measuring about 150 cm at the shoulder, and have a wider spread of horns. Gayals may be a domesticated form of gaur.

Gay Liberation. *See* homosexuality.

Gay-Lussac, Joseph Louis (1778–1850) French chemist and physicist. He discovered the element boron (1808) and the law that gases combine in a simple ratio by volume (**Gay-Lussac's law**). He also discovered *Charles' law independently of Charles and published his results first.

Gaza (Arabic name: Ghazzah) 31 30N 34 28E The largest town in the *Gaza Strip. Gaza has been inhabited continuously for over 3000 years; in biblical times it was a Philistine centre, where Samson was killed (Judges 16). Its products now include **pottery and textiles. Population (1979): 120 000.**

Gazankulu. *See* Bantu Homelands.

Gaza Strip A strip of coastal territory, 50 km (30 mi) long, on the SE corner of the Mediterranean Sea. Following the Arab-Israeli War of 1948–49, the only part of Palestine held by Egypt was a strip of land on the coast that became known as the Gaza Strip. Egypt did not integrate the Strip into its own state, but established a military governorship here. Held by the Israelis for a short time in 1956–57, it was taken by them again in 1967, and is now under Israeli military administration. Under the Camp David agreement (1979) between Israel and Egypt, eventual self-government for the area was planned. The Gaza Strip suffers from extreme overpopulation, many Palestine refugees being housed in squalid camps, and violent protests against Israeli occupation continue to occur (1987–88). Population (1981): 451 400, including North Sinai.

gazelle A slender antelope of the genus *Gazella* (about 12 species), of Africa and Asia. 50–90 cm high at the shoulder, gazelles are distinguished from other antelopes by light and dark horizontal stripes on the face. Brown to grey in colour, gazelles may also have a dark band along the sides above the lighter belly. In most species both sexes have horns, which are generally lyre-shaped, ridged, and backward-curving with a forward-pointing tip.

Gaziantep 37 04N 37 21E A city in S Turkey, near the Syrian border. Known for its Hittite remains, Gaziantep is situated near ancient trade routes and has changed hands frequently. It is an important market town. Population (1980): 808 697.

GBE. *See* Order of the British Empire.

Gdańsk (German name: Danzig) 54 22N 18 41E A port in N Poland, on the Baltic Sea. It is an industrial centre with shipbuilding, metallurgy, chemicals, and food processing; exports include coal, grain, and timber. Its university was founded in 1970. *History*: it developed as an important trade centre during the Renaissance. It was under Prussian control (1793–1807 and 1814–1919), becoming a free city under the League of Nations in 1919. In 1939 it was annexed by Germany, an act that precipitated World War II; the city was returned to Poland in 1945. Population (1982): 462 000.

GDP (gross domestic product). *See* gross national product.

Gdynia 54 31N 18 30E A port in N Poland, on the Baltic Sea. Originally a fishing village, it was developed (1924–39) to replace Danzig (*see* Gdańsk) as Poland's port, becoming Poland's main shipbuilding centre and naval base. Population (1982): 237 000.

Ge A group of South American Indian peoples of Brazil and N Paraguay who speak languages of the Macro-Ge group. Its numerous different tribes are very diverse in their range of cultural patterns. They are largely hunters and gatherers but some have adopted cultivation. Their social organization tends to be complex. Besides clan divisions, there is a variety of associations based on age, sex, occupation, etc., each autonomous in its respective sphere.

gean. *See* cherry.

Geber (14th century) Spanish alchemist, whose suggestion that different metals consist of mercury and sulphur in different proportions laid the foundation for the belief in the *philosopher's stone. He was also an experimental chemist, preparing nitric and acetic acids and white lead. He assumed the name Geber, which is the Latin form of Jabir, in honour of the 8th-century Arab alchemist Jabir ibn Hayyan.

gecko A slender long-tailed nocturnal lizard belonging to the widely distributed family *Gekkonidae* (650 species), found in a wide range of habitats including deserts and rain forests. 3–35 cm long, many geckos have fleshy toe pads covered with microscopic hooks enabling them to cling to smooth surfaces, such as ceilings. They feed on insects and have well-developed vocal cords producing a variety of chirps and barks. The tokay (*Gekko gecko*) of E Asia is a large arboreal gecko and lays its eggs in crevices (□reptile).

Gediminas (c. 1275–1341) Grand Duke of Lithuania (1316–41). One of Lithuania's greatest rulers, he founded the state by unifying the Lithuanian tribes. He extended his dominions, which he defended against the *Teutonic Knights. He was converted to Christianity in 1323. Gediminas made Vilnius the capital of Lithuania.

Geelong 38 10S 144 26E A city and major port in Australia, in S Victoria on Corio Bay. Wool, wheat, and oil are the principal exports. Population (1981): 125 279.

gegenschein (German: counterglow) A very faint glow in the night sky that can sometimes be seen on the *ecliptic in a direction directly opposite the sun's position. It is part of the *zodiacal light.

Gehenna In the Bible, the Valley of Hinnom, outside Jerusalem. At one time it was apparently the site of human sacrifices and was therefore considered an unclean place. In Jewish thought it came to represent a place where sinners are punished and in the New Testament it is a name for hell.

Geiger, Hans (1882–1945) German physicist, who in 1913 invented the *Geiger counter for detecting ionizing radiation in connection with his work on cosmic rays. During World War II he participated in Germany's unsuccessful attempt to build an atomic bomb.

GEIGER COUNTER *The radiation entering the tube causes an electrical discharge through the gas between the anode and cathode, sending an electrical pulse to the counter.*

Geiger counter A device that detects and counts ionizing radiation and particles. Essentially it consists of a metal cylinder containing low-pressure gas and a wire anode running along its central axis. The anode is held at a potential difference just less than that required to produce a discharge in the gas. Ionizing particles passing into the tube through a window at one end induce discharges, which can be counted by a suitable circuit. Named after Hans *Geiger.

geisha A Japanese woman whose profession is to entertain men in a restaurant. Geishas, who are not prostitutes, sing and dance or engage their clients in conversation. In modern Japan geishas are employed primarily for the benefit of the tourist trade.

gel. *See* colloid.

Gela 37 04N 14 15E A town in Italy, in Sicily. Founded by Greek colonists in 689 BC, it flourished under the rule of Hippocrates in the 5th century BC. Abandoned in 281 BC, it was refounded in 1233. Its industries include fishing and petrochemicals. Population (1981 est): 71 739.

gelada A large *Old World monkey, *Theropithecus gelada*, of the Ethiopian mountains. 120–150 cm long including the tufted tail (70–80 cm), it has a cape of dark-brown hair with two bare patches on the chest and lives in large groups, feeding on roots, leaves, and fruit.

gelatin A protein derived from bones and skins. In solution it forms a reversible gel that becomes fluid as the temperature rises and solidifies on cooling. Because of this property it is widely used in the food industry as a stabilizer in jellies and confectionery, in drug preparations, and in photographic emulsions.

Gelderland A province in the E Netherlands, bordering on West Germany. Predominantly rolling upland, the fertile soils of the Rhine Valley produce vegetables, fruit, and dairy products while the poorer soils in the N produce fodder crops. The NW is also an important tourist area. Manufactured products include cotton and paper. Area: 5131 sq km (1981 sq mi). Population (1981 est): 1 708 860. Capital: Arnhem.

Geldof, Bob (1952–) Irish rock musician. Born in Dublin, Geldof made several successful recordings with the Boomtown Rats before becoming involved in fund raising for the starving in Africa in 1984. His efforts, culminating in a massive concert held simultaneously in the UK and the USA in 1985, generated unprecedented donations to charity. He received an honorary knighthood in 1986.

gelignite A high explosive consisting of nitroglycerin, cellulose nitrate, potassium nitrate, and woodpulp.

Gell-Mann, Murray (1929–) US physicist, who won the 1969 Nobel Prize for his theoretical work on elementary particles. In 1953 he introduced the concept of *strangeness to account for the absence of certain expected interactions. He also formulated the theory of *unitary symmetry and introduced the concept of quarks (*see also* particle physics).

Gelsenkirchen 51 30N 7 05E A city in NW West Germany, in North Rhine-Westphalia. A *Ruhr coalmining centre and port on the Rhine-Herne Canal, it has a moated palace (16th-18th centuries). Its manufactures include steel, chemicals, and glass. Population (1980 est): 305 600.

Gemini (Latin: Twins) A conspicuous constellation in the N sky near Orion, lying on the *zodiac between Cancer and Taurus. The brightest stars are *Pollux and the somewhat fainter *Castor.

gemsbok. *See* oryx.

gemstones Minerals or mineral fragments used for decorative purposes, particularly jewellery. Desirability is usually based on the gem's beauty (in terms of colour, transparency, and lustre), its durability (gemstones must be hard), and rarity. Diamond, ruby, sapphire, and emerald are precious stones, the others (amethyst, agate, jasper, onyx, aquamarine, topaz, garnet, etc.) are semiprecious. Not all are crystalline; for example, opal and jade are amorphous. Gemstones are usually artificially cut (either faceted or rounded) and polished; some, such as onyx, are suitable for engraving, as cameos for instance. Many can be synthetically produced. *See* Plate III.

gene A unit of the hereditary material of an organism that provides the genetic information necessary to fulfil a single function. The term was first coined by W. L. *Johannsen in 1909.

Genes were initially conceived as a string of beads comprising the *chromosome; they were later defined as lengths of the chromosome that were physically indivisible during the exchange of chromosomal material that occurs during *meiosis. Alternatively, a gene was defined as the shortest length of the chromosome that could undergo *mutation. However, with the discovery of the structure of *DNA and the molecular basis of heredity, a gene is now regarded as being a functional unit (cistron) corresponding to a specific sequence of the *genetic code. Structural genes code for individual polypeptides (*see* peptides), while regulator genes control the activity of the structural genes.

General Agreement on Tariffs and Trade (GATT) A set of trade agreements, in operation from January, 1948, establishing procedures and tariffs for international trading. Signatories agree to favourable tariffs between members and the reduction of trade restrictions, on condition that home producers do not suffer losses as a result. During the negotiations of 1964–67 the principle of a single tariff for all industrial manufactures was agreed upon, with a resulting reduction in trade costs. There are more than 80 member countries, which are responsible for 80% of world trade. The secretariat of GATT, which is a specialized agency of the *United Nations, is in Geneva.

General Strike (1926) A national stoppage of work by members of Britain's major industries, lasting from 3 to 12 May. The General Strike began when the Trades Union Council (TUC) called out its members in support of the miners, who had refused to accept a reduction in wages. The Strike affected transport, the iron and steel industries, the building and printing trades, and gas and electricity services. Over two million men were out. However, the government under Stanley *Baldwin kept essential services going and the TUC called off the Strike. The miners gained nothing and trade unions were worse off after the Trade Union Act was passed in 1927.

Genesis The first book of the Bible, traditionally ascribed to Moses. It recounts the creation of the universe and of man (Adam), the fall of Adam and his exclusion from the Garden of Eden, the Flood, and the scattering of the nations at *Babel. The remainder of the book focuses on the lives of Abraham, Isaac, Jacob, and Joseph. It also introduces the Old Testament theme of the *covenant between God and Israel.

genet A carnivorous mammal of the genus *Genetta* (9 species) of Africa and Europe. Genets range in size from the 50-cm Abyssinian genet (*G. abyssinica*) to the 100-cm African giant genet (*G. victoriae*). They have retractile claws, long tails (up to 50 cm), foxlike heads, and pale fur with dark spots or stripes. Genets are nocturnal hunters. Family: *Viverridae.

Genet, Jean (1910–86) French novelist and dramatist. His autobiographical *A Thief's Journal* (1948) tells of his life in reformatories and prisons and among the criminals and prostitutes of various European cities. In his novels, which include *Our Lady of the Flowers* (1944) and *Miracle of the Rose* (1946), he describes this underworld with poetic intensity. His plays are *Deathwatch* (1947), *The Maids* (1947), *The Balcony* (1956), *The Blacks* (1958), and *The Screens* (1961).

genetic code The means by which information for the organization and function of living cells is carried by *DNA and *RNA molecules. Evidence for the nature of the genetic code was provided in the 1960s by the work of *Crick, M. W. Nirenberg (1927–), *Khorana, and many others. They found that the basic symbol of the code was a sequence of three consecutive bases of the DNA molecule. Therefore, according to the combination of the four possible bases—adenine, guanine, cytosine, and thymine (DNA) or uracil (RNA)—the different triplet sequences (or codons) could specify the 20 or so amino acids commonly used by cells for protein synthesis and give start and stop signals for the process.

genetic engineering Alteration of the genetic constitution of organisms, usually bacteria in order to obtain gene products beneficial to man. Typically, a sequence of desirable genes is inserted into the DNA of a host bacterium. This altered DNA (or recombinant DNA) then directs the bacterial cell to synthesize the desired gene product. As bacteria can be cultured quickly and easily, large quantities of products, such as insulin and interferon, can be obtained. Genetic engineering can also be used to improve crop plants.

genetic fingerprinting A recently developed identification technique based on DNA examination. DNA is extracted from sample cells (e.g. from blood or semen) and broken into fragments using enzymes. These fragments, containing the genetic code unique to each individual, are graded for size and com-

pared with fragments obtained from a blood sample of the test subject. In 1987 the technique was used for the first time in the UK as forensic evidence.

genetics The study of heredity and variation in living organisms. The science of genetics is founded on the work of Gregor *Mendel, who, in 1865, established the basic laws of inheritance. In the early 20th century *chromosomes and their *genes were established as the carriers of information determining inheritable characteristics, and with the discovery of the structure of *DNA in 1953, the molecular basis of genetics was revealed. Genetics is important in plant and animal breeding and in understanding inherited diseases and abnormalities. □ p. 494.

Geneva (French name: Genève; German name: Genf) 46 13N 6 09E A city in SW Switzerland, on the SW corner of Lake Geneva. It is a cultural and commercial centre with over two-thirds of the population employed in the service sector, banking and international finance being particularly important. Industries include the production of watches, precision instruments, and chemicals. It is the base of many international organizations including the International Red Cross, the World Health Organization, and the International Labour Organisation. The European headquarters of the United Nations occupy buildings that formerly housed the League of Nations. It has a cathedral (12th–13th centuries) and a university (1559). *History*: originally a prehistoric lake dwelling, it was later a Roman city. It became the centre of the Calvinist Reformation and a refuge for persecuted Protestants. Population (1980 est): 156 505.

Geneva, Lake (French name: Lac Léman; German name: Genfersee) A lake on the River Rhône lying partly in Switzerland and partly in France. Geneva (at its W end) and Lausanne and Montreux are on the Swiss N shore; the French resort of Evian lies on its S shore. It is dominated by the Alps to the N. Area: 577 sq km (223 sq mi).

Geneva Bible An English translation of the Bible published in 1560 by Puritan exiles in Geneva. It is also called the Breeches Bible because the word is used in translating Genesis 3.7.

Geneva Conferences 1. (1932–34) An international conference on *disarmament. Representatives of 59 states attended the opening meeting, chaired by the British foreign secretary Arthur *Henderson, but the major powers were unable to come to an agreement and in 1933 Hitler withdrew Germany from both the conference and the *League of Nations. Continuing deadlock led to the postponement of the conference, which did not reassemble. 2. (1954) A conference convened following the conclusion of the *Korean War. Discussions on the settlement of Korea, attended by representatives of the USA, Soviet Union, the UK, France, North Korea, South Korea, and the People's Republic of China ended without agreement. The war in *Indochina was also discussed by representatives of the USA, the Soviet Union, the UK, France, China, Vietnam, Cambodia, Laos, and the *Viet Minh; a ceasefire line was settled along the *seventeenth parallel.

Geneva Conventions International agreements covering the care and protection of noncombatants and wounded troops in wartime. Inspired by the establishment of the International *Red Cross, the first conference, attended by representatives from 16 countries, met in Geneva in 1864 to formulate a code of practice for the treatment of wounded soldiers. Later conventions (1906, 1929) ratified further agreements, covering assistance for forces at sea and treatment of *prisoners of war. In 1949 a fourth convention concerning the protection of civilians was incorporated and the others revised. Most states accept the conventions as morally binding. Neutral countries and the International Red Cross have a supervisory role in wartime but enforcement is difficult as violation cannot be punished.

Genghis Khan (c. 1162–1227) The founder of the Mongol empire. Originally called Tamujin, he adopted the title

GENETICS

single-factor inheritance

two-factor inheritance

GENETICS *When a purebred (homozygous) black guinea pig (BB) mates with a purebred white one (bb) all the offspring (F₁ generation) will be black (Bb), since the gene for black is dominant. Mating of this heterozygous F₁ generation will produce both black and white guinea pigs (F₂ generation) in the ratio 3:1, since each of the parents carries a white recessive gene. The same principle applies to the inheritance of two factors – seed colour and texture – in pea plants. When a plant with round yellow seeds (RRYY– dominant) is crossed with one producing wrinkled green seeds (rryy – recessive) the offspring will all have round yellow seeds (RrYy – heterozygous). Crossing of this generation results in the segregation and reassortment of the genes so that their offspring will show all four possibilities of seed colour and texture in the proportions 9:3:3:1. Both these examples of single- and two-factor inheritance obey Mendel's laws.*

Genghis Khan (Emperor of All) in 1206 after uniting under his command the nomadic Mongol tribes of the Siberian steppes and destroying Tatar power. Organizing his horsemen into highly mobile and disciplined squadrons called *ordus* (hence "hordes"), he attacked China's frontiers. Although his armies breached the Great Wall and captured Peking, they failed to conquer China completely. Advancing westwards, Genghis, by ruthless massacres and pillage, crushed all resistance in Afghanistan, Persia, and S Russia. After his death his son Ogadai (1185–1241) executed Genghis' plans for the empire's organization.

genipap The fruit of *Genipa americana*, a small West Indian tree. Resembling a brown orange, it is used in preserves and beverages. Family: *Rubiaceae* (madder family).

Genk 50 58N 5 30E A town in Belgium. The centre of an important coalmining region, its manufactures include mining machinery. Population (1981 est): 61 399.

Gennesaret, Lake of. *See* Galilee, Sea of.

Genoa (Italian name: Genova) 44 24N 08 56E A port in NW Italy, the capital of Liguria on the Gulf of Genoa. A major maritime city during the middle ages, it possesses many notable buildings dating from then. These include the cathedral of San Lorenzo (1118) and a university (1471). Genoa is Italy's chief port and also a major industrial centre with shipbuilding, heavy engineering, steel processing, and oil refining. Population (1980 est): 774 643.

genotype The genetic constitution of an individual organism, which comprises its *genes and determines the physical characteristics (*see* phenotype) of that individual.

genre painting A type of painting representing some aspect of everyday life. Although earlier examples exist, genre painting first became popular in 17th-century Holland, where it was developed by such painters as *Vermeer, *Steen, and de *Hooch. Notable 18th-century examples are the works of *Hogarth and *Chardin. Genre painting became widespread in the 19th century, when the impressionists and Victorian painters enthusiastically adopted it. Although now overshadowed by abstract art it is still practised by such artists as John *Bratby.

Genseric (*or* Gaiseric; d. 477 AD) King of the *Vandals (428–77), who played a major role in bringing about the fall of the *Roman Empire. He led the Vandals from Spain to N Africa, which he conquered after seizing Carthage from the Romans in 439. In 455 he sacked Rome.

Gent. *See* Ghent.

gentian A herbaceous plant of the widely distributed genus *Gentiana* (about 400 species), which includes many alpine perennials. The leaves are opposite and unstalked. The flowers have four or five petals, usually blue, arranged to form a bell or funnel with spreading lobes. The fruit of most species is a capsule. Many gentians are cultivated in rock gardens. Family: *Gentianaceae*.

gentian violet A purple dye derived from *aniline. It is used as an antiseptic, a chemical indicator, and as a dye.

Gentile, Giovanni (1875–1944) Italian philosopher. Gentile held to Hegelian theories about the dominance of the will; a thinking person had a spiritual unity that was realized in the *pure act*—hence his doctrine of "actualism." As Mussolini's minister of public education he purged the educational system of teachers suspected of democratic or liberal tendencies depite the protests of his former collaborator *Croce.

Gentile da Fabriano (Niccolo di Giovanni di Massio; c. 1370–1427) Florentine painter of the *international gothic style. His fresco cycles (completed by *Pisanello) for the Doge's Palace, Venice, and the Lateran Basilica, Rome, have perished. The *Adoration of the Magi* (Uffizi) shows his richly decorated style.

gentrification Upgrading a former working-class street or district for habitation by the middle classes. For example, Is-lington in London was gentrified in the 1960s by converting terraces of artisans' cottages into small but smart (bijou) residences, usually by knocking down walls to enlarge rooms and adding modern bathrooms and kitchens.

geocentric system. *See* Ptolemaic system.

geochemistry The study of the chemical composition of the earth. It involves estimating the absolute and relative abundance of the constituent elements and their isotopes, as well as their distribution and migration in the various geochemical environments (lithosphere, atmosphere, biosphere, hydrosphere) and in the rocks and minerals that make up the earth. In the earth's crust, oxygen (47%), silicon (28%), and aluminium (8%) are the most abundant elements.

geochronology The study of dating geological events, rocks, sediments, and organic remains, either absolutely or relatively. Absolute dating involves radioactive *dating techniques giving an actual date BP (before present). Relative dating establishes the order of geological events in relation to each other, using fossil correlation, pollen analysis, archaeological evidence, etc.

geodesy The science of determining the exact shape and size of the earth or portions of it, using precise surveying and exact calculations of gravitational force. Related topics, such as the earth's rotational effects and tides, are also studied. Geodetic surveying is the large-scale surveying of the earth's surface, taking into account its curvature. This provides the data for fixing exact control points for more detailed surveying (triangulation and levelling).

Geoffrey Martel (1006–60) Count of Anjou (1040–60). Through his marriage (1032) to Agnes the widow of the Duke of Aquitaine he unsuccessfully claimed Aquitaine for his heirs. However, Geoffrey subsequently acquired Touraine and much of Maine.

Geoffrey of Monmouth (c. 1100–54) English chronicler. His major work, *Historia Regum Britanniae*, was the main source for the whole body of medieval European literature concerned with the Arthurian legend and included the stories of King Lear, Cymbeline, and other legendary figures.

Geoffroy Saint-Hilaire, Étienne (1772–1844) French naturalist, who originated the concept that all animals conformed to the same basic structural plan or "unity of composition." Geoffroy saw modern species as unchanging but derived from ancestral species through the appearance of successful "monstrosities."

geography The study of the features of the earth's surface, together with their spatial distribution and interrelationships, as the environment of man. The Greeks, notably Herodotus, Eratosthenes of Cyrene, and Ptolemy, studied the shape of the earth and the location of land and sea. Modern geography was founded as a discipline in the early 19th entury by the German scholars Humboldt and Ritter. During the 20th century geography has moved away from a regional approach, in which different areas were studied and compared, to a more systematic approach. The discipline is now divided between the physical and social sciences. Physical geography includes geomorphology (the study of the landforms of the earth), biogeography (the study of soils and the distribution of animals and plants), and climatology (*see* climate). The main branches of human geography are historical geography (studying spatial change in an area over a period of time or reconstructing past landscapes), economic geography, urban geography, and political geography.

geological time scale A time scale covering the whole of the earth's history from its origin about 4600 million years ago to the present. The largest divisions are eras (Palaeozoic, Mesozoic, and Cenozoic); these are subdivided into periods and the Tertiary and Quaternary periods are further subdivided into epochs; epochs consist of several ages, and ages can be divided into chrons. A number of eras together is an eon. This is known as the chronomeric standard scale of chronostratigraphic classification. The stratomeric standard scale refers to the bodies of rocks formed in these time intervals; the corresponding terms are group (era), system (period), series (epoch), stage (age), and chronozone (chron). The divisions are not uniform time intervals but are based mainly on major evolutionary changes. For example, at the beginning of the Cambrian, about 570 million years ago, marine organisms suddenly became abundant and varied.

geology The study of the earth: its origin, history, structure, composition, and the natural processes acting on it. The branches of geology are historical (including geochronology, stratigraphy, and palaeontology); physical (including geomorphology, geophysics, petrology, mineralogy, crystallography, and geochemistry); and economic, involving the distribution and occurrence of the economically important rocks and minerals, such as petroleum. *See* Plate II.

geomagnetic field The earth's magnetic field, causing a compass needle to align north-south. It is believed to be caused by the liquid-iron core acting as a dynamo resulting from the convection currents moving in it. The magnetic poles do not coincide with the geographic poles, and their positions vary with time. Complete reversals of the earth's magnetic field have occurred in the past; relic magnetism in rocks, which coincides with the magnetic alignment adopted at the time of their formation, provides strong evidence for the theory of sea-floor spreading and continental drift (*see* plate tectonics). The three **magnetic elements** of the earth's field are the *magnetic dip, the *magnetic declination, and the horizontal field strength, which together completely define the earth's field at any point on its surface.

geometrid moth A moth of the family *Geometridae*, occurring in Europe, Asia, and North America. The name is derived from the looping method of locomotion of the caterpillars, which are known as inch worms, loopers, or measuring worms. The adults, known as pugs, umbers, carpet moths, etc., have slender bodies, a weak flight, and camouflaging coloration, often resembling dead leaves.

geometry A branch of mathematics concerned with the properties of space and shapes. In *Euclidean geometry the space corresponds to common notions of physical space and the shapes are idealizations of the common shapes that occur in real life. Other branches of geometry include *non-Euclidean geometry, such as the geometry of the surface of a sphere; *Riemannian geometry, which is used in *relativity theory; and *analytic geometry, in which algebra is used to solve geometrical problems. *See also* topology.

geophysics The study of the physical forces acting on, and particularly within, the earth. Sophisticated equipment is used to study the properties, structure, composition, and evolution of the earth. Important branches of geophysics are seismology, geomagnetism, vulcanology, natural radioactivity, and the earth's rotation and gravitational field. Much geophysical data has been collected in recent years as a result of geophysical prospecting, particularly for petroleum.

geopolitics The study of the influence of geographical factors upon international politics. It suggest that a state's foreign policy is influenced by its desire to obtain, for example, sufficient agricultural land. The term was coined by the Swedish political scientist Rudolf Kjellen (1864-1922) and was used by the Nazis, who justified their expansionist ambitions as the seeking of *Lebensraum* (living space). As a result geopolitics was discredited and has become outdated by technological developments.

George I (1660-1727) The first Hanoverian King of Great Britain and Ireland (1714-27) and Elector of Hanover (1698-1727). He divorced his wife, Sophia Dorothea, for infidelity (1694) and imprisoned her for 32 years. A successful soldier and a shrewd diplomat, he was none the less unpopular in Britain because he seemed to subordinate British to Hanoverian interests. He never learnt English and

left government to his Whig ministers, particularly after they saved George and his mistresses from disgrace in connection with the *South Sea Bubble.

George II (1683-1760) King of Great Britain and Ireland and Elector of Hanover (1727-69), succeeding his father George I. He married *Caroline of Ansbach in 1705. His reliance on such ministers as Sir Robert *Walpole influenced the development of constitutional monarchy. In the War of Austrian Succession he fought at Dettingen (1743), the last British king to appear in battle. He was a patron of musicians, notably Handel.

George III (1738-1820) King of Great Britain and Ireland (1760-1820) and Elector (1760-1815) and King (1815-20) of Hanover, succeeding his grandfather George II. He married Charlotte Sophia of Mecklenburg-Strelitz (1744-1818) in 1761. The political instability of the 1760s was blamed by the Whigs unjustly on George's alleged attempts to influence parliament through corrupt "king's friends." He shared with Lord *North the blame for the loss of the American colonies but was more astute in backing William *Pitt the Younger as prime minister (1783-1801). From the 1780s he suffered periods of madness and was permanently insane by 1811, after which the Prince of Wales (later George IV) acted as regent (*see also* Regency style).

GEORGE IV   *An engraving of the king by James Gillray entitled A Voluptiary under the Horrors of Digestion.*

George IV . (1762-1830) King of the United Kingdom and of Hanover (1820-30), succeeding his father George III, for whom he was regent (1811-20). He secretly married a Roman Catholic, Maria Fitzherbert, in 1785 but the marriage was invalid and in 1795 he married *Caroline of Brunswick. They were separated in 1796. Although intelligent and artistic, George's dissipation and extravagance and his heartless treatment of Caroline undermined the prestige of the monarchy.

George V (1865-1936) King of the United Kingdom (1910-36), second son of Edward VII, whose heir he became on the death (1892) of his elder brother Albert Victor. In

GEOLOGY

stages in the evolution of the geological strata of a small area

1 *Desert conditions resulted in the lowest rock layer being sandstone.*

2 *The advance of a warm sea over much of the area saw the deposition of chalk.*

3 *Following the retreat of the sea the area was covered with a fine sediment eventually forming clay and an igneous intrusion of granite was forced up by volcanic activity into the overlying strata.*

4 *The area was then subjected to folding, faulting, and erosion to form the present day landscape.*

geological map

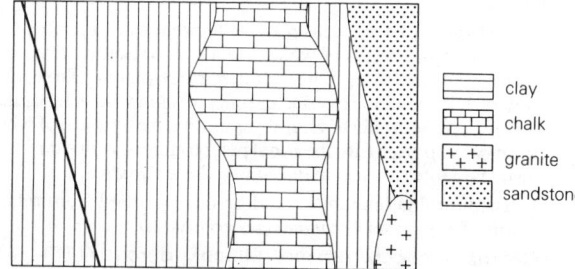

The map of the same area shows the rock types that would be exposed if the overlying soil and vegetation were stripped away.

geological time scale

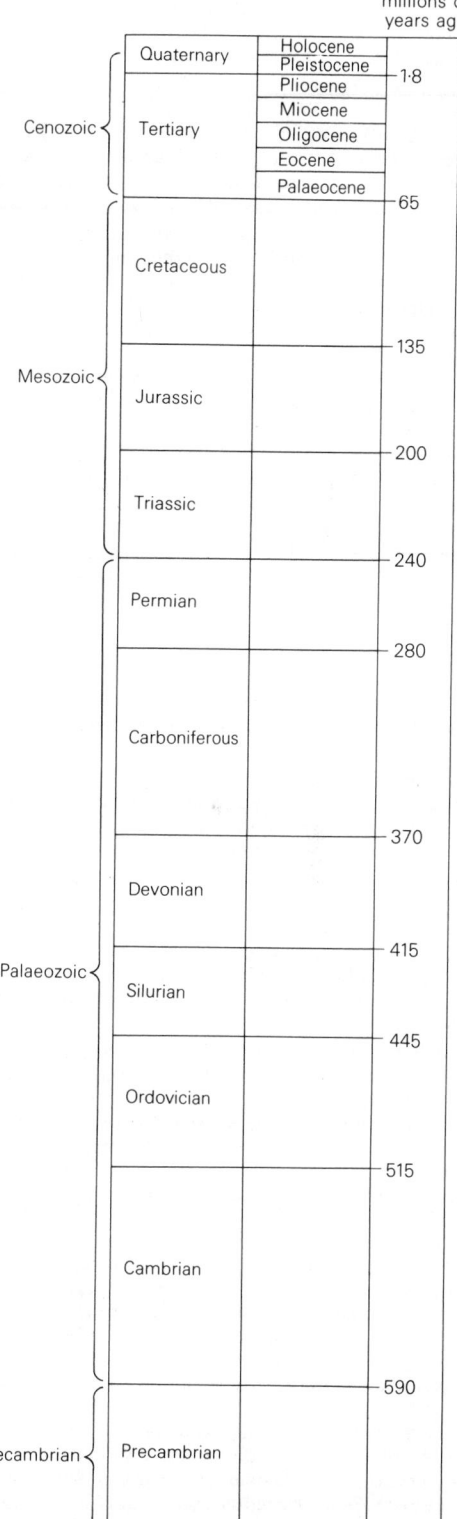

			millions of years ago
Cenozoic	Quaternary	Holocene	
		Pleistocene	1·8
	Tertiary	Pliocene	
		Miocene	
		Oligocene	
		Eocene	
		Palaeocene	
Mesozoic	Cretaceous		65
			135
	Jurassic		
			200
	Triassic		
Palaeozoic	Permian		240
			280
	Carboniferous		
			370
	Devonian		
			415
	Silurian		
			445
	Ordovician		
			515
	Cambrian		
			590
Precambrian	Precambrian		
			4500

clay
chalk
granite
sandstone

1893 George married *Mary of Teck. He gave valuable political advice during the many crises of his reign.

George VI (1895–1952) King of the United Kingdom (1936–52). Second son of George V, he succeeded to the throne when Edward VIII abdicated. He married (1923) Lady Elizabeth Bowes-Lyon (see Elizabeth the Queen Mother). His example inspired Britain in World War II.

George, St The patron saint of England and of soldiers. His cult was brought to England by Crusaders returning from Palestine, where he was believed to have been martyred during Emperor Diocletian's rule. In art he is usually portrayed slaying a dragon to rescue a maiden, a legend that probably derives from the *Pegasus myth. Feast day: 23 April.

George, Stefan (1868–1933) German poet. He studied in Paris, where he was associated with the Symbolist poets, and in Germany, where he assembled and dominated a group of disciples. In his manifesto *Über Dichtung* (1894) he advocated rigid formal perfection and metrical regularity, goals that he achieved in *Das Jahr der Seele* (1897) and *Der Teppich des Lebens* (1899). His later work glorified a godlike youth, Maximin. The Nazis favoured him, but he rejected them, voluntarily exiling himself in 1933.

George-Brown, Baron (1914–85) British statesman, born George (Alfred) Brown; vice chairman and deputy leader of the Labour Party (1960–70) and foreign secretary (1966–68). He entered parliament in 1945, representing Belper until created a life peer after electoral defeat in 1970. His disagreement with government policies led to his resignation as foreign secretary and in 1976 he left the Labour Party. Later he helped found the *Social Democratic Party.

George Cross The highest British decoration for civilian bravery, awarded since 1940. A silver cross superscribed *For Gallantry*, its recipients include the island of Malta (1942). The **George Medal**, the second highest decoration for civilian bravery, was also instituted in 1940.

Georgetown (or Penang) 5 26N 100 16E A city in NW Peninsular Malaysia, the capital of Penang state. The first British Malayan settlement, it is now Malaysia's chief port, exporting tin, rubber, and copra. Population (1980): 250 578.

Georgetown 6 46N 58 10W The capital and main port of Guyana, on the Atlantic Ocean at the mouth of the River Demerara. Founded by the British in 1781, it was later occupied by the French and the Dutch. It has twice in recent years (1945, 1951) been badly damaged by fire. Exports include sugar, rice, and bauxite. Its university was founded in 1963. Population (1980): 183 000.

Georgia A state on the SE coast of the USA. It can be divided into two physical regions: the higher elevations of the Appalachian Mountains in the N and a rolling coastal plain with forests and swamps in the S. Manufacturing is important although largely rurally orientated. It is the major textile producer in the USA; other industries include motor-vehicle and aircraft assembly, chemicals, and food processing. The state is also a major source of building stone. Agriculture is important; poultry has replaced cotton as the major item and Georgia is a leading producer of peanuts. Other products include tobacco, water melons, and other fruits (especially peaches) with some cattle and pig raising. Forest products are produced throughout the state. Its capital Atlanta is the cultural and economic centre of the SE and the state has a rich traditional folk culture. *History*: named after George II, it was founded in 1732, the youngest of the 13 original colonies. Settlement of the state expanded after the American Revolution with the development of agriculture. A supporter of the Confederate cause in the US Civil War, it suffered considerable damage during Gen Sherman's March to the Sea (1864). During the 20th century it has experienced many of the problems of the S, such as the decline in the cotton

industry and troubled race relations. Area: 152 488 sq km (58 876 sq mi). Population (1980): 5 464 265. Capital: Atlanta.

Georgian The language spoken by the Georgian peoples of the Georgian SSR, the Azerbaidzhan SSR, NE Turkey, and Isfahan province in Iran. It belongs to the Kartvelian or *South Caucasian group and is written in a script derived from Aramaic with Greek influences and has a literature dating from the 5th century AD. It is the official language of the Georgian SSR.

Georgian Bay A large bay in central Canada, in NE Lake Huron in Ontario. Its many islands and irregular coastline make it a popular recreational area.

Georgian Soviet Socialist Republic (or Georgia) A constituent republic in the SW Soviet Union. It is a mountainous region with many holiday resorts on the Black Sea coast. The population is predominantly Georgian. Georgia is rich in minerals, especially manganese and coal, and a gold field was discovered in 1941. The region also has vast hydroelectric resources. The main crop is tea; citrus fruits, grapes, and tobacco are also important to agriculture. *History*: Christianity was introduced in the 4th century AD. An independent kingdom for most of the middle ages, Georgia was divided between Persia and Turkey in 1555, passing to Russia in the 19th century. It became independent in 1918 but subsequently formed part of the Transcaucasian Soviet Federated Republic (see Transcaucasia). It became a separate republic in 1936. Area: about 69 700 sq km (26 900 sq mi). Population (1981 est): 5 100 000. Capital: Tbilisi.

Georgian style A style of British architecture prevalent during the reigns of George I to George IV (1714–1830). The period was subject to several different influences but was dominated by *Palladianism and *neoclassicism. Well-proportioned elegance was the keynote of Georgian architecture, characterized by the symmetrical use of twelve-paned sash windows in domestic architecture and the restrained use of classical features in public buildings.

geostationary orbit. See communications satellite.

geothermal energy Heat produced in the earth's interior, which may provide a source of usable energy. Volcanoes, geysers, and hot springs are all sources of geothermal energy, although only the latter two provide convenient energy sources. Countries that make use of geothermal energy include Iceland (where it is an important source of power), Italy, New Zealand, and the USA. Although geothermal energy is being actively explored as an alternative energy source, it currently supplies only about 0.1% of the world's energy requirements.

Gera 50 53N 12 6E A city in S East Germany, on the Weisse Elster River. Its manufactures include machinery, textiles, and furniture; there are uranium mines nearby. Population (1980 est): 124 146.

Geraldton 28 49S 114 36E A port in W Western Australia, on Champion Bay. Gold, copper, sandalwood, and wool are the main exports; crayfishing is important. Population (1983 est): 19 610.

geranium A herbaceous plant of the genus *Pelargonium* (250 species), most species of which are native to South Africa and widely cultivated as house and garden plants. They have roundish leaves and rounded clusters of showy flowers, usually red or pink. Most horticultural geraniums are hybrids, of which the most important are the zonal pelargoniums, with a dark ring near the centre of each leaf. Family: *Geraniaceae*.

Horticultural geraniums should be distinguished from related plants of the genus *Geranium* (see cranesbill).

Gérard, François (Pascal Simon), Baron (1770–1837) French painter, born in Rome. He was the pupil of *David but later rivalled him at the court of Napoleon with his elegant portraits, e.g. *Josephine Bonaparte* (Louvre), and history paintings. After Napoleon's fall, he became painter to Louis XVIII, who ennobled him in 1819.

gerbil A small *rodent belonging to the subfamily *Gerbillinae* (over 100 species) of Africa and Asia, also called jird and sand rat. Ranging in size from 5-20 cm, gerbils have long hind legs. They inhabit dry open country and spend the day in underground burrows, feeding at night on seeds and roots. Chief genera: *Gerbillus, Tatera*; family: *Cricetidae*.

GEORGIAN STYLE *The Royal Crescent (1767–1775) in Bath, designed by John Wood the Younger.*

gerenuk A long-necked antelope, *Litocranius walleri*, of E African bush country. About 100 cm tall at the shoulder, gerenuks are bright chestnut with white underparts; only males have the curved backward-pointing horns. They feed by rearing up on their hind legs and cropping leaves from thorny shrubs.

geriatrics The medical specialty that deals with the diseases and problems of old age. With improved standards of living and medical care, the number of people surviving to old age has increased and the suitable care of elderly patients is of great importance. In the past little active treatment was given, the patients being virtually bedridden in hospitals, almshouses, etc. Now, however, the aim is to restore as much function and activity as possible, by encouraging patients to engage in suitable activities with the aid of physiotherapy and occupational therapy.

Géricault, (Jean Louis André) Théodore (1791-1824) French painter, born in Rouen. His famous *Raft of the Medusa* (1819; Louvre), for which he used corpses in the morgue as models, was based on a contemporary shipwreck, which had become a political issue. While visiting England (1820-22), he produced a number of lithographs depicting poor people. He also painted his favourite subject—horses (e.g. *Derby at Epsom*; Louvre). His last works, inspired by a psychiatrist friend, were five portraits of the insane. Despite his early death after a riding accident, he greatly influenced French Romantic painters, especially *Delacroix.

German A language of the West *Germanic language group. It is the official language of Germany and Austria and one of the four official languages of Switzerland. High German, the official and written form, developed from dialects of the highland areas of Germany and Austria. Old High German was spoken before 1100 AD when Middle High German, based on Upper German dialects, became the standard form. Modern High German developed from the 16th-century dialect of Luther, whose biblical translations

spread this form. Low German exists only in a spoken form in the lowland areas of N Germany and is derived from Old Saxon and Middle Low German speech. The main difference between Low and High German is the sound system, especially the consonants.

germander A herbaceous plant of the worldwide genus *Teucrium* (300 species), with square stems and simple toothed leaves. The small tubular two-lipped flowers, borne in groups in the axils of leaflike bracts, are usually pinkish-purple. The perennial water germander (*T. scordium*) is a Eurasian species. Family: *Labiatae*.

Germanic languages A subgroup of the *Indo-European language group. Its member languages are spoken in Britain, Scandinavia, Germany, the Netherlands, and Iceland. There are three recognized subgroups: East Germanic, North Germanic, and West Germanic. The first of these is now extinct but it included Gothic, one of the earliest Germanic languages. North Germanic covers the *Scandinavian languages. West Germanic includes modern English and German among its descendants as well as *Dutch (Netherlandic) and *Frisian. These developed from their earlier forms High and Low German, Anglo-Saxon, Middle English, and Old Saxon. Also developed from Germanic origins are *Yiddish and Afrikaans (*see* Afrikaner). All three branches can be traced back to an unrecorded Proto-Germanic language, which has been reconstructed by philologists by comparing and tracing back similar modern languages using such generalizations as those stated in Grimm's Law (*see* Grimm).

Germanicus Julius Caesar (15 BC-19 AD) Roman soldier, who was adopted by his uncle, Emperor Tiberius, in 4 AD. In 17 he was appointed to govern Rome's eastern provinces and died mysteriously in Antioch, perhaps as a result of poison. Germanicus married *Agrippina the Elder and was the father of Caligula.

germanium (Ge) A brittle grey-white metalloid, discovered by C. A. Winkler (1838-1904) in 1886. Like *gallium it is present in coal and is concentrated in chimney soot as well as in the flue dusts of zinc smelters, from which it is obtained commercially. The element is a *semiconductor and its most important uses are in the electronics industry. Germanium compounds include the volatile tetrachloride ($GeCl_4$) and the dioxide (GeO_2), which has a high refractive index and is used in lenses. At no 32; at wt 72.59; mp 937.4°C; bp 2830°C.

German literature Little vernacular German literature earlier than the 12th century survives. The fragmentary *Hildebrandslied* (c. 800) is the only extant example of early heroic verse. The major works of medieval German literature were the epics the *Nibelungenlied* and *Gudrun*, several court epics based on French models, and the love lyrics of the wandering minnesingers, notably those of Walther von der Vogelweide. The Reformation had a great influence, especially through Luther's translation of the Bible (1522; 1534); Lutheran ideals were often expressed in the poetry of the *Meistersingers, the best known of whom was Hans Sachs. The Thirty Years' War, portrayed in Grimmelhausen's novels, resulted in cultural insecurity in the 17th and early 18th centuries and adherence to French models. An upsurge of national feeling in the 18th century resulted in a literary revival; the literature of the Enlightenment, represented most notably by Lessing, was succeeded by the *Sturm und Drang* movement and at the end of the century by Romanticism.

Goethe and Schiller outgrew *Sturm und Drang* emotionalism and espoused classicism instead, although Goethe's *Faust* remains balanced by warmth of feeling. The poets Hölderlin and Heine, the novelist and dramatist Kleist, and the dramatist Büchner were not associated with particular literary movements.

The aestheticism of the late 19th and early 20th centuries, found in the poems of George and the plays of Hofmannsthal, was paralleled by the realism of Fontane's novels. The social malaise of Germany at the time of World War I was reflected in Expressionism, elements of which appear in the works of various writers, influencing the mysticism in Rilke's poetry, the nightmare visions in Kafka's novels, and the search for new social and aesthetic values in the novels of Thomas Mann and Hesse and the dramas of Brecht.

The economic and political character of West Germany after World War II has been analysed in the novels of Böll and Grass. The Swiss playwrights Max Frisch and Friedrich Dürrenmatt have written a number of influential plays. In East Germany postwar literature has suffered from an official insistence on a restrictive form of socialist realism; only recently have poets and novelists emerged who show signs of being able to develop their individual talents.

German measles A common contagious disease of children and young adults caused by a virus. Known medically as rubella, it is a mild infection producing a pink rash and a sore throat. If a woman is infected in early pregnancy she may give birth to a malformed child; for this reason immunization of schoolgirls is encouraged.

German shepherd dog (or Alsatian) A breed of large strongly built ⌐dog originating in Germany. It has a coarse coat that can range in colour from white to black but is often black and tan. German shepherds are used as working dogs, especially for police work, as guard dogs, and as guide dogs for the blind. Height: 61-66 cm (dogs); 56-61 cm (bitches).

Germany A country in central Europe, now comprising (see below) the German Democratic Republic (East Germany) and the Federal Republic of Germany (West Germany). The region was occupied by German tribes from about 500 BC and came repeatedly into conflict with the Romans from the 2nd century BC. Overrun by the Huns in the 4th and 5th centuries, the area was dominated by the *Franks from the 6th century and was christianized in the late-7th to 8th centuries. After the death of the Carolingian Louis the Pius his empire was divided (843), the E part becoming the eastern Frankish kingdom, the nucleus of Germany. After the failure of the Frankish dynasty the German kings became nominally elective (see electors) but medieval Germany was in practice ruled by a series of hereditary dynasties. The first of these, the Saxons, was founded by Henry the Fowler in 919 and from the election (963) of his son as Holy Roman Emperor (see Otto (I) the Great), the German kings claimed the imperial title by right. The 11th to 13th centuries were dominated by struggle between the emperors and popes over the *investiture controversy, which with the conflict between *Guelfs and Ghibellines gave rise to a sustained period of civil strife. In the 13th century, following the fall of the *Hohenstaufen dynasty, the first *Habsburg emperor was elected and from the 15th century the imperial title remained almost continuously in the family. In the later middle ages the power of the princes was challenged by the *Hanseatic League of northern ports, which wielded political as well as commercial power. The 16th and 17th centuries were dominated by religious strife, following Luther's inception of the *Reformation at Wittenberg in 1520 and the subsequent division of Germany into a predominantly Protestant N and Roman Catholic S. The religious conflict was not resolved until the conclusion (1648) of the *Thirty Years' War. In the 17th century the Hohenzollern Electors of Brandenburg acquired Prussia, which, as a kingdom from 1701, became the dominant German state and, under *Frederick (II) the Great, a major European power. In 1806 the Holy Roman Empire was brought to an end by Napoleon, who formed the *Confederation of the Rhine in its place. The post-Napoleonic German confederation was dominated by Austria and Prussia and in 1834 the latter was the moving influence behind the formation of the *Zollverein (customs union). Prussian power increased further with victory in the *Austro-Prussian War (1866), which permanently destroyed

Austrian influence in Germany, and in the *Franco-Prussian War (1870-71). In 1871 Bismarck achieved his cherished ambition of creating a German Empire. The late 19th and early 20th centuries saw rapid industrialization, an aggressive armaments programme, and the rise of Germany as a colonial power, especially in Africa; its international aspirations were a major cause of *World War I. Defeated in 1918, the Empire came to an end (1919) and was replaced by the *Weimar Republic, which was plagued by the economic difficulties that facilitated *Hitler's rise to power in the early 1930s. His aggressive foreign policy, aimed at the establishment of a new German empire, led to the annexation of Austria and the Sudetenland (1938) and then of Czechoslovakia (1939). Finally, his invasion of Poland precipitated World War II. Following Germany's defeat the country was divided into British, French, Soviet, and US occupation zones before the subsequent formation of the two separate states, the German Democratic Republic and the Federal Republic of Germany.

German Democratic Republic (GDR; German name: Deutsche Demokratische Republik) The N part of the country, which borders on the Baltic Sea and includes the island of *Rügen, is generally low lying and contains many lakes. The Harz Mountains rise in the W, the Thuringian Forest in the SW, and the Erzgebirge in the SE. The main rivers are the Elbe and the Oder. *Economy*: highly industrialized and planned in close cooperation with the Soviet Union. Almost all industry is state-owned and includes precision engineering (including optical instruments), electronics, shipbuilding, machinery, and chemicals. However, the growth of light industries, such as textiles and food products, has slowed down recently. The main mineral resource is lignite, which supplies over half of the country's basic energy. It has two nuclear power stations. Oil and coal (all East German coalmines were largely exhausted and closed by the end of 1977) are supplied by the Soviet Union. The agricultural sector, which is organized in collectives and state farms, is gradually declining in importance although forestry remains an important source of revenue. Exports include lignite, potash, textiles, and photographic paper. *History*: formed from the Soviet-occupied zone of Germany following World War II, it was given a provisional constitution as the German Democratic Republic in 1949, becoming independent in 1954. The leading architect of the new state was Walter Ulbricht; in 1960, following the death of President Wilhelm Pieck, he became chairman of the newly established Council of State. The early years of economic austerity and curbs on civil liberties led to much discontent and in 1953 serious riots, particularly in East Berlin, were suppressed by Soviet troops, but the flow of refugees to West Germany continued until 1961, when the *Berlin Wall was erected. Since the early 1970s there has been a marked improvement in living standards and relations with West Germany have eased slightly with a treaty calling for closer relations being ratified by both countries in 1973. In 1984 West Germany extended a loan to the GDR, and, in turn, the GDR eased foreign exchange requirements for West Germany. Trade between the two countries also increased greatly. East Germany is a member of COMECON and in 1973 was admitted to the UN as a separate state. Chairman of the council of state: Erich Honecker. Official language: German. Official currency: (GDR) Mark of 100 Pfennige. Area: 108 178 sq km (41 757 sq mi). Population (1983 est): 16 724 000. Capital: East Berlin. Chief port: Rostock.

Germany, Federal Republic of (German name: Bundesrepublik Deutschland) For administrative purposes, West Germany is divided into 11 *Länder* (German *Land*, state). Extensive plains in the N, which border on the North Sea, rise to a central hilly area with the peaks of the Alps in the extreme S. The chief rivers are the Rhine, Danube, Ems, Weser, and Elbe. *Economy*: rapid reconstruction, particularly of the industrial sector, followed World War II. There is a large amount of heavy industry, especially in the centre and the N, including electrical engineering, iron and steel, motor vehicles, shipbuilding, and chemicals. The manufacture of photographic equipment and optical and other scientific instruments is also important. Considerable mineral resources include coal, iron ore, lead and zinc, and potash. Although the agricultural sector has declined in importance, there is a considerable amount of forestry (now mainly under state control) and an important wine industry, especially in the Rhine and Moselle Valleys. Tourism is an important source of revenue. The main exports include motor vehicles, machinery, chemicals, and electrical-engineering products; in 1978 West Germany superseded the USA as the world's principal exporter. *History:* formed from the British-, French-, and US-occupied zones following World War II, it became fully independent in 1955. The capital was transferred to Bonn although West Berlin remained a part of the Federal Republic. In the postwar years it enjoyed a spectacular economic recovery making it the most prosperous country in W Europe. The import of foreign labour became increasingly essential to the continued industrial expansion, although the total number of *Gastarbeiter* (guest workers; *see* migration) has varied according to the fortunes of the economy. Christian Democratic governments under Adenauer and Ehrhard were followed in the early 1970s by the Social Democrats under Willi Brandt, and this contributed to better relations with East Germany and other E European countries. In 1982 the coalition government of Social Democrats and Free Democrats led by Helmut Schmidt collapsed and a new coalition was formed. Federal President: Richard von Weizsäcker (1920–   ). Chancellor: Helmut Kohl. Official language: German. Official currency: Deutsche Mark of 100 Pfennige. Area: 248 620 sq km (95 989 sq mi). Population (1985): 61 022 000. Capital: Bonn. Main port: Hamburg.

germination The process by which an embryo plant within a seed is transformed into a recognizable plant with roots, stem, and leaves. Water, warmth, and oxygen stimulate germination, which begins with the emergence of the root (radicle) and is followed by the shoot (plumule). Energy for the process is provided by the *cotyledons (seed leaves), which either remain below ground (hypogeal germination, as in the broad bean) or form the first leaves of the seedling (epigeal germination, as in the marrow).

Germiston 26 15S 28 10E A city in South Africa, in the S Transvaal. It contains the world's largest gold refinery and serves the Witwatersrand mines. It is an important railway junction and has extensive railway-engineering industries. Population (1980 est): 155 435.

Gerona 41 59N 2 49E A city in NE Spain, in Catalonia. It was besieged several times in the 17th–18th centuries. The fine gothic cathedral (1312–1598) has an exceptionally wide single nave. Industries include textiles, paper, and food processing. Population (1981): 87 648.

Geronimo (1829–1909) US Apache Indian chief. He led several raids, resisting resettlement of his people on a barren reservation in Arizona, but surrendered in 1886. Eventually they became farmers in Oklahoma. He dictated his autobiography *Geronimo: His Own Story* shortly before he died.

Gershwin, George (Jacob Gershvin; 1898–1937) US composer and songwriter. He wrote many songs for musical shows and films, perhaps the best-remembered being "The Man I Love," "I Got Rhythm," and "Lady Be Good." His jazz-inspired orchestral works include *Rhapsody in Blue* (1924) and *An American in Paris* (1928); the opera *Porgy and Bess* (1935) is still widely performed. His brother **Ira Gershwin** (1896–1983) wrote the lyrics to many of his songs.

Gerson, Jean de (1363–1429) French theologian and chancellor of the University of Paris. He was one of the earliest advocates of restricting papal power (*see* Galli-

canism). His efforts to end the *Great Schism of the Western Church by calling a general council were rewarded at the Council of *Constance (1415), of which he was a leading member.

Gesner, Conrad (1516–65) Swiss physician, who was a founder of modern zoology and botany. He compiled a survey of knowledge of animal life, the *Historiae animalium* (5 vols, 1551–87), and described many plant species, often in the form of woodcut illustrations. His other works include a bibliography of authors and their works, a survey of world languages, and a compendium of the recorded knowledge of the world.

Gestalt psychology A school of *psychology that originated in Germany in the early 20th century: Wolfgang *Köhler and Kurt *Koffka were its founders. It regards mental processes as wholes (gestalts) that cannot be analysed into smaller components. According to this theory, when something is learned the individual's entire perception of the environment has been changed.

Gestapo (German: *Geheime Sta*atspolizei, secret state police) The Nazi secret police formed in 1933 under Göring. Administered from 1936 by the *SS, the two organizations were the chief instruments of atrocities carried out by the Nazi Party in Germany and German-occupied Europe.

gestation. *See* pregnancy.

Gesualdo, Carlo, Prince of Venosa (c. 1560–1613) Italian composer. His madrigals employ extraordinary harmonic effects. He was also famous for his lute playing and notorious for the murder of his first (unfaithful) wife.

Getty, J(ean) Paul (1892–1976) US businessman, who lived in the UK. He made his fortune in oil, becoming a millionaire at the age of 22. He founded the J. Paul Getty Museum at Malibu, California.

Gettysburg, Battle of (1–3 July, 1863) The most significant battle of the US *Civil War, fought in S central Pennsylvania as part of the Confederacy's second invasion of the North. The battle was joined unintentionally at Gettysburg, both armies having been uncertain of the other's position. The first day ended with a slight Southern advantage but a delayed attack by the Confederates on the second day shifted the advantage to the Federal troops. On the third day the Confederates charged the enemy's centre, holding their line briefly despite massive fire, but ultimately withdrawing in defeat. The North lost 23 000 men and the South, 25 000. The **Gettysburg Address**, one of the shortest and most famous of modern speeches, was delivered (19 November, 1863) by President Abraham Lincoln at the dedication of a cemetery at the Gettysburg battlefield.

Geulincx, Arnold (1624–69) Belgian-born philosopher. He was converted to Protestantism and settled in Holland. In response to *Descartes' mind-body relationship problem Geulincx originated the "two clock" theory, whereby body and mind are conceived of as keeping perfect time, side by side, without interaction. For Geulincx, when a mental or physical process takes place, God occasions it, hence the term "occasionalism" applied to this doctrine (*see also* Malebranche).

geysers Jets of hot water and steam issuing intermittently from holes in the earth's crust, some reaching heights of up to 70 m. Geysers are found in volcanically active or recently active regions, for example, in Iceland. They occur when water from deep within the crust becomes superheated and suddenly boils, gushing up to the surface like a fountain. Cones of sinter (deposits of silica) frequently build up around the vents of geysers. □ p. 502.

Gezira, El (*or* al-Jazirah) A triangular plain in the Sudan, between the Blue and White Nile Rivers. The Gezira irrigation scheme using water from the Makwar Dam (completed 1925) makes possible the production of cotton, millet, fodder crops, and groundnuts.

Ghana, Republic of A country in West Africa, on the Gulf

GEYSERS *The Pohutu geyser, North Island, New Zealand.*

cessor, Lt Gen Fred Akuffo (1937–79), was executed following a military coup (1979) led by Fl Lt Jerry Rawlings (1942–). A new civilian government was formed (1979) with Dr Hilla Limann (1934–) as president but this was overthrown in another military coup led by Fl Lt Rawlings in December, 1981. To stem smuggling activities all borders were closed in 1982. The expulsion from Nigeria of one million Ghanaians forced Ghana to reopen its borders and created a national emergency. In 1982 and 1983 there were four abortive coups. Official language: English. Official currency: cedi of 100 pesawas. Area: 238 305 sq km   (92 010 sq mi). Population   (1983   est): 13 367 000. Capital: Accra. Main port: Takoradi.

gharial. *See* gavial.

Ghats Two mountain ranges lying along the W and E coasts of India. The **Western Ghats**, which extend about 1500 km (932 mi) from N of Bombay to Cape Comorin, are the higher, rising to 2693 m (8840 ft). With the plentiful rain brought by the W winds, they have dense natural vegetation and are used for tea planting. The **Eastern Ghats** extend, with several breaks, about 1400 km (880 mi) from near Cuttack to the Nilgiri Hills.

Ghaznavids A Turkish dynasty that ruled in E Iran, Afghanistan, and N India (977–1186). The Ghaznavids created the first powerful Muslim state in India and prepared the way for the spread of Islam there. Founded by Sebuktigin (d. 997), a Turkish soldier, the dynasty's territories centred on Ghazna (Afghanistan) and reached its peak with *Mahmud of Ghazna. Following the battle of Dandanqan in 1040, the Ghaznavids lost their lands in Persia to the Seljuqs.

Ghazzah. *See* Gaza.

Ghegs One of the two major ethnic divisions of the Albanian people (*see also* Tosks). The Ghegs live N of the Shkumbi River and differ from the Tosks in dress and other customs.

Ghent (Flemish name: Gent; French name: Gand) 51 02N 3 42E A city in Belgium, at the confluence of the canalized Rivers Scheldt and Lys. One of Belgium's oldest cities, it has a university (1816) and a gothic cathedral. It is a major port and the textile centre of the country; other economic activities include metallurgy, chemicals, and banking. Population (1981 est): 239 959.

gherkin A trailing West Indian vine, *Cucumis anguria*, with lobed leaves and small yellow flowers. It is cultivated for its prickly edible fruit, 2.5–7.5 cm long, which is borne on a crooked stalk and used when immature for pickling. The "gherkins" sold in pickle mixtures are immature *cucumbers. Family: *Cucurbitaceae* (gourd family).

ghetto Any slum area occupied by an ethnic minority. Originally a ghetto was that quarter of a city to which Jews were restricted by law. Originating in Italy in the middle ages, ghettos were established during the *Counter-Reformation in many European cities. During the 19th century legal restrictions fell into disuse in W Europe and the communities became bound solely by customs and religion. However, in the 20th century ghettos were revived by the Nazis, for example in *Warsaw.

Ghibellines. *See* Guelfs and Ghibellines.

Ghiberti, Lorenzo (c. 1378–1455) Florentine Renaissance sculptor. Ghiberti trained as a goldsmith and painter but made his name as a sculptor in 1402, when he won the competition for the bronze relief sculptures for the north doors of the Baptistry of the Florentine Duomo. Finished in 1424, these New Testament scenes, mainly in the *international gothic style, were followed by Old Testament scenes in the Gates of Paradise (1425–52), strongly influenced by antique sculpture. Simultaneously he wrote *I commentarii*, which included histories of ancient and early Renaissance art and an autobiography. His other works include three statues of saints (1416–25) for Orsanmichele.

Ghirlandaio, Domenico (Domenico di Tommaso Bigordi;

of Guinea. Coastal plains rise to undulating country around Accra, and, in the centre, the basin of the River Volta rises to plateaus, especially in the N and W. The inhabitants are chiefly of Black Sudanese stock but there are a large number of tribal units. *Economy*: chiefly agricultural. Food crops are varied, and increased production is being encouraged through such schemes as "Operation Feed Yourself". The main cash crop is cocoa, of which Ghana is the world's chief producer. Such crops as rubber and cotton are produced to provide raw material for industry, in an effort to diversify the economy. Gold and diamonds are mined, as well as manganese, bauxite, and limestone. Hydroelectricity is being developed, particularly through the Volta Dam, and oil was found offshore in 1978. Forestry is also important. Fishing limits were extended from 48 km to 322 km (30 mi to 200 mi) in 1977. In spite of government efforts, economic difficulties continue, exacerbated by crop failures and also by such problems as large-scale smuggling. The main export is cocoa; others include timber and gold. *History*: from the middle ages several small kingdoms flourished in what is now Ghana. In 1472 the Portuguese and subsequently other Europeans set up trading posts in the region, which they called the Gold Coast. It became a centre of the slave trade and the scene of rivalry between the British and Dutch. The British abolition of slavery led to prolonged wars with the Ashanti slave-traders in the 19th century. The area became the British colony of the Gold Coast in 1874. In 1957, together with the British part of Togo, it became independent, its new name, Ghana, being that of a medieval N African empire. In 1960 it became a republic within the British Commonwealth, with Dr Kwame Nkrumah as its first president. His government became increasingly dictatorial and in 1966 he was overthrown in a military coup. Military rule continued until 1969, when civilian government was re-established. In 1972, however, a second military coup took place under Col Ignatius K. Acheampong (1931–79). He was forced to resign in 1978 and, with his suc-

1449–94) Florentine painter of the early *Renaissance. From 1481 to 1482 he worked on a fresco in the Sistine Chapel but his major undertaking was the fresco cycle (1486–90) in Sta Maria Novella, Florence. These scenes from the life of the Virgin and St John the Baptist are notable for their portrayal of Florentine personalities in contemporary dress. The tenderly painted *Old Man and Boy* (Louvre) is a fine example of his portraiture.

ghost The disembodied spirit of a dead person, believed in many cultures to be capable of manifesting itself to the living. Ghosts are still venerated in tribal societies in Africa, Asia, and Polynesia (*see* ancestor worship). Certain feasts in the Roman calendar were devoted to their propitiation. Post-Reformation ghosts exhibited more secular interests, demanding revenge or restitution of such wrongs as misappropriated inheritances. Scepticism grew in the 18th century but the *gothic revival initiated a revival in ghost stories. Hauntings continue to be reported (*see also* spiritualism).

ghost shark. *See* chimaera.

Giacometti, Alberto (1901–66) Swiss sculptor and painter. Working chiefly in Paris after 1922, he was influenced initially by *cubism and primitive art and later by *surrealism, particularly in his abstract construction of sticks, glass, wire, etc., entitled *The Palace at 4 am* (New York). After breaking with surrealism in 1935, he developed a unique figure style, featuring spindly elongated forms.

Giambologna (Giovanni da Bologna *or* Jean de Boulogne; 1529–1608) Italian mannerist sculptor of Flemish birth. Working from 1557 in Florence, where he was patronized by the Medici, he produced fountains, religious sculptures, and small bronze statues. His works include *Samson and a Philistine* (1567; Victoria and Albert Museum).

giant planet. *See* planet.

Giant's Causeway 55 14N 6 32W A promontory in N Northern Ireland, in Antrim on the North Channel. It consists of several thousand closely packed basaltic columns, mainly hexagonal in shape, formed by an outpouring of lava into the sea. According to legend it was built as a bridge for the giants to cross between Ireland and Scotland.

giant star A large very luminous star that has a very tenuous atmosphere but a dense core. It is in a late stage of evolution, having exhausted the normal source of energy in its core (hydrogen), and must obtain energy from other nuclear fusion reactions. This causes its size and temperature to alter as it evolves. *See also* red giant.

giant tortoise. *See* Galápagos giant tortoise.

giant water bug A large brown *water bug of the family *Belostomatidae* (up to 200 species), found in tropical and temperate regions. Sometimes over 10 mm long, they are strong fliers and are often attracted to light. In some species, such as *Belostoma plumineum*, the female forcibly lays her eggs onto the back of the male, attaching them with a glue.

gibberellins A group of organic compounds that stimulate plant growth. First isolated from the fungus *Gibberella fujikuroi*, over 30 gibberellins are now known. When applied to plants they stimulate the growth of leaves, stems, flowers, and fruit and break the dormancy of seeds and tubers; hence their importance in horticulture and agriculture.

gibbon A small *ape belonging to the genus *Hylobates* (7 species), of S Asia. 45–65 cm long, they have long arms with slender hands and hooked fingers used to swing through trees. On the ground they walk upright or run on all fours. They live in family groups, feeding chiefly on fruit and leaves, and have a loud whooping call. Family: *Hylobatidae*. *See also* siamang.

Gibbon, Edward (1737–94) British historian. Sent to Lausanne in 1753 by his father because of his conversion to Roman Catholicism, which he soon renounced, he travelled in Switzerland and later (1764–65) in Italy. His ironic treatment of Christianity in his monumental *The History of the Decline and Fall of the Roman Empire* (1776–88) aroused contemporary controversy, but the work gained acceptance as successive volumes

appeared.

Gibbon, Lewis Grassic (James Leslie Mitchell; 1901–35) Scottish writer. He published *Stained Radiance* (1930) and *Spartacus* (1933) under his own name. The trilogy *Scots Quair* (1932–34), for which he is best known, was published under his pseudonym. *Scottish Scene*, with Hugh *MacDiarmid, is a celebration of Scottish prose and verse.

Gibbons, Grinling (1648–1721) English wood carver and sculptor, born in Rotterdam. Patronized by Charles II and subsequent British monarchs, he produced decorative carvings of flowers, swags of fruit, etc., in wood and occasionally stone, for Windsor Castle, Kensington Palace, Blenheim Palace, and Petworth House. His best-known works, however, are the choir stalls and organ screen in St Paul's Cathedral.

Gibbons, Orlando (1583–1625) English composer, organist, and virginalist. He became organist of the Chapel Royal at the age of 21. His church music includes services and anthems. Of his madrigals, "The Silver Swan" is the best known. He also wrote three- and four-part string fantasias and contributed pieces to *Parthenia* (1611), the first anthology of keyboard music to be printed in England.

GIBBON *These apes are noted for their agility in trees. This individual* (Hylobates lar) *from Borneo manipulates a twig while clinging to a tree branch.*

Gibbs, James (1682–1754) British architect. Gibbs trained under Carlo Fontana (1634–1714) at Rome, where he was influenced by the Italian *baroque style. His notable works include St Mary-le-Strand (1714–17) and St Martin's in the Fields (1722–26) in London and the circular Radcliffe Camera (1737–49) in Oxford.

Gibbs, Josiah Willard (1839–1903) US physicist, who was a professor at Yale University (1871–1903). Gibbs founded chemical thermodynamics, which is largely based on the function known as the Gibbs free energy. He is also known for his phase rule, relating the number of parameters that can be varied in a system of more than one phase. His papers, published in the USA between 1876 and 1878, did not become known in Europe until the 1890s.

Gibraltar A British crown colony occupying a tiny peninsula at the southern tip of Spain. The sandy isthmus that links it to the Spanish mainland rises sharply to the 427 m (1400 ft) limestock Rock of Gibraltar, which contains numerous caverns and galleries. The population is mainly of Spanish, Genoese, and Portugese descent. *Economy*: its strategic position makes it a naval and air base of great importance; British defence expenditure together with tourist earnings and fees for services to shipping form the basis of its economy. Tourist attractions include the colony's barbary apes, the only monkeys native to Europe. *History*: settled by the Moors in 711 AD, the Rock of Gibraltar was taken by Castile in 1462, becoming part of united Spain. It was captured in 1704 by the British to whom it was formally ceded by the Treaty of Utrecht (1713). The colony became an important British naval base. Claims to Gibraltar have long been made by Spain but a UN proposal to end British occupation was defeated in a referendum in 1967. In 1969 Spain closed its frontier with Gibraltar leading to a man-power shortage (as much of its workforce was Spanish) and the subsequent import of Moroccan labour. The border was reopened in 1985. Official languages: English and Spanish. Official currency: Gibraltar pound of 100 pence. Area: 6.5 sq km (2.5 sq mi). Population (1980 est): 29 787.

Gibraltar, Strait of A strait between Europe (Spain and Gibraltar) and Africa (Morocco), joining the Atlantic Ocean and the Mediterranean Sea, of which it is the only outlet. It narrows to 13 km (8 mi) and is of great strategic importance.

Gibran, Khalil (1883-1931) Lebanese mystic and poet. He studied in Beirut and Paris and settled in New York in 1912. His major work in English is *The Prophet* (1923), a romantic blending of religion and philosophy.

Gibson Desert A desert in central Western Australia. It consists of a vast arid area of active sand dunes and desert grass. Area: 220 000 sq km (85 000 sq mi).

Gide, André (1869-1951) French novelist and critic. Much of his work is semiautobiographical and deals with the conflict between desire and discipline, reflecting his homosexuality and consequent conflict with conventional morality. His visits to North Africa from 1893 to 1896 gave him a sense of freedom, celebrated in *Fruits of the Earth* (1897). In 1895 he married his cousin Madeleine Rondeaux, the inspiration of two short works, *The Immoralist* (1902) and *Strait Is the Gate* (1909). In 1908 he was one of the founders of the important literary journal, *La Nouvelle Revue française*. His longer novels are *The Vatican Cellars* (1914) and *The Counterfeiters* (1926). For a short time he was drawn to communism but soon became disillusioned. His *Journal*, which he kept from 1885 until his death, is a major work of literary autobiography. He won the Nobel Prize in 1947.

Gielgud, Sir (Arthur) John (1904-) British actor. He is noted for his distinguished speaking voice and for his many fine performances in Shakespearian productions. His *Hamlet*, first performed in 1929, received especial acclaim. During the 1970s he also acted in plays by modern dramatists, such as Harold Pinter and Edward Bond, and in many films.

Gierek, Edward (1913-) Polish statesman, who succeeded *Gomułka as first secretary of the Polish United Workers' Party (1970-80). Born in Poland, he lived in France and Belgium from 1923 to 1948. A communist from 1931, he became a member of the politburo in 1956 and came to power following the demonstrations against food prices in 1970.

Giessen 50 35N 08 42E A town in central West Germany, in Hessen on the River Lahn. The university (1607) contains the chemist Liebig's laboratory. Its manufactures include rubber, machine tools, leather, and tobacco. Population (1983 est): 74 757.

Gifu 35 27N 136 46E A city in Japan, in central Honshu. It was *Nobunaga's headquarters in the 16th century. Manufactures include paper lanterns and textiles. Population (1980): 410 000.

Gigantes In Greek mythology, the giant sons of *Uranus

(Heaven) and *Gaea (Earth), whose rebellion against the Olympian gods was defeated with the help of Heracles. They were subsequently associated with earthquakes and volcanoes.

Gigli, Beniamino (1890-1957) Italian tenor. He became a world-famous opera singer and was regarded as the successor to Caruso. Toscanini brought him to La Scala, Milan, in 1920, where he made his debut as Faust in Boito's *Mefistofele*. He gave his final concert in 1955.

Gijón 43 32N 5 40W A port in NW Spain, in Asturias on the Bay of Biscay. Its many ancient buildings include Roman baths and medieval palaces. It is an important manufacturing centre with metallurgical and chemical industries. Population (1981): 255 969.

Gila monster A rare venomous lizard, *Heloderma suspectum*, occurring in the SW USA and N Mexico. 50 cm long, it has a stout black body with pink blotches and bands and small beadlike scales and feeds at night on eggs. It has a strong bite and grooved teeth that inject a nerve poison. Family: *Helodermatidae*.

gilbert (Gb) The unit of magnetomotive force in the *c.g.s. system equal to the magnetomotive force produced by a current of 40π amperes passing through a single coil. Named after William *Gilbert.

Gilbert, Sir Humphrey (c. 1539-83) English navigator. Halfbrother of Sir Walter *Raleigh, Gilbert had a notable career as a soldier in Ireland (1567-70, 1579) and the Netherlands (1572). His first attempt to reach North America was a failure (1578) but in 1583 he landed at St John's, Newfoundland, which he claimed for Elizabeth I. He was lost at sea on his return voyage.

Gilbert, William (1544-1603) English physicist and physician to Elizabeth I. One of the early adherents of the experimental method, his *De magnete* (1600) listed many experimental observations concerning magnets, including the discovery of magnetic dip. He suggested that the earth is a spherical magnet, that other magnets point towards its poles, and that the planets are held in their orbits by magnetic attraction. He was the first English scientist to accept the ideas of *Copernicus; he was also responsible for many new terms, including *electricity* and *magnetic pole*.

Gilbert, Sir William Schwenk (1836-1911) British comic dramatist. He wrote comic verses, published as *Bab Ballads* (1869), while studying law. In 1870 he met Arthur *Sullivan, the composer for whom he wrote the libretti for 14 popular operas. His plays written after Sullivan's death in 1900 were less successful.

Gilbert Islands. *See* Kiribati, Republic of.

Gilbert of Sempringham, St (c. 1083-1189) English priest, who founded the Gilbertines, the only indigenous religious order of medieval England, at Sempringham, Lincolnshire. It was composed of nuns, lay sisters and brothers, and canons. It was dissolved by Henry VIII. Feast day: 4 Feb.

Gilded Age In the USA, an era (1865-1900) marked by ostentatious materialism and governmental corruption. *The Gilded Age* (1873) by Mark *Twain (with Charles Dudley Warner; 1829-1900) described and named the period.

Giles, Carl Ronald (1916-) British cartoonist. Working for the *Daily Express* and *Sunday Express* from 1943, he has satirized the activities of a typical British family, his best-known character being the fearsome Grandma.

Gilgamesh An ancient Mesopotamian hero whose adventures are related in the collection of fragmentary texts known as the *Epic of Gilgamesh*. These are inscribed on 12 tablets discovered in the library of the Assyrian king, Ashurbanipal (reigned 669-626 BC), at Nineveh. They relate how Gilgamesh defeats and then befriends the savage man Enkidu, rejects the love goddess *Ishtar, journeys to consult an immortal wise man, Utnapishtim, about the secret of eternal life, and gains and then loses the plant of immortality.

Gill, (Arthur) Eric (Rowton) (1882–1940) British sculptor, engraver, and typographer. Gill's best-known sculptures are the *Stations of the Cross* (1914–18) for Westminster Cathedral and *Prospero and Ariel* (1931) on Broadcasting House, London. He illustrated many books and designed two new printing typefaces, Perpetua (1928) and Gill Sans (1929).

Gillespie, Dizzy (John Birks G.; 1917–) US Black jazz trumpeter, band leader, and composer, who was one of the originators of *bop. Gillespie played with many different bands in the 1930s and 1940s before forming his own band in 1945. In later years Gillespie incorporated singing and comedy into his performances. His recordings include *Groovin' High* and *Hot vs Cool*; in 1980 he published his autobiographical *To Be or Not to Bop*. □ p. 644.

Gillingham 51 24N 0 33E A town in SE England, in Kent on the Medway estuary. The largest of the Medway towns, it has extensive dockyards at Chatham and various light industries. Locally fruit growing is important. Population (1981): 93 741.

Gillray, James (1756–1815) British caricaturist. After training as a letter engraver and at the Royal Academy, he specialized in political and social cartoons. Targets included George III, whom Gillray called "Farmer George," □George IV, Burke, Napoleon, and Pitt.

gills The respiratory organs of aquatic animals: specialized thin-walled regions of the body surface through which dissolved oxygen is taken into the blood and carbon dioxide released into the water. The gills of fish lie in gill slits on each side of the gullet. Each gill consists of many leaflike gill filaments, which provide a large surface area over which water is pumped. The gills of molluscs (such as the mussel) and fanworms are ciliated and trap food particles in the respiratory currents. The external gills of amphibian larvae (tadpoles) are feathery structures projecting from the body wall.

gillyflower (*or* gilliflower) A name given to various clove-scented flowers, originally applied to plants of the pink family (*Caryophyllaceae*), such the carnation.

gilt-edged security A UK government fixed-interest stock. Some, such as *Consols, are irredeemable (no date is stipulated for the return of the capital); others are redeemable at par on a specified date. Short-term gilts ("shorts") are redeemable within 5 years, "mediums" in 5–15 years, and "longs" in over 15 years. The price of gilts depends upon prevailing interest rates, the price rising as interest rates fall and vice versa. Most gilts are issued in units of £100 (the par value) although the issue price may be above or below this figure, depending on the interest rate offered and the redemption date. The *flat yield* of a stock is the interest rate calculated on the market price rather than the par value. The *yield to redemption* takes into account any capital loss or gain between the market price and the par value, averaged over the years remaining to redemption. Gilts may be purchased through a bank or a stockbroker.

gin A *spirit distilled usually from grain flavoured with juniper berries (the name is derived from the Dutch *jenever*, juniper). Gin is almost pure alcohol, with little flavour. It is generally drunk with tonic water, *vermouth, fruit juice, etc. Martini cocktails are a mixture of gin and dry vermouth served very cold with ice. Dry or London Dry gin is the gin most frequently used for mixed drinks.

ginger A perennial herbaceous plant, *Zingiber officinale*, native to SE Asia and widely grown in the tropics for its pungent underground stems (rhizomes), used as a spice, food, and flavouring and in medicine. Its leafy stems grow about 1 m high; the leaves are 15–30 cm long and the flowers grow in dense conelike spikes. The plants are sterile, and propagation is by cuttings from the rootstocks. Family: *Zingiberaceae*.

gingivitis Inflammation of the gums. It may be caused by ill-fitting dentures or by infection in debilitated people or those taking antibiotics.

Ginkel, Godert de, 1st Earl of Athlone (1644–1703) Dutch general. As William III's commander in chief in Ireland after the king's victory at the Boyne, he crushed the remaining Roman Catholic resistance and was created Earl of Athlone (1692). He later fought under Marlborough.

ginkgo A deciduous *gymnosperm tree, *Ginkgo biloba*, also called maidenhair tree, that is the sole living representative of a group of trees that flourished in the Carboniferous period (370–280 million years ago). Growing to a height of 30 m, it has lobed fan-shaped leaves, 12 × 10 cm, which are pale green and turn yellow in autumn, and fleshy plumlike yellow fruits containing edible kernels. The ginkgo is native to China and widely planted for ornament. Family: *Ginkgoaceae*.

Ginsberg, Allen (1926–) US poet. His first book, *Howl* (1956), a rambling attack on contemporary America, was a popular work of the *Beat movement. In the 1960s he travelled in Asia, India, and South America. His later work, in *The Change* (1963), *The Fall of America* (1973), and other books, is fragmentary and rhapsodic.

ginseng An extract of the forked roots of either of two herbs, *Panax quinquefolium* or *P. schinseng*, used as a stimulant drug in the Far East and to make aromatic bitters. It is said to have aphrodisiac and life-prolonging properties. *P. quinquefolium* is grown commercially in North America; *P. schinseng* in Korea and Japan. Family: *Araliaceae* (ivy family).

Giordano, Luca (1632–1705) Neapolitan painter, nicknamed Luca fa presto (Luca works quickly). His enormous output of religious and mythological paintings, at first influenced by *Ribera but later by Venetian art, includes ceiling frescoes in the ballroom of the Palazzo Medici-Riccardi, Florence, and in El Escorial, Spain, where he was court painter (1692–1702).

Giorgione (c. 1477–1510) Italian painter of the Venetian school, born in Castelfranco. He trained under Giovanni *Bellini and worked with *Titian, whom he influenced, on frescoes for the façade of the German Exchange in Venice (1508). Most of his paintings are small-scale secular pictures of a type previously unknown. Their subject matter is often inexplicable, particularly in the *Tempest* (Accademia, Venice), notable for its atmospheric landscape. *The Sleeping Venus* (Gemäldegalerie, Dresden), completed by Titian, and *The Three Philosophers* (Kunsthistorisches Museum, Vienna) show the romantic and dreamlike mood of his paintings. His portraits, e.g. *Laura* (Vienna), influenced many Venetian painters. He probably died of the plague.

Giotto (Giotto di Bondone; c. 1266–1337) Italian painter and architect, who laid the foundation for *Renaissance painting. He was probably the pupil of *Cimabue. The fresco cycle of St Francis, in the upper church of S Francesco, Assisi, is thought to be an early work. He painted the innovative frescoes of scenes from the lives of Joachim and Anne and the Virgin and Christ in the Arena Chapel, Padua, and frescoes in Sta Croce, Florence. In 1334 he became architect of the city and surveyor of Florence Cathedral, for which he designed the campanile.

Gipsies A wandering people found on most continents. The name "Gipsy" is derived from "Egyptian," but they probably originated in India. One group is thought to have migrated through Egypt and North Africa and another through Europe reaching NW Europe during the 15th and 16th centuries. They travel by motorized caravan and live largely by seasonal work, itinerant trade, entertaining, and fortune telling. They have been persecuted frequently, half a million being killed by the Nazis during World War II. Their native language is *Romany.

Gir A breed of *zebu cattle originating from the Gir forest of W India. They have characteristic domed foreheads with backward-curving horns and long ears and are yellowish red to black in colour. Traditionally a dairy breed, they are also used for draught purposes.

giraffe A hoofed *mammal, *Giraffa camelopardalis*, of tropical African grasslands. Measuring 3 m at the shoulder, with a neck 2.5 m long, giraffes are marked with a patchwork of reddish-brown blotches on a buff-coloured background. They feed on leaves, using their long necks and prehensile lips and tongues. Both sexes have permanent skin-covered horns. Giraffes live in small groups led by a mature male and can go for long periods without drinking. They usually sleep standing up. Family: *Giraffidae*.

Giraldus Cambrensis (c. 1146–c. 1223) Welsh chronicler. His chronicles of Ireland and Wales, *Expugnatio Hiberniae* (c. 1189) and *Itinerarium Cambriae* (1191), written while in the service of Henry II, contain a number of interesting folk tales. His unfulfilled ambition to become bishop of St David's, Pembrokeshire, is recorded in his autobiography, *De rebus a se gestis* (c. 1204).

Giraudoux, Jean (1882–1944) French dramatist, novelist, and diplomat (from 1910 to 1940). His early literary reputation was established by a series of poetic novels, including *Elpénor* (1919) and *Suzanne et le Pacifique* (1921). His stylized plays, often blending elements of tragedy, comedy, and fantasy, include *Amphitryon 38* (1929), *Tiger at the Gates* (1935), *Ondine* (1939), and *The Madwoman of Chaillot* (1949).

Girl Guides Association An association founded by Robert and (his sister) Agnes *Baden Powell in 1910 to encourage the physical, mental, and spiritual development of girls. The three classes of members are Brownie Guides (for girls aged between 7 and 10), Guides (10–15), and Ranger Guides (14–20). Its counterpart for boys is the *Scout Association. There are some 7 million Girl Guides throughout the world, of which 853 000 are in the UK.

giro A low-cost system for transferring money. It originated in Austria in 1883 and the British National Giro was set up by the Post Office in 1968. All accounts are held at the Giro Centre (in Bootle, Lancashire), which transfers money from one account to another on receipt of a completed form. Bank giro operates similarly, but accounts are held at bank branches.

Gironde, River A wide estuary in SW France, on the Bay of Biscay. Formed by the confluence of the Rivers Garonne and Dordogne near Bordeaux, it is used by oceangoing vessels. Length: 72 km (45 mi).

Girondins A French Revolutionary political group. Named from the Gironde, where their support was strong, the Girondins were moderate republicans. They became prominent in the newly formed Legislative Assembly (1791), where, suspicious of counter-revolution and seeking to unite the Revolution's supporters, they involved France in war against Austria and Prussia. Military failure undermined their influence and, after the overthrow of the monarchy, they were themselves ousted by the more radical *Jacobins (1793). Many Girondins were subsequently executed.

Girtin, Thomas (1775–1802) British landscape painter, famous for being among the first to perfect watercolour technique. His use of broad transparent washes without the old monochrome underpainting produced heightened atmospheric effects, as in *White House at Chelsea* (Tate Gallery). Other works include his etchings of Paris during a visit (1801–02) and drawings for a lost painting of a panoramic view of London.

Gisborne 38 41S 178 02E A port in New Zealand, in E North Island on Poverty Bay. It serves an agricultural region; the chief exports are wool, meat, and dairy produce. Population (1984 est): 31 300.

Giscard d'Estaing, Valéry (1926–) French statesman; president (1974–81). He was minister of finance and economic affairs from 1962 until 1966, when he established

the Independent Republican Party. He returned to this post (1969) under Pompidou, whom he succeeded as president. In the 1981 presidential elections he was defeated by Mitterrand. His attempts at liberal reform were thwarted by his party's dependence on Gaullist support.

GLACIER *The Surprise Glacier in the Chugach Mountains of Alaska.*

Gish, Lillian (1899–) US actress, who began her career as a child actress on stage with her sister **Dorothy Gish** (1898–1968). Both acted for the director D. W. *Griffith in several early silent films, including *Birth of a Nation* (1916) and *Intolerance* (1916), and subsequently worked in both films and the theatre. The later films of Lillian Gish include *Duel in the Sun* (1946) and *The Night of the Hunter* (1955).

Gislebertus (early 12th century) French *romanesque sculptor. Probably trained in the workshop associated with the Abbey of Cluny, Gislebertus developed an original and powerfully expressive style. His best-known sculptures are those around the west doorway and on the capitals of columns at the Cathedral of St Lazarus, Autun (c. 1125–35).

Gissing, George Robert (1857–1903) British novelist. Of 20 novels written between 1880 and his death, the best known are the autobiographical *New Grub Street* (1891) and *The Private Papers of Henry Ryecroft* (1903). He specialized in realistic portrayals of poverty and never attained popular success. His two marriages to uneducated working-class girls were both unhappy. He separated from his second wife and from 1899 lived with his French mistress in France, where he completed *By the Ionian Sea* (1901), a travel book that contains some of his best writing.

gittern An early type of guitar with four gut strings, played with a plectrum. It is known to have been a popular instrument for accompanying the voice at various periods between the 13th and 17th centuries but it lost favour after the Restoration.

Giulini, Carlo Maria (1914–) Italian conductor, musical director of the Los Angeles Philharmonic since 1978. He is well known in the UK for his work at Covent Garden and with the Philharmonia Orchestra; he is particularly noted as a conductor of Verdi.

Giulio Romano (Giulio Pippi; c. 1499–1546) Italian mannerist painter and architect, born in Rome (*see* mannerism). He was the pupil of *Raphael, whom he assisted in the decoration of the Vatican apartments and the Villa Farnesina. After Raphael's death, Giulio completed some of his works. In 1524 he settled in Mantua, where he designed and decorated the Palazzo del Tè, notable for its Room of the Giants, completely covered with illusionistic frescoes.

Giza, El (*or* al-Jizah) 30 01N 31 12E A city in N Egypt, forming a suburb of Cairo on the River Nile. Nearby are the great pyramids of *Khafre, *Khufu, and Menkaure, one of the Seven Wonders of the World, and the Sphinx. Tourism is important and it has textile and film industries. Population (1983 est): 1 509 600.

Glace Bay 46 11N 59 58W A town in E Canada, on the coast of *Cape Breton Island. Located over coal seams that have been mined since 1858, it is now chiefly a fishing centre. From here Marconi sent his first wireless message (1902). Population (1981): 21 466.

glacier A mass of ice and *firn of limited width lying chiefly, or completely, on land and moving downslope from its source. Different glacier forms exist; **cirque glaciers** are contained in depressions on mountain slopes or valley heads. **Valley glaciers** are contained within pre-existing valleys and are frequently tongue-shaped in plan, originating either from cirque glaciers as an alpine type or from an icesheet as an outlet type. The longest of these is the Lambert Glacier, 400 km (250 mi) long. Where a glacier emerges from a valley onto a lowland area, a lobe-shaped **piedmont glacier** results; an example is the Malaspina Glacier in Alaska (USA). **Glaciation** is the action of glacier ice on the land surface. The most recent period of extensive glaciation took place during the Pleistocene epoch, when about 30% of the world's surface area was ice covered. The main landforms resulting from glaciation are either erosional or depositional. Erosional features include the formation of U-shaped valleys and *cirques. Those of depositional origin include glacial *drift and *till. When water is also involved in the formation of glacial landforms the term fluvioglacial is used; fluvioglacial deposits include *eskers and *kames.

gladiators The slaves, prisoners of war, condemned criminals, or volunteers who fought in amphitheatres for the entertainment of the ancient Roman people. Gladiatorial combats began as a feature of funeral games but their popularity was soon so great that statesmen sponsored shows to enhance their political prestige. Pairs of gladiators would fight to the death unless the audience spared the loser. Several Roman writers condemned gladiatorial shows.

Gladiolus A genus of ornamental perennial herbaceous plants (300 species), native to Europe, Africa, and the Mediterranean regions and widely cultivated. Growing from a corm, the flowering stem reaches a height of 1.2 m, with funnel-shaped flowers, usually red, yellow, orange, or white, grouped on one side. The leaves are sword-shaped. Gladioli cultivated for cut flowers have been developed mainly from South and East African species. Principal garden forms are *G. cardinalis*, *G. primulinus*, *G. psittacinus*, *G. purpurea-auratus*, and *G. saundersii*. Family: *Iridaceae*.

Gladstone, W(illiam) E(wart) (1809–98) British statesman; Liberal prime minister (1868–74, 1880–85, 1886, 1892–94). Elected to parliament in 1832, he was initially a Tory, becoming president of the Board of Trade (1843) under *Peel. He supported the Peelites in the repeal of the *Corn Laws, which split the Tories with the Peelites joining the Whigs (shortly to be termed Liberals). As chancellor of the exchequer (1852–55, 1859–66) Gladstone introduced a series of budgets that reduced tariffs and government expenditure. In 1867 he succeeded Lord *Russell as leader of the Liberal Party. His first ministry disestablished the Irish Church (1869) and introduced the *Education Act (1870), the first Irish *Land Act (1870), and the Ballot Act (introducing secret ballots). Defeated in the 1874 election, he resigned the Liberal leadership. In 1875 he re-emerged to criticize the apathetic attitude of his rival *Disraeli to the Turkish atrocities in Bulgaria. He again became an MP and prime minister in 1880. His second ministry achieved a second Irish Land Act (1881) and further parliamentary reform (1884) but its failure to save *Gordon from Khartoum led to Gladstone's resignation. His last ministries followed his conversion to Irish *Home Rule but both his Home Rule bills were rejected (1886, 1893).

WILLIAM EWART GLADSTONE   *Detail from a photograph taken during his last premiership.*

An impressive speaker, Gladstone with his Conservative opponent Disraeli dominated British politics in the second half of the 19th century.

Glamis 56 37N 3 01W A village in E Scotland, in Tayside Region. Macbeth was thane of Glamis. Nearby Glamis Castle was the childhood home of Queen Elizabeth the Queen Mother and birthplace of Princess Margaret.

Glamorgan A former county of South Wales. Under local government reorganization in 1974 it was divided to form parts of *Mid Glamorgan, *South Glamorgan, *West Glamorgan, and *Gwent.

gland An organ or group of cells that is specialized for synthesizing a specific chemical substance (secretion) from constituents of the blood and releasing its secretion for use by the body. Man and higher animals have two kinds of glands. The *endocrine glands lack ducts and release their secretions (which are hormones) directly into the bloodstream. The exocrine glands have ducts through which their products are secreted. Exocrine glands include the salivary glands, the sweat and sebaceous glands in the skin, and the pancreatic cells that secrete digestive enzymes.

Plants also have glands, which secrete a variety of products including latex, resin, nectar, and tannin.

glanders A highly contagious disease of horses, donkeys, and related animals caused by the bacterium *Pfeifferella mallei*, which can also infect other animals and man. Onset of symptoms can occur several months after infection and include the formation of nodules in the lungs, liver, spleen, etc., ulceration of the mucous membranes, enlarged lymph nodes, nasal discharge, and pus-filled blisters. The disease is usually chronic. There is no known cure and slaughter of infected animals is compulsory in most countries.

Glanville, Ranulf de (d. 1190) English jurist; chief minister (1180–89) under Henry II. He assisted Henry with his extensive legal reforms and reputedly wrote the *Tractatus de legibus et consuetudinibus regni Angliae*, the earliest treatise on English common law. He died at the siege of Acre during the third Crusade.

Glaser, Donald Arthur (1926–) US physicist, who was awarded the 1960 Nobel Prize for his invention of the *bubble chamber (1952), an instrument that makes visible the tracks of ionizing particles. His first bubble chamber measured only 15 cm across and contained ether.

Glasgow 55 53N 4 15W The largest city in Scotland, the administrative centre of Strathclyde Region on the River Clyde. The third largest city in the UK, it is Scotland's chief commercial and industrial centre. An important port with a tradition of shipbuilding, Glasgow also has major engineering, textile, chemical, brewing, and whisky-blending industries. *History*: of early religious and educational importance (St Mungo's cathedral dates from the 12th century and the university was founded in 1451), Glasgow's wealth grew rapidly through trade after the union with England (1707), especially in tobacco and sugar from the New World, and through industry in the industrial revolution. Population (1981): 762 288.

glasnost A policy of increased freedom in social and cultural matters introduced in the Soviet Union by Mikhail *Gorbachov in 1986. A Russian word meaning openness, glasnost was adopted by the Soviet government in conjunction with *perestroika* (meaning progress), which heralded a new (though still limited) flexibility in the organization of the economy of the USSR, and facilitated the improvement of relations with the West.

glass A translucent and usually transparent noncrystalline substance that behaves as a solid although it has many of the properties of a liquid. Glass itself was known in the 3rd millennium BC and glass objects survive from Egypt's 18th dynasty (1570–1320 BC), but glassblowing was not invented until about 100 BC (in Syria) and windows, which were originally made of blown glass, were not in use until about 100 AD. Ordinary soda glass, used for windows, etc., consists of silica (sand), sodium carbonate, and calcium carbonate (limestone). Flint glass, used for crystal glassware, contains silica, potassium carbonate, potassium nitrate, and lead oxide. Heat-resistant glass also contains borates and alumina; optical glass contains additional elements to control the refractive index and other optical properties, homogeneity being obtained by repeated heating and slow cooling. Blown glass is melted and blown inside a mould until it fills the mould; bottles and lightbulbs are made in this way by a fully automatic process. Flint glass is also blown to make glassware, but this is usually done by hand. Pressed glass, to make domestic bowls and headlamp lenses, is made by pressing the molten glass into a mould. Plate glass, for windows, etc., was formerly made by pouring molten glass onto a flat table and rolling it through heated rollers into sheets, which were then polished. Since 1959 the last stage has been replaced by floating the rolled sheet of glass on molten tin. *See also* fibreglass; stained glass.

glassfish A fish of the family *Centropomidae* (about 24 species), especially the genus *Chanda*, having a transparent body and a cleft dorsal fin. Glassfish occur along coastlines, in estuaries, and in fresh waters from Africa to the Indian and Pacific regions. Order: *Perciformes*.

glass harmonica. *See* harmonica.

glass snake A legless lizard belonging to the genus *Ophisaurus*, occurring in Europe, S and E Asia, N Africa, and North America. Glass snakes feed on insects, lizards, mice, and birds' eggs. Unlike true snakes, they have ears and eyelids. When attacked, they shed their tail. Family: *Anguidae*.

glasswort (*or* marsh samphire) An annual or perennial plant of the genus *Salicornia* (at least 7 species), native to European salt marshes, with jointed succulent stems that turn red in autumn. The fleshy leaves sheath the stem and the flowers are inconspicuous. It was once used in glassmaking as a source of soda. Family: *Chenopodiaceae*.

Glastonbury 51 09N 2 43W A market town in SW England, in Somerset. Here by tradition Joseph of Arimathea founded England's first Christian church; Glastonbury is also the reput-

ed burial place of King Arthur. There are the ruins of an early Benedictine abbey and the site of an excavated iron age lake village. Population (1981): 6773.

glaucoma An eye disease caused by raised pressure inside the eye. Acute glaucoma is often caused by a sudden block to the drainage of the watery fluid (aqueous humour) inside the eye. It leads to pain and disturbed vision, which will result in blindness without treatment. Chronic glaucoma, a common cause of blindness, comes on slowly and painlessly.

Glazunov, Aleksandr Konstantinovich (1865–1936) Russian composer and pupil of Rimsky-Korsakov. He became director of the St Petersburg conservatoire in 1906 but left Russia in 1928 and died in Paris. Glazunov's works, which were influenced by Wagner and Liszt, included eight symphonies, concertos, ballets, and string quartets.

Gleiwitz. *See* Gliwice.

Glencoe A glen in W Scotland, in the Highland Region extending to Loch Leven. It was the scene of the massacre of the Macdonalds by the Campbells and English (1692). Today it is a major rock-climbing centre.

Glendower, Owen (Welsh name: Owain Glyndwr; c. 1359–c. 1416) Welsh rebel. He led a Welsh rising that became a national war of independence. Allying with Henry IV's opponents, Glendower controlled most of Wales by 1404 but was subsequently defeated and turned to guerrilla warfare. He disappeared in 1416.

Glenn, John (1921–) US astronaut and politician, who on 20 February, 1962, became the first American to orbit the earth. Previously a test pilot, he became an astronaut in 1959. He remained in orbit in Friendship 7 for 4 hours 56 minutes, reaching a height of about 261 km (162 mi). He subsequently entered politics, becoming a US senator in 1974.

Glenrothes 56 12N 3 10W A town in E central Scotland, in Fife Region. Developed since 1948 as a new town, its industries include light and electronic engineering, food processing, and plastics. Population (1981): 32 700.

gliders Light fixed-wing engineless aircraft, sometimes called sailplanes. They are launched into the air by a winch or catapult or by being towed by a car or powered aircraft. Once airborne a glider slowly loses height unless it is lifted by a rising air current created by warm air rising from the ground (a thermal), a ground contour, or a thunderstorm. These air currents enable a skilful pilot to remain airborne for several hours. The height record is 14.1 km (P. F. Bickle; 1961) and the distance record 1460.8 km (H. W. Grosse; 1972).

Pioneered by Otto *Lilienthal in the USA, gliders were used by the *Wright brothers in designing their powered aircraft. Gliders towed by aircraft were used in World War II to carry men and equipment, notably by the British in the ill-fated Arnhem expedition. Gliding is a popular sport, controlled in the UK by the British Gliding Association (1924). *See also* hang-gliding.

Glinka, Mikhail Ivanovich (1804–57) Russian composer. He studied with John Field, made many journeys abroad, and is regarded as the founder of Russian musical nationalism. He composed the first truly Russian opera *Ivan Susanin* (*A Life for the Tsar*; 1836), various works in a Spanish style, piano music, songs, and a second opera, *Russlan and Ludmilla* (1842).

Gliwice (German name: Gleiwitz) 50 20N 18 40E A town in S Poland. Within Upper Silesia, its industries include coalmining, steel processing, chemicals, and food processing. Population (1982): 202 000.

globe artichoke. *See* artichoke.

globefish. *See* puffer.

globeflower A herbaceous plant of the genus *Trollius* (about 15 species), found throughout Europe. It has lobed toothed leaves and globe-shaped flowers, yellow or orange, borne on stems 10–70 cm high. Family: *Ranunculaceae*.

Globe Theatre An Elizabethan theatre, in Southwark, in

which most of Shakespeare's plays were first produced. A cylindrical wooden building open to the sky, it was built in 1599, burnt down in 1613, rebuilt in 1614, and finally demolished in 1644. In 1987 plans were accepted for a £13 million project to rebuild the Globe.

globe thistle A stout perennial *thistle of the genus *Echinops* (about 15 species), of central and S Europe. 50–200 cm high, it has lobed leaves, often white and woolly beneath, and large spherical flower heads, usually blue and sometimes woolly. They are often planted in gardens.

Globigerina A genus of protozoan animals that are common components of marine plankton. Ranging in size from 0.3 to 2 mm, their chalky skeletons are a major constituent of the grey mud on some sea beds, forming globigerina ooze. Order: *Foraminifera*.

globular cluster. *See* star cluster.

globulin A type of protein that is generally insoluble in water. Serum (gamma) globulins of the blood include the immunoglobulins (antibodies), which are manufactured by the animal to combat infections. Newborn mammals receive these immunoglobulins in maternal milk. Other globulins occur in eggs, nuts, and seeds.

glockenspiel (German: bell play) A tuned percussion instrument having a keyboard-like arrangement of steel bars played with two small hammers. The notes of its two-and-a-half-octave compass above bottom G of the bass stave sound two octaves higher.

Glomma, River (Norwegian name: Glåma) A river in SE Norway and the longest river in Scandinavia. Flowing S from a small lake SE of Trondheim, it enters the Skagerrak at Fredrikstad. It is important for hydroelectric power and for transporting timber. Length: 588 km (365 mi).

Glorious Revolution (1688) The overthrow of James II of England and the establishment of his daughter Mary and her husband William of Orange on the throne. The opposition to James' pro-Catholic and absolutist policies requested William's armed intervention; James panicked and, offering no resistance, fled to France. William and Mary accepted the *Bill of Rights, which is held to have established constitutional monarchy in England.

glory pea. *See* Clianthus.

glottis. *See* larynx.

Gloucester 51 53N 2 14W A market town in W England, the administrative centre of Gloucestershire on the River Severn. First developed under the Romans (Glevum) in the 1st century AD, its principal building is its cathedral, noted for its inventions in the Perpendicular style. Gloucester has engineering (aircraft components, agricultural machinery) and match-making industries. Population (1983 est): 92 200.

Gloucester, Humphrey, Duke of (1391–1447) The youngest son of Henry IV and brother of John, Duke of *Bedford, with whom he was protector during the minority of Henry VI. Despite his political incompetence and quarrelsome nature his patriotism and patronage of literature earned him the nickname, the Good Duke Humphrey. He died, apparently naturally, shortly after being arrested for treason.

Gloucestershire A county of W England, bordering Wales. Under local government reorganization in 1974 it lost the SW part to the new county of Avon. It consists of three distinct regions: the Cotswold Hills, the Severn Valley, and the Forest of Dean. It is predominantly agricultural; wheat and barley are the chief arable crops and dairy farming is increasing in importance. Industry includes engineering and timber production. Coal is mined in the Forest of Dean. Area: 2638 sq km (1019 sq mi). Population (1983 est): 506 100. Administrative centre: Gloucester.

glowworm. *See* firefly.

gloxinia An ornamental herb, *Sinningia speciosa*, native to Brazil. Gloxinias have rosettes of large simple velvety leaves and large bell-shaped velvety flowers, usually violet, purple, or pink. New plants can regenerate from the base of the leafstalks. There are many hybrids, which are popular house plants. Family: *Gesneriaceae*.

The genus *Gloxinia* (6 species) of the same family is not cultivated.

Glozel An archaeological site SE of Vichy (central France). During the 1920s finds here included engraved pebbles and clay tablets with an alphabetic script. An international commission investigated the site (1927) and cast grave doubts on its authenticity. Scientific dating of Glozel artefacts in the 1970s revived the puzzle, as some objects are undoubtedly ancient.

glucagon A polypeptide hormone, produced by the islets of Langerhans in the *pancreas, that increases the level of glucose in the blood by stimulating the breakdown of *glycogen in body tissues and promoting the utilization of protein and fat as energy sources. At high levels in the blood glucagon stimulates the secretion of *insulin.

Gluck, Christoph Willibald (1714–87) German composer. He reformed *opera seria, making it less artificial. Inspired by Calzabigi's librettos, he composed the operas *Orfeo ed Euridice* (1762) and *Alceste* (1767) in which the music reflected the dramatic situation and merely musical repetition and vocal ornamentation were excluded. He composed over 40 dramatic works as well as other music.

glucose (*or* dextrose) A simple sugar ($C_6H_{12}O_6$) and an essential substance in the carbohydrate metabolism of living organisms. Carbohydrates (such as starch and glycogen) in food or tissue reserves are broken down to glucose, which is easily transported to cells where it undergoes *glycolysis to provide energy for the cell. Organisms can also manufacture glucose from fats and proteins. Glucose levels in blood are regulated by the hormones *insulin and *glucagon and small amounts of glucose are normally present in urine. Fruits and honey are good sources of glucose.

gluten A protein mixture derived from wheat. In bread making, dough rises because the gluten in wheat flour expands, trapping the carbon dioxide bubbles in an elastic network. The properties of gluten vary according to the mixture of the proteins, chiefly gliadin and glutenin. *See also* coeliac disease.

glutton. *See* wolverine.

glycerol (*or* glycerine; $CH_2OHCHOHCH_2OH$) A colourless syrupy liquid with a sweet taste. It is made from fats and oils or by fermentation and is used in explosives, cosmetics, and antifreeze solutions.

glycogen A starchlike carbohydrate found in animal tissues as a reserve energy source. Chemically, it consists of branched chains of *glucose molecules: when required to provide energy, glycogen is broken down to glucose under the influence of hormones, chiefly *adrenaline and *glucagon.

glycolysis The sequence of chemical reactions occurring in most living cells by which glucose is partially broken down to provide usable energy for the cell in the form of *ATP. Glycolysis can take place in the presence or absence of oxygen but only a small amount of the available energy is released, the major proportion being released via the *Krebs cycle.

Glyndebourne An estate near Lewes, in East Sussex, home of an annual international festival of opera. The opera house was built on the estate by its owner John Christie (1882–1962), a British patron of music, who founded the Glyndebourne Festival in 1934 for his wife, the opera singer Audrey Mildmay (1900–53).

Glyptodon An extinct giant *armadillo, whose remains have been found in South America. Glyptodons had a rigid bony shell (unlike the jointed modern armadillo shell) and some had a spiky macelike knob at the end of the tail. They became extinct about 100 000 years ago.

GMT. *See* Greenwich Mean Time.

gnat Any of the smaller delicate species of two-winged flies, the males of which fly in dancing swarms. The term is applied to the less virulent mosquitoes and phantom gnats (family *Culicidae*), winter gnats (family *Trichoceridae*), fungus gnats (family *Mycetophilidae*), craneflies (family *Tipulidae*), and several others.

gnatcatcher A small active songbird belonging to a family (*Polioptilidae*; 11 species) ranging from S Canada to Argentina. 10 to 14 cm long, gnatcatchers have long wagging tails and fine pointed bills used to pick insects from leaves and crevices. The plumage is typically greyish blue above with lighter underparts and white outer tail feathers.

Gneisenau, August (Wilhelm Anton), Graf Neithardt von (1760-1831) Prussian field marshal, who was instrumental in effecting major reforms in the Prussian army following its defeat by Napoleon (1807). He subsequently played an important part in the wars of liberation (1813-14) and in the defeat of Napoleon at Waterloo (1815).

gneiss A coarse-grained metamorphic rock consisting predominantly of bands of quartz and feldspar alternating with bands of micas and amphiboles. These bands are often irregular or poorly defined. Gneisses are formed during regional metamorphism; those derived from igneous rocks are termed **orthogneiss**, those from sedimentary rocks **paragneiss**.

Gniezno 52 32N 17 32E A city in W central Poland. One of the oldest cities in Poland, it contains many notable historical buildings, including its 10th-century cathedral. It is a commercial centre specializing in food processing. Population (1982 est): 63 500.

Gnosticism A religious movement that flourished in the early Christian era. It manifested itself in many ways and contained many elements of pagan thought and magic, but is most fully recorded as a group of heretical Christian sects, attacked by Church Fathers, such as *Tertullian. The Gnostics' defining characteristic was their belief in *gnosis* (Greek: knowledge)—a special revelation from God to initiates, which would ensure their salvation (*compare* mysteries). Their world view was dualistic: God and the spirit were good and matter evil. They interpreted Christ (whose humanity they denied) as being sent to rescue particles of spirit (souls) entrapped in matter. Gnosticism influenced *Manichaeism and several medieval heresies. *See also* Mandaeanism.

GNP. *See* gross national product.

gnu A large ungainly antelope belonging to the genus *Connochaetes* (2 species), also called wildebeest, of African plains. The brindled gnu (*C. taurinus*) grows to 140 cm high at the shoulder and is blue-grey with a long black mane, black facial tufts, and a black-tufted tail. The smaller white-tailed gnu (*C. gnou*) has a long white tail and is very rare, surviving only in game reserves.

go (*or* i-go) A board game that originated in China (as *Wei-ch'i*), possibly in the 3rd millennium BC, and is especially popular in Japan. The board is marked with a grid of 19 vertical and 19 horizontal lines, making 361 intersections. There are 361 counters: 181 black "stones" for one player and 180 white for the other. Black begins by placing a stone on any intersection of the empty board. Play alternates, one stone being placed at a time; once played a stone may not be moved except to remove it from the board. The object is to conquer territory by enclosing empty points with one's own stones. Opposing stones that are encircled are captured and removed. The score is calculated by deducting the number of stones a player has lost from the number of intersections he has captured.

Goa The 25th state of India, formerly part of Goa, Daman, and Diu Union Territory. A Portuguese overseas territory from 1510 until annexed by India in 1961, it has many fine examples of Portuguese colonial architecture, including the church in which St Francis Xavier is buried. Area: 3496 sq km (1363 sq mi).

Goa, Daman, and Diu A former Union Territory of W India. Goa is on the central W coast; Daman lies inland N of Bombay; Diu is an island off the coast of Gujarat. They depend economically on agriculture, fishing, and tourism. Area: 3813 sq km (1472 sq mi). Population (1981): 1 082 117. Capital: Panaji. *See also* Daman and Diu.

goat A hoofed *ruminant mammal belonging to the genus *Capra* (5 species). Related to sheep, goats are 60-85 cm tall at the shoulder and have hollow horns, less curled than those of sheep; males have a scent gland beneath the tail and a beard. Wild goats, found in mountainous regions of Eurasia, are greyish in winter, reddish in summer, and live in herds of 5-20 individuals. Goats were first domesticated over 10 000 years ago and are still used to provide milk, meat, and hides in many semiarid regions of the world. Family: *Bovidae*. *See also* ibex; markhor; Rocky Mountain goat; tahr.

goat moth A large moth, *Cossus cossus*, of Europe, Asia, and N Africa. Mottled grey and brown, it has a wingspan of 70 mm. The reddish caterpillar bores under the bark of trees and emits a characteristic strong odour. It may hibernate for up to four years.

goatsbeard A perennial herb, *Aruncus dioicus* (or *A. sylvestris*), native to N temperate wooded regions, especially Siberia. Often grown as a border plant, goatsbeard is 120-180 cm tall and has fine compound leaves and branched plumes of small stalkless hay-scented creamy-white flowers. Family: *Rosaceae*.

Gobbi, Tito (1915-84) Italian baritone. He sang in all the world's major opera houses and was a well-known teacher. His most famous parts included the title roles in Mozart's *Don Giovanni* and Verdi's *Falstaff* and Scarpia in Puccini's *Tosca*. He also produced opera.

Gobelins, Manufacture nationale des A French state-controlled tapestry factory, founded in Paris as a dyeworks in the 15th century by Jean and Philibert Gobelin. Manufacturing tapestries from 1529, it was incorporated by Henry IV in 1607. In 1662 Louis XIV purchased it and it was directed from 1663 to 1690 by his First Painter Charles *Le Brun. Since 1826 carpets have also been made here.

Gobi Desert A vast desert of SE Mongolia and N China, one of the largest in the world. On a plateau 900-1500 m (2950-4920 ft) high, it is largely rocky with salt marshes and streams that disappear into the sand. It is rich in prehistoric remains including fossils and stone implements. Area: about 1 295 000 sq km (500 000 sq mi).

Gobind Singh (*or* Govind S.; 1666-1708) The tenth and last Guru of the Sikhs (1675-1708). As a religious reformer he remodelled the Sikh religious belief and practice and renounced social inequality and caste distinctions. He was assassinated by a Muslim.

Gobineau, Joseph Arthur, Comte de (1816-82) French writer and diplomat. He wrote novels, notably *Les Pléiades* (1874), short stories, and scholarly studies, including *La Renaissance* (1877). His influential *Essai sur l'inégalité des races humaines* (1853-55) argued that the continuing strength of the Aryan race depended on its racial purity.

goblin shark A carnivorous *shark, *Scapanorhynchus owstoni*. Up to 4.2 m long, it has long upper teeth that overlap the lower set, a long paddle-shaped nose, and a very long tail fin. It has been found in deep water off Japan, India, and Portugal and is probably the only member of its family, *Scapanorhynchidae*.

goby A fish of the suborder *Gobioidei* (over 800 species), especially the family *Gobiidae* (true gobies). True gobies have smooth elongated bodies, two dorsal fins, and a suction disc formed from fused pelvic fins. Most are 5-10 cm long, although *Pandaka pygmaea* of the Philippines is the smallest known vertebrate at under 13 mm long. They are chiefly marine and inhabit sand or mud burrows in tropical coastal regions, sometimes in association with other animals. Order: *Perciformes*.

God The supreme being that is the creator and ruler of the universe. The concept of God perhaps originated in primitive animistic belief, which attributed souls to natural objects and phenomena. It may then have developed into *polytheism, as in India and ancient Greece and Rome. In some religions, principally Judaism, Christianity, and Islam, God is seen as not only the architect of the universe but also as being actively involved with its inhabitants and its destiny (*see* theism). In *deism, God is seen as the creator of the universe who leaves its destiny to natural forces and the will of its inhabitants. In *Hinduism, Brahman, the supreme spirit and ultimate reality, is conceived as operating through the triad Brahma, Vishnu, and Shiva (*see* Trimurti). *Buddhism is, strictly speaking, nontheistic, being concerned more with the attainment of *nirvana than with the nature of a supreme being. The concept of a single supreme deity (*see* monotheism) originated with the ancient Jews (*see* Yahweh). Jews, Christians, and Muslims believe that God reveals himself with supernatural authority in their holy scriptures (*see* Bible; Koran). However, theologians and philosophers have also tried to prove the existence of God by rational means or by means of observed facts about the universe (natural theology). Most of the traditional arguments are associated with St Thomas *Aquinas; these include: the argument from design or the teleological argument (there is an observable design, order, and regularity in the universe and therefore it must have been designed, which argues a designer); the cosmological argument (the mere fact that there is a universe demands further explanation); the degrees of perfection argument (if every thing or quality in the universe can be traced back to a more perfect thing or quality, there must be some ultimate perfect being, i.e. God); the First Cause argument (if everything is caused by something else, at the beginning there must have been an uncaused First Cause). Another important argument is the ontological argument (*see* Anselm of Canterbury, St). ǀ

Godalming 51 11N 0 37W A residential town in SE England, in Surrey on the River Wey. Charterhouse (a famous public school established in 1611) was moved here from London in 1872. Population (1981): 18 209.

Godard, Jean-Luc (1930–) French film director. During the 1950s he wrote for the magazine *Cahiers du Cinéma* and became a member of the *New Wave. His films, which are characterized by experimental narrative and editing techniques and by his Marxist political convictions, include *À bout de souffle* (1960), *Alphaville* (1965), *Week-End* (1967), *Tout va bien* (1972), and *Je Vous Salue, Marie* (1985).

Godavari, River A river, in central India. Rising in the Western Ghats, it flows ESE across the Deccan, through the Eastern Ghats, and into the Bay of Bengal. Its delta has an extensive canal irrigation system, which is linked to the Krishna delta. It is sacred to the Hindus. Length: 1500 km (900 mi).

Goddard, Robert Hutchings (1882-1945) US physicist, who pioneered the technology of rockets. His first liquid-fuelled rocket (petrol and liquid oxygen) was launched in 1926. Throughout the 1920s and 1930s he continued to make improvements to his rockets but was largely ignored by the US Government. During World War II he' invented the *bazooka but died before the space-rocket age, although the German *V-2 was largely based on his work.

Gödel, Kurt (1906-78) US mathematician, born in Austria, who derived probably the most important proof in modern mathematics. Known as **Gödel's proof**, it states that, in a mathematical system based on a finite number of axioms, there will always exist statements that can be neither proved nor disproved. Gödel's proof, published in 1931, thus ended the search by mathematicians for a complete and self-consistent system.

Goderich, George Frederick Samuel Robinson, Viscount (1827-1909) British politician and colonial administrator; governor general of India (1880-84). Elected a Liberal MP in 1852, he served under Gladstone before succeeding *Lytton in India. There, he ended the second Afghan War (1878-80) and pursued an enlightened policy of reform, increasing the powers of local government and relaxing restrictions on the vernacular press. He was subsequently colonial secretary (1892-95). He became the 2nd Earl of Ripon at the death of his father **Frederick John Robinson, Viscount Goderich and 1st Earl of Ripon** (1782-1859), who had been Tory prime minister from 1827 to 1828.

Godesberg (*or* Bad Godesberg) 50 41N 7 10E A spa in W West Germany, in North Rhine-Westphalia on the River Rhine; since 1968 a district of Bonn. The site of ministries and embassies, it has a pharmaceutical industry. Population (1970 est): 6100.

Godfrey of Bouillon (c. 1060-1100) Crusader and Duke of Lower Lorraine. In 1096 Godfrey joined the first Crusade and played a major role in the siege and capture of Jerusalem. He then became defender of the Holy Sepulchre and effective King of Jerusalem. His exploits were celebrated in the medieval song cycle, the *Chansons de Geste*.

Godiva, Lady (d. ?1080) The English woman who, according to the chronicler Roger of Wendover (d. 1236), rode naked through the market place of Coventry in order to persuade her husband Leofric, Earl of Mercia, to reduce the taxes he had imposed on the town. The story was later embellished with a Peeping Tom who, ignoring Godiva's request that the townspeople remain indoors, was struck blind.

Godolphin, Sidney, Earl of (1645-1712) British Whig politician; Lord Treasurer (1685-88, 1700-01, 1702-10). Under Anne (reigned 1702-14) he and *Harley were the most powerful men in politics until the unpopularity of their pursuit of the War of the *Spanish Succession caused their downfall. Godolphin was also a noted importer of racehorses, including the famous Godolphin Arabian.

Godoy, Manuel de (1767-1851) Spanish statesman; chief minister (1792-97, 1801-08) of Charles IV of Spain. He rose to power through the influence of Charles' wife María Luisa (1751-1819), whose lover Godoy became. He allied Spain with France during the Napoleonic War and, extremely unpopular, was overthrown together with Charles.

Godthåb 64 10N 51 40W The capital of Greenland, a port at the mouth of Godthåb Fjord. Founded in 1721, it is the site of a radio station, hospital, and college. Chief occupations are reindeer and sheep raising, hunting, and fishing. Population (1981): 9423.

Godunov, Boris (Fedorovich) (c. 1551-1605) Russian statesman and tsar (1598-1605). Godunov rose to power in the reign of *Ivan the Terrible and became regent for Fyodor I, whose younger brother and heir, Dimitrii, Godunov may have murdered in 1591. After Fyodor's death (1598), Godunov was elected tsar. His authority was challenged by the first False Dimitrii, a pretender who succeeded Godunov (*see* *Time of Troubles). Godunov was the subject of a play by Pushkin, on which Mussorgsky based his famous opera.

Godwin (*or* Godwine; d. 1053) Earl of Wessex. An Anglo-Danish noble, he rose to power under Canute, after whose death Godwin supported the accession of Edward the Confessor and became a dominant figure in royal government. In 1045 his daughter Edith married Edward. He was overthrown in 1051 but regained his position by force in 1052. He was succeeded by his son Harold (later Harold II).

Godwin, William (1756-1836) British political philosopher and novelist. A utilitarian of the extreme radical kind, Godwin in *Political Justice* (1793) advocated anarchy and communism. As a determinist, he held that the notion of moral desert was irrelevant; Christianity was also a harmful influence, distracting men with bogus promises of immortality. His major novel, *Caleb Williams* (1794), propagates his views on justice. He married Mary *Wollstonecraft (1797).

Godwin Austen, Mount. *See* K2.

godwit A long-legged long-billed migratory bird belonging to a genus (*Limosa*; 4 species) that breeds in N Eurasia and North America. The black-tailed godwit (*L. limosa*) is 40 cm long and has a distinctive black-banded white tail, white wing stripe, and, in summer, a chestnut neck and breast. Family: *Scolopacidae* (plovers, sandpipers, etc.).

Goebbels, (Paul) Joseph (1897–1945) German Nazi politician. From 1926, when he became Nazi Party leader in Berlin, he was well known for his skilful propagandist techniques. In 1928 he entered the Reichstag and in 1933 was appointed minister of propaganda by Hitler. He established a vast and complex machine for the control of public information, the arts, cinema, and theatre, all of which he manipulated with a cynical disregard for truth to achieve Nazi aims. He committed suicide with his wife after taking the lives of his six children during the collapse of the Third Reich.

Goes, Hugo van der (c. 1440–82) Flemish painter, who worked in Ghent until about 1478. He spent the rest of his life in a monastery near Brussels. His *Portinari Altarpiece* (Uffizi), painted for a Florentine patron, is uncharacteristically large for Flemish paintings. The unharmonious colours and emotional intensity of his last work, *The Death of the Virgin* (Bruges), are perhaps related to mental illness, from which he suffered in the last years of his life.

JOHANN WOLFGANG VON GOETHE *After a portrait by Friedrich Bury, drawn when Goethe was about 51 years old.*

Goethe, Johann Wolfgang von (1749–1832) German poet, scholar, and statesman. He studied law at Leipzig and Strasbourg, where his discovery of Shakespeare inspired him to write an epic drama, *Götz von Berlichingen* (1773). The autobiographical novel *The Sorrows of Young Werther* (1774) won him international fame. In 1775 he settled at the court of the Duke of Saxe-Weimar, whom he served as prime minister until 1785 as well as directing the state theatre and scientific institutions. At Weimar he fell in love with Charlotte von Stein, who inspired some of his greatest lyric poetry. A visit to Italy (1786–88) made him an enthusiastic

advocate of classicism, influencing such plays as *Iphigenia on Tauris* (1787) and *Torquato Tasso* (1790). After the novel *Wilhelm Meister's Apprentice Years* (1795–96) he published the first part of his greatest work *Faust* (1808), a poetic drama of the aspirations of man. Other novels and scientific publications followed, until in 1829 he published *Wilhelm Meister's Journeyman Years*. The second, more philosophical, part of *Faust* he completed shortly before his death. A friend of the dramatist Schiller, Goethe's wide interests included stagecraft, biology, physics, astrology, and philosophy both orthodox and occult; he knew six languages well and translated many works into German.

Gog and Magog In Revelation and other books of the Bible, attendant powers of Satan. In British folklore they appear as the survivors of a race of giants destroyed by Brutus, the legendary founder of Britain. A famous pair of statues depicting them are located in the Guildhall, London.

Gogol, Nikolai Vasilievich (1809–52) Russian novelist and dramatist. Early ambitions to become a poet and an actor and to emigrate to the USA all failed, but two volumes of stories based on his Ukrainian childhood won him acclaim from *Pushkin and other leading writers. To escape the controversy aroused by his satirical play *The Government Inspector* (1836) he went to Rome, where he wrote his best-known work, *Dead Souls* (1842), a grotesque lampoon of Russian feudalism. In his last years he became a depressive and a religious maniac.

Goiânia 16 43S 49 18W A city in central Brazil, the capital of Goiás state on the Pan-American Highway. Founded in 1933 to replace the old capital, it serves a cattle-raising and coffee-growing area and has two universities. Population (1980 est): 703 263.

Goidelic languages. *See* Celtic languages.

goitre Swelling in the neck caused by enlargement of the thyroid gland. A goitre is called simple if the thyroid is functioning normally; this occurs in areas where iodine is deficient in the water supply and it may occur sporadically in adolescent girls. A goitre may also be seen when the thyroid is overactive (*see* hyperthyroidism) or underactive (*see* cretinism; myxoedema).

Golan Heights A range of hills in SW Syria, under Israeli administration. They are of great strategic importance; Syrian artillery positioned here was able to fire into the upper Jordan and Hula Valleys in Israel. Israeli forces stormed the heights in June, 1967, when most of the local populace fled; Jewish settlements have since been established.

Golconda 17 24N 78 23E A ruined city in S India, in Andhra Pradesh near Hyderabad city. The impressive tombs of the Qutb Shahi dynasty and the fortress, built on a granite ridge, stand as reminders of the city's former status as capital of one of the five Islamic kingdoms of the Deccan (1518–1687).

gold (Au) A soft dense yellow metal known and valued since ancient times. It occurs in nature as the element and in compounds with tellurium, in rock veins and alluvial deposits. The metal is the most malleable and ductile known. It alloys with other metals, is a good conductor of heat and electricity, and is chemically unreactive. The major uses for the element are for jewellery (*see* Plate III), electrical contacts, and as a currency standard (*see* gold standard). Gold dissolves in aqua regia (a mixture of one-third nitric acid and two-thirds hydrochloric acid) and the most common compound is the chloride ($AuCl_3$). Purity is measured in *carats. At no 79; at wt 196.967; mp 1064.43°C; bp 2966°C.

Gold, Thomas (1920–) Austrian-born astronomer, who spent 20 years in England (at Cambridge University) before emigrating to the USA in 1956 and becoming a professor at Cornell University. With *Bondi and *Hoyle he proposed the *steady-state theory of the universe. He is also known for describing (1948) pulsars as spinning neutron stars.

Gold Coast The name applied by Europeans to the coastal

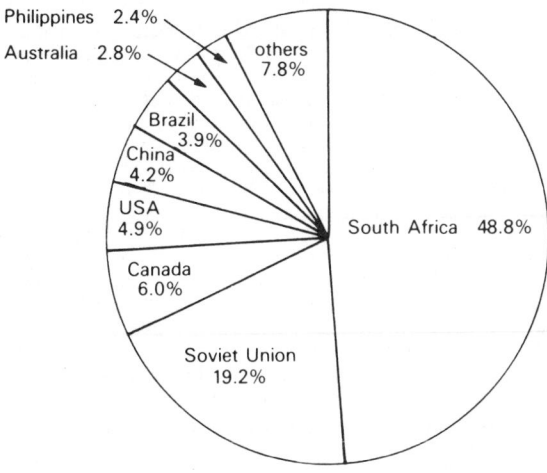

Philippines 2.4%
Australia 2.8%
others 7.8%
Brazil 3.9%
China 4.2%
USA 4.9%
Canada 6.0%
South Africa 48.8%
Soviet Union 19.2%

GOLD *World production (1984).*

zone in West Africa between Axim and the River Volta on the Gulf of Guinea. An important source of gold, it came under British control in the 19th century as part of the British colony of Gold Coast (present-day Ghana).

Gold Coast, City of 27 58S 153 20E A resort city of Australia, on the coast of Queensland. It stretches 32 km (20 mi) S of Brisbane, from Southport, the administrative centre, to the New South Wales border. Population (1980 est): 112 900.

goldcrest A tiny agile songbird, *Regulus regulus*, occurring chiefly in coniferous woodland of N Europe and Asia and feeding on insects and spiders. It is about 9 cm long and has a yellow-green plumage with white wing stripes and an orange crest, brighter in the male than the female. Family: *Muscicapidae* (Old World *flycatchers).

Golden Age, Latin The period (70 BC–18 AD) during which some of the highest achievements of Latin literature were produced. The first part of the period (70–43 BC) was dominated by *Cicero. The major writers of the subsequent Augustan age (43 BC–18 AD) include *Virgil, *Horace, *Livy, and *Ovid.

Golden Bull of 1222 A charter of liberties granted by Andrew II of Hungary (1175–1235) that curbed monarchical powers and confirmed the rights of the nobility. The nobles gained important concessions on military service, taxation, and the administration of justice. They had the right to resist if the king violated the Charter's articles.

golden calf An idol made by Aaron for the Israelites to worship when they believed that Moses would not return from Mt Sinai, where he was receiving the tables of the Law (Exodus 32). Moses destroyed the idol upon his return. A similar idol was made by King Jeroboam I (937–915 BC) and set up at Bethel and Dan (I Kings 12.28).

golden cat A small *cat of SE Asia and Sumatra, *Felis temmincki*, also called Temminck's cat. It is about 125 cm long, with a plain golden coat and strikingly marked head; it lives among rocks preying on rodents and ground-dwelling birds. The closely related African golden cat (*aurata*) is found on the fringes of forests in West Africa.

golden chain (*or* golden rain). *See* laburnum.

golden eagle A large dark-brown *eagle, *Aquila chrysaetos*, occurring in mountainous regions of North America and Eurasia. It is 70–85 cm long and has golden neck feathers, a grey beak, fully feathered legs, large yellow feet, and powerful talons. Golden eagles have a wingspan of up to 230 cm and catch small mammals, rabbits, and gamebirds.

goldeneye A *diving duck, *Bucephala clangula*, that breeds in forested areas of N Eurasia and winters in more southerly regions. It is 41–45 cm long and males are black and white with a greenish head and a circular white patch on the cheek; females are grey with white markings and a brown head.

Golden Fleece The fleece of a sacred winged ram, the recovery of which was the goal of *Jason and the *Argonauts. Athamas, King of Thebes, had two sons, Phrixus and Helle, by his first wife Nephele. His second wife, Ino, hated her stepsons and plotted their death. They escaped across the sea on the golden ram and, having reached Colchis, sacrificed the ram to Zeus and hung the fleece in a grove sacred to Ares, where it was guarded by a dragon.

Golden Fleece, Order of the A chivalric order founded by *Philip the Good, Duke of Burgundy, in 1430, taking as its badge the fleece captured by Jason in Greek mythology. When Burgundy was united to the Habsburg empire (1477) the Order became increasingly aristocratic and was eventually confined to Austria and Spain.

Golden Gate bridge A suspension bridge for road traffic over the Golden Gate strait near San Francisco (USA). Completed in 1937, its total length of 1280 m (4200 ft) made it the longest bridge in the world until the completion of the Verrazano-Narrows bridge (1964) across New York Harbor.

Golden Horde The western part of the Mongol Empire following its fragmentation on the death (1227) of *Genghis Khan. The Horde, which adopted Islam, controlled all of Russia between the Urals and the River Danube until defeated by the Turk, *Timur, in the late 14th century.

Golden Horn (Turkish name: Haliç) An inlet of the Bosporus in NW Turkey, on the N side of the peninsula upon which the old quarter of Istanbul stands. It is 7 km (4.5 mi) long and serves as the city's harbour.

golden mole A burrowing insect-eating mammal belonging to the African family *Chryochloridae* (15 species). 7–23 cm long, they are stout-bodied, blind, and almost tailless, with two of the four digits on each forefoot greatly enlarged. Their fur is an iridescent golden-brown. Order *Insectivora.

golden pheasant A small *pheasant, *Chrysolophus pictus*, native to mountainous regions of E Asia but widespread as an ornamental bird. Its plumage is gold, scarlet, black, and green and the male has a large ruff of broad feathers.

goldenrain tree. *See* lacquer tree.

golden retriever A large strongly built breed of □dog whose ancestors possibly included labradors, setters, and spaniels. The dense water-resistant wavy coat is gold or cream and these dogs are strong swimmers. They are used as gun dogs, guide dogs, and police dogs. Height: 56–61 cm (dogs); 51–56 cm (bitches).

goldenrod A perennial herb of the genus *Solidago* (about 120 species), up to 2.5 m tall and mostly native to North America. The stem bears one-sided cylindrical heads of small yellow flowers, forming a branching plumelike inflorescence. Canadian goldenrod (*S. canadensis*) is often grown as a garden ornamental. Family: *Compositae.

goldfinch A Eurasian *finch, *Carduelis carduelis*, once popular as a cagebird. About 12 cm long, it has a brown back, black wings with a broad yellow stripe, black-and-white tail and head, and a red face. It uses its pointed bill to extract seeds from thistles and dandelions and flocks of goldfinches (called charms) are commonly seen on farmland.

goldfish A freshwater fish, *Carassius auratus*, also called golden carp, of E Asian origin but introduced elsewhere as an ornamental fish. In its natural state it is greenish brown or grey and up to 30 cm long. However, the breeding of abnormal specimens, originally in China and Japan, has produced over 125 varieties, such as the "pop eye," "veiltail," and "lionhead," often with a characteristic red-gold coloration. The goldfish requires cold well-oxygenated water and is omnivorous.

Golding, William (1911–   ) British novelist. He served in the Royal Navy and became a schoolteacher. His best-known novel, *Lord of the Flies* (1954), concerns a group of schoolboys who are isolated on a desert island and revert to savagery. His other novels include *Pincher Martin* (1956), *The Spire* (1964), *Darkness Visible* (1979), *Rites of Passage* (1980), which won the 1980 Booker prize, *A Moving Target* (1982), *The Paper Men* (1984), and *Close Quarters* (1987). His *An Egyptian Journal* was published in 1985. He won the Nobel Prize in 1983.

Goldoni, Carlo (1707–93) Italian comic playwright. A prolific writer of over 250 plays, he revolutionized the rigid conventions of the *commedia dell'arte with his realistic characters and witty dialogue. His plays include *The Liar* (1759), *Mine Hostess* (1753), and *The Fan* (1764). In 1762 he went to Paris, where he wrote his *Mémoires* (1787) and was from 1769 tutor to the daughters of Louis XV.

Gold Rush The transcontinental journey of eastern profiteers after the discovery of gold in California (1848). Those (some 80 000) who arrived in the first year were called forty-niners. Harsh living conditions and the violent life of the gold fields took many lives and only a few made fortunes. There were gold rushes in Australia, South Africa, and the Klondike, Canada, in the next half century.

Goldschmidt, Richard Benedict (1878–1958) US geneticist. His view of the chromosome as a large-chain molecule led to advances in genetic research. He demonstrated that differences between races were genetically determined and showed how drastic changes in environmental factors could cause changes in the external appearance of fruit flies.

Goldschmidt process The reduction of a metal oxide to the metal by reacting it with aluminium to form aluminium oxide and metal. The process, which produces a great deal of heat, is used to extract chromium from chromium ore. Named after Hans Goldschmidt (1861–1923).

Goldsmith, Oliver (1730–74) Anglo-Irish writer. Born in Ireland, he was sent to study medicine in Edinburgh and arrived penniless in London in 1756. A friend of Johnson and Boswell, he was inarticulate in conversation and a compulsive gambler. His best-known works are the poem *The Deserted Village* (1770), the novel *The Vicar of Wakefield* (1776), and the play *She Stoops to Conquer* (1773).

gold standard A monetary system in which paper money was convertible on demand into gold. Banknotes were issued fractionally backed by gold (i.e. gold reserves were a fixed proportion of the value of the notes in circulation). Rates of exchange between countries were fixed by their currency values in gold. In classical economics imbalances in international trade were rectified automatically by the gold standard. A country in deficit would have depleted gold reserves and would therefore have to reduce its money supply. The resulting fall in demand would reduce imports and the lowering of prices would boost exports; thus the deficit would be rectified. Most financially important countries were on the gold standard from 1900 until its suspension during World War I because of the problems of transporting gold. It was reintroduced in 1925 but finally abandoned in 1931. *See also* International Monetary Fund.

Goldwyn, Samuel (S. Goldfish; 1882–1974) US film producer, born in Poland. In 1916 he cofounded Goldwyn Pictures, a production company that merged with other concerns to become Metro-Goldwyn-Mayer (MGM) in 1924. His many successful films as an independent producer include *Wuthering Heights* (1939) and *Guys and Dolls* (1955).

golem In medieval Jewish folklore, an image or automaton that can be brought to life by a charm. They were supposed to have been used as servants by rabbis. The word originally referred to anything incomplete or embryonic.

golf A club-and-ball game for two or four players played on a golf course. It was well established in Britain by the 15th century and almost certainly originated in Scotland. A standard course is usually between 4572 m (5000 yd) and 6400 m (7000 yd) and is divided into 18 holes (9 on a small course), each of which is between 90 m (100 yd) and 540 m (600 yd) long. A "hole" comprises the flat starting point, called the "tee," a strip of mown grass about 27–90 m (30–100 yd) wide, called the "fairway," and a smooth putting green. On the green is the actual hole, which has a diameter of 10.8 cm (4.25 in). There are also obstacles around the course, such as trees, ditches, and sand bunkers. The object of the game is to hit the ball from each tee into each hole with as few strokes as possible ("par" for a hole is the standard number of strokes needed by a first-class player; one stroke less than par is called a "birdie," and an "eagle" is two strokes less). To achieve this a player has a set of clubs of which there are three basic types: woods, irons, and putters. The rubber-cored ball must not be less than 41.15 mm (1.62 in) in diameter or weigh more than 45.93 g (1.62 oz).

Golgi, Camillo (1843–1926) Italian cell biologist, whose staining technique using silver nitrate revealed fine details of cells. Golgi distinguished different types of nerve cells in the brain (Golgi cells) and demonstrated a network of tubules and granules within cells (the *Golgi apparatus). He shared the 1906 Nobel Prize with *Ramon y Cajal.

Golgi apparatus (*or* Golgi complex) A structure present in the cytoplasm of nearly all cells, composed of stacks of flattened sacs bounded by membranes and associated with vesicles. Discovered by Camillo *Golgi, it is thought to function in the synthesis and concentration of certain materials, especially secretory products, which are then packaged into the vesicles and transported within the cell.

Golgotha. *See* Calvary.

goliards Wandering scholars (often students or lesser clerics) of medieval Europe who were notorious for their scurrilous verses. Frequently condemned by the Church for their poetry and riotous behaviour, by the 14th century the term had lost its earlier connotations, being applied to all minstrels. The largest collection of goliard poetry was published as the *Carmina Burana* in the 19th century.

goliath beetle A large beetle belonging to the group of flower *chafers. The African goliath beetle (*Goliathus giganteus*) has the largest body of all the insects, measuring about 96 mm in length. It is white with black stripes and brown wing cases. The larvae are found in rotten logs.

goliath frog The largest known living frog, *Rana goliath*, which grows up to 35 cm long. This rare shy frog inhabits deep river pools in Africa. Its bones are supposed to have magical properties.

Gollancz, Victor (1893–1967) British publisher and writer. In 1928 Gollancz founded his publishing company in Henrietta Street, London. During the 1930s he campaigned vigorously against fascism, setting up the Left Book Club, and in 1951 he founded the charity War on Want.

Golovkin, Gavril Ivanovich, Count (1660–1734) Russian statesman. A relative of *Peter the Great, he accompanied the tsar on his early visits to western Europe. In 1706 he became foreign minister and in 1709, state chancellor. In the reign (1725–27) of Catherine I (?1684–1727), he became a member of the supreme privy council. In the 1730 accession crisis, he supported *Anna Ivanovna.

Gomel 52 25N 31 00E A port in the W Soviet Union, in the Belorussian SSR on the River Sozh. It is an important railway junction and industrial centre, producing fertilizers, machinery, timber products, foodstuffs, and textiles. Population (1981 est): 405 000.

Gómez, Juan Vicente (1857–1935) Venezuelan soldier and statesman, who was brought to power in 1908 by a military coup. Elected president in 1910, he governed, either directly or through puppets, until his death. He did much to modernize Venezuela, simultaneously accumulating a vast

GOLF *Irons are numbered according to the angle of the face; the greater the angle of inclination, the higher the ball is hit into the air. Thus a good player, under normal conditions, knows the range of each iron. The Number One wood (driver) is used from the tee for the maximum distance and the putter is used on the green.*

personal fortune. His power base was in the army and he brutally suppressed all opposition to his regime.

Gomułka, Władysław (1905-82) Polish statesman. Gomułka was secretary general of the Polish Workers' Party from 1945 until 1948, when his criticism of the Soviet Union led to his demotion and imprisonment (1951-54). Following the *Poznan Riots, which gave Poland more independence from the Soviet Union, Gomułka became first secretary of the Party. In 1970 he resigned after demonstrations over price increases.

gomuti A *palm tree, *Arenga pinnata* (or *A. saccharifera*), also called sugar palm, occurring in SE Asia. The sap yields palm sugar and the fermented juice (palm wine) is distilled to produce arrack. A form of sago is obtained from the pith and the leaf fibres are used to make cord, ropes, etc.

gonad. *See* ovary; testis.

gonadotrophin One of several hormones that control the activity of the testes and ovaries (the gonads) in mammals. The pituitary gland, under the influence of the hypothalamus, produces three gonadotrophins: luteinizing hormone (LH), which stimulates ovulation and *oestrogen production by the ovaries and the production of *androgens by the testes; follicle-stimulating hormone (FSH), which promotes ovulation and sperm production; and *prolactin, which triggers lactation. LH and FSH are glycoproteins and are usually released together. Human chorionic gonadotrophin (HCG) is produced by the placenta, reaching a peak level in the urine in early pregnancy. Measurement of urinary HCG is the basis of pregnancy tests. Gonadotrophins are also used in *fertility drugs.

Gonaïves 12 29N 72 42W A port in W Haiti, on the Gulf of Gonaïves. Exports include coffee, bananas, and mangoes. Population (1982 est): 34 209.

Goncharov, Ivan Aleksandrovich (1812-91) Russian novelist. Apart from a voyage to Japan (1852-55), he led an uneventful life as a civil servant. The conflict between traditionalism and pragmatism is a recurrent theme of his work, most notably of *Oblomov* (1859), in which the inactive aristocratic hero loses his beloved to his more prosaic, practical friend, and sinks deeper into absurd idleness.

Goncourt, Edmond de (1822-96) French writer, who collaborated with his brother **Jules de Goncourt** (1830-70) on art criticism, social histories of France, and a series of carefully researched naturalistic novels, most notably *Germinie Lacerteux* (1864) and *Madame Gervaisais* (1869). They are best known for their *Journal*, a lively record of French literary life from 1851 to 1895, and for Edmond's legacy, the Académie Goncourt, which awards France's most prestigious annual literary prize, the Prix Goncourt.

Gondar 12 40N 37 45E A town in central Ethiopia. A former capital of Ethiopia, Gondar was built after the Portuguese Jesuits had been expelled in the 16th century and is now a tourist attraction. Population (1980): 76 932.

Gondomar, Diego Sarmiento de Acuña, Conde de (1567-1626) Spanish diplomat. He twice served as ambassador to England (1613-18, 1619-22), becoming a close friend of James I. He encouraged the proposed marriage between the Prince of Wales and the Spanish princess, thereby contributing to James' poor relations with parliament.

Gondwanaland The supercontinent in the S hemisphere believed to have existed prior to 200 million years ago, when the drift of the continents to their present positions began. It probably consisted of South America, Africa, Australia, Antarctica, Arabia, and India. *See also* Laurasia.

gong A percussion instrument of indefinite pitch. The orchestral gong (*or* tam-tam) is a disc of metal about 1 m (3 ft) in diameter with a turned-over edge, hanging in a wooden frame.

gong chimes A set of gongs tuned to different pitches, used in many countries of the Far East. The instrument exists in a number of forms, the most elaborate of which, found in Burma and Thailand, consists of 15-20 small gongs set in a circular wooden frame. The player kneels inside the frame and plays the gongs with hammers. □musical instruments.

Góngora y Argote, Luis de (1561-1627) Spanish poet. Son of a judge, he was court chaplain in Madrid from 1617. He wrote many conventional sonnets and satirical verses but is best known for his longer works, *Polifemo* (1612) and *Soledades* (1613), in which he used esoteric allusions and elaborate diction and syntax to create a deliberately obscure and artificial style.

gonorrhoea An acute venereal infection caused by a bacterium (the gonococcus). It is now one of the commonest infections in developed societies. Symptoms in men are discharge from the penis and a burning pain on passing urine. Women may have vaginal discharge and pain on urinating, but half have no symptoms at all. Gonorrhoea can be treated with penicillin.

Gonzaga   An Italian dynasty that ruled Mantua (1328–1707) and Montferrato and Casale (1536–1707). The family was established in Mantua by **Luigi Gonzaga** (c. 1268–1360). His distinguished successors included **Gianfrancesco Gonzaga** (?1394–1444), a soldier and patron of learning under whom *Vittorino da Feltre established a famous school at Mantua, and **Francesco Gonzaga** (1466–1519), who commanded Italian forces against the French invasion in 1494 and was the husband of the distinguished patron of arts Isabella d'Este (*see* Este).

González de Mendoza, Pedro   (1428–95) Spanish churchman; cardinal, Archbishop of Toledo, and Primate of Spain (from 1482). He was the most powerful supporter of Isabella in her successful claim to the Spanish throne and in her subsequent attempts to strengthen the monarchy. He took part in the conquest of Granada.

Good Friday   The Friday before *Easter, when Christ's crucifixion is commemorated. It is a fast day, and in the Roman Catholic Church the Mass is not celebrated. In the Anglican Church Holy Communion is rarely held, although provided for in the Book of *Common Prayer.

Good Hope, Cape of.   *See* Cape of Good Hope.

Goodman, Benny   (Benjamin David G.; 1909–   ) US clarinettist, prominent in the development of *swing. A versatile player, he led big bands and played in small jazz groups from the 1930s to the 1950s. Also active in classical music, Bartok and Copland wrote works for him.

Good Neighbor Policy   A US policy between World Wars I and II intended to allay Latin American fears of US domination. Initiated by President F. D. Roosevelt in 1933, its measures included the withdrawal of troops, the lifting of trade barriers, and the preparation of common defences.

Goodwin Sands   A range of dangerous sandbanks off the SE coast of England, in the Strait of Dover. At low tide large areas of sand are exposed; the sands shelter the Downs roadstead but are a hazard to shipping.

Goodyear, Charles   (1800–60) US inventor of a method of treating rubber with sulphur at a high temperature to make it strong and elastic (the *vulcanization process). Patented in 1844, his process led to the development of the rubber-manufacturing industry.

Goolagong, Evonne.   *See* Cawley, Evonne.

Goole   53 42N 0 52W An important port in E England, in Humberside at the confluence of the Rivers Ouse and Don. Its industries include flour milling, boatbuilding, chemicals, and machinery. Population (1981): 17 127.

goosander   A large migratory *duck, *Mergus merganser*, that breeds in North America and N Eurasia, also called sawbill because of its long toothed bill. The male is 75 cm long and has a green head, black back, and white body; females are 57 cm long and have a chestnut head and grey body. Goosanders feed chiefly on fish.

goose   A large long-necked waterbird belonging to the family *Anatidae* (ducks, geese, and swans), occurring in the N hemisphere. Geese have short bills, humped at the base and tapering towards the tip, and short webbed feet. They chiefly feed inland on grass, grain, roots, etc., and are highly migratory, flying in characteristic V-formations and honking loudly in flight. The several breeds of domesticated goose are probably descended from the *greylag goose. Genera: *Anser* (grey geese), *Branta* (black geese); order: *Anseriformes*. *See also* barnacle goose; brent goose; Canada goose; Hawaiian goose.

gooseberry   A fruit bush of the genus *Ribes*, especially *R. uva-crispa* (or *R. grossularia*), which is widely cultivated in the Old World for its hairy prickly-coated berries used for preserves, wine, and in desserts. The bush, 1–1.5 m high, may be upright, spreading, or drooping, with three-lobed toothed

leaves and spiny stems. The small greenish flowers arise in the axils of the leaves. Family: *Grossulariaceae*.

goosefish.   *See* anglerfish.

goosefoot   A herb or small shrub of the genus *Chenopodium* (110 species), of temperate regions, also called pigweed. The stem, 15–1500 cm high, is grooved or angular and the leaves are often fleshy. The whole plant may have a whitish mealy appearance. The small greenish flowers are borne on a branched inflorescence. Family: *Chenopodiaceae*.

goosegrass.   *See* cleavers.

Goossens, Sir Eugene   (1893–1962) British conductor and composer of Belgian descent. He was well known for his performances of modern music and wrote an oboe concerto for his brother **Leon Goossens** (1896–1988), who was principal oboist in several leading British orchestras. He was also a prominent soloist and a noted teacher. Vaughan Williams wrote an oboe concerto for him.

gopher.   *See* pocket gopher; souslik.

Gorakhpur   26 45N 83 23E A city in N India, in Uttah Pradesh. It served as an army recruitment centre for Gurkhas while under British rule. The main industries are sugar refining and fertilizer production and it has a university (1956). Population (1981): 306 000.

goral   A small hoofed mammal, *Naemorhedus goral*, of mountainous regions in S Asia. About 65 cm high at the shoulder, gorals have short horns and a woolly coat, which varies from grey to foxy red. They graze in small herds at dawn and dusk. Family: *Bovidae*. *See also* serow.

Gorbachov, Mikhail Sergeevich   (1931–   ) Soviet statesman and general secretary of the Soviet Communist Party (1985–   ). Born in the Stavropol region into a peasant family, he studied law at Moscow university before entering politics. He progressed from first secretary of the Party in Stavropol to Central Committee Secretary for Agriculture before becoming a member of the Politburo in 1980. He has responded to outside pressures on human rights by relaxing some repressive measures (*see* glasnost). In 1987 he broke new ground when he signed a major arms limitation treaty with President Reagan (*see* disarmament).

Gorbals   A district of Glasgow, Scotland, notorious for its 19th-century slum tenements, which are now being cleared and redeveloped with buildings designed by Sir Basil Spence.

Gordian knot   A knot binding the yoke and beam of the chariot of Gordius, a legendary king of Phrygia. The knot was extremely complex. According to legend, whoever could unloose the knot would become the ruler of Asia. In 333 BC Alexander the Great is said to have cut the knot with his sword and so laid claim to Asia.

Gordon, Charles George   (1833–85) British general. Gordon served in the Crimean War and then in China, where he earned the nickname Chinese Gordon after suppressing the *Taiping Rebellion (1864). In 1874 he was employed by the Khedive of Egypt to open up the country and from 1877 to 1880 was British governor of the Sudan. In 1884 he was sent back to the Sudan to evacuate Europeans and Egyptians, following al *Mahdi's revolt. Gordon was besieged for ten months in Khartoum, which was taken two days before a relief force arrived. Gordon himself was murdered.

Gordon Riots   (1780) Anti-Roman Catholic riots in London fomented by Lord George Gordon (1751–93), who opposed the Roman Catholic Relief Act (1778). The riots were crushed; Gordon was arrested but acquitted of treason.

Gorgon   In Greek legend, an underworld monster. Hesiod refers to three Gorgons, the sisters Stheno, Euryale, and *Medusa. They were usually portrayed as winged females with snakes for hair and boars' tusks for teeth.

Gorgonzola   45 32N 9 23E A town in N Italy, in Lombardy, famous for Gorgonzola cheese. Population (1981 est): 14 571.

gorilla   The largest living *ape, *Gorilla gorilla*, of tropical

African forests. Male gorillas can grow to 1.8 m with a weight of 300 kg. They walk on their feet and knuckles, feeding on plant stems and also climbing to reach fruit. Troops are led by a dominant adult male and are generally not aggressive, preferring retreat to attack, although they will fight when cornered. Three races are recognized: the rare shaggy mountain gorilla and two lowland forms—light-coloured in the west and black in the east.

Göring, Hermann Wilhelm (1893-1946) German Nazi politician. He served in the air force in World War I and became a Nazi in 1922, taking command of Hitler's Brownshirts. He was elected to the Reichstag in 1928 and became its president in 1932. When Hitler came to power in 1933, Göring was appointed air minister of Germany and prime minister of Prussia. He established the *Gestapo and *concentration camps and probably engineered the Reichstag fire (1933). He directed the development of the Luftwaffe and in 1936 was given charge of mobilizing the economy for war. Hitler declared Göring his successor in 1939 but expelled him from the party shortly before the Nazi collapse. "When I hear the word culture I reach for my gun" was an appropriate epigram for a Nazi who looted occupied Europe for some £20 million worth of art treasures. Condemned to hang at Nuremberg, he committed suicide before the execution could take place.

Gorizia (German name: Görz; Serbo-Croat name: Gorica) 45 57N 13 37E A town in Italy, in Friuli-Venezia Giulia on the Yugoslav border. It was a noted cultural centre under Habsburg rule. Industries include tourism, textiles, and machinery. Population (1981 est): 42 955.

Gorki, Maksim (Aleksei Maksimovich Peshkov; 1868-1936) Russian novelist. His hard nomadic early life is recounted in his autobiographical trilogy *Childhood* (1913-14), *In the World* (1915-16), and *My Universities* (1923). He established his literary reputation with romantic short stories and followed these with several novels and plays, including *Mother* (1906) and *The Lower Depths* (1906). He lived in exile in Italy from 1906 to 1913 and again from 1921 to 1928. He then returned to Russia, becoming first president of the Soviet Writers Union and an exponent of Stalinism.

Gorkii (Gorki *or* Gorky; name until 1932: Nizhnii Novgorod) 56 20N 44 00E A city in the central Soviet Union, in the RSFSR on the Rivers Oka and Volga. It is one of the country's most important industrial cities, whose manufactures include machinery, chemicals, and textiles. Gorkii's trade fair was the most important in Russia until it was discontinued in 1917. The city was renamed in 1932 in honour of the writer Maksim Gorki. Population (1981 est): 1 367 000.

Gorky, Arshile (Vosdanig Adoian; 1905-48) US painter, born in Armenia, who emigrated to the USA in 1920. He worked in most 20th-century styles before adopting, in about 1940, an individual and abstract form of *surrealism. Such works as *The Liver Is the Cock's Comb* (1944; New York) anticipate *action painting in their free application of paint. His promising career was cut short by his suicide.

Görlitz 51 11N 15 0E A town in SE East Germany, on the *Neisse River where it marks the boundary with Poland. Famous since the middle ages for clothmaking, its many industries also include vehicle and machinery manufacture and lignite mining. Population (1983): 80 492.

Gorlovka 48 17N 38 05E A city in the SW Soviet Union, in the Ukrainian SSR in the *Donets Basin. It is one of the largest coalmining and industrial centres of the area. Population (1981 est): 338 000.

Gorno-Altai An autonomous region (*oblast*) in the S Soviet Union, in the RSFSR. Formed in 1922 for the Turkic-speaking Altaian peoples, it is now inhabited mostly by Russians. Gold and mercury are mined and livestock breeding is the main agricultural activity. Area: 92 600 sq km

(35 740 sq mi). Population (1980 est): 173 000. Capital: Gorno-Altaisk.

Gorno-Badakhshan An autonomous region (*oblast*) in the S Soviet Union, in the Tadzhik SSR. It was formed in 1925 and its population consists mainly of *Tadzhiks. Chiefly agricultural, it produces wheat, fruit, and fodder crops; cattle and sheep are bred. Area: 63 700 sq km (24 590 sq mi). Population (1983): 140 000. Capital: Khorog.

gorse (*or* furze) A very spiny densely branched shrub, *Ulex europaeus*, up to 4 m high, with bright-yellow sweet-scented flowers. The leaves, which consist of three leaflets, are reduced to spines or scales on mature plants. The fruit is a black hairy pod that splits open explosively to release the seeds. Gorse is native to grassy areas and heaths throughout Europe and has been introduced elsewhere. Family: *Leguminosae*.

Gorton, Sir John Grey (1911-) Australian statesman; Liberal prime minister (1968-71). His administration was responsible for greater federal government intervention in the field of education, and he fostered Australia's involvement in the Vietnam War. In 1971 he lost a vote of no confidence and resigned.

goshawk A large powerful *hawk, *Accipiter gentilis*, ranging throughout forests of the N hemisphere and formerly used in falconry. It is 60 cm long with a wingspan of 130 cm and a finely barred grey plumage. It feeds chiefly on birds.

Goslar 51 57N 10 28E A city in NE West Germany, in Lower Saxony. An imperial residence in the middle ages, the palace remains. Silver has been mined here since the 10th century. Population (1983 est): 52 104.

Gospels (Old English: good news) The four New Testament accounts of Christ's life, ascribed to *Matthew, *Mark, *Luke, and *John. The word originally referred to the message of Christ's redemptive work rather than to the writings. The first three are known as the Synoptic Gospels, since they report approximately the same synopsis of the events. According to some biblical scholars Mark is the oldest of these and was used as a source by the authors of Matthew and Luke. Material that is not found in Mark but is common to Matthew and Luke is believed to derive from a single lost source, known as Q. The fourth Gospel, John, emphasizes the divinity of Christ and may presuppose a knowledge of the Synoptic Gospels.

Gosport 50 48N 1 08W A port in S England, in Hampshire on Portsmouth Harbour. It is a naval base, linked with Portsmouth by ferry, and has yacht-building and marine-engineering industries. Population (1981): 77 276.

Gossaert, Jan (c. 1478-c. 1532) Flemish painter, whose popular surname, Mabuse, derives from his birthplace Maubeuge. As one of the first Flemish artists to work in the Italian Renaissance style, after visiting Italy (1508) he painted sculptural nudes against Italian architectural backgrounds, e.g. *Neptune and Amphitrite* (Berlin). As a portraitist he was noted for his expressive treatment of hands.

Gosse, Sir Edmund (1849-1928) British critic. His autobiographical *Father and Son* (1907) recounts his painful self-emancipation from his dominating Victorian father. He translated plays by Ibsen, and his many critical books include studies of French literature and biographies of Donne (1899) and Ibsen (1908).

Göta Canal A canal in S Sweden, linking Göteborg on the Kattegat in the W with Stockholm in the E. Opened in 1832, it enters the Baltic Sea near Söderköping. Length: 93 km (58 mi).

Göteborg (English name: Gothenburg) 57 45N 12 00E An important ice-free port in SW Sweden, at the mouth of the River Göta. Sweden's second largest city, it expanded through Napoleon's Continental System and with the opening of the Göta Canal (1832). Notable buildings include the town hall (1750), cathedral (1633), and university (1891). Industries include shipbuilding, oil refining, and the manufacture of cars. Population (1983): 424 186.

Gotha 50 56N 10 42E A town in SW East Germany, on the N edge of the Thuringian Forest, former capital of the duchy of Saxe-Coburg-Gotha. It is noted for the *Almanac de Gotha* (an annual record of the royal and noble houses of Europe, published here from 1764 to 1944). Gotha manufactures machinery, vehicles, textiles, and chemicals. Population (1983): 57 876.

Gothenburg. *See* Göteborg.

Early English   Decorated

Perpendicular

GOTHIC ART AND ARCHITECTURE *In England the three phases of gothic architecture are characterized by distinctive window designs.*

gothic art and architecture The styles flourishing in Europe from the mid-12th to the end of the 15th centuries. "Gothic" originated as a derisory term used by Renaissance artists, who blamed the destruction of classical art on the Goths who invaded the Roman Empire. The gothic is most closely associated with church architecture, the hallmarks of gothic design being the rib and shaft ceiling, the pointed arch, the flying buttress, and later great height and the impression of weightlessness. Gothic architecture was initiated in France in the chevet of the Abbey of Saint-Denis, near Paris. It was followed by the cathedrals of *Notre-Dame (begun 1163), Chartres (begun c. 1194), Reims (begun 1211), etc. (*see also* Flamboyant). In England it has been subdivided into three phases named by the architect and antiquarian Thomas Rickman (1776-1841) as *Early English (c. 1200-c. 1300; e.g. Lincoln Cathedral),

*Decorated (c. 1300-70; e.g. Exeter Cathedral), and *Perpendicular (c. 1370-1540; e.g. Winchester Cathedral). Although used during the *romanesque period, *stained glass was only fully developed in the gothic period, being characterized by elaborate tracery, brilliant colours, and the reduction of stonework between the windows to very thin stone bars. Gothic sculpture mirrored the development of the architecture it adorned, renouncing its early naturalism for a stylized elegance and an emphasis on line and silhouette. In painting, the early gothic manifested itself chiefly in manuscript illumination. In the 14th century elements of it appear in the art of Simone *Martini, Rogier van der *Weyden, and others, but its full flowering in panel and manuscript painting came with the *international gothic style of the early 15th century. The gothic was revived in the 19th century by the Victorians, who considered it a perfect embodiment of religious intensity (*see* gothic revival).

gothic novel An English genre, popular in the late 18th and early 19th centuries, characterized by a prevailing atmosphere of mystery and terror and pseudomedieval—"gothic"—settings. Examples include Horace Walpole's *Castle of Otranto* (1765), Ann Radcliffe's *The Mysteries of Udolpho* (1794), and Matthew Gregory Lewis' *The Monk* (1796). The genre wilted under parodies, such as Jane Austen's *Northanger Abbey* (1818), but influenced later writers, among them the Brontë sisters, Poe, and Bram Stoker, in *Dracula* (1897).

gothic revival An architectural style. Initially associated with *Romanticism, the revived popularity for *gothic architecture began in England in the late 18th century, with such buildings as *Fonthill Abbey. Common throughout W Europe and the USA, it was particularly dominant in Britain after 1818, when parliament voted £1 million to be spent on building 214 new Anglican churches. Of these over 170 were built in the gothic style. The culmination of the gothic revival was perhaps the new Houses of Parliament (1834-45) built by Charles *Barry and *Pugin. Other leaders of the revival were George Gilbert *Scott, *Ruskin, *Butterfield, and *Waterhouse. One of the last important gothic-revival buildings in London was the Law Courts (1882) by G. E. Street (1824-81).

Goths Germanic peoples who originated in Scandinavia (Gotland) and had moved into the Ukraine by the end of the 2nd century AD. Shortly afterwards they invaded the Roman Empire N of the Danube and expanded into the Balkans. Converted to Arian Christianity (*see* Arianism) in the mid-4th century, their empire was soon destroyed by the *Huns and their two groups, the *Ostrogoths and *Visigoths, separated.

Gotland (Gothland *or* Gottland) The largest of the Swedish islands, in the Baltic Sea. Long disputed between Denmark and Sweden, it was finally ceded to Sweden in 1645. Its economy is based chiefly on agriculture (cattle and sheep raising) and tourism. Area: 3140 sq km (1225 sq mi). Population (1980 est): 55 346, including associated islands. Capital: Visby.

Gottfried von Strassburg (13th century) German poet. Nothing is known of his life apart from what can be inferred from the erudition and poetic skill of his epic *Tristan und Isolde*, a retelling of the original Celtic legend according to the conventions of courtly love. It inspired Wagner's famous opera.

Göttingen 51 32N 9 57E A city in E West Germany, in Lower Saxony. With its famous university, founded in 1734 by George II of Great Britain, and the Max Planck Association for the furtherance of science, it is a noted educational centre. Its manufactures include precision instruments and aluminium goods. Population (1980 est): 128 500.

Gottsched, Johann Christoph (1700-66) German critic, who introduced French classical and rationalist critical principles into German literature. His dramatic academy in Leipzig and his own plays, such as *Der sterbende Cato* (1732), and translations helped to raise the literary standards of German theatre.

gouache. *See* watercolour.

Gouda 52 01N 4 43E A town in the W Netherlands, in South Holland province. Its most notable church, the Grote Kerk (1552), has exceptional stained-glass windows (1556–1603). It is famous for its gouda cheese. Population (1984): 60 026.

Goujon, Jean (c. 1510–68) French Renaissance sculptor. His best-known works are the marble relief of the *Deposition* (Louvre) for St Germain l'Auxerrois, Paris, *The Tribune of the Caryatids* supporting a gallery in the Louvre, and reliefs of nymphs for the Fontaine des Innocents. The first two were produced in collaboration with the architect Pierre *Lescot.

Goulburn 34 47S 149 43E A city in Australia, in SE New South Wales. It is the commercial centre of an agricultural region. Population (1983): 22 400.

Gounod, Charles François (1818–93) French composer. A pupil of Halévy, he began serious composition after studying theology and deciding not to become a priest. His most successful works were the operas *Faust* (1852–59) and *Romeo and Juliet* (1864). Towards the end of his life he composed a large quantity of sacred music, including oratorios and masses.

gourami One of several freshwater tropical *labyrinth fishes, especially *Osphronemus goramy*. It has a brown or grey oval body, up to 60 cm long, and a filamentous ray extending from each pelvic fin. Native to the E Indies, it has been introduced elsewhere and cultivated for food.

gourd The fruit of certain plants of the family *Cucurbitaceae*, especially the white-flowered bottle gourd (*Lagenaria siceraria*), a trailing annual herb widely grown in the tropics. Its fruits have woody shells used locally as bottles, pipes, and utensils. Other gourds are grown as ornamentals, having attractive shapes, colours, and surface patterns. The dishcloth gourd (*see* loofah) is used as a bath sponge and the *snake gourd is grown for food.

gout Sudden attacks of arthritis caused by the presence of uric acid crystals in the joints. The big toe is most commonly affected, becoming hot, red, and very painful. Gout is commonest in older men and tends to recur; if not treated (by drugs to reduce the uric acid in the blood) it may lead to destruction of the joint. Gout is associated with an increased incidence of heart disease.

Government of India Acts The laws passed by the British parliament from 1773 to 1935 concerning the government of India prior to the establishment of independence (1947). The Acts of 1773, 1780, 1784, 1786, 1793, and 1830, known as the East India Company Acts, regulated the administration of India by the Company and vested supreme power in a government-appointed board of control. In 1833 the Company lost its monopoly of trade and gradually also lost its administrative functions (1833, 1853, 1858). The 1919 Act set up a central parliament in Delhi and provincial parliaments, which were strengthened by the 1935 Act to favour a federal form of government.

Govind Singh. *See* Gobind Singh.

Gower, David Ivon (1957–) British cricketer, who has played for Leicestershire and England (1978–). An excellent left-hand batsman, he has captained England since 1984.

Gower, John (c. 1330–1408) English poet. He was a friend of Chaucer and enjoyed the patronage of Henry IV. His works are moral allegories. They are *Miroir de l'homme* (1376–79), written in French; the Latin *Vox clamantis* (c. 1382), in which he attacks the government of Richard II; and his major work, the English *Confessio amantis* (1390), illustrating the virtues of Christian and courtly love.

Gower Peninsula A peninsula in South Wales, in West Glamorgan to the W of Swansea. Agriculture (especially dairy farming) and tourism are the principal economic activities. The National Trust owns some of the picturesque S coast as well as stretches of sand dunes in the W.

Gowon, Yakubu (1934–) Nigerian statesman; head of state (1966–76). An army officer, in the 1966 military coup he became chief of staff and then head of state. He was ousted in a bloodless coup in 1976 and now lives in England.

Goya (y Lucientes), Francisco (Jose) de (1746–1828) Spanish painter, born near Saragossa. After studying in Italy, he settled in Madrid (1775), where he painted gay scenes of Spanish life for the royal tapestry factory. As court painter from 1789 he produced realistic unflattering portraits of the royal family. He became deaf in 1792, and his works grew pessimistic and sometimes nightmarish, as in his etchings of *Los Caprichos* and *The Disasters of War*, condemning the French invasion of Spain. He settled in France in 1824. Among his best-known paintings are *Maja Clothed*, *The Shootings of 3 May 1808*, and the so-called black paintings, such as *Satan Devouring His Children* (all Prado).

Goyen, Jan Josephszoon van (1596–1656) Dutch landscape painter and etcher, who was born in Leiden but after 1630 lived in The Hague. His river and winter scenes were characterized by large expanses of sky and near-monochrome colours.

Gozzi, Carlo (1720–1806) Italian dramatist. He opposed the theatrical reforms of *Goldoni and attempted to revive the techniques of the *commedia dell'arte. His plays, often including elements of fantasy and the grotesque, include *Turandot* (1762), on which Puccini's opera is based, and *L'Augellin Belverde* (1764).

Gozzoli, Benozzo (Benozzo di Lese; 1420–97) Florentine painter. His major works are the frescoes of the *Journey of the Magi* (Palazzo Medici-Riccardi, Florence), which are noted for their detailed landscapes, and portraits of his contemporaries.

W. G. GRACE *Painting by an unknown artist (National Portrait Gallery; London).*

stock

scion

whip and tongue

scion

stock

saddle

GRAFTING *Two commonly used grafting methods. After stock and scion are fitted together they are held securely by tape, string, etc., and protected from desiccation by covering the point of union with wax or moist material.*

Graafian follicle. *See* ovary.

Gracchus, Tiberius Sempronius (163–133 BC) Roman reformer, who as tribune (133) proposed land reforms intended to create a class of small landowners. He was killed in a riot. His brother **Gaius Sempronius Gracchus** (153–121 BC) was tribune in 123 and renewed Tiberius' attempts at land reform. He was killed in riots over his proposal to grant Roman citizenship to Latins. The Gracchi's attempts at reform polarized the aristocracy into hostile factions and thereafter change was difficult to achieve without violence.

grace In Christian theology, God's freely offered forgiveness to his sinful creatures. The nature of divine grace and the conditions on which it is offered and accepted were central to the controversy between *Pelagius and St *Augustine, and between the Calvinists and their opponents at the Reformation. *See also* free will; predestination.

Grace, W(illiam) G(ilbert) (1848–1915) British cricketer, who captained Gloucestershire (1871–98), London County, and England in 13 Test matches. In his long career (1865–1908) he scored 54 896 runs, including 126 centuries, took 2876 wickets, and held 877 catches. No other cricketer has ever approached this achievement. □ p.519.

Graces In Greek mythology, the three daughters of Zeus and Hera, representing beauty, grace, and charm. They were named Aglaia, Euphrosyne, and Thalia.

grackle An omnivorous black bird of the North American genus *Quiscalus*. Grackles are about 30 cm long and have strong pointed bills used to dig for insect larvae, to kill small vertebrates, and to crack open nuts. They often feed in large flocks, causing damage to crops. Family: *Icteridae* (American orioles).

gradient A measure of the inclination of a slope, often expressed as the rise in height divided by the length of the slope, i.e. the sine of the angle of the slope. Mathematically, however, the gradient is the ratio of the vertical rise to the horizontal distance covered, i.e. the tangent of the angle. For gentle gradients the difference between the sine and the tangent is small. In *calculus the gradient is the slope of the *tangent at any point on a curve in a Cartesian *coordinate system. If the curve is represented by the function f(x), then the gradient is the first derivative of this function.

grafting 1. (horticulture) The transfer of part of one plant, usually a shoot or a bud, onto another plant. It is often used as a means of vegetative propagation, particularly for fruit trees and roses. The *cambium (a region of actively dividing cells) of the transplanted piece (called the scion) is aligned with that of the recipient plant (called the stock): the wound tissue formed by the two cambia binds the graft together. Grafts will "take" only if the scion and stock are closely related. Genetically identical scions on different stocks may differ considerably, but this is due solely to environmental effects and there is no transfer of genetic material between stock and scion. Occasionally graft hybrids (*see* chimaera) arise from the graft junction, but these are mixtures of the two cell types rather than true hybrids. 2. (surgery). *See* transplantation.

Grafton 29 40S 152 56E A city in Australia, in NE New South Wales. It is an agricultural trading centre. Population (1983): 17 300.

Graham, Billy (1918–) US evangelist. He began as an evangelist with the Youth for Christ movement before forming the Billy Graham Evangelistic Association (1950) and conducting worldwide crusades. His association with prominent personalities and carefully staged meetings, in which the audience are invited to "take a decision for Christ," have attracted very large crowds.

Graham, Martha (1893–) US ballet dancer and choreographer. Following the establishment of her own academy in 1927 she became one of the most influential teachers of modern dance. Her ballets, often concerned with the psychological exploration of mythological themes, include *Primitive Mysteries* (1931), *Night Journey* (1947), *Circe* (1963), and *Acts of Light* (1981).

Graham, Thomas (1805–69) British physicist, who investigated gaseous diffusion, discovering **Graham's law** (1831), which states that the rates at which gases diffuse are inversely proportional to the square roots of their densities. After being appointed Master of the Royal Mint (1854), he continued to study diffusion, investigating the flow of solutions through semipermeable membranes. He coined the terms osmosis, crystalloids, and colloids.

Grahame, Kenneth (1859–1932) British children's writer. His best-known book is the children's classic, *The Wind in the Willows* (1908), concerned with Toad, Mole, Rat, and other animal characters that inhabit an ideal riverside world. It was adapted as a play, *Toad of Toad Hall* (1929), by A. A. *Milne.

Graham Land A mountainous peninsula in Antarctica, bordering on the Weddell Sea and comprising part of *British Antarctic Territory. It was formerly a dependency of the Falkland Islands.

Grahamstown (Afrikaans name: Grahamstad) 33 19 S 26 32E A town in South Africa, in SE Cape Province. It was the focus of British settlement in 1820. It is an important religious and educational centre with a Roman Catholic procathedral and an Anglican cathedral; Rhodes University was founded here in 1904. Population (1985 est): 75 000.

Graiae In Greek legend, three goddesses personifying old age, the sisters and protectors of the *Gorgons. They shared one eye and one tooth. *Perseus stole the eye in order to take the Gorgons by surprise.

Grainger, Percy Aldridge (1882–1961) Australian composer and pianist, trained in Germany. He lived in London (1900–15) and thereafter in the USA, becoming a US citizen. Grainger was a friend of Grieg and Delius and studied and recorded English folksong. Many of his compositions incorporate folk-music intervals and rhythms; they include the orchestral *Shepherds' Hey* (1913), *English Dance* (1925), and *Harvest Hymn* (1933), as well as the "clog dance" *Handel in the Strand* (1913).

gram (g) A unit of mass equal to 1/1000 of a *kilogram. The gram is itself one of the basic units in the *c.g.s. system, but in *SI units the basic unit is the kilogram.

grammar The study of the forms of the words of a language (morphology) and their relationships with one another (syntax). Until 1957 there were two basic types of grammar: **prescriptive grammar**, which expressed value judgments about the correctness of particular expressions, and **descriptive grammar**, which aimed to give an accurate account of the structures observable in recorded texts of a language. The earliest known descriptive grammar is by *Panini (c. 5th century BC) of *Sanskrit. Many grammars of the ancient Greek and Latin languages are still influential today; for example, the traditional parts of speech—noun, verb, adjective, etc.—were invented by Greek grammarians. Descriptive grammarians have been able to show that the judgments of prescriptivists are founded on no more objective basis than the willingness of the community to accept their judgments. Each language has its own patterns; attempts to resolve disputes or difficulties by appealing to authority, history, logic, or the structure of some other language are at best irrelevant, at worst confusing.
Publication in 1957 of *Syntactic Structures* by Noam *Chomsky introduced a new view of the study of grammar—namely that it should be predictive. Chomsky argued that, since the potential number of grammatical sentences in a language is literally infinite, a grammar must predict whether any given utterance is or is not a grammatical sentence of a particular language. Chomsky invented the concept of **generative grammar**, the finite set of linguistic rules that generate an infinite number of grammatical sentences in the language. Every speaker of a language acquires these rules at a very early age in a form to some degree idiosyncratic and different from those of other speakers. The raw material from which sentences are generated (words, phrases, etc.) form in a speaker's memory a store the exact nature of which is disputed. The concept of **transformational** (*or* transformational-generative) **grammar** seeks to explain the relationships among words in a sentence and among sentences themselves by logical structural analysis. Ambiguities and certain other problems are explained by postulating that behind the "surface structure" of a sentence lies a "deep structure," an abstract underlying form that determines the sentence's meaning. The surface structure is generated from the deep structure by generative rules, some of which are similar to the transformations of theoretical *logic.

grammar schools Secondary schools in the UK providing a largely academic education for children between the ages of 11 and 18, in preparation for further education or the professions. Most of the grammar schools that existed in England and Wales in the 1960s were established following the Education Act (1944) and a large number of the longer-established schools date only from the beginning of this century, created after the Education Act (1902). The original grammar schools, established in the middle ages, were preparatory institutions for university or for jobs in which a knowledge of Latin was essential. Their role expanded during the Renaissance to provide a broader education, and academic standards were generally high. The standard of instruction subsequently fell, however, and by the early 19th century comparisons with the USA, France, Germany, and especially Scotland led many legal and political reformers to conclude that the English secondary schools were among the most backward in Europe. The main emphasis of the reform movement of the 19th century was one of high moral tone and self-discipline (*see* public schools); only in the years immediately following World War II, with the

growing demand for academic excellence as the key to success in an increasingly meritocratic and complex technological society, were grammar schools compelled to restrict entry to those passing the *eleven-plus examination. Most grammar schools have been replaced by *comprehensive schools.

gramophone. *See* recording of sound.

Grampian Region An administrative region in NE Scotland, bordering on the North Sea. It was created under local government reorganization in 1975 from the counties of Aberdeen, Banff, Kincardine, and Moray. It consists of fertile lowlands in the NE rising to the Cairngorm and Grampian Mountains in the SW. Agriculture is important with sheep farming, stock raising, pigs, and arable farming. The famous breed of Aberdeen-Angus cattle originated in the region. Fishing is also a major source of income. Industries include fish processing, whisky distilling, and those associated with North Sea oil production. Tourism is a thriving industry. Area: 8708 sq km (3361 sq mi). Population (1981): 470 596. Administrative centre: Aberdeen.

Grampians A range of mountains in central Scotland, mainly in the Grampian and Tayside Regions. It extends generally SW–NE, bordered in the S by the Central Lowlands; the Cairngorm Mountains form a northerly extension. Its chief summits include Ben Nevis at 1343 m (4406 ft) and Ben Macdhui at 1309 m (4296 ft).

Grampians A mountain range in Australia. It extends SW from the Great Dividing Range, in SW central Victoria, reaching 1166 m (3827 ft) at Mount William.

grampus A small toothed *whale, *Grampus griseus*, of warm and temperate waters, also called Risso's dolphin. About 3.7 m long, dark-grey with a pale belly, grampuses live in small herds and migrate towards the Poles in summer and the equator in winter.

Gramsci, Antonio (1891–1937) Italian politician and Marxist theorist. In 1914 he joined the Italian Socialist Party but, dissatisfied with its moderation, broke away in 1921 to form the Italian Communist Party. In 1924 he became its leader in the chamber of deputies. The party was banned by the fascists in 1926 and Gramsci was imprisoned from 1928 until shortly before his death. His voluminous Marxist writings, mostly the work of his prison years, were publishd posthumously as *Prison Notebooks* (1947).

Granada 37 10N 3 35W A city in S Spain, in Andalusia. Formerly the capital of the kingdom of Granada, the last Moorish stronghold in Spain, it was conquered in 1492. Much frequented by tourists, its splendid architecture includes many Moorish buildings (notably the □Alhambra), a cathedral (1523–1703), and the 16th-century Capilla Real, containing the tombs of Ferdinand and Isabella. Population (1981): 262 182.

Granada 11 58N 85 59W A town in SW Nicaragua. It is the centre of an area producing cotton, sugar, and coffee; manufactures include furniture, soap, and rum. Population (1981): 72 640.

granadilla. *See* passionflower.

Granados, Enrique (1867–1916) Spanish composer and pianist. His music was influenced by Spanish folk music. He and his wife were drowned during World War I when HMS *Sussex*, on which they were returning from the USA, was torpedoed. Granados is best remembered for the two sets of piano pieces entitled *Goyescas* (1911), inspired by *Goya. These became the basis for an opera of the same name (1916).

Granby, John Manners, Marquess of (1721–70) British soldier. As a cavalry officer in the *Seven Years' War, he made amends for his commander's disgrace at Minden (1759) by his part in the victory of Warburg (1760). Promotion and popular acclaim followed.

Gran Chaco A vast plain in S central South America,

mainly in N Argentina, E Bolivia, and Paraguay. It consists of a vast alluvial lowland region, drained by the W tributaries of the Rivers Paraguay and Paraná. It was the cause of the *Chaco War between Paraguay and Bolivia (1932–35). Area: 780 000 sq km (300 000 sq mi).

Grand Alliance, War of the (1689–97) The war in which a grand alliance led by England, Austria, Spain, and the Netherlands attempted to curb the expansionist policy of Louis XIV of France. Precipitated by the French invasion of the Palatinate (1688), the war was fought mainly in Flanders. Exhausted by the inconclusive battles and sieges, the participants accepted the Treaty of *Rijswijk in 1697. The conflict was renewed, however, in 1701, with the War of the *Spanish Succession.

Grand Banks A section of the North American continental shelf in the N Atlantic Ocean, extending SE of Newfoundland with a depth of about 40–100 m (130–330 ft). It is an internationally important fishing ground in which cod is especially plentiful. Area: about 1 280 000 sq km (494 000 sq mi).

Grand Canal (Chinese name: Da Yunhe) A canal in E China, the longest in the world, extending about 1600 km (1000 mi) N–S from Peking to *Wuhan. Begun possibly in the 4th century BC, it was built in sections over two millenniums. 30–61 m (100–200 ft) wide and 0.6–4.6 m (2–15 ft) deep, it is still used, chiefly in the S.

Grand Canyon A vast gorge in the USA, in Arizona on the Colorado River. It has been eroded through a varied series of virtually horizontal beds of multicoloured rock, creating spectacular steps and rock formations. A popular tourist area, it was designated the **Grand Canyon National Park** in 1919. Length: 451 km (280 mi). Width: 6–29 km (4–18 mi). Greatest depth: over 1.5 km (1 mi).

Grand Coulee Dam A large gravity *dam on the Columbia River in Washington (USA). Completed in 1942, it is 1272 m long at its crest, 108 m high, and has a reservoir capacity of 11 600 million cubic metres for irrigation, flood control, and hydroelectric power.

Grande Dixence Dam A gravity *dam on the River Dixence (Switzerland). Until 1970 it was the tallest dam in the world (284 m high). It is 670 m wide at the crest and has a reservoir of 400 million cubic metres.

Grand Guignol A type of popular sensational drama, exploiting situations of violence and terror, that flourished in Paris in the late 19th century. The term derives from the name of a theatre at which these plays were performed, and from Guignol, a stock character in French puppet shows.

grand mal. *See* epilepsy.

Grand National Steeplechase The world's most famous and exacting *steeplechase, run in March at Aintree near Liverpool (England), over a course of 7.2 km (4 mi 856 yd) with 30 assorted obstacles of considerable severity. It was first run in 1839.

Grand Pré A village in E Canada, in Nova Scotia. It was the centre of French-speaking *Acadia until Britain deported its inhabitants for refusing to swear allegiance to the Crown (1755), an event romanticized in Longfellow's *Evangeline*.

Grand Rapids 42 57N 86 40W A city in the USA, in W central Michigan on the Grand River. Founded in the 1820s, its industries include the manufacture of furniture, motor bodies, paper, and paint. Population (1980): 181 843.

Grand Remonstrance (1641) A list of grievances drawn up by the *Long Parliament on the eve of the English *Civil War. It itemized the past faults of Charles I, the reforms achieved by the Long Parliament, and grievances outstanding.

Grand Tour The tourist journey through continental Europe that was fashionable among wealthy English in the 18th and 19th centuries. Taking advantage of improved travelling conditions, the tour, which completed a gentleman's education, could last two years.

Grangemouth 56 01N 3 44W A port in Scotland, in Central Region lying on the Firth of Forth at the E end of the

Forth–Clyde Canal. Its industries include oil refining, engineering, shipbuilding, saw milling, and chemicals. Population (1981): 21 666.

granite A coarse-grained plutonic rock of acid composition resulting from the high silica content. Granites contain quartz, feldspar (usually alkali), and mafic (dark-coloured) minerals, usually muscovite and biotite (micas). Most granites crystallize from magma in large igneous intrusions known as batholiths, but some are produced by granitization, which is the transformation of pre-existing rocks into granite by the action of granitic fluids rising from great depths. There are many different types of granite with different modes of formation and mineral content.

Gran Paradiso 45 33N 7 17E The highest mountain entirely in Italy, in the Alps. The surrounding area has been made into a national park. Height: 4061 m (13 323 ft).

Grant, Cary (Archibald Leach; 1904–86) US film actor, born in England. He went to Hollywood in 1932 and established his reputation as an actor of debonair sophistication in such films as *Holiday* (1938) and *The Philadelphia Story* (1940). He acted in more than 70 films, including several directed by Alfred Hitchcock, notably *To Catch a Thief* (1955) and *North By Northwest* (1959).

Grant, Duncan James Corrowr (1885–1978) British painter and designer. He was influenced by the postimpressionists and was associated with Roger *Fry and the *Bloomsbury group. His work includes designs for rugs and fabrics, murals, stage costumes and scenery, and, among his paintings, a portrait of Vanessa Bell (Tate Gallery).

Grant, Ulysses S(impson) (1822–85) US general and statesman; Republican president (1869–77). He was a brilliant Civil War strategist but as president, although popular, showed no talent for leadership. As supreme commander of the Federal armies (1864–65) he defeated the Confederates by means of strategy and battering them into submission. The consequently great losses to his own side earned him the nickname Grant the Butcher. As president, he acquiesced in Reconstruction attempts to enfranchise Blacks, fought inflation, and unsuccessfully planned to annex the Dominican Republic. Subsequently he became so poor that he had to sell his swords and war souvenirs.

Grantham 52 55N 0 39W A town in E central England, in Lincolnshire. Sir Isaac Newton was born nearby and attended the grammar school (1528) here. An important agricultural centre, Grantham has agricultural and general engineering industries. Population (1981): 30 084.

Granville, Granville George Leveson-Gower, 2nd Earl (1815–91) British Liberal politician; foreign secretary (1870–74, 1880–85) under Gladstone. He was one of the few Liberals to support Gladstone on Irish *Home Rule.

Granville, John Carteret, 1st Earl (1690–1763) British statesman; prime minister (1742–44). A bitter opponent of Robert *Walpole, Granville became prime minister after Walpole's fall. During the War of the *Austrian Succession he was criticized for putting George II's Hanoverian interests above Britain's and George was forced to dismiss him.

Granville-Barker, Harley (1877–1946) British theatre director, critic, and dramatist. As comanager of the Royal Court Theatre from 1904 to 1907 he produced many plays by G. B. Shaw and by modern European dramatists. His most influential practical criticism is contained in *Prefaces to Shakespeare* (1927–47). His own plays include *The Voysey Inheritance* (1905) and *The Madras House* (1910).

grape The fruit of vines of the genus *Vitis* (about 60 species), especially *V. vinifera*, native to N Asia but cultivated throughout Mediterranean regions. The grapevine is up to 30 m long, twining by means of tendrils, with lobed toothed leaves and dense clusters of small greenish flowers. The fruit—a berry—is green, red, or blue-black and used to make *wine, brandy, and liqueurs or eaten fresh or dried (in the form of raisins, sultanas, and currants).

grapefruit A tree, *Citrus paradisi*, 6–12 m high, cultivated in the tropics and subtropics. It has shiny oval leaves and clusters of white flowers that mature into fleshy yellow-skinned fruits, 10–15 cm in diameter. Grapefruits are eaten fresh, tinned, or crushed to make beverages. *See* Citrus.

grape hyacinth A perennial herbaceous plant of the genus *Muscari* (50 species), mostly native to the Mediterranean region and widely grown as spring-blooming garden bulbs. The leaves are long and narrow and the blue, pink, or white urn-shaped flowers are borne in a dense cluster at the tip of a leafless flower stalk, up to 15 cm high. *M. botryoides*, with blue flowers, is a popular species. Family: *Liliaceae*.

graph A method of providing a visual representation of relationships between quantities, usually in the Cartesian *coordinate system. In mathematics graphs are used to solve equations, represent functions, etc. Histograms, in which the height of columns represents the frequency of a result in each of a series of ranges, and pie charts, which show percentages as segments of a circle, are also sometimes referred to as graphs.

graphite An iron-grey to black form of pure carbon, found in many metamorphic rocks, especially metamorphosed coals or other carbonaceous sediments. It occurs in a laminar or massive form. It is very soft, flaky, and greasy to the touch. Graphite is used for making metallurgical crucibles, as a lubricant, in paint, rubber, and pencil leads, in batteries and for other electrical purposes, and as a moderator in nuclear reactors. It has often been called plumbago or black lead, since it was formerly mistaken for lead.

Grappelli, Stephane (1908–) French jazz violinist, who played in the quintet of the Hot Club de France (1934–39). He has made many recordings, with Earl Hines and Yehudi *Menuhin among others.

graptolite A small colonial marine animal belonging to the extinct class *Graptolithina*, possibly related to *coelenterates. Their fossils, in the form of carbonaceous impressions, occur in rocks of the Upper Cambrian to Carboniferous periods, about 420–250 million years ago. Graptolites were floating animals, individual polyps living in the cuplike tips of simple or branched hollow tubes.

Grasmere 54 28N 3 02W A village in NW England, in Cumbria on Lake Grasmere. It is famous for its associations with William Wordsworth (whose cottage is now a museum) and other Lakeland poets. Population (1985 est): 1100.

grass A monocotyledonous annual or perennial herbaceous plant belonging to the family *Poaceae* (or *Gramineae*; 6000–10 000 species), distributed worldwide. The leaves consist of a basal sheath, which encircles the stem, and a long narrow blade. The flowering stems (culms) bear spikelets of inconspicuous flowers; each spikelet has two basal bracts (glumes) and each flower is enclosed by two other bracts—a lower lemma and an upper palea. The hard single-seeded fruit (the grain) is known botanically as a caryopsis, with the ovary wall (pericarp) and seed coat fused. Many species are important in agriculture as a source of food (*see* cereals; sugar cane) and as pasture grasses.

Grass, Günter (1927–) German novelist, poet, and political activist. His first novel, *The Tin Drum* (1959), an epic picaresque treatment of modern German history, established him as a moral spokesman for his generation. His other works include the play *The Plebeians Rehearse the Uprising* (1966) and the novels *Dog Years* (1963), *The Flounder* (1978), *The Meeting at Telgte* (1981), and *Headbirths or The Germans are Dying Out* (1982).

Grasse 43 40N 6 56E A town and resort in SE France, in the Alpes-Maritimes department. It is the centre of the French perfume industry. Population (1982): 38 360.

grassfinch A songbird belonging to a subfamily of

*weaverfinches, occurring chiefly in arid regions of Australasia. About 10 cm long, grassfinches have long tails and stout bills. The group includes a number of colourful popular cagebirds, such as the Gouldian finch (*Poephila gouldiae*) and the *zebra finch.

grasshopper A jumping insect belonging to the family *Acrididae* (about 5000 species). Grasshoppers, 24–110 mm long, are usually green or brown and have short stout antennae and tail appendages. Both sexes produce sound by rubbing the hind legs against the front wings. Some species can fly, sometimes forming dense migratory swarms (*see* locust). Grasshoppers live and feed on grass and low vegetation and the females lay eggs in the soil. Order: *Orthoptera.

grass monkey A small African *guenon monkey, *Cercopithecus aethiops*, inhabiting thinly wooded regions. The West African green monkey, the East African grivet monkey, and the South African vervet or blue monkey are all local races of grass monkey.

grass of Parnassus A tufted perennial herb of the genus *Parnassia* (about 50 species), especially *P. palustris*, found in wet places throughout Europe and temperate Asia. The basal leaves are stalked and heart-shaped. The solitary white five-petalled flower is borne on an erect stalk with a single unstalked leaf near the base. Family: *Parnassiaceae*.

grass snake A nonvenomous snake, *Natrix natrix*, also called water snake, occurring throughout Europe, usually near ponds, streams, and marshes. 75–95 cm long, it has a green back with two rows of black spots, vertical black bars along its sides, and a yellow neck patch. It can be distinguished from the *adder, which has a black zigzag line along its back. Its prey includes frogs, tadpoles, fish, lizards, and small mammals. Family: *Colubridae*.

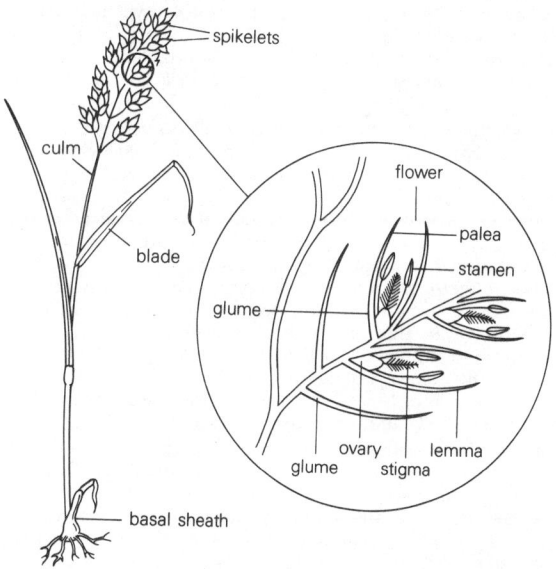

GRASS *The typical structure of a grass is seen in the meadow fescue (Festuca pratensis). The flowers are grouped into spikelets and each consists only of male and female parts; petals and sepals are absent.*

grass tree A woody plant of the genus *Xanthorrhoea* (about 5 species), native to E Australia. They often have palmlike stems, 5 m tall, that end in a tuft of rigid grasslike leaves, from which extend flower spikes resembling those of the *reedmace, about 3 m tall. A red or yellow gumlike resin, used for varnishes, exudes from the bases of old leaves. Family: *Xanthorrhoeaceae*.

Gratian(us), Flavius

524

Gratian(us), Flavius (359-83 AD) Western Roman emperor (367-83). He was a Christian and abandoned (382) the pagan title *pontifex maximus* (supreme priest). He was deposed by Magnus Maximus (d. 388) and murdered.

Grattan, Henry (1746-1820) Irish politician, who with *Flood was one of the greatest orators in the Irish parliament. From 1775 he led the patriot party and in 1782 obtained Irish free trade and legislative independence from Britain. He opposed, unavailingly, the union of England and Ireland and in 1805 sat in the British parliament, where he pressed for *Catholic emancipation.

gravel Unconsolidated rock fragments ranging between 2 and 60 mm in particle size, or between coarse sand and cobbles. The term is loosely used for any unconsolidated material coarser than sand, for instance river gravels and glacial gravels.

Gravenhage, 's. *See* Hague, The.

Graves, Robert (Ranke) (1895–1985) British poet, critic, and novelist. His early autobiography, *Goodbye to All That* (1929), recounts his experiences in World War I. In 1929 he emigrated to Majorca. He published several editions of *Collected Poems*, historical novels including *I Claudius* (1934) and *Claudius the God* (1934), and studies of mythology, notably *The White Goddess* (1948). His more recent works include *They Hanged My Saintly Billy* (1980).

Gravesend 51 27N 0 24E A port in SE England, in Kent on the River Thames. It is a customs and pilot station for the Port of London and has printing, engineering, and paper-making industries. Population (1981): 52 963.

Gravettian A culture of the Upper *Palaeolithic, succeeding the *Aurignacian in W Europe. Named after the cave at La Gravette in the Dordogne (SW France), the Gravettian is characterized by small pointed stone blades with one blunted edge (Gravette points) and dates from between 26 000 and 20 000 BC. The well-known small female figurines called Venuses are of Gravettian origin. The term Eastern Gravettian is applied to similar material from mammoth hunters' camp sites in Russia and E Europe. *Compare* Périgordian.

gravitation An attractive force that occurs between all bodies that possess mass. It was first described by Sir Isaac *Newton in a law stating that the force between two bodies is directly proportional to the product of their masses and inversely proportional to the square of the distance between them. The constant of proportionality is called the universal gravitational constant, G, which has the value 6.673×10^{-11} newton metre squared per kilogram squared. Gravitation is now more accurately described by the general theory of *relativity. In this theory a mass distorts the *space-time continuum around it so that the geometry of the space is locally no longer Euclidean. The force of gravity and the *acceleration of free fall are the result of the attractive force between a body and the earth.

gravitational collapse The sudden collapse of the core of a *star when thermonuclear fusion eventually ceases. The star's internal gas pressure can no longer support the weight of the star and the initial result may be a *supernova explosion. The gravitational pull of all the constituents of the star, or its remains, causes it to contract. The extent of the contraction depends on the mass of the object, producing a *white dwarf, *neutron star, or *black hole.

gravitational interaction One of the four kinds of interaction that occur between elementary particles (*see* particle physics) and by far the weakest (about 10^{40} times weaker than the *electromagnetic interaction). The interaction occurs between all particles with mass and can be explained as the exchange of *virtual particles called gravitons. Such particles have not yet been detected.

gray (Gy) The *SI unit of absorbed dose of ionizing radiation equal to the energy in joules absorbed by one kilogram of irradiated material.

Gray, Asa (1810-88) US botanist, who compiled *Flora of North America* (2 vols, 1838-43), a comprehensive taxonomic guide to the region's plants. He also wrote many popular books on botany, including a *Manual of the Botany of the Northern United States* (1848). Gray was a firm supporter of Darwin's theories of evolution, although he believed that the process of natural selection was controlled by God.

Gray, Thomas (1716-71) British poet. The only survivor of 12 children, he was educated at Eton and Cambridge, where he spent most of his life in scholarly retirement. He published only a few odes apart from his most famous poem, *Elegy Written in a Country Churchyard* (1751), a classical meditation on the graves of the humble villagers of Stoke Poges, Buckinghamshire.

grayling A troutlike fish of the genus *Thymallus*, sometimes placed in a distinct family (*Thymallidae*). Graylings have a silvery-purple scaly body, up to 50 cm long, with a sail-like dorsal fin, and live in cold clear fresh waters of Eurasia and N North America, feeding on aquatic insects. They are important food and game fish. Family: *Salmonidae*.

Gray's Inn. *See* Inns of Court.

graywacke. *See* greywacke.

Graz 47 05N 15 22E The second largest city in Austria, the capital of Styria. Its numerous historical buildings include a cathedral (1438-62) and a notable clock tower (1561). It has a university (1586). An industrial centre, it produces iron and steel, textiles, and chemicals. Population (1981): 243 166.

Great Artesian Basin An artesian basin of E Australia. The largest area of artesian water in the world, it extends S from the Gulf of Carpentaria in Queensland into South Australia and New South Wales, underlying the catchments of both the Darling River and Lake Eyre. Area: 1 750 000 sq km (676 250 sq mi).

Great Australian Bight A wide bay of the Indian Ocean, in S Australia situated between Capes Pasley and Carnot. Width: 1159 km (720 mi).

Great Awakening A religious revival in the American colonies in the 18th century. It began in the 1720s among members of the Dutch Reformed Church of New Jersey but flourished in New England in 1740-43, after which it spread to other colonies. It was largely inspired by the preaching of George *Whitefield and Jonathan *Edwards, who, however, disapproved of the excessive enthusiasm or hysteria that was often manifested by those claiming to be converted.

Great Barrier Reef The largest coral reef in the world, situated in the Coral Sea off the coast of NE Australia. Approximately 15 000 years old, it consists of a complex of coral reefs, shoals, and islets extending for 2012 km (1250 mi) from Breaksea Spit to the Gulf of Papua. Its many fish, crustaceans, birds, exotic plant life, and some 350 species of colourful corals make it popular with tourists.

Great Basin A large semiarid area in the USA. Situated between the Sierra Nevada and the Wasatch Mountains, it extends over most of Nevada, Utah, and parts of California and Oregon. It consists of a series of basins, mountain ranges, deserts (including the *Mojave Desert), and salt lakes (including the *Great Salt Lake).

Great Bear. *See* Ursa Major.

Great Bear Lake A lake in N Canada, in Mackenzie district on the Arctic Circle. Frozen eight months of the year, it is the fourth largest lake in North America. It drains into the Mackenzie River via the Great Bear River, 112 km (70 mi) long. Area: 31 792 sq km (12 275 sq mi).

Great Belt (Danish name: Store Bælt) A channel between the Danish islands of Fyn and Sjælland, linking the Kattegat and the Baltic Sea.

Great Britain The largest island in the British Isles and in Europe, separated from the mainland of W Europe by the North Sea and the English Channel. Containing *England,

*Scotland, and *Wales, it includes the islands governed with the mainland but excludes the Isle of Man and the Channel Islands. Area: 229 523 sq km (88 619 sq mi). Population (1981): 54 285 422.

great circle A circle that is the intersection on the surface of a sphere of a plane passing through the centre of that sphere. On the earth, each meridian of longitude is half of a great circle; the equator is the only parallel of latitude that is a great circle.

great crested grebe A large *grebe, *Podiceps cristatus*, occurring in Eurasia. It is dark brown above with a white face, neck, and underparts, a black two-horned crest and neck frill, and chestnut patches at the sides of the face. Mating pairs perform an elaborate courtship display. *See* Plate V.

Great Dane A breed of large dog originating in Germany, where they were developed for hunting boar. The Great Dane has a large powerful frame with long legs and a large head with a square muzzle. The short sleek coat can be golden, black, streaked brown, blue-grey, or white with black patches. Height: 76 cm minimum (dogs); 71 cm minimum (bitches).

Great Dividing Range (Great Divide *or* Eastern Highlands) The E highlands of Australia, comprising a complex of mountains and plateaus. It extends for about 3700 km (2300 mi) from Cape York Peninsula to the Grampians of Victoria and includes the *Blue Mountains and Australian Alps, where it reaches 2230 m (7316 ft) at Mount *Kosciusko.

Greater Antilles The four largest West Indian islands, in the N Caribbean Sea, comprising Cuba, Hispaniola, Jamaica, and Puerto Rico.

Greater Manchester A metropolitan county of NW England, created in 1974 from SE Lancashire and parts of NE Cheshire and SW Yorkshire. It comprises the districts of Wigan, Bolton, Bury, Rochdale, Salford, Oldham, Manchester, Trafford, Stockport, and Tamesside. Area: 1285 sq km (496 sq mi). Population (1981): 6 696 008. Administrative centre: Manchester.

Great Exhibition (1851) A display of the products of industrial Britain and Europe, planned by Prince Albert and held in the *Crystal Palace. It contained about 13 000 exhibits and showed the technical progress and industrial supremacy of Britain.

GREAT BARRIER REEF

Great Glen (*or* Glen More) A rift valley extending across N Scotland from Fort William to Inverness. A number of lochs lie along the valley, including Loch Ness and Loch Linhe; the *Caledonian Canal was constructed along its length.

Great Indian Desert. *See* Thar Desert.

Great Lake A shallow freshwater lake in Australia. It lies on the central plateau of Tasmania, at an altitude of 1030 m (3380 ft), and is used as a storage reservoir for hydroelectric power. Area: 114 sq km (44 sq mi).

Great Lakes Five large lakes in E central North America, mostly along the US-Canadian border: Lakes *Superior, *Michigan, *Huron, *Erie, and *Ontario. The world's largest freshwater surface, they drain into the *St Lawrence River and form part of the *St Lawrence Seaway. Canals also link them to the Mississippi River, making them a major transportation route. Their basin is an important economic region, with agriculture, fishing, forestry, mining, hydroelectricity, manufacturing, commerce, and tourism. Recently water pollution has become a major problem, compounded by the many governments with jurisdiction over the lakes.

Great Leap Forward A nationwide campaign in China to promote economic and industrial growth. The movement started in 1958 and aimed to increase industrial production dramatically by using manpower rather than capital in large-scale rural communes and backyard steel furnaces and factories. Ambitious production targets were reached but it proved impossible to coordinate production and control quality, and the movement was revoked in 1960.

Great Ouse River (*or* R. Ouse) A river in E England, rising in Northamptonshire and flowing NE across the Fens to the Wash near King's Lynn. Length: 257 km (160 mi).

Great Plains An extensive area in North America. It consists of a system of rolling plains extending from the Mackenzie River Delta in Canada in the N to the Rio Grande in the S. It is chiefly agricultural with livestock raising and grain production. Length: about 4828 km (3000 mi). Average width: about 644 km (400 mi).

Great Red Spot An immense reddish oval feature in the atmosphere of *Jupiter, lying S of the equator. Observed for over a century, its prominence, colour, and size (14 000 km N-S by up to 40 000 km E-W) have been found to fluctuate. Pioneer planetary probes showed it to be a vortex of cold anticlockwise-rotating clouds elevated above the surrounding cloud layer and coloured possibly by traces of phosphorus.

Great Rift Valley (*or* East African Rift System) An extensive rift valley in the Middle East and East Africa. It extends from the Jordan Valley in Syria along the Red Sea into Ethiopia and through Kenya, Tanzania, and Malawi into Mozambique. It is marked by a chain of lakes (Lakes Turkana (formerly Rudolf) and Natron) and volcanoes (Mount Kilimanjaro). Length: about 6400 km (4000 mi).

Great Salt Lake A salt lake in the USA, in NW Utah in the Great Basin. It is bordered by the Wasatch Mountains and the Great Salt Lake Desert and has no outlet. A salt extraction industry exists along its shores. Its area has fluctuated from less than 2500 sq km (1000 sq mi) to over 5000 sq km (2000 sq mi).

Great Sandy Desert A desert of N Western Australia. It consists of a vast arid region of sand dunes and salt marshes stretching SE from Eighty Mile Beach on the Indian Ocean to the Gibson Desert. Area: 415 000 sq km (160 000 sq mi).

Great Schism (1378-1417) The split in the Roman Catholic Church following the election of two rival popes to succeed Gregory XI. Criticisms of the residency of the papacy in Avignon (*see* Avignon papacy) forced its return to Rome and the election of an Italian, Urban VI. He determined to reform the College of Cardinals, which responded by electing an *antipope at Avignon, Clement VII. The Schism was ended by the Council of *Constance (1414-18) and the election of Martin V in 1417. (For the schism in 1054 between the E and W Christian churches, *see* Filioque.)

Great Slave Lake A very deep lake in N Canada, in Mackenzie district. The fifth largest lake in North America, it drains into the Mackenzie River. Area: 28 438 sq km (10 980 sq mi).

great tit The largest of the *tits, *Parus major*: a common European bird of woodland, farmland, and gardens feeding on caterpillars, aphids, scale insects, and other pests. It is about 14 cm long and has a black head with white cheeks, a green back, and a black stripe down its yellow breast.

Great Trek The movement from the mid-1830s to mid-1840s of Dutch settlers (Afrikaners) in South Africa northwards across the Orange and Vaal Rivers from the Cape. The so-called Voortrekkers, under such leaders as Andries *Pretorius, moved away from British rule at the Cape in search of more farmland that they could administer themselves. They are considered by Afrikaners to be the founding fathers of South Africa. They established the republics of the Transvaal and the Orange Free State.

Great Victoria Desert A desert of Western and South Australia, between the Gibson Desert and Nullarbor Plain. It consists of a vast arid region of sand hills and salt marshes. Area: 323 750 sq km (125 000 sq mi).

Great Vowel Shift The phrase coined by *Jespersen to describe the change in English pronunciation that took place mainly during the 15th century; it accounts for many of the existing anomalies in English spelling and pronunciation. The highest Middle English long vowels became diphthongized (e.g. ī originally pronounced as in *machine* came to be pronounced like the *i* in *mice*) and other vowels, affected by this, shifted to higher positions.

Great Wall of China A medieval defensive fortification in N China. Stretching from the Yellow Sea N of Peking nearly 2400 km (1500 mi) inland, the Great Wall is the world's largest building achievement. Originally begun in 214 BC as a defence against nomadic tribes, it was improved and largely rebuilt of stone in the 15th and 16th centuries. It is about 9 m (30 ft) high, with numerous higher watch towers along its length.

Great Yarmouth. *See* Yarmouth.

GREAT ZIMBABWE *A picture of the ruins of a large round tower, part of the so-called Elliptical Building, published in the* Proceedings of the Royal Geographical Society *(London), in 1892.*

Great Zimbabwe The largest of the ruined Bantu royal centres on the Zambezian plateau in Zimbabwe. The word *zimbabwe* is derived from the Bantu for "revered houses." Great Zimbabwe reached its zenith in the late 14th century but suffered abrupt decline after about 1440. Traces of widespread trade, based on local gold, have been discovered, including Chinese pottery. Parts of the so-called Elliptical

Building (a compound enclosing now vanished huts) stand 10.5 m (35 ft) high and consist of regular dry stone courses of dressed granite.

grebe A bird belonging to a primitive family (*Podicipitidae*; 21 species) occurring in rivers and lakes worldwide. Grebes are adapted for swimming and diving by having short wings, a very small tail, and partially webbed feet with lobed toes. They have a long neck and a long pointed bill and feed chiefly on fish and aquatic invertebrates. Grebes are grey, black, or brown, usually with white underparts, and in the breeding season many have brightly coloured erectile crests and ear tufts. Order: *Podicipediformes. See also* dabchick; great crested grebe.

Greece, Republic of (Greek name: Ellás) A country in SE Europe, occupying the S section of the Balkan Peninsula between the Mediterranean and Aegean Seas. Numerous islands, which comprise about one-fifth of the total area of Greece, lie to the S, E, and W; the largest is *Crete. The mainland is largely mountainous, with plains in Thrace and Macedonia in the N and Thessaly in the centre. *Economy*: since the early 1970s industry has replaced agriculture as the mainstay of the economy. The rapid expansion of the industrial sector (especially metallurgy, chemicals, textiles, rubber, plastics, and electrical machinery) began in the 1960s. Mineral resources, including lignite, bauxite, and iron ore, have been intensively exploited and processed and there has been a dramatic increase in electricity output. The first nuclear power station is expected to be in operation by the 1980s. Recent plans include incentives for the decentralization of industry, which has led to a rapidly changing pattern of growth in N Greece aided by the discovery of natural gas and oil near the island of Thásos. There has been considerable diversification of agriculture and the principal crops include wheat, barley, maize, tobacco, sugar beet, tomatoes, and dried and fresh fruits. Tourism is also an important source of revenue. *History*: the centuries following the collapse of the *Mycenaean civilization (c. 1200 BC) saw the rise of the Greek city states. From the 8th century, trading activities led to the establishment of colonies around the Mediterranean, in Asia Minor, N Africa, S Italy and Sicily, and in S France. The first half of the 5th century was dominated by the ultimately abortive attempt of the Persians to annex Greece (*see* Greek-Persian Wars) and the late 5th century, by the Peloponnesian War between rival Athens and Sparta. Sparta's subsequent supremacy in Greece lasted until its defeat by Thebes in 371. Greece fell to Philip of Macedon in 338 and was incorporated in the empire of his son Alexander the Great. Following the division of Alexander's possessions at his death (323), the Greek city states remained within the Macedonian orbit but repeatedly attempted to assert their independence until the last Macedonian War (171-168) allowed Rome to dominate Greece. Roman rule lasted until 395 AD, when the Roman Empire was divided between W and E and Greece became part of the Byzantine (Eastern Roman) Empire, centred on Constantinople. In the middle ages Greece was subject to invasions by the Franks, Normans, and the Latin Crusaders. In the early 14th century Byzantium reasserted its control over the area but in 1453 Constantinople fell to the Ottoman Turks; by 1460 they controlled all Greece. Apart from a brief period (1686-1715) of partial Venetian occupation, Greece remained under Ottoman rule until achieving independence in 1829 (*see* Greek Independence, War of). In 1832 the Greek Crown was offered to a Bavarian prince, who became Otto I (1815-67), but his despotic rule precipitated his deposition in 1862. In 1863 a Danish prince became king as George I (1845-1913). In the same year Greece acquired the Ionian Islands from Britain and in 1881, in the aftermath of the Congress of Berlin, Thessaly and part of Epirus from Turkey. Greek demands for Crete led to a disastrous war with Turkey in 1897, but in the Balkan Wars (1912-13) Greece gained the island together with territory in Thrace and Macedonia. In 1917 Venizelos took Greece into World War I on the Allied side and the immediate postwar period saw renewed territorial conflict with Turkey, in which Greece lost Smyrna. In 1924 Greece became a republic, which lasted until George II was restored in 1935. In World War II an unsuccessful Italian invasion (1940) was followed by the German occupation (1941–44), after which Greece was plunged into a civil war between monarchists and communists that lasted until 1949. The 1950s were dominated by the question of union with Cyprus, which Greece supported (*see* EOKA), and the 1960s saw a military coup (1967), which exiled Constantine II and established the rule of the colonels under Papadopoulos. He was overthrown in 1973 and succeeded by Gen Phaedon Ghizikis (1917–   ). The government's involvement in the coup against Makarios in Cyprus led to its collapse (1974). A republican constitution (1975) saw the reintroduction of democratic government. Greece became a member of the EEC in 1981. In 1987 a law was passed depriving the Orthodox church of its land, and tension increased with Turkey over rights to oil in the Aegean. Head of state: President Christos Sartzetakis. Prime minister: Andreas Papandreou (1919–   ). Official language: Greek. Official religion: Greek Orthodox. Official currency: drachma of 100 lepta. Area: 131 986 sq km (50 960 sq mi). Population (1983): 9 898 000. Capital: Athens. Main port: Piraeus.

Greek art and architecture   The arts of ancient Greece from the 8th century BC until Greece's absorption in the Roman Empire after 27 BC, conventionally divided into three main periods: archaic (before c. 550), classical (550–323), and Hellenistic (323–27). Most extant paintings are on pottery. Nonfigurative all-over designs of the earliest period gradually gave way to the more naturalistic black-figure technique in the 7th and 6th centuries BC. The greatest achievements are the Athenian red-figure vases (530–400 BC). As is also the case with sculptors, the work of many Greek painters (e.g. *Zeuxis) is known only through Roman copies, but magnificent Hellenistic wall paintings have recently been uncovered at Vergina. In sculpture, the monumental Egyptian-influenced solidity of the early *kore and *kouros statues yielded to the idealized naturalism of the classical period (480–323 BC). This is exemplified in the *Elgin marbles and in the work of *Phidias and *Praxiteles. In the subsequent Hellenistic period sculpture is characteristically represented by dramatic subject matter and highly complex figure poses and groupings. The small-scale arts of coin engraving, gem carving, jewellery making, and the sculpting of bronze and terracotta figures (*see* Tanagra figurines) also reached a peak of perfection in the Hellenistic era. Greek architecture is perhaps the greatest legacy that the ancient Greeks have left us, for almost all subsequent European architecture is indebted to it. Although the Egyptians invented the colonnade (c. 2500 BC) and the Romans were the first to make use of arches, domes, and vaults as structural features, it was the Greeks who invented the entablature to surmount the colonnade in order to support a hipped roof. They also perfected the design of columns and created the concept of an architect as an artist, engineer, and town planner. Archaic Greek architecture had its roots in Crete (the first palace at Knossos was built about 2000 BC) and in Mycenae (the famous Lion Gate was erected about 1450 BC). However, classical (*or* Hellenic) Greek architecture did not emerge until about 700 BC, when the Greeks began to build in stone (limestone or marble) instead of wood, rubble, and mud bricks. This development followed slightly different courses on opposite sides of the Aegean Sea. During the 6th century BC the Doric order (*see* orders of architecture; architecture) emerged as a consistent style in mainland Greece; at about the same time the Ionic order developed on the eastern shores of the Aegean. Both styles reached their zenith in the time of Pericles (490–429 BC); on the Athenian Acropolis the *Parthenon is the prime example of a Doric temple, while the Erechtheum (built by Mnesicles in 405 BC) contains three different Ionic orders. During the Hellenistic period the Doric gave way to the Ionic, and this in turn yielded to the

third order of Greek architecture, the Corinthian. This style is exemplified by the Olympieium at Athens, built by Cossutius in 174 BC.

Greek Independence, War of   (1821–32) The war that established a Greek state independent of the Ottoman Empire. The rebels had some initial success until in 1825 the Ottomans were strengthened by Egyptian help. The UK, France, and Russia offered to mediate and when rebuffed by the Ottomans defeated the Ottoman and Egyptian fleet at the battle of *Navarino (1827). The Ottomans fought on briefly but peace negotiations were begun in London in 1829 and independence was proclaimed, being recognized by the Ottoman Empire in 1832, when a Greek monarchy was established. European sympathizers for the Greek cause included Lord Byron.

Greek language   An Indo-European language spoken chiefly in Greece and the E Mediterranean islands. Well documented since the 14th century BC (*see* Linear B), ancient Greek was a highly complex inflected language. It had many dialect forms, the main groupings being Ionic (E Greece and Asia Minor), Aeolic (Boeotia and Thessaly), and Doric (the Peloponnese). From Ionic developed the Attic dialect, centred on Athens, which became the chief literary language of classical Greece. When the Greek city states lost their independence (4th century BC), their dialects gave way to a new common dialect (*koine*), which became the language of Hellenistic Greece and the New Testament. During the Byzantine Empire, Greek diverged from classical forms, with simplified pronunciations and foreign borrowings. Modern Greek has two widely differing forms: the classically based Katharevusa (purified tongue) used in official publications, and Demotic, the living language of speech, poetry, and fiction.

Greek literature   The epics of *Homer date from the 8th century BC, though their echoes of *Mycenaean civilization suggest that they may have existed in oral form for considerably longer. A little later (c. 700) *Hesiod's poems portray the lives and concerns of farmers. *Archilochus of Paros and Alcman (both 7th century) were early masters of lyric verse; they were followed by *Alcaeus, *Sappho, *Solon, and *Anacreon in the 6th century and *Pindar in the early 5th century. Incipient philosophical speculation in 6th-century Ionia stimulated the development of prose, but the earliest prose work to survive entire is the mid-5th-century history of *Herodotus. After the defeat of the Persians (480 BC) Attic writers brought about the flowering of classical Greek literature; major figures were the tragedians *Aeschylus, *Sophocles, and *Euripides, the comedian *Aristophanes (*see* Old Comedy), and the historian *Thucydides. Prose achieved its acme in the 4th century with the works of *Plato, *Xenophon, and the orators *Isocrates and *Demosthenes. During the Hellenistic age Alexandria became the cultural centre of the Greek world; it was the home of the poets *Apollonius of Rhodes and *Callimachus, as well as of mathematicians, astronomers, and others who enhanced the status of Greek as a scientific and scholarly medium. Notable among Hellenistic writers elsewhere were the Sicilians *Theocritus and Moschus (c. 150 BC). Under the Roman Empire Greek remained an international literary language, as the works of *Marcus Aurelius, *Plutarch, and the Greek Church Fathers testify. After the 6th century AD, when Byzantium became the centre of Greek culture, histories (*see* Procopius), theological works, and scholarly commentaries became the main output. The 10th-century compilation known as the Greek Anthology comprises over 6000 poems ranging in date from the 7th century BC to the 10th century AD. A popular (demotic) tradition also survived, which expressed itself in folksong and epic (e.g. the late 10th-century epic, *Digenis Akritas*) and led eventually to modern Greek literature. *See also* Greek language.

Greek Orthodox Church   Strictly, the Orthodox Church in Greece, although the term is often applied to the Orthodox Churches as a whole, to distinguish them from the Latin

Church of the West. The Church in Greece dates from the 1st century and St Paul's activities, especially at Corinth. Under the patriarchate of Constantinople Greece was, from the acceptance of Christianity by *Constantine, one of the main Christian centres. With the eventual fall of Constantinople to the Turks, it ceased to be identified with the Byzantine Empire and is now a self-governing Church, the see of Athens holding a primacy of honour after the separation from the patriarchate of Constantinople in 1833.

Greek-Persian Wars An intermittent conflict between the Greeks and Persians. Persian encroachment on Greek territory began in 499 BC, when the Greek cities of *Ionia revolted against their Persian overlords and were crushed by *Darius I. In 490 the Persians were defeated by a small force of Athenians at *Marathon. Darius died in 486 and in 480 *Xerxes I crossed the Hellespont with a large force. The Greeks and Persians fought at *Thermopylae, where the Spartans (under *Leonidas I) heroically held the pass. Xerxes now attacked Attica and Athens was evacuated. At the battle of *Salamis the Persians were defeated by the Greek fleet commanded by *Themistocles and were again defeated at *Plataea (479). Intermittent warfare continued until 449, when the Persians abandoned hope of annexing Greece.

Greek religion The polytheistic religion of ancient Greece. From at least the time of Homer (9th century BC) the myths and deities of the various Greek states were integrated into a more or less coherent system, with a pantheon of 12 anthropomorphic gods who lived on Mount Olympus: *Zeus, *Hera, *Poseidon, *Athena, *Apollo, *Artemis, *Hephaestus, *Aphrodite, *Ares, *Demeter, *Hermes, and *Hestia. All these had appropriate festivals and observances throughout Greece. The orgiastic rites of *Cybele and *Dionysus were slightly later imports from Asia Minor. Deified heroes, such as *Heracles, were also worshipped and there were innumerable local cults for lesser supernatural beings, such as the *nymphs. For those who found the traditional eschatology of *Hades unsatisfactory, the *mysteries held a powerful attraction. During the Hellenistic age king-worship, another oriental import, became important. Religious centres honoured throughout Greece included *Delphi, *Delos, Dodona, *Epidaurus, and *Olympia. The forms of the ancient religion were not finally abolished until the Christian emperors closed these shrines (4th century AD), and even today local saints sometimes retain some of the attributes of the pagan gods.

Greeley, Horace (1811–72) US political journalist, who in 1841 founded the *New York Tribune*, championing temperance, liberal reforms, and protectionism; Karl Marx was a contributor. In the 1860s he vigorously opposed slavery. He made several attempts to enter politics, unsuccessfully standing as presidential candidate for the Liberal Republican Party in 1872.

Green, Henry (Henry Vincent Yorke; 1905–73) British novelist. He worked for his family engineering business for many years, eventually becoming managing director. His novels, satires of English social life written in a distinctive impersonal style, include *Living* (1929), *Loving* (1945), *Back* (1946), and *Concluding* (1948).

green algae *Algae of the division *Chlorophyta* (about 6000 species), which are bright green, owing to the predominance of the green pigment chlorophyll. Green algae range from simple unicellular plants, for example *Chlamydomonas*, to complex seaweeds, for example *sea lettuce. They are aquatic (mainly freshwater) or terrestrial in moist areas. Reproduction can be sexual or asexual.

Greenaway, Kate (1846–1901) British artist and book illustrator. The daughter of an engraver and draughtsman, she is famous for her charming representation of children in such books as *Kate Greenaway's Birthday Album* and *The Language of Flowers*.

Green Bay 44 32N 88 00W A city and port in the USA, in E Wisconsin at the head of an inlet of Lake Michigan. Its main industries are paper manufacture and food and dairy processing. Green Bay is the home of the National Railroad Museum. Population (1980): 87 889.

green belt A zone of open, mostly agricultural, land surrounding a town to prevent it from spreading uncontrollably. The concept, which has biblical origins, has been cherished, usually unsuccessfully, by utopians throughout the centuries. Sir Ebenezer *Howard's *garden cities of the early 1900s provided the first practical examples; in 1935 the London County Council initiated the steps towards a London green belt that were realized in the Green Belt Act (1938) and the Town and Country Planning Act (1947). Since the 1950s, however, successive governments have been made aware of the shortcomings of the concept—an unacceptably high density for the poorer sections of the community inside the belt combined with spacious acres for the privileged within it. Planners now favour a selective approach, preserving the more desirable areas of the countryside and permitting urban development in others.

greenbrier A green-stemmed often evergreen vinelike plant, *Smilax rotundifolia*, that grows in North American woods and thickets, also called catbrier. The leaves are heart-shaped and leathery, and the plant climbs by means of tendrils. The six-part flowers are borne in stalked clusters in the leaf axils and produce blue-black berries. Family: *Liliaceae*.

Greene, (Henry) Graham (1904–) British novelist. After the publication of his first novel *The Man Within* (1929), he devoted himself to full-time writing. He was converted to Roman Catholicism in 1927, and an intense concern with questions of morality is central in many of his novels, including *Brighton Rock* (1938), *The Power and the Glory* (1940), *The End of the Affair* (1951), *The Human Factor* (1978), *Dr Fischer of Geneva or The Bomb Party* (1980), and *Monsignor Quixote* (1982). He also wrote a number of literary thrillers, which he labelled "entertainments," including *The Ministry of Fear* (1943), *The Third Man* (1950), and *Our Man in Havana* (1958). His other works include plays, film scripts of several of his books, short stories, essays, and a biography, *Getting to Know the General* (1984). He was awarded the OM in 1986.

Greene, Nathaneal (1742–86) American general, who commanded the southern army in the American Revolution in succession to *Gates (1780–83). Greene conducted a strategic retreat into Virginia and by long marches and skilful deployments so exhausted the pursuing British that he was able to retake the Carolinas.

Greene, Robert (c. 1558–92) English pamphleteer and dramatist. A prolific writer, his best-known works include *Pandosto* (1588), a prose pastoral, which is the source of Shakespeare's *A Winter's Tale*, and the romantic comedy *Friar Bacon and Friar Bungay* (c. 1591). His pamphlet, *A Notable Discovery of Cosenage* (1592), contains a vivid account of Elizabethan low life. *Greene's Groatsworth of Wit* (1592), in which he repented of his dissolute life, contains interesting references to his contemporaries, including Shakespeare.

greenfinch A Eurasian *finch, *Carduelis chloris*, about 14 cm long with an olive-green body and a pale bill. The male has a bright yellow-green breast and both sexes show bright-yellow wing flashes in flight.

greenfly. *See* aphid.

greengage A bush or small tree, *Prunus italica*, related to the *plum, probably native to Asia Minor and widely cultivated. It bears round green fruits, often tinged with red, which are scented and used in preserves and for canning.

Greenham Common A US airbase near Newbury in England, designated as the first UK site for cruise missiles. A protest peace camp (1981–85) set up by women, who organized demonstrations of up to 30 000 people, failed to prevent the deployment of the missiles in 1983 and the camp was closed by the police in 1985; a few protesters remain.

greenheart An evergreen South American timber tree, *Nectandria rodiaei*, native to Guiana, also called sweetwood or bebeeru. Up to 30 m tall, it has inconspicuous flowers and the fruit is surrounded by an acorn-like cup. The wood, which is extremely hard, is used for underwater construction and ships. Family: *Lauraceae* (laurel family).

greenhouse effect An atmospheric effect in which some of the energy of ultraviolet radiation and visible light from the sun is retained by the earth as heat. The radiation is transmitted through the atmosphere to the earth's surface, where it is re-adiated as longer wavelength infrared radiation. The atmosphere only partially transmits the infrared back into space and so a heating effect occurs. The phenomenon takes its name from a greenhouse, in which a similar effect occurs.

Greenland (Danish name: Grønland; Greenlandic name: Kalaallit Nunaat) A large island off NE North America bounded by the N Atlantic Ocean and the Greenland and Norwegian Seas. Lying chiefly within the Arctic Circle, it is largely covered by a vast ice cap through which nunataks protrude around its rim. Many glaciers emerge from this, including the Humboldt Glacier, breaking off to form icebergs along the coast. Eskimos form about 80% of the population, the remainder being chiefly Danish. *Economy*: fishing is the chief occupation, principally for cod and halibut but other catches include shrimps and sea trout. Whaling and seal hunting have declined in recent years. The harsh environment makes agriculture difficult but sheep are reared in the SW. Greenland possesses potentially important mineral resources, notably lead and zinc, which have been exploited since the early 1970s; uranium is also present. *History*: in about 986 AD the Norwegian Eric the Red discovered the island, which he named Greenland to attract settlers. Norse colonies on the island disappeared during the 15th century and until 1721, when a new Danish settlement was established, the Eskimoes were the sole inhabitants. A Danish colony from 1721, Greenland became an integral part of Denmark in 1953. In 1979 it gained self-government under Danish sovereignty with its own parliament. In 1985 Greenland left the EEC. In 1987 a coalition government was formed from the Siumut and Invit Ataqatigitt parties. Prime minister: Jonathan Motzfeldt (1939–). Official language: Greenland Eskimo. Official currency: Danish krone of 100 øre. Area: 2 175 600 sq km (840 000 sq mi). Population (1981): 50 643. Capital: Godthaab.

Greenland Sea An extension of the Arctic Ocean, between Greenland, Svalbard, and Iceland. Covered by drifting ice, it links with the Atlantic Ocean.

Greenland shark An omnivorous *shark, *Somniosus microcephalus*, up to 7 m long, found in shoals in the deeper waters of the N Atlantic and Arctic Oceans. Family: *Squalidae*.

green monkey disease An acute, often fatal, viral infection first described in Marburg, West Germany, and therefore sometimes called Marburg disease. It occurs in vervet monkeys and may be transmitted to laboratory workers by contact with infected animals.

Green Mountain Boys An association of irregular forces formed (1770) and originally commanded by Ethan *Allen to oppose colonial New York's claim to control the Green Mountain region (now Vermont). They fought in the American Revolution, notably at the capture of Fort Ticonderoga (1775) and at Bennington (1777). Their purpose was attained in 1791 when Vermont was granted statehood.

Greenock 55 57N 4 45W A town in W central Scotland, in Strathclyde Region on the Clyde estuary. Shipbuilding is its principal industry; others include engineering and chemicals. James Watt was born here. Population (1981): 57 324.

Greenough, Horatio (1805–52) US neoclassical sculptor. A pupil of *Thorvaldsen, Greenough worked mainly in Rome. His most important sculpture was of George Washington in a toga (Smithsonian Institution, Washington, DC) commission-

ed by Congress in 1832.

Greenpeace movement An international environmental pressure group founded in 1971 to protest at nuclear tests in the Aleutian Islands. It campaigns primarily against nuclear power, dumping nuclear waste, and commercial whaling and sealing. Its use of direct action has sometimes led to confrontation, notably with the Soviet navy over whaling in 1983. In 1985 French saboteurs sank a Greenpeace vessel in New Zealand, killing one crew member.

Green Revolution. See agriculture; arable farming.

Greensboro 36 03N 79 50W A city in the USA, in North Carolina. It is a major centre of the cotton, textile, and rayon industries. Population (1980): 155 642.

greenshank A bird, *Tringa nebularia*, that breeds in N Eurasian moorland and tundra and winters in South Africa and S Eurasia. It is 30 cm long and greyish in colour with greenish legs, a white rump, and a long slightly upturned blue-grey bill. Family: *Scolopacidae* (sandpipers).

green turtle A large brown-green marine turtle, *Chelonia mydas*, which has green fat and is used to make turtle soup. Up to 1 m long and weighing up to 140 kg, they occur in warm Atlantic coastal waters feeding on marine algae and migrate to lay their eggs on Central American beaches. ⌐reptile.

Greenwich A borough of E Greater London, on the S bank of the River Thames. Created in 1965 from the former metropolitan boroughs of Greenwich and *Woolwich, it has important royal and maritime connections. The first Renaissance building in England, the Queen's House designed by Inigo *Jones (1616), was completed in 1637. The Greenwich Royal Hospital, designed by *Wren, became the Royal Naval College in 1873. Wren also designed the original *Royal Greenwich Observatory. The tea clipper *Cutty Sark* and Sir Francis Chichester's *Gipsy Moth IV* are at Greenwich Pier. Population (1981): 211 806.

Greenwich Mean Time (GMT) The local time at Greenwich, London, located on the 0° meridian (*see* longitude), from which the standard times of different areas of the globe are calculated, 15° longitude representing one hour in time.

Greenwich Village A residential section of New York City (USA), in Manhattan. It became a haunt of authors and artists early in the 20th century, acquiring a reputation for bohemianism. It is the site of the campus of New York University.

Greenwood, Walter (1903–) British novelist. His best-known book is *Love on the Dole* (1933), based on his own experience of unemployment. Later novels include *Standing Room Only* (1936) and *How the Other Man Lives* (1959).

Greer, Germaine (1939–) Australian feminist writer and lecturer. A leading figure in the women's movement since the 1970s, her books include *The Female Eunuch* (1970) and *Sex and Destiny* (1984).

Gregorian calendar. See calendar.

Gregorian chant The official liturgical plainchant of the Roman Catholic Church as codified during the papacy of Gregory I (590–604 AD). It consists of single unaccompanied melodic lines based on a system of *modes and sung to flexible rhythms. See plainchant.

Gregory I, St (c. 540–604 AD) Pope (590–604), known as Gregory the Great. Of senatorial rank, he gave himself to charitable works and was a monk before becoming a papal official. As pope he reorganized and increased papal power in Italy, making peace with the Lombards and limiting imperial authority over the Church. He reformed the papal states and sponsored *Augustine (of Canterbury) in his mission to convert England. Gregory's many pastoral and doctrinal works were of considerable influence, and he introduced the use of *Gregorian chant into the liturgy. He was canonized on his death. Feast day: 12 March.

Gregory VII, St (Hildebrand; c. 1021-85) Pope (1073-85). Before his election he worked closely with *Leo IX and Alexander II to reform the Church. As pope, he condemned simony, lay investiture, and clerical marriage. He was ultimately largely successful in asserting the independence of the Church from lay control but during his lifetime he created considerable opposition, especially in France and Germany, where Emperor *Henry IV declared his deposition (1076). He in turn excommunicated Henry and released his subjects from allegiance. Henry was soon forced to accept the pope's reforms and submitted to him at Canossa (1077). The conflict continued, however, when the emperor appointed Wibert, Archbishop of Ravenna, antipope (1080), invaded Italy, and captured Rome (1084). Gregory was rescued by Norman troops whom he had summoned but was nevertheless forced to flee from Rome. He died at Salerno. Feast day: 25 May.

Gregory IX (Ugolino of Segni; c. 1148-1241) Pope (1227-41). He was employed as a papal legate by his uncle, *Innocent III, and preached the fifth Crusade (1217). On his election as pope, he immediately excommunicated Emperor *Frederick II for his delay in fulfilling crusading vows. His papacy was marked by conflict with the emperor, and he died while Frederick was besieging Rome. He was a noted canon lawyer and was a friend of St *Francis of Assisi, whom he canonized.

Gregory XIII (Ugo Buoncompagni; 1502-85) Pope (1572-85). His pontificate was marked by support of the *Counter-Reformation and the sponsorship of colleges and reformed orders, especially the *Jesuits and the Oratorians. He founded the English College at Rome (1579) and was responsible for instituting the Gregorian *calendar (1582).

Gregory, James (1638-75) Scottish mathematician and astronomer. He was the first to investigate converging number series, which have an infinite number of terms but a finite sum. He also designed a reflecting *telescope, but failed in an attempt to build it because the glass could not be ground accurately enough. Similar types of telescope are still in use.

Gregory, Lady Augusta (1852-1932) Irish theatre patron and dramatist. With W. B. Yeats, in 1899 she founded the Irish Dramatic Movement, a national theatre company that moved into the Abbey Theatre in 1904. She collaborated with Yeats on *The Pot of Broth* (1902) and *Cathleen ni Houlihan* (1902) and wrote many comedies and translations, notably of Molière.

Gregory of Nazianzus, St (c. 330-c. 389 AD) Cappadocian Father of the Church, son of the Bishop of Nazianzus. He was educated in Athens, where he became a friend of St *Basil the Great. With Basil and St *Gregory of Nyssa he became a leading defender of orthodox Christianity against *Arianism. He was Bishop of Caesarea from 370 to 379 and briefly served as Patriarch of Constantinople in 380. Feast Day: 9 May.

Gregory of Nyssa, St (c. 335-c. 394 AD) Cappadocian Father of the Church. A leader of the orthodox party, which opposed *Arianism, he was made Bishop of Nyssa in 372 by his brother, St *Basil the Great. He was deposed in 376 but reinstated in 378 on the death of the Arian emperor, Valens. He wrote many theological works. Feast day: 9 March.

Gregory of Tours, St (c. 538-594 AD) French churchman and historian; Bishop of Tours (573-94). He is best known for his *Historia Francorum*, which is a history of the world from its creation to the 6th century AD. It is a valuable source of information on early European history. Feast Day: 17 Nov.

Greig, Tony (Anthony William G.; 1946-) Rhodesian-born cricketer, who played for Sussex and was captain of

England (1975-77). A fine all-rounder, he scored 3695 runs and took 152 wickets in Test cricket.

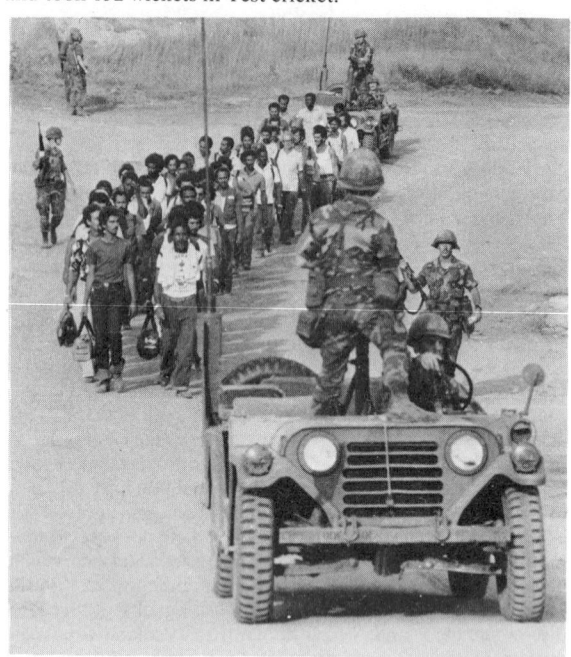

GRENADA *When the USA invaded in 1983, they expelled a number of Cubans, Soviet citizens, East Germans, and Libyans.*

Grenada, State of An island country in the West Indies, in the Windward Islands in the E Caribbean Sea off the NE coast of Venezuela. It also includes some of the Grenadine Islands, the largest of which is Carriacou. The majority of the population is of mixed European and Indian descent. *Economy*: largely agricultural, the chief products are cocoa, bananas, citrus fruits, sugar, and nutmeg (the main export). *History*: discovered by Columbus in 1493, it was colonized by the French and ceded to the British in 1763. In 1967 it became an Associated State under the West Indies Act and in 1974, an independent state within the British Commonwealth. In March, 1979, the government of Sir Eric Gairy (1922-) was overthrown in a nearly bloodless coup by the New Jewel Movement (NJM) led by Maurice Bishop (1944-83), who subsequently became prime minister. Following an uprising of armed forces in 1983, during which Bishop was killed, the USA invaded the country to protect US interests. Prime minister: Herbert Blaize (1922-). Official language: English. Official currency: East Caribbean dollar of 100 cents. Area: 344 sq km (133 sq mi). Population (1981 est): 100 000. Capital: St George's.

grenadier A carnivorous bottom-dwelling fish, also called rat-tail or torpedo, belonging to a family (*Macrouridae*; about 300 species) found in deep warm and temperate marine waters. It has a stout body, usually 30-60 cm long, with a long ratlike tail and a large head.

Grenadine Islands A chain of West Indian islets, extending for about 100 km (60 mi) between St Vincent and Grenada and administratively divided between the two.

Grenoble 45 11N 5 43E A city in SE France, the capital of the Isère department. The capital of the Dauphiné until 1341, it has a cathedral (12th-13th centuries) and a university (1339). It is the principal tourist centre of the French Alps and has metallurgical, textile, cement, and paper industries. Population (1982): 159 503.

Grenville, Sir Richard (?1541-91) British sailor. In 1585 Grenville commanded the seven ships taking Sir Walter

Raleigh's colonists to Virginia. In 1591, as commander of the *Revenge*, he refused to withdraw before a Spanish fleet off the Azores and put four Spanish ships out of action. Eventually prevailed upon to surrender, he died aboard a Spanish ship. The exploit is the subject of Tennyson's ballad *The Revenge*.

Grenville, William (Wyndham), Baron (1759-1834) British statesman; prime minister (1806-07). He was foreign secretary (1791-1801) under his cousin William *Pitt the Younger, with whom he resigned when George III rejected Catholic emancipation. As prime minister he led the coalition Ministry of All the Talents, which took office after Pitt's death and was notable for its abolition of the slave trade (1807). His government fell owing to royal opposition to the Catholic Relief bill. His father **George Grenville** (1712-70) was prime minister from 1763 to 1765. His government, which was hindered by George III's continued reliance on Grenville's predecessor *Bute, was noted for its *Stamp Act (1765) and prosecution of John *Wilkes.

Gresham, Sir Thomas (c. 1519-79) English financier and philanthropist. He founded Gresham College and the Royal Exchange, both in London, but is best known for the so-called **Gresham's Law**, attributed to him in the 19th century, that "bad money drives out good": if there are two different types of coin in circulation, and one sort of coin is suspected of being debased and is falling in value relative to the other, the more valuable coin will be hoarded and will eventually disappear from circulation.

Gretna Green 55 00N 3 04W A village in S Scotland, in Dumfries and Galloway Region on the English border. It is famous as the scene of marriages of eloping English couples following the prohibition of clandestine marriages in England (1753). From 1856 three weeks residence in Scotland was required and in 1939 these marriage ceremonies were declared illegal.

Grétry, André Ernest Modeste (1741-1813) Belgian composer, who lived and died in France. One of the leading opera composers of his time, he was an exponent of *opera comique. Of his large output little is known today, although Beecham made well-known arrangements of some of his music.

Greuze, Jean-Baptiste (1725-1805) French painter, born in Tournus. Settling in Paris, he achieved early acclaim with his *Father Reading the Bible to His Children* (1755; Louvre). After an unsuccessful attempt at history painting (1769), he concentrated on sentimental and vaguely erotic portraits of girls, e.g. *The Broken Pitcher* (Louvre).

Greville, Fulke, 1st Baron Brooke (1554-1628) English poet and biographer. He served as a diplomat and administrator and was chancellor of the exchequer from 1614 to 1622. He wrote a collection of sonnets, *Caelica* (1633), but is now mainly remembered as the author of *The Life of the Renowned Sir Philip Sidney* (published 1652), a memoir of his lifelong friend.

Grey, Charles, 2nd Earl (1764-1845) British statesman, who as Whig prime minister (1830-34) secured the passage of the parliamentary *Reform Act of 1832 by persuading William IV to create sufficient new peers to carry the bill through the House of Lords. His son **Henry George, 3rd Earl Grey** (1802-94) was Whig colonial secretary (1846-52) and, in advance of his time, advocated colonial self-government. The 2nd earl's nephew **Edward, 1st Viscount Grey of Fallodon** (1862-1933) was Liberal (formerly termed Whig) foreign secretary from 1905 to 1916. He negotiated the *Triple Entente of Britain, France, and Russia (1904-07) and supported France against Germany in the Morocco crises of 1905-06 and 1911. At the outbreak of World War I he remarked: "The lamps are going out all over Europe; we shall not see them lit again in our lifetime."

Grey, Sir George (1812-98) British colonial administrator. After serving as governor of South Australia (1841-

45) he was governor of New Zealand (1845-53), where he suppressed the initial hostilities of the *Maori Wars. He subsequently fostered good relations with the Maoris before being posted to Cape Colony, where as governor (1854-61) he dealt effectively with hostilities between Africans and Europeans. He was again governor of New Zealand (1861-68) following the resumption of the Maori Wars and was later prime minister of New Zealand (1877-79). He retired to Britain in 1894.

Grey, Lady Jane (1537-54) Queen of England for nine days (1553) and the great-granddaughter of *Henry VII. The Duke of *Northumberland had her proclaimed queen when Edward VI died but Mary, the rightful heiress, had popular support and Jane abdicated. She was executed for treason with her husband Lord Guildford Dudley, Northumberland's son.

greyhound An ancient breed of dog used for hare coursing and racing. It has a slender deep-chested streamlined body with long legs and a long muscular neck. The short smooth coat can be of various colours. Greyhounds can reach speeds of up to 70 km per hour. Height: 71-76 cm (dogs); 68-71 cm (bitches).

greyhound racing (*or* dog racing) A form of racing popular for betting, in which greyhounds pursue an electrically propelled mechanical hare round a circular or oval track. The sport evolved from *coursing in the USA in the early 20th century and is especially popular in the UK and Australia. Races may be on the flat or over hurdles, with distances ranging from 210 m (230 yd) to 1100 m (1200 yd).

greylag goose A grazing *goose, *Anser anser*, occurring in N and E Europe and central Asia. 75-87 cm long, it has a heavy orange bill and is dark grey above with pale wings, a finely barred neck, and pink legs.

greywacke (*or* graywacke) A dark-coloured sedimentary rock with sand-sized angular rock particles in a finer matrix. Greywackes display a wide range of sedimentary structures and are commonly found in geosynclines.

gribble A wood-boring marine crustacean of the genus *Limnoria* (about 20 species). It feeds on algae, driftwood, and the submerged sections of docks and piers. *L. lignorum*, common in the N hemisphere, has a grey body up to 5 mm long. Order: *Isopoda*.

Grieg, Edvard Hagerup (1843-1907) Norwegian composer, who studied in Leipzig and Copenhagen. He spent the latter part of his life in a house near the Troldhaugen fjord and was buried there. The influence of Norwegian folk music is apparent in many of his works, which include the *Lyric Pieces* (for piano; 1867-1901), a very popular piano concerto (1868), incidental music to Ibsen's play *Peer Gynt* (1876), chamber music, and many songs.

Grierson, John (1898-1972) British film director. He developed the concept of *documentary film and helped to establish film production units in Britain, Canada, and the USA. His own documentary films include *Drifters* (1929), *Industrial Britain* (1933), and *Granton Trawler* (1934).

griffin A mythological creature with the head and wings of an eagle, the body of a lion, and often a serpent's tail. It is common in many ancient eastern mythologies.

Griffith, Arthur (1872-1922) Irish journalist and nationalist, who organized *Sinn Féin in 1905. He was imprisoned three times (1916, 1918-19, 1920-21) by the British authorities. In 1918 Sinn Féin won the majority of parliamentary seats in Ireland and declared a republic, which Griffith headed from 1919 to 1920. In 1921 he led the Irish delegation to the conference that determined the treaty establishing the Irish Free State. On *De Valera's rejection of the terms, Griffith was elected (1922) president of the Irish assembly (the Dáil Éireann) but died later that year.

Griffith, D(avid) W(ark) (1875-1948) US film director. His intuitive understanding of the artistic potential of the cinema and his innovations in editing and narrative techniques made him the most influential pioneer of the cinema in the USA. His major films include *The Birth of a Nation* (1915), an ambitious epic concerning the Civil War, *Intolerance* (1916), *Broken Blossoms* (1919), and *Isn't Life Wonderful* (1924).

griffon (dog) A breed of toy dog originating in Belgium and of terrier ancestry. It has a square compact body, a docked tail, and a large head covered with long coarse hair. The coat is either rough and wiry or short and tight and may be red, black, or black and tan. Weight: 2–5 kg.

griffon vulture One of the largest Old World *vultures, *Gyps fulvus*. It is 100 cm long and occurs in mountainous regions of S Europe, South Africa, and Asia. It is grey-brown with darker wingtips and a white head and ruff.

Grignard reagents Organomagnesium compounds, discovered by F. A. V. Grignard (1871–1935) and usually prepared by adding an organic halide to magnesium under ether. They are invaluable in a host of organic syntheses, giving addition products with almost all groups.

Grillparzer, Franz (1791–1872) Austrian dramatist. He worked in government service until his retirement in 1856 and was appointed court dramatist at the Hofburgtheater after the success of his first tragedy, *Die Ahnfrau* (1817). His tragedies ranged from adaptations of Greek myth, such as *The Golden Fleece* (1821), to fantasy plays, such as *A Dream Is Life* (1834).

Grimaldi, Joseph (1779–1837) British clown. His popular success at Covent Garden between 1806 and 1823 was based on his skills as a dancer, acrobat, and singer, as well as his instinct for pathos and comedy.

Grimm Two brothers, German philologists and folklorists. After early work on medieval German texts, **Jakob Grimm** (1785–1863) and **Wilhelm Grimm** (1786–1859) set about collecting German folktales, published in 1812–14 as *Kinder- und Hausmärchen*. The *Deutsche Grammatik* (1819, 1822) is a historical and descriptive German grammar containing observations on the regularity of sound changes in Indo-European languages, known as **Grimm's law**. Their *Deutsches Wörterbuch* is a historical and descriptive German dictionary.

Grimmelshausen, Hans Jacob Christoph von (c. 1625–76) German novelist. Orphaned when a child, he served in the Imperial and Swedish armies during the Thirty Years' War and later worked as a steward, bailiff, and innkeeper. His picaresque *Simplicissimus* novels (1669–72) are a realistic and satirical record of his unsettled times.

Grimond, Jo(seph), Baron (1913–) British politician; leader of the Liberal Party (1956–67). He campaigned for British membership of the EEC and developed the idea of a "copartnership in industry" of management and labour, contributing to Liberal successes in the elections of 1959 and 1964. He resigned the leadership following electoral reverses in 1966 and was created a life peer in 1983.

Grimsby 53 35N 0 05W A seaport in NE England, in Humberside near the mouth of the Humber estuary. Although it is the largest fishing port in England, the extension of Iceland's fishing limits (1975–76) combined with overfishing in many of the traditional grounds has led to a considerable reduction in the size of the fishing fleet. Population (1981): 92 147.

Grindelia A genus of herbaceous plants (about 50 species), native to temperate North and South America and sometimes cultivated as garden plants. They have yellow aster-like flowers, solitary or in clusters, and usually rigid toothed leaves. The dried plants of some species, e.g. *G. camporum*, have medicinal properties. Family: *Compositae*.

Grindelwald 46 38N 8 03E An alpine village in central Switzerland, in the Grindelwald Valley. It is a major mountaineering centre and a summer and winter resort at the foot of the Wetterhorn and Eiger mountains at a height of 1037 m (3402 ft). Population (1980): 3555.

Gris, Juan (José Victoriano González; 1887–1927) Spanish-born cubist painter, who worked in Paris from 1906. In contrast to *Picasso and *Braque, his approach to *cubism was mathematical; his starting points were abstract shapes from which he developed real objects in geometrically constructed still lifes, landscapes, and portraits. He also promoted the art of collage and wrote an influential study of painting entitled *Les Possibilités de la peinture* (1924).

grison A mammal belonging to the genus *Grison* (2 species) of Central and South America. Grisons are about 60 cm long and greyish black, hunting through forest and grassland for invertebrates and small mammals. Family: *Mustelidae* (weasels, stoats, etc.).

Grivas, Georgios (1898–1974) Greek general, born in Cyprus. Known as Dighenis, he was the leader of *EOKA, which fought for the union of Cyprus with Greece.

grizzly bear. *See* brown bear.

Grodno 53 40N 23 50E A port in the W central Soviet Union, in the Belorussian SSR on the River Neman. Possessed by Lithuania and then by Poland, it includes a medieval castle and *Stephen Báthory's 16th-century palace. It is an important railway centre and major industrial city, producing fertilizers, textiles, food products, and tobacco. Population (1981 est): 212 000.

Gromyko, Andrei (1909–) Soviet diplomat; foreign minister (1957–85) and president of the Soviet Union (1985–). Gromyko began his diplomatic career in 1939 and served as ambassador to the USA (1943–46) and the UK (1952–53). He was Soviet representative at the UN between 1946 and 1949.

Groningen 53 13N 6 35E A city in the N Netherlands, the capital of Groningen province. It has a notable church (the 15th-century Martinikerk) and a university (1614). An important commercial and market centre, its industries include textiles, clothing, and sugar refining. Population (1983): 166 942.

Groningen A province in the Netherlands, bordering on the North Sea and West Germany. Low lying and fertile, it is intensively cultivated and agriculture forms the chief occupation. Natural gas is extracted at Slochteren. Area: 2350 sq km (900 sq mi). Population (1983): 560 708. Capital: Groningen.

Groote Eylandt 12 20S 135 15E An Australian island, in the Gulf of Carpentaria off the coast of the Northern Territory. It forms part of the Arnhem Land Aboriginal Reserve. Manganese deposits have recently been discovered and exploited. Area: 2460 sq km (950 sq mi). Population (1981 est): 1961.

Gropius, Walter (1883–1969) German architect, one of the pioneers of the international modern style of architecture. Gropius was influenced by William *Morris and Frank Lloyd *Wright and trained under *Behrens until 1910. His first major building, a factory at Alfeld (1911) is a very early example of the new style. As director of the *Bauhaus (1919–28) he was able greatly to influence all aspects of contemporary design. The rise of Nazi power forced him to leave Germany (1934) for England. In 1937 he moved to America, where he spent 14 influential years teaching at Harvard. He continued to design a few buildings, for example the US Embassy in Athens (1960), and to influence European architecture.

Gros, Antoine Jean, Baron (1771–1835) French painter. A pupil of *David, he later travelled with Napoleon's armies, painting such scenes as *Napoleon Visiting the Plague-Stricken at Jaffa* (1804; Louvre). Although initially successful under the restored Bourbons, he fell into obscurity in the 1820s and finally drowned himself. His style, influenced by *Rubens, anticipates the work of *Delacroix and *Géricault.

grosbeak A finch with a particularly heavy bill used to crack open hard seeds and nuts. The name is given to birds of several genera found in N Eurasia, America, and the tropics. The reddish-brown Eurasian pine grosbeak (*Pinicola enucleator*) uses its bill as a hammer to obtain seeds from pine cones.

gross domestic product. *See* gross national product.

Grosseteste, Robert (c. 1175-1253) English ecclesiastical reformer and scholar; Bishop of Lincoln (1235-53). Grosseteste brought about many reforms in his diocese and was a regular and stringent visitor of monasteries. His opposition to clerical laxity and nepotism led him to quarrel with both his chapter and the papacy. His writings included translations of the church fathers and philosophical commentaries. His scientific experiments inspired Roger *Bacon.

Grossglockner 47 05N 12 44E The highest mountain in Austria, in the Alps. The Grossglockner Road (built 1930-35) crosses it, rising to 2576 m (7852 ft). Height: 3797 m (12 457 ft).

Grossmith, George (1847-1912) British singer and entertainer. From 1877, he played in many of the main roles in the operas of Gilbert and Sullivan. His brother **Weedon Grossmith** (1854-1915) wrote and acted in social comedies. They collaborated on an extremely successful novel, *Diary of a Nobody* (1892), which satirized lower-middle-class pretensions.

gross national product (GNP) A measure of the total annual output of a country, including net income from abroad; it provides a measure of the economic strength of that country. GNP can be calculated in three ways: based on income, output, or expenditure. If income is used as the basis, all incomes accruing to residents of the country as a result of economic activity (excluding, for instance, pensions) are summed (national income is thus synonymous with GNP calculated in this way). On the basis of output, the value added to a product at each stage of production is summed. If expenditure is used, the value of all consumption products is calculated. All three methods should give the same result. **Gross domestic product** (GDP) is GNP excluding net income from abroad and gives some indication of the strength of industry within a country. **Net national product** differs from GNP in that it makes a provision for *depreciation, i.e. the using up of the country's capital stock.

Grosz, George (1893-1959) German painter and draughtsman, born in Berlin. A member of the *Dada art movement, he is famous for his bitter satirical depictions of war, the bourgeoisie, the church, and German social evils. He was fined and charges of blasphemy were brought against him because of his work. He emigrated to the USA in 1932.

Grotefend, Georg Friedrich (1775-1853) German philologist. He did important work on ancient *Italic languages, but after 1800 was increasingly occupied with attempts to decipher Persian *cuneiform inscriptions. He established several facts, including the alphabetic (as opposed to syllabic) nature of the characters, which facilitated their successful decipherment by *Rawlinson.

Grotius, Hugo (*or* Huig de Groot; 1583-1645) Dutch jurist and diplomat, the founder of international law. Sentenced to life imprisonment in 1619 by Prince Maurice of Nassau for his support of the Arminian faith in the religious controversies of the time, he escaped to France in 1621. There he wrote his famous *De jure belli et pacis* (1625), arguing that natural law should be applied to nations as well as individuals and that war should only be waged for justified causes. He was Swedish ambassador to France from 1635 until his death.

ground beetle A heavily armoured long-legged beetle belonging to a family (*Carabidae*; 25 000 species) that is particularly common in temperate regions. Ground beetles are dark in colour or have a metallic sheen and are from 2 to 85 mm long. Most are nocturnal and can be found under stones, logs, and debris during the day. The adults and most

larvae are active carnivores, preying on insects, slugs, and snails. *See also* bombardier beetle.

ground bug A *plant bug belonging to the worldwide famiy *Lygaeidae* (about 3000 species). Ground bugs have elongated brown or black bodies, 3-15 mm long, often with red markings. They live in moss or rubbish or under stones or low bushes and feed on a variety of plants, in many cases becoming serious pests (*see* chinch bug).

ground elder A perennial herbaceous plant, *Aegopodium podagraria*, also called goutweed, bishop's weed, or herb Gerard, common in Europe on waste ground and as a garden weed. 49-100 cm tall, it has compound leaves with three leaflets (like those of elder) and umbrella-like clusters of small white flowers. The leaves may be eaten as a salad or vegetable. Family: *Umbelliferae*.

groundhog. *See* marmot.

ground ivy A creeping perennial herb, *Glechoma hederacea* (or *Nepeta glechoma*), found in woods and grasslands across Eurasia. It has long-stalked heart-shaped toothed leaves and its stems, 10-30 cm high, bear groups of tubular violet two-lipped flowers. Family: *Labiatae*.

groundnut The fruit of *Arachis hypogea*, also called peanut or earthnut, native to tropical South America but widely cultivated in the tropics. The plant is an erect or creeping annual, 30-45 cm high, with compound leaves and yellow flowers. After fertilization the flower stalk elongates, pushing the developing pod below the soil to ripen under ground. The pod has a thin spongy wall and contains one to three seeds (the nuts), which are highly nutritious. They are used in cookery, canned, and made into peanut butter and groundnut oil (used in margarine). Family: *Leguminosae*.

groundsel A weedy herbaceous plant of the genus *Senecio*, especially *S. vulgaris*, 8-45 cm high and common in Eurasia and N Africa. It has lobed toothed leaves and small yellow flower heads, which lack ray florets and are almost enclosed by the sepals. Family: *Compositae*.

ground squirrel A *squirrel that lives in an underground burrow rather than in a tree. Ground squirrels have short strong legs, small ears, and shorter tails than tree squirrels, inhabiting open country in North America, Eurasia, and Africa. Chief genera: *Citellus* (34 species), *Lariscus* (2 species), *Xerus* (4 species). *See also* prairie dog; chipmunk; souslik; marmot.

groundwater The water that has percolated into the ground and become trapped within pores, cracks, and fissures. It is important in *weathering processes through its chemical effects. With depth the *water table is reached, below which all pore spaces are filled.

grouper One of several sedentary food and game fish of the family *Serranidae* (*see* sea bass), especially the genera *Epinephelus* and *Mycteroperca*, widely distributed in warm seas. Groupers have a dull-green or brown heavy body, up to or exceeding 2 m long, and a large mouth. Some are poisonous when consumed.

Group Theatre 1. A US theatre company founded in 1929 and dedicated to the production of socially relevant plays and the development of *Stanislavsky's theories of "method" acting. It produced many of the plays of the US playwright Clifford Odets (1906-63), notably *Waiting for Lefty* (1935), before disbanding in 1940. 2. A British theatre society founded in 1933. Among its experimental productions of the 1930s were plays by *Auden and *Isherwood, T. S. *Eliot, and Stephen *Spender.

group therapy A form of *psychotherapy in which several patients meet together to understand and overcome their problems, usually with the help of a therapist. There are many forms of group therapy: sometimes the aim is to increase patients' insight in psychoanalytic terms, sometimes to teach social skills, sometimes to act out distressing events from the past, and sometimes to support one another in overcoming a common problem (such as alcoholism).

GROUSE *The male sage grouse* (Centrocercus urophasianus) *in courtship display, during which it fans out its tail and inflates a pouch on its chest to attract females.*

grouse A fowl-like game bird, 30–88 cm long, belonging to a family (*Tetraonidae*; about 18 species) of the N hemisphere. Grouse are mostly ground-living, with short round wings, a short strong bill, and feathered legs. They are noted for their spectacular courtship displays (called *leks*). The family includes the *black grouse, *red grouse, and *capercaillie of N Europe (including Britain); the *ptarmigans; and the North American ruffed grouse (*Bonasa umbellus*) and *sage grouse. In Britain the grouse-shooting season is from 12 Aug to 10 Dec. Order: *Galliformes*. *See also* gamebird.

Grove, Sir George (1820–1900) British musicologist, founder and first editor of *Grove's Dictionary of Music and Musicians* (1879–89). A Londoner, he trained and practised as a civil engineer. His interest in the arts led to extensive musical and biblical research during which he travelled widely. He was founder and first director (1883–94) of the Royal College of Music and was knighted in 1883. *The New Grove Dictionary of Music and Musicians* was published in 1980.

Groves, Sir Charles (1915–) British conductor. Trained at the Royal College of Music, he became successively conductor of the BBC Northern Symphony Orchestra, the Bournemouth Symphony Orchestra, and the Royal Liverpool Philharmonic Orchestra. He was musical director of English National Opera from 1978 to 1979 and was knighted in 1973.

growth hormone (*or* somatotrophin) A protein hormone that promotes the metabolic processes involved in growth of bone and muscle. It is secreted by the pituitary gland and stimulates protein synthesis, mobilizes fat reserves, increases glucose levels in the blood, and affects mineral metabolism. Lack of growth hormone in children causes dwarfism.

Grozny 43 21N 45 42E A city in the S Soviet Union, the capital of Checheno-Ingush ASSR in the RSFSR. It is one of the country's oldest and richest oil-producing areas. Population (1984): 389 000.

Grub Street A street, now renamed Milton St, in Moorfields, London, associated in the 18th century with writers of little talent, who earned their livings by whatever literary work they could obtain. *Pope satirized such hacks in *An* *Epistle to Dr Arbuthnot* (1755) and the name is referred to in the title of George *Gissing's novel *New Grub Street* (1891).

Grünewald, Matthias (Mathis Gothardt; d. 1528) German painter, born in Würzburg. His earliest known work is *The Mocking of Christ* (c. 1503; Alte Pinakothek, Munich). For much of his career, he was court painter at Mainz. His favourite subject was the crucifixion, of which perhaps his most tragic treatment is the *Isenheim Altarpiece* (Colmar, France), noted also for its dazzling colour. His style, characterized by a distortion of form, influenced 20th-century German expressionists (*see* expressionism).

grunt A small food fish, belonging to the family *Pomadasyidae* (about 75 species), that can produce piglike grunts. It has a colourful elongated body and a large mouth; it occurs in the warm and tropical coastal waters. Order: *Perciformes*.

Gruyère A district in Switzerland, in the middle Saane Valley, famed for its cheese and cattle.

Guadalajara 20 30N 103 20W The second largest city in Mexico, at an altitude of 1650 m (5413 ft). Founded by the Spanish (1530), it has several notable buildings including the cathedral (16th–17th centuries) and the Governor's Palace (begun 1763); there are two universities (1792, 1935). Its key position as a communications centre across the Sierra Madre Occidental has led to its rapid expansion in recent years and it now has a large industrial complex. Its handicraft industries (especially glassware and pottery) also remain important. Population (1980): 2 244 715.

Guadalajara 40 37N 3 10W A town in NE Spain, in New Castile. Its notable palace was virtually destroyed during the Spanish Civil War but has since been restored. Industries include textiles and tanning. Population (1981): 56 922.

Guadalcanal 9 30S 160 00E The largest of the Solomon Islands, in the S Pacific Ocean. During World War II the first major US offensive in the Pacific against the Japanese took place here; it was captured after six months of jungle fighting (1942–43). Copra, rubber, and some gold are produced. Area: 6475 sq km (2500 sq mi). Population (1984): 63 335. Chief settlement: Honiara.

Guadalquivir, River The main river of S Spain. It flows mainly WSW from the Sierra de Segura to the Gulf of Cádiz and is navigable to Seville by oceangoing vessels. Length: 560 km (348 mi).

Guadalupe Hidalgo (name from 1931 until 1971: Gustavo A. Madero) 19 29N 99 07W A city in central Mexico, a NE suburb of Mexico City. The Basilica of the Virgin of Guadalupe, which was built after an Indian convert reported seeing a vision of the Virgin Mary here in 1531, is a famous place of pilgrimage. The Treaty of *Guadalupe Hidalgo was signed here.

Guadalupe Hidalgo, Treaty of (1848) The treaty that ended the *Mexican War. In exchange for $15 million and the payment of the claims of US citizens, the USA received what are now the states of California, Nevada, Utah, parts of Colorado, Wyoming, and Arizona and most of New Mexico.

Guadeloupe A French overseas region in the West Indies, in the E Caribbean Sea. It comprises two main islands, Grande Terre and Basse Terre, together with the island dependencies of Marie Galante, La Désirade, Îles des Saintes, St Barthélemy, and the N part of *St Martin. The economy is based on agriculture; sugar cane is the chief crop. Area: 1702 sq km (657 sq mi). Population (1984 est): 329 400. Capital: Basse-Terre.

guaiacum A small evergreen tree of the genus *Guaiacum*, especially *G. officinale* of tropical America, also called lignum vitae. It has blue flowers, yellow heart-shaped fruits, and very dense hard wood, used to make pulleys, axles, and bowling balls. The greenish resin is distilled for medicinal use. Family: *Zygophyllaceae*.

Guam 13 30N 144 40E An island and US unincorporated territory in the West Pacific Ocean, the largest of the

FRANCESCO GUARDI *An architectural caprice, depicting the vaulted arcade of the Doge's Palace, Venice (c. 1780; Wallace Collection, London).*

Mariana Islands. Mountainous in the S, it is mantled by jungle. Spanish from 1565 to 1898, it was occupied by the Japanese (1941–44). It is a major naval and air base, especially important during the Vietnam War. Industries include ship repairing. Area: 450 sq km (210 sq mi). Population (1980): 105 821. Capital: Agaña.

guanaco A hoofed mammal, *Lama guanacoe*, closely related to the *llama and found at altitudes of up to 5000 m in W South America. Red-brown with a pale face and pale underparts, guanacos grow up to 110 cm high at the shoulder and live in small herds on open grassland. Family: *Camelidae*.

Guan Di (*or* Kuan Ti) In Chinese mythology, the god of war. A historical figure and hero of numerous romantic exploits, he was captured and executed in 219 AD. His popularity with both common people and the aristocracy grew until he was pronounced a god in 1594. Various professions and trades, including writers, adopted him as patron and hundreds of temples were built in his honour.

Guangdong (Kuang-tung *or* Kwangtung) A mountainous province in S China, including Hainan and other islands. Heavily populated, it produces rice, sugar cane, tobacco, silk, fish, timber, and minerals. *History*: Chinese from 222 BC, it only came under Chinese cultural influence in the 12th and 13th centuries AD. As China's main trading area, it later had considerable contact with the West and from the mid-19th century overpopulation led to overseas emigration. During the 19th and early 20th centuries it was a centre of revolutionary movements. Area: 231 400 sq km (90 246 sq mi). Population (1980 est): 56 810 000. Capital: Canton.

Guangxi Zhuang Autonomous Region (*or* Kwangsi Chuang AR) A mountainous administrative division in S China, on the North Vietnamese border. It has seen great economic growth since 1949, producing sugar cane, rice, timber, manganese, and tin. *History*: its non-Chinese minorities have rebelled

periodically and the *Taiping Rebellion started here (1851). It became a centre of communist opposition to *Chiang Kaishek's government and heavy fighting against the Japanese invasion took place here during World War II. Area: 220 400 sq km (85 956 sq mi). Population (1980 est): 34 700 000. Capital: Nanning.

Guang Xu (*or* Kuang-hsü; 1871–1908) The title of Cai Tian (*or* Tsai-t'ien) of the Qing dynasty, who became emperor (1875) at the age of four with his aunt *Zi Xi as regent. When after coming of age he sponsored the *Hundred Days of Reform she imprisoned him for the rest of his life.

Guangzhou. *See* Canton.

guano The accumulated excrement of certain animals, especially seabirds, seals, and bats. It contains 10–18% nitrogen, 8–12% phosphoric acid, and 2–3% potash, according to the age and origin of the deposit. Large amounts have been found on islands off the Peruvian and other coasts and it has been widely used as a fertilizer.

Guantánamo 20 09N 75 14W A city in SE Cuba, N of Guantánamo Bay. It is the centre of an agricultural area producing sugar cane and coffee. Industries include coffee roasting, sugar refining, and chocolate manufacture. Population (1981): 246 739.

Guan Yin (*or* Kuan Yin) In Chinese Buddhism, the goddess of compassion. She is the same *bodhisattva who was worshipped in India in male form as Avalokiteshvara and in Japan as the multiheaded or multiarmed Kannon. In Chinese art Guan Yin only took on female form during the 12th and 13th centuries.

guarana A climbing plant, *Paullinia cuparia*, of the Amazon Basin, with large compound leaves and clusters of short-stalked flowers. The fruit is about 2 cm long and contains one seed. The seeds are roasted to produce a stimulant drink containing more caffeine than coffee or ground to make bread. Guarana is also a source of starch, gum, saponin, oils, and drugs. Family: *Sapindaceae*.

Guarani A group of South American Indian peoples of Paraguay and neighbouring areas of Brazil and Argentina who speak languages of the Tupian group. About a million Paraguayans speak Guarani. Few now retain their original culture, typical of the tropical forest, based on hunting and maize cultivation, warfare, and cannibalism.

Guardi, Francesco (1712–93) Venetian painter, who studied under and sometimes collaborated with his elder brother, **Giovanni Antonio Guardi** (1699–1760). His souvenir views of Venice were sometimes copied from *Canaletto but they are distinguished by their romantic style and impressionistic technique.

guardian angels Divine beings that figure in several religions. They derive from the belief that every individual has an angel assigned by God as his guardian. In the Roman Catholic Church they may be invoked as intercessors; feast day: 2 Oct.

Guarini, Giovanni Battista (1538–1612) Italian poet. He served at the court of the Duke of Ferrara and in Rome and Florence. His best-known work, *The Faithful Shepherd* (1590), emulating Torquato *Tasso's *Aminta* (1573), helped to establish the genre of pastoral drama.

Guarini, Guarino (1624–83) Italian baroque architect, philosopher, and mathematician. Most of Guarini's work was done in his native Piedmont. Although influenced by *Borromini, his work shows great originality and technical skill. Probably his most successful building is the church of S Lorenzo, Turin (1668–87).

Guarneri An Italian family of violin makers, famous in the 17th and 18th centuries. The first of the line was **Andrea Guarneri** (d. 1698), who was a pupil (with Stradivari) of Amati in Cremona. Andrea's grandson **Giuseppe Guarneri** (1698–1744), known as "del Gesù," was the most famous member of the family; influenced by the makers of the Brescian school, he produced violins with a characteristically powerful tone, signing them "Guarnerius."

Guatemala, Republic of A country in Central America, on the Pacific Ocean, with a small outlet on the Caribbean Sea. The tropical forests of the Petén in the N and a narrower plain on the Pacific rise to a central mountainous region, containing a fertile plateau. The country is subject to hurricanes and earthquakes, which have caused havoc throughout its history. About half the population are *Maya Quiché Indians and most of the rest are of mixed Spanish and Indian descent. *Economy*: mainly agricultural, the land being fertile but subject to erosion. Since the 1950s a new system of land development has been introduced, largely on a cooperative basis. The main crops are coffee, sugar, bananas, and cotton, which are the principal exports. Rubber and essential oils are being developed as well as forest products (chicle and timber). Minerals include zinc and lead concentrates, and nickel mining is being introduced. Oil was discovered in 1974 and production is increasing. Efforts are being made to promote industrial growth in plastics, as well as the more traditional food processing and textile industries. *History*: there is extensive archaeological evidence of pre-Spanish civilizations, especially that of the Maya, and, from the 12th century, the Aztecs. From 1524 to 1821 the area was part of the Spanish captaincy general of Guatemala, which included most of Central America. It formed the nucleus of the Central American Federation until 1839, when it became independent. In recent years periods of democratic government have alternated with military dictatorships, accompanied by considerable political unrest. In 1976 it suffered a serious earthquake in the centre. Guatemala's claims to Belize have intensified in recent years. Following a military coup in 1983 Gen Oscar Humberto Mejia Victores (1930–   ) became president; in 1986 civilian rule returned with the election of Vinicio Cerezo as president. Official language: Spanish. Official religion: Roman Catholic. Official currency: quetzal of 100 centavos. Area: 108 889 sq km (42 042 sq mi). Population (1983 est): 7 714 000. Capital: Guatemala City. Main port: Puerto Barrios.

Guatemala City 14 38N 90 22W The capital of Guatemala, situated in the S of the country in a high valley. Founded in 1776, it was the capital of the captaincy general of Guatemala and later of the Central American Federation. It has four universities; the oldest was founded in 1776. Population (1983 est): 1 300 000.

guava A tropical American tree, *Psidium guajava*, about 10 m tall. Its white four-petalled flowers develop into yellow pear-shaped fruits with white or pink pulp containing many small seeds. Guava fruits, rich in vitamin C, are used to make jam and jelly, stewed for desserts, or canned. Family: *Myrtaceae* (myrtle family).

Guayaquil (*or* Santiago de Guayaquil) 2 13S 79 54W The largest city and chief port of Ecuador, on the River Guayas. It is a major commercial centre; industries include food processing, tanning, and textile manufacture. Its university was founded in 1867. Population (1982): 1 300 868.

Gudbrandsdal The fertile valley of the River Lågen, in S central Norway. Farming is important and it has been a trade route for many centuries. Ibsen's *Peer Gynt* is set here.

gudgeon A freshwater shoaling fish, *Gobio gobio*, related to *carp, found in Europe and N Asia. It has a slender greenish or greyish body, up to about 20 cm long, with a row of blackish spots along each side and a pair of barbels at the corners of the mouth. It is used as food and bait.

guelder rose A small tree or shrub, *Viburnum opulus*, 4–5 m high, found throughout Eurasia. It has three-lobed leaves and flat-topped clusters of flowers, 5–10 cm across, in which the outer flowers are large and sterile and the inner ones are small and fertile. The fruits are clusters of red translucent berries. The cultivated form, grown as a garden shrub, is

sterile: it has rounded heads of flowers and is called snowball tree. Family: *Caprifoliaceae* (honeysuckle family).

Guelfs and Ghibellines The propapal and proimperial factions respectively in medieval Germany and Italy. Commencing in a German struggle between rival claimants to the Holy Roman Empire, the Guelfs (named after Welf, the family name) and Ghibellines (after Waiblingen, a *Hohenstaufen castle), their conflict acquired an Italian context because of papal opposition to the Hohenstaufen. The Italian city states were led by Florence (Guelf) and Pisa (Ghibelline). Both sides, however, had factions within each city. Defeat of the Hohenstaufen (1268) contributed to Ghibelline decline, while the Guelfs espoused the *Angevin cause in Italy. By the end of the 14th century the factions had only local significance, reflecting urban rivalries.

Guelph 43 34N 80 16W A city in central Canada, in SW Ontario. Founded in 1827, it is an agricultural research and farming centre, especially at the University of Guelph (1964). Numerous factories produce electric motors, wire, metal and rubber products, and many other goods. Population (1981): 71 207.

guenon An *Old World monkey belonging to the genus *Cercopithecus* (10 species), of African forests. They are 83–160 cm long including the tail (50–88 cm) and move through the trees in troops, feeding on leaves, fruits, insects, and snails. The mona monkey (*C. mona*), dark with creamy-white underparts and rump patches, is a strikingly marked guenon. *See also* grass monkey.

Guercino (Giovanni Francesco Barbieri; 1591–1666) Italian painter, born at Cento, near Bologna. His masterpiece, the ceiling frescos in the Casino Ludovisi, Rome, commissioned by Pope Gregory XV in 1621, were influenced by the *Carracci, under whom he had studied. While in Rome (1621–23) he also painted the *Burial of St Petronilla* (Capitoline Museum, Rome), which his later work never equalled.

Guericke, Otto von (1602–86) German physicist, renowned for his investigation of vacuums. In 1650 he invented the air pump, which he used to perform a series of experiments culminating in a demonstration in which two teams of horses failed to separate a pair of large hemispheres (called the Magdeburg hemispheres after his home town) placed together and evacuated. When air was admitted to the hemispheres they fell apart on their own.

Guernica 43 19N 2 40W A historic Basque town in N Spain, on the Bay of Biscay. During the Spanish Civil War it was bombed and virtually destroyed by German planes supporting the Nationalists on 27 April, 1937. This event is depicted in a painting by Picasso. Population (1981): 17 836.

Guernsey 49 27N 2 35W The second largest of the Channel Islands, in the English Channel. Roughly triangular in shape, it is low lying in the N and hilly in the S with rugged coastal cliffs. Agriculture and horticulture are important, especially dairy farming (the Guernsey breed of cattle originated here) and the production of tomatoes and flowers for export. Guernsey's mild climate, scenery, and beaches contribute to its popularity as a tourist resort. Area: 63 sq km (24.5 sq mi). Population (1981): 53 303. Capital: St Peter Port.

Guernsey cattle A breed of dairy cattle originating from Guernsey. They have a yellowish coat with a white tail switch and produce high-quality creamy milk.

guerrilla warfare (Spanish: small war) Military action by small irregular armed forces, often supported by a hostile foreign power, intended to erode the war potential and political stability of a country. Relying on hit-and-run techniques and avoiding combat with better equipped regulars, guerrillas usually attempt to gain local support rather than territory. The word was first adopted in reference to the Spanish-Portuguese action against the

French conquest in the *Peninsular War. In the 20th century, guerrilla warfare has been employed by many movements for national liberation.

Guesclin, Bertrand du (c. 1320–80) French commander in the *Hundred Years' War. As constable of France from 1370 he was instrumental in recovering the territory previously lost to the English in S and W France.

Guevara, Che (Ernesto G.; 1928–67) Argentine revolutionary and theorist of guerrilla warfare, who became the hero of left-wing youth in the 1960s. A doctor by training, he joined *Castro's invasion of Cuba (1956) and became one of his chief lieutenants in the subsequent guerrilla war. After Castro's victory, Che Guevara influenced Cuba's procommunist foreign relations and directed the land-reform policies. Guevara was an exponent of exporting revolution and in 1967 he was captured and killed by government troops while attempting to instigate a revolt in Bolivia.

Guicciardini, Francesco (1483–1540) Florentine statesman and historian. He was Florentine ambassador to Aragon (1512–14) and then active in Florentine politics before entering the service of the papacy and becoming governor of Modena (1516) and Reggio (1517). After the sack of Rome (1527) by the imperial army, Guicciardini concentrated on his writings, including his famous *Storia d'Italia*, which deals with contemporary events in Italy between 1494 and 1534.

guided missiles Rocket-powered missiles without wings or other lift surfaces that are guided throughout their flight. They comprise a power unit, a guidance system, and a warhead. In most, propulsion is by solid-fuel rocket. Of the many guidance systems the most common methods of controlling the missile depend on a trailing wire or a radio, radar, or laser beam. Some have preset on-board computers, others depend on *inertial guidance, and some home on sources of infrared radiation. Warheads range from relatively small antitank high explosives to nuclear devices in the kiloton range. All missiles are vulnerable to electronic countermeasures (ECM), although cruise missiles, driven by turbofan engines, have a range of over 3000 km (2000 miles) and can change course and direction according to a preset-computer program to confuse defence measures. Missiles may be launched from aircraft (air-to-air or air-to-surface) or from the land or sea (surface-to-air or surface-to-surface). *See also* MX missile; Polaris missile; Trident missile.

guide dogs Dogs that are specially selected and trained to guide the blind. The first training schools were established in Germany (1911–18) and the British Guide Dog Association was founded in 1931. Among the most suitable breeds for the four-month training course are German Shepherd dogs (Alsatians), Labradors, and golden retrievers.

Guido d'Arezzo (c. 990–c. 1050) Italian monk and musical theorist. He developed the hexachord, a six-note scale used to facilitate sight-singing. The notes of the hexachord were named after the first syllables of the first six lines of a Latin hymn: ut, re, mi, fa, sol, and la. The hexachord became the basis of later systems of *solmization. Guido also developed the Guidonian hand, a mnemonic device that gave note names to the tips and joints of the fingers, and popularized the use of coloured lines in written music to indicate pitch.

Guildford 51 14N 0 35W A city in SE England, in Surrey on the River Wey. A market and residential town, it is the site of the University of Surrey (1966). Guildford Cathedral (founded in 1936 and designed by Sir Edward Maufe; 1883–1974) is one of the three entirely new Anglican cathedrals to be built in England since the Reformation. Population (1981): 56 652.

guilds (*or* gilds) Associations formed in medieval Europe to further their members' common purposes. Originally religious or social in character, the first such guilds are recorded in the 9th century. Merchant guilds were created in

many towns in the 11th century to organize local trade and became a powerful force in local government. Craft guilds, confined to specific crafts or trades, were formed from the 12th century and these too became very powerful, exercising a monopoly over both production and trade and controlling recruitment by the apprenticeship system. In the later middle ages and beyond, their activities were largely superseded by the development of capitalism. The *livery companies of London are descended from the craft guilds.

Guild Socialism A movement, influential from about 1906 to 1925 in Britain, which sought the abolition of capitalism and the establishment of guilds of workers to control industry within broad guidelines set down by the government. The National Guilds League was formed in 1915 but the doctrine had greatest support immediately after World War I, when the National Building Guild was formed. However, this only lasted until 1922 and in 1925 the National Guilds League was dissolved.

Guillaume de Lorris (13th century) French poet, author of the first 4000 lines of the verse allegory *Roman de la rose* (c. 1230–40), one of the most influential of medieval poems, translated into English by *Chaucer. Nothing certain is known about Guillaume.

guillemot A bird, *Uria aalge*, occurring in coastal regions of the N hemisphere. It is 40 cm long and has a dark-brown plumage with a white belly and wing stripe and a slender bill, feeding on fish, shellfish, and worms. The eggs are shaped so that they do not roll off the cliff ledges where they are laid (*see* Plate V). Family *Alcidae* (auks).

guillotine A device with which a person may be beheaded. It consists of two vertical posts and a horizontal knife that is dropped onto the victim's neck. Joseph Ignace Guillotin (1738–1814) introduced it as a method of capital punishment in France in 1792, during the French Revolution.

Guimarães 41 26N 8 19W A town in NW Portugal. It was Portugal's first capital (12th century) and the birthplace of Alfonso I (1112–85), Portugal's first king. An industrial centre, its manufactures include cutlery. Population (1981): 22 092.

Guinea, Gulf of A large inlet of the E Atlantic Ocean, bordering on the *Guinea Coast of West Africa, between Cape Palmas, Liberia, and Cape Lopez, Gabon.

Guinea, People's Republic of A country on the coast of West Africa. A coastal plain, partly swamp, rises steeply to plateaus and mountains. The population is mainly Fulani and Mandingo. *Economy*: chiefly agricultural, now largely collectivized. The chief crops are rice and palm oil and nuts, as well as coffee, peanuts, and fruits. Livestock, especially cattle, is also important. The principal mineral resources are diamonds, iron ore, and bauxite (alumina is the principal export). Most trade and industry is now nationalized. *History*: the N formed part of Ghana from the 5th to the 8th centuries AD and of the Mali empire in the 16th century. From the mid-15th century European traders were active along the coast. In 1849 the French established a protectorate over part of Guinea, which became a colony in 1891. In 1895 it became part of French West Africa. In 1958 French Guinea became an independent republic, with Ahmed Sékou *Touré as its first president, rather than joining the French Community. A treaty of cooperation re-established economic relations with France in 1963. Guinea is a single-party state, and in recent years accusations have been made of violations of human rights. The army took over after Touré's death in 1984. President: Col Lansana Conté. Official language: French and the languages of eight ethnic groups. Official currency: syli of 100 cauris. Area: 245 857 sq km (95 000 sq mi). Population (1983 est): 5 430 000. Capital and main port: Conakry.

Guinea-Bissau, Republic of (name until 1974: Portuguese Guinea) A small country on the coast of West Africa, including the archipelago of Bijagós. It consists chiefly of a coastal plain, cut by wide river estuaries and rising to savanna-covered plateau inland. The majority of the population are Fulani, Mandyako, and Mandingo. *Economy*: chiefly agricultural, the principal crops being groundnuts (the main export), rice, palm oil, and nuts. Cattle breeding is important in the interior. Land has been nationalized and cooperative farming introduced. Important bauxite deposits have been discovered and there are plans for a major hydroelectric scheme to power an aluminium plant. Other smaller industries are also being developed. *History*: explored by the Portuguese in the mid-15th century, the area became a centre of the slave trade. It became a Portuguese colony in 1879 and an overseas province of Portugal in 1951. In 1974 it became an independent republic. Luis de Almeida Cabral (1931–   ) became the first president; he was replaced by Maj João Bernardo Vieira following a coup in 1980. Constitutional rule returned in 1984, with Vieira as elected head of state. Official language: Portuguese; Crioulo is widely spoken. Official currency: Guinea-Bissau peso of 100 centavos. Area: 36 125 sq km (13 948 sq mi). Population (1984 est): 844 000. Capital: Bissau.

Guinea Coast The coastlands of West Africa extending from Gambia to Cape Lopez in Gabon.

guinea fowl A bird belonging to an African family (*Numididae*; 7–10 species). About 50 cm long, domesticated guinea fowl are descended from the helmet guinea fowl (*Numida meleagris*), which has a large bony crest, a bare face with red and blue wattles, and a grey white-spotted plumage. Guinea fowl scratch for seeds and insects, especially termites. Order: *Galliformes* (pheasants, turkeys, etc.).

guinea pepper The spicy aromatic fruit of a West African tree, *Xylopia aethiopica*, source of the condiment "Negro pepper." The tree has fragrant flowers producing aggregates of berries. Family: *Annonaceae*.

guinea pig A domesticated rodent, *Cavia porcellus*, descended from the *cavy. Guinea pigs were originally bred for food but are now popular as pets. They should be fed on grain, roots, green food, and hay.

guinea worm A parasitic *nematode worm, *Dracunculus medinensis*, that is a serious parasite of man in Africa, India, and the Middle East. The larvae are carried by water fleas (genus *Cyclops*) often present in drinking water. When swallowed by the human host, they burrow into the tissues and grow to maturity: the females reach a length of up to 120 cm, causing ulcers on the feet and legs.

Guinevere In *Arthurian legend, the wife of King Arthur and lover of *Lancelot. She features in various medieval romances. Malory's *Morte d'Arthur* (1485) describes her abduction by Modred, Arthur's nephew, and her adulterous love for Lancelot.

Guinness, Sir Alec (1914–   ) British actor. He established his reputation as a stage actor in repertory in the late 1930s and played Hamlet in modern dress in 1938. After World War II he achieved success as a character actor in films, including *Oliver Twist* (1948), *Kind Hearts and Coronets* (1949), *The Bridge on the River Kwai* (1957), for which he received an Academy Award, *The Comedians* (1967), and *Star Wars* (1977).

Guiscard, Robert (c. 1015–85) Norman knight, who took part in the Norman invasions of S Italy and Sicily. He established himself in Calabria and gained papal recognition as Duke of Apulia (1059). He died while campaigning in the Balkans. His brother and nephew later ruled Sicily as Roger I (1031–1101; reigned c. 1071–1101) and *Roger II.

Guise A French noble family prominent during the 16th century. The duchy of Guise was the reward (1528) of **Claude I, Duke of Aumale** (1496–1550) for services to France. His daughter **Mary of Guise** (1515–60) married James V of Scotland and was the mother of Mary, Queen of Scots. Claude's sons **François, 2nd Duke of Guise** (1519–63) and **Charles, Cardinal of Lorraine** (1524–74) led the Roman Catholic party in the French *Wars of Religion. François was assassinated by a

Huguenot and the Catholic leadership passed to his son **Henri I, 3rd Duke of Guise** (1550–88), who directed the *St Bartholomew Day's Massacre of Huguenots in 1572. Following Henri's assassination the Guise's influence on French politics diminished.

guitar A plucked stringed instrument of Moorish origin, which came to Europe via Spain. The modern Spanish guitar has a flat back, a round sound hole, a fretted fingerboard, and six strings tuned chiefly in fourths. It has a range of over three octaves from the E below the bass stave. Music for it is written an octave higher than it sounds. Guitar technique was developed by Fernando Sor (1778–1839) and in the 20th century by Andrés *Segovia.

guitar fish A *ray fish, belonging to the family *Rhinobatidae*, that has a pointed flattened head with fused pectoral fins and a long muscular sharklike tail. Guitar fish live in shallow waters of tropical and temperate seas and feed on bottom-dwelling animals, especially crustaceans.

Guitry, Sacha (1885–1957) French actor and dramatist. He wrote many light comedies, often concerning the lives of famous men, such as Napoleon and Mozart. He acted in these and occasionally in films, including *Le Comédien* (1949) and *Napoléon* (1955).

Guiyang (or Kuei-yang) 26 35N 106 40E A city in S China, the capital of Guizhou province. Industries, developed since 1949, include steel, machinery, and aluminium. Population (1983 est); 1 314 000.

Guizhou (Kuei-chou or Kweichow) A province in S China, a rather infertile high plateau. There were frequent rebellions among the minority non-Chinese groups, which have rich folk cultures. Rice, maize, tobacco, tea, and timber are grown and silk and minerals produced. Area: 174 000 sq km (69 278 sq mi). Population (1980 est): 27 310 000. Capital: Guiyang.

Guizot, François (Pierre Guillaume) (1787–1874) French statesman and historian. A professor of history at Paris University (1812–30), he was prominent in the revolution that brought Louis Philippe to the throne in 1830 and served as foreign minister (1840–48). He was forced by the Revolution of 1848 to resign and devoted the rest of his life to historical writing.

Gujarat A state in W India, on the Arabian Sea SE of Pakistan. Lowlands merge into hills in the S and E and into marshes in the NW. Cotton, tobacco, peanuts, and other crops are raised. An industrial area, Gujarat produces textiles, machinery, and chemicals. *History*: a flourishing area under Muslim princes (13th–17th centuries), Gujarat was conquered by the Maratha in the 18th century before passing to Britain. Area: 195 984 sq km (75 650 sq mi). Population (1981): 33 960 905. Capital: Gandhinagar.

Gujarati An Indo-Aryan language spoken by 20 million people in Gujarat and Maharashtra in India. It is related to Rajasthani, uses a modified Devanagari script, and has a long literary tradition.

Gujranwala 32 06N 74 11E A city in NE Pakistan. The Sikh ruler Ranjit Singh was born here. Manufactures include textiles and leather goods and it has a famous ceramics industry. Population (1981): 597 000.

Gulf States The nations situated on the Persian Gulf. They are Oman, the United Arab Emirates, Qatar, Bahrein, Saudi Arabia, Kuwait, Iraq, and Iran. They comprise the world's major oil-producing area.

Gulf Stream One of the major ocean currents of the world, flowing from the Florida Strait parallel to the North American coast as far as the Newfoundland banks. It bears NE across the Atlantic as the North Atlantic Drift, branching into two main directions, one flowing N towards Spitsbergen and the other flowing S to form the Canary Current. Water from the North and South Equatorial Currents builds up in

GULF STREAM

the Gulf of Mexico and escapes with force through the Florida Strait as the Florida Current, one of the strongest major ocean currents. The water is warm and has an ameliorating effect on the climate of NW Europe.

Gulf War (1980–) An indecisive conflict in the Persian Gulf, between Iran and Iraq. The war began when Iraqi forces invaded Iran shortly after the Iranian revolution in pursuit of claims over border territory. A war of attrition developed, costing (by 1987) Iran 250 000 and Iraq 150 000 dead and much in material and financial resources. The conflict has also seen the use of toxic gas (by Iraq), the bombing of major cities, and missile attacks on international shipping (despite the 'reflagging' of vessels in order to gain protection from the US, UK, and other naval powers).

gulfweed Tropical *brown algae, also called rockweed or sea holly, of the genus *Sargassum*, especially *S. natans*, which forms huge free-floating masses of seaweed in the Sargasso Sea. They have serrated fronds, with berry-like gas-filled floats or bladders, and most reproduce sexually.

gull A seabird belonging to the subfamily *Larinae* (about 40 species), ranging throughout the world's coastal regions and also found inland. Up to 75 cm long, gulls are well built and have long pointed wings and a strong slightly hooked bill. Gulls are typically grey and white, often with dark markings, and some have a dark mask or hood in summer. Some gulls feed on fish but most are scavengers, feeding on invertebrates, eggs, chicks, and refuse. Family: *Laridae* (gulls and terns); order: *Charadriiformes* (gulls, plovers, etc.).

gullet. See oesophagus.

gum arabic. See gums.

gums Adhesive substances exuded by plants. They are odourless tasteless amorphous *carbohydrates that form either clear liquid solutions or gelatinous mixtures with water. **Gum arabic** (*or* gum acacia), the most widely used of the water-soluble gums, is obtained from trees of the genus *Acacia*, although the name is also applied to substitute gums from other plants. It is used for making sweets, cosmetics, gummed labels, and textile finishes. **Gum tragacanth** is extracted from shrubs of the genus *Astragalus*: it is not completely water-soluble, but forms a thick mucilage. It is used as an adhesive in pills and as a sauce thickener.

gum tree A tree of the genus *Eucalyptus* (about 600 species), so called because it is rich in resin and aromatic oils.

gun metal A type of *bronze containing about 90% copper and sometimes a little zinc. Being easy to cast, it was originally used for making cannons. Admiralty gun metal (88% copper, 10% tin, 2% zinc) is used in shipbuilding.

Gunn, Thom(son William) (1929–) British poet, usually considered one of the leading contemporary British poets. His books include *Fighting Terms* (1954), *The Sense of Movement* (1957), *My Sad Captains* (1961), *Positives* (1966; with photographs by his brother Ander Gunn), and *Jack Straw's Castle* (1976). He lives in California.

Gunn effect The effect used in solid-state *semiconductor microwave generators (Gunn diodes). When a sufficiently high steady electric field (typically several thousand volts per centimetre) is applied across a sample of n-type gallium arsenide, microwave frequency current oscillations are set up. Named after J. B. Gunn (1928–).

gunnel An eel-like fish of the family *Pholididae* (about 8 species), found usually among seaweed or rocks in N Atlantic and N Pacific coastal waters, feeding on invertebrates. The rock gunnel (*Pholis gunnellus*), also called butterfish, is 30 cm long and brownish with 9–13 black spots along the dorsal fin. Order: *Perciformes*.

gunpowder An explosive mixture of saltpetre (potassium nitrate), sulphur, and powdered charcoal. Invented by the Chinese many centuries before its description by Roger *Bacon in the 13th century it has had a profound effect on human conflict (*see* firearms). Replaced for most purposes by safer explosives, it is still used in fireworks.

Gunpowder Plot. See Fawkes, Guy.

guns *Artillery firearms that discharge high-velocity shells with a relatively flat trajectory. A modern breech-loading gun has a rifled barrel. Its sliding or interrupted screw-thread breech blocks contain linked levers activating the firing pin, which strikes the primer, located either in the round or the block. Buffers absorb the firing shock and recuperators return the barrel to its firing position. Controls elevate and traverse the gun, sometimes electronically. Most ammunition is fused to burst before, on, or after impact. Specialized shells are used in *antitank guns and *anti-aircraft guns. Some shells have nuclear warheads. Guns may be towed or mounted on vehicles or in aircraft or ships. *See also* small arms.

Gunter's chain. See chain.

Guntur 16 20W 80 27E A city in S India, in Andhra Pradesh. It is an agricultural trading and processing centre. Population (1981): 367 000.

Guomindang (or Kuomintang) The National People's Party of *Taiwan (Republic of China). Organized in 1912, following the overthrow of the imperial government, from *Sun Yat-sen's Alliance Society, it formed, under Soviet influence, an alliance with the new Chinese Communist Party (CCP) in 1924 (*see* United Fronts). Following Sun's death (1925), the Guomindang was led by *Chiang Kai-shek and with the CCP had gained control of most of China from the *warlords by 1926. A break between the two parties (1927) led to civil war until Japanese conquests in China (*see* Sino-Japanese Wars) necessitated renewed cooperation in 1937. After Japan's defeat (1945), civil war was resumed until a communist victory in 1949 drove Chiang Kai-shek and his Guomindang followers into exile in Taiwan.

guppy A freshwater fish, *Lebistes reticulatus*, native to N South America and the West Indies. Male guppies are up to 4 cm long and brightly coloured, marked with black eyespots and having variably shaped and coloured fins. Females, slightly larger and less colourful, are prolific breeders, producing live young (rather than eggs) at monthly intervals. Guppies are popular aquarium fish and—in their native regions—control mosquitoes. Family: *Cyprinodontidae*.

Gupta A powerful Indian dynasty founded in the late 4th century AD. Its founder *Chandra Gupta I was succeeded by *Samudra Gupta and the throne then passed to *Chandra Gupta II. His son Kumara (d. 455; reigned c. 415–55) was followed by Skanda Gupta (reigned 455–67), during whose reign foreign invaders began to conquer parts of the empire. The early Gupta kings fostered Buddhism and presided over a golden age of artistic and cultural achievement. The dynasty was overthrown by the Huns in the 6th century.

Gurdjieff, George Ivanovitch (1873-1943) Russian occultist of Greek parentage, who travelled widely in Europe and Asia before establishing a teaching centre near Paris in the 1920s. Believing that man is not usually fully conscious, his students were required to perform a stylized dance to assist them to attain a higher level of perception. Part mystic, part bon viveur, and reputedly part charlatan, this enigmatic man had a considerable following, including P. D. Ouspensky, whose books have outlived Gurdjieff's own *All and Everything, Beelzebub's Tales to his Grandson.*

gurdwara A Sikh place of worship, housing a copy of the *Adi Granth. Although every Sikh home contains one, public gurdwaras are used for meetings, weddings, and services. The most sacred is the Golden Temple or Harimandir at Amritsar.

Gurkhas Soldiers of Nepalese origin who served in the British Indian Army from 1815 until 1947. The Brigade of Gurkhas now serves in the British Army, Hong Kong. The name derives from that of the ruling dynasty of Nepal.

gurnard A carnivorous bottom-dwelling fish, also called sea robin, belonging to a family (*Triglidae*; about 40 species) found in temperate and tropical seas. It has a tapering body, up to 70 cm long, a large armoured head, and finger-like pectoral fin rays and produces sound by vibrating its swim bladder. The flying gurnards belong to the family *Dactylopteridae*. Order: *Scorpaeniformes.*

guru In *Hinduism, a venerated spiritual teacher who personally instructs and guides the disciple. In Tibetan Buddhism the guru embodies the Buddha himself and is correspondingly revered. In Sikhism, guru is the title of the first ten patriarchs (*see* Nanak).

Gustavus II Adolphus (1594-1632) King of Sweden (1611-32), who displayed military genius in the *Thirty Years' War. He inherited wars with Denmark, Russia, and Poland, which he successfully terminated in 1613, 1617, and 1629 respectively. He simultaneously, with the help of his chancellor *Oxenstierna, consolidated his internal position and in the 1620s instituted important administrative and educational reforms. In 1630 he entered the Thirty Years' War on the Protestant side, inspired by religious aims as well as a desire for Sweden to dominate the Baltic. He defeated Tilly at *Breitenfeld (1631) and at the Lech (1632) and Wallenstein at *Lutzen, in which Gustavus Adolphus was mortally wounded.

Gustavus I Vasa (1496-1560) King of Sweden (1523-60), who achieved Swedish independence of Denmark and founded the Vasa dynasty. He was taken captive in the 1517-18 war against Denmark but escaped and on returning to Sweden led a successful rebellion against the Danes (1521-23). As king, he dealt effectively with the political and economic consequences of war and established Lutheranism as the state religion (1527-29).

Gutenberg, Johann (c. 1400-c. 1468) German printer, who invented the method of printing with movable metal type (*see* typesetting). Gutenberg worked on his printing process from the 1430s. In 1448 he received the financial backing of *Fust and by 1455 had produced his great 42-line Bible (the Gutenberg Bible). Fust successfully sued Gutenberg in 1455 for the repayment of his loan and the impoverished Gutenberg was forced to relinquish his machinery, with which Fust set up a printing business. He produced a famous psalter (1457), which was largely Gutenberg's work.

Guthrie, (William) Tyrone (1900-71) British theatre director. He directed the Old Vic and other British companies and frequently worked abroad, notably at Stratford, Ontario, where he founded the Shakespeare Festival in 1953. He is best known for his inventive productions of Shakespeare, often in modern dress.

Guthrie, Woody (Woodrow Wilson G.; 1912-67) US folksinger and songwriter, many of whose songs reflected the social injustice of the Depression. His most famous song was "This Land Is Your Land." His son, **Arlo Guthrie** (1947-), is also a singer and songwriter.

gutta percha A brownish leathery material obtained from the *latex of various trees of the family *Sapotaceae*, especially those of the SE Asian genus *Palaquium*. It was once extensively used, for example as an electrical insulator, in golf balls, and in chewing gum, but it has now largely been replaced by synthetics.

Guyana, Cooperative Republic of (name until 1966: British Guiana) A country in the NE of South America, on the Atlantic Ocean. Narrow fertile coastal plains give way to higher undulating areas, rich in minerals and forests. The main rivers, the Demerara, Essequibo, and Berbice give their names to its three counties. Most of the population is of African and East Indian descent. *Economy*: agriculture is important, the main crops being rice and sugar. Fishing, livestock, and cotton growing are being developed as part of a campaign to "feed, house, and clothe" the nation. The most important minerals were formerly gold and diamonds, but these have now been overtaken by bauxite. A local aluminium smelter is planned for the mid 1980s with the assistance of Jamaica and Trinidad and Tobago. By 1976 nearly all foreign economic interests had been nationalized. Most power comes from hydroelectric sources. *History*: the coast was first explored by the Spanish in 1499 and settlements were founded by the Dutch in the 17th century. The area was occupied by the British (1796-1802, 1803-14) and then formally ceded to Britain, becoming a colony as British Guiana in 1831. In 1961 it gained internal self-government under *Jagan. In 1966, as Guyana, it became independent within the British Commonwealth. It is also a member of CARICOM. Marxist forces in political life led to the formation of a Cooperative Republic in 1970. In 1978 an agricultural commune (Jonestown) 240 km (150 mi) NW of Georgetown was the scene of the mass suicide of some 900 members of the People's Temple Sect led by James Warren Jones. President: Desmond Hoyte. Official language: English. Official currency: Guyana dollar of 100 cents. Area: 210 000 sq km (83 000 sq mi). Population (1983 est): 834 000. Capital and main port: Georgetown.

Guyenne A former region of SW France. Ruled by the English kings in the late middle ages, it was regained by France after the Hundred Years' War. The scene of fierce fighting in the 16th-century Wars of Religion and the 17th-century Fronde, Guyenne was later merged with Gascony.

Guzmán Blanco, Antonio (1829-99) Venezuelan statesman. He was president three times (1870-77, 1879-84, 1886-88) but retained despotic power throughout the period 1870-88. He helped Venezuela's economy, encouraging foreign investment and building public works, including the country's first railway.

Gwalior 26 12N 78 09E A city in India, in Madhya Pradesh. Strategically important, it developed around its impressive fortress, which is believed to date from the 6th century AD. Gwalior is an important commercial and industrial centre manufacturing a variety of goods. Jiwaji University was established here in 1964. Population (1981): 560 000.

Gwelo. *See* Gweru.

Gwent A county of SE Wales, on the English border. It was created under local government reorganization in 1974 from most of Monmouthshire and part of Breconshire. It is generally hilly and is drained by the Rivers Wye, Usk, Monnow, Ebbw, and Rhymney. There are varied agricultural activities including sheep farming on the uplands and market gardening in the valleys; but the county is better known for its traditional coalmining in the upland valleys of the NW and for the manufacture of iron and steel. Despite a sharp decline in these activities, W Gwent remains heavily industrialized and the modern stripmill at Llanwern continues the tradition of steelmaking. Area: 1376 sq km (532 sq mi). Population (1981): 439 684. Administrative centre: Newport.

Gweru (name before 1982: Gwelo) 19 25S 29 50E A town in central Zimbabwe. It is the centre of a mining area (with chrome-ore and asbestos deposits) and a cattle-rearing area. Industries include ferrochrome processing. Population (1980 est): 72 000.

Gwyn, Nell (1650–87) English actress. Originally an orange seller in Drury Lane, she achieved fame as an actress and became Charles II's mistress, bearing him two sons. "Let not poor Nellie starve," are said to have been his last words. She helped to establish the Royal Hospital at Chelsea.

Gwynedd A county of NW Wales, bordering on the Irish Sea. It was created under local government reorganization in 1974 from the former counties of Anglesey, Caernarfonshire, Merionethshire, and part of W Denbighshire. It is predominantly mountainous rising to 1086 m (3563 ft) in Snowdon. Most of Gwynedd lies within the *Snowdonia National Park which makes it a popular tourist area. Slate quarrying, formerly a major occupation, has declined seriously. Area: 3868 sq km (1493 sq mi). Population (1981): 230 468. Administrative centre: Caernarfon.

gymkhana 1. An event with a number of different games and contests on horseback. Gymkhanas originated among British soldiers in India during the 19th century. In England the Prince Philip Cup (instituted in 1957) is the *Pony Club gymkhana championship. 2. A timed event, especially in the USA, testing the skill of a car driver over an obstacle course.

gymnastics Exercises designed to perfect balance, strength, and coordination, popular as a sport for individual performers and teams. The modern sport developed in Germany and Sweden in the 19th century from **calisthenics**, rhythmical exercises performed without apparatus or weights. The ancient Persians, Chinese, Indians, Greeks, and Romans also exercised in this way. Competitions consist of prescribed programmes of exercises and optional routines, the apparatus being for men the horizontal bar, parallel bars, pommel horse, vaulting horse, and rings and for women the balance beam, asymmetrical bars, and vaulting horse; both men and women do floor exercises. The sport's popularity increased dramatically, especially among girls, after the victories of Olga Korbut (1972) and Nadia *Comaneci (1976) in the Olympics. The world governing body is the Fédération internationale de Gymnastique (founded in 1881).

gymnosperms A group of plants, most of which are trees, forming one of the two classes of seed-bearing plants (*compare* angiosperms). The sole consistent characteristic of this variable class is that their seeds are not enclosed within a fruit but are borne naked, in many species on *cone scales. Gymnosperms originated in the late Devonian period (about 380 million years ago) and the principal orders are as follows: *Coniferales* (*see* conifer); *Ginkgoales* (*see* ginkgo); *Cycadales* (*see* cycad); *Gnetales* (e.g. *welwitschia); and several extinct orders, including the *Pteridospermales* (*see* seed fern) and the *Cordaitales*.

gymnure An insectivorous mammal belonging to the family *Erinaceidae* of SE Asia, also called hairy hedgehog. There are four species, including the *moon rat. Short-legged and flat-footed, 15–60 cm long, they resemble *hedgehogs without spines. They are shy, usually living in thick undergrowth and hunting mainly at night.

gynaecology The branch of medicine and surgery concerned with diseases of women and girls, particularly those affecting the reproductive system. The closely related specialty of **obstetrics** deals with the care of women during pregnancy, childbirth, and the period immediately after delivery. Doctors specializing in these fields (gynaecologists

NELL GWYN *Detail from portrait (c. 1675; National Portrait Gallery, London) from the studio of Sir Peter Lely.*

and obstetricians) work in close association: a gynaecologist is often also an obstetrician.

Györ 47 41N 17 40E A city in NW Hungary, near the confluence of the Rivers Rába and Danube. Györ's many old buildings include a 12th-century cathedral (rebuilt in the 18th century). It has heavy engineering and lies in an area famous for horse breeding. Population (1980): 125 000.

Gypsies. *See* Gipsies.

Gypsophila A genus of slender annual or perennial herbs (about 120 species), native to the Mediterranean area. Up to 1.5 m high, they have grey-green strap-shaped leaves and large clusters of white or pink flowers. Some species are grown in rock gardens; others are popular for flower arrangements. Family: *Caryophyllaceae* (pink family).

gypsum A colourless or white mineral consisting of hydrated calcium sulphate found in clays, shales, and limestones. It occurs mainly as a result of the evaporation of saline water. Rock gypsum is often red-stained, granular, and found in layers. Gypsite is impure and earthy, occurring as surface deposits. *Alabaster is a pure compact fine-grained translucent form. Satin-spar is fibrous and silky. Selenite occurs as transparent crystals in clays and mudstones. Gypsum is used in the manufacture of cement, rubber, paper, plaster of Paris, and blackboard chalk.

gypsy moth A moth, *Lymantria dispar*, distributed throughout the N hemisphere. Males are brownish grey and females white. The greyish larvae, which feed on a variety of trees, were introduced to North America in 1869 and have become a serious pest. *See also* tussock moth.

gyrfalcon The largest *falcon, *Falco rusticolus*, which breeds in N Eurasia, North America, and mountainous regions of Asia. It is 60 cm long and its plumage varies from pure white speckled with black to dark grey with dense black barring. It hunts for hares, rodents, and ground-dwelling birds.

gyrocompass. *See* compass.

H

Haakon IV Haakonsson (1204–63) King of Norway (1217–63), who added Iceland and Greenland to Norwegian territories (1262). He subdued rebellions and strengthened the monarchy by improving royal administration and by extensive legislation. In 1247 he was crowned by the pope's legate. He died in an invasion of the Isle of Man and the Hebrides.

Haakon VII (1872–1957) The first King of Norway (1905–57) following the restoration of Norwegian independence. In 1896 he married Maud (d. 1938), the daughter of Edward VII of the UK. His refusal to abdicate during the German occupation (1940–45), during which he was in England, encouraged Norwegian resistance.

Haarlem 52 23N 4 38E A city in the W Netherlands, the capital of North Holland province. Surrounded by flower fields, it is a major trade centre for bulbs. Industries include textiles and printing. It is noted for its Frans Hals museum and its fine cathedral (14–15th centuries). Population (1981 est): 157 556.

Habakkuk An Old Testament prophet of Judah, who lived at the time when a Babylonian invasion was imminent (c. 605 BC). **The Book of Habakkuk** records his perplexity that a just God should make use of an evil nation to inflict punishment on his own people, but the prophet is told to trust in God, who will see to it that all evil will eventually be punished.

habeas corpus (Latin: have the body) A remedy against unlawful confinement, which takes the form of a writ ordering the person alleged to have unlawful custody of a prisoner to produce him before the court issuing the writ and to submit to whatever the court directs. The writ may be used to test the legality of imprisonment but not to appeal against a lawful conviction or sentence. Applications for habeas corpus, made to the Lord Chief Justice's court, take precedence over all others, the counsel interrupting the court by the cry: "My Lord, I have a matter concerning the liberty of the subject."

Haber, Fritz (1868–1934) German chemist and inventor of the Haber process (*see* Haber-Bosch process). The Haber process, developed in 1908, enabled atmospheric nitrogen to be combined with hydrogen to form ammonia, which could then be converted into nitrates. The process was essential to Germany's supply of explosives and fertilizers during World War I. For this work, Haber was awarded the 1918 Nobel Prize. *See also* Bosch, Carl.

Haber-Bosch process A method for the bulk production of ammonia from nitrogen and hydrogen. The pure gases are passed over an iron catalyst at about 500°C and a pressure of 500 atmospheres. Ammonia is chiefly used in the manufacture of fertilizers and *explosives. The process was devised by Fritz Haber (1868–1934) and adapted by Carl Bosch (1874–1940), who added a process for making the hydrogen from *water gas and steam.

Habsburgs (*or* Hapsburgs) The most prominent European royal dynasty from the 15th to 20th centuries. The family originated in Switzerland in the 10th century. In 1273 *Rudolf I was elected Holy Roman Emperor and consolidated through marriage and conquest his family's possession of Austria, Carniola, and Styria. After Rudolf's death (1291) the Habsburgs lost the imperial title until 1438 but thereafter kept it until 1740, holding it again from 1745 to 1806. In 1516 *Charles V inherited the Spanish Crown, adding Spain with its European and American possessions to the Habsburg domains. When he abdicated in 1556 he left the Spanish Crown to his son, *Philip II, and his Austrian possessions to his brother, *Ferdinand I. The Spanish branch ruled until 1700, when it died out and was re-placed by the Bourbons. The Austrian Habsburgs continued to rule, becoming emperors of Austria in 1804 and of *Austria-Hungary in 1848, which they ruled until the end of World War I.

Hackney A borough of N central Greater London, created in 1965 from the former metropolitan boroughs of Hackney, Shoreditch, and Stoke Newington. Hackney Marsh, a former haunt of highwaymen, is now one of London's largest playing fields. Population (1983 est): 186 700.

hackney coach A four-wheeled vehicle drawn by two horses, containing seats for six people. Hackney coaches, which appeared in England in the early 17th century, were hired out for town journeys. The phrase "hackney carriage" still appears on the municipal licence plate of English taxis. *See also* cab.

Hackney horse An English breed of trotting horse developed from Norfolk trotters. It has a compact body with strong short legs and powerful shoulders, a full tail, and a fine chestnut bay, brown, or black coat. Hackneys were once fashionable carriage horses and are now used mainly for shows. Height: 1.50–1.60 m (14¾–15¾ hands). A smaller version of the Hackney horse is the **Hackney pony**. Standing at 1.22–1.42 m (12–14 hands), it is bred mainly for the show ring.

hadal zone. *See* abyssal zone.

Haddington 55 58N 2 47W A town in E Scotland, in Lothian Region. It has an important agricultural market and manufactures woollens and hosiery. John Knox was born here. Population (1981): 8117.

haddock A carnivorous food fish, *Melanogrammus aeglefinus*, related to *cod, that usually occurs in shoals near the bottom of N Atlantic coastal waters. It has an elongated body, up to 1 m long, grey or brown above and silvery below with a black spot behind each pectoral fin, two anal and three dorsal fins, a small chin barbel, and a dark lateral line. It is eaten both fresh and smoked, Finnan haddock from Scotland being especially well known.

Hades (*or* Pluto) The Greek god of the dead; also the name of the underworld he ruled. He was the brother of Zeus and Poseidon and husband of *Persephone, whom he abducted. The souls of the dead were ferried to Hades across the River Styx by *Charon.

Hadhramaut A region in central South Yemen. It consists of a mountain range parallel to the coast rising to over 2000 m (6562 ft) and the valley, further inland, of an intermittent stream that turns towards the sea E of the mountains. With irrigation, the production of dates, grain, and tobacco is the main industry, and the chief town is Mukalla, on the coast.

Hadith (Arabic: tradition) Traditional records of sayings and deeds attributed to Mohammed that are not contained in the Koran but are accepted as authoritative sources of moral, ritual, and religious law. Extensive compilations of such traditions were made after the Prophet's death. The chief collection is that made by al-*Bukhari.

Hadrian (76–138 AD) Roman emperor (117–38). He was admitted to the imperial household as *Trajan's ward in 85 and a successful military career included special responsibility in Trajan's Parthian campaign. On Trajan's death he became emperor, crushed a conspiracy against him (118), and from 120 to 131 toured the provinces. His foreign policy was generally defensive (he sponsored the building of *Hadrian's Wall in Britain) but he subdued a Jewish revolt (132–35) with considerable severity. From 131 until his death he lived in Rome, instigating building projects, including the *Pantheon and the mausoleum (Castel Sant' Angelo) in which he was buried.

Hadrian IV. *See* Adrian IV.

Hadrian's Wall A Roman frontier defence work. Begun in 122 AD, it was the N frontier of Roman Britain for 250 years. Designed to control the Scottish tribes, it stretched 120 km (75 mi) from Tyne to Solway. It eventually comprised ditch, stone and turf wall (incorporating 16 forts, smaller forts every mile, and signalling turrets), road system, and "vallum" (earthworks delimiting the military area), with supporting troop installations. Temporarily superseded by the *Antonine Wall and several times overrun and rebuilt, it was finally abandoned in 383 AD. Substantial portions still stand.

hadron Any elementary particle that takes part in *strong interactions. The group thus includes all baryons and mesons but not leptons or the photon. *See* particle physics.

Haeckel, Ernst Heinrich (1834–1919) German zoologist, noted for his speculative theories concerning the origin of life and evolution. A firm advocate of *Darwin's theories, Haeckel went even further. He suggested that life originated through spontaneous combination of the elements and he drew genealogical trees to represent the course of evolution. His recapitulation theory (i.e. that stages in the embryological development of an individual reflect stages in the evolution of the species) did much to stimulate embryological research, although the theory is now regarded as unsound.

haematite (*or* hematite) The principal ore of iron, ferric oxide, varying in colour from red to grey to black. It contains over 70% iron. It occurs either in crystalline form (specular iron ore) or in massive form. Most ore deposits are derived from altered iron carbonates and silicates in sedimentary rocks.

haematology The study of blood and its diseases. This medical specialty is concerned particularly with treating *leukaemias, *haemophilia, and rare kinds of anaemia.

haemoglobin The substance, contained within the red blood cells (*see* erythrocyte), that is responsible for the colour of blood. In humans haemoglobin consists of a protein (globin) combined with an iron-containing pigment (haem). Haem combines with oxygen, which is absorbed into the blood at the lungs, to form oxyhaemoglobin, which gives arterial blood its bright-red colour and is the means by which oxygen is transported around the body. Oxygen is released at the tissues and the pigment acquires a bluish tinge, responsible for the bluish-red colour of venous blood.

haemophilia A hereditary disease in which the blood does not clot properly due to absence of one of the clotting factors. Some of the children of both Queen Victoria and Tsar Nicholas II had this disease, which is almost entirely restricted to boys but is transmitted through the mother. If an affected person (a haemophiliac) cuts himself seriously he may bleed to death without appropriate plasma transfusions. Haemophiliacs also bleed easily into their joints and other parts of the body and must therefore restrict their activities.

haemorrhage Bleeding. Large amounts of blood may be lost in severe injuries, from bleeding peptic ulcers, during operations, in childbirth, or if the patient has a clotting disorder (such as *haemophilia). In these circumstances it may be necessary to give a blood transfusion to avoid *shock and death. If haemorrhage occurs in a confined space, such as the brain or the eye, damage results from destruction of normal tissue.

haemorrhoids (*or* piles) Swollen (varicose) veins in the anal canal, which may enlarge sufficiently to hang down outside the anus. They are very common, usually resulting from chronic constipation, and tend to run in families. Piles may cause bleeding from the anus and itchiness, but rarely severe pain. In severe cases they may need to be surgically removed or injected with a sclerosing agent, which makes them shrivel up. External haemorrhoids are painful swellings at the side of the anus, caused by rupture of an anal vein.

Ha-er-bin (English name: Harbin) 45 45N 126 41E A port in NE China, the capital of Heilongjiang province on the Songhua River. A trading and industrial centre, the site of Heilongjiang University, it was developed by Russia and was a haven for refugees from the Russian Revolution (1917). Population (1982): 2 550 000.

Hafiz, Shams al-Din Muhammad (?1326–90) Persian lyric poet, born at Shiraz, where he lived and worked as a religious teacher and copyist of manuscripts. He subsequently became court poet. He is the acknowledged master of the *ghazal*, a short lyric poem on the traditional subjects of love and wine, which are often treated symbolically (the beloved, whether male or female, representing God, and wine symbolizing ecstasy). About 500 *ghazals* are attributed to him. They have been widely translated; Goethe's German versions are perhaps the best known.

hafnium (Hf) A dense ductile metal, first detected in zircon ($ZrSiO_4$) in 1923 and named after the Latin (Hafnia) for Copenhagen, where it was discovered. It is chemically similar to zirconium and the two elements are difficult to separate. The capacity of hafnium to absorb neutrons is used to control nuclear reactors, especially in submarines. Its compounds include the chloride ($HfCl_4$) and other halides, the oxide (HfO_2), the carbide (HfC), and the nitride (Hf_3N_4). At no 72; at wt 178.49; mp 2150°C; bp 5400°C.

Haganah (Hebrew: defence) The irregular organization of the early Jewish settlers in Palestine established in 1920 to

HADRIAN'S WALL *One of the largest Roman remains in the UK.*

counteract the attacks of the Palestinian Arabs. After the partition of Palestine in 1947, the Haganah became the defence force of the Jewish state, coordinating opposition to the Palestinian and British forces, and in 1948 the national army of the state of Israel.

Hagen 51 22N 7 27E A city in NW West Germany, in North Rhine-Westphalia in the *Ruhr. It has iron and steel, textile, and paper industries. Population (1980 est): 220 100.

Hagen, Walter Charles (1892-1969) US professional golfer, who did much to popularize the game with his exhibition matches and his extrovert personality. Between 1914 and 1929 he won four British and two US Open championships and five US Professional Golfers Association championships.

hagfish A fishlike vertebrate, 40-80 cm long, sometimes called slime eel, belonging to a family (*Myxinidae*; about 20 species) of *cyclostomes. The eel-like body has 5-16 pairs of gill slits and a sucking mouth surrounded by several thick barbels. They occur on or near the sea bottom in cold regions and feed on dead or dying fish. Hagfishes are initially hermaphrodites but develop either male or female sex organs; fertilization is internal and the eggs hatch to produce young that resemble adults.

haggadah (*or* aggadah) **1.** Nonlegal portions of the Jewish *Midrash, as opposed to *halakhah. **2.** The liturgy recited in the Jewish home over the *Passover meal (*seder*). It contains a narrative of the Exodus from Egypt and various commentaries and hymns.

Haggai An Old Testament prophet. **The Book of Haggai** contains four addresses delivered after the *Babylonian exile (c. 520 BC). Their purpose is to encourage the completion of the Temple; the prophet rebukes the people's failure to complete the rebuilding of it, but prophesies a return of divine favour when it is rebuilt.

Haggard, Sir H(enry) Rider (1856-1925) British adventure novelist. His five years in government service in South Africa provided the background of his first and most popular novel, *King Solomon's Mines* (1885), notable for a sympathetic treatment of Black Africans, reflecting his own liberal views. Of his many later romances, *She* (1887) is the best known.

haggis A traditional Scottish meat dish, called by Burns "great chieftain o' the puddin' race" and eaten especially on Burns' Night (25 Jan). Haggis is made from minced sheep's heart, liver, and lungs with onion, oatmeal, suet, seasonings, lemon juice, and stock. The ingredients are stuffed into a bag, made from the sheep's stomach or a substitute, and boiled for several hours.

Hague, The (Dutch name: 's Gravenhage *or* Den Haag) 52 05N 4 16E The seat of government of the Netherlands and capital of South Holland province. It developed as a settlement surrounding a 13th-century hunting lodge and became the seat of the States General of the seven United Provinces of the Netherlands in the 16th century. It is the residence of the court and the International Court of Justice is located here. Notable buildings include the 13th-century Binnenhof, in which the government is housed. It is chiefly a commercial and residential centre with some light industry. Its port, Scheveningen, is a major herring-fishing centre and the most popular Dutch seaside resort. Population (1981 est): 456 726.

Hague Agreement (1949) A treaty ending the hostilities between the Netherlands and the Republic of Indonesia that had erupted after the establishment of the Republic in 1945. A federal government composed of the Republic and 15 autonomous states was created to administer the former Dutch East Indies, excluding West New Guinea. The treaty proved unacceptable to Indonesian nationalists and was finally revoked by the Indonesian parliament in 1956.

Hague Peace Conferences (1899, 1907) Two international congresses on *disarmament, held at The Hague (Netherlands). The first conference, attended by representatives of 26 countries, codified some of the rules of war as recommended by the *Geneva Convention and instituted the permanent Court of Arbitration at The Hague. However, no agreement was reached on disarmament. The second conference, attended by 44 delegates, adopted further conventions on war (*see* neutrality) but again failed to limit armaments.

HAITI *Cane sugar ready for export at Cité Simone.*

Hahn, Kurt (1886-1974) German progressive educationalist. The headmaster of Salem school in Germany (1920-33), Hahn was arrested by the Nazis. He fled to Britain, where he founded Gordonstoun school and was instrumental in establishing the Duke of Edinburgh's Award and the Outward Bound schemes for young people.

Hahn, Otto (1879-1968) German chemist and physicist. With Lise *Meitner he discovered protactinium in 1918. He continued to work with Meitner until she was forced to leave Germany in 1938. Together they discovered the process of nuclear fission. Hahn was unwilling to publish the results of this work, but Meitner did so from Sweden in 1939 and *Bohr took the information to the USA. Although Hahn remained in Germany for the rest of his life, he did not work on Germany's unsuccessful attempt to make an atom bomb. In 1944 he was awarded the Nobel Prize for Chemistry.

Hahnemann, Samuel Christian Friedrich (1755-1843) German physician and founder of *homeopathy. Hahnemann's methods aroused controversy among his contemporaries and he was forced to leave his practice in Leipzig, eventually settling in Paris.

hahnium (Ha; element 105) An artificial transuranic element, synthesized in the USA in 1970 by bombarding californium-249 with nitrogen-15 in a particle accelerator and possibly also in the Soviet Union in 1967 by a different method. Named after Otto Hahn. At no 105; at wt (260).

Haifa 32 49N 34 59E A town in NE Israel, on the Mediterranean coast by Mount Carmel. It was the scene of fighting in the 1948-49 Arab-Israeli conflict and has since developed into a manufacturing town based on the deepwater port (opened 1933). Haifa University was founded in 1963. Population (1983): 225 800.

Haig, Douglas, 1st Earl (1861-1928) British field marshal. After service in N Africa and India, Haig in World War I became commander of the first army corps in France and later commander in chief of the British Expeditionary Force (1915). Haig has been criticized for the appalling losses of the Somme and Passchendaele campaigns but his task was made difficult by the lack of support from ▢Lloyd George's War Cabinet. Under the supreme command of *Foch, Haig directed the final victorious assault on the Hindenburg line with distinction. He organized the *Royal British Legion after the war.

hail The approximately spherical ice pellets that fall from cumulonimbus clouds. These have been known to weigh almost 1 kg (2.2 lb). They originate within clouds as small ice particles around which layers of ice freeze. Hailstorms occur most frequently in the continental interiors of temperate latitudes.

Haile Selassie I (Ras Tafari Makonnen; 1892–1975) Emperor of Ethiopia (1930–36, 1941–74). In 1916 he became regent and heir to Empress Zauditu, succeeding her in 1930 and adopting the name Haile Selassie (Might of the Trinity). He led the resistance to the Italian invasion (1935) and gained world sympathy by taking his case to the League of Nations. In 1936 he had to flee to England but was restored to the throne by the Allies in 1941. An autocratic ruler, who did much to modernize Ethiopia, he was deposed by a military coup and died in captivity. *See also* Rastafarianism.

Hailsham of St Marylebone, Quintin McGarel Hogg, Baron (1907–   ) British lawyer and Conservative politician; Lord Chancellor (1970–74, 1979–87). A fellow of All Souls College, Oxford (1931–38), he entered parliament in 1938. From 1959 to 1963 he was minister for science and technology. In 1950 he succeeded his father **Douglas McGarel Hogg, 1st Viscount Hailsham** (1872–1950), Lord Chancellor (1928–29, 1935–38), but disclaimed his viscountcy in 1963, when he made an unsuccessful bid for the Conservative Party leadership. In 1970 he became a life peer. His grandfather **Quintin Hogg** (1845–1903), a philanthropist, founded the Regent Street Polytechnic in 1882.

Hailwood, Mike (Stanley Michael Bailey H.; 1940–81) British racing motorcyclist, who between 1961 and 1967 won nine world championships and 12 TT races. He later switched to motor racing (1969) and in 1973 was awarded the George Medal for saving another driver.

Hainan Island A Chinese island, the largest in the South China Sea, apart from Taiwan, and separated from the mainland by **Hainan Strait**. Sparsely populated, it is one of China's least developed regions. The aboriginal population has moved into the mountainous forested centre and S as Chinese farmers have settled the N coastal plain. Rubber and timber are produced and iron ore and other minerals are mined. Area: 33 991 sq km (13 124 sq mi). Capital: Haikou.

Hainaut (Flemish name: Henegouwen; French name: Hainault) A province in SW Belgium, bordering on France. It contains important coalfields and industries include iron and steel processing. Area: 3997 sq km (1466 sq mi). Population (1980 est): 1 305 163. Capital: Mons.

Haiphong 20 50N 106 41E A city in N Vietnam, on the Red River delta. As Hanoi's outport and an industrial centre much developed after 1954 with Soviet and Chinese aid, it was severely bombed during the Vietnam War. Textiles, phosphates, and plastics are manufactured and minerals and rice exported. Population (1979): 1 279 067.

hair The threadlike structures forming the body covering of mammals. Each hair grows from the base of a sheath (hair follicle) embedded in the inner layer (dermis) of the ▢skin but only a few cells at its root are living. The rest consists of scaly dead cells made largely of *keratin and other proteins. Colour is determined by the amount of *melanin pigment in hair. In most mammals hair forms an insulating and protective coat (the pelage), which reduces heat loss from the body and often provides camouflage. In humans hair is important only for personal adornment and display.

Similar structures in lower animals (e.g. insects) often have a sensory function, and plants possess hairs on roots, stems, and leaves.

hairstreak A butterfly belonging to the family *Lycaenidae* and characterized by fine white streaks on the underwings and a small "tail" on each hindwing. Both Old and New World species show a great variety of coloration.

hairy frog A *frog, *Astylosternus robustus*, of the Cameroons. In the breeding season the skin on the sides and thighs of male frogs develops hairlike filaments, containing many blood vessels, that assist in breathing and compensate for its much reduced lungs. The females grow no hairs.

Haiti, Republic of A country in the Caribbean Sea, occupying the W third of the island of Hispaniola (the Dominican Republic occupies the E two-thirds). Much of the country is mountainous and forested, with fertile plains lying between the three main mountain ranges. It is subject to hurricanes. The majority of the population is of African descent, with a minority of mulattoes. *Economy*: mainly agricultural, mostly organized in small farms. The main crops are coffee (the principal export), sugar, rice, bananas, and sisal. Mineral resources are largely unexploited although some bauxite and copper are mined. Hydroelectricity is an important source of power. Small industries are being encouraged, particularly manufactures for export. *History*: the island was discovered by Columbus in 1492 and became a Spanish colony. The Spanish virtually wiped out the native Indian population and large numbers of African slaves were imported. The W part was ceded to France in 1697, becoming the most prosperous of the French colonies, and the remainder was temporarily ceded between 1795 and 1809. The slave leader *Toussaint L'Ouverture briefly extended his rule over the whole island and in 1804, under Gen *Dessalines, Haiti gained its independence. A period of unrest was followed by union with the rest of the island (1822–44). For most of the time since it has been a republic; there was a brief period of occupation by the USA (1915–34). After a series of coups Dr François *Duvalier came to power in 1957 and was succeeded in 1971 by his son, Jean-Claude Duvalier. In 1986 Duvalier's brutal regime fell in a military coup and he fled to France; a provisional government was then set up under Lt-Gen Henri Namphy. In 1988 a general election resulted in the army-backed candidate, Leslie Manigat, becoming president. Official language: French; Creole is widely spoken. Offical religion: Roman Catholic. Area: 27 750 sq km (10 700 sq mi). Population (1983 est): 5 566 000. Capital and main port: Port-au-Prince.

Haitink, Bernard (1929–   ) Dutch conductor. He was appointed permanent conductor of the Amsterdam Concertgebouw Orchestra in 1964 and conductor of the London Philharmonic Orchestra in 1967. He became musical director at Glyndebourne (1978) and Covent Garden (1986).

hajj The pilgrimage to Mecca that every able Muslim is required to make, if means permit, at least once in his lifetime during the first half of the last month of the Islamic year. The pilgrimage includes circumambulations of the *Kaaba.

hake A food fish, of the genus *Merluccius*, that is related to *cod and occurs off European, African, and American coasts. Its elongated body, up to about 1 m long, is dark grey above and lighter below, with two dorsal fins, the second running to the tail and matching the anal fin.

Hakka A Chinese ethnic minority group found in the provinces of Canton and Fujian and in Taiwan and Chinese settlements in East Asia. The Hakkas (guest people) migrated S from N China in the unrest of the 12th and 13th centuries and for several centuries were social outcasts, having brought with them the different dialect and customs that they still retain.

Hakluyt, Richard (c. 1553–1616) English geographer. As a clergyman he served in various posts, but his chief interest was in exploration, navigation, and the establishment of a colony in Virginia. His major work, *The Principal Navigations, Voyages, Traffics, and Discoveries of the English Nation . . .* (1 vol, 1589; 3 vols, 1598–1600), stimulated English overseas trade and colonization.

Hakodate 41 46N 140 44E A port in Japan, in SW Hokkaido on the Tsugaru Strait. It contains Japan's only western-style fort (1855). Industries include fishing and shipbuilding. Population (1980): 320 000.

halakhah Jewish law. The Hebrew word is used in different ways, either for the law as a whole or an individual regulation. The main halakhic sources are the *Torah, *Mishnah and *Talmuds, the gaonic responsa (*see* gaon), and the medieval codes (e.g. those of *Maimonides and Joseph *Caro). The halakhah embraces more than law: it governs every aspect of life and also embodies theological ideas. The authority of halakhah is one of the main points of disagreement between traditional and *Reform Judaism.

Halberstadt 51 53N 11 2E A town in W East Germany. Many of its historic buildings, including the gothic cathedral, survived the bombing during World War II. Its varied industries include sugar refining, engineering, and chemicals. Population (1983): 47 255.

Halcyone In Greek legend, daughter of *Aeolus. She threw herself into the sea after her husband, Ceyx of Thrachis, drowned, and they were both transformed into kingfishers.

Haldane, Richard Burdon, 1st Viscount (1856–1928) British army reformer. A Liberal MP (1885–1911) until becoming a peer, he was secretary for war from 1905 to 1912. He created a general staff on the German model (1906), formed the Territorial Force (*see* Territorial Army), and facilitated the mobilization of the British Expeditionary Force at the outbreak of World War I. Becoming Lord Chancellor in 1912 he was dismissed in 1915 because his knowledge of Germany brought accusations that he was pro-German. Also a philosopher, he wrote a study of the philosophical implications of *relativity, *The Reign of Relativity* (1921). He helped to found the London School of Economics (1895). His brother **John Scott Haldane** (1860–1936) was a physiologist, noted for his investigations of human respiration. Haldane established that the rate of breathing was regulated according to the concentration of carbon dioxide in the blood. He also investigated the effects of high altitude and deepsea pressures on respiration and improved mine safety by demonstrating the toxic effects of carbon monoxide. J. S. Haldane's son **John Burdon Sanderson Haldane** (1892–1964) was a geneticist and philosopher, who contributed to many aspects of biology, including evolution and population genetics. Haldane was a Marxist and during the 1930s edited the communist *Daily Worker* (London). He left the Communist Party because of his disillusionment with the prominence given to the theories of *Lysenko in the Soviet Union. In 1957 Haldane emigrated to India in protest against aspects of British policy.

Hale, Sir Matthew (1609–76) English lawyer and judge. Hale defended such royalists as Archbishop *Laud during the Civil War but nevertheless became a judge and MP under Cromwell. After the Restoration he was appointed chief baron of the Exchequer (1660) and later chief justice of the King's Bench (1671). He was the author of an important legal work, *The History of the Common Law of England* (1713).

Hale Observatories The group of observatories comprising the Palomar Observatory, Mount Wilson Observatory, Big Bear Solar Observatory, all in California, and Las Campanas Observatory, near La Serena, Chile. They are sponsored by the Californian Institute of Technology and the Carnegie Institution, Washington. The principal telescopes are the famous 5 m (200 in) reflector and a 1.2 m (48 in) *Schmidt telescope (Palomar), the oldest 2.5 m (100 in) reflector (Mount Wilson), and a new 2.5 m reflector (Las Campanas). They are named after the US astronomer G. E. Hale (1868–1938), who helped to devel-

op the Mount Wilson and Palomar Observatories.

Halévy, Jacques François (Fromental Elias Levy; 1799–1862) French composer of Jewish origin. A pupil of Cherubini at the Paris conservatoire, he won the Prix de Rome in 1819. He composed ballets, incidental music, cantatas, and over 30 operas, including *La Juive* (1835).

half-life The time taken for half the atoms in a sample of a radioactive isotope to decay. It is therefore a measure of the activity of an isotope. A very active isotope may have a half-life of only a millionth of a second, whereas some more stable isotopes have half-lives of millions of years.

half-timber work A building technique used since ancient times. It involves constructing a wooden skeleton for a building, which is then filled out with either plasterwork or brick. Frequently the frame is left exposed. A quickly built and strong structure, it is best suited to temperate climates. The technique was frequently used in 15th- and 16th-century England.

halibut A *flatfish of the genus *Hippoglossus*, especially *H. hippoglossus*—a large food fish, up to about 2 m long, found in N Atlantic coastal waters. The eyed (right) side is brown or dark green with mottling. Family: *Pleuronectidae*.

Other halibuts include the Greenland halibut and the California halibut, which belong to the family *Bothidae*.

Haliç. *See* Golden Horn.

Halicarnassus (modern name: Bodrum) An ancient city of *Caria on the SW coast of Asia Minor. Its rulers included *Artemisia and Mausolus, who made Halicarnassus his capital (c. 370 BC) and is remembered chiefly for his tomb, the *Mausoleum. Herodotus, the Greek historian, was born here.

Halidon Hill, Battle of (19 July, 1333) The battle between English forces under *Edward III and Scots attempting to relieve Berwick-upon-Tweed. Using archers to great effect, the English victory ensured the temporary success of Edward's vassal, Edward de *Balliol, in his claims to the Scottish throne.

Halifax 53 44N 1 52W A town in N England, in West Yorkshire on the River Calder. Halifax has a strong wool textile tradition going back to the 13th century. Carpets, woollens, and worsteds are manufactured as well as machine tools and textile machinery. Population (1981): 87 488.

Halifax 44 38N 63 35W A city and major port in E Canada, the capital of Nova Scotia on the Atlantic Ocean. Founded as a British naval base (1749), it dominates the cultural life, commerce, and industry of the *Maritime Provinces. Its industries include shipbuilding, oil refining, steel, and food processing. Population (1981): 114 594.

Halifax, Charles Montagu, 1st Earl of (1661–1715) English statesman. A Whig MP (1689–95), as a lord of the treasury (1692–94) he initiated the national debt and set up the *Bank of England (1694) and as chancellor of the exchequer (1694–95) he introduced a new coinage. In 1697 he became first lord of the treasury but in 1699 was forced by the Tories to resign; he again held the post in 1714–15. He was a patron of writers, including the playwright *Congreve.

Halifax, Edward Frederick Lindley Wood, 1st Earl of (1881–1959) British politician and colonial administrator. As viceroy of India (1925–31) he was sympathetic to the nationalists, collaborating with Gandhi. As foreign secretary (1938–40), he supported Neville Chamberlain's policy of *appeasement. He was passed over as Chamberlain's successor (Churchill became prime minister) and served as ambassador to the USA (1941–46).

Halifax, George Savile, 1st Marquess of (1633–95) English politician, nicknamed the Trimmer because of the inconsistency of his views. He became a privy councillor in 1672 but was dismissed in 1676 for opposing Charles II's pro-French and pro-Roman Catholic policies. Again a privy councillor in 1679, he opposed the exclusion of the Catholic

A typical hallmark, from an article assayed in London in 1796.

London

Birmingham

A leopard's head introduced in 1300 (crowned between 1478 and 1821).

An anchor introduced in 1773.

Sheffield

Glasgow

The crown introduced in 1773.

A tree embellished with bell, bird, and fish, introduced in 1681.

Edinburgh

Dublin

The castle introduced in mid-16th century. The thistle was introduced in 1759.

The crowned harp introduced in mid-17th century. In 1731 the figure of Hibernia was added.

marks of some other halls

Chester   Newcastle-on-Tyne   York

Norwich   Exeter

HALLMARKS   *A set of typical hallmarks and the marks of the different assay offices.*

Duke of York (later James II) from the succession. He lost office at James' accession (1685) and supported the *Glorious Revolution, which brought William III and Mary II to the throne. He was the author of *The Character of a Trimmer* (1688).

halitosis   Bad breath. Very foul-smelling breath may be caused by infection in the mouth, teeth, tonsils, or lungs and sometimes by stomach disease. The mild odour that many people have needs no treatment except regular cleaning of the teeth.

Hall, Sir Peter   (1930–   ) British theatre director. He was director of the Royal Shakespeare Company from 1960 to 1968 and became director of the National Theatre Company in 1973. He is best known for his Shakespearian productions, but he has also directed plays by Harold Pinter and other contemporary playwrights, as well as operas and films. He was formerly married to the actress and dancer Leslie Caron (1931–   ).

Halle   51 30N 11 59E A city in SW East Germany, on the River Saale. The birthplace of Handel, Halle has many fine old buildings. Its diverse industries include sugar refining and coalmining. The university was founded in 1694. Population (1980 est): 232 217.

Hallé, Sir Charles   (Karl Hallé; 1819–1895) German conductor and pianist. He settled in Britain in 1848 and in 1857 established a series of concerts in Manchester, for which he founded and conducted the **Hallé Orchestra**. *See also* Barbirolli, Sir John.

Hall effect   If a conductor carrying an electric current is placed in a magnetic field, so that the field and the current are at right angles to each other, an electric field appears across the material. The electric field is perpendicular to both the current and the magnetic field. The effect is due to the force experienced by all moving charges in a magnetic field: the charges flowing in the material are displaced to one side thus creating a potential difference. Named after Edwin H. Hall (1855–1938).

Haller, Albrecht von   (1708–77) Swiss biologist, poet, and one of the founders of modern physiology. Haller showed how the stimulation of a nerve caused contraction of the muscle to which it was attached. He also studied the brain, heart, breathing mechanisms, and embryology; his works include *Elementa physiologiae corporis humani* (8 vols, 1757–66) and four large bibliographies of botany, anatomy, surgery, and medicine. His best-known poem is *Die Alpen.*

Halley, Edmund   (1656–1742) British astronomer, who was appointed professor of geometry at Oxford University in 1703. He was the first to realize that *comets do not appear randomly but have periodic orbits. In 1705 he identified a particular comet, now known as **Halley's comet**, as having a period of 76 years (appearing 1986, 2062, etc.). In 1986 it was intercepted and photographed at close range by the European probe Giotto. He also discovered that stars have a proper motion of their own (1718) and was appointed astronomer royal to succeed *Flamsteed (1720). A friend of Sir Isaac Newton, he had earlier financed the publication of Newton's *Principia* from an inheritance.

hallmarks   A set of marks stamped onto gold or silver objects manufactured in the UK, as a guarantee of purity. Each article has up to five marks: the mark of the assay office, an assay mark to indicate quality, a date mark, the sovereign's head (between 1784 and 1890), and the maker's mark. Gold articles also have a mark to indicate their purity in *carats.

Hallowe'en   Oct 31, the eve of All Saints' Day. The name is a contraction of All Hallows (hallowed or holy) Eve. In pre-Christian Britain, 31 Oct was the eve of New Year, when the souls of the dead were thought to revisit their homes. After it became a Christian festival supernatural associations continued; customs include the shaping of a demon's face from a hollow turnip or pumpkin, in which a candle is then placed. Children go from door to door on Hallowe'en demanding "treats" on penalty of "tricks."

Hallstatt   The phase of the central European Iron Age (700–500 BC) preceding *La Tène. It is named after the site in the Salzkammergut in Austria, which is famous for its salt mines. Earlier Bronze Age (*see* Urnfield) people in the same area (1200–700 BC) are often included under the term. The wealth of Iron Age Hallstatt depended on extensive trade. Characteristic artefacts were iron swords and elaborate bronze vessels decorated with geometric patterns, solar symbols, or ducks. Wagon burial of chieftains was practised, e.g. at Vix (France).

hallucination   A vivid but false perception of something that is not really there. Any sense can be affected. It may be a result of mental illness, especially *psychosis, when the commonest forms are hearing voices and seeing frightening visions. It can also be caused by drugs, epilepsy, disease of the brain, and sensory deprivation. Transient hallucinations can be experienced by normal people, especially when they are falling asleep (hypnagogic hallucinations) or waking up (hypnopompic hallucinations) or if they have been bereaved (grief hallucinations, of the person who has been lost).

hallucinogens   Drugs that produce hallucinations due to their stimulant action on the brain. Such drugs are also described as psychedelic. Hallucinogens, which include *cannabis and *LSD, tend to lead to some form of *drug dependence. The ability of any given hallucinogen to produce a hallucination depends very much on the personality of the individual. Some unlikely drugs (e.g. digitalis) may provoke hallucinations in susceptible individuals.

halogens The elements forming group VII of the *periodic table: fluorine, chlorine, bromine, iodine, and astatine. In chemical reactions they tend to form negative ions or covalent bonds and they have a valence of 1. All are reactive, particularly fluorine and chlorine. They produce salts on contact with metals ("halogen" means salt-yielding) and react with other nonmetals and many organic compounds.

Hals, Frans (c. 1581–1666) Dutch painter of portraits and scenes of everyday life. He was born in Antwerp but worked mainly in Haarlem. Apart from his *Laughing Cavalier* (1624; Wallace Collection, London), he is best known for his group portraits, such as those of the companies of archers and musketeers, which are characterized by lively expressions and gestures. Later works, such as *Lady-Governors of the Almshouse at Haarlem* (1664; Frans Hals Museum, Haarlem), influenced by *Rembrandt, are more sombre and show a greater sympathy for character.

Halsey, William F(rederick) (1882–1959) US admiral. A naval aviator, he commanded the South Pacific area (1942–44) and the Third Fleet (1944–45). He contributed significantly to the battles of Guadalcanal, the Coral Sea (1942), *Leyte Gulf (1944), and Okinawa (1945), which marked the transition in naval warfare from guns to aircraft as the decisive weapons.

Hälsingborg (or Helsingborg) 56 05N 12 45E A seaport in S Sweden, on the Sound opposite Helsingor, Denmark. It changed hands several times between Denmark and Sweden before finally becoming Swedish in 1710. An industrial centre, it has an important shipbuilding industry. Population (1983): 103 870.

Hama 35 09N 36 44E A town in W Syria. It dates from Hittite times and still possesses the medieval water-wheels up to 27 m (89 ft) in diameter used for irrigation. It is mainly an agricultural and commercial centre. Population (1982): 177 208.

Hamadan 34 46N 48 35E A town in W central Iran. Hamadan lies at a high altitude, and visitors are attracted by the cool summers; the winters, however, are severe. A university was founded here in 1973. Population (1985 est): 262 200.

hamadryas A small *baboon, *Papio hamadryas*, of NE Africa and Saudi Arabia. 100–140 cm long including the tail (40–60 cm), hamadryas baboons have a long silvery-brown mane, pinkish face, and red buttocks and live in groups with a complex social structure. They were sacred animals to the ancient Egyptians.

Hamamatsu 34 42N 137 42E A city in Japan, in S central Honshu. A commercial and industrial centre, its manufactures include musical instruments, textiles, and motor cycles. Population (1980): 491 000.

Hamburg 53 33N 10 00E A city in N West Germany, on the Rivers Elbe and Alster. A major port and the largest city in West Germany, it is also an important cultural centre, with a university (1919), art gallery, and opera house (1678). It is the birthplace of Mendelssohn and Brahms. Its many industries include shipbuilding, engineering, and food processing. *History*: in 834 AD it was made the seat of a missionary archbishop. Its alliance with Lübeck (1241) became the basis of the Hanseatic League. It was a trading centre from the middle ages and the first German stock exchange was established here (1558). It was severely bombed during World War II. Population (1980 est): 1 645 095.

Hamburg A small *Land* in NE West Germany, comprising the city of *Hamburg, its surrounds, and two islands in the Elbe estuary. Area: 748 sq km (289 sq mi). Population (1980 est): 1 648 800.

Hamelin (German name: Hameln) 52 06N 9 21E A town in

N West Germany, in Lower Saxony on the River Weser. Its many Renaissance houses include the Ratcatcher's House (1602–03), associated with the legendary Pied Piper. Manufactures include carpets and chemicals. Population (1984): 56 000.

Hamersley Range A mountain range of N Western Australia. It extends W–E between the Fortesque and Ashburton Rivers, reaching 1227 m (4024 ft) at Mount Bruce, and contains large deposits of iron ore.

Hamhŭng (or Hamheung) 39 54N 127 35E A city in E central North Korea. Its industry was bombed by US forces during the Korean War (1950–53) but has been restored and developed. The principal manufactures are synthetic textiles, chemicals, and machinery. Its seaport, Hungnam, lies to the SE of the city. Population (1980 est): 775 000.

Hamilcar Barca (died c. 229 BC) Carthaginian general and Hannibal's father. Commander in Sicily during the first *Punic War, he negotiated peace in 241. After suppressing rebellious mercenaries in Carthage, he invaded Spain, accompanied by the young Hannibal. He was drowned after the siege of Helice.

Hamilton 43 15N 79 50W A city and port in central Canada, in S Ontario on Lake Ontario. Canada's main centre of heavy industry, it is particularly important for iron and steel, motor vehicles, machinery, chemicals, and electrical goods. Hamilton is also a financial, agricultural, transportation, and educational centre. McMaster University (1887) was moved here from Toronto in 1930. Population (1981): 306 434.

Hamilton 37 46S 175 18E A city in New Zealand, in N North Island on the Waikato River. It is the most important inland centre and serves a pastoral and lumbering region. The University of Waikato was established in 1964. Population (1983 est): 164 600.

Hamilton 55 47N 4 03W A town in W central Scotland, in Strathclyde Region in the Clyde valley. Metal goods, carpets, and electrical equipment are manufactured, local coalmining having declined. Population (1981): 51 529.

Hamilton, Alexander (?1755–1804) US statesman; the first US secretary of the treasury (1789–95); leader of the *Federalist Party. He established the first national bank (1791) and set up the national debt. He believed in representative central government and collaborated in the *Federalist* (1788), which was influential in securing ratification of the Constitution. He was killed in a duel by Aaron *Burr, a long-standing political opponent, after denouncing him as candidate for the governorship of New York.

Hamilton, Lady Emma (c. 1761–1815) The mistress of Horatio *Nelson. She was the mistress of Charles Greville (1749–1809) and then of his uncle Sir William Hamilton (1730–1803), envoy to the court of Naples (1764–1800). She married Hamilton in 1791 and met Nelson in Naples in 1793. They became lovers and in 1801 their daughter Horatia (d. 1881) was born. After Nelson's death (1805), Lady Emma squandered her inheritance and fled, a bankrupt, to Calais (1814), where she died. *Romney painted many portraits of her.

Hamilton, James, 1st Duke of (1606–49) Scottish royalist in the English Civil War. As Charles I's commissioner in Scotland (1638–41) he tried to moderate the king's unpopular religious policy and opposed his minister Strafford. After the outbreak of the Civil War, however, he joined Charles. Defeated by Cromwell at Preston, he was executed.

Hamilton, Sir William Rowan (1805–65) Irish mathematician. A child prodigy, he had mastered 13 languages by the age of 13 and at 22 was appointed professor of astronomy at Trinity College, Dublin. His most important work was the discovery of quaternions, three-dimensional equivalents of *complex numbers. He also made important contributions to the mathematics of light rays and helped to establish the wave theory of light.

Hamito-Semitic languages A language family spoken in N Africa and S Asia. It is more appropriately known as Afro-Asiatic, especially since the Hamitic section of the name describes no particular characteristics. It has five branches that descend from an ancestor language, Proto-Hamito-Semitic, which was spoken between the 6th and 8th millenniums BC. The five branches are Egyptian, Berber, Cushitic, Semitic, and Chadic. There is some doubt about the membership of the Chadic languages in this group.

Hamm 51 40N 7 49E A city in NW West Germany, in North Rhine-Westphalia. The rail centre of the *Ruhr, it has the largest marshalling yards in the country. Its chief manufactures are wire, cable, and machinery. Population (1980 est): 171 600.

Hammarskjöld, Dag (Hjalmar Agne Carl) (1905–61) Swedish international civil servant; the son of Hjalmar Hammarskjöld (1862–1953), who was a prime minister of Sweden (1914–17). As deputy foreign minister (1951–53) he headed the Swedish delegation to the UN and in 1953 succeeded Trygve *Lie as secretary general of the UN. He dealt with the Suez crisis (1956) and the civil war arising from the grant of independence to the Congo (1960). He was killed in a plane crash and awarded the Nobel Peace Prize posthumously in 1961. His diary *Markings* was published in 1964.

Hammerfest 70 40N 23 44E A port in N Norway, on the W coast of the island of Kvaløya (*or* Kväloy). It is the most northerly town in the world. Its ice-free harbour permits fishing all year. Population (1983): 7208.

hammerhead A dark-brown bird, *Scopus umbretta*, that is the only member of its family (*Scopidae*) and occurs in marshes and mangrove swamps of tropical Africa, Madagascar, and the Arabian Peninsula. It has a large bill and a long backward-pointing crest. Hammerheads feed on frogs, fish, and aquatic invertebrates and build a large domed nest of sticks cemented together with mud. Order: *Ciconiiformes* (herons, storks, etc.).

hammerhead shark A *shark of the family *Sphyrnidae*, found in warm and temperate salt waters. Up to 4.5 m long, the head is flattened and extended laterally into two hammer- or spade-shaped lobes, which bear the eyes and nostrils. They feed primarily on fish but may attack other animals, including man.

Hammersmith A borough of W Greater London, on the River Thames. It was created in 1965 from the former metropolitan boroughs of Hammersmith and *Fulham. It contains Olympia (an exhibition centre) and the BBC television centre. Population (1981): 148 054.

Hammerstein II, Oscar (1895–1960) US lyricist and librettist, who collaborated with several well-known musical comedy composers. With Richard Rodgers he wrote *Oklahoma!* (1943), *Carousel* (1945), *South Pacific* (1949), *The King and I* (1951), and *The Sound of Music* (1959).

hammer throw A field event for men in athletics. The hammer is an iron or brass sphere weighing 16 lb (7.26 kg) attached to a spring-steel wire handle and grip. It is thrown with both hands from within a circle 7 ft (2.13 m) in diameter. A competitor has six tries in which to throw the hammer the furthest. World record: 86.34 m (1984) by Yuri Sedykh (Soviet Union).

Hammett, Dashiell (1894–1961) US novelist. He worked as a private detective for eight years before writing his first detective stories. His novels, the realistic and economical style of which influenced Raymond *Chandler and other detective-story writers, include *The Maltese Falcon* (1930) and *The Thin Man* (1932), both of which were made into successful films. He was a close friend of Lillian *Hellman.

Hammond, Dame Joan (1912–   ) British soprano, born in New Zealand. She studied in Sydney, London, and Vienna, making her operatic debut in Vienna in 1929 and thereafter appearing in the principal opera houses of the world. She was created a DBE in 1974.

Hammond, Wally (Walter Reginald H.; 1903–65) British cricketer, who played for England and Gloucestershire. A great all-rounder, he played in 85 Test matches and in his career hit 167 centuries (22 in Tests).

Hammurabi (d. 1750 BC) King of Babylon (1792–1750). After defeating the kingdoms of Eshunna, Elam, and Ashur, Hammurabi turned against his former allies, the kingdoms of Larsa and Mari. The Code of Hammurabi, a collection of Babylonian laws, has survived in the Akkadian language.

Hampden, John (1594–1643) English parliamentarian, who opposed the policies of Charles I. Elected an MP in 1621, he was imprisoned (1627–28) for refusing to pay a forced loan. In 1636 he was tried for failing to pay *ship money but the king only narrowly won the case and the widespread opposition to the tax was intensified. A vocal critic in the *Long Parliament (summoned in 1640), he was one of the five MPs whom Charles tried to arrest in 1642. Hampden was killed near Thame in a minor battle of the Civil War.

Hampshire A county of S central England, bordering on the English Channel. Under local government reorganization in 1974 it lost part of the SW, including Bournemouth, to Dorset. It consists mainly of gently undulating lowlands, rising to chalk downlands in the N and E. The chief rivers, the Test and Itchen, drain into the Solent, which separates the Isle of *Wight from the mainland. It is predominantly agricultural with dairy and arable farming. Industries, centred on Southampton, include shipbuilding and oil refining and there are important naval bases at Portsmouth and Gosport. Tourism is important in the *New Forest and coastal resorts. Area: 3772 sq km (1456 sq mi). Population (1981): 1 456 367. Administrative centre: Winchester.

Hampstead A district in the Greater London borough of Camden. It contains Hampstead Heath, an extensive open space, and the exclusive residential area of Hampstead "village."

Hampton 37 02N 76 23W A port in the USA, in SE Virginia on Hampton Roads Harbour. Founded in 1610, it has large fish-packing and shipping industries. Several military installations are situated nearby. Population (1980): 122 617.

Hampton, Lionel (1913–   ) US Black jazz band leader and vibraphone player, who played with Benny Goodman before forming his own orchestra in 1940. Hampton was the first jazz musician to popularize the vibraphone; one of his biggest successes was the record *Flyin' Home* (1942).

Hampton Court A Tudor and Stuart palace on the River Thames near London. Built by Cardinal Wolsey, it was given in the 1520s to Henry VIII, who made substantial alterations, including the addition of the Great Hall. In the 1690s *Wren began a further rebuilding project for William III, which included the Fountain Court and the east and south fronts. The palace, now open to the public, has an important collection of paintings. In 1986 it was damaged by fire, causing considerable loss to the King's Audience Chamber.

hamster A small *rodent of the family *Cricetidae*. The common hamster (*Cricetus cricetus*), native to Europe and W Asia, is solitary and aggressive and has a red-brown coat with white patches on the flanks, neck, and cheek. It feeds on seeds and grains, storing them in underground burrows. The golden hamster (*Mesocricetus auratus*) is a domestic pet and all are thought to have descended from a single family found at Aleppo, Syria, in 1930.

Hamsun, Knut (1859–1952) Norwegian novelist. His early novels, *Hunger* (1890), *Mysteries* (1892), and *Pan* (1894), reflected his interest in nature and the irrational. Much of his subsequent work was influenced by Nietzsche and Strindberg and revealed a distrust of society and civilization; it includes the novels *Vagabonds* (1927) and *Markens gróde* (*The Growth of the Soil*; 1917). He won the Nobel Prize in 1920. He was accused of pro-Nazi tendencies after World War II but was not tried; his own attitude towards the war is commented on in the autobiographical *På gjengrodde stier* (1949).

Han (206 BC–220 AD) A Chinese dynasty founded by the general Liu Bang (*or* Liu Pang; 256–195 BC), who overthrew the preceding Qin dynasty. The power of the Han was consolidated by the emperor, Wu Di (*or* Wu Ti; 157–87 BC; reigned 140–87), who completed the conquest of a vast empire. Confucianism was recognized as the state philosophy, Chinese export of silk increased, and a vast canal-building programme was started. Paper was invented by the Han Chinese, who also produced early forms of porcelain and kept detailed historical records. The programme of expansion led to financial difficulties that enabled Wang Mang to usurp the throne in 8 AD. However, he was toppled in turn and the Han dynasty was restored for a second period, known as the Later Han (23–220 AD).

Hancock, Tony (1924–68) British comedian. He is best known for his radio series of the 1950s, *Hancock's Half Hour*, which was characterized by his unique style of lugubrious humour. He also appeared on television and in several films, including *Those Magnificent Men in Their Flying Machines* (1965).

hand The terminal part of the arm. The human hand contains 27 bones. There are 8 carpal bones, which form the wrist and articulate with the forearm at a hinge joint; 5 metacarpals, in the palm of the hand; and 14 phalanges (the bones of the fingers and thumb). The thumb of man and other primates is unique in being opposable, i.e. it can be rotated to touch each of the other fingers, making possible a wide range of manual skills (including using tools and writing). This—combined with its sensitive skin—has produced a manipulative and exploratory organ that has contributed to the success of man as a species. *See* Plate IV.

handball 1. A court game related to *pelota and *fives that probably originated in the Roman baths. It is played in a court against one, three, or four walls with a small rubber ball that is hit with the gloved hand. 2. An 11-a-side field game (or seven-a-side indoor game) introduced in about 1890 and adapted to Association football rules, played by catching and throwing the ball.

Handel, George Frederick (1685–1759) German composer. He studied in Halle and travelled to Italy, where he became famous as a harpsichordist and as a master of the Italianate style of composition. In 1710 he became kapellmeister to the Elector of Hanover but did not return there after visiting England in 1712. He received a court pension from Queen Anne, which was doubled by the forgiving elector when be became George I of Great Britain on Anne's death in 1714. Handel became musical director to James Brydges, first duke of Chandos (1673–1744), in 1718. He subsequently became music master to the family of the Prince of Wales and director of the Royal Academy of Music on its foundation in 1720. His Italian operas were successfully produced in London and Handel triumphed over his greatest rival, Giovanni Bononcini (1670–1747). The effort needed to sustain his position affected his health and from 1739 he turned from opera to oratorio, producing such masterpieces as *Saul* (1739), *Israel in Egypt* (1739), and *Messiah* (1742), which maintained his public popularity. In 1751, however, he began to be afflicted with loss of sight and despite operations for cataract became completely blind, although he continued to compose with the aid of an amanuensis until his death. His mastery of composition is reflected in the range of his works, which include the *Water Music* (1717), a favourite of the king's, *Music for the Royal Fireworks* (1749), concerti grossi, sonatas, organ concertos,

harpsichord suites, and anthems. He was buried in Westminster Abbey.

Handley Page, Sir Frederick. *See* Page, Sir Frederick Handley.

Handy, William Christopher (1873–1958) US Black jazz musician, remembered chiefly for the song "St Louis Blues" (1914). In later life he became a music publisher, continuing to work until his death, even after becoming blind.

Han fei zi (d. 233 BC) Chinese diplomat and philosopher of law. Although an author of antiquity, he has been studied, along with the Taoists, in the modern period in China. He is best known for his conception of government by law and his advocacy of statecraft.

Hangchow. *See* Hangzhou.

hang-gliding Unpowered flight in a hang-glider, consisting of a large bat-shaped cloth wing on a light metal framework from which the pilot hangs in a harness, holding a horizontal control bar. In flight, the wing fills to form an aerofoil (*see* aeronautics). The first hang-glider was built by Otto *Lilienthal, but the prototype for modern design was the sail-wing invented by Frances Rogallo (1912–) as a means of recovering space vehicles. Hang-gliding became popular in the late 1960s, acquiring a reputation as a dangerous sport largely because hang-gliders are relatively easy to attempt to fly without instruction. A powered hang-glider was first used to cross the English Channel in 1979.

hanging. *See* capital punishment.

Hanging Gardens of Babylon Ancient gardens in the palace of Nebuchadnezzar II (604–562 BC) on the E side of Babylon. One of the Seven Wonders of the World, they were built on top of stone arches 23 m (75 ft) above ground and watered from the Euphrates by a complicated mechanical system.

Hangzhou (Hang-chou *or* Hangchow) 30 18N 120 07E A city in E China, the capital of Zhejiang province on Hangzhou Bay, an inlet of the East China Sea. It was the capital (1132–1276) of the Southern *Song dynasty. A picturesque tourist centre, it is the site of three universities. Its varied industries include silk production. Population (1982): 3 120 000.

haniwa Japanese terracotta sculptures, originally cylindrical in shape, placed on the outside of tomb mounds between about 330 and 552 AD. By the 5th century modelled houses and later horses and human figures were placed on top of the cylinders.

Hankou (*or* Hankow). *See* Wuhan.

Hannibal (247–c. 183 BC) Carthaginian general. Appointed commander in Spain in 221, he deliberately provoked the second *Punic War with Rome. Advancing swiftly, in 218 he crossed the Alps in winter, reaching N Italy after a heroic trek in which he lost about 10 000 of his 35 000 men. For two years he devastated Italy but, after disastrous Roman defeats at Trasimene and *Cannae, Hannibal lost ground in the face of *Fabius' guerrilla tactics. Recalled to defend Carthage after *Scipio Africanus' invasion of Africa, Hannibal was defeated at Zama (202). Domestic politics occupied him until, suspected of rebellion, he was forced to flee Roman retribution. He committed suicide to avoid capture.

Hanoi 20 57N 105 55E The capital of Vietnam, situated in the NE of the country on the Red River. The capital of the Vietnamese empire from the 11th until the 17th centuries, it was occupied by the French in 1873 and became the capital of French Indochina. Following the Japanese occupation in World War II, it became the capital of the Democratic Republic of Vietnam. Despite the frequent bombing by the USA during the Vietnam War, many ancient buildings in the Vietnamese quarter remain, together with several imposing buildings in the European quarter built by the French. Its university was established in 1956. Population (1983 est): 2 674 400.

Hanover (German name: Hannover) 52 23N 9 44E A city in N West Germany, the capital of Lower Saxony on the River Leine. It is a transshipment port and a commercial and industrial centre, where an important industrial fair is held annually. After the destruction of World War II it was largely rebuilt and some buildings, such as the old town hall (1435–80), were reconstructed. The Leine Palace (founded 1636) is now the *Land* parliament building. Hanover's manufactures include machinery, rubber, textiles, and motor vehicles. *History*: in 1638 Hanover became the capital of an area of Brunswick that was later the electorate and then the kingdom of Hanover. In 1714 Elector George Louis became George I of Great Britain, inheriting the British throne through his mother Sophia (*see* Settlement, Act of). He is buried in Hanover. The Kings of Great Britain were Electors (later Kings) of Hanover until 1837. Population (1980 est): 535 100.

Hanoverian A breed of horse developed in Hanover and originally used for draught purposes. During the 19th and 20th centuries crosses with English Thoroughbreds produced the strong but elegant modern Hanoverian, which is popular for showjumping and hunting. Height: 1.63-1.73 m (16-17 hands).

Han River A river in E central China, rising in S Shenxi province and flowing SE to join the Yangtze River at Wuhan. Length: about 1450 km (900 mi).

Hansard The official reports of debates in the UK *parliament. The name, which was officially adopted in 1943, is that of the family that first printed the reports. From 1774 the House of Commons' journals were printed by **Luke Hansard** (1752-1828). From 1807 his son **Thomas Curson Hansard** (1776-1833) printed the unofficial reports of parliamentary debates that Cobbet had begun to compile in 1804. Hansard continued to print the reports until 1890.

Hanseatic League An association of N German trading towns (the Hanse) formed in the 13th century to protect their economic interests overseas. By the mid-14th century, the League, comprising some hundred towns, had become a powerful corporate body and was able to establish trading monopolies in much of NE Europe. It faced considerable opposition from Denmark and England, with which it conducted a number of trade wars. The rise of the non-German Baltic states during the 15th and 16th centuries, as well as changing trade routes, contributed to the League's declining influence. It was finally dissolved in 1669.

hansom cab. *See* cab.

Hanukka A Jewish festival, commemorating the revolt of the *Maccabees. It falls in midwinter and is celebrated by lighting of lamps or candles.

Hanuman In Hindu mythology, a monkey god and one of the principal characters in the *Ramayana*, in which he helps Rama to recover his wife Sita from the demon Ravana. There are many temples dedicated to him in India and Japan.

Hanyang. *See* Wuhan.

Hapsburgs. *See* Habsburgs.

hara-kiri The honourable way of death for Japanese *samurai who wished to avoid shame or demonstrate sincerity. In its strict form it involved ceremoniously cutting one's stomach open with a dagger before one's head was struck off by the single blow of another samurai's sword. In later times, however, there was often only a token gesture of disembowelment before decapitation. It is still sometimes practised by Japanese suicides, although it is now illegal.

Harappa The site in the Punjab in Pakistan of a great city of the *Indus Valley civilization. Its cemeteries and brick buildings (excavated 1920s, 1946) equal *Mohenjo-Daro in importance.

Harar (*or* Harer) 9 20N 42 10E A city in E Ethiopia, the capital of Harar province. Situated at 1800 m (6000 ft), it is Ethiopia's only walled city. Its capture by British forces (1941) led to the eventual collapse of Mussolini's African

colonial empire. Trade is based on coffee and grain. Population (1982 est): 70 289.

Harare (name until 1982: Salisbury) 17 50S 31 02E The capital of Zimbabwe, on a plateau in the NE. Founded in 1890 it was the capital of the Federation of Rhodesia and Nyasaland (1953–63). The University of Zimbabwe (formerly Rhodesia) was founded here in 1970 and Harare has Anglican and Roman Catholic cathedrals. The centre of a tobacco-growing area, it has an important trade and industry in tobacco. Other industries include textiles and engineering. Population (1980 est): 654 000.

Harbin. *See* Ha-er-bin.

harbour seal The common *seal, *Phoca vitulina*, of coastal Pacific and Atlantic waters. Up to 1.8 m long, with a blotchy grey coat, harbour seals inhabit sandbanks and river estuaries, feeding on fish. Family: *Phocidae*. □mammal.

Hardanger Fjord A fjord in SW Norway, S of Bergen, penetrating inland from the North Sea for 110 km (68 mi). It is edged by spectacular mountains and many waterfalls.

Hardecanute (*or* Harthacnute; c. 1019–42) The last Danish King of England (1040–42), succeeding his illegitimate half-brother Harold I Harefoot, and King of Denmark (1035–42). As the legitimate son of Canute, he ordered Harold's corpse to be disinterred and thrown into the Thames as a revenge for Harold's seizure of the throne after Canute's death. He razed Worcester after a riot against his tax collectors. He died of a seizure at a marriage feast.

Hardenberg, Karl (August), Fürst von (1750–1822) Prussian statesman. He was foreign minister under Frederick William III from 1804 to 1806 and prime minister in 1807, when Prussia was subjected to Napoleonic rule. Again prime minister from 1810 until his death, he introduced reforms that enabled Prussia to break away from French control in 1813. However, monarchist opposition resulted in his declining influence after 1815.

Hardie, J(ames) Keir (1856–1915) British politician, who was an important figure in the early parliamentary Labour Party. Born in Scotland, he became a coalminer at the age of ten and was active in the trades-union movement before founding (1888) the Scottish Parliamentary Labour Party. As an Independent Socialist MP (1892–95) he helped to found (1893) the Independent Labour Party. Again an MP (1900–15), he became chairman of the parliamentary Labour Representation Committee in 1906, shortly before it was renamed the *Labour Party. He was an ardent pacifist.

Hardinge of Lahore, Henry, 1st Viscount (1785–1856) British soldier and colonial administrator; governor general of India (1844–48) after 24 years as an MP (1820–44), during which time he was twice secretary for war (1828–30, 1841–44). He became commander in chief of the British army in 1852 but was demoted in 1855 during the Crimean War. His grandson **Charles, 1st Baron Hardinge of Penshurst** (1858–1944) was viceroy of India (1910–16).

Hardouin-Mansart, Jules (1646–1708) French *baroque architect, who succeeded Le Vau as court architect to Louis XIV. He built Les Invalides, Paris (1680–91), but is most famous for his huge extensions to *Versailles, begun in 1678. These include the Galérie des Glaces (Gallery of Mirrors) and the orangery. He was also a town planner and designed the Place Vendôme (1699) in Paris.

Hardwar 29 58N 78 09E A town in N India, in Uttar Pradesh. One of the most sacred Hindu pilgrimage centres, its bathing ghat (or steps) along the River Ganges is believed to contain the footprint of the god Vishnu. Population (1981): 115 513.

hardware. *See* computer.

Hardy, G(odfrey) H(arold) (1877–1947) British mathematician, who championed pure mathematics and despised its applied aspects. He discovered one of the fundamental results in population *genetics, which gives the proportion of dominant and recessive genes in a large mixed population, but he regarded the work as unimportant.

THOMAS HARDY

Hardy, Thomas (1840–1928) British novelist and poet. The son of a mason, he went to London in 1862 to study architecture. His major novels, which include *The Return of the Native* (1878), *The Mayor of Casterbridge* (1886), and *Tess of the D'Urbervilles* (1891), are tragic tales set in his native Dorset (called "Wessex" in the novels). After the public outrage caused by the alleged immorality of *Jude the Obscure* (1895) he published only verse, beginning with *Wessex Poems* (1898), and an epic drama, *The Dynasts* (1903–08). After the death of his first wife, Emma, he married his secretary, Florence Dugdale, in 1914. He was awarded the OM in 1910.

hare A mammal belonging to the widely distributed family *Leporidae* (which also includes the *rabbits). Hares are typically larger than rabbits (the European hare (*Lepus europaeus*) weighs up to 4 kg) and have long black-tipped ears. They live and breed in the open (rather than in burrows) and are mainly nocturnal, feeding on grass and bark. The young are born fully furred with open eyes. Chief genus: *Lepus* (about 26 species); order: *Lagomorpha*.

Hare, William. *See* Burke, William.

harebell A herbaceous perennial plant, *Campanula rotundifolia*, of N temperate regions, growing to a height of 60 cm. It has rounded leaves and blue nodding bell-shaped flowers on slender stems. Harebell grows in a variety of open habitats. Family: *Campanulaceae*.

Hare Krishna movement (Sanskrit: hail Krishna) An international religious community, the International Society for Krishna Consciousness (ISKCON), founded in New York in 1966 on Hindu principles by an Indian, Swami Prabhupada (1895–   ). Members live according to a strict vegetarian regime that also prohibits gambling, extramarital sex, and the use of drugs. They dress in saffron linen robes and the men have shaved heads. Daily worship includes the chanting of the Hare Krishna mantra and dancing in the streets. The movement is financed by begging, the sale of literature and incense, and donations.

harelip A defect, present at birth, in which there is a cleft in the upper lip. There is often a simultaneous defect in the roof of the mouth (*see* cleft palate). Both defects interfere with speech and feeding but can be repaired surgically.

Harfleur 49 31N 0 12E A port in N France, in the Seine-Maritime department on the Seine estuary. A major port in the middle ages, it declined with the rise of Le Havre. Its manufactures include metal goods and flour. Population (1982): 8125.

Hargeisa 9 20N 43 57E A town in N Somalia, near the Ethiopian border. It was the summer capital of former British Somaliland (1941–60). It is a watering and trading place for nomadic herdsmen. Population (1980 est): 70 000.

Hargreaves, James (d. 1778) English inventor, who around 1764 invented the spinning jenny, a machine (named after his daughter) with which several threads could be spun simultaneously. After local spinners, believing that their jobs were threatened by the jenny, broke into his home near Blackburn, Lancashire, and broke up his machines, Hargreaves set up (1768) a small mill in Nottingham.

haricot bean A variety of *French bean (*Phaseolus vulgaris*) grown in warm climates. The seeds, which are dried for storage and soaked before use, are either brown or light-coloured and are used for making baked beans.

Haringey A mainly residential borough of N Greater London, created in 1965 from the former municipal boroughs of Hornsey, Tottenham, and Wood Green. Population (1981): 203 175.

Harishchandra (1850–85) Hindi poet, dramatist, and essayist, also known as Bharatendu. He founded two literary Hindi magazines and through his writings and patronage of other writers he contributed to the literary development of Hindi, which eventually became the official language of India. In *Bharat durdasa* (1880) and other plays he attributed the decline of Indian civilization to Muslim and western influences.

Harlan, John Marshall (1833–1911) US jurist. As associate justice of the US Supreme Court from 1877 until his death, he became famous for his opposition to many of the court's rulings. He was an ardent supporter of civil rights, particularly those of Blacks. In the case of *Plessy versus Ferguson* (1896) he vigorously opposed the Supreme Court's decision that racial segregation in US schools was justified on the principle of "separate but equal."

Harlech 52 52N 4 07W A historic town in NW Wales, in Gwynedd on Cardigan Bay. It is a resort with a famous ruined castle (□Wales) begun in 1285 by Edward I. Population (1986 est): 1110.

Harlem 40 49N 73 57W A residential district of New York City, USA, in Manhattan. It is a political and social focus for Blacks. The poets Langston Hughes (1902–67) and Countee Cullen (1903–46) were part of the "Harlem renaissance" of the 1920s.

Harlem Globetrotters A Black American professional basketball team formed by Abraham Saperstein (1903–66) in 1927. They play exhibition matches all over the world.

Harlequin A stock character of the □commedia dell'arte. Known as Arlecchino in Renaissance Italy, Harlequin began as a comic and covetous servant but developed by the 18th century into the agile and capricious lover of Columbine and the central comic figure of the harlequinade. Dressed in a bright diamond-patterned costume, masked, and carrying a wooden club (called a slapstick), he was played in England by such leading actors as John Rich and David Garrick. The rise of Pierrot and pantomime in the 19th century led to a decline in the harlequinade.

harlequin duck A short-billed *diving duck, *Histrionicus histrionicus*, occurring in coastal waters of Iceland and Greenland. The female is brown with white patches around the eyes; the male is grey-blue with black-edged white markings and chestnut flanks.

Harley, Robert, 1st Earl of Oxford (1661–1724) English statesman under Queen Anne. An MP from 1688, he was a Tory but allied with the Whigs, becoming speaker of the House of Commons (1701) and then secretary of state (1704). Intriguing against his Whig colleagues *Godolphin and *Marlborough, he was dismissed in 1708 and rejoined the Tories. After the fall of the Whigs, he became Anne's chief minister as chancellor of the exchequer (1710–11) and Lord Treasurer (1711–14). The machinations of his rival

*Bolingbroke brought his dismissal and after the accession of George I he was imprisoned (1714-17) for his Tory (and, by implication, *Jacobite) views.

Harlow 51 47N 0 08E A town in SE England, in Essex. It is a new town, developed since 1947 as a satellite town of London with light industries (surgical and scientific instruments, electronics, engineering, furniture, glass). Population (1981): 79 253.

Harlow, Jean (Harlean Carpentier; 1911-37) US film actress. Her well-publicized sex appeal and her talent for comedy won great popularity during the 1930s in such films as *Platinum Blonde* (1931) and *Bombshell* (1933). She died from kidney failure while making *Saratoga* (1937).

harmonica 1. The mouth organ: the smallest member of the reed-organ family; its invention is attributed to Sir Charles *Wheatstone in 1829. Notes and chords are obtained by blowing or sucking rows of parallel reeds. It is used mainly in light music, although *Vaughan Williams and *Milhaud have written works for the instrument's main exponent, Larry *Adler. 2. The glass harmonica: an obsolete instrument consisting of tuned glasses rubbed with a damp finger.

harmonic analysis A procedure, developed in 1822 by Joseph *Fourier, by which complicated periodic functions, such as sound waves, can be written as the sum of a number of simple wave functions known as a Fourier series. One wave function, called the fundamental, has the same frequency as the original function. Those that have frequencies that are integral multiples of the fundamental are called harmonics.

harmonium A keyboard instrument of the reed organ family, patented in 1848 by Alexandre Debain (1809-77) in Paris. It is a free *reed instrument, the air being blown by a bellows activated by foot pedals. It may have several stops (*see* organ).

harmony In music, the combining of notes into chords, so that they are heard simultaneously. Harmony can be defined as the "vertical" aspect of music in contrast to melody, its "horizontal" aspect; it has greater importance in western music than in any other musical tradition. Before about 1650 composers made use of *polyphony, in which the combination of a number of melodic lines based on *modes was of prime importance. Between about 1650 and about 1900 (the **harmonic period**) a system of harmony evolved based on diatonic chords (*see* scale). Such chords consist of three notes sounded simultaneously; a note of the scale of the *tonality of the composition and the notes a third and a fifth above it. The constituent notes of any chord can be rearranged to provide variety. A **harmonic progression** consists of a particular sequence of chords, especially one leading (*or* modulating) into another tonality. When chords are subject to increasing *chromaticism the harmony becomes more complex and the tonality of the music becomes ambiguous. During the last half of the 19th century the music of Wagner, Liszt, and Richard Strauss became increasingly chromatic. In the early years of the 20th century Schoenberg first adopted *atonality and later invented *serialism as a substitute for traditional harmony. Debussy developed novel harmonic practices, such as harmonizing melodies with chords from unrelated tonalities and chords derived from whole-tone and pentatonic scales. Composers of the 20th century have made use of a wide range of harmonic styles, some following Schoenberg, some deliberately cultivating dissonance, and others modifying traditional harmonic practice in various ways.

Harmsworth, Alfred. *See* Northcliffe, Alfred Harmsworth, 1st Viscount.

Harmsworth, Harold. *See* Rothermere, Harold Harmsworth, 1st Viscount.

Harnack, Adolf von (1851-1930) German Protestant theologian. A professor at the Universities of Leipzig, Marburg, and Berlin, Harnack was considered the greatest scholar of his day on the early Church Fathers. His influential *History of Dogma* (1886-90), which traced the history of Christian doctrine down to the Reformation, was strongly criticized by conservative theologians.

harness racing A form of horse racing in which each horse pulls a light two-wheeled *sulky with a single driver. The races are of two sorts, according to the pace that the horses are trained to use: trotting (a two-beat gait with legs moving in diagonal pairs) or pacing (a two-beat gait with legs moving in lateral pairs). Races are usually run over 1.6 km (1 mi) on oval dirt tracks. The sport is particularly popular in the USA and Australia.

Harold I Harefoot (d. 1040) Danish King of England (1037-40). The illegitimate son of Canute, he became king while Hardecanute, Canute's legitimate son, was preoccupied in Denmark. Before Hardecanute could oust him, Harold died.

Harold II (c. 1022-66) The last Anglo-Saxon King of England (1066), reputedly designated heir by the dying Edward the Confessor. He was the son of Earl *Godwin. After becoming king, he crushed the forces of his brother *Tostig and *Harold III Hardraade of Norway, who claimed the throne, at Stamford Bridge (1066). Harold was killed in the battle of *Hastings by the army of another, successful, claimant to the throne, *William the Conqueror.

Harold III Hardraade (1015-66) King of Norway (1047-66). His nickname means Hard Ruler. Until 1045 he served in the Byzantine army, his exploits in which became the subject of Norse sagas. After his return to Norway he briefly shared the throne with Magnus I (d. 1047); when he became sole ruler, he tried unsuccessfully to conquer Denmark. In 1066 he invaded England in support of *Tostig against Harold II and died at Stamford Bridge.

harp A plucked stringed instrument of ancient origin, consisting of an open frame with strings of varying length and tension. The modern orchestral harp is triangular in shape with about 45 strings stretched between the long soundbox, which rests against the player's body, and the curved neck, which takes the tuning pegs. The pillar, which completes the triangle, contains a mechanism invented in 1810 by Sébastien Érard (1752-1831). This enables the player to raise each string by one or two semitones by means of pedals at the base. It gives the harp a full chromatic range of six and a half octaves from the B below the bass stave. ⌐musical instruments.

Harpers Ferry Raid (1859) The capture of the Federal arsenal at Harpers Ferry, West Viriginia, by John *Brown. An abolitionist (*see* Abolition Movement), Brown seized the arsenal as a base for a slave insurrection. Robert E. *Lee assaulted and captured Brown's position. Brown was hanged, a martyr to the abolitionist cause.

Harpies In Greek mythology, malicious spirits, originally conceived as winds, who carried off their victims to their deaths. They were later portrayed as rapacious birds with ugly women's faces.

harpsichord A keyboard instrument with strings plucked by quills, rather than hit by hammers (*see* spinet; virginals; *compare* clavichord; piano). In the 16th, 17th, and 18th centuries it was an instrument of great importance and it has been successfully revived in the 20th century. It lacks the sustaining power and dynamic variation of the piano; the tone can be changed by the addition of stops, which sound strings an octave below or above the note depressed. A muted effect can be obtained by use of the lute stop.

harpy eagle A tropical South American *eagle, *Harpia harpyja*, that lives in rain forests. It is the largest of the eagles, 100 cm long, and has a huge hooked bill and extremely powerful feet for gripping prey, which includes monkeys, sloths, opossums, and parrots. Mottled grey with a dark-banded tail, it has a large erectile crest.

harquebus

harquebus (*or* arquebus). *See* musket.

harrier (bird) A slender long-legged *hawk belonging to a widely distributed genus (*Circus*). Harriers are about 50 cm long and are usually brown (in some species the males are grey), with a small bill and a long tail. They fly low over fields and marshes, searching for frogs, mice, snakes, and insects. *See also* marsh harrier.

harrier (dog) A breed of hound used for hunting hares. It is similar to the *foxhound but smaller. The short smooth coat is usually black, tan, and white but may be mottled blue-grey. Height: 46–56 cm.

Harriman, W(illiam) Averell (1891–1986) US diplomat; ambassador to the Soviet Union (1943–46) and to the UK (1946). He was governor of New York (1955–58) and then helped to negotiate the *Nuclear Test-Ban Treaty (1963). He was ambassador to the Paris peace talks on Vietnam (1968–69).

Harrington, James (1611–77) English republican, an admirer of *Hobbes and *Machiavelli. He believed a nation's distribution of land was the factor determining the form of its government, but ignored mercantile and financial influences. His ideal form of government was a "commonwealth," for which he worked out a scheme in his *Oceana* (1656).

Harris. *See* Lewis with Harris.

Harris, Joel Chandler (1848–1908) US novelist and short-story writer. His Uncle Remus stories, drawing on his knowledge of Negro folklore gained from his work as a journalist and on plantations, were published in several volumes, beginning with *Uncle Remus, His Songs and His Sayings* (1880).

Harris, Roy (1898–1979) US composer. He studied with Nadia Boulanger in Paris and held various university teaching posts. His compositions, which include 11 symphonies, concertos, chamber music, and choral music, show the influence of Gregorian chant and folk music.

Harrisburg 40 17N 76 54W A city in the USA, the capital of Pennsylvania on the Susquehanna River. An important rail centre, its manufactures include bricks, steel, and clothing. In March, 1979, a failure in the cooling system at the nuclear power plant at nearby Three Mile Island caused widespread concern. Population (1980): 53 264.

Harrison, George (1943–) British rock musician, formerly a member of the *Beatles. When the group disbanded, Harrison embarked on a solo career and made four albums influenced by his interest in eastern mysticism, notably *All Things Must Pass* (1970) and *Extra Texture* (1975).

Harrison, William Henry (1773–1841) US soldier and statesman; president for one month in 1841. As governor of the Indiana Territory (1800–11) he secured it for White settlement by defeating an Indian uprising led by *Tecumseh (1811). He served in the *War of 1812 with Britain and died a month after a demagogic campaign had made him a "frontiersman president." His grandson **Benjamin Harrison** (1833–1901) was Republican president (1889–93). His administration secured passage of the Sherman Anti-Trust Act (1890).

Harrogate 54 00N 1 33W A residential town and spa in N England, in North Yorkshire. It is a holiday resort, noted for its parks and open spaces. Harrogate has also become an important centre for conferences and trade fairs. Population (1981): 66 475.

Harrow A residential borough of NW Greater London, created in 1965 from the former municipal borough. It is the site of one of England's oldest public schools, founded by John Lyon in 1571. Population (1983 est): 199 400.

Harsa (*or* Harsha; c. 590–c. 647 AD) King of N India (c. 606–47). He ruled an extensive empire from his capital of Kanauj. In later life he became a devout Buddhist and combined his successful rule with the pursuit of poetry and

the arts. His life and reign were well documented by the author *Bana.

Hart, Moss (1904–61) US dramatist. He collaborated with George S. *Kaufman on a great number of successful Broadway comedies, including *You Can't Take It with You* (1936) and *The Man Who Came to Dinner* (1939). He also wrote librettos for musicals by Irving *Berlin and Kurt *Weill, notably *Lady in the Dark* (1941).

Harte, (Francis) Bret(t) (1836–1902) US short-story writer. He gained international fame with stories about the miners, gamblers, and prostitutes of California, collected in *The Luck of the Roaring Camp* (1870). He collaborated with Mark Twain on the play *Ah Sin* (1877).

hartebeest A long-faced antelope, *Alcephalus busephalus*, of African plains. About 120 cm high at the shoulder, hartebeests are slender fast-running animals. There are several races, ranging in colour from dark chestnut to fawn; their horns are united at the base and are generally lyre-shaped. Hartebeests live in small herds, grazing by day.

Hartford 41 45N 72 42W A city in the USA, the capital of Connecticut. Founded in 1633, it has many notable buildings. Trinity College (1823) and the law and insurance schools of the University of Connecticut are situated here. A commercial, industrial, and financial centre, Hartford is one of the leading insurance centres in the world. Population (1980): 136 392.

Hartington, Lord. *See* Devonshire, Spencer Compton Cavendish, 8th Duke of.

Hartlepool 54 41N 1 13W A port in NE England, in Cleveland, including West Hartlepool and the resort of Seaton Carew since 1967. Originally an old fishing port and medieval walled town, Hartlepool's main industries are engineering, clothing manufacture, and timber working. Population (1983 est): 93 400.

Hartley, L(esley) P(oles) (1895–1972) British novelist. His most ambitious achievement is a trilogy of novels (*The Shrimp and the Anemone*, 1944; *The Sixth Heaven*, 1946; *Eustace and Hilda*, 1947) concerning the growth to adulthood of a brother and sister. His other novels include *The Boat* (1949) and *The Go-Between* (1953).

Hartmann, (Karl Robert) Eduard von (1842–1906) German philosopher. He wrote a massive and eclectic work, *Philosophy of the Unconscious* (1869), which sought to reconcile all previous systems and all sciences by means of the hypothesis of the unconscious mind.

Hartmann, Nicolai (1882–1950) Russian-born German philosopher. He was troubled by the problem of cultural relativism pervading all branches of philosophy. Ideas, and even the concepts of logic, were historically conditioned, so that no thinker could begin without preconceptions. Systematic metaphysics, as presented by 19th-century idealists, was impossible, and the task of the philosopher was to draw the boundary between the rational and the irrational.

Hartnell, Sir Norman (1901–79) British fashion designer. He designed new uniforms for the WRAC and for Red Cross nurses and was appointed official dressmaker to Queen Elizabeth II and Elizabeth the Queen Mother. He was knighted in 1977.

Harun ar-Rashid (?766–809 AD) The fifth caliph (786–809) of the 'Abbasid dynasty of Islam. He relied greatly on the support of the powerful Barmecide family until it fell from power in 803. His reign was troubled by revolts in subject territories and saw the beginning of Tunisian independence. Harun sent expeditions against the Byzantines and forced them to accept a humiliating treaty in 806. He has become an almost legendary figure because of the references to him in *The Arabian Nights*. Muslim sources, however, say nothing of his alleged close relations with Charlemagne.

Harvard classification system A system, introduced in the 1890s by astronomers at the Harvard College Observatory (USA), by which stars are classified according to features in their spectra. Stellar spectral differences arise mainly from differing surface and atmospheric temperatures, and the stars are grouped accordingly into seven major spectral types: O, B, A, F, G, K, and M, in order of decreasing temperature. These types range in colour from blue (O and B) through white, yellow, and orange, to red (M). There are 10 subdivisions for each spectral type, indicated by a digit (0–9) placed after the letter. Stars of one spectral type can be further classified into supergiants, giants, etc., according to their *luminosity. *See also* Hertzsprung-Russell diagram.

Harvard University The oldest university in the USA (founded 1636), located at Cambridge, Massachusetts. It is named after a clergyman, John Harvard (1607–38), who bequeathed his books to the college. The associated women's college, Radcliffe College, dates from 1879.

harvestman An *arachnid, also called harvest spider, belonging to the order *Opiliones* (or *Phalangida*; 2200 species), found in tropical and temperate regions. It has an undivided body, 1–22 mm long, and very long delicate legs. It is found in fields, woods, and buildings, feeding on insects and plant materials, and is particularly common in late summer in temperate regions.

harvest mite A *mite, also called chigger and scrub mite, belonging to the genus *Trombicula*. Its larvae are parasitic on vertebrates, including man, feeding on skin to cause intense itching and inflammation. Certain species transmit diseases, including scrub typhus.

HARVEST MOUSE   *These rodents are small enough to be able to climb cornstalks, with the aid of their prehensile tails, and feed on the grain.*

harvest mouse A tiny *mouse, *Micromys minutus*, of Europe and Asia. Light red-brown with white underparts, harvest mice are about 4 cm long with a prehensile tail of the same length. They weave a nest of grass among the stems of plants in cornfields and reedbeds, but are becoming rarer as a result of mechanical farming methods.

Harvey, William (1578–1657) English physician and anatomist, who discovered the circulation of the blood. Harvey studied under the great anatomist *Fabricius ab Aquapendente and later became physician to James I and Charles I. From his numerous dissections and experiments on animals, Harvey concluded that blood flowed from the heart to the lungs, returned to the heart, and was pumped out via the arteries to the limbs and viscera, returning to the heart through the veins. His findings, published in *On the Motion of the Heart and Blood in Animals* (1628), aroused controversy, but by his death the circulation of blood was generally accepted. Harvey also made valuable studies of the development of chick embryos.

Harwell 51 37N 1 18W A village in S central England, in Oxfordshire, site of an atomic research station built in 1947.

Harwich 51 57N 1 17E A seaport in E England, in Essex on the estuary of the Rivers Stour and Orwell. It has passenger services to Scandinavia and the Continent. Population (1981): 15 076.

Haryana A state in N India, mostly in the fertile Upper Ganges plain. Predominantly rural, it produces wheat, other grains, cotton, sugar cane, and oilseeds. There is some light industry, including textiles, agricultural implements, and sugar refining. *History*: an important centre of Hinduism, Haryana lies on the migration route into India. Britain merged it with the Punjab, but it was separated in 1966. Area: 44 222 sq km (17 070 sq mi). Population (1981): 12 850 902. Capital: Chandigarh.

Harz Mountains A mountain range extending about 90 km (56 mi) across the East German-West German border W of Halle. They are the northernmost range of the European mountain system. The highest peak is the *Brocken.

Hasan al-Basri, al- (d. 728) Muslim ascetic and religious thinker. He was active in Basra in Iraq and is important in the development of Muslim theology, although little is known about him. He is said to have supported the idea of human free will against that of divine predetermination.

Hasdrubal (Barca) (d. 207 BC) Carthaginian general; the son of *Hamilcar Barca and the brother of *Hannibal. Hasdrubal commanded the Carthaginian army in Spain following Hannibal's departure to campaign in Italy but was recalled to Africa after being defeated by the Romans in 217. He returned to Spain in 212, campaigning successfully before following Hannibal across the Alps in 207. He was defeated at Metaurus and died in battle.

Hašek, Jaroslav (1883–1923) Czech novelist, who established an early reputation as a satirist and anarchist. During World War I he was captured by the Russians, joined the Czech liberation army, and became a communist. His unfinished novel sequence *The Good Soldier Schweik* (1920–23) is a bawdy and irreverent satire upon bureaucracy and bourgeois values.

Haselrig, Sir Arthur. *See* Hesilrige, Sir Arthur.

Hashemites The Arab descendants of the prophet Mohammed, including the fourth caliph *Ali and the line of hereditary emirs of Mecca. King Hussein of Jordan is a modern representative of the line.

hashish. *See* cannabis.

Hasidism A Jewish religious movement, founded by the *Ba'al Shem Tov. Essentially a blend of *kabbalah and popular pietism, Hasidism spread, against strong opposition, throughout the Jewish communities of E Europe in the 18th and 19th centuries. Led by charismatic teachers (*zaddikim*), the Hasidim stressed simple piety and ecstatic prayer and denounced what they saw as the arid scholasticism of the talmudic academies. A more intellectual approach was adopted by the Habad Hasidim, whose leader is the Lubavitch Rabbi, now based in New York. Most of the Hasidic communities in Europe were wiped out during the *holocaust, but Hasidism still thrives in North America and Israel.

Haskalah (Hebrew: enlightenment) The intellectual

movement for spreading modern European culture among the Jews. It began in Germany in the 18th century, largely under the influence of Moses *Mendelssohn, and spread to Russia in the 19th century. Linked to the movement for the political emancipation of the Jews, it attempted to provide them with a modern Hebrew culture of their own and rejected the previous alternatives of the medieval ghetto culture or total assimilation. In its day it exercised an enormous influence, giving birth to modern *Judaism, *Zionism, and the modern Hebrew language and literature. In the West it succumbed to linguistic and cultural assimilation; in Russia, after enjoying a period of government support, it yielded, in the face of the growing *antisemitism of the 1880s, to attempts to find a political solution to the Jewish problem.

Hassall, John (1868-1948) British artist. After studying in Antwerp and Paris, he exhibited paintings at the Royal Academy and worked as a newspaper cartoonist. He is best known for his humorous theatre and trade posters, of which the most famous is *Skegness Is So Bracing.*

Hassan II (1929-) King of Morocco (1961-). Educated in France, Hassan maintains autocratic rule in Morocco. He introduced some reforms in 1971 following an attempted coup.

Hasselt 50 56N 5 20E A town in NE Belgium. It was the site of a Dutch victory over the Belgians in 1831. Industries include brewing and distilling. Population (1981 est): 64 818.

Hassi Messaoud 32 10N 6 10E A town in E Algeria. It is an oil-producing centre; its oilfield was opened in 1957.

Hastings 39 39S 176 42E A city in New Zealand, in E North Island. Rebuilt after an earthquake (1931), it is the centre of a fruit-growing district and is known as "The Fruit Bowl of New Zealand." Population (1984 est): 37 800.

Hastings 50 51N 0 36E A town on the S coast of England, in East Sussex, including the resort of St Leonards. Formerly a port (chief of the Cinque Ports), it is now a resort and residential town with a ruined castle built by William the Conqueror, who landed at nearby Pevensey in 1066 (*see* Hastings, Battle of). Population (1981): 74 803.

BATTLE OF HASTINGS *The three lines of Norman troops were led by archers, including crossbowmen (making their first recorded appearance in battle), who were able to undermine the advantage of the English position on a ridge above.*

Hastings, Battle of (14 October, 1066) The battle between the Normans and the English at Senlac Hill (*see* Battle), near Hastings, in which William, Duke of Normandy, claiming the English throne, defeated Harold II of England. The battle was dominated by the Norman use of archery supported by cavalry to break through the defensive ranks of infantry, which alone made up the English army. Both sides suffered heavy losses but the death of Harold allowed William to conquer England (*see* Norman conquest) and become its king.

Hastings, Francis Rawdon-Hastings, 1st Marquess of (1754-1826) British soldier and colonial administrator; governor general of Bengal (1813-23). He joined the army in 1771 and fought (1775-82) in the American Revolution. In India he asserted British control over the Maratha states of W and central India and in 1819 negotiated the purchase of Singapore. He was subsequently governor of Malta (1824-26).

Hastings, Warren (1732-1818) British colonial administrator; the first governor general of India (1774-85). He first went to India in 1750 in the employ of the East India Company and by 1761 had become a member of its Calcutta council. In 1769 he became second in council in Madras, in 1771, governor of Bengal, and then governor general of India. His outstanding administration consolidated British control of India and introduced administrative, legal, and financial reforms that provided the basis of subsequent British government there. In 1782 he negotiated peace with the Maratha states and in 1784 with Mysore. Hastings failed, however, to maintain good relations with his colleagues, especially Sir Philip *Francis, with whom he fought a duel in 1779. He was also criticized for the hanging for forgery of one Maharaja Nandakumar and on his return to England was impeached for corruption. The trial before the House of Lords, which lasted until 1795, cost Hastings £70,000 but ended in his acquittal.

hatchetfish A carnivorous hatchet-shaped fish, up to 10 cm long, belonging to one of two unrelated groups. Deepsea hatchetfish (family *Sternoptychidae*; 15 species) are related to *salmon and occur in warm and temperate waters down to about 1000 m. The freshwater or flying hatchetfish (family *Gasteropelecidae*; about 9 species) of South America are related to *carp. They swim near the surface and are able to leap out of the water and "fly" short distances by flapping their large pectoral fins. □oceans.

Hatfield 51 46N 0 13W A market town in SE England, in Hertfordshire, extended as a new town since 1948. The old town contains the 17th-century Hatfield House and remains of the 15th-century Hatfield Palace used by Elizabeth I, where she received the news of her accession to the throne. Industries include aircraft manufacture and light engineering. Population (1981): 25 160.

Hathaway, Anne (c. 1556-1623) The wife of William *Shakespeare. She was born at Shottery, near Stratford. She married Shakespeare in 1582 and bore him three children. Her cottage may still be seen in Stratford.

Hathor An Egyptian sky goddess, worshipped as goddess of fertility and of love, happiness, and beauty. She was usually portrayed as a cow or with a cow's horns and is sometimes identified with *Isis.

Hatshepsut Queen of Egypt (c. 1490-1468 BC) of the 18th dynasty. The half-sister and widow of *Thutmose II, she overshadowed the young *Thutmose III, and assumed the status of pharaoh. During her reign direct communications with Punt (now S Eritrea) were reopened. Illustrated accounts of her expedition there and of the transport of her obelisks from Aswan are carved on her funerary temple at Dayr al-Bahri. After her death Thutmose III attempted to obliterate her memory by defacing her monuments.

Hatteras, Cape 35 14N 75 31W A low sandy promontory in the USA, in North Carolina on Hatteras Island. Its shallows are a danger to navigation.

Hattusas The ancient capital of the *Hittite empire (c. 1700-1230 BC) situated at Boğazköy (*or* Boğazkale) in central Turkey. The massive fortifications still visible date from the reign of *Suppiluliumas (c. 1375-c. 1335 BC). Thousands of tablets, forming part of the royal archives, have been found here and provide invaluable evidence for diplomatic and commercial activity in the period.

Haughey, Charles (1925–) Irish statesman; prime minister of Ireland (1979–81, 1982, and 1987–). He has been president of the Fianna Fáil party since 1979 and has served in several ministerial posts.

Hauptmann, Gerhart (1862–1946) German dramatist. After studying sculpture he turned to writing plays, establishing his reputation with *Before Dawn* (1889). His early work was influenced by *naturalism, as in *The Weavers* (1892). This element later alternated with a mystical and *Symbolist strain, as in *The Assumption of Hannele* (1893). He also wrote novels (*The Fool in Christ*, 1910), novellas (*Flagman Thiel*, 1888), and poetry (*Der grosse Traum*, 1942). He was awarded a Nobel Prize in 1912.

Hauraki Gulf A large inlet of the South Pacific Ocean, in New Zealand on the E coast of North Island. Waitemata Harbour, on which stands Auckland, is situated in the SW. Area: about 2290 sq km (884 sq mi).

Hausa A people of NW Nigeria and S Niger, numbering about nine million. Their language belongs to the Chadic subgroup of the *Hamito-Semitic family, but has absorbed many Arabic words and influences. It is an official language of Nigeria and a second language in much of West Africa. The Hausa are mainly Muslim. There were once several Hausa states ruled on feudal lines by emirs and titled office holders who held villages as fiefs. Slavery was practised but slaves could attain high office. The economy is based on the cultivation of maize, millet, sorghum, and other crops. Crafts are highly developed and trade is extensive. Cities, such as *Kano, date from precolonial times but most Hausa live in small rural settlements.

Haussmann, Georges-Eugène, Baron (1809–91) French town planner, responsible for extensive rebuilding in Paris under *Napoleon III. Haussmann's long avenues and dramatic vistas, for example the avenues radiating from the *Arc de Triomphe, form much of the city's character. His schemes, while improving sanitation and public utilities, destroyed many remnants of the medieval town.

Havana (Spanish name: La Habana) 23 00N 82 30W The capital of Cuba, a port in the NW. It exports sugar, cotton, and tobacco. The city has been considerably modernized during the Castro regime but much of the Spanish-colonial element remains, including the cathedral. The university was founded in 1728. *History*: the original settlement was on the S coast, but the inhabitants moved to the city's present site in 1519. It became the capital of Cuba in the late 16th century. Because of its excellent natural harbour, Havana has long been of strategic and commercial importance and during the early 19th century it was among the wealthiest commercial centres in the New World. Population (1981): 1 924 886.

Havana cat A breed of short-haired cat, formerly known as Chestnut Brown Foreign. The Havana has a lithe slender body with a long tail, a long head, and large ears. The coat is chestnut-brown and the eyes are green and slanting.

Havering A borough of NE Greater London, created in 1965 from the former municipal borough of Romford and the urban district of Hornchurch. Population (1981): 240 318.

Hawaii (former name: Sandwich Islands) A state in the USA, occupying a chain of over 20 volcanic islands in the central Pacific Ocean. These include the islands of Hawaii (the largest), Maui, Oahu, Kauai, and Molokai. Its population, concentrated mainly on Oahu, is more ethnically diverse than that of any other US state, the largest groups being White Americans and Japanese. Its industry relies heavily on imported raw materials; manufactures include oil and chemical products, steel, textiles, and food. Agriculture is important, the main crops being sugar and pineapples. The principal industry, however, is tourism. There is some lumbering and fishing. There are many US military bases. Hawaii's cultural and scientific institutions

reflect both Western and Pacific cultures. *History*: first discovered by Capt Cook in 1778, Hawaii remained a kingdom until becoming a republic in 1893. It was annexed by the USA in 1894 and became a territory in 1900. The Japanese attack on Pearl Harbor in 1941 precipitated the entry of the USA into World War II. Hawaii became a state in 1959. Area: 16 641 sq km (6425 sq mi). Population (1980): 965 000. Capital: Honolulu.

Hawaiian goose A rare *goose, *Branta sandvicensis*, native to Hawaii and Maui, where it is called néné. It has a grey-brown plumage barred with white and an orange neck. Its numbers are now increasing by breeding programmes.

Hawaiian guitar (or steel guitar) A type of guitar held flat on the player's lap. The strings are stopped by a sliding steel bar, which produces a characteristic glissando.

Hawarden 53 11N 3 02W A market town in NE Wales, in Clwyd. Gladstone lived at Hawarden Castle, built in 1752, and founded St Deiniol's library and hostel for theological students here in 1895. Population (1981): 44 373.

hawfinch A large *finch, *Coccothraustes cocothraustes*, of Eurasia and N Africa. 18 cm long, it has a reddish-brown plumage with paler underparts, a black bib, and black-and-white wings. Its massive bill is used to crack open the stones of cherries, sloes, and damsons to extract the seeds.

Haw-Haw, Lord. *See* Joyce, William.

Hawick 55 25N 2 47W A town in SE Scotland, in the Borders Region on the River Teviot. The site of a 12th-century castle, it produces knitwear and high-quality tweeds and is an important market town for livestock. Population (1981): 16 333.

hawk A bird of prey belonging to a widely distributed family (*Accipitridae*; 205 species) that includes buzzards, eagles, harriers, kites, and vultures. Hawks range in size from small *sparrowhawks to the *harpy eagle and have down-curved pointed bills, powerful gripping feet, and highly developed eyesight. Hawks typically fly fast in pursuit of live prey, using their strong claws for killing, and have broad rounded wings; they usually nest in trees or crags. Order: *Falconiformes. Compare* falcon. *See also* falconry.

Hawke, Edward, 1st Baron (1705–81) British admiral, who destroyed the French fleet in Quiberon Bay in 1759. He thus prevented the French invasion of England.

Hawke, Robert (James Lee) (1929–) Australian statesman; Labor prime minister (1983–). A trade unionist, he was president of the Australian Council of Trade Unions (1970–80) before becoming president (1973–78) and leader (1983–) of the Labor Party.

Hawke Bay An inlet of the SW Pacific Ocean, in New Zealand in E North Island. The surrounding land area of Hawke's Bay is important for sheep rearing. Length: 80 km (50 mi).

Hawkesbury River A river in SE Australia, rising in the Great Dividing Range in New South Wales and flowing generally NE to enter the Tasman Sea at Broken Bay. Length: 472 km (293 mi).

Hawking, Stephen William (1942–) British physicist, a leading figure in the field of general relativity and the theory of black holes. Although a victim of a progressive nervous disease since the 1960s and forced to rely upon mental calculation, he has described the particle emission of black holes (1974) and shown that general relativity supports the big-bang theory.

Hawkins, Sir John (1532–95) English navigator. In 1562 he became the first English slave trader, transporting slaves from West Africa to the Spanish West Indies. His third expedition (1567–69), in which Drake participated, met with the Spaniards on its way home and only the ships of Drake and Hawkins escaped. In 1577 he became treasurer of the navy, instituting reforms that greatly contributed to England's victory against the Spanish *Armada (1588), and died at Puerto Rico on a new expedition with Drake. His son **Sir Richard Hawkins** (c. 1562–1622) served against the Armada and in a subsequent round-the-world plundering expedition was seized by the Spanish and imprisoned (1594–1602). His *Observations in His Voyage into the South Sea* (1622) influenced Charles Kingsley's *Westward Ho!* (1855).

hawk moth A moth belonging to the widespread family *Sphingidae* (about 1000 species), also called sphinx moth or hummingbird moth. They have large bodies with relatively small wings (spanning 5–20 cm), which they beat rapidly, hovering over flowers and sipping nectar through their long proboscis. The leaf-eating larvae pupate in soil or litter.

HAWK OWL *Unlike many owls, this species is active by day. Its swooping flight and long tail resemble those of a hawk.*

hawk owl An *owl, *Surnia ulula*, that occurs in coniferous forests of Eurasia and North America. It is 40 cm long and has a long tail, a small head, and short pointed wings, which give a hawklike silhouette in flight. It hunts by day.

Hawks, Howard (1896–1977) US film director. He started as a writer but from 1938 produced and directed numerous comedies and fast-paced action dramas such as *Sergeant York* (1941) and *The Big Sleep* (1946).

hawksbill turtle A small sea turtle, *Eretmochelys imbricata*, found in warm waters worldwide. It has hooked jaws, feeds on algae, fish, and invertebrates, and is usually 40–55 cm long. The polished translucent mottled brown shell is the tortoiseshell used to make combs, etc.

Hawksmoor, Nicholas (1661–1736) English baroque architect. Hawksmoor was trained by *Wren and collaborated with *Vanbrugh at *Blenheim Palace and Castle Howard. He was easily Vanbrugh's superior in technical skill. His finest individual work was at Easton Neston (1702), All Souls', Oxford (1729), and St Anne's, Limehouse (1714).

hawkweed A perennial herb of the genus *Hieracium* (about 1000 species), of temperate regions and tropical mountains. It grows to a height of about 60 cm and usually has yellow flower heads. The name derives from the old belief that hawks ate these plants to improve their eyesight. Family: *Compositae*.

Haworth 53 50N 1 57W A village in N England, in West Yorkshire on the edge of the Pennine moorland. Haworth parsonage (now a museum) was the home of the Brontë family from 1820; Emily and Charlotte are buried in the church. Population (1981): 3271.

Haworth, Sir Walter Norman (1883–1950) British biochemist, who first synthesized artificial vitamin C (ascorbic acid), thus enabling its cheap production for medical use. He shared a Nobel Prize (1937) with the Swiss chemist Paul Karrer (1889–1971).

hawthorn A thorny shrub or tree of the N temperate genus *Crataegus* (about 200 species). Hawthorns have lobed leaves, usually about 4 cm long, white spring-blooming flowers, and yellow, black, or red fruits. The common hawthorn, or may (*C. monogyna*), is found in hedgerows and thickets in Europe and the Mediterranean. Up to 10 m high, it has red fruits (haws). Horticultural forms include double-flowered varieties. Family: *Rosaceae*.

Hawthorn, Mike (John Michael H.; 1929–58) British motor-racing driver, who had many successes in the 1950s and was world champion in 1958. He was killed in a road accident after retiring.

Hawthorne, Nathaniel (1804–64) US novelist and short-story writer. His two best-known novels, *The Scarlet Letter* (1850) and *The House of the Seven Gables* (1851), concern the psychological effects of Puritanism in New England. He was a friend of Herman *Melville, who visited him in England after his appointment as consul at Liverpool in 1853. In 1857 he travelled in Italy, the setting of *The Marble Faun* (1860).

Hay, Will (1888–1949) British comedian. After many years as a music-hall comedian he began acting in films in 1934. His films include *Oh, Mr Porter!* (1937) and *Ask a Policeman* (1939).

Haya de la Torre, Victor Raúl (1895–1979) Peruvian politician. In exile following an attempt at revolution in 1923, he founded the radical Alianza Popular Revolucionaria Americana (APRA). He ran for the presidency in 1931 and, successfully, in 1962, only to have the result cancelled by a military coup.

Haydn, Franz Joseph (1732–1809) Austrian composer, born in Rohrau. He became a cathedral chorister in Vienna at the age of eight and subsequently worked as a freelance musician and music teacher, studying the works of C. P. E. Bach. He later studied with the Italian composer Nicola Porpora (1686–1768) and in 1760 made an unfortunate marriage. In 1761 he became kapellmeister to the Esterházy family, a post he held for the rest of his life. In 1791 and 1794 he visited London and wrote his last 12 symphonies, which include the *Oxford* and *London* symphonies. Haydn's compositions include piano sonatas, piano trios, string quartets, masses, concertos, 104 symphonies, operas, and the oratorios *The Creation* (1798) and *The Seasons* (1801).

Hayek, Friedrich August von (1899–   ) British economist, born in Austria. A historian of economic doctrine, Hayek argues for the free-market economy and the reduction of trade-union and government power. His works include *The Road to Serfdom* (1944). He shared the 1974 Nobel Prize.

Hayes, Rutherford B(irchard) (1822–93) US statesman; Republican president (1877–81) who ended southern *Reconstruction after the Civil War. As governor of Ohio (1868–72, 1876–77) Hayes had pressed for social reforms and ratified the 15th Amendment protecting Black suffrage. As president he continued to support the welfare of minority groups and initiated civil-service reform.

hay fever An *allergy to pollen, which leads to sneezing, a streaming nose, and inflamed eyes. If the sufferer is allergic to only one kind of pollen it may be possible to desensitize him (*see* desensitization); otherwise treatment is with *antihistamines or, in severe cases, steroids.

hazard A dice game of great antiquity, played in Europe since the middle ages and popular among gamblers since the 17th century. William *Crockford's famous gambling club (opened 1827) was a favourite venue for the game. Two dice are used. The person throwing the dice calls a number between 5 and 9; to win he must throw either this number or a 12 if he has called 6 or 8, or an 11 if he has called 7. An ace loses him the throw, as does an 11 if he has called 5, 6, 8, or 9, or a 12 if he has called 5, 7, or 9. He continues to throw until he either wins or loses. *See also* craps.

hazel A hardy shrub or tree of the N temperate genus *Corylus* (15 species), cultivated since ancient times for its

559

heat

edible nuts, also called cob nuts. Flowers appear in early spring, before the leaves (which are rounded and toothed). The male flowers are attractive yellow catkins; each female flower, which consists only of two bright-red stigmas, develops into a nut partly enclosed in a green fringed husk. The best-known species is the European hazel (*C. avellana*), up to 12 m high. Family: *Betulaceae* (birch family) or, according to some authorities, *Corylaceae*.

Hazlitt, William (1778–1830) British critic and essayist. The son of a Unitarian minister, he studied art and philosophy before becoming a journalist on various dailies and periodicals, including the *Edinburgh Review*. A friend of Wordsworth and Coleridge, Hazlitt held independent opinions in politics and literary matters and expressed them in a style notable for its brilliant invective. He also wrote vivid sketches on diverse subjects, such as prize fighting. His best-known collections of essays and lectures are *Lectures on the English Poets* (1818) and *The Spirit of the Age* (1825).

Healey, Denis (Winston) (1917–) British Labour politician; chancellor of the exchequer (1974–79). He was secretary of the Labour Party's international department from 1945 until entering parliament in 1952 and from 1964 to 1970 was defence minister. He presented more budgets than any other chancellor in British history. He was deputy leader of the Labour Party (1981–83).

health physics The study of the problems that arise from the use of radiation of various kinds, especially those emitted by radioactive substances. Particular areas of study include *radioactive waste disposal, the maximum levels of radiation to which workers may reasonably be exposed, and the causes and effects of *radiation sickness. Health physics is a multi-disciplinary subject involving physics, medicine, mathematics, chemistry, biology, and hygiene.

Heard and MacDonald Islands A group of uninhabited subantarctic islands in the S Indian Ocean, under Australian control since 1947. Heard Island is mountainous and chiefly ice covered; its elephant seals and penguins were hunted in the 19th century. The MacDonald Islands consist of a group of rocky islets.

hearing aid A device used by the partially deaf to increase the loudness of sounds. A simple form of hearing aid is the ear trumpet, which by its conical shape increases the sound pressure at the ear. Modern hearing aids are electronic and, since the advent of microcircuitry, can be made sufficiently small to be unobtrusive. An electronic hearing aid consists of a microphone to convert the sound into electrical signals, which are passed into an amplifier. The amplified signal is then fed into an earphone to convert the signal back into a sound wave of increased intensity.

Hearst, William Randolph (1863–1951) US newspaper proprietor. Beginning with the *San Francisco Examiner*, which he took over from his father, and the New York *Morning Journal*, which he bought, he built up a vast newspaper empire whose commercial success was based on popular sensationalism. His career inspired Orson *Welles' film *Citizen Kane* (1941).

heart A four-chambered muscular organ that pumps blood around the body (*see* Plate IV). Two chambers—the left and right atria—dilate to receive oxygen-rich blood from the lungs and oxygen-depleted blood from the rest of the body, respectively (this is called diastole). Contraction of the heart (called systole) starts in the atria, forcing blood into the two ventricles. The left ventricle then contracts to force blood into a large artery—the aorta, which leads from the heart and feeds all the other arteries. The right ventricle pumps blood into the pulmonary artery and to the lungs, where it receives oxygen. Valves between the atria and ventricles and at the arterial exits of the heart prevent the backflow of blood. The rhythm of the heartbeat is maintained by the electrical activity of a group of specialized cells within the heart (*see* pacemaker). The muscle of the heart is supplied with blood

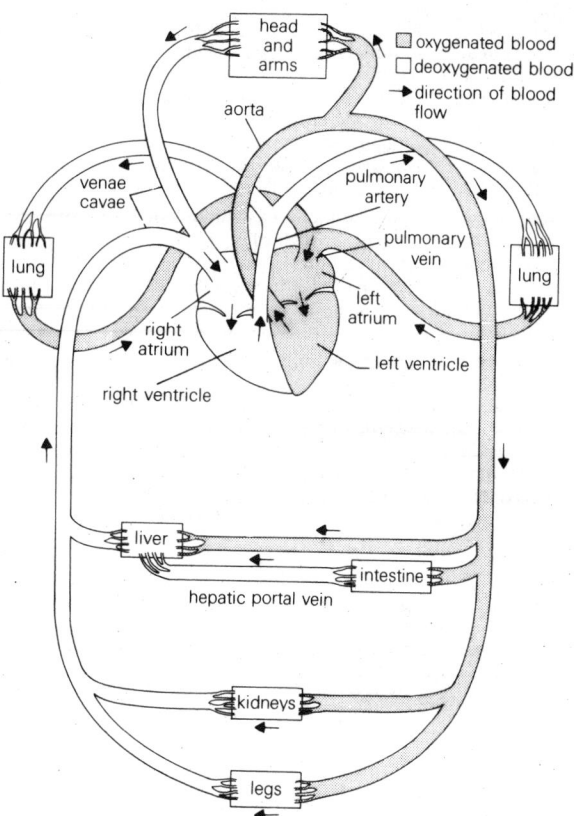

HEART *In man and other mammals the right and left chambers of the heart are completely separate from each other. This ensures that oxygenated and deoxygenated blood do not mix and enables oxygen-depleted blood to receive a fresh supply of oxygen from the lungs before circulating to the rest of the body.*

by the coronary arteries. *Atherosclerosis of these arteries is the most common form of heart disease in industrial societies: it may lead to a heart attack (*see* coronary heart disease; myocardial infarction). Other disorders affecting the heart include disease of the valves (which may result from rheumatic fever) and congenital heart disease—defects present at birth. *See also* circulation of the blood.

heartburn A burning pain felt behind the breastbone. It is usually due to regurgitation of the contents of the stomach into the gullet and may be associated with inflammation of the gullet. It is relieved by antacids (drugs that neutralize stomach acids).

heart-lung machine An apparatus that temporarily replaces the functions of the heart and the lungs during heart surgery. Blood from two main veins is drained from the body through tubes to an apparatus that bubbles oxygen through it. The oxygenated blood is then returned to a large artery in the body by a mechanical pump.

heartsease. *See* pansy.

heart urchin A marine invertebrate animal belonging to an order (*Spatangoida*) of *echinoderms. It typically has a rigid heart-shaped body, covered with short fine spines used for locomotion and defence. It lives in burrows lined with mucus and uses long tentacles (modified tube feet) to pick up particles of food from the surrounding sand. Class: *Echinoidea*.

heat The form of energy that is transferred from one body or region to another at a lower temperature. The amount of heat gained or lost by a body is equal to the product of its *heat capacity and the temperature through which it rises or falls. Heat is transferred by conduction, convection, or radiation (see heat transfer). The heat contained by a body is equal to the *total* *kinetic energy of its component atoms and molecules; its temperature is the *average* of their kinetic energies. Heat is measured in joules, but older units, such as calories and British thermal units, are still sometimes used.

heat capacity The amount of heat needed to raise the temperature of a body through one degree Celsius (symbol: C). It is measured in joules per kelvin. For a gas, the heat capacity may be measured under conditions of either constant pressure or constant volume. See also specific heat capacity.

heat death of universe A hypothetical final state of the universe in which its *entropy is at a maximum and no heat is available to do work. In any closed system the total entropy can never decrease during any process. Thus the entropy of the universe will eventually reach a maximum value and when that happens all matter will be totally disordered and at a uniform temperature. This assumes that the universe can be treated as a closed system.

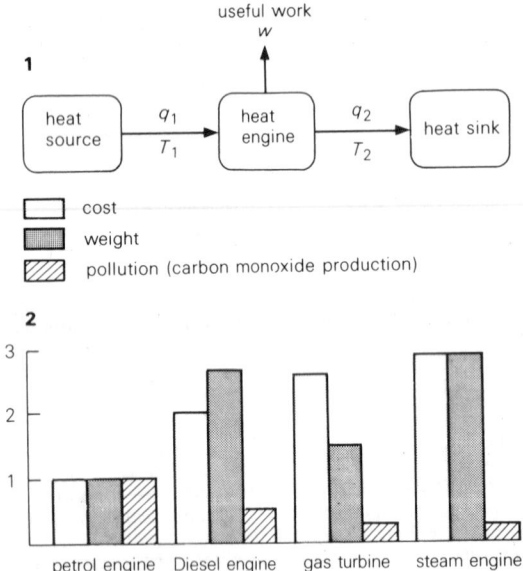

HEAT ENGINE *The efficiency of a heat engine depends on the temperature T_1 at which heat is fed to it and the temperature T_2 at which waste heat is discharged (1). A comparison of cost, weight, and pollution for various types of heat engine is shown at (2).*

heat engine A device that converts heat energy into work. Examples are petrol and Diesel engines, gas turbines, and steam engines. In terms of *thermodynamics, the heat engine converts a quantity of heat q_1 at temperature T_1 into work w; but the conversion can never be complete, some of the heat q_2 will be wasted and can be regarded as being discharged into a heat sink at a temperature T_2. The efficiency of the engine is defined as the work output divided by the heat input (w/q_1). As the work, w, is equal to q_1-q_2 (according to the first law of thermodynamics), the efficiency is $1-q_2/q_1$, or $1-T_2/T_1$. It is therefore important to make T_1 as high as possible and T_2 as low as possible. See also Carnot cycle; internal-combustion engine.

heath An evergreen shrub or tree of the genus *Erica* (about 500 species) of Europe and Africa (about 470 species are native to South Africa). Heaths have small whorled often needle-like leaves and spikes of bell-shaped or tubular flowers, white, pink, purple, or yellow in colour. Dwarf heaths, such as the European species *E. tetralix* (bog heather) and *E. cinerea* (bell heather), are abundant on acid peaty soils, such as moorlands. There are many cultivated varieties, which are popular in rock gardens. Some tree heaths grow to a height of 6 m. Family: *Ericaceae*.

Heath, Edward (Richard George) (1916-) British statesman; Conservative prime minister (1970-74), who took the UK into the EEC (1973). He entered parliament in 1950 and assumed cabinet office as minister of labour in 1959. He was Lord Privy Seal (1960-63) and secretary of state for industry (1963-64) and in 1965 succeeded Douglas-Home as leader of the Conservative Party. His Industrial Relations Act (1971) was badly received by the trade unions and his government was twice challenged by miners' strikes: in 1972 he was forced to submit to their demands but in 1974 went to the country. Defeated in both the elections of that year (February, October), in 1975 he relinquished the party leadership to Margaret Thatcher. He refused her offer of the post of ambassador to the USA following the Conservative electoral victory in 1979. He is an enthusiastic yachtsman and musician.

heather (or ling) An evergreen shrub, *Calluna vulgaris*, up to 60 cm high, with scaly leaves and clusters of pale-purple bell-shaped flowers. It grows—often with *heath—on acid soils of heaths, moors, and bogs throughout Europe and in parts of N Africa and North America (where it was probably introduced). Family: *Ericaceae*.

Heathrow (or London Airport) 51 28N 0 27W The chief air terminal for the UK, in the Greater London borough of Hounslow. Begun in 1944, it was opened to passengers in 1946. An underground railway connection covering the 24 km (15 mi) from central London was opened in 1977.

heat pump A device that extracts heat from one substance at a low temperature and supplies it to another substance at a higher temperature. Such a process would violate the second law of *thermodynamics if it occurred spontaneously; therefore the heat pump necessarily consumes energy in the process. Heat pumps are used to extract the low temperature heat from rivers that flow through towns and to convert it to a higher temperature so that use can be made of it, for example in space- and water-heating units. See also refrigeration.

heatstroke A rise in body temperature associated with *dehydration and exhaustion, caused by overexposure to high temperatures. The emergency treatment is to cool the patient down with water or fans, but medical treatment may be needed in addition.

heat transfer The transference of energy between two bodies or regions by virtue of the difference in temperatures between them. The three methods of transference are: *convection, *conduction, and *radiation. In convection the heat is transferred by a hotter region flowing into a colder region, either as a result of density differences (natural convection) or by using a fan (forced convection). In conduction, on the other hand, the heat is transferred by direct contact without any apparent relative motion. In radiation the heat is transferred by means of either *infrared radiation or *microwave radiation. Radiation is the only method of transferring heat through a vacuum. The *Dewar (Thermos) flask is designed to minimize heat transfer, whereas the heat exchanger or radiator is designed to maximize it.

heat treatment The process of heating a metal to a temperature below its melting point and then cooling it in order to change its physical properties. Metals are made up of tiny crystals (grains). Their hardness, strength, and ductility is determined by the concentration and distribution of irregularities (dislocations) in the crystal lattice. In response to stress the dislocations move and change the shape and orientation of the grains. Heating creates and redistributes dislocations, relieving any internal stresses that have built up. This makes the metal softer and more ductile; a process known as annealing. Dislocation movement is restricted by the boundaries between grains and by the presence of impurities, which "pin" the dislocations making the metal harder and less ductile. Because both the impurity distribution and the grain structure are affected by heating and the rate of cooling, so also is the metal's strength. In steel manufacture, rapid cooling (quenching) by immersion in water or oil hardens the steel, leaving it brittle. Slow cooling makes it soft and ductile. The process of heating steel to around 900°C and quenching it, followed by warming to about 300°, is known as hardening and tempering. This results in a tough springy steel. *See also* case hardening; work hardening.

heaven In Christian belief, the abode of God and the angels, in which the souls of the virtuous will be rewarded with everlasting life. The iconography of heaven is based upon the account in the Book of Revelation. The peace, light, and harmony of heaven are generally interpreted as metaphors for the bliss enjoyed by beings in the uninterrupted praise and contemplation of God (*compare* hell). Analogous concepts exist in other major religions.

Heaviside, Oliver (1850-1925) British physicist, who pioneered the mathematical study of electric circuits and helped to develop vector analysis. Independently of *Kennelly, he predicted and then discovered a charged layer of the upper atmosphere that was capable of reflecting radio waves. This region, now known as the E-region of the *ionosphere, was formerly called the Heaviside layer or Heaviside-Kennelly layer.

heavy water Deuterium oxide (D_2O), the form of water containing the isotope of hydrogen with mass number 2. It is chemically less reactive than normal water and has a relative density of 1.1; its boiling point is 101.42°C. It is present to an extent of 1 part in 5000 in natural water and it is used as a moderator and coolant in some nuclear reactors.

Hebbel, (Christian) Friedrich (1813-63) German dramatist. Coming from a poor family in Holstein, he was largely self-taught. His pessimistic plays, all tragedies, often have historical or legendary settings, *Maria Magdalena* (1844) being the only exception. Among his other plays are *Herodes und Marianne* (1850), *Gyges und sein Ring* (1856), and *Die Nibelungen* (1862).

Hebe In Greek mythology, the personification of youth. She was the daughter of Zeus and Hera and is described by Homer as cupbearer to the gods and the wife of Heracles.

Hebei (Ho-pei *or* Hopeh) A province in NE China, on the Yellow Sea. Its fertile S plain is one of the earliest areas of civilization. Chief products are cereals, cotton, coal, and iron. Area: 202 700 sq km (79 053 sq mi). Population (1980 est): 51 040 000. Capital: Shijiazhuang.

Hébert, Jacques-René (1757-94) French journalist and revolutionary. With his newspaper *Le Père Duchesne* he attained a wide following among the Parisian working class (*see* sans-culottes), becoming their leading demagogue. In 1792 he helped engineer the overthrow of the monarchy and became the procurator general of the Paris Commune. His unsuccessful attempt to incite a popular uprising against the Committee of *Public Safety resulted in his execution.

Hebrew A Semitic language. It is written from right to left in an alphabet of 22 letters, all consonants, with vowels indicated by subscript and superscript diacritical marks. The oldest and best-known works of Hebrew literature are those preserved in the *Bible (Old Testament). Mishnaic Hebrew is a somewhat different language, spoken in Palestine until the 2nd century AD. It is the language of the *Mishna and the oldest extant Jewish prayers. Hebrew continued to be a literary language throughout the middle ages, with a particularly rich poetic tradition, besides prose writing. The

study of Hebrew grammar was developed by the *Masoretes, and by the *gaon Saadya and later grammarians. In more modern times the *Haskala movement led to a renaissance in Hebrew writing, and from the late 19th century Hebrew was revived as a spoken language, particularly in Russia and Palestine. The *Ashkenazim and *Sephardim differ in their pronunciation of Hebrew. In 1948 it became an official language of Israel.

Hebrew literature A body of literature originating as early as 1200 BC in Old Testament writings and still flourishing in the modern secular idiom of Israel. Not synonymous with Jewish literature (which was frequently composed in other languages, e.g. Arabic or Yiddish), Hebrew literature reflects the vicissitudes of the Hebrew language, being confined after about 200 AD to religious and legal texts and commentaries (*see* Mishna; Talmud). Medieval Spain produced some original talents, including the poets *Judah ha-Levi and *Ibn Gabirol and the philosopher *Maimonides. The 18th-century Haskala (enlightenment) in E Europe initiated the renaissance of secular literature, and the rise of Zionism encouraged the novelist *Agnon and the poet *Bialik, among others, to mould Hebrew into a modern literary language.

Hebrews, Epistle to the A New Testament book by an unknown author (formerly believed to be Paul), probably written between 62 and 69 AD. The book asserts that Christ is the high priest and greater than any of the *Levites and that his work fulfils and renders obsolete the old *covenant between God and Israel. The book is obviously addressed to readers who had a thorough knowledge of Judaism and is intended to confirm such converts in their new faith.

Hebrides, the A group of about 500 islands off the W coast of Scotland. The islands are subdivided into the Inner and Outer Hebrides, separated by the Minch. The chief islands of the Outer Hebrides include Lewis with Harris and the Uists; those of the Inner Hebrides include Skye, Mull, Islay, and Jura. The Outer Hebrides now comprise an island authority (*see* Western Isles Islands Area) while the Inner Hebrides are divided between the Highland and Strathclyde Regions. The main occupations are stock rearing, fishing, and crofting (producing fodder crops, potatoes, and vegetables). Harris tweed is produced, especially in the Uists.

Hebron (Arabic name: Al Khalil) 31 32N 35 06E A town in the S of the *West Bank of the River Jordan. It is one of the oldest continuously inhabited cities in the world and is revered by both Jews and Muslims as the burial place of Abraham. Population (1984 est): 75 000.

Hecate A primitive Greek fertility goddess and a ruler of the underworld. She was associated with witchcraft and magic and was worshipped at crossroads. She witnessed the abduction of *Persephone and accompanied *Demeter in her search for her daughter.

hectare (ha) A unit of area in the *metric system equal to 100 ares or 10 000 square metres. 1 ha = 2.471 acres.

Hector In Greek legend, the eldest son of Priam, King of Troy, and the chief Trojan warrior. He was the husband of Andromache. He fought Ajax in single combat, killed *Patroclus, and was killed in revenge by *Achilles. Priam pleaded for the return of his body, which was buried with great ceremony.

Hecuba In Greek legend, the wife of Priam, King of Troy, and mother of *Hector. She was captured by the Greeks after the fall of Troy, but in revenge for the death of her son Polydorus, she blinded King Polymestor of Thrace and killed his sons.

hedgehog A nocturnal prickly-coated insectivorous mammal belonging to the subfamily *Erinaceinae* (15 species), of Africa, Europe, and Asia. The European hedgehog (*Erinaceus europaeus*) grows up to 30 cm long and has brown and cream spines and soft grey-brown underfur. It feeds on worms, beetles, slugs, and snails, hunting mainly by scent and hearing along ditches and hedgerows. Hedgehogs hibernate in colder climates. Family: *Erinaceidae.* ⌐mammal.

hedgehog cactus A cactus of the North American genus *Echinocactus* (10 species), some species of which are cultivated as pot plants. They have round or cylindrical strongly ribbed woolly stems bearing many spines and—at the top—mainly yellow flowers.

hedge sparrow. *See* dunnock.

hedging A commercial operation enabling a trader or speculator to protect himself against unpredictable changes in price. In *commodity markets, trading in futures (goods for delivery in the future) provides a hedging facility. For example, a manufacturer may wish to purchase a year's supply of a commodity for regular deliveries throughout the year but may expect the price to fall over the period. In this case he could hedge his purchase by selling short (i.e. selling without buying) on a futures market so that he could cover (buy back) the sales at a lower price if there was a fall in prices.

hedonism The ethical theory holding that pleasure is the greatest good. Varying definitions of pleasure distinguished the classical hedonistic schools but all considered individual rather than communal happiness. *Utilitarianism, the most important modern form of hedonism, uses a social criterion: "The greatest good of the greatest number." *Compare* Epicureanism.

Heenan, John Carmel, Cardinal (1905-75) British Roman Catholic prelate; Archbishop of Westminster (1963-75). Ordained in 1930, he worked as a priest in the East End of London until 1947. He was appointed Bishop of Leeds (1951-57) and Archbishop of Liverpool (1957-63) before being created cardinal in 1963. He was the author of several books, including an autobiography entitled *Not the Whole Truth* (1971).

Hefei (*or* Hofei) 31 55N 117 18E A city in E China, capital of Anhui province. The capital of a 10th-century kingdom, it is now a fast-growing industrial centre with an industrial university and a scientific university. Population (1983 est): 815 000.

Hegel, Georg Wilhelm Friedrich (1770-1831) German philosopher, one of the greatest and most influential thinkers of the 19th century. He followed *Kant, *Fichte, and *Schelling but exceeded them all in the scale and erudition of his work. He developed his ideas slowly and steadily; his first major work, *The Phenomenology of Mind*, was published in 1807, the *Encyclopedia of the Philosophical Sciences* in 1817, and *The Philosophy of Right* in 1821. Besides these major works, he left voluminous lecture notes on history, religion, and aesthetics. He became an eminent and respected figure, collecting disciples, appointments, and decorations before dying, in Berlin, of cholera. *See also* Hegelianism.

Hegelianism The idealist school of thought based on the philosophy of *Hegel. His followers built on his idea that philosophy is the highest available form of knowledge and that all other forms (scientific, religious, etc.) must be referred to it. Ambiguity in Hegel's own thought has encouraged considerable diversity in interpreters of Hegelianism. The so-called Old Hegelians thought religion could be brought into harmony with philosophy, while the Young Hegelians saw philosophy as essentially critical of religion. *Marx was influenced by the Young Hegelians, especially *Feuerbach.

Hegira (Arabic *hijrah*: migration) The usual English name for the Muslim era. Based on lunar months, it is reckoned from 622 AD (or 1 AH, from Latin *anno hegirae*), the date of Mohammed's migration from Mecca to Medina. Most Muslim countries now use both the Hegira calendar and the Christian or Common Era calendar.

Heidegger, Martin (1889-1976) German philosopher. His main philosophical work was *Sein und Zeit* (*Being and Time*;

1927). As rector of Freiburg University (1933-34) he supported Hitler and this association, together with logical flaws in his work, has damaged his reputation. Although his preoccupation with *Angst* (dread) as a fundamental part of human consciousness is typical of *existentialism, Heidegger himself denied that he was an existentialist.

Heidelberg 49 25N 08 42E A city in SW West Germany, in Baden-Württemberg on the River Neckar. A tourist centre, it has a ruined castle (mainly 16th-17th centuries) and the oldest university in Germany (1386), famed for its student prison. Its varied manufactures include printing presses, cigars, and electrical appliances. *History*: the capital of the Palatinate until 1685, it was devastated during the Thirty Years' War and later by the French. During the 19th century it was the student centre of Germany. In 1952 it became the European headquarters of the US army. Population (1980 est): 131 900.

Heifetz, Jascha (1901-87) Russian-born violinist. A child prodigy, he entered the St Petersburg conservatoire in 1910, and at the age of 12 toured Russia, Germany, and Scandinavia, the beginning of a worldwide career. He commissioned important works for the violin, including Walton's violin concerto. He became a US citizen in 1925.

Heilbronn 49 08N 9 14E A city in SW West Germany, in Baden-Württemberg on the River Neckar. Many historic buildings, including the town hall (1540), were reconstructed after World War II. It is a transshipment point and a centre for electrical engineering. Population (1980 est): 111 500.

Heilongjiang (Hei-lung-chiang *or* Heilungkiang) A province in NE China, bordering on the Soviet Union, comprising N Manchuria. The Da Hinggan Ling (mountains) provide valuable timber, while wheat is grown on the S plain. Oil, coal, and gold are produced. Area: 464 000 sq km (179 000 sq mi). Population (1982): 32 665 546. Capital: Ha-er-bin.

Heilungkiang. *See* Heilongjiang.

Heimdall The Norse god of light and dawn, who guarded the Bifrost bridge between *Asgard (the home of the gods) and *Midgard (the earth). He possessed miraculously sharp sight and hearing.

Heine, Heinrich (1797-1856) German Jewish poet and writer. Before establishing himself as a writer, he worked in banking and studied law. His early works include *Buch der Lieder* (1827), a collection of poetry, and his prose *Reisebilder* (1826-31), in which accounts of his travels are mixed with satirical comment. Sympathetic to revolutionary politics, he moved to Paris in 1831 and remained there until his death. In this period he wrote essays on French and German culture and some satirical poetry, notably *Atta Troll: Ein Sommernachtstraum* (1847).

Heisenberg, Werner Karl (1901-76) German physicist, who, with *Schrödinger, was the main architect of quantum mechanics. In 1927 Heisenberg created a mathematical system, known as matrix mechanics, to explain the structure of the hydrogen atom. *Dirac soon showed that matrix mechanics and Schrödinger's wave mechanics were equivalent. In the same year he put forward the theory known as the *Heisenberg uncertainty principle, which has had a profound effect on both physics and philosophy. For this discovery he was awarded the Nobel Prize in 1932. Heisenberg was one of the few major physicists to remain in Germany during the Nazi period; during World War II he was in charge of Germany's unsuccessful attempts to make an atom bomb at the Max Planck Institute in Berlin. After the war he became director of the Max Planck Institute for Physics in Göttingen.

Heisenberg uncertainty principle If a simultaneous measurement is made of the position and momentum of a particle then, no matter how accurate the measurements, there is always an uncertainty in the values obtained. The product of the uncertainties is of the same order as *Planck's constant. A similar uncertainty exists with the simultaneous measurement of energy and time. The uncertainty arises because the act of observing the system interferes with it in an unpredictable way. Uncertainty is only important at the atomic and subatomic levels and at this level throws the principle of causality into doubt. Named after Werner *Heisenberg.

Hejaz (*or* Western Province) A province in Saudi Arabia, bordering on the Red Sea. Hilly inland, its coastal plain supports some agriculture; significant income is also derived from light industry and from pilgrims to the holy Muslim cities of Mecca and Medina. The largest town is Jidda. Hejaz, formerly independent, joined *Najd in a dual kingdom in 1926, and both became part of Saudi Arabia in 1932. Area: about 350 000 sq km (135 107 sq mi). Population (1973 est): 2 000 000.

Hel In Norse mythology, the underworld; also called Nifleheim. It was covered with ice and guarded by the dog Garm. It is also the name of the goddess of death and ruler of the underworld, who was the daughter of the giant *Loki.

Helder, Den. *See* Den Helder.

Helen In Greek legend, the daughter of Zeus and *Leda, famed for her supreme beauty. She married Menelaus, King of Sparta, but later fled to Troy with *Paris, thus precipitating the *Trojan War. After the fall of Troy she was reunited with Menelaus.

Helena 46 35N 112 00W A city and resort in the USA, the capital of Montana. It is the commercial centre for an agricultural and mining region. Population (1980): 23 938.

Helena, St (c. 248–c. 328 AD) Roman empress, mother of Constantine the Great. A Christian from 313, she made a pilgrimage to the Holy Land (c. 326), where she founded several churches and, according to tradition, rediscovered the cross used at the crucifixion. Feast day: 18 Aug. Emblem: the cross.

Helgoland (*or* Heligoland) 54 09N 7 52E A West German island in the North Sea, in the North Frisian group. Ceded to Britain in 1814, it was transferred to Germany in exchange for Zanzibar (1890) and was a major German naval base during both World Wars. With the end of World War II its fortifications were destroyed. Area: about 150 ha (380 acres).

Heliconia A genus of perennial herbaceous plants (about 120 species), native to tropical America and cultivated for ornament in the tropics. They have stout or reedlike stems and the leaves are often coppery with an ivory and pink midrib. The small flowers are contained within brightly coloured pointed bracts: *H. psittacorum* has green-yellow black-spotted flowers and red bracts. Family: *Heliconiaceae.*

helicopter An aircraft that obtains both its lift and its thrust from aerofoils (rotors) rotating about a vertical axis (*compare* autogiro). The principle was known to Leonardo da Vinci, but the first successful helicopter was made in 1939 by Igor *Sikorsky in the USA (his 1909 model, made in Russia, failed to lift a man). A helicopter using a single rotor requires an anti-torque tail propeller and some models also use a vertical propeller for forward thrust. Helicopters can rise and drop vertically, hover, and move backwards, forwards, and sideways by control of the pitch of the rotors. First used in World War II, helicopters were widely employed for military purposes in the Korean War. They have since been developed for rescue services, police observation, and urban passenger services.

heliocentric system Any model of the solar system in which the planets move around the sun. The geocentric *Ptolemaic system was accepted for centuries until the heliocentric system of *Copernicus was published in 1543 and, after much religious and scientific controversy, shown to be true in essence (although not in detail).

Heliopolis An ancient Egyptian city near present-day Cairo dedicated to the cult of the sun god Re. *Cleopatra's Needles came from here.

Helios The Greek sun god, usually represented as a charioteer driving the sun across the sky each day. In later legends he was identified with Hyperion or Apollo. Because he was all-seeing he was called to witness oaths and promises.

heliotrope A herb or shrub of the genus *Heliotropium* (220 species), found in tropical and temperate regions and having heads of blue or white flowers. Many will withstand cold, but none will survive frost. Many horticultural varieties of the cherry-pie plant (*H. peruvianum*) and *H. corymbosa* are used as bedding plants in cooler climates. Family: *Boraginaceae.*

helium (He) The lightest noble gas, first detected in 1868 by Janssen (1838–1904) as an unexpected line in the spectrum of the sun. The term is derived from Greek *helios*, sun. Helium was discovered on earth in 1895 in the uranium mineral, clevite, as a radioactive decay product (*see* radioactivity). Because of its low density and chemical inertness, it is extensively used for filling balloons. It is also used as a gas shield in arc welding, and to replace nitrogen in the breathing mixture used by divers. Helium has the lowest melting point of any element. At no 2; at wt 4.0026; mp −272.2°C; bp −268.9°C.

helium dating A method of dating materials that utilizes the production of helium in the form of *alpha particles during the radioactive decay of uranium-235, uranium-238, or thorium-232. The amount of helium trapped in the sample may be used to measure its age, after correction to allow for diffusion. The method is used mainly for rocks, minerals, and fossils.

hell In Christian belief, the place in which the fallen *angels under *Lucifer and the souls of the wicked are imprisoned in everlasting torment. The concept of hell as a dark and fiery pit derives from the Book of Revelation and opinions have differed widely regarding its nature. Some Christians insist upon the physical reality of hellfire; others consider it a metaphor for the misery of a soul deprived forever of the vision of God (*compare* heaven). According to the doctrine often condemned as a heresy and known as apocatastasis, hell is not everlasting but will eventually be destroyed and all creatures, even the fallen angels, will be restored to God's grace. *Compare* purgatory.

hellbender The largest North American *salamander, *Cryptobranchus alleganiensis.* Growing to over 60 cm, it is dark olive-green with a wrinkled shiny skin. Hellbenders inhabit fast-moving oxygen-rich water, emerging from under rocks to feed at night on small animals and carrion. Family: *Cryptobranchidae.*

hellebore A poisonous perennial herb of the genus *Helleborus* (20 species), of Europe and W Asia. The stinking hellebore (*H. foetidus*) grows to a height of 30–50 cm and bears clusters of cup-shaped purple-edged green flowers. Family: *Ranunculaceae. See also* Christmas rose.

helleborine A terrestrial *orchid of either of the genera *Cephalanthera* (about 14 species) or *Epipactis* (about 24 species), native to N temperate regions. They have tall thin stems, crinkled leaves, and clusters of flowers, which are either small, stalked, and drooping (*Epipactis*) or larger, stalkless, and held erect (*Cephalanthera*). The white helleborine (*C. damasonium*) and the marsh helleborine (*E. palustris*) are two Eurasian species.

Hellen In Greek mythology, the grandson of Prometheus and eponymous ancestor of the Greeks, who called themselves the Hellenes and their country Hellas. The four subgroups of the Hellenes, the Aeolians, Dorians, Ionians, and Achaeans, were named after his sons and grandsons.

Hellenistic age The period, between the death of Alexander the Great of Macedon (323 BC) and the accession of the Roman emperor Augustus (27 BC), when Greek culture spread throughout the Mediterranean. Alexander's conquests took Greek ideas to the East and in the political confusion that followed his death city states became cosmopolitan and Greek colonists, following in Alexander's footsteps, implanted Greek ideas in their new environments. In the Hellenistic period Alexandria in Egypt was the major commercial city and centre of intellectual life, including scholarly literature and grandiose art, *Epicureanism, *Neoplatonism, Stoic philosophy, *gnosticism, and Christianity. The Koine, common Greek, was the universal language.

Heller, Joseph (1923–) US novelist. He served in the Air Force during World War II and subsequently worked in advertising. His best-known novel, *Catch-22* (1961), is a satirical portrayal of modern warfare and bureaucracy. He has also written three other novels, *Something Happened* (1974), *Good as Gold* (1979), *God Knows* (1984), and a play, *We Bombed in New Haven* (1968).

Hellespont. *See* Dardanelles.

Hellman, Lillian (1905–84) US dramatist. Her plays, often concerning political themes, include *The Little Foxes* (1939) and *The Searching Wind* (1944). She was a close friend of Dashiell *Hammett and published volumes of memoirs, including *An Unfinished Woman* (1969), *Pentimento* (1973), and *Scoundrel Time* (1976).

Helmand, River (R. Helmund *or* R. Hilmand) The longest river in Afghanistan. Rising in the E of the country, it flows generally SW then N to enter the marshy lake of Halmun Helmand on the Afghan-Iranian border. Length: 1400 km (870 mi).

helmet shell A *gastropod mollusc belonging to the family *Cassidae* (about 60 species), also called bonnet shell. Found in shallow tropical seas and measuring 2–25 cm long, they feed mainly on sea urchins. □shells.

Helmholtz, Hermann Ludwig Ferdinand von (1821–94) German physicist and physiologist, who made contributions to many fields of science. In physiology his main interest was the sense organs, discovering the function of the cochlea in the inner ear and developing T. *Young's theory of colour vision (now known as the Young-Helmholtz theory). This work was published in his *Physiological Optics* (1856). His study of muscle action led him to formulate a much more accurate theory concerning the conservation of energy than that earlier proposed by Julius *Mayer and James *Joule. He played a considerable part in the development of thermodynamics, especially in formulating the concept of free energy.

Helmont, Jan Baptist van (1580–1644) Belgian alchemist and physician, who discovered the gas now called *carbon dioxide. Although Helmont was an alchemist he was a skilled and careful experimenter and helped to transform alchemy into chemistry.

Heloise. *See* Abelard, Peter.

helots Indigenous Peloponnesian Greeks who lost their lands and freedom under the repressive state control of Sparta. They formed the farming communities of Messenia and Laconia.

Helpmann, Sir Robert (1909–86) Australian ballet dancer, choreographer, and actor. He went to England in 1933 and worked mainly with Sadler's Wells Ballet until 1950. He became artistic director of the Australian Ballet in 1955. His ballets include *Comus* (1942) and *Hamlet* (1942), and he also acted in films and plays, including several productions of Shakespeare.

Helsingborg. *See* Hälsingborg.

Helsingfors. *See* Helsinki.

Helsingør (*or* Elsinore) 56 03N 12 38E A seaport in Denmark, in NE Sjælland situated on the *Sound opposite Hälsingborg in Sweden. It contains the fortress of Kronborg (1580), famous as the scene of Shakespeare's play *Hamlet*. Its industries include shipbuilding, brewing, and food processing. Population (1981 est): 56 280.

Helsinki (Swedish name: Helsingfors) 60 13N 24 55E The capital of Finland, a port in the S on the Gulf of Finland. It is the country's commercial and administrative centre; industries include metals, textiles, food processing, and paper. Among its fine pale granite buildings are the 18th-century cathedral and the old senate house. The city is well laid out and spacious in appearance and is renowned for its 20th-century architecture. The university was moved here from Turku in 1828. *History*: founded by Gustavus I Vasa of Sweden in 1550 it was largely rebuilt following a fire in 1808. It replaced Turku as capital of Finland (then under Russian rule) in 1812. It was badly bombed in World War II. Population (1980): 483 036.

Helvellyn 54 32N 3 02W A mountain in NW England, in Cumbria, in the Lake District. It lies between the lakes of Thirlmere and Ullswater; a sharp ridge, Striding Edge, descends E of the summit. Height: 950 m (3118 ft).

Helvetia. *See* Switzerland, Confederation of.

Helvetii A Celtic tribe that settled about 200 BC in what is now Switzerland. Defeated by Caesar as they migrated southwards, they nevertheless retained their former territory, which was a buffer state between Rome and the Germans for over 400 years.

Helvétius, Claude Adrien (1715–71) French philosopher. He followed Hume in holding that self-interest was the only motive of human action. His principle of the artificial identity of interests (i.e. interests manipulated by government) influenced *Bentham. *De l'esprit* (1758), expounding these views, was furiously denounced and burned by the public hangman.

Hemel Hempstead 51 46N 0 28W A market town in SE England, in Hertfordshire. Designated a new town in 1946, the principal industries include light engineering (aircraft components, scientific, electronic, and photographic equipment), paper, and pyrotechnics. Population (1981): 76 776.

HENBURY CRATERS

Hemichordata A phylum of marine invertebrate animals (about 100 species), found in coastal sand or mud and on the sea bed. The gill slits and nervous system show similarities with those of chordates—hence their name. The group comprises the *acornworms and the pterobranchs (class *Pterobranchia*). These are up to 7 mm long and have tentacle-bearing arms. They often form colonies and reproduce both sexually and by budding.

Hemingway, Ernest (1899–1961) US novelist. After serving in the Red Cross during World War I he joined the American expatriate community in Paris. His first successful novel was *The Sun Also Rises* (1926). He was a keen sportsman, and in his short stories and his later novels, including *For Whom the Bell Tolls* (1940), about the Spanish Civil War, and *The Old Man and the Sea* (1952), he celebrated the virtues of courage and stoicism in a forceful economical style. Other works include *A Farewell to Arms* (1929), *To Have and Have Not* (1937), and *Islands in the Stream* (1970). He won the Nobel Prize in 1954. Subject to severe depressions after leaving his home in Cuba in 1960, he committed suicide. In 1985 the Ritz Paris Hemingway prize of $150,000 was instituted for fiction that continues the Hemingway tradition of excellence. The prizewinning author receives $50,000 and the rest is shared by educational institutions.

hemiplegia. *See* paralysis.

Hemiptera An order of insects (about 50 000 species)—the true bugs—having piercing mouthparts for sucking the juices from plants or animals. The suborder *Heteroptera* includes plant and animal feeders (*see* plant bug; water bug). The forewings of these insects have both a leathery and a membranous region and are held flat over the body at rest. The suborder *Homoptera*, including the *froghoppers, *aphids, *cicadas, and *scale insects, are all plant feeders and have uniform front wings, held over the body at rest.

hemlock 1. A poisonous biennial plant, *Conium maculatum*, native to Europe, W Asia, and N Africa. It grows in damp places to a height of 2 m and has branching purple-spotted stems that bear much divided leaves and clusters of tiny white flowers. The plant is notorious as the means by which Socrates died. Family: *Umbelliferae.* **2.** A coniferous tree of the genus *Tsuga* (15 species), native to S and E Asia and North America. The narrow bladelike leaves, up to 2 cm long, are grouped in two rows along the stems and the brown egg-shaped cones are 2–3 cm long. The western hemlock (*T. heterophylla*) of W North America, up to 60 m tall, is grown for timber and ornament. Family: *Pinaceae.*

hemp An annual herb, *Cannabis sativa*, native to central Asia. It grows to a height of 5 m and bears small yellow flowers. Hemp is cultivated in many temperate regions (e.g. Italy and the Soviet Union) for its fibre, obtained from the inner stem bark and used for ropes, sacking, and sailcloth. The flowers, bark, twigs, and leaves contain a narcotic resin (*see* cannabis), source of marihuana and related drugs. Family: *Moraceae. See also* Indian hemp.

Henan (*or* Honan) A province in E central China. The Yellow and the Huai Rivers irrigate the E fertile plain. Densely populated, it has been a centre of Chinese culture since about 2000 BC. Chief products are cereals, cotton, silk, and coal. Area: 167 000 sq km (65 000 sq mi). Population (1980 est): 71 890 000. Capital: Zhengzhou.

henbane A strong-smelling poisonous annual or biennial herb, *Hyoscyamus niger*, native to Europe and N Africa. Up to 80 cm high, it has funnel-shaped yellow flowers, veined with purple, and grows in sandy places. It contains the medicinal alkaloid hyoscyamine. Family: *Solanaceae.*

Henbury Craters A group of 13 craters in the central Australian desert near Henbury. They are meteorite craters, the three largest believed to have been formed by explosions and the others by impact. The meteoritic fragments in the area are composed of nickel-iron and some have been shown to be of great age.

Henderson, Arthur (1863-1935) British Labour politician; foreign secretary (1929-31). An iron moulder, he became an MP in 1903 and later led the parliamentary Labour Party (1908-1910, 1914-1917). He served in Asquith's coalition government (1915-16) and then in Lloyd George's war cabinet (1916-17). As foreign secretary under MacDonald, he ardently supported the League of Nations and the Disarmament Conference, of which he became chairman in 1932. In 1934 he won the Nobel Peace Prize.

Hendon A district in the Greater London borough of Barnet. There is a famous boys' public school (1807) at Mill Hill. Hendon airfield, from which the first UK aerial postal delivery was made, was an important flying centre (1909-57) and is now the site of an RAF museum (1972).

Hendrix, Jimi (James Marshall H.; 1942-70) US rock singer and guitarist. With his group, the Jimi Hendrix Experience, Hendrix recorded such hits as "Purple Haze" and "Foxey Lady" and became famous for his virtuoso electric-guitar playing. He died as a result of a drug overdose.

henequen A perennial herbaceous plant, *Agave fourcroydes*, native to Mexico and cultivated for its leaf fibres called Yucatan, or Cuban, sisal. The plant stems grow to an average height of 90 cm in cultivation and the lance-shaped leaves form a dense rosette. Each plant yields 25 leaves annually from 5 to 16 years after planting. The fibres, which have an average length of 1.3 m, are made into twines used in agriculture, shipping, and rope. Family: *Agavaceae.*

Hengist and Horsa Legendary leaders of the first Anglo-Saxon settlers in Britain. According to the Anglo-Saxon Chronicle (late 9th century AD) Horsa was killed in 455 AD and his brother Hengist ruled over Kent from 455 to 488.

Hengyang 26 58N 112 31E A city in S China, in Hunan province on the Xiang (*or* Siang) River. A long-established communications, commercial, and cultural centre, many historic buildings survive. Chemicals and machinery are manufactured. Population (1980): 507 000.

Henley-on-Thames 51 32N 0 56W A town in S central England, in Oxfordshire on the River Thames. It is chiefly a residential and recreational town with an annual Royal Regatta (first held in 1839). Population (1981): 10 976.

henna A shrub, *Lawsonia inermis*, occurring in Egypt, India, and the Middle East. Up to 2 m high, it has fragrant white-and-yellow flowers. The leaves are powdered and used for tinting the hair and nails a reddish colour. It also has medicinal uses. Family: *Lythraceae.*

Henrietta Maria (1609-69) The wife of Charles I of England. Her marriage was happy but as a French Roman Catholic she was unpopular in England. During the Civil War she negotiated abroad for men, money, and munitions for the Royalist cause. Impeached by parliament, she escaped to France in 1644 and settled there.

henry (H) The *SI unit of inductance equal to the inductance of a closed circuit such that a rate of change of current of one ampere per second produces an induced e.m.f. of one volt. Named after Joseph *Henry.

Henry (I) the Fowler (c. 876-936) Duke of Saxony (912-36) and German king (919-36), founder of the Saxon dynasty (918-1024). In 925 he recovered Lotharingia for Germany, in 933 he defeated the Hungarians, and in 934, after invading Denmark, he won Schleswig for Germany.

Henry I (1069-1135) King of England (1100-35); the youngest son of *William (I) the Conqueror. Henry became king on the death of his brother William Rufus, successfully defending his throne against the claims of his eldest brother Robert II Curthose, Duke of Normandy, from whom he won the duchy in 1106. In England his reign is notable for important legal and administrative reforms, especially in the Exchequer, and for the final resolution of the *investiture controversy involving Archbishop *Anselm. Abroad, Henry waged several campaigns against Louis VI of France (1081-1137; reigned 1108-37), Fulk V, Count of Anjou (1092-1143), and Norman rebels in order to consolidate and expand his continental possessions.

Henry (II) the Saint (973-1024) German king and Holy Roman Emperor (1002-24; crowned 1014). After a protracted conflict with Poland he was forced to cede Lusatia but in Italy he successfully defended the papacy against the Greeks and Lombards. He sponsored Church reform, founding monasteries and schools. He was canonized in 1145.

Henry II (1133-89) King of England (1154-89); the son of Matilda and Geoffrey of Anjou and the grandson of Henry I. Henry succeeded Stephen. Married (1152) to *Eleanor of

Aquitaine, he ruled an empire that stretched from the River Tweed to the Pyrenees (*see* Angevins). In spite of frequent hostilities with the French king, his own family, and rebellious barons (culminating in the great revolt of 1173-74) and his quarrel with Thomas *Becket, Henry maintained control over his possessions until shortly before his death. His judicial and administrative reforms, which greatly increased royal control and influence at the expense of the barons, were of great constitutional importance.

Henry II (1519-59) King of France (1547-59); the husband from 1533 of *Catherine de' Medici. He concluded war against the Emperor *Charles V at Cateau-Cambrésis (1559), after winning the bishoprics of Metz, Toul, and Verdun. An ardent Roman Catholic, he began the systematic persecution of Huguenots, which ultimately led to the *Wars of Religion. He died of blood poisoning following injury in a tournament.

Henry III (1017-56) German king and Holy Roman Emperor (1039-56; crowned 1046), who greatly enhanced the power of the Empire. He became interested in Church reform under the influence of his second wife, Agnes, and at the synod of Constance (1043) announced his desire to reform the Church. His suppression of heresy, however, was unpopular and towards the end of his reign he faced rebellions in Germany, Hungary, and S Italy.

Henry III (1207-72) King of England (1216-72), succeeding his father John. Hubert de *Burgh controlled the government from 1119 until dismissed in 1232 and Henry's personal government began in 1234. Baronial discontent simmered, boiling over in 1258, when Henry, facing financial disaster, attempted to raise large sums from his magnates. Reforms—the Provisions of *Oxford—were agreed upon but then renounced by Henry. Simon de *Montfort led a rebellion against the king (*see* Barons' Wars), which was defeated after initial success. Thereafter, the aged Henry ceded much power to his son, the future Edward I.

Henry III (1551-89) King of France (1574-89) during the *Wars of Religion. Elected King of Poland in 1573, he abandoned that country on succeeding to the French throne. In France he was caught between the Huguenot and Roman Catholic parties and after fleeing Paris following an uprising (1588) allied with the Huguenot Henry of Navarre (the future *Henry IV). He was assassinated while besieging Paris.

Henry IV (1056-1106) German king (1056-84) and Holy Roman Emperor (1056-1106; crowned 1084), famous as the opponent of Pope Gregory VII in the *investiture controversy. The conflict over Henry's right to appoint bishops led him in 1076 to depose Gregory, who proceeded to excommunicate Henry. In 1077, however, Henry did penance at Canossa but was then dethroned by the German princes (1078-80). Again excommunicated, in 1084 he entered Rome, deposed Gregory, and nominated the antipope Clement III (d. 1100) by whom he was crowned emperor. He subsequently faced a further rebellion of the German princes and his sons Conrad and the future Emperor Henry V.

Henry IV (1366-1413) King of England (1399-1413); the eldest son of *John of Gaunt. As Henry Bolingbroke, he seized the throne from Richard II. In the early years of his reign Henry faced considerable opposition from Richard's supporters, led by the Earl of Northumberland and his son Hotspur (*see* Percy, Sir Henry), and from the Welsh under *Glendower. Successful in defeating his enemies, the costs of these wars and resultant taxation led to protracted struggles between king and parliament for control of royal expenditure. Increasingly incapacitated by illness, Henry's last years were marked by bitter factional struggles within his council.

Henry IV (1553-1610) The first Bourbon King of France (1589-1610), who restored peace and prosperity following

the *Wars of Religion. A Protestant, he succeeded his mother to the throne of Navarre in 1572. Shortly afterwards he married Charles IX's sister *Margaret of Valois and was forced to renounce his religion and confine himself to court. In 1576 he escaped and became a *Huguenot (Protestant) leader in the Wars of Religion. His succession to the throne was only secured in 1594, when he became a Roman Catholic, and civil war continued until he granted the Huguenots freedom of worship by the Edict of *Nantes (1598). Thereafter he sponsored the efforts of his minister *Sully to restore France's shattered economy. Henry died at the hands of an assassin.

Henry V (1081-1125) German king (1089-1125) and Holy Roman Emperor (1106-25; crowned 1111); son of Emperor *Henry IV and first husband of Matilda of England. His reign saw the settlement of the *investiture controversy with the papacy by the Concordat of Worms (1122), which brought him control of the German Church but antagonized his bishops.

Henry V (1387-1422) King of England (1413-22); the eldest son of Henry IV. He vigorously resumed the *Hundred Years' War, partly as a distraction from domestic tensions. His first campaign culminated in the battle of *Agincourt (1415) and by 1420, in alliance with Burgundy, he controlled much of N France. He married Catherine of Valois and gained recognition (1420) as the heir of her father *Charles VI (1420). He was noted by contemporaries as much for his personal piety and love of justice as for military prowess.

Henry VI (1165-97) German king (1169-97) and Holy Roman Emperor (1190-97). Son of *Frederick Barbarossa, he acquired Sicily through his marriage (1189) to Constance of Sicily (1152-98). His reign was dominated by his attempts to secure Sicily and to subdue *Henry the Lion. In 1193 he imprisoned the English king, Richard the Lionheart, and received a large ransom in return for his release.

Henry VI (1421-71) King of England (1422-61, 1470-71), succeeding his father Henry V. He married (1445), and was dominated by, *Margaret of Anjou. His inability to govern led to bitter struggles that culminated in the Wars of the *Roses. Deposed and imprisoned by the Yorkists (1461), he was briefly restored to power (1470-71), only to be again defeated and probably murdered. He was a notable patron of learning and religion: he founded Eton College (1440) and King's College, Cambridge (1447).

Henry VII (c. 1275-1313) Holy Roman Emperor (1309-1313; crowned 1312) and, as Henry VI, Count of Luxembourg (1288-1313). He became King of the Lombards in 1313 but had to contend with *Guelf (anti-imperial) opposition in Italy. He arranged a brilliant match between his son John, the future Count of Luxembourg, and Elizabeth of Bohemia.

Henry VII (1457-1509) King of England (1485-1509). As Henry Tudor, Earl of Richmond, he defeated Richard III at *Bosworth (1485) and his marriage (1486) to Richard's niece Elizabeth of York (1465-1503) united the Houses of *Lancaster and *York, effectively ending the Wars of the *Roses. Until 1499, however, he faced Yorkist plots, such as those of *Simnel and *Warbeck. His domestic rule was noted for its harsh financial exactions, efficient royal administration, and growing prosperity. His foreign policy temporarily put an end to war with France (on favourable terms, 1492), while treaties with Burgundy and the Holy Roman Empire resulted in a new pattern of European alliances.

Henry VIII (1491-1547) King of England (1509-47), who initiated the English *Reformation. In 1512 he joined a European alliance against France, which he defeated at the battle of the *Spurs (1513), gaining Tournai, and in the same year his army thwarted a Scottish invasion at *Flodden. His desire to make England a notable European power was pursued from 1515 by his Lord Chancellor, Cardinal

567

.HENRY VIII *The imposing figure of Henry, in an engraving (1824) by T. A. Dean after a painting derived from a cartoon by Holbein, symbolizes the strength of the Tudor monarchy.*

*Wolsey, who arranged the meeting between Henry and *Francis I of France at the *Field of the Cloth of Gold, near Calais (1520). From 1527 Henry was preoccupied by his wish to divorce *Catherine of Aragon, who had been the widow of his elder brother Arthur (d. 1502). He blamed her failure to produce a son (she had given birth to the future Mary I in 1516) on the canonical prohibition against marrying one's brother's widow, a conviction that was enforced by his love affair with Anne *Boleyn. Wolsey's failure to gain a papal annulment of Henry's marriage brought about the cardinal's fall in 1529 but only in 1533, after Thomas *Cromwell had initiated the legislation that made the English Church, under Henry's supreme headship, independent of Rome, could the king marry Anne. In the same year she gave birth to the future Elizabeth I. In 1535 Thomas *More was executed for refusing to acknowledge royal supremacy over the Church and in the following year Anne met the same fate for adultery. Henry then married Jane *Seymour, who died shortly after giving birth to the future Edward VI (1537). His next marriage, arranged by Cromwell, to *Anne of Cleves was short lived, ending in divorce and the execution of Cromwell (1540). Shortly afterwards Henry married Catherine *Howard, who was executed in 1542, and finally, in 1543, Catherine *Parr, who outlived him. Henry's last years were dominated by war with France and Scotland, consequent economic problems, and his attempts to hold back the forces of Protestantism, which "the King's great matter" had unleashed.

Henry, Joseph (1797-1878) US physicist, who made important contributions to the investigation of electromagnetism. He built the largest electromagnet then known, which could lift over 300 kilograms; he also discovered electromagnetic induction independently of *Faraday. Henry invented an early form of the telegraph and the electrical relay. In 1846 he was appointed secretary of the

Smithsonian Institution and he was one of the founders of the National Academy of Sciences. The unit of inductance (*see* henry) is named after him.

Henry, O. (William Sidney Porter; 1862-1910) US short-story writer. He adopted his pseudonym while serving a prison sentence for embezzlement. He subsequently worked in New York, where he published *Cabbages and Kings* (1904), the first of many volumes of short stories characterized by the use of coincidence and unexpected endings.

Henry, Patrick (1736-99) American Revolutionary orator; first governor of Virginia (1776-79). As a lawyer and member of the Virginia assembly (the House of Burgesses), Henry defended colonial rights against British rule. The mobilization of a Virginia militia on the eve of the American Revolution was ensured by Henry's famous speech ending "give me liberty or give me death." He was again governor of Virginia from 1784 to 1786.

Henryson, Robert (15th century) Scottish poet. A schoolmaster at Dunfermline Abbey, he was, with *Dunbar and Gavin *Douglas, one of the Scottish disciples of Chaucer (the Scottish Chaucerians). His works include *The Testament of Cresseid* (a sequel to Chaucer's *Troilus and Criseyde*) and 13 *Moral Fables of Esope the Phrygian*, noted for their colloquial style.

Henry the Lion (?1129-95) Duke of Saxony (1142-81), whose wealth and power brought him into conflict with the Holy Roman Emperors. He gave support to *Frederick Barbarossa in return for regaining Bavaria (1154) but when he broke with Frederick in 1176 most of his lands were confiscated and he was exiled. In 1194, after further conflict, he was reconciled with Frederick's son and successor Emperor *Henry VI.

Henry the Navigator (1394-1460) Portuguese patron of explorers; the fourth son of John I. He won a military reputation at the capture of Ceuta (1415) in N Africa, which kindled his interest in the exploration of the continent. Becoming governor of the Algarve (1419) he set up a school of navigation at Sagres and inspired and sponsored explorers. Under his auspices Madeira, the Azores, and the Cape Verde Islands were colonized, the W coast of Africa was explored, probably as far as Sierra Leone, and many trading stations were established.

Henze, Hans Werner (1926-) German composer, a pupil of Wolfgang Fortner (1907-). His piano concerto won the Schumann Prize in 1951 and he settled in Italy in 1953. He has organized an annual festival at Montepulciano since 1977. Henze has made use of a number of different styles of composition, including serialism and neoromanticism. His Marxist sympathies are evident in such works as the oratorio *The Raft of the Medusa* (1968), for which Schnabel wrote the text. He has composed symphonies; concertos for piano, violin, viola, and double bass; ballet music; and the operas *Elegy for Young Lovers* (1961) and *The Bassarids* (1966).

heparin An *anticoagulant that occurs naturally in the tissues and is also used in medicine. Heparin is a complex carbohydrate produced and secreted by special cells (mast cells) in connective tissues, especially in the lungs. It inhibits the enzymes responsible for blood clotting.

hepatitis Inflammation of the liver, most commonly caused by viruses. The two main types are infectious hepatitis, usually contracted by ingesting the virus from food or drink, and serum hepatitis, contracted mainly from dirty hypodermic needles or blood products. Some chemicals (e.g. alcohol) can also cause hepatitis. The patient usually has a fever, loses his appetite, and later becomes jaundiced. Hepatitis usually resolves without specific treatment, but sometimes chronic disease develops.

Hepburn, Katherine (1909-) US actress. Her performances in both films and the theatre are distinguished by her intelligence and versatility. She made several films with Spencer *Tracy, and her other films include *The Philadelphia Story* (1940), *The African Queen* (1952), *The Lion in Winter* (1968), and *On Golden Pond* (1981).

Hephaestus The Greek god of fire and crafts, the son of Zeus and Hera. According to Hesiod he created *Pandora, the first woman. He is identified with the Roman *Vulcan.

Hepplewhite, George (d. 1786) British furniture designer and cabinetmaker, who established a business in London. His neoclassical furniture is a simplified and more functional version of the designs of Robert *Adam, with whom he sometimes collaborated. Usually in inlaid mahogany or satinwood, it is characterized by straight tapering legs and heart- or oval-shaped chairbacks filled with openwork designs.

heptane (C_7H_{16}) A colourless flammable liquid *alkane. It is obtained from *oil and is used as a solvent and to make other chemicals. Heptane is also a standard in determining the *octane rating of petrol.

DAME BARBARA HEPWORTH *In her garden with the plaster model of her bronze sculpture* The Meridian.

Hepworth, Dame Barbara (1903–75) British sculptor. She studied in Leeds and at the Royal College of Art. A friend of Henry *Moore, she was also influenced by *Brancusi and *Arp. Her abstract carving in wood and stone developed after *Pierced Form* (1931), creating massive shapes broken by holes with wires stretched across their openings. Twice-married, to sculptor John Skeaping (1901–80) and painter Ben *Nicholson, she received the DBE in 1965.

Hera In Greek mythology, the daughter of Cronus and Rhea and the sister and wife of Zeus. She was jealous of Zeus' many mistresses and cruel to their children but gave loyal support to *Jason and *Achilles. She was worshipped as a goddess of women and marriage. She is identified with the Roman *Juno.

Heracles (or Hercules) A Greek legendary hero, famed for his strength and courage. He was the son of Zeus and Alcmene (see Amphitryon). After killing his wife and children in a fit of madness inflicted by Hera, he went to the court of King Eurystheus of Tiryns, where he performed the Twelve Labours in expiation: he killed the Nemean lion and the *Hydra of Lerna, captured the Hind of Ceryneia and the Boar of Erymanthus, cleaned the Augean stables, chased away the Stymphalian birds, captured the Cretan bull and the horses of Diomedes, stole the girdle of Hippolyte, captured the oxen of Geryon, stole the apples of the *Hesperides, and finally captured and bound *Cerberus in Hades.

Heraclitus (c. 535–c. 475 BC) Greek philosopher of *Ephesus. His treatise *On Nature* postulates that fire is the universe's basic constituent. Rejecting *Parmenides' doctrine of a unitary static reality, Heraclitus maintained that reality is transitory and every object "a harmony of opposite tensions." Everything was always changing ("you cannot step into the same river twice") and wisdom consisted in seeking to understand this eternal principle (see logos).

Heraclius (c. 575–641 AD) Byzantine emperor. Between 613 and 628 he faced the Persians, who took Syria, Palestine, and Egypt and besieged Constantinople (626). Following a campaign in 626–28, Heraclius restored the Holy Cross to Jerusalem (629), a deed that was immortalized in medieval legend. His success was short-lived for in 634 the Arabs attacked the empire, defeating the Byzantines at Yarmuk (636) and taking Palestine, Syria, and Egypt. He divided Anatolia into military units, from which peasants were enlisted for military service in return for land.

Herakleion. See Iráklion.

heraldry A system of pictorial devices on shields originally used to identify individuals when wearing armour. Personal devices on shields are of great antiquity but in the early 12th century armorial devices became hereditary in Europe. They were also used as *seals. Coats of arms are also granted to institutions. In England heraldry is controlled by the *College of Arms. The Court of the Lord Lyon has a similar function in Scotland. Coats of arms comprise the shield, a helmet surmounted by a crest, a mantling (stylized drapery behind the shield), a wreath, and a motto. The shield bears the heraldic signs (charges), which have ancient fixed meanings. From these heralds can determine the genealogy and status of the bearer.

Herat (or Harat) 34 20N 62 10E A city in W Afghanistan. Near the site of several ancient cities, including one built by Alexander the Great, Herat developed as a scientific and cultural centre under the rule of the Turkish conqueror Timur, who seized the city in 1393. An agricultural and commercial centre, Herat's industries include flour milling and textiles. Population (1982 est): 155 858.

herbaceous plant A plant that lacks woody stems and the aerial parts of which die each winter. Many herbaceous plants are *annuals but some are *perennials, surviving the winter as underground bulbs, corms, rhizomes, etc.

Herbart, Johann Friedrich (1776–1841) German educational theorist, who pioneered the application of psychology to teaching. Rejecting *Fichte's philosophy with its emphasis on freedom, he preferred *Kant's pluralism, believing that beyond the phenomenal world there existed many real "things-in-themselves," which are inaccessible to the mind. Herbart, like Kant, wasted time developing fruitless systems that had no experimental foundation.

Herbert, Sir A(lan) P(atrick) (1890–1971) British writer and politician. Notable as a humourist, he wrote *Misleading Cases in the Common Law* (1927), *Holy Deadlock* (1934), and a novel, *The Water Gypsies* (1930). As an MP (1935–50) he worked for reform of the marriage laws.

Herbert, George (1593–1633) English poet. A member of a distinguished Anglo-Welsh family, Herbert had a brief

569

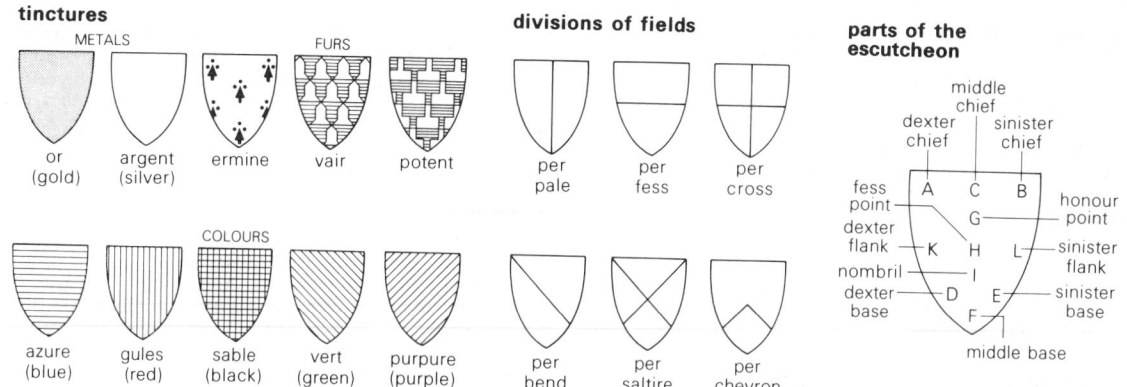

HERALDRY *The terminology of heraldry, of which a few terms are illustrated, reveals the science's French origins.*

career in secular life as Public Orator at Cambridge and as MP for Montgomery before pursuing a religious vocation. In 1630 he was appointed rector of Bemerton, Wiltshire. A friend of Francis *Bacon and *Donne, he wrote religious lyrics, collected in *The Temple* (1633), which rank among the finest in the language. He died of consumption. His brother **Edward, 1st Baron Herbert of Cherbury** (1583-1648) was a philosopher and poet. He was appointed ambassador to France (1619-24), during which time he completed a philosophical treatise, *De veritate* (1624), a controversial work that had wide contemporary influence. His *Autobiography* (1764) covers his life to 1624. His poems are collected in *Occasional Verses* (1665).

herbicide (*or* weedkiller) A chemical used to kill unwanted plants (*see* weed). Selective weedkillers kill the target without harming the plants among which it is growing. Some of these act by interfering with the growth of the weed and are often based on plant hormones. An example is 2,4-D, a synthetic *auxin, which is used to control broadleaved weeds in cereal crops. Herbicides used to clear waste ground are nonselective and kill every plant with which they come into contact. An example is *Paraquat.

herb Paris A perennial herbaceous plant, *Paris quadrifolia*, native to woodlands of Europe and Asia. Up to 30 cm high, it has a whorl of usually four leaves and a solitary flower with prominent sepals and narrow yellow petals. The fruit is a fleshy capsule. Family: *Trilliaceae*.

herb Robert An annual or biennial herb, *Geranium robertianum*, growing up to 50 cm high and found in woods and hedgerows throughout temperate Eurasia and introduced to North and South America. The small flowers are pink or red. Family: *Geraniaceae*.

herbs and spices The fresh or dried parts of aromatic or pungent plants used in food, drink, medicine, and perfumery. Herbs are generally the leaves of plants and are best used fresh. They grow in temperate zones. Common culinary herbs are *basil, *bay leaves, *marjoram, *mint, *parsley, and *thyme. Spices generally grow in hot countries. They were formerly a valuable trade commodity; the Roman Empire's spice trade extended to Indochina and Zanzibar and the quest for spice routes motivated 15th-century European exploration of the East and the Americas. Spices are usually dried and may be obtained from the root (e.g. *ginger), bark (e.g. *cinnamon), flower (e.g. *clove), seed pod (e.g. *chilli), or, most commonly, from the seed itself (e.g. *coriander, *cumin, *pepper).

Hercegovina. *See* Bosnia and Hercegovina.

Herculaneum An ancient Italian city near *Naples in Italy. It was destroyed by the same eruption as *Pompeii (79 AD). It was smaller, better planned, and wealthier than Pompeii. Entombment beneath solidified volcanic mud makes excavation there very difficult and much remains buried.

Hercules. *See* Heracles.

hercules beetle A giant green and black beetle, *Dynastes herculeus*, occurring in Central and South America. The male may reach a length of 15 cm, nearly two-thirds of which is taken up by an enormous pair of horns, extending from the thorax and head. Family: *Scarabaeidae* (*see* scarab beetle).

hercules moth A large Australian *saturniid moth, *Coscinoscera hercules*. The adult has broad dark-brown wings, spanning about 28 cm, with a wing area that is possibly the largest of any insect.

Herder, Johann Gottfried (1744-1803) German philosopher and poet. At first a disciple and later a critic of *Kant, he developed a form of religious humanism based on his readings of Shakespeare, Homer, and the Bible. His works include *A Treatise upon the Origin of Language* (1772) and *Outline of a Philosophy of the History of Man* (1784-91).

Hereford · 52 04N 2 43W A city in W England, in Hereford and Worcester on the River Wye. Situated in an important agricultural area, Hereford deals mainly in agricultural produce, manufacturing cider, beer, leather goods, and chemicals. It has given its name to a famous breed of cattle. The cathedral, begun in 1079, contains one of the oldest maps in the world (about 1314). Population (1981): 47 652.

Hereford and Worcester A county of W England, bordering Wales. It was created in 1974 from the former counties of Herefordshire and Worcestershire. It consists chiefly of two lowland plains, separated by the Malvern Hills, with the Black Mountains in the W. The chief rivers are the Wye in the W and the Severn in the E. It is predominantly agricultural; hop production is surpassed only by Kent; soft fruit and vegetables are grown in the S of the Avon Valley, known as the Vale of Evesham; and the Hereford breed of cattle is renowned throughout the world. Industries include engineering, chemicals, and food processing. Salt is produced near Droitwich. Area: 3927 sq km (1516 sq mi). Population (1983 est): 640 400. Administrative centre: Worcester.

Hereford cattle A breed of beef cattle originating from Herefordshire and surrounding areas in W England. They are large and stocky with red coats and white faces. Hardy and maturing quickly, Herefords are often mated with dairy breeds to produce a white-faced beef cross.

Herefordshire A former county of W England. Under local government reorganization in 1974 it became part of the new county of *Hereford and Worcester.

Herero A group of Bantu-speaking peoples of SW Africa, Botswana, and Angola. They are traditionally cattle, sheep, and goat herders but some adopted agriculture after European contact. Their social organization is based on the common principle of counting descent in the male line for some purposes and in the female line for others.

Hereward the Wake (11th century) Anglo-Saxon thegn, who led a raid on Peterborough Abbey (1070) as a protest against William I's appointment of a Norman abbot. He and other disaffected Anglo-Saxon nobles took refuge on the Isle of Ely, until its capture by William (1071) forced Hereward to flee.

Hermann von Reichenau (1013–54) German poet and chronicler, known as Hermann the Lame. He was a monk at the monastery at Reichenau. One of the most gifted thinkers of his age, he wrote on theology, mathematics, and astronomy. He may have written *Salve Regina* and *Alma Redemptoris Mater*, among many other hymns and antiphons.

hermaphrodite (*or* bisexual) A plant or animal possessing both male and female reproductive organs. Such organisms may show cross- or self-*fertilization: the latter method is particularly common when the opportunity of finding a mate is remote, for example in parasitic invertebrates and deepsea fish. True hermaphroditism rarely occurs in humans. More common is **pseudohermaphroditism**, in which an individual develops secondary characteristics appropriate to the opposite sex (e.g enlarged external genitals in a woman or breasts in a man), due to hormone imbalance.

Hermes In Greek mythology, the messenger and herald of the gods and the guide of travellers. He was regarded as the god of riches and good luck, the protector of merchants and thieves, and the god of dreams. He was usually portrayed as an athletic youth wearing a cap and winged sandals and carrying a golden staff. He was the son of Zeus and Maia. He conducted the souls of the dead to Hades and is credited with the invention of the lyre, which he gave to Apollo. He is identified with the Roman *Mercury.

Hermes Trismegistos (Greek: Hermes the thrice great) The name applied by Greek Neoplatonists to the Egyptian god *Thoth. It is also the name given, after the third century AD, to the author of certain Neoplatonic writings.

Hermeticism An Italian literary movement of the early 20th century. Its leading writers were the poets Ungaretti, Quasimodo, and Montale, whose early poetry was influenced by the theories of the French *Symbolists and characterized by verbal experiment and esoteric symbolism. After World War II all three poets developed more accessible styles.

hermit crab A *crab with a soft unprotected abdomen, belonging to the worldwide families *Paguridae* and *Coenobitidae*. It lives in portable hollow objects, such as snail shells, for protection and changes these for successively larger ones as it grows. Hermit crabs are found in sandy or muddy-bottomed waters and occasionally on land and in trees. Tribe: *Anomura*.

Hermite, Charles (1822–1901) French mathematician, who (in 1873), discovered the first transcendental number: e, the base of natural *logarithms. Such numbers cannot be expressed as a root of a polynomial equation, i.e. an equation of the form $a_0 + a_1x + \ldots + a_nx^n = 0$, where n and the a's are integers. *Liouville had already shown that such numbers exist but could not identify any.

Hermon, Mount 33 24N 35 50E A mountain on the Syrian-Lebanese border, at the S end of the Anti-Lebanon Mountains. It is the highest point near the E coast of the Mediterranean Sea. Height: 2814 m (9232 ft).

Hermosillo 29 15N 110 59W A city in NW Mexico. It is an important commercial centre for the surrounding agricultural areas and has a university (1938). Population (1980): 340 779.

Herne 51 32N 7 12E A city in NW West Germany, in North Rhine-Westphalia on the Rhine-Herne Canal. It is a coalmining and industrial centre. Population (1980 est): 183 000.

hernia The protrusion of an organ or tissue through a weak spot in the wall that normally contains it. The most common types are the inguinal hernia (popularly called a rupture), which is a swelling in the groin caused by the protrusion of the abdominal contents, and the hiatus hernia, in which part of the stomach protrudes into the chest cavity. Other common hernias are femoral (also in the groin) and umbilical (at the navel). Hernias should usually be surgically repaired or they may become painful and cut off from their blood supply (strangulated).

Hero and Leander Legendary lovers whose story was recounted by the Greek poet Musaeus (4th or 5th century AD). Hero was a priestess of Aphrodite at Sestos and Leander swam to her each night across the Hellespont from Abydos. After a stormy night Hero found her lover's drowned body and in despair drowned herself.

Herod (I) the Great (c. 73–4 BC) King of Judaea (37–4); the son of *Antipater the Idumaean. Supported by Mark Antony, he became the Romans' king in Judaea. A Jew of Arab origins, he was regarded as a usurper by nationalists, who resented his encouragement of Greek culture; he retained power by control of the religious establishment and rigorous suppression of opposition. His jealousy and cruelty were exacerbated by feuds among his ten wives and their sons. Shortly before his death he ordered the massacre of the infants of Bethlehem.

Herod Agrippa I (c. 10 BC–44 AD) King of Judaea (41–44); the grandson of *Herod the Great. An impecunious adventurer, he was educated at the Roman imperial court after the execution of his father by Herod the Great. He intrigued in imperial family politics and helped Emperor *Claudius to power, for which he was made King of Judaea. He was a popular ruler but persecuted Christians, executing St James, the son of Zebedee, and imprisoning St Peter.

Herod Agrippa II (died c. 100 AD) King of Chalcis (50–c. 100) in S Lebanon; the son of *Herod Agrippa I. In 60 he heard the case of the arrested St Paul and found him innocent. He attempted to prevent the Jewish rebellion of 66, during which his troops fought on the Roman side, and helped to take Jerusalem in 70.

Herod Antipas (21 BC–39 AD) Tetrarch (governor) of Galilee (4–39 AD) after the partition of the realm of his father *Herod the Great. He divorced his wife to marry his niece Herodias, for which he was censured by John the Baptist. Herodias persuaded her daughter Salome to ask for John's head in return for dancing at Antipas' birthday celebration and John was executed. Jesus Christ, as a Galilean, was brought before Antipas after his arrest, but Antipas returned him to Pontius Pilate of Judaea without passing judgment. After the death of Antipas' friend Emperor *Tiberius, religious riots gave *Caligula an excuse to exile Antipas.

Herodotus (c. 484–c. 425 BC) Greek historian. Born at Halicarnassus, he was exiled for political reasons and moved to Samos. He subsequently moved to Athens and then to the Athenian colony of Thurii in S Italy, where he died. Called "the father of history" by Cicero, he was the first historian to subject his material to critical evaluation and research. His narrative account of the wars between Greece and Persia in nine books contained much incidental anthropological and geographical information gathered on his travels in the Mediterranean countries, Egypt, and Asia, and was written in a lively dramatic style.

heroin (*or* diamorphine) A pain-killing drug with a stronger action and fewer side effects than *morphine, from which it is made. Heroin is used to alleviate the suffering of terminal illness. Because the regular use of heroin readily leads to physical dependence its use in medicine has been restricted. *See* drug dependence.

heron A wading bird belonging to a subfamily (*Ardeinae*; 60 species) occurring on lakes and rivers worldwide, especially in the tropics. 75–150 cm long, herons have a slim body, longish legs, long toes, broad wings, a short tail, and a loose plumage coloured grey, blue, greenish, white, purple, or reddish. Herons hunt by standing at the water's edge and seizing fish and insects with the long pointed bill. In the breeding season herons may develop ornamental plumes and perform elaborate courtship displays. Family: *Ardeidae* (herons and bitterns). *See also* egret; night heron.

Hero of Alexandria (mid-1st century AD) Greek engineer and mathematician, best known for his invention of the aeolipile, the earliest known steam engine. It consisted of a sphere containing water with two bent tubes extending from it. When heated, steam issued from the tubes, causing the sphere to rotate. However, the device was only used for trivial purposes, such as controlling doors and causing statues to move. He also discovered the well-known formula for calculating the area of a triangle from the lengths of its sides.

Herophilus (c. 335–c. 280 BC) Greek physician, who founded one of the earliest medical schools in Alexandria. Herophilus performed public dissections of human cadavers, distinguished between sensory and motor nerve trunks, and described parts of the brain, duodenum, and several other organs.

herpes A virus of which there are several forms. Herpes zoster causes chickenpox in children and shingles in adults. Herpes simplex causes cold sores. Herpes simplex II causes the sexually transmitted genital herpes, which produces painful blisters in the genital area.

Herrera, Juan de (1530–97) Spanish architect. After having studied in Italy, Herrera designed a palace in Aranjuez (1569) and the Exchange in Seville (1582) in an Italianate style that had great influence on Spanish architecture. He is best known for his completion of the *Escorial.

Herrera the Younger, Francisco de (1622–85) Spanish baroque painter and architect, born in Seville, the son and pupil of the painter and engraver **Francisco de Herrera the Elder** (1576–1656). After leaving his father's tutelage, he studied in Italy. On his return to Seville, he introduced the dramatic style of Italian baroque in such religious works as *Triumph of St Hermengild* (Prado). He later worked in Madrid, where he designed the high altar of the church of Montserrat.

Herrick, Robert (1591–1674) English poet. A friend of Jonson and other members of London literary society, he was ordained (1623) after graduating from Cambridge and served as rector of Dean Prior, Devonshire, from 1630 to 1646 and again after the Restoration. The majority of his secular and religious poems, collected in *Hesperides* (1648), are short lyrics influenced by classical models.

herring An important food fish, *Clupea harengus*, found mainly in cold waters of the N Atlantic and the North Sea. It has a slender silvery blue-green body, up to about 40 cm long, with a single short dorsal fin and swims in large shoals, feeding on plankton. A related species (*C. pallasi*) occurs in the N Pacific. Many other small silvery fish of the family *Clupeidae* are called herring. Herrings have long been fished in N Europe, where they are eaten fresh, pickled, and smoked. In the UK, smoked herring are known as kippers, and are produced mainly in Scotland. Overfishing and pollution have greatly reduced catches of herring in European waters in recent years. Order: *Clupeiformes. See also* whitebait.

herring gull A large grey and white *gull, *Larus argentatus*, occurring around coasts in the N hemisphere. It is omnivorous and is commonly seen scavenging at refuse tips. Adults are 57 cm long and have pink legs and a yellow bill with a red spot on the lower mandible.

Herriot, Édouard (1872–1957) French statesman and writer; prime minister of a Radical-Socialist coalition (1924–25, 1926 (for two days), 1932). During World War II, he opposed the Vichy Government and spent the years 1942–45 in prison. From 1947 to 1953 he served as president of the national assembly.

Herschel, Sir William (1738–1822) British astronomer, born in Germany. Working with his sister **Caroline Herschel** (1750–1848), he became expert in grinding lenses and built the largest telescopes then known. In 1781 Herschel discovered the planet *Uranus, the first such discovery since prehistoric times. His other discoveries include binary stars, two new satellites of Saturn, and *infrared rays from the sun (1800). His son **Sir John Herschel** (1792–1871) was also an astronomer. Using his father's telescope, he continued with the work of mapping binary stars and nebulae. In order to observe stars in the S hemisphere, he set up an observatory in Capetown in 1834. He was also greatly interested in photography, using it for astronomical purposes. He was the first to use sodium thiosulphate (hypo) as a fixer and he developed a sensitized photographic paper.

Herstmonceux (*or* Hurstmonceux) 50 53N 0 20E A village in SE England, in East Sussex. Its castle (built in 1440) has housed the *Royal Greenwich Observatory since 1950. The Isaac Newton telescope was moved to the Canary Islands in 1979 and the observatory will move to Cambridge by 1990.

Hertford 51 48N 0 05W A market town in SE England, the administrative centre of Hertfordshire on the River Lea. Industries include printing, flour milling, brewing, and brush manufacturing. The castle remains include a Norman tower. Population (1981): 21 412.

Hertfordshire A county of S England, bordering on Greater London. It lies mainly in the Lower Thames Basin rising to the Chiltern Hills in the NW and is drained by the Rivers Lea, Stort, and Colne. The chief agricultural activity is arable farming, producing barley for the brewing industry. Dairy farming, market gardening, and horticulture are also important. Industries include paper and printing at Watford, and tanning. It has four new towns including Hemel Hempstead and Stevenage. Area: 1634 sq km (632 sq mi). Population (1981): 954 535. Administrative centre: Hertford.

Hertogenbosch, 's. *See* 's Hertogenbosch.

hertz (Hz) The *SI unit of frequency equal to one cycle per second. Named after Heinrich *Hertz.

Hertz, Heinrich Rudolf (1857–94) German physicist, who first produced and detected *radio waves (1888). *Maxwell's equations had predicted the existence of *electromagnetic radiation over a wide spectrum of frequencies but, until Hertz's discovery, radio-frequency radiation was unknown. The unit of frequency is named after him.

Hertzog, James Barry Munnik (1866–1942) South African statesman; prime minister of the Union of South Africa (1924–39). In the second *Boer War he led the Orange Free State forces. He was a member of Botha's government from 1910 to 1912 but formed the Afrikaner Nationalist Party in 1914 in opposition to Botha, becoming prime minister in 1924. In 1933 he formed a coalition government with *Smuts but resigned in 1939, when his motion against entering World War II was defeated. With *Malan he then revived the Nationalist Party but retired in 1940.

Hertzsprung-Russell diagram A graphic representation of the classification of stars according to spectral type (*see* Harvard classification system) and brightness—usually absolute *magnitude. The stars are not uniformly distributed. Most, including the sun, lie on a diagonal band, the main sequence, the brightest stars of which are spectral types O and B and the faintest are M stars. Main-sequence stars are normal stars, obtaining their energy from the nuclear fusion of hydrogen in their cores. The somewhat brighter *giant stars, the even brighter *supergiants, and the faint *white dwarfs fall into their own distinct groupings and are at later stages of evolution. The diagram was originally produced, indepen-

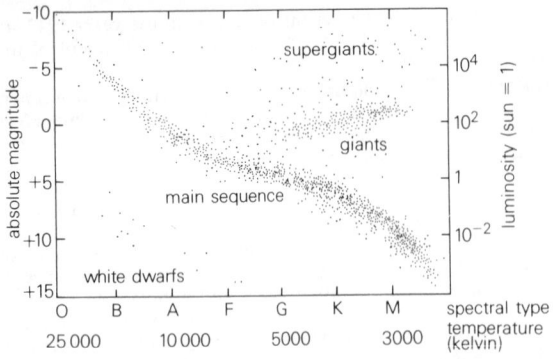

HERTZSPRUNG-RUSSELL DIAGRAM *This graph for bright stars is important in studies of stellar evolution and in determining distance.*

dently, in 1911 by E. Hertzsprung (1873–1967) and in 1913 by H. N. Russell (1897–1957).

Herzen, Aleksandr (Ivanovich) (1812–70) Russian political philosopher. The illegitimate son of a nobleman, he was exiled to the provinces from 1834 to 1842 for his political activities. After 1848 he lived mostly in Paris and London, where he founded several emigré political journals. His early enthusiasm for W European progressive ideals dwindled as he came to believe in Russian peasant communes as a basis for a socialist society. His major literary work was his memoirs, *My Past and Thoughts* (1861–67).

Herzl, Theodor (1860–1904) Hungarian-born journalist and playwright, who founded the movement to establish a Jewish nation (*see* Zionism). Living mostly in Vienna, he published the pamphlet *The Jewish State* (1896), calling for a world council to discuss the problem of finding a Jewish homeland. At a world congress of Zionists in Basle (1897) the World Zionist Organization was established, Herzl becoming the first president. This congress advocated Palestine as the homeland and set up the Jewish National Fund to buy land there.

Herzog, Werner (1942–) German film director. In *Fata Morgana* (1971), *Aguirre, Wrath of God* (1973), *The Enigma of Kaspar Hauser* (1975), and *Nosferatu* (1979) he uses an allegorical or historical framework to express his bleak vision of human society. His latest films include *Wozzeck* (1979) and *Fitzcarraldo* (1982).

Hesilrige, Sir Arthur (*or* Haselrig; d. 1661) English parliamentarian. He played a prominent part in the *Long Parliament (summoned in 1640) and was one of the five MPs whom Charles I attempted to arrest (1642). He fought through the Civil War but opposed the *Protectorate. At the Restoration of Charles II (1660), he was imprisoned in the Tower of London, where he died.

Hesiod (8th century BC) Greek poet, the earliest known after Homer. He was a farmer near Mount Helicon in Boeotia in central Greece and was involved in a long dispute with his brother Perses concerning their inheritance. His two major works are the *Theogony*, concerning the gods and their myths, and *Works and Days*, a realistic and personal account of farming life.

Hesperides (Greek: daughters of evening) In Greek mythology, three nymphs who guarded the sacred golden apples of Hera in a garden in the far west. The apples were stolen by *Heracles as one of his Twelve Labours.

Hesperornis A genus of extinct flightless seabirds whose fossils date from the Cretaceous period (125–60 million years ago). It was 2 m long and adapted for swimming and catching fish in shallow seas, having large powerful feet and legs, a long slender neck, a small head, and a long bill (possibly with teeth), but only tiny wing bones and reduced flight muscles.

Hess, Dame Myra (1890–1965) British pianist. She made her London debut in 1907. During World War II she initiated daily lunchtime concerts at the National Gallery and was created a DBE in 1941. She was famous for her performances of Mozart.

Hess, Rudolf (1894–1987) German Nazi politician. Hess joined the Nazi Party in 1920, becoming Hitler's close friend and deputy party leader (1933). However, his declining influence in the late 1930s led to his unsuccessful secret mission to Scotland to negotiate a separate peace with Britain in 1941. There, he was imprisoned until 1946, when he was convicted at the Nuremberg war trials and sent to Spandau prison. The only prisoner there from 1966, he committed suicide.

Hess, Victor Francis (1883–1964) US physicist, born in Austria. Using a balloon to investigate atmospheric background radiation, he discovered that the radiation increased with altitude. This was contrary to expectation, because background radiation was then believed to emanate from rocks. This work led to the discovery of *cosmic rays, for which he shared a Nobel Prize in 1936 with Carl *Anderson.

Hesse (German name: Hessen) A *Land* in central West Germany. Formed in 1945, it consists of the former duchies of Hesse-Darmstadt and Nassau. Hilly and forested, it is chiefly agricultural, producing potatoes, sugar beet, and wheat. Industry, concentrated in the S, includes publishing and the manufacture of machinery and chemicals. Iron ore, salt, and coal are mined. Area: 21 112 sq km (8150 sq mi). Population (1980 est): 5 587 300. Capital: Wiesbaden.

Hesse, Hermann (1877–1962) German novelist and poet. He rejected traditional schooling and worked as a bookseller until publication of his first novel, *Peter Camenzind* (1904). His early themes of art and self-knowledge were later extended by his interest in Indian mysticism and Jungian psychology, reflected in *Siddharta* (1922). His other major novels are *Steppenwolf* (1927) and *Narziss und Goldmund* (1930). After publication of his last novel, *The Glass Bead Game* (1943), he was awarded a Nobel Prize (1946). From 1911 until his death he lived in Switzerland.

Hestia The Greek goddess of the hearth, daughter of Cronus and Rhea and the oldest of the Olympian deities. She vowed to remain a virgin, rejecting both Apollo and Poseidon as consorts. She is identified with the Roman *Vesta.

Hevesy, George Charles von (1885–1966) Hungarian-born chemist, who worked in Denmark and Sweden. He discovered the use of *radioactive tracers to follow the course of compounds in a system, for which he received the 1943 Nobel Prize. He also discovered the element *hafnium in 1923, by analysing zirconium ores.

Heyerdahl, Thor (1914–) Norwegian ethnologist, who led the *Kon-Tiki* expedition (1947). The *Kon-Tiki* was a balsawood raft that Heyerdahl built and sailed with five companions from the Pacific coast of South America to Polynesia to show that the pre-Incan inhabitants of Peru might thus have migrated to Polynesia. In 1969–70 he attempted to cross the Atlantic Ocean from Morocco to South America in a papyrus boat—the *Ra*; he reached Barbados, showing the possibility of Egyptian influence on the Precolumbian civilization of America. Heyerdahl wrote accounts of both expeditions. In 1978, on his way from Iraq to India, he burnt his reed boat, the *Tigris*, in protest against the war in the Horn of Africa.

Heysham. *See* Morecambe.

Heywood, Thomas (c. 1574–1641) English dramatist. An actor as well as a prolific and versatile writer, he wrote numerous comedies, chronicle plays, and scripts for pageants and masques. His best-known work is the domestic tragedy *A Woman Killed with Kindness* (1607).

Hezekiah King of Judah (c. 715–c. 686 BC), noted as a religious reformer. Allied with Egypt, he rebelled against *Sennacherib of Assyria, against Isaiah's advice, and was defeated and forced to pay huge indemnities.

Hiawatha The legendary chief of the Onondaga tribe of American Indians, who was said to have formed the *Iroquois League. His story is the subject of Longfellow's *Song of Hiawatha* (1855).

hibernation A state of *dormancy in winter experienced by many fish, amphibians, reptiles, and mammals of temperate and Arctic regions: it is an adaption to avoid death by heat loss, freezing, or food scarcity. True hibernation is seasonal and not simply a reaction to a drop in temperature. It occurs in a few mammals, including bats and hedgehogs, and some birds. Hibernation involves a period of sleep during which the body temperature drops almost to that of the surroundings, the body processes are slowed, and the hibernator lives on a reserve of body fat until it awakens in the spring.

Hibiscus A genus of tropical and subtropical herbs, shrubs, and trees (about 150 species). Several species are cultivated for their showy five-petalled flowers; two popular shrubs, up to 3 m high, are the Chinese *H. rosa-sinensis* (rose of China), which has red, pink, or yellow flowers with prominent stigmas, and the Syrian *H. syriacus* (rose of Sharon), which has pink, blue, or white hollyhock-like flowers. Both can be grown as pot plants. The genus also includes plants cultivated for their food value and for their fibre (*see* okra; roselle). Family: *Malvaceae*.

hiccup (*or* hiccough) A sudden involuntary intake of breath interrupted by closure of the glottis (in the larynx), producing a characteristic sound. Hiccups are commonly due to indigestion or eating too quickly, but they may be associated with kidney disease or alcoholism.

Hickok, James Butler (1837–76) US lawman, known as Wild Bill Hickok. He was celebrated for his skill and speed as a gunman. After army service in the Civil War and against the Indians he was appointed marshal in Kansas (1869–71). He was shot dead from behind while playing poker in a saloon.

hickory A tree of the genus *Carya* (20 species), native to E North America and Asia and cultivated for timber, nuts, and ornament. They grow to a height of about 30 m and have compound leaves consisting of paired leaflets. Commercially important species are the shagbark (*C. ovata*), which yields hard durable timber, and the pecan (*C. illinoensis*), which produces thin-shelled nuts resembling walnuts. Both species are North American. Family: *Juglandaceae*.

hide A unit of land measurement in Anglo-Saxon England based on the approximate area of land needed to support a peasant household. Tax assessments were often calculated on the basis of the number of hides comprising an estate. The size of the hide varied, ranging in different areas from 40 to 120 acres.

Hideyoshi (1536–98) Japanese military ruler, who brought feudal Japan under his dominance. Of humble birth, Hideyoshi became by sheer ability a leading commander of *Oda Nobunaga, aiding him to become master of central Japan. Succeeding to Oda's power in 1582, he achieved national hegemony by 1590 but then wasted his energy on an unsuccessful invasion of Korea.

hieroglyphics Originally, an Egyptian system of picture writing in use from about 3000 BC to 300 AD; the term now denotes any *pictographic or *ideographic writing system. The Egyptians used hieroglyphics largely for monumental inscriptions. The characters are careful reproductions of people, animals, and objects and may be interpreted as representing either the objects they portray or the sounds that are featured in the pronunciation of the referent. Hieroglyphic records are coextensive with hieratic, a more cursive stylized form appropriate to brush and ink and the smooth surfaces of papyrus and wood.

eye   to fly   old age

HIEROGLYPHICS *A picture was used to represent objects, related ideas, and sounds.*

hi-fi. *See* high-fidelity sound systems.

Higgins, Alex (1949–) Northern Irish snooker player, known as "Hurricane" Higgins. He won the world professional championship in 1972 and 1982.

high-fidelity sound systems (*or* hi-fi) Systems of recording and reproducing sound in which the quality of the reproduced sound is as close as possible to that of the original source. A typical reproducing system consists of a record player or *cassette player, a stereophonic amplifier, and two loudspeakers. To achieve high fidelity, total distortion in such a system must be less than 2%, the frequency response must be constant between 20 and 20 000 hertz, and the system must be able to reproduce stereophonic or quadraphonic recordings. While two frontal stereophonic speakers can reproduce the spatial pattern of the sound source, reproduction of the reverberation characteristics of the place at which the recording was made can be reproduced more fully by a quadraphonic system with two additional rear speakers. The term high fidelity is commonly applied to a wide range of domestic record- and tape-reproducing systems, many of which do not fulfil the requirements of true high fidelity. Stereophonic and quadraphonic radio broadcasts can also be used in many hi-fi systems.

Highgate A residential district mainly in the Greater London borough of Haringey. It derived its name from the tollgate erected by the Bishop of London in the 14th century. Highgate Cemetery contains the graves of several famous people, including Karl Marx, George Eliot, and Herbert Spencer. Highgate School for boys was founded in 1565. The Whittington Stone and nearby Whittington Hospital mark the point at which Dick *Whittington is popularly supposed to have turned back to London.

high jump A field event in athletics in which jumpers compete to clear a horizontal bar. A competitor is allowed three attempts at a height and is eliminated if he fails to clear it. The height is increased until there is only one jumper left. World records: men: 2.42 m (1987) by Patrik Sjöberg (Sweden); women: 2.09 m (1987) by Stefka Kostadinova (Bulgaria).

Highland dress The traditional male costume (since the 17th century) of the Scottish Highlands. It consists of the kilt (a wrapover skirt pleated at the back) and the plaid (a cloak worn over one shoulder). Accessories include the sporran (a goatskin pouch), cap, kilt pin, and dagger (worn in the right sock). This form of dress was probably preceded by "trews" (close-fitting trousers), often checkered, and then by the plaid, a long length of woollen cloth, half of which was pleated round the waist, the other half forming a cloak. Highland dress was banned for civilian wear (1746–82) following the Jacobite rebellions.

Tartan, the material used for the kilt and plaid, is a woollen cloth woven of differently coloured threads at regular intervals both in the weft and the warp; this gives a design of large-meshed cross stripes. The tradition of each clan having its own tartan probably dates from the 17th century.

Highland Games Scottish athletics meetings, usually professional, held in the Highlands. Events include standard track and field events as well as such Scottish sports as *caber tossing, and there are also competitions in highland dancing and playing the bagpipes. The modern games date from the early 19th century but they originated far earlier in clan assemblies. The most famous meeting, the Braemar Games, can be traced back to the 8th century AD.

Highland pony A breed of pony originating in the Highlands of Scotland. There are two varieties, both with a deep muscular frame, strong legs, and a profuse mane. The Western Isles variety is smaller and more finely built than the mainland variety, which is also known as the Garron. The Highland is usually black, brown, or grey and is now used for pony trekking as well as for pack work. Height: 1.27–1.47 m (12½–14½ hands).

Highland Region An administrative region in N Scotland, created in 1975 under local government reorganization from the N part of Argyll, Caithness, Inverness, Nairn, Ross and Cromarty, and Sutherland. The region consists chiefly of glaciated highlands divided from NE to SW by the fault valley, Great Glen, and includes part of the Inner Hebrides. Sheep farming is the main agricultural activity. Industries associated with North Sea oil are developing, especially on the coast, and aluminium smelting, pulp and paper production, and distilling are all important, although the manufacturing sector is underdeveloped by national standards. Tourism is a major source of revenue. Area: 25 425 sq km (9814 sq mi). Population (1981): 200 030. Administrative centre: Inverness.

high priest The chief official of the ancient Jerusalem *Temple. The office was hereditary in the family of Aaron. The Hasmonean rulers (*see* Maccabees) claimed the title themselves, and in the last century of the temple the high priests were appointed by political rulers. With the destruction of the temple (70 AD) the office ceased to exist.

Highsmith, Patricia (1921–) US author of crime fiction. Her novels are characterized by great suspense and tension, although she is less concerned with traditional formulae of detection than with psychological exploration of the characters involved. Her novels include *Strangers on a Train* (1950) and *Ripley's Game* (1974).

High Wycombe 51 38N 0 46W A town in SE England, in Buckinghamshire. It has a long tradition of furniture making and also produces paper, precision instruments, and clothing. Hughenden Manor was the home of Disraeli. At nearby **West Wycombe** are the Hell Fire caves (*see* Wilkes, John), excavated in the 18th century. Population (1981): 60 516.

Hilary of Poitiers, St (c. 315–c. 367 AD) French churchman; bishop and Doctor of the Church. A leading opponent of *Arianism, he was converted to Christianity from Neoplatonism and became Bishop of Poitiers in about 353. His works include *De trinitate* and *De synodis*. Feast day: 14 Jan.

Hilbert, David (1862–1943) German mathematician, who gave geometry a mathematically rigorous foundation. In a book entitled *Foundations of Geometry* (1899), he defined such concepts as the point, the line, and the parallel relationship, which *Euclid in his *Elements* had assumed to be intuitively obvious. Hilbert then developed geometry from a much more rigorous set of axioms than those of Euclid. He also studied the properties of infinite-dimensional space, known as Hilbert space, which is used in the mathematics of quantum theory.

Hildebrand. *See* Gregory VII, St.

Hildesheim 52 09N 9 58E A city in NE West Germany, in Lower Saxony. The romanesque 11th-century cathedral escaped the destruction of World War II. A notable collection of Roman silver plate was found nearby in 1868. Its manufactures include machinery, textiles, and carpets. Population (1980 est): 102 700.

Hill, Archibald Vivian (1886-1977) British physiologist, noted for his work on muscle contraction. Hill found that oxygen was needed not for the contraction of a muscle but for its recovery, which provided a clue to the underlying biochemistry involved. Hill shared the 1922 Nobel Prize with Otto *Meyerhoff.

Hill, David Octavius (1802-70) Scottish painter and photographer. He first collaborated with **Robert Adamson** (1821-48) in 1843, when Hill was commissioned to paint a portrait of the founders of the Free Church of Scotland. For greater accuracy Hill and Adamson, a chemist by training, photographed each clergyman, using the calotype method developed by *Talbot. Numerous portrait photographs and views of Edinburgh followed until Adamson's death, when Hill returned to landscape painting.

Hill, Graham (1929-75) British motor-racing driver, who was world champion in 1962 and 1968 and was runner-up from 1963 to 1965. Despite breaking both legs in an accident (1969) he continued to race. He was killed in a flying accident.

Hill, Octavia (1838-1912) British philanthropist and leader of the open-space movement, which resulted in the establishment of the *National Trust. With an inheritance left to her by John *Ruskin she financed housing projects in London.

Hill, Sir Rowland (1795-1879) British postal expert. In *Post Office Reform* (1837) he advocated a single postage rate within the British Isles that would be prepaid by purchase of an adhesive stamp (which he invented). His efforts achieved the introduction in 1840 of the penny postage stamp. He was secretary to the Post Office (1854–64).

Hillary, Sir Edmund (Percival) (1919–) New Zealand mountaineer and explorer. In 1953 he and *Tenzing Norgay were the first to reach the summit of Mount Everest, for which achievement he was knighted. In 1958–59 he participated in the Commonwealth Trans-Antarctic Expedition, preparing the way for the last part of *Fuchs' crossing of Antarctica. In 1984 he was appointed New Zealand High Commissioner in Delhi.

Hillel (1st century BC) Jewish teacher, lawyer, and biblical scholar. Many of his teachings subsequently became authoritative in rabbinic Judaism. His tolerant character and views are often contrasted with those of his contemporary Shammai.

Hillery, Patrick (John) (Gaelic name: Pádraig Óhírighile; 1923–) Irish statesman; president (1976–). In 1951 he entered the Dáil and in 1959 he assumed office as minister for education, becoming minister for industry in 1965, for labour in 1966, and for foreign affairs in 1969. From 1973 he was vice president of the EEC Commission.

Hilliard, Nicholas (1547-1619) English portrait miniaturist, born in Exeter. Like his father, he trained as a jeweller, later becoming court painter to Elizabeth I and James I. His high reputation among his contemporaries led many prominent Elizabethans to have their portraits done by him; many of these are in the royal collection at Windsor Castle. In his *Treatise on the Art of Limning* (c. 1600), he describes his style and technique of painting miniatures. The elegance and symbolism of his *Unknown Man Against a Background of Flames* (Victoria and Albert Museum, London) is typical of his best work.

Hillingdon A borough of W Greater London, created in 1965 from the former municipal borough of Uxbridge together with several urban districts, all in Middlesex. Population (1981): 229 183.

hill mynah A glossy black songbird, *Graculus religiosa*, native to India and the East Indies. 25-37 cm long, it has a yellow bill and yellow wattles on the neck and beneath the eyes. It is a popular cagebird with a remarkable ability to mimic human speech. Family: *Sturnidae* (starlings). *See also* mynah.

Hilton, James (1900-54) British novelist. His two most popular novels are *Lost Horizon* (1933), set in the Tibetan monastery of Shangri-La, and *Goodbye, Mr Chips* (1934).

From 1935 he worked as a scriptwriter in Hollywood, where he died.

Hilversum 52 14N 5 10E A town in the central Netherlands, in North Holland province. It is a summer resort and commuter town for Amsterdam and is the country's main radio and television broadcasting centre. Population (1981 est): 92 141.

Himachal Pradesh A state in NW India, in the W Himalayas beside Tibet's border. Long part of the *Punjab, it was formed by the combination of various hill states (1948). Most of the inhabitants are Pahari-speaking Hindus who farm grains, potatoes, maize, and livestock. The forests yield timber and bamboo. Himachal Pradesh has enormous hydroelectric potential. Area: 55 673 sq km (21 490 sq mi). Population (1981): 4 237 569. Capital: Simla.

Himalayas A vast mountain system, the highest in the world, structurally the southern edge of the great plateau of central Asia. They extend about 2400 km (1550 mi) along the N Indian border in a W–E arc, 200–400 km (125–250 mi) wide, reaching 8848 m (29 028 ft) at Mount *Everest. The region is the subject of dispute between China and India.

Himeji 34 50N 134 40E A city in Japan, in SW Honshu. It developed around its famous 16th-century castle, one of the few remaining castles in Japan. Its industries include textiles and steel. Population (1980): 446 000.

Himmler, Heinrich (1900–45) German Nazi politician, infamous for his direction of the *SS. He joined the Nazi Party in 1925 and became head of the SS in 1929. From 1936 he also directed the Gestapo and supervised the extermination of Jews in E Europe. After the Nazi collapse he was captured by the Allies and committed suicide.

NICHOLAS HILLIARD A Youth Leaning against a Tree with Roses (c. 1588), miniature painting in the Victoria and Albert Museum, London.

Hims. See Homs.

Hinckley 52 33N 1 21W A town in central England, in Leicestershire. It has an engineering industry and manufactures footwear, cardboard boxes, and hosiery. Population (1981): 55 273.

Hincmar of Reims (c. 806–82) French theologian, archbishop of Reims (845–82). He came into conflict with the emperor Lothair I and successive popes over the extent of his jurisdiction. He also engaged in controversy with the Benedictine monk Gottschalk (d. 868) over the doctrine of predestination.

Hindemith, Paul (1895–1963) German composer and viola player. From the age of 11 he supported himself by playing in dance halls and later studied in Frankfurt am Main, where he led the opera orchestra (1915–23). He also played the viola in the Amar Quartet. In 1927 he began teaching in Berlin. His music was banned by the Nazis in 1933; he moved to Turkey and in 1939 went to the USA. His early works were highly dissonant; he later evolved his own system of tonal harmony. Many of his compositions are neoclassical in character (see neoclassicism); they include the operas Cardillac (1926) and Mathis der Maler (1938), the ballet Nobilissima Visione (1938), many concertos, instrumental sonatas, and much Gebrauchsmusik (German: utility music).

Hindenburg, Paul von Beneckendorff und von (1847–1934) German general, who was recalled from retirement at the outbreak of World War I and with *Ludendorff won a great victory at *Tannenberg (1914). In 1916 Hindenburg became commander in chief and, again with Ludendorff, effectively controlled Germany. He directed the German retreat to the **Hindenburg line** (fortified defence on the Western Front). After Germany's defeat he again retired but became president in 1925. Re-elected in 1932, he was forced to appoint Hitler as chancellor early in 1933.

Hindi The national language of India and the most widely spoken, having approximately 134 million speakers. It is an *Indo-Aryan language, showing strong *Sanskrit influence in its written form but with a much simpler grammar. The standard form, written in Devanagari script, is based on the Khari Boli dialect of Delhi. This belongs to the western dialect division from which *Urdu also developed.

Hinduism The religious beliefs and institutions of about 400 million inhabitants of India and parts of neighbouring countries. Hinduism is not a religion with a formal creed, but the complex result of about 5000 years of continuous cultural development. It includes a number of extremely diverse traditional beliefs and practices and over the centuries it has influenced and been influenced by younger religions, including Buddhism, Jainism, Christianity, Islam, and Sikhism. One of its central concepts is that the necessary result of one's actions in life leads to *reincarnation at a higher or lower level of life (see karma), a belief that has given rise both to the system of *castes and to a deep respect for all forms of life (see ahimsa). The goal of the religion is to find a release from the cycle of rebirth and to return to the ultimate unchanging reality, *Brahman. Release may be sought through good works, devotion to a particular god, such as the popular deity *Krishna, or through various types of meditation and asceticism (see samadhi; yoga). The principle gods are Brahma, Vishnu, and Shiva, together known as the *Trimurti; the last two are especially venerated by the two major sects, the Vaishnavas and the Shaivas. These and all the innumerable lesser gods and spirits are seen by many Hindus as manifestations of one reality (Brahman). Popular devotion consists mainly of temple worship and the celebration of numerous festivals. Hinduism originated in early *animism and *totemism (before 2750 BC) and developed a sacrificial worship of a pantheon of nature gods, such as *Indra, during the period of the *Vedas (c. 1500-500 BC). *Brahmanism was the dominant form of Hinduism in the 6th century BC, when Buddhism and Jainism were established in reaction to it. The great Hindu texts, the *Mahabharata* and the *Ramayana*, were composed at this time. Vishnu and Shiva became the prominent deities in the medieval period (after 800 AD). New schools have continued to emerge in recent times, most of them concerned with universalizing Hindu thought. *See also* Arya samaj; Brahmo samaj; Ramakrishna; Vedanta; Vivekananda.

Hindu Kush A mountain range in central Asia, extending about 800 km (500 mi) W from the Pamirs to the Koh-i-Baba Mountains of central Afghanistan. Its highest peak is Tirich Mir, at 7692 m (25 236 ft).

Hindustani An *Indo-Aryan language that originated in the dialect of the Delhi district. The Moguls and the British promoted its use as a lingua franca throughout India. *Urdu and *Hindi are the literary forms developed from it.

Hines, Earl (Fatha) (1905-83) US Black jazz pianist and songwriter, who trained as a concert pianist but formed his own jazz band in 1928. He worked with Louis Armstrong from 1948-51 and was well known for his complex and virtuosic piano playing. He wrote the songs "The Earl" and "I Got It Bad."

Hinkler, Herbert John Lewis (1892-1933) Australian aviator. He went to England in 1912, served in the Royal Naval Air Service in World War I, and in 1928 made a solo flight to Australia in a record 15½ days. He died in a crash in the Apennines (Italy).

hinny The sterile offspring of a female ass and a male horse. Smaller than a *mule, hinnies are used as pack animals, especially in hot climates, but are less common than mules.

Hinshelwood, Sir Cyril Norman (1897-1967) British chemist, who became professor at Oxford University in 1937. He pioneered the investigation of reaction kinetics and discovered several chain reaction mechanisms. He shared the Nobel Prize with N. N. Semyonov (1896-) in 1956. He was knighted in 1948.

hip The part of the body where the legs are joined to the trunk (*see* Plate IV). The skeleton of the hip consists of the *pelvis and the part of the spine (the sacrum) to which it is attached. The hip joint—the articulation between the pelvis and femur (thigh bone)—is a common site for arthritis: in severe cases the whole joint may be replaced by an artificial one or pins or other devices may be inserted into the damaged parts.

Hipparchus (c. 190-c. 120 BC) Greek astronomer, born in Nicaea. He produced the first accurate map of over 1000 stars, indicating their positions by means of latitude and longitude. He also discovered the precession of the equinoxes and accurately measured the distance to the moon by parallax. In mathematics he invented trigonometry by constructing a table of the ratios of the sides of right-angle triangles.

Hipparion An extinct *horse that lived in the Pliocene epoch (about seven million years ago). It was slender and fast-running, about the size of a modern pony, and lived on open plains. Its foot had a distinct hoof, the remaining toes being small and not touching the ground. *See also* eohippus.

Hippeastrum A genus of herbaceous plants (60 species), native to tropical and subtropical America and cultivated as ornamental garden and pot plants. They have large bulbs (about 10 cm in diameter), broad straight-sided leaves, and a stout flower stem terminating in a cluster of white, pink, or red flowers, each 10 cm across. The genus includes the Barbados lily (*H. equestre*), with scarlet flowers. Family: *Amaryllidaceae*.

Hippocrates (c. 460-c. 377 BC) Greek physician and founder of the Hippocratic school of medicine, which greatly influenced medical science until the 18th century. Hippocrates seems to have been a prominent physician, who travelled widely in Greece and Asia Minor. His followers believed that health was governed by the balance of four body fluids, or humours: phlegm, blood, black bile, and yellow bile. The Hippocratic Collection of 60 or so medical works is ascribed to various authors and the Hippocratic Oath, taken by medical students, was probably not written by Hippocrates.

Hippolytus In Greek legend, the bastard son of *Theseus and Hippolyta, Queen of the Amazons. A devotee of *Artemis, his dedication to chastity led him to reject the advances of Theseus's wife *Phaedra, and he was destroyed by a bull from the sea sent by Poseidon.

hippopotamus A large hoofed mammal, *Hippopotamus amphibius*, of tropical Africa. About 150 cm high at the shoulder and weighing around 3.5 tonnes, hippos have virtually naked dark-brown skin and continuously growing tusks up to 60 cm long. They spend the day in rivers or waterholes, emerging at night to graze on surrounding pasture. Herds usually number 10-15 individuals. Hippos are highly territorial, marking the boundaries of their grazing ground with piles of dung. Family: *Hippopotamidae*. *See also* pygmy hippopotamus.

hire purchase The buying of goods on credit terms. The buyer pays a deposit, contracts to make periodic payments, and obtains possession of the goods on hire. The seller retains ownership until the full price plus interest and costs have been paid, and can repossess the goods if the buyer defaults on his payments; however, in England and Wales a court order has to be obtained if the buyer has paid more than one-third of the value of the goods. Government control of the minimum deposit and the maximum repayment period has frequently been used as an instrument of *monetary policy as a means of regulating consumer demand.

Hirohito (1901-) Emperor of Japan (1926-), having previously been regent for five years after his father Yoshihito (1879-1926) had been declared insane. He married (1924) Princess Nagako Kuai. Ruling as divine emperor until Japan's defeat in World War II, he became no more than a constitutional monarch under the 1946 constitution (introduced under US pressure). The author of several books on marine biology, he is believed to have played a reluctant role in Japan's prewar expansionist aspirations.

Hiroshige (Ando Tokitaro; 1797-1858) Japanese colour-print artist of the *ukiyo-e movement. Trained under another ukiyo-e master, Toyohiro (1774-1829), Hiroshige first specialized in prints of women. From about 1830 he turned to landscapes, which he often depicted in snow, rain, or moonlight. His best-known print series is *Fifty-Three Stages of the Tokaido Highway* (1833).

Hiroshima 34 23N 132 27E A city in Japan, in SW Honshu on the delta of the River Ota. A former military base and important seaport, it was largely destroyed (6 August, 1945) by the first atomic bomb to be used in warfare; over 130 000 people were killed or injured. Many leading architects helped design the rapid rebuilding of the city and it is now a major industrial centre. An international conference is held here annually to oppose nuclear weapons. Its university was established in 1949. Population (1983): 898 000.

Hispaniola The second largest West Indian island, in the Greater Antilles. It is politically divided between the *Dominican Republic and the Republic of *Haiti. Area: 18 703 sq km (29 418 sq mi).

histamine An amine, derived from the amino acid histidine, that is released from body tissues after injury or in an allergic reaction, such as asthma or hay fever. It dilates blood vessels, producing inflammation; contracts smooth muscle, which in the lungs leads to breathing difficulties; and stimulates the secretion of gastric juice. Its effects can be counteracted with *antihistamine drugs.

histology The study of *tissues. Originally histology was limited to the study of tissues by light microscopy, but the development of such techniques as electron microscopy, immunofluorescence, and autoradiography has enabled the details of subcellular structure to be revealed. *See also* cytology.

history The story of the past. The student of history discovers, examines, and interprets the records of past human societies. Records of events are found in the inscriptions of the ancient Egyptians but history as a literary activity is generally regarded as beginning with the ancient Greeks, among whom *Herodotus, *Thucydides, and *Xenophon were outstanding. The desire of ancient historians for accuracy was sometimes subordinated to their purely literary ambitions and the Romans (notably *Sallust, *Cicero, *Livy, and *Tacitus) were also concerned to glorify Rome. Early Christian history writing (historiography) was influenced by Jewish historians, such as *Josephus, and Christian preconceptions and subject matter continued to influence the writing of history throughout the middle ages. Medieval historiography consisted largely of chronicles, such as those of *Bede, Matthew *Paris, and Jean *Froissart. The later middle ages were influenced by Byzantine historians, including *Anna Comnena, and by such Arabs as *Ibn Khaldun and al-*Tabari. The classical interests of early Renaissance scholars (*see* humanism) led to a new concern for textual criticism, which led to the outstanding work of *Machiavelli and *Guicciardini in the early 16th century. Their critical approach to sources was continued by 17th-century historians but the 18th-century Enlightenment enlarged the interests of historians to include a more fundamental study of the pattern of change in human societies. This concern is reflected in the work of the 18th-century British historian Edward Gibbon, who tried to show that the history of mankind is one of continuous progress. In the 19th century, under the influence of the German school of historians, which included von *Ranke and *Mommsen, history was established as an academic discipline in the universities. Outstanding British historians of the 19th century included William Stubbs and F. W. Maitland (1850–1906) and the more literary—and more widely read—Macaulay and Carlyle. The scope of historiography has greatly widened in the 20th century under the influence of sociology, anthropology, and psychiatry, and new techniques, such as the use of computers to analyse statistics, have been introduced.

Hitachi 36 35N 140 40E A city in Japan, in E Honshu on the Pacific Ocean. Copper has been mined here since 1591 and the city is Japan's leading producer of electrical equipment. Population (1982 est): 205 763.

Hitchcock, Sir Alfred (1899–1980) British film director. He worked almost exclusively in Hollywood from 1940. He specialized in sophisticated thrillers, using calculated cinematic effects to create an atmosphere of tension and suspense. His technique was appreciated by and influenced directors of the *New Wave. His films include *Notorious* (1946), *Strangers on a Train* (1951), *Psycho* (1960), and *The Birds* (1963).

Hitler, Adolf (1889–1945) German dictator. Born in Austria, the son of a customs officer, his youth was spent in poverty in Vienna and Munich (he worked as a housepainter although he aspired to be an artist). He fought in World War I, rising to the rank of lance corporal and winning the Iron Cross. In 1919 he joined the German Workers' Party, renamed the National Socialist (abbreviated to *Nazi) Party in 1920. He became its president in 1921 and two years later staged an abortive coup—the Munich Putsch—against the Bavarian Government. During a brief imprisonment he wrote most of *Mein Kampf* (*My Struggle*), setting out his political philosophy, based on a notion of the innate superiority of the Aryan race, the culpability of the Jews for Germany's defeat in World War I, and a violent anticommunism. In the eco-

nomic crisis of the late 1920s and early 1930s Hitler's powers of oratory and his propaganda machine (headed by *Goebbels) brought the Nazis increasing support, especially from German industrialists, and in 1930 they won 107 Reichstag seats. In 1933, aided by von *Papen, Hitler was offered the chancellorship by *Hindenburg, the German president. The *Reichstag fire enabled him to discredit the opposition, gain a majority in the subsequent elections (in coalition with the Nationalists), and acquire the dictatorial powers he sought; following Hindenburg's death in 1934 he assumed the title of Führer (leader). He proceeded to crush his opponents, institute his fanatical persecution of the Jews by the establishment of *concentration camps, and launch a massive rearmament programme in preparation for the wars of conquest that he planned for the Third Reich. He lent his support to Mussolini in Italy and Franco in Spain, precipitating *World War II by invading Austria (1938) and then Czechoslovakia and Poland (1939). Military reverses in 1943 led to Stauffenberg's unsuccessful attempt (1944) to assassinate Hitler, but as the Third Reich collapsed in the face of Allied victory the Führer committed suicide with Eva *Braun (whom he had married shortly before) in the bunker of the chancellory in Berlin. How Hitler was able, unchecked for over a decade, to implement policies of an unparalleled atrociousness is a question that continues to plague mankind.

ALFRED HITCHCOCK

Hittites An *Indo-European people who appeared in Anatolia around the beginnning of the second millennium BC. By 1340 BC they had emerged as a major power, with their capital at *Hattusas (*or* Boğazköy) from which they conquered much of Anatolia and also Syria (*see* Carchemish). In their polytheistic religion, their king was believed to be the representative of god on earth and became a god himself on death. The society was feudal in organization and also upheld the institution of slavery. Their language is extinct, but is known from cuneiform tablets and inscriptions (*see* Indo-Hittite languages).

hives. *See* urticaria.

HMSO. *See* Stationery Office, Her Majesty's.

Hoad, Lewis Alan (1934–) Australian tennis player,

who was Wimbledon singles champion in 1956 and 1957 and doubles champion in 1953, 1955, and 1956 but then became a professional (1957).

Hoare-Laval Pact. *See* Laval, Pierre.

hoatzin A primitive bird, *Opisthocomus hoazin*, that occurs in tropical South American swamps. It is 65 cm long and has a small head with a wispy crest and a long tail. Its plumage is streaked brown with yellowish underparts and it feeds chiefly on flowers and fruit. It is the only member of its family (*Opisthocomidae*). Order: *Galliformes* (pheasants, turkeys, etc.).

Hobart 42 54S 147 18E A city in Australia, the capital and chief port of Tasmania on the Derwent River estuary. It has an excellent natural harbour with small tidal changes. Industries include zinc refining and food processing; the chief exports are apples, wool, timber, and dairy produce. The University of Tasmania was established here in 1890. Population (1983 est): 173 700.

Hobbema, Meindert (1638-1709) Dutch landscape painter, born in Amsterdam. He often sketched with *Ruisdael but, unlike him, Hobbema specialized in peaceful woodland and rural scenes with watermills. Through his marriage (1668) he gained a minor post in the local excise department but continued with his painting, producing in this period perhaps his best work, *The Avenue, Middelharnis* (1689; National Gallery, London).

Hobbes, Thomas (1588-1679) English political philosopher. Hobbes was a vigorous proponent of scientific *materialism, particularly with regard to human nature. His interests lay in mathematics, geography, and the classics until the breakdown of English political and social order in the 1640s inspired him to devise his own political theory. *Leviathan* (1651) argues that because people are inherently selfish they need to be ruled by an absolute sovereign, whose function is to enforce public order. Contemporary theories of natural rights, and the civil rights thought to derive from them, were anathema to him. His theories made him a loyalist both to the English monarchy and, during the Interregnum, to its parliamentary opponents.

Hobbs, Jack (Sir John Berry H.; 1882-1963) British cricketer. The world's greatest batsman between *Grace and *Bradman, he played for Surrey and for England in 61 Test matches. During his career (1905-34) he scored 61 237 runs and 197 centuries (98 made after the age of 40). He was the first cricketer to be knighted (1953).

hobby A *falcon, *Falco subbuteo*, occurring in open regions of Eurasia and NW Africa. It is 33 cm long and has a darkgrey back, whitish underparts streaked with black, and red "trousers." It feeds on large insects and small birds caught in flight.

Hochhuth, Rolf (1933-) Left-wing Swiss dramatist, who writes in German. His controversial documentary plays include *The Representative* (1962), criticizing the attitude of Pius XII to the Nazi persecution of the Jews, and *The Soldiers* (1966), accusing Winston *Churchill of complicity in the death of the Polish general Sikorski. His novel *German Love Story* (1980) analyses the extent of the involvement of the German people in Nazi atrocities.

Ho Chi Minh (Nguyen That Thanh; 1890-1969) Vietnamese statesman, who led Vietnam in its struggle for independence from the French. As a young man he lived in England (1915-17) and then in France (1917-23), where in 1920 he joined the French Communist Party. In 1924 he went to communist-controlled Canton, where he formed the Association of Young Vietnamese Revolutionaries (Thanh Nien), the forerunner of the Indochinese Communist Party (1930). Returning to Vietnam in 1941, following the French defeat by the Germans in World War II, he formed the *Viet Minh, which waged the long and ultimately victorious colonial war against the French (1945-54; *see* Indochina). According to the Geneva Accords, which Ho Chi Minh

attended, Vietnam was divided on either side of the 17th parallel into North Vietnam, of which Ho became president, and South Vietnam. In 1959 he extended support to the *Viet Cong guerrilla movement in the South (*see also* Vietnam War) with the aim of Vietnamese unification, which was achieved after his death.

Ho Chi Minh City (name until 1976: Saigon) 10 46N 106 43E A city in S Vietnam, on the River Saigon. The University of Saigon (now Ho Chi Minh City) was established in 1917. It is the major commercial and industrial centre of the S, with shipbuilding, metalworking, textile, and chemical industries. *History*: an ancient Khmer town, it was the capital of *Cochinchina and then of French Indochina (1887-1902). During the *Vietnam War, as the capital of South Vietnam, US presence brought an economic boom but left problems of prostitution, crime, and drug addiction. Population (1981): 3 500 000.

HOCKEY *The dimensions of the pitch.*

hockey An 11-a-side field game for men and women, the object of which is to score goals. It has been played in various forms for at least 4000 years. A team comprises a goalkeeper, two full-backs, three half-backs, and five forwards (left wing, inside left, centre, inside right, and right wing), each of which carries a curved stick for hitting the ball. Play is started at the beginning of the two 35-minute periods (and after each goal) with a bully-off in the centre of the field. In this brief ritual two opposing players cross their sticks and tap the ground three times. Play proceeds by dribbling the ball with the stick and passing it by hitting it along the ground or through the air. *See also* ice hockey.

Hockney, David (1937-) British painter, draughtsman, and printmaker, born in Bradford. After studying at the Royal College of Art (1959-62), he travelled widely in the USA, where he developed his realistic but witty style, his favourite subjects being figure studies and aquatic themes. The latter play a prominent part in a quasi-documentary film about him entitled *A Bigger Splash* (1974). He has also designed stage sets and illustrated books.

Hoddinott, Alun (1929-) Welsh composer. He became professor of music at University College of South Wales in 1967. His works include four symphonies, concertos for piano, organ, clarinet, oboe, and harp, and much chamber music.

Hodeida (*or* Hudaydah) 14 50N 42 58E A town in North Yemen, on the Red Sea coast. It is the country's principal port, exporting cotton and mocha coffee. Population (1980): 126 386.

Hodgkin, Alan Lloyd (1914–) British physiologist, who discovered the chemical changes associated with the propagation of a nerve impulse (*see* action potential) along a nerve fibre. He wrote *Conduction of the Nervous Impulse* (1964) and shared a Nobel Prize (1963) with A. F. Huxley (his colleague) and Sir John Eccles.

Hodgkin, Dorothy Mary Crowfoot (1910–) British biochemist, who determined the structure of several complex molecules by means of *X-ray diffraction. She helped to determine the structure of penicillin (in the 1940s) and of vitamin B_{12} (in the early 1950s). She was awarded the Nobel Prize in 1964.

Hodgkin, Thomas (1798-1866) British physician, who described the disease of the lymphatic system now known as **Hodgkin's disease** (*see* lymphoma). Hodgkin made a considerable contribution to the pathology of diseases.

Hofei. *See* Hefei.

Hoffman, Dustin (1937–) US film actor. He made his reputation in the films *The Graduate* (1967) and *Midnight Cowboy* (1969). In 1980 he was awarded an Oscar for his performance as a divorced man bringing up his son in *Kramer vs Kramer*. Other films include *Lenny* (1974) and *Tootsie* (1982).

Hofmann, Joseph Casimir (1876-1957) Polish-born pianist. A performer from the age of six, he was a pupil of Anton Rubinstein. He also composed under the name "Michael Dvorsky." He toured extensively and became a US citizen in 1926.

Hofmannsthal, Hugo von (1874-1929) Austrian poet and dramatist. In 1901, after studying law and philology, he devoted himself to writing. His influential essay "The Letter of Lord Chandos" (1902), expressing his loss of confidence in language, divides the lyrical aestheticism of his short early plays from the social concern of his later ones, such as *Der Turm* (1925). He was librettist for several Richard *Strauss operas, including *Der Rosenkavalier* (1911) and *Ariadne auf Naxos* (1912). He was a cofounder of the Salzburg Festival in 1920.

Hofmeister, Wilhelm Friedrich Benedict (1824-77) German botanist, who pioneered the science of comparative plant morphology. His major work established the relationship between the cryptogams (algae, mosses, ferns, etc.), the gymnosperms (e.g. conifers), and the angiosperms (flowering plants). Hofmeister also discovered that regular alternation between sexual and asexual generations occurs in mosses, ferns, and seed plants.

Hogan, Ben (William Benjamin H.; 1912–) US professional golfer, most of whose major successes, including winning the Masters Tournament in 1951 and 1953, came after a car accident that was expected to cripple him (1949).

Hogarth, William (1697-1764) British painter and engraver. He studied under a silverplate engraver and later under Sir James Thornhill (whose daughter he married), before establishing his reputation with the paintings and engravings of *A Harlot's Progress* (1731-32). He excelled in moralizing social satires in such narrative series as *A Rake's Progress, Industry and Idleness, Gin Lane*, and the paintings of *Marriage à la Mode* (Tate Gallery), works that led him to campaign for an Engraving Copyright Act (the so-called Hogarth's Act, 1734). As a portraitist the naturalism and vivacity of *Captain Coram* (Foundling Hospital, London) and *Hogarth's Servants* (National Gallery, London) were influential, although unpopular with his contemporaries. His artistic theories are expressed in his treatise *The Analysis of Beauty* (1753).

hogfish A beautifully coloured tropical marine fish belonging to a genus (*Bodianus*) of *wrasses. They change colour while growing and are very popular in aquaria.

Hogg, James (1770-1835) Scottish poet and writer. Originally a shepherd (hence his nickname "The Ettrick Shepherd"), he was self-educated and became famous as a writer of ballads and narrative poems under the patronage of Sir Walter Scott. His modern reputation rests chiefly on the novel *The Confessions of a Justified Sinner* (1824).

Hogg, Quintin. *See* Hailsham, Quintin McGarel Hogg, Baron.

Hoggar Mountains. *See* Ahaggar Mountains.

hogweed A biennial herb, *Heracleum sphondylium*, also called cow parsnip, native to Eurasia and N Africa and introduced to North America. Up to 2 m high, it has hollow ridged stems, divided leaves, and umbrella-like clusters of white or pinkish flowers. The giant hogweed (*H. mantegazzianum*) may reach a height of 3.5 m and is grown as an ornamental. Family: *Umbelliferae*.

WILLIAM HOGARTH   *Portrait attributed to J. A. Rouquet (National Portrait Gallery, London).*

Hohenlinden, Battle of (3 December, 1800) The battle in the Napoleonic Wars in which the French under Jean Victor *Moreau defeated the Austrians. It was fought 31 km (16 mi) E of Munich. The French victory brought the collapse of the second coalition against Napoleon. *See* Revolutionary and Napoleonic Wars.

Hohenlohe-Schillingsfürst, Chlodwig Karl Viktor, Fürst zu (1819-1901) German statesman; chancellor (1894-1900). He came to prominence during the 1860s as a vigorous supporter of Bismarck's policy of German unification. He served as ambassador to Paris (1874-78) and as governor of Alsace-Lorraine (1885-94) before becoming chancellor, when he attempted to exercise a moderating influence on William II. He was succeeded by his protégé Bernhard von Bülow.

Hohenstaufen A German dynasty, founded by Frederick,

Duke of Swabia (d. 1105), that ruled the Holy Roman Empire from 1138 to 1254. *Conrad III was the first Hohenstaufen emperor and of his successors the most important were *Frederick (I) Barbarossa and *Frederick II. Frequently in conflict with Italian city states and the papacy, the dynasty was destroyed by its defeat at Tagliacozzo by a papal alliance (1268).

Hohenzollern   A dynasty, originating in Swabia, that ruled *Brandenburg, then *Prussia, and later Germany. First prominent in the late 12th century, the Hohenzollerns became Electors of Brandenburg in the 15th century. During the next 300 years they acquired other territories, including Prussia, of which *Frederick I became king in 1701. From 1871 they ruled the German Empire until its collapse in 1918.

Hohhot (or Huhehot)   40 49N 111 37E A city in NE China, the capital of Inner Mongolia AR. An old frontier trading town, its industry was developed after 1949. The university was established in 1957. Population (1983): 747 000.

Hojo   Hereditary holders of the regency for the military overlordship (see shogun) of Japan between 1204 and 1333. Hojo Tokimasa (1138-1215) became the first regent in 1204 although he had held actual power from the death (1199) of his son-in-law, the first shogun *Minamoto Yoritomo. The Hojo regents were notable for their codification of feudal law, their encouragement of Zen Buddhism, and their repulse of the Mongols (1274, 1281). Their power was destroyed in 1333 by a combination of other feudal lords and the emperor *Daigo II.

Hokan languages   An American Indian language group spoken mainly in the NW of the USA and in California. Some Hokan languages are found in Mexico, including the most widely spoken, Tlapanecan and Tquistlatecan. The Yuman subdivision found in Colorado and California also has a comparatively large number of speakers. The Mohave language is a member of this subgroup.

Hokkaido (former name: Yezo)   The second largest and northernmost of the four main islands of Japan, separated from Honshu by the Tsugaru Strait and from the Soviet island of Sakhalin by La Perouse Strait. Mountainous, volcanic, and forested, with a relatively cool climate, it is popular for winter sports. It has a sizable aboriginal population and the N is largely uninhabited. Main industries are coalmining, agriculture, and fishing. History: the Japanese began to settle on the island in the 16th century but did not develop it seriously until after 1868. It became administratively autonomous in 1885. Area: 78 508 sq km (30 312 sq mi). Population (1984 est): 5 667 000. Capital: Sapporo.

Hokusai (Katsushika H.; 1760-1849)   Japanese painter and book illustrator, the most famous *ukiyo-e designer of colour prints. He began as a wood engraver, becoming in 1778 a pupil of the painter and printmaker Shunsho (1726-92). From the 1790s he illustrated historical novels, verse anthologies, etc., and designed greeting and announcement cards. His early prints were chiefly of women and actors but he is best known for his later landscapes, which deeply influenced the impressionists and postimpressionists. His most famous works include his Views of Mount Fuji (1835) and his collection of sketchbooks, the Hokusai Manga, published from 1814 onwards.

Holbein the Younger, Hans (c. 1497-1543)   German painter, born in Augsburg. In 1515 he settled in Basle, where he designed woodcuts of the Dance of Death. Through his friend Erasmus he obtained the patronage of Sir Thomas More in England (1526-28). Settling in England in 1532, he painted portraits of merchants before becoming court painter and designer to Henry VIII (1536). His portrait of Henry VIII in a wall painting (destroyed) for Whitehall Palace became the prototype for other paintings of the king. He was also commissioned to paint Henry's prospective wives,

Christina, Duchess of Milan (National Gallery, London) and Anne of Cleves (Louvre) and established a thriving portrait-painting business, e.g. The Ambassadors (National Gallery, London). Many of the preparatory drawings for his English portraits are in the Royal Collection, Windsor. Holbein died of the plague. His father **Hans Holbein the Elder** (c. 1465-1524) was also a painter, whose major work is the S Sebastian Altar (Alte Pinakothek, Munich).

Holberg, Ludvig, Baron (1684-1754)   Danish playwright, poet, and historian, the founder of modern Danish literature. Born in Norway, he was educated in Copenhagen and settled in Denmark after travelling throughout Europe. After publishing historical and legal works, he wrote a satirical poem, Peder Paars (1719), one of the earliest classics in modern Danish, and subsequently (1722-27) wrote over 30 comedies for the first Danish-language theatre, including Jeppe paa Bjerget, Erasmus Montanus, and Henrik og Pernille. Much of his later work is historical and philosophical with the exception of the comic satire Nicolai Klimii iter subterraneum (Journey of Niels Klim to the World Underground; 1741).

Hölderlin, (Johann Christian) Friedrich (1770-1843)   German poet. Trained as a Lutheran minister, he found Christianity incompatible with his enthusiasm for Greek mythology. While working as a private tutor, he fell in love with his employer's wife, who is portrayed in his novel Hyperion (1797-99). After her death in 1802 his life was dominated by his schizophrenia, from which he never recovered. His great lyrical talent was unrecognized until the 20th century, when a comprehensive edition of his poetry was published.

hole.   See semiconductors.

Holguín   20 54N 76 15W A city in E Cuba. It is an important commercial centre; the chief exports through its port Gilbara (to the NE) are sugar and tobacco. Population (1982 est): 189 604.

BILLIE HOLIDAY

Holiday, Billie (Eleanora Gough McKay; 1915-59)   US Black jazz singer, known as "Lady Day." She was discovered in Harlem by John Hammond and made her first recording in 1933. She subsequently sang with the bands of Count Basie and Artie Shaw. Addiction to heroin caused her death.

Holinshed, Raphael (d. 1580)   English chronicler. A translator in the printing office of Reginald Wolfe, Holinshed continued the compilation of their universal history after Wolfe's death (1573). Pared down to cover only the British Isles, the *Chronicle* was published in 1578. Lucid, patriotic, and uncritical, it inspired many Elizabethan dramatists, including Shakespeare.

holistic medicine An approach to therapy in which all the physical, mental, and social aspects of the patient's life are taken into account in understanding and curing his disease, as opposed to merely treating his symptoms. A basic tenet of—and often used as a synonym for—*alternative medicine, the principle is gaining acceptance among orthodox practitioners.

Holland The low-lying NW region of the Netherlands, now comprising the provinces of *North Holland and *South Holland. A county of the Holy Roman Empire from the 12th century, Holland came under Burgundy in the 15th century and then (1500) under the Habsburgs. Prominent in the 16th-century *Revolt of the Netherlands against Spanish Habsburg rule, Holland became the chief province of the independent United Provinces of the Netherlands. When the kingdom of the *Netherlands was established in 1814, its importance diminished. Nevertheless the whole country is still commonly called Holland.

Holland, Henry (1745–1806) British architect. Trained under Capability *Brown, Holland began his career by designing Brooks's Club in London (1776). His best work, Carlton House, London (1783), exemplified his style—an unoriginal but dignified neoclassicism.

Holland, Parts of. *See* Lincolnshire.

Holland, Sir Sidney (George) (1893–1961) New Zealand statesman; National Party prime minister (1949–57). His government was repressive in industrial disputes and unable to control inflation. His party was defeated shortly after his retirement in 1957.

Hollar, Wenceslaus (1607–77) Bohemian etcher, born in Prague. He worked in Germany and Antwerp before settling permanently in England (1652), where he produced book illustrations and views of London before the Great Fire.

Holles, Denzil, Baron (c. 1599–c. 1680) English politician. Prominent in the parliamentary opposition to Charles I, he was imprisoned (1628–30) for helping to hold the speaker in his chair to prevent the adjournment of parliament until the three resolutions of Sir John *Eliot had been passed. Holles fought in the Civil War but, a moderate, fled to France (1648) when the army gained the upper hand. He returned in 1653 and participated in the Restoration of Charles II, becoming a member of his Privy Council (1661).

Holliger, Heinz (1939–) Swiss oboist, conductor, and composer. He is a leading performer of modern music; Berio and Henze have written works for him.

holly A tree or shrub of the widely distributed genus *Ilex* (300 species). The evergreen English holly (*I. aquifolium*) grows to a height of 15 m and has spiny lustrous dark-green leaves and small white male and female flowers growing on separate trees: the female flowers develop into red berries. It is widely cultivated for hedging and used for Christmas decorations. Family: *Aquifoliaceae. See also* maté.

hollyhock A perennial herb, *Althaea rosea*, native to China but widely cultivated (garden hollyhocks are usually treated as biennials). Up to 3 m high, it bears tall spikes of large white, yellow, or red flowers. Family: *Malvaceae.*

holly oak. *See* holm oak.

Hollywood 26 01N 80 09W A NW suburb of Los Angeles, in California in the USA. Founded in the 1880s, it has been the centre of the US film industry since 1911.

Holmes, Oliver Wendell (1809–94) US essayist and poet. He became dean of the Medical School at Harvard and wrote several important medical works. He is best remembered for his occasional verse, especially "Old Ironsides" (1830) and "The Chambered Nautilus" (1858), and for his collections of conversational essays beginning with *The Autocrat of the Breakfast Table* (1857). His son **Oliver Wendell Holmes** (1841–1935) was a jurist, known as the Great Dissenter. He became a pro-

fessor at Harvard University in 1882 and served as a judge in the Supreme Court of Massachusetts from 1882 until 1902, when he was appointed to the US Supreme Court. He opposed legislative restriction of individual rights but dissented from the famous 14th Amendment to the constitution, which specifically restricted state interference with private citizens. His best-known work is *The Common Law* (1881).

holmium (Ho) A metallic lanthanide element, discovered in 1879 by P. T. Cleve (1840–1905) and named after his native city, Stockholm. Holmium occurs in rare-earth minerals, such as monazite ($CePO_4$). It forms an oxide (Ho_2O_3) and halides (HoX_3), but has few uses. At no 67; at wt 164.9304; mp 1474°C; bp 2695°C.

holm oak An evergreen *oak tree, *Quercus ilex*, also called holly oak, native to S Europe and cultivated for ornament and for its wood. Growing to a height of 30 m, it has a dense crown and the leaves of young trees resemble holly leaves.

holocaust The extermination of European *Jews by the Nazis (1939–45). Some six million Jews from many countries, approximately two-thirds of European Jewry, were killed in Auschwitz and other *concentration camps. The holocaust has raised serious theological problems and questions about the nature of European civilization.

Holocene epoch The present, or Recent, epoch in *geological time, including the last 10 000 years from the end of the Pleistocene. It is sometimes called the Postglacial, although some authorities consider it to be only an interglacial phase of the Pleistocene. At the beginning of the Holocene the general rise in sea level resulting from the melting of the ice isolated Britain from the rest of Europe.

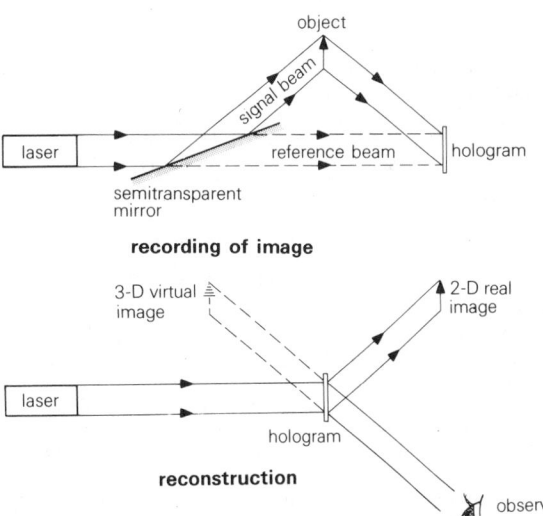

HOLOGRAPHY *A three-dimensional image formed by two beams of light is recorded as an interference pattern on a single plate. The two images, giving a 3-D effect, are reconstructed by shining two similar beams through the hologram.*

holography A method of producing a stereoscopic image without using a camera. A monochromatic beam of *coherent radiation from a laser is split into two using a semitransparent mirror; one beam falls directly onto a photographic film or plate and the other is reflected by the subject onto the film. The two beams form *interference patterns on the film, which is called a hologram. To reconstruct the image, light of the same wavelength from a laser is shone onto the hologram. The interference pattern on the hologram diffracts the beam and splits it into two parts. One part gives a real two-dimensional image and the other a virtual three-dimensional image. The theory of holography was suggested by Dennis *Gabor in 1947 but could not be put into practice until the laser was invented 16 years later.

Holst, Gustav (Theodore) (1874–1934) British composer and teacher. He studied composition with Charles Villiers Stanford (1852–1924) at the Royal College of Music, where he met his lifelong friend Vaughan Williams. He taught at the Royal College of Music, Morley College, and St Paul's Girls' School, for whose string orchestra he wrote the *St Paul's Suite* (1913). His interest in oriental philosophy inspired the chamber opera *Savitri* (1908) and other works. Among his most famous compositions are the choral work *The Hymn of Jesus* (1917), the tone poem *Egdon Heath* (1927), and the orchestral suite *The Planets* (1914–16).

Holt, Harold (Edward) (1908–67) Australian statesman; Liberal prime minister from 1966 until his death, apparently by drowning. His administration relaxed immigration and citizenship laws and supported involvement in the Vietnam War.

Holy Grail In medieval legend and romance, a vessel or dish having supernatural power. Originally the grail may have had some significance in pre-Christian Celtic mythology; but by the 12th century, in romances by *Chrétien de Troyes and Robert de Boron's *Joseph d'Arimathie*, it was associated with the chalice used by Christ at the Last Supper and later given to *Joseph of Arimathea, who received the blood of Christ in it at the crucifixion. Chrétien had combined the grail legend with the *Arthurian legend, and the knightly quest for the Holy Grail, undertaken by Percival, Galahad, and other Knights of the Round Table, is a dominant theme in many Arthurian romances. According to a passage in *William of Malmesbury, Joseph brought the Holy Grail to Glastonbury, where he also allegedly built the first church in England.

Holyhead 53 20N 4 38W A port and resort in North Wales in Anglesey, Gwynedd, on Holy Island. It has steamer services to Dun Laoghaire in the Republic of Ireland. Extensions to its fine harbour were completed in 1977. The major London–Holyhead road (A5) was built by Telford. Population (1981): 10 467.

Holy Island (*or* Lindisfarne) 55 41N 1 48W An island, in NE England off the NE coast of Northumberland. Its monastery was founded by St Aidan (635 AD); St Cuthbert was a bishop here (685–87).

Holy Lance The lance said to have pierced Christ's side at the crucifixion. This relic was discovered (1098) after a visionary revelation to a peasant, Peter Bartholomew, at the siege of Antioch during the first *Crusade. Accepted as genuine by most, but not all, of the Crusaders, its discovery raised morale and inspired the capture of Antioch from the Muslims.

Holy League Any of several alliances formed in the 15th, 16th, and 17th centuries usually for the furtherance of papal or Roman Catholic interests. The best known are those formed against the French invasion of Italy (1494) and against the Huguenots in the French *Wars of Religion (1576).

Holyoake, Sir Keith Jacka (1904–83) New Zealand statesman; National Party prime minister (1957; 1960–72). He entered parliament in 1932, became deputy leader of the National Party in 1947, and was deputy prime minister and minister for agriculture from 1949 until Sir Sidney Holland's resignation in 1957. He was governor general of New Zealand (1977–80).

Holy of Holies The central shrine of the Jewish *tabernacle (Exodus 25–31, 35–40) and later of the *Temple of Jerusalem. Originally it contained the Ark of the Covenant (the receptacle of the two tablets of the law) and other cultic objects. In the second Temple it was apparently empty. The

*high priest entered it once a year, on *Yom Kippur, to make atonement for the people.

holy orders In Christian Churches, specifically those accepting *episcopacy, the ranks of bishop, priest, etc., conferred by a bishop. They are traditionally divided into major and minor orders, the former being the ranks of bishop, priest, deacon, and (in the Roman Church) subdeacon. In the Roman Catholic Church, there are four minor orders: porters (or doorkeepers), lectors (or readers), exorcists, and acolytes. Holy orders are considered a *sacrament by the Orthodox and Roman Catholic Churches; they are also held to impose an "indelible character" on the recipient, so that they remain valid after the most serious sin and can be conferred only once.

Holy Roman Empire The successor to the western *Roman Empire of antiquity. The name itself was not employed until the mid-13th century but the institution dates from 800, when *Charlemagne was crowned emperor of the West by Pope Leo III. Its territory came to comprise much of W and central Europe, being centred on Germany and Austria and including areas of E France and N Italy. After the failure of Charlemagne's *Carolingian dynasty the imperial title, which was nominally elective (*see* electors), passed (962) to the German kings, who retained it until the Empire's abolition in 1806; from the 13th century the emperors were almost always *Habsburgs. Between the 11th and 13th centuries the emperors (especially those of the *Hohenstaufen dynasty) vied with the popes for dominance in Europe (*see* investiture controversy; Guelfs and Ghibellines), a conflict from which the Empire emerged much weakened. It was further undermined by the Protestant *Reformation in the 16th century, the *Thirty Years' War in the 17th century, and the rise of Prussia and was finally broken by Napoleon's conquest of imperial territories in the early 19th century.

Holyrood House A palace in Edinburgh, which is the Scottish residence of the British monarch. A medieval building, it was substantially modified in the classical style from 1671 onwards by Sir William Bruce (d. 1710).

Holy Spirit (*or* Holy Ghost) In Christian theology, the third person of the Trinity, coequal and of one substance with the Father and the Son. Old Testament references to the spirit of God are given a more specific application in the New Testament Gospels; in St John's Gospel the Holy Spirit is seen as the "Paraclete" or Comforter, sent to inspire Christ's followers after the *Ascension. In Acts, the descent of the Holy Spirit upon the Apostles is described, an event commemorated at the Feast of Pentecost (the 50th day after Easter). In art, the Holy Spirit is usually symbolized by a dove.

Home, Daniel Douglas (1833–86) British spiritualist and medium. In 1868 he astonished a distinguished group of witnesses by appearing to float out of one third-storey window and into another, but their testimony is not now regarded as proof of his paranormal faculties.

Home Counties The counties in England nearest to London, consisting of Buckinghamshire, Essex, Hertfordshire, Kent, Berkshire, and Surrey; Middlesex was formerly included.

Home Guard A World War II British defence force of unpaid volunteers between the ages of 17 and 65, first recruited in 1940 as the Local Defence Volunteers (LDV). Originally formed to provide a local defence force in case of invasion, its responsibilities included guard duties, patrolling key areas, and manning anti-aircraft guns and searchlights. It was disbanded at the end of World War II but was raised again between 1951 and 1957. At its highest, its strength reached 1.75 million.

Home Office The government department, headed by the home secretary, that is responsible for domestic affairs in England and Wales. It was formed in 1782, when the secretary of state for the southern department became the secretary of state for home affairs (*compare* Foreign and Commonwealth Office). The Home Office's responsibilities include immigration and race relations, broadcasting regulation, prisons, and some aspects of police administration.

Home of the Hirsel, Alec Douglas-Home, Baron (Alexander Frederick D.-H.; 1903-) British statesman; Conservative prime minister (1963-64). He was an MP (1931-45, 1950-51) before becoming the 14th Earl of Home. He was foreign secretary (1960-63) and then, to widespread surprise, succeeded Macmillan as prime minister, renouncing his peerages. Following the Conservative electoral defeat (1964) he resigned the party leadership (1965). He received a life peerage in 1974.

homeomorphism In mathematics, a one-to-one correspondence. In *set theory it is a property of two sets in which every member of one set is capable of being paired with one member of the other set and vice versa. In *topology, two shapes are homeomorphic if one can be transformed into the other by a continuous deformation, without being cut; for example, the surfaces of a sphere and a cube are homeomorphic.

homeopathy The system of treating illness developed by Samuel *Hahnemann at the end of the 18th century and based on the principle of "like cures like." To treat a particular disease homeopathists prescribe small doses of a drug that in larger quantities would cause the symptoms of the disease in a healthy person.

homeostasis The self-regulating process by which living organisms tend to maintain their bodies in a constant physiological state regardless of environmental extremes. The extent to which this independence is achieved by a particular group is a measure of its success: protozoans, for instance, are affected by many external factors, whereas man is relatively independent. In man, reflex activity of the nervous system and the action of hormones are important means of achieving homeostatic control. Claude *Bernard was one of the first to recognize the importance of this kind of regulation.

Homer (8th century BC) Greek epic poet, presumed author of the *Iliad* and *Odyssey*. He is believed to have lived in Ionia in Asia Minor and according to legend was blind. Working within a primitive oral tradition, his achievement lay in ordering a wealth of traditional material into a monumental and unified poetic structure. The *Iliad* concerns the Trojan War, and its basic tragic theme is enlivened by the variety and human sympathy of its individual episodes. The *Odyssey* relates the various adventures of *Odysseus during his voyage home from the Trojan War to his kingdom of Ithaca. Both poems were revered by the ancient Greeks for their moral as well as their literary value and have had a profound influence on western culture.

Homer, Winslow (1836-1910) US painter of everyday life, landscapes, and seascapes. In his native Boston he trained under a lithographer. In New York he worked as an illustrator and as an artist-correspondent of the Civil War, achieving prominence with his painting *Prisoners from the Front* (1866; Metropolitan Museum). After a visit to England (1881-83), he settled in the Maine fishing village of Prouts Neck, where he painted a number of watercolours of fishermen and the sea, often in dramatic conflict, as in *The Gulf Stream* (1899; Metropolitan Museum).

Home Rule An Irish political movement to repeal the Act of *Union with Britain and give Ireland a legislature responsible for domestic affairs. Founded by Isaac Butt (1813-79) in 1870, the Home Rule movement achieved parliamentary prominence under the leadership of *Parnell from 1880. *Gladstone's conversion to Home Rule produced the Home Rule bills of 1886 and 1893 but both were defeated. In 1914 the third Home Rule bill was passed but suspended for the

duration of the war. A modified act was passed in 1920 providing separate parliaments for northern and southern Ireland. This was accepted by the north but rejected by the south, which in 1922 gained dominion status as the Irish Free State.

homing instinct. *See* migration, animal.

hominid A member of the *Hominidae* family of primates, to which man belongs. Besides man, there are no surviving hominids: the others are known only from fossil remains. The *Hominidae* include the genera *Ramapithecus, *Australopithecus,* and **Homo.* The hominids appeared between five and one million years ago in Africa and Asia. The first to appear in Europe date from between 600 000 and 800 000 years ago.

Homo A genus of *hominids characterized by a large cranial capacity, erect posture, bipedal gait, a thumb capable of a precision grip, and the ability to make and use tools. The genus includes the species *Homo erectus* (*see* Pithecanthropus), which may have been ancestral to modern man. This species, which first appeared more than one million years ago during the middle *Pleistocene, includes specimens from Java, Peking, Heidelberg, and elsewhere. *Neanderthal man also belongs to the genus *Homo,* as does *Cro-Magnon man, who was probably an early form of the species *Homo sapiens* (modern man). *See also* Australopithecus. □ p. 584.

homoiothermy The condition of being warm-blooded, i.e. of maintaining a fairly constant body temperature by physiological mechanisms. Birds and mammals are warm-blooded: in cold climates body heat is conserved and also produced by muscle activity, such as shivering, while in hot weather body heat is lost by sweating and panting. *Compare* poikilothermy.

homosexuality Sexual attraction or relations between persons of the same sex. It is known as lesbianism when the persons involved are females. Homosexuality is an ancient and widespread phenomenon that can involve moral stigma and even punishment, as in the Judaeo-Christian tradition, but just as often is regarded as neither abnormal nor immoral, as in ancient Greece. Related phenomena are bisexuality (when an individual is attracted by people of both sexes) and transsexuality (*see* transvestism). Many European countries have in recent years liberalized their laws concerning homosexuality (*see* Wolfenden, John). Contemporary movements, such as Gay Liberation, seek to alleviate any residual social problems that may persist for homosexuals in a predominantly heterosexual society.

Homs (Arabic name: Hims) 34 44N 36 43E A town in Syria, on the River Orontes close to the border with N Lebanon. There is a large Crusader fortress here, and Homs is an important trading and industrial town. Population (1982 est): 354 508.

Honan. *See* Henan.

Honduras, Republic of A country in Central America, with a N coastline on the Caribbean Sea and a short S one on the Pacific Ocean. Narrow coastal plains rise to mountainous country, dissected by river valleys. The majority of the population is of mixed Indian and Spanish descent. *Economy*: mainly agricultural, the chief crops are bananas and coffee (the principal exports). Almost half-the land is forested, with valuable hardwoods in the NE and pine in the interior. Fishing is important, especially shrimps for export. The considerable mineral resources, some as yet unexploited, include gold, silver, lead, tin and zinc, and mercury. Hydroelectricity is being developed. *History*: the area was a centre of Mayan culture from the 4th to the 9th centuries AD and was later occupied by the Lenca Indians. Discovered by Columbus in 1502, it became part of the Spanish captaincy general of Guatemala. It gained independence from Spain in 1821 and then formed part of the Central American Federation (1823-38). Honduras has suffered much internal unrest as well as a long conflict with Guatemala and, more

thousands of years ago

8000 5000 4000 2000 500 100 50 10

HYLOBATIDAE
GIBBONS
ORANGUTANS
CHIMPANZEES
GORILLAS
PONGIDAE

Propliopithecus (Egypt)

Proconsul (Kenya)

Ramapithecus (India)

skull 1470 (Lake Turkana)

Homo habilis

HOMO ERECTUS (PITHECANTHROPUS)

Peking man (Choukoutien)

Java man (Trinil)

A. afarensis ('Lucy') (Ethiopia)
A. africanus
A. robustus (Lake Turkana)

AUSTRALOPITHECUS

Heidelberg man

Vertesszöllös

Swanscombe

Steinheim

HOMO NEANDERTHALENSIS

HOMO SAPIENS

Cro-Magnon (Les Eyzies)

MODERN MEN

Boskop

Omo

Broken Hill

Le Moustier

Saldanha

Gibraltar

Mt Carmel

Neanderthal

HOMINIDAE

evolution of Homo sapiens *The picture of man's evolution is constantly changing as new fossil evidence comes to light. The fossil* Propliopithecus *represents the apparent divergence of the gibbons (Hylobatidae), great apes (Pongidae), and humans (Hominidae) from the monkeys, but palaeontologists are still debating many of the other classifications and relationships shown on this chart.*

sites of important discoveries of fossil Hominidae

recently, with El Salvador: in 1969 war broke out following El Salvador's defeat of Honduras in a World Cup football match. In 1972 a former (1966–71) president, Gen Oswaldo López (1921–   ), seized power in a bloodless coup but was overthrown in 1975. There was a further coup in 1978 but military rule did not end until 1982, when Dr Roberto Suazo Córdova took office as president. In the 1985 elections he was succeeded by José Azcona Hoya. Honduras is a member of the OAS and the Organization of Central American States. Official language: Spanish. Official currency: lempira of 100 centavos. Area: 112 088 sq km (43 227 sq mi). Population (1980 est): 3 691 027. Capital: Tegucigalpa. Main ports: Amapala on the Pacific and La Ceiba on the Atlantic.

Honecker, Erich (1912–   ) East German statesman; first secretary of the Socialist Unity Party (1971–   ). After his release from Nazi imprisonment', Honecker led a German youth group (1946–1955). From 1958 to 1971 he was responsible for security matters.

Honegger, Arthur (1892–1955) French composer, born in Switzerland. He was a pupil of Widor and d'Indy and one of Les *Six. He developed his own polyphonic and dissonant style. His compositions include five symphonies, the stage works *King David* (1921) and *Joan of Arc at the Stake* (1934–35), an orchestral depiction of a large steam locomotive entitled *Pacific 231* (1923), chamber music, and piano music.

honesty A herbaceous plant of the European genus *Lunaria* (3 species). Up to 1 m high, it is often grown in gardens for its decorative disc-shaped papery seed heads. *L. annua* has white to purple flowers while *L. variegata* has crimson flowers and variegated foliage. Family: *Cruciferae*.

honey A sweet thick yellow syrup collected from the honeycomb of bee hives. Bees suck nectar from flowers and empty it into the cells of their hives, where they convert the sugar it contains from sucrose into dextrose and laevulose. Honey from heather is golden and that from white clover is greenish-white. It is commercially extracted by heating the honeycomb. Honey consists of about 70% sugars, 18% water, and small amounts of minerals, pollen, and wax. Honey was used for embalming in ancient Egypt and was a favourite food of the ancient Greeks. Mildly antiseptic on account of its acidity, it has also been used medicinally.

honey ant An *ant belonging to subfamilies (*Camponotinae* or *Dolichoderinae*) occurring in North America, Africa, Australia, and New Guinea. Certain members of the colony, called repletes, gorge themselves with honeydew (mainly from aphids and scale insects) gathered by other workers. They then hang from the ceiling of their underground chamber and regurgitate this food store when stimulated by the other ants.

honey badger. *See* ratel.

honeybee A social *bee, *Apis mellifera*, also called hive bee. Native to SE Asia, it is reared worldwide for its *honey and *beeswax. Honeybees have large colonies with 50 000–80 000 workers during the summer and a well-defined caste system. Workers attend to nest building, food gathering, and brood care; they use dances to communicate the location of food sources to other colony members. The queen lays her eggs in wax chambers (cells). Developing drones and workers are fed on protein-rich "royal jelly" for a few days and then changed to a diet of pollen and honey. Larvae hatching from fertilized eggs and fed on royal jelly throughout their development become queens, rather than workers. New colonies are formed by a swarm of workers led by the old queen (*compare* bumblebee); a young queen continues the established colony. Family: *Apidae*.

honeycreeper A songbird belonging to a family (*Drepanididae*; 22 species) restricted to the Hawaiian Islands, where they appear to have evolved from a single species. Honeycreepers are of two types: nectar feeders with colourful plumage and long slender curved bills and drab-green

seed eaters with short bills. Some honeycreepers face extinction due to man's destruction of their specialized habitats.

honeyeater An arboreal songbird belonging to a family (*Meliphagidae*; 160 species) occurring chiefly in SE Asia and Australasia. They are 10 to 35 cm long and have a drab plumage with wattles or naked patches on the face. The slender bill is down-curved and the long extensible tongue has a central trough, through which nectar is drunk, and a brushlike tip for collecting pollen and small insects.

honey fungus A fungus, *Armillaria mellea*, also called bootlace fungus, that forms clusters of toadstools on or near old trees or stumps, to which it is attached by thick black rootlike structures resembling bootlaces. These may be found beneath the bark of an infected tree. The toadstool is 3–10 cm in diameter and may be yellowish, green, brown, grey, or pink. Honey fungus is a serious pest of trees. Family: *Tricholomataceae*; class: *Basidiomycetes*.

honey guide An arboreal bird belonging to a tropical Old World family (*Indicatoridae*; 12 species). Honey guides are 11.5–20 cm long and dull-brown, grey, or greenish in colour. They feed mainly on bees and wasps and certain species are known to guide honey badgers or men to bees' nests by chattering and flying in the direction of the nest; the mammal robs the nest and the bird feeds on the remains. Order: *Piciformes* (woodpeckers, etc.).

honey locust A tree of the genus *Gleditschia* (11 species), occurring in warm parts of America, Africa, and Asia. The American species *G. triacanthos* is planted for ornament in Europe. It has stout thorns, compound leaves with paired leaflets, and small green flowers producing long pods. Family: *Leguminosae*.

honey mouse A small marsupial, *Tarsipes spenserae*, of SW Australia, also called honey possum or phalanger. It has a grey-brown body (70–85 mm long) with three dark stripes along the back; a long snout; and a very long prehensile tail (88–100 mm). It climbs shrubs to extract nectar from the flowers, using its long bristly tongue. Family: *Phalangeridae*.

honeysuckle A shrub or twining plant of the genus *Lonicera* (100 species). The common European honeysuckle (*L. periclymenum*), also called woodbine, is a trailing shrub with clusters of tubular yellowish flowers. Some species are cultivated as ornamentals, including the fragrant climbing honeysuckle (*L. japonica*). Family: *Caprifoliaceae*.

Hong Kong A British crown colony lying off the S coast of China. It consists of the island of Hong Kong, the mainland peninsula of Jiulong, the New Territories, and Stonecutters Island. Much of the land is steep and barren. The majority of the population is Chinese. *Economy*: owing to its strategic position and fine natural harbour, it is an important entrepôt port and banking centre. Much of China's foreign trade passes through Hong Kong. The export of manufactured goods has become increasingly important following the rapid industrial expansion since World War II and the textile and clothing industry (developed by immigrants from Shanghai) accounts for over half the total domestic exports. Electronics and plastics are also important and there is some heavy industry, such as ship building and repair and iron and steel manufacture. There is a certain amount of cultivation, although agricultural land is scarce and the reclamation of land from the sea has long been important in the colony's history. Tourism is also a major source of revenue. *History*: the island was ceded to Britain by China at the end of the first Opium War (1842) and Kowloon was added in 1860. In 1898 the New Territories were granted on a 99-year lease. Hong Kong was occupied by the Japanese during World War II. The return of the colony to Chinese control in 1997 was agreed between Britain and China in 1984. Official language: English; Cantonese is widely spoken. Official currency: Hong Kong dollar of 100 cents. Area: 1031 sq km (398 sq mi). Population (1987): 5 500 000. Capital and main port: Victoria.

Hong-wu (or Hung-wu; 1328-98) The title of Chu Yuan-zhang (or Chu Yüan-chang), who became the first emperor (1368-98) of the Ming dynasty. A monk, he became a rebel leader and outstanding military tactician, ousting the Yuan dynasty and declaring himself emperor. He made Nanjing his capital and by 1382 he had united China.

Hong Xiu Quan (or Hung Hsiu-ch'uan; 1814-64) Chinese religious leader and revolutionary. After failing to get a place in the civil service, he espoused a strongly political Protestant Christianity, declaring himself God's second son and saviour of China. He led the *Taiping Rebellion, but eventually ceased to take part in politics and committed suicide in Nanjing shortly before it fell.

Honolulu 21 19N 157 50W A city in the USA, the capital of Hawaii on SE Oahu in the central Pacific Ocean. Famed for its beauty, it is the economic centre of the islands and a transpacific route stop. It is the site of three universities and of Iolani Palace, the former royal residence. *Pearl Harbor is still an important naval base. Population (1980): 681 004.

Honorius II (Lamberto Scannabecchi; d. 1130) Pope (1124-30). An architect of the Concordat of Worms, which ended the *investiture controversy (1122), he re-established relations between the papacy and Empire, supporting the claims of Lothair II against Conrad III. Fearing the growing strength of the Normans under Roger II in Sicily, he led an army against him and was defeated and forced to accept Roger as Duke of Apulia.

Honshu The largest of the four main islands of Japan, situated between the Pacific Ocean and the Sea of Japan. It is mountainous, volcanic, and prone to earthquakes, with a great difference in climate between the subtropical S and the cooler N. The historic centre of Japan, it has been the site of its capital since earliest times. Most of Japan's major ports and cities are here, although agriculture is also very important; rice, fruit, cotton, and tea are grown. Mineral wealth includes oil, zinc, and copper. The traditional industry is silk but the many modern industries include shipbuilding, iron and steel, chemicals, and textiles. Area: 230 448 sq km (88 976 sq mi). Population (1970): 82 559 580. Chief town: Tokyo.

Honthorst, Gerrit von (1590-1656) Dutch painter. Working in Rome (c. 1610-1620), Utrecht, London (1628), and The Hague, he painted biblical, mythological, and everyday scenes, which were influenced by *Caravaggio in their use of candlelight. His portraits include one of Charles I and Henrietta Maria (Hampton Court).

Hooch, Pieter de (1629-c. 1684) Dutch painter, born in Rotterdam. Working in Delft, Leiden, and Amsterdam, he excelled in small paintings, such as The Pantry (Rijks-museum, Amsterdam), depicting household tasks in courtyards or dark interiors that open into sunlit rooms.

Hood, Samuel, 1st Viscount (1724-1816) British admiral, who achieved eminence in the American Revolution, when he defeated the French off Dominica (1782). In the French Revolutionary Wars he captured Toulon (1793) and destroyed the defences of Corsica (1794).

Hood, Thomas (1799-1845) British poet. He became a friend of *Hazlitt and *Lamb through his work for various periodicals. He followed his successful Odes and Addresses (1825) with further volumes of humorous verse, and also wrote serious poems of social and political protest, such as The Song of the Shirt (1843).

hooded crow A crow, Corvus corone cornix, identical to the *carrion crow except for its grey back and underparts. It is found in N and E Europe, where the carrion crow does not occur, but in the narrow zone where the two races overlap they hybridize, producing birds of mixed coloration.

hooded seal A *seal, Cystophora cristata, of deep Arctic waters, also called bladdernose, or crested seal. About 3 m

long, pale grey with dark blotches, hooded seals have a red inflatable bladder on top of the nose. In males the inflated bladder may be used to frighten enemies. Hooded seals are solitary except when breeding. Family: Phocidae.

Hooft, Pieter Corneliszoon (1581-1647) Dutch poet and historian, who travelled in France and Italy, where he was influenced by Renaissance art and literature. He gathered a circle of writers, artists, and musicians at the castle at Muiden, of which he was made steward in 1609. Hooft expressed his humanistic and pacifist philosophy in the pastoral play Granida (1605), while his love poetry echoed that of Petrarch. His history of the Dutch revolt against Spain, Nederlandsche Historien (1628-47), remained a model of Dutch prose for over 200 years.

Hooghly, River (R. Hoogli or R. Hugli) A river in India, rising in West Bengal. The W stream of the Ganges delta, it flows S through Calcutta to the Bay of Bengal. Length: 233 km (145 mi).

Hooke, Robert (1635-1703) British physicist and instrument maker, who became professor of geometry at Gresham College, London, in 1665. In 1660 he discovered *Hooke's law. His work on springs led him into horology and he claimed to have invented the hair spring (also claimed by *Huygens). He was one of the first scientists to examine vegetable matter with a microscope, in 1667 discovering the existence of cells in cork. Many of his microscope studies were published in Micrographia (1665). Appointed a city surveyor after the Fire of London, he designed several buildings, including the College of Physicians.

Hooker, Richard (c. 1554-1600) English churchman and theologian. Educated at Oxford, becoming a Fellow of Corpus Christi College, and later a parish priest, Hooker emerged as the chief apologist of his day of Anglican doctrine. His most famous work, On the Laws of Ecclesiastical Polity (from 1594), strongly influenced Anglican theology and the theory of both church and state government.

Hooker, Sir William Jackson (1785-1865) British botanist and first director of Kew Gardens. Under his directorship (1841-65) Kew became a world centre for the study of plants. His son **Sir Joseph Dalton Hooker** (1817-1911) achieved equal distinction as a botanist. He travelled widely, making important contributions to plant geography and providing supporting evidence for Darwin's theories of evolution. His many works include a world flora, Genera plantara (3 vols, 1862-83), written with George Bentham (1800-84). Hooker succeeded his father as director of Kew Gardens (1865-85) and was president of the Royal Society (1872-77).

Hooke's law For an elastic body, the *stress is directly proportional to the *strain. For example, if a heavy mass is hung from a wire, the fractional extension is directly proportional to the mass. The law applies only up to the elastic limit (see elasticity). Named after its discoverer Sir Robert *Hooke, who stated it in the form ut tensio, sic vis.

Hook of Holland (Dutch name: Hoek van Holland) 51 59N 4 07E A port in the SW Netherlands, in South Holland province at the North Sea end of the Nieuwe Waterweg (New Waterway). A ferry service operates from here to Harwich, England.

hookworm A parasitic *nematode worm inhabiting the intestine of animals and man. About 1 cm long, hookworms attach themselves to the gut lining and feed by sucking blood and body fluids. The two main species infecting man are Necator americanus, of the southern USA and Africa, and the Eurasian Ancylostoma duodenale. Both cause lowered resistance to disease, anaemia, and malnutrition. The larvae enter the body through the skin, usually the feet, and migrate to the intestine. Infection can be prevented by wearing shoes and improving sanitation.

hoopoe A bird, Upupa epops, of S Eurasia and Africa. 28

587

cm long,' it has a pink-brown plumage with black and white barred wings, a long tail, and a long black-tipped crest. It feeds on insects and larvae with its long downcurved bill. It is the only member of its family (*Upupidae*). Order: *Coraciformes* (hornbills, kingfishers, etc.).

Hoover, Herbert (Clark) (1874-1964) US statesman; Republican president (1929-33). As secretary of commerce (1921-29) he was chairman of commissions that initiated construction of the Hoover Dam (named after him) and the St Lawrence Seaway. Although chief of Allied World War I programmes for relief of famine, Hoover's belief in individual freedom led him to reject federal relief for urban unemployment during the Depression and he was defeated in the 1932 election by F. D. Roosevelt.

Hoover, J(ohn) Edgar (1895-1972) US lawyer, director of the Federal Bureau of Investigation (FBI) from 1924 to 1972. He fought the gangsters of the 1930s with his reformed FBI and established the first fingerprint file and crime-detection laboratory.

ROBERT HOOKE *The microscope he used (1664).*

hop A perennial climbing herb, *Humulus lupus*. Native to Eurasia, where it grows to a length of 3-6 m in hedges and thickets, it is widely cultivated for its pale yellow-green female flowers ("cones"), which are used in brewing to flavour beer. The male flowers are smaller. The young shoots have been eaten as a vegetable. Family: *Cannabiaceae*.

Hope, Anthony (Sir Anthony Hope Hawkins; 1863-1933) British novelist. He gave up careers in law and politics after the immediate popular success of *The Prisoner of Zenda* (1894), a tale of adventure set in the imaginary country of Ruritania. He wrote many other successful romances of this kind.

Hope, Bob (Leslie Townes Hope; 1903-) US comedian, born in Britain. He starred in a number of popular films during the 1940s, including *Road to Zanzibar* (1941) and other "Road" films in which he partnered Bing *Crosby. He

gave many performances for US troops both in and after World War II; he has also acted as compère of the Academy Award presentations.

Hopeh. See Hebei.

hop-hornbeam A tree of the N temperate genus *Ostrya* (7 species). Related to hornbeams, they have hard wood, furrowed bark, flowers in catkins, and conelike fruits resembling those of the hop. The European hop-hornbeam (*O. carpinifolia*) may grow to a height of over 20 m. Family: *Corylaceae*. See also ironwood.

Hopi North American Indians of NE Arizona whose language belongs to the Uto-Aztecan family (*see* Aztec-Tanoan languages). They live in stone and adobe houses forming small towns built on rocky plateaus (mesas). They are peaceful cultivators and sheep farmers, much given to religious practice and ceremonial. There are about 6000 now living. *See also* Pueblo Indians.

Hopkins, Sir Frederick Gowland (1861-1947) British biochemist, who discovered that certain substances—now known as *vitamins—are essential in the diet in trace amounts. He also showed that some amino acids (called essential amino acids) cannot be manufactured by certain animals. He shared a Nobel Prize (1929) with *Eijkman and was president of the Royal Society (1930-35).

Hopkins, Gerard Manley (1844-89) British poet. He was converted to Roman Catholicism in 1866 and ordained as a Jesuit priest in 1877. In verse of daring originality he rejected conventional metres in favour of a flexible "sprung rhythm." "The Wreck of the Deutschland" and "The Windhover" are among his best-known poems, which were published posthumously in 1918.

Hopkins, Harry (Lloyd) (1890-1946) US administrator. His interest in social welfare projects culminated in his administration of *New Deal relief programmes during the Depression. As aide to President Roosevelt during World War II he negotiated with Churchill and Stalin and headed the US lend-lease programme (*see* Lend Lease Act).

Hopkinson, John (1849-98) British physicist and electrical engineer, who devised the three-phase system for the transmission of electricity. He was killed mountaineering in the Alps.

Hoppner, John (1758-1810) British portrait painter, born in London of German descent. He was rumoured to be the illegitimate son of George III, one of his chief patrons. His portraits of famous contemporaries, e.g. Nelson and Wellington, were strongly influenced by Reynolds.

Horace (Quintus Horatius Flaccus; 65-8 BC) Roman poet. He was the son of a freed slave. Although he was reduced to poverty after fighting for Brutus in the Civil War, he became a leading poet under the emperor Augustus and acquired a farm near Rome, celebrated in his poetry. His *Odes* and his more informal *Satires* and verse *Epistles* vividly portray contemporary Roman society and express his own humane and tolerant personality.

Horae Greek goddesses of the seasons. They were originally three in number, the daughters of Zeus and Themis, and associated with the concepts of order, justice, and peace. They later became the four seasons, daughters of Helios and Selene (the sun and moon).

Horatii and Curiatii In Roman legend, two sets of three brothers who fought on opposing sides in the war between Rome and Alba in the reign of Tullus Hostilius, legendary king of Rome. The single survivor, Horatius, killed his grief-stricken sister on finding she had been engaged to one of the Curiatii, but was acquitted after appealing to the people of Rome.

Hordern, Sir Michael (Murray) (1911-) British actor. He has acted in a wide range of plays, including Ibsen's *Ghosts*, Pinter's *The Collection*, Stoppard's *Jumpers*, and Shakespeare, often portraying eccentrics.

Hore-Belisha, (Isaac) Leslie, 1st Baron (1893-1957)

horehound

588

British politician. A National Liberal, he was minister of transport (1934-37), introducing belisha beacons to mark pedestrian crossings. As secretary for war (1937-40) he introduced conscription in 1939. His unpopularity with the army establishment brought about his dismissal.

horehound (*or* hoarhound) Either of two Eurasian perennial herbs growing in dry waste places and waysides. White horehound (*Marrubium vulgare*) reaches a height of 3 m and has whorls of white flowers while black horehound (*Balleta nigra*) has whorls of purple flowers and a disagreeable odour. Both have been used medicinally. Family: *Labiatae.

hormone A substance that is secreted into the blood in small quantities to cause a response in a specific target organ or tissue of the body. Hormones are produced and secreted by *endocrine glands and by specialized nerve cells (*see* neurohormone) under the control of the nervous system or in response to changes in the chemical composition of the blood. Hormones regulate short-term physiological processes, such as digestion, and long-term changes, such as those associated with growth and reproduction; they also help to maintain a constant internal environment in the body (*see* homeostasis). The first demonstration of hormone activity was made in 1905, by *Bayliss and Starling, working with the digestive hormone secretin. The following are some of the more important hormones now known in man: *ACTH, *gonadotrophin, *growth hormone, and *prolactin (secreted by the pituitary); *corticosteroids, *aldosterone, and *adrenaline (from the adrenal glands); *androgens and *oestrogens (from the sex glands); thyroid hormone (from the *thyroid gland); *insulin and *glucagon (from the pancreas). Chemically, most hormones are proteins or steroids. The study of hormones—and the diseases caused by their under- or over-production—is called endocrinology. Substances that regulate plant growth, e.g. *auxins, *gibberellins, and *kinins, are sometimes known as plant hormones.

Horn, Filips van Montmorency, Graaf van (*or* Hoorne; ?1524-68) Flemish statesman and admiral, who played a leading part in the resistance to Philip II's religious and domestic policies in the Netherlands. He served his Spanish rulers in military, naval, and administrative capacities, becoming stadholder (chief magistrate) of Gelder and Zutphen in 1555. However, he joined *Egmont and William the Silent in resigning from the state council (1565) and demanding the abolition of the Inquisition. He was executed for treason and heresy by the Duke of *Alba. *See also* Revolt of the Netherlands.

hornbeam A tree of the genus *Carpinus* (26 species), of N temperate regions. The common Eurasian hornbeam (*C. betulus*) grows to a height of 30 m in the wild (cultivated trees are up to 19 m tall); it has smooth grey bark, oval pointed leaves with prominent veins, and small nuts with conspicuous winged bracts. It is planted for ornament and for its hard fine-grained timber. Family: *Corylaceae.

hornbill A bird belonging to a family (*Bucerotidae*; 45 species) occurring in Old World tropical regions. 38-150 cm long, hornbills are characterized by a huge bill, often bearing a large bony "helmet," and feed on fruit and berries. Most hornbills nest in treeholes in which the female imprisons herself by plastering the entrance with mud, leaving only a small hole through which the male feeds her, until the young hatch. Order: *Coraciiformes* (kingfishers, etc.).

hornblende A mineral of the *amphibole group, which occurs widely in igneous and metamorphic rocks. It consists mainly of silicates of sodium, calcium, magnesium, and iron. It is black or greenish black and occurs in crystalline or massive form. Hornblende schist is a rock consisting mainly of orientated hornblende crystals.

horned lizard. *See* horned toad.

horned poppy One of two herbs belonging to the *poppy

family and having slender hornlike seed pods. The perennial or biennial yellow horned poppy (*Glaucium flavum*) of Eurasia grows to a height of 90 cm and is found mainly on seashores. The red horned poppy (*G. corniculatus*) is an annual of the Mediterranean region.

horned toad A desert-dwelling lizard, also called horned lizard, belonging to the genus *Phrynosoma*, occurring in Central and North America and characterized by hornlike spines on its head. 8-13 cm long, they have a flattened oval body with a fringe of scales along the sides and hide by wriggling sideways until buried in sand. In defence, they may squirt blood from their eyes. Family: *Iguanidae.

horned viper A mildly venomous desert *viper, *Cerastes cornutus*, that occurs in Africa and the Middle East and has a hornlike scale over each eye. Up to 60 cm long, it has a broad head and is pale with dark spots and bars.

hornet A social *wasp, *Vespa crabro*, that is common throughout Europe and has spread to North America and elsewhere. 35 mm long, it is tawny-yellow with brown markings and nests in hollow trees. It feeds chiefly on insects, nectar, and fruit juices and its painful sting can be dangerous to man.
Members of the genera *Dolichorespula*, *Paravespula*, and *Vespula* may also be known as hornets.

hornpipe A traditional British dance, originally accompanied by a wooden pipe. It retains its popularity with sailors as it requires no partners and little space. Like the jigs and reels to which it is related, it was often danced in clogs. Handel composed a hornpipe for his *Water Music*.

horntail A *wasp, also called wood wasp, belonging to the family *Siricidae* (about 60 species), having a hornlike projection on its abdomen. Horntails are usually brown, blue, or black with yellow bands and can be up to 37.5 mm long. The females have strong ovipositors to insert their eggs into hardwood trees, particularly elm, beech, and maple, in which the larvae develop.

hornwort 1. A plant of the widely distributed genus *Ceratophyllum* (3 species), which grows submerged in ponds and streams. *C. demersum* is rootless, with a stem 20-100 cm long and simple forked leaves, 1-2 cm long. The small flowers produce a three-spined nutlike fruit. Family: *Ceratophyllaceae*. 2. A thallose *liverwort of the order *Anthocerotales*, also called horned liverwort and often classified as a separate class of bryophytes—the *Anthocerotae*. Distributed worldwide, they consist of a flat leaflike gamete-producing plant from which arises a long-lived spikelike spore-producing structure, 2-5 cm long.

horoscope. *See* astrology.

Horowitz, Vladimir (1904-) Russian pianist. He settled in the USA in 1940. Horowitz excels in Russian music and in his own transcriptions. He has twice made a triumphant return to the concert platform after periods of illness during 1936-39 and 1953-65.

horse A hoofed mammal, *Equus caballus*, domesticated worldwide for pack and draught work, riding, and sport (*see* equestrianism). The earliest horse is believed to have been *eohippus, which is thought to have originated in North America and spread to Asia. Successive larger forms evolved, in which the central toe became enlarged as the hoof and the remaining toes became smaller and fewer (*see* Hipparion). These horses developed from forest browsers to become grazing animals of the plains with well-developed senses to detect predators.
The many breeds of modern horse—thought to have evolved from several different Asian and European forms, including *Przewalski's horse and the *tarpan—are commonly grouped into ponies, light horses, and draught horses. They range in size from the tiny *Falabella to the massive *Shire horse and are measured in hands (1 hand = 4 in = 10.16 cm) to the top of the shoulders (withers). According to breed, horses mature at 3½-5 years of age and the lifespan

589

HORSE

Percheron

Arab horse

Thoroughbred

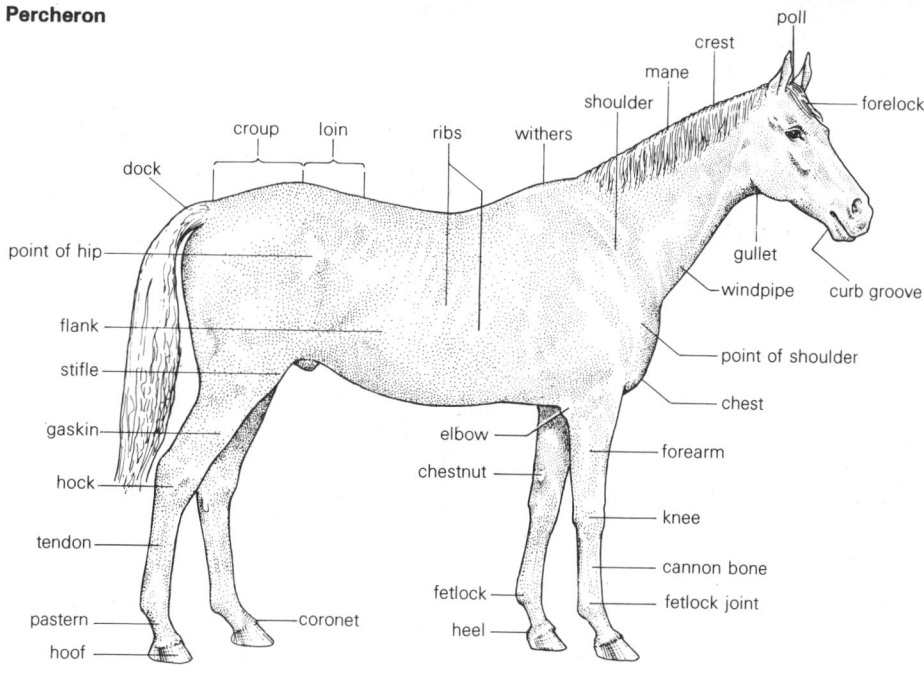

points of the horse

Exmoor pony

Lipizzaner

Tennesee Walking Horse

is usually 20–35 years. Mares have a gestation period of 11 months, producing usually a single foal. Except for breeding stallions, males are usually castrated, being called geldings. Horses belong to the family *Equidae*, which also includes *asses and *zebras.

horse chestnut A broad spreading □tree, *Aesculus hippocastanum*, native to SE Europe and widely planted as an ornamental. It grows to a height of 25 m, producing large compound leaves and erect clusters of white flowers; the green spiny fruits ripen to release large brown shiny seeds (conkers). The red horse chestnut (*A. × carnea*) is similar but has red flowers. It is a hybrid between the horse chestnut and *A. pavia*. Family: *Hippocastanaceae*.

horse fly A stout-bodied fly of the genus *Tabanus* (the term is also used loosely for the other genera—*Chrysops* (deerflies) and *Haematopota* (cleg flies)—of the family *Tabanidae*; 2500 species). Male horse flies feed on nectar but the females are bloodsuckers and inflict painful bites on man, horses, cattle, etc. A few species transmit diseases, such as tularemia and anthrax. The carnivorous larvae live in damp soil.

horsehair worm A long thin hairlike aquatic invertebrate of the phylum *Nematomorpha* (about 80 species), found mostly in fresh water. They range in length from 1–100 mm, with a diameter of only 0.3–2 mm. Their larvae are parasitic in beetles, crickets, and grasshoppers.

horsepower (hp) A unit of power equal to 550 foot-pounds per second. It was devised by James *Watt, who found that a strong horse could raise a weight of 150 pounds 4 feet in 1 second. *See also* watt.

horse racing A form of contest in which horses are ridden or driven. Its three main forms are *flat racing, *steeplechase and hurdling (known collectively in England as National Hunt racing), and *harness racing.

horseradish A perennial herb, *Armoracia rusticana*, probably native to SE Europe and W Asia and widely cultivated. Growing to a height of 125 cm, it has thick fleshy pungent roots from which horseradish sauce is made and it bears small white flowers. Family: *Cruciferae*.

horseshoe bat An insect-eating *bat belonging to the genus *Rhinolophus* (74 species), found in temperate and tropical regions of the Old World. Horseshoe bats are named after the fleshy structure surrounding the nostrils, which focuses the ultrasonic signals that the bat emits when navigating. They also have large ears for receiving the echoes. Family: *Rhinolophidae*.

horseshoe crab A large nocturnal marine *arthropod (up to 50 cm long), also called king crab, belonging to the subclass *Xiphosura*, most members of which are now extinct. The two living genera, *Limulus* and *Tachypleus*, are found in shallow waters on the E coasts of North America and Asia respectively. They have a hinged body covered by a brown horseshoe-shaped carapace and a long tail spine. They can swim but usually burrow in sand, feeding on worms and thin-shelled molluscs. Class: *Meristomata*.

horsetail A rushlike perennial *pteridophyte plant, also called scouring rush, belonging to the only living genus (*Equisetum*; about 30 species) of the class *Sphenopsida* (which includes such giant extinct forms as *Calamites). Horsetails grow in moist soils everywhere except Australasia. Their creeping rhizomes give rise to aerial jointed stems of two kinds—green sterile stems, often branched in whorls, and fertile stems, bearing cone-shaped clusters of spore capsules. The leaves are sheaths encircling each stem joint. Tropical horsetails grow to a height of 6 m, but temperate species are smaller. They are used in folk medicine.

horse trials Contests to test a horse's abilities and the rider's skill in horsemanship. The three-day event is an Olympic sport involving on successive days: *dressage; speed, endurance, and jumping tests on *steeplechase and cross-country courses; and *showjumping. The one-day event is a reduced version.

Horsham 51 04N 0 21W A market town in SE England, in West Sussex. Shelley's birthplace and Christ's Hospital School are both nearby. Horsham's industries include tanning, flour milling, and the manufacture of bricks and tiles. Population (1981): 25 438.

horst. *See* fault.

Horta, Victor (1861–1947) Belgian architect. His early work, particularly the Hôtel Tassel (1892) and the Maison du Peuple (1896) in Brussels, are fine examples of *Art Nouveau. He later abandoned Art Nouveau for classicism.

Horthy de Nagybánya, Miklós (1868–1957) Hungarian admiral and statesman. After the collapse of *Austria-Hungary (1919), he organized an army against Béla *Kun's communist government. Elected regent of Hungary in 1920, he preserved an independent constitutional system, despite alliance with Nazi Germany. When he attempted to surrender to Russia (1944) the Germans deposed him.

horticulture The cultivation of vegetables (also known as market gardening) and fruit for food and of trees, shrubs, and other plants for ornament. Traditionally practised in small gardens and orchards, horticulture is now both a popular domestic pastime and an important commercial activity using large field and glasshouse acreages. Higher-yielding and more disease-resistant plant varieties, increased mechanization, the use of new cultivation techniques, such as *hydroponics, and the application of fertilizers and pesticides have all contributed to improved productivity and quality. Also, modern refrigeration, storage, and transport mean that many crops are now available throughout the year.

Horus The Egyptian sun-god, usually portrayed as a falcon or with a falcon's head. He was the son of *Osiris and *Isis and avenged his father's death by killing *Set. The pharaohs were conceived as the incarnations of Horus as earthly ruler and added the god's name to their titles.

Hosea (8th century BC) An Old Testament prophet of Israel. In the **Book of Hosea** the unfaithfulness of Israel to God is presented in terms of a spiritual adultery. This familial analogy was later developed in the Christian concepts of the Fatherhood of God and of the Church as the bride of Christ.

hospice movement A movement that provides care for the terminally ill. Originally conceived by religious orders in medieval Europe, hospices specialize in easing the physical and mental distress of the patients and providing support for their families. Most modern hospices are modelled on St Christopher's hospice, founded in London in 1967 by Dame Cicely *Saunders.

hospital An institution providing diagnostic and therapeutic services for the sick on a residential (in-patient) or nonresidential (out-patient) basis. In the ancient world such medical services as existed were provided by religious organizations (e.g. the Temple of Aesculapius at Epidaurus in Greece). In Europe in the middle ages many institutions for the care of the sick were founded by monastic orders and later, during the Crusades, by orders of knighthood. St Bartholomew's (1123) and St Thomas's (1207) in London date back to this period. In the UK, during the 18th and 19th centuries, many new voluntary hospitals were founded by philanthropists and staffed by doctors who gave their services free. Municipal hospitals arose alongside the voluntary hospitals and were based on Elizabeth I's Poor Law relief system; they had paid medical staff. The two systems existed side by side until they were both nationalized by the National Health Service Act (1946). Since then all National Health hospitals have provided free services for all who want them, although some have a small number of paybeds for those willing to pay for private rooms and the privilege of being able to choose their doctors (*see* private medical insurance). Since 1974 the NHS hospitals in England have been organized into 15 Regional Health Authorities with at least one teaching hospital in each region. In Scotland and

Wales administration is controlled by Area Health Authorities. *See also* National Health Service.

Hospitallers (Order of the Hospital of St John of Jerusalem) A religious order of knighthood that began as a hospital for pilgrims to Jerusalem (c. 1070) and during the *Crusades took on a military function. Immensely wealthy, the Hospitallers were the great rivals of the *Templars. After the fall of Acre (1291) they established themselves in Cyprus, Rhodes, and finally Malta.

Hosta A genus of perennial herbaceous plants (10 species), native to China and Japan and widely planted in gardens. They are grown chiefly for their foliage—the leaves are large (12-25 cm long), oval, and pointed and come in a variety of colours, often variegated—but they also produce attractive spikes of purplish or white funnel-shaped flowers. Family: *Liliaceae*.

hot spring A spring from which hot water flows continuously from deep within the earth's crust. Like *geysers, hot springs normally occur in areas that are (or have recently been) volcanically active. A distinction is sometimes made between hot springs (at a temperature above that of the human body) and *thermal springs* (above the mean annual temperature of the place where they emerge). The water is charged with minerals and deposits of travertine or sinter usually build up.

Hotspur. *See* Percy, Sir Henry.

Hottentot fig A perennial herb, *Carpobrotus edulis*, native to South Africa but naturalized in many warm temperate regions. It has creeping woody stems, fleshy leaves, showy magenta or yellow flowers, and edible fruits. Family: *Aizoaceae*.

Hotter, Hans (1909-) German baritone, formerly a church organist and choirmaster. He is famous for his interpretation of the roles of Hans Sachs in *Die Meistersinger* and Wotan in *Der Ring des Niebelungen*.

HARRY HOUDINI *Posing with a submersible canister from which he would escape under water.*

Houdini, Harry (Erich Weiss; 1874-1926) US magician. His ability to escape from handcuffs, straitjackets, and locked containers, even when under water, gained him an international reputation. He wrote articles and books on magic and was deeply interested in spiritualism.

Houdon, Jean Antoine (1741-1828) French sculptor. Houdon's highly successful career began in Rome (1764-68) with his *St Bruno* (1767; Sta Maria degli Angeli, Rome). Although he made many religious and mythological sculptures, he was most popular as a portrait sculptor; famous sitters included Voltaire, Benjamin Franklin, Catherine the Great, and Napoleon. He visited the USA (1785) to make a statue of George Washington.

Hounslow A borough of W Greater London, bordering on the River Thames in the S. Created in 1965 from parts of Middlesex, it contains Hounslow Heath, a former haunt of highwaymen. Population (1981): 199 782.

Houphouët-Boigny, Félix (1905-) Ivory Coast statesman; president (1960-). In 1946 he founded the Ivory Coast branch of the Rassemblement démocratique africain and was a member of the French Constituent Assembly (1945-46) and National Assembly (1946-59). In 1959 he became prime minister and, on independence in 1960, president.

housecarl A member of the household bodyguard of the Danish kings of England (1016-51). Originally warriors from the Scandinavian army, the housecarls performed strictly organized military and administrative services for which they were rewarded with gifts of money and land.

housefly A dull-grey fly, *Musca domestica*, that is a worldwide household pest. The adult is 5-7 mm long, with mouthparts used for sucking up organic liquids of all kinds. Through the contamination of food it spreads many serious diseases, such as typhoid, tuberculosis, and dysentery. The scavenging larvae grow quickly on practically any decaying organic matter, especially dung. Family: *Muscidae*.

houseleek A European perennial herb, *Sempervivum tectorum*, that has a basal rosette of fleshy leaves and bears heads of dull-red flowers on stems up to 60 cm long. Growing on walls and roofs, it was formerly believed to guard against fire, sorcery, and death and had many medicinal uses. Family: *Crassulaceae*.

house sparrow A Eurasian *sparrow, *Passer domesticus*, that originated in Africa and spread north with Neolithic man: it is now also found in the New World. The male has a black-streaked brown plumage with grey underparts and a black bib and eye stripe; the female has a paler drabber plumage. *See* Plate V.

Housman, A(lfred) E(dward) (1859-1936) British poet and scholar. Although he failed his degree at Oxford, his classical erudition was eventually rewarded with professorships at London and Cambridge. His two volumes of lyrics, *A Shropshire Lad* (1896) and *Last Poems* (1922), are concerned with themes of human vanity and transience and are imbued with an atmosphere of romantic pessimism. He also published editions of the Roman poets Juvenal and Manilius.

Houston 29 45N 95 25W A city in the USA, the main port in Texas. Founded in 1836, it is named after the Texan leader Sam(uel) Houston (1793-1863). It expanded rapidly following the building of a canal (1912-14), linking it to the Gulf of Mexico, and the development of coastal oilfields. Today it is one of the world's major oil and petrochemical centres; other industries include shipbuilding and the manufacture of steel. Among its many educational institutions is Texas medical centre, and the Lyndon B. Johnson Space Center is nearby. Population (1980): 1 594 086.

Hove 50 49N 0 10W A town in S England, on the East Sussex coast. It is a resort and residential town adjoining Brighton. Sussex county cricket ground is situated here. Population (1981): 66 612.

Hovell, William Hilton. *See* Hume, Hamilton.

hovercraft (*or* air-cushion vehicle) A shiplike vehicle equipped with powerful horizontal blowers capable of lifting it off a surface so that it rides on a cushion of air, which is contained within a rubber skirt. It can navigate on almost stationary air cushion   skirt   stationary air cushion

air inlet

plenum-chamber type   **annular-chamber type**

thrust of propellor

aerodynamic lift

drag

weight   centre of gravity

air cushion lift   skirt

HOVERCRAFT *In the plenum chamber the air cushion is produced by a horizontal fan; the cushion in the centre is almost at rest and is surrounded by a fast-moving ring of turbulent air. In the annular chamber the cushion is formed within an annular ring of jets, the nozzles of which are sloped inwards. The lower figure shows the forces acting on a Hovercraft.*

any kind of surface (water, swamp, or land) and is moved forward at high speed by vertical propellers. The first hovercraft was built by Christopher *Cockerell in 1959. Hovercraft are used as ferries between England and France, Hong Kong and Macao, between ports in Scandinavia, and elsewhere.

hoverfly A fly, also called a flowerfly or syrphid fly, belonging to the family *Syrphidae* (about 4000 species). Many species are black and yellow, resembling bees and wasps, but they do not sting. The larvae of many hoverflies are scavengers in decaying organic matter or the nests of ants, termites, or bees. Others eat aphids and plant lice, while a few are plant pests. *See also* maggot. ▯insect.

Howard, Catherine (c. 1520–42) The fifth wife (1540–42) of Henry VIII of England. She was beheaded for treason when Henry learnt of her premarital love affairs.

Howard, Sir Ebenezer (1850–1928) British theorist of town planning. His book *Garden Cities of Tomorrow*, first published under this title in 1902, propounds his concept of ideal spacious suburbs. This was first realized in the planning of Letchworth (1903), *Lutyens' design for Hampstead (1908), and Welwyn Garden City (1920). His ideas continue to be influential, both in Britain and abroad. *See also* garden city.

Howard, Henry. *See* Surrey, Earl of.

Howard, John (c. 1726–90) English prison reformer. Horrified by conditions in Bedford gaol, which he inspected while high sheriff of Bedfordshire, Howard campaigned for sanitary improvements and wages, rather than prisoners' fees, for gaolers. An act of 1774 achieved his aims. The **Howard League for Penal Reform**, founded in 1866 as the Howard Association, was named after him.

Howard, Leslie (Leslie Howard Stainer; 1890–1943) British actor of Hungarian descent. He became famous for his performances as the romantic leading man in both British and US films, including *The Scarlet Pimpernel* (1935), *Pygmalion* (1938), and *Gone with the Wind* (1939). He was killed when the aeroplane in which he was travelling was shot down by German aircraft in 1943. ▯Leigh, Vivien.

Howard, Trevor (1916–88) British actor. After working in the theatre in the 1930s he concentrated on films from the 1940s, often appearing in leading romantic roles. His films include *Brief Encounter* (1946), *The Third Man* (1949), *Mutiny*

on the Bounty (1962), *Ryan's Daughter* (1970), *Conduct Unbecoming* (1975), and *White Mischief* (1987).

Howard of Effingham, Charles, 2nd Baron (1536–1624) English Lord High Admiral (1585–1618), who commanded the English victory against the Spanish *Armada (1588). He was a commander of the expedition that sacked Cádiz (1596), for which he was created 1st Earl of Nottingham.

Howe, Elias (1819–67) US inventor, who invented a lockstitch sewing machine, patented in 1846. It was not at first well received but by the 1850s large numbers were being manufactured in infringement of Howe's patent rights. Successful in a series of legal suits, he subsequently earned a fortune from royalties.

Howe, Sir (Richard Edward) Geoffrey (1926–) British Conservative politician; chancellor of the exchequer (1979–83); foreign secretary (1983–). He was formerly solicitor general (1970–72) and minister for trade and consumer affairs (1972–74).

Howe, Richard, Earl (1726–99) British admiral. In the Seven Years' War (1756–63) he fought with distinction off the N French coast. In 1776 he became commander of the British fleet in the American Revolution. He is best known for the victory in the French Revolutionary Wars of the Glorious *First of June (1794). His brother **William, 5th Viscount Howe** (1729–1814) gained fame in the army. He fought under *Wolfe in North America during the Seven Years' War and in the American Revolution commanded at *Bunker Hill (1775), after which he became commander in chief in America. Although he scored successes, notably at *Brandywine (1777), his career ended in anticlimax after the failure at *Valley Forge (1778). He resigned, maintaining that he had lacked support from home.

Howel Dda. *See* Hywel the Good.

howitzer A low-velocity *artillery firearm with a shorter barrel and a larger bore than a *gun but a smaller bore and longer barrel than a *mortar. They are often mounted on carriages that enable them to fire either flat gun-type trajectories or arched mortar-type trajectories. They were widely used in World War I but the distinction between a gun and a howitzer in modern practice is now much reduced. The word comes from the Dutch *houwitzer*, catapult.

howler monkey A large monkey belonging to the genus *Alouatta* (6 species), of Central and South American forests. Howlers are 115–180 cm long including the tail (58–91 cm) and are named after their loud voices. They have beards over their enlarged throats, prehensile tails, and live in groups of up to 40 individuals. Family: *Cebidae*.

Howrah 22 35N 88 20E A city and port in India, in West Bengal situated on the River Hooghly opposite Calcutta. The focal point of rail and road routes, its industries include shipbuilding, jute milling, engineering, and chemicals. Population (1981): 744 429.

Hoxha, Enver (1908–85) Albanian leader (1946–85). In World War II Hoxha led Albania's struggle against Italy and founded the country's Communist Party (1941), becoming (1943) its general secretary. He was prime minister (1946–54) and then first secretary (1954–85) of the newly named Party of Labour. After the Sino-Soviet disagreement in 1961, Hoxha supported China until 1978.

Hoya. *See* waxplant.

Hoyle, Edmond (1672–1769) British authority on card games. His book *A Short Treatise on the Game of Whist* (1742) was highly successful and his revised rules of 1760 governed whist until 1864. The idiom "according to Hoyle" (meaning according to the rules) is an allusion to this book.

Hoyle, Sir Fred (1915–) British astronomer, who with H. *Bondi and T. *Gold proposed the *steady-state theory of the universe. His other theoretical studies have mainly been concerned with stellar evolution. He is also one of the foremost of today's science writers, his *Galaxies, Nuclei and*

Quasars (1965) being a standard work, and a notable science-fiction writer.

Hradec Králové (German name: Königgratz) 50 13N 15 50E A town in NW Czechoslovakia, in E Bohemia on the confluence of the Rivers Elbe (Labe) and Orlice. Industries include the manufacture of musical instruments and photographic equipment. Population (1980 est): 93 000.

Hsia Kuei. *See* Xia Gui.

Hsiang-t'an. *See* Xiangtan.

Hsi Chiang. *See* Xi Jiang.

Hsin dynasty. *See* Wang Mang.

Hsi-ning. *See* Xining.

Hsiung-nu. *See* Xiong Nu.

Hsuan-tsang. *See* Xuan Cang.

Hua Guo Feng (*or* Hua Kuo-feng; 1921–) Chinese communist statesman; chairman of the Chinese Communist Party (1976–81). A communist from boyhood, he became Party secretary in Hunan, which he made one of the most efficiently run provinces in China. He survived a *Red Guard attack during the Cultural Revolution to succeed Chou En-lai as prime minister (1976–80) and Mao Tse-tung as chairman, the victor of a power struggle with the radicals led by Mao's widow, *Jiang Qing. The pragmatic policies pursued by China under Hua are regarded as being in part the result of the influence of *Deng Xiao Ping.

Huainan 32 41N 117 06E A city in E China, in Anhui province. Situated on a rich coalfield, it has been developed during the 20th century. Industries include iron and steel and chemicals. Population (1982): 561 000.

Huambo (name until 1973: Nova Lisboa) 12 47S 15 44E A town in W Angola. It is a commercial centre with a trade in agricultural produce and has important railway industries. Population (1970): 61 885.

Huancayo 12 05S 75 12W A city in W Peru, the chief commercial centre of the central Andes. It has a cathedral and a university (1962). Population (1981): 321 549.

Huang Hai. *See* Yellow Sea.

Huang Ho. *See* Yellow River.

Huari An ancient city in the central Peruvian Andes that was briefly the centre of an empire (c. 600–800 AD). Huari itself remained prosperous until abandoned about 1000 and the influence of its pottery styles prevailed over most of its central Peruvian neighbours until the rise of the *Chimú.

Huascar (c. 1495–1532) Ruler of the Incas, who was defeated in civil war by his half-brother *Atahuallpa in 1532. Their conflict helped *Pizarro to conquer the Incas.

Huascarán (*or* Nevado Huascarán) 9 08S 77 36W The highest mountain in Peru, in the Andes. In 1962 an avalanche buried the village of Raurahirca killing about 3500 people. Height: 6768 m (22 205 ft).

Hubble, Edwin Powell (1889–1953) US astronomer, who used the 100-inch telescope at Mount Wilson Observatory to show that there were celestial bodies (*galaxies) lying beyond our own Galaxy and that these were receding from us, thus confirming the idea of an expanding universe. He discovered that the velocity of recession of the galaxies is proportional to their distance from the earth, which led to the evaluation of the *Hubble constant.

Hubble constant (H_o) The rate at which the velocity of expansion of the universe changes with distance. It relates the recessional velocity, V, of a distant galaxy to its distance, D. **Hubble's law**, proposed in 1929 by Edwin *Hubble, states that recessional velocity and distance are directly proportional: $V = H_o D$. One value for H_o is 55 km s^{-1} megaparsec^{-1}, although higher values are and have been used.

Hubei (*or* Hupei) A province in E central China. Its fertile E plain has many lakes and rivers, including the Yangtze River. It was devastated during the Taiping Rebellion (1851–64) and

the 1911 revolution began here. Products include wheat, rice, cotton, fish, and steel. Area: 187 500 sq km (72 394 sq mi). Population (1980 est): 46 320 000. Capital: Wuhan.

Hubli 15 20N 75 14E A city in India, in Karnataka. Together with Dharwar, it forms one of the state's most populous areas. Industries include cotton and newspapers. Population (1981): 526 000.

hubris (*or* hybris) The ancient Greek concept of human pride or arrogance that results in the transgression of the natural order and subsequent retribution by the gods. The concept is important in Greek tragedies, the protagonists of which, being talented and powerful, were especially prone to this fault.

Huddersfield 58 39N 1 47W A town in N England, in West Yorkshire at the confluence of the Rivers Colne and Holme. One of the major wool textile towns of West Yorkshire, Huddersfield produces various fabrics and has important engineering (tractors, textile machinery) and metalworking industries. Population (1981): 123 888.

Huddleston, Trevor (1913–) British missionary and bishop. While a missionary in South Africa (1943–56) he wrote *Naught for Your Comfort* (1952), highlighting the dilemma of the Church under apartheid. He has been Bishop of Massai, in Tanzania (1960–68), Suffragan Bishop of Stepney, London (1968–77), and since 1978 Bishop of Mauritius.

Hudson, Henry (d. 1611) English navigator. In 1607, in a small ship with ten sailors, he sailed in search of the *Northeast Passage to China, reaching Spitzbergen. He tried again, unsuccessfully, in 1608. On a third voyage, under the auspices of the Dutch East India Company, he sailed some 240 km (150 mi) down what came to be called the Hudson River, establishing Dutch claims to the area. His fourth voyage (1610–11), in the *Discovery*, took him to what is now Hudson Bay (NE Canada), where his men mutinied and cast him adrift. Nothing more was heard of him.

Hudson, W(illiam) H(enry) (1841–1922) British naturalist and writer. Born in Argentina, he came to England in 1869. His books, which achieved little popular success, include ornithological studies, works on the English countryside, and several prose romances, of which the best known is *Green Mansions* (1904).

Hudson Bay A huge shallow oceanic bay in N central Canada, linked to the Atlantic Ocean by Hudson Strait and to the Arctic Ocean by Foxe Channel. Frozen during winter, in summer it carries grain ships from W Canada to Europe.

Hudson River A river in the NE USA, flowing from the Adirondack Mountains to New York Bay, where it forms part of New York Harbor. An important commercial waterway, it is linked by canals with the *Great Lakes and the *St Lawrence Seaway. Length: 492 km (306 mi).

Hudson's Bay Company A fur-trading company, formed in 1670, that was given settlement and trading rights in Canada; its first governor was Prince *Rupert (*see also* Rupert's Land). The company engaged in bitter rivalry with the *Northwest Company from the 1780s until 1821, when they were united under the name of the Hudson's Bay Company. It maintained a monopoly of the fur trade in Rupert's Land until 1859. In 1870 it sold its territories to Canada but remained a major fur-trading agency with headquarters in London.

Hue 16 28N 107 35E An ancient city in central Vietnam, on the Huong estuary. The University of Hue was established in 1957. A commercial centre, Hue has textile, timber, and cement industries. *History*: a Chinese military stronghold from about 200 BC, Hue later fell to Champa and after 1635 was the capital of *Annam and after 1802 of the short-lived Vietnamese empire. It suffered heavily during the Vietnam War, in which it was a part of South Vietnam, and lost many of the historic buildings and treasures of the imperial citadel. Its population was also increased sixfold by refugees. Population (1979): 165 865.

Huelva 37 15N 6 56W A port in SW Spain, in Andalusia on the Odiel estuary. It ships copper from the Riotinto mines and also iron, manganese, and wine. Population (1981): 127 806.

Huesca 42 08N 0 25W A town in NE Spain, in Aragon. Quintus Sertorius (c. 123–72 BC) founded his school here in 77 BC. It has a cathedral (13th–16th centuries). Population (1982 est): 42 554.

Huggins, Sir William (1824–1910) British astronomer, who pioneered the application of spectroscopy to astronomy, using the technique to discover that stars consist of the same elements as those found on the earth. He also discovered the *red shift in the lines of a star's spectrum. He was knighted in 1897.

Hugh Capet (c. 940–96 AD) The first *Capetian King of France (987–96). Son of the Count of Paris, Hugh seized the throne after the failure of the *Carolingian line.

Hughes, Howard (Robard) (1905–76) US aviator, film producer, and entrepreneur. After founding the Hughes Aircraft Company he broke the landplane speed record in 1935, reaching a speed of 352 mph in a craft of his own design. His films include *Hell's Angels* (1930), *Scarface* (1932), and *The Outlaw* (1944), the last of which he also directed. From 1950 until his death he lived in seclusion.

Hughes, Richard (1900–76) British novelist. His best-known novel is *A High Wind in Jamaica* (1929), concerning a family of children captured by pirates. *The Fox in the Attic* (1961) and *The Wooden Shepherdess* (1973) are the first two parts of an unfinished work concerning British and German society during the interwar years.

Hughes, Ted (1930–) British poet. His first volume, *The Hawk in the Rain* (1957), contained many poems concerned with the natural world written in a forceful energetic style. The poems in *Crow* (1970) and subsequent volumes are characterized by increased violence of language and subject matter. He married Sylvia *Plath in 1956 and became poet laureate in 1984.

Hughes, Thomas (1822–96) British writer. *Tom Brown's Schooldays* (1857), his best-known novel, is a celebration of the public-school ethos formulated by Thomas *Arnold. He was a Christian Socialist and a Liberal MP (1865–74).

Hughes, William M(orris) (1864–1952) Australian statesman, born in London; prime minister (1915–23) as leader of the Labor Party (1915–16) and then of the newly founded Nationalist Party. An advocate of Australian federation in the 1890s, he was attorney general (1908–09, 1910–13, 1914–21, 1939–41). As prime minister he attended the Paris Peace Conference (1919) after World War I.

Hugh of Saint-Victor (1096–1141) French theologian. He joined the abbey of St Victor in Paris as a canon regular and, under his direction, its school became a major centre of learning. His best-known book is *The Sacraments of the Christian Faith*.

Hugo, Victor (Marie) (1802–85) French poet, dramatist, and novelist. After several early novels and volumes of poetry, his leadership of the Romantic movement was confirmed by the success of his drama *Hernani* (1831). During the 1840s he became increasingly involved in politics as a champion of republican ideals and, after the coup d'état by the future Napoleon III in 1851, he went into exile in the Channel Islands until 1870. His later major works included *Les Contemplations* (1856), a volume of poems, and the novel *Les Misérables* (1862). The greatest French poet of the 19th century, during his last years he was honoured as a national literary figure. He died in Paris and was buried in the Panthéon.

Huguenots French Protestants. Their name is derived from the Swiss-German *Eidgenoss*, confederate. The Huguenots, chiefly followers of John Calvin, were soon an influential national minority. The rivalry of their leaders, especially the *Condé, with the prominent Roman Catholic *Guise family gave rise to the *Wars of Religion (1562–94). The Edict of Nantes (1598) guaranteed the Huguenots freedom of worship but in Louis XIV's reign they were increasingly persecuted and after the revocation of the Edict (1685) over 250 000 Huguenots emigrated. Persecution continued until the French Revolution.

Huhehot. *See* Hohhot.

Hui Chinese Muslims of NW China, mainly in the provinces of Hebei, Xinjiang, Gansu, and Qinghai. Numbering about 3.5 million, they are descended from Chinese who were converted as a result of contact and intermarriage with *Turkic peoples during the 14th and 15th centuries. They are also known as Dungan (*or* T'ung-kan).

huia An extinct New Zealand songbird, *Heteralocha acutirostris*, 45 cm long, that had a glossy black plumage with a white-tipped tail and orange wattles at the base of the bill. The bill of the male was strong and straight; that of the female was long, slender, and curved. Huias were hunted for the feathers by Maoris but their extinction was caused by the destruction of their habitat and excessive collection of specimens as curios by European settlers. Family: *Callaeidae* (wattlebirds).

Huitzilopochtli The Aztec sun- and war-god. He was portrayed as a hummingbird, or with armour of hummingbird feathers, and dead warriors were believed to be reincarnated as this bird. His temple at Tenochtitlan, founded in 1325 in the Valley of Mexico, was the principal Aztec religious structure. He was identified with the sun as a warrior who defeated the night stars, was reborn each day, and depended for nourishment on the blood of human sacrificial victims.

Huizinga, Johan (1872–1945) Dutch historian. Huizinga was professor of history, first at Groningen and then at Leyden University. His best-known book, *The Waning of the Middle Ages* (1919), was a study of life, thought, and art in late medieval France and the Netherlands. He also wrote *Erasmus* (1924), *In the Shadow of Tomorrow* (1935), an analysis of the malaise of contemporary western society, and *Homo Ludens* (1938).

Hull (official name: Kingston-upon-Hull) 53 45N 0 20W A city and port in NE England, the administrative centre of Humberside, situated on the Humber estuary. An important fishing port, Hull has vast docks and serves as a port for much of the North and Midlands, with passenger services to the Continent. Its industries include vegetable-oil extraction, saw-milling, flour-milling, paints, chemicals, and engineering, as well as fish-related industries. Its university was established in 1927. William Wilberforce was born here and his house is now a museum. Population (1981): 268 302.

Hull 45 26N 75 45W A city in E Canada, in SW Quebec on the Ottawa River opposite Ottawa. One of North America's main pulp-and-paper and timber centres, it has acquired many federal government offices in recent years. Population (1980): 59 100.

Hull, Cordell (1871–1955) US Democratic politician; secretary of state (1933–44) under F. D. Roosevelt. He did much to foster good relations with Latin America (*see* Good Neighbor Policy), attending the important Montevideo Conference in 1933, and supported China against Japanese ambitions in East Asia. He was instrumental in the foundation of the UN, for which he won the Nobel Peace Prize in 1945.

humanism **1.** The intellectual movement that formed the inspiration and the basis of Renaissance culture. Humanist scholars based their programme upon the rediscovery and study of classical Greek and Roman authors, which had been initiated in Italy by such men as *Petrarch and *Boccaccio. They turned away from the exclusively theological bias of their medieval forerunners and concentrated instead upon human achievements in the arts and sciences. *Erasmus was the greatest N European humanist. For him and the other Renaissance thinkers humanism by no means implied rejection of Christianity. **2.** A 20th-century philosophical viewpoint that is based on a policy of *atheism, holding religion to be a superstition unworthy of serious thought.

human rights Privileges claimed or enjoyed by a human being simply by virtue of being human. The concept developed from Roman ideas of "natural law" entailing "natural rights," via *Locke, *Paine, and the American Declaration of Independence (1776), to 20th-century liberal acceptance of the idea that human beings should have certain equal civil, political, and economic rights. Since the horrors of World War II, moves have been made to ensure international enforcement of human-rights agreements as embodied in the UN Charter. The UN Universal Declaration of Human Rights (1948), itself not a legally binding code, has spawned various subsequent agreements, such as the Covenants on Civil and Political Rights and on Economic, Social, and Cultural Rights (1966), which have been accepted as binding by 35 states.

Humber An estuary in N England, flowing from the confluence of the Rivers Ouse and Trent to the North Sea past the ports of Hull, Immingham, and Grimsby. The **Humber Bridge** (opened 1981), the world's longest single-span suspension bridge with a main span of 1410 m (4626 ft), links N and S Humberside. Length: 64 km (40 mi).

Humberside A county in NE England, bordering on the North Sea. It was created in 1974 from N Lincolnshire and parts of the East and West Ridings of Yorkshire. It consists mainly of lowlands, divided by the Humber Estuary, with uplands in the NW. It is a rich agricultural region producing cereals, root crops, and livestock. There are important fishing industries at Hull and Grimsby. Other industrial activities include iron and steel manufacture at Scunthorpe, and an expanding petrochemical and chemical complex on the S bank of the Humber. Area: 3512 sq km (1356 sq mi). Population (1981): 847 666. Administrative centre: Hull.

Humboldt, (Karl) Wilhelm von (1767-1835) German scholar and statesman; friend of Schiller and Goethe. As minister of education he founded Berlin University (1809) and was subsequently employed as a diplomat. His writings on language are especially profound: he saw language as a generative process rather than a lifeless structure. He perceived that language and thought are inseparable and identified various kinds of structures by which languages may be differentiated. His brother (**Friedrich Wilhelm Karl Heinrich) Alexander von Humboldt** (1769-1859) was a scientist and explorer. In 1799 he set off with Aimé Bonpland (1773-1858) to explore Central and South America and in the following five years the two men collected a large number of samples and much data relating to earth sciences. He subsequently explored central Asia, again collecting scientific material of great importance. In his great work *Kosmos* (5 vols, 1845-62) he set out his views on the whole universe. The *Humboldt Current and Glacier were named after him.

Humboldt Current (*or* Peru Current) An ocean current constituting part of the South Pacific oceanic circulation system. It flows N off the Peruvian coast of South America. Because of its Antarctic origins and the upwelling of cold water along the W coast of South America, it is a cold current rich in plankton and the fish that feed on them, giving rise to Peru's prosperous fishing industry.

Humboldt Glacier The largest known glacier in the N hemisphere, in NW Greenland. At its end in Kane Basin it is 100 km (60 mi) wide and 91 m (300 ft) high.

Hume, Basil George, Cardinal (1923-) British Roman Catholic churchman. He joined the Benedictine order and taught languages at Ampleforth College in Yorkshire from 1952 until 1963, when he became Abbot of Ampleforth. He succeeded Cardinal Heenan as Archbishop of Westminster

in 1976, the first monk to hold this office, and was created a cardinal in the same year.

Hume, David (1711-76) Scottish philosopher and historian. He spent three years in France (1734-37) but for the rest of his life lived in either London or Edinburgh. In *A Treatise of Human Nature* (1739-40) he developed his influential distinction between impression and ideas, claiming that impressions have more force than ideas. We receive impressions from an unknown source and ideas derive from them through the operations of memory and imagination. For Hume almost nothing about existence was demonstrable; regarding the existence of God, his position throughout his numerous works is an incisive *agnosticism. Although an empiricist like *Locke and *Berkeley, Hume modified problematic aspects of their philosophies in favour of psychological explanations. Another aspect of Hume's thought that is influential among 20th-century philosophers is his analysis of cause and effect as no more than "constant conjunction": we can *observe* that one thing follows another but we can never *know* that it must follow, because of the limitations in the nature and scope of human understanding. Hume's *History of England* (1754-62), written while he was librarian of the Advocates' Library in Edinburgh, was a bestseller for many years.

Hume, Hamilton (1797-1873) Australian explorer. His most important journey (1824-25) was with an English immigrant **William Hilton Hovell** (1786-1875) with whom he travelled from Sydney to Port Phillip, Victoria, discovering the Murray River. The Hume Highway (Melbourne to Sydney) is named after him.

Hume, Joseph (1777-1855) British radical politician. After early employment by the East India Company he briefly became an MP (1812). Re-elected in 1818, he advocated free trade, opposed flogging in the army, and consistently questioned public expenditure.

humerus. *See* arm.

humidity A measure of the amount of water vapour in the atmosphere. Absolute humidity is the mass of water vapour in unit volume of air, measured in kilograms per cubic metre. Relative humidity is the ratio of the absolute humidity at a given temperature to the maximum humidity without precipitation at the same temperature, usually expressed as a percentage.

Hummel, Johann Nepomuk (1778-1837) Hungarian pianist and composer. He numbered Mozart and Haydn among his teachers. He toured Europe as a concert pianist and was famous as an improviser. His compositions include concertos and many piano solos.

hummingbird A brightly coloured bird belonging to a New World family (*Trochilidae*; 320 species). Hummingbirds are 5.5-20 cm long and have a slender often downcurved bill and a brush-tipped tongue for feeding on nectar and small insects. Hummingbirds can hover, fly backwards, and produce a humming noise by the rapid vibration of their wings during flight. Order: *Apodiformes* (swifts, etc.). □ p. 596.

humpback whale A *rorqual whale, *Megaptera novaeangliae*, found in coastal waters throughout the world. It is 15 m long with long flippers and a large dorsal fin with lobes down to the tail. It is an acrobatic swimmer and lives in communities, feeding on crustaceans and small fish. □oceans.

Humperdinck, Engelbert (1854-1921) German composer. He assisted Wagner with the score of *Parsifal* in 1880-81. Of his many operas only *Hänsel und Gretel* (1893) is still popular: it blends German folklore with Wagnerian operatic techniques.

Humphrey, Hubert Horatio (1911-1978) US Democratic politician; vice president (1965-69) under President Johnson. A liberal democrat, he championed civil rights but his defence of Johnson's Vietnam policies cost him liberal

humus

support. He was 1968 presidential candidate but lost to Nixon.

humus The black organic matter in soil resulting from the *decomposition of dead plants and animals (humification). It is rich in such elements as carbon, nitrogen, phosphorus, and sulphur, which are useful in maintaining soil fertility and hence in promoting plant growth. Humus also improves water absorption and workability of the soil.

Hunan A province in S central China, mountainous and forested in the S and W. The population includes an aboriginal minority. The chief products are rice, cereals, tea, cotton, timber, and such minerals as lead, zinc, tungsten, and gold. *History*: it was devastated during the Taiping Rebellion (1851–64). Mao Tse-tung was born here. Area: 210 500 sq km (82 095 sq mi). Population (1982): 54 008 851. Capital: Changsha.

HUMMINGBIRD *Gould's long-tailed sylph hummingbird (Aglaiocercus kingi) extracting nectar while hovering by a flower. This species is found in the Andes and from Venezuela to Peru and Bolivia.*

hundred A subdivision of the shire in England, first mentioned in the 10th century. Of varying size, it may originally have consisted of a hundred *hides. It corresponded to the *wapentake in the areas under Danish law. An administrative and judicial unit, it had its own court sitting every four weeks until the 13th century, when its importance began to decline. Hundreds survived, however, until the 19th century. *See also* Chiltern Hundreds.

Hundred Days (20 March–28 June, 1815) The period from *Napoleon Bonaparte's return to France, after his escape from Elba, until his final defeat by the allies at *Waterloo.

Hundred Days of Reform (1898) A programme of reforms announced by the Chinese emperor *Guang Xu, with the help of the reformer *Kang You Wei, to modernize the educational system, administration, and the armed forces and to develop trade, commerce, and industrialization on a western model. Most of the reforms were repealed by Guang Xu's mother *Zi Xi, who with the support of the army imprisoned her son and became regent, thus frustrating a reform movement that might have prevented the overthrow of the *Qing dynasty.

Hundred Flowers A Chinese government campaign to allow greater freedom of speech, particularly among intellectuals. It began in 1956 under the slogan "Let a hundred flowers bloom together, let a hundred schools of thought contend." It led to much open criticism of the government and was harshly suppressed a year later.

Hundred Years' War (1337–1453) A war between England and France. It was precipitated by Edward III's claim to the French throne, although there had long been hostility occasioned by disputes over English territory in

France and French support for the Scots. The Treaty of *Brétigny (1360) recognized initial English successes at *Sluys (1340), *Crécy (1346), and Poitiers (1356) but thereafter the war was waged intermittently with frequent truces. Conditions were exacerbated by growing French and Burgundian rivalry, the Burgundians supporting Henry V of England, who achieved recognition as heir to the French throne after his victory at *Agincourt (1415). His early death, the accession of the weak *Henry VI, and more vigorous French prosecution of the war (inspired by *Joan of Arc) reversed his triumph and by 1453 England had been expelled from all French territory except Calais.

Hungarian A language of the *Finno-Ugric branch of the *Uralic family. It is spoken by 14 million people mainly in Hungary, where it is the official language, and in Czechoslovakia, Romania, and Yugoslavia. It uses a modified Latin alphabet and has borrowed many words from surrounding languages. Vowel harmony is characteristic of its sound system and its grammar is based on the use of suffixes. *See also* Magyars.

Hungarian National Council (1918–19) A political coalition formed in October, 1918, by *Károlyi and dedicated to establishing constitutional government in Hungary. In November, after Károlyi had become prime minister, it proclaimed Hungary a republic but the decline of the economy and the opposition of Hungary's minority nationalities forced its resignation (March, 1919) in favour of the communists under *Kun.

Hungarian Revolution (1956) An uprising against Soviet dominance of Hungary. Following the Soviet acceptance of *Gomułka as leader in Poland, a demonstration of students and workers in Budapest demanded the end of the Soviet presence in Hungary and of one-party government. The protestors were joined by army units. Imre *Nagy formed a coalition government, withdrew Hungary from the *Warsaw Pact, and sought UN help. An opposition government was formed by János *Kádár, and Soviet troops attacked Budapest and crushed the rebellion; Nagy and his associates were captured and executed. About 190 000 people left Hungary as a result of the Revolution.

Hungary, People's Republic of (Hungarian name: Magyar Népköztársasag) A country in central Europe. It lies mainly in the basin of the middle Danube, which forms the NW boundary with Czechoslovakia before running N–S across the centre of the country. To the E of the Danube lies the Great Hungarian Plain, crossed by the River Tisza; to the W an undulating plain rises to some low hills in the SW and in the NW to the hilly Bakony Forest, S of which lies Lake *Balaton. The people are mainly Magyars, with minorities of Germans, Slovaks, and others. *Economy*: agriculture is now organized collectively, though individuals can still own small plots. The main crops are wheat and maize as well as fruit and vegetables. The wine industry is being encouraged, including the redevelopment of the Takaj region in the NE. The only mineral resource of significance is bauxite. Oil and natural gas have been found but most supplies come by pipeline from the Soviet Union. All industry is nationalized and there has been considerable expansion since World War II, particularly in engineering and chemicals. Since 1968 there has been a new system of economic planning, aiming at a certain amount of decentralization and encouragement of individual initiative, while still maintaining overall state control. The considerable volume of exports (largely to communist countries) includes transport equipment, machinery, fruit and vegetables, and meat. *History*: the Magyars reached the Danube area in the 9th century AD and settled there under the Árpád dynasty. In the 11th century St *Stephen I converted the country to Christianity and became the first Hungarian king. After a long period of dynastic struggles and threats from foreign powers, Hungary was conquered by the Turks in 1526 and in the 17th century it became part of the Habsburg Empire.

The 19th century saw the rise of Hungarian nationalism. A revolt under *Kossuth in 1848 was suppressed by the Austrians but in 1867 Hungary gained internal self-government as part of the Dual Monarchy of *Austria-Hungary. Following the collapse of the Dual Monachy in 1918 Hungary became a republic but, after a short period of communist rule, a constitutional monarchy was formed with *Horthy de Nagybanya as regent. Although allied to the Germans in World War II, it was occupied by them in 1944 and liberated by Soviet troops in 1945. After the war it became a republic and in 1949 the communists gained control. In 1956 an anti-Stalinist uprising was crushed by Soviet forces. In 1967 a treaty of friendship with the Soviet Union was renewed and in recent years a certain amount of liberalization has taken place. A sign of Hungary's nonconformist status within the Eastern Bloc is the recent adoption (1987) of income tax and VAT. Effective power is in the hands of János *Kádár, first secretary of the Central Committee. Official language: Hungarian (Magyar). Official currency: forint of 100 fillér. Area: 93 035 sq km (35 911 sq mi). Population (1980): 10 710 000. Capital: Budapest.

Hung Hsiu-ch'uan. *See* Hong Xiu Quan.

Hungnam. *See* Hamhŭng.

Hung-wu. *See* Hong-wu.

Huns Nomadic peoples, originating in Mongolia, who overran much of SE Europe in the late-4th and 5th centuries, overthrowing the *Ostrogoths and then invading the Roman Empire. Renowned and feared for their military prowess, especially their use of cavalry, the failure of the Empire to continue payment of tribute to them inspired *Attila, under whom the Huns were now united and controlled, to invade Greece, Gaul, and finally Italy (452). The death of Attila (453) fragmented their empire and after defeat by a coalition of tribes at Nedao (455) they ceased to be of importance.

Hunt, Henry (1773–1835) British radical, known as Orator Hunt, who presided over the demonstration that ended in the *Peterloo Massacre (1819). He was imprisoned (1820–23) but was subsequently elected to parliament (1830), where he campaigned for parliamentary reform.

Hunt, James (1947–) British motor-racing driver, who became world champion in 1976 and won ten Grand Prix races. He retired in 1979.

Hunt, (Henry Cecil) John, Baron (1910–) British army officer and mountaineer, who led the successful 1953 expedition to climb Mount Everest. Teamwork and meticulous planning enabled *Hillary and *Tenzing to reach the summit.

Hunt, (James Henry) Leigh (1784–1859) British poet and journalist. In essays and criticism for many periodicals he supported Keats and other Romantic poets and promoted various political reforms. In 1813 he was imprisoned for his attacks on the Prince Regent. His books include *Imagination and Fancy* (1844) and *Autobiography* (1850).

Hunt, William Holman (1827–1910) British painter. After studying in the Royal Academy, he helped found the *Pre-Raphaelite Brotherhood, to the principles of which he alone remained faithful. His symbolic but technically realistic paintings include *The Light of the World* (Keble College, Oxford) and *The Scapegoat* (Port Sunlight), inspired by a visit to Syria and Palestine (1854).

Hunter, John (1728–93) British physician and one of the founders of modern surgery. Hunter learnt anatomy under his elder brother William and qualified as a physician, becoming surgeon extraordinary to George III. Hunter also investigated various diseases, most notably venereal diseases, inoculating himself in the process. His brother **William Hunter** (1718–83) was a leading anatomist and obstetrician, attending Queen Charlotte during three pregnancies. He bequeathed his collection of coins, pictures, medals, etc., to Glasgow University.

Hunter River A river in SE Australia, in New South Wales.

It rises in the Eastern Highlands and flows generally S through Glenbawn Reservoir to enter the Pacific Ocean at Newcastle. Length: 467 km (290 mi).

Huntingdon 52 20N 0 12W A town in E England, in Cambridgeshire on the Great Ouse River. A market town with printing, brewing, and knitwear industries, Huntingdon is the birthplace of Oliver Cromwell, who attended the grammar school (now a Cromwell museum), as did Samuel Pepys. Population (1981): 17 477, with Godmanchester.

Huntingdon, Selina Hastings, Countess of (1707–91) British Methodist leader. She was an early member of the Wesleys' Methodist society but supported the Calvinistic beliefs of George *Whitefield rather than the Arminianism of the Wesleys. After being widowed in 1746, she founded many chapels, known collectively as the Countess of Huntingdon's Connexion.

Huntingdon and Peterborough A former county of E England, formed in 1965 from Huntingdonshire and the Soke of Peterborough (an administrative county; 1888–1965). In 1974 it became part of Cambridgeshire.

Huntsville 34 44N 86 35W A city in the USA, in NE Alabama. Founded in 1805, it is a centre for rocket and guided-missile research. Industries include textiles and agricultural implements. Population (1980): 142 513.

Hunyadi, János (c. 1387–1456) Hungarian military leader and statesman. Following his successful Long Campaign against the Turks (1443–44), he was elected (1446) governor and regent for King Ladislas (1440–57). In 1456, shortly before dying of the plague, he routed the Turkish forces before Belgrade, thus securing a 70-year peace.

Hupa An Athabascan-speaking North American Indian people of the lower Trinity River region of N California. They lived along the river banks in villages consisting of women's houses and men's lodges. They hunted elk and deer, fished for salmon, and gathered acorns. Wealth consisted of dentalium shells and woodpecker scalps. Their religion was characterized by *shamanism and the performance of seasonal ceremonies.

Hupei. *See* Hubei.

Hurd, Douglas (Richard) (1930–) British Conservative politician; home secretary (1985–). After service overseas with the Foreign Office, he became an MP in 1974 and Secretary of State for Northern Ireland in 1984. He is also known as a writer of political thrillers.

hurdling A track event in athletics in which sprinters jump ten hurdles in the course of each race. The standard distances are 110 m and 400 m for men and 100 m for women. For the 110 m the height of the hurdles is 106.7 cm (3.5 ft), for the 400 m it is 91.4 cm (3 ft), and for the 100 m, 84 cm (2.75 ft). Racers are not normally disqualified for knocking hurdles over. World records: men's 110 m: 12.93 seconds (1981) by Renaldo Nehemiah (USA); men's 400 m: 47.02 seconds (1983) by Edwin Moses (USA); women's 100 m: 12.29 seconds (1986) by Jordanka Donkova (Bulgaria); women's 400 m: 54.02 seconds (1983) by A. Ambrosene-Kastetskaia (USSR).

hurdy-gurdy A stringed instrument sounded by a rosined wheel, turned by the right hand, and stopped by a set of keys played by the left hand; there are also two drone strings. It was very popular in medieval times and survives as a folk instrument in parts of Europe. □ p. 598.

hurling (*or* hurley) An Irish 15-a-side stick-and-ball field game similar to *hockey, over 3000 years old. The ball is hit or carried through the air with a broad-bladed curved stick, the hurley (Gaelic word: *caman*), and may be caught in the hand. A standard field measures 137 × 82 m (150 × 90 yd). A goal, hit under the crossbar, scores three points; a hit between the posts but above the bar scores one.

Huron An Iroquoian-speaking North American people of the St Lawrence River region. They cultivated maize, beans, squashes, and tobacco. Families of matrilineal descent occupied villages of bark-covered dwellings. Groups of villages formed bands governed by a council of village chiefs and band chief. Band chiefs formed a tribal council. Women were prominent in public affairs and the appointment of chiefs. The Huron were attacked and displaced by the *Iroquois during the 17th century.

HURDY-GURDY

Huron, Lake The second largest of the Great Lakes in North America, situated between the USA and Canada. It is an important shipping route carrying iron ore, coal, grain, and oil. Area: 59 570 sq km (23 000 sq mi).

Hurrians A people living in E Anatolia and N Mesopotamia during the 2nd millennium BC. The Hurrians probably originated in the Armenian mountains before their expansion. Their language, which is extinct, was neither Indo-European nor Semitic, but may be related to *Georgian and the Caucasian languages. It is largely known from cuneiform tablets from Hattusas, the capital of their neighbours, the *Hittites, whose civilization the Hurrians greatly influenced. There was never a Hurrian empire, but the powerful kingdom of Mitanni (1550–1400 BC) was largely Hurrian in population. *See also* Nuzi.

hurricane 1. A tropical *cyclone with surface-wind speeds in excess of 64 knots (32.7 m per second) that occurs around the Caribbean Sea and Gulf of Mexico. Tropical cyclones also occur in the W Pacific Ocean, Bay of Bengal, and Queensland but are identified by their own local names (*see* typhoon). The centre (eye) of a hurricane is an area of light winds around which strong winds, cloud, and rain bands spiral. 2. Any wind reaching force 12 on the *Beaufort scale (in excess of 64 knots or 32.7 metres per second) whether or not it is related to a tropical cyclone.

Hurstmonceux. *See* Herstmonceux.

Hus, Jan (c. 1369–1415) Bohemian religious reformer and martyr. Ordained as a priest in 1401, he became a university teacher in Prague and a popular preacher. Under the influence of the writings of *Wycliffe, he criticized the ecclesiastical establishment, chiefly on moral grounds, emphasizing the role of the Scriptures. In 1415, while defending his beliefs at the Council of *Constance, where he had been lured by a promise of safe conduct, he was tried, condemned, and burnt at the stake. His followers in Bohemia became known as *Hussites.

Husák, Gustáv (1913–) Czechoslovak statesman. Husák, a lawyer, took part in the Slovak uprising against the Germans in 1944. In April, 1969, after the fall of *Dubček, he became first secretary of the Czechoslovak Communist Party.

Husaynids The ruling dynasty of Tunisia from 1705 to 1957. Their founder, al-Husayn ibn Ali, was recognized as governor of Tunisia by the Ottomans, but he and his successors, who had the title of *bey*, were practically independent. In 1883 their land became a French protectorate. The *beys* lost popularity because it was thought they were too servile to the French and in 1957, when Tunisia became a republic, the dynasty came to an end.

husky One of several breeds of compact sturdy deep-chested dogs used for pulling sledges in Arctic regions. The Siberian husky has small erect ears, a long muzzle, and a brushlike tail curved over the back. The dense double-layered coat may be of various colours and provides insulation against the severe climate. The Eskimo dog, bred in Greenland, closely resembles the Siberian husky, from which it is probably descended. The Alaskan malamute is a similar breed of sledge dog. Height: 51–63 cm. *See also* Samoyed.

hussars Light-cavalry regiments originating in Hungary in the 15th century. Most European armies have used hussars for reconnaissance and raids. Their uniform included the characteristic dolman, a cloak worn hanging from the left shoulder. The name hussar has now been adopted by some armoured units.

Hussein (ibn Talal) (1935–) King of Jordan (1952–). He became king following the deposition because of mental illness of his father Talal. Of his four wives, his second (1961–72) was an Englishwoman, Antoinette Gardiner, who took the name Muna. Hussein led Jordan into the 1967 Arab-Israeli War, in which its possessions on the West Bank of the River Jordan were occupied by Israel. The large Palestinian population of the area moved to the East Bank, where al-*Fatah guerrillas established themselves, posing a threat to Hussein's government. In 1970 he ruthlessly crushed the guerrillas in the fighting of "Black September" but in 1974, under pressure from other Arab countries, accepted the claims of the Palestine Liberation Organization to the West Bank.

Husserl, Edmund (1859–1938) German philosopher, influential in the phenomenological tradition (*see* phenomenology). He taught at Halle, Göttingen, and Freiburg Universities. Husserl's philosophy rejected presuppositions about what actually exists (and why it does) and studied instead purely "subjective" data.

HURRICANE *A house at Bonnet Shores, Rhode Island, USA, after being struck by a 200 km per hr (125 mph) hurricane.*

Hussites The followers of the Bohemian heretic, Jan *Hus (1372-1415). They demanded a reformed national Church with a vernacular liturgy. In spite of papal and imperial crusades led by the Holy Roman Emperor *Sigismund, the Hussites, who were supported by many of the Bohemian aristocracy, remained undefeated until a compromise was reached at the Council of *Basle in 1433. Their more radical wing, the Taborites, rejected this but were quickly defeated. The moderate Utraquists gained many of their demands and, in spite of frequent schisms, survived until the 17th century. *See also* Moravian Brethren.

Huston, John (1906-87) US film director. He began his career as a scriptwriter. His first film as director was *The Maltese Falcon* (1941), and subsequent films included *The Treasure of the Sierra Madre* (1948), for which he wrote the script and in which he also acted, *The African Queen* (1951), *The Misfits* (1960), *The Man Who Would Be King* (1975), *Annie* (1982), *Prizzi's Honour* (1985), and *The Dead* (1987).

Hutcheson, Francis (1694-1746) Scottish philosopher. He was a professor at Glasgow University (1729-46) and author of works on ethics and aesthetics. The posthumously published *System of Moral Philosophy* (1755) holds that man has an innate moral sense, so that he is born knowing what is good and right. Hutcheson's phrase, "the greatest happiness of the greatest number," as the criterion of virtuous action, was taken up by the exponents of *utilitarianism.

hutia A large *rodent of the family *Capromyidae* (which also includes the *coypus), found in Cuba and the West Indies. Hutias are 20-60 cm long excluding the naked tail (3-30 cm). They are mainly vegetarian and are either diurnal and arboreal (genus *Capromys*; 4 species) or nocturnal and terrestrial (genus *Geocapromys*; 3 species).

Hutten, Ulrich von (1488-1523) German humanist, who became poet laureate of the Holy Roman Empire in 1517. His reputation was established as a wit and satirist before he devoted himself to the cause of the Reformation and German nationalism. Joining the war against the German princes, he was driven into exile shortly before his death.

Hutton, James (1726-97) Scottish physician, generally regarded as the founder of geology. His investigations led him to believe that the earth was very much older than generally believed at that time. These views were expressed in his book *Theory of the Earth* (1795) which met with strong objections from those who accepted the view of creation contained in Genesis.

Hutton, Len (Sir Leonard H.; 1916-) British cricketer, who played for Yorkshire and England and became the first professional English captain (1953). He made a record Test score against Australia of 364 (1938) and in his career (1934-60) hit 129 centuries.

Huxley, Thomas Henry (1825-95) British biologist, whose impact spanned both biology and philosophy. A qualified surgeon, Huxley developed his interest in natural history while serving as a ship's surgeon in the Far East. He was a staunch supporter and friend of Charles *Darwin and led the debate against opponents of Darwinism at Oxford in 1860. After valuable work in palaeontology Huxley held numerous public posts and was instrumental in bringing enlightened change to educational methods. From 1880 onwards he challenged orthodox theology and coined the term agnosticism to describe his own position. He served as president of the Royal Society (1883-85). Three of his grandsons achieved fame in the fields of science and literature. **Sir Julian Huxley** (1887-1975) was a zoologist and scientific administrator, who also made valuable contributions to the philosophy of science. He was involved in the improvement of the London Zoo at Regent's Park and in developing its offshoot at *Whipsnade and was appointed first director general of UNESCO (1946-48). His brother **Aldous Huxley** (1894-1964) was a novelist and writer. During the 1920s he lived mostly in Italy and in 1937 settled in California. The

witty satirical novels *Antic Hay* (1923) and *Point Counter Point* (1928) were followed by *Brave New World* (1932), *Eyeless in Gaza* (1936), and *After Many A Summer Dies the Swan* (1939). His later essays, including *The Doors of Perception* (1954) and *Heaven and Hell* (1956), explore such subjects as mysticism and the use of drugs. **Sir Andrew Fielding Huxley** (1917-), half-brother to Sir Julian and Aldous, is a biologist noted for his researches into the mechanisms of nerve-impulse conduction and muscle contraction. For their work on nerve impulses Huxley and his collaborator A. L. *Hodgkin shared a Nobel Prize (1963) with Sir John *Eccles. He was awarded the OM in 1983.

Huygens, Christiaan (1629-95) Dutch astronomer and physicist, who discovered Saturn's rings in 1656. He also built the first pendulum clock and designed an arrangement of lenses called a Huygens eyepiece, which is still in use on some telescopes and microscopes. He devised a wave theory of light to explain double refraction. He claimed to have invented the hairspring (a claim also made by *Hooke).

Huysmans, Joris Karl (1848-1907) French novelist. In his best-known novel, *À rebours* (1884), he epitomized the contemporary taste for decadent aestheticism in the character of Des Esseintes, who devoted his life to the sensual indulgence of his esoteric tastes. He also wrote art criticism and a series of partly autobiographical novels, including *Là-bas* (1891), that charted his spiritual progress and ultimate acceptance of Roman Catholicism.

hyacinth A perennial herbaceous plant of the genus *Hyacinthus* (about 30 species), native to the Mediterranean region and tropical Africa and widely planted as ornamental garden and pot plants. Growing from bulbs, the flower stems, up to 35 cm high, bear a dense head of bell-shaped flowers, varying from white and yellow to deep purple. The plants have slender leaves, up to 30 cm long. The common garden hyacinths are derived from *H. orientalis*. Family: *Liliaceae*.

Hyades A young open *star cluster in the constellation Taurus, the brightest stars forming a V-shaped group that can be seen with the naked eye. The star *Aldebaran lies in the direction of the cluster but is actually much nearer the sun.

hyaena. *See* hyena.

hybrid The offspring resulting from the mating of two unrelated individuals. The hybrid offspring often shows greater general fitness than either of the two parents, a phenomenon called hybrid vigour (or heterosis). This is commonly used by plant breeders to produce a generation of crop plants giving higher yields and showing improved resistance to disease. Hybrid vigour cannot be maintained in subsequent generations and new hybrids have to be produced for each season.

Hyde, Douglas (1860-1949) Irish scholar, whose translations of Irish literature influenced such writers as Yeats and Synge. He was also a senator in the Irish parliament (1925, 1938) and was the first president of Eire (1938-45). He founded, and was first president (1893-1915) of, the Gaelic League. His books include *The Love Songs of Connacht* (1893), *A Literary History of Ireland* (1899), and *Legends of Saints and Sinners* (1915).

Hyde Park An extensive park in the Greater London borough of the City of Westminster. Adjoining Kensington Gardens, it is divided by the Serpentine, a popular boating lake, and crossed by Rotten Row, a horse-riding track. The Great Exhibition (1851) was held here and the park remains a venue for open-air meetings with Speakers' Corner in the NE, opposite Marble Arch. Area: about 1.4 sq km (0.55 sq mi).

Hyderabad 17 22N 78 26E One of the largest cities in India, the capital of Andhra Pradesh situated on the River Musi. Formerly the capital of the princely state of Hyderabad, it was founded in 1590 by the Muslim Qutb

Shahi sultans. The old city was planned around the Char-minar (1594), a rectangular building surmounted by four minarets; other notable buildings include the Mecca Masjid, a mosque modelled on the one at Mecca. An educational centre, Hyderabad is the site of Osmania University (1918), an agricultural university, and several research institutes. There has been considerable industrial growth in recent years, giving Hyderabad a higher standard of living than many other Indian cities. The chief manufactures include bus and railway equipment, textiles, and pharmaceutical goods. Population (1981): 2 528 000.

Hyderabad 25 23N 68 24E A city in SW Pakistan, on the River Indus. A focal point of rail and road routes, it has light industries and several institutions of higher education, includ-ing the University of Sind (1947). Population (1981): 795 000.

Hyder Ali (1728–82) Muslim Indian ruler of Mysore. A volunteer in the Mysore raja's army from 1749, he became a commander (1759) and in about 1761 deposed the raja. When the British refused to support him against his Indian enemies, he invaded British territory and was narrowly defeated near Madras, coming closer than any other Indian ruler to ousting the British from S India.

Hydra In Greek legend, a monster with many heads who grew two more whenever one was cut off. It was killed by *Heracles, whose own death was later caused by the mon-ster's poisonous blood or gall.

Hydra A widely distributed genus of solitary freshwater invertebrate animals belonging to an order (*Hydroida*) of *coelenterates. They are flexible *polyps, 10–30 mm long, with the mouth at the top surrounded by 6–10 tentacles. Hydras are usually attached to stones, sticks, or aquatic vegetation and feed on small animals. Reproduction is asexual in summer and sexual in winter. Class: *Hydrozoa*.

Hydrangea A genus of shrubs (about 80 species) native to Asia and North and South America, including several popular ornamentals. The showy heads of white, pink, or blue flowers may be sterile and sometimes change colour according to the acidity or alkalinity of the soil. *H. macro-phylla* is a popular pot plant. Family: *Hydrangeaceae*.

hydraulics The study of the applications of *hydrostatics and *hydrodynamics to design problems. In civil engineer-ing it is used to study the flow of water in pipes, rivers, canals, etc., especially with reference to the construction of dams, reservoirs, and hydroelectric power stations. In mechanical engineering, applications include the design of machinery involving fluids, such as hydraulic presses, *tur-bines, propellers, etc. Hydraulics is concerned with the bulk properties of fluids, such as density, viscosity, elasticity, and surface tension, rather than their molecular properties.

hydraulis (Greek: water pipe) An early type of *organ in which the air pressure was maintained by water. A clay model found in the ruins of Carthage has three ranks of pipes and suggests an actual height of about 3 m (10 ft). The loud sound it produced made it useful for signalling in battle; it was also played in Roman amphitheatres, Emperor Nero being a keen performer.

hydrocarbons Compounds containing carbon and hydro-gen. The saturated hydrocarbons are classified as *alkanes. Unsaturated hydrocarbons include the *alkenes and *alkynes. *Aromatic hydrocarbons include *benzene and its many derivatives.

hydrocephalus An excess of fluid in the brain. The brain is normally bathed in cerebrospinal fluid, which is constantly being produced and reabsorbed. A block in the flow or reabsorption of the fluid will result in hydrocephalus. In a baby, the bones of whose skull are not yet joined, the head becomes enlarged. Congenital defects, meningitis, tumours, and injury can all be causes. Hydrocephalus may resolve spontaneously or may require surgical treatment.

hydrochloric acid A solution in water of the colourless pungent gas hydrogen chloride (HCl). It is made by the action of sulphuric acid on salt or by the direct recom-bination of hydrogen and chlorine from the electrolysis of sea water. It is very soluble in water and forms a strong acid. Concentrated hydrochloric acid contains about 40% HCl by weight and is a clear fuming corrosive liquid. The acid in the human stomach is dilute hydrochloric acid (0.4%).

ladder foils

V-shaped foils

short submerged foils

HYDROFOIL

hydrocyanic acid (*or* prussic acid; HCN) A highly toxic colourless liquid. It is made from ammonia and methane reacted with air in the presence of a catalyst. HCN forms weakly acidic solutions in water and is used in making synthetic fibres and as a fumigant.

hydrodynamics (*or* fluid dynamics) The branch of mechanics concerned with the study of ideal fluids in motion. An ideal fluid is assumed to be incompressible and to be free from frictional forces. Although never achieved, this simplification is often necessary to analyse a complex situation. The velocity, acceleration, and pressure at each point in the flow of an ideal liquid gives an indication of what will happen in a real liquid. *See also* aerodynamics; hydraulics.

hydroelectric power Electricity generation using the energy of falling water. The water turns a *turbine con-nected to an alternator, generating electricity with an effi-ciency of over 90% at full load and generally over 60% at quarter-load. Water is led through pipes from high-level natural or artificial reservoirs to the power station. Lower-level reservoirs and dammed rivers are also used in some situations. The higher the reservoir, the less water is needed for the same power output. Hydroelectric power is, there-fore, a cheap power source in mountainous areas with high rainfall. Unfortunately these are not usually near the industrial communities that consume the most power. Also, because it depends on rainfall, hydroelectricity has to be backed by other power sources (*see* power station). In pumped storage stations, electricity is stored by using it to drive pumps that raise the water to a high-level reservoir. In times of high demand this water is run back through the turbines. Hydroelectric power stations can have an output of 10 000 megawatts but in the UK most produce less than 100 MW.

hydrofoil A ship the hull of which is raised out of the water by foils as its speed increases. The foils provide lift in much the same way as an aerofoil; once the hull is clear of the water the drag is greatly reduced and the speed can be increased far above that of a normal ship of the same size and weight. The first hydrofoil was built in 1906 by Enrico Fortanini (1848-1930); this had a stack of foils arranged like a ladder. Modern craft use a large V-shaped foil, to provide stability in turns or in rough seas, or small totally submerged foils, which support the hull on streamlined struts. Propulsion is by propeller or by pumped-water jet. Hydrofoils of 150 tonnes are in use in many parts of the world, including a cross-Channel service; some are capable of reaching speeds of up to 112 km per hour (70 mph).

hydrogen (H) The lightest of all gases, recognized as an element by Cavendish in 1766 and named by Lavoisier after water (Greek *hudro*, water). Hydrogen makes up about three-quarters of the mass of the universe. It is the simplest element, its nuclei consisting of one proton. Heavier elements are formed by nuclear fusion (*see* nuclear energy) from hydrogen in stars. The heavier isotope of hydrogen, *deuterium (D *or* ^2H), occurs as about one part in 6000 of ordinary hydrogen. *Tritium (^3H) also occurs but is unstable. As well as the gaseous element (H_2) and water (H_2O), hydrogen occurs in organic compounds and in all inorganic *acids and *alkalis. The gas itself is used as a fuel for rockets, in welding, for filling balloons, and in chemical manufacture. It combines (explosively if in the right proportions) with oxygen to form water and can be obtained from water by electrolysis. Liquid hydrogen is used for experiments in low-temperature physics. At no 1; at wt 1.00797; mp −259.14°C; bp −252.87°C.

hydrogen bomb. *See* nuclear weapons.

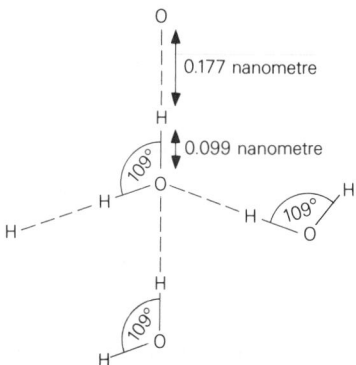

HYDROGEN BOND *The hydrogen bonding between water molecules (H_2O) in ice crystals.*

hydrogen bond A weak attraction (much weaker than a covalent or ionic *chemical bond but much stronger than *Van der Waals forces) between an oxygen, nitrogen, or fluorine atom in one molecule and a hydrogen atom in a neighbouring molecule. The hydrogen atom must itself be linked to a similar electronegative atom by a covalent bond. The attraction arises because the atom bonded to the hydrogen atoms exerts a strong pull on the shared electrons and thus confers a partial positive charge on the hydrogen. Consequently electrostatic attraction occurs between this hydrogen atom and the oxygen, fluorine, or nitrogen in the other molecule. Hydrogen bonding is responsible for the anomalous physical properties of many compounds, including water. It is particularly important in biological

systems, being responsible for maintaining the structure of proteins and nucleic acids.

hydrography The description, measurement, and charting of the waters of the earth's surface (oceans, seas, lakes, rivers, and streams), particularly for navigational purposes. Tides, currents, and waves are also involved. The term is sometimes used for the shape of the sea floor and the deposits covering it.

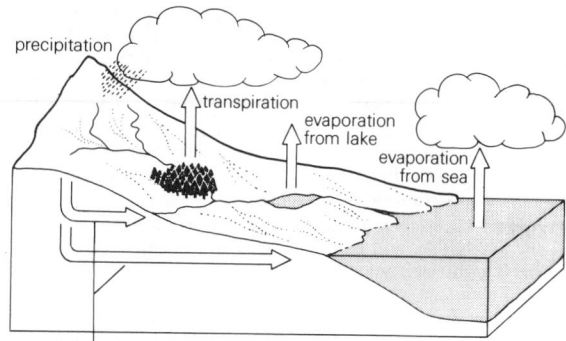

HYDROLOGY *The hydrological cycle.*

hydrology The science that studies the occurrence and movement of water on and over the surface of the earth. The **hydrological cycle** is the cyclic movement of water from the sea to the atmosphere and back, via precipitation, streams, and rivers. The main processes with which hydrology is concerned are precipitation, evaporation and transpiration, stream flow, and groundwater flow. It has many important applications, such as flood control and the supply of water for domestic and industrial purposes, irrigation, and hydroelectric power. □water table.

hydrolysis The reaction of a chemical compound with water; usually water is the solvent in which the reaction occurs. A common example is the hydrolysis of *esters to form alcohols and carboxylic acids.

hydrometer An instrument for measuring the relative *density of a liquid. It consists of a weighted and sealed glass bulb with a long neck on which a scale is calibrated. The relative density is measured by placing the hydrometer in the liquid and noting the level to which it sinks.

hydrophobia. *See* rabies.

hydrophone A type of *microphone that converts underwater sound waves into electrical signals. It consists essentially of a diaphragm, a *transducer, and an *amplifier. It is used in *sonar equipment, depth sounding, and underwater communications.

hydroponics The cultivation of plants in a liquid nutrient solution instead of soil. A carefully prepared aqueous solution of all the nutrients required for healthy growth is used, usually in conjunction with an inert medium, such as sand or gravel, which provides support for the plant-root system. On a small scale, the solution is simply poured over the substrate and the excess allowed to drain into containers for re-use. On a commercial scale, this is done by an automatic pumping system in which the solution is monitored to maintain nutrient levels and acidity.
Hydroponics enables crops to be produced in arid regions or where the soil is infertile or toxic, but its high cost restricts its use to high-value crops, such as flowers and vegetables.

hydrostatics The branch of mechanics concerned with fluids at rest (*compare* hydrodynamics). It is generally considered to have been instigated by Archimedes. Applications include the design of storage tanks, gates, and valves for hydraulic structures, dams, etc.

Hydrozoa A class of aquatic invertebrate animals (3700 species)—*coelenterates—whose life cycle usually alternates between generations of mainly marine sessile colonial *polyps and free-swimming solitary *medusae. *See also* Hydra; Obelia; Portuguese man-of-war.

hyena (*or* hyaena) A carnivorous □mammal of the family *Hyaenidae*. There are three species: the African spotted hyena (*Crocuta crocuta*); the Asian striped hyena (*Hyaena hyaena*); and the brown hyena (*H. brunnea*) of South Africa, also called strandwolf. Hyenas are doglike in appearance, up to 1.5 m long including the tail, and stand about 90 cm high at the shoulder. They hunt in packs, feeding on carrion and killing young or sick animals.

Hyères 43 07N 6 08E A resort and spa in S France, in the Var department on the French Riviera. It has a notable beach and offshore are the Îles d'Hyères, a small group of islands (Porquerolles, Port-Cros, I'Île du Levant, and two islets). Population (1982): 41 739.

Hygiea The Greek goddess of health, worshipped together with *Asclepius, god of medicine, and sometimes identified as his daughter or wife. She was usually portrayed in the act of feeding a serpent from a dish.

hygrometer An instrument that measures the relative *humidity of the atmosphere. In mechanical hygrometers, a material (usually human hair) is used, the length of which varies with the humidity; the variations being transformed into the movement of a pointer along a scale. In the wet-and-dry bulb hygrometer, two thermometers are placed side by side, one having its bulb covered by a moist cloth. The cooling caused by the evaporation from this wet bulb depends on the atmospheric moisture and thus the difference between the two thermometer readings can be related by standard tables to the relative humidity.

Hyksos A nomadic Asiatic tribe, known to the ancient Egyptians as Shepherd Kings or Princes of Foreign Lands. Moving southwards about 1750 BC through Palestine and Syria, the Hyksos invaded Egypt and, until driven northwards again by the Egyptians about 1570 BC, ruled the Delta area, introducing metallurgy, bronze weapons, the wheel and, traditionally, the use of horse and chariot.

Hymen The Greek god of marriage. He was the son of Apollo or of Dionysus and Aphrodite.

Hymenoptera A large worldwide order of insects (over 100 000 species) including the ants, sawflies, ichneumons, wasps, and bees. Many species show a high degree of social organization. Typically they have two pairs of membranous wings and the first segment of the abdomen is constricted to form a "waist." A tubular egg-laying structure (ovipositor) is generally present and in higher groups is modified for sawing, piercing, or stinging. The larvae (except the sawflies) are legless and have well-developed heads. The males develop from unfertilized eggs. Many species are of benefit to man because they pollinate flowering plants and prey on or parasitize insect pests.

Hymettus, Mount (Modern Greek name: Imittós Óros) 37 57N 23 49E A mountain ridge in SE Greece, running N-S for about 15 km (9 mi) immediately E of Athens. The Kara marble used in ancient times was quarried here. Height: 1026 m (3366 ft).

hymn A song of praise in honour of a deity or saint, often in a metrical verse form. Hymns have been an important part of Christian congregational worship since the end of the 4th century. During the middle ages polyphonic settings became common but after the Reformation Lutheran chorale became the basis of the German and English hymn traditions. Famous hymn writers include Martin Luther, Charles Wesley, and Isaac Watts (1674-1748); many of the hymns sung in the Anglican church today were written in the 19th century.

hyoscine (*or* scopolamine) A drug with similar uses and actions to *atropine. It also has a depressant effect on the

brain and is therefore used to prevent travel sickness and for sedation before surgery.

Hypatia (d. 415 AD) Neoplatonist philosopher and mathematician. She lectured on philosophy at *Alexandria, where her wisdom and learning endeared her to both pagans and Christians. The patriarch Cyril resented her influence, and she was brutally murdered by a Christian mob.

hyperbola The curve, or pair of curves, formed by a *conic section and defined in Cartesian coordinates (*see* coordinate systems) by the equation $x^2/a^2 - y^2/b^2 = 1$, where a and b are constants. Its two parts have a common axis and are separated by a minimum distance $2a$ along this axis. As it goes out to *infinity, the curve becomes increasingly close to two straight lines, called *asymptotes.

hyperbolic functions A set of mathematical functions written $\sinh x$, $\cosh x$, $\tanh x$, and their inverses $\operatorname{csch} x$, $\operatorname{sech} x$, and $\coth x$ respectively. Sinh x is defined as $\frac{1}{2}(e^x - e^{-x})$, where e is the base of natural logarithms; cosh x is $\frac{1}{2}(e^x + e^{-x})$, and tanh x is sinh x/cosh x. Hyperbolic functions are defined by analogy with the trigonometric functions sin x, etc., and are so named because they are related to the *hyperbola in much the same way as the trigonometric functions are related to the circle.

Hyperboreans In Greek mythology, a people who lived in the far north, beyond the north wind (Boreas), in a land of sunshine and luxury. According to *Herodotus, they were devotees of Apollo and sent offerings to him at Delos but did not come themselves.

hyperglycaemia A high concentration of sugar in the blood. This occurs in *diabetes mellitus and may, if severe and uncontrolled, lead to coma.

Hyperion In Greek mythology, one of the *Titans, the son of Uranus and Gaea and father of *Eos, *Helios, and *Selene. He was himself a sun god and was often identified with his son Helios.

hypermetropia. *See* longsightedness.

hypersensitivity. *See* allergy.

hypertension High *blood pressure. This is a common condition, which can be caused by kidney disease, hormonal disorders, and some congenital diseases; for most cases, however, no cause can be found (this is known as essential hypertension). Usually there are no symptoms, with the consequent danger that untreated hypertension may lead to heart failure, kidney failure, cerebral haemorrhage, and blindness. In some cases surgery can be curative, but usually only drug treatment is necessary and must continue indefinitely.

hyperthyroidism Overactivity of the thyroid gland, which occurs most commonly in women. It may lead to the syndrome of thyrotoxicosis: restlessness, irritability, heat intolerance, weight loss, and palpitations, sometimes with protruding eyes and swelling of the neck (*see* goitre)—this is called exophthalmic goitre (*or* Graves's disease). It can be treated by surgery, radioactive iodine to destroy part of the gland, or drugs that suppress the production of thyroid hormones.

hypnosis The production of a trance state by means of firm suggestion, with the cooperation of the subject. People who have been deeply hypnotized can carry out instructions that would not be possible in a normal waking state; for instance, they can become insensible to pain or regress to childish behaviour. First used for therapeutic purposes by *Mesmer in the 18th century, it was developed (and given the name hypnosis) by James Braid in the 19th century. In France it was used by *Charcot (under whom *Freud studied), and by the turn of the century it was established as a means of treating certain psychiatric disorders (especially those of psychosomatic origin). It has, however, always been regarded as somewhat disreputable, first because of its misuse on the stage as a form of entertainment and second because the mechanism is still not understood. Although it is

HYPNOSIS *Mesmer demonstrating his powers at his home in Paris.*

alleged that a hypnotist cannot force a patient under hypnotism to do anything he would not be willing to do when awake (e.g. commit a crime), the dangers inherent in one person controlling another's actions are obvious.

hypnotics Drugs that cause sleep. Although most drugs that depress the brain's activity have this effect, the ideal hypnotic produces natural sleep without "hangover" effects on awakening. Some drugs of the *benzodiazepine group come closest to this ideal and have now almost entirely replaced *barbiturates as hypnotics.

hypoglycaemia A low concentration of sugar in the blood. This may occur in otherwise healthy people who have eaten little and exercised considerably, but is more often seen in diabetics who have taken too much insulin. The patient feels weak, sweaty, and shaky. *See* diabetes.

hypothalamus A part of the *brain, surrounding the lower part of the third ventricle, that is an important coordinating centre for the functions of the autonomic *nervous system. It is particularly involved with the control of body temperature, with regulating how much is eaten and drunk, and with the emotions. It also releases *neurohormones affecting other organs, especially the *pituitary gland.

hypothermia Lowering of the body temperature. This is most commonly seen in old people and young babies—whose body temperature is less well controlled—if they are living in poorly heated rooms. If the body temperature falls very low severe internal changes may occur, but otherwise gentle

warming will help the patient to recover. Hypothermia may be deliberately induced for heart surgery.

hyrax An African *mammal belonging to the order *Hyracoidea* (6 species), also called coney. 30-60 cm long, hyraxes are related to ungulates (hooved mammals), having hooflike toes and a two-chambered stomach for digesting their vegetable diet. They are nimble and live in small colonies in trees or among rocks, being most active at twilight.

hyssop A perennial herbaceous plant, *Hyssopus officinalis*, native to S Europe, Asia, and Morocco. It is grown elsewhere as a garden ornamental and was formerly cultivated as a medicinal herb. Growing to a height of 60 cm, it has whorls of violet-blue flowers along the stem. Family: *Labiatae*.

hysterectomy The surgical removal of the womb. A subtotal hysterectomy involves removing the body of the womb but leaving the neck (cervix); in total hysterectomy (or panhysterectomy) the entire womb is removed. It is most commonly performed when the womb contains large fibroids—benign tumours that cause heavy menstrual periods. Other conditions that may require hysterectomy include cancer of the womb or the presence of precancerous cells in the cervix. The operation is usually performed through an incision made in the abdominal wall: it invariably precludes subsequent pregnancy but does not affect sexual activity.

hysteresis Any of several physical phenomena in which an induced effect lags behind the inducing cause. The term is most often applied to magnetic hysteresis in which magnetic induction produced in a ferromagnetic material lags behind the magnetic field. Thus a graph of magnetic induction plotted against a magnetizing field is a closed S-shaped loop (hysteresis loop). The area within the loop is equal to the energy dissipation per unit volume during one cycle of magnetization. Other forms of hysteresis include thermal, dielectric, and elastic hysteresis.

hysteria A neurotic condition of emotional instability and immaturity in which patients are vulnerable to suggestion and develop physical symptoms. Hysterical symptoms are unconsciously adopted by the individual because they bring some gain. The symptoms may be of "conversion hysteria," characterized by physical symptoms, such as paralysis; or of "dissociative hysteria," with changes in thinking, such as multiple personality. Treatment is usually by *psychotherapy.

Hythe 51 05N 1 05E A resort in SE England, in Kent on the English Channel. It is an ancient Cinque Port, long silted up. A light railway, claimed to be the world's smallest, runs to Dymchurch and Romney. Population (1981): 12 723.

Hywel the Good (Howel Dda; d. 950 AD) Welsh prince (c. 909-50 AD). A friend of the English king Athelstan, Hywel eventually united S and N Wales in his remarkably peaceful reign. His famous codification of Welsh law remained effective for over three hundred years.

I

iamb In verse, a metrical foot consisting of an unstressed syllable (or in verse based on quantity, a short syllable) followed by a stressed (or long) syllable. It was developed in quantitative verse by the ancient Greeks, who used it in dramatic dialogue because of its affinity to the natural rhythm of speech, and is the commonest type of metrical foot in English poetry.

Iapetus In Greek mythology, one of the *Titans, the son of Uranus and Gaea and father of Atlas and Prometheus. When the rebellion of the Titans was defeated by Zeus, he was imprisoned in Tartarus.

Iaşi (German name: Jassy) 47 09N 27 38E A city in NE Romania, near the Soviet border. The former capital of Moldavia, it possesses many historic buildings and academic institutions, including a university (1860). It has metal, chemical, and pharmaceutical industries. Population (1983): 265 176.

Ibadan 7 23N 3 56E The second largest city in Nigeria. The arrival of the railway (1901) aided its commercial development and it is now an important industrial, commercial, and administrative centre although there are few modern industries. Cocoa, palm products, and cotton are traded. It contains the University of Ibadan (1962). Population (1983 est): 1 060 000.

Ibagué 4 35N 75 30W A city in central Colombia, on the E slopes of the Central Cordillera. The surrounding area produces cocoa, tobacco, rice, and sugar cane. Tolima University was founded here in 1945. Population (1980): 238 000.

Ibarruri, Dolores (1895–) Spanish politician. The foremost Spanish communist in the 1930s, her oratory earned her the name La Pasionaria. She went into exile in 1939 and lived in the Soviet Union until the legalization of the Communist Party allowed her to return to Spain (1977). She is now a member of the Cortes.

Iberian Peninsula A peninsula in SW Europe, occupied by Portugal and Spain. It is separated from the rest of Europe by the Pyrenees and its flora and fauna are similar to those of N Africa. Area: 593 250 sq km (229 054 sq mi).

Iberians A Bronze Age people of S and E Spain in the 1st millennium BC. Their non-Indo-European language, which was displaced by Latin, is known from a variety of inscriptions on stone and other materials. The culture of the tribes of the coastal region of Valencia and in the NE showed considerable Greek influence while that of the SE tribes owed much to the Carthaginians. This is shown, for example, in differences in the alphabets used in each area. The economic basis was agriculture, mining, and metalworking. They lost their identity by cultural assimilation to the *Celts in Roman times.

Ibert, Jacques (1890–1962) French composer. A pupil of Fauré, he won the Prix de Rome in 1919. He directed the Academy of Rome from 1937 to 1955. His compositions include operas, chamber and orchestral music, and songs. His best-known work is the humorous orchestral *Divertissement* (1930).

Iberville, Pierre le Moyne, Sieur d' (1661–1706) French-Canadian explorer. After serving in the French navy he returned to Canada and led raids on the English fur-trading posts on Hudson Bay (1686–97). In 1699 he founded a colony at present-day Biloxi (Mississippi) and in 1700, the first French colony in Louisiana (near present-day New Orleans).

ibex A rare wild *goat, *Capra ibex*, of Eurasian and N African mountains. About 85 cm high at the shoulder, ibexes have backward-curving horns up to 65 cm long and their coat is brownish-grey with variable markings.

Other species known as ibex include the tur (*C. caucasica*) of Russia and the Spanish ibex (*C. pyrenaica*).

ibis A long-necked wading bird belonging to the subfamily *Threskiornithinae* (20 species), distributed worldwide in warm regions. 55–75 cm long, ibises have a characteristic slender downcurved bill, and unfeathered face or head and neck, which may be black or brightly coloured. They feed on small fish and aquatic invertebrates. Family: *Threskiornithidae* (ibises and spoonbills); order: *Ciconiiformes* (herons, storks, etc.).

IBIS *The sacred ibis* (Threskiornis aethiopica) *was revered by the ancient Egyptians as a symbol of the god Thoth: mummified birds have been found in the tombs of the pharaohs. Today the species is restricted to Africa S of the Sahara.*

Ibiza (Iviza *or* Ivica) A Spanish island in the Mediterranean Sea, in the Balearic Islands. Its climate and fine beaches have made it a popular tourist centre. Exports include almonds, dried figs, apricots, and salt. Area: 541 sq km (209 sq mi). Population (1981): 59 933. Chief town: Ibiza.

Iblis The Muslim name for the devil, perhaps derived from Greek *diabolos*. He is also called *al-Shaytan* (Satan). Because of his disobedience and pride, the devil was expelled from Paradise by God, but given power to lead astray those who do not serve God. Muslim tradition gives him a number of names before his fall, such as Azazil. It is disputed whether he was an angel, as in the Koran, or a jinni.

Ibn al-'Arabi, Muhyi-l-din (1165–1240) Muslim mystic and poet born in Murcia (Spain). The leading mystic of his age, he was one of the great geniuses of *sufism. In philosophy, he was a Neoplatonist. Some scholars believe that Islamic sufism, as represented by Ibn al-'Arabi, was an imitation of Christian monastic mysticism.

Ibn Battutah (1304–?1368) Arab traveller. From 1325 to 1354 he travelled extensively in Asia Minor, the Near and Far East, Europe, and Africa. He then settled at Fez and wrote an invaluable and amusing account of his work—the *Rihlah*.

Ibn Ezra, Abraham Ben Meir (1093–1167) Hebrew poet and scholar, born in Toledo, who travelled to England, Italy, France, North Africa, and perhaps to Palestine. His works include a set of famous commentaries on the Hebrew Bible, poems, riddles, and epigrams.

Ibn Gabirol, Solomon (c. 1021–c. 1058) Jewish philosopher and poet, born in Málaga (Spain). He was one of the earliest philosophers of Moorish Spain and a leading Neoplatonist. His outstanding philosophical work, *The Fountain of Life*, influenced generations of western medieval thinkers. *The Kingly Crown* is the summit of his poetic achievement.

Ibn Khaldun (1332–1406) Arab historian and philosopher, who held court posts in Spain and was chief judge in Cairo, where he died. In the *Kitab al-'ibar* (*Book of Examples*) he outlined the history of Islam and a historical theory of cyclical progress and regression in which nation states develop out of, and are subsequently destroyed by, nomadic communities.

Ibn Saud (c. 1880–1953) The first King of Saudi Arabia (1932–53). With the military help of al-*Ikhwan, he extended his territory from the Sultanate of Najd, which he reconquered in 1902, to encompass much of Arabia by 1924, when he took Hejaz. The name Saudi Arabia was adopted in 1932. In 1933 Ibn Saud came to an agreement with a US oil company, which discovered oil in his country in 1936, and used the resultant revenues to introduce modernization programmes.

Ibo (*or* Igbo) A people of SE Nigeria who speak Igbo, a language of the Kwa subgroup of the *Niger-Congo family. Subsistence cultivators of yams, cassava, and taro, they traditionally lived in scattered small holdings or village clusters of patrilineal kin headed by the eldest male descendant of the founder. Small federations of villages were the largest political units before colonial times. Many have now adopted Christianity. A growing sense of ethnic identity led to the proclamation of the short-lived Ibo secessionist republic of *Biafra (1967–70).

Ibrahim Pasha (1789–1848) Ottoman general; the son (or adopted son) and right-hand man of the viceroy of Egypt, *Mehemet Ali. In Egypt from 1805, he was given various offices by his father, culminating in the command of the Egyptian army after Mehemet Ali had quarrelled with the Ottomans (1831). Ibrahim occupied Syria, becoming governor general (1833), until forced to withdraw by the European powers (1840). His modernizing policies were severely imposed and provoked much opposition. In 1848 he succeeded his infirm father as viceroy of Egypt but died after only 40 days in office.

Ibsen, Henrik (1828–1906) Norwegian playwright and poet, the founder of modern prose drama. The son of a rich merchant who became bankrupt when his son was eight, Ibsen was preparing to study medicine when he wrote his first, unsuccessful, play. After working in theatres in Bergen and Kristiania and continuing to write plays, none of which was outstanding, he wrote *Kongsemnerne* (*The Pretenders*; 1864), for which he was granted a scholarship. He travelled to Rome and from 1864 to 1891 lived in Italy and Germany, with occasional visits to Norway. His fame as a dramatist grew with *Brand* (1865) and *Peer Gynt* (1867). In his next several plays he turned to the presentation of social issues: women's emancipation in *A Doll's House* (1879), inherited disease and guilt in *Ghosts* (1881), and public corruption in *An Enemy of the People* (1882), plays which earned him a wide and controversial reputation. Subsequent works, such as *The Wild Duck* (1884) and *Hedda Gabler* (1890), dealt with the problems of individuals. In his last plays, *The Master Builder* (1892), *John Gabriel Borkman* (1896), and *When We Dead Awaken* (1899), he turned to the treatment of autobiographical themes in a symbolic manner.

Icarus (astronomy) A very small (about 1 km diameter) *minor planet with the smallest known *perihelion (0.19 astronomical units). It passed only 600 000 km from earth in 1968.

Icarus (mythology). *See* Daedalus.

Ice Age A period in the earth's history when ice spread towards the equator with a general lowering of temperatures. The most recent of these was the *Pleistocene epoch ending about 10 000 years ago, during which four major ice advances occurred. Other ice ages occurred in Permo-Carboniferous times about 250 million years ago and in Pre-Cambrian times about 500 million years ago. Between 1550 and 1850 the **Little Ice Age** occurred, with a significant lowering of temperatures in the N hemisphere.

iceberg A large mass of ice in the sea that has originated on land. Many result from the breaking off, or calving, of ice from glaciers. In the N hemisphere icebergs originate chiefly from Greenland, in the S hemisphere most break off from the Antarctic ice. A large part of an iceberg is submerged, causing a hazard to shipping (e.g. the loss of the *Titanic* in 1912).

icefish A name given to several unrelated fish including the family *Chaenichthyidae* (175 species) of the order *Perciformes*, also called white-blooded fish, which occur in Antarctic waters. Others include the semitransparent icicle or glass fish of E Asia (family *Salangidae*) and certain species of *smelt. Order: *Salmoniformes*.

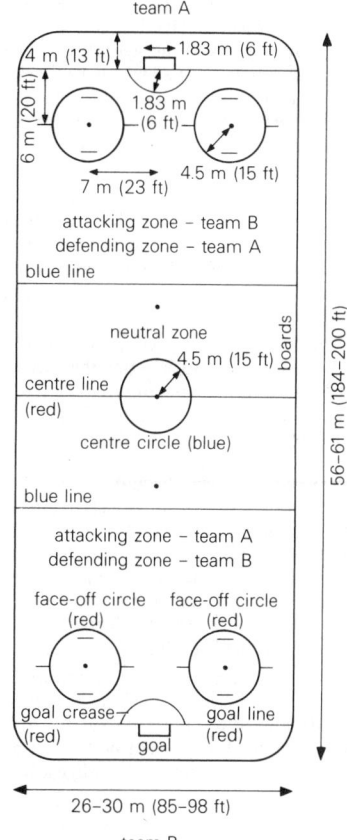

ICE HOCKEY *The dimensions of the rink.*

ice hockey A six-a-side team game played with stick and puck on a rink. It derives from field hockey and was first played by Englishmen on the frozen Kingston Harbour, Ontario (c. 1860). Canada is the true home of the game, but it is widely played in the USA, the Soviet Union, Sweden, Czechoslovakia, West Germany, and Finland. Each team consists of a goalkeeper, right and left defence, centre, and right and left wing and each team is allowed eight reserves.

The premier competition is the National Hockey League (NHL) of North America (instituted 1917). The premier trophy is the Stanley Cup, won by the Montreal Canadiens more than any other team. The Canada Cup is an international tournament, and ice hockey is also played at the Winter Olympics.

Iceland, Republic of (Icelandic name: Island) An island country in the N Atlantic, just S of the Arctic Circle, off the SE coast of Greenland. It consists mainly of an uninhabited plateau of volcanoes, lava fields, and glaciers; most of the population live around the deeply indented coast. *Economy*: some crops and livestock are produced for local needs, but the basis of the economy is fishing. Hydroelectricity and geothermal power (from the numerous geysers and thermal springs) are important sources of energy. There is also a tourist industry. The main exports are fish products and aluminium. *History*: the Vikings reached Iceland about 874 AD and by the 10th century it had become an independent state with its own parliament, the Althing, considered to be the oldest in the world. In 1264 it came under Norwegian rule and, with Norway, passed to the Danish Crown in 1381. In the late 19th century it gained a degree of self-government and in 1918 became an independent state under the Danish Crown, attaining full independence as a republic in 1944. In recent years, following extensions of its fishing limits, it has been involved in several *Cod Wars with the UK. President: Vigdis Finnbogadottir. Official language: Icelandic. Official religion: Evangelical Lutheranism. Official currency: króna of 100 aurar (100 old króna = 1 new króna introduced 1981). Area: 103 000 sq km (39 758 sq mi). Population (1983 est): 236 000. Capital and main port: Reykjavik.

Icelandic A North Germanic language of the Western Scandinavian subgroup. It is the official language of Iceland. Developed from the *Old Norse spoken by the original settlers of Iceland during the 9th and 10th centuries, Icelandic remains the most conservative of the Scandinavian languages in vocabulary, grammar, and orthography, but there has been much change in pronunciation.

Icelandic literature The greatest period of Icelandic literature was between 1100 and 1350, when the language was a dialect of *Old Norse and the Roman alphabet had only recently replaced the indigenous *runic script. Much of the material then written down drew upon considerably older oral sources. *Skaldic poetry, originating in the pre-Christian (pre-1000) era, remained an important form throughout the middle ages (*see also* Eddas). In prose, stories previously recited were written down for reading aloud (*see* sagas) and the influence of this classical prose has remained a strong conservative force in subsequent Icelandic writing. Despite the small number of Icelandic speakers there was a considerable revival in prose and poetry during the 19th century. In 1955 the Icelandic novelist Halldor *Laxness won the Nobel Prize for Literature.

Iceland moss An edible *lichen, *Cetraria islandica*, that grows on moors and alpine areas of the N hemisphere and on lava slopes and plains of Iceland. Up to about 10 cm high, it has a dark-brown to grey-white upright body with numerous flattened branches. It contains about 70% digestible starch and a brown dye.

Iceland spar A variety of *calcite consisting of pure colourless transparent crystals having the property of double refraction. It is therefore used for optical purposes and formerly for the nicol prisms in polarizing microscopes. It occurs in large steam cavities in basalt lava in Iceland.

Iceni A British tribe that inhabited the area that is now Norfolk and Suffolk. Under *Boadicea (60 AD) their revolt against Roman rule was brutally suppressed.

ice plant A succulent annual or biennial plant, *Cryophytum crystallinum*, that is covered in glistening papillae and has long prostrate stems reaching 75 cm. Native to South Africa, it is naturalized in California and the Mediterranean region and

widely grown as a garden or pot plant. It is easily propagated from seed. Family: *Aizoaceae*.

ice skating The recreation and sport of sliding over ice on steel-bladed skates. It originated over 2000 years ago and was widely practised in the middle ages in Scandinavia and on Dutch canals. The main forms of the sport, which is governed by the International Skating Union and is predominantly amateur, are speed skating (long-distance outdoor racing) and two events judged on style—figure skating (compulsory exercises followed by a freestyle performance to music, either singly or in pairs) and ice dancing (a combination of dancing and pairs figure skating). *See also* ice hockey.

I-ch'ang. *See* Yichang.

I CHING   *The* pa kua *are the basis of the 64 hexagrams of the* I Ching, *each of which has a particular significance.*

I Ching A Chinese classic work on divination, also called the Book of Changes, attributed to Wen Wang (12th century BC). It is based on eight named trigrams (*bagua* or *pa kua*) made up of broken and unbroken lines (representing *yin and yang respectively) and arranged in different sequences. Study of the I Ching and its cosmology has exercised many Chinese philosophers.

ichneumon An insect, also called ichneumon fly and ichneumon wasp, belonging to a family (*Ichneumonidae*; about 40 000 species) occurring in Europe, North America, and elsewhere. About 12 mm long, ichneumons resemble wasps but have longer antennae. They are parasitic upon other insects thereby controlling many insect pests. The female uses a long tubular ovipositor to lay eggs on or in the host. The larvae feed on the host's body fluids and eventually cause its death. Order: *Hymenoptera*.

Ichthyornis A genus of extinct seabirds whose fossils date from the Cretaceous period (125–60 million years ago). It was 20 cm long and was probably an active flier, having a large-keeled breastbone and strong wing bones.

ichthyosaur An extinct dolphin-like marine reptile that lived through much of the Mesozoic era but was most abundant in the Jurassic period (200–135 million years ago). 1–12 m long, it had broad flexible paddles, a large tail fin, and a triangular dorsal fin. Most ichthyosaurs had a long snout and jaws armed with sharp teeth and hunted fish near the surface of the sea but some had few or no teeth and fed on molluscs. □fossil.

Icknield Way A prehistoric trackway in SE England. Like its westward extension, the *Ridgeway, it follows high ground and runs NE from the Thames Valley along the Chilterns towards the East Anglian coast.

Icon A painted or mosaic image of Christ or a saint, peculiar to the Byzantine and Orthodox churches. Reverence of icons was castigated as idolatry by the Byzantine iconoclasts (*see* iconoclasm) and they were temporarily banned (730–843 AD). The decree reinstating them proclaimed that an icon must be a recognizable portrait of its subject with his accepted attributes, a formula resulting in a high degree of standardization. Unlike other paintings, therefore, icons have undergone little stylistic development and are characterized by a symbolic rather than realistic approach to colour, perspective, etc. *See also* Rublyov.

Iconium. *See* Konya.

iconoclasm The rejection of the veneration of *icons in the Byzantine Church. The movement gained much support, especially in Asia Minor, during the 8th and 9th centuries. Imperial prohibition of icons lasted from 730 to 787 and from 815 to 843, during which times icon worshippers were severely persecuted. Iconoclasm was an expression both of long-standing Christological disputes and of the antagonism towards the portrayal of divinity that was also common to Islam and Judaism in the Near East.

iconography The branch of art history dealing with the interpretation of images and symbols associated with a particular subject in art. Although the term was first used in the 18th century in the study of engravings, it was largely promoted by Aby Warburg (1866-1929) and Erwin Panofsky (1892-1968). *See also* iconology.

iconology The interpretation of the content of a picture in relation to its historical context. The term was adopted by Erwin Panofsky (1892-1968) from the title, *Iconologia*, of a 16th-century book on symbols. Iconology attempts to place *iconography in a broader context and to study visual imagery as a bridge to wider aspects of history and civilization.

Ictinus (5th century BC) Greek architect. With *Callicrates, Ictinus designed the *Parthenon, the most perfect of classical Greek buildings. He also helped rebuild the Telesterion for the temple at Eleusis and possibly designed the temple of Apollo Epicurius at Bassae.

id In *psychoanalysis, the part of the unconscious mind that is governed by irrational instinctive forces, such as *libido and *aggression. These forces seek immediate (actual or symbolic) relief and the id is therefore said to be ruled by the pleasure principle and not by reality or logic. *See also* ego; superego; unconscious.

Ida, Mount (Turkish name: Kaz Daği) A mountain range in NW Asian Turkey, rising to 1767 m (5797 ft). It was important in classical times as it overlooks the plain on which Troy was built.

Idaho A state in the NW USA, dominated by the N Rocky Mountains. The valley of the Snake River, famous for its canyons and cataracts, lies in the S of the state. It is primarily agricultural. On the better soils potatoes, wheat, and sugar beet are grown while the poorer lands support herds of beef cattle and sheep. Rich in minerals, Idaho is a leading US producer of silver and antimony. Natural gas and oil are increasingly exploited. The forested uplands make lumbering an important activity. *History*: first settled in the early 19th century, it became a state in 1890. Area: 216 412 sq km (83 557 sq mi). Population (1980): · 943 935. Capital: Boise.

ide. *See* orfe.

ideal gas A hypothetical gas that exactly obeys the ideal gas equation (*see* gas laws). Such a gas has no intermolecular forces and the volume of its molecules is negligible. Also known as a perfect gas, it is closely approximated by real gases at low pressure.

idealism Any doctrine that equates reality with mind, spirit, person, soul, thought, or, as in *Plato, archetypal ideas. *Berkeley was an idealist in holding that all we perceive is sensible ideas. He escaped from *solipsism on the ground that other people were, like himself, spirits—ideas in the mind of God, perceivers of the collections of ideas that were "material objects." In the early 18th century the term came to be used for the belief that the world of common sense was only a projection of our minds. Later it was publicized by *Kant, who called his theory of knowledge "transcendental idealism," the view that the synthetic knowable is confined to the world of phenomena as contrasted with the real world of ideas, or things-in-themselves. *Hegel's absolute idealism conceived the real as being perfect, whole, and complete. *Bradley and *Bosanquet developed this in England, and it is Hegelian idealism that

has led to the organic theory of the state (*see also* Hegelianism).

Identikit and Photofit Systems for reconstructing the facial appearance of a suspect from details recollected by witnesses. Identikit, which was developed by Hugh McDonald (1913-) and first used in Los Angeles, is based on artists' drawings of portions of the face (hair line, nose, eyes, etc.), put together to make up a composite picture. It was successfully used in Britain in 1961. Photofit, based on photographs of various features, produces a more realistic picture and has replaced Identikit. More sophisticated computerized systems are now being developed. *See also* fingerprint.

ideographic writing systems (*or* ideography) Writing systems in which each concept is represented by a symbol. All ideographic systems were probably derived from *pictographic writing systems, stylized representations of abstract concepts being added to the list of symbols. Languages such as Chinese still use ideographic writing systems. However, the huge number of symbols required to represent even a practical selection of the words in a language places a great strain on a person's memory, and hinders the acquisition of literacy skills. Moreover, ideographic systems are inflexible and cannot easily represent new coinages, words borrowed from foreign languages, etc. They have, therefore, been largely replaced by the more efficient phonetic writing systems (*see* alphabets).

Idi Amin Dada, Lake. *See* Edward, Lake.

Idomeneus In Greek legend, a king of Crete, grandson of *Minos. He was a suitor of *Helen and fought in the *Trojan War. On returning to Crete he killed his son, having sworn to Poseidon to sacrifice the first being he met. Thereafter he lived in exile in Italy.

If A French islet in the Gulf of Lyons. Its 16th-century fortress, Château d'If, was used as a state prison and made famous by Alexandre Dumas in *The Count of Monte Cristo*.

Ife 7 33N 4 34E A town in SW Nigeria. It is the holy city of the Yoruba tribe and is famed for its terracotta and bronze pieces. Today it is primarily an agricultural trade centre, the chief products being cocoa and cotton. It contains the University of Ife (1961). Population (1983 est): 214 500.

Ifni An area in Morocco, on the Atlantic coast. First settled by the Spanish (1476), it formed part of Spanish West Africa (1946) and was returned to Morocco in 1969. Chief town : Sidi Ifni.

Igarka 67 31N 86 33E A port in the N Soviet Union, in the RSFSR on the River Yenisei. It is one of the country's largest sawmilling centres and a major timber port. Population (1973 est): 39 000.

igloo A temporary dome-shaped dwelling made from blocks of snow by Eskimos of the region between the MacKenzie River delta and Labrador in N Canada. The blocks are cut with a long knife and the joints filled with snow. The igloo is entered by a low and narrow semicylindrical passageway about three metres long.

Ignatiev, Nikolai Pavlovich, Count (1832-1908) Russian diplomat, who was instrumental in expanding Russian interests into the Far East and the Balkans. After successful diplomatic missions to Bukhara and China (1858-60), Ignatiev served as ambassador to Turkey (1864-77). In 1878 he negotiated the Treaty of *San Stefano, which ended the Russo-Turkish War. He was subsequently minister of the interior (1881-82).

Ignatius of Antioch, St (1st century AD) Christian martyr; Bishop of Antioch. Little is known of his life apart from a series of famous letters to Churches in Rome and Asia Minor, written while he was a prisoner on his way to Rome to be executed. They are a valuable source of information on the beliefs and organization of the early Church. Feast day: 1 Feb.

Ignatius Loyola, St (1491-1556) Spanish founder of the

ST IGNATIUS LOYOLA *An engraving after a painting by Rubens. The Latin motto is* Ad Maiorem Dei Gloriam *(To the greater glory of God).*

*Jesuits. Of noble birth, his deep interest in religion dated from 1521, after reading the life of Christ while convalescing from a war wound. After visiting the Holy Land (1523), he studied in Spain and in Paris. There, in 1534 he made vows of poverty, chastity, and obedience, with St *Francis Xavier and other followers. He was ordained in 1537 and then moved to Rome, where he founded the Society of Jesus with the approval of Pope Paul III in 1540. As its first superior general, he sent out missionaries to Japan, India, and Brazil and founded Jesuit schools. His *Spiritual Exercises* (1548) has had lasting influence on the Roman Catholic Church. Feast day: 31 July.

igneous rock   One of the three major categories of rock (*compare* metamorphic rock; sedimentary rock) consisting mostly of crystalline rocks cooled directly from magma. That cooled at the surface forms extrusive rocks—volcanic lavas with small crystals because they have cooled rapidly (*see also* pyroclastic rock). Some extrusive rocks, such as obsidian, are like glass. Igneous rocks cooled at depth are called intrusive or plutonic. They have larger crystals, granite being a common example. A third category contains the hypabyssal rocks, cooled in dykes or sills at intermediate depth and usually having intermediate crystal sizes, for example dolerite. Silica is the dominant chemical constituent of igneous rocks and the silica content, resulting from the chemical composition of the magma from which the rock cooled, determines whether the rock is acidic (over 66% silica), intermediate (55–66%), basic (45–55%), or ultrabasic (under 45%). See Plate II.

ignis fatuus (*or* will-o'-the-wisp)   A phenomenon sometimes observed on marshy ground or graveyards, appearing as a small bluish light. It is believed to be the flame of burning marsh gas (mostly methane), ignited by traces of hydrogen phosphide sometimes found near decaying organic matter.

Iguaçú Falls (*or* Iguassú Falls)   25 35S 54 22W A waterfall in South America, on the border between Brazil and Argentina on the Rio Iguaçú. The spectacular falls are divided by forested rocky islands and are a major tourist attraction. Height: 82 m (269 ft). Width: about 4 km (2.5 mi).

iguana   A lizard belonging to the predominantly New World family *Iguanidae* (700 species), comprising desert-dwelling, arboreal, and amphibious species. The green common iguana (*Iguana iguana*) reaches a length of 1.8 m including the long tail (about 1.3 m) and has a short spiny crest along the back; males have a dewlap beneath the throat. They feed on vegetation and are excellent swimmers. The marine iguana (*Amblyrhynchus cristatus*) of the Galapagos is the only lizard that feeds in the sea. *See also* anole; basilisk; chuckwalla.

Iguanodon   A large dinosaur that lived in the Jurassic and Cretaceous periods (200–65 million years ago). It stood on powerful hind legs about 5 m tall and measured 11 m from its head to the tip of its heavy balancing tail. Iguanodons were herbivorous, tearing off leaves with their tongues and cutting them with bladelike teeth. Order: *Ornithischia.

Iguvine tablets   Nine inscribed bronze plaques, discovered (1444) at Gubbio (ancient Iguvium) in central Italy. Seven survive, containing ritual records of a priestly brotherhood between 400 and 90 BC. They are important evidence for ancient Italian religion as well as the extinct Umbrian language.

IJmuiden   52 28N 4 38E A port in the central Netherlands, in North Holland province on the North Sea. It is connected to Amsterdam by canal and has major iron and steel and fishing industries. Population (1974): 66 474.

IJsselmeer (*or* Ysselmeer)   A freshwater lake in the NW Netherlands, formed from the S part of the *Zuider Zee by the dam completed in 1932. Out of the original area of 3440 sq km (1328 sq mi) approximately 1400 sq km (540 sq mi) will remain under water. In 1986 the area reclaimed from the IJsselmeer became the province of Flevoland.

Ik   A small tribe of N Uganda, also known as the Teuso. They are one of the remnants of the original East African hunter-gatherers of Palaeolithic times. Their language is unrelated to any other. Recently resettled and forbidden to hunt game they adopted farming but unsuitable conditions and lack of agricultural knowledge have resulted in rapid social and moral disintegration.

ikebana   The art of Japanese flower arrangement, first practised in Japan in the 6th century for Buddhist rituals. Thereafter it evolved into a formal art, being practised only by men until the 19th century. Famous styles of ikebana include the *shoka*, developed in the 18th century and using three asymmetrically arranged branches.

Ikhnaton.   See Akhenaton.

Ikhwan, al- (Arabic: the Brethren)   Arabian tribesmen united to extend the power of *Ibn Saud in Arabia between 1912 and 1930. Ibn Saud organized the Ikhwan in encampments and with their military help conquered most of Arabia. They then attempted revolt but were defeated by Ibn Saud at the battle of Sabala (1929). He later incorporated the Ikhwan into the National Guard of Saudi Arabia.

Île-de-France   A former province in N France, surrounding Paris and enclosed by the Rivers Seine, Marne, Beuvronne, Thève, and Oise. It was made a dukedom during the 9th century AD. Following the French Revolution it was divided into departments.

Ilesha   7 38N 4 45E A city in SW Nigeria. Cocoa is exported from here and it is the centre of a gold-mining area. Population (1983 est): 273 400.

Ilhéus   14 50S 39 06W A port in E Brazil, in Bahía state on the Atlantic Ocean. Fomerly an important export centre for cocoa, chief exports now include timber and piassava. Population (1980 est): 132 600.

Ilipa, Battle of (206 BC)   A battle in S Spain between *Scipio Africanus and the Carthaginians. Scipio's victory established Roman control of Spain, opening the way for his invasion of Africa.

Ilkeston 52 59N 1 18W A town in central England, in Derbyshire. Situated in a former coalmining region, some opencast mining remaining, Ilkeston has engineering, iron founding, textile, clothing, plastics, furnishings, and pipe-making industries. Population (1981): 33 031.

Ilkley 53 55N 1 50W A town in N England, in West Yorkshire on the River Wharfe. The parish church (13th century) is built on the site of a Roman fort. **Ilkley Moor**, reaching 403 m (1321 ft), lies to the S. Population (1981): 24 082.

Illich, Ivan (1926–) Austrian educationalist and radical social critic. A former Roman Catholic priest, who worked in Latin America, Illich seeks a "convivial" society brought about by a cultural revolution. In books such as *Deschooling Society* (1971) he attacks technology, capitalism, and the values of the consumer society that dominate rather than serve human life.

Illinois A group of Algonkian-speaking North American Indian tribes of Wisconsin, Illinois, Missouri, and Iowa. Their villages were of rush-mat-covered dwellings, each housing several families. Separate chiefs were responsible for matters of war and for civil affairs. Men hunted forest game and prairie bison. Women cultivated maize and corn. The Illinois were much reduced in population through wars with other tribes and eventually dispersed from their territory.

Illinois A state in the USA, in the Midwest. It consists largely of flat prairies crossed by the Illinois and Kaskaskia Rivers. Approximately half its population is concentrated in the Chicago metropolitan area, the principal grain market of the US interior. Primarily an agricultural state, its farmers are major producers of soya beans, as well as maize, corn, pork, beef, and dairy products. Manufacturing includes machine tools, electrical machinery, printing and publishing, chemicals, iron and steel, motor vehicles, and food processing. It is also an important coalmining state. A deep division exists between upstate Illinois, which contains the Chicago metropolitan area, and the predominantly rural area to the S. *History*: the first Europeans to visit Illinois were the French in the 17th century. It formed part of the French province of Louisiana but was ceded to Britain (1763). It came under US control (1783), becoming a territory in 1809 and a state in 1818. The Illinois and Michigan Canal (1848) ensured its importance as a national transport centre by linking Lake Michigan with the Mississippi River. Area: 146 075 sq km (56 400 sq mi). Population (1980): 11 418 461. Capital: Springfield.

illiteracy The inability to read or write. The ever-increasing demands of a technological society and the concomitant need for a numerate and literate population has led to a growing awareness of the scale of the problem: although exact numbers are difficult to determine there are an estimated two million adults with reading and writing problems in the UK. Between 1973 and 1976 there was a tenfold increase in the number of adults having tuition and in the three years ending 31 March, 1978, some 125 000 adults had received literacy tuition. The campaign has since been extended to include help with numeracy problems. The anti-illiteracy campaign is run by voluntary helpers and coordinated by a small agency of central government, the Adult Literacy Unit, and Local Education Authorities.

illuminated manuscripts Manuscripts of gospels, books of hours, prayers, etc., decorated with designs in opaque or transparent watercolour and frequently gold leaf. The art was first practised by monastic scribes in the early middle ages, as in the 8th-century Book of Kells. Although it began as the elaboration of capital letters and decoration of margins, by the time printing was invented (mid-15th century) it had become a form of miniature painting, perfected by professional illuminators. The Duke of Berry's book of hours by the de *Limburg brothers is

ILLUMINATED MANUSCRIPTS *An elaborate capital C from an English writing master's copy sheet (c. 1600).*

an outstanding example of late medieval illumination. Such illumination laid the basis for medieval panel painting.

Illyria The Adriatic coastal region W of the Balkans. Inhabited from the 10th century BC by warlike independent tribes, Illyria constantly harassed Macedonia and Epirus, expanding when their power declined. Piratical raids in the Adriatic provoked Roman intervention from 228 BC; Illyria became the Roman province of Illyricum in 167 BC.

ilmenite A black metallic mineral of composition $FeTiO_3$, found in basic igneous rocks, in veins, and as a detrital mineral in sands. It is an ore of titanium.

Iloilo 10 41N 122 33E A port in the central Philippines, in SE Panay. The island's commercial centre, famed for its fabrics, it exports sugar and rice. Population (1980): 244 827.

Ilorin 8 32N 4 34E A city in W Nigeria. It is an important trading centre for local agricultural and manufactured products, with modern industries producing sugar, matches, and cigarettes. Its university was founded in 1976. Population (1983 est): 343 900.

Ilyushin, Sergei Vladimirovich (1894–1977) Soviet aircraft designer. He first became known for the Il-2 Stormovik, a dive bomber widely used by the Soviet Union during World War II. He later worked on commercial aircraft, designing the jet airliner Il-62.

imaginary number. *See* numbers; complex numbers.

Imagism A literary movement begun in Britain in 1912, dedicated to composing poetry characterized by the concise expression of pure visual images. It profoundly influenced British and American poetry for a decade. It derived from the criticism of T. E. Hulme, who rejected the prevailing sentimental romanticism in favour of clarity and hardness. *Des Imagistes* (1914), an anthology edited by Ezra Pound, included poems by Richard Aldington, Hilda Doolittle (H. D.), John Gould Fletcher, and Amy Lowell, who succeeded Pound as leader of the movement.

imago (zoology) The sexually mature adult form of any insect.

imam (Arabic: leader) A Muslim title. **1.** Among Shiite Muslims, the title of the successors of Mohammed, who must be descendants of the fourth caliph *Ali. The imams were regarded as infallible and exercised complete authority. Various Shiite sects recognize different lines of imams and believe that the last of the line (usually considered either the 7th or the 12th after Ali) will return at the end of time. **2.** A title often used by the caliphs and also honorifically given to certain religious leaders, such as *Abu Hanifah. **3.** The title of the leader of prayers in a mosque.

Imbros. *See* Imroz.

Imhotep (c. 2600 BC) Egyptian physician, architect, and

adviser to pharaoh *Djoser of the 3rd dynasty. Revered in later times as a healer and magician, Imhotep was eventually deified. He was identified with Asclepius by the Greeks.

Immaculate Conception A dogma of the Roman Catholic Church stating that the Virgin Mary was conceived free from *original sin. It had long been a belief, connected with the feast of the Conception of the Blessed Virgin Mary (8 Dec), which had been celebrated since 1471; but it was the subject of controversy and was opposed by prominent theologians, such as St Bonaventure and St Thomas Aquinas. It was promulgated as dogma in 1854 by Pope Pius IX.

immigration. *See* migration, human.

Immingham 53 37N 0 12W A port in NE England, in Humberside on the Humber estuary. The docks, built in 1912, have been expanded to incorporate a petrochemical complex with bulk handling facilities for the import of iron ore. Exports include chemicals, iron and steel, and petroleum products. Population (1985 est): 11 630.

immortelle. *See* everlasting flowers.

immunity In medicine, resistance to infection. Nonspecific immunity is achieved by such agents as polymorphic white blood cells (which engulf invading bacteria) and *interferon, but the term immunity usually refers to that specifically acquired due to the presence of *antibodies. This may be passive, when antibodies derived from another individual are introduced into the body. For example, newborn babies have a temporary passive immunity from antibodies transferred from the mother's blood through the placenta. Active immunity is produced when an individual forms his (or her) own antibodies after exposure to an antigen, such as occurs following an infection. There are two different kinds of immune response produced by antibodies derived from two populations of lymphocytes (white blood cells). Cell-mediated immunity is due to activity of the T-lymphocytes (produced by or dependent on the *thymus). In the presence of antigens these lymphocytes produce cells with antibody bound to their surface. They can attack whole cells and are responsible for such reactions as graft rejection, allergic responses, and delayed hypersensitivity reactions. Humoral immunity is produced by the B-lymphocytes, so called because they are formed in an organ in chickens called the bursa of Fabricius. In man they are probably formed by lymphatic tissue in the gut. B-lymphocytes produce cells that release free antibody into the blood, neutralizing bacterial toxins and coating bacteria to facilitate their ingestion by the polymorphic blood cells.

Immunization is the production of immunity by artificial means. This may be achieved by injecting antibodies against specific diseases (e.g. tetanus and diphtheria), providing temporary passive immunity, or by *vaccination to produce active immunity.

immunology The study of the biological processes by which the body reacts to foreign substances. This includes the action of *antibodies both in protecting the body against infection (*see* immunity) and in rejecting foreign tissues (*see* transplantation). Immunologists are also concerned with disorders of the immune system, including *allergy and *autoimmunity.

immunosuppression The condition in which the *immunity of the body is reduced. This can occur in various diseases (e.g. leukaemia and severe infections) or it may be deliberately induced by certain drugs (e.g. azathioprine and cyclophosphamide). Immunosuppressive drugs are administered after transplant surgery to enable the body to accept the foreign tissue or organ; they are also used to treat rheumatoid arthritis and other conditions associated with *autoimmunity.

impala A common antelope, *Aepyceros melampus*, of central and S African savanna. About 100 cm high at the shoulder, impalas have a red-brown coat and white underparts; males have lyre-shaped ridged horns. In the rutting season the herds, numbering several hundreds, break up into smaller groups, each led by a mature male. Impalas are known for their agile springing leaps, which are most marked when the animals are alarmed.

INCAS *The Inca* quipu, *or knotted string device, was used by the* quipucamayoc, *the* quipu *keeper, for keeping accounts.*

Impatiens A genus of annual and perennial herbaceous plants (about 700 species), widely distributed in temperate and tropical regions. They have irregular often spurred flowers and (usually) fleshy stems. The genus includes *touch-me-not and various cultivated species, such as the garden *balsam and busy Lizzies—red-, pink-, purple-, and orange-flowered hybrids that are popular pot plants. Family: *Balsaminaceae*.

impeachment A prosecution brought by the House of Commons as prosecutor and tried by the House of Lords as judge, especially against a minister of the Crown for a serious public offence. Although still legal, the last impeachment was that of the 1st Viscount Melville (1742–1811) in 1804, tried in 1806 for alleged financial mismanagement of the Admiralty. In the USA impeachments (e.g. of the president) are brought by the House of Representatives and tried by the Senate.

impedance A measure of the ability of a circuit to resist the flow of an alternating current. It is given by $Z = R + iX$, where Z is the impedance, R is the *resistance, and X is the reactance. The reactance of an inductance L is ωL and that of a capacitance C is $1/\omega C$, where ω is the angular frequency. Impedance and reactance are measured in *ohms.

imperial cities The German cities of the Holy Roman Empire subject directly to the Emperor (by whose officials they were governed). They grew in number during the middle ages, when cities took advantage of political disturbance to assert their freedom. Those that survived flourished, forming themselves into leagues (of which the *Hanseatic League was the most important) and from 1489 were represented in the imperial diet (assembly). In subsequent centuries most cities lost their free status and were incorporated into the provinces; only Hamburg and Bremen maintain their free status today.

Imperial College of Science and Technology A school of the University of London formed in 1907 by the amalgamation of three institutions: the Royal College of Science (1845), the Royal School of Mines (1851), and the City and Guilds College (1884). Since the 1950s the college has more than doubled in size, several of its college buildings being replaced. It is the premier academic institution in the UK for science and engineering.

Imperial Conferences Meetings between the British Government and representatives of the self-governing dominions held between 1907 and 1937 to discuss questions of common interest. Imperial Conferences, which replaced the Colonial Conferences of 1887, 1897, and 1902, discussed such matters as migration, naturalization (1911), defence (1917-18, 1921, 1923), trade (1923), intraimperial relations (1926), and dominion status (1930). The last Conference (1937) discussed the foreign policy of the newly established *Commonwealth of Nations. The Conferences gave way during World War II to the meetings of Commonwealth prime ministers. *See also* Ottawa Agreements.

imperialism The territorial expansion of a nation and its domination over other countries. Powerful nations generally formed their empires by conquest until the 19th century, when imperialism became an economic policy. European powers, especially Britain (*see* Empire, British), ambitious for prestige and anxious for new industrial trading outlets, established their rule over countries in other continents (⊡Africa). Until World War I ended such imperialism these countries depended on their rulers for government, commerce, and protection. Since World War II imperialism has been used to describe the efforts of world powers to impose, by persuasion or force, their political ideologies on less prosperous nations.

Imperial War Museum A British museum founded in 1917 to house collections of military equipment, uniforms, insignia, and art, relating mainly to the two World Wars. It also has a photograph collection and a reference library. It occupies what was formerly *Bedlam (the Bethlem Royal Hospital) in S London.

impetigo A highly infectious skin disease, usually caused by staphylococci. Children are most commonly affected and epidemics may occur in crowded schools. Usually occurring on the face, hands, and knees, it starts with a red mark that develops into a blister, which later forms yellow crusts. Antibiotics, applied locally or internally, will cure the condition.

Imphal 24 47N 93 55E A city in India, the capital of Manipur. During World War II, Imphal was the scene of an Anglo-Indian victory over the Japanese. Population (1981): 156 622.

impotence Sexual inadequacy in men, with failure to achieve or maintain an erection or to ejaculate at orgasm. It may be temporary, resulting from tiredness, illness, drunkenness, depression, or taking certain drugs. Long-term impotence is likely to have a deeper cause reflecting the sufferer's fear of women or of castration. It can usually be treated by specialist counselling or by psychotherapy.

impressionism A French art movement that flourished from the late 1860s to the late 1880s. Its name was derived from Monet's painting *Impression: Sunrise* (1872; Musée Marmottan, Paris), shown at the first of the eight impressionist exhibitions (1874, 1876, 1877, 1879, 1880, 1881, 1882, 1886). The leading impressionists were *Monet, *Pissarro, *Sisley, and *Renoir. Among their many forerunners were *Constable, *Turner, *Boudin, *Daubigny, and *Corot. *Manet shared some of their aims and *Degas, although stylistically independent of them, participated in their exhibitions. Painting mainly in the open air, the impression-

ists aimed to capture fleeting effects of light and weather in paint with dabs of bright colour and a minimum of drawing.

imprinting In *ethology, a rapid and irreversible form of learning that takes place in some animals in the first hours of life. Animals attach themselves in this way to whatever creatures they are exposed to at that time—usually, but not necessarily, their mothers. This type of behaviour was first described by Konrad *Lorenz working with newly hatched ducks and geese.

Imroz (*or* Imbros) A Turkish island close to the Gallipoli Peninsula. It was occupied by Britain (1914-23) and used as a base in the Dardanelles campaign (*see* World War I). Area: 280 sq km (108 sq mi). Population (1980): 4802.

inbreeding Mating between closely related individuals. (The term is also used for self-fertilization in plants.) Inbreeding often occurs in small isolated populations of organisms. The effect is to increase the tendency for harmful *recessive genes to express themselves among the population, thus affecting the fitness and survival of individuals. For example, inbreeding in rats reduces fertility and increases mortality. In human societies close inbreeding is prevented by custom and law (*see* incest).

incandescent lamp An electric lamp in which light is produced by passing an electric current through a filament, usually inside a glass bulb containing an inert gas. The filament, of tungsten in the common light bulb, is heated to over 2600°C so that it glows with a white light.

Incarnation A central tenet of Christian belief, that the second person of the Trinity took human form and became man. Although in other religions gods temporarily appear in human form (i.e. a theophany), in Christianity the Incarnation is a unique event occurring at a particular time; the union of the divine and human in Christ is permanent and the integrity of both the divine and human natures is maintained. The doctrine is stated in the opening of the Gospel of St John and in St Paul's Epistle to the Colossians and was further defined by the Councils of *Nicaea (325) and *Chalcedon (451).

Incas A Quechua-speaking South American Indian people of the Peruvian Andes. From their capital of *Cuzco, they established, during the 15th century, an empire extending from Ecuador to central Chile. It was destroyed in the 16th century by the Spaniards. The Incas assimilated much of the culture of such people as the *Chimu, whom they conquered. Their hierarchical society, ruled by the King of Inca and a class of aristocratic officials, was highly centralized. Although the wheel and writing were unknown, imperial messengers and an extensive road system enabled the ruler to maintain contact with all parts of his empire. The complex religion was concerned with the propitiation of the sun god Inti, object of the state cult, the creator god Viracocha (*see also* Kon-Tiki), the rain god Apu Ilapu, and others. *See also* Machu Picchu.

incense A mixture of gums and spices (especially gum benzoin) that is burnt for its aroma (*see also* frankincense). It was employed in pagan rituals in ancient Egypt, Greece, and Rome as well as in Judaic ritual and was a valued trade commodity. In the Book of Revelation it is a symbol of the prayers of saints and has been used in Christian worship since the 6th century AD. It is used predominantly by the Orthodox and Roman Catholic Churches, but in England it enjoyed a limited revival initiated by the *Oxford Movement. The vessel for burning incense is called a censer or thurible.

incense cedar A conifer, *Calocedrus* (or *Libocedrus*) *decurrens*, native to W North America and planted for ornament in Europe, where it is usually narrow and columnar and may reach a height of 45 m. It has small scalelike leaves covering the twigs and branches and bright-yellow pointed cones, 2 cm long, which split open to release the seeds. Family: *Cupressaceae* (cypress family).

incest Proscribed sexual relations between close kin. Such proscriptions are universal, but vary considerably in terms of the categories of kin to which they apply. For instance, the table of kindred and affinity in the Anglican prayerbook sets out the list of partners prohibited by the Church of England. The most common and universal prohibitions, however, apply to members of the same nuclear family, such as relations between parents and children and between brothers and sisters. These taboos, founded in folklore, have a sound basis in genetics (unfavourable recessive genes can become dominant when consanguineous relatives breed). However, folklore is not always a reliable guide to what constitutes consanguinity, as in the case of taboos forbidding marriage between a man and his mother-in-law.

Inchcape Rock. *See* Bell Rock.

Inchŏn 37 30N 126 38E A city in NW South Korea, Seoul's main seaport on the Yellow Sea. It has a private university (1954). A UN attack here (1950) during the Korean War halted the North Korean invasion. Population (1980): 1 084 730.

incomes policy. *See* prices and incomes policy.

income tax A direct tax on income and a major source of government revenue in many countries. In most countries, including the UK and the USA, it is a progressive tax (the rate charged increasing with the taxable income) in which a certain amount can be earned without attracting tax. Thus, those with higher incomes pay more tax in proportion to their incomes than the lower paid; therefore the tax, to a certain extent, balances unequal distribution of incomes in the community. However, it acts as a disincentive to increasing income and makes it difficult for the low paid to escape from the *poverty trap (compare tax-credit system). Income tax makes no distinction between income that is spent and income that is invested (furthering the productive potential of the economy); higher indirect taxation and lower direct taxation is advocated as a remedy for this disadvantage.

incunabula Books printed during the infancy of modern printing (before 1500) after the invention of movable type by *Gutenberg. N European incunabula have a heavy type design known as black letter; Italian books have a more elegant roman typeface; both were based on current manuscript writing. Paper leaves and a binding of calf leather over wooden boards were usual. Editions were small (200–500), the preferred subjects being religious or scientific.

Independence 39 04N 94 27W A city in the USA, in Missouri. Situated in an agricultural area, its industries include oil refining and cement. It was the home of President Harry S. Truman. Population (1980): 111 806.

Independence Day The national holiday in the USA that marks the anniversary of the adoption of the *Declaration of Independence by the Continental Congress on 4 July, 1776.

Independents In English ecclesiastical history, the members of groups in the 17th century and later who believed in self-government for each congregation and advocated toleration of Nonconformity. The term was at first synonymous with *Congregationalism; after the Restoration and the Act of Uniformity (1662), it was more widely applied to dissenting bodies the ministers of which were expelled from the Church of England for refusing to subscribe to the Act.

indeterminacy principle. *See* Heisenberg uncertainty principle.

indexation. *See* price index.

Index Librorum Prohibitorum (Latin: *Index of Prohibited Books*) In the Roman Catholic Church, a list of publications considered dangerous to spiritual wellbeing and not to be read without a bishop's permission. The first formal list of this sort was produced under Pope Paul IV (1555–59); a more comprehensive guide was issued in 1564. The Second *Vatican Council (1962–65) resolved that no new revisions should be undertaken, and the specific limitation on suitable reading is no longer in effect.

India, Republic of (Hindi name: Bharat) A country in S Asia, the seventh largest in the world and the second most populous. Bordering on Pakistan, China, Nepal, Bhutan, and Burma, it comprises 23 states and 8 Union Territories, reorganized since 1946 according to linguistic groupings. The Himalayas, in which the River Ganges rises, form a natural barrier to the N. Central India consists of a plateau (the Deccan), flanked by the mountains of the Western and Eastern Ghats. N of this lies the Indo-Gangetic plain, with the Thar Desert in the W. The population comprises many ethnic and cultural groups and about 1600 languages and dialects are spoken. The chief religions are Hinduism (83% of the population) and Islam (11%). The *caste system still survives, although untouchability has been abolished. *Economy*: helped by foreign aid, 70% of the workforce is engaged in agriculture, with rice, pulses, and cereals as the main food crops; tea, jute, cotton, and tobacco are also important. Despite land irrigation and reclamation, production is hampered by floods, droughts, insufficient mechanization, and the small size of agricultural units; food supplies are therefore inadequate for the country's needs. Fishing and forestry are also important. India's large mineral resources include iron ore, manganese, bauxite, mica, and ilmenite. Coal is mined, oil is produced from the Arabian Sea, and India also has nuclear power. Industry, much of it state owned, employs only 10% of the workforce, but India is the world's tenth greatest industrial power. Industries include steel, chemicals, electronics, cotton and silk textiles, and handicrafts. The new economic policy of 1977 channelled resources into agriculture and aimed to stimulate rural employment by allowing new capital intensive industries to be established only for goods that could not be produced by cottage or small-scale industries. Chief exports are cotton goods, tea, leather, iron ore, and jute, while chief imports are petroleum, wheat, and machinery. *History*: the *Indus Valley was the site of a civilization for a millennium before the invading Aryans established theirs (c. 1500 BC) between the Indus and the Ganges. From this

INDIA *The distribution of major language groups in the Indian subcontinent.*

civilization Hinduism evolved and it has remained India's dominant religion. The Mauryan Empire followed (c. 320 BC–c. 185 BC), which unified most of India. The 4th–6th centuries AD saw a flowering of Hindu culture in the N under the *Gupta dynasty. Muslim raids on the N from the 10th century culminated in the establishment of a Muslim sultanate based on Delhi (1129), under which much of India was again unified. A later Muslim invasion resulted in the magnificent *Mogul Empire (established 1526). At this time Europeans were also arriving. The British *East India Company, grown powerful in the 17th century, fought with French traders in the 18th century for a monopoly as the Mogul Empire declined. With Robert Clive's victory at *Plassey (1757), the British established their supremacy and from 1784 a series of *Government of India Acts shifted power from the East India Company to the British Government. Some of the territory was directly administered by Britain and came to be called British India. The rest of India was administered by Indian princes, with Britain only exercising general supervision; such areas were called princely states. The Indian economy suffered under British trading arrangements, which allowed British goods into India duty free but barred Indian goods from Great Britain by high tariffs, thus provoking social and political unrest. After the *Indian Mutiny (1857–59) reforms were introduced, including the transfer of the East India Company's administrative powers to the India Office, represented by a viceroy and provincial governors. Subsequent reforms allowed greater Indian involvement in government, and in 1919 a parliament was created, the majority of members of which were elected. However, the nationalist movement (see Indian National Congress) became increasingly forceful in its demand for home rule and, under the leadership of Mahatma *Gandhi, pursued a policy of civil disobedience. During World War II Gandhi and other Nationalist leaders were imprisoned for refusing to support Britain unless independence was immediately granted. This was finally achieved in 1947 on condition that a Muslim state should be established to satisfy the Muslim faction, active since the late 19th century (see Muslim League). The creation of *Pakistan (1947) was followed by violent upheavals in which 500 000 people were killed and by war between the two countries over Kashmir. Trouble between Hindus and Muslims has continued, with riots in 1978, while hostility between India and Pakistan erupted again in 1965 and 1971 (see also Bangladesh). India, which became a sovereign state in 1950, has been consolidated by the incorporation of former French and Portuguese territories (1956 and 1961) and the inclusion of Sikkim (1975), although the Kashmir border dispute with Pakistan continues. Nevertheless, economic problems coupled with inefficient or corrupt administrations encouraged separatist terrorist movements. Indira *Gandhi (prime minister 1966–77, 1980–84) dealt forcibly with the problems, suppressing a militant Sikh movement, advocating autonomy for the Punjab, in 1984. Later that year she was assassinated by Sikhs in her bodyguard; she was succeeded by her son, Rajiv Gandhi. In foreign affairs India has followed a policy of nonalignment, although it became the world's sixth nuclear power (1974). Zail Singh was elected president of the republic in 1982. Prime minister: Rajiv Gandhi. Official languages: Hindi and English. Official currency: Indian rupee of 100 paise. Area: 3 287 590 sq km (1 269 072 sq mi), including Jammu and Kashmir. Population (1983 est): 740 009 000. Capital: New Delhi.

Indiana A state in the USA, in the Midwest, forming part of the Mississippi Basin. It is largely undulating prairie with glacial lakes in the N. Agriculture is important in the central plain, the major crops being soya beans, maize, wheat, and vegetables (especially tomatoes); pigs are the primary livestock. Its industry produces steel, diamond tools, agricultural machinery, motor vehicles, and domestic appliances. Coal and building stone are also exploited. It is a transport centre with the Ohio River linking Indiana with the Mississippi River. *History*: explored by the French in the 17th century, the area was ceded to Britain in 1763, passing to the USA in 1783. Increased settlement followed the defeat of the Indians (1794) and Indiana became a state in 1816. Area: 93 993 sq km (36 291 sq mi). Population (1980): 5 490 179. Capital: Indianapolis.

Indianapolis 39 45N 86 10W A city in the USA, the capital of Indiana. A rail, road, and air centre, its varied manufactures include car and aircraft parts and chemicals. It is the scene of annual speedway races, including the **Indianapolis 500**, a 500-mile race for 33 cars first held in 1911. Population (1980): 700 807.

Indian art and architecture The styles evolved in the Indian subcontinent. Evidence for many older art forms is incomplete, as the hostile climate militates against the survival of objects in perishable materials, such as wood. The art of the *Indus Valley civilization is best represented by carved steatite sealstones and miniature sculptures and its architecture by the massive brick ruins at *Harappa and *Mohenjo-Daro. Between about 324 and 185 BC the characteristic Buddhist *stupa appeared, decorated with stone or stucco reliefs depicting scenes from the Buddha's life. Greek and Roman influence is apparent in the art of the N Indian Buddhist kingdom of Gandhara (1st–7th centuries AD). The 10th-century Muslim invasions drove indigenous art to the S. The central spire of Hindu temples became increasingly massive, symbolizing the mythological cosmic mountain; luxuriant carvings, often of erotic scenes, covered every surface, as in the 13th-century Sun Temple at Konarak (Orissa). The Tamil kingdom of Cola (c. 850–1279) is famous for its small bronzes. With the spread of Mogul dominance, *Mogul art and architecture became the main tradition until its decline under British rule.

Indian corn. *See* maize.

Indian hemp A North American perennial herb, *Apocynum cannabinum*, that grows to a height of 1.5 m and bears small greenish-white flowers. The stem fibres were used by Indians to make matting and ropes and the dried roots have medicinal properties. Family: *Apocynaceae*.

True *hemp is also sometimes called Indian hemp.

Indian languages Languages of widely differing origins spoken in the Indian subcontinent. The two major language families to be found are the *Indo-European and the *Dravidian. On the NW borders of India, Baluchi and *Pashto, members of the *Iranian subgroup of the Indo-European family, are spoken. Most of the other Indo-European languages of India are of the *Indo-Aryan subgroup. This includes the lingua franca Hindustani; *Hindi, the official national language; Rajasthani, *Punjabi, *Gujarati, and *Sindhi in the west; *Bengali and *Bihari in the east; and Kashmiri. Most of S India is covered by the Dravidian language family. In addition to these two large families, there are scattered languages of the *Munda group in the NE, and languages of *Sino-Tibetan origins are spoken in the Himalayas.

Indian liquorice An Indian plant, *Abrus precatorius*, the roots of which have been used as a substitute for liquorice although they contain poisonous resins. The poisonous red and black seeds are used to make necklaces and as weights. Family: *Leguminosae*.

Indian literature Sanskrit literature, the most important division of ancient Indian literature, is divided into three periods: the Vedic period (c. 1500–c. 200 BC), during which the vast and complex sacred literature of Hinduism was accumulated (see Vedas; Upanishads); the Epic period (c. 400 BC–c. 400 AD), in which the great Indian epic, the *Mahabharata*, which includes the *Bhagavad-gita*, and the shorter epic, the *Ramayana*, were composed; and the Classical period (from c. 200 AD), characterized by various literary forms including romances, drama, and lyric poetry. *Kalidasa is considered the greatest writer of this period. During the 19th century various regional vernacular literatures of India developed, adopting new western forms and reviving traditional ones. Leading writers of this period include the Bengali poet Rabindranath *Tagore and the Urdu poet Muhammad *Iqbal.

Indian Mutiny (1857-59) A revolt of about 35 000 sepoys (Indian soldiers in the service of the British East India Company), which developed into a bloody Anglo-Indian War. It began with a massacre of Europeans at Meerut in May, 1857, following which the mutineers captured Delhi. The sepoys then rose in many other N Indian towns and were joined by local princes. Extensive British reinforcements were able under Colin *Campbell to regain Delhi in Sept and relieve besieged Lucknow in Nov; by July, 1858, the revolt had largely been contained. The consequent Government of India Act (1858) transferred the administrative powers of the East India Company to the British Crown.

Indian National Congress The political party, founded in 1885, that governed India after the declaration of independence in 1947. Though earlier a moderate party, a section of it took up the cause of home rule in 1917. For the next 20 years, chiefly under the guidance of Mahatma *Gandhi, it advocated noncooperation with the British and in World War II refused to support Britain without being promised Indian independence. The party was led by Jawarhalal *Nehru from 1951 to 1964, by Lal Bahadur Shastri (1904-66) until 1966, and then by Mrs Indira *Gandhi until her assassination in 1984, when the leadership passed to her son Rajiv Gandhi.

Indian Ocean The world's third largest ocean, extending between Asia, Africa, Australia, and Antarctica. Lying mainly in the S hemisphere, most is within the tropical and temperate zones. It contains coral and volcanic islands while others, such as the Seychelles, are the peaks of underwater ridges or, like Madagascar, are continental. The ocean floor is extremely rich in minerals.

Indian pipe A fleshy waxy-white to pinkish herb, *Monotropa uniflora*, of North America and Asia, also called corpse plant. Up to 30 cm high, it has tiny scalelike leaves, lacks chlorophyll, and obtains nutrients from woodland humus. The stem and single cup-shaped flower resemble a small pipe. Family: *Monotropaceae*.

Indian Territory The land W of the Mississippi, corresponding to present-day Oklahoma, set aside (1834) for settlement of Indians ejected, sometimes forcibly, from the E. These included the Cherokee, whose journey was known as the Trail of Tears because so many died on the way.

indicator A substance used to indicate through changes in colour, fluorescence, etc., the presence of another substance or the completion of a chemical reaction. Indicators are usually weak organic acids or bases that yield ions of a different colour to the unionized molecule. For example, litmus is red in the presence of acids but blue in the presence of alkalis.

indigestion (*or* dyspepsia) Abdominal discomfort due to disordered digestion. Most people experience indigestion at some time and there is usually no serious cause, but peptic ulcers, a hiatus hernia, and gall bladder disease may all give symptoms that are described as indigestion.

indigo A blue *dye formerly obtained from plants, particularly of the genus *Indigofera*, and present in the woad plant (*Isatis tinctoria*). It is now synthesized from *aniline.

indium (In) A soft silvery metal, named after the bright indigo line in its spectrum. It is used in making transistors, rectifiers, thermistors, and alloys of low melting point. At no 49; at wt 114.82; mp 156.6°C; bp 1450°C.

Indo-Aryan languages A subgroup of the *Indo-Iranian language group, spoken in India, Sri Lanka, and Pakistan.

Sometimes called the Indic group, it descends from *Sanskrit, and the earliest Indo-Aryan language dates from about 1100 AD. The most important languages of the group are *Hindi and *Urdu, which are the national languages of India and Pakistan respectively; these are both literary languages with many borrowings of Persian and Arabic words dating from the Mogul period. More colloquial *Hindustani is also a member of this group, as are the widely spoken *Sindhi, *Bengali, *Gujarati, *Punjabi, and Sinhalese. The Dardic (*see* Dards) languages of Pakistan, Afghanistan, and Kashmir, of which the best known is Kashmiri, are often included in the Indo-Aryan group.

INDIGO *This ornamental shrub* (Indigofera gerardiana) *is closely related to the species formerly used as a source of indigo. It has red flowers and silvery branches.*

Indochina The area of SE Asia comprising *Vietnam, *Kampuchea (Cambodia), *Burma, *Thailand, *Malaysia, and *Laos. It was so called by Europeans because it has been influenced by both Indian and Chinese culture. During the 19th century the French established control over the E part of the region, forming (1887) the Union of Indochina from *Cochinchina, Cambodia, *Tonkin, and *Annam; Laos was added in 1893. Its capital was Saigon (now Ho Chi Minh City). Except in Cochinchina the royal families were retained, although most power lay with the French federal government. During World War II the Japanese occupied Tonkin (1940) and then all Indochina (1941–42). Following Japan's defeat France established the Federation of Indochina, to which Laos and Cambodia submitted while nationalists in Annam, Tonkin, and Cochinchina demanded complete independence for a new state of Vietnam (*see* Ho Chi Minh). In 1946 fighting broke out between nationalists (*see* Viet Minh) and the French, bitter conflict continuing until 1954, when the *Geneva Conference ended the French presence in Indochina.

Indo-European languages The largest language family of the world, sometimes called Indo-Germanic. They are spoken throughout Europe as well as in India, Iran, and in parts of the central and E Soviet Union, and the family is generally thought to include the following subgroups: *Germanic; *Italic; *Indo-Iranian; *Celtic; *Baltic; Slavic (*see* Slavonic); *Albanian; *Greek; *Armenian; *Tocharian; and *Anatolian. Of these, the oldest recorded is Anatolian and the most recent Albanian. Armenian and Greek are single languages rather than subdivided groups like Indo-Iranian or Germanic. Anatolian and Tocharian are now extinct. The only living languages of Europe that do not come from Indo-European origins are *Turkish, *Finnish, *Hungarian, and *Basque. The Indo-European group relates languages as apparently separate as English, a subgroup of Germanic, and *Sanskrit, an ancestor of modern Indian languages. Most of the research needed to support this wide grouping was done by German philologists in the 19th century. *See also* Indo-Hittite languages.

Indo-Hittite languages A language family proposed by some scholars to include the *Indo-European and *Anatolian languages as subgroups. There has been some confusion about the relation of *Hittite, an Anatolian language, to the Indo-European group. Indo-Hittite has been suggested as an ancestor of both Indo-European and Anatolian. It is more generally accepted that Indo-European is the parent language and Anatolian a subgroup on the same level as the *Celtic or the *Germanic languages.

Indo-Iranian languages A subgroup of the *Indo-European language group, spoken in India, Pakistan, Bangladesh, Nepal, and Sri Lanka. It is subdivided into two branches: *Indo-Aryan and *Iranian. These are among the oldest of the Indo-European group, spoken originally in Turkistan, and there is still much debate about the relation of these languages to the Hittite languages of Anatolia. *Sanskrit was a language of Indo-Iranian origin and the *Romany language spoken by *Gipsies is a member of this group.

Indonesia, Republic of (name from 1798 until 1945: Dutch East Indies) A country in SE Asia, consisting of a series of islands extending E–W for some 5150 km (3200 mi) in the Pacific and Indian Oceans. The main islands are Sumatra, Java and Madura, Bali, Sulawesi, Lombok, the Moluccas, and Timor together with part of Borneo (Kalimantan), and Irian Jaya (the W half of New Guinea). Plans to link Sumatra, Java, and Bali by tunnels and bridges were approved in 1986. Most of the islands are mountainous and volcanic. Its ethnically diverse population, which belongs mainly to the Malaysian race, may be broadly divided into three groups: the Hindu rice growers of Java and Bali (who make up over half the population), the Islamic coastal peoples, and a group of tribal peoples. The Chinese are the largest nonindigenous group. *Economy*: although rich in natural resources, with large deposits of oil, natural gas, and other minerals as well as some of the richest timber stands in the world, it is a mainly agrarian economy of which the staple crop is rice; cash crops include rubber, palm oil, copra, sugar cane, and coffee. Agricultural output, however, is generally low. The manufacturing sector, which includes shipbuilding, textiles, chemicals, and glass, has been slow to develop. The main exports include oil, timber, sand, and rubber. *History*: in the middle ages kingdoms and empires flourished, including the Hindu Srivijaya empire (7th–13th centuries), based on Palembang, and the Majapahit, which, centred on Java, ruled most of the area in the 15th century. In the 16th century it was occupied successively by the Portuguese, the British, and the Dutch, and from 1602 to 1798 it was ruled by the Dutch East India Company. It became a colony of the Netherlands and, after Japanese occupation during World War II, declared itself a republic in 1945 under the leadership of Dr Sukarno. Dutch colonial interests continued in conflict with the Indonesian nationalists until the country was formally granted independence (1949–50) as a single state. In 1956 ties with the Netherlands were broken off. During the period 1957–65 Sukarno pursued an essentially nationalist policy; Irian Jaya was incorporated in 1963 and there

was confrontation with Malaysia (1963–66). A military coup in 1966 under the leadership of Gen Suharto overthrew Sukarno's moderately right-wing authoritarian government replacing it with a harsh military dictatorship; left-wing elements were virtually eliminated. Despite subsequent moves to increase the number of civilian cabinet ministers, the regime remains predominantly military. Changes in foreign policy have led to an influx of capital from the West and Japan and an improvement in relations with Malaysia, but despite the substantial increases in revenue from oil there has been little change in the standard of living for the majority of the population. Separatist movements have continued in Irian Jaya and East Timor, which was formally incorporated as a province in 1976. President: Gen Suharto. Official language: Bahasa Indonesia. Official currency: rupiah of 100 sen. Area: 1 903 650 sq km (735 000 sq mi). Population (1983): 160 932 000. Capital and main port: Jakarta.

Indore 22 42N 75 54E A city in India, in Madhya Pradesh. Formerly the capital of the princely state of Indore, it is an important trading centre with cotton mills and engineering works. Its university was established in 1964. Population (1981): 827 000.

Indra The principal Hindu deity of the Vedic period, god of war and storm, who slew the dragon Vritra, releasing the fertile water and light necessary to create the universe. He is portrayed as wielding a thunderbolt. In later Hinduism, he is supplanted by *Vishnu, *Shiva, and *Krishna and appears as the relatively powerless ruler of the firmament and the east.

indri The largest Madagascan woolly lemur, *Indri indri*. Up to 70 cm long, it is grey and black, with long hind legs, a short tail, and a doglike head. It lives in treetops, eating leaves, and has a loud howling cry. Indris are threatened by the destruction of their forest habitats. Family: *Indriidae*.

induction (electromagnetism). *See* electromagnetic induction.

induction (embryology) The process by which an embryonic tissue influences adjacent cells to develop in a certain way, i.e. to differentiate into a particular adult tissue. Absence of the inducer tissue may result in abnormal development or nondevelopment of the induced cells.

induction (logic) The process of making an empirical generalization by observing particular instances of its operation. The conclusion goes beyond the facts, since not all possible instances can be examined. From induction predictions can be made but they are always liable to falsification. *Compare* deduction.

indulgences In the Roman Catholic Church, remissions of the temporal penalties incurred for sins already forgiven by God in the sacrament of penance. Indulgences are based on the belief that a sin, although forgiven, must still have a penalty on earth or in purgatory. The Church may remit these penalties by virtue of the merits of Christ and the saints. The practice of indulgences arose in the early Church when confessors and those about to be martyred were permitted to intercede for penitents and so mitigate the discipline imposed on them. During the later middle ages, indulgences came to command a financial value, which led to widespread abuse and was one of the chief causes of Luther's attack on the Church at the Reformation. Their sale was prohibited in 1567. Today the grant of indulgences, to encourage piety and good works, is largely the prerogative of the pope.

Indus, River A river in S central Asia, one of the longest in the world. Rising in SW Tibet in the Himalayas, it flows NW through Kashmir, then SSW across Pakistan to its large delta near Karachi on the Arabian Sea. Its main tributary is the Panjnad, which is formed from the Rivers Jhelum, Chenab, Ravi, Beas, and Sutlej. The Indus carries large amounts of sediment and it is also· subject to severe flooding but it is an important source of irrigation and hydroelectric power. Waterlogging and salinization have threatened cultivation on the Indus plain and projects have been undertaken to provide an effective drainage system. The Indus contained one of the earliest organized cultures, which lasted from about 2500 until 1700 BC (*see* Indus Valley civilization). Length: 2900 km (1800 mi).

industrial democracy The participation of workers in decisions regarding their work, factory, or company. Various forms of industrial democracy are used in different countries. In the USA, the method widely advocated is an extension of *collective bargaining. In West Germany, workers' representatives sit on supervisory boards, which vet the decisions of the board of directors. German experience has been that the supervisory boards have had little effect on decision making; this led the Bullock Report on industrial democracy (by a committee chaired by Lord (Alan) Bullock; 1914-) in the UK to advocate trade-union representation on a single board. In Yugoslavia, there is full worker representation, and at least three-quarters of a management board must consist of production workers. Other methods of encouraging workers' participation include *profit-sharing schemes and *works' councils.

industrial relations Relations between the two sides of industry, employers and employees, usually represented respectively by management and trade unions. In industries with good industrial relations, strikes and lockouts are rare or nonexistent and both sides cooperate to achieve, and to share in, their objectives, whether they be profits, the provision of an efficient service, or simply job satisfaction. Poor industrial relations are easily recognized by frequent and damaging strikes. The key to good industrial relations is probably some measure of *industrial democracy, *profit sharing, and unacrimonious *collective bargaining.

industrial revolution The name given to the process of change that transformed Britain and then other countries from agricultural to industrial economies. The industrial revolution began about 1750 when the *agricultural revolution was well under way. Inventions were made in the textile industry by such men as James *Hargreaves, Richard *Arkwright, and Samuel *Crompton, which made the production of cloth much faster and the yarn produced of better quality. These new machines could not be used in the home and necessitated the building of factories to house them, at first near rivers for water power and then, when the steam engine was invented, near coalfields. In the factories working conditions were usually intolerable: long hours were worked for low wages and the employment of children was common. Industrial towns sprang up, where living conditions were pitiable, but the current belief in *laissez-faire meant little was done to interfere with the progress of industrial growth. Advances were also made in the production of iron, especially by Henry *Cort, and in communications. The *canals were extended and from about 1830 *railways were built. By the mid-19th century British industrial methods had spread to continental Europe and the USA, laying the foundations for further progress in the 20th century.

Indus Valley civilization A homogeneous culture flourishing between about 2500 and 1700 BC in the area of modern Pakistan. Excavations from the 1920s onwards in the great centres of *Mohenjo-Daro and *Harappa have revealed grid-planned streets, municipal drainage, workmen's barracks, granaries and other large public buildings of baked brick, and a standardized system of weights and measures, all testifying to effective centralized administration. Sealstones bearing undeciphered hieroglyphics have also been found. The economy was primarily agricultural but there was some trade with *Sumer and *Akkad. The final downfall of the civilization (c. 1500 BC) was probably because of the *Aryans' incursion.

Ine (died c. 726) King of Wessex (688-726), whose code of law provides valuable information on economic and social life in his time. A patron of the Church, he abdicated (726) to retire to Rome.

inequality A mathematical statement that one quantity is greater or less than another.
$a<(>)b$ means a is less (greater) than b.
$a\leq(\geq)b$ means a is less (greater) than or equal to b.

inert gases. *See* noble gases.

inertia A property of a body that causes it to resist changes in its velocity or, if stationary, to resist motion. When the body resists changes in its linear motion its mass is a measurement of its inertia (*see* mass and weight). When it resists changes in rotation about an axis its inertia is given by its *moment of inertia.

INDUS VALLEY CIVILIZATION *A seal, probably used for trading purposes, showing a humped bull and pictographic letters. It was found at Mohenjo-Daro (Pakistan).*

inertial guidance A means of guiding a missile or submarine without communicating with its destination or point of departure. It consists of a set of three gyroscopes, with their axes mounted mutually perpendicular to each other, connected to a computer. The gyroscopes provide a frame of reference, which enables the computer to adjust the controls of the vehicle to steer a preset course.

infallibility A dogma of the Roman Catholic Church promulgated at the first *Vatican Council (1870). It stated that the pope cannot err in defining the Church's teaching in matters of faith and morals when speaking *ex cathedra* (Latin: from the throne), i.e. when intending to make such a pronouncement. The pope is not held thereby to be inspired by God but only to be preserved from error when making such a pronouncement.

infanticide The killing of newborn children. In advanced societies it is generally considered a crime but in many communities, especially in India and China, it has been used to limit population numbers in circumstances of poverty, overpopulation, or famine. Frequently female children and the weak or deformed were at greater risk because they were considered unproductive. In some societies, for instance among the ancient Phoenicians, a firstborn child would be offered as a sacrifice to the gods.

infant mortality The number of deaths that occur in infants under one year of age. This includes neonatal mortality, occurring in the first four weeks of life, from such causes as asphyxia and other birth injuries, prematurity, and developmental abnormalities. Neonatal deaths account for about two-thirds of infant mortalities in prosperous countries. The quality of a country's obstetric and antenatal care is reflected in its perinatal mortality rate: the number of stillbirths and deaths occurring in the first week of life per 1000 births. In Europe, the Scandinavians have the lowest perinatal mortality rates, e.g. 10.7 in Sweden (1976). In the same year the UK rate was 18.0. *See also* cot death.

infantry   A force of soldiers who fight on foot, even though they may be transported to the battle by air, sea, or mechanized transport. Infantry was predominant in ancient warfare, declined when the emphasis shifted to cavalry (c. 400 AD), and became important again with the development of firearms in the late middle ages. World War I, with its trench warfare, was still essentially an infantry war. The development of fast-moving armour, air power, and the landing craft made World War II a war of combined operations in which infantry played a decisive but not exclusive role. In modern warfare the extensive use of armour and guided missiles has turned the emphasis away from confrontation between massed infantry towards infiltration and *guerrilla warfare.

infection   Illness caused by microorganisms, including bacteria, viruses, fungi, and protozoa. Examples of bacterial infections are diphtheria, plague, pneumonia, scarlet fever, tuberculosis, venereal disease, and whooping cough. Viruses cause chickenpox, the common cold, influenza, measles, polio, rabies, and smallpox (among others); malaria and sleeping sickness result from protozoan infection, and fungi cause ringworm. Infectious diseases (also called contagious or communicable diseases) are the commonest cause of sickness and—except in modern industrial societies—have always been the main cause of death. Infections flourish in dirty crowded impoverished conditions, where the inhabitants are malnourished. Methods of transmission include direct contact with an infected person, contact with a human or animal carrier or contaminated objects, and contact with infected droplets produced by coughing and sneezing. The spread of infectious diseases can be prevented by such measures as improving public health, isolation of infected persons, and *vaccination. *Antibiotics are active against a wide range of disease-causing organisms, but as yet there are few effective drugs for viral diseases.

inferiority complex   An unconscious belief, first described by Alfred *Adler, that one is severely inadequate in some particular way. This leads to defensive behaviour and often to an overcompensation, such as open aggressiveness. *See also* complex.

infinity   In mathematics, a quantity larger than any that can be specified. The symbols $+\infty$ and $-\infty$ are read as "plus infinity" and "minus infinity" respectively. They indicate infinitely large positive and negative values. $x \to +\infty$ means that the value of a variable quantity, x, continues to increase and has no maximum.

inflammation   The reaction of the body's tissues in response to injury, infection, chemicals, and poisons, which is characterized by redness, heat, swelling, and pain. Blood flow to the inflamed area increases and white blood cells infiltrate the tissues and begin to engulf the invading bacteria (or other foreign particles). This may result in the accumulation of dead cells and bacteria, which form pus. Inflammation is an essential part of the healing process.

inflation   A general sustained increase in prices resulting from excessive demand for goods (demand-pull inflation), increased pricing by sellers in the absence of increased demand (cost-push inflation), or an expansion of the money supply (monetary inflation). **Deflation** is the opposite process and causes a reduction in both output and employment. In the 19th century periods of deflation and inflation alternated regularly in Europe. However, the abnormal

length and severity of deflation in the 1930s has been followed in the postwar years by a protracted period of inflation, rising in the 1970s to over 10% per annum in many countries, including the UK. Remedies vary according to the importance ascribed to each contributory factor: control of wages and prices (*see* prices and incomes policy), increased taxation, reduced government spending, and a controlled money supply are among current policies. However, none of them is likely to succeed when the basic cause is an increase in the cost of imported raw materials, such as oil. *Compare* depression.

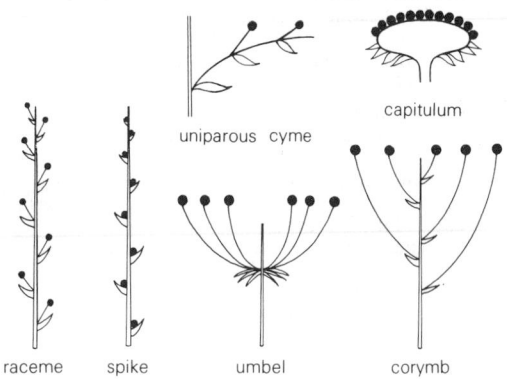

INFLORESCENCE   *All plants except those with solitary flowers show characteristic arrangements of their flowers on the main flowering stalk. All the types shown here, with the exception of the uniparous cyme, are racemose inflorescences.*

inflorescence   The arrangement of a group of flowers borne on the same main stalk, of which there are two basic types. In a racemose (or indefinite) inflorescence the tip of the main stem continues to grow and flowers arise below it. Examples are the raceme (e.g. foxglove) and the spike, which is similar but the flowers lack stalks (e.g. wheat). Flat-topped racemose inflorescences include the umbel (*see* Umbelliferae), the capitulum (e.g. daisy), and the corymb (e.g. candytuft). A cymose (or definite) inflorescence, or cyme, is one in which a flower is produced at the tip of the main stem, which then ceases to grow. Growth—and further flower production—is continued either by one lateral bud below the tip, to produce a monochasium (e.g. buttercup), or by a pair of buds, giving a dichasium (e.g. stitchwort).

influenza   An acute viral infection characterized by chills, fever, headache, and a slight cough. Muscle weakness, aching joints, and loss of appetite may follow. Cases vary from mild to very severe and possibly fatal (particularly if a secondary bacterial infection occurs). Bed rest, aspirin, and fluids provide the only treatment. Usually small outbreaks of influenza occur regularly in winter, but occasionally epidemics sweep across the world. The worst epidemic in the 20th century occurred in 1918-19, when as many as 20 million people died. These epidemics occur because of the development of new strains of influenza viruses, which are not recognized by the body's immune system. Because of this, it is difficult to produce a vaccine, although new ones are constantly produced and are partially effective.

information theory   The mathematical theory of communication, involving analysis of the information content of messages and the processes used in their transmission, reception, storage, and retrieval. Statistical concepts, such as probability, are used to assess the extra information (redundancy) necessary to compensate for spurious signals (noise) occurring during communication. The *bit is the basic unit of information and the channel capacity is a measure of the ability of the transmission medium, e.g. a telegraph line, to carry information.

Information theory was developed in the 1940s by Claude E. Shannon (1916–). It has been applied widely in such fields as computer science and *cybernetics and has greatly aided the understanding of many processes, ranging from the laws of thermodynamics to the use of language.

infrared radiation Electromagnetic radiation with wavelengths between about 750 nanometres and 1 millimetre. In the electromagnetic spectrum it lies between the red end of visible light and microwaves. It was discovered in 1800 by William *Herschel, who noticed that the solar spectrum contained invisible rays with a heating effect. Infrared radiation is emitted by all bodies at temperatures above absolute zero and is the predominant radiation emitted up to temperatures of about 3000°C. See Plate VII.

infrared telescope A reflecting *telescope for detecting and studying infrared radiation from astronomical sources, such as stars enveloped in dust clouds or cool *molecular clouds of gas and dust. Semiconductor detectors are used, and these (and in some cases the telescope optics) must be cooled to very low temperatures. Infrared telescopes are normally sited at high altitudes to reduce infrared absorption by the atmosphere or are carried on satellites. Several major telescopes are located at the summit of Mauna Kea (4200 m) in Hawaii.

infrasonics The study of sound waves with a frequency below the threshold of human hearing, i.e. below about 20 hertz. They are produced naturally by earthquakes and tidal waves; in cars travelling at high speeds they have been suspected of having adverse effects on the drivers.

Inge, William Ralph (1860–1954) British Anglican churchman, nicknamed the "Gloomy Dean." He was professor of divinity at Cambridge (1907–11), Dean of St Paul's (1911–34), and a widely read author of a number of theological works. His books include *Christian Mysticism* (1899), *Outspoken Essays* (1919; 1922), and *The Platonic Tradition in English Religious Thought* (1926).

Ingenhousz, Jan (1730–99) Dutch physician and plant physiologist, who discovered the process of *photosynthesis in green plants. Ingenhousz found that plants took in carbon dioxide and gave off oxygen, but only when exposed to light. This oxygen replenished that used by animals and plants in respiration.

Ingleborough 54 10N 2 23W A hill in N England, in North Yorkshire. Ingleborough Cave in the S contains stalagmites and stalactites. Height: 723 m (2373 ft).

Ingres, Jean-Auguste-Dominique (1780–1867) French painter, born in Montauban, the son of an artist. He became a pupil of *David in Paris in 1797. His three paintings of the Rivière family (Louvre) established him as a skilled portraitist. From 1806 to 1820 he lived in Rome, where he produced numerous pencil portraits as well as paintings. Many of his historical and mythological paintings aroused criticism but, on returning to Paris in 1824, his *Vow of Louis XIII* (Cathedral, Montauban) established him as an opponent of the Romantic movement (see Romanticism). After teaching at the Ecole des Beaux-Arts, he returned to Rome as the director of the French Academy (1835–41). He is noted for his nudes, e.g. *Valpinçon Bather* (Louvre); his draughtsmanship influenced *Degas and *Picasso.

inheritance tax A UK tax introduced in the 1986 Budget to replace capital-transfer tax. The first £90,000 of an inheritance is tax-free, thereafter the tax rises in tranches from 30% to 60% (for an inheritance of £330,000 or more). The tax on lifetime gifts was replaced with a tapered charge on gifts made within seven years of death.

inhibitor A substance that retards a chemical reaction; often called a negative *catalyst. Examples include antioxidants, enzyme inhibitors, and antipolymerization agents.

initiation rites Rituals performed on the transition from childhood to adult status or on joining certain professions or associations. During this period adolescents among primitive peoples are often educated in the duties of adulthood. *Circumcision may be practised at this time. Initiation rites are frequently performed on admission to religious orders, secret societies, and guilds. See also passage rites.

initiative. See referendum and initiative.

JEAN-AUGUSTE-DOMINIQUE INGRES *Detail from a self-portrait (1804; Musée Condé, Chantilly).*

injection The introduction of medicinal fluids into the body using a syringe and hollow (hypodermic) needle. The three basic injection routes are under the skin (subcutaneous), for example for insulin; into a muscle (intramuscular), for drugs to be slowly absorbed; and into a vein (intravenous), for drugs to be rapidly absorbed. Drugs are injected when high concentrations are needed or when they are poorly absorbed by the intestines.

injection moulding A process, similar to die-casting, for moulding thermoplastic materials (plastics that soften on heating and harden on cooling). Injection-moulding machines are often fully automatic; the plastic is heated in a cylinder until it has melted and is then forced under pressure into a cooled moulding chamber.

ink A coloured fluid for writing or printing. Ordinary permanent blue-black writing ink contains ferrous sulphate, mineral organic acid, and other dyes. Coloured inks contain only synthetic dyes, while washable inks use water-soluble synthetic dyes. Marking ink is a mixture of inorganic and organic salts that precipitates aniline black on the surface being marked. Indian ink, used mainly for drawing, is a black waterproof ink containing carbon black and *shellac. Printing ink consists of pigments suspended in linseed oil, resins, and solvents, the composition depending on the printing process. Ballpoint pen ink is more like printing ink than writing ink since it consists of synthetic dye dissolved in organic liquids with a resinous binder.

ink cap A *mushroom belonging to the genus *Coprinus*, the gills of which are digested after release of the spores to form an inky fluid that drips from the cap. The common ink cap (*C. atramentarius*) grows in tight clusters, usually at the base of trees and shrubs, and has a pale brownish-grey cap, 3–7 cm high, and a whitish stalk.

Inkerman, Battle of (5 November, 1854) A decisive battle of the Crimean War, in which the French and British defeated the Russians at Inkerman, near Sevastopol. In spite of poor direction the Anglo-French force withstood the Russian attack: the Russians lost about 12 000 men, the British, about 2 500, and the French, about 1 000.

Inland Sea A shallow section of the NW Pacific Ocean between the Japanese islands of Honshu, Shikoku, and Kyushu.

Inner Mongolia Autonomous Region (Chinese name: Nei Menggu AR) An administrative division in NE China, bordering on Mongolia and the Gobi Desert in the W. Its steppes are now partly irrigated and cultivated, producing mainly wheat, and the nomadic Mongol herdsmen, now comprising only 7% of the population, are beginning to settle. Some coal is mined. Area: 1 177 500 sq km (459 225 sq mi). Population (1980 est): 18 510 000. Capital: Hohhot.

Inner Temple. *See* Inns of Court.

Innocent III (Lotario de' Conti di Segni; 1160-1216) Pope (1198-1216). He was an outstanding canon lawyer, and as pope his policy was directed to the extension of papal power in all areas of temporal and spiritual government. He successfully intervened in the disputed imperial succession in Germany. In France he condemned the marital behaviour of *Philip II Augustus and in England forced the submission of King *John, who recognized the pope as feudal overlord. He also proclaimed the fourth *Crusade (1204). The fourth *Lateran Council (1215) represents the climax of his spiritual rule. In its proclamation of the supremacy of spiritual over temporal power, his pontificate marks the apogee of the medieval papacy.

Innocent IV (d. 1254) Pope (1243-54). Before election to the papacy he was a renowned teacher of canon law at Bologna. Much of his pontificate was taken up with attempts to resolve the conflict between the papacy and Emperor *Frederick II. Innocent was forced to flee Rome (1244) and at the Council of Lyon (1245) condemned and deposed the emperor. Only after Frederick's death, however, did Innocent return to Rome (1253).

Innsbruck 47 17N 11 25E A city in W Austria, the capital of the Tirol on the River Inn. Chartered in 1239, it developed as the junction of several important trade routes, including the *Brenner Pass. It has many fine medieval buildings, and a university (1677). It is a popular tourist and winter-sports centre and the 1964 Olympic Winter Games were held here. Industries include glass and textiles. Population (1981): 117 287.

Inns of Court Assocations with the exclusive right to confer the rank or degree of barrister-at-law, known as "calling to the Bar." For the English bar, the Inns are the Honourable Societies of Lincoln's Inn (established 1310), Middle Temple (1340), Inner Temple (1340), and Gray's Inn (1357). They are administered by a body of senior barristers and judges known as "benchers," who have absolute discretion as to admission of students to the Bar. Their previous disciplinary functions and power to deprive a barrister of his status, "disbarring," is now exercised by the Senate of the Inns of Court and the Bar, which has six benchers of each Inn among its membership of 94. Most barristers' offices (known as chambers) in London are in one of the Inns. An Inn of Court of Northern Ireland was established in Belfast in 1926.

inoculation. *See* vaccination.

Inönü, Ismet (1884–1973) Turkish statesman; prime minister (1923–37, 1960–65) and president (1938–50). After a successful military career he joined *Atatürk and commanded the fighting against the Greeks in Anatolia (1921). He was prime minister under Atatürk and succeeded him as president. Following defeat in the elections of 1950 he led the Republican People's Party opposition to the Democratic Party government and after the 1960 coup formed three successive coalition governments (1961–65).

inorganic chemistry. *See* chemistry.

inquilinism An animal relationship in which one species lives in the nest of another species or makes use of its food. For example, some termites live only in the mounds of certain other termite species, although in completely separate compartments.

Inquisition (*or* Holy Office) An institution of the medieval and early modern Church designed to combat heresy and moral offences. Formally instituted (1231) by Pope *Gregory IX in response to the growing threat of heresy, especially of the *Cathari and *Waldenses, it attempted to place all control of heresy in papal hands. Inquisitors, appointed by the pope, especially from the Dominican and Franciscan orders, and possessing considerable powers, often merited their reputation for cruelty. The use of torture was authorized in 1252 and trials were held in secrecy; fines and various penances were imposed on those who confessed, while those who refused were imprisoned or executed by burning. Almost entirely confined to S Europe, the Inquisition lapsed during the 14th and 15th centuries but was revived in Spain in 1478 against apostate Jews and Muslims. Operating with great severity, especially under the first grand inquisitor, de *Torquemada, the Spanish Inquisition later operated against Protestants in Spain and (with little success) the Netherlands, and achieved some notoriety for its arrest of St *Ignatius Loyola. The growth of Protestantism led to the establishment (1542) of a Roman Inquisition by Pope Paul III. It was given complete independence in matters of doctrine and control of heresy and among its victims was *Galileo. In 1965 the Holy Office became a branch of papal bureaucracy and was renamed the Sacred Congregation for the Doctrine of the Faith; it is now concerned with maintaining Roman Catholic discipline.

INRI Abbreviation for *Iesus Nazarenus Rex Iudeorum* (Jesus of Nazareth King of the Jews). According to St John (19.19-20) this inscription, written in Hebrew, Greek, and Latin, was placed by order of Pilate on the cross upon which Jesus was crucified. The initials often appear on the representation of the cross in Christian painting and sculpture.

insanity In law (although not a legal term), defect of reason caused by disease of the mind, making a person not responsible for his acts. A person is presumed sane until the contrary is proved. If a jury finds an accused person committed an act as charged but was insane, it must return a verdict of not guilty by reason of insanity. According to **M'Naghten's Rules** (established following the acquittal in 1843 on the ground of insanity of Daniel M'Naghten, charged with murder) an accused person is insane if he was unaware of the nature or quality of his act or did not know it was morally wrong. Insanity may affect a person's capacity to make binding contracts or a will or his fitness to plead, i.e. answer to a criminal charge and therefore to stand trial. An insane person contracting with someone unaware of his insanity is only bound by contracts for necessaries, such as food, but is liable to pay only a reasonable price irrespective of the contract price. In cases of a person with partial insanity, i.e. with intermittent periods of lucidity, a defence must show that at the relevant time the person was insane.

insect An invertebrate animal, 0.2-350 mm long, belonging to the largest class in the animal kingdom (*Insecta*; about a million known species). Insects occur throughout the world and account for 83% of all animal life. An insect's body, covered by a waterproof cuticle, is divided into three sections: the head, which bears a pair of antennae; the thorax, with three pairs of legs and typically two pairs of wings; and the abdomen. With biting or sucking mouthparts they feed on almost all plant or animal materials. The majority of insects lay eggs, which go through a series of changes (*see* metamorphosis) to reach the adult stage. In the more primitive orders, for example *Orthoptera* and *Hemiptera*, the young (called nymphs) resemble the adults, but in the higher orders, for example *Hymenoptera*, *Diptera* (flies), and *Coleoptera* (beetles), the young (called larvae)

INSECT

silverfish

swallowtail butterfly

hoverfly

mayfly

cranefly

springtail

earwig

hawthorn shield bug

aphid

damselfly

ocelli (simple eyes)

head

thorax

forewing

hindwing

compound eye

antenna

abdomen

mandible

hind leg

foreleg

middle leg

lacewing

scorpion fly

leaf beetle

flea

termite

green bush cricket

mantis

stick insect

sucking louse

American cockroach

bumblebee

ant

INSECT *The structure of a typical insect (centre), with representatives from all the principal insect orders.*

are unlike the adults, often have a different diet, and go through a resting pupal stage.

Insects play an important role in nature as predators, parasites, scavengers, and as prey. Many are plant or animal pests and disease carriers. Others are useful in pollinating crops or killing insect pests and some produce useful substances, such as honey, beeswax, and silk. Phylum: *Arthropoda*.

insecticides Substances used to kill insects by chemical action. Previously, strong inorganic poisons, such as arsenic compounds and cyanides, were used but these were also toxic to humans and livestock. Synthetic organic substances, beginning with DDT in 1945 and including aldrin, endosulphan, and parathion, are now widely used, mainly because of their selectivity, but also because of their cheapness and ease of application. Insecticides are classified according to mode of action or application; for example, **contact insecticides** are applied directly to the insects, while **residual insecticides** are sprayed on surfaces that the insects touch. Problems of insect immunity and environmental pollution have encouraged research into alternative methods involving *biological control.

Insectivora The order of *mammals, comprising about 375 species, that includes *shrews, *tenrecs, *hedgehogs, *moles and *desmans, *golden moles, and *solenodons. Feeding mainly on invertebrates, insectivores are fairly primitive mammals with narrow snouts and sharp simple teeth; their eyes and brains are generally small. Inconspicuous and frequently nocturnal, insectivores are found in nearly all regions; they are absent from the Poles and Australasia.

insectivorous plant. *See* carnivorous plant.

insolvency The inability of a person or company to pay their debts. A creditor may petition a court to declare an insolvent debtor bankrupt (*see* bankruptcy), in which case all his property is sold and the proceeds distributed to his creditors. An insolvent company or partnership is put into liquidation, the court appointing a liquidator, who realizes its assets for distribution to creditors.

insomnia. *See* sleep.

instinct 1. A complex pattern of behaviour, the form of which is determined by heredity and is therefore characteristic of all individuals of the same species. Although the behaviour may be released and modified by environmental stimuli, its basic pattern does not depend on the experience of the individual. Birdsong and the complex behaviour of social insects (such as bees) are striking examples. It is doubtful whether any human activities are, in this sense, instinctive. 2. An innate drive, such as hunger or sex, that urges the individual towards a particular goal.

insulator A material that is a poor conductor of electric current and therefore has a high resistivity. Solids, such as glass, rubber, ceramics, and PVC, are used in electric circuits to separate conducting wires and prevent current loss. In overhead power transmission, air acts as the insulator between high-voltage lines. *See also* energy band.

insulin A protein hormone that is secreted by the islets of Langerhans in the *pancreas in response to a high concentration of glucose in the blood, which occurs, for example, after a meal. It stimulates the uptake of glucose and amino acids from the blood by the tissues and the formation of *glycogen. Its effects are counteracted by the hormone *glucagon. Insulin was first isolated in 1921 by *Banting and *Best and its amino acid composition and three-dimensional structure were revealed by Frederick *Sanger and Dorothy *Hodgkin. A deficiency of insulin causes the symptoms of *diabetes mellitus.

insurance A method of providing monetary compensation for a misfortune or loss that may not occur. Events that must occur at some time, such as death, are provided for by *assurance. In the UK and some other countries insurance against unemployment, sickness, and retirement is provided

by the government (*see* National Insurance). Other types of insurance are undertaken by the private sector, either by insurance companies or by *Lloyd's. Almost any risk can be insured against, the most common being *marine and aviation insurance; *motor insurance; fire, burglary, and household insurance; *private medical insurance; and weather insurance. The public does not deal directly with the underwriters (insurers) but arranges to cover a risk through an insurance broker, who works for a commission paid by the insurer and advises the client as to the best cover available, taking into account the cost and reliability of the insurer. Claims are also settled through brokers. The cost to the insured of covering the risk (premium) is calculated by the insurer's *actuary on the basis of the probability of the risk occurring. If the event occurs the insured's claim is paid by the insurer, as calculated by an insurance assessor or as stipulated in the insurance policy. *See also* credit insurance.

intaglio The production of a sunken image, especially in metal or stone, by etching or engraving. It is used in sculpture, gems, and seals, and for making the plates for gravure printing, in which ink is transferred to the paper from only the sunken areas of the plate, the rest having been wiped clean.

integers. *See* numbers.

integrated circuit (IC) A solid-state *semiconductor circuit contained in a single wafer of semiconductor. ICs are made by a process of etching and diffusing a pattern of impurities into the semiconductor surface, forming tiny p-n junctions, which make up individual diodes, *transistors, etc. Since the 1970s computers have been used to make ICs smaller and more complex, in spite of the fact that further reducing the size makes the doping pattern imprecise. A silicon chip (*or* microchip) is covered with circuits, and computer-controlled microscopic probes search out the best points for connections for each specific device. The application of this technique has revolutionized many areas of industry and commerce, making cheap *microprocessors available for the automation of production processes.

intelligence The ability to reason and to profit by experience. An individual's level of intelligence is determined by a complex interaction between his heredity and environment; the Swiss psychologist Jean *Piaget greatly contributed to present-day understanding of intellectual development. The first **intelligence tests** were devised by Alfred *Binet in 1905 and there are now many tests for assessing intellectual ability. An individual's performance in a test is represented by his **intelligence quotient** (IQ), the product of 100 and the ratio of mental age (obtained from the test results) to actual age. Tests are constructed so that the average IQ is 100 and over 95% of the population come between 70 and 130. However, since it is now widely thought that true intelligence can be expressed only through speech and writing (and is therefore inaccessible to testing) and since each test reflects the constructor's view of the nature of intelligence, the predictive value of the tests as a basis for selection for secondary education is questionable. Tests that measure a wide range of abilities, such as the Weschler Intelligence Scale for Children (WISC), are now regarded as the most useful and relevant for diagnosing educational difficulties.

intelligence service The government department responsible for obtaining information about the military and economic capabilities and political intentions of another country (intelligence) or for thwarting the attempts of a foreign country to get such information for itself (counter-intelligence). Sources of intelligence information may be open, such as diplomatic reports, newspapers, and radio broadcasts, or secret, such as aerial reconnaissance, "bugging," and the fieldwork of spies. Intelligence services existed in antiquity and the first known treatise on the subject is Sun Tzu's *The Art of War* (c. 400 BC). Elizabeth I of England had a notable intelligence service, organized by

Sir Francis *Walsingham, as did Cardinal de Richelieu in 17th-century France and Frederick the Great in 18th-century Prussia. The first specifically military service was established in France under *Fouché (1802) during the Napoleonic Wars, which the British countered (1808) with the Peninsular Corps of Guides in Spain. This was disbanded after Napoleon's fall but a similar corps was set up (1855) during the Crimean War. The subsequent Intelligence Department was active in the second *Boer War (1899–1902), using balloons for reconnaissance and pigeons for the speedy relaying of messages. In 1909 and 1912 respectively the army general staff's Directorate of Military Operations organized MO-5 (counterintelligence) and MO-6 (intelligence), which soon became MI(Military Intelligence)-5 (the Security Service) and MI-6 (the Secret Intelligence Service). Elsewhere, the best-known intelligence services are the *Central Intelligence Agency, the *Federal Bureau of Investigation (counterintelligence), and the National Security Agency (dealing with cryptology) in the USA and the *KGB in the Soviet Union.

The development of intelligence services since World War II is linked with technological advances. Modern methods of obtaining secret information about a foreign state, including photoreconnaissance by such aircraft as the U-2 and by satellites, as well as the work of spies, depend on the use of microfilm, recording machines, and computers. The activities of spies have become less significant but remain an enduringly popular theme for books and films and those real-life agents who have been uncovered, such as *Mata Hari, the *Rosenbergs, Burgess and *Maclean, and *Philby, have attracted enormous interest.

Intelsat. *See* communications satellite.

Inter-American Development Bank An international bank founded in 1959 to provide assistance to developing countries in Latin America and the Caribbean by making loans at very low *interest rates. The UK joined in 1974.

interest The amount of money charged by a lender to a borrower for the use of a loan. The principal (P) is the amount on which interest is calculated; the term (t), the length of time in years for which the money is lent; and the interest rate (r), the annual rate of return per 100 units of principal. In simple interest, the principal each year is the sum originally lent. The lender is paid $Prt/100$ in interest and repaid P after t years. In compound interest, the interest each year is not paid to the lender but is added to the principal, so that the principal for the next year becomes $P + r/100$. After t years the lender is paid $P(1 + r/100)^t$.

interference A wave phenomenon in which two waves combine either to reinforce each other or to cancel each other out, depending on their relative phases. The pattern of light and dark strips so produced is called an **interference pattern** (*or* interference fringe). The effect occurs when the two beams have the same frequency and have approximately the same amplitude. Interference was discovered in 1801 by Thomas *Young and provided strong evidence for the wave theory of light.

An **interferometer** is used to produce interference patterns, mainly for the accurate measurement of wavelengths. Several different types are in use, the older instruments being devices for splitting a beam into two parts and then recombining them to form interference patterns after each part has travelled a different distance. In the Michelson interferometer (□Michelson-Morley experiment) the beam is split by a half-silvered mirror in which part of the beam is reflected and the rest transmitted. In the Fabry-Perot interferometer two parallel half-silvered mirrors are placed close to each other. In more modern instruments two lasers are used as separate coherent sources.

interferon A protein that appears in the plasma during viral infections: it is released from infected cells and inhibits the growth of the viruses. Interferon plays an important role in *immunity because it can enter uninfected cells and

render them immune to all viral infections. It was discovered in 1957 by a British virologist, Alick Isaacs (1921–67). Attempts are being made to produce human interferon in bulk in bacterial cells, which could be used to treat viral diseases.

interior design The part of architectural design that deals with the placing and layout of rooms within a building. It chiefly involves the decoration of walls and ceilings and design of normally immovable types of furniture, such as mirrors and fireplaces. Since Robert *Adam it has increasingly concerned movable furniture as well, a field previously left to the skill of the individual craftsman. In the 20th century greater attention has been given to creating a harmonious and functional style for buildings, down to the smallest object of furniture. A notable practitioner of this was Arne *Jacobsen, who sometimes specified exact positions for his furniture.

Interlaken 46 42N 7 52E A resort in central Switzerland in the Bernese Oberland between Lakes Brienz and Thun. One of Switzerland's oldest tourist resorts, it is surrounded by spectacular mountain scenery with a fine view of the Jungfrau mountain. Population (1985 est): 13·000.

intermediate vector boson (*W*) A hypothetical elementary particle thought to be exchanged by particles undergoing a *weak interaction. It would be an unstable *boson, either charged or neutral, and have a mass greater than about 800 MeV. *See also* particle physics.

internal-combustion engine A *heat engine in which fuel is burnt inside the engine, rather than in a separate furnace (*see* steam engine). This category includes all piston engines, *jet engines, and *rockets. The first practical internal-combustion engine was patented by N. *Otto in 1876. This was a four-stroke engine using gas as a fuel. It was the invention of the □carburettor and the development of the *oil industry that made the liquid-fuelled Otto engine a practical source of power for the horseless carriages emerging in the late 19th century (*see* car). Since then the petrol engine has powered most road vehicles.

The modern petrol engine has a compression ratio of 8 or 9 to 1, which requires special fuels (*see* tetraethyl lead) to avoid *knocking. A simpler but less efficient variety of the petrol engine is the two-stroke. This does not have the complicated inlet and exhaust valves of the Otto engine, the explosive mixture entering and leaving the cylinder through ports in its walls that are covered and uncovered by the movements of the piston. Two-stroke engines are used where low power is required and in some cars and motorcycles.

The main alternative to the petrol engine is the oil engine, based on a cycle invented by the German engineer Rudolf Diesel (1858–1913). In the Diesel engine, air is compressed alone inside the engine, causing its temperature to rise to over 550°C; oil is then pumped into the combustion chamber as a fine spray and ignites on contact with the hot air. In this case the compression ratio has to be 15 or 16 to 1, making the engine considerably heavier and more expensive than the petrol engine. The efficiency of both Otto and Diesel engines is limited by their compression ratios and thus their working temperatures (□heat engines). Also, combustion is intermittent and therefore incomplete, causing pollution problems. Moreover, both being reciprocating engines, they have inherent vibrations. This last problem is overcome to some extent in the *Wankel engine. The *gas turbine, however, uses continuous combustion and with a compression ratio of up to 30:1 can reach a working temperature of 1200°C. It is therefore more efficient and creates less pollution than piston engines. Jet engines based on the gas turbine are used widely in aircraft and as an easily started and shut down prime mover in some power stations.

International An association of national socialist or labour parties formed to promote socialism or communism. The **First International** was an organization of labour and socialist groups founded in London in 1864 as the

ideal Otto cycle

working stroke (4-5)

decompression (5-2)

ignition (3-4)

compression stroke (2-3)

inlet   exhaust

induction stroke (1-2)

exhaust stroke (2-1)

pressure

working
ignition
decompression
compression
exhaust
induction

volume

ideal Diesel cycle

working stroke (4-5)

decompression (5-2)

ignition (3-4)

compression stroke (2-3)

inlet   exhaust

induction stroke (1-2)

exhaust stroke (2-1)

pressure

ignition
working
compression
decompression
exhaust
induction

volume

INTERNAL-COMBUSTION ENGINE   *In the ideal Otto-cycle (four-stroke) engine, there are four piston strokes (movements up and down) for each explosion. The petrol-air mixture is drawn into the cylinder by the induction stroke (1-2) and compressed by the compression stroke (2-3). A spark then ignites (3-4) the mixture causing the pressure to rise from P_3 to P_4 before the piston descends (combustion at constant volume). The piston then descends in the working stroke (4-5) and rises again in the exhaust stroke (2-1), when the burnt gases are pushed out of the cylinder through the exhaust valve. The graph illustrates the pressure and volume changes during the cycle. In the Diesel cycle, ignition is caused by the high compression achieved by the compression stroke (2-3) and the piston descends, increasing the volume of the burning gas from V_3 to V_4, before the pressure has time to rise (combustion at constant pressure).*

International Working Men's Association. Karl Marx soon assumed its leadership and its first congress was held in Geneva in 1866. Although the First International was successful in disseminating socialist ideas among workers, it failed to make any political changes, largely because of the conflicting socialist views of its members, especially those of Marx and *Bakunin. Its last meeting was held in 1876 in Philadelphia.

The **Second International** was founded in Paris in 1889; its headquarters were in Brussels. The organization was composed primarily of European, North American, and Japanese social democratic parties, which believed in parliamentary democracy, and of trade unions. Its leaders included Ramsay *Macdonald. At the outbreak of World War I, the organization collapsed because of division between pro- and anti-war groups. A postwar attempt to revive it failed.

The **Labour and Socialist International** was founded in Vienna in 1921; its goal was to create a socialist commonwealth. It has been called the "second and a half International" because it was composed of those out of sympathy with the Second and Third Internationals. It opposed fascism and also communist dictatorship while supporting the Soviet Union. The organization came to an end following Hitler's invasions in W Europe in 1940.

The **Third International** (*or* Comintern), an organization of world Communist Parties, was founded by Lenin in March, 1919, to encourage worldwide proletariat revolution. Throughout its existence it adjusted its programme to political exigencies and to the power struggles within the Soviet party leadership. As a gesture of reconciliation with his western allies, Stalin dissolved the International in 1943 (*see also* Cominform).

The **Fourth International** was founded by *Trotsky in Mexico City in 1937 in opposition to Stalin and the Third International. It held its first conference in France in 1938 and was composed primarily of those who supported Trotsky's transitional programme, which aimed to undermine capitalism in preparation for its revolutionary overthrow.

The **Socialist International** was founded in 1951 as an association of socialist parties that believe in parliamentary democracy and oppose communism. Its headquarters are in London.

International Bank for Reconstruction and Development (IBRD) A specialized agency of the *United Nations, known as the World Bank, with headquarters in Washington, DC. It finances development in member countries by making loans to governments or under government guarantee. It was set up by the 1944 *Bretton Woods agreements to facilitate reconstruction after World War II. All members must belong to the *International Monetary Fund.

International Brigades A volunteer army recruited during the Spanish Civil War (1936–39) by the Comintern to aid the Republicans against Franco. Comprising at its largest some 20 000 volunteers, of which about 60% were communists, it was organized by nationality into 7 brigades. Ill-armed and badly led, it was disbanded in 1938.

International Civil Aviation Organization (ICAO) A specialized agency of the *United Nations established in 1947 to promote high operating standards and fair competition among international airlines. With headquarters in Montreal, it formulates agreed standards in telecommunications, personnel training, and air-traffic protocols. Its council of representatives of 27 of the member countries implements the decisions of the assembly, its legislative body, and when necessary settles disputes between members.

international commodity agreements Agreements between producers of primary products to regulate their production and sale in order to stabilize prices and conserve supplies; examples include the Tin Agreement (1956), Coffee Agreement (1962), and Rubber Agreement (1976). Natural factors, such as crop failures, and the discovery of new mineral deposits cause fluctuations in the supply and hence the price of commodities. Producers, which are mostly developing countries, have agreed to limit production, fix minimum prices, and establish marketing organizations to build up buffer stocks by buying surpluses, which are sold when prices exceed a specific ceiling.

International Confederation of Free Trade Unions (ICFTU) An international body of national trades-union federations formed in 1949 by federations that had withdrawn from the *World Federation of Trade Unions (WFTU) following disagreements with the communist members of the WFTU.

International Court of Justice The judicial body set up by the UN to pass judgment on disputes between states. The court, which normally sits at The Hague, comprises 15 judges, each from a different state, elected by the UN General Assembly. The court may only hear disputes between states that have agreed to be brought before it by any other state, either generally or in a specific case. Judgments of the court are enforced by application to the UN Security Council. The court also advises the UN and other specified bodies on questions of public *international law.

International Criminal Police Organization. *See* Interpol.

International Date Line A line following the 180° meridian, deviating to avoid some land areas. The date immediately E of the line is one day earlier than to the W since 180°E is 12 hours ahead of *Greenwich Mean Time and 180°W is 12 hours behind.

Internationale The national anthem of the Soviet Union until 1944, originally composed by P. Degeyter (1848–1932).

international gothic A style of painting and sculpture dominant in W Europe between about 1375 and 1425. Originating in France and Burgundy, it later spread to Italy, Bohemia, and other German states. International gothic retained the figure stylizations of *gothic but introduced naturalism in the depiction of landscape, animals, and costume. Leading exponents were the de *Limburg brothers and Claus *Sluter in Burgundy and *Gentile da Fabriano and *Pisanello in Italy.

International Labour Organisation (ILO) A specialized agency of the *United Nations dedicated to the improvement of working conditions and living standards. It was first convened in 1919, when it was affiliated to the *League of Nations, and its headquarters are in Geneva. The organization advocates a world labour code to protect the interests of workers, supports labour research projects, monitors labour legislation, and provides technical assistance to developing nations. In 1977 the USA withdrew from the ILO on the grounds that it had come to be dominated by political interests but rejoined in 1980.

international law The rules that determine the legal relationship between independent states (public), or the method of resolving disputes between individuals concerning transactions to which two or more legal systems may be relevant, as when a contract made in one country is to be performed in another (private). Public international law, also called the law of nations and administered by the *International Court of Justice, is based on: (1) natural law, being laws recognized by civilized nations; (2) agreements between states, i.e. conventions; (3) customs followed in practice; and, to a lesser extent (4) the writings and opinions of respected jurists. Private international law, also called conflict of laws, determines the laws of which country should apply and which courts should have jurisdiction.

International Monetary Fund (IMF) A specialized agency of the *United Nations, with headquarters in Washington, DC, set up by the 1944 *Bretton Woods agreements to stabilize exchange rates and facilitate international trade. Each member country contributes to the fund in both gold and its own currency. A member with balance-of-payments difficulties can obtain foreign currency from the fund in exchange for its own, which it must repurchase within five years. The higher a member's contribution the greater its voting rights. Dr Herman Ruding of the Netherlands was elected chairman in 1985. *See also* Special Drawing Rights.

International Organization for Standardization (ISO) An organization, situated in Geneva, for establishing and controlling international scientific, industrial, and commercial standards of measurement and design. It was founded in 1946. The *British Standards Institution is a member.

International Phonetic Alphabet (IPA) An augmented Roman alphabet, developed by the International Phonetic Association in the late 19th century and kept under continuous revision since. It attempts to symbolize, on phonetic principles, every sound used in human language. Many dictionaries represent the pronunciation of words in IPA.

international style The predominant architectural style of the 20th century, so called because it was the first style effectively to breach all national and cultural barriers. Originating in W Europe and the USA with such architects as *Gropius, *Wright, *Behrens, and *Le Corbusier, the international style evolved from the new tastes, materials, and advanced technology produced by industrialization. It is chiefly characterized by the use of concrete, often roughcast, a tendency towards monolithic uniformity in the use of undecorated cubic forms, and a functional asymmetry.

International Telecommunication Union (ITU) A specialized agency of the *United Nations founded in 1934 to promote international agreement on standards of use and development of telecommunications systems. It makes recommendations on the regulation and use of radio frequencies, general operating procedures, and the establishment of telecommunications systems in developing countries, including radio, telegraph, telephone, cable, and television. Its headquarters are in Geneva.

International Working Men's Association. *See* International.

Interpol (*Inter*national Criminal *Police* Organization) An association of about 120 national *police forces formed in 1923 to provide a means of international cooperation in the prevention of crime. Its constitution strictly precludes activities of a political, military, religious, or racial nature. Its major concerns are the exchange of police information and the arrest of those who are the subject of an extradition order. Interpol has been most effective in the control of smuggling, particularly of gold and narcotics, and of currency offences and counterfeiting.

Interregnum. *See* Commonwealth.

interstellar medium The matter, mainly hydrogen gas and some dust, contained in the region between the stars of the *Galaxy and concentrated in the spiral arms. It can exist, for example, as hot ionized clouds, cooler and more tenuous neutral areas, or dense clouds of molecular hydrogen and other molecules. Small dust particles are found throughout the interstellar region. The gas and dust is probably material cast off from old stars, with young stars forming out of the dense clouds.

interstitial An atom that exists in the spaces (interstices) between the atoms or molecules in a crystal lattice. Some interstitial compounds are important *alloys and some are *semiconductors.

intestine The part of the digestive tract, in the abdomen, that extends from the stomach to the anus. It is divided into two parts. The small intestine, which includes the duodenum, jejunum, and ileum, is the principal site of digestion and absorption of food. It secretes digestive enzymes and mucus and its inner surface is thrown into finger-like processes, which increase the absorptive area. The duodenum is a common site for a *peptic ulcer, since it receives the acid contents from the stomach. The large intestine consists of the colon, caecum, rectum, and anus. It is largely concerned with the absorption of water from digested food and the formation of *faeces, which are expelled from the anus. The intestines contain specialized muscle whose rhythmic contractions (called peristalsis) propel food towards the anus. *See* Plate IV.

intimism A branch of postimpressionist painting, specializing in domestic interiors having an atmosphere of intimacy. The chief practitioners were the *Nabis painters Pierre *Bonnard and Édouard *Vuillard.

Intolerable Acts (*or* Coercive Acts; 1774) British parliamentary Acts intended to enforce stricter control over the American colonies following the *Boston Tea Party. The Boston Port Bill (1774) closed the port until reparation for the lost tea had been made. The Massachusetts Government Act repealed the colony's charter and imposed a military government on Massachusetts; the Administration of Justice Act allowed British officials to return home for trial in a criminal case; and the Quebec Act gave the lucrative fur trade between Ohio and Mississippi to Quebec. The Acts contributed to the outbreak of the *American Revolution.

intoxication Any form of acute poisoning: in popular language it usually refers to alcoholic poisoning. This is characterized by excited, often abusive, behaviour, unsteady gait, confused memory, flushed skin, and poor coordination. In the past doctors were needed to diagnose drunkenness in those suspected of drunken driving, but the law in the UK now states that it is illegal to drive with an alcohol concentration in the blood greater than 80 mg/100 ml, which can be determined by means of a simple chemical test (*see* Breathalyzer). Most other countries have a similar law.

intra-uterine device (IUD). *See* contraception.

introversion (*or* intraversion) A quality of personality characterized by interest in oneself rather than in the outside world: it is the opposite of *extroversion. Introverts are reflective and introspective, with a tendency to have a small circle of friends. They are good at persisting for a long time at one task; their interests tend to be philosophical; and they are highly susceptible to permanent *conditioning.

intrusive rock. *See* igneous rock.

intuitionism Any doctrine in which what appears to be self-evident is regarded as the basis of knowledge ("I just *know* that such-and-such is the case"). From the model of mathematics, the Pythagoreans believed that intuition is superior to observation and in modern times the mathematical school of *Brouwer was called intuitionist regarding its views about the nature of mathematics. In contemporary philosophy, intuitionism has been most emphasized in *ethics; the so-called Oxford Intuitionists regarded the faculty of moral judgment (the individual's conscience) as nonrational and autonomous and opposed *utilitarianism and teleology in ethics.

Inuvik 68 16N 133 40W A settlement in N Canada, in the Northwest Territories on the Mackenzie River delta. Built (1954-62) as the regional administration headquarters, it has a largely Eskimo population. Population (1982): 3511.

Invar An *alloy of iron with 36% nickel, which expands by only 0.9 mm per km for each centigrade degree temperature rise. This is about one-tenth the expansion of platinum and titanium and less than one-twentieth of that of most other metals. It was discovered in 1896 and since then has been used for accurate measuring tapes and chronometer parts.

Inveraray 56 13N 5 05W A town in W Scotland, in Strathclyde Region on Loch Fyne. Inveraray Castle, seat of the dukes of Argyll, was built around 1780 on the site of an earlier castle. Population (1981 est): 949.

Invercargill 46 26S 168 21E A city in New Zealand, in S South Island on the Waihopai River. It is the centre of a sheep- and dairy-farming region. Population (1983 est): 54 000.

Inverness 57 27N 4 15W A city in N Scotland, the administrative centre of the Highland Region, at the head of the Moray Firth. Inverness is a tourist centre and has boatbuilding, distilling, iron-founding, and woollen industries. It has a 19th-century cathedral and castle, which occupies the site of an earlier castle destroyed in 1746. Population (1981): 39 736.

Inverness (*or* Inverness-shire) A former county of N Scotland. Under local government reorganization in 1975 its boundaries were adjusted to form Inverness District, in the Highland Region.

invertebrate Any animal without a backbone. All animals except vertebrates belong to this category, including the *protochordates—animals that possess a rodlike skeletal notochord. Although widely used, the term is seldom employed in taxonomic systems.

invert sugar A mixture of the sugars glucose and fructose resulting from the action of heat or the enzyme invertase on cane or beet sugar (sucrose). It is sweeter than sucrose and widely used in foods and confectionery.

investiture controversy A dispute between the papacy and the Holy Roman Empire during the late 11th and early 12th centuries concerning the right of secular rulers to appoint bishops and invest them with their office in return for pledges of loyalty. The conflict arose between Pope *Gregory VII and the Holy Roman Emperor *Henry IV and later also involved the Norman kings of England. Compromise was reached with England in 1106 and with the Emperor in 1122. This issue focused the struggle for supremacy between lay and ecclesiastical powers.

investment 1. The purchase of capital goods (plant and machinery) used in the production of consumer goods and services. Investment and consumption together comprise the national income. A high level of investment is a necessary part of a nation's economic wellbeing and helps to promote *economic growth. In most countries incentives, in the form of tax relief, are available on investment expenditure. What actually motivates investment is a matter of debate: some economists believe the rate of interest is the most important factor, while others assign more importance to the level of demand in the economy. Certainly investment varies a great deal over the *trade cycle. **2.** The use of money to obtain an income or a capital gain in the future. This can be achieved by depositing it with a bank or building society to provide income without capital growth; government stocks and bonds will provide certain limited gains and income; while shares, unit trusts, etc., provide an opportunity for larger capital gains (or losses) and some income, with an element of speculation. Investment also includes the purchase of any asset that can be expected to increase in value and can also be linked with insurance policies.

investment bank. *See* issuing house.

investment company (*or* investment trust) A company that buys and sells *securities to make profits for its shareholders. The company has a fixed capital and its shares are bought and sold on the *stock exchange. Investors (shareholders) thus become part owners of a professionally managed portfolio of securities. In the USA it is called a closed-end investment company. *Compare* unit trust.

in vitro fertilization. *See* test-tube baby.

Io (astronomy). *See* Galilean satellites.

Io (Greek legend) A priestess of Hera, loved by Zeus, who transformed her into a heifer to protect her from discovery. Hera ordered Argus, a herdsman with eyes covering his entire body, to guard her, but she escaped with the help of Hermes and was finally restored to Zeus in Egypt.

Ioánnina (*or* Yannina) 39 40N 20 51E A town in NW Greece, in Epirus on Lake Ioánnina. Conquered by the Turks in 1430, it became the seat (1788–1822) of Ali Pasha. It was captured by the Greeks in 1913. The university was founded in 1970. Population (1981): 44 829.

iodine (I) A purple-black lustrous solid *halogen that evaporates slowly at room temperature to give a purple gas. It was discovered in 1811 by B. Courtois (1777–1838). It is insoluble in water but dissolves readily in organic solvents, such as chloroform ($CHCl_3$) or carbon tetrachloride (CCl_4), to give pink-purple solutions. Iodine is present in sea water and concentrated by seaweeds; it also occurs in saltpetre deposits, such as those in Chile. Potassium iodide (KI) is widely used in photography. The radioactive isotope ^{131}I, with a half-life of 8.1 days, is produced in nuclear reactors; its accidental release into the atmosphere would cause serious problems. It is also used in the diagnosis and treatment of thyroid disorders as it is concentrated in the thyroid gland. Tincture of iodine is used as an antiseptic. At no 53; at wt 126.904; mp 113.5°C; bp 184.35°C.

io moth A large common American *saturniid moth, *Automeris io*. Males are yellow and the larger females reddish brown, with a wingspan of 70 mm. The greenish spiny larvae feed on trees and are poisonous to touch.

ion An atom or group of atoms that has lost or gained one or more electrons and consequently has an electric charge. Positively and negatively charged ions are called **cations** and **anions** respectively. The sign and magnitude of the charge is indicated by a superscript, as in the potassium ion, K^+, or the doubly charged sulphate ion, SO_4^{2-}. Many compounds (electrovalent compounds) are combinations of positive and negative ions; sodium chloride, for example is formed from sodium ions (Na^+) and chloride ions (Cl^-). *See also* chemical bond; ionization.

IONA *The 13th-century abbey. Two Celtic crosses can be seen in the foreground.*

Iona 56 19N 6 25W A small sparsely populated island in NW Scotland, in the Inner Hebrides. It has many religious associations; St Columba landed here in 563 AD, establishing a monastery that became the centre of the Celtic Church. It later became a burial ground for Scottish, Irish, and Norwegian kings. In the early 1900s work began on restoring the abbey; the Iona Community (founded 1938) continues this work. Area: 854 ha (2112 acres).

Ionesco, Eugène (1912–) French dramatist, born in Romania of French and Romanian parents; he settled permanently in France in 1938. He inaugurated the *Theatre of the Absurd with his first play, *The Bald Prima Donna* (1950), which exposed the poverty of language as a means of communication. His later plays, which include *The Lesson* (1951), *The Chairs* (1951), *Rhinoceros* (1960), *Exit the King* (1962), and *Man With Bags* (1977), use a variety of surrealistic techniques to express a nihilistic vision of society.

Ionia In antiquity, the central W coast of Asia Minor and the adjacent islands, settled by Greeks about 1000 BC. Between the 8th and 6th centuries BC *Miletus, *Samos, *Ephesus, and other Ionian cities led Greece in trade, colonization, and culture. The first Greek philosophers, including *Thales, *Pythagoras, and *Anaximander, were Ionian. After 550 BC Ionia passed under the domination of *Lydia and later Persia. The Ionian revolt against Persian rule (499–494 BC) resulted in defeat, economic ruin, subjugation by outsiders, and comparative eclipse.

Ionian Islands A group of Greek islands in the Ionian Sea, extending from Corfu in the N to Zacynthus in the S and including Páxos, Lévkas, Ithaca, and Cephalonia. They belonged to Britain from the Treaty of Paris (1815) until 1864, when they were ceded to Greece. Several were devastated by earthquakes in 1514, 1893, and 1953. Total area: 2307 sq km (891 sq mi). Population (1981): 182 651.

Ionian Sea The section of the central Mediterranean Sea, bounded by Italy, Sicily, and Greece, that contains the Ionian Islands.

Ionic order. *See* orders of architecture.

ionization The process of producing *ions from neutral

atoms or molecules. Solvation (surrounding of an ion by polar solvent molecules), heating (thermal ionization), or bombardment with particles or radiation provides the necessary energy for the process. The minimum energy required to ionize an atom A (i.e. $A \rightarrow A^+ + e^-$) is called its **ionization potential**, which is usually measured in electronvolts.

ionization chamber An instrument used for measuring the intensity of *ionizing radiation. It consists of a gas-filled chamber containing two electrodes with a large potential difference between them. When radiation enters the chamber it ionizes some of the gas atoms or molecules. The ions flow towards the electrodes creating a current, the magnitude of which is a measure of the intensity of the radiation. The *Geiger counter is an example of an ionization chamber.

ionizing radiation Any radiation that ionizes the atoms or molecules of the matter through which it passes. It may consist of particles (such as *electrons) or it may be electromagnetic radiation (*see* ultraviolet radiation; X-rays; gamma radiation). Ionizing radiation occurs naturally in *cosmic rays and is emitted by radioactive substances. It is also produced artificially in X-ray machines, particle accelerators, nuclear reactors, etc. Ionizing radiations are used in medical diagnosis and therapy and in sterilization of food. In biological tissue these radiations create reactive free radicals, especially by ionizing water molecules, which attack proteins, nucleic acids, etc., and can cause damage by changing their structure and function.

ionosphere A region of the upper ▫atmosphere that reflects short radio waves, enabling transmissions to be made round the curved surface of the earth by sky waves. The gases in the ionosphere are ionized by absorption of radiation from the sun. Its existence was suggested in 1902 by A. E. Kennelly and independently by O. Heaviside. Sir Edward Appleton (1892–1925) provided proof by bouncing radio waves off the different layers of the ionosphere, which vary in behaviour with the position of the sun and with the sunspot cycle. The ionization of the D region, at between 50 and 90 kilometres altitude, disappears during the day. The E region is between 90 and 160 kilometres high and the F region (sometimes called the Appleton layer) is from 160 kilometres up to about 400 kilometres. The lower part of the ionosphere (E region) is sometimes called the Kennelly-Heaviside layer. The gas particles in the F region do not lose their charge as quickly as those below because the gas is less dense and therefore ions and electrons are subject to fewer collisions. This enables radio transmissions to continue at night.

Iowa A state in the USA, in the Midwest bounded on the E by the Mississippi River and by the Missouri River in the W. The land rises slowly from the Mississippi Valley to form a gentle rolling landscape, with the higher land in the NW. Iowa is predominantly an agricultural state and has associated industries, particularly the manufacture of agricultural machinery and food processing. It is famed for its livestock, particularly pigs. Major crops are corn, oats, soya beans, and other fodder crops. There is also some mining for portland cement and gypsum. The scattered population and lack of urban areas limit the cultural institutions the state can support. *History*: explored by the Frenchmen Jolliet and *Marquette in 1673, it formed part of the Louisiana Purchase (1803) by the USA. It became a territory (1838) and then a state (1846). The end of the US Civil War and the arrival of the railway opened up the state to immigrants. Area: 145 790 sq km (56 290 sq mi). Population (1983 est): 2 905 000. Capital: Des Moines.

Ipatieff, Vladimir Nikolaievich (1867–1952) US physicist, born in Russia. While working in Germany he discovered the structure of *isoprene (1897); returning to Russia in 1899 he investigated the catalytic breakdown of *hydrocarbon molecules at high temperatures. In 1930 he emigrated to the USA, where he worked on the development of high-octane fuels for internal-combustion engines.

ipecacuanha A South American herbaceous plant, *Uragoga ipecacuanha*, cultivated in the tropics for its root, which yields medicinal alkaloids used as an expectorant and emetic. Large doses cause vomiting and diarrhoea. Family: *Rubiaceae*.

Iphigenia In Greek legend, the eldest daughter of *Agamemnon and *Clytemnestra. When the Greek fleet was delayed at Aulis at the beginning of the *Trojan War, Agamemnon was told that Artemis demanded the sacrifice of his daughter before the fleet could sail to Troy. He was about to comply when Artemis took pity on Iphigenia and transported her to Tauris, where she became a priestess of Artemis. The story is the subject of two plays by *Euripides.

I-pin. *See* Yibin.

Ipoh 4 36N 101 02E A city in NW Peninsular Malaysia, the capital of Perak state. The tinmining centre of Malaysia, it has noted Chinese rock temples. Population (1980): 300 727.

Ipswich 52 04N 1 10E A town in SE England, the administrative centre of Suffolk at the head of the Orwell estuary. It is a port with engineering, printing, brewing, flour-milling, plastics, fertilizers, tobacco, and textile industries. Cardinal Wolsey was born here. Population (1982 est): 120 908.

Ipswich 27 38S 152 40E A city in Australia, in SE Queensland. It is the state's second largest coal producer. Population (1984 est): 73 680.

Iqbal, Mohammed (?1875–1938) Indian Muslim poet and philosopher, born in Sialkot (Punjab). He came to England in 1905 (already a noted romantic poet and promoter of Indian nationalism) to read philosophy and law at Cambridge University. From 1908 Iqbal lived in Lahore where he became a leading member of the *Muslim League. He is generally credited with the formulation of the political theory of Pakistan as a separate Muslim state in the Indian subcontinent.

Iquique 20 15S 70 08W A port in N Chile, on the Pacific Ocean. Industries include fishmeal plants and canneries; the chief exports are nitrates, iodine, and fishmeal. Population (1983 est): 112 872.

Iquitos 3 51S 73 13W A port in NE Peru, on the River Amazon 3700 km (2300 mi) from its mouth. The furthest point upstream accessible to oceangoing vessels, it exports rubber, timber, and nuts. Its university was founded in 1962. Population (1981): 173 629.

IRA. *See* Irish Republican Army.

Iráklion (*or* Herakleion; Italian name: Candia) 32 20N 25 08E The chief port of the Greek island of Crete, on the N coast. It is picturesque, possessing many Venetian fortifications, and has become a tourist centre. Exports include raisins, grapes, and olive oil. Population (1981): 101 634.

Iran (name until 1935: Persia) A country in the Middle East lying between the Caspian Sea and the Persian Gulf. Its central plateau, containing deserts and marshes, is surrounded by mountains, the *Zagros Mountains in the W, the *Elburz Mountains and the Kopet Mountains in the N, and a barren region of peaks and sand in the E. It suffers great extremes of temperature and severe earthquakes. The most populous areas are the NW and the Caspian coast, which have the greatest rainfall. The population is mainly Persian with groups of Turks, Kurds, Armenians, Arabs, and such tribes as the Bakhtyari. *Economy*: agriculture supports 75% of the population, although lack of rain hampers productivity and much food has to be imported. The development of irrigation has been a high priority. Wheat, rice, tobacco, fruit, sugar beet, and tea are grown; sheep and goats are kept. Iran's chief source of revenue is its oil; it possesses 10% of the world's reserves and has profited greatly from the oil price increases of the 1970s. The main oilfields are in the

Zagros Mountains, where oil was first discovered (1908). Other minerals include coal, copper, iron ore, lead, natural gas, and precious stones. The textile industry uses local cotton and silk, and carpet manufacture is an important handicraft. Among Iran's other industries, its steel industry is the largest in the Middle East. Oil revenues have been used to diversify the economy; to this end many capital goods, such as machinery, are imported. *History*: the Caspian coast and the plateau are among the earliest centres of civilization. Early Persian dynasties include the *Achaemenians and the *Sasanians (*see also* Greek-Persian wars). Arab domination, which established Islam in the area, was followed by that of the Turks and Mongols before the Persian Safavid dynasty (1502–1736) came into power. Following a period of great prosperity (1587–1629) Persia again declined, encroached on by Uzbeks, Arabs, Afghans, Turks, and Russians. The next great dynasty, the Kajar dynasty (1794–1925), was marked largely by rivalry for domination between Britain and Russia. Western influence was felt increasingly during the latter half of the 19th century. Repressive rule provoked opposition that became open in about 1900 and was intensified by resentment against the concessions granted to Britain and Russia, made necessary by the Shah's financial difficulties. The Shah was forced to grant a constitution and National Assembly (the Majlis; 1906); his successor disbanded this and was then deposed and replaced (1909). Further disorders resulted in the army coup that established Reza Khan in power (1921), from 1925 as *Reza Shah Pahlavi. Under his virtual dictatorship order returned and the country was industrialized and extensively westernized; he was forced to abdicate in favour of his son *Mohammed Reza Pahlavi (1941). Iran's oil has been a major source of political unrest. In 1945 the Soviet Union supported an Azerbaidzhan and Kurdish revolt to gain oil concessions (later withdrawn). Oil was also a major issue for the militant National Front movement, which nationalized the oil industry (1951); the British responded with a blockade resulting in serious economic difficulties and the Shah was forced to flee the country temporarily. Martial law was ended after 16 years in 1957 but economic and political instability continued; the Shah's reform programme, which included in 1963 the enfranchisement of women, the redistribution of land, and compulsory education, was opposed by major religious and political groups. There were riots in the early 1960s and unrest was further provoked by harsh repression, with many dissidents executed or imprisoned; Savak, the secret police, were notorious for their use of torture and imprisonment. By 1978 different opposition groups, including Muslims, politicians, intellectuals, students, communists, and human-rights supporters had united under the exiled Muslim leader Ayatollah Ruholla *Khomeini. Demonstrations and riots in 1977–78 were reinforced by strikes, despite the imposition of martial law in the cities, concessions, and a change of administration; by February, 1979, an estimated 10 000 people had died in political violence, while anti-US and anti-British feeling had forced foreigners to leave the country. The Shah then left the country, later dying in exile (1980), and Ayatollah Khomeini took over the government in the so-called Islamic Revolution. Unrest continued, with Khomeini's strict Muslim administration opposed by progressive groups and Kurdish rebels. In 1979 students occupied the US embassy in Tehran and took 52 of the personnel hostage, only releasing them in January, 1981, after lengthy negotiations. Abolhassan Bani-Sadr, elected Iran's first president in 1980, was dismissed and forced to flee the country in 1981. In the continuing violence his successor, Muhammad Ali Radjai, was killed in a bomb explosion (1981). Hojatoleslam Ali Khamenei was later elected president in October, 1981. War with Iraq broke out in September, 1980 (*see* Gulf War). Official language: Persian (Farsi). Official currency: Iranian rial of 100 dinars.

Area: 1 648 000 sq km (636 160 sq mi). Population (1987): 49 700 000. Capital: Tehran.

Iranian languages A subgroup of the *Indo-Iranian language family. Iranian languages are spoken in Iran, Afghanistan, Turkey, and parts of the Caucasus. Like its counterpart the *Indo-Aryan group, the Iranian languages are closely related to *Sanskrit. Modern Iranian languages include Persian, Kurdish, *Pashto, and *Ossetic.

Iraq, Republic of A country in the Middle East, bordering on the Persian Gulf. The SE consists of an alluvial plain around the delta of the Rivers Tigris and Euphrates; this floods in spring. The W is a vast desert while the N is mountainous. The population is about 90% Muslim divided evenly between Shiite and Sunnite sects. The Kurds, who live in the mountainous NE, form about 15–20% of the population. *Economy*: mainly agricultural, the chief crops being wheat, barley, rice, maize, sorghum, sesame, dates, and cotton. Since 1958 cooperative and collective farms have been set up and mechanization and irrigation schemes have increased production. The main industry is oil (first discovered at Kirkuk in 1927) and Iraq is a member of OPEC. Natural gas is also produced, as are textiles, processed foods, cement, and electrical and leather goods. Cereals, meat, machinery, vehicles, chemicals, and consumer goods are imported, chiefly from Japan, Germany, the USA, France, and the Soviet Union. *History*: as *Mesopotamia, Iraq was the site of the world's first civilization; it is extremely rich in archaeological remains. It was conquered by Arabia and became Muslim in the 7th century AD and was part of the Ottoman Empire from 1534 until World War I, when UK troops expelled the Turks. As a British mandate (1920–32), Iraq became a kingdom (1921). From this period on it has been politically unstable, with ethnic and religious unrest and frequent coups; the monarchy was overthrown in 1958. During the 1960s and 1970s the Kurds have been in intermittent rebellion and there has been opposition to the socialist government (in power since 1968) from Muslims and communists. Although a member of the *Arab League and formerly of the *Baghdad Pact it has been in dispute with Iran and Syria during the 1960s and 1970s, although in 1978 an agreement on military union was signed with Syria. In 1980, following a build up of tensions, war broke out against Iran (*see* Gulf War). President: Sadam Hussein (1935–   ). Official language: Arabic. Official currency: Iraqi dinar of 1000 fils. Area: 438 446 sq km (169 248 sq mi). Capital: Baghdad. Population (1983): 14 509 000.

Irbil (Arbil *or* Erbil) 36 12N 44 01E A town in N Iraq close to the Turkish and Iranian borders. It was important in Assyrian times and is now a trading centre for a productive agricultural region. Population (1980 est): 368 000.

Ireland The second largest island in the British Isles, separated from Great Britain by the North Channel, the Irish Sea, and St George's Channel. It consists of a central lowland area of fertile plains, bogs, and moorland, rising to hills and mountains in the N and S. The River Shannon is the chief river, draining N–S, and Ireland contains many lakes, particularly in the N and W, including Lough Neagh. Since 1920 Ireland has been politically divided, the NE part forming Northern Ireland in the UK and the remainder comprising the Republic of Ireland. *History*: rich in archaeological remains, Ireland was invaded in the 4th century BC by the Celts. The country came to be divided into the five tribal kingdoms (the Five Fifths) of Ulster, Meath, Leinster, Munster, and Connaught, which nominally acknowledged the overlordship of the High Kings of Ireland (the rulers of Tara). In the 5th century the country was converted to Christianity—a process in which St Patrick was the outstanding figure—and in the following centuries the Irish Church fostered scholarship, art, and missionary work. The 9th and 10th centuries saw Viking invasions, which were brought to an end by Brian Boru's great victory at Clontarf (1014). In the mid-12th century Ireland was invaded by the

Norman conquerors of England and Henry II gained the allegiance of the Irish kings. English law and administration were introduced in the 13th century, a series of viceroys was appointed to represent the king's interests, and an Irish parliament (composed of the Anglo-Irish and subordinate to the English Crown) began to meet. However, English rule was restricted to the area around Dublin (called the Pale) until the 16th century, when the subjection of the Irish became the aim of the Tudor monarchs of England. Revolts, inspired in part by Roman Catholic opposition to the Reformation, were suppressed and the *Plantation of Ireland by English and later by Scottish settlers was begun, being most successful, in terms of permanence, in Ulster. Irish resistance continued, culminating in the rebellion of 1641, which, centred on the NE, was not suppressed until Oliver Cromwell's notorious expedition in 1649-50. The subsequent confiscation of the rebels' land and its redistribution among English colonists established the economic and political ascendancy of the Protestant minority in Ireland. It was strengthened by the Restoration settlement, which extended Protestant landholdings, and by events after William of Orange's defeat (1690) of the Irish supporters of the deposed Catholic king, James II: the usual land confiscations were accompanied on this occasion by new anti-Catholic penal laws. In the 18th century Ireland's subservience to England came to be opposed by many Irish Protestants and in 1782, under the leadership of Henry Grattan, the Irish parliament obtained legislative independence. However, the abortive Irish rebellion of 1798 (see United Irishmen, Society of) persuaded Pitt the Younger of the need for the complete union of Britain and Ireland (1800; see Union, Acts of). It also convinced him of the need for *Catholic emancipation, which was not fully obtained until 1829 (see also O'Connell, Daniel). The appalling social conditions suffered by the majority of Irish renewed Catholic militancy in the 19th century. Attempts by the Young Ireland group to repeal the Act of Union failed, and nationalist agitation was taken up after the Irish (potato) famine first, abortively, by the *Fenians and then by the *Home Rule movement. While the *Land League pursued agrarian reform with some success, Home Rule, in spite of Gladstone's conversion to the cause, was delayed. It was nominally obtained in 1914 but was opposed both by the Republicans, who wanted a greater degree of independence, and the Protestant Ulster Unionists, who feared for their future in a self-governing country with a Catholic majority. Following the proclamation of an Irish republic by Sinn Fein (1919) and virtual civil war Britain proposed partition (1920), with the establishment of separate parliaments in the predominantly Protestant NE and Catholic S and W. The formula was unacceptable to the Republicans and in 1921 the Irish Free State, with dominion status, came into being. The NE (Northern Ireland) immediately withdrew, accepting self-government within the UK.

Northern Ireland The province comprises 26 districts replacing the former counties of Antrim, Armagh, Down, Fermanagh, Londonderry, and Tyrone. *Economy*: there has been a significant change since the 1950s, the traditional industries of shipbuilding and linen manufacture as well as agriculture having declined in importance. Diversification of industry has taken place (chemicals, rubber products, man-made fibres, and engineering) and there has been a large rise in the number of people employed in the service sector. The economy has suffered, however, from the political upheavals of the last decade. *History*: the Government of Ireland Act (1920) established a parliament, which met at Stormont Castle in Belfast and had legislative responsibility for most matters other than foreign affairs. Executive power lay with a prime minister and cabinet. Some 17 MPs are now returned to the UK parliament. The Protestant majority in Northern Ireland predominantly supports the union with Great Britain, while many of the Roman Catholic minority, dissatisfied with Protestant po-

litical dominance, seek union with the Republic of Ireland. Violent conflict broke out between the two groups in 1969, since when the British army has maintained a peacekeeping force in Northern Ireland. Terrorist activities both in Ireland and Great Britain led to the imposition (1972) of direct rule of Northern Ireland by the UK parliament. In 1973 a Northern Ireland Executive, comprising Protestant and Catholic representatives and responsible to an Assembly, was established but, following a general strike in 1974, this arrangement was replaced with rule by a secretary of state for Northern Ireland and, until 1976, a Constitutional Convention. Bombings and shootings, both by the Irish Republican Army and Protestant paramilitary groups (e.g. the Ulster Volunteer Force), continue to occur. During 1981 violent reprisals followed the deaths of a number of hunger strikers at Belfast's Maze Prison. In 1985 the Anglo-Irish Agreement gave the Republic of Ireland a voice in the province's affairs, leading to further controversy. Area: 14 121 sq km (5452 sq mi). Population (1981 est): 1 481 959. Capital: Belfast.

Republic of Ireland (Irish name: Éire) The country is administratively divided into 26 counties. *Economy*: predominantly agricultural, cattle rearing being of major importance, especially in the E lowlands, where cattle are fattened for beef production. Dairy farming is also extensively practised, particularly in the S. Arable crops produced include barley, wheat, oats, potatoes, and sugar beet. Tourism is the second major source of revenue. Industries have expanded considerably since the 1950s, largely under foreign companies, and are oriented to the export market. They include food processing, brewing, distilling, textiles, and clothing. Peat is extensively cut as a fuel for power stations and as a household fuel. In 1977 Europe's largest lead-zinc mines were opened at Navan. Although the Republic has an extensive coastline its fishing industry is relatively small. *History*: Republican opposition to partition continued immediately after the establishment of the Irish Free State but was quelled by 1923. In 1932 De Valera, leader of Fianna Fáil, became prime minister and, in 1937, introduced a new constitution by which the Irish Free State was renamed Éire. In 1949 a coalition led by Fine Gael took the country, as the Republic of Ireland, out of the British Commonwealth. Since 1969 Irish politics have been dominated by the violent conflict in Northern Ireland and successive Irish governments have declared their desire to see the establishment there of a form of government acceptable to both Roman Catholics and Protestants. In 1973 Ireland became a member of the EEC. Charles J. *Haughey who, as Jack Lynch's successor, led a Fianna Fáil government (1979–81; 1982), was ousted in November, 1982, and Dr Garret *Fitzgerald became prime minister, heading a Fine Gael–Labour coalition. This collapsed over the issue of spending cuts and Haughey was elected prime minister for the third time in 1987. President: Patrick Hillery (1923–). Official languages: Irish and English. Official religion: Roman Catholic. Official currency: Irish pound of 100 pence. Area: 68 893 sq km (26 599 sq mi). Population (1981 est): 3 443 405. Capital and main port: Dublin.

Ireland, John Nicholson (1879-1962) British composer, a pupil of Stanford and teacher of Britten and E. J. Moeran (1894-1950). His works include orchestral and chamber music, songs, and piano pieces. Many of these, including *The Forgotten Rite* (for orchestra; 1913) and *Sarnia* (for piano; 1941), were inspired by the history of the Channel Islands.

Irene (c. 752-803 AD) Byzantine empress and saint of the Greek Orthodox Church. After the death of her husband Leo IV (reigned 775-80), Irene ruled jointly with her son Constantine VI (771-?797) until 790, when she was banished from court. In 797 she returned, blinded and imprisoned Constantine, and ruled alone. She fought against the iconoclasts (see iconoclasm) for the restoration of icons in Christian worship. In 802 she was overthrown and exiled to Lesbos.

Ireton, Henry (1611-51) English soldier, who fought for the parliamentarians in the *Civil War. Ireton fought at the battles of Edgehill (1642), *Marston Moor, and *Naseby (1645). In 1646 he became Cromwell's son-in-law. Initially favouring negotiations with Charles I, he proposed a constitutional solution to the conflict of power (Heads of the Proposals, 1647) but in 1649 he was a signatory to the king's death warrant. During the Commonwealth, Ireton served in Ireland, where he died of fever at the siege of Limerick.

Irian Jaya. *See* West Irian.

iridium (Ir) A hard brittle metal, discovered in 1803 by C. Tennant (1768-1838), in the residue left after dissolving platinum in aqua regia. Its salts are highly coloured, whence its name (Latin *iris*, rainbow). Its principal use is as a hardening agent for platinum and in electrical contacts. At no 77; at wt 192.22; mp 2410°C; bp 4130°C.

iris (anatomy) The muscular tissue in the □eye that surrounds the pupil and is situated immediately in front of the lens: it is responsible for eye colour. Reflex contraction of the muscles in the iris cause it to become smaller in dim light (which enlarges the pupil and allows more light to enter the eye) and larger in bright light (thus decreasing the size of the pupil).

Iris (botany) A genus of perennial herbaceous plants (about 300 species), native to N temperate regions and widely planted in gardens. Irises grow from bulbs or rhizomes (underground stems) and their flowers, which have three erect inner petals and three drooping outer sepals, can be three or more colours, often with a contrasting "beard" on the lower petals. Many garden varieties are derived from *I. germanica*: up to 1 m high, they have purple, white, or yellow flowers and grow from rhizomes. Family: *Iridaceae*. *See also* flag.

Iris (mythology) The Greek goddess of the rainbow and messenger of the gods, especially of *Hera. She is portrayed as carrying a herald's staff and often bearing water that could put perjurers to sleep.

Irish elk A large extinct European *deer belonging to the genus *Megaloceros*, which was abundant during the Pleistocene epoch (2.5 million-10 000 years ago). It stood 1.8 m at the shoulder and its massive palmate antlers spanned up to 4 m. Several species are known and remains of the largest have been found in Irish bog deposits.

Irish famine (1846-51) The starvation and death of almost a million Irish following a blight that ruined the potato crop (the staple diet of most Irish) in 1846. Another million emigrated.

Irish Hospitals' Sweepstakes The world's largest international lottery, sponsored since 1930 by the government of the Republic of Ireland. It is held on three races a year and derives most of its income from the USA, where it is illegal and tickets are smuggled into the country. A quarter of the takings are distributed as prizes, which may exceed £40,000. The remainder is given to the Hospitals' Trust Board.

Irish Literary Renaissance A period of literary activity in Ireland in the late 19th and early 20th centuries inspired by the contemporary resurgence of political nationalism and of interest in traditional Gaelic culture. The strongest individual influence was that of W. B. *Yeats, especially through his *The Wanderings of Oisin* (1889) and *The Celtic Twilight* (1893). Other writers included the poet George Russell (pseudonym AE; 1867-1935), the novelist George Moore (1852-1933), and the dramatist J. M. *Synge.

Irish literature The Gaelic literature of Ireland. The earliest literature, as in other parts of the Celtic world, was the responsibility of an official learned class, the *filid* (or *Druids), who transmitted orally the ancient traditions of the people. The earliest written literature, however, dates from the 7th to 10th centuries. Of most interest in this period are the heroic sagas, written in prose and preserved mainly in three 12th-century manuscript collections, the Book of the Dun Cow, the Book of Leinster, and the Yellow Book of Lecan. These epics, which are shorter than Icelandic sagas, deal with both heroic (warfare, voyages, etc.) and romantic elements. They were grouped in the middle ages into two cycles, the early pagan Ulster cycle and the much later *Fenian cycle. *Deirdre and *Cuchulain are the prominent figures in the Ulster cycle and appear in the two most famous stories, the *Longes Mac Nusnig* (*Exile of the Sons of Usnech*) and the *Táin Bó Cúalnge* (*Cattle-Raid of Cooley*). From the 13th century bardic poets preserved Gaelic culture from the impact of Norman English; their main productions were panegyrics written for aristocratic patrons, but they also responded to influences introduced by the Normans and English, such as, for example, the theme of courtly love. Despite a revival of Gaelic poetry in the 16th century, it declined with the submergence of the Irish aristocracy, particularly after the coming of Cromwell (1649). The work of the poet and historian Geoffrey Keating (c. 1580-c. 1645) is the most important prior to this date; the two outstanding poets of the period were David O'Bruadair (1625-98) and Egan O'Rahilly (1670-1728). Gaelic literature was at its lowest ebb during the 18th century, but was revived in the 19th century, having splintered in the meantime into several dialects. Such 20th-century writers as Liam *O'Flaherty and Brendan *Behan have produced distinguished work in Gaelic, but generally there has been nothing to equal the work of the major modern Irish poets and writers in English. *See also* Irish Literary Renaissance.

Irish moss. *See* carragen.

Irish Republican Army (IRA) A militant organization established in 1919. It fought a successful war against British forces (1919-21) but the subsequent partition treaty was rejected by many IRA members. The antitreaty faction (keeping the name IRA) was defeated by 1923 and declared illegal but continued to press for an all-Ireland republic. A bombing campaign against England in 1939 and an "offensive" against Northern Ireland (1956-62) both failed. The movement was then quiescent until the present troubles began in 1968. In 1969 both the IRA and *Sinn Féin, to which many IRA members belong, split into the Officials, desiring a socialist 32-county republic, and the Provisionals, concerned only with expelling the British from the North. Recent campaigns by the IRA have included the murder of Lord Mountbatten (1979), bombings in London, and the attempted assassination of the British prime minister in Brighton (1984). The Irish National Liberation Army is a breakaway terrorist group.

Irish Republican Brotherhood. *See* Fenians.

Irish Sea A section of the Atlantic Ocean, separating England, Scotland, and Wales from Ireland. Area: about 100 000 sq km (40 000 sq mi). Maximum width: 240 km (149 mi).

Irish terrier A breed of dog originating in Ireland and used for hunting. It has a sturdy streamlined body, a long head, and an alert appearance. The hard wiry coat is red to yellowish-red. Height: 41-46 cm.

Irish wolfhound An ancient breed of large hunting dog originating in Ireland. It has a powerful body and a long narrow head with small ears. The rough wiry coat is long on the brow and under the jaw and can be grey, brindle, red, black, white, or fawn. Height: 78 cm minimum (dogs); 71 cm minimum (bitches).

Irkutsk 52 18N 104 15E A city in the S Soviet Union, in the RSFSR. It is a major railway junction and is the industrial, cultural, and educational centre of E Siberia. Its industries include ship, aircraft, and vehicle production and repair; machinery, chemicals, textiles, and food are also produced. Population (1981 est): 568 000.

iron (Fe) A metallic transition element that has been known and used since prehistoric times. It is the fourth most

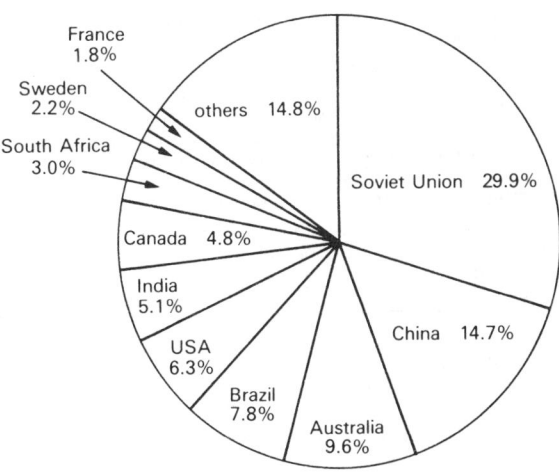

IRON *World production of iron ore (1984).*

France 1.8%
Sweden 2.2%
South Africa 3.0%
others 14.8%
Soviet Union 29.9%
Canada 4.8%
India 5.1%
USA 6.3%
China 14.7%
Brazil 7.8%
Australia 9.6%

abundant element in the earth's crust, occurring in the ores haematite (Fe_2O_3), magnetite (Fe_3O_4), and siderite ($FeCO_3$). It is widely used in toolmaking, construction, shipbuilding, car manufacture, and a host of other applications, almost always alloyed with other elements, such as carbon, manganese, chromium, titanium, and vanadium (*see* steel). It is obtained from its ores by smelting in a *blast furnace to give pig iron, which is then converted into cast iron, wrought iron, or steel. Iron has two important valence states forming iron II (ferrous) and iron III (ferric) compounds. Common compounds include the sulphates ($FeSO_4$, $Fe_2(SO_4)_3$), chlorides ($FeCl_2$, $FeCl_3$), and oxides (FeO, Fe_3O_4, Fe_2O_3). Iron is vital to animal life owing to its presence in *haemoglobin. Studies of meteorites and of the magnetic and seismic properties of the earth suggest that the earth has an iron-nickel core, molten on the outside but solid in the interior. At no 26; at wt 55.847; mp 1535°C; bp 2750°C. *See also* ferromagnetism.

Iron Age The cultural phase during which iron replaced bronze metal technology (*see* Bronze Age). Despite spasmodic earlier use of meteoric iron, it was not until about 1500 BC that iron-working techniques were perfected by the *Hittites. Initially a prestige metal, the superior hardness of which was prized for weapons, iron gradually spread throughout the Middle East after about 1100 BC. It was used in *Hallstatt Europe in the 7th century BC. The Chinese were both forging and casting iron about 500 BC, preceding Europe by about 1700 years in casting. Australia and pre-Columbian America never developed iron metallurgy but African societies moved directly from stone to iron technologies.

ironclad A wooden warship protected by iron armour, the forerunner of the modern battleship. Both the French and the British used ironclad barges against the Russians in the Crimean War (1854-56) but the first ironclad warship, the *Gloire*, was built by France in 1859. The first battle between ironclads occurred in 1862 in the US Civil War.

Iron Cross The highest German decoration for bravery in battle, instituted by Frederick William III of Prussia in 1813. An iron Maltese cross edged in silver, it was reinstituted by Hitler in 1939.

Iron Curtain The ideological differences that divided the democratic and communist countries after World War II. The term was first used by Winston Churchill in 1946.

Iron Gate (Romanian name: Porţile de Fier; Serbo-Croat name: Gvozdena Vrata) 44 40N 22 30E The deepest gorge in Europe, on the Romanian-Yugoslav border, through

which the River Danube flows. A canal, which is used by larger shipping, bypasses the gorge on the Romanian side. A Romanian-Yugoslav hydroelectric plant was opened here (1972). Length: about 3 km (2 mi).

iron lung. *See* respirator.

Ironside, William Edmund, 1st Baron (1880-1959) British field marshal. Disguised as a railwayman he was a secret agent in the second Boer War. In World War I he commanded the Allied forces against Soviet Russia at Archangel (1918). In World War II he was chief of the imperial general staff (1939-40) and commander in chief of the home forces (1940).

ironwood One of several unrelated trees with very hard wood, including *Mesurea ferrea* of India and Malaysia (family *Guttiferae*), used in cabinetwork, and a *hop-hornbeam, *Ostrya virginiana*, of E North America.

Iroquois North American Indian tribes of the NE region, between the Hudson River and Lake Erie, who spoke the Iroquois language belonging to the Iroquois Caddoan family. They were cultivators and hunters who lived in villages of longhouses that housed many families, organized into matrilineal clans. These were grouped into tribes and nations ruled by councils of delegates chosen by the senior clanswomen. The *Mohawk, Oneida, Onondaga, Cayuga, and Seneca tribes formed the famous **Iroquois League** during the 16th century, which was allied with the British in wars against the French and, except for the Oneida and Tuscarora, against the colonists in the American Revolution (1775-83). The League collapsed following the second Treaty of *Fort Stanwix (1784).

irrational numbers. See numbers.

Irrawaddy River The chief river in Burma, flowing SSW across the entire country. Joined by the River Chindwin at Mandalay, it enters the Andaman Sea through a swampy delta (one of the great rice bowls of Asia). Length: 2010 km (1250 mi).

Irredentists Italians who sought to bring all Italian-speaking areas into newly unified Italy in the late 19th century, in particular the Austrian-controlled Trentino in the NE. The Irredentists, so called from *Italia irredenta* ("unrecovered Italy"), urged Italy to join the UK and France in World War I. The postwar distribution of territories, giving Italy the Trentino and the Istrian peninsula on the N Adriatic, realized their chief ambitions.

irrigation The artificial watering of land for crop production. Irrigation was practised in ancient Egypt; traditional systems linked to seasonal changes in river level, using earth banks and channels with water-lifting devices, are still used in many areas. Modern methods involve artificial reservoirs, canals, and pumping systems; the entire field may be flooded, as in rice growing, or the water may run in channels between the rows of the crop. High-pressure sprinklers are also used, especially where the land is undulating. Irrigation may be essential for crop production in arid regions but is also used to supplement rainfall in other regions.

Irtysh, River (*or* R. Irtish) A river in central Asia. Rising in the Altai Mountains of China, it flows W and NW to join the River Ob in the Soviet Union. Length: 4444 km (2760 mi).

Irvine 55 37N 4 40W A port in W Scotland, in Strathclyde Region at the mouth of the River Irvine on the Firth of Clyde. It was scheduled for development as a new town in 1966. Population (1984 est): 57 000.

Irving, Sir Henry (John Henry Brodribb; 1838-1905) British actor and manager. He established his reputation in London during the early 1870s and remained the leading actor of the London stage for the next 30 years. From 1878 to 1902 he was manager of the Lyceum Theatre, where, with Ellen *Terry as his leading lady, he acted in a notable series of Shakespearian productions. He made several tours in the

SIR HENRY IRVING *As Shylock in* The Merchant of Venice, *one of his most famous roles.*

USA, and in 1895 became the first actor to receive a knighthood.

Irving, Washington (1783-1859) US short-story writer and historian. From 1815 to 1832 he lived mostly in Europe, where he wrote *The Sketch Book* (1819-20), which contains his best tales, including "Rip Van Winkle" and "The Legend of Sleepy Hollow." After returning to the USA he reinforced his reputation as the first American professional man of letters with several biographies, notably one of *George Washington* (5 vols, 1855-59).

Isaacs, Jorge (1837-95) Colombian novelist of British Jewish origin, who worked as a journalist and later became a diplomat. He is chiefly remembered for *María* (1867), a romantic novel set in the Colombian countryside.

Isabella (*born* Elizabeth Farnese; 1692-1766) The second wife of Philip V of Spain, whom she dominated throughout their marriage (1714-46). Her ambitions centered on the acquisition of Italian possessions for her sons, the eldest of whom ruled Naples and Sicily before becoming *Charles III of Spain.

Isabella (I) the Catholic (1451-1504) Queen of Castile (1474-1504). Her marriage (1469) to Ferdinand of Aragon brought about the union of the two major Spanish kingdoms, to which Granada was added following its reconquest from the Moors in 1492. The introduction of the Inquisition (1480) and the expulsion of the Jews (1492) were largely due to Isabella's influence. She also supported Columbus' voyages of discovery. *See also* Ferdinand V and II.

Isabella II (1830-1904) Queen of Spain (1833-68). Isabella's reign saw almost continual political turmoil. Her succession was contested by her uncle Don Carlos and only secured in 1839, after the first Carlist War (*see* Carlism).

Her governments became increasingly unpopular and she was deposed.

Isabella of France (1292-1358) The wife (1308-27) of Edward II of England; the daughter of *Philip (IV) the Fair. Increasingly isolated by Edward's favourites, she left England in 1325. She became the mistress of Roger *Mortimer and together they returned to overthrow and murder Edward (1327). In 1330 her son Edward III executed Mortimer and confined Isabella to a nunnery.

Isabey, Jean Baptiste (1767-1855) French portrait painter and miniaturist, born in Nancy. He trained under *David and was patronized successively by Marie Antoinette, Napoleon, and the restored Bourbon kings. His son **Eugène Isabey** (1804-86) was also a painter.

Isaiah (8th century BC) Old Testament prophet. He was influential at the court of the rulers of Judah until the Assyrian invasion (701 BC) and, according to tradition, was later martyred.

The Book of Isaiah contains his prophecies, although some scholars attribute chapters 40-66 to others. The prophecies condemn the corruption of both Judah and the surrounding nations, counsel against entering foreign political alliances, and predict the captivity of the nation in Babylon and its return. Several sections announce the coming of a Messiah. These passages formed the basis of the messianic expectations of the Jews and were interpreted by the Christian writers of the New Testament as referring to Jesus.

ISBN (International Standard Book Number). *See* library.

Ischia, Island of 40 44N 13 57E A volcanic island in Italy, at the entrance to the Bay of Naples. A popular resort, it is noted for its picturesque scenery and mineral springs. Area: 47 sq km (18 sq mi). Population (1981 est): 15 914. Chief town: Ischia.

Ise 34 29N 136 41E A city in Japan, in S Honshu on the Pacific Ocean. It is the site of Japan's most sacred Shinto shrines, some of which possibly date back to the 1st century BC. Population (1982 est): 106 453.

Isfahan (*or* Esfahan) 32 41N 51 41E A town in central Iran. It has some fine examples of Persian architecture, including the 17th-century royal mosque. An industrial quarter was established in the 1930s, and a university was founded in 1950. The city was prominent in the unrest that preceded the Shah's departure from Iran in February, 1979. Population (1985 est): 1 121 200.

Isherwood, Christopher (1904-86) British novelist. His experiences while teaching in Berlin in the 1930s are described in the novel *Mr Norris Changes Trains* (1935) and in the stories, *Goodbye to Berlin* (1939), featuring the memorable Sally Bowles, portrayed in the film *Cabaret* (1968). He collaborated with his friend W. H. *Auden on several plays. In 1939 he moved to California, where he cultivated an interest in Vedanta. His other works include the novels *The World in the Evening* (1954), *Down There on a Visit* (1962), and *A Single Man* (1964). In these and several autobiographical works, including *Christopher and His Kind* (1977), homosexuality is a recurrent theme.

Ishtar The supreme Babylonian and Assyrian goddess, the daughter of the sky god Anu or of the moon god Sin. She combined aspects of a beneficent mother goddess and fierce goddess of war and fertility. She descended to the underworld in search of her lover *Tammuz.

Isidore of Seville, St (c. 560-636 AD) Spanish churchman; Doctor of the Church and the last of the western Fathers of the Church. Archbishop of Seville from about 600, he is famous for his encyclopedia of knowledge, the *Etymologiae*, which was much used by medieval scholars. In dealing with such subjects as grammar, mathematics, history, and theology Isidore included etymological explanations of words (hence the title), but these were allegorical rather than scientific. Feast day: 4 April.

isinglass A form of gelatin, about 90% pure, made from the swim bladders of fish. It is used in glues and to clarify jellies and alcoholic drinks.

Isis An Egyptian goddess, the sister and wife of *Osiris, whose dismembered body she magically restored to life, and mother of *Horus. She was usually portrayed as holding the child Horus and wearing on her head the solar disc and a cow's horns, the same attributes as *Hathor. She was essentially a goddess of protection, being the perfect mother and having magical powers of healing. Her cult eventually spread throughout the Roman Empire.

Iskenderun (former name: Alexandretta) 36 37N 36 08E A port in central S Turkey. Its main activities are fishing and trading in tobacco, silk, bananas, and cereals. Until 1939 it was in Syria. Population (1980): 124 824.

Islam (Arabic: submission to God) A major world religion, which originated in Arabia in the 7th century AD. The essential creed of Islam, whose adherents are called Muslims, is that there is one God, Allah, and that *Mohammed is his prophet. The revelations received by Mohammed are recorded in the *Koran, which is the basis of Islamic belief and practice and the source of a complex legal and social system (see also Islamic law). Islam shares a number of beliefs with Judaism and Christianity and accepts the Books of Moses and the Gospels of Jesus as parts of the same divine scripture that is definitively expressed in the Koran. There is no formally organized church or priesthood. Instead, five fundamental duties are incumbent upon the individual Muslim: expression of belief in the one God, Allah, and in the prophethood of Mohammed; observance at set times of five daily prayers, which are recited facing towards Mecca; fasting during the month of *Ramadan; payment of a special tax for charitable purposes; and performance of the pilgrimage to Mecca (see hajj) at least once, if means permit. Given the impetus of the *jihad* or holy war against unbelievers originally prescribed as a duty, the Muslim armies of Arabia extended Islam through the Middle East and N Africa in the 7th and 8th centuries AD. It later spread to sub-Saharan Africa, India, China, SE Asia, parts of Russia, the Balkans, and Spain. It early divided into sects, which originally differed as to who should be the leader of Islam and what should be his powers. The main sects are the *Sunnites (or Sunni) and the *Shiites (or Shiah; see also Ahmadiya; Wahhabiya). There are an estimated 450 million Muslims.

Islamabad 33 40N 73 08E The capital of Pakistan, situated in the N of the country on the Potwar Plateau. The site was chosen in 1959 and construction began in 1961. The government's first cabinet meeting was held in 1967. The Quaid-i-Azam University was founded in 1965 and the People's Open University in 1974. Population (1981): 201 000.

Islamic art and architecture A distinctive style of art and architecture created and developed by the Muslims in the countries they conquered. Islamic art is generally classified by scholars into five regional groupings: Syrian-Egyptian; Persian; Ottoman-Turkish; Moorish (i.e. North African and Spanish); and Indian. Its most distinctive feature is its elaborate patterning in architecture, painting, ceramics, metalwork, woodwork, glassware, textiles, and carpets. Of all these arts architecture is the most individual, its main characteristics being the dome and the horseshoe □arch. Religious objections to the depiction of human and animal forms inhibited the development of sculpture. Islamic painting is usually associated with Persian, Mogul, and Turkish miniatures, although there were many schools of painting during the middle ages and later. Calligraphy, particularly in decoration, is regarded as an art form in a class of its own. See also Mogul art; Persian art.

Islamic law The sacred law of Islam, *shari'ah*, prescibes not only religious duties (see Islam) but covers every aspect of the life of a Muslim. Its basic principles were elaborated in the 9th century AD, when the *Koran and the practice of

Mohammed (the *sunna*) came to be generally accepted as the main sources of the law. The law covers marriage, divorce, and inheritance; it forbids usury, the depiction of living beings, the drinking of alcohol, the eating of pork, etc., and prescribes penalties and punishments for crimes. When a problem could not be solved by reference to the Koran or *sunna*, other sources were allowed and different legal interpretations developed. Thus among the *Sunnite majority, four equally orthodox schools have arisen, which agree on fundamentals but differ in their interpretation of specific points. In modern times most Muslim states have adopted secular legal systems at least in part and especially with regard to criminal, financial, and property law.

island A piece of land surrounded by water (excluding the continents). The world's largest island is Greenland (2.2 million sq km, 840 000 sq mi). Continental islands, such as Britain, lie on the continental shelves, separated usually by a narrow shallow stretch of water from the mainland. Oceanic orogenic islands, such as the Japanese islands, frequently occur in island arcs at the junction of two lithospheric plates (see plate tectonics); they are volcanic in origin. Oceanic volcanic islands, such as the Hawaiian islands, occur in the central parts of the deep oceans, particularly the Pacific. They are believed to be formed over "hot spots" in the earth's crust, where molten magma rises to the surface. Many coral islands have a volcanic base. See also reef.

Islay An island in the Atlantic Ocean, off the W coast of Scotland. One of the more prosperous islands of the Inner Hebrides, its economy is based on whisky distilling, tourism, agriculture, and fishing. Area: 606 sq km (234 sq mi). Population (1981): 3792.

Islington A borough of N Greater London, created in 1965 from the former metropolitan boroughs of Islington and Finsbury. Many of the 19th-century squares and terraces in Highbury, Canonbury, and Barnsbury are being improved by gentrification. Population (1981): 159 754.

Ismaili A *Shiite Muslim sect. In the 8th century AD a group of Shiites recognized Ismail the son of Jafar al-Sadiq as *imam, while the rest of the Shiites supported his brother Musa. In 909 the Fatimid caliphate was established, the rulers of which were Ismaili imams. The Ismaili Fatimids ruled in Egypt and N Africa until 1171, contesting control of the Muslim world with the *Abbasid dynasty of Baghdad. They developed several doctrines that diverge considerably from non-Ismaili Islam and eventually split into many subsects. Today the best-known Ismaili sect is that headed by the *Aga Khan.

Ismailia (Arabic name: al Isma'iliyah) 31 36N 32 15E A city in NE Egypt, midway along the Suez Canal on Lake Timsah. Dependent on the canal trade, much of the population moved elsewhere during the canal's closure (1967–75). It is the centre of an irrigated area producing market-garden crops. Population (1983 est): 145 478.

Isma'il Pasha (1830–95) Viceroy of Egypt for the Ottoman Empire (1863–79). He introduced important reforms but the huge foreign debts that his policies incurred eventually led to his deposition (1879) by the Ottomans, and ultimately to the British occupation of Egypt (1882). Under Isma'il the *Suez Canal was opened in 1869.

ISO. See International Organization for Standardization.

Isocrates (436–338 BC) Athenian teacher of rhetoric and political pamphleteer. After developing his highly polished style as a professional speechwriter, Isocrates opened a school, where his method of teaching rhetoric as a preparation for life began the literary tradition of education. His appeals to successive military leaders to unite the feuding Greek states against Persia culminated in the *Philippus* (346 BC), addressed to *Philip of Macedon.

isolationism The policy that opposes participation in world affairs, except in self-defence. The term is most usually used to describe policies pursued after World War I in the USA, where isolationism reached its peak in the Neutrality Acts (1935-37). The Japanese attack on Pearl Harbor in World War II ended isolationism.

ethanol   dimethyl ether

structural isomers *Ethanol and dimethyl ether have the same atoms in the molecule but different functional groups.*

maleic acid   cis   trans   fumaric acid

cis-trans isomers *A form of stereoisomerism occurring as a result of a double bond.*

optical isomers *Another form of stereoisomerism in which two forms of tartaric acid have different optical properties.*

ISOMERS

isomers Chemical compounds that have the same molecular formulae but different arrangements of atoms in their molecules. In **structural isomerism** the molecules have different molecular formulae. Thus, ethanol (C_2H_5OH) and dimethyl ether (CH_3OCH_3) both have the formula C_2H_6O, although they are quite different compounds. A form of structural isomerism is that in which functional groups occur at different positions in the molecule. For example, there are two alcohols derived from propane: propan-1-ol ($CH_3CH_2CH_2OH$) and propan-2-ol ($CH_3CH(OH)CH_3$), which differ in the position of the OH group on the chain. In **stereoisomerism** the molecules have the same structure and groups but the isomers differ in their spatial arrangements. **Cis-trans isomerism** occurs as a result of the positioning of groups in a planar molecule. A common type occurs in organic molecules with double bonds. Since rotation cannot occur about the bond it is possible to have two isomers: one with groups on both sides of the bond (the cis isomer) and the other with groups on opposite sides of the bond (trans isomer). Similar types of isomer are found in square inorganic complexes depending on opposite (trans) or adjacent (cis) positioning of ligands. Another form of stereoisomerism is **optical isomerism**, in which the two isomeric forms of the molecule are asymmetric and differ in that one molecule is a mirror image of the other. Asymmetric molecules of this type exhibit optical activity, i.e. they rotate *polarized light passed through their solutions. One isomer rotates the light in one sense, the other rotates the light the same amount in the opposite sense. Many naturally occurring organic compounds are optically active. Isomers of all types have different physical properties and, to a greater or lesser ' extent, different chemical properties. In some cases isomers can exist in equilibrium, a phenomenon known as **tautomerism**.

isomorphism The existence of different chemical compounds with the same crystal structure. Usually it is a reflection of analogous chemical bonding patterns. The *alums, for instance, are all isomorphic compounds.

Isopoda A widely distributed order of *crustaceans (4000 species). The group includes the most successful terrestrial crustacean—the *woodlouse—as well as aquatic forms, such as the *gribble; some marine species are parasites. Isopods have oval flattened bodies, covered by armour-like plates, and—usually—seven pairs of walking legs. The young develop within a brood pouch on the female.

isoprene ($CH_2:C(CH_3)CH:CH_2$) A colourless volatile liquid. It is made from chemicals extracted from oil, coal, or tar and is used to make synthetic rubber. Natural rubber consists mainly of a polymer of isoprene. *See also* polymerization.

isostasy The principle that segments of the earth's outer crust of equal area have the same mass; the higher the feature rises, the deeper the sial of which it is composed extends into the denser sima below. If a change in this equilibrium condition occurs, movements of the crust occur to restore the equilibrium (this is called isostatic compensation). For example, areas of deposition sink, while areas of erosion rise.

isotherm A line on a map joining points of equal temperature. Corrections are usually made to compensate for the effect of altitude on temperature.

isothermal process Any process that occurs without a change in the temperature of a system (*compare* adiabatic process).

isotopes Atoms of the same element that contain equal numbers of *protons but different numbers of *neutrons in their nuclei. They have identical chemical properties but different physical properties. An isotope is indicated by combining its nucleon number and its name or symbol in various ways, for example uranium-235, U-235, ^{235}U. All naturally occurring elements are mixtures of isotopes; hydrogen, for example, consists mainly of ^1H(98.44%) with small amounts of ^2H (deuterium). A third isotope, ^3H (tritium), also exists in nature in minute quantities (1 part in 10^{17}) but can be made artificially. Radioactive isotopes (radioisotopes) are important in nuclear reactors and nuclear weapons. For these purposes sophisticated methods of separation have had to be devised, based on differences in their physical properties. Methods used depend on different rates of gaseous and thermal diffusion, centrifuging, electrolysis, and electric or magnetic effects.

isotopic spin (*or* isospin) A *quantum number used to distinguish between elementary particles (*see* particle physics) having the same properties, except that of electric charge. The concept is not based directly on the idea of rotation but it is analogous in mathematical terms to angular momentum, different charge states of the same particle (e.g. the nucleon) being regarded as having different orientations in a fictitious "isotopic space."

isotropy Any property of a body or medium that is independent of the direction in which it is measured. A body or medium that is not isotropic is said to be anisotropic.

Israel, State of A country in the Middle East, bordering on the Mediterranean Sea. There are mountains in the N, a narrow coastal plain in the W, and the Negev Desert in the S. The River Jordan flowing through the *Great Rift Valley forms part of the E border. The population varies greatly in language and culture, as it consists largely of Jews who have immigrated since 1948. Many Palestinian Arabs left the area when Israel was created but some have since returned. The remaining Arab population lives mainly in the N, with some nomadic Bedouins in the Negev Desert. In 1948 the population consisted of 650 000 Jews and 155 000 Arabs; the population since then has more than quadrupled, with Jews now forming 85% and Arabs 11%; immigration is now decreasing. Some 3% of the population live in *kibbutzim* (*see* kibbutz) and about 5% live in *moshavim*; rural settlements established since 1948 are usually on these lines. *Economy*: both industrial and agricultural output has increased rapidly since 1948, boosted by investments and gifts of capital from abroad. There are resources of copper ore and phosphates; potash and bromine from the Dead Sea are also exploited. One of the chief centres of diamond cutting and polishing, Israel also has food-processing, textile, chemical, and electronics industries and exports finished diamonds and light manufactures. Fishing and tourism are also important. 6% of the work force is employed in agriculture, which depends heavily on artificial irrigation. Between 1949 and 1970 the area of irrigated land increased by six times, with a corresponding increase in production. There has also been extensive reafforestation, with a land reclamation scheme in the Negev Desert. Thus, although in 1948 Israel produced only 30% of its food requirements, it now imports only grain in large quantities and exports citrus and other fruit, vegetables, and flowers. *History*: Israel's history prior to 1948 is that of *Palestine, in which Jewish Zionists had demanded the creation of a Jewish state since the late 19th century. According to a UN recommendation and against Arab opposition, Palestine was to be divided into a Jewish state, an Arab state, and a small internationally administered zone around Jerusalem. As soon as the state of Israel was proclaimed following British withdrawal (1948), however, Arab forces (those of Egypt, Transjordan, Iraq, Syria, and Lebanon) invaded; by early 1949 Israeli forces had not only repulsed them but had gained control of 75% of Palestine, while the rest had been annexed by Jordan (the *West Bank of the River Jordan) and Egypt (the *Gaza Strip). Jerusalem was divided between Jews and Arabs. In 1956, following Nasser's nationalization of the Suez Canal, Israeli forces occupied the Gaza Strip and the *Sinai Peninsula and gained access to the Red Sea, which boosted its international trade. In the Six Day War (1967) Israel defeated Egypt, Syria, and Jordan and again occupied the Gaza Strip and the Sinai Peninsula as well as the *Golan Heights, the West Bank, and the Arab sector of Jerusalem, which it administered thereafter as a single unit. A peace agreement with Egypt after the Yom Kippur War (1973; in which the Israelis were taken unawares by Egyptian forces on the Day of Atonement—Yom Kippur), was finally achieved in 1979 at the Camp David talks, following which Israel withdrew from Sinai (1980–82). In 1982 Israel invaded Lebanon and forced the Palestinian Liberation Organization to leave West Beirut. The war was unpopular and Israel finally withdrew from Lebanon in 1985. Because of the war and astronomical inflation, a coalition government was formed in 1984. Inflation is now more controlled, due to a policy of economic austerity. In 1988 Israel was criticized for its treatment of Palestinian protestors in Israeli-occupied territories. Head of State: President Chaim Herzog (1918–). Prime minister: Yitzhak Shamir. Official languages: Hebrew and Arabic. Official currency: Israeli shekel of 100 new agorot. Area: 20 770 sq km (8018 sq mi). Population (1983 est): 3 957 000. Capital: Jerusalem. Main port: Haifa.

Issachar, tribe of One of the 12 *tribes of Israel. It claimed descent from Issachar, son of Jacob and Leah. It occupied territory to the S and SE of the Sea of Galilee.

Issas. *See* Somali.

issuing house A financial institution in the UK (often a *merchant bank) that acts as an intermediary between a company seeking to raise capital on a stock exchange and those wishing to invest. It advises a client on when and how to make a new issue of *securities, advertises it to the public, and often underwrites the issue (i.e. guarantees to buy all the securities that have not been applied for). In the USA this function is performed by an investment bank.

Issus, Battle of (333 BC) The battle in which Alexander

the Great of Macedon defeated an enormous Persian army under Darius III, which was caught in a narrow pass and outmanoeuvred. Victory here opened Alexander's way from Asia Minor into Persia proper.

Issyk Kul, Lake A lake in the S Soviet Union, in the Kirgiz SSR in the N Tien Shan. It is 702 m (2303 ft) deep, lying 1609 m (5279 ft) above sea level, and never freezes. Area: about 6220 sq km (2401 sq mi).

Istanbul (*or* Stamboul) 41 02N 28 57E A city in W Turkey, on both sides of the Bosporus. There are many ancient buildings in the city, including the mainly 6th-century Hagia Sophia (originally a church and now a museum), the Blue Mosque, and the Topkapi Palace (the former sultans' harem). It is a major port and industrial centre and has three universities (15th century, 1773, and 1971); tourism is a major source of revenue. *History*: ancient Byzantium was renamed Constantinople in 330, when the emperor Constantine I declared it the capital of the Eastern Roman Empire. It was the capital of the Byzantine Empire until its capture by the Ottoman Turks in 1453, although it had been held by Crusaders from 1204 to 1261. The Ottomans renamed it Istanbul and made it the capital of their empire in 1457. After having been taken by the Allies in World War I, Istanbul became the largest city of the Turkish Republic (established in 1923). Population (1985): 5 475 982.

Isthmian Games In ancient Greece, the biennial festival held near Corinth in Poseidon's honour. Established in 581 BC these games, more lighthearted than the other major Greek festivals, included music and poetry competitions as well as the more usual athletic events and horse racing. The victor's prize was a crown of wild celery.

Istria A peninsula in NW Yugoslavia, in Croatia between the Gulf of Trieste and the Bay of Kvarner. Passing to Italy at the end of World War I, it was ceded to Yugoslavia (1947) except for the Territory of Trieste, which was divided between Italy and Yugoslavia in 1954.

Itaipu Dam. *See* Paraná, Rio.

Italian A language of the *Romance family spoken in Italy. The standard literary and official form is based upon the Tuscan dialect of Florence, the dialect used by *Dante.

Italian art The style of art found in Italy after the collapse of the Roman Empire. Antique motifs continued but were gradually replaced by Christian imagery and the influence, especially in Ravenna and Venice, of *Byzantine art and architecture. The *romanesque style of the 11th and 12th centuries gave way to the *gothic in the 13th century. A truly Italian art developed in the late-13th and 14th centuries, when the foundations of *Renaissance art were laid by *Giotto, *Duccio, and the sculptor Nicola *Pisano. Independent styles arose in the regional centres of Italy, especially in Florence (which dominated the 15th century), Venice (where the Venetian school was founded by the *Bellini family), and Rome. The giants of the Renaissance, *Leonardo, *Michelangelo, *Raphael, and the Venetians *Giorgione and *Titian dominated the late 15th and early 16th centuries. Their work merged into ▢mannerism, exemplified by the architect *Giulio Romano, the painter *Parmigianino, and in Venice the painters *Tintoretto and *Veronese. Mannerism gave way around 1600 to the *baroque, the outstanding Italian exponents of which worked in Rome: the architects *Bernini (also a sculptor) and *Borromini and the painter *Caravaggio. After the 17th century Italian art lost its impetus, except in Venice, where it briefly flowered in the 18th century with the work of *Canaletto, *Guardi, and *Tiepolo. A revival occurred in the early 20th century under the influence of *futurism and the outstanding Italian painters of the modern period are *Modigliani and de *Chirico.

Italian East Africa. *See* Somaliland.

Italian literature Latin remained the literary language of Italy until the 13th century, when poets at the Sicilian court of Frederick I (later Emperor Frederick II) began to imitate the poetry of Provence in native Italian. The delicate love poetry of the *dolce stil nuovo school of Florentine poets was followed in the 14th century by the allegorical works of *Dante, the love sonnets of *Petrarch, and the prose tales of *Boccaccio. The gradual development of the Italian language culminated in the Renaissance works of *Ariosto, *Machiavelli, and *Tasso. There followed a long period of decadence until, in the late 18th century, a literary revival was brought about by the dramatists *Alfieri and *Goldoni and the poet *Foscolo. In the 19th century the influence of Romanticism, epitomized in the poetry of *Leopardi, was followed by a reaction represented by the classicism of the poet *Carducci and the realism of the novelist and dramatist Giovanni Verga (1840–1922). Major writers of the early 20th century include the poet *D'Annunzio, the dramatist *Pirandello, and the critic Benedetto *Croce. Literary exploration of social and moral themes was curbed during the fascist regime from 1922 to 1943, but recommenced after World War II, with such writers as Alberto *Moravia, Cesare *Pavese, and Italo Calvino (1923–85).

Italic languages A subgroup of the *Indo-European language family spoken in central and NE Italy in the thousand years before the rise of Rome. A parent of modern *Romance languages, this group comprised four related dialects: *Latin, Faliscan, Osco-Umbrian, and Venetic. At the beginning of the 1st millennium BC Osco-Umbrian was the most widely spoken, but with the growth of Roman civilization, Latin quickly came to dominate other dialects, which are now known only through Latin sources.

italic script A style of handwriting adopted in 15th-century Italy by papal scribes and later (c. 1500) adapted for printing. Italic cursive letters eliminate unnecessary lifts of the pen, permitting rapid legible handwriting. *In print its characteristic sloped letters, such as those used in this sentence, are used mainly for display, emphasis, or to indicate that a word is in a foreign language.*

Italy, Republic of A country in S Europe, occupying a peninsula bordered by the Tyrrhenian Sea (W), the Ionian Sea (S), and the Adriatic Sea (E). The principal offshore islands are Sicily and Sardinia. Except for small coastal areas and the Po Valley in the N, the country is generally rugged and mountainous. The main rivers are the Po, Tiber, Arno, and Adige. *Economy*: agriculture is still important, the main crops being wheat, maize, grapes, and olives. Industry, however, has expanded considerably since World War II and is now the most important sector. The principal manufactures are textiles (including silk) and clothing, and machinery, motor vehicles, and chemicals, which together with fruit and vegetables are the principal exports. The wine industry is growing in importance and exports have increased in recent years. Mineral resources are not large and Italy is heavily dependent on imported fossil fuels, although oil is now being extracted, especially in Sicily, and hydroelectricity has been considerably developed. There are also plans to develop nuclear energy. Tourism is an important source of revenue. During the 1970s, however, Italy was faced with severe problems of inflation and economic stagnation and the long-standing problem of integrating the poorer predominantly agricultural S with the industrial N remained unresolved. *History*: pre-Roman Italy was inhabited from the 7th century BC by the *Etruscans in the N, Italics (including the Samnites) and Latins in central Italy, and Greek colonists in the southern mainland and Sicily. By 275 BC most of the peninsula had come under the rule of Rome (*see* Roman Republic). As the western *Roman Empire declined from the 4th century AD, Italy was invaded by a succession of barbarian tribes, including the Visigoths and the Vandals. The last Roman emperor was deposed in 476 by the German king, Odoacer, who in 493 was in turn overthrown by the Ostrogoths. They were expelled in the early 6th century by the Eastern (Byzantine)

Roman Empire, the position of which was threatened from the mid-6th century by successive invasions: the Lombards were followed by the Franks in the 8th and 9th centuries, a period that also saw the origins of the pope's temporal power (*see* papal states); the Muslims invaded the S in the 9th and 10th centuries, Magyars, the N in the 10th century, and Normans, the S in the 11th century. The claim of the German kings to rule Italy was established in 962, when Otto the Great was crowned Holy Roman Emperor in Rome. The conflict from the 11th century between successive popes and emperors over the *investiture controversy embroiled the Italian city states (notably Milan, Pisa, Genoa, Venice, and Florence), which in the 12th century were further divided by the struggle between *Guelfs and Ghibellines. The economic and political development of the city states in the first half of the 14th century was facilitated by the removal of the papacy to Avignon and the preoccupation with German affairs of the Holy Roman Emperors. Many of the Italian cities came to be dominated by single families, such as the *Visconti and then the Sforza in Milan and the *Medici in Florence, who during the Renaissance were often outstanding patrons of culture and learning. Following the French invasion of Italy in 1494 Italy became the scene of conflict between France and Spain and from the 16th to early 18th centuries was largely dominated by the latter. Spain ruled Milan, Naples, Sicily, and Sardinia directly and influenced Savoy, Genoa, and Tuscany; of the major Italian states only the papal states and Venice remained independent. During the 18th century Spanish hegemony was destroyed, passing to Austria until 1796, when Italy was conquered by the French Revolutionary armies under Napoleon. The French occupation gave Italy the experience of unity. After Napoleon's fall and the restoration of Austrian rule this developed into the movement for independence and unification (the *Risorgimento). By 1861, under the leadership of Victor Emmanuel II of Sardinia-Piedmont and his chief minister Cavour, aided by Garibaldi in the S, the Austrians had been expelled and the kingdom of Italy proclaimed with Victor Emmanuel as its first king; unification was virtually complete by 1870. In the late 19th century Italy acquired a colonial empire, notably Somaliland and Eritrea in East Africa, but its attempt to seize Ethiopia was defeated at Adowa in 1896. In 1915 Italy entered World War I on the side of the Allies, obtaining the Trentino and the Istrian peninsula (*see* Irredentists). The postwar rise of fascism brought Mussolini to power in 1922. In 1936 he conquered Ethiopia and in 1939, Albania. In 1940, loyal to his alliances (1936, 1939) with Hitler, Mussolini took Italy into World War II on Germany's side (1940). The Allied conquest of Sicily (1943) brought Mussolini's fall and in 1946 Umberto II abdicated following a referendum rejecting the monarchy. Since the establishment of the Republic there have been nearly 50 governments. The repeated failure of the Christian Democrats to deal effectively with a stagnating economy, widespread corruption, and growing lawlessness exacerbated by such groups as the *Red Brigades and fascists led to an increase in the strength of the Communist Party in the late 1970s. Following the general elections of 1983 Bettino Craxi (1934–) became Italy's first socialist prime minister, heading a coalition government. He resigned in early 1987 and was succeeded by Giovanni Goria (1943–), who headed the 47th government since World War II. Italy was a founder member of the EEC. President: Francesco Cossiga (1929–). Official language: Italian. Official religion: Roman Catholic. Official currency: lira of 100 centesimi. Area: 301 425 sq km (116 350 sq mi). Population (1983 est): 56 345 000. Capital: Rome. Main port: Genoa.

itch mite A parasitic *mite, *Sarcoptes scabei*, that produces *scabies in man and mange in domestic animals. The female burrows into the skin, where it lays eggs and causes intense itching and irritation. Family: *Sarcoptidae*.

Ithaca (Modern Greek name: Itháki) A Greek island in the Ionian Sea, one of the Ionian Islands. It is widely believed to have been the home of Homer's Odysseus. Area: 85 sq km (33 sq mi). Population (1981): 3646.

Ito Hirobumi (1841–1909) Japanese statesman, who played a leading part in the abolition of feudalism and the adoption of modern methods and institutions. During the 1880s he assumed responsibility for drafting the Meiji constitution (1889) and between 1885 and 1901 he was prime minister four times. During his second ministry Japan defeated China in the *Sino-Japanese War (1894–95). Ito was assassinated by a Korean nationalist.

Itúrbide, Agustín (1783–1824) Mexican soldier prominent in the independence movement; emperor (1822–23). He used the general unrest in Mexico to further his own advancement in the army. Appointed commander of the combined rebel forces when Mexico declared itself independent of Spain (1820), he subsequently proclaimed himself emperor. Within months *Santa Anna forced his abdication; Iturbide returned from exile in 1824 but was executed.

Ivanovo 57 00N 41 00E A city in the central Soviet Union, in the RSFSR on the River Uvod. It played an important part in both the 1905 and 1917 Russian Revolutions. It is one of the country's major textile centres. Population (1981 est): 470 000.

Ivan (III) the Great (1440–1505) Grand Prince of Muscovy (1462–1505). Ivan greatly expanded Muscovite territory and ended Russian subordination to the Tatars. In 1497 he introduced a new legal code. Ivan married (1472) Zoë Palaeologus (d. 1503), the niece of the last Byzantine emperor, and adopted the Byzantine two-headed eagle as his arms.

Ivan (IV) the Terrible (1530–84) Grand Prince of Muscovy (1533–84), who was crowned tsar in 1547. Ivan reformed the legal code and local administration (1555), conquered Kazan and Astrakhan, and established commercial relations with England. After 1560 his reign was marred by his brutality: thousands were executed and in a fit of rage Ivan murdered his son (1581). The effects of his tyranny were aggravated by the financial strains resulting from the abortive *Livonian War (1558–82).

Ives, Charles (Edward) (1874–1954) US composer. An early experimenter with polyrhythms, polytonality, quarter tones, and the superimposition of disparate musical styles, he composed four symphonies, five violin sonatas, songs, and other works. His second piano sonata, subtitled *Concord, Mass* (1909–15), was inspired by US writers associated with the town of Concord. Its movements were subtitled "Emerson," "Hawthorne," "The Alcotts," and "Thoreau." One of his best-known works is *Central Park in the Dark* (1898–1907). Of the more than 500 works he composed, most remained unpublished. For his Symphony No. 3 (1904) he was awarded a Pulitzer Prize. He was also senior partner of the insurance firm of Ives and Myrick.

ivory The close-grained white tissue forming the tusks of elephants, walruses, and narwhals and the teeth of hippos. So-called fossil ivory is obtained from mammoths. Plastics have now generally replaced ivory for such mundane domestic artefacts as knife handles, but, being easy to carve and polish, ivory is still such a valuable commodity that its main source, the African elephant, is threatened with extinction. Ivory carving is a very ancient art; objects from France date to Palaeolithic times and fine examples survive from Egyptian, Minoan, Mycenaean, Assyrian, Greek, and Roman civilizations. In Europe ivory plaques with relief carving became important during the early middle ages for small religious icons, book covers, caskets, etc. India, SE Asia, China, and Japan (*see* netsuke) have ancient traditions of skilled ivory carving. American Eskimo carvings in walrus ivory are greatly prized by connoisseurs.

ivory-billed woodpecker A rare black-and-white *woodpecker, Campephilus principalis, occurring in North American forests. 45 cm long, it has a white bill and the male has a red crest. It feeds on woodboring insects and requires a large feeding territory, hence its decline due to the expansion of the timber industry.

Ivory Coast, Republic of (official name: Côte d'Ivoire) A country in West Africa, on the Gulf of Guinea. Swamps and tropical forests give way to savanna on higher land to the N. The diverse African population includes Baule, Bete, Senufo, and Malinke. *Economy*: chiefly agricultural, livestock being important as well as crops, including maize, yams, and other tropical plants. The main cash crop is coffee, of which, together with timber (particularly mahogany), Ivory Coast is Africa's leading exporter. Other exports include cocoa, pineapples, and rubber. Mineral resources are on the whole sparse, although some manganese is mined, diamond fields are being exploited, and some oil was found in 1977. Industry is being developed, including tourism. *History*: explored by the Portuguese in the late 15th century, the area was disputed by several European trading nations over the centuries, becoming a French colony in 1893. It became part of French West Africa in 1904 and an overseas territory in 1946. It possessed internal self-government as a member of the French Community from 1958 and became fully independent in 1960. President: Félix Houphouët-Boigny. Official language: French. Official currency: CFA (Communauté financière africaine) franc of 100 centimes. Area: 322 463 sq km (124 470 sq mi). Population (1983 est): 8 890 000. Capital: Yamoussoukro. Main port: Abidjan.

ivy An evergreen woody climbing plant, *Hedera helix*, that has glossy three- to five-lobed leaves, aerial roots (with which it clings to supports), clusters of small greenish-yellow flowers, and small round fruits ripening from green to black. Native to Europe and W Asia, it is widely cultivated (ornamental ivies often have variegated foliage). Family: *Araliaceae*.

Ivy League A number of universities in the NE USA of high academic and social prestige. They include *Harvard, *Yale, and *Princeton and are all members of an athletic conference for intercollegiate sports known as the Ivy League, which dates back to the 1870s.

Iwo 7 38N 4 11E A town in SW Nigeria. Its main activity is the export of agricultural products, especially cocoa. Population (1983 est): 261 600.

Iwo Jima 24 47N 141 19E A Japanese island in the W Pacific Ocean, the largest of the Volcano Islands. Captured by US forces after a severe struggle (1945), it was returned in 1968. Sulphur and sugar are produced. Area: 20 sq km (8 sq mi).

Izanagi and Izanami In Japanese mythology, the male and female creator deities of Japan. They stirred the sea with a spear and drops from its tip formed the Japanese islands, for which they then created other *kami* (spirits) as inhabitants and guardians (*see* Amaterasu).

Izhevsk 56 49N 53 11E A city in the W central Soviet Union, the capital of Udmurt ASSR in the RSFSR. It is a major metallurgical centre. Population (1981 est): 574 000.

Izmir (former name: Smyrna) 38 25N 27 10E A port in W Turkey, on the Aegean Sea. Much was destroyed by fire in 1922, the rebuilt town being a modern commercial centre with a university (1953). There is trade in silk, cotton, carpets, figs, raisins, and sponges. Population (1980): 1 976 763.

Izmit 40 47N 29 55E A town in NW Turkey, on the Sea of Marmara. As ancient Nicomedia it was the seat of the kings of Bithynia, and it is now a naval port. Population (1980): 190 423.

J

Jabalpur (*or* Jubbulpore) 23 10N 79 59E A city in India, in Madhya Pradesh. An important railway junction and industrial centre, its manufactures include cement, textiles, and military equipment. Its university was established in 1957. Population (1981): 758 000.

Jabir. *See* Geber.

jabiru A large *stork, *Jabiru mycteria*, ranging from Mexico to Argentina. 140 cm long, it is white with a dark-blue head and neck with a red patch at the base and has a long slightly upturned heavy bill.

jaborandi A tropical American plant of the genus *Pilocarpus* (22 species), the dried leaves of which yield an alkaloid, pilocarpine, used medicinally in eyedrops to constrict the pupil and to treat glaucoma. Family: *Rutaceae*.

jacamar A bird belonging to a family (*Galbulidae*; 15 species) occurring in tropical American forests. 12–27 cm long, jacamars have a large head tapering to a long narrow tail and iridescent blue, green, or bronze plumage. They feed on insects. Order: *Piciformes* (woodpeckers, etc.).

jacana A waterbird belonging to a family (*Jacanidae*; 7 species) occurring in tropical regions worldwide, also called lily trotter. Jacanas are characterized by long legs with elongated toes and claws, which enable them to run over floating vegetation. 25–32 cm long, they are commonly reddish to dark-brown in colour and can swim and dive well. Order: *Charadriiformes* (gulls, plovers, etc.).

Jacaranda A genus of □trees and shrubs (50 species) of South and Central America and the West Indies, often grown as ornamentals. *J. mimosifolia*, up to 15 m tall, has compound leaves and blue or violet tubular flowers. In cooler climates it can be cultivated in greenhouses. Some species yield valuable timber. Family: *Bignoniaceae*.

jackal A carnivorous mammal of the genus *Canis*, found in Asia and Africa. Jackals are closely related to dogs and have pricked ears and bushy tails. The African black-backed jackal (*C. mesomeles*) is up to 110 cm long including the tail (25–33 cm) and often hunts in packs for carrion. The African side-striped jackal (*C. adustus*) is smaller and shyer.

jackdaw An intelligent Eurasian crow, *Corvus monedula*, about 32 cm long, having a black plumage with a grey nape, an erectile crest, and pale-blue eyes. Often found in colonies, jackdaws may be seen flying around cliffs, ruins, and large buildings. They feed on insects, grain, and carrion and may rob nests of eggs and chicks.

Jacklin, Tony (1944–) British professional golfer, whose successes include the British open championship (1969), the US open championship (1970), and the British Professional Golfers Association championship (1972, 1982). He captained two victorious European Ryder Cup teams (1985 and 1987).

Jack Russell terrier A breed of dog developed in England from the fox terrier by the Rev John Russell (1795–1883) for flushing foxes from earth. It has a stocky body and a strong muscular head with small drooping ears. The short coat is white, black, and tan. Height: up to 38 cm.

Jackson 32 20N 90 11W A city in the USA, the capital of Mississippi on the Pearl River. Founded in 1821, it was virtually destroyed by Gen Sherman in 1863. More recently (1960s) it has been the scene of considerable racial tension. Its industries include the production of oil and gas, textiles, and glass. Population (1980): 202 895.

Jackson, Andrew (1767–1845) US statesman and military hero; Democratic president (1829–37). A Tennessee frontiersman and self-made man, he became the "Hero of New Orleans" when his defence of the city boosted US morale at the end of the

*War of 1812. Jacksonian democracy, the political movement that made him president, relied on support from the masses and advocated universal White male suffrage, instead of rule by a few aristocratic professional politicians. He supported *states' rights; his distribution of federal deposits from the Bank of the United States to local banks resulted in land speculation and inflation.

GLENDA JACKSON *As Cleopatra (1979).*

Jackson, Glenda (1936–) British actress. She has acted in many Royal Shakespeare Company stage productions, but first achieved popular success with her portrayal of Elizabeth I in a television series (1971). Her films include *Women in Love* (1969), *Hedda* (1976), *Stevie* (1978), and *Hopscotch* (1980); in 1986 she returned to the stage in *The House of Bernarda Alba*.

Jackson, Stonewall (Thomas Jonathan J.; 1824–63) US Confederate general in the Civil War. In the first battle of *Bull Run, he and his brigade were described as standing "like a stone wall" in the face of the Federal advance. Jackson was a master of rapid tactical movement, shown particularly in the Shenandoah valley campaign (1862). His untimely accidental death at Chancellorsville left a gap in the Confederate command that was never filled.

Jacksonville 30 20N 81 40W A city and port in the USA, in NE Florida on the St Johns River near its mouth on the Atlantic Ocean. Named after President Jackson (formerly the first territorial governor of Florida), it is the state's largest city and main commercial centre. A major naval base, its industries include ship repairing, paper, and chemicals. Population (1980): 540 898.

Jack the Ripper An unidentified murderer who killed and mutilated at least six prostitutes in the East End of London in late 1888. One recent theory suggests that he was Vassily Konovalov, a Russian who committed similar murders in Paris and St Petersburg and who died in a Russian asylum.

Jacobins An extremist group in the *French Revolution. The Jacobin Club was founded in 1789 and (meeting in a Dominican (*or* Jacobin) monastery) became increasingly radical. Helped by *Danton's rabble-rousing speeches, they proclaimed the republic, had the king executed, and overthrew the *Girondins (1792–93). Through the Committee of *Public Safety, the Jacobins, under the influence of *Robespierre, instituted the *Reign of Terror. They collapsed after Robespierre's execution.

Jacobites Supporters of the exiled *Stuart king, James II

(Latin name: Jacobus), and his descendants. Between 1688, when the Glorious Revolution overthrew James II, and 1745, the Jacobites (mainly Roman Catholics and/or Tories), were the rallying point for opposition to the Hanoverian monarchs. Two Jacobite rebellions, in 1715 (the "15 Rebellion" led by *James Edward Stuart, the Old Pretender) and 1745 (the "45 Rebellion" led by *Charles Edward Stuart, the Young Pretender), were suppressed and thereafter the movement lost its political force.

Jacobsen, Arne (1902–71) Danish architect and designer of furniture, wallpaper, etc. The foremost modern Danish architect, Jacobsen's style is characterized by neat clear lines and elegant masses. His most important buildings were Rødovre Town Hall (1955) and the SAS Hotel, Copenhagen (1960). In England he designed St Catherine's College, Oxford (1960–64).

Jacob's ladder A perennial herb, *Polemonium caeruleum*, native of Eurasia and widely cultivated as a garden flower. Growing to a height of 90 cm, it has bright-blue flowers and leaves consisting of paired ladder-like leaflets. Family: *Polemoniaceae*.

Jacopo della Quercia (c. 1374–1438) Italian Renaissance sculptor, who was the Sienese counterpart to *Donatello. His Sienese works include the Fonte Gaia (1416–19), the now dismantled fountain for the Piazza del Campo, and the Baptistry font, on which he collaborated with *Ghiberti. However, Jacopo's most powerful works are the marble reliefs (1425–35) of scenes from Genesis, which surround the portal of S Petronio, Bologna.

Jacopone da Todi (c. 1236–1306) Italian religious poet. On the death of his wife, he joined the Franciscans as a member of the "Spirituals," the strictest group of the order. In 1298 he was imprisoned by Pope Boniface VIII, whom he had attacked in verse, but was released on the pope's death in 1303. The famous Latin poem *Stabat mater dolorosa* is attributed to him, but most of his poetry was written in the Umbrian dialect of Italian. His *laudi spirituali* (spiritual praises) are vivid devotional poems.

Jacquard, Joseph-Marie (1752–1834) French inventor of the Jacquard loom, completed in 1801. Its design allowed for the weaving of figured patterns by means of punched cards, which were later employed in the calculator developed by Charles *Babbage and in subsequent computers.

Jacquerie (1358) A peasant revolt in NE France during the Hundred Years' War with England. Its name refers to the aristocrats' contemptuous nickname for a peasant, Jacques Bonhomme. Caused by famine, plague, and war, the rebellion was rapidly suppressed.

jade An extremely hard semiprecious stone, usually green or greenish white, consisting of a tough compact variety of either jadeite (a pyroxene, $NaAlSi_2O_6$) or nephrite (an amphibole). Many highly prized stones come from Upper Burma, where they are found in river beds. *See* Plate III.

Jadotville. *See* Likasi.

Jaén 37 46N 3 48W A town in S Spain, in Andalusia. It has a fine Renaissance cathedral. Once famous for silk, it now produces chemicals and has rich leadmines nearby. Population (1981): 96 424.

Jaffa. *See* Tel Aviv-Jaffa.

Jagan, Cheddi Berrat (1918–) Guyanese statesman, who as leader (since 1950) of the People's Progressive Party (PPP) was the first prime minister (1961–64) of British Guyana. His wife **Janet Jagan** (1920–) was general secretary of the PPP (1950–70).

Jagannatha A Hindu deity in some contexts synonymous with Krishna. Devotees of Jagannatha have been known to throw themselves under the massive chariot on which his idol is annually wheeled during a festival at Puri, in Orissa, and from which the term "juggernaut" is derived.

Jagger, Mick (1944–) British rock singer, who studied at the London School of Economics before joining the *Rolling Stones. He became notorious for his aggressive performances on stage and was arrested in 1967 for possessing drugs. He acted in the films *Ned Kelly* (1969) and *Performance* (1970).

Jagiellons The ruling dynasty of Poland and Lithuania (1386–1572), Hungary (1440–1441, 1490–1526), and Bohemia (1471–1526). The dynasty was founded by Jagiełło (1350–1434), Grand Duke of Lithuania, who became King of Poland as Władysław II in 1386, when he married Queen Jadwiga of Poland (1370–99; reigned 1384–99). His son, Władysław III (1424–44), also became King of Hungary (1440). Władysław III's nephew Władysław (1456–1516) became Vladislav II of Bohemia in 1471 and of Hungary in 1490. After defeat by the Turks at the battle of *Mohacs (1526), the Jagiellons lost the thrones of Hungary and Bohemia to the Habsburg *Ferdinand I. The last Jagiellon ruler was Sigismund II Augustus (1520–72; ruled Poland 1548–72), under whom a Polish-Lithuanian commonwealth was created by the Union of *Lublin.

jaguar The largest New World *cat, *Panthera onca*, found in the southern USA and Central and South America. Up to 2.5 m long including the tail (70–90 cm), it has dark rosette-shaped spots on its yellow coat. Jaguars inhabit forest and scrub and can swim well and may catch fish. They also hunt peccaries, turtles, and capybaras and attack livestock.

jaguarundi A weasel-like *cat, *Felis yagouaroundi*, of Central and South America. Up to 110 cm long, it stands only 28 cm high at the shoulder. It has a red or grey coat, long tail, and small ears. In addition to birds, jaguarundis eat such fruits as grapes, figs, and bananas.

Jahangir (1569–1627) Emperor of India (1605–27); the son of *Akbar the Great, from whom he inherited a powerful empire. After expanding it further he ruled wisely and justly, fostering sport and the arts. He enjoyed good relations with the British *East India Company.

Jainism The religion of between two and three million Indians, followers of *Mahavira. Founded in the 6th century BC in opposition to Vedic religion, Jainism stresses *ahimsa, asceticism, and meditation. Right belief, knowledge, and conduct are the means of release from the perpetual round of rebirth caused by *karma. This release is possible only for monks; the laity aim only for a better rebirth. Jainism is atheistic, although lesser spirits and demons proliferate. The universe, containing heavens and hells revolving eternally in ascending and descending cycles, is seen as the mechanistic interaction of six principles: souls, space, time, matter, right, and wrong.

Jaipur 26 53N 75 50E A city in India, the capital of Rajasthan. Formerly the capital of the princely state of Rajasthan, it has many fine buildings built in pink sandstone, an 18th-century observatory, and a university (1947). Jaipur is famous for its enamel work and jewellery, textile printing, and stone, marble, and ivory carving. Population (1981 est): 1 004 669.

Jajapura (or Djajapura; former name: Sukarnapura) 2 37S 140 39E A port in E Indonesia, the capital of West Irian province on the Pacific Ocean. Liberated from Japanese occupation by US forces in 1944, it became Gen MacArthur's headquarters. Population (1980): 149 618.

Jakarta (or Djakarta; name until 1949: Batavia) 6 09S 106 49E The capital of Indonesia, in NW Java linked by canal to its port, Tanjung Priok. The Dutch set up a fort here in the early 17th century and it became a major commercial centre as the headquarters of the Dutch East India Company. The University of Indonesia was founded in 1950. Population (1980): 6 503 449.

jalap A climbing plant *Ipomoea purga*, of Mexico and South America, that has crimson flowers. The dried tubers yield a resin that is used as a laxative. Family: *Convolvulaceae*.

Jamaica, State of An island country in the Caribbean Sea, off the S coast of Cuba. A high plateau is crossed by the

Jambi 640

Blue Mountains, which reach 2255 m (7400 ft). The population is mainly of African and mixed African and European descent. *Economy*: sugar, bauxite, and tourism form the basis, although the tourist trade was badly affected for several years by domestic unrest. Jamaica is the world's second largest producer of bauxite and alumina although a decline in the demand for bauxite has put pressure upon Jamaica's foreign exchange reserves and contributed to the devaluation of the Jamaican dollar. There is an agreement between Guyana and Jamaica to build two alumina-processing smelters by 1981, and a bauxite and alumina complex is being jointly constructed by Jamaica and Mexico. Other recent industrial developments include the construction of an oil refinery with Mexican aid. *History*: discovered by Columbus in 1494, it was occupied by the Spanish, who exterminated the original Arawak inhabitants. Captured by the British in 1655, it became a colony and a centre of the slave trade until the abolition of slavery in 1833. Self-government was introduced in 1944 and extended in 1959, and in 1962 Jamaica became an independent state within the British Commonwealth. There has been considerable political unrest in recent years between the Labour Party (JLP) and the People's National Party (PNP) led by Michael *Manley, an advocate of democratic socialism and republican status for Jamaica. A state of emergency existed in 1976–77 following riots. Jamaica is a member of the OAS and CARICOM. Prime minister: Edward Seaga. Official language: English. Official currency: Jamaican dollar of 100 cents. Area: 10 991 sq km (4244 sq mi). Population (1983 est): 2 535 000. Capital and main port: Kingston.

Jambi (Djambi *or* Telanaipura) 1 36S 103 39E A port in Indonesia, in SE Sumatra. It is a commercial centre producing chiefly rubber and oil. Its university was established in 1963. Population (1980): 230 373.

James (I) the Conqueror (1208–76) King of Aragon (1213–76). James, who became effective ruler in 1227, was the greatest medieval Aragonese monarch. He reconquered the Balearic Islands and Valencia from the Moors and thus laid the basis for Aragonese expansion in the Mediterranean in the next century. James also contributed to the cultural achievements of his reign, prompting the compilation of the *Chronicle* of his exploits.

James I (1394–1437) King of the Scots (1406–37), whose actual rule began on his release (1424) from English imprisonment. He strengthened royal authority at the expense of the nobles, whom he treated with some harshness, and extended royal control over the administration of justice and commerce. He was assassinated by a group of disaffected nobles. He is believed to be the author of the poem "The Kingis Quair" ("The King's Book").

James I (1566–1625) The first Stuart King of England and Ireland (1603–25) and, as James VI, King of the Scots (1567–1625). He succeeded to the Scottish throne after the abdication of his mother Mary, Queen of Scots, and was brought up, a Presbyterian, by a series of regents. As king he reasserted royal authority against the encroachments of the nobility and, less successfully, of the Presbyterians. In 1589 he married *Anne of Denmark. In England, James encountered opposition from his parliaments (1604–10, the 1614 "Addled" Parliament, 1621–22), which resented his assertion of the *divine right of kings and attempted to make financial grants dependent on the king's redress of its constitutional grievances. James was also unpopular for his choice of favourites—after the death (1612) of Robert Cecil, 1st Earl of Salisbury (*see* Burghley, William Cecil, Lord), he was influenced by Robert Carr, Earl of *Somerset, and then by George Villiers, Duke of *Buckingham—and for his attempts to obtain a Spanish marriage for his son. One of the great achievements of his reign was the publication (1611) of the *King James or Authorized version of the Bible.

James II (1430–60) King of the Scots (1437–60). He established his authority over rival factions and continued the extension of royal control and justice begun by his father James I. He was killed while besieging the English at Roxburgh Castle.

James II (1633–1701) King of England, Scotland, and Ireland (1685–88). The second son of Charles I, James (as Duke of York) escaped to Holland (1648) after his father's defeat in the Civil War and during the 1650s fought for the French and then the Spanish. In 1659 he married the daughter of the Earl of Clarendon, Anne Hyde (1637–71), by whom he had two daughters (later Queens Mary II and Anne). At the Restoration (1660) of his brother Charles II, James became Lord High Admiral. In about 1669 he became a Roman Catholic and when this became public was forced to resign (1673). Successive attempts to exclude him from the succession failed and in 1684 he was reappointed Lord High Admiral and in 1685 became king. The Protestant rebellion of the Duke of *Monmouth was suppressed, Roman Catholics were admitted to public office, and religious freedom for all denominations was announced (1687). In 1688 James prosecuted the Archbishop of Canterbury and six bishops who refused to proclaim religious toleration from the pulpit but lost the case. This defeat and the threat of a Roman Catholic succession with the birth of a son (*see* James Edward Stuart, the Old Pretender) to his second wife, Mary of Modena (1658–1718), precipitated his overthrow in the *Glorious Revolution. James was forced to flee and his subsequent attempt to regain the Crown from Ireland failed with his defeat by William III's forces at the *Boyne (1690) and *Aughrim (1691). He died an exile in France.

James III (1452–88) King of the Scots (1460–88). Until 1469 Scotland was ruled by a regency and his personal rule was marked by baronial revolts. He was killed after defeat by rebel barons near Stirling.

James IV (1473–1513) King of the Scots (1488–1513). In 1503 he married *Margaret Tudor. He defeated the rebels who had killed his father James III, procuring internal stability and respect for the monarchy. Recurrent hostility with England culminated in the invasion of Northumberland (1513) and his defeat and death, with most of his nobles, at *Flodden. He encouraged literature and was a patron of the Scottish Chaucerians, William *Dunbar and Gavin *Douglas.

James V (1512–42) King of the Scots (1513–42). During his minority (1513–28) Scotland was controlled by rival pro-French and pro-English factions. James favoured the French, to whom he was allied by his marriage to Mary of Guise (1515–60). He died shortly after the failure of an invasion of England and was succeeded by his daughter Mary, Queen of Scots.

James VI (King of the Scots). *See* James I (King of England).

James, Henry (1843–1916) US novelist and critic. Much of his childhood was spent in Europe, and in 1875 he moved to Paris, where he met Turgenev, Flaubert, and others who influenced his concern with the technique of fiction. From 1876 he lived mainly in England, becoming a British citizen in 1915. His novel *Roderick Hudson* (1875) introduced the international theme of Americans confronting European culture that he was to develop in many other novels, such as *The Portrait of a Lady* (1881), although he occasionally returned to strictly American settings, as in *Washington Square* (1881) and *The Bostonians* (1886). He wrote more than a hundred shorter works of fiction, of which *The Turn of the Screw* (1898) is perhaps the best known. In his later novels, *The Wings of the Dove* (1902), *The Ambassadors* (1903), and *The Golden Bowl* (1904), action is subordinated to a searching psychological analysis rendered in a highly elaborate style. He was an influential critic; the Prefaces to his novels are important theoretical statements on the novel. He also wrote plays, but they were not successful, although many of his works have been adapted for dramatic performance. His brother **William James** (1842–1910) was a psychologist and philosopher, who developed the theory of *pragmatism in ethics. He held that the truth or falsity of classical philosophical systems made little difference to everyday life and that the function of a theory should be to solve practical difficulties: thus a theory was only true in so far as it successfully helped to solve problems. Religious and moral beliefs were treated in the same nondogmatic way, especially in his influential *Varieties of Religious Experience* (1902) and *The Meaning of Truth* (1909).

James, Jesse (Woodson) (1847–92) US outlaw. After fighting with southern guerrilla groups during the Civil War he formed the James gang and by 1867 was robbing banks, stagecoaches, and trains in his native Missouri and surrounding states. He was shot and killed by Robert Ford, a James gang member who claimed the $10 000 reward offered by the state of Missouri.

James, St In the New Testament, the name of three followers of Christ. **1.** A leader, with St Peter, of the early Christians of Jerusalem. He is described as "the Lord's brother" (Mark 6.3), but the exact relationship is uncertain. He was a devout follower of Jewish practice, being converted to Christianity at the time of the resurrection. He was condemned to death by the Sanhedrin in 62 AD. The **Epistle of James** in the New Testament was traditionally attributed to him and was possibly written early in the 1st century AD. **2.** The Apostle, known as St James the Great, son of Zebedee and brother of *John. He was present with his brother at many events in the life of Christ recounted in the Gospels. He was beheaded by Herod Agrippa I in 44 AD. In the middle ages it was believed that he had preached in Spain and was buried at Santiago de Compostela. Feast day: 25 July. **3.** The Apostle, known as St James the Less, son of Alphaeus. Feast day: 1 May.

James Edward Stuart, the Old Pretender (1688–1766) The son of James II, the deposed Roman Catholic King of England. In exile, he was urged by his supporters, known as *Jacobites, to claim the English throne. After their invasion of Scotland failed in 1715, James abandoned his claim and lived in permanent exile in Rome.

Jameson, Sir Leander Starr (1853–1917) South African statesman, born in Scotland, who worked closely with Cecil *Rhodes; prime minister of Cape Colony (1904–08). In 1895 he led the **Jameson Raid** into the Transvaal to support British immigrants against the Afrikaners. Imprisoned for three months in England he returned to Cape Colony to become a member of parliament and, on Rhodes' death, leader of the Progressive Party.

James River A river in the central USA, flowing generally ESE through Virginia to *Chesapeake Bay. Jamestown was established along its lower course in 1607. Length: 547 km (340 mi).

Jamestown The first permanent English colony in America, established in 1607 on a peninsula in the James River (Virginia) by Captain John Smith. It is preserved as a colonial historical park.

Jammu and Kashmir A state in N India, forming part of the disputed area of *Kashmir. Area: 100 569 sq km (38 820 sq mi). Population (1981): 5 981 600. Capital: Jammu (winter); Srinagar (summer).

Jamnagar 22 28N 70 06E A city in India, in Gujarat on the Gulf of Kutch. Formerly the capital of the princely state of Nawanagar, it has a fine palace. Industries include textiles and cement. Population (1981): 317 000.

Jamshedpur 22 47N 86 12E A city in India, in Bihar. Founded in 1907 by the industrialist Dorabji Jamsetji Tata, it is the site of India's principal iron and steel works. Population (1981): 670 000.

Janáček, Leoš (1854–1928) Czech composer. He studied at the Leipzig and Vienna conservatoires and became professor of composition at Brno conservatoire in 1919. He was over 60 before he gained wide recognition as a composer. In his vocal works he attempted to reproduce natural speech rhythms; he was also influenced by folk music. His works include the operas *Jenufa* (1894–1903), *The Excursions of Mr Brouček* (1908–17), and *The Makropulos Case* (1923–25), two string quartets, and the *Glagolitic Mass* (1926).

Janissaries The elite troops of the Ottoman sultans. First raised by Sultan Orkhan (1279–1359; reigned 1326–59) about 1330, and organized by his successor Murad I (1319–89; reigned 1359–89) as a professional army, the Janissaries were carefully selected from the Ottoman subject peoples, especially from Christian families. Highly trained, powerful, and close to palace politics, during the 17th and 18th centuries they engineered palace coups, murdering two sultans, and forcing others to abdicate. After their insurrection in 1826 *Mahmud II killed the entire corps.

Jan Mayen 70 10N 9 00W A volcanic island in the Arctic Ocean. It was annexed to Norway in 1929 and has a meteorological station and a NATO radio and navigation station. Area: 373 sq km (144 sq mi).

Jansen, Cornelius Otto (1585–1638) Dutch Roman Catholic theologian and founder of *Jansenism. The director of episcopal colleges in Bayonne (1612–14) and Louvain (1617–30), he became dean of the University of Louvain in 1635 and Bishop of Ypres in 1636. His major work, *The Augustinus* (1640), is the basis of Jansenist doctrine and was condemned as heretical by Pope Innocent X in 1653.

Jansenism A movement in the Roman Catholic Church in the 17th and 18th centuries based on the teaching of Cornelius *Jansen. Stressing the more rigorously predestinarian aspects of St *Augustine's teaching, it brought the Jansenists into conflict with the Jesuits and was condemned by the Church as constituting a threat to traditional sacramentalism. Among other points, Jansenists argued that the efficacy of the sacraments depended on the moral character of the recipient. One of the most famous Jansenists was *Pascal. *See also* Port Royal.

Jansky, Karl Guthe (1905–50) US radio engineer, who discovered a source of radio waves outside the solar system (1932), while investigating static interference. Jansky's discovery led to the new science of *radio astronomy.

Januarius, St (Italian name: San Gennaro; d. ?305) Italian churchman; Bishop and patron saint of Naples. He was probably martyred during the persecution of *Diocletian. The phial of solidified blood in the cathedral in Naples, believed to liquefy miraculously several times each year, is revered as one of his relics. Feast day: 19 Sept.

January Insurrection. *See* Congress Kingdom of Poland.

Janus The Roman god of doors, thresholds, and beginnings, after whom the month January is named. He is usually portrayed as having two heads facing forwards and backwards. His blessing was invoked for the sowing of crops and the beginning of any other major activity.

Japan (Japanese name: Nippon *or* Nihon) A country in E Asia, consisting of a series of islands lying between the Pacific Ocean and the Sea of Japan. The four main islands are *Honshu, *Kyushu, *Hokkaido, and *Shikoku. They have long indented coastlines and much of the land is mountainous, with the highest mountain, *Fujiyama, rising to 3778 m (12 399 ft). The country has long been subject to earthquakes. The population is of mixed Malay, Manchu, and Korean descent; the original inhabitants, the *Ainu, survive in small numbers on Hokkaido. *Economy*: during the past two decades Japan has developed into a highly industrialized country, manufacturing electrical goods, motor vehicles, and petrochemicals; it now produces about half the world's ships. The electronics, paper, and textile industries are also important. Mineral resources, which include limestone, copper, chromite, and coal, are on the whole sparse and Japan relies heavily on imports. There is some oil and natural gas; hydroelectricity is an important source of power. Agriculture is intensive: rice is still the main crop, but wheat, barley, and soya beans are also grown. Vast forests cover over half the land and there is considerable timber production. Although fishing is proportionately less important than before World War II, Japan is still one of the world's leading fishing nations and in 1977 fishing limits were extended to 200 miles. Exports include machinery, motor vehicles, metals, textiles, and chemicals. Japan is now one of the foremost financial centres of the world, which accounts for an important part of the economy. *History*: about 200 BC the country was united under the *Yamato dynasty, already rulers of one of its component kingdoms for about 500 years. Their religion formed the basis of *Shinto, the native religion of Japan, and until 1946 Japanese emperors were regarded as divine descendants of the sun goddess. From 1186 AD real power was in the hands of the military *shoguns until Emperor *Mutsuhito regained power for the House of Yamato in 1867. 1871 saw the end of Hoken Seido (the feudal system) and from the mid-19th century the country was once again opened up to western communications and ideas, from which it had been virtually isolated for 200 years. It expanded colonially, especially in successful wars against China and Russia, and it occupied several Asian countries. It fought against the Allies in World War II and surrendered after the dropping of atomic bombs on Hiroshima and Nagasaki in 1945. Until the peace treaty of 1951 it was under US occupation. In 1956 Japan joined the UN and in 1972 regained the Ryukyu Islands. By a new constitution of 1947 the emperor renounced his former claim to divinity and became a constitutional monarch. The Liberal Democratic Party has been in power since 1955. Head of state: Emperor Hirohito. Prime minister: Noboru Takeshita (1924–). Official language: Japanese. Official currency: yen of 100 sen and 1000 rin. Area: 372 480 sq km (143 777 sq mi). Population (1986): 120 720 542. Capital: Tokyo. Main port: Yokohama.

Japan, Sea of A section of the NW Pacific Ocean between Japan and the Asian mainland.

Japanese The language of the Mongoloid people of Japan. Its relationship to other languages is uncertain but it is probably related to *Korean. It is polysyllabic and tonal. There are many very different regional dialects; the standard and official form is based on the speech of Tokyo. Japanese writing systems are extraordinarily complex. The basic kana system has about 1850 characters (c. 2nd century AD) from *Chinese script but used to indicate both a syllabic value (the *on*) and a conceptual value (the *kun*). This has two forms, each with 50 characters, developed in the 9th to 10th centuries: the formal hiragana style used for literary works and the katakana or cursive style used for practical purposes and for loanwords.

Japanese art Neolithic Japanese art consisted of crudely executed terracotta figurines and some ceramic ware. The introduction of Buddhism via Korea in the 6th century and the influence of Chinese culture initiated a great period of temple building, sculpture (chiefly of the Buddha), and the development of the art of flower arrangement (*see* ikebana). In the Kamakura period (12th-14th centuries) the refined *Fujiwara style was replaced in sculpture by a vigorous naturalism. In painting, a uniquely Japanese style developed in continuous narrative paintings on horizontal scrolls and realistic landscapes. Another entirely Japanese art form was the coloured woodblock print of the Tokugawa period (1630-1867). These prints, portraying the transient world of theatre, teahouse, etc., and produced by such artists as *Hokusai and *Kitagawa Utamaro, enjoyed a popularity in Europe in the late 19th century, being particularly influential among impressionist painters (*see* ukiyo-e). Examples of Japanese applied arts are the small wood and ivory carvings (called netsuke) and the gold inlaid sword guards (tsuba). Japanese ceramic art is best illustrated by the *cha-no-yu wares.

JAPANESE ART   Fuji from the Village of Sekiya on the Banks of the Sumida (1835) by Hokusai, colour print from wood blocks (Victoria and Albert Museum, London).

Japanese cedar A conifer, *Cryptomeria japonica*, native to China and Japan, where it is an important timber tree reaching a height of 55 m; elsewhere it is grown for ornament and rarely exceeds 35 m. Japanese cedar has narrow curved leaves that point towards the tips of the branches and globular spiny cones, 2 cm across, ripening from green to brown. Family: *Taxodiaceae*.

Japanese literature Before the mid-8th century AD Chinese was the more prestigious language in Japan and in the 8th century Chinese characters were adapted to render spoken Japanese (*see* Japanese). Vernacular Japanese folksongs, however, gave rise to a type of lyric poem, the *waka*, which remained a standard poetic form for over a millennium. This native form appears in the earliest Japanese anthology, the *Manyoshu* (compiled after 759), which contains about 4500 poems. The emperors of the Heian period (794-1185) encouraged literature, and further anthologies were published, as well as prose tales (*monogatari*) and fictionalized diaries (*nikki*). Fiction writing was particularly the province of women; its most famous practitioner was *Murasaki Shikibu, the author of the *Genji Monogatari* (*Tale of Genji*; c. 1015). Unsettled conditions in the following 500 years led to a decline in this essentially aristocratic literary output. The last official anthology appeared in 1439. The *no drama, mainly Buddhist in inspiration, however, flowered during the late 14th and early 15th centuries, and the *haiku* (an epigram comprising 17 syllables) was a product of the early 16th century.

In the Tokugawa period (1603-1867) literature of all kinds enjoyed a renaissance under the patronage of the leisured warrior class and the new mercantile middle class. The *haiku* reached its peak in the hands of *Matsuo Basho. Fiction encompassed many forms and moods, and nationalistic pride led to official encouragement for writers of philosophy, history, and other learned works. The *joruri* (puppet theatre) at first prospered with playwrights of the calibre of Monzaemon writing for it but during the late 18th century it declined in competition with the popular *kabuki* theatre.

After 1868 European influence manifested itself in every branch of literature, mainly with adverse effects as writers strove to imitate western models. In the years after World War II, however, several novelists and poets have established international reputations, including *Kawabata Yasunari and Yukio *Mishima.

Japanese maple A *maple tree, *Acer palmatum*, up to 13 m tall, the 5-11 lobed leaves of which turn scarlet in autumn. Native to Japan, it is a popular ornamental in many cultivated varieties, including purple-leaved and dwarf types. They require shelter in cooler climates.

japonica A shrub or tree of the genus *Chaenomeles* (or *Cydonia*), native to Japan but widely cultivated as an ornamental. Flowering quince (*C. japonica*) and Japanese quince (*C. speciosa*) are the most popular species. These have toothed oval glossy leaves and clusters of scarlet five-petalled flowers, 5 cm across. The apple-like fruit is used in marmalade and jelly. Family: *Rosaceae*.

Japurá, River A river in NW South America, rising as the Rio Caquetá in SW Colombia and flowing generally SE to join the River Amazon near Tefé in Brazil. Length: 2800 km (1750 mi).

Jaques-Dalcroze, Émile (1865–1950) Swiss composer and educationalist. While professor of harmony at the Geneva conservatoire he developed *eurhythmics, a system of coordinating musical rhythms and bodily movement. The London School of Dalcroze Eurythmics was founded in 1913.

jarrah A shrub or tree, *Eucalyptus marginata*, of W Australia, that has extremely durable weather-resistant timber, known as West Australian mahogany. It can grow to a height of 16 m and is found in dry areas. Family: *Myrtaceae*.

Jarrow 54 59N 1 29W A town in NE England, in Tyne and Wear on the S bank of the River Tyne. The Venerable Bede lived in the monastery here. The Jarrow hunger marches, in protest against high local unemployment and poverty, took place in the 1930s when the shipbuilding industry declined. Jarrow has shipyards, foundries, oil installations, and chemical works. Population (1981): 27 074.

Jarry, Alfred (1873–1907) French dramatist. His play, *Ubu Roi* (1896), is an outrageous satire on bourgeois conventions of respectability. He wrote several sequels and also novels and poems and is regarded as a precursor of *surrealism and the *Theatre of the Absurd.

Jaruzelski, Wojciech (1923–) Polish general and statesman; prime minister (1981–85); first secretary of the Communist Party (1981–); head of state (1985–). Coming to power to halt the liberal reforms obtained by the independent trade union Solidarity, he instituted martial law (1981–83), detained Lech *Walesa and other union leaders (1981–82), and dissolved Solidarity (1982).

jasmine A shrub of the genus *Jasminum* (about 300 species), native to tropical and subtropical regions and widely cultivated. Many species yield an essential oil used in perfumery. Two species suitable for temperate gardens are the common jasmine (*J. officinalis*) from S Asia, up to 6 m tall with fragrant white flowers, and the Chinese winter jasmine (*J. nudiflorum*), 3–6 m tall, the yellow flowers of which open in winter before the leaves. (Winter jasmine can be distinguished from *Forsythia* by its green stems.) Family: *Oleaceae*.

Jason A legendary Greek hero, heir to the throne of Iolcos in Thessaly. Sent by his uncle, the usurper Pelias, to fetch the *Golden Fleece, he and the *Argonauts underwent many adventures before finally recovering the Fleece from Colchis with the help of *Medea. After many years of wandering he died at Corinth.

jasper An impure variety of *chalcedony, usually red or reddish brown. It is slightly translucent and is regarded as a semiprecious stone. It is an abundant mineral, occurring mainly in veins and in cavities in volcanic rocks.

Jaspers, Karl (Theodor) (1883–1969) German philosopher, a forerunner of *existentialism. He studied medicine and psychology and believed philosophers should be acquainted with the scientific method. His philosophy, expounded in *Philosophie* (1932), is about the possibilities and quality of human choice. He thought *Kierkegaard and *Nietzsche were exceptional in exhibiting the variety of possibilities open to man.

Jassy. See Iaşi.

Jatakas In the Pali Buddhist canon, a collection of 550 moral tales describing previous existences of the Buddha before his enlightenment. Each story is related to an event in the Buddha's present life.

jaundice Yellowing of the skin and whites of the eyes due to the presence of *bile pigments. Bile pigments are normally produced by the liver from the breakdown of red blood cells and then excreted in bile into the gut. Jaundice may result if there is excessive breakdown of red blood cells, as in haemolytic anaemia, or in disease of the liver, such as *hepatitis, or blockage of the bile duct by *gallstones.

Jaurès, Jean (1859–1914) French socialist leader and journalist; a proponent of the international unity of the working class. He was a vehement supporter of Dreyfus and advocated the separation of church and state. In 1905 he was instrumental in founding the French socialist party (the Section française de l'internationale Ouvrière). He helped found *L'Humanité* in 1904 and was its editor until 1914, when he was assassinated.

Java An Indonesian island, the smallest of the Greater *Sunda Islands. Its chain of volcanic mountains has formed exceptionally fertile soil, and its many rivers feed its intensive wet-rice agriculture. Other food crops, sugar cane, and kapok are grown and forest products include teak. Indonesia's administrative and industrial centre, Java has its three largest cities and is heavily overpopulated. The textile industry is of particular importance, especially synthetic textiles, although the village batik industry has declined. Java is subsidized by other islands, which has provoked much unrest. *History*: Indian colonies in the early centuries AD developed into Hindu and Buddhist kingdoms, with Hindu-Javanese culture reaching its height in the 14th century. Later Islamic control barely influenced the culture. The Dutch East India Company was centred here from 1619. During the anticommunist purges (1965–67) between 500 000 and 1 000 000 people were killed. Area: 132 174 sq km (51 032 sq mi). **Population** (1980): 91 269 528, with Madura. Capital: Jakarta.

javelin throw A field event in athletics in which a spearlike javelin is thrown as far as possible. The men's javelin is 2.6–2.7 m (8.5–8.9 ft) long and weighs 800 g (1.8 lb). The women's measures 2.2–2.3 m (7.2–7.5 ft) and weighs a minimum of 600 g (1.3 lb). It is thrown with one hand, over the shoulder, after a run-up of approximately 36 m (120 ft), and the metal head must hit the ground first. Each competitor has six tries. World records: men: 87.66 m by Jan Zelezny (Czechoslovakia); women: 78.90 m by Petra Felke (East Germany).

jaw One of the two bones of the face that form a framework for the mouth and provide attachment for the teeth. The lower jaw (or mandible) is a horseshoe-shaped bone with a vertical process at each end that forms a joint with the temporal bone of the skull, just in front of each ear. The upper jaw consists of two closely connected bones (maxillae) each containing an air *sinus.

Jawara, Sir Dawda (1924–) Gambian statesman; president (1970–). A Muslim, he became minister of education in 1960 and prime minister in 1962, in which post he led his country to independence in 1965. When The Gambia became a republic in 1970 Jawara became president.

Jawlensky, Alexey von (1864–1941) Russian expressionist painter, who spent most of his life in Germany (*see* expressionism). His chief influences were *Kandinsky, with whom he was associated in several artistic groups, notably *Neue Kunstlervereinigung, and *Matisse. Typical of his vibrantly coloured and heavily outlined style is his series of heads resembling icons.

jay A crow, *Garrulus glandarius*, of Eurasia and N Africa. It is about 34 cm long and brownish pink, with a black tail, white rump, black-barred blue wing patches, and a black-and-white erectile crest. Jays are found mainly in woodland, feeding on insects and larvae in summer and storing acorns, beechmast, and other seeds for winter food.

Jay, John (1745–1829) US Revolutionary patriot; the first chief justice of the USA (1789-95). He led peace negotiations with Britain after the American Revolution and negotiated the so-called **Jay Treaty** averting war with Britain and securing favourable commercial terms. As chief justice he affirmed the subordination of states to the federal government.

Jaya, Mount (*or* Mount Sukarno) 4 05S 137 09E The highest mountain in Indonesia, in West Irian in the Sudirman range. Height: 5029 m (16 503 ft).

Jayawardene, J(unius) R(ichard) (1906-) Sri Lankan statesman; prime minister (1977-78) and then president (1978-). He became a significant politician in the years before Ceylon (Sri Lanka from 1972) obtained independence in 1948 and as a member of the United National Party, which he led from 1970, held various posts before becoming prime minister.

jazz A form of popular music that originated in New Orleans around 1900, characterized by improvisation and syncopated rhythms. The musical influences responsible for its creation included French and Spanish popular music, ragtime, blues, brass-band music, and African slave songs. It first became popular in the Storyville district of New Orleans and as an accompaniment to funerals, weddings, and country outings. Early jazz bands featured improvised solos on such instruments as the cornet, clarinet, and trombone. Louis Armstrong and Jelly Roll Morton are associated with New Orleans jazz (*see* New Orleans style). In the 1920s jazz spread to larger US cities, such as New York and Chicago; the original band was enlarged with saxophones and additional cornets and trumpets. Large dance bands emerged in the era of *swing (the 1930s), in which the bandleaders Paul Whiteman (1891-1967), Benny Goodman, Glenn Miller, and Count Basie were especially important. In the 1940s Dizzy Gillespie and Charlie "Bird" Parker revolted against swing with *bop, using a smaller band and introducing harmonic and rhythmic innovations. *Cool jazz of the late 1940s and 1950s adopted a relaxed behind-the-beat approach as in the playing of Miles Davis and Stan Getz (1927-). In the 1960s and 1970s such musicians as Gunther Schuller (1925-) and John Lewis (1920-) integrated jazz idioms with classical forms and techniques to form *third stream. Ornette Coleman (1930-) and John Coltrane (1926-) expanded the boundaries of jazz to include atonality in a style called *free-form jazz.

Jean de Meun (c. 1240-c. 1305) French poet. His conclusion (18 000 lines) of the verse allegory *Roman de la rose*, contrasting in both style and content with the earlier part written by *Guillaume de Lorris, is valued chiefly for its lengthy and informative digressions on topics of contemporary interest.

Jean Paul (Johann Paul Friedrich Richter; 1763-1825) German Romantic novelist. His novels, such as *Hesperus* (1795) and *Das Leben des Quintus Fixlein* (1796), combine fantasy with humour and psychological realism and later influenced *Keller and *Mörike.

Jeans, Sir James Hopwood (1877-1946) British mathematician and astronomer. His early work was on the kinetic theory of gases and on the quantum theory. Later he concentrated on cosmogony, putting forward a now discredited theory of planetary formation. After 1928 he devoted himself to writing books popularizing science: *The Universe around Us* (1930), *Science and Music* (1937), and *The Growth of Physical Science* (1947) are examples. He was knighted in 1928 and awarded an OM in 1939.

Jedburgh 55 29N 2 34W A town in SE Scotland, in the Borders Region. The royal castle was destroyed in 1409 but the abbey (founded 1118) remains. Jedburgh's chief industries are textiles (tweeds, woollens, and rayon) and precision tools. Population (1981): 4168.

Jedda. *See* Jiddah.

Jeeps, Dickie (Richard Eric Gantry; 1931-) British

Rugby Union footballer, who played for Northampton, England, and the British Lions. An outstanding scrum half, he played 24 times for England (1956-62) and 13 times for the British Lions. He became chairman of the Sports Council (1978).

Jefferies, Richard (1848-87) British novelist and naturalist. He published several collections of essays and sketches about rural life, notably *Hodge and His Masters* (1880). In his autobiography *The Story of My Heart* (1883) and other later works he developed a personal philosophy of mysticism.

Jeffers, Robinson (1887-1962) US poet. From 1916 he lived in isolation near Carmel on the coast of California. *Tamar and Other Poems* (1924) and other volumes of long narrative poems and short lyrics express a bleak view of mankind. He also wrote plays, notably an adaptation of Euripides' *Medea* (1946).

JAZZ *Dizzy Gillespie seen here in 1985.*

Jefferson, Thomas (1743-1826) US statesman; the third president (1801-09) of the USA. A lawyer, Jefferson began his political career (1769) in Virginia's House of Burgesses. He was elected a delegate to the second *Continental Congress in 1775 and was the chief author of the *Declaration of Independence. Jefferson served as governor of Virginia (1779-81), minister to France (1785-89), secretary of state (1789-93), and vice president (1797-1801) under John Adams. During Jefferson's two terms as president, he approved the *Louisiana Purchase (1803) and encouraged US neutrality in the Napoleonic Wars. In private life after 1809, Jefferson founded the University of Virginia. Both he and John Adams died on 4 July, 1826, the 50th anniversary of American independence.

Jefferson City 38 33N 92 10W A city in the USA, the capital of Missouri on the Missouri River. Primarily an administrative centre, it is the site of Lincoln University (1866). Population (1980): 33 619.

Jeffrey, Francis, Lord (1773–1850) Scottish literary critic and judge. He is best known as cofounder (1802) and editor (1802–29) of the *Edinburgh Review*. For this brilliant and controversial periodical Jeffrey wrote essays denouncing the work of the Romantics, particularly Wordsworth.

Jeffreys of Wem, George, 1st Baron (c. 1645–89) English judge. A staunch supporter of the Crown, he became a leading prosecutor of suspected traitors following the *Popish Plot and, in 1685, James II's Lord Chancellor. He is notorious for the harsh punishments and death sentences that he imposed during the Bloody Assizes, which followed Monmouth's rebellion (1685). He was imprisoned and executed after the downfall of James II.

Jeffries, John. *See* Blanchard, Jean Pierre François.

Jehol. *See* Chengde.

Jehovah. *See* Yahweh.

Jehovah's Witnesses A religious movement, first known as Bible Students, organized in the early 1870s by Charles Taze Russell (1852–1916) in Pittsburgh. From 1884 the Watch Tower Bible and Tract Society became their legal publishing agency. Jehovah's Witnesses accept the Bible as their sole authority, worshipping the Creator, Jehovah, and acknowledging Jesus Christ to be God's son and spokesman. They look for the end of wickedness and of the present world order in the near future. They believe that 144 000, the Christian congregation, will rule with Christ Jesus in his heavenly kingdom over the rest of obedient mankind, who will live on a paradise earth. Following the example of the first Christians, they do not engage in politics and are conscientious objectors.

Jellicoe, John Rushworth, 1st Earl (1859-1935) British admiral; commander of the grand fleet (1914-16) in World War I. He was criticized for his command at the battle of *Jutland, in which the German fleet escaped relatively unscathed.

jellyfish A free-swimming aquatic invertebrate animal belonging to a class (*Scyphozoa*; about 200 species) of *coelenterates. The translucent gelatinous body, 1.5-2000 mm in diameter, is bell- or umbrella-shaped, with a central tubular projection that hangs down and bears the mouth. Jellyfish occur in all oceans, especially in tropical regions, and usually propel themselves through the water by contracting muscles around the edge of the bell. Stinging tentacles are used to capture and paralyse prey, ranging from plankton to small fish, and can seriously affect man. The term jellyfish is also used for the free-swimming sexual form of any other coelenterate (*see* medusa).

Jena 51 00N 11 30E A town in S East Germany, on the River Saale. Its university (1558) became famous in the 18th century when Fichte, Hegel, Schelling, Schiller, and August Schlegel taught there. As well as the Zeiss optical works, founded in 1846, Jena has chemical and engineering industries. Population (1980): 103 263.

Jena and Auerstädt, Battles of (14 October, 1806) Simultaneous battles in which Napoleon defeated the Prussians. Following Prussia's challenge to Napoleon after his defeat of Austria at *Austerlitz, Auerstädt and Jena broke Prussia as a military power and left Russia to face Napoleon alone. Prussia remained in the orbit of the French Empire until 1813, when it rejoined the alliance against Napoleon.

Jenkins, Roy (Harris) (1920–) British politician and historian, leader of the Social Democratic Party (1982–83). He entered parliament in 1948 as a Labour member and from 1957 to 1958 was chairman of the Fabian Society. He was chancellor of the exchequer (1967–70) and then deputy leader of the Labour Party until resigning in 1972 over Harold Wilson's position on the EEC. After serving as home secretary (1974–76) he became president of the EEC Commission (1977–81). He was instrumental in founding the *Social Democratic Party in 1981. His publications include a biography of Asquith. In 1987 he was elected Chancellor of Oxford University.

Jenkins' Ear, War of (1738–48) A war that arose out of Britain's illicit trade in Spanish America and merged into the War of the *Austrian Succession (1740–48). It followed the accusation of Capt Robert Jenkins that his ear had been cut off by Spanish coastguards in the West Indies.

Jenner, Edward (1749–1823) British physician, who developed the first effective vaccine–against smallpox. Jenner noticed that people who caught the mild disease cowpox never contracted smallpox. In 1796 he inoculated a small boy with cowpox and, two months later, with smallpox. The boy did not get smallpox. Jenner published his findings in 1798 and vaccination–a word that Jenner coined–became a widespread protective measure against smallpox.

Jensen, Johannes (Vilhelm) (1873–1950) Danish novelist and poet, many of whose works were inspired by his travels in the USA and the Far East. His most important work was the novel sequence *Den lange Rejse* (*The Long Journey*; 1908–22), a Darwinian account of the origin of mankind.

Jenson, Nicolas (c. 1420–80) French printer, who produced the first distinctive roman typeface, which replaced Gothic (*or* black letter) type. After studying printing under Gutenberg, Jenson opened a printing shop in Venice in 1470.

jerboa A small hopping *rodent belonging to the family *Dipodidae* (25 species) of Asian and N African deserts, also called desert rat. Jerboas are 4–15 cm long and have kangaroo-like hind feet, a long balancing tail, large eyes and ears, and soft sandy-coloured fur. They spend the day in burrows and emerge at night to feed on seeds and tubers.

Jeremiah (7th century BC) An Old Testament prophet. He is believed to have been born about 650 BC in a village near Jerusalem. The **Book of Jeremiah** contains his prophecies relating to the fall of Judah, its conquest by Nebuchadnezzar, and the *Babylonian exile of the Jews. A Messiah is prophesied, who will rule over Jews and Gentiles.

Jerez de la Frontera 36 41N 6 08W A city in SW Spain, in Andalusia. It is renowned for its wine industry and gave its name to sherry. It is also famous for its horses. Population (1981): 176 238.

Jericho 31 52N 35 27E A village in the Jordan Valley (Israel), N of the Dead Sea, now in the Israeli-occupied West Bank area. The nearby site of the old city was excavated by Kathleen *Kenyon, revealing one of the earliest known towns (before 8000 BC), with massive stone fortifications surrounding circular brick-built houses. Later Neolithic burials yielded skulls with features modelled in plaster and shells inset for eyes. Of the biblical Bronze Age city attacked by *Joshua (Joshua 6) nothing remains. The extensive ruins of the magnificent palace, Khirbat al-Mafjar, built (739–44 AD) by the Umayyad caliph Hisham (d. 743) can still be seen.

Jerome, Jerome K(lapka) (1859–1927) British humorist, novelist, and playwright. His plays include *The Passing of the Third Floor Back* (1908) but he is best known for his novel *Three Men in a Boat* (1899).

Jerome, St (c. 342–420 AD) Italian biblical scholar; Doctor of the Church and author of the *Vulgate Bible, the first Latin translation of the Bible from the Hebrew. After a period as a hermit, he was ordained by St *Paulinus of Nola in Antioch. A secretary to Pope Damasus I (reigned 366–94) from 382 until 385, he later settled in Bethlehem, where he established a monastery. He also wrote biblical commentaries and theological works, which are famous for their prose style. Feast day: 30 Sept.

Jersey 49 13N 2 07W The largest of the Channel Islands, in the English Channel. Colonized from Normandy in the 11th century, French influence remains strong and French is the official language. It consists chiefly of a plateau incised by deep valleys. Agriculture, particularly dairy farming, is important and the famous Jersey cattle are bred for export.

Tourism is also a major source of income. In 1959 the Jersey Zoological Park was founded by Gerald Durrell to protect rare species of wildlife. Area: 116 sq km (45 sq mi). Population (1981): 77 000. Capital: St Helier.

Jersey cattle A breed of dairy cattle originating from Jersey. Relatively small and fine-boned, Jerseys are golden-brown to black in colour, adaptable, and mature rapidly. They produce high-quality creamy milk.

Jersey City 40 44N 74 04W A city in the USA, in New Jersey. Founded in 1629, it is connected to nearby New York City by the Hudson River tunnels. Its 20 km (12 mi) of waterfront forms part of the port of New York. A major industrial and commercial centre with oil refineries, its products include paper and cigarettes. Population (1980): 223 532.

JERSALEM *At the ancient Western Wall, men and women each have their own areas of worship.*

Jerusalem (Arabic name: El Quds) 31 47N 35 13E The capital of Israel, in the Judaea Heights between the Mediterranean and the Dead Seas. Jerusalem is a religious centre for three major world religions: Christianity, Judaism, and Islam. Most employment is found in government and the city's main industry, tourism. The Hebrew University of Jerusalem was founded in 1918. The modern city spreads out extensively on the W side of the Old City, which is walled (1537–40) and contains most of the religious shrines, including the Western (Wailing) Wall (Jewish), the Dome of the Rock (begun 661 AD; Islamic), and the Church of the Holy Sepulchre, which was founded in about 335 on the traditional site of Christ's burial and resurrection, although most of the present structure is 19th-century. *History*:

Jerusalem was conquered by King David in 1005 BC and the first *Temple was built by his son, Solomon, in 969 BC; it became the capital of Judah in 930 BC. Nebuchadnezzar, King of Babylon, destroyed the city in 586 BC, when the Jewish inhabitants were exiled to Babylon. In 538 BC, 40 000 Jews returned to the city, whose walls were rebuilt under Nehemiah in 445 BC. It was occupied by Alexander the Great (4th century BC) and the Romans (63 BC), under whose fifth procurator, Pontius Pilate, Jesus Christ was put to death. Occupation by the Arabs and Turks was succeeded by the establishment of the Kingdom of Jerusalem, a feudal state created in 1099 following conquest by the Crusaders. It was enlarged in the early 12th century by *Baldwin I and his successors, but fell to Saladin in 1187. The Ottoman Turks took the city in 1516 and in 1538 *Suleiman the Magnificent rebuilt the city walls, which are those still standing. The Ottoman period lasted until 1917, when it was taken by the British, who held it under mandate until 1948. Jerusalem was then divided between the new state of Israel, of which it became the capital (1950), and Jordan. Israel occupied the whole city in June, 1967. Population (1982 est): 424 400.

Jerusalem artichoke A North American perennial herb, *Helianthus tuberosus*, that grows to a height of 2 m, and has edible sweet-tasting tubers up to 10 cm long. Their yellow flowers appear only in hot summers. Family: *Compositae*.

Jerusalem cherry A small shrub, *Solanum pseudocapsicum*, probably of Old World origin, growing to a height of 1.3 m and bearing cherry-sized red or yellow highly poisonous fruits. The false Jerusalem cherry (*S. capsicastrum*) of Brazil is similar. Both are grown as ornamentals. Family: *Solanaceae*.

Jervis Bay An inlet of the Tasman Sea, in SE Australia. It forms a fine natural harbour and was transferred to the Australian Capital Territory (1915) for development as an outlet port. It contains the Royal Australian Naval College (1915). Area: about 73 sq km (28 sq mi).

Jespersen, Otto (1860–1943) Danish linguist. His principal works are *Growth and Structure of the English Language* (1905), *A Modern English Grammar on Historical Principles* (1909–31), *The Philosophy of Grammar* (1924), and *Analytic Syntax* (1937). His approach to language is traditional and historical; his writing is noted for its lucidity.

Jesselton. *See* Kota Kinabalu.

Jesuits Members of the Society of Jesus, an order founded by St *Ignatius Loyola in 1533 to propagate the Roman Catholic faith. The order was organized along military lines; in addition to the traditional vows of chastity, poverty, and obedience, Jesuits were sworn to go wherever the pope might send them. They quickly established themselves as educators and missionaries, becoming one of the dominant forces of the *Counter-Reformation; their argumentative subtlety was proverbial. They also played a prominent role in missions to the New World and the East. Their power and rigorous organization eventually brought them into conflict with civil authorities throughout Europe, and they were expelled from several states. In 1773 Pope Clement XIV suppressed the order, and it was not reinstated until 1814. Today Jesuits are active in most countries and are noted for their schools and universities, including the Gregorian University in Rome. In 1986 the Pope appointed Fr Paolo Dezza to lead and especially to impose discipline upon the order.

Jesus (c. 6 BC–c. 30 AD) The founder of *Christianity; called by his followers the Messiah or Christ (Greek *khristos*, anointed one). Most of the information concerning Jesus comes from the New Testament *Gospels of Matthew, Mark, and Luke. This material was arranged in order to proclaim and interpret his life and teachings to early Christians and therefore does not provide neutral biographical detail, although it is based on historical facts. According to these sources, Jesus was born at Bethlehem in the last years of the reign of *Herod the Great; he was the son of the Virgin *Mary, of Nazareth in Galilee, who belonged to the tribe of Judah and the family of David. Mary's husband, Joseph, was a carpenter, and Jesus was apparently trained as a carpenter in Nazareth. About 27 AD, *John the Baptist, who was related to Jesus, began to preach that the Kingdom of God (a divine last judgment) was approaching and to urge repentance and baptism as a preparation for it. Jesus was baptized by John and shortly (after John had been imprisoned by Herod Antipas) began his public ministry, travelling in Galilee and in the area NW of Lake Gennesaret. He taught in synagogues and in the open, not using sacred texts but adopting a popular style by preaching in parables and proverbial expressions. His teaching, which is summarized in the Sermon on the Mount (Matthew 5-7), emphasized the approaching kingdom of God, the need for repentance, and the importance of such virtues as charity, faith, and humility instead of the ceremonial observance of the Law. Miracles were attributed to him, including healing, driving out demons, and miraculously feeding a multitude of 5000. The beginnings of a movement are evident in Galilee when Jesus summoned the disciples, traditionally 12 in number, instructing them to leave their families and their work in order to preach the imminence of the Kingdom of God. The Gospels devote most attention to the last week of Jesus' life. He went with the disciples to Jerusalem for Passover, apparently aware of the serious opposition that awaited him. There he was acknowledged as the Messiah by many people, but, after betrayal by Judas, was arrested and condemned to death by the chief Jewish tribunal, the Sanhedrin, for the blasphemous claim to Messiahship. The Gospels tend to exonerate Pontius *Pilate in the proceedings against Jesus, but he was executed according to Roman law as a criminal (see crucifixion). In the New Testament his death is presented as the fulfilment of a divine purpose that was made clear to the disciples only at the resurrection (on the next day but one after the crucifixion) and by a number of appearances to individuals and groups of disciples. His ascension into heaven is mentioned in the Gospels and in Acts (1.3), where it is said to have occurred 40 days after the resurrection.

jet engine A form of *gas turbine (see also internalcombustion engine) in which part of the energy released by burning the fuel is used to drive a turbine, which in turn drives a compressor to increase the pressure of the air required for combustion, and part is used as a high-velocity jet to provide thrust to drive an aircraft. The jet engine was patented in 1930 in the UK by Sir Frank *Whittle, the first practical Whittle engine powering a Gloster aircraft in 1941. Except for light aircraft, all military and commercial aircraft are now powered by jet engines. Thrust in these engines is equal to the mass of the gas produced multiplied by its acceleration and is due to the forward reaction of the gas jet on the engine itself rather than on the air through which it is flying. It is therefore more efficient at higher altitudes, where the atmosphere is thinner and drag is less.

Early postwar commercial aircraft (e.g. the Vickers Viscount) used a turboprop engine, in which a propeller is driven by the turbine shaft—strictly, therefore, these are not jet engines. For greater speed and economy the turboprop has now been replaced by the turbojet (with reheat) or the turbofan. At over twice the speed of sound (Mach 2), the forward pressure of the air is sufficient for the compressor, and therefore the turbine, to be dispensed with. The resulting engine is called a ramjet or, colloquially, a flying drainpipe. The main drawback of the ramjet is that it needs a rocket-assisted take-off to attain a speed of Mach 2 before it starts to operate. Turboshaft engines, similar to the turboprop, are also in use for driving helicopters, hovercraft, ships, trains, turbogenerators in power stations, and (experimentally) cars. In these the turbine shaft is used to provide all the working power. See also rockets.

Jevons, William Stanley (1835-1882) British economist, logician, and statistician. The best-known economist of his day, Jevons' reputation was established by his writings on contemporary economic questions. His *Theory of Political Economy* (1871) sets out his theory of utility. He also wrote on logic and science.

Jewel, John (1522-71) Anglican churchman. From 1547 a leading Protestant reformer, Jewel fled to the Continent during Queen Mary's reign. As Bishop of Salisbury (1560-71) he defended Anglicanism against both Puritan and Roman Catholic criticisms, most notably in his treatise *Apologia Ecclesiae Anglicanae* (1562).

Jewish autonomous region (*or* Birobidzhan) An autonomous region (*oblast*) in the E Soviet Union, in the RSFSR. Formed in 1934 for Soviet Jews, the harsh climate discouraged settlers, and Russians and Ukrainians outnumber Jews, although there is a Yiddish theatre, newspaper, and broadcasting service. Industries include metallurgy, timber, and engineering. Area: 36 000 sq km (13 895 sq mi). Population (1980 est): 193 400. Capital: Birobidzhan.

Jews A predominantly Semitic people, claiming descent from the ancient Israelites. The Jews spread or were dispersed in antiquity from the land of Israel, and there are now communities in most countries (*see* Ashkenazim; diaspora; Sephardim). Although they do not share distinctive racial characteristics, they have a strong sense of cultural identity (*see* Bene Israel; Falashas). Their religion is *Judaism (but in recent times some Jews have professed an attachment to the people while rejecting the religion). Under Persian, Greek, and Roman rule the Jews gradually evolved a system of internal self-government and communal administration that enabled them to survive as minority communities through many centuries of Christian and Muslim domination, despite adverse discrimination and frequent persecution (*see* antisemitism). Since the late 18th century they have gradually achieved equal rights as citizens in most countries, although the Nazi slaughter of six million Jews in Europe (*see* holocaust) is one of the ugliest episodes in human history. It did, however, provide the Zionist claim for a national home for the Jews with unanswerable force (*see* Israel; Zionism).

Jew's harp A musical instrument consisting of a metal tongue set in a small frame, held between the teeth. The tongue vibrates when plucked; different notes are produced by varying the size of the mouth cavity.

Jezreel, Valley of. See Esdraelon, Plain of.

Jhansi 25 27N 78 34E A city in India, in Uttar Pradesh. The heroism of the Rani (female ruler) of Jhansi during the Indian Mutiny has become legendary in modern Indian history. Primarily an agricultural trading centre, Jhansi also has a steel-rolling mill. Population (1981): 281 000.

Jhelum 32 58N 73 45E A town in Pakistan, on the River Jhelum. It has a thriving timber industry and there are several oilfields in the surrounding district. Population (1981): 106 000.

Jhelum, River A river in India and Pakistan, the most westerly of the five rivers of the Punjab. Rising in Kashmir it flows generally SSW to join the River Chenab. Its lower course is a source of irrigation and hydroelectric power. Length: about 720 km (450 mi).

Jiang Jing Guo *See* Chiang Kai-shek.

Jiang Qing (*or* Chiang Ch'ing; 1912–) Chinese communist politician; the third wife (from 1939) of Mao Tse-tung. A former actress, she attempted with three associates (Zhang Chunjao, Wang Hungwen, and Yao Wenyuan) to seize power on Mao's death. Known as the **Gang of Four**, they were arrested within a month. She remained in prison after a public trial at which she refused to recant.

Jiangsu (Chiang-su *or* Kiangsu) A low-lying province in E China on the Yangtze delta. It is the most densely populated area and one of the richest agricultural regions. It was the centre of European trade after 1842 and was badly damaged by Japanese occupation (1937–45). It produces wheat, rice, tea, cotton, salt, fish, and silk. Area: 102 200 sq km (39 860 sq mi). Population (1980 est): 58 930 000. Capital: Nanjing.

Jiangxi (Chiang-hsi *or* Kiangsi) A mountainous province in SE China. It was a centre of Confucianism (960–1279), and in the 20th century the Communist-Nationalist conflict originated here (*see* Jiangxi Soviet). One of China's main rice-producing areas, it has mineral resources, including coal and uranium, and is known for its porcelain. Area: 164 800 sq km (64 300 sq mi). Population (1980 est): 32 290 000. Capital: Nanchang.

Jiangxi Soviet (*or* Kiangsi Soviet; 1931–34) A communist republic proclaimed in the Chinese province of Jiangxi. It was a revolutionary base from which Mao Tse-tung and *Zhu De were able to build up their forces in the civil war with the *Guomindang under Chiang Kai-shek. They withstood four encirclement campaigns by the Guomindang but in 1933 Chiang Kai-shek launched a massive fifth campaign in response to which Mao evacuated the base and set off on the *Long March.

Jiddah (*or* Jedda) 21 30N 39 10E A town in Saudi Arabia, on the Red Sea coast. It is a modern industrial city and the chief port for Muslim pilgrims to Mecca. The King Abdulaziz University was opened here in 1967. Population (1983): 1 500 000.

Jilin (Chi-lin *or* Kirin) A province in NE China, in Manchuria. The E is mountainous, while the W lies on the fertile Manchurian plain. Soya beans, cereals, timber, and minerals are produced. Area: 187 000 sq km (72 930 sq mi). Population (1980 est): 21 850 000. Capital: Changchun.

Jilong (Chi-lung *or* Keelung) 25 10N 121 43E A port and naval base in N Taiwan. It was developed under Japanese occupation (1895–1945). Industries include fishing, chemicals, coal- and gold-mining, and shipbuilding. Population (1982 est): 348 200.

Jim Crow Laws Legislation passed by southern US states in the late 19th century to enforce racial segregation; the name derives from that of a Black character in a popular song. Legislation in Oklahoma, for example, provided separate telephone booths for Blacks and Whites and in Arkansas separate gambling tables were required. Most of the laws were invalidated by the civil-rights legislation of the 1950s and 1960s.

Jiménez, Juan Ramón (1881–1958) Spanish poet. His early works, such as *Sonetos espirituales* (1915), were influenced by French symbolism but he later developed a pure abstract style in such works as *La estación total* (1946). He also wrote *Platero y yo* (1914), a portrait of a boy and his donkey.

Jimmu The legendary first ruler of Japan. According to the oldest Japanese writings, Jimmu was descended from the sun-goddess Amaterasu and embarked upon the unification of Japan in 660 BC. This legend was intended to glorify the imperial dynasty and anticipated the dynasty's actual establishment by about seven centuries.

jimsonweed. *See* thorn apple.

Jinan (Chi-nan *or* Tsinan) 36 41N 117 00E A city in E China, the capital of Shandong province. A city since the 8th century BC, it is a cultural centre. Industries include textiles, chemicals, and machine building. Population (1983 est): 1 320 000.

jinja A Shinto shrine dedicated to a deity or nature spirit, situated in a place of exceptional natural beauty. It consists of three parts: the *haiden*, a hall where the laity pray and worship; the *heiden*, where religious ceremonies are performed; and the *honden*, the main inner sanctuary usually accessible only to priests. Before the jinja is a sacred gateway. The architecture is simple and traditional. Larger

jinja may incorporate other elements, such as a dance platform, an ablution basin, and animal statues.

Jinja 0 27N 33 14E The second largest city in Uganda, on the N shore of Lake Victoria. Founded by the British (1901), it has developed as an industrial centre since the opening of the Owen Falls Dam (1954) with steel rolling, copper smelting, and other industries. Population (1980 est): 45 060.

Jinjiang (Chen-chiang *or* Chinkiang) 32 15N 119 20E A port in E China, in Jiangsu province at the junction of the Yangtze River and the *Grand Canal. It is a major trading centre, its industries including food processing. Population (1982): 150 000.

Jinmen (Chin-men *or* Quemoy) 24 26N 118 20E A Taiwanese island in Taiwan Strait. It is near the Chinese mainland and was bombed from there in 1958, an event that caused an international incident. Area: 130 sq km (50 sq mi). Population (1982): 57 847.

Jinnah, Mohammed Ali (1876–1948) Indian statesman, who was largely responsible for the creation of Pakistan. Born in Karachi, he studied law in England and embarked on an extremely successful legal practice in India before becoming involved in politics. As a member of both the *Muslim League and the *Indian National Congress he championed Hindu-Muslim unity until 1930, when he resigned from the Congress in opposition to Gandhi's policies. He was president of the League in 1916 and 1920 and from 1934, and came to advocate the establishment of a separate state for Indian Muslims. This was achieved with the creation in 1947 of Pakistan, of which he was the first governor general.

Jiulong (*or* Kowloon) 22 20N 114 15E A port in SE China, on the Jiulong peninsula, opposite Hong Kong island and part of the British colony (ceded 1860). Population (1971): 716 272.

Joachim, Joseph (1831–1907) Hungarian violinist and composer. A child prodigy, he studied with Ferdinand David (1810–73) at the Leipzig conservatoire. His interpretations of Bach and Beethoven and his musical perfectionism influenced many composers: Brahms dedicated his violin concerto to him.

Joachim of Fiore (c. 1132–1202 AD) Italian mystic and abbot. He is best known for his philosophy of history, which divided history into three periods: The Age of the Father (Old Testament), The Age of the Son (New Testament and 42 subsequent generations), and The Age of the Spirit, in which all humanity would be converted. Joachim's monastic order, which he founded at San Giovanni in Fiore, was dissolved in 1505.

Joan, Pope A legendary female pope first referred to in the 13th century. She is said to have been elected pope in male disguise about 1100 or earlier, to have ruled for more than two years, and then to have given birth to a child while in a procession, dying immediately thereafter. The legend may be based on a Roman folktale.

Joanna the Mad (1479–1555) Queen of Castile (1504–16). The death of her husband, Philip the Handsome of Castile in 1506, drove her mad. Her father Ferdinand (V and II) of Aragon ruled for her until his death, when he was succeeded by her son, later Emperor *Charles V. He kept Joanna imprisoned in the castle of Tordesillas, where she died.

Joan of Arc, St (French name: Jeanne d'Arc; c. 1412–31) French patriot, known as the Maid of Orléans, whose courageous military and moral leadership against the English invaders led to a reversal of French fortunes in the *Hundred Years' War. Of peasant origin, she claimed to have been told by Saints Michael, Catherine, and Margaret that it was her divine mission to expel the English from France and enable Charles VII to be crowned. She persuaded Charles to allow her to lead an army to relieve the besieged city of Orléans.

649

John (II) the Good

JOAN OF ARC   *This portrait of the great French heroine dates to 1584.*

Her success resulted in Charles' coronation at Rheims (July, 1429). Other victories followed but she failed to recapture Paris and was subsequently seized by the Burgundians, who sold her to their English allies. They tried her and burned her as a heretic. She was canonized in 1920.

João Pessoa (name until 1930: Paraíba)   7 06S 34 53W A port in E Brazil, the capital of Paraíba state near the mouth of the Rio Paraíba do Norte. The chief exports are cotton, sugar, and coffee. Population (1980): 290 424.

Job   An Old Testament figure. **The Book of Job**, probably written between the .5th and 2nd centuries BC, develops the theme of the suffering of the innocent. Job experiences the loss of his family, property, and health, but adamantly denies his friends' suggestions that sin is the cause of his misfortunes, for he knows himself to be innocent. No final explanation of the dilemma is reached, but Job is brought to see that man cannot understand the ways of God. Humbled by this knowledge, he prays for his friends and is ultimately granted greater prosperity, etc., than he formerly had.

Jocasta.   *See* Oedipus.

Jochho   (d. 1057) Leading Japanese sculptor of the Fujiwara period (*see* Fujiwara style). His serene and refined statues of the Buddha for the Fujiwara family temple and his joined-wood technique were influential.

Jochum, Eugen   (1902–   ) German conductor. He studied piano and organ at the Augsburg conservatoire and has held appointments in Berlin, Hamburg, Munich, and Amsterdam (with the Concertgebouw Orchestra). He was made conductor laureate of the London Symphony Orchestra in 1975.

Jodhpur   26 18N 73 08E A city in India, in Rajasthan. Formerly the capital of the princely state of Jodhpur, the city is noted for its handicraft industries, such as ivory carvings and lacquerware. It also gave its name to a style of riding breeches that were introduced into Britain during the 19th century. Jodhpur University was established in 1962. Population (1981): 494 000.

Jodl, Alfred   (1890–1946) German general, who was responsible for much of German strategy in World War II. He was executed as a war criminal.

Jodrell Bank   The site, at Macclesfield, Cheshire (UK), of the Nuffield Radio Astronomy Laboratories of Manchester University. The principal instrument is the 76.2 m (250 ft) fully steerable radio-telescope dish.

Joel   An Old Testament prophet of Judah. **The Book of Judah** records his prediction of a plague of locusts and other disasters as punishment for Judah's sins, followed eventually by a restoration of God's favour and the nation's final triumph over its enemies.

Joffre, Joseph Jacques Césaire   (1852–1931) French marshal; commander in chief of the French armies (1915–16) in World War I. As chief of staff he won the victory of the Marne (1914) but the French failure at Verdun (1916) led to his resignation. ▯Lloyd George, David, 1st Earl.

Jogjakarta (*or* Djokjakarta)   7 48S 110 24E A city in Indonesia, in S Java. It was the capital of the 1945–49 Indonesian Republic. A cultural centre, its university was established in 1949. It is rich in Buddhist monuments, notably the temple of Borobudur. Population (1980): 398 727.

Johannesburg   26 10S 28 02E The largest city in South Africa, in the Transvaal on the Witwatersrand. It was founded in 1886 following the discovery of gold in the area and developed rapidly as the centre of the gold-mining industry. During the second Boer War it was taken by the British (1900). Today it is a major industrial, commercial, and banking centre containing the South African Stock Exchange (1887). Its industries include engineering, chemicals, diamond cutting, and textiles. Linked to the city is the complex of towns known as *Soweto, inhabited by Black Africans. Johannesburg has a number of cultural and educational institutions, notably the University of Witwatersrand (1922) and the Rand Afrikaans University (1966). The fine Johannesburg Art Gallery (1911) was designed by Sir Edwin Lutyens. Population (1980 est): 1 536 457.

Johannsen, Wilhelm Ludvig   (1857–1927) Danish geneticist, whose work with plants demonstrated that the physical appearance (phenotype) of individuals was the result of the interaction of their hereditary constitution (genotype) and their environment. He also provided supporting evidence for the mutation theory of *de Vries. Johannsen coined the word *gene* for a unit of heredity as well as the terms phenotype and genotype.

John   (1167–1216)   King of England (1199–1216), nicknamed John Lackland; the youngest son of Henry II, he succeeded his brother Richard I. His reign saw the renewal of war with *Philip II Augustus of France, to whom he had lost several continental possessions, including Normandy, by 1205. Struggles with Pope Innocent III over John's objection to the election of *Langton as Archbishop of Canterbury led to the imposition of an interdict over England (1208) and the king's excommunication (1212). He came into conflict with his barons and was forced to grant the *Magna Carta at Runnymede. His subsequent repudiation of the Charter led to the first *Barons' War (1215–17), during which John became ill and died.

John I   (1357–1433) King of Portugal (1385–1433). The head of the military order of Aviz, John led the nationalist opposition to the succession to the Portuguese throne of John I of Castile (1358–90; reigned 1379–90). After securing the throne, John soundly defeated the Castilians at Aljubarrota. In 1415 he captured Ceuta, the first possession of any European nation in Africa.

John I Tzimisces   (925–76 AD) Byzantine emperor (969–76). He increased the power of the Byzantine empire by subjecting the Bulgarians and defeating the Russians (971) and by conquering cities in Syria (974–75).

John (II) the Good   (1319–64) King of France (1350–64), who was taken prisoner by the English at the battle of Poitiers (1356) during the *Hundred Years' War. He remained in captivity in London, where he was forced to sign the unfavourable Treaty of *Brétigny, until 1360. Released in 1360, he was unable to raise the ransom demanded by the English and was forced to return to London, where he died.

John (II) the Perfect (1455-95) King of Portugal (1481-95). John encouraged Portugal's overseas expansion, supporting Bartolomeu Dias, and concluded the Treaty of Tordesillas with Spain (1494), which demarcated their respective fields of action in the New World. His home policies reduced the power of the aristocracy.

John II Casimir (1609-72) King of Poland (1648-68), whose reign is known as the Deluge. John faced a revolt of the Ukrainian Cossacks, on whose behalf Russia invaded Poland in 1654, and in 1667 John Casimir was forced to cede the eastern Ukraine. Sweden's invasion of Poland in 1655 resulted in the loss of N Livonia (1660). John Casimir abdicated and died in France.

John III (1502-57) King of Portugal (1521-57). John's reign saw the flourishing of culture in the works of Camoens and others. Spending his country's wealth on his lavish court (rather than economic development), he was responsible for the start of Portugal's decline.

John III Sobieski (1624-96) King of Poland (1674-96), famous as an adversary of the Turks. A brilliant military commander, John Sobieski was elected king after defeating the Turks at Khotin (1663). In 1683 he saved Vienna from the Turks in the great victory at Kahlenberg. His subsequent failure to conquer Moldavia and Wallachia led to a loss of personal prestige, which aggravated the domestic unrest that was a feature of his reign.

John (IV) the Fortunate (1604-56) King of Portugal (1640-56). As Duke of *Bragança, John led a revolt in 1640 against Spanish rule that brought him to the throne. He revived the Cortes and formed foreign alliances against Spain but lost most of Portugal's Asian possessions to the Dutch.

John VI (?1769-1826) King of Portugal (1816-26), having been prince regent from 1799. John lived in Brazil during Napoleon's occupation of Portugal. Returning to Portugal in 1821, he faced a revolt of the reactionaries against constitutional monarchy, which was only defeated with French and British help. In 1825 John recognized the independence of Brazil, which was ruled by his son *Pedro I.

John XXII (Jacques d'Euse; c. 1249-1334) Pope (1316-34) during the *Avignon papacy, a man of great administrative and financial ability. In 1317 he dissolved the austere group of the *Franciscans known as Spirituals, whose cause was taken up by Emperor Louis IV. Aided by the philosophers Marsilius of Padua and William of Ockham, Louis denounced papal supremacy and in 1328 set up an antipope in Rome. John's last years were dominated by theological disputes.

John XXIII (Baldassare Cossa; d. 1419) Antipope (1410-15), one of three claimants to the papacy during the *Great Schism. In 1414 John summoned the Council of *Constance to end the Schism but fled when it demanded his resignation. He was arrested, imprisoned, and deposed.

John XXIII (Angelo Roncalli; 1881-1963) Pope (1958-1963). A papal diplomat and then patriarch of Venice (1953-58) before his election at the age of 77, John was the most popular and innovative pope of modern times. In 1962 he summoned the second *Vatican Council, which marked the climax of John's pursuit of Church reforms and Christian unity. His best-known encyclical, *Pacem in Terris* (*Peace on Earth*; 1963), advocated reconciliation between the western democracies and eastern communist countries. His diary was published as *The Journal of a Soul* (1965).

John, Augustus (Edwin) (1878-1961) British painter, born in Wales. He studied at the Slade School, London

(1894-98), displaying a precocious drawing talent, and exhibited at the *New English Art Club from 1903. A flamboyantly unconventional character, he travelled widely, often in Gipsy style. His strongly characterized portraits of contemporaries, such as James Joyce and T. E. Lawrence, are indebted to tradition. His sister **Gwen John** (1876-1939) was also a painter.

John, Barry (1945-) Welsh Rugby Union footballer, who played for Llanelli, Cardiff, Wales, and the British Lions. A brilliant fly half, he won 25 international caps and scored a record 180 points for the British Lions against New Zealand (1971).

John, Elton (Reginald Kenneth Dwight; 1947-) British rock pianist and singer, who became popular in Britain and the USA with such songs as "Rocket Man" and "Daniel." He is well known for wearing large and colourful spectacles on stage.

John, St In the New Testament, one of the 12 Apostles, son of Zebedee and brother of James. He was present at a number of events in the life of Jesus as recounted in the Gospels and is also thought to be the anonymous disciple "whom Jesus loved" present at the crucifixion. Tradition states that he escaped martyrdom and died at Ephesus. Feast day: 27 Dec.

The Gospel according to St John is the fourth book of the New Testament traditionally ascribed to St John and probably written in the late 1st century AD. It is markedly different in a number of details from the other three synoptic Gospels and was specifically written with the intention of inspiring faith in Jesus as the Son of God. It begins with a prologue portraying Jesus as the *Logos* or Word, a theme familiar to current Greek philosophy. Having spoken of his incarnation, it concentrates on his public ministry and especially on claims made in a number of discourses and conversations not recorded in the other Gospels. Over half the book is devoted to the events and teaching occurring during the last week before the crucifixion.

The Epistles of John are three New Testament books traditionally ascribed to St John and written towards the end of the 1st century. The first is addressed to the Churches at large and defines the distinctive marks of a true Christian. The others are brief personal letters. The second warns an unnamed lady against false teachers, while the third commends and encourages a certain Gaius. Tradition also ascribes the Book of *Revelation to John.

John Birch Society A right-wing group in the USA, founded in 1958. John Birch was a US Army intelligence officer who was killed by the Communist Chinese in August, 1945, and is represented by the Society as the first hero of the *Cold War.

John Bull The personification of England or the English national character. The character first appeared in *The History of John Bull* (1712) by John Arbuthnot, and was popularized in 18th- and 19th-century political cartoons. He is usually portrayed as a stocky countryman noted for his honesty and stubbornness.

John Dory (*or* dory) A fish of the family *Zeidae*, found worldwide in moderately deep marine waters. It has a round narrow body with deep sides, each having a black spot surrounded by a yellow ring, and spiny-rayed fins extended into filaments. *Zeus faber*, up to 90 cm long, is a food fish of the Atlantic and Mediterranean. Order: *Zeiformes*.

John Frederick (I) the Magnanimous (1503-54) Elector of Saxony (1532-47), who led the Protestant Schmalkaldic League against Emperor *Charles V. John Frederick was imprisoned (1547-52) after the League's defeat at the battle of Mühlberg and was deprived of his territory and electoral rank.

John of Austria, Don (1545-78) Spanish soldier. The illegitimate son of Emperor *Charles V, his half-brother *Philip II entrusted him with major military commands. He suppressed the revolt of the Moriscos (Moors converted to Christianity) in S Spain in 1569 and in 1571 he commanded the combined fleets of Spain, Venice, and the papacy against the Turks, winning a great victory at *Lepanto. In 1573 he conquered Tunis and in 1576 became governor general of the Netherlands, where he died.

John of Damascus, St (c. 675–c. 749 AD) Greek Orthodox theologian and Doctor of the Church, born in Damascus. While a tax official at the caliph's court at Damascus he wrote several treatises defending the use of images in church worship against *iconoclasm. In about 716 he retired to a monastery near Jerusalem, where he was ordained. There he wrote his most influential work, *The Fount of Wisdom*, which deals with philosophy, heresies, and the Orthodox faith. Feast day: 27 March.

John of Gaunt (1340–99) The fourth son of Edward III of England, born at Ghent; Duke of Lancaster from 1362. After a distinguished career in the *Hundred Years' War he assumed an increasingly important role in domestic government during the senility of Edward and the minority of Richard II. Never popular, John, who supported *Wycliffe and the *Lollards, was opposed by a clerical group led by *William of Wykeham. From 1386 to 1389 he attempted without success to realize his claim, through his second wife Constance, the daughter of *Pedro the Cruel, to Castile. In 1396 he married his mistress Catherine Swynford, and in 1397 their descendants were legitimized but excluded from the royal succession. They included Margaret *Beaufort, the mother of Henry VII.

John of Leiden (Jan Beuckelszoon; 1509–36) Dutch *Anabaptist leader. In 1534 he pronounced himself King of Münster, an Anabaptist stronghold in Germany that had expelled its civil and religious authorities. During his brief rule he legalized polygamy and made property communal. The town was recaptured in 1535 and he was executed.

John of Luxembourg (1296–1346) Count of Luxembourg (1310–46) and, by marriage, King of Bohemia (1311–46); son of Emperor Henry VII. His almost constant warfare and consequent levy of high taxes made him unpopular in Bohemia. He died at Crécy fighting for the French.

John of Nepomuk, St (c. 1340–93) The patron saint of Bohemia. As vicar general of Prague, he opposed Wenceslas IV's plans to create a second bishopric in the city. At the king's instigation he was tortured and drowned. Feast day: 16 May.

John of Salisbury (c. 1115–80) English churchman, philosopher, and a leading classical scholar of his age. After studying in Paris under *Abelard he became secretary to Thomas Becket and later Bishop of Chartres (1176). His principal works are the *Polycraticus*, a treatise criticizing contemporary political and courtly life, and the *Metalogicon*, a defence of the study of grammar, logic, and rhetoric.

John of the Cross, St (Juan de Yepes y Alvarez; 1542–91) Spanish mystic, poet, and since 1926 Doctor of the Church. With St *Teresa he founded the Discalced *Carmelites, a reformed branch of the Carmelite order. His poems, which include *Cántico espiritual* and *Noche oscura del alma*, are regarded as the finest examples of Spanish mystical literature. Feast day: 24 Nov.

John O'Groats 58 39N 3 02W A village at the NE tip of Scotland, site of the house of John de Groot, a 16th-century Dutch immigrant. John O'Groats is 970 km (603 mi) in a straight line from Land's End, Cornwall.

John Paul II (Karol Wojtyła; 1920–) Pope (1978–). A Pole, he is the first non-Italian pope since 1522. He taught at Lublin and Kraków Universities before becoming Archbishop of Kraków (1964). He has outspokenly defended the Church in communist countries and has condemned the politicization of the Church. His visits to Poland (1979 and 1987) made him the first pope to go to a communist state. In 1981 he survived an assassination attempt. Extensive over-

JOHN PAUL II   *At the Jasna Góra monastery, Częstochowa, during his 1979 visit to Poland. The monastery, a famous place of pilgrimage, contains the image of the Virgin known as The Black Madonna.*

seas tours have not always been popular. In Holland in 1985 he was booed for his condemnation of homosexuality and his uncompromising position on contraception, abortion, and a celibate clergy. He succeeded **John Paul I** (Albino Luciani; 1912–78; reigned August–September, 1978), who took the names of his two predecessors, John XXIII and Paul VI, thus symbolizing his desire to combine the charismatic and intellectual qualities for which they were respectively known.

Johns, Jasper (1930–) US artist, who was a major influence on *pop art. He worked as a commercial artist before establishing his reputation at a one-man show in New York (1958) with paintings of targets and flags. The collages and constructions that followed made a similar use of everyday objects, for example the bronze *Beer Cans* (1960).

Johnson, Amy (1903–41) British aviator. She established several long-distance records with her solo flights to Australia in 1930, to Tokyo in 1932, and to the Cape of Good Hope and back in 1936. In 1932 she married Jim Mollison (1905–59), another pilot, with whom she flew the Atlantic in 1936. She was killed in an air crash near London.

Johnson, Andrew (1808–75) US statesman; Democratic president (1865–69), who saw himself as a spokesman for ordinary people. He became president after Lincoln's assassination. Despite his veto, the largely Republican Congress passed *Reconstruction measures after the Civil War ensuring Republican domination of the South. Impeachment proceedings were begun when Johnson defied the Tenure of Office Act limiting presidential power but he was acquitted.

Johnson, Cornelius (Janssen van Ceulen; 1593–1661) English portrait painter, born in London of Dutch parents. Until Van Dyck's arrival (1632), Johnson was the leading portraitist at the courts of James I and Charles I, where he specialized in oval-shaped bust portraits. He settled in Holland in 1643.

Johnson, Lyndon Baines (1908–73) US statesman; Democratic president (1963–69). A Texan, he succeeded to the presidency after Kennedy's assassination. His Great Society programme initiated broad social reform including a tax-reduction Act to stimulate economic growth and various civil-rights Acts. He became unpopular for increasing US military involvement in the *Vietnam War.

Johnson, Samuel (1709-84) British poet, critic, and lexicographer. He left Oxford without taking a degree, married a wealthy widow in 1735, and went to London in 1737. His early publications include a biography of his friend Richard *Savage (1744) and a long didactic poem, *The Vanity of Human Wishes* (1749). From 1750 to 1752 he produced the weekly *Rambler* almost single handed. His *Dictionary* appeared in 1755 after nine years' work and was well received, but he still relied on hackwork for money, writing *Rasselas* (1759), a moral fable, in a week to pay for his mother's funeral. His last major works were an edition of Shakespeare (1765) and his *Lives of the Poets* (1779-81). From the early 1760s he enjoyed the security of a pension and the friendship of Reynolds, Goldsmith, Burke, and other men of letters, including his biographer *Boswell, who met him first in 1763 and became a close friend in the 1770s. His last years were clouded by the deaths of friends and his estrangement from his companion, Mrs Thrale (*see* Piozzi, Hester Lynch).

Johnson, Virginia Eshelman. *See* Masters, William Howell.

John the Baptist, St In the New Testament, the son of a priest, Zacharias, and Elizabeth, a relative of the Virgin *Mary; known as the "Forerunner of Christ". Born in his mother's old age, he was six months older than Jesus. After living in the desert, he began about 27 AD preaching on the banks of the River Jordan, urging repentance and baptism because of the imminent approach of the Kingdom of God (Matthew 3.2). He baptized Christ, recognizing him as the Messiah. He was beheaded by *Herod Antipas, at the request of *Salome, for denouncing his second marriage to Herodias as illicit. Feast days: 24 June (birth); 29 Aug (beheading).

John the Fearless (1371-1419) Duke of Burgundy (1404-19), a great military leader who earned his nickname on a Crusade in 1396. He competed with the Armagnacs for control over the mad Charles the Well-Beloved of France and arranged the assassination (1407) of their leader (and his cousin) Louis, Duc d'Orléans. His own death, however, was at the hands of an Armagnac assassin.

Johor A swampy forested state in S Peninsular Malaysia. It is economically linked to Singapore, depending on it for trading facilities and supplying it with water. Chief products are rubber, copra, pineapples, palm oil, tin, and bauxite. Area: 18 958 sq km (7330 sq mi). Population (1980): 1 601 504. Capital: Johor Baharu.

Johor Baharu 1 29N 103 44E A city in S Peninsular Malaysia, the capital of Johor state. A trading centre with a notable sultan's residence, it is linked to Singapore by a causeway across the Johor Strait. Population (1980): 249 880.

joint The point at which two or more bones are connected to each other. There are three broad categories. Immovable joints allow no movement of the bones; examples are the sutures between the bones of the skull. Slightly movable joints allow a certain degree of movement, as in the joints connecting the individual bones of the spine. Freely movable joints (diarthrodial, or synovial, joints) permit a variety of movements. They include the hinge joints at the knee and elbow, the ball-and-socket joints at the hip and shoulder, and the gliding joints at the wrist and ankle. The bone ends at movable joints are covered by *cartilage and enveloped in a tough capsule thickened in parts to form *ligaments. The inside of the capsule is lined by synovial membrane, which secretes a lubricating fluid. *See* Plate IV.

Joinville, Jean de (c. 1224-1317) French chronicler. His record of the seventh Crusade (1248-54), on which he accompanied Louis IX and shared his captivity, constitutes the main part of his *Histoire de Saint Louis*. His work is noted for its vivid descriptions and its honesty and human sympathy.

Joliot, Frédéric, and Irène Joliot-Curie. *See* Curie, Marie.

Jolliet, Louis. *See* Marquette, Jacques.

Jolson, Al (Asa Yoelson; 1886-1950) US popular singer and songwriter, born in Russia. He sang in circuses, vaudevilles, and minstrel shows, becoming famous for his blacked-up face and the song "Mammy." In 1927 he appeared in the first full-length sound film *The Jazz Singer* and subsequently made the films *The Singing Fool* (1928) and *Swanee River* (1940).

Jonah (8th century BC) An Old Testament figure. The Book of Jonah was probably written after the *Babylonian exile of the Jews. It relates how Jonah was commanded by God to preach to the Gentiles in Nineveh, the Assyrian capital. Attempting to escape this task, he fled by ship, but was thrown overboard, swallowed by a great fish (probably a whale), and after three days was safely cast ashore. He repented of his disobedience and fulfilled God's commandment. The purpose of the story was to emphasize that God was the God of the Gentiles as well as the Jews.

Jones, (Alfred) Ernest (1879-1958) British psychoanalyst. A follower and friend of Sigmund *Freud, Jones helped to establish psychoanalysis in Britain and North America. He wrote many papers, especially on the psychology of literary works, including a famous analysis of *Hamlet* in *Hamlet and Oedipus* (1949). In 1920 he founded the *International Journal of Psychoanalysis* and he also wrote *Sigmund Freud: Life and Work* (3 vols, 1953-56).

Jones, Bobby (Robert Tyre J.; 1902-71) US amateur golfer. Between 1923 and 1930 he won four US and three British Open championships, five US amateur championships, and one British amateur championship. In 1930 he won all four championships, after which he entered no more competitions.

Jones, Daniel (1881-1967) British phonetician. His most influential work was the description (or prescription) of "Received Pronunciation"—the socially prestigious dialect of English spoken especially in public schools and the BBC. It is set out in his *English Pronouncing Dictionary* (1917) frequently revised since its first publication. He also established a system of cardinal vowels, by reference to which individual variations may be described.

Jones, Daniel (1912-85) Welsh composer. His large output contains symphonies, chamber music, and a sonata for three kettledrums (1947).

Jones, David (1895-1974) Anglo-Welsh writer and artist. His major writings, combining prose and free verse, dense with allusions to Anglo-Welsh history and folklore, Arthurian legend, and Christian symbolism, are *In Parenthesis* (1937), based on his experience of World War I, and *The Anathemata* (1952).

Jones, Henry. *See* Cavendish.

Jones, Inigo (1573-1652) English classical architect. He was closely associated with the courts of James I and Charles I, for whom he designed masques and many major buildings. One of the first Englishmen to study architecture in Italy and to understand the rules of classicism, Jones was particularly influenced by *Palladio in his two best-known buildings, the Queen's House, Greenwich (1616-35), and the Banqueting Hall, Whitehall (1619-22). His career effectively ended with the outbreak of the Civil War in 1642, and his style only became strongly influential in England in the 18th century, when it was adopted by Lord *Burlington and others.

Jones, Jack (James Larkin J.; 1913-) British trade unionist; general secretary of the Transport and General Workers' Union (1968-78) and a member of the TUC general council (1968-78).

Jones, John Paul (1747-92) American naval commander, born in Scotland. He went to America after working in mercantile shipping and on the outbreak of the American Revolution was commissioned into the American navy

(1775). Jones captured and sank a number of ships in American and British waters (1776, 1778). In 1779 in the *Bon Homme Richard* Jones defeated the British frigate *Serapis* in a desperate battle lasting almost four hours. He subsequently became a rear admiral in the Russian navy, fighting in the Black Sea against the Turks (1788–89).

Jones, LeRoi (1934–) US dramatist and poet. In *Dutchman* (1964) and other plays and volumes of poetry he deals with social relationships between Blacks and Whites in the USA. As a leading Black editor and publisher he has encouraged many other Black writers. He changed his name to Imamu Baraka to emphasize his identity with his Black heritage and culture.

Jones, Sir William (1746–94) British jurist, linguist, and orientalist. He was a supreme-court judge in Calcutta (1783–94) and published a Persian grammar (1771). He is noted for his observation in 1786 that the resemblances between Sanskrit, Latin, Greek, Gothic, Persian, and Celtic languages might be accounted for by their common descent from an earlier language, now lost. This insight inaugurated the study of *Indo-European languages.

Jongkind, Johan Barthold (1819–91) Dutch landscape painter and etcher, who settled in Paris in 1846. He was influenced by the Dutch landscape tradition but the atmospheric effects he achieved in his seascapes and watercolours anticipate *impressionism.

Jönköping 57 45N 14 10E A town in S Sweden, at the S end of Lake Vättern. Its manufactures include matches, paper, textiles, footwear, and machinery. Population (1982 est): 107 134.

jonquil. *See* Narcissus.

Jonson, Ben (1572–1637) English dramatist and poet. In *Every Man in His Humour* (1598) he introduced the "comedy of humours," each character being driven by a particular obsession. Other major satirical plays include *Volpone* (1606), *The Alchemist* (1610), and *Bartholomew Fair* (1614). In collaboration with Inigo *Jones he produced many court masques. He also published two collections of poems and translations. Ranked above Shakespeare in the 17th century, Jonson based his finest work on classical principles and influenced a number of younger poets known as "the Tribe of Ben." He is buried in Westminster Abbey.

Joplin, Scott (1868–1917) US Black pianist and composer of *ragtime music. One of the first to write down such music, Joplin is remembered for his skilful syncopation in such rags as "Maple Leaf Rag" and "The Entertainer." The revival of the latter, in the film *The Sting* (1973), sparked off a renewed interest in Joplin's music. His ragtime operas *A Guest of Honour* (1903), now lost, and *Treemonisha* (1907) were failures and Joplin, having known success, died in an asylum in poverty.

Jordaens, Jakob (1593–1678) Flemish painter, born in Antwerp. Although he painted numerous religious altarpieces, influenced by *Rubens, he is best known for his allegorical and everyday scenes of merrymaking peasants, such as *The King Drinks* (Brussels). His commissions from the House of Orange included murals for their country house near The Hague.

Jordan, Dorothy (1761–1816) British actress. She was a brilliant comic actress and her first London appearance in *The Country Girl* at Drury Lane in 1785 was a popular success. She became mistress of the Duke of Clarence, the future William IV, and bore him ten children.

Jordan, Hashemite Kingdom of A country in the Middle East, its only sea outlet being on the tip of the Gulf of Aqaba. It is mainly desert but more fertile in the W and N, where the population is concentrated. The people are Arab, and most are Sunnite Muslims, with Christian and other minorities. *Economy*: Jordan's major industries are the extraction and some processing of phosphates, which are exported from Aqaba and also used locally in fertilizers. Agriculture is concentrated in the irrigated Jordan Valley.

JORDAN *Camels on the Gulf of Aqaba, the country's only sea outlet.*

Produce includes cereals, vegetables, wool, and such fruit as melons and olives. Potash from the shore of the Dead Sea is also exploited and some copper is mined. *History*: the area that is now Jordan appears to have flourished in the Bronze Age and was part of the Roman Empire by 64 BC. It was controlled by Arabs from the 7th century, Crusaders in the 11th and 12th centuries, and Turks from the 16th century until 1916, when the part E of the River Jordan was named Transjordan and a League of Nations mandate for its control was given to the UK. It became an independent kingdom in 1946 and was named the Hashemite Kingdom of Jordan in 1949. In the Arab-Israeli War of 1948–49, Jordan overran the *West Bank, but it was occupied by Israel in the Six-Day War of 1967. Palestinians, many of whom were refugees from the West Bank, then began raids on Israel from the East Bank; they were, however, subdued by Jordanian forces in the civil war of 1970–71 to avoid Israeli retaliation against Jordan. This brought Jordan into disfavour with other Arab states, which was only temporarily alleviated by Jordanian participation in the Arab-Israeli War of 1973. Under Arab pressure, Jordan has recognized the *Palestine Liberation Organization as the body entitled to govern the West Bank. The present monarch, King Hussein, succeeded to the throne in 1952. Prime minister: Ahmad Ubdayat (1938–). Official·language: Arabic. Official currency: Jordanian dinar of 1000 fils. Area: about 97 740 sq km (37 738 sq mi), including the West Bank. Population (1983 est): 3 436 000, including the West Bank. Capital: Amman.

Jordan, River A river in the Middle East. It rises in Syria and Lebanon and flows due S through the Sea of Galilee, finally entering the Dead Sea. It forms for some of its course part of the border between Israel and Jordan. Length: 320 km (199 mi).

Jos 9 54N 8 53E A city in central Nigeria. It developed following the discovery of tin (1903); tinmining remains important and it is the world's chief source of the mineral columbite. It has a university (founded 1975). Population (1983 est): 149 000.

Joselito (José Gómez; 1895–1920) Spanish matador, regarded as one of the greatest. At 17, he was the youngest ever to qualify; together with *Belmonte, he introduced the current style of fighting, working very close to the bull. He died in the ring.

Joseph, Sir Keith (Sinjohn) (1918–) British Conservative politician; secretary of state for industry (1979–81); secretary of state for education and science (1981–86). He entered parliament in 1956, becoming minister of housing and local government (1962-64) and for social services (1970-74).

Joseph, Père (François le Clerc du Tremblay; 1577-1638) French Franciscan friar and diplomat, known as the Éminence Grise (Grey Eminence), who as Richelieu's secretary (from 1611) became an active proponent of French participation against Protestant forces in the Thirty Years' War.

Joseph, St In the New Testament, the husband of the Virgin *Mary. He was a devout Jew belonging to the line of David but worked humbly as a carpenter. He eventually settled in Nazareth. *Jesus grew up there and remained in his house for at least 12 years. He was certainly dead by the time of the crucifixion. Feast day: 19 March.

Joseph II (1741-90) Holy Roman Emperor (1765-90), ruling with his mother *Maria Theresa until 1780. As sole ruler, Joseph, an enlightened despot (*see* Enlightenment), introduced religious freedom and reforms in education, law (issuing a legal code in 1786), and administration, and emancipated the serfs. His sweeping reforms encountered some opposition, especially in Hungary and the Austrian Netherlands, and his attempt to subject church to state involved the dissolution of over 700 monasteries and much hardship for monks.

Joséphine (1763-1814) The wife (1796-1809) of Napoleon Bonaparte and Empress of the French from 1804. Her first husband was Alexandre, Vicomte de *Beauharnais, who was guillotined in the French Revolution. She presided over a brilliant court until divorced by Napoleon because of their childlessness.

Joseph of Arimathea, St In the New Testament, a man described as a councillor. He asked Pontius Pilate for the body of Christ after the crucifixion and arranged for its burial on the same day. According to medieval legend, he came to England after the crucifixion, bringing with him the *Holy Grail, and built the first English church, at Glastonbury. Feast day: 17 March.

Josephson, Brian David (1940-   ) British physicist, who shared the 1973 Nobel Prize for his work on tunnelling effects in superconductors and semiconductors. He discovered that when two superconductors are separated by a thin dielectric an oscillating current is set up if a steady potential difference is applied between them (Josephson effect).

Josephus, Flavius (Joseph ben Mattityahu; c. 38-c. 100 AD) Jewish historian and apologist. During the Jewish revolt of 66 AD against the Romans he helped organize the defence of Galilee, but was captured and subsequently accompanied *Vespasian to Rome. Here he wrote his surviving works: a history of the Jewish war, a history of the Jews from the creation up to the war, a defence of Judaism (*Against Apion*), and an autobiography.

Joshua In the Old Testament, the successor of Moses as leader of the Israelites in the period shortly after the *Exodus. **The Book of Joshua**, which follows Deuteronomy in the Old Testament, relates the history of the Israelites between the death of Moses and the death of Joshua. It describes the invasion and conquest of Canaan (Palestine) and its division among the 12 tribes. Among the well-known episodes in the narrative are the Israelites' miraculous crossing of the River Jordan and the capture of Jericho, the walls of which collapsed at the blast of the Israelites' trumpets.

Joshua tree A treelike plant, *Yucca brevifolia*, native to desert regions of the SW USA. Growing to a height of more than 10 m, its branching stem can assume unusual shapes: the name is said to derive from its supposed resemblance to the prophet Joshua extending his arms in blessing. It has stiff sword-shaped leaves and bears waxy white flowers in dense clusters at the tips of the branches.

Josquin des Prez (c. 1450-1521) Flemish composer. A pupil of Ockeghem, he served at the courts of Milan, Ferrara, and Rome and sang in the papal choir between 1486 and 1494. He was choirmaster at Cambrai Cathedral from 1495 to 1499. His compositions were either elaborately contrapuntal or expressively homophonic; they include masses, motets, and chansons.

Jotunheimen A mountain range in S central Norway. It rises to 2472 m (8110 ft) at Glittertinden, the highest mountain in the country.

Joubert, Piet (Petrus Jacobus J.; 1831-1900) Afrikaner general and politician. He commanded the Transvaal's forces in the first *Boer War and negotiated the consequent *Pretoria Convention, which restored independence to the Transvaal. He became vice president (1883) and supported the English-speaking people against the dominance of the Afrikaners. He also held command at the start of the second Boer War.

joule (J) The *SI unit of work or energy equal to the work done when the point of application of a force of one newton moves through a distance of one metre. Named after James *Joule.

Joule, James Prescott (1818-89) British physicist, who performed a series of experiments during the 1840s to determine the mechanical equivalent of heat. His result, announced in 1847, attracted little attention at first but, supported by Lord *Kelvin, his work greatly contributed towards *Helmholtz's formulation of the law of conservation of energy. He also investigated the heating effect of an electric current (*see* Joule's law) and, with Lord Kelvin, discovered the fall in temperature that occurs when a gas expands adiabatically (*see* Joule-Kelvin effect). The unit of energy is named after him.

Joule-Kelvin effect (*or* Joule-Thomson effect) The change in temperature of a gas when it is expanded adiabatically. In most gases it produces a cooling as energy is needed to overcome the attractive forces between molecules when the gas is expanded. The effect is utilized in *refrigeration and in the *liquefaction of gases. It was discovered by James *Joule and William Thomson (later Lord *Kelvin).

Joule's law A law formulated by James *Joule describing the rate at which a resistance in an electrical circuit converts energy into heat. The heat energy produced per second (in watts) equals the product of the resistance (in ohms) and the square of the current (in amperes).

journalism The gathering, writing, and publication or broadcasting of news. Journalism developed together with *newspapers and *periodicals and its modern origins lie in the 17th century. Most early English journalists were essentially propagandists for political parties, although a campaign for freedom from government control was hotly fought throughout the 18th century. The role of journalists became that of objective reporters and investigators only after newspapers became independent of direct political control in the mid-19th century, a period that saw the work of some of the most celebrated journalists, including Sir Henry Morton *Stanley and William Howard *Russell. The late 19th century saw the introduction of sensational journalism (the "yellow" press) in the USA, which greatly increased circulation. The first academic courses providing training in journalism were established around the beginning of the 20th century. Awareness of the social responsibilities of journalists and the new specialized demands of radio and television broadcasting increased this trend towards professionalism. *See also* Press Council.

Jouvet, Louis (1887-1951) French actor and theatre director. As a director of the Comédie Française from 1936, he directed the first productions of most of the plays of Jean *Giraudoux and gave notable performances in productions of Molière. He published *Réflexions du comédien* in 1939.

Jovian, Flavius (c. 331-64 AD) Roman emperor (363-64). He served with the emperor *Julian the Apostate in

Persia. After Julian's death (363), Jovian was named emperor by the army. He made an unpopular peace with the Persians and died before his return to Constantinople.

Jowett, Benjamin (1817-93) British theologian and classical scholar. Jowett's *Epistles of St Paul* (1855) provoked a storm of theological prejudice from the Anglican establishment, which regarded biblical criticism as tantamount to heresy. His classical works include the translation of Plato's *Dialogues* (1871). Master of Balliol College at Oxford from 1870, he was called "the great tutor" and was renowned for his kindness to undergraduates.

Joyce, James (1882-1941) Irish novelist and poet. After a distinguished student career at a Jesuit college, Joyce graduated from University College, Dublin, in 1902, having decided to devote himself to writing. Accompanied by Nora Barnacle (whom he did not marry until 1931), he left Ireland in 1904, living first in Trieste (until 1915) and later in Zurich during World War I and Paris (1920-40). *Dubliners* (1914), a volume of short stories, was followed by the semiautobiographical novel *Portrait of the Artist as a Young Man* (1916). In 1922 he published *Ulysses*, a stream-of-consciousness epic portraying a single day in the lives of several Dubliners. He carried linguistic experiment to further extremes in *Finnegans Wake* (1939), a dream recounted in puns and word play. Joyce died in Zurich.

Joyce, William (1906-46) Nazi broadcaster, known as Lord Haw-Haw. Born in the USA of Irish parents, he became a supporter of the British fascist Sir Oswald *Mosley and in 1939, having obtained a British passport, went to Germany. He broadcast Nazi propaganda to Britain throughout World War II and was subsequently tried as a British subject for treason and executed.

JP. *See* justice of the peace.

Juan Carlos (1938-) King of Spain (1975-). The grandson of Alfonso XIII, he was designated heir to the throne by Francisco *Franco and became king when he died, presiding over Spain's peaceful transition to democracy. In 1962 he married Sophia (1938-), daughter of King Paul of Greece.

Juan de Fuca Strait A strait between *Vancouver Island (SW Canada) and the Olympic Peninsula (USA), linking the Pacific Ocean to Puget Sound and Georgia Strait.

Juan Fernández Islands A Chilean group of three volcanic islands, in the S Pacific Ocean. Alexander Selkirk, who inspired Daniel Defoe's *Robinson Crusoe* (1719), lived on the largest island Más-a-Tierra (1704-09). Area: about 180 sq km (70 sq mi).

Juantorena, Alberto (1951-) Cuban middle-distance runner, who in the 1976 Olympic Games set a world record for the 800 metres and ran the 400 metres in 44.26 seconds, the fastest nonaltitude time.

Juárez. *See* Ciudad Juárez.

Juárez, Benito (Pablo) (1806-72) Mexican statesman, who was the first Indian president of Mexico (1861-65, 1867-72). He became acting president in 1857 but was forced by conservative opposition to flee from Mexico City. In 1861 he returned and was elected president, winning popularity by nationalizing ecclesiastical property. He led the successful opposition (1864-67) to the French invasion (*see* Maximilian) and was re-elected president in 1867 and 1871, dying in office.

Juba, River A river in East Africa. Rising in S central Ethiopia, it flows S across Somalia to enter the Indian Ocean near Kismayu. Length: 1660 km (1030 mi).

Jubbulpore. *See* Jabalpur.

Juchen Nomadic tribes that originated in the area N of Korea and around the Liaodong peninsula. The Juchen became especially powerful in *Song times, when they founded their own dynasty (1122-1234) modelled on the Chinese system of government.

Judaea The southern division of ancient Palestine. The Old Testament kingdom of Judah survived Syrian, Assyrian, and Philistine attacks following Solomon's death but came to an end after conquest by *Nebuchadnezzar II of Babylon, when its capital, Jerusalem, was destroyed (586 BC) and the Jews were exiled. Judaea came next under Persian domination, when the Jews were allowed to return and rebuild Jerusalem, but under the Seleucids Antiochus IV Epiphanes' desecration of the temple in 167 BC instigated the *Maccabees' revolt. Judaea achieved a shortlived independence until the Roman conquest in 63 BC. After years of unrest the Roman province of Syria absorbed it in 135 AD.

Judah ha-Levi (*or* Halevy; c. 1075-1141) Jewish poet and philosopher. He was born and spent most of his life in Spain, living in both Christian (Toledo) and Muslim (Cordoba) centres, where he practised as a physician. Some 1100 of his poems, on religious and secular subjects, are extant and he is considered one of the greatest of Jewish poets and the most important one to emerge from medieval Arabic culture. His major prose work, *Sefer ha-Kuzari*, is a philosophical dialogue on Judaism and the nature of religious truth. According to tradition, he left Spain in the last year of his life on a pilgrimage to Jerusalem; he was enthusiastically received by the Jews of Alexandria and Cairo but died before reaching the Holy Land.

Judah, tribe of One of the 12 *tribes of Israel. It claimed descent from Judah, the son of Jacob and Leah, and occupied territory W of the Dead Sea, which included Jerusalem and Bethlehem. It became the royal house of David in fulfilment of Jacob's dying prophecy. After the division of Israel (*see* Ten Lost Tribes of Israel), it formed with the tribe of *Benjamin the southern kingdom of Judah.

Judaism The religion of the *Jews. Its fundamental tenet is trust in a single, eternal, invisible God, who created the world and desires its welfare. Man's duty is to serve God, with all his being. Judaism's most sacred text is the *Torah, which, according to tradition, contains not only a record of history and revealed law but a complete guide to human life and the mysteries of the universe. Judaism has no official creed and no central authority; it lays stress on right behaviour (*see* halakhah) rather than on doctrine.

There is no agreement as to when Judaism began. Tradition attaches importance to the early figures of *Abraham and *Moses, but many of the characteristic ideas and institutions emerged during the *Babylonian exile and the period of the Second *Temple. After the destruction of the temple the *rabbis codified and elaborated the traditional teachings (*see* Midrash; Mishnah; Talmud), and in the middle ages philosophy and the *kabbalah exerted a great influence. The modern enlightenment (*see* Haskalah) undermined traditional values and gave rise to several conflicting movements. Orthodox Judaism asserts the supernatural authority of Torah and halakhah, which is challenged by *Reform Judaism. Conservative Judaism and Reconstructionism, which are strongest in the USA, attempt to reach a compromise between these extreme views.

Judas tree A shrub or small tree of the genus *Cercis* (7 species), also called redbud, native to S Europe, Asia, and North America, and cultivated for ornament. The pinkish-red clusters of flowers appear before the heart-shaped leaves have opened. The name is used particularly for *C. siliquastrum*, from which Judas Iscariot is said to have hanged himself. Family: *Leguminosae*.

Jude, St In the New Testament, one of the 12 Apostles. He is generally identified with Thaddeus and also known as Judas Thaddeus. Referred to as "Judas of James," he was probably the brother of *James ("the Lord's brother") and therefore a half-brother of Jesus. According to tradition he was martyred in Persia with St *Simon, whose feast is held on the same day. Feast day: 28 Oct.

The Epistle of Jude in the New Testament is ascribed to

him. Of uncertain date, it is a brief warning against certain immoral teachers who were currently infiltrating the Church.

judge An officer who decides legal disputes and passes sentence on offenders. In England and Wales judges try cases in the House of Lords (the Lords of Appeal in Ordinary, or law lords), the Court of Appeal (the Lords Justices), the High Court of Justice (high-court judges), the Crown Court (high-court judges and circuit judges), and County Courts (circuit judges). A judge is appointed by the Crown on the recommendation of the Lord Chancellor (*see* chancellor; Lord Chief Justice; Master of the Rolls) and must be a barrister (or in some cases a *solicitor) of at least ten years' standing. (A part-time recorder, who must also be a solicitor or barrister of ten years' standing, may be appointed to serve in the Crown Court; a *justice of the peace or stipendiary magistrate serves in Magistrates' Courts.)

A judge is not answerable for anything he says or does in his judicial capacity unless he exceeds his jurisdiction. He can only be removed from office for bad behaviour on the recommendation of both Houses of Parliament. *See also* courts of law.

Judges An Old Testament book of unknown authorship, but ascribed by Jewish tradition to Samuel. It covers the history of the Israelites from the death of Joshua to shortly before the commencement of the monarchy under Saul (11th century BC). The book introduces a philosophy of history in which God repeatedly causes nations to oppress Israel, as punishment for its apostasy, and then delivers it through the "judges" or virtuous leaders, such as Gideon and Samson, each time it repents.

Judith A Jewish widow who deceived and assassinated a general of Nebuchadnezzar's invading army and thus caused the Assyrian army to flee from her home city. The incident is recorded in the **Book of Judith**, a book of the *Apocrypha. Its purpose was probably to inspire Jewish resistance to the policy of *Antiochus IV Epiphanes.

JUDO *Black-belt contestants compete in judo championships.*

judo An international form of wrestling developed from *jujitsu in Japan by Jigoro Kano (1860–1938). It was included in the Olympic Games for the first time in 1964. Contestants wear kimonos and belts to indicate their proficiency. The six *kyu* (pupil) grades wear white, yellow, orange, green, blue, or brown belts in order of increasing skill, the 12 *dan* (master) grades all wear black belts. Contests take place on a mat 9 m (30 ft) square and usually last two to ten minutes. The contestants score points by executing prescribed throws, ground holds, and locks. Balance, speed, surprise, and the ability to use an opponent's strength characterize the skilful judoka. *See also* martial arts.

Jugendstil The German equivalent of the *Art Nouveau style. Named after the magazine *Jugend* (*Youth*), which was first published in 1896, Jugendstil originated in about 1894 in the embroideries of curving plant forms by Hermann Obrist (1863–1927). Other leading exponents were the architects Peter *Behrens and Henry *van der Velde.

juggernaut. See Jagannatha.

jugular vein A vein that drains blood from the head and neck regions to the larger veins passing to the heart. There are two jugular veins on each side of the neck: a large internal and a smaller external jugular, the latter lying just beneath the skin. *See* Plate IV.

Jugurtha (c. 160–104 BC) King of Numidia (118–105). He was the illegitimate grandson of Masinissa (d. 148) and initially ruled with Masinissa's legitimate grandsons Hiempsal and Adherbal. He assassinated Hiempsal and the Romans divided Numidia, a Roman dependency, between Jugurtha and Adherbal. Jugurtha's attack (112) on Adherbal caused Rome to declare war (the Jurgurthine War), which continued intermittently until 105, when Jugurtha was captured. He was taken to Rome and executed.

Juiz de Fora 21 47S 43 23W An industrial city in SE Brazil, in Minas Gerais state on the Rio Paraibuna. It specializes in the manufacture of textiles, especially of knitted goods, and has a university (1960). Population (1980): 299 728.

jujitsu (Japanese name: *yawara*) The form of self-defence, usually unarmed, used by the Japanese *samurai. The object was to disable, cripple, or kill an opponent by using his own momentum and strength against him. It evolved in about the 16th century and was taught in many forms in different schools. It was misused and fell into disrepute in the late 19th century, when the activities of the samurai were curtailed, but *judo, *aikido, and *karate developed from it.

jujube A small thorny tree of the genus *Zizyphus* that produces sweet edible fruit. *Z. jujuba*, native to China, has been widely introduced to other hot dry regions. It grows up to a height of 9 m and has small yellow flowers; blood-red berries are collected and eaten fresh or made into glacé fruits. Family: *Rhamnaceae. See also* crown of thorns.

Juliana (1909–) Queen of the Netherlands (1948–80) following the abdication of her mother Wilhelmina. In 1937 she married Prince Bernhard von Lippe-Biesterfeld (1911–). In 1980 Queen Juliana abdicated in favour of her eldest daughter *Beatrix. Her other daughters are Princess Irene (1939–), whose marriage in 1964 to a Spanish prince involved her conversion to Roman Catholicism and renunciation of her right of succession to the Dutch throne; Princess Margriet (1943–); and Princess Maria (1947–).

Julian calendar. *See* calendar.

Julian of Norwich (c. 1342–c. 1413) English mystic. As a recluse in Norwich, she wrote her famous *Revelations of Divine Love*, describing her many visions.

Julian the Apostate (Flavius Claudius Julianus; 332–63 AD) Roman emperor (360–63). Julian was the only non-Christian emperor after Constantine. The army proclaimed Julian emperor (360) and he attained power after the death in 361 of Constantius II. In spite of a Christian upbringing, Julian embraced paganism and as emperor restored pagan temples and deprived Christian churches of subsidy. He was killed fighting the Persians.

Julius II (Giuliano della Rovere; 1443–1513) Pope (1503–13). The protégé of his uncle, *Sixtus IV, Julius became a cardinal in 1471 but lived in exile during the pontificate of his rival Alexander VI. Following his election he restored and extended the papal states in Italy. In 1511 he formed a Holy League against the invading Louis XII of France, who, after trying to depose Julius, was forced to withdraw. Julius is best known as a patron of artists, especially Michelangelo and Raphael; he began the building of St Peter's, Rome.

Jullundur   31 18N 75 40E A city in India, in Punjab. An important communications and agricultural centre, it manufactures sporting goods. Population (1981): 408 196.

July Revolution   Three days of rioting in Paris in July, 1830, which brought *Louis Philippe to the French throne. Rebelling against *Charles X's reactionary ordinances, bourgeoisie and workers alike barricaded the streets. Charles abdicated, and the Chamber of Deputies elected Louis Philippe as king.

Jumna, River (R Jamuna *or* R Yamuna)   A river in N India. Rising in Uttar Pradesh, it flows S and SE past Delhi to join the River Ganges near Allahabad. This confluence is sacred to the Hindus. Length: 1385 km (860 mi).

jumping bean   A Mexican shrub, *Sebastiana pringlei*, the seeds of which may contain the caterpillars of a moth, *Carpocapsa saltitans*. When warmed (for example, when held in the hand) the caterpillars wriggle, causing the seed to jump. The seeds of some species of *Colliguaja* of South America may also contain these caterpillars. Family: *Euphorbiaceae*.

jumping mouse   A small long-legged rodent belonging to the subfamily *Zapodinae* (5 species), of North America and Asia. 8–10 cm long, jumping mice have long tails (10–15 cm) and are grey, golden, or yellow-brown in colour. Living either in nests on the ground or in very shallow burrows, they feed at night on fruit, seeds, and insects. They hibernate in winter. Family: *Zapodidae*.

Junagadh   21 32N 70 32E A town in India, in Gujarat. An agricultural trading centre, it is famous for its Buddhist caves (3rd century BC) and temples. Population (1981): 120 416.

junction transistor. *See* transistor.

Juneau   58 20N 134 20W A city in the USA, the capital of Alaska on the Gastineau Channel. A supply centre for a fur-trading and mining region, it is also an ice-free port. Industries include salmon fishing and sawmilling. Willow South is planned to replace Juneau as the state capital in the 1980s. Population (1980): 19 528.

June beetle   A brown beetle, also called May beetle or June bug, belonging to a genus (*Phyllophaga*) of *chafers. 12–25 mm long, June beetles are commonly seen during early summer evenings, being attracted to lights. They can sometimes be serious pests, destroying crops of corn, potato, and strawberry. The adults feed on the foliage and flowers, while the larvae (white grubs) attack the roots.

Jung, Carl Gustav (1875–1961) Swiss psychiatrist and pioneer psychoanalyst. Jung worked in Zurich and collaborated with Sigmund *Freud until, in 1912, their differences became irreconcilable. Jung originated the concept of introvert and extrovert personalities and made valuable studies of mental disorders, including schizophrenia. In his major work, *Psychology of the Unconscious* (1912), Jung regarded the unconscious part of the mind as containing both the personal experiences of the individual and the common inherited cultural experiences (*see* collective unconscious) of the particular social group to which he belongs. Jung later applied his theories to historical studies of religion and to the way in which the layers of the unconscious become manifest in dreams. He also developed psychiatric methods for the treatment of the elderly.

Jungfrau   46 33N 7 58E A mountain peak in S central Switzerland, in the Bernese Oberland. It forms a massif with the Eiger and the Mönch. A railway climbs to 3454 m (11 333 ft) at the **Jungfraujoch**, the pass between the Jungfrau and the Mönch. Height: 4158 m (13 632 ft).

Junggar Pendi (English name: Dzungarian Basin) A region in NW China, in Xinjiang Uygur Autonomous Region. A semidesert plateau among mountains, it is

inhabited chiefly by nomadic herdsmen. There are some state farms and oil and coal are produced.

jungle fowl   An Asian forest bird belonging to the genus *Gallus* (4 species). The males have a large fleshy comb and wattles at the sides of the bill and, in the breeding season, fight fiercely using their sharp leg spurs. The red jungle fowl (*Gallus gallus*) is the ancestor of the domestic *fowl. Family: *Phasianidae* (fowl and pheasants).

juniper   A coniferous tree or shrub of the genus *Juniperus* (60 species), widely distributed in the N hemisphere. Junipers have two kinds of leaves: needle-like and scalelike. All species have needles when young and some have both needles and scales when mature. Male and female flowers grow on separate trees and the cone is a fleshy "berry." The common juniper (*J. communis*) is native to N Europe, North America, and SW Asia; it rarely exceeds 4 m in height and is often planted for ornament. It has needle-like leaves and blue-black cones, 6–9 mm in diameter, used for flavouring gin and foods, as a source of oil, and as a diuretic. Family: *Cupressaceae*. *See also* cade; pencil cedar; savin.

Junius, Letters of   A series of letters, written by a still unidentified author, criticizing the government of George III. They appeared in the *Public Advertiser* between 21 January, 1769, and 21 January, 1772. Sir Philip *Francis is thought to be the most likely author, although the names of Edmund Burke and Tom Paine, among others, have also been suggested.

Junkers   A class of Prussian aristocrats. From small landowners the Junkers rose from the 15th century to control land, industry, and trade. Encouraged by Frederick the Great and Bismarck, they became notorious for arrogance and privilege, enjoying a monopoly of power in the army and civil service that remained unbroken until the 1930s.

Juno (astronomy)   A *minor planet (247 km diameter), the orbit of which lies between those of Mars and Jupiter.

Juno (mythology)   A principal Roman goddess, the wife of Jupiter. She was concerned with all aspects of women's life, especially marriage and childbirth, and is usually portrayed as a matronly figure. In 390 BC the warning given by her sacred geese on the Capitoline hill saved Rome from an attack by the Gauls. She was identified with the Greek *Hera.

Jupiter (astronomy)   The largest and most massive planet, orbiting the sun every 11.86 years at a mean distance of 778.3 million km. Its rapid axial rotation (in less than 10 hours) has produced a nonspherical shape: equatorial diameter 142 800 km, polar diameter 135 500 km. In a telescope light and dark bands of clouds are visible, running parallel to the equator, together with spots and streaks. Jupiter is composed mainly (99%) of hydrogen and helium (in the ratio 82:17). Ammonia, methane, and other compounds are present in the cloud layers. The gaseous atmosphere is 1000 km thick. The planetary interior is liquid hydrogen with possibly a small rocky core. Jupiter radiates, as heat, about twice as much energy as it receives from the sun, suggesting an internal energy reservoir. It is also a source of radio waves. It has a magnetic field and radiation belts of great intensity. The planet has 16 known satellites, including the four large *Galilean satellites, and a satellite ring of rocks, discovered in 1979. *See also* planetary probe.

Jupiter (mythology)   The principal Roman god, identified with the Greek *Zeus. Originally a sky god, he controlled the weather and used the thunderbolt as his weapon. His temple on the Capitoline hill was the principal Roman religious structure. He was a protective god and the guardian of honour, being concerned with oaths, treaties, and marriages.

Jura   An island in NW Scotland, in the Inner Hebrides, separated from the mainland by the Sound of Jura. It is mountainous and sparsely populated. Area: 381 sq km (147 sq mi). Population (1971): 343, with Colonsay.

Jura Mountains A mountain range in E France and NW Switzerland. It extends along the border in a NE–SW arc between the Rivers Rhine and Rhône, rising to 1723 m (5653 ft) at Crêt de la Neige. The area is chiefly agricultural.

Jurassic period A geological period of the Mesozoic era, between about 200 and 135 million years ago, following the Triassic and preceding the Cretaceous periods. The dinosaurs and other reptiles flourished and diversified in this period. Fossils of the earliest birds and mammals have also been found in Jurassic rocks.

Juruá, Rio A river in South America, rising in E central Peru and flowing NE through NW Brazil to join the River Amazon. Length: 1900 km (1200 mi).

jury A body of people, usually 12, who have taken an oath to decide questions of fact arising in a court case (now usually a criminal case but occasionally a civil case) according to the evidence before them. The English jury developed under the Normans as a body of people familiar with the case. The modern civil jury developed as the jurors became differentiated from witnesses and constituted an impartial body ignorant of the facts and sworn to decide solely on the evidence produced in court. To qualify for jury service a person must be a registered elector between 18 and 65 years old (21 and 60 in Scotland) and resident in the UK for at least 5 years since the age of 13. Persons ineligible for jury service are members of the judiciary and anyone involved in administering justice, the clergy, and the mentally ill. Others (MPs, medical personnel, etc.) have a right to be excused from jury service, while those who have received certain types of convictions are disqualified. Before being empanelled, jurors may be "challenged" (rejected) for various reasons by either side in a court case. They may claim compensation for loss of income while serving and are also paid travel expenses and subsistence. By the Criminal Justice Act (1967) a majority verdict (normally ten to two) was permitted in criminal trials and the Courts Act (1971) permitted similar verdicts in civil proceedings in the High Court.

Jussieu A French family of botanists. **Antoine de Jussieu** (1686–1758) was a physician, who wrote many papers on natural history and made a collection of European plants. He became director of the Jardin des Plantes, Paris. His brother **Bernard de Jussieu** (1699–1777) originated a method of classifying plants that was developed by his nephew **Antoine-Laurent de Jussieu** (1748–1836). The youngest brother of Antoine, **Joseph de Jussieu** (1704–79), spent many years in South America and introduced the garden heliotrope to Europe.

justice of the peace (JP) An unpaid *magistrate appointed by the Lord Chancellor to keep the peace within a county, with statutory power to try summarily certain cases in a Magistrates' Court and to commit other more serious cases for trial by a higher court. Justices have the power to grant licences to sell intoxicating liquor, to deal in gaming, and to rule on certain matrimonial matters, such as maintenance.

justiciar The royal deputy in the late 12th and 13th centuries, having full powers to govern England during the king's absence. The office became pre–eminent under Henry II, especially with the appointment (1180) of Ranulf Glanville (d. 1190). The justiciar's duties were chiefly administrative but might also include presiding over courts in the king's name, issuing writs, and controlling finance.

Justinian I (482–565 AD) Byzantine emperor (527–65). His reign saw chiefly defensive wars on the eastern frontier but in the west his general *Belisarius crushed the Vandals in Africa (533) and the Ostrogoths in Italy (535–53). Justinian, who was greatly influenced by his wife *Theodora, reformed provincial administration and codified *Roman law, which he issued in the *Corpus Juris Civilis* (Body of Civil Law), informally known as the Justinian Code. An orthodox Christian, he attempted to wipe out paganism and built the great church of St Sophia at Constantinople. □Ravenna.

Justinian II (c. 669–711 AD) Byzantine emperor (685–95, 705–11), the last of the Heraclian dynasty. He was a notoriously harsh ruler and after a revolt in 695 his nose was cut off (hence his nickname Rhinotmetus) and he was banished to the Crimea. With Bulgar support he returned to Constantinople as emperor, instigating savage reprisals. He was killed in a second revolt.

Justinian Code. *See* Roman law.

Justin Martyr, St (c. 100–c. 165 AD) Christian apologist and martyr, born in Samaria. After his conversion (c. 130) he taught in Ephesus and founded a school of Christian philosophy at Rome, where he was later beheaded. His only certain works are two *Apologies* addressed to the emperor Marcus Aurelius and the Roman Senate and the *Dialogue*, defending Christianity against Judaism. Feast day: 14 April.

jute Either of two Indian annual plants, *Corchorus capsularis* or *C. olitorius*, cultivated in India, Pakistan, and Thailand for their fibres. Growing to a height of 3 m, they have straight spearlike stems and small yellow flowers. The stems are cut, soaked in water, and beaten to remove the fibres, which are processed into cloth. There are many grades, used for ropes, sacks, carpet backings, hessian, and tarpaulin. Blending jute with man-made fibres has increased its uses. Family: *Tiliaceae.* □Bangladesh.

Jutes A Germanic people, probably from Jutland, who invaded Britain together with the *Angles and *Saxons in the 5th century AD. Archaeological evidence supports *Bede's statement that the Jutes settled in what are now Kent, the Isle of Wight, and Hampshire.

Jutland (Danish name: Jylland) A peninsula in N Europe, between the North Sea, the Skagerrak, the Kattegat, and the Little Belt. It is occupied by the continental part of Denmark and part of the West German *Land* of Schleswig-Holstein.

Juvenal (Decimus Junius Juvenalis; c. 60–c. 130 AD) Roman satirist. The biographical records are unreliable, but it is probable that he was born in Aquinum, SE of Rome, and that he was exiled to Egypt under the emperor Domitian but later became relatively prosperous under the emperor Hadrian. His 16 *Satires*, probably written in the period 98–128 AD, are savage indictments of the corruption and immorality of contemporary Roman society and of the absurd follies of mankind in general.

juvenile delinquency Offences against the law by persons under 17 years old. In the UK special punishments exist for these in the *criminal law and some are dealt with by care proceedings in special Juvenile Courts, to which the press and public are not admitted and in which the terms "sentence" and "conviction" may not be used. In these courts the juvenile offender may be bound over to his parents, put under the supervision of a local authority or probation order, or committed to the care of a local authority. Juvenile delinquency appears to be a problem only of the developed countries. Although it was formerly believed to be the result of poverty, delinquency, especially in the urban West, is now thought to be related to the breakdown of stable family life.

Jylland. *See* Jutland.

K

K2 (*or* Mt Godwin Austen) 35 53N 76 32E The second highest mountain in the world (after Mount Everest), in N Pakistan in the Karakoram Range. As it was the second peak to be measured in the range it was given the symbol, K2. The summit was first reached on 31 July, 1954, by an Italian team. Height: 8611 m (28 250 ft).

Kaaba The cube-shaped building at the centre of the great mosque at Mecca. Muslims believe that it was built by Abraham and Ishmael for the worship of God, was corrupted by Arab paganism, but was then purified and adopted for Islam by Mohammed. In the annual pilgrimage the Muslims circumambulate it and kiss the Black Stone, supposedly brought to Abraham by Gabriel, which is fixed in the interior in the southeast corner.

kabaddi A seven-a-side team game played in India, in which each player in turn tries to catch and touch members of the other team while holding his breath.

Kabardino-Balkar Autonomous Soviet Socialist Republic An administrative division in the S Soviet Union, in the RSFSR on the N side of the Caucasus Mountains. A large part of this mountainous region is unsettled and without roads. The population is 45% Kabardinian, 10% Balkar, and 40% Russian. The Kabardinians, most of whom are Muslims, speak a Northwest Caucasian language, while the Balkars are Turkic-speaking. The principal industries of the region are mining, timber, engineering, and food processing. The main crops are cereals, and livestock, poultry, and dairy farming are also important. *History*: the Kabardinians were associated with the Russians from 1557 and, although the Balkars resisted Russian rule, the region was annexed by Russia in 1827. It became an autonomous republic in 1936. In 1943 the Balkars, accused of collaborating with the Germans, were deported; they were returned in 1956. Area: 12 500 sq km (4825 sq mi). Population (1981 est): 688 000. Capital: Nalchik.

kabbalah (Hebrew: tradition) An esoteric Jewish theosophical system. The classical kabbalistic text is the *Zohar (*Book of Splendour*), written in Aramaic in 13th-century Spain, but kabbalah has much older roots. It has strong connections with *gnosticism and also with magical practices. An important 16th-century kabbalistic school flourished at Safed, in Galilee, around Isaac *Luria, and Christian interpretations of the kabbalah blended with *Neoplatonism in the 16th and 17th centuries. In modern times a thirst for occult teachings has revived considerable amateur interest in the kabbalah.

Kabinda. See Cabinda.

Kabuki A form of Japanese popular theatre that developed from the aristocratic *No theatre during the 17th century. The earliest notable dramatist was Chikamatsu Monzaemon (1653–1724). The plays are performed with musical accompaniment on a wide revolving stage and emphasize visual effects and acting skills. The conventional scenery, costumes, and the actors' make-up are elaborate. Female roles are played by male actors. A traditional programme consists of both historical and domestic dramas separated by dance plays. □ p. 660.

Kabul 34 30N 69 10E The capital of Afghanistan, situated in the NE of the country at an altitude of 1830 m (6000 ft) on the River Kabul. It is over 3000 years old, with a strategic position commanding high mountain passes. It has been destroyed and rebuilt many times, being in the path of the great invasions of India by Alexander the Great, Genghis Khan, and others. It was capital of the Mogul Empire (1504–1738), becoming capital of Afghanistan in 1773. The university was founded in 1932. Population (1982 est): 1 036 407.

Kabwe (former name: Broken Hill) 14 29S 28 25E A town in central Zambia. The first Rhodesian (Zambia was formerly Northern Rhodesia) railway was built here to serve the mines that now produce some of the world's highest grades of lead, zinc, and vanadium. In 1921 prehistoric hominid fossils were discovered here (*see* Homo). Population (1980): 143 635.

Kabyle A *Berber people of NE Algeria. They are Muslims and speak the Sanhajah dialect of the Berber language. The Kabyle are mainly settled cultivators living in autonomous villages (firquahs) occupied by patrilineal clans and governed by assemblies of adult males. There are also several castelike groups of inferior status, such as smiths and butchers.

Kádár, János (1912–) Hungarian leader. Head of the Hungarian secret police (1948–50), in 1956 Kádár led the opposition in the *Hungarian Revolution to Imre *Nagy's government and after the Soviet invasion became first secretary of the Hungarian Socialist Workers' Party. He was also prime minister (1956–58, 1961–65).

Kaduna 10 28N 7 25E A city in Nigeria. Formerly a colonial administrative centre, it developed as a railway junction and is a major textile and local trade centre. Population (1983 est): 202 000.

Kaesŏng 37 59N 126 30E A city in SW North Korea, a former Korean capital (938–1392). Many historic buildings here were destroyed during the Korean War (1950–53). Population (1980 est): 259 000.

kaffir corn A variety of sorghum, *Sorghum vulgare var. *cafforum*, originating in S Africa and cultivated here and in the USA for its grain. It has stout short-jointed stems, up to 5 m high, and a whitish bloom to stems and leaves.

Kaffirs The former collective name for the Pondo and Xhosa peoples of the E Cape Province of South Africa, with whom the advancing White settlers fought a series of wars (the *Cape Frontier Wars) in the late 18th and 19th centuries.

Kafirs A people of the Hindu Kush mountains of Afghanistan and Pakistan, who speak a Dardic language (*see* Dards). Their name (Arabic *kafir*: infidel) was acquired from their Muslim neighbours on account of their traditional religion, which is polytheistic and involves sacrifice and divination by shamans.

Kafka, Franz (1883–1924) Czech writer. Born in Prague (then in Bohemia), the son of German Jewish parents, he studied law and worked in an insurance company until tuberculosis forced him to leave. His own inner conflicts are reflected in fantasies and parables that portray the individual isolated in an incomprehensible and uneasy environment. Most of his work was published posthumously, against his instructions, by his friend Max Brod. Among his best-known writings are the stories *Metamorphosis* (1912) and *In the Penal Settlement* (1919) and the novels *The Trial* (1925) and *The Castle* (1926).

Kafuan stone tools Quartz pebbles apparently flaked by human agency, found along the Kafue River (Zambia). They are now considered to be of natural origin.

Kafue River A river in Zambia, rising on the Zaïre frontier and flowing generally S and E to join the Zambezi River. Length: 966 km (600 mi). The **Kafue Dam** (1972) provides about two-thirds of Zambia's hydroelectric power.

Kagoshima 31 37N 130 32E A port in Japan, in S Kyushu on Kagoshima Bay. It was the site of *Francis Xavier's

KABUKI *The interior of a theatre, from a print by Utagawa Toyokuni. The performers enter and leave the stage from the back of the theatre along the "flower path," a section of which extends from the stage at the bottom left. Music and sound effects are produced by the group behind the lattice at the right of the stage.*

landing in Japan (1549). Its university was established in 1949. It has porcelain and textile industries, a naval yard, and a rocket base. Population (1983): 512 000.

kagu A rare virtually flightless bird, *Rhynochetus jubatus*, occurring on remote forested mountains of New Caledonia. 55 cm long, it has a dark-barred grey plumage, an erectile crest, and reddish eyes, legs, and downcurved bill. It feeds at night on insects and snails. It is the only member of its family (*Rhynochetidae*). Order: *Gruiformes* (cranes, rails, etc.).

Kahn, Herman (1922–83) US scientist and futurologist. Originally a physicist and military analyst (1948–61), Kahn won recognition for his dispassionate analysis of nuclear war in his books *On Thermonuclear War* (1960) and *Thinking About the Unthinkable* (1962). Later books included the optimistic *The Year 2000* (1967) and *Why ABM?* (1969). In 1961 he founded the influential Hudson Institute in New York to make reasoned predictions on world affairs.

Kahn, Louis I(sadore) (1901–74) US architect. Kahn's first major building was the Yale University Art Gallery (1951–53). He then developed a striking and individual form of *functionalism, for example at the Medical Research Building, University of Pennsylvania (1957–60). Other designs include the Kimbell Art Museum in Fort Worth, Texas (1966–72), and the Yale Center for British Art, New Haven, Connecticut (1969–74).

Kaieteur Falls 5 09N 59 29W A waterfall in central Guyana, on the River Potaro. It is an important feature of the Kaieteur National Park. Height: 226 m (741 ft). Width: about 107 m (350 ft).

Kaifeng 34 47N 114 20E A city in E China, in Henan province. It was a *Song dynastic capital, and a Jewish colony was established here (12th–19th centuries). It is a commercial and industrial centre. Population (1980 est): 700 000.

Kaikoura Ranges Twin mountain ranges in New Zealand, comprising the Inland and the Seaward Kaikouras. They extend SW–NE in NE South Island, reaching 2885 m (9465 ft) at Tapuaenuku in the Inland Kaikouras, and are separated by the Clarence River.

Kairouan (*or* Qairouan; Arabic name: al Qayrawan) 35 42N 10 01E A city in N central Tunisia. An ancient holy city of Islam, it is now a local trade centre producing carpets and other craft goods. Population (1984): 72 254.

kaiser The title (derived from the Latin: Caesar) adopted by the German kings as Holy Roman Emperors (800–1806). It was assumed by William I of Prussia in 1871 and borne by the German emperors until 1917.

Kaiser, Georg (1878–1945) German dramatist. His carefully structured expressionist plays reveal a conflict between his desire for spiritual regeneration and his inherent pessimism. They include *Von Morgens bis Mitternachts* (1916), *Gas I* (1919), and *Gas II* (1920).

Kaiserslautern 49 27N 7 47E A city in SW West Germany, in Rhineland-Palatinate. The site of Barbarossa's ruined castle (1153–58), it shares a university with Trier (1970). Its manufactures include car parts, machinery, and textiles. Population (1983 est): 98 774.

kakapo A rare nocturnal New Zealand *parrot, *Strigops habroptilus*, also called owl parrot. It is the largest and only flightless parrot, having discs of stiff feathers around the eyes resembling an owl. Its green plumage is barred with yellow and brown and it has a heavy bill for grinding plant material.

Kakinomoto Hitomaro (c. 680–710) Japanese poet. He is considered the greatest of the poets whose works appear in the Man'yo-shu, an 8th-century anthology of lyric poetry. He was poet to the court of Empress Jito and Emperor Mommu and many of his poems describe court life.

kala-azar. *See* leishmaniasis.

Kalahari Desert A semiarid area in S Africa, chiefly in Botswana. It is sparsely inhabited by nomadic Bushmen, and although its few rivers are generally dry there is some vegetation. Wildlife is concentrated in the game reserves in the S. Area: about 250 000 sq km (96 505 sq mi).

Kalamazoo 42 17N 85 36W A city in the USA, in Michigan on the Kalamazoo River. It produces paper, fishing tackle, and stoves. Population (1980): 79 722.

Kalanchoe A genus of small tropical shrubs (over 100 species) having fleshy leaves and clusters of colourful flowers on tallish stems. They are popular house plants, requiring good draining and warm water supply and warm temperatures. Most flower in winter, having white, red, yellow, or pink flowers. Family: *Crassulaceae*.

Kalat (*or* Khelat) A division of SW Pakistan, in S Baluchistan. A former princely state, it was incorporated into Pakistan in 1948. Area: 65 610 sq km (25 332 sq mi). Population (1981 est): 333 000. Capital: Kalat.

kale A variety of *cabbage, also called borecole, grown for its large edible leaves, which are used as a winter vegetable and as livestock food. Curly kales, which have curled crimped leaves, are the most popular as vegetables. Some produce tender spring shoots. They are more hardy.than most other brassicas.

Kalemie (name until 1966: Albertsville) 5 57S 29 09E A city in Zaïre, on Lake Tanganyika. A port, it handles the Indian Ocean and Zaïre–Tanzania trade. Industries include fishing and textiles. Population (1976): 172 297.

Kalgan. *See* Zhangjiakou.

Kalgoorlie-Boulder 30 49S 121 29E A city in S central Western Australia. It is the centre of Australia's largest gold- and nickel-mining region. Because of the arid climate water is piped 563 km (250 mi) from Mundaring Weir in the Darling Range. Population (1983 est): 21 800.

Kali In Hindu mythology, the goddess of death. The wife of *Shiva in her destructive aspect, she is represented as a hideous four-armed black woman, adorned with skulls, and is propitiated by nocturnal sacrifices of animals.

Kalidasa (5th century AD) Indian poet, considered to be the greatest writer in classical Sanskrit. Almost nothing is known of his life, but he is traditionally associated with the court of Chandra Gupta II. The seven works attributed to him include two epics, two shorter poems, and three dramas, of which the most famous is the *Sakuntala*, concerning the love of King Dusyanta for a semidivine nymph.

Kalimantan The Indonesian part of *Borneo, comprising the SE two-thirds of the island. It is little developed, but its dense forests provide valuable timber. Small-scale agriculture includes the growing of rice, tobacco, sugar cane, coffee, and rubber. It is a long-standing source of gold and also produces oil and coal. Since Indonesian independence in 1949 separatism against the Java-based government has remained strong with active guerrilla activity. Area: 550 203 sq km (212 388 sq mi). Population (1980): 6 723 086. Chief towns: Banjarmasin and Pontianak.

Kalinin (name until 1931: Tver) 56 49N 35 57E A port in the central Soviet Union, in the RSFSR on the River Volga. The city was renamed Kalinin in 1931 in honour of the revolutionary M. I. *Kalinin. It is a major industrial and administrative centre, with industries that include engineering and textiles. Population (1981 est): 422 000.

Kalinin, Mikhail Ivanovich (1875–1946) Soviet statesman. A loyal supporter of Stalin, he was formally head of state (1919–46) as chairman of what came to be called the presidium of the Supreme Soviet.

Kaliningrad (name until 1946: Königsberg) 54 40N 20 30E A port in the W Soviet Union, in the RSFSR on the River Pregolya near its mouth at the Baltic Sea. Founded in 1255 as a fortress for the Teutonic Knights, it passed to Prussia in the 16th century and became a major German naval base. It was ceded to the Soviet Union in 1945. Its industries include shipbuilding, timber, paper, textiles, and food processing. Population (1981 est): 366 000.

Kalisz 51 46N 18 02E A town in W central Poland. Originally called Calissia, it is one of the oldest towns in Poland, being mentioned by Ptolemy in the 2nd century AD. Population (1982 est): 100 910.

Kalmar 56 39N 16 20E A port in E Sweden, on Kalmar Sound. The Union of Kalmar (1397) united Sweden, Denmark, and Norway under one ruler. It has a notable 13th-century castle, Kalmar Slott. Shipbuilding is important and nearby are the famous Orrefors glassworks. Population (1984 est): 53 516.

Kalmyk Autonomous Soviet Socialist Republic An administrative division in the S Soviet Union, in the RSFSR on the Caspian Sea. The Kalmyk people, who speak a Mongolian language, are traditionally Buddhists. Industries include fish processing, canning, and manufacture of building materials, but the economy is predominantly agricultural and cattle breeding and fodder crops are particularly important. The Kalmyks were deported to Siberia for collaborating with the Germans in World War II but some

were returned in 1957. Area: 75 900 sq km (29 300 sq mi). Population (1981 est): 301 000. Capital: Elista.

Kaluga 54 31N 36 16E A port in the central Soviet Union, in the RSFSR on the River Oka. It produces railway equipment, electrical equipment, textiles, and consumer goods. Population (1981 est): 276 000.

Kama In Hindu mythology, the god of love. He is the son of *Shiva and his popular epithet of Ananga (bodiless) derives from his having been reduced to ashes by a glance from his father's eye when Kama playfully shot his arrows at him.

Kama, River A river in the E Soviet Union, rising in the Ural Mountains and flowing mainly SW to the River Volga. It is a main waterway. Length: 2030 km (1260 mi).

Kamakura 35 19N 139 33E A city in Japan, in SE Honshu on an inlet of the Pacific Ocean. A former Japanese capital (1192–1333), it is now a religious centre, noted for its shrines and temples and for its bronze ⌐Buddha, 13 m (43 ft) high. Population (1982 est): 218 508.

Kamchatka A peninsula in the extreme E Soviet Union. It is about 1200 km (746 mi) long and separates the Sea of Okhotsk from the Bering Sea. There are many lakes, rivers, and forests, two mountain chains, and about 20 active volcanoes. Area: about 270 000 sq km (104 225 sq mi).

kame A mound consisting chiefly of stratified sands and gravels, deposited by meltwater from a glacier or icesheet. *See also* esker.

Kamehameha I (c. 1758–1819) King of Hawaii (1810–19), who founded the Kamehameha dynasty. Ruler of part of Hawaii from 1782, by 1810 he had united all the Hawaiian islands. He maintained Hawaiian independence despite the arrival of European explorers following James Cook's discovery of Hawaii in 1779. His encouragement of foreign trade established Hawaiian prosperity.

Kamehameha IV (1834–63) King of Hawaii (1854–63). He instituted social reforms, including free medical care, and encouraged greater commercial activity. He successfully opposed annexation by the USA in 1853–54 and curbed the political influence of US missionaries by inviting representatives of the Church of England to share their educational work.

Kamenev, Lev Borisovich (1883–1936) Soviet politician. Kamenev failed to win a favourable position in the power struggle after Lenin's death and he was arrested for participating in *Kirov's assassination (1934). He was tried in the first public purge trial and executed.

Kamet, Mount 30 55N 79 36E A mountain in N India, in the Himalayas. It was first climbed in 1931. Height: 7756 m (25 446 ft).

Kamikaze A Japanese aircraft crashed deliberately by its pilot into its target. Such suicide missions were first flown at the battle of Leyte Gulf (1944) in World War II; at Okinawa (1945) some 3000 sorties sunk 21 US ships. Kamikaze means divine wind and refers to the typhoon that scattered Kublai Khan's invasion fleet in 1281.

Kampala 0 20N 32 30E The capital of Uganda, N of Lake Victoria. Founded by the British in the late 19th century, it became the capital in 1962. In 1979 its fall to the combined forces of Tanzanians and exiled Ugandans effected the end of President Idi Amin's regime. It has two cathedrals and Makerere University (1970). It is chiefly an administrative centre with some small industries. Population (1980 est): 458 423.

Kampuchea, Democratic (former name: Cambodia) A country in SE Asia, in the Indochina Peninsula on the Gulf of Thailand. It consists mainly of an alluvial plain drained by the River Mekong and enclosed by mountains. Most of the inhabitants are Khmers, with small minorities of Vietnamese and Chinese. *Economy*: predominantly agricultural, the staple crop being rice. Production has been severely reduced by the recent political upheavals and there is little industry. Kampuchea is rich in forests, and phosphates, gemstones, and gold are produced; there are also known quantities of unexploited iron ore and manganese. There is an abundance of freshwater fish. Exports include rubber and dried fish. *History*: the kingdom of Funan (1st–6th centuries AD) was conquered by the Buddhist *Khmers. Following the collapse of their empire in the 15th century, Cambodia was prey to attack from the Thais and Vietnamese until 1863, when it became a French protectorate. In 1887 it became part of the Union of *Indochina. In 1949 it achieved self-government as a member of the French Union, gaining full independence in 1953. Under Prince *Sihanouk Cambodia was used as a base by North Vietnamese (communist) forces (*see* Vietnam War) and, following the failure of his attempts to negotiate their withdrawal, he was deposed (1970) by Gen Lon Nol (1913–85), who was supported by the USA. Shortly afterwards US and South Vietnamese troops invaded the renamed Khmer Republic to support Lon Nol against the communist Khmer Rouge guerrillas. In the ensuing civil war the Khmer Rouge was finally victorious in 1974 and, after the formation of a new constitution in 1975, the Khmer Republic became Democratic Kampuchea. The Khmer Rouge Government, led by Pol Pot (1925–   ), attempted to reshape the country's economy on cooperative lines by driving the Kampucheans out of the towns, depriving them of their property, and killing some three million of the aged, sick, or dissenting. Although Pol Pot's regime maintained relations with the Chinese, they failed to come to its aid when the Vietnamese invaded on 25 December, 1978. Pol Pot was overthrown and a People's Revolutionary Council was set up under the pro-Vietnamese Heng Samrin (1935–   ). The retreating Khmer Rouge devastated the land leaving behind them a trail of famine and disease. Fighting between the Khmer Rouge and Vietnam has continued on the Kampuchea–Thai border. In 1988, after peace talks between Hun Sen (1951–   ), the pro-Vietnamese prime minister, and Sihanouk, leader of the anti-Vietnam resistance coalition, early withdrawal of Vietnamese forces seemed possible. Official language: Khmer; French is widely spoken. Official currency: riel of 100 sen. Area: 181 000 sq km (71 000 sq mi). Population (1981 est): 5 756 141. Capital and main port: Phnom Penh.

Kananga (name until 1966: Luluabourg)   5 53S 22 26E A city in central Zaïre, on the River Lulua. A major commercial centre, it serves an agricultural and diamond-producing area. Population (1982 est): 704 211.

Kanarese   A *Dravidian language of SW India, also called Kannada. It is the official language of Mysore. Texts written in the Kanarese alphabet date from the 6th century.

Kanazawa   36 35N 136 38E A city in Japan, in central Honshu. It is renowned for its landscape garden. Its university was established in 1949. Industries include textiles, porcelain, and lacquerware. Population (1983): 412 000.

Kanchenjunga, Mount.   *See* Kangchenjunga, Mount.

Kanchipuram (*or* Conjeeveram)   12 50N 79 44E A city in India, in Tamil Nadu. It is one of the oldest cities in S India and is sacred to the Hindus. It is noted for its silk and cotton fabrics. Population (1981): 145 254.

Kandahar (*or* Qandahar)   31 36N 65 47E A city in S Afghanistan. Situated on main routes to central Asia and India, it is built on the site of several ancient cities. It was the first capital (1747) of a unified Afghanistan. Kandahar is a major commercial centre. Population (1982 est): 198 161.

Kandinsky, Wassily (1866–1944) Russian expressionist painter and art theorist, born in Moscow, where he graduated in law. In 1896 he moved to Munich to study. Here he painted the first purely abstract pictures in European art (c. 1911). These are characterized by freely applied paint and dazzling colours, from which he drew analogies to music in his book *Concerning the Spiritual in Art* (1911). He was a founder of the

*Neue Kunstlervereinigung (1909) and Der *Blaue Reiter (1911); following a stay in Russia (1914–21), he taught at the *Bauhaus school, where his style became more geometrical. He settled in France in 1933.

Kandy   7 17N 80 40E A city in central Sri Lanka. Capital of the kingdom of Kandy from 1480 until 1815, when it was occupied by the British, it has a famous Buddhist temple, Dalada Malagawa. Kandy is the commercial centre for Sri Lanka's major tea-producing region. Population (1981): 101 281.

Kanem Bornu   An African empire that controlled the area around Lake Chad. Kanem, situated on the eastern trade routes, became a centre of Muslim civilization in the 11th century. The king was expelled in 1389 and founded a new dynasty in Bornu, which in the 16th century conquered Kanem and expanded the empire. Torn by internal strife, the empire collapsed in about 1800.

kangaroo   The largest *marsupial mammal. There are two species, the red kangaroo (*Macropus rufus*) of Australia and the grey kangaroo (*M. kanguru*) of Australia and Tasmania. Red kangaroos can reach a height of 2 m and a weight of 90 kg. Kangaroos have short front legs and long hind legs and feet: they travel by a succession of leaps. When moving slowly, they use their long heavy tail as a prop. The red kangaroos graze across the plains while grey kangaroos live in open woodland. Family: *Macropodidae. See also* wallaby; wallaroo; tree kangaroo. □mammal.

kangaroo paw   A stiff hairy plant of the Australian genus *Anigozanthos* (10 species), also known as Australian sword lilies and sometimes planted in gardens in warm regions. The flowers, borne in short branched terminal clusters, are long, tubular, and hairy, with six pointed flaring lobes, usually yellow, green, or red. Unopened flowers resemble kangaroos' paws. Family: *Haemodoraceae*.

kangaroo rat   A North American desert rodent of the genus *Dipodomys* (22 species). Up to 20 cm long, kangaroo rats have long back legs and very long hairy tails. They do not need to drink as they obtain water from their food (seeds, tubers, and other vegetation). They spend the day in relatively cool humid burrows, in which they also store food during droughts. □mammal.

Kangchenjunga, Mount (*or* Mt Kanchenjunga) 27 44N 88 11E The third highest mountain in the world (after Mount Everest and K2), on the Sikkim (India)–Nepal border in the Himalayas. It was first climbed in 1955 by a British expedition; however, George Band and Joe Brown (1930–   ) stopped just short of the actual summit in deference to the religious wishes of the Sikkimese. On 16 May, 1979, a British team of four climbed it without oxygen-breathing equipment. Height: 8598 m (28 208 ft).

KaNgwane.   *See* Bantu Homelands.

Kang Xi (*or* K'ang-hsi; 1654–1722) Chinese emperor (1661–1722) of the Qing dynasty, who completed the Qing conquest of China started by *Nurhachi. He was a powerful ruler, who led his armies in person against the Mongols and carried out tours of inspection of his vast empire. He built the imperial summer palace at Jehol (now Chengde) and sponsored engineering works to prevent the Yellow River from flooding and to improve communications. His greatest achievement was probably in his sponsorship of the arts.

Kang You Wei (1858–1927) Chinese reformer. A major influence on the *Hundred Days of Reform (1898), he was subsequently forced to flee China and in 1907, in British Columbia, founded the China Reform Association. Back in China (1914), he opposed Sun Yat-sen.

Kano   12 00N 8 31E A city in N Nigeria. It was an important trade centre for caravans crossing the Sahara. It was captured by the British (1903) and trade developed with the S. It is now an important trade centre, particularly for groundnuts and cattle, with some local industries. Population (1983): 487 100.

Kanpur (former name: Cawnpore)   26 27N 80 14E A city in India, in Uttar Pradesh on the River Ganges. Ceded to the British East India Company (1801), it became an important British frontier station and during the Indian Mutiny was the scene (1857) of a massacre of British soldiers. Today Kanpur is one of India's largest cities and a major communications and industrial centre; the chief manufactures are wool, cotton, jute, leather goods, plastics, and chemicals. Several educational institutions are located here, including a university (1966) and an Institute of Technology (1960). Population (1981): 1 688 000.

Kansas   A state in the centre of the USA. It consists mainly of undulating prairie, forming part of the Great Plains, and is crossed by the Kansas and Arkansas Rivers. Manufacturing is significant with aircraft production, food and meat processing, and a range of different processing industries. Its large mineral resources yield oil, natural gas, coal, sand and gravel, cement, stone, chalk, zinc, and lead. Kansas is the USA's main wheat-growing area; other crops include sorghum grains and hay. Beef production is especially important. *History*: first explored by the Spanish in the 16th century, it was claimed by the French (1682) and formed part of the Louisiana Purchase (1803) by the USA. It became a state (1861) and the arrival of the railway in the late 1860s and 1870s brought many cattlemen. The *Mennonites introduced wheat into the area (1874). Area: 213 063 sq km (82 264 sq mi). Population (1980): 2 363 679. Capital: Topeka.

Kansas City   39 05N 94 37W A city in the USA, in Missouri at the confluence of the Missouri and Kansas Rivers. Settled in 1821, it expanded rapidly with the arrival of the railways in the mid-18th century. A major trading and distribution centre for a vast agricultural region, it is the site of the annual Royal Livestock and Horse Show. Industries include food processing, metals, chemicals, and machinery and there are several military installations nearby. Population (1980): 448 033.

Kansu.   *See* Gansu.

Kant, Immanuel   (1724–1804) German philosopher, who made many original and influential contributions to thought. He spent much of his life (1755–97) teaching at the university in his native Königsberg (now Kaliningrad in the Soviet Union). His early works, notably *Theory of the Heavens* (1755), sought to examine metaphysics in the light of the work of *Newton and *Leibniz. Acquaintance with Hume's *empiricism, however, initiated his so-called "critical period" in which he evolved his doctrine of transcendental idealism. In the famous *Critique of Pure Reason* (1781) he explored the limitations of reason by which mankind interprets experience. The *Critique of Practical Reason* (1788) and the *Critique of Judgment* (1790) deal respectively with *ethics and aesthetic and teleological judgments. Reason makes experience possible by imposing upon the raw data supplied by the senses the forms of understanding. Kant identified 12 of these basic forms (which he called "categories"), such as causality; they were transcendental in as much as they were found in pure reason independently of experience. But reason is also practical and as such he identified it with morality. He maintained that there was an absolute moral law, which can never be modified by expediency (it can never be right to tell a lie), and called the obligation to obey this moral law the "categorical imperative."

Kao-hsiung.   *See* Gaoxiong.

kaolin   A group of clay minerals consisting of hydrous aluminium silicates. It includes kaolinite (the most important), nacrite, and dickite. Kaolin is the main constituent of *china clay. It has many industrial uses apart from the ceramic industry, particularly as a mineral filler in the manufacture of paper, paint, textiles, rubber, plastics, and cosmetics. It is also used in medicine.

Kapil Dev   (Kapil Dev Ramlal Nikhanj; 1959–   )   Indian cricketer, who has played for Haryana, Northamptonshire, Worcestershire, and India (1978–   ). The youngest player to

have scored 2000 runs and taken 200 wickets in Test matches, he has also captained India (1983–84).

Kapitza, Peter Leonidovich   (1894–1984) Soviet physicist, who went to Cambridge in 1921 and worked with *Rutherford on high transient magnetic fields. Returning to the Soviet Union in 1934 he transferred his attention to low-temperature physics, which led him to the discovery of superfluid helium (1941). For this work he was awarded the 1978 Nobel Prize.

KAPOK   *The fruit pods of the silk-cotton tree ripen in about two months. They split open to release masses of white kapok, which surrounds the black seeds.*

kapok   The fine silky hairs covering the seeds of the silk-cotton tree (*Ceiba pentandra*), which are used for stuffing mattresses, etc. Impervious to water, kapok can also be used to fill life jackets and oil from the seeds is used in soap making and is edible. The tree is native to tropical America and widely cultivated in the tropics. Growing to 35 m, it has large buttresses at the base of the trunk and clusters of white or red flowers. Family: *Bombacaceae*.

Kara-Bogaz-Gol   A shallow gulf in the SW Soviet Union, on the E Caspian Sea. Its water evaporates fast, drawing more in from the Caspian and creating the richest natural deposits of marine salts in the world. Area: about 13 000 sq km (5018 sq mi).

Karachai-Cherkes   An autonomous region (*oblast*) in the W Soviet Union, in the RSFSR. It was formed in 1922 for the Muslim Karachai and Cherkes peoples. Mining, engineering, and chemical industries are important, and the chief agricultural activities are livestock raising and cereal production. Area: 14 100 sq km (5440 sq mi). Population (1980 est): 370 000. Capital: Cherkessk.

Karachi   24 51N 67 02E The largest city and chief seaport in Pakistan, situated on the Arabian Sea just NW of the Indus delta. A modern city, it developed rapidly from the mid-19th century as a port. It became the capital of Pakistan (1947) following partition, which brought a further influx of refugees to an already overcrowded city. The removal of the capital to Islamabad (1959) and the building of new satellite towns has eased the housing situation. The University of Karachi was established here in 1957. The city is Pakistan's principal naval base and its port is a major outlet for the agricultural produce of the Sind and Punjab provinces. Industries include textiles, chemicals and plastics, and engineering. Population (1981): 5 103 000.

Karafuto.   *See* Sakhalin.

Karaganda   49 53N 73 07E A city in the SW Soviet Union, in the Kazakh SSR. Founded in 1857, Karaganda grew rapidly in the 1920s and 1930s as the Karaganda coal basin was exploited. Today it is one of the largest producers of bituminous coal in the Soviet Union. Although coalmining and the production of coalmining equipment dominate the city's industries, it also produces building materials and has light industries. Population (1981 est): 583 000.

Karageorge (George Petrović Karadordević; c. 1762–1817) Serbian revolutionary leader. In 1804 he led a successful revolt against Turkey and in 1808 became the "Supreme Serbian hereditary leader." Turkey regained control of Serbia in 1813 and after a five-year exile in Austria Karageorge was murdered, probably by his rivals, the *Obrenović family.

Karajan, Herbert von (1908–) Austrian conductor. Educated at Vienna and the Salzburg Mozarteum, he was musical director of the Vienna State Opera (1957–64). He founded the Salzburg Easter Festival in 1967 and conducted the Berlin Philharmonic Orchestra (1955–).

Kara-Kalpak Autonomous Soviet Socialist Republic (or Kara-Kalpakia) An administrative division in the S Soviet Union, in the Uzbek SSR on the Aral Sea. The population consists mainly of Kara-Kalpaks, a Turkic-speaking people closely related to the Kazakhs. Kara-Kalpakia's main industries are the manufacture of bricks, leather goods, and furniture and canning and wine making. It is the Soviet Union's chief producer of alfalfa, and other crops grown include cotton, rice, corn, and jute. Cattle and karakul sheep are raised. *History*: the Kara-Kalpaks were under the rule of the *Kazakhs, passing under Russian rule in the late 19th and early 20th centuries. Kara-Kalpakia was within the Kazakh SSR (1925–30) before being incorporated in the RSFSR. It became an autonomous republic in 1932. Area: 165 600 sq km (63 900 sq mi). Population (1981 est): 957 000. Capital: Nukus.

Karakoram Range A mountain range mainly in SW China, NE Pakistan, and NW India. It extends about 450 km (280 mi) between the Pamirs and the Himalayas and includes *K2, the second highest mountain in the world. In 1978 the **Karakoram Highway** was opened connecting China with Pakistan over the Khunjerab Pass, 4933 m (16 188 ft) high.

Karakorum The former Mongol capital founded (c. 1220) by *Genghis Khan in the upper valley of the River Orhon Gol (Outer Mongolia). It replaced the nearby Uighur capital of the same name. After *Kublai Khan moved the capital from Karakorum (1267) the city declined and was eventually destroyed (1388).

karakul A breed of sheep originating in central Asia. The young lambs bear a coat of fine tightly curled black wool, known as Persian lamb.

Kara Kum A desert in the SW Soviet Union, between the Caspian Sea to the W and the River Amu Darya to the E, comprising most of the Turkmen SSR. Area: about 300 000 sq km (115 806 sq mi).

Karamanlis, Constantine (1907–) Greek statesman; prime minister (1955–63, 1974–80), president (1980–85). Karamanlis resigned in 1963 and went into exile, returning in 1974, after the fall of the military dictatorship, to form a civilian government. He resigned the presidency in 1985.

Kara Sea A section of the Arctic Ocean off the N coast of the Soviet Union, between Novaya Zemlya and Severnaya Zemlya. It is frozen for much of the year but is used to reach the port of Novy Port some 600 km (373 mi) inland on the Gulf of Ob.

karate An oriental form of unarmed combat that was systematized in Okinawa, one of the Ryukyu Islands, in the 17th century and spread to Japan in the 1920s, where it absorbed elements of *jujitsu. Breath-control techniques as well as philosophical attitudes, such as the necessity of mental calm, were taken from Zen Buddhism. The aim is to focus the body's total muscular power in one instant. Hands, feet, elbows, etc., are toughened in stylized training sequences against padded or

wooden blocks, and karate fighters also perform feats of strength, such as wood breaking. In actual fights, however, which last two or three minutes, blows are stopped short before impact. As in *judo, grades are distinguished by coloured belts and points are awarded in combat. *See also* martial arts.

KARAKORUM RANGE *These mountains form the border between Pakistan and China.*

Karatepe A fortified hilltop site near Adana (S Turkey), founded (c. 740 BC) by Asitawandas, King of the Danuna (possibly the same people as the Danaoi, mentioned by Homer). King Sanduarri of Karatepe was beheaded by *Esarhaddon (676 BC). A palace with sculptured reliefs and an important bilingual Phoenician and Hittite hieroglyphic inscription have been found.

Karbala (or Kerbela) 32 37N 44 03E A town in central Iraq, S of Baghdad. Muslim pilgrims are attracted to the tomb of Husan (the son of *Ali), who was martyred here. It is a trading centre for dates and other agricultural produce. Population (1980 est): 136 000.

Karelian Autonomous Soviet Socialist Republic (or Karelia) An administrative division in the NW Soviet Union, in the RSFSR. Comprising largely forest, it also possesses thousands of lakes and rivers. The Karelians speak a Finno-Ugric language, and W Karelia has formed part of Finland for much of its history, but was finally ceded to Russia in 1940. Industries include mining, timber, and chemicals. Some cereals, potatoes, and fodder crops are grown and fishing is very important. Area: 172 400 sq km (66 560 sq mi). Population (1981 est): 746 000. Capital: Petrozavodsk.

Karelian Isthmus A land bridge in the NW Soviet Union, situated between the Gulf of Finland in the W and Lake Ladoga in the E. It connects Finland with the Soviet Union to which it was ceded in 1944. It is 40–113 km (25–70 mi) wide and 145 km (90 mi) long and its principal cities are Leningrad and Vyborg.

Karen A group of peoples of S Burma who speak tonal languages distantly related to those of the Tibeto-Burman branch of the *Sino-Tibetan family. There are many different and distinct groups and languages broadly divided into the White Karens (including Sgaw and Pwo) and the Red Karens (including Bre, Padaung, Yinbaw, and Zayein). Only Sgaw and Pwo have written forms and all are much influenced by surrounding languages. Their religion is animistic.

Kariba, Lake A reservoir in Zambia and Zimbabwe. It is formed by the Zambezi River above the **Kariba Dam** (completed 1959) and is used for generating hydroelectric power. Length: 282 km (175 mi).

Karl-Marx-Stadt (name until 1953: Chemnitz)   50 49N 12 50E A city in S East Germany, on the River Chemnitz. A textile centre since the 14th century, it became famous for machine construction in the 19th century, when the first German machine tools and the first German locomotive were made here. Population (1980 est): 316 937.

Karloff, Boris (William Pratt; 1887–1969) British character actor, who worked mostly in US films. Following his great success as the monster in *Frankenstein* (1931), he was typecast in a number of sinister and gruesome roles in horror films.

Karlovy Vary (German name: Karlsbad)   50 14N 12 53E A spa town in W Czechoslovakia, in W Bohemia. It has many hot sodium sulphate springs, including the Vřidlo (Sprudel) at a temperature of 72°C (162°F). Population (1980 est): 61 000.

Karlsbad. *See* Karlovy Vary.

Karlsburg. *See* Alba Iulia.

Karlskrona   56 10N 15 35E A seaport in S Sweden, on the Baltic coast. It has been the main naval station of Sweden since 1680. Its industries include the manufacture of naval equipment, quarrying, and sawmilling. Population (1983): 59 696.

Karlsruhe   49 00N 8 24E A city in SW West Germany, in Baden-Württemberg. The capital of the former *Land* of Baden, it is the site of the federal court of justice and a university (1825). It has a harbour on the Rhine; industries include oil refining and machinery manufacturing. It is a centre for nuclear research and development. Population (1983 est): 270 300.

Karlstad   59 24N 13 32E A port in SW Sweden, on the N shore of Lake Vänern, at the outlet of the River Klar. Its industries are based on timber and heavy machinery and it has a university (1967). Population (1983): 73 939.

karma (Sanskrit: action) The sum of all human actions, which according to Hinduism and Jainism are passed from one individual existence to the next and determine the nature of the individual's rebirth. In *Buddhism, karma is associated with mental and physical elements passed on in the cycle of rebirth until the personal self is annihilated in attaining *nirvana.

Karnak   25 44N 32 39E A village near *Thebes (Upper Egypt), the site of the huge temple of *Amon, built (c. 1320–1237 BC) mainly by the pharaohs Seti I (reigned 1313–1292) and *Ramses II. *See also* Luxor.

Karnataka (name until 1973: Mysore)   A state in SW India, on the Arabian Sea stretching E over the Western Ghats onto the Deccan plateau. Rice and sugar cane are grown along the coast, coffee and tea on the Ghats, and rice, cotton, and fruit on the Deccan. Hill forests provide teak and most of the world's sandalwood. Iron ore, gold, manganese, and bauxite are mined. Industries include iron and steel, food products, and silk. Most of the population are Kanarese-speaking Hindus. *History*: long ruled by Hindu dynasties, Karnataka was conquered (1761) by a Muslim, Hyder Ali, whose son Britain dispossessed (1799). Area: 191 773 sq km (74 024 sq mi). Population (1981): 37 043 451. Capital: Bangalore.

Károlyi, Mihály, Count (1875–1955) Hungarian statesman. Károlyi led the campaign for Hungarian independence during World War I and became (January, 1919) the provisional president of the new Hungarian Democratic Republic. In a confrontation between conservatives and communists, he was forced in March to resign and was succeeded by Béla Kun.

Karpov, Anatoly (1951–   ) Soviet chess player, who became an International Grandmaster at 19 and subsequently world champion (1975). He successfully defended his title against *Korchnoi in 1978 and 1981 but was defeated by *Kasparov in 1985 (after a tournament in 1984–85 had been abandoned as indecisive), 1986, and 1987.

karri A tree, *Eucalyptus diversicolor*, native to SW Australia and cultivated elsewhere. It grows to a height of over 35 m in moist areas and produces excellent timber. The attractive leaves are dark green above and lighter below.

Karroo A plateau in S South Africa, divided by the Groot-Swartberge range into the **Great Karroo** and, to the S, the **Little Karroo**. Seasonal rains turn them into rich pasture for sheep.

Kars   40 35N 43 05E A town in NE Turkey. It was fortified in the 16th century and captured by Russians three times during the 19th century before being restored to Turkey after World War I. Population (1980): 58 799.

karst region An area of the earth's surface typified by sink holes, uvalas (depressions), and underground drainage, produced by the solution of limestone or dolomite. Such features are notable in the Karst region of Yugoslavia.

karting (*or* go-karting) A form of *motor racing that originated in the USA in the 1950s. A kart usually has a tubular chassis, no body or suspension system, and a single driving seat. It has a maximum wheelbase of 50 in (1.27 m) and is usually powered by a single-cylinder two-stroke engine. 100 cc, 200 cc, and 270 cc are among the more common engine capacities. Most karts are capable of about 160 km per hour (100 mph).

Kasai, River A river in central Africa. Rising in Angola, it flows N into Zaïre to join the Zaïre River as its main tributary. It forms part of the Angola–Zaïre border and is rich in alluvial diamonds. Length: 2100 km (1300 mi).

Kasavubu, Joseph (c. 1917–69) Congolese statesman; president (1960–65). A teacher, Kasavubu joined with *Lumumba to lead the Congo (now Zaïre) to independence. In 1961, helped by *Mobutu, he deposed Lumumba, until then prime minister, but was himself deposed in Mobutu's coup in 1965. He retired to his farm, where he died.

Kashi (K'a-shih *or* Kashgar)   39 29N 76 02E A city in NW China, in Xinjiang Uygur AR on a fertile oasis. It is a centre of trade with the Soviet Union and the Middle East. Chinese rule has been intermittent here since the 2nd century BC and rebellion among the Muslim population was common in the period 1862–1943. Cloth is manufactured and handicrafts include rug-making. Population (1980 est): 100 000.

Kashmir The northernmost region of the Indian subcontinent, bordered by China to the NE and Afghanistan to the NW. The S Jammu lowlands rise into the Himalaya and Karakoram Mountains. Except for the Indus Valley and the beautiful Vale of Kashmir, the valleys are small. Rice, other grains, silk, cotton, fruits, and sheep are farmed. Embroidery and other crafts help tourism to thrive. *History*: most Kashmiris became Muslims in the 14th century but in the 19th century Hindu princes won power under British control. Britain's withdrawal (1947) was followed by a Muslim revolt; the Hindu maharajah acceded to India but Pakistan intervened and fighting between the two sides resulted in the partition of the region. Pakistan rules 78 932 sq km (30 468 sq mi) of the W and barren N. China occupies 42 735 sq km (16 496 sq mi) in the E. The remainder forms the Indian state of *Jammu and Kashmir. Fighting continues between Indian and Pakistani forces around the border. Area (all Kashmir): 222 236 sq km (85 783 sq mi).

Kasparov, Gary (Gary Weinstein; 1963–   ) Soviet chess player of Armenian-Jewish origin, born in Azerbaidzhan. At 22 he became the youngest ever world champion, beating *Karpov in 1985, 1986, and 1987.

Kassala   15 24N 36 30E A city in the NE Sudan. It has declined as a centre for cotton but has an important fruit trade. Population (1980 est): 149 000.

Kassel   51 18N 9 30E A city in E West Germany, in Hessen. Notable buildings include the Orangery Palace (1701–11). Its manufactures include railway engines and textiles. Population (1983 est): 190 400.

Kassem, Abdul Karim (1914–63) Iraqi soldier and statesman; prime minister (1958–63) after leading an army coup that overthrew the monarchy. An opponent of Arab unity, he survived a rebellion (1959) of those who wanted federation with the United Arab Republic but was killed in a revolt led by army officers.

Kassites A people of mysterious racial origins who moved SW from the Zagros Mountains to overrun *Babylonia in the 16th century BC. Although Indo-European gods were apparently worshipped, the Kassite language is neither Indo-European nor Semitic. The Kassites ruled Babylon for about 400 years until overthrown by *Assyria.

Kästner, Erich (1899–1974) German novelist and poet, best known for his children's books, such as *Emil and the Detectives* (1929). His satirical poetry, novels, and later plays combine humour with social concern.

Katanga. See Shaba.

Kathiawar Peninsula A peninsula in W India, in Gujurat, roughly 190 km (118 mi) square, projecting into the Arabian Sea between the Gulfs of Kutch and Cambay.

Kathmandu (*or* Katmandu) 27 42N 85 19E The capital of Nepal, near the confluence of the Rivers Baghmati and Vishnumati. Founded in the 8th century AD, it possesses numerous historical buildings and a university (1959) and is the site of several religious festivals. Its development as the country's main commercial centre has been assisted by a programme of road building. Population (1982 est): 195 260.

Katmai, Mount An active volcano in the USA, in S Alaska in the Aleutian Range. Following its violent eruption in 1912, the *Valley of Ten Thousand Smokes was formed. Height: 2100 m (7000 ft). Depth of crater: 1130 m (3700 ft). Width of crater: about 4 km (2.5 mi).

Katowice (former name (1953–56): Stalinograd) 50 15N 18 59E A city in S central Poland. It is an important industrial centre within the Upper Silesia coalfield; manufactures include iron and steel. The Silesian University was established here in 1968. Population (1982): 366 000.

Katrine, Loch A lake in Scotland, in the NW Central Region. Noted for its beautiful scenery, it also supplies Glasgow with water. Length: 15 km (8 mi). Maximum width: 1.6 km (1 mi).

Katsina 13 00N 7 32E A city in N Nigeria. From its early foundation (c. 1100), it was an important centre for trans-Saharan trade. Active until the 18th century, it has now declined in importance. Population (1983 est): 149 300.

Katsura Taro (1847–1913) Japanese soldier and statesman, who was instrumental in introducing into the Japanese army a general-staff system on German lines. He was prime minister three times (1901–06, 1908–11, 1912–13) and presided over the victorious *Russo-Japanese War (1904–05) and the annexation of Korea (1910).

Kattegat A strait between Denmark and Sweden linking the Skagerrak with the Baltic Sea. Length: about 240 km (149 mi).

katydid A *bush cricket of the subfamily *Pseudophyllinae*, common in the tropics and E North America. It takes its name from the repetitive song—"katy-did, katy-didn't"—of male katydids of the genus *Pterophylla*. Katydids are generally green and have long wings but never fly. They are mainly herbivorous, although some species eat insects.

Katyn Massacre The execution during World War II of 4250 Polish officers in the Katyn forest, near Smolensk in the Soviet Union. The bodies of the Poles, who had been interned by the Russians following the Soviet occupation of Polish territory in 1939, were discovered by the Germans in 1943. The Russians denied responsibility, countercharging the Germans with the massacre. The Soviet Union forbade the Red Cross investigation requested by the Polish Government in exile, with which it broke diplomatic relations. The weight of evidence points to Soviet accountability.

Kauffmann, Angelica (1741–1807) Swiss painter, who divided her career between London and Rome. In England (1765–81) she painted portraits influenced by *Reynolds and was employed on decorative work in country houses designed by Robert and James *Adam.

Kaufman, George S(imon) (1889–1961) US dramatist. He worked as a newspaper columnist while collaborating, especially with Moss *Hart, on an enormous number of Broadway comedy hits, including *Bandwagon* (1931) and *The Man Who Came to Dinner* (1939). With George *Gershwin he wrote *Of Thee I Sing* (1932), and he also wrote the scripts of two *Marx brothers films.

Kaunas (Russian name: Kovno) 54 52N 23 55E A port in the Soviet Union, in the S central Lithuanian SSR at the confluence of the Rivers Neman and Viliya. It was held successively by Lithuania, Poland, and Russia before becoming (1918) the capital of Lithuania; it was occupied by German forces during World War II. A major educational and industrial centre, its industries include chemicals, textiles, and iron production. Population (1984): 400 000.

KENNETH KAUNDA

Kaunda, Kenneth (David) (1924–) Zambian statesman; president (1964–). He trained as a teacher and joined the African National Congress in 1949. In 1958 he founded the more militant Zambia African National Congress and was imprisoned for subversion. On his release in 1960 he became president of the United National Independence Party, which took Northern Rhodesia to independence as Zambia in 1964. Under his leadership Zambia became a one-party state in 1972. In 1984 he hosted a conference on Namibia, between South Africa and Angola.

Kaunitz, Wenzel Anton, Count von (1711–94) Austrian statesman. As chancellor (1753–92) he controlled Habsburg foreign policy under Empress Maria Theresa and her son Emperor Joseph and was also influential in the reform of internal administration. His most striking achievement was to reverse (1756–57) the European alliances of the War of the *Austrian Succession, making France and Russia Austria's allies in the *Seven Years' War against Prussia.

kauri pine A coniferous tree, *Agathis australis*, from New Zealand. Growing to a height of 46 m, it has oblong leaves, 5 cm long and 2 cm wide, and spherical cones, 5–8 cm in diameter. It yields a resin (kauri copal or gum) used in making varnishes; the best resin is fossilized, derived from extinct trees and dug out of the ground. Its timber is used for building purposes. Family: *Araucariaceae*. *See also* dammar.

kava A shrub, *Piper methysticum*, of the Pacific Islands and Australia, the ground and fermented roots of which are made into a narcotic drink. The roots are also chewed, and continued use produces inflammation and ulcers of the mouth. It has been used medicinally and as a local anaesthetic. Family: *Piperaceae*.

Kaválla (*or* Kavála; ancient name: Neopolis) 40 56N 24 24E A port in NE Greece, in Macedonia on the Aegean Sea. A Roman naval base, it was visited by St Paul (50–51 AD). It was ceded by Turkey to Greece in 1912. Tobacco is the chief export. Population (1981): 56 260.

Kawabata Yasunari (1899–1972) Japanese novelist. He was one of a group known as the Neo-Impressionists, which opposed the preceding realist movement in Japanese literature. His novels, which include *Snow Country* (1935–47) and *The Sound of the Mountain* (1949–54), are characterized by melancholy and loneliness, probably related to his being orphaned at an early age. In 1968 he was awarded the Nobel Prize. He committed suicide.

Kawasaki 35 32N 139 41E A city in Japan, in SE Honshu. Part of the Tokyo-Yokohama industrial complex, it has shipbuilding, iron and steel, and chemical industries. Population (1980): 1 041 000.

Kay, John (1704–c. 1764) British inventor of the flying shuttle (patented in 1733), which contributed to the mechanization of weaving. Kay was defrauded of most of the royalties due to him and died in poverty in France.

kayak A native Eskimo canoe consisting of waterproofed animal skins stretched over a light framework and having one or two openings in the top with flexible watertight closures for one or two occupants.

Kayseri 38 42N 35 28E A town in central Turkey on the site of ancient Caesarea Mazaca. Kayseri has remains of the Seljuq civilization, notably the Great Mosque built in 1136. Population (1980): 281 320.

Kazakh A Turkic people of the Kazakh SSR and Xinjiang Uygur AR in China. With the Kirgiz, *Bashkir, and *Tatars they form the Kipchak division of the Turkic peoples. They were traditionally nomadic herders of horses, sheep, and goats who lived on milk products and mutton. Their movable dome-shaped dwellings (yurts) were constructed of wooden frames across which skins were stretched. Except in Xinjiang Uygur AR they are now settled stock breeders. Clan units, comprising extended-family groups and headed by chiefs, were the main social organization. *See* Turkic languages.

Kazakh Soviet Socialist Republic (*or* Kazakhstan) A constituent republic in the S Soviet Union. The *Kazakhs comprise some 30% of the population, which includes Russians (43%) and Ukrainians (7%). The area is rich in mineral resources, especially coal, oil, copper, and iron ore. The atomic power station on the Mangyshlak peninsula has the world's first industrial fast-breeder reactor. An important agricultural area, it produces cereals, cotton, rice, and fruit. Kazakhstan is also noted for its sheep, from which excellent quality wool is obtained. *History*: conquered by Mongols in the 13th century, the region came under Russian rule in the 18th and 19th centuries. It became a constituent republic in 1936. Area: 2 715 100 sq km (1 048 030 sq mi). Population (1981 est): 15 000 000. Capital: Alma Ata.

Kazan (*or* Kasan) 53 45N 49 10E A city in the E Soviet Union, since 1920 the capital of the Tatar ASSR in the RSFSR on the River Volga. It is a major historic, cultural, educational, and commercial centre and has oil refining, electrical engineering, chemical production and food processing industries. *History*: founded in the 14th century by the *Tatars, it became the capital of an independent khanate and was captured (1552) by Ivan the Terrible. Its trade and industry developed during the 19th century. It became the capital of the Tatar ASSR in 1920. Lenin and Tolstoi studied at Kazan's university (1804). Population (1981 est): 1 011 000.

Kazan, Elia (E. Kazanjoglous; 1909–) US stage and film director and novelist, born in Turkey of Greek parentage. He helped to found the *Actors' Studio in 1947. For the stage he directed *The Skin of Our Teeth* (1942), *A Streetcar Named Desire* (1947), *Death of a Salesman* (1949), and other outstanding plays. His films include *Viva Zapata* (1952), *On the Waterfront* (1954), *East of Eden* (1955), and *The Arrangement* (1969), which is based on his own novel. Other novels include *America, America* (1963) and *The Anatolian* (1982).

Kazantzakis, Nikos (1885–1957) Greek novelist and poet, who also wrote plays, travel books, and essays. His epic poem *I Odysseia* (1938), a continuation of Homer's *Odyssey*, embodies many of his ideas. He is best known for the novels *Zorba the Greek* (1946) and *Christ Recrucified* (1954).

Kazvin (*or* Qazvin) 36 16N 50 00E A town in NW Iran. It is the trading centre for a fertile plain and was the national capital in the 16th century. Population (1982 est): 244 265.

KBE. *See* Order of the British Empire.

Kean, Edmund (c. 1787–1833) British actor. He was particularly successful as Shylock in *The Merchant of Venice*, his first London success in 1814, Richard III, Macbeth, Iago in *Othello*, and Barabas in Marlowe's *The Jew of Malta*, all roles suited to his passionate style of acting.

Keating, Tom (1918–84) British artist, who won notoriety in 1976 when he confessed to painting fake old masters. Trained as a picture restorer, Keating imitated the style of Turner, Constable, Gainsborough, and others to produce some 2000 paintings and drawings, which he then sold as originals as a protest against art-dealing. Charges against him were dropped in 1979 due to ill health, after which he made a TV series demonstrating his technique and his paintings became sought after in their own right.

Keaton, Buster (Joseph Francis K.; 1895–1966) US comedian of silent films. He worked with his parents in vaudeville before starting his film career in 1917. He developed his character of the unsmiling and resilient clown in a series of classic silent comedies, including *The Navigator* (1924), *The General* (1926), and *The Cameraman* (1928). He was awarded a special Academy Award in 1959. His autobiography is *My Wonderful World of Slapstick* (1962).

Keats, John (1795–1821) British poet. The son of a London ostler, he trained as a surgeon before being encouraged by Leigh *Hunt to devote himself to poetry. Despite the failure of his first volume, *Poems* (1817), which contained the sonnet "On First Looking into Chapman's Homer," and the savage criticism directed at his second, *Endymion* (1818), Keats persisted and between 1819 and 1820 wrote most of his best-known poems. His short life was dogged by tragedies, especially the death of his brother from tuberculosis in 1818 and his unrequited love for Fanny Brawne. Such poems as *La Belle Dame Sans Merci*, *The Eve of Saint Agnes*, and the great odes ("To a Nightingale," "On a Grecian Urn," etc.), all published in 1820, eventually established his reputation. He died in Rome in search of a cure for his tuberculosis and was buried there.

Keble, John (1792–1866) British churchman. While professor of poetry at Oxford (1831–41) he preached a famous sermon, entitled "National Apostasy," which effectively began the *Oxford Movement. His book of poetry, *The Christian Year* (1827), was widely read in the 19th century. Keble College, Oxford, was founded in his memory (1870).

Kebnekaise A mountain range in N Sweden. It rises to 2123 m (6965 ft) at Kebnekaise Sydtopp, the highest mountain in Sweden.

Kecskemét 46 56N 19 43E A town in central Hungary. It lies on a wide fertile plain that is Hungary's most important agricultural area, notably for such fruit as apricots. Population (1980): 93 000.

Kedah A state in NW Peninsular Malaysia, bordering on Thailand. Rice is grown on the W coastal plain; other products include rubber, tin, tungsten, and iron. Area: 9425 sq km (3639 sq mi). Population (1980): 1 102 200. Capital: Alor Star.

Keegan, Kevin (1951–) British footballer. A forward, he played for Liverpool (1971–77), England (1972–84), Hamburg (1977–80), Southampton (1980–82), and Newcastle United (1982–84). In 1978 and 1979 he was elected European Footballer of the Year. He retired in 1984.

Keeling Islands. *See* Cocos Islands.

Keelung. *See* Jilong.

Keene, Charles Samuel (1823–91) British artist and illustrator, famous for his gentle satirization of lower- and middle-class characters in *Punch* (1851–90). He also illustrated Charles Reade's *The Cloister and the Hearth* and George Meredith's *Evan Harrington* in the periodical *Once a Week*.

Keeshond A breed of dog traditionally used by the Dutch as barge dogs. It has a compact body with a foxlike face and a long thick grey coat with black-tipped hairs. The tail is carried over the back and a dense ruff surrounds the neck. Height: 43–45 cm.

Keewatin A district of N Canada, in the *Northwest Territories. It consists of the mainland E of 102°W and N of 60°N plus most islands in Hudson Bay. Part of the Canadian Shield, it is mostly tundra. Some fur trapping takes place. Area: 590 934 sq km (228 160 sq mi). Population (1981): 4327. *See also* Barren Grounds.

Kefallinía. *See* Cephalonia.

Keflavík 64 01N 22 35W A town and fishing port in SW Iceland. It has a NATO air base. Population (1980): 6622.

Keighley 53 52N 1 54W A town in N England, in West Yorkshire on the River Aire. The main products are woollens and worsteds, textile machinery, and machine tools. It is the N terminus of the Worth Valley Railway (steam trains). Population (1981): 57 451.

Keitel, Wilhelm (1882–1946) German field marshal, who was Hitler's chief military adviser throughout World War II. In 1945 in Berlin he confirmed the German surrender. He was hanged for war crimes.

Kekulé von Stradonitz, (Friedrich) August (1829–96) German chemist, whose main interest was in valence. He was the first chemist to establish the valence of the elements and to introduce the notion of single, double, and triple bonds. He went on to deduce the structural formulae of many organic molecules, including that of benzene (**Kekulé formula**), which he claimed to have thought of in 1865 while dozing on a bus. *See also* aromatic compound.

Kelantan A state in central Peninsular Malaysia, bordering on Thailand. It was ruled by Siam (now Thailand) from the early 19th century until 1909. Rice is grown on the NE coastal plain, and rubber, copra, and minerals are produced. Area: 14 931 sq km (5765 sq mi). Population (1980): 877 575. Capital: Kota Baharu.

Keller, Gottfried (1819–90) German-Swiss poet and novelist. His early poetry (1846) won him a scholarship to study in Germany. His works include the novel *Der grüne Heinrich* (1854–55) and short stories, including *Die Leute von Seldwyla* (1856–74), describing life in a small town.

Keller, Helen Adams (1880–1968) US social worker and writer. At the age of 19 months she lost her sight and hearing through an illness. Despite these handicaps she learnt to speak, read, and write and finally graduated from Radcliffe College, Cambridge (Massachusetts), in 1904. She lectured in many countries and raised money for the education of handicapped people. Her books include *The Story of My Life* (1902).

Kellogg-Briand Pact (1928) An international agreement that condemned war as a means of settling disputes. The pact of perpetual friendship, negotiated by the US secretary of state, Frank B. Kellogg (1856–1937) and French foreign

minister, *Briand, was signed in Paris in 1928 by representatives of 15 nations, and later by 48 others. Some success in South American disputes was achieved by invoking the treaty, but it proved ineffective against the Japanese invasion of Manchuria (1931), the Italian invasion of Ethiopia (1938), and against Hitler's aggression.

Kells (Irish name: Ceanannus Mór) 54 48N 6 14W A market town in the Republic of Ireland, in Co Meath. A monastery was founded here in the 6th century AD by St Columba in which *The Book of Kells*, an 8th-century illuminated manuscript of the Gospels, is reputed to have been written. Population (1981): 2623.

Kelly, Grace (1929–82) US film actress. Her films include *High Noon* (1952), *The Country Girl* (1955), *To Catch a Thief* (1955), and *High Society* (1956). She retired from acting when she married Prince Rainier III of Monaco in 1956. She died following a road accident.

NED KELLY *A contemporary engraving of the famous bushranger during his final battle (1880). All members of the gang wore heavy home-made armour.*

Kelly, Ned (1855–80) Australian outlaw. He and his brother Dan formed a gang in 1878 that became notorious for its daring robberies in Victoria and New South Wales. He was captured and hanged in 1880 after a gunfight with the police in which the other gang members were killed.

Kelmscott Press A private printing press established in Hammersmith, London, by William *Morris in 1890. Of the 52 books issued by the press, the best known was an edition of Chaucer (1896) celebrated for its design, its typography, and its illustrations by *Burne-Jones.

kelp A large brown *seaweed belonging to the order *Laminariales* (about 30 genera), found in cold seas, usually below the level of low tide, and often covering large areas. The giant kelp *Macrocystis*, of the E Pacific coast, reaches a length of 65 m. Its branching fronds are kept afloat by air bladders. The name kelp is also used for the ashes of seaweed, from which potassium and sodium salts and iodine were once obtained. *See also* Laminaria.

kelpie A breed of short-haired dog developed in Australia from the Border Collie and used for herding sheep and cattle. Named after a champion sheepdog of the 1870s, the kelpie has a long muzzle and pricked ears. The coat may be black or red (with or without tan), fawn, chocolate, or smoke-blue. Height: 43–50 cm.

kelvin (K) The *SI unit of *thermodynamic temperature equal to 1/273.16 of the thermodynamic temperature of the triple point of water. Named after Lord *Kelvin.

Kelvin, William Thomson, 1st Baron (1824–1907) Scottish physicist, who was professor at Glasgow University (1846–99). Kelvin was the first physicist to take notice of *Joule's work on heat and to press for its recognition. The two physicists then worked together, discovering the *Joule-Kelvin effect; both also made great contributions to the new science of thermodynamics. In 1848 Kelvin postulated that there is a temperature at which the motions of particles cease and their energies become zero. He called this temperature *absolute zero and suggested a scale of temperature, now known as the Kelvin scale, in which the zero point is absolute zero. In 1852 he suggested that a *heat pump was a feasible device. Kelvin was also active in the study of electricity; during the 1860s he worked on the electrical properties of cables in conjunction with the laying of the first transatlantic cable in 1866. Kelvin was knighted for his contribution to this work in the same year and was created baron in 1896. The unit of temperature (see kelvin) is named after him.

Kemal, (Mehmed) Namik   (1840–88) Turkish poet, novelist, and dramatist. He was strongly influenced by European Romanticism and became one of the founders of modern Turkish literature. He was a member of a literary group known as the "Young Ottomans" and was imprisoned for the liberal and patriotic ideas he expressed in his most famous play, *Vatan yahnut Silistre (Fatherland or Silistria;* 1871).

Kemble, Roger   (1722–1802) British travelling actor and founder of a famous family of actors. His eldest daughter was the tragic actress Sarah *Siddons. His sons included **John Philip Kemble** (1757–1823), who played many classical tragic roles and managed both the Drury Lane and the Covent Garden theatres, and **Charles Kemble** (1775–1854), who played supporting roles and managed the Covent Garden Theatre from 1822. Charles' daughter **Frances Ann Kemble** (1809–93), known as Fanny Kemble, made a successful debut at Covent Garden in 1829, where she appeared in order to save her father from bankruptcy. She toured the USA several times. Three daughters of Roger were also well-known actresses in London and New York.

Kemerovo   55 25N 86 05E A city in the S Soviet Union, in the RSFSR on the River Tom. It is the centre of the *Kuznetsk Basin coalfield and is one of the country's major chemical-producing cities. Population (1984): 502 000.

Kempe, Margery   (c. 1373–c. 1440) English mystic. After experiencing a conversion following a period of insanity, she undertook a series of pilgrimages in Europe and Palestine. These and her mystical experiences are recounted in her autobiography, *The Book of Margery Kempe*, which she dictated between about 1432 and 1436.

Kempe, Rudolf   (1910–76) German conductor, formerly an oboist. He was conductor of the Royal Philharmonic Orchestra from 1961 to 1963 and from 1964 until his death. He was particularly well known for his performances of Wagner and Richard Strauss.

Kempis, Thomas à.   *See* Thomas à Kempis.

Kendal   54 20N 2 45W A town in NW England, in Cumbria, called the Gateway to the Lakes. It manufactures footwear, textiles, and Kendal mint cake. Catherine *Parr was born in the Norman castle. Population (1981): 23 411.

Kendall, Edward Calvin   (1886–1972) US biochemist, who shared the 1950 Nobel Prize in medicine and physiology with Phillip Hench (1896–1965) and Tadeus Reichstein (1897–   ) for their work on hormones. In 1916 he isolated the hormone thyroxine produced by the thyroid gland and later isolated several hormones from the adrenal cortex. This work laid the basis for modern endocrinology.

Kendall, Henry   (1841–82) Australian poet. He held a succession of menial jobs in Melbourne and Sydney. In three volumes of poetry, including *Leaves from Australian Forests* (1869) and *Songs from the Mountain* (1880), he vividly described the landscape and atmosphere of Australia.

kendo   A Japanese *martial art deriving from *samurai sword fighting. Combatants using bamboo staffs or wooden swords try to deliver blows on specified target areas of each other's bodies. Two hits constitute a win.

Kendrew, Sir John Cowdery   (1917–   ) British biochemist, who shared the 1962 Nobel Prize for Chemistry with Max

*Perutz for his discovery of the structure of the myoglobin molecule. Kendrew, working at Cambridge University, used the technique of *X-ray diffraction, analysing his results with a computer. He was knighted in 1974.

Keneally, Thomas Michael   (1935–   ) Australian writer. A schoolteacher until 1965, he published 16 novels before writing *Schindler's Ark* (1982), which won the 1982 *Booker Prize. His other works include *The Chant of Jimmie Blacksmith* (1972), *Gossip from the Forest* (1975), *Confederates* (1979), *A Family Madness* (1985), and *The Playmaker* (1987).

Kenilworth   52 21N 1 34W A town in central England, in Warwickshire. Kenilworth Castle, built in the 12th century, was presented to Robert Dudley, Earl of Leicester, by Elizabeth I in 1563 and described in Sir Walter Scott's novel *Kenilworth*. The town has motor and agricultural engineering and tanning industries. Population (1981): 19 315.

Kenitra (former name: Port Lyautey; Arabic name: Mina Hassan Tani)   34 20N 6 34W A port in NW Morocco, on the Atlantic Ocean. It handles agricultural products, minerals, and timber. **Population (1982): 188 194.**

Kennedy, Cape.   *See* Canaveral, Cape.

Kennedy, Joseph Patrick   (1888–1969) US businessman and diplomat. A millionaire by the age of 30, he was ambassador to Britain (1937–40). He had five daughters and four sons, three of whom entered public life. **Joseph Patrick Kennedy, Jr** (1915–44), a naval pilot, was killed in World War II. **John Fitzgerald Kennedy** (1917–63), a Democrat, was the first Roman Catholic president of the USA (1961–63). His liberal domestic polices—the so-called New Frontier—involved tax and social reforms and an extension of racial integration. He also established the *Peace Corps. Abroad, he presided over the *Bay of Pigs invasion (1961), planned under his predecessor Eisenhower, and confronted the Soviet Union over its installation of missile bases in Cuba (1962). In 1963, however, he negotiated the *Nuclear Test-Ban Treaty with Khrushchev and Macmillan, which eased relations between the superpowers. Kennedy's presidency also saw the beginning of US military involvement in Vietnam. He was assassinated in Dallas, apparently by Lee Harvey *Oswald. In 1953 he married Jacqueline Bouvier (1929–   ), who became the wife of Aristotle *Onassis in 1968. **Robert Francis Kennedy** (1925–68), attorney general (1961–64) and then a senator (1965–68), campaigned for the Democratic presidential nomination in 1968, during which he too was assassinated. **Edward Moore Kennedy** (1932–   ) is a lawyer and Democratic Senator. In 1980 he competed for the presidential nomination.

Kennelly, Arthur Edwin   (1861–1939) US electrical engineer. On learning that *Marconi had succeeded in transmitting radio waves across the Atlantic, despite the earth's curvature, Kennelly guessed that the waves were being reflected by an electrically charged layer in the upper atmosphere. The existence of this layer was confirmed independently by Oliver *Heaviside and was known as the Kennelly-Heaviside layer (now known as the E-layer of the *ionosphere).

Kenneth I MacAlpine   (died c. 858) King of the Scots of Dalriada (c. 844–c. 858). He formed the kingdom of Alba, the foundation of modern Scotland.

Kensington and Chelsea   A royal borough of W central Greater London, created in 1965 from the metropolitan boroughs of *Chelsea and Kensington. The grounds of Kensington Palace now form Kensington Gardens, a public park, which contains the famous Peter Pan statue by *Frampton. South Kensington is a centre for museums and colleges, including the Victoria and Albert Museum and the Imperial College of Science and Technology. Population (1983 est): 134 100.

Kent   A county of SE England, bordering on the English Channel and Greater London. It consists chiefly of undulating lowlands, crossed by the North Downs from W to E, and rising to the The Weald in the SW. The chief rivers are the Thames, Medway, and Stour. There are impressive chalk cliffs, notably at Dover. Often called the Garden of England, it is the country's leading fruit and hop-growing area. Other important agricultural activities include market gardening and arable, cattle, and sheep farming. The main industries are paper manufacture, shipbuilding, and oil refining. Area: 3730 sq km (1440 sq mi). Population (1983 est): 1 486 300. Administrative centre: Maidstone.

Kent, William (1685-1748) English architect, landscape gardener, and interior designer. Kent is possibly the most famous exponent of English *Palladianism. Starting as a painter in Rome, he returned to England in 1719 as the protégé of Lord Burlington, with whom he frequently worked. His most notable buildings were Holkham Hall, Norfolk (1734), the Horse Guards, London (built after his death), as well as several London townhouses. His furniture and interior designs were noticeably influenced by the *baroque. Kent's greatest contribution to English art was his development of *landscape gardening, later continued by such designers as Capability *Brown.

Kentucky A state in the central USA, lying to the E of the Mississippi River. It consists of the Appalachian Mountains in the E, the Bluegrass region in the centre, an undulating plain in the W, and the basins of the Tennessee and Ohio Rivers in the SW. Manufacturing in the state includes machinery, iron and steel products, paints, varnishes, textiles, whiskey, and food products. It is an important coal-mining state and also produces petroleum and natural gas. Local timber is used in the furniture and wood industries. The principal agricultural products are tobacco, corn, hay, soya beans, cattle, sheep, and pigs. It is also an important region for the breeding of thoroughbred horses. Kentucky is a rural state with a strong rural tradition and folk culture. *History*: Daniel Boone explored the area (1769) and after rapid settlement it became a state (1792). Area: 104 623 sq km (40 395 sq mi). Population (1980): 3 661 433. Capital: Frankfort.

Kenya, Mount 0 10S 37 30E An extinct volcano in Kenya, the second highest mountain in Africa. It includes 12 small glaciers. Height: 5200 m (17 058 ft).

Kenya, Republic of A country in East Africa, on the Indian Ocean. The land rises gradually from the coast to the highlands of the interior reaching heights of over 5000 m (17 000 ft). In the W the Great Rift Valley runs N–S. Most of the inhabitants are Africans, including *Kikuyu, *Luo, *Masai, and Kamba. *Economy*: agricultural production and processing forms the basis of the economy. A variety of subtropical and temperate crops are grown. The chief cash crops are coffee, tea (of which Kenya is Africa's leading producer), sisal, and pineapples; livestock rearing and dairy farming are also important. Forestry is being developed and mineral resources include soda ash, gold, limestone, and salt. Hydroelectricity is a valuable source of power and industries include food processing, with oil refining at Mombasa. Tourism is an important source of income with Kenya's abundant big game; wildlife reserves include the huge Tsavo National Park. *History*: some of the earliest known fossil *hominid remains have been found in the region by the *Leakey family. The coastal area was settled by the Arabs from the 7th century AD and was controlled by the Portuguese during the 16th and 17th centuries. It became a British protectorate (East Africa Protectorate) in 1895 and a colony (Kenya) in 1920. In the 1950s independence movements, especially among the Kikuyu, led to the *Mau Mau revolt. Kenya gained independence in 1963 and in 1964 became a republic within the British Commonwealth, with Jomo *Kenyatta as its first president. In the late 1980s tension escalated with neighbouring Uganda, leading to border clashes. President: Daniel Arap Moi (1924–   ). Official languages: Swahili and English. Official currency: Kenya shilling of 100 cents. Area: 582 600 sq km (224 960 mi). Popu-

WILLIAM KENT *The Palladian portico on the south front of Holkham Hall in Norfolk.*

lation (1983 est): 18 580 000. Capital: Nairobi. Main port: Mombasa.

Kenyatta, Jomo (c. 1891-1978) Kenyan statesman; president (1964-78). Son of a poor farmer of the Kikuyu tribe, Kenyatta studied anthropology in London, where his doctoral thesis on the Kikuyu was published in 1938 as *Facing Mount Kenya*. On his return to Kenya he became (1947) president of the Kenya African Union and in 1953 was imprisoned for seven years by the colonial government for his part in the *Mau Mau rebellion (complicity in which he always denied). While in gaol he was elected leader of the Kenya African National Union (1960), which achieved Kenya's independence in 1963. Kenyatta was prime minister before becoming president of a one-party state.

Kenyon, Dame Kathleen (1906-78) British archaeologist. Under the influence of Sir Mortimer *Wheeler she promoted sophisticated excavation techniques. Her excavations at *Jericho (1952-58), through which the site's great age was revealed, and at *Jerusalem (1961-67) are renowned.

Kepler, Johannes (1571-1630) German astronomer, who was one of the first supporters of *Copernicus' heliocentric theory of the solar system. In 1597 he went to Prague to study under Tycho *Brahe; on Tycho's death, Kepler inherited his astronomical observations. Kepler used this data to deduce the shape of planetary orbits, discovering that they were elliptical. He published this discovery, the first of *Kepler's laws, together with his second law in *Astronomia Nova* (1609). In 1619 he published his third law relating a planet's year to its distance from the sun. In 1610 he received a telescope built by *Galileo, which he used to observe Jupiter. In 1611 he constructed an improved version, now known as a Keplerian *telescope.

Kepler's laws Three laws of planetary motion proposed by Johannes Kepler in 1609 and (third law) 1619. They state that: (1) each planet moves round the sun in an elliptical orbit with the sun at one focus of the ellipse; (2) the line joining a planet to the sun sweeps out equal areas in equal times, i.e. orbital velocity decreases as distance from the sun increases; (3) the square of the *sidereal period (P) of a planet is directly proportional to the cube of its mean distance (a) from the sun. For P in years and a in *astronomical units, $P^2 = a^3$.

Kerala A state in SW India, extending along the W coastal plain and Western Ghats to India's S tip. Tropical, beautiful, and poor, it is India's most densely populated state, with little industry or mining. Rice, tea, coffee, pepper, rubber, nuts, and fruit are farmed. Fishing is also important. *History*: a civilization separate from Aryan N India, Malayalam-speaking Kerala has traded with the Near and Far East since ancient times, flourishing in the 9th and 10th centuries. Area: 38 855 sq km (14 998 sq mi). Population (1981): 25 403 217. Capital: Trivandrum.

keratin An insoluble fibrous protein that is the major constituent of hair, nails, feathers, beaks, horns, and scales. Keratin is also found in the outer protective layers of the skin.

Kerbela. *See* Karbala.

Kerch 45 22N 36 27E A port in the SW Soviet Union, in the Ukrainian SSR on the Black Sea on the Strait of Kerch. Founded in the 6th century BC by Greek colonists, it was captured from the Tatars by Russia in 1771. Fishing is important, and related activities, together with iron and steel production, form the basis of its industry. Population (1981 est): 159 000.

Kerenski, Aleksandr Feodorovich (1881–1970) Russian revolutionary. A member of the Socialist Revolutionary Party, after the outbreak of the Russian Revolution in February, 1917, Kerenski became minister of justice and then minister of war in *Lvov's provisional government. In July, after Lvov's fall, he became prime minister. His insistence that Russia remain in World War I, and his mismanagement of internal economic affairs, led to the Bolshevik coup d'état in October. Kerenski fled to Paris and in 1940 to the USA.

Kerguelen Islands 49 30S 69 30E An archipelago in the S Indian Ocean, in the French Southern and Antarctic Territories. Kerguelen Island, the largest, is mountainous and glacial and the site of several scientific bases. Area: 7215 sq km (2786 sq mi).

Kérkira (*or* Kérkyra). *See* Corfu.

Kerman 30 18N 57 05E A town in E Iran. It is an agricultural trading centre and carpet-making town. Kerman University was founded in 1974. Population (1985 est): 266 800.

Kermanshah. *See* Bakhtaran.

kermes A scale insect of the genus *Kermes*, especially *K. ilices* of Europe and W Asia, the dried bodies of which were formerly used to produce a red dye. They feed on the small evergreen kermes oak (*Quercus coccifera*), which is native to S Europe, N Africa, and W Asia and grows to a height of 7 m.

Kern, Jerome (David) (1885–1945) US composer of musical comedies, the most famous of which was *Show Boat* (1927), written in collaboration with Oscar *Hammerstein II. After 1939 he devoted himself to film music. Two of his best-known songs are "Ol' Man River" and "Smoke Gets in Your Eyes."

kerosene. *See* paraffin.

Kerouac, Jack (1922–69) US novelist. He was a leading figure of the *Beat movement, of which his novel *On the Road* (1957) was a seminal work. His other loosely structured autobiographical works include *The Dharma Bums* (1958), *The Subterraneans* (1958), *Big Sur* (1962), and *Desolation Angels* (1965).

Kerr effects Two effects concerned with optical changes produced by magnetic or electric fields. In the magneto-optical effect, plane-polarized light is slightly elliptically polarized when reflected by the pole of an electromagnet. In the electro-optical effect, the plane of polarization of a beam of light is rotated when passed through certain liquids or solids across which a potential difference is applied. This effect is utilized in the **Kerr cell**, which consists of a transparent cell containing a liquid, such as nitrobenzene; two parallel plates immersed in the liquid enable a field to be applied so that the passage of a beam of polarized light can be interrupted. The cell is used as a high-speed shutter and to modulate *laser beams. Named after the discoverer John Kerr (1824–1907).

Kerry (Irish name: Chiarraighe) A county in the SW Republic of Ireland, in Munster bordering on the Atlantic Ocean. Chiefly mountainous with a deeply indented coastline, it rises in the S to *Macgillycuddy's Reeks and contains the famous Lakes of Killarney, noted for their beauty. The chief occupations are fishing, farming, and tourism. Area: 4701 sq km (1815 sq mi). Population (1981): 122 770. County town: Tralee.

Kertanagara (d. 1292) King of Java (1268–92). Honoured as Java's greatest leader, he took advantage of the disunited Malay world in the 13th century to unite Java and became the most powerful ruler in SE Asia. He protected Indonesia from Kublai Khan's efforts to exact tribute and upheld Buddhism and Javanese culture.

Kesey, Ken (1935–) US novelist. His best-known novel, *One Flew Over the Cuckoo's Nest* (1962), a satire based on his own experience in a mental hospital, was made into a successful film by Miloš *Forman. Later works include *Sometimes a Great Notion* (1964) and *Kesey's Garage Sale* (1973).

Kesselring, Albert (1885–1960) German general, who commanded the Luftwaffe in World War II. He held the air command in the invasions of Poland (1939) and France (1940) and in the battle of Britain (1940). In 1943 he became commander of land and air forces in Italy and in 1945 on the Western Front. His death sentence as a war criminal was commuted to life imprisonment and he was released in 1952.

Kesteven, Parts of. *See* Lincolnshire.

kestrel A small *falcon characterized by a long tail and the ability to hover, with the tail fanned out, before diving on its prey. The common kestrel (*Falco tinnunculus*), 32 cm long, is widespread in Eurasia and Africa and hunts small rodents, birds, and insects. The female has a brown streaked plumage; the male is blue-grey with black-streaked pale-brown underparts, a black-tipped tail, and a black eye stripe.

Keswick 54 37N 3 08W A town in NW England, in Cumbria. One of the main tourist centres of the Lake District, it is situated on the River Greta close to Derwentwater and Skiddaw. It has many associations with the Lakeland poets; for example, Robert Southey is buried here. Population (1981): 5635.

ketch A fore-and-aft-rigged □sailing vessel with two masts, a taller one set approximately one-third of the boat's length from the bows, a shorter one just forward of the rudder post. Ketches are a favoured rig for yachts, for the split rig reduces the area of each sail, making handling easier. Ketches do not sail as well towards the wind as *sloops do. *See also* yawl.

Ketch, Jack (d. 1686) English hangman, notorious for his cruelty. He was appointed public hangman in 1663, and was responsible for the executions of Lord William *Russell (1683) and the Duke of *Monmouth (1685), both of which he badly bungled. Subsequently all English executioners were popularly known by his name.

ketone A class of organic chemicals having the general formula RCOR′, where R and R′ are hydrocarbon groups. Ketones are prepared by the oxidation of secondary alcohols. *Acetone (dimethyl ketone) is a common example.

Kettering, Charles Franklin (1876–1958) US engineer, whose inventions, notably the electric starter (1912), greatly improved motor cars. He also pioneered the use of leaded petrol and antiknock compounds; in 1951 he developed a high-compression car engine.

kettledrums. *See* timpani.

Kew Gardens The Royal Gardens at Kew, near Richmond, Surrey, which occupy land once owned by the royal family. The first botanic garden was created there in 1759, by Augusta (d. 1772), Princess of Wales, and in the late 18th and early 19th centuries Kew became internationally famous as an advisory centre, with many exotic plants, largely due to the efforts of Sir Joseph *Banks. Between 1848 and 1876 William and Joseph *Hooker founded the Museum of Economic Botany, the Library, Herbarium, and Jodrell Laboratory. Kew has played a major role in the distribution of many economic plants, notably the transfer of the rubber plant from its native South America to the Far East, and is now renouned as a scientific institute. In Oct 1987 hurricane-force winds caused extensive damage, destroying many irreplaceable trees.

key. *See* tonality.

Keynes, John Maynard, 1st Baron (1883–1946) British economist, whose ideas continued to exert influence on modern government economic policies (*see* Keynesianism). After attending the Versailles peace conference as a Treasury representative, Keynes published *The Economic Consequences of the Peace* (1919), which attacked the war reparations imposed on Germany. In his greatest work, *General Theory of Employment, Interest and Money* (1936), written during the Depression years, he argued that unemployment can only be alleviated by increased public spending. During World War II he worked for the government on war finance and in 1944 was the chief British representative at the Bretton Woods conference, at which the *International Monetary Fund was established.

Keynesianism The economic theories of the British economist J. M. *Keynes, whose *General Theory of Employment, Interest and Money* (1936) has had a pervasive influence. Keynes' central departure from established theory was the premise that what is rational for the individual and the firm is not necessarily rational for the government, and that rather than reinforcing the *trade cycle the government should counter it by public spending with money raised by *deficit financing. This has been developed by later thinkers, not all of whose ideas Keynes himself would have agreed with, into a doctrine of expansive *fiscal policy and government interventionism.

Keystone Kops A zealous but incompetent police force that featured in the silent film comedies produced by Mack *Sennett for the Keystone Film Company between 1912 and 1917. They were the butt of much irreverent slapstick comedy, preserving their imperturbable masks of dignity even during the absurd accelerated chase sequences.

Key West 24 34N 81 48W A city in the USA, in Florida situated at the tip of the Florida Keys. A naval, air, and coastguard base, Key West is a tourist centre and was the home of Ernest Hemingway. Population (1980): 24 382.

KGB (Committee of State Security) The Soviet secret police concerned with internal security and intelligence. It was founded in 1954, after the fall of *Beria, and replaced the more brutal MGB (Ministry of State Security; 1946–53).

Khabarovsk 48 32N 135 08E A port in the E Soviet Union, in the RSFSR on the River Amur. Situated on the Trans-Siberian Railway, it is an important transport centre. Industries include engineering, machine building, and oil refining. Population (1981 est): 545 000.

Khachaturian, Aram Ilich (1903–78) Soviet composer of Armenian birth. He studied composition at the Moscow conservatoire. His music was deeply influenced by the scales and rhythms of Caucasian folk music. His compositions include concertos for piano (1936) and violin (1940) and the famous ballets *Gayaneh* (1942) and *Spartacus* (1954).

Khafre (Greek name: Chephren) King of Egypt (c. 2550 BC) of the 4th dynasty. He emerged victorious from the dynastic strife that followed the death of his father *Khufu. Khafre built the second pyramid and (probably) the Sphinx at *Giza.

Khakass An autonomous region (*oblast*) in the S Soviet Union, in the RSFSR. It was formed in 1930 for the Turkic-speaking Khakass people, who are Orthodox Christians. Khakass is rich in minerals, including gold, coal, iron ore, and copper, and timber and woodworking industries are also important. Livestock is raised. Area: 61 900 sq km (23 855 sq mi). Population (1980 est): 503 000. Capital: Abakan.

khaki (Hindi-Urdu: dust-coloured) A yellowish-brown fabric of cotton, wool, or synthetic fibre used chiefly for military uniforms. Khaki was first worn by British troops in India as a form of camouflage. From about 1900 it became the regular British uniform for battle and has since been adopted by most other nations.

Khalid Ibn Abdul Aziz (1913–82) King of Saudi Arabia (1975–82). Son of *Ibn Saud, the founder of Saudi Arabia, Khalid had a traditional Muslim education. He succeeded his brother, *Faisal Ibn Abdul Aziz.

Khalifa. *See* Abd Allah.

Khama, Sir Seretse (1921–80) Botswana statesman; president (1966–80). Trained as a barrister in London, Seretse Khama married Ruth Williams, an Englishwoman, as a result of which he had to renounce the chieftaincy of the Bamangwato tribe before returning to what was then Bechuanaland in 1956. In 1961 he founded the Bechuanaland Democratic Party, which gained independence for Botswana in 1966.

khamsin A hot dry southerly wind that blows across Egypt from the Sahara Desert. Most common in April and June, it precedes *depressions moving E along the N African coast. According to Arab tradition it blows for 50 days.

Kharga, El (*or* al-Wahat al-Kharijah) A large oasis in Egypt, in the Libyan Desert. It produces dates, figs, olives, and vegetables; efforts have been made to increase irrigation by sinking deep wells. Chief town: El Kharga.

Kharkov 50 00N 36 15E A city in the Soviet Union, in the E Ukrainian SSR. It was almost totally destroyed in World War II, when its importance as a road and railway junction led to bitter fighting. Today, it is the third (after Moscow and Leningrad) largest railway junction in the country. The nearby Donets Basin coalfield supports a major engineering industry. Population (1981 est): 1 485 000.

Khartoum (*or* al-Khurtum) 15 40N 32 52E The capital of the Sudan, at the confluence of the Blue and the White Nile Rivers. An Egyptian army camp in the early 19th century, it later became a garrison town. In 1885 *Gordon was besieged and killed here and the town destroyed by the forces of the Mahdi (*see* Mahdi, al-) but was recaptured by Anglo-British forces in 1898 and rebuilt. It has several cathedrals and two mosques; its university was founded in 1956 and it also houses part of Cairo University (1955). An important trading centre, it produces textiles and glass. Population (1983): 476 218.

Khazars A Turkic people who inhabited the lower Volga basin from the 7th to 13th centuries. Noted for their laws, tolerance, and cosmopolitanism, the Khazars were the main commercial link between the Baltic and the Muslim empire. In the 8th century the Khazars embraced Judaism. Slavonic and nomadic Turkic invaders brought the downfall of the Khazars in the 11th century. Itil, near modern Astrakhan, was their capital.

khedive The title bestowed in 1867 by the sultan of the Ottoman Empire on the hereditary viceroy of Egypt. It was used until 1914, when Egypt became a British protectorate.

Kherson 46 39N 32 38E A port in the Soviet Union, in the S Ukrainian SSR on the River Dnepr. It is 25 km (15 mi) from the Black Sea and, founded in 1778, was Russia's first naval base on the Sea. Shipbuilding remains the chief industry. Population (1984): 340 000.

Khiva 41 25N 60 49E A town in the S Soviet Union, in the Uzbek SSR on the River Amu Darya. It may have existed in the 6th century AD and was the centre of the khanate of Khiva from the 16th century until 1873, when it was captured by Russia. Its architectural remains attract many tourists. Cotton spinning is also important.

Khlebnikov, Velimir (Victor K.; 1885-1922) Russian poet, who founded the Russian futurist movement (see futurism) with *Mayakovskii. His poetry was characterized by verbal experimentation and technical virtuosity; much of it was written on scraps of paper during his many travels. He died of typhus and starvation while returning from Persia.

Khmer A people of Kampuchea (Cambodia), Thailand, and Vietnam who speak the Khmer language, belonging to the Mon-Khmer Division of the *Austro-Asiatic languages, which includes Vietnamese, *Mon, and Palaung. They are rice cultivators and fishers, living in village communities headed by an elected chief. Their religion is Theravada Buddhism, but magical beliefs and practices survive from pre-Buddhist times. The Khmer empire was founded in 616 AD and between the 9th and 13th centuries Khmer kings presided over the advanced civilization that was responsible for the great stone buildings of *Angkor. The name Khmer was adopted by the anti-French nationalist movement of Cambodia (which was called the Khmer Republic from 1971 to 1975) and the name continues in the communist Khmer Rouge movement (see Kampuchea).

Khoisan The racial grouping comprising the Hottentot and Bushmen people of S Africa. The Khoisan languages, of which the Hottentot Nama and the Bushman Kung have been most studied, are noted for their click sounds. Formerly widespread S of the Zambezi River, the Khoisan tribes have been decimated by Bantu and European encroachments since 1700 and their traditional culture and racial integrity almost exterminated. The Hottentots were nomads, herding sheep and cattle. They were divided into clans, each with its own territory and chief, but with no overall political coherence. The Bushmen were traditionally hunters and gatherers, but most are now farm workers. Some groups in the desert regions of W Botswana still roam in small bands, with the women collecting roots and berries and the men hunting with bows and poisoned arrows. Bushman rock paintings survive in many areas of South Africa.

Khomeini, Ayatollah Ruholla (1900-) Iranian Shiite Muslim leader (ayatollah). Following the overthrow of the shah (1979) he returned from 16 years of exile to lead the so-called Islamic Revolution.

Khorana, Har Gobind (1922-) US biochemist, born in India, who was responsible for deciphering the *genetic code, i.e. the hereditary information carried by DNA molecules. Khorana shared a Nobel Prize (1968) with R. W. Holley (1922-) and M. Nirenberg (1927-). In 1976 Khorana and his team were responsible for constructing the first entirely synthetic yet biologically active gene.

Khosrow I King of Persia (531-79 AD), who came to the throne after prolonged social disturbance and took measures to restore prosperity and to reform the state. He reorganized the army, strengthened his frontiers, and expanded his territory. His only serious rival, the Byzantine empire, was forced to concede tribute and territory but remained hostile. Khosrow's firm yet benevolent rule over an empire stretching from the River Oxus (now Amu Darya) to the Yemen marked the summit of *Sasanian power.

Khosrow II (d. 628 AD) King of Persia (590-628) of the Sasanian dynasty, who accepted Byzantine aid to secure his throne, conceding territory in return. Its subsequent recovery and the conquest of Anatolia, Syria, and Egypt overtaxed Persian resources. The Byzantine counterattack reached his capital, Ctesiphon, and Khosrow was assassinated; the Sasanian empire disintegrated and was soon overrun by the Arabs.

Khrushchev, Nikita S(ergeevich) (1894-1971) Soviet statesman; first secretary of the Soviet Communist Party (1953-64) and prime minister (1958-64). Khrushchev was a close associate of Stalin and emerged victorious from the power struggle that followed his death. In 1956 Khrushchev began a programme of destalinization and the degree of liberalization that ensued within the Soviet Union gave rise to revolts in other communist countries, such as the *Poznan Riots in Poland and the *Hungarian Revolution. Owing to the failure of his economic policies and his unsuccessful foreign policy, notably his attempt to install missiles in Cuba (1962) and his antagonism towards China, he was ousted by *Brezhnev and *Kosygin.

Khufu (or Cheops) King of Egypt (c. 2600 BC) of the 4th dynasty; the father of *Khafre. He built the Great Pyramid at *Giza, which was said to have taken 20 years to construct. Khufu's funeral barge has been discovered in good condition.

Khulna 22 49N 89 34E A city in S Bangladesh, on the Ganges delta. An agricultural trading centre, its industries include shipbuilding and the manufacture of cotton cloth. Population (1981 est): 623 184.

Khyber Pass (Khaybar Pass or Khaibar Pass) 34 06N 71 05E A mountain pass in the Safid Kuh range of the Hindu Kush, connecting Kabul in Afghanistan with Peshawar in Pakistan. Rising to 1072 m (3518 ft) in barren country, it is of strategic importance, having been used many times over the centuries by invading armies, the progress of which has often been impeded by hostile Afridi tribesmen.

kiang A wild *ass, Equus hemionus kiang, of the Himalayas. It is the tallest wild ass, 1.4 m at the shoulder, and has a chestnut-coloured coat. See also onager.

Kiangsi. See Jiangxi.

Kiangsi Soviet. See Jiangxi Soviet.

Kiangsu. See Jiangsu.

kibbutz An Israeli collective settlement in which land and property are owned or leased by all its members and work and meals are organized collectively. Adults generally have private quarters but children are housed together. About 3% of the population live in kibbutzim. A moshav is a smallholders' cooperative in which machinery is shared but land and property is generally privately owned. About 5% of the Israeli population live in moshavim.

Kicking Horse Pass A pass through the Canadian Rocky Mountains, NW of Banff. It is the highest point on the Canadian Pacific Railway. Height: 1627 m (5339 ft).

Kidd, William (c. 1645-1701) Scottish sailor. He spent his youth privateering for the English against the French off the North American coast and in 1695 he was given a royal commission to suppress pirates in the Indian Ocean. He reached Madagascar, a pirates' centre, where he seems to have joined them. He was arrested on his return to Boston, sent to England, and executed (possibly unjustly).

Kidderminster 52 23N 2 14W A market town in W central England, in Hereford and Worcester on the River Stour. It is famous for carpet manufacture, begun in 1735. Woollen and worsted yarn, textile machinery, and beet sugar are also produced here. Population (1981): 51 261.

Kidinnu (4th century BC) Babylonian mathematician and astronomer, who discovered the precession of the equinoxes, an effect that causes the position of the sun at equinox to move slowly backwards through the zodiac. He also calculated the interval of time between successive new moons to within a second.

kidneys The two organs of excretion in vertebrate animals

KILLER WHALE   *A specimen at Windsor Safari Park. Killer whales are known for their spectacular jumps, during which they may cover a distance of 12-13.5 m.*

and man, which also regulate the amount of salt and water in the blood. The human kidneys are bean-shaped, each about 12 cm long and weighing about 150 g, and situated on either side of the spine below the diaphragm. They contain millions of tubules, the outer parts of which filter water and dissolved substances from blood supplied by the renal artery. Most of the water and some substances are reabsorbed back into the blood further down the tubules: the remaining fluid (*see* urine) contains waste products of protein metabolism and passes on to the pelvis of the kidneys and out through the ureters to the *bladder. The reabsorption of water is controlled by a hormone (vasopressin) from the pituitary gland. The kidneys also secrete a hormone (*see* renin) that assists in controlling blood pressure.

If one kidney ceases to function or is removed the other will enlarge and take over its function. Removal of both kidneys requires the use of an artificial kidney machine (*see* dialysis) unless a suitable donor kidney is available for *transplantation.

Kiel   54 20N 10 08E A city in NE West Germany, the capital of Schleswig-Holstein. A Baltic port, famed for its annual regatta, it was the chief naval port of Germany by the late 19th century. The naval mutiny here in 1918 sparked off revolutions throughout Germany. It has a university (1665) and a 13th-century palace, restored after World War II. Its chief industries are shipbuilding and engineering. Population (1983 est): 248 400.

Kiel Canal (German name: Nord-Ostsee Kanal; former name: Kaiser Wilhelm Kanal)   A canal in West Germany, in Schleswig-Holstein *Land*, linking Kiel on the Baltic Sea with the Elbe estuary on the North Sea.

Kielce   50 51N 20 39E A town in S central Poland. During World War II it contained four German concentration camps. Notable buildings include its cathedral (12th century). It is a major industrial centre. Population (1982): 192 000.

Kierkegaard, Søren   (1813–55) Danish philosopher. Although critical of *Hegel, particularly in *The Concept of Irony* (1841), he remained under his influence. Kierkegaard was a prolific writer; much of his work is poetic and paradoxical even in its titles, for example *Either-Or* (1843) and *Concluding Unscientific Postscript* (1846). Suspicious of both science and the established Church, he saw man as existing in isolation and relating only to God. Among his specifically religious books is *Works of Love* (1847). His journal reveals him as a deeply religious, if unorthodox, thinker. He greatly influenced 20th-century *existentialism.

Kiev   50 28N 30 29E A city in the SW Soviet Union, the capital of the Ukrainian SSR on the River Dnepr. It is the third (after Moscow and Leningrad) largest city in the country and a major economic and cultural centre. Industries include metallurgy, the manufacture of machinery and instruments, chemicals, and textiles. Among its many educational institutions is the Kiev State University (1833), and its opera and ballet companies have a worldwide reputation. Outstanding buildings include the 11th-century St Sophia cathedral, now a museum, and the Golden Gate of Kiev. *History*: Kiev, "the mother of cities," was probably founded in the 6th or 7th century AD and from the 9th to the 13th centuries was the centre of a feudal state ruled by the Rurik dynasty—Kiev-Rus, the historical nucleus of Russia. Tatar attacks virtually destroyed the city, which subsequently passed to Lithuania. Russian rule was established in the 17th century. After the Russian Revolution Kiev became the capital of the short-lived Ukrainian republic and in 1934, the capital of the Ukrainian SSR. In World War II the city was occupied after a long siege by the Germans and thousands of its inhabitants were massacred. Its postwar reconstruction has been spectacular; in 1986 it absorbed many inhabitants of Chernobyl after the nuclear disaster. Population (1984): 2 409 000.

Kigali   1 58S 30 00E The capital of Rwanda (since 1962). It is the centre of the country's mining industry and has a trade in coffee. Population (1981): 156 650.

Kikuyu   A Bantu-speaking tribe of Kenya. They cultivate cereals and sweet potatoes and keep considerable numbers of livestock, particularly cattle. Small groups of patrilineal kin occupy scattered homesteads of conical-shaped huts. These kin groups are organized into clans but there is little hierarchical organization or centralization of authority. Age grades are an important basis of social organization, boys being initiated by circumcision. Political authority is held by a council of members of the senior age grade. The largest tribe in Kenya, the Kikuyu were deeply involved in the anticolonial *Mau Mau movement during the 1950s and have had a dominant voice in postindependence government.

Kilauea   A volcanic crater in the USA, in Hawaii on the E side of Mauna Loa. It is one of the largest active craters in the world. Height: 1247 m (4090 ft). Width: 3 km (2 mi).

Kildare (Irish name: Contae Chill Dara)   A county in the E Republic of Ireland, in Leinster. It consists chiefly of a low-lying fertile plain containing part of the Bog of Allen in the N and the Curragh, an area noted for its racehorse breeding and race track. Cattle rearing and arable farming are also important. Area: 1694 sq km (654 sq mi). Population (1981): 104 122. County town: Naas.

Kilimanjaro, Mount   3 02S 37 20E A volcanic mountain in Tanzania on the Kenyan border, the highest mountain in Africa. It has two volcanic peaks: Kibo at 5895 m (19 340 ft) and Mawenzi at 5273 m (17 300 ft).

Kilkenny (Irish name: Contae Chill Choinnigh)   A county in the SE Republic of Ireland, in Leinster. Chiefly hilly, it is drained by the Rivers Suir, Barrow, and Nore. Agriculture is the chief occupation with cattle rearing and dairy farming. Area: 2062 sq km (796 sq mi). Population (1981): 70 806. County town: Kilkenny.

Kilkenny (Irish name: Cill Choinnigh)   52 09N 7 15W A city in the Republic of Ireland, the county town of Co Kilkenny. One of Ireland's oldest towns, it has two cathedrals and a 12th-century castle. Population (1981): 9466.

Killarney (Irish name: Cill Airne)   52 03N 9 30W A town in the Republic of Ireland in Co Kerry. A tourist centre near the three Lakes of Killarney, it is famous for its lake, mountain, and forest scenery. Population (1981): 7693.

killer whale A large toothed whale, *Orcinus orca*, common in Pacific and Antarctic waters but found in all other oceans. Up to 9 m long, killer whales are black above and pure white beneath, with an erect dorsal fin as tall as a man. They are notorious for their voracious appetites, hunting in packs and tackling even sharks and other whales. Like other dolphins, they are intelligent and trainable in captivity. Family: *Delphinidae* (dolphins).

Killiecrankie, Pass of 56 43N 3 40W A pass in the Grampian Mountains, Scotland, in Tayside Region. It was the scene of a massacre of William III's troops by Jacobite Highlanders (1689).

killifish One of several small elongated fish, also called egg-laying top minnows, belonging to the family *Cyprinodontidae*, especially the genus *Fundulus*. Killifish occur chiefly in tropical America, Africa, and Asia in fresh, brackish, or salt water and feed at the surface on plant or animal material. Up to 15 cm long, many are brightly coloured and kept as aquarium fish. Similar related fish are the live-bearing top minnows of the family *Poeciliidae*. Order: *Atheriniformes*.

Kilmarnock 55 37N 4 30W An industrial town in SW Scotland, in Strathclyde Region on Kilmarnock Water. Industries include engineering, carpets, woollens, lace, whisky, footwear, and earthenware. The Burns museum contains many of his manuscripts. Population (1981): 52 080.

kilogram (kg) The *SI unit of mass equal to the mass of the platinum-iridium prototype kept at the International Bureau of Weights and Measures near Paris.

kiloton A measure of the explosive power of a nuclear weapon. It is equivalent to an explosion of 1000 tons of trinitrotoluene (TNT).

kilowatt-hour (kW-hr) A unit of energy used in charging for electricity. It is equal to the work done by a power of 1000 watts in 1 hour.

kilt. *See* Highland dress.

Kilvert, Francis (1840–79) British clergyman and diarist. His diary, vividly recording scenes of rural life in the Welsh marches in the 1870s, was discovered in 1937 and published in three volumes (1938–40).

Kimberley 28 45S 24 46E A city in South Africa, in N Cape Province. It was founded (1871) following the discovery of diamonds and is today the world's largest diamond centre. The famous Kimberley Open Mine, 1.6 km (1 mi) in circumference, was closed in 1915. Industries include engineering, clothing, and diamond cutting. Population (1980): 144 923.

Kimberleys. *See* Western Australia.

Kim Il Sung (Kim Song Ju; 1912–) North Korean statesman; prime minister (1948–72) and then president (1972–). He became leader of the Soviet-dominated N in 1945 and with the establishment there of the Democratic People's Republic of Korea in 1948, its first prime minister and chairman of the Korean Workers' Party. In 1950 he ordered the invasion of South Korea in an unsuccessful attempt to reunite Korea (*see* Korean War).

kimono The traditional costume of Japan for men and women from the 7th century AD, now worn mainly by women for formal occasions. It is an ankle-length wide-sleeved robe, often silk, wrapped over at the front and tied with an *obi* (sash) in a large bow at the back of the waist.

Kincardine (*or* Kincardineshire) A former county of NE Scotland. Under local government reorganization in 1975 it became part of Grampian Region.

kindergarten A school for young children aged three to five years. The term kindergarten, a German word meaning "children's garden," was originated by the German educationalist Friedrich *Froebel but the education of young children in the UK is now generally referred to as nursery education.

kinematics. *See* mechanics.

kinetic energy Energy possessed by a body by virtue of its motion. If the body, mass m, is moving in a straight line with velocity v, its kinetic energy is $\frac{1}{2}mv^2$. If it is rotating its rotational kinetic energy is $\frac{1}{2}I\omega^2$, where I is its moment of inertia and ω its angular velocity.

kinetics. *See* mechanics.

kinetic theory A theory developed in the 19th century, largely by *Joule and *Maxwell, in which the behaviour of gases is explained by regarding them as consisting of tiny dimensionless particles in constant random motion. Collisions, either between the particles or between the particles and the walls of the container, are assumed to be perfectly elastic. The theory explains the pressure of a gas as being due to collisions between the particles and the walls, its temperature as a measure of the *average* *kinetic energy of the particles, and the heat of the gas as the *total* kinetic energy of the particles. The kinetic theory is based on the concept of an *ideal gas obeying ideal *gas laws; real gases consist of molecules having a finite volume (*see* Van der Waals). The kinetic theory is extended to all matter and regards the heat of a body as the total of the translational, rotational, or vibrational energy of its constituent particles.

King, Billie Jean (*born* Moffitt; 1943–) US tennis player, who was Wimbledon singles champion in 1966, 1967, 1968, 1972, 1973, and 1975. She won many other titles and took her 20th Wimbledon title in 1979 for the women's doubles, thus beating the previous record of 19 held by Elizabeth Ryan (1892–1979).

MARTIN LUTHER KING *Holding the gold medal of the Nobel Peace Prize (Oslo, 1964).*

King, Jr, Martin Luther (1929–68) US Black civil-rights leader. An outstanding orator, he followed principles of nonviolent resistance in organizing demonstrations against racial inequality and was one of the leaders of the great

March on Washington (1963), joined by over 250 000 people. His campaigns contributed to the passing of the Civil Rights Act (1964) and the Voting Rights Act (1965) and earned him the Nobel Peace Prize in 1964. He was assassinated in Memphis, Tennessee, by James Earl Ray.

King, William Lyon Mackenzie (1874-1950) Canadian statesman; Liberal prime minister (1921-26, 1926-30, 1935-48). His administration enacted moderate welfare legislation and increased Canadian trade with the USA and UK. His chief political aim was national unity, achieved by enlisting the support of Progressives and French Canadians.

King Charles spaniel A breed of *spaniel having a compact body, short legs, a short neck, and a large head with a short upturned nose. There are four colour varieties: Blenheim, ruby, tricolour, and black and tan, the last being associated with King Charles II. Weight: 3.5-6 kg; height: about 25 cm. The Cavalier King Charles spaniel has a similar coloration but is lighter bodied, with relatively longer legs and a longer muzzle. Weight: 5-8 kg; height: about 30 cm.

kingcup. See marsh marigold.

kingfisher A bird belonging to a family (*Alcedinidae*; 85 species) divided into two subfamilies: the *Alcedininae* are narrow-billed and live near water, feeding on small fish; the *Dacetoninae* are broad-billed insectivorous birds not closely associated with water. Kingfishers are 12-45 cm long, mostly compact with a bright plumage of blues, greens, purples, and reds, and are often crested; they have large heads with often brightly coloured bills and usually nest in burrows in banks. Order: *Coraciiformes* (hornbills, etc.).

King George's War (1744-48) An indecisive conflict between Britain and France for control of North America. It was an aspect of the War of the *Austrian Succession.

King James Version The Authorized Version of the English *Bible that appeared in 1611 under the patronage of James I. A scholarly translation from the original languages, it preserved the best from previous versions. It was based on the earlier Bishops' Bible (1568), but the translators also consulted and made use of the *Geneva Bible and the *Douai Bible. It was much indebted to the translations of William *Tyndale. Its rich and vigorous language has had a unique influence on English prose style.

King Philip's War (1675-76) A war of resistance on the part of the Indians, led by King Philip of the Wampanoags, to the westward expansion of English settlers in Massachusetts, Connecticut, and Rhode Island. War broke out when three Wampanoags were executed by the settlers for the murder of an informer. The fighting was savage, lasting until Indian resistance collapsed after the death of King Philip, and the war toll was enormous.

Kings, Books of Two Old Testament books of unknown authorship. They are the major source for the history of the Hebrew kings after David, continuing the narrative from the point where the Books of Samuel end. The first book traces the reign of Solomon (c. 970-933 BC) and his building of the Temple at Jerusalem. After his death, the kingdom was divided into Judah and Israel, the histories of which are continued alternately in the second book. The work of the prophets Elisha and Elijah is treated in detail. After the fall of Israel to Assyria in 722 BC the narrative is devoted to the history of Judah alone up to the *Babylonian exile (586 BC).

king's evil. See scrofula.

Kingsley, Charles (1819-79) British clergyman and writer. A supporter of "Christian socialism," in many works, such as *Alton Locke* (1850), he championed various social reforms. He became chaplain to Queen Victoria (1859) and canon of Westminster (1873). His works include the popular children's book *The Water Babies* (1863), historical romances, and a volume of lectures on history, *The Roman and the Teuton* (1864). His niece **Mary Henriette Kingsley** (1862-1900) was a noted traveller, chiefly in W Africa, and wrote perceptive accounts of her experiences, including *Travels in West Africa* (1897). She died in Africa, nursing sick Boer prisoners.

King's Lynn (Lynn or Lynn Regis) 52 45N 0 24E A historic market town in E England, in Norfolk on the Great Ouse River near its mouth on the Wash. Its importance as a port has declined since the middle ages. There are food canning and refrigeration, sugar-beet refining, brewing, engineering, and inshore fishing industries. Population (1981): 33 340.

King's Medals Two awards instituted in 1945 to recognize the work of foreign civilians in the British interest during World War II. They are awarded for service and courage, respectively, in the cause of freedom.

Kingston 17 58N 76 48W The capital and main port of Jamaica, in the SE. Founded in 1692, it became the capital in 1872. In the early 20th century it suffered much damage from hurricanes and an earthquake. The University of the West Indies was founded nearby in 1962. Most industry is associated with agriculture. Population (1982 est): 100 637.

Kingston 44 14N 76 30W A city and port in central Canada, in SE Ontario at the point where Lake Ontario becomes the St Lawrence River. Founded as a fort (1673), it has Canada's Royal Military College, as well as numerous prisons and Queen's University (1841). Kingston's industry includes ship repairing, aluminium, chemicals, and food processing. Population (1981): 52 616.

Kingston-upon-Hull. See Hull.

Kingston-upon-Thames A royal borough of SW Greater London, on the S bank of the River Thames. Created in 1965 from several former Surrey boroughs, it is mainly residential. Population (1981): 132 411.

Kingstown 13 12N 61 14W A port in SW St Vincent, in the West Indies in the E Caribbean Sea. Exports include bananas, copra, arrowroot, and cotton. Population (1980): 32 600.

kinkajou A nocturnal arboreal mammal, *Potos flavus*, of Central and South American forests. Up to 110 cm long including the prehensile tail (40-55 cm), it has a soft woolly golden-brown coat and feeds mainly on fruit and honey. Family: *Procyonidae* (see raccoon).

Kinneret, Lake. See Galilee, Sea of.

Kinnock, Neil (Gordon) (1942-) British Labour politician. He became a member of the National Executive Committee of the Labour Party in 1978 and Labour leader (1983-) following Michael Foot's resignation.

kinnor A musical instrument, the ancient Jewish form of the *kithara. A type of *lyre, it is the biblical instrument traditionally reputed to have been played by David.

Kinross A former county of SE Scotland. Under local government reorganization in 1975 it became part of Perth and Kinross District, in Tayside Region.

Kinsey, Alfred (1894-1956) US zoologist and sociologist, who initiated surveys of human sexual behaviour. His reports *Sexual Behaviour in the Human Male* (1948) and *Sexual Behaviour in the Human Female* (1953) aroused great publicity and helped create more open attitudes to sex.

Kinshasa (name until 1966: Léopoldville) 4 18S 15 18E The capital of Zaïre, on the Zaïre River on the S shore of Malebo Pool. It has a long history of human settlement and was occupied by the Humbu when *Stanley discovered it in the late 19th century. A campus of the National University was founded in 1954. One of Africa's largest cities, it is an important industrial and commercial centre with food-processing, woodworking, and textile industries. Population (1979): 2 242 297.

kinship The social recognition of real or ascribed blood relationship. It is usually distinguished from affinity (relationship by marriage). Kinship implies genetic relationship but this is defined very differently in different societies. Many people deny the genetic contribution of either the father or the mother to the child and count the kin of only one parent as their own. These are known respectively as matrilineal and patrilineal systems. Different societies recognize relationships of very different degrees of distance, some counting as kin those descended from common ancestors many generations back. In primitive societies kinship systems are the fundamental basis of social organization.

Kintyre A peninsula in W Scotland, in Strathclyde Region between the Atlantic Ocean and the Firth of Clyde. The **Mull of Kintyre** headland forms its most southerly point.

Kioga, Lake. *See* Kyoga, Lake.

Kiowa A North American Indian people of Oklahoma. With the *Comanche, they were among the most warlike tribes, raiding settlers in Texas during the 19th century. They also fought against the US Government and were one of the last tribes to be subdued. Their culture was typical of the Plains region. Their language forms part of the *Aztec-Tanoan family.

Kipling, (Joseph) Rudyard (1865–1936) British writer and poet. Born in Bombay, he was educated in England, returning to India in 1882 to work as a journalist. When Kipling returned to London in 1889, he was already famous for his satirical verses and for stories, such as those in *Plain Tales from the Hills* (1888). His popularity was confirmed with *Barrack Room Ballads and Other Verses* (1892), a volume that includes such well-known poems as "The Road to Mandalay," "If," and "Gunga Din." From 1892 to 1896 he lived with his American wife in New England, where he wrote *The Jungle Books* (1894, 1895). *Kim* (1901) is his best novel and the last he wrote with an Indian setting. Among his many other works are *Just So Stories* (1902) and *Puck of Pook's Hill* (1906), both for children, and the story collections *Debits and Credits* (1926) and *Limits and Renewals* (1932). He won the Nobel Prize in 1907.

kipper. *See* herring.

NEIL KINNOCK *With his wife Glenys in 1987.*

Kipp's apparatus A laboratory apparatus for producing a gas as a result of a reaction between a liquid and a solid. It is often used to produce hydrogen sulphide by reacting hydrochloric acid with sticks of ferrous sulphide ($2HCl + FeS = FeCl_2 + H_2S$). The device is named after its Dutch inventor, Petrus Jacobus Kipp (1808–64).

Kirchhoff, Gustav Robert (1824–87) German physicist, who was appointed professor at Heidelberg University in 1854. There, working with Robert *Bunsen, he invented the technique of spectroscopy. Using this technique, Kirchhoff

and Bunsen discovered the elements caesium and rubidium in 1861. Kirchoff, working alone, also discovered several elements in the sun, by investigating the solar spectrum. He is also known for his work on thermal radiation and on networks of electrical wires (*see* Kirchhoff's laws).

Kirchhoff's laws Two laws applying to electrical networks, discovered by G. R. *Kirchhoff. The first states that the net current flowing into and out of any point in the network is zero. The second states that the algebraic sum of the voltages in any closed loop of the network is equal to the algebraic sum of the products of the currents and the resistances through which they flow.

Kirchner, Ernst Ludwig (1880–1938) German expressionist painter and printmaker, who helped found the art movement called Die *Brücke (The Bridge) in 1905 (*see also* expressionism). His diverse influences ranged from *Grünewald to *Munch and African art in paintings notable for their eroticism, vibrant colours, and angular outlines. He painted many satirical street scenes in ·Berlin (1911–17) before moving to Switzerland, where he concentrated mainly on landscapes. After Nazi condemnation of his work he committed suicide.

Kirghizia (*or* Kirghiz Soviet Socialist Republic) A constituent republic in the S Soviet Union, bordering on China. The Kirghiz, a traditionally nomadic Turkic people, comprise over one-third of the population. Kirghizia, which is mountainous, has important deposits of coal, lead, mercury, and antimony, as well as oil and natural gas. Industries include the manufacture of machinery and building materials and food processing. Wheat, cotton, and tobacco are grown and livestock, especially cattle, sheep, horses, and yaks, are important. *History*: the Kirghiz came under Russian rule in the 19th century and fought the new Soviet Government after the Russian Revolution. As a result they suffered a famine in 1921–22, in which over 500 000 Kirghiz died. Kirghizia became an SSR in 1936. Area: 198 500 sq km (76 460 sq mi). Population (1985 est): 3 976 000. Capital: Frunze.

Kiribati, Republic of (name until 1979: Gilbert Islands) A country in the S Pacific Ocean comprising the Gilbert Islands, the Phoenix Islands, and some of the Line Islands together with Ocean Island. The majority of the inhabitants are Micronesians. *Economy*: chiefly fishing and subsistence agriculture, including crops such as coconuts, pandanus palm, and breadfruit. Ocean Island is rich in phosphates, which, with copra, are the chief exports. *History*: first sighted by the Spanish in the 16th century, the islands became a centre for sperm whale hunting in the 19th century. Part of the British protectorate of the Gilbert and Ellice Islands from 1892, they became a colony in 1915. Links with Ellice Islands (*see* Tuvalu, State of) were severed in 1975 and they became independent in 1979 as the Republic of Kiribati. The Banabans of Ocean Island are seeking independence from Kiribati to become an associate state of Fiji. Chief minister: Ieremia Tabai. Official languages: English and Gilbertese. Official currency: Australian dollar of 100 cents. Area: 861 sq km (332 sq mi). Population (1983): 60 000. Capital and main port: Tarawa.

Kirin. *See* Jilin.

Kirk, Norman (Eric) (1923–74) New Zealand statesman; Labour prime minister (1972–74). He implemented social-welfare and housing measures and recognized the People's Republic of China.

Kirkcaldy 56 07N 3 10W A town in E central Scotland, in Fife Region on the Firth of Forth. It is a port, mainly for coastal trade, and manufactures linoleum and coarse textiles, such as canvas. It is the birthplace of Adam Smith. Population (1981): 46 314.

Kirkcudbright A former county of SW Scotland. Under local government reorganization in 1975 it became part of Dumfries and Galloway Region.

Kirkuk 35 28N 44 26E A town in NE Iraq, in a rich oilfield. It is the origin of pipelines to Syria, Lebanon, and, until it was cut in the war of 1948, Haifa (Israel). Population (1979): 500 000.

Kirkwall 58 59N 2 58W A town in NE Scotland, the administrative centre and main port of the island authority of Orkney, on the island of Mainland. It has fishing and distilling industries. Population (1981): 5947.

Kirov (name from 1780 until 1934: Vyatka) 58 38N 49 38E A port in the Soviet Union, in the NW RSFSR on the River Vyatka. Founded in 1181, it fell to the Russians in the 15th century and became important as a stopping place on the Moscow–Siberia route. It was renamed in honour of S. M. Kirov. Population (1981 est): 396 000.

Kirov, Sergei Mironovich (1888–1934) Soviet politician. As one of Stalin's closest associates Kirov quickly rose to power and became first secretary of the Leningrad branch of the Communist Party. His assassination, which Stalin claimed to be part of a plot against the entire Soviet leadership and led to the Great Purge trials (1934–38), was probably instigated by Stalin himself.

Kirovabad (name until 1813 and from 1920 until 1935: Gandzha; name from 1813 until 1920: Yelisavetpol) 40 39N 46 20E A city in the Soviet Union, in the NW Azerbaidzhan SSR. A medieval commercial centre, it is now an important industrial centre, producing especially textiles, building materials, and wine. Population (1981 est): 243 000.

Kirov Ballet A Soviet ballet company based at the Kirov State Theatre of Opera and Ballet (formerly the Maryinsky Theatre) in Leningrad. The theatre was renamed in honour of S. M. *Kirov in 1935. The company's style of dancing owes much to the Imperial Russian Ballet, founded in 1935, of which *Nijinsky was a product. Some of the Kirov's leading dancers, including Rudolf *Nureyev, Natalia Makarova (1940–), and Mikhail Baryshnikov (1948–), have defected to the West and earned international reputations.

Kirovograd (name until 1924: Yelisavetgrad; name from 1924 until 1936: Zinoviyevsk) 48 31N 32 15E A city in the Soviet Union, in the S central Ukrainian SSR. It is a major agricultural trading centre. Population (1981 est): 246 000.

kirsch (*or* kirschwasser) A *spirit distilled from fermented liquor of wild cherries (German *Kirsch*, cherry). It is drunk neat, or used in cooking, especially in cheese fondue or poured over pineapple.

Kiruna 67 53N 20 15E A town in N Sweden, within the Arctic Circle. In area, it is the largest town in the world. It has vast iron-ore deposits. Population (1984 est): 27 754.

Kisangani (name until 1966: Stanleyville) 0 33S 25 14E A riverport in NE Zaïre, on the Zaïre River. It is an agricultural centre and industries include furniture, brewing, and clothing. Zaïre University was founded here in 1963. Population (1982 est): 339 210.

Kish A city of ancient *Sumer, near Babylon. Built on Mesopotamia's fertile alluvial plains, Kish was one of the oldest centres of civilization, retaining its pre-eminence until eclipsed by *Ur (c. 2600 BC). Under the Babylonian empire Kish became obscure but remained inhabited until the 2nd century AD. Excavated between 1923 and 1933, its site has produced valuable evidence of Sumerian civilization, including the earliest known example of writing—pictograms on a limestone tablet dating to soon after 3500 BC.

Kishinev (Romanian name: Chişinău) 47 00N 28 50E A city in the SW Soviet Union, the capital of the Moldavian SSR. Founded in the 15th century, it passed from the Turks to the Russians (1812), becoming the capital of Bessarabia; it was under Romanian rule (1918–40). It is an important food-processing centre. Population (1981 est): 539 000.

Kissinger, Henry (Alfred) (1923–) US diplomat and political scientist, born in Germany; secretary of state (1973–76). Appointed adviser to President Nixon on national security (1969), Kissinger and *Le Duc Tho were jointly awarded the Nobel Peace Prize (1973) for helping to negotiate an end to the Vietnam War. Under President Ford he became well known for his flying-shuttle style of diplomacy while negotiating a truce between Syria and Israel (1974). His publications include *Nuclear Weapons and Foreign Policy* (1956), *The White House Year* (1979), and *Years of Upheaval* (1982).

Kisumu 0 03S 34 47E A town in W Kenya, on the NE shore of Lake Victoria. It is an important commercial and industrial centre with trade links with Mombasa. Population (1983 est): 167 100.

kit A tiny high-pitched violin used by dancing masters in the 18th century. Its neck, to accommodate the fingers, is disproportionately large.

Kitagawa Utamaro (1753–1806) Japanese artist of the *Ukiyo-e movement, whose colour woodblock prints were the first to be popularized in Europe. His book of *Insects* (1788) introduced naturalistic observation into the art of colour print. However, he specialized chiefly in scenes of women engaged in everyday tasks or pastimes and half-length portraits of women, such as the series of *Ten Physiognomies of Women* and *Beauties of the Gay Quarters*. In 1804 his prints of the military ruler's wife and mistresses so offended the government that he was handcuffed for 50 days.

Kitakyushu 33 52N 130 49E A city in Japan, in N Kyushu on the Shimonoseki Strait. Formed in 1963 from the cities of Wakamatsu, Yawata, Tobata, Kokura, and Moji, it is one of Japan's leading trade and deepsea fishing ports as well as an important centre of heavy industry. Population (1980): 1 065 000.

Kitasato, Shibasaburo (1852–1931) Japanese bacteriologist, who, during an epidemic of bubonic plague in Hong Kong, identified the bacillus responsible. In Berlin Kitasato worked with *Behring on tetanus and diphtheria, demonstrating the value of antitoxin in conferring passive immunity. Kitasato founded a laboratory near Tokyo that was incorporated with the university in 1899. In 1914 he founded the Kitasato Institute.

Kitchener 43 27N 80 30W A city in central Canada, in SW Ontario. Established by German-speaking settlers after 1800, it was called Berlin until 1916. Kitchener is a financial, distribution, and manufacturing centre, producing furniture, foods, and leather and rubber goods. Population (1981): 139 734.

Kitchener of Khartoum, Horatio Herbert, 1st Earl (1850–1916) British field marshal. After service with the Royal Engineers, he was appointed to the Egyptian army (1883), becoming commander in chief in 1892. By 1898, with the battle of Omdurman, he had reconquered the Sudan, becoming its governor general (1899). In the second *Boer War he suppressed the guerrillas by a scorched-earth policy and the internment of civilians in concentration camps. In 1914, as war secretary, his recruitment campaign was successful but he lost power in the direction of strategy to *Haig and (Sir) William Robertson (1860–1933). He was drowned on his way to Archangel.

kite A *hawk belonging to the subfamily *Milvinae*, which occurs throughout the world, most commonly in warm regions. Typically reddish brown and 52–57 cm long, kites have long narrow wings, a long often forked tail, and a narrow bill and feed on insects, small mammals, and reptiles; some are scavengers.

kithara An ancient Greek plucked instrument, traditionally believed to have been invented by Apollo. It was a large wooden-framed *lyre; Greek vases show it held against the player's body. It was used to accompany epic song and declamation.

Kitimat 54 05N 128 38W A port in W Canada, in British Columbia on the Pacific Ocean. It was built (1951–54) to house a vast aluminium smelter using cheap local hydroelectricity. Fishing, timber, and pulp and paper are also important. Population (1981): 12 814.

kittiwake A North Atlantic *gull, *Rissa tridactyla*, that is adapted for nesting on narrow cliff ledges. It is 40 cm long and has a white plumage with black-tipped grey wings, short black legs, dark eyes, and a yellow bill. It feeds at sea on fish and offal, going ashore only to breed. Kittiwakes nest in dense colonies, anchoring their seaweed nests with mud.

Kitt Peak National Observatory An observatory near Tucson, Arizona, with an assembly of optical telescopes, notably a 4 m (158 in) reflector, and some radio telescopes.

Kitwe 12 48S 28 14E A town in N central Zambia. It is the chief commercial, industrial, and communications centre of the *Copperbelt. Population (1980 est): 341 000.

Kitzbühel 47 27N 12 23E A town in W Austria, in the Tirol in the Kitzbühel Alps. A famous winter-sports centre, it is also a health and tourist resort. Population (1981): 7872.

Kivi, Alexis (A. Stenvall; 1834–72) Finnish poet, dramatist, and novelist, who was chiefly responsible for establishing the western dialect as the modern literary language of Finland. His greatest work was the novel *Seitsemän veljestä* (*Seven Brothers*; 1870), a naturalistic portrayal of rural life.

Kivu, Lake 1 50S 29 10E A lake between Zaïre and Rwanda. It is 96 km (60 mi) long and drained by the River Ruzizi S into Lake Tanganyika.

kiwi (bird) A secretive flightless bird belonging to a family (*Apterygidae*; 3 species) occurring in forested regions of New Zealand. 25–40 cm long, kiwis have tiny wings hidden in coarse grey-brown plumage and strong legs with large claws. Kiwis are nocturnal and have weak eyes but well-developed hearing; the long bill is used to probe the soil for worms, insect larvae, etc. The kiwi is the national emblem of New Zealand. Order: *Apterygiformes*.

kiwi (plant) A Chinese climbing shrub, *Actinidia chinensis*, also called Chinese gooseberry. It has white or yellow flowers and an edible rough-skinned fruit, up to 5 cm long, with a gooseberry-like flavour. Family: *Actinidiaceae*.

Klagenfurt 46 38N 14 20E A city in S Austria, the capital of Carinthia. It has a cathedral (1578–91) and is a tourist centre. Industries include metals, clothing, and shoe production. Population (1981): 86 221.

Klaipeda (German name: Memel) 55 43N 21 07E A port in the W Soviet Union, in the Lithuanian SSR on the Baltic Sea. It has shipyards and other industries include fish canning, textiles, and fertilizers. *History*: dating from the 7th century AD, it was conquered by the Teutonic Knights in 1252, subsequently passing under Prussian rule. In 1919, after World War I, the Allies imposed a French administration over the region, which was seized by Lithuania in 1923. The Memel Statute (1924) recognized Lithuanian possession. It was occupied by the Germans in World War II. Population (1981 est): 181 000.

Klaproth, Martin Heinrich (1743–1817) German chemist, who pioneered the techniques of analytical chemistry. He isolated the oxides of uranium, zirconium, and titanium from minerals and investigated the rare-earth metals.

Klausenburg. *See* Cluj.

Kléber, Jean Baptiste (1753–1800) French general in the Revolutionary Wars distinguished for his suppression of the uprising in the Vendée (1793). He was recalled from retirement in 1798 and given command in Napoleon's Egyptian campaign. He became governor of Alexandria (1799) but was assassinated after recapturing Cairo.

Klebs, Edwin (1834–1913) Prussian bacteriologist, who, with Friedrich *Loeffler in 1884, isolated the bacillus responsible for diphtheria (the **Klebs-Loeffler bacillus**). He also demonstrated the presence of bacteria in infected wounds and showed that tuberculosis could be transmitted via infected milk.

Klee, Paul (1879–1940) Swiss painter and etcher, born in Berne. After training in the Munich Academy, he worked initially as an etcher, influenced by *Beardsley and *Goya in the grotesque and symbolic character of his works. Returning to Germany (1906), he became associated with Der *Blaue Reiter and taught at the *Bauhaus school of design (1920–33), but remained an original and independent talent. Inspired by a visit to Tunisia (1914), he turned to painting. Initially he produced small watercolours in brilliant colours; after 1919 he used oils, incorporating signs and hieroglyphs to create a fantasy world influenced by children's art.

Klein, Melanie (1882–1960) Austrian psychiatrist, who moved to England in 1926. She is noted for her psychoanalytical studies of children, which were influenced by Sigmund *Freud and his associates. Using children's play in place of free association, she analysed the behaviour of children in terms of their desires and anxieties, their relationship with their parents, and the significance of their experiences in their emotional and sexual development.

KLEIN BOTTLE *A solid with no edges and only one side.*

Klein bottle In *topology, a surface that has no edges and only one side. It is made by putting the small end of a tapering tube through the side of the tube, stretching it, and joining it to the large end. It was discovered by the German mathematician Christian Felix Klein (1849–1925).

Kleist, Heinrich von (1777–1811) German dramatist. Coming from an old Prussian family, he gave up his early career in the army. His plays vary in mood between the comedy of *Der zerbrochene Krug* (1808), the demonic violence of *Penthesilea* (1808), the romanticism of *Das Käthchen von Heilbronn* (1810), and the spirit of self-discipline of *Prinz Friedrich von Homburg* (1821). A unifying theme, also present is his short stories, is the confusion between illusion and reality. Always unstable, he committed suicide.

Klemperer, Otto (1885–1973) German conductor. He studied in Berlin and became conductor of the German Opera in Prague on the recommendation of Mahler in 1907. He was expelled by the Nazis in 1933 and became first a US and subsequently an Israeli citizen. He was principal conductor of the Philharmonia Orchestra from 1959 until his death and is particularly remembered for his performances of Beethoven's symphonies.

Klimt, Gustav (1862–1918) Viennese Art Nouveau artist, who founded the Vienna Sezession (1897), an avantgarde exhibiting society. He achieved notoriety with the pessimistic and erotic symbolism of his murals for Vienna University (1900–03). Subsequent paintings and mosaics, allegories or female portraits, are characterized by large patterned areas often predominantly in gold, as in *The Kiss* (Vienna).

Klinger, Friedrich Maximilian von (1752–1831) German dramatist. After touring with a troupe of actors, he made a career in the Russian army. From his tempestuous play *Der Wirrwarr, oder Sturm und Drang* (1776), the *Sturm und Drang* movement took its name.

Klint, Kaare (1888–1954) Danish furniture designer, the originator of the contemporary Scandinavian style of design. Trained as an architect, he founded the Danish Academy of

Arts in 1924 and became its first professor of furniture. His pioneering designs in natural unvarnished wood combined craftsmanship with modern functional needs and were influenced by *Chippendale as well as 20th-century styles.

klipspringer A small antelope, *Oreotragus oreotragus*, of rocky regions of S and E Africa. 60 cm high at the shoulder, klipspringers have a matted bristly yellowish-brown speckled coat with white underparts; males have short horns, ringed at the base. They are agile and aptly named "cliff-springers."

Klondike The valley of the Klondike River in NW Canada, in the central *Yukon, where gold was discovered in 1896. The subsequent gold rush opened up the Yukon, although the population dwindled when the gold started to run out (1900). The Klondike has passed into Canadian literature and song.

Klopstock, Friedrich Gottlieb (1724–1803) German poet. Inspired by what he felt to be his divine mission as a poet, he achieved success with his early epic *Der Messias* (1745–73) and later with his odes (*Oden*, 1771). In reacting against rationalism by emphasizing emotion and in his enthusiasm for nature, religion, and German history, he anticipated Romanticism. He also wrote plays.

klystron An electronic device used to generate or amplify *microwaves. It consists of a sealed evacuated tube in which a steady beam of electrons from an electron gun is alternately accelerated and retarded by high-frequency radio waves (velocity *modulation) as it passes through a cavity. The resultant radio-frequency pulses are picked up at a second cavity, either as a voltage oscillation or, if connected to a *waveguide, as electromagnetic waves. The second cavity can be tuned to the input frequency or a harmonic of it. *See also* magnetron.

knapweed One of several plants of the genus *Centaurea*, of Eurasia and N Africa, having knoblike purplish flower heads. The lesser knapweed (*C. nigra*), also called hardheads, is a plant of grasslands and open places and has been introduced to New Zealand and North America. Family: *Compositae*.

Knaresborough 54 00N 1 27W A town in N England, in North Yorkshire on the River Nidd. It has a ruined 14th-century castle and the Dropping Well, in which objects are petrified with lime. Population (1981): 13 375.

Kneller, Sir Godfrey (1646–1723) Portrait painter of German birth. He trained in Holland and Italy, before beginning a successful career in England (1674), working successively for Charles II, William III, Queen Anne, and George I, and founding the first English academy of painting (1711). His best portraits, those of the Whig Kit Cat Club (c. 1702–17; National Portrait Gallery), established a standard British portrait type, known as the kit cat (less than half-length but including a hand).

Knight, Dame Laura (1877–1970) British painter, famous for her scenes of circus, gipsy, and ballet life. She exhibited frequently at the Royal Academy, becoming a member in 1936. She was married to the portraitist **Harold Knight** (1874–1961).

knighthood, orders of Societies, found in many countries, to which persons are admitted as a mark of honour. In medieval Europe, companies of knights (e.g. the *Hospitallers) bound by monastic vows fought to defend Christendom (*see* Crusades). Subsequently, secular orders were instituted, usually by rulers who sought the sworn loyalty of their nobles. The most distinguished British orders are those of the *Garter, the *Thistle, and the *Bath.

knitting The chain looping of yarn to form a network fabric that is more elastic than woven fabric; it is very suitable for clinging garments, such as sweaters and stockings. Hand knitting, using two or three needles, is an old craft. In addition to shaped flatwork in various relief patterns, tubular shapes can be knitted. Since the 19th century knitting machines have been developed. The Cotton machine can make shaped work like hand knitting, but the Tompkins system is more versatile and well adapted to modern manufacture using synthetic yarns.

Knock A village in the Republic of Ireland, in Co Mayo. Visions of the Virgin Mary were allegedly seen here, the first in 1879, and it has become a place of pilgrimage. A new church was opened in 1976 and in 1979 the village was visited by Pope John Paul II.

knocking A metallic knock heard in petrol engines as a result of combustion of the explosive charge ahead of the flame front. This is caused by local areas of high pressure in the combustion chamber. It greatly reduces the efficiency of the engine and is controlled by additives, such as *tetraethyl lead. Antiknock compounds that do not contain lead are being sought, owing to pollution of the atmosphere by lead.

Knossos The principal city of Minoan Crete, near present-day Heraklion. It was occupied between about 2500 and 1200 BC. Excavated and reconstructed (1899–1935) by Sir Arthur *Evans, the Palace of Minos was luxurious and sophisticated. It is the probable original of the labyrinth in which, according to legend, *Theseus fought the *Minotaur. Frescoes showing processions, bull sports, and seascapes decorated its walls, there was an elaborate water system, and goods were imported from Egypt. About 1450 BC the palace was burnt down. □Minoan civilization.

knot (bird) A short-legged bird, *Calidris canutus*, that breeds in Arctic tundra and winters on southern coasts. 25 cm long, it has a short black bill and its plumage is mottled grey in winter and reddish in summer. In winter, knots feed in flocks, probing mud and sand for snails, worms, and crabs. Family: *Scolopacidae* (sandpipers, snipe, etc.).

knot (unit) A unit of speed, used for ships and aircraft, equal to 1 nautical mile per hour (i.e. 1.15 miles per hour).

knots Fastenings formed by looping and tying pieces of rope, cord, etc.
The mathematical theory of knots, a branch of *topology, was developed mainly in the 20th century, and draws on *matrix theory, algebra, and geometry. A simple closed curve in space may be knotted in various ways, each with specific topological properties. These are classified by knot theory and can be expressed in matrix form.

Knox, John (c. 1514–72) Scottish Protestant reformer. He adopted the reformed faith under the influence of *Wishart in the 1540s. In 1547 he joined the Protestants who had murdered Cardinal Beaton in revenge for Wishart's execution in St Andrew's Castle. The castle was stormed by the French, who imprisoned Knox as a galley slave. After his release (1549) he became a chaplain to Edward VI in England and contributed to the revision of the Second Book of Common Prayer. On Queen Mary's accession he escaped to the Continent, where he met *Calvin in Geneva. Returning to Scotland in 1559, he became its leading reformer. In 1560 the Scottish parliament adopted the *Confession of Faith* that Knox had compiled. His *First Book of Discipline* (1561) outlined a structure for the reformed Church of Scotland that included education and poor relief.

Knox, Ronald (Arbuthnott) (1888–1957) British Roman Catholic priest and author, son of an Anglican bishop. He wrote about his faith and his conversion to Roman Catholicism (1917) in such works as *A Spiritual Aeneid* (1918). The Catholic chaplain at Oxford University from 1926 to 1939, he is best known for his modern translation of the *Vulgate (1945–49). He also published several detective novels.

Knox-Johnston, Robin (William Robert Patrick K.-J.; 1939–) British yachtsman; the first person to sail alone around the world nonstop (1968–69). In 1981 he set the British transatlantic sailing record (11 days 7 hours 45 mins).

Knoxville 36 00N 83 57W A city in the USA, in Tennessee on the Tennessee River. It is the site of the University of Tennessee (1794) and the headquarters of the Tennessee Valley Authority. An inland port and agricultural trading

overhand knot *This is used either to make a knob in a rope or as the basis for another knot.*

reef knot *A non-slip knot for joining ropes of similar thickness.*

quick release knot *A tug on* a *will quickly unfasten this knot.*

surgeon's knot *The extra twist in the first part of the knot prevents it from slipping loose while the second part is tied.*

Hunter's bend *A strong, easily tied knot invented in 1978 by Dr Edward Hunter.*

bowline *A knot to form a non-slip loop.*

running bowline *A knot for making a running noose.*

sheepshank *A means of temporarily shortening a rope.*

sheet bend *A knot for securely joining two ropes of different thickness.*

double sheet bend *This follows the same principles as the sheet bend.*

fisherman's knot *Used especially for joining lengths of fishing gut.*

carrick bend *A knot well suited to tying heavy ropes together.*

clove hitch *A simple knot for attaching a rope to a ring, rail, etc.*

round turn and two half hitches *Used for similar purposes as the clove hitch, this knot does not easily work loose.*

anchor bend *A secure means of attaching a cable to an anchor.*

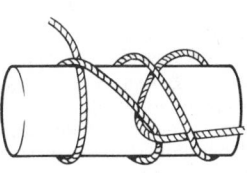

rolling hitch *A quickly made and quickly unfastened knot for attaching a rope to a rail or another, standing rope.*

centre, its industries include meat packing and marble processing. Population (1980): 476 517.

Knutsford 53 18N 2 23W A town in N England, in Cheshire, serving as a dormitory town for Manchester. Mrs Gaskell lived here and it is the setting for her novel *Cranford*. Population (1981): 13 675.

koala An arboreal *marsupial, *Phascolarctus cinereus*, of E Australia. About 60 cm high, koalas have thick greyish fur, tufted ears, a small tail, and long claws. Groups of koalas move slowly through eucalyptus forests, each adult eating more than 1 kg of the leaves every day. The pouch opens towards the female's tail and the young are weaned on half-digested eucalyptus soup from their mother's anus. Family: *Phalangeridae*.

kob An antelope, *Kobus kob*, of African savanna regions, also called Buffon's kob. Males stand about 90 cm high at the shoulder; females are smaller. The coat ranges from orange-red to nearly black, with white markings on the face, legs, and belly and a black stripe down the foreleg.

Kobarid (Italian name: Caproetto) 46 16N 13 35E A village in NW Yugoslavia, in Slovenia. Part of Italy until 1947, it was the site of the defeat of the Italians by the Austro-German army in 1917.

Kobayashi Masaki (1916-) Japanese film director. He established his international reputation with *The Human Condition* (1959-61), a trilogy of films concerned with the dignity of the individual in modern society. His other films include *Kwaidan* (1964), an anthology of ghost stories, *Rebellion* (1967), and *Kaseki* (1974).

Kobe 34 40N 135 12E A major port in Japan, in S Honshu on Osaka Bay. It forms the W end of the Osaka-Kobe industrial area and has two of the biggest shipbuilding yards in the country. Other industries include engineering, sugar, chemicals, and rubber. Its university was established in 1949. Population (1980): 1 367 000.

København. *See* Copenhagen.

Koblenz (English name: Coblenz) 50 21N 7 36E A city in W West Germany, in Rhineland-Palatinate at the confluence of the Rivers Rhine and Moselle. The seat of Frankish kings during the 6th century AD, it was annexed by France in 1798, passing to Prussia in 1815. Notable buildings, many rebuilt after World War II, include the Ehrenbreitstein fortress (c. 1000) and the birthplace of Metternich. It is a wine-trading centre and manufactures furniture, pianos, and clothing. Population (1980 est): 113 900.

Koch, Robert (1843-1910) German bacteriologist, who was responsible for major discoveries in the study of disease-causing bacteria. As a young doctor, Koch successfully cultured the bacillus causing anthrax in cattle and determined its life cycle. Devising new and better culture methods, Koch succeeded in 1882 in identifying and isolating the bacillus responsible for tuberculosis. Koch investigated many other diseases including cholera, bubonic plague, and malaria. He was awarded a Nobel Prize (1905).

Köchel, Ludwig von (1800-77) Austrian naturalist and musical bibliographer. He compiled a thematic catalogue of Mozart's works, which was published in 1862; a particular work is referred to by a **Köchel number**, consisting of the letter K followed by the appropriate catalogue number.

Kodály, Zoltan (1882-1967) Hungarian composer. He was educated at Budapest University and conservatoire, where he developed an interest in Magyar folk music. In collaboration with *Bartók he collected and edited Hungarian peasant songs, which influenced his style of composition. He achieved international recognition with his *Psalmus Hungaricus* (1923); other works include the opera *Háry János* (1926), *Dances of Galanta* (1933), a mass, chamber music, and orchestral music.

Kodiak 57 20N 153 40W An island in the USA, off the S coast of Alaska in the Gulf of Alaska. First settled by Russians in 1784, it became a base for seal hunting and whaling. In 1964 it suffered an earthquake that lowered it by about 1.8 m (6 ft). Area: 8974 sq km (3465 sq mi). Population (1984): 13 389.

Kodiak bear. *See* brown bear.

Kodok (former name: Fashoda) 9 51N 32 07E A small town in the S central Sudan, on the White Nile River. The *Fashoda incident took place here (1898), causing a crisis between Britain and France. Population: about 3000.

Koestler, Arthur (1905-83) British writer, born in Hungary and educated as an engineer in Vienna. As a journalist in Berlin, he joined the Communist Party (1931) but left it in 1938. He settled in Britain in 1940, writing in English thereafter. His novel *Darkness at Noon* (1940), depicting the Moscow purge trials, calls on his own experience as a prisoner in the Spanish Civil War. His other novels include *Thieves in the Night* (1946) about Palestine and *The Call Girls* (1972). His nonfiction was concerned with politics (*The Yogi and the Commissar*, 1945), scientific creativity (*The Sleepwalkers*, 1959; *The Act of Creation*, 1964; *The Ghost in the Machine*, 1967), and parapsychology (*The Roots of Coincidence*, 1972). His autobiographical volumes include *Arrow in the Blue* (1952) and *The Invisible Writing* (1954). An active member of the Voluntary Euthanasia Society, he and his wife Cynthia committed suicide when his Parkinson's disease became intolerable.

Koffka, Kurt (1886-1941) US psychologist, born in Germany, who was one of the founders of *Gestalt psychology. Among his works was *Growth of the Mind* (1921). He made an influential distinction between the behavioural and the geographical environments—the perceived world of common sense and the world studied by scientists.

Koh-i-noor A famous diamond of 108 carats owned by the Mogul dynasty until the Shah of Iran looted it from Delhi (1739). Although reclaimed for India by the Sikhs, it became Crown property in 1849, when Britain annexed the Punjab. It was set in the coronation crown of George VI's consort, Queen Elizabeth.

Kohl, Helmut (1930-) West German statesman; chancellor (1982-). A member of the Christian Democrat Party, he was leader of the opposition in the Bundestag (1976-82).

Köhler, Wolfgang (1887-1967) US psychologist and a founder of *Gestalt psychology. Kohler's experiments on problem solving in apes (*The Mentality of Apes*, 1917) led to his exploration of the physiological basis of perception and the process of learning.

kohlrabi A variety of *cabbage, sometimes called turnip-rooted cabbage. The green or purple stem base, which swells like a turnip, is used as a vegetable and as livestock food.

Kokand 40 33N 70 55E A city in the Soviet Union, in the NE Uzbek SSR in the Fergana Valley. Fertilizers and chemicals are produced. Population (1983 est): 161 000.

Koko Nor. *See* Qinghai, Lake.

Kokoschka, Oskar (1886-1980) Austrian expressionist painter and writer (*see* expressionism). In Vienna and Berlin, he specialized in probing portraits and allegorical poems, plays, and paintings, expressing the struggle of life. After World War I he taught at the Dresden Academy and travelled widely, painting landscapes and city views, particularly of London, where he lived (1938-53). From 1953 he lived and worked in Switzerland.

Kokura. *See* Kitakyushu.

kola (*or* cola) Either of two trees, *Cola nitida* or *C. acuminata*, native to West Africa and widely grown in the tropics, that produce **kola nuts**. These are rich in caffeine and chewed in Africa and the West Indies for their stimulating effects. Family: *Sterculiaceae*.

Kola Peninsula A promontory in the NW Soviet Union, between the Barents Sea to the N and the White Sea to the

S. The area is largely granite but is mined for apatite (for its phosphorus) and nephelinite (for its aluminium). Tundra is extensive with some swampy pine and other forests in the S. The chief town is Murmansk. Area: about 130 000 sq km (50 182 sq mi).

Kolar 13 10N 78 10E A town in India, in Karnataka. To the NW lie the Kolar Gold Fields, which produce almost all India's gold output. Population (1981): 77 679.

Kolarovgrad (*or* Shumen) 43 17 N 26 55E A town in NE Bulgaria. It was an important fort under Turkish rule (15th-19th centuries) and has a notable brewing industry. Population (1982): 99 642.

Kolbe, (Adolf Wilhelm) Hermann (1818-84) German chemist, who became professor at Marburg University in 1851. He was one of the first chemists to synthesize organic compounds, his most important discovery being the Kolbe reaction, for synthesizing salicylic acid. This led to the large-scale manufacture of aspirin.

Kolchak, Alexander Vasilievich (1874-1920) Russian admiral. After the Russian Revolution (1917) he became leader of anti-Bolshevik elements at Omsk, clearing Siberia and linking with *Denikin in the south. However, Bolshevik counterattacks, discontent in his territories, and divisions among his followers destroyed Kolchak's forces. He was betrayed by the Allied powers to the Bolsheviks and shot.

Koldewey, Robert (1855-1925) German archaeologist. After digging at several classical sites (e.g. *Baalbek), Koldewey excavated *Babylon (1899-1917). Here his training as an architect greatly facilitated recovery of the ancient street plan and reconstruction of the mud-brick buildings.

Kolhapur 16 40N 74 15E A city in India, in Maharashtra. An early centre of Buddhism, its industries include sugar processing and textiles and it has a university (1962). Population (1981): 351 000.

Kolmogorov, Andrei Nikolaevich (1903-) Soviet mathematician, who has made notable contributions to many fields of mathematics, particularly topology, probability theory, functional analysis, and geometry. His work in the branch of probability theory known as stochastic processes has found applications in the science of *cybernetics. He is the foremost Soviet mathematician of the 20th century and his influence on younger generations of mathematicians in the Soviet Union has been considerable.

Köln. *See* Cologne.

Koloszvár. *See* Cluj.

Kolyma, River A river in the NE Soviet Union. Rising in the Kolyma Range of NE Siberia, it flows mainly NE to the East Siberian Sea. Length: 2600 km (1615 mi).

Komeito A Japanese political party, known in English as the Clean Government Party, formed in 1964 by the Soka-gakkai, a branch of the extreme Nichiren Buddhists. It advocates the establishment of a nonaligned Japan free from extremes of wealth and poverty. Komeito rapidly increased its parliamentary representation to become Japan's third strongest political party. Accused of wishing to impose Nichiru Shoshu as the state religion and of reviving fascism, Komeito severed its links with the Soka-gakkai in 1970.

Komi Autonomous Soviet Socialist Republic An administrative division in the NW Soviet Union, in the RSFSR. It comprises chiefly tundra (in the NE) and coniferous forests. The administrative region was established in 1921 for the Komi people, who speak a Finno-Ugric language, and became an ASSR in 1936. Timbering and mining (notably of coal and oil) are the most important economic activities; livestock raising is the main branch of agriculture. Area: 415 900 sq km (160 540 sq mi). Population (1981 est): 1 147 000. Capital: Syktyvkar.

Kommunizma Pik. *See* Communism Peak.

Komodo dragon A rare *monitor lizard, *Varanus*

komodoensis, which, at 3 m long and weighing 135 kg, is the largest living lizard. It has a stout neck and body, a long powerful tail, and short strong legs and is powerful enough to attack and kill a man. Komodo dragons feed mainly on carrion but also eat smaller monitors. They occur only on Komodo Island and some of the Lesser Sunda Islands of Indonesia. □reptile.

KOMSOMOL (All-Union Leninist Communist League of Youth) A Soviet youth organization. Organized in 1918, its members fought in the civil war (1918-21). In 1922 it became a social organization to promote communist ideology through social activities. Membership, which is for those aged between 14 and 28, gives good employment opportunities.

Komsomolsk-na-Amur 50 32N 136 59E A city in the Soviet Union, in the W RSFSR on the River Amur. It is named after the *KOMSOMOL, members of which built much of the city (founded 1932). Its industries, including engineering and machine building, are based on the Amurstal steelworks, located here; oil from Sakhalin is refined. Population (1981 est): 274 000.

Konakry. *See* Conakry.

Koniecpolski, Stanislaw (1591-1646) Polish soldier and statesman. Koniecpolski fought many victorious battles against the Turks, Tatars, and Swedes. In 1632 he became commander in chief and subsequently influenced the government of Władysław IV (1595-1648; reigned 1632-48). Koniecpolski was extremely wealthy and acquired huge estates in the Ukraine.

Koniev, Ivan Stepanovich (1897-1973) Soviet marshal. A commander in World War II in the Ukraine and the southern front, he ended the war encircling Berlin from the south. He commanded all Warsaw Pact forces in Europe (1955-60).

Königsberg. *See* Kaliningrad.

Konoe Fumimaro, Prince (1891-1945) Japanese noble, who was prime minister three times. His first cabinet (1937-39) escalated the conflict between Japan and China; his second (1940-41) took Japan into alliance in World War II with Germany and Italy; and his third (1941) made the decision to attack the USA. After Japan's surrender he avoided trial as a war criminal by committing suicide.

Konstanz. *See* Constance.

Kon-Tiki The name given by Thor *Heyerdahl to the raft built of nine balsawood logs on which, between 28 April and 7 August, 1947, he and five companions travelled the 5000 miles between Peru and the Tuamotu islands near Tahiti. The purpose of the voyage was to demonstrate the possibility that ancient peoples of South America could have reached Polynesia. Kon-Tiki was an older name for the Inca creator god, Viracocha, allegedly known in Polynesia as Tiki.

Konya (ancient name: Iconium) 37 51N 32 30E A town in SW central Turkey. It is the centre of the Whirling Dervish sect, and the monastery around the tomb of its founder is a religious museum. The town was visited by St Paul and was the capital of the Seljuq kingdom of Rum. Population(1980): 329 139.

kookaburra A large grey-brown Australian *kingfisher, *Dacelo novaeguineae*, also called laughing jackass because of its chuckling call. 43 cm long, it is arboreal and pounces on snakes, lizards, insects, and small rodents from a perch.

Köprülü A family, of Albanian origin, of viziers (public servants) of the Ottoman Empire. **Köprülü Mohammed** (c. 1583-1661), grand vizier (1656-61), reformed the Ottoman navy and economy. His son **Köprülü Ahmed** (1635-76), grand vizier (1661-76), conquered Crete. Ahmed's brother **Köprülü Mustafa** (1637-91), grand vizier (1689-91), instituted many financial and military reforms. Their cousin **Köprülü Hussein** (d. 1702), grand vizier (1697-1702), negotiated the Treaty of Karlowitz (1699), in which the Ottoman Empire lost much territory to Austria.

Koran (*or* Quran) The sacred scripture of Islam. According to tradition, the divine revelations given to *Mohammed (d. 632 AD) were preserved by his followers and collected as the Koran under the third caliph, Uthman (d. 656). Written in classical Arabic, they were arranged in 114 suras or chapters according to length, the longer ones first. Admonitions to worship God alone and legal prescriptions predominate. The Koran is one of the main sources of the comprehensive system of *Islamic law. Although the revelations were given to Mohammed piecemeal, Muslims believe that they exist complete in a heavenly book, which contains all that has happened and will happen in the universe.

KOREAN WAR   *Refugees near Inchon; young and old indiscriminately suffer the consequences of conflict between ideologies that barely concern them.*

Korçë 40 38N 20 44E A town in SE Albania. It is the commercial centre of a large wheat-growing area. Population (1980 est): 54 300.

Korchnoi, Victor (1931-   ) Soviet chess player. An International Grandmaster, he became Soviet champion in 1960, 1962, and 1964. He left the Soviet Union (1976) and later took part in a much publicized match with *Karpov (1978).

Korda, Sir Alexander (Sandor Kellner; 1893–1956) British film producer and director, born in Hungary. After settling in London in 1930, he greatly boosted the British film industry during the 1930s and 1940s with a series of extravagant productions, including *The Private Life of Henry VIII* (1932), *The Scarlet Pimpernel* (1934), and *Anna Karenina* (1948).

kore (Greek: maiden) In archaic Greek sculpture, a draped standing female figure, derived originally (c. 650 BC) from Egyptian models. During the next two centuries the drapery, pose, and expression became increasingly naturalistic. *Compare* kouros.

Korea A country in NE Asia, occupying a peninsula

between the Sea of Japan and the Yellow Sea, now divided (*see* below) into the Democratic Republic of Korea (North Korea) and the Republic of Korea (South Korea). Plains in the W rise to mountains in the N and E. Both North and South Koreans are ethnically related to the Mongoloid race. From the 1st century AD three kingdoms flourished in the peninsula: the Koguryo in the N, the Paechke in the SW, and the Silla in the SE. In 668 they were united under Silla and Buddhism subsequently became the state religion. The country long had ties with China but in 1905 became a Japanese protectorate, coming formally under Japanese rule in 1910. In 1945, following Japan's defeat in World War II, the Allies divided Korea at the *thirty-eighth parallel. The communist Democratic People's Republic of Korea under *Kim Il Sung was established in the Soviet-occupied N and the Republic of Korea under Syngman Rhee, in the US-occupied S (1948). Soviet and US troops had withdrawn by 1949 and in 1950 the *Korean War broke out between North and South Korea, ending in 1953 with the country still divided.

Korea, People's Democratic Republic of (Korean name: Chosŏn) The division of Korea left the North with almost all the country's mineral wealth (coal, iron ore, lead, zinc, molybdenum, gold, graphite, and tungsten) and a large proportion of the industries, which had been developed by the Japanese. Although many of the industries were destroyed during the Korean War, reconstruction proceeded rapidly. Textiles, chemicals, machinery, and metals are among the principal manufactures and all industry is nationalized. The rather sparse agricultural land was collectivized in the 1950s and is now almost all farmed in large cooperatives. Exports, mainly to communist countries, include metals and metal products. President: Kim Il Sung. Official language: Korean. Official currency: won of 100 jun. Area: 122 370 sq km (47 225 sq mi). Population (1983 est): 18 802 000. Capital: P'yŏngyang.

Korea, Republic of (Korean name: Han Kook) The repressive government led by the first president of South Korea, Syngman *Rhee, was ended by a military coup in 1961, followed by the rise to power of Gen *Park Chung Hee, who was assassinated in 1979. The more densely populated South was primarily agricultural when separated from the North but the injection of US aid and other international assistance led to the predominance of the industrial sector. Mineral resources are not large, although it has one of the world's largest deposits of tungsten. The main exports include clothes, plywood, textiles, and electrical goods. The restrictive government of President Chun Doo Hwan led to increasing political unrest in the mid-1980s and in Dec 1987 Roh Tae Woo (1932-   ), leader of the Democratic Justice Party, was elected president. South Korea will host the Olympic Games in 1988. Official language: Korean. Official currency: won of 100 chon. Area: 98 447 sq km (38 002 sq mi). Population (1983 est): 41 287 000. Capital: Seoul. Main port: Pusan.

Korean The language of the Mongoloid people of Korea. It is probably distantly related to *Japanese and has a somewhat similar grammatical structure. The standard and official form is based on the dialect of Seoul. It is written in a phonetic script called onmun, devised in the mid-15th century to replace the Chinese characters in use before then. Korean literature also dates from about this time, with a royal college of literature being founded in 1420.

Korean War (1950-53) An indecisive conflict between communist and noncommunist forces in Korea. In 1948 two Korean states were established on either side of the *thirty-eighth parallel: the communist Democratic People's Republic in the N and the Republic of Korea in the S. Growing friction led to the invasion of South Korea by Northern forces in 1950. The UN condemned the invasion, and 16 member nations sent troops, under the supreme command of the US general, Douglas *Macarthur, to support South Korea. The North Koreans were joined by

Chinese Communist troops. An armistice was eventually signed on 27 July, 1953, by which time some five million people had died.

Kórinthos. *See* Corinth.

Kornberg, Arthur (1918-) US biochemist, who discovered how DNA is replicated in bacterial cells. Kornberg and associates were able to reproduce the conditions necessary for DNA replication in a test tube. They found that the "building blocks" (nucleotides) of the new DNA strand were joined together by an enzyme—DNA polymerase I—using existing DNA as a template.

Kornilov, Lavrentia Georgievich (1870-1918) Russian general. After the Russian Revolution (1917) he led the anti-Bolshevik White armies in S Russia. After his death in action, the command was assumed by *Denikin.

Koroliov, Sergei Pavlovich (1906-66) Soviet aeronautical engineer, who designed missiles, rockets, and spacecraft. During the 1930s he headed development of the Soviet Union's first liquid-fuel rocket. After World War II he worked on ballistic missiles and later supervised the Vostok and Soyuz manned spaceflight programmes.

Kortrijk. *See* Courtrai.

Koryŏ An ancient Korean kingdom founded and ruled by the Wang dynasty (935-1392). Both Buddhism and Confucianism were influential and Koryŏ was divided by rivalry between pacifist Confucianists and militarist nationalists. The weakened state succumbed to Mongol invasions in the 13th century and virtually became a Mongol dependency in 1231. The last Wang ruler was deposed by the *Yi in 1392.

Kos. *See* Cos.

Kosciusko, Mount 36 28S 148 17E The highest mountain in Australia, in SE New South Wales in the Snowy Mountains. It lies within the Kosciusko National Park, a popular area for winter sports. Height: 2230 m (7316 ft).

Kosciuszko, Tadeusz Andrezei Bonawentura (1746-1817) Polish general and statesman, who served in the American Revolution with George Washington (1776-83). Returning to Poland (1784), he distinguished himself in the war against the Russian invasion, which ended in the partition of Poland. Kosciuszko withdrew to Saxony but returned in 1794 to lead the revolt against the occupation. He was defeated and captured at Maciejourice and imprisoned until 1796.

Košice (German name: Kaschau; Hungarian name: Kassa) 48 44N 21 15E A city in E Czechoslovakia, in E Slovakia. It has a 13th-century cathedral and a university (1959). One of the largest integrated iron and steel complexes in E Europe is situated here. Population (1983): 213 000.

Kossuth, Lajos (1802-94) Hungarian statesman, who was one of the leaders of the Hungarian *Revolution of 1848. In March, 1848, when Hungary was granted a separate government by Austria, Kossuth was appointed finance minister. He became governor of an independent Hungarian republic in April, 1849. When Russia destroyed the republic in August, he left Hungary and lived in exile in Turkey, England, and Italy. After his death, his body was returned to Hungary.

Kosygin, Aleksei Nikolaevich (1904-80) Soviet statesman; prime minister (1964-80). Kosygin rose in the Communist Party hierarchy in the 1940s as an expert in economic affairs. He served in the politburo from 1948 to 1952, when he was demoted. In 1960 he was again elected to what was now the presidium and after Khrushchev's fall he became prime minister. He initially shared power with *Brezhnev but in the late 1960s Kosygin's influence declined.

Kota Baharu 6 07N 102 15E A town in NE Peninsular Malaysia, the capital of Kelantan state on the Kelantan delta. It has a major power station. Population (1980): 170 559.

Kota Kinabalu (former name: Jesselton) 5 59N 116 04E A port in Malaysia, the capital of Sabah state on the South China Sea. Industries include fishing and rice milling; rubber is exported. Population (1980): 108 725.

koto A Japanese stringed instrument of the *zither family. The narrow 2-metre sound board has 13 strings, which the player, sitting on his heels, plucks with plectra attached to two fingers and the thumb of the right hand. ⌐musical instruments.

Kotor 42 27N 18 46E A port in S Yugoslavia, on the Gulf of Kotor. The oldest town in Montenegro with a remarkable 12th-century cathedral, it is now protected as a monument. The town was damaged during an earthquake in April, 1979. Population (1981 est): 20 455.

Kottbus. *See* Cottbus.

Kotzebue, August von (1761-1819) German dramatist and novelist. He was a prolific writer of popular sentimental plays, most notably the comedy *Die deutschen Kleinstädter* (1803). He was assassinated as a suspected spy while working for the Russian tsar.

KOUROS *The* Rampin Head *(Louvre, Paris), part of an equestrian statue from the Acropolis, Athens. Its "archaic smile" is typical of Greek sculpture of the second quarter of the 6th century* BC.

kouros (Greek: youth) In archaic Greek sculpture, a nude standing male figure, often more than life-size, derived (c. 650 BC) from Egyptian models. The modelling of the face and body became increasingly naturalistic. *Compare* kore.

Koussevitsky, Sergei (1874-1951) Russian composer. Originally a virtuoso double-bass player, he conducted the State Symphony Orchestra in Petrograd (now Leningrad) but left Russia in 1920. He worked in Paris and subsequently in the USA, where he directed the Boston Symphony Orchestra from 1924 to 1949. He was an advocate of contemporary music and founded the Koussevitsky Music Foundation, which continues to commission new musical works.

Kovno. *See* Kaunas.

Kowloon. *See* Jiulong.

Koxinga. *See* Zheng Cheng Gong.

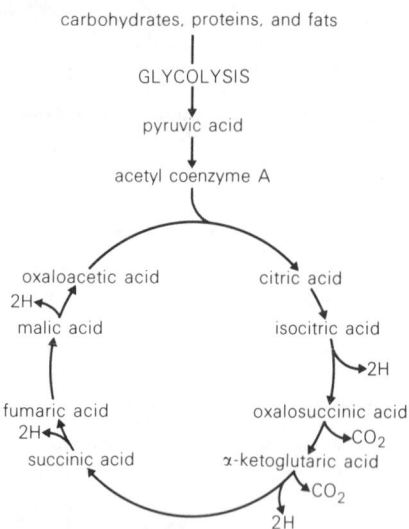

carbohydrates, proteins, and fats

GLYCOLYSIS

pyruvic acid

acetyl coenzyme A

oxaloacetic acid

2H

malic acid

citric acid

isocitric acid

fumaric acid

2H

succinic acid

oxalosuccinic acid

CO_2

α-ketoglutaric acid

CO_2

2H

2H

KREBS CYCLE   *For every two atoms of hydrogen transferred, three ATP molcules are generated.*

Kozhikode (former name: Calicut)   11 15N 75 45E A seaport on the W coast of India, in Kerala. Formerly famous as a cotton-manufacturing centre (Calicut gave its name to calico), it was visited by the Portuguese explorer Vasco da Gama (1498) and in 1664 the British East India Company established a trading post here. Tea, coffee, coconut products, and spices are exported. Population (1981): 394 447.

Kozirev, Nikolai Aleksandrovich   (1908–   ) Soviet astronomer, who first observed volcanic activity on the moon. In 1958 he observed a cloud in one of the moon's craters. Kozirev discovered that the cloud contained carbon and deduced that it was formed by volcanic activity.

Kra, Isthmus of   The neck of the Malay Peninsula connecting it to the Asian mainland. It is occupied by Burma and Thailand and is 64 km (40 mi) across at its narrowest point.

Krafft-Ebing, Richard von   (1840–1902) German psychiatrist, who studied many aspects of mental and nervous disorders. He established the link between syphilis and general paralysis of the insane and made pioneering studies of sexual aberrations in *Psychopathia sexualis* (1886).

kraft process   An industrial process for producing cellulose for paper manufacture from pine-wood chips by digestion with alkali. Rosin and fatty-acid soaps are by-products. The pulp produced is especially strong, hence the name (German *kraft*, strong).

Kragujevac   44 01N 20 55E A town in E Yugoslavia, in Serbia. A former centre of the Serbian struggle against the Turks, it was the capital of Serbia (1818–39). Its industries include a large car factory. Population (1981): 164 823.

krait   A highly venomous snake belonging to the genus *Bungarus* (12 species) occurring in S Asia. Kraits have shiny scales and are usually patterned with blue-and-white or black-and-yellow bands; they prey chiefly on other snakes. The common blue krait (*B. caeruleus*) of India and China is 1.5 m long and its venom can be fatal to humans. Family: *Elapidae* (cobras, mambas, coral snakes).

Krakatoa   (Indonesian name: Krakatau)   6 11S 105 26E A small volcanic Indonesian island in the Sunda Strait. During its eruption in 1883, one of the greatest ever recorded, 36 000 people were killed, many by the tidal waves that swept the coasts of Java and Sumatra. Today the island remains uninhabited.

Kraków (*or* Cracow)   50 03N 19 55E The third largest city in Poland, on the River Vistula. It was the capital of Poland from 1305 to 1609 and remains famous as a cultural centre. The Jagiellonian University, one of the oldest in Europe, was founded here in 1364. Other notable buildings include the cathedral (14th century) and many architecturally distinguished churches. Its industry is based at Nowa Huta 10 km (6 mi) to the E. Population (1982): 723 000.

Kramatorsk   48 43N 37 33E A city in the Soviet Union, in the E Ukrainian SSR in the Donets Basin. An iron-and-steel centre, it manufactures machinery and machine tools. Population (1984): 189 000.

Krasnodar (name until 1920: Ekaterinodar)   45 02N 39 00E A city in the Soviet Union, in the SW RSFSR on the River Kuban. It is the centre of an agricultural region and food processing is the most important industry. Population (1984): 603 000.

Krasnoyarsk   56 05N 92 46E A city in the Soviet Union, in the E central RSFSR on the River Yenisei. It was founded in 1628, developing greatly after the discovery of gold in the region in the 19th century. It produces aluminium, having one of the largest outputs in the country, and has a notable hydroelectric station. Population (1984): 857 000.

Krebs, Sir Hans Adolf   (1900–81) British biochemist, born in Germany. Working in Germany until 1933, Krebs discovered the cycle of reactions by which waste nitrogenous products are converted to *urea by the body. After his move to Britain came his major achievement—the *Krebs cycle. Krebs was awarded a Nobel Prize (1953) with Fritz Lipmann (1899–   ).

Krebs cycle (citric acid cycle *or* tricarboxylic acid cycle)   The sequence of chemical reactions, taking place in the mitochondria of cells, that is central to the metabolism of virtually all living organisms. Named after its principal discoverer, Sir Hans *Krebs, the cycle involves the conversion of acetyl coenzyme A, derived from the carbohydrates, proteins, and fats of food, into hydrogen atoms or electrons, from which usable energy in the form of *ATP is produced by the *cytochrome electron transport chain. Intermediate products of the Krebs cycle are used for the manufacture of carbohydrates, lipids, and proteins by cells.

Krefeld   51 20N 6 32E A city in NW West Germany, in North Rhine-Westphalia on the River Rhine. It is known especially for its silk and velvet industries. It was the site of a Prussian victory (1758) during the Seven Years' War. Population (1983 est): 222 100.

Kreisky, Bruno   (1911–   ) Austrian statesman; Socialist chancellor (1970–83). After Austria fell to Nazi Germany, he escaped to Sweden (1938), where he lived until 1945. He was foreign minister (1959–66) before becoming chancellor.

Kreisler, Fritz   (1875–1962) Austrian violinist. A child prodigy, he studied at the Vienna and Paris conservatoires and toured the USA in 1889, the beginning of a brilliant career. He frequently played his own compositions, written in the style of older composers and (until 1935) ascribed to them.

Kremenchug   49 03N 33 25E A city in the Soviet Union, in the E central Ukrainian SSR on the River Dnepr. It has a large hydroelectric station and metallurgical and engineering industries. Population (1984): 222 000.

Kremlin   The citadel of any Russian city, now referring usually to that of Moscow. Built in 1156 but continually extended, it contains the Cathedral of the Assumption (1475–79), the Cathedral of the Annunciation (1484–89), the Great Kremlin Palace (1838–49), etc. Except for the period between 1712 and 1918 it has served continually as the seat of the Russian government and is now also a public museum of Russian architecture.

Křenek, Ernst   (1900–   ) Austrian composer, a pupil of Franz Schreker (1878–1934) in Berlin. His jazz-influenced opera, *Jonny spielt auf* (1925–26), is atonal; he later made use of *serialism. He became a US citizen in 1954.

Kreutzer, Rodolphe (1766–1831) French violinist and composer, renowned for his violin studies. Beethoven's *Kreutzer Sonata* for violin and piano (1803) was dedicated to him.

Krewo, Union of (1385) The union of Poland and Lithuania under Jagiello, Grand Duke of Lithuania (*see* Jagiellon), whose rule there was threatened by rivals in the ducal family and by the *Teutonic Knights. He agreed to marry the young Polish queen and to accept Christianity while Lithuania was to be annexed to Poland. The union was only made permanent by the Union of *Lublin (1569).

krill Shrimplike marine *crustaceans, 8–60 mm long, of the order *Euphausiacea* (82 species). Periodically krill swarms occur in certain regions, for example the Arctic and Antarctic Oceans, to become an important source of food for fishes, birds, and especially baleen whales.

Krishna A popular Hindu deity, the eighth incarnation of *Vishnu and the subject of much devotional worship, art, and literature. In the *Bhagavadgita* he is revealed as the creator, sustainer, and destroyer of the universe (*see* Trimurti). Elsewhere he is worshipped as a fertility god, whose flute playing entrances all and whose erotic love for young maidens expresses God's love for man. He is commonly represented as a beautiful youth with bluish skin wearing a crown of peacock feathers.

Krishna Menon. *See* Menon, Krishna.

Kristiansand 58 8N 08 01E A major seaport in S Norway, on the *Skagerrak. Its numerous industries include shipbuilding, textiles, smelting, and food processing. Population (1981 est): 60 938.

Kristianstad 56 02N 14 10E A town in Sweden, on the River Helge. Originally a Danish fortress (1614), it finally became part of Sweden in 1678. Its industries include textiles and engineering. Population (1984): 61 704.

Krivoi Rog 47 55N 33 24E A city in the Soviet Union, in the SE Ukrainian SSR. Founded by the Cossacks in the 17th century, it is now an important ironmining centre. Population (1984): 680 000.

Krochmal, Nachman (1785–1840) Jewish philosopher and historian, born in Poland. His *Guide to the Perplexed of Our Time* (published posthumously in 1851) offers an original philosophy of Jewish history and marks a significant achievement in the early modern study of Jewish history and literature.

Kronstadt 60 00N 29 40E A port in the NW Soviet Union, in the RSFSR on Kotlin Island in the Gulf of Finland. The *Kronstadt Rebellion (1921) of sailors was instrumental in the Soviet Government's decision to inaugurate the New Economic Policy. Kronstadt is still an important naval base. Population (1970): 39 477.

Kronstadt Rebellion (1921) An uprising among Soviet sailors in Kronstadt. The sailors, who had supported the Bolsheviks in the Russian Revolution, demanded economic reforms and an end to Bolshevik political domination. The Red Army crushed the rebels and Lenin's *New Economic Policy (1921) was introduced to relieve the privations that had given rise to the revolt.

Kropotkin, Peter, Prince (1842–1921) Russian anarchist. A noted geographer and geologist, Kropotkin joined the anarchist movement in the 1870s, was arrested, and escaped abroad. He settled in England in 1886 and later wrote his famous autobiography, *Memoirs of a Revolutionist* (1899). In 1917, Kropotkin returned to Russia but, unsympathetic to the authoritarianism of the Bolsheviks, retired from politics.

Kruger, (Stephanus Johannes) Paul(us) (1825–1904) Afrikaner statesman; president (1883–1902) of the South African Republic (Transvaal). A farmer of Dutch descent, Kruger settled with his parents in the Transvaal after taking part in the *Great Trek. He led the struggle to regain independence for the Transvaal from the British, achieved in 1881, after the first *Boer War. As president he resisted Uitlander (British immigrant) demands for political equality with the Afrikaner, a poli-

cy that led to the second Boer War (1899–1902). In the course of the war he went to Europe to seek aid for the Afrikaner cause. Unsuccessful, he settled in Holland and then Switzerland, where he died.

KREMLIN   *Red Square in Moscow; the Kremlin is on the left and the cathedral on the right.*

Kruger National Park A game and plant reserve in NE South Africa, adjacent to the border with Mozambique. About 325 km (202 mi) long and 20–50 km (12–31 mi) wide, it serves to protect most species found in the area, including lions, leopards, zebras, and elephants. Area: about 21 000 sq km (8106 sq mi).

krugerrand A South African coin containing one troy ounce of gold, minted since 1967 for overseas issue and bought for investment purposes. It has never been a true currency coin and was minted to enable investors to escape restrictions on the private ownership of gold. Since 1975 an import licence has been required to bring them into the UK. In the late 1980s they lost popularity for political reasons and because other countries produced similar coins.

Krugersdorp 26 06S 27 46E A town in South Africa, in the S Transvaal. Founded in 1887, it is an important mining and industrial centre producing gold, uranium, and manganese. Population (1980 est): 102 940.

Krum (d. 814 AD) Khan of the Bulgars (802–14). After defeating a Byzantine army in 811, Krum besieged Constantinople in 813 and 814, dying during the campaign. Krum introduced a state administrative system to Bulgaria.

Krupp A German family of arms manufacturers. Under **Arndt Krupp** (d. 1624), the family settled in Essen, where in 1811 **Friedrich Krupp** (1787–1826) established a steel factory. His son **Alfred Krupp** (1812–87) diversified the family business into arms manufacture, contributing to Prussian victory in the *Franco-Prussian War (1870–71). Under Alfred's son-in-law **Gustav Krupp von Bohlen und Halbach** (1870–1950), the company developed Big Bertha, the World War I artillery piece named after Gustav's wife **Bertha Krupp** (1886–1957). Their son **Alfried Krupp** (1907–67) developed Gustav's ties with the Nazis, using concentration-camp internees in his factories. After World War II he was imprisoned for war crimes and his property was confiscated until 1951, when he was granted an amnesty.

krypton (Kr) A noble gas discovered in 1898 by Sir William Ramsay and M. W. Travers (1872–1961), in the residue left after boiling liquid air. Compounds include KrF_2 and some *clathrates. It is used for filling some fluorescent light bulbs and the *metre was (1960–83) defined in terms of the wavelength of a specified transition of one of its isotopes. At no 36; at wt 83.80; mp 156.6°C; bp -152.2°C.

Kuala Lumpur 3 10N 101 40E The capital of Malaysia, in central Peninsular Malaysia. It became capital of the Federated Malay States in 1895. Formerly also capital of the state of Selangor, it became a federal territory in 1974. The University of Malaya was founded in 1962 and the Technological University of Malaysia in 1972. It is a major commercial centre serving an important tinmining and rubber-growing area. Population (1980): 937 875.

Kuang-chou. *See* Canton.

Kuang-hsü. *See* Guang Xu.

Kuan Ti. *See* Guan Di.

Kuan Yin. *See* Guan Yin.

Kuban, River A river in the S central Soviet Union. Rising in the Caucasus Mountains, it flows mainly NW into a swampy delta that enters the Sea of Azov. Its main port is Krasnodar. Length: 906 km (563 mi).

Kubelik, Rafael (1914-) Czech conductor. His career in Prague ended in 1948, when he went to live first in the UK and subsequently in the USA. He was music director of the Royal Opera, Covent Garden (1955-58), and of the New York Metropolitan Opera (1972-74). In 1973 he took Swiss citizenship. His father **Jan Kubelik** (1880-1940) was a famous violinist.

Kublai Khan (1215-94) Emperor of China (1279-94), who founded the Yuan dynasty. Genghis Khan's grandson, Kublai established himself (1259) as chief of the Mongols after years of conflict with his brother Mangu (d. 1259). The conqueror and acknowledged ruler of all China from 1279, he administered from Peking an empire extending from the River Danube to the East China Sea. More humane than his predecessors and much influenced by Chinese culture and civilization, he opened up trade and communications with Europe, largely through Marco *Polo. However, his preoccupation with China and attempts to conquer SE Asia weakened the rest of the empire.

Kubrick, Stanley (1928-) US film writer, director, and producer working mainly in the UK. His first major film, *Paths of Glory* (1957), which he wrote and directed, concerned an unjust courtmartial. His subsequent films, mainly satirical and highly imaginative, include *Lolita* (1962), *Dr Strangelove* (1963), *2001: A Space Odyssey* (1968), *A Clockwork Orange* (1971), *Barry Lyndon* (1975), and *The Shining* (1980).

Kuching 1 32N 110 20E A port in Malaysia, the capital of Sarawak state on the River Sarawak. It exports rubber, sago, and pepper. It has Anglican and Roman Catholic cathedrals. Population (1980): 120 000.

kudu A large antelope, *Tragelaphus strepsiceros*, of African bush regions. About 130 cm high at the shoulder, kudus are red-brown with thin white vertical stripes on the flanks. Males have long corkscrew-shaped horns, a fringe on the lower side of the neck, and a mane along the back. The lesser kudu (*T. imberbis*) is smaller and found only in NE Africa.

kudzu A climbing vine, *Pueraria lobata*, with entire or lobed leaves and fragrant purple flowers. Native to E Asia, it has been introduced to North America for its edible tubers, fibre, and as a quick-growing ornamental along highways, etc. Family: *Leguminosae.*

Kuei-yang. *See* Guiyang.

Kufah A town 145 km (90 mi) S of Baghdad, in Iraq. Founded as an Arab garrison town in 638 AD, Kufah became one of the most important centres of Islam. From the 10th century it began to decline and it is now an archaeological site. Its suburb of Najaf is the burial place of *Ali and a flourishing centre of *Shiite Islam.

Kuibyshev (name until 1935: Samara) 53 10N 50 10E A port in the SW central Soviet Union, in the RSFSR on the River Volga. Oil refining is a major industrial activity and

market gardening is also important. Population (1981 est): 1 238 000.

Kukai (774-835) Japanese Buddhist monk, famous as a scholar and artist. The founder of the Kongobuji monastery on Mount Koya, Kukai reputedly invented hiragana, the character system of *Japanese writing.

Ku Klux Klan (KKK) A US secret society active against the Blacks. It originated in Tennessee after the Civil War to deter newly enfranchised Blacks from voting. Klansmen in white cloaks and hoods, burning fiery crosses, killed Blacks and destroyed their property. It was revived in 1915, supporting White protestants in business and politics against immigrants, Catholics, Jews, and Blacks. Membership dropped during the Depression and the KKK became quiescent. Bitterness in the South against the *civil-rights movement led to another revival in the 1950s. The Un-American Activities Committee investigated its leaders in 1965, after a civil-rights demonstrator was murdered. Recently Klansmen have violently opposed desegregation orders.

kulaks Wealthy peasants in late imperial and early Soviet Russia. Before the Russian Revolution (1917) they were prominent in village affairs. After the Revolution, they were favoured by the *New Economic Policy (1921) until 1927, when Stalin raised their taxes and then transformed their lands into *collective farms. The dekulakization programme led to the exile of many kulaks to remote regions.

Kulturkampf (German: conflict of beliefs) The struggle between *Bismarck and the German Roman Catholic Church during the 1870s and 1880s. Bismarck opposed the church's involvement in politics and subordinated it to the state. However, opposition to the persecution of priests had forced Bismarck to restore the church's rights by 1887.

Kumamoto 32 50N 130 42E A city in Japan, in W Kyushu on the River Shira. One of the strongest centres in feudal Japan, it has a 17th-century castle. Its university was established in 1949. It is an agricultural centre, with bamboo, pottery, and textile industries. Population (1980): 526 000.

Kumasi 6 45N 1 35W The second largest city in Ghana. Formerly the capital of Ashanti, it was taken by the British in 1874. It is the commercial and transportation centre of Ghana's chief cocoa-growing area. The University of Science and Technology was founded here in 1961. **Population** (1982 est): 436 069.

kumquat A shrubby plant of the genus *Fortunella* (6 species), of E and SE Asia, with fruits resembling small oranges. They are acid-tasting and mainly used for pickling and preserves and kumquats can be grown farther N than citrus trees. Family: *Rutaceae.*

Kun, Béla (1886-?1939) Hungarian revolutionary. Kun founded the Hungarian Communist Party in 1918 and led the Soviet Republic that succeeded *Károlyi's government in March, 1919. The populace's reluctance to accept his nationalization programme led to a reign of terror, which with his unsuccessful campaigns against Romania forced him to flee in August to Vienna and then to Russia. He reportedly died in Stalin's purges.

kung fu An ancient Chinese form of combat, mainly for self-defence. Among the other *martial arts it is most closely related to *karate, which possibly developed from it. In the second half of the 20th century the *wing chun* style (according to tradition devised as a means of self-defence for women) has become particularly well known, partly because of the publicity given it by Bruce *Lee. Like other martial arts, it embodies a philosophy as well as a method of combat.

Kunlun Mountains A mountain system in W China, separating Tibet from the Tarim Basin. It extends 1600 km (1000 mi) E-W, reaching 7723 m (25 378 ft) at Ulugh Muztagh.

Kunming 25 04N 102 41E A city in S China, the capital of

Yunnan province. A major commercial and cultural centre, it is noted for its Ming bronze temple and is the site of Yunnan University. Industries include iron and steel, engineering, and chemicals. Population (1983): 1 430 000.

Kuomintang. *See* Guomindang.

Kuo Mo-jo (1892–1978) Chinese man of letters, translator of many western classics. Born in Szechwan, he went to Japan in 1913, where in 1921 he founded the Creation Society, dedicated to the reform of Chinese language and literature. He produced a vast amount of work as a poet, novelist, playwright, and critic. He returned to China in 1937 a committed communist and held many major cultural posts under Mao.

Kura, River A river in W Asia. Rising in NE Turkey, it flows N into the Soviet Union, through the Georgian and Azerbaidzhan SSRs to enter the Caspian Sea near Baku. It is used for hydroelectric power and irrigation. Length: 1515 km (941 mi).

KUBLAI KHAN *Marco Polo with his father Niccolò and his uncle Maffeo offering papal letters to Kublai Khan on their return to China in 1271 (from a 14th-century manuscript).*

Kurchatov, Igor Vasilievich (1903–60) Soviet physicist, who headed his country's research into nuclear fission during World War II. His team constructed a nuclear reactor in 1946 and built the Soviet Union's first atomic bomb in 1949 and its first hydrogen bomb in 1952. The element kurchatovium is named after him.

kurchatovium (Ku) An artificial transuranic element and the first transactinide. It was first detected by Soviet scientists in 1964 and named after I. V. *Kurchatov. The claim is disputed by scientists at Berkeley, USA, who proposed the name **rutherfordium** (Rf) after Lord *Rutherford, following their independent synthesis. At no 104.

Kurdistan An area in the Middle East inhabited by *Kurds, comprising parts of SE Turkey, N Syria, N Iraq, and NW Iran, including the Iranian province of Kordestan. The Turkish part includes a plateau that supports some agriculture, the remainder being mainly mountainous; the chief towns are Diyarbakir (Turkey), Kirkuk (Iraq), and Kermanshah (Iran). The area was split between different countries on the dissolution of the Ottoman Empire at the end of World War I, and subsequent attempts to form a Kurdish state have been only partially or temporarily successful. Area: 192 000 sq km (74 600 sq mi).

Kurds The major population group in *Kurdistan. Their language, Kurdish, is one of the *Iranian languages and is written in either a modified Arabic or a modified Cyrillic script.

The Kurds grow cereals and cotton and are now mostly detribalized but a few nomadic groups still exist. They are Muslims but do not restrict their women to the same extent as other Islamic peoples. Known from Assyrian records (6th century BC), the Kurds have never enjoyed political unity, and nationalistic aspirations issuing in rebellions in the 19th and 20th centuries have led to reprisals, especially in Turkey (1925), Iraq, and Iran.

Kure 34 14N 132 32E A port in Japan, in SW Honshu on Hiroshima Bay. An important naval base since 1886, an enormous battleship, the *Yamato*, was built here during World War II. Other industries include engineering and steel. Population (1982 est): 233 675.

Kurgan 55 30N 65 20E A city in the W central Soviet Union, in the RSFSR on the River Tobol. Machinery is produced and food processed. Population (1984): 339 000.

Kuria Muria Islands A group of five islands off the coast of Oman, in the Arabian Sea. Area: 72 sq km (28 sq mi).

Kuril Islands A Soviet chain of 56 islands extending 1200 km (746 mi) NE–SW between Kamchatka (Soviet Union) and Hokkaido (Japan) and separating the Sea of Okhotsk and the main body of the Pacific Ocean. Discovered in 1634 by the Dutch, the islands were Japanese until seized by the Soviet Union in 1945; in 1986 Japan demanded their return. The largest are Paramushir, Urup, Iturup, and Kunashir. There are 38 active volcanoes. About 200 km (124 mi) to the E is the **Kuril Trench**, which has a maximum depth of 10 542 m (34 587 ft). Total area: about 15 600 sq km (6022 sq mi).

Kurosawa, Akira (1910–) Japanese film director. His best-known films are action costume dramas such as *Rashomon* (1950) and *Seven Samurai* (1954). Working usually with the actor Toshiro Mifune (1920–), he has also made films on contemporary themes of social injustice and several literary adaptations, notably *Throne of Blood* (1957) and *Ran* (1985) (from Shakespeare's *Macbeth* and *King Lear*, respectively) and *Kagemusha* (1980).

kuroshio A warm ocean current forming part of the N Pacific circulation. Analogous to the Gulf Stream of the Atlantic, it flows NE along the Pacific coast of Japan, then veers across the N Pacific as the North Pacific Drift.

Kursk 51 45N 36 14E A city in the W central Soviet Union, in the RSFSR. Food processing and metallurgy are important. Population (1984): 413 000.

Kusunoki Masashige (1294–1336) Japanese samurai. His steadfast loyalty to Emperor *Daigo II and heroic defence of Chihaya castle became one of the most famous examples of *bushido* (the way of the warriors).

Kut. *See* Al Kut.

Kutaisi 42 15N 42 44E A city in the Soviet Union, in the W Georgian SSR on the River Rioni. It is a historic Transcaucasian city and the 11th-century Bagrati Cathedral survives. It is a major industrial centre, producing especially consumer goods. Population (1984): 210 000.

Kutch, Rann of An area of salt waste in central W India, near the border with S Pakistan. It consists of the Great Rann in the N and the Little Rann in the SE. It was a navigable lake in the 4th century BC, but is now salt marsh in the wet season and salt desert in the dry. Total area: about 23 000 sq km (8878 sq mi).

Kutenai A North American Indian people of the plateau region between the Rocky and Cascade Mountains of British Columbia. They were a hunting and fishing people, occasionally moving on to the Plains to hunt buffalo. Their language is distantly related to the *Algonkian family.

Kutná Hora (German name: Kuttenberg) 49 58N 15 15E A mining town in Czechoslovakia, in E Bohemia, famous during the 13th century as a silvermining centre. It contains the fine gothic Cathedral of St Barbara (13th century), in the form of an **imperial crown**. Population (1983 est): 21 316.

Kutuzov, Mikhail Ilarionovich, Prince of Smolensk
(1745–1813) Russian field marshal. After service in Poland, Austria, and against the Turks, he commanded the forces opposing Napoleon's invasion of Russia. When Napoleon withdrew from Moscow, Kutuzov's army harassed his retreat until barely 100 000 French soldiers remained.

Kuwait 29 20N 48 00E The capital of the sheikdom of Kuwait, on the Persian Gulf. It has a good natural harbour, and its livelihood was based on sea trade, fishing, and boatbuilding until oil became the major industry in the early 1950s and the traditional Islamic town began to develop into a metropolis with modern facilities including a university (1962). Population (1980): 60 525.

Kuwait, State of A country in the Middle East, in Arabia situated at the head of the Persian Gulf. The country is flat, sandy, and barren and has a harsh climate with extremes of temperature. The inhabitants are predominantly Arab, although about half are foreigners, and the Kuwaitis are mainly Sunnite or Shiite Muslim. *Economy*: Kuwait is one of the largest oil producers in the world and has one of the highest per capita incomes; oil revenues account for over half the gross national product and oil-related services for most of the remainder, as the country has almost no other natural resources. Kuwait is a member of OPEC. There are some manufacturing industries, such as plastics and fertilizers, and the traditional fishing (especially for shrimp) and the building of dhows (Arab sailing craft) continue. *History*: Kuwait was originally settled in the early 18th century by nomads from the Arabian interior, who established a sheikdom in 1756. In 1899, to counter German and Ottoman expansionism, Kuwait made an agreement giving Britain control over its foreign affairs and on the outbreak of World War I it became a British protectorate. Its borders were fixed in 1922–23, including those of a neutral zone, the oil revenues from which are shared by Saudi Arabia and Kuwait. Oil was discovered in 1938 and transformed the Kuwaiti economy after World War II. On gaining independence in 1961, Kuwait had to request troops from Britain to avert the threatened annexation by Iraq; in the 1980s the *Gulf War increased tension within Kuwait. Head of state: Sheik Jabir al-Ahmad al-Jabir as-Sabah (1928–   ). Prime minister: Sheik Saad al-Abdullah as-Salim as-Sabah. Official language: Arabic. Official currency: Kuwait dinar of 1000 fils. Area: 24 286 sq km (9375 sq mi). Population (1985): 1 697 301. Capital: Kuwait.

Kuznets, Simon (1901–   ) US economist, born in Russia. His theory of the *gross national product as a measure of economic output is contained in his major work *National Income and Its Composition (1919–1938)* (1941). Other works include *Economic Growth of Nations* (1971). Kuznets was awarded the Nobel Prize in 1971.

Kuznetsk Basin An area in the central S Soviet Union comprising the river basin of the Tom from Novokuznetsk to Tomsk. It has vast coal deposits, which have brought heavy industry to the area, notably iron- and steel-works.

Kwa A major division of the *Niger-Congo language family that includes many languages of West Africa, such as Yoruba, Igbo (*see* Ibo) *Ewe, Twi, and Anyi.

Kwajalein 9 15N 167 30E The largest atoll of the Marshall Islands, in the W Pacific Ocean. It was the first Pacific territory captured by US forces in World War II and is now a US military base.

Kwakiutl A North American Indian people of the coastal region of British Columbia. They speak a *Wakashan language. Their vigorous traditional culture was typical of the NW coast and characterized by extreme competition for status and rank through ostentatious disposal and even destruction of wealth (*see* potlatch). There was an elaborate religious and ceremonial life and a distinctive artistic tradition based upon carving of wooden totem poles, masks, and other objects. Their economy was based on an abundance of salmon and other fish, game, and wild fruits and agriculture was not practised.

Kwangju 35 07N 126 52E A city in SW South Korea. An ancient commercial and administrative centre, it has industries that include motor-vehicle manufacture. Its university was established in 1952. Population (1980): 727 627.

Kwangsi Chuang Autonomous Region. *See* Guangxi Zhuang Autonomous Region.

Kwangtung. *See* Guangdong.

kwashiorkor Severe protein deficiency in children under five years. **Marasmus** is deficiency of not only protein but also of carbohydrate and fat. Kwashiorkor and marasmus often occur together in some combination. Kwashiorkor, which develops in babies soon after they are weaned, occurs in poor countries, especially parts of West Africa, where the diet does not contain sufficient protein (the name derives from a Ghanaian word). The children fail to grow, are apathetic, have swollen stomachs and ankles, sparse hair, diarrhoea, and enlarged livers. The slightest infection is usually fatal but the children recover rapidly with a good diet.

KwaZulu. *See* Bantu Homelands.

Kweichow. *See* Guizhou.

Kwinana. *See* Fremantle.

Kyd, Thomas (1558–94) English dramatist. A friend of *Marlowe, Kyd inaugurated the genre of revenge tragedy with *The Spanish Tragedy* (1592). Among his probable works is a play about Hamlet, now lost, which influenced Shakespeare.

Kyoga, Lake (*or* Lake Kioga) A lake in central Uganda. Formed by the Victoria Nile River, it is shallow and reedy and has many arms. Length: about 130 km (81 mi).

Kyoto 35 2N 135 45E A city in Japan, in S Honshu. It has been a leading cultural centre since early times, when it was the Japanese capital (794–1192 AD) and the old imperial palace and ancient Buddhist temples still remain. Kyoto university was established in 1897. It is also the centre of Japanese Buddhism. Situated within the Osaka-Kobe industrial complex, it is famed for its silk, porcelain, and handicrafts. Population (1980): 1 473 000.

Kyprianou, Spyros (1932–   ) Cypriot statesman; president (1977–88). When Cyprus became independent in 1960 he was appointed minister of justice and then foreign minister (1960–72). In 1976 he founded the Cyprus Democratic Party.

Kyushu The southernmost of the four main islands of Japan, separated from Korea by the Korea Strait and from Honshu by Shimonoseki Strait. Mountainous and volcanic, it has hot springs and a subtropical climate and is the most densely populated of the Japanese islands. There is a large rice-growing area in the NW, drained by the River Chikugo, while heavy industry is centred on the N coalfield. Other important products are silk, fish, timber, fruit, and vegetables. It is noted for its Satsuma and Hizen porcelain. Area: 35 659 sq km (13 768 sq mi). Population (1984): 13 230 000. Chief cities: Kitakyushu, Fukuoka, and Nagasaki.

Kyzyl Kum A desert in the W central S Soviet Union, lying between the Rivers Amu Darya and Syr Darya in the Kazakh and Uzbek SSRs. Area: about 300 000 sq km (115 806 sq mi).

L

Laaland. *See* Lolland.

Labanotation. *See* illustration at ballet.

labelled compounds. *See* radioactive tracer.

Labiatae A family of herbaceous plants and shrubs (about 3500 species), widely distributed but particularly abundant in the Mediterranean region. They typically have square stems, hairy simple leaves, and clusters of tubular two-lipped flowers. Many of the plants are aromatic and yield useful oils (lavender, rosemary, etc.) and many are used as culinary' herbs (marjoram, mint, sage, thyme, etc.).

Labiche, Eugène (1815–88) French dramatist. His numerous popular farcical comedies include *The Italian Straw Hat* (1851) and *The Journey of Mr Perrichon* (1860). They are characterized by intricate plots and the satirical portrayal of contemporary bourgeois conventions.

Labor Party The Australian democratic socialist party. It was formed in New South Wales in 1891 and first held federal office in 1904. World War I provoked a split in the party with the Labor prime minister W. M. *Hughes leading the proconscription majority out of the party to form the National Party (1916). The Labor Party did not regain power until 1929 and in 1931 policies in dealing with the Depression caused another split. In power from 1939 to 1949, the party introduced important social legislation but in opposition in the 1950s another split occurred over attitudes to communism. Labour were again in power from 1972 until 1975 under Gough *Whitlam and from 1983, when Bob *Hawke became prime minister.

Labour Day The day on which the labour movement is celebrated. In 1889, the Second International declared an international labour holiday on *May Day, which has since been thus celebrated in many countries. In Britain, Labour Day was the first Sunday in May until 1977, when the first Monday of the month was declared a public holiday. It is celebrated in Australia at different times in different states, in New Zealand on the fourth Monday in October, and in the USA on the first Monday in September.

Labour Party The democratic socialist party in the UK. The party was formed in 1900 as the Labour Representation Committee, being renamed the Labour Party in 1906. Its origins lie in the trades-union movement of the 19th century, and the trade unions continue to provide over three-quarters of its funds. The *Fabian Society was also a powerful influence on its formation and political beliefs. In 1922 the Labour Party replaced the divided Liberal Party as one of the two major UK parties (*compare* Conservative Party) and in 1924 and 1929–31 Labour formed a minority government under Ramsay *MacDonald. It was not until after World War II, when under Clement *Attlee the party won a huge majority in the general election of 1945, that it was able to introduce radical policies. In office from 1945 to 1951, the Labour administration undertook widespread *nationalization and set up a comprehensive system of *social security. The party was in office again from 1964 to 1970 and from 1974 to 1979, under Harold *Wilson (1964–76) and then James *Callaghan. The increasing prominence of the left caused splits within the party and in 1981 four members from the right defected to form the *Social Democratic Party. Michael *Foot turned out to be an ineffectual leader (1980–83) and was succeeded by Neil *Kinnock.

labour relations. *See* industrial relations.

labour theory of value The economic theory that the value of a product can be determined by the amount of labour needed to produce it, e.g. a product needing twice as many man hours (of equal skill) to produce as another is

worth twice as much.

labour union. *See* trade union.

Labrador (*or* Coast of Labrador) A district of NE Canada, on the Atlantic Ocean. Although the coast has belonged to Newfoundland for several centuries, the interior was finally awarded to Newfoundland in 1927 by a judicial decision, which is still not recognized by Quebec. Labrador is mostly a rolling swampy plateau within the Canadian Shield. Generally barren except for forested river valleys, it has vast reserves of high-grade iron ore, which are being mined. Its hydroelectric potential is enormous. Churches and missions are very influential in Labrador, especially in the sphere of education. Area: 258 185 sq km (99 685 sq mi). Population (1976): 33 052. *See also* Churchill Falls.

Labrador Current A major ocean current of the N Atlantic, flowing S from the polar seas down the W coast of Greenland and past Newfoundland, until it meets the Gulf Stream and, being cold and dense, sinks beneath it. The Labrador Current carries icebergs S and is a cause of frequent fogs in the region of Newfoundland.

Labrador retriever A breed of dog originating in Newfoundland and brought to Britain by fishermen in the early 19th century. It is solidly built with a tapering otter-like tail and a short dense water-resistant coat, usually black or yellow-brown. Height: 56–57 cm (dogs); 54–56 cm (bitches).

La Bruyère, Jean de (1645–96) French satirist. He studied law and then served in the Bourbon household of Louis II, Prince of Condé. His single work, *Caractères de Théophraste, avec les caractères ou les moeurs de ce siècle* (1688), consisted chiefly of satirical portrait sketches (often of real persons under disguised names) and contemporary illustrations of vices; it achieved lasting popularity.

Labuan A Malaysian island in the South China Sea. It became part of the state of Sabah in 1946. Copra, rubber, and rice are produced. Area: 98 sq km (38 sq mi). Population (1980): 12 219. Chief town: Victoria.

laburnum A tree of the genus *Laburnum*, especially *L. anagyroides*, which is native to mountainous regions of central Europe and widely grown for ornament. Up to 7 m high, it has smooth olive-green or brown bark and its leaves each consist of three dark-green leaflets. The bright-yellow flowers grow in hanging clusters, 10–30 cm long, and produce slender brown pods. All parts of the plant are poisonous, especially the seeds. Family: *Leguminosae.

labyrinth fish A small elongated laterally compressed fish of the family *Anabantidae* (about 70 species), found in fresh waters of tropical Asia and Africa. They have an accessory respiratory organ (labyrinth) with which they obtain oxygen from air gulped at the surface—of benefit in poorly oxygenated water. The males often build a floating nest of bubbles to protect the eggs. Some species are popular aquarium fish. Order: *Perciformes. See also* climbing perch; fighting fish; gourami.

Laccadive, Minicoy, and Amindivi Islands. *See* Lakshadweep.

lace An ornamental network of threads of silk, linen, etc., used mainly for dress collars, cuffs, altar cloths, etc. Needlepoint lace, originating in Italy in the early 16th century, is made with a needle on parchment or fabric. Pillow or bobbin lace, reputedly invented by Barbara Uttmann (b. 1514) in Saxony, is formed by twisting threads around pins stuck in a pillow. The best work was done in Italy, Flanders, France, and England in the 17th and 18th centuries, famous types of lace being Brussels, Valenciennes,

LACE *An example of bobbin lace from Brussels made in the first half of the 18th century.*

Mechlin, and Honiton. Lace making as an art declined in the 19th century after machine manufacture was introduced.

La Ceiba 15 45N 86 45W A port in N Honduras, on the Gulf of Honduras. It is a major port exporting chiefly coconuts, abaca fibre, and oranges. Population (1982): 68 911.

lacewing An insect belonging to one of several families of the suborder *Plannipennia*. Lacewings have delicate net-veined wings and are carnivorous, with biting mouthparts. Green lacewings (*Chrysopidae*), also called golden-eyed lacewings, are about 10 mm long and occur worldwide near vegetation. Eggs are laid individually on hairlike stalks and the larvae feed on aphids, scale insects, etc. The brown lacewings (*Hemerobiidae*) are smaller and often have spotted wings. Order: *Neuroptera*. ⌐insect.

Lachish An ancient city in *Canaan, W of Hebron (Israel), occupied from before 1580 BC. The Israelites held it from about 1220 until its destruction by the Babylonians (588). Inscriptions discovered here are important evidence for the early evolution of the alphabet.

Lachlan River A river in SE Australia, in New South Wales. Rising in the Great Dividing Range it flows generally NW to join the Murrumbidgee River. Length: 1483 km (922 mi).

lac insect An insect of the family *Lacciferidae*, found mainly in tropical and subtropical regions. The legless females have globular bodies covered with a layer of hardened resin. In the Indian species, *Laccifer lacca*, the females become encrusted on twigs to form sticklac, from which *shellac is produced. Suborder: *Homoptera*; order *Hemiptera*.

Laclos, Pierre Choderlos de (1741–1803) French novelist. He was a professional soldier and died while serving as a general under Napoleon in Italy. His novel, *Les Liaisons dangereuses* (1782), written in the form of letters between the main characters, concerned sexual corruption and intrigue in aristocratic society. The seducer Valmont, his accomplice Mme de Merteuil, and their victims are depicted with keen psychological insight.

La Condamine, Charles Marie de (1701–74) French geographer. After service in the army he travelled widely and joined a geographical expedition to Peru (1735–43). He later went down the River Amazon on a raft, studying the region, and brought the drug curare to Europe.

Laconia (modern Greek name: Lakonía) The SE region of the Peloponnese. Once a prosperous Mycenaean kingdom, Laconia was conquered by invading *Dorians about 1000 BC. Settling in *Sparta, the newcomers became rulers of Laconia, using the indigenous inhabitants as serf labourers, called *helots.

La Coruña (*or* Corunna) 43 22N 8 24W A port in NW Spain, in Galicia on the Atlantic Ocean. The Spanish Armada sailed from here on 26 July, 1588, and in 1589 the

city was sacked by Sir Francis Drake. During the Peninsular War Sir John *Moore was mortally wounded here after ensuring a British victory against the French. An important fishing centre, it also manufactures tobacco and linen. Population (1981): 232 356.ʼ

lacquer Coloured and often opaque varnish applied to metal or wood for protection and decoration. In Chinese and Japanese artwork, the sap of the *lacquer tree is used as wood lacquer. Other types of lacquer consist of *shellac dissolved in alcohol, which dries to form a protective film.

lacquer tree A tree, *Rhus vernicifera*, of SE Asia, also called varnish tree. Up to 30 m tall, it has compound leaves each with up to nine pairs of leaflets, which turn red in autumn. Japanese *lacquer is obtained from the milky resin that oozes from cuts in the bark. Family: *Anacardiaceae*.

The optimum dimensions of the women's ground, although the game is played with no boundaries.

The dimensions of the men's ground.

LACROSSE

lacrosse A 10-a-side field game (12 for women) played with a ball and a long-handled stick (the crosse), which has a triangular head with a raw-hide strung pocket for catching, throwing, and picking up the ball. Of North American Indian origin, it is played mainly in the USA, Canada, Britain, and Australia. The object is to score goals by running with the ball and passing it. Each team consists of a goalkeeper, three defensive players (point, cover point, and first defence), three attackmen (first attack, in home, and out home) and three midfielders (second defence, centre, and second attack). Tackling and striking an opponent's stick to dislodge the ball are allowed, and protective clothing is worn.

lactation The secretion of milk from the breasts or mammary glands. In women lactation is controlled by hormones released from the ovary, placenta, and pituitary gland (*see* prolactin) and starts shortly after childbirth, in response to the sucking action of the baby at the nipple: it will continue for as long as the baby is breastfed. A protein-rich fluid called colostrum is secreted in the first few days of lactation, before the milk has been produced. It contains antibodies that give the baby temporary immunity to disease.

lactic acid (*or* 2-hydroxypropanoic acid) A carboxylic acid $(CH_3CH(OH)COOH)$ that is the end product of *glycolysis in animal muscles and of *fermentations (such as the souring of milk) by certain bacteria. A commercial preparation is used as a flavouring and preservative in pickles and salad dressings and in tanning leather.

lactose (*or* milk sugar) A disaccharide carbohydrate $(C_{12}H_{22}O_{11})$ consisting of one molecule of glucose linked to one of galactose. Lactose is found in the milk of all animals and is less sweet than sucrose.

Ladakh Range A mountain range mainly in NW India, extending about 370 km (230 mi) between the Karakoram Range and the Himalayas and rising to over 6000 m (19 685 ft).

Ladin A language spoken in the Dolomite region of Italy that belongs to the Rhaetian branch of the *Romance family. It is related to French and the Occitan dialects, to Romansh, and to Friulian, which is spoken around Udine in N Italy.

Ladino A *Romance language originally spoken by Sephardic Jews in Spain but taken by them after their exile in 1492 to the Balkans, the Near East, N Africa, Greece, and Turkey. It is an old form of Castilian Spanish mixed with Hebrew elements and written in Hebrew characters.

Ladoga, Lake A lake in the NW Soviet Union in the RSFSR, the largest lake in Europe. It discharges via the River Neva into the Gulf of Finland. A canal forming part of the water route from the Gulf of Finland to the River Volga and the White Sea has been built parallel to its S shore to avoid the storms on the lake. *See also* Leningrad. Area: about 17 700 sq km (6836 sq mi).

ladybird beetle A small round beetle, 8-10 mm long, that belongs to the widely distributed family *Coccinellidae* (5000 species). Most species are red or yellow with black spots and are of great benefit to man. Both the larvae and adults feed on a variety of plant pests, including aphids, scale insects, mealybugs, and whiteflies. When attacked, ladybirds exude a toxic fluid.

Lady Day The Christian feast of the *Annunciation of the Virgin Mary. Celebrated on 25 March, it began the calendar year in England from 1155 to 1752 and is still a quarter day.

lady fern A delicate *fern, *Athyrium filix-femina*, found in moist shady temperate regions. It has a short stout scaly rhizome that produces a circular cluster of large light-green feathery branched fronds, usually 50-70 cm long. The clusters of spore capsules (sori) are curved or horseshoe-shaped. Family: *Aspidiaceae*.

Ladysmith 28 34S 29 47E A town in South Africa, in NW Natal. Founded in 1850, it was besieged for four months (1899-1900) by the Boers during the second Boer War, with the death of 3200 British soldiers. Population (1985): 43 200.

lady's slipper A terrestrial orchid, *Cypripedium calceolus*, native to N Europe and Asia. Up to 45 cm high, it has broad leaves and the flowers are grouped singly or in twos and threes. Each flower has small twisted red-brown petals and an inflated yellow slipper-like lip. The lady's slipper is nearly extinct in Britain. *See also* slipper orchid.

lady's smock A perennial herb, *Cardamine pratensis*, also called cuckoo flower, found in damp meadows of N temperate regions. 15-60 cm high, it has compound leaves and a tall spike of pink or violet four-petalled flowers on slender stalks. Family: *Cruciferae*.

Laënnec, René Théophile Hyacinth (1781-1826) French physician and inventor of the stethoscope. Laënnec listened to the chest sounds of his patients using a foot-long wooden cylinder, from which he was able to diagnose diseases of the heart and respiratory system.

Lafayette, Marie Joseph Gilbert Motier, Marquis de (1757-1834) French general and politician, prominent at the beginning of the French Revolution. His early career was distinguished by his military successes (1777-79, 1780-82) against the British in the *American Revolution. In France as a representative in the *States General, he presented the Declaration of the *Rights of Man (1789) and after the storming of the Bastille he became commander of the new National Guard. In 1792 the rising power of the radicals threatened his life and he gave himself up to France's enemy, Austria. Lafayette was also prominent in the July Revolution (1830), which overthrew Charles X.

La Fayette, Mme de (Marie Madeleine, Comtesse de L. F.; 1634-93) French novelist. She was a friend of *La Rochefoucauld and many other prominent writers. Her best-known novel is *La Princesse de Clèves* (1678), a study of the conflict between passion and duty in marriage.

Lafontaine, Henri-Marie (1854-1943) Belgian jurist and statesman. A senator (1894-1936) and president of the International Peace Bureau (1907-43), he is best known for his contribution to international law. In 1913 he received the Nobel Peace Prize.

La Fontaine, Jean de (1621-95) French poet. He was a friend of many prominent writers and patrons. His major work was the *Fables* (1668-94), sophisticated verse treatments of traditional fables from the collections of *Aesop, *Phaedrus, and later writers. His many other works included the bawdy verse tales, *Contes* (1664), which he is said to have repudiated after his religious conversion in 1692.

Laforgue, Jules (1860-87) French poet, one of the *Symbolists. He was born in Montevideo (Uruguay) and wrote most of his poetry in Berlin while serving as reader to the Empress Augusta (1858-1921). His ironic and slangy poetry in *vers libre* greatly influenced several later French and foreign poets, notably T. S. Eliot.

LAFTA. *See* Latin America.

Lagash A city of ancient *Sumer, N of *Ur, flourishing about 2500 to 2100 BC. *Cuneiform tablets found here bear witness to social, legal, and commercial conditions in Sumer.

Lagerkvist, Pär (Fabian) (1891-1974) Swedish novelist, poet, and dramatist. His early works were pessimistic in tone and influenced by expressionism. In the novels *Bödeln* (*The Hangman*; 1934) and *Dvärgen* (*The Dwarf*; 1944) he explored the problems of evil and human brutality. His best-known work is the novel *Barabbas* (1950), after which he achieved a worldwide reputation, winning the Nobel Prize in 1951.

Lagerlöf, Selma Ottiliana Lovisa (1858-1940) Swedish novelist, who drew her inspiration from myth, legend, and her early life in Värmland. Her works include *Gösta Berlings Saga* (1891) and the children's storybook *The Wonderful Adventures of Nils* (1907). She was the first woman to be awarded the Nobel Prize (1909).

Lagomorpha An order of mammals (66 species) comprising *pikas, *rabbits, and *hares. Lagomorphs have teeth similar to rodents, with four continuously growing incisors. They are vegetarians and eat their own faecal pellets, thus obtaining the maximum value from their food. Lagomorphs are found all over the world except Antarctica.

Lagos 6 27N 3 28E The main port and former capital (until 1982) of Nigeria, on the Bight of Benin. First settled by Yoruba fishermen in the 17th century, it became the centre of the Portuguese slave trade in West Africa and was ceded to Britain in 1861. Its university was founded in 1962. One of Africa's largest cities, it is an important commercial and industrial centre. Exports include palm oil and kernels and groundnuts. Population (1983 est): 1 097 000.

Lagrange, Joseph Louis, Comte de (1736–1813) Mathematician and astronomer, born in Italy of French parents. In 1788, he published a book entitled *Mechanique analytique*, in which mechanics is developed algebraically and a wide variety of problems are solved by the application of general equations. In astronomy he solved the problem of predicting how two or more bodies move under each other's gravitational force and worked with *Laplace on planetary perturbations. Lagrange also headed the commission that produced the metric system of units in 1795.

La Guardia, Fiorello Henry (1882–1947) US politician; mayor of New York City (1933–45). As a lawyer and Congressman (1917–21, 1923–33) La Guardia helped initiate such laws as the Norris-La Guardia Act (1932), which allowed organized labour to strike, boycott, and picket. As mayor of New York he fought municipal corruption and supported action for civic improvement.

Lahore 31 34N 74 22E The second largest city in Pakistan, near the River Ravi. Traditionally the chief city of the Punjab, Lahore is situated close to the Indian border and has been the scene of much bloodshed and violence. It is a major railway, commercial, and political centre and the headquarters of the Muslim League. The famous Shalimar gardens lie to the E of the city. An important educational centre, it is the site of the University of the Punjab (1882) and Pakistan University of Engineering and Technology (1961). *History*: founded about the 7th century AD, it fell to the Moguls in 1524 and in 1798 it became the seat of Ranjit Singh's Sikh empire. It came under British rule in 1849. Population (1981): 2 922 000.

Lahti 61 00N 25 40E A town in S Finland. A winter-sports resort and growing industrial centre, it has sawmilling, furniture, and textile industries and is the site of Finland's main radio and television stations. Population (1980): 94 767.

Laibach. See Ljubljana.

Laing, R(onald) D(avid) (1927–) British psychiatrist. He is best known for regarding schizophrenia as a defensive façade and madness as a journey of self-realization (*The Divided Self*, 1960). *The Politics of Experience* (1967) became influential among the radical movements of that period and his views on family life (*Sanity, Madness and the Family*, 1965 and *The Politics of the Family*, 1971) aroused controversy. His poetry includes *Knots* (1970).

Laird, Macgregor (1808–61) Scottish explorer. In 1830 he formed a merchant company to trade with Africa and took the first oceangoing vessel (*Alburkah*) up the lower Niger, with a loss, however, of 39 lives. He also sailed up the Niger's tributary, the Benue. In 1854 he promoted an expedition that advanced 240 km (150 mi) up the Niger; the use of quinine prevented any loss of life.

laissez-faire The economic theory that governments should not interfere with market forces based on self-interest and the profit motive. The concept, originally proposed by the 18th-century French economists led by François *Quesnay (*see also* Physiocrats), was advocated by Adam *Smith and widely accepted until the beginning of the 19th century. By then the growth of capitalism had exposed its principal weaknesses: the rise of monopolies, the grossly inequitable distribution of wealth, and the exploitation of labour. In the 20th century, in western economies, laissez-faire policies have been largely abandoned for *mixed economies.

lake (landform) An extensive body of water occupying a hollow in the earth's surface. Rivers generally flow both into and out of lakes although some are landlocked with no outlet. An **oxbow lake** is crescent shaped and is formed when a river *meander is cut off by the river flow breaching its neck. The larger saline lakes form inland seas, such as the *Caspian Sea.

Many lakes are man made, for water supply, hydroelectric-power generation, and irrigation; Lake *Kariba in S Africa is an example.

lake (pigment) An insoluble pigment formed by the combination of an organic dyestuff with a metallic compound (salt, oxide, or hydroxide). Lakes are used in paints and printing *inks.

Lake District (*or* Lakeland) An area in NW England, in Cumbria, a national park since 1951. It consists of a high dome incised by a radial system of glaciated valleys, many of which contain ribbon lakes including Derwentwater, Ullswater, and Windermere. High mountains rise between the valleys, the highest being *Scafell Pike and *Helvellyn. Its spectacular scenery, popularized by the Lakeland poets (notably Wordsworth), is now a major tourist attraction, together with facilities for hill walking, rock climbing, and water sports. Other traditional occupations include hill farming, forestry, and quarrying. Area: about 1813 sq km (700 sq mi).

Lakeland terrier A breed of dog originating in the English Lake District and used to flush foxes from cover. It has a robust body and a long flat head with small folded triangular ears. The rough dense coat may be black or blue (with or without tan), red, or dark brown. Height: up to 36 cm.

Lakshadweep (name until 1973: Laccadive, Minicoy, and Amindivi Islands) A Union Territory of India comprising 27 islands in the Indian Ocean, 300 km (186 mi) W of Kerala. Ruled by Britain from 1792, it was handed over to India in 1956 and depends economically on fish, coconuts, grains, bananas, and vegetables. Area: 32 sq km (12 sq mi). Population (1981): 40 237. Administrative headquarters: Kavaratti Island.

Lakshmi In Hinduism, the goddess of wealth and happiness, the benign aspect of Shakti, the supreme goddess. As the wife of Vishnu she appears in various forms according to his several incarnations. Many festivals are held in her honour (*see* Diwali). Lakshmi is also revered by the Jains.

Lalande, Joseph-Jérôme Le Français de (1732–1807) French astronomer, who published (1801) the most complete catalogue of the stars then known. It listed some 47 000 stars, one of which was found by *Leverrier a hundred years later to be the planet Neptune.

La Línea 36 10N 5 21W A town in SW Spain, in Andalusia on the Strait of Gibraltar. Many of its inhabitants work in Gibraltar. Industries include textiles and cork. Population (1981): 56 282.

Lalique, René (1860–1945) French *Art Nouveau jeweller and glassmaker. His jewellery is usually asymmetric with motifs of plants, snakes, etc. He later designed glassware with frosted patterns in relief, establishing a factory at Wingen-sur-Moder (1920).

Lallans The dialect of the lowlands of Scotland, in which Robert *Burns wrote. A movement to re-establish it as a literary medium occurred after World War I (*see also* MacDiarmid, Hugh).

Lally, Thomas, Comte de (1702–66) French general of Irish ancestry. He took part in the *Jacobite rebellion of 1745 and subsequently became commander in chief in the French East Indies (1756), coming into conflict with the British. Forced to surrender in 1761, his action was construed as treason and he was beheaded.

Lalo, (Victor Antoine) Édouard (1823–92) French composer of Spanish descent. He is best remembered for his *Symphonie espagnole* (for violin and orchestra; 1873), a cello concerto (1876), and the ballet *Namouna* (1882).

Lalor, Peter (1827–89) Australian engineer and politician, born in Ireland, who led the *Eureka Stockade uprising (1854). He was subsequently postmaster general (1875), commissioner of trade and customs (1875, 1877–80), and speaker of the Legislative Assembly of Victoria (1880–87).

lamaism. *See* Tibetan Buddhism.

Lamarck, Jean-Baptiste de Monet, Chevalier de (1744–1829) French naturalist, noted for his speculations about the evolution of living things, particularly his theory ·of the inheritance of acquired characteristics (*see* Lamarckism). Lamarck studied botany under Bernard de *Jussieu and published a flora of France in 1778. In 1793 he became professor of invertebrate zoology at the Museum of Natural History, Paris. Here Lamarck worked on a system of classification for invertebrate animals, published in his *Histoire naturelle des animaux sans vertebres* (7 vols, 1815–22). In 1809 Lamarck published his theory of evolution (in *Philosophie zoologique*). Lamarckism has generally been rejected in favour of Charles *Darwin's theory of evolution by natural selection, although some attempts have been made to revive it, most notably by *Lysenko. Lamarck's speculations about the physical and natural world found little favour among his contemporaries and he died blind and poverty stricken.

Lamarckism The first theory of *evolution as proposed by Jean-Baptiste *Lamarck in 1809, based on his concept of the inheritance of acquired characteristics. He suggested that an ·organism develops structural changes during its lifetime as an adaptation to its particular environment and that these features are then inherited by successive generations through sexual reproduction. A classic example of these acquired characteristics are the forelegs and neck of a giraffe, which he believed became longer through its habit of browsing on tall trees. There is now little support for Lamarck's theory, although it was revived in a slightly modified form (neo-Lamarckism) by the Soviet geneticist T. D. *Lysenko.

Lamartine, Alphonse de (1790–1869) French poet, one of the major figures of the Romantic movement. He established his reputation with *Méditations poétiques* (1820), a volume of lyrical poetry inspired by an unsuccessful love affair. During the 1820s he served as a diplomat in Naples and Florence and in the 1830s he became an active political champion of republican ideals. He was briefly head of the provisional government after the Revolution of 1848. His other major works include the narrative poems *Jocelyn* (1836) and *La Chute d'un ange* (1836).

Lamb, Charles (1775–1834) British essayist and critic. He worked as a clerk for the East India Company, devoting his private life to caring for his sister Mary (1764–1847), who had killed their mother in 1796 during one of her recurrent fits of insanity. He collaborated with Mary on *Tales from Shakespeare* (1807), a children's book. He is best remembered for his *Essays of Elia* (1822).

Lamb, Henry (1885–1960) Australian-born British painter, the son of the mathematician and engineer **Sir Horace Lamb** (1849–1934). After studying medicine, he became a painter of portraits, notably the much acclaimed *Lytton Strachey* (1914; Tate Gallery), and was official war artist during World War II.

Lambaréné 0 41S 10 13E A town in W Gabon, on an island in the River Ogooué. Its hospital (1913) was founded by the missionary Albert *Schweitzer. Industries include palm products. Population (1978 est): 26 257.

lambert A unit of luminance equal to the luminance of a surface that emits one lumen per square centimetre. Named after J. H. *Lambert.

Lambert, Constant (1905–51) British composer and conductor, a pupil of Vaughan Williams. Diaghilev commissioned his ballet *Romeo and Juliet* (1925–26) and he was musical director of the Sadler's Wells from 1928 to 1947. His most famous composition is the choral work *Rio Grande* (1929). He wrote a famous book about music entitled *Music Ho!* (1934).

Lambert, Johann Heinrich (1728–77) German mathematician and astronomer, who first derived the *hyperbolic functions and proved that π is an irrational *number. As an astronomer he measured the luminosities of stars and planets

and introduced the term *albedo; a unit of luminance (*see* lambert) is named after him.

Lambert, John (1619–83) English parliamentary general in the *Civil War. He commanded the cavalry at *Marston Moor (1644) and against the Scots at Preston (1648), Inverkeithing (1650), and Worcester (1651). He was largely responsible for the overthrow of Richard Cromwell (1659) and was one of the rulers of the country until *Monck engineered the Restoration of Charles II (1661). Convicted of treason, he was imprisoned until his death.

Lambeth A borough of S central Greater London, on the River Thames. Created in 1965 from the former metropolitan borough and E Wandsworth, it contains the Royal Festival Hall (*see* Festival of Britain), the *National Theatre (1976), and Lambeth Palace (London residence of the Archbishop of Canterbury). Population (1981): 245 739.

Lambeth Conferences Assemblies normally convened every ten years under the chairmanship of the Archbishop of Canterbury at Lambeth Palace, London, to which all bishops of the Anglican Church are invited. The first Lambeth Conference was held in 1867. Although their decisions have no binding power, the conferences are important indications of the Anglican episcopate's views and policies.

Lambeth walk A British ballroom dance popularized in the 1930s by the musical *Me and My Girl* (1937). It purported to imitate the strutting walk of the Lambeth cockney.

lamb's lettuce. *See* corn salad.

Lamentations of Jeremiah An Old Testament book, a sequel to the Book of *Jeremiah and traditionally attributed to him, although it is more likely a work of the 5th century BC. It consists of a series of five dirgelike chapters concerned with the capture and destruction of Jerusalem and its Temple by the Babylonians in 586 BC. The event is graphically described, as are the accompanying slavery and famine. Jeremiah sees it as a divine judgment and closes with a prayer for mercy.

Lamerie, Paul de (1688–1751) English silversmith of French Huguenot parents. Establishing his shop in 1712, he progressed from an unornamented Queen Anne style to *rococo designs, for which he is most famous. □ p. 696.

Lamian War (323–322 BC) The conflict that confirmed Macedon's supremacy in Greece after Alexander the Great's death. *Antipater, the Macedonian regent, was besieged in Lamia by rebellious Greek forces but eventually crushed the city states and reimposed his authority more firmly.

laminar flow Fluid flow in which the particles move in parallel layers. A fluid moving slowly along a horizontal straight pipe flows in this way. Above a certain velocity, given by the *Reynolds number, the layers no longer remain parallel and the flow becomes turbulent.

Laminaria A genus of large brown seaweeds (*see* kelp), also called oarweed, that occurs in abundance along British and Pacific coasts. *L. digitata* (tangle) is a fan-shaped seaweed that may grow to a length of 50 m. *Laminaria* is a good source of alginic acid and alginates, used in the manufacture of ice cream, tyres, etc.

lammergeier A large *vulture, *Gypaetus barbatus*, also called bearded vulture because of the long bristles on its chin. It is over 1 m long with a wingspan of 3 m and occurs in mountainous regions of S Europe, central Asia, and E Africa. It is brown with tawny underparts and a black-and-white face. Lammergeiers feed on bones and other carrion.

Lammermuir Hills A range of hills in SE Scotland, in the Lothian and Borders Regions. It extends NE between the Vale of Gala Water and the North Sea, reaching 535 m (1755 ft) at Meickle Says Law.

Lampedusa, Giuseppe Tomasi di (1896–1957) Italian novelist. He lived an adventurous early life as a wealthy Sicilian aristocrat. During his last years he wrote *The Leopard* (1958), a panoramic historical novel concerning Sicily in the late 19th century.

PAUL DE LAMERIE *One of his silver-gilt ewers (London, 1736).*

Lampeter (Welsh name: Llanbedr Pont Steffan) 52 07N 4 05W A market town in SW Wales, in Dyfed on the River Teifi. St David's College (founded in 1822 as a theological college) is part of the University of Wales. Population (1981): 1908.

lamprey A fishlike vertebrate belonging to a family (*Petromyzonidae*; about 22 species) of *cyclostomes. 15–100 cm long, lampreys have an eel-like body with one or two dorsal fins and seven pairs of gill slits. They occur in fresh or salt water and many are parasitic on fish, attaching themselves with a circular sucking mouth and feeding on the blood and flesh. Sexually mature adults move into fresh water to breed and then die after the eggs are laid. The burrowing larvae (ammocoetes) feed on microorganisms and take three to seven years to grow before their metamorphosis into adults and return to the sea. □fish.

lamp shell. *See* Brachiopoda.

Lanark 55 41N 3 48W A town in S central Scotland, in Strathclyde Region overlooking the middle Clyde Valley. Nearby New Lanark, founded as a cotton-spinning centre in 1784 by David Dale and Richard Arkwright, is well known for the social experiments carried out there by Robert □Owen. Population (1981 est): 9804.

Lanark (*or* Lanarkshire) A former county of W Scotland. Under local government reorganization in 1975 its boundaries were adjusted to form Lanark District, in Strathclyde Region.

Lancashire A county of NW England, bordering on the Irish Sea. It consists of lowlands in the W rising to the high level plateaus of the Pennines in the E, with the chief river, the Ribble, flowing SW to the Irish Sea. The lowlands are important agricultural regions, especially for dairy farming and market gardening. Industry is based chiefly on textiles, mining, and engineering. Tourism is important in the coastal towns of Blackpool, Southport, and Morecambe. *History*: it became a county palatine in 1351. With industrialization, exploitation of the coalfields accelerated and by the 19th century Lancashire had become the greatest cotton-manufacturing centre in the world. Under local government reorganization in 1974 it lost the S (including Liverpool and Manchester) to Merseyside and Greater Manchester, and the Furness Peninsula to Cumbria. It gained part of the former West Riding of Yorkshire. Central Lancs New Town (1970) comprising Preston, Fulwood, Bamber Bridge, Leyland, and Chorley is the new county focus. Area: 3043 sq km (8191 sq mi). Population (1983 est): 1 377 600. Administrative centre: Preston.

Lancaster 54 03N 2 48W A town in NW England, in Lancashire on the River Lune, superseded by Preston as the administrative centre of Lancashire. The castle, partly 13th-century and enlarged by Elizabeth I, stands on the site of a Roman garrison. Port trade, of considerable importance during the Georgian period, has declined. Lancaster manufactures textiles (rayon, cotton), floor coverings, and plastic goods. The university was founded in 1964. Population (1983 est): 126 400.

Lancaster 40 08N 76 18W A city in the USA, in SE Pennsylvania. Settled by German Mennonites in the early 18th century, it developed as an armaments centre during the American Revolution. Today it is an agricultural and industrial centre, producing tobacco, grain, livestock, and electrical products. Population (1980): 54 725.

Lancaster A ruling dynasty of England descended from Edmund, the second son of Henry III, who was created Earl of Lancaster in 1267. In 1361 the title passed by marriage to the third son of Edward III, *John of Gaunt. His son seized the throne from Richard II and ruled (1399–1413) as Henry IV. He was succeeded by Henry V, whose son Henry VI led the Lancastrians against the Yorkists (*see* York) in the Wars of the □Roses (1455–85), in which their emblem was a red rose. Following Henry VI's death (1471) the royal dynasty came to an end.

Lancaster, Duchy of A territory with its own courts and administration created in 1267 by Henry III for his son Edmund (1245–96). After the last Duke of Lancaster became Henry IV in 1399 the Duchy was attached to the Crown, retaining its own jurisdiction. The Crown continues to hold the Duchy's revenues and the chancellor of the Duchy of Lancaster is usually a member of the cabinet.

Lancaster, Sir Osbert (1908–86) British cartoonist. He graduated from Oxford before studying painting and stage design at the Slade School. Although also a writer on architecture, he is best known for his *Daily Express* cartoons (from 1939), satirizing the upper classes.

lancelet. *See* amphioxus.

Lancelot In *Arthurian legend, a knight of the Round Table, the son of King Ban and Queen Helaine of Benoic. While a child he was kidnapped by the Lady of the Lake, who educated him and later sent him to serve King Arthur. He was a celebrated warrior but failed in the quest of the *Holy Grail because of his adulterous love for *Guinevere.

lancers Originally foot soldiers armed with a lance, they subsequently became cavalrymen belonging to one of the regiments called lancers, both on the continent and in the UK. The name is retained in some armoured regiments.

lancewood Dense strong straight-grained wood obtained from various trees of the family *Annonaceae*, especially *Oxandra lanceolata*, native to the West Indies and South America. It is used in whip handles, fishing rods, etc., for which an elastic wood is essential. Australian lancewood comes from several trees, including *Acacia doratoxylon* (family *Leguminosae*).

Lanchester, Frederick William (1868–1946) British engineer, who built the first British car in 1896. He formed the Lanchester Engine Company producing high-quality vehicles. He later became interested in aeronautics.

Plate I   **Butterflies and Moths**

The normal pale-coloured form of the peppered moth (below) is conspicuous against trees blackened by pollution in industrial areas and is readily taken by predators. In such areas it has largely been replaced by a dark (melanic) form (bottom), which is better camouflaged.

Camouflage

Camouflaging coloration in two Trinidad moths. Manduca florestan (top) – a hawk moth – can barely be distinguished from the tree bark on which it rests. The geometrid moth below (genus Aeschropteryx) closely resembles the foliage among which it is found, even down to the veinlike marking on its wings.

The underside of the wings of this West Indian butterfly (top) resembles a frog's head; the upper surface is plain. A bird predator will be startled by the sudden change when the butterfly folds its wings. If it attacks, the eyespot on the wing will draw its attention from the insect's more vulnerable body.

Life Cycle

American monarch butterflies mate during their northerly migrations in spring.

The eggs are laid on milkweed.

A caterpillar hatches from an egg and begins to feed on the milkweed.

eggs laid within 7 to 10 days

hatching 10 to 15 days

mating within 3 days

larval development 1 month

emergence 90 secs to 30 mins

pupal stage 9 to 15 days

A butterfly, just emerged from the chrysalis, rests until its wings are expanded.

The developing butterfly.

A fully grown caterpillar about to be transformed into a chrysalis.

Zones of seismic and volcanic activity, as well as the major structural features of the earth, are now known to be directly related to the movements of the rigid lithospheric plates (see plate tectonics). When a continental plate and an oceanic plate collide (1), the oceanic plate is forced to plunge into the mantle, forming deep oceanic trenches. Along the continental margin, magma is forced up to form chains of volcanoes around which earthquakes occur. The compression of a continental plate (2), or the collision of two continental plates, intensely folds and deforms the sedimentary rock strata into mountain chains. When two plates are pulling apart (3), oceanic ridges are formed in a process known as sea-floor spreading. Basaltic lava welling up from below pours out and forms the new oceanic crust, causing oceanic volcanoes and earthquakes.

About 200 million years ago the large land-mass named Pangaea (right, above) began to break up into the continents, which have since drifted to their present-day positions.

igneous rock *Formed when molten rock (magma) cools, the most common intrusive rock is granite. Hard and resistant, with a crystalline composition, it has long been used as a building material and in road construction.*

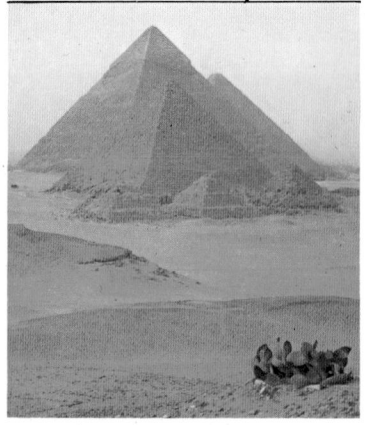

sedimentary rock *Formed at the earth's surface by mechanical, chemical, or organic deposition, sedimentary rocks include limestone (such as the above oolitic variety) which is often used as a building stone, as in the famous El Giza pyramids, Egypt.*

metamorphic rock *Formed when existing rocks are subjected to intense pressure and heating, metamorphic rock includes marble, which is easily cut and polished. Marble has been used since classical times in architecture and sculpture: Michelangelo's Pietà (St Peter's, Rome) is a fine example.*

Plate III　　　　　　　　　　　　　　　　　　　　　　　　　**Minerals**

Gold, shown here as small deposits in calcite, is malleable enough to be worked in fine detail as in this Charles I tobacco box (1640).

opal

Silver ore seen beside the finished product: a 19th-century silver medal (1838) commemorating a French victory.

beryl

topaz

corundum
(purple sapphire)

labradorite

apatite

tourmaline

beryl
(morganite)

topaz

quartz
(citrine)

moonstone

spinel

garnet
(pyrope)

black opal

fluorite

garnet
(hessonite)

Jade, first used and highly prized by the Chinese, can be carved and polished into intricate designs as shown in this Chinese pendant.

danburite

A 7.2 carat rough diamond (left) in its natural octahedral shape, still embedded in its host rock, beside a 3 carat polished "emerald-cut" diamond.

lumbar vertebra

spinal cord

spinal nerves

slipped disc pressing on spinal cord

normal intervertebral disc

cranium

clavicle

scapula

humerus

ribs

radius

ulna

hip bone

carpus

metacarpus

phalanges

femur

patella (kneecap)

fibula

tibia

tarsus

metatarsus

phalanges

spine

abdominal muscles

scapula (shoulder bone)

pectoral muscle

deltoid

triceps

biceps

sartorius

quadriceps femoris

gastrocnemius

soleus

peroneal muscle

biceps contracts

triceps contracts

humerus

elbow joint

triceps relaxes

biceps relaxes

radius

ulna

The bones (vertebrae) of the backbone are separated by intervertebral discs made of cartilage. If a crack develops in a disc, the softer core may bulge out and press on the spinal cord or a spinal nerve, causing pain. This is called a slipped disc and it most commonly occurs in the lower back (lumbar) region. When the slipped disc presses on the spinal cord the pain may be felt in the neck, chest, or back.

Two muscles are needed to move the arm at the elbow. Contraction of the biceps, attached at one end to the shoulder bone and at the other to the radius, causes the arm to be bent towards the shoulder. The triceps is attached to the shoulder and humerus at one end and to the elbow at the other. When it contracts the arm is straightened.

ball-shaped head of femur

acetabulum

hip bone

femur (thigh bone)

vas deferens

bladder

seminal vesicle

prostate gland

pubic bone

penis

urethra

erectile tissue

testis

scrotum

epididymis

anus

The type of joint between the femur (thigh bone) and the hip bone is called a ball-and-socket joint. The head of the femur fits into a cup-shaped socket (called the acetabulum) in the hip bone. The joint itself is lined with cartilage and synovial membrane, which secretes a fluid that lubricates the joint.

The skeleton – a framework of over 200 connected bones – gives form to the body, protects its soft tissues and organs, and provides attachment for muscles. It also forms a system of levers, which are worked by contractions of the muscles attached to them. The muscles themselves are responsible for all movements of the body. In men the muscles are relatively larger, accounting for about 42% of body weight (compared with 36% in women). There are also differences in the skeleton; for example a woman's pelvic cavity is wider to accommodate the baby during labour.

In males the reproductive system is very closely associated with the urinary system. The urethra provides a route both for urine from the bladder and for semen. Sperms are carried in the vas deferens from the testis to the prostate gland, which contributes to the fluid part of the semen.

Plate IV

Human Body

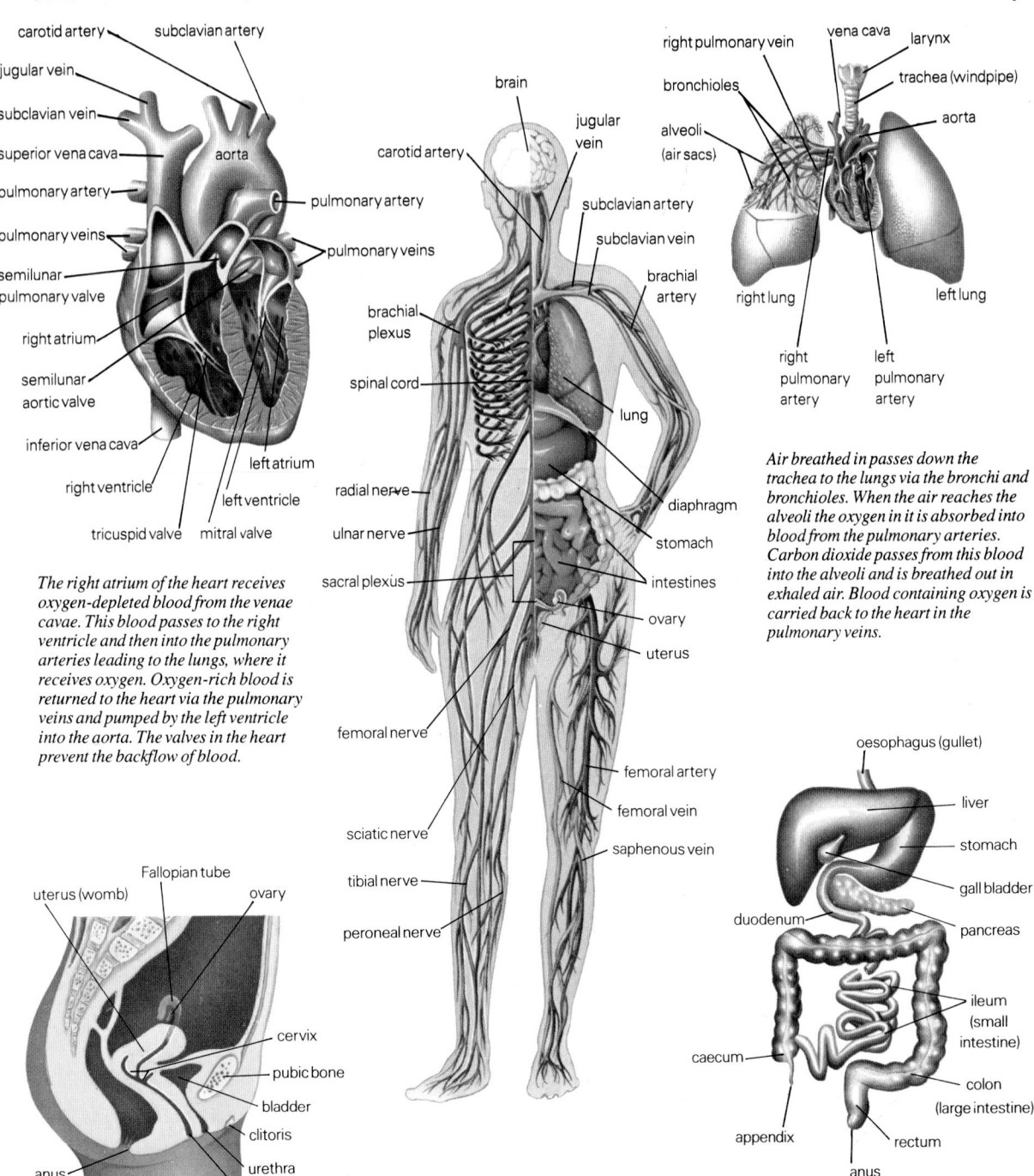

carotid artery
subclavian artery
jugular vein
subclavian vein
superior vena cava
aorta
pulmonary artery
pulmonary artery
pulmonary veins
pulmonary veins
semilunar pulmonary valve
right atrium
semilunar aortic valve
inferior vena cava
left atrium
right ventricle
left ventricle
tricuspid valve
mitral valve

The right atrium of the heart receives oxygen-depleted blood from the venae cavae. This blood passes to the right ventricle and then into the pulmonary arteries leading to the lungs, where it receives oxygen. Oxygen-rich blood is returned to the heart via the pulmonary veins and pumped by the left ventricle into the aorta. The valves in the heart prevent the backflow of blood.

brain
jugular vein
carotid artery
subclavian artery
subclavian vein
brachial artery
brachial plexus
spinal cord
lung
radial nerve
diaphragm
ulnar nerve
stomach
sacral plexus
intestines
ovary
uterus
femoral nerve
femoral artery
femoral vein
sciatic nerve
saphenous vein
tibial nerve
peroneal nerve

right pulmonary vein
vena cava
larynx
bronchioles
trachea (windpipe)
alveoli (air sacs)
aorta
right lung
left lung
right pulmonary artery
left pulmonary artery

Air breathed in passes down the trachea to the lungs via the bronchi and bronchioles. When the air reaches the alveoli the oxygen in it is absorbed into blood from the pulmonary arteries. Carbon dioxide passes from this blood into the alveoli and is breathed out in exhaled air. Blood containing oxygen is carried back to the heart in the pulmonary veins.

oesophagus (gullet)
liver
stomach
gall bladder
duodenum
pancreas
ileum (small intestine)
caecum
colon (large intestine)
appendix
rectum
anus

Food passes down the oesophagus to the stomach, where digestion begins. This process is continued in the duodenum and ileum, where digested food is absorbed into the bloodstream. Undigested remains pass through the colon, where water is absorbed from them, and the resulting semisolid faeces are channelled into the rectum and out through the anus.

uterus (womb)
Fallopian tube
ovary
cervix
pubic bone
bladder
clitoris
urethra
anus
vagina

The female reproductive system is quite separate from the urinary system. The womb (uterus) is connected to the exterior via the vagina, through which the baby passes during labour, while urine is conveyed from the bladder via the urethra.

The brain and spinal cord together constitute the central nervous system (above left). From them arise pairs of nerves that carry messages between the central nervous system and the different parts of the body they supply. A part of the nervous system called the autonomic nervous system (ANS) controls the heart, intestines, lungs, reproductive system, and other internal organs (right). The ANS is not under conscious control (one cannot, for example, consciously control heart rate and intestinal movements), but thoughts and emotions often influence the ANS: fear, for instance, makes the heart beat faster.

When identifying birds it is important to note the exact position of patches of colour and other distinguishing marks. For this it is helpful to know the names of the precise areas involved, as shown in this picture of a female reed bunting, Emberiza schoeniclus. The only feature not exhibited by the reed bunting is a dark line through the eye, called the eyestripe (not to be confused with the line over the eye, the supercilium).

The shape of a bird's bill often indicates its feeding habits: the boatbill, for instance, scoops up its prey from shallow water. The colourful sheath of the puffin's bill is part of its breeding display, being shed in winter.

Many birds, including the great crested grebe, adopt a special breeding plumage. In a few species (e.g. the ruff) plumage varies between individual males during the breeding season, while others, such as the great spotted woodpecker, show different plumage according to sex and age.

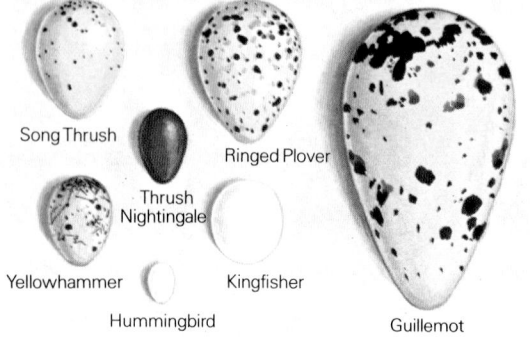

Nests vary enormously, from the elaborate feather-lined structure of the long-tailed tit to the shallow scrape of the ringed plover. Eggs too vary greatly in size and colour, and those that are vulnerable to predators are often patterned and coloured so as to match their background. Their shape is also significant: guillemots' eggs are shaped so that they do not roll off the narrow cliff ledges.

Plate V   **Birds**

Scarlet Macaw

House Sparrow ♂

Osprey

Lady Amherst's Pheasant ♂

Lesser Bird of Paradise ♂

Little Owl

Emperor Penguin

Mallard ♂

*The size, shape and plumage of birds is of astonishing variety, and
is largely governed by their environment*

Exhaustible

Most (90%) of the world's energy comes from fossil fuels – coal, oil and natural gas. These fuels are buried beneath the land or the sea in exhaustible deposits. Once they have been used up, other forms of energy will have to be found for powering motor vehicles and aircraft. Estimates of known stocks vary, but most experts agree that the diminishing reserves will be exhausted within the next few hundred years, although new deposits of oil and coal are continuously being discovered.

oil *Oil burns and expands, producing a large volume of gas which drives car and aircraft engines. It is a source of many important chemicals.*

coal *Most easily burnt in stationary installations like power stations, coal is essential for making coke, used to extract iron from its ores and to make steel.*

gas *Clean and efficient for domestic use, natural gas is piped all over the country. It is widely used in industry, as in this gas-fired kiln for making bricks.*

nuclear *All nuclear power stations now in use depend on the fission of uranium fuels. They provide only 3.9% of the world's energy. Although reserves of uranium in the earth's crust are exhaustible, estimates suggest that stocks will not be depleted for many centuries. In the future, nuclear fusion, based on deuterium fuels, may become feasible. The supply of fuel for this type of power station is virtually unlimited, as about 15 hydrogen atoms in every thousand consist of deuterium and water is 5.6% hydrogen (by weight).*

coal-fired power station

energy

CITY

coal

oil

gas

coal seam

gas deposit

oil deposit

Plate VI

Renewable

Unlike fossil fuels and uranium, some energy supplies are inexhaustible. The sun indirectly controls the weather and the winds, which power wind generators, and the hydrological cycle, which provides hydroelectric and wave power. It is also a source of direct solar energy.

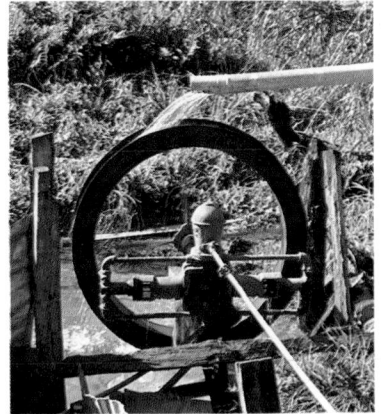

water *Falling water is an important source of energy, schemes utilizing reservoirs and dams providing some 6.7% of the world's energy. But it is also useful for small local applications – here is a generator run by a water wheel on the Amazon.*

wind *Large aerogenerators are a practical source of economic renewable energy, but here is a local generator supplying a house at the National Centre for Alternative Technology in Wales.*

solar *(above) The giant parabolic reflector of the solar power station at Odeillo, France, is one successful large-scale application of solar energy. (below) A smaller domestic use is this house (with Sizewell nuclear power station in the background) with solar panels for domestic water heating.*

Other renewable energy sources are the tides and geothermal energy. The tides derive their energy from the gravitational forces between the moon and earth. Geothermal energy comes from the heat of the earth's core (magma) and from radioactive decay in the crust. Currently about 0.1% of the earth's energy is supplied by tapping hot rocks beneath the surface.

ergy

nuclear power station

wind

hydroelectric

geothermal

wave

tidal

magma

Plate VII

Infrared radiation is electromagnetic radiation having longer wavelengths than red light. Warm surfaces that are not hot enough to glow visibly emit infrared radiation. In this photograph, taken with an infrared thermographic system, the warmest surfaces of the house show up as yellow.

When exposed to ultraviolet radiation, the minerals in this piece of uranium ore emit visible light – a process called fluorescence. In this way different minerals can be identified: autunite is seen here as greenish-yellow, calcite as pink.

Refracted colour

White light contains a continuous range of all the colours (wavelengths) in the visible spectrum. When light passes from one transparent medium to another, for example, from air to glass, the light waves change their velocity; if the rays cross the surface at an angle, this causes a change in direction. A beam of white light passing through a glass is refracted in this way twice, causing it to split into the colours of the rainbow. The wavelengths at the red end of the spectrum are longer than those at the blue end.

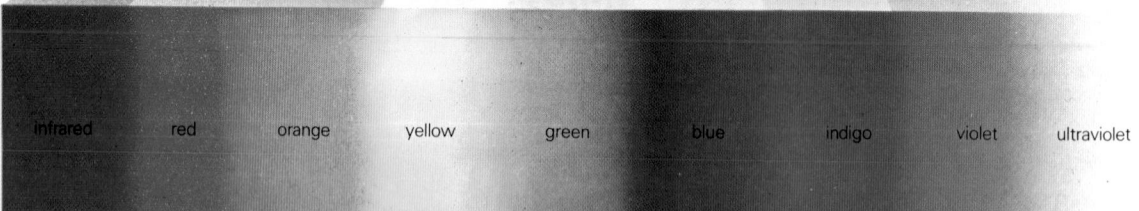

| infrared | red | orange | yellow | green | blue | indigo | violet | ultraviolet |

RED + YELLOW = ORANGE

RED + BLUE = PURPLE

YELLOW + BLUE = GREEN

The Cook (c. 1658) by Jan Vermeer shows his skill in mixing pigments to give paints of exactly the desired colour.

Pigment colour

Surfaces appear coloured because they reflect some wavelengths and absorb others. Red pigment, for example, reflects red light and absorbs the rest. Blue pigment mixed with yellow reflects mostly the green light that is not absorbed by either. Similarly, mixed red and blue pigments reflect mostly purple and mixed red and yellow reflects mostly orange. Mixing paints or pigments is a subtractive process, so that a mixture of all the colours of the spectrum produces black.

World – Physical

Scale at the Equator

Kilometres 1000 2000 3000

Metres: 3 200 · 1 600 · 400 · 200 · 0 · Land below Sea Level · 200 · 5 000

The World – Geographical Facts

Highest peaks		Height in m
Mt Everest	Nepal	8 848
K2	India	8 611
Kangchenjunga	Nepal-India	8 598
Mt Makalu	Nepal-China	8 475
Dhaulagiri	Nepal	8 172
Nanga Parbat	India	8 126
Annapurna	Nepal	8 078
Gasherbrum	India	8 072
Gosainthan	Nepal-China	8 013
Nanda Devi	India	7 817
Rakaposhi	India	7 788
Mt Kamet	India	7 756
Namcha Barwa	China	7 756

Longest rivers		Length in km
Nile	Africa	6 741
Amazon	South America	6 440
Yangtze	China	6 380
Mississippi-Missouri	USA	6 050
Zaire	Africa	4 820
Irtysh	Soviet Union	4 444
Amur	Soviet Union	4 350
Yellow River	China	4 350
Lena	Soviet Union	4 271
Niger	Africa	4 183
Mekong	Asia	4 025
Yenisei	Soviet Union	4 000

Principal seas	Area in sq km	Greatest depth in m
Pacific Ocean	165 723 100	11 033
Atlantic Ocean	81 662 384	9 187
Indian Ocean	73 426 216	7 001
Arctic Ocean	14 352 888	5 441
Mediterranean Sea	2 965 538	4 399
Caribbean Sea	2 718 200	7 686
South China Sea	2 318 041	5 016
Bering Sea	2 274 011	4 091
Gulf of Mexico	1 812 993	3 707
Sea of Okhotsk	1 507 374	3 847
East China Sea	1 243 195	3 200

Principal lakes		Area in sq km
Caspian Sea	Soviet Union	370 000
Superior	Canada-USA	82 362
Victoria	East Africa	69 485
Aral Sea	Soviet Union	66 000
Huron	Canada-USA	59 570
Michigan	USA	58 000
Great Bear	Canada	31 792
Baikal	Soviet Union	31 500
Malawi	Malawi-Mozambique	31 000
Great Slave	Canada	28 438
Erie	Canada-USA	25 718
Winnipeg	Canada	24 514

Flags

Argentina

Australia

Austria

Bahamas

Bangladesh

Belgium

Bolivia

Brazil

Bulgaria

Burma

Canada

Chile

China

Colombia

Cuba

Cyprus

Czechoslovakia

Denmark

Ecuador

Egypt

Ethiopia

Finland

France

German F R

German D R

Ghana

Greece

Guyana

Hungary

Iceland

India

Indonesia

Iran

Iraq

Ireland (Republic)

Israel

Italy

Jamaica

Japan

Jordan

Kenya

Lebanon

Liberia

Libya

Luxembourg

Malaysia

Malta

Mexico

Morocco

Netherlands

New Zealand

Nigeria

Norway

Pakistan

Philippines

Poland

Portugal

Saudi Arabia

Sierra Leone

Singapore

South Africa

Spain

Sri Lanka

Sweden

Switzerland

Taiwan

Tanzania

Thailand

Trinidad

Turkey

Uganda

USSR

UK

USA

Uruguay

Venezuela

Vietnam

Yugoslavia

Zaire

Zambia

Flags of some recently independent countries and international organizations

Dominica

Fiji

Saint Lucia

St Vincent

Seychelles

Surinam

Zimbabwe

NATO

Olympics

UN

World – Political

Scale at the Equator

1000   0   1000   2000   3000 Kilometres

International Boundary ——
Capital City ■
Other Town ○

ARCTIC OCEAN

Melville I.
Banks I.
Victoria I.
Baffin Bay
Baffin I.
Davis Str.
Arctic Circle
Denmark Str.

GREENLAND (Denmark)

Jan Mayen I. (Nor.)
Spitsb (No

ALASKA (U.S.A.)
Fort Yukon
Anchorage
To Tokyo
Bering Sea

Godthåb
ICELAND
Reykjavik
Faeroe Is. (Den.)

UNITED KINGDOM   Edinburgh   DENM
Dublin
REP. OF IRELAND   London
Paris
FRANCE S

CANADA
Gt. Bear L.
Gt. Slave L.
Churchill
Hudson Bay

Yukon
Vancouver I.
Vancouver
Winnipeg
Seattle
Quebec
Montreal
Ottawa
Toronto
St. John's
Halifax
Newfoundland

UNITED STATES OF AMERICA
Salt Lake City
Chicago
New York
San Francisco
Philadelphia
Washington
Los Angeles
Houston
New Orleans
Miami
Gulf of Mexico
Havana

PORTUGAL   Madrid
Lisbon   SPAIN
Azores (Port.)
Gibraltar
Madeira (Port.)
Canary Is. (Sp.)
Aíun
WESTERN SAHARA
MOROCCO   Rabat   Algiers   Mediterra
ALGERIA

NORTH ATLANTIC OCEAN
Bermuda Is. (Br.)
Tropic of Cancer

Hawaiian Is. (U.S.A.)
To Honolulu

PACIFIC OCEAN

MEXICO
Mexico City
CUBA
BAHAMAS
HAITI   DOM. REP.
JAMAICA
Puerto Rico (U.S.A.)
Caribbean Sea

BELIZE
GUATEMALA   HOND.
EL SALVADOR
NICARAGUA
COSTA RICA
PANAMA
Panamá
Caracas
VENEZUELA
Bogotá
COLOMBIA
Georgetown
GUYANA
SURINAME
FR. GUIANA

BARBADOS
TRINIDAD & TOBAGO

CAPE VERDE IS.
MAURITANIA
Nouakchott
SENEGAL   Dakar
THE GAMBIA
GUINEA BISSAU   GUINEA
Conakry   Freetown
SIERRA LEONE
Monrovia   LIBERIA
MALI
Bamako
BURKINA
IVORY COAST   GHANA
Accra
Niamey
N'D
NIGER
Lagos
BENIN
Yaoun
EQ. GUINE
Libreville
Brazz
Lua

Galapagos Is. (Ecuador)
Quito
ECUADOR
Guayaquil

Equator

PERU
Lima
Belém
Manaus
Amazon
BRAZIL
Recife
Ascension (Br.)

SOUTH ATLANTIC OCEAN

Marquesas Is. (Fr.)
To Fiji
Tuamotu Arch. (Fr.)
Pitcairn I. (Br.)
Easter I. (Chile)

BOLIVIA
La Paz
Brasilia
Salvador
St. Helena (Br.)

Tropic of Capricorn

PARAGUAY
Asunción
São Paulo
Rio de Janeiro

OCEAN

Tristan da Cunha (Br.)
Gough I. (Br.)

Valparaiso
Santiago
ARGENTINA
Buenos Aires
Bahia Blanca
URUGUAY
Montevideo

Falkland Is. (Br.)
S. Georgia (Br.)

Punta Arenas
Str. of Magellan

Abbreviations

ALB.	Albania	**ISR.**	Israel
Aust.	Australia	**LEB.**	Lebanon
AUST.	Austria	**NETH.**	Netherlands
BEL.	Belgium	*N.Z.*	New Zealand
Br.	British	*Nor.*	Norway
COMM.	Commonwealth	**P.D.R. YEMEN**	People's Democratic Republic of the Yemen
CZECH.	Czechoslovakia		
Den.	Denmark	**REP.**	Republic
DOM. REP.	Dominican Republic	**SW.**	Switzerland
Fr.	France	**U.A.E.**	United Arab Emirates
FR. GUIANA	French Guiana	*U.S.A.*	United States of America
HOND.	Honduras	**YEMEN A.R.**	Yemen Arab Republic
HUNG.	Hungary	**ZIMB.**	Zimbabwe

West of Greenwich

2 352   Principal Sea Route
5 243   Principal Air Route

Distances in kilometres

ARCTIC OCEAN

Severnaya
Zemlya

New Siberian Is.

80

Novaya
Zemlya

Verkhoyansk

Arctic Circle

Murmansk

Arkhangelsk

North C.

orth C.

sinki

Leningrad

Perm

Sverdlovsk

Omsk

Novosibirsk

Okhotsk

Bering
Sea

60

To Anchorage

Moscow

ev

Rostov

Volga

Caspian Sea

L. Balkhash

Aral Sea

2 816

2 816

2 012

Ob

Ob

Lena

Yenisey

1 529

Irkutsk

L. Baykal

Amur

Sakhalin

Kamchatka

Kuril Is.

Aleutian Is.

To Vancouver

5 584

6 888

40

UNION OF SOVIET SOCIALIST REPUBLICS

Tashkent

Ulan Bator

MONGOLIA

Harbin

Shenyang

Vladivostok

690

NORTH

Pyongyang

KOREA

Seoul

SOUTH

Tokyo

Osaka

JAPAN

7 300

To San Francisco

Black Sea

Istanbul

Ankara

TURKEY

Baku

CYPRUS

LEB.

SYRIA

Baghdad

Damascus

ISR.

JORDAN

IRAQ

Cairo

EGYPT

KUWAIT

Tehran

AFGHANISTAN

Kabul

Islamabad

Lahore

IRAN

PAKISTAN

Karachi

TIBET

CHINA

Beijing

Chongqing

Yellow River

Wuhan

Nanjing

Shanghai

Yangtze Kiang

T'ai-pei

TAIWAN

3 010

3 203

PACIFIC

Tropic of Cancer

To Honolulu

OCEAN

5 451

QATAR

U.A.E.

Muscat

OMAN

SAUDI

Riyadh

ARABIA

Makkah

2 482

Delhi

NEPAL

BHUTAN

Ganges

BANGLA-
DESH

2 189

INDIA

Calcutta

Bombay

Arabian Sea

2 624

BURMA

Rangoon

Hanoi

Hong Kong
(Br.)

Hai-nan Tao

5 243

20

Wake I.
(U.S.A.)

To Honolulu
3 718

YEMEN

P.D.R.

A.R.S.

Aden

YEMEN

Socotra
(P.D.R. Yemen)

artoum

SUDAN

DJIBOUTI

Djibouti

ETHIOPIA

Addis Ababa

SOMALIA

Lakshadweep
(India)

Madras

Andaman and Nicobar
Is. (India)

THAILAND

Bangkok

VIETNAM

KAMPUCHEA

Ho Chi
Minh City

China Sea

Manila

Quezon City

PHILIPPINES

4 989

7 660

Mariana Is.
(U.S.A.)

Caroline Is.
(U.S.A.)

Marshall Is.
(U.S.A.)

SRI LANKA

Colombo

MALDIVES
REP.

2 522

W. MALAYSIA

Kuala Lumpur

SINGAPORE

MALAYSIA

SARAWAK

BRUNEI

SABAH

2 881

Kalimantan

Equator

0

UGANDA

Kampala

KENYA

Nairobi

ANDA

RUNDI

Mogadishu

SEYCHELLES

7 145

INDIAN OCEAN

Sumatra

Jakarta

Java

INDONESIA

Sulawesi

Irian Jaya

PAPUA
NEW
GUINEA

Port Moresby

SOLOMON IS.

6 070

Coral
Sea

VANUATU

TANZANIA

Dodoma

Dar es Salaam

Cocos Is.
(Aust.)

Christmas I.
(Aust.)

Timor

Darwin

AMBIA

ZIM.

MOZAMBIQUE

Lilongwe

MALAWI

Harare

Antananarivo

MADAGASCAR

MAURITIUS

Réunion
(Fr.)

9 092

5 021

Tropic of Capricorn

Alice Springs

New Caledonia
(Fr.)

To Fiji

To Fiji

20

ka

Maputo

SWAZILAND

sburg

LESOTHO

Durban

2 558

9 357

9 036

2 177

AUSTRALIA

Perth

Fremantle

Adelaide

Melbourne

Darling

Murray

Sydney

Canberra

Brisbane

3 186

Norfolk I.
(Aust.)

2 050

Auckland

To
Panama

NEW

ZEALAND

Wellington

Christchurch

40

Tasmania

Hobart

Kerguelen I.
(Fr.)

Antipodes
(N.Z.)

60

East of Greenwich

30

60

90

120

150

180

60   90   120   150   180   150

World – Time Zones

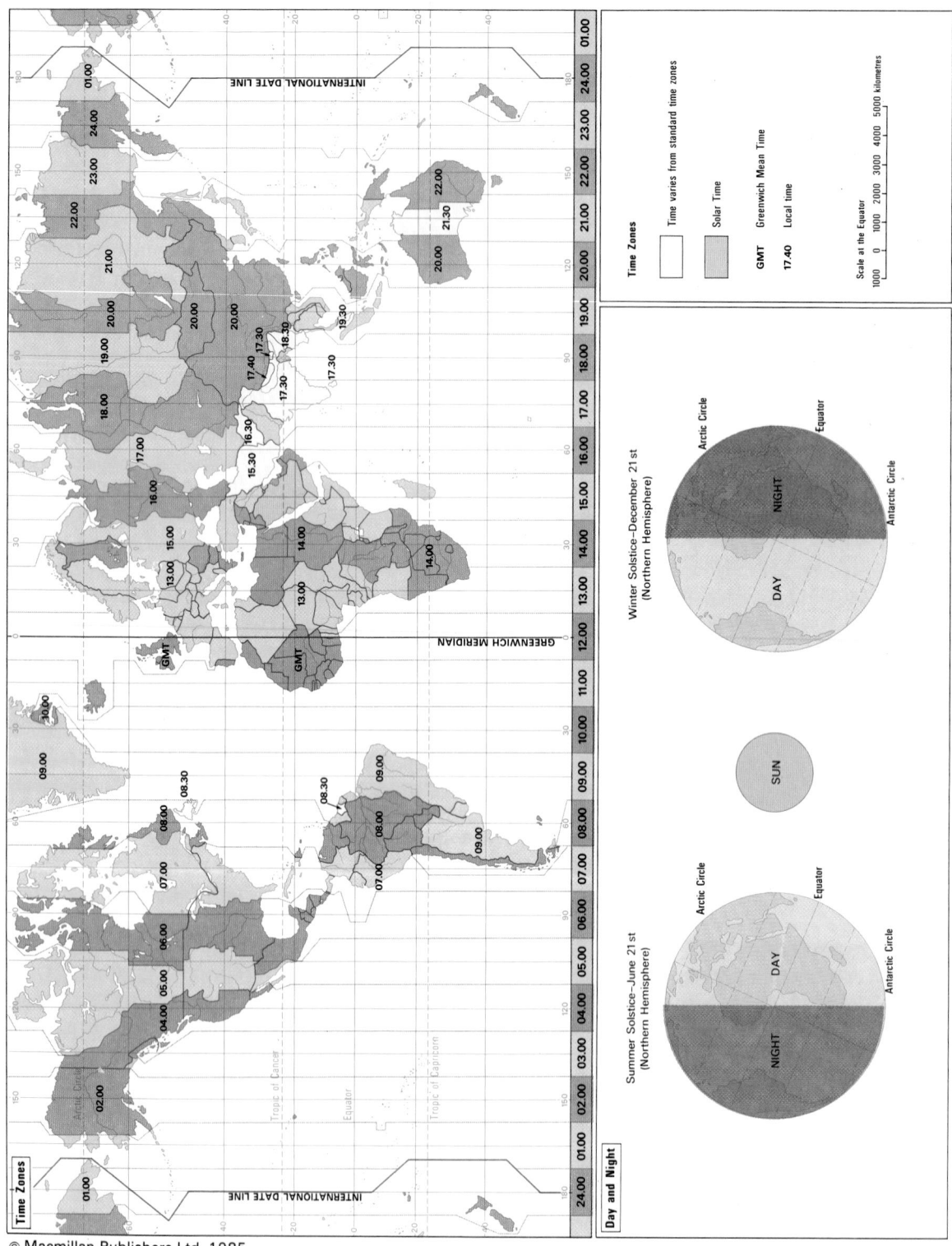

Time Zones

| | Time varies from standard time zones |
| | Solar Time |

GMT — Greenwich Mean Time
17.40 — Local time

Scale at the Equator

1000 0 1000 2000 3000 4000 5000 kilometres

INTERNATIONAL DATE LINE

GREENWICH MERIDIAN

INTERNATIONAL DATE LINE

Tropic of Cancer

Equator

Tropic of Capricorn

Time Zones

Day and Night

Winter Solstice – December 21st (Northern Hemisphere)

Arctic Circle
Equator
Antarctic Circle
NIGHT
DAY

SUN

Summer Solstice – June 21st (Northern Hemisphere)

Arctic Circle
Equator
Antarctic Circle
DAY
NIGHT

Scale at the Equator
1000 0 1000 2000 3000 Kilometres

Density (persons per sq. km.)
Over 100
50–100
25–50
10–25
1–10
Under 1
• Towns over 2 000 000

Tropic of Cancer
Equator
Tropic of Capricorn
Arctic Circle

West of Greenwich   East of Greenwich

Cities of North-East USA.
1 Baltimore
2 Boston
3 Chicago
4 Cleveland
5 Detroit
6 New York
7 Pittsburgh
8 Philadelphia
9 Washington

Selected Population Figures, (in millions)   (Latest available census figures or estimates, usually 1980)

World	4 124.0
China	982.6
India	683.8
Soviet Union	265.5
USA	227.6
Brazil	123.0
Nigeria	77.1
UK	55.9
Australia	14.7

China, India, Soviet Union, and USA
have the four highest populations in the world.

© Macmillan Publishers Ltd, 1980. Revised 1985.

Scale at the Equator
1000 0 1000 2000 3000 Kilometres

Industrial/Urban
Agricultural
Ranching
Grazing (Open and Commercial)
Lumbering
Forests
Unproductive

Tropic of Cancer
Equator
Tropic of Capricorn
West of Greenwich East of Greenwich

Countries with GNP per capita over 11 000 US dollars, 1982

UAE	24080	Sweden	13840
Brunei	22150	USA	13160
Qatar	22060	Burmuda	12770
Kuwait	19610	Denmark	12350
Switzerland	16960	West Germany	12300
Saudi Arabia	15820	Iceland	12110
Norway	14270	France	11540
Luxembourg	14010	Greenland	11380
		Canada	11330
		Australia	11140

Countries with GNP per capita below 300 US dollars, 1982.

Somalia	290	Malawi	210
Tanzania	270	Burma	190
India	260	Zaire	180
Rwanda	260	Mali	170
Burundi	240	Nepal	170
Uganda	240	Bangladesh	140
Guinea-Bissau	220	Ethiopia	140
Burkina	210	Chad	80

1982 GNP data are not available for all countries.

© Macmillan Publishers Ltd, 1980 Revised 1985.

Scale at the Equator

1000   0   1000   2000   3000 Kilometres

Frequent Earthquakes and Active Volcanoes

Paths of Tropical Storms

Mean Annual Rainfall of less than 100mm

Lack of Rainfall causes disaster

Less than 80 days with minimum temperatures above 0°C

The World's Hottest and Coldest Recorded Places

Arouane, Mali
Cloncurry, Australia
Abadan, Iran
Wadi Halfa, Sudan
Fort Flatters, Algeria
Aswan, Egypt
Mosul, Iran
Cufra, Libya

Eismitte, Greenland
Yakutsk, Soviet Union
Fairbanks, USA
Aklavik, Canada
Ulan Bator, Mongolia
Ha-er-bin, China
Kuusamo, Finland
Haparanda, Sweden

°C

55   45   35   25   15   5   -5   -15   -25   -35   -45   -55   -65

Scale at the Equator

1000   0   1000   2000   3000 Kilometres

- - - - Columbus 1492–93
──── Bering 1728–41
──── Vasco da Gama 1497–99
──── Cook 1768–71
──── Magellan 1519–22
──── Cook 1772–75
- - - - Barents 1594–95
- - - - Amundsen 1903–06

Christopher Columbus
(1451–1506) Spanish.
Founded the first European city in the New World – Isabella – in the Dominican Republic.

Vasco da Gama
(c1469–1524) Portuguese.
First discoverer of a continuous sea route from Europe to India via Cape of Good Hope.

Ferdinand Magellan
(c1480–1522) Portuguese.
First European to navigate in the Pacific Ocean. Began the first circumnavigation, completed by Del cano.

Willem Barents
(c1550–97) Dutch.
Explorer of the Arctic. Remembered for his charting of northern waters.

Vitus Bering
(1681–1741) Danish.
Discoverer of Alaska as he sailed through the strait named after him.

James Cook
(1728–79) British.
Pacific Ocean explorer. Charted coasts of New Zealand and East Australia.

Metres	Metres	Metres	Metres		International Boundaries		Capital Cities
3 200	400	Land below Sea Level	4 000		Internal Boundaries		Important Towns
1 600	200	1 000			Main Roads		Other Towns
800	0	2 000			Railways		Airports
					Mountain Peaks		

50 0 50 100 150 200 Kilometres

British Isles – Counties

ORKNEYS
Kirkwall

SHETLANDS
Lerwick

Stornaway

WESTERN
ISLES

ATLANTIC
OCEAN

North
Sea

HIGHLAND
Inverness

GRAMPIAN
Aberdeen

TAYSIDE
Dundee

SCOTLAND

CENTRAL
Stirling
Cupar
FIFE
Edinburgh
Glasgow
LOTHIAN
Newtown
St. Boswells
BORDERS

STRATHCLYDE

NORTHERN
IRELAND

DUMFRIES &
GALLOWAY
Dumfries

NORTHUMBERLAND
Newcastle-upon-Tyne (also headquarters for Northumberland)
TYNE & WEAR

DONEGAL
Lifford
DERRY
ANTRIM
TYRONE
Belfast
FERMANAGH
ARMAGH
DOWN
Monaghan
MONAGHAN
Dundalk

Carlisle
Durham
DURHAM
CLEVELAND
Middlesbrough
Northallerton

CUMBRIA

Sligo
SLIGO
Carrick-on-Shannon
LEITRIM
CAVEN
Caven

ISLE
OF
MAN
Douglas

NORTH YORKSHIRE

ENGLAND

MAYO
Castlebar
ROSCOMMON
Roscommon
LONGFORD
Longford
Mullingar
Naven
CAVEN
LOUTH

HUMBERSIDE
Kingston upon Hull

LANCASHIRE
Preston
WEST
YORKS.
Wakefield
Barnsley
S. YORKS.

GALWAY
Galway
WEST MEATH
MEATH
Dublin
Tullamore
KILDARE
DUBLIN
OFFALY
Naas

Liverpool
MERSEYSIDE
G.M.
Manchester
Lincoln
LINCOLNSHIRE

Caernarfon
GWYNEDD

Mold
CHESHIRE
Chester
CLWYD

DERBYSHIRE
NOTTS.
Matlock
Nottingham

REPUBLIC
OF
IRELAND

CLARE
Ennis
Port Laoise
LAOISE
Carlow
CARLOW
Kilkenny
KILKENNY
Wicklow
WICKLOW

STAFFS
Shrewsbury
SHROPSHIRE
Stafford

NORFOLK
Norwich

Limerick
LIMERICK
TIPPERARY
Clonmel
WEXFORD
Wexford

POWYS
Llandrindod
Walls
WALES

W.M.
Birmingham
WARWICK
Warwick

LEICS.
Leicester

NORTHANTS.
Northampton
CAMBS.
Cambridge
BEDS.
Bedford
Hertford
HERTS.

SUFFOLK
Ipswich

Worcester
HEREFORD & WORC.

ESSEX
Chelmsford

KERRY
Tralee
CORK
Cork

Waterford
WATERFORD

DYFED
Carmarthen

GWENT
Gloucester
GLOS.

Oxford
OXON.
Aylesbury
BUCKS.

GREATER
LONDON

W.G.
Swansea
M.G.
S.G.
Cardiff
(also headquarters for M.G.)
Newport
AVON
Bristol
Trowbridge
WILTS.

Reading
BERKS.
Kingston
upon Thames
SURREY

Maidstone
KENT

SOMERSET
Taunton

HAMPSHIRE
Winchester

WEST SUSSEX
Chichester

EAST SUSSEX
Lewes

DEVON
Exeter

DORSET
Dorchester

Newport
ISLE OF
WIGHT

Isles of
Scilly

CORNWALL
Truro

English Channel

FRANCE

	Boundary / Symbol
———	International Boundary
– – –	National Boundaries
———	County/Regional Boundaries
– – –	Historic counties in Northern Ireland
•	Administrative Headquarters
G.M.	Greater Manchester
W.M.	West Midlands

W.G. West Glamorgan
M.G. Mid Glamorgan
S.G. South Glamorgan

20 0 20 40 60 80 Kilometres

Asia – Physical and Political

Metres

6 400	
3 200	
1 600	
800	
400	
200	
0	
Land below Sea Level	
1 000	
2 000	
4 000	
8 000	

200 0   400   800   1 200   1 600 Kilometres

——— International Boundaries
– – – European Turkey Boundary
–·–·– European USSR Boundary
——— Railways
■ Capital Cities
● Major Towns
○ Other Towns
▲ Mountain Peaks

Population (in millions) of South and East Asia 1982

World	4 586.0
China	1 013.6
India	711.7
Indonesia	153.0
Japan	118.4
Bangladesh	92.6
Pakistan	87.1
Vietnam	56.2
Philippines	50.7
Thailand	48.5
S. Korea	39.3
Burma	37.1
N. Korea	18.7
Taiwan	18.3
Nepal	15.4
Sri Lanka	15.2
Malaysia	14.8

1 giant represents 500 million people
1 man represents 10 million people

© Macmillan Publishers Ltd, 1980. Revised 1985.

Population of the Soviet Union and Europe (in millions) 1982

Soviet Union	270.0
West Germany	61.6
Italy	56.3
United Kingdom	55.8
France	54.2
Spain	37.9
Poland	36.2
Yugoslavia	22.7
Romania	22.6
East Germany	16.9
Czechoslovakia	15.4
Netherlands	14.3
Hungary	10.7
Portugal	10.1
Belgium	9.9
Greece	9.8
Bulgaria	9.1
Sweden	8.3
Austria	7.6
Switzerland	6.5
Denmark	5.1
Finland	4.8
Norway	4.1
Ireland	3.5
Albania	2.9

1 giant represents 50 million people

1 man represents 1 million people

(European countries below 1 million are not included)

Metres
6 400
3 200
1 600
800
400
200
0
Land below
Sea Level
1 000
2 000
4 000
8 000

0 200 400 600 800 1000 1200 Kms

International Boundaries
Capital Cities
Major Towns
Other Towns
Major Roads
Major Railways
Mountain Peaks
Sea Depths
European Soviet Boundary

© Macmillan Publishers Ltd, 1980. Revised 1985.

Middle East – Physical and Political

Land below Sea Level
International Boundaries
Main Roads
Tracks
Railways
Oil Pipelines
Gas Pipelines
Airports
Airfields
Capital Cities
Major Towns
Other Towns
Mountain Peaks
Dams
Canals

World Petroleum Production –
Major Production Areas (1983)

USSR 22%	Iran 5%	Canada 3%
USA 18%	UK 4%	Indonesia 2%
Saudi Arabia 9%	China 4%	Nigeria 2%
Mexico 5%	Venezuela 4%	Kuwait 2%

World Petroleum Distribution

△ Petroleum

Australia – Physical and Political

Key:

- Major Towns
- Other Towns
- Mountain Peaks
- Sea Depths

- International Boundaries
- State Boundaries
- Roads
- Railways
- Capital Cities

Australia
100 0 100 200 300 400 500 600 Kilometres

South East Australia
100 0 100 200 300 400 500 Kilometres

New Zealand – Physical and Political

Auckland 26m above sea level

Wellington 126m above sea level

Hokitika 4m above sea level

Christchurch 10m above sea level

Metres	Metres	Metres	Metres
3 200	400	200	6 000
1 600	200	0	4 000
800			2 000

- - - - Provincial Boundaries   ——— Main Roads   ■ Capital City
N.P. National Parks   -------- Railways   ● Provincial Towns
▲ Mountain Peaks   ✈ Airports   ● Major Towns
○ Other Towns

50 0 50 100 Kilometres

Africa – Physical and Political

© Macmillan Publishers Ltd, 1980. Revised 1985.

North America – Physical and Political

Capital City
State Capitals
Other Important Towns

International Boundaries
State Boundaries
Major Roads
Major Railways

400 Kilometres

200

0

200

COMM.
OF THE
BAHAMAS

Hawaii

100 Kilometres

100 50 0

Alaska

600 Kilometres

300 0 300

South America – Physical and Political

Area of Countries (% of total area)

Uruguay
Surinam
Guyana
French Guiana
Paraguay
Ecuador
Colombia
Chile
Venezuela
Peru
Argentina
Bolivia
Brazil

**Gross National Product
(per head of population 1979)**

US Dollars

	500	1 000	1 500	2 000	2 500
Argentina					
Bolivia					
Brazil					
Chile					
Colombia					
Ecuador					
French Guiana			2690		
Guyana					
Paraguay					
Peru					
Surinam					
Uruguay					
Venezuela			3440		

**Population (in millions) of
South America 1982**

Brazil	126.8	
Argentina	28.4	
Colombia	27.0	
Peru	18.8	
Venezuela	14.7	
Chile	11.5	
Ecuador	9.0	
Bolivia	6.0	
Paraguay	3.4	
Uruguay	3.0	
Guyana	0.9	
Surinam	0.4	
French Guiana	0.1	

1 giant represents 10 million people

1 man represents 1 million people

1 dot represents less than 500,000 people

Lanchow. *See* Lanzhou.

Land. *See* Germany, Federal Republic of.

Land, Edwin Herbert (1909-) US inventor of *Polaroid, who set up the Polaroid Corporation in 1937 for its manufacture. He also invented the Polaroid Land Camera in 1947, in which pictures are printed inside the camera.

Land Acts, Irish A series of laws passed between 1870 and 1903 to deal with Irish agrarian problems. The three Fs (freedom to sell, fixity of tenure, and fair rents) were obtained in Gladstone's acts of 1870 and 1881. Later acts (especially those of 1885 and 1903) provided means for the tenant to buy his holding and Ireland thus became a land of owner occupiers.

landau A four-wheeled coach drawn by two or four horses. Landaus, first made in Landau (Germany) in the late 18th century, have fully collapsible tops and are still used in European royal processions.

Landau, Lev Davidovich (1908-68) Soviet physicist, who pioneered the mathematical theory of magnetic domains (*see* ferromagnetism). Working with Peter *Kapitza on *super-fluid helium he was able to explain its properties in terms of quantum theory. For this work on superfluidity he was awarded the Nobel Prize in 1962.

land crab A large square-bodied *crab of the tropical family *Gecarcinidae*, specialized for a terrestrial existence. It feeds on plant and animal materials. *Cardiosoma guanhumi*, 11 cm across the back, is found in the West Indies and S North America. It lives in fields, swamps, and mangroves, sometimes several miles inland. Tribe: *Brachyura*.

Landes An area of heath and marshland in SW France, bordering on the Bay of Biscay and consisting chiefly of the Landes department. It is bordered by a strip of sand dunes, many over 45 m (148 ft) high, that have been fixed by the planting of pine forests. Area: 14 000 sq km (5400 sq mi).

landing craft Amphibious craft used for military assaults on beaches. Developed mainly by the US Marine Corps in World War II, they were first used on a large scale in the Anglo-American invasion of Sicily (June, 1943), and later were important in the D-Day invasion of Normandy (1944) and in the Pacific campaign from Guadalcanal onwards.

Land League An Irish agrarian organization established by Michael *Davitt in 1879 to press for land reforms. Its most famous tactic was one of organized ostracism (boycotting; *see* Boycott, Charles). After Gladstone's 1881 Land Act, the League's immediate aims were achieved and it was forced to disband.

landlord and tenant The relationship arising from a grant (lease) of exclusive possession of land by a landlord to a tenant for a fixed period and, usually, for a regular payment of rent. The relationship is defined by a *contract, which is contained in the lease or, for short terms, in a tenancy agreement. Security of tenure in England has been protected by a series of Acts, culminating in the controversial Rent Act (1974), by which tenants in furnished premises were given security similar to those in unfurnished. These Acts, now largely re-enacted in the Rent Act (1977), have had the effect of reducing the amount of property available for rent.

Rents are controlled in England to prevent exploitation of tenants in a period of housing shortage. A fair rent is decided by a rent officer, taking into account the age, character, and locality of the accommodation; any objection on either side is referred to a rent assessment committee.

Landor, Walter Savage (1775-1864) British poet and prose writer. He lived for many years on the Continent, chiefly in Florence. He wrote poems and dramas based on classical models, and is best known for his *Imaginary Conversations of Literary Men and Statesmen* (1824-28).

Landowska, Wanda (1877-1959) Polish-born harpsichordist and authority on its technique and repertoire. She established a school for advanced performers in Paris and later lived in the USA.

Landrace A breed of pig originating in Denmark, where it has been intensively developed as a producer of high-quality lean bacon. It has a relatively small head and neck with light shoulders and long flanks. It can also produce good-quality pork.

Land Registry, HM An official registry of titles to land, established in 1862. The purpose of establishing a registry of land is to simplify conveyancing when the property is sold: by searching in the Registry, outstanding leases, mortgages, etc., may be discovered. Not all land in the UK is yet subject to compulsory registration.

landscape gardening The theory and practice of designing and planting a pleasing garden or park. Landscape gardening was carried out in the ancient Middle East, Greece, and Rome. In Europe, geometric formality in rigidly organized enclosed spaces predominated until the mid-18th century, when William *Kent and Capability *Brown demonstrated the possibilities of large-scale remoulding of the landscape to achieve a naturalistic impression. Apparently random planting of trees, strategic siting of focal points, and sinuous expanses of water, as at *Blenheim Palace, are key components. With the 20th-century decline of the *country house estate, landscape gardening principles (harmony, variety, etc.) have come to be applied on a smaller scale.

Landseer, Sir Edwin Henry (1802-73) British artist, the son of an engraver. He first exhibited at the Royal Academy at the age of 12, becoming a member in 1831. He achieved success, particularly with Queen Victoria, with his sentimental animal and Highland subjects, notably *Dignity and Impudence*. As a sculptor he is famous for the four bronze lions in Trafalgar Square.

Land's End (Cornish name: Pednanlaaz) 50 03N 5 44W The extreme western point of England. A granite headland in Cornwall, it lies at a distance of 970 km (603 mi) from John o'Groats at the N tip of Scotland. The southernmost point of England is the Lizard nearby.

Landshut 48 31N 12 10E A town in SE West Germany, in Bavaria on the River Isar. It is an industrial centre and the site of a 13th-century castle. The Bavarian university was sited here (1800–26). Population (1983 est): 56 326.

Landskrona 55 53N 12 50E A seaport in SW Sweden, on the Sound. A centre for shipping and trade, it has flour milling, sugar refining, and chemical industries. Population (1984 est): 35 656.

landslide (*or* landslip) The sudden downward movement of a mass of rock or earth. This may be triggered by an earthquake, or be due to an increase in the weight borne by a steep slope as a result of water soaking into it. Landslides may also occur as a result of undercutting of a slope by water, as in a riverbank or sea cliff.

Landsteiner, Karl (1868-1943) Austrian immunologist, who (in 1900) discovered human *blood groups and devised the ABO system of classification. Landsteiner's discovery enabled safe blood transfusions: by matching the blood groups of donor and recipient the immunological rejection of "foreign" blood by the recipient was avoided. He also discovered, in 1940, the *rhesus (Rh) factor in blood and made valuable contributions to poliomyelitis research. He was awarded the Nobel Prize (1930).

Lane, Sir Allen (1902-70) British publisher, who founded Penguin Books Ltd in 1935 to produce the first paperbacks in Britain.

Lanfranc (c. 1010-89) Italian churchman and theologian; Archbishop of Canterbury (1070-89). In about 1043 he founded and became prior of a Benedictine abbey at Bec in Normandy; under the direction of his pupil St Anselm, the abbey became one of the most famous medieval schools. As archbishop under William the Conqueror from 1070, he launched a programme of Church reform, which included appointing Normans as abbots of English monasteries and

LILLIE LANGTRY *As Rosalind in* As You Like It, *one of her most successful roles.*

enforcing celibacy among the clergy. His famous tract, *De Corpore et sanguine Domini* (1079), is a defence of the doctrine of transubstantiation against the teachings of Berengar of Tours (c. 998–1088).

Lang, Andrew (1844–1912) Scottish writer and literary critic. One of the most versatile writers of his day, Lang published historical and anthropological works, in addition to journalistic articles. He also wrote poetry and compiled several books of fairytales. As a classical scholar he is known for his translations of Homer.

Lange, David Russell (1942–) New Zealand politician; Labour prime minister (1984–). Trained as a lawyer, he became an MP in 1977 and two years later was appointed deputy leader of the opposition. Becoming leader in 1983, he led his party to victory in the 1984 elections. Controversy surrounded his refusal to allow nuclear armed ships to dock in New Zealand.

Lang, Fritz (1890–1976) German film director. The best known of a number of influential silent films are *Dr Mabuse the Gambler* (1922), *Metropolis* (1926), a nightmare vision of the future, and *M* (1931), a study of a psychopathic murderer. He left Germany in 1933 for Hollywood, where he made commercially successful thrillers and westerns.

Langland, William (c. 1330–c. 1400) English poet and probably a minor cleric. He is generally credited with the authorship of the allegorical Middle English alliterative poem, *The Vision of Piers Plowman*. Its theme of spiritual pilgrimage is combined with a depiction of 14th-century English society and criticisms of ecclesiastical abuse.

Langley, Samuel Pierpont (1834–1906) US astronomer, whose work on aerodynamics contributed to the design of early aircraft. Langley himself failed to build a working aircraft, in spite of a $50,000 grant from the US Government.

Langmuir, Irving (1881–1957) US chemist, whose early work on gases led to the invention of the Langmuir condensation pump. He also developed gas-filled filament lamps. He was awarded the 1932 Nobel Prize for his work on monomolecular layers and surface chemistry.

Langton, Stephen (c. 1150–1228) English theologian; Archbishop of Canterbury (1207–28). A student and later the chancellor at the University of Paris, he was appointed Archbishop of Canterbury by Pope Innocent III. However, he was unable to occupy the see until 1213 because King John opposed

his election. He sided with the barons against John and supported the Magna Carta.

Langtry, Lillie (Emilie Charlotte le Breton; 1853–1929) British actress, known as the Jersey Lily. After marrying a wealthy husband and becoming well known in London society, she made her stage debut in 1881. She was the first woman in Britain to prove that high social position was not incompatible with an acting career, although her fame was based more on her beauty than her acting talents. She was an intimate friend of the Prince of Wales, later Edward VII.

language The chief means by which human beings communicate with one another. Among the features that distinguish human language from other animals' communication systems are that it is learned, not inborn; the connection between a word or expression and that to which it refers is in principle arbitrary; it can be used to talk about itself, about events, objects, etc., not immediately present, or about any novel or unforeseen situation; and it is organized in recognizable patterns on two levels: *grammar and phonology. The origins of language are unknown, but since it is unique to man and all speech organs have some other more basic physiological function it is probably of quite recent origin in evolutionary terms. It is estimated that there are some 4000 languages spoken in the world today; countless thousands of others have perished, generally without trace. *See also* dialect; linguistics.

languages, classification of The division of languages into groups. There are three methods of classification. The first method is that of geographical or political division, in which languages are grouped together according to the continent or country in which they occur. Examples of the former include *Indian languages and European languages. The latter is represented by the similar but politically distinct languages *Swedish, *Danish, and *Norwegian. Such divisions do not always follow the genetic relationships that exist between languages. This relationship forms the basis for the second method of classification, which maps the historical development from one form of the language to another, as in the relation between Old English and modern *English. Further back both these and other languages can be traced to their common *Indo-European ancestor. However, some languages, such as *Basque, have no discoverable ancestry or relations. The third possible method of classification is on typological evidence, which depends on the grammatical structure of the language. The original three classes were devised by W. von *Humboldt: analytic (or isolating), agglutinative, and inflecting languages. **Analytic languages** (e.g. English, Chinese) show little variation in the forms of words but rely on strict word order to express grammatical relations (compare "The speaker thanked the chairman" with "The chairman thanked the speaker"; the words are the same in both sentences and the subject-object relations are understood purely by the order). In **agglutinative languages** (e.g. Turkish) words have the capacity to be split up into individual components with separate grammatical roles (in Turkish *sev/mek* means "to love"; *sev/dir/il/mek* means "to be made to love"; *sev/ish/mek/* means "to love one another"; and *sev/ish/dir/il/mek* means "to be made to love one another"). In **inflecting languages** (e.g. Latin, Sanskrit) words are characteristically built up of a root plus a component (morpheme) that represents several different grammatical categories (the Latin word *lavo* (I wash) consists of the root *lav-* and a suffix *-o*, the suffix here indicating the distinct grammatical elements of first person, singular number, present tense, indicative mood, and active voice. No language is entirely in one or other of these categories and the system itself has been modified and expanded by 20th-century linguists, but it is possible, on the grounds of predominant characteristics, to make general classifications.

Languedoc A former province in S France, on the Gulf of Lions. Its name derived from *langue d'oc*, the language of its inhabitants (*see* Provençal). In the 10th–12th centuries it flourished as an important cultural centre. It is now incor-

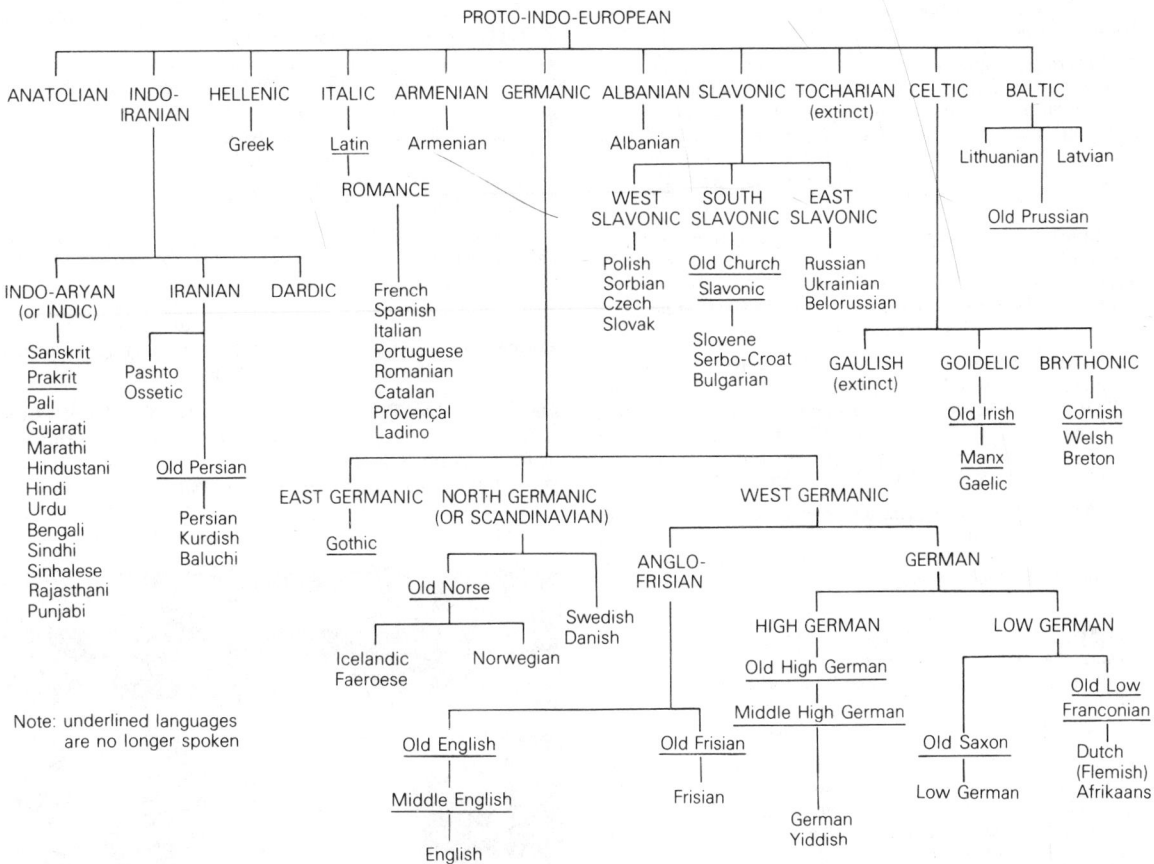

CLASSIFICATION OF LANGUAGES *A simplified family tree shows the relationships of the Indo-European languages, spoken by about half the world's population.*

porated chiefly into the planning region of **Languedoc-Roussillon** and is a very important wine-producing area. Area: 27 447 sq km (10 595 sq mi). Population (1982): 1 926 514.

langur A leaf-eating *Old World monkey of tropical Asia. Langurs have specially adapted stomachs to digest their food. The largest is the hanuman, or entellus langur (*Presbytis entellus*), 75 cm long with a 95-cm tail. The douc langur (*Pygathrix nemaeus*) of Vietnam is mainly grey with white forearms and is now an endangered species. Chief genera: *Presbytis* (14 species), *Rhinopithecus* (4 species).

Lanier, Sidney (1842-81) US poet. As a Confederate soldier in the Civil War he was imprisoned and contracted tuberculosis, from which he eventually died. His poetry, notably "Corn" (1875), "The Symphony" (1875), and "The Marches of Glyn," was greatly influenced by his musical skills.

Lankester, Sir Edwin Ray (1847-1929) British zoologist, whose wide-ranging contributions to biology included work on protozoan parasites of vertebrate animals and the embryology of invertebrates. He was director of the British Museum of Natural History (1898-1907) and helped found the Marine Biological Association.

lanner falcon A large *falcon, *Falco biarmicus*, occurring in SE Europe and Africa. Up to 45 cm long, it has a grey-brown back, white underparts flecked with black on the breast, a tawny head, and a black moustache. Lanner falcons feed chiefly on birds and are used in falconry.

lanolin A purified *wax extracted from wool. It is a mixture of cholesterol and other sterols, aliphatic alcohols,

and esters. Because it is easily absorbed by the skin, lanolin is used as a base for creams, soaps, and other skin preparations.

Lansbury, George (1859-1940) British Labour politician. He became an MP in 1910 but resigned in 1912 to fight a by-election on a women's suffrage ticket. Mayor of Poplar (1919-20), he was imprisoned (1921) together with most of the borough council for refusing to raise the rates. Again an MP from 1922 to 1940 he led the Labour Party in opposition (1931-35), resigning because, as a pacifist, he opposed the party's militant response to Mussolini's seizure of Ethiopia.

Lansdowne, Henry Charles Keith Petty-Fitzmaurice, 5th Marquess of (1845-1927) British politician and colonial administrator. After holding office under Gladstone he was governor general of Canada (1883-88) and then viceroy of India (1888-94). As secretary for war (1895-1900) he was criticized for early British failures in the second Boer War but was nevertheless appointed foreign secretary in 1900. In 1917, during World War I, he wrote the notorious **Lansdowne Letter** to the *Daily Telegraph*, in which he advocated a negotiated peace with Germany.

Lansing 42 44N 85 34W A city in the USA, the capital of Michigan on the Grand River. The site of the Michigan State University (1855), it contains part of the Detroit motor-vehicle industry, manufacturing car components. Population (1980): 130 414.

lantern fish A deepsea *bony fish belonging to the family *Myctophidae* (about 150 species). 2.5-15 cm long, lantern fish have large mouths and eyes and numerous light-producing organs on the head, underside, and base of the tail. At night, many species migrate towards the surface. Order: *Myctophiformes*.

lanthanides (*or* rare-earth metals) A group of 15 *transition-metal elements, atomic numbers 57–71, which all have remarkably similar physical and chemical properties as a result of their electronic structures. They occur together in monazite and other minerals. They are used as catalysts in the petroleum industry, in iron alloys and permanent magnets, and in glass polishes. The **rare earths** are the oxides of these metals.

lanthanum (La) The first of the series of rare-earth metals (*see* lanthanides), all of which have similar chemical properties. It is used in *misch metal to make lighter flints. Its compounds include an oxide (La_2O_3) and a chloride ($LaCl_3$). At no 57; at wt 138.9055; mp 921°C; bp 3457°C.

Lanzhou (Lan-chou *or* Lanchow) 36 01N 103 45E A city in N China, the capital of Gansu province at the confluence of the Yellow and Wei Rivers. It is an ancient trade and communications centre and the site of a university. Industries include oil refining, plutonium processing, and the manufacture of chemicals and machinery. Population (1983 est): 1 430 000.

Laocoon In Greek legend, a Trojan priest of Apollo who warned against accepting the Greek gift of the *Trojan Horse. He and his two sons were killed by sea serpents sent by Apollo, and the Trojans then opened their gates to the wooden horse.

Laodicea 37 46N 29 02E An ancient city of Asia Minor, near present-day Denizli (SW Turkey), founded by *Antiochus II about 250 BC. On an important trade route Laodicea soon prospered; early Christians condemned its worldliness. Under Diocletian it became Phrygia's metropolis (mother city). Its Roman remains include theatres and an aqueduct.

Laoighis (*or* Leix; former name: Queen's County) A county in the E central Republic of Ireland, in Leinster. Predominantly low lying with bogs and drained chiefly by the Rivers Barrow and Nore, it rises to mountains in the NW. Agriculture is the main occupation with dairy farming and cattle rearing. Area: 1719 sq km (664 sq mi). Population (1981): 51 171. County town: Portlaoise.

Laon 49 34N 3 37E A town in N France, the capital of the Aisne department. A former leading town of the kingdom of the Franks, notable buildings include the cathedral (begun in the 12th century) and the bishop's palace. It has metallurgical and sugar-refining industries. Population (1982): 29 074.

Laos, People's Democratic Republic of A landlocked country in SE Asia, in the Indochina peninsula between Vietnam and Thailand. Except for the valley of the River Mekong along its western border, the country is mountainous and forested. Over half the population are Lao (descendants of the Thai) and there are minorities of Vietnamese, Chinese, and others. *Economy*: predominantly agricultural, the difficult terrain combined with recent political upheavals has hindered production and Laos remains the least developed of the nations of the Indochina peninsula. The main crops are rice, corn, coffee, cotton, tea, and tobacco. The valuable mineral resources (tin, iron ore, gold, and copper) have yet to be fully exploited. There is little industry. Hydroelectricity is an important source of power, especially since the opening of the Nan Ngum Dam in 1971. Communications are difficult; there are no railways and river traffic is hindered by rapids and waterfalls. Meagre exports include timber and tin. *History*: the origins of the area as a nation date from the rule of Fa Ngum in the 14th century. European contacts were initiated in the 17th century and in 1893 Laos became a French protectorate. It was occupied by the Japanese from 1941 to 1945, when the Lao Issara (Free Lao) proclaimed an independent government. This movement collapsed when the French returned in 1946 and a constitutional monarchy was formed in 1947. In 1949 Laos became independent within the French Union. In 1953 civil war, which was to last for 20 years, broke out between the government (supported by

the USA and by Thai mercenaries) and the communist-led Pathet Lao movement (supported by the North Vietnamese). In 1974 a provisional coalition government was formed but following the collapse of the South Vietnamese the Pathet Lao gained power (December, 1975) and the People's Democratic Republic of Laos was formed with Prince Souphanouvong (1902–) as president; he resigned because of illness in 1986 and was succeeded by Phoumi Vongvichit. Prime minister: Kaysone Phoumvihan (1920–). Official language: Laotian; French is widely spoken. Official currency: kip of 100 at. Area: 235 700 sq km (91 000 sq mi). Population (1984 est): 3 500 000. Capital: Vientiane.

Laotian A language of SE Asia belonging to the Thai language family. It is a tonal and monosyllabic language and written in an alphabet derived from *Khmer.

Lao Zi (*or* Lao Tzu; ?6th century BC) The founder of *Taoism. A shadowy, possibly legendary, figure, he was eventually deified. His purpose, propounded mainly in books compiled about 300 years after his likely date of death, was to reach harmony with the *Tao* (way) by dwelling on the beauty of nature, by being self-sufficient, and by desiring nothing.

LAOCOON *Marble by Hagesandros, Athenodoros, and Polydoros of Rhodes. (c. 25 BC; Vatican Museum, Rome).*

La Paz 16 30S 68 00W The administrative capital of Bolivia, situated in the W of the country. At an altitude of 3577 m (11 735 ft), it is the world's highest capital. Founded by the Spanish in 1548, it became the seat of government in 1898. The University of San Andrés was founded here in 1830. Population (1982 est): 881 404. *See also* Sucre.

lapis lazuli A blue semiprecious stone composed mainly of a sulphur-rich variety of the mineral haüyne (a feldspathoid) called lazurite. It is formed by the metamorphism of limestone. It often contains specks or threads of yellow iron pyrites. Lapis lazuli has been mined in Afghanistan for over 6000 years. The pigment ultramarine was formerly made by grinding up lapis lazuli.

Laplace, Pierre Simon, Marquis de (1749–1827) French mathematician and astronomer. Laplace worked with *Lagrange on the effects, known as perturbations, of the small gravitational forces that planets exert on each other. (Newton's work considered only the gravitational force of the sun on the planets.) They deduced that the perturbations only cause small oscillations in the planets' motions and not any permanent movement, thus proving the stability of the solar system. Laplace published their results, without giving Lagrange credit, in a five-volume work, *Mécanique céleste* (1799–1825). At the end of the work, Laplace speculated that the solar system was formed from a condensing rotating cloud of gas.

Lapland (*or* Lappland) A vast region in N Europe, inhabited by the *Lapps and extending across northern parts of Norway, Sweden, Finland, and into the extreme NW of the Soviet Union. Lying mainly within the Arctic Circle, it consists of tundra in the N, mountains in the W, and forests in the S; there are many lakes and rivers. For many centuries the Lapps were reduced to virtual slavery by their more powerful neighbours. Subsistence farming, fishing, trapping, and hunting are the principal occupations and reindeer are a particularly important source of income. There are rich deposits of iron ore in Swedish Lapland. High unemployment, however, has led to considerable emigration S although there are plans to develop Lapland's fishing potential and to establish fur farms (especially the silver fox). Recent industrial successes include the new steel works at Tornio on the border between Finland and Sweden.

La Plata (name from 1952 until 1955: Eva Perón) 34 52S 57 55W A city in E Argentina, near the Río de la Plata. Its industries include meat packing and oil refining and it has a university (1884). Population (1980 est): 455 000.

Lapps A people of N Scandinavia and the Kola peninsula of the Soviet Union. They speak a *Finno-Ugric language, which differs from the related Finnish and *Estonian mainly in its sound system. There are three major Lapp dialects, which are very different from one another. The mountain Lapps are nomadic reindeer herders who follow their herds on their seasonal migrations using them as pack animals or to pull sledges. Other Lapps are seminomadic hunters and fishers.

Laptev Sea A section of the Arctic Ocean off the coast of the Soviet Union, between the Taimyr Peninsula and the New Siberian Islands. Half of its supply of fresh water comes from the River Lena and it is frozen for most of the year.

lapwing A Eurasian *plover, *Vanellus vanellus*, also called peewit and green plover. It occurs commonly on farmland, where it feeds on harmful insects, such as wireworms and leatherjackets. 28 cm long, it has a greenish-black and white plumage, a long crest, short rounded wings, a short tail, and pink legs. In spring, lapwings perform acrobatic courtship displays.

Laramie 41 20N 105 38W A city in the USA, in SE Wyoming on the Laramie River. Founded in 1868 with the arrival of the Union Pacific Railroad, it is a commercial and industrial centre for a timber, mining, and livestock region. The University of Wyoming was established here in 1886. Population (1980): 24 339.

larceny. *See* theft.

larch A deciduous conifer of the genus *Larix* (10 species), native to the cooler regions of the N hemisphere. Larches are graceful trees, with needles growing in bunches on short spurs and producing small woody cones. The common European larch (*L. decidua*), from the mountains of central Europe, is widely cultivated both for timber and ornament. It reaches a height of 40 m and its cones, 2–4 cm long, ripen from pinkish-

red to brown. The Japanese larch (*L. kaempferi*) is commonly grown on plantations. Family: *Pinaceae*. □tree.

Lardner, Ring (1885–1933) US short-story writer. He worked as a sports reporter and his early stories concern the life of a baseball player. His best-known stories are collected in *How to Write Short Stories* (1924) and *The Love Nest and Other Stories* (1926).

Laredo 27 32N 99 22W A city in the USA, in Texas on the Rio Grande. Situated opposite Nuevo Laredo (Mexico), it was founded by the Spanish in 1755 and is a centre for US and Mexican trade. It has a thriving tourist industry and is the commercial centre for an oil-producing and agricultural region. Population (1980): 91 229.

Lares and Penates Roman household gods. The Lares were originally gods of cultivated land who were worshipped at crossroads and boundaries. The Penates were gods of the storeroom. Together with the *Manes, they were later worshipped in private homes as guardian spirits of the family, household, and state.

Large White A breed of pig originating in Yorkshire, England, also called the Yorkshire. Relatively large-framed, Large Whites are white-skinned with a sparse coat of fine hair. They are extensively used for bacon production. A smaller derivative breed, the Middle White, was formerly popular as a porker.

Lárisa (*or* Larissa) 39 38N 22 25E A town in E Greece, in Thessaly. It is a commercial centre; products include silk cloth and tobacco. Population (1981): 102 048.

lark A slender long-winged songbird belonging to a family (*Alaudidae*; 75 species) found mainly in mudflats, marshes, grasslands, and deserts of the Old World and characterized by a beautiful song. Larks commonly have a brown or buff streaked plumage that often matches the local soil colour. They have long slender bills and feed on seeds and insects. The only New World lark is the horned lark, or shorelark (*Eremophila alpestris*) of North America. *See also* skylark.

Larkin, Philip (1922–85) British poet. His poetry expresses a resigned but honest acceptance of the limitations of daily existence. His volumes include *The Whitsun Weddings* (1964) and *High Windows* (1974). He became librarian at Hull University in 1955, edited *The Oxford Book of Twentieth Century English Verse* (1973), and published two novels and a volume of jazz criticism.

larkspur An annual herb of the genus *Consolida*, especially *C. ajacis*, *C. ambigua*, or *C. orientalis*, native to Eurasia but commonly grown for ornament. Larkspurs have feathery leaves and tall stems with branching spikes of white or blue spurred flowers. The name is also applied to species of the genus *Delphinium*. Family: *Ranunculaceae*.

Larne 54 51N 5 49W A port in Northern Ireland, in Co Antrim at the entrance to Lough Larne. Larne is a tourist centre and has the shortest searoute between Ireland and Britain (Stranraer). Population (1981): 18 222.

La Rochefoucauld, François, Duc de (1613–80) French moralist. He was born into an ancient aristocratic family and played an active part in intrigues against Richelieu and in the *Fronde revolts against Mazarin (1648–53). Thereafter he lived in retirement, writing his *Mémoires* (1664) and compiling his celebrated *Maximes* (1665), a collection of cynical epigrammatic observations on human conduct.

La Rochelle 46 10N 1 10W A port in W France, the capital of the Charente-Maritime department on the Bay of Biscay. A major seaport (14th–16th centuries), it was a Huguenot stronghold until its capture by Richelieu in 1628. Industries include fishing, shipbuilding, fertilizers, and plastics. Population (1982): 74 728.

Larousse, Pierre (1817–75) French lexicographer, encyclopedist, and publisher. In 1852 he founded the publishing firm of Larousse, which specialized in dictionaries, encyclopedias, and other works of reference. His major work was the *Grand Dictionnaire universel du XIXe siècle* (15 vols, 1866–76). His firm continues as a major French publisher, with such reference works as the *Grand Larousse Encyclopédique* (1960–64).

Lars Porsena (*or* Porsenna; 6th century BC) Etruscan king of Clusium (now Chiusi, near Siena). According to legend, when *Tarquin the Proud, the last Etruscan king of Rome, was deposed, Porsena successfully attacked Rome on his behalf. In another version of the story, Porsena made peace with the Romans from admiration of their bravery.

Lartet, Édouard Armand Isidore Hippolyte (1801–71) French archaeologist, who was one of the founders of palaeontology. Following his first discoveries of fossil remains in SW France, Lartet excavated many cave sites, finding important evidence for dating the various phases of human culture in the region.

larva The immature form of many animals, which hatches from the egg and often differs in appearance from the adult form. Larvae usually avoid competing for food, etc., with the adults by occupying a different habitat or adopting a different lifestyle. For example, adult barnacles, which are sessile, produce motile larvae, whose role is distribution of the species. Other larvae are responsible for gathering food reserves for the production of a fully formed adult, whose primary function is to breed. Caterpillars and maggots are types of insect larvae with this function. *See also* metamorphosis; tadpole.

Larwood, Harold (1904–) British cricketer, known as "Lol", who played for Nottinghamshire and England. A miner at the age of 14, Larwood was a fast bowler who was at the centre of the bodyline controversy during the 1932–33 tour of Australia. His 33 wickets from fast short-pitched balls made him disliked in Australia, although he emigrated there after World War II.

larynx An organ, situated at the front of the neck above the windpipe (*see* trachea), that contains the **vocal cords**, responsible for the production of vocal sounds. The larynx contains several cartilages (one of which—the thyroid cartilage—forms the Adam's apple) bound together by muscles and ligaments. Within are the two vocal cords: folds of tissue separated by a narrow slit (glottis). The vocal cords modify the flow of exhaled air through the glottis to produce the sounds of speech, song, etc.

La Salle, Robert Cavelier, Sieur de (1643–87) French explorer in North America. La Salle settled in Montreal in 1666 and in 1669 set out on his first expedition, exploring the Ohio region. From 1679 he concentrated on achieving his ambition to descend the Mississippi River to the Gulf of Mexico. In 1682, after two arduous years, he reached the Gulf and named the area watered by the Mississippi and its tributaries Louisiana, after Louis XIV of France. While attempting to found a permanent colony, he was murdered by mutineers.

La Scala (*or* Teatro alla Scala) The principal Italian opera house, opened in Milan in 1776. It is noted for its varied repertoire of new and classical works, and attained its highest reputation under Arturo *Toscanini, director from 1898 to 1907 and from 1921 to 1931.

Las Campanas Observatory. *See* Hale Observatories.

Las Casas, Bartolomé de (1474–1566) Spanish priest, known as the Apostle of the Indies. As a planter on Hispaniola, Las Casas was horrified by the treatment to which the Indians were subjected. He became a priest (1510) and entered the Dominican order, becoming the defender of the Indians at the Spanish court. His agitation included the publication of *The Brief Relation of the Destruction of the Indies* (1552) and bore fruit with the abolition of Indian slavery in 1542.

Las Cases, Emmanuel, Comte de (1776–1842) French writer. He held political office under Napoleon and shared his

exile on St Helena. His *Mémorial de St Hélène* (1823) recorded Napoleon's final conversations and opinions on politics and religion and greatly influenced his posthumous reputation.

Lascaux Upper *Palaeolithic cave site in the Dordogne (France), discovered in 1940. Lascaux contains rock paintings and engravings of horses, oxen, red deer, and other animals, dating from about 18 000 BC; traps and arrows depicted nearby suggest that the pictures had magical significance in a hunting ritual. Atmospheric changes resulting in deterioration of the paintings caused the cave to be closed again (1963).

Lasdun, Sir Denys (1914–) British architect. One of the foremost contemporary British architects, Lasdun's most important works are East Anglia University (1963) and, in London, the National Theatre (1968–76) and the School of African and Oriental Studies (1970–73).

ruby laser

helium-neon gas laser

LASER *In the solid-state ruby laser, chromium ions are excited by an intense flash of light and then stimulated by weak light of one wavelength to emit a pulse of photons. In the helium-neon gas laser, a continuous laser beam is produced from an electrical discharge through low-pressure gas.*

laser (*light amplification by stimulated emission of radiation*) A device that produces a beam of high-intensity coherent monochromatic radiation (light, infrared, or ultraviolet). Stimulated emission is the emission of a photon when an atomic electron falls from a higher energy level to a lower level as a result of being stimulated by another photon of the same frequency. In the laser large numbers of electrons are "pumped" into a higher energy level, an effect called population inversion, and then stimulated to produce a high-intensity beam. Laser beams have been produced from solids, liquids, and gases. The simplest type is the ruby laser, consisting of a cylinder of ruby, silvered at one end and partially silvered at the other. A flash lamp is used to excite chromium ions in the ruby to a high energy level. When the ions fall back to their ground state photons (wavelength 694.3 nanometres) are emitted. These photons collide with other excited ions producing radiation of the same wavelength (monochromatic) and the same phase (coherent), which is reflected up and down the ruby crystal and emerges as a narrow beam from the partially silvered end. Lasers are used in civil engineering to aid alignment, in eye surgery, in laser interferometers to measure very small displacements, in *holography, and in scientific research.

Lashio 22 58N 97 48E A town in NE central Burma. It is a railway terminus and the starting point of the Burma Road to Chongqing, China.

Lasker, Emanuel (1868-1941) German chess player, who became world champion in 1894 and remained champion until he conceded the title to *Capablance in 1921. A Jew, he left Germany in 1933 to settle in the Soviet Union and finally the USA.

Laski, Harold Joseph (1893-1950) British political theorist. Laski became professor of political science at the London School of Economics in 1926. A socialist, he was influenced by the theories of *Burke and *Mill but became progressively more Marxist in outlook. His writings include *Authority in the Modern State* (1919) and *Faith, Reason, Civilization* (1944). His niece **Marghanita Laski** (1915-88) was a novelist and critic.

Las Palmas 28 08N 15 27W The largest city in the Canary Islands, the capital of Las Palmas province in Gran Canaria. It is a popular resort noted for its palms and is a major fuelling port between Europe and South America. Population (1981): 366 454.

La Spezia 44 07N 9 48E A port and resort in Italy, in Liguria on the Gulf of Spezia. It is a major naval base, with the largest harbour in Italy. Its industries include shipbuilding, textiles, and the manufacture of porcelain. Population (1980 est): 116 719.

Lassa fever A severe virus disease occurring in West Africa and first described in 1969 in Lassa, a village in Nigeria. It is a rare and often fatal disease that is transmitted to man by certain species of rat.

Lassalle, Ferdinand (1825-64) German socialist politician and theorist. Although deeply influenced by Karl Marx, Lassalle developed a distinctive theory of socialism, stressing the formation of workers' cooperatives as a peaceful way to socialism. He headed working-class opposition to Bismarck and helped to found the General German Workers' Association (1863), the precursor to the Social Democratic party. He was killed in a duel.

Lassus, Roland de (Italian name: Orlando di Lasso; c. 1532-94) Flemish composer. He was born in Mons, where he became a chorister. He obtained appointments in Rome (choirmaster at St John Lateran), Antwerp, and with the Bavarian court in Munich. His madrigals, chansons, and motets exhibit great contrapuntal skill. He was afflicted with depression in later life.

Las Vegas 36 10N 115 12W A city in the USA, in SE Nevada. Founded in 1855, it grew rapidly after construction of the nearby Hoover Dam. It is famous for its nightclubs and the Strip (a row of luxury hotel and gambling casinos). Population (1980): 164 674.

László I, Saint (1040-95) King of Hungary (1077-95). In 1091, László conquered Croatia, to which he introduced Roman Catholicism, founding the bishopric of Zagreb. He also reformed the criminal code, bringing peace and security to Hungary.

Latakia (Arabic name: Al Ladhiqiyah) 35 31N 35 47E A town in NW Syria, on the Mediterranean coast. It dates from Phoenician times and is now Syria's principal port. It is also famous for its tobacco. Population (1981): 196 791.

La Tène The second phase of the European Iron Age, succeeding *Hallstatt from the 5th century BC. Named after the site at La Tène (Switzerland), this recognizably Celtic culture spread throughout Europe, coming into contact with the civilizations of Greece and Rome. Aristocratic chariot burials replaced wagon burials and the geometric patterns of Hallstatt metalwork were superseded by the intricate curvilinear designs of *Celtic art. By the 1st century BC Roman expansionism effectively ended coherent La Tène culture. *See also* Celts.

latent heat The amount of heat absorbed or released by a substance when it undergoes a change of state. For example, a liquid absorbs heat (**latent heat of vaporization**) from its surroundings on evaporation, since energy is needed to overcome the forces of attraction between the molecules as the liquid expands into a gas. Similarly a solid absorbs heat (**latent heat of fusion**) when it melts. The heat absorbed or released per unit mass of substance is called the **specific latent heat**; per amount of substance it is the **molar latent heat**.

Lateran Councils Five ecumenical councils of the Roman Catholic Church convened in the Lateran Palace, Rome. **1.** (1123) The council that confirmed the settlement of the *investiture controversy. **2.** and **3.** (1139, 1179) The councils that were principally concerned with the papal-election procedure. **4.** (1215) The council, attended by most major European ecclesiastical and secular powers, that proclaimed the fifth Crusade (1217-21) and was enormously influential in its formulations of doctrine and Church organization and law. **5.** (1512-17) The council that endeavoured to counteract hostility to papal power on the eve of the Reformation.

Lateran Treaty (1929) An agreement between the Italian government of Mussolini and the Vatican. The Vatican City state was created and the papacy abandoned its claims to the former *papal states.

laterite A deposit formed from the weathering of rocks in humid tropical conditions. It consists mostly of iron and aluminium oxides. It occurs either under ground, where it is soft, or as a hardened reddish surface capping where the overlying material has been eroded. Most laterites developed in the Tertiary period.

latex A liquid, often milky, emulsion found in certain flowering plants. It has a complex composition and its function in the plant is not fully understood. The latex of the *rubber tree is used in rubber manufacture, while opium and morphine are obtained from the latex of the *opium poppy.

lathe A machine for turning wood, plastic, or metal into cylindrical or conical parts or for cutting holes or screwthreads in them. The piece to be worked is held in a rotating plate or chuck so that a cutting tool can be held against it. The **turret lathe** has a turret containing a set of cutting tools, which can be used independently or simultaneously. Automatic turret lathes perform a sequence of operations on the workpiece without manual interference and are extensively used in mass-production processes.

Latimer, Hugh (c. 1485-1555) Anglican reformer and martyr. While a university preacher, he was converted to Protestantism (1524) and declared against the legality of Henry VIII's marriage to Catherine of Aragon. He became Bishop of Worcester in 1535, but his opposition to Henry's Six Articles upholding Roman Catholic doctrine resulted in his resignation and imprisonment (1539). A popular preacher under Edward VI, he was arrested at Mary's accession, tried for heresy at Oxford, and burnt at the stake.

Latimeria. *See* coelacanth.

Latin America The countries of Central and South America lying S of the US-Mexican border, including those islands of the West Indies where a Romance language is spoken. Spanish is the most widely used language but Portuguese is spoken in Brazil, the largest country, and

French is spoken in Haiti and French Guiana. The population is mainly mestizo (people of mixed Indian and European—usually Spanish—parentage), with minorities of pure Indians and Europeans. The **Latin American Free Trade Association** (LAFTA) was formed in 1961 with the aim of removing all restrictions on trade among its member countries (Argentina, Brazil, Bolivia, Chile, Colombia, Ecuador, Mexico, Paraguay, Peru, Uruguay, and Venezuela).

Latini, Brunetto (c. 1220–c. 1294) Florentine scholar and politician. A friend of *Dante, Latini contributed to the spread of French learning in Italy and wrote an encyclopedia entitled *Li Livres dou trésor*.

Latin language An Italic Indo-European language, the ancestor of modern Romance languages. First spoken on the plain of Latium near Rome, Latin spread throughout the Mediterranean world as Roman power expanded. An inflected and syntactically complex language, written Latin was gradually moulded to express with equal power Cicero's rhetoric and philosophy, Martial's epigrams, and Virgil's subtle poetry. Educated conversational Latin developed contemporaneously with literary Latin, although, with its freer syntax and vocabulary, it remained less static than the formalized written language. Colloquial Vulgar Latin used prepositions and conjunctions freely to replace inflected forms and had a simpler word order; it became the Latin of the provinces, contributing to the early development of the Romance languages. As the western Roman Empire's official language, Latin was used in W Europe for religious, literary, and scholarly works until the middle ages and beyond, and remained the Roman Catholic Church's official language until the mid-20th century.

Latin literature The earliest Latin literature dates from after the conclusion of the first *Punic War (241 BC). Writers such as *Ennius, Naevius, and *Plautus (*see* Roman comedy) translated Greek epic, tragedy, and comedy and adapted them to Roman themes. Prose, particularly legal and historical writing, developed along more independent lines until the 1st century BC, when *Cicero conclusively established Latin as a mature literary medium. His contemporary *Lucretius perfected the Latin hexameter and, together with the lyric poet *Catullus, they inaugurated the *Golden Age of Latin literature. Their achievements were consolidated in the subsequent Augustan age (43 BC–18 AD), during which the emperor Augustus' adviser *Maecenas was patron to *Virgil, *Horace, and *Propertius. Among their important contemporaries were the poets *Ovid and *Tibullus and the historian *Livy. The spirit of the succeeding *Silver Age is encapsulated in *Seneca's highly rhetorical tragedies. *Juvenal and *Martial were the major poets and *Tacitus, *Suetonius, *Quintilian, and *Petronius contributed notable prose works. Imitations, anthologies, and commentaries later predominated over original work. In the 4th and 5th centuries the Latin Church Fathers set Latin on course for becoming the lingua franca of Christian intellectuals. As the literature of learning, Latin literature's characteristic products were encyclopedias and theological texts. Exceptions to this were the medieval Latin lyrics, which have the spontaneity of their vernacular counterparts. *See also* Latin language.

Latinus A legendary ancestor of the Romans, who gave his name to their language. *Aeneas arrived from Troy in his kingdom of Latium, an area S of Rome, and married his daughter Lavinia.

latitude and longitude Imaginary lines on the earth's surface, enabling any point to be defined in terms of two angles. **Parallels of latitude** are circles drawn round the earth parallel to the equator; their diameters diminish as they approach the Poles. These parallels are specified by the angle subtended at the centre of the earth by the arc formed between a point on the parallel and the equator. All points on the equator therefore have a latitude of 0°, while the North Pole has a latitude of 90°N and the South Pole of

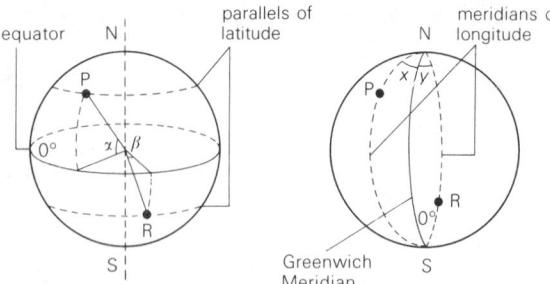

The latitude of P is given by the angle α. *In this case it would be* α° N. *The latitude of R is* β° S.

The longitude of P is given by the angle x. *In this case it would be* x° W. R *has a longitude* y° E.

LATITUDE AND LONGITUDE

90°S. Parallels of latitude 1° apart are separated on the earth's surface by about 100 km (63 mi).

Meridians of longitude are half great circles passing through both Poles; they cross parallels of latitude at right angles. In 1884 the meridian through Greenwich, near London, was selected as the prime meridian and given the designation 0°. Other meridians are defined by the angle between the plane of the meridian and the plane of the prime meridian, specifying whether it is E or W of the prime meridian. At the equator meridians 1° apart are separated by about 112 km (70 mi).

latitudinarianism An attitude originating with certain 17th-century Anglican clergymen, who deprecated sectarian squabbles over Church government and forms of ritual and considered such matters unimportant in comparison with personal piety and practical morality. Latitudinarian principles characterized the *Cambridge Platonists. Between the 1690s and the rise of the *Oxford Movement in the 1830s latitudinarianism was the predominant tendency in the Church of England.

Latium. *See* Lazio.

La Tour, Georges de (1593–1652) French painter, a native of Lorraine. He excelled in candlelit religious scenes, influenced by such Dutch followers of Caravaggio as *Honthorst. His works include *St Joseph the Carpenter* (Louvre) and *The Lamentation over St Sebastian* (Berlin). La Tour's reputation has only been re-established in the 20th century.

La Tour, Maurice-Quentin de (1704–88) French portrait pastellist, born in Saint-Quentin. He settled in Paris, where he enjoyed an immense and lasting popularity. His sitters included Voltaire, Madame de Pompadour, and Louis XV.

Latter-Day Saints, Church of Jesus Christ of. *See* Mormons.

Latvian A language belonging to the E division of the *Baltic languages division of the Indo-European family, spoken by about two million Latvians. Most live in the Latvian SSR, where Latvian is the official language. Also known as Lettish, it is closely related to *Lithuanian. It is written in a Latin alphabet and written texts date from the 16th century.

Latvian Soviet Socialist Republic (*or* Latvia) A constituent republic in the NW Soviet Union, on the Baltic Sea. It is a fertile lowland with extensive forests. Latvians, who comprise approximately 60% of the population, are mainly Lutheran Christians. Industries include shipbuilding, engineering, chemicals, and textiles. Fishing plays an important part in the economy and Riga, the capital, is an important seaport. *History*: the Latvians were conquered by the Livonian Knights (a German order of knighthood) in the 13th century, passing to Poland in the 16th century, to

Sweden in the 17th century, and to Russia in the 18th century. Latvia gained independence in 1918, which was recognized by Soviet Russia in 1920. In 1940 it was incorporated into the Soviet Union as an SSR. It was occupied by Germany in World War II. The USA does not recognize Latvia's status as a Soviet republic. Area: 63 700 sq km (25 590 sq mi). Population (1984): 2 600 000. Capital: Riga.

Laud, William (1573–1645) Anglican churchman, with *Strafford the chief adviser to Charles I immediately before the *Civil War. Successively Bishop of St David's, Bath and Wells, and London, and then Archbishop of Canterbury (1633–45), he supported Charles I's personal rule and his attempt to enforce liturgical uniformity among both Roman Catholics and Puritans. His pressure on the Scots to accept the Book of Common Prayer led to the *Bishops' Wars and paved the way for the Civil War and his own downfall. He was impeached for high treason by the Long Parliament in 1640. Although found not guilty by the Lords, he was executed by a bill of attainder passed by the Commons.

Lauda, Niki (1949–) Austrian motor-racing driver, who was world champion in 1975, 1977, and 1984 and won numerous Grand Prix races. Badly burnt in a crash in 1976, he finally retired in 1985.

laudanum. *See* opium.

Lauder, Sir Harry (Hugh MacLennan; 1870-1950) Scots singer and famous music-hall comedian. He always appeared on stage wearing a glengarry and kilt and carried a crooked stick. His most famous songs included "I Love a Lassie" and "Roamin' in the Gloamin'." He toured in Australia and the USA and gave concerts for the troops during World War I.

Lauderdale, John Maitland, Duke of (1616-82) Scottish statesman; a member of the political faction called the *Cabal under Charles II. He supported parliament in the English Civil War until changing sides in 1647; in 1651 he was captured by the English army and imprisoned until the Restoration (1660). Under Charles II he was an unpopular high commissioner for Scotland from 1667 until 1680.

Laue, Max Theodor Felix von (1879-1960) German physicist, who became professor at the University of Berlin in 1919. His early investigations of X-rays led him to discover the technique of *X-ray crystallography, now widely used for determining crystal structures. For this work he won the 1914 Nobel Prize. In 1943 he resigned his chair in protest against the Nazis. After the war he was appointed director of the Max Planck Institute for Physical Chemistry.

Laugharne 51 47N 4 28W A small town in SW Wales, in Dyfed on the estuary of the River Taff near Carmarthen Bay. The poet Dylan Thomas lived and was buried here.

laughing jackass. *See* kookaburra.

laughing owl A ground-nesting New Zealand *owl, *Sceloglaux albifacies*, probably now extinct due to the introduction of predatory mammals. It was 37 cm long and had a speckled and barred brown plumage with whitish facial feathers.

Laughton, Charles (1899-1962) British actor. His international reputation was based on his numerous films, which included *The Private Life of Henry VIII* (1933), *Mutiny on the Bounty* (1935), and *Rembrandt* (1936). He was married to the actress Elsa Lanchester (1902-86) and lived for many years in Hollywood, but made several late appearances in the English theatre, notably as King Lear in 1959.

Launceston 41 25S 147 07E A city and port in Australia, in N Tasmania situated at the confluence of the North and South Esk Rivers. It is an important commercial centre; industries include aluminium smelting, heavy engineering, textiles, and sawmilling. Population (1981): 64 555.

Laura The subject of Petrarch's love sonnets and other poems. She has been variously identified, traditionally as Laura de Noves (?1308-48), a married woman living in Avignon. The poems suggest that Petrarch's love for her was not returned.

LAUREL AND HARDY   *Oliver Hardy is on the left.*

Laurasia The supercontinent of the N hemisphere that is believed to have existed prior to 200 million years ago, when the drift of the continents to their present positions began. It probably consisted of Greenland, Europe, Asia (excluding India), and North America. *See also* Gondwanaland.

laurel One of several unrelated aromatic shrubs or small trees with attractive evergreen leaves. The so-called true laurels (genus *Laurus*) include the *bay tree. Other laurels include the ornamental *cherry laurels, the spotted laurels (genus *Aucuba*; family *Cornaceae*), and the mountain laurel (*Kalmia latifolia*; family *Ericaceae*). The spurge laurel is a species of *Daphne.

Laurel and Hardy US film comedians. **Stan Laurel** (Arthur Stanley Jefferson; 1890-1965), the thin member of the team and originator of the gags, was born in Britain. He joined with **Oliver Hardy** (1892-1957), who played the pompous fat partner, in 1926. They made numerous outstanding two-reel and feature-length comedy films in the 1920s and 1930s, including *The Music Box* (1932), *Our Relations* (1936), and *Way Out West* (1937).

Laurentian Shield. *See* shield.

Laurier, Sir Wilfrid (1841-1919) Canadian statesman; the first French-Canadian prime minister of Canada (1896-1911). His Liberal government was notable for the settlement of the West and the defence of Canadian autonomy within the British Empire.

laurustinus An ornamental evergreen shrub, *Viburnum tinus*, native to the Mediterranean region and up to 3 m tall. It has pointed oval leaves, reddish twigs, and round heads of tiny five-petalled pink-and-white flowers, borne on red stalks and producing blue-black berries. It is often grown as a pot plant. Family: *Caprifoliaceae*.

Lausanne 46 32N 6 39E A city and resort in W Switzerland, on the N shore of Lake Geneva. A cultural and intellectual centre, it has a notable cathedral (13th century) and a university (1891) founded as a college in the 16th century. Lausanne is the seat of the Swiss Supreme Court and the headquarters of the International Olympic Committee. Industries include chocolate, precision instruments, and clothing. Population (1980 est): 127 349.

Lausanne, Conferences of 1. (1922-23) A conference between the Allied Powers and Turkey that modified the post-World War I Treaty of Sèvres (1920), which had been unacceptable to Turkey. By the Treaty of Lausanne, Turkey regained territory from Greece and the Allies recognized Turkey's right to control its own affairs. 2. (1932) A conference between the UK, France, Belgium, and Italy, which ended the payment by Germany of World War I reparations.

Lautréamont, Comte de (Isidore Ducasse; 1846-70) French writer, born in Montevideo. Sent to Paris to study, he died after three years and little is known of his life. His prose poems, *Les Chants de Maldoror* (1868), concern a blasphemous misanthropic hero, and fantastic episodes are described with hallucinatory intensity. Lautréamont was later acknowledged as an important precursor by the surrealists.

lava Magma that has reached the earth's surface through volcanic vents and from which the volatile material has escaped, either molten or cooled and solidified. Basic lavas tend to be liquid and flow over large areas, while acid lavas are viscous.

Laval 45 33N 73 43W A city in E Canada, in Quebec on the island next to *Montreal. Primarily a suburb, it has some industry, including electronics, paper, and metal goods. Population (1980 est): 262 300.

Laval, Pierre (1883-1945) French statesman, whose collaboration with Germany during the German occupation of France in World War II resulted in his execution as a traitor. A socialist, Laval was prime minister in 1930, 1931, 1932, 1935, and 1936 and foreign minister in 1934, 1935, and 1936. In 1935, with Sir Samuel Hoare (1880-1959), the British foreign minister, he proposed an unsuccessful plan (the Hoare-Laval Pact) for the settlement of Mussolini's claims in Ethiopia. After the collapse of France (1940) he joined Marshal *Pétain's Vichy government. Increasingly powerful, he was dismissed and briefly imprisoned by Pétain (December, 1940) but the support of Germany secured Laval the virtual leadership of the Vichy government in 1942. After the liberation of France (1944) he fled to Germany and then to Spain but later gave himself up for trial in France (July, 1945).

La Vallière, Louise de Françoise de la Baume le Blanc, Duchesse de (1644-1710) The mistress of Louis XIV of France from 1661 until 1667, when she was replaced by Mme de Montespan. In 1674 she retired to a convent.

Lavalloisian A Middle *Palaeolithic technique of making stone tools by flaking pieces away from a specially shaped lump (prepared core). It is often associated with *Mousterian sites.

lavender A small shrub of the genus *Lavandula* (about 8 species), especially *L. vera* and *L. angustifolia* (or *L. officinalis*). 30-80 cm high, it has aromatic narrow grey-green leaves and long-stemmed spikes of small mauve or violet flowers. Native to the Mediterranean area, it is widely cultivated for its flowers, which retain their fragrance when dried, and for its oil, which is used in perfumes. Family: *Labiatae.

laver An edible red *seaweed of the genus *Porphyra*, found growing at the high tide mark in both hemispheres. It has wide irregular membranous fronds, which are dried to provide an important food source in the Orient. In the British Isles it is fried and known as laverbread (*or* sloke).

Laver, Rod(ney George) (1938-) Australian tennis player, who was Wimbledon singles champion in 1961, 1962, 1968, and 1969. In 1962 he took all four major singles titles (Australian, French, US, and Wimbledon) as an amateur and repeated the feat as a professional in 1969.

Laveran, Charles Louis Alphonse (1845-1922) French physician, who (in 1880) first recognized the protozoan parasite responsible for malaria while stationed with the army in Algeria. Laveran investigated other diseases caused by protozoa, including trypanosomiasis and leishmaniasis. He was awarded the 1907 Nobel Prize.

Lavoisier, Antoine Laurent (1743-94) French chemist, regarded as the founder of modern chemistry. Born into an aristocratic family, he became wealthy by investing his money in a private company hired by the government to collect taxes. With his wealth he built a large laboratory where he discovered in 1778 that air consists of a mixture of two gases, which he called oxygen and nitrogen. He then went on to study the role of oxygen in combustion, finally disposing of the *phlogiston theory. Lavoisier also discovered the law of conservation of mass and devised the modern method of naming compounds, which replaced the older nonsystematic method. Lavoisier was arrested during the French Revolution and tried for his involvement with the tax-collecting company. He was found guilty and guillotined.

law The body of rules that govern and regulate the relationship between one state and another (*see* international law), a state and its citizens (public law), and one person and another when the state is not directly involved (*see* civil law). Two great legal systems are dominant in the western world: *Roman law, as used in most countries of continental Europe and South America, and English law. The laws of England, which are enforceable by judicial process, can be divided into: (1) the *common law, based on judicial decisions, as opposed to law enacted by parliament; (2) *equity, the principles originally applied by the Court of *Chancery; and (3) statute law, embodied in specific Acts of Parliament. *See also* courts of law; criminal law.

Law, (Andrew) Bonar (1858-1923) British statesman; Conservative prime minister (1922-23). Colonial secretary (1915-16), he fostered the revolt against *Asquith's coalition and in the subsequent coalition led by *Lloyd George became chancellor of the exchequer and leader of the House of Commons. Bonar Law became prime minister after Lloyd George's resignation.

Law, William (1686-1761) Anglican divine. Deprived of his Cambridge fellowship for refusing to take the oath of allegiance to George I, Law later became a private tutor. His most famous work, *A Serious Call to a Holy and Devout Life* (1728), became a classic of Protestant spirituality, influencing, among others, the *Wesleys.

Lawes, Sir John Bennet (1814-1900) British agriculturalist, who pioneered the production of artificial fertilizers. Lawes patented a method for chemically improving phosphate rock and in 1842 opened the first fertilizer factory. In 1843 Lawes began a long association with Sir Henry Gilbert (1817-1901), with whom he investigated aspects of crop fertilization and animal nutrition. This marked the foundation of Rothamsted Experimental Station.

Lawler, Ray (1921-) Australian dramatist. He worked as actor and producer for the National Theatre Company in Melbourne. He won international fame with his plays *The Summer of the Seventeenth Doll* (1955) and *The Piccadilly Bushman* (1959).

Lawrence, D(avid) H(erbert) (1885-1930) British novelist, poet, and painter. The son of a Nottinghamshire miner, he was encouraged by his mother to become a teacher; he published his first novel *The White Peacock*, in 1911. The semiautobiographical *Sons and Lovers* (1913) established his reputation. In 1912 he eloped with Frieda Weekley, the German wife of a professor at Nottingham University College and a cousin of Baron von *Richthofen.

Their extensive travels provided material for the novels *Kangaroo* (1923), reflecting a stay in Australia, and *The Plumed Serpent* (1926), set in Mexico and published after they had lived several years in Taos, New Mexico. Lawrence explored marital and sexual relations in *The Rainbow* (1915) and *Women in Love* (1921); he treated this subject in more explicit detail in *Lady Chatterley's Lover* (privately printed, Florence, 1928). As a result, an exhibition of his paintings was banned in 1929. The novel was not published in Britain in its unexpurgated form until 1961, after a long trial. Lawrence's collected poems were published in 1928. *Fantasia of the Unconscious* (1922) develops ideas that become increasingly prominent in the novels. A number of his critical writings are collected in *Selected Literary Criticism* (1955). He died of tuberculosis in Vence (France). An autobiogaphical novel *Mr Noon* (1920) was published posthumously in 1984.

Lawrence, Ernest Orlando (1901–58) US physicist, who in 1930, at the University of California, designed and built the first *cyclotron, a type of particle *accelerator upon which almost all subsequent models have been based. For his invention he received the Nobel Prize in 1939.

Lawrence, Gertrude (1898–1952) British actress. She performed in many revues and was especially successful in Noel *Coward's *Private Lives* (1930) and *Tonight at 8.30* (1935–36). She went to the USA and made her final appearance in the musical *The King and I* in 1951.

Lawrence, John Laird Mair, 1st Baron (1811–79) British colonial administrator. As chief commissioner in the Punjab (1853–57) he helped to suppress the *Indian Mutiny, for which he received a life pension of £2,000 a year and the nickname Saviour of the Punjab. He was subsequently governor general of India (1864–69).

Lawrence, St (d. 258) Roman deacon martyred during the reign of Emperor Valerian. According to tradition he distributed ecclesiastical treasure to the poor and was condemned to death by being roasted on a gridiron, which has become his emblem. Feast day: 10 Aug.

T. E. LAWRENCE *Drawing by Augustus John (1919).*

Lawrence, T(homas) E(dward) (1888–1935) British soldier and writer, known as Lawrence of Arabia. He learned Arabic while excavating Carchemish (1911–14) and after the outbreak of World War I worked for army intelligence in N Africa. In 1916 he joined the Arab revolt against the Turks, leading the Arab guerrillas triumphantly into Damascus in October, 1918. His exploits, which brought him almost legendary fame, were recounted in his book *The Seven Pillars of Wisdom* (subscription edition, 1926). Disillusioned by the failure of the Paris Peace Conference to establish Arab independence, in 1922 he joined the ranks of the RAF, assuming the name John Hume Ross, and then the Royal Tank Corps (1923), as T. E. Shaw. In 1925 he rejoined the RAF, about which he wrote in *The Mint* (1955). He died in a motorcycle accident in Dorset. His house at Bovington is now owned by the National Trust.

Lawrence, Sir Thomas (1769–1830) British painter, born in Bristol. He achieved immediate success in London (from 1787) with his portrait of *Queen Charlotte* (c. 1789; National Gallery, London). He became painter to George III (1792) and president of the Royal Academy (1820), establishing a European reputation with his portraits of the statesmen and military leaders of the Congress of *Vienna, all now in the Waterloo Chamber, Windsor Castle.

lawrencium (Lr) A synthetic transuranic element discovered in 1961 and named after E. O. *Lawrence. Chemical tests on a few atoms suggest a dominantly trivalent chemistry. At no 103; at wt (257).

Law Society The body that governs solicitors in England and Wales. It controls the training and examination of solicitors, investigates complaints against solicitors, and manages *legal aid. Membership of the Society is voluntary but all solicitors contribute to its fund to compensate persons who have been defrauded by solicitors.

Lawson, Nigel (1932–) British Conservative politician; chancellor of the exchequer (1983–). He became an MP in 1974 and was secretary of state for energy (1981–85).

laxatives (*or* purgatives) Drugs used to treat constipation. Such laxatives as magnesium sulphate (Epsom salts) mix with the faeces and cause them to retain water, which increases their bulk and makes them easier to pass. Irritant laxatives, such as castor oil, senna, and cascara, stimulate the bowel directly. Another group, which includes bran, both lubricates the faeces and increases their bulk.

Laxness, Halldór (Kiljan) (1902–) Icelandic novelist and essayist. He spent much of his early life travelling in Europe, where he became a Roman Catholic. The novel *Vefarinn mikli frá Kasmir* (*The Great Weaver from Kashmir*; 1927) marked his abandonment of Catholicism and adoption of socialism, a theme of subsequent works written after his return to Iceland in 1930. These include *Salka Valka* (1934) and *Sjalfstaet folk* (*Independent People*; 1934–35). He was awarded the Nobel prize in 1955.

Layamon (early 13th century) English poet and priest. His alliterative verse chronicle *Brut*, based on the *Roman de Brut* by *Wace, relates the history of England from the arrival of Brutus (a legendary Trojan) to the defeat of the Britons by the Saxons in 689 AD and includes original detail in its treatment of *Arthurian legend.

Layard, Sir Austen Henry (1817–94) British archaeologist and diplomat. As excavator of □Nimrud and *Nineveh (1845–51), Layard stimulated popular interest in Mesopotamian archaeology by his book *Nineveh and Its Remains* (1848) —actually about Nimrud, as he had at first misidentified the site —and by his feat of transporting colossal statues of winged bulls to Britain.

Lazarists A Roman Catholic order of lay priests known more formally as the Congregation of the Mission. Established by St *Vincent de Paul at St Lazare Priory, Paris, in 1625, the Lazarists now have teaching and missionary communities all over the world.

Lazio (Latin name: Latium) A region in W central Italy. It consists of an extensive coastal plain in the W and mountains in the E, separated by volcanic hills. The majority of the population live in urban centres, such as Rome. Agriculture is important producing cereals, olives, wine, fruits, sheep, and cattle. Rome is an important centre for manufacturing industries, such as food processing, chemicals, textiles, and paper; there is also a sizable service industry. Area: 17 204 sq km (6642 sq mi). Population (1983 est): 5 056 119. Capital: Rome.

L-dopa (*or* levodopa) A drug used to treat *parkinsonism, which is caused by a deficiency of dopamine (a chemical secreted at nerve endings when an impulse passes) in the brain. L-dopa is converted to this compound in the brain. It is taken by mouth, combined with carbidopa (Sinemet), which prevents its breakdown in the body.

Lea, River (*or* R. Lee) A river in S England, rising in S Bedfordshire and flowing SE and S past Luton to join the River Thames at Blackwall. Its valley is being developed as a recreational park. Length: 74 km (46 mi).

Leach, Bernard (Howell) (1887–1979) British potter, born in Hong Kong. After training in Japan (1909–20), he established a pottery at St Ives in Cornwall (1920) and began producing simple designs indebted to Japanese *raku* ware (moulded rough earthenware with a thick lead glaze). His pottery and writings, notably *A Potter's Book* (1940), have been very influential.

Leacock, Stephen (Butler) (1869–1944) English-born Canadian humorist. He was educated and taught economics and political science at Canadian universities. *Literary Lapses* (1910) and *Nonsense Novels* (1911) were the first of over 30 popular humorous books.

lead (Pb) A dense soft bluish-grey metal, known from prehistoric times. It occurs in nature chiefly as the sulphide *galena (PbS) but also as cerussite ($PbCO_3$), anglesite ($PbSO_4$), and occasionally as the native metal. The metal is very resistant to corrosion and some lead pipes installed by the Romans are still intact. Lead is used in plumbing (although it is now being replaced by plastics). It is also used to shield X-rays, as ammunition, as cable sheathing, in crystal glass (as lead oxide), and as an antiknock (as *tetraethyl lead; $(C_2H_5)_4Pb$). Other common compounds include the sulphate ($PbSO_4$), chromate ($PbCrO_4$), and the oxides red lead (Pb_3O_4) and litharge (PbO). These are coloured white, yellow, red, and orange respectively and were formerly extensively used as paint pigments. Most lead salts are insoluble, with the exception of the nitrate, ($Pb(NO_3)_2$), and acetate ($Pb(CH_3COO)_2$). Acute lead poisoning causes diarrhoea and vomiting, but poisoning is more often chronic and characterized by abdominal pain, muscle pains, anaemia, and nerve and brain damage. Children are particularly vulnerable to excess lead levels from car exhaust fumes. At no 82; at wt 207.19; mp 327.50°C; bp 1740°C.

Leadbelly (Huddie Ledbetter; 1888–1949) US Black folksinger and songwriter, whose blues and work songs foreshadowed the folk revival of the 1960s.

leaf An outgrowth from the stem of a ▢plant in which most of the green pigment chlorophyll, used for *photosynthesis, is concentrated. Foliage leaves are typically thin and flat, providing a large surface area for absorbing the maximum amount of light, and they contain pores (stomata) through which exchange of gases and water occurs. They may be simple or compound (composed of a number of leaflets) and with a branching vein system (in *dicotyledons) or parallel veins (in *monocotyledons). Other kinds of leaves include seed leaves (*see* cotyledon) and *bracts. The spines of cacti and the thorns of gorse are modified leaves.

leaf beetle A beetle belonging to a large family (*Chrysomelidae*; 26 000 species) occurring in tropical and temperate regions. Leaf beetles are generally small (less than 12 mm) and brightly coloured. Both the adults and larvae feed on leaves and flowers, although the larvae may also eat roots and stems. Leaf beetles have a wide range of habits: one group is aquatic; in others the larvae carry excrement on their backs (*see* tortoise beetle); and many are serious pests, including the notorious *Colorado potato beetle. ▢insect.

leaf arrangements on the stem

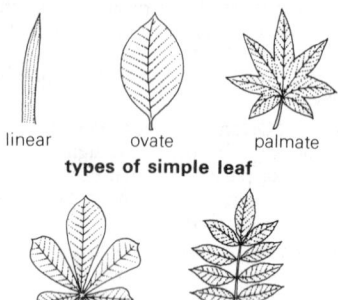

types of simple leaf

types of compound leaf

LEAF *The type and arrangement of the leaves are characteristic for a particular species of plant. For example, the pear has alternate ovate leaves; the horse chestnut has opposite palmate leaves.*

leafcutter ant An *ant, also called a parasol ant, belonging to the genus *Atta* and related genera and occurring in tropical and subtropical America. Armies of leafcutter ants damage crops by cutting pieces of leaf and carrying them to their large underground nests. The leaves are used as a medium on which the ants cultivate their diet of fungi. Subfamily: *Myrmicinae*.

leafcutter bee A solitary *bee, about 10 mm long, belonging to a genus (*Megachile*) of the family *Megachilidae*. It nests in rotten wood and soil, lining the chamber and egg cells with pieces of leaf cut with its strong jaws. Leafcutters are similar to *honeybees in appearance and have pollen-carrying brushes on the underside of their abdomens.

leaf hopper A small slender insect (up to 15 mm long) belonging to the family *Cicadellidae*. Leaf hoppers are often brightly coloured and are powerful jumpers. They feed by sucking plant juices and exude honeydew. Some species are serious pests of plants causing discoloration and weakening or spreading disease. Suborder: *Homoptera*; order: *Hemiptera*.

leaf insect A plant-eating insect, also called a walking leaf, belonging to the family *Phyllidae*. It is excellently camouflaged against foliage, having a broad leaflike body and wings and leaflike flaps on the legs. The female is much larger than the male and lacks hindwings. Order: *Phasmida*.

League of Nations An international organization created (1920) after World War I with the purpose of achieving world peace. The League's Covenant was incorporated into the postwar peace treaties and the USA's failure to ratify the Treaty of *Versailles meant its exclusion from the League. Before 1930 the League, from its Geneva headquarters, organized international conferences, settled minor disputes, and did much useful humanitarian work. However, it failed to deal effectively with the aggression during the 1930s of Japan in China, Italy in Ethiopia (in which the League's use of *sanctions was ineffectual), and Germany, which withdrew from the League in 1933. The UN superseded the League after World War II.

Leakey, Louis Seymour Bazett (1903–72) Kenyan palaeontologist. His work at *Olduvai Gorge uncovered crucial evidence for man's early evolution, notably the *Zinjanthropus* skull dating from 1.75 million years ago. In 1974 his wife **Mary Leakey** (1913–) unearthed hominid remains at Laetolil (N Tanzania) dating back 3.75 million years. Their son **Richard Leakey** (1944–) has made significant fossil finds around Lake Turkana (N Kenya).

Leamington 52 18N 1 31W A spa town in central England, in Warwickshire, noted for its mineral springs. It was named Royal Leamington Spa in 1838 as a result of an earlier visit by Queen (then Princess) Victoria. Motor-car components and gas cookers are manufactured here. Population (1981): 42 953.

Lean, Sir David (1908–) British film director. His early films in collaboration with Noel Coward include *In Which we Serve* (1942), *Blithe Spirit* (1945), and *Brief Encounter* (1946). Adaptations of Charles Dickens' *Great Expectations* (1946) and *Oliver Twist* (1947) were followed by the classic *The Bridge on the River Kwai* (1957). Later films include *Lawrence of Arabia* (1962), *Dr Zhivago* (1965), and *A Passage to India* (1984). He was knighted in 1984.

Leander. *See* Hero and Leander.

leap year. *See* calendar.

Lear A legendary British king, probably invented by Geoffrey of Monmouth, who recounts the story of the old king's division of his kingdom among his three daughters. This story is the basis of Shakespeare's *King Lear* (c. 1605) and is referred to in other works of Elizabethan literature.

Lear, Edward (1812–88) British artist and poet. After 1837 he lived mainly abroad, working as a landscape painter. He died in Italy. He showed great inventiveness in his four books of nonsense verse for children, beginning with *The Book of Nonsense* (1846), and he popularized a form of the limerick.

leasehold. *See* estate.

leasing back An operation to raise liquid cash from a capital asset. The owner of a property, such as a house, sells it on the condition that the buyer leases it back to the seller for a fixed period for a specified rent.

leather Specially treated animal skin. Although any skin can be made into leather, that of domesticated animals, such as cows, sheep, goats, and pigs, is chiefly used. Animals killed exclusively for their skins, such as crocodiles and lizards, produce beautiful but very expensive leather. The skin is first stripped of the fleshy inner and hairy outer layers and then tanned by steeping it in tannin, a preservative. Various finishing processes include rubbing to bring out the grain, as in Morocco leather (goatskin); dyeing; oiling; lacquering for patent leather; and sueding to raise a nap. The uses of leather, which is strong, flexible, and waterproof, range from shoes to saddles. Synthetic leather, made since about 1850, is now usually made from vinyl polymers. *See also* fur; parchment.

leatherback turtle The largest living turtle, *Dermochelys coriacea*, found worldwide. Up to 2.1 m long with a weight of 540 kg, it has no horny external shell and its bones are buried in a ridged leathery brown-black skin. It is a strong swimmer and feeds on marine invertebrates, especially large jellyfish. It is the sole member of its family, *Dermochelyidae*.

Leatherhead 51 18N 0 20W A residential town in SE England, in Surrey. It is the home of the Royal School for the Blind (1799). Population (1981): 40 473.

Leavis, F(rank) R(aymond) (1895–1978) British literary critic. The moral value of the study of literature was the theme of his teaching at Cambridge University and of his critical journal *Scrutiny* (1932–53). His books include *The Great Tradition* (1948), *The Common Pursuit* (1952), and studies of D. H. *Lawrence (1955) and *Dickens (1970).

Lebanon A country in the Middle East, on the E coast of the Mediterranean Sea. It contains two mountain ranges (the Lebanon and Anti-Lebanon Mountains) extending N–S separated by the Beqaa Valley. The population is mixed, having Arab, Phoenician, Crusader, and Greek origins. Roughly half are Christian and half Muslim; political and official posts are rigorously divided between the two religions. *Economy*: Lebanon was once heavily forested and famous for its cedars, but much has been converted to arable use. The fertile Beqaa Valley is the main area of production but has suffered through fighting in the area. The extensive grazing of goats has also seriously depleted the forests and has caused widespread erosion. Industries include traditional crafts and there are two oil refineries, which process oil from Iraq and Saudi Arabia. Until the civil war of 1975–76, international trade, banking, and insurance were the major sources of income. *History*: Lebanon was an early convert to Christianity but in the 7th century broke away from the rest of the Church (*see* Maronite Church) and was invaded by Muslims. Crusaders received support from the Maronites in the 12th and 13th centuries, and Lebanon was held by the Mamelukes during the 14th and 15th centuries and by the Ottoman Turks from the early 16th century to 1918. France was given the mandate over Greater Lebanon after World War I. Lebanon became independent in 1941, although France retained control until 1945. In 1958, at the request of President Camille Chamoun (1900–), US troops were sent to quell a rebellion against his pro-Western policies. Lebanon did not fight in the 1967 and 1973 Arab-Israeli Wars, but Israel has made raids across the border to eliminate Palestinian guerrillas. In 1975, civil war broke out between Christians and Muslims, which after 19 months was brought to an end by intervention from a Syrian-backed Arab Deterrent Force but unrest continued, especially in the S. In 1982 Israel invaded S Lebanon, clashing with Syrian forces in the Beqaa Valley and, after besieging Beirut, forced the Palestine Liberation Organization to leave. Bashir Gemayel (1947–82), the president-elect, was killed in a bomb explosion and his brother, Amin Gemayel (1942–) succeeded him. Violence continued with the United Nations Interim Force in Lebanon (UNIFIL) suffering casualties in separate terrorist bomb attacks (1983). Israel withdrew her forces in 1985 leaving UNIFIL to maintain peace between the Israeli-armed Christians, the Muslims, Druses, and Palestinian guerrillas. Since 1986 various groups have taken foreign hostages. In early 1987 Syrian troops moved into Beirut hoping to end the intermilitia wars. They drove the dominant Shia Muslim Amal militia out of the Muslim sector, but have since clashed with other groups. The former prime minister, Rashid Karami, was killed by a bomb within a month of resigning (1987). Prime minister: Salim Hoss (1930–). Official language: Arabic. Official currency: Lebanese pound of 100 piastres. Area: 10 173 sq km (3927 sq mi). Population (1984 est): 3 500 000. Capital: Beirut.

Lebowa. *See* Bantu Homelands.

Le Brun, Charles (1619–90) French history and portrait painter and designer. During Louis XIV's reign he helped to make Paris the artistic centre of Europe. He became First Painter to Louis XIV, for whom he decorated rooms in Versailles. He became director of the Gobelins tapestry works (1664) and of the French Academy (1683).

Le Carré, John (David Cornwell; 1931–) British novelist. He served in the foreign service in Germany (1961–64). His novels *The Spy Who Came in from the Cold* (1963), *Tinker, Tailor, Soldier, Spy* (1974), and *Smiley's People* (1980), are realistic studies of espionage. Other spy novels include *The Little Drummer Girl* (1983) and *A Perfect Spy* (1986).

Lecce 40 21N 18 11E A town in SE Italy, in Apulia. It has Roman remains, a 12th-century cathedral, and a university (1956). It has a wine industry. Population (1981 est): 91 265.

Lech, River A river in central Europe. Rising in SW Austria, it flows mainly N through S West Germany and joins the River Danube. Length: 285 km (177 mi).

Le Châtelier, Henri-Louis (1850–1936) French chemist, who discovered (1888) **Le Châtelier's principle**, that a chemical system will react to a disturbance of its equilibrium by tending to compensate for the disturbance. He used this principle to assist in the foundation of chemical thermodynamics. He was also the first to use a thermocouple to measure high temperatures and invented an optical pyrometer.

Leconte de Lisle, Charles Marie René (1818–94) French poet. He was born on Réunion Island in the Indian Ocean and settled in Paris in 1846. His poetry, especially in *Poèmes antiques* (1852) and *Poèmes barbares* (1862), contains powerful descriptions of natural physical beauty. His disciples were known as the *Parnassians.

Lecoq de Boisbaudran, Paul-Émile (1838–1912) French chemist, who used the technique of spectroscopy, newly developed by *Bunsen and *Kirchhoff, to discover the element gallium (1874). He also discovered samarium (1879) and dysprosium (1886).

LE CORBUSIER

Le Corbusier (Charles-Édouard Jeanneret; 1887–1965) French architect, born in Switzerland, one of the most inventive artists of the 20th century. The influence of Le Corbusier's buildings and writings has been enormous. He trained under Auguste Perret (1874–1954) and *Behrens. His career falls into two parts. Until World War II he pioneered a rational, almost cubist, form of design, especially with his villas at Garches (1927) and Poissy (1929). Afterwards he became more individual, for example at his extraordinary chapel at Ronchamp (1950; □architecture). He was also concerned with town planning (e.g. *Chandigarh, 1950s) and large-scale housing projects (L'Unité, Marseilles, 1945). As a member of the architectural panel, he also contributed much to the UN buildings in New York (1946).

Le Creusot 46 48N 4 27E A town in E central France, in the Saône-et-Loire department. A major metallurgical centre, it produced the first French locomotives and armour plate. Population (1982): 32 309.

Leda In Greek myth, the wife of Tyndareus, King of Sparta, and mother, either by her husband or by Zeus, of Clytemnestra, Helen, and Castor and Pollux. Helen was born from an egg after Zeus had visited Leda as a swan.

Lederberg, Joshua (1925–) US geneticist, who discovered the phenomenon of transduction in bacteria. Lederberg found that fragments of bacterial DNA could be transmitted from one bacterium to another by a virus. For this, together with his earlier work on bacterial sex factors, Lederberg shared a Nobel Prize (1958) with George *Beadle and Edward *Tatum.

Le Duc Tho (1911–) Vietnamese politician. He was a founder member of the Indochinese Communist Party (1930) and the Viet Minh (1945). His negotiations with Henry Kissinger towards the close of the *Vietnam War were instrumental in securing the ceasefire of 1973; the two men were jointly awarded the Nobel Peace Prize (1974) but Le Duc Tho refrained from accepting it.

Lee, Bruce (Lee Yuen Kam; 1940–73) US film actor and *kungfu expert, whose films include *Enter the Dragon*. He became famous for films made in Hong Kong, after only moderate success in Hollywood.

Lee, Gypsy Rose (Rose Louise Hovick; 1914–70) US entertainer, who brought grace and sophistication to the art of striptease. She appeared in the Ziegfeld Follies in 1936 and in several films. A film and a musical were based on her autobiography, *Gypsy* (1957).

Lee, Robert E(dward) (1807–70) US Confederate commander in the Civil War. He initially saw his role as one of defending his native state of Virginia, using superior mobility to defeat Federal attacks in the Seven Days' battles (1862), and subsequently as one of advance to keep the enemy outside Virginia. Losses at *Gettysburg (1863), however, again forced a defensive strategy. Lee was the first to use fixed field defences to assist manoeuvre, quick to understand his opponents' intentions and capabilities, and an outstanding leader of men.

Lee, Tsung-Dao (1926–) US physicist, born in China, who (working with his countryman Chen Ning *Yang) showed that parity is not conserved in *weak interactions. For this discovery the two shared the 1957 Nobel Prize.

leech A carnivorous aquatic *annelid worm of the class *Hirudinea* (about 300 species). Leeches inhabit fresh and salt water throughout the world and also occur in wet soil and cloud forest. They have one sucker around the mouth and a second at the rear. Leeches can move by "looping," using their suckers. Most feed on the blood of animals and man, using specialized piercing mouthparts, but some species feed on insect larvae and earthworms.

Leech, John (1817–64) British caricaturist, born in London. He studied medicine before publishing his first caricatures, *Etchings and Sketches by A. Pen*, in 1835. He is famous as the principal cartoonist to *Punch* from 1841 until his death and as an illustrator of such books as Dickens' *Christmas Carol*.

Leeds 53 50N 1 35W A city in N England, the largest city in West Yorkshire on the River Aire. Canal links with Liverpool and Goole and the local outcropping of coal assisted in promoting Leeds as an important industrial and commercial centre. Its main industries are clothing, textiles, printing, engineering, chemicals, and leather goods. The university was founded in 1904. Among Leeds' principal buildings is the imposing town hall, built in 1858 in the classical style. The Leeds international piano competition is held here every three years. Population (1981): 448 528.

leek A hardy biennial plant, *Allium porrum*, native to SW Asia and E Mediterranean regions and widely grown in Europe as a vegetable. The bulb is hardly differentiated from the stem, which bears long broad leaves. Cultivated leeks are grown from seed and the stems and leaves are eaten in the first year, before flowering. They are set deep in the soil to ensure blanching. The leek is the national emblem of Wales.

Lee Kuan Yew (1923–) Singaporean statesman; prime minister (1959–). As leader of the People's Action Party (PAP) from 1954, he advocated Singaporean self-government within the British Commonwealth and in 1958–59 helped to draft a constitution in preparation for independence. He agreed, in 1963, to lead Singapore into the

Federation of Malaysia but constant dissensions led to Singapore's withdrawal in 1965. His government is authoritative and pro-Western.

Leeuwarden 53 12N 5 48E A town in the N Netherlands, the capital of Friesland province. An economic centre with trade in cattle and dairy produce, its industries include engineering and glass production. It contains the notable Frisian museum. Population (1981 est): 84 367.

Leeuwenhoek, Antonie van (1632–1723) Dutch scientist, noted for his microscopic studies of living organisms. He was the first to describe protozoa, bacteria, and spermatozoa and he also made observations of yeasts, red blood cells, and blood capillaries. Among his many other achievements, Leeuwenhoek traced the life histories of various animals, including the flea, ant, and weevil, refuting many popular misconceptions concerning their origin. Leeuwenhoek ground over 400 lenses during his lifetime, achieving magnifications of up to 300 times with a single lens.

Leeward Islands 1. A West Indian group of islands in the Lesser Antilles, in the Caribbean Sea extending SE from Puerto Rico to the Windward Islands. 2. A former British colony in the West Indies (1871–1956), comprising Antigua, St Kitts-Nevis-Anguilla, Montserrat, and the British Virgin Islands. 3. A group of islands in French Polynesia, in the Society Islands in the S Pacific Ocean.

Le Fanu, (Joseph) Sheridan (1814–73) Irish novelist. He studied law before becoming a journalist and writer. His best-known books are stories of mystery and suspense, notably the novel *Uncle Silas* (1864) and the collection of stories *In a Glass Darkly* (1872).

leg In human anatomy, the lower limb, which extends from the hip to the foot. The bone of the thigh (*see* femur) is connected by a ball-and-socket joint to the pelvis, permitting a wide range of movements. It forms a hinge joint at the knee with the bones of the lower leg—the shin bone (tibia) and the smaller fibula. This joint is overlain at the front by a bone (the patella, or kneecap) embedded in the tendon of the quadriceps muscle of the thigh. *See* Plate IV.

legal aid A UK scheme enabling a person to have all or part of the costs connected with legal proceedings (including solicitors' and barristers' fees) paid from public funds. In civil proceedings it is available if the applicant's disposable income and capital are less than amounts fixed by government orders. Eligibility is decided by a committee of the Law Society on the basis of means and the reasonableness of the case. In criminal cases, a defendant is eligible if his means are insufficient to pay for his defence, which is a matter decided by the courts. For legal advice and assistance, other than proceedings, a separate arrangement, known as the 'green-form scheme', is available. In practice, legal aid has made civil litigation available to poor individuals; they, and large companies, are now virtually the only litigants to be able to afford it. Legal aid is expected to cost some £600 million p.a. by 1990; proposals are being examined to make it available to a wider section of the community.

Legaspi 13 10N 123 45E A port in the E Philippines, in SE Luzon. It was severely damaged by the eruption of Mount *Mayon in 1815. Hemp and copra are exported. Population (1980): 99 766.

Legendre, Adrien Marie (1752–1833) French mathematician, who made important contributions to number theory and mathematical physics. Due to the jealousy of *Laplace, then the foremost mathematician in France, Legendre never in his lifetime received the recognition that he deserved.

Léger, Fernand (1881–1955) French painter, born in Argentan. He settled in Paris (1900) where, associated with *cubism, he produced robotlike figure paintings, followed by an abstract series entitled *Contrasts of Forms* (1913), consisting of brightly coloured tubes. His experiences in World War I inspired the machine imagery of such paintings as *The City* (1919; Philadelphia) but later he often returned to the human figure.

Broad areas of bright colours are the most characteristic feature of his work. He also painted murals, designed ballet sets, and made the first non-narrative film, *Le Ballet mécanique* (1924).

Leghorn (bird) A breed of domestic fowl originating in Italy and widely used in breeding commercial hybrids for egg laying. It has a full rounded breast, a flat sloping back, a short stout beak, long wattles, and a prominent comb in the male. The plumage can be of various colours, including black, blue, reddish brown, white, and black and white. Weight: 3.4 kg (cocks); 2.5 kg (hens).

Leghorn (port). *See* Livorno.

legionnaires' disease An acute severe pneumonia, caused by the bacterium *Legionella pneumophila*, first described in 1976 after an outbreak among US legionnaires in Philadelphia. Over 30 people died in Stafford, England, as a result of an outbreak in 1985. The treatment is with the antibiotic erythromycin. The route of transmission is not definitely known but air-conditioning systems are suspected.

Legion of Honour (French name: Légion d'Honneur) A French order of knighthood, established by Napoleon in 1802. Its five ranks, to which foreigners are admitted, are knight of the grand cross, grand officer, commander, officer, and chevalier. Its grand master is the president of France.

Legnica (German name: Liegnitz) 51 12N 16 10E An industrial town in SW Poland. Its manufactures include metal products, textiles, and chemicals. Population (1982 est): 91 400.

Leguminosae A worldwide family of herbs, shrubs, and trees (about 7000 species), which includes many important crop plants, such as peas, beans, clovers, and alfalfa. They all have compound leaves and the fruit is a pod containing a single row of seeds. Both pods and seeds are rich in protein. Most species possess root nodules that contain nitrogen-fixing bacteria and leguminous crops replenish nitrogen in the soil (*see* nitrogen cycle).

Lehár, Franz (Ferencz L.; 1870–1948) Hungarian composer. He studied at the Prague conservatoire and after a period as a military band conductor (1894–99) turned to the composition of operettas, of which *The Merry Widow* (1905) was his greatest success. Others include *The Count of Luxembourg* (1911) and *Land of Smiles* (1923).

Le Havre 49 30N 0 06E A port in N France, in the Seine-Maritime department on the English Channel at the mouth of the River Seine. Severely damaged in World War II, its harbour was subsequently rebuilt and now maintains an important transatlantic cargo service and a car-ferry service to England. Population (1982): 198 700.

Lehmann, Lilli (1848–1929) German operatic soprano. She was taught by her mother. During a long career she sang many roles, including Brünnhilde in *Die Walküre*, Isolde, Donna Anna in *Don Giovanni*, and Leonora in *Fidelio*.

Lehmann, Lotte (1885–1976) German soprano, a US citizen from 1938. She studied in Berlin with Mathilde Mallinger (1847–1920) and became a renowned dramatic soprano; her most famous role was the Marschallin in Richard Strauss' opera *Der Rosenkavalier*.

Leibniz, Gottfried Wilhelm (1646–1716) German philosopher and mathematician. He put forward a coherent philosophy, which is summarized in his two philosophical books, *New Essays on the Human Understanding* (c. 1705) and *Theodicy* (1710), and numerous essays. Leibniz' best-known doctrine is that the universe consists of an infinite set of independent substances (monads) in each of which a life force is present. In creating the world, God took account of the wishes of monads and this led to a rational harmony in the "best of all possible worlds"—a view satirized in *Voltaire's *Candide*. As a rationalist Leibniz founded the distinction between the logically necessary and the merely contingent truth. His claim to have invented the calculus was disputed by *Newton.

Leicester 52 38N 1 05W A city in central England, the

administrative centre of Leicestershire. Ancient Ratae Corita-norum on the Fosse Way, Leicester has many Roman remains including the Jewry Wall and sections of the forum and baths. Parts of the Norman castle also remain. St Martin's Church became a cathedral in 1927 and the university was established in 1957. The principal industries are hosiery, knitwear, foot-wear, engineering, printing, plastics, and electronics. Popula-tion (1983 est): 282 300.

Leicester, Robert Dudley, Earl of (c. 1532–88) English courtier; the fifth son of the Duke of *Northumberland. Dud-ley's good looks attracted the attention of Elizabeth I, who made him Master of the Horse (1558) and then a privy council-lor (1559). It was rumoured that he might marry the queen after the death (for which some believed him responsible) of his wife Amy Robsart (c. 1532–60). His incompetent command (1585–87) of an English force in support of the Revolt of the Netherlands against Spain led to his recall but he retained Eliz-abeth's favour until his death. A strong supporter of the Protes-tant cause, he was attacked, probably by a Roman Catholic, in *Leicester's Commonwealth* (1584).

VIVIEN LEIGH *In* Gone with the Wind *(1939), with Leslie How-ard.*

Leicestershire A county in the East Midlands of England. Since 1974 it has included the former county of Rutland. The River Soar, flowing N, separates Charnwood Forest from the uplands of the E. Its fertile soil makes it an important agricul-tural county with dairy and livestock farming in the E and ara-ble farming in the W. Stilton cheese is produced in the E. Coal is extracted in the W; there are also reserves in the Vale of Belvoir. Hosiery has long been the county's staple industry; others in-clude footwear at Leicester and bell founding at Loughbor-ough. Area: 2553 sq km (986 sq mi). Population (1983 est): 863 700. Administrative centre: Leicester.

Leichardt, (Friedrich Wilhelm) Ludwig (1813–48) German explorer in Australia. In 1844–45 he led an expedition from Moreton Bay, near Brisbane (Queensland), to the Gulf of Car-pentaria. He subsequently disappeared while trying to cross Australia from E to W. His unusual character was used by Pat-rick White in the novel *Voss* (1957).

Leiden (English name: Leyden) 52 10N 4 30E A city in the W Netherlands, in South Holland province. In 1574 it survived a Spanish siege by cutting the dykes and flooding the country-side. Its famous university was founded in 1575 as a reward for this heroic defence. During the 17th and 18th centuries it was an artistic and educational centre. The painters Rembrandt and

Lucas van Leyden were born here. Industries include textiles and metallurgy. Population (1981 est): 103 246.

Leif Eriksson (11th century) Icelandic explorer; the son of *Eric the Red. He was converted to Christianity by Olaf I Tryggvason of Norway around 1000 and on his way to promote the faith in Greenland Leif, off course, became the first Europe-an to reach America. He landed in a region he called Vinland (perhaps Newfoundland or Nova Scotia). His story is told in Icelandic sagas.

Leigh, Vivien (Vivien Hartley; 1913–67) British actress. In the theatre, she played many leading Shakespearian roles, fre-quently appearing with Laurence *Olivier, her husband from 1937 to 1960. Her films include *Gone with the Wind* (1939), in which she played the heroine Scarlett O'Hara, and *A Streetcar Named Desire* (1951).

Leighton of Stretton, Frederic, Baron (1830–96) British painter and sculptor of classical subjects, born in Scarborough. He studied in Europe and established his reputation with *Cimabue's Madonna Carried in Procession* (1855), which was purchased by Queen Victoria. In 1860 he settled in London. He became president of the Royal Academy in 1878 and was enno-bled in 1896.

Leinster A province in the SE Republic of Ireland. It consists of the counties of Carlow, Dublin, Kildare, Kilkenny, Laoighis, Longford, Louth, Meath, Offaly, Westmeath, Wexford, and Wicklow. It incorporates the ancient kingdoms of Meath and Leinster. Area: 19 632 sq km (7580 sq mi). Population (1981): 1 790 521.

Leipzig 51 20N 12 21E A city in S East Germany, near the confluence of the Rivers Elster, Pleisse, and Parthe. Important international trade fairs have been held in Leipzig since the middle ages. It was also the centre of the German book and publishing industry until World War II. Notable buildings in-clude the 15th-century Church of St Thomas and Auerbach's Keller, an inn that provided the setting for Goethe's *Faust*. A famous musical centre, the city has associations with J. S. Bach and Mendelssohn. The university was founded in 1409 and renamed Karl Marx University in 1952. Leipzig is the country's second largest city and one of its chief industrial and commer-cial centres. Its industries include iron and steel, chemicals, printing, and textiles. Population (1982): 558 994.

Leipzig, Battle of (*or* Battle of the Nations; 16–19 October, 1813) The battle in which Napoleon was defeated by an alliance including Prussia, Russia, and Austria. The engagement culminated in the allies driving the French into Leipzig and then storming the city. The French army was shattered and its remnants retreated westwards across the Rhine, ending Napo-leon's empire in Germany and Poland.

leishmaniasis A tropical disease caused by infection with parasitic protozoans of the genus *Leishmania* (see Flagellata), which are transmitted to man by the bite of sandflies. The dis-ease may affect the skin, causing open sores or ulcers, or the internal organs, principally the liver and spleen (this form of leishmaniasis is called **kala-azar**). Treatment is by means of drugs that destroy the parasites.

Leith 55 59N 3 10W A port in E central Scotland, in Lothian Region on the Firth of Forth, now an integral part of Edin-burgh. There are shipbuilding, engineering, and chemical in-dustries.

leitmotif (German: leading theme) A short musical phrase characterizing an object, person, state of mind, event, etc. *Wagner developed the technique of constructing large-scale compositions from leitmotifs in his mature operas, such as the cycle *Der Ring des Nibelungen*.

Leitrim (Irish name: Contae Liathdroma) A county in the NW Republic of Ireland, in Connacht bordering on Donegal Bay. Mainly hilly, descending to lowlands in the S, it con-tains several lakes, notably Lough Allen. Agriculture consists chiefly of cattle and sheep rearing; potatoes and oats are also grown. Area: 1525 sq km (589 sq mi). Population (1981): 27 609. County town: Carrick-on-Shannon.

Leix. *See* Laoighis.

Leland, John (c. 1506–52) English antiquary. He served as chaplain and librarian to Henry VIII. The manuscripts and antiquities he collected during an extensive tour of England, recorded in his *Itinerary* (1710), were used by many later antiquaries.

Lely, Sir Peter (Pieter van der Faes; 1618–80) Portrait painter, born in Germany of Dutch parents. He studied and worked in Haarlem before settling in London (1641), where he was patronized by Charles I and later Cromwell. As court painter to Charles II from 1661, he produced his best-known works, including his *Windsor Beauties* (Hampton Court) and *Admirals* (National Maritime Museum, London).

Lemaître, Georges Édouard, Abbé (1894–1966) Belgian priest and astronomer, who originated the *big-bang theory of the universe (1927). Lemaître based his theory on *Hubble's suggestion that the universe is expanding; it went unnoticed until *Eddington drew attention to it.

Léman, Lac. *See* Geneva, Lake.

Le Mans 48 00N 0 12E A city in NW France, the capital of the Sarthe department. Its many historical buildings include the cathedral (11th–15th centuries) in which Queen Berengaria (died c. 1290), the wife of Richard the Lionheart, is buried. The Le Mans Grand Prix, a 24-hour motor race, is held here annually. Le Mans is an agricultural, industrial, and commercial centre. Population (1982): 150 331.

Lemberg. *See* Lvov.

lemming A *rodent belonging to the subfamily *Microtini* (which also includes voles), found in northern regions of Asia, America, and Europe. They range from 7.5 to 15 cm in length and have long thick fur. When their food of grass, berries, and roots is abundant, they breed at a great rate but when food is scarce they migrate southwards, often in large swarms crossing swamps, rivers, and other obstacles. Although able to swim, they sometimes drown through exhaustion. (Contrary to popular belief, they do not deliberately drown themselves.) Chief genera: *Dicrostonyx* (collared lemmings; 4 species), *Lemmus* (true lemmings; 4 species). Family *Cricetidae*. □mammal.

Lemnos (Modern Greek name: Límnos) A Greek island in the N Aegean Sea. Remains of the most advanced Neolithic communities in the Aegean have been found here. Area: 477 sq km (184 sq mi). Population (1981): 15 721.

lemon A small tree or shrub, *Citrus limon*, 3–6 m high, probably native to the E Mediterranean but widely cultivated in subtropical climates for its fruit. Its fragrant white flowers produce oval fruits with thick yellow skin and acid-tasting pulp rich in vitamin C. The juice is used as a flavouring in cookery and confectionery and as a drink. Family: *Rutaceae*.

lemon sole A *flatfish, *Microstomus kitt*, also called lemon dab, found in the NE Atlantic and North Sea. Up to 45 cm long, its upper side is red-brown or yellow-brown with light or dark marbling. It is an important food fish. Family: *Pleuronectidae*.

lemur A small *prosimian primate belonging to the family *Lemuridae* (16 species), found only in Madagascar and neighbouring islands. Lemurs are mostly arboreal and nocturnal and often live in groups, feeding mainly on fruit, shoots, and leaves and also insects. The ring-tailed lemur (*Lemur catta*) is 70–95 cm long including the tail (40–50 cm) and is mainly terrestrial, sheltering among rocks and in caves. Dwarf lemurs (subfamily *Cheirogaleinae*) are only 25–50 cm long including the tail (12–25 cm).

Lemures In Roman religion, maleficent spirits of the dead. They haunted their former homes and were ritually appeased at the annual festival of the Lemuria, held in May.

Lena, River The longest river in the Soviet Union. Rising

in S Siberia, W of Lake Baikal, it flows mainly NE to the Laptev Sea. Its large delta, about 30 000 sq km (11 580 sq mi) in area, is frozen for about nine months of the year. Length: 4271 km (2653 mi).

Le Nain A family of French painters, natives of Laon, who established a workshop together in Paris (c. 1680). The individual contributions of **Antoine Le Nain** (c. 1588–1648), **Louis Le Nain** (c. 1593–1648), and **Mathieu Le Nain** (1607–77) are uncertain, since their works were not signed and some were probably joint efforts. Louis probably painted the dignified peasant scenes, such as *The Peasant's Meal* (Louvre); small-scale works on copper, often of family life, are credited to Antoine. All three became members of the newly established French Academy in 1648.

Lenclos, Ninon de (Anne de L.; 1620–1705) French courtesan, whose salon was the meeting place for many prominent literary and political figures of her day. She herself was much interested in Epicurean philosophy. Her lovers included *La Rochefoucauld and *Sévigné.

Lendl, Ivan (1960–) Czech tennis player. He won the US Open championship in 1985 and 1986 but was beaten in the Wimbledon final (1986) by *Becker.

Lend-Lease Act (1941) Legislation introduced by President Roosevelt enabling Congress to lend or lease information, services, and defence items to any country vital to US defence. Britain and its World War II allies immediately received planes, tanks, raw materials, and food.

L'Enfant, Pierre-Charles (1754–1825) US architect and town planner of French birth. His principal achievement was his design for Washington, DC (1791), with its traditional French layout of long parallel avenues and dramatic focal points. It was executed in 1901.

Lenglen, Suzanne (1899–1938) French tennis player. She won the Wimbledon singles seven times between 1919 and 1926, when she turned professional. Her grace and daring dress helped to make tennis a spectator sport.

LENIN *Sitting at the centre, surrounded by his colleagues in the St Petersburg Union for the Struggle for the Liberation of the Working Class (1895).*

Lenin, Vladimir Ilich (V. I. Ulyanov; 1870–1924) Russian revolutionary and first leader of communist Russia. Lenin became a Marxist after the execution (1887) of his brother Aleksandr for attempting to assassinate the tsar, Alexander III. In 1893 Lenin joined a revolutionary group in St Petersburg (subsequently renamed *Leningrad), where he practised as a lawyer. In 1895 he was imprisoned and in 1897, exiled to Siberia, where he married (1898) Nadezhda Krupskaya, a fellow Marxist, with whom he worked closely throughout his career. In 1902 he published *What Is to Be Done?*, in which he emphasized the role of the party in effecting revolution. This emphasis led to a split in the

Russian Social Democratic Workers' Party between the *Bolsheviks under Lenin and the *Mensheviks. After the failure of the *Revolution of 1905, Lenin again went into exile, settling in Zurich in 1914, where he wrote *Imperialism, the Highest Stage of Capitalism* (1917). In April, 1917, after the outbreak of the *Russian Revolution, Lenin returned to Russia. Calling for the transfer of power from the Provisional Government to the soviets (workers' councils), he was forced into hiding and then to flee to Finland. Lenin returned in October to lead the Bolshevik revolution, which overthrew the Provisional Government and established the ruling Soviet of People's Commissars under Lenin's chairmanship. He made peace with Germany and then led the revolutionaries to victory against the Whites in the civil war (1918–20). He founded (1919) the Third *International and initiated far-reaching social reforms, including the redistribution of land to the peasants, but in response to the disastrous economic effects of the war he introduced the *New Economic Policy (1921), which permitted a modicum of free enterprise.

In 1918 Lenin was injured in an attempt on his life and a series of strokes from 1922 led to his premature death. *See also* Leninism.

Leninabad (name until 1936: Khodzhent) 59 55N 30 25E A city in the S central Soviet Union, in the Tadzhik SSR on the River Syr Darya. Located on the ancient *Silk Road, it supports a major silk industry. Consumer goods are also produced. Population (1981 est): 130 000.

Leninakan (name from 1840 until 1924: Aleksandropol) 40 47N 43 49E A city in the Soviet Union, in the NW Armenian SSR. Its textile industries are of major importance. Population (1981 est): 213 000.

Leningrad (name from 1703 until 1914: St Petersburg; name from 1914 until 1924: Petrograd) 59 55N 30 25E The second largest city in the Soviet Union and the capital of the Leningrad autonomous region (*oblast*), at the head of the Gulf of Finland on the River Neva. It is a major industrial and commercial centre and its port, although frozen between January and April, is one of the largest in the world. Industries include heavy engineering (particularly shipbuilding), metallurgy, electronics, chemicals, car manufacture, and light industries; the city is an important railway junction. Leningrad is rich in baroque and neoclassical buildings and is noted for its broad boulevards and many bridges and canals. The most notable buildings include the Peter-Paul Fortress (Leningrad's oldest building, founded in 1703), the Winter Palace (1754–62, rebuilt 1839), the Gostiny Dvor (1761–85), and Kazan cathedral (1801–11). The city is an important cultural centre; it has a university (1918) and many museums, of which the Hermitage Museum, founded by Catherine the Great in 1764, is the most famous with its fine collection of European paintings. *History*: the city was founded (1703) by Peter the Great as a "window on Europe" and was the capital of Russia from 1712 until 1918, replacing Archangel as Russia's main seaport. In the late 19th century it developed as an important industrial centre and from its labour force emerged several revolutionary parties, later united by Lenin to form the St Petersburg Union for the Struggle for the Liberation of the Working Class. In 1905 a general strike took place and on Bloody Sunday (9 January, 1905) more than a thousand people were killed in a march on the Winter Palace. Leningrad was also prominent in the 1917 revolution (*see* Russian Revolution). During World War II the city withstood a siege by the Germans (8 September, 1941–27 January, 1944), in which nearly a million people perished. In 1941 a road was constructed across frozen Lake Dadoga over which supplies could be brought. Leningrad was awarded the status of "Hero City" in recognition of its ordeal. Population (1981 est): 4 676 000.

Leninism Developments in the theory of scientific socialism (*see* Marxism) by V. I. *Lenin. His theory of imperialism is an account of the final stage of capitalism, in which it dominates the entire world, decisive control resting with finance capital

(banks) as opposed to industrial capital. Because of the worldwide nature of capitalism, socialist revolution becomes possible even in economically underdeveloped countries, the "weak link" of imperialism. According to his theory of the revolutionary party, the most conscious element of the proletariat provides the leadership for the rest of the working class and the peasantry in organizing the overthrow of the capitalist class.

Lenin Peak (Russian name: Pik Lenina) 39 21N 73 01E The second highest mountain in the Soviet Union, in the Trans-Altai range. Height: 7134 m (23 406 ft).

Leninsk-Kuznetskii (name from 1864 until 1925: Kolchugino) 40 37N 72 15E A city in the central S Soviet Union, in the RSFSR in the Kuznetsk Basin. Coalmining has been the most important industrial activity since its foundation in 1864. Population (1980 est): 133 000.

Lennon, John (1940–80) British rock musician and founding member of the *Beatles. After the Beatles disbanded Lennon recorded solo albums, several of which featured his second wife, **Yoko Ono** (1933–). His most distinctive recording was *Imagine* (1971). He was assassinated in 1980.

Le Nôtre, André (1613–1700) French landscape gardener. Le Nôtre perfected the French version of the formal garden with his use of imposing vistas and was imitated throughout Europe. His first complete garden was at Vaux-le-Vicomte (1656–61) but his largest and most perfect was for Louis XIV at *Versailles, on which he worked for nearly 30 years.

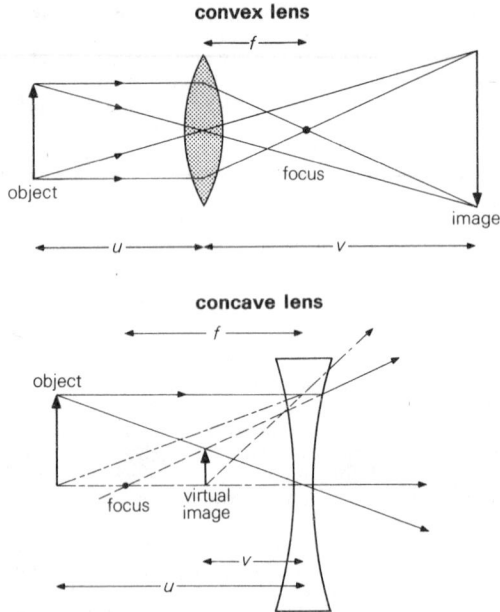

LENS *The lines representing light rays show how a convex lens gives a real inverted image and how a concave lens gives an upright virtual image.*

lens A piece of transparent material, usually glass, quartz, or plastic, used for directing and focusing beams of light. The surfaces of a lens have a constant curvature; if both sides curve outwards at the middle the lens is called convex, if they curve inwards it is concave. The image formed by a lens may be real, in which case the rays converge to the image point (a converging lens), or virtual, in which the rays diverge from the image point (a diverging lens). The focal length of a lens is the distance from the lens at which a parallel beam of light is brought to a focus. If the focal length of the lens is f, the rays from an object distance u from the lens are focused at a distance v from the lens, where $1/f = 1/u + 1/v$ and u, v, and f all obey certain sign conventions.

Lens 50 26N 2 50E A town in N France, in the Pas-de-Calais department. It was badly damaged in both World Wars, especially in World War I. The centre of an important coalmining area, it has metallurgical and chemical industries. Population (1982): 38 307.

Lent The Christian period of fasting and penance preceding Easter. Beginning on *Ash Wednesday, the Lenten fast covers 40 days, in emulation of Christ's 40 days in the wilderness (Matthew 4.2). In the middle ages the fast was more or less strictly observed, especially with regard to the prohibition on eating meat, but since the Reformation the rules have been generally relaxed in both Roman Catholic and Protestant Churches.

lentil An annual herb, *Lens culinaris*, native to the Near East but widely cultivated. Each pod produces 1-2 flat round green or reddish seeds, which are rich in protein and can be dried and stored for use in soups, stews, etc. Family: *Leguminosae*.

Lenya, Lotte (Caroline Blamauer; 1900-81) Austrian singer and character actress, famous for her interpretations of the songs by her husband, the composer Kurt *Weill.

Lenz's law The direction of an induced current in a conductor is such as to oppose the cause of the induction. For example, a current induced by a conductor cutting the lines of flux of a magnetic field would produce a magnetic field of its own, which would oppose the original magnetic field. Named after Heinrich Lenz (1804-65).

Leo (Latin: Lion) A large conspicuous constellation in the N sky near Ursa Major, lying on the *zodiac between Virgo and Cancer. The brightest stars are the 1st-magnitude Regulus, which lies at the base of the **Sickle of Leo**, and the 2nd-magnitude Denebola and Algeiba.

Leo (I) the Great, St (d. 461 AD) Pope (440-61). One of the greatest medieval popes, Leo was largely successful in his attempts to extend papal control in the West after the fall of the western Roman Empire, but he failed to find support in the East. His treaties with the invading *Huns (452) and *Vandals (455) protected Rome from their onslaughts. His Christology, expressed in the *Epistola Dogmatica* (or *Tome of Leo*; 449), defined the doctrine of the Incarnation and was accepted at the Council of Chalcedon (451). Feast day: 11 April.

Leo (III) the Isaurian (c. 675-741 AD) Byzantine emperor (717-41). He repulsed a Muslim attack on Constantinople in 718 and finally secured Asia Minor in 740 after a great victory over the Muslims at Acroïnon. In 730 he issued a decree that established the policy of *iconoclasm (the destruction of Christian images).

Leo III, St (d. 816 AD) Pope (795-816). After his election he was opposed by a Roman faction and was forced to flee to *Charlemagne, who supported his return to Rome. There, in 800, Leo crowned Charlemagne Emperor of the West—an act that marks the start of the Holy Roman Empire. His rule was noted for its munificent church building. He was canonized in 1673. Feast day: 12 June.

Leo IX, St (Bruno of Egisheim; 1002-54) Pope (1049-54), the first of the great medieval reforming popes. At successive councils clerical marriage and simony were condemned and, assisted by Hildebrand (later *Gregory VII) and Humbert of Moyenmoutier (c. 1000-61), he attempted to free the papacy from imperial control. Rival claims with the Normans to gain control of S Italy resulted in Leo's defeat at the battle of Civitella (1053). His conflict with the Eastern Church led to the schism between Rome and Constantinople (1054; see Filioque). Feast day: 19 April.

Leo X (Giovanni de' Medici; 1475-1521) Pope (1513-21), the second son of Lorenzo the Magnificent (*see* Medici), by

whose influence Giovanni was made a cardinal in 1489. His pontificate was marked by political vacillation and financial disasters but lavish patronage of the arts. He negotiated the Concordat of Bologna (1516) with Francis I, giving the French Crown almost total control over ecclesiastical appointments in France.

Leo XIII (Vincenzo Gioacchino Pecci; 1810-1903) Pope (1878-1903). Elected after a long career as a papal diplomat, Leo fostered relations between the papacy and European powers, the USA, and Japan. He also encouraged learning, foreign missions, and lay piety. His encyclical *Rerum novarum* (*Of New Things*; 1891), while condemning socialism, emphasized the duty of the Church in matters of social justice.

Leoben 47 23N 15 06E A town in central Austria, in Styria. A lignite-mining centre, it has a university of mining and iron-founding industries (1840). Population (1981): 32 131.

León (*or* León de los Aldamas) 21 10N 101 42W A city in central Mexico. It is a commercial and distribution centre; industries include the manufacture of footwear and leather goods. Population (1980): 655 809.

León 42 35N 5 34W A city in NW Spain, in León. Formerly capital of the kingdom of León, it declined after the 13th century. Medieval in atmosphere, it has a notable gothic cathedral. Population (1981): 131 134.

León 12 24N 86 52W A city in W Nicaragua. Moved to its present site after the original city near Lake Managua was destroyed by an earthquake in 1610, it was the capital of Nicaragua until 1855. It is the country's cultural centre and has a university (1812). Industries include textiles, distilleries, tanneries, and food processing. Population (1981): 158 577.

LEONARDO DA VINCI *This head of an old man, drawn after 1515, is possibly a self-portrait of the artist.*

Leonardo da Vinci (1452-1519) Italian artistic and scientific genius of the *Renaissance, born in Vinci, the illegitimate son of a notary. He trained in Florence under *Verrocchio and painted the *Adoration of the Magi* (Uffizi) for the monks of S Donato a Scopeto (1481). In 1482 he became painter, engineer, and designer to Duke Ludovico Sforza in Milan, where he painted the fresco of the *Last Supper* (Sta Maria delle Grazie) and the first version of the *Virgin of the Rocks* (Louvre). His promised equestrian sculpture glorifying the Duke was never cast but the studies of horses for the project have survived. After the French invasion of Milan (1499), he returned to Florence, becoming military engineer and architect (1502) to Cesare *Borgia. Paintings in this period include the *Battle of Anghiari* for the Palazzo Vecchio, *The Virgin and Child with St John the Baptist and St Anne* (painting, Louvre; cartoon, National Gallery, London) and the *Mona Lisa* (Louvre). Some of his paintings were left unfinished and others, because of his experimental techniques, failed to survive. After working again in Milan (1506-13) and in Rome (1513-15), he was invited by Francis I to France (1516), where he spent his last years in Cloux near Amboise. His notebooks reveal his wide range of interests, including anatomy, botany, geology, hydraulics, and mechanics. □ p. 715.

Leoncavallo, Ruggiero (1858-1919) Italian composer of operas. Only *I Pagliacci* (1892) has met with continuing success, although he composed over 15, including a trilogy on Italian historical subjects and, a year after Puccini, his own *La Bohème* (1897).

Leonidas I (d. 480 BC) King of Sparta (?490-480), following the suicide of his half-brother Cleomenes. Leonidas was the hero of the battle of *Thermopylae, in which with indomitable courage he and a small force held the pass for three days before being killed by the Persians.

Leonov, Leonid (1899-) Soviet novelist and playwright. His moral and psychological themes were most powerfully expressed in his early novels, notably *Barsuki* (*The Badgers*; 1924) and *Vor* (*The Thief*; 1927). His later novels are politically and stylistically more orthodox.

leopard A large spotted *cat, *Panthera pardus*, found throughout Africa and most of Asia. Leopards are slender, up to 2.1 m long including the 90-cm tail, having a yellow coat spotted with black rosettes. Colour variations, such as the *panther, sometimes occur. Leopards are solitary and nocturnal, typically lying in wait in a tree for their prey, which includes monkeys, dogs, and antelopes.

Leopardi, Giacomo (1798-1837) Italian poet. His pessimistic philosophy, which is most fully expressed in the long poem *La ginestra* (1836), was largely conditioned by his unhappy home background, his poor health, and his failure in love. He is best known for the intense lyric poetry of *I canti* (1831). He died of cholera in Naples.

leopard lily A perennial herbaceous plant, *Belamcanda chinensis*, also called blackberry lily, native to E Asia and widely planted as a garden ornamental. Growing over 1 m tall from an underground stem (rhizome), it has sword-shaped leaves, orange-spotted red flowers, and blackberry-like clusters of seeds. Family: *Iridaceae*.
The name is also given to several other garden flowers, including the snake's head *fritillary and a North American lily (*Lilium pardalinum*).

leopard seal A solitary Antarctic *seal, *Hydrurga leptonyx*, of the pack ice. Leopard seals are fast agile hunters, feeding mainly on penguins. Grey, with dark spots and blotches, females grow to 3.7 m and males to 3.2 m. Family: *Phocidae*.

Leopold I (1640-1705) Holy Roman Emperor (1658-1705). Leopold was ultimately successful against the Turks, who had besieged Vienna in 1683, freeing most of Hungary from Turkish dominance by 1699. He also came into conflict with Louis XIV of France, whose claims to the Spanish throne he opposed in the War of the *Spanish Succession. Under Leopold, Vienna became a great European centre.

Leopold I (1790-1865) The first King of the Belgians (1831-65). He defended Belgium against William III of the Netherlands (1817-90; reigned 1849-90), who refused to recognize Belgian independence until 1838. A leading diplomat in Europe, at home he encouraged educational and economic reforms. A member of the House of Saxe-Coburg-Saalfield (previously Gotha), he helped to negotiate the marriage of his niece Queen Victoria to Prince Albert. He was briefly (1816-17) married to Charlotte (1796-1817), the daughter of George IV of Great Britain.

Leopold II (1797-1870) Grandduke of Tuscany (1824-59). Initially a liberal who granted a constitution in 1848, he became increasingly reactionary after a brief period in exile in 1849 and was forced by radical opposition to abdicate.

Leopold II (1835-1909) King of the Belgians (1865-1909), who sponsored Stanley's exploration of the Congo region of Africa. In 1885 he obtained European recognition of his sovereignty over the Congo Free State, which was annexed as the Belgian Congo in 1908.

Leopold III (1901-83) King of the Belgians (1934-51). He surrendered to the Germans in *World War II, provoking opposition to his return to Belgium in 1945 and forcing his abdication in favour of his son *Baudouin.

Léopoldville. *See* Kinshasa.

Lepanto, Battle of (7 October, 1571) A naval battle off Lepanto, Greece, in which the *Holy League routed the Ottoman navy, which was threatening to dominate the Mediterranean. The Christian force, commanded by *John of Austria, was composed of about 30 000 fighting men, of which over 7000 died. Some 15 000 Turks were killed or captured and 10 000 Christian galley slaves were freed.

Lepidodendron An extinct genus of treelike pteridophytes that—with *Calamites—were dominant forest trees of the Carboniferous period (370-280 million years ago), their fossilized remains forming coal seams. Some species were over 30 m high and 1 m wide. Class: *Lycopsida* (clubmosses, etc.).

Lepidoptera. *See* butterflies and moths.

Lepidus, Marcus Aemilius (died c. 13 BC) Roman politician and protégé of Julius Caesar. After Caesar's death, Lepidus joined Antony and Octavian in the second Triumvirate (43), which divided responsibility for the empire, but in 42 they deprived him of his provincial governorships. In 36 Lepidus attempted to secure Sicily and was forced by Octavian to retire.

leprosy A chronic disease, occurring almost entirely in tropical countries, caused by the bacterium *Mycobacterium leprae* (which is related to the tuberculosis bacillus). The incubation period is usually one to three years and—contrary to popular belief—leprosy is contracted only after close personal contact with an infected person. In the lepromatous form of the disease lumps appear on the skin, which—together with the nerves—becomes thickened and progressively destroyed, resulting in disfigurement and deformity. Eyes, bones, and muscles may also be affected. Tuberculoid leprosy usually produces only discoloured patches on the skin associated with loss of sensation in the affected areas. There are now potent drugs—sulphones—available to cure the disease.

Leptis Magna An ancient trading centre near present-day Homs (Libya). Founded by the Phoenicians (6th century BC) Leptis' importance increased during Roman imperial times; ruins of unusually splendid public buildings attest its former grandeur.

lepton A group of elementary particles, consisting of the *electron, *muon, *tau particle, *neutrinos, and their antiparticles. They take part only in the *weak and *electromagnetic interactions; together with *quarks and photons they are thought to be the only truly elementary particles. *See* particle physics.

Le Puy 45 03N 3 53E A town in S France, the capital of the Haute-Loire department. It has a 12th-century cathedral and is famous for its lace making. Population (1975): 29 024.

Lérida 41 37N 0 38E A town in NE Spain, in Catalonia. It possesses two cathedrals and a massive Moorish castle. An agricultural centre, its industries include glass and silk. Population (1981): 109 573.

Lermontov, Mikhail (1814–41) Russian poet and novelist. His early Romantic poetry, published while he was a student at Moscow University, was greatly influenced by *Byron. As an army officer and an observer of high society he developed the cynical attitudes expressed in his novel *A Hero of Our Time* (1840). He was twice exiled to the Caucasus, the first time for a poem attacking the court, and was killed in a duel.

Lerner, Alan Jay (1918–86) US lyricist and librettist, who collaborated with the composer Frederick *Loewe in the musicals *Brigadoon* (1947), *My Fair Lady* (1956), and *Camelot* (1960). Lerner also wrote the film scripts for *An American in Paris* (1951) and *Gigi* (1958).

Lerwick 60 09N 1 09W A town in N Scotland, the administrative centre and chief port of the island authority of Shetland, on the E coast of Mainland. The most northerly town in the UK, it has fishing and hand-knitting industries. Population (1985 est): 8000.

Lesage, Alain-René (1668–1747) French novelist. His best-known work is the picaresque novel *Gil Blas* (1715–35). He also made translations and satirical adaptations of Spanish plays as well as writing over 60 plays and librettos of his own.

lesbianism. *See* homosexuality.

LEPROSY *Mother Teresa in her leprosy hospital in Calcutta.*

Lesbos (Modern Greek name: Lésvos) A Greek island in the E Aegean Sea, situated close to the mainland of Turkey. Settled by Aeolians about 1000 BC, it is associated with the development of Greek lyric poetry (especially through the work of Alcaeus and Sappho). Lesbos was a member of the Delian League and the chief town, Mytilene, was made a free port in the era of Roman power. Olives, grapes, and cereals are grown here and there is sardine fishing. Area: 1630 sq km (629 sq mi). Population (1981): 104 620.

Leschetizky, Theodor (1830–1915) Polish pianist and piano teacher. His method influenced a generation of pianists, including Paderewski. He was a pupil of Czerny in Vienna and

moved to St Petersburg in 1852, becoming head of the piano department at the conservatoire.

Lescot, Pierre (c. 1510–78) French architect. Lescot's most influential work was the square court of the *Louvre (1546), the proportions and ornamentation of which set the style of French classicism. Little else of his work has survived.

Lesotho, Kingdom of (name until 1966: Basutoland) A small country in SE Africa, enclosed by South Africa. It is largely mountainous, rising to 3350 m (11 000 ft). Most of the inhabitants are *Sotho. *Economy*: chiefly agricultural, the main crops being maize, wheat, and sorghum. Livestock is important but soil erosion due to overgrazing is a serious problem. The main exports, along with diamonds, are cattle, wool, and mohair. Some industry, including tourism, is being developed, but a large proportion of the male population still work in South African mines. *History*: in 1868, following warfare with the Orange Free State, Basutoland came under British protection on the request of the Sotho chief, Moshesh. In 1871 it was annexed by the Cape Colony but came under direct British administration in 1884. In 1910 it was placed under the authority of the British High Commission in South Africa and in 1966 became an independent kingdom within the Commonwealth under King Moshoeshoe II (1939–   ). A state of emergency existed from 1970 to 1973 and the political climate continued to be unsettled; Chief Leabua Jonathan (1914–87) was deposed as prime minister in a military coup in 1986. Official languages: Sesotho and English. Official currency: South African rand of 100 cents. Area: 30 340 sq km (11 716 sq mi). Population (1983): 1 438 000. Capital: Maseru.

Lesseps, Ferdinand de (1805–94) French diplomat, who supervised the construction of the Suez Canal, which was completed in 1869. A subsequent project to construct the Panama Canal ended in disaster when Lesseps was prosecuted for embezzling funds.

Lesser Antilles (former name: Caribbees) A West Indian group of islands, comprising a chain extending from Puerto Rico to the·N coast of Venezuela. They include the Leeward and Windward Islands, Barbados, Trinidad and Tobago, and the Netherlands Antilles.

Lessing, Doris (1919–   ) British novelist. Born in Iran and brought up in Rhodesia, she came to England in 1949. Political and social themes predominate in her fiction, notably the sequence of five novels entitled *Children of Violence* (1952–69) and *The Golden Notebook* (1962). Later novels include *Memoirs of a Survivor* (1974), a series of science-fiction works (1979–83), and *The Good Terrorist* (1985).

Lessing, Gotthold Ephraim (1729–81) German dramatist and writer. After studying theology and medicine, he worked as a translator and critic. His *Miss Sara Sampson* (1755) was the first successful German tragedy to reject the classical French model and to use middle-class protagonists, while his comedy *Minna von Barnhelm* (1767) demonstrates the *Enlightenment ideal of reason. In 1765 he was involved in an unsuccessful attempt to create a German national theatre; in his influential essays, the *Hamburgische Dramaturgie* (1767–69), he developed his dramatic theories.

Letchworth 51 58N 0 14W A town in SE England, in Hertfordshire. Built in 1903 as England's first garden city, preserving the original village, Letchworth has engineering, printing, and rubber industries. Population (1981): 32 835.

Le Tellier, Michel. *See* Louvois, Michel Le Tellier, Marquis de.

Lethbridge 49 43N 112 48W A city in W Canada, in S Alberta. Founded in 1870 as a coalmining centre, it has become an agricultural, distribution, and research centre, housing the University of Lethbridge (1967). Most industry is agriculturally based. Population (1984): 58 586.

Lethe In Greek and Roman mythology, a river in the underworld, the water of which caused those who drank it to forget their former lives.

Leto In Greek mythology, a daughter of the *Titans loved by Zeus. During her pregnancy she 'was not welcomed anywhere because of the fear of Hera and was forced to give birth to Apollo and Artemis on the barren island of Delos.

letter of credit A letter from a bank to a foreign bank authorizing the payment of a specified sum to the person or company named. They are widely used as a means of paying for goods in foreign trade. An **irrevocable letter of credit** cannot be cancelled by the purchaser or the issuing bank. A **confirmed letter of credit** guarantees payment to the beneficiary should the issuing bank fail to honour it. A confirmed irrevocable letter of credit opened at a first-class bank is a safe basis for trading, although it must be negotiated before its expiry date. Unconfirmed or revocable letters of credit do not have great value.

Lettish. See Latvian.

lettres de cachet (French: letters of the seal) Administrative and judicial orders issued by the Kings of France. They were much misused during the 17th and 18th centuries to authorize arrest and imprisonment without trial or appeal. As symbols of the monarchy's despotism they were abolished (1790) during the French Revolution.

lettuce An annual herb, *Lactuca sativa*, probably from the Near East and widely cultivated as a salad plant. It has a tight rosette of juicy leaves, rich in vitamin A, and is usually eaten fresh or cooked in soups. Cos lettuce has long crisp leaves and oval heads while cabbage lettuce has round or flattened heads and often curly leaves. Family: *Compositae.

Leucippus (5th century BC) Greek philosopher. He developed from the teachings of *Parmenides the theory that there are two ultimate realities: (1) an infinite number of tiny irreducible particles (atoms), randomly circulating in (2) empty space. This theory is remarkably close to modern *atomic theory. See also Democritus of Abdera.

leucite A feldspathoid mineral of composition KAl(SiO₃)₂, occurring as whitish or greyish crystals in some volcanic rocks deficient in silica. Where sufficiently concentrated it is a source of potash.

Leuckart, Karl Georg Friedrich Rudolph (1822-98) German zoologist, who founded the science of parasitology. Leuckart described the life cycles of tapeworms and the liver fluke and revealed the importance of wormlike parasites in causing diseases in man.

leucocyte (*or* white blood cell) A colourless □blood cell, up to 0.02 mm in diameter, of which there are normally 4000-11 000 per cubic millimetre of blood. There are several kinds, all involved in the body's defence mechanisms. Granulocytes (*or* polymorphs), which have granules in their cytoplasm, and monocytes ingest and feed on bacteria and other microorganisms that cause infection (*see also* phagocyte). The lymphocytes are involved with the production of *antibodies. Cancer of the white blood cells is called *leukaemia.

leucotomy The surgical operation of interrupting the course of white nerve fibres within the brain. It is performed to relieve uncontrollable pain or emotional tension in very severe and intractable psychiatric illnesses, such as severe depression, chronic anxiety, and obsessional neurosis. The original form of the operation—prefrontal leucotomy (*or* lobotomy)—had the serious complications of epilepsy, apathy, and irresponsibility. Modern procedures make small and selective lesions and side effects are uncommon. See also psychosurgery.

Leuctra, Battle of (371 BC) The battle in which the reorganized Theban army under *Epaminondas crushed the Spartan invasion of Boeotia in Sparta's first major defeat on land. Sparta's resultant loss of influence allowed Thebes a short-lived ascendency in Greece.

leukaemia A disease in which the blood contains an abnormally large number of white blood cells (*see* leucocyte). Leukaemia is a type of cancer of the blood-forming tissues, which undergo uncontrolled proliferation to produce many immature and abnormal white blood cells that do not function properly. Leukaemias may be acute or chronic, depending on the rate of progression of the disease. They are also classified according to the type of white cell affected. For example acute lymphocytic leukaemia (affecting the lymphocytes) occurs most commonly in children and young adults; it can now often be controlled by means of radiotherapy or *cytotoxic drugs. Chronic leukaemias occur more often in old people and may not need any treatment.

Leuven. See Louvain.

Levant A former name for the lands on the E coast of the Mediterranean Sea, now within Turkey, Syria, Lebanon, and Israel. The French mandates (1920-46) of Syria and Lebanon were known as the Levant States.

Le Vau, Louis (1612-70) French *baroque architect. His first building, the Hôtel Lambert, Paris (1642), was remarkable for its ingenious room planning. As first architect to the Crown from 1654, he completed the Louvre, built the Collège des Quatre Nations (begun 1661), and designed the first extension of *Versailles (1669), which was later obliterated by the work of *Hardouin-Mansart. His most famous building is Vaux-le-Vicomte (begun in 1657), a chateau outside Paris built for Nicolas Fouquet.

level 1. An instrument (also called a spirit level) for indicating whether or not a surface is level. It consists of a sealed glass tube containing spirit (alcohol) and a bubble of gas. The tube is mounted so that the wooden or metal frame supporting it is level when the bubble is in the centre of the tube. **2.** An instrument for obtaining a horizontal line of sight. It consists of a telescope with cross hairs on both sights together with a parallel tubular spirit level, mounted on a tripod. Levelling is achieved by means of screw legs on the tripod table.

Levellers An extremist English Puritan sect, active 1647-49. Led by the pamphleteer John *Lilburne, they were drawn mainly from the lower ranks of the army. They campaigned for a written constitution, radical extension of the franchise, and abolition of the monarchy and of other social distinctions (hence their name). Cromwell's refusal to execute this programme led to mutinies (1647, 1649). After suppression of the last of these, the Levellers lost their identity and influence. See also Diggers.

Leven, Alexander Leslie, 1st Earl of (1580-1661) Scottish general. After over 30 years with the Swedish army, he led the Scots against Charles I of England in the *Bishops' Wars. In the English Civil War he had charge of Charles between the king's surrender to the Scots (1646) and his delivery to the English (1647).

Leven, Loch A lake in Scotland, in SE Tayside Region. It has seven islands, one of which contains the ruins of a castle in which Mary, Queen of Scots, was imprisoned (1567-68). Length: 6 km (3.7 mi). Width: 4 km (2.5 mi).

Leverhulme, William Hesketh Lever, 1st Viscount (1851-1925) British soap manufacturer and the founder with his brother James Lever of the Lever Brothers company. He introduced profit-sharing, pensions, medical care, and other benefits for his employees and in 1888 established the model industrial town *Port Sunlight. He was an MP from 1906 to 1910.

Leverkusen 51 02N 6 59E A city in NW West Germany, in North Rhine-Westphalia on the River Rhine. It is the site of the large Bayer chemical works. Population (1983 est): 157 400.

Leverrier, Urbain Jean Joseph (1811-77) French astronomer, who predicted the existence of the planet *Neptune (1846) after investigating anomalies in the orbit of Uranus. John *Adams had made similar calculations but the planet was actually first observed by Johann Galle (1812–1910), the German astronomer, in 1846 on information supplied by Leverrier.

Lévesque, René (1922–   ) French Canadian politician. An advocate of French separatism, in 1968 he founded the Parti Québecois and in 1976 became Quebec's prime minister. He is the author of *Option Quebec* (1968).

Leviathan An animal mentioned in several passages (Job, Isaiah, Psalms) of the Old Testament and variously interpreted as referring to the whale or crocodile. Leviathan was mythologically associated with evil and the devil.

Lévi-Strauss, Claude (1908–   ) French anthropologist, the founder of structural anthropology. After teaching in America, Lévi-Strauss became professor of ethnology at the University of Paris (1948) and professor of anthropology at the Collège de France (1959). His works include *The Elementary Structures of Kinship* (1949), *Structural Anthropology* (1958), and *From Honey to Ashes* (1967).

Levites In ancient Israel, the descendants of Levi, the son of Jacob and Leah, who formed one of the 12 *tribes of Israel and became the priestly caste. They were not allocated territory in Palestine but only scattered settlements with grazing rights and they were partly supported by offerings. After the *Babylonian exile, the priesthood was confined to Levites descended from Aaron.

Leviticus The third book of the Old Testament, attributed to Moses and concerned with religious and ceremonial law. Its purpose is to give instruction in the laws governing sacrifice and purification, in which the priestly caste of *Levites officiate. It also relates the laws governing diet, hygiene, the five annual national feasts, the use of land, and personal chastity.

Lewes 50 52N 0 01E A market town in SE England, the administrative centre of East Sussex, on the River Ouse. At the battle of Lewes (1264) Henry III was defeated by the rebel barons under Simon de Montfort. *Glyndebourne is nearby. Population (1981): 77 507.

Lewes, George Henry (1817–78) British author and literary critic. His most successful work was his *Life of Goethe* (1855), but he did much to publicize Comte's positivism in his *Biographical History of Philosophy* (1845–46) and *Comte's Philosophy of the Sciences* (1853). From 1854 he lived with the novelist George *Eliot.

Lewis, Carl (Frederick Carleton L.; 1961–   ) Black US athlete, who won four gold medals (long jump, 100 m, 200 m, 4 × 100 m relay) at the 1984 Olympics, equalling Jesse *Owens' 1936 performance.

Lewis, C. Day. *See* Day Lewis, C(ecil).

Lewis, C(live) S(taples) (1898–1963) British scholar and writer. He taught at Oxford University from 1925 to 1954 and was professor of medieval and Renaissance English at Cambridge University from 1954 to 1963. He wrote science-fiction including *Out of the Silent Planet* (1938), children's books chronicling the land of Narnia, and works on religious themes, notably *The Problem of Pain* (1940), *The Screwtape Letters* (1942) and *Mere Christianity* (1952).

Lewis, Matthew Gregory (1775–1818) British novelist, known as Monk Lewis. His major work is the influential gothic novel, *The Monk* (1796), written while he was in the diplomatic service in Germany. In 1817 he visited his inherited estates in Jamaica and died on the return voyage.

Lewis, (Harry) Sinclair (1885–1951) US novelist. He established his reputation with *Main Street* (1920), a satire on provincial materialism. His other social satires include *Babbitt* (1922), in which he portrayed the archetypal well-meaning but dehumanized businessman, *Arrowsmith* (1925), and *Elmer Gantry* (1927). He was the first US writer to win the Nobel Prize (1930).

Lewis, (Percy) Wyndham (1882–1957) British novelist and painter. After studying art in London and Paris, he helped

found □vorticism, the manifestos of which were published in *Blast*, a journal he cofounded with Ezra Pound in 1914. In many polemical works and brilliant satirical novels, which include *The Apes of God* (1930) and the trilogy *The Human Age* (1928–55), he sustained a continual attack on the liberal cultural establishment.

Lewis and Clark expedition (1804–06) A journey of exploration across the American continent by Meriwether Lewis (1774–1809) and William Clark (1770–1838). They ascended the Missouri, crossed the Rockies, and went down the Columbia River to the Pacific, exploring the Yellowstone River on the return journey. Promoted by Thomas Jefferson, the expedition established the US claim to the Louisiana Purchase.

Lewisham A borough of SE Greater London, created in 1965 from the former metropolitan boroughs of Deptford and Lewisham. Population (1983 est): 231 900.

lewisite (*or* chlorovinyl dichloroarsine; $ClCH:CHAsCl_2$) A colourless volatile liquid that causes blistering of the skin and is used as a war gas. It can be destroyed by oxidizing agents such as *bleaching powder. Named after the US chemist W. L. Lewis (1878–1943).

Lewis with Harris The largest island of the Outer Hebrides, separated from the coast of NW Scotland by the Minch. Often referred to as separate islands, Lewis in the N is linked with Harris by a narrow isthmus; its most northerly point is the Butt of Lewis. The main occupations are crofting, sheep farming, fishing, and the weaving of the famous Harris tweed. Area: 2134 sq km (824 sq mi). Population (1981): 23 390. Chief town: Stornoway.

lexicography The compilation of dictionaries. Dictionaries can be monolingual (dealing with only one language) or bi- or multi-lingual (giving equivalents of words in other languages). Both were known in antiquity. Monolingual dictionaries differ in the style and fullness of the definitions, in the audience for which they are intended (e.g. for native speakers or foreign learners), and in the principles on which they are compiled. Some are on historical principles (listing definitions of a word in historical order) while others take the language as it is at the time of compilation (listing definitions in order of current usage). Some dictionaries are prescriptive in that they set out to tell the user how the language should be used; most modern dictionaries tend to be only descriptive, recording without comment the way words are currently used. Almost all dictionaries contain information about spelling and meaning; many also offer guidance on pronunciation, usage, inflected forms of words, *etymology, etc.

The earliest English dictionary was *A Table Alphabeticall of Hard Words* (1604) by Robert Cawdrey; the most famous are Samuel *Johnson's *Dictionary* (1755) and the *Oxford English Dictionary on Historical Principles* (1884–1928; chief editor Sir James *Murray). Both the latter works contain illustrative quotations. The best-known American dictionary is Noah *Webster's *American Dictionary of the English Language* (1828). Both the Oxford and Webster's have several updated and shortened modern versions. The most recent dictionary of the English language is the *Collins English Dictionary* (1979).

Lexington 38 02N 84 37W A city in the USA, in Kentucky. A major horse-breeding centre, Lexington is the market and distribution centre for E Kentucky's farm produce, oil, and coal. The University of Kentucky was established here in 1865. Population (1980): 204 165.

Lexington and Concord, Battle of (19 April, 1775) The first battle in the *American Revolution. British troops intending to destroy American stores were attacked at Lexington by militiamen alerted by Paul *Revere. Going on to Concord they destroyed the stores but were then attacked and forced to retreat to Boston.

Leyden. *See* Leiden.

Leyden jar An early form of *capacitor, consisting of a

glass jar coated with tinfoil on part of its inner and outer surfaces. Named after Leiden (*or* Leyden), the town in the Netherlands in which it was invented.

Leyland 53 42N 2 42W A town in NW England, in Lancashire. Leyland has an important commercial motor vehicle industry and also produces tyres, paints, carpets, and cottons. Population (1981): 26 567.

Leyte Gulf, Battle of (23-26 October, 1944) The battle in World War II in which a US armada of 250 000 men defeated almost the entire Japanese navy. It initiated the reconquest of the Philippines and US command of the Pacific.

Lhasa 29 41N 91 10E A city in W China, the capital of Tibet, surrounded by mountains. As the traditional centre of *Tibetan Buddhism, it is the site of many temples, monasteries, and of the Potala, the former palace of the Dalai Lama, the priest-ruler. Tibet's trading centre, it has many traditional handicrafts and some light industry. *History*: the Tibetan capital since 1642, it was closed to foreigners in the 19th century. Before the Chinese occupation (1951) monks comprised half the population. Since then many Tibetans have fled, including the Dalai Lama following the 1959 uprising, while much Chinese immigration has taken place. Population (1982 est): 110 000.

Liaodong Peninsula (*or* Liaotung Peninsula) A mountainous peninsula in NE China, in Liaoning province. After rivalry with Russia (1895-1905; *see* Sino-Japanese War; Russo-Japanese War) Japan occupied its strategic S harbours (1905-45).

Liaoning A province in NE China, on the Yellow Sea in S Manchuria. The Japanese controlled it (1905-45) and developed its industry. Rich in coal and iron, it is an important industrial area. Area: 150 000 sq km (58 500 sq mi). Population (1982): 35 721 693. Capital: Shenyang.

Liaoyang 41 16N 123 12E A city in NE China, in Liaoning province, one of the oldest Chinese settlements in Manchuria. Industries include food processing, textiles, and engineering. Population (1980 est): 347 000.

Libau. *See* Liepaja.

Libby, Willard Frank (1908-80) US chemist, who was awarded the Nobel Prize in 1960 for his discovery of *radiocarbon dating. He also perfected a similar technique in which water is dated from its tritium content.

libel. *See* defamation.

Liberal Party (Australia) A conservative political party, formed in 1944 from the *United Australia Party, which had performed disastrously in the 1943 election. A Liberal-Country Party (*see* National Country Party) coalition won the election of 1949 and under the leadership successively of Robert *Menzies, Harold *Holt, John *Gorton, and William *McMahon held office until 1972. Under Malcolm *Fraser the Liberals again held power from 1975 until 1983.

Liberal Party (UK) A political party that grew out of the *Whig party. The heyday of the party was from the mid-19th century to World War I, under the prime ministers *Gladstone, *Campbell-Bannerman, *Asquith, and *Lloyd George. Conflict between Asquith and Lloyd George led to a split in the party after World War I, and in 1922 the Labour Party replaced the Liberals as the official opposition. The Liberals enjoyed a small revival under the leadership of *Grimond (1956–67) and then Jeremy *Thorpe (1967–76). Under the leadership of David *Steel, the party came to an agreement (the Lib-Lab pact) to support the Labour government in return for consultation (1977–78) and in 1981 formed the Liberal-SDP Alliance with the Social Democratic Party, which led to merger discussions after a poor showing in the 1987 election.

Liberec (German name: Reichenberg) 50 48N 15 05E A town in Czechoslovakia, in Bohemia on the River Neisse. In 1938 it was a centre of the Sudeten-German movement. Population (1980 est): 85 000.

Liberia, Republic of A country in West Africa, on the Atlantic Ocean. Coastal plains rise to higher ground inland and to mountains in the N; much of the land is covered with tropical rainforest. Most of the population belongs to indigenous tribes, including the Kpelle, Bassa, and Kru, with a minority who are descended from American slaves. *Economy*: agriculture is extensive, the main food crops being rice and cassava. There have been considerable efforts to increase rice production, including the growing of swamp as well as hill rice and there has been large-scale development in the sugar industry with aid from China. The main cash crop is rubber, some of it grown under concession to US companies. Foreign investment in other areas includes the exploitation of Liberia's rich mineral resources, which form the basis of the country's economy, especially high-grade iron ore and diamonds. These, together with rubber and timber, are the main exports. Ships are easily registered in Liberia and, with many foreign vessels, its merchant fleet is the largest in the world. *History*: it was founded in 1822 by the American Colonization Society as a settlement for freed American slaves. In 1847 it became the Free and Independent Republic of Liberia with a constitution based on that of the USA. It has had considerable US aid, and from the 1920s the Firestone Company, developing rubber resources, played an important part in the economy, as have many other foreign companies. Liberia also has close economic ties with Sierra Leone. In 1980 the president Dr William R. Tolbert, Jr (1913–80), was assassinated in a military coup led by Master Sergeant Samuel Doe, who won a general election in 1985. Official language: English. Official currency: Liberian dollar of 100 cents. Area: 111 400 sq km (43 000 sq mi). Population (1983 est): 2 091 000. Capital and main port: Monrovia.

libido The sexual drive. In *psychoanalysis the libido (like the death instinct) is a fundamental source of energy for all mental life, and changes in psychosexual development are responsible for many distortions of the adult personality.

Libra (Latin: Scales) A constellation in the S sky, lying on the *zodiac between Scorpius and Virgo. The brightest star is of 2nd magnitude.

library A collection of books, gramophone records, photographic materials, etc., organized for private or public consultation or borrowing. In ancient Mesopotamia libraries were offshoots of royal archives (*see* Nineveh). Aristotle's teaching library at his *Lyceum inspired the Ptolemaic rulers of Egypt to found a library at Alexandria that became the cultural centre of Hellenism. Sizable private libraries were assembled by Roman scholars, such as *Cicero, and Roman and Byzantine emperors founded large public libraries. With the growth of Christian literature it became customary to attach libraries to churches. Monastic libraries grew from the requirement of daily study of religious treatises, especially among the *Benedictines. Late medieval and Renaissance nonecclesiastical collections form the basis of many of today's great libraries, such as the *Bodleian, the Vatican (present building opened in 1571), the *Bibliothèque Nationale, the *British Library, and the US *Library of Congress. In response to increasing literacy in the 19th century most European countries developed a municipal library network.

The explosion in the numbers both of items held by libraries and of library users has placed increasing demands on **library science**, a discipline that is concerned chiefly with the acquisition, classification, and cataloguing of items in a library. The acquisition of materials is dictated by a library's selection policy, which is influenced by its budget, storage space, and readers' requirements. The systems of classification of materials into subject fields that are most widely used today are the *Universal Decimal Classification, based on the *Dewey Decimal Classification. and the Library of Congress system. Catalogues, or lists, of holdings generally consist of an alphabetized author catalogue and a subject catalogue. The practice of printing catalogues, with regularly issued supplements, has been complemented since the late 19th century by card catalogues, which facilitate the incorporation of new items. More recent developments include the use of *microcopy systems for recording holdings and of automatic *data processing, which aid the centralization on a regional, national, or international scale of library information. Centralization demands standardization and all publications now bear an International Standard Book Number (ISBN) or an International Standard Serial Number (ISSN), by which an item may be quickly identified.

Formal training for libraries was pioneered by the American Library Association (founded 1876). The sister organization in the UK (founded 1877) campaigned for the first school of librarianship, established within London University in 1917. Technical and other specialist libraries have their own association, ASLIB (Association of Special Libraries and Information Bureaux), formed in 1925. The International Library Committee was set up in 1927 to try to achieve internationally accepted conventions in such matters as the transliteration of Cyrillic characters into the Roman alphabet, and UNESCO has a division concerned with libraries.

Library of Congress The national library of the USA founded in 1800. First housed in the Capitol, it was moved to its present site in Washington in 1897. It contains over 60 million items, and its system of classification is widely used in academic libraries.

libretto (Italian: little book) The text of an opera or operetta. The most notable early librettists were the Italians Apostolo Zeno (1668–1750) and Pietro Metastasio (1698–1782), whose elevated style eventually provoked a reaction in favour of greater realism. Dramatists whose plays have been used as libretti include von *Hofmannsthal, *Maeterlinck, and Oscar *Wilde. *Wagner and *Berlioz wrote their own libretti. Notable partnerships between librettists and composers include Calzabigi (1714–95) and Gluck, da Ponte (1749–1838) and Mozart, Boito and Verdi, and Gilbert and Sullivan.

Libreville 0 25N 9 25E The capital of Gabon, a port in the NW on the Gabon Estuary. It was founded by the French in the 19th century, when freed slaves were sent there. The National University was established in 1970. Population (1983): 350 000.

Librium. See benzodiazepines.

Libya (official name: Popular Socialist Libyan Arab Jamahiriya) A country in N Africa, on the Mediterranean Sea. It consists chiefly of desert, with a narrow coastal plain, rising to the Tibesti Mountains along its southern border and is divided into the three main areas (provinces until 1963) of Cyrenaica, Tripolitania, and Fezzan. The population is mainly of Berber and Arabic origin. *Economy*: between 1955 and 1970 considerable prospecting for oil took place during which time major deposits were discovered, notably at Zelten (1959). Libya is now one of the world's major oil producers and oil constitutes about 95% of exports in value; liquefied natural gas is also exported. Subsistence agriculture is important, livestock farming of sheep, goats, and cattle being the main agricultural occupation, nomadic in the S. The aridity of the land restricts crop production to the narrow coastal areas and scattered oases; barley, wheat, and olives are grown here and esparto grass in semidesert areas. Recently programmes have been implemented to improve agriculture, such as in the Fezzan. Manufacturing industry is based largely on traditional crafts. *History*: the area was important within the Roman Empire. During the 16th century it came under Turkish domination and in 1912 was annexed by Italy. It was the scene of heavy fighting in World War II; the French occupied Fezzan and the British occupied Cyrenaica and Tripolitania. In 1951 the United Kingdom of Libya was formed from the federation of these three areas and the Emir of Cyrenaica, Mohammed Idris Al-Senussi (1889–1983), became its first king. He was deposed in a coup led by Col Moammar al-*Gaddafi in 1969 and Libya was pro-

claimed a republic. The Revolutionary Command Council was established to rule the country. In 1973 Gadafi introduced a cultural revolution based on Islamic principles. Since 1969 Libya has been firmly aligned against Israel and has been accused of using terrorist methods abroad; in 1986 such terrorist activity prompted punitive bombing raids on Tripoli and Benghazi by US planes. Official language: Arabic; English and Italian are also spoken. Official currency: Libyan dinar of 1000 millemes. Area: 1 759 540 sq km (679 216 sq mi). Population (1982 est): 3 500 000. Capital: Tripoli.

lichee. See litchi.

lichens A large group of plants (*Lichenes*; about 15 000 species) consisting of two components, an alga and a fungus, in a mutually beneficial association. Millions of algal cells (the phycobiont) are interwoven with fungal filaments (the mycobiont) to form the lichen body (a thallus), which may be crusty, scaly, leafy, or stalked and shrublike in appearance. Lichens occur in almost all areas of the world, mainly on tree trunks, rocks, and soil, and can survive in extremely harsh conditions. They normally reproduce asexually by fragmentation, *budding, or by producing special structures (soredia), consisting of a few algal cells enmeshed with fungal threads. Lichens are an important source of food for browsing animals of tundra regions (*see* reindeer moss) and they are used by man for food, dyes, medicine, in perfume, and as pollution indicators. *See also* crottle; oak moss; orchil; rock tripe.

Lichfield 54 42N 1 48W A city in central England, in Staffordshire. Lichfield cathedral (13th–14th centuries) is noted for its three spires. Dr Johnson was born here. Population (1981): 25 600.

Lichtenstein, Roy (1923–) A leading US painter of *pop art. His one-man show of comic-strip paintings in 1962 pioneered the use of mass-media techniques in the context of noncommercial art. His works include *Whaam* (1963; Tate Gallery).

Liddell Hart, Sir Basil Henry (1895–1970) British soldier and military theorist. He served throughout World War I and wrote the official manual on infantry training (1920). In 1927 he became a military journalist and his advocacy of mechanized warfare and airpower led to his appointment as adviser (1937–38) to the secretary for war *Hore-Belisha.

Lidice 50 03N 14 08E A small mining village in W Czechoslovakia. On 10 June, 1942, it was destroyed by the Nazis in revenge for the assassination of Reinhard Heydrich, their local administrative head. The 400 or so inhabitants were either shot or deported to concentration camps. The site is now a memorial garden.

Lie, Trygve (Halvdan) (1896–1968) Norwegian Labour politician and international civil servant; the first secretary general of the UN (1946–52). At the UN he dealt with the first Arab-Israeli War and UN armed aid to South Korea in the *Korean War. Soviet opposition to his Korean policies resulted in his resignation.

Liebig, Justus, Baron von (1803–73) German chemist; one of the earliest investigators of organic compounds. His work on fulminates (1920) was followed by the development of a technique for measuring the proportion of carbon and hydrogen in a compound by burning it and determining the amount of carbon dioxide and water released (1831). His later work was concerned with biochemistry and agricultural chemistry. His name is also connected with the Liebig condenser, a much used piece of laboratory equipment.

Liebknecht, Wilhelm (1826–1900) German socialist. He participated in the *Revolution of 1848 and was forced to flee Germany, living in Britain, where he worked with Karl Marx. Returning to Germany in 1862, he was expelled from Prussia in 1865 for his socialist activities but in 1867 became a member of the North German Reichstag. His opposition to the Franco-Prussian War (1870-71) brought imprisonment but he subsequently became a leader of what became (1891) the Social Democratic Party. His son **Karl Liebknecht** (1871-1919) was among the few socialists who refused to support the war effort in 1914. In 1915 he helped to found the revolutionary *Spartacus League, which he led with Rosa *Luxemburg. They were both murdered following the unsuccessful communist revolt of 1919.

Liechtenstein, Principality of A small country in central Europe, between Switzerland and Austria. Mountains rise from the Rhine Valley to heights of over 2500 m (8000 ft). *Economy*: although there is still a considerable amount of farming, the balance of the economy has shifted since World War II to light industry, including textiles, ceramics, tools, instruments, and food processing. Tourism and the sale of postage stamps are also important sources of revenue. *History*: the principality was formed from the union of the counties of Vaduz and Schellenberg in 1719 and was part of the Holy Roman Empire until 1806. It formed a customs union with Switzerland in 1923. Until 1984 women were banned from voting in national elections. Head of state: Prince Francis Joseph II (1906-). Head of government: Hans Brunhart. Official language: German. Official religion: Roman Catholic. Official currency: Swiss franc of 100 centimes (*or* Rappen). Area: 160 sq km (62 sq mi). Population (1980): 25 215. Capital: Vaduz.

lie detector An instrument designed to detect whether a person is lying by measuring such factors as blood pressure, respiration rate, skin conductivity, and pulse rate. A sudden change in these factors in a person being questioned is taken to indicate that he is under stress and may be telling a lie. Lie detectors are not usually accepted in a court of law.

Liège (Flemish name: Luik) 50 38N 5 35E A city in E Belgium, on the River Meuse. It has many old churches, including St Martin's (692 AD). Its university was founded in 1817. The centre of a former coalmining area, its industries include the manufacture of armaments, iron, textiles, and paper. Population (1985 est): 250 000.

Liegnitz. See Legnica.

Liepaja (German name: Libau) 56 30N 21 00E A port in the Soviet Union, in the W Latvian SSR on the Baltic Sea. It was founded by the Teutonic Knights (1263), passing to Russia in 1795. The independent Latvian Government met here in 1918. A naval base, it has shipbuilding and metallurgy industries. Population (1981 est): 108 000.

Lif and Lifthrasir In Norse mythology, a man and woman destined to sleep during the destruction of the world (*see* Ragnarök), awaking afterwards to found a new race.

Lifar, Serge (1905-) Russian ballet dancer and choreographer. He joined Diaghilev's Ballets Russes in 1923 and from 1932 to 1958 was ballet master at the Paris Opéra Ballet, which he revitalized with his experimental choreography. His ballets include *Prométhée* (1929), *Icare* (1935), and *Phèdre* (1950).

life The property that enables a living organism to assimilate nonliving materials from its environment and use them to increase its size and complexity (the process of growth), to repair its existing tissues, and to produce new independent organisms that also possess the properties of life (the process of reproduction). *See also* animal; plant.

Life on earth is thought to have originated between 4500 and 3000 million years ago. The atmosphere then consisted chiefly of methane, hydrogen, ammonia, and water vapour, from which simple organic molecules (such as amino acids, proteins, and fatty acids) were formed as a result of energy supplied by solar radiation, lightning, and volcanic activity. The first "cells" may have arisen spontaneously as simple envelopes of protein and fat molecules. However, the crucial steps towards life would probably have been the inclusion in such a cell of both the enzyme molecules necessary to

perform primitive fermentations and the nucleic acid molecules, such as RNA and DNA, capable of directing the metabolic processes of the cell and of self replication, i.e. passing on this information to succeeding generations. These early cells are thought to have arisen in the sea, deriving their energy from the fermentation of simple organic molecules. In the course of time increasingly efficient biochemical pathways evolved, including the process of trapping light energy in cellular pigments, enabling the first simple green plants to develop the process of photosynthesis. This led to the gradual build-up of oxygen in the atmosphere, which started about 2000 million years ago; by about 400 million years ago the *ozone layer in the upper atmosphere was sufficiently dense to shield the land from harmful ultraviolet radiation, enabling plants and animals to survive. With increasing oxygen levels, aerobic respiration—the most efficient method of energy utilization—was adopted by most living organisms.

The factors involved in the origination of life on earth have prompted a search for similar conditions on other planets and in other solar systems, but so far no evidence of life elsewhere in the universe has been discovered. *See* astrobiology.

lifeboat 1. In the UK, a powerful motorboat, especially designed to right itself in the event of capsize and equipped with safety devices, used by the *Royal National Lifeboat Institution (RNLI) as an emergency vessel in the event of a disaster near the shore. 2. A boat carried aboard a ship, used for accommodating passengers and crew if the ship has to be abandoned.

life cycle The progressive series of stages through which a species of organism passes from its *fertilization or production by asexual means to the same stage in the next generation. The simplest life cycles occur by asexual *reproduction, producing offspring similar to the parent. Life cycles involving sexual reproduction are much more complex and the young do not necessarily resemble the adults: marine crustaceans, for example, pass through several different larval stages before becoming adult. In many plants and animals there is a succession of individuals showing an alternation of sexual and asexual reproduction before completing the cycle (*see* alternation of generations).

Liffey, River A river in the E Republic of Ireland, rising in the Wicklow Mountains and flowing mainly W and NE through Dublin to Dublin Bay. Length: 80 km (50 mi).

ligament A strong fibrous tissue that joins one bone to another at a *joint. Ligaments are flexible but inelastic: they increase the stability of the joint and limit its movements to certain directions. Unusual stresses on a joint often damage ("pull") a ligament, as occurs in a "twisted" ankle.

ligature Any material, such as silk, gut, cotton, or wire, used to tie a blood vessel (to stop bleeding) or the base of a tumour (to constrict it). Ligatures are widely used in surgery and are available in various thicknesses.

liger. See tigon.

Ligeti, György (1923-) Hungarian composer. He worked in the West German Radio's studio for electronic music in Cologne (1957-58) and settled in Vienna. His compositions are largely experimental, often involving indeterminacy of pitch and rhythm, and include *Volumina* (1961-62) for organ, a Requiem (1963-65), *Continuum* (1968) for harpsichord, and *Melodien* (1971) for orchestra.

light The form of *electromagnetic radiation to which the eye is sensitive. It forms the part of the electromagnetic spectrum from 740 nanometres (red light) to 400 nanometres (blue light), white light consisting of a mixture of all the colours of the visible spectrum. The nature of light has been in dispute from earliest times, *Newton supporting a corpuscular theory in which a luminous body was believed to emit particles of light. This theory adequately explained reflection and geometric optics but failed to explain *interference and *polarized light. The wave theory, supported in the 19th century by *Fresnel and *Foucault, adequately explains these phenomena and achieved a mathematical basis when *Maxwell showed that light is a form of electromagnetic radiation. The wave theory, however, does not explain the *photoelectric effect and *Einstein reverted to a form of the corpuscular theory in using the *quantum theory to postulate that in some cases light is best regarded as consisting of energy quanta called photons. The present view, expressing *Bohr's concept of complementarity, is that both electromagnetic theory and quantum theory are needed to explain this phenomenon. Light travels at a velocity of $2.997\,925 \times 10^8$ m per second in free space, this being, according to the special *relativity, the highest attainable velocity in the universe.

light-emitting diode. *See* semiconductor diode.

lighthouse A tall structure, built on a coastal promontory or cape or on an island at sea, equipped with a powerful beacon, visible at some distance, to mark an obstruction or other hazard. Modern lighthouses are also equipped with radio beacons. Both light and radio signals are emitted in a unique pattern to enable vessels to identify the lighthouse producing them.

lightning An electrical discharge in the atmosphere caused by the build up of electrical charges in a cloud by such methods as friction between the particles in the cloud. The potential difference causing the discharge may be as high as one thousand million volts. The electricity then discharges itself in a lightning flash, which may be between the cloud and the ground or, much more commonly, between two clouds or parts of a cloud. Thunder is the noise made by the discharge or its reverberations. *See also* ball lightning; thunderstorm.

lightning conductor An earthed conducting rod placed at the top of buildings, etc., to protect them from damage by lightning. It acts by providing a low-resistance path to earth for the lightning current.

lightship A vessel, anchored at sea, used as a lighthouse. In wide use until the mid-20th century, most lightships have now been replaced by fixed structures or, because of advances in sophisticated navigation devices, have been eliminated entirely.

light year A unit of distance, used in astronomy, equal to the distance travelled by light in one year. 1 light-year = 9.46×10^{15} metres or 5.88×10^{12} miles.

lignin A complex chemical deposited in plant cell walls to add extra strength and support. It is the main constituent of *wood cells, allowing the trunk to support the heavy crown of leaves and branches.

lignum vitae Wood from trees of the genus *Guaiacum*, especially *G. officinale*, a tropical evergreen of the New World. Lignum vitae is hard, dense, greenish-brown, and rich in fat (making it waterproof). It is used for shafts, pulleys, and bowling balls. Lignum vitae was formerly thought to have medicinal properties: its name (from the Latin) means "wood of life." Family: *Zygophyllaceae*.

Liguria A region in NW Italy. It consists of a narrow strip of land between the Apennines and Maritime Alps in the N and the Gulf of Genoa in the S. It is an important industrial region, concentrating on engineering, shipbuilding, metals, petroleum products, and chemicals. Tourism is a major source of revenue, the region more or less corresponding to the Italian Riviera. Agricultural products include vegetables, olives, and flowers. Area: 5415 sq km (2091 sq mi). Population (1983 est): 1 789 225. Capital: Genoa.

Ligurian Sea A section of the NW Mediterranean Sea, between Italy (N of Elba) and Corsica.

Li Hong Zhang (*or* Li Hung-chang; 1823–1901) Chinese soldier and statesman of the *Qing dynasty. His armies helped suppress the *Taiping Rebellion in 1864 and, as the trusted adviser of the empress *Zi Xi, he encouraged com-

merce and industry, attempting to introduce modernizing projects, and conducted China's foreign affairs. He amassed a huge personal fortune.

Likasi (name until 1966: Jadotville) 10 58S 26 47E A city in SE Zaïre. Founded in 1917, near the site of old copper workings, it is a major mineral-processing centre refining copper and cobalt. Other industries include chemicals and brewing. Population (1975): 185 328.

lilac A deciduous bush or small tree of the genus *Syringa* (30 species), especially *S. vulgaris*, native to temperate Eurasia and often grown as a garden ornamental. It has heart-shaped leaves arranged in opposite pairs and dense terminal clusters of white, purple, or pink tubular fragrant flowers with four flaring lobes. The fruit is a leathery capsule. Family: *Oleaceae*.

Lilburne, John (c. 1614–57) English pamphleteer; leader of the radical Puritan sect called the *Levellers. Imprisoned (1638–40) for his Puritan activities, he joined the parliamentarians in the Civil War but resigned from the army in 1645 to organize the Levellers. Between 1645 and 1647 he was mostly in prison and was twice tried and acquitted for treason (1649, 1653) but a popular demonstration in his favour led to further imprisonment from 1653 until 1655.

Liliaceae A family of monocotyledonous plants (about 250 species), mostly herbaceous and native to temperate and subtropical regions. They usually grow from bulbs or rhizomes to produce six-lobed flowers and three-chambered capsular fruits. The family includes many popular garden plants, including the lilies, tulip, hyacinth, and lily-of-the-valley. A few are economically important, for example *Asparagus*. Some authorities enlarge this family to include related plants, such as the onion, leek, etc., (*see* Allium), *Agave*, and *Yucca*.

Lilienthal, Otto (1848–96) German aeronautical engineer, who pioneered the construction of gliders. A student of bird flight, Lilienthal demonstrated the superiority of a curved wing over a flat wing. He made some 2000 flights before being killed in a crash.

Lilith In Jewish folklore, a female demon, traditionally the first wife of Adam, who refused to recognize his authority over her. An amulet bearing the names of the three angels who tried to persuade her to return to Adam was worn as protection against her evil powers.

Liliuokalani (1838–1917) The only queen and last sovereign of Hawaii (1891–95). Hawaiian resistance to US attempts to annex the islands led to an insurrection after which she abdicated. She composed the song "Aloha Oe," as a farewell gift to her people.

Lille 50 39N 3 05E A city in N France, the capital of the Nord department on the River Deûle. The centre of a large industrial and commercial complex, its industries include textiles, machinery, chemicals, distilling, and brewing. Notable buildings include the citadel (built by Vauban) and the university (1887). *History*: following a prosperous period under the Dukes of Burgundy (14th century), Lille later passed to Austria and then Spain before returning to France in 1668, and was badly damaged in both World Wars. Gen de Gaulle was born here. Population (1982): 174 039.

Lillie, Beatrice (Constance Sylvia Munston, Lady Peel; 1898–) British actress, born in Canada. The sophisticated comedy of her performances in revues and cabaret was successful in both London and New York. She also made several films, notably *Exit Smiling* (1926) and *On Approval* (1943).

Lilongwe 13 58S 33 49E The capital of Malawi. It replaced Zomba as the capital in 1975. Tobacco production is important. Population (1983 est): 158 000.

lily A perennial herbaceous plant of the genus *Lilium* (80–100 species), native to N temperate regions and widely grown for ornament. Lilies grow from bulbs to produce leafy stems with terminal clusters of showy flowers, usually with backward-curving petals. Some popular species are the tiger lily (*L. tigrinum*), from China and Japan, 60–120 cm high with purple-spotted golden flowers; the Japanese golden ray lily (*L. auratum*), 90–180 cm high, whose white flowers are marked with yellow and crimson; the Eurasian Madonna lily (*L. candida*), 60–120 cm high with pure-white flowers; and the turk's-cap or martagon lily (*L. martagon*), also from Eurasia, 90–150 cm high, the purplish-pink flowers of which are marked with darker spots. There are numerous varieties and hybrids of these and other species. Family: *Liliaceae*.

The name is also applied to numerous other unrelated plants, such as the *arum lily, *day lily, and *leopard lily.

lily-of-the-valley A fragrant perennial herbaceous plant, *Convallaria majalis*, native to Eurasia and E North America and a popular garden plant. Growing from creeping underground stems (rhizomes), it has a stem, 13–20 cm long, bearing a cluster of white nodding bell-shaped flowers. Family: *Liliaceae*.

Lima 12 06S 77 03W The capital of Peru, situated in the E of the country near its Pacific port of Callao. Founded by Pizarro in 1535, it became the main base of Spanish power in Peru. Notable buildings include the 16th-century cathedral and the National University of San Marcos (1551). Lima has expanded rapidly in recent years and now has considerable industry; the main manufactures include motor vehicles, textiles, paper, paint, and food products. Approximately one-third of the population live in the shanty-town settlements that surround the city. Population (1983): 5 258 600.

Lima bean A herb, *Phaseolus lunatus*, also called butter bean or Madagascar bean, native to South America but widely cultivated in the tropics and subtropics as a source of protein. It is easily stored when dry. Family: *Leguminosae*.

Limassol (modern Greek name: Lemesós; Turkish name: Limasol) 34 40N 33 03E A town in Cyprus, on the S coast. It is the island's second largest town and a major port, exporting notably wine and fruit. Population (1980 est): 105 200.

limbo In medieval Christian theology, the state of existence of souls that merit neither heavenly bliss nor the torments of hell after death. The two categories of soul destined for limbo were unbaptized babies and the patriarchs and prophets of the Old Testament.

Limburg 1. A former duchy in W Europe, divided in 1839 between Belgium and the Netherlands. 2. (French name: Limbourg) A province in NE Belgium, bordering on the Netherlands. In the N, the Kempen heath area has rich coalfields and industries include chemicals and glass. The S is chiefly agricultural (especially dairy farming). Area: 2422 sq km (935 sq mi). Population (1980 est): 716 059. Capital: Hasselt. 3. A province in the SE Netherlands. Its traditional coalmining industry has declined in recent years. Agriculture is varied producing cereals, fruit, vegetables, and sugar beet; cattle, pigs, and poultry are raised. Area: 2208 sq km (852 sq mi). Population (1976 est): 1 073 403. Capital: Maastricht.

Limburg, de (*or* de Limbourg) A family (active c. 1400–c. 1416) of manuscript illuminators comprising three brothers Pol, Herman, and Jehanequin, born in Nijmegen (Netherlands), the sons of a sculptor. They worked for the Duke of Burgundy (1402–04) and later for the Duke of Berry, for whom they illuminated the *Très Riches Heures* (Chantilly, France), a fine example of the *international gothic style. They influenced the development of Flemish landscape painting.

lime (botany) 1. A large deciduous tree of the genus *Tilia* (about 30 species), also called linden. Growing to a height of 30 m, it has toothed heart-shaped leaves and fragrant pale-yellow flowers that hang in small clusters on a long winged stalk. The small round fruits remain attached to the papery wing when shed. Family: *Tiliaceae*. 2. A tree, *Citrus aurantifolia*, growing to a height of about 4 m and cultivated in the tropics for its fruit.

Lime fruits are pear-shaped, 4 cm in diameter, with a thick greenish-yellow skin and acid-tasting pulp; the juice is used to flavour food and drinks.

lime (chemistry) Calcium oxide (*or* quicklime; CaO), calcium hydroxide (*or* slaked lime; Ca(OH)$_2$), or, loosely, calcium salts in general. Ca(OH)$_2$ is prepared by reacting CaO with water and is used in *cement. CaO is used in making paper, as a *flux in *steel manufacture, and in softening water.

limerick A short form of comic and usually bawdy verse having five lines of three or two feet and usually rhyming aabba, as in:

> There was a young lady of Lynn
> Who was so uncommonly thin
> That when she essayed
> To drink lemonade,
> She slipped through the straw and fell in.

The form, the origin of which is uncertain, was popularized by Edward *Lear in the 19th century and practised by several notable poets, but the best-known limericks are by anonymous authors. The name is said to have originated in the chorus of an Irish soldiers' song, "Will you come up to Limerick?"

Limerick (Irish name: Luimneach) 52 40N 8 38W A port in the Republic of Ireland, the county town of Co Limerick on the Shannon estuary. It was besieged by William III (1691). Notable buildings include two cathedrals. Its industries include flour milling, tanning, and brewing. Population (1981): 75 520.

Limerick (Irish name: Luimneach) A county in the SW Republic of Ireland, in Munster bordering on the River Shannon estuary. It consists chiefly of lowlands rising to hills in the S. Lying mainly in the fertile Golden Vale, it is important for dairy farming. Area: 2686 sq km (1037 sq mi). Population (1981): 100 925. County town: Limerick.

limestone A common sedimentary rock consisting largely of carbonates, especially calcium carbonate (calcite) or dolomite. Most limestones were deposited in the sea in warm clear water, but some limestones were formed in fresh water. Organic limestones, including *chalk, consist of fossil skeletal material. Precipitated limestones include evaporites and *oolites (spherically grained calcite). Clastic limestones consist of fragments of pre-existing limestones. Marble is metamorphosed limestone. Limestone is used as a building stone, in the manufacture of cement and glass, for agricultural lime, for road metal, and as a flux in smelting.

limitation, statutes of The Acts of Parliament that specify a time (period of limitation) within which legal proceedings must be started by any person seeking to enforce a right; failing this, the right of action is barred. If the specified time has passed, some rights, such as those over land, cease to exist, whereas others, for example the right to receive payment of a debt, continue for all purposes, except that there is no right to enforce them by legal action. Proceedings must be started within six years to recover debts on simple *contracts and in most civil wrongs (torts).

limited liability The restriction of a shareholder's obligation to meet company debts in the event of its *insolvency. In the UK those who engaged in business ventures before 1855 (when the concept was introduced) risked losing all their personal property. The *Companies Act allows the formation of corporations the liability of whose shareholders is restricted either to the nominal amount of their shares ("company limited by shares") or to the amount that they have respectively undertaken to contribute if the company is wound up ("company limited by guarantee").

Limoges 45 50N 1 15E A city in W France, the capital of the Haute-Vienne department on the River Vienne. The centre of the French porcelain industry, it has Roman remains, a cathedral (13th–16th centuries), and a university (1808). It is the birthplace of Pierre Auguste Renoir. Population (1982): 144 082.

limonite A naturally occurring mixture of hydrated iron oxides and iron hydroxides, both amorphous and cryptocrystalline, derived from the weathering of minerals containing iron. It ranges in colour from yellow to brown to black and occurs in bog iron ore, in gossan, and in *laterite.

Limosin, Léonard (or Limousin; c. 1505–c. 1577) French artist, born in Limoges. As court painter to Francis I and later Henry II he was popular chiefly for his enamel portraits, although he also painted plates, vases, etc., and worked in oils.

Limousin A planning region and former province in central France, on the W Massif Central. It was in the possession of the English from 1152 until 1369. Area: 16 932 sq km (6536 sq mi). Population (1982): 737 153.

limpet A marine *gastropod mollusc with a flattened shell and powerful muscular foot for clinging to rocks and other surfaces. The true limpets (superfamily *Patellacea*; about 400 species) are oval-shaped and up to 10 cm long whereas the keyhole limpets (superfamily *Fissurellacea*; several hundred species) have an opening in the shell for expelling wastes and tend to be smaller.

Limpopo River A river in SE Africa. Rising as the Crocodile River in the Witwatersrand, South Africa, it flows generally NE through Mozambique, to the Indian Ocean, forming part of the border between the Transvaal and Botswana. Length: 1770 km (1100 mi).

Linacre, Thomas (c. 1460–1524) English physician and humanist, who (in 1518) founded the Royal College of Physicians in London. This was intended to control the indiscriminate practice of medicine by introducing a system of examining and licensing would-be physicians. Linacre translated the medical works of *Galen from Greek to Latin. He also taught at Oxford, where Erasmus and Sir Thomas More were among his pupils.

Lin Biao (or Lin Piao; 1908–71) Chinese communist soldier and statesman. Lin received military training under *Chiang Kai-shek at the Whampoa Military Academy. He became a Guomindang (Nationalist People's Party) colonel but led his regiment to join the communist uprising in Nanchang. He became commander of the First Red Army Corps and played a major part in the communist victory against the Guomindang (1949). In 1959 he became defence minister and in 1969, vice chairman of the Chinese Communist Party. Lin seemed destined to become Mao Tse-tung's successor but he was killed in a mysterious aircrash in Outer Mongolia, when he may have been attempting to flee China after making an unsuccessful bid for power.

Lincoln 53 14N 0 33W A city in E central England, the administrative centre of Lincolnshire on the River Witham. The British settlement became Lindum Colonia under the Romans, at the intersection of the important routeways Fosse Way and Ermine Street. The castle was begun in 1068 and the cathedral in 1075. The principal manufactures are machinery, radios, metal goods, vehicle components, and cattle feed. Population (1983 est): 78 000.

Lincoln 40 49N 96 41W A city in the USA, the capital of Nebraska. It is the centre of a region producing grain and livestock. The University of Nebraska was established here in 1869. Population (1980): 171 932.

Lincoln, Abraham (1809–65) US statesman; Republican president (1861–65). A self-educated man, who had been born in a log cabin, Lincoln became a lawyer and, in 1847, member of Congress for Illinois. Holding long-standing convictions against slavery, he opposed its extension to the new western states and in 1856 joined the newly formed antislavery Republi-

ABRAHAM LINCOLN *The US president being shot at by John Wilkes Booth in a box at Ford's Theatre, Washington DC. Lincoln's wife is on the right. He died next morning.*

can Party. Elected president on the slavery issue just before the outbreak of the *Civil War, in 1863 Lincoln proclaimed the freedom of slaves in the South (the Emancipation Proclamation) and gave his famous *Gettysburg Address recalling the principles of equality established by America's founding fathers. He oversaw the 13th amendment prohibiting slavery (1865) and advocated magnanimous *Reconstruction measures but was assassinated a few days after the South surrendered.

Lincolnshire A county in E England, bordering on the North Sea. It is generally low lying, with the Lincolnshire Edge (a limestone escarpment) in the W and the Lincolnshire Wolds in the E. It is mainly agricultural producing arable crops and livestock; horticulture is also important. *History*: under Roman occupation drainage of the Fens was attempted. This was achieved in the 17th century, increasing its importance as an agricultural region. In 1974, under local government reorganization, Lincolnshire lost the N part to Humberside. It formerly comprised the administrative regions of Lindsey, Holland, and Kesteven. Area: 5885 sq km (2272 sq mi). Population (1983 est): 554 300. Administrative centre: Lincoln.

Lincoln's Inn. *See* Inns of Court.

Lind, Jenny (1820–87) Swedish soprano, known as "the Swedish nightingale." Her brilliant career in opera and on the concert platform took her all over Europe and to the USA. She endowed many charities in England and Sweden.

Lindbergh, Charles A(ugustus) (1902–74).US aviator who made the first solo nonstop flight across the Atlantic Ocean, from New York to Paris (1927), in the monoplane *Spirit of St Louis*. After the kidnapping and murder of his two-year-old son in 1932 he and his wife moved to Europe to escape the ensuing publicity. He advocated US neutrality at the start of World War II but subsequently contributed to the Allied cause. His book *The Spirit of St Louis* (1953) won a Pulitzer Prize.

Lindemann, Frederick Alexander, 1st Viscount Cherwell (1886–1957) German-born British physicist, who became Churchill's scientific adviser in World War II. Criticized for advocating mass bombing of civilians, Lindemann was highly praised by Churchill, who made him paymaster-general (1951–53).

linden. *See* lime.

Lindisfarne. *See* Holy Island.

Lindsay, (Nicholas) Vachel (1879–1931) US poet. After an unsuccessful attempt to be a painter he became an itinerant poet, earning his living by reciting his poems. His best-known volumes, *General William Booth Enters into Heaven and Other Poems* (1913) and *The Congo and Other Poems* (1914), owe much to his interest in regional folklore and his mastery of ballad-like verse.

Lindsey, Parts of. *See* Lincolnshire.

Lindwall, Raymond Russell (1921–) Australian

cricketer, who played for New South Wales, Queensland, and Australia. One of the greatest fast bowlers, he took 228 wickets in 61 Test matches (1946-59).

Linear A A syllabic script used (c. 1700-1450 BC) to write the lost language of the *Minoan civilization of Crete. It evolved from a pictographic script. Known from fewer than 400 inscriptions, it is still undeciphered, but, like its successor, *Linear B, was mainly used on clay tablets to record inventories.

linear accelerator An *accelerator in which charged elementary particles are repeatedly accelerated along a long straight tube by a radio-frequency electric field. In modern linear accelerators the field is supplied by the electric component of a travelling radio wave in a waveguide. The particles are confined in the tube by a series of magnetic lenses, which focus the beam. The maximum energy attained by a linear accelerator is about 10 GeV for electrons and 2 GeV for protons.

Linear B A syllabic script apparently adapted (c. 1450-1400 BC) from *Linear A by the invading Mycenaeans at *Knossos to write their own language (see Mycenaean civilization). In 1952 Michael *Ventris deciphered this language as an early form of *Greek. Several thousand Linear B clay tablets, mainly containing inventories, survive from Knossos, *Pylos, and elsewhere, dating between about 1400 and 1100 BC.

linear motor A form of electric induction motor in which the stator and the rotor are linear instead of cylindrical and parallel instead of coaxial. The development of linear motors as a method of traction for monorail intercity trains has been proposed by E. R. Laithwaite (1921-). In this arrangement one winding would be in the train and the other on the single rail, thus obviating the need for rotating parts.

Line Islands A chain of coral atolls in the W central Pacific Ocean. Of the N islands, Palmyra and Jarvis Islands are US territories while Washington, Fanning, and Christmas Islands, the only permanently inhabited ones, form part of Kiribati. Copra is produced.

linen A fabric manufactured from *flax (Linum usitatissimum). Probably the first textile of plant origin, specimens 4500 years old have been found in Egyptian tombs. Flax growing was brought to Britain by the Romans and in the 16th century a flourishing trade grew up, especially in Scotland and Northern Ireland. Greatly reduced by the 18th-century expansion of the cotton trade, and even more so by the advent of man-made fibres, these strong absorbent fibres now constitute less than 2% of world fibre production, being reserved for luxury household fabrics and summer garments.

line of force. See field.

ling A deep-sea fish, belonging to a genus (Molva; 3 species) related to cod, that is cured and dried for food. The common ling (M. molva) has a long slim body, up to about 2 m long, mottled brown or green, a long chin barbel, and two dorsal fins.

lingua franca Any language that is used as a means of communication between speakers with different native languages. It may be a hybrid of other languages, such as *pidgin English, or it may refer to an already existing language, such as French, which was formerly the lingua franca of diplomacy. Lingua franca, meaning Frank language, was originally a pidgin used by Mediterranean traders in the middle ages (Frank being the Arabic word for European).

linguistics The scientific study of *language. The earliest recorded studies of particular languages include the Sanskrit grammar of *Panini (6th/4th century BC) and the Greek grammar of Dionysius Thrax of Alexandria (2nd century BC). In the 19th century the study of language (then called *philology) was mainly concerned with establishing the history and relationships of the *Indo-European languages.

The chief influences in broadening the scope of linguistics to its present range were Ferdinand de *Saussure, Leonard *Bloomfield, and Noam *Chomsky. Modern linguistics has three main branches, corresponding to the three main components of language: *semantics, *grammar, and *phonetics. Many linguists at present see it as their task to contribute to the building of a formal model of language, in which the theoretical problems are resolved, the components and processes accurately identified, and the relationships among the components and between linguistic systems and other worlds are plausibly described. Other linguists believe that a coherent one-piece model is simply not possible.

Various specialized interests exist within the field of linguistics. **Comparative linguistics** compares languages either to establish the history of and relationships among related languages (e.g. the Indo-European family) or to test theories about linguistic universals by comparing unrelated languages (see also etymology). The main contribution of **structural linguistics**, which developed in the early 20th century, was to free linguistics from the historical and comparative approach, viewing language as a unique relational structure. **Sociolinguistics** deals with social aspects of language, including such matters as how language affects and reflects the role and status of individuals within the community, attitudes to dialect and "correctness," linguistic taboos and preferences, bilingualism, etc. **Psycholinguistics** is the comparatively recent branch of linguistics that deals with psychological aspects of language, including how children acquire language, how language is stored in and generated by the brain, the relationship between meaning and memory, etc. **Neurolinguistics**, a branch of psycholinguistics, is concerned with the relationship between language and the physiology of the brain, especially with speech disorders that arise from brain damage.

Linklater, Eric (1889-1974) Scottish novelist. Born in Orkney, he studied and later taught English literature at Aberdeen and in the USA. His many satirical and picaresque novels include Juan in America (1931), Judas (1939), and The House of Gair (1953).

Linköping 58 25N 15 35E A town in SE Sweden. It has a notable romanesque cathedral and its university was established in 1970. Industries include railway engineering and the manufacture of cars and textiles. Population (1983): 114 681.

Linlithgow 55 59N 3 37W A town in central Scotland, in Lothian Region. The palace (now in ruins) was the birthplace of Mary, Queen of Scots. The chief industries are paper making, footwear, and whisky distilling. Population (1984 est): 10 000.

Linnaeus, Carolus (Carl Linné; 1707-78) Swedish botanist, who established the principles for naming and classifying plants and animals. As a result of his botanical studies, Linnaeus proposed a system for classifying plants based on their flower parts. He published Systema naturae in 1735 followed by Genera plantarum (1737) and Species plantarum (1753). In his system, Linnaeus defined each type of plant by two names: a generic name and a specific name (see binomial nomenclature). Furthermore he grouped related genera into classes and combined related classes into orders. Linnaeus also applied his system to the animal kingdom. His was the first major attempt to bring systematic order to the great array of living things and provided a valuable framework that *Cuvier and others were able to modify and improve. Linnaeus' manuscripts and collections are kept at the Linnaean Society, London, which was founded in his honour in 1788.

linnet A small Eurasian *finch, Acanthis cannabina, occurring in dry open regions, where it feeds on the seeds of common weed plants. The female has a dull brown-streaked plumage; the male has a crimson crown and breast, a greyish head, and a red-brown back with darker wings and tail.

Male linnets have a beautiful flutelike voice and were popular cagebirds in the 19th century.

LINEAR B   *A clay tablet from Knossos, Crete (c. 1400 BC; British Museum).*

linotype.   *See* typesetting.

linsang   A carnivorous mammal belonging to the genus *Prionodon* (2 species) of SE Asia. Linsangs are short-legged, about 75 cm long including the tail (30-35 cm), and have short velvety fur. Nocturnal, with large ears and eyes, they prey on lizards, small mammals, birds, frogs, and insects. Family: *Viverridae*.

linseed   The flat oval seed of cultivated *flax, which is a source of linseed oil, used in paints, inks, varnishes, oilcloth, and sailcloth. The crushed seed residues form linseed meal, an important protein feed for ruminants and pigs.

Linz   48 19N 14 18E The third largest city in Austria, the capital of Upper Austria on the River Danube. Its many historical buildings include two 13th-century baroque churches and a cathedral (1862-1924). A cultural centre, it has art galleries, libraries, and theatres. Its industries include iron and steel processing using local hydroelectric power. Population (1981): 201 421.

Lin Ze Xu   (*or* Lin Tse-hsü; 1785-1850) Chinese statesman and scholar. Lin Ze Xu served as governor of several provinces. While imperial commissioner of Canton (1839-41) he confiscated opium and tried to put an end to its trafficking through British merchants, thus provoking the *Opium War (1839-42). He is also known for his efforts to introduce western defence techniques to China.

lion   A large carnivorous □mammal *Panthera leo*, one of the big *cats. Lions are found mainly in Africa (there are a few in India). They are heavily built with sandy-coloured coats: the shaggy-maned males grow to 2.8 m while females lack a mane and are more lightly built. Both sexes have a thin tail with a tuft at the end.
Lions inhabit grasslands, living in groups (prides) containing between four and 30 individuals dominated by a supreme male. They hunt mainly at twilight.

Lions, Gulf of   (French name: Golfe du Lion)   An inlet of the NW Mediterranean Sea, on the coast of central S France between Marseille and the Spanish border.

Liouville, Joseph   (1809-82) French mathematician, who proved that there exists a class of numbers, called transcendental numbers, that cannot be expressed as a solution of a polynomial equation (i.e. one of the form $a_0 + a_1 x + \ldots + a_n x^n = 0$, where n and the a's are integers). Liouville could not identify any transcendental numbers, a feat first achieved by *Hermite.

Lipari Islands   (*or* Aeolian Is; Italian name: Isole Eolie)   An Italian group of seven volcanic islands in the Tyrrhenian Sea, off the N coast of Sicily. The largest is Lipari and the islands of Stromboli and Vulcano have active volcanoes. Exports include pumice stone, grapes, wine, and figs. Area: 114 sq km (44 sq mi). Population (1981 est): 10 208. Chief town: Lipari, on Lipari.

lipase   An enzyme that splits the glycerides of fats in food and fatty tissue into their component fatty acids and glycerol. Digestive lipases are secreted by the pancreas and small intestine.

Lipchitz, Jacques   (1891-1973) Lithuanian cubist sculptor, who lived in Paris from 1909 and New York after 1941. Producing his first cubist sculpture in 1914, Lipchitz developed heavy angular forms in such characteristically cubist subjects as bathers and musicians. In 1925 he began experimenting with the use of voids in bronze sculptures, which he entitled "transparents." His later mythological and religious sculptures explored themes of love, evil, and conflict.

Lipetsk   52 37N 39 36E A city in the central Soviet Union, in the RSFSR on the River Voronezh. Industries include iron and steel and engineering. Its mud spa attracts health devotees. Population (1984): 440 000.

lipids   A group of compounds, generally insoluble in water but soluble in organic solvents, that includes *fats, *oils, *waxes, phospholipids, sphingolipids, and *steroids. Fats and oils function as energy reserves in plants and animals and form a major source of dietary energy in animals. Phospholipids are important structural components of cell membranes, and sphingolipids are found predominantly in nerve tissues. Steroids have many important derivatives, including cholesterol, bile salts, and certain hormones. *Prostaglandins, *carotenoids, and *terpenes are also classified as lipids. Lipids often occur in association with proteins as lipoproteins.

Lipizzaner   A breed of □horse long associated with the Spanish Riding School in Vienna, where they are trained for spectacular displays. It is named after the stud founded by Archduke Charles at Lipizza, near Trieste, in 1580. The Lipizzaner has a short back, strong hindquarters, a powerful neck, and a small head. Born black, they mature to a grey colour. Height: 1.47-1.52 m (14½-15 hands).

Li Bo   (Li Po *or* Li T'ai Po; 705-62) Chinese poet. Li Po and *Du Fu together are often considered China's greatest poets. Li Po's poetry is mostly light-hearted and romantic and has its stylistic origins in folk ballads and other old traditions. Legend has it that he drowned trying to embrace the reflection of the moon from a boat.

Lippe, River   A river in NW Germany, rising in the Teutoburger Wald (forest) and flowing generally W to join the River Rhine at Wesel. **The Lippe Canal** (1929), which runs parallel to the river, is the more important waterway. Length: 240 km (150 mi).

Lippershey, Hans   (died c. 1619) Dutch lens grinder, who built the first *telescope. The Dutch Government tried to keep the invention a secret but news of it eventually reached *Galileo, who built his own telescope, which he used for astronomical observations.

Lippi, Fra Filippo   (c. 1406-69) An early Renaissance Florentine painter, who was a Carmelite monk from 1421 to about 1432. During this time he probably trained under *Masaccio. He was frequently patronized by the Medici but his greatest works are his fresco decorations for the choir of Prato Cathedral (1452-64), showing scenes from the lives of St John the Baptist and St Stephen. He is also noted for his idealized Madonnas, e.g. *The Madonna and Child with Two Angels* (Uffizi). He abducted and later married a nun, Lucrezia Buti; their son, **Filippino Lippi** (1457-1504), was also a painter. Filippino trained under *Botticelli after his father's death and completed Masaccio's fresco cycle in the Brancacci Chapel. His paintings, such as *The Vision of St*

Bernard (Badia, Florence), influenced the Florentine mannerists of the 16th century.

Lipscomb, William Nunn (1919-) US chemist, who won the 1976 Nobel Prize for his elucidation of the structure of *boranes. He discovered the arrangement of atoms inside borane molecules by means of X-ray diffraction and showed how groups of three such atoms are bonded by a single pair of electrons.

liquefaction of gases Gases are liquefied in several ways. If the temperature of the gas is below its critical temperature (*see* critical state), it can be liquefied simply by compressing it. If the critical temperature is too low for this, the cascade process can be used. In this a gas with a high critical temperature is first liquefied by compression and then allowed to cool by evaporation under reduced pressure. This gas cools a second gas below its critical temperature, so that it in turn can be liquefied, evaporated, and cooled still further. Thus the temperature is reduced in stages. Other methods include cooling by the *Joule-Kelvin effect, which is used industrially in the Linde process (named after Carl von Linde; 1842-1934), and by adiabatic expansion in which a compressed gas is cooled by performing external work. This is the basis of the Claude process (named after Georges Claude; 1870-1960).

Liquefied Petroleum Gas (LPG) Propane, propene, butane, butene, or a mixture of any of these. LPG is a product of *oil refining and is also produced from *natural gas. It is transported by pipeline or in specially built tankers by road, rail, or sea.
Most of the LPG produced is sold in low-pressure cylinders for heating or used as a raw material for chemical manufacture, although it is also used as engine fuel.

liqueurs Alcoholic *spirits flavoured with herbs or other ingredients, usually heavily sweetened. Liqueurs are generally sipped, neat, from small glasses after dinner. Some liqueurs, such as Benedictine, were originated by monks; the yellow or green Chartreuse is still made by the Carthusians. Other liqueurs include Curaçao, Cointreau, and Grand Marnier, which are made with brandy and oranges; Kümmel made with cumin and caraway seeds; Maraschino made with marasca cherries; and Drambuie made with whisky and honey. Aged high-quality brandy and whisky, drunk neat, are sometimes described as liqueurs.

liquid crystal A substance exhibiting some liquid properties, especially fluidity, and some crystalline properties, in that large clusters of molecules are aligned in parallel formations. As liquid crystals change their reflectivity when an electric potential is applied to them, they are used in the digital display of electronic calculators, etc.

liquidity preference The proportion of an individual's total assets held in cash. Liquidity preference is determined chiefly by the general price level (if prices are high people need more cash to finance their purchases) and the rate of interest (if interest rates are high people will wish to invest their assets in interest-bearing bonds rather than in money). The concept was originated by J. M. *Keynes to explain the demand for money.

liquids A state of matter between that of *gases and the *solid state. Liquids assume the shape of a container in the same way as gases but being incompressible do not expand to fill the container. Intermolecular forces are considerably stronger than in gases but weaker than in solids. Molecules are only maintained in an orderly arrangement by intermolecular forces over relatively small groups of molecules. The theory of liquids is much less well established than that of gases and solids.

liquorice A perennial herb, *Glycyrrhiza glabra*, native to S Europe but cultivated throughout warm temperate regions. It bears clusters of blue flowers and long flat pods and its sweet roots, up to 1 m long, are a source of flavouring for confectionery, tobacco, and medicines. The thickened juice of the roots is made into liquorice paste (*or* black sugar). Family: *Leguminosae*.

lira 1. Another name for the *hurdy-gurdy. 2. A bowed string instrument of the late middle ages. The **lira da braccio** (Italian: lyre for the arm) resembled the *violin but had a flatter body; it was held against the shoulder. The larger **lira da gamba** (Italian: lyre for the leg) was held like a *cello or viola da gamba. Both instruments had between 7 and 15 strings, some of which were sympathetic strings.

Lisbon (Portuguese name: Lisboa) 38 44N 9 08W The capital of Portugal, in the SW on the River Tagus. The country's chief seaport, it has one of the finest harbours in Europe; main exports include wine, olive oil, and cork. Lisbon is also a major industrial and commercial centre. Historic buildings include the Tower of Belém and the Jerónimos Monastery; its university was founded in 1290. *History*: a settlement from very early times, it was an organized community under the Roman Empire but was later overrun by German tribes. Occupied by the Moors in the 8th century AD, it was captured by the Portuguese in the 12th century and became their capital in 1256. It flourished in the 15th and 16th centuries, the great age of Portuguese exploration and colonization, but later suffered a decline. In 1755 it was almost totally destroyed by an earthquake. It has expanded considerably in the 20th century and in 1966 one of the world's longest suspension bridges was opened across the River Tagus, linking Lisbon with Almada. Population (1981): 817 627.

Lisburn 54 31N 6 03W A market town in Northern Ireland, in Co Antrim. The Irish fine-linen industry was begun here by immigrant Huguenots in the 17th century. Furniture is also manufactured. Population (1985 est): 87 900.

Lisieux 49 09N 0 14E A town in N France, in the Calvados department. The shrine of Ste Thérèse (1873-1917) attracts large numbers of pilgrims to Lisieux. An agricultural trading centre (especially in dairy products), its manufactures include textiles and car components. Population (1982): 25 823.

Lismore 52 08N 7 55W A market town in the Republic of Ireland, in Co Waterford. There is a castle (1185) and two cathedrals, one built on the site of a 6th-century monastery that was a centre of learning. Population (1981): 919.

Lissajous figures Patterns arising from the addition of two *simple harmonic motions at right angles to each other, first studied by Jules Lissajous (1822-80). The shape of the pattern depends on the periods of the two motions and the initial conditions. If one of the two periods is an exact multiple of the other the curve is closed, otherwise the curve is open. Lissajous figures are displayed on a *cathode-ray oscilloscope when two sinusoidal signals control the vertical and horizontal motion of the electron beam.

Lissitzky, El (Eliezer L.; 1890-1941) Russian painter, typographer, designer, and architect, known particularly for his work in advertising and exhibition design. While teaching architecture at Vitebsk (1919-21) he painted his series of abstract geometrical paintings, *Proun*. Between 1922 and 1929 he lived in the West, where he was instrumental in spreading Russian ideas on design (*see* constructivism).

List, Friedrich (1789-1846) German economist, who was exiled in 1825 and emigrated to the USA. In *Outlines of American Economy* (1827), he argued the need for tariffs to encourage the growth of industry, especially in a developing country. He also wrote *The National System of Political Economy* (1841).

Lister, Joseph, 1st Baron (1827-1912) British surgeon, who pioneered antiseptic techniques in surgery. In 1865, while surgeon at Glasgow Royal Infirmary, Lister realized the significance of *Pasteur's germ theory of disease in trying to prevent the infection of wounds following surgical operations. Lister devised a means of eliminating contamination and introduced carbolic acid as an antiseptic to

JOSEPH LISTER *He introduced a carbolic spray to reduce infection in surgery. Before an operation his students used to say "Let us spray." Although surgeons operated through a carbolic mist they still wore ordinary clothes.*

dress wounds. Mortality arising from infected wounds declined sharply in Lister's ward and his antiseptic procedures eventually became standard practice in hospitals everywhere. Lister was appointed president of the Royal Society (1895–1900) and was awarded the OM (1902).

Liszt, Franz (Ferencz L.; 1811–86) Hungarian pianist and composer. He made his debut at the age of nine. After studying the piano with Czerny and studying composition he began a career as a virtuoso. From 1835 to 1839 he lived with the Comtesse d'Agoult (1805–76); their daughter Cosima married Wagner, of whose works Liszt was an early champion. From 1848 to 1861 Liszt lived with the Princess Sayn-Wittgenstein. In 1865 he took minor orders in the Roman Catholic Church; he spent most of the rest of his life in Weimar, Budapest, and Rome. As a pianist Liszt was considered the greatest performer of his time. As a composer he invented the symphonic poem and made use of advanced harmonies and original forms. His compositions include much piano music (including a sonata in B minor and operatic paraphrases), the *Faust Symphony* (1854–57) and *Dante Symphony* (1855–56), and the symphonic poem *Les Préludes* (1854).

litchi (lychee *or* lichee) A Chinese tree, *Litchi chinensis*, cultivated in the tropics and subtropics for its fruits. The fruit is almost globular, 2.5 cm in diameter, with a warty deep-pink rind and is borne in branched clusters. The white translucent watery flesh has a sweet acid flavour and encloses a single large brown seed. The fruit is eaten fresh, canned, or dried as litchi nuts. Family: *Sapindaceae*.

litharge. *See* lead.

lithium (Li) The lightest metal (relative density 0.534), discovered by Arfvedson in 1817. It is an alkali metal and gives a crimson-red colour to flames. It occurs in nature in lepidolite, spodumene ($LiAlSi_2O_6$), and other minerals; as well as in brine, from which it is extracted commercially by electrolysis of the molten chloride (LiCl). The metal has the highest specific heat capacity of any solid element. It is corrosive, combustible, and reacts with water. Because of its efficiency in reflecting neutrons, lithium has imp   ant applications as a blanketing material in both the hydrogen bomb and proposed *thermonuclear reactors. It forms salts, like the other alkali metals, and the hydride LiH. Lithium salts are used in the treatment of some forms of mental depression. At no 3; at wt 6.941; mp 180.54°C; bp 1347°C.

lithography. *See* printing.

Lithops A genus ·of succulent South African desert plants (about 50 species), with no stems and leaves partly buried in the soil. The tips of the leaves are smooth, with a deep cleft across the top, camouflaged to resemble pebbles. The daisy-like flowers are white or yellow. Family: *Aizoaceae*.

Lithuanian A language belonging to the E division of the Baltic languages division of the Indo-European family, spoken mainly by the Lithuanians of the Lithuanian SSR, where it is the official language. The total population of Lithuanian speakers, including those in America, is about 2 750 000. Lithuanian is closely related to *Latvian. It is written in a Latin alphabet and written texts date from the 16th century.

Lithuanian Soviet Socialist Republic (*or* Lithuania) A constituent republic in the NW Soviet Union, on the Baltic Sea. Most of Lithuania comprises a central lowland and is a particularly fertile region, with forests and peat reserves. The Lithuanians comprise about 80% of the population. Lithuania has large fertilizer, textile, and metalworking industries. Agriculture, especially livestock breeding, has been intensified in the postwar period. *History*: one of the largest states in medieval Europe, in the 14th century Lithuania united with Poland under the *Jagiellon dynasty, passing after the partition of Poland in the 18th century to Russia. It became independent in 1918 but was incorporated into the Soviet Union as an SSR in 1940. It was occupied by Germany during World War II, during which the large Jewish minority was virtually exterminated. The USA does not recognize Lithuania's status as a Soviet republic. Area: 65 200 sq km (25 170 sq mi). Population (1984 est): 3 500 000. Capital: Vilnius.

litmus A soluble compound obtained from certain lichens. Litmus turns red in an acid solution and blue in an alkaline solution. It is therefore used as an *indicator, often in the form of **litmus paper**, strips of paper impregnated with litmus.

litre A unit of volume in the *metric system formerly defined as the volume of one kilogram of pure water under specified conditions. This definition still applies for purposes of the UK Weights and Measures Act (1963), but in *SI units the litre is a special name, not recommended for high-precision measurements, for the cubic decimetre.

Little America 78 11S 162 10W The main US Antarctic base, near the coast of Ross Dependency. It was established in 1928 as the headquarters for the polar expeditions of Richard *Byrd.

Little Belt (Danish name: Lille Bælt) A strait in SW Denmark, between the mainland and the island of Fyn. It links the Kattegat with the Baltic Sea and narrows to 1 km (0.6 mi) wide.

Little Bighorn, Battle of the (25 June, 1876) The battle fought on the S bank of the Little Bighorn River in which Gen *Custer and his men were massacred by Sioux Indians led by *Crazy Horse and *Sitting Bull (Custer's Last Stand). It was one of the battles fought to seize the American West for White settlement.

little owl A small *owl, *Athene noctua*, occurring in Eurasia and North Africa. 20 cm long, it has a white-mottled brown plumage with heavily barred underparts, rounded wings, and bright-yellow eyes and hunts over open country at dawn and dusk, feeding on insects, worms, and occasionally mice. *See* Plate V.

Little Rock 34 42N 92 17W A city in the USA, the capital of Arkansas. In 1957, when Black pupils entered the high school for the first time, it was the scene of major race riots protesting against desegregation. Population (1980): 158 915.

Littlewood, Joan (1914–) British theatre director. In 1945 she founded Theatre Workshop, a company dedicated to the production of plays for working-class audiences. It moved into the Theatre Royal, Stratford, in the East End of London, in 1953. Her best-known productions include *The*

Hostage (1958) and *Oh What a Lovely War!* (1963). The company disbanded in 1964.

Litvinov, Maksim Maksimovich (1876-1951) Soviet diplomat; foreign minister (1930-39). Litvinov, who believed in cooperation between the Soviet Union and the West, obtained US recognition of his country in 1934. In the League of Nations he advocated action against the Axis powers and was dismissed shortly before the German-Soviet nonaggression treaty of 1939. After the German invasion of the Soviet Union, Litvinov was ambassador to the USA (1941-43).

Liu Shao Qi (*or* Liu Shao-ch'i; 1898-1974) Chinese communist statesman. He joined the Communist Party in Moscow in 1921 and later became a leader of the trades union movement in the *Jiangxi Soviet. In 1959 he succeeded *Mao Tse-tung as chairman of the People's Republic of China but was condemned as a reactionary during the *Cultural Revolution and disappeared from public view.

liver A large glandular organ, weighing 1.2-1.6 kg, situated in the upper right region of the abdomen, just below the diaphragm (*see* Plate IV). The liver has many important functions concerned with the utilization of absorbed foods. It converts excess glucose into glycogen, which it stores and reconverts into glucose when required; it breaks down excess amino acids into *urea; and it stores and metabolizes fats. The liver forms and secretes *bile, which contains the breakdown products of worn-out red blood cells, and synthesizes blood-clotting factors, plasma proteins, and—in the fetus—red blood cells. It also breaks down (detoxifies) poisonous substances, including alcohol. *Cirrhosis of the liver is commonly caused by a combination of sensitivity to, and excess of, alcohol.

liver fluke A parasitic *flatworm that inhabits the bile duct of sheep, cattle, and man. The common liver fluke (*Fasciola hepatica*) passes its larval stages in a marshland snail before infecting grazing animals (or, rarely, man). The Chinese liver fluke (*Opisthorchus sinensis*), 1-2 cm long, passes two larval stages in a freshwater snail and fish before maturing in a human host.

Liverpool 53 25N 2 55W A major city in NW England, the administrative centre of Merseyside, on the estuary of the River Mersey. It is the UK's fourth most important port and the foremost for Atlantic trade. It is linked with Birkenhead and Wallasey on the Wirral Peninsula by two tunnels under the Mersey. The most famous landmark is the Royal Liver Building (1911) at the Pier Head, alongside the Cunard and Mersey Docks buildings. There is a Roman Catholic cathedral constructed (1962-67) in a modern design of Sir Frederick Gibberd (1908-84); the original design (1929) in modern classical style was by Sir Edwin Lutyens (only the crypt and sacristy were completed before World War II prevented further building). The Anglican cathedral (1904-78), designed by Sir G. G. Scott, is the country's largest ecclesiastical building. Other notable buildings include St George's Hall (1854). Liverpool has one of the largest provincial universities in the UK (1903). Exports include all kinds of manufactured goods, especially textiles and machinery, from a hinterland covering most of the North and Midlands. The main imports are petroleum, grain, ores, nonferrous metals, sugar, wood, fruit, and cotton. These are reflected in some of Liverpool's industries: flour milling, sugar refining, electrical engineering, food processing, chemicals, soap, margarine, tanning, and motor vehicles. *History*: originally trading with Ireland, Liverpool grew rapidly in the 18th and 19th centuries, superseding Bristol as the chief west coast port as a result of trade with the Americas (sugar, tobacco, slaves, cotton) and the industrialization of S Lancashire (raw cotton came through Liverpool). Britain's first wet dock was built here in 1715. Liverpool developed also as a cultural centre, with the Walker Art Gallery (built 1877) and the Royal Liverpool Philharmonic Orchestra, the home of

which is the Philharmonic Hall (1939). Population (1987 est): 476 500.

Liverpool, Robert Banks Jenkinson, 2nd Earl of (1770-1828) British statesman; Tory prime minister (1812-27). He became an MP in 1790 and held office continuously from 1793 until 1827 except for 14 months in 1806-07; he was foreign secretary (1801-04), home secretary (1807-09), and secretary for war and the colonies (1809-12). As prime minister he is remembered for his unenlightened response to the unrest that followed the Napoleonic Wars (1803-15). In 1817 he suspended *Habeas Corpus and following the *Peterloo Massacre introduced the repressive Six Acts (1819). He also opposed *Catholic emancipation but the last years of his government saw the development of Tory reform under the influence of George *Canning and William *Huskisson.

liverwort A *bryophyte plant of the class *Hepaticae* (10 000 species), found growing on moist soil, rocks, trees, etc. There are two groups: leafy liverworts, in which the plant body is differentiated into stems and leaves; and thallose liverworts, which have a flat lobed liverlike body (thallus). The liverwort plant is the gamete-producing phase (gametophyte) and gives rise to a capsule, the spore-producing phase (sporophyte), which is sometimes borne on a slender erect column (*see* hornwort).

livery companies Descendants of the medieval craft *guilds, so called because of the distinctive dress (livery) worn by their members on ceremonial occasions. Some occupy notable buildings in the City of London and, in addition to their ceremonial duties, some, such as the Mercers, Haberdashers, and Merchant Taylors, have educational interests. In 1878 the livery companies joined the Corporation of the *City of London in setting up the City and Guilds of London Institute to promote technical education.

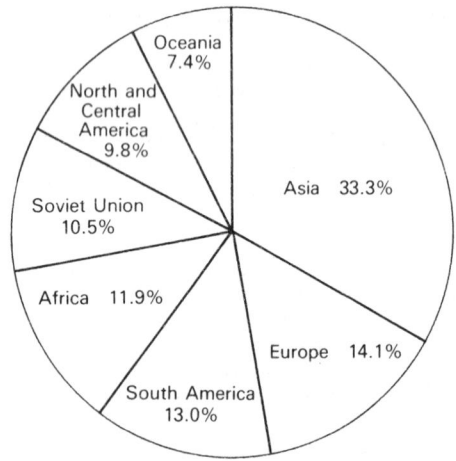

LIVESTOCK FARMING *Distribution of the world's livestock (1984; cattle, sheep, pigs, horses, asses, and mules).*

livestock farming The maintenance and management of domesticated animals for the production of milk, meat, eggs, fibres, skins, etc. Farming methods vary widely throughout the world and modern improvements in livestock breeds and husbandry techniques have enabled dramatic increases to be made in productivity, nutrition and disease control being essential aspects of management.

Cattle produce milk (*see* dairy farming) and beef. Under European conditions, a cow may breed at any time of the year. The gestation period is about 9 months, followed by about 10 months of lactation and a 2-month dry period before calving again. A cow is known as a heifer until her second lactation. Heifers are reared either for beef or as dairy replacements and bull calves are generally castrated and reared for beef, being known as bullocks or steers. Age at slaughter depends on the breed and level of feeding but is generally about 18 months. Calves for veal are reared on a milk-based diet and are slaughtered at about 14 weeks.

Sheep are farmed worldwide for meat and wool (and in some countries for milk), often grazing on poor mountainous or arid pastures. Under European conditions, the one or two lambs per ewe are born in early spring. Males are castrated and reared for slaughter at weights of 20–45 kg. Selected females are reared as replacement ewes. Each sheep yields 2–5 kg of wool.

Pigs have traditionally been kept outdoors, foraging for roots, seeds, etc. In modern intensive systems, they are housed under controlled conditions. Young females (gilts) are first mated at 7–8 months. Following the gestation period of 115 days, an average of 7–9 piglets are born per litter. Pork pigs are slaughtered at 40–50 kg; those reared for bacon are slaughtered at 80–100 kg.

Poultry are now kept indoors in an artificially controlled environment. Chicks are hatched artificially, the female birds starting to lay after about 20 weeks and producing about 250 eggs per year. Laying flocks are kept in "batteries" of cages with 3–5 birds per cage, feeding, cleaning, and egg collection being automatic. Table birds are fed ad lib and reach a weight of around 2 kg in 8–12 weeks. Turkeys are also reared for meat under intensive conditions.

Apart from producing food, many livestock, especially horses, mules, and donkeys, provide important means of transport and motive power. Goats provide milk in many traditional agricultural systems.

Livia Drusilla (58 BC–29 AD) The wife of Octavian (Emperor *Augustus) from 39 BC and the mother by her first husband of Emperor *Tiberius. As Augustus' consort Livia's image was one of matronly dignity and reports of her machinations on Tiberius' behalf are probably exaggerated. After Augustus' death (14 AD) she received the honorific name Julia Augusta.

living fossil A living organism whose closest relatives are all extinct, being known only as fossils. Such organisms were thought—before their discovery in modern times—to be extinct themselves. Examples of living fossils are the *coelacanth and the *dawn redwood, discovered in 1938 and 1941, respectively.

Livingston 55 51N 3 31W A town in central Scotland, in Lothian Region. Designated for development as a new town in 1962, it is planned to accommodate an eventual population of 100 000. Population (1985): 40 000.

Livingstone (or Maramba) 17 50S 25 53E A city in S Zambia, on the Zambezi River. It was the former capital of Northern Rhodesia (1907–35). It is a tourist centre for the nearby Victoria Falls. Population (1980): 71 987.

Livingstone, David (1813–73) Scottish missionary and explorer of Africa. Livingstone qualified as a physician at Glasgow University and after his ordination as a missionary in 1840 set out for Bechuanaland (now Botswana). He traced long stretches of the Zambezi, Shire, and Rovuma Rivers, and discovered Lake Ngami (1849), the Victoria Falls (1855), and Lake Nyasa (now Malawi). During an attempt to trace the source of the Nile (1866–73) his famous encounter with Sir Henry Morton *Stanley occurred. He died near Lake Bangweulu in Old Chitambo village, where his heart is buried. His body lies in Westminster Abbey.

Living Theatre An experimental theatre company founded in New York City in 1947 by Julian Beck (1925–) and Judith Malina (1926–). Their best-known productions include Jack Gelber's *The Connection* (1959), a play about

DAVID LIVINGSTONE   *"Found" by Stanley (on the right) at Ujiji.*

drug addiction, and *Paradise Now* (1968), in which they developed controversial experiments in audience participation. They have made several successful tours of Europe.

Livonian Knights (Livonian Brothers of the Sword) A German military and religious order of knighthood founded in 1202 to conquer and christianize the region, notably Livonia, around the Baltic Sea. They merged with the Teutonic Knights in 1237 and were disbanded in 1561.

Livonian War (1558–83) A confrontation over Russian expansion towards the Baltic Sea. In 1558 *Ivan the Terrible invaded Livonia and defeated its rulers, the Livonian Knights, who placed Livonia under Lithuanian protection. Russia was eventually defeated by the Polish-Lithuanian commonwealth (see Lublin, Union of) and Sweden, losing its Livonian conquests and some border towns on the Gulf of Finland.

Livorno (English name: Leghorn) 43 33N 10 18E A port in central Italy, in Tuscany on the Ligurian Sea. It has a 16th-century cathedral. Its industries include shipbuilding, oil refining, and engineering. Straw (Leghorn) hats are produced. Olive oil, copper products, and marble are exported. Population (1983 est): 176 298.

Livy (Titus Livius; 59 BC–17 AD) Roman historian. He was born in Patavium (Padua) in N Italy and settled in Rome about 29 BC. His monumental history of Rome from its legendary foundation to the death of Drusus in 9 BC, written in an elevated style and emphasizing the moral examples of individual lives, was immediately popular. Only 35 of the original 142 books survive, covering the early history up to the 4th century BC, the second Punic War against Hannibal, and the wars against Macedonia up to 166 BC.

lizard A *reptile belonging to the suborder *Sauria* (3000 species), occurring worldwide but most abundant in tropical regions. They are mainly terrestrial with cylindrical or narrow scaly long-tailed bodies, some with limbs reduced or absent (see glass snake; skink), and often with crests, spines, and frills. They range in size from the smallest *geckos to the formidable *Komodo dragon. Lizards lay leathery-shelled eggs although certain species of colder regions and many skinks bear live young. The female builds a simple nest and may guard her eggs until the young hatch and disperse. Some lizards reproduce by parthenogenesis, i.e. unfertilized eggs develop into races of females. Lizards eat chiefly insects and vegetation and have been known to live for 25 years in captivity.

Lizard Point (or Lizard Head) 49 56N 5 13W The most southerly point of the British Isles, in SW Cornwall on the Atlantic Ocean. It possesses magnificent coastal scenery with distinctive green- and purple-coloured serpentine rock.

Ljubljana (German name: Laibach) 46 04N 14 30E A city in NW Yugoslavia, the capital of Slovenia. Under foreign rule until 1918, it is the centre of Slovene culture with a university (1595). It was largely destroyed by an earthquake in 1895. Population (1981): 305 211.

llama A hoofed mammal, *Lama glama*, of S and W South America. Up to 120 cm high at the shoulder, llamas are surefooted, nimble, and hardy, with thick warm coats. They are now only found in the domesticated state, being used for meat, wool, and as pack animals. Family: *Camelidae* (camels, etc.).

Llanberis 53 07N 4 06W A small town in NW Wales, in Gwynedd at the W end of Llanberis Pass. A mountain railway (opened 1896) to the summit of Snowdon starts from here. Population (1981): 1863.

Llandaff 51 30N 3 14W A district of Cardiff, in South Wales on the River Taff. It is the oldest bishopric in Wales (6th century). The 12th-century cathedral, severely bombed in World War II, was restored in 1960 with inclusion of a prestressed concrete arch supporting Epstein's *Majestas*.

Llandrindod Wells 52 15N 3 23W A town in central Wales, the administrative centre of Powys. It is the largest Welsh spa and a tourist centre. Population (1981): 4186.

Llandudno 53 19N 3 49W A resort in North Wales, in Gwynedd on Conway Bay. Two limestone promontories, the Great Orme's Head and the Little Orme's Head, lie on either side of the town. Population (1981): 18 991.

Llanelli 51 42N 4 10W A port in South Wales, in Dyfed on the Burry Inlet of Carmarthen Bay. It is a tinplate manufacturing centre besides producing steel, copper, chemicals, and bricks. Population (1981): 24 079.

Llanfair PG (or Llanfairpwll) 53 13N 4 12W A village in NW Wales, in Anglesey, famous for its 58-letter full name (lengthened in the 18th century): Llanfairpwllgwyngyllgogerychwyrndrobwllllantysiliogogogoch (St Mary's Church in the hollow of the white hazel near to the rapid whirlpool of St Tysilio's Church by the red cave). The Women's Institute began here in 1915.

Llangollen 52 58N 3 10W A town in North Wales, in Clwyd. It is a tourist centre on the River Dee, spanned by a famous 14th-century bridge. An international musical Eisteddfod is held here each summer. Population (1981): 3058.

llanos The treeless grasslands of South America that cover about 570 000 sq km (220 000 sq mi) of central Venezuela and N Colombia. Drained by the River Orinoco and its tributaries, the llanos are traditionally a cattle-rearing region but the discovery of oil in the 1930s led to considerable population growth and economic development.

Llewellyn, Harry (Lt Col Sir Henry Morton L.; 1911–) British show jumper and equestrian, who won over 150 international competitions. At the 1948 Olympic Games he won a team bronze medal and in the 1952 Olympics won the team gold medal. His horse Foxhunter became world famous.

Llewellyn, Richard (R. D. V. L. Lloyd; 1907–83) Welsh novelist. After working in films and journalism, he achieved success with his novel about a Welsh mining village, *How Green Was My Valley* (1939). His other novels include the sequel *Up,*

Into the Singing Mountains (1960).

Lleyn Peninsula A peninsula in NW Wales, in Gwynedd between Caernarfon Bay and Cardigan Bay. It is a popular tourist area with several coastal resorts, including Pwllheli and Criccieth.

Lloyd, Chris(tine) (*born* Evert; 1954–) US tennis player who was Wimbledon singles champion in 1974, 1976 and 1981 and doubles champion in 1976. She won the US singles title 1975–78, 1980, and 1982.

Lloyd, Clive Hubert (1944–) West Indian cricketer. A batsman, he captained his country's team (1974–78; 1979–85) in 74 tests. He became a UK citizen in 1986.

Lloyd, Harold (1893–1971) US film comedian. He developed the character of the dogged little man in conventional suit and spectacles in numerous early silent comedies, most of them characterized by his use of dangerous stunts. His films include *Just Nuts* (1915), *Safety Last* (1923), and *The Freshman* (1925).

Lloyd, Marie (Matilda Wood; 1870–1922) British music-hall entertainer. She began her career on stage in 1885. Her songs, characterized by cockney humour, include "Oh! Mr Porter" and "A Little of What You Fancy."

DAVID LLOYD GEORGE   *Haig (left) and Joffre (centre) argue a point with the British prime minister on the Western Front (1916).*

Lloyd George, David, 1st Earl (1863–1945) British statesman; Liberal prime minister (1914–22). Born in Manchester of Welsh parents, he entered parliament in 1890 and gained a reputation for radicalism as a Welsh nationalist and a supporter of the Afrikaners in the second Boer War (1899–1902). He was president of the Board of Trade (1905–08) and then chancellor of the exchequer (1908–15), in which post he is best known for the so-called People's Budget (1909). This proposed higher death duties, a land value tax, and a supertax; the rejection of this budget by the House of Lords led ultimately to the 1911 Parliament Act, which removed the Lords' veto power. Lloyd George also introduced old-age pensions (1908) and national insurance (1911). In World War I he served as minister of munitions (1915–16) and secretary for war (1916) before succeeding Asquith as prime minister. His energetic war policy conducted by a small war cabinet included the introduction of the convoy system to thwart the German U-boat aggression. After the war he continued to lead a coalition government increasingly dominated by the Conservatives. He was criticized for negotiating with Irish militants in the establishment of the Irish Free State (1921) and his government fell when Britain came close to war with the Turkish nationalists. Lloyd George never regained prominence in British politics, although he held his parliamentary seat until 1945. After the death of his first wife **Dame Margaret Lloyd George** (1864–1941) he married his secretary **Frances Stevenson** (1888–1972), who published (1971) *Lloyd George: A Diary*.

Lloyd's An association of *insurance underwriters named after the 17th-century London coffee house, owned by Edward Lloyd, where underwriters used to meet. Lloyd's was incorporated by Act of Parliament in 1871. The corporation itself does not underwrite insurance business, which is all undertaken by syndicates of private underwriters, who are wholly responsible for losses and who are required to deposit a substantial sum of money with the corporation before being admitted as underwriters. There are over 6000 underwriters, none of whom are permitted to deal with the public, all insurance policies with the public being transacted by Lloyd's insurance brokers. Although Lloyd's is situated in London (its new building in Lime St (1986) was designed by Richard Rogers) its business in marine and aircraft insurance is worldwide. In addition to marine business (both hulls and cargoes), Lloyd's will undertake all other kinds of insurance. **Lloyd's Register of Shipping** is an organization formed by Lloyd's to inspect and list all oceangoing vessels over 100 tonnes. The *Register*, published annually, gives up-to-date reports on these ships by Lloyd's surveyors. The highest classification, "A1 at Lloyds," indicates that the hull and the trappings are both in first-class order.

Lloyd Webber, Andrew (1948–) British composer. His early musicals, with lyrics by Tim Rice (1944–), include *Jesus Christ Superstar* (1970) and *Evita* (1978); later works include *Cats* (1981), *Song and Dance* (1982), *Starlight Express* (1983), and *Phantom of the Opera* (1986). His brother **Julian Lloyd Webber** (1951–) is a cellist.

Llywelyn ap Gruffudd (d. 1282) The only native Prince of Wales (1258–82) to be recognized as such by England. He aided the English barons against Henry III (1263–67) and refused homage to Edward I (1276), who forced Llywelyn into submission but allowed him to remain Prince of Wales by title. Llywelyn was killed in another revolt.

Llywelyn ap Iorwerth (d. 1240) Prince of Gwynedd, N Wales (1194–1238), who achieved supremacy over most other Welsh princes. He supported the barons against his father-in-law, King John of England (1215), obtaining recognition for Welsh rights in Magna Carta.

loach A small freshwater *bony fish of the family *Cobitidae* (over 200 species), found mainly in Asia, but also in Europe and N Africa. Loaches feed at night on bottom-dwelling invertebrates detected by the three to six pairs of barbels around the mouth. The intestine can serve as a respiratory organ using swallowed air. Order: *Cypriniformes*.

loam A type of soil containing approximately equal proportions of sand, silt, and clay. It is an ideal soil for agriculture since it can retain some moisture and plant nutrients but is well aerated and drained and easily worked.

Lobachevski, Nikolai Ivanovich (1793–1856) Russian mathematician, who (in 1829) produced the first *non-Euclidean geometry by examining what is possible if the fifth axiom in Euclid's *Elements* is neglected. In Lobachevski's geometry the angles of a triangle always add up to less than 180°.

Lobelia A genus of annual and perennial herbs (about 250 species), found in most warm and temperate regions. The leaves are simple and the flowers are tubular, with a two-lobed upper lip and a larger three-lobed lower lip, and are arranged in a terminal spike. Ornamental species, called cardinal flowers, are usually blue or red. Family: *Lobeliaceae*.

Lobengula (c. 1836–94) King (1870–94) of the Matabele (*or* Ndebele) kingdom in S Rhodesia. Son of *Mzilikazi, Lobengula granted land and mineral rights to the British South Africa Company but this was no protection against the conquest of his kingdom in 1893.

Lobito 12 20S 13 34E A port in W Angola, on the Atlantic coast. Its fine natural harbour has made it the country's busiest port. Population (1976 est): 70 000.

lobotomy. *See* leucotomy.

lobster A large marine *crustacean of the section *Macrura* that has a long abdomen ending in a tailfan. True lobsters (family *Homaridae*) have segmented bodies, a pair of pincers, four pairs of walking legs, and several pairs of swimming legs (swimmerets). They live on the ocean bottom and are mainly nocturnal, feeding on seaweed and animals. Eggs are carried on the swimmerets and hatch into free-swimming larvae that later descend to the bottom. Species used as food include *Homarus vulgaris* and *H. americanus*. Order: *Decapoda*.

local government The administration of a locality. In the UK local government has developed from the Anglo-Saxon division of the country into *shires, *hundreds, and *boroughs. However, local administration only became systematized in the 19th century, when the industrial revolution brought social problems demanding local attention. The Municipal Corporation Act (1835) established 178 municipal councils, elected by ratepayers, which in the following decades grew in number and took over a wide range of responsibilities, including the police and public health. County councils were established in 1888. In 1894 the work of local government was distributed by the creation of borough and urban district councils in urban areas and parish councils in rural areas. The Local Government Act (1972) divided England and Wales into 53 *counties. These are divided into districts, and they in turn into parishes or, in Wales, communities. District councils are responsible for a number of important services, including education, housing, and refuse collection. Parish and community councils exercise such minor functions as the provision of allotments and bus shelters. A similar system was established in Scotland in 1973 but in Northern Ireland there are 26 district councils. Local government is financed by *rates, rent, borrowing, and central-government grants. *See also* poll tax.

Local Group The small irregularly shaped *cluster of galaxies to which our *Galaxy belongs. Other members include the *Andromeda galaxy, the Triangulum Spiral, and both *Magellanic Clouds. There are 30 or more members.

Locarno (German name: Lugarrus) 46 10N 8 48E A resort in S Switzerland, on Lake Locarno. Its church of Madonna del Sasso (1480) is a place of pilgrimage. The *Locarno Pact was signed here. Population (1983 est): 14 224.

Locarno Pact (1925) A series of treaties between Germany, France, Belgium, Poland, Czechoslovakia, the UK, and Italy. The most important was an agreement between France, Germany, and Belgium, guaranteed by the UK and Italy, to maintain the borders between Germany and France and Belgium respectively and the demilitarized zone of the Rhineland. The latter was violated by Hitler in 1936.

Lochner, Stefan (c. 1400–51) German painter of the Cologne School, born in Meersburg on Lake Constance. He probably trained in the Netherlands before settling in Cologne. His *Madonna of the Rose Bower* (Wallraf-Richartz Museum, Cologne) combines the delicacy of the *international gothic with the naturalism of Flemish painting.

Loch Ness 57 15N 4 30W A lake in the Glen More valley, NW Scotland. Inverness is located at its junction with the sea. Length: 36 km (22.5 mi). Depth: 229 m (754 ft). The **Loch Ness monster**, alleged to inhabit the lake, is a persistent but unconfirmed phenomenon.

lock A section of a canal or river, enclosed by gates, that is used to regulate the water level and raise or lower vessels wishing to navigate the waterway. The more common pound lock consists of two sets of mitred gates set a distance apart pointing into the downward force of the water. A vessel wishing to pass from the lower water level to the higher level enters the lock, the lower gates are closed behind it, and water from the upper level is allowed to flow into the lock through gaps in the upper gates. When the two levels are

vessel about to   vessel being raised   vessel emerging
enter lock   inside lock   from lock at higher level

LOCK

equal the upper gates are opened and the vessel leaves. The reverse procedure enables vessels to travel from the higher to the lower level.

Locke, John (1632-1704) English philosopher. His greatest work, the *Essay concerning Human Understanding* (1690), reveals him as a pioneer of *empiricism. It maintains, contrary to received tradition, that every one of our ideas comes from sense impressions; at birth the human mind is a *tabula rasa* (blank tablet). The *Essay* also attempts to sustain the distinction between primary qualities (found without exception in all bodies) and secondary qualities (originating in the impressions these bodies make on our senses). Locke's two works *Of Government* (1690) were enormously influential in moulding modern concepts of liberal democracy. He dismissed any divine right to kingship and advocated liberal government, the function of which was, he thought, to preside over the exchange of "natural" for "civil" rights. He held that, in virtue of the occurrence of some form of *social contract in antiquity, political rulers were obliged to guarantee as civil rights any liberties that their subjects' ancestors might be supposed to have surrendered. However, there were some inalienable rights that could never be given up to a citizen's ruler.

Locke, Matthew (c. 1622-77) English composer. He became Composer in Ordinary to Charles II. His works include the masque *Cupid and Death* (with Christopher Gibbons; 1653). He wrote a pamphlet defending his "modern" church music.

Lockhart, Sir (Robert Hamilton) Bruce (1887-1970) British diplomat and writer, born in Scotland. He was acting consul general in Moscow (1915-17) and led a mission to the newly established Soviet Government in 1918, when he was briefly imprisoned in the Kremlin. He subsequently worked on the *Evening Standard* (London), returning to the Foreign Office in World War II. Among his books is *Memoirs of a British Agent* (1932).

Lockhart, John Gibson (1794-1854) Scottish biographer and journalist. His best-known work is his biography of Sir Walter Scott (1837-38), whose daughter he married. He also wrote a biography of Robert Burns (1828) and edited the *Quarterly Review* from 1825 to 1853.

lockjaw. See tetanus.

lockout The closure of a workplace by an employer to prevent employees from working, in an attempt to persuade them to accept the employer's terms of employment. In the interests of good industrial relations, the measure is now rarely used.

Lockyer, Sir Joseph Norman (1836-1920) British astronomer, who in 1868 first recognized the existence of an unknown element, which he called helium, in the sun's spectrum. Terrestrial helium was eventually discovered nearly 40 years later by Sir William *Ramsay. Lockyer also founded the scientific journal *Nature*.

locomotive An engine that draws a train on a *railway. The first locomotives, designed by *Trevithick and *Stephenson were driven by steam engines and steam dominated the railways until the end of World War II. Even in the mid-1970s, it was estimated that over 25 000 steam locomotives were still in use throughout the world.

However, the steam engine has a low efficiency (about 8% in a locomotive, which does not use a condenser), it takes a long time to become operational while steam is raised, it uses an awkward and dirty solid fuel (which it has to pull with it in a tender immediately behind the engine), and it creates pollution. For these reasons steam locomotives have largely been replaced in the industrial countries by electric, Diesel-electric, or Diesel trains, all of which have efficiencies of about 22%.

Where the traffic justifies the cost of installing overhead wires or a conductor rail, electric trains are usually preferred, as it is more efficient to generate electricity centrally than in the locomotive. Various configurations have been tried, but series-wound direct-current motors are the most widely used, with rectification in the locomotive when the supply is alternating current. In some cases a three-phase supply is used, with *thyristor control. For lines in which a permanent installation is not economic, Diesel engines are used as a prime mover. These are either coupled hydraulically to the wheels, using a hydraulic torque converter (or fluid flywheel) and a gearbox, or to an electric generator or alternator, which produces current to power electric motors that drive the wheels. The first Diesel-electric train was used in Sweden in 1912 and the first Diesel-hydraulic in Germany a year later. Because the Diesel provides a very low torque at low speeds, it cannot be used without a hydraulic coupling, but even these units are usually restricted to small trains.

The use of *gas turbines on the railways began in 1934, when a turbine powered a Swedish experimental train. A gas turbine-electric train was first tried in Switzerland in 1941. Although the gas turbine is lighter than the Diesel, it is only efficient at high power, and most of the long runs that could utilize its smooth full-power output are already electrified. The outlook for gas turbines is therefore not regarded as very promising.

Locri 38 14N 16 15E A city founded by Dorian Greek colonists about 700 BC on the E of the toe of Italy. Well governed by oligarchic rulers, Locri possessed in Zaleucus' legal code (c. 650 BC) Europe's earliest written laws. Its strategic position inevitably brought involvement in Rome's wars with Pyrrhus and Hannibal, and Scipio Africanus conquered it in 205 BC. Locri subsequently declined and was destroyed by Muslims in 915 AD. Excavations in 1889-1900 and the 1950s revealed a temple and many 5th-century terracotta plaques.

locus In mathematics, a set of points that satisfy certain conditions. For example, in two dimensions the set of points a fixed distance from a particular point is a circle.

locust (botany) An evergreen Mediterranean tree, *Ceratonia siliqua*, also called carob tree or St John's bread. 12-15 m in height, it has catkins of petalless flowers and produces leathery pods containing a sweet edible pulp and small flat beans. The black locust (*Robinia pseudoacacia*), also called false acacia, is a North American tree widely cultivated for ornament (it is common in streets and parks). Up to 24 m tall, it has deeply ridged dark-brown bark, paired pale-green leaves, hanging clusters of white flowers, and black pods. Family: *Leguminosae*.

locust (zoology) A *grasshopper that undergoes sporadic increases in population size to form huge swarms, which migrate long distances and devour all the crops and other vegetation on which they settle. When the population density is high, due to favourable environmental conditions, the nymphs (immature forms), called hoppers, are brightly coloured and crowd together—the gregarious phase, maturing into gregarious swarming adults. Solitary-phase nymphs, whose coloration is that of their surroundings, mature in uncrowded conditions into solitary nonswarming adults. Economically important species include the migratory locust (*Locusta migratoria*), about 55 mm long (all locusts are relatively large), found throughout Africa and S

Stephenson's "Rocket" *The first locomotive to combine a multi-tubular boiler and a blast pipe, the "Rocket" ran on the earliest public railway, between Stockton and Darlington (NE England), in 1829.*

"General" *Typical of the commonest type of US locomotive in the 19th century, the "General" was involved in a dramatic sabotage incident in 1862 during the Civil War. One of this class was the first to run at 100 mph (1893).*

C.R. No. 123 *Caledonian Railway's famous locomotive, designed by Dugald Drummond, ran the difficult 100.6 miles between Carlisle and Edinburgh in 102.5 minutes in August 1888.*

"Mallard" *This locomotive, designed by Sir Nigel Gresley, took the world steam traction speed record in July 1938, achieving 126 mph on a brake-test run.*

S.N.C.F. BB 9004 *For many years France held the world rail speed record. In 1955, the electric BB 9004 reached a speed of 205.6 mph, hauling three carriages weighing 100 tons.*

High Speed Train (HST) *British Rail's diesel-electric HST set a world record in 1985 for diesel-powered trains by reaching 144.8 mph. The HST powers the highly successful Inter-City 125 services.*

Eurasia and eastward to Australia and New Zealand; and the desert locust (*Schistocerca gregaria*), occurring from N Africa to the Punjab. In 1986 African food crops were threatened by the simultaneous swarming of five different species: the migratory and desert locusts, the red locust (*Nomadacris septemfasciata*), the brown locust (*Locusta pardalina*), and the Senegalese grasshopper.

Lod (*or* Lydda) 31 57N 34 54E A town in central Israel, between Jerusalem and Tel Aviv-Yafo. Lydda was the scene of many biblical events. Allocated to the Arabs by the UN in 1947, it fell to Israeli forces and is now the site of Israel's international airport. Population (1982 est): 40 700.

lodestone. *See* magnetite.

Lodge, Henry Cabot (1850–1924) US Republican politician; a senator from 1893 to 1924. An isolationist, he led the group of Republican senators who rejected the Treaty of *Versailles (1919) and prevented US membership of the League of Nations (1920).

Lodge, Sir Oliver Joseph (1851–1940) British physicist; one of the pioneers in the study of radio waves and radio communication, for which he was knighted in 1902. After 1910 he became increasingly involved in attempting to reconcile science and religion, which led him into a serious investigation of psychical phenomena. His books include the spiritualist *The Survival of Man* (1909) and the more scientific *Atoms and Rays* (1924).

Lodge, Thomas (1558–1625) English poet, dramatist, and writer. His works are very varied. Notable among them is the pastoral romance *Rosalynde* (1590), the source of Shakespeare's *As You Like It*. After studying medicine at Avignon he published medical treatises and translations.

Lodi 45 19N 9 30E A town in Italy, in Lombardy on the River Adda. It has a 12th-century cathedral. Manufactures include iron, maiolica, silk, and linen. Situated in a rich dairy-farming district, it has a large trade in cheese, especially Parmesan. Population (1980): 35 221.

Łódź 51 49N 19 28E The second largest city in Poland. It developed rapidly during the 19th century and is now a leading industrial centre specializing in textiles, chemicals, and electrical goods. Its university was founded in 1945. Population (1982 est): 845 000.

Loeb, Jacques (1859–1924) US zoologist, born in Germany, who demonstrated that unfertilized eggs of sea urchins and frogs could develop to maturity by means of controlled changes in their environment, which influenced cell division (*see* parthenogenesis). Loeb also worked on brain physiology, animal *tropisms, and tissue regeneration.

Loeffler, Friedrich August Johannes (1852–1915) German bacteriologist, who (with Edwin *Klebs in 1884) first isolated the diphtheria bacillus (the Klebs-Loeffler bacillus). Loeffler also showed how some animals were immune to diphtheria, which helped *Behring to develop an antitoxin.

loess A deposit consisting of wind-born dust from desert or vegetation-free areas at the margins of ice sheets. Vast thick deposits occur in NW China; in Europe loess occurs in Germany (the Bördeland), Belgium, and NE France. Deep well-drained soils develop from loess.

Loewe, Frederick (1904–88) Austrian composer of musical comedies, resident in the USA after 1924. He is famous for such musicals as *Brigadoon* (1947), *Paint Your Wagon* (1950), *My Fair Lady* (1956), *Gigi* (1958), and *Camelot* (1960), written with the librettist Alan *Lerner.

Loewi, Otto (1873–1961) US physiologist, who demonstrated that stimulation of nerves releases a chemical transmitter that affects the muscle concerned. He identified it as *acetylcholine—a substance first isolated by Sir Henry *Dale, with whom Loewi shared the 1936 Nobel Prize.

Lofoten Islands A large group of islands off the NW coast of Norway, within the Arctic Circle. There are rich cod and herring fisheries in the surrounding waters, to which many Norwegian fishermen come during spring. Area: about 5130 sq km (1980 sq mi). Population (1970): 56 066.

log **1.** A book containing a detailed record of the events occurring in and navigation of a vessel. **2.** A device, towed behind or fastened to a vessel, that records the speed of the vessel through the water. Its name comes from chip log, the device formerly used, which consisted of a chip tossed overboard, at the bow of a vessel; the time required to pass the chip and the distance covered were used to calculate the speed of the vessel.

Logan, Mount 60 31N 140 22W The highest mountain in Canada, in SW Yukon in the St Elias Mountains. Its huge mass towers 4200 m (13 780 ft) above glaciers. Height: 6050 m (19 850 ft).

loganberry A trailing bramble-like shrub that is a cross between a raspberry and a blackberry. It bears heads of juicy wine-red tart-tasting fleshy berries, which are used for preserves, puddings, and wine. It originated in California and is named after James H. Logan (1841–1928), who first grew it in 1881. Family: *Rosaceae*.

logarithms A mathematical function used to facilitate multiplication and division. Based on the law that $a^x \times a^y = a^{x+y}$, two numbers p and q can be multiplied together by writing them in the form $p = a^x$ and $q = a^y$ and then adding together the values of x and y (the exponents). x is called the logarithm of p to the base a, i.e. $x = \log_a p$. Thus $p \times q$ is found by looking up their logarithms in books of tables, adding them together, and looking up the antilogarithm of the result. Division is carried out in a similar way using subtraction, based on the law $a^x \div a^y = a^{x-y}$. The base of common logarithms is 10 (i.e. $a = 10$); Naperian or natural logarithms use the base e. Pocket calculators have obviated the need for logarithms as a method of computation but they remain useful mathematical functions.

logic In the widest sense, the science of reasoned argument. As a mental discipline, it is concerned not so much with the application of argument in specific instances as with the general rules covering the construction of valid inferences. The dialogues of *Plato present *Socrates as pursuing wisdom through rational discourse, but *Aristotle was the first to make a systematic study of the principles governing such discourse (*see also* syllogism). His six logical treatises, known collectively as the *Organon*, were the sourcebooks for such medieval logicians as *Abelard. After the Renaissance philosophers became increasingly aware of limitations in the Aristotelian approach. *Leibniz, for instance, was worried by the difference between the logical and grammatical structure of sentences; two grammatically identical sentences may be very different logically. (Suppose, for example, that Jemima is a cat and compare the following two sentences: "Jemima is a cat; Jemima is mine; therefore Jemima is my cat." "Jemima is a mother; Jemima is mine; therefore Jemima is my mother.") Rules must therefore be found to formalize ordinary language in such a way as to make plain its underlying logical structure, before further rules for the construction of valid arguments can be drawn up. Since the 19th century formulation of such rules has become mainly the province of mathematicians. *Boole and *Frege were important pioneers in what is now called "mathematical logic" to differentiate it from the wider still current sense. *Russell, whose work had important repercussions for *set theory, called "logic . . . the youth of mathematics, and mathematics . . . the manhood of logic."

logical positivism A philosophical movement that arose from the *Vienna Circle in the 1920s. Influenced by *Mach and *Wittgenstein, it insisted that philosophy should be scientific, regarding it as an analytical (rather than a speculative) activity, the purpose of which was clarification of thought. Any assertion claiming to be factual has meaning only if its truth (or falsity) can be empirically tested. Metaphysical propositions and those of ·aesthetics and religion are consequently meaningless, since it is impossible to say how they can be verified. A secondary goal of logical positivism was the analysis and unification of scientific terminology. After the Nazi invasion of Austria, members of the Circle emigrated to Britain and the USA, where the movement continued to be influential.

logos (Greek: word)   A term with several different philosophical interpretations. *Heraclitus used it to mean the pervading rational underpinning of the universe. For the *Sophists logos could simply mean an argument. For the Stoics it was the kind of god from whom stems all the rationality in the universe. Students of St John's Gospel tend to interpret its occurrence there in the Stoic sense. *See also* Stoicism.

logwood   A thorny tropical American tree, *Haematoxylon campechianum*, 9–15 m tall, with a short twisted trunk, compound leaves comprising many paired leaflets, and clusters of small yellow flowers. The blood-red heartwood yields the black to purple dye haematoxylin, used in the textile industry and as a biological stain. Family: *Leguminosae*.

Lohengrin   In *Arthurian legend, the son of Percival (Parzival). He champions a young noblewoman, Elsa of Brabant, whom he agrees to marry on condition that she does not enquire into his origins. When her curiosity overcomes her, he is taken back by his swan guide to the castle of the *Holy Grail, whence he came. The story was adapted by *Wagner in the opera *Lohengrin* (1850).

Loire, River   The longest river in France. Rising in the Cévennes Mountains, it flows mainly W to the Bay of Biscay at St Nazaire, passing through Orléans, Tours, and Nantes. Its tributaries include the Allier, Vienne, and Maine and it drains an area of 119 140 sq km (40 000 sq mi), one–fifth of the area of France. The Loire Valley is renowned for its vineyards and chateaux (Amboise, Blois, Chambord, Chaumont, Chenonceaux). It is linked by canal with the River Seine. Length: 1020 km (634 mi).

Loki   In Norse mythology, a mischief-making giant with the ability to change his shape and sex, who lived among the gods until imprisoned in a cave for the murder of Balder. His offspring—Hel, the goddess of death, Jörmungandr, the evil serpent surrounding the earth, and Fenris, the wolf—are among the forces of evil, which he leads against the gods at doomsday (□Ragnarök).

Lolland (*or* Laaland)   A Danish island in the Baltic Sea, S of Sjælland. Produce includes cereals, hops, apples, and sugar beet. Area: 1240 sq km (480 sq mi). Population (1976): 77 957. Chief town: Maribo.

Lollards   The followers of the English reformer *Wycliffe. Until his retirement from Oxford in 1378, the preaching of his doctrines attacking the Church hierarchy and transubstantiation and advocating the primacy of Scripture was largely confined to the University. Thereafter his teachings were taken up by nonacademics, including merchants, lesser clergy, and a few members of Richard II's court. Henry IV's reign saw considerable repression of the Lollards culminating in the defeat of *Oldcastle's rebellion in 1414. The movement then went underground and became increasingly proletarian. Many of its tenets were adopted by the early Protestants.

Lomax, Alan (1915–   ) US compiler of folksongs. With his father **John Avery Lomax** (1867–1948), he compiled *American Ballads and Folk Songs* (1934), *Negro Folk Songs As Sung by Lead Belly* (1936), and *Our Singing Country* (1941).

Lombard League   A confederacy of Lombard towns formed with papal support in 1167 against attempts by the Holy Roman Empire to weaken their communal liberties. These were confirmed by Frederick (I) Barbarossa at the Peace of Constance (1183). Renewed against the threat of Frederick II the League was disbanded after his death (1250).

Lombardo, Pietro (c. 1438–1515) Italian sculptor and architect. Lombardo worked mainly in Venice, where he was the

leading sculptor of his generation. His works include the Pietro Mocenigo monument (c. 1476–81; SS Giovanni e Paolo) and the design and sculptural decoration of Sta Maria dei Miracoli (1481–89). He was frequently assisted by his two sons **Antonio Lombardo** (c. 1458–c. 1516) and **Tullio Lombardo** (c. 1460–1532).

Lombards (Latin name: Langobardi)   A Germanic people who, under *Alboin, invaded Italy and established a kingdom centred on Pavia (572 AD). When *Aistulf and then Desiderius (reigned 756–74) threatened Rome, the pope sought Carolingian assistance and in 773–74 the Lombards lost their independence to Charlemagne.

Lombardy (Italian name: Lombardia)   A region in N Italy, consisting mainly of mountains in the N and lowlands in the S. Italy's most industrialized region, its economic prosperity has attracted workers from other parts of the country. The industrial area containing Milan is dominated by textile, chemical, and engineering industries; metal manufacture is also important. Agriculture is the most mechanized in Italy, producing a wide range of foods. There are natural-gas fields and hydroelectric plants. Area: 23 834 sq km (9191 sq mi). Population (1983 est): 8 891 318. Capital: Milan.

Lombok   An Indonesian island in the Nusa Tenggara group. The N and S are mountainous, while on the central fertile plain intensive cultivation produces rice, coffee, and tobacco. Under Hindu-Buddhist rule until the 15th century, it resisted later Islamic influence and came under Dutch control in 1894. Area: 4730 sq km (1826 sq mi). Population (1980): 1 957 128. Chief town: Mataram.

Lombroso, Cesare (1835–1909) Italian criminologist. His theories that some criminals can be recognized by physical characteristics are no longer considered valid, but his major work, *L'uomo delinquente* (1876), initiated a new emphasis in criminology on the study of the criminal mind.

Lomé 6 10N 1 21E The capital and chief port of Togo, on the Gulf of Guinea. The Lomé Convention, providing trade concessions with EEC countries for 46 African and Caribbean states, was signed here in 1975, as were its successors in 1979 and 1984. It has a university (1970). Population (1980): 283 000.

Lomond, Loch   The largest lake in Scotland, in E Strathclyde Region. It is a picturesque tourist area. Length: about 38 km (24 mi). Width: 8 km (5 mi).

Lomonosov, Mikhail Vasilievich (1711–65) Russian poet and scientist. The son of a fisherman, his work in the natural sciences led to a professorship at the St Petersburg Academy. In 1755 he founded Moscow University. He also wrote classical poetry and works on grammar and rhetoric.

London (Latin name: Londinium)   51 30N 0 10W The capital of the UK, in SE England on the River Thames. One of the six largest cities in the world, it comprises a succession of village communities that counterbalance its overall size, bustle, and complexity. It is also exceptional in its large number of parks, gardens, and leafy squares.

London's financial hub is to be found in its original nucleus, the **City of London**, on the N bank of the Thames between Blackfriars Bridge and Tower Bridge. The City comprises some 2.6 sq km (1 sq mi) and its large daytime population dwindles to a mere 4234 at night. Attempts to halt its depopulation have included new residential developments, notably the Barbican (1973), designed for about 6500 people. London's **East End**, centring on the borough of *Tower Hamlets, has long provided a home for successive immigrant groups and acquired in the 19th century a reputation for harbouring Britain's leading criminal families. The **West End** comprises the district around Oxford Street (constructed in the 19th century) and is the city's shopping and entertainment centre. The **government** of the City is the responsibility of the Corporation of the *City of London, which is administratively separate from the two-tier structure

LONDON *A view in 1616 of the first stone London Bridge, begun by Peter de Colechurch in 1176. The Southwark gatehouse (foreground) bears the heads of traitors.*

devised in 1963 for the 32 (12 Inner London and 20 Outer London) boroughs—the Greater London Council (GLC) and the borough councils. The Labour-controlled GLC was abolished by the Conservative government in 1986, its functions being transferred to the borough councils and to specially constituted residuary bodies.

London's **cultural life** is outstanding. In addition to the small private art galleries found around Bond Street in Mayfair, London is enhanced by the remarkable collections housed in the *National Gallery, the National Portrait Gallery, the *Tate Gallery, and the *Courtauld Institute. Its museums include the *British Museum (in Bloomsbury), the Natural History Museum—properly the British Museum (Natural History), the *Science Museum, the *Victoria and Albert Museum (all in South Kensington), and the *Imperial War Museum. Most of London's commercial theatres are in the West End but the subsidized National Theatre Company in 1975 moved to Lasdun's building on the South Bank of the Thames, where a remarkable complex of buildings has been constructed since World War II: this comprises the Royal Festival Hall (*see* Festival of London), the Queen Elizabeth Hall, the Purcell Room (all concert halls), the Hayward Gallery, and the British Film Institute. The Barbican Centre (opened 1982) in the City of London houses the Royal Shakespeare Company and the London Symphony Orchestra. Other concert halls include the Royal Albert Hall and the Wigmore Hall. London's rich musical life is enhanced by four symphony orchestras—the BBC Symphony, the London Philharmonic, the London Symphony, and the Royal Philharmonic Orchestras. The Royal Opera House at *Covent Garden also houses the *Royal Ballet, which with the English National Opera (now at the London Coliseum) was founded at *Sadler's Wells. The University of London (1836) comprises a number of colleges scattered throughout the city; the City University (1966) and Brunel University (1966) also lie within Greater London and other educational institutions include the *Royal Academy, the Royal Academy of Music, the Royal College of Music, the Guildhall School of Music and Drama, the *Royal Academy of Dramatic Art, and several teaching hospitals and polytechnics.

Economy: the City of London is one of the world's greatest banking, commodity, shipping, and insurance centres: the *Bank of England is to be found in Threadneedle Street with the *Stock Exchange nearby, while *Lloyd's is in Lime Street, near Leadenhall Market. Other markets include *Billingsgate (for fish), *Smithfield (the largest meat market in the world), and Nine Elms in Vauxhall, which replaced the colourful fruit and vegetable market at Covent Garden. London's commercial development depended to a large extent on its port, on which a vast entrepôt trade was based. However, apart from Tilbury Docks, most of the port area has been redeveloped for residential and commercial purposes. The Docklands Light Railway provides a link with the City, and London City Airport has frequent flights to the continent.

Many industries have now moved from central London to the suburbs but a wide variety of light industries remain. Activities are often localized: for example, the bespoke tailoring trade is centred on Savile Row, diamonds on Hatton Garden, and Harley Street (in Marylebone) is synonymous with private medicine. London's public-transport system is the responsibility of London Regional Transport (since 1984), which administers an extensive bus service as well as the *underground railway (the "tube"). London has the chief railway terminuses in the UK (stations include Euston, Paddington, Victoria, King's Cross, and Waterloo); it is served by airports at *Heathrow and (subsidiary ports) at *Gatwick in Surrey and Stansted in Essex.

History: the foundations of London Wall are the chief reminder of the City's origins under the Romans, who built London at the highest point at which the Thames could be forded and at the river's tidal limit—on what was later Cornhill and Ludgate Hill. It was sacked by Boadicea in 61 AD and subsequently, on several occasions, by the Vikings. During the reign of William the Conqueror the famous White Tower (*see* Tower of London) was built, and as London prospered in the middle ages both the Church and the *guilds sponsored exceptional building programmes. Parts of St Bartholomew the Great (1123), St John of Jerusalem at Clerkenwell (c. 1150), and the Temple Church (1185), among others, survive from the 12th century; □Westminster Abbey dates from the 11th century, being largely rebuilt in the 13th century, when Southwark Cathedral was begun. To the 15th century belong Westminster Hall, the Guildhall, and Lambeth Palace and to the 16th century, when London began to extend westwards, *St James' Palace. The early Stuart period witnessed the great work of Inigo Jones, notably the Queen's House at Greenwich (1617-35) and the Banqueting Hall in Whitehall (1619-22), its ceiling painted by Rubens. London's population was decimated by the Plague (1665) and much of its fabric was destroyed in the calamitous Fire of the following year. The greatest loss—Old St Paul's (□St Paul's Cathedral)—was replaced by Wren, who was responsible for much of the work of reconstruction: of his 49 parish churches, probably the finest is St Stephen Walbrook (1679), the Lord Mayor's church. Many of London's finest squares were built in the late 17th and early 18th centuries—Grosvenor and Berkeley Squares in Mayfair, Hanover and Cavendish Squares off Oxford Street, and St James's Square, S of Piccadilly all belong to this period. In the second half of the 18th century the Adam brothers designed the Adelphi estate near the Strand and also Portland Place; the early 19th century witnessed the work of Nash: Regent's Park (in which the zoological gardens are now to be found) and the terraces around it. London's other parks include *Hyde Park, Kensington Gardens, St James's Park (in which *Buckingham Palace is located), and Battersea Park in S London. New bridges were also being built at this time: Westminster was completed in 1750, Blackfriars in 1769, Waterloo in 1817, and Southwark in 1819. The 19th century produced the *Palace of Westminster, the Law Courts, such railway stations as St Pancras, and the Byzantine-style Westminster Cathedral. London, especially the City and the East End, was seriously damaged by bomb attacks during World War II and subsequent rebuilding has consisted largely of high offices and flats, including the National Westminster building (1977), which at 183 m (600 ft) is the tallest building in London. Area: 1580 sq km (610 sq mi). Population (1983): 6 754 500.

London 42 58N 81 15W A city in central Canada, in

Ontario. Founded in 1826, it has become SW Ontario's centre for transportation, manufacturing, finance, and education. London's industries include textiles, printing, food processing, chemicals, electrical and metal goods, motor vehicle parts, and engines. It houses the University of Western Ontario (1878). Population (1981): 254 280.

London, Jack (1876-1916) US novelist. After childhood poverty and imprisonment for vagrancy he embarked on a course of self-education from which he emerged as a committed socialist and best-selling author. His best-known novel, *The Call of the Wild* (1903), was written after his experience of the Klondike gold rush in 1897. His other novels include *White Fang* (1906) and the autobiographical *Martin Eden* (1909).

London Bridge A bridge spanning the River Thames from the SE region of the City of London to the borough of Southwark. Bridges on this site date back to Roman times but the most famous London Bridge was built in stone between 1176 and 1209, had 19 pointed arches and a draw-bridge, and was surmounted by shops and houses. It was replaced by a new bridge in the 1820s, designed by John *Rennie. The present bridge was completed in 1973.

London clubs Establishments, chiefly in and around the London streets of St James and Pall Mall, in which men or women gather for companionship or to pursue a common interest. Most have restaurants and provide accommodation for short stays. Membership to a London club is by election; subscriptions and entrance fees provide for the maintenance of the buildings and the staff. The origins of the modern club lie in the regular gathering of men over coffee in the 17th and 18th centuries; the first London club was White's, which began as a Chocolate House in 1698. Others include Boodle's (founded 1762), the Athenaeum (1824), *Crockford's (1827), the Garrick (1831), the Carlton (1832), the Reform (1836), and the Royal Automobile (1897). Women's clubs include the University Women's (1887) and the Forum (1919).

Londonderry (former name: Derry) 55 00N 7 19W A city and port in Northern Ireland, the county town of Co Londonderry on the River Foyle. The City of London Corporation was granted Londonderry and the Irish Society established (1610) to administer it. In a famous siege (1688-89) it held out for 105 days against the forces of James II. Industries include shirt manufacture, light engineering, and food processing. Population (1981): 62 697.

Londonderry (*or* Derry) A former county in N Northern Ireland, bordering on the Atlantic Ocean. It consists of central uplands bordered by lowlands with Lough Neagh in the SE. It is drained by the Rivers Foyle, Bann, and Roe. Londonderry is predominantly agricultural producing flax, cereals, and dairy produce. Fishing is also an important source of income. Industries include textiles, chemicals, and light engineering. Area: 2108 sq km (814 sq mi). County town: Londonderry.

London pride A succulent herb, *Saxifraga umbrosa*, also called St Patrick's cabbage, native to Ireland and Portugal and widely grown as an ornamental. It has a basal rosette of fleshy leaves with wavy edges and small white or pinkish five-petalled flowers in branching clusters on slender stems, 30-50 cm tall. The garden form is a hybrid, *S.* × *urbium*. Family: *Saxifragaceae*.

Londrina 23 18S 51 13W A city in S Brazil, in Paraná state. Founded in 1930, it is the centre of a coffee-growing area and has a university (1971). Population (1980): 258 084.

Long Beach 33 47N 118 06W A city and port in the USA, in California on San Pedro Bay. It is a major tourist centre, with a beach 13.5 km (8.5 mi) long. Other attractions include the former British liner *Queen Mary*, which has been converted into a hotel and conference centre. Industries

include the manufacture of aircraft and oil refining. Population (1980): 361 334.

longbow A bow of straight-grained yew used from about 1400 to about 1600. Originally Welsh, longbows were up to 1.8 m (6 ft) long and could fire a 110 cm (37 in) arrow capable of piercing chainmail and some plate armour at 183 m (200 yd) every 10 seconds.

Longfellow, Henry Wadsworth (1807-82) US poet. He travelled extensively in Europe and was professor of modern languages at Harvard (1834-54). He achieved enormous popularity with such narrative poems as *Evangeline* (1847) and *The Song of Hiawatha* (1855). He also produced an undistinguished translation of Dante's *Divine Comedy* (1865-67).

Longford (Irish name: Longphort) A county in the N central Republic of Ireland, in Leinster. Chiefly low lying with areas of bog, it contains part of Lough Ree in the SW. Agriculture consists of cattle and sheep rearing and the production of oats and potatoes. Area: 1043 sq km (403 sq mi). Population (1981): 31 140. County town: Longford.

Longhi, Pietro (Pietro Falca; 1702-85) Venetian painter, who specialized in historically interesting scenes of upper-class life. Small in scale, they are distinguished by their doll-like figures and humorous approach, notably in *Exhibition of a Rhinoceros* (National Gallery, London). His son **Alessandro Longhi** (1733-1813) was a portrait painter.

Longinus (1st century AD) Greek rhetorician, supposed author of *On the Sublime*. This treatise, a critical analysis of the quality of excellence in literature with illustrative quotations from numerous Greek writers, greatly influenced many later neoclassical writers, including Dryden, Pope, and Gibbon; it was first translated (1674) into a modern language by the French critic Boileau.

Long Island An island in the USA, in New York state separated from the mainland by Long Island Sound. Chiefly residential with many resorts, it contains the New York City boroughs of *Brooklyn and *Queens and the international John F. Kennedy Airport. Its farming provides the city with market-garden produce. Area: 4462 sq km (1723 sq mi).

longitude. *See* latitude and longitude.

long jump A field event in athletics. Competitors sprint up a runway and leap as far as possible into a sandpit from a take-off board. The competitor who makes the longest jump in three or six tries is the winner. World records: men: 8.9 m (1968) by Robert Beamon (USA); women: 7.43 m (1983) by A. Cusmir (Romania).

Longleat An English country house near Warminster, in Wiltshire, owned by the Marquess of Bath. Begun in the 1550s, burned down in 1567, and rebuilt from 1572 for Sir John Thynne (d. 1580), Longleat typifies the Elizabethan style of architecture. The house and its grounds, originally laid out by Capability *Brown and now containing a lion safari park, are open to the public.

Long March (1934-35) The flight of the Chinese communists from the *Jiangxi Soviet, which they were forced by the *Guomindang to abandon, to Yan'an, a distance of 10 000 km (6000 mi). Over 100 000 people, led by Mao Tse-tung, took part in the heroic march but only about 30 000 reached Yan'an. The Long March established Mao as the leader of the Chinese Communist Party. □ p. 740.

Long Parliament (1640-60) The parliament that was summoned by Charles I of England following his defeat in the second *Bishops' War. In 1640 it impeached the king's ministers, *Strafford and *Laud, and in 1641 expressed its grievances against Charles in the *Grand Remonstrance. Following his attempt to impeach five MPs by force it assumed control of the militia (1642). Charles' rejection of its demands for reform (Nineteen Propositions) precipitated the outbreak of the Civil War. Its power declined as that of the *New Model Army increased and in 1648 it was purged

LORD'S CRICKET GROUND *Engraving of a match between Middlesex and Notts. (1892).*

of its moderate members (*see* Pride, Thomas). The remaining Rump Parliament was dismissed in 1653 by Oliver □Cromwell, who established the *Protectorate. The Rump was reinstated in 1659 and the full membership of the Long Parliament was restored by *Monck in 1660. Shortly afterwards it dissolved itself, being replaced by the Convention Parliament, which effected the *Restoration.

longship A large sailing vessel equipped with a bank of oars on each side. Longships were used by Scandinavian maritime peoples until the mid-18th century. They had square sails and very high prows and were steered by a long tiller attached to a large rudder. Larger longships could carry about a hundred people and are said to have carried the Vikings from Scandinavia as far as Greenland and to the coast of North America.

longsightedness (*or* hypermetropia) Inability to see close objects clearly, because the lens of the eye focuses light to a point behind the retina (light-sensitive layer). This is less common than shortsightedness among young people, but, owing to changes in the lens with age, many people need glasses for reading by the time they are 50. This type of longsightedness is known as **presbyopia**.

long-tailed tit An acrobatic Eurasian tit, *Aegithalus caudatus*, about 14 cm long, with a black, pink, and white plumage and a long (7 cm) black-and-white tail. It feeds on insects and spiders and builds an elaborate nest from lichens, animal hair, cobwebs, and feathers. *See* Plate V.

Lonsdale, Gordon Arnold (Konon Trofimovich Molody;' 1924–) Russian secret agent. He worked in Britain from 1954, posing as a Canadian businessman. Arrested in 1961, he' was exchanged in 1964 for the British agent Greville Wynne.

Lonsdale, Dame Kathleen (1903–71) Irish physicist. One of the foremost X-ray crystallographers of her time, she used this technique to prove the ring structure of benzene compounds (1929). In 1945 she became the first woman to be elected to the Royal Society.

loofah The fibrous skeleton of the fruit of the tropical dishcloth gourd, or vegetable sponge (genus *Luffa* (6 species), especially *L. cylindrica*). These vines produce cucumber-like fruits, about 30 cm long. When mature, the pulp and seeds are removed leaving a dense network of fibrous conducting tissue, which is used as a bath sponge, dish washer, and industrial filter. Family: *Cucurbitaceae*.

loom. *See* weaving.

looper. *See* geometrid moth.

Loos, Adolph (1870–1933) Austrian architect. One of the pioneers of modern architecture, Loos was influenced by the styles of Otto *Wagner and Louis *Sullivan. His austere plain style, evident in the Steiner House, Vienna (1910), influenced *Gropius and the development of *functionalism. Later in his career, however, he became less dogmatic, designing buildings with classical motifs.

loosestrife Either of two perennial herbs occurring in marshes, ditches, and along river banks. Purple loosestrife, *Lythrum salicaria* (family *Lythraceae*), native to Eurasia, N Africa, and North America, grows to a height of 60–120 cm and bears spikes of purple flowers. The Eurasian yellow loosestrife, *Lysimachia vulgaris* (family *Primulaceae*), grows to a height of 1 m and bears clusters of yellow flowers.

Lope de Vega. *See* Vega (Carpio), Lope Félix de.

López, Carlos Antonio (?1790–1862) Paraguayan statesman. As president (1844–62) he attempted to modernize the country and to end its isolation. He was succeeded by his son **Francisco Solano López** (1826–70), who led Paraguay into the disastrous War of the *Triple Alliance.

López de Ayala, Pero (c. 1332–c. 1407) Spanish poet and chronicler, who became chancellor of Castile in 1399. His works include translations of Livy, Boethius, and Boccaccio, as well as *Rimado de palacio*, a collection of satirical poetry, and *Cronicas de los reyes de Castilla*.

Lop Nor An area of salt marsh and shallow shifting lakes in NW China, in the *Tarim Basin. Nuclear tests have been carried out here. Formerly a large salt lake, its area now varies widely.

loquat A small evergreen tree *Eriobotrya japonica*, native to China and Japan but cultivated in Mediterranean countries. 6–9 m high, it bears clusters of white flowers. The pear-shaped orange fruit has a woolly skin and is eaten fresh, in preserves, or in stews. · Family: *Rosaceae*.

Lorca, Federico Garcia. *See* Garcia Lorca, Federico.

Lord Chief Justice The presiding judge of the Queen's Bench Division of the High Court of Justice and the Criminal Division of the Court of Appeal; he is second in the judicial hierarchy to the Lord Chancellor (*see* chancellor). The present incumbent (since 1980) is Geoffrey Dawson, Baron Lane (1918–).

Lord Lyon King of Arms The highest authority in the deciding of heraldic matters in Scotland. Originally a herald in the 14th century, the Lord Lyon now heads four heralds and two pursuivants at the Lyon Office where, since 1677, all claims to arms must be registered. Also a judge, the Lord Lyon has jurisdiction over issues of clan chieftainship and pedigrees.

Lords, House of. *See* parliament.

Lord's cricket ground The world's most famous cricket ground, owned by the *Marylebone Cricket Club and situated in St John's Wood, London. It was founded by Thomas Lord (1757–1832) in Dorset Square and was moved to its present site in 1814. It has been the home of the Middlesex County Cricket Club since 1877.

Lorelei A rock in the Rhine River in W Germany noted for its echo and its association with a legend concerning a water nymph whose singing lured sailors to destruction. The legend first appears in the works of Clemens *Brentano.

Loren, Sophia (S. Scicoloni; 1934–) Italian film actress. From working as an extra and then as a supporting actress, she progressed to international stardom in such films as *Two Women* (1961), *The Millionairess* (1961), *Marriage Italian Style* (1964), and *The Cassandra Crossing* (1977). She was married to the Italian film producer Carlo Ponti (1913–).

Lorentz, Hendrick Antoon (1853–1928) Dutch physicist, who was awarded the 1902 Nobel Prize, with his pupil *Zeeman, for their work on the relationship between magnetism and radiation. Independently of *Fitzgerald, he suggested that bodies become shorter as their velocity increases, in order to explain the negative result of the *Michelson-Morley experiment. This phenomenon, now known as the **Lorentz-Fitzgerald** contraction, was later incorporated into Einstein's theory of *relativity. The mathematical treatment for transforming a set of coordinates from one frame of reference to another was worked out by Lorentz (**Lorentz transformations**) and also formed part of Einstein's theory of relativity.

Lorenz, Konrad (1903–) Austrian zoologist, who was one of the founders of modern ethology (the study of animal behaviour). In the 1930s Lorenz identified the phenomenon of *imprinting in young chicks. He was concerned with determining the elements of behaviour, how they were stimulated, their development in an individual, and their evolutionary significance. Lorenz has written several popular books about his work, including *King Solomon's Ring* (1949) and *Man Meets Dog* (1950). He has applied his theories to the human species, with controversial implications (*On Aggression*, 1963). He was awarded a Nobel Prize (1973) with Karl von *Frisch and Niko *Tinbergen.

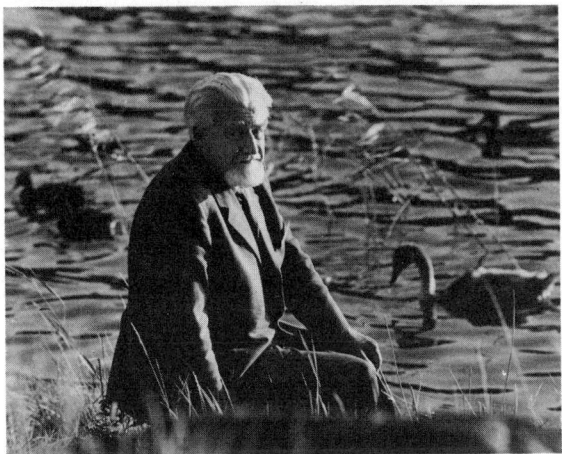

KONRAD LORENZ *A pioneer of the science of ethology (the behaviour of animals in their natural surroundings). Lorenz is pictured here in 1973, the year he received a Nobel Prize.*

Lorenzetti Two brothers, both Italian painters of the Sienese school, who were influenced by Giovanni *Pisano and *Giotto. They probably both died in the plague of 1348. **Pietro Lorenzetti** (c. 1280–?1348) was probably the pupil of *Duccio; he introduced a new humanity into his master's style in such works as *The Birth of the Virgin* (Duomo, Siena). His brother **Ambrogio Lorenzetti** (c. 1290–?1348) is renowned for his frescoes of *Good and Bad Government* (1337–39; Palazzo Pubblico, Siena). They are among the first Italian paintings to show scenes of contemporary life and are remarkable for their early mastery of perspective.

Lorenzo Monaco (Piero di Giovanni; c. 1370–1425) Italian painter, born in Siena. He settled in Florence, becoming a monk in 1391. Influenced by both the Sienese school and the Florentine tradition of *Giotto, his *Coronation of the Virgin* (Uffizi) is his major work.

Lorestan. *See* Luristan.

Loreto 43 26N 13 36E A small town in central Italy, in Marche. Pilgrims travel here to see the Santa Casa (Holy House), which is said to have been the home of the Virgin Mary in Nazareth and to have been brought to Loreto by angels in the 13th century. Population (1981 est): 10 622.

Lorient 47 45N 3 21W A port in NW France, in the Morbihan department on the Bay of Biscay. Formerly the principal naval shipyard in France, it was destroyed in World War II. Today it has important fishing and car component industries. Population (1982): 64 675.

loris A nocturnal Asian *prosimian primate belonging to the subfamily *Lorisinae* (5 species). Lorises are 20,–35 cm long with almost no tail and very large dark eyes. They are generally slow-moving and arboreal, feeding on insects and fruit. Family: *Lorisidae*. *See also* angwantibo; potto.

Lorrain, Claude. *See* Claude Lorrain.

Lorraine (German name: Lothringen) A planning region and former province in NE France, bordering on Belgium, Luxembourg, and West Germany. Its valuable iron-ore deposits are the largest in Europe outside Sweden and the Soviet Union. *History*: it was frequently the scene of conflict between France and Germany. In the 9th century AD it formed part of the kingdom of Lotharingia, later becoming a duchy under the Holy Roman Empire. Disputed between France and the Habsburgs, it was finally incorporated into France, as a province, in 1766. Following the Franco-Prussian War (1871) part of Lorraine (now Moselle department) was lost to Germany and united with *Alsace to form the imperial territory of Alsace-Lorraine. Area: 23 540 sq km (9087 sq mi). Population (1982): 2 319 905.

Lorraine, Charles, Cardinal de. *See* Guise.

lory A small brightly coloured *parrot belonging to the subfamily *Loriinae* (62 species), occurring in Australia, New Guinea, and Polynesia. Lories have a slender bill with a brush-tipped tongue and feed on pollen and nectar.

Los Alamos 28 54N 103 00W A town in the USA, in New Mexico. Chosen by the US government (1942) for atomic research, the first atom bombs were made here during World War II. The H-bomb was later developed here by the scientific laboratory of the University of California, which now covers an area of 199 sq km (77 sq mi). Government control of Los Alamos ended in 1962. Population (1980): 11 039.

Los Angeles 34 00N 118 15W A city and seaport in the USA, in S California on the Pacific coast. Founded in 1781 by Franciscan missionaries, it was made the capital of Mexican California in 1845 but was captured by US forces in the following year. Over the years it has incorporated many neighbouring towns so that today it comprises a large industrial and urban complex, with the third largest population in the USA. It is the centre of the US film industry, which attracts many tourists to the city, and more recently several television and radio stations have been established here. Other major industries include the manufacture of aircraft and oil refining. Industrial pollution, augmented by the high density of cars (Los Angeles is the only major US city without a public system of transport), is a serious problem. An educational centre, it is the site of several universities. Population (1980): 2 968 579.

Los Angeles, Victoria de (1923–) Spanish soprano. She studied at Barcelona conservatoire, made her London and New York debuts in 1950, and established herself as a popular prima donna, particularly in the title roles of Massenet's *Manon Lescaut* and Puccini's *Madame Butterfly*.

Losey, Joseph (1909–84) US film director. Accused during the McCarthy era of having communist sympathies, he went to Europe in 1952. His fascination with English class structure is evident in *The Servant* (1963), *Accident* (1967), and *The Go-Between* (1971), all scripted by Harold *Pinter. His other films included *The Romantic Englishwoman* (1975) and *Mr Klein* (1976).

Lossiemouth 57 43N 3 18W A town in NE Scotland, in Grampian Region on the Moray Firth. It is a small fishing port, resort, and the birthplace of Ramsay MacDonald. Population (1983 est): 7065.

Lost Generation A term applied to the expatriate US writers of the 1920s whose works expressed their sense of spiritual alienation. The term derives from a remark attributed to Gertrude Stein and used as an epigraph to Ernest Hemingway's novel *The Sun Also Rises* (1926).

Lot, River A river in S France, flowing mainly W through the departments of Lozère, Aveyron, Lot, and Lot-et-Garonne to the River Garonne. Length: 483 km (300 mi).

Lothair (c. 835-69 AD) King (855-69) of an area W of the Rhine, inherited from his father Lothair I, that came to be called Lotharingia. His attempts to divorce his childless wife Theutberga developed into a struggle with Pope Nicholas I.

Lothair I (795-855 AD) Coemperor of the West; eldest son of *Louis (I) the Pious, whose coemperor he became in 817. On Louis' death in 840 Lothair's position was challenged by his brothers Louis the German (d. 876) and Charles the Bald and in 843 the Frankish territories were divided between them.

Lothair II (1075-1137) Holy Roman Emperor (1133-37) and, as Lothair III, German king (1125-37). He became Duke of Saxony in 1106 in return for supporting Emperor Henry V against his father in 1104 but subsequently turned against Henry, defeating him at the battle of Welfesholz (1115). The Hohenstaufen family contested his election as king until 1135. As emperor, he tried to expel Roger II of Sicily from Italy.

Lothian Region An administrative region in SE Scotland, created under local government reorganization in 1975 from the counties of East Lothian, Midlothian, and West Lothian. It consists of lowlands bordering on the Firth of Forth in the N and rising gently to the S. The fertile lowlands are important agriculturally, especially for vegetables and pigs. Coal is extracted from the Midlothian coalfield. Other industry includes distilling and engineering. Area: 1756 sq km (677 sq mi). Population (1983 est): 744 802. Administrative centre: Edinburgh.

Loti, Pierre (Julien Viaud; 1850-1923) French novelist. He served as a naval officer and wrote numerous novels of romance and adventure with exotic settings and several travel books. His best-known novels include three studies of Breton sailors, *Mon frère Yves* (1883), *Pêcheur d'Islande* (1886), and *Matelot* (1893).

Lotto, Lorenzo (c. 1480-1556) Venetian painter. He travelled extensively in Italy and his work is consequently marked by a number of influences; he frequently visited Venice but, unable to compete with Titian's success, worked chiefly in Bergamo. He is noted for his altarpieces, e.g. the *Crucifixion* (Monte San Giusto, Bergamo), and the psychological insight of such portraits as *A Young Man* (Kunsthistorisches Museum, Vienna), and *Andrea Odoni* (Hampton Court). He spent his last years in a monastery in Loreto.

lotus Any of several different water plants. The sacred lotus of ancient Egypt was probably *Nymphaea lotus*, a sweet-scented white night-flowering *water lily with broad petals, or *N. caerulea*, a blue-flowered species. The sacred Indian lotus, *Nelumbo nucifera* (family *Nelumbaceae*), has roselike pink flowers and its seeds, called lotus nuts, are eaten raw or in soups. The genus *Lotus* contains about 70 species of herbs, including the birdsfoot *trefoils.

loudspeaker A device for converting electrical signals into sound. It usually consists of a small coil fixed to the centre of a movable diaphragm or cone. The coil is in an annular gap between the poles of a strong *magnet. An audio-frequency electrical signal fed to the coil creates a varying magnetic field, which interacts with the steady field in the gap. This causes the coil, and the attached cone, to vibrate and produce sound waves of the same frequencies as the electrical signal. Generally, larger cones give a better response at low frequencies and the smaller cones are best at high frequencies; for the best results two or more different-sized cones are therefore used, either in the same or in separate cabinets. The loudspeaker cabinet is also an important part of the system since it can act as a sound baffle and improve the frequency response.

Loughborough 52 47N 1 11W A town in central England, in Leicestershire on the River Soar. Industries include footwear, hosiery, pharmaceuticals, electrical equipment, and bell founding (the great bell of St Paul's, London, was cast here). Loughborough University of Technology was incorporated in 1966. Population (1981): 50 673.

Louis (I) the Pious (778-840 AD) Emperor of the West (813-40); son of Charlemagne. He fostered Christianity but imperial unity was undermined by his rebellious sons and after his death the Empire was partitioned.

Louis (I) the Great (1326-82) King of Hungary (1342-82) and Poland (1370-82). Louis encouraged commerce and the arts and in 1367 he founded Hungary's first university at Pécs. His campaigns against Venice had brought Hungary most of Dalmatia by 1381.

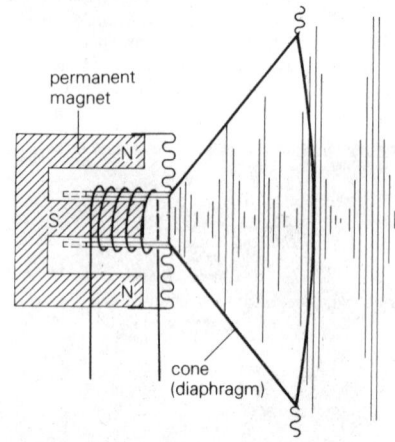

permanent magnet

cone (diaphragm)

LOUDSPEAKER *A moving-coil loudspeaker with a pot-shaped permanent magnet.*

Louis II (1845-86) King of Bavaria (1864-86) renowned for his extravagant castles, especially Neuschwanstein, and patronage of the composer Richard Wagner. His hopes for Bavaria in the newly founded German empire (1871) were disappointed and he subsequently withdrew from politics. In 1886 he was pronounced mad and shortly afterwards drowned himself.

Louis (IV) the Bavarian (?1283-1347) German king and Holy Roman Emperor (1314-47; crowned 1328). In 1324 Pope John XXII excommunicated Louis in support of Frederick III of Austria (c. 1286-1330), who contested the German throne. Louis deposed John in 1327 and in 1328 was crowned emperor by the antipope Nicholas V. From 1294 Louis was Duke of Bavaria, for which he devised a legal code (c. 1335).

Louis (V) le Fainéant (967-87 AD) The last Carolingian King of France (986-87), whose frivolity (his nickname means "feckless") helped to discredit the dynasty, bringing the Capetian *Hugh Capet to power.

Louis (VII) le Jeune (c. 1120-80) King of France (1137-80). He was engaged in a bitter struggle with Henry II of England between 1152, when Henry acquired Aquitaine through his marriage to Louis' former wife *Eleanor of Aquitaine, until 1174.

Louis VIII (1187-1226) King of France (1223-26), known as the Lionheart. He was offered the English throne by King John's baronial opponents but his invasion of England was defeated in 1217. He gained Toulouse and Languedoc for the French Crown and in 1226 launched a crusade against the *Albigensians.

Louis IX, St (1214-70) King of France (1226-70), regarded as the model medieval Christian king. After defeating Henry III of England (1242) he set out as leader of the sixth *Crusade (1248), during which he was captured by the Egyptians. On his return to France he introduced administrative reforms and fostered learning and the arts. He died on a Crusade in Tunisia and was canonized in 1297.

Louis XI (1423-83) King of France (1461-83), who united most of France under his rule. In 1447 his father, Charles VII exiled him to Dauphiné for his part in a conspiracy. After becoming king Louis overcame the aristocratic opposition of the League of the Public Weal (1465) and in 1477 finally defeated Charles the Bold of Burgundy. He extended royal authority over the church and encouraged commerce, gaining the support of the middle classes.

Louis XII (1462-1515) King of France (1498-1515). His reign was dominated by the wars that his father Charles VIII had initiated in Italy, and Louis suffered major defeats (1511-13) on several fronts at the hands of the Holy League.

Louis XIII (1601-43) King of France (1610-43), whose reign was dominated by his chief minister Cardinal de *Richelieu. He was the son of the assassinated Henry IV and of *Marie de' Medici, who was regent during his minority. In 1617 he exiled Marie from court and she raised two revolts against him but mother and son were later reconciled by Richelieu, her adviser, who in 1624 became Louis' chief minister. The king defeated two *Huguenot uprisings (1622, 1628), taking their fortress of La Rochelle in 1628.

Louis XIV (1638-1715) King of France (1643-1715), known as the Sun King because of the splendour of his reign. His minority was dominated by Cardinal *Mazarin, after whose death in 1661 Louis allowed no single minister to dominate. He was ably served by such men as *Colbert, who revived French trade, industry, and agriculture, and *Louvois, who with his father made France's army the best in Europe, but insisted that *L'état c'est moi* ("I am the state"). He was a firm advocate of the *divine right of kings and subdued the aristocrats, whose rebellion known as the *Fronde had threatened the Crown during his minority, by providing diversions at his great palaces—outstandingly

LOUIS XIV   *The Sun King portrayed in all his glory.*

*Versailles. His patronage of artists, including the writers Molière and Racine, further enhanced the magnificence of his court. In 1660 he married Maria Theresa (1638-83), the daughter of Philip IV of Spain (1605-65; reigned 1621-65). His mistresses included Mme de *Montespan and then Mme de *Maintenon, whom he secretly married after Maria Theresa's death. Abroad, France became the dominant power in Europe during Louis' reign. His ambitions in the Spanish Netherlands sparked off the War of *Devolution (1667-68) and were renewed by a second invasion in 1672. From this, the third *Dutch War, France emerged (1678) at the pinnacle of its power, a position Louis was unable to retain through the subsequent Wars of the *Grand Alliance (1689-97) and *Spanish Succession (1701-14). France was further weakened by Louis' revocation (1685) of the Edict of Nantes, ending toleration of Protestants and driving many of France's most productive citizens into exile. He left a country weakened by the economic demands of his wars and a monarchy that was to prove unequal to the enormous demands placed on it by his personal rule. His reign was nevertheless one of incomparable brilliance.

The **Louis Quatorze style** of late 17th-century interior design was developed in a deliberate attempt by Louis XIV and his designers to establish a French national idiom. The formal baroque furniture made in the new royal workshops derived from Italian antiquity and was sumptuously gilded or veneered for such regal settings as *Versailles. The most resplendent items were made of cast silver.

Louis XV (1710-74) King of France (1715-74), whose weak rule discredited the Crown and contributed to the outbreak of the French Revolution of 1789. His early reign was dominated by *Fleury, after whose death in 1743 Louis' indecisiveness and the influence of his mistresses, especially Mme de *Pompadour and, later, Mme *Du Barry, fostered faction and intrigue. The loss of almost all France's colonies in the *Seven Years' War (1756-63) increased his unpopularity, which hasty judicial and financial reforms at the end of his reign did nothing to alleviate.

The **Louis Quinze style** of French interior decoration and furnishing lasted from about 1723 until Louis' death. A sophisticated and informal style, it was a reaction to the formal baroque pomp of Louis XIV's court. The rococo, with its lighthearted use of eccentric scrolls, replaced symmetrical antique and Renaissance motifs. Chairs, formerly ranged around the walls of large rooms, were designed and arranged for ease of conversation in the new, smaller, and more intimate rooms.

Louis XVI (1754-93) King of France (1774-93), who was guillotined during the *French Revolution. The opposition of Louis' wife *Marie Antoinette and the aristocracy thwarted the attempted reforms of his ministers *Turgot and *Necker. The consequent economic crisis forced the king to summon (1789) the States General, the disaffected Third Estate of which precipitated revolution. The royal family was confined to the Tuileries Palace from which they attempted to flee in 1791, reaching Varennes. Brought back to the Tuileries, Louis was deposed after it had been stormed by the Paris mob. In 1793 he was guillotined and was followed to the scaffold by his wife.

The **Louis Seize style**, a neoclassical French style of furnishing, came into fashion after Louis XVI's accession. It was characterized by rejection of the rococo with straight lines replacing curves and a continuing tendency towards lightness and utility. The predominant idiom was restrained classicism (key patterns, caryatids, garlands, trophies). After the French Revolution (1789-99) this style remained in vogue for some time.

Louis XVII (1785-95) King of France in name (1793-95) following the execution of his father Louis XVI during the French Revolution. He died in prison.

Louis XVIII (1755-1824) King of France, in name from 1795, following the death in prison of his nephew *Louis

XVII, and in fact from 1814, following the overthrow of Napoleon. He fled Paris when Napoleon returned from Elba, being restored with diminished prestige after Waterloo "in the baggage train of the allied armies." His attempts to be a moderate constitutional monarch were thwarted by the ultraroyalists.

Louis, Joe (Joseph Louis Barrow; 1914–81) US boxer, called the Brown Bomber, who was world heavyweight champion from 1937 to 1948, when he retired. He defended his title 25 times and has been regarded as the world's greatest boxer.

Louisiana A state in the S USA, on the Gulf of Mexico. Chiefly low lying, it is crossed by the Mississippi River, the delta of which dominates the coastal lowlands in the S. The main upland area in the state is found in the NW along the Red River Valley. The increasingly urban population lives mainly in the S. The state produces chemicals and petrochemicals, paper and food products. Oil is exploited throughout the state and there are major deposits of natural gas, sulphur, and salt. New Orleans and Baton Rouge are important ports and tourism is a growing industry. Its favourable climate and fertile soils make it an important agricultural state; the chief products are beef cattle, rice, soya beans, dairy products, sugar cane, and cotton. It is an important cultural region, famous for its jazz music centred on New Orleans. *History*: although discovered by the Spanish, it was claimed for France and named after Louis XIV in 1682. It was ceded to Spain (1762) but was restored to France (1800). It was acquired by the USA as part of the Louisiana Purchase (1803), becoming a state in 1812. It was a supporter of the Confederate cause in the US Civil War. Area: 125 675 sq km (48 523 sq mi). Population (1980): 4 203 972. Capital: Baton Rouge.

Louisiana Purchase (1803) About 2 144 250 sq km (828 000 sq mi) of land between the Mississippi River and the Rocky Mountains, purchased by the USA from France for $27,267,622. The purchase doubled the size of the USA and established US dominance in North America.

Louis of Nassau (1538–74) A leader of the *Revolt of the Netherlands against Spain. His opposition to the Spanish led to his exile in 1567 but, after gaining support in Germany and France, he invaded the Netherlands with a Protestant army (1568). The campaign was indecisive and in the second invasion, in 1574, Louis and his younger brother were killed.

Louis Philippe (1773–1850) King of the French (1830–48), the son of the Duke of *Orléans. He supported the *French Revolution until 1793, when he deserted to the Austrians, living abroad until 1814. He joined the liberal opposition to the restored Louis XVIII and came to the throne after the July Revolution had ousted Louis' successor Charles X. Styled King of the French rather than of France and described by Thiers as the Citizen King, Louis Philippe relied on the support of the middle class. His initial moderation turned to repression in the face of the many rebellions against his rule and he abdicated in the Revolution of 1848. He retired to England, dying at Claremont, in Surrey.

Louisville 38 13N 85 48W A city and port in the USA, in N Kentucky on the Ohio River. The state's largest city, it has many historical buildings and is the site of the University of Louisville (1798). The American Printing House for the Blind is situated here. Since 1875 the famous Kentucky State Derby has been held in Louisville at the Churchill Downs racecourse. Industries include tobacco manufacture, whiskey distilling, milling, and chemicals. Population (1980): 298 451.

Lourdes 43 06N 0 02W A town in SW France, in the Hautes-Pyrénées department situated at the foot of the Pyrenees. It is a major pilgrimage centre for Roman Catholics (*see* Bernadette of Lourdes). Population (1982): 17 619.

Lourenço Marques. *See* Maputo.

louse A wingless □insect parasitic on warm-blooded animals. The sucking lice (order *Anoplura*; 225 species) suck the blood of mammals. They have hairy flattened bodies, 0.5–6 mm long, and claws for attachment to the host. The eyes are often reduced or absent. One of the most important species is the human louse (*Pediculus humanus*), of which there are two varieties—the head louse (*P. humanus capitis*) and the body louse (*P. humanus humanus*). Both are transmitted by direct contact and lay their eggs ("nits") on hair or clothing. Body lice are carriers of typhus and related diseases. Biting lice (order *Mallophaga*; 2600 species) resemble sucking lice but have biting mouthparts for feeding on the skin, feathers, etc., of birds—their principal hosts.

Louth (Irish name: Contae Lughbhaidh) The smallest county in the Republic of Ireland, in Leinster bordering on the Irish Sea. It is chiefly low lying. Agriculture is important with cattle rearing and arable farming producing oats and potatoes. Area: 821 sq km (317 sq mi). Population (1981): 88 514. County town: Dundalk.

Louvain (Flemish name: Leuven) 50 53N 04 42E A town in central Belgium. It was a centre of the cloth trade in the middle ages and the capital of the duchy of Brabant. It possesses a gothic town hall and a university (1426). Much of the town was destroyed in World War I. Industries include leather and chemicals. Population (1983 est): 84 908.

Louvois, Michel Le Tellier, Marquis de (1641–91) French statesman; minister for war (1666–77). With his father **Michel Le Tellier** (1603–85), war minister (1643–66), he reorganized the French army. Their success was demonstrated by Louis IV's many military victories. Louvois was the king's chief minister after 1683.

Louvre The national museum of France containing the art collection of the French kings and housed in the former royal palace and Tuileries palace in Paris. It was opened to the public in 1793. Napoleon exhibited his war loot here, of which the celebrated Venus de Milo still remains. Other highlights are Leonardo da Vinci's *Mona Lisa* and a collection of impressionist paintings, housed separately in the Jeu de Paumes in the Tuileries gardens.

lovage A perennial herb, *Ligusticum scoticum*, that grows 15–90 cm high and has large compound leaves with pairs of divided toothed leaflets and clusters of greenish-white flowers. It is native to Europe and used as a pot herb and salad plant. Family: *Umbelliferae*.

lovebird A small brightly coloured *parrot belonging to a genus (*Agapornis*; 9 species) occurring in Africa and Madagascar. 10–16 cm long, lovebirds typically have a short tail, a red bill, and a prominent eye ring. Lovebirds often feed in large flocks and may damage crops. They are popular cagebirds because they are long-lived, can be taught tricks, and appear to have great affection for each other.

Lovecraft, H(oward) P(hilips) (1890–1937) US novelist and short-story writer. He lived virtually as a recluse and wrote science-fiction stories and tales of macabre fantasy, such as *The Case of Charles Dexter Ward* (1928) and *At the Mountains of Madness* (1931).

love-in-a-mist An annual herb, *Nigella damascena*, also called fennel flower, native to S Europe and grown as an ornamental in temperate regions. It has fernlike leaves and blue or white flowers, 4 cm across, with many clawed petals surrounded by the leaves. The fruit is a globular head of capsules. Family: *Ranunculaceae*.

Lovelace, Richard (1618–57) English Cavalier poet. During the Civil War, although he was not actively involved, he was committed to and spent nearly all his fortune in the royalist cause, and was twice imprisoned. In prison he wrote one of his best-known poems "To Althea, from Prison." *Lucasta* (1649) contains most of his best lyrics.

love-lies-bleeding. *See* Amaranthus.

Lovell, Sir Bernard (1913-) British astronomer. After working on radar during World War II he became interested in *radio astronomy and supervised the construction of a 250-foot radio telescope at *Jodrell Bank Experimental Station, a part of Manchester University. His books include *The Exploration of Outer Space* (1961) and *Out of the Zenith* (1973).

Lovett, William (1800-77) British Chartist leader. He helped to found the London Working Men's Association in 1836 and to draft the People's Charter in 1838. He was imprisoned (1839-40) following riots in Birmingham. His moderate views subsequently alienated him from other Chartist leaders. *See* Chartism.

Low, Sir David (Alexander Cecil) (1871-1963) New Zealand-born cartoonist. Self-taught, he was employed by the *Sydney Bulletin* (1911) and in England by the *Star* (1919-27) and the *Evening Standard* (1927-50). He created world-famous characters, notably Colonel Blimp, and cartoons, satirizing Hitler, Mussolini, Churchill, etc., with a uniquely simple drawing technique. He later worked for the *Daily Herald* (1950-53) and the *Guardian* (1953-63).

Low Countries The Netherlands, Belgium, and Luxembourg. The Low Countries originally comprised numerous small states, controlled by major powers. In 1568 the N Protestant states revolted against Spanish rule, becoming the independent United Provinces of the Netherlands (*see* Revolt of the Netherlands). Belgium and Luxembourg gained independence in 1830 and 1867 respectively.

Lowell 42 38N 71 19W A city in the USA, in NE Massachusetts at the confluence of the Concord and Merrimack Rivers. Its growth began with the establishment of textile mills here in 1822 and it became one of the most famous textile centres in the USA. Population (1980): 92 418

Lowell, Amy (1874-1925) US poet and critic. After meeting Ezra *Pound in London in 1913, she became the leading propagandist for *Imagism. Her *Collected Poetical Works* was published in 1955. She also wrote criticism and a biography of *John Keats* (1925).

Lowell, James Russell (1819-91) US poet, critic, and diplomat. He published literary criticism, political works, and poetry ranging from the satirical *Fable for Critics* (1848) to the dialect *Biglow Papers* (1848, 1867). He edited the *Atlantic Monthly* (1857-61). He served as minister to Spain (1877-80) and Britain (1880-85).

Lowell, Percival (1855-1916) US astronomer, who first predicted the existence of the planet *Pluto, because of certain irregularities in the orbit of Uranus. Lowell never discovered Pluto despite intense searching and it was not found until 14 years after his death. He also made a detailed study of the "canals" on Mars.

Lowell, Robert (1917-77) US poet. In 1943 he was imprisoned as a conscientious objector. *Life Studies* (1959) marked a change from his complex and allusive early poetry, such as *Lord Weary's Castle* (1946), to a looser, more personal style. His left-wing political involvement during the 1960s is reflected in *For the Union Dead* (1964). He also published free translations, collected in *Imitations* (1962), and verse dramas. His last book was *Day by Day* (1977).

Lower California (Spanish name: Baja California) A peninsula in NW Mexico, between the Gulf of California and the Pacific Ocean. It is chiefly mountainous and arid. Within irrigated areas, especially in the N near the US border, cotton, fruit, vegetables, and vines are grown. There are important mineral deposits; these include copper, silver, and lead. Length: 1223 km (760 mi).

Lower Hutt 41 12S 174 54E A city in New Zealand, in S North Island on Port Nicholson (an inlet of Cook Strait).

An important industrial centre, Lower Hutt has meat freezing, engineering, and textile industries. Population (1983 est): 62 900.

Lower Saxony (German name: Niedersachsen) A *Land* in N West Germany, bordering on the North Sea, the Netherlands and East Germany. Formed in 1946 from four former states, it lies on the N German plain, with mountains in the S. It is chiefly agricultural but some minerals are extracted, including oil and iron ore. Area: 47 430 sq km (18 301 sq mi). Population (1983 est): 7 250 900. Capital: Hanover.

lowest common denominator The smallest common multiple of the denominators of two or more fractions. For example, the group 2/3, 1/6, 5/8 have the lowest common denominator 24.

Lowestoft 52 29N 1 45E A fishing port in E England, in Suffolk. It suffered considerable damage in both World Wars and the Royal Naval Patrol Service Memorial stands in Belle Vue Park. Besides fishing and associated industries, Lowestoft is concerned mainly with yachting and tourism. Population (1981): 55 231.

L. S. LOWRY   The Pond *(1950; Tate Gallery, London).*

Lowry, L(awrence) S(tephen) (1887-1976) British painter, born in Manchester. He worked as a clerk until his retirement at 65, using his spare time for art lessons and painting. He exhibited regularly in Manchester from the 1920s, when he began his most characteristic works, bleak industrial landscapes and towns dotted with matchstick figures. These first attracted serious attention in the 1940s. A large retrospective exhibition was held at the Royal Academy in 1976.

Lowry, (Clarence) Malcolm (1909-57) British novelist. His first novel *Ultramarine* (1933) was based on his experience as a deckhand on a voyage to China. After studying at Cambridge he lived in Paris before going to Mexico, the setting of his novel *Under the Volcano* (1947), the semiautobiographical account of the self-destruction of an alcoholic ex-consul. He lived in Canada from 1940 to 1954. Further stories and fragments were published posthumously.

Loyalists. *See* United Empire Loyalists.

Lo-yang. *See* Luoyang.

Lozi A Bantu-speaking people of Zambia, also known as Barotse. They are cereal cultivators on the fertile flood plain of the upper Zambezi, but hunting and animal husbandry are also important. Political authority is vested in a divine king and subordinate queen who rule from separate northern and southern capitals with a council of ministers and regional chiefs drawn from the aristocracy. There is an elaborate system of taxation, centralization, and redistribution of reserves.

LPG. *See* Liquefied Petroleum Gas.

LSD (lysergic acid diethylamide) A drug that—in very small doses—produces hallucinations, altered sensory perception, and a sense of happiness and relaxation or, in some people, fear and anxiety. Long-term use of LSD can cause a schizophrenia-like illness and—if taken by pregnant women—may produce deformities in the developing fetus.

Lualaba, River A river in SE Zaïre, the headstream of the Zaïre River. Rising in the Shaba region, it flows N to join the River Luvua and becomes the Zaïre River at the Boyoma Falls. Length: 1800 km (1100 mi).

Luanda 8 58S 13 09E The capital of Angola, a port in the NW on the Atlantic Ocean. Founded by the Portuguese in 1575, it became a centre of the slave trade to Brazil. Oil was discovered nearby in 1955 and a refinery was established; main exports include coffee, cotton, diamonds, iron, and salt. The University of Luanda was established in 1963. Population (1982): 700 000.

Luang Prabang 19 53N 102 10E A town in N Laos, a port at the head of navigation on the River Mekong. The royal capital of Laos (1946–75), it has many Buddhist pagodas and is the trading centre for the surrounding agricultural region. Population (1975): 46 000.

Lubbock 33 35N 101 53W A city in the USA, in NW Texas. Settled by Quakers in 1879, it is an important market centre for cotton, grain, cattle, and poultry. Population (1980): 173 979.

Lübeck 53 52N 10 40E A city in NE West Germany, in Schleswig-Holstein on the Trave estuary. A leading city of the Hanseatic League, it has a cathedral (1173) and city hall (13th–15th centuries), both restored after World War II. Buxtehude lived here (1668–1707) and it is the birthplace of Thomas and Heinrich Mann. West Germany's largest Baltic port, its industries include shipbuilding and metal founding. Population (1980 est): 221 500.

Lubitsch, Ernst (1892–1947) US film director, born in Germany. Following the success of *Madame Dubarry* (1919), a historical romance, he went to Hollywood, where he made a series of sophisticated comedies during the 1920s and 1930s. These include *Forbidden Paradise* (1924), *Bluebeard's Eighth Wife* (1938), and *Ninotchka* (1939).

Lublin 51 18N 22 31E A city in E Poland. The Union of *Lublin, between Poland and Lithuania, was signed here in 1569. Notable buildings include the 16th-century cathedral; its university was founded in 1944. It is an important commercial and industrial centre; manufactures include farm machinery, motor vehicles, and beer. Population (1982): 314 000.

Lublin, Union of (1569) The act that created a Polish-Lithuanian commonwealth. Poland and Lithuania were to share a common monarch and diet (parliament) but each maintained its own laws, administration, treasury, and army.

Lubumbashi (name until 1966: Elizabethville) 11 30S 27 31E A city in SE Zaïre. Founded in 1910 as a copper-mining settlement, it is the industrial centre of an important mining area. It has a cathedral and a campus (1955) of the Université Nationale du Zaïre. Population (1976 est): 451 332.

Lucan (Marcus Annaeus Lucanus; 39–65 AD) Roman poet, nephew of the Stoic philosopher Seneca. He was born in Spain. The *Pharsalia*, his single surviving work, is an epic poem in ten books concerning the civil war between Caesar and Pompey. He committed suicide after the discovery of his involvement in a conspiracy against the emperor Nero.

Lucas van Leyden (Lucas Hugensz *or* Jacobsz; c. 1494–1533) Northern Renaissance artist. His early paintings include everyday subjects, notably *The Chess Players* (Berlin), but he mainly painted religious works, his masterpiece being the triptych of *The Last Judgment* (Leiden). Best known as an engraver, he was influenced by Dürer, whom he met in Antwerp

(1521). He was probably the first to etch on copper rather than iron and to combine *etching with *engraving; his portrait of Emperor Maximilian I (1521) uses these techniques.

Lucca 43 50N 10 30E A town in NW Italy, in Tuscany on the River Serchio. It has Roman remains, an 8th-century church, and a cathedral (11th–15th centuries). Industries include chemicals, engineering, and food processing. It is the birthplace of Puccini. Population (1983 est): 90 686.

Luce, Henry R(obinson) (1898–1967) US publisher, who was a cofounder of the magazine *Time* (1923), which he edited and published. He also founded *Fortune* (1930), *Life* (1936), and *Sports Illustrated* (1954). His wife **Clare Booth Luce** (1903–87), a playwright, wrote the satire *Kiss the Boys Goodbye* (1938). She sat in the US House of Representatives (1943–47) and was subsequently ambassador to Italy (1953–56) and Brazil (1959).

lucerne. *See* alfalfa.

Lucerne (German name: Luzern) 47 03N 8 17E A town in central Switzerland, on Lake Lucerne. The Lion of Lucerne, a monument to the Swiss guards who fell in Paris (1792), is a notable feature and Lucerne also has a 17th-century cathedral. It is a major tourist centre. Population (1980 est): 63 278.

Lucerne, Lake (German name: Vierwaldstättersee) A lake in N central Switzerland. It has four arms formed from deep winding glaciated valleys. Area: 114 sq km (44 sq mi).

Lucian (c. 120–c. 180 AD) Greek rhetorician. He was born in Syria and travelled during his early life as a public lecturer in Asia Minor, Greece, Italy, and Gaul (France). He eventually settled in Athens but also held an administrative post in Alexandria. His many lively satirical works attacking contemporary superstitions and religious fanaticism include *Dialogues of the Dead* and *Dialogues of Courtesans*.

Lucifer In Christian tradition, the leader of the angels expelled from heaven for rebelling against God. Known thereafter as Satan (Hebrew: adversary) or the Devil, he presides over the souls condemned to torment in *hell. He is identified with the serpent that tempted Eve (Genesis 3.1–6) and the great red dragon cast out of heaven by Michael (Revelation 12.3–9). The exact nature of Lucifer's sin was much debated; the commonest view is that his sin was pride.

Lucknow 26 50N 80 54E A city in India, the capital of Uttar Pradesh. Capital of the nawabs of Oudh (1775–1856), it has many notable buildings including the Great Imambara (1784), which is a Muslim meeting place, and the British Residency (1800), which was besieged in 1857 during the Indian Mutiny. The University of Lucknow was established here in 1921. An agricultural trading centre, its industries include food processing, railway engineering, and the manufacture of chemicals, carpets, and copper and brass products. Population (1981 est): 1 006 943.

Lucretia A legendary Roman heroine, wife of Tarquinius Collatinus. After being raped by Sextus, son of Tarquinius Superbus, the Etruscan King of Rome, she committed suicide. Junius Brutus then led a rebellion that expelled the Tarquins and established the Roman Republic.

Lucretius (Titus Lucretius Carus; c. 95–c. 55 BC) Roman philosopher and poet. The biographical records are unreliable, including St Jerome's statements that he became insane but in moments of sanity wrote books that were edited by Cicero and that he committed suicide. His single work, *De rerum natura*, consists of six books that give the most complete exposition of the philosophy of *Epicurus, including his atomic theory of phenomena and the belief that the soul was material (and mortal). His style blends moral intention with poetic sensitivity to the physical world.

Lucullus, Lucius Licinius (died c. 57 BC) Roman general. After service with *Sulla, he successfully conducted the third war against *Mithridates until his troops mutinied and

Pompey took command in 67. Lucullus retired to private life and luxury; the splendours of "Lucullan" feasts became proverbial.

Lüda (*or* Lü-ta) 38 53N 121 37E A port complex in NE China, at the end of the *Liaodong Peninsula. It comprises the two cities **Lüshun** (English name: Port Arthur) and **Dalian** (*or* Talien; English name: Darien). Industries include shipbuilding, railway engineering, and fishing. *History*: Lüshun, a major naval base from 1878, was the base of the Russian Pacific fleet during the Russian occupation (1898–1905). The Russians began the construction of the commercial port at Dalian, completed under Japanese occupation (1905–45). Population (1983 est): 4 500 000.

Luddites A group of Nottingham frameworkers, named after their probably mythical leader, Ned Ludd, who destroyed labour-saving machinery in 1811. Luddism, which spread to other parts of industrial England, showed the hostility of the handicraftsmen to the new machines that were taking their livelihood from them. They were severely repressed.

Ludendorff, Erich (1865–1937) German general in World War I. He became chief of staff under *Hindenburg in 1914 and was largely responsible for the German victory at *Tannenberg. After being appointed quartermaster general (1916) Ludendorff exerted considerable political as well as military influence, forcing the resignation of *Bethmann-Hollwegg. He himself resigned after the German defeat and from 1924 to 1928 sat in the Reichstag as a Nazi.

Lüderitz (former name: Angra Pequena) 26 38S 15 10E A port in SW Namibia, on the Atlantic coast. It was the first German settlement in SW Africa (1883). The major industry is rock-lobster fishing. Population (1978 est): 6460.

Ludhiana 30 56N 75 52E A city in India, in Punjab. An important grain market, its manufactures include textiles, machinery, and agricultural tools. It is the site of Punjab Agricultural University (1962). Population (1981): 606 000.

Ludlow 52 22N 2 43W A market town in W central England, in Shropshire on the River Teme. Its historical importance resulted from its proximity to the Welsh border and its castle, which has a massive Norman keep. Population (1983 est): 8130.

Ludwigshafen 49 29N 8 27E A city in SW West Germany, in Rhineland-Palatinate on the River Rhine. It is a transshipment point and centre of the chemical industry. Population (1983 est): 157 400.

Luftwaffe The German air force. The Luftwaffe, which fought in World War I, was developed by Göring in the 1930s. In *World War II, countries destined for Nazi invasion were first pounded by aerial bombardment (*see* Blitzkreig) but the Luftwaffe's failure in the battle of Britain was disastrous to German plans to invade Britain.

Lugano 46 01N 8 57E A town in S Switzerland, on Lake Lugano. Noted for the beauty of its scenery, it is a popular tourist centre. It is also a centre of international finance. Population (1980): 27 815.

Lugansk. *See* Voroshilovgrad.

Lugard, Frederick Dealtry, 1st Baron (1858–1945) British colonial administrator. After army service he joined the British East Africa Company (1890), gaining control of Buganda. He was high commissioner for Northern Nigeria (1900–06) and then, after uniting N and S, of all Nigeria (1914–19), where he laid the foundations of the modern state.

Luger pistol A German automatic *pistol developed from a Borchard design by George Luger in 1902. The Parabellum 9-mm model was the standard sidearm of the German navy (1904) and army (1908) until 1938.

Lugus One of the principal Celtic gods. In Ireland he was called Lug and was skilled in many fields, being a warrior, poet, musician, craftsman, magician, etc. His Welsh counterpart was

Lleu Llaw Gyffes (skilful hand). Many European placenames, notably, Lyon, Laon, and Leiden, derive from his name.

lugworm A burrowing *annelid worm, *Arenicola marina*, of Atlantic shores, also known as the lobworm. Up to 40 cm long, lugworms have about 20 segments, with tufts of red gills on all but the last few. They feed on organic material in the mud, leaving casts of egested mud on the surface. Class: *Polychaeta*.

Lu Hsün (*or* Chou Shu-jen; 1881–1936) Chinese writer, famous for his short stories criticizing traditional Chinese thought and government. Among the best known are *The True Story of Ah Q* (1921) and those collected in *Call to Arms* (1923) and *Wandering* (1924–25). Although he never joined the Communist Party, the Chinese regard him as a revolutionary hero.

Luik. *See* Liège.

Lukacs, Giorgi (1885–1971) Hungarian Marxist philosopher. Having shown the resemblance between the philosophies of *Hegel and the young *Marx in *History and Class Consciousness* (1923), he disowned the book, which was also condemned by Soviet orthodoxy. For Lukacs, a cultural relativist, the dynamic of all art is the historical movement of its time; in the 20th century this is socialist realism.

Luke, St A New Testament evangelist, traditionally the author of the third Gospel and of the Acts of the Apostles. Although information about him is scarce, he seems to have been a Gentile doctor and to have accompanied *Paul on numerous missions, notably to Greece, Macedonia, and Jerusalem. He is the patron saint of doctors and artists. Feast day: 18 Oct.

The Gospel according to St Luke was written in the latter part of the 1st century AD. It was written in idiomatic Greek and with Gentile readers in mind. It contains the most complete account of the life of Jesus. Many historic hymns, such as the *Ave Maria, Magnificat, Benedictus, Gloria in Excelsis*, and *Nunc Dimittis*, are taken from it.

Luleå 65 35N 22 10E A seaport in N Sweden, on the Gulf of Bothnia. It is icebound in the winter, but exports iron ore from *Gällivare and *Kiruna during the rest of the year. Its university was established in 1971. Population (1983): 66 512.

Lull, Ramón (English name: Raymond Lully; c. 1235–c. 1315) Catalan mystic and poet. After an early secular career, he became a Franciscan and devoted himself to missionary work among the Muslims. His mystical writings foreshadow those of St *Teresa and St *John of the Cross. His important theological work, *Ars magna*, was condemned by Pope Gregory XI in 1376 for its attempt to show that the mysteries of faith could be proved by reason. According to tradition, he was stoned to death in N Africa.

Lully, Jean Baptiste (Giovanni Battista Lulli; 1632–87) French composer of Italian birth. The son of a miller, he worked as a scullion in an aristocratic French household but subsequently became composer, violinist, and dancer to Louis XIV. He composed ballets, incidental music to Molière's plays, and operas, being granted a monopoly of operatic production in 1684. He died from gangrene as a result of striking his foot with a pointed stick while conducting.

Luluabourg. *See* Kananga.

lumbago Chronic backache. Almost everybody experiences backache at some time and many biologists regard it as the price man pays for walking upright. More serious backache may be caused by arthritis, a slipped disc, muscle strain, or strained ligaments.

lumbar puncture A procedure in which *cerebrospinal fluid is withdrawn using a hypodermic needle inserted through the spine and into the spinal cord in the region of the lower back. Examination of the fluid assists in the diagnosis of various conditions, for example the presence of blood may indicate a brain haemorrhage.

Lumbini A park and Buddhist shrine in the modern village of Rummindei, in S Nepal. According to legend, the Buddha was born here in about 563 BC.

lumen (lm) The *SI unit of luminous flux equal to the light emitted per second in a cone of one steradian solid angle by a point source of one candela.

Lumière, Auguste (1862-1954) French photographer, who, with his brother **Louis Lumière** (1864-1948), manufactured photographic equipment and made innovations in the techniques of photography, especially in motion pictures. In 1895 they invented the *cinématographe*, which had a camera and projector combined into one. In the same year they used their invention to film and show the first motion picture, *La Sortie des usines Lumière*, which was an immediate success. They went on to make a great number of short films, especially comedies. They also greatly improved existing methods of colour photography.

luminance The *luminous intensity of a surface in a given direction per unit of orthogonally projected area of that surface. It is measured in candela per square metre.

luminescence The emission of light by a substance for any reason except high temperature. It occurs as a result of the emission of a *photon by an atom of the substance when it decays from an excited state to its ground state. The atom may be excited by absorbing a photon (photoluminescence), colliding with an electron (electroluminescence), etc. If the luminescence stops as soon as the exciting source is removed, it is known as fluorescence; if it persists for longer than 10^{-8} seconds it is called phosphorescence. The photons emitted may have a different energy (in visible light, a different colour) from the absorbed energy. Fluorescent dyes in washing powders make clothes look brighter. Luminous paint is phosphorescent. Other examples of luminescence include triboluminescence, caused by friction, chemiluminescence, caused by chemical reaction. Bioluminescence, which is seen in glow worms, seaweeds, and other organisms, is a form of chemiluminescence. Radioluminescence is caused by radioactive decay.

luminosity The intrinsic brightness of an object, such as a star, equal to the total energy radiated per second from the object. A star's luminosity increases both with surface temperature and with surface area: the hotter and larger a star, the greater its luminosity. Stellar luminosity is related (logarithmically) to absolute *magnitude.

luminous flux The rate of flow of light energy, taking into account the sensitivity of the observer or detector to the different wavelengths. For example, the human eye is most sensitive to the colour green. Luminous flux is measured in *lumens.

luminous intensity The amount of light emitted per second by a point source per unit solid angle in a specified direction. It is measured in *candela.

lumpsucker A slow-moving carnivorous *bony fish, also called lumpfish, belonging to the family *Cyclopteridae*, found in cold northern seas. They have a thickset body, sometimes studded with bony tubercles, a cleft dorsal fin, and a ventral sucking disc formed from fused pelvic fins. *Cyclopterus lumpus* is the largest species, reaching 60 cm long. The roe is used as a substitute for caviar. Order: *Scorpaeniformes*.

Lumumba, Patrice (Hemery) (1925-61) Congolese statesman; prime minister (1960-61) of the Congo (now Zaïre). Mission-educated, Lumumba was active in trades unionism before entering national politics. He became prime minister of the newly independent Congo under president *Kasavubu in 1960 and opposed the secession of Katanga province under *Tshombe. The following year he was deposed and murdered.

luna moth A large North American saturniid moth, *Actias luna*. It is pale green with a long "tail" on each hindwing, moonlike markings on the forewings, and a wingspan of about 150 mm. The pale-green larvae feed on trees.

Lund 55 42N 13 10E A town in S Sweden, near Malmö. It has a university (1668) and an 11th-century cathedral. Its varied industries include printing, publishing, and sugar refining. Population (1983): 80 458.

Lunda A group of Central Bantu tribes speaking languages of the Benne-Congo division of the *Niger-Congo family. Historically they were united under a paramount chief but their customs and culture vary considerably. Cultivation, hunting and gathering, and trade are all important economic factors.

Lundy 51 11N 4 40W An island in SW England in the Bristol Channel, off the N coast of Devon. Once the haunt of smugglers and pirates, it is now a bird sanctuary, owned by the National Trust (since 1969). Area: 4 sq km (1.5 sq mi). Population (1981): 52.

Lüneburg 53 15N 10 24E A spa in NE West Germany, in Lower Saxony. There are many fine medieval buildings. **Lüneburg Heath** was the site of the surrender of German troops to Montgomery in 1945 at the end of World War II. Population (1985 est): 61 000.

lungfish A freshwater *bony fish belonging to the formerly abundant order *Dipnoi*, now reduced to six species including *Lepidosiren paradoxa* of South America, *Protopterus annectens* of Africa, and the Australian *Neoceratodus forsteri*. Up to 2 m long, lungfish have slender bodies, narrow paired fins, and tapering tails. Their swim bladders are modified for breathing air, an adaptation for droughts, when some make burrows in the bottom mud, leaving air vents above the mouth. They re-emerge in the rainy season to feed on bottom-dwelling fish, snails, mussels, etc., and to spawn. Subclass: *Sarcopterygii*. ☐fish.

lungs The respiratory organs of many air-breathing animals and man. The human lungs are situated within the rib cage on either side of the heart. Each lung is enclosed by a smooth moist membrane (the pleura), which permits it to expand without friction, and contains many tiny thin-walled air sacs (alveoli), through which exchange of oxygen and carbon dioxide takes place during breathing (*see* respiration). Air to the lungs passes through the *trachea (windpipe) to the two main airways (bronchi), which subdivide into progressively smaller branches that terminate (as respiratory bronchioles) in the alveoli. *See* Plate IV. Diseases most commonly affecting the lungs and airways are virus infections and bronchitis; cancer and tuberculosis are less common.

lungworm One of several species of parasitic *nematodes that inhabit the lungs and bronchial passages of cattle, pigs, deer, sheep, and other animals. They damage lung tissue, causing coughing, distress, and debilitation, and may act as reservoirs of such diseases as swine influenza.

lungwort A perennial herb of the genus *Pulmonaria* (about 10 species), especially *P. officinalis*, native to woods of Eurasia. The leaves are heart-shaped or oval, often white-spotted, and the tubular five-lobed flowers, borne in drooping terminal clusters, are pink when young, turning blue later. The plant grows to a height of 30 cm. Family: *Boraginaceae*.

Lunt, Alfred (1892-1977) US actor, who worked with **Lynne Fontanne** (1887-1983) after their marriage in 1922. They were most successful in sophisticated comedies, such as Noel Coward's *Design for Living* (1933) and Terence Rattigan's *Love in Idleness* (1944), but they also performed in more serious productions, notably Dürrenmatt's *The Visit* (1959).

Luo A Nilotic people of N Uganda and Kenya, who moved into this area from the SE Sudan after about 1500. They speak a Sudanic language. The Luo cultivate cereal crops and herd cattle. For lakeside groups fishing is important. They lack centralized political institutions or chiefs.

Luoyang (or Lo-yang) 34 47N 112 26E A city in E central China, in Henan province. A commercial and cultural centre, it was the Tang dynastic capital. Manufactures include machinery and ball bearings. Population (1983 est): 978 000.

Lupercalia An ancient Roman festival of purification and fertility held annually on 15 Feb. After performing sacrifices, priests carrying whips of goat hide made a circuit of the Palatine. Women struck by their whips were ensured fertility. The ceremony was suppressed in 494 AD by Pope Gelasius.

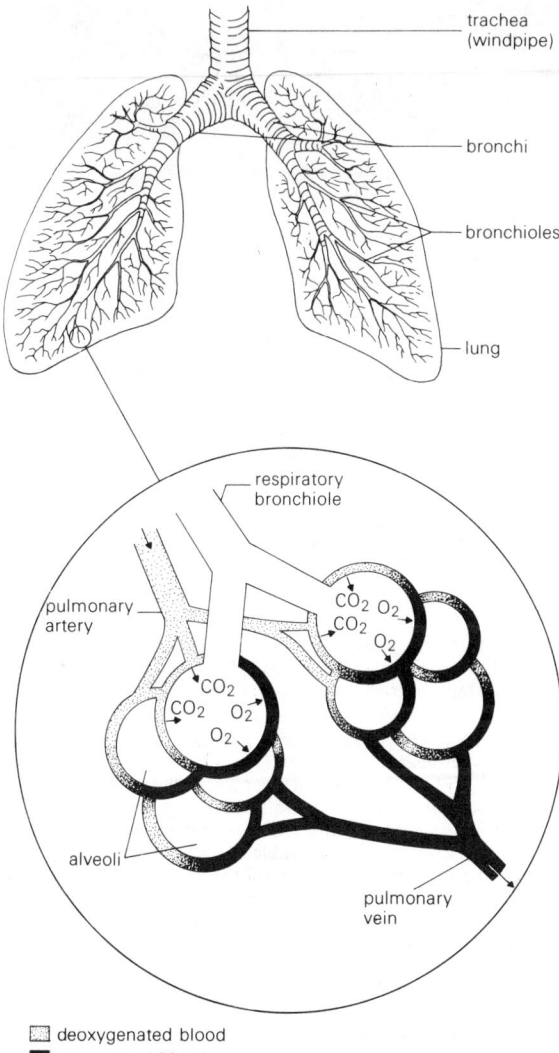

LUNGS *The air passages in the lungs terminate in millions of tiny air sacs (alveoli), into which blood from the pulmonary artery releases its carbon dioxide. Inhaled oxygen in the alveoli is absorbed by the blood, which is carried back to the heart by the pulmonary vein.*

lupin An annual or perennial herb of the genus *Lupinus* (about 200 species), native to the N hemisphere and widely cultivated for ornament. They grow 30-120 cm high and have compound leaves with up to 18 radiating leaflets. Lupins produce dense spikes of blue, purple, white, pink, or yellow flowers. Family: *Leguminosae.*

lupus A skin disease of which there are two forms. Used alone, the term usually refers to **lupus vulgaris**, which is a

tuberculous infection of the skin. Without treatment the infection will progress to erode the face (hence the name, which is Latin for wolf, implying a gnawing disease), but it is now readily cured by drugs. **Lupus erythematosus** (LE) is a disease in which inflammation of tissues is brought about by the body's own antibodies. Discoid LE is a chronic condition of scaling and scarring of the skin. Systemic LE affects the connective tissues and so can have serious effects in almost any part of the body, particularly the joints, skin, kidneys, heart, lungs, and brain. LE can be controlled with steroid drugs.

Lurçat, Jean (1892-1966) French tapestry designer. A painter in the cubist style until 1936, he established a tapestry factory at Aubusson in 1939, where he played a major part in the 20th-century revival of tapestry weaving and design.

Luria, Isaac (1534-72) Jewish mystic of Safed (Galilee); the founder of an important school of *kabbalah. He attracted a large band of disciples who, after his early death in an epidemic, collected and developed his teachings, which became extremely influential, especially later in *Hasidism.

Luristan (*or* Lorestan) A province in W Iran, comprising part of a larger historical region in which many important archaeological finds have been made since 1929.

Lusaka 15 03S 28 30E The capital of Zambia, lying on the Tanzam Railway. It became the capital of Northern Rhodesia in 1935 and of Zambia on independence in 1964. The University of Zambia was founded here in 1965. The centre of an important agricultural region, it has expanded rapidly and industries include food processing, paint, clothing, and plastics. Population (1980): 538 469.

Lüshun. *See* Lüda.

Lusitania A British liner that, although unarmed, was sunk by a German submarine off the Irish coast on 7 May, 1915, during World War I. Of the 1195 lives lost, some 128 were Americans and the incident contributed to the anti-German feeling in the USA that ultimately brought the country into the war.

Lü-ta. *See* Lüda.

lute A plucked stringed instrument of Moorish origin; the name derives from the Arabic *al'lud.* The European lute, popular during the 15th, 16th, and 17th centuries, had a body in the shape of a half pear, six or more courses of double strings and a fretted fingerboard. The round sound hole was often intricately carved. Music for the lute was written in tablature, a system of notation using letters or numbers to indicate the position of the fingers. The lute was used chiefly as a solo instrument and to accompany singers; it has been revived in the 20th century.

luteinizing hormone. *See* gonadotrophin.

lutetium (Lu) The heaviest *lanthanide element, separated from ytterbium by G. Urbain (1872-1938) in 1907 and named after Paris (Latin name: *Lutetia*), his native city. It was also discovered independently by C. A. von Welsbach, who called it **cassiopeium**, a name used until the 1950s, especially in Germany. It is present in small amounts in monazite ($CePO_4$) and extracted by reduction of $LuCl_3$ or LuF_3 by alkali metals (e.g. sodium). It is separated from the other lanthanides by ion-exchange techniques. At no 71; at wt 174.97; mp 1663°C; bp 3395°C.

Luther, Martin (1483-1546) German Protestant reformer, founder of *Lutheranism. An Augustinian monk and from 1507 a priest, he became professor of theology at Wittenberg University in 1511. After experiencing a personal revelation he came to believe that salvation could be attained by faith alone. Several visits to Rome convinced him of the corruption of the papacy, the Dominican monk *Tetzel, who sold *indulgences on behalf of papal funds, being a particular target for his hostility. In 1517 he nailed his 95 theses against this practice to the church door at Wittenberg. He disobeyed the papal summons to Rome (1518) and further attacked the papal system in such writings as *On the Babylonian Captivity* of the Church of God (1520). His public burning of a papal bull condemning his theses and writings resulted in his excommunication in 1521. He appeared before Charles V's imperial diet (legislative assembly) at Worms but refused to recant and was declared an outlaw. While in hiding at Wartburg, under the protection of the Elector of Saxony, he completed a German translation of the New Testament. In 1522 he returned openly to Wittenberg, where he led the reform of its church and in 1525 married the former nun Catherina van Bora (1499-1552). At the same time he lost much popular support because of his opposition to the Peasants' Revolt (1524-25). His contention that human will was incapable of following the good resulted in his rift with *Erasmus and in 1529 he also broke with *Zwingli, maintaining his belief in *consubstantiation. His original intention was reform not schism, but with the *Augsburg Confession (1530) a separate Protestant church emerged. Subsequently the leadership of the German Reformation was gradually taken over by *Melanchthon.

Lutheranism The belief and practice of the Protestant Churches that derive from the teaching of Martin *Luther, especially as formulated in the *Augsburg Confession (1530). There is a wide divergence in matters of belief among Lutherans. Essentially Scripture is taken to be the only rule of faith and conservative Lutherans accept Luther's basic doctrine of justification by faith alone, i.e. that redemption is only through faith in Christ. Lutheranism is the national faith in all Scandinavian countries, where there are some 19 million Lutherans. It is the principal Protestant Church in Germany (about 40 million adherents) and is also strong in North America (over 8 million). The Lutheran World Federation, based in Geneva, claims authority over some 80 million Lutherans world wide, which makes it the largest Protestant body.

Lutine bell The ship's bell taken from the *Lutine*, a ship that sank in the North Sea in 1799 with a cargo of bullion. The bell now hangs in the underwriting room at *Lloyd's and is rung when news arrives of a ship previously posted "missing, fate unknown." One ring is for bad news and two for good news; after the bell has rung, business stops and a message is read. The ringing of the bell ensures that all underwriters receive the news simultaneously.

Luton 51 53N 0 25W A town in SE England, the largest in Bedfordshire. It has an important motor-vehicle industry and also manufactures household appliances, engineering components, and chemicals. A straw-plaiting industry has survived from the 17th century. Nearby is Luton Airport. Population (1981): 164 049.

Lutoslawski, Witold (1913-) Polish composer. His early works, such as his first symphony, were influenced by Bartók. From the orchestral *Venetian Games* (1961) onwards most of his works contain *aleatoric sections. They include a second symphony (1967), a cello concerto (1970), and *Preludes and Fugue for 13 Solo Strings* (1972).

Lutuli, Albert (John Mvumbi) (1898-1967) South African Black leader, whose advocacy of nonviolent opposition to racial discrimination won him the Nobel Peace Prize in 1960. A Zulu chief, in 1952 he became president of the African National Congress, formed in 1912 to further the Black cause in South Africa. In 1956 he was arrested for treason and although acquitted in 1957 continued to suffer social and political restrictions.

Lutyens, Sir Edwin Landseer (1869-1944) British architect. Known as the last English designer of country houses, a notable example of which is Middlefield, Cambridgeshire (1908), he combined classicism with the influence of Norman *Shaw and the *Arts and Crafts movement. He designed the central square of Hampstead Garden Suburb (1908-10) and the Cenotaph (1919-20) but his most spectacular commission was the layout and viceregal palace of New Delhi (1912-30). His daughter, **Elisabeth**

SIR EDWIN LUTYENS *The President's House (formerly Viceroy's House) in New Delhi combines classical features with decoration in the Indian idiom.*

Lutyens (1906-83), a composer, studied in London and Paris and adopted *serialism as a basis for composition. Her works include *O Saisons, O Chateaux* (1963) for soprano and strings, concertos for horn and viola, operas, and chamber music.

Lutzen, Battles of 1. (16 November, 1632) The battle in the *Thirty Years' War in which the Swedes under Gustavus II Adolphus clashed with imperial forces in a costly and indecisive battle. Gustavus Adolphus was killed. 2. (May, 1813) A battle in which Russian and Prussian forces were defeated by Napoleon.

lux (lx) The *SI unit of intensity of illumination equal to the illumination resulting from a flux of one lumen falling on an area of one square metre. Former name: metre candle.

Luxembourg A province in SE Belgium, bordering on the Grand Duchy of Luxembourg and France. The *Ardennes is an important tourist area. Area: 4416 sq km (1705 sq mi). Population (1980 est): 223 396. Capital: Arlon.

Luxembourg, Grand Duchy of A small country in central Europe, between France and Germany. The generally undulating S with its wide valleys rises to the rugged uplands of the Ardennes Plateau in the N. *Economy*: predominantly industrial, the manufacture of iron and steel is especially important although considerable economic diversification has taken place (e.g. chemicals, rubber, and synthetic fibres). Agriculture remains important, especially livestock raising, and wine is produced from the vineyards of the Moselle Valley. The city of Luxembourg is an important international centre with the headquarters of the European Parliament and the European Coal and Steel Community, as well as many international companies. *History*: with the Netherlands and Belgium it formed part of the so-called Low Countries. It became a duchy in 1354 and passed to Burgundy in 1443 and to the Habsburgs in 1482. It became a grand duchy in 1815 under the Dutch Crown. In 1830 it joined the Belgian revolt against the Netherlands, W Luxembourg joining independent Belgium and the E forming part of the Netherlands until obtaining independence in 1867. It was occupied by the Germans in both World Wars. In 1921 it formed an economic union with Belgium and in 1948 both joined with the Netherlands to form the *Benelux Economic Union. Luxembourg is now a member of the EEC. Head of state: Grand Duke Jean (1921-). Head of Government: Jacques Santer. Official languages: Luxembourgish, French, and German. Official currency: Luxembourg franc of 100 centimes. Area: 2586 sq km (999 sq mi). Population (1980 est): 365 100. Capital: Luxembourg.

Luxemburg, Rosa (1871-1919) German revolutionary,

born in Poland. She was converted to communism in 1890, helped to found the Polish Social Democratic party (later the Communist Party), and from 1898 was a leader of the left wing of the German Social Democratic party. Upon the outbreak of World War I she broke with the majority of German socialists and formed, with Karl *Liebknecht, the *Spartacus League. She spent most of the war in prison and after her release participated in the abortive uprising of 1919, following which she and Liebknecht were murdered.

Luxor (*or* El Aksur)   25 40N 32 38E A town in central Egypt, on the River Nile. It occupies the S part of the ancient city of *Thebes. Its numerous ruins and tombs include the temple built by Amenhotep III to the god Ammon. The town is a winter resort. Population (1983 est): 113 400.

Luzern.   *See* Lucerne.

Luzon   A volcanic island in the N Philippines, the largest and most important. Largely mountainous, its central fertile plain is a major grain growing area with rice terraces to the N. Other products include sugar cane, hemp, timber, and minerals, notably chromite. Most industry is concentrated around Manila. *History*: power struggles for the Philippines have been centred here, including the Japanese invasion during World War II (*see* Corregidor). Area: 108 378 sq km (41 845 sq mi). Population (1980): 23 900 796. Chief town: Manila.

Lvov (German name: Lemberg)   49 50N 24 00E A city in the Soviet Union, in the W Ukrainian SSR. A major industrial and cultural centre of the W Ukraine, Lvov supports machine building, food processing, and chemical and textile industries, and has a notable university (1661). *History*: founded in the 13th century, it subsequently passed to Poland. Under Austrian rule from 1772, it became the capital of Galicia. It was ceded to Poland after World War I and to the Soviet Union in 1939. It was occupied by the Germans in World War II. Population (1984): 728 000.

Lvov, Georgi Yevgenievich, Prince   (1861–1925) Russian statesman. Lvov was the first leader of the provisional government in the *Russian Revolution. His unrealistic policies led to the Petrograd uprising in July, 1917, and he resigned. He emigrated to Paris, where he died.

Lyallpur.   *See* Faisalabad.

Lyautey, Louis Hubert Gonzalve   (1854–1934) French marshal and colonial administrator. He served in Indochina and then in Madagascar, where he reformed the colonial government. In 1912 he became resident general of the French protectorate of Morocco, where he again reorganized the administration, maintaining the French position there during World War I. He was briefly war minister (1917–18).

Lyceum   The gardens and gymnasium in ancient Athens in which *Aristotle lectured and which gave their name to the school and research foundation that he established there in about 335 BC. The name is now applied particularly to Aristotle's philosophical doctrines.

Lycurgus   A legendary Spartan statesman credited with establishing the constitution and military regime of Sparta after a slave rebellion in the 7th century BC. He is mentioned by *Herodotus and his biography was written by *Plutarch. The name refers to several other figures in Greek legend, notably a king of Thrace who opposed the cult of *Dionysus and was subsequently blinded or driven mad.

Lydda.   *See* Lod.

Lydgate, John   (c. 1370–c. 1450) English poet. He lived at the monastery of Bury St Edmunds. A prolific writer, his major works include the long narrative poems *The Troy Book* (1412–21), written at the request of Henry V, and *The Fall of Princes* (1431–38).

Lydia   In antiquity, a region of W Asia Minor with its capital at *Sardis. Its last native king, *Croesus (ruled 560–546 BC), enriched by Lydia's alluvial gold, controlled Anatolia eastwards to the River Halys, until his defeat by *Cyrus the Great. The Lydians invented coined money (c. 700 BC).

Lyell, Sir Charles   (1797–1875) British geologist, who was

mainly responsible for the acceptance of the view that rocks are formed by slow continual processes, such as heat and erosion. Lyell popularized this theory in his *The Principles of Geology* (3 vols, 1830–33). Lyell's work had a great influence on Charles *Darwin and, in turn, Lyell became one of the earliest supporters of Darwin's theory of natural selection.

Lyly, John   (c. 1554–1606) English dramatist and writer. From the elaborate artificial style of his two didactic prose romances *Euphues, the Anatomy of Wit* (1578) and *Euphues and His England* (1580) was derived the term "euphuism." He wrote several comic dramas, courtly precursors of later Elizabethan comedies.

Lyme Regis   50 44N 2 57W A resort in S England, in Dorset on Lyme Bay. Once an important port, the picturesque harbour was the scene of Monmouth's landing (1685). Important prehistoric fossils have been found here. Population (1981): 3447.

lymph   A clear colourless fluid, consisting of water and dissolved substances, that is contained in a network of vessels called the **lymphatic system**. It is derived from blood and bathes the cells, supplying them with nutrients and absorbing their waste products, before passing into the lymphatic vessels. Here the lymph passes through a series of small swellings called **lymph nodes**, which filter out bacteria and other foreign particles, before draining into the main lymphatic vessels—the thoracic duct and the right lymphatic duct—in the neck. These two vessels are connected to veins in the neck and so drain the lymph back into the bloodstream. The lymph nodes, which also produce lymphocytes (a type of white blood cell), sometimes become enlarged during infections. The lymphatic system is one of the routes by which cancer is spread.

lymphocyte.   *See* leucocyte.

lymphoma   Cancer of the lymph nodes, which is one of the commonest cancers of young people. There are several different types but the most common is Hodgkin's disease, which can now often be controlled by chemotherapy.

Lynch, Jack   (1917–   ) Irish statesman; prime minister (1966–73, 1977–79). A former hurling star, in 1948 he was elected Fianna Fáil MP for Cork, enjoying enormous popular support in that city.

Lynd, Robert Staughton   (1892–1970) US sociologist. Lynd taught at Columbia University from 1931 to 1961. He collaborated with his wife **Helen Lynd** (1896–1982) on the field study of Muncie, Indiana, their findings being published in *Middletown: A Study in Contemporary American Culture* (1929) and *Middletown in Transition* (1937).

Lynn   42 29N 70 57W A city in the USA, in Massachusetts. A long-established industrial centre, it was the site of the first ironworks (1643) and the first fire engine (1654) in the USA. A shoe-manufacturing centre since 1636, Lynn also manufactures jet engines and marine turbines. Population (1980): 78 471.

lynx   A short-tailed *cat, *Felis lynx*, that inhabits forests of Eurasia and North America. Lynxes are about 1 m long with faintly spotted yellow-brown thick fur; their ears are tipped with black tufts. The rare Spanish race has especially bright spots.
Lynxes hunt at night, usually for small mammals (such as lemmings) but sometimes catching moose or reindeer, especially in deep snow. □mammal.

Lyon (English name: Lyons)   45 46N 4 50E The third largest city in France, the capital of the Rhône department at the confluence of the Rivers Rhône and Saône. Notable buildings include the cathedral (12th–15th centuries) and the *hôtel de ville* and Palais des Arts (both 17th century). The university was founded in 1808. A *métro* (underground railway) was opened here in 1978. The focal point of road and rail routes, Lyon is an important financial centre and has been a leading textile centre since the 15th century. Manufactures include synthetic fibres, cars, chemicals, and hosiery. Population (1982): 418 476.

Lyons, Joseph Aloysius (1879–1939) Australian states-man; prime minister (1931–39). At first a Labor politician, he resigned over financial policy in 1931 and with the Nationalist Party formed the *United Australia Party. He died in office.

Lyra (Latin: Lyre) A constellation in the N sky near Cygnus. The brightest star is *Vega. The constellation con-tains the **Ring nebula** (a *planetary nebula) and the *variable stars **RR Lyrae** (a pulsating variable) and **Beta Lyrae** (an eclipsing binary).

lyre An ancient plucked string instrument. It consists of a sound box with two symmetrical arms supporting a cross piece from which strings are stretched to a bridge on the belly. Greek vases often show players holding a lyre in the left hand and a large plectrum in the right.

LYREBIRD *The underside of the tail of the male superb lyrebird forms a silvery shimmering veil during display.*

lyrebird A primitive ground-dwelling passerine bird be-longing to a family (*Menuridae*; 2 species) restricted to forests of E Australia. The male superb lyrebird (*Menura superba*), about 130 cm long, is brown with grey underparts. Its magnifi-cent tail is spread out into a lyre shape during the courtship display, which is performed on a mound of mud and debris. The smaller Prince Albert's lyrebird (*M. alberti*) does not build display mounds and has a smaller tail. All lyrebirds sing loudly and are excellent mimics.

Lysander (d. 395 BC) Spartan general and politician. He commanded the fleets that defeated the Athenians at Notium (407) and Aegospotami (405) towards the end of the *Pelo-ponnesian War. His plot to make the Spartan throne elective rather than hereditary was thwarted by the government but

Lysander escaped punishment. He was subsequently killed in action in Boeotia.

Lysenko, Trofim Denisovich (1898–1976) Soviet biolo-gist, who achieved notoriety for his maverick ideas and dam-aging influence on Soviet biology. He claimed that changes induced in wheat by his vernalization experiments could be inherited, thus endorsing *Lamarck's discredited theory of evolution through inheritance of acquired characteristics. This led him to attack Mendelian genetics and the chromo-some theory of inheritance, which, in the 1930s, were widely accepted elsewhere. With the backing of Stalin, Lysenko's in-fluence grew. In 1939 he attacked the Soviet geneticist *Vavilov, who was later exiled to Siberia, and by 1948, Soviet scientific opposition to his views had been stifled. Lysenko's influence was eclipsed after Stalin's death although he re-tained his post as director of the Institute of Genetics until 1965, after the fall of Khrushchev.

lysergic acid diethylamide. *See* LSD.

Lysias (c. 459–c. 380 BC) Greek orator. He escaped from Athens during the reign of terror of the Thirty Tyrants (404 BC), but returned to prosecute one of them in his speech "Against Eratosthenes". About 35 of his legal speeches in plain unadorned style survive. He and his family are por-trayed in Plato's *Republic*.

Lysippus (4th century BC) The court sculptor of Alexander the Great. Long-lived, original, and prolific, Lysippus worked in bronze and was noted for his portraiture and new system of proportions for human figures. Surviving copies of his works (e.g. the Vatican statue of the athlete scraping oil from his arm) indicate his naturalism.

lysosome A membrane-bounded structure occurring in large numbers in nearly all animal cells and containing en-zymes responsible for the breakdown of materials both within and outside the cell. Functions of lysosomes include the de-struction of bacteria in white blood cells, the digestion of food by protozoa, and the breakdown of cellular material after death.

lysozyme An enzyme, present in tears, nasal secretions, and egg white, that destroys bacteria by breaking down their cell walls. It was one of the first enzymes whose molecular struc-ture and mode of action were analysed by X-ray diffraction techniques.

Lyttelton, Humphrey (1921–   ) British jazz trumpeter and band leader, who influenced the revival of New Orleans jazz in England. Lyttelton, an Old Etonian, played with George Webb's Dixielanders, formed his own group in 1948, and has written several books on jazz.

Lytton, Edward George Earle Bulwer-Lytton, 1st Baron (1803–73) British novelist and politician. His long career as a Liberal and then a Tory MP culminated in his peerage in 1866. The best known of his many popular volumes of fiction, verse, and drama are his historical novels, which include *The Last Days of Pompeii* (1834). His son **(Edward) Robert Bulwer-Lytton, 1st Earl of Lytton** (1831–91) was viceroy of India (1876–80), initiating the second Afghan War (1878–80) against Russian influence in Afghanistan. An able adminis-trator, he abolished internal customs duties. He was also a poet and his publications, under the pseudonym Owen Mere-dith, include *Clytemnestra . . . and Other Poems* (1855) and *The Wanderer* (1858).

M

Maas, River. *See* Meuse, River.

Maastricht 50 51N 5 42E A city in the SE Netherlands, the capital of Limburg province on the River Meuse. It has the Netherlands' oldest church (founded in the 6th century AD) and is a cultural centre. Industries include pottery and textiles. Population (1984): 113 277.

Maazel, Lorin (1930–) US conductor, formerly a violinist. He directed the German Opera in West Berlin from 1965 to 1971 and was appointed conductor of the Cleveland Orchestra in 1972. He was musical director of the Vienna State Opera (1982–84).

Mabinogion, the A collection of eleven medieval Welsh folk-tales. Drawing on Celtic, Norman, and French legends, it was compiled in the 14th century and contains the earliest known Arthurian romance, *Culhwch and Olwen* (c. 1100). The four best-known tales are known as "The Four Branches of the Mabinogi"; others parallel French stories.

Mabuse. *See* Gossaert, Jan.

McAdam, John Loudon (1756–1836) British inventor of the macadam road surface. It consisted of rocks interspersed with small chips, bound together with slag or gravel and raised to facilitate drainage. In 1823 McAdam's methods were adopted by the British Government and in 1827 he became general surveyor of roads.

Macadamia A genus of bushy evergreen trees, 9–15 m tall, native to Australia and often grown as ornamentals. *M. ternifolia* has long stiff leaves and small white or lilac flowers. The round hard-shelled fruit contains a single edible seed. Called macadamia or Queensland nuts, they are used as dessert nuts. Family: *Proteaceae*.

Macao (Portuguese name: Macáu; Chinese name: Aomen) 22 13N 113 36E A port in S China, administered by Portugal, across the Zhu estuary from Hong Kong. The population is mainly Chinese, but has Portuguese cultural traditions. Chief industries are textiles and fishing; tourism, gambling, and gold smuggling are also important. *History*: it was a major trading centre until the 19th century. Immigration of refugees from Communist China was stopped after procommunist riots (1966–67). Sovereignty will pass to China in 1999. Area: 16 sq km (6 sq mi). Population (1981): 261 680.

Macapá 9 30S 67 29W A port in N Brazil, the capital of Amapá territory on the N channel of the Amazon delta. Exports include manganese, iron and cassiterite ores, and rubber. Population (1980 est): 135 100.

macaque An *Old World monkey belonging to the genus *Macaca* (12 species), found mainly in the forests of S Asia. 35–78 cm long (the tail is absent or up to 90 cm long), macaques have short legs and areas of hard bare skin on the rump. Intelligent and sociable, they are mainly terrestrial, feeding on plant and animal matter. *See also* Barbary ape; rhesus monkey.

MacArthur, Douglas (1880–1964) US general. One of the outstanding strategists of World War II, he directed the recapture of the SW Pacific as Allied commander (1942–45). He commanded the occupation of Japan (1945–51) and then commanded the UN forces in the Korean War. After defeating the North Korean army, he advocated active operations against China. This was contrary to US policy and President Harry S. Truman dismissed him (1951).

Macarthur, John (1767–1834) Australian sheep farmer, who helped develop Australia's wool industry. Born in Britain, he went to Australia in 1789 and became a wealthy landowner. His experiments in sheep breeding led him to import (1797) the Merino sheep on which the development of Australia's wool industry was to be based. In 1808 Macarthur instigated the

*Rum Rebellion against William *Bligh, the governor of New South Wales, and was in exile in Britain from 1811 to 1817.

Macassar. *See* Ujung Pandang.

Macaulay, Dame Rose (1881–1958) British novelist. She published her first novel while an undergraduate at Oxford. Subsequent novels, such as *Dangerous Ages* (1921), established her reputation as a social satirist. Her best-known novel is *The Towers of Trebizond* (1956).

Macaulay, Thomas Babington, 1st Baron (1800–59) British essayist and historian. From 1825 he was a leading contributor to the *Edinburgh Review*. He had a long career in parliament (1830–34, 1839–47, 1852–56) and worked in India from 1834 to 1838. His Whig sympathies are evident in his immensely successful *History of England* (5 vols, 1849–61).

macaw A large brightly coloured *parrot belonging to one of two genera (*Ara* and *Anodorhynchos*), ranging from Mexico to Paraguay. Up to 100 cm long, macaws have a characteristically long loose tail and a huge hooked bill that is used to crack open large nuts. *See* Plate V.

Macbeth (d. 1058) King of Scots (1040–58), after killing Duncan I in battle at Bothnagowan. He was killed by Duncan's son Malcolm.

MacBride, Seán (1904–88) Irish diplomat. The son of the nationalist, Maud Gonne (1866–1953), he belonged to the IRA before becoming a member of the Irish assembly (1947). He was chairman of Amnesty International (1961–75) and UN commissioner for Namibia (1973–77). He shared the Nobel Peace Prize in 1974.

DOUGLAS MACARTHUR *General MacArthur, in command of the UN forces in Korea, seen here with the commander of the US Eighth Army, General Matthew Ridgway, in February, 1950.*

McBride, Willie John (1939–) Irish Rugby Union footballer, who played for Ballymena, Ireland, and the British Lions. A lock forward, he won 63 caps for Ireland and made a record 17 appearances for the British Lions (1962–74). He captained the British Lions team that toured South Africa unbeaten (1974).

Maccabees The name applied loosely to the Hasmonean dynasty, founded in Jerusalem by Judas Maccabee (d. 161 BC) after a revolt against Syrian (Seleucid) rule. It continued until the capture of Jerusalem by the Romans in 63 BC. In Christian usage it is applied to seven young brothers martyred during the revolt. In 1895 it was revived in the name of a Jewish athletics organization, Maccabi, the World Union of which was formed in 1921.

The **Books of Maccabees** are four books of the *Apocrypha. I and II Maccabees record the revolt (168 BC) of the Maccabees against the Seleucid king Antiochus Epiphanes and the establishment of an independent Jewish kingdom. They date from the late second century BC. III and IV Maccabees are unrelated works, written probably at the beginning of the Christian era. III Maccabees describes a (probably imaginary) persecution of Jews by Ptolemy IV Philopator of Egypt (late 3rd century BC), while IV Maccabees is a philosophical treatise, with a Stoic flavour, on the superiority of intellect over passions.

McCarthy, Joseph R(aymond) (1908–57) US Republican senator, who led Senate investigations of supposed communists during the Cold War. His claim to have the names of communist infiltrators into the State Department was not proved and in 1954, after he had been censured by the Senate, his anticommunist witchhunt—commonly known as McCarthyism—came to an end.

McCarthy, Mary (1912–) US novelist and critic. Her novels deal with aspects of American society and include *The Groves of Academe* (1952), *The Group* (1963), *Birds of America* (1971), and *Cannibals and Missionaries* (1974). She has published criticism, travel books, the autobiographical *Memories of a Catholic Girlhood* (1957), and journalism, notably *Vietnam* (1967).

McCartney, Paul (1942–) British rock musician, formerly a member of the *Beatles. His solo career was launched with the hit "Maybe I'm Amazed" (1970). With his wife **Linda McCartney** (1942–) he formed (1971) Wings, the band with which he recorded such albums as *Band on the Run* (1973) and toured the world (1975–76). A multimillionaire, he financed and starred in a film *Give My Regards to Broad Street* (1984).

McClellan, George B(rinton) (1826–85) Federal general in the US *Civil War. His 1861 campaign preserved Kentucky and separated W Virginia from the Confederacy. He then fortified Washington, rebuilding the Federal forces there. In 1862 he was defeated before Richmond. Despite superior strength he did not counterattack at Antietam and President *Lincoln dismissed him (1862).

Macclesfield 53 16N 2 07W A town in N England, in Cheshire on the W edge of the Pennines. Traditionally a centre of the silk industry, it also produces clothing in other fabrics as well as textile machinery, paper, and plastics. Population (1981): 46 832.

McClure, Sir Robert John Le Mesurier (1807–73) Irish naval officer and explorer. In 1850, in search of Sir John *Franklin, missing in the Arctic, McClure entered the Beaufort Sea from the Pacific and was marooned in the strait named after him. He was rescued, returning home via the Atlantic (1854), and was thus the first to traverse the *Northwest Passage.

McCullers, Carson (1917–67) US novelist and playwright. Her novels, which include *The Heart Is a Lonely Hunter* (1940), *Reflections in a Golden Eye* (1941), and *A Member of the Wedding* (1946), are set in her native South and describe a grotesque and violent world. Other works include *The Ballad of the Sad Café* (1951), *The Square Root of Wonderful* (1958), and *Clock Without Hands* (1961).

MacDiarmid, Hugh (Christopher Murray Grieve; 1892–1978) Scottish poet. Active both as a nationalist and Marxist, he virtually created the "Scottish Renaissance" in literature. His early poetry, notably in *A Drunk Man Looks at the Thistle* (1926), was written in a Scots language drawn from regional dialects and Middle Scots writers. A number of later poems, however, such as *In Memoriam James Joyce* (1955), are written in English.

MacDonald, Flora (1722–90) The Scottish gentlewoman who, after the battle of Culloden in 1746, smuggled the defeated *Charles Edward Stuart, the Young Pretender, disguised as her maid, to Skye whence he sailed to permanent exile in Europe.

Macdonald, Sir John (Alexander) (1815–91) Canadian statesman; prime minister (1857–58, 1864, 1867–73, 1878–91). Macdonald was a member of the British America League, the proposals of which formed the basis of the British North America Act giving Canada dominion status within the British Empire (1867). As prime minister, he promoted the expansion of Canada to include Manitoba, British Columbia, and Prince Edward Island.

MacDonald, (James) Ramsay (1866–1937) British statesman; the first Labour prime minister (1924, 1929–31, 1931–35). He joined the Independent Labour Party in 1894 and became secretary of the Labour Representation Committee in 1900. Elected an MP (1906) he became leader of the parliamentary *Labour Party (1911) but resigned in opposition to World War I (1914) and lost his seat in the 1918 election. Re-elected to parliament in 1922 he again led the Labour Party, becoming prime minister in 1924. His minority government was defeated in an election held after a vote of no confidence in his administration in the House of Commons. His 1929–31 government, failing to deal with current economic problems, was broadened into a coalition (1931–35) that was increasingly dominated by the Conservatives and he was replaced by Baldwin in 1935.

Macdonnell Ranges A system of mountain ranges in Australia. They extend for about 65 km (40 mi) E and 320 km (200 mi) W of Alice Springs, across S Northern Territory reaching 1510 m (4955 ft) at Mount Ziel.

mace. *See* nutmeg.

Macedonia The central region of the Balkans. Inhabited from Neolithic times, Macedonia was settled by many migrating northern tribes. About 640 BC Perdiccas I became the first ruler of the kingdom of Macedon. *Philip II (359–336 BC) quelled the warlike tribes and founded Macedon's military and economic power, which under his son *Alexander the Great was extended to the East. Alexander's successors were harassed by rebellious uprisings and, after defeat (168 BC) in the *Macedonian Wars, Macedonia became a Roman province (146), losing its independence but remaining a centre of Hellenistic culture. The region is now divided between S Yugoslavia (a constituent republic), N Greece, and SW Bulgaria.

Macedonian Wars The three campaigns that secured Roman control of the kingdom of Macedon. The first Macedonian War (214–205 BC) coincided with the intervention of Philip V of Macedon (237–179; reigned 220–179) against Rome in the second *Punic War. The second Macedonian War (200–196) ended with the Roman victory at Cynoscephalae, in Thessaly. Rome instigated the third Macedonian War (171–168) against Philip's son Perseus (reigned 179–168) and finally crushed the Macedonians at the battle of Pydna.

Maceió 9 40S 35 44W A city in NE Brazil, the capital of Alagoas state. It contains many colonial buildings and has sugar-refining, distilling, sawmilling, and textile industries. Population (1980): 375 771.

McEnroe, John (Patrick, Jr) (1959–) US tennis player. He won the US singles title in 1979, 1980, 1981 and 1984, and the doubles title in 1979. An intense competitor noted for his tempestuous court behaviour, he became Wimbledon singles champion in 1981 (defeating Bjorn *Borg), 1983, and 1984, and doubles champion in 1979, 1981, and 1984, partnered by Peter Fleming.

Macgillicuddy's Reeks A mountain range in the Republic of Ireland, in Co Kerry. It extends W of the Lakes of Killarney, reaching 1041 m (3414 ft) at Carrantuohill.

McGonagall, William (1830–1902) Scottish poet. Convinced of his own genius, he wrote memorably bad poetry characterized by naive sincerity and lack of rhythm. He published *Poetic Gems* in 1890.

Mach, Ernst (1838–1916) Austrian physicist and philosopher, after whom the *Mach number is named in recognition of his researches into airflow and his observation that as the velocity of sound is reached the airflow changes. Philosophically he was a positivist and as such argued strongly against the concept of atoms, which he regarded as mystical entities since their existence could not be detected but only inferred. *See also* logical positivism.

Machaut, Guillaume de (c. 1300–77) French poet and composer, who held a number of court and ecclesiastical appointments in Bohemia and France before becoming canon of Rheims in 1337. He wrote a number of allegorical poems and developed the *ballade* and *rondeau*. He was one of the leading composers of the *ars nova* style and was the first composer to write a complete musical setting of the mass.

Machel, Samora Moïses (1933–86) Mozambique statesman; president (1975–86). Machel led the FRELIMO (Front for the Liberation of Mozambique) forces against Portugal (1966–74) and on independence became Mozambique's first president. He died in a plane crash.

Machen, Arthur (Llewellyn) (1863–1947) Welsh novelist. His novels of the supernatural include *The Great God Pan* (1894) and *The Hill of Dreams* (1907). His short story "The Bowmen" (1914) gave rise to the World War I legend of the angels of Mons.

Machiavelli, Niccolò (1469–1527) Italian political theorist. He served the Florentine republic as statesman and diplomat from 1498 to 1512, when the restoration of the Medici family forced him into exile. In *The Prince* (1532), written in 1513, he argued that all means are permissible in the realization of a stable state, and in the *Discorsi* (written 1513–19) he used the example of the ancient Roman Republic to reinforce his arguments. The adjective Machiavellian describes the view, or a supporter of the view, that opportunist or amoral means justify politically desirable ends.

machine gun A *small arm that fires repeatedly without reloading. The first was Puckle's rotating cylinder flintlock (1718). By 1862 the Gatling, named after Richard Jordan Gatling (1818–1903), was firing six rounds in a second by means of its several barrels and a hand-rotated breech. Modern weapons are derived from the recoil-operated belt-fed water-cooled weapons designed by Sir Hiram *Maxim towards the end of the 19th century, some of which are still in service. Ammunition from pan, box, belt, or drum is loaded, fired, extracted, and reloaded automatically by recoil or in later models by gas and piston (*see* Bren gun). Classes are: light machine gun (LMG), developed from the rifle; medium machine gun (MMG), normally having a two-man crew and using belt-fed rifle ammunition; and heavy machine gun (HMG), with calibres up to 20 mm. *Submachine guns using pistol ammunition are light derivatives.

machine tools Power-driven mechanical tools used to turn, form, drill, mill, shape, or plane metal or other materials. In *lathes the material to be worked (workpiece) is rotated and the tool is applied to it, whereas in other types of machine tool the workpiece is held stationary and a rotating cutter (milling machine), drill (drilling machine), or reciprocating cutter (shaping machine) is applied to it. In a planing machine the workpiece is reciprocated past the tool. In mass-production techniques a number of operations are carried out on the workpiece without human intervention, often by using a transfer machine to convey it from one machine tool to anoth-

er. Computer-controlled machine tools are a further step in the automation of production lines.

Mach number The ratio of the velocity of a body in a fluid to the velocity of sound in that fluid. The velocity is said to be supersonic if the Mach number is greater than one. If it exceeds five the velocity is said to be hypersonic. Named after Ernst *Mach.

MACHU PICCHU   *The real name of this fortified Inca retreat is unknown, Machu Picchu being the name of the mountain that rises above it.*

Machu Picchu A well-preserved *Inca town in the Urubamba valley (Peru), discovered in 1911. Sited on a precipitous ridge, Machu Picchu is flanked by extensive agricultural terraces. It contains a central plaza, royal palace, and sun temple, all built of polygonal dressed stone blocks.

Equatorial Guinea, Republic of.

McIndoe, Sir Archibald Hector (1900–60) New Zealand surgeon, who pioneered techniques in plastic surgery. He is particularly noted for his work in Britain with badly burnt RAF airmen during World War II.

Macintosh, Charles (1766–1843) Scottish chemist, who invented the waterproof garment known as the "mackintosh." He made his discovery in 1823 by noting that rubber dissolved in naphtha could be used to stick together two pieces of cloth, producing a waterproof layer between them. He also patented a steel-making process (1825).

Macke, August (1887–1914) German painter. During visits to France he was successively influenced by *impressionism, *fauvism, and *cubism. A member of Der *Blaue Reiter group, he became known for his light-hearted subjects, particularly parks and zoos, although his best works were watercolours painted in Tunis (1914), shortly before his death in World War I.

McKenna, Siobhán (1923–86) Irish actress. She acted at the Abbey Theatre, Dublin, from 1943 to 1946 and made her London debut in 1947. She was particularly successful in the roles of St Joan in G. B. Shaw's play and of Pegeen in Synge's *The Playboy of the Western World*, a role she also played in the film (1962).

Mackenzie A district of N Canada, the westernmost district of the *Northwest Territories. Mountains straddle the W border with the Yukon, the *Mackenzie River valley runs N through the centre, and barren plains cover the E. The Territories' most populous district, it produces zinc, lead, gold, and oil. Area: 1 366 199 sq km (527 490 sq mi). Population (1981): 29 869.

Mackenzie, Sir (Edward Montague) Compton (1883–1972) British novelist. His early novels include the semiautobiographical *Sinister Street* (1913). He served at Gallipoli in World War I and later settled on a Hebridean island. All of his later work is in a lighter vein and includes several volumes of memoirs and many humorous novels, notably *Whisky Galore* (1947).

Mackenzie River The longest river in Canada, flowing from Great Slave Lake in the North West Territories W and NNW through sparsely settled country to an extensive delta on the Beaufort Sea. Navigable in summer, it carries oil and minerals from the Arctic Ocean to S Canada. Its tributaries generate cheap hydroelectricity. Length: 1705 km (1065 mi).

mackerel An important food and game fish belonging to the genus *Scomber*, related to tuna. Mackerels live in shoals in tropical and temperate oceans, feeding on fish and invertebrates. They have a streamlined body, two dorsal fins, and a series of finlets running in front of the forked tail. The common Atlantic mackerel (*S. scombrus*), about 30 cm long, is marked with black and green bands above and is silvery-white below.

mackerel shark A medium to large carnivorous oceanic *shark of the family *Isuridae*, which includes the *porbeagle and the *white shark. They are heavy bodied and have large keels along both sides of the crescent-shaped tail for stability during fast swimming.

Mackerras, Sir Charles (1925–) US-born Australian conductor. He studied conducting in London and Prague. He was director of the Hamburg State Opera from 1965 to 1969 and director of the English National Opera from 1970 to 1978. He is particularly well known for his performances of Janáček's operas.

Mackinder, Sir Halford John (1861–1947) British geographer. Mackinder developed what he called the "new geography," a discipline that bridged the natural sciences and the humanities. In 1899 he became director of the newly founded Oxford school of geography and subsequently director of the London School of Economics. Mackinder's *Democratic Ideas and Reality* (1919) was an astute and far-sighted treatise on the balance of world power. His later theories on the Atlantic Community anticipated NATO. Mackinder was a Conservative MP from 1910 to 1922.

McKinley, Mount A mountain in the USA, in S central Alaska in the Alaska Range. The highest peak in North America, it was first successfully climbed in 1913 by the US explorer, Hudson Stuck (1863–1920). Height: 6194 m (20 320 ft).

McKinley, William (1843–1901) US statesman; Republican president (1897–1901). An Ohio congressman, and later governor of Ohio (1891–96), he introduced the McKinley Tariff Act (1890), which established protective duties. Dominated by the war with Spain to protect Cuban investments, his administration, under which business boomed, opened an era of US imperialism, annexing the Philippines and intervening in the Boxer Rising in pursuit of the *Open Door trading policy. He died shortly after being shot by an anarchist.

Mackintosh, Charles Rennie (1868–1928) Scottish architect and designer. One of the most brilliant exponents of *Art Nouveau, Mackintosh evolved an austere version of the style, which was highly influential throughout Europe, though less so in Britain. All his best work was in Glasgow, in particular the School of Art (1897–1909) and four tearooms (1897–1912). In

1923 he moved to London, where his practice collapsed, resulting in his retirement.

Maclean, Alistair (1923–87) Scottish writer. After five years in the Navy he wrote *HMS Ulysses* (1955). Other novels include *The Guns of Navarone* (1956), *Where Eagles Dare* (1967), and *The Lonely Sea* (1985).

Maclean, Donald (1913–83) British Foreign Office official and Soviet secret agent. He fled to Russia in company with Guy Burgess (1911–63) in 1951. They had been warned of the British authorities' growing suspicion by Kim Philby. In 1979 it was revealed that Anthony Blunt (1907–83), a distinguished art historian, was implicated in the affair.

Macleish, Archibald (1892–1982) US poet. An expatriate writer in France during the 1920s, he later worked in the US government service. Much of his *Collected Poems* (1952) was influenced by his liberal politics. He wrote verse dramas including *Panic* (1935) and *J.B.* (1958), which was awarded a Pulitzer Prize, and a collection, *Six Plays* (1980).

Maclennan, Robert (1936–) British politician. Formerly a Labour MP, he joined the Social Democratic Party in 1981, becoming its leader in 1987.

Macleod, Iain (Norman) (1913–70) British Conservative politician. After serving as minister of health (1952–55) and minister of labour (1955–59) he was a notable colonial secretary (1959–61). Appointed chancellor of the exchequer in 1970, he died in office. He was also a notable bridge theorist.

Macleod, John James Rickard (1876–1935) British physiologist, noted for his work on carbohydrate metabolism. He was professor of physiology at Toronto University (1919–28), where F. G. *Banting and C. H. *Best first isolated the hormone insulin. Macleod was awarded the 1923 Nobel Prize with Banting.

McLeod gauge An instrument that uses *Boyle's law to measure the pressure of a near vacuum. A sample of the vacuum is compressed into a small volume thus raising its pressure, which may then be measured. It is accurate down to about 10^{-6} millimetre of mercury.

Mac Liammóir, Micheál (1899–1978) Irish actor and dramatist. In 1928 he was a founder of the Gate Theatre in Dublin, a platform for international drama and young Irish dramatists. He is best known for his one-man show, *The Importance of Being Oscar* (1960–61), based on Oscar Wilde.

Maclise, Daniel (1806–70) Irish portrait and history painter, born in Cork. He moved to London (1827), where he painted his celebrated *Death of Nelson* (Liverpool) and *The Meeting of Wellington and Blücher*.

McLuhan, (Herbert) Marshall (1911–81) Canadian sociologist and literary critic, best known for his controversial views on the effects of technology on society. His books include *The Gutenberg Galaxy* (1962), *The Medium Is the Massage* (1967), and *The City as Classroom* (1977).

MacMahon, Marie Edme Patrice Maurice, Comte de (1808–93) French marshal and statesman; president (1873–79). He came to prominence in the Crimean War (1854–56) and in Italy, where his victory at Magenta (1859) brought him the title Duc de Magenta. He helped to suppress the Commune of Paris (1871) succeeding Thiers as president, he attempted to break the influence of the republican party by appointing a royalist cabinet in defiance of the chamber of deputies. The chamber's successful resistance to this move forced MacMahon to resign.

McMahon, William (1908–) Australian statesman; prime minister (1971–72) of a coalition of Liberal and Country Parties. He became Liberal deputy leader in 1966 and minister for foreign affairs in 1969.

Macmillan, Daniel (1813–57) Scottish bookseller and publisher, who with his brother **Alexander Macmillan** (1818–96) founded (1843) Macmillan and Company, which became one of the world's largest publishing houses.

Apprenticed to a bookseller in Irvine, Scotland, in 1824, Daniel moved (1833) to Cambridge, where he opened his own shop in 1843. The first publications appeared in 1844.

McMillan, Edwin Mattison (1907–) US physicist, who shared the 1951 Nobel Prize with Glenn *Seaborg for their discovery of transuranic elements. The first such element, *neptunium, was discovered by McMillan in 1940 by bombarding uranium with neutrons.

HAROLD MACMILLAN *Photographed by Patrick Lichfield on his 90th birthday.*

Macmillan, (Maurice) Harold, 1st Earl of Stockton (1894–1986) British statesman; Conservative prime minister (1957–63). The grandson of Daniel *Macmillan, who founded the family publishing business (in which Harold Macmillan worked from World War I), he was an MP from 1924 to 1929 and again from 1931. During the 1930s he opposed *appeasement and in World War II held office under Churchill. In 1951 he became a successful minister of housing and local government and then minister of defence (1954) and foreign secretary (1955). As chancellor of the exchequer (1955–57) he introduced Premium Bonds (1957). He succeeded Sir Anthony Eden as prime minister. His "wind of change" speech in Africa in 1958 marked his government's support of independence for African states; he is also remembered for his speech during the 1959 election asserting "you've never had it so good." His second ministry failed to deal with inflation and suffered a major blow when de Gaulle frustrated Britain's attempt to join the EEC (1963). However, he improved relations with the USA and helped to achieve the *Nuclear Test-Ban Treaty (1963). The last year of his government was marred by the *Profumo affair. Macmillan resigned because of ill health and was awarded the OM in 1976. He became chancellor of Oxford University in 1960 and was granted an earldom in 1984.

MacMillan, Sir Kenneth (1929–) British ballet dancer and choreographer. He choreographed many ballets for companies in Europe and the USA, notably *Romeo and Juliet* (1965), *Anastasia* (1967), and *Sleeping Beauty* (1973). He was director of the Royal Ballet from 1970 to 1977.

Macmillan, Kirkpatrick (d. 1878) Scottish blacksmith, who in 1839 built the first *bicycle. It was an adaptation of the hobby-horse and was propelled by pedals.

MacNeice, Louis (1907–63) Irish-born British poet. A friend of *Auden, *Spender, and *Day Lewis at Oxford in the 1930s, he published his first volume of poetry, *Blind Fireworks*,

in 1929. Among his other volumes are *Autumn Journal* (1939), *The Burning Perch* (1963), and a distinguished collection of plays for radio, *The Dark Tower* (1947).

Macon 32 49N 83 37W A city in the USA, in Georgia on the Ocmulgee River. It is the industrial centre of a large agricultural area. Population (1980): 116 860.

Mâcon 46 18N 4 50E A town in E France, the capital of the Saône-et-Loire department on the River Saône. An important trading centre for Burgundy wines, its manufactures include textiles, vats, and agricultural machinery. Population (1982): 38 719.

Maconchy, Elizabeth (1907–) British composer. She studied with Vaughan Williams and in Prague. Her works include 12 string quartets and other chamber music, operas, choral music, and ballet music.

Macquarie, Lachlan (1761–1824) Scottish colonial administrator; governor of New South Wales (1810–21). He encouraged construction and exploration in the colony but his liberal policies towards the *Emancipists and the Aborigines made him enemies and he resigned.

Macquarie Island A subantarctic volcanic island in the S Pacific Ocean, in the Australian Antarctic Territory. The site of a meteorological research station, it is the only known breeding ground of the royal penguin. Area: about 168 sq km (65 sq mi).

McQueen, Steve (1930–80) US film actor. Following his success in *The Magnificent Seven* (1960) he was usually associated with the roles of tough laconic heroes. His later films include *The Cincinnati Kid* (1965) and *Bullitt* (1968), *Papillon* (1973), and *An Enemy of the People* (1976).

Macready, William Charles (1793–1873) British actor and theatre manager. One of the most distinguished of 19th-century tragedians, he was particularly successful in the roles of Lear, Hamlet, and Macbeth, and was regarded as the chief rival of Edmund *Kean. He reformed production standards and advocated fidelity to the original texts of Shakespeare.

Madagascar, Democratic Republic of (name until 1975: Malagasy Republic) An island country in the Indian Ocean, off the SE coast of Africa. A narrow coastal plain in the E and a broader one in the W rise to central highlands, reaching heights of over 2800 m (9000 ft). Most of the inhabitants are Merina, Betsimisaraka, and Betsileo, all speaking *Austronesian dialects. *Economy*: chiefly agricultural, now developed on a cooperative basis. Livestock is important and the main crops include rice and manioc as well as coffee, sugar, and spices, the main exports. Forests produce not only timber, but also gums, resins, and dyes. Clearing of the forests has, however, seriously depleted the unique indigenous fauna, especially the lemurs. Minerals include graphite, chrome, and ilmenite. Industry, previously based mainly on food processing and tobacco, now includes metals, plastics, paper, and oil refining. *History*: settled by Indonesians from the 1st century AD and by Muslim traders from Africa from the 8th century, the Portuguese visited the island in the 16th century. It remained a native kingdom until the late 19th century, when the French laid claim to Madagascar and, after much bloodshed, established a protectorate (1896). It became a French overseas territory in 1946 and a republic within the French Community in 1958, gaining full independence in 1960. A military government took over in 1972 but was overthrown in 1975. A new socialist constitution was then approved by a referendum and Madagascar became a democratic republic, with Lt Cdr Didier Ratsiraka (1936–) as its first president. Official languages: Malagasy and French. Official currency: Malagasy franc of 100 centimes. Area: 587 041 sq km (229 233 sq mi). Population (1983 est): 9 389 000. Capital: Antananarivo. Main port: Tamatave.

Madariaga y Rojo, Salvador de (1886–1978) Spanish historian and diplomat, who was ambassador to the USA (1931) and to France (1932–34). His historical writings include *The Rise and Fall of the Spanish American Empire* (1947) and *Bolívar* (1952).

madder A perennial herb of the genus *Rubia* (about 38 species), especially *R. tinctorum*, native to Eurasia. It has trailing stems with whorls of narrow leaves, clusters of small yellow flowers, and blackish berry-like fruits. A red dye is extracted from the roots. Family: *Rubiaceae*.

Madeira, Rio A river in W Brazil, formed by the union of the Ríos Beni and Mamoré and flowing generally NE to join the River Amazon. Length: 3241 km (2013 mi).

Madeira Islands (*or* Funchal Islands) A Portuguese archipelago in the Atlantic Ocean, about 640 km (398 mi) off the coast of Morocco. It comprises the inhabited islands of Madeira and Porto Santo and two uninhabited island groups. Madeira, the largest and most important island, is densely vegetated and its mild climate attracts many holiday-makers. Its products include basketwork, fruit (such as mangoes), sugar, and the famous Madeira wine. Area: 777 sq km (300 sq mi). Population (1981): 252 844. Capital: Funchal.

Maderna, Carlo (1556-1629) Roman architect. A precursor of the Roman *baroque style of architecture, Maderna's vigorous style first gained full expression in the façade of Sta Susanna (1597-1603). His major work was the completion of St Peter's Basilica, adding the nave and façade to Michelangelo's design.

Madhya Pradesh A state in central India, stretching N over highlands to the S edge of the Ganges plain. The largest state, it is predominantly agricultural, producing grains, cotton, and sugar cane. Its huge hydroelectric potential is harnessed for a few industries, including steel, aluminium, and cement. Coal, iron ore, and other minerals are mined. *History*: under Islamic (11th-18th centuries) and Maratha (18th-19th centuries) rule until Britain established control, Madhya Pradesh became a state in 1956. Area: 442 841 sq km (170 937 sq mi). Population (1981): 52 131 717. Capital: Bhopal.

Madison 43 04N 89 22W A city in the USA, the capital of Wisconsin situated on an isthmus between Lakes Mendota and Monona. The commercial and industrial centre of a rich agricultural region, it is the site of the University of Wisconsin (1848). Population (1980): 170 616.

Madison, James (1751-1836) US statesman; president (1809-17). His influence at the *Constitutional Convention (1787), which drew up the US constitution, earned him the title "father of the American constitution." Madison urged its ratification and defended federal powers over *states' rights in the essays published as *The Federalist Papers*. As secretary of state under Jefferson he promoted the *Louisiana Purchase. While president he declared the expansionist *War of 1812 on Britain, described as "Mr Madison's War."

Madras 13 05N 80 18N A city and major seaport in India, the capital of Tamil Nadu on the Coromandel Coast. Founded (1639) by the British East India Company, the city developed around the small fort, Fort St George, which now contains state government offices and is the site of the first English church built in India (1678-80). The University of Madras was established here in 1857. An important industrial centre, Madras manufactures cars, bicycles, and cement and its chief exports are leather, iron ore, and cotton textiles. Population (1981 est): 4 276 635.

Madras. *See* Tamil Nadu.

Madrid 40 27N 3 42W The capital of Spain, situated on a high plateau in the centre of the country on the River Manzanares. Madrid is the focal point of rail, road, and air routes and is the financial centre of Spain. Its industries include the manufacture of leather goods, textiles, chemicals, engineering, glassware, and porcelain and the processing of agricultural products. A cultural centre, Madrid possesses a university (transferred from Alcalá de Henares in 1836), notable art galleries (especially the *Prado), and the national

library (founded in 1712). Fine buildings include the former royal palace, the parliament, many churches, and the 17th-century cathedral. *History*: Madrid was captured from the Moors in 1083 by Alfonso VI. Philip II established it as the capital in 1561. The citizens' uprising against Napoleon's army of occupation in 1808 provided inspiration for the rest of Spain. In the Spanish Civil War Madrid was a Republican stronghold until it fell to the Nationalists in March, 1939, after being besieged for over two years. Population (1981): 3 188 297.

madrigal A secular polyphonic composition (*see* polyphony) for voices, often a setting of a love poem. Its first flowering was in 14th-century Florence, where Landini wrote madrigals in two and three parts for voices and instruments. The Italian madrigal of the 16th and 17th centuries developed as an aristocratic art form of great expressiveness in the complex and often chromatic compositions of Marenzio, Monteverdi, and Gesualdo. The English school (Byrd, Morley, Weelkes, etc.) wrote in a simpler but idiomatic style; many sets of madrigals were composed in praise of Elizabeth I.

Madura An Indonesian island in the Java Sea, off NE Java. Largely infertile, its chief industries are cattle rearing and fish farming. It is known for its bull races. The population is Muslim and there is a notable mosque at Bangkalan. Area: 5472 sq km (2113 sq mi). Chief town: Pamekasan.

Madurai 9 55N 78 07E A city in India, in Tamil Nadu. Capital of the Pandya kings (4th-11th centuries AD), it is the site of a large Hindu temple (rebuilt 16th-17th centuries). Its university was established in 1966. Industries include brassware and textiles. Population (1981): 904 000.

Maeander, River. *See* Menderes, River.

Maecenas, Gaius (d. 8 BC) Roman statesman, who was a close adviser of Emperor *Augustus. Also noted as a literary patron, Maecenas included in his circle the three most important Augustan poets, Virgil, Horace, and Propertius.

Maelstrom A violent whirlpool in a channel in the Norwegian Lofoten Islands, a notorious shipping hazard. The word (uncapitalized) is also used for any whirlpool, particularly one of tidal origin occurring in a narrow irregular channel, as between islands.

Maes, Nicolas (*or* N. Maas; 1634-93) Dutch painter of domestic scenes and portraits, born in Dordrecht. Initially influenced by his teacher *Rembrandt, in such paintings as *Girl at the Window* (c. 1655; Rijksmuseum, Amsterdam), he later adopted the style of Flemish portraiture, after visiting Antwerp in the 1660s.

Maeterlinck, Maurice (1862-1949) Belgian poet and dramatist. Having established his reputation as a poet he became the leading dramatist of the *Symbolist movement with such plays as *Pelléas et Mélisande* (1892), on which Debussy based his opera of the same name, and *L'Oiseau bleu* (1908). He also wrote several philosophical and mystical prose works. From 1890 he lived mostly in France. He won the Nobel Prize in 1911.

Mafeking (*or* Mafikeng) 25 53S 25 39E A town in South Africa, in Bophutha Tswana. It was besieged for 217 days by Boers during the second Boer War (1899-1902) but was held by Col *Baden-Powell until relieved. Although outside the territory, it was the capital of the protectorate of Bechuanaland (now Botswana) until 1965. The town was officially surrendered to Bophutha Tswana by South Africa in 1980. Population (1980): 6775.

Mafia A criminal organization that originated as a secret society in 13th-century Sicily. The word (meaning "swank") was coined in the 19th century, when the Mafia was employed by the great landowners of Sicily to manage their estates. By extortion, "protection," ransom, and blackmail, the Mafia formed an organization so powerful that it virtually ruled Sicily. Repeated attempts to end its power, including the almost successful efforts of the fascists, have been hampered by the code of absolute silence enforced by reprisals. Italian emigrants took the Mafia to the USA in the early 20th century, where as Cosa Nostra (Our Affair), it has flourished.

Magadha An ancient kingdom in NE India, now absorbed by Bihar state. Its early kings included Bimbisara (reigned c. 543–c. 491 BC) and Ajataśatru (reigned c. 491–c. 459). Under *Chandragupta Maurya, *Aśoka, and later the *Gupta kings Magadha, and its capital Pataliputra, became a great cultural and political centre.

Magdalena, Río A river in Colombia, rising in the SW of the country and flowing generally N to enter the Caribbean Sea near Barranquilla. Length: 1540 km (956 mi).

Magdalenian A culture of the Upper *Palaeolithic, succeeding the *Solutrean in W Europe. Named after La Madeleine cave in the Dordogne (SW France), the Magdalenian is marked by an abundance of bone and antler tools, notably barbed harpoons and spear throwers, both new additions to man's toolkit. Dating from about 15 000 to 10 000 BC, it was the heyday of prehistoric art with magnificent cave paintings (e.g. at *Altamira) and carved and engraved decoration on bone artefacts.

Magdeburg 52 8N 11 35E A city in W East Germany, on the River *Elbe. It achieved fame in the middle ages for its judicial system, the "Magdeburg Law," which was used as a model by many other European cities. It was also a leading member of the Hanseatic League. Bombs destroyed much of the city during World War II, including the town hall (1691), but the cathedral (begun in the 13th century) survived. An important inland port, its industries include iron, oil and sugar refining, chemicals, and textiles. Population (1982): 289 075.

Magellan, Ferdinand (c. 1480–1521) Portuguese explorer. He undertook many expeditions to India and Africa for Portugal between 1505 and 1516. In 1519, under Spanish patronage, he set off to seek a passage W to the Moluccas. The expedition of five ships—Magellan's flagship *Trinidad* with *San Antonio*, *Concepción*, *Victoria*, and *Santiago*—crossed the Pacific and late in 1520 sailed through the strait that was named after him. In the spring of 1521, after severe privations, they reached the East Indies, where Magellan was killed. Only the *Victoria* returned to Spain, thus completing under del *Cano the first circumnavigation of the world. *See also* Magellanic Clouds.

Magellan, Strait of A channel separating the mainland of South America from Tierra del Fuego. Discovered in 1520 by the Portuguese explorer Magellan, it is an important passage between the S Atlantic and the S Pacific Oceans. Length: 600 km (370 mi). Maximum width: 32 km (20 mi).

Magellanic Clouds Two relatively small irregular *galaxies, the Small and Large Magellanic Clouds, that are close neighbours of our *Galaxy. They can be seen, by eye, from the S hemisphere and were first recorded by Ferdinand *Magellan in 1519.

Magendie, François (1783–1855) French physiologist, noted for his work on the nervous system. He investigated the finding, first made by the anatomist Sir Charles Bell (1774–1842), that the anterior roots of the spinal cord carry motor nerves and the posterior roots carry sensory nerves. Magendie also experimented on nutritional requirements and studied the effects of drugs on the body.

Magenta 43 28N 8 52E A town in N Italy, in Lombardy. A decisive battle in the struggle for Italian national independence was fought here in 1859, in which the French and Sardinians defeated the Austrians; Magenta dye was named in honour of the event. Population (1981 est): 23 694.

Maggiore, Lake (Latin name: Lacus Verbanus) A long narrow lake in Italy and Switzerland. Sheltered from the N by the Alps, it enjoys a mild climate: the holiday resorts at its edge include Locarno, in Switzerland. Area: 212 sq km (82 sq mi).

maggot The legless soft-bodied larva of many two-winged flies, such as the *blowfly and *housefly. Rat-tailed maggots are the aquatic larvae of certain *hoverflies, so called because of their long respiratory siphons.

Maghrib (*or* Maghreb; Arabic: west) The area in NW Africa occupied by the states of Morocco, Algeria, Tunisia, and Libya, so called on account of its geographical position in the Arab world. It formerly included Moorish Spain. Its inhabitants are of mixed *Arab and *Berber stock. Although the peoples of the Maghrib have their own distinctive customs and Arabic and Berber dialects they have always formed an integral part of the Arabic cultural tradition. *Compare* Mashriq.

Magi 1. In antiquity, the priests of Zoroaster, renowned for their astronomical knowledge (*see* Zoroastrianism). 2. The sages who came from the East, following a star, to worship the infant Christ at Bethlehem (Matthew 2.1–12). Early Christian tradition embroidered the New Testament account, giving them the title of kings and the names of Caspar, Melchior, and Balthazar. Symbolic significance was ascribed to their gifts: gold (kingship), frankincense (divinity), and myrrh (death). Honoured as saints during the middle ages, they became the patron saints of *Cologne, and their adoration of Christ was a favourite theme in Christian art.

magic A system of beliefs and practices by which it is believed that man may control the natural and supernatural forces that affect his life. Generally regarded as "superstition" in industrial societies, magic still lingers in such popular rituals as touching wood to avert ill luck. In many preindustrial societies, magic plays an important social role. Its practitioners may rank next to the chief in prestige and authority, being credited with the ability to communicate with good and evil spirits to ensure success in war and hunting and the fertility of land and livestock. Some primitive rituals, such as pouring water on the ground to bring rain, are purely magical. They differ from religious rituals (praying for rain) because they rely on the naive belief that the poured water can in some way directly affect the mechanics of precipitation.

Maginot line Fortifications built (1929–38) to protect the E frontier of France. They were named after André Maginot (1877–1932), French minister of war (1929–32), who authorized its construction. Outflanked in World War II by the invading Germans (1940), the line was never tested.

magistrate An officer who administers the law. In England magistrates are either *justices of the peace or stipendiary magistrates, who are appointed to try cases in some metropolitan Magistrates' Courts, have wider powers than justices, and are salaried.

Maglemosian A *Mesolithic culture of N Europe, dating from about 8000 to 5000 BC. Named after a site at Mullerup on Sjaelland (Denmark), the Maglemosian extended from E England to NW Russia. Hunters of forest game and fishers in the lakes by which they preferred to live, the Maglemosians used wood, stone, antler, and bone artefacts, including dug-out canoes, but lacked domestic animals (apart from dogs), cultivated crops, and pottery.

magma Molten rock lying beneath the earth's surface, either in the crust or upper mantle. It may rise to the surface through volcanic fissures and be extruded as lava; if it solidifies under ground it forms intrusive *igneous rock. Magma is a hot largely silicate liquid, containing dissolved gases and sometimes suspended crystals.

Magna Carta (1215) The Great Charter that was sealed at Runnymede by King John of England in response to the baronial unrest that resulted from his disastrous foreign policy and arbitrary government. The Charter defined the barons' feudal obligations to the monarch, opposed his arbitrary application of justice, and confirmed the liberties of the English Church; its enforcement was to be supervised by 25 men elected by the barons. Although it failed to avert the outbreak of the first *Barons' War and was annulled by the pope, it was reissued, with some changes, in 1216, 1217, and 1225. The Charter was subsequently upheld, especially by the parliamentarians in the 17th century, as a statement of fundamental civil rights, a claim that went beyond its contemporary significance as a definition of the limitations of royal power. Of the four extant originals, two are in the British Library, one is in Salisbury Cathedral, and one is in Lincoln Cathedral.

Magnani, Anna (1908–73) Italian film actress, born in Egypt. She began her career as a nightclub singer in Rome. She appeared in Rossellini's *Rome, Open City* (1945), Renoir's *The Golden Coach* (1953), and, after she went to Hollywood, *The Rose Tattoo* (1955).

magnesite A white or colourless mineral consisting of magnesium carbonate. It results from the alteration of magnesium-rich rocks, as in the veins of magnesite in serpentine, and as replacement deposits in limestone and dolomite. It is an important ore of magnesium and is used in the manufacture of refractory material, fertilizers, abrasives, etc.

magnesium (Mg) A light silvery-white reactive metal, first isolated by Sir Humphry Davy in 1808. Magnesium is the eighth most common element in the earth's crust and is a major constituent of the earth's mantle as the minerals olivine (Mg_2SiO_4) and enstatite ($MgSiO_3$). It is extracted by electrolysis of lead chloride ($MgCl_2$), which is obtained from sea water and is responsible for the stickiness of unrefined table salt, since magnesium chloride is deliquescent. Magnesium forms many other ionic salts, such as the sulphate ($MgSO_4$; Epsom salts), the oxide (MgO), the nitrate ($Mg(NO_3)_2$), and the hydroxide ($Mg(OH)_2$; milk of magnesia). It also plays a central role in plant life, occurring in *chlorophyll. It has important commercial uses when alloyed with aluminium to make the strong light alloys used in aircraft construction. It is also used in flares, incendiary bombs, and as magnesium oxide in refractory furnace linings. At no 12; at wt 24.312; mp 648.8°C; bp 1090°C.

magnet A body that has an appreciable external *magnetic field (*see also* magnetism). Every magnet has two distinct areas around which the field is greatest—these areas are called the north and south poles. If two magnets are brought together, the like poles repel each other and the opposite poles attract each other. Ferromagnetic materials (*see* ferromagnetism) are attracted to magnets because the magnet induces a field in the material in line with its own field. **Permanent magnets** are made of ferromagnetic materials and retain their magnetism unless they are heated above a certain temperature or are demagnetized by a strong opposing field. **Electromagnets** only function when an electric current flows through their coils. The field strength along the axis of the coil is proportional to the number of turns of the coil and the current flowing through it.

magnetic bottle An arrangement of magnetic fields designed to contain a *plasma. Usually the fields are linear with strong magnetic fields called **magnetic mirrors** at both ends so that the plasma is confined within a cylinder. They are used in experimental *thermonuclear reactors.

magnetic constant (μ_0) A constant frequently occurring in magnetic equations in SI units. Also known as the *permeability of free space, its value is $4\pi \times 10^{-7}$ henry per metre. It is related to the *electric constant (ε_0) by $\mu_0\varepsilon_0 = 1/c^2$, where c is the velocity of light.

magnetic declination The angle between geographical north and the horizontal component of the *geomagnetic field at the same point. It is also known as the magnetic variation.

magnetic dip The angle formed between the horizon and a compass allowed to swing freely in the vertical plane. It thus indicates the direction of the vertical component of the *geomagnetic field. It is measured with a **dip circle**, a vertically mounted magnetic needle surrounded by a circular scale.

magnetic domain. *See* ferromagnetism.

magnetic field The concept, devised by *Faraday, to explain the action-at-a-distance forces produced by a *magnet. The magnet is thought of as being surrounded by a field of force, within which its magnetic properties are effective. The strength and direction of the field is indicated by the lines of force that join the magnet's north and south poles. These lines of force can be seen if a card is laid over a magnet and iron filings sprinkled onto the card; when the card is tapped, the filings congregate along the lines of force. A wire carrying an electric current is also surrounded by a magnetic field, with concentric lines of force. An electromagnet usually consists of a coil of wire, in which the lines of force run through the centre of the coil and around its circumference. The strength of the field at the centre of the coil is proportional to the current and the number of turns, and inversely proportional to the radius of the coil. *See also* electromagnetic field.

magnetic flux A measure of the current-inducing properties of a magnetic field (*see* flux). It is measured in *webers.

magnetic moment A measure of the strength of a *magnet in terms of the torque or twisting force it experiences in a uniform magnetic field. It is equal to the product of the strength of a magnet's poles and the distance between them.

magnetic monopole A hypothetical particle that would carry a magnetic charge equivalent to either a north pole or a south pole. Such particles would be analogous to charged elementary particles and would provide a complete symmetry between electricity and magnetism. Unlike an electrically charged particle, a stationary magnetic monopole would give rise to a magnetic field and, when moving, an additional electric field. No monopole has ever been discovered.

magnetic tape. *See* cassette; tape recorder.

magnetism A phenomenon in which one body can exert a force on another body with which it is not in contact (action at a distance). The space in which such a force exists is called a *magnetic field. Stationary charged particles are surrounded by an *electric field; when these charged particles move or spin, an associated effect, the magnetic field, is created. Thus, an electric current, consisting of a flow of electrons, produces a magnetic field around the conductor carrying the current. The behaviour of materials when placed in such a field depends on how the spinning electrons inside its atoms align themselves to reinforce or oppose the external field. *See also* antiferromagnetism; diamagnetism; ferrimagnetism; ferromagnetism; paramagnetism.

magnetite (*or* lodestone) A black magnetic mineral, a form of iron oxide (Fe_3O_4). It often has distinct north and south magnetic poles and was known around 500 BC for its use as a compass. It is one of the ores from which iron is extracted.

magneto An alternating-current *electric generator that uses a permanent *magnet, rather than an electromagnet, to create the magnetic field. It usually consists of one or more conducting coils rotating between a number of pairs of *magnetic poles. The induced voltage has a frequency equal to the number of magnets times the speed of rotation of the coils. It is used in some small internal-combustion engines to produce the ignition spark, often combined with the flywheel.

magnetohydrodynamics (MHD) A method of generating electricity in which current carriers in a fluid are forced by an external magnetic field to flow between electrodes placed in the fluid. Usually the fluid is a hot ionized gas or plasma in which the current carriers are electrons. The electron concentration is increased by adding substances of low ionization potential (e.g. sodium or potassium salts) to the flame. The method has been used to increase the efficiency of generation of a gas turbine, the exhaust flame of which is used for MHD generation.

magnetomotive force (mmf)   A measure of the magnetic effect of an electric current in a coil. It is analogous to *electromotive force and is measured in ampere-turns, being dependent on the number of turns in the coil.

magnetosphere   A region surrounding a planet in which charged particles are controlled by the magnetic field of the planet rather than by the interplanetary magnetic field carried by the *solar wind; beyond a magnetosphere, solar-wind particles flow undisturbed. Its shape arises from the interaction between solar wind and planetary magnetic field. The earth's magnetosphere, which includes the *Van Allen radiation belts, extends 60 000 km from the sunward side of the planet but is drawn out to a much greater extent on the opposite side.

magnetostriction   The mechanical deformation of a ferromagnetic material (*see* ferromagnetism) when it is subjected to a magnetic field. The effect is the result of internal mechanical stress that arises because the energy required to magnetize the crystal domains varies with their orientation in the field. The converse effect, mechanical stress causing a change in magnetization, also occurs. Magnetostriction is used in *echo-sounding oscillators to produce the ultrasonic sound wave.

magnetron   An electronic device used to generate and amplify *microwaves. It consists of a sealed evacuated tube containing a central cylindrical cathode (source of electrons) inside a cylindrical anode to which electrons are drawn by an electrostatic field. A steady magnetic field applied along the axis of the tube deflects the electrons from their radial path and, if strong enough, will cause them to rotate around the cathode setting up microwave-frequency oscillations. It is widely used in radar generators.

magnification   In optical systems, the ratio of the width of an object to the width of its image, both being measured perpendicular to the axis of the system. For a single lens this reduces to the ratio of the distances of the image and the object from the lens when the image is in focus. For optical instruments the magnification is defined as the ratio of the size of the image on the retina produced by an object with and without the instrument.

Magnitogorsk   53 28N 59 06E A city in the central Soviet Union, in the RSFSR on the River Ural. It is an important metallurgy centre and also possesses the largest iron and steel plant in the country. Population (1981 est): 413 000.

magnitude   A measure of the brightness of stars and other astronomical objects. An object's **apparent magnitude** is its brightness as observed from earth and depends primarily on its *luminosity and its distance. An object's **absolute magnitude** is its apparent magnitude if it lay at a distance of 10 parsecs (32.616 light years). Both apparent and absolute magnitude are measured at various specific wavebands in the visible, ultraviolet, and infrared regions of the electromagnetic spectrum. Magnitude values range from about +25 for the faintest objects so far detected through zero to negative values for the brightest objects. Magnitude is proportional to the logarithm of the brightness. One star 5 magnitudes less than another is 100 times brighter; a difference of one magnitude thus denotes a brightness ratio of $\sqrt[5]{100}$, i.e. 2.512. The difference between the absolute and apparent magnitudes of a body is related to its distance from earth.

Magnolia   A genus of evergreen or deciduous shrubs and trees (35 species), native to North America and Asia and widely grown as ornamentals. Up to 45 m high, they have large simple leaves and big showy flowers, with a whorl of white, yellow, greenish, or pink petals and many stamens. These produce papery conelike structures containing winged fruits. A popular ornamental magnolia is the Chinese hybrid *M.* × *soulangeana*, which has pink-tinged flowers. Family: *Magnoliaceae*. *See also* umbrella tree.

magpie   A noisy black-and-white crow, *Pica pica*, occurring in Eurasia, NW Africa, and W North America. 44 cm long, it has a long wedge-shaped tail and an iridescent blue sheen on the wings. Magpies are omnivorous and notorious predators of eggs and nestlings; they are also attracted to bright objects. The name is also given to Australian songbirds of the family *Cracticidae*, which includes the *currawongs.

Magritte, René   (1898–1967) Belgian surrealist painter. Initially a wallpaper designer and commercial artist, he became associated with the Paris surrealists (*see* surrealism) in the late 1920s. Using a realistic but deadpan technique, he made everyday images appear menacing by the use of unusual juxtapositions.

Magyars   The largest ethnic group in Hungary. There are substantial Magyar minorities in neighbouring countries. They originated from mixed Ugric and Turkic stock, who migrated from Siberia during the 5th century and reached their present location during the late 9th century. They subjugated the local *Slavs and *Huns and for 50 years raided far into Europe causing widespread disruption. Today they are chiefly peasant farmers. *See also* Hungarian.

Mahabharata (Sanskrit: great epic of the Bharatas)   A Hindu epic poem in 18 books. Probably composed about 300 BC, it may record actual events of a thousand years earlier. The main story relates the feud between the Pandava and Kaurava clans and is interwoven with many myths and other episodes, including the *Bhagavadgita* in the sixth book. The *Mahabharata* and *Ramayana* form the two great classics of Sanskrit literature.

Mahalla el-Kubra   30 59N 31 10E A city in N Egypt, on the Nile Delta. In a region producing rice, cereal, and cotton, it is an important cotton-manufacturing centre. Population (1983 est): 345 800.

Maharashtra   A state in W central India, on the Arabian Sea. Rising from its coastal plain eastwards over the Western *Ghats, it lies mostly on the *Deccan plateau. Cotton, millet, wheat, and rice are farmed. The second most industrialized state, it produces cotton textiles, chemicals, machinery, and oil products. Bauxite, manganese, and iron ore are mined. *History*: conquered by Muslims (1307), the Marathas regained their freedom (16th century) and maintained it until Britain established control (19th century). Maharashtra became a state in 1960. Area: 307 762 sq km (118 796 sq mi). Population (1981): 62 693 898. Capital: Bombay.

Mahavira, title of **Vardhamana**   (?599–527 BC) The 24th and final *Tirthankara and founder of *Jainism. Born a member of the warrior caste, at the age of 30 he left his family to become an ascetic, following the teaching of the previous Tirthankara. After 12 years of austere self-mortification, he gained the spiritual knowledge he sought. He devoted the rest of his life to teaching Jaina doctrine.

Mahayana (Sanskrit: Great Vehicle)   The school of Buddhism dominant in Tibet, Mongolia, China, Korea, and Japan. More evolved, adaptable, and less conservative and academic than the rival school, the *Theravada, the Mahayana teaching differs from it primarily in promulgating the ideal of the *Bodhisattva–the one who, having gained enlightenment, remains in the world in order to help other beings to their release.

Mahdi, al- (Arabic: the guided one)   In Islamic tradition, a messianic leader who will appear shortly before the end of the world and, for a few years, restore justice and religion. According to some *Shiite Muslims, the 12th *imam (9th century AD), who is now hidden, will return as the Mahdi. Of a number of claimants to the title, the best known was the Sudanese leader **Muhammad Ahmad** (1844–85). After a religious experience, he proclaimed himself the Mahdi and led an uprising against the Egyptian Government. In 1884 he attacked Khartoum, which was defended by General *Gordon, and captured it in January, 1885, after a ten-months siege. He died at Omdurman, near Khartoum, in June, 1885, probably of typhus. His rule was continued by *Abd Allah, the Khalifa.

mahjong An ancient Chinese game. It is usually played by 4 people using 2 dice and 136 tiles of bone, ivory, or plastic. 108 of the tiles are arranged in 3 suits: circles, bamboos, and characters. Each suit comprises tiles numbered one to nine, with four of each type of tile. There are also four each of red, white, and green dragons and four each of east, south, west, and north winds. Many sets have eight additional tiles, the flowers and seasons. The tiles are built into a square of four walls, symbolizing a walled city. Players score by collecting sequences of tiles according to complex rules.

Mahler, Gustav (1860–1911) Austrian composer and conductor. He studied at the Vienna conservatoire and directed the Viennese Court Opera from 1897–1907, where he acquired a brilliant reputation. In 1909 he became conductor of the New York Philharmonic Society, but met resistance to his advocacy of modern music. He died of heart disease, aged 50.
His nine large-scale symphonies (and uncompleted tenth) were written during brief vacations. The second (*Resurrection Symphony*), third, fourth, and eighth (*Symphony of a Thousand*) employ vocal soloists. He also wrote the song cycles *Kindertotenlieder* (1901–04) and *Das Lied von der Erde* (1907–10).

Mahmud II (1785–1839) Sultan of the Ottoman Empire (1808–39). He continued and increased the modernization and westernization of the Empire that had begun under Selim III (1761–1808; reigned 1789–1807). He destroyed the *Janissaries in 1826 and in 1829 was forced to recognize Greek independence (*see* Greek Independence, War of).

Mahmud of Ghazna (971–1030) The third sultan (997–1030) of the Ghaznavid dynasty, which ruled a kingdom comprising modern Afghanistan. During his reign Mahmud led about 17 expeditions into India, conquering Kashmir and the Punjab, and also expanded his state in Iran. He is regarded as the greatest of his dynasty.

mahogany An evergreen tree of the genus *Swietenia* (7 species), native to tropical America and the West Indies and widely cultivated for timber. Up to about 20 m high, it has large compound leaves with 2–6 pairs of leaflets, greenish-yellow flower clusters, and fruit capsules containing winged seeds. *S. macrophylla* and *S. mahagoni* are the most important species: their hard red-brown wood is highly valued for furniture. Similar wood is obtained from members of other genera (*Khaya*, *Trichilia*, etc.). Family: *Meliaceae*. *See also* jarrah.

Mahón (*or* Puerto de Mahón) 39 54N 4 15E A port on the Spanish island of Minorca, on the Mediterranean Sea. It is the site of an important air and naval base. Population (1981): 22 926.

Mahonia A genus of evergreen shrubs (70 species), native to N temperate regions and South American mountains and often grown as ornamentals. They have leaves with paired, sometimes spiky, leaflets, and bunches of yellow or orange flowers that produce berries; only those of the Oregon grape (*M. aquifolium*) are edible. Family: *Berberidaceae*.

Mahratta. *See* Maratha.

Maiden Castle The 115-acre site on Fordington Hill, near Dorchester, Dorset (UK), of a prehistoric fortress that may date back to 2000 BC. Excavations (1934–37) by Sir Mortimer *Wheeler provided evidence that an Iron Age fortified village occupied the site in the 4th century BC. It was captured by the Romans in 43 AD and abandoned in about 70.

maidenhair fern An ornamental *fern of the genus *Adiantum* (about 200 species), especially *A. capillus-veneris*, found worldwide in moist warm places. From a creeping rhizome arise delicate brown or black stalks, about 2.5–30 cm high, bearing fan-shaped green leaflets. Clusters of spore capsules (sori) are situated on the leaf margins, which are folded onto the underside. Family: *Adiantaceae*.

maidenhair tree. *See* ginkgo.

Maidenhead 51 32N 0 44W A town in SE England, in Berkshire. It is mainly residential and its situation on the River Thames makes it a popular tourist centre. Several light industries have been established since World War II. Population (1981): 49 038.

Maidstone 51 17N 0 32E A town in SE England, the administrative centre of Kent on the River Medway. It is an ancient town and the centre of an important fruit-and-hop-growing region. There are brewing, paper, cement, confectionery, and engineering industries. Population (1981): 72 311.

Maiduguri (*or* Yerwa) 11 53N 13 16E A city in NE Nigeria. It comprises the towns of Yerwa and Maiduguri. It exports livestock, crocodile skins, and leather goods. It has a university (1960). Population (1983 est): 230 900.

Maikop 44 37N 40 48E A city in the SW Soviet Union, the capital of the Adygei autonomous region in the RSFSR. It is the centre of an oil-producing region and is also important for timber and food processing. Population (1980 est): 128 000.

Mailer, Norman (1923–   ) US novelist and journalist. He established his reputation with the World War II novel *The Naked and the Dead* (1948). His concern with American society, which provided the themes for novels such as *An American Dream* (1965), is more directly expressed in later works, such as *The Armies of the Night* (1968), concerned with a protest march on the Pentagon, and *The Executioner's Song* (1979), about a convicted murderer, both of which were awarded a Pulitzer Prize. More recent works include *Pieces and Pontifications* (1982), *Ancient Evenings* (1983), and *Tough Guys Don't Dance* (1984).

Maillol, Aristide (1861–1944) French sculptor. Originally a painter and tapestry designer influenced by the *Nabis and *Gauguin, Maillol turned to sculpture in 1896. He made his name in the early 1900s with his monumental female nudes, the best known being *Mediterranean* (c. 1901; New York) and *Night* (1902; Paris). Although influenced by classical Greek models, their extreme simplicity anticipated modern abstract sculpture. Maillol's later works included war memorials and monuments to Cézanne and Debussy.

mail-order business A method of retail trading in which members of the public purchase goods (clothes, household goods, etc.) direct from mail-order houses through the post, either in response to individual advertisements or from large highly illustrated catalogues. As no retailers' mark-up has to be paid, items can usually be purchased by mail order more cheaply than they can in shops. The customer, however, usually has to pay a delivery or postage charge. This method of trading was pioneered in the USA, being especially appropriate to people living in remote areas, but has become popular in the UK.: newspaper colour magazines carry extensive mail-order advertising.

Maimonides, Moses (Mosheh ben Maymun; 1135–1204) Jewish philosopher and physician. He was born in Córdoba (Spain), then under Moorish rule. After the fall of that city to the *Almohads and the subsequent religious persecution of Jews, Maimonides and his family left Spain. They settled in Cairo about 1165, where he later became physician to the Egyptian court. Maimonides' medical theories were advanced for his age. His celebrated philosophical work, *The Guide of the Perplexed*, which attempts to reconcile faith with reason, led to bitter controversy between orthodox Judaism and science.

Main, River A river in central West Germany, flowing

generally W through Frankfurt to join the River Rhine at Mainz. It is linked by canal with the River Danube. Length: 515 km (320 mi).

Maine A coastal state in the extreme NE USA. The largest of the New England states, it consists of uplands in the W and NW and lowlands along the deeply indented coast in the E. Four-fifths of the state is forested although the famous white pine is now almost extinct. It is the most sparsely populated state E of the Mississippi, most of its inhabitants living in the original settlements along the coast and river valleys. Manufacturing is most important and the major products are paper and pulp, leather goods, food, timber, and textiles. An area of considerable mineral wealth, limestone, building stone, and sand and gravel are exploited. The state's major agricultural products are potatoes, poultry, dairying, apples, and beef. *History*: although claimed by both Britain and France, it became a British possession (1763). It entered the Union as part of Massachusetts (1788) and later became a separate state (1820). Area: 86 027 sq km (33 215 sq mi). Population (1980): 1 124 660. Capital: Augusta.

Maine A former province in NW France, approximating to the modern departments of Mayenne and Sarthe. United with Anjou in 1126, Maine became English territory in 1154. It was reconquered by Philip II Augustus in 1204 and was a province from about 1600 until divided into departments in 1789.

Mainland 1. (*or* Pomona) The largest of the Orkney Islands, divided into two main parts by Kirkwall Bay and *Scapa Flow. Area: 492 sq km (190 sq mi). Population (1981): 14 279. Chief town: Kirkwall. 2. The largest of the Shetland Islands. Area: about 583 sq km (225 sq mi). Population (1986): 19 236. Chief town: Lerwick.

main sequence. *See* Hertzsprung-Russell diagram.

Maintenon, Mme de (Françoise d'Aubigné, Marquise de M.; c. 1635–1719) The second wife of Louis XIV of France. In 1652 she married the writer Paul *Scarron and after his death became the governess of Louis' illegitimate children (1669) and the king's mistress. She became his wife secretly after the death of Queen Marie Thérèse (1683).

Mainz (French name: Mayence) 50 00N 8 16E A city and port in SW West Germany, the capital of Rhineland-Palatinate at the confluence of the Rivers Rhine and Main. Originally a Celtic settlement, it was the first German archbishopric and in the 15th century Gutenberg set up his printing press here. Its cathedral was founded in 975 AD and its university in 1477 (discontinued 1816–1946). It is a wine-trading centre with varied industries. Population (1980 est): 186 700.

maiolica Italian pottery originating in the 15th century. Made from calcareous clay, the soft buff body is coated with white tin glaze and brilliantly painted in lustre and rainbow colours. Motifs include narrative pictures, botanical and zoological subjects, grotesques, arabesques, and armorial designs. Items made include tableware, drug jars, and display ornaments. Principal centres of manufacture were Gubbio (famous for lustres by Maestro Giorgio), Deruta (yellow and blue designs on orange backgrounds), Faenza (*see* faience), and *Caffaggiolo. The manufactures of the first quarter of the 16th century, which are sought after and valuable, were often financed by noble patronage. Imitations and forgeries abound.

Maistre, Joseph de (1753–1821) French monarchist. Settling in Lausanne, he became prominent as an opponent of Revolutionary France with his advocacy of absolutist government, faith in the divine right of kings, and belief, expounded in *Du pape* (1819), that an infallible pope can depose rulers who disregard the laws of God.

Maitland 32 33S 151 33E A town in Australia, in E New South Wales on the Hunter River. It is an agricultural, industrial, and coalmining centre. Population (1981): 38 865.

maize An annual *cereal grass, *Zea mays*, also called Indian corn, sweet corn, or corn, native to the New World and widely cultivated in tropical and subtropical regions. 1–4.5 m high, it bears a tassel of male flowers at the top of the stem and spikes of female flowers in the leaf axils; these develop into cobs, each comprising long parallel rows of grains. Maize is used as a vegetable, in breakfast cereals, flour, and livestock feed and for the extraction of corn oil. Cultivated as a grain crop in Central America since at least 2000 BC, maize is a staple food in Latin America and many other countries throughout the world. In terms of world production, it is the third most important cereal crop (after wheat and rice), the USA being the chief producing country.

Majorca (Spanish name: Mallorca) A Spanish island in the Mediterranean Sea, the largest of the Balearic Islands. The chief occupations are agriculture and tourism; cereals, legumes, oranges, olives, and figs are produced and marble is quarried. Area: 3639 sq km (1465 sq mi). Population (1981): 561 215. Capital: Palma.

MAIOLICA *An enamelled earthenware dish, made in Savona in the 17th century.*

Majuba Hill A mountain in South Africa, on the border between the Transvaal and Natal in the Drakensberg range. In 1881 it was the scene of a Boer victory over the British. Height: 1981 m (6500 ft).

Makarios III (Mikhail Khristodolou Mouskos; 1913–77) Cypriot churchman and statesman; archbishop of the Orthodox Church of Cyprus (1950–77) and president of Cyprus (1960–74, 1974–77). In 1956 he was deported to the Seychelles by the British because of his support for Greek-Cypriot union (*see* EOKA). He subsequently abandoned this aim, thus facilitating the attainment of Cypriot independence. In 1974 he was deposed in a coup that was backed by the Greek military regime but resumed the presidency before the end of the year.

Makassar. *See* Ujung Pandang.

Makeevka (*or* Makeyevka) 48 01N 38 00E A city in the Soviet Union, in the SE Ukrainian SSR in the Donets Basin. Its industry is based on coalmining and metallurgy. Population (1981 est): 442 000.

Makhachkala (name until 1921: Petrovsk)   42 59N 47 30E A port in the S Soviet Union, the capital of the Dagestan ASSR on the Caspian Sea. It has oil-refining, engineering (especially aircraft), and textile industries. Population (1981 est): 269 000.

Malabar Coast (*or* Malabar)   The W coast of India from Goa in the N to Cape Comorin in the S. In 1498 Vasco da Gama landed here, making it the first part of India to be brought into contact with Europe. The shore is fringed by sand dunes and coconut palms, while further inland there are long shallow lagoons and paddy fields.

Malabo (name until 1973: Santa Isabel)   3 45W 8 48E The capital of Equatorial Guinea, a port in the N of the island of Bioko (formerly Macías Nguema), founded by the British in 1827. Population (1984): 37 500.

Malacca   02 14N 102 14E A historic port in W Peninsular Malaysia, the capital of Malacca state. It was colonized successively by the Portuguese, Dutch, and British after 1511; many Portuguese and Dutch buildings remain. Population (1980): 88 073.

Malacca   A state in W Peninsular Malaysia, on the Strait of Malacca. Consisting chiefly of a low-lying coastal plain, it produces rice, rubber, copra, tin, and bauxite. Area: 1650 sq km (637 sq mi). Population (1980): 453 153. Capital: Malacca.

Malacca, Strait of   A channel between Sumatra and Peninsular Malaysia, linking the Indian Ocean with the Pacific Ocean. It is one of the world's most important shipping lanes. Length: about 800 km (500 mi).

Malachi   An Old Testament prophet who rebuked religious hypocrites and the various social evils of the time, predicted a day of judgment, and urged the people to observe the Law of Moses. **The Book of Malachi** is the last book of the Old Testament.

malachite   An ore of copper consisting of hydrated copper carbonate, $Cu_2(OH)_2CO_3$. It is bright green and is found in the oxidized zone of deposits of copper minerals. It occurs in massive form, often with a smooth surface.

malachite green (aniline green *or* China green; $C_{23}H_{25}ClN_2$) A dye that occurs as lustrous green crystals and is soluble in alcohol. It is used medicinally in dilute solution as an antiseptic and in fish breeding to kill fungus and bacteria. It is also used to dye leather and natural fabrics.

Malachy, St   (1094–1148) Irish prelate, whose Church reforms initiated a religious revival in Ireland. He became Bishop of Connor in 1124 and Archbishop of Armagh in 1132. On his way to Rome (1139) he visited St *Bernard of Clairvaux, with whose encouragement he founded the first Cistercian abbey in Ireland, at Mellifont (1142). Feast day: 3 Nov.

Málaga   36 43N 4 25W A city in S Spain, in Andalusia on the Mediterranean Sea. Founded by the Phoenicians (12th century BC), it passed successively to the Romans, the Visigoths, and the Moors, before falling to Ferdinand and Isabella in 1487. It has a cathedral (begun 16th century) and is the birthplace of the painter Picasso. A major tourist centre and port, it exports olives, almonds, and dried fruits. Population (1981): 503 521.

Malagasy   A language of the *Austronesian family, related to Malay, spoken in Madagascar. The standard form, written in Roman characters, is based on the Merina dialect. It has been influenced by Swahili and Arabic.

Malagasy Republic.   *See* Madagascar, Democratic Republic of.

Malamud, Bernard   (1914–86) US novelist. With such witty and ironic novels as *The Assistant* (1957) and *A New Life* (1961) he built a reputation as a skilful chronicler of Jewish characters and themes. His other works include the story collections *The Magic Barrel* (1958) and *Pictures of Fidelman* (1969) and the novels *The Fixer* (1966), *The Tenants* (1971), *Dubin's Lives* (1979), and *God's Grace* (1982).

Malan, Daniel F(rançois)   (1874–1959) South African politician; prime minister (1948–54). Founder in 1939 with *Hert-zog of the Nationalist Party, which won the 1948 elections, Malan instituted *apartheid in South Africa. A minister of the Dutch Reformed Church, he was a right-wing Afrikaner nationalist.

Malang   07 59S 112 45E A city in Indonesia, in E Java. It is the site of ancient ruined royal palaces and Indonesian army and air-force bases. Its university was established in 1961. An agricultural centre, it has soap, ceramics, and cigarette industries. Population (1980): 511 780.

Malaparte, Curzio   (Kurt Erich Suckert; 1898–1957) Italian political journalist, novelist, and dramatist. He was an active but unorthodox adherent of fascism from the 1920s to the 1940s. His best-known novels are *Kaputt* (1944) and *The Skin* (1949), which drew on his experience as a war correspondent on the Russian front and as a liaison officer with the Allies in Naples during World War II.

malaria   An infectious disease caused by protozoa of the genus *Plasmodium*. Malaria is transmitted by the female *Anopheles* mosquito, which lives only in the tropics. There are four species of *Plasmodium* that infect man and cause different types of malaria. Malignant tertian malaria (caused by *P. falciparum*) is the most severe; benign tertian malaria (caused by *P. vivax*) is less often fatal but there are repeated attacks. The parasites invade the red blood cells and cause them to burst. There is always fever but, depending on the type of parasite and the number of cells affected, there may also be fits, diarrhoea, shock, and jaundice. Chronic infection causes enlargement of the liver and spleen. There are drugs (such as chloroquine) to treat the disease and these can also be taken to prevent it. Attempts by the World Health Organization to limit malaria, which is a major cause of death and ill health in the tropics, by destroying the mosquito have not yet achieved complete success.

Malatesta   A family that ruled Rimini (Italy) from 1295 to 1500. **Malatesta da Verrucchio** (d. 1312) led the local Guelf (papal) faction and came to power in 1295 after ousting the Ghibellines (imperial party; *see* Guelfs and Ghibellines). In the 15th century the family lost papal support and its most famous member, **Sigismondo Pandolfo Malatesta** (1417–68), was expelled from Rimini by Pope Pius II (1461). The family's temporary recovery of Rimini (1469–1500) ended when it was taken by Cesare *Borgia.

Malatya   38 22N 38 18E A town in SE central Turkey dating from 1838. It is in a fertile area producing cotton, tobacco, apricots, and grapes and has a university (1975). Population (1980): 179 074.

Malawi, Lake (former name: Lake Nyasa)   A lake in Malawi, Tanzania, and Mozambique. Discovered for Europeans by Livingstone in 1859, it is 595 km (370 mi) long and is drained by the Shiré River S into the River Zambezi. Area: about 31 000 sq km (11 966 sq mi).

Malawi, Republic of (name until 1963: Nyasaland)   A country in SE Africa, between Tanzania, Zambia, and Mozambique. Lake Malawi lies at its E border and the land consists mainly of high plateaus reaching heights of over 3000 m (9800 ft). The majority of the population is Bantu. *Economy*: chiefly agricultural. The main subsistence crop is maize, and cash crops include tobacco, tea, sugar, and groundnuts, which are the chief exports. Mineral resources are sparse and most power comes from hydroelectric sources, which are now being intensively developed. *History*: the area was visited by the Portuguese in the 17th century and, after Livingstone's exploration, became a British protectorate in 1891. In 1953, in spite of African opposition, it was joined with Northern and Southern Rhodesia to form the Federation of *Rhodesia and Nyasaland. This was dissolved in 1963 and Nyasaland gained internal self-government, becoming independent in 1964. In 1966 it became a republic within the British Commonwealth with Dr Hastings *Banda

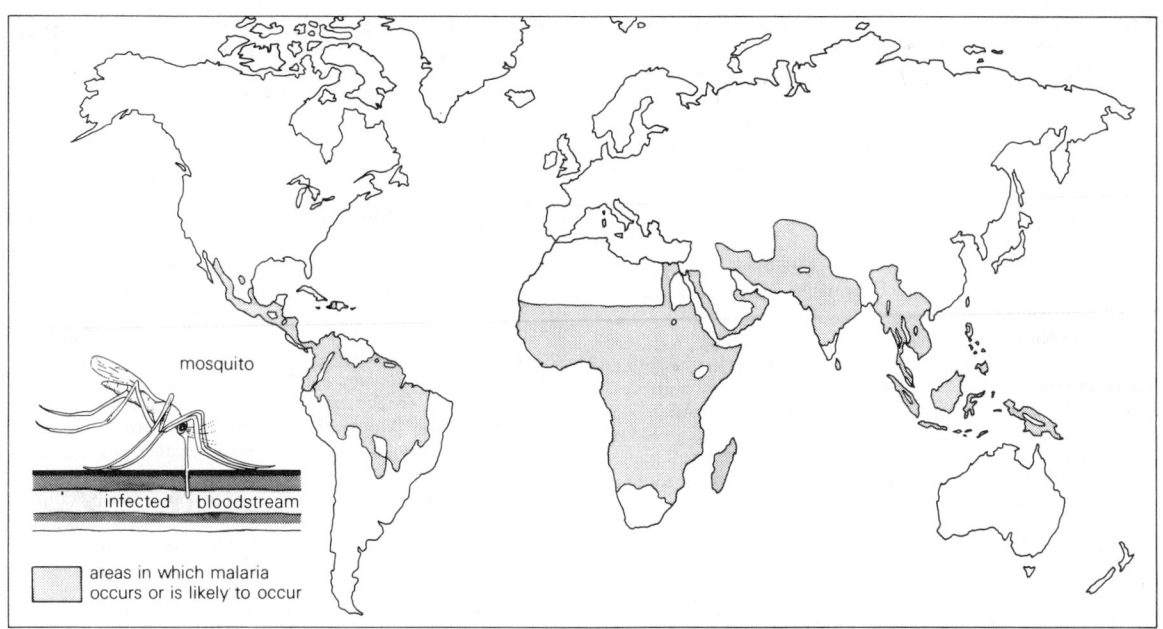

MALARIA *Despite eradication programmes, malaria is still endemic in many parts of the tropics. By sucking the blood of an infected person, the female* Anopheles *mosquito can transmit the malarial parasite to an uninfected person.*

as its first president. The Malawi Congress Party is the only political party. Official language: English. Official currency, since 1971: kwacha of 199 tambala. Area: 94 079 sq km (36 324 sq mi). Population (1980 est): 5 900 000. Capital: Lilongwe.

Malay A language of the Indonesian branch of the *Austronesian family spoken in SE Asia and Indonesia. The dialect of the S Malay peninsula is the basis of standard Malay. It can be written in Roman or Arabic script. The Malay people probably migrated to this area from China between 2500 and 1500 BC. They became great seafarers, colonizing as far as Madagascar. Predominantly village dwellers, they live in nuclear families in houses raised on piling. Rice and rubber are the main crops. Distinction between noble and commoner social groups is important. Since the 15th century Islam has been the accepted religion, but vestiges of former Hinduism survive.

Malayalam A *Dravidian language of SW India. It is the official language of Kerala. It is related to Tamil from which its script, Koleluttu, is derived.

Malay Archipelago (former name: East Indies) An island group in SE Asia, the largest in the world. It lies between the Pacific and Indian Oceans and between the Asian and Australian continents. It comprises the Indonesian, Malaysian, and Philippine islands; New Guinea is sometimes included.

Malay Peninsula (*or* Kra Peninsula) A narrow peninsula in SE Asia, between the Andaman Sea and the South China Sea and separated from Sumatra by the Strait of Malacca. Politically it comprises SW Thailand, Peninsular Malaysia, and Singapore. Length: about 320 km (200 mi). *See also* Malaysia, Federation of.

Malaysia, Federation of A country in SE Asia, consisting of the 11 states of Peninsular Malaysia (formerly the Federation of Malaya) and the states of *Sabah and *Sarawak in N Borneo. Peninsular Malaysia consists of coastal plains rising to mountains in the interior, reaching heights of 2100 m (7000 ft). Most of the inhabitants are Malays and Chinese with minorities of Indians, Pakistanis,

and others. *Economy*: Malaysia is a major exporter of rubber, tin, and palm oil. Agriculture is the chief occupation; besides the cash crops of rubber and palms, rice (the chief food crop) is extensively produced. Much of the land area is under dense forest producing considerable quantities of timber; fishing is also important. Other than tin, minerals exploited include iron ore, bauxite, ilmenite, and gold. The tourist industry is expanding, an added attraction being Malaysia's ethnic cultures. *History*: from the 9th to the 14th centuries the Srivijaya empire dominated the area. In the 14th century it was overrun by Hindu Javanese from the Majapahit kingdom and in about 1400 Malacca was established as an Islamic centre. The spice trade flourished, centred on Malacca, attracting the attention of Europeans. In 1511 the port was taken by the Portuguese and in 1641 by the Dutch. British interest in the Malay states began in the 18th century; the East India Company established stations on Penang, Malacca, and Singapore Island, which became the Straits Settlements (1826). With the opening of the Suez Canal, British trade interests increased and in 1909 British protection was extended over the Federated Malay States (Selangor, Negri Sembilan, Perak, and Pahang) and the remaining five unfederated states. Following occupation by the Japanese during World War II, the Federation of Malaya was established (1948). Malaya became independent in 1957 and in 1963 part of the federal state of Malaysia, together with Sabah, Sarawak, and Singapore (which left the federation in 1965). There has been considerable unrest in recent years caused mainly by Chinese resentment of Malay dominance in the government. A resurgence of communist guerrilla activities has taken place leading to strong measures against communism. In foreign policy Malaysia has moved away from its previous pro-Western stand to a more neutral position. Supreme head of state: Sultan Mahmood Iskandar. Prime minister: Datuk Seri Mahathir Muhammed. Official language: Bahasa Malaysia. Official religion: Islam. Official currency: Ringgit of 100 cents. Area: 329 749 sq km (127 289 sq mi). Population (1983 est): 14 995 000. Capital: Kuala Lumpur. Main port: Georgetown.

Malcolm, George (John) (1917–) British harpsichordist, educated at Oxford and the Royal College of Music.

From 1947 to 1959 he was Master of Music at Westminster Cathedral. He was created a CBE in 1965.

Malcolm III (c. 1031–93) King of the Scots (1057–93). He became king after killing *Macbeth, the murderer of his father Duncan I (d. 1040; reigned 1034–40). Malcolm married St *Margaret. He became a vassal of William the Conqueror (1072) and was murdered during the last of frequent raids into N England.

Malcolm X (1925–65) US militant Black leader. Formerly a member of the *Black Muslims, he founded the rival militant Organization of Afro-American Unity (1964), which supported violent means of achieving racial equality. He was assassinated while addressing a rally.

Maldives, Republic of (Divehi name: Divehi Raajje; name until 1969: Maldive Islands) A small country in the Indian Ocean, to the SW of Sri Lanka. It consists of a large number of small coral islands, grouped in atolls, of which just over 200 are inhabited. Most of the population is of mixed Indian, Sinhalese, and Arabic descent. *Economy*: coconuts, along with fish, are the main export. Other sources of revenue are shipping, tourism, and copra production. *History*: adherents of Islam since the 12th century, the islands were ruled by a sultan. Formerly a dependency of Ceylon, they were officially under British protection from 1887 to 1965. They were ruled by an elected sultan until 1968, when they became a republic. An agreement allowing the UK staging facilities on the island of Gan ended in 1976. The Republic of Maldives became a special member of the Commonwealth of Nations in 1982. Head of state: President Maumoon Abdul Gayoon (1937–   ). Official language: Divehi. Official religion: Islam. Official currency: Maldivian rupee of 100 larees. Area: 298 sq km (115 sq mi). Population (1983): 168 000. Capital and main port: Malé.

Malebo Pool (former name: Stanley Pool) 4 15S 15 25E A broad section of the Zaïre River in West Africa, on the Congo–Zaïre border. It contains the island of Bamu, which divides the river channel into N and S branches. Area: 450 sq km (174 sq mi).

Malebranche, Nicolas (1638–1715) French philosopher and theologian. Like *Descartes, whose work he publicized, Malebranche was concerned with the mind-body relation. In *De la recherche de la vérité* (1674) he held that the two could not interact causally. God brought about all events, including bodily movements, by direct intervention, a doctrine known as occasionalism.

maleic acid (or *cis*-butenedioic acid; HOOCCH:CHCOOH) A colourless crystalline toxic *fatty acid. It is an *isomer of **fumaric acid** (*trans*-butenedioic acid) and both are used in making dyes and synthetic resins.

Malenkov, Georgi Maksimilianovich (1902–88) Soviet statesman; prime minister (1953–55). A close associate of Stalin, Malenkov became first secretary of the Soviet Communist Party and prime minister after Stalin's death. Shortly afterwards, he was replaced in the former post by Khrushchev but continued as prime minister until forced, owing to agricultural failures, to resign. He was expelled from the Communist Party in 1961.

Malesherbes, Chrétien Guillaume de Lamoignon de (1721–94) French statesman, a leading figure of the pre-revolutionary era of reform in France. In 1750 he became director of censorship and gained a reputation for his liberal attitude, permitting, for example, the *Philosophes to publish their work. Criticism of the monarchy led to his banishment from court in 1771 but he was executed as a royalist during the French Revolution.

Malevich, Kazimir (1878–1935) Russian painter and art theorist, born in Kiev. He worked in most modern styles before exhibiting (1915) his *Black Square on White Ground*, which launched the art movement called *suprematism and made a significant contribution to *abstract art.

Malherbe, François de (1555–1628) French poet and critic. In 1605 he became court poet to Henry IV. In his criticism, mostly contained in letters and commentaries, he anticipated classicism by advocating principles of harmony, regularity, and propriety. His poetry consisted chiefly of conventional verses on political and religious themes.

Mali, Republic of (name until 1959: French Sudan) A large landlocked country in West Africa. It consists largely of desert, extending into the Sahara in the N, and is crossed by the River Niger, the flood plains of which provide most of the fertile land. The majority of the population are Bambara, Fulani, and Senufo. *Economy*: chiefly subsistence agriculture, especially livestock, including cattle, camels, and sheep. The main crops are rice, millet, cassava, cotton, and groundnuts, but all agriculture has been badly affected by droughts (1968–74). River fishing is important and dried and smoked fish, together with cattle and groundnuts, are the main exports. Industry is based mainly on the processing of food and hides and skins. Mineral reserves of bauxite, uranium, and oil are present but only salt and small quantities of gold are exploited. Tourism is being developed, the main attractions being hunting, fishing, and the ancient city of Timbuktu. *History*: from the 4th century AD the area was occupied by successive empires, including those of Ghana, Mali (the most famous ruler of which was Mansu Musa), and Gao. In the late 19th century it was conquered by the French and, as French Sudan, it became part of French West Africa. It achieved internal self-government as part of the French Community in 1958. It briefly formed with Senegal the Federation of Mali in 1959, becoming a fully independent republic in 1960. It broke away from the French Community but, because of economic problems, rejoined the franc zone in 1967. In 1968 the government was overthrown in a military coup led by Lt Moussa Traoré (1936–   ), who became president in 1969. In 1985 war broke out with Burkina Faso over the disputed Agacher area. Official language: French. Official currency: Mali franc of 100 centimes. Area: 1 204 021 sq km (464 752 sq mi). Population (1983 est): 7 393 000. Capital: Bamako.

malic acid (or 2-hydroxybutanedioic acid) A dicarboxylic acid ($C_4H_6O_5$) that occurs widely in fruits (including apples, plums, and grapes) as the free acid or its salts. The anion malate is an intermediate compound in the *Krebs cycle.

Malik-Shah (1055–92) The last of the three great Seljuq Sultans of Turkey (1073–92), succeeding his father *Alp Arslan. Malik-Shah, a noted patron of science and the arts, built the famous mosques of Isfahan (his capital) and sponsored the poet *Omar Khayyam. His government owed its distinction to the work of the vizier *Nizam al-Mulk.

Malines. *See* Mechelen.

Malinke A people of West Africa, also known as Mandingo, who speak a language of the Mande division of the *Niger-Congo family. During the 7th century AD one group founded a state with its capital at Kangaba. This spread to become the empire of Mali, which flourished from about 1250 to 1500. The Malinke are agriculturalists, who live in villages of round huts. Descent is patrilineal.

Malinowski, Bronislaw (1884–1942) Polish anthropologist, regarded as the founder of social anthropology. Between 1914 and 1918 Malinowski lived among the natives of New Guinea and the Trobriand Islands, making a detailed study of their culture. A professor at London University from 1927, he became famous for his functional theory of anthropology, which saw every ritual and belief of a society as fulfilling a particular function. Malinowski's published work includes *The Natives of Mailu* (1915) and *The Father in Primitive Psychology* (1927).

Malipiero, Gian Francesco (1882–1973) Italian composer and teacher. His style owes much to the study of 17th- and 18th-century Venetian composers; his works include operas and orchestral, vocal, and chamber music. He published an edition of the works of Monteverdi.

mallard A *dabbling duck, *Anas platyrhynchos*, common on ponds and lakes in the N hemisphere. About 55 cm long, females are mottled brown and males greyish with a green head, white collar, reddish breast, black rump, and a curly tail. Both sexes have a broad yellow bill and a purple wing speculum. The mallard is the ancestor of most domestic breeds of duck. *See* Plate V.

Mallarmé, Stéphane (1842-98) French poet. He visited England frequently and until 1871 taught English in schools in the French provinces and in Paris. Influenced by Baudelaire and Poe, he became a major figure of the *Symbolist movement, believing that the function of poetry was to evoke the ideal essences that lay behind the world of actual appearances. His best-known works include *Hérodiade* (1864), *L'Après-Midi d'un faun* (1865), and his obscure final poem, *Un Coup de dés jamais n'abolira le hasard* (1897).

mallee Scrubland vegetation of the coastal regions of S Australia, dominated by small trees and shrubs of the genus *Eucalyptus. Most are 2-3 m high, with leathery grey-green leaves and many thick roots that store water.

mallee fowl A white-spotted light-brown bird, *Leipoa ocellata*, occurring in semiarid interior regions of Australia. 65 cm long, it feeds on seeds and flowers and builds a large nest mound of fermenting plant material and sand, which may reach 4.5 m across. Throughout the incubation period the male maintains the mound at a constant temperature by adding and taking away sand as necessary. Family: *Megapodidae* (megapodes).

Mallorca. *See* Majorca.

mallow A herbaceous plant of the genus *Malva* (30 species), native to N temperate regions. Mallows, which may be creeping or erect, grow up to 90 cm tall. They have hairy lobed leaves and five-petalled flowers, which are usually purple, pink, or white and 1.5-6 cm across. The name is also given to other plants of the same family. The tree mallow (*Lavatera arborea*) is a shrublike biennial, up to 3 m high, with rose-purple flowers. Family: *Malvaceae*. *See also* marsh mallow.

Malmédy. *See* Eupen-et-Malmédy.

Malmö 55 38N 12 57E A city and port in S Sweden, on the *Sound opposite Copenhagen. It was a prominent trade and shipping centre in the middle ages. Malmö's varied industries include shipbuilding, textiles, and food processing. Population (1983): 229 380.

malnutrition Ill health resulting from an inadequate diet, usually associated with poverty. The body needs certain amounts of protein, carbohydrate, fat, vitamins, and minerals. Insufficient protein causes *kwashiorkor in children, and a diet deficient in all nutrients causes marasmus. Lack of vitamins causes a wide variety of diseases, including *scurvy, *rickets, *beriberi, and *pellagra. *Obesity can be considered as a form of malnutrition resulting from overeating.

Malory, Sir Thomas (?1400-1471) English writer. He was the author of *Morte d'Arthur* (c. 1469), a narrative in 21 books of the legendary court of King Arthur, drawn mostly from French sources. The work was printed by Caxton in 1485. Malory's identity remains uncertain, but he was probably a Warwickshire knight who had fought in France, became an MP in 1445, and was several times imprisoned.

Malpighi, Marcello (1628-94) Italian anatomist, whose microscopical studies of living organisms provided new insights into their function. In 1661 he discovered the fine capillaries that connect arteries with veins, substantiating William *Harvey's theory of blood circulation. Malpighi made numerous studies of body organs—the kidney glomeruli (Malpighian corpuscles) and a layer of skin tissue (Malpighian layer) are named after him. He also made valuable early studies of embryology and comparative plant anatomy.

Malplaquet, Battle of (11 September, 1709) A battle in the War of the *Spanish Succession in which the French faced the armies, under Marlborough and Prince Eugene of Savoy, of Britain, the Netherlands, and Austria, fought 16 km (10 mi) S of Mons. By a strategic retreat the French inflicted severe casualties upon the allies, who, although victorious, were checked in their advance upon Paris.

Malraux, André (1901-76) French novelist and essayist. His career included active service with communist revolutionaries in China in the 1920s, with the Republican forces in the Spanish Civil War, and with the French Resistance in World War II. His novels, which are notably objective treatments of the issues involved in these conflicts, include *Man's Estate* (1933) and *Days of Hope* (1938). He was minister for cultural affairs under de Gaulle from 1959 to 1969. He also wrote on art, notably in *Voices of Silence* (1953) and *Museum without Walls* (1967), and a volume of memoirs, *Antimémoires* (1967).

malt Barley or other grain prepared for brewing or distilling. The grain is softened by soaking in water, then either heaped on the malting floor and turned by hand or put in revolving drums to encourage germination. Germ growth is stopped by drying the malt by heat, after which it is ready for brewing. Alternatively, after eight to ten days' germ growth the malt may be used for malt *whisky.

Malta, Republic of A small country in the Mediterranean Sea, to the S of Sicily comprising the two main islands of Malta and Gozo and several islets. *Economy*: previously heavily dependent on foreign military bases, Malta has made efforts to diversify the economy in recent years. The naval dockyards have been converted to commercial use and port facilities are being developed to encourage the use of Malta as a transit centre for Mediterranean shipping. Shipbuilding and repair are important and the development of other varied industries is aided by foreign investment (especially from Libya, Algeria, and Saudi Arabia). There is some agriculture, both crops and livestock, and fishing. Tourism is an important source of revenue. Exports include clothing, textiles, machinery, and food. *History*: occupied successively by the Phoenicians, Greeks, Carthaginians, and Romans, the island was conquered by the Arabs in 870 AD. In 1090 it was united with Sicily and in 1530 was granted to the Knights Hospitallers. In 1798 the island was occupied by the French and then by the British, to whom it was formally ceded in 1814. As a crown colony it became an important naval and air base. In World War II Malta's heroic resistance to German attack (1940-42) gained it the George Cross. In 1947 and 1961 it acquired increasing self-government, becoming fully independent in 1964. In 1974 under Dom *Mintoff it became a republic within the British Commonwealth. President: Agatha Barbara (1923-). Prime minister: Dr Fenech Adami. Official languages: Maltese and English; Italian is widely spoken. Official religion: Roman Catholic. Official currency: Maltese pound of 100 cents and 1000 mils. Area: 316 sq km (122 sq mi). Population (1983 est): 363 000. Capital and main port: Valletta.

Malthus, Thomas Robert (1766-1834) British clergyman and economist, famous for his population theories. In his *Essay on the Principle of Population* (*First Essay*, 1798; *Second Essay*, 1803) Malthus argued that mankind is doomed to remain at near-starvation level as growth in food production, which increases at an arithmetical rate, is negated by the geometrical increase in population. Elaborating ideas from Plato, Aristotle, and Hume, Malthus called for positive efforts to cut the birth rate, preferably by sexual restraint but, failing that, by birth control.

Maluku. *See* Moluccas.

Malvern 52 05N 2 20W A town in W central England, in Hereford and Worcester, consisting of Great Malvern and several villages incorporating the name. Lying on the E slopes of the Malvern Hills, it is a spa town with a famous public school (Malvern College, founded 1863), the Royal

Radar Establishment, and an annual drama and music festival associated with Elgar and G. B. Shaw. Edward Elgar lived and is buried here. Population (1981): 30 187.

Malvinas, Islas. *See* Falkland Islands.

mamba A large agile highly venomous snake belonging to the African genus *Dendroaspis* (4–5 species). The aggressive black mamba (*D. polylepis*) is 4.3 m long, lives in open rocky regions, and preys on birds and small mammals. The smaller arboreal green mamba (*D. angusticeps*) reaches a length of 2.7 m and is much less aggressive. Mambas are egg-laying snakes. Family: *Elapidae* (cobras, mambas, coral snakes).

Mamelukes (Arabic: *mamluk*, slave) The rulers of Egypt and Syria (1250–1517). The Mamelukes were slave soldiers who seized power and then provided a succession of rulers from their own ranks. They drove back the Mongols and finally expelled the Crusaders from Syria. In 1517 the Ottoman Turks conquered Syria and Egypt but the Mamelukes survived as a class and were frequently the effective rulers of Egypt until destroyed by *Mehemet Ali in 1811.

mammal A warm-blooded animal belonging to the class *Mammalia* (about 4250 species). The evolution of mammals from reptiles involved the development of a temperature-regulation system with an insulating layer of fur and sweat glands in the skin for cooling. This enabled mammals to become highly active, with well-developed sense organs and brains, and to colonize cold climates. The survival of the young was improved by the evolution of milk-secreting *mammary glands, and in placental mammals a specialized nourishing membrane (the *placenta) in the uterus (womb) enabled the young to be born at an advanced stage of development. The stages involved in this evolution can still be seen in such primitive mammals as the egg-laying *monotremes and the *marsupials, which produce young at an early developmental stage.

The majority of modern mammalian species are terrestrial, ranging in size from tiny shrews to the elephant. However, bats are flying mammals and whales have adapted to a wholly marine existence. □ pp. 770–71.

mammary gland The gland in female mammals that secretes milk. Believed to have evolved from sweat glands, there are one or more pairs on the ventral (under) side of the body. The number of glands is related to the number of young produced at one birth; for example, rats and mice have five or six pairs; whales and humans have one pair. Each gland consists of branching ducts leading from milk-secreting cells and opening to the exterior through a nipple. In the most primitive mammals (*Monotremata*) there are no nipples and the milk is secreted directly onto the body surface. The secretion of milk (*see* lactation) is under hormonal control. *See also* breast.

mammoth An extinct elephant belonging to the genus *Mammuthus*, whose remains have been found in India, Europe, and North America. Of the four types known, the imperial mammoth (*M. imperator*) was the largest, 4.5 m at the shoulder. The woolly mammoth (*M. primigenius*) had thick body hair and tusks up to 2.5 m long. The well-preserved remains of woolly mammoths, which died out about 10,000 years ago, have been found frozen in the permafrost of Siberia. └fossil.

Mammoth Cave A large cavern in the USA, in W central Kentucky in the Mammoth Cave National Park. It consists of a series of limestone caves with spectacular stalactites and stalagmites. The largest cave reaches 38 m (125 ft) in height and a width of 91 m (300 ft).

Mamoré, Río A river in South America, rising in the Andes in central Bolivia and flowing generally N. It forms part of the Bolivia–Brazil border before joining the Río Beni to become the Rio Madeira. Length: about 1500 km (930 mi).

Ma'mun, al- (786–833 AD) The seventh *caliph (813–833) of the 'Abbasid dynasty. A son of Harun ar-Rashid, al-Ma'mun seized the caliphate from his half-brother al-Amin (c. 785–813). As caliph he was inclined towards Shiite ideas and encouraged philosophical and scientific work.

Man, Isle of An island in the Irish Sea, between England and Ireland. It has been a British Crown possession since 1828 but is virtually self-governing with its own parliament, the Court of Tynwald, comprising the lieutenant governor (representing the Crown), the Legislative Council, and the elected House of Keys. It consists of central hills rising to 620 m (2034 ft) at Snaefell, with lowlands in the N and S. Tourism is the main source of revenue; attractions include its mild climate, scenery, and the famous annual Tourist Trophy (TT) motorcycle races. The island's low taxation levels encourage a steady influx of retired people. Its agriculture is varied; sheep and cattle are raised and produce includes cereals, turnips, and potatoes. Some manufacturing industry exists including light engineering. *History*: originally inhabited by Celts, the derivative Manx language survived in common usage until the 19th century. The island became a dependency of Norway in the 9th century AD and was ceded to Scotland (1266), coming under English control after 1406. Area: 588 sq km (227 sq mi). Population (1981): 64 679. Capital: Douglas.

Manado. *See* Menado.

Managua 12 06N 86 18W The capital of Nicaragua, on the S shore of Lake Managua. Formerly an Indian settlement, it became capital in 1857. It suffered severe damage from earthquakes in 1931 and 1972 and from the civil war (1979). The Nicaragua campus of the Central American University was founded in 1961. It is the country's principal industrial centre. Population (1981): 615 000.

manakin A small stocky bird belonging to a family (*Pipridae*; 59 species) occurring in tropical forests of South and Central America. Male manakins are generally dark with bright patches and decorative crests and tail feathers; the females are usually green. Males perform elaborate courtship displays, either on the ground in specially cleared territories or in the trees.

Manama (Arabic name: Al Manamah) 26 12N 50 38E The capital of Bahrain since 1971, situated at the N end of Bahrain Island. An important free port, its economy is based on oil. Population (1981): 121 986.

Manasseh, tribe of One of the 12 *tribes of Israel. It claimed descent from Manasseh, King of Judah, son of Joseph and grandson of Jacob. Manasseh's lands lay E and W of Jordan, midway between Galilee and the Dead Sea.

Manasseh ben Israel (Manoel Dias Soeiro; 1604–57) Rabbi of Amsterdam. His *Hope of Israel* (1650) dealt with the supposed discovery of the ten lost tribes in South America. Encouraged by English mystics, he presented a petition to Oliver *Cromwell (1655), asking for the readmission of the Jews to England (they had been expelled in 1290). He died before he could witness the success of his mission.

manatee A herbivorous aquatic □mammal belonging to the genus *Trichechus* (3 species), of warm Atlantic waters and coastal rivers of Africa and America. Up to 4.5 m long, manatees have a rounded body with tail fin and flippers and a squarish snout. The American manatee (*T. manatus*) of Florida feeds mainly at night. Slow and placid, it rests on the bottom during the day, rising regularly to breathe. Family: *Trichechidae*; order: *Sirenia*. *See also* dugong.

Manaus (*or* Manáos) 3 06S 60 00W A city in NW Brazil, the capital of Amazonas state on the Rio Negro. Founded in 1660, it became the centre of the rubber boom (1890–1920). It remains the chief inland port of the Amazon basin and is accessible to oceangoing steamers. Exports include rubber, brazil nuts, timber, and other forest products. Notable buildings include the Teatro Amazonas (the opera house, 1896) and the University of Amazonas (1965). Population (1980): 613 098.

Manawatu River A river in New Zealand, in SW North Island flowing generally W and SW to the Tasman Sea NE of Wellington. The surrounding plain is one of New Zealand's most productive farming areas. Length: 182 km (113 mi).

Mancha, La An area and former province in Spain. It consists of an extensive sparsely populated arid plateau. Windmills, used to pump water from under ground, are a distinctive feature. It became famous as the setting of Cervantes' *Don Quixote de la Mancha*.

Manchester 53 30N 2 15W A city in NW England, the administrative centre of Greater Manchester, situated on the River Irwell and forming part of a large conurbation. Linked with the Mersey estuary by the Manchester Ship Canal (opened 1894), it is an important port as well as England's second largest commercial centre (banking, insurance). It is the centre of Lancashire's traditional cotton industry, although most of the cotton mills lie outside the city itself. Other industries include chemicals, engineering, clothing, printing, publishing, paper, rubber, food products, and electrical goods. Manchester is the cultural centre of the North. It has well-known art galleries, libraries, the Hallé Orchestra, Manchester Grammar School (1519), the University of Manchester (1851), and the Institute of Science and Technology (1824) and Manchester Business School (now both part of the university). The national newspaper the *Guardian* was founded here as the *Manchester Guardian* in 1821. The 15th-century parish church became Manchester Cathedral in 1847. *History*: the Roman fort of Mancunium, Manchester developed as a regional market place for raw wool and flax and finished pieces. From the mid-18th century onwards a number of factors, such as new technology, the humid climate, and the availability of labour, combined to make it the world's main cotton-manufacturing town. It became the centre of a network of roads, canals, and railways but its rapid growth led to industrial discontent and political agitation (*see* Peterloo Massacre). It also nurtured the basic principles of economic and political liberalism, embodied in the **Manchester School** (a group of political economists, the most famous being John *Bright and Richard *Cobden). Population (1981): 449 168.

Manchu A nomadic people of Manchuria who conquered China during the 16th and 17th centuries and established the *Qing dynasty.

Manchukuo A puppet state set up by the Japanese in Manchuria in 1932 in a bid to occupy all China. It was administered by Chinese with the last Chinese emperor, Henry P'u-i (1906–67), as ruler, and lasted until Japan's defeat in 1945.

Manchuria A region in NE China bordering on the Soviet Union, roughly comprising the provinces of Heilongjiang, Jilin, and Liaoning. It is mountainous in the E and W with a large central fertile plain. The densely populated plain is a major industrial and agricultural area. Products include timber, minerals, such as coal and iron, and fish. *History*: the area was for centuries inhabited and fought over by the Manchu, Mongols, and Chinese. Their power struggles resulted in empires established over China by the Mongols (1279–1368; *see* Yuan) and Manchus (1644–1912; *see* Qing). Although the S had long been colonized by the Chinese, immigration into the whole area increased greatly under the Qing because of land hunger in China. In the late 19th century this fertile area was dominated by Russia (1898–1904) and then by Japan (1905–45), which developed industrial centres in the region. In 1931, following the Mukden Incident (*see* Shenyang), Japanese forces invaded Manchuria and established a puppet state (*see* Manchukuo). After 1945 the area, staunchly communist, received much aid from the Soviet Union until the 1960s, when the break between China and the Soviet Union took place. Since then military forces have been massed along the border. Area: about 1 300 000 sq km (502 000 sq mi).

Manchu-Tungus A group of languages of the *Altaic language family, related to *Mongolian and *Turkic. It comprises only a few languages, of which only the almost extinct Manchu has any literary tradition.

Mandaeanism A Gnostic sect surviving in S Iraq and SW Iran (*see* Gnosticism). It originated in the 1st or 2nd century AD, but its place of origin and its relationship to Christianity, Judaism, and indigenous Iranian religions, on all of which it draws, are disputed. Mandaeans are hostile to Christ but revere John the Baptist. Their most important rite is frequent baptism. The sacred *Ginza* described their cosmology, which envisages a universe in which hostile spirits (*archons*) endeavour to prevent the soul's ascent to God.

mandala A Buddhist painted or sometimes metal-wrought symbol used in meditation and other religious practices and particularly associated with Tibetan and Japanese Buddhism. It usually consists of a series of concentric circles, representing universal harmony and containing religious figures, the Buddha being represented in the centre.

Mandalay 21 57N 96 04E A city in Burma, on the Irrawaddy River. The last capital of the Burmese kingdom, it fell to the British in 1885. It has numerous monasteries, temples, and pagodas and is the site of a university (1964). Mandalay is the principal commercial centre of Upper Burma. Population (1983): 417 266.

mandarin (fruit). *See* tangerine.

mandarin (official) A Chinese bureaucrat, whose appointment to salaried posts in the civil service was from early Han times until the 1911 revolution by examination. Mandarins occupied a privileged position in society, wore special embroidered robes, and spoke the Mandarin dialect of *Chinese, which in its standard, Peking, form is now spoken by 70% of the population.

mandarin duck A brilliantly coloured *duck, *Aix galericulata*, native to China—where it was the symbol of marital fidelity—and widespread as an ornamental bird. It is 43 cm long. The female is grey-brown with a bluish head, a white eye stripe, and a black bill; the male has a red bill, black-and-white head, purple breast, white underparts, and distinctive chestnut wing fans and whiskers at the sides of the face.

mandate The authority given by the League of Nations to the Allied Powers, after World War I, to administer the former German colonies and Turkish territories (including *Palestine). After the UN was established those that had not become self-governing became *trust territories.

Mandela, Nelson (Rolihlahla) (1918–) South African lawyer and politician, now imprisoned on Robben Island, near Cape Town. A Black, Mandela practised law in Johannesburg and was active in the *African National Congress. He was acquitted of treason in 1961 but retried (1963–64) and sentenced to life imprisonment. With his wife, **Winnie Mandela** (1934–), he was awarded the 1985 Third World Prize in recognition of their struggle against *apartheid; many nations have called for his release.

Mandelstam, Osip (1891–?1938) Russian poet, a friend of Akhmatova and a leading poet of *acmeism. His second volume, *Tristia* (1922), contains poems noted for their classical form and spiritual intensity. Arrested in 1934 and 1938, he is presumed to have died in a labour camp.

Mandeville, Sir John (14th century) The professed author of the immensely popular *Travels* (1356–57), an account that mixes factual and fantastic information about the Middle East, Africa, and Asia. He claimed to be from St Albans but was probably fictional and never existed. The book is a translation of a French work itself compiled from other sources.

mandolin A plucked musical instrument, generally having four double courses of wire strings tuned in the same way as

MAMMAL

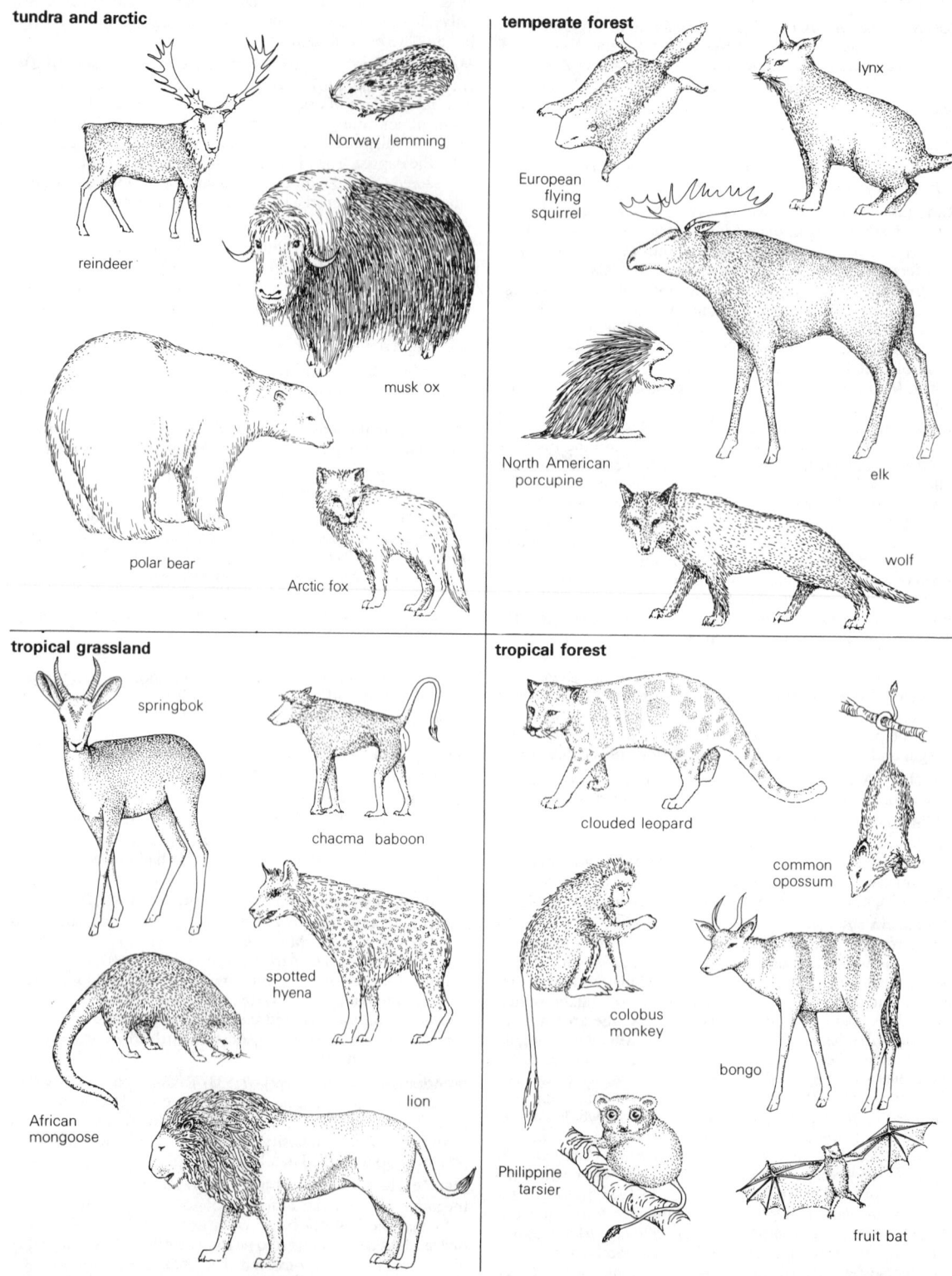

tundra and arctic

Norway lemming

reindeer

musk ox

polar bear

Arctic fox

temperate forest

European flying squirrel

lynx

North American porcupine

elk

wolf

tropical grassland

springbok

chacma baboon

spotted hyena

African mongoose

lion

tropical forest

clouded leopard

common opossum

colobus monkey

bongo

Philippine tarsier

fruit bat

MAMMAL   *This large and diverse group of animals has succeeded in colonizing almost every available habitat on earth, even the most inhospitable. Representative mammals are shown from eight of the world's major habitats (the animals depicted in each habitat are not necessarily from the same geographical region).*

MAMMAL

temperate grassland

American bison

prairie dog

Eurasian hedgehog

saiga antelope

giant anteater

fresh water

beaver

American mink

muskrat

giant otter

desert

Arabian camel

addax

kangaroo rat

fennec fox

red kangaroo

salt water

Florida manatee

blue whale

bottlenose dolphin

walrus

harbour seal

mandrake

the violin. It is played with a plectrum, using a tremolo effect to sustain longer notes. It is used in informal music making and more rarely as a solo or orchestral instrument.

mandrake A herb of the genus *Mandragora*, especially *M. officinarum*, native to Europe. It has large simple leaves, white flowers, and a thick forked root, which resembles the human form and was formerly believed to have healing and aphrodisiac properties. Family: *Solanaceae*.

mandrill A large *Old World monkey, *Mandrillus sphinx*, of West African coastal forests. They are 66–84 cm long, including the tail (5–7.5 cm), with red and blue muzzle and buttocks and shaggy yellow-brown hair. They live in small family groups and forage for plants and insects, sometimes climbing for berries. *See also* drill.

Manes In Roman religion, the spirits of the dead. The word, a euphemism meaning "the kindly ones," also referred to the underworld and its gods.

Manet, Edouard (1832–83) French painter, born in Paris. After overcoming parental opposition, he trained under the classical painter Thomas Couture (1815–79) between 1850 and 1856. By 1860 he was painting contemporary scenes, but throughout his career he remained indebted to the Old Masters, particularly to Velázquez and Hals. He exhibited mainly at the Paris Salon, where such paintings as *Olympia* and *Déjeuner sur l'herbe* (both Louvre) became targets for considerable scorn and derision. However, his friend Émile *Zola spiritedly defended his work in an article published in 1867. In the 1870s he adopted the technique of the impressionists, although he refused to participate in their exhibitions (*see* impressionism). Such paintings as *The Balcony* (Louvre) and *The Luncheon* (Neue Staatsgaleries, Munich) anticipate 20th-century painting by making brushwork, colour, and design more important than the subject matter. His last great work was *A Bar at the Folies-Bergère* (Courtauld Institute, London).

mangabey A large long-tailed *Old World monkey belonging to the genus *Cercocebus* (4 species), of central African forests. Mangabeys are 80–165 cm long including the tail (43–75 cm) and have long limbs and muscular bodies. They live in troops, feeding on fruit high in the trees.

Mangalore 12 54N 74 51E A port in India, in Karnataka on the Malabar Coast. Its manufactures include textiles and tiles. Population (1981): 306 000.

manganese (Mn) A hard grey brittle transition element that resembles iron, first isolated in 1774 by J. G. Gahn (1745–1818). It occurs in nature in many minerals, especially pyrolusite (MnO_2) and rhodochrosite ($MnCO_3$), in addition to the extensive deposits of manganese nodules discovered on the deep ocean floors. It is extracted by reduction of the oxide, with magnesium or aluminium, or by electrolysis. The metal is used in many alloys, particularly in steel, in which manganese improves the strength and hardness. Manganese forms compounds in a number of different *valence states: for example MnO, Mn_3O_4, MnO_2. The permanganate ion (MnO_4^-) is a well-known oxidizing agent. At no 25; at wt 54.9380; mp 1244°C; bp 1962°C.

mange A contagious skin disease, caused by mites, that can affect domestic livestock, pets, and man (*see* scabies). The parasites bite or burrow into the skin causing hair loss, scaly dry skin, pimples, blisters, and intense itching. Treatment is with a suitable insecticide, such as gamma benzene hexachloride.

mangel-wurzel. *See* beet.

mango A large evergreen tropical tree, *Mangifera indica*, native to SE Asia but cultivated throughout the tropics for its fruit. Growing 15–18 m high, it has long narrow leaves and large clusters of pinkish flowers. The oblong fruit, up to 2.3 kg in weight, has a green, yellow, or reddish skin and contains a stony seed, surrounded by juicy orange edible flesh that has a spicy flavour. Mangos are eaten fresh and used in preserves or for canning. Family: *Anacardiaceae*.

mangosteen A tropical fruit tree, *Garcinia mangostana*, native to SE Asia and reaching a height of 9.5 m. The round or oval fruit, up to 8 cm in diameter, has a thick hard purple rind and contains a few seeds surrounded by juicy white edible flesh, which is divided into separate segments and has a slightly sharp taste. Family: *Guttiferae*.

MANGROVES *A young specimen of* Rhizophora stilosa *with conspicuous prop roots, growing in Singapore.*

mangroves Shrubs and trees forming dense thickets and low forests on coastal mudflats, salt marshes, and estuaries throughout the tropics. Many are evergreen, with shiny leathery leaves, aerial supporting (prop) roots, and breathing roots with "knees" that protrude above the water or mud. The main species are the common or red mangrove (*Rhizophora mangle*), the black mangrove (*Avicennia nitida*), and *Sonneratia* species.

mangrove snake A mildly venomous snake belonging to the genus *Boiga* (30 species) occurring in mangrove swamps and lowland forests of Africa, Asia, Australia, and Polynesia. They live on the ground or in trees and prey on frogs, birds, lizards, crabs, fish, etc. The black-and-yellow mangrove snake (*B. dendrophila*) of E Asia can reach a length of 2.5 m. Family: *Colubridae*.

Manhattan An island in the USA, situated at the N end of New York Bay, between the Hudson, East, and Harlem Rivers, comprising one of the five boroughs of New York City. It is a major commercial and financial centre focused on Wall Street. Other notable features include the famous Broadway theatre district, *Greenwich Village, and its many skyscrapers, including the Empire State Building (1931). Area: 47 sq km (22 sq mi). Population (1980): 1 427 533.

Manhattan Project The code name for a US project set up in 1942 to develop an atomic bomb. Research culminated in the construction of the bombs at Los Alamos, New Mexico. In 1945 a uranium bomb and a plutonium bomb were dropped on Hiroshima and Nagasaki respectively (*see* World War II; nuclear weapons).

manic-depressive psychosis A severe mental illness causing repeated episodes of severe *depression, mania (excessive euphoria, overactivity, irritability, and impaired judgment), or both. These episodes can be precipitated by upsetting events but are out of proportion to them. There is a genetically inherited predisposition to this psychosis; long-term treatment with lithium salts can prevent or reduce the frequency and severity of attacks.

Manichaeism A religion influenced by both *Gnosticism and Christianity. It originated in Persia (c. 230 AD), spread throughout Asia and the Roman Empire, and survived in Chinese Turkistan until the 13th century. It influenced several dualistic medieval heresies (see Cathari). Its founder, Mani (c. 216-c. 276), was martyred by the adherents of *Zoroastrianism. Fundamental to his creed was the belief that matter is entirely evil, but within each individual is imprisoned a soul, which is a spark of the divine light. By strict abstinence and prayer man can recover consciousness of the light and be liberated at death from material entanglement. Mani's followers were divided into the elect, teachers who lived in poverty and celibacy, and the hearers, who cared for the elect's material needs and could only achieve salvation after a cycle of reincarnation.

Manila 14 30N 121 12E The capital and main port of the Philippines, on Manila Bay in Luzon. Founded by the Spanish in 1571, it suffered several foreign occupations over the centuries and the old town was destroyed in World War II. The official capital was transferred to Quezon City on the outskirts (1948-76). An educational centre, it has over 20 universities, including the University of Santo Tomas founded in 1611. It has one of the finest harbours in the world and is also an important industrial centre; its industries include textiles, pharmaceuticals, and food processing. Manila suffers from severe traffic congestion; highly decorated jeeps left by US forces provide the main form of transport. Population (1980): 1 626 249.

Manila Bay An inlet of the South China Sea, in the Philippines in SW Luzon. One of the world's finest natural harbours, it was important before the ports of Manila and Cavite were founded. In the battle of Manila Bay in 1898 the US navy defeated the Spanish fleet, and there was again bitter fighting here during World War II. Area: 1994 sq km (770 sq mi).

Manila hemp A strong fibre obtained from a treelike herb, the *abaca, grown in the Philippines. It is largely used to make rope, matting, and strong paper. Finer grades are made into hats and local fabrics.

Manin, Daniele (1804-57) Italian patriot, born in Venice. His opposition to Austrian rule of Venice resulted in his imprisonment in 1847. He was released on the outbreak of the Revolution of 1848, appointed president of the newly restored Venetian Republic, and led a courageous defence of Venice against an Austrian siege. On its surrender (August, 1849) he went into exile in Paris.

manioc. See cassava.

Manipur A state in NE India, on the hilly Burmese border. Its largely Mongoloid inhabitants speak many languages. Rice, fruits, sugar cane, and mustard are grown. There is some silk weaving. The jungles yield bamboo and teak. History: Burmese threats caused the raja to seek British aid (1824), which became British rule (1891). Manipur became a state in 1972. Area: 22 356 sq km (8629 sq mi). Population (1981 est): 1 433 691. Capital: Imphal.

Manisa (ancient name: Magnesia) 38 36N 27 29E A town in W Turkey. Founded in the 12th century BC, Manisa is a commercial town with trade in such crops as tobacco, olives, and raisins. The Romans defeated Antiochus the Great here in 190 BC. Population (1970): 70 022.

Manitoba A province of W Canada, in the centre of North America. Although it is one of the *Prairie Provinces, only the SW is true prairie. Further to the NE lies the *Red River Valley and three large lakes (Winnipeg, Winnipegosis, and Manitoba) with extensive forests in the N and tundra near Hudson Bay. Manitoba's economy is based on large mechanized farms producing grains and livestock. Forests, fisheries, and hydroelectricity are also important. Manitoba produces copper, gold, zinc, silver, nickel, and oil.

Manufacturing is based on natural resources and agriculture. The province boasts a rich cultural life centred around Greater *Winnipeg, which contains over half the population. History: originally exploited for furs, Manitoba (then known simply as the Red River Settlement) first attracted dispossessed Scots Highlanders as settlers (1812). Acquisition of the area by Canada (1869) provoked the Riel Rebellion (1869-70), an uprising of French-speaking halfbreeds (Métis). Manitoba became a province in 1870. The transcontinental railway (1882) and steady immigration (especially 1900-14) brought a prosperity that has been interrupted only between the World Wars. Area: 548 495 sq km (211 774 sq mi). Population (1981): 1 026 241. Capital: Winnipeg.

Manitoulin Islands A group of Canadian islands in N Lake *Huron. Timber, farming, and tourism are economically important. The main island, Manitoulin Island, is the largest freshwater lake island in the world. Area (Manitoulin Island): 2766 sq km (1068 sq mi).

Manizales 5 03N 75 32W A city in central Colombia, in the Central Cordillera. It is the commercial centre of the country's chief coffee-growing area. Manufactures include textiles, chemicals, and leather products and it has a university (1943). Population (1980): 302 000.

Manley, Michael (1924-) Jamaican statesman, who, as leader of the People's National Party, was elected prime minister of Jamaica in 1972 and re-elected in 1976. His socialist policies included nationalizing 51% of the bauxite industry, developing close ties with Cuba, and speaking out for the Third World. He was defeated in the 1980 elections

Mann, Thomas (1875-1955) German novelist. Born into a wealthy merchant family, he chose a similar family as the subject of his first novel, *Buddenbrooks* (1901). Art and the artist are his main themes, however, in the novella *Death in Venice* (1912), *The Magic Mountain* (1924), in which a sanatorium is a microcosm of society, and *Doctor Faustus* (1947), a novel about a modern composer of genius. His other works include *Joseph and His Brothers* (1933-44), a series of four novels based on the biblical story of Joseph, and the picaresque *Felix Krull* (1954). Mann opposed Nazism and was forced to emigrate to the USA in the 1930s. He was awarded a Nobel Prize in 1929. His brother **Heinrich Mann** (1871-1950), also a novelist and opponent of fascism, is best known for his novel *Professor Unrat* (1905; filmed as *The Blue Angel*, 1928).

manna 1. In the Bible, the miraculous food that fell with the dew to sustain the Israelites in the wilderness (Exodus 16.14-15). This phenomenon has been variously identified as an exudation from the tamarisk tree or a form of lichen. 2. A sugary substance obtained from the ash tree and used in medicine.

Mannerheim, Carl Gustaf Emil, Baron von (1867-1951) Finnish general and statesman. He led the antisocialist forces to victory against the Finnish Bolsheviks in 1918 and then retired until 1931. In 1939, at the outbreak of the *Russo-Finnish War, he became commander in chief and, although defeated, was able to obtain good terms for Finland (1941). He re-embarked on war with the Soviet Union (June, 1941) and as president (1944-46) negotiated peace.

mannerism An art movement dominant in Italy from about 1520 to 1600. Mannerism developed out of the *Renaissance style, some of its characteristics being evident in the late work of *Raphael and *Michelangelo. It aimed to surpass the Renaissance style in virtuosity and emotional impact. In architecture this resulted in a clever and playful misuse of the rules of classical architecture, notably in the buildings of *Giulio Romano. In painting it led to a distortion of scale, an elongation of form, and dissonance of colour, which frequently resulted in an effect of tension. Leading mannerist painters were *Pontormo, *Parmigianino, *Vasari, and *Bronzino. Features of mannerism also

MANNERISM *Detail from* The Madonna with the Long Neck *(1532–40; Palazzo Pitti, Florence) by Parmigianino. The elongated proportions of the Madonna's neck and fingers and the baby's body are typical of the reaction against naturalism.*

appeared in the work of *Tintoretto and *El Greco. Although largely confined to Italy, it appeared in France in the school of *Fontainebleau and in Bohemia in the work of *Arcimboldo and Bartholomeus Spranger (1546–1611).

Mannheim 49 30N 8 28E A city in SW West Germany, in Baden-Württemberg at the confluence of the Rivers Rhine and Neckar. It was the seat of the Electors Palatine (1720–98) and has a notable baroque castle. It is a major port with an oil refinery and its manufactures include motor vehicles and agricultural machinery. Population (1980 est): 303 600.

mannikin A *waxbill of the genus *Lonchura* (30 species) occurring in Africa, S Asia, and Australasia. Mannikins are typically small (about 11 cm long) and brown or black with paler underparts. The chestnut mannikin (*L. ferruginosa*) of the Philippines has become a pest to rice growers.

Manning, Henry Edward, Cardinal (1808–92) British churchman. A prominent member of the *Oxford Movement, he was converted to Roman Catholicism in 1851. As Archbishop of Westminster (1865–75) he became a leading defender of papal infallibility at the *Vatican Council (1870). He was made a cardinal in 1875 and later was active in social reform and the temperance movement.

Manolete (Manuel Laureano Rodríguez Sánchez; 1917–47) Spanish matador, who became a professional at 17 and achieved a reputation as a bullfigher of great style. He died of injuries received in the ring.

manometer An instrument for measuring pressure differences. The simplest form consists of a U-shaped tube containing mercury, one arm of which is connected to a source of pressure and the other is open. The difference in height of the liquid in the arms is a measure of the pressure difference.

manor The most common unit of agrarian organization in medieval Europe, introduced into England by the Normans. The manor was essentially the lord's landed estate, usually consisting of the lord's own farm (the demesne), and land let out to peasant tenants, chiefly *villeins, who worked for the demesne and were legally dependent upon their lord.

Manpower Services Commission (MSC) A statutory body that organizes the British government's employment and training services. Set up under the Employment and Training Act (1973), it consists of two agencies (the Employment Services Agency and the Training Services Agency) and has ten members, representing employers, employees, local government, and educational interests.

Manresa 41 43N 1 50E A town in NE Spain, in Catalonia. Below its 17th-century church is the Holy Cave of St Ignatius of Loyola, where he composed his *Spiritual Exercises*. Population (1981): 67 014.

Mansart, François (*or* Mansard; 1596–1666) French classical architect. His first achievement, the north wing of the chateau at Blois (1635–38), featured the double-angled (Mansard) roof. He built or remodelled several houses in Paris, notably the Hôtel de la Vrillière (1635), but his best-known building was Maisons-Laffitte near Paris (1642). He also designed the church of Val-de-Grâce, Paris (1645), but his arrogance, reputed dishonesty, and extravagance resulted in his dismissal.

Mansell, Nigel (1954–) British racing driver. Since winning the European Grand Prix in 1985 he has been Britain's top Formula One driver.

Mansfield 53 09N 1 11W A town in the Midlands of England, in Nottinghamshire. Coalmining is the chief industry; others are cotton textiles, shoe manufacturing, engineering, and chemicals. Population (1981): 58 949.

Mansfield, Katherine (Kathleen Mansfield Beauchamp; 1888–1923) New Zealand short-story writer. She came to Europe in 1908, published her first collection of stories in 1911, and in 1918 married John Middleton *Murry. *Bliss* (1920) and *The Garden Party* (1922) contain her best-known stories. She died of gonorrhoea and tuberculosis in France.

Mansfield, William Murray, 1st Earl of (1705–93) British judge and politician. He was elected to parliament in 1743 and later became a cabinet minister. As chief justice of the King's Bench from 1756 to 1788 he incurred public hostility because of his views on seditious libel. His London house was a principal target during the *Gordon Riots (1780). He transformed the diverse customs of commerce into a code of legal practice.

Mansholt, Sicco (1908–) Dutch politician and economist. During World War II he worked secretly to maintain the food supplies of the W Netherlands during the German occupation. After the war he held a number of ministerial posts and was then vice president (1958–72) and president (1972–73) of the EEC Commission. In 1953 he prepared the **Mansholt Plan** for a common EEC agricultural policy.

manslaughter The crime of killing a person either (1) accidentally by an unlawful act or by culpable negligence or (2) in the heat of passion, after provocation. The second case is closely related to murder, and is possible only if there is no evidence of premeditation.

Mansur, Abu Ja'far al- (c. 712–75 AD) The second *caliph (754–75) of the 'Abbasid dynasty and its effective founder. He built Baghdad (begun 762) and made it the 'Abbasid capital. Influenced by Persia, he developed the bureaucracy.

Mansura, El (*or* al-Mansurah) 31 03N 31 23E A city in N Egypt, on the Nile Delta. In 1250 it was occupied by Crusaders under Louis IX (St Louis) of France, who was taken and held for ransom by Muslim forces. A market centre, it has cotton-ginning and flour-milling industries. Population (1983 est): 310 900.

the family *Mobulidae*. 60–660 cm long, they swim near the surface of warm-temperate and tropical waters, feeding on plankton and small animals swept into the mouth by horn-like feeding fins projecting from the front of the head.

Mantegna, Andrea (c. 1431–1506) Italian Renaissance painter and engraver, born near Vicenza. He was trained in Padua by his adopted father Francesco Squarcione, an artist and archaeologist. His marriage (1453) to the daughter of Jacopo *Bellini connected him with the Venetian school. As court painter to the Duke of Mantua from 1459, he painted nine panels depicting *The Triumph of Caesar* (Hampton Court, London). His fresco decorations for the bridal chamber of the ducal palace include portraits of members of the Mantuan court and an illusionistic ceiling, which anticipates the *baroque.

mantis An insect belonging to the family *Mantidae* (2000 species), found in tropical and warm temperate regions. Up to 125 mm long, mantids blend with the surrounding vegetation and are voracious carnivores, using their forelegs to capture insects and other small animals. The "praying" position held by the forelegs at rest accounts for the name praying mantis, applied in particular to *Mantis religiosa* but also to all other mantids. Eggs are laid in capsules (oothecae) on rocks and plants. Order: *Dictyoptera*. □insect.

mantis shrimp A marine *crustacean of the widely distributed order *Stomatopoda* (over 250 species), especially the genus *Squilla*. 1–300 mm long, it has a short carapace and stalked eyes and the second pair of legs form large pincers for catching prey. Mantis shrimps live in sand burrows or crevices in coastal waters up to depths of 1300 m.

Mantua (Italian name: Mantova) 45 10N 10 47E A city in N Italy, in Lombardy on the River Mincio. Its history dates from Etruscan and Roman times and from 1328 to 1708 it was ruled by the Gonzaga family. It has several notable buildings, including a cathedral (10th–18th centuries), the 15th-century church of S Andrea (designed by Alberti), a 14th-century castle, and a ducal palace. The poet Virgil was born nearby. An important tourist centre, Mantua's industries also include tanning, printing, and sugar refining. Population (1983 est): 60 468.

Manu In Hindu mythology, the ancestor of mankind. Like the biblical *Noah, he survives a flood because supernatural intervention warns him in time to build an ark. He is the reputed author of a Sanskrit code of laws, the *Manusmriti*, probably compiled between 500 and 300 BC.

Manuel I (1469–1521) King of Portugal (1495–1521) during the great period of Portuguese overseas exploration. The Crown was greatly enriched by the voyages of Vasco da *Gama and *Cabral, which opened up eastern markets to Portugal. Manuel's reign also saw a revision of the legal code and the expulsion of the Jews (1497–98).

Manukau 37 03S 174 32E A city in New Zealand, in N North Island on Manukau Harbour (an inlet of the Tasman Sea). It serves as the W coast harbour for *Auckland. Population (1982 est): 163 700.

Manutius, Aldus (Aldo Manucci *or* A. Manuzio; 1449–1515) Italian printer and classical scholar, who founded the famous Aldine Press in Venice in about 1490. He specialized in inexpensive compact editions of the Greek and Latin classics, many of them first printed editions. His edition of *Virgil* (1501) was the first book in italic type. After his death the Press was carried on by his brothers-in-law and later by his son **Paulus Manutius** (1512–74) and grandson **Aldus Manutius the Younger** (1547–97).

Manx An extinct language of the Goidelic branch of the *Celtic family. An offshoot of Irish Gaelic, it was spoken on the Isle of Man until the 19th century.

Manx cat A breed of short-haired tailless cat originating from the Isle of Man. The Manx has a short body with deep flanks and a large head. The soft coat has a thick undercoat and may be of any colour.

Manzini (former name: Bremersdorf) 26 30S 31 22E A town in central Swaziland. It has a cathedral and nearby is the University of Swaziland (1964). It is an important commercial centre serving an agricultural area; industries include meat processing and cotton. Population (1983): 18 818.

Manzoni, Alessandro (1785–1873) Italian poet and novelist. After living in France from 1805 to 1810 he returned to Italy and established his reputation with the Catholic poems *Inni sacri* (1815), an ode to Napoleon, and two verse dramas. His patriotism and religious convictions are most fully expressed in his masterpiece, *The Betrothed* (1821–27), a historical novel set in 17th-century Milan during the Spanish occupation.

Maoism The theories developed by *Mao Tse-tung. Mao's strategy for revolution in China gave central importance to peasant armies rather than to the action of the industrial working class in urban centres. Similarly, on a world scale, he believed that the socialist revolutions would develop first in the underdeveloped countries rather than in advanced capitalist countries (*compare* Marxism). Mao laid great stress on moral exhortation, indoctrination, and willpower in overcoming objective obstacles and problems in socialist construction. Like Stalin, Mao defended the system of one-party rule and the view that socialism could be constructed in a single country.

Maori A Polynesian people of New Zealand, who make up about 10% of the population. They trace their origins to migrants, probably from the Cook Islands, who came in canoes around 1350. They were an agricultural people who lived mainly in the North Island in large fortified villages of timber dwellings. Descent was counted in both lines and a person could attach himself to either his mother's or father's descent group (hapu) to obtain rights to land and residence. The traditional arts of wood carving and dancing still survive but urbanization and Christianization have largely destroyed the Maoris' way of life.

Maori Wars The wars between the colonial government of New Zealand and the Maoris, fought intermittently between 1845 and 1848 and between 1860 and 1872. They were caused by the enforced sale of Maori lands in infringement of the Treaty of *Waitangi. They resulted in the loss of much Maori land to European settlers.

MAO TSE-TUNG   *The cult of Mao finds expression in a portrait on silk measuring 3.6 m (12 ft) by 6 m (20 ft).*

Mao Tse-tung (*or* Mao Ze Dong; 1893–1976) Chinese communist statesman. Born into a peasant family in Hunan province, he was a Marxist by 1920 and helped to form the Chinese Communist Party (CCP) in 1921. In the late 1920s he became a guerrilla leader against the *Guomindang (Nationalist Party) and in 1931 he became chairman of the

*Jiangxi Soviet. Forced to evacuate Jiangxi in 1934, Mao led the communist forces on the *Long March with a price of $250,000 on his head. His arrival in Yan'an in 1935 marked his emergence as a leader of the CCP. Following the defeat of Japan in the *Sino-Japanese War of 1937-45, in which the communists and Guomindang joined forces, civil war was resumed, ending in communist victory. In 1949 Mao, as chairman of the Communist Party, proclaimed the establishment of the People's Republic of China. Mao's political writings formed the theoretical basis of the new government and led to the founding of communes and the *Great Leap Forward. He stepped down as chairman in 1958, purportedly due to ill health, but reappeared with greater standing during the *Cultural Revolution. Following his death, his third wife (from 1939) *Jiang Qing attempted unsuccessfully to seize power and Mao was succeeded by *Hua Guo Feng. *See also* Maoism.

maple   A shrub or tree of the genus *Acer* (over 200 species), widespread in N temperate regions and often grown for timber and ornament. Growing 6-35 m high, maples usually bear lobed leaves, which turn yellow, orange, or red in autumn, and small yellow or greenish flowers, which give rise to paired winged fruits (samaras). Popular ornamental species are the *sycamore, *Japanese maple, and *box elder. The sugar maple (*A. saccharum*) of E North America is the source of maple sugar (obtained from the sap). Family: *Aceraceae.*

map projection   The representation of the curved surface of the earth on a plane surface. The parallels of latitude and meridians of longitude (*see* latitude and longitude) are represented on the plane surface as a network or graticule of intersecting lines. It is not possible to produce a projection of the earth's surface without some distortion of area, shape, or direction and a compromise between these has to be reached. The basic map projections include conical, cylindrical, and azimuthal (*or* zenithal) projections. In the conical form the globe is projected onto a cone with its point above either the North or the South Pole. In the cylindrical projection the globe is projected onto a cylinder touching the equator; the *Mercator projection is of this type. Part of the globe is projected upon a plane from any point of vision in the azimuthal projection; all points have their true compass bearings. Peters' projection is a modified form of cylindrical projection (see illustration).

Maputo   (name until 1975: Lourenço Marques)   25 58S 32 35E   The capital and chief port of Mozambique, on Delagoe Bay. It became the capital of Portuguese East Africa in 1907. It has a university (1962). A major East African port, its exports include minerals from South Africa, Swaziland, and Zimbabwe. Population (1982 est): 785 512.

Maquis   Groups of provincial guerrillas of the French resistance to the Germans in World War II, as distinct from the urban underground groups. The maquisards took their name from the scrubland (French word: *maquis*) in which they hid. Their operations were usually limited to attacks upon enemy patrols and depots.

marabou   A large African *stork, *Leptoptilus crumeniferus.* It is 150 cm tall with a wingspan of 2.6 m and has a grey-and-white plumage, a bare black-spotted pink head and neck with a pendulous inflatable throat pouch, and a huge straight pointed bill. It feeds chiefly on carrion.

maraca   A percussion instrument originating in Latin America, consisting of a dried gourd filled with beads, shot, or dried seeds. Maracas are usually played in pairs, chiefly in jazz bands. □musical instruments.

Maracaibo   10 44N 71 37W   The second largest city in Venezuela, a port on the NW shore of Lake Maracaibo. Its economic importance is based on oil production; industries include petrochemicals. The University of Zulia was founded here in 1891. Population (1981 est): 929 000.

Maracaibo, Lake   A lake in NW Venezuela. Oil is drilled both in and around the lake, providing about 70% of Venezuela's total oil production. It is connected with the Gulf of Venezuela by a waterway (completed in 1956). Area: about 13 000 sq km (5000 sq mi).

Maracay   10 20N 67 28W   A city in N Venezuela, NE of Lake Valencia. A military centre with two airfields, its chief industry is textiles. Population (1981 est): 355 000.

Maradona, Diego   (1960–   ) Argentinian footballer, who captained the team that won the World Cup in 1986; he has also played for Barcelona and Naples.

Marajó Island   (Portuguese: Ilka de Marajó)   The world's largest fluvial island, in NE Brazil in the Amazon delta. Area: 38 610 sq km (15 444 sq mi).

Marañón, Río   The headstream of the River Amazon, in South America. Rising in the Peruvian Andes, it flows generally NE forming the Amazon at its confluence with the Río Ucayali. Length: 1450 km (900 mi).

Maraş   37 34N 36 54E   A town in central S Turkey. Founded by Hittites, it used to manufacture guns and swords but now exports carpets and embroidery. Population (1980): 178 557.

marasmus.   *See* kwashiorkor.

Marat, Jean Paul   (1743–93) French politician, journalist, and physician, who devoted himself to radical journalism during the French Revolution. He became editor of *L'Ami du peuple*, supporting the *Jacobin cause of radical reform. Elected to the National Convention in 1792, he was murdered by Charlotte *Corday, a member of the *Girondins, whom Marat had helped to overthrow (1793).

Maratha   (*or* Mahratta)   A people of India, who live mainly in Maharashtra and speak the *Indo-Aryan Marathi language. Marathas are strictly the high-ranking castes of this region, who are cultivators, landowners, and warriors. During the 17th century there was a Maratha kingdom, and a confederacy of Maratha leaders resisted the British between 1775 and 1818.

marathon   A long-distance running race over 42 195 m (26 mi 385 yd). The marathon derives its name from the story of a soldier who ran from the Battle of Marathon to Athens with news of the Greek victory. As courses vary, there is no official world record; the fastest time is 2 hours 8 minutes 13 seconds (1982) by Alberto Salazar (USA). In the Olympic Games there are marathon races for both men and women.

Marathon, Battle of   (490 BC) The battle during the *Greek-Persian Wars in which the Athenians under *Miltiades defeated the Persians. *Phidippides was sent to summon Spartan help but the Spartans arrived too late.

marble   A rock consisting of metamorphosed limestone, although the term is often used of any rock, particularly limestone, that can be cut and polished for ornamental use. Pure marble is white recrystallized calcite, but impurities, such as dolomite, silica, or clay minerals result in variations of colour. Certain quarries in Greece and Italy have been producing large quantities of marble since pre-Christian times. The flawless white marble from Carrara in Tuscany, Italy, is particularly prized by sculptors.

Marburg   50 49N 8 36E   A town in central West Germany, in Hessen on the River Lahn. It has a gothic castle and an important library and is the site of the country's first Protestant university (1527). Population (1983 est): 79 300.

Marburg disease.   *See* green monkey disease.

Marc, Franz   (1880–1916) German expressionist painter, born in Munich. A member of *Neue Künstlervereinigung and a founder of Der *Blaue Reiter art group, Marc is known for his symbolic animal paintings, such as *Blue Horses* (1911; Walker Art Center, Minneapolis). He was killed in World War I.

marcasite   A pale bronze mineral form of *pyrite. It occurs as nodules in sedimentary rocks as a replacement mineral, particularly in chalk. Marcasite jewellery is sometimes pyrite but more often polished steel or white metal.

MAP PROJECTION

Mercator projection

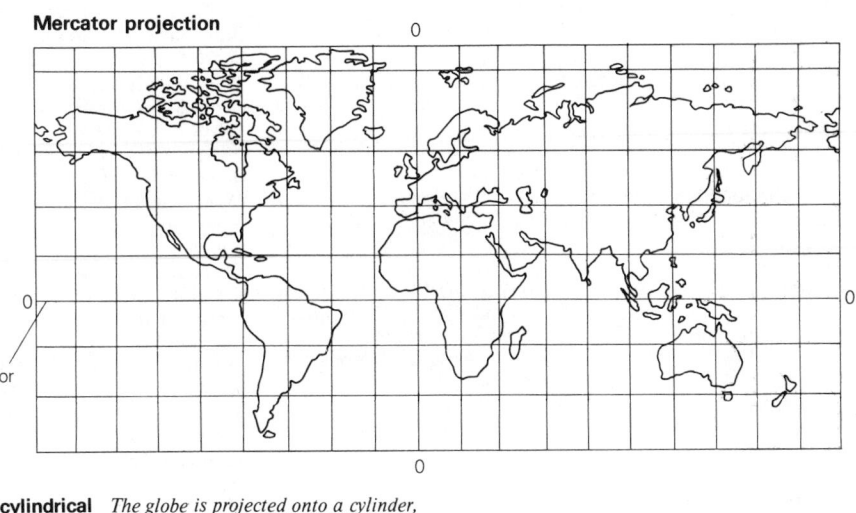

cylindrical *The globe is projected onto a cylinder, the Mercator projection being the best known.*

conical *The globe is projected onto the cone as if it contained a source of light casting a shadow of its features onto the cone, resulting in a flat projection when the cone is unfurled. The cone may touch the globe along one parallel of latitude or intersect along two parallels.*

Peters' projection *Designed by the German historian, Arno Peters, in 1973, this modified cylindrical equal-area projection draws attention away from Europe, focusing instead on the Third World countries, which are placed prominently in the centre of the map. It aims to show countries more accurately in relation to their true size but has an odd appearance in that landsurfaces close to the equator are elongated and those in high latitudes are compressed.*

orthographic projection

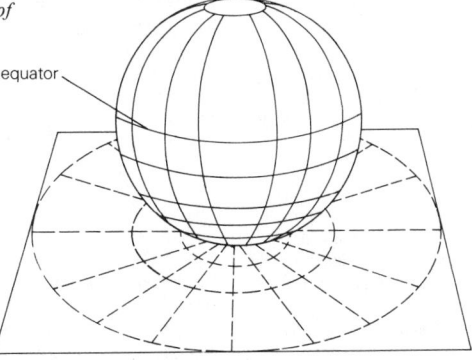

azimuthal *(or zenithal) The globe is pictured as a flattened disc. It may be projected as if it were seen from a point in the centre of the earth (gnomonic), from a point on the far side of the earth (stereographic), or from a point in space (orthographic).*

Lambert's azimuthal projection

Marceau, Marcel (1923–   ) French mime. He began to study mime in 1946, gradually developing the original character Bip, a white-faced clown derived from the traditional pantomime figure of Pierrot. As well as giving solo performances, he formed his own mime company.

Marcellus, Marcus Claudius (d. 208 BC) Roman general in the second *Punic War. After Roman defeats at Trasimene and Cannae, he was chosen to check Hannibal's advance through Italy. After capturing Syracuse, he harassed the Carthaginian armies in S Italy until his death.

Marchand, Jean Baptiste (1863–1934) French soldier and explorer. After exploring the Niger, W Sudan, and the Ivory Coast, he narrowly avoided causing a war with the British by occupying Fashoda (*see* Fashoda incident).

Marche (*or* the Marches) A region in central Italy, consisting of a narrow undulating coastal plain and a large hilly or mountainous interior. It produces wheat, maize, wine, fruit, vegetables, and cattle. Area: 9692 sq km (3742 sq mi). Population (1980 est): 1 420 443. Capital: Ancona.

Marches The border areas of England and Wales, conquered between 1067 and 1238 by vassals of the English kings. The so-called **marcher lords** enjoyed enormous powers until the union of Wales and England in the 1530s.

March on Rome (1922) The display of armed strength by Mussolini's *Blackshirts that established fascist government in Italy. Using threats of violence to support his demands for representation in the government, Mussolini organized the Blackshirts in a march against Rome. They entered unopposed by government or army and Mussolini was asked by Victor Emmanuel III to form a cabinet.

Marciano, Rocky (Rocco Francis Marchegiano; 1923–69) US boxer. He took the world heavyweight championship from Joe Walcott in 1952 and retired undefeated in 1956, after 6 defences. Unbeaten in his 49 professional fights, a record among world heavyweight champions, he was killed in an aircrash.

Marconi, Guglielmo (1874–1937) Italian electrical engineer, who invented, independently of *Popov, communication by radio. On reading about the discovery of radio waves, Marconi built a device that would convert them into electrical signals. He then experimented with transmitting and receiving radio waves over increasing distances until, in 1901, he succeeded in transmitting a signal across the Atlantic Ocean. For this work he shared the Nobel Prize for Physics in 1909. In 1929 he was made a marchese and an Italian senator; during the 1930s he was a fascist supporter.

Marcos, Ferdinand E(dralin) (1917–   ) Philippine statesman; president (1965–86). He declared martial law and assumed dictatorial powers in 1972. The murder in 1983 of opposition leader Begnino Aquino Jr, with alleged government complicity, caused further unrest and Marcos was overthrown in 1986 by the supporters of Aquino's widow, Corazon Aquino, who succeeded him as president. He fled into exile.

Marcus Aurelius (121–180 AD) Roman emperor (161–180), in association with Lucius Verus (130–169) from 161 and alone from 169. Although he is known as the philosopher emperor on account of his *Meditations* (12 books of aphorisms in the Stoic tradition), his rule was active: from 170 he fought on the Danube frontier, where he died.

Marcuse, Herbert (1898–1979) German-born US thinker. His radical anti-authoritarian philosophy evolved from the Frankfurt School of social research. Marcuse attacked both western positivism and orthodox Marxism, the former because it led to analysis rather than action, the latter because it lacked relevance to 20th-century conditions. His books include *The Ethics of Revolution* (1966) and *Counter-Revolution and Revolt* (1973).

Mar del Plata 38 00S 57 32W A resort in E Argentina, on the Atlantic Ocean. It possesses extensive beaches, hotels, and a casino. The National University of Mar del Plata was founded in 1961. Population (1980): 423 989.

Marduk The supreme god in Babylonian mythology. He created order out of the universe after defeating the sea dragon Tiamat and the forces of chaos. This victory, recounted in the Babylonian and Assyrian creation myth, *Enuma Elish*, was celebrated in a festival at the start of each year.

Marengo, Battle of (14 June, 1800) A battle, fought 5 km (3 mi) SE of Alessandria, in Napoleon's Italian campaign (*see* Revolutionary and Napoleonic Wars). Napoleon was surprised by the Austrians with his forces divided and only the timely arrival of reinforcements made French victory possible.

Marenzio, Luca (1553–99) Italian composer, noted for his nine volumes of madrigals containing over 200 works. Some, published in London, influenced English madrigalists. He spent his life in service to various Italian noble families and lived for a time in Warsaw.

mare's tail An aquatic perennial herb, *Hippuris vulgaris*, found in lakes and ponds throughout N temperate regions. It resembles the unrelated *horsetails in having stems, rising up to 30 cm above the water surface, bearing whorls of small slender leaves with minute greenish flowers at their bases. Family: *Hippuridaceae*.

Margaret (1353–1412) Queen of Denmark, Norway, and Sweden. Daughter of Valdemar IV Atterdag of Denmark, in 1363 she married Haakon VI of Norway (1339–80; reigned 1355–80). Their son Olaf (1370–87) succeeded Valdemar in Denmark (1375) and Haakon in Norway; after Olaf's death Margaret became queen of both countries, which remained united until 1814. In 1388 she was proclaimed Queen of Sweden by discontented Swedish nobles. The union of the three countries was formalized in 1397, when her heir Erik of Pomerania (1382–1459) was crowned at Kalmar. Margaret remained effective ruler until her death.

Margaret (Rose) (1930–   ) Princess of the United Kingdom; the younger daughter of George VI and sister of Elizabeth II, she is ninth in succession to the throne. In 1955 she abandoned her plan to marry Group Captain Peter Townsend (1914–   ), a divorcé, in response to public opposition and in 1960 married Antony Armstrong-Jones (later Lord *Snowdon); they were divorced in 1978. Their children are David, Viscount Linley (1961–   ), and Lady Sarah Armstrong-Jones (1964–   ).

Margaret, Maid of Norway (?1282–90) Queen of the Scots (1286–90), succeeding her grandfather *Alexander III; she was the daughter of Eric II of Norway (reigned 1280–99). Betrothed to the future Edward II of England, she died while travelling to England and Edward I promptly declared himself overlord of Scotland.

Margaret, St (1045–93) The wife of *Malcolm III of Scotland and the sister of *Edgar the Aetheling. She was noted for her piety and reform of the Scottish Church in accordance with Gregorian principles, for which she was canonized in 1250.

Margaret of Angoulême (1492–1549) An outstanding patron of Renaissance artists and writers; wife of Henry II of Navarre (1503–55). Her own writings include a collection of tales (*Heptaméron*, 1558) and of poetry (*Miroir de l'âme pécheresse*, 1531).

Margaret of Anjou (1430–82) The wife (1445–71) of Henry VI of England; their marriage constituted an attempt to cement peace between England and France during the Wars of the *Roses, in which she was one of the most formidable Lancastrian leaders. She was captured and imprisoned after the Lancastrian defeat in the battle of *Tewkesbury (1471), in which her son Edward was killed. Her husband died, probably murdered, shortly afterwards and she returned to France (1476) after Louis XI had paid a ransom for her release.

Margaret of Valois (1553–1615) The wife of Henry IV of France, famous for her *Mémoires* (1628). Daughter of Henry II and Catherine de' Medici, her marriage, which took place in 1572, was dissolved in 1599 to enable Henry to marry Marie de Médicis.

Margaret Tudor (1489–1541) Regent of Scotland (1513–14) for her son James V. The elder daughter of Henry VII of England and the wife of James IV of the Scots (d. 1513), she was ousted from the regency by the English but continued to play an active role in politics until 1534. Her great-grandson, James VI of the Scots, succeeded to the English throne as James I in 1603.

margarine A butter substitute that does not contain dairy-product fat. A type of margarine was first produced in France in 1869 from beef tallow. However, vegetable oils were only able to be used extensively after 1910, when a hydrogenation process was developed to solidify the liquid vegetable oils by adding hydrogen to saturate some of the unsaturated fatty-acid residues in the oils. In modern margarine, pasteurized fat-free milk powder is emulsified with water and such refined vegetable oils as soya-bean oil, groundnut oil, and palm-kernel oil. Vitamins A and D are also added. The resulting emulsion is cooled, solidified, and kneaded to remove air. Soft margarines contain only lightly hydrogenated oils, retaining a large part of their unsaturated nature to comply with medical opinion that they are less likely to form damaging *cholesterol in the blood than saturated fats.

Margarita Island A Venezuelan island in the S Caribbean Sea. Pearl and deepsea fishing are of importance. Area: 1150 sq km (444 sq mi). Population (1979 est): 117 700. Capital: La Asunsión.

Margate 51 24N 1 24E A resort in SE England, on the N Kent coast, including the resorts of Westgate-on-Sea and Cliftonville. It developed as a resort in the late 18th century, when Benjamin Beale, a local Quaker, invented the bathing machine. Population (1981): 53 280.

margay A spotted *cat, *Felis wiedi* of Central and South America. It is 90 cm long including the tail (30 cm), and is found in forests and brush, hunting small mammals and reptiles in trees and on the ground.

Margrethe II (1940–) Queen of Denmark (1972–), who succeeded her father Frederick IX after the Danish constitution had been altered to permit the accession of a woman to the throne. In 1967 she married a French diplomat Henri de Laborde de Monpezat (Prince Henrik; 1934–); they have two sons, Prince Frederick (1968–) and Prince Joachim (1969–).

marguerite A perennial herb, *Chrysanthemum frutescens*, also called Paris daisy, native to the Canary Isles. Each stem bears a large daisy-like flower. The name is also applied to the *oxeye daisy. *See also* Chrysanthemum.

Mari An ancient city on the middle Euphrates River in Syria. Commanding major trade routes, Mari throve during the early Sumerian period (*see* Sumer) and under the rule of *Akkad (c. 2300 BC). Excavated buildings of Mari's final period of prosperity include the palace of the last king, Zimrilim, killed when *Hammurabi destroyed the city (c. 1763). Its archive of 25 000 cuneiform tablets throws light on contemporary diplomacy, administration, and trade.

maria (Latin: seas) Large dark fairly smooth areas on the surface of a planet or satellite. The moon's maria consist of iron-rich basaltic lava that erupted onto the moon's surface (primarily on the nearside) some 3000–3900 million years ago. The lava flooded the immense basins produced by earlier impacts of bodies from space, creating both circular and irregularly shaped maria.

Mariana Islands (*or* Ladrone Islands) A group of mountainous islands in the W Pacific Ocean, comprising the US unincorporated territory of *Guam and the US commonwealth territory of the Northern Marianas. Strategically important, they include the islands of Tinian and *Saipan. Discovered in 1521, the islands were colonized by Spanish Jesuits after 1668. Guam was ceded to the USA after the Spanish-American War, while the Northern Marianas were sold to Germany (1899) and occu-

pied by Japan (1914–44) until taken by the USA. They voted in 1975 to leave the UN Trust Territory of the *Pacific Islands. Sugar cane, coffee, and coconuts are produced. Area: 958 sq km (370 sq mi). Population (1980): 16 780. Administrative centre: Garapan, on Saipan.

MARIANAS TRENCH

Marianas Trench A deep trench in the earth's crust in the W Pacific; it is the greatest known ocean depth (11 033 m). It marks the site of a plate margin (*see* plate tectonics), where one plate is being submerged beneath another.

Mariánské Lázně (German name: Marienbad) 49 59N 12 40E A town in Czechoslovakia, in W Bohemia. During the 18th and 19th centuries it was a popular spa, patronized by such famous people as Edward VII of the UK and the composer Richard Wagner. Population (1981 est): 17 950.

Maria Theresa (1717–80) Archduchess of Austria (1740–80). Her father Emperor Charles VI issued the *Pragmatic Sanction (1713) to enable Maria Theresa, as a woman, to succeed to his Austrian territories. Her accession nevertheless precipitated the War of the *Austrian Succession (1740–48), with European powers, especially Prussia, which seized Silesia, hoping to expand their possessions at her expense. In 1745 her husband Francis (whom she married in 1736) became Holy Roman Emperor. Under the influence of *Kaunitz, and determined to regain Silesia, Maria Theresa substituted her English alliance with a French coalition but in the subsequent *Seven Years' War (1756–63) Austria suffered resounding defeat. At home she combined absolutism with a measure of reform, anticipating the Enlightened Despotism (*see* Enlightenment) of her son and successor, Emperor Joseph.

Mari Autonomous Soviet Socialist Republic An administrative division in the W central Soviet Union, in the RSFSR. It is heavily forested. The Mari people, who speak a Finno-Ugric language, are known for their wood and stone carving and embroidery; they came under Russian rule in the 16th century and the region became an autonomous republic in 1936. Industries include machine building, metalworking, timber, paper and food processing; agriculture comprises mainly cereal production. Area: 23 200 sq km (8955 sq mi). Population (1981 est): 711 000. Capital: Yoshkar-Ola.

Maribor (German name: Marburg) 46 35N 15 40E A town in N Yugoslavia, in Slovenia on the River Drava. A former Habsburg trading centre, it is now one of Yugoslavia's largest industrial centres. Its university was established in 1975. Population (1981): 185 699.

Marie (1875–1938) The wife of *Ferdinand of Romania. Marie was instrumental in affiliating Romania with the

Allies in World War I. A granddaughter of Queen Victoria, Marie wrote several books in English, including an autobiography (1934–35).

Marie Antoinette (1755–93) The wife of Louis XVI of France, whose uncompromising attitude to the *French Revolution contributed to the overthrow of the monarchy. The daughter of Emperor Francis I and Maria Theresa, she married the dauphin Louis in 1770. Her extravagance and alleged immorality contributed to the unpopularity of the Crown. After the outbreak of the Revolution she is said to have remarked of the Paris mob: "If they have no bread, let them eat cake." After the overthrow of the monarchy and Louis' execution, she was herself guillotined.

Marie Byrd Land (*or* Byrd Land) An area in Antarctica, between the Ross Ice Shelf and Ellsworth Land. The USA, although laying no claim to it, has long been active in the area and has established a research station.

Marie de France (12th century AD) French poet. Her identity is uncertain, although it has been suggested that she was a daughter of Geoffrey Plantagenet and half-sister of Henry II of England. Her works include several *lais*, verse narratives based on traditional Celtic stories of love, adventure, and the marvellous.

Marie de Médicis (1573–1642) The wife (1600–10) of Henry IV of France and regent (1610–14) for her son Louis XIII. Banished by Louis from court in 1617 she raised two revolts (1619, 1620) and was readmitted to the king's council in 1622. She persuaded Louis to make her protégé Richelieu chief minister in 1624 but she subsequently tried to oust him and in 1631 fled to Brussels. She built the Luxembourg Palace in Paris, the galleries of which were decorated by Rubens (1622–24).

Marie Louise (1791–1847) The second wife of Napoleon Bonaparte, who married her (1810) following the dissolution of his marriage to Empress Josephine. Their son, his longed-for heir, was entitled King of Rome (*see* Napoleon II). After her husband's fall she became Duchess of Parma (1816).

Marienbad. *See* Mariánské Lázně.

Mariette, Auguste Ferdinand François (1821–81) French Egyptologist. Abandoning art teaching, he went to Egypt (1850) to buy Coptic manuscripts for the Louvre, but embarked instead on the excavation of *Saqqarah. He established the Egyptian Antiquities Service (1858) and Cairo Museum (1864) and initiated excavations at *Abydos, *Memphis, *Thebes, and elsewhere.

marigold One of several annual herbaceous plants of the family *Compositae*, popular as garden ornamentals. The pot marigold (*Calendula officinalis*), native to S Europe, bears orange or yellow flowers, which can be eaten in salads. The African and French marigolds (genus *Tagetes*), native to Mexico, have single or double flowers with large outer florets; there are several dwarf varieties. Cape marigolds (genus *Dimorphotheca*) are more daisy-like. *See also* marsh marigold.

marihuana. *See* cannabis.

marine biology The study of the organisms that live in the sea and on shore and the features of the environment that influence them. Marine biology is of great economic importance to man in view of his dependence upon the oceans for food, in the form of fish and shellfish, and the effects of pollution upon these organisms. *See also* fishing industry.

marine insurance *Insurance against the perils of the sea, including storm, collision, theft, stranding, fire, and piracy. Marine insurance, which is underwritten by insurance companies or by Lloyd's, falls into three categories: hull, cargo, and freight. Hull. insurance provides cover against losses arising from the perils of the sea as well as accidents caused by the crew, faulty machinery, etc., to the ship itself. Cargo insurance is arranged for each cargo and for each voyage; it is the respon-

sibility of the seller in cif (cost, insurance, and freight) contracts and of the buyer in c & f (cost and freight) and fob (free on board) contracts. Cargo is either insured free of particular *average (FPA) or with average (WA). FPA insurance covers against total loss and any contribution to general average; WA covers these risks in addition to partial losses or damage. Cargo insurance throughout the world is usually based on the clauses drawn up by the Institute of London Underwriters. Freight insurance is the form of marine insurance enabling a buyer or a seller to cover himself against loss for sums paid out in chartering a ship or hiring cargo space.

Mariner probes A series of highly successful US *planetary probes. Mariners 2 and 5 approached Venus in 1962 and 1967, while Mariner 10 flew past Venus in 1974 and then three times past Mercury in 1974–75. Mariners 4 (1965), 6 and 7 (1969), and 9 (1971–72) investigated Mars, with Mariner 9 going into Martian orbit. Mariners 11 and 12 were renamed the *Voyager probes. Mariners 1, 3, and 8 did not achieve their missions.

Marinetti, Filippo Tommaso (1876–1944) Italian poet and novelist. His manifesto published in Paris in 1909 calling for the destruction of traditional literary goals and the creation of new means of expression inaugurated the literary and artistic movement of futurism. His glorification of warfare and technology resulted in his commitment to fascism, which he defended in *Futurism and Fascism* (1924).

Marini, Marino (1901–80) Italian sculptor, born in Pistoia. Originally a painter, he turned to sculpture in the late 1920s, becoming professor of sculpture at the Brera Academy, Milan, in 1940. Marini, under the influence of ancient Etruscan and Roman sculpture, continued the figural tradition of European art with his bronze horse-and-rider and dancer series.

Maritain, Jacques (1882–1973) French Roman Catholic thinker. He was interested in applying St Thomas *Aquinas' methods to contemporary social problems. *Les Degrés du savoir* (1932) treats mystical, metaphysical, and scientific knowledge as complementary. When the metaphysical pretensions of the sciences are abandoned, Maritain thought they would not conflict with Christian faith. He was for a time associated with the reactionary group Action Française.

Maritime Alps (French name: Alpes Maritimes) A range of mountains in SE France and NW Italy, running about 130 km (81 mi) along the border and constituting the southernmost arm of the Alps. It reaches 3297 m (10 817 ft) at Punta Argentera.

maritime law The branch of law relating to ships and shipping. It evolved from the local customs of certain dominant ports. The Romans, borrowing from the customs of Rhodes, imposed a code in the Mediterranean that was international and uniform in character. This uniformity was preserved until 17th-century nationalism gave rise to various individual codes. The French *Code de Commerce* (1807) treated maritime law as a branch of commercial law and has been widely adopted by other European countries. Outside the Mediterranean the most important early code was the 12th-century Rolls of Oléron (an island off the W coast of France), which codified the customary laws of the Atlantic ports and formed the basis of the maritime law of England, Scotland, France, Flanders, and other countries. The laws of Wisby, the seat until 1361 of the Hanseatic League, were also important and contained the mercantile code of the Baltic. The English **Admiralty Court**, established in the 14th century, developed very broad powers in deciding questions of commercial law, but in the 17th century was restricted to matters "done upon the sea." Today the Admiralty Court is mainly concerned with cases involving *salvage and collisions at sea, while other types of cases, such as those involving marine insurance, are referred to the Commercial Court. A certain international uniformity has been achieved by the Comité maritime international (CMI), in which 31 member states have agreed and ratified a number of maritime conventions.

Maritime Provinces (Maritimes *or* Atlantic Provinces) The easternmost provinces of Canada, on the Atlantic coast and the Gulf of St Lawrence. They consist of *New Brunswick, *Nova Scotia, *Prince Edward Island, and usually *Newfoundland and lie in the Appalachian Highlands.

Maritime Trust A UK organization established in 1970 "to discover, repair and preserve, for the benefit of the nation, vessels of historic, scientific, or technical interest and to arrange for their berthing at sites ashore or afloat."

Maritsa, River A river in SE Europe. Rising in the Rila Mountains in W Bulgaria, it flows E then S forming part of the Greek-Turkish border, before entering the Aegean Sea. Length: 483 km (300 mi).

Mariupol. See Zhdanov.

Marius, Gaius (c. 157–86 BC) Roman general; an opponent of *Sulla. Military ability outweighing his undistinguished origins and educational deficiencies, he entered Roman politics after campaigns in Numantia, becoming associated with the popular party. After reorganizing the Roman army, he quelled *Jugurtha and crushed Gallic uprisings. In competition with Sulla for the command against *Mithridates, he was forced to flee Italy but in 87 returned with *Cinna and captured Rome, massacring his political opponents. He died shortly afterwards.

Marivaux, Pierre Carlet de Chamblain de (1688–1763) French dramatist. His popular comedies, mostly witty and sophisticated treatments of romantic themes, include *La Surprise de l'amour* (1722) and *Le Jeu de l'amour et du hasard* (1730). He also wrote two unfinished novels and much literary journalism.

marjoram One of several aromatic perennial herbs or small shrubs of the Eurasian genera *Origanum* (about 13 species) or *Majorana* (about 4 species). Wild marjoram (*O. vulgaris*), is a hairy plant, 30–80 cm tall, bearing clusters of small tubular pinkish-purple flowers. Sweet marjoram (*M. hortensis*), is widely cultivated for its aromatic leaves and flowers, which are used as culinary flavouring. Family: *Labiatae*.

Mark, St A New Testament evangelist, traditionally the author of the second Gospel. A cousin of *Barnabas, he went with him and Paul on their first mission. Subsequently he seems to have assisted Paul in Rome, where he also acted as interpreter for Peter. He was believed to have founded the Church in Alexandria and is also associated with Venice, of which he is patron saint. Feast day: 25 April.

The Gospel according to St Mark is the earliest of the Gospels and is thought to have been written about 65–70 AD. It is a brief record of the life of Jesus and is believed to have been used by Matthew and Luke in the compiling of their Gospels.

Mark Antony (Marcus Antonius; c. 83–31 BC) Roman general and statesman. Antony fought under Julius *Caesar in Gaul (54–50) and held command in Caesar's civil-war victory at *Pharsalus (48). Following Caesar's assassination, Antony came into conflict with Octavian (*see* Augustus) but they were later reconciled and formed the second *Triumvirate with Lepidus (43). In 42 Antony defeated his opponents, Brutus and Cassius, at *Philippi. In 41 he met *Cleopatra for the first time; not until 37 did Antony abandon his wife Octavia (Octavian's sister) to live with Cleopatra in Egypt. His strained relations with Octavian were finally severed in about 33. In the following year the Senate declared war on Egypt and Antony was defeated at *Actium. Both he and Cleopatra committed suicide.

market forces. See supply and demand.

market gardening. See horticulture.

markhor A large wild *goat, *Capra falconeri*, of the Himalayas. Over 100 cm tall at the shoulder, markhors are red-brown in summer and grey in winter and have massive corkscrew-like horns. The species is subdivided into four geographical races, which show variations in the horns.

Markiewicz, Constance, Countess of (?1868–1927) Irish nationalist, who married a Polish count. She fought in the 1916 Easter rising and was imprisoned. She was the first woman to be elected to the British parliament (1918, as a Sinn Féin Member) but did not take her seat.

Markov, Andrei Andreevich (1856–1922) Russian mathematician, who did important work in probability theory, notably on the type of event series known as the Markov chain. In such series the probability of an event occurring depends upon previous events. His work led to the theory of *stochastic processes.

Markova, Dame Alicia (Lilian Alicia Marks; 1910–) British ballet dancer. She joined Diaghilev's Ballets Russes in 1925 and the Vic-Wells Ballet in 1931. Her dancing was noted for its lightness and delicacy, particularly evident in her performances in *Giselle*, *Swan Lake*, and *Les Sylphides*. She retired in 1962.

Marks, Simon, 1st Baron (1888–1964) British businessman, who expanded the company Marks and Spencer, a chain of retail stores selling high-quality clothes, household goods, and food at reasonable prices. The firm was founded by his father **Michael Marks** (d. 1907) and **Thomas Spencer** (d. 1905) in 1887 as a penny bazaar.

marl A calcareous clay that is soft and plastic when wet; consolidated marl is usually called marlstone. Marls are deposited in water, either fresh or marine. The word is also used for any friable clayey soil. Marls and marlstones are used in the manufacture of cement.

Marlborough 51 26N 1 43W A market town in S central England, in Wiltshire on the River Kennet. It has engineering and tanning industries and is the site of Marlborough College, a famous public school founded in 1843. Population (1981): 5771.

Marlborough, John Churchill, 1st Duke of (1650–1722) British general. He suppressed *Monmouth's rebellion against James II (1685) but subsequently supported the *Glorious Revolution (1688) against James. In 1691 he lost favour when suspected of Jacobite sympathies but was reinstated (1701) at the beginning of the War of the *Spanish Succession. As commander in chief under Queen Anne, he won the great victories of *Blenheim (1704), Ramillies (1706), Oudenaarde (1708), and Malplaquet (1709). A *Whig, his political importance owed much to the influence of his wife **Sarah Churchill** (*born* Jennings; 1660–1744), a confidante of Anne. Following Sarah's fall from favour, he was charged with embezzlement and dismissed (1711), living in Holland until 1714. *See also* Blenheim Palace.

marlin A large game fish, also called spearfish, belonging to the genus *Tetrapturus* (or *Makaira*). It has an elongated body, up to 2.5 m long, a cylindrical spearlike snout, and a long rigid dorsal fin, which extends forwards to form a crest. Marlins are fast swimmers, occurring in all seas and hunting shoals of small fish. Family: *Istiophoridae*; order: *Perciformes*.

Marlowe, Christopher (1564–93) English dramatist and poet. His involvement in secret political activity while a student at Cambridge may have had some bearing on his death in a tavern fight in Deptford. His development of blank verse and dramatic characterization in his plays *Tamburlaine the Great* (written about 1587), *The Jew of Malta* (about 1590), *Faustus* (probably 1592), and *Edward II* (1592), prepared the way for the achievements of Shakespeare. His poetry included lyrics, translations, and the narrative *Hero and Leander* (unfinished; completed by Chapman, 1598).

Marmara, Sea of A sea lying between European and Asian Turkey and between the Bosporus and the Dardanelles. In it lies the island of Marmara, where marble (from which the name Marmara comes) and granite have long been quarried. Area: 11 474 sq km (4429 sq mi).

marmoset A small South American monkey belonging to the genus *Callithrix* (9 species), with claws instead of fingernails. Marmosets are 20-90 cm long including the tail (10-38 cm) and have silky fur, often strikingly coloured and marked, and long balancing tails. They feed on fruit, insects, eggs, and small birds and have a twittering call. Family: *Callithricidae*.

marmot A large *ground squirrel belonging to the genus *Marmota* (8 species), also called groundhog, of Europe, Asia, and North America. Marmots are 30-60 cm long and inhabit mountainous or hilly country, feeding on vegetation during the day and living in burrows at night. The woodchuck (*M. monax*) lives in North American woodlands. Marmots live in colonies; at any sign of danger, the whole colony will bolt under ground.

Marne, River A river in NE France. Rising on the Plateau de Langres, it flows N and W to join the River Seine near Paris. Linked by canal to the Rivers Rhine, Rhône, and Aisne, it was the scene of two unsuccessful German offensives during *World War I (1914, 1918). Length: 525 km (326 mi).

Maronite Church A Lebanese Christian *uniat church named after St Maro (died c. 410). The Maronites apparently originated in a Syrian Orthodox Church group that embraced *Monothelite doctrines in the 7th century and were consequently excommunicated. In the 12th century Crusader influences caused them to enter into full communion with the Roman Catholic Church and in 1584 a Maronite college was established at Rome. Although Catholic in doctrine, the Maronites retain their own Syriac liturgy and Church hierarchy.

Maros, River. See Mureş, River.

Marot, Clément (1496-1544) French poet. He served in the households of Marguerite of Navarre and of her brother Francis II. Suspected of being a Lutheran, he took refuge several times in Italy and died in Turin. He is best known for his metrical translations of the *Psalms* (1539-43), which received the encouragement of John Calvin. He was one of the first French poets to adopt the sonnet. His work marks the transition from the middle ages to the Renaissance.

Marprelate Tracts (1587-89) Pamphlets, published under the assumed name Martin Marprelate, in London, attacking the bishops (mar a prelate). The work of extreme Puritans, John Penry (1559-93) was charged with their authorship and executed. They intensified government hostility towards Puritanism.

Marquand, J(ohn) P(hillips) (1893-1960) US novelist. His best-known novels are satirical studies of upper-middle-class New England families adrift in an era of social change. These include *The Late George Apley* (1937), *Wickford Point* (1939), and *H. M. Pulham Esq.* (1941). Another of his characters was Mr Moto, the Japanese detective.

Marquesas Islands A group of 12 volcanic islands in the S Pacific Ocean, in French Polynesia (annexed 1842). Nuku Hiva is the largest and Hiva Oa, where Gauguin is buried, the second largest. Since the 1850s European diseases have reduced the population to a quarter. Mountainous and fertile, the islands export copra, cotton, and vanilla. Area: 1287 sq km (497 sq mi). Population (1983): 6548. Capital: Atuona on Hiva Oa.

marquetry A technique of veneering furniture with different woods, ivory, tortoiseshell, and metals cut into interlocking shapes, which form ornamental or pictorial compositions. It is frequently used on European 17th- and 18th-century fine furniture. *See also* parquetry.

Marquette, Jacques (1637-75) French explorer. A Jesuit, he worked among the Indians in Canada from 1666 and in 1673, with **Louis Jolliet** (1645-1700), he descended the Mississippi River as far as the mouth of the Arkansas

River, establishing that it flows into the Gulf of Mexico rather than the Gulf of California.

Marrakech (*or* Marrakesh) 31 49N 8 00W The second largest city in Morocco. Founded in 1062, it was for a time the capital of the Moorish kingdom of Morocco. Its notable buildings include the 12th-century Kotubai Mosque. It is an important commercial centre, producing carpets and leather goods, and it is also a tourist centre. Population (1982): 439 728.

marram grass A coarse perennial *grass of the genus *Ammophila* (2 species), also called beach grass or sand reed, which grows on sandy coasts of temperate Europe, North America, and N Africa. About 1 m high, it has spikelike leaves and tough scaly underground stems, which can spread over large areas. It is used to stabilize sand dunes.

marriage The socially, and sometimes legally, acknowledged union between a man or men and a woman or women, such that the resulting children are recognized as legitimate offspring of the parents. Although societies vary greatly in the rules that govern marriage, such legitimacy is always important in determining rights to property, position, rank, group membership, etc. Monogamy, in which each spouse may have only one partner, is general in Christianized societies. Most churches treat marriage as an important rite and in the Roman Catholic and Greek Orthodox Churches it is accounted a *sacrament. Polygyny, in which a man may be married to more than one woman simultaneously, is widespread and sanctioned by Islam. A few societies allow polyandry, in which a group of men, usually brothers, have a wife between them, as in traditional Nayar communities in India. Polygyny and polyandry are collectively known as polygamy. Many societies proscribe certain unions (*see* incest). Others insist on marriage within a particular group (endogamy) or outside it (exogamy). In most countries, social customs and tax laws presuppose some form of marriage as the basis of family life. However, in industrialized societies there has been a marked decline in both the insistence upon strict monogamy and the penalization of unmarried cohabiting couples. Furthermore, changes in the educational and economic status of women, the widespread use of *contraception, and the need for more than one income to support a family have combined to alter the economic structure of marriage. *See also* divorce.

marrow (botany) A trailing or climbing vine, *Cucurbita pepo*, probably native to the Americas and including several varieties widely cultivated as vegetable crops. Marrows bear yellow or orange cup-shaped flowers and large elongated fleshy fruits, which have orange, green, or yellow skins and are eaten as cooked vegetables. Family: *Cucurbitaceae*. *See also* courgette.

marrow (zoology) The soft tissue contained in the central cavities of bones. In early life the marrow of all bones is engaged in the manufacture of blood cells: it is called red marrow. In adult life the marrow of the limb bones becomes filled with fat cells and ceases to function: this is yellow marrow.

Marryat, Captain Frederick (1792-1848) British novelist. His novels based on his long naval career include *Mr Midshipman Easy* (1836) and *Masterman Ready* (1841). He also wrote children's books, notably *The Children of the New Forest* (1847).

Mars (astronomy) The fourth planet from the sun, orbiting the sun every 687 days at a mean distance of 227.9 million km. Its diameter is 6794 km and its period of axial rotation 24 hours 37 minutes 23 seconds. It has two small *satellites. The Martian atmosphere is 95% carbon dioxide and is very thin (surface pressure 7 millibars). The dry reddish dust-covered surface is heavily cratered in the S hemisphere while N regions show signs of earlier volcanic activity: there are several immense volcanoes, the largest being **Olympus Mons** (25 km high), and extensive lava plains. Huge canyons and smaller valleys occur in equatorial regions; the valleys are evidence of running water in the past. *See* Viking probes.

Mars (mythology) The Roman war god, the son of Juno. He was identified with the Greek *Ares and is usually portrayed as an armed warrior. Originally a god of agriculture, he was later worshipped at Rome as a major deity and protector of the city. The temple of Mars Ultor (Mars the Avenger) was erected by Augustus after the battle of *Philippi and dedicated in 2 BC.

Marsala (ancient name: Lilybaeum) 37 48N 12 27E A port in Italy, in W Sicily. Founded in 397 BC as a Carthaginian stronghold, it has ancient remains and a baroque cathedral. Marsala wine, grain, and salt are exported. Population (1981 est): 79 093.

Marseillaise, La The French national anthem, written in April, 1792, by *Rouget de l'Isle. It was originally a patriotic song entitled "Le Chant de guerre de l'armée du Rhin". It was taken up by a group of republican soldiers from Marseille, who were prominent in the storming of the Tuileries, and became the revolutionary anthem.

Marseille (English name: Marseilles) 43 18N 5 22E The principal seaport in France, the capital of the Bouches-du-Rhône department. Flanked on three sides by limestone hills, it stands on a bay overlooking the Gulf of Lions. Founded about 600 BC, it was destroyed by the Arabs in the 9th century AD, redeveloped during the Crusades, and came under the French Crown in 1481. Most industry is associated with its large world trade and includes oil refining at Fos, which lies to the W and is being developed as an industrial centre. The city has few ancient buildings but is noted for Le Corbusier's L'Unité (multiple dwellings). A *métro* (underground railway) was opened in 1978. Population (1982): 878 689.

Marsh, Dame Ngaio (1899–1981) New Zealand detective-story writer. She came to England in 1928. Her detective novels, which feature Roderick Alleyn of Scotland Yard and often drew on her experience of art and the theatre, include *Final Curtain* (1947) and *Last Ditch* (1977).

Marshall, George C(atlett) (1880-1959) US general and statesman. As army chief of staff (1939-45), and President Franklin Roosevelt's strategic adviser, he organized the build-up of US forces, ensuring that recruitment, training, weapons, and strength allocations conformed. He thus contributed greatly to the Allied victory. As secretary of state (1947-49) he devised the **Marshall Plan**, or European Recovery Programme, in which the USA undertook to provide economic aid to Europe after World War II. For this he won a Nobel Peace Prize (1953).

Marshall, John (1755-1835) US judge. He began his legal career after serving in the American Revolution. As a staunch Federalist, he supported a strong federal government and was elected to Congress in 1799, becoming secretary of state in 1800. As chief justice of the Supreme Court from 1801 until his death, he was instrumental in shaping US law since he had to interpret the recently drafted constitution and his decisions created several precedents. Among his most famous cases was that of *Marbury versus Madison* (1803), in which he firmly established the Supreme Court's right to review the constitutionality of federal and state laws.

Marshall Islands An archipelago in the central Pacific Ocean in the UN Trust Territory of the *Pacific Islands. It consists of the Ralik (W) and Ratak (E) chains; the chief islands are Kwajalein, Majuro, and Jaluit. Self-government was achieved in 1979 and free association with the USA in 1986, with the USA retaining control of military matters. Area: 158 sq km (61 sq mi). Population (1980): 31 042.

marsh gas. *See* methane.

marsh harrier A temperate Eurasian *hawk, *Circus aeruginosus*, that hunts low over reedbeds and marshes, preying chiefly on water voles, waterbirds, and frogs. It is

53 cm long and its plumage is dark brown; the male has a paler streaked breast, bluish wing patches, and a grey tail and the female has a pale head and throat.

marsh mallow A stout perennial herb, *Althaea officinalis*, of marshy coastal areas of Eurasia. Its velvety stems, 60–90 cm high, bear lobed leaves and clusters of flesh-coloured flowers, 5 cm in diameter. The fleshy roots yield a mucilage that was formerly used to make marshmallows (spongy sweets). Family: *Malvaceae*.

marsh marigold A stout perennial herb, *Caltha palustris*, also called kingcup, growing in marshes and wet woods throughout arctic and temperate Eurasia and North America. It has erect or prostrate stems, up to 80 cm long, bearing round leaves and bright golden flowers, 2-5 cm across. Family: *Ranunculaceae*.

Marsilius of Padua (c. 1280-1342) Italian critic of papal imperialism. Marsilius argued in his *Defensor Pacis* (1324) that since the Church is concerned entirely with faith through revelation, and not reason, which belongs to the secular world, it should be regulated by the civil power and should not interfere with government.

Mars-la-Tour and Gravelotte, Battles of (16-18 August, 1870) ·Successive battles in the *Franco-Prussian War in which the French were defeated. These engagements led to the encirclement of the French in Metz, allowing Prussian forces to march on Paris.

Marston, John (1576-1634) English dramatist. Initially a verse satirist, he was involved in a literary feud with Ben *Jonson until they collaborated (with *Chapman) on the satirical comedy *Eastward Ho!* (1605), for which they were both imprisoned. His best-known play is *The Malcontent* (1604). He was ordained priest in 1609.

Marston Moor, Battle of (2 July, 1644) The battle in the English *Civil War in which the parliamentarians and the Scots decisively defeated the royalists at Marston Moor, W of York. The parliamentary victory, which owed much to Oliver Cromwell's cavalry, destroyed the king's hold on N England.

MARSUPIAL *The newly born young of all marsupials are incapable of independent existence. After a gestation period of only 12½ days, newly born opossums, the size of bees, climb into their mother's pouch, where they remain for nine to ten weeks feeding on milk from the nipples.*

marsupial A primitive *mammal belonging to the order *Marsupialia* (176 species). Most marsupials are found in Australia and New Guinea and include the *kangaroos, *wallabies, *marsupial moles, *dasyures, *bandicoots, and *phalangers. The only New World marsupials are the *opossums.

Marsupials have relatively small brains and they lack a placenta (through which—in other mammals—the embryos are nourished). Young marsupials, which are born in a very immature state, complete their development in a pouch of skin on the mother's belly surrounding the teat, from which they are fed until fully formed. In general, the pouch of herbivorous marsupials opens forwards and that of carnivorous ones opens to the rear.

marsupial mole An insectivorous burrowing *marsupial, *Notoryctes typhlops*, of Australia. It is molelike and has short velvety golden fur, powerful forelimbs with digging feet, tiny eyes, a sensitive nose, and a cylindrical body. Family: *Notoryctidae*.

Marsyas In Greek mythology a Phrygian satyr who discovered the flute that Athena had invented and discarded, and challenged Apollo, who played the lyre, to a musical contest. He lost and was bound and flayed alive by Apollo for his presumption.

Martello towers Fortifications containing cannon built in S Britain, Ireland, and Guernsey from 1804 to 1812. The towers were intended to check the potential invasion of Britain by Napoleon—which never materialized. Their construction was proposed after observation of the single tower mounting cannon at Mortella Point, Corsica, whence the term Martello was derived.

marten A carnivorous mammal belonging to the genus *Martes* (8 species), of Eurasian and North American forests. Up to 90 cm long including the tail (15-30 cm), martens are arboreal agile hunters with dark lustrous fur: they prey largely on squirrels but also take sitting birds and their eggs. The two European species are the *pine marten and the smaller stone marten (*M. foina*). The fur of the American marten (*M. americana*) is called American *sable. Family: *Mustelidae*. *See also* fisher.

martensite The hard brittle form of *steel produced after rapid quenching in *heat treatment. When steel is heated to red heat (750°C), the carbon in it forms a solid solution in the iron. On quenching the carbon is frozen into this configuration and the crystal structure of the steel has internal strains, which cause its hardness. Named after Adolph Martens (1850-1914).

Martha's Vineyard An island in the USA, off the coast of SE Massachusetts. A former whaling and fishing centre, it is now known chiefly as a summer resort. Area: about 260 sq km (100 sq mi).

Martí, José Julián (1853-95) Cuban poet and patriot. He worked for Cuban independence as a journalist in France, Mexico, Venezuela, and the USA and died during a military expedition to Cuba. He published many essays on social and literary topics and several volumes of poetry, notably *Versos sencillos* (1891) and *Versos libres* (1913).

Martial (Marcus Valerius Martialis; c. 40-c. 104 AD) Roman poet. Born in Spain, he went to Rome in about 64 AD and gained the patronage of his fellow Spaniards Seneca and Lucan. His best-known works are his 12 books of epigrams, comprising about 1500 short poems describing the contemporary social scene with concise satirical wit and occasional lyricism. Shortly before his death he returned to Spain.

martial arts Styles of armed and unarmed combat developed in the East. The Japanese forms, such as *karate, *judo, *aikido, kendo, and sumo, derive largely from the fighting skills of the *samurai. Since the late 19th century they have become forms of sport, some popular worldwide, as has the Chinese style, *kung fu. They are closely associated with Eastern philosophies, especially Zen Buddhism. *See also* Bushido.

martin A bird belonging to the *swallow family (*Hirundidae*; 78 species). The widely distributed brown sand martin (*Riparia riparia*) is about 12 cm long and has white underparts with a brown breast band. It nests in colonies in tunnels excavated in sand or clay banks. The black-and-white Old World house martin (*Delichon urbica*), about 13 cm long, commonly nests beneath the eaves of houses.

Martin V (Oddone Colonna; 1368-1431) Pope (1417-31), whose election at the Council of *Constance ended the *Great Schism. He attempted to increase papal power by condemning the view that Church councils have supreme authority and by limiting the power of the national Churches. His attempts to suppress the *Hussites were largely unsuccessful.

Martin, Archer John Porter (1910-) British biochemist, who shared the 1952 Nobel Prize with Richard Synge (1914-) for their development of the technique of paper *chromatography (1944), which they used for separating amino acids. Martin went on to develop gas chromatography in 1953.

Martin, John (1789-1854) British painter. His large and grandiose paintings, often on biblical themes, including *The Fall of Babylon* (1819), *Belchazzar's Feast* (1826), and *The Deluge* (1834), brought him fame throughout Europe.

Martin, Pierre-Émile (1824-1915) French engineer, who invented the Siemens-Martin process of producing steel. In this process Martin employed the open-hearth furnace developed in 1856 by Sir William *Siemens but adopted his own steel-producing process, which utilized pig iron and scrap steel. The Siemens and the Siemens-Martin processes largely replaced the *Bessemer process but the Siemens-Martin eventually became the more widespread.

Martin, Richard (1754-1834) Irish politician. He was an MP in the Irish (1776-'83, 1798-1800) and British (1801-26) parliaments. Nicknamed Humanity Dick by his friend George IV, he was a founder of the RSPCA.

Martin, St (c. 316-97 AD) A patron saint of France; Bishop of Tours (372-97). A soldier in the imperial army, he later settled at Poitiers and nearby founded the first monastery in Gaul. After becoming Bishop of Tours, he continued to live as a monk at a monastery that he established outside Tours. His military cloak, part of which he reputedly gave to a naked beggar, has become a symbol of charity. Feast day: 11 Nov.

Martin du Gard, Roger (1881-1958) French novelist. After active service in World War I he devoted his life entirely to writing. His major work was *Les Thibault* (1922-40), a cycle of novels analysing contemporary society through family relationships. His other works include the outspoken *Notes sur André Gide* (1951). He won the Nobel Prize in 1937.

Martineau, Harriet (1802-76) British writer. Despite deafness and ill health, she was a leading figure in intellectual life. Her work includes novels, books on religion and economics, and the influential *History of England during the Thirty Years' Peace, 1816-46* (1849).

Martini, Simone (c. 1284-1344) Italian painter, born in Siena and probably the pupil of *Duccio. In 1317 he worked for Robert of Anjou (reigned 1309-43) in Naples, where he was influenced by French gothic art. His *Guidoriccio da Fogliano* (1328), commissioned for the town hall of Siena, is probably the first commemorative equestrian portrait in European art. The *Annunciation* (1333; Uffizi) is the best example of his decorative style and graceful use of line. In about 1340 he moved to Avignon (France), where he worked for the papal court.

Martinique A French overseas region in the West Indies, in the Windward Islands of the Lesser Antilles. It consists of a mountainous island of volcanic origin. Agriculture is of importance, the chief exports being sugar, bananas, and rum. Tourism is being developed. *History*: colonized by the French in 1635, it became a French overseas department in 1946. The volcanic eruption of Mont Pelée (1902) destroyed the town of St-Pierre. Area: 1090 sq km (420 sq mi). Population (1980 est): 308 169. Capital: Fort-de-France.

Martinmas The feast of St *Martin (11 Nov), traditionally the date for slaughtering livestock to be salted as winter food. Fairs, at which servants could be hired, were also held at Martinmas, and in Scotland it is a quarter day recognized in common law.

Martinů, Bohuslav (1890–1959) Czech composer. He was largely self-taught apart from a period of study with Roussel in Paris from 1923. During World War II he settled in the USA. He composed many works, including symphonies, concertos, the ballet *La Revue de cuisine* (1927), the opera *Julietta* (1936–37), and a concerto for double string orchestra and timpani (1938).

Marvell, Andrew (1621–78) English poet. He was employed as tutor by Cromwell and Fairfax and as secretary by Milton. From 1659 until his death he served as MP for Hull. He published several satires and pamphlets attacking religious intolerance and government corruption. His poetry, most of which was published posthumously, is noted for its combination of intelligent argument and lyricism. "To his Coy Mistress" and "The Garden" are among his best-known poems.

marvel of Peru. *See* four o'clock plant.

KARL MARX *Photographed (c. 1880) towards the end of his life.*

Marx, Karl (Heinrich) (1818–83) German philosopher, economist, and revolutionary. While studying at the University of Berlin, Marx became a member of the Young Hegelians, an antireligious radical group. Unable to obtain a university post because of his radical views, Marx turned to journalism, becoming the editor of a radical paper in 1842. After its suppression Marx left Germany and spent the rest of his life in exile. He stayed first in Paris (until his expulsion in 1845), where he met several leading socialists including Friedrich *Engels, who later collaborated in many of Marx's writings and provided him with substantial financial support. While in Brussels, Marx's association with a group of German handicraftsmen led to the writing of *The Communist Manifesto* (1848). In 1849 Marx moved to London, where he remained for the rest of his life, publishing *The Class Struggles in France* (1850), *The Eighteenth Brumaire of Louis Bonaparte* (1852), and *A Contribution to the Critique of Political Economy* (1859). Following the establishment of the International Working Men's Association in 1864, Marx devoted many years to the affairs of the First *International, gaining wide recognition among socialists. The first volume of *Das Kapital* was published in 1867 but the rest of his work did not appear until after his death. *See also* Marxism.

Marx brothers A US family of comic film actors: **Chico** (Le-

onard M.; 1891–1961), **Harpo** (Adolph M.; 1893–1964), **Groucho** (Julius M.; 1895–1977), and, until 1933, **Zeppo** (Herbert M.; 1900–79). Their original vaudeville act also included **Gummo** (Milton M.; 1901–77). Their film comedies, characterized by irreverent comic interplay between the fast-talking Groucho, the incompetent Chico, and the dumb harp-playing Harpo, included *Horse Feathers* (1932), *Duck Soup* (1933), and *A Night at the Opera* (1935). The team disbanded in 1949.

Marxism The theory of scientific socialism introduced by Marx and Engels, which explains the origin, historical development, and demise of the capitalist economic system. It relies heavily on the philosophy of Hegel, in particular Hegel's thesis that change has to be explained in terms of contradiction (*see* dialectical materialism). Class analysis, the central component of Marxism, is not peculiar to Marx but was shared by contemporary political economists, such as Adam Smith and Ricardo. Marxism is distinct in that it developed the theory of proletarian revolution. The transition to a socialist and eventually a classless society would not be a gradual evolution but would involve the violent overthrow of the state power (army, police, bureaucracy, etc.) of the bourgeois class. The working class would have to establish its own state power, which would be more democratic because it would be the rule of the majority of the population, the working class. As classes gradually disappeared, however, state power would also wither away since the state was fundamentally an instrument by which one class ruled over other classes. The classless society of the future would allow the fullest developments of individuals through social cooperation. Since World War I many different versions of Marxism have been expounded (*see also* Leninism; Maoism; communism).

Mary 37·42N 61·54E A city in the S Soviet Union, in the Turkmen SSR. Located in a cotton-growing oasis of the Kara Kum Desert, it has important textile industries. Population (1979): 81 000.

Mary I (1516–58) Queen of England and Ireland (1553–58), succeeding her younger half-brother *Edward VI. The daughter of Henry VIII and Catherine of Aragon, Mary's life after her parent's divorce in 1533 was one of extreme uncertainty until her rehabilitation in the line of succession in 1544. She became queen after the failure of a conspiracy to place Lady Jane *Grey on the throne. Her singleminded aim was to restore Roman Catholicism in England: Edward's Protestant legislation was repealed and in 1554 the heresy laws were reintroduced, resulting in almost 300 deaths at the stake and the queen's nickname, Bloody Mary. Her marriage (1554) to Philip II of Spain, the announcement of which had incited the unsuccessful rebellion (1553) of Sir Thomas *Wyatt, led to England's entanglement in Philip's foreign policy and the loss in 1558 of its last possession on the Continent, Calais. This disaster, coupled with a series of false pregnancies, hastened Mary's death.

Mary II (1662–94) Queen of England, Scotland, and Ireland (1689–94), joint monarch with her husband William III. Daughter of James II, she was brought up as a Protestant and came to the throne after the enforced abdication of her Roman Catholic father during the *Glorious Revolution. She was a popular ruler, governing during William's absences abroad, and died prematurely of smallpox.

Mary, Queen of Scots (1542–87) The daughter of James V and the French noblewoman Mary of Guise (1515–60) and the great-niece of Henry VIII of England; she succeeded to the throne shortly after her birth. Her mother became regent and from 1547 Mary, a Roman Catholic, lived at the French court, where in 1558 she married the dauphin (later Francis II). After Francis' death (1561) Mary returned to Scotland and in 1565 married, unpopularly, her cousin Lord *Darnley. In 1566 he murdered out of (probably unfounded) jealousy her secretary David *Riccio. In that year Mary gave birth to the future James VI (James I of

England). In 1567 Darnley was murdered by *Bothwell, who abducted Mary (so she later alleged) and then married her. The question whether Mary was already the mistress of Bothwell remains unsettled, resting on the evidence of the much debated Casket Letters. A rebellion of Scottish nobles defeated Mary and Bothwell at Carberry Hill (1567) and Mary, imprisoned at Loch Leven, was forced to abdicate in favour of her son. She escaped and raised an army that was defeated at Langside (1568). Fleeing to England, where her claim to the English succession had long been an embarrassment to Elizabeth I, she was held prisoner for the rest of her life. She became the focus of a series of plots against Elizabeth and was finally tried for complicity in the conspiracy of Anthony *Babington (*see also* Ridolfi, Roberto; Throckmorton, Sir William) and executed at Fotheringhay Castle, near Peterborough. Her remains were moved to Westminster Abbey by her son.

Mary, the Virgin In the New Testament, the mother of *Jesus Christ. The fullest accounts of Mary are contained in the birth stories in *Luke and *Matthew. *John (19.25) reports that she was present at the crucifixion, and she appears to have been present at the growth of the early Church in Jerusalem (Acts 1.14). Luke records the Annunciation (the announcement by the Angel Gabriel that she was to conceive the Son of God by the Holy Spirit); her betrothal to *Joseph; her meeting with her cousin Elizabeth; and her song of praise (the Magnificat) when Elizabeth had greeted her as the mother of the Lord. The Gospels also state that she was and remained a virgin. Mary's *Immaculate Conception has been recognized as a dogma of the Roman Catholic Church since 1854 and the belief that she was taken up bodily into heaven (the Bodily Assumption) was defined as doctrine in 1950. In the Orthodox and Roman Catholic Churches Mary is venerated as having a secondary mediating role between God and man.

Mary Magdalene, St In the New Testament, the first person to see Jesus after the resurrection. Jesus cured her of possession by evil spirits. She aided his work in Galilee and was present at the crucifixion and burial. Medieval scholars associated her with the repentant sinner who annointed Jesus' feet, mentioned in Luke's Gospel. Feast day: 22 July. Emblem: an ointment jar.

Mary of Teck (1867-1953) The wife of George V of England. Previously engaged to Albert, Duke of Clarence (1864-92), George's elder brother, she married George in 1893, following Albert's death. She was noted as a needlewoman and for her interest in art and antique furniture.

Maryborough 25 32S 152 36E A port in Australia, in SE Queensland. The main industries are timber milling, and the manufacture of heavy machinery; exports include sugar, tropical fruits, coal, and timber. Population (1980 est): 21 800.

Maryborough (Ireland). *See* Portlaoise.

Maryland A state on the E seaboard of the USA. It consists of two physical regions: the Atlantic Coastal Plain, which is split by Chesapeake Bay into a low flat plain in the E and uplands in the W, and an area of higher ground, part of the Alleghenies in the N and W. Manufacturing is the most important sector of the economy, with primary metals, metal products, food processing, transportation and electrical equipment, printing and publishing, and textiles. There is an important service sector. The state's farmers produce livestock, poultry, and dairy products as well as some corn, tobacco, soya beans, and vegetables. *History*: one of the 13 original colonies, it was first settled by the English. It was granted (1632) to George Calvert, 1st Baron Baltimore by Charles I and named after his wife, Henrietta Maria. Under the 2nd Baron Baltimore, it became a refuge for Roman Catholics. Area: 27 394 sq km (10 577 sq mi). Population (1980): 4 216 446. Capital: Annapolis. Chief port: Baltimore.

Marylebone Cricket Club (MCC) A cricket club founded

in London in 1787. Its headquarters are at *Lord's Cricket Ground. The MCC became the leading authority on the laws of cricket and was responsible for the control of English cricket until 1969, when this became the responsibility of the Cricket Council.

Mary Rose A Tudor warship (Henry VIII's flagship), which sank in 1545 in Portsmouth Harbour while sailing into battle. A search for the wreck was begun in 1965 by underwater archaeologists and it was positively identified in 1971. The ship's contents, most of which were remarkably preserved, were raised during the following ten years and the hull itself was lifted in 1982 and placed in a dry-dock in Portsmouth. The Mary Rose Trust, of which the Prince of Wales is president, was formed in 1979.

Masaccio (Tommaso di Giovanni di Simone Guidi; 1401-28) Florentine painter of the early Renaissance. He collaborated with *Masolino on the *Madonna and Child with St Anne* (Uffizi) and on the fresco cycle in the Brancacci Chapel in Sta Maria del Carmine. His independent paintings include the *Trinity* (Sta Maria Novella, Florence). Influenced by *Giotto and the innovations of *Brunelleschi and *Donatello, Masaccio initiated the use of linear perspective and a single light source in painting.

MASAI *Warriors decorated with body paint.*

Masada 31 19N 35 21E A precipitous rocky hilltop near the W shore of the Dead Sea, in S Israel. The site of one of *Herod the Great's fortified palaces, it was later a centre of the *Essene sect and a stronghold of the Jews in their revolt against Rome (66 AD). In the last action of the war (73 AD), after a siege lasting almost two years, the defenders, on the eve of the final assault by the Roman besiegers, committed mass suicide rather than surrender. The site is an Israeli national monument.

Masai A Nilotic people of Kenya and Tanzania who speak a Sudanic language. They are nomads with little centralized political organization. Age sets are the basis of social organization, with three principal stages for every male: boy, warrior, and elder. This system allowed the Masai to form large raiding parties to increase their stock of cattle, which are the basis of their economy. Milk and blood from cattle form an important part of their diet, the blood being drawn from a vein in the animal's neck without killing it. Tall and active, the Masai highly value courage in their warriors.

Masaryk, Tomáš (Garrigue) (1850-1937) Czechoslovak statesman, who was one of the founders of Czechoslovakia. In Paris, during World War I, he and Beneš founded the Czechoslovak National Council, which the Allies recognized in 1918. When Austria-Hungary fell in November, 1918,

Masaryk was elected Czechoslovakia's first president; he was re-elected in 1920, 1927, and 1934. His administration was marked by a major land reform. He resigned, owing to his age, in 1935. His son **Jan (Garrigue) Masaryk** (1886–1948), a diplomat, was Czechoslovak minister to Britain (1925–38) and foreign minister in Czechoslovakia's provisional government in London (1940–45). Following World War II he returned to Prague but after the communists came to power in 1948 he died in a fall from a window, allegedly a suicide.

Mascagni, Pietro (1863–1945) Italian opera composer. His fame rests chiefly on his one-act opera *Cavalleria Rusticana* (1889), written as an entry for a competition in which it won first prize. He wrote many other operas, including *L'amico Fritz* (1891).

Mascara 35 28N 0 02E A town in NW Algeria. In 1832 Abdelkader chose the town as his headquarters but it was razed by the French in 1835. It is noted for the production of red and white wines. Population (1977 est): 62 301.

Mascarene Islands (French name: Îles Mascareignes) The heavily populated islands of Mauritius, Réunion, and Rodrigues in the W Indian Ocean. Discovered by the Portuguese in the early 16th century, they were known earlier to the Arabs.

mascons Disc-shaped masses that are located beneath the lunar surface in the younger *maria and are denser than their surroundings. They were discovered when lunar-satellite orbits were found to be slightly perturbed as a result of the higher gravitational attraction over these regions.

Masefield, John (1878–1967) British poet. Having served briefly in the merchant navy, he captured the fascination of the sea in his first volume, *Salt-Water Ballads* (1902). He also wrote narrative poems, such as *Reynard the Fox* (1919), and several adventure novels, including *Sard Harker* (1924) and *Odtaa* (1926). He became poet laureate in 1930.

maser (*m*icrowave *a*mplification by *s*timulated *e*mission of *r*adiation) A device that works on the same principle as the *laser, the radiation produced being in the *microwave region instead of in the visible spectrum. Masers are used as oscillators (e.g. the *ammonia clock) and amplifiers.

Maseru 29 19S 27 29E The capital of Lesotho, near the South African border. It was founded in 1869. The University of Botswana, Lesotho, and Swaziland was established nearby in 1966. Population (1976 est): 45 000.

Mashhad (*or* Meshed) 36 16N 59 34E A town in NE Iran, close to the Afghan and Soviet borders. It is a pilgrimage centre for Shiite Muslims; the shrine of the *imam* 'Ali ar-Rida is a magnificent structure. Mashhad is famous for carpets and turquoise; its university was founded in 1956. Population (1985 est): 1 103 300.

Mashonaland An area in central and NE Zimbabwe, inhabited by the Shona, a Bantu people. Mashonaland was administered by the British South Africa Company from 1889 to 1923, when it became a part of the new colony of Southern Rhodesia.

Mashriq (Arabic: east) The Arab countries of SW Asia (the Middle East) as compared with the *Maghrib countries of N Africa. Egypt and the Sudan are included in the Mashriq.

Masinissa (c. 240–148 BC) Ruler of Numidia in North Africa. With the support of Rome, whom he had helped against Carthage in the second Punic War (208–201), he established a strong state among the diverse Numidian tribes.

masochism Sexual pleasure obtained from the experience of pain. The condition is named after an Austrian writer, Leopold von Sacher-Masoch (1835–95), whose novels depict it. It is often associated with a pathologically strong need to be humiliated by and submissive to one's sexual partner. Frequently, masochistic and sadistic desires are combined in the same individual.

Masolino (Tommaso di Cristoforo Fini; 1383–?1447) Italian painter, born in Panicale but active mainly in Florence. He was strongly influenced by *Masaccio, particularly while working with him on the fresco cycle in the Brancacci Chapel, Florence. Later he painted in the *international gothic style. Independent works include *The Miracle of the Snow* (Sta Maria Maggiore, Rome).

Mason, A(lfred) E(dward) W(oodley) (1865–1948) British novelist. After several popular adventure stories, notably *The Four Feathers* (1902), he wrote detective novels featuring Inspector Hanaud of the Sûreté, starting with *At the Villa Rose* (1910). He was MP for Coventry and served in naval intelligence during World War I.

mason bee A solitary *bee belonging to the genus *Osmia* and related genera, occurring in Europe, Africa, and elsewhere. It builds nests of soil cemented together with saliva in hollows in wood or stones. Family: *Megachilidae*.

Mason–Dixon line A line drawn in 1767 by two surveyors, Charles Mason and Jeremiah Dixon, to settle the conflict over borders between Pennsylvania and Maryland. Until the Civil War it also represented the division between southern proslavery and northern free states. It has remained a symbolic boundary between the North and South.

masoretes Transmitters of the textual tradition (*masorah*) of the Hebrew Bible. The textual study of the Bible goes back to antiquity (*see* scribes); in the gaonic period (*see* gaon) various schools of masoretes laboured to establish a correct text and to mark the pronunciation with the help of accents. The text of Aaron ben Asher (930 AD) was recognized as authoritative by *Maimonides. The masoretic text is the basis of all Hebrew Bibles printed today.

masque A form of dramatic court entertainment popular in England during the late 16th and early 17th centuries. It consisted of a combination of verse, dance, and music, usually with a slight dramatic plot based on a mythological theme. The form was perfected in the collaborations of Ben *Jonson and Inigo *Jones, whose elaborate costumes and scenery were vastly expensive. Other writers of masques include Sir Philip *Sidney and Samuel *Daniel.

mass (physics). *See* mass and weight.

mass (religion). *See* Eucharist.

Massachusetts A state on the NE coast of the USA, in New England. The uplands in the W, which are cut N–S by the Connecticut River, are separated from the lowlands of the Atlantic Coastal Plain and Cape Cod Peninsula by the rolling country of central Massachusetts. The mainly urban population is concentrated along the coast and river valleys. A major manufacturing state, its industries produce electrical and communications equipment, high-quality instruments, chemicals, textiles, and metal and food products. Boston is an important financial and service centre. Its farmers produce dairy products, eggs, poultry, cranberries, and horticultural goods. Massachusetts is an important centre in the educational and cultural life of the USA. *History*: one of the 13 original colonies, the arrival of the Pilgrim Fathers on the *Mayflower* (1620) heralded major settlement. It was a centre for opposition to British colonial policy leading to the American Revolution and became prominent following statehood (1788), although it lost much of its industrial influence in the 20th century. Area: 21 386 sq km (8257 sq mi). Population (1980): 5 737 037. Capital: Boston.

Massachusetts Bay Company. A colony of English Puritans established at Salem in 1628. The main body of colonists arrived in 1630 under the leadership of John *Winthrop. The Company's charter was withdrawn in 1684.

Massachusetts Institute of Technology (MIT) A university in the USA, situated at Cambridge, Massachusetts. Founded in 1861 at Boston, it moved to its present site in 1916. It is world famous for scientific education and research.

mass action, law of The rate of a chemical reaction for a uniform system at constant temperature varies as the concentration of each reacting substance, raised to the power equal to the number of molecules of the substance appearing in the balanced equation. Thus, for the reaction $2H_2 + O_2 = 2H_2O$ the speed of the forward reaction is proportional to the concentration of O_2 (written $[O_2]$) and to $[H_2]^2$; the reverse reaction depends on $[H_2O]^2$. The law is thus useful for calculation of equilibrium concentrations when reaction speeds are known, and vice versa. It was first proposed in the period 1864–79 by two Norwegian scientists C. M. Guldberg (1836–1902) and P. Waage (1833–1900).

massage Manipulation of the soft tissues of the body for therapeutic purposes. This includes rhythmic stroking (effleurage), kneading (petrissage), and repeated tapping (tapotement); it is used to relieve muscular spasm and pain, improve blood circulation in the skin, and reduces swelling due to accumulation of fluid in the tissues. *See also* physiotherapy.

mass and weight Two physical quantities used to express the extent to which a substance is present; they are sometimes confused. The mass of a body was defined by *Newton as the ratio of a force applied to the body to the acceleration it produces. This is now called the **inertial mass**, as it is a measure of the extent to which a body resists a change in its motion. **Gravitational mass** is defined in terms of the gravitational force between two bodies in accordance with Newton's law of gravitation. Lóránt Eotvos (1848–1919) showed experimentally that inertial mass and gravitational mass are equal, a result used by Einstein in his general theory of relativity.

Mass was also shown by Einstein, in his special theory of relativity, to be a form of energy, according to the relationship $E = mc^2$ (where c is the velocity of light). The total of the mass and the energy of a closed system remains unchanged under all circumstances (the law of the conservation of mass and energy). Weight is proportional to gravitational mass, being the force by which an object is attracted to the earth. It is therefore equal to the product of the mass and the *acceleration of free fall (i.e. $W = mg$). Thus, the weight of a body may vary according to its position; the mass is a constant. In scientific terms mass and weight are different, mass being expressed in units of mass (e.g. kilograms) and weight in units of force (e.g. newtons). *See also* amount of substance.

Massawa (*or* Mitsiwa) 15 37N 39 28E A port in N Ethiopia, in Eritrea on the Red Sea. It was occupied (1885) by the Italians, who used it as a base for their offensive against Ethiopia in 1935. With good communications to Asmara, 64 km (40 mi) WSW, Massawa is an important outlet for Ethiopia's exports and has a naval base. Population (1982 est): 36 839.

mass defect The difference between the total mass of the constituent protons and neutrons in an atomic nucleus and the mass of the nucleus. This defect is equal to the *binding energy of the nucleus.

Masséna, André (?1756–1817) French marshal. He fought in Napoleon's Italian campaign, winning an important victory at Rivoli (1797). He subsequently defeated the Russians in Switzerland (1799), fought again in Italy, and against the Austrians (1809–10). He was defeated by Wellington in the *Peninsular War and lost his command.

mass-energy equation. *See* relativity.

Massenet, Jules (1842–1912) French composer. He studied at the Paris conservatoire and won the Prix de Rome in 1863. Massenet catered for the Parisian musical taste of his day, writing 27 operas, of which *Manon* (1884) and *Werther* (1892) are still performed today.

Massey, Raymond (1896–1983) Canadian actor. He first acted on the stage in 1922 and thereafter appeared in a number of films, including *The Scarlet Pimpernel* (1934), *Abe Lincoln in Illinois* (1939), *Arsenic and Old Lace* (1944), and *East of Eden* (1955). He also appeared in the television series *Dr Kildare* (1961–65). His son **Daniel Massey** (1933–   ) and daughter **Anna Massey** (1937–   ) are also actors.

Massey, William Ferguson (1856–1925) New Zealand statesman; prime minister (1912–25). He entered parliament in 1894 and became (1903) leader of the Conservative opposition, which in 1909 he named the Reform Party. His administration, in coalition (1915–19) with the Liberals during World War I, supported agrarian interests.

Massif Central A plateau area in S central France. Generally considered to be that area over 300 m (984 ft) high, it rises to 1885 m (6188 ft) at Puy de Sancy. The central N area is also known as the Auvergne and the SE rim as the Cévennes. There is dairy and arable farming as well as heavy industry. Area: about 90 000 sq km (34 742 sq mi).

Massine, Léonide (Leonid Miassin; 1896–1979) Russian ballet dancer and choreographer. He joined Diaghilev's company in Paris in 1914 and choreographed his first ballet, *Soleil de nuit*, in 1915. He choreographed for many companies, notably the Ballet Russe de Monte Carlo. Most controversial were his innovatory symphonic ballets *Les Présages* (1933) and *Symphonie Fantastique* (1936).

Massinger, Philip (1583–1640) English dramatist. He collaborated with several other writers before succeeding John *Fletcher in 1625 as chief dramatist for the leading theatrical company, the King's Men. His best-known plays are the satirical comedies *A New Way to Pay Old Debts* (1621) and *The City Madam* (1632).

mass number (*or* nucleon number) The total number of protons and neutrons in the *nucleus of an atom.

Massys, Quentin (*or* Matsys, Messys, Metsys; c. 1466–1530) Flemish painter, born in Louvain but active in Antwerp. He was influenced by Italian Renaissance artists, particularly *Leonardo. In portraits, such as *Erasmus* (Galleria Nazionale, Rome), he anticipated *Holbein by depicting his sitter at work. He also painted scenes of daily life, notably *The Banker and His Wife* (Louvre).

mastectomy Surgical removal of a breast, usually for the treatment of breast cancer. There are several varieties of the operation. In a partial mastectomy (or lumpectomy) only the tumour is removed, while in a total mastectomy the entire breast is removed. A radical mastectomy involves removal of the breast together with the lymph nodes in the armpit and the chest muscles associated with it.

Master of the Queen's (*or* King's) **Music** An English court post established in the reign of Charles I. Originally the holder presided over the monarch's private band. It is now an honorary position held by a composer who may be called upon to write music for ceremonial occasions. The present holder is Malcolm Williamson (since 1975).

Master of the Rolls The presiding judge of the Civil Division of the Court of Appeal. The office originated as the guardian of all charters, patents, etc., entered upon parchment rolls. They were stored from 1290 in a chapel founded by Henry III in 1233 for receiving Jewish rabbis converted to Christianity. The Master of the Rolls also advised the Lord Chancellor in the judicial work of the old Court of *Chancery, becoming a full judge in 1729 and a member of the Court of Appeal in 1881. As his legal responsibilities increased he became less involved in record-keeping. Since the 19th century the rolls have been kept in the Public Record Office. He also admits solicitors to practice, and appoints the members of the Solicitors Disciplinary Tribunal.

Masters, Edgar Lee (1868–1950) US poet. His best-known work is *Spoon River Anthology* (1915), a collection of free-verse epitaphs spoken as monologues by the inhabitants of a small provincial town, successfully staged in 1963.

Masters, William Howell (1915–   ) US physician, noted for his studies of human sexual behaviour using volunteer subjects under laboratory conditions. Masters and his colleague, the psychologist **Virginia Eshelman Johnson** (1925–   ), measured physiological changes associated with sex and published their findings in *Human Sexual Responses* (1966). Although criticized, their work established a body of knowledge that is useful in such areas as marriage guidance.

mastic An evergreen shrub, *Pistacia lentiscus*, up to 1.8 m high, native to the Mediterranean region. An aromatic yellowish-green resin is obtained from the bark and used to make varnishes for coating metals and paintings and as an adhesive. Family: *Anacardiaceae*. The name is also applied to other resin-yielding trees, including the related American mastic (*Schinus molle*) and *Sideroxylon mastichodendron* (family: *Sapotaceae*).

mastiff An ancient Eurasian breed of large dog long used as a guard dog and for bull- and bear-baiting. It is powerfully built with a large head and a short deep muzzle. The short smooth coat may be apricot, silver, or fawn; the muzzle, ears, and nose are black. Height: 76 cm (dogs); 69 cm (bitches). *See also* bull mastiff.

mastodon An extinct elephant that originated in Africa 34 million years ago and spread throughout Europe, Asia, and America. Early mastodons were small and had two pairs of tusks; later forms were larger and more elephant-like. The American mastodons survived until about 8000 years ago and were painted in hunting scenes by early man.

mastoid bone A nipple-shaped process of the temporal bone of the skull, situated behind the ear and containing many air spaces. Infection of the middle ear may spread through these spaces to affect the mastoid bone. Formerly treated surgically, this infection is now readily cured with antibiotics.

Mastroianni, Marcello (1924–) Italian actor. He became one of the best-known international film stars of the 1960s, a representative European leading man. He appeared in Visconti's *White Nights* (1957), Fellini's *La dolce vita* (1960), and Antonioni's *La notte* (1961).

Matabeleland An area in W Zimbabwe, between the Limpopo and Zambezi Rivers. It was named after the Ndebele, a tribe that was driven across the Limpopo by the Voortrekkers in 1837. Consisting chiefly of extensive plains, the area has important gold deposits. Area: 181 605 sq km (70 118 sq mi).

Matadi 5 50S 13 32E The chief port in Zaïre, on the Zaïre River. It was founded in 1879 by *Stanley. It has one of central Africa's largest harbours and is accessible to oceangoing vessels. Population (1976 est): 162 396.

Mata Hari (Margaretha Geertruida Zelle; 1876–1917) Dutch courtesan and secret agent. She lived in Indonesia with her husband, a Dutch colonial officer, from 1897 to 1902. She became a professional dancer in Paris in 1905 and probably worked for both French and German intelligence services. She was executed by the French in 1917.

matamata. *See* snake-necked turtle.

Matamoros 25 50N 97 31W A city in N Mexico, on the Rio Grande on the US border. It is the manufacturing centre for a region producing cotton and sugar cane and is an important point of entry for US tourists. Population (1980 est): 238 840.

Matanzas 23 04N 81 35W A port in Cuba, on Mantanzas Bay on the N coast. Its chief export is sugar. It is also a popular tourist centre. Population (1981): 421 272.

Matapan, Cape (Modern Greek name: Ákra Taínaron) 36 23N 22 29E The southernmost point of mainland Greece, off which (March, 1941) the British Mediterranean fleet scored a decisive victory over the Italians during World War II.

matches Small lengths of wood, cardboard, etc., tipped with an ignitable substance. The friction match was invented in 1816 (by Dérosne). Modern strike-anywhere matches are usually tipped with phosphorus sesquisulphide, potassium chlorate, and zinc oxide. Safety matches, invented in 1844, have their ignitable substances divided between the tip and a special striking surface. Usually the surface contains red phosphorus and the tip a mixture of antimony sulphide and such oxidizing agents as potassium chlorate and manganese dioxide.

matchlock. *See* musket.

maté The dried leaves of a *holly shrub or tree, *Ilex paraguariensis*, native to Paraguay and Brazil. They are roasted, powdered, and infused with water to make the stimulating greenish tealike beverage, popular in many South American countries.

materialism In classical metaphysics, materialism is the doctrine of *Democritus and *Leucippus that everything in the universe is matter or stuff. All events were explicable in terms of the movements and alterations initiated by this matter. By contrast *Plato sought to establish the existence of some incorporeal objects, called by him Forms. *Aristotle also did not confine himself to a completely materialist explanation of the world, believing that the soul was immaterial. His doctrines nevertheless led to more refined materialistic views than those of the Presocratics, but *Hobbes' uncompromising materialism owed nothing to Aristotle. *Marx's economic materialism, whereby human actions and beliefs are explained solely in terms of economic forces was developed by *Lenin in *dialectical materialism. Some recent materialist philosophers studying the body-mind relationship have reduced thought to (physical) neural processes. In all these senses materialism is a metaphysical doctrine. More popularly, the term has also been used to signify worldly outlooks and behaviour.

mathematics The logical study of numerical and spatial relationships. It is usually divided into pure and applied mathematics. In pure mathematics the general theoretical principles are studied, often in abstract. Its branches are *arithmetic, *algebra, *calculus, *geometry, and *trigonometry. Some form of mathematical calculation is an indispensable part of all financial transactions and all measurements. The ancient Egyptians, Sumerians, and Chinese were all using a form of *abacus to carry out these calculations for thousands of years before the Christian era. But it was not until the 9th century AD that *al-Khwarizmi introduced the idea of writing down calculations instead of carrying them out on an abacus. The Venetian mathematicians of the 11th and 12th centuries were largely responsible for the introduction of these methods to the West; indeed it was they who showed that commercial calculations based on algorisms (a word derived from al-Khwarizmi's name) were superior to those performed on an abacus. However, the application of mathematics to the physical sciences (including astronomy) was largely a 16th-century development inspired by *Galileo. It was from this development that applied mathematics grew. It is now largely concerned with *mechanics and *statistics. *See also* new maths.

Mathura 27 30N 77 42E A city in India, in Uttar Pradesh on the River Jumna. A pilgrimage centre, it is the traditional birthplace of the Hindu god, Krishna. Population (1981): 159 458.

Matilda (*or* Maud; 1102–67) The daughter of Henry I of England, who designated her his heir. On his death (1135), his nephew Stephen, seized the throne and Matilda invaded England (1139) inaugurating a period of inconclusive civil war. She and her second husband Geoffrey, Duke of Anjou (1113–51), captured Normandy and in 1152 the Treaty of Wallingford recognized her son Henry as Stephen's heir. Her first husband was Emperor *Henry V (d. 1125).

Matisse, Henri (1869–1954) French painter and sculptor. Having abandoned his legal studies he became a pupil of the painter Gustave *Moreau in the 1890s. Matisse initiated *fauvism in the early 1900s with his boldly patterned and vibrantly coloured still lifes, portraits, and nudes, notably the controversial *Woman with the Hat* (1905). He was the only artist to continue fauvist principles after the development of *cubism. He was also inspired by Islamic art. By 1909 he had achieved worldwide recognition and he remained inventive until his death, a stained glass design for the Dominican chapel at Vence (S France) being among his last works.

Matlock 53 08N 1 32W A town in England, in Derbyshire on the River Derwent. Nearby Matlock Bath was a noted spa during Victorian times. Population (1981): 20 750.

Mato Grosso A plateau area in SW central Brazil. It extends across the states of Mato Grosso and Goias, separating the Amazon and Plata river systems. Its height varies between about 100 m (328 ft) and 900 m (2953 ft). It is an important cattle-raising area.

Matopo Hills A range of hills in SW Zimbabwe, S of Bulawayo. Cecil Rhodes is buried here at a point named World's View.

$$\begin{pmatrix} a & b \\ c & d \\ e & f \end{pmatrix} + \begin{pmatrix} p & q \\ r & s \\ t & u \end{pmatrix} = \begin{pmatrix} a+p & b+q \\ c+r & d+s \\ e+t & f+u \end{pmatrix} \quad \textbf{addition}$$

$$k \times \begin{pmatrix} a & b \\ c & d \\ e & f \end{pmatrix} = \begin{pmatrix} ka & kb \\ kc & kd \\ ke & kf \end{pmatrix} \quad \textbf{multiplication by a constant}$$

$$\begin{pmatrix} a & b \\ c & d \\ e & f \end{pmatrix} \times \begin{pmatrix} p & q & r \\ s & t & u \end{pmatrix} =$$

matrix multiplication

$$\begin{pmatrix} (ap+bs) & (aq+bt) & (ar+bu) \\ (cp+ds) & (cq+dt) & (cr+du) \\ (ep+fs) & (eq+ft) & (er+fu) \end{pmatrix}$$

the **determinant** of $\begin{pmatrix} a & b \\ c & d \end{pmatrix} = \begin{vmatrix} a & b \\ c & d \end{vmatrix} = ad - bc$

MATRIX *Examples of matrix algebra.*

matrix A set of numbers, called elements, arranged in rows and columns to form a rectangular array. It is used to assist in the solution of certain mathematical problems. The *commutative, *associative, and *distributive laws of matrix arithmetic and algebra are different from those of ordinary arithmetic. The **determinant** of a square matrix is a number, or algebraic expression, that is obtained by multiplication and addition of the elements in a specified way. It has properties that are useful for simplifying and solving sets of simultaneous equations. Single column matrices may represent *vectors, enabling them to be handled algebraically and processed by computer.

Ma-tsu. *See* Mazu.

Matsuo Basho (Matsuo Munefusa; 1644-94) Japanese poet. Born near Kyoto, he moved to Edo (Tokyo) in 1667 and in 1680 became a recluse. He transformed the traditional 17-syllable lyric verse form, the haiku, introducing the characteristic concentrated elliptical imagery and the philosophical spirit of *Zen Buddhism. He also wrote travel diaries, of which *The Narrow Road to the Deep North* (1694) is outstanding.

Matsuyama 33 50N 132 47E A port in Japan, in NW Shikoku on the Inland Sea. It is an agricultural and industrial centre, with a university (1949). Population (1980): 402 000.

Matteotti, Giacomo (1885-1924) Italian Socialist politician, who was assassinated by fascists after denouncing their party in the Chamber of Deputies. His murder almost

brought the fall of Mussolini's government. Three of his assassins were imprisoned following the reopening of the case after World War II.

Matterhorn (French name: Mont Cervin; Italian name: Monte Cervino) 45 59N 7 39E A mountain in Europe, on the Swiss-Italian border in the Alps near Zermatt. First climbed in 1865 by the British mountaineer, Edward Whymper, it is conspicuous because of its striking pyramidal shape. Height: 4478 m (14 692 ft).

Matthew, St In the New Testament, one of the 12 *Apostles. He was a tax collector until he became a follower of Jesus. According to tradition, he preached in Judaea, Ethiopia, and Persia and suffered martyrdom. Feast day: 21 Sept. Emblem: a man with wings. **The Gospel according to St Matthew,** is generally believed to have been written sometime after St Mark's Gospel, from which it drew material. It is a narrative of the life and ministry of Jesus that seeks to convince the Jews that he is the Messiah predicted by the Old Testament. It contains the Sermon on the Mount (chapters 5-7).

Matthew Paris (c. 1200-59) English chronicler. He became a monk of the Benedictine abbey of St Albans in 1217 and was a member of the court of Henry III. His careful coverage of the years 1235-59 form the second part of his major work, the *Chronica majora*, a history of the world from the Creation to 1259.

Matthews, Sir Stanley (1915-) British Association footballer, who played for Stoke City (1931-47; 1961-65), Blackpool (1947-61), and England, for which he played 54 times. A skilful winger, he played in 886 first-class matches, his last at the age of 50.

Matthias (1557-1619) Holy Roman Emperor (1612-19). He became King of Hungary (1608) and of Bohemia (1611) following revolts against his brother Rudolph II and was in turn forced to cede these crowns to Ferdinand of Styria (later Ferdinand II) in 1618 and 1617 respectively. Matthias then tried unsuccessfully to moderate Ferdinand's harsh policies against the Bohemian Protestants.

Matthias I Corvinus (?1443-90) King of Hungary (1458-90). The son of János Hunyadi, Matthias brought Hungary to a peak of greatness before its fall in 1526 to the Turks. His reforms embraced administration, law, and the army. He also imposed high taxes, which greatly benefited the treasury but precipitated revolts. His foreign policy was dominated by conflict with Emperor *Frederick III and in 1485 Matthias occupied Vienna. He also added Bosnia, Moravia, and Silesia to his domains but failed in his efforts to take Bohemia. A great patron of Renaissance art and scholarship, Matthias founded the great Corvina library.

Mauchly, John W. *See* Eckert, John Presper.

Maud. *See* Matilda.

Maudslay, Henry (1771-1831) British engineer, who invented the metal lathe. After working under Joseph *Bramah, Maudslay established his own machine-tools business. His other inventions include the slide rule and a method of desalinating seawater. He also designed marine engines.

Maugham, W(illiam) Somerset (1874-1965) British novelist and dramatist. Born in Paris, he studied and qualified in medicine but abandoned it after the success of his first novel, *Liza of Lambeth* (1896). His later fiction includes *Of Human Bondage* (1915), *The Moon and Sixpence* (1919), *Cakes and Ale* (1930), and *The Razor's Edge* (1944). He wrote popular comedies of manners, such as *The Circle* (1921), and many short stories with Far Eastern or other exotic settings. From 1928 he lived in the South of France. His nephew **Robin Maugham** (1916-81) became famous with a controversial first novel, *The Servant* (1948), which was filmed in 1965. His later novels, often with homosexual themes, include *The Last Encounter* (1972) and *Lovers in Exile* (1977).

Mau Mau A secret organization among the Kikuyu people of Kenya, which led a revolt (1952–57) against the British colonial government. Secret oaths were administered to participants, who committed appalling atrocities against Whites and un-cooperating Blacks. Jomo *Kenyatta was thought to be a Mau Mau leader and was imprisoned from 1953 to 1961.

Maundy Thursday The Thursday before *Good Friday. Its name derives from Latin *mandatum*, commandment, and its traditional foot-washing and almsgiving ceremonies originated at the Last Supper, when Christ washed the disciples' feet and commanded them to follow his example (John 13). The British sovereign's distribution of special Maundy money in Westminster Abbey and other sites is a survival of these rites.

Maupassant, Guy de (1850–93) French short-story writer and novelist. He was introduced into literary circles by Flaubert, his literary mentor, met Zola, and joined his group of naturalist writers (*see* Naturalism). Following the phenomenal success of the first story he published under his own name, "Boule de Suif" (1880), he wrote about 300 short stories and 6 novels, including *Une Vie* (1883) and *Bel-Ami* (1885). He suffered from syphilis and died in an asylum.

Maupertuis, Pierre Louis Moreau de (1698–1759) French mathematician, best known for his principle of least action, by which the paths of moving bodies, rays of light, etc., are such that the action (momentum multiplied by distance) is a minimum. A quarrelsome and dislikeable man, Maupertuis argued with *Voltaire over his principle and became involved with the controversy between *Newton and *Leïbniz over who first discovered the calculus.

Mauretania The coastal area N of the Atlas Mountains in ancient N Africa. Inhabited by Moorish tribes, who retained their independence while permitting settlements of Phoenician traders and later Italian colonists, Mauretania was incorporated in the Roman Empire in 40 AD. It was conquered by the Muslims in the 7th century. *See also* Moors.

Mauriac, François (1885–1970) French novelist. He was born into a middle-class Roman Catholic family near Bordeaux. His novels, which include *Le Désert de l'amour* (1925), *Thérèse Desqueyroux* (1927), and *Le Noeud de vipères* (1933), characteristically portray the conflict between worldly passions and religion in provincial marital and family relationships. He also wrote plays and polemical criticism and journalism. He won the Nobel Prize in 1952.

Maurice of Nassau (1567–1625) Stadholder (chief magistrate) of the United Provinces of the Netherlands (1584–1625), succeeding his father William the Silent. A great military leader and a master of siege warfare, Maurice instituted army reforms that enabled the United Provinces to withstand Spanish attempts to destroy the newly established Protestant republic (*see* Revolt of the Netherlands). He failed to draw the Roman Catholic provinces of the S into the union and was forced to negotiate a 12-year truce with Spain in 1609. His career was marred by the arrest and execution of his colleague *Oldenbarnevelt in 1619.

Mauritania, Islamic Republic of (French name: Mauritanie; Arabic name: Muritaniyah) A country in West Africa, with a coastline on the Atlantic Ocean. The N part is desert while the S is mainly fertile. Most of the inhabitants are Arabs and Berbers with a Negro population, mainly Fulani, in the S. *Economy*: chiefly agricultural. Livestock, especially cattle, are particularly important and the main crops are millet, sorghum, beans, and rice. All agriculture was severely affected by the droughts of the late 1960s and early 1970s. Fishing is important and fish processing is one of the main industries. Iron ore and copper are exploited and, together with dried and salt fish, are now the main exports. *History*: dominated by Muslim Berber tribes from about 100 AD, the coast was visited by the Portuguese in the 15th century and by the Dutch, English, and French in the

17th century. The area became a French protectorate in 1903 and a colony in 1920. It achieved internal self-government within the French Community in 1958 and became fully independent in 1960 with Mokhtar Ould Daddah (1924–) as its first president. It moved from French to Arab ties in international relations, joining the Arab League and the Arab Common Market. In 1976, with Morocco, it took over Western Sahara, part of the former Spanish Sahara territories, prompting guerrilla attacks from the Polisario, the Western Saharan independence movement. In 1979 Mauritania withdrew from all but the southern tip of Western Sahara. In 1978 Daddah was overthrown and Lt Col Mustapha Ould Mohamed Salek (1935–) became president until his resignation in 1979. He was succeeded by Lt Col Khouna Ould Kaydalla (1940–), who was ousted in a coup in 1984. Prime minister: Moäuya Ould Sidi-Ahmad Iaya. Official language: French; Arabic, known as Hassaniya, is widely spoken. Official religion: Islam. Official currency: ougiya of 5 khoums. Area: 1 030 700 sq km (397 850 sq mi). Population (1983 est): 1 591 000. Capital and main port: Nouakchott.

Mauritius, State of An island country in the Indian Ocean, about 800 km (500 mi) to the E of Madagascar. It is mainly hilly and subject to tropical cyclones, which cause severe damage. Dependencies are the Agalega and St Brandon Islands. The majority of the population are of Indian descent, with European, African, and mixed minorities. *Economy*: sugar production plays an important role although manufacturing now provides over 50% of its total exports. Fishing is being developed, as well as subsistence agriculture and tourism, in an effort to reduce unemployment. *History*: visited by the Arabs in the 10th century and by the Portuguese in the 16th century, the island was settled by the Dutch in 1598. In 1715 it came under French rule as Île de France and in 1814 it was ceded to Britain. After riots in 1968 it became independent within the British Commonwealth, with Dr Sir Seewoosagur Ramgoolam (1900–85) as its first prime minister. In the 1970s there was considerable political unrest. Rangoolam was ousted in the 1982 elections and succeeded by Anerood Jugnauth. Official languages: English and French; Creole is widely spoken. Official currency: Mauritius rupee of 100 cents. Area: 1843 sq km (720 sq mi). Population (1980 est): 969 522. Capital and main port: Port Louis.

Maurois, André (Émile Herzog; 1885–1967) French biographer, novelist, and critic. He served in the British army in World War I and had a lifelong affection for English culture. He wrote several novels and short stories but is best known for his biographical studies of Shelley (*Ariel*, 1923), Disraeli (1927), Byron (1930), Voltaire (1935), Chateaubriand (1937), Proust (1949), and Hugo (1954).

Maurras, Charles (1868–1952) French political theorist and essayist. In 1899 he helped found L'Action Française, a political group dedicated to extreme monarchist, antisemitic, and Roman Catholic principles (although condemned and excommunicated by the Church). *Au signe de Flore* (1931) contains his memoirs of his political activities. After World War II, during which he supported the government of Pétain, he was condemned to life imprisonment, but was released because of ill health shortly before his death.

Mauser rifle The first successful metallic-cartridge breech-loading rifle, designed by Paul von Mauser (1838–1914) in 1868. The Model-98 rifle and Model-98a/b carbine were standard in the German infantry in World War I; the Model-98k (1938) was standard in World War II.

Mausoleum of Halicarnassus An ancient Greek tomb built (363–361 BC) as a monument to Mausolus of Caria by his widow, *Artemisia. The building, designed by Pythius, was probably a standard temple form with adorning sculptures, fragments of which are in the British Museum, but raised on a high base and with a stepped pyramid-like roof. It was one of the *Seven Wonders of the World.

Maxim, Sir Hiram Stevens (1840–1916) British inventor, born in the USA, who in 1884 invented the first fully automatic *machine gun. The Maxim gun led him to discover cordite, which being smokeless increased the gun's efficiency. He also discovered a method of manufacturing carbon filaments, which were then being used in light bulbs.

Maximilian (1832–67) Emperor of Mexico (1864–67). Maximilian, the brother of Emperor Francis Joseph I, was the Archduke of Austria. He was offered the Mexican Crown by France following its invasion of Mexico in 1863. He had no popular support and when in 1867 the French army withdrew under US pressure Maximilian was captured by the forces of Benito *Juarez and executed.

Maximilian I (1459–1519) Holy Roman Emperor (1493–1519). His ambition to rule all W Europe led him into unsuccessful wars, especially with France. However, his marriage (1477) to Mary of Burgundy (1457–82), and that of his son Philip the Handsome to Joanna the Mad of Castile, provided his grandson *Charles V with a vast empire.

Maximilian I (1756–1825) King of Bavaria (1806–25); formerly Elector of Bavaria (1799–1806) as Maximilian IV Joseph. In 1799 he joined the second coalition against France (see Revolutionary and Napoleonic Wars) but in 1801 negotiated peace. Until abandoning the French alliance in 1813 Maximilian gave military aid to Napoleon, acquiring in return extensive new territories. His government was noted for its liberalism.

maxwell The unit of magnetic flux in the *c.g.s. system equal to the flux through one square centimetre perpendicular to a field of one gauss. Named after James Clerk *Maxwell.

Maxwell, James Clerk (1831–79) Scottish physicist, who achieved the unification of electricity, magnetism, and light into one set of equations (known as **Maxwell's equations**). These equations, first published in their final form in 1873, enabled Faraday's lines of force to be treated mathematically by introducing the concept of the electromagnetic field. Maxwell observed that the field radiated outwards from an oscillating electric charge at the speed of light, which led him to identify light as a form of electromagnetic radiation. Maxwell also made important advances in the kinetic theory of gases, by introducing Maxwell-Boltzmann statistics developed independently by *Boltzmann). See also Maxwell's demon.

Maxwell, Robert (Robert Hoch; 1923–) British publisher, born in Czechoslovakia. He founded Pergamon Press in 1948 and was a Labour MP from 1964 to 1970. Although declared unfit to run his company in 1971, he became a leading force in British publishing. As chairman of the Mirror Group Newspapers, he controls several national newspapers; he also has an interest in several top football clubs.

Maxwell's demon A hypothetical creature, postulated by *Maxwell in 1871 as a theoretical construct to disprove the second law of *thermodynamics. The demon was visualized as being able to separate a gas into a hot region and a cold region by opening and closing a shutter to allow only fast-moving molecules to enter the hot region. No violation of the second law on these or any other grounds has ever been observed.

may. See hawthorn.

maya (Sanskrit: illusion) In the Vedas maya is the magic power of a god or spirit. In the *Upanishads, maya is illusion or the mundane world, which is ultimately unreal because of its impermanence. Elsewhere maya is seen as the play of *Brahma, who splits himself into innumerable parts, thereby forgetting himself.

Maya An American Indian people of Yucatán (Mexico) Guatemala, and Belize. There are a number of languages in the Totonac-Mayan language family (see Mesoamerican languages). Today the Maya live mainly in farming villages and are nominally Roman Catholic, but between 300 and 900 AD they had established an advanced civilization. They developed hieroglyphic writing and had considerable knowledge of astronomy and mathematics. They devised a precise calendar, which regulated an elaborate ritual and ceremonial life centred on such sites as *Chichén Itzá, *Tikal, Copan, and Palenque, where large pyramid temples were constructed for the worship of the sun, moon, and rain gods. After 900 the influence of the *Toltecs led to a mixed Toltec-Maya culture in cities such as Mayapan.

MAYA *The Temple of the Sorcerer at Uxmal in Yucatán (Mexico).*

Mayagüez 18 13N 67 09W A port in W Puerto Rico, in the West Indies. It has an important needlework industry; other manufactures include beer, rum, and soap. An experimental station operated here by the US Department of Agriculture has possibly the largest tropical-plant collection in the W hemisphere. Population (1980 est): 95 886.

Mayakovskii, Vladimir (1893–1930) Russian poet. He was a leading member of the futurist movement (see futurism) and a prolific propagandist for Bolshevism. Revolutionary politics and his frustrated private life are the main themes of his poetry, which is characterized by aggressive vitality and experimentation. He also wrote two satirical dramas, *The Bedbug* (1929) and *The Bath-House* (1930). He committed suicide.

May Day May 1, traditionally a festival associated with spring fertility rites, celebrated in Britain by such customs as dancing round the Maypole. See also Labour Day.

Mayence. See Mainz.

Mayer, Julius Robert von (1814–78) German physicist, who (in 1842) was the first to calculate the mechanical equivalent of heat and formulated a form of the law of conservation of energy. However, his work went virtually unrecognized; *Joule received credit for the first achievement and *Helmholtz for the second.

Mayer, Louis B. (1885–1957) US film producer, born in Russia. He helped to create the Hollywood star system. With Samuel *Goldwyn in 1924 he founded the Metro-Goldwyn-Mayer (MGM) production company, whose films were largely determined by his personal taste for lavish but uncontroversial entertainment. He retired in 1951.

Mayer, Sir Robert (1879-1985) German-born British businessman and patron of music. He founded the Robert Mayer Concerts for Children.

Mayfair A fashionable residential district in the Greater London borough of the City of Westminster. It was named after the annual fair held from the 16th century until 1809.

Mayflower The ship that carried the *Pilgrim Fathers to America. They had intended to settle in Virginia but the *Mayflower* was blown off course and reached Plymouth (Massachusetts) in December, 1620. There, the Pilgrims drew up the **Mayflower Compact**, which based their government on the will of the colonists rather than the English Crown.

mayfly A slender □insect of the order *Ephemeroptera* (1500 species), found near fresh water. Up to 40 mm long, mayflies are usually brown or yellow with two unequal pairs of membranous wings. The adults do not feed and only live long enough to mate and lay eggs. The aquatic nymphs feed on plant debris and algae.

May Fourth Movement (1917-21) A Chinese movement for social and intellectual reform that culminated in a student demonstration in Peking on 4 May, 1919, against government acceptance of the allocation of Chinese territory to Japan by the Paris Peace Conference following World War I. The movement aimed to throw off foreign dominance and to build a new modern China.

Mayhew, Henry (1812-87) British journalist. His best-known work is *London Labour and the London Poor* (4 vols, 1851-62), a combination of vivid reportage and amateur social and economic analysis. He was a founder of *Punch* in 1841 and the author of many plays and novels.

Mayo (Irish name: Contae Mhuigheo) A county in the W Republic of Ireland, in Connacht bordering on the Atlantic Ocean. Mountainous in the W it contains several large lakes. Cattle, sheep, and pigs are raised and potatoes and oats are grown. Area: 5397 sq km (2084 sq mi). Population (1981): 114 766. County town: Castlebar.

Mayo A family of US physicians, who pioneered the concept of group practice and established the Mayo Clinic in Rochester, Minnesota, along these lines. The family included **William Worrall Mayo** (1819-1911), his sons **William James Mayo** (1861-1939) and **Charles Horace Mayo** (1865-1939), and Charles' son **Charles William Mayo** (1898-1968). The Mayos also made a number of contributions to medical research.

mayor The chief officer of a municipal council. In the UK a mayor or mayoress is the chairman or chairwoman of a district council having *borough status. The mayor's counterpart in Scotland is called a provost. The mayor of the City of London (*see* City of London, Corporation of the) and certain other cities is called a **Lord Mayor** (Lord Provost in Scotland). In the City of London he presides over the three courts that comprise the Corporation and attends all civic functions:

mayor of the palace An officer of the royal household and later a viceroy appointed by the Merovingian kings of the early middle ages. The most famous were *Pepin of Herstel and his grandson *Pepin the Short, who overthrew the Merovingians and founded the Carolingian dynasty.

Mayotte An island in the W Indian Ocean, in the Comoro Islands group. After the other islands declared independence from France (1975), Mayotte decided by a referendum to remain a French territory. Area: 374 sq km (144 sq mi). Population (1984 est): 56 000. Chief town: Dzaoudzi.

maypole dance A folk dance of ancient origin, traditionally performed on 1 May as part of the May Day festival. Participants circle round a tall pole, often adorned with ribbons, which they weave into patterns.

Mazarin, Jules, Cardinal (1602-61) French statesman. A papal diplomat, he rose to prominence as a protégé of Cardinal de Richelieu and shortly after Richelieu's death (1642) became chief adviser to the regent Anne of Austria, Louis XIV's mother. The era of Mazarin witnessed a great expansion in the power of the monarchy, achieved largely through his suppression of rebellious aristocrats during the *Fronde. Abroad, he enhanced French supremacy in Europe by the Treaties of *Westphalia (1648) and the *Pyrenees (1659).

Mazatlán 23 11N 106 25W A port and resort in W Mexico, on the Gulf of California. The chief industries are textiles manufacture and sugar refining; exports include tobacco and minerals. Population (1980): 249 988.

Mazu (*or* Ma-tsu) 26 10N 119 59E A Taiwanese island in the East China Sea. It is near the Chinese mainland, from which it was bombed in 1958, causing an international incident. Area: 44 sq km (17 sq mi). Population (1982 est): 8199.

Mazurian Lakes Several hundred lakes in NE Poland, around which Germany inflicted two heavy defeats on the Russians in 1914 and 1915.

Mazzini, Giuseppe (1805-72) Italian patriot, who was a leader of the movement for Italian unification (*see* Risorgimento). Forced to live mostly in exile in France, Switzerland, and England, he planned with his *Young Italy movement a rising in Piedmont and an invasion of Savoy in the 1830s but both failed. Mazzini was in Italy during the Revolutions of 1848 in Milan, Piedmont, Tuscany, and Rome, where he became head of a short-lived Roman republic. Although a united kingdom of Italy was finally established in 1861, he never realized his ideal of an Italian republic.

Mbabane 26 30S 31 30E The capital of Swaziland, in the Mdimba Mountains. It was founded in the late 19th century. Tourism is important and nearby is a large iron mine. Population (1984 est): 23 109.

MBE. *See* Order of the British Empire.

Mbini. *See* Equatorial Guinea, Republic of.

Mboya, Tom (1930-69) Kenyan politician. Mboya was from the Luo tribe and was an active trades unionist and general secretary of the Kenyan Federation of Labour. He was a founder member and general secretary (1960-64) of the Kenya African National Union and after the achievement of independence became, under Kenyatta, minister of justice (1963) and later minister of economic planning and development (1964-69). He was assassinated.

Mbuji-Mayi (name until 1966: Bakwanga) 6 10S 23 39E A city in central Zaïre. Diamonds were discovered here in 1909 and the region now produces about 75% of the world's industrial diamonds. Population (1976 est): 382 632.

Mc-. Names beginning Mc are listed under Mac.

MCC. *See* Marylebone Cricket Club.

mead An alcoholic drink of fermented honey and water. The honey is dissolved in water and boiled with spices. When cool, after brewer's yeast has been added, the mead ferments in barrel. It should be stored in bottle for at least six months before serving. It was drunk in Anglo-Saxon England, and called hydromel, by the ancient Romans.

Mead, Margaret (1901-78) US anthropologist. Margaret Mead's anthropological work centred on the study of child rearing and the family. Her field work was done in New Guinea, Polynesia, and other Pacific islands. Her books include *Coming of Age in Samoa* (1929), *Sex and Temperament in Three Primitive Societies* (1935), and *Male and Female* (1949). She also wrote on education, science, and culture. A significant amount of her work was in the field of mental health.

Meade, Richard (1938-) British three-day-event horse rider. He won gold medals in the 1968 and 1972 Olympic Games and retired in 1986.

meadowsweet A perennial herb, *Filipendula* (or *Spiraea*) *ulmaria*, common in damp places throughout temperate Eurasia. 60-120 cm high, it has large compound leaves, with

8-20 pairs of toothed leaflets and fluffy terminal clusters of small, creamy-white fragrant flowers, with long stamens. An oil distilled from the flower buds is used in perfumes. Family: *Rosaceae*.

Meads, Colin Earl (1935-) New Zealand Rugby Union footballer, who played for King Country and the All Blacks. A huge lock forward, he won a record 55 New Zealand caps (1957-71).

mealworm. *See* darkling beetle.

mealybug An insect of the worldwide family *Pseudococcidae*, closely related to the *scale insects. The female is covered with a white sticky powder, which may be extended into filaments. The species *Pseudococcus citri* is a serious pest of citrus trees in America.

mean. *See* average.

meander A sinuous curve in a river. The velocity of flow in a meandering river is highest on the outside of the meander bends; erosion is concentrated here with deposition occurring on the inside of the bend. The meander will become increasingly looped until the river eventually breaks through its narrow neck creating an oxbow *lake.

mean free path The average distance travelled by a molecule between successive collisions with other molecules. According to the *kinetic theory, the mean free path is directly proportional to the viscosity of the substance and inversely proportional to the average velocity of the molecules.

mean life (*or* lifetime) The average time for which a radioactive isotope, elementary particle, or other unstable state exists before decaying. *See* radioactivity.

means test An inquiry into a person's resources to establish his entitlement to a welfare benefit. In the UK between 1931 and 1934 a means-tested benefit was paid to the long-term unemployed who had exhausted their *National Insurance rights. Introduced as an economy measure and operated by local councils, it was discontinued because of its unpopularity. Means tests are still applied in the UK to certain benefits, e.g. supplementary benefit, legal aid, and students' maintenance grants. Their defenders claim that they lower the cost of a benefit, while their opponents assert that they are expensive to apply, represent an invasion of privacy, and stigmatize a section of the population.

measles A highly infectious viral disease, which usually affects children. After an incubation period of about two weeks the child becomes irritable and fevered and has a running nose and inflamed eyes. Two or three days later a rash appears on the head and face and spreads over the body. Usually the child recovers after a week, but sometimes pneumonia or encephalitis may develop. There is no specific treatment, but vaccine has reduced the incidence of the disease. *Compare* German measles.

Meath (Irish name: Contae na Midhe) A county in the E Republic of Ireland, in Leinster bordering on the Irish Sea. Consisting chiefly of fertile glacial drifts it is important for agriculture; cattle are fattened and oats and potatoes grown. Area: 2338 sq km (903 sq mi). Population (1981): 95 419. County town: Trim.

Meaux 48 58N 2 54E A town in N France, in the Seine-et-Marne department on the River Marne. The commercial and industrial centre of the Brie region, it supplies Paris with agricultural produce. Population (1982): 45 873.

Mecca (Arabic name: Makkah) 21 26N 39 49E A city in W Saudi Arabia, in a narrow valley surrounded by barren hills. Mecca and Riyadh are joint capitals of the kingdom, but it is famous as the holiest Muslim city, which every Muslim is expected to visit at least once in his lifetime; nonbelievers are not allowed to enter the city. It has been a holy city since ancient times, but was also the birthplace of Mohammed (c. 570). Inside the court of the al-Haram Mosque in the centre of the city are located the chief shrines: the Kabaa (a small windowless building) and the sacred well

MECCA *The court of the Al-Haram Mosque in the centre of the city, showing the black stone of the Kabaa.*

of Zamzam. In November, 1979, the al-Haram Mosque was seized by armed militants, who held a number of worshippers hostage before being overpowered by the military forces. Population (1980 est): 550 000.

mechanical advantage The ratio of the force output of a machine to the force input, i.e. the ratio of load to effort. It is useful only as an analysis of simple machines, such as levers, pulleys, jacks, etc., as no account of friction is taken. The **velocity ratio** of the machine is the distance moved by the effort divided by the distance moved by the load; the **mechanical efficiency** of a machine is the ratio of its mechanical advantage to its velocity ratio.

mechanical engineering The branch of *engineering concerned with the application of scientific knowledge to dynamical structures and systems, rather than the static structures of civil engineering. This branch encompasses the design, manufacture, and maintenance of machines of all kinds, engines, vehicles, and many aspects of industrial manufacturing. The subject has numerous specialized subdivisions, including *aeronautics, motor engineering, machine-tool design, etc. In the UK the professional body is the Institute of Mechanical Engineers.

mechanics The study of the motion of bodies and systems and the forces acting on them. The subject is traditionally divided into statics, the study of bodies in equilibrium, and dynamics, the study of forces that affect the motion of bodies. Dynamics is further divided into kinetics, the effects of forces and their moments on motion, and kinematics, the study of velocity, acceleration, etc., without regard to the forces causing them. Aristotelian (*see* Aristotle) mechanics was based on the erroneous concept that a force is required to maintain motion. *Newtonian mechanics recognizes that once a body is moving a force is required to stop it but no force is needed to keep it moving. Newtonian mechanics is the mechanics of classical systems, i.e. large-scale systems moving at relatively low velocities. The more general relativistic mechanics is also applicable to systems moving at speeds comparable to that of light (it reduces to Newtonian mechanics at velocities that are small compared to that of light). *Fluid mechanics is the application of mechanical principles to fluids, both stationary (hydrostatics) and flowing (hydrodynamics).

Mechelen (French name: Malines; English name: Mechlin) 51 02N 4 29E A town in N Belgium, on the River Ryle. Its 12th-century cathedral contains an altarpiece by

Van Eyck and there are Rubens masterpieces in two other churches. Once famous for Mechlin lace, industries now include textiles and tinned vegetables. Population (1981 est): 77 377.

Mechnikov, Ilya. *See* Metchnikov, Ilya.

Mecklenberg A former German state on the SW Baltic coast, now the Rostock, Schwerin, and Neubrandenburg districts of East Germany. Thinly populated, with many lakes and forests, Mecklenberg was frequently partitioned until its permanent division in 1701 into the Duchies of Mecklenberg-Schwerin and Mecklenberg-Strelitz. After the Congress of Vienna in 1815, both duchies formed part of the German Confederation under Austria's leadership, but in 1866 joined Prussia's North German Confederation; thereafter Mecklenberg's history is linked with Prussia's.

medals Pieces of metal fashioned as coins or crosses to commemorate individuals or special occasions, or awarded in recognition of service to a state or institution. During the Renaissance personal medals, usually bearing a portrait of the owner with an emblem and motto on the reverse, achieved high artistic standards. *Pisanello, *Dürer, and *Cellini were notable medallists. Military medals multiplied in Britain during the imperialist expansion of the 18th and 19th centuries. They usually portray the sovereign's head or insignia of the awarding body, bear a commemorative legend, and are worn suspended on a special ribbon. Many are individual rewards for bravery, such as the *Victoria Cross and *George Cross, but some are general medals to commemorate campaigns and state occasions, such as coronations.

Medan 03 35N 98 39E A city in Indonesia, in N Sumatra. Its state and Islamic universities were established in 1952. An agricultural and trade centre that grew around tobacco plantations, it has a seaport (Belawan). Population (1980): 1 378 955.

Medawar, Sir Peter Brian (1915-87) British immunologist, noted for his investigation of the development of the immune system in embryonic and young animals, including the phenomenon of acquired immunological tolerance to foreign tissue grafts. He also showed how genetically determined "markers" (antigens) enable the immune system to discriminate between host cells and foreign cells. Medawar shared the 1960 Nobel Prize with Sir Macfarlane *Burnet.

Medea In Greek legend, a sorceress, the daughter of King Aeetes of Colchis and niece of *Circe. She helped *Jason steal the *Golden Fleece and fled with him to Iolcus. When Jason deserted her for Glauce, daughter of the Corinthian King Creon, she killed Glauce, Creon, and her own two children and fled to Athens.

Medellín 6 15N 75 36W The second largest city in Colombia, in the Central Cordillera. It is the country's leading industrial centre; steel processing and the manufacture of textiles are especially important. Its university was founded in 1822. Population (1980): 1 812 000.

Media An ancient region SW of the Caspian Sea settled by seminomadic tribes of Medes. Between the 8th and 6th centuries BC they began to unite against Assyria and in 612 under their sovereign Cyaxares (625-585) destroyed Nineveh with the help of Chaldea and overthrew the Assyrian empire. But in 550 the Medes were amalgamated with the Persians in Cyrus the Great's expanding empire.

median 1. The line joining the vertex of a triangle to the midpoint of the opposite side. 2. The middle value of a set of numbers arranged in order of magnitude. For example, the median of {2, 3, 3, 4, 5} is 3.

medical jurisprudence (*or* forensic medicine) The legal aspects of medical practice. This includes the application of a country's laws to such practices as the termination of pregnancy, transplantation of organs, sterilization, and artificial insemination. It also covers investigations of the causes of sudden *death and the giving of medical evidence

in courts of law, for example in cases of murder, assault, infanticide, etc.

Medici A family that dominated Florence from 1434 to 1494, from 1512 to 1527, and from 1530 to 1737 (as grand dukes from 1532). The Medici, who were merchants and bankers, dominated the government of Florence in the 15th century by manipulating elections to the key magistracies. The family's power was established by **Cosimo de' Medici** (1389-1464), entitled Pater Patriae (Father of His Country), who also initiated the Medici tradition of artistic patronage: Brunelleschi, Ghiberti, and Donatello, among others, were employed by Cosimo. His son **Piero de' Medici** (1416-69) succeeded to his position, which then passed to **Lorenzo the Magnificent** (1449-92). Following the *Pazzi conspiracy (1478), in which his brother **Giuliano de' Medici** (1453-78) died, Lorenzo's political prestige was greatly enhanced. An outstanding patron of Renaissance artists (Botticelli, Ghirlandaio, Michelangelo) and scholars (Ficino, Pico della Mirandola, Politian), Lorenzo tended to neglect the family business, which declined in the late 15th century. He was succeeded by his son **Piero de' Medici** (1472-1503), who was forced to flee Florence in a revolt incited by *Savonarola. Piero's brother **Giovanni de' Medici** (1475-1521) was restored to Florence in 1512, a year before he became Pope *Leo X. The Medici were again ousted, in 1527, but the combined efforts of Emperor Charles V and Pope Clement VII (previously Giulio de' Medici, the illegitimate son of Lorenzo's brother Giuliano) established Clement's illegitimate son **Alessandro de' Medici** (1511-37) as the first Duke of Florence. Subsequent grand dukes included **Cosimo I** (1519-74), **Francesco I** (1541-87), and **Ferdinando I** (1549-1609).

medicine The science and practice of preventing, diagnosing, and treating disease. The term is also used specifically for the management of disease by nonsurgical methods, for example by drugs, diet, etc. (*compare* surgery). Medicine involves study of the anatomy, physiology, and biochemistry of the body in health as well as the changes that occur in disease (pathology). It is closely connected with pharmacology (the study of drugs).

Medicine has its origins in ancient Greece. The medical school at Cnidos, established in the 7th century BC, was concerned purely with the description of symptoms, whereas that founded later by *Hippocrates considered the causes of symptoms in relation to the patient and the environment. In the Alexandrian school the emphasis was on the effects of disease rather than the causes. All existing knowledge of medicine was coordinated and supplemented in the 2nd century AD, by *Galen, whose influence prevailed until the Renaissance. Landmarks in the development of modern medicine were the publication of *Vesalius' major work on anatomy (1543) and of William Harvey's discovery of the circulation of the blood (1628). The nature, treatment, and prevention of infectious diseases were illuminated by the researches of *Pasteur, *Koch, and *Klebs in the 19th century; their work directed *Lister to the discovery of antiseptics, by means of which wound healing and hospital sanitation were greatly improved. Chemotherapy (the treatment of disease by chemical agents) was revolutionized in 1911, when *Ehrlich introduced salvarsan for treating syphilis. The late 1930s saw the development of the sulphonamides—the first powerful general antibacterial drugs—and World War II provided the stimulus for the widespread production and use of antibiotics (the first of which was penicillin). Together these drugs have enabled most infectious diseases to be cured. Viruses, however, do not succumb to antibiotics and the control of viral diseases has relied on immunological methods derived from *Jenner's discovery of vaccination in 1798. With infectious diseases under control, medical research since World War II has concentrated on the organic diseases, especially coronary artery disease, strokes, etc., and cancer. The emphasis has also been on preventive medicine, with the establishment of the *World Health Organization in 1948, campaigns to eradicate epidemic diseases, and the establishment of pre- and ante-natal clinics, medical inspections for schoolchildren, dental clinics, welfare centres, etc., in many parts of the world. *See also* alternative medicine.

medick An annual or perennial herb of the genus *Medicago* (about 120 species), native to Eurasia and N Africa. The stems are creeping or erect, 5–90 cm tall, bearing compound leaves with three toothed leaflets, dense yellow or purple flower heads, and curved or spirally twisted pods. Family: *Leguminosae*.

Medina (Arabic name: Al Madinah) 24 30N 39 35E A city in W Saudi Arabia, N of Mecca. The tomb of Mohammed is in the mosque at Medina, the second most holy Muslim city after Mecca. Husayn ibn Ali, with the assistance of T. E. *Lawrence, expelled the Turks during World War I by putting the railway from Damascus out of commission. Date-packing supplements the city's income from pilgrims, and the Islamic University was founded in 1961. Population (1980 est): 290 000.

Mediterranean Sea An almost landlocked sea extending between Africa and Europe to Asia. It connects with the Atlantic Ocean at Gibraltar, the Black Sea via the Sea of Marmara, and the Red Sea via the Suez Canal. It loses twice as much water through evaporation as it receives from rivers and thus is fed continuously by the Atlantic and to a lesser extent by the Black Sea. Although its waters return to the Atlantic in a ten-year cycle, it is saltier and warmer than the oceans; pollution is a serious problem because of the large quantities of waste discharged into its waters. Tidal variation is insignificant.

medlar A thorny shrub or tree, *Mespilus germanica*, native to SE Europe and central Asia and cultivated for its fruit. Growing to a height of 6 m, it bears oblong toothed leaves, 15 cm long, and white five-petalled flowers. The globular brownish fruit, 5–6 cm across, has an opening at the top, surrounded by the remains of the sepals, through which the five seed chambers can be seen. Medlars are eaten when partly decayed and have a pleasant acid taste; they can also be made into jelly. Family: *Rosaceae*.

Médoc An area in SW France, bordering on the left bank of the Gironde estuary. Producing some of France's finest red wines, it contains some famous vineyards including Château Latour.

medulla oblongata. *See* brain.

medusa The free-swimming sexual form that occurs during the life cycle of many animals of the phylum *Coelenterata*. Medusae resemble small *jellyfish and have separate sexes, releasing eggs and sperm into the water. The ciliated larvae settle and develop into the sedentary asexual forms (*see* polyp). *See also* coelenterate.

Medusa In Greek mythology, the only mortal *Gorgon. Athena, angered by her love affair with Poseidon, made her hair into serpents and her face so ugly that all who saw it were turned to stone. She later sent *Perseus to behead her. From her blood sprang *Pegasus and Chrysaor, her children by Poseidon.

Medway, River A river in SE England. Rising in Sussex, it flows N and E through Kent to join the River Thames by a long estuary. It passes through Tonbridge, Maidstone, Rochester, Chatham, and Gillingham. In 43 AD, near Rochester, the invading Romans defeated the British under Caractacus in the battle of the Medway. Length: 113 km (70 mi).

Meegeren, Hans van (1889–1947) Dutch painter, notorious for his *Vermeer forgeries. He successfully misled the art world, notably with works such as *Christ at Emmaus*, bought by the Boymans Museum, Rotterdam, as an early Vermeer painting. In 1945 he was arrested as a Nazi

collaborator, confessed his deceptions, was imprisoned, and died in poverty.

meerkat A small carnivorous mammal, *Suricata suricata*, also called suricate, of South African grasslands. It is about 60 cm long including the tail (17–25 cm), and lives in large colonies of shallow burrows, emerging to sunbathe in the early morning. Meerkats stay close to home, feeding on insects, grubs, reptiles, birds, and small mammals. Family: *Viverridae*.

meerschaum A white mineral consisting of hydrated magnesium silicate, $H_4Mg_2Si_3O_{10}$, found in some magnesium-rich rocks, such as serpentine. Turkey has famous deposits of meerschaum; it also occurs in East and S Africa. It is used for making tobacco pipes.

Meerut 29 00N 77 42E A city in India, in Uttar Pradesh. The scene of the first uprising (1857) of the Indian Mutiny, Meerut is an important army headquarters and has diverse industries. Population (1981): 538 000.

megalith (Greek: large stone) A large stone particularly favoured for building monuments in the *Neolithic and *Bronze Age (in Britain, about 3500 BC to 1500 BC). Megaliths could be placed singly, as in Rudston (N Yorkshire) churchyard; or in lines, as on Dartmoor or at *Carnac; or in simple or complex circles as at *Stonehenge. Megaliths were also used for tombs and temples in Malta, Egypt, and elsewhere. Stones weighing many tons were set up using simple tackle of timbers and ropes.

Megaloceros. *See* Irish elk.

megapode A bird belonging to a family (*Megapodiidae*; 12 species) ranging from Australia to the Peninsular Malaysia. 48–68 cm long, megapodes are fowl-like and ground-dwelling with brownish plumage and build a large nest mound in which the eggs are incubated by the heat of fermenting plant material, the sun's rays, or volcanic heat. Order: *Galliformes* (pheasants, turkeys, etc.). *See also* brush turkey; mallee fowl.

Mégara 38 00N 23 20E A town in E central Greece. It was an important city state from the 8th century BC fostering many colonies, including *Chalcedon and Byzantium, before its decline in the 5th century BC. Population (1981): 17 719.

Megatherium A genus of extinct giant ground sloths that lived in North and South America about a million years ago. *Megatherium* was about the size of a modern elephant and probably ate leaves. Giant mammals like this were common in South America before the Panama isthmus closed at the end of the Ice Age, when most of them—including *Megatherium*—became extinct.

megaton A measure of the explosive power of a nuclear weapon. It is equivalent to an explosion of one million tons of trinitrotoluene (TNT).

Meghalaya A state in NE India, NE of Bangladesh on a beautiful plateau falling N to the Brahmaputra Valley. One of the world's wettest areas, it has rich forests but little industry. Rice, potatoes, cotton, and fruits are grown. Meghalaya was separated from Assam in 1972. Area: 22 489 sq km (8681 sq mi). Population (1981 est): 1 327 824. Capital: Shillong.

Megiddo An ancient site in N Israel. Continuously occupied between about 3000 and 350 BC, Megiddo was strategically positioned on the route between Egypt and Syria and was the scene of many battles. Excavations (1925–39) unearthed hundreds of Phoenician ivories (13th–12th centuries BC) and stabling for about 450 horses, built probably by King Solomon. Megiddo is identified with the biblical Armageddon, where, according to St John the Divine (Revelation 16.16), the last battle will be fought.

Mehemet Ali (1769–1849) Viceroy of Egypt for the Ottoman Empire (1805–48). An Albanian in the Ottoman army, he was recognized as viceroy after he had seized power in Cairo. His important military, agricultural, and educational reforms have led some to see him as the founder of modern Egypt. In 1840 the Ottomans recognized him as hereditary ruler of Egypt and he was succeeded by his son *Ibrahim Pasha. His dynasty survived until 1952.

Meiji. *See* Mutsuhito.

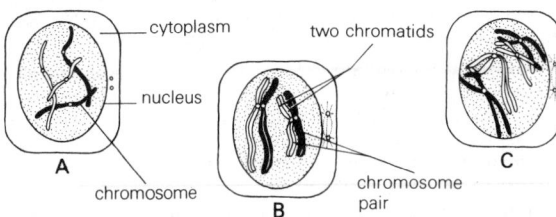

prophase I *The four chromosomes appear as thin threads (A), which from pairs (B). Each chromosome divides into two chromatids and exchange of genetic material occurs between the chromatids of each pair (C).*

metaphase I *The chromosomes of each pair separate from each other and move to opposite poles of the spindle.*

metaphase II *Two new spindles form and the chromatids of each group separate from each other.*

telophase II *Four new nuclei form, each containing two chromosomes.*

MEIOSIS *The formation of four egg or sperm cells from one parent cell takes place in two divisions, each of which is divided into several phases. Only four phases are shown here.*

meiosis The process by which the nucleus of a germ cell divides prior to the formation of gametes (such as sperm, pollen, or eggs). Meiosis consists of two successive divisions during which one cell with the normal duplicate (diploid) set of chromosomes gives rise to four cells each with only one chromosome of each type (haploid). Meiosis differs from *mitosis in that the chromosomes of each pair become closely associated, enabling the interchange of genetic material between maternal and paternal chromosomes. There is no duplication of chromosomes between the two divisions of meiosis.

Meir, Golda (1898-1978) Israeli stateswoman, born in Russia; prime minister (1969-74). Brought up in the USA (1906-21), she emigrated to Palestine in 1921. A founder member of the Israeli Workers' Party (Mapai) she was its secretary general (1966-68). She was minister of labour (1949-56) and minister of foreign affairs (1956-66) before becoming prime minister. She was committed to the establishment of peace in the Middle East and resigned after Israel had been taken unawares in the 1973 *Arab-Israeli War.

Meissen 51 11N 13 23E A town in SE East Germany, on the River Elbe. Meissen is famous for porcelain manufac-

ture, moved here from Dresden in 1710. The process of production of the porcelain (known as Dresden china) was discovered by J. F. Böttger in 1709. Population (1983 est): 38 908.

Meissen porcelain The first hard-paste porcelain made in Europe following discovery (1710) of the technique by the alchemist Böttger (1682-1719) under the patronage of the Elector of Saxony. Initially, the Elector's oriental collection at Dresden was copied. There followed extensive ranges of domestic ware, figures (shepherdesses, monkey bands, Italian comedy, etc.), chinoiseries, small boxes, seals, and ornaments painted with landscapes, flowers, and insects. The styles were extensively copied by all 18th-century factories.

Meissonier, Jean-Louis-Ernest (1815-91) French painter, born in Lyons. He achieved great success at the Paris Salon exhibitions from the 1840s onwards with his small, minutely detailed history and military paintings, particularly of Napoleonic battles, for example *Campagne de France, 1814* (1864; Louvre).

Meistersingers (German: master singers) German singing guilds, which flourished from the 14th to the 17th centuries. As the *Minnesingers declined in Germany, song guilds developed in the artisan class, the first being established in Mainz in 1311. They flourished in most German towns; their contests were regulated by a superabundance of rules, as depicted by Wagner in his opera *The Mastersingers of Nuremberg.*

Meitner, Lise (1878-1968) Austrian physicist. After studying in Vienna under *Boltzmann, she worked with Otto *Hahn in Berlin (1907-38) until expelled by the Nazis. Together they discovered protactinium (1918) and caused the first fission of a uranium atom by neutron bombardment (1934). Hahn did not publish the results of this work and it was first published by Meitner from Stockholm in 1939. In Stockholm she worked with Karl Manne Georg Siegbahn (1886-1978), becoming a Swedish citizen in 1949. In 1958 she moved to Cambridge.

Meknès 33 53N 5 37W A city in N Morocco. It became known as the "Moroccan Versailles" under Mawlay Isma'il (?1645-1727; reigned 1672-1727), when several palaces were built. It is a trade centre for agricultural produce and carpets. Population (1982): 319 783.

Mekong, River A major SE Asian river, rising in Tibet and flowing generally SE through China, Laos, Kampuchea, and Vietnam to the South China Sea. It is navigable for about 550 km (340 mi). The extensive delta is one of the greatest Asian rice-growing areas. Length: about 4025 km (2500 mi).

Melanchthon, Philip (P. Schwarzerd; 1497-1560) German Protestant reformer, who succeeded *Luther as leader of the German Reformation movement. Professor of Greek at the University of Wittenberg, Melanchthon was a convinced humanist, influenced by *Erasmus, and a supporter of Luther in public confrontations, including the debate with *Zwingli over the Eucharist. He was largely responsible for the *Augsburg Confession (1530), the main Lutheran statement of belief.

Melanesia A division of Oceania in the SW Pacific Ocean, consisting of an arc of volcanic and coral islands NE of Australia. It includes the Bismarck Archipelago, the Solomon, Admiralty, and D'Entrecasteaux Islands, Vanuatu Republic, New Caledonia, and Fiji. *See also* Micronesia; Polynesia.

Melanesians The people of the Melanesian islands. The term also covers similar peoples of New Guinea, though these are also often known as Papuan. They are of Oceanic Negroid race and speak languages of the *Austronesian family. There are a great many very different languages mostly spoken by only small numbers. The Melanesians cultivate yams, taro, and sweet potatoes and live in small, usually dispersed, homesteads. In coastal areas fishing is important. Pigs play a major role in the economy, being used in the ceremonial exchanges of valuables to establish status that are a common cultural trait.

melanin A pigment, varying from brown-black to yellow, that occurs in hair, skin, feathers, and scales. Derived from the amino acid tyrosine, its presence in the skin helps protect underlying tissues from damage by sunlight. Melanin is also responsible for colouring the iris of the eye.

melanoma A form of cancer, mainly affecting the skin, that arises in the cells producing the pigment *melanin. Most melanomas develop from an existing *mole, and excessive exposure to sunlight is known to be a contributory factor.

Melba, Dame Nellie (Helen Porter Armstrong; 1861–1931) Australian soprano, whose professional name was derived from her native city, Melbourne. She studied in Paris, making her debut in 1887 as Gilda in Verdi's opera *Rigoletto*. Her worldwide career culminated in a number of farewell performances in 1926.

Melbourne 37 45S 144 58E The second largest city of Australia, the capital of Victoria on Port Phillip Bay. It is a major commercial centre and contains about two-thirds of the state's population. Port Melbourne is sited 4 km (2.5 mi) away, on the mouth of the Yarra River; exports include wool, scrap metal, and dairy products. The chief industries are heavy engineering, food processing, and the manufacture of textiles and clothes. A cultural centre, Melbourne possesses three universities (including the University of Melbourne founded in 1853), and the new Arts Centre of Victoria (first stage completed in 1968). Other notable buildings include the State Parliament House and the Anglican and Roman Catholic cathedrals. The Melbourne Cricket Ground, founded in 1853 and the main arena of the 1956 Olympic Games, is world famous. *History*: founded in 1835, it developed rapidly following the 1851 gold rush. It was the capital of the Commonwealth of Australia from 1901 until 1927. Population (1983 est): 2 864 600.

Melbourne, William Lamb, 2nd Viscount (1779–1848) British statesman; Whig prime minister (1834, 1835–41), who exerted an early influence on Queen Victoria. He was chief secretary for Ireland (1827–28) and then home secretary (1830–34), when he dealt harshly with the *Tolpuddle Martyrs. During his second ministry his attempted resignation (1839) precipitated Victoria's *Bedchamber Crisis. In 1805 he married Lady Caroline Ponsonby (1785–1828), who had a love affair with Lord Byron (1812–13); in 1825 they formally separated and he was subsequently named in two divorce cases.

Melchett, Alfred Mond, 1st Baron. *See* Mond, Ludwig.

Melchior, Lauritz (1890–1973) Danish tenor. He studied at the Royal Opera School in Copenhagen and made his debut in 1913. His performances in the roles of Tristan and Siegfried marked him as the leading Wagnerian tenor of the 20th century.

Melchites Christians of the Orthodox Churches in Syria and Egypt who, during the 5th-century *Monophysite controversy, adhered to the anti-Monophysite doctrine supported by the Byzantine emperor. Their name was therefore derived from a Syriac word meaning "imperial."

Meleager In Greek legend, the son of Oeneus, King of Calydon. He killed the Calydonian boar, sent by Artemis because Oeneus had neglected to sacrifice to her.

Melilla 35 17N 2 57W A Spanish port forming an enclave on the Mediterranean coast of N Morocco. Iron ore is the principal export. Population (1981): 58 449.

melilot A herb belonging to the genus *Melilotus* (25 species), also called sweet clover, occurring in temperate and subtropical Eurasia. The leaves consist of three leaflets and the small yellow or white flowers grow in clusters along the stems. The biennial common melilot (*M. officinalis*) grows to a height of 130 cm. Family: *Leguminosae.

Melitopol 46 51N 35 22E A city in the Soviet Union, in the SE Ukrainian SSR. The centre of a fruit-growing region, it has food-processing industries. Nearby is the site of ancient Merv, an Islamic centre at its height under the Seljuq Turks in the 12th century. Population (1981 est): 165 000.

Melk 48 14N 15 21E A town in N Austria, in Lower Austria on the River Danube. Its Benedictine abbey is one of the finest baroque buildings. Population (1981): 5074.

Mellon, Andrew William (1855–1937) US financier and philanthropist. As secretary of the treasury (1921–32) he played a major role in the US Government's postwar tax reforms. He was also ambassador to Great Britain (1932–33). An art collector, he donated his collection and $15 million to the National Gallery of Art in Washington, DC.

melon An annual trailing vine, *Cucumis melo*, native to tropical Africa but widely cultivated for its edible fruits. Melon plants have coarse hairy five- to seven-lobed leaves, yellow or orange cup-shaped flowers, and round or oval fruits, up to 4 kg in weight, with tough skins and sweet juicy flesh surrounding a core of seeds. There are several varieties including the muskmelon, with a net-veined skin and pinkish orange flesh; the honeydew melon, with smooth whitish or greenish skin and light-green flesh; the canteloupe, with rough warty skin and orange flesh; and a newer variety produced in Israel with a green skin and sweet green flesh. Family: *Cucurbitaceae*. *See also* watermelon.

Melos (*or* Milos) A Greek island in the Aegean Sea, one of the Cyclades. Successive Minoan cities have been excavated here and the famous statue, the *Venus de Milo*, was discovered here in 1820. Area: 150 sq km (58 sq mi). Population (1981): 4554.

Melpomene In Greek religion, one of the nine Muses, the patron of tragedy and lyre playing. She was the mother of the *Sirens.

Melrose 55 36N 2 44W A market town in SE Scotland, in the Borders Region on the River Tweed. It is famous for its associations with Sir Walter Scott and for its 12th-century ruined abbey, where the heart of Robert the Bruce is interred. Population (1981 est): 2221.

melting point The temperature at which the solid form of a substance becomes a liquid, usually at atmospheric pressure.

Melton Mowbray 52 46N 0 53W A market town in central England, in Leicestershire on the River Eye and Wreak. It lies in a stock-raising area and is renowned for its pork pies and as a fox-hunting centre. Population (1981): 23 554.

Mélusine (*or* Melusina) In French legend, a fairy who was punished for imprisoning her father in a mountain by being changed into a serpent from the waist down every Saturday. When her husband, Count Raymond of Lusignan, broke his promise not to see her on Saturdays, she vanished but her cries were heard at Lusignan castle shortly before the death of each of her descendants.

Melville, Herman (1819–91) US novelist. In 1841 he joined the crew of a whaler; his experiences in the South Seas form the raw material of *Typee* (1846), *Omoo* (1847), *Mardi* (1849), *Redburn* (1849), and *White Jacket* (1850). His masterpiece, *Moby Dick* (1851), is a narrative about whaling with the underlying philosophical theme on the nature of evil. After the failure of *Pierre* (1852), Melville abandoned professional writing. *Billy Budd*, published in 1924 after his death, formed the basis of a libretto for an opera by Benjamin Britten.

Memel. *See* Klaipeda.

Memling, Hans (*or* Memlinc; c. 1430–1494) Painter of portraits and religious subjects, born in Seligenstadt (Germany). He settled in the Netherlands, where he probably studied under Rogier van der *Weyden. About 1465 he moved to Bruges, where his best-known works, *The Shrine of St Ursula* and *The Mystic Marriage of St Catherine*, were painted for the Hospital of St John.

HANS MEMLING *Triptych:* The Virgin and Child with Saints and Donors *(c. 1477). Sir John Donne (d. 1503) and his wife Elizabeth are kneeling in front of Sts Catherine and Barbara. The figures on the extreme left and right are St John the Baptist and St John the Evangelist.*

memory The recollection of experiences from the past. Three processes are required: registration, in which an experience is received into the mind; retention, in which a permanent memory trace, or engram, is preserved in the brain, probably in the form of a chemical molecule; and recall, in which a particular memory is brought back into consciousness. Short-term memories are vivid but are forgotten with the passage of time unless they are registered in the long-term memory. Once in the long-term memory, they remain available unless they are interfered with by a similar memory. Failure of memory (*see* amnesia) is a common consequence of diseases of the brain, especially those caused by *alcoholism and those affecting the hippocampus (*see also* Alzheimer's disease). An abnormally good memory (hypermnesia) can sometimes be produced by hypnosis and is sometimes found in *autism.

memory, computer The part of a computer that stores information. It usually refers to the computer's internal store, in which the programs and data needed to run the computer are held; this is under the direct control of the central processing unit. In large computers, a high-speed buffer store holds information in active use by the central processing unit, while longer-term storage is provided by the slower main store. Solid-state electronic memory devices operate at very high speeds and are used for the internal memory. Magnetic tapes and disks form the external memory, available to the computer through peripheral devices; it contains information that is not needed frequently.

Memphis 35 10N 90 00W A city and port in the USA, in Tennessee situated above the Mississippi River. Founded in 1819, it was so called because of the similarity of its riverside position to that of the ancient Egyptian city of Memphis. A major cotton, timber, and livestock market, its manufactures include textiles and chemicals. Memphis State University was established in 1912. Population (1980): 646 356.

Memphis An ancient city of Lower Egypt, S of modern Cairo. A centre for *Ptah worship, Memphis was founded as the capital of all Egypt after its unification by *Menes (c. 3100 BC), remaining the capital until supplanted by *Thebes (c. 1570 BC). The necropolis of *Saqqarah and the *pyramids and sphinx at Giza formed part of its extensive complex of monuments.

Menado (*or* Manado) 01 32N 124 55E A port in Indonesia, in N Sulawesi on the Celebes Sea. A trading centre, it exports copra, coffee, and spices. Its university was established in 1961. Population (1980): 217 159.

Menai Strait A channel separating the island of Anglesey from the mainland of NW Wales. It is crossed by a suspension bridge designed by Thomas Telford (1819–26). The Britannia railway bridge, built by Robert Stevenson (1850), was damaged by fire in 1970. It has been rebuilt to carry a road track above the railway (1980).

Menander (c. 341–c. 290 BC) Greek dramatist. The most celebrated dramatist of the *New Comedy, he wrote sophisticated comedies on romantic and domestic themes. His single surviving complete play is the *Dyscolus*, recovered from an Egyptian papyrus in 1958, but many of his plays are known from their adaptations by the Roman dramatists Plautus and Terence.

Menander (c. 160–c. 20 BC) Greek King of the Punjab and one of the heirs to *Alexander the Great's conquests. His capital was at Sakala (probably present-day Sialkot, Pakistan) and he commanded an extensive empire over NW India. He became a devout Buddhist.

menarche. *See* puberty.

MENCAP A British charity founded in 1946, as the Association of Parents of Backward Children, to improve understanding of mental handicap. It became the National Society for Mentally Handicapped Children in 1955, being authorized to add Royal to its title in 1981. It provides homes and training for the mentally handicapped and support for their families.

Mencius (Mengzi *or* Meng-tzu; 371–289 BC) Chinese moral philosopher. He was taught by pupils of *Confucius and produced the *Mencius*, an exposition of Confucian thought read by Chinese schoolchildren until the 20th century. Mencius made benevolence (*ren* or *jen*) the keynote of his political philosophy. He travelled extensively, advocating that rulers should treat their subjects humanely.

Mencken, H(enry) L(ouis) (1880–1956) US journalist and critic. As editor of *The Smart Set* (1914–23) and *American Mercury* (1924–33) he boldly attacked both the political and the literary establishments and championed many young novelists. His miscellaneous essays were collected in *Prejudices* (6 vols, 1919–27). In *The American Language* (1919) he surveyed the development of English in America. *Newspaper Days 1899–1908* (1914) and *Heather Days 1890–1936* (1943) are autobiographical.

Mendel, Gregor Johann (1822–84) Austrian botanist, who discovered the fundamental principles governing the inheritance of characters in living things (*see* genetics). Mendel was a monk with a scientific education and an interest in botany. In 1856 in the monastery garden at Brünn, Moravia, he began to inbreed lines of pea plants by means of repeated self-pollination. All the dwarf plants produced dwarf offspring only, but of tall plants, only about one third were true-breeding. The majority each produced both tall plants and dwarf plants in the ratio 3:1. Mendel then crossed pure-bred tall and dwarf plants and found that all the resulting hybrids were tall. Crossing these hybrids resulted in a mixture of pure-bred dwarf, hybrid tall, and pure-bred tall plants in the ratio 1:2:1. Mendel concluded that such characteristics were determined by factors of inheritance that were contributed equally by both parents and that sorted themselves among the offspring according to simple statistical rules. He summarized these findings in two principles (*Mendel's laws). Mendel reported his findings in 1865 but his achievement was not appreciated until the rediscovery of his work by C. E. *Correns, Hugo *de Vries and E. von Tschermak (1871–1962) in 1900.

mendelevium (Md) A synthetic element, first produced in 1955 by Ghiorso and others, by bombarding einsteinium with helium ions; it is named after the chemist Mendeleyev. At no 101; at wt (256).

Mendeleyev, Dimitrii Ivanovich (1834–1907) Russian chemist, who was professor at St Petersburg (now Leningrad) from 1866 to 1890. He became interested in the subject of atomic weights after hearing *Cannizzaro lecture on the subject and, in 1869, succeeded in arranging the elements in order of increasing atomic weights so that those with similar properties were grouped together (*see* periodic table). Mendeleyev recognized that the rows of the table were not all of equal length and that there were gaps in the table, representing undiscovered elements.

Mendel's laws The basic principles governing the inheritance of characters, first proposed by Gregor *Mendel in 1865. His first law, the Law of Independent Segregation, states that the factors of inheritance (now called *alleles of the gene) that determine a particular characteristic segregate into separate sex cells. His second law, the Law of Independent Assortment, states that the segregation of factors for one character occurs independently of that for any other character. (This is true except for alleles of genes located on the same chromosome, which are segregated together.)

Mendelssohn, Felix (Jacob Ludwig Felix Mendelssohn-Bartholdy; 1809–47) German composer; the grandson of Moses Mendelssohn. A child prodigy, his education was strictly supervised by his father. His string octet (1825) and the overture to *A Midsummer Night's Dream* (1826) demonstrated his precocious brilliance. In 1836 he became conductor of the Leipzig Gewandhaus orchestra and subsequently founded the Leipzig conservatoire. His music was popular in Britain and he was entertained by Queen Victoria. His compositions include five symphonies, overtures, the oratorios *St Paul* (1836) and *Elijah* (1846), chamber music, and piano music. He revived Bach's *St Matthew Passion* in 1829.

Mendelssohn, Moses (1729–86) German Jewish philosopher and literary critic. He was admired by *Kant and *Lessing and sought civil rights for the Jews. He also advocated the separation of church and state, the immortality of the soul, in *Phaedon* (1767), and the existence of a personal God, in *Morgenstunden* (1785).

Menderes, Adnan (1899–1961) Turkish statesman; prime minister (1950–60). His repressive policies led to an army coup in 1960 and his execution.

Menderes, River (ancient name: R. Maeander; Turkish name: Büyük Menderes) A winding river in W Turkey, flowing WSW into the Aegean Sea. Its ancient name gave rise to the term *meander. Length: 400 km (249 mi).

Mendès-France, Pierre (1907–82) French statesman; prime minister (1954–55). A Radical Socialist, Mendès-France was forced to resign because of his unpopular policies, which aimed to restore the failing Fourth Republic; these included strengthening the executive, ending the war with Indochina, and granting independence to Tunisia.

Mendip Hills (*or* Mendips) A range of limestone hills in SW England, in Somerset. It extends NW–SE between Axbridge and the Frome Valley, reaching 325 m (1068 ft) at Blackdown. Its many limestone features include Cheddar Gorge and the caves of Cheddar and Wookey Hole.

Mendoza 32 48S 68 52W A city in W Argentina. It is the commercial centre of an irrigated area specializing in wine production and has a university (1939). Population (1980): 597 000.

Mendoza, Antonio de (?1490–1552) Spanish colonial administrator. Mendoza was the first viceroy (1535–50) of New Spain (Mexico), where he fostered economic development and education, bringing the first printing press to the New World. He subsequently became viceroy of Peru (1551–52), where he died.

Menelaus A legendary Spartan king and husband of *Helen. He served under his brother Agamemnon in the *Trojan War and after the fall of Troy won Helen back.

Menelik II (1844–1913) Emperor of Ethiopia (1889–1913). He greatly expanded Ethiopia, limited the power of the nobility, and modernized the administration. In 1896 he was able to repel an Italian invasion.

Menes The first ruler of a united Egypt (c. 3100 BC); the founder of the 1st dynasty. Perhaps a legendary figure, he was said to have founded *Memphis.

Mengelberg, William (1871–1951) Dutch conductor. He studied at the Cologne conservatoire and was conductor of the Amsterdam Concertgebouw Orchestra from 1895 to 1941. He was famous for his performances of Beethoven.

Mengele, Josef (1894–?1979) German medical scientist who became notorious for atrocities committed in the Nazi concentration camp at Auschwitz. Known as "the Angel of Death", he was camp doctor at Auschwitz from 1943 to 1945 and was subsequently held responsible for the deaths of 400 000 people, mostly Jews, many of whom died in bizarre medical experiments. After World War II he was reported to be in hiding in South America and probably died from drowning in Brazil in 1979. In 1985 a body was exhumed and identified as his; to the end of his life he denied that he had ever done anything wrong.

Mengs, Anton Raphael (1728–79) German painter, born in Aussig, Bohemia. An early exponent of *neoclassicism, he achieved a high reputation particularly in Rome, where he settled (1755), and in Spain, where he worked for Charles III. Apart from numerous portraits, his best-known work is the *Parnassus* fresco (1761; Villa Albani, Rome).

menhir (Breton: long stone) A prehistoric *megalith set upright either by itself or with others in circles (e.g. *Stonehenge) or alignments (e.g. *Carnac).

Ménière's disease A disease of the inner ear causing progressive deafness, tinnitus (ringing in the ear), and vertigo. The disease normally occurs in the middle-aged and elderly and treatment (medical or surgical) is not altogether successful.

Menindee Lakes A series of lakes and reservoirs in Australia. They lie in SW New South Wales, forming part of the Darling River Conservation Scheme, and provide water for irrigation and industrial and domestic purposes.

meningitis Inflammation of the meninges—the membranes that surround the brain. This is usually caused by bacteria or viruses and occurs most commonly in children. Symptoms include headache, vomiting, stiff neck, intolerance to light, tiredness, irritability, and fits. Treatment for bacterial meningitis is with antibiotics and the patient usually recovers rapidly. Viral meningitis is often mild but may have serious effects. Tuberculous meningitis comes on more slowly and –before modern drugs were developed–was always fatal. Complications such as mental handicap, deafness, and weak limbs may occasionally occur.

Mennonites A Christian sect that originated in Holland and adjacent areas in the 16th century. Their name derives from Menno Simons, who reorganized persecuted *Anabaptist groups after 1536. There are sizable Mennonite communities in Holland and in North America, where the first colony settled in 1683. Common ground between the doctrinally diverse Mennonite groups is their rejection of hierarchical Church organization and of infant baptism. In secular life Mennonites are pacifists and avoid public office.

Menno Simons (c. 1496–1561) Dutch Anabaptist leader. A former Roman Catholic priest, Menno became the travelling shepherd of scattered *Anabaptist groups in N Europe, persecuted by both Roman Catholics and Reformers. His preaching of total pacifism became the mark of the *Mennonites, one section of the Anabaptist movement.

Menon, Krishna (Vengalil Krishnan Krishna Menon; 1896–1974) Indian diplomat. In England from 1924 to 1927, he was secretary of the India League from 1929 and a major figure in the campaign for Indian independence. After this was achieved in 1947 he was high commissioner for India to the UK (1947–52) before becoming a member of the Indian legislature; he was a delegate at the UN (1952–62) and defence minister (1957–62).

menopause The change of life: the time in a woman's life when the menstrual periods become irregular and finally cease because egg cells are no longer produced by the ovaries. The menopause can occur at any age between the late 30s and late 50s. Some women may experience symptoms, including flushing ("hot flushes"), palpitations, and irritability, due to reduced secretion of oestrogens.

Menorca. *See* Minorca.

Menotti, Gian Carlo (1911–) Italian-born US composer, living in the USA since 1928. He studied and later taught at the Curtis Institute, Philadelphia. Among his compositions are the operas *The Medium* (1946) and *The Saint of Bleecker Street* (1954), which both won a Pulitzer Prize, *The Consul* (1950), and the television opera *Amahl and the Night Visitors* (1951). In 1958 he founded the Spoleto Festival.

Mensa International An international organization, founded in the UK in 1945, the members of which are admitted on the basis of a high score in a standard intelligence test.

Mensheviks One of the two factions into which the Russian Social Democratic Workers' Party split in 1903 in London. Unlike the rival *Bolsheviks, the Mensheviks (meaning those in the minority) believed in a large and loosely organized party. They supported Russia's participation in World War I and were prominent in the Russian Revolution until the Bolsheviks seized power in October, 1917. They were finally suppressed in 1922.

menstruation The monthly discharge of blood and fragments of womb lining from the vagina. This is part of the **menstrual cycle**–the sequence of events, occurring in women from puberty to the menopause, by which an egg cell is released from the ovary. Menstruation is the stage at which the egg cell (with blood, etc.) is expelled from the womb if conception has not occurred. Ovulation occurs at around the middle of the cycle: it may be associated with abdominal pain. Depression and irritability are common shortly before menstruation (premenstrual tension).

mental retardation A state of arrested or incomplete development of the intellect. Mildly retarded people (with an IQ of approximately 50–70) usually make a good adjustment to life

after special help with education; their condition is usually caused by inherited disorders or psychological disturbances. Severely retarded people (with an IQ of less than 50) usually require permanent help from other people and may need care in a special home or a hospital. Severe retardation is nearly always caused by physical diseases affecting the brain, but good education improves the outcome. *See also* intelligence.

menthol ($C_{10}H_{20}O$) A white crystalline solid. It is a constituent of peppermint oil and is responsible for the characteristic smell of the mint plant, but can also be prepared synthetically. Menthol is used as an analgesic in medicine as well as in flavouring for sweets and cigarettes.

Menton 43 47N 7 30E A town in SE France, in the Alpes-Maritimes department on the French Riviera near the Italian border. A popular holiday resort, it produces fruit and flowers. Population (1982): 25 449.

Menuhin, Sir Yehudi (1916–) British violinist, of Russo-Jewish parentage. A pupil of Georges Enesco, he became famous in boyhood; Elgar coached him for performances of the composer's violin concerto. From 1959 to 1968 Menuhin was director of the Bath Festival, where he also participated as a conductor. He founded the Yehudi Menuhin School for musically gifted children in 1963. He was frequently partnered in recitals by his sister, the pianist **Hephzibah Menuhin** (1920–81); another sister **Yaltah Menuhin** (1921–) and his son **Jeremy Menuhin** (1951–) are also pianists. He was made a KBE in 1965 and an OM in 1987.

YEHUDI MENUHIN *Seen here with the Chinese conductor Muhai Tung during rehearsals.*

Menzies, Sir Robert Gordon (1894–1978) Australian statesman; prime minister as leader of the United Australia Party (1939–41) and then of the Liberal Party (1949–66). Elected to the federal parliament in 1934, he was attorney general (1934–39) before becoming prime minister as leader of the United Australia party. He resigned in 1941 and formed the Liberal Party in 1944. As Liberal prime minister he increased US influence in Australian affairs and was strongly anticommunist, attempting to disband the Australian Communist Party in 1951 and later supporting the USA in the Vietnam War. He encouraged immigration from Europe and developed the Australian universities. Loyal to the British Commonwealth, he became Lord Warden of the Cinque Ports in 1965.

Merca 1 45N 44 47E A town in Somalia, on the Indian Ocean. Merca has a deepwater harbour and exports agricultural produce. Population (1980 est): 60 000.

mercantilism An economic doctrine that flourished in the 17th and 18th centuries. Primarily concerned with international trade, mercantilism attempted to maximize national wealth, which it identified with a nation's bullion reserves.

To this end, tariffs were applied to imports in the hope of creating a *balance-of-trade surplus and adding to bullion reserves. Mercantilism was replaced by *free trade, after *Hume and Adam *Smith had shown that mercantilism merely served the self-interest of the merchant classes.

Mercator, Gerardus (Gerhard Kremer; 1512-94) Flemish geographer, best known for his method of mapping the earth's surface, known as the *Mercator projection. He worked at Louvain, but was prosecuted for heresy in 1544 and emigrated to Protestant Germany in 1552, where he was appointed cartographer to the Duke of Cleves. In later life he prepared a book of maps, which, since it had a picture of Atlas supporting the earth on its cover, became known as an atlas.

Mercator projection A cylindrical □map projection, originally used (1569) by Gerardus Mercator. The parallels of latitude are represented as being straight lines of equal length to the equator. The meridians are equally spaced and intersect at right angles. The correct ratio between latitude and longitude is maintained by increasing the distance between the parallels away from the equator causing increased distortion towards the Poles. Compass bearings are accurately shown and the projection is commonly used for navigation charts. The **Transverse Mercator projection** is a development of the Mercator projection but in this case the cylinder is tangential to a meridian rather than to the equator. It is used chiefly for small areas with a N-S orientation and is used in all British *Ordnance Survey maps.

Mercer, David (1928-80) British dramatist. His plays for both television and the theatre generally concern political disillusion, insanity, and sexual relationships. He also wrote scripts for the films *Morgan, a Suitable Case for Treatment* (1965), *Family Life* (1970), and *Providence* (1977).

mercerization A finishing process for cotton fabrics and yarns. Named after John Mercer (1791-1866), who investigated the process (1844), mercerization involves treating the cotton by immersion, while under tension, in a caustic soda solution, later neutralized by acid. This process causes the fibres to swell permanently; cotton thus treated dyes better and is stronger and more lustrous.

merchant banks Financial institutions that became *acceptance houses as a result of their foreign trading as merchants. They are now involved in a variety of other businesses, including: the issue, placing, and underwriting of shares and debentures for firms (*see* issuing house); the issue of long-term loans for governments and institutions abroad; advising on the investment of funds and the management of portfolios; advising on and managing takeover bids; and dealings in foreign exchange.

Merchants Adventurers An English trading company, incorporated in 1407, which controlled the export of cloth to the Continent. Its continental centre was at Bruges until 1446, when it moved to Antwerp; in 1567 it transferred to Hamburg but returned to a series of Dutch marts after 1580. The Adventurers, which rivalled the *Hanseatic League, were criticized for furthering their own interests at the expense of the English economy and lost their charter in 1689.

Merchant Staplers (*or* Company of the Merchants of the Staple) The company of between 26 and 38 English merchants that controlled the export and sale of wool from the late 13th to late 16th centuries. Exports were sold at one market (the staple), which from 1363 was Calais. At its height in the 15th century, the company declined with the growth of English manufacturing.

Mercia A kingdom of Anglo-Saxon England. The Mercians were *Angles and their territory embraced most of central England south of the Humber between Wales and East Anglia. Mercia became a formidable power under *Penda (c. 634-55) and achieved pre-eminence under *Offa (757-96), who controlled all England S of the Humber.

Thereafter it declined and was merged in the 9th century into a united England under Wessex.

Mercouri, Melina (1925-) Greek actress and politician; minister of culture and science (1981-). Her best-known films were made with the US director Jules Dassin (1911-), whom she married, and include *Never on Sunday* (1960) and *Topkapi* (1964). She campaigned in exile against the military junta (1967-74) and returned to Greece when civilian government was restored.

mercury (botany) An annual or perennial herb of the genus *Mercurialis* (8 species), native to Eurasia and N Africa. The perennial dog's mercury (*M. perennis*) of woodland areas has an evil smell and is poisonous to grazing animals. Growing 15-40 cm high, it has large toothed leaves arranged in pairs and clusters of small green male and female flowers borne on separate plants. The annual mercury (*M. annua*) occurs on wasteland and as a garden weed. Family: *Euphorbiaceae*.

mercury (Hg) The only common metal that is liquid at room temperature (it has a high relative density of 13.546). It occurs chiefly as the sulphide cinnabar (HgS), from which mercury is obtained simply by heating in a current of air. The element was known in ancient Egypt, India, and China and occurs rarely in nature in the metallic state. It is used in thermometers, barometers, and batteries and as an amalgam in dentistry. Compounds include the oxide (HgO), mercurous and mercuric chlorides (Hg_2Cl_2, $HgCl_2$), and the explosive mercury fulminate ($Hg(ONC)_2$), which is widely used as a detonator. Mercury and its compounds are highly poisonous and are only slowly excreted by the human body. Organo-mercury compounds, such as dimethyl mercury, $(CH_3)_2Hg$, are particularly toxic (*see* Minimata disease). At no 80; at wt 200.59; mp -38.87°C; bp 356.58°C.

Mercury (astronomy) The innermost and second smallest (4880 km diameter) planet, orbiting the sun every 88 days at a mean distance of 57.9 million km. Its long period of axial rotation, 58.6 days, is two-thirds of its orbital period. Mercury can only be seen low in the twilight and early morning sky and, like the moon, exhibits *phases. Its surface is heavily cratered, with intervening lava-flooded plains. It has only a very tenuous atmosphere, mainly helium and argon. *See also* planetary probe.

Mercury (mythology) The Roman god of merchants and commerce and patron of astronomy. He is usually portrayed as holding a purse, and also with a cap, winged sandals, and staff, the attributes of the Greek *Hermes, with whom he was identified.

Meredith, George (1828-1909) British poet and novelist. Educated in Germany, he returned to England to study law but embarked on a literary career instead. For many years he was dependent on literary hackwork. His long poem *Modern Love* (1862) was partly based on his unhappy marriage to Mary Ellen Nicholls, daughter of Thomas Love *Peacock. With his novels, including *The Egoist* (1879) and *The Tragic Comedians* (1880), he achieved critical acclaim and financial security.

Meredith, Owen. See Lytton, Edward George Earle Bulwer-Lytton, 1st Baron.

merganser A *duck belonging to a genus (*Mergus*) of the N hemisphere, also called sawbill. It occurs on inland lakes in summer and coastal regions in winter. 40-57 cm long, mergansers have a long serrated bill for feeding on worms, fish, and eels. Males have a dark-green double-crested head, a chestnut breast, and a grey-and-white back; females are brown with a white wing bar. *See also* goosander.

merger The amalgamation of two or more companies to form one new company; usually the shareholders of the old companies exchange their old shares for shares in the new company. **Vertical mergers** involve the amalgamation of companies specializing in different parts of the production process (e.g. a car manufacturer and a steelmaker); **horizon-**

tal **mergers** involve the amalgamation of related product manufacturers (e.g. car and truck manufacturers); and **conglomerate mergers** are between firms unrelated in production. Mergers usually require government approval, as they can lead to *monopolies. In the UK the Monopolies Commission has, since 1965, been empowered to investigate selected mergers; in the USA the antitrust laws must be observed.

Mérida (Latin name: Augusta Emerita) 38 55N 06 20W A town in W Spain, in Estremadura on the River Guadiana. Founded by the Romans in 25 BC, it has numerous Roman remains, including an aqueduct, temples, two bridges, and a triumphal arch. Population (1981): 41 783.

Mérida 20 59N 89 39W A city in E Mexico. It is the commercial and industrial centre for an agricultural area specializing in henequen (a fibre) production. It has a 16th-century cathedral and is the site of the University of Yucatán (refounded 1922). Population (1980): 424 529.

meridian. *See* latitude and longitude.

meridian circle (*or* transit circle) An instrument for determining very accurately the position of a celestial body by measuring the body's altitude and the time as it crosses the observer's meridian (which passes through the observer's zenith and N and S celestial poles). It consists of a telescope pivoted on a horizontal E–W axis so that the telescope's line of sight follows the meridian plane.

Mérimée, Prosper (1803–70) French novelist. His first published works were fake translations of plays and ballads that deceived many leading scholars. His best-known works are his short novels, especially *Columba* (1841) and *Carmen* (1843), the source of Bizet's opera. He was also a distinguished historian and archaeologist, and a friend of the empress Eugénie.

Merino A breed of sheep originating from Spain and noted for its long thick high-quality white fleece. Merinos are well adapted to hot arid climates and have been exported to many parts of the world, especially Australia, where the Australian Merino has been developed for its superior fleece.

Merionethshire A former county of NW Wales. Under local government reorganization in 1974 it became part of *Clwyd and *Gwynedd.

meristem An area of actively dividing plant cells responsible for growth in the plant. The main meristematic regions in dicotyledon plants are the shoot tip and root tip (apical meristems) and the *cambium (lateral meristem). A damaged meristem produces distorted growth, but it can be used for plant propagation.

Merleau-Ponty, Maurice (1908–61) French philosopher. He was interested in the nature of human consciousness and its interaction with matter, problems that he examined in *Le Structure du comportement* (1942) and *Phénoménologie de perception* (1945). In his eyes, causal and behaviouristic theories misinterpreted consciousness, as did dualism, and he accepted the Marxist view of the dependence of consciousness upon material conditions.

merlin A small *falcon, *Falco columbarius*, occurring in moorland and heathland regions of the N hemisphere. The female is 32 cm long and is dark brown with heavily streaked underparts; the male is 26 cm long and has a grey-blue back and tail. Merlins feed chiefly on small birds, which are caught in flight.

Merlin In *Arthurian legend, the wizard who counsels and assists Arthur and his father, Uther Pendragon. There are various accounts of Merlin's life in *Geoffrey of Monmouth and later writers. He helped Uther to win Igraine, Arthur's mother, made the Round Table, cared for Arthur as a child, and gave him, or arranged for him to be given, the sword Excalibur. In old age Merlin fell in love with Nimue (*or* Vivien), who tricked him into a cave or hollow tree and left him there forever imprisoned by a spell.

mermaid A legendary creature whose form is that of a beautiful woman above the waist and a fish below. A mermaid's male counterpart is called a **merman**. They are generally represented as malicious to man. Such aquatic mammals as dugongs may account for mermaid stories in mythology and folklore.

Merneptah King of Egypt (c. 1236–1223 BC) of the 19th dynasty. His father *Ramses II had neglected frontier defence in his old age and Merneptah faced the aggression of Libya and the Sea Peoples, against whom he scored a victory in 1232.

Meroë The capital of an ancient Nubian kingdom in the area that is now the Sudan. After ruling Egypt (c. 730–670 BC), Nubian kings established Meroë in about 600 BC. Its temples and pyramids show Egyptian influence. Before its abandonment (7th century AD), Meroë may have been the route by which iron technology reached sub-Saharan Africa.

Merovingians The first Frankish ruling dynasty (*see* Franks). It was founded by Merovech, King of the Salian Franks, in the mid-5th century AD. His grandson *Clovis (reigned 481–511) greatly extended Merovingian possessions and the kingdom reached its zenith in the mid-6th century. The last Merovingian king, Childeric III, was deposed in 751 by the *Carolingian Pepin the Short.

Merseburg 51 22N 12 0E A town in S East Germany, on the River Saale just S of Halle. Founded in 800 AD, there is a 15th-century castle and a 13th-century cathedral. Industries include tanning, brewing, engineering, lignite mining, and the manufacture of machinery and paper. Population (1983 est): 50 078.

Mersey, River A river in NW England. Formed by the confluence of the Rivers Goyt and Tame at Stockport, it flows W to enter the Irish Sea by way of a 26 km (16 mi) long estuary, with the ocean ports of *Liverpool and Birkenhead on its banks. Length: 113 km (70 mi).

Merseyside A metropolitan county of NW England, created in 1974 from SW Lancashire and NW Cheshire. It comprises the districts of Sefton, Liverpool, St Helens, Knowsley, and Wirral. Area: 648 sq km (250 sq mi). Population (1981): 1 513 070. Administrative centre: Liverpool.

Mersin 36 47N 34 37E A port in central S Turkey, the major port on the S coast. It has an oil refinery and exports wool, cotton, and agricultural produce. Population (1980): 216 308.

Merthyr Tydfil (Welsh name: Merthyr Tudful) 51 46N 3 23W A town in South Wales, in Mid Glamorgan on the River Taff. Formerly a world iron and steel centre based on the surrounding coalfields, the main industries are now light and electrical engineering. Population (1981): 53 843.

Merton A mainly residential borough of SW Greater London, created in 1965 from the former urban district and adjacent boroughs, including *Wimbledon. Population (1981): 164 912.

Meru, Mount In Hindu mythology, the cosmic mountain at the centre of the universe. It is symbolized in the massive pyramidal towers of Hindu shrines.

Merv. *See* Melitopol.

mesa An isolated flat-topped hill occurring in areas of long-continued erosion of horizontally bedded strata, usually in semiarid climates. The upper slopes are steep, and gentle lower slopes merge into the surrounding plain. The cap rock is of resistant material. Further erosion may reduce the mesa to a *butte.

Mesa Verde A high plateau in the USA, in SW Colorado. It contains the remains of numerous cliff dwellings, spanning four archaeological periods.

mescaline A hallucinogenic drug obtained from the *peyote cactus of Mexico, where it was once widely used in religious ceremonies. The effect of mescaline varies from individual to individual; it does not cause serious dependence and the hallucinations are mostly visual.

Mesembryanthemum. *See* fig marigold.

Meshed. *See* Mashhad.

Mesmer, Franz Anton (1734–1815) German physician, who claimed to cure diseases by correcting the flow of "animal magnetism" in his patients' bodies during séance-like group sessions. Investigation of "mesmerism" by a commission of his contemporaries concluded that any cures were due to the powers of suggestion. Mesmer's claims stimulated serious study of hypnosis by such men as James *Braid.

Mesoamerican languages A geographical classification of the languages spoken by the American Indian peoples of Mexico, Guatemala, Honduras, Belize, El Salvador, and Nicaragua. It includes around 70 languages belonging to a number of families. The main families are: the Totonac-Mayan (e.g. Mayan); Uto-Aztecan (e.g. *Nahuatl) the Otomangean (e.g. Mixtec); the Hokan-Coahuiltecan; and Tarascan.

Mesolithic The middle division of the *Stone Age, especially in N Europe, where a distinct cultural stage, the *Maglemosian, intervened between the last ice age and the evolution of farming communities. Generally, the Mesolithic is characterized by production of microliths (very minute stone tools), which were hafted into wooden, bone, or other handles. The dog was the only domesticated animal. Outside Europe the Mesolithic distinction is less useful: for example, the Middle Eastern transition between *Palaeolithic and *Neolithic was more rapid and less definable and in Japan pottery, a Neolithic characteristic, coexisted with microlith manufacture.

mesons A group of unstable elementary particles (lifetimes between 10^{-8} and 10^{-15} second) that are classified as hadrons; each meson is believed to consist of a quark-antiquark pair (*see* particle physics). The muon was originally called the mu-meson as it was thought to be a meson but is now classified as a lepton.

Mesopotamia The region between the Rivers Tigris and Euphrates, "the land between two rivers." The Sumerians (*see* Sumer) settled in S Mesopotamia about 4000 BC to cultivate the alluvial land left by flooding. They established the world's first civilization and founded city states, such as *Ur, *Kish, and *Uruk. *Babylon became Mesopotamia's capital under *Hammurabi, whose code of laws shows the development of civilized conduct and government. After his death Mesopotamia, overrun successively by Kassites, Assyrians, and Persians, was no longer the most advanced civilization, being overtaken by Egypt.

Mesosaurus A small slender freshwater reptile of the late Carboniferous and early Permian periods (around 280 million years ago). It was 1 m long and had a long narrow skull with numerous teeth for straining crustaceans from water.

Mesozoic era The geological era following the Palaeozoic and preceding the Cenozoic. It contains the Triassic, Jurassic, and Cretaceous periods, and lasted from about 240 to 65 million years ago. The reptiles were at their greatest development during this era but became extinct before the end of it. The Alpine orogeny began at the end of the Mesozoic.

mesquite A spiny shrub or small tree, of the genus *Prosopis*, with deep penetrating roots, native to the SW USA and Mexico. Up to 15 m tall, it has compound leaves, with many narrow leaflets, and creamy flower catkins producing long narrow pods, which are used as cattlefeed. The hard wood is sometimes used in furniture. Family: *Leguminosae*.

Messager, André (Charles Prosper) (1853–1929) French composer and conductor. His compositions include the operetta *Véronique* (1898) and the ballet *Les Deux Pigeons* (1886). He directed the first performance of Debussy's *Pelléas et Mélisande* in 1902.

Messalina, Valeria (c. 26–48 AD) The third wife of Emperor Claudius and mother of Britannicus (41–55) and Octavia (the wife of Nero). Messalina was notorious for her promiscuity and, according to Roman scandal, contracted a bigamous and treacherous marriage to the senator Gaius Silius, for which they were both executed.

Messerschmitt, Willy (1898–1978) German aircraft designer. He is best known for his World War II military planes, particularly the Me-109 fighter (1935) and the Me-262, the first jet fighter. In 1927 he was appointed chief designer at the Bayerische Flugzeugwerke, which was later renamed Messerschmitt-Aktien-Gesellschaft.

Messiaen, Olivier (1908–) French composer, organist, and teacher. Messiaen was a pupil of Paul Dukas and Marcel Dupré. In 1931 he was appointed organist of La Trinité in Paris. His music has been heavily influenced by Catholic mysticism and the rhythms of eastern music. His works include *La Nativité du Seigneur* (for organ; 1935), the symphony *Turangalîla* (1948), the *Quatuor pour la fin du temps* (for violin, cello, clarinet, and piano; 1941), and *La Transfiguration* (for chorus and orchestra; 1965–69). His opera *St Francis d'Assise* had its British premiere in 1986.

Messier, Charles (1730–1817) French astronomer. In 1760 he began making a list of what he thought were nebulae. The result was the **Messier catalogue**, which listed 109 bright nonstellar celestial objects and was published in 1784–86. The objects were given a number preceded by the letter M, as in M31—the Andromeda galaxy. They are mainly galaxies and star clusters together with some nebulae.

Messina 38 13N 15 33E A port in Italy, in NE Sicily on the Strait of Messina. Originally known as Zancle, after the sickle shape of its harbour, it was successively occupied by Greeks, Carthaginians, Mamertines, Romans, Saracens, Normans, and Spaniards. In 1860 it became the last city in Sicily to be made part of a united Italy. Most of its old buildings were destroyed by severe earthquakes in 1783 and 1903. It has a university (1549) and its manufactures include macaroni, chemicals, and soap. Population (1980): 273 810.

Messina, Strait of A channel in the central Mediterranean Sea, between Italy and Sicily and narrowing to 3 km (2 mi). The rocks on the Italian side and the whirlpool on the Sicilian are possibly the origin of the myth of *Scylla and Charybdis.

Meštrović, Ivan (1883–1962) Yugoslav sculptor. Trained at the Vienna Academy, Meštrović enjoyed an international reputation with his religious and portrait sculptures. His sitters included Herbert Hoover, Pope Pius XI, and Sir Thomas Beecham. Moving to the USA (1947), he adopted US citizenship in 1954.

metabolism The sum of the processes and chemical reactions that occur in living organisms in order to maintain life. It can be divided into two components. **Anabolism** involves building up the tissues and organs of the body using simple substances, such as amino acids, simple sugars, etc., to construct the proteins, carbohydrates, and fats of which they are made. These processes require energy, which is provided by the oxidation of nutrients or the body's own food reserves. Oxidation and all other processes involving the chemical breakdown of substances with the production of waste products are known collectively as **catabolism**. Basal metabolism is the energy required to maintain vital functions (e.g. respiration, circulation) with the body at rest. It is measured by estimating the amount of heat produced by the body and is controlled by hormones from the thyroid gland.

metal An element that is usually a hard crystalline solid, opaque, malleable, a good conductor of heat and electricity, and forms a salt and hydrogen when reacted with an acid and a salt and water when reacted with an alkali. Not all metals have all these properties, however: mercury is a liquid at normal temperatures, sodium is soft, and antimony is brittle. Of the 70 odd metals known, the most important are the heavy metals (iron, copper, lead, and zinc) used in engineering and the rarer heavy metals (nickel, chromium, tungsten, etc.) used in *alloys. Other commercially important metals are the *noble metals (gold, silver, platinum, and mercury) and the light metals (aluminium and magnesium). Chemically important metals include the *alkali metals (sodium, potassium, and lithium), the *alkaline-earth metals (calcium, barium, etc.), and the rare-earth metals (see lanthanides). Uranium is an important metal in the nuclear power industry (see nuclear energy).

Most metals occur in the earth's crust in the combined state and have to be mined (see mining and quarrying) before being extracted from their ores (see metallurgy). The extracted metal is then usually formed into an alloy (see also steel) before being ready for use.

metal fatigue   The deterioration of metal caused by repeated stresses. Fatigue, which eventually leads to failure, occurs in vibrating parts of machinery, but only when the stresses are above a critical value, known as the endurance limit. It is an important consideration in the design of aircraft, where high engine speeds and high stresses are unavoidable.

metallography   The study of the crystalline structure of metals. It includes various techniques and is used to test the quality of steel after *heat treatment. Usually a small sample is taken from a batch and polished before being examined under a microscope for cracks, impurities, or holes. The polished surface may also be treated chemically to show up the different constituents of an alloy or to highlight cracks. In 1911 Max von *Laue used X-rays to show that the atoms in metals are arranged in a regular geometrical fashion, i.e. they are crystalline. His technique of *X-ray diffraction is still used to examine metallic crystals.

metalloids   Elements displaying the physical and chemical properties both of *metals and nonmetals. Examples of metalloids are arsenic and germanium, which both have metallic and nonmetallic allotropes. Chemically, their behaviour is intermediate between metals and nonmetals in that they may form positive ions as well as covalently bonded compounds. The metalloid elements are often *semiconductors.

metallurgy   The science and technology of producing metals. It includes the extraction of metals from their ores, alloying to form materials with specific properties, and *heat treatment to improve their properties. The art of working metals was known as early as 3500 BC, when copper, lead, tin, gold, and silver were in use in various parts of the world. Modern metallurgy is concerned with all metals, but primarily with those, such as iron, that are abundant and useful (see steel). Metallurgy originally developed by finding new *alloys and treatments by trial and error. Techniques, such as *metallography, have reduced the element of chance by identifying the factors in the microscopic structure of metals that contribute to hardness, strength, and ductility.

metamorphic rock   One of the three major rock categories (compare igneous rock; sedimentary rock) consisting of rocks produced by the alteration (in the solid state) of existing rocks by heat, pressure, and chemically active fluids. Contact (or thermal) metamorphism occurs around igneous intrusions and results from heat alone. Regional metamorphism, extending over large areas, results from the heat and pressure created by crustal deformation. Dislocation metamorphism results from localized mechanical deformation, as along fault planes. Metamorphic rocks tend to be resistant to denudation and often form upland masses. Marble is a metamorphic rock formed from recrystallized limestone. See Plate II.

metamorphosis   The process in animals by which a *larva changes into an adult. This radical change of internal and external body structures may be gradual or abrupt. Certain insects, such as dragonflies, undergo incomplete metamorphosis, during which successive stages (known as nymphs) become increasingly like the adult through a series of moults. In complete metamorphosis, seen in such insects as butterflies and houseflies, the larva passes into a quiescent pupal stage, during which the adult tissues are developed. Metamorphosis also occurs in amphibians (see frog). The process in insects and amphibians is controlled by hormones.

metaphor   A figure of speech in which one thing is described in terms of another. The comparison is implicit, lacking such words as like or as (see simile). The metaphor is a common feature of ordinary language, as in such phrases as "time flies" and "to lose one's head," and is a fundamental poetic device. This example is from Shakespeare's Macbeth (act 5, scene 3):

Life's but a walking shadow, a poor player
That struts and frets his hour upon the stage.

metaphysical painting   A style of painting practised by Carlo Carrà (1881–1966) and Giorgio de *Chirico in the second decade of the 20th century. Together they established a school in Ferrara in 1917. They illustrated the mystery behind everyday reality by depicting dreamlike illusions, characterized by hallucinatory lighting with stark shadows, incongruous juxtapositions of objects, sharply plunging perspectives of empty streets, and the use of mannequins rather than people. *Surrealism adopted many of their ideas and devices.

metaphysical poets   A group of 17th-century English poets whose work was characterized by intellectual wit and ingenuity, especially in their use of elaborate figures of speech. The leading poet was John *Donne, and his successors included George *Herbert, Henry *Vaughan, Andrew *Marvell, and Abraham *Cowley. They frequently employed colloquial speech rhythms in both their secular and their religious verse. The influential criticism of T. S. Eliot, who praised their union of intellect and emotion, helped to establish their high reputation in the 20th century.

metaphysics   The study of existence or being in general. The term derives from the title given to a group of Aristotle's writings by the philosopher Andronicus of Rhodes (1st century BC). The status of metaphysics has been much debated; *Kant thought this kind of investigation impossible because our minds can only cope with the phenomenal world or the world of appearances and *Ayer used the word in Language, Truth and Logic (1936) as a pejorative term to indicate the meaninglessness of much traditional philosophy. However, with *ethics and *epistemology, metaphysics is still held to be one of the main divisions of philosophy.

Metastasio, Pietro   (Pietro Antonio Domenico Trapassi; 1698–1782) Italian poet and librettist. In 1730 he was appointed court poet in Vienna, where he wrote numerous classical libretti. These include L'Adriano (1731) and La clemenza di Tito (1732), which has been set to music by many composers.

Metaxas, Ioannis   (1871–1941) Greek general; dictator (1936–41). After the monarchy was re-established in 1935, he became premier and then, with George II's support, dictator. He led Greek resistance to the Italian invasion in World War II.

metayage   A type of land tenure in which rent is paid in kind. Metayage, a French word (from Latin medietas, half), was at one time the dominant form of tenure in S France, involving payment of approximately half the tenant's output to the landowner.

Metazoa   A subkingdom of animals whose bodies consist of many cells differentiated and coordinated to perform specialized functions. The Metazoa includes all animals except the single-celled *Protozoa and the Parazoa (see sponge).

Metchnikov, Ilya Ilich (*or* I. I. Mechnikov; 1845-1916) Russian zoologist, who discovered that certain cells in animals could surround and engulf foreign particles, such as disease-causing bacteria. He called these cells *phagocytes and was awarded, with Paul *Ehrlich, the 1908 Nobel Prize.

metempsychosis. *See* reincarnation.

meteor A streak of light seen in the night sky when a **meteoroid**—an interplanetary rock or dust particle, usually with a mass from 10^{-7} to 10^{-3} gram but sometimes weighing over 10 kg—enters and burns up in the earth's atmosphere. A decaying *comet gradually produces a **meteor stream** of meteoroids around its orbit. When the earth passes through a meteor stream, an often spectacular **meteor shower** is observed, usually at the same time each year. The August Perseids and December Geminids are examples. A **meteorite** is a large piece of interplanetary debris (mass usually over 100 kg) that falls to the earth's surface, usually breaking up in the process. It produces a brilliant meteor. Meteorite composition is either principally iron or stone, or an intermediate mixture. Meteorites were formed early in the history of the solar system and most are believed to be fragments of minor planets. The rare fragile stony carbonaceous chondrites are possibly cometary fragments.

meteorology The study of the physics, chemistry, and movements of the *atmosphere and its interactions with the ground surface. The troposphere and stratosphere, the lower layers of the atmosphere in which most weather phenomena occur, are the chief focuses of meteorology and much attention has been paid to the explanation of surface weather and to weather forecasting. **Weather** is the state of atmospheric conditions (including temperature, sunshine, wind, clouds, and precipitation) at a particular place and time. A **weather forecast** is a prediction of what weather conditions will be over a stated future period; it is made by studying weather maps, especially those obtained from satellites (often feeding the observations into a computer). Short-term forecasts are made usually for a period of 24 hours (less for specialized uses) and long-range forecasts may be made for a month ahead although they are considerably less accurate. Weather forecasts are essential to shipping and aviation and are of use to many other bodies, including power authorities (predicting cold spells) and transport authorities (predicting snow, ice, and fog), as well as to farmers. Attempts have been made to modify weather, including cloud seeding, hurricane steering, and fog clearance, but success has been limited. *See also* climate.

methane (CH_4) A colourless odourless flammable gas that is the main constituent of *natural gas. It is the simplest member of the *alkane series and is used as a fuel and a source of other chemicals. Methane is produced in nature by the decay of vegetable matter under water, rising in bubbles from marshes as **marsh gas**. Coal gas also contains methane and is found in coalmines. Recently the generation of methane from sewage has been investigated as an *alternative energy source. It burns with a clear blue flame.

methanol (methyl alcohol *or* wood alcohol; CH_3OH) A colourless poisonous flammable liquid. Originally produced by distillation of wood, it is now usually made from hydrogen and carbon monoxide by high-pressure *catalysis. It is used as a solvent, antifreeze, and a raw material for making other chemicals. *See also* methylated spirits.

Methodism The Christian denomination that developed out of the religious practices advocated by the *Wesley brothers. Although not conceived initially as an institution separate from the Church of England, to which it is very close in doctrinal matters, Methodism evolved its own church organization during the 1790s. The supreme decision-making body is the Conference; local societies (congregations) are highly organized and pastoral and missionary work are major concerns. Methodism in the USA, where it dates from the 1780s and is the second largest Protestant denomination (after the Baptists), accounts for 80% of all Methodists, but there are thriving communities elsewhere.

Methodius, St. *See* Cyril, St.

methyl alcohol. *See* methanol.

methylated spirits A form of *ethanol (ethyl alcohol) that has been made unsuitable for drinking (and is therefore duty free) by the addition of about 9.5% of methanol (methyl alcohol), about 0.5% of pyridine, and a methyl violet dye (as a warning that it is dangerous to drink). In this form it has many household uses, especially as a fuel for spirit burners. It is sometimes drunk by desperate alcoholics, in whom it can cause blindness and other serious medical conditions. Industrial methylated spirits (IMS) consists of ethanol with about 5% of methanol and no pyridine. It is used as a solvent for varnishes, etc.

metre (m) The unit of length in the *metric system. Originally defined in 1791 as one ten-millionth of the length of the quadrant of the earth's meridian through Paris, it was redefined in 1927 as the distance between two marks on a platinum-iridium bar. It is now defined (General Conference on Weights and Measures, 1983) as the length of the path travelled by light in a vacuum in 1/299 792 458 second, which replaces the 1960 definition based on the emission of a krypton lamp.

metre (poetry) The rhythmic pattern of a line of verse measured in terms of basic metrical units or feet. In accentual verse, as in English, a foot consists of various arrangements of stressed (´) and unstressed (˘) syllables. In classical Greek and Latin verse, the quantity or length rather than the stress of syllables determines the foot. In English the most common feet are the *iamb (˘´), the trochee (´˘), the anapaest (˘˘´), the dactyl (´˘˘), and the spondee (´´). A typical line of *blank verse consisting of five iambs is known as an iambic pentameter. Most traditional poetic forms, such as the *sonnet, are written according to strict metrical patterns. Many poets of the late 19th and 20th centuries have written in free verse, which has no regular metre or line length, or syllabic verse, in which each line has a fixed number of syllables but no regular pattern of stress.

metric system A system of measurement based on the decimal system. First suggested in 1585 by Simon Stevin (1548-1620), an inspector of dykes in the Low Countries, it was not given formal acceptance until 1795, when a French law provided definitions for the *metre, *are, *stere, *litre, and gram. In 1799 a subsequent law established legal standards, made of platinum, for the metre and the kilogram. However, this form of the metric system was not widely used, even in France, until the third decade of the 19th century; during this period it was also adopted by most European countries.

Although the metric system was authorized in the UK in 1864, bills for its compulsory adoption were defeated in parliament in 1871 and again in 1907. British reluctance to abandon its own "Imperial units" did not weaken until 1963, when the Imperial yard and pound were given legal definitions in terms of metric units (e.g. the yard is now defined as 0.9144 metre exactly). By 1969 the **Metrication Board** had been set up with the target of completing the metrication of British industry and commerce by 1975. This target was not met and the Metrication Board was disbanded in April 1980, metrication proceeding thereafter on a voluntary basis. A review of some of the major units will take place before 1989.

For scientific purposes, former metric systems (such as the *c.g.s. system and the *m.k.s. system) have been replaced by *SI units, a coherent system of metric units.

metrology The science of measurement. The scientific method is based on making accurate measurements, i.e. of

weather conditions

- • rain
- ❋ snow
- ⌒ dew
- ⌐ drizzle
- ▲ hail
- = fog
- ▽ showers
- △ ice pellets
- Ⓚ thunderstorm

cloud cover

- ◯ clear
- ⬤ 1 okta
- ◕ 2
- ◔ 3
- ◑ 4
- ◕ 5
- ⬤ 6
- ◑ 7
- ⬤ 8
- ⊗ sky obscured
  (1 okta = $\frac{1}{8}$ of the sky)

wind
The arrow points in the direction from which the wind is blowing.

knots

- ◎ calm
- ○— 1–2
- ○—⌐ 3–7
- ○—/ 8–12
- ○—// 13–17
- ○—// 18–22
- ○—/// 23–27
- ○—/// 28–32
- ○—//// 33–37
- ○—//// 38–42
- ○—///// 43–47
- ○—▲ 48–52

weather map
The numbers at the stations show temperature (0°C). Isobars show atmospheric pressure in millibars.

fronts

- ▼▼▼ **cold front** *boundary between overtaking cold air mass and warm air mass.*
- ●●● **warm front** *boundary between overtaking warm air mass and cold air mass.*
- ▼●▼● **stationary** *boundary between air masses of similar temperature.*
- ▲▲●● **occluded** *line where a cold front overtakes a warm front.*

METEOROLOGY *Internationally agreed symbols are used throughout the world by meteorological stations to represent current weather conditions. These are plotted on weather maps from which forecasts can be made.*

expressing the magnitude of a physical quantity (say, length) in terms of a number and a unit (say, metres). Metrologists study methods of making these accurate measurements and of deciding what units should be used and how they should be defined. Modern metrology is based on *SI units and the methods of defining the system's seven basic units. The decision to adopt this system was taken in 1960 by metrologists from 30 nations meeting at the Conférence Générale des Poids et Mesures.

metronome A small device consisting of a pendulum with a small sliding weight on it, which can be regulated to make the pendulum beat at a desired number of beats per minute. The most common type is the clockwork metronome invented by J. N. Maelzel (1770-1838); electric metronomes also exist. Metronome markings are often given in musical scores to indicate the exact speed of the music.

Metropolitan Museum of Art The principal museum in New York City and one of the most important in the world. Founded in 1870, it was opened in its present premises in Central Park in 1880. Its enormous collection comprises paintings, drawings, sculptures, ceramics, furni-

ture, etc., from many periods and countries, including China, ancient Egypt, Greece, and Rome. Since 1938 its collection of medieval art has been housed in the Cloisters, built in Fort Tyron Park, Manhattan, from fragments of medieval monasteries and churches.

Metropolitan Opera Association The principal US opera company, founded in New York in 1883. *Caruso sang regularly with the company from 1904 to 1921. The general manager from 1950 to 1972 was Sir Rudolph *Bing. The company occupied the Metropolitan Opera House until 1966, when it moved into the Lincoln Centre for the Performing Arts, the original building being demolished.

Metsu, Gabriel (1629-67) Dutch painter, who was born in Leyden but lived in Amsterdam from about 1650. His early subjects were often religious but he is better known for his interiors showing middle-class life in such paintings as *The Duet* (National Gallery, London).

Metternich, Klemens Wenzel Nepomuk Lothar, Fürst von (1773-1859) Austrian statesman, the leading figure in European diplomacy from the fall of Napoleon (1815) until the Revolutions of 1848. As foreign minister (1809–48) he sought to maintain the balance of power in Europe, supporting dynastic monarchies and suppressing liberalism. His policies dominated the great Congresses of *Vienna (1814–15), *Aix-la-Chapelle (1818), Troppau (1820), Laibach (1821), and Verona (1822). The Revolution of 1848 forced him to seek refuge in Britain, the constitutional monarchy of which he had always condemned.

Metz (Latin name: Divodorum)   49 07N 6 11E A city in NE France, the capital of the Moselle department on the River Moselle. The centre of the Lorraine coal and metal industries, it trades in wine and agricultural products and has varied manufacturing industries. It has a fine cathedral (13th–16th centuries) and a university (1971). *History*: part of the Holy Roman Empire until seized by France (1552), it fell to Germany (1871) but returned to France after World War I. Population (1982): 118 502.

Meuse, River (Dutch and Flemish name: Maas)   A river in W Europe. Rising in NE France and flowing mainly N past Liège in Belgium and Maastricht in the S Netherlands, it enters the North Sea at the Rhine Delta. It was the scene of heavy fighting in World War I (1914) and World War II (1940). Its lower course is an important commercial waterway. Length: 926 km (575 mi).

Mewar. *See* Udaipur.

Mexicali   32 36N 115 30W A city in the extreme NW of Mexico, on the US border. It is the commercial centre for a rich irrigated agricultural area. Population (1980): 510 554.

Mexican War   (1846–48) The war between Mexico and the USA over disputed border territory. Military operations began when Gen Zachary *Taylor invaded New Mexico and ended with the fall of Mexico City (1847). Peace was concluded with the Treaty of *Guadaloupe-Hidalgo.

Mexico, United States of   A country in Central America between the Gulf of Mexico and the Pacific Ocean. Narrow coastal plains rise to high mountain ranges in the interior, which include the volcano Popocatépetl. Much of the N is arid with tropical forest in the S, especially in the Yucatán Peninsula in the SE (the only extensive low-lying area). Most of the population is of mixed Indian and Spanish descent. *Economy*: Mexico now ranks among the world's main oil-producing countries following substantial finds in several areas, the most recent being along the E coastline of the states of Tamaulipas and Veracruz. Some 80% of exported oil went to the USA in 1978. Mexico also has large reserves of natural gas and there are substantial deposits of uranium, although in 1979 only one nuclear-power plant was under construction. Other minerals extracted include iron ore, zinc, sulphur, silver, and copper, and Mexico is the world's largest producer of fluorite and graphite. Agriculture remains relatively underdeveloped and during the mid-1970s a programme to collectivize smallholdings was launched in an effort to increase food production. Maize is the main food crop; cash crops include cotton, sugar, coffee, and fruit and vegetables, as well as sisal in Yucatán. Fishing has been developed considerably in recent years and important catches include sardines, shrimps, and oysters. Tourism is an important source of foreign currency. *History*: Mexico was the site of the Mayan civilization from the 2nd to the 13th centuries AD, and between the 8th and the 12th centuries the *Toltecs flourished. The 14th century saw the rise of the *Aztecs, whose capital was at Tenochtitlán, the site of present-day Mexico City. The Aztecs were conquered by the Spanish under Cortés in 1521 and Mexico became part of the viceroyalty of New Spain. The struggle for independence from Spain began in 1810 and was achieved in 1821. A turbulent period dominated by *Santa Anna was followed by the *Mexican War (1846–48), in which territory was lost to the USA. In 1864 *Maximilian, Archduke of Austria, was installed as emperor by the French, but in 1867 he was shot in the successful anti-French revolution led by Benito Juá-

rez. In 1911 the long dictatorship of Porfirio Díaz ended in an uprising under Francisco Madera. The Mexican Revolution culminated in the constitution of 1917, the democratic goals of which have been the declared aims of subsequent governments. Mexico is now a one-party state dominated by the Party of Institutionalized Revolution (PRI), serious demonstrations against which have occurred. Economic pressures in the 1980s have led to high inflation, devaluation of the peso, austerity measures, and rescheduling of Mexico's debts by the International Monetary Fund. Mexico is a member of the OAS. President: Miguel de la Madrid Hurtado (1935–   ). Official language: Spanish; Indian languages, especially Nahuatl, are widely spoken. Official currency: Mexican peso of 100 centavos. Area: 1 967 183 sq km (761 530 sq mi). Population (1982 est): 75 702 000. Capital: Mexico City. Main port: Veracruz.

Mexico City (Spanish name: Ciudad de México)   19 25N 99 10W The capital of Mexico, in the S of the high central plateau at a height of 2380 m (7800 ft), surrounded by mountains. The 14th-century Aztec city of Tenochtitlán (built on a lake, since filled in) had a population of almost half a million when it was destroyed by Cortés in 1521. A new Spanish city was built on the site and it rapidly became the most important in the New World. It was captured by the USA and then by France in the 19th century and in the 20th century was the centre of several revolutions. It now has considerable industry. It is the site of the National Autonomous University of Mexico (founded in 1551), the national library, a famous school of mining engineering, the museum (containing the Aztec Calendar Stone), and the Palace of Fine Arts Theatre. Other famous landmarks include the cathedral (16th–19th centuries) and the 17th-century Palacio Nacional. In 1985 the city and surrounding areas were devastated by an earthquake in which some 20 000 people are thought to have died. Population (1980): 12 932 116.

Meyerbeer, Giacomo   (Jacob Liebmann Beer; 1791–1864) German composer and pianist. A child prodigy, he studied the piano with Clementi and composition with Abbé Vogler (1749–1814). His early German operas failed while those in the more superficial Italian style were more successful. In Paris he composed the spectacular works by which he is remembered: *Robert le Diable* (1831), *Les Huguenots* (1836), and *L'Africaine* (performed posthumously; 1865).

Meyerhof, Otto Fritz   (1884–1951) US biochemist, born in Germany, who showed that glycogen in muscles is broken down anaerobically into lactic acid when the muscle is working. He shared the 1922 Nobel Prize with Archibald *Hill.

Meyerhold, Vsevolod Emilievich   (1874–?1943) Russian theatre director. He joined the Moscow Art Theatre in 1898, but rejected the naturalism of *Stanislavsky and experimented with a symbolic and abstract drama in which the actor's individual role was reduced. He supported the Revolution and joined the Bolshevik Party in 1918. In the 1920s he was the first director to specialize in producing Soviet plays, but fell out of favour with the government in the 1930s. He died probably in a Soviet labour camp.

Mezzogiorno (Italian: midday)   Southern Italy; the name refers to the heat of the region, which is economically, socially, and politically backward. After the unification of Italy in the 19th century the development of the N received greater attention from the central government than the S, where local government was ineffectual, the *Mafia flourished, and the gulf between landowners and peasants was considerable. Despite special government aid during the 20th century, the problems are still largely unsolved.

mezzo-soprano. *See* soprano.

mezzotint   A technique of printing tonal areas (as opposed to lines), invented by a German officer, Ludwig von Sieger (1609–?1680). It was thus particularly suitable for reproducing paintings, being popular in 18th- and 19th-century

England for printing Reynolds' portraits, Constable's landscapes, etc. The technique involves roughening and indenting a copper or steel plate with a serrated edged tool (rocker). Some of the roughened parts are then scraped away before the plate's surface is coated with ink. The indentations create the dark tones of the print, while the polished parts produce the lighter accents. Mezzotint is often combined with *etching and line engraving.

Mfecane (1818-28) A period of wars and upheaval among Bantu peoples of southern Africa. The Zulu, under their warrior king *Shaka, turned on neighbouring tribes, causing them to abandon their cattle and grain stores and to flee into the territory of other tribes. This movement of peoples radically altered tribal groupings and led to the formation of new groupings, such as the Swazi, Basuto, Kololo, and Ndebele.

Miami 25 45N 80 15W A city and port in the USA, in □Florida on Biscayne Bay. A major tourist resort and retirement centre, it grew during the Florida land boom of the 1920s and includes Coral Gables (site of the University of Miami, established in 1925) and Miami Beach. It is famous for its citrus fruit and winter vegetables. Industries include aircraft repairing, sponge fisheries, clothing, and concrete. Population (1980): 346 931.

Micah (8th century BC) An Old Testament prophet of Judah and contemporary of Isaiah. **The Book of Micah** records his condemnation of a number of specific sins in the corrupt nation and predicts the fall of Jerusalem, the renewal of the people, and the coming of a Messiah.

micas A group of common rock-forming silicate minerals with a layered structure and complex composition. Muscovite, $K_2Al_4(Si_6Al_2)O_{20}(OH,F)_4$, is a white mica and economically the most important; it occurs in granitic rocks (often pegmatites), gneisses, and schists. The other principal micas are *phlogopite (amber), biotite (dark), paragonite, margarite, zinnwaldite, and lepidolite (a source of lithium). Their perfect cleavage is reflected in the layered structure. In its commercial form it is sold in blocks (sheets), books (flakes resembling the pages of a book), and splittings (loose flakes). Since it is a good insulator and can withstand high temperatures, mica has many electrical uses and is used for furnace windows. Splittings bonded together with shellac or synthetic resins are used to make Micanite.

Michael (1596-1645) Tsar of Russia (1613-45) and founder of the *Romanov dynasty. Michael's election as tsar ended the *Time of Troubles. Michael was a weak ruler, relying upon his father Patriarch Philaret (c. 1553-1633). Serfdom was intensified during his reign.

Michael (1921-) King of Romania (1927-30, 1940-47). Michael succeeded his grandfather in 1927 but lost the crown in 1930, when his father *Carol II returned from exile. After Carol's abdication in 1940, Michael again became king. In 1944 he overthrew the dictatorship of Ion Antonescu and declared war on Germany. He abdicated in 1947.

Michael. *See* archangels.

Michael VIII Palaeologus (1224-82 AD) Byzantine emperor (1259-82), who founded the Palaeologan (the last Byzantine) dynasty (1259-1453). In 1261 Michael captured Constantinople from the Latins and re-established the Byzantine empire there after its 57-year exile. His subsequent policies were determined by the fear of another attack from the West. An alliance with the papacy against Charles I of Naples and Sicily led to the union (1274) of the Greek and Roman Churches, for which he was vilified after his death.

Michaelmas daisy. *See* Aster.

Michaelmas Day The feast of St Michael the archangel (29 September). It is one of the four quarter days in traditional English business practice.

Michelangelo Buonarroti (1475-1564) Italian sculptor, painter, architect, and poet, born at Caprese, in Tuscany. Michelangelo was trained in Florence under the painter *Ghirlandaio and in the school in the Medici gardens, under the patronage of Lorenzo de' Medici. Working in Rome from 1496 until 1501, he produced his first major sculptures, notably the *Pietà* (St Peter's, Rome). This was followed (1501-05) by his work in Florence, including *David* (Accademia, Florence), the painting of the *Holy Family* (Uffizi), and the influential cartoon of the *Battle of Cascina*. The last was commissioned as a fresco for the Palazzo Vecchio but was never finished and was painted over by Vasari. Michelangelo's productive but stormy association with Pope Julius II began in 1505, when the pope commissioned Michelangelo to produce his tomb. Although this proved to be his most chequered and lengthy project, it resulted in such masterpieces as the *Slaves* (Accademia, Florence). The celebrated Sistine Chapel ceiling (1508-12), in the Vatican, established his reputation as the greatest painter of his day. Returning to Florence (1516), Michelangelo became the architect and sculptor of the Medici funerary chapel (1520-34) in S Lorenzo and he also designed the Laurentian Library. These architectural projects and the fresco of the *Last Judgment* (1534-41) for the Sistine Chapel were his first major works in the new mannerist style (*see* mannerism). In his last years he worked mainly as an architect, becoming in 1547 chief architect of St Peter's, Rome, in which capacity he designed its great dome. His last sculptures included the *Rondanini Pietà* (Milan, Castello).

Michelet, Jules (1798-1874) French historian. He established his academic reputation while still young and was appointed Keeper of the National Archives in 1831. His *Histoire de France* (6 vols, 1833-43; 11 vols, 1855-67) and *La Révolution française* (7 vols, 1847-53) were unashamedly nationalist works, written with romantic imagination. During the Second Empire (1852-70) he retired from public life and wrote works on natural science.

Michelin, André (1853-1931) French tyre manufacturer, who founded, with his brother **Édouard Michelin** (1859-1940), the Michelin Tyre Company (1888). In 1895 they became the first to demonstrate the feasibility of using pneumatic tyres on motor cars. The company is now also famous for its maps and guidebooks.

Michelozzo di Bartolommeo (1396-1472) Florentine *Renaissance sculptor and architect. As a sculptor he collaborated first with *Ghiberti and then with *Donatello, but after 1433 he turned to architecture. He designed several buildings for the Medici, including the Palazzo Medici (1444-59), which was the first Renaissance palace.

Michelson, Albert Abraham (1852-1931) US physicist, born in Germany. He designed a highly accurate interferometer known as the Michelson interferometer and used it to measure precisely the speed of light. He also used it in an attempt to measure the velocity of the earth through the ether. This work, carried out in conjunction with Edward *Morley and known as the *Michelson-Morley experiment, eventually led *Einstein to his theory of relativity. Michelson received the Nobel Prize in 1907.

Michelson-Morley experiment An experiment performed by A. A. *Michelson and E. W. *Morley in 1881 in an attempt to demonstrate the existence of the luminiferous ether by measuring the earth's velocity relative to it. They used a Michelson interferometer to obtain interference fringes and then rotated the apparatus through 90° expecting to find a shift in the fringes, since the velocity of light would be different in the two directions. This difference would result from the earth's motion through the ether. However, no shift was detected. This negative result led to the downfall of the ether theory and was explained by Einstein's theory of *relativity in 1905 (*see also* Lorentz, Hendrick Antoon). □ p. 810.

Michigan A state in the N central USA, bordered largely

by water (Lakes Superior, Huron, Michigan, Erie, and St Clair). It is divided by the Straits of Mackinac into the Lower Peninsula in the S (an area of lowlands) and the Upper Peninsula in the N (lowlands in the E and uplands in the W). Michigan is also divided demographically and economically, with most of its population and industry concentrated in the Lower Peninsula. Manufacturing is very important, especially the production of motor vehicles at Detroit; other industries include machinery, iron and steel, and chemicals. The state exploits its large mineral reserves of gypsum, calcium, and magnesium compounds, natural gas and oil. Tourism is the state's second largest industry. It is also an important agricultural state producing vegetables, maize, beans, fruit, and livestock. *History*: first explored by the French in the 17th century, it remained under French control until it was acquired by the British (1763) as part of Canada. It came under American control (1783), becoming a state in 1837. Area: 150 779 sq km (58 216 sq mi). Population (1980): 9 258 344. Capital: Lansing.

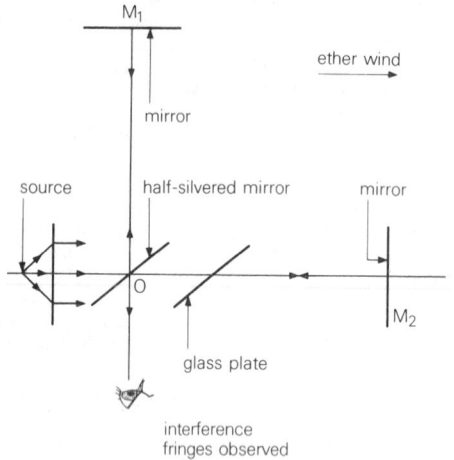

Michelson interferometer

MICHELSON-MORLEY EXPERIMENT *The Michelson interferometer was used in an attempt to detect changes in the velocity of light of the earth's motion through the ether. Distances OM_1 and OM_2 are equal. The glass plate compensates for the thickness of the half-silvered mirror.*

Michigan, Lake The third largest of the Great Lakes in North America, the only one wholly in the USA. It is linked with Lake Huron via the Straits of Mackinac; the city of Chicago is on its S bank. Area: 58 000 sq km (22 400 sq mi).

Mickiewicz, Adam (1798–1855) Polish poet. His early poetry was strongly influenced by the Romantics, especially Byron. In 1823 he was arrested with other students of Vilna University and deported to Russia, where he became a friend of Pushkin. He left Russia in 1829 and settled in Paris in 1832. His works include the Romantic drama *Dziadzy* (1823–32) and the epic poem *Pan Tadeusz* (1832–34).

microbiology The study of microorganisms, or microbes —organisms that are invisible to the naked eye, including bacteria, small fungi (e.g. yeasts and moulds), algae, protozoa, and viruses. Microorganisms, which are abundant everywhere, are of immense importance to all living things. They bring about *decomposition and the recycling of nutrients. They are vital to numerous industries, including brewing, baking, dairying, and food processing, and they have revolutionized medical treatment with the discovery of antibiotics. Some microorganisms, however, are parasites that cause disease in plants, animals, and man (*see* infection).

microchip. *See* integrated circuit.

microcomputers Small sophisticated *computers designed for a single user and often for a specific application. The tiny central processing unit is a *microprocessor. Microcomputers were introduced in the 1970s for industrial, commercial, and domestic applications. They have had a great impact in speeding automation.

microcopy A greatly reduced photographic copy of a printed page, drawing, or other image. **Microfilm** is a strip of standard-width film containing microcopies. It was introduced in the 1920s for use in banks and is now widely used for compact storage and ready reference to documents. Special enlarging viewers can rapidly wind the film to the correct page. **Microfiche** is a similar system on cards holding a single film negative, with even greater reduction of the pictures. The viewers often have a printer attached to reproduce paper copies. Microfiche is widely used in data-processing systems as an alternative to paper computer printout, and in libraries to store periodicals, etc.

micrometer An instrument for measuring small lengths with great accuracy. The object to be measured is held between the jaws of a C-shaped metal piece, one jaw of which can be adjusted by a screw. The screw is turned by rotating a drum with a *vernier scale marked on it, from which the required dimension can be read.

micron (μm) An obsolete name for one-millionth of a metre. The correct name is now the **micrometre** (*see* SI units).

Micronesia A division of Oceania in the W Pacific Ocean, consisting of an arc of islands E of the Philippines. It includes the Belau, Kiribati, Mariana, Caroline, and Marshall archipelagos. *See also* Melanesia; Polynesia.

Micronesia, Federated States of An island group within the UN Trust Territory of the *Pacific Islands, comprising Truk, Yap, Ponape, and Yosrae. Self-government was achieved in 1979. Population (1980): 116 974.

microphone A device that converts sound into electrical signals. It acts like a *loudspeaker in reverse and some microphones may also be used as loudspeakers. Most consist of a thin diaphragm, the mechanical vibration of which is converted to an electrical signal proportional to the sound pressure. A telephone mouthpiece usually consists of a carbon microphone in which the sound waves exert a varying pressure on carbon granules, so varying their electrical resistance. In capacitor microphones, the most commonly used type in music recording, the diaphragm forms one plate of a capacitor, across which the sound waves produce a fluctuating potential difference. Crystal microphones rely on the *piezoelectric effect. Other types use magnetic induction, and less commonly magnetostriction or other electromagnetic effects. Ribbon microphones have a highly directional response. They consist of a thin strip of aluminium alloy in a strong magnetic field. The ribbon vibrates in the sound waves, inducing in itself an electromotive force proportional to its velocity.

microprocessor The central processing unit of a *microcomputer. Its development was made possible in the 1970s by advances in solid-state electronics, in particular the design of integrated circuits of such complexity that all the main calculating functions can be carried out by a single silicon chip (*see* integrated circuit).

microscope An optical instrument used for producing a magnified image of a small object. There are several distinct types, the most common being the compound microscope, which contains an objective lens system and an eyepiece system. It was invented in 1609 by a Dutch spectacle maker Zacharias Janssen (1580–c. 1638) and his father, but Robert *Hooke gave the first extensive description of its use in biology in his *Micrographia* (1665). In a compound microscope the objective produces a real magnified image, which is further magnified by the eyepiece. At low *magnifications the system is illuminated by a source the light of which is reflected through the specimen by a mirror. At high magnifications special illuminating systems are needed. The magnification, which may be up to a thousand, is limited by the *resolving power of the lenses; the smallest detail capable of resolution by an optical microscope is about 0.2 micrometre. This can be increased by using an *oil-immersion lens (*see also* ultramicroscope). Still higher magnifications are obtained by using shorter wavelength radiations as in the *electron microscope.

A **photomicrograph** is a photograph of the image obtained using a microscope. This enables a permanent record to be kept and also enables ultraviolet radiation to be used for illumination of the specimen.

microsurgery. *See* surgery.

microwave background radiation. *See* big-bang theory.

microwaves Electromagnetic radiation with wavelengths between 1 and 300 millimetres, lying between infrared rays and radio waves in the electromagnetic spectrum. They are used in *radar and **microwave heating**. This method is used in the rapid cooking of food as the radiation penetrates to the interior of the food. The microwave photon is the same order of magnitude as the vibrational energy of atoms and molecules and therefore heats the interior directly, rather than by conduction from the surface. It is also used in sterilization and in drying wood, etc. Microwaves are generated by such devices as *magnetrons and *klystrons.

Midas In Greek legend, a king of Phrygia whose wish that everything he touched be turned to gold was granted by Dionysus in gratitude for his hospitality to the satyr *Silenus. Because he was therefore unable to eat or drink, he was released from this handicap by bathing in the River Pactolus. In another legend, Midas was asked to judge between the music of Pan and Apollo and chose the former. Apollo punished his tactlessness by changing his ears into those of an ass.

Mid-Atlantic Ridge The submarine ridge extending N–S through the Atlantic Ocean. It forms part of the mid-ocean ridge system that crosses all the major oceans. Much of it is over 1000 km (621 mi) wide and rises to between 1 and 3 km (0.6–1.9 mi) above the ocean basin, in places rising above sea level to form islands. Along the crest are rift mountains and a fractured plateau. *See* plate tectonics.

Middelburg 51 30N 3 36E A town in the SW Netherlands, the capital of Zeeland province on Walcheren Island. Badly damaged in World War II, a 12th-century abbey survives. Population (1981 est): 38 619.

middle ages The period of European history that is generally regarded as commencing in the 5th century with the fall of the western Roman Empire and ending with the Renaissance. This period begins with the creation of the barbarian kingdoms, which developed into the nation states of W Europe. In Church history, the period covers the rise to supremacy of the Roman Catholic Church, centred on Rome, and the development of the papacy as an international religious and political power. Socially and economically the period saw the rising power of the great landed magnates and the creation of a feudal society, while urban growth and the development of trade reached unprecedented heights. The period can be said to end with the fall of Constantinople to the Turks (1453), the discovery of America (1492), and the successful challenge to the papacy of the national reform movements.

Middleback Range A range of hills in S South Australia. It extends N–S for 64 km (40 mi) in the Eyre Peninsula and possesses rich deposits of iron ore; these are worked at Iron Knob, Iron Monarch, and Iron Baron.

Middle Comedy The transitional period of Greek comic drama, lasting from about 400 BC to about 320 BC. Its characteristics are evident in the last two plays of Aristophanes, *Ecclesiazusae* (392) and *Plutus* (388). A more

oblique humour replaced the exuberant and scurrilous wit of earlier comedy, perhaps reflecting the Athenians' loss of confidence in themselves after their defeat (404) in the Peloponnesian War. *See also* Old Comedy; New Comedy.

Middle East The area comprising Iran and the countries of the Arabian peninsula and the Mediterranean seaboard. The Middle East, sometimes called the cradle of civilization, is the birthplace of three major world religions, Judaism, Christianity, and Islam, and their attendant cultures. A world crossroads, its troubled history has been dominated at different times by the Jews, Assyrians, Babylonians, Tatars, Macedonians, and Arabs. The present unrest derives from the conflict between superpowers to influence an area that produces 40% of the world's oil, by conflict between Arab countries and Israel (exacerbated by the displaced Palestinians), and by the recent revolution in Iran.

Middlesbrough 54 35N 1 14W A town in NE England, the administrative centre of Cleveland on the Tees estuary. Local iron ore (in the Cleveland Hills) and local coking coal (from the Durham coalfield) gave Middlesbrough early industrial advantages. Iron and steel, chemicals, constructional engineering, and shipbuilding are the major industries and almost all the traffic through the port of Middlesbrough is related to the steel and chemical industries. Population (1981): 149 770.

Middlesex A former county of SE England. In 1965 it was for the most part absorbed by Greater London, the boundaries of which were reorganized in that year. Staines and Sunbury-on-Thames were transferred to Surrey and Potters Bar to Hertfordshire.

Middle Temple. *See* Inns of Court.

Middleton, Thomas (1580–1627) English dramatist. He wrote and collaborated on many comedies and pageants, and achieved popular success with his political satire *A Game at Chess* (1624), which was suppressed after complaints from the Spanish ambassador. His best-known plays are the tragedies *Women Beware Women* (c. 1621) and, in collaboration with William *Rowley, *The Changeling* (1622).

Middle West, the. *See* Midwest, the.

Midgard In Norse mythology, the earth, which lies between Hel or Niflheim, the land of ice, and Muspelheim, the land of fire, and is reached from *Asgard (the home of the gods) by Bifrost, the rainbow bridge. It was formed by the gods from the dead body of the giant Aurgelmir, his flesh being the land, his blood the oceans, etc.

midge A small fly, also called a nonbiting midge, belonging to the family *Chironomidae* (over 2000 species). It resembles a mosquito but is harmless. Midges are found near fresh water, often in large swarms. The wormlike aquatic larvae are often red (*see* bloodworm) and live in gelatinous or sand tubes, feeding on algae.

The term is also applied loosely to similar but unrelated flies, including the biting or bloodsucking midges (family *Ceratopogonidae*) and the *gall midges.

Mid Glamorgan A county of SE Wales. It was created in 1974 from central Glamorgan and a small part of Breconshire and Monmouthshire. It consists of uplands dissected by the deep parallel valleys of the Rivers Taff, Rhymney, and Ogmore. There is sheep farming on the uplands. Coalmining remains an important activity in the inner valleys but the traditional iron industry has been replaced by light industry since World War II, especially around Merthyr Tydfil and Aberdare. Area: 1019 sq km (393 sq mi). Population (1981): 537 866. Administrative centre: Cardiff.

Midlands A collective term for the central counties of England. The area includes the counties of Derbyshire, Leicestershire, Northamptonshire, and Nottinghamshire, which are frequently referred to as the **East Midlands**, and the counties of Staffordshire, Warwickshire, Hereford and Worcester, and the metropolitan county of West Midlands, which comprise the **West Midlands**. The term **South Midlands** is sometimes used to refer to the counties of Buckinghamshire, Bedfordshire, and Oxfordshire.

Midlothian A former county (once called Edinburghshire) of SE Scotland. Under local government reorganization in 1975 its boundaries were adjusted to form a district of the same name, in Lothian Region.

midnight sun The sun when it is seen on or above the horizon at midnight at places within the Arctic or Antarctic circles. At the polar circles it is seen only at the summer *solstice. At the Poles it is seen for the six months between the summer and winter solstices.

Midrash (Hebrew: enquiry, exposition) Exposition of the Bible, and more particularly a book consisting of such exposition. There are many Midrashim, mostly dating from the early middle ages, and they are a valuable source for the religious ideas of the Jews of the time. The *Talmuds also contain a great deal of Midrash.

midshipman A fish, also called singing fish, belonging to a genus (*Porichthys*) of *toadfishes. It is able to produce a whistling sound and has rows of light-producing organs on its underside.

Midway Islands 28 15N 177 25W A small group of US islands in the central Pacific Ocean. A military base, they are unpopulated apart from US military personnel. The air battle that took place here (3-6 June, 1942) resulted in a major Allied victory. Area: 5 sq km (2 sq mi).

Midwest, the (*or* Middle West) An area in the N central USA. Its boundaries are indefinite but it is generally accepted to be N of the Ohio River, W of Lake Eyre, and E of the Great Plains. One of the world's most fertile agricultural areas, it produces chiefly maize and wheat.

midwifery The nursing specialty concerned with the care of women during pregnancy and childbirth. Midwives assist in monitoring the health of the mother and baby during labour and deliver the baby in the absence of complications. Midwives undergo extensive training beyond basic nursing training and are usually registered with a supervisory body.

MIDWIFE TOAD *Mating takes place on land. Soon after fertilization the male twines the eggs around his legs and carries them about, thus protecting them from the predators they would otherwise encounter if laid in water.*

midwife toad A *toad, *Alytes obstetricans*, found in W Europe up to 2200 m above sea level. Pale grey and slow-moving, it has an unusual breeding habit. As the eggs are laid, the male winds the two egg strings around his hind legs. He keeps the eggs for about a month, frequently

moistening them with dew and finally takes them to hatch in a pool.

Mies van der Rohe, Ludwig (1886-1969) German architect. A pioneering architect of the 1920s and 1930s, Mies first achieved fame with his glass skyscrapers (1919-21). However, his most influential building was the glass, steel, and marble German pavilion at the Barcelona international exhibition (1929; □furniture). After a short period running the *Bauhaus, he moved (1937) to the USA, where he designed such buildings as the Illinois Institute of Technology (1939) and the Seagram building, New York (1958; □architecture). His last design, an executed controversial tower block for Mansion House Square in the City of London, was finally rejected in 1985.

mignonette A bushy annual herb, *Reseda odorata*, native to N Africa and widely grown as an ornamental. Up to 60 cm high, it bears dense terminal clusters of tiny yellow or white flowers, which have a musky fragrance and are used in perfumery. The name is also applied to other species of *Reseda*. Family: *Resedaceae*.

migraine Recurrent headaches, usually affecting one side of the head and thought to be caused by contraction and then dilation of the arteries in the brain. The attacks are often preceded by blurring of vision and flickering lights (called an aura). During the headache itself vomiting commonly occurs. Some drugs reduce the incidence of attacks and others relieve the severity of an attack.

migration, animal The periodic movement of animal populations between one region and another, usually associated with seasonal climatic changes or breeding cycles. Migration is best known among birds. Many European species travel to S Africa to avoid the harsh winter weather and the Arctic tern makes a spectacular migration of 17 600 km (11 000 mi) between its breeding grounds in the Arctic and the Antarctic. The phenomenon is seen in many other animals, including fish (notably salmon), which return each year from the sea to spawn in the same river that they themselves were spawned, butterflies, bats, lemmings, and whales. The mechanism of navigation and homing is not completely understood. In birds it seems to involve sighting of visible landmarks, such as mountains and vegetation, as well as a compass sense, using the sun or the stars as bearings. Other animals are thought to use similar methods. Land mammals may lay scent trails for local direction finding.

migration, human The movement of groups of people from one country to another in which they intend to settle. Religious persecution has led many (e.g. the *Pilgrim Fathers, the French *Huguenots following the revocation of the Edict of *Nantes, and the Jews) to flee their homelands and settle elsewhere. The 19th century was a period of migration on a large scale, often prompted by severe population pressures, rural unemployment, and the economic opportunities in the country of destination as well as racial persecution. Many of the major countries able to absorb large numbers of immigrants have had historic policies favouring Europeans (e.g. Australia, South Africa, and the USA). Even European immigration in these countries was severely restricted by legislation in the 1920s. Since World War I governments have been more active in controlling migration and this applies also to controls exercised in the sending countries.

Traditionally, Commonwealth citizens have been allowed to enter the UK freely. Immigration increased in the 1950s, when British public services, faced with shortages of labour, began recruiting West Indians to work in the UK. Despite the net fall in population due to emigration the continuation of immigration from Asia and the Caribbean led to demands for controls, which caused a temporary surge in the number of immigrants before they were enforced. Controls were introduced in 1962, since when approximately 20 000 migrants have entered the UK annually. Official statistics show that in the decade 1974–83 there was an average annual net outflow from the UK of 37 000.

A specific feature of the postwar period has been the temporary migration of approximately 11 million unskilled "guest workers" (German word: *Gastarbeiter*) from such countries as Turkey and Algeria to the industrial countries of Europe, especially France and Germany.

Mihajlović, Draža (*or* D. Mihailović; (1893–1946) Yugoslav general. After Germany occupied Yugoslavia in World War II he organized the *Chetniks. In 1943 he was appointed minister of war by Peter II (1923–70; reigned 1934–45) but lost the king's confidence and Allied support to *Tito. After the liberation he was shot for treason.

Míkonos (*or* Mykonos)   A Greek island in the S Aegean Sea, one of the Cyclades. It is popular with tourists and is noted for having a large number of churches. Area: 90 sq km (35 sq mi). Population (1981): 5503.

Milan (Italian name: Milano; Latin name: Mediolanum) 45 28N 9 12E A city in N Italy, the capital of Lombardy on the River Olona. Milan is the focal point of rail and road routes and is the chief commercial and industrial centre of Italy. Its manufactures include motor vehicles, machinery, silk and other textiles, and chemicals and it is a major publishing centre. Milan has a gothic cathedral (duomo), two universities (both founded in the 1920s), the Brera Palace (containing the city's chief art collection), a library, and the opera house of *La Scala. The convent of Sta Maria delle Grazie contains Leonardo da Vinci's fresco *The Last Supper*. *History*: founded by the Gauls about 600 BC, it was captured by the Romans in 222. Later devastated by the Huns and the Goths, it was involved in much warfare until the 12th century, after which time it enjoyed considerable economic prosperity. It was ruled by the Visconti family from 1310 until 1447, after which it passed to the Sforza family, who ruled until the fall of Milan to Spain (1535). It was under Austrian rule (1713–96) and in 1797 Napoleon made it capital of the Cisalpine Republic (1797) and the kingdom of Italy (1805–14). It grew in industrial importance after its unification (1861) with Italy. Population (1980 est): 1 655 599.

Mildenhall   52 21N 0 30E A market town in E England, in Suffolk on the River Lark. Nearby, relics have been found from Stone Age, Roman, and Saxon times. Population (1983 est): 12 040.

mildew   Any fungus that grows as dense filaments forming visible white patches. Many fungal diseases of plants are called mildews: powdery mildews are infestations by fungi of the order *Peronosporales*, while downy mildews are due to infection by fungi of the family *Erysiphaceae*.

Mildura   34 14S 142 13E A city in Australia, in NW Victoria on the Murray River. It is the centre of the Mallee, an irrigated region producing chiefly fruit, vegetables, and wheat. Population (1981): 15 763.

mile   A unit of length traditionally used in the UK and USA. A statute mile is equal to 1760 yards. A nautical mile (UK) is equal to 6080 feet; a nautical mile (international) is equal to 1852 metres (6076.12 ft). The unit is based on the Roman mile of 1000 paces.

Miles, Bernard, Baron   (1907–   ) British theatre director and actor. He founded the Mermaid Theatre, which opened at its present riverside site in Blackfriars, London, in 1959. He has contributed as writer, director, and actor to many of its productions.

Miles Gloriosus (Latin: boastful soldier)   A stock character in comic drama who boasts of brave deeds yet is easily shown to be a fool or coward. The term derives from the title of a play by *Plautus.

Miletus   An ancient Greek city in *Ionia, founded about 1000 BC. Centre of the wool trade, early colonizer of the Black Sea area, and commercially active from Italy to Egypt, Miletus exemplified Ionian energy and enterprise. Milesians were prominent among the 6th-century Ionian thinkers, and even after destruction by Persia (494 BC) Miletus remained commercially important until its harbours silted up.

milfoil.   *See* yarrow.

Milford Haven   51 44N 5 02W A port in SW Wales, in Dyfed on the Milford Haven estuary. It was developed as a major oil terminal capable of accommodating large oil tankers. There are oil refineries and a long-established fishing industry. Population (1981): 13 934.

Milhaud, Darius   (1892–1974) French composer, a member of Les *Six. He made use of polytonality and jazz in many of his compositions. With Jean Cocteau he wrote the ballets *Le Boeuf sur le toit* (1919) and *Le Train bleu* (1924); with Paul Claudel he wrote the opera *Christophe Colomb* (1928). His other works include 12 symphonies, 15 string quartets (the last 2 of which can be played simultaneously as an octet), concertos, and Jewish liturgical music.

Militant Tendency   A faction formerly within the *Labour Party advocating Trotskyist policies, which emerged in the 1970s around the newspaper *Militant*. It attracted notoriety after 1979 in the controversy over reform of the party. In 1982 it was judged to have broken the rules for groups within the party. In 1986 members of the Militant Tendency were expelled from the party.

militia   A military force composed of reservists enlisted in emergencies to reinforce a standing army. The militia is descended from the Anglo-Saxon *fyrd*, to which all free men were compulsorily recruited for short-term local service. This general levy survived the introduction to England of the feudal levy by William I and under the Tudors responsibility for raising so-called "trained bands" fell to the parishes. The militia declined with the establishment (1661) of a standing army and was reorganized in 1757. In the 19th century the militia became voluntary and militiamen served abroad for the first time. It lasted until the Territorial and Reserve Forces Act (1907). *See also* Territorial Army.

milk   A fluid secreted by the *mammary glands of mammals to feed their young. Cows' milk consists typically of about 87% water, 3.6% fat, 3.3% protein, 4.7% lactose (milk sugar), small quantities of minerals (mainly calcium and phosphorus), and vitamins (mainly vitamins A and B). (Human milk, in contrast, contains less protein and more lactose.) Although its composition depends on the breed of animal, its diet, and the season, milk forms a well-balanced and highly nutritious food. In the UK most milk is sold, after *pasteurization, in bottles or cartons, with daily doorstep deliveries. Sterilized and UHT (ultraheat-treated) milk both have a longer shelf-life (about one month) but sterilized milk has a distinctive flavour. Long-life UHT milk will keep for up to six months in sealed containers. Homogenized milk is processed so that the fat globules are uniformly sized. *See also* dairy farming; dairy products.

milk of magnesia   A suspension of magnesium hydroxide $(Mg(OH)_2)$ in water. It is a white milky fluid used as an antacid and a mild laxative.

milkweed   A herb of the genus *Asclepias* (120 species), native to North America and often grown in the tropics and subtropics for ornament. Up to 1.2 m high, it bears umbrella-shaped clusters of orange, purple, pink, or red flowers and yields a milky latex. The seeds have long silky hairs ("vegetable silk"), often used in upholstery padding or as insulation. Family: *Asclepiadaceae*.

milkweed butterfly   A butterfly belonging to the widely distributed mainly tropical family *Danaidae*. The adults are typically large and colourful and may fly long distances (*see* monarch). The caterpillars feed on milkweed and other plants, which makes them taste unpleasant to predators.

milkwort   A perennial herb or small shrub of the genus *Polygala* (500–600 species), native to Europe and North America. The common European milkwort (*P. vulgaris*) has slender branching stems, 7–25 cm long, and spikes of irregular flowers, white, pink, or blue in colour. Family: *Poly-galaceae*.

Milky Way   The diffuse band of light that is seen, on a clear moonless night, stretching across the sky. It is composed of innumerable stars that are too faint to be seen individually. They lie around the sun in the flattened and densely populated disc of our *Galaxy.

Mill, James   (1773–1836) Scottish writer, historian, and philosophical radical. In the course of a busy journalistic career he met *Bentham (1808), whose enthusiastic disciple he became. Mill's *History of India* (1818) secured him an official post at India House for the remainder of his life. His *Elements of Political Economy* (1821) influenced *Marx and his philosophical stance is reflected by his son **John Stuart Mill** (1806–73), one of the greatest 19th-century thinkers. In economics, J. S. Mill was influenced by the theories of Adam *Smith, *Ricardo, and *Malthus, and his *Principles of Political Economy* (1848) is little more than a restatement of their ideas. He was also the last of the English philosophers in the empirical tradition of Locke. He was a proponent of *utilitarianism, publishing a book under that title (1863). *On Liberty* (1859) shows that he was concerned for the rights of the individual, yet sympathetic to the ideas of contemporary socialists. He believed strongly in the equality of the sexes, publishing his views in *Subjection of Women* (1869). He edited the *London Review* (1835–40).

Millais, Sir John Everett   (1829–96) British painter, born in Southampton. He was one of the founders of the *Pre-Raphaelite Brotherhood, the principles of which he applied to his best paintings, notably the controversial *Christ in the House of His Parents* (1850) and *Ophelia* (1852; both Tate Gallery). After abandoning Pre-Raphaelitism in the 1860s, he painted more popular and sentimental works, such as *Bubbles* (1886).

Millay, Edna St Vincent   (1892–1950) US poet. The bohemianism of her early lyrical poetry matured into a more profound disillusion, especially in *The Buck in the Snow* (1928) and *Fatal Interview* (1931), a sonnet sequence. *The Harp Weaver and Other Poems* (1923) won a Pulitzer Prize.

millenarianism   A belief, widespread among early Christians, that Christ will soon return to reign on earth with his elect for a period of a thousand years preceding the Last Judgment. The idea was fostered by literal interpretations of the Book of Revelation (especially chapter 20) but was rejected by *Origen, whose views on the matter became generally accepted. At the Reformation millenarianism flourished among persecuted minorities, such as the *Anabaptists. Puritan millenarian sects, notably the *Fifth Monarchy Men, proliferated in the mid-17th-century turmoils in England. The political frustrations of colonial rule, combined with fundamentalist biblical teaching, fostered millenarianism among the indigenous peoples of Africa and Polynesia, where it sometimes took the form of *cargo cults. Contemporary millenarian groups include the *Adventists and *Mormons.

Miller, Arthur   (1915–) US dramatist. As a Jewish liberal intellectual he has played an active role in political life, and one of the main themes of his plays is social responsibility. His plays include *All My Sons* (1947), *Death of a Salesman* (1947), which won a Pulitzer Prize, *The Crucible* (1953), concerning the Salem witch trials of the 1690s, *A View from the Bridge* (1955), and *After the Fall* (1964), which is in part a portrait of his late wife Marilyn ◻Monroe.

Miller, Glenn   (1904–44) US jazz trombonist, band leader, and composer of the popular songs "Moonlight Serenade" and "In the Mood." Miller's band, assembled in 1938, recorded many hit swing tunes and entertained the troops during World War II. He died when his plane disappeared on a routine flight between England and France.

Miller, Henry   (1891–1980) US novelist. During the 1930s he lived in Paris, where he became a close friend of Lawrence *Durrell; he lived in California from 1944. He first gained notoriety with the sexually explicit novels *Tropic of Cancer* (1934)

and *Tropic of Capricorn* (1939). Later writings include *The Rosy Crucifixion* (1949–60) and *My Life and Times* (1972). His works, which are mostly autobiographical, are anarchic celebrations of life and liberty.

Miller, Jonathan (Wolfe)   (1934–) British theatre director, who studied medicine at Cambridge and appeared in the successful Footlights revue *Beyond the Fringe* (1960). As a director, his productions include Sheridan's *The School for Scandal* (1972), Ibsen's *Ghosts* (1974), Chekhov's *Three Sisters* (1976), and Shakespeare. His opera productions include *Don Giovanni* (1985), *The Mikado* (1986), and *Tosca* (1986).

miller's thumb.   *See* bullhead.

millet   One of various *grasses or their seeds, cultivated in Asia and Africa as a cereal crop and in parts of Europe and North America chiefly as a pasture grass and fodder crop. It grows 30–130 cm high and the flowers form spikes or branched clusters. Common or broomcorn millet (*Panicum miliaceum*) is used for poultry feed or for flour milling. Pearl millet (*Pennisetum glaucum*) is grown in arid and infertile soils as a food grain; Italian millet (*Setaria italica*) has been cultivated as a grain crop in Asia since ancient times; and Japanese millet (*Echinochloa crus-galli* var. *frumentacea*) is grown for fodder. A variety of sorghum (*see* durra) is also known as millet.

Millet, Jean François   (1814–75) French painter of peasant origin. He studied under *Delaroche, achieving acclaim in 1844, although later his works were criticized for expressing socialist ideas. After settling in Barbizon (1849), he became associated with the *Barbizon school and painted melancholy and sometimes sentimental agricultural scenes, notably *The Gleaners* (1857) and *The Angelus* (1859; both Louvre).

millibar.   *See* bar.

Millikan, Robert Andrews   (1868–1953) US physicist, who first measured the charge on the electron. For this and other work, he was awarded the Nobel Prize in 1932. In **Millikan's oil-drop experiment**, he balanced the effects of an upward electromagnetic attraction and the downward pull of gravity on an electrically charged droplet. As changes in the drop's charge (caused by bombardment with X-rays) occur in whole numbers of units of electronic charge, the size of the unit can be calculated from the movement of the drop. Millikan also studied cosmic rays and hoped to reconcile religion and science.

millipede   A slow-moving *arthropod of the widely distributed class *Diplopoda* (about 8000 species). Its slender cylindrical body, 2–280 mm long, is covered by a calcareous cuticle and consists of 20–100 segments, most of which bear two pairs of legs (*compare* centipede). Millipedes live in dark humid places as scavengers of dead plant and animal materials. In defence they secrete a toxic fluid containing cyanide and iodine. Eggs are usually sheltered in a nest of excrement.

Mills, Sir John   (1908–) British actor. He appeared in the roles of quiet but gallant heroes in *This Happy Breed* (1944) and other war films and later in character roles, as in *Ryan's Daughter* (1971). His daughters **Hayley Mills** (1946–) and **Juliet Mills** (1941–) are both actresses.

Milne, A(lan) A(lexander)   (1882–1956) British novelist and dramatist. He contributed to *Punch* and wrote several popular comedies, but is best known for his books for and about his son Christopher Robin. These include *When We Were Very Young* (1924), a collection of verse, and two books about toy animals, *Winnie-the-Pooh* (1926) and *The House at Pooh Corner* (1928).

Milner, Alfred, Viscount   (1854–1925) British colonial administrator. After serving in Egypt (1889–92) and as chairman of the Board of Inland Revenue (1892–97) he was high commissioner in southern Africa (1897–1906) and governor of Cape Colony (1897–1901). His inflexibility towards Kruger at the Bloemfontein Conference (1899) precipitated the second *Boer War. However, he was a distinguished administrator as governor (1902–06), after their annexation, of the Orange River Colony (previously the Orange Free State) and the Transvaal.

Milo (late 6th century BC) Greek wrestler of legendary strength, who won six Olympic prizes. He is said to have carried a calf on his shoulders once every day from its birth and eventually to have carried the grown cow round the Olympic stadium.

MIME   *Marcel Marceau in the role of Bip, at the Théâtre des Champs-Élysées, Paris.*

Miloš (1780–1860) Prince of Serbia (1815–39, 1858–60), who led a successful revolt against the Ottoman Empire (1815) and founded the *Obrenović dynasty. Miloš was the alleged assassin of *Karageorge. He was forced to abdicate in 1839 but was recalled in 1858.

Milstein, Nathan (1904–   ) US violinist, born in Russia, resident in the USA since 1929. A pupil of Leopold Auer (1843–1930) and Eugène Ysaÿe (1858–1931), Milstein gave recitals with Vladimir Horowitz in Russia before establishing a European reputation in 1925. He has published a number of violin transcriptions.

Miltiades (c. 550–489 BC) Athenian general and statesman. Sent to govern the Thracian peninsula in Athenian interests, he ruled as tyrant and fought with *Darius I of Persia in Scythia. Later, after joining the Ionian cities' unsuccessful revolt against the Persians, he had to flee to Athens (493) but escaped punishment. Appointed a general in 490, he devised the strategy by which the Greeks decisively defeated the Persians at the battle of *Marathon.

Milton, John (1608–74) English poet. After leaving Cambridge University he studied privately at his father's house, where he wrote the poems *L'Allegro* and *Il Penseroso* (1632), the masque *Comus* (1633), and the elegy *Lycidas* (1637). In 1638 he travelled in France and Italy. During the 1640s and 1650s he actively supported the Puritan revolution and wrote many polemical pamphlets, notably *Areopagitica* (1644), a defence of free speech. He also wrote a series of pamphlets justifying divorce in cases of incompatibility, a position reflecting his own unhappy marriage (1642) to Mary Powell. In 1649 he was appointed Latin Secretary to the Council of State, but his eyesight

began to fail and he had become totally blind by 1652. After the Restoration he retired from public life to write his great epic poem *Paradise Lost* (1667), its sequel *Paradise Regained* (1671), and the dramatic poem *Samson Agonistes* (1671).

Milton Keynes 52 02N 0 42W A town in S England, in Buckinghamshire. Developed since 1967 as a new town around the old village of Milton Keynes, the eventual population is planned to be 200 000. It is the headquarters of the Open University (1969) and has varied light industries. Population (1982 est): 133 900.

Milwaukee 43 03N 87 56W A city and port in the USA, in Wisconsin on Lake Michigan. Originally a fur-trading post, it grew after an influx of German refugees in 1848. The state's largest city and a major shipping centre, Milwaukee is a leading producer of heavy machinery, electrical equipment, and diesel and petrol engines. Population (1980): 636 212.

mime Acting without words by physical gestures alone. It was practised in ancient Greek and Roman drama and was an important constituent of the *commedia dell'arte in the 16th century. Modern mime was developed during the early 19th century in France by *Debureau and was revived in the 1920s by Etienne Decroux (1898–   ), whose pupils included Jean-Louis *Barrault and Marcel *Marceau.

mimesis (Greek: imitation)   A philosophical concept introduced by *Aristotle in the *Poetics*. He argues that imitation is the basis of all the arts but they differ as to the means they use and the objects they imitate. Thus, drama is the imitation of an action and the dramatic genres, tragedy and comedy, may be differentiated by their characters, who are either better (in tragedy) or worse (in comedy) than average humanity. Imitation in the arts does not refer to a simple realistic rendering of detail but to the poet's (or artist's) ability to select and present his material so as to express essential truth.

mimicry The phenomenon of two or more organisms (commonly different species) resembling each other closely, which confers an advantage—usually protection—to one or both of them. In **Batesian mimicry**, named after H. W. *Bates, a poisonous or inedible species (the model) has a conspicuous coloration, which acts as a warning to predators. This coloration is adopted by a harmless edible species (the mimic), which derives protection against the same predators. In **Müllerian mimicry**, first described by the German naturalist Fritz Müller (1821–97), two or more species—all inedible—have the same warning coloration. After a predator has associated this pattern with an inedible species it will learn not to select similarly coloured species, resulting in a reduction in total mortality.

Mimosa A genus of trees, shrubs, and herbs (450–500 species), mostly native to tropical and subtropical America. They have feathery compound leaves and fluffy round catkins of yellow flowers. The genus includes the sensitive plants, *M. pudica* and *M. sensitiva*, of which the leaflets fold upwards and the leafstalks droop at the slightest touch. Florists' mimosas are species of *Acacia* (*see* wattle). Family: *Leguminosae*.

Mina Hassan Tani. *See* Kenitra.

Minamata disease A form of mercury poisoning that killed 43 people in the Japanese town of Minamata between 1953 and 1956. The disease was contracted by eating fish contaminated with dimethyl mercury, derived from an effluent from a local PVC factory. The symptoms of mercury poisoning include tremors, paralysis, severe anaemia, and bone deformities.

Minamoto Yoritomo (1147–99) Japanese military leader descended from a 9th-century emperor, who as the first *shogun (military overlord, 1192–99) laid the foundations of feudal government in Japan. After the defeat (1185) of the dominant *Taira clan, Yoritomo built up an extensive vassal network based on Kamakura, near modern Yokohama. In 1192 he obtained the title of shogun from the emperor and his administrative organization gradually moved from coexistence with the imperial government to dominance over it. His half-brother **Minamoto Yoshitsune** (1159–89) was a warrior whose flair and valour contributed greatly to the Minamoto triumph against the Taira but who subsequently incurred the suspicion or jealousy of Minamoto Yoritomo. His adventures before he was finally hunted down and committed suicide have captured the imagination of succeeding generations.

minaret A tall slender tower attached to a mosque from which the muezzin calls Muslims to prayer five times a day.

Minch, the A channel in the E Atlantic Ocean. It consists of the **North Minch** between Lewis and the mainland of NW Scotland and the **Little Minch** between Harris, North Uist, and Skye.

mind A philosophical term for whatever it is in a person that thinks, feels, wills, etc. Whether it is immaterial or not is controversial. *Materialism denies its existence as an incorporeal entity. For *Aristotle mind was *nous* (intellect), the only part of the soul to survive death. For *Descartes it is his starting point, an incorporeal mental substance by virtue of whose activity (thought) he knew he existed (*cogito ergo sum*—I think therefore I am). Until recently it has been usual to suppose that nonhuman animals do not have minds, the possession of mind being perhaps a defining characteristic of human beings. A more modern view identifies mental attitudes with brain states (*see* behaviourism).

Mind (National Association for Mental Health) A voluntary British organization founded in 1946 to provide for the needs of the mentally ill and handicapped. It has 130 local associations and campaigns for better services for the mentally ill, runs advice centres, generally encourages an understanding of mental illness, and promotes mental health. Since 1970, when the name Mind was adopted as part of a successful publicity campaign, the organization has increased its role as a political lobbying group. Director: Christopher Heginbotham.

Mindanao An island in the S Philippines, the second largest. Volcanic and rugged, soil erosion caused by indiscriminate tree felling is a serious problem. Hemp, maize, pineapples, timber, nickel, and gold are the chief products. *History*: the Muslim population has resisted Spanish, US, and now Philippine rule. Separatism, aggravated by rapid economic development in the 1960s, resulted in heavy fighting in 1975. A tribe with a Stone Age culture was discovered here in 1971. Area: 101 919 sq km (39 351 sq mi). Population (1980 est): 10 905 243. Chief towns: Davao and Zamboanga.

Minden 52·18N 8·54E A town in NW West Germany, in North Rhine-Westphalia on the River Weser. In 1759 the English and Hanoverians defeated the French here. Its cathedral (11th–13th centuries) was rebuilt after World War II. Its varied manufactures include chemicals and glass. Population (1985 est): 80 000.

Mindoro A mountainous island in the central Philippines, S of Luzon. The chief products are timber and coal. Area: 10 236 sq km (3952 sq mi). Population (1980): 669 369. Chief town: Calapan.

Mindszenty, József, Cardinal (J. Pehm; 1892–1975) Hungarian Roman Catholic churchman. He was a vehement opponent of the Nazis and later the Communists, who imprisoned him in 1948. Released by the insurgents in the 1956 Hungarian Revolution, he gained asylum at the US legation in Budapest and eventually settled in Rome in 1971.

minerals Naturally occurring substances of definite chemical composition (although this may vary within limits). Some consist of a single element but most are compounds of at least two. Strictly defined, minerals are solid (except native mercury) and are inorganically formed, although the constituents of organic limestones, for instance, are considered minerals. The term is used loosely for any naturally occurring material that is of economic value, especially if it is obtained by mining, and the fossil fuels (of organic origin) are in this broader sense minerals. Almost all true minerals are crystalline; a few, such as opal, are amorphous. Minerals are identified by the following properties: crystal system (e.g. cubic) and habit or form (e.g. fibrous), hardness (*see* Mohs' scale), relative density, lustre (e.g. metallic), colour, streak (colour when finely divided), *cleavage, and fracture. *Rocks are composed of mixtures of minerals. If a rock contains an economically extractable quantity of a mineral of commercial value, it constitutes a mineral deposit (*see* mining and quarrying). **Mineralogy** is the study of minerals (in the strict sense): their identification, classification, and formation.

Minerva A Roman goddess originally of the arts and crafts of wisdom, later identified with the Greek *Athena. As goddess of war her importance almost equalled that of Mars. Her annual festival was the Quinquatrus, held in March.

minesweeper A powerful fast vessel equipped to cut the cables of floating mines. Partially submerged cables, attached to paravanes that keep them taut and at a desired angle to the boat, are towed through a minefield so that the cable, passing under the mines, cuts their anchor chains, allowing the mines to float so that they can be detonated by gunfire.

Ming (1368–1644) A native Chinese dynasty, which succeeded the Mongol Yüan dynasty. It was founded by *Hong Wu, the first of 17 Ming emperors. The Ming provided an era of stable government personally controlled by the emperor. The examination system to select bureaucrats was restored and overseas expeditions were encouraged. Painting and pottery, especially blue and white porcelain, flourished under the Ming, who built the Forbidden City in Peking in the 15th century.

Mingus, Charlie (1922–79) US Black jazz musician, who experimented with atonality and dissonance in jazz. A double-bass player, he played with Louis Armstrong, Lionel Hampton, and others. He also led his own band and appeared in films.

Minho, River. *See* Miño, River.

miniature painting The art of painting on a very small scale, using watercolour on a vellum, card, or (from the 18th century) ivory base. The medieval Persian and Indian miniatures are the first great examples of the art. In Europe it flourished in the form of oval, circular, and occasionally rectangular portraits from the 16th to mid-19th centuries. There it developed from the medieval art of manuscript illumination (sometimes also called miniature painting) and *Renaissance portrait medals. Although *Holbein the Younger produced some miniatures, Nicholas *Hilliard was the first major specialist of the art in England. His portraits were often worn as jewellery. Other famous British miniaturists were Isaac *Oliver, Samuel *Cooper, and Richard *Cosway.

minicomputer A small *computer, especially one that fits into a single cabinet. Compared with a large mainframe computer it is slower, has a smaller memory, and is considerably cheaper. The term is no longer used specifically and predates the more usual word, *microcomputer, for a small personal device.

Minicoy Islands. *See* Lakshadweep.

minimal art An abstract style of painting and sculpture developed in New York in the late 1960s. In reaction against the personal character of *action painting, it aims to eliminate artistic self-expression by reducing creativity to a minimum. This has been achieved by using simple hard-edged geometrical shapes and unmodulated vibrant colours. Leading minimalists include the painters Kenneth Noland (1924–) and Frank Stella (1936–) and the sculptor Carl André (1935–).

mining and quarrying The extraction of useful minerals from the earth's crust. Quarrying is usually regarded as the extraction of stone, sand, gravel, etc., from surface workings. Mining is the extraction by opencast or underground workings of ores producing metals (gold, silver, zinc, copper, lead, tin, iron, and uranium) and other valuable minerals (coal, limestone, asbestos, salt, precious stones, etc.); mining also includes the extraction of oil from wells and the extraction of alluvial deposits. Some 70% of mineral ores come from surface workings, which using modern equipment can reach down to depths of 500 m (1640 ft). After the overburden of rock or sand has been removed, the underlying mineral is blasted by explosives or broken up by machinery and excavated by power shovels, which load it onto conveyors or trucks. To comply with environmental requirements the overburden is often backfilled (deposited behind the current working face). In underground workings many factors have to be taken into account, such as the size, shape, and hardness of the deposit, the nature of the surrounding rock and the surface terrain, and the risk of subsidence. Ores are loosened and excavated by blasting, drilling, and mechanical shovelling. The waste material after the valuable ore has been extracted is often fed back into the mine (sometimes hydraulically, as a slurry) to reduce the risk of subsidence. *See also* coalmining; oil.

minivet An Asian songbird of the genus *Pericrocotus* (10 species), occurring in forests, where it hunts for insects in small flocks. Male minivets, about 17 cm long, have a black-and-red plumage; the females are yellowish grey. Family: *Campephagidae* (cuckoo-shrikes and minivets).

MINOAN CIVILIZATION *Detail of the* Blue Ladies Fresco *(c. 1600 BC; Heraklion Museum) from the Palace of Minos at Knossos (Crete).*

mink A small carnivorous ▫mammal belonging to the genus *Mustela* (weasels, stoats, etc.), prized for its fur. The American mink (*M. vison*) is the largest species (about 70 cm long) and has the most valuable fur. It is bred in captivity in many parts of the world, and escaped animals readily adapt to life in the wild. They are nocturnal, semi-aquatic, and efficient hunters both on land and in water, preying on fish, rodents, and waterfowl. Family: *Mustelidae*.

Minneapolis 45 00N 93 15W A city in the USA, in Minneso-

ta on the Mississippi River. Adjacent to St Paul, the Twin Cities comprise the commercial, industrial, and financial centre of a large grain and cattle area; flour milling is the main industry. Minneapolis is noted for its wide streets, many lakes, and parks. The University of Minnesota was established here in 1851. Population (1980): 370 951.

Minnelli, Liza. *See* Garland, Judy.

Minnesingers (German: singers of love) Aristocratic German singing guilds that flourished in the 12th and 13th centuries; the German equivalent of the French *troubadours. Their decline coincided with the rise of the *Meistersingers.

Minnesota A state in the USA, bordering on Canada in the N and Lake Superior in the NE. It consists of rolling prairies rising to the heavily forested Superior Highlands in the N and contains many lakes, the largest being the Lake of the Woods. Manufacturing industries (especially food processing) now form the most important sector of the economy. The high-grade iron ores, of which it was a major source, are virtually exhausted but mining remains important following new finds of copper and nickel. Agriculture, concentrated chiefly in the S, produces maize and soya beans. Tourism is an important source of revenue. *History*: part of the Louisiana Purchase in 1803, it became a state in 1858. During the 1880s many Scandinavians settled in Minnesota and their influence remains strong today. Area: 217 736 sq km (84 068 sq mi). Population (1980): 4 077 148. Capital: St Paul.

minnow One of several fish of the family *Cyprinidae*, especially *Phoxinus phoxinus*, found in clear fresh waters of Europe and N Asia. Its slim body is usually about 7.5 cm long, has small scales, and ranges in colour from gold to green. Order: *Cypriniformes*.

The name is also applied to various other small fish, including mudminnows (family *Umbridae*; order *Salmoniformes*) and *killifish.

Miño, River (Portuguese name: Minho) A river in SW Europe. Rising in NW Spain, it flows mainly SSW, forming part of the border between Spain and Portugal, to the Atlantic Ocean. Length: 338 km (210 mi).

Minoan civilization The civilization of Bronze Age Crete, named by Sir Arthur *Evans after the legendary King *Minos. The most advanced Aegean civilization, the Minoan arose after 2500 BC. It is conventionally divided into three phases: Early (2500–2000), Middle (2000–1700), and Late (1700–1400). During the Middle Minoan period palace building at *Knossos, Mallia, and Phaistos attests Crete's growing wealth. Around 1700 these structures were destroyed and replaced by grander ones, the centres of power in a marine empire covering the S Aegean. A catastrophic eruption on *Thera (c. 1450) ended Minoan prosperity as the sterile volcanic fallout temporarily ruined Crete's agriculture. Subsequent occupation levels show increasing Mycenaean influence (*see* Mycenaean civilization).

Excavated frescoes and artefacts show that Minoan material culture was highly sophisticated; craftsmen included skilled architects, potters, painters, stone cutters, goldsmiths, and jewellers. Three scripts were used: hieroglyphics (c. 1900–1700), *Linear A (c. 1700–1450), and *Linear B (c. 1450–1400). A prominent deity was a snake goddess; religious symbols of bulls' horns suggest ritual significance for the famous bull sports.

Minorca (Spanish name: Menorca) A Spanish island in the Mediterranean Sea, the second largest of the Balearic Islands. It is generally low lying and dry and agriculture is limited, with livestock raising. Shoe manufacture is important and it has an expanding tourist industry. Area: 702 sq km (271 sq mi). Population (1981): 58 727. Chief town: Mahón.

minor planet (*or* asteroid) A small nonluminous rocky body that orbits a star. Over 100 000 orbit the sun, mostly (probably 95%) in a main belt between the orbits of Mars and Jupiter, 2.17–3.3 astronomical units from the sun. Of the remainder, some, such as Icarus, have highly elliptical orbits that bring them close to the sun while others, including the *Trojan group, lie far beyond the main belt. The smallest minor planets are less than 1 km across with only about 200 exceeding 100 km: the largest is *Ceres (1003 km). They are probably debris from collisions of bodies that formed between Mars and Jupiter. In turn, most meteorites (*see* meteor) are considered fragments of minor planets.

Minos A legendary king of Crete, son of Zeus and Europa. His wife was Pasiphae, by whom he had two daughters, *Ariadne and *Phaedra. Although usually regarded as a good ruler, the Athenians portrayed him as a tyrant, who exacted an annual tribute of seven youths and seven maidens who were fed to the *Minotaur. According to Herodotus, he was killed in Sicily while pursuing *Daedalus after his escape from Crete. He is, with Rhadamanthus and Aeacus, one of the judges of the dead in Hades.

Minotaur In Greek legend, a Cretan monster with a bull's head and a man's body. It was the offspring of Pasiphae, wife of *Minos, and a bull with which Poseidon had caused her to become enamoured. It was kept in the labyrinth built by *Daedalus and fed on Athenian youths and maidens sent in tribute to Minos. *Theseus killed it with the help of Ariadne.

Minsk 53 51N 27 30E A city in the W Soviet Union, the capital of the Belorussian SSR. Dating from at least the 11th century, it came under Lithuanian and then Polish rule; it was restored to Russia in 1793. It was virtually destroyed in World War II, and its large Jewish population, exterminated during the German occupation. Its varied industries include machine and vehicle manufacturing, textiles, and food processing. It boasts a lively cultural life. Population (1981 est): 1 333 000.

mint An aromatic perennial herb of the genus *Mentha* (about 25 species), native to Eurasia and Australia and widely distributed throughout temperate and subtropical regions. It has creeping roots from which arise square stems, bearing simple toothed leaves and terminal clusters of purple, pink, or white flowers. Many species are grown in gardens for their fragrance or as culinary herbs, especially *peppermint and *spearmint: their leaves are used fresh or dried as flavouring. An oil extracted from mint stems and leaves is used in perfumes and medicines. Family: *Labiatae.

Mint. *See* Royal Mint.

Mintoff, Dom(inic) (1916-84) Maltese statesman; Labour prime minister (1955-58, 1971-   ). He was an active proponent of Maltese independence from British rule, which was achieved in 1964.

Minton ware Porcelain produced at the pottery founded (1796) by Thomas Minton (1765-1836) at Stoke (England). Famous for artistic and technical innovation, the Minton works still make fine porcelain. Remarkable products included imitation *maiolica, tiles, and Parian (imitation marble) statuary.

minuet A court dance of the 17th and 18th centuries in triple time. Of rustic origin, it was often included in the instrumental suite and became part of the sonata and symphony in the works of Haydn, Mozart, etc. The first statement of the minuet was followed by a second minuet in a related key (called a trio), after which the first minuet was repeated.

Minya, El 28 06N 30 45E A port in N central Egypt, on the River Nile. It is an important link between the left bank of the Nile and the Bahr Yusuf Canal and trade includes cotton and flour. Population (1983 est): 197 000.

Miocene epoch. *See* Tertiary period.

Miquelon Island. *See* St Pierre et Miquelon.

Mirabeau, Honoré Gabriel Riquetti, Comte de (1749-91) French statesman. In the years before the *French Revolution he gained notoriety as a libertine and profligate.

In 1789 he was elected to the States General, championing the cause of the Third Estate at the outbreak of the Revolution. However, he was out of sympathy with the growing republicanism, advocating the establishment of a constitutional monarchy on the British model. By 1790 he was coming under increasing attack from the *Jacobins but died of natural causes before a crisis was reached.

Mira Ceti A *red giant in the equatorial constellation Cetus that is a *variable star with a mean period of 331 days. Long known to vary considerably in brightness (by 5-6 magnitudes on average), it is the prototype of the **Mira stars**, which are all long-period pulsating variables.

miracle plays Medieval European dramas based on religious themes. In England, they flourished particularly in the 14th and early 15th centuries. A distinction between mystery plays (based on episodes in the Bible) and miracle plays (based on the lives of saints) is often made with regard to French examples of the genre, but in England the plays were almost invariably based on scriptural stories. They were originally performed in churches on religious holidays, especially Corpus Christi and Whitsuntide. They became increasingly secular in form and content and were eventually performed on mobile stages by trade guilds in public marketplaces. Almost complete cycles of plays from York, Coventry, Wakefield, and Chester have survived.

mirage An optical illusion sometimes observed on hot days. It is caused by the air near the ground being considerably hotter than the air above, causing refraction of light rays from the sky, since the refractive index of air depends on its density and therefore on its temperature. Thus rays near the horizon can be bent upwards sufficiently to appear to be coming from the ground, creating the illusion of a lake.

Miró, Joan (1893-1983) Surrealist painter, born in Barcelona. He moved to Paris (1919), where he participated in the first surrealist exhibition (1925) and began painting in a childlike style under the influence of dreams and poetry. The gaiety of his painting disappeared in the late 1930s with his "savage" paintings, expressing the horrors of the Spanish Civil War; it reappeared, however, in his *Constellations*, painted (during World War II) with his characteristic amoebic shapes intertwined with threadlike lines. He is also known for his ballet sets, murals, and sculptures.

mirrors Devices for reflecting light, usually consisting of a sheet of glass with one surface silvered. A plane mirror, in which the sheet is flat, forms a laterally inverted virtual image. Spherical mirrors, concave or convex, magnify or reduce the image. If the distances of the object and image from the mirror surface are u and v, then $1/u + 1/v = 1/f$, where f is the focal length of the mirror, taking all distances as positive in front of the mirror and negative behind it. To avoid spherical aberration, parabolic mirrors are used in reflecting *telescopes.

miscarriage. *See* abortion.

misch metal An *alloy of between 15% and 40% iron with cerium and other rare metals. When rubbed with an abrasive it produces sparks and it is used for flints in cigarette lighters. The name comes from the German *Mischmetall*, mixed metal.

misdemeanour. *See* felony.

Mishima, Yukio (Kimitake Hiraoka; 1925-70) Japanese novelist and playwright of international fame. He also acted in several films. His novels, which include *Confessions of a Mask* (1948) and *Sun and Steel* (1970), dealt with homosexuality, death, suicide, and the importance of traditional Japanese military values. He organized his own military group, the Shield Society, and in 1970 shocked the world by committing harakiri as a protest against the weakness of postwar Japan.

Mishnah (Hebrew: instruction) An early code of Jewish law. Written in Hebrew, it is traditionally thought to have been based on earlier compilations and edited in Palestine by the ethnarch Judah I in the early 3rd century AD. It consists of *halakhah on a wide range of subjects, derived partly from biblical law as interpreted by the early rabbis (called *Tannaim*) and partly from customs that had grown up over a long period of time. *See also* Talmud.

Miskolc 48 07N 20 47E A city in NE Hungary. It has much fine architecture including a 13th-century gothic church and the National Theatre. The Technical University of Heavy Industry was established here in 1949. A major industrial centre, its manufactures include iron, steel, and chemicals. Population (1984): 212 000.

missiles. *See* antiballistic missiles; ballistic missiles; guided missiles; Pershing missile; Polaris missile; Trident missile.

missions, Christian Enterprises to spread the Christian faith among those who profess other religions or none. The missionary journeys of St *Paul and the Apostles set an example that Christian individuals and organizations have followed ever since. St *Patrick, St *Columba, and St *Augustine of Canterbury were outstanding early missionaries in the British Isles. Isolated medieval missions reached as far as China, but concentrated activity began only with the discovery of the Americas and the sea route round Africa in the late 15th century. Roman Catholic orders, such as the *Dominicans, *Franciscans, and *Jesuits, made substantial conversions, especially in the 17th century, but Protestant denominations, with the exception of the *Moravian Brethren, did not enter the field in force until the 1790s. The 19th century was the peak period of activity with mission stations being established in even the most inaccessible regions. Developing countries frequently recognize the value of this work, which generally includes training in literary, practical, and medical skills, and allow missions to remain in the postcolonial period, although sometimes facing hardship and danger. Missionary attempts are now felt, ironically, to be necessary against the indifference and materialism of the western world.

Mississippi A state in the S central USA, on the Gulf of Mexico. Mainly low lying, it consists of the cotton-producing alluvial plain of the Mississippi River in the W, an area of extensive swamps in the SW, and a generally infertile region of low hills in the E and NE. The predominantly rural population has a large Black community. Still an important agricultural state, its main products are cotton (although this is no longer the mainstay of the economy), soya beans, poultry, eggs, and livestock. Manufacturing has increased in importance, with ship construction and repair the main industry. Timber and paper products, textiles, chemicals, and food processing are also important. Petroleum is the main mineral but natural gas, clay, and sand and gravel are also exploited. Mississippi remains, however, one of the country's poorest states. *History*: explored by the Spanish, it was later claimed for France and was ceded to Britain (1763). Colonization followed and the area came under US control (1783). Made a state in 1817, it became a leading cotton producer and slave state until the US Civil War. Area: 123 584 sq km (47 716 sq mi). Population (1980): 2 520 638. Capital: Jackson.

Mississippian period. *See* Carboniferous period.

Mississippi River A river in the central USA, the second longest river in North America. Rising in N Minnesota, it flows generally S into the Gulf of Mexico, through several channels (known as the Passes). Together with its chief tributary, the Missouri River, it forms the third longest river system in the world, at 6050 km (3759 mi) long with the world's third largest drainage basin, covering 3 222 000 sq km (1 243 753 sq mi). Because of the danger of flooding, the lower course has high artificial embankments (levees). Famous for its steamboats, celebrated by Mark Twain, it is now one of the world's busiest commercial waterways, with

major ports at St Louis and New Orleans. Length: 3780 km (2348 mi).

Missolonghi (Modern Greek name: Mesolóngion) A town in W Greece, on the Gulf of Patras. It is famous for its defence against the Turks during the War of Greek Independence (1821-29). Lord Byron died here in 1824. Population (1981): 10 164.

Missouri A state in the central USA, lying immediately W of the Mississippi River. It is divided by the Missouri River into fertile prairies and rolling hills in the N and W and the hills of the Ozark plateau in the S. Highly urbanized, much of its population lives in the two main cities of St Louis and Kansas City. Manufacturing dominates the economy, with transport and aerospace equipment, food processing, chemicals, and printing and publishing. The leading lead producer in the USA, it also exploits barytes, iron ore, and zinc deposits. Agriculture is diversified producing livestock and dairy products, soya beans, corn, wheat, cotton, and sorghum grains. *History*: explored by the French from Canada and claimed for France (1682), it was ceded to Spain (1783) before returning to France in 1800. It formed part of the Louisiana Purchase (1803) by the USA, becoming a state in 1821. Area: 180 486 sq km (69 686 sq mi). Population (1980): 4 917 444. Capital: Jefferson City.

Missouri River A river in the central USA, the longest river in North America and chief tributary of the Mississippi River. Rising in the Rocky Mountains, it flows N and E through Montana, then SE across North and South Dakota before joining the Mississippi at St Louis. A series of dams provides irrigation and has considerably reduced the danger of flooding along its lower course. Length: 4367 km (2714 mi).

Mistinguett (Jeanne-Marie Bourgeois; 1875-1956) French singer and comedienne. She was a leading star of the Moulin Rouge, the Folies-Bergère, and other Paris music halls between the wars. She performed with elaborate costumes and settings, often in company with Maurice *Chevalier.

mistle thrush A heavily built thrush, *Turdus viscivorus*, of Eurasia and NW Africa. It is about 28 cm long and has a greyish-brown upper plumage with a thickly speckled yellowish breast and white underwings. It feeds on berries (especially mistletoe—hence its name), snails, and worms.

mistletoe A semiparasitic evergreen shrub of the temperate and tropical family *Loranthaceae* (1300 species), growing on the branches of many trees. The Eurasian mistletoe (*Viscum album*) occurs mainly on apple trees, poplars, willows, and hawthorns. It has rootlike suckers, which penetrate into the host tissues, and woody branching stems, 60-90 cm long, bearing oval leathery leaves and yellow male and female flowers borne on separate plants. The female flowers give rise to white berries, which are eaten by birds (which thereby disperse the seeds).
Mistletoe was once believed by the Druids to have magic powers and medicinal properties and is a traditional Christmas decoration.

mistral A cold dry northerly wind that is funnelled down the Rhône Valley in S France to the Mediterranean Sea. Thick hedges and tree screens orientated E-W protect crops from its force.

Mistral, Frédéric (1830-1914) French poet. In 1854 he helped found the Félibrige, a movement dedicated to the regeneration of Provençal language and culture. His many works in the Provençal vernacular include the epic verse narratives *Mirèio* (1859) and *Lou Pouèmo dóu Rose* (1897). He won the Nobel Prize in 1905.

Mistral, Gabriela (Lucila Godoy Alcayaga; 1889-1957) Chilean poet, who worked as a teacher and cultural ambassador. Her volumes of poetry include *Desolación* (1922), published after the suicide of her fiancé, *Tala* (1938), and *Lagar* (1954). She was awarded the Nobel Prize in 1945.

Mitchell, Margaret (1909-49) US novelist. Her single

novel, the international bestseller *Gone with the Wind* (1936), is a historical romance set in Georgia during and after the Civil War. It won a Pulitzer Prize (1937) and was made into one of the cinema's most successful films in 1939.

Mitchell, R(eginald) J(oseph) (1895–1937) British aeronautical engineer. He joined Vickers in 1916 and was a leading designer of seaplanes entered for the Schneider Trophy in the 1920s. His seaplane designs led to his design for the first Spitfire (1936), although he did not live to see its supremacy as a fighter in World War II. □aircraft.

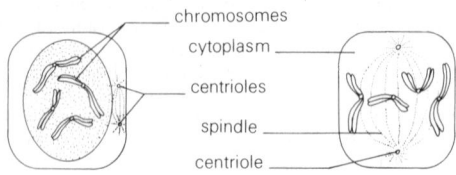

prophase *The genetic material becomes visible in the form of chromosomes and the nuclear membrane disappears.*

metaphase *The chromosomes become attached to the equator of a fibrous spindle.*

anaphase *The two chromatids of each chromosome move to opposite poles of the spindle.*

telophase *Nuclear membranes form around the two groups of chromatids, which become less distinct.*

MITOSIS *Division of the nucleus of an animal cell takes place in four phases, which grade into each other.*

mite A tiny *arachnid (up to 6 mm long) comprising—with the *ticks—the worldwide order *Acarina* (or *Acari*; over 20 000 species). It has an unsegmented body and eight bristly legs. Mites occur in great abundance in a wide range of habitats, including soil, stored foods, fresh and salt water, plants, and decaying organic material; some are parasitic on animals. They can become serious pests and may also transmit diseases (including *typhus). *See also* harvest mite; itch mite; spider mite.

Mitford, Nancy (1904–73) British writer; one of four famous daughters of the eccentric Lord Redesdale. Her books include *The Pursuit of Love* (1945) and *Love in a Cold Climate* (1949). Her sister, **Lady Diana Mosley** (1910–), was the wife of the notorious British Fascist Sir Oswald *Mosley. Another sister, **Unity Mitford** (1914–48), was an admirer and friend of Hitler; she committed suicide. Her youngest sister, **Jessica Mitford** (1917–), is also a writer, the author of *Hons and Rebels* (1960) and *The American Way of Death* (1963).

Mithra A Persian god of light, truth, and justice. He killed a cosmic bull, whose blood was the source of all animals and plants. The cult of *Mithraism flourished in the Roman Empire from the 2nd century AD, especially in the army, until the official adoption of Christianity in the 4th century.

Mithraism A mystery religion (*see* mysteries) that worshipped Mithra, the Persian god of the sun who represented justice and goodness. It spread through Asia Minor, finally reaching Rome in about 68 BC. Here Mithra was known as Mithras and was worshipped widely among Roman soldiers. He was regarded as the eternal enemy of evil, whose sacrifice of

a bull symbolized the regeneration of life. Part of the cult's initiation ceremony was a bath in a sacrificed bull's blood. Mithraism rivalled Christianity until its decline in the 3rd century AD. Remains of a Roman temple to Mithras were discovered (1954) in the City of London; parts of it can still be seen.

Mithridates VI Eupator (120–63 BC) King of Pontus and one of Rome's most persistent enemies. Mithridates extended his kingdom by invading Colchis and Lesser Armenia, antagonizing Rome by proceeding to Paphlagonia, Cappadocia, and Greece. Sulla, Lucullus, and Pompey in turn opposed him in three Mithridatic Wars (88–84, 83–81, 74–64) and he finally committed suicide.

mitochondria Granular rod-shaped structures that occur in the cytoplasm of nearly all □cells. They contain various enzymes that function in cellular *respiration and the metabolism of fat, glycogen, proteins, etc., to produce energy. Therefore in very active cells (i.e. those requiring more energy), such as heart muscle, mitochondria are large and numerous.

mitosis The process by which the nucleus of a somatic cell (i.e. any cell that is not a germ cell) duplicates itself exactly, producing two daughter nuclei with chromosomes that are identical to those of the parent nucleus. This nuclear division involves the separation of the two chromatids of each chromosome, which move apart to form two groups at opposite ends of the cell. In the final phase each group becomes enclosed in a new nuclear membrane. After this the cytoplasm usually divides to form two new cells. Mitosis occurs in most animals and plants during the normal growth and repair of tissues. *Compare* meiosis.

Mitsiwa. *See* Massawa.

Mittelland Canal (*or* Ems-Weser-Elbe-Kanal) A canal in central Europe. Opened in 1938, it links the Dortmund-Ems Canal in West Germany with the River Elbe in East Germany. Length: 325 km (202 mi).

Mitterrand, François (Maurice) (1916–) French socialist politician; president (1981–). He held ministerial posts from 1947. He was president of a democratic-socialist union (1965–68) and in 1971 assumed leadership of the newly unified Socialist Party. After two unsuccessful runs for the French presidency (1965, 1974) he defeated Giscard d'Estaing in 1981 to become the first socialist president in 35 years.

mixed economy An economy in which there is neither complete capitalist control of resources, nor complete government control. Examples are the democracies of W Europe.
The aim is to temper the "unacceptable face" of capitalism with its incentives and its efficient allocation of resources. Although some critics assert that mixed economies maintain the worst evils of capitalism, their undeniable capacity for economic growth has substantially improved the lot of the poorer sections of society. In mixed economies, governments seek to control the public services, the basic industries, and those enterprises that cannot raise adequate capital investment from private sources. This arrangement enables a measure of economic planning to be combined with a measure of free enterprise.

Mixtecs An American Indian people originating in W Oaxaca province (S Mexico). After the 10th century they gradually absorbed the neighbouring *Zapotecs. The Mixtecs were excellent craftsmen, whose skill in gold working, mosaics, pottery, and painting spread over much of Mesoamerica, influencing both *Maya and *Aztec art styles.

Mizoguchi Kenji (1898–1956) Japanese film director. His films are characterized by a controlled visual style and by a persistent concern with the psychology of women. They include *The Life of O'Haru* (1952), *Ugetsu Monogatari* (1953), and *Street of Shame* (1956).

Mizoram A state (since 1986) in NE India, in tropical hills between Bangladesh and Burma. Its largely Christian tribes are subsistence farmers of rice, sugar, and potatoes. Mizoram was separated from Assam (1972), following the activities of secessionist factions. Area: 21 230 sq km (8195 sq mi). Population (1981): 487 774. Capital: Aijal.

m.k.s. system A system of *metric units based on the metre, kilogram, and second. It has now been replaced for scientific purposes by *SI units, which are derived from it. The main difference between the two systems is that in SI units, the m.k.s. electrical units are rationalized (i.e. the factor 4π or 2π is introduced when it is demanded by the geometry).

M'Naghten's Rules. *See* insanity.

Mnemosyne In Greek mythology, a daughter of the *Titans Uranus and Gaea. She is the personification of memory. After sleeping with Zeus for nine consecutive nights she gave birth to the *Muses.

moa An extinct flightless bird belonging to an order (*Dinornithiformes*; about 25 species) that occurred in New Zealand. Moas were 60–300 cm tall and had a small head, a long neck, and long stout legs. They were fast runners but were hunted by early Polynesian settlers for food. Members of some smaller species may have survived until the 19th century.

Moabites A highly civilized Semitic tribe living E of the Dead Sea from the late 14th century BC. Closely associated ethnically with their neighbours and rivals the Israelites, they successfully rebelled against Israelite occupation in the 9th century BC. In 582 BC, according to Josephus, they were conquered by the Babylonians. The Moabite Stone, found at Dibon near Amman (Jordan) in 1868 and dating to the 9th century BC, bears an inscription (in the Moabite alphabet) celebrating a Moabite victory against the Israelites.

Mobile 30 12N 88 00W A seaport in the USA, in Alabama on Mobile Bay at the mouth of the Mobile River. Founded in 1710, it was occupied by the French, British, and Spanish before being seized for the USA in 1813. Industries include shipbuilding, oil refining, textiles, and chemicals. Population (1980): 200 452.

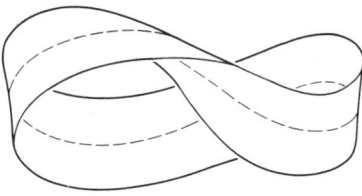

MÖBIUS STRIP   *A surface with one side and one edge.*

Möbius strip In *topology, a one-sided surface with only one edge, made by taking a strip of paper, twisting it once, and joining the ends. If cut in two lengthwise, it remains in one piece but with a double twist. It was discovered by the astronomer August Ferdinand Möbius (1780–1868).

Mobutu, Lake (former name: Lake Albert) A lake in Uganda and Zaïre. Discovered for Europeans by Baker in 1864, it is some 160 km (100 mi) long and is drained to the N by the Albert Nile River. Area: about 5346 sq km (2064 sq mi).

Mobutu, Sese Seko (Joseph Désiré M.; 1930–) Zaïrese statesman; president (1970–), having come to power in '965 in a coup. In 1967 he founded the country's only political party—the Popular Movement of the Revolution—and the stability of his authoritarian government is fostered by his personal cult, Mobutuism.

Moçambique. *See* Mozambique, People's Republic of.

Moçâmedes. *See* Namibe.

moccasin (snake). *See* water moccasin.

Mocenigo A Venetian family from which came many of the *doges of the Venetian Republic. They included **Tommaso Mocenigo** (1343–1423), doge (1414–23); his nephew **Pietro Mocenigo** (1406–76), who was a distinguished admiral as well as doge (1474–76); Pietro's brother **Giovanni Mocenigo** (1408–85), doge (1478–85); and Giovanni's grandson **Andrea Mocenigo** (1473–1542), a historian.

Mocha (*or* Al Mukha) 13 20N 43 16E A town in SW North Yemen, on the Red Sea coast. It was famous for its export of high-quality coffee but declined following the rise of coffee growing in South America and Java in the early 18th century. Population (1977): 1163.

mock epic A form of satiric verse that exposes the absurdity or worthlessness of a trivial subject or theme by treating it in the elevated style appropriate to a genuine *epic. The form originated in classical literature and was practised by neoclassical writers in the late 17th and early 18th centuries. Examples include *Le Lutrin* (1674–83) by *Boileau and *The Rape of the Lock* (1712–14) and the *Dunciad* (1728–43) by *Pope.

mockingbird A songbird that belongs to an American family (*Mimidae*; 30 species) and is noted for its ability to mimic sounds. Mockingbirds live on or near the ground, feeding on insects and fruit. They were once prized as cagebirds. The common mockingbird (*Mimus polyglottus*), which ranges from S Canada to S Mexico, is about 25 cm long with a grey plumage and white wing bars.

mock orange A shrub, also called syringa, belonging to the genus *Philadelphus* (75 species), native to N temperate regions and commonly cultivated for ornament. They have simple leaves and fragrant white flowers resembling orange blossom. *P. coronarius* is the only native European species. Family: *Philadelphaceae*.

Modena (ancient name: Mutina) 44 39N 10 55E A city in N Italy, in Emilia-Romagna. Ruled by the Este family (1288–1860), it has an 11th-century romanesque cathedral, several palaces, and an ancient university (1175). The centre of a rich agricultural area, its industries include agricultural engineering, textiles, and motor vehicles. Population (1980 est): 180 526.

modern art The art of the late 19th and 20th centuries, which has largely abandoned traditional subjects, aesthetic standards, and techniques of art. The development of modern art was stimulated by the decline of artistic patronage by church and state, giving the artist more freedom to experiment. These experiments have largely centred round the use of colour and form as properties in their own right and not only as a means to mirror the real world (*see* photography). They can be traced back to *Manet and the impressionists. *Cézanne began the dissolution of one of the main foundations of western painting since the Renaissance—the use of linear *perspective. It was completed by *cubism in the early 20th century. Variations of cubism were *futurism in Italy and *vorticism in England but in Russia it developed into a completely nonrepresentational geometric art in the form of *suprematism and *constructivism. Suprematism, constructivism, and neoplasticism (*see* Stijl, de) were highly influential in the 1920s at the German *Bauhaus school of design and geometric abstraction is still a leading artistic trend today in the form of *op art and *minimal art. Colour used for its own sake was a major feature of French *fauvism in the early 1900s. Die *Brucke, the German counterpart of fauvism, was also part of another modern movement—*expressionism. However, these two trends were fused in the first abstract painting, which was produced by Kandinsky in about 1910. His heir in the 1940s, when the centre of modern art shifted to New York, was Jackson *Pollock, the inventor of *action painting. Other movements have explored modern concerns, such as the value of art (*see* dada), the world of dreams and the subconscious (*see* surrealism), and the role of the mass media in society (*see* pop art). *See also* abstract art; sculpture.

Modern Art, Museum of An art gallery in New York City devoted to late 19th- and 20th-century painting. It was opened in 1929.

modern dance A form of theatrical dance developed in central Europe and the USA in the early 20th century in reaction to the technical virtuosity and fairytale subjects of *ballet. The early pioneers were the German dancers Kurt Joos (1901–79) and Mary Wigman (1886–1973) and the US dancers Isadora *Duncan and Martha *Graham.

Modern dance has developed new kinds of movement to express feeling, particularly jerking, thrusting, and contracting movements. It is usually performed in simple clothing against austere scenery. In England it has been promoted by the London School of Contemporary Dance, founded in 1969. Some of today's leading ballet choreographers, notably *Béjart and *Robbins, have been influenced by modern dance.

Modernism A movement among Roman Catholic theologians that arose independently in several countries in the late 19th century. Its adherents sought to bring Roman Catholic thinking into harmony with modern philosophical and scientific trends and in particular with the new critical approach to the Bible. The historical accuracy of the Bible and the problems of dogmatic theology were held to be relatively unimportant. Pope Pius X condemned the movement officially in 1907 and many Modernist clergy were excommunicated.

modes Musical scales derived from ancient Greek music, on which European music was based up to the 16th century. Each mode consists of a different pattern of the five tones and two semitones of the octave; the patterns can be clearly demonstrated using the white notes of the piano keyboard. Some of the most common modes were the Ionian (C-C), the Dorian (D-D), the Lydian (F-F), and the Aeolian (A-A). The Ionian and Aeolian modes became the basis of the major and minor scales of the 17th century and after.

Modigliani, Amedeo (1884–1920) Italian painter and sculptor, born in Livorno of Jewish origin. His mature work, executed in Paris (1906–20), was influenced by *Cézanne and *Brancusi and, in its angular and elongated character, by Negro masks. From 1909 to 1915 he worked chiefly on sculptures; from 1915 until his death from tuberculosis, aggravated by drink and drug addiction, he painted many nudes and portraits.

modular construction A method of building construction in which large components of the building are prefabricated for assembly on the site. Where low-cost buildings or many buildings of repeated design are required it has an economical advantage. The modules are usually made of prestressed or precast concrete and may be simply bolted into place, usually around an iron girder frame.

modulation A method of carrying information (the signal) on an electromagnetic wave or an oscillating electric current. In **amplitude modulation** (AM) the amplitude of a carrier wave is changed according to the magnitude of the signal. This is used in medium-wave sound broadcasting in which audio-frequencies (50–20 000 hertz) are carried on radio waves with a frequency of about one megahertz. In **frequency modulation** (FM) the frequency of the carrier wave is changed within a small bandwidth of the reference frequency. FM is used in VHF *radio (about 100 megahertz). Its main advantage over AM is its better signal-to-noise ratio.

In **pulse modulation** the carrier is a series of pulses. It is used in digital equipment, such as computers, and in telegraphy and telemetry. A continuous signal alters the height in pulse-amplitude modulation, the width in pulse-duration modulation, or the time between pulses in pulse-position

modulation. Pulse-code modulation uses a coded pattern of pulses to carry the signal, e.g. in *Morse code.

Moers 51 27N 6 36E A city in NW West Germany, in North Rhine-Westphalia in the *Ruhr. It grew rapidly in the 20th century as a coalmining centre. Population (1980 est): 100 300.

Mogadishu (*or* Mogadiscio) 2 01N 45 25E The capital and main port of Somalia, on the Indian Ocean. It was founded as an Arab settlement in the 10th century and sold to Italy in 1905 becoming the capital of Italian Somaliland. It has a university (1969). It is the chief commercial centre of the republic. Population (1980 est): 400 000.

Mogilev 53 54N 30 20E A city in the Soviet Union, in the E Belorussian SSR on the River Dnepr. Founded in 1267, it passed to Lithuania and then to Poland before being annexed by Russia (1772). It produces metal goods, machinery, and chemicals. Population (1981 est): 308 000.

MOGUL ART AND ARCHITECTURE *An example of late Mogul painting, depicting dancers and musicians performing a nautch, a traditional Indian dance, inside a European palace.*

Mogul art and architecture A style that developed in N India under the patronage of the Mogul emperors. Originally much indebted to *Persian art, Mogul painting developed a more naturalistic style with small-scale scenes of court life and natural history as favoured subjects. Book illustration was highly developed. Architecture reached its peak during the reign (1556–1605) of *Akbar, when attempts were made to fuse the opposing traditions of the indigenous Hindu architecture, characterized by solid rocklike masses and use of beams in building, with the Islamic tradition of mathematical clarity in design and use of true arches and internal spaces in construction (*see* Fatehpur Sikri). *See also* Indian art and architecture; Taj Mahal.

Moguls An Indian Muslim dynasty, descended from the Mongol leader *Genghis Khan, that ruled from 1526 until 1858. Its founder was *Babur (reigned 1526–30); he and the first 5 of his 18 successors, Humayun (1508–56; reigned 1530–56), *Akbar (reigned 1556–1605), *Jahangir (1605–27), *Shah Jahan (1627–58), and *Aurangzeb (1658–1707), are known as the Great Moguls, and by the time of Aurangzeb the Empire spread from the far N to the far S of India. During the late 17th and the 18th centuries Mogul power declined in the face of opposition from Hindus to religious intolerance and of European commercial expansion. The last emperor, Bahadur Shah II (1775–1862; reigned 1837–58), was deposed after the *Indian Mutiny and exiled to Burma.

Mohács, Battle of (29 August, 1526) The battle in which the Ottoman Turks under *Suleiman the Magnificent defeated a vastly outnumbered Hungarian and Bohemian army. The battle led to the submission of Hungary to Ottoman overrule.

mohair A wool-like fabric or yarn manufactured from the hair of *Angora goats. Warm, light, and durable and frequently blended with wool, silk, or cotton, mohair is used for light-weight suiting, upholstery, and fluffy fashion knitwear.

Mohammed (*or* Muhammad; c. 570–632 AD) According to Muslims, the last of the prophets and preacher of *Islam to the Arabs. Mohammed is said to have been born in Mecca, a member of the Quraysh clan, which dominated the town. In 610, when he was about 40, he received revelations from God and called upon his pagan fellow townsmen to prepare for the Last Day and to repent. The Meccans rejected him and threatened his life and in 622 he fled to Yathrib (*see* Hegira), where he established the first Muslim community and began to spread Islam. Yathrib now came to be called Medina, "City of the Prophet." By 629 the Muslims in Medina were strong enough to defeat the still pagan Meccans and obtained control of Mecca. By the time of Mohammed's death, Islam had begun to spread throughout Arabia. Mohammed's revelations were collected after his death to form the *Koran. His tomb is venerated in the mosque at Medina.

Mohammed I Askia (d. 1538) Ruler of the West African empire of Songhai (1493–1528), which reached its greatest extent under his rule. He controlled the trade routes to North Africa and was an able administrator. An enthusiastic Muslim, he made the pilgrimage to Mecca in 1495–97.

Mohammed II (1430–81) Sultan of the Ottoman Empire (1451–81). Known as the Conqueror, his fame rests mainly on his conquest in 1453 of Constantinople, which as *Istanbul became the Ottoman capital. He also extended Ottoman territories in the Balkans and Asia Minor.

Mohammed Reza Pahlavi (1918–80) Shah of Iran (1941–79). He became shah when the Allies forced his father *Reza Shah Pahlavi, to abdicate in World War II. In 1979 civil war forced him into exile and an Islamic republic was established in Iran under the leadership of Ayatollah Khomeini.

Mohawk An Iroquoian-speaking American Indian tribe of New York state. They were one of the five tribes that formed the league of the *Iroquois, said to have been founded by the Mohawk chief *Hiawatha. Their culture was typical of that of the neighbouring Iroquois tribes.

Mohenjo-Daro The site in Sind (Pakistan) of a great city of the ▢Indus Valley civilization. First excavated in the 1920s, it has extensive brick-built remains. *See also* Harappa.

Mohican An Algonkian-speaking American Indian tribe of New England. Primarily cultivators, they lived in fortified communities of 20 to 30 houses or in enclosed villages, but were displaced by wars with the Mohawks. Each of their five tribal sections was governed by a chief (sachem) together with an elected council.

Mohole An unsuccessful research project embarked upon with US government funds but abandoned in 1966 because of its enormous cost. The aim was to obtain samples of the rocks of the earth's upper mantle by drilling down from the ocean floor through the crust to the *Mohorovičić discontinuity. Drilling was undertaken off W Mexico but the technological difficulties proved enormous.

Moholy-Nagy, László (1895–1946) Hungarian artist. His most influential work was produced while teaching at the *Bauhaus (1923–29), where his experimental abstract paintings and photographs culminated in his *Light-Space Modulators*, plastic mechanical constructions designed to show continuously changing effects of light. His last years were spent teaching in Chicago.

Mohorovičić discontinuity The boundary between the earth's crust and upper mantle, marked by a sudden increase in velocity in seismic waves as the denser mantle is reached. It lies at a depth of 33–35 km (20–22 mi) beneath the continents and

5–10 km (3–6 mi) beneath the oceans. It is named after the Croatian scientist, Andrija Mohorovičić (1857–1936), who discovered it in 1909.

Mohs' scale A scale of hardness of minerals named after the mineralogist Friedrich Mohs (1773–1839). The ten standard minerals in the scale, in ascending order of hardness, are: 1. talc, 2. gypsum, 3. calcite, 4. fluorite, 5. apatite, 6. orthoclase feldspar, 7. quartz, 8. topaz, 9. corundum, and 10. diamond. Each can be scratched by any mineral higher up the scale, and other minerals can be assigned numbers in the scale according to which materials will scratch them.

moiré pattern A wavy cloudy fabric design. Originally applied to mohair (hence its name), this watered effect is obtained by steam pressing the material, usually silk or rayon, between engraved rollers.

Mojave Desert (*or* Mohave Desert) A desert area in the USA, in S California. It comprises part of the *Great Basin. Area: 38 850 sq km (15 000 sq mi).

Moji. *See* Kitakyushu.

Mold 53 10N 3 08W A market town in North Wales, the administrative centre of Clwyd on the River Alyn. Population (1981): 8589.

Moldavia A former principality in SE Europe. It was occupied by the Mongols in the 13th century, becoming independent in the 14th century and encompassing Bukovina and Bessarabia. It became an Ottoman vassal state in the 16th century, losing Bukovina to Austria in the 18th century and Bessarabia to Russia in the 19th century. In 1859 Moldavia and Walachia formed Romania. Russian Moldavia became the *Moldavian Soviet Socialist Republic in 1940.

Moldavian Soviet Socialist Republic A constituent republic in SW Soviet Union. It was formed in 1940, mainly from areas of *Bessarabia (*see also* Moldavia). Its main industries are wine making, tobacco processing, and food canning, for it is very fertile, producing wheat, maize, fruit, and vegetables, as well as having many vineyards. Area: 33 670 sq km (13 000 sq mi). Population (1981 est): 4 000 000. Capital: Kishinev.

mole (medicine) An area of darkly pigmented skin, known medically as a naevus. Many people have moles and the only reasons for doing anything about them are cosmetic unless they enlarge, bleed, or become painful, any of which may indicate malignant change (*see* melanoma).

mole (metrology; symbol mol) The *SI unit of amount of substance equal to the amount of substance that contains the same number of entities as there are atoms in 0.012 kg of carbon-12. One mol of any substance contains $6.022\,52 \times 10^{23}$ entities (*see* Avogadro's number). The entities may be atoms, molecules, ions, electrons, etc.

mole (zoology) A burrowing mammal belonging to the family *Talpidae*, of Europe, Asia, and North America. The common Eurasian mole (*Talpa europaea*) is about 14 cm long including its small bristly tail. It is thickset, with velvety-black fur, and has long-clawed digging forefeet. Moles make an extensive system of underground tunnels, feeding on earthworms and storing surplus worms in a "larder." Practically blind above ground, moles rapidly starve when prevented from digging. Order: *Insectivora. See also* desman.

mole cricket A large *cricket belonging to the family *Gryllotalpidae* (about 50 species). 35–50 mm long, mole crickets are brown and have enlarged and toothed front legs, which are used for digging long shallow tunnels under damp ground. The female lays large numbers of eggs in an underground nest and the young (like the adults) feed on plant roots and insect larvae.

molecular biology The scientific discipline that deals with the molecular basis of living processes. Molecular biology involves both *biochemistry and *biophysics: its growth since the 1930s has been made possible by the development of such techniques as *chromatography, *electron microscopy, and *X-ray diffraction, which have revealed the structures of biologically important molecules, such as DNA, RNA, and enzymes. Heredity, and the development, organization, function, and malfunction of living cells, all depend on the physical and chemical properties of the molecules involved.

molecular cloud An immense cloud of cool dense matter in the *interstellar medium, composed mainly of molecular hydrogen with a very small proportion of other molecules and dust grains. A typical cloud is 130 light years across, has a mass of 500 000 solar masses, and a temperature of 10–20 K. Stars form in these regions and have been detected by radio astronomers in our Galaxy and others. Several thousand molecular clouds are thought to exist in the Galaxy.

molecule The smallest portion of a compound that can exist independently and retain its properties. The atoms that make up a molecule are either bonded together covalently, e.g. CO_2, or electrovalently, e.g. NaCl. However, in crystalline substances the bonds extend throughout the whole crystal structure and the molecule has only a notional existence. In covalent gases and liquids, however, the molecule actually exists as a small group of atoms. **Molecular weight** (or relative molecular mass) is the ratio of the average mass per molecule to one-twelfth of the mass of an atom of carbon-12. It is thus the sum of the *atomic weights of the atoms comprising a molecule.

mole rat A burrowing *rodent superficially resembling a mole. Mole rats belong to three families found in Africa and Eurasia: *Bathyergidae* (16 species), *Spalacidae* (3 species), and *Rhizomyidae* (14 species). Mole rats of all three families have small eyes and ears, a small tail, and powerful digging feet. They feed on roots and tubers.

Molière (Jean-Baptiste Poquelin; 1622–73) French dramatist, the father of modern French comedy. He left home in 1643 to establish a theatrical company and toured the provinces from 1645 to 1658. *Les Précieuses ridicules* (1659) was the first of a series of Paris productions for both court and public audiences that included *Tartuffe* (1664), *Dom Juan* (1665), *Le Misanthrope* (1666), *L'Avare* (1668), *Le Bourgeois Gentilhomme* (1670), and *Le Malade imaginaire* (1673). His ridicule of hypocrisy and his vigorous satire of contemporary manners and types brought him into constant conflict with the religious authorities. He frequently acted in his own productions and died after collapsing on stage.

Molina, Luis de (1535–1600) Spanish *Jesuit theologian. A professor at Évora in Portugal and later at Madrid, he is best known for his *Concordia liberi arbitrii cum gratiae donis* (1588), which founded Molinism. This was an attempt to reconcile divine grace with man's free will. It precipitated a dispute between Molina's Jesuit supporters and the *Dominicans, which lasted for several centuries.

Molinos, Miguel de (c. 1640–97) Spanish mystic and priest, who was a leading advocate of *Quietism. From 1669 he lived chiefly in Rome, where he wrote his famous *Spiritual Guide* (1675). He was condemned to life imprisonment by the *Inquisition in 1687.

Molise A mountainous region in S central Italy, part of Abruzzi e Molise until 1963. It is a poor underdeveloped agricultural region producing wheat, potatoes, maize, sheep, and goats. Area: 4438 sq km (1713 sq mi). Population (1982 est): 329 745. Capital: Campobasso.

mollusc An invertebrate animal belonging to the phylum *Mollusca* (about 100 000 species). Molluscs occupy marine, freshwater, and terrestrial habitats, being especially common on rocky coasts. They have a soft unsegmented body with a muscular foot, variously modified for crawling, burrowing, or swimming, and a thin dorsal mantle that secretes a shell of one, two, or eight parts. The shell is usually external, as in snails, but it may be internal, as in cuttlefish, or absent, as in slugs. All except bivalves feed using a ribbon-shaped rasping tongue (rad-

ula). Most molluscs are herbivorous with some carnivorous and scavenging species. In the more primitive molluscs there are separate male and female sexes and eggs and sperm are released into the water, where fertilization takes place. Some of the more advanced gastropods and bivalves are hermaphrodite and in some gastropods and all cephalopods fertilization is internal. *See also* bivalve; cephalopod; chiton; gastropod.

molly An attractive tropical fish of the genus *Mollienesia*. 5–13 cm long, several colour varieties have been bred for use in aquaria, including the well-known sailfin mollies (*M. latipinna* and *M. velifera*), which have a bluish sheen and, in the male, a sail-like dorsal fin. Family: *Poeciliidae*; order: *Atheriniformes*.

Molnár, Ferenc (1878–1952) Hungarian dramatist known for his romantic and witty plays, notably *The Devil* (1907) and *The Red Mill* (1923). He also wrote novels and short stories. He emigrated to the USA in 1940.

moloch A grotesque desert-dwelling Australian lizard, *Moloch horridus*, also called thorny devil. Its yellow-and-brown body is covered in thorny spines, which provide good camouflage. Ants are its chief food and a network of microscopic channels on its head collect dew, which drips into its mouth. Family: *Agamidae*.

Moloch A Semitic god whose worship was characterized by the sacrificial burning of children. There are several biblical references to his worship by the Israelites during the period of the Kings (c. 961–c. 562 BC).

Molokai A mountainous US island in the N Pacific Ocean, in Hawaii. Father Damien worked in its leper colony. Pineapples and cattle are exported. Area: 676 sq km (261 sq mi). Population (1980): 6076. Chief settlement: Kaunakakai.

Molotov. See Perm.

Molotov, Vyacheslav Mikhailovich (V. M. Scriabin; 1890–1986) Soviet statesman, who assumed his name in 1906 to escape from the Imperial police. As prime minister (1930–41) and foreign minister (1939–49, 1953–56), Molotov signed the Soviet-German nonaggression treaty in 1939; after the German invasion in 1941, he negotiated alliances with the Allies. His subsequent attitude to the West (the frequency with which he said *niet* (no) in the UN was renowned) contributed to the Cold War. Disagreements with Khrushchev led to demotion in 1956 but in 1984/5 he was rehabilitated. The **Molotov cocktail**, named after him, is an incendiary hand-grenade.

Moltke, Helmuth, Graf von (1800–91) Prussian field marshal; chief of the general staff (1858–88). His reorganization of the Prussian army led to victories against Denmark (1864) and Austria (1866) and in the Franco-Prussian War (1870–71). His nephew **Helmuth Johannes Ludwig von Moltke** (1848–1916) was chief of the German general staff (1906–14), directing at the outbreak of World War I the strategy devised by *Schlieffen. Held responsible for the defeat at the Marne, he was relieved of his command.

Moluccas (or Maluku) An Indonesian group of islands between Sulawesi and West Irian. It includes the islands of Ambon, Halmahera, and Ceram. Mountainous and volcanic, most are fertile and humid. The indigenous population fishes, hunts, and collects sago, while along the coasts the tropical rain forest is giving way to shifting cultivation; spices, fish, and copra are exported. *History*: before the Portuguese arrival (1512), the islands were ruled by Muslims and already famed for their cloves and nutmeg from which they gained the name of Spice Islands. After great European rivalry, Dutch control was established in the 19th century. With Indonesian independence (1949) the S Moluccas fought to secede but were subjugated by the new government (1950–56). Since 1966 S Moluccans in the Netherlands have drawn attention to their cause with violent protests. Area:

about 74 504 sq km (28 766 sq mi). Population (1980): 1 411 006. Chief town: Ambon.

molybdenum (Mo) A very hard silvery-grey metal of high melting point, it was first prepared in 1782 by P. J. Hjelm (1746–1813). It occurs in nature as molybdenite (MoS_2) and as wulfenite (lead molybdenate; $PbMoO_4$). It is extracted by the reduction of molybdenum trioxide (MoO_3). Molybdenum is used in high-temperature filaments and as an alloying agent in the production of high-strength steels. Trace quantities of molybdenum are important for plant nutrition. At no 42; at wt 95.94; mp 2617°C; bp 4612°C.

Mombasa 4 04S 39 40E A port in Kenya, on an island in an inlet of the Indian Ocean. It was an important port for Arab traders and was taken in the 16th and 17th centuries by the Portuguese; the Arab influence remains strong. The modern deepwater port at Kinlindini handles most of Kenya's trade; industries include oil refining and a pipeline (opened 1977) supplies Nairobi. Population (1983 est): 409 616.

moment The product of a force and its perpendicular distance from the axis about which it acts. A moment produces a turning effect and is sometimes called a torque. The inertia of a body to a torque is called its **moment of inertia**. This quantity is equal to mr^2 for a single mass (m) rotating about an axis at a distance r from the axis. The moment of inertia of a system of masses is equal to the sum of these products.

momentum The linear momentum of a body is the product of its mass and its linear velocity. The angular momentum of a body is the product of its *moment of inertia and its angular velocity. Momentum is an important quantity in physics as during any process, for example a collision between two bodies, the total momentum of the system always remains constant (the law of conservation of momentum).

Mommsen, Theodor (1817–1903) German historian and politician. In his major historical work, *The History of Rome* (1854–85), Mommsen adopted a modern critical approach, effectively demythologizing Roman history. He also wrote on law and archaeology.

Mon A people of lower Burma and central Thailand. They speak an *Austro-Asiatic language, also known as Talaing. It is written in a script derived from *Pali, which the Burmese subsequently adopted. Between about 600 and 1000 AD Mon kingdoms dominated the area. After the fall of rival *Pagan the Mons recovered independence (late 13th to mid-16th centuries) but were subjugated by the Burmese in the 18th century and now survive only as minority groups. They are village-dwelling rice farmers, whose Theravada Buddhism is tinged with earlier pagan beliefs.

Mona. See Anglesey.

Monaco, Principality of A small country on the Mediterranean Sea, an enclave within French territory. It consists of three principal localities: the business district around the ports, Monte Carlo with its famous casino, and the capital Monaco. *Economy*: the main sources of revenue are tourism and the sale of postage stamps. *History*: ruled by the house of Grimaldi since 1297, it has been under French protection since 1641 (except for a period, 1815–61, of Sardinian protection). Executive power lies with the hereditary prince and the State Council and legislative power, with the prince and the National Council. Head of state: Prince Rainier III. Official language: French; Monégasque, a mixture of French and Italian, is also spoken. Official currency: French franc of 100 centimes. Area: 189 hectares (467 acres). Population (1980 est): 28 000.

Monadhliath Mountains (or Grey Hills) A mountain range in N Scotland, in the Highland Region. It lies between Loch Ness and the River Spey and reaches 941 m (3087 ft) at Carn Mairg.

Monaghan (Irish name: Contae Mhuineachain) A county in the NE Republic of Ireland, in Ulster bordering on Northern Ireland. It is generally low lying and undulating. Agricultural produce includes oats and potatoes; cattle rearing and dairy farming are also important. Area: 1551 sq km (499 sq mi). Population (1981): 51 192. County town: Monaghan.

mona monkey. See guenon.

monarch A widespread American *milkweed butterfly, *Danaus plexippus* (see Plate I). Light brown with black borders and white dots, the adults migrate southwards to overwinter in semihibernation. In spring they move north, breeding on the way. Occasionally, individuals may reach Europe. The caterpillars are green with black and yellow bands.

monasticism A system under which men or women devote themselves to a religious life either in solitude or in special communities removed from society. St *Anthony of Egypt probably inaugurated Christian monasticism by organizing ascetic hermits under a rule (c. 305). They were, however, essentially solitaries; communal monastic life was introduced by Anthony's disciple, *Pachomius. Between 358 and 364 St *Basil drew up the rule that still governs the Orthodox Churches' religious communities. In the 6th century St *Benedict of Nursia introduced a monastic rule in Italy that remained the basic system in the West (see Benedictines). It underwent periodic reform, first at *Cluny in the 10th century. The rules of three orders founded in the 11th century—the Camaldolese (1012), *Carthusian (1084), and *Cistercian (1098)—were also stricter variants of the Benedictine rule. The mendicant friars (see Augustinians; Carmelites; Dominicans; Franciscans) also took vows and lived according to a rule, but not in seclusion: they continued to perform duties in the world. They had corresponding rules for women, however, who lived enclosed lives as nuns. Two military orders, the *Hospitallers and *Templars, followed monastic discipline. Both monks and nuns were required to take vows of poverty, chastity, and obedience and to devote their lives to prayer and work. Until the Renaissance revived secular learning, the monasteries were the main cultural centres, preserving and transmitting the learning of antiquity. Monasticism was also practised by the ancient Jews (see Essenes), and there is a strong monastic tradition in Buddhism (see sangha; tri-ratna).

Monastir. See Bitola.

monazite A rare-earth mineral of composition $(Ce,La,Y,Th)PO_4$ and yellow to reddish-brown colour, found as an accessory in acid igneous rocks and as placer deposits. Monazite is usually obtained as a by-product of titanium and zircon mining; it is the most common source of the rare earths.

Mönchengladbach (or München Gladbach) 51 12N 6 25E A city in NW West Germany, in North Rhine-Westphalia. The site of a 13th-century cathedral, it is the centre of the German textile industry and headquarters of the NATO forces in N central Europe. Population (1980 est): 258 000.

Monck, George, 1st Duke of Albemarle (1608–70) English general. Initially a royalist in the Civil War, he was captured and imprisoned (1644–46). Won over to the parliamentary cause, he defeated the Scots at Dunbar (1650) and pacified Scotland. In the first *Dutch War he became a successful general at sea. In command of Scotland from 1654, he supported the overthrow of Richard Cromwell (1659) but opposed the subsequent military government and was largely responsible for the Restoration of Charles II.

Moncton 46 04N 64 50W A city and river port in E Canada, in New Brunswick. The railway and transportation hub of the *Maritime Provinces, it also has light industry and the French-language University of Moncton (1864). Population (1981): 54 743.

Mond, Ludwig (1839–1909) German industrial chemist, who lived in Britain from 1862. He discovered nickel carbonyl and its application to the extraction of platinum from its ores, a method now known as the **Mond process**. He also made improvements to the *Solvay process. His son **Alfred Mond, 1st Baron Melchett** (1868–1930) was a British industrialist and Liberal politician, who helped to found Imperial Chemical Industries Ltd.

Mondrian, Piet (Pieter Cornelis Mondriaan; 1872–1944) Dutch painter, born in Amersfoot. His early still lifes and landscapes became increasingly architectural; however, while in Paris (1912–14) he came under the influence of *cubism. His first abstract compositions (1917) used only horizontal and vertical lines, primary colours, and black and white. During this period he helped to launch the art movement of de *Stijl. After 1919 his style, known as neoplasticism, influenced both the *Bauhaus school and the *international style in architecture. In New York after 1940 his style became more relaxed with such paintings as *Broadway Boogie Woogie*.

Monet, Claude (1840–1926) French impressionist painter, born in Paris (*see* impressionism). He spent his childhood in Le Havre, where his teacher *Boudin encouraged him to paint in the open air. After military service in Algeria (1860–62) he met *Sisley and *Renoir in Gleyre's studio. Initially influenced by the *Barbizon school, in the late 1860s he developed the impressionist technique in views of Paris and in the 1870s in boating scenes at Argenteuil. He excelled in his series of the same scenes painted at different times of day, e.g. *Gare St Lazare, Haystacks, Rouen Cathedral*, and the *Poplars*, the last of which anticipates *abstract art. His last works were his famous murals of water lilies (Orangerie, Paris).

monetarism A revision of old-established economic theories that rivals *Keynesianism. Monetarism's most celebrated proponent is the US economist Milton *Friedman. Monetarists believe that with the exception of *monetary policy government economic policy does not achieve its aims and is harmful. They regard responsible regulation of the money supply as essential to the wellbeing of the economy, advocating a gentle expansion of the money supply at roughly the rate of growth of the economy. Monetarists blame *inflation on overexpansion of the money supply. The essential difference between neo-Keynesians and monetarists is that the former believe in government regulation of the economy, whereas the latter do not.

monetary policy An economic policy in which the money supply is managed by the government, in order to influence the economy. During the 1950s and 1960s in the UK, government attention was focused on *fiscal policy and, to a lesser extent, on *prices-and-incomes policy to the neglect of monetary policy. Following the inflation of the 1970s and the impact of monetarist ideas (*see* monetarism), more attention is being paid to monetary policy (*see also* open-market operations).

money A medium of exchange. To be an efficient medium of exchange, money should be divisible (for small transactions), have a high value-to-weight ratio (to make it easy to carry about), be readily acceptable, and not easily counterfeited. Money also functions as means of credit and a store of wealth, for which purposes its value must remain stable. The depreciation in the value of money (*see* inflation) is an economic problem, at present besetting the West. Money was reputedly invented by the Lydians in the 7th century BC. It originally took the form of something intrinsically valuable (such as a precious metal) but, so long as it is generally acceptable and retains confidence, this is not necessary. Indeed, most money is now in the form of paper, which is itself almost worthless. Individual countries have their own form of money (currency), which cannot be used in other countries; to be used in another country currencies have to be exchanged (*see* exchange rates).
The total stock of money in the economy is known as the **money supply**. In the UK two definitions of the money

supply are used: the narrow M1 (essentially, the total amount of cash and current accounts) and the broad M3 (essentially, the total amount of cash plus both current and deposit accounts). Government regulation of the money supply, known as *monetary policy, is one of the means by which it attempts to control an economy.

money market A market in which money is borrowed and lent for short periods. Participants in the UK money market, in the City of London, include *discount houses, the *commercial banks, and the *Bank of England conducting *open-market operations for the government and acting as lender of the last resort.

money spider A tiny *spider of the family *Liniphiidae* (over 250 species). It has a reddish or black body and occurs in enormous numbers in fields, etc. Money spiders build sheetlike webs on vegetation to which they cling upside down, waiting to catch insects that drop onto the web. Immature spiders may be seen drifting considerable distances in the air, attached to silken gossamer threads.

moneywort A perennial herb, *Lysimachia nummularia*, also called creeping jenny, native to damp places in Europe. It has a creeping stem, up to 60 cm long, shiny heart-shaped leaves, and yellow flowers borne individually on short stalks. Family: *Primulaceae*.
The Cornish moneywort (*Sibthorpia europaea*) is a small trailing perennial with minute pink flowers. Family: *Scrophulariaceae*.

Monge, Gaspard (1746–1818) French mathematician. He was one of the founders of descriptive geometry, the mathematics of projecting solid figures onto a plane, upon which modern engineering drawing is based. He became a close friend of Napoleon and was appointed minister for the navy (1792–93), but was stripped of all honours on the restoration of the Bourbons. He died in poverty.

Mongolian languages A group of languages that, together with *Turkic and *Manchu-Tungus, constitute the Altaic language family. Western Mongolian languages are spoken in parts of the Soviet Union, the Mongolian People's Republic, and Afghanistan; Eastern Mongolian is spoken in China and the Mongolian People's Republic. There are more than three million speakers of these languages, the majority of which remain unwritten.

Mongolian People's Republic A large sparsely populated country in NE central Asia, between the Soviet Union and China. It is mainly high plateau, rising to the Altai and Khangai Mountains in the W and extending into the Gobi Desert in the S. *Economy*: with its nomadic-pastoral tradition, it is still mainly dependent on livestock rearing, now organized in collectives and state farms. In recent years there have been attempts to increase crop growing. Copper mining is being introduced and other minerals include coal, oil, gold, tungsten, lead, and uranium. There is some light industry, mainly based on Ulan Bator. Exports, mainly to communist countries, include cattle and horses, wool, and hair. *History*: in the 13th century Genghis Khan ruled the Mongol empire from Karakoram in the N. As Outer Mongolia, the area was a province of China from 1691 to 1911, when it became an autonomous monarchy under Russian protection. Again under Chinese influence from 1919 to 1921, it then became independent and the Mongolian People's Republic was declared in 1924. Persecution of lama priests (*see* Tibetan Buddhism) precipitated the Lama Rebellion (1932), when several thousand Mongolians with several million head of livestock crossed the border into Inner Mongolia. After World War II its independence was guaranteed by the Soviet Union and China. Head of state: Jambyn Batmunkh. Official language: Khalkha Mongolian. Official currency: tugrik of 100 möngö. Area: 1 565 000 sq km (604 095 sq·mi). Population (1981 est): 1 732 000. Capital: Ulan Bator.

mongolism. *See* Down's syndrome.

Mongoloid The racial grouping comprising the populations of E Asia and the Arctic region of North America. They are characterized by medium skin pigmentation, the epicanthic fold of the upper eyelid, straight coarse black hair, a rather flat face with high cheekbones, slight facial and body hair, and a high percentage of B blood type. The American Indian peoples used to be classified as Mongoloid but now only the Eskimo peoples are included.

Mongols An Asiatic people united in the early 13th century by *Genghis Khan, who built up an empire that encompassed much of central Asia. Under his grandson *Kublai Khan the Mongols conquered China and ruled there as the *Yuan dynasty until 1368. They were subsequently confined to the area approximating to the present-day Mongolian People's Republic.

mongoose A carnivorous □mammal belonging to the family *Viverridae* (which also includes civets and genets), found in warm regions of the Mediterranean, Africa, and Asia. There are about 40 species, ranging in size from 50 to 100 cm including the long tapering furry tail (25–50 cm), with short legs, small ears, and long coarse grey-brown fur. Mongooses are renowned for catching snakes and rats and also eat eggs, small mammals, frogs, and birds. Chief genera: *Galidictis, Herpestes, Helogale*.

monism. *See* dualism.

monitor A class of ironclad US warship of the mid-19th century, especially the *Monitor*, a Federal ship that engaged its Confederate counterpart, the *Merrimack*, at Hampton Roads, Virginia (1862). In 1978 the wreck of the victorious *Monitor* was identified in 75 m (230 ft) of water outside the harbour, but was found to be in too fragile a condition to be raised.

MONITOR LIZARD *The Australian lace monitor, or goanna (Varanus varius), about 1.8 m long, is mainly black and yellow.*

monitor lizard A lizard belonging to the Old World family *Varanidae* (30 species), occurring in tropical and subtropical regions. 0.2–3 m long, monitors have an elongated body and well-developed legs. They feed on mammals, snakes, lizards, eggs, and carrion. The rare Bornean earless monitor (*Lanthanotus borneensis*) lives in subterranean tunnels and is a good swimmer, feeding on fish and worms. *See also* Komodo dragon.

Moniz, Antonio Egas (1874–1955) Portuguese surgeon, who pioneered the use of brain surgery in the treatment of severe mental illness. In 1935 he performed the first operation of prefrontal lobotomy (*see* leucotomy) and shared the 1949 Nobel Prize with Walter Rudolf Hess (1881–   ).

Monk, Thelonius (Sphere) (1920–82) US Black jazz pianist and composer, influential in the development of *bop. He developed a characteristic pianistic style and played alone or in small groups; his compositions include "Off Minor" and "Blue Monk."

monkey A tree-dwelling *primate. Monkeys are 20–110 cm long and most have a long balancing tail of up to 100 cm used in climbing, although some are tailless. Agile and intelligent, they have fingernails and an opposable thumb enabling manual dexterity. Most monkeys are omnivorous but they prefer fruit, nuts, and other vegetation. *See also* New World monkey; Old World monkey.

monkey flower A fragrant annual or perennial herb or shrub of the mostly North American genus *Mimulus* (100 species), growing near streams and rivers. *M. guttatus* is a naturalized European species. Up to 60 cm tall, it has simple toothed leaves and showy yellow tubular flowers with red spots, each with a two-lobed upper lip and a larger three-lobed lower lip. Family: *Scrophulariaceae*. *See also* musk.

monkey puzzle A coniferous tree, *Araucaria araucana*, also called Chile pine, native to Chile and Argentina and widely grown as an ornamental. Up to 30 m high (ornamental trees are much smaller), it has whorled horizontal branches covered with leathery prickly overlapping leaves, 3–4 cm long. The globular spiny cones, 10–17 cm long, ripen from green to brown and break up to release large seeds, which are edible when roasted. Family: *Araucariaceae*.

monkfish A *shark belonging to the family *Squatinidae*. It has a broad flattened head, an elongated tapering body, winglike pectoral fins, two dorsal fins, and no anal fin. Monkfish occur in tropical and temperate seas and feed on bottom-dwelling fish, molluscs, and crustaceans. A species of *anglerfish, *Lophius piscatorius*, is also called monkfish.

monkshood. *See* aconite.

Monmouth, James Scott, Duke of (1649–85) The illegitimate son of Charles II of England and Lucy Walter (d. 1658), who led the Monmouth rebellion against his uncle James II. In 1662 he married, and took the name of, Anne Scott, Countess of Buccleuch. A Protestant, he became a focus of the opposition to the succession of the Roman Catholic James and was banished (1684) after being implicated in the *Rye House Plot. After James' accession (1685), Monmouth landed at Lyme Regis to raise a rebellion and was defeated at *Sedgemoor, captured, and beheaded.

Monmouthshire A former county of SE Wales. Under local government reorganization in 1974 it became part of *Mid Glamorgan, *South Glamorgan, and *Gwent.

Monnet, Jean (1888–1979) French economist and public official, known for his contribution to European unity. He was deputy secretary general of the League of Nations (1919–23). In 1946 he inaugurated the Monnet Plan for the modernization of French industry and later drafted the *Schuman Plan for the establishment of the European Coal and Steel Community, of which he was president (1952–55). His efforts culminated in the establishment of the EEC.

monoclonal antibody A type of pure antibody that can be produced artificially in large quantities and used, for example, to distinguish the major blood groups. Mouse lymphocytes producing the required antibody are fused with mouse cancer cells; the resulting hybrid cells multiply rapidly and all produce the same type of antibody as their parent lymphocytes.

monocotyledons The smaller of the two main groups of flowering plants, which includes the palms, bananas, orchids, grasses, lilies, and many garden bulbs and corms—daffodils, irises, tulips, crocuses, etc. (*compare* dicotyledons). Monocots have a single seed leaf (cotyledon) in the embryo. Typically the flower parts are in threes (or multiples of three) and the leaves have parallel veins. Very few monocots produce true wood. *See also* angiosperms.

Monod, Jacques-Lucien (1910-76) French biochemist, who proposed a mechanism for the regulation of gene activity. Monod and his colleague F. Jacob (1920-) postulated a regulatory gene that controlled the activity of a neighbouring gene for protein synthesis. Their theory was later found to be largely true. Monod and Jacob shared the 1965 Nobel Prize with A. Lwoff (1902-).

monomer A simple molecule or group of atoms forming a repeated unit in a dimer (two molecules), trimer (three molecules), or polymer (*see* polymerization).

Monophysites (Greek *monos physis*: one nature) Supporters of the doctrine that the incarnate Christ had only a single divine nature. They opposed the orthodox teaching that he possessed two natures, human as well as divine. The doctrine was provoked by the dogmatic formulations of the Council of Chalcedon (451) and, despite attempts at reconciliation by the Byzantine emperors, the *Coptic and several other Eastern Churches were irrevocably schismatic by the mid-6th century.

monopoly An industry in which the market is supplied by one supplier. The monopolist can obtain a high profit by restricting supply and demanding a high price. Consumers are thus penalized and it is likely that with a secure market there will also be inefficiency in production. In the public sector of a mixed economy monopolies for the supply of public services (electricity, gas, transport, etc.) are commonplace. In the private sector they are usually restricted by legislation, which in the UK is set out in the Fair Trading Act (1973). The **Monopolies Commission**, the duties of which are set out in the Act, conducts detailed investigations into monopolies and mergers. In the USA the *antitrust laws perform a similar function.

monosaccharide (*or* simple sugar) A *carbohydrate consisting of a single sugar unit and possessing either a keto group (C=O) or an aldehyde group (CHO). Monosaccharides are classified according to the number of carbon atoms they possess—the most common being pentoses (with five) and hexoses (with six)—and they can exist as either straight-chain or ring-shaped structures. The most widely occurring monosaccharides are *glucose and *fructose.

monosodium glutamate The sodium salt of the amino acid glutamic acid, used widely in the food industry as a flavouring agent, especially in tinned preserved foods.

monotheism Belief in only one God. The great monotheistic religions are Judaism, Christianity, and Islam. Earlier views that monotheism evolved out of *polytheism are now discredited, as Judaism and Islam in particular seem to have grown from conscious opposition to polytheistic systems.

Monothelites (Greek *monos, thelein*: one, (to) will) Supporters of the doctrine that the incarnate Christ possessed only one divine will. Monothelitism was conceived in 624 as a formula for reconciling the *Monophysite churches but failed in its purpose and was formally branded a heresy in 680.

monotreme A primitive *mammal belonging to the order *Monotremata*, found only in Australia (including Tasmania) and New Guinea. The name means "single hole," and monotremes have the reptilian characteristic of a single vent for passing urine, faeces, and eggs or sperm. Monotremes lay eggs, suckling their young after these hatch. The only living monotremes are the *echidnas and *duck-billed platypus.

Monroe, James (1758-1831) US statesman; president (1817-25). He fought in the American Revolution and was later minister to France (1794-96) and Britain (1803-07) before becoming secretary of state (1811). His two peaceful terms as president, known as the "era of good feelings," saw the opening of the West and the acquisition of Spanish Florida. The **Monroe Doctrine** (1823), largely the work of John Quincy *Adams, became a basic principle of US foreign policy; it warned European powers not to intervene in the Americas and declared that the USA would likewise refrain from interference in Europe.

Monroe, Marilyn (Norma Jean Baker *or* Mortenson; 1926-62) US film actress. Her childhood was spent in an orphanage and foster homes. Promoted as a sex symbol, in such films as *Niagara* (1952) and *Gentlemen Prefer Blondes* (1953), she later developed a real acting talent and ability as a comedienne. Her third husband was Arthur *Miller, and her last film appearance was in *The Misfits* (1961), which he wrote. She died from an overdose of barbiturates.

MARILYN MONROE *With Arthur Miller.*

Monrovia 6 20N 10 46W The capital and main port of Liberia, on the Atlantic Ocean. Founded in 1822 as a settlement for freed North American slaves, it was named after President Monroe of the USA. The University of Liberia was founded in 1851. Population (1984): 425 000.

Mons (Flemish name: Bergen) 50 28N 3 58E A town in Belgium, situated between two important coalmining regions. Notable buildings include the town hall (1443-67) and the Church of Ste Waudru (1450-1621). The battle of Mons took place here on 23 August, 1914, at the beginning of World War I. Principally a commercial centre, its industries include oil, cotton, porcelain, and tobacco. Population (1981 est): 96 336.

Monsarrat, Nicholas (John Turney; 1910-79) British novelist. His best-known novel, *The Cruel Sea* (1951), was based on his naval experiences in World War II. Other novels include *The Tribe That Lost its Head* (1956) and *The Pillow Fight* (1965).

monsoon A seasonal large-scale reversal of winds in the tropics, resulting chiefly from the differential heating of the land and oceans. It is best developed in India, SE Asia, and China; N Australia and East and West Africa have similar wind reversals. The term is derived from the Arabic word *mawsim*, originally applied to the seasonal winds of the Arabian Sea. It is now commonly applied to the rainfall that accompanies the wind reversals, especially the period of heavy rainfall in S Asia extending from April to September, in which the winds are southwesterly.

Monstera A genus of large tropical American herbaceous plants (50 species) that climb by means of aerial roots. *M. deliciosa* is often grown as a house plant for its foliage and in the tropics for its edible green fruits. The leaves, up to 60 cm long, are perforated with slits or holes and the flowers resemble those of the *arum lily. Family: *Araceae.*

Montagu, Lady Mary Wortley (1689–1762) English writer. Her best-remembered works are her letters, especially those written from Constantinople, where her husband was ambassador and from where she introduced into England the practice of inoculation against smallpox. A friend of many prominent writers, she lived in Italy from 1739 to 1761.

Montaigne, Michel de (1533–92) French essayist. Soon after the death of his father, a wealthy merchant, in 1568, he resigned his position as magistrate in Bordeaux and began composing his *Essais.* In 1580 he travelled extensively in Europe and was mayor of Bordeaux from 1581 to 1585. His *Essais,* which inaugurated a new literary genre, expressed his mature humanistic philosophy and constitute a moving self-portrait. They were published in two editions in 1580 and 1588, and a posthumous edition incorporated his final revisions. The *Essais* were translated into English by John Florio in 1603 and influenced the development of the English essay.

Montale, Eugenio (1896–1981) Italian poet. The stoic pessimism and symbolic imagery of his early poetry, especially in *Ossi di seppia* (1925), contrasts with the personal warmth of such later volumes as *Satura* (1971) and *Xenia* (1972). He was an opponent of fascism, and from 1947 literary editor of the newspaper *Corriere della Sera.* He published many translations and literary essays and won the Nobel Prize in 1975.

Montana The fourth largest state in the USA, bordering on Canada. It is mountainous and forested in the W, rising to the Rocky Mountains, with the rolling grasslands of the Great Plains in the E. Its economy is predominantly agricultural, cattle ranching and wheat production being of greatest importance. Other crops include barley and sugar beet. It possesses important mineral resources, notably copper (at Butte) and coal. The extraction of the latter is possible through strip mining but this has caused environmental problems. There are several Indian reservations within the state, notably the Crow reservation. *History*: it formed part of the Louisiana Purchase in 1803. During the mid-19th century a gold rush caused an influx of immigrants to the state; the capital, Helena, originated as a mining camp called Last Chance Gulch. During the Indian wars the battle of *Little Bighorn (Custer's Last Stand) took place (1876). Area: 377 070 sq km (145 587 sq mi). Population (1980): 786 690. Capital: Helena.

Montanism An early Christian sect founded by a shadowy individual called Montanus in Asia Minor in the mid-2nd century. It spread to N Africa, where *Tertullian became an adherent. It was characterized by *millenarianism, prophesying, and insistence upon strict asceticism.

Montauban 44 01N 1 20E A town in SW France, the capital of the Tarn-et-Garonne department. It has textile and porcelain industries. Population (1982): 53 147.

Mont Blanc (Italian name: Monte Bianco) 45 50N 6 52E The highest mountain in the Alps, on the French–Italian border. It was first climbed in 1786. A road tunnel (1958–62) beneath it, 12 km (7.5 mi) long, connects the two countries. Height: 4807 m (15 771 ft).

montbretia A perennial herb, *Crocosmia crocosmiflora* (a hybrid between *C. pottsii* and *C. aurea*), native to South Africa but naturalized in Europe and often grown as a garden ornamental. Up to 1 m high, it has long stiff sword-shaped leaves and clusters of orange-red funnel-shaped flowers, up to 7.5 cm across, with spreading petals. The name is also applied to the similar and related flowering herbs of the South African genus *Montbretia* (or *Tritonia*). Family: *Iridaceae.*

Montcalm, Louis Joseph de Montcalm-Grozon, Marquis de (1712–59) French general distinguished for his command (1756–59) against the British in Canada during the Seven

Years' War. In 1756 he regained control of Ontario for the French, in 1757 he took Fort William Henry, and in 1758 repulsed the much larger British force from Ticonderoga. He died defending Quebec from assault by Gen James *Wolfe, who, although victorious, was also mortally wounded.

Monte Bello Islands 20 30S 115 30E A group of uninhabited coral islands in the Indian Ocean, off the W coast of Western Australia. They were used for testing British nuclear weapons in 1952 and 1956.

Monte Carlo 43 44N 7 25E A resort in the principality of Monaco, on the Riviera. It is famous for its casino, motor rally, and other cultural and sporting events. Population (1982): 27 063.

Monte Cristo An Italian islet in the Tyrrhenian Sea. It is associated with the novel by Dumas, *The Count of Monte Cristo.*

Montefeltro An Italian noble family that ruled the city of Urbino between the 13th and 16th centuries. Originally rulers of the town of Mons Feretri from which they derived their name, the Montefeltri gave military support to the Holy Roman Emperor in his struggle against the pope (*see* Guelfs and Ghibellines). The best-known member of the family is the illegitimate **Federigo Montefeltro, Duke of Urbino** (1422–82), who distinguished himself as a military leader and as an art patron, especially of *Piero della Francesca. Urbino passed into the hands of the Rovere family in the 16th century because there were no Montefeltro heirs.

Montefiore, Sir Moses (1784–1885) British philanthropist, born in Italy, who campaigned for Jewish rights. He travelled widely throughout Europe and the Middle East, furthering with some success the cause of persecuted Jews. He also endowed many hospitals.

Montego Bay 18 27N 77 56W A port and tourist resort in NW Jamaica. Its chief exports are bananas and sugar. Population (1982): 59 614.

Montélimar 44 33N 4 45E A town in SE France, in the Drôme department. Famous for its nougat, it is an agricultural centre and has light industry. Population (1982): 30 213.

Montenegro (Serbo-Croat name: Crna Gora) The smallest constituent republic of Yugoslavia, bordering on the Adriatic Sea. It is predominantly mountainous and forested. Stock raising is important, especially of sheep, goats, and pigs. *History*: it was declared a kingdom in 1910, becoming a province of the kingdom of the Serbs, Croats, and Slovenes (later Yugoslavia) in 1918. Area: 13 812 sq km (5387 sq mi). Population (1982): 593 000. Capital: Titograd.

Monterey 36 39N 121 45W A city in the USA, in California on Monterey Bay. One of California's oldest cities, it is a well-known retreat of artists and writers. It forms the background for several of John Steinbeck's novels. Population (1980): 27 558.

Monte Rosa 45 57N 7 53E A massif in S Europe, on the Swiss–Italian border in the Alps. The highest peak, the Dufourspitze, is, at 4634 m (15 203 ft), the highest in Switzerland.

Monterrey 25 40N 100 20W The third largest city in Mexico. Founded in 1579, it has many notable buildings including the 18th-century cathedral. Monterrey is a major industrial centre specializing in metallurgy. Population (1980): 1 916 472.

Montespan, Françoise Athénaïs de Rochechouart, Marquise de (1641–1707) The mistress of Louis XIV of France from 1667 until replaced by the governess of their seven children—Mme de *Maintenon. Mme de Montespan remained at court until 1691, when she retired to a convent.

Montesquieu, Charles Louis de Secondat, Baron de (1689–1755) French historical philosopher and writer. Montesquieu's first work, the *Lettres persanes* (1721), was a brilliant satirical portrait of French institutions and society. It was a forerunner of the *Enlightenment. There followed the *Considérations sur les causes de la grandeur et de la décadence des romains* (1734) and the famous *Esprit des lois* (1748). This latter work, a comparative study of ideas on law and government, was perhaps the most important book of 18th-century France. It impressed even *Voltaire, who disliked Montesquieu intensely.

Montessori system A system of education for young children devised by the Italian doctor Maria Montessori (1870–1952). It places emphasis on development of the senses and envisages a limited role for the teacher as the child learns by itself through the use of didactic materials. Her first school opened in Rome in 1907 and her methods continue to be influential in infant schools today.

Monteux, Pierre (1875–1964) French conductor. He became conductor of Diaghilev's Ballets Russes in 1911 and gave the first performances of Stravinsky's *Petrushka* and *The Rite of Spring*. He subsequently held various posts in Europe and the USA and was principal conductor of the London Symphony Orchestra from 1961 to 1964.

Monteverdi, Claudio (1567–1643) Italian composer, a pupil of Marco Ingegneri (1545–92). From about 1590 to 1612 Monteverdi was court musician to the Duke of Mantua. From 1613 until his death he was maestro di cappella at St Mark's Cathedral, Venice. Monteverdi was the first great composer of *opera; enlarging the orchestra, he employed a new range of instrumental effects and made use of an innovatory harmonic style to achieve dramatic effects. He also influenced the development of the madrigal as an expressive form. His works include the operas *Orfeo* (1607) and *The Coronation of Poppea* (1642), a set of *Vespers* (1610), and many madrigals.

Montevideo 34 55S 56 10W The capital and main port of Uruguay, in the S on the Río de la Plata. Founded in 1726 by the Spanish as a defence against Portuguese attacks from Brazil, it suffered several occupations in the early 19th century before becoming capital of the newly independent Uruguay in 1828. In the 20th century it has developed rapidly, as both an industrial and a communications centre, and it is now one of South America's largest cities. It is also a popular summer resort. The University of Uruguay was founded here in 1849. Population (1980 est): 1 314 129.

Montez, Lola (Marie Gilbert; 1818–61) Irish dancer and mistress of Louis I of Bavaria (1786–1868; reigned 1825–48). The hostility aroused by her influence led to the abdication of Louis in 1848 and her own expulsion. She later lived for several years in the USA.

Montezuma II (1466–c. 1520) The last Aztec Emperor of Mexico (1502–20). During his reign his empire was weakened by tribal warfare, which enabled the Spaniards, led by Hernán *Cortés, to establish themselves in Mexico. The emperor was captured by Cortés and was killed either by the Spaniards or by his own people during the Aztec attack on Cortés' force as it tried to leave Tenochtitlán.

Montfort, Simon de, Earl of Leicester (c. 1208–65) English statesman, born in Normandy; the son and namesake of the leader of the Crusade against the *Albigenses. After serving Henry III of England in Gascony, he joined the antiroyalist faction that demanded greater control of the government, becoming the barons' leader in the subsequent *Barons' War. Initially successful, he became virtual ruler of England, summoning a parliament in 1265. In the same year, however, he was defeated and killed at Evesham.

Montgolfier, Jacques-Étienne (1745–99) French balloonist, who with his brother **Joseph-Michel Montgolfier** (1740–1810) invented the hot-air balloon. The hot-air balloon, so called because it derived its buoyancy from air heated by a fire, was publicly launched in 1782. A much larger balloon, which rose 2000 m, was demonstrated in June 1783 and in

October a series of passenger-carrying ascents were made. Jacques-Étienne (who himself never made an ascent) then launched a free-flying balloon and in 1784 Joseph-Michel with five companions ascended in a steerable balloon. Their experiments aroused enormous interest in flying.

Montgomery 32 22N 86 20W A city in the USA, the capital of Alabama on the Alabama River. Montgomery was the first capital (1861) of the Confederate states during the American Civil War. In the mid-1950s it was the scene of a bus boycott by Blacks, which played an important part in the growth of the civil-rights movement and brought Martin Luther King to the nation's attention. Montgomery is an industrial city and agricultural trading centre. Population (1980): 178 157.

Montgomery of Alamein, Bernard Law, 1st Viscount (1887–1976) British field marshal. In World War II he became commander of the Eighth Army (1942) and after the battle of Alamein drove *Rommel back to Tunis and surrender (1943), an achievement that brought him enormous popularity. Having played a major role in the invasion of Italy (1943), he became chief of land forces in the 1944 Normandy invasion. He helped plan the Arnhem disaster (September, 1944), but restored his reputation by pushing back the subsequent German offensive, receiving Germany's surrender. After the war he was chief of the imperial general staff (1946–48) and deputy commander of NATO forces (1951–58).

Montgomeryshire A former county of NE Wales. Under local government reorganization in 1974 it became part of *Powys.

month The time taken by the moon to complete one revolution around the earth. The complicated motion of the moon requires the starting and finishing points of revolution to be specified. The length of the month depends on the choice of reference point. The **sidereal month**, of 27.32 days, is measured with reference to the background stars. The **synodic month**, of 29.53 days, is measured between two identical phases of the moon. The month is one of the basic time periods used in *calendars.

Montherlant, Henry de (1896–1972) French novelist and dramatist. He was born in Paris into an aristocratic family. His works celebrate the virtues of austerity and virility and concentrate on physical pursuits and relationships. His novels include *Les Célibataires* (1934), the tetralogy *Les Jeunes Filles* (1936–39), and *Le Chaos et la nuit* (1963), and his plays include *Malatesta* (1946) and *Port-Royal* (1954).

Montmartre. *See* Paris.

Montparnasse. *See* Paris.

Montpellier 43 36N 3 53E A city in S France, the capital of the Hérault department. A Huguenot stronghold, it was besieged and captured by Louis XIII in 1622. Notable buildings include the gothic cathedral, the university (founded 1289), and the Musée Fabre. Montpellier trades in wine and brandy and has numerous manufacturing industries. Population (1982): 201 067.

Montreal 45 30N 73 36W A city and port in E Canada, in Quebec on Montreal Island at the junction of the Ottawa and St Lawrence Rivers. Canada's largest city, it is also the greatest transportation, trade, and manufacturing centre. Montreal employs cheap hydroelectricity for many industries, including oil refining, meat packing, brewing and distilling, food processing, textiles, and aircraft. It is the headquarters of banks, insurance companies, airlines, and railways. Housing two English-speaking and two French-speaking universities, Montreal is a forum for politics, broadcasting, theatre, film, and publishing. Two-thirds of the population is French speaking, making it the second largest French-speaking city in the world. Among its many beautiful buildings are Notre Dame Church, Christ Church Cathedral, and St James Cathedral. *History*: founded as Ville-Marie (1642), Montreal quickly became a commercial centre. Captured by Britain (1760), it acquired an English-speaking merchant community that has dominated Quebec's economy ever since. Recently Montreal was the venue of the world fair, Expo '67, and the 1976 Olympics. Population (1981): 980 354.

Montreux   46 27N 6 55E A winter resort in W Switzerland, on Lake Geneva. Its 13th-century Château de Chillon is immortalized in Byron's poem, the "Prisoner of Chillon". It holds an annual television festival awarding the Golden Rose of Montreux. Tourism is an important source of income. Population (1983 est): 19 292.

Montrose   56 43N 2 29W A resort in E Scotland in Tayside Region. It has fishing, canning, chemical, and distilling industries besides services for the North Sea oil industry. Population (1981): 12 286.

Montrose, James Graham, 1st Marquess of   (1612–50) Scottish general. In 1637 he signed the Covenant in support of Presbyterianism but became a rival of the antiroyalist *Argyll, who secured his imprisonment in 1641. Montrose fought for Charles I in the English Civil War but after a series of victories (1644) against the Scottish covenanters his army of Highlanders was defeated at Philipaugh (1645) and he fled to the Continent. He returned in 1650 but was defeated, captured, and executed by the parliamentarians.

Montserrat   A British crown colony comprising one of the Leeward Islands, in the Caribbean Sea to the SE of Puerto Rico. It is largely mountainous with active volcanoes. *Economy*: chiefly agricultural, the main crops are cotton, coconuts, and fruit and vegetables, which with cattle are the main exports. Forestry is being developed. *History*: discovered by Columbus in 1493, it was colonized by the Irish in the 17th century. Formerly administratively joined to the Leeward Islands, it became a separate colony in 1960. It was part of the Federation of the West Indies (1958–62). Official language: English. Official currency: East Caribbean dollar of 100 cents. Area: 106 sq km (40 sq mi). Population (1980): 12 073. Capital and main port: Plymouth.

Montserrat   41 36N 1 48E An isolated mountain in NE Spain, NW of Barcelona. On its E slope is a Benedictine monastery housing a well-known carving, supposedly by St Luke, of the Virgin and Child. Height: 1235 m (4054 ft).

Mont St Michel   48 38N 1 30W A granite islet in NW France, in the Manche department in the Bay of St Michel. The islet is connected to the mainland by a causeway. It is about 78 m (256 ft) high and is crowned by a Benedictine monastery (founded 966 AD), which was used as a prison from the French Revolution until 1863.

Monument.   *See* Fire of London.

Monza   45 35N 9 16E A city in Italy, in Lombardy. An important commercial city in the 13th century, it has a gothic cathedral. Umberto I was assassinated here in 1900. Its manufactures include machinery and textiles. It is noted for its motor-racing circuit. Population (1981 est): 124 362.

Moody, Dwight Lyman   (1837–99) US evangelist. As a successful businessman in Chicago in the 1850s, he was an active lay worker in a Congregational Church. He first achieved fame as a preacher in England (1873–75), and together with his musical colleague Ira David Sankey (1840–1908) compiled a popular collection of hymns, the *Sankey and Moody Hymn Book* (1873). He founded the Moody Bible Institute in 1899.

Moog synthesizer.   *See* synthesizer.

moon   The natural satellite of the earth. The moon orbits the earth every 27.32 days at a mean distance of 384 400 km, keeping more or less the same face (the nearside) towards the earth. As it revolves, different *phases can be seen from earth, together with up to two or three lunar *eclipses per year. The moon is only 81 times less massive than the earth and has a diameter of 3476 km.

The major surface features are the light-coloured highlands on the southern nearside and most of the farside, and the much darker lava plains—the *maria. The maria and more especially the highlands are heavily cratered. These roughly circular walled depressions, ranging greatly in size, were produced by impacting bodies from space. The extremely tenuous atmosphere exposes the surface to considerable temperature extremes (−180°C to +110°C).

Much of our information about the moon has been derived from photographs and other measurements taken from orbiting US and Soviet satellites and later from moonrock samples brought back (1969–72) by the Apollo astronauts (and the unmanned Soviet Luna landers) and from experiments set up on the moon by the astronauts. The first landing on the moon was made by Neil *Armstrong and Edwin *Aldrin on 20 July, 1969. *See* Apollo moon programme.

moonfish   A deep-bodied fish, also called opah, belonging to the genus *Lampris* and family *Lamprididae*, widely distributed in warm seas. Up to 2 m long, its body is coloured blue above, rose-pink below, and is spotted with white; the fins are scarlet. It is uncommon and is valued as food. Order: *Lampridiformes*.

moonflower.   *See* morning glory.

Moonies.   *See* Unification Church.

moon rat   The largest living mammal of the order *Insectivora*, *Echinosorex gymnurus*, of Sumatra, Borneo, and S Asia. It is a *gymnure about 60 cm long, black with a white head and long whiskery snout. A secretion of the anal glands gives it a characteristic smell.

moonstone   A gem variety of feldspar, usually transparent or translucent orthoclase, albite, or labradorite. It shows a play of colours resembling that of opal. *See* Plate III.

Moore, Bobby   (Robert Frederick M.; 1941–   ) British Association footballer, who played for West Ham United (1958–74) and Fulham (1974–76). He also played for England a record number of 108 times. A fine defender, he captained West Ham United and led the England team that won the 1966 World Cup.

Moore, G(eorge) E(dward)   (1873–1958) British philosopher. Moore's work centred around language and the analysis of its meaning. He maintained that the common usage of words is often profoundly different from their analytical meaning. Much of his published work is in the field of ethics and is concerned with the analysis of concepts of goodness. His books include *Principia Ethica* (1903) and *Ethics* (1912). He was professor of mental philosophy and logic at Cambridge (1925–39) and editor of the journal *Mind* (1921–47).

Moore, Gerald   (1899–1987) British pianist. He became one of the leading accompanists of such singers as Dietrich Fischer-Dieskau and Elizabeth Schwarzkopf and such instrumentalists as Pablo Casals. He wrote several books

HENRY MOORE   *In the indoor studio at his home in Much Hadham, Hertfordshire (England).*

of reminiscences and on the art of accompanying.

Moore, Henry (1898–1986) British sculptor. Moore was born at Castleford, Yorkshire, and studied at Leeds and the Royal College of Art (1921–24). His fascination with primitive African and Mexican art moulded the development of his two characteristic themes: mother and child sculptures and reclining figures. The latter, a lifelong preoccupation, reached its apogee in the sculpture for UNESCO in Paris (1956–57). After devoting himself to abstract work in the 1930s, Moore reverted to the humanist tradition in the early 1940s with his celebrated drawings of sleeping figures in air-raid shelters. These, his *Madonna and Child* (1943–44; St Matthew's, Northampton), and family groups brought him international fame. His later output continued in this vein, together with more experimental abstract works, such as *Atom Piece* (1964–66; University of Chicago). □ p. 831.

Moore, Sir John (1761–1809) British general, whose fame rests on his command (1808–09) in the *Peninsular War. Forced to retreat from Valladolid to Coruña over hazardous terrain and in bad conditions, he then repulsed a French attack but was mortally wounded.

Moore, Marianne (1887–1972) US poet. Her first volume, *Poems* (1921), contained poems contributed to the English Imagist magazine *Egoist*. She edited the literary magazine *Dial* from 1925 to 1929. *Collected Poems* (1951) won the Pulitzer Prize. Her poetry is noted for its qualities of irony and sharply observed detail. She also published a verse translation of *The Fables of La Fontaine* (1954).

Moore, Thomas (1779–1852) Irish poet. He went to London in 1799 and won great popular success with his *Irish Melodies* (1807–34) and his oriental romance *Lalla Rookh* (1817). While living abroad after 1819 he met *Byron and was responsible, with the publisher John Murray, for the burning of Byron's memoirs in 1824.

moorhen A grey-brown waterbird, *Gallinula chloropus*, also called common gallinule and waterhen, occurring worldwide except for Australia. It is 32 cm long and has a red bill and forehead and a white patch beneath the tail. It breeds in thick vegetation near ponds and marshes and feeds on seeds, water plants, and aquatic invertebrates. Family: *Rallidae* (rails, etc.).

Moorish idol A deep-bodied tropical fish, *Zanclus canescens*, found in shallow Indo-Pacific waters. It has a black and yellow vertically striped body, about 18 cm long, a beaklike mouth, and a greatly extended dorsal fin. It is the only member of its family (*Zanclidae*). Order: *Perciformes*.

Moors The conventional European name for the *Arab and *Berber inhabitants of NW Africa and, by extension, for the 8th-century Muslim conquerors of the Iberian peninsula, whose armies consisted of both Arab and Berber troops. The word originates in the Roman name for that region of Africa –Mauretania. The Moors were the dominant power in Spain until the 11th century, after which they fell gradually under Christian rule (*see* Mudéjars). A highly civilized people, the Moors played a major role in transmitting classical science and philosophy to W Europe.

moose. *See* elk.

Moose Jaw 50 23N 105 35W A city in W Canada, in S Saskatchewan. Founded in 1882, it is a railway and farming centre. Food processing, building materials, and oil refining are economically important. Population (1984 est): 35 118.

moped. *See* motorcycles.

Moradabad 28 50N 78 45E A city in India, in Uttar Pradesh. Founded in 1625, it is an agricultural trading centre and has metalworking, cotton-weaving, and printing industries. Population (1981): 348 000.

moraine The clay, stone, boulders, etc. (*see* till), carried along or deposited by glaciers. It may have been deposited by former glaciers as particular landforms or be actively transported on the ice surface, within the ice, or beneath the ice.

morality plays A form of vernacular religious drama popular in England and France from the late 14th to late 16th centuries. Similar in content and purpose to medieval sermons, morality plays were dramatized allegories of good and evil fighting for man's soul. They include *The Pride of Life*, *The Castle of Perseverance*, and *Everyman*, which is best known. They influenced Elizabethan drama and at the Reformation in England provided a vehicle for dramatizing the religious issues at stake. *See also* miracle plays.

moral philosophy. *See* ethics.

Moral Rearmament (MRA) An evangelical movement founded by a US evangelist and former Lutheran pastor, Frank Nathan Daniel Buchman (1878–1961), in the 1920s. It initially received most support at Oxford University and was called the Oxford Group until 1938. It seeks the regeneration of national and individual spirituality through conversion, God's personal guidance, and living in purity, unselfishness, honesty, and love.

Morandi, Giorgio (1890–1964) Italian still-life painter and etcher, born in Bologna. Although he also painted landscapes and flowerpieces, he is noted for his austere compositions of bottles and jars. He was associated with the school of *metaphysical painting.

Moravia (Czech name: Morava; German name: Mähren) An area and former province (1918–49) of central Czechoslovakia. Lying chiefly in the basin of the River Morava, it rises in the N to the Sudeten Mountains and in the E to the Carpathian Mountains. It contains important mineral deposits, including coal and iron ore. *History*: settled by Slavic tribes in the late 8th century AD, it formed the centre of an important medieval kingdom (Great Moravia) until incorporated into the kingdom of *Bohemia in 1029; in 1849 it was made an Austrian crownland. It became part of the Republic of Czechoslovakia in 1918. Chief town: Brno.

Moravia, Alberto (Alberto Pincherle; 1907–) Italian novelist. His early novels, beginning with *The Time of Indifference* (1929), criticized fascism and the corrupt middle-class society that allowed it to flourish. His later works, which include *The Woman of Rome* (1947), *Roman Tales* (1954), *Two Women* (1957), *The Lie* (1966), *1934* (1983), and *Erotic Tales* (1985) concern themes of social alienation and the futility of sexual relationships. His literary and political essays are collected in *Man As an End* (1963).

Moravian Brethren A Protestant denomination that continues the ideals of the earlier Bohemian Brethren, a 15th-century group centred in Prague that practised a simple unworldly form of Christianity. The Moravians date from the establishment of a community in 1722 by Count von *Zinzendorf on his estates in Saxony. In doctrine they are close to *Lutheranism but have a simplified Church hierarchy and liturgy. Hymn singing is important in their services. From the 1730s they were active missionaries; John *Wesley was among those whom they influenced. Many now live in North America.

Moray (or Morayshire) A former county of NE Scotland. Under local government reorganization in 1975 its boundaries were adjusted to form Moray District, in Grampian Region.

Moray, James Stuart, Earl of (or Murray; c. 1531–70) Regent of Scotland (1567–70) after the abdication of his half-sister Mary, Queen of Scots. The illegitimate son of James V, he was exiled (1565–66) after opposing Mary's marriage to Darnley. As regent he defeated Mary and Bothwell at Langside (1568). He was assassinated by a supporter of Mary.

moray eel A thick-bodied *eel of the family *Muraenidae* (over 80 species). Up to 1.5 m long, it is brightly coloured and lacks pectoral fins. Moray eels live in rock crevices and reefs of warm and tropical seas and can be dangerous when disturbed. The flesh can be poisonous.

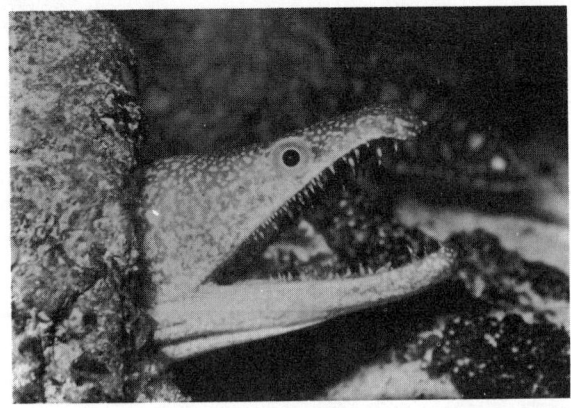

MORAY EEL   *The long jaws of a moray eel are armed with very sharp strong teeth, which are capable of inflicting a severe bite.*

Moray Firth An inlet of the North Sea in NE Scotland, extending SW from a line between Tarbat Ness in the Highland Region and Burghead in Grampian Region. Length: about 56 km (35 mi).

Mordvinian Autonomous Soviet Socialist Republic (*or* Mordovian ASSR) An administrative division in the W central Soviet Union, in the RSFSR. It is heavily forested. The majority of the population is Russian, 35% being Mordvinians, who speak a Finno-Ugric language. The area was annexed by Russia in the 16th century and became an autonomous republic in 1934. The region supports a wide range of industries, including timber, manufacturing of building materials, and textiles, but is predominantly agricultural: the main crops are cereals; sheep and dairy farming are also important. Area: 26 200 sq km (10 110 sq mi). Population (1981 est): 984 000. Capital: Saransk.

More, Henry (1614–87) English philosopher. One of the *Cambridge Platonists, More shared the group's interest in *Neoplatonism. *Descartes, whose work he helped publicize in England, was an early influence, but More later found his philosophy too materialistic. Although he was an opponent of religious fanaticism, More's own writings, such as *The Immortality of the Soul* (1659) and *Divine Dialogues* (1668), are more poetical and mystical than philosophical.

More, Sir Thomas (1477–1535) English lawyer, scholar, and saint, whose martyrdom horrified his contemporaries and has captured the imagination of succeeding generations. He joined Henry VIII's Privy Council in 1518 and succeeded Wolsey as chancellor in 1529. He resigned the chancellorship in 1532 in opposition to Henry's assumption of the supreme headship of the English Church. In 1534 More was imprisoned after refusing to swear to the new Act of Succession because it repudiated papal authority in England, and he was brought to trial for treason in 1535. In spite of a brilliant self-defence, he was convicted on false evidence and beheaded. He was canonized by the Roman Catholic Church in 1935.

His best-known scholarly work is *Utopia* (1516), in which he discussed an ideal social and political system; he also wrote (c. 1513–c. 1518) an unfinished *History of King Richard III*.

Moreau, Gustave (1826–98) French symbolist painter, best known for his detailed and brilliantly coloured biblical and mythological fantasies and as the enlightened teacher of *Matisse and *Rouault at the École des Beaux Arts. Most of his works are in the Musée Gustave Moreau, Paris.

Moreau, Jean Victor (1763–1813) French general. He fought in the Revolutionary Wars and, after Napoleon came to power (1799), became commander of the Rhine army, defeating the Austrians at Hohenlinden (1800). In 1804 he was arrested after becoming involved with anti-Bonapartists and was exiled. In 1813 he joined the coalition army formed to oppose Napoleon and died in the battle of *Dresden.

Morecambe 54 04N 2 53W A resort in NW England, in Lancashire on Morecambe Bay (a wide shallow inlet of the Irish Sea between NW Lancashire and the Furness district of Cumbria). The adjacent port of Heysham forms part of the borough known as Morecambe and Heysham. Population (1981): 41 187.

morel A fungus belonging to the genus *Morchella*. Morels are typically club-shaped with the surface of the cap pitted like a honeycomb. The edible common morel (*M. esculenta*) has a yellowish-brown cap, 4–8 cm high, and a stout whitish stalk. It is found in clearings and hedgerows. Class: *Ascomycetes.

Morelia (name until 1828: Valladolid) 19 40N 101 11W A city in Mexico, situated on the central plateau. It has a notable cathedral (17th–18th centuries) and is the centre of a cattle-raising area. Population (1980): 353 055.

Morgagni, Giovanni Battista (1682–1771) Italian anatomist and founder of pathological anatomy. His great work, *On the Seats and Causes of Diseases as Investigated by Anatomy* (1761), was based on over 600 postmortem dissections. Morgagni was professor of anatomy at Padua University for nearly 60 years until his death.

Morgan An American all-purpose breed of horse descended from a stallion with some Thoroughbred and Arabian ancestry, born in about 1790 and named after its owner, Justin Morgan. The Morgan has a compact deep-chested body, powerful hindquarters, and a long crested neck and is usually bay. Height: 1.42–1.52 m (14–15 hands).

Morgan, Charles (1894–1958) British novelist and dramatist. With his novels, which include *The Fountain* (1932) and *The Voyage* (1940), he achieved a considerable reputation in Europe, becoming a member of the French Academy. In England he won greater success with his plays, especially *The River Line* (1949).

Morgan, Sir Henry (c. 1635–88) Welsh buccaneer. Said to have been kidnapped and taken to Barbados, he joined the buccaneers then raiding the Spanish in the Caribbean. In 1671 he led a band over the Isthmus of Panama and sacked the city (1671), thus opening the way to plunder in the S Pacific. He was knighted in 1674 and made lieutenant general of Jamaica.

Morgan, John Pierpont (1837–1913) US financier, who founded (1895) J. P. Morgan and Co, one of the most powerful banking corporations in the USA. During the 1880s he reorganized many foundering railway companies and later financed such consolidations as the US Steel Corporation and General Electric. His son **John Pierpont Morgan, Jr** (1867–1943) succeeded him and helped to organize the credit requirements of the Allies in World War I.

Morgan, Thomas Hunt (1866–1945) US geneticist, who established that *chromosomes carried the units of inheritance proposed by Gregor *Mendel. Morgan was sceptical about Mendelian theory until he began his breeding experiments with the fruit fly *Drosophila*. He discovered that a number of genetic variations were inherited together and demonstrated that this was because their controlling genes occurred on the same chromosome (the phenomenon of linkage). Morgan was awarded a Nobel Prize (1933).

Morgan le Fay In *Arthurian legend, an evil sorceress who plotted the overthrow of her brother King Arthur. According to Malory's *Morte d'Arthur* (1485) she betrayed *Guinevere's adultery to Arthur. However, in the earlier *Vita Merlini* (c. 1150) by *Geoffrey of Monmouth she is a benevolent figure who lives in Avalon, where she once healed the wounded Arthur.

Mörike, Eduard Friedrich (1804–75) German poet and novelist. A rural clergyman, he found inspiration in country life, which supplied the subjects of his first distinguished collection of lyrics (*Gedichte*, 1838). The best of his prose works is the novella *Mozart auf der Reise nach Prag* (1856).

Moriscos Muslims forced to profess Christianity in Spain. Many Muslims continued to live in Spain after the formerly Muslim areas came under Christian rule and by the 15th century they were forced to become Christians or go into exile. Many chose to remain in Spain while privately remaining Muslims and eventually the government ordered their expulsion. Between 1609 and 1614 about 500 000 Moriscos were forced into exile, settling mainly in Africa.

Morison, Stanley (1889-1967) British typographer, editor, and historian of printing. As typographic adviser to the Monotype Corporation (from 1923), the Cambridge University Press (1923-59), and *The Times* (1929-44), he helped to adapt traditional typefaces to machine composition. He is best known for designing the Times New Roman typeface (first used in 1932).

Morisot, Berthe (1841-95) French painter, granddaughter of the artist *Fragonard. The first female impressionist and an outstanding painter of women and children, she was strongly encouraged by *Corot. *Manet, whose brother Eugène she married (1874), was influenced by her.

Morland, George (1763-1804) British painter, born in London. The son and pupil of the painter Henry Morland (c. 1730-97), he exhibited sketches at the Royal Academy when aged only ten. Popularized through engravings, his work, which included such picturesque rustic scenes as *The Inside of a Stable* (Tate Gallery), declined after 1794. His dissolute life finally resulted in imprisonment (1799-1802).

Morley, Edward Williams (1838-1923) US chemist, who investigated the relative atomic weights of hydrogen and oxygen. However, he is best known for his collaboration with Albert *Michelson in the *Michelson-Morley experiment.

Morley, Robert (1908-) British stage and film actor. His long career as a character actor dates from 1929, and his films include *Major Barbara* (1940), *Beat the Devil* (1953), and *Oscar Wilde* (1960). Other films are *The Trygon Factor* (1967), *Theatre of Blood* (1973), and *The Blue Bird* (1976). Many of his later roles have been those of pompous eccentrics. He was the son-in-law of Dame Gladys Cooper (1888-1971).

Morley, Thomas (1557-1603) English composer, music printer, organist of St Paul's Cathedral, and member of the Chapel Royal. A pupil of Byrd, he wrote madrigals, canzonets, songs, church music, and the textbook *A Plaine and Easie Introduction to Practicall Musicke* (1597).

Mormons Adherents of the Christian sect that is formally called the Church of Jesus Christ of Latter-Day Saints, founded in 1830 by Joseph Smith in New York state. A series of visions culminated in Smith's claim that he had discovered golden tablets that contained the Book of Mormon, a sacred book named after a primitive American prophet who had compiled it. After Smith's murder by a mob, the persecuted Mormons moved W under Brigham Young, establishing their headquarters at Salt Lake, Utah, in 1847. Attempting to revert to the simple sanctity of the early Christians, Mormons have no professional clergy, reject infant baptism, emphasize self-help to avoid want, abstain from alcohol and other stimulants, and run educational and missionary programmes. Polygamy (*see* marriage), for which Mormons were once notorious, has been disallowed since 1890.

Mornay, Philippe de, Seigneur du Plessis-Marly (1549-1632) French Huguenot (Protestant) leader during the *Wars of Religion. Escaping the *St Bartholomew's Day Massacre (1572), he rose to a position of considerable influence as one of the chief confidants of Henry of Navarre, later Henry IV of France. When Henry was converted to Roman Catholicism, Mornay retained his Huguenot sympathies and lost the king's favour.

morning glory A trailing or twining plant of the genus *Ipomoea*, native to tropical America and Australia and cultivated for its beautiful flowers. The leaves are often heart-shaped and the trumpet-shaped flowers, up to 12 cm across, are deep blue, purple, pink, or white. Popular species are *I. purpurea* and *I. alba* (the moonflower). The seeds of certain varieties contain hallucinogens. Family: *Convolvulaceae*.

Moro, Aldo (1916-1978) Italian statesman; Christian Democratic prime minister (1963-68, 1974-76) and foreign minister (1965-66, 1969-72, 1973-74). He included socialists in his first cabinet and in 1976 was instrumental in gaining communist support for the minority Christian Democratic government. In 1978 he was kidnapped and then murdered by the *Red Brigades.

Morocco, Kingdom of A country in NW Africa, bordering on the Atlantic Ocean and Mediterranean Sea. The Atlas Mountains crossing the centre of the country rise to 4165 m (13 665 ft) at Mount Toubkal and separate the Atlantic coastal area from the Sahara. The population is mainly of Berber and Arabic origin. *Economy*: the chief occupations are agriculture and mining. Wheat, barley, maize, and citrus fruits are grown, mainly in the coastal areas N of the mountains; livestock, especially sheep and goats, is also important. Morocco is a leading exporter of phosphates having about 40% of the world's known phosphate reserves. Other mineral resources are iron ore, coal, lead, zinc, cobalt, and manganese. Industries include food processing, textiles, and traditional handicraft industries; a major phosphoric acid plant has been developed. There is a thriving fishing industry, sardines and tuna being the chief catch. Morocco's hot sunny climate and Atlantic and Mediterranean beaches make it a popular tourist centre. *History*: part of the Roman province of Mauretania, it fell to the Vandals in the 5th century AD. Conflict between Arabs and Berbers was virtually continuous; in the 15th and 16th centuries Morocco came under attack from Spain and Portugal and until the 19th century was a base for Barbary pirates. Its strategic importance was recognized by the European powers in the 19th century, French and Spanish interests conflicting with those of Germany. The Algeciras Conference was held (1906) to consider the Moroccan question. The French increased their control in the area and the appearance of a German warship at Agadir (1911) was interpreted by the French as a threat of war. Following the Agadir incident Morocco was partitioned into French and Spanish protectorates (1912) and the international zone of Tangier (1923). In 1956 the protectorates were relinquished and Morocco became a sultanate, later a kingdom (1957) under King Mohammed V; his son, Hassan II, acceded to the throne in 1961. In 1975 agreement was reached providing for the partition of Spanish Sahara (*see* Western Sahara) between Morocco and Mauretania; in 1979 Mauretania withdrew from Western Sahara and it came under Moroccan occupation. Prime minister: Azeddine Laraki (1919-). Official religion: Islam. Official language: Arabic. Official currency: dirham of 100 centimes. Area: 458 730 sq km (144 078 sq mi). Population (1984 est): 21 160 000. Capital: Rabat.

Moroni 11 40S 43 16E The capital of the Comoro Islands, a port in the SW of Grande Comore island. Population (1980 est): 20 112.

Moroni, Giovanni Battista (c. 1525-78) Italian painter, born near Bergamo. Although he painted many altarpieces in Bergamo, he is best known for his portraits, notably *The Tailor* (National Gallery, London).

Morosini A noble Venetian family, prominent from the 10th century, that produced four *doges as well as distinguished generals, admirals, and churchmen. Best known is **Francesco Morosini** (1618–94), who was doge of Venice from 1688 until his death. As commander in chief of the Venetian fleet, he defeated the Turks, Venice's enemies, at sea and in Greece.

MORRIS DANCE   *The Wheatley Morrismen (and boys) performing their processional dance at the Towersey Folk Festival in Oxfordshire. Each group performs its own unique dances.*

Morpheus   In Greek mythology, a god of dreams, a son of Somnus, the god of sleep. He sent human forms into the dreams of sleeping men, while his brothers Phobetor and Phantasus sent animal and inanimate forms.

morphine   A *narcotic analgesic drug obtained from *opium and used in medicine for the relief of severe pain. Its depressant effect on the brain accounts for the pain-killing properties; in high doses it also inhibits the breathing and cough centres. Other side effects include constipation, nausea, and vomiting. Morphine is an addictive drug and readily leads to severe physical dependence. Nalorphine is a specific antidote to morphine overdosage. *See also* drug dependence.

morphology (biology)   The study of the form and structure of plants, animals, and microorganisms. *Anatomy is often used synonymously with morphology but in the former the emphasis is on the gross and microscopic structure of organs and parts.

morphology (language).   *See* grammar.

Morphy, Paul Charles   (1837–84) US chess player, who between 1858 and 1860 was regarded as the world's best player and whose games still fascinate chess enthusiasts. He travelled to Europe, defeating all opponents, but gave up chess to follow his legal career. This was unsuccessful and he became mentally unstable.

Morris, Desmond John   (1928–   ) British zoologist, noted for his popularization of biology, especially in his books on human behaviour. *The Naked Ape* (1967), *The Human Zoo* (1969), and *Manwatching* (1977) all set out to prove that human beings are still subject to the basic laws of animal behaviour.

Morris, William   (1834–96) British designer, artist, and poet. Associated with the *Pre-Raphaelite Brotherhood, he later started a firm of decorators and designers (1861), who placed great importance on preindustrial crafts. He designed stained glass, carpets, and furniture, and his wallpaper designs are still used. His Kelmscott Press, founded in 1890, influenced book design and printing generally. The 19th-century *Arts and Crafts movement drew much of its inspiration from his work. He was also one of the founders of British socialism.

Morris dance   A ritual English folk dance performed by groups of white-clad men wearing bells and often carrying sticks or handkerchiefs. A common theme is fertility through death and rebirth, symbolized by the carrying of green branch-

es. Similar dances are found throughout Europe, India, and the Americas, often featuring animal characters or the black-faced Morisco (Moor), whence the name Morris is thought to derive. Morris dancing is a popular pastime, many groups existing in both town and country.

Morris Jesup, Cape   83 40N 34 00W The N tip of Greenland, the world's most northerly land point, 708 km (440 mi) from the North Pole.

Morrison, Herbert Stanley, Baron   (1888–1965) British Labour politician, who was prominent as a member of the London County Council from 1922 to 1945. He was also minister of transport (1929–31) and, in World War II, minister of supply (1940) and then home secretary (1940–45), serving in the war cabinet (1942–45). He became deputy leader of the Labour Party in 1951 but resigned when Gaitskell won the leadership in 1955.

Morse, Samuel Finley Breese   (1791–1872) US inventor, who erected the first telegraph line, between Washington and Baltimore (1844). Messages were sent by a system of dots and dashes that he had invented for the purpose (*see* Morse code).

Morse code   The code invented by Samuel *Morse for transmitting telegraph messages. Each letter of the alphabet and number has a characteristic sequence of dots and dashes (short and long pulses), a dash being three times as long as a dot.

mortar (building material)   A mixture of sand, hydrated lime, and Portland cement, used to bind together building bricks, etc. It is applied wet as a paste, which sets to a durable solid.

letters

A	·—	N	—·
B	—···	O	———
C	—·—·	P	·——·
D	—··	Q	——·—
E	·	R	·—·
F	··—·	S	···
G	——·	T	—
H	····	U	··—
I	··	V	···—
J	·———	W	·——
K	—·—	X	—··—
L	·—··	Y	—·——
M	——	Z	——··

numbers

1	·————
2	··———
3	···——
4	····—
5	·····
6	—····
7	——···
8	———··
9	————·
0	—————

punctuation marks

·	·—·—·—
,	——··——
:	———···
?	··——··
'	·————·
-	—····—
/	—··—·
(or)	—·——·—
"	·—··—·

MORSE CODE

mortar (weapon)   A short-barrelled muzzle-loading artillery piece with a low-velocity high-angled trajectory. Although modern designs date from 1915, it originated before 1600. In World War II the largest Allied mortar had a calibre of 4.2 inches (107 mm), the German version being 8.3 inches (210 mm) with six barrels. Used against an enemy behind cover, mortars are principally used to fire high-explosive and smoke bombs.

mortgage Rights in property (usually land, buildings, etc.) given by a borrower (mortgagor) to a lender (mortgagee) as security for a loan. In the UK *building societies lend money for house purchase in return for a legal charge on the property, which gives them the right to sell it to recover their debt if the borrower defaults. Successive mortgages may be taken out on the same property for further loans. Mortgages normally require registration at the Land Registry. When all the money borrowed and the interest due under the mortgage have been repaid, it is redeemed.

Mortier, Édouard Adolphe Casimir Joseph, Duc de Trévise (1768–1835) French marshal, who fought in the Revolutionary and Napoleonic Wars. In 1803 he occupied Hanover but in 1805 was defeated at Dürnstein by the Russians. He subsequently served in the campaign against Prussia (1806–07) and in the *Peninsular War, winning at Ocaña (1809). He was Louis-Philippe's prime minister (1834–35) and died in an attempt on the king's life.

Mortimer, John Clifford (1923–) British barrister and playwright. He was called to the bar in 1948, a year after his first novel, *Charade*, was published. He is best known for the televised tales of Horace Rumpole, a fictional barrister. The first of his many plays was *The Dock Brief* (1958); his novels include *Paradise Postponed* (1985). He was married (1949–72) to the writer **Penelope Mortimer** (1918–), whose novels include *The Pumpkin Eater* (1962).

Mortimer, Roger de, 1st Earl of March (c. 1287–1330) English magnate. He led the baronial opposition to Edward II (1320–22) and was imprisoned before fleeing to France. There he became the lover of Edward's queen *Isabella with whom he secured Edward's deposition and murder in 1327. He then ruled England in the name of Edward's son, Edward III, until the latter had him executed.

Morton, James Douglas, 4th Earl of (c. 1516–81) Regent of Scotland (1572–78) for James VI (later James I of England). Under Mary, Queen of Scots, he was involved in the murder of Riccio (1566) and then, for which he was eventually executed, of Darnley (1567).

Morton, Jelly Roll (Ferdinand Joseph La Menthe; 1885–1941) US Black jazz pianist and composer, who began his career playing the piano in New Orleans' Storyville brothels and made recordings in the 1920s with the group Morton's Red Hot Peppers. Claiming that he "invented jazz in 1902," his reputation has been the subject of controversy.

Morton, John (c. 1420–1500) English churchman. A supporter of the Lancastrian cause, under Henry VII he became Archbishop of Canterbury (1486), chancellor (1487), and cardinal (1493). He is remembered for his argument—**Morton's Fork**—that both rich and poor could afford to contribute to royal funds: the rich obviously had the money to spare, while those who lived less extravagantly must have saved money by their modest way of life.

mosaic A picture or ornamental design made from small coloured cubes of glass, stone, tile, etc. Mosaics were common in ancient Greece, where they were principally used for floors and made from coloured pebbles. During the Roman Empire mosaics of opaque glass and glass covered with gold leaf became popular for wall and vault decoration, a development that reached its peak in the early Christian churches in Byzantium and Italy. The 6th-century decorations in S Vitale, in Ravenna, are among the most famous mosaics of the middle ages. During this period mosaics were no longer stylistically dependent on painting but, instead, led artistic trends with their use of two-dimensional forms, rich colour, and lavish use of gold. During the Renaissance frescoes became the preferred form of church decoration but mosaics have been revived during the 20th century.

Mosaic law The collective name for the laws contained in the *Torah. They purport to have been revealed by God to Moses on Mount Sinai and in *Judaism they form the basis of

*halakhah. In Christianity some of them are accepted, but most are rejected or interpreted allegorically.

mosasaur A member of an extinct family of huge marine lizards that lived during the Cretaceous period (135–65 million years ago). Up to 10 m long, mosasaurs had broad paddle-like limbs and a long flexible tail and were efficient swimmers, feeding on fish, cuttlefish, and squid.

moschatel A perennial herbaceous plant, *Adoxa moschatellina*, also called townhall clock, native to Eurasia and North America. Up to 10 cm high, it has compound leaves and greenish flowers. It has a musky smell and is the sole member of its family (*Adoxaceae*).

Moscow (Russian name: Moskva) 55 45N 37 42E The capital of the Soviet Union and of the Moscow autonomous region (*oblast*), in the RSFSR on the River Moskva. It is the economic and political centre of the Soviet Union and an important transportation centre. Industries include heavy engineering, cars, textiles, electronics, chemicals, publishing, and food processing. Moscow is at the centre of the Soviet railway system and is an important riverport. Its underground railway (begun 1935) is of note. The city is based on a radial plan; the *Kremlin (citadel) and Red Square are at its heart. The Kremlin, triangular in shape, encloses a number of notable ecclesiastical buildings including the Cathedral of the Assumption (1475–79) and the Cathedral of the Annunciation (1484–89). Red Square is the traditional setting for military parades and demonstrations. Beyond its historical centre Moscow is a modern city. It is a major cultural centre; its many educational institutions include the University of Moscow (1755), the People's Friendship University (1960) for foreign students, and the Academy of Sciences of the USSR. The Tretyakov Gallery of Russian Art (1856) is the most notable of its many museums. Other famous institutions include the Bolshoi Theatre of Opera and Ballet (1780), the *Moscow Art Theatre, and the Moscow State Circus. *History*: first documented in 1147, settlement actually dates back to prehistoric times. By the beginning of the 13th century it was the centre of the Muscovy principality and became the seat of the Russian Church containing the Kremlin (1326). In 1712–13 the capital was transferred to St Petersburg (Leningrad) but Moscow remained significant. The city was invaded by Napoleon (1812) and the ensuing fire, started either by looting French soldiers or the Moscow people themselves, destroyed much of the city. The workers' movements in Moscow played an important role in the Revolution of 1905. In March, 1918, it became the capital of the RSFSR and following the arrival of Lenin and other communist leaders (1922) the capital of the Soviet Union. Development resumed after World War II, during which the German invasion of the city was only halted by severe weather and strong resistance. Since the war, Moscow has developed an important tourist industry. It was the site of the 1980 Olympic Games. Population (1981 est): 8 203 000.

Moscow Art Theatre A Russian theatre company founded in 1898 by Konstantin *Stanislavsky and Vladimir Nemirovich-Danchenko (1859–1948). Its first success was a production of *The Seagull* by Chekhov, whose plays suited the naturalistic acting style developed by Stanislavsky. Other dramatists whose plays were produced include Gorky, Tolstoy, and Maeterlinck. The company gained international acclaim on its tour of Europe and the USA in 1922 and has continued to maintain high standards of ensemble acting.

Moseley, Henry Gwyn Jeffries (1887–1915) British physicist, who, working under *Rutherford, discovered the connection between the frequency of the X-rays emitted by an atom and its atomic number. This discovery provided a theoretical basis for the periodic classification of the elements. He was killed at Gallipoli in World War I.

Moselle, River (German name: R. Mosel) A river in W Europe, flowing N from NE France to join the River Rhine at Koblenz. It forms part of the border between West Germany and Luxembourg. Its valley is one of the main wine-growing areas of West Germany. Length: 547 km (340 mi).

Moses In the Old Testament, the lawgiver of Israel, who led the people from slavery in Egypt (Exodus) and, after wandering in the desert for 40 years, brought them to an area E of the River Jordan, the border of the Promised Land. He is the central figure in most of the Pentateuch (the first five Old Testament books). As a child in Egypt (according to the Old Testament), Moses was saved from the slaughter of all Hebrew male children ordered by Pharaoh by being hidden in bulrushes on the Nile; he was found and brought up by one of Pharaoh's daughters. On Mt Sinai he was given the Ten Commandments by Jehovah. He died at the age of 120, before the Israelites entered the Promised Land, which he was allowed to see from a distance (Mt Pisgah).

Moses, Grandma (Anna Mary Robertson M.; 1860-1961) US primitive painter, born in Greenwich, New York (*see* primitivism). Entirely self-taught, she only turned seriously to painting at the age of 67 after a life as a farmer's wife. She specialized in naive and nostalgic scenes of farm life, popularized through prints and Christmas cards.

Mosley, Sir Oswald Ernald (1896-1980) British fascist. He was a Conservative MP (1918-22), an Independent MP (1922-24), and then a Labour MP (1924, 1926-31), serving as chancellor of the Duchy of Lancaster (1929-30). In 1932 he established the British Union of Fascists, which incited antisemitic violence, especially in the East End of London. In World War II he was interned (1940-43) and in 1948 founded the Union Movement. He married (1936) Diana Mitford (1910-).

mosque A Muslim place of worship. It evolved in various styles from a simple rectangular building, such as the first mosque built by Mohammed at Medina in 622 AD. Larger mosques are usually built around a courtyard, which is surrounded by arcades on all four sides. Prayers are said in a large covered area on the side facing Mecca, the direction being indicated by a niche (*mihrab*) in the wall. Mosques are often domed and have *minarets. Painting and sculpture of living beings are forbidden, but elaborate geometrical designs and Arabic calligraphy frequently adorn both exterior and interior walls. The mosque has traditionally been the centre of Muslim life, intellectual and social as well as religious. The three most sacred mosques are those of Mecca, Medina, and Jerusalem.

Mosque of Islam. *See* Black Muslims.

mosquito A small fly belonging to a family (*Culicidae*; about 2500 species) of almost worldwide distribution, being especially abundant in the tropics. It has long legs, elongated mouthparts, and a long slender abdomen. In most species the males feed on plant juices, while the females bite and suck the blood of mammals, often transmitting serious human and animal diseases. The three important genera are *Anopheles, *Aedes, and *Culex (including the common gnat, *C. pipiens*). The active larvae live in fresh water, feeding on algae, bacteria, and organic debris. Most breathe through a siphon at the rear end.

Mosquito Coast (*or* Miskito Coast) A coastal belt in Central America, bordering on the Caribbean Sea and extending from E Honduras into E Nicaragua. Its name derives from the former inhabitants of the area, the Mosquito (Miskito) Indians. The cultivation of bananas is the chief occupation. Average width: 60 km (40 mi).

moss A *bryophyte plant of the class *Musci* (or *Bryopsida*; about 15 000 species), growing worldwide (except in salt water) on moist soil, trees, rocks, etc. The moss plant is differentiated into stems and leaves and produces sex cells (gametes), which give rise to a spore capsule that grows from the plant on a long stalk. Mosses help control erosion by providing surface cover and retaining water. *Sphagnum,

responsible for peat formation, is the only economically important moss.

The name is also applied to several unrelated plants, for example *Spanish moss.

Moss, Stirling (1929-) British motor-racing driver, who had innumerable successes on the track in the 1950s, including 16 Grand Prix wins, but never won the world championship—being runner-up from 1955 to 1958.

moss animal. *See* Bryozoa.

Mössbauer effect The emission of a gamma ray (*see* gamma radiation) by an excited nucleus in a solid. Generally such an emission causes the nucleus to recoil, thus reducing the energy of the gamma ray. In the Mössbauer effect the recoil is distributed throughout the solid. The gamma ray therefore loses no energy and may then raise other nuclei into the same excited state. It was discovered by the German physicist Rudolph Mössbauer (1929-) and enables the structure of nuclei and molecules to be examined.

moss pink. *See* Phlox.

Mostaganem 36 04N 0 11E A port in NW Algeria, on the Mediterranean Sea. Founded in the 11th century, it has an 11th-century citadel. It trades in wine, fruit, and vegetables, and is at the head of a natural gas pipeline from Ḥasse R'Mel in the Sahara. Population (1980 est): 806 606.

Mostar 43 20N 17 50E A town in W central Yugoslavia, in Bosnia and Hercegovina on the River Neretva. A centre for Serbian culture with a university (1977), it is situated amid mountainous wine-growing country. Population (1981): 110 377.

most-favoured-nation clause A clause in a trade agreement between two countries in which each country agrees that any more favourable agreement either may make with a third country shall also apply to the other country. The mechanism is at the heart of the *General Agreement on Tariffs and Trade (GATT), although GATT allows the clause to be waived in treaties with *developing countries, in certain cases involving the formation of a *customs union, and formerly for Commonwealth preference arrangements.

Mosul 36 21N 43 08E A town in N Iraq, close to the Turkish border. From 1534 to 1918 it was an important trading centre in the Ottoman Empire, and Turkey continued to claim the town until 1926. Mosul's modern prosperity is derived from nearby oilfields. Its former Faculties of the University of Baghdad became Mosul University in 1967. Population (1979): 906 000.

motet A polyphonic composition (*see* polyphony) for voices, generally unaccompanied. In the medieval motet the fundamental tenor (holding) part was based on a slow-moving plainchant or popular song while the upper triplex (treble) and motetus (worded) parts had a different text and a quicker rhythm. The 16th-century motet with Latin text, used during church services but not a part of the liturgy, is found in its purest form in the works of Palestrina. In England a Latin motet was distinguished from an English *anthem. Since the 17th century the word has been used to describe a serious though not necessarily religious choral work.

mother-of-pearl. *See* pearl.

Motherwell, Robert (1915-) US abstract painter. Largely self-taught, he turned to painting during World War II, under the influence of the European surrealists. He became a leading exponent of *action painting with his use of dripped and splattered paint, notably in his black and white series entitled *Elegy to the Spanish Republic*. His painting after this period became more structured, showing the influence of *Rothko.

Motherwell and Wishaw 55 48N 4 00W A town in central Scotland, in Strathclyde Region on the River Clyde. Formed by the union of the two towns in 1920, its industries include iron and steel and engineering. Population (1982 est): 150 059.

moth orchid An epiphytic *orchid of the genus *Phalaenopsis* (about 40 species), native to SE Asia and E Australia. It has a very short stem bearing several broad leathery leaves and larger clusters of flowers. Moth orchids are popular hothouse ornamentals; hybrids produced usually have white or pink long-lasting flowers.

moths. *See* butterflies and moths.

motmot A bird of the tropical American family *Motmotidae* (8 species). 16–50 cm long, motmots have short rounded wings, short legs, and long tails with elongated central feathers. The bill is broad and serrated and the plumage is green, blue, brown, and black. Motmots live in forests and prey on insects, spiders, worms, etc. Order: *Coraciiformes* (kingfishers, etc.).

moto-cross (*or* scrambling) A form of *motorcycle racing invented in the UK in 1927. It takes place on a circuit marked out across rough country. International events are for 250 cc and 500 cc machines.

motorcycle racing Racing single-seater motorcycles or sidecar combinations, in classes according to engine capacity. In **road racing**, run usually on special circuits, the main classes are 125, 250, 350, and 500 cc. World championships are awarded according to points won in Grand Prix and other races, such as the Tourist Trophy (TT) races on the Isle of Man (first held in 1907). **Motorcycle trials** are usually events in which a cross-country course has to be completed within a certain time, with points lost in observed sections of the course for stopping, touching the ground, etc. *See also* drag racing; moto-cross; rally; speedway.

motorcycles Two-wheeled engine-powered vehicles. The evolution of the motorcycle has been closely associated with the development of the *bicycle, *steam engine, and *car. The muscle-powered bicycle was in use by the mid-19th century but the concept of a steam-powered bicycle was first realized by S. H. Roper in the USA in the 1860s. Similar machines were being built in Paris at about the same time by Pierre and Ernest Michaux. However, the true forerunner of the modern motorcycle was Gottlieb *Daimler's 1885 bicycle powered by an *Otto four-stroke engine. The first production model was Hildebrand and Wolfmüller's 1894 *Pétrolette*. By 1900 there were some 11 000 motorcycles in France and by the start of World War I over 100 000 were registered in the UK (many of which were powered by continental engines). By then the invidious belt drive (which slipped in wet weather) had been replaced by the chain, hot-tube ignition (which often set the whole machine alight) had given way to the sparking plug, and the battery had been augmented by the magneto. During the war, motorcycles (often in combination with sidecars) were extensively used by both sides. The interwar period—the great era of the motorcycle—saw the development of many classic designs: the Harley-Davidson in the USA; the Brough Superior, Triumph Speed Twin, and Ariel Square Four in the UK; and the German DKW two-stroke and BMW four-stroke. All these were in military use in World War II. During and after the war some innovations were made, such as telescopic forks, sprung near wheels, disc brakes, and starter motors, but the basic design remained unchanged. In the 1950s and 1960s interest in motorcycles in Europe and the USA declined; their inherent danger and the status symbol of car ownership forced most European manufacturers out of business. The motor scooter, a low-powered Italian-originated version of the motorcycle, and the moped, an engine-assisted bicycle, acquired some popularity. In the 1970s, the Japanese, exploiting the closure of European factories, developed a whole new range of motorcycles, based on European designs. These machines now dominate world markets.

motor insurance *Insurance against the risks to people and property arising from the use of motor vehicles. It is of two kinds: insurance against damage caused to a third party or his property and insurance against damage to the insured or his own property. Third-party insurance has been compulsory in the UK since the Road Traffic Act (1930) and in most other countries from about the same time. Comprehensive insurance covers both kinds and is considerably more expensive than third-party insurance, although some insurers offer an intermediate policy covering third-party, fire, and theft insurance. In the UK most policies include a no-claims bonus, which considerably reduces the cost of the premium and discourages the insured from making small claims. In most parts of the world, motor insurance claims are settled on a "knock-for-knock" basis, each insurer settling his own client's claims without attempting to establish blame for an accident.

motor racing Racing in cars, from family saloons at club level to highly specialized Grand Prix vehicles. Early races, such as the 1895 race from Paris to Bordeaux and back, were held on roads, but since 1903 they have usually been held on closed-circuit courses, the first of which in England was Brooklands (1907) in Surrey. (Racing round-the-houses (on roads) was revived in Birmingham (1986).) The most prestigious form of racing is Grand Prix (Formula One) racing, for which specially built single-seater vehicles are raced by professional drivers for manufacturers or private owners. The Drivers' World Championship (instituted in 1950) is awarded according to points won in certain Formula One races. Formula One cars must weigh at least 530 kg, must not have more than 12 cylinders or an engine capacity in excess of 3000 cc (or 1500 cc if they are supercharged). Formulas Two (minimum weight 450 kg for 4 cylinders, 475 kg for 6 cylinders, or 500 kg in excess of 6; engine capacity less than 2000 cc) and Three (maximum of 4 cylinders and 1600 cc) function largely as training grounds for Formula One drivers. **Sports-car racing** is for production-type or modified sports cars; the most famous sports-car race is the Le Mans 24 Hours. **Autocross** races are amateur races over grass, while **rallycross** is a more professional form held on circuits that are half grass and half tarmac. *See also* drag racing; karting; rally; stock-car racing.

Mo-tzu. *See* Mo-Zi.

mouflon A wild sheep, *Ovis musimon*, native to Corsica and Sardinia and introduced to other parts of Europe and to North America. Mouflons are about 65 cm high at the shoulder and males have large curved horns, a distinctive rump patch, and a white saddle on the back.

mould Any fungus that forms a fine woolly mass growing on food, clothing, etc. Examples are the *bread mould and species of *Aspergillus* and *Penicillium*. *See also* slime mould.

Moulins 46 34N 3 20E A town in central France, the capital of the Allier department on the River Allier. Its manufactures include leather, metal goods, and textiles. Population (1982): 25 548.

Moulmein 16 30N 97 39E A port in Burma, on the River Salween. The chief town of British Burma from 1826 until 1852, Moulmein has an important teak trade and exports rice. Population (1983): 202 967.

mountain. *See* orogeny.

mountain ash A tree, *Sorbus aucuparia*, also called rowan, native to temperate Eurasia and commonly cultivated as an ornamental. Up to 15 m high, it has long leaves with numerous paired leaflets and large clusters of small cream flowers, which give rise to bright-scarlet berries with a bitter acid taste, used to make wine and jelly. The similar and related American species is *S. americana*. Family: *Rosaceae*. The Australian mountain ash (*Eucalyptus regnans*), up to 105 m high, is the world's tallest broad-leaved tree.

mountain beaver. *See* sewellel.

mountaineering A sport that developed in the mid-19th century. Interest in exploring mountains first grew in the

1860s S.H. Roper Velocipede *One of the earliest steam-powered cycles, this machine survives in the Smithsonian Institute, Washington, USA.*

1885 Daimler *The forerunner of the modern motorcycle, it had a wooden frame, iron tyres, and a 264 cc four-stroke engine.*

1894 Hildebrand and Wolfmüller "Pétrolette" *The first production motor cycle, it had direct rearwheel drive, pneumatic tyres, and a 1488 cc engine. Production was ten machines a day.*

1917 Harley-Davidson *This 989 cc Vee-twin chaindrive machine had the first twist-grip throttle control.*

1930 Brough Superior *Built from 1919 to 1940 this Rolls Royce of motorcycles had a 980 cc Vee-twin JAP engine. Only 3000 were ever made.*

1938 Triumph 500 cc Speed Twin *Capable of over 100 mph, it was widely used by the police.*

1949 Ariel Square Four *The compact arrangement of the four cylinders gave the machine its name. It had telescopic front forks and a sprung rear wheel.*

1988 Honda Goldwing Aspencade *A Japanese tourer with a flat four 1182 cc engine, 5-speed gearbox, drive shaft, and transistorized ignition.*

18th century; after Mont Blanc was climbed in 1786 by Michel Paccard and Jacques Balmat interest gradually extended to other areas of the Alps. The English Alpine Club, founded in 1857, was quickly followed by continental clubs. The Matterhorn was climbed in 1865 by Edward *Whymper's expedition, Mount Kilimanjaro in 1889 by Hans Meyer and Ludwig Purtscheller, and Mount Kenya in 1899 by Sir Halford Mackinder (1861-1947) and two guides. No peak over 7817 m (25 646 ft) was climbed until after World War II, when modern equipment and generous funding made high-altitude climbing possible. Annapurna I was climbed in 1950 by Maurice Herzog and Louis Lachenal and Mount Everest in 1953 by Sir Edmund *Hillary and *Tenzing Norgay. Now that the world's highest peaks have been conquered, mountaineering is largely a matter of finding new routes and new methods. Rock climbing and ice climbing, skills always intrinsic to mountaineering, have become independent sports; like mountaineering in general, they make use of such equipment as nylon ropes, eiderdown suits, and crampons and are organized through clubs.

mountain lion. *See* cougar.

LORD MOUNTBATTEN *His outstanding contribution to public life was to oversee, as last viceroy of India, the establishment of Indian independence, and here he is greeted by Y. B. Chavan (1913-), India's defence minister (1962-66), at celebrations for Independence Day.*

Mountbatten of Burma, Louis, 1st Earl (1900-79) British admiral and colonial administrator; son of Prince Louis of Battenberg (1854-1921), who took the name Mountbatten and was created Marquess of Milford Haven in 1917, and of Princess Victoria of Hesse-Darmstadt, the granddaughter of Queen Victoria. He entered the Royal Navy in 1913 and in World War II was supreme Allied commander in SE Asia (1943-45), retaking Burma. As viceroy of India (1947) he presided over the transfer of power to India and Pakistan and was then governor general of India (1947-48). He was subsequently commander in chief of the Mediterranean fleet (1952-54) and first sea lord (1955-59), becoming an admiral in 1956. He died in Ireland, the victim of an IRA bomb.

Mounties. *See* Royal Canadian Mounted Police.

Mount Isa 20 50S 139 29E A town in Australia, in NW Queensland. Zinc, lead, silver, and copper are mined. Population (1980 est): 26 000.

Mount Lofty Ranges A range of hills in SE South Australia. It consists of an extension of the *Flinders Range and reaches 934 m (3063 ft) at Mount Byron.

Mount of Olives The highest point in a small range of four summits situated just E of Jerusalem. It features in the Old and New Testaments. Its W slope was the site of the Garden of *Gethsemane. According to the Acts of the Apostles

(1.2-12), Christ ascended to heaven from the Mount of Olives. Many churches and convents of various denominations have been built here since the 4th century AD or earlier.

Mount Rushmore National Memorial The gigantic sculpture of the heads of four US presidents—Washington, Jefferson, Lincoln, and Theodore Roosevelt—carved (1927-41) to the design of the sculptor Gutzon Borglum (1871-1941) on the NE cliffs of Mount Rushmore, South Dakota. Each head is about 18 m (60 ft) high.

Mount Vernon A national shrine in the USA, in Virginia S of Washington, DC, on the Potomac River. It was the home (1759-99) of George Washington, whose tomb lies in the grounds of the 18th-century mansion. The house, outbuildings, and gardens have been carefully restored and preserved.

Mount Wilson Observatory. *See* Hale Observatories.

Mourne Mountains A mountain range in Northern Ireland, in Co Down. It extends SW-NE between Carlingford Lough and Dundrum Bay, reaching 853 m (2798 ft) at Slieve Donard.

mourning dove A common North American *pigeon, *Zenaidura macroura*, that is adapted for survival in hot deserts; it can endure high body temperatures and dehydration and can fly long distances, enabling it to live far from water. 30 cm long, it has a long pointed tail and grey-brown plumage with pink and violet patches on the neck.

mouse A *rodent belonging to the suborder *Myomorpha*. The house mouse (*Mus musculus*) is common in buildings worldwide and has long been associated with man. Greyish brown, it is 14-16 cm long including its tail (7-8 cm) and feeds on a variety of foods, from sugar and grain to oil-based paints and putty.
Most mice—together with their larger relatives, the *rats—are grouped into the subfamilies *Murinae* of the Old World and *Cricetinae* of the New World (which also includes hamsters). There are separate subfamilies for African tree mice (*Dendromurinae*; 7 species), jumping mice (*Zapodinae*; 3 species), dormice, and other small groups.

mousebird. *See* coly.

mouse deer. *See* chevrotain.

Mousterian A stone-tool industry of the Middle *Palaeolithic, associated with *Neanderthal man. Named after caves at Le Moustier in the Dordogne (SW France), the Mousterian occurs, with variants, throughout Eurasia from France to China and in N Africa. Spanning roughly the period of 70 000 to 35 000 BC, it is characterized by a wide variety of hand axes, scrapers, points, and blades, often made by the *Lavalloisian technique. Mousterian sites have provided the earliest evidence for formal burial of the dead.

mouthbrooder A fish belonging to one of several genera of *cichlid fishes. The eggs are carried in the mouth of the parent, usually the female, until they hatch. Chief genera: *Tilapia*; *Haplochromis*; *Pelmatochromis*. Other mouthbrooders include certain *fighting fish, *catfish, and cardinal fish.

mouth organ. *See* harmonica.

Mozambique, People's Republic of (Portuguese name: Moçambique) A country in S East Africa, bordering on the Indian Ocean. Extensive coastal plains, at their widest in the S, rise to plateaus inland then mountains reaching over 2000 m (6500 ft). The chief rivers, notably the Zambezi and Limpopo, flow E and provide both irrigation and hydroelectric power. Most of the population is African, mainly Bantu, with diminishing minorities of Europeans and others. *Economy*: chiefly agricultural, the staple food crops being rice and maize. The main cash crops of cashew nuts (of which Mozambique is the world's largest producer), cotton, and sugar are also the principal exports. Industry is, at present, based largely on food processing and textiles but there are plans to develop heavy industry. Mineral resources, including natural gas and high-grade iron ore, are largely unexploited except for coal and bauxite. The transit trade provides an important source of income and Mozambique was compensated for closing its routes to Rhodesia (now Zimbabwe) in 1976. *History*: the N coast was settled by Arabs from the 10th century and was explored by Vasco da *Gama in 1498, becoming a Portuguese colony in the early 16th century. In 1951 it became an overseas province of Portugal. From 1963 FRELIMO (Frente de Libertação de Moçambique) waged a guerrilla campaign that achieved the establishment (1975) of an independent socialist republic. Mozambique provided a base for *Mugabe's arm of the Zimbabwe guerrilla organization, the Patriotic Front, and its borders with Rhodesia (now Zimbabwe) were closed from 1976 until 1980. The South African-backed Mozambique National Resistance (MNR) has applied military pressure in Mozambique with raids on guerrillas in Maputo. In 1985 two US petroleum companies contracted with Mozambique to explore for oil. President: Joaquim Chissano (1939–   ). Official language: Portuguese; the main African language is Makua Lomwe. Official currency: Mozambique escudo of 100 centavos. Area: 784 961 sq km (303 070 sq mi). Population (1983 est): 13 047 000. Capital and main port: Maputo.

Mozarabs   Christians living in Spain under Muslim rule. The Mozarabs (meaning "almost Arabs") were so called because in spite of their Christianity they adopted the Arabic culture of their Muslim rulers. They formed autonomous communities within the Muslim state.

MOZART   *Detail from lithograph by Jab from a painting by Hamman. Many of Mozart's piano compositions were written to display his abilities as an instrumentalist.*

Mozart, Wolfgang Amadeus   (1756–91) Austrian composer, born in Salzburg, the son of the violinist and composer Leopold Mozart (1719–87). Mozart exhibited extraordinary musical talent at the age of four; in 1762 his father took him on a tour of Germany and to Paris and London, where he received adulation for his abilities. In 1770 in Rome Mozart was able to write out the entire score of a *Miserere* by Gregorio Allegri (1582–1652) after hearing the work twice; he earned the highest praise for his talents as performer, improviser, and composer. He continued to tour, composing piano sonatas, symphonies, and his early operas but failing to find a permanent position worthy of his exceptional talents.

After a period of unhappy service with the Archbishop of Salzburg (1779–81) he settled in Vienna as a freelance musician and

teacher, composing such masterpieces as the operas *The Marriage of Figaro* (1786) and *Don Giovanni* (1787). The success of the latter obtained him belated recognition from the emperor but constant travelling, poverty, and frequent overwork contributed to his early death, possibly from typhus. Mozart achieved a fusion of the Germanic and Italianate styles of composition and his immense productivity enriched almost every musical genre. He composed 49 symphonies, over 40 concertos (of which those for piano (25), horn, violin, and clarinet are best known), 6 string quintets, 26 string quartets, numerous divertimenti, piano sonatas, violin sonatas, and much other music. Some of his finest works, such as the operas *Cosi fan tutte* (1790) and *The Magic Flute* (1791) and the *Jupiter* symphony (1788), were written in the last years of his life. His unfinished *Requiem* was completed after his death by Franz Süssmayr (1766–1803). The "Odense Symphony" (1768), was found in 1982 and first performed in 1984. *See also* Köchel, Ludwig von.

Mo-Zi   (*or* Mo-tzu; ?470–?391 BC) Chinese philosopher. Originally a follower of Confucius, Mo-Zi criticized him for stressing ritual rather than virtue. In his chief work, the *Mo-Zi*, he taught universal love, pacifism, and simplicity, principles that formed the basis of a short-lived religious movement, Moism. Although Moism as a religion had ceased to be practised by the 2nd century BC, as a philosophy it is still highly regarded.

Mtwara   10 17S 40 11E A deepwater port in S Tanzania, on the Indian Ocean. It exports chiefly local produce, mainly cashew nuts. Population (1978): 48 510.

Mu'awiyah I   (c. 602–80 AD) The first *caliph (661–80) of the Umayyad dynasty. He participated in the conquest of Syria, where he was made governor in 640. He fought against *Ali, after whose assassination he himself became caliph. Renowned for his tactful control of the Arabs, Mu'awiyah is blamed by Islam for turning the caliphate into a worldly kingship.

Mubarak, (Mohammed) Hosni (Said)   (1928–   ) Egyptian statesman; president (1981–   ). A general, he commanded (1972–75) the Egyptian air force in the *Yom Kippur War (1973). He became vice president to Anwar *Sadat in 1975 and succeeded him on his assassination. A cautious conservative, he has contained inflation and improved relations with the USA and Arab countries.

mucous membrane   A moist membrane that lines the digestive and respiratory tracts and the nasal sinuses. It is a type of *epithelium containing cells that secrete **mucus**, a slimy substance that protects its surface and—in the digestive tract—also lubricates the passage of food and faeces. In the bronchi the mucus traps particles that are inhaled with air.

Mudéjars   (Arabic: vassal)   The Muslims (*see* Moors) of Spain who had, by the 13th century, become subject to Christian rule during the reconquest of the Iberian peninsula. Many were of mixed *Berber and Spanish descent and continued to preserve their Islamic religion and customs. They created an architectural style notable for its ornamental brickwork and use of ceramic tiling. Many examples survive in Castile and Aragon. *Compare* Mozarabs.

mudfish.   *See* bowfin.

mudpuppy   A salamander, *Necturus maculosis*, of North America. Grey-brown, with four well-developed limbs, mudpuppies retain their dark-red gills throughout their lives, even when mature at about five years old and 20 cm long. They are slow moving and generally hunt fish, snails, and other invertebrates at night. The female guards her eggs until they hatch. Family: *Proteidae*. *See also* olm.

mudskipper   A fish of the subfamily *Periophthalminae*, especially the genus *Periophthalmus*, found in swamps, estuaries, and mud flats of Africa, Polynesia, and Australia. Mudskippers have an elongated body, up to 30 cm long, a blunt head, and   dorsally   protruding   eyes.   They   are   able   to climb and walk over land using their limblike pectoral fins. Family: *Gobiidae* (*see* goby).

mufti A Muslim legal expert. They assist judges or private citizens by writing their opinions (*futwas*) on legal matters. These only become precedents in cases of marriage, divorce, and inheritance. In the Ottoman Empire muftis were state officials, the grand mufti being the chief spiritual authority.

Mugabe, Robert (Gabriel) (1925–) Zimbabwe statesman; prime minister (1980–87); president (1987–). A teacher, he helped found the Zimbabwe African National Union (ZANU) in 1963 and, after ten years' (1964–74) detention in Rhodesia, formed the *Patriotic Front (PF) with Joshua Nkomo, leader of the Zimbabwe African People's Union (ZAPU). Based in Mozambique and Zambia respectively, they waged guerrilla warfare against the governments of Ian Smith and then Bishop Muzorewa until agreeing at the Lancaster House talks (1979–80) to disarm (*see* Zimbabwe). His party's election victory (1980) brought Mugabe the leadership of newly independent Zimbabwe. Since then he has consolidated his power and restricted political opposition.

mugger A broad-snouted *crocodile, Crocodylus palustris*, found in India, Sri Lanka, and Burma. It was formerly a sacred animal, kept in temples and tended by priests.

mugwort. *See* wormwood.

Muhammad. *See* Mohammed.

Muhammad Ahmad. *See* Mahdi, al-.

Mühlhausen 51 14N 10 26E A town in SW East Germany, on the River Unstrut. The headquarters of Thomas *Müntzer in the Peasants' War, it has several fine medieval churches. Industries include the manufacture of textiles, machinery, and furniture. Population (1983 est): 43 471.

Muir, Edwin (1887–1959) Scottish poet. Born in Orkney, he moved to Glasgow in 1901 and to London in 1919. During the 1930s he and his wife Willa moved to Prague, where they translated the novels of Franz *Kafka and other major German writers. His reputation as a poet was established rather late in life with *The Voyage* (1946) and *The Labyrinth* (1949), in which he made distinctive use of traditional metres and diction. His *Autobiography* (1954) contains much of his best prose.

Mujibur Rahman, Sheik (1920–75) Bangladesh statesman; prime minister (1972–75). He was gaoled in 1968 by *Ayub Khan's regime in Pakistan for campaigning for the independence of East Pakistan. Following the victory of his party, the Awami League, in the 1970 elections and victory in the subsequent civil war (1971), he became prime minister of the independent state of Bangladesh. Shortly before his assassination he assumed dictatorial powers.

Mukden. *See* Shenyang.

mulberry A tree of the genus *Morus* (12 species), native to N temperate and subtropical regions. The black mulberry (*M. nigra*) is the species most commonly cultivated for its fruit. About 12 m high, it has toothed heart-shaped leaves and round green male and female flower clusters (catkins), borne usually on separate trees. The female flowers give rise to a blackberry-like fruit, which has a pleasant slightly acid taste and is used in jellies, desserts, etc. The leaves of the white mulberry (*M. alba*) are the staple food of silkworms. Family: *Moraceae*. *See also* paper mulberry.

mule The sterile offspring of a female horse and a male ass. Mules are useful pack and draught animals, being hardy, sure-footed, and strong but smaller than a horse and requiring less food. *See also* hinny.

Mülheim an der Ruhr 51 25N 6 50E A city in NW West Germany, in North Rhine-Westphalia on the River Ruhr. There is a 13th-century castle. Its manufactures include power-station generators, pipes and tubes, and machinery. Population (1980 est): 182 100.

Mull An island off the W coast of Scotland, in the Inner Hebrides. It is chiefly mountainous; some sheep and cattle are raised. Other occupations include fishing, forestry, and tour-ism. Area: 909 sq km (351 sq mi). Population (1981): 2605. Chief town: Tobermory.

mullein A biennial or perennial herb of the genus *Verbascum* (about 300 species), native to N temperate Eurasia. The biennial common mullein (*V. thapsus*), also called Aaron's rod, occurs in dry limy regions. 0.6–2 m tall, it bears large woolly leaves and pale-yellow flowers. Some species, including the European dark mullein (*V. nigrum*), are grown as garden plants. Family: *Scrophulariaceae*.

Muller, Hermann Joseph (1890–1967) US geneticist, who discovered the ability of X-rays to induce changes (mutations) in genetic material. Although useful as an experimental tool, Muller recognized the danger of X-radiation to man. He was awarded a Nobel Prize (1946).

Müller, Paul Hermann (1899–1965) Swiss chemist, who discovered the insecticidal properties of *DDT (1939). Müller found it was relatively harmless to other forms of life and DDT became widely used to combat insect pests. Müller was awarded the 1948 Nobel Prize for Medicine.

mullet A food fish, also called grey mullet, belonging to the genus *Mugil* (about 70 species), found in temperate and tropical coastal waters and estuaries. It has a slender silvery-green or grey large-scaled body, 30–90 cm long, with two dorsal fins. It feeds in large schools on algae and small invertebrates. Family: *Mugilidae*; order: *Perciformes*. *See also* red mullet.

Mulliken, Robert Sanderson (1896–1986) US chemist and physicist, who developed *Schrödinger's theory of wave mechanics to provide a mathematical explanation of chemical bonding in terms of electron probabilities, orbitals, and energy levels. He received the 1966 Nobel Prize.

Mullingar (Irish name: Muileann Cearr) 53 32N 7 20W A market town in the Republic of Ireland, the county town of Co Westmeath. Trade includes cattle and it has a cathedral. Population (1981): 7854.

Mulready, William (1786–1863) British painter, born in Ireland, best known for his everyday scenes of cottages, schoolrooms, etc., and as the designer of the first penny postage envelope (1840).

Mulroney, (Martin) Brian (1939–) Canadian statesman and lawyer; prime minister (1984–). After practicing law in Montreal he became leader of the Progressive Conservative Party in 1983 and prime minister a year later, promising to strengthen Canada's economy, extend social services, and improve relations with the USA.

Multan 30 10N 71 36E A city in central Pakistan. An ancient settlement on the key route to S India, it has often been besieged and occupied. It has textile and noteworthy cottage industries. Population (1981): 730 000.

multinational corporations Large business enterprises with headquarters (the parent company) in one country and operating divisions (subsidiaries) in one or more other countries. Strategic decision making usually takes place at the head office. Their command of large resources and ability to manoeuvre around local legislation and taxation have led to demands for international legislation to restrain their activities when these conflict with national interests.

multiple sclerosis A chronic and usually progressive disease of the nervous system in which the fatty sheaths that surround the nerves in the brain or spinal cord are destroyed, which affects the function of the nerves. The disease is also called disseminated sclerosis, as its effects are disseminated in different parts of the body. It usually begins in young adults, and the commonest initial symptoms are sudden severe blurring of the vision or weakness in one limb. The initial symptoms often resolve completely but later the disease returns, causing permanent handicap.

multiple star A system of two or more stars that move in complex orbits under mutual gravitational attraction. *See also* binary star.

multiplexer In *telecommunications, a device that combines several signals so that they can be sent along a single transmission path, or channel, and reconstructed at the receiver. One method is to superimpose carrier waves of different frequencies (*see* modulation) on the signals. Multiplexers are used with radio transmissions, telephone lines, etc.

multiplier A number used in economic theory to indicate how many times a specific increase in income, demand, etc., will be multiplied to produce an increase in the overall income, demand, etc., in a nation's economy. For example, if an individual's income is increased by £10 as a result of a cut in direct taxation, half of this increase may be spent in such a way that it becomes income for others, who may in turn also spend half of their increased income. Thus the original £10 could be multiplied to produce a total of £20 of additional income, in which case the multiplier has a value of 2. Opinions differ as to the practical impact of the multiplier, depending on the prevailing view of what motivates consumption.

Mumford, Lewis (1895-) US social philosopher. Mumford's academic posts included research professorships at the Universities of Stanford (1942-44) and Berkeley (1961-62). He wrote widely on architecture and cities, arguing that technological society was repressive. His books include *Sticks and Stones* (1924), *Technics and Civilization* (1934), *Values for Survival* (1946), *In the Name of Sanity* (1954), and *The City in History* (1961).

mummers' play An English folk drama based on the legend of St George and the Seven Champions of Christendom; it was a dumb show (*mummer*, from Middle English *mum*, silent), traditionally enacted on Christmas Day by masked performers. Its plot largely consists of a duel between St George and an infidel knight, in which one of them is killed but is later revived by a doctor. The play is still performed in a few villages in England and N Ireland.

mummy A human or animal body prepared and embalmed for burial according to ancient Egyptian religious practice. The internal organs were extracted and sealed in *Canopic jars and the body was desiccated by packing in dry natron, anointed, and encased in linen bandages.

mumps An acute virus infection that usually occurs in children. After an incubation period of 12 to 20 days the child develops headache and fever; later, the parotid salivary glands (situated under the ear) become tender and swollen. The disease is usually mild and resolves rapidly, but sometimes mild *meningitis develops. In adult male patients the infection may spread to the testicles, which may occasionally lead to sterility.

Munch, Charles (1892-1968) French conductor. He made his debut in Paris in 1932 and directed the Boston Symphony Orchestra from 1949 to 1962. In 1967 he founded the Orchestre de Paris but died on its first US tour.

Munch, Edvard (1863-1944) Norwegian painter and printmaker, who was a major influence on 20th-century German *expressionism. Largely self-taught, he developed his mature style in Berlin, following visits to Paris where he was influenced by *Gauguin and *Van Gogh. His symbolic paintings of love, death, and despair, including the famous *Cry* (1893; Nasjonalgalleriet, Oslo), reflect the pessimism caused by family tragedy. After 1910 he lived in Norway, where he painted murals for the festival hall of Oslo University (1913).

München. *See* Munich.

München Gladbach. *See* Mönchengladbach.

Münchhausen, Karl Friedrich, Freiherr von (1720-97) German soldier famous as a raconteur. His hyperbolic accounts of his feats passed into legend and were the subject of a series of adventure tales, *The Adventures of Baron Munchhausen* (1793), written by R. E. Raspe (1737-94).

Muncie 40 11N 85 22W A city in the USA, in E Indiana on the White River. It is the "typical American" town of the classic sociological study *Middletown* (1929) by Robert and Helen Lynd. An agricultural trading centre, Muncie's varied manufactures include machine tools and glass. Population (1980): 77 216.

Munda Aboriginal tribes living mainly in the hills and forests of central and NE India. Munda languages form a subgroup of the *Austro-Asiatic language family. The northern branch of the Munda languages includes Santali, the most important. The Munda peoples are mainly slash-and-burn cultivators.

mung bean A *bean plant, *Phaseolus aureus*, also known as green gram, native to India and cultivated in tropical and subtropical regions chiefly as a vegetable crop. The slender pods contain up to 15 small edible seeds, which can be dried and stored or germinated in the dark to produce bean sprouts. Family: *Leguminosae*.

Munich (German name: München) 48 08N 11 35E A city in S West Germany, the capital of Bavaria on the River Isar. It has a 15th-century cathedral and many baroque and rococo buildings, including Nymphenburg Palace (1664-1728). Its university was moved here from Landshut in 1826. It is also noted for its technical university, opera, art galleries, and for its annual Oktoberfest (beer festival). A centre of commerce, industry, and tourism, its manufactures include precision instruments, electrical goods, chemicals, and beer. *History*: Munich was from 1255 the residence and from 1506 the capital of the Dukes of Bavaria (from 1806 Kings). During the late 19th and early 20th centuries it flourished culturally, attracting such figures as the composer Wagner. The Nazi movement began here in the 1920s. Munich was severely bombed during World War II. Population (1980 est): 1 298 900.

Munich Agreement (1938) The settlement, resulting from the conference between Neville Chamberlain (UK), Daladier (France), Hitler (Germany), and Mussolini (Italy), that recognized Hitler's territorial claims to the *Sudetenland. Described by Chamberlain as achieving "peace in our time," it was followed in March, 1939, by Hitler's invasion of Czechoslovakia and in Sept by World War II.

Munich Putsch (1923) The attempt by *Hitler to seize power in Germany. Hitler planned to form a national government after first seizing power in Bavaria. This attempt at revolution (German word: *Putsch*) failed and Hitler was imprisoned.

Munnings, Sir Alfred (1878-1959) British painter. His immaculate paintings of horses were first exhibited at the Royal Academy in 1898. He was president of the Royal Academy from 1944 to 1951.

Munro, Hector Hugh. *See* Saki.

Munsell colour system A method of classifying *colours based on three parameters: hue (dominant colour), luminosity (brightness), and saturation or chroma (strength, i.e. the degree to which it is a pure spectral colour). The various colours are set out in a chart known as the colour tree, in which the different gradations of colour are exhibited according to the three parameters. The Munsell colour system is widely used in the paint industry. Named after Albert H. Munsell (1858-1918).

Münster 51 58N 7 37E A city and port in NW West Germany, in North Rhine-Westphalia on the Dortmund-Ems Canal. It was an important member of the Hanseatic League and the capital of the former province of Westphalia. It has a 13th-century cathedral, restored after the damage of World War II, and a university (1773). Service industries provide employment for most of the workforce. Population (1980 est): 267 600.

Munster A province and ancient kingdom of the SW Republic of Ireland. It consists of the counties of Clare,

MURAL PAINTING   *A mural by Diego Rivera on the Hôtel del Prado depicting the history of Mexico from the conquest to the 1910 revolution.*

Cork, Kerry, Limerick, Tipperary, and Waterford. Area: 24 125 sq km (9315 sq mi). Population (1981): 998 315.

Munthe, Axel (1857–1949) Swedish physician and author. Munthe practised in Paris and Rome before retiring to Capri, where he built the Villa San Michele. *The Story of San Michele* (1929) described his early life and the building of the villa. It has been translated into 44 languages.

muntjac A small deer belonging to the subfamily *Muntiacinae* (6 species), occurring in forests of Asia, Sumatra, Java, and Borneo. The Indian muntjac (*Muntiacus muntjak*), also called barking deer or rib-faced deer, is 55 cm high at the shoulder, chestnut above and paler beneath with short unbranched antlers and short sharp fangs. Muntjacs are solitary and nocturnal, feeding on grass, leaves, and shoots.

Müntzer, Thomas (c. 1490–1525) German Protestant reformer and *Anabaptist leader. He began preaching reformed doctrines at Zwickau in 1520 but soon diverged from Luther's teachings. Claiming direct inspiration from the Holy Spirit, he called for radical social, political, and religious reform. A leader of the *Peasants' Revolt (1524–25), he was captured at the battle of Frankenhausen (1525) and executed.

Muntz metal A relatively hard strong type of *brass containing 60% copper and 40% zinc. It is not easily worked at room temperature and is usually shaped while hot or by casting. Named after G. F. Muntz (d. 1847).

muon A negatively charged unstable elementary particle (lifetime 2×10^{-6} second; mass 207 times that of the electron) that decays into an electron and two *neutrinos. It has a corresponding antiparticle. It was originally thought to be a meson (and was called the mu-meson) but is now classified as a lepton. *See* particle physics.

mural painting The decoration of walls and ceilings by such varied techniques as *encaustic, *tempera, and *fresco painting. The design of murals is largely dependent on their architectural settings. *Renaissance painters often used perspective and architecture in their murals to create the illusion that the painted walls or ceilings were space extensions of the real architecture. Mural painting was revived during the 20th century, principally by the Mexican painters *Rivera, *Orozco, and *Siqueiros, who used it to reach a wider public with their social and political subject matter.

Murasaki Shikibu (?978–?1014) Japanese writer. She is most famous for her great saga, *The Tale of Genji*, which is probably the world's earliest novel. It deals chiefly with the love

life of Prince Genji and is remarkable for its observations of nature and understanding of human emotions.

Murat, Joachim (1767–1815) French marshal and King of Naples (1808–15). He served in Napoleon's campaigns in Italy (1796–97) and Egypt (1798–99) and fought at *Marengo (1800) and *Austerlitz (1805). In Naples, Murat introduced important administrative reforms. He treated with the Austrians after Napoleon's defeat (1813) but subsequent attempts to regain his throne ended first in defeat at Tolentino and then in his capture and execution.

Murcia 38 59N 1 08W A city in SE Spain, in the province of Murcia. It was formerly the capital of the Moorish kingdom of Murcia and possesses a cathedral and university (founded 1915). Industries include silk and textiles. Population (1981): 288 631.

Murdoch, Dame Iris (1919–) British novelist. Born in Dublin, she studied and taught philosophy at Oxford. Her first publication was a philosophical study, *Sartre* (1953). Her novels include *Under the Net* (1954), *The Bell* (1958), *A Severed Head* (1961), *The Black Prince* (1974), *The Sea, the Sea* (1978), for which she won the Booker Prize, *Nuns and Soldiers* (1980), *The Good Apprentice* (1985), and *The Book and the Brotherhood* (1987).

Murdoch, (Keith) Rupert (1931–) US publisher and entrepreneur, born in Australia. His company, News International, runs several British national papers and the only national Australian newspaper. He attracted notoriety after sacking 5500 printing staff in the Wapping dispute; he also owns US newspapers, 20th Century Fox, and US TV networks.

Murdock, William (1754–1839) British inventor, who pioneered the use of coal-gas for lighting. In 1802–03 he used it to light Matthew Boulton's Soho engineering works, where he was an employee.

Mureş, River (Hungarian name: Maros) A river in E Europe, flowing W from the Carpathian Mountains in Romania across the Transylvanian Basin to join the Tisza River in Hungary. Length: 803 km (499 mi).

murex A *gastropod mollusc belonging to the family *Muricidae* (about 1000 species), mainly of tropical seas. Murex shells are elaborately ornamented with spines and frills; the snail feeds on other molluscs by drilling holes in their shells and extracting the flesh with its long proboscis. *Murex trunculus* was the source of the dye Tyrian purple.

Murillo, Bartolomé Esteban (1617–82) Spanish painter. He spent most of his life in Seville, working for the religious orders and helping to found the Spanish Academy (1660), of which he became first president. After abandoning his early realism, he painted urchins and religious scenes, particularly the Immaculate Conception, in an idealized style influenced by Rubens and the Venetians. In the 20th century there has been a reaction against the sentimentality of such works as *The Two Trinities* (National Gallery, London).

Murmansk 68 59N 33 08E A port in the NW Soviet Union, in the RSFSR on the Kola inlet of the Barents Sea. Its ice-free harbour was used by the Allied expedition against the Bolsheviks in 1918 and is an important fishing base. Population (1981 est): 394 000.

Murray, Gilbert (1866–1957) British classical scholar. He was professor of Greek at Glasgow (1889–1908) and Oxford (1908–36). His verse translations of Aeschylus, Sophocles, Euripides, and Aristophanes kindled both academic and popular interest in ancient Greek drama.

Murray, Sir James (Augustus Henry) (1837–1915) British lexicographer. Largely self-educated, he became a teacher at Mill Hill School in 1870. After joining the Philological Society and editing some early English texts, he was in 1878 appointed editor of the *New English Dictionary on Historical Principles* (later called the *Oxford English Dictionary*), to which he devoted the rest of his life. There were other editors, but it was Murray who made a practical reality of this project and set the standards of its scholarship.

Murray, Len (Lionel M.; 1922–) British trades-union leader; general secretary of the Trades' Union Council (TUC; 1973–84). He was involved in union management from 1947, heading the economic department of the TUC (1954–69). In 1974 he became vice president of the European Trade Union Confederation.

Murray cod A carnivorous food and game fish, *Maccullochella macquariensis*, found in fresh waters of Australia. Up to 2 m long, it has a deep broad olive-green body with brown spots and a long dorsal fin.

Murray River The chief river in Australia. Rising near Mount Koscuisko, in New South Wales, it flows generally W and S forming the boundary between Victoria and New South Wales. It enters Encounter Bay on the Indian Ocean through Lake Alexandrina. The main tributaries are the Darling and Murrumbidgee Rivers; it also receives water from the Snowy Mountains hydroelectric scheme. Length: 2590 km (1609 mi).

Murrow, Edward R(oscoe) (1908–65) US radio and television journalist. He joined CBS in 1935 and became head of the European Bureau in 1937. After World War II he became a CBS vice president but continued to broadcast regularly and in the 1950s was a fearless critic of Senator Joseph *McCarthy. In 1961 he became director of the US Information Agency.

Murrumbidgee River A river in SE Australia, rising in the Eastern Highlands in New South Wales and flowing through the Australian Capital Territory before entering the Murray River. The Burrinjuck Dam provides water for irrigation. Length: 1690 km (1050 mi).

Murry, John Middleton (1889–1957) British literary critic. He married Katherine *Mansfield and was a friend of D. H. *Lawrence. He edited the literary magazines *Athenaeum* (1919–21) and *Adelphi* (1923–48). His many books include studies of Keats (1925, 1930, 1949) and Blake (1933) as well as an autobiography, *Between Two Worlds* (1935).

Muscat 23 37N 58 38E The capital of Oman, on the Gulf of Oman. Most port traffic is now handled at Matrah to the NW. There is an oil terminal to the W. Population (1981): 50 000.

Muscat and Oman. *See* Oman, Sultanate of.

muscle Tissue that is specialized to contract, producing movement or tension in the body. It contains long spindle-shaped cells (muscle fibres) that convert chemical energy (*see* ATP) into mechanical energy. Most of the body's musculature consists of voluntary muscle, which is consciously controlled via the central nervous system. It is also known as skeletal muscle (because it is attached to the bones) and striated (or striped) muscle (because of its banded appearance under the microscope). Individual muscles are made up of bundles of fibres enclosed in a strong fibrous sheath and attached to bones by tendons. Involuntary muscle occurs in the walls of hollow organs, such as blood vessels, intestines, and the bladder. It is responsible for movements not under conscious control and is regulated by the autonomic nervous system. Cardiac muscle is a special type of muscle found only in the heart: its rhythmic contractions produce the heartbeat. *See* Plate IV.

muscovite. *See* micas.

Muscovy Company The first important English joint-stock company. Founded in 1553 to discover a northeast passage to the Orient, it was chartered in 1555 and granted a Russian trade monopoly, which it lost in 1698. It was dissolved in 1917.

Muscovy duck A large tropical American *perching duck, *Cairina moschata*. It has a glossy black plumage with white wing patches. The domesticated form is larger with a grey, white, or speckled plumage and a large scarlet caruncle on the bill.

muscular dystrophy A group of chronic and progressive disorders characterized by wasting and weakening of the muscle fibres. The disease is inherited and the commonest type, Duchenne muscular dystrophy, affects predominantly boys. The muscles affected and the rate of progress of the disease are both very variable. There is no specific treatment but physiotherapy and orthopaedic measures can help those who suffer from the disease.

Muses In Greek mythology, the nine patrons of the arts and sciences, daughters of Zeus and *Mnemosyne. Calliope was the muse of epic poetry; Clio, history; Euterpe, flute playing and music; Erato, love poetry and hymns; Terpsichore, dancing; Melpomene, tragedy; Thalia, comedy; Polyhymnia, song and mime; and Urania, astronomy.

Musgrave, Thea (1928–) Scottish composer. She was a pupil of Nadia Boulanger in Paris. Her works include concertos for horn, viola, and clarinet as well as operas and choral, orchestral, and chamber music.

Musgrave Ranges A range of rocky granite hills in NW South Australia. It runs parallel to the Northern Territory border, reaching 1516 m (4970 ft) at Mount Woodruffe.

mushroom The umbrella-shaped spore-forming body produced by many fungi. (Sometimes the word toadstool is used for those species that are inedible or poisonous, mushroom being restricted to the edible species.) It consists of an erect stem (stipe) and a cap, which may be flat, conical, spherical, or cylindrical and has numerous radiating gills on its undersurface in which the spores are produced. The well-known edible mushrooms belong to the genus *Agaricus*; they have a smooth white or scaly brown cap with gills that are white, grey, or pink when immature and become deep brown at maturity. The field mushroom (*A. campestris*) has a white cap 4–8 cm in diameter and deep-pink to brown gills.

music The art of organizing sounds, which usually consist of sequences of tones of definite *pitch, to produce melody, harmony, and rhythm. Musical cultures based on *scales evolved in such ancient civilizations as those of China, Persia, India, etc., as well as in Europe. Within each culture both *folk music and classical (*or* "art") music traditions exist. In western music both traditions evolved from the Greek system of *modes established by Pythagoras and codified during the middle ages. In classical music modes became the basis for *plainchant and subsequently for *polyphony, which reached its peak in the 15th and 16th centuries. With the development of the major and minor scales in the early 17th century harmonic composition for instrumental ensembles and in *opera began to evolve. During the 17th and 18th centuries increasing attention was given to the development of musical form in classical music. By the beginning of the 19th century the dominant musical forms were the *sonata, *symphony, *concerto, and string quartet. Opera continued to flourish and *oratorio, invented during the 18th century, remained popular. The influence of Romanticism in music gave rise to the tone poem (*see* symphonic poem) and an increasingly free attitude to traditional forms. *Chromaticism in the music of the late 19th and early 20th centuries led to *atonality and the adoption by some composers of *serialism. In the later 20th century composers have used unpitched sounds, electronic generators, tape recordings, synthesizers, and unconventional instrumental techniques to create music, as well as experimenting widely with musical forms. The 20th century has also seen the development of other important forms of popular music in the western tradition, heavily influenced by African folk music. *See* jazz; rock; pop music.

musica ficta (Latin: false music) A modification of the pitch of certain notes, which, during the 11th to 16th centuries, was made in the course of musical performance. For instance, the harsh tritone F–B, known as *diabolus in*

MUSICAL INSTRUMENTS

trumpet

flute

clarinet

grand piano

viola

violin

triangle

double bass

castanets

harp

range of some musical instruments

flute
oboe
cor anglais
clarinet
bassoon
horn
trumpet
tenor trombone
tuba
timpani
piano keyboard

C''' C'' C' C C' C'' C''' C''''

harp
violin
viola
cello
double bass

timpani

cymbals

vibraphone

sitar

maracas

koto

gong chimes

In the matchlock, a slow-burning match was forced into the powder pan by the arm when the trigger was pressed.

In the wheellock, the flint or iron pyrites was lowered onto a serrated wheel when the trigger was pressed. The sparks produced ignited the charge in the pan. The wheel, wound up by a key, also rotated when the trigger was pressed.

In the flintlock, pressing the trigger caused the flint to strike a hinged steel plate, forcing it back to expose the powder in the pan to the sparks.

The percussion cap, containing mercury fulminate, was struck by the hammer when the trigger was pressed. The flame produced passed through the hollow nipple into the vent, where it fired the main charge.

MUSKET　　*The types of lock mechanism used in muzzle-loaders.*

musica (Latin: the devil in music), was avoided by sharpening the F or flattening the B.

musical instruments Devices used to produce music. The chief characteristics of a musical instrument are its *timbre and range (i.e. the highest and lowest notes it can produce). In the *orchestra musical instruments are grouped into families. The *stringed instruments (*or* strings) include the violin, viola, cello, double bass, and harp (*see also* piano). The *wind instruments are divided into the woodwind (flute, clarinet, oboe, and bassoon) and brass (horn, trumpet, trombone, and tuba). The *percussion instruments include a whole range of instruments from the triangle and cymbals to the xylophone and timpani. Many instruments are used chiefly in jazz or pop (e.g. guitar, vibraphone, and maracas) while others, such as the Indian sitar, the Japanese koto, and the Spanish castanets, feature predominantly in the music of particular countries.

musicals Light dramas combined with songs and dances. The genre evolved in the USA in the late 19th century and was developed during the 1920s and 1930s by George *Gershwin, Cole *Porter, and Irving *Berlin. In *Oklahoma!* (1943) and other musicals of the 1940s, Richard *Rodgers and Oscar *Hammerstein attempted to integrate the dramatic and musical elements, a trend culminating in Leonard Bernstein's *West Side Story* (1957). Successful British musicals include *Jesus Christ Superstar* (1971), *Evita* (1978), *Cats* (1981), and *Phantom of the Opera* (1986) by Andrew Lloyd Webber.

music drama. *See* opera.

music hall A type of popular entertainment featuring a variety of performers including singers, dancers, comedians, conjurors, jugglers, and acrobats. It developed from entertainments given in taverns, attained its greatest popularity in 19th-century England, and declined in the 1920s and 1930s with the rise of the rival attractions of cinema and the radio. Notable music-hall performers were Marie *Lloyd, Vesta *Tilley, Harry *Lauder, and Gracie *Fields. Revivals of music-hall entertainments are occasionally featured on television and have great nostalgic appeal. The US equivalent is known as vaudeville. Celebrated vaudeville performers include W. C. *Fields and Will Rodgers (1879–1935), both of whom later became film actors.

Musil, Robert (1880–1942) Austrian novelist. He studied engineering and later philosophy and psychology and served as an officer in World War I. His fame was posthumous and due chiefly to his one major work, *The Man Without Qualities* (1930–43), a long novel describing life during the declining years of the Habsburg empire. Of his other works, only the novel *Young Törless* (1906) is noteworthy.

musique concrète A type of musical composition invented by Pierre Schaeffer (1910–　) in 1948. Natural or man-made sounds are recorded on tape and arranged, often in an altered or distorted form, to form a composition made up of "concrete" or already existing sounds, as opposed to "abstract" musical tones.

musk (botany) A perennial plant, *Mimulus moschatus* (a species of *monkey flower), native to North America and grown as an ornamental for its musky fragrance. 20–60 cm tall, it has oval leaves and tubular yellow flowers. The name is also applied to several other plants with a musky odour including the *moschatel, musk mallow (*Malva moschata*), musk rose (*Rosa moschata*), and musk stork's bill (*Erodium moschatum*).

musk (perfumery) An odorous substance obtained from the male *musk deer. It is included in perfumes because of the strength and persistence of its odour and it has been used as an aphrodisiac and stimulant.

musk deer A small solitary deer, *Moschus moschiferus*, found in mountain forests of central Asia. Musk deer are about 60 cm high at the shoulder with long hind legs; males have no antlers but grow long fangs. They have been widely hunted for the secretion of their musk gland, which is used in the manufacture of perfumes.

musket A smoothbore firearm fired from the shoulder. The earliest form, known as a harquebus (*or* arquebus from Middle Dutch *hakebusse*, hook gun), evolved in the 15th century as the first hand-held form of the *cannon—a development that depended on the matchlock as a means of igniting the charge. With a range of only 110 m (120 yd), the ball from the harquebus was unable to penetrate armour. In the second half of the 16th century a Spanish general invented a heavy shoulder weapon with a sufficiently large charge to penetrate even the finest armour—this musket still relied on the matchlock, essentially a fair-weather device. It was not until the mid-17th century that wheellocks (working on much the same principle as a flint lighter) and flintlocks were adopted for military use. The next landmark in the development of the musket was the *percussion cap at the beginning of the 19th century, which led to the breech-loading musket with cartridge and percussion-cap ammunition. Muskets were superseded by *rifles in the mid-19th century.

musk ox A large hoofed □mammal, *Ovibos moschatus*, inhabiting the Arctic tundra of North America. About 150 cm high at the shoulder, musk oxen have long dark shaggy hair and prominent curved horns. They live in herds of 20–30 and feed on grass, etc. Bulls have a strong musky scent in the rutting season. Family: *Bovidae.

muskrat A large North American water *vole, *Ondatra zibethica*, also called musquash. It grows up to 35 cm long, excluding its black hairless tail, and its soft glossy coat is used in the fur trade. Muskrats inhabit marshland and feed on water plants, mussels, and crayfish. Family: *Cricetidae*. □mammal.

Muslim League An organization of Indian Muslims created to safeguard their rights in British India. Formed in 1906 as the All-India Muslim League, it generally supported British rule. In 1940, under the leadership of *Jinnah and with the prospect of Indian independence, the League began to press for a separate state for Indian Muslims. In 1947, after the founding of Pakistan, it became Pakistan's dominant political party. Supported mainly by the westernized middle class, it split into three factions in the 1960s.

muslin A smooth delicately woven cotton fabric. Originally made in Mosul in Mesopotamia (hence its name), it is used for dresses and curtains. In the USA coarser cotton fabrics used for shirts and sheeting are also called muslins.

musquash. *See* muskrat.

mussel A *bivalve mollusc belonging either to the family *Mytilidae* (marine mussels) or the superfamily *Unionacea* (freshwater mussels). Marine mussels have wedge-shaped shells measuring 5–15 cm, which are anchored to rocks by strands (byssus threads). Some species burrow into sand or wood. The edible mussel (*Mytilus edulis*) is an important seafood. Freshwater mussels inhabit ponds, lakes, and streams, embedded in mud or wedged between rocks.

Musset, Alfred de (1810–57) French poet and dramatist, one of the major figures of the Romantic movement. He published his first volume of poetry, *Contes d'Espagne et d'Italie*, at the age of 20. He lived extravagantly, and wrote satires on the excesses of the Romantic movement. His autobiographical *La Confession d'un enfant du siècle* (1836) includes an account of his love affair with George *Sand.

MUSSOLINI

Mussolini, Benito (Amilcare Andrea) (1883–1945) Italian fascist dictator. Initially an ardent socialist, his support of Italian participation in World War I led to his expulsion from the Socialist Party (1915). In 1919 he formed the Fasci di combattimento (*see* Blackshirts) in Milan and came to power following the *March on Rome (1922). He was prime minis-

ter until the murder of *Matteotti persuaded him to establish (1924–29) a dictatorship. As *duce* ("leader") his social policies, programme of public works, maintenance of law and order, and conciliatory policies towards the Roman Catholic Church (*see* Lateran Treaty) initially impressed the Italian people. However, his expansionist foreign policy, especially his invasion of Ethiopia (1935), and his alliance with Hitler (the Rome-Berlin Axis, 1936) brought him increasing unpopularity. In 1939 he annexed Albania and after the outbreak of World War II he declared war on France and Britain (June, 1940). The Italian war effort was disastrous, leading to defeats in E and N Africa and in Greece. Following the Allied invasion of Sicily, Mussolini was forced by the Fascist Grand Council to resign (July, 1943). Rescued by the Germans to head a new fascist republic in N Italy, he was subsequently captured and shot by Italian partisans. His body was brought to Milan and hung up in a public square before burial.

Mussorgski, Modest Petrovich (1839–81) Russian composer. An army officer and civil servant, he had little formal training beyond a few lessons with Balakirev. He developed a highly personal style, reproducing Russian speech rhythms in such works as the song cycles *The Nursery* (1868–72) and *Songs and Dances of Death* (1875–77). His masterpieces are the opera *Boris Godunov* (1868–72), the piano work *Pictures at an Exhibition* (1874), and the orchestral tone poem *A Night on the Bare Mountain* (1860–66).

mustang The wild horse of North America. Mustangs are descended from the domesticated European stock of Spanish settlers and have become tough and small in the harsh conditions. Many were caught and tamed by cowboys and Indians, including the Mustang tribe, which was noted for its horse breeding. Wild herds were rapidly declining until protective legislation was passed in 1971.

mustard Any of various annual herbs of the genus *Brassica* and closely related genera, native to Europe and W Asia and cultivated chiefly for their seeds–source of the condiment mustard. They have branched stems, up to 1.5 cm high, deeply lobed leaves, and terminal clusters of yellow flowers. The leaves may be used as fodder, fertilizer, vegetables, or herbs. The main species are the white or yellow mustard, *Sinapis alba* (or *B. hirta*), black or brown mustard (*B. nigra*), and Indian mustard (*B. juncea*).

Mustelidae A family of mammals of the order *Carnivora. It includes the stoats, weasels, martens, badgers, skunks, and others. Mustelids typically have a long body and tail, short legs, and glands that secrete a musky fluid.

Mutanabbi, Abu At-Tayyib Ahmad Ibn Husayn al- (915–65 AD) Arab poet. From a poor but noble family, he learned his craft from the Bedouins and at Damascus, becoming a court poet in N Syria (948) and later in Egypt. He brought elaborate rhetorical innovations to the traditional odes (*qasidahs*) addressed to his patrons.

Mutare (name until 1982: Umtali) 19 00S 32 40E A town in E Zimbabwe. Situated on the main railway to Mozambique from Harare, it is an important market centre for an area producing fruit and timber. Industries include papermills, textiles, and food canning. Nearby national parks attract tourists. Population (1980 est): 64 000.

mutation A change in the hereditary material (*see* DNA) of an organism, which results in an altered physical characteristic. A mutation in a germ cell is inherited by subsequent generations of offspring; a change in any other cell (somatic cell) affects only those cells produced by division of the mutated cell. Gene mutations result from a change in the bases of the DNA molecule; chromosome mutations may be due to the addition or subtraction of bases and can usually be seen under a microscope. Both types of mutation affect the *genetic code and hence the corresponding function of the genes.
Very occasionally, mutations occur spontaneously and at random. They can also be induced by certain chemicals, ionizing radiation (such as X-rays), and by ultraviolet light. Most

nonlethal mutations are of no benefit to the organism, but they do provide an important source of genetic variation in the population on which natural selection can act, which eventually results in the *evolution of new species.

Mutesa I (c. 1838–84) King of *Buganda in East Africa. An absolute ruler, Mutesa tried to play off the Arab intruders into his kingdom against the Europeans so that neither would become too powerful. He traded with both and encouraged Islam and Christianity.

mute swan An Old World *swan, *Cygnus olor*, found in marshy areas and estuaries and, as a semidomesticated ornamental bird, on rivers and lakes. It is 160 cm long and has a long neck, white plumage, black legs, and an orange bill with a black base. Less vocal than other swans, it is also silent in flight.

Mutsuhito (1852–1912) Emperor of Japan (1867–1912), who presided over Japan's transformation into a modern state. The Meiji (Mutsuhito's title as emperor) restoration (1866–68) ended seven centuries of feudal rule and nominally returned full power to the throne, a change that culminated in the constitution promulgated by Mutsuhito in 1889.

muttonbird A bird whose chicks are collected for meat and oil. The name is used especially for the slender-billed shearwater (*Puffinus tenuirostris*) of Australia and the sooty shearwater (*Procellaria griseus*) of New Zealand. Both belong to the family *Procellariidae* (petrels).

mutualism. *See* symbiosis.

Muybridge, Eadweard (Edward James Muggeridge; 1830–1904) US photographer, born in Britain. He was a pioneer of action photography with his series of animals and humans photographed in consecutive stages of motion. He showed that a trotting horse momentarily raises all four legs simultaneously.

Muzorewa, Bishop Abel (Tendekayi) (1925–   ) Zimbabwe statesman and bishop of the Methodist Church. One-time president of the African National Congress and the All Africa Conference of Churches, Muzorewa negotiated a new constitution with Ian *Smith's government in 1978 and headed a nominally Black government in *Zimbabwe until 1980, when Robert *Mugabe became prime minister.

MYCENAE *The entrance to the citadel of Mycenae is by the Lion Gate, set between massive walls of Cyclopean stonework.*

MX missile A US nuclear strategic missile with a range of 9650 km (6000 m). Carrying 10 warheads, the MX missile was developed in response to the vulnerability of the concrete un-

derground silos in which other ICBMs are housed. The MX missile can be launched from ships, aircraft, submarines, mobile land launchers, or from specially reinforced silos. A controversial weapon, the MX programme was begun in 1979 under Jimmy *Carter and continued, although reduced by Congress in 1985, under Ronald *Reagan.

Mycenae An ancient citadel in the Peloponnese (S Greece). Famed in legend as the home of *Agamemnon, Mycenae attained its zenith between 1600 and 1200 BC. Massive fortifications, including the famous Lion Gate, attest Mycenae's military readiness and exquisite bronze daggers, gold masks, and silver drinking vessels from its royal graves indicate accompanying affluence.

Mycenaean civilization The civilization of Bronze Age Greece. It developed after about 1650 BC in mainland centres, such as *Mycenae and *Pylos, but after the collapse of the Minoan civilization (c. 1450 BC) its influence and political control extended to Crete. The Mycenaeans were a warrior aristocracy, identifiable with Homer's *Achaens. They spoke a form of Greek, used *Linear B script, and lived in palaces decorated with frescoes and equipped with luxury stone and metal goods. About 1200 BC the palaces were destroyed, either by invaders or in internecine struggles, but recognizably Mycenaean culture survived in debased form until about 1100 BC.

mycology The branch of biology dealing with the study of fungi. Mycology was established as a separate discipline in the early 19th century, when the Swedish botanist Elias Fries (1794–1878) published the first scientifically based classification of the fungi (1821–32).

mycoplasma A minute organism that lacks a cell wall and belongs to the class *Mollicutes*, also called pleuropneumonia-like organisms (PPLOs). Regarded by some authorities as bacteria, mycoplasmas may be rounded, 150–300 nanometres in diameter, or filamentous, up to several micrometres long (*see* SI units). They are the cause of several plant and animal diseases; for example *Mycoplasma mycoides* causes pleuropneumonia in cattle.

myelin A white fatty material that forms a sheath around the large nerve fibres of vertebrates and some invertebrates. Myelin acts as an insulator, thereby increasing the speed of conduction of impulses along the nerve fibre.

Myers, F(rederic) W(illiam) H(enry) (1843–1901) British essayist and poet. As well as poetry and literary criticism, he published several books concerning psychical research, including *Phantasms of the Living* (1886) and *Human Personality and Its Survival of Bodily Death* (1903). He helped to found the Society for Psychical Research in 1882.

Mylae, Battle of (260 BC) A battle in the first *Punic War in which the Romans destroyed the Carthaginian fleet off Sicily. It was Rome's first naval victory.

My Lai A village in S Vietnam, where a massacre of about 347 civilians by US soldiers took place (16 March, 1968) during the Vietnam War. The incident was only investigated after it had been disclosed by an ex-serviceman (1969) and provoked much criticism of the role of the USA in Vietnam.

Mylodon A genus of extinct South American ground sloths dating from the Pleistocene epoch (one million years ago). About 300 cm long, they had a specialized toe on the hind limb that was probably used for gripping branches or digging up tubers. *See also* Megatherium.

mynah A songbird belonging to a genus (*Acridotheres*) native to SE Asia. Mynahs usually have a dark plumage with bright wattles on the face. They feed chiefly on the ground and eat the insects found on cattle. The common mynah (*A. tristis*) lives in close proximity to man and has become a pest in some regions. The Chinese crested mynah (*A. cristatellus*) has been introduced to North America. Family: *Sturnidae* (starlings). *See also* hill mynah.

myocardial infarction Death of part of the heart muscle: the cause of what is popularly described as a heart attack.

This is the commonest cause of death in advanced societies and usually results from *atherosclerosis. The patient usually experiences sudden severe central chest pain, which may spread to the neck and arms and is usually accompanied by sweating and nausea. Most people who recover from heart attacks can eventually lead a full and active life: many have survived for as long as 40 years.

myopia. *See* shortsightedness.

Myrdal, Gunnar (1898–1987) Swedish sociologist and economist. Joint recipient of the 1974 Nobel Prize, Myrdal is best known for his study of the US racial problem, published as *An American Dilemma* (1944). His wife **Alva Myrdal** (1902–86) won the 1982 Nobel Peace Prize for her work for disarmament.

Myriapoda A group of terrestrial arthropods comprising the *centipedes, *millipedes, *pauropods, and *symphylids. They have elongated bodies and numerous walking legs.

Myrmidons A legendary Greek people from Thessaly. According to one legend, they originated on the island of Aegina when Zeus turned the ants (Greek *myrmex*, ant) into people. They are best known as the loyal warriors commanded by *Achilles in the Trojan War.

Myron (5th century BC) Athenian sculptor. His *Discus-Thrower* and *Marsyas*, described by ancient critics, are known through Roman copies. These free-standing figures show the new stances (made possible by the novel techniques of bronze working) that superseded the stylized poses derived from *kouros and *kore figures.

myrrh An aromatic yellow to red gum resin obtained from small tropical thorny trees of the genus *Commifera*, especially *C. myrrha*, *C. molmol*, and *C. abyssinica*, native to Africa and SW Asia. Myrrh exudes from the bark through slits and hardens on exposure to air. It is used in incense, perfumes, cosmetics, dentistry, and pharmaceuticals. Family: *Commiphoraceae*.

myrtle An evergreen shrub of the genus *Myrtus* (over 100 species). The common myrtle (*M. communis*), native to the Mediterranean area and W Asia, may grow to a height of 5 m. It has aromatic dark-green shiny leaves, fragrant five-petalled white flowers, 2–3 cm across, with numerous stamens, and blue-black berries. An oil obtained from the leaves, flowers, and fruit is used in perfumery. Family: *Myrtaceae*. Other plants known as myrtle include the *sweet gale.

Mysore 12 18N 76 37E A city in India, in Karnataka. Industries include textiles, chemicals, and food processing and it has a university (1916). Population (1981): 476 000.

mysteries Secret religious cults in the ancient Mediterranean world that revealed their mystical rites only to initiates and promised them a life after death. Their initiation ceremonies, of which the details are often vague, involved purification, assimilation of occult knowledge, and acting out a sacred drama. The Egyptian cult of *Isis, the Greek *Eleusinian and *Orphic mysteries, and Roman *Mithraism are the most famous.

mystery plays. *See* miracle plays.

mysticism Belief in a type of religious experience in which the individual claims to achieve immediate knowledge of or temporary union with God. Mysticism is an element in most theistic traditions and the validity of the experience is often claimed to be established by the similarity of the accounts by mystics from totally different cultures of their visions, trances, and ecstasies. The usual preliminary is strict *asceticism. Christianity insists that a mystic should demonstrate his spiritual grace by practical works of charity. St *Francis of Assisi, St *Catherine of Siena, St *Teresa of Avila, St *John of the Cross, and *Julian of Norwich are among the many famous Christian mystics. Official Church attitudes have alternated between regarding mysticism as a special spiritual grace and suspecting it of verging on *Gnosticism, *pantheism, *Neoplatonism, or simply dangerous individualism. *See also* Sufism.

mythology Imaginative poetic stories, traditions, etc., concerning religious beliefs, gods, and supernatural and heroic human beings. Mythology often involves a cosmogony—an attempted explanation of the origin of the universe, of mankind, or of a particular race or culture. The term also refers to the formal study of such stories, traditions, etc. Myths have been interpreted in several ways. One ancient theory, first advanced by the Greek Euhemerus (300 BC) and called euhemerism, holds that there is an element of historical truth in myths and that mythical characters are only kings or other heroes given the honour of deification by the populace. *Plato also adopted a critical view of Greek mythology because of its immorality and sought to introduce worthier ideals by inventing more rational myths. Anthropology and psychoanalysis have thrown new light on the function of myths. Among primitive peoples they serve to provide an explanation or justification for social institutions. They also appear to embody universal values or patterns with regard to human psychology, as in Freud's interpretation of the child's relationship to its parents in terms of the *Oedipus myth. The mythologies of particular cultures have provided the material of most of the world's great literature and art, as in Egypt, Greece and Rome, and in Hinduism.

Mytilene (Modern Greek name: Mitilíni) 39 06N 26 34E The chief town of the Greek island of Lesbos, on the Aegean Sea. It is a port trading chiefly in olive oil, citrus fruits, and cereals. Population (1981): 24 115.

myxoedema Underactivity of the *thyroid gland. Patients are slow, tired, dislike the cold, and have a slow pulse and reflexes. The skin may be thick and swollen. Myxoedema can be easily treated with thyroxine, the hormone produced by the thyroid gland.

myxomatosis An infectious disease of rabbits and hares that is caused by a virus. Symptoms include swollen eyes, nose, and muzzle, closed eyelids, and fever. The disease is usually fatal although some strains of rabbits show resistance. A vaccine is available to protect domestic rabbits. The disease was introduced to the UK and Australia during the 1950s as a pest-control measure.

Mzilikazi (c. 1790–1868) Zulu warrior, who in about 1840 founded the Matabele (*or* Ndebele) kingdom in S Rhodesia. A great military leader and an able administrator, Mzilikazi organized his new kingdom on military lines and withstood attacks from neighbouring tribes and from the Afrikaners. Not long after his death his kingdom, under his son *Lobengula, was overwhelmed by the Whites.

N

Naas (Irish name: Nás na Riogh) 53 13N 6 39W A town in the Republic of Ireland, the county town of Co Kildare. It is a centre for horse racing and hunting. Population (1981): 8345.

Nabis (Hebrew: prophets) A group of French artists formed in Paris in 1888. The leading members—Paul Sérusier (1863-1927), *Denis, *Bonnard, and *Vuillard—were united by their admiration for *Gauguin and Japanese prints. They applied their famous tenet that "a picture is ... essentially a flat surface covered by colours in a certain order" to their activities as painters, poster and stained-glass designers, book illustrators, etc., thus influencing many branches of art. They disbanded in 1899.

Nablus 32 13N 35 16E A town on the *West Bank of the River Jordan. Nablus is the Shechem of the Old Testament: Jacob's Well is nearby. Population (1984 est): 80 000.

Nabokov, Vladimir (1899-1977) US novelist. Born into an aristocratic Russian family, he was educated at Cambridge University and lived in France and Germany before emigrating to the USA in 1948. He achieved popular success with *Lolita* (1955), whose academic antihero lusts after young girls. His novels, noted for their elegant and witty word play, include *The Defence* (1930), one of several originally written in Russian, *Pale Fire* (1962), and *Ada* (1969). His other works include the autobiographical *Speak, Memory* (1967) and a translation of Pushkin's *Eugene Onegin* (4 vols, 1964).

nacre. *See* pearl.

Nadar (Gaspard Felix Tournachon; 1820-1910) French photographer, caricaturist, and writer, born in Paris. Although better known by his contemporaries as a novelist and essayist, his reputation now rests on his photographs of writers and artists, such as Baudelaire and Delacroix, and his pioneering aerial photographs taken from a balloon (1858).

Na-Dené languages An American Indian language group covering the northern USA, NW Canada, and Alaska. It includes the Athabascan, Tlingit, Haida, and Eyak subgroups. Athabascan is the largest group, with more than 20 languages, and is also the most widespread, extending from the Yukon almost to the US border. Another Athabascan subgroup, spoken on the N American Plains, includes *Navajo and several *Apache languages.

Nader, Ralph (1934–) US lawyer. His book, *Unsafe at Any Speed* (1965), which criticized the safety standards of the car industry, resulted in the passing of a car safety act in 1966. Among the many consumer issues he has investigated are advertising, nuclear power, and meat processing. He founded the Centre for the Study of Responsive Law in 1969.

Nader Shah (1688-1747) Shah of Persia (1736-47). Of Turkoman origin, he overthrew the Safavid dynasty to become shah. He had military successes but his internal policies led to many revolts. His attempt at introducing a new rite of Sunni Islam (*see* Sunnites) into Shiite Persia, and forcing his subjects to join it, failed. He was assassinated.

nadir. *See* zenith.

Naevius, Gnaeus (c. 270-c. 200 BC) Roman poet. He wrote a number of tragedies and comedies and an epic on the first Punic War, in which he related the mythical origins of Rome (making Romulus a grandson of the Trojan Aeneas). Only fragments of his work are extant.

naevus. *See* birthmark.

naga In Hindu mythology, one of a race of minor serpent deities inhabiting an underworld region called Patala, which is filled with gems. They are associated with water and may be regarded as demons and a possible source of evil, but are

NAGA   *A 10th-century sandstone panel from a temple in central India depicting a naga encircled by a 5-headed cobra.*

also worshipped as companions of the gods. □Vishnu is often portrayed sleeping on the naga Sesha, and there is a Buddhist legend of a naga raising the Buddha on its coils above a flood sent to prevent his attaining enlightenment. Nagas are variously depicted as half-snake and half-human, as many-headed cobras, or in human form posed beneath a canopy of cobras.

Nagaland A state in NE India, on the Burmese border. Mostly in the forested Naga Hills, it produces rice, other grains, pulses, sugar cane, and vegetables. Mahogany and other forest products are important. Local industries include weaving. *History*: after 1947 the Naga tribes resisted Indian rules as fiercely as they had Britain, winning statehood in 1963. Further talks with the Naga underground movement led to the Shillong Peace Agreement in November, 1975. Area: 16 527 sq km (6379 sq mi). Population (1981): 773 281. Capital: Kohima.

Nagarjuna (c. 150-c. 250 AD) Indian Buddhist monk and philosopher. Probably originally a brahmin from S India, he founded the Madhyamika (Middle Way) school of Mahayana Buddhism, noted for its highly intellectual approach to defining the nature of reality. Works attributed to him survive only in Tibetan and Chinese.

Nagasaki 32 45N 129 52E A port in Japan, in W Kyushu on the East China Sea. The first Japanese port to deal with European traders, it became a centre of Christianity following its introduction by the Portuguese in the 16th century. On 9 August, 1945, the second of the two atomic bombs used against Japan was dropped on Nagasaki, killing or wounding about 75 000 people, although the damage was not as extensive as at Hiroshima. Rapid rebuilding followed and the city is now an important centre of the shipbuilding industry. Its university was established in 1949. Population (1980): 447 000.

Nagorno-Karabakh An autonomous region (*oblast*) in the W Soviet Union, in the Azerbaidzhan SSR. It was formed in 1923 and its population comprises chiefly Azerbaidzhani and Armenians. It has metal and mineral deposits and supports many light industries but is chiefly agricultural: cotton, grapes, and wheat are grown. Area: 4400 sq km (1700 sq mi). Population (1981 est): 164 000. Capital: Stepanakert.

Nagoya 35 8N 136 53E A port in Japan, in SE Honshu on Ise Bay. The fourth largest city in the country, it was founded in 1610 and by World War II had developed into an important centre for the manufacture of aircraft and ammunition. It was largely rebuilt following heavy bombing in 1945 and its industries now include steel and textiles. Its universities were established in 1939 and 1950. Population (1980): 2 088 000.

Nagpur 21 10N 79 12E A city in India, in Maharashtra. Founded in the early 18th century, it fell under British control in 1853. It grew with the arrival of the Peninsula Railway (1867) and now has cotton, transport equipment, and metallurgical industries. Its university was established in 1923. Population (1981 est): 1 297 977.

Nagy, Imre (1896-1958) Hungarian statesman, who led the revolutionary government of 1956. As prime minister (1953-55) Nagy promised such reforms as an end to the forced development of heavy industry and agricultural collectivization, more consumer goods, occupational mobility, and the closure of labour camps. Opposed by Hungary's Stalinists, he was demoted and in 1956 expelled from the Communist Party. In the subsequent *Hungarian Revolution Nagy again became prime minister but was abducted by Soviet troops and executed.

Naha 26 10N 127 40E A port in Japan, the main city of the *Ryukyu Islands and capital of Okinawa. It is the site of the University of the Ryukyus. Population (1983): 302 000.

Nahuatl The most widely used American Indian language of the Uto-Aztecan family, spoken in Mexico. It was the language of the *Aztecs and *Toltecs. A distinctive characteristic is the extensive use of the *tl* sound. The Nahua people are slash-and-burn cultivators, growing maize, beans, tomatoes, and chilis. Crafts, especially weaving, are well developed. The Nahua are nominally Roman Catholic, but pagan beliefs continue to flourish.

Nahum An Old Testament prophet who predicted the imminent destruction of the Assyrian capital of Nineveh by the Medes in 612 BC. **The Book of Nahum** describes this event in detail and interprets it as divine retribution.

naiads In Greek mythology, a class of *nymphs or female spirits of nature associated with rivers, lakes, and springs.

Naipaul, V(idiadhur) S(urajprasad) (1932-) West Indian novelist. He was educated at Oxford and now lives in England. A witty ironic tone characterizes his early comic novels, such as *A House for Mr Biswas* (1961), concerning the life of the poor in his native Trinidad. His later more sombre novels include *In a Free State* (1971), *Guerrillas* (1975), and *A Bend in the River* (1979). He has also published two travel books and a history of Trinidad, *The Loss of El Dorado* (1969). Other works include *Among the Believers* (1981) and a collection of essays, *The Return of Eva Perón* (1980).

Nairn A former county of N Scotland. Under local government reorganization in 1975 it formed a new district of the same name, in the Highland Region.

Nairobi 1 17S 36 50E The capital of Kenya, situated on a plateau just S of the equator. It was founded as a trading and railway centre in the late 19th century. Its varied manufactures include chemicals, textiles, glass, and furniture. The Nairobi National Park lies on the city's outskirts. The University of Nairobi was established in 1970. Population (1985 est): 1 200 000.

naive art. *See* primitivism.

Najd (*or* Nejd) A province in Saudi Arabia, occupying the centre of the country. It is largely desert and much of the population is nomadic. Formerly an independent kingdom, it became part of Saudi Arabia in 1932. Area: about 1 100 000 sq km (424 621 sq mi). Population (1970 est): 4 000 000. Capital: Riyadh.

Nakhichevan Autonomous Soviet Socialist Republic An administrative division in the S Soviet Union, in the Azerbaidzhan SSR. It is populated mainly by Azerbaidzhani. The economy is predominantly agricultural, producing mainly cereals, cotton, and tobacco. Industries include textiles and food processing. Area: 5500 sq km (2120 sq mi). Population (1983 est): 257 000. Capital: Nakhichevan.

Nakuru 0 16S 36 04E A town in Kenya, on the N shore of Lake Nakuru. It has a large European community and is the trading centre of an agricultural area producing wheat, maize, and coffee. Population (1983 est): 101 700.

Namaqualand (*or* Namaland; Afrikaans name: Namakwaland) An arid coastal area in SW Africa, extending S from near Windhoek (Namibia) into Cape Province (South Africa), divided by the Orange River into Little Namaqualand (S) and Great Namaqualand (N). It is occupied chiefly by Namas (Hottentots) and has important diamond reserves.

Namib Desert A desert chiefly in W Namibia, extending some 1600 km (994 mi) along the Atlantic coast. It is arid and almost devoid of population.

Namibe (name until 1982: Moçâmedes) 15 09S 40 34E A port in SW Angola, on the Atlantic Ocean, noted for its fishing industry. Population (1982 est): 100 000.

Namibia (name until 1968: South West Africa) A territory in SW Africa, on the Atlantic Ocean. The narrow coastal plains of the Namib Desert rise to the central plateau, with the Kalahari Desert to the N. The Orange River forms its S boundary, and the Rivers Kunene and Okavango form part of its N boundary. The majority of the population is African, the largest group being the Ovambo. *Economy*: chiefly subsistence agriculture with emphasis on stock raising, and some dairy farming. Fishing is important, especially for pilchards. Rich mineral resources include diamonds (the main export), copper, lead, zinc, tin, vanadium, and uranium. Hydroelectricity is a valuable source of power. *History*: a German protectorate from 1884, during World War I it surrendered (1915) to South Africa, which administered South West Africa under a League of Nations mandate. In 1966 South Africa refused to acknowledge the declaration by the League's successor, the UN, that the mandate was at an end and has been condemned by both the UN and the South West Africa People's Organization (SWAPO) as illegally occupying the territory. A constitutional solution put forward by South Africa in 1976 proved unacceptable to SWAPO; in 1985 South Africa installed an interim administration as a step towards Namibian independence. Official languages: Afrikaans and English. Official currency: South African rand of 100 cents. Area: 824 269 sq km (318 261 sq mi). Population (1983 est): 1 018 000. Capital: Windhoek. Main port: Walvis Bay (an enclave of South Africa).

Namier, Sir Lewis Bernstein (1888-1960) British historian. Born in Poland, he emigrated to England (1906) and was professor of modern history at Manchester University (1931–53). Among his works on 18th-century politics is *The Structure of Politics at the Accession of George III* (1929).

Namur (Flemish name: Namen)   50 28N 04 52E A town in S Belgium, strategically positioned at the confluence of the Rivers Sambre and Meuse. It was besieged and captured many times. Notable buildings include the 18th-century cathedral. Its chief manufactures are glass, paper, and leather and steel goods. Population (1981 est): 100 670.

Nanaimo   49 08N 123 58W A city and port in W Canada, in British Columbia on the E coast of Vancouver Island. With the main ferry links to the mainland, it is Vancouver Island's distribution centre and the site of primary industries. Population (1983): 49 347.

Nanak   (1469–1539) Indian founder of *Sikhism. Born near Lahore, a member of the mercantile Hindu class he travelled within and perhaps beyond India, visiting both Hindu and Muslim centres in search of spiritual truth. He settled finally in Kartarpur, where he attracted a large community of disciples. His teachings are contained in a number of hymns, many of which are extant.

Nana Sahib   (Dandhu Panth; c. 1825–c. 1860) A leader of the *Indian Mutiny (1857). Adopted into a noble family, he led the revolt at Cawnpore, in which the British were massacred. When defeated in 1859 he was driven into the Himalayan foothills, where he probably died.

Nanchang   28 38N 115 56E A city in SE China, the capital of Jiangxi province and the site of its university. China's first commune was briefly established here in 1927. An ancient commercial centre, it has varied manufactures. Population (1983 est): 1 046 000.

Nancy   48 42N 6 12E A town in NE France, the capital of the Meurthe-et-Moselle department on the River Meurthe. The former capital of the Dukes of Lorraine, it passed to France in 1766. It has a fine collection of 18th-century buildings and is the site of a university (1572). Its varied industries include iron, salt, sodium, machinery, and textiles. Population (1982): 99 307.

Nanda Devi, Mount   30 21N 79 50E A mountain in NW India, close to the Tibetan border in the Himalayas. Height: 7817 m (25 645 ft).

Nanga Parbat, Mount   35 15N 74 36E A mountain in NE Pakistan, in the Himalayas. Height: 8126 m (26 660 ft).

Nanhai.   *See* South China Sea.

Nanjing (Nan-ching *or* Nanking)   32 05N 118 55E A port in E China, the capital of Jiangsu province on the Yangtze River. An ancient cultural centre, it was a Chinese capital (1368–1421, 1928–37) and the centre of the Taiping Rebellion (1851–64). The university was established in 1902. It is a centre of heavy industry. Population (1983 est): 2 130 000.

Nanking.   *See* Nanjing.

Nanning   22 50N 108 19E A city in S China, the capital of Guangxi Zhuang AR. The commercial centre of a rich agricultural area, it has many industries, including food processing and the manufacture of paper and agricultural machinery. Population (1983 est): 866 000.

Nansen, Fridtjof   (1861–1930) Norwegian explorer, zoologist, and statesman. In 1888 he led an expedition across the Greenland icefield and in 1893, in the *Fram*, specially designed to resist icepacks, set sail across the Arctic. He allowed the vessel to drift attached to an icefloe. In 1895, with F. J. Johansen (1867–1923), he left the ship and reached 18 14N, the nearest point to the North Pole then attained. He subsequently contributed greatly to the League of Nations, becoming its high commissioner for refugees in 1920; he pioneered the **Nansen passport**, an identification card for displaced persons (1922). He won the Nobel Peace Prize (1923).

Nantes   47 14N 1 35W A major port in W France, the capital of the Loire-Atlantique department on the Loire estuary. Its commercial importance dates back to Roman times and it was here that the Edict of Nantes was signed in 1598. It has a 15th-century cathedral and a university (1961). Its port is accessible to oceangoing vessels and its industries include shipbuilding, oil refining, and tanning. Population (1982): 247 227.

Nantes, Edict of   (1598) A decree that guaranteed the French Protestants (*see* Huguenots) religious liberty. The edict, proclaimed by Henry IV, established the principle of religious toleration; by permitting the Huguenots freedom of worship and limited civil equality, Henry hoped to prevent further wars of religion in France. The Edict was revoked in 1685 by Louis XIV.

Nantucket   An island in the USA, off the coast of SE Massachusetts. A former whaling centre, it is now chiefly a resort. Length: 24 km (15 mi). Width: 5 km (3 mi).

napalm   An inexpensive jelly consisting of a mixture of the aluminium salts of *na*pathenic acid and *palm*itic acid used to thicken petrol so that it can be used in incendiary bombs and flame-throwers. It was used in World War II, the Korean War, and in Vietnam. It ignites easily, burns at temperatures up to 1000°C, and is particularly effective against humans.

Naphtali, tribe of   One of the 12 *tribes of Israel. It claimed descent from Naphtali, the son of Jacob by his concubine Bilhah. Its territory was NW of the Sea of Galilee.

naphthalene ($C_{10}H_8$)   A white crystalline aromatic hydrocarbon that occurs in coal tar. It is used in the manufacture of dyes, synthetic resins, and mothballs. **Naphthol** ($C_{10}H_7OH$) is the hydroxy derivative. It consists of two isomers; the most important, beta-naphthol, is used in antioxidants for rubbers and dyes and in drugs.

Napier   39 29S 176 58E A port in New Zealand, in E North Island on Hawke Bay. It is the most important centre of New Zealand's wool trade. Population (1983 est): 49 200.

Napier, Sir Charles James   (1782–1853) British general and colonial administrator. After service in the Peninsular War (1808–10), against the USA (1813–14), in Greece (1822–30), and at home, he was sent (1841) to Sind (now in Pakistan). By 1843 he had gained control of the country and as governor (until 1847) he established a civil administration.

Napier, John   (1550–1617) Scottish mathematician, who invented *logarithms. In 1614 he published a table of logarithms to the base e, now known as Napierian logarithms. Logarithms to the base ten (common logarithms) were later adopted, following a suggestion by Henry *Briggs. Napier also produced an elementary calculating machine using a series of rods, known as **Napier's bones**.

Napier of Magdala, Robert Cornelis, 1st Baron   (1810–90) British field marshal. He fought in the *Sikh Wars in India (1845–49) and during the Indian Mutiny helped to relieve Lucknow (1857). In 1868 he led the expedition to release British diplomats imprisoned in Ethiopia, capturing Magdala.

Naples   (Italian name: Napoli; ancient name: Neapolis) 40 50N 14 15E A city in S Italy, the capital of Campania situated on volcanic slopes overlooking the Bay of Naples. It is an important port and a centre of commerce and tourism. As well as traditional industries, such as textiles, food processing, and oil refining, newer industries (including the manufacture of cars and ball bearings) have grown up in recent years as a result of central government assistance. Its many historic buildings include medieval castles, a gothic cathedral (13th–14th centuries), the 17th-century Royal Palace, and the university (1224). The National Museum houses remains from Pompeii and Herculaneum. *History*: founded by Greek colonists about 600 BC, it fell to Rome in 326 but retained its Greek culture. It was under Byzantine rule (6th–8th centuries AD) and in 1139 it became part of the Norman kingdom of Sicily. It prospered under Charles I, the first Angevin King of Sicily, who made Naples his capital. Following the revolt known as the *Sicilian Vespers (1282), the island of Sicily passed to the House of Aragon and the Italian peninsula S of the Papal States became known as the kingdom of Naples (with Naples as its capital) until it fell to Garibaldi (1860) and was united with the rest of Italy (see also Sicily). From this time Naples lagged economically behind the N, resulting in considerable poverty. The city suffered further hardships during World War II, when it was badly damaged. Central government assistance during the postwar period has led to improvements in roads, port installations, transport, and communications. Existing industries have been modernized and new industries added. Many thousands of its inhabitants, however, continue to live in slum conditions. Population (1980 est): 1 219 362.

NAPOLEON I   David's portrait (1821; Versailles) of the emperor crossing the Alps evokes the glory of the Napoleonic legend.

Napoleon I (1769–1821) Emperor of the French (1804–15). Born Napoleon Bonaparte in Corsica, he became an artillery officer and rose to prominence in 1795, when he turned the guns of the Paris garrison—"a whiff of grapeshot"—on a mob threatening the government of the National Convention. Shortly afterwards he married *Josephine de Beauharnais and in January, 1796, was appointed to command the French army in Italy (see Revolutionary and Napoleonic Wars). His Italian campaign (1796–97) took the army from the brink of defeat by the Austrians to the conquest of Milan and Mantua. After Sardinia, Naples, and the papacy had sued for peace Napoleon obtained the Directory's support for his plan to break British imperial power by conquering Egypt and India. In Egypt his great victory of the *Pyramids was undermined by Nelson's annihilation of a French fleet at the Battle of the *Nile (1798) and in 1799 he returned unobtrusively to France, where he joined a conspiracy against the tottering Directory. In the coup d'état of 18 Brumaire (9–10 November, 1799) he became first consul in a consulate formed on the Roman model; in 1802 he became consul for life and in 1804, emperor.

His outstanding domestic achievement was the legal codification, the *Code Napoléon, that remains the basis of French law, but Napoleon achieved immortality with his exploits abroad. He negotiated the Treaty of Lunéville (1801), which marked his defeat of the Austrians at *Marengo, and the Treaty of Amiens (1802) with the British; however, his designs upon Italy, Germany, and Switzerland led to a renewal of war in 1805. Despite the disaster at *Trafalgar (1805), which forced him to abandon his plan for the invasion of Britain, his land victories, especially at *Austerlitz (1805), *Jena (1806), and *Friedland (1806), drew almost every continental power within the French orbit.

Napoleon's supremacy was short lived. The *Continental System failed to break the British by blockade and the protracted *Peninsular War (1808–14) drained French resources. In 1812 Napoleon invaded an increasingly recalcitrant Russia with half a million men, of whom nearly 400 000 died in the brutal Russian winter. In 1813 Europe rose against Napoleon, inflicting a massive defeat at Leipzig that forced his abdication and subsequent exile to Elba, of which he was given sovereignty. In 1815, however, he escaped, returned to a rapturous welcome in France, and attempted in the *Hundred Days to regain his former greatness. He suffered a decisive defeat at *Waterloo and spent the remainder of his life confined to the island of St Helena. Napoleon's claim to the French Crown was pursued after his death by the son of his second marriage, to Marie Louise of Austria (see Napoleon II), and then by his nephew, Emperor *Napoleon III. See also Bonaparte.

Napoleon II (1811–32) The title accorded by supporters of the Bonapartist claim to the French throne to the son of Napoleon I and Empress Marie Louise. At birth entitled King of Rome, he was brought up, after his father's fall (1814), in Austria, with the title Duke of Reichstadt.

Napoleon III (1808–73) Emperor of the French (1852–70); son of Louis Bonaparte and Hortense de Beauharnais and nephew of Napoleon I. Pretender to the French throne during the reign of Louis Philippe (1830–48), Napoleon used the enormous prestige of his name to win the presidential election after the Revolution of 1848. By a coup d'état at the end of 1851, he dissolved the legislative assembly and, a year later, declared himself emperor. His domestic policies fostered industry and, with the planning work of Baron *Haussmann, transformed the face of Paris. Abroad, his diplomacy embroiled France in the Crimean War (1854–56), in war against the Austrians in Italy (1859), and in a desultory conflict in Mexico (1861–67). Finally, his aggressive stance towards Bismarck helped to cause the *Franco-Prussian War, in which the Second Empire was destroyed and Napoleon was driven into exile.

Napoleonic Code. See Code Napoléon.

Napoleonic Wars. See Revolutionary and Napoleonic Wars.

Nara 34 41N 135 49E A city in Japan, in S Honshu. Japan's first capital (710–84 AD), it contains many historic monuments, including a bronze Buddha 16 m (72 ft) high. Population (1983 est): 316 924.

Narayan, R(asipuram) K(rishnaswamy) (1906–) Indian novelist and short-story writer. Writing in English and setting his stories in Malgudi, an imaginary version of his hometown Mysore, Narayan drew upon his experiences as a teacher for his first novel, Swami and Friends (1935). Later works, such as The Financial Expert (1952), The Man-Eater of Malgudi (1961), Under the Banyan Tree (1985), and numerous short stories are witty and ironic portrayals of Indian daily life.

Narayanganj 23 36N 90 28E A city in Bangladesh, the chief riverport of Dhaka. It is a major trading centre and together with Dhaka forms the largest industrial region in the country. Population (1981 est): 196 139.

Narbonne 43 11N 3 00E A market town in SE France, in the Aude department. An important Roman settlement, it was formerly a port (silted up in the 14th century). Population (1982): 42 657.

Narcissus (botany) A genus of perennial herbaceous plants (about 40 species), native to Eurasia and N Africa and widely planted in gardens and parks. Growing from bulbs, they produce strap-shaped or rushlike leaves and erect flower stalks, usually up to 30 cm high. The flowers are usually yellow, orange, or white, with a ring of petal-like segments surrounding a central crown. The *daffodils (*N. pseudonarcissus*) have large solitary yellow flowers with trumpet-shaped crowns; the sweet-scented jonquils (*N. jonquilla*) have clusters of smaller pale-yellow flowers with small cuplike crowns; and the poet's narcissus (*N. poeticus*) has solitary flowers with white petals surrounding a short fringed orange-tipped crown. Family: *Amaryllidaceae*.

Narcissus (Greek mythology) A beautiful youth who was punished for rejecting the love of the nymph Echo by being made to fall in love with his own reflection in a pool. He died and was transformed into a flower.

narcotics Drugs that cause stupor or sleep and relieve pain by depressing activity of the brain. The term is used particularly for *opium and its derivatives (opiates), including morphine and codeine. Synthetic narcotics include heroin, methadone, and pethidine. The main medical use of narcotics is for the relief of severe pain, but their use is strictly controlled by law in most countries because they carry the risk of *drug dependence. The term narcotics is also used more loosely for any addictive drug.

Narita 35 46N 140 20E A town in Japan, NE of Tokyo in central Honshu. It is the site of an international airport, which was for several years the scene of angry protests by the local farming population, student groups, and environmentalists; although completed in 1972 it did not become operational until May, 1978. Population (1980): 68 418.

Narraganset An Algonkian-speaking North American Indian people of Rhode Island. They were a woodland people who cultivated maize, hunted, and fished. There were eight divisions of the Narraganset, each headed by a chief. In 1675, after wars with White settlers, they were dispersed.

Narragansett Bay A bay in the USA, in SE Rhode Island state. It contains many islands including Rhode Island, Prudence Island, and Conanicut Island.

Narses (c. 480–574 AD) Byzantine general. Originally a slave in Emperor *Justinian I's household, Narses rose to become the emperor's confidant. In 551 he replaced *Belisarius as commander in Italy. He recaptured Rome and eventually subdued the Ostrogoths, governing Italy until 567.

Narva 59 22N 28 17E A port in the W Soviet Union, in the Estonian SSR on the River Narva near the Gulf of Finland. Peter the Great was defeated by the Swedes in a famous battle here in 1700. It is an important textile centre and has food-processing industries. Population (1983 est): 78 000.

Narvik 68 26N 17 25E An ice-free port in N Norway. Two naval battles between the British and Germans were fought here in 1940 and the port was occupied by the Allies from 10 May until 9 June. It exports iron ore from the Kiruna-Gällivare mines in N Sweden. Population (1983 est): 19 080.

narwhal A gregarious Arctic toothed *whale, *Monodon monoceros*, up to 5 m long and feeding on fish and squid. Male narwhals have a long straight spirally twisted tusk that is derived from a tooth and grows to a length of 3 m; its function is unknown. Family: *Monodontidae*.

NASA (National Aeronautics and Space Administration) The US civilian agency, formed in 1958, that is responsible for all nonmilitary aspects of the US space programme. Its major projects have included the manned *Apollo moon programme, *Skylab, reusable *space shuttles, and successful *planetary probes. In addition it has launched many artificial *satellites belonging to the USA and other nations.

Naseby, Battle of (14 June, 1645) The battle in the English Civil War that decided Charles I's defeat. The *New Model Army under Fairfax and Oliver Cromwell routed Prince *Rupert's royalist forces at Naseby, near Market Harborough, Leicestershire, and in the following year Charles surrendered.

Nash, John (1752–1835) British architect of the Regency period. An unsuccessful speculative builder in London, he went bankrupt in 1783 and retired to Wales. There he built up a new practice as an architect specializing in large country houses. Returning to London at the end of the century, he attracted the patronage of the Prince of Wales (later George IV). When the prince became regent (1811) he employed Nash to redevelop parts of London. Central to Nash's plan was the laying out of Marylebone Park (later called Regent's Park) as a formal park surrounded by curved terraces of houses with stucco façades. Regent's Street (1825) was designed to link the park with Westminster. Nash's colonnades were removed later but his All Souls, Langham Place, remains. In London Nash also built Carlton House Terrace (1833), laid out Trafalgar Square and St James's Park (1829), and redesigned *Buckingham Palace with the triumphal Marble Arch (1828) as its gateway (it was moved to its present position in 1851). In *Brighton he redesigned the Royal Pavilion for the king as an oriental fantasy. His career ended with the death of the king.

Nash, Ogden (1902–71) US humorous writer. He wrote witty comments on social and domestic life expressed in doggerel verse. He contributed to the *New Yorker* magazine, and his books include *Free Wheeling* (1931), *I'm a Stranger Here Myself* (1938), *You Can't Get There From Here* (1957), *Collected Verse* (1961), and *Marriage Lines* (1964). He collaborated with Kurt Weill and S. J. Perelman on the musical *One Touch of Venus* (1943).

Nash, Paul (1889–1946) British painter. After studying at the Slade School, he became known for his symbolic war landscapes during World Wars I and II, the finest example being *Totes Meer* (1940–41; Tate Gallery). Nash was also a leading member of Unit One (1933), a group of artists, including Barbara *Hepworth and Henry *Moore, dedicated to promoting modern art (particularly *abstract art) in the UK. His brother **John Nash** (1893–1977) produced fine watercolour landscapes and botanical illustrations.

Nash, Richard (1674–1762) English gentleman, known as Beau Nash. In 1705 his fondness for gambling led him to Bath, where he became Master of Ceremonies and which he developed into the most fashionable spa town in England. He opposed duelling, smoking, and casual clothes.

Nash, Sir Walter (1882–1968) New Zealand statesman; Labour prime minister (1957–60). Born in Britain, he introduced successful anti-Depression policies while minister of finance (1934–49) and was also a member of the Pacific War Council (1942–44).

Nashe, Thomas (1567–c. 1601) British pamphleteer and dramatist. In *Pierce Penilesse* (1592) and other satiric pamphlets he attacked the Puritans and defended the theatres against them. Among other works are the comic masque *Summer's Last Will and Testament* (1592) and the pioneering picaresque novel *The Unfortunate Traveller* (1594). He collaborated with Ben Jonson and others on the satirical play *The Isle of Dogs* (1597).

Nashville 36 10N 86 50W A city in the USA, the capital of Tennessee on the Cumberland River. Founded in 1779, it is the site of Vanderbilt University (1873) and is a major centre for religious education. A centre of the recording industry for country and western music, the Country and Western Music Hall of Fame and Museum are situated here. Since the 1930s, cheap electric power from the Tennessee Valley Authority has made it an important commercial and industrial city. Industries include railway engineering, glass, printing and publishing, and clothing. Population (1980): 455 651.

Nasik 20 00N 73 52E A city in India, in Maharashtra on the River Godavari. It is a major Hindu pilgrimage centre. Industries include printing and distilling. Population (1981): 429 000.

Nassau A former duchy, now in Hesse and Rheinland-Pfalz (West Germany). In 1544 William the Silent, Count of Nassau, inherited the principality of *Orange, thus linking the two states. Nassau joined Napoleon's Confederation of the Rhine in 1806 and in 1866 came under Prussia.

Nassau 25 2N 77 25W The capital of the Bahamas, a port on New Providence Island. Built in 1729, it is an important tourist centre. Population (1982 est): 135 000.

Nasser, Gamal Abdel (1918–70) Egyptian statesman; prime minister (1954–56) and president (1956–70). An army officer, he helped to found the nationalist Free Officers group, which overthrew the monarchy in 1952. He became prime minister and then president of the Republic of Egypt (United Arab Republic from 1958). His nationalization of the Suez Canal led to an unsuccessful Israeli and Anglo-French attack on Egypt (1956), after which he was established as a leader of the Arab world. His socialist and Arab nationalist policies brought him into frequent conflict with the West and the more conservative Arab states.

Nasser, Lake. *See* Aswan High Dam.

nasturtium An annual garden plant of the genus *Tropaeolum* (90 species), also called Indian cress, native to Central and South America. It has round parasol-like leaves with central stalks, and orange, yellow, pink, or red flowers, which are funnel-shaped with a long spur containing nectar. *T. majus* is the most popular ornamental species and its seeds may be used in salads. The canary creeper (*T. peregrinum*) has twining leaf-stalks. Family: *Tropaeolaceae*.

Natal 5 46S 35 15W A port in NE Brazil, the capital of Rio Grande do Norte state near the mouth of the Rio Potengi. The chief exports are sugar, cotton, and carnauba wax; industries include salt refining and textiles. It has a university (1958). Population (1980): 376 552.

Natal The smallest province in South Africa. The land rises sharply from the Indian Ocean in the E to the Drakensberg Mountains in the W. Economic growth has been rapid. Agriculture and forestry are important. Along the coast sugar cane is the major crop and inland pine, eucalyptus, and wattle plantations supply the timber and paper industries. Other products are tropical fruits, maize, and beef and dairy cattle. Industries include shipping, food processing, chemicals, and sugar and oil refining. Durban is the main industrial centre and port. Coal is the chief mineral. *History*: the Boers attempted to establish a republic in Natal (1838) but this was annexed by Britain in 1843 and with additions became a province of the Union of South Africa (1910). Area: 86 967 sq km (33 578 sq mi). Population (1980): 2 676 340. Capital: Pietermaritzburg.

Nataraja In Hinduism, *Shiva in his aspect as lord of the cosmic dance, which symbolizes constant creation and dissolution. During the middle ages, in imitation of this dance, dancing became an important part of temple ritual.

Natchez A Muskogean-speaking North American Indian tribe of the Lower Mississippi. They were cultivators who, like the *Creeks, built mound temples and worshipped the sun. They were ruled by a despotic chief known as the Great Sun and had an elaborate system of social classes. The highest caste, the "suns," were obliged to marry members of the lowest caste, the commoners.

National Aeronautics and Space Administration. *See* NASA.

national anthem The official patriotic song of a country, sung or played on ceremonial occasions. The British national anthem, "God Save the King," was adopted in the mid-18th century. Its musical origin is much earlier and its authorship is unknown.

National Book League A British society founded in 1925 to promote general interest in books. As well as providing library and information facilities, it publishes book lists, organizes exhibitions, and administers literary prizes, notably the annual Booker Prize for fiction.

National Country Party An Australian political party, formed in 1919 as the Country Party, that represents the interests of farmers. It has held office only in coalition with the *Liberal Party. Since 1971 it has been led by John Douglas Anthony (1929–).

national debt The money that a government borrows; together with the revenue from *taxation it makes up the government's income. In the UK, the internal debt consists of two parts, the funded debt and the unfunded debt. The funded debt consists of money that the government does not have to repay on a fixed date (e.g. war loan); it makes up about 10% of the national debt. The unfunded debt consists of the floating debt (e.g. treasury bills), *gilt-edged securities, and such small savings as Savings Bonds. Money borrowed as unfunded debt has to be repaid on a fixed date. The external debt consists mainly of money borrowed from the USA and Canada after World War II. In the USA the national debt is known as the public debt.

National Economic Development Council (NEDC *or* Neddy) A UK body set up in 1962 to advise the government on economic policy, particularly with a view to increasing economic growth. Its members are drawn from government, industry, and trade unions. The **Economic Development Committees**, set up under its management, study particular industries.

National Enterprise Board (NEB) A UK body set up in 1975 to promote industrial efficiency. Given access to £1 billion, it made investments in British Leyland and other firms. In 1981 it merged with the National Research and Development Corporation to form the British Technology Group.

National Front An extreme right-wing political party in the UK, formed in 1966. In May, 1979, it polled only 1.6% of the total vote with its 303 candidates.

National Gallery An art gallery in Trafalgar Square (London), containing the largest collection of paintings in the UK. Founded for the nation in 1824, it originally contained only 38 paintings, bought by parliament from the merchant John Julius Angerstein (1735–1823). These and others added subsequently were housed in a building in Pall Mall until William Wilkins (1778–1839) built the present premises (1832–38). A proposed extension of the building has caused considerable controversy.

National Health Service (NHS) A comprehensive medical service in the UK, financed primarily by national government and local taxation. The National Health Service Act (1946), implemented in 1948, covered all aspects of health care except that of the school child, which was primarily the responsibility of the local education authorities, and that of the worker, which was covered by a series of Factory Acts. Progress was slow during its first ten years with a virtual ban on the building of new hospitals and little relocation of adequate resources to areas of deprivation. It also became apparent that Aneurin Bevan's initial hope that the Service would be a self-eliminating expense was based on a fallacy. The success of the Service in keeping people alive into old age and new treatments resulting from advances in medical science have caused costs to escalate. Complaints during the late 1950s and 1960s that the structure and policies of the NHS did not facilitate medical advance led to substantial reorganization of the Service in 1974 and again in 1982. In England and Wales overall responsibility lies with the secretary of state for the social services. Administration is based on a system of delegation downwards and accountability upwards through a hierarchy of Regional Health Authorities (RHAs) and District Health Authorities (DHAs). In Scotland and Northern Ireland responsibility lies with the appropriate secretary of state and administration with Area Health Boards.

National Insurance A compulsory UK insurance scheme providing funds to pay for the National Health Service and *social security benefits. Benefits are related to contributions, unlike supplementary benefits, which are paid from state funds on the basis of need. Contributions from employees, employers, the self-employed, and the government are paid into the National Insurance Fund, from which the benefits (including unemployment, sickness, maternity, and child benefits as well as retirement pensions) are paid. Lloyd George introduced old-age pensions in 1908 and sickness and unemployment benefits in 1911. Plans for a comprehensive insurance scheme, however, first appeared in the *Beveridge Report (1942), becoming law in the National Insurance Act (1946).

nationalism A doctrine that claims to determine the unit of population entitled to have government of its own. In its revolutionary form it regards existing state boundaries as arbitrary. The doctrine developed in Europe around 1800. The Latin word *Natio* had simply meant a group, regardless of frontiers, as in *Montesquieu's reference to monks as the "pietistic nation." After the French Revolution nationalists, such as *Fichte and *Mazzini, sought to make the boundaries of states coextensive with those of national habitation. Nations were supposed to be recognizable by certain distinguishing characteristics—for Fichte this was the use of a particular language. *Kant's doctrine of the autonomy of the will was used to provide philosophical backing for nationalism. While it was hoped that nationalism would make for peace, nationalistic aspirations in practice have often resulted in xenophobia, rivalry, and war.

nationalization The policy of taking into public ownership industries that were formerly privately owned. Nationalization is the aim of *socialism. In the UK after World War II, *Attlee's Labour government (1945–51) nationalized the "commanding heights" of the economy: those industries in which competition appeared wasteful (e.g. the gas and electricity supplies) and those war-damaged enterprises needing huge injections of capital (e.g. coal, railways). In the 1980s Thatcher's Conservative government reversed the trend, returning several industries to the private sector to restore competition and efficiency. *See* privatization.

National Parks Areas that are set aside to be maintained as far as possible in their natural state. In England and Wales National Parks were first established in 1949. The ten parks (in England, Dartmoor, Exmoor, Lake District, Northumberland, North York Moors, Peak District, and Yorkshire Dales and, in Wales, Brecon Beacons, Pembrokeshire Coast, and Snowdonia) are the responsibility of the Countryside Commission (established in 1968). In the USA the National Park Service (established in 1916) is responsible for 38 national parks, the largest of which is *Yellowstone National Park. The many Australian National Parks include the *Simpson Desert and the Kosciusko National Park.

National Physical Laboratory An establishment financed by the UK government, founded in 1900 at Teddington, Middlesex, which carries out research and special investigations into subjects connected with physics and monitors standards of measurements.

National Portrait Gallery An art gallery in London founded in 1856 to house portraits that are authentic likenesses of famous personalities in British history. Its collection includes works by Holbein, Rubens, Reynolds, and Augustus John and an increasing number of photographs. The main gallery is in St Martin's Place, adjacent to the National Gallery, and there are annexes in Carlton House Terrace and at Montacute House, Somerset.

National Service. *See* conscription.

National Socialist German Workers' Party. *See* Nazi Party.

National Society for the Prevention of Cruelty to Children (NSPCC) A British charity, incorporated in 1884, that investigates reports of cruelty to or neglect of children. In 1986 its annual caseload was 30 000 cases. Its inspectors work closely with the social services and the Society also runs over 70 playgroups of its own in the UK; in 1974 it established the National Advisory Centre on the Battered Child.

National Theatre Company A British government-subsidized theatre company established in 1963. Sir Laurence *Olivier, its first director, was succeeded by (Sir) Peter *Hall in 1973 and Richard Eyre in 1987. The company's new building, designed by Sir Denys Lasdun and opened in 1976, comprises an open-stage theatre called the Olivier, a proscenium-stage theatre called the Lyttelton, and a studio theatre for experimental plays called the Cottesloe.

National Trust An independent charity in the UK, founded in 1895, that acquires and preserves country houses (e.g. Knole, Kent), castles (e.g. Bodiam, East Sussex), gardens (e.g. Hidcote, Gloucestershire), and places of interest or natural beauty. Properties bequeathed to the Trust are exempt from *inheritance tax but to be accepted by the Trust they must be self-supporting or accompanied by an endowment.

Nation of Islam. *See* Black Muslims.

NATO. *See* North Atlantic Treaty Organization.

Natron, Lake 2 20S 36 05E A lake in N Tanzania, in the *Great Rift Valley. It measures about 56 km (30 mi) by 24 km (15 mi) and contains salt and soda.

natterjack A short-legged European *toad, *Bufo calamita*. About 7 cm long when fully grown, the natterjack has a yellow stripe down its back. It runs in a series of short spurts and if alarmed raises its inflated body on its hind legs to appear larger to the enemy.

natural gas A naturally occurring mixture of gaseous hydrocarbons consisting mainly of methane with smaller amounts of heavier hydrocarbons. It is obtained from underground reservoirs, often associated with *oil deposits. Like oil it originates in the bacterial decomposition of animal matter. It is a relatively cheap effective fuel, although in short supply (the present known reserves will be exhausted early next century). It also contains nonhydrocarbon impurities, the most important being helium, which is extracted commercially. It has to a large extent replaced coal gas in town gas supplies.

Natural History Museum. *See* British Museum.

Naturalism A literary and artistic movement of the late 19th century characterized by the use of realistic techniques to express the philosophical belief that all phenomena can be explained by natural or material causes. It was influenced by the biological theories of *Darwin, the philosophy of *Comte, and the deterministic theories of the historian *Taine. Its literary manifesto was *Le Roman expérimentale* (1880) by *Zola, whose sequence of 20 novels known as *Le Rougon-Macquart* (1871–93) was intended to demonstrate, by its concentration on the history of a single family, how human life is determined by heredity and environment. Writers influenced by Naturalism include the dramatists *Hauptmann, *Ibsen, *Strindberg, and, in the 20th century, the US novelist Theodore *Dreiser. Its influence is also apparent in the work of such painters as *Courbet and *Van Gogh.

naturalization In law, the process by which an *alien, on taking an oath of allegiance, acquires the rights of a natural-born citizen of a country. In the UK, the requirements for naturalization are governed by the British Nationality Act (1981) and include a period of residence or service abroad with the Crown, good character, a knowledge of English, and the intention to reside in the UK or to be in the service abroad of the Crown or a UK company.

natural selection. *See* Darwinism.

Naukratis (*or* Naucratis) An ancient town on the W side of the Nile delta in Egypt. A community of Greek traders with considerable autonomy flourished here by permssion of the pharaohs from the 7th century BC.

Nauplia (Modern Greek name: Návplion) 37 34N 22 48E A port in S Greece, in the E Peloponnese. It was the capital of Greece from 1829 to 1834. Exports include fruit, vegetables, tobacco, and cotton. Population (1981): 10 609.

Nauru, Republic of (*or* Naoero; former name: Pleasant Island) A small country in the central Pacific Ocean, NE of Australia comprising a coral island. The small population consists mainly of Naurians and other Pacific islanders. *Economy*: based entirely on the mining of phosphates, the only export. Deposits are expected to run out in the 1990s, but it is hoped to derive sufficient revenue by developing the island as a transport centre and tax haven. *History*: discovered by the British in 1798, it was under British mandate from 1920 to 1947, when it came under the joint trusteeship of Australia, New Zealand, and the UK. In 1968 it became an independent republic and a special member. of the British Commonwealth, with Hammer De-Roburt (1922–) as its first president. Replaced by Bernard Dowigogo (1946–) in 1976, DeRoburt was re-elected in 1978. In 1983 he was forced to resign after defeats in a libel suit and over the issue of the dumping of nuclear waste in the Pacific, but was re-elected 4 days later. Official language: English. Official currency: Australian dollar. Area: 21 sq km (8 sq mi). Population (1983 est): 8000. Capital and main port: Yaren.

Nausicaa In Greek legend, the daughter of Alcinous, King of Phaeacia. She gave help to the shipwrecked *Odysseus, and was offered by her father in marriage, but Odysseus, loyal to his wife, refused.

nautical mile. *See* mile.

nautilus One of several cephalopod molluscs with external shells. The pearly nautiluses (genus *Nautilus*; 3 species) live near the bottom of the Pacific and Indian Oceans. Up to 20 cm across, they have 60–90 tentacles surrounding a horny beak and live in the outermost chamber of their flat coiled shells. The others serve as buoyancy chambers from which gases can be absorbed, thus enabling the animals to float at different depths. The paper nautilus (*Argonauta argo*) is found in the Atlantic and Pacific Oceans. The female, 20 cm long, secretes from one of its tentacles a papery boat-shaped shell in which the eggs are laid and fertilized and develop. The male is much smaller (about 2 cm long).

Navajo A North American Indian Athabascan-speaking people of New Mexico, Arizona, and Utah. Like their relatives, the *Apache, they migrated from the far north, probably during the 17th century. Unlike the Apache, they learned farming and adopted many traits from the *Pueblo Indians. Their social organization is based on the matrilineal principle and they live in small dispersed settlements. They are farmers and herders and now the most numerous North American Indian tribe.

Navarino, Battle of (20 October, 1827) A naval battle arising from European intervention on behalf of Greece in the War of *Greek Independence from the Ottoman Empire. French, Russian, and British ships destroyed the Ottoman-Egyptian fleet in the Bay of Navarinou in the Peloponnese. This was the last fleet action fought wholly under sail.

Navarre A former kingdom in N Spain, corresponding to the present-day Spanish province of Navarre and part of the French department of Basses-Pyrénées. Known as Pampalona until the late 12th century, it was ruled by Muslims until the late 9th century, when a Basque dynasty established control over the kingdom. In 1234 it passed to a French dynasty but in 1512 S Navarre was conquered by Ferdinand the Catholic of Aragon

and united with Castile in 1515. French Navarre passed to the French Crown in 1589.

navel A depression in the centre of the abdomen that represents the site of attachment of the *umbilical cord of the fetus. Its medical name is the umbilicus. Occasionally babies are born with an umbilical hernia, in which the intestines protrude through the navel.

Navigation Acts A series of Acts originally to foster English shipping (1382, 1485, 1540) but subsequently to protect England's colonial trade, especially against its Dutch rivals. During the Commonwealth (1649–53) two ordinances (1650, 1651) respectively banned foreign trading in the colonies and restricted such trade to English or colonial ships, manned by predominantly English crews. These and similar Acts of 1660, 1672, and 1696 were repealed in 1849.

Navratilova, Martina (1956–) Czech-born tennis player who defected to the USA in 1975. She was Wimbledon singles champion in 1978, 1979, and 1982–86 and doubles champion in 1976, 1979, and 1981–86. She also holds a record of 74 consecutive wins.

navy A nation's warships (*see* ships), together with their crews and supporting administration. Navies were built by the ancient Greek city states at first to protect their Mediterranean trade routes from pirates and later to undermine the sea power of their rivals and enemies. The first recorded sea battle took place between Corinth and Corcyra (*or* Corfu) in 664 BC and navies—typically comprising triremes—played an important part in both the Greek-Persian and Peloponnesian Wars. The first permanent naval administration was organized (311 BC) in ancient Rome, which was the supreme Mediterranean power by the early 2nd century BC (*see* Punic Wars). Rome's naval power passed after the collapse of the western Empire in the 5th century AD to the Byzantine (Eastern Roman) Empire. Meanwhile, the Vikings marauded northern waters, provoking Alfred the Great of England to create (9th century) the origins of the *Royal Navy. The later middle ages saw the rise of Italian navies, outstandingly those of Venice and Genoa, and the decline of the Byzantine fleet, under the threat of the Ottoman Turks. By 1571, when, at Lepanto, the Turkish control of the Mediterranean was finally destroyed, Spain had emerged as the supreme naval power. England's defeat of the Spanish *Armada (1588) anticipated its subsequent emergence as a great naval power: by the late 17th century it had overtaken the Netherlands (*see* Dutch Wars) and by the early 19th century, France (*see* Revolutionary and Napoleonic Wars). British naval supremacy was threatened in the early 20th century by the German navy, which in spite of defeat in World War I again became a power to be reckoned with in the 1930s. By the end of World War II command of the seas had passed to the US navy. The navies of the USA and the Soviet Union now dominate the seas and with their nuclear-powered missile-armed submarines also dominate most of the earth's surface. *See also* Admiralty, Board of; Royal Marines.

Naxalites An extremist communist movement centring on the town of Naxalbari in W Bengal (India). Dedicated to Maoist principles, it attempted a violent seizure of land for the landless in 1967.

Náxos A Greek island in the S Aegean Sea, the largest in the Cyclades. Náxos is traditionally the place where Theseus abandoned Ariadne. It was an ancient centre of the worship of Dionysius. Area: 438 sq km (169 sq mi). Population (1981): 14 037. Chief town: Náxos.

Nazareth 32 41N 35 16E A town in N Israel, between Haifa and the Sea of Galilee. The chief attractions of the city are the many churches, which commemorate its associations with the early life of Jesus Christ. Population (1982 est): 44 900.

Nazi Party (*N*ationalso*zi*alistische Deutsche Arbeiterpartei) The National Socialist German Workers' Party, founded in

NAZI PARTY *Hitler's exploitation of the techniques of mass propaganda, notably at party rallies such as the one pictured here, helps explain his rise to power in prewar Germany.*

1919 as the German Workers' Party and led from 1921 until his suicide in 1945 by Adolf *Hitler. *See also* fascism.

Nazirites (*or* Nazarites) In the Old Testament, a group of Israelites who consecrated themselves to God by taking special vows, originally perhaps for life but later for a certain period only. The vows were to abstain from wine, not to cut the hair, and to avoid contact with dead bodies. Samson and Samuel were Nazirites from birth.

N'djamena (name until 1973: Fort Lamy) The capital of Chad, a port in the SW on the River Chari. It was founded by the French in 1900. The University of Chad was established in 1971. Population (1983): 225 000.

Ndola 13 00S 28 39E A city in N Zambia, near the Zaïre border. It is an important commercial and distribution centre for the *Copperbelt and has copper and cobalt refineries. Population (1980 est): 323 000.

Neagh, Lough A lake in Northern Ireland, divided between Co Antrim, Co Armagh, and Co Tyrone. It is the largest lake in the British Isles. Area: 388 sq km (150 sq mi).

Neanderthal man An extinct *hominid race that inhabited Europe and the adjacent areas of Africa and Asia between about 115 000 and 40 000 years ago. Characterized by heavy brow ridges, receding forehead, heavy protruding jaw, and robust bone structure, Neanderthal man nonetheless had a large cranial capacity and upright posture. They were cave-dwelling hunters who made tools and buried their dead in a manner implying some sort of cult and ritual (*see* Mousterian). Their status as a distinct species (*Homo neanderthalensis*) is now questioned and some palaeontologists prefer to see them as a subspecies of *Homo sapiens* (*see* Homo).

neap tide A □tide of comparatively small range that occurs near the time of the moon's quarters. The range falls below the average range by 10 to 30% (high low tides and low high tides). *Compare* spring tide.

Nebraska A state in the N central USA, lying W of the Missouri River. Part of the Central Lowlands cover the eastern third of the state, with the higher Great Plains in the W. Traditionally an agricultural state, it is still a leading producer of cattle, corn, and wheat. Most of the population is situated in the industrial E. Food processing (especially meat) is a major industry; machinery, fabricated metal, transport equipment, chemicals, and printing and publishing are also important. *History*: explored by the French and Spanish, it formed part of the Louisiana Purchase (1803). It became a state in 1867 and, with the arrival of the railways in the same year, it began to develop

rapidly as a cattle-ranching region. Area: 200 018 sq km (77 227 sq mi). Population (1980): 1 570 006. Capital: Lincoln.

Nebuchadnezzar II (*or* Nebuchadrezzar; c. 630–562 BC) King of *Babylon (605–562). Nebuchadnezzar defeated the Egyptians at Carchemish (605 BC) and extended Babylonian power in Elam, N Syria, and S Asia Minor. He captured Jerusalem in 597 and again in 586, when he destroyed the city and forced the Jews into exile (*see* Babylonian Exile). He restored Babylon to its former glory. Daniel's story of his madness is probably unhistorical.

nebula A cloud of interstellar gas and dust that becomes visible for one of three reasons. In an **emission nebula** the gas is ionized by ultraviolet radiation, generally from a hot star within the cloud; the ions interact with free electrons in the cloud, and light (predominantly red and green) is emitted. In a **reflection nebula** light from a nearby star is reflected in all directions by dust in the cloud, thus illuminating the cloud. The dust in a **dark nebula** reduces quite considerably the amount of light passing through it (by absorption and scattering) and a dark region is seen against a brighter background.

NEBULA *The Orion nebula, one of the brightest emission nebulae.*

Neckar, River A river in SW West Germany, flowing mainly N from the Black Forest past Stuttgart and Heidelberg to join the River Rhine at Mannheim. Length: 394 km (245 mi).

Necker, Jacques (1732–1804) French statesman. A successful banker, in 1768 he became a director of the French East India Company. In 1776 he was appointed director of the treasury and in 1777, director general of finance. In retirement from 1781 to 1788, he was recalled to his former post on the eve of the French Revolution in the hope that he would deal with the economic crisis. He persuaded Louis XVI to summon the States General and suggested reforms that aroused the enmity of the aristocrats, who secured his dismissal. Reappointed after the storming of the Bastille, he resigned in 1790. His daughter was Mme de Staël.

nectar A sugary solution produced by glandular structures (nectaries) in animal-pollinated flowers. Nectar attracts insects, birds, or bats to the flower and encourages pollination as the animal collects nectar from different sources.

nectarine. *See* peach.

needlefish A carnivorous fish, also called garfish, belonging to the family *Belonidae* (about 60 species), that occurs in tropical and warm-temperate seas. It has a slender

JAWAHARLAL NEHRU *On a visit to Peking in 1954 with his daughter Indira Gandhi, who was assassinated in 1984.*

silvery-blue or green body, up to 1.2 m long, with elongated jaws and numerous sharp teeth. Species include the European garfish (*Belone belone*). Order: *Atheriniformes*.

Needles, the   50 39N 1 34W A group of chalk rocks in S England, off the W coast of the Isle of Wight. A lighthouse stands on the most westerly rock.

Neer, Aert van der   (c. 1603–77) Dutch landscape painter, famous for his moonlight, sunset, and firelight scenes. He also painted ice-bound canals and other winter landscapes.

Nefertiti   (died c. 1346 BC) The cousin and chief wife of *Akhenaton of Egypt. She is depicted with her six daughters and the king in many scenes of personal and domestic life, a unique exception to the priestly conventions of Egyptian royal portraiture. Her portrait bust is perhaps the best-known work of Egyptian art.

negative income tax.   *See* tax-credit system.

Negev   A desert in S Israel. In recent years large areas have been irrigated by pipeline from the River Jordan and many farming communities established, including over a hundred *kibbutzim*. Area: about 12 000 sq km (4632 sq mi).

Negrín, Juan   (1889–1956) Spanish politician. A moderate socialist, Negrín became prime minister of the Republic in 1937 during the *Spanish Civil War. He centralized the military forces of the Republic but Negrín's dependence on the Communist Party brought opposition that forced his resignation.

Negri Sembilan   A state in W Peninsular Malaysia, on the Strait of Malacca. It is hilly, producing mainly rubber, rice, coconuts, and tin. Area: 6605 sq km (2550 sq mi). Population (1980): 563 955. Capital: Seremban.

Negro, Río   1. (Portuguese name: Rio Negro) A river in NE South America. Rising in E Colombia as the Guainía, it flows generally E into Brazil, joining the River Amazon about 16 km (10 mi) below Manaus. Length: about 2250 km (1400 mi). 2. A river in S Argentina, rising in the Andes and flowing generally SE across Patagonia to the Atlantic Ocean. Length: 1014 km (630 mi).

Negroid   The racial grouping comprising populations of sub-Saharan Africa. They are characterized by heavy skin pigmentation, curly to kinky dark hair, broad nose and lips, slight body hair, and high frequency of blood type Ro in the Rh system. Two subtypes exist: the taller darker Congoloid race and the shorter and lighter pygmies, Bushmen, and Hottentots, collec-

tively known as Capoids.

Negros   A volcanic island in the central Philippines, in the Visayan Islands. The chief industry is sugar production. Area: 13 670 sq km (5278 sq mi). Population (1980): 2 749 700. Chief town: Bacolod.

Nehemiah   In the Old Testament, a Jewish leader of the 5th century BC. He was cupbearer to the Persian king but was granted permission to return to Jerusalem in 444 BC, where, despite opposition, he planned and supervised the restoration of the city walls. In 432 he visited Jerusalem a second time and initiated a number of religious and social reforms. **The Book of Nehemiah**, recording his activities, is by the author of *Chronicles and *Ezra.

Nehru, Jawaharlal   (1889–1964) Indian statesman; the first prime minister of independent India (1947–64). Educated in England, he returned to India in 1912 to practise law but soon left his profession to follow Mahatma *Gandhi; in 1929 he was elected president of the *Indian National Congress in succession to his father Motilal Nehru (1861–1931). Between 1921 and 1945 he served nine prison sentences for participating in the movement of noncooperation against the British. After World War II he was a central figure in the negotiations for the creation of an independent India. Throughout his long premiership he was held in high esteem both in his own country and abroad. He carried through many social reforms and maintained a policy of nonalignment with foreign powers, although he was finally forced to enlist US support against Chinese border attacks in 1962. His sister is Vijaya *Pandit and his daughter was Indira *Gandhi.

Neill, A(lexander) S(utherland)   (1883–1973) Scottish educationalist, child psychologist, and writer. The best-known British exponent of child-centred education, Neill founded Summerhill (1921), a coeducational boarding school, famous for its informal atmosphere and liberal educational techniques. His books include *Hearts, Not Heads* (1945) and *Talking of Summerhill* (1967).

Neisse, River   1. (*or* Glatzer Neisse; Polish name: Nysa) A river in SW Poland, flowing NE to join the River Oder near Brzeg. Length: 244 km (159 mi). 2. (*or* Lusatian Neisse) A river rising in NW Czechoslovakia and flowing mainly N to the River Oder near Gubin in Poland. It forms part of the border between East Germany and Poland. Length: 225 km (140 mi).

Nejd.   *See* Najd.

Nekrasov, Nikolai Alekseevich   (1821–78) Russian poet. After rejecting the military career proposed by his father, he became a successful editor and manager of various literary periodicals. The main theme of his poetry is the oppression and character of the Russian peasants. He frequently drew on traditional folksongs, especially in his poems for children.

nekton   An ecological division of aquatic animals that includes all those swimming actively, i.e. by their own efforts, in the open waters of a sea or lake (*compare* plankton). The nekton includes fishes, squids, turtles, seals, and whales.

Nelson   53 51N 2 13W A town in N England, in E Lancashire. It developed in the 19th century around the Lord Nelson Inn. Cotton and rayon weaving and engineering are the chief industries. Population (1981): 30 435.

Nelson   41 18S 173 17E A port and resort in New Zealand, in N South Island on Tasman Bay. It contains the Cawthron Institute, a notable agricultural research centre. Population (1980 est): 42 900.

Nelson, Horatio, Viscount   (1758–1805) British admiral. While serving in the West Indies, he married (1787) Mrs Frances Nisbet (1761–1831). At the outbreak of the French Revolutionary Wars he was given command of the *Agamemnon* in the Mediterranean. In 1794, at Calvi, he lost the sight in his right eye but went on to play an important part in the victory off Cape St Vincent (1797), for which he

HORATIO NELSON   *Portrait (1798-1800) by Guy Head.*

was knighted. Shortly afterwards he lost his right arm in action but in 1798 he destroyed France's naval power in the Mediterranean by his great victory in the battle of the *Nile. Nelson spent the following year in Naples, where he fell in love with Emma, Lady *Hamilton. Returning to England in 1800, Nelson, now Baron Nelson of the Nile, received a hero's welcome but his affair with Emma Hamilton, who gave birth to their daughter Horatia late in 1800, caused considerable scandal. Given command in the Baltic, he was responsible for the victory at Copenhagen (1801) and was created a viscount on his return. In 1803 he became commander in the Mediterranean. He blockaded Toulon for 18 months but in 1805 the French escaped, with Nelson hot in pursuit, and the ensuing chase culminated in the battle of *Trafalgar (1805). Nelson directed this British triumph from aboard the *Victory* (□ships) but was himself mortally wounded. He is buried in St Paul's.

Neman, River (*or* R. Nyeman)   A river in the W Soviet Union. Rising in the Belorussian SSR, it flows mainly NW through the Lithuanian SSR to enter the Baltic Sea. Length: 937 km (582 mi).

nematode   A spindle-shaped colourless worm, also called roundworm, belonging to the phylum *Nematoda* (over 10 000 species). Most nematodes are less than 3 mm long and have a mouth at one end, sometimes containing teeth or stylets, and usually a short muscular pharynx leading to the intestine. The sexes are generally separate. Nematodes live almost everywhere in soil, fresh water, and the sea. Some are parasites of plants or animals; others feed on dead organic matter. Many damage crops or parasitize domestic animals and man. *See also* Ascaris; eelworm; filaria; guinea worm; hookworm; pinworm; vinegar eel.

Nemertina.   *See* ribbonworm.

Nemery, Jaafar Mohammed al   (1930–   ) Sudanese states-man; president (1971–85). An army officer, Nemery came to power in a coup in 1969 as chairman of a revolutionary council. In 1972 he negotiated an end to the 17-year revolt of the non-Muslims in the S. After a coup in 1985, he went into exile in Egypt.

Nemesia   A genus of annual herbs native to South Africa. They are up to 30 cm tall, with narrow leaves and showy white, yellow, red, pink, or purple two-lipped flowers, sometimes spurred, with spotted centres. Many species are popular ornamentals, especially *N. strumosa*, *N. floribunda*, and *N. versicolor*. Family: *Scrophulariaceae*.

Nemesis   In Greek mythology, a goddess personifying the gods' anger at and punishment of human arrogance or *hubris. According to Hesiod, she is the daughter of night. She is associated with just vengeance and especially the punishment that befalls the impious.

Nemi, Lake   41 43N 12 43E A small crater lake in W central Italy, SE of Rome. Two large pleasure ships from the time of the Roman emperor Caligula were raised from the bottom (1930–31) but burned by the retreating German army in 1944.

Nennius   (9th century AD) Welsh antiquary. He is traditionally held to be the author of *Historia Britonum*, a summary of Roman, Saxon, and Celtic legends concerning the early history of Britain. It contains the earliest reference to King *Arthur and mentions the poets *Aneirin and *Taliesin.

neoclassicism   **1.** In art and architecture, a style dominant in Europe from the late 18th to mid-19th centuries. Originating in Rome in about 1750, it later spread throughout Europe and to the USA. Although essentially a revival of classical art and architecture, it was distinguished from similar revivals by its new scientific approach to the recreation of the past. This was largely stimulated by archaeological discoveries at *Pompeii, *Herculaneum, and elsewhere. Key figures in the early development of neoclassicism were the art historian *Winckelmann, who promoted enthusiasm for Greek art, and *Piranesi, who did the same for Roman art. Early neoclassical painters included *Mengs and Benjamin *West but the best known were Jacques Louis *David and *Ingres, who worked in France. Here neoclassicism developed under the stimulus of the *Enlightenment as a reaction to the frivolity of the *rococo style. The neoclassical penchant for themes of self-sacrifice in painting made it popular during the French Revolution. Other leading neoclassicists were the sculptors *Canova and *Thorvalsden and the architects Robert *Adam, *Soufflot, Claude-Nicholas Ledoux (1736–1806), and Friedrich Gilly (1772–1800). *See also* Empire style:
2. A style of composition originating in the 1920s. It was characterized by the use of counterpoint, small instrumental forces, and the use of such 18th-century forms as the concerto grosso. The leading practitioners of musical neoclassicism were *Stravinsky and *Hindemith.

neodymium   (Nd)   A *lanthanide element, occurring in the mineral monazite. It is used with lanthanum in *misch metal in lighter flints and, as the oxide (Nd_2O_3), together with praseodymium, to produce special dark glasses used in welding goggles. At no 60; at wt 144.24; mp 1021°C; bp 3068°C.

neoimpressionism.   *See* pointillism.

Neolithic   The final division of the *Stone Age. It is characterized by the development of the earliest settled agricultural communities and increasing domestication of animals, apparently occurring first in the Middle East during the 9th millennium BC (*see* Catalhüyük; Jericho). Although man still used only stone tools and weapons, he evolved improved techniques of grinding (as opposed to flaking) stone and the invention of pottery facilitated food storage and preparation.

Neo-Melanesian   The form of *pidgin English widely used in Melanesia and New Guinea as a trade and mission language, which has become the native language of some communities. It has a more restricted vocabulary than that of English, on which it is based, a simplified grammar, and a modified sound system.

neon (Ne) A noble gas present in very small amounts in the earth's atmosphere, discovered in 1898 by Ramsay and M. W. Travers (1872-1961) by fractional distillation of liquid air. In an electrical discharge tube, neon glows orange-red and it is commonly used in advertising signs and voltage indicator lamps. Although some ion-pairs have been reported (for example NeH^+), no stable compounds similar to those of krypton and xenon are yet known. At no 10; at wt 20.179; mp $-248.67°C$; bp $-246.048°C$.

neoplasticism. *See* Stijl, de.

Neoplatonism The philosophy, formulated principally by *Plotinus that emphasizes an eternal world of order, goodness, and beauty, of which material existence is a weak and unsatisfactory copy. The chief influences were Plato's concept of the Good, the analysis of love in the *Symposium*, and the speculations about the soul and immortality in the *Phaedo*; Plotinus had little interest in Plato's political and other systems. Neoplatonism helped to shape both medieval Christian theology and Islamic philosophy. *See also* Platonism.

Neoptolemus In Greek legend, King of Epirus, the son of *Achilles. He took part in the *Trojan War after his father's death and killed *Priam at the altar of Zeus.

Neorealism An Italian literary movement that originated during the early years of the fascist regime in the 1920s and flourished openly after its fall in 1943. Notable writers included the novelists Cesare *Pavese, Alberto *Moravia, and Ignazio *Silone, all of whom suffered political persecution for their accurate portrayal of social conditions. The term Neorealism has also been applied to certain Italian films made after World War II. Often using nonprofessional actors and shot on real locations, Neorealist films include *De Sica's *Bicycle Thieves* (1948).

neoteny The condition in which larval characteristics persist in an animal when it reaches sexual maturity. The *axolotl is a neotenous salamander that rarely assumes the typical adult form under natural conditions, although metamorphosis can be triggered by injection of thyroid hormone. Neotony is also known in certain tunicates (primitive marine chordates).

Nepal, Kingdom of A landlocked country in the Himalayas, between China (Tibet) and India. Most of the country consists of a series of mountain ranges and high fertile valleys, with some of the world's highest peaks, including Mount Everest, along its northern border and a region of plain and swamp in the S. Its predominantly Hindu population is of Mongoloid stock, the Gurkhas having been the dominant group since 1769. *Economy*: chiefly agricultural, the main crops are rice, maize, millet, and wheat. Forestry is also important. Mineral resources are sparse, although some mica is being mined. Hydroelectricity is being developed on a large scale and some industry is being encouraged, including jute and sugar. Tourism is an important source of revenue. Exports, mainly to India, include grains, jute, and timber, as well as medicinal herbs from the mountains. *History*: the independent principalities that comprised the region in the middle ages were conquered by the Gurkhas in the 18th century and Nepal was subsequently ruled by the Shah family and then by the Rana, who continue to reign. In 1959 a new constitution provided for an elected parliament, but in 1960 the king dismissed the new government and in 1962 abolished the constitution. There is now a pyramidal structure of government by local and national councils (*panchayat*) and executive power lies with the king. In international relations Nepal tries to keep a balance between the two neighbouring great powers. Head of state: King Birendra Bir Bikram Shah Dev. Prime minister: Marich Man Singh Shrestha. Official language: Nepali.

Official currency: Nepalese rupee of 100 paisa. Area: 141 400 sq km (54 600 sq mi). Population (1980 est): 11 700 000. Capital: Kathmandu.

nephritis (*or* Bright's disease) Inflammation of the kidneys. It may result from infection, as in *pyelitis, or from a disorder of the body's system that affects the kidneys (called glomerulonephritis), which causes protein, cells, and blood to appear in the urine and swelling of the body tissues (*see* oedema). This sometimes occurs in children after a streptococcal infection of the throat and often resolves, but other types of glomerulonephritis, occurring more often in adults, may become chronic and result eventually in kidney failure or *uraemia.

Neptune (astronomy) The most distant giant planet, orbiting the sun every 165 years at a mean distance of 4497 million km. It is somewhat smaller (48 600 km in diameter) and more massive (17.2 earth masses) than *Uranus, exhibits a similar featureless greenish disc in a telescope, and is thought to be almost identical to Uranus in atmospheric and internal structure. It has three *satellites. Neptune's existence was predicted by John Couch Adams and Urbain Leverrier. It was discovered in 1846 by J. G. Galle, using Leverrier's predicted position.

Neptune (mythology) An early Italian god associated with water. When seapower became important to Rome, he became the principal Roman sea god and was identified with the Greek *Poseidon. He is usually portrayed holding a trident and riding a dolphin.

neptunium (Np) The first synthetic transuranic element, produced in 1940 at Berkeley, USA, by bombarding uranium with neutrons. Trace quantities are produced in natural uranium ores by the same reaction. It is available in small quantities in nuclear reactors and forms halides (for example NpF_3, $NpCl_4$) and oxides (for example NpO_2). At no 93; at wt 237.0482; mp 640°C; bp 3902°C.

nereids In Greek mythology, a class of *nymphs or female spirits of nature associated with the sea. They were the daughters of the sea god Nereus and Doris, daughter of Oceanus. The best-known Nereids were *Amphitrite, wife of Poseidon, and *Thetis, mother of Achilles.

Nereus A primitive Greek sea god, father of the *Nereids. He had prophetic powers and was capable of changing his form.

Nergal A Mesopotamian god of hunger and devastation and ruler of the underworld. He is also described as a protective god capable of restoring the dead to life and features in the *Epic of Gilgamesh*.

Neri, St Philip (1515-95) Italian mystic, who founded the Congregation of the Oratory (*see* Oratorians). Settling in Rome (c. 1533), he organized a body of laymen dedicated to charitable works. He was ordained in 1551, becoming a priest at the Church of San Girolamo. Over its nave he built an oratory to hold religious meetings and concerts of sacred music, from which both the name of Neri's order and the word *oratorio* derive. He later ordained his followers, finally installing them in Sta Maria at Vallicella in 1575. Feast day: 26 May.

Nernst, Walther Hermann (1864-1941) German physical chemist, who first stated the third law of *thermodynamics. He also explained the ionization of certain substances when dissolved in water and showed that hydrogen and chlorine combine, when exposed to light, as a result of a chain reaction involving free radicals. He won the 1920 Nobel Prize for Chemistry.

Nero (Claudius Caesar) (37-68 AD) Roman emperor (54-68), notorious for his cruelty. His early reign was dominated by his mother *Agrippina the Younger, *Seneca, and Sextus Afranius Burrus but by 62 Nero had thrown off these influences: Agrippina was murdered (59), Burrus died, perhaps by poison (62), and Seneca retired (62). Also in 62, he murdered his wife Octavia in order to marry Poppaea, who herself died in 65 after being kicked by her husband. Nero ruled with a vanity and irresponsibility that antagonized most sectors of society. A conspiracy to assassinate him, after which Seneca was forced to kill himself, failed in 65. In 68, however, revolts in Gaul, Spain, and Africa and the mutiny of his palace guard forced him to flee Rome and precipitated his suicide.

Neruda, Pablo (Neftalí Ricardo Reyes; 1904-73) Chilean poet. He served in the diplomatic service from 1927 to 1943, was elected a Communist senator in 1943, and was appointed ambassador to France by Salvador *Allende in 1970. The nihilism of his early poetry, such as *Residencia en la tierra* (1925-31), was later replaced by social commitment in *Canto general* (1950) and other works. He won the Nobel Prize in 1971.

Nerva, Marcus Cocceius (c. 30-98 AD) Roman emperor (96-98), chosen by the Senate to succeed Domitian. Nerva's brief rule was enlightened: land was allotted to poorer citizens, treason charges were abolished, and administration was improved.

Nerval, Gérard de (Gérard Labrunie; 1808-55) French poet. His childhood interest in the occult was furthered by travels in the Near East, described in *Voyage en Orient* (1851). His best-known works, which anticipate the techniques of symbolism (*see* Symbolists) and *surrealism, include the story *Sylvie* (1854), the sonnets *Les Chimères* (1854), and the collection of prose and poetry, *Le Rêve et la vie* (1855). His writing was affected by his thwarted love for an actress and by his mental breakdowns, which recurred from 1841 until his suicide in 1855.

nerve. *See* neurone.

nerve gases War gases that inhibit the action of the enzyme acetylcholinesterase, which is essential for the transmission of impulses from nerve to nerve or muscle. Death results from paralysis of the diaphragm leading to asphyxiation. Most nerve gases are derivatives of phosphoric acid and they are toxic in minute quantities (1 mg can be lethal). *See* chemical warfare.

Nervi, Pier Luigi (1891-1979) Italian engineer and architect, famous for his inventive use of reinforced concrete. His first major building, a stadium in Florence (1930-32), features a concrete cantilevered spiral staircase and curved roof. It was followed between 1935 and 1941 by a series of aircraft hangars (now destroyed) with vaults of lattice-patterned beams. In 1949 he designed the great exhibition hall in Turin and in 1953 was one of the architects of the UNESCO building in Paris. Among his later works were two sports stadiums for the 1960 Rome Olympics and San Francisco Cathedral (1970). He was a professor at Rome University from 1947 to 1961.

nervous system The network of nervous tissue in the body. This comprises the central nervous system (CNS), i.e. the *brain and *spinal cord, and the peripheral nervous system. The latter includes the cranial and spinal nerves with their *ganglia and the autonomic nervous system (ANS). The ANS controls unconscious body functions, such as digestion and heartbeat, and is coordinated by the *hypothalamus. The nervous system is chiefly responsible for communication both within the body and between the body and its surroundings. Incoming information passes along sensory *neurones to the brain, where it is analysed and compared with *memory; nerve impulses then leave the central nervous system along motor nerves, carrying signals to all parts of the body and enabling it to respond continuously. Man's success as a species is largely due to the complexity of his nervous system. *See* Plate IV.

Nesbit, Edith (1858-1924) British children's writer. Among her best-known books, noted for their realistic characterization of children, are *The Treasure Seekers* (1899), *The Would-be Goods* (1901), and *The Railway Children* (1906).

Ness, Loch A deep lake in N Scotland, in the Highland Region in the Great Glen. The sight of a monster (the **Loch Ness monster**) has frequently been reported. Length: 36 km (22 mi). Depth: 229 m (754 ft).

Nesselrode, Karl Robert, Count (1780-1862) Russian statesman. He represented Russia at the Congress of Vienna (1814-15) and became foreign minister in 1822, dominating the formation of Russian foreign policy until his death. Nesselrode's intransigent policy in the Balkans contributed largely to the outbreak of the *Crimean War in 1853.

Nessus In Greek legend, a centaur who attempted to rape Deianira, the wife of *Heracles, who killed him with an arrow tipped with the *Hydra's poisonous blood. Before he died, Nessus deceitfully told Deianira that she should save some of his own infected blood as a potion to win-back Heracles' love. She smeared the centaur's blood on Heracles' shirt and thus caused his death.

nest A structure built or taken over by animals to house their eggs, their young, or themselves. The greatest variety is found among birds, whose nests are typically bowl-shaped and constructed of twigs, leaves, moss, fur, etc., woven or glued together. The nests of certain swifts are made entirely of saliva and form the major ingredient of bird's nest soup. Some birds nest on the ground, without using any nesting material; others use holes, either naturally occurring or excavated in trees. Nest building in birds is a complex behaviour, triggered by hormones, in which some components are instinctive and others learnt. Nests are also built by ants, termites, bees, and wasps, which construct elaborate tunnel systems, and by fish, amphibians, reptiles, and small mammals.

Nestor In Greek legend, a king of Pylos. His 11 brothers were killed by *Heracles. As a commander in the *Trojan War during his old age, he acted as a wise counsellor to the quarrelling Greek leaders.

Nestorians The adherents of the Christological doctrines of the Syrian bishop Nestorius (died c. 451). Appointed Patriarch of Constantinople (428), he maintained, probably in overreaction to *Monophysite theories, that there were two persons, not merely two natures, in the incarnate Christ, and that the Virgin Mary could not therefore properly be called the Mother of God. He was accused of heresy and deposed (431). His supporters in his E Syrian homeland formed their own church, centred on Edessa. Expelled from Edessa (489), they established themselves in Persia until virtually annihilated by the 14th-century Mongol invasions.

netball A seven-a-side court game adapted from *basketball and played almost exclusively by girls and women, mainly in English-speaking countries. The court is 100×50 ft (30.5×15.25 m), divided into three equal zones. The goal is a net mounted 10 ft (3.05 m) above the ground. A team consists of a goal shooter, goal attack, wing attack, centre, wing defence, goal defence, and goalkeeper, who are all restricted to particular areas of the court. The game is played by throwing the ball; players may not run with it.

Netherlandic A subgroup of the Western *Germanic languages. It first appears in documents in the 12th century. It is now spoken in Holland and Belgium, where it is called Dutch and Flemish respectively, although the two are in fact the same language. It is the parent language of Afrikaans and is also spoken in parts of Indonesia as a result of Dutch colonization.

Netherlands, Kingdom of A country in NW Europe, on the North Sea. It is almost entirely flat except for some low hills in the SE, and considerable areas of land have been reclaimed from the sea. Rivers, including the Scheldt, Maas, and Rhine, together with the many canals form an efficient system of inland waterways. *Economy*: although popularly considered to be an agricultural nation, industry and commerce are the principal sources of income. Highly developed industries include oil and gas, chemicals, electronics, printing, metals, and food processing. The production of coal, once important, ceased in 1975, when all mines were closed. Agriculture is highly mechanized and market gardening is important. There is also considerable livestock farming, dairy produce being one of the principal exports together with flower bulbs, fuels, chemicals, textiles, and machinery. There is a thriving fishing industry and oysters are a valuable product. Tourism is an important source of revenue as is the Europort at *Rotterdam. *History*: until 1581 the Netherlands formed with present-day Belgium and Luxembourg the region often referred to as the Low Countries. It was under Roman occupation from the 1st century BC to the 4th century AD. It was then overrun by German tribes, of which the Franks had established dominance over the area by the mid-5th century. After the partition of the Frankish empire in 843 the region formed (855) part of Lothair's inheritance and was called Lotharingia. The following centuries saw the rise of powerful principalities, notably the bishopric of Utrecht and the counties of Holland and Guelders, which were fiefs of the German kings before coming under the influence of Burgundy from the 14th century and the Habsburg Emperor Charles V in the early 16th century. Commercial prosperity and the persecution of Protestants fostered a growing movement for independence from the rule of Charles' son Philip II of Spain. In 1581, during the *Revolt of the Netherlands, the seven northern provinces—Holland, Zeeland, Utrecht, Overijssel, Gröningen, Drenthe, and Friesland—proclaimed their independence as the United Provinces of the Netherlands under the leadership of William the Silent. War with Spain continued intermittently until, at the conclusion of the Thirty Years' War, Spain recognized the independence of the Dutch Republic in the Peace of Westphalia (1648). In the 17th century, under the rule of the House of Orange-Nassau, from which the stadholder (chief magistrate) was elected until 1795, the Netherlands reached a peak of prosperity (based on trade and fishing) and international prestige, forming a considerable overseas empire. In the 18th century, however, after the death of William III of Orange, who in 1688 had become King of England, the Netherlands declined. In 1795 it fell to Revolutionary France and in 1806 Napoleon made his brother Louis Bonaparte King of Holland. Following Napoleon's defeat the former Dutch Republic was reunited with the southern provinces (the Spanish Netherlands until 1713 and then the Austrian Netherlands), which had remained loyal to the Habsburgs in the 16th century, to form the Kingdom of the Netherlands (1814). In 1830 the S revolted against the union, forming Belgium (1831), and in 1867 Luxembourg became an independent state. The Netherlands, which flourished economically in the second half of the 19th century, remained neutral in World War I but in World War II was occupied by Germany (1940–45) in spite of fierce Dutch resistance. In 1948 the Netherlands joined with Belgium and Luxembourg to form the *Benelux economic union; it was a founder member of the EEC. The immediate postwar period was dominated by the Dutch colony of Indonesia's fight for independence, achieved in 1950 after bitter and bloody conflict. The peaceful assimilation of non-White immigrants from the former colonies was marred in the 1970s following terrorist activities by the South Moluccans, who were protesting against the Indonesian occupation of their country. In 1980 Queen Juliana abdicated and was succeeded as head of state by her daughter Princess Beatrix. In the 1980s much argument surrounded the Dutch decision to allow deployment of nuclear weapons on its soil under a 1979 NATO agreement. Prime minister: Ruud Lubbers (1939–). Official language: Dutch. Official currency: guilder of 100 cents. Area: 41 160 sq km (15 892 sq mi). Population (1983 est): 14 347 000. Capitals: Amsterdam (legal and administrative); The Hague (seat of government). Main port: Rotterdam.

Netherlands Antilles (Dutch name: Nederlandse Antillen) Two groups of West Indian islands in the Lesser Antilles, in the Caribbean Sea some 800 km (497 mi) apart. The S group lies off the N coast of Venezuela and consists of *Curaçao, *Aruba, and Bonaire; the N group (geographically part of the Leeward Islands) consists of St Eustatius, Saba, and the S part of *St Martin. Under Dutch control since the 17th century, the islands became self-governing in 1954. The economy is based chiefly on oil refining, centred on Curaçao and Aruba. Area: 996 sq km (390 sq mi). Population (1983): 260 000. Capital: Willemstad.

net national product. *See* gross national product.

Neto, Agostinho (1922–79) Angolan statesman; president (1975–79). A physician, he led the MPLA (Popular Movement for the Liberation of Angola) in the struggle against Portuguese rule (1962–74) and on independence became Angola's first president.

nettle An annual or perennial herb of the genus *Urtica* (about 30 species), found in temperate regions worldwide. Up to 1.5 m in height, it has simple leaves with toothed margins and bears clusters of small green unisexual flowers. Stems and leaves may have stinging hairs. Family: *Urticaceae*. Dead nettles are annual or perennial herbs of the genus *Lamium* (about 40 species), occurring in Europe, temperate Asia, and N Africa. They bear clusters of tubular two-lipped flowers. Family: *Labiatae*.

nettle rash. *See* urticaria.

Neuchâtel (German name: Neuenburg) 47 00N 6 56E A city in W Switzerland, on Lake Neuchâtel. It possesses a university (1909) and the Swiss Laboratory of Horological Research. Industries include watchmaking and chocolate production; wine trading is important. Population (1980): 34 478.

Neue Kunstlervereinigung (New Artists' Association) An organization of artists founded in Munich in 1909 by *Kandinsky and *Jawlensky, among others. Its aim to provide more favourable exhibiting conditions for modern art in Munich was largely fulfilled in its large exhibition of international contemporary art in 1910. Disagreements among the members resulted in the defection in 1911 of Kandinsky and Marc, who then founded Der *Blaue Reiter.

Neumann, (Johann) Balthasar (1687–1753) German architect, born in Bohemia. One of the greatest rococo architects, Neumann was a military engineer before being appointed court architect to the Bishop of Würzburg (1719), for whom he built his most famous palace. He also designed churches, notably the church of Vierzehnheiligen (1743–72), with its complex plan and lavish ornamentation.

Neumann, John von (1903–57) US mathematician, born in Hungary. He invented *game theory, the branch of mathematics that analyses strategy and is now widely employed for military purposes. He also set quantum theory upon a rigorous mathematical basis.

neuralgia Sharp or burning pain arising from nerves. Causalgia, one form of neuralgia, is pain arising from a single nerve and is usually caused by an injury to that nerve. The commonest form is trigeminal neuralgia, in which paroxysms of pain affect one side of the face, particularly the cheek, along the course of the trigeminal nerve.

neuritis Inflammation of the nerves. This can be caused by leprosy and multiple sclerosis. However, most diseases of peripheral nerves are caused not by inflammation but by degeneration of the nerve, and the word **neuropathy** is used to describe this. Neuropathies can be caused by a variety of conditions, including diabetes, alcoholism, lead poisoning, and vitamin deficiencies, such as beriberi and pellagra.

neurohormone A chemical (*see* hormone) that is secreted by nerve cells and modifies the function of other organs in the body. The *hypothalamus, for example, releases several hormones that cause the *pituitary gland to secrete its own hormones, the kidney to retain water in the body, and the breast to produce milk.

neurology The study of the structure (neuroanatomy),

function (neurophysiology), and diseases (neuropathology) of the *nervous system. A neurologist is a physician who specializes in the diagnosis and treatment of nervous diseases.

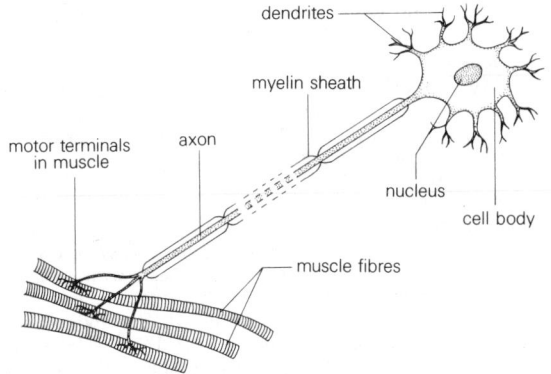

NEURONE *When a nerve impulse transmitted down the axon of a neurone reaches the motor terminals in muscle fibres, the muscle is stimulated to contract.*

neurone (*or* nerve cell) The functioning unit of the *nervous system. A neurone consists of a cell body, containing the nucleus; small irregular branching processes called dendrites; and a single long nerve fibre, or axon, which may be ensheathed by layers of fatty material (myelin) and either makes contact with other neurones at *synapses or ends at muscle fibres or gland cells. When a neurone is stimulated from outside or by another neurone, a nerve impulse is transmitted electrochemically down the axon (*see* action potential). The frequency of these impulses is the basis for the control of behaviour. Bundles of nerve fibres are bound together to form **nerves**, which transmit impulses from sense organs to the brain or spinal cord (sensory nerves) or outwards from the central nervous system to a muscle or gland (motor nerves).

Neuroptera An order of slender carnivorous insects (4500 species) with long antennae and two similar pairs of net-veined wings. The order includes the *alderflies, *snakeflies, and *dobsonflies (suborder *Megaloptera*) and the *lacewings and *antlions (suborder *Plannipennia*).

neurosis A mental illness in which insight is retained but there is a disordered way of behaving or thinking that causes suffering to the patient (*compare* psychosis). The symptoms of neurosis vary considerably: they include a pathologically severe emotional state, as in *anxiety or *depression; distressing behaviour and thoughts, as in *phobias or *obsessions; and physical complaints, as in *hysteria. A neurosis with psychological symptoms is known as a **psychoneurosis**. Neurotic symptoms usually arise through a complex interaction between *stress and a vulnerable personality. Treatment for neurosis can include *tranquillizers, *psychotherapy, and *behaviour therapy.

Neusiedl, Lake (German name: Neusiedlersee) A lake in Austria and Hungary. Having no natural outlet, its area varies with the rainfall. Many species of bird are to be found on its reedy shore. Area: about 350 sq km (135 sq mi).

Neuss 51 12N 06 42E A city in NW West Germany, in North Rhine-Westphalia near the River Rhine. Known for its annual rifle-shooting contest, it is a canal port and industrial centre. Population (1980 est): 149 300.

Neustria The western Frankish kingdom created by the partition in 511 of the possessions of *Clovis I. Approximating in area to N France, it was the rival to *Austrasia (the eastern kingdom) until 687, when *Pepin of Herstal, mayor of the palace (viceroy) of Austrasia, defeated the Neustrians at Tertry.

neutrality The legal status of a country that remains impartial in relation to other countries that are at war (belligerents). In *international law the rights and obligations of a neutral state are mainly contained in the Hague Conventions V and XIII (1907; *see* Hague Peace Conferences) on neutrality in land war and on the sea, respectively. A neutral state must treat belligerents in the same way in matters not relating to war and must not assist either side in furthering its war aims. In particular it must prohibit the use of its territory for the purpose of equipping for war or recruiting men, and it may use force if necessary to prevent any violation of its neutrality. The most important right conferred by neutrality is inviolability of territory: belligerents may not carry on warfare in a neutral state's territory, which includes its water and air space. The term "nonbelligerence" is used when a state that is theoretically neutral is, in fact, sympathetic to one belligerent, for example the relationship between the USA and the UK between 1939 and 1941.

neutrinos A group of three elementary particles and their antiparticles. They are classified as leptons, have no charge, and are probably massless. One type of neutrino is associated with the *electron, one with the *muon, and one with the *tau particle.

neutron An elementary particle that is a constituent of all atomic nuclei except hydrogen-1. It has no electric charge and its mass is slightly greater than that of the *proton. Inside the nucleus the neutron is stable but when free it decays by the *weak interaction to a proton, an electron, and an antineutrino (*see* beta decay). Its mean life is about 12 minutes. The neutron was discovered by *Chadwick in 1932. *See also* particle physics.

neutron bomb. *See* nuclear weapons.

neutron star A star that has undergone *gravitational collapse to the extent that most of the protons and electrons making up its constituent atoms have coalesced into neutrons. The density is extremely high (about 10^{17} kg m^{-3}) and the pressure exerted by the densely packed neutrons can support the star against further contraction. Neutron stars are thought to form when the mass of the stellar core remaining after a *supernova exceeds about 1.4 times the sun's mass. *See also* pulsar.

Neva, Battle of the (15 July, 1240) The battle in which Sweden was defeated by the forces of Prince Aleksandr Yaroslavich of Novgorod (who thus received the name Nevsky; *see* Alexander Nevsky). His victory ended the expansionist ambitions of Sweden into NW Russia.

Nevada One of the mountain states in the W USA. Lying almost wholly within the Great Basin, most of the state consists of a vast plateau with several high mountain ranges rising to well over 1600 m (5249 ft). The only major river is the Colorado in the SE. It is the most arid state in the USA. Most of its population and manufacturing industry is located in the two main cities of Las Vegas and Reno. Copper smelting is a major industry; others include stone, clay, and glass products, cement, food processing, and more recently space, electronics, and the atomic industries. A mineral-rich state, it produces metallic ores and other minerals. Tourism is by far the most important industry. Livestock, especially cattle and sheep, are the principal agricultural products. *History*: ceded by Mexico to the USA in 1848, it became a state (1864) during a mining boom (1860–80). Area: 286 297 sq km (110 540 sq mi). Population (1980): 799 184. Capital: Carson City.

Nevers 47 00N 3 09N A town in central France, the capital of the Nièvre department on the River Loire. It has a 13th-century cathedral and a palace (15th–16th centuries) and its industries include light engineering and pottery. Population (1982): 42 768.

Nevis. *See* St Kitts-Nevis.

New Amsterdam 6 18N 57 30W A port in NE Guyana, on the River Berbice. It serves an area producing sugar cane, rice, and cattle. Population (1976 est): 19 200.

Newark 40 44N 74 11W A city in the USA, in New Jersey on Newark Bay, part of the Greater New York Metropolitan Area. Founded in 1666, it attracted several inventors, whose developments included patent leather (1818), malleable cast iron (1826), the first photographic film (1888), and electrical measuring instruments (1888). It is the focus of air, road, and rail routes. Industries include cutlery, jewellery, and chemicals. Population (1980): 329 248.

Newark (official name: Newark-on-Trent) 53 05N 0 49W A market town in the Midlands of England, in Nottinghamshire on a branch of the River Trent. King John died in the Norman castle, which was later besieged three times in the Civil War. Engineering, building materials, and brewing are important industries. Population (1981): 24 091.

New Britain A volcanic island in the SW Pacific Ocean, in Papua New Guinea, the largest of the Bismarck Archipelago. Copra and some minerals are exported. Area: 36 520 sq km (14 100 sq mi). Population (1984 est): 227 100. Chief town: Rabaul.

New Brunswick A province of E Canada, on the Gulf of St Lawrence. Heavily forested, it consists of rugged uplands with fertile river valleys; the population is concentrated in the *St John River Basin. There is some mixed farming and fishing is important along the Bay of Fundy. Lead, zinc, and some copper are mined at Bathurst. Forestry was a major activity during the last century but overcutting and the loss of protected British markets led to a decline in the industry. In an attempt to encourage industrial development the federal government has spent considerable sums of money on improving the infrastructure (factories, roads, etc.). *History*: slow settlement by French peasants, beginning in the 17th century, ended shortly after Britain's control of the coastal areas was confirmed in 1713. Colonization from Britain and New England followed, and New Brunswick became a separate colony (1784). It prospered and was a founding member of the Dominion of Canada (1867). Area: 72 092 sq km (27 835 sq mi). Population (1981 est): 696 403; approximately 30% are French speaking. Capital: Fredericton.

Newbury 51 25N 1 20W A market town in S England, in Berkshire on the River Kennet. Two indecisive Civil War battles were fought here. Newbury has a famous racecourse. Population (1981): 26 396.

New Caledonia (French name: Nouvelle Calédonie) A French island in the SW Pacific Ocean. With its dependencies (the Isle of Pines, the Loyalty Islands, and others) it forms a French overseas territory. The main industries are nickel mining and meat preserving. Nickel, copra, and coffee are exported. In 1984 violence broke out in response to plans for independence, and in a national referendum (1987) the people voted to remain under French sovereignty. Area: 19 103 sq km (7374 sq mi), including dependencies. Population (1983): 145 368. Capital: Nouméa.

Newcastle 32 55S 151 46E A city in Australia, in New South Wales on the mouth of the Hunter River. Iron and steel industries are important, using coal from the Newcastle-Cessnock field. Population (1983 est): 414 300.

Newcastle, Thomas Pelham-Holles, 1st Duke of (1693–1768) British statesman; Whig prime minister (1754–56, 1757–62). He was secretary of state (1724–54; until 1742 under Sir Robert Walpole). He resigned as prime minister in 1756 because of early reverses in the *Seven Years' War but returned in 1757 with foreign affairs in the hands of Pitt the Elder. His brother **Henry Pelham** (1696–1754) was prime minister (1743–54) in the Broad-Bottom administration, which included members of opposing political factions.

Newcastle, William Cavendish, Duke of (1592–1676) British soldier, author, and patron of the arts. He fought for the royalists in the Civil War and after their defeat at *Marston Moor (1644) he went into exile. Returning at the Restoration, he became a patron of writers, including Jonson and Dryden. He wrote books on horsemanship and such plays as *The Triumphant Widow* (1677).

Newcastle disease. *See* fowl pest.

Newcastle-under-Lyme 53 00N 2 14W A town in the Midlands of England, in Staffordshire. There are traces of a 12th-century castle built by John of Gaunt. The principal industries are coalmining, bricks and tiles, clothing, paper, and machinery. Nearby is Keele University (1962). Population (1981): 72 853.

Newcastle upon Tyne 54 59N 1 35W A city in NE England, the administrative centre of Tyne and Wear on the N bank of the River Tyne opposite Gateshead, with which it is linked by tunnel and five bridges. It is the principal port and commercial and cultural centre of NE England, with a 14th-century cathedral and a university (1852). The principal industries include shipbuilding, marine and electrical engineering, chemicals, flour milling, soap, and paints. *History*: on the site of a Roman settlement (Pons Aelius), Newcastle derives its name from the castle (1080) built as a defence against the Scots. Newcastle's well-known trade in coal developed in the 13th century. The first locomotives for the Stockton–Darlington Railway were made at George Stephenson's iron works, established here in 1823. Population (1981): 192 454.

Newchang. *See* Yingkou.

Newcombe, John (1944–) Australian tennis player, who was Wimbledon singles champion in 1967, 1970, and 1971 and US singles champion in 1967 and 1973. Also an outstanding doubles player, he had three successive wins at Wimbledon (1968–70).

New Comedy The final period of Greek comic drama, lasting from c. 320 BC to the mid-3rd century BC and characterized by well-constructed plays on domestic themes. The role of the chorus diminished as the plots became more complicated. The leading writers of this period were *Menander and *Philemon, whose plays influenced the development of comedy in Rome and later in W Europe. *See also* Middle Comedy; Old Comedy.

Newcomen, Thomas (1663–1729) English blacksmith, who in 1712 constructed an early steam engine. It was based on Thomas *Savery's engine and was widely used for pumping water out of mines. It was extremely inefficient, however, and it was not until *Watt invented the separate condenser that steam engines became suitable for use in transportation.

New Deal (1933–41) Legislation introduced by the US president, F. D. Roosevelt, to ameliorate the effects of the Depression and to initiate social and economic reforms. Emergency legislation enabled sound banks to reopen and regulated credit, currency, and foreign exchange; the gold standard was abandoned and the dollar devalued. Loans on crops, credit, and refinancing of debts and mortgages supported farmers, while the unemployed were helped by direct relief and civil-works programmes. Labour legislation protected the rights of unions to organize and bargain and provided federal agencies to mediate disputes. Ostensibly set up for flood control, the Tennessee Valley Authority (*see* Tennessee River) improved the social and economic status of the backward valley area by developing farming and industry.

New Economic Policy (NEP) An economic policy adopted by the Soviet Union between 1921 and 1929. Introduced by Lenin, the NEP replaced War Communism, a period during the civil war of forced labour and brutal requisitioning of food supplies. The NEP, by contrast, gave concessions to private enterprise in agriculture, trade, and industry and aimed at the political neutralization of the peasants. Although the NEP met with considerable success, it was followed under Stalin by more radical policies and the *five-year plans.

New England An area in the extreme NE USA, bordering on the Atlantic Ocean. It consists of the states of Maine, New Hampshire, Vermont, Massachusetts, Rhode Island, and Connecticut. Explored and named by Capt John Smith (1614), it was first settled by the Puritans (1620). Poor agriculturally, it developed industry early, especially fishing and textiles. Despite the decline of its textile industry the area is now of major economic importance with a flourishing tourist industry. Area: about 164 000 sq km (63 300 sq mi).

New England A district of Australia, in New South Wales. Predominantly agricultural, it occupies the N Tableland between the Moonbi Range and the Queensland border. A separatist movement has existed since the early 20th century but so far has been unsuccessful in making the district a separate state.

New English Art Club A society of British artists founded in London in 1886 to provide an alternative exhibiting organization to the Royal Academy. Largely catering for avantgarde painters influenced by *impressionism, it attracted such artists as *Sickert and *John. It still exists but is now more conservative.

New Forest A woodland area in S England, in Hampshire. Originally an ancient hunting forest it was extended considerably by William the Conqueror during the 11th century. Today it consists chiefly of oak and beech woodland, coniferous afforestation, and open heathland and is a popular tourist area, noted for its ponies. Area: 336 sq km (130 sq mi).

New Forest pony A breed of pony native to the New Forest in S England. Different breeds have been introduced to the wild herds over the years producing marked variations. The smaller ponies tend to be more finely built than the larger ones. They are usually bay or brown and make good childrens' mounts. Height: 1.22–1.47 m (12–14½ hands).

Newfoundland A province of E Canada, consisting of the sparsely populated Coast of *Labrador on the Atlantic Ocean and the triangular island of Newfoundland, lying between the Ocean and the Gulf of St Lawrence. The island consists of a low forested plateau rolling gently to the NE. Its interior is fairly infertile and most of the population lives along the irregular coast, especially in the SE. Pulp and paper has replaced the declining fisheries as the major industry. Iron, lead, zinc, and copper are mined. *History*: discovered by John Cabot (1497), Newfoundland became an English fishing station where settlement was actively discouraged until the 19th century. The island won representative government (1832) and developed steadily until World War I, when it became a dominion. In 1927 it won possession of Labrador's interior and in 1949 became the newest Canadian province. In the last 50 years Newfoundland has not been very prosperous. The island still has a rich tradition of folksong and story-telling. Area: 370 485 sq km (143 044 sq mi). Population (1981 est): 567 681. Capital: St John's.

Newfoundland dog A breed of working dog originating in Newfoundland. Massively built and strong swimmers, Newfoundlands have been used for life-saving at sea. The heavy dense black, brown, or black-and-white coat enables them to withstand icy water. Height: 71 cm (dogs); 66 cm (bitches).

New France The French colonies in E Canada. From about 1600 French trading posts extended along the St Lawrence River to the Great Lakes. France lost these colonies to Britain in the *Seven Years' War (1756–63).

Newgate A prison that formerly stood on the present site of the *Old Bailey. Originally a gatehouse at the wall of the City of London, it was established as a prison under Henry I. It was twice rebuilt, after the Great Fire (1666) and after the Gordon Riots (1780). Last used as a prison in 1881, it was pulled down in 1902.

New Granada A Spanish colony in South America, which in 1717 became a viceroyalty comprising modern Colombia, Ecuador, Panama, and Venezuela (which was later detached). It was liberated by Simón *Bolívar in 1819. From 1830 to 1858 Colombia and Panama formed the Republic of New Granada.

New Guinea An island in the SW Pacific Ocean, the second largest island in the world, separated from Australia by the Torres Strait. It consists of the Indonesian province of *West Irian in the W and *Papua New Guinea in the E. Mountainous and forested, it is largely undeveloped and is famed for its unique species of butterflies and birds. Its linguistically diverse tribal population consists of Melanesian, Negrito, and Papuan ethnic groups. *History*: known to Europeans from 1511, the island was colonized by the Dutch in the 18th century. In 1828 the Dutch controlled the W part; this became part of Indonesia in 1963. The SE was colonized by Britain and the NE by Germany in the late 19th century. Area: 775 213 sq km (299 310 sq mi). Population (1971 est): 1 795 602.

Newham A borough of E Greater London, created in 1965 from the former county boroughs of East Ham and West Ham, and parts of Barking and Woolwich. Population (1981): 209 290.

New Hampshire A state in the NE USA, in New England. It is generally hilly, with many lakes; a low-lying area adjoins the Atlantic Ocean in the SE. Manufacturing is the principal source of employment, centred mainly in the S. Electrical and other machinery together with paper and wood are the principal products. Tourism is the other major industry. The state's farmers produce livestock, dairy and poultry products, and vegetables. Mining is of minor importance and the large deposits of granite are no longer quarried to any great extent. *History*: one of the 13 original colonies, it was first settled by English colonists about 1627, becoming a royal province in 1679. One of the first states to declare its independence, it became a state in 1788. Area: 24 097 sq km (9304 sq mi). Population (1980): 920 610. Capital: Concord.

New Haven 41 18N 72 55W A city and seaport in the USA, in Connecticut on Long Island Sound. It is best known as the site of Yale University (1701). It was here that Charles Goodyear invented vulcanized rubber. Industries include hardware, watches, and firearms. Population (1980): 126 109.

New Hebrides. *See* Vanuatu Republic.

Ne Win (1911–) Burmese statesman; president (1974–82). From 1943 he fought for Burmese independence and, when this was achieved in 1948, became defence minister. In 1958 he became prime minister after forcing U *Nu's resignation and, after leaving office in 1960, again seized power in 1962. In 1972 the 1947 constitution was abolished and replaced (in 1974) by one introducing a single-party assembly and the presidency of Ne Win.

New International Economic Order A series of economic measures adopted by the United Nations General Assembly in 1974, aimed at achieving an international distribution of wealth, income, and political power comparable to that of western Europe. Because the existing world economy favours the industrial nations, the most important measures concern the control of basic raw materials supplied by the developing nations, especially by *international commodity agreements. Other measures include curbs on multinational companies and taxing nonterritorial airways and waterways.

New Ireland A volcanic island in the SW Pacific Ocean, in Papua New Guinea in the Bismarck Archipelago. Copra is exported. Area: 8650 sq km (3340 sq mi). Population (1980): 66 028. Chief town: Kavieng.

New Jersey A state in the NE USA, on the mid-Atlantic coast. The Kittatinny Mountains extend across the NW corner of the state, SE of which lies a belt of lowland containing most of New Jersey's major cities. The remaining area to the S consists of coastal plains, which cover more than half the state. One of the most highly urbanized and densely populated states, it is a major industrial centre. The chief manufactures are chemicals, textiles, electrical machinery, and food products. Although mining is relatively unimportant, New Jersey is a centre for copper smelting and refining as well as a major producer of titanium concentrate. Agriculture is also well developed and a variety of crops are grown, including asparagus, tomatoes, peppers, sweet corn, potatoes, and peaches. Its beaches, forests, and mountain regions form the basis of a thriving tourist industry. *History*: one of the original 13 colonies, it was first settled by the Dutch in the 1620s, coming under British control in 1664. It became a state in 1787 and the construction of canals, roads, and railways aided its industrial development. Area: 20 295 sq km (7836 sq mi). Population (1980): 7 364 158. Capital: Trenton.

New London 41 21N 72 06W A city and seaport in the USA, in Connecticut at the mouth of the Thames River on Long Island Sound. The US Coast Guard Academy and a US naval submarine base (1916) are located here. The annual Harvard-Yale boat race is held here on the Thames River. Industries include shipbuilding and textiles. Population (1980): 28 842.

Newman, John Henry, Cardinal (1801-90) British churchman and a leader of the *Oxford Movement, until his conversion to Roman Catholicism (1845). He was educated at Oxford, later becoming a fellow and tutor there. While vicar of St Mary's, Oxford (1827-43), he published *Parochial and Plain Sermons* (1834-42) and began the series entitled *Tracts for the Times* in 1833. He wrote many of these, including the most controversial one, *Tract 90*, which argued that the Thirty-Nine Articles were not incompatible with Roman Catholicism. In Rome (1846) he joined the *Oratorians and later established his own Oratorian congregation at Edgbaston. Of his later works the most famous are *Idea of a University* (1852), his poem, *Dream of Gerontius* (1866), and a theological work, *Grammar of Assent* (1870). His spiritual autobiography, *Apologia pro vita sua* (1864), was a reply to Charles Kingsley's criticisms of Roman Catholicism. He was made a cardinal in 1879.

Newman, Paul (1925–) US film actor and political activist. He has frequently played the roles of cynical and witty heroes, notably in *Hud* (1963), *Butch Cassidy and the Sundance Kid* (1969), and *The Sting* (1973); among his recent films are *Absence of Malice* (1981), *The Verdict* (1982), and the Oscar-winning *The Color of Money* (1986). From 1968 he also directed and produced films. He is married to the US actress Joanne Woodward (1930–).

Newmarket 52 15N 0 25E A market town in E England, in Suffolk. It is the centre of British horse racing; many racehorses are bred and trained here and several important racing events take place annually. Caravans and electronic equipment are manufactured. Population (1981): 16 235.

new maths A method of teaching mathematics and presenting mathematical relationships that incorporate some of the concepts of formal logic. *Set theory and *vectors, for example, formerly considered advanced and abstract, are sometimes taught at an early stage in school mathematics in the UK and form part of the logical basis of further learning. New applications of mathematics are being developed to deal with computers, automation, and their effect upon social organization, for example operational research.

New Mexico One of the mountain states in the SW USA. There are three main physical regions: a flat tableland in the E, a central mountainous region cut N-S by the Valley of the Rio Grande, and a region of mountains and plains in the W. The relatively sparse population is mainly concentrated in the urban centres, especially in Albuquerque. Its oil and natural-gas deposits are important, and it is a leading producer of uranium ore, manganese ore, and potash. There are also large commercial forests. Livestock is the main agricultural product, and crops include hay, cotton, wheat, and sorghum grains. Problems of irrigation are mitigated by the Rio Grande and the Pecos rivers. There is limited manufacturing. Tourism is an important source of revenue. *History*: a Spanish possession from the 16th century, it was under Mexican rule when it was annexed by the USA in 1848. Following a period of Indian wars and land disputes typical of the Far West at this time, it became a state (1912). Area: 315 113 sq km (121 666 sq mi). Population (1980): 1 299 968. Capital: Santa Fe.

New Model Army The parliamentary army formed in 1645 during the English *Civil War. Organized by Sir Thomas *Fairfax, it united the various local armies; its core comprised the forces of the Eastern Association led by Oliver *Cromwell. It wielded increasing political power after its success at *Naseby (1645), emerging the victor from its power struggle with the *Long Parliament. In 1650 Cromwell became its commander in chief.

New Netherland A Dutch colony in North America. Established in 1613, the colony was centred on New Amsterdam, which after its conquest by the English (1664) was renamed New York.

New Orleans 30 00N 90 03W A city and major port in the USA, in Louisiana. Known as the Crescent City because of its location on a bend in the Mississippi River, it is one of the leading commercial and industrial centres of the South with food processing, oil, chemical, shipbuilding, and ship repairing industries. The Vieux Carré (French Quarter) has many historic buildings, including St Louis Cathedral (1794) and the Cabildo (1795). An educational centre, New Orleans possesses several universities. The famous Mardi Gras festival is held here annually. *History*: founded in 1718, New Orleans became the capital of the French colonial region of Louisiana before passing to Spain in 1763. It returned briefly to France in 1803 but passed to the USA in the same year. Jazz had its origins among the Black musicians of New Orleans during the late 19th century. Population (1980): 557 482.

New Orleans style The original style of jazz, which developed in the Storyville district of New Orleans. The New Orleans style began around 1890 with the band of Buddy Bolden (1868-1941) and continued until the 1920s when *swing bands gained popularity. In New Orleans jazz, the melody of a song was treated as a basis for improvisation by the cornet, clarinet, or trombone, supported by double bass, drums, guitar, and piano. Important New Orleans jazz musicians include Louis Armstrong and Jelly Roll Morton. *Compare* Dixieland.

New Plymouth 39 03S 174 04E A port in New Zealand, in W North Island on North Taranaki Bight. An important dairy centre, it is known for its export of cheese. New Zealand's chief natural gas field is nearby, at Kapuni. Population (1983): 45 000.

Newport 50 42N 1 18W A market town and port in S England, the chief town of the Isle of Wight on the River Medina. Nearby are Carisbrooke Castle and Parkhurst Prison. Population (1981): 23 570.

Newport (Welsh name: Casnewydd ar Wysg) 51 35N 3 00W A port in South Wales, the administrative centre of Gwent near the mouth of the River Usk. Iron and steel, engineering, chemicals, and fertilizers are important industries. Its parish church became the cathedral for the Monmouth diocese in 1921. Population (1981): 105 374.

Newport News 36 59N 76 26W A city and seaport in the USA, in SE Virginia on the James River estuary. A major shipbuilding and ship-repair centre, its manufactures include metal products and building materials. Population (1980): 144 903.

Newry 54 11N 6 20W A port in Northern Ireland, in Co Down on Carlingford Lough. A market town and resort, Newry manufactures clothing, electrical equipment, and food products. Population (1981): 19 426.

news agency An organization that gathers news and sells it to newspapers, broadcasting companies, etc. The four largest international news agencies are Reuters (*see* Reuter, Paul, Baron von), Associated Press, Agence France-Presse, and TASS (Telegrafnoie Agentsovo Soiuza).

New Siberian Islands (Russian name: Novosïbirskiye Ostrova) A Soviet archipelago off the N coast, between the Laptev Sea and the East Siberian Sea. Kotelny, Faddeyevskii, and New Siberia are the largest islands and the Lyakhov Islands to the S are sometimes considered part of the group. There is no permanent population. Total area: 35 100 sq km (13 549 sq mi), including the Lyakhov Islands.

New South Wales A state of SE Australia, bordering on the Pacific Ocean. It consists of extensive plains in the W, separated from the narrow coastal belt by the *Great Dividing Range with the *Snowy Mountains and part of the Australian Alps in the SE. The chief rivers are the Murray, Darling, and Murrumbidgee. It is the most populous and economically important state of Australia. Agricultural products include beef cattle, cereals (of which wheat is the most important), fruit and vegetables (especially in the southern *Riverina district), wool, and dairy produce, which includes large quantities of butter and milk products processed at cooperative factories along the coast. Fishing, including oyster farming, and forestry are also important. Minerals extracted include coal, silver, lead, zinc, and copper. Over half the population live in Sydney, where most of the industries are located; these include the manufacture of iron and steel, textiles, electrical goods, and chemicals. Separatist movements, resenting the domination of the state, exist in the districts of *New England and Riverina. Area: 801 428 sq km (309 433 sq mi). Population (1980 est): 5 146 200. Capital: Sydney.

New Spain, Viceroyalty of (1535-1821) A Spanish colony in the New World comprising modern Mexico, the SW USA, and parts of Central America. It was established under Antonio de *Mendoza.

newspaper A publication issued at regular intervals and containing information and opinion about current affairs. The earliest newspaper may have been the ancient Roman *Acta Diurna* (59 BC) but newspapers in their modern form originated in Europe in the 17th century. Early English newspapers include the *Oxford Gazette* (founded in 1665), which became the *London Gazette* in 1668, and the *Daily Courant* (founded in 1702), the first daily newspaper. In 1785 John *Walter founded the *Daily Universal Register*, which became *The Times* in 1788. The political influence of newspapers was quickly appreciated by governments, which introduced such legislation as the Stamp Act (1712), imposing a duty of a halfpenny on each half-sheet and a penny on each whole sheet. The most notable victory in the campaign for press freedom was made in the 18th century by John *Wilkes, who obtained the right to publish parliamentary reports, but not until 1855 was the Stamp Act repealed. The rapid expansion of newspapers during the 19th century was influenced by improvements in printing technology, the establishment of international *news agencies, and the increase in literacy. In 1903 the first tabloid, the *Daily Mirror*, was founded by Alfred Harmsworth (*see* Northcliffe, Alfred Harmsworth, 1st Viscount) and introduced to England the popular *journalism pioneered in the USA by such newspapers as the *San Francisco Examiner* (1880) and the *Morning Journal* (1895), both founded by William Randolph *Hearst.
The emergence of the great press families (e.g. Beaverbrook,

Thomson) has led to the multiownership of newspapers, on which two Royal Commissions have reported critically. Controversy has also focused recently on the scope of the Official Secrets Acts (1911, 1920, 1939) and the system for issuing D-notices to restrict publication of sensitive material. The advent of computer-aided typesetting in the newspaper industry and the threat it poses to manning levels has caused dissension between management and trade unions, most seriously at *The Times*, where conflict led to its closure in 1978-79. Other great newspapers of the world include the *New York Times* and *Washington Post* in the USA, the *Asahi Shimbun* and *Mainichi Shimbun* in Japan, the *Age* in Melbourne (Australia), the *Corriere della Sera* in Milan (Italy), *Le Figaro* in France, the *Neue Zürcher Zeitung* in Zürich (Switzerland), and the *Frankfurter Allgemeine Zeitung* in Germany. *See also* periodical; Press Council.

ISAAC NEWTON   *A portrait attributed to John Vanderbank (c. 1726; National Portrait Gallery).*

newt A salamander belonging to a family (*Salamandridae*) occurring in Europe, Asia, and North America. The European smooth newt (*Triturus vulgaris*) is greenish brown with dark-brown spots and has a black-spotted orange belly. It grows to a length of 10 cm (including a 5 cm tail). Newts live mainly on land, hibernating under stones in winter and returning to water to breed in spring. The European fire salamander (*Salamandra salamandra*) bears live young and produces a poisonous skin secretion when harmed.

New Testament The 27 books that constitute the second major division of the Christian *Bible. The title is intended to convey the belief that the books contain the fulfilment of prophecies made in the *Old Testament. Written in Greek, the New Testament has four divisions: the four Gospels (Matthew, Mark, Luke, and John); the *Acts of the Apostles; the *Epistles, mainly written by St Paul; and the Book of *Revelation. It covers a period from the birth of *Jesus to the spread of Christianity throughout the Roman Empire and was written between about 50 and 100 AD.

newton (N) The *SI unit of force defined as the force required to give a mass of one kilogram an acceleration of one metre per second per second. Named after Sir Isaac *Newton.

Newton, Sir Isaac (1642-1727) British physicist and mathematician, who was a professor at Cambridge University (1669-1701), MP for the university (1689-90), and Master of the Mint (1699-1727). One of the greatest scientists of all time, Newton did much of his original work in his parents' Lincolnshire home immediately after his graduation, while the university was closed (1665-67) during the Great Plague. His first discovery was the law of gravitation, apocryphally inspired by the realization that an apple falling from a tree is attracted by the same force that holds the moon in orbit. Gravitation required a precise definition of force, this Newton also supplied in his laws of motion (*see* Newtonian mechanics). Newton's second major work in this period was the invention of the calculus; *Leibniz and Newton bickered unbecomingly for some years as to who had the idea first. Probably they both invented the method independently. His third contribution was in optics: he recognized that white light is a mixture of coloured lights, which can be separated by refraction. His incorrect belief that this effect could not be corrected, when it occurs as the chromatic aberration of a lens, inspired him to invent the reflecting telescope. Newton's principal publications were *Philosophiae naturalis principia mathematica* (1686–87) and *Optics* (1704), which held that light is a corpuscular phenomenon.

Although Newton became a Whig MP he made little impact in politics; he did, however, reform the coinage when he was Master of the Mint. He was president of the Royal Society from 1703 until his death and was knighted in 1705. A considerable amount of Newton's later life was spent delving into alchemy, astrology, and theological speculation. From biblical chronology he calculated the day of the earth's creation to be about 3500 BC. Newton is buried in Westminster Abbey. Einstein said of him: "in one person, he combined the experimenter, the theorist, the mechanic and, not least, the artist in exposition."

Newton Abbot 50 32N 3 36W A market town in SW England, in Devon at the head of the Teign estuary. William of Orange was first proclaimed king here in 1688. Population (1981): 20 927.

Newtonian mechanics The branch of *mechanics concerned with systems in which the results of *quantum theory and the theory of *relativity can be ignored. Also known as classical mechanics, it is based on *Newton's three laws of motion. The first law states that a body remains at rest or moves with constant velocity in a straight line unless acted upon by a *force. This law thus defines the concept of force. The second law, which defines mass, states that the *acceleration (a) of a body is proportional to the force (f) causing it. The constant of proportionality is the mass (m) of the body: $f = ma$. The third law states that the action of a force always produces a reaction in the body. The reaction is of equal magnitude but opposite in direction to the action.

Newton's rings A series of light and dark rings formed in a plano-convex lens if monochromatic light is shone onto the lens when it rests on a plane mirror. First observed by *Newton, they are caused by *interference between light reflected by the mirror and light reflected at the curved surface of the lens.

Newtown 52 32N 3 19W A market town in central Wales, in Powys on the River Severn. Designated a new town in 1967, it has a number of light industries. It is the birthplace of Robert Owen. Population (1981): 8660.

new towns Planned towns built in one phase, as opposed to towns that have evolved gradually in response to economic and social pressures. Under the guidance of Ebenezer Howard *garden cities, e.g. Letchworth (1903), were built in the UK to provide an alternative way of life to that in the crowded cities. After World War II new towns were built, as part of larger economic and social plans, to cater for the expanding populations of large towns, e.g. *Milton Keynes, Buckinghamshire, or to provide economic growth centres in declining areas, e.g. Peterlee, Co Durham.

Newtown St Boswells 55 34N 2 40W A town in SE Scotland, the administrative centre of the Borders Region on the River Tweed. Population (1981): 1086.

New Wave (*or* Nouvelle Vague) A group of French film directors in the late 1950s whose films were characterized by their informal and highly original individual styles. The directors, most of whom were associated with the magazine

Cahiers du Cinéma and the *auteur theory of film criticism, included *Truffaut, *Chabrol, *Resnais, and *Godard.

New Westminster 49 10N 122 58W A city and port in W Canada, in British Columbia on the Fraser River. Bordering on E Vancouver, it manufactures wood products, foods, and oil. Population (1981): 38 550.

New World A name for the American continent, used especially by early emigrants from Europe and in describing the geographical distribution of plants and animals. *Compare* Old World.

New World monkey A *monkey native to the Americas. There are two families: the *Cebidae* (37 species) including *uakaris, *sakis, *titis, *howlers, *capuchins, *squirrel monkeys, *spider monkeys, *woolly monkeys, and the *douroucouli; and the *Callithricidae* (33 species) containing *marmosets and *tamarins. New World monkeys are restricted to Central and South America and are largely arboreal and vegetarian.

New York A state in the NE USA. It is basically an upland region, dissected by the valleys of the Mohawk and Hudson Rivers. Traffic flowing from the Great Lakes to the major port of New York City has provided many opportunities for industrial development and today New York is the chief manufacturing state in the USA. Its varied products include clothing, electrical machinery, and processed foods and printing and publishing are among the most notable industries. The presence of New York City also makes it the commercial, financial, and cultural centre of the nation. The most important agricultural activity is dairying; other leading products include apples, grains, and potatoes. *History*: one of the 13 original colonies, it was first settled by the Dutch in the early 17th century. It became an English colony in 1664 and later played a prominent role in the American Revolution. The completion of the Erie Canal in 1825 facilitated rapid commercial expansion in the 19th century. Area: 128 402 sq km (49 576 sq mi). Population (1980): 17 557 288. Capital: Albany.

New York 40 45N 74 00W The largest city in the USA, situated in New York state on New York Bay at the mouth of the Hudson River. Divided into five boroughs—*Manhattan, *Brooklyn, the *Bronx, *Queens, and Richmond (coextensive with *Staten Island), it is the nation's leading seaport and one of the most important business, manufacturing, communications, and cultural centres in the country. As one of the world's financial centres (*see* Wall Street), it is the site of many large corporations and the New York and American Stock Exchanges. The principal manufactures include furs, jewellery, chemicals, metal products, and processed foods. New York is also the main centre of US television and radio and book publishing. Its most notable features include Central Park, the fashionable shops of Fifth Avenue, the *Statue of Liberty, Times Square, *Greenwich Village, the Brooklyn Bridge (1883), Rockefeller Center, St Patrick's Cathedral (1858–79), and a large number of extremely tall buildings (□skyscrapers), such as the Empire State Building (1931), the World Trade Centre (1973), and the United Nations Headquarters (1951), which give Manhattan its characteristic skyline. As well as the famous Broadway theatre district and the Lincoln Center for the Performing Arts, which houses two opera companies, a symphony orchestra, and a ballet company, there are numerous museums, art galleries, and libraries. The most notable educational institutions include Columbia University (founded as King's College in 1754); the City University of New York (1847), and New York University (1831). *History*: on 3 September, 1609, Henry Hudson sailed into New York Bay. and his glowing reports attracted its founding Dutch colonists, who arrived in 1620. In 1625 New Amsterdam, situated at the S tip of Manhattan, became the capital of the newly established colony of New Netherland and the following year the whole island of Manhattan was bought from the Indians for the equivalent of $24. In 1664 the city was captured by the English for the Duke of York and promptly renamed. In the 17th century it became a base for prosperous merchants and such pirates as Capt Kidd. From 1789 until 1790 it was the first capital of the USA. The opening of the Erie Canal in 1825 ensured its pre-eminence as a commercial city and seaport. Following the US Civil War, it began to merge with neighbouring towns, such as Brooklyn, and the metropolis began to form. Early in the 20th century the arrival of millions of European immigrants supplied New York with limitless cheap labour. In recent years many of its middle-class inhabitants have moved to the suburbs of the metropolis and the city subsequently lost a considerable amount of tax revenue. During the mid-1970s New York's financial crisis worsened and the city was narrowly saved from bankruptcy by emergency loans. Population (1980): 7 071 030.

New Zealand, Dominion of A country in the Pacific Ocean, to the SE of Australia. It consists of two main islands, *North Island and *South Island, together with several smaller ones, including *Stewart Island to the S. *Ross Dependency and the *Tokelau Islands are dependencies, and the *Cook and Niue Islands are self-governing. Most of the population is of British descent with a large Maori minority. *Economy*: the main basis of the economy is livestock rearing, especially sheep farming. Farms are highly mechanized and there is considerable research into agricultural science and technology. Meat, wool, and dairy products are the main exports, which were adversely affected when the UK joined the EEC in 1973. However the effects were less than had been feared and New Zealand has opened up markets in other parts of the world. Mineral resources include coal, gold, limestone and silica sand, and oil and natural gas have been found. New Zealand's swift-flowing rivers make hydroelectricity a valuable source of power. Timber production has increased in recent years and there is a growing pulp and paper industry. Other industries, such as food processing and textiles, have also been expanding and tourism is of growing importance. *History*: from about the 14th century the islands were inhabited by the Maoris, a Polynesian people. The first European to discover New Zealand was *Tasman in 1642, who called it Staten Land, later changed to Nieuw Zealand; in 1769 the coast was explored by *Cook. During the early part of the 19th century it was used as a whaling and trading base. By the Treaty of *Waitangi in 1840 the Maori chiefs ceded sovereignty to Britain and a colony was established. British settlement increased rapidly and sheep farming developed on a large scale. After two wars with the Maoris over land rights, peace was reached in 1871. New Zealand was made a dominion in 1907 and became fully independent by the Statute of Westminster in 1931. By the early part of the 20th century its social administration policy was one of the most advanced in the world. Free compulsory primary education was introduced in 1877 and in 1893 New Zealand became the first country in the world to give women the vote. A comprehensive social security system was established in 1898. Since World War II New Zealand has played an increasing role in international affairs, especially in the Far East. Its economy has suffered from the recent world recession and efforts to curb inflation have included a prices and wages policy. In 1985 relations with the USA became strained when the new Labour government prohibited nuclear vessels from entering New Zealand waters. Prime Minister: David Lange. Official language: English. Official currency: New Zealand dollar of 100 cents. Area: 268 704 sq km (103 719 sq mi). Population (1983 est): 3 142 000. Capital: Wellington. Main port: Auckland.

Nexø, Martin Andersen (1869–1954) Danish novelist. His upbringing in the slums of Copenhagen led him to become a socialist and subsequently a communist. He achieved worldwide fame with his novels *Pelle erobreren* (*Pelle the Conqueror*; 1906–10) and *Ditte menneskebarn* (*Ditte: Daughter of* *Man*; 1917–21), depicting the struggles of the working class. In 1949 he settled in East Germany.

Ney, Michel, Prince of Moscow (1769-1815) French marshal, whom Napoleon described as "the bravest of the brave." He served throughout the Revolutionary Wars and, under Napoleon, won the great victory at Elchingen (1805) and fought at *Jena (1806) and *Friedland (1807). His extraordinary courage in the French retreat from Moscow (1812-13) prompted Napoleon's accolade. When Napoleon returned from Elba, Ney rallied to the former emperor's cause and after his defeat at Waterloo was shot as a traitor.

Nez Percé A North American Indian people of the plateau region of Idaho. Their culture, typical of this area, was based on salmon fishing. After acquiring horses in the 18th century, they frequently left their riverside villages to hunt buffalo on the Plains and thus acquired many Plains Indian traits. They became expert horse breeders possessing large herds. Their language belongs to the Sahaptin division of the *Penutian family.

Ngo Dinh Diem (1901-63) Vietnamese statesman; president of South Vietnam (1955-63). Unsympathetic to Ho Chi Minh's *Viet Minh, he went into exile during the war of independence against France. Returning just before the partition of Vietnam, he was appointed prime minister (1954) under US influence and in the following year abolished the monarchy and became president. His government was threatened by the guerrilla activities of the *Viet Cong against whom he sought US aid (*see* Vietnam War). He was assassinated, together with his brother Ngo Dinh Nhu, in a military coup in 1963.

Nguni A division of the *Bantu-speaking peoples of S Africa. It includes the *Swazi, *Xhosa, and *Zulu.

Nha Trang 12 15N 109 10E An ancient port in S Vietnam, at the mouth of the River Cai. Nearby are four shrines dating from the 7th to 12th centuries. The chief industry is fishing. Population (1979): 172 663.

Niagara Falls Two waterfalls on the US-Canadian border, on the Niagara River between Lakes Erie and Ontario. The American Falls, 51 m (167 ft) high and 300 m (1000 ft) wide, are straight while the Horseshoe Falls (Canada), 49 m (162 ft) high and 790 m (2600 ft) wide, are curved. Much of their flow is diverted to generate electricity but they remain spectacular tourist attractions. Shipping between the two lakes is diverted past the Falls by way of the Welland Ship Canal.

Niamey 13 32N 2 05E The capital (since 1926) of Niger, on the River Niger. It has grown rapidly as the country's administrative and commercial centre. Its university was founded in 1973. Population (1981 est): 343 600.

Niarchos, Stavros Spyros (1909-) Greek businessman and the owner of one of the largest independent shipping lines in the world. In rivalry with his brother-in-law, Aristotle *Onassis, he pioneered the construction of supertankers during the 1950s.

Nibelungenlied (German: *Song of the Nibelungs*) A Middle High German epic poem composed in the 13th century but drawing on much earlier material. Its main theme is the disastrous rivalries following *Siegfried's killing of the Burgundian princes called Nibelungs and his seizure of their treasure. A variant of the story also occurs in the Old Norse *Volsungasaga* (*see* sagas), in which Siegfried is called Sigurd. *Wagner's operatic cycle, *The Ring of Nibelung*, makes use of elements from both the Germanic and Old Norse versions.

Nicaea, Councils of Two ecumenical councils of the Christian Church held at Nicaea, now Iznik (Turkey). **1.** (325) The council that was summoned by the Byzantine emperor Constantine to establish Church unity and suppress *Arianism. The number of participating bishops was, according to later reports, 318. The *Nicene Creed was the major doctrinal formulation. **2.** (787) The council that was summoned by the Byzantine empress Irene to condemn *iconoclasm. Its initial assembly at Constantinople (786) was disrupted by iconoclasts, but the following year at Nicaea it approved a formula for restoring the veneration of icons.

Nicaragua, Republic of A country in Central America between the Caribbean Sea and the Pacific Ocean. Swamp and dense tropical forest on the Caribbean coast, and a broader plain with lakes to the W rise to a central mountain range. Lake Nicaragua in the SW is the largest in Central America. The population is mainly of mixed Indian and Spanish descent, with minorities of African and other descent. *Economy*: chiefly agricultural, the main crops are maize, rice, cotton, coffee, and sugar. Production of bananas in the E has been reduced in recent years. There is considerable livestock rearing, and meat packing is an important industry. Minerals include gold, silver, and copper, and large quantities of natural gas were found in 1974. Oil deposits are being explored. Industries, on a small scale, include food processing, textiles, and oil refining. The main exports are cotton, coffee, sugar, beef, and timber. In the late 1980s economic hardship resulted from the internal war. *History*: sighted by Columbus in 1502, it was colonized by Spain from 1522, becoming part of the captaincy general of Guatemala. It broke away from Spain in 1821 and formed part of the Central American Federation until 1838, when Nicaragua became a republic. A treaty with the USA in 1916 gave the latter an option on a canal route through Nicaragua as well as naval-base facilities. From 1933 the government was dominated by the Somoza family, opposition to which culminated in a civil war that forced (1979) the resignation and exile of the president, Gen Anastasio Somoza (1925–80). The victorious Sandinista National Liberation Front (FSLN) instituted socialist policies. Accusing the Sandinistas of supplying arms to the rebels in El Salvador, the USA has supported an army of 'Contras' that attacks Nicaragua from Honduras and Costa Rica, attracting worldwide criticism. A disunited rebel force complicates attempts to end the war. Nicaragua is a member of the OAS and the Central American Common Market. Official language: Spanish. Official currency: córdoba of 100 centavos. Area: 148 000 sq km (57 143 sq mi). Population (1980 est): 2 568 000. Capital: Managua. Main ports: Corinto (on the Pacific) and Bluefields (on the Caribbean).

Nice 43 42N 7 16E A city in SE France, the capital of the Alpes-Maritimes department on the Baie des Anges. Ceded by Sardinia to France in 1860, it is one of the leading resorts of the French Riviera. Notable landmarks include the Promenade des Anglais and it has a university (1965). It is famous for its many carnivals and fêtes and it has a large trade in fruit and flowers. Population (1982): 338 486.

Nicene Creed The statement of Christian belief accepted by the first Council of *Nicaea (325). The Nicene Creed used in the *Eucharist service of Orthodox, Roman Catholic, and Protestant Churches is a version of this creed, with the sections on Christ (*see* Filioque) and the Holy Spirit expanded.

Nichiren Buddhism A popular Japanese Buddhist school named after its founder, a 13th-century monk and prophet. He militantly opposed other Buddhist sects and held that *The Lotus Sutra* contained the true teaching and that the historical Buddha was identical with eternal Buddha-nature, in which all men participate. The sincere invocation of the mantra of homage to *The Lotus Sutra* is sufficient to gain enlightenment. Among the subsects of the school, the Nichiren-sho-shu and the related lay group, the Soka-gakkai, are the largest.

Nicholas I, St (d. 867) Pope (858–67 AD). In the West Nicholas successfully defended and expanded papal authority against both secular rulers, such as *Lothair, and local bishops, notably *Hincmar of Reims. In the East Nicholas strongly opposed the appointment of *Photius to the patriarchate of Constantinople and declared him deposed. Photius, in his turn, declared the deposition of Nicholas (867) but Photius' overthrow prevented further hostilities. Feast day: 13 Nov.

Nicholas I (1796–1855) Emperor of Russia (1825–55), notorious as an autocrat. Nicholas' accession was followed by the *Dekabrist revolt, which though unsuccessful hardened his conservatism. His ambitions in the Balkans precipitated the *Crimean War.

Nicholas II (1868–1918) The last Emperor of Russia (1894–1917). Nicholas' ambition in Asia led to the unpopular *Russo-Japanese War, which in turn precipitated the *Revolution of 1905. Forced to accept the establishment of a representative assembly (*see* Duma), Nicholas nevertheless continued attempts to rule autocratically. In 1915 he took supreme command of Russian forces in World War I, leaving Russia to the mismanagement of the Empress *Alexandra and *Rasputin. After the outbreak of the Russian Revolution in 1917, Nicholas was forced to abdicate (March). He and his family were imprisoned by the Bolsheviks and executed at Ekaterinburg (now Sverdlovsk).

Nicholas, St (4th century AD) The patron saint of Russia, sailors, and children. He is thought to have been Bishop of Myra in Asia Minor and his alleged relics are in the Basilica of S Nicola, Bari. Legends telling of his gifts of gold to three poor girls for their dowries gave rise to the practice of exchanging gifts on his feast day, 6 Dec. As he is also identified with the legendary Santa Claus this now happens on 25 Dec in most countries.

Nicholas of Cusa (1401–64) German prelate and scholar. He was made a cardinal in 1448, appointed bishop of Brixen (present-day Bressanone) in 1450, and became a papal legate. He wrote important works on mysticism, mathematics, biology, and astronomy.

Nicholson, Ben (1894–1982) British artist. He studied at the Slade before holding his first one-man exhibition (1922), which reflected the influence of *cubism and de *Stijl. Some of his best abstract works were produced in the 1930s, while a member of the British art group Unit One (*see* Nash, Paul). These include white-painted plaster reliefs of rectangles combined with circles. He was the son of **Sir William Nicholson** (1872–1949), a poster artist.

Nicholson, Jack (1937–) US film actor. After success in *Easy Rider* (1969), he became a star of the 1970s. His films include *Chinatown* (1974), *One Flew Over the Cuckoo's Nest* (1976), *Prizzi's Honour* (1985), and *The Witches of Eastwick* (1987). He won an Oscar for *Terms of Endearment* (1983).

Nicholson, William (1753–1815) British chemist, who in 1800 discovered *electrolysis by passing a current from a Voltaic pile through water and noting the bubbles of gas given off.

Nicias (c. 470–413 BC) Athenian general and politican. An aristocratic opponent of the demagogue *Cleon, Nicias negotiated a temporary peace with Sparta in the Peloponnesian War (peace of Nicias, 421). He opposed Alcibiades' imperialist designs and only reluctantly commanded the ill-fated Athenian campaign to Sicily, during which he and nearly his entire force perished.

nickel (Ni) A hard silvery metal similar to iron, discovered in 1751 by A. F. Cronstedt (1722–65). It occurs in nature chiefly as pentlandite, NiS, and pyrrhotite, $(Fe,Ni)S$, which are found in Canada and Australia. Iron meteorites typically contain from 5 to 20% nickel. It is chemically similar to cobalt and copper, and forms a green oxide (NiO), the chloride $(NiCl_2)$, the sulphate $(NiSO_4)$, and other compounds. It is used widely in alloys, such as stainless steel, Invar, Monel, armour plating, and in coinage. Finely divided nickel is also used as a catalyst for hydrogenation reactions in organic chemistry. At no 28; at wt 58.71; mp 1453°C; bp 2732°C.

Nicklaus, Jack William (1940–) US golfer, who has won more major championships than any other. Between 1959 and 1981 he won two US amateur championships, four US and three British Open championships, five US

JACK NICKLAUS

Professional Golfers Association championships, and five Masters championships.

Nicobar Islands. *See* Andaman and Nicobar Islands.

Nicolai, Otto Ehrenfried (1810-49) German conductor and composer of operas. He held posts in Rome and Vienna and is remembered for *The Merry Wives of Windsor* (1849).

Nicolson, Sir Harold (George) (1886-1968) British diplomat and literary critic. Born in Iran and educated at Oxford, he worked in the diplomatic service until 1929 and was later an MP (1935-45). In 1913 he married the novelist Victoria Sackville-West (1892-1962). He published political studies, critical appreciations of Verlaine, Byron, Tennyson, and others, and several volumes of his *Diaries*.

Nicopolis, Battle of (25 September, 1396) The battle in which a coalition of Crusaders under Emperor *Sigismund, at the request of the Byzantine emperor, Manuel II Palaeologus (1350-1425; reigned 1391-1425), were decisively defeated by the Turks under Sultan Bayezid I (1347-1403; reigned 1389-1403). It contributed greatly to further Turkish advances and the ultimate fall of the Eastern Roman (Byzantine) Empire.

Nicosia (Greek name: Leukosía; Turkish. name: Lefkosa) The capital of Cyprus, on the River Pedieas. Originally known as Ledra it has been successively under Byzantine, Venetian, Turkish, and British control. It possesses many old buildings, including the Cathedral of St Sophia (completed 1325), now the main mosque in Nicosia. Its industries include textiles, food processing, and cigarettes. Population (1980 est): 161 200.

nicotine ($C_{10}H_{14}N_2$) A toxic colourless oily liquid alkaloid that rapidly turns brown on exposure to air. It is obtained from the dried leaves of the tobacco plant and is present in small quantities in cigarettes.

nicotinic acid. *See* vitamin B complex.

Niebuhr, Barthold Georg (1776-1831) German historian. Niebuhr served as Prussian ambassador in Rome from 1816 to 1823, when he joined the staff of Bonn University. His *History of Rome* (1811-32) was significantly different from previous works on the ancient world, as he adopted a more critical approach and stressed the importance of external factors in the development of Rome. His ideas and methods influenced many scholars, including Theodor *Mommsen.

Niedersachsen. *See* Lower Saxony.

Nielsen, Carl (August) (1865-1931) Danish composer and conductor. He began his musical career as a violinist. Nielsen developed the principle of progressive tonality (beginning in one *tonality and ending in another) in his six

symphonies, of which the fourth, entitled *The Inextinguishable* (1914-16), and the fifth (1922) are the best known. He also composed concertos for the violin, flute, and clarinet, the operas *Saul and David* (1900-02) and *Maskarade* (1904-06), chamber music, and choral music.

Niemeyer, Oscar (1907-) Brazilian architect. A disciple of Le Corbusier with whom he collaborated on the Ministry of Education (1937-43) in Rio de Janeiro, Niemeyer has made a major contribution to the development of modern architecture in Brazil. His first independent buildings included a casino, club, and church at Pampulha in Bel Horizonte. He has achieved international fame for his designs for □Brasília, notably the president's palace (1959) and the cathedral (1964).

Niemöller, Martin (1892-1984) German Lutheran pastor and Protestant leader. A U-boat commander in World War I, he was ordained in 1924. In 1933 he became head of the Pastors' Emergency League, which became the *Confessing Church, and opposed the nazification of the Church in Germany. Niemöller was dismissed from his pastorate in Berlin in 1934 and in 1937 was sent to a concentration camp, where he remained until the end of the war. After the war he served (1947-64) as the first bishop of the newly established Evangelical Church of Hesse.

Nietzsche, Friedrich (1844-1900) German philosopher. A friend of Wagner, Nietzsche was influenced by the writings of *Schopenhauer and *Goethe. His first book, *The Birth of Tragedy* (1872), argued that Wagnerian opera was the successor to Greek drama. Nietzsche rejected Christianity and its morality and attempted a "transvaluation of all values." He argued that the "will to power" (the title of his posthumously edited notebooks) was the crucial human characteristic. In *Thus Spake Zarathustra* (1883-92), he eulogizes the man who is free, titanic, and powerful, an ideal adopted by the Nazis for the Aryan superman. After 1889 he was permanently insane.

Niger, Republic of A large landlocked country in West Africa. Lying mainly in the Sahara, it consists of desert in the N merging to semidesert in the S and rising to the central Aïr mountains. In the extreme SW it is drained by the River Niger, bordered by fertile flood plains. Approximately half the population are Hausa, with large porportions of Zerma, Songhai, and Fulani. *Economy*: agriculture, particularly livestock raising, is important but it suffered badly from the droughts of the late 1960s and early 1970s in the Sahel. Crops include groundnuts, millet, beans, and cassava, with cotton and rice being grown in the wetter river districts. Mineral resources include salt, natron, and tin, and important uranium deposits in the N are being exploited. The main exports are uranium and groundnuts. *History*: occupied by France (1883–99), it became a territory of French West Africa in 1904. It was made an autonomous republic within the French Community in 1958 prior to gaining full independence in 1960 with Hamani Diori as president. Diori was overthrown in a military coup (1974) led by Maj Gen Seyni Kountché (1931–87), who became president. Upon his death Col Ali Seybou took control. In the same year a referendum approved a charter to end the 13-year military rule. Official language: French. Official currency: CFA (Communauté financière africaine) franc of 100 centimes. Area: 1 186 408 sq km (458 075 sq mi). Population (1981 est): 5 619 000. Capital: Niamey.

Niger, River The third longest river in Africa. Rising in the S highlands of Guinea, near the Sierra Leone border, it flows NE and then SE through Mali, Niger, and Nigeria to enter the Gulf of Guinea. It has one of the largest hydroelectric-power schemes in Africa. Length: 4183 km (2600 mi).

Niger-Congo languages An African language family spoken in central and S Africa. It is subdivided into six groups: the *West Atlantic languages; the Mande languages spoken in Guinea, Mali, and Sierra Leone; the Voltaic languages spoken in Upper Volta, Ghana, and the Ivory Coast; the *Kwa languages of West Africa, such as Yoruba and Igbo; the Benue-Congo group, which includes the *Bantu languages; and the Adamawa-Eastern group spoken in Nigeria. The whole family is sometimes included in the larger Niger-Kordofanian classification, which relates it to the Kordofanian languages of the Sudan.

Nigeria, Federation of A large country in West Africa, on the Gulf of Guinea. Mangrove swamps along the coast give way to tropical rain forest inland rising to open savanna-covered plateaus, with mountains in the E reaching heights of over 2000 m (5000 ft). The N is semidesert and the River Niger flows through the W. The inhabitants are mainly Hausa and Fulani in the N, Yoruba in the W, and Ibo in the E. *Economy*: since the discovery of oil in the 1960s and 1970s there has been a dramatic expansion in the economy and a shift away from agriculture to industry. Oil production accounts for about 90% of exports although production has declined in recent years; Nigeria is a member of OPEC and the world's eighth largest producer. There are also important reserves of natural gas and other minerals, including tin, coal, iron ore, and columbite (of which Nigeria is the world's main supplier). Manufacturing industries to have undergone rapid expansion include brewing, aluminium, motor vehicles, textiles, and cement. Hydroelectricity is a valuable source of power, particularly since the opening of the Kainji Dam on the River Niger (1969). Agriculture is still important and diverse although output has declined in recent years and it suffered severely through the prolonged drought in the Sahel. The main cash crops are groundnuts and cotton in the N and palms, coconut, and rubber in the S. Livestock, fishing, and forestry for timber are also important. *History*: in the middle ages there were highly developed kingdoms in the area, such as those of the Hausa in the N and the Yoruba (e.g. Oyo, Benin) in the SW; the Ibo occupied the SE. The coast was explored in the 15th century by the Portuguese, who developed the slave trade, in which the Dutch and English also participated. In 1861 Lagos was annexed by Britain and in 1886 the Royal Niger Company was incorporated to further British interests. By 1906, the British were in control of Nigeria, which was divided into the protectorate of Northern Nigeria and the colony (of Lagos) and protectorate of Southern Nigeria. These were united in 1914. Nigeria became a federation in 1954, gained independence in 1960, and became a republic within the Commonwealth in 1963. The government was overthrown in a violent military coup in 1966 and, after a further coup, a new government was formed under Lt Col Gowon. In 1967 the eastern region, which contained the homeland of the Ibo, withdrew to form the Republic of *Biafra under Lt Col Odumegwu Ojukwu's (1933–   ) leadership. Civil war followed, lasting until Biafra's surrender in 1970. Gowon was overthrown in a coup in 1975. In 1979 Alhaji Shehu Shagari (1925–   ) became president. He was re-elected in 1983 but the failure of his government to combat escalating corruption and the worsening economy led to his overthrow in December, 1983, in a military coup led by Maj Gen Mohammed Buhari (1942–   ). A further coup in 1985 brought Maj Gen Ibrahim Babangida to power. Official currency: naira of 100 kobo. Area: 923 773 sq km (356 669 sq mi). Population (1983 est): 85 219 000. Capital: Abuja. Main port: Lagos.

nightblindness Inability to see in dim light. This is the earliest sign of vitamin A deficiency and is seen most commonly in young children in poor countries. Vitamin A is found in fruit, vegetables, and fish-liver oil. Preparations of vitamin A and cod-liver oil are used in treatment.

night heron A nocturnal *heron belonging to a subfamily (*Nycticoracini*; 9 species) occurring worldwide. Night herons are comparatively short-legged and squat, with a short neck and a broad bill. Birds of the main genus (*Nycticorax*) are

mostly black-headed with long white ornamental head plumes.

nightingale A plump woodland bird, *Luscinia megarhynchos*, that winters in tropical Africa and breeds in S Europe and Asia Minor during the summer. It is about 16 cm long with reddish-brown plumage and pale underparts and feeds on ground insects and spiders. Nightingales are noted for their beautiful song and were popular as cagebirds. The thrush nightingale (*L. luscinia*) is a closely related similar species. Family: *Turdidae* (thrushes). *See* Plate V.

FLORENCE NIGHTINGALE *The legendary Lady with the Lamp tending patients in the hospital at Scutari, during the Crimean War.*

Nightingale, Florence (1820–1910) British hospital reformer and founder of the nursing profession. With strong religious convictions, Florence Nightingale trained as a nurse and was appointed as a nursing superintendent in London in 1853. On the outbreak of the Crimean War, in 1854, she volunteered to lead a party of nurses to work in the military hospitals. She set about transforming the appalling conditions, earning herself the title Lady with the Lamp from her patients. After the war she was instrumental in obtaining improved living conditions in the army and, in 1860, from a Nightingale Fund subscribed by the public, she established the Nightingale School for Nurses at St Thomas's Hospital—the first of its kind. In 1907 Florence Nightingale became the first woman to receive the OM.

nightjar A nocturnal bird belonging to a subfamily (*Caprimulginae*; 60–70 species) occurring in most temperate and tropical regions, also called goatsucker. About 30 cm long, nightjars have a soft mottled grey, brown, and rufous plumage with spotted and barred underparts and a long tail. Its short bill has a wide gape surrounded by long sensitive bristles enabling it to catch insects in flight. Family: *Caprimulgidae*; order: *Caprimulgiformes* (frogmouths, nightjars, etc.).

nightmares Frightening *dreams, from which the sufferer often wakes with a feeling of suffocation. They are distinguished from **night terrors**, in which a child wakes suddenly in panic but later cannot remember the incident. Nightmares are more common during states of anxiety and depression and in people taking certain sleeping tablets. *See also* sleep.

nightshade One of several plants of the family *Solanaceae. The most notorious is *deadly nightshade (or belladonna). The **woody nightshade**, or bittersweet (*Solanum dulcamara*), is a scrambling shrubby perennial, up to 2 m tall, of Eurasia and N Africa. It has oval leaves, the lower ones much divided, and loose clusters of flowers with five spreading purple lobes and conspicuous yellow stamens. The red berries are poisonous. The **black nightshade** (*S. nigrum*) is an annual, up to 50 cm high, widely distributed as a weed. It has oval pointed leaves, small yellowish flowers, and poisonous black berries.

The unrelated **enchanter's nightshade** (*Circaea lutetiana*), of Eurasia, is a herbaceous perennial of shady places. Up to 60 cm tall, it has large heart-shaped leaves and a terminal spike of tiny white flowers. Family: *Onagraceae*.

nihilism A view that rejects all traditional values and institutions. *Turgenev invented the label in *Fathers and Sons* (1861) for the philosophy of the character of Basarov, which was based on that of Dmitrii Pisarev (1840–68). The political expression of nihilism is anarchy; its 19th-century Russian proponents held that progress is impossible without the destruction of all existing organizations. Nihilism also undermines accepted standards in *ethics and *aesthetics.

Niigata 37 58N 139 2E A city in Japan, in NW Honshu. The main port for the Sea of Japan, its industries include chemicals and oil refining. Its university was established in 1949. Population (1980): 458 000.

Nijinsky, Vaslav (1890–1950) Russian ballet dancer. In 1909 he joined Diaghilev's company in Paris, and quickly achieved an international reputation for his daring and sensitive dancing. Michel *Fokine created *Petrushka*, *Scheherazade*, and other ballets for him, and from 1913 he also began to choreograph. He retired in 1919 suffering from schizophrenia and was cared for by his wife until his death.

Nijmegen (German name: Nimwegen) 51 50N 5 52E A city in the E Netherlands, in Gelderland province. The Treaties of *Nijmegen (1678–79) were signed here. Its university was founded in 1923. It is an important industrial centre with chemicals and engineering. Population (1981 est): 147 346.

Nijmegen, Treaties of (1678–79) The peace treaties between France and, respectively, the Netherlands (1678), Spain (1678), and the Holy Roman Empire (1679) that ended the third *Dutch War. Terms were least favourable to Spain, Louis XIV securing Franche-Comté and a naturally defensible frontier with the Spanish Netherlands.

Nike The Greek personification of victory, often portrayed as an aspect of *Athena. Among larger representations is the famous statue discovered in Samothrace in 1836 and now in the Louvre, Paris.

Nikisch, Arthur (1855–1922) Hungarian conductor. A brilliant student at the Vienna Conservatoire, he directed the Leipzig Opera (1879–87), the Boston Symphony Orchestra (1889–93), and then the Leipzig Gewandhaus and Berlin Philharmonic Orchestras concurrently (1895–1922).

Nikko 36 45N 139 37E A town in Japan, in central Honshu. Situated within Nikko National Park its beautifully ornamented temples and shrines are a place of pilgrimage and attract a large number of tourists. Population (1980): 23 885.

Nikolaev 46 57N 32 00E A port in the Soviet Union, in the S Ukrainian SSR at the confluence of the Rivers Bug and Ingul about 64 km (40 mi) from the Black Sea. Long a naval base, it has important shipbuilding and flour-milling industries. Population (1984): 480 000.

Nikopol 47 34N 34 25E A city in the SW Soviet Union, in the Ukrainian SSR on the River Dnepr. It is important as the centre of a region having the world's largest manganese reserves. Population (1983 est): 153 000.

Nile, Battle of the (1 August, 1798) A naval battle in which the British, under *Nelson, defeated the French during *Napoleon's invasion of Egypt (*see* Revolutionary and Napoleonic Wars). This engagement severed communications between France and Napoleon's army in Egypt and gave Britain control of the Mediterranean.

Nile, River A river in N Africa, the longest river in the world. The longest of its three main tributaries, the White Nile, rises in Burundi as the River Luvironza before joining the River Kagera to enter Lake Victoria, the chief reservoir of the Nile. It emerges as the Victoria Nile at Jinja to flow northwards through Lake Mobutu becoming the White Nile at its confluence with the Bahr el Ghazal. At Khartoum it is joined by the Blue Nile (which rises in the Ethiopian highlands) and later by the River Atbara before flowing through a broad delta into the Mediterranean Sea. The Nile's annual floodwaters have supported cultivation on its floodplains since ancient times. To provide the increasing amounts of water required for irrigation vast dams have been constructed, including the Aswan Dam and *Aswan High Dam. Length: 6741 km (4187 mi).

nilgai A large antelope, *Bosephalus tragocamelus*, inhabiting Indian forests and plains. Up to 140 cm high at the shoulder, male nilgais have a slate-grey coat with white underparts and develop short horns and a throat tuft. Females are smaller and tawny brown. They live in small herds, browsing on shrubs and fruit.

Nilo-Saharan languages A family of African languages that covers the smallest geographical area of all the African language groups. It is also the least clearly defined group, there being very great variety within its constituent languages. It includes the Nilotic languages of the Chari-Nile group, such as Dinka and Nuer.

Nilsson, Birgit Marta (1918–) Swedish soprano, who studied at the Stockholm Royal Academy, making her debut in 1946 as Agathe in Weber's opera *Der Freischütz*; now retired, she was well known in the roles of Brunnhilde, Salome, Elektra, and Turandot.

nimbostratus A form of *cloud common in temperate latitudes. Dark grey and solid in appearance it has a low base but may show extensive vertical development. Precipitation of snow or rain is often prolonged although not usually heavy.

Nîmes 43 50N 4 21E A city in S France, the capital of the Gard department. An important Roman settlement, it was a Protestant stronghold (16th–17th centuries). It has several notable Roman remains, including an amphitheatre and the temple of Diana; the Pont du Gard lies to the NE. A trading centre for wine and brandy, its manufactures include textiles, footwear, and agricultural machinery. Population (1982): 129 924.

Nimitz, Chester W(illiam) (1885–1966) US admiral. In World War II, as commander of the Pacific Fleet after Pearl Harbor (1941), he complemented General Douglas *MacArthur's command of the SW Pacific. His victories along the island chains from Japan to New Guinea, which destroyed the Japanese fleet, were made possible by his use of aircraft carriers as support bases.

Nimrod A legendary biblical figure described in Genesis as a mighty hunter. He founded a Mesopotamian kingdom that included the cities of Babel, Erech, and Akkad and is credited with building the cities of Nineveh and Kalhu (modern Nimrud).

Nimrud An Assyrian capital (ancient Kalhu) near Mosul (Iraq). Founded about 1250 BC it was destroyed by the Medes in 612 BC. *Layard's excavations (1845–51) of the 9th-century city yielded gigantic sculptures of winged bulls and a library of *cuneiform tablets. *See also* Nineveh. □ p. 876.

ninety-five theses. *See* Luther, Martin.

Nineveh An Assyrian capital (modern Kuyunjik) near Mosul (Iraq). Nineveh was made cocapital with □Nimrud by *Sennacherib (c. 700 BC). The Medes sacked it in 612 BC. Sculptures, reliefs, and inscriptions illuminate Assyrian life at this period, but *Layard's great find was the library of *Ashurbanipal, which preserved masterpieces of *cuneiform literature, including the epic of *Gilgamesh.

Ningbo (*or* Ning-po) 29 54N 121 33E A river port in E China, in Zhejiang province near the East China Sea. Important for overseas trade (5th–9th centuries), it was also a religious centre and has many temples. Its industries include textiles and food processing. Population (1980): 900 000.

NIMRUD. *Layard directing the excavation and removal of the statue of the winged bull, now in the British Museum. He at first believed this to have been the site of Nineveh.*

Ningxia Hui Autonomous Region (*or* Ningsia Hui AR) An administrative division in N China. It occupies a plateau and is largely desert, with nomadic herdsmen in the N and some cultivation in the S. Area: 66 400 sq km (25 896 sq mi). Population (1980 est): 3 640 000. Capital: Yinchuan.

Niobe In Greek mythology, the daughter of Tantalus and wife of the King of Thebes. She took great pride in her many children and arrogantly urged the Thebans to worship her instead of Leto, the mother of only two children, Apollo and Artemis. When the Thebans consented to this, Apollo and Artemis avenged their mother's honour and killed Niobe's children. Overcome by grief, Niobe wandered to Mount Sipylus in Lydia, where Zeus changed her into a stone column or statue, the face of which was said continually to shed tears.

niobium (Nb) A soft ductile white metal, discovered in 1801. It was formerly known as columbium in the USA. Niobium is used in specialist alloys in spacecraft, and at low temperatures it has superconducting properties. Its compounds include the white oxide (Nb_2O_5), which has interesting structural properties, and the volatile fluoride and chloride (NbF_5, $NbCl_5$). At no 41; at wt 92.9064; mp $2468 \pm 10°C$; bp $4742°C$.

nipa A small *palm tree, *Nipa fruticans*, of brackish waters and estuaries of SE Asia. It has a creeping trunk and large feathery foliage, which is used for thatching and basket making. The fruits are sometimes eaten and the flowers are used commercially as a source of sugar.

Nippur A city of ancient *Sumer (modern Niffer in central Iraq). From about 2600 BC it was Sumer's chief religious centre with a *ziggurat dedicated to Enlil (built c. 2000 BC) and temples to *Ishtar (Inanna). Quantities of tablets bearing religious, literary, and other texts have been discovered.

Nirenberg, Marshall Warren (1927–) US biochemist, who developed a technique for breaking the genetic code. Nirenberg used synthetic RNA of known base sequence and determined for which amino acid it coded. He shared a

Nobel Prize (1968) with *Khorana and Robert W. Holley (1922–) for this work.

nirvana The supreme goal of Buddhism, in which liberation from the limitations of existence and rebirth are attained through the extinction of desire. Whereas the *Theravada school sees nirvana as the negation of the mundane, the *Mahayana regards it as the ultimate achievement of man's essential Buddha-nature. In Hinduism nirvana also means spiritual release in the sense of freedom from reincarnation or union with God or the Absolute.

Niš 43 20N 21 54E A city in E Yugoslavia, in Serbia on the River Nišava. For five centuries to 1877 it was a centre for Serbian resistance to Turkish control. Its products include locomotives and textiles, and it has a university (1965). Population (1981): 230 711.

Nishinomiya 34 44N 135 22E A city in Japan, in S Honshu on Osaka Bay. A heavy industrial centre, it is traditionally known for its *sake* (a Japanese rice wine). Population (1980): 410 000.

Niterói 22 54S 43 06W A city in SE Brazil, in Rio de Janeiro state on Guanabara Bay opposite the city of Rio de Janeiro. Although largely residential, it has shipbuilding and textile industries and is a popular resort. Population (1980): 386 185.

Nithsdale, William Maxwell, 5th Earl of (1676–1744) Scottish Jacobite. He was captured during the 1715 *Jacobite rising and condemned to death. His wife helped him to escape from the Tower of London dressed as a woman and he fled to France.

nitric acid (HNO_3) A fuming corrosive liquid made by the oxidation of ammonia by air in the presence of a platinum catalyst or the action of sulphuric acid on sodium or potassium nitrate. It is widely used in the manufacture of fertilizers and explosives and in other chemical processes.

nitrocellulose. *See* cellulose nitrate.

nitrogen (N) A colourless odourless gas, discovered by D. Rutherford (1749–1819) in 1772. It makes up 78% of the earth's atmosphere by volume. The element exists as diatomic molecules (N_2) bonded very strongly together. This bond must be broken before nitrogen can react, which accounts for its chemical inertness. It forms a range of chemical compounds including ammonia (NH_3), the oxides (N_2O, NO, N_2O_3, NO_2, N_2O_5), nitric acid (HNO_3), and many nitrates (for example $NaNO_3$). Liquid nitrogen has a wide range of cryogenic applications. Ammonia (NH_3) and nitrates are of great importance as fertilizers. Nitrates are also used in explosives as a source of oxygen, which they liberate when heated. Sodium and potassium nitrates occur naturally in some desert areas. Nitrogen gas is used to provide an inert gas blanket in some welding applications. At no 7; at wt 14.0067; mp -290.86°C; bp -195.8°C.

nitrogen cycle The sequence of processes by which nitrogen and its compounds are utilized in nature. Nitrogen gas in the air is converted (fixed) to ammonia by lightning, cosmic radiation, certain soil bacteria, and fertilizer manufacturers (*see* nitrogen fixation). Nitrifying bacteria in the roots of leguminous plants convert ammonia to nitrites and then to nitrates. Some nitrates are reduced by denitrifying bacteria to nitrogen, but most are used by plants to manufacture amino acids and proteins. When animals eat plants some of this nitrogenous plant material is incorporated into animal tissues. Nitrogenous excretory products and dead organic matter decompose to produce ammonia, so completing the cycle.

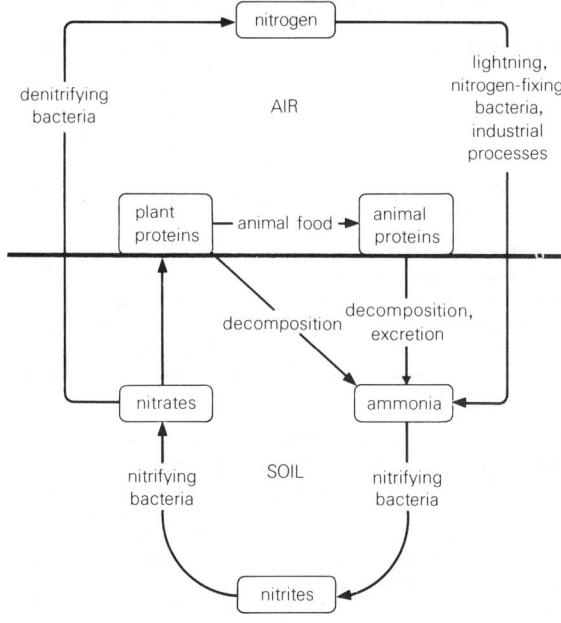

NITROGEN CYCLE

nitrogen fixation The conversion of atmospheric nitrogen gas into nitrogen compounds. The process occurs naturally by the action of bacteria in the roots of leguminous plants (*see* nitrogen cycle). Industrial methods of fixing nitrogen are of immense importance in the manufacture of nitrogen fertilizers. One method is the reaction of nitrogen with oxygen to give nitric oxide in an electric arc. The process is only economical in regions in which cheap hydroelectric power is available. The major method of fixing nitrogen is the *Haber-Bosch process for making ammonia.

nitroglycerin ($C_3H_5(NO_3)_3$) A yellow oily highly *explosive liquid. It is used as an explosive either alone or as *dynamite or *gelignite.

Niue 19 02S 169 55W A fertile coral island in the S Pacific Ocean, belonging to New Zealand. Copra and bananas are exported. Area: 260 sq km (100 sq mi). Population (1980 est): 3288. Chief town: Alofi.

Niven, David (1909–83) British film actor. His early films include *The Prisoner of Zenda* (1937) and *Wuthering Heights* (1939), and he later appeared in many stylish comedies and action films, including *Separate Tables* (1958), *The Guns of Navarone* (1961), and *Candleshoe* (1977). He published two highly successful volumes of autobiography, *The Moon's a Balloon* (1972) and *Bring on the Empty Horses* (1975).

Nixon, Richard Milhous (1913–) US statesman; Republican president (1969-74). A Californian-born lawyer, he contributed to McCarthy's anticommunist investigations and achieved early political power partly by discrediting Democratic opponents as communist sympathizers. He was Eisenhower's vice president from 1953 until 1960, when he became the Republican presidential candidate. He was defeated by Kennedy, and when in 1962 he failed to win the governorship of California his political career seemed over. However, he returned to national politics in the mid-1960s and in 1968 narrowly defeated Hubert Humphrey for the presidency. As president he reduced US troop commitments abroad and in 1973 ended US military involvement in Vietnam. In 1972 he visited the People's Republic of China, a move that was to lead to the establishment of diplomatic relations between the USA and China. Participation in illegal efforts to ensure re-election in 1972 and the subsequent cover-up attempt led to the *Watergate scandal. Under threat of impeachment he became the first president to resign office. President *Ford granted him a free pardon after succeeding him as president. He wrote *RN: The memoirs of Richard Nixon* (1978) and *The Real War* (1980).

Nizam al-Mulk (c. 1018–92) Persian statesman, who was vizier (minister; 1063–92) to the *Seljuq sultans *Alp-Arslan and Malik-Shah. Wielding almost absolute power, he governed the Seljuq empire at its zenith. He was the author of *The Book of Government*, in which he expressed his political and orthodox religious views. Shortly before Malik-Shah's death, Nizam al-Mulk was assassinated.

Nizhnii Novgorod. *See* Gorkii.

Nizhnii Tagil 58 00N 59 58E A city in the Soviet Union, in the W RSFSR on the River Tagil and on the E slopes of the Ural Mountains. Its metallurgical industries arise from the surrounding ironmining region. Population (1981 est): 404 000.

Nkomo, Joshua (1917–) Zimbabwean politician. Secretary general of the Rhodesian African Railway Union in Rhodesia (1945-50), Nkomo became president of the Zimbabwe African People's Union (ZAPU) in 1961. With headquarters in Zambia, it allied with Robert Mugabe's Zimbabwe African National Union (ZANU) in 1976 to form the *Patriotic Front (PF) against the government of Ian Smith in Rhodesia (*see also* Zimbabwe). Nkomo became a minister in Mugabe's government in 1980 but was dismissed (1982) when arms caches were found on his farms; he returned to the Cabinet in 1988.

Nkrumah, Kwame (1909–72) Ghanaian statesman; prime minister (1957–60) and then president (1960–66). A student in the USA and the UK, after returning home he formed (1949) the Convention People's Party, which with a policy of noncooperation with the British took the Gold Coast to independence as Ghana in 1957. Nkrumah was deposed by a military coup in 1966. He sought exile in Guinea, where Sékou Touré made him cohead of state. An advocate of African unity, he wrote *Towards Colonial Freedom* (1947) and *Handbook of Revolutionary Warfare* (1968).

No A form of Japanese theatre, the early development of which is associated with the work of the actor and dramatist *Zeami Motokiyo (1363-1443). Originating in religious ritual and folk dances and strongly influenced by Zen Buddhism, it is performed with a minimum of scenery and

	1984	1985	1986	1987
Physics	C. Rubbia S. van der Meer	Klaus von Klitzing	Ernst Ruska Gerd Binning Heinrich Rohrer	Alex Müller Georg Bednorz
Chemistry	R. Bruce Merrifield	Herbert Hauptman Jerome Karle	Dudley Herschbach Yuan Tseh Lee John Polanyi	Donald Cram Jean-Marie Lehn Charles Pedersen
Medicine	N. Jerne G. Koehler C. Milstein	Joseph Goldstein Michael Brown	Stanley Cohen Rita Levi-Montalcini	Susumu Tonegawa
Literature	Jaroslav Seifert	Claude Simon	Wole Soyinka	Joseph Brodsky
Peace	Bishop Desmond Tutu	International Physicians for the Prevention of Nuclear War	Elie Wiesel	Oscar Arias Sánchez
Economics	Sir Richard Stone	Franco Modigliani	James Buchanan	Robert M. Solow

NOBEL   *Recent prizewinners*

properties and is characterized by the use of dance, mime, and masks. The acting is highly stylized. A traditional No programme lasts several hours and consists of five plays separated by three comic interludes known as *Kyogen*. It has remained an aristocratic form, contrasting with the more realistic *Kabuki* drama.

Noah An Old Testament figure. After God had determined to destroy the human race because of its wickedness (Genesis 6–8), he made a covenant with Noah as the only man worthy of being saved from the coming flood. Noah was instructed to build an ark for his family and representatives of each animal species, and they would be preserved after the flood subsided. Noah and his sons Ham, Shem, and Japheth and their wives became the ancestors of the present human race. Several other cultures have similar legends about a catastrophic primeval flood.

Nobel, Alfred Bernhard (1833–96) Swedish chemist and businessman. From his invention of dynamite (1867) and a smokeless gunpowder (1889) and his exploitation of the Baku oilfields he amassed a considerable fortune, leaving £1.75 million as a foundation for the **Nobel Prizes**. Five of the annual awards (for physics, chemistry, physiology or medicine, literature, and peace) are made by various Swedish academies, except for the Peace Prize, which is awarded by a committee elected by the Norwegian parliament. A sixth prize, for economics, instituted in memory of Alfred Nobel, has been financed by the Swedish National Bank since 1969.

nobelium (No) A synthetic transuranic element discovered in 1957 by bombarding curium with carbon ions in an accelerator. Five isotopes with short half-lives have been discovered. Named after Alfred Nobel. At no 102; at wt (255).

Nobile, Umberto (1885–1978) Italian aeronautical engineer and aviator. He designed the airships *Norge* and *Italia*, piloting the *Norge* in *Amundsen's flight over the North Pole (1926). In 1928 he flew the *Italia* across the Pole but crashed on the return journey, being rescued after 40 days.

Noble, Sir Andrew (1831–1915) British physicist, who founded the science of ballistics. In conjunction with Sir Frederick *Abel he improved the quality of gunpowder and made many innovations in artillery design.

noble gases (*or* inert gases) The elements forming group O of the *periodic table: helium, neon, argon, krypton, xenon, and radon. All are colourless odourless tasteless gases, which are slightly soluble in water. They are virtually inert chemically owing to their filled outer electron shells, although complexes of xenon and krypton have recently been isolated (e.g. XeF_4). Helium is commercially obtained from natural gas, the others (apart from radon) from the distillation of air. Their inertness suits them for such applications as arc welding and filling incandescent lamps.

noble metals Metals, such as gold, silver, and platinum, that do not rust or tarnish in air or water and are not easily attacked by acids.

Nobunaga Oda (1534–82) Japanese general, hero of many legends. As the emperor's chief military commander, Nobunaga was virtual ruler of central Japan from 1568. Thereafter he built up his own regular forces, bringing much of Japan under imperial rule. His work of unification was brought to an end by his assassination.

Noctiluca A genus of minute single-celled animals (□Protozoa) found in coastal waters throughout the world. They are pinkish, about the size of a pinhead, have a single flagellum that wafts food particles towards the mouth, and are luminescent. Class: *Flagellata*.

noctuid moth A moth belonging to the family *Noctuidae* (about 20 000 species), also called owlet moth, widespread in Eurasia and North America. The adults are usually dull brown or grey and fly at night. The caterpillars, which are also known as *army worms and *cutworms, are active at night, eating plant roots and stems.

noctule An insect-eating *bat, *Nyctalus noctula*, of Eurasia. About 12 cm long, it has bright-chestnut fur and long narrow wings. Noctules hibernate only from Dec to Jan. Family: *Vespertilionidae*.

noddy. *See* tern.

Noel-Baker, Philip John (1889–1982) British campaigner for disarmament and Labour politician. He worked at the League of Nations (1919–22) and helped to draft the UN Charter; he was an MP (1929–31, 1936–50). The author of *The Arms Race: A Programme for World Disarmament* (1958), in 1959 he was awarded the Nobel Peace Prize.

Noguchi, Hideyo (1876–1928) Japanese bacteriologist, who discovered that paralysis in syphilitic patients was caused by spirochaete organisms in the central nervous system. Noguchi also investigated snake venoms, poliomyelitis, and trachoma. He died of yellow fever while investigating the disease in Africa.

Nolan, Sir Sidney (1917–) Australian painter. Largely self-taught, he first painted abstract works, influenced by *Klee and *Moholy-Nagy but is internationally known for his paintings of Australian historical figures, such as Ned *Kelly, and landscapes of the outback. Knighted in 1981, he became a member of the OM in 1983.

Nolde, Emil (E. Hansen; 1867–1956) German expressionist painter and printmaker. Although briefly associated

(1906-07) with Die *Brucke, he developed an independent style characterized by his distorted forms and clashing colours. Deeply religious, he painted many biblical scenes, bleak landscapes of the Baltic coast, and still lifes of flowers.

Nollekens, Joseph (1737-1823) British neoclassical sculptor (*see* neoclassicism). After executing several portrait busts in Rome (1760-70), he became highly successful with his portrait sculptures in England. His sitters included George III, Benjamin West, William Pitt the Younger, and Charles James Fox. He was also a sculptor of tombs and mythological subjects.

nomads Peoples who live in no fixed place but wander periodically according to the seasonal availability of food, pasture, or trade and employment. Hunters and gatherers (e.g. Australian Aborigines) usually live in small bands that spend anything from a few days to a few weeks in a vicinity, moving within a loosely defined territory. Pastoralists (e.g. many central Asian tribes) often move between summer and winter pastures (*see* transhumance). Traders, tinkers, entertainers, and those who provide certain crafts and services, such as the *gipsies, often travel widely seeking custom.

Nome 64 30N 165 30W A port in the USA, in W Alaska on the S shore of the Seward Peninsula. Founded as Anvil City during the gold rush of 1868, it has fishing and handicraft industries. Population (1980): 2301.

SIDNEY NOLAN Dead Duck Mine, *private collection.*

nominalism The medieval philosophical theory that general terms (called universals) have no real existence, that is, there is no abstract entity corresponding to a universal. Thus, there exists no such thing as blueness, but only individual blue things (called particulars). Nominalism, therefore, contrasts with *realism. *William of Ockham, *Hobbes, and certain modern analytic philosophers have all made varying statements of nominalist theory.

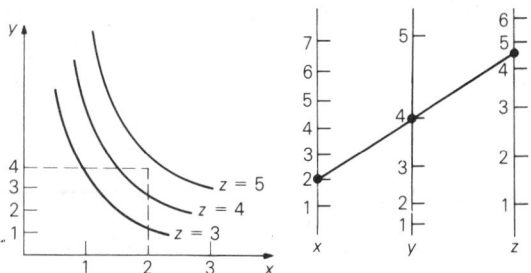

NOMOGRAPH   *If* x = 2 *and* y = 4, *a value of approximately* 4.5 *for* z *is obtained from the two forms of nomograph shown.*

nomograph (*or* nomogram) A *graph showing the relationship between three variable quantities, enabling the value of one variable to be read off if the other two are known. It can take the form of a series of curves on a graph of two quantities, corresponding to constant values of a third. Or it can consist of three straight lines calibrated with the values of the variables. A fourth line is drawn between two known points on two of the straight lines: the point at which this fourth line cuts the third straight line gives the value of the unknown quantity.

Nonconformists In its original early-17th-century sense, the term referred to members of the Church of England who did not conform with its rituals. After the Act of Uniformity (1662), the term's scope widened to include members of dissenting Protestant sects, such as the Quakers and Methodists.

non-Euclidean geometry A form of *geometry in which *Euclid's postulates are not satisfied. In *Euclidean geometry if two lines are both at right angles to a third they never meet (i.e. they remain parallel). In, for example, hyperbolic (or elliptic) geometry they eventually diverge (or converge). Non-Euclidean geometry was developed independently by *Lobachevski (published 1831) and *Bolyai (published 1836). *See also* Riemannian geometry.

Nonjurors Four hundred Church of England clergy who were deprived of their livings in 1690 for refusing to swear allegiance to William III and Mary II on the grounds that they had usurped the throne from James II. In Scotland most ministers of the Episcopal Church, which was disestablished in 1689, were Nonjurors.

Nono, Luigi (1924-   ) Italian composer. A pupil of Francesco Malipiero (1882-1973), he married Schoenberg's daughter Nuria. Nono's compositions frequently employ serialism; many of them consist of settings of texts by Marxist writers. They include *La fabbrica illuminata* (for mezzo-soprano and tape; 1964) and *Non consumiamo Marx* (for voices and tape; 1969).

Nonproliferation of Nuclear Weapons, Treaty on the. *See* disarmament.

nonsense verse A genre of comic verse that is structured according to a kind of surreal logic that defies rational interpretation. It is characterized by strict rhyme schemes and the use of meaningless neologisms. The genre, predominantly English, is usually dated from the publication of *The Book of Nonsense* by Edward *Lear in 1846. Other outstanding writers of nonsense are Lewis *Carroll and Hilaire *Belloc. *See also* limerick.

Nootka A North American Indian people of the NW Pacific coast region who speak a *Wakashan language. They were traditionally hunters, fishers, and expert whale catchers, using large canoes and harpoons. They practised the *potlatch as did their neighbours, the *Kwakiutl.

noradrenaline (*or* norepinephrine) A hormone that is secreted by the central core (medulla) of the adrenal glands.

It is a *catecholamine, structurally similar to *adrenaline but produces different effects in certain target organs, especially the heart, the rate of which it decreases. Noradrenaline is taken up and stored by cells of the sympathetic nervous system and subsequently released by nerve endings to excite adjacent nerves in the transmission of impulses. In the hypothalamus it is thought to inhibit transmission of impulses.

Nordenskjöld, Nils Adolf Erik, Baron (1832-1901) Swedish navigator. After exploration in Spitsbergen he became the first, in the *Vega*, to navigate the *Northeast Passage (1878-79).

Nore, the A sandbank in SE England, at the mouth of the River Thames near Sheerness. A naval mutiny occurred near here (1797).

Norfolk 36 54N 76 18W A seaport in the USA, in Virginia on Hampton Roads. Founded in 1682, it suffered considerable damage in the American Revolution and the US Civil War. It is the headquarters of the US Atlantic Fleet. Norfolk's industries include textiles, cars, and shipbuilding. Population (1980): 266 979.

Norfolk A county of E England, in *East Anglia bordering on the North Sea. It is mainly low lying, with fens in the W and the Norfolk *Broads in the E. It is mainly agricultural with arable farming and intensive turkey rearing. Fishing is centred on Great Yarmouth. Tourism is important, especially in Great Yarmouth and on the Norfolk Broads. Under local government reorganization in 1974 it gained a small part of NE Suffolk. Area: 2763 sq km (1067 sq mi). Population (1981): 693 490. Administrative centre: Norwich.

Norfolk, Thomas Howard, 3rd Duke of (1473-1554) English statesman; the uncle of two of Henry VIII's wives, Anne Boleyn and Catherine Howard. He became president of the privy council in 1529 and in 1536 suppressed the *Pilgrimage of Grace. He lost power after Catherine Howard's execution (1542) and was imprisoned under Edward VI for involvement in the treason (1546) of his son Henry Howard, Earl of *Surrey. Surrey's son **Thomas Howard, 4th Duke of Norfolk** (1538-72) was imprisoned (1559-60) by Elizabeth I for planning to marry Mary, Queen of Scots. He subsequently participated in *Ridolfi's plot against Elizabeth and was executed.

Norfolk Island 29 05S 167 59E A mountainous Australian island in the SW Pacific Ocean. Formerly a British penal colony, some of the descendants of the *Bounty* mutineers were resettled here from *Pitcairn Island (1856). Area: 36 sq km (14 sq mi). Population (1984 est): 2000. Chief town: Kingston.

Norman art and architecture The styles that flourished in Normandy and the lands that the Normans had conquered in the 11th and 12th centuries, notably the *romanesque architectural style. First appearing in England before the Norman conquest in Westminster Abbey (consecrated 1065), Norman architecture later developed into a distinctive native style. Characteristic Norman features include massive walls, rounded arches, two-tower church façades and abstract geometrical ornamentation on columns, etc. In S Italy the Norman style was fused with the native Saracen and Byzantine traditions. In the other arts the most notable Norman achievement was the *Bayeux tapestry.

Norman conquest (1066-72) The conquest of England by William, Duke of Normandy (*see* William the Conqueror). After defeating Harold II at the battle of Hastings (1066), William captured London and was crowned. English risings in the SW, N, and on the Welsh border were suppressed by 1070 and with the defeat of the Scots in 1072 the conquest was complete. The Norman influence on Anglo-Saxon England was fundamental. Although structures of government continued virtually unaltered, the English lay and ecclesiastical aristocracy was replaced by Normans and

other continentals and *feudalism was introduced. Latin became the language of government and Norman French, the literary language; the Norman influence was also felt in church organization and architecture.

Normandy (French name: Normandie) A former province in N France, on the English Channel. It now comprises the planning regions of **Basse-Normandie**, with an area of 17 583 sq km (6787 sq mi) and a population (1975 est) of 1 303 600, and **Haute-Normandie**, with an area of 12 258 sq km (4732 sq mi) and a population (1975 est) of 1 595 400. A fertile agricultural area with sheep and dairy farming, it also produces flax, hemp, and apples. *History*: during the medieval period Normandy flourished as a major state. William II, Duke of Normandy, conquered England (1066) to become William I of England. Disputed between England and France during the following centuries, it finally reverted to France in 1449. During World War II it suffered severe damage, the Normandy invasion taking place in 1944.

Norman French The dialect spoken in Normandy during the early middle ages and by the Norman invaders of England. Their speech influenced English and introduced new words to the language.

Normans Viking settlers in N France (later Normandy) whose rule, under their leader Rollo, was formally recognized (911) by Charles the Simple (879-929; reigned 898-923). Further expansion in Normandy followed and by the end of the 11th century they had also conquered England (*see* Norman conquest) and much of S Italy and Sicily and had established crusading states in the E, besides gaining a foothold in Wales and Scotland. Noted for their military dynamism and inventiveness (they introduced the castle into England) they adopted and adapted existing administrative practices in countries they conquered with great success, normally possessing a stable government working in close harmony with the Church.

Norns In Norse mythology, the fates, three females who shape the life of man. They are Urth (the past), Verthandi (the present), and Skuld (the future).

Norrköping 58 35N 16 10E A port in SE Sweden, on an inlet of the Baltic Sea. Its industries include shipbuilding, engineering, and textiles. Population (1983): 118 064.

Norsemen. *See* Vikings.

North, Frederick, Lord (1732-92) British statesman; prime minister (1770-82). He was a Lord of the Treasury (1759-65) and chancellor of the exchequer (1767-70) before becoming prime minister, as which his policies were largely dictated by George III. He was severely criticized for precipitating the *American Revolution (1775-83), and for British defeats in the conflict, and eventually resigned.

North, Sir Thomas (c. 1535-c. 1601) English translator. His famous translation of Plutarch's *Lives of the Noble Grecians and Romans* (1579) was based on that of the classical scholar Jacques Amyot (1513-93) but was more vivid and descriptive. It was widely read in Elizabethan times and used by Shakespeare. Other translations by North include the beast fables of Doni (1580).

Northallerton 54 20N 1 26W A market town in N England, the administrative centre of North Yorkshire. The battle of the Standard took place nearby in 1138, in which the English defeated the Scots. Northallerton has light engineering and trailer-manufacturing industries. Population (1981): 9622.

North America The third largest continent in the world, in the N of the W hemisphere bordering on the Arctic Ocean, the N Pacific Ocean, the N Atlantic Ocean, the Gulf of Mexico, and the Caribbean Sea. The Isthmus of Panama links it with South America. It is generally accepted as consisting of *Canada, the *United States of America, *Mexico, *Central America, *Greenland, and the *West Indies. The mountains of the Western Cordillera extend down its entire W coast descending E to the Great Plains before rising to the Appalachian Mountains further E, which are separated from the Canadian Shield by the Great Lakes. Area: over 24 000 000 sq km (9 500 000 sq mi). Population (1981 est): 323 250 000.

North American Indian languages A geographical classi-fication of the languages of the indigenous peoples of North America. It is estimated that these languages originally numbered about 300; at least a third of these are dead or dying out, but the number of speakers of a few, such as *Navaho, is increasing. Highly diverse, these languages have been classified in various ways and about 57 families have been identified. *Sapir arranged these into six phyla (1929): *Eskimo-*Aleut; *Algonkian-*Wakashan; *Na-Dené; *Penutian; *Hokan-*Siouan; and *Aztec-Tanoan.

Northampton 52 14N 0 54W A town in central England, the administrative centre of Northamptonshire on the River Nene. Notable buildings include St Peter's Church and the Church of the Holy Sepulchre (one of the few round churches in the country), both dating from the 12th century. A centre of the footwear industry, Northampton also manufactures shoe machinery, cosmetics, leather goods, and motor-car accessories and has undergone considerable expansion since its designation as a new town in 1968. Population (1981): 156 853.

Northamptonshire (*or* Northants) A county in the East Midlands of England. An escarpment runs NE–SW across the county, dipping gently to the SE. It is predominantly agricultural producing livestock, cereals, potatoes, and sugar beet. Industrial activities include shoemaking, printing, food processing, and engineering. Area: 2367 sq km (915 sq mi) Population (1981): 527 532. Administrative centre: Northampton.

North Atlantic Drift One of the major ocean currents of the world, flowing NE across the Atlantic from the *Gulf Stream.

North Atlantic Treaty Organization (NATO) An alliance formed in 1949 by Belgium, Canada, Denmark, France, Iceland, Italy, Luxembourg, the Netherlands, Norway, Por-tugal, the UK, and the USA; Greece and Turkey joined in 1952, West Germany in 1955, and Spain in 1982 (confirmed by referendum in 1986). It was formed during the *Cold War to protect the western world against possible Soviet aggres-sion. All member states are bound to protect any member against attack. The strategic areas of NATO are divided into three great commands covering the Atlantic, Europe, and the English Channel and North Sea. NATO also seeks to en-courage economic and social cooperation among its member states. Its secretariat headquarters is in Brussels and its mili-tary headquarters near Mons.

North Borneo. *See* Sabah.

North Brabant (Dutch name: Noord-Brabant) A province in the S Netherlands, bordering on Belgium. Its fertile coastal lowlands were badly flooded in 1953; these produce wheat and sugar beet. Area: 4911 sq km (1896 sq mi). Population (1981 est): 2 071 885. Capital: 's Hertogenbosch.

North Cape (Norwegian name: Nordkapp) 71 11N 25 40E A promontory in Norway, on the island of Magerøy. It is the most northerly point in Europe.

North Carolina A state in the USA, on the S Atlantic coast. The extensive coastal plain stretches westwards from the indented coastline to the Piedmont Plateau and the Appalachian Mountains in the E. It is heavily populated and the leading industrial state in the South, producing textiles, furniture, and processed foods. It is the nation's major producer of tobacco and tobacco products. *History*: one of the 13 original colonies, it shares its early history with South Carolina. It was made a separate colony in 1713 and it became a state in 1789. It was a supporter of the Con-federate cause in the US Civil War. Area: 136 197 sq km (52 586 sq mi). Population (1983): 5 874 429. Capital: Ra-leigh.

Northcliffe, Alfred Charles William Harmsworth, 1st Viscount (1865–1922) British newspaper proprietor, born in Ireland, who pioneered popular journalism in Britain. After founding several periodicals he and his brother (*see* Rothermere, 1st Viscount) bought the *Evening News* (Lon-don) in 1894. Two years later he founded the *Daily Mail*, which was immediately the most widely circulated daily in the world. In 1903 he founded the *Daily Mirror* and in 1908 acquired control of *The Times*, which was sold after his death.

North Dakota A state in the N central USA. It comprises three main physical regions: the Red River Valley along the E border, the Central Lowlands just W of this strip, and the Great Plains in the SW. The population is sparse, parti-cularly in the W. Agriculture and mining are the two principal economic activities; its coal and oil reserves are among the country's largest and it is a major producer of wheat. The small manufacturing sector is growing, especially food processing. *History*: early attempts to settle were made by Scottish and Irish families at Pembina in 1812, although major settlements did not occur until after 1871 and the arrival of the railway. It formed part of the territory of Dakota from 1861 until 1889 when it was made a separate state. Area: 183 022 sq km (70 665 sq mi). Population (1980): 652 695. Capital: Bismarck.

Northeast Caucasian languages A group of about 25 languages of the NE region of the Caucasus, also called the Nakho-Dagestanian family. Chechen, the most important, is part of the Nakh subdivision. The Dagestanian subdivision may be further divided into the Avar-Ando-Dido languages of which Avar is the most important and the only one that is written; the Lakk-Dargwa languages; and the Lezgian languages. Most of these languages fall within the boun-daries of the Dagestan ASSR.

North-East Frontier Agency. *See* Arunachal Pradesh.

Northeast Passage (Russian name: Severny Morskoy Put) The sea route along the N Eurasian coast, kept open in summer by Soviet icebreakers. It was first traversed by the Swedish explorer, Niels Nordenskjöld (1878–79). *See also* Northwest Passage.

Northern Areas The northernmost districts administered by, although technically not part of, Pakistan, principally Baltistan, Hunza, and Gilgit.

Northern Ireland. *See* Ireland.

Northern Marianas. *See* Mariana Islands.

Northern Rhodesia. *See* Zambia.

NORMAN ARCHITECTURE *The highly ornamental south door-way (c. 1140) of the Norman church at Kilpeck near Hereford.*

Northern Territory An administrative division of N central Australia, bordering on the Timor and Arafura Seas. It consists chiefly of a plateau with Arnhem Land in the N (containing Australia's largest Aborigine reservation) and the Macdonnell Ranges in the S. SW of Alice Springs and close to the geographical centre of the continent stands *Ayers Rock. The main agricultural activity is the rearing of beef cattle; these are transported in trains of trailers (road trains) along the highways, the chief means of transport. Minerals are important, especially iron ore, manganese, copper, gold, and bauxite. There are also large deposits of uranium, as yet unexploited, but possibly containing a quarter of all the world's known resources of high-grade ore. In 1978 the Northern Territory became an independent state, although the federal government retained control over uranium. Area: 1 346 200 sq km (519 770 sq mi). Population (1980 est): 121 300. Capital: Darwin.

Northern War, Great (1700-21) The war fought between Russia, Denmark, and Poland, on one side, and Sweden, on the other. *Charles XII of Sweden, whose Baltic supremacy was opposed by his neighbours, defeated Denmark, then Russia at Narva (1700), and Poland (1706). He was subsequently overcome by the Russians under Peter the Great (Poltava, 1709) and fled to the Turks, who defeated the Russians at Pruth River (1711). After returning to Sweden Charles suffered a series of setbacks and was forced to initiate peace negotiations. At the same time he continued hostilities in the course of which he died (1718). The war between Denmark, Poland, and Sweden was ended by the Treaties of Stockholm (1719-20). The Treaty of *Nystad (1721) between Russia and Sweden marked Russia's emergence as the major Baltic power.

North German Confederation (1867-71) An alliance of German states under Prussian leadership formed by Bismarck following victory in the Austro-Prussian War (1866). It formed the basis of the German Empire, proclaimed in 1871.

North Holland (Dutch name: Noord-Holland) A province in the W Netherlands, between the North Sea and the IJsselmeer. Much of it lies below sea level. The province contains major urban centres, including Amsterdam, and its industrial activities include shipbuilding, textiles, and motor vehicles. Its farms produce mainly dairy and livestock products. Area: 2912 sq km (1124 sq mi). Population (1981 est): 2 315 676. Capital: Haarlem.

North Island The most northerly of the two principal islands of New Zealand, separated from South Island by Cook Strait. It consists chiefly of a central volcanic plateau with fertile coastal and valley lowlands. Area: 114 729 sq km (44 281 sq mi). Population (1980 est): 2 289 300.

North Ossetian Autonomous Soviet Socialist Republic An administrative division in the S Soviet Union, in the RSFSR. The Ossetians are a Caucasian people, known for their wood and silver carving. The region has metal and oil deposits and industries include textiles and food processing. The main crops are grain, cotton, and grapes. Area: 8000 sq km (3088 sq mi). Population (1981 est): 601 000. Capital: Ordzhonikidze.

North Rhine-Westphalia (German name: Nordrhein-Westfalen) A *Land* in W West Germany, bordering on the Netherlands and Belgium. It was formed in 1946. Rich in minerals, including coal, it contains the vast Ruhr industrial region and is one of the world's most densely populated areas. Its many industries include steel, textiles, and chemicals. Area: 34 057 sq km (13 147 sq mi). Population (1980 est): 17 040 700. Capital: Düsseldorf.

North Riding. *See* Yorkshire.

Northrop, John Howard (1891–1987) US biochemist, who isolated and purified various digestive enzymes and showed that they were all proteins. He received the 1946 Nobel Prize.

North Sea A section of the Atlantic Ocean in NW Europe, between the British Isles and the continent N of the Strait of Dover. The entire floor is part of the continental shelf, with an average depth of about 300 m (914 ft). It is fished for over 5% of the world's catch, consisting especially of cod, herring, and mackerel; recent exploitation of *North Sea oil and natural-gas finds have further increased its economic importance. Freak high tides have flooded large areas of coastal lowlands, especially in the Netherlands and E England.

North Sea oil The *oil deposits that were discovered under the North Sea in the 1960s. Exploration and development has been carried out by multinational companies from the USA and Europe. The area is divided into UK, West German, Norwegian, Danish, and Dutch sectors. The UK has the largest of these sectors and became self-sufficient in oil in 1980, since when oil revenues have aided the UK's balance of payments. In 1978 some 54 million tonnes of oil were produced by the UK; by 1984 total output had reached 125 million tonnes. By comparison, world production of oil was nearly three billion tonnes in 1984. Discovered reserves in the North Sea contain an estimated 2.5 billion tonnes but exploration is still continuing.

North Star. *See* Polaris.

North Uist. *See* Uist.

Northumberland The northernmost county of England, bordering on Scotland and the North Sea. It consists of a coastal plain rising to the Cheviot Hills in the N and the Pennines in the W. The main river, the Tyne, flows SE. The county also includes Kielder Water (opened 1982), the largest man-made lake in N Europe. There are outstanding Roman remains, notably Hadrian's Wall. The main agricultural activity is sheep farming. In 1974 the industrial SE became part of Tyne and Wear. Area: 5033 sq km (1944 sq mi). Population (1981): 299 905. Administrative centre: Newcastle-upon-Tyne.

Northumberland, John Dudley, Duke of (1502-53) English statesman, who was virtual ruler of England (1549-53) under Edward VI. On the accession of Edward (a minor) in 1547, Dudley (as Earl of Warwick) became a member of the regency council dominated by the Duke of *Somerset. He replaced Somerset in 1549, securing his execution in 1552. In 1553 he married his son Guildford Dudley to Lady Jane *Grey, whom he persuaded the king to name as his heir. On Edward's death Jane was proclaimed queen but lack of support forced Northumberland's surrender to Mary (I) and he was executed.

Northumbria A kingdom of Anglo-Saxon England north of the Humber, formed in the 7th century by the union of the kingdoms of Deira and Bernicia. Northumbria became politically pre-eminent in England in the 7th century under *Edwin, Saint *Oswald, and *Oswin. Northumbrian scholarship was also unrivalled, boasting such great names as *Bede and *Alcuin. By 829, however, Northumbria had recognized the overlordship of Wessex and in the late 9th century its unity was destroyed by the Danes.

Northwest Caucasian languages A group of languages of the NW region of the Caucasus, also called the Abkhazo-Adyghian family. It includes Abkhaz, Abaza, Adyghian, Kabardian (Circassian), and Ubykh. All but Ubykh are written. A distinctive feature is the small number of vowel sounds and great number of consonants.

Northwest Company A Canadian fur-trading company, founded in 1783, that became a bitter rival of the *Hudson's Bay Company. Conflict between them ended in their forced merger in 1821.

North-West Frontier Province A province in NW Pakistan, SE of Afghanistan in the Himalayas and lower mountains. Its Pathan inhabitants mostly herd livestock or cultivate grains, fruit, sugar cane, and tobacco. There is little industry, but the province controls the strategic Khyber Pass to Afghanistan. Over the centuries each great power in the region has sought to control the province, but it has usually remained semiautonomous because of its rugged terrain and fierce inhabitants. Area: 74 522 sq km (28 773 sq mi). Population (1981): 11 061 000. Capital: Peshawar.

Northwest Passage   The sea route along the coast of North America, between the Atlantic and Pacific Oceans. It was first traversed by Roald Amundsen (1903–06) and since 1969 has been used for transporting Alaskan oil. *See also* Northeast Passage.

Northwest Territories   A territory of N Canada, stretching from 60°N to the North Pole. It consists of the districts of *Franklin, *Keewatin, and *Mackenzie. One of the most sparsely populated areas in the world, two-thirds of the people are Indians and Eskimos, who traditionally live nomadically by hunting, trapping, and fishing. The Eskimos are increasingly settling in larger communities around cooperatives and government institutions. Rich in mineral resources, the economy is dominated by mining; pitchblende, silver, zinc, lead, tungsten, and gold are all extracted. The territory's vast oil reserves are being explored. Plans to divide the territory on ethnic lines—into the Eskimo E (Nunavut) and mixed-race W (Denendeh) —were agreed in 1987. Area: 3 246 389 sq km (1 253 432 sq mi). Population (1981): 45 471. Capital: Yellowknife.

Northwich   53 16N 2 32W A town in N England, in Cheshire on the River Weaver. Salt is extracted and there are large chemical works. Population (1981): 17 126.

North Yorkshire.   A county in N England, bordering on the North Sea. It was created in 1974 from most of the North Riding and parts of the West and East Ridings of Yorkshire. It consists of two upland areas separated by the Vale of York. The Pennines rise to the W of the Vale, while the Cleveland Hills, North York Moors, and Tabular Hills rise to the E. The River Ouse flows SE to the Humber Estuary. It is chiefly agricultural with cereals in the Vale of York, dairy farming in the Pennine Dales, and sheep farming on the moorlands. There is some industrial activity in the larger towns, such as York, primarily associated with agriculture. Coal is mined from a new field centred on Selby (opened 1983). Tourism is centred on Harrogate and Scarborough. Area: 8321 sq km (3213 sq mi). Population (1981): 666 610. Administrative centre: Northallerton.

Norway, Kingdom of (Norwegian name: Norge)   A country in N Europe occupying the W part of the Scandinavian Peninsula. It borders on the Arctic Ocean (N), the Norwegian Sea (W), and the Skagerrak (S). It is largely mountainous, reaching heights of almost 2500 m (8000 ft), with a heavily indented coastline. There are numerous glaciers and forests cover approximately one-quarter of the country. The archipelago of Svalbard and Jan Meyen Island are also part of Norway together with the dependencies of Bouvet Island, Peter I Island, and Queen Maud Land. Norway is one of the most sparsely populated countries on the Continent. *Economy*: abundant hydroelectric power has enabled Norway to develop as an industrial nation. Chemicals, engineering, shipbuilding, and food processing are all important while forestry is a major source of wealth, especially for the pulp and paper industry. Norway is one of the world's great fishing nations and fish is one of the principal exports. It also has one of the world's largest merchant fleets. Revenues from tourism are important. Minerals include iron ore, limestone, coal, copper, zinc, and lead. Heavy borrowing to finance the development of offshore oil and gas deposits (discovered 1968), which have proved to be considerably less than was first thought, has led to a balance-of-payments deficit. *History*: its early history was dominated by the Vikings. The many local chieftains were not subjected to a single ruler until the reign of Harold I Haarfager (died c. 930). Christianity was introduced in the 10th century and became established under Olaf II Haraldsson (reigned 1015–28). During the reign (1204–63) of Haakon IV Haakonsson Norway acquired Iceland and Greenland and in the 14th century, under Margaret, was united with Sweden and Denmark. Sweden broke free in

1523 but Norway remained under Danish domination until 1814, when it was united with Sweden under the Swedish Crown, while maintaining internal self-government. Only in 1907 was full independence achieved. Norway declared its neutrality in both World Wars but from 1940 to 1944 was occupied by the Germans, who established a government under Quisling. Abandoning isolationism after World War II, Norway joined the UN (of which the Norwegian Trygve Lie was first secretary general) and NATO. In 1972 Norwegians rejected membership of the EEC in a referendum. In common with other Scandinavian countries Norway has a highly developed social-welfare system. Head of state: Olav V. Prime minister: Kaare Isaachsen Willoch (1928–   ). Official language: Norwegian. Official religion: Evangelical Lutheran. Official currency: krone of 100 øre. Area: 323 886 sq km (125 053 sq mi). Population (1983): 4 131 000. Capital and main port: Oslo.

Norwegian   A North Germanic language of the West Scandinavian division, spoken in Norway. There are two distinct forms known as Dano-Norwegian (Bokmål or Riksmål) and New Norwegian (Nynorsk or Landsmål). Bokmål derives from written Danish, the language used during the union with Denmark (1397–1814). Nynorsk was created by the scholar Ivar Aasen (1813–96) to revive the tradition of Old Norwegian, which was closely related to *Old Norse speech. Bokmål is more widely used.

Norwegian Antarctic Territory   The area in Antarctica claimed by Norway, lying S of latitude 60°S and between longitudes 20°W and 45°E. It consists of the end of Coats Land, Queen Maud Land, and islands. There have been many European, South African, and Soviet research stations along the mountainous coast.

Norwich   52 38N 1 18E A city in E England, the administrative centre of Norfolk on the River Wensum. Towards the end of the 16th century many weavers from the Netherlands settled in the city and it became a major textile centre. It has a Norman cathedral (1096) and keep, many medieval churches, and is the site of the University of East Anglia (1963). Industries include shoe manufacturing, electrical and other machinery, food and drink, chemicals, printing, and bookbinding. Population (1981): 122 270.

Norwich school   A school of regional landscape painters active in Norwich in the first half of the 19th century. Founded as the Norwich Society in 1803, it held regular exhibitions until 1834. Its leading members were *Cotman and *Crome.

nose   The organ of smell, which is also an entrance to the respiratory tract. The external nose, which projects from the face, has a framework of bone and cartilage and is divided into two nostrils by the nasal septum. It leads to the nasal cavity, which is lined by *mucous membrane, extends back to the pharynx and windpipe, and is connected to the air *sinuses of the skull. Hairs in the nostrils filter particles from inhaled air, which is further cleaned, warmed, and moistened in the nasal cavity. The membrane at the top of the nasal cavity contains olfactory cells, which are sensitive to different smells and are connected to the brain via the olfactory nerve.

Nostradamus (Michel de Notredame; 1503–66) French physician and astrologer, who became famous with his publication of *Centuries* (1555–58), in which he made a number of prophecies in the form of rhyming quatrains. Some of his prophecies, which are obscure and open to various interpretations, appeared to come true and Charles IX appointed him his physician on his accession (1560).

nothosaur   A primitive marine reptile of the Jurassic period (200–135 million years ago). 0.3–6 m long, nothosaurs had a long neck and tail and long limbs partly modified into paddles. They fed on fish, which were gripped tightly with long sharp teeth.

notochord A flexible skeletal rod that runs along the length of the body in the embryos of all animals of the phylum Chordata (including vertebrates). In primitive chordates, such as the lancelets and lampreys, the notochord remains the main axial support, but in vertebrates it is incorporated into the backbone as the embryo develops.

Notoungulata An extinct order of mammals whose remains have been found mainly in South America. Notoungulates ranged from small rabbit-like forms to the massive *Toxodon*, which stood over 2 m high at the shoulder. They had three-toed feet, with either claws or hooves, and lived from the Paleocene epoch to the Pleistocene epoch (about 70 million to 2.5 million years ago).

Notre-Dame de Paris The gothic cathedral built (1163–1345) on the Île de la Cité, Paris, to replace two earlier churches. The nave, choir, and west front were completed by 1204; the innovatory flying buttresses and the great rose windows, which still retain their 13th-century stained glass, are notable features. Damaged during the French Revolution, Notre-Dame was saved from demolition and redecorated for Napoleon's coronation (1804) and was subsequently fully restored (1845–64) by *Viollet-le-Duc.

Nottingham 52 58N 1 10W A city in N central England, the administrative centre of Nottinghamshire on the River Trent. Charles I raised his standard here in 1642 at the outbreak of the Civil War. Notable buildings include the castle (built by William the Conqueror and restored in 1878) and the "Trip to Jerusalem," reputed to be the oldest inn in England. Formerly a lace-making centre, Nottingham's chief industries are now hosiery, bicycles, cigarettes, pharmaceuticals, engineering, brewing, and printing. The university dates from 1948. Population (1981): 271 080.

Nottinghamshire A county in the East Midlands of England. It consists mainly of lowlands, crossed by the River Trent, with the Pennine uplands in the W and the remnants of Sherwood Forest (famous for the Robin Hood legend) in the SW. Agriculture is important with arable and dairy farming, orchards, and market gardening. It contains important coalfields. Gypsum, limestone, and gravel are also extracted. The main industrial town is Nottingham. Area: 2164 sq km (835 sq mi). Population (1981): 982 631. Administrative centre: Nottingham.

Nouakchott 18 09N 15 58W The capital of Mauritania, in the W near the Atlantic coast. A small village until the 1950s, it was developed as the capital after independence in 1960. Its modern port is situated 6.4 km (4 mi) from the city. Population (1981 est): 250 000.

Nouméa 22 16S 166 26E The capital of New Caledonia. A port, it exports nickel, chrome, manganese, and iron. Population (1983): 60 112.

nouveau roman An experimental type of the novel pioneered by French writers in the 1950s. The leading exponents include Nathalie *Sarraute, Alain *Robbe-Grillet, and Michel *Butor. Reacting against traditional realistic concepts of character and narrative, their works are characterized by a distrust of psychological motives, detailed descriptions of external reality, and the avoidance of any kind of value judgment.

Nouvelle Vague. *See* New Wave.

nova A *binary star that suddenly increases in brightness by perhaps 10 000 times or more and then fades over months or years, usually to its original brightness. Nova eruptions occur in close binary systems comprising a *white dwarf with a nearby companion star that is expanding and is losing matter to the white dwarf. Gaseous material flowing from the large star forms a disc around the white dwarf and gradually spirals down to and accumulates on its surface. When enough has accumulated a thermo-nuclear explosion occurs, observed as the nova eruption.

Novalis (Friedrich Leopold, Freiherr von Hardenberg;

1772–1801) German Romantic poet and writer. After studying law, he became an auditor. The death of his fiancée (1797) inspired his celebration of death and love in the *Hymnen an die Nacht* (1800); he himself died prematurely of tuberculosis. His unfinished novel *Heinrich von Ofterdingen* (1802) typifies the Romantic belief in the transforming power of art.

Nova Lisboa. *See* Huambo.

Novara 45 27N 08 37E A town in NW Italy, in Piedmont. It has several notable buildings, including a 13th-century town hall. As well as a rice-milling industry, there are textile and chemical plants. Population (1980 est): 102 039.

Nova Scotia A province of E Canada. It consists of a peninsula protruding into the Atlantic Ocean and *Cape Breton Island. Mostly rolling hills and valleys, Nova Scotia was originally covered by mixed forest but has been largely replanted with conifers. Economic growth is restricted by limited resources and the distance from important markets. Coal output is down significantly, but Nova Scotia also mines gypsum, salt, and copper. Agriculture includes dairying, mixed farming, livestock, and fruit. Iron and steel, pulp and paper, fishing, and tourism are also economically important. *History*: from the first colonization (1605), Britain and France contested the area, Britain eventually gaining possession (confirmed by the Treaty of Paris in 1763). Largely settled by Scots, Nova Scotia prospered in the 19th-century age of sail. But since joining Canada (1867), its economy has lagged. Area: 52 841 sq km (20 402 sq mi). Population (1981 est): 847 442. Capital: Halifax.

Novaya Zemlya A Soviet archipelago off the N coast, between the Barents and the Kara Seas. It is a continuation of the Ural Mountains and consists almost entirely of two islands separated by a narrow strait. There is no permanent population, and the N island is always icebound. Total area: about 83 000 sq km (32 040 sq mi).

novel An extended work of prose fiction dealing with the interaction of characters in a real or imagined setting. The term derives from Italian *novella*, meaning a short tale or anecdote. Latin forerunners of the novel are the picaresque *Satyricon* of Petronius (1st century AD) and *The Golden Ass* by Apuleius (2nd century AD). Cervantes' *Don Quixote* (1605) is considered the most important early novel. In England, a particular combination of social, economic, and literary conditions led to the development of the novel in the 18th century. The first notable English novelists included *Richardson, *Fielding, and *Defoe. The novels of the great 19th-century writers, notably *Dickens in England, *Tolstoy and *Dostoievsky in Russia, and *Balzac and *Flaubert in France, together constitute one of the great achievements of world literature. In the 20th century the novel has been strongly influenced by developments in psychology and philosophy, and the various proliferating categories of novel—such as *science fiction, the *detective story, and the *nouveau roman—appeal to all levels of readership. *See also* picaresque novel.

Novello, Ivor (David Ivor Davies; 1893–1951) British composer, dramatist, and actor. He composed the World War I song "Keep the Home Fires Burning," and is best known for his series of romantic musicals including *Careless Rapture* (1936) and *The Dancing Years* (1939).

November Insurrection. *See* Congress Kingdom of Poland.

Novgorod 58 30N 31 20E A city in the Soviet Union, in the NW RSFSR on the River Volkhov. It has varied manufacturing industries and is a famous tourist centre, although many of its magnificent buildings, including the St Sofia Cathedral (1045–50), were badly damaged during World War II. *History*: it is one of Russia's oldest towns, dating at least to the 9th century, and was a notable trading centre in the middle ages. Self-governing from 1019, it was forced to acknowledge Tatar overrule in the 13th century and that of Moscow in the 15th century. It was held by the

Swedes from 1611 to 1619 and subsequently declined. Population (1981 est): 198 000.

Novi Sad 45 15N 19 15E A port in N central Yugoslavia, in Serbia on the River Danube. It is a centre of Serbian culture with a university (1960). Population (1981): 257 685.

Novosibirsk 55 04N 83 05E A city in the Soviet Union, in the W central RSFSR on the River Ob and the Trans-Siberian Railway. The most important economic centre in Siberia, it has machine-building, textile, chemical, and metallurgical industries. Nearby is the Academic Community (Akademgorodk), a complex of science research institutes. Population (1984): 1 384 000.

Novotný, Antonín (1904–75) Czechoslovak statesman. One of the founding members of the Czechoslovak Communist Party (1921), he was first secretary of the Party (1953–68) and president of Czechoslovakia (1957–68). He was forced to resign by *Dubček, after whose fall Novotný was reinstated as a Party member.

Noyes, Alfred (1880–1958) British poet. He wrote patriotic verse about the sea and several epic narrative poems including *Drake* (1906–08) and *The Torchbearers* (1922–30). His traditional views on literature and politics were expressed in his literary criticism and his autobiography, *Two Worlds for Memory* (1953).

NSPCC. *See* National Society for the Prevention of Cruelty to Children.

Nu, U (*or* Thakin Nu; 1907–) Burmese statesman; prime minister (1948–56, 1957–58, 1960–62). A leading nationalist from the 1930s, he became prime minister on the achievement of independence. He sought to establish parliamentary democracy but when his Anti-Fascist People's Freedom League split in 1958 he was forced by *Ne Win to resign. He was restored, together with parliamentary government, in 1960 but was again deposed in 1962 and in 1966 withdrew into exile. He returned to Burma in 1980.

Nubia A region of NE Africa, in the Nile valley, approximately between Aswan (Egypt) and Khartoum (Sudan). Much of Nubia is now drowned by Lake Nasser. From about 2000 BC the Egyptians gradually occupied Nubia, which they called Cush. Trade, especially in gold, flourished. By the 15th century BC Nubia had an Egyptian viceroy. As Egyptian power waned, Nubian kings, based at Napata and *Meroë, became influential, even dominating Egypt itself (c. 730–670). Their independent nation, culture, and language lasted until the 4th century AD.

Nubian Desert A desert in the NE Sudan, between the River Nile and the Red Sea. It consists of a sandstone plateau with peaks of up to 2259 m (7411 ft) near the coast. Area: about 400 000 sq km (154 408 sq mi).

nuclear energy The energy evolved by nuclear fission or nuclear fusion. The energy is liberated in fission when a heavy atomic nucleus, such as uranium, splits into two or more parts, the total mass of the parts being less than the mass of the original nucleus. This difference in mass is equivalent to the *binding energy of the nucleus and most of it is converted into kinetic energy (i.e. the increased velocity with which the parts move) according to Einstein's law, $E = mc^2$. In a fusion reaction, two light nuclei, such as hydrogen or deuterium, combine to form a stable nucleus, such as helium; as the nucleus formed is lighter than the sum of the component nuclei, again energy is released in accordance with Einstein's law.

In the case of fission, when the nucleus of a uranium-235 atom is struck by a neutron, a U-236 nucleus is formed, which immediately splits into two roughly equal parts, two or three neutrons being liberated at the same time. As these neutrons can then cause further fissions, a chain reaction builds up and a lump of U-235 will disintegrate almost instantaneously with enormous explosive power, provided that it is in excess of the critical mass (*see* nuclear weapons).

In nuclear power stations the fission reaction is harnessed to produce heat at a controlled rate (to raise steam to drive a tur-

bine) in one of two ways. Both use natural uranium, which contains only 0.7% of the fissionable U-235 isotope, nearly all of the rest being the isotope U-238. The U-238 isotope absorbs the fast-moving neutrons emitted by the fission of U-235 and prevents a chain reaction from occurring in natural uranium. There are, however, two ways of producing a chain reaction. One is to use a moderator to slow down the fast neutrons so that they are not absorbed by U-238 nuclei (*see* thermal reactor). The other is to enrich the natural uranium with extra quantities of U-235 (or plutonium-239) so that there are sufficient neutrons to sustain the chain reaction in spite of absorption by U-238 (*see* fast reactor). All present commercial reactors are thermal, although the fast reactor is under development.

The fusion process is the basis of the hydrogen bomb (*see* nuclear weapons) and the □thermonuclear reactor, which is unlikely to be a source of energy until the 21st century.

The importance of nuclear energy is that it will almost certainly be increasingly needed to supply world energy requirements as reserves of fossil fuels diminish. It is also important as a source of energy to power submarines, a very small quantity of nuclear fuel providing a very large amount of energy–about 7×10^{13} joules per kilogram, compared to about 4×10^7 J/kg for coal. □p. 886.

nuclear fission. *See* fast reactor; nuclear energy; nuclear weapons; thermal reactor.

nuclear fusion. *See* nuclear energy; nuclear weapons; thermonuclear reactor.

nuclear magnetic resonance (NMR) An effect observed when an atomic nucleus is exposed to radio waves in the presence of a magnetic field. A strong magnetic field causes the magnetic moment of the nucleus to precess around the direction of the field, only certain orientations being allowed by quantum theory. A transition from one orientation to another involves the absorption or emission of a photon, the frequency of which is equal to the precessional frequency. With magnetic field strengths customarily used the radiation is in the radio-frequency band. If radio-frequency radiation is supplied to the sample from one coil and is detected by another coil, while the magnetic field strength is slowly changed, radiation is absorbed at certain field values, which correspond to the frequency difference between orientations. An NMR spectrum consists of a graph of field strength against detector response. This provides information about the structure of molecules and the positions of electrons within them, as the orbital electrons shield the nucleus and cause them to resonate at different field strengths.

nuclear power The generation of electricity using nuclear energy. Some 15% of the world's electricity in 1985 was generated by 374 nuclear reactors. France has 41 reactors generating 58.7% of its electricity, the UK has 37 reactors (13%), the USA 85 (13.5%), and the USSR 46 (9%). The Soviet disaster in 1986 (*see* Chernobyl) caused considerable public concern over nuclear safety, leading several countries to postpone plans for nuclear expansion. The Chernobyl graphite-moderated light-water reactor, a unique Soviet design, is now regarded as unsafe, especially as it is contained in a single-shell building, unlike the US water-cooled reactors (*see* thermal reactor), which are contained in double-walled buildings. This prevented disaster in the Three Mile Island incident in the USA in 1979. *See also* fast reactor; nuclear energy; thermonuclear reactor.

nuclear reactor A device for producing *nuclear energy in a usable form. *See* fast reactor; thermal reactor; thermonuclear reactor.

Nuclear Test-Ban Treaty (1963) A treaty banning nuclear testing by its signatories on the ground, in the atmosphere, in space, and under water. The signatories were the Soviet Union, the UK, and the USA; many other countries agreed to adhere to the treaty. It made no attempt to limit nuclear stockpiling and therefore was rejected as ineffectual by France, which performed atmospheric tests until 1974, and China. Underground nuclear tests continue, although proposals for a total ban feature in *disarmament talks.

NUCLEAR ENERGY

neutron

U-235 atom

fission products

neutrons

nuclear fission

| uranium purification | enriched uranium | uranium oxide fuel | uranium metal fuel | thermal nuclear power stations | irradiated fuel reprocessing | recovered uranium | plutonium for fast reactors |

radioactive waste

nuclear fuel cycle

Magnox reactor

advanced gas-cooled reactor (AGR)

pressurized-water reactor (PWR)

fast reactor

NUCLEAR ENERGY   *Natural uranium metal fuel clad in Magnox (magnesium alloy) is used in Magnox thermal reactors. Enriched uranium dioxide pellets clad in steel are used in AGR and PWR fuel elements. Plutonium for fast reactors and recycled enriched uranium is obtained by reprocessing spent fuel from thermal reactors. The electricity generating plant is similar with all reactor types.*

nuclear waste. *See* radioactive waste.

nuclear weapons Missiles, bombs, shells, or land mines that use fission or fusion of nuclear material (*see* nuclear energy) yielding enormous quantities of heat, light, blast, and radiation. The first **atomic bomb** (*or* fission bomb), manufactured by the USA in World War II, was dropped on Hiroshima in 1945. It consisted of two small masses of uranium-235 forced together by a chemical explosion to form a supercritical mass, in which an uncontrolled chain reaction occurred. Below the critical mass (estimated at between 16 and 20 kg) a chain reaction does not occur, as too many neutrons escape from the surface. The bomb had an explosive power equivalent to 20 000 tons of TNT. Later models used plutonium-239 to even greater effect.

The **hydrogen bomb** (fusion bomb *or* thermonuclear bomb) consists of an atom bomb surrounded by a layer of hydrogenous material, such as lithium deuteride. The atom bomb creates the necessary temperature (about 100 000 000°C) needed to ignite the fusion reaction (*see* thermonuclear reactor). Hydrogen bombs have an explosive power measured in tens of megatons (millions of tons) of TNT. The first hydrogen bomb was exploded by US scientists on Eniwetok Atoll in 1952 and although it has never been used in war, hydrogen bombs have been tested by the Soviet Union, Britain, France, and China. Further testing was prohibited by the *Nuclear Test-Ban Treaty of 1963.

The **neutron bomb** (*or* enhanced radiation bomb) is a nuclear weapon designed to maximize neutron radiation. It is lethal to all forms of life but, having reduced blast, leaves buildings, etc., relatively undamaged.

nucleic acids Organic compounds, found in the cells of all living organisms, that consist of a mixure of nitrogenous bases (purines and pyrimidines), phosphoric acid, and a pentose sugar. The sugar is ribose in the ribonucleic acids (*see* RNA) and deoxyribose in the deoxyribonucleic acids (*see* DNA). Nucleic acids store genetic information in living organisms and interpret that information in protein synthesis. *See also* nucleoprotein.

nucleolus A small dense body, one or more of which can be seen within the *nucleus of a nondividing cell. It contains RNA and protein and is involved in the synthesis of *ribosomes.

nucleon A collective name for a proton or neutron. *See also* mass number.

nucleoprotein A compound consisting of a *nucleic acid associated with one or more proteins. The nucleoprotein of cell nuclei—the chromosomes—consists of DNA and proteins, mainly histones; cytoplasmic nucleoproteins—the *ribosomes—are ribonucleoproteins comprising some 60% protein and 40% RNA. *Viruses also consist of nucleoprotein.

nucleus (biology) A large granular component of nearly all □cells. It is usually spherical or ovoid in shape and is surrounded by a nuclear membrane, which is perforated with pores to allow exchange of materials between the nucleus and cytoplasm. The nucleus contains the *chromosomes, made up of the hereditary material (DNA), and is therefore essential for the control and regulation of cellular activities, such as growth and metabolism. During cell division the chromosomes are involved in the transfer of hereditary information (*see* meiosis; mitosis).

nucleus (physics) The central core of the atom (*see* atomic theory) discovered by Lord Rutherford in 1911. All nuclei consist of protons and neutrons (jointly called nucleons), except for hydrogen, which consists of a single proton. The constituent nucleons are held together by the *strong interaction, which at the minute distances within the nucleus (of the order 10^{-15} m) is some one hundred times stronger than the electromagnetic interaction between protons. The number of protons in the nucleus determines its charge and atomic number; the number of neutrons (in addition to the number of protons) determines the mass number and the isotope. **Nuclear physics** is the study of the structure and reactions of the nucleus. *See also* particle physics.

Nuevo Laredo 27 30N 99 30W A city in N Mexico, on the Rio Grande. It is an important point of entry into Mexico from the USA. Population (1980): 203 286.

Nuffield, William Richard Morris, 1st Viscount (1877–1963) British car manufacturer and philanthropist. Starting with a small bicycle shop, he established a car factory in Cowley, near Oxford, which in 1913 produced the first Morris Oxford, soon followed by the Morris Cowley. He founded Nuffield College, Oxford, the Nuffield Trust, and the Nuffield Foundation.

Nu Jiang. *See* Salween River.

Nuku'alofa 21 09S 175 14W The capital of Tonga in the S Pacific, in N Tongatabu. It is the site of the Royal Palace (1865–67) and Royal Tombs. Copra and bananas are exported. Population (1984): 21 716.

Nukus 42 28N 59 07E A city in the S Soviet Union, the capital of the Kara-Kalpak ASSR in the Uzbeck SSR on the River Amu Darya. Its industries include food processing. Population (1981 est): 113 400.

Nullarbor Plain A plain of SW South Australia and SE Western Australia, bordering on the Great Australian Bight. It consists of a treeless arid plateau with extensive limestone areas and is crossed by the Trans-Australian Railway. Area: 260 000 sq km (100 000 sq mi).

NUCLEAR WEAPONS *A test firing of a US ground-launched cruise missile.*

humbat A rat-sized *marsupial, *Myrmecobius fasciatus*, of open eucalyptus woods in SW Australia, also called marsupial (*or* banded) anteater. It is slender and rust-coloured, with white stripes across the back and a long tail, and it feeds on ants and termites with its long sticky tongue. Numbats have no pouch. Family: *Dasyuridae*.

numbers Mathematical symbols used to denote quantity. The natural numbers, 1, 2, 3, 4, 5..., etc., were developed first by the Hindus and Arabs for simple counting. Subtraction led to negative numbers and to zero, which together with natural numbers make up the set of integers ... -3, -2,

-1, 0, 1,.... Division of whole numbers results in fractions or rational numbers. Some numbers, such as $\sqrt{2}$, cannot be expressed as the ratio of two integers. These are called irrational numbers and they occur as the solutions to simple algebraic equations. They can be calculated to any required accuracy but cannot be written as exact values. Other numbers, called transcendental numbers, do not come from algebraic relationships. Some of these occur as basic properties of space, for example π, the ratio of a circumference of a circle to its diameter. Real numbers include all rational and irrational numbers. The equation $x^2 = -1$ can have no real solution for x, since the square of any number is positive. The imaginary number, $i = \sqrt{-1}$, was introduced to overcome this problem. *See* complex numbers; number theory.

Numbers The fourth book of the Old Testament, attributed to Moses. It derives its name from the two records of a census that it mentions. The narrative covers the Israelites' journey from Mt Sinai to the borders of Canaan and gives the reasons for their failure to enter Canaan. It recounts the subsequent 40 years wandering in the wilderness and includes miscellaneous laws relevant to the eventual occupation of the Promised Land.

number theory The study of the properties of *numbers. It includes various theorems about *prime numbers, many of which are unproved but apparently true, and the study of Diophantine equations (named after *Diophantus of Alexandria), i.e. equations that have only integer solutions. *Fermat's last theorem deals with the solution of one of these equations and is a famous unproved theorem. Although number theory has existed for thousands of years, its development has been continuous and it now includes analytic number theory, originated by *Euler in 1742; geometric number theory, which uses such geometrical methods of analysis as Cartesian coordinates (*see* coordinate systems), *vectors, and *matrices; and probabilistic number theory, based on *probability theory.

Numidia An ancient kingdom of N Africa, W of *Carthage. Its *Berber population was nomadic until Masinissa (c. 240-149 BC), Rome's ally during the second and third *Punic Wars, promoted agriculture and urbanization. After supporting Pompey against Julius Caesar (46 BC), Numidia lost its monarchy and became part of the Roman province of Africa.

numismatics (*or* coin collecting) Collecting and studying coins, medals, or banknotes as a hobby or as a form of historical research. Collecting Greek and Roman coins became popular among aristocrats in Renaissance Italy, although collections then often included copies. During the 19th century numismatics became popular among a wider public; catalogues were produced and societies formed. Museums are now the greatest collectors, while private collectors usually specialize in one field. Coins in good condition are a form of investment, the best being "proof" coins, struck especially for sale to collectors.

Nummulites A genus of protozoan animals, sometimes called money fossils, that was abundant during the Eocene epoch (about 54-38 million years ago) although only one species has survived. Some limestones are almost entirely composed of their shells, which were disc-shaped and biconvex. Order: *Foraminifera.

nunatak A rock peak protruding above the surface of an ice sheet. Nunataks occur in Greenland, the word originating from the Eskimo language.

Nuneaton 52 32N 1 28W A town in central England, in Warwickshire. Besides its coalmining industry, Nuneaton manufactures textiles, cardboard boxes, and bricks. Its name refers to the 12th-century Benedictine nunnery, now in ruins. Population (1981): 71 530.

Nuremberg (German name: Nürnberg) 49 27N 11 05E A city in SE West Germany, in Bavaria on the River Pegnitz. It was severely bombed during World War II because of its

engine industry and is now a major centre of the metalworking and electrical industries. It shares a university with Erlangen. *History*: a medieval trading centre, it became the centre of the German Renaissance, when the mastersingers' contests were held here. It was the site of the Nazi Party congresses (1933-38) and the war-crime trials following World War II. It is the birthplace of Albrecht Dürer and Hans Sachs. Population (1980 est): 483 900.

Nuremberg Trials (1945-46) The trials of *Nazi criminals after World War II. An international military court was set up by the Allied Powers in Nuremberg to try Nazi individuals or groups who had violated the rules of war or committed crimes against humanity, such as the mass murders of Jews in *concentration camps. 12 men were sentenced to hang (including Göring, who committed suicide before the sentence could be carried out, Ribbentrop, Frank, Streicher, and Jodl) and six others were imprisoned for various terms (including Hess, who still remains in Spandau). The trials of the war criminals created precedents, chiefly that war crimes are the responsibility not merely of the state but also of the individual.

Nureyev, Rudolf (1938-) Russian ballet dancer. He danced with the Leningrad Kirov Ballet from 1958 until 1961, when he defected from Russia. In 1962 he joined the Royal Ballet, where he frequently partnered Margot *Fonteyn in such ballets as *Giselle* and *Swan Lake*. In 1977 he starred in the film *Valentino*. He became an Austrian citizen in 1982.

Nurhachi (1559-1626) Manchu chieftain, who founded the Qing dynasty of China. He unified the Juchen tribes of Manchuria to found the Manchu state. He organized all his subjects under the *Banner System, creating a powerful base from which his successors conquered all China.

Nurmi, Paavo Johannes (1897-1973) Finnish middle-distance and long-distance runner. He broke over 20 world records and won 12 Olympic medals, 9 gold and 3 silver. He was Olympic 10 000 metres champion in 1920 and 1928 and in 1924 won both the 1500 metres and the 5000 metres. He was in the habit of running carrying a stopwatch.

nursery rhymes Traditional verses said or sung to small children. They are usually for amusement only, although some, such as counting rhymes, are also instructional. They vary greatly in age and origin: some probably originate in ancient folklore, while others were first composed as popular ballads in the 19th century. The earliest known collection, *Tommy Thumb's Song Book* (1744), includes such perennial favourites as "Sing a Song of Sixpence" and "Who Killed Cock Robin?".

nurse shark A *shark, *Ginglymostoma cirratum*, that occurs in warm shallow waters of the Atlantic Ocean. Yellowbrown or grey-brown and up to 4.2 m long, it is considered dangerous to man only when provoked. Live young are born. Family: *Orectolobidae*.

nursing The medical specialty concerned with the care of the sick. Nursing originated in the religious orders, becoming increasingly secularized in Protestant countries after the Reformation; the standards of professional nursing were established by Florence *Nightingale after her work in the Crimea. Nurses are responsible for the day-to-day welfare of patients and for carrying out routine medical and surgical procedures under the supervision of a doctor. In Britain nursing training is given in a hospital approved by the General Nursing Council and student nurses must pass examinations to qualify as a state enrolled nurse (SEN) after a two-year course or a state registered nurse (SRN) after a three-year course. The professional organization for British nurses is the Royal College of Nursing. Apart from nursing in hospitals, the profession includes the work of midwives, health visitors, and home and school nurses.

Nusa Tenggara (former name: Lesser *Sunda Islands) A volcanic Indonesian island group E of Java, the chief islands being Bali, Lombok, Sumbawa, Sumba, Flores, and Timor. Area: 73 144 sq km (28 241 sq mi). Population (1971): 7 706 561.

nut Loosely, any edible nonsucculent fruit, including the peanut and brazil nut. Botanically, a nut is a large dry fruit containing a single seed that is not released from the fruit at maturity. An example is the chestnut.

nutcracker A songbird of the genus *Nucifraga* found in coniferous forests of E Europe and Asia. The common nutcracker (*N. caryocatactes*) is dark brown speckled with white, about 32 cm long, and cracks open pine cones with its sharp bill to extract the seeds. Clark's nutcracker (*N. columbianus*) is grey with a black tail and wings patched with white. Family: *Corvidae* (crows, jays, magpies).

nuthatch A small stocky bird belonging to a family (*Sittidae*: 30 species) occurring everywhere except South America and New Zealand. Nuthatches have long straight bills, for hammering open nuts, and long-clawed toes, for running up and down tree trunks in search of insects. The European nuthatch (*Sitta europaea*), about 14 cm long, has a blue-grey upper plumage with paler underparts and a black eyestripe.

nutmeg A fragrant tropical evergreen tree, *Myristica fragrans*, native to Indonesia but widely cultivated in SE Asia and the West Indies. Growing to 20 m high, it has oval pointed leaves and tiny male and female flowers borne on separate trees. The yellow fleshy fruit, about 3 cm across, splits when ripe to expose the seed, which has a red fleshy covering (aril). The dried aril (mace) and whole or ground seeds (nutmeg) are used as spices. Family: *Myristicaceae*.

nutria. *See* coypu.

nux vomica A poisonous evergreen tree, *Strychnos nux-vomica*, also called the koochla tree, native to lowlands of Burma and India. It has simple leaves and clusters of tubular flowers, each with five spreading lobes. The seeds of the orange-like fruits contain the highly poisonous substances strychnine and curare. Family: *Strychnaceae*.

Nuzi An ancient *Hurrian city SW of Kirkuk (N Iraq). Nuzi flourished in the 15th century BC before being absorbed into the Assyrian Empire. Excavations here in the 1920s revealed a prosperous trading centre with archives detailing legal, commercial, and military activities.

nyala An antelope, *Tragelaphus angasi*, of SW Africa. About 100 cm high at the shoulder, nyalas are shy and nocturnal, inhabiting dense undergrowth, and have spiral-shaped horns and a greyish-brown coat with vertical white stripes on the flanks. The mountain nyala (*T. buxtoni*) lives in mountainous regions of S Ethiopia.

Nyasa, Lake. *See* Malawi, Lake.

Nyasaland. *See* Malawi, Republic of.

Nyeman, River. *See* Neman, River.

Nyerere, Julius (Kambarage) (1922–   ) Tanzanian statesman; president (1962–85). Educated at Makerere College (Uganda) and Edinburgh University, in 1954 Nyerere formed the Tanganyika African National Union, which led the fight for independence (achieved in 1960). He became chief minister (1960), prime minister (1961), and then president of Tanganyika, which was renamed Tanzania in 1964 after union with Zanzibar. Nyerere, who defends the one-party state as being more appropriate for a developing country, is a prominent advocate of African unity. Under his leadership Tanzania was instrumental in the overthrow of Amin in Uganda in 1979.

Nyköping 58 45N 17 03E A seaport in E Sweden, on the Baltic coast. A centre of commerce and industry, its manufactures include machinery and textiles. Population (1983): 64 746.

nylon A synthetic material with a translucent creamy white appearance, widely used both in fibre form and in solid blocks because of its lightness, toughness, and elasticity. It is made by *polymerization of diamine with *fatty acid or by polymerizing a single monomer, in both cases to form a polyamide. Nylon is used to make small engineering components, such as bearings and gears, because it is hard wearing and easy to machine. It is also spun and woven into fabrics for clothing, etc., and can be coloured with pigments. Introduced commercially in 1938, nylon was the first truly synthetic fibre.

nymph A stage in the life cycle of insects that show incomplete *metamorphosis, including dragonflies, grasshoppers, and bugs. The egg hatches into a nymph, which undergoes a series of moults to form a line of nymphs that show increasing similarity to the adult.

nymphalid butterfly A butterfly belonging to the widely distributed family *Nymphalidae*, also called brush-footed butterfly. Nymphalids are characterized by small hairy forelegs, useless for walking. Many, including the migratory *red admiral and *painted lady, are strong fast fliers. The adults are generally orange or brown with black markings and the caterpillars are commonly brown or black and covered with branched spines.

Nymphenburg porcelain Porcelain produced at a factory established (1753) near Munich. It is famed for rococo figures designed by F. A. Bustelli (1723–64). They include Italian comedy, chinoiserie, and mythological models. After Bustelli died table wares, particularly tea services, were made, often based on Meissen. The factory still copies its early models.

nymphs In Greek mythology, female spirits of nature, often portrayed as youthful and amorous dancers or musicians. They were long lived, though not immortal, and usually benevolent. The several classes of nymphs associated with particular natural phenomena include the *dryads, the *naiads, and the *nereids.

Nyoro A Bantu-speaking people of the western lakes region of Uganda. They were traditionally divided into three distinct groups: the Bito clan from whom the hereditary paramount chief (Mukama) always came, the aristocratic Huma pastoralists, and the subordinate Iru cultivators. The Bito and Huma are thought to have originally come from the north as conquering invaders. They are a patrilineal people who live in small scattered settlements.

Nysa, River. *See* Neisse, River.

Nystad, Treaty of (1721) The peace treaty between Russia and Sweden that concluded the Great *Northern War. Sweden was obliged to cede large tracts of territory, including Livonia, and Russia gained its long-coveted access to the Baltic Sea, thus becoming a European power.

Nyx (Latin name: Nox) A Greek goddess, the personification of night. She was the daughter of Chaos and her offspring included Thanatos (Death), Hypnos (Sleep), the *Fates, and *Nemesis. She lived in Tartarus, from which she emerged as Hemera, the goddess of day.

O

Oahu A US island in Hawaii, the most populous and the administrative centre. The Japanese attack on *Pearl Harbor (1941) was decisive in bringing the USA into World War II. Area: 1584 sq km (608 sq mi). Population (1980): 761 964. Chief town: Honolulu.

oak A deciduous or evergreen □tree or shrub of the genus *Quercus* (over 800 species), found in N temperate and subtropical regions. The simple leaves usually have lobed or toothed margins and the yellow male catkins and tiny green female flowers are borne on the same tree. The fruit—an acorn—is a hard oval nut partly enclosed by a round cup. Often 30–40 m high, many species are important timber trees, especially the common or pedunculate oak (*Q. robur*) and the *durmast oak (both Eurasian) and the North American white oak (*Q. alba*) and live oaks. Several are planted for ornament, including the Eurasian Turkey oak (*Q. cerris*), the North American red oak (*Q. rubra*), which has a red autumn foliage, and the Mediterranean *holm oak. The cork oak (*Q. suber*) is the main commercial source of *cork. Family: *Fagaceae*.

Oakham 52 40N 0 43W A market town in central England, in Leicestershire. It was the county town of the former county of Rutland and has a 12th-century castle and a school founded in 1584. The main industries are plastics, engineering, footwear, and hosiery. Population (1981): 7996.

Oakland 37 50N 122 15W A port in the USA, in California on San Francisco Bay and connected with San Francisco by the San Francisco–Oakland Bay Bridge (1936). Oakland's industries include chemicals and shipbuilding. Population (1980): 339 288.

Oakley, Annie (Phoebe Anne Oakley Mozee; 1860–1926) US gunshooter. From 1885 she and her husband, Frank Butler, performed daring acts of marksmanship in Buffalo Bill's Wild West Show. A musical, *Annie Get Your Gun* (1948) with music by Irving Berlin, was based on her life.

oak moss An edible *lichen, *Evernia prunastri*, found in mountainous regions of the N hemisphere. It has a pale greenish-grey body, 3–8 cm long, with numerous pointed branches. Its heavy fragrance makes it of value in perfumery and it is used in the preparation of drugs for treating wounds and infections.

Oak Ridge 36 02N 84 12W A town in the USA, in Tennessee. It contains the Oak Ridge National Laboratory (1943) for nuclear research. Population (1980): 27 662.

Oaks A flat race for three-year-old fillies only, run over the *Derby course (2.4 km; 1.5 mi) at Epsom, three days after the Derby in early June. One of the English *Classics, it was first run in 1779 and was named after the 12th Earl of Derby's hunting lodge.

Oakville 43 27N 79 41W A town in central Canada, in S Ontario. A dormitory suburb of Toronto, it houses a major motor-vehicle factory and produces plastics, paints, and electrical appliances. Population (1981): 76 720.

oarfish A *ribbonfish of the genus *Regalecus*, especially *R. glesne*, found in all seas. It has a long silvery ribbon-like body, up to 9 m long, a long red dorsal fin that extends forwards to form a crest, long red oarlike pelvic fins situated near the pectoral fins, and no anal or tail fins. □oceans.

OAS. *See* Organisation de l'Armée secrète; Organization of American States.

oasis An area within a desert where water is available for vegetation and human use. It may consist of a single small spring around which palms grow or be an extensive area where the water table is at or near the ground surface.

Oastler, Richard (1789–1861) British social reformer. He attacked the employment of children in factories and campaigned for a ten-hour working day, which was achieved in the act of 1847.

Oates, Lawrence Edward Grace (1880–1912) British explorer. A professional soldier, he was given leave to participate in R. F. *Scott's expedition to the Antarctic (1910–12). They reached the Pole but on the return journey Oates, fearing that his lameness (resulting from frostbite) might hinder the already struggling expedition, walked out into the blizzard to die. His gallant act, related in Scott's diaries, failed to save his companions.

Oates, Titus. *See* Popish Plot.

oat grass A perennial *grass of either of the genera *Arrhenatherum* (about 6 species), native to temperate Eurasia, and *Danthonia* (over 100 species), native to S temperate regions. Tall oat grass (*A. elatius*) has been introduced as a pasture grass to many countries; *Danthonia* species are important forage grasses.

oats Annual *grasses belonging to the genus *Avena* (10 species), native to temperate regions. The common oat (*A. sativa*) was first cultivated in Europe and is grown widely in cool temperate regions. Up to 1 m high, it has a branching cluster of stalked flowers; the grain is used as a livestock feed, especially for horses, and for oatmeal, breakfast cereals, etc. The straw is used for livestock fodder and bedding. Wild oats, especially *A. fatua*, can be a serious weed in cereal crops.

OAU. *See* Organization of African Unity.

Oaxaca (*or* Oaxaca de Juárez) 17 05N 96 41W A city in S Mexico, in the Atoyac Valley. Founded in 1486 by the Aztecs, it has flour-milling, cotton, textile, and handicraft industries. Its university was established in 1827. Population (1980): 157 284.

Ob, River A river in the N central Soviet Union, flowing N from the Altai Mountains to the **Gulf of Ob** on the Kara Sea. One of the world's largest rivers, its drainage basin covers an area of about 2 930 000 sq km (1 131 000 sq mi). Length: 3682 km (2287 mi).

Obadiah An Old Testament prophet who predicted the downfall of Edom, the traditional enemy of Israel. **The Book of Obadiah** records his prophecy and is the shortest book of the Old Testament.

Oban 56 25N 5 29W A port and resort in W Scotland, in Strathclyde Region on an inlet of the Firth of Lorne. Tweeds and whisky are manufactured. Population (1981): 8134.

OBE. *See* Order of the British Empire.

Obelia A genus of marine invertebrate animals belonging to a suborder (*Leptomedusae*) of *coelenterates. Their life cycle alternates between a sedentary asexual phase (*see* polyp) and a free-swimming sexual phase (*see* medusa). The polyps occur in small whitish or brownish colonies attached to the sea bottom, rocks, shells, etc., of shallow coastal waters. Order: *Hydroida*; class: *Hydrozoa*.

obelisk A stone monument generally shaped as a tall tapering rectangular column of stone, ending in a pyramid-like form. First used by the Egyptians, they have also been employed in the modern age. They were normally made of a single piece of stone and erected for religious or commemorative purposes. Perhaps the most famous are those known as *Cleopatra's Needles.

Oberammergau 47 35N 11 07E A town in S West Germany, in the Bavarian Alps. It is noted for its passion play, performed every ten years following a vow made by the

891

villagers (1633) when they were saved from the plague. Population (1976 est): 5000.

Oberhausen 51 27N 6 50E A port in NW West Germany, in North Rhine-Westphalia on the Rhine-Herne Canal in the *Ruhr. Population (1980 est): 229 300.

oboe A woodwind instrument with a double reed, made in three jointed sections and having a conical bore and small belled end. It derives from the ancient shawm. It has a range of about three octaves above the B flat below middle C and because of its constant pitch usually gives the A to which other orchestral instruments tune.

Obote, (Apollo) Milton (1925–) Ugandan statesman; prime minister (1962–66) and president (1966–71, 1980–85). He formed (1958) the Uganda People's Congress, which opposed the existence of the kingdom of *Buganda within Uganda. On independence he became prime minister and in 1966 deposed Mutesa II of Buganda (1924–69). Overthrown by *Amin in 1971, he was re-elected in 1980 but deposed in a military coup in 1985.

Obrenović A Serbian ruling dynasty that came to power in 1815, when *Karageorge was assassinated, probably by *Miloš Obrenović. The subsequent feud between the Karadordević and Obrenović families lasted until *Alexander, the last Obrenović monarch, was assassinated in 1903.

O'Brien, Conor Cruise (1917–) Irish diplomat, who was the UN representative in the Congo (1961). He then held posts at the Universities of Ghana and New York. In 1969 he became a Labour MP in Ireland and served in the coalition government of 1973–77. He became a senator (1977–79) in the Irish parliament and was editor of the *Observer* newspaper (London) from 1979 to 1981.

O'Brien, Edna (1936–) Irish author. Her novels include *The Country Girls* (1960), *The Lonely Girls* (1962; filmed as *The Girl With Green Eyes*, 1965), *Casualties of Peace* (1966), *Night* (1972), *The Dazzle* (1981), and *Returning* (1982). She has also written plays, film scripts, and short stories.

O'Brien, Fiann (Brian O'Nolan; 1911–66) Irish novelist and journalist. His best-known novel is *At Swim-Two-Birds* (1939), an exuberant comic mixture of folklore, farce, and lyricism that was praised by James Joyce and Dylan Thomas. Other novels include *The Dalkey Archive* (1964) and *The Third Policeman* (1967). He wrote a satirical column for the *Irish Times* under the name Myles na Gopaleen.

O'Brien, William (1852–1928) Irish nationalist politician and journalist. He made a great impression as a fiery MP (from 1883) in the *Home Rule party. He later became more moderate, forming (1910) a short-lived political party that attempted to reconcile different opinions in Ireland.

O'Brien, William Smith (1803–64) Irish politician. An MP (1828–48), he was at first a moderate constitutionalist but in the 1840s became a prominent member of the *Young Ireland group and led the abortive 1848 rebellion. O'Brien was transported to Australia but subsequently pardoned.

obscenity. *See* censorship.

observatory A collection of optical, *infrared, or *radio telescopes together with ancillary equipment and housing. Observatories for optical and infrared studies are now sited at high altitudes so that atmospheric disturbance is minimized. Space observatories, orbiting above the earth's atmosphere, permit X-ray, gamma-ray, ultraviolet, and infrared studies to be made and improve optical measurements.

obsidian A black glassy volcanic rock with a conchoidal fracture. It is of rhyolitic composition (*see* rhyolite) and contains less water and less crystalline material than pitchstone, a similar volcanic glass. Obsidian is formed by the rapid cooling of acid lava.

obstetrics. *See* gynaecology.

O'Casey, Sean (1880–1964) Irish dramatist and nationalist. Born into a poor Protestant family in Dublin, he was largely self-educated. His early realistic tragicomedies, such as *The Shadow of a Gunman* (1923) and *Juno and the Paycock* (1924),

were produced at the Abbey Theatre and dealt with Ireland in the time of the "Troubles." In 1926 he went to live in England. His later work includes the antiwar play *The Silver Tassie* (1929), *Red Roses for Me* (1943), *The Bishop's Bonfire* (1955), and *The Drums of Father Ned* (1958). He published six volumes of autobiography (1939–54).

Occitan. *See* Provençal.

occultation The temporary disappearance of one astronomical body behind another, as when the moon passes in front of and obscures a star. *See also* eclipse.

occultism Theories and practices based on a belief in hidden supernatural forces that are presumed to account for phenomena for which no rational or scientific explanation can be provided. Occultists set great store by ancient texts, secret rituals, esoteric traditions, and the powers of the human mind as keys to the understanding of the universe. *See also* theosophy; satanism; alchemy; astrology; Kabbalah; gnosticism; I Ching.

occupational therapy The ancillary medical specialty concerned with restoring the physical and mental health of the sick and disabled. It plays an important role in keeping long-stay hospital patients interested and usefully occupied, in helping them gain confidence to return to work, and in training disabled persons for new employment. *See also* geriatrics.

oceanarium A large display tank in which species of marine animals and plants are maintained in the conditions of their natural environment. The first public oceanarium was founded in 1938 at Marineland, Florida (USA).

Oceania The islands of the Pacific Ocean, usually taken to exclude Japan, Indonesia, Taiwan, the Philippines, and the Aleutian Islands, but often including Australasia.

Ocean Island (*or* Banaba) 00 52S 169 35E An island in the SW Pacific Ocean, in Kiribati. Rich in phosphate, it was mined by the UK from 1900 to 1979, when supplies were exhausted. After a long legal battle the Banabans accepted £5 million compensation for the loss of their island. Resettled on Rabi Island in Fiji during World War II, they are demanding independence from the government of Kiribati. Area: about 5 sq km (2 sq mi). Population (1980 est): 300.

oceanography The study of the oceans, particularly their origin, structure, and form, the relief and sediments of the sea floor, and the flora and fauna they contain. The physical and chemical properties of sea water, waves, currents, and tides are also involved. The structural geology of the oceans is a major element in the theory of *plate tectonics. Underwater techniques, such as GLORIA (geological long-range incline ASDIC), based on *echo sounding are being developed, especially in the USA, to obtain information about the sea floor and the minerals it contains.

oceans The large areas of water (excluding lakes and seas) covering about 70% of the earth's surface. The whole water mass is known as the hydrosphere. The oceans are the Pacific (covering about one-third of the world), Atlantic, Indian, and Arctic; the Southern Ocean (waters south of 40°S) is sometimes distinguished. Major structural features are the continental margins (continental shelf and slope), mid-ocean ridges, ocean basins, and trenches. □ p. 892.

Oceanus In Greek mythology, a river issuing from the underworld and encircling the earth. It was personified as a *Titan, a son of Uranus and Gaea and father of the gods and nymphs of the seas and rivers.

ocelot A *cat, *Felis (Panthera) pardalis*, also called painted leopard, of Central and South American forests. 100–150 cm long including the tail (30–50 cm), it has a black-spotted buff coat with stripes on the legs—an attractive target for hunters. It frequently hunts by night, searching for small mammals and reptiles.

ochre A natural pigment, either red or yellow, consisting of hydrated ferric oxide with various impurities. It is therefore a type of *limonite deposit. It has been used as a pigment since prehistoric times and was important in medieval frescoes.

OCEANS

diving petrel

sea surface

crabeater seal

plankton

anchovies

ocean bonito

southern
bluefin tuna

Portuguese
man-of-war

humpback whale

1000 m

hatchetfish

giant squid

oarfish

3000 m

anglerfish

deep-sea
jellyfish

abyssal
sea cucumber

deep-sea
shrimp

brittle star

OCEANS *A selection of animals and plants found at different depths of the ocean.*

Ockham's Razor The metaphysical principle, associated with the English medieval philosopher *William of Ockham, that "Entities should not be multiplied unnecessarily." In analysing a problem one should always choose the hypothesis that makes the least number of assumptions; only indispensible concepts are real.

O'Connell, Daniel (1775–1847) Irish politician, who aroused popular support in the 1820s for the right of Roman Catholics to sit in the British parliament. Himself a Catholic, his election as MP for Clare in 1828 forced the government to concede *Catholic emancipation. Thereafter O'Connell was dubbed the Liberator. He subsequently worked for the repeal of union with Britain but lost the backing of the more revolutionary *Young Ireland group.

O'Connor, Feargus (1794–1855) Irish politician. From 1832 to 1835 he was a radical MP for Cork. He then became a leading Chartist (*see* Chartism), editing the radical newspaper *Northern Star*. He was elected MP for Nottingham in 1847 and presented the 1848 Chartist petition. In 1852 he was pronounced insane.

O'Connor, Frank (Michael O'Donovan; 1903–66) Irish short-story writer. During the 1930s he was director of the Abbey Theatre and a friend of W. B. *Yeats. He published many collections of stories, from *Guests of the Nation* (1931) to *My Oedipus Complex* (1964), and translations from Gaelic.

OCR (*optical character recognition*). *See* computer.

octane number A measure of the extent to which a fuel causes *knocking in a petrol engine. It is the percentage by volume of *iso*-octane (C_8H_{18}) in a mixture of *iso*-octane and *n*-heptane (C_7H_{16}), which has the same knocking characteristics as the fuel under specified conditions.

Octavia (d. 11 BC) The sister of Emperor Augustus, who married her to Mark Antony (40) to seal their reconciliation. Antony divorced her in 32, when he returned to Egypt and Cleopatra.

Octavian. *See* Augustus.

octopus An eight-armed *cephalopod mollusc belonging to the genus *Octopus*, found in most oceans. Octopuses are 5–540 cm long and a large species may have an armspan of 900 cm. The common octopus (*O. vulgaris*), weighing up to 2 kg, has a pair of well-developed eyes, a ring of tentacles around its horny beak, and a saclike body. Octopuses feed mainly on crabs and lobsters and may eject a cloud of ink when alarmed. Family: *Octopodidae*; order: *Octopoda*.

Oda Nobunaga (1534–82) Japanese feudal lord, who began the reunification of feudal Japan. By careful administration, skilful diplomacy, the selection of able generals, and the adoption of novel military tactics based on formations of infantry armed with the newly introduced arquebus, Nobunaga achieved domination between 1560 and 1582 over Kyoto and central Japan. He was treacherously assassinated.

Odense 55 24N 10 25E A seaport in S Denmark, on the island of Fyn. Its gothic cathedral was founded by *Canute II and contains his tomb and shrine. Odense University was established in 1964. It is the birthplace of Hans Christian Andersen. Its varied industries include shipbuilding, sugar refining, textiles, and iron founding. Dairy produce is the main export. Population (1981 est): 169 183.

Oder, River (Polish and Czech name: Odra) A river in E Europe. Rising in the Oder Mountains of Czechoslovakia, it flows N and W through Poland and enters the Baltic Sea at Szczecin. Linked by canals to both E and W Europe, it is of great commercial importance. Length: 886 km (551 mi).

Oder-Neisse Line The boundary between Germany and Poland confirmed by the Allies at the *Potsdam Conference (1945) at the end of World War II. The line ran S from Swinoujście on the Baltic Sea to the Czechoslovak border, following the Rivers Oder and Neisse. It was recognized by East Germany and Poland in 1950 but not by West Germany until 1970.

Odessa 46 30N 30 46E A port in the Soviet Union, in the S Ukrainian SSR on the Black Sea. Fishing and whaling as well as ship repairing are important activities and industries include engineering, chemicals, and oil refining. *History*: founded in the 14th century as a Tatar fortress, it passed to Russia in 1791 and became a naval base. It was the scene in the Revolution of 1905 of the mutiny on the *Potemkin*, as filmed by Eisenstein. Population (1981 est): 1 072 000.

Odets, Clifford (1906–63) US dramatist. He joined the Communist Party in 1934 and was a founding member of the Group Theatre, which produced his first successful play, *Waiting for Lefty* (1935). He later became a Hollywood scriptwriter. His other plays include *Awake and Sing* (1935), *Golden Boy* (1937), *The Big Knife* (1949), and *The Country Girl* (1950).

Odin The principal god of the Teutonic peoples, the husband of *Frigga and, according to some legends, the father of *Thor. Also known as Woden and Wotan, he was the god of war, learning, and poetry and possessed great magical powers. He was the protector of slain heroes, who were brought to *Valhalla by his servants the *Valkyries. His desire for learning was so great that he gave up his right eye to drink from Mimir's well of knowledge. The Old English form of his name, *Woden*, is preserved in *Wednesday*. □Ragnarök.

Odoacer (c. 433–93 AD) King of Italy (476–93). A German chieftain, he served with various Roman commanders before rebelling and deposing the last western Roman emperor, *Romulus Augustulus. After acknowledging the overlordship of the Eastern Roman emperor, Zeno (reigned 474–91), he ruled Italy competently until overthrown and treacherously killed by the Ostrogothic king, *Theodoric the Great.

Odontoglossum A genus of epiphytic *orchids (about 250 species) native to mountainous areas of tropical America. Each large swollen stem base bears one or more leaves, and the flowers, which are borne on a spike, vary greatly in colour and size. Many *Odontoglossum* species have been crossed both within the genus and with other orchid genera to produce hundreds of beautiful hybrids, prized by orchid growers.

Odo of Bayeux (c. 1036–97) Bishop of Bayeux (1049–97). The half-brother of William the Conqueror, he took part in the Norman conquest of England and helped rule the country during William's absences but subsequently rebelled against William II. He died on the first Crusade.

Odysseus (*or* Ulysses) A legendary Greek king of Ithaca and hero of Homer's *Odyssey*, notable for his cunning. His many adventures during his voyage home from the *Trojan War included encounters with the Cyclops *Polyphemus, the cannibalistic Laestrygones, the enchantress *Circe, and the goddess Calypso, with whom he lived for eight years. Having reached Ithaca, he was reunited with his faithful wife *Penelope after killing her suitors with the help of his son Telemachus.

OECD. *See* Organization for Economic Cooperation and Development.

oedema The accumulation of fluid in body tissues, leading to swelling, popularly known as dropsy. There are many causes of oedema, including heart failure, kidney failure, liver failure, and malnutrition. Fluid in the lungs (pulmonary oedema) will cause breathlessness. *Diuretic drugs can usually resolve oedema by causing the patient to pass more urine. Swelling of the ankles occurs quite commonly: for example, in hot weather and in women before menstruation. It is usually relieved by resting with the legs raised.

Oedipus In Greek legend, a king of Thebes who unwittingly fulfilled the prophecy of the oracle at Delphi that he would kill his father and marry his mother. He was brought up by Polybus, King of Corinth. He killed his true father, Laius, in a roadside quarrel, and after winning the throne of Thebes by solving the riddle of the *sphinx he married his mother, the widowed Jocasta. When they discovered the truth, Jocasta committed suicide and Oedipus blinded himself and went into exile. The story is the subject of Sophocles' best-known tragedy.

Oedipus complex The unconscious sexual feelings of a boy for his mother, which are accompanied by aggressive feelings for his father. According to psychoanalysis this is a normal desire, made unconscious by *repression. The female equivalent (in which a girl desires her father) is called the **Electra complex**.

Oehlenschläger, Adam (Gottlob) (1779–1850) Danish poet and playwright. Greatly influenced by Goethe, Fichte, Schelling, and the Schlegels, Oehlenschläger was the founder of Danish Romanticism and Denmark's greatest poet. His works include the blank-verse tragedies *Hakon Jarl* and *Baldur hin Gode* (*Balder the Good*), based on Norse legend and published in *Nordiske Digte* (1807). He also wrote lyric poetry and a ballad cycle based on the poetic Edda, *Nordens Guder* (*The Gods of the North*; 1819).

Oersted, Hans Christian (1777–1851) Danish physicist; professor at Copenhagen University. He discovered the magnetic effect of an electric current and thus established the relationship between electricity and magnetism. He did not, however, take an active part in the elucidation of this discovery. The c.g.s. unit of magnetic field strength is named after him.

oesophagus The gullet: a muscular tube, about 25 cm long, running from the pharynx at the back of the mouth to the stomach. Contractions of the oesophagus propel swallowed food towards the stomach: the food is lubricated with mucus secreted by the walls of the oesophagus.

oestrogens A group of steroid hormones that function principally as female sex hormones. The most important oestrogens in mammals are oestradiol and oestrone. Produced by the ovaries under the influence of pituitary *gonadotrophins, they promote the development of the reproductive organs and secondary sexual characteristics (such as enlargement of breasts) at puberty and regulate the changes of the menstrual cycle (*see* menstruation). Oestrogens are also produced by the placenta, adrenal glands, and testes. Synthetic oestrogens are used in medicine to treat menstrual and menopausal disorders; they are also constituents of *oral contraceptives.

oestrus The period of "heat" in the sexual cycle of female mammals, when the female will attract males and permit copulation. It corresponds to the time of ovulation, so that mating is most likely to result in pregnancy. The oestrous cycle is similar to the menstrual cycle of women, except that the lining of the womb is not shed during oestrus.

Offa (d. 796) King of Mercia (757–796) and overlord of all England S of the Humber. He engaged in trade with Charlemagne, although Charlemagne had refused to marry his daughter to Offa's son. He accepted greater papal control of the Church, introduced a new currency, and devised a code of laws. **Offa's Dyke**, an earthwork dividing England from Wales, built c. 784–c. 796, marks the frontier established by his wars with the Welsh.

Offaly (Irish name: Uabh Failghe) A county in the central Republic of Ireland, in Leinster bordered in the W by the River Shannon. It is chiefly low lying containing part of the Bog of Allen in the N. Agricultural produce includes oats, barley, and wheat; cattle are reared. Area: 2000 sq km (770 sq mi). Population (1981): 58 312. County town: Tullamore.

Off-Broadway theatres Small-scale professional theatres in New York City that specialize in noncommercial and experimental productions. They were responsible for the most lively drama in the USA in the 1950s and 1960s.

Offenbach (am Main) 50 06N 8 46E A city in S central West Germany, in Hessen on the River Main. It is noted for its leather industry. Population (1980 est): 111 200.

Offenbach, Jacques (J. Eberst; 1819–80) German composer of French adoption and Jewish descent. He adopted the name of the town in which his father lived. A professional cellist, at the age of 30 he began writing a series of popular operettas, including *Orpheus in the Underworld* (1858), *La Belle Hélène* (1864), and *La Vie Parisienne* (1866). He also composed one grand opera, *The Tales of Hoffman* (produced posthumously; 1881).

O'Flaherty, Liam (1897–1984) Irish novelist. Born in the Aran Islands, he worked his way round the world before starting his literary career in London in 1922. His novels, chiefly concerned with themes of violence and terrorism, include *The Informer* (1925) and *The Assassin* (1928). *The Pedlar's Revenge and Other Stories* was published in 1976.

Ogaden, the A semidesert area in E Ethiopia, enclosed by Somalia except to the W. The nomadic inhabitants are chiefly Muslim Somalis and in the 1960s a claim to the area by Somalia provoked border clashes. Somalia invaded the Ogaden in 1977 but withdrew (1978) in the face of counteroffensives launched by Ethiopia with Cuban and Soviet aid. Guerrilla fighting has continued.

Ogam (*or* Ogham) A script found in about 400 Celtic inscriptions in Ireland and W Britain, dating from the 5th to the 7th centuries AD. It is alphabetic and consists of 20 letters, each made from a number of oblique or straight strokes on either side of a central dividing line.

Ogbomosho 8 05N 4 11E The third largest city in Nigeria, on the Yorubaland plateau. Agricultural trade is important and there are local craft industries, including textiles and wood working. There are also shoe and tobacco factories. Population (1983 est): 527 400.

Ogden, C(harles) K(ay) (1889–1957) British writer and scholar. With I. A. *Richards he wrote *The Meaning of Meaning* (1923). From 1925 he developed *Basic English, with a restricted vocabulary of 850 words, intended as a practical medium of international communication.

Ogdon, John (1937–) British pianist. He was joint winner with Vladimir Ashkenazy of the 1962 Tchaikovsky Competition in Moscow. He is particularly well known for his championship of such composers as Scriabin, Busoni, and Messiaen.

Oglethorpe, James Edward (1696–1785) English general and colonizer. While an MP, he promoted the establishment of a colony in North America for indigent debtors and persecuted Protestants and in 1733 he led the first group of settlers to the colony that was to become Georgia. He repulsed a Spanish attack against it (1742).

Ogooué, River (*or* R. Ogowe) A river in W central Africa. Rising in the SW Congo, it flows mainly NW and W through Gabon to enter the Atlantic Ocean. Length: 970 km (683 mi).

O'Hara, John (Henry) (1905–70) US novelist. He was a journalist before publishing ironic stories about middle-class life in the 1930s. His novels include *Appointment in Samarra* (1934), *Butterfield 8* (1935), *Pal Joey* (1940), *Ten North Frederick* (1955), and *From the Terrace* (1958).

O'Higgins, Bernardo (?1778–1842) Chilean national hero. The son of an Irish-born soldier who became Spanish colonial governor, he fought with José de *San Martin against Spain and liberated Chile. He was made dictator of the country in 1817 but his wide-ranging reforms created much resentment and he was deposed after a revolt in the provinces.

Ohio A state in the USA, in the Midwest situated to the S of Lake Erie. The flat or rolling land of W Ohio gives way in the E to the hill and valley region of the Appalachian Plateau. A major industrial state, it lies at the centre of the most industrialized area of the USA and is strategically located near many rich markets. The principal manufactures are transportation equipment and raw and fabricated metals. It also exploits its abundant natural resources, including clay and stone, lime, coal, natural gas, and oil. Agriculture is important, especially livestock. *History*: disputed by the French and British, it was eventually ceded to Britain in 1763 and to the USA in 1783. It became a state in 1802. Area: 106 764 sq km (41 222 sq mi). Population (1980): 10 797 419. Capital: Columbus.

Ohio River A river in the USA flowing mainly.SW from Pittsburgh in W Pennsylvania to join the Mississippi (in Illinois) as its main E tributary. Length: 1577 km (980 mi).

ohm (Ω) The *SI unit of electrical resistance equal to the resistance between two points on a conductor when a potential difference of one volt between the points produces a current of one ampere. This definition replaced the former definition, which was based on the resistance of 'a specified column of mercury. Named after Georg *Ohm.

Ohm, Georg Simon (1787-1854) German physicist, who discovered in 1827 that the current flowing through a wire is proportional to the potential difference between its ends (*see* Ohm's law). Ohm also found that the electrical resistance of a wire is proportional to its length and inversely proportional to its cross-sectional area. The unit of electrical resistance is named after him.

Ohm's law The basic law of electric current, named after its discoverer Georg *Ohm. The current, I, flowing through an element in a circuit is directly proportional to the voltage drop, V, across it. It is written as $V = IR$, where R is the resistance of the circuit element.

oil There are three types of oil: lipids (*see* fats and oils), *essential oils, and mineral oil.
Petroleum (*or* rock oil) is the thick greenish mineral oil that occurs in permeable underground rock and consists mainly of *hydrocarbons, with some other elements (sulphur, oxygen, nitrogen, etc.). It is believed to have derived from the remains of living organisms deposited many millions of years ago with rock-forming sediments. Under the effects of heat and pressure this organic material passed through a number of chemical and physical changes ending up as droplets of petroleum, which migrated through porous rocks and fissures to become trapped in large underground reservoirs, often floating on a layer of water and held under pressure beneath a layer of natural gas (mostly methane).
Mineral oil was used in the 4th millennium BC by the Sumerians to reinforce bricks, and the Burmese were burning it in oil lamps in the 13th century AD. However, the modern oil industry began when oil was discovered in Pennsylvania in 1859 and has grown with the development of the internal-combustion engine, which is entirely dependent on it as a fuel.
The presence of oil in underground reservoirs is detected by geologists, who seek evidence of the type of structures in which oil is known to occur and measure the gravitational force in likely areas to identify variations of rock density; depth is determined by such measures as the behaviour of sound waves produced by small surface explosions. Exploratory narrow-bore drillings are then made to determine the extent of a reservoir. The actual oil well is made by drilling through the rock with a rotating bit supported in a wider shaft; a specially prepared mud is pumped through the hollow bit to collect the debris, which is forced back up the shaft around the drilling bit. When the oil is reached, the pressure of the mud is used to control the pressure of the oil so that none is wasted by "gushers"; when the mud has been removed from the shaft the flow is controlled by valves. This method of sinking wells enables oil over 5 km (3 mi) below the surface to be mined. Drilling for oil below the sea is achieved in a similar manner, except that the drilling rig has to be supported on a base, which has legs sunk into the sea bed.
Petroleum has no uses in its crude form and has to be refined by fractional distillation (i.e. separating the components

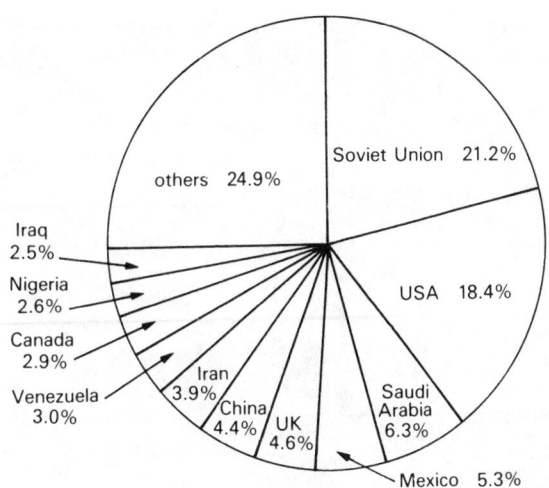

OIL   *World crude petroleum production (1985).*

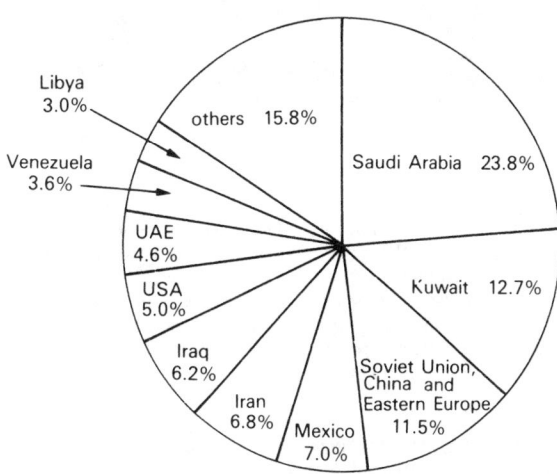

OIL   *World crude petroleum reserves (1985).*

according to their boiling points) before it is of commercial value. Natural gas is widely used as a substitute for coal gas and as a source of power in the refinery. Products made by blending the distillation fractions include aviation spirit, petrol, kerosene, Diesel oil, lubricating oil, paraffin wax, and petroleum jelly. In addition to fractional distillation, other processes, such as catalytic cracking, are used to split the larger molecules into smaller ones to increase the yield of petrol and to reduce the viscosity of heavier oils. Catalytic reforming is used to make a number of valuable chemicals (petrochemicals), which are required to manufacture detergents, plastics, fibres, fertilizers, drugs, etc.

As one of the world's primary energy sources, the price, conservation, and political significance of oil are extremely controversial issues. In 1961 the *Organization of Petroleum Exporting Countries (OPEC) was set up to protect producing countries from exploitation. Its advent ended the era of cheap energy and prices for petroleum products rose sharply during the ensuing decade. In 1974 the International Energy Agency (IEA) was established to protect consumers. Since then various factors, including the flow of North Sea oil, have helped to stabilize prices, although the Iranian

OKAPI   *The closest living relative of the giraffe, this nocturnal animal becomes very docile and breeds readily in captivity.*

revolution of 1979 and the *Gulf War have led to world shortages and further price increases. World oil reserves are as difficult to estimate as future world consumption. Reserves depend on undiscovered sources, while consumption depends on the projected usage, the price of oil in relation to its competitors, and the extent to which nuclear energy will be utilized. Possible sources of oil in the future include shale, tar sands, and coal.

oil beetle   A heavy-bodied flightless beetle belonging to the family *Meloidae* (about 2000 species). If disturbed, it discharges evil-smelling oily blood—an example of reflex bleeding—as a defence mechanism. It has a similar lifestyle to the *blister beetle.

oilbird   A South American cave-dwelling bird, *Steatornis caripensis*, also called guacharo. It is 30 cm long and has a fan-shaped tail, a white-spotted black-barred brown plumage, and a hook-tipped bill surrounded by long bristles. It lives in colonies, uses echolocation inside caves, and feeds on fruit. It is the only member of its family (*Steatornithidae*); order: *Caprimulgiformes* (frogmouths, nightjars, etc.).

oil-immersion lens   A lens system used in some *microscopes in which the gap between the objective lens and the specimen is filled with oil (usually cedar-wood oil). It increases the amount of light entering the system.

oil palm   A *palm tree, *Elaeis guineensis*, native to tropical West Africa and cultivated in Africa, Indonesia, Malaysia, and tropical America as the source of palm oil. Growing to a height of 15 m, the palms produce fleshy fruits, 3 cm long, containing a white kernel within a hard black shell. Palm oil is extracted from the pulp and kernel and used in making soaps, margarine, lubricants, etc. The residual meal from the kernels is a valuable livestock feed.

oilseeds   Oil-bearing seeds of plants from which the edible oil is extracted for making margarine, soaps, etc. Examples include rapeseed, cottonseed, groundnuts, and soya beans. The oil is

obtained from the seeds by expelling it under pressure or by extracting it using a solvent (with a solvent recovery cycle); the **oilcake** remaining after most of the oil has been removed is called expellers or extractions, respectively. Both forms of oil-cake are widely used as animal feeds.

Oise, River   A river in N France, flowing mainly SW from the Belgian Ardennes to join the River Seine at Conflans. Length: 302 km (188 mi).

Oistrakh, David   (1908–75) Russian violinist. He made his debut in Moscow in 1933 and won the International Violin Competition in Brussels in 1937. He played frequently in the West, and was well known for his performances of the Brahms, Tchaikovsky, and Prokofiev violin concertos. His son and pupil, the violinist **Igor Oistrakh** (1931–   ), often gave joint recitals with him and has also conducted.

Oita   33 15N 131 36E A port in Japan, on the NE coast of Kyushu. An important town in the 16th century, it is now an expanding industrial centre with an oil refinery and iron and steel industries. Population (1980): 360 000.

Ojibwa   A North American Indian people of the Great Lakes region, who speak a language of the Algonkian family. They are also known as Chippewa; those who now live near Lake Winnipeg in Canada are called Saulteaux. They were traditionally hunters, fishers, and gatherers, who wandered in small bands and sheltered in simply made dome-shaped wigwams. Shamans exercised considerable influence.

Ojos del Salado   27 05S 68 05W A mountain peak on the border between Argentina and Chile, the second highest peak in the Andes. Height: 6873 m (22 550 ft).

okapi   A hoofed mammal, *Okapia johnstoni*, of central African rain forests. Okapis are about 150 cm high at the shoulder and have a dark-brown coat with horizontal black and white stripes on the legs and rump, which provide camouflage. The smaller male has short bony backward-pointing horns. They were unknown to science until 1901. Family: *Giraffidae* (giraffes).

Okavango Swamp   A marshy area in NE Botswana, into which the River Okavango drains. It supports a rich and varied wildlife.

Okayama   34 40N 133 54E A town in Japan, in SW Honshu. A commercial and industrial centre, it has a 16th-century castle and a traditional Japanese garden (1786). Its university was established in 1949. Population (1980): 546 000.

Okeechobee, Lake   A large freshwater lake in the USA, in S Florida. It drains into the Atlantic Ocean through the *Everglades. Area: 1813 sq km (700 sq mi).

O'Keeffe, Georgia   (1887–1986) US painter. Her first one-person show was presented in 1917 by the photographer Alfred *Stieglitz, whom she married in 1924. Thereafter she specialized in semiabstract paintings of flowers, bones, architecture, and landscapes inspired by the countryside of New Mexico.

Okefenokee Swamp   A swamp area in the USA, extending through SE Georgia and NE Florida. In 1937 a large proportion of it was designated the Okefenokee National Wildlife Refuge; the wildlife includes alligators, snakes, and birds.

Okeghem, Jean d'   (c. 1425–c. 1495) Flemish composer, noted for his innovatory counterpoint. He was composer to Charles VII, Louis XI, and Charles VIII of France and his pupils included Josquin des Prez. He wrote much church music, including 16 masses and 9 motets.

Okhotsk, Sea of   A section of the N Pacific Ocean off the E coast of the Soviet Union, separated from the main ocean by Kamchatka and the Kuril Islands.

Okinawa   A mountainous Japanese island, the main one of the *Ryukyu group. During World War II it was captured by the USA in a major amphibious operation and was only returned to Japan in 1972, the USA retaining military bases there. Chief products are fish, rice, sugar cane, and sweet potatoes. Area: 1176 sq km (454 sq mi). Population (1983 est): 1 146 000. Capital: Naha.

Oklahoma A state in the S central USA. It has a diverse landscape, with uplands in the W, the lowlands of the Arkansas River Valley and coastal plain in the centre and S, and wooded hills in the E. An oil-rich state, agriculture (especially cattle) remains a major source of revenue. Most industry is located around Oklahoma City and Tulsa (one of the world's leading oil centres). The most important manufacturing industries are food processing, nonelectrical machinery, fabricated metal products, and electrical and transport equipment. *History*: first explored by the Spanish, it formed part of the Louisiana Purchase in 1803. It was reserved as Indian territory (1828) but after the US Civil War White settlement began and it became a state in 1907. Area: 181 089 sq km (69 919 sq mi). Population (1980): 3 025 266. Capital: Oklahoma City.

Oklahoma City 35 28N 97 33W A city in the USA, the capital of Oklahoma on the North Canadian River. Founded in 1889, it expanded rapidly following the discovery of oil (1920s). Today it is a commercial, industrial, and distribution centre for an oil-producing and agricultural area. Oklahoma City University was established in 1904. Population (1980): 403 213.

okra An annual African herb, *Hibiscus esculentus*, also called lady's fingers or gumbo, widely cultivated in the tropics and subtropics. It grows 1–2 m high and has heart-shaped leaves and five-petalled yellow flowers with a crimson centre. The pods are picked before they are ripe and eaten fresh, canned, dried, or pickled. They may be used to thicken stews and soups. The seeds are a coffee substitute. Family: *Malvaceae*.

Olaf I Tryggvason (c. 964–c. 1000) King of Norway (995–c. 1000). He took part in the Viking attacks on England (991–94) but the English king, Ethelred the Unready, became his godfather when Olaf was confirmed as a Christian at Andover (994). Olaf subsequently imposed Christianity on Norway. A hero of Scandinavian literature, he died at the hands of the Danes in the battle of Svolder.

Olaf II Haraldsson, Saint (c. 995–1030) King (1015–28) and patron saint of Norway. Baptized in 1013, he attempted to complete the conversion of Norway to Christianity. He was overthrown by Canute II of England and Denmark and died, attempting to regain his kingdom, at the battle of Stikelstad.

Olaf V (1903–) King of Norway (1957–). A talented sportsman, he took part as a yachtsman in the 1928 Olympic Games. In 1929 he married Princess Märtha of Sweden (1901–54) and his heir is his son Prince Harald (1937–).

Öland A long narrow island in Sweden, in the Baltic Sea separated from the mainland by the Kalmar Sound. Area: 1347 sq km (520 sq mi). Population (1984 est): 23 874. Chief town: Borgholm.

Olbers, Heinrich Wilhelm Matthäus (1758–1840) German astronomer, who was the first to point out the paradoxical nature of the night sky (*see* Olbers' paradox). He was also one of the first astronomers to detect and study the asteroids, discovering Pallas in 1802 and Vesta in 1804.

Olbers' paradox Why is the sky dark at night? Heinrich *Olbers argued, in 1826, that if the universe were infinite, uniform, and unchanging, with innumerable stars, then the night sky would be covered in stars and appear as bright as the average star, i.e. the sun. The paradox is resolved by the facts that the universe does not extend infinitely in space and time and is expanding rather than remaining static and unchanging: as the galaxies recede, their radiation suffers a *redshift (i.e. is diminished in energy), which increases with distance.

Old Bailey A street in the City of London in which the *Central Criminal Court is situated. The street takes its name from the Bailey, originally an outwork outside the city wall. The Court is now also called the Old Bailey and occupies the site of the former *Newgate prison. The old courthouse, built in 1773, was replaced by E. W. Mountford's building in 1907, which was extended in 1970.

Old Believers A schismatic sect of the Russian Orthodox Church that rejected the liturgical reforms of the Patriarch of Moscow (1667). Its members were mainly peasants, who suffered much persecution. The majority, who evolved their own Church hierarchy, was eventually recognized by the state (1881), but the remainder split up into small and often eccentric sects.

Oldcastle, Sir John (c. 1378–1417) English soldier and leader of the *Lollards. An ardent supporter of *Wycliffe, whose works he distributed, he was arrested for heresy and imprisoned in the Tower of London (1413). He escaped but was recaptured four years later and hanged. Shakespeare's character Falstaff is partly based on him.

Old Catholics Christian Churches from several European countries that separated from the Roman Catholic Church at various times and in 1932 entered into communion with the Church of England. They comprise the Church of Utrecht, which supported *Jansenism against Roman Catholic orthodoxy (1724), the Old Catholic Churches of Germany, Switzerland, and Austria, which rejected papal infallibility (1870), the National Polish Church (established 1897), and the Yugoslav Old Catholic Church (1924).

Old Comedy The first period of Greek comic drama, lasting up to the end of the 5th century BC. The episodic choral plays of this period contained elements of song, dance, topical satire, and political criticism and ranged in style from bawdy slapstick to lyrical grace. All the surviving examples are by *Aristophanes. *See also* Middle Comedy; New Comedy.

Oldenbarneveldt, Johan van (1547–1619) Dutch statesman. He supported William the Silent in the *Revolt of the Netherlands against Spain and, with *Maurice of Nassau, became (from 1586) the leading statesman of the newly formed United Provinces of the Netherlands. He presided over a vast expansion of Dutch trade and the formation of the Dutch East India Company. His moderate Protestantism brought him into conflict with Maurice, whose imprisonment and execution of Oldenbarneveldt was a shameful blot on the early history of the United Provinces.

Oldenburg 53 08N 8 13E A city in NW West Germany, in Lower Saxony on the River Hunte. The capital of the former duchy of Oldenburg, it has a 17th-century palace. It is an agricultural and industrial centre. Population (1983 est): 138 800.

Oldenburg, Claes (Thure) (1929–) US sculptor, born in Sweden. He became a leading exponent of *pop art in the 1960s, first with his re-creation of ordinary environments, notably *The Store* (1960–61), and later with his "soft sculptures," in which vinyl and stuffed canvas are shaped into everyday objects, such as bathtubs, typewriters, etc.

Old English sheepdog A breed of working ⬚dog originating in England. It has a compact body, a characteristic ambling gait, and a long dense shaggy coat that may be grey or blue-grey with white markings. These dogs are also known as bobtails because their tails are docked at birth. Height: 55–66 cm.

Oldham 53 33N 2 07W A town in N England, in Greater Manchester. Traditionally a cotton-spinning town, Oldham now also has electronics, textile machinery, plastics, and clothing industries. The town hall is a copy of Ceres' Temple in Athens. Population (1981): 95 467.

old man cactus A succulent desert *cactus of the genus *Cephalocereus* (50 species), especially *C. senilis*, native to tropical and subtropical America. Its sturdy stems are coated with long strands of white hair at maturity and may reach a height of 12 m. It is a popular house plant.

old man's beard. *See* Clematis.

Old Norse A North Germanic language formerly spoken in Iceland and Norway (c. 1150–c. 1350). It is the language of the Norse *sagas and was closely related to the contemporary speech of Denmark and Sweden. From this group the modern Scandinavian languages are derived.

Old Sarum. *See* Salisbury.

Old Testament The collection of 39 books constituting the sacred scriptures of *Judaism. Together with the *New Testament they also form the first of the two major divisions of the Christian *Bible. The title derives from the Latin word for *covenant and refers to the pact between God and Israel, a concept that underlies the authors' view of history and is the major theme throughout. The books claim to cover the period from the creation of the universe and man (Adam) to about 400 BC. They are traditionally divided into three parts: the Law or *Torah, the first five books, traditionally ascribed to Moses and often called the Pentateuch by scholars; the Prophets, which are most of the books bearing the names of individual prophets and containing much historical information; and the Writings .or Hagiographa (Hebrew: *Kethubim*), the latest books admitted to the Hebrew Old Testament (c. 100 AD), i.e. Psalms, Proverbs, Job, Ruth, Lamentations, the Song of Solomon, Ecclesiastes, Esther, Daniel, Chronicles, Ezra, and Nehemiah.

Olduvai Gorge A site in N Tanzania yielding an important sequence of Lower *Palaeolithic fossils and tools. Here L. S. B. *Leakey found remains of the *Australopithecus he called *Zinjanthropus* (c. 1 750 000 years old) and the *hominid *Homo habilis* (c. 2 000 000 years old), one or both of which manufactured crude pebble choppers.

Old Vic A London theatre built in 1818 and named the Royal Victoria in 1833. It became famous for its music-hall entertainments and, after Lilian *Baylis became manager in 1912, its productions of Shakespeare. It was the temporary home of the *National Theatre Company from 1963 to 1976 and in 1979 became the home of the Prospect Theatre Company.

Old World A name for Europe, Africa, and Asia, used especially by early emigrants from Europe. *Compare* New World.

Old World monkey A *monkey belonging to the family *Cercopithecidae* (58 species), native to Africa or Asia. There are both terrestrial and arboreal species, active mainly by day and either omnivorous or vegetarian. They inhabit forest, savannah, swamps, and rocks. *See also* baboon; colobus; guenon; langur; macaque.

oleander A poisonous evergreen shrub, *Nerium oleander*, also called rosebay, native to the Mediterranean region and widely cultivated in warm regions for its attractive flowers. Up to 7 m high, it has long narrow leaves, clusters of white, pink, or purplish five-petalled flowers (up to 7.5 cm across), and dangling pods. Family: *Apocynaceae*.

oleaster A shrub or tree, *Elaeagnus angustifolia*, also called Russian olive, found throughout S Europe and sometimes cultivated for its ornamental silvery foliage. It grows 2–12 m high and bears small fragrant yellowish flowers. The olive-shaped yellowish fruits have a silvery scaly coat and are dried and used in cakes as Trebizond dates. Family: *Elaeagnaceae*.

olefines. *See* alkenes.

Oligocene epoch. *See* Tertiary period.

oligopoly An economic market structure in which there is imperfect competition between a few suppliers. Oligopoly is common in western economies today. Economic theory is not as successful at predicting the market trends in an oligopoly as it is under the extremes of *monopoly and *perfect competition, because the action of each firm in an oligopoly affects the policies of the others.

olingo A mammal belonging to the genus *Bassaricyon* (3 species), found in tropical forests of South America. Olingos are 75–95 cm long including the tail (40–48 cm), with buff-coloured or golden fur. They apparently nest in hollow trees and feed chiefly on fruit. Family: *Procyonidae* (raccoons, kinkajous, etc.); order: *Carnivora*.

Oliphant, Sir Mark Laurence Elwin (1901–) Australian physicist, who in 1934 discovered *tritium while bombarding deuterium with deuterons. His work contributed to the development of the hydrogen bomb. He also designed the first proton synchrotron accelerator.

Olivares, Gaspar de Guzmán, Conde-Duque de (1587–1645) Spanish statesman. The chief minister of Philip IV (1621–43), he combined reform, especially economic, with a grand imperial vision and attempted to make all the Spanish kingdoms provide him with men and money. Dissatisfaction exploded under the strain of Spain's participation in the *Thirty Years' War into revolt in Portugal and Catalonia and led to his downfall. Olivares supported the painters Rubens and Velázquez and the writer Lope de Vega.

olive An evergreen tree, *Olea europaea*, native to W Asia but cultivated throughout Mediterranean and subtropical regions for its fruits. Up to 12 m high, it has a gnarled grey trunk and lance-shaped leathery grey-green leaves. Small greenish-white flowers produce fleshy oval berries containing a hard stone. Unripe green olives and ripe black olives are usually pickled for use in hors d'oeuvres and other dishes. **Olive oil,** pressed from the fruit, is one of the finest edible oils and can be consumed without refining or processing. It is also used in making soaps, cosmetics, and textiles. Olive wood resists decay and is used for furniture and ornaments. Family: *Oleaceae*.

Oliver, Isaac (?1556–1617) Portrait miniaturist, born in Rouen (France). In about 1568 he moved to London with his Huguenot parents to escape religious persecution. Although he studied under *Hilliard, his naturalistic style was influenced by Italian and Flemish art. He successfully rivalled his master at James I's court, where he painted many portraits of the queen and Henry Frederick, Prince of Wales (1594–1612). □Donne, John.

Olives, Mount of (*or* Olivet) 31 47N 35 15E A hill to the E of the old city of Jerusalem. Near its foot is the Garden of Gethsemane, the scene of the betrayal of Christ (Mark 14.26–50) and it is the traditional site of Christ's Ascension (Acts 1.2–12). Height: 817 m (2686 ft).

olive shell A *gastropod mollusc of the family *Olividae* (300 species) of warm shallow seas. The shiny □shell, 1–12 cm long, is roughly cylindrical with a short spire and is covered by the mantle. The animals prey on smaller molluscs on sandy seabeds.

Olivier, Laurence (Kerr), Baron (1907–) British actor. He played many Shakespearian roles while with the Old Vic Theatre Company from 1937 to 1949 and a number of outstanding modern roles, including Archie Rice in *The Entertainer* (1957). His films include the Shakespeare adaptations *Henry V* (1944), *Hamlet* (1948), and *Richard III* (1956). He was director of the National Theatre Company from 1961 to 1973, during which time he played many leading roles, including Shakespeare's Othello (filmed 1965) and in plays by Chekhov, O'Neill, and Ionesco. His second marriage to Vivien *Leigh ended in divorce; in 1961 he married his third wife, Joan *Plowright. He was knighted in 1947 and created a life peer in 1970. The Olivier Theatre, part of the National Theatre, was named in his honour.

olivine A group of rock-forming silicate minerals, varying in composition between the end-members forsterite (Mg_2SiO_4) and fayalite (Fe_2SiO_4). Olivines are green, brownish green, or yellowish green, with a conchoidal fracture. Those rich in magnesium occur in basic and ultrabasic igneous rocks, while fayalite occurs in acid igneous rocks. Peridot is a pale green gem variety. Olivine is believed to be a major constituent of the earth's upper mantle.

olm A cave-dwelling salamander, *Proteus anguineus*, found in the Carpathian Mountains. Growing to about 30 cm, it is white and has bright-red gills throughout its life. The eyes are covered with skin but are clearly visible in young larvae. Although sightless, olms prey on small worms and can survive for long periods without feeding. Family: *Proteidae. See also* mudpuppy.

Olmecs An ancient American Indian people of the Gulf Coast of Mexico. Between about 1200 and 400 BC they evolved the first important Mesoamerican culture, with great ceremonial centres at La Venta and San Lorenzo. They invented a hieroglyphic script and a calendar. Outstanding stone carvers, they produced both monumental basalt heads and small jade figures.

Olomouc (German name: Olmütz) 49 48N 17 15E An industrial town in central Czechoslovakia, in N Moravia. Its notable historic buildings include the gothic cathedral and town hall with a 15th-century astronomical clock. The university was founded in 1576. Population (1980 est): 103 000.

LAURENCE OLIVIER *As Lord Marchmain in the dramatization of Evelyn Waugh's* Brideshead Revisited.

Olsztyn (German name: Allenstein) 53 48N 20 29E A market town in NE Poland. It was founded in 1334 by the Teutonic Knights. Industries include the manufacture of leather. Population (1982 est): 140 000.

Olympia A sanctuary of *Zeus, established about 1000 BC in the NW *Peloponnese, in W Greece. From 776 BC until at least 261 AD it was the venue of the *Olympic Games. Extensive excavations from 1881 have revealed no important buildings before the 6th century BC, when the temple of Hera and the stadium were built. In 457 BC the temple of Zeus in the Altis (sacred grove), which later held *Phidias' famous statue, was completed. Public buildings and monuments, a gymnasium, wrestling area, baths, and guest houses for officials and competitors were built later. The sanctuary was closed by the Christian Emperor Theodosius (390 AD).

Olympia 47 03N 122 53W A seaport in the USA, the capital of Washington on Puget Sound. Founded in 1850, it possesses a fine capitol building (1893). Industries include timber, fishing, and mining. Population (1980): 27 447.

Olympic Games A quadrennial international amateur sports contest. The modern games derive from the ancient Greek athletic festival held at *Olympia, first recorded reliably in 776 BC; however, the games probably date back to the 14th century BC and originated in a religious ceremony. Corrupted in Roman times, they were banned by *Theodosius the Great (393 AD). They were revived at Athens in 1896, largely through the efforts of Baron Pierre de Coubertin (1863–1937), a French educator, who wished to improve national and international understanding through sport. The Winter Olympics were first held in 1924. The Games are governed by the International Olympic Committee, a self-elected international body. Although officially a contest between individuals, hosted by a particular city, the Games are often seen as a competition between countries; they have recently been disrupted by international political tensions, with a US boycott of the Moscow games in 1980, and an East bloc boycott of the Los Angeles games in 1984.

Olympus, Mount (Modern Greek name: Óros Ólimbos) 40 05N 22 21E A small group of mountains in NE central Greece, held in ancient times to be the home of the gods. Highest point: 2917 m (9570 ft).

Om In Indian religions, the greatest of the mantras or mystical sounds embodying spiritual power. In Sanskrit *Om* comprises three sounds *A*, *U*, *M* (the vowels being equivalent to *O*), which represent the three Vedic scriptures, the three worlds (earth, atmosphere, heaven), the *Trimurti or some other triple, and ultimately the essence of the universe.

OM. *See* Order of Merit.

Omagh 54 36N 7 18W A market town in Northern Ireland, the county town of Co Tyrone. Dairy products and shirts are manufactured. Population (1981): 14 627.

Omaha 41 15N 96 00W A city in the USA, in Nebraska on the Missouri River. The state's main commercial centre, industries include meat processing and agricultural machinery. Omaha is a centre for medical research. Population (1980 est): 311 681.

Oman, Sultanate of (name until 1970: Muscat and Oman) A country in the Middle East, in E *Arabia. It is mainly flat but rises to 3107 m (10 194 ft) near the coast in the N. The majority of the population is Arab, Ibadhi Muslim by religion, nomadic, and illiterate. *Economy*: oil, which has been extracted since 1967, accounts for about 90% of the country's revenue. There is also beef production, fishing for sardines, tuna, and sharks, and the growing of such produce as cereals, tobacco, and dates; dates, limes, and pomegranates are the chief export crops. *History*: Oman was settled by the Portuguese, Dutch, and English in the 16th century. Since the 19th century Britain has been influential in Oman. It supported the present sultan's overthrow of his father in 1970 and has helped fight the guerrillas in *Dhofar. Head of State: Sultan Qaboos ibn Sa'id. Official language: Arabic. Official currency: Rial Omani of 1000 baiza. Area: 300 000 sq km (120 000 sq mi). Population (1980 est): 890 000. Capital: Muscat.

Omar (*or* Umar) (d. 644 AD) The second *caliph (634–44), who is regarded by Islam as the founder of the Muslim state. Omar continued the Muslim conquests and in 638 visited Jerusalem after its capture. He was murdered in Medina by a discontented slave.

'Omar Khayyam (?1048–?1122) Persian poet, who was famous as a mathematician and made astronomical observations for the reform of the calendar. His poems, characterized by an agnostic and hedonistic philosophy, were written in the form of *ruba'is* (quatrains). The free translation of 75 of them by Edward *Fitzgerald in 1859 became widely popular; more recent translations have been made by the British poets Robert Graves and John Heath Stubbs (1918–).

Omayyads. *See* Umayyads.

ombres chinoises (French: Chinese shadows) A form of

OMDURMAN   *A painting of the Battle of Omdurman (1898) showing the first charge of the Dervishes.*

shadow puppet drama introduced into 18th-century Europe by travellers returning from the Far East. It was popularized in France by the opening of a shadow theatre at Versailles in 1774. The technique involved the representation of brief amusing episodes by black silhouettes cast from solid puppets.

ombudsman   A person appointed to investigate grievances against maladministration. The post originated in Sweden in 1809 and exists in most Scandinavian countries. New Zealand has had an ombudsman since 1962. In the UK an ombudsman (the parliamentary commissioner for administration) was first appointed in 1967 to investigate complaints against central government departments; complaints against health authorities are investigated by Health Service Commissioners, appointed since 1973; and there have been ombudsmen for local government since 1974.

Omdurman   15 37N 32 29E A city in the Sudan, on the River Nile. The Mahdi made it his capital in 1885 but his successor, the Khalifa, was defeated by Anglo-Egyptian forces under Lord Kitchener in the battle of Omdurman (1898). The Islamic University of Omdurman was founded in 1961. It has trade in hides, textiles, agricultural produce, and handicrafts. Population (1983): 526 287.

Omsk   55 00N 73 22E A port in the Soviet Union, in the W central RSFSR at the confluence of the Rivers Irtysh and Om. Also on the Trans-Siberian Railway, it is a significant transportation centre and has important engineering industries and oil refineries. Population (1981 est): 1 044 000.

onager   A small wild *ass, *Equus hemionus onager*, of Iran. Onagers have a yellow-brown summer coat, which becomes darker in winter, and roam dry grassland in small herds.

Onassis, Aristotle Socrates   (1906–75) Greek businessman, who owned one of the largest independent shipping lines in the world. He started his business in 1932 and during the 1950s became one of the first to construct supertankers. In 1968 he married Jacqueline *Kennedy, his second wife, after a long relationship with Maria *Callas.

Oñate, Juan de   (d. 1630) Spanish conquistador. In about 1595 he settled the territory NW of Central America, New Mex-

ico, and in 1601 sought the mythical kingdom of Quivira. Later, seeking a strait to the Pacific, he reached the Colorado River and Gulf of California.

oncogene   A gene responsible for turning a normal cell into a cancerous cell. Several viruses (called oncogenic viruses) are known to carry oncogenes; when such a virus infects a host cell the oncogene directly transforms it into a cancer cell without altering the host cell's genes.

Ondes Martenot   (French: Martenot waves)   An electronic musical instrument invented in 1928 by Maurice Martenot (1898–   ). It consists of oscillators that produce signals, which are then mixed, amplified, and emitted through a loudspeaker. The frequency of the notes is determined by a keyboard and a special metal ribbon, by means of which glissandi can be produced. The keys can also be moved laterally to produce microtonal variations in pitch. The instrument plays an important part in Messiaen's symphony *Turangalîla* (1948).

Onega, Lake   A lake in the NW Soviet Union, the second largest in Europe. It forms part of the water route from the Gulf of Finland to the White Sea. Area: 9887 sq km (3817 sq mi).

Oneida   43 04N 75 40W A city in the USA, in New York state. A religious society, the Oneida Community, was established nearby in 1848. Its members, who made silverware and steel traps, held all property in common, but social experiments ceased when it became a joint stock company in 1881. Population (1980): 10 810.

O'Neill, Eugene   (1888–1953) US dramatist. The son of actors, he began writing one-act plays while recovering from tuberculosis in a sanatorium and won critical recognition with *Beyond the Horizon* (1920), *Emperor Jones* (1920), *Anna Christie* (1921), and *Desire Under the Elms* (1924). *Mourning Becomes Electra* (1931) transplants Aeschylus' trilogy to Civil War New England. His finest plays, including *The Iceman Cometh* (1946) and *Long Day's Journey into Night* (1956; written 1940–41), were written while he was suffering from Parkinson's disease and alcoholism. He won the Nobel Prize in 1936.

O'Neill, Terence, Baron   (1914–   ) Northern Irish statesman, who became prime minister in 1963. In 1969 his acceptance of civil rights for the Roman Catholic minority forced his resignation from the Unionist Government. He became a life peer in 1970.

One Thousand Guineas A flat race for three-year-old fillies only, run each spring at Newmarket over the Rowley Mile course. It was the last of the English *Classics to be instituted (1814).

onion A hardy herbaceous perennial plant, *Allium cepa*, probably native to central or W Asia but now cultivated worldwide, mainly in temperate regions, for its edible bulb. The mature plant has a leafless stalk, about 1 m high, which bears a round head of small white flowers, and six long slender leaves growing directly from the bulb. Onions are grown either from seed or from tiny bulbs called sets, produced in the flower head. Immature bulbs, together with their leaves, are eaten raw in salads, etc.: these are spring, or green, onions (*see* scallion). Family: *Liliaceae*.

Onitsha 6 10N 6 47E A port in S Nigeria, on the River Niger. It suffered damage during the civil war (1967–71). It is an important trading centre. Agricultural products are the main exports and manufacturing is being developed, including textiles, printing, and tyre retreading. Population (1983 est): 268 700.

Onsager, Lars (1903–76) US chemist, born in Norway. His study of the thermodynamics of irreversible processes helped to solve the problems of separating uranium-235 from uranium-238 by gaseous diffusion, which was essential to the production of nuclear fuel. For this work Onsager was awarded the Nobel Prize in 1968.

Ontario The second largest province of Canada, stretching from the Great Lakes N to Hudson Bay. It lies mainly on the mineral-rich Canadian Shield, a rocky forested plateau with many lakes and rivers. Most of the population live in the gentle fertile lowlands near the S Great Lakes, dominated by the highly industrialized belt stretching from Toronto to Windsor. Manufacturing is very important, especially the production of motor vehicles, steel, pulp and paper, textiles, machinery, petrochemicals, and food products. Ontario is Canada's leading mining province, producing half the world's nickel as well as copper, iron, zinc, gold, and uranium. The province's farmers produce tobacco, fruit, vegetables, and dairy products. Ontario is the wealthiest and most populous Canadian province, the country's political and economic heartland, and the cultural and educational centre of English-speaking Canada. *History*: penetrated by French explorers and fur traders in the 17th century, Ontario became British (1763) and was settled by *Loyalists after the American Revolution. The province benefited greatly from the formation of Canada (1867), which provided it with a vast hinterland and a larger domestic market. Area: 891 194 sq km (344 090 sq mi). Population (1981): 8 625 107. Capital: Toronto.

Ontario, Lake A lake in E North America, the smallest and easternmost of the Great Lakes. It is fed by the Niagara River and empties into the St Lawrence River. Area: 18 941 sq km (7313 sq mi).

ontogeny. *See* phylogeny.

ontology The branch of philosophy that deals with the theory of being and considers questions about what is and what is not. Ontological theories may assert that only minds exist (extreme *idealism), or that only physical objects do (*see* materialism). The term was introduced by *Wolff to cover one of the chief concerns of *metaphysics.

o'nyong-nyong An acute viral infection occurring in East Africa. The disease, transmitted by mosquitoes, is characterized by a rash, aching joints, headache, and fever. Patients usually recover with rest and drugs to relieve the pain and fever.

onyx A semiprecious stone consisting of a variety of *chalcedony characterized by straight parallel bands, often

distinctly coloured. Onyx occurs in the lower part of steam cavities in igneous rocks. **Sardonyx** (birthstone for August) is a variety with reddish bands.

oolite A variety of *limestone consisting mainly of beds of ooliths, approximately spherical concretions of calcite accumulated in concentric layers around a nucleus (for example a grain of sand or fragment of a shell). Ooliths of greater diameter than 2 mm are called pisoliths and the resultant rocks pisolites. Although most oolites are calcareous, oolitic ironstones also occur.

Oort cloud A cloud of ten million or more comets, thought to move around the sun in orbits whose aphelia (greatest distance from sun) lie in a zone far beyond Pluto's orbit. A comet can be perturbed out of the cloud by, say, a passing star and sent closer to the sun, taking many thousands of years to complete its orbit. The cloud is named after the Dutch astronomer Jan Hendrik Oort (1900–   ).

opah. *See* moonfish.

opal A semiprecious stone consisting of a hydrous amorphous variety of silica. Common opal is a dull-white or milky-blue colour, with yellow, brown, or red tinges due to impurities. The precious variety, used as a gem, shows a characteristic internal play of colours (opalescence) resulting from internal reflection and refraction of light passing through adjacent thin layers of different water content. It occurs in cavities in many rocks, deposited by percolating silica-bearing water; geyserite is a variety deposited from hot springs. The variety diatomite, made up of diatom skeletons, is used industrially as an insulator, abrasive, and filtering agent. The main sources of opal gems are Australia and Mexico. Birthstone for October. *See* Plate III.

Op art A form of abstract art, developed in the 1950s and 1960s, that exploits optical techniques to produce dramatic effects, such as the illusion of movement. Violent colour contrasts and subtly distorted patterns are commonly used. Notable exponents include Victor *Vasarely in the USA and Bridget *Riley in the UK.

OPEC. *See* Organization of Petroleum Exporting Countries.

Open Door A policy promulgated by the USA in 1899 to ensure equal trading rights in China for all countries. Its own trade with China threatened by the growing influence there of the other major powers, the USA sought and received the guarantee by Britain, France, Germany, Italy, and Japan of the maintenance of Chinese integrity.

open-hearth process A technique for making *steel from *pig iron, scrap steel, and iron ore. It was developed in the 1850s and is still used, although *electric-arc furnaces are being used increasingly, especially for high-grade steel. The process uses gaseous fuel, which is preheated by the exhaust gases from the furnace. The molten metal lies in a shallow pool at the bottom or hearth of the furnace.

open-market operations The mechanism by which the *Bank of England controls domestic credit and interest rates. When conducting a credit squeeze the Bank sells *treasury bills to the public (via the *discount houses), thus reducing *commercial bank assets (as a result of cheques drawn on them by the buyers of the bills) and making the banks call for funds from the discount houses. The discount houses. The discount houses in turn must borrow from the Bank at a high rate. This encourages the discount houses to sell bills, thus repeating the cycle until the commercial banks, faced with a drop in their liquid assets, are forced to cut back their advances in order to maintain the statutory ratio of liquid assets to total assets.

Open University (OU) A nonresidential university in the UK, established in 1969 to provide further education on a part-time basis for adults by means of correspondence courses and radio and television programmes, supported by a tutor-counselling service at regional centres throughout the country. While in many respects a revolutionary step in the social and educational history of the UK (a university open to anyone regardless of previous qualifications, age, or school attended), it was at the same time a further step in the tradition of *adult education in the UK. First mooted by the Advisory Centre for Education, it came to fruition under the administration (1964-70) of Harold Wilson, who made Jennie Lee responsible for the project. The first courses started in 1971 and by 1979 some 70 000 undergraduates and associate students from all walks of life were following OU courses. The project has earned international esteem, giving those who did not have the chance early in life the opportunity to undertake a university education. More recently the OU has moved into nondegree forms of continuing education, providing a variety of courses, ranging from in-service education for teachers to short courses on such subjects as "energy in the home" and "health choices."

opera A staged dramatic work in which all or most of the text is set to music. Opera originated in Florence in the early 17th century as the result of attempts to revive Greek tragedy and to reproduce its musical elements. These became the aria, recitative, and chorus of operatic convention. Opera began in the court but quickly became a popular public entertainment. The earliest opera still in the modern repertory is Monteverdi's *Orfeo* (1607). In *opera seria, the Italian style of opera developed by such composers as Scarlatti, Lully, and Handel, vocal ability became the dominant feature until Gluck reaffirmed the importance of the dramatic element in the mid-18th century. *Opera buffa developed in the early 18th century and was originally performed between the acts of opera seria. At the end of the 18th century Mozart perfected opera buffa, giving it greater depth and expression. In the early 19th century the influence of Romanticism gave rise to the works of Weber and Meyerbeer, while the Italian *bel canto tradition was maintained by Bellini, Rossini, and Donizetti. In the mid-19th century Wagner evolved the theory of music drama, in which the musical and dramatic elements of opera were integrated. He applied it to his opera cycle *Der Ring des Nibelungen* (1869-1876) and his subsequent operas, which embodied his theory of the *gesamtkunstwerk* (German: complete work of art). Verdi extended the emotional and dramatic range of Italian opera and in his late works assimilated the Wagnerian technique of continuous music in each act in place of the traditional division into separate numbers. The realism of Bizet's *Carmen* (1875) influenced Leoncavallo, Mascagni, and Puccini. In the 20th century a wide variety of operatic styles have flourished, including the dramatic realism of Janáček and the neoclassicism of Stravinsky. Richard Strauss's operas were greatly influenced by Wagner, as was Debussy's opera *Pelléas et Mélisande* (1902). Schoenberg and Berg applied atonal and serial techniques to opera. Other important operatic composers of the 20th century include Prokofiev, Britten, Henze, and Tippett. *See also* opéra comique; comic opera; operetta.

opera buffa A form of comic *opera containing some spoken dialogue. It evolved in Italy in the 18th century, an early example being *Pergolesi's *La serva padrona* (1733). The French genre, *opéra bouffe*, evolved from it in the 19th century and is typified by *Offenbach's operettas.

opéra comique 1. A type of French comic opera of the 18th century with spoken dialogue. 2. In the 19th century, any French opera with spoken dialogue, a category including Bizet's *Carmen* and Gounod's *Faust*.

opera seria A type of *opera common in the 18th century, characterized by a mythological or heroic plot, an Italian libretto, and a formal musical scheme of recitatives and arias.

operetta A light or comic *opera, usually with spoken dialogue. Lehar's *The Merry Widow* (1905) is a typical example.

Ophites (Greek *ophis*: serpent) A Gnostic sect that wor-

shipped the serpent who brought about man's fall (Genesis 3) as the source of wisdom. *See* Gnosticism.

ophthalmia The old name for inflammation of the eye (*see* conjunctivitis). **Ophthalmia neonatorum** is conjunctivitis in newborn babies due to gonorrhoea that they have caught from their mothers during birth. The babies are treated with antibiotics and silver nitrate eyedrops.

ophthalmology The medical specialty concerned with the study, diagnosis, and treatment of diseases of the eye. Ophthalmologists are doctors specializing in this. **Optometry** is the assessment and correction of visual defects, and opticians are not doctors: ophthalmic opticians both test eyesight and prescribe suitable lenses; dispensing opticians make and fit glasses.

Ophüls, Max (M. Oppenheimer; 1902-57) German film director. He worked mostly in France, Italy, and the USA. His stylish and elaborate romantic films include *La Ronde* (1950), *Madame De* (1953), and *Lola Montes* (1955).

Opie, John (1761-1807) British portrait and history painter, born in St Agnes, Cornwall. He was introduced to London (1781) as a prodigy by his teacher John Wolcot (1738-1819) and later became professor of painting at the Royal Academy (1805). His best work was done in the early part of his career.

Opitz (von Boberfeld), Martin (1597-1639) German poet and man of letters. Educated at Heidelberg, he served in the courts of various German nobles until he was appointed historiographer to Ladislaus IV of Poland. His own verse, for example *Teutsche Poemata* (1624), lacks originality but was, with his translations and critical works, especially *Buch von der teutschen Poeterey* (1624), extremely influential in providing a model for German verse and in introducing the work of the *Pléiade, Sidney's *Arcadia*, and other foreign writers.

opium The dried juice obtained from the seed capsule of the *opium poppy. A narcotic drug, opium has been used for centuries in medicine for the relief of pain. Although still sometimes given in the form of laudanum (tincture of opium), its main legitimate uses today include the extraction of its active ingredients—*morphine (first isolated in 1803), codeine, papaverine, etc.—and preparation of their derivatives (e.g. heroin). Because opium causes *drug dependence and overdosage can be fatal, its preparation and use are strictly controlled (in spite of this, illegal trading in opium continues). India and Turkey are the main opium-producing countries.

opium poppy An annual *poppy, *Papaver somniferum*, cultivated since ancient times in N temperate and subtropical regions as the source of *opium. 30-60 cm tall, it has large white to purple flowers with dark centres and the fruit is a round capsule. Opium is extracted from the latex of the plant, which exudes from notches made in the half-ripened capsule and hardens on exposure to air.

Opium Wars 1. (1839-42) The war between Britain and China precipitated by the confiscation by the Chinese Government of British opium stores in Canton and the murder of a Chinese by British sailors. The British victory was confirmed by the Treaty of Nanking in which five *treaty ports were opened to British trade and residence. 2. (1856-60) The war between Britain and France, on one side, and China. Its immediate ·cause was the boarding of the British *Arrow* by Chinese officials. The allied victory opened further ports to western trade (Treaty of Tientsin, 1858, to which the Chinese agreed in the Peking Convention, 1860) and led to the legalization of opium.

Opole (German name: Oppeln) 50 40N 17 56E A town in SW Poland, on the River Oder. It was the capital (1919-45) of the German province of Upper Silesia. Industries include the manufacture of machinery, chemicals, cement, and textiles. Population (1982 est): 119 342.

Oporto (Portuguese name: Pôrto) 41 09N 8 37W The

second largest city in Portugal, on the River Douro near the Atlantic coast. Built on terraces, it has many tall granite houses and a modernized 13th-century cathedral; its university was founded in 1911. It is famous for the export (chiefly to Britain) of its port wine; other exports include fruit, olive oil, and cork. Population (1981): 335 916.

OPOSSUM *Young common opossums cling to their mother's fur after emerging from the pouch and remain close to her for about three months before leading an independent existence.*

opossum A New World *marsupial belonging to the family *Didelphidae* (65 species). Opossums are the only marsupials outside Australasia. The common, or Virginian, opossum (*Didelphys marsupialis*) is cat-sized, with a large pouch containing up to 16 teats; it produces at least two litters of young every year. After about three months the young ride on their mother's back, leaving the pouch free for another litter. Opossums live in crevices and abandoned burrows, feeding on both animal and vegetable matter. □mammal.

Oppeln. *See* Opole.

Oppenheimer, J. Robert (1904–67) US physicist, who contributed to quantum mechanics and particle physics. In 1943 he was put in charge of the development of the atom bomb at Los Alamos, New Mexico. After the war he was appointed chairman of the advisory committee to the Atomic Energy Commission but as a result of his opposition to the development of the hydrogen bomb, he lost his post in 1954 and was labelled a security risk by Senator Joseph *McCarthy's committee.

opposition An alignment of two celestial bodies in the solar system, usually the sun and a planet, that occurs when they lie directly opposite each other in the sky. The angle planet-earth-sun is then 180°. Venus and Mercury cannot come to opposition with the sun. For the other planets, opposition is the most favourable time for observation.

Ops A Roman fertility goddess, wife of Saturn, identified with the Greek *Rhea. She was usually worshipped together with a primitive rustic god, Consus.

optical activity The rotation of the plane of polarization of plane *polarized light as it passes through certain solutions and crystals. The angle through which the plane is rotated is directly proportional to the path length of the light in the substance and, in the case of a solution, to its concentration. If the plane is rotated clockwise (looking at the oncoming light) the substance is said to be dextrorotatory and is indicated by the prefix *d*–. Laevorotatory substances, indicated by *l*–, rotate the plane anticlockwise.

optics The branch of physics concerned with *light and vision. Optics is divided into two major branches: geometrical optics and physical optics. Geometrical optics studies the geometry of light rays as they pass through an optical system.

Physical optics concerns light's properties (e.g. *diffraction, *interference, and polarization) and its interaction with matter (e.g. in *refraction, *scattering, and absorption).

option The right to buy or sell something at an agreed price by a specified date. Usually the option costs a sum of money (the option money), which is not returned if the option is not taken up; and in the UK (except Scotland) option money is necessary to render an option enforceable, unless it is granted by deed. Options are sought for such diverse assets as the right to buy a house, the film rights of a book, or a line of shares. On the London Stock Exchange and on many commodity exchanges options to buy shares or commodities (a call option) or to sell them (a put option) are regular features of trading.

Opuntia. *See* prickly pear.

Opus Dei (Latin: God's work) **1.** In Benedictine monasticism, the monk's primary duty of prayer. It specifically refers to the recitation of prescribed prayers (the Divine Office) at set times known as the canonical hours, namely matins, lauds, prime, terce, sext (noon), nones, vespers, and compline. **2.** An international Roman Catholic organization (full name: Prelature of the Holy Cross and Opus Dei) founded by the Spanish priest Josemaría Escrivá de Balaguer (1902–75) in 1928 to spread Christian ideals to all spheres of society. In 1987, the Prelature had 1000 priests and 72 000 lay members.

orache An annual branching herb or small shrub of the genus *Atriplex* (about 100 species), occurring worldwide on sea shores and waste land and growing 1–1.5 m high. The leaves are narrow or triangular and, in some species, may be used as a vegetable. Tiny green flowers are borne in a branching cluster and the fruit is surrounded by a winglike membrane. Family: *Chenopodiaceae.*

oracle A response given by a deity, usually through the medium of a priest or priestess, to an individual's inquiry; also, the sacred place at which such responses were sought. Although occurring in Egyptian and other ancient civilizations, the best-known oracles were those of classical Greece. The oldest was that of Zeus at Dodona, where the oracle was interpreted from the rustling of the leaves of oak trees. At the oracle of Apollo at Delphi, which attained great political influence during the 6th and 7th centuries BC, the oracular pronouncements made by the Pythian priestess in a state of frenzy were interpreted in verse by the priests.

Oracle. *See* teletext.

Oradea 47 03N 21 55E A city in NW Romania, on the River Crişul Repede. It is situated in a wine-producing area where many Neolithic, Roman, and other artefacts have been found. Its varied industries include the manufacture of machine tools, chemicals, and food products. Population (1983): 197 968.

oral contraceptive A hormonal drug—usually a mixture of an *oestrogen and a synthetic *progesterone—taken in the form of tablets ("the Pill") by women to prevent conception. Oral contraceptives act by preventing the monthly release of an egg cell from the ovary. They are taken every day from the 5th to the 26th day of the menstrual cycle (menstruation occurs during the week in which they are not taken). The Pill may cause fluid retention (therefore swelling of the ankles), depression, high blood pressure, weight gain, and in rare cases thrombosis.

Oran (Arabic name: Wahran; French name: Ouahran) 35 45N 0 38W A port in Algeria, on the Mediterranean Sea. Under intermittent Spanish occupation from the 16th to the 18th centuries, it was occupied by France from 1831 until Algerian independence (1962). It has a university (1965). Exports include cereals, wine, wool, and esparto grass. Population (1983 est): 663 504.

orange One of several small evergreen □trees or shrubs of the genus *Citrus*, native to SE Asia but cultivated throughout the tropics and subtropics. The thick oval shiny leaves have winged stalks and the fragrant white five-petalled flowers are borne in clusters. The globular fruit has a dimpled orange or yellow rind and a juicy pulp, rich in sugars, acids, and vitamin C. Fruit of the sweet orange (*C. sinensis*) is eaten fresh while that of the Seville orange (*C. aurantium*) is used to make marmalade. Oranges are also used in soft drinks and confectionery. Family: *Rutaceae*. *See also* tangerine.

Orange The ruling dynasty of the Netherlands since 1815. In the 16th century the Princes of Orange, in S France, married into the House of *Nassau, a member of which, *William the Silent, became Prince of Orange-Nassau (1544) and led the Revolt of the Netherlands against Spain. He and his descendants (one of whom became William III of England) were *stadholders (chief magistrates) of the United Provinces of the Netherlands until its collapse in 1795. In 1815 the family were restored as monarchs of the newly established kingdom of the Netherlands. The principality of Orange was seized by Louis XIV in 1660.

Orange 44 08N 4 48E A town in SE France, in the Vaucluse department. It was the capital of the principality of Orange in the middle ages, the descendants of which formed the House of Orange. There are several notable Roman remains. Population (1982): 27 502.

Orange 33 19S 149 10E A city in Australia, in E central New South Wales. It is the centre of a fruit-growing and sheep-rearing region. Its industries include woollen mills and electrical engineering. Population (1983 est): 31 950.

Orange Free State (Afrikaans name: Oranje Urystaat) An inland province in South Africa. Much of the province consists of the undulating plain of the Highveld. It is predominantly rural, with agriculture as the leading economic activity. Wheat, maize, and stock rearing are important. Mining has developed recently; diamonds, gold, uranium, and coal are produced. Chemicals, fertilizers, and oil from coal are manufactured. The province has a strong Afrikaner culture. *History*: first settled by Voortrekkers in the early 19th century, it was under British rule as the Orange River Sovereignty from 1848 until an independent Orange Free State was recognized in 1854. It joined the Union of South Africa in 1910. Area: 129 152 sq km (49 886 sq mi). Population (1980): 1 931 860. Capital: Bloemfontein.

Orange Order An Irish sectarian society, named after William III of England (previously William of Orange), pledged to maintain the Protestant succession. Formed in 1795, following William's defeat of the Roman Catholic former king James II, it provided the backbone of Ulster resistance to the *Home Rule movement. The embodiment of Protestant Unionism, its parades and paraphernalia have been seen as contributing to the political unrest of Northern Ireland.

Orange River A river in SW Africa. Rising in NE Lesotho, it flows mainly W across the South African plateau to the Atlantic Ocean. The largest river in South Africa, it forms part of the border between South Africa and Namibia. In 1963 the **Orange River Project** was begun to provide, through a series of dams, irrigation and hydroelectric power. Length: 2093 km (1300 mi).

orang-utan A long-armed great *ape, *Pongo pygmaeus*, of Borneo and Sumatra. Orang-utans grow up to 120 cm tall, with arms spanning more than 200 cm, and have long coarse reddish-brown hair. Mainly vegetarian, they are especially fond of durian fruit. They are the only great apes outside Africa and there are fewer than 5000 individuals in the wild.

Oratorians Communities of Roman Catholic priests who live together without taking vows and who devote themselves to teaching, preaching, prayer, and administration of the sacraments. There are two orders: the Italian Oratory of St Philip Neri (founded 1564) and the French Oratoire de Jésus-Christ (1611). The former has oratories in England founded by Cardinal Newman. The latter runs seminaries for the training of priests.

oratorio A musical composition, usually on a religious subject, for soloists, chorus, and orchestra. The name derives from the Oratory of St Philip Neri in 16th-century Rome (*see* Oratorians), where semidramatized versions of biblical stories were performed with musical accompaniment. Among notable oratorios are the *St Matthew* and *St John Passions* of J. S. Bach, Handel's *Messiah*, Haydn's *The Creation*, Mendelssohn's *Elijah*, Berlioz's *Childhood of Christ*, Elgar's *Dream of Gerontius*, and Tippett's *A Child of Our Time*.

orbital An atomic orbital is the region around the nucleus in which there is an appreciable probability that an electron will be found. In *wave mechanics an electron does not have a fixed orbit as it does in the *Bohr atom; it has instead an orbital in which there is a probability distribution, given by a wave function, that it will be found in a particular region. Each orbital has a fixed energy and a shape determined by three *quantum numbers, one (*n*) indicating the most probable distance of the electron from the nucleus, one (*l*) giving its angular momentum, and one (*m*) giving the orientation of the orbital if it is not spherical. In the formation of a covalent bond between two atoms, a molecular orbital containing two electrons is formed.

orb weaver A *spider belonging to a widely distributed family (*Argiopidae*; over 2500 species), noted for its geometrically designed web. For example, the web of the orange garden spider (*Miranda aurantia*), common in grass and bushes, has a zigzag band and reaches 60 cm across.

Orcagna, Andrea (Andrea di Cione; c. 1308–c. 1368) Florentine artist. His only certain surviving painting is the altarpiece in the Strozzi Chapel of Sta Maria Novella, Florence; as a sculptor he is known for his marble tabernacle in Orsanmichele. He became architect to Orsanmichele (1355) and to the Duomo in Florence (1357 and 1364–67) and in Orvieto (1358).

orchestra A body of instrumentalists playing music written or arranged for a specific combination of instruments. The modern **symphony orchestra** evolved from the small and variously constituted orchestras of the 18th century; its original instrumentation (first and second violins, violas, cellos, double basses, bassoons, oboes, flutes, horns and timpani) being that of the typical symphony. Such orchestras were directed from a continuo keyboard instrument or by the leader of the first violin section. In the 19th century the orchestra was enlarged and the range of instruments widened by the addition of clarinets, trumpets, trombones, and percussion instruments; later the harp, cor anglais, piccolo, bass clarinet, contra bassoon, and tuba were added. In the late 19th century the number of woodwind and brass was increased, and such instruments as the saxophone, saxhorn, Wagner tuba, glockenspiel, and xylophone were occasionally used. The role of the conductor became increasingly important from the early 19th century onwards. In the 20th century the piano, guitar, mandolin, marimba, vibraphone, as well as various electric and electronic instruments have all had orchestral parts written for them. The modern symphony orchestra comprises at least a hundred players. The **chamber orchestra** corresponds in size to the smaller orchestras of the 18th century.

orchid A herbaceous perennial plant of the family *Orchidaceae* (about 20 000 species), found worldwide, especially in damp tropical regions. Most temperate orchids grow normally in the soil (i.e. they are terrestrial), while tropical orchids tend to grow nonparasitically on trees (i.e. as epiphytes) and form pseudobulbs (storage organs) at the base of the stem. Orchid flowers vary greatly in shape, colour, and size and occur usually in clusters. Each flower consists of three petal-like sepals and three petals—the lowest (labellum) being very distinctive. The one or two stamens and stigma are fused to form a central column that bears pollen grains grouped into masses (pollinia), which are transferred to other flowers by insects. The flowers of many species are adapted to receive only a particular species of insects in order to restrict natural hybridization; examples are the bee, fly, and spider orchids (genus *Ophrys*). The fruit is a capsule containing enormous numbers of tiny seeds, which are dispersed by wind. Many orchids are cultivated for ornament, both commercially for the florist trade and by amateur growers (*see* Cattleya; Cymbidium; Odontoglossum; slipper orchid); one genus—*Vanilla*—is of commercial importance as the source of vanilla flavouring.

orchil (*or* archil)   One of several *lichens (Umbilicaria, Roccella, Evernia, Lecanova,* and *Ochrolechia*) from which a violet dye can be extracted by fermentation. The name is also applied to the dye itself.

Orczy, Baroness Emmusca   (1865–1947) British novelist. Born in Hungary, she went to London to study art. Her best-known novel is *The Scarlet Pimpernel* (1905), concerning the adventures of an English nobleman who smuggles aristocrats out of Revolutionary France.

Order in Council   A command or direction issued by the queen with the advice of the *Privy Council, although in fact it is issued only with the advice of the cabinet. Apart from the Crown's inherent right (royal prerogative) to issue Orders, for example declarations of war, some Acts of Parliament (statutes) authorize them to give legal force to administrative regulations made by government departments. Only Orders authorized by act of parliament can make or alter the law.

Order of Merit (OM)   A British order of chivalry, instituted in 1902. It comprises the sovereign and not more than 24 men and women of great eminence.

Order of the British Empire, The Most Excellent   A British order of knighthood, instituted in 1917 and having five classes: Knights or Dames Grand Cross (GBE); Knights or Dames Commanders (KBE or DBE); Commanders (CBE); Officers (OBE); and Members (MBE). Its motto is *For God and Empire*.

orders of architecture   The fundamental elements of classical □architecture, comprising five main types of supportive column—Doric, Tuscan, Ionic, Corinthian, and Composite. The column was first employed by the Egyptians but it was developed by the Greeks and Romans to such an extent that the proportions between the column's constituent parts determined the proportions of the entire building.

Each order usually consists of four main parts, the base, shaft, *capital, and entablature, these having individual shapes and types of decoration. The first order to be developed, the Doric, takes two forms: the Greek Doric, which has no base, and the Roman Doric, more slender in proportion and with a base. Roman Doric's unadorned and unfluted counterpart is the Tuscan order. The Ionic first appeared in Asia Minor in about the 6th century BC and was adopted by the Greeks in the 5th century BC. It has slender proportions and a capital adorned with four spiral scrolls (volutes), two at the front and two at the back. The most decorative order, the Corinthian, was developed by the Romans, although it was occasionally used in ancient Greece. The Romans also combined the Corinthian capital of *acanthus leaves with the volutes of the Ionic capital to form the Composite order.

A **pilaster** is a rectangular column attached to the wall. It conforms to the system of orders but, unlike the cylindrical column, is usually only decorative in function.

Ordnance Survey   The official map-making body of the UK. Established in 1791, following the mapping of Scotland by Gen William Roy (1726–90), it published its first map in 1801. Maps ranging from the large-scale 1:1250 (used for major urban areas) to the small-scale 1:1 000 000 (covering the entire UK in two parts) have since been produced. The original scale to be used, the 1:63 360 (1 in:1 mi) was converted to the metric scale of 1:50 000 in the 1970s and remains the most widely used

scale. The First Series of the 1:50 000 was completed in 1976 and is gradually being replaced by a Second Series with redrawn maps. Other major scales include the 1:10 000 (formerly 6 in:1 mi) and the 1:625 000 (formerly ¼ in:1 mi). Some maps are produced for specialized uses, such as the archaeological maps. Revisions are produced by the Ordnance Survey Department based in Southampton. *See also* digital maps.

Ordovician period   A geological period of the Lower Palaeozoic era, between the Cambrian and Silurian periods. It lasted from about 515 to 445 million years ago. It is divided into the Upper and Lower Ordovician, based on the graptolite fossils that are abundant in the deepwater deposits.

Ordzhonikidze (name until 1944: Vladikavkaz; name from 1944 until 1954: Dzaudzhikau)   43 02N 44 43E A city in the S Soviet Union, the capital of the North Ossetian ASSR in the RSFSR. An important road and rail junction, it has a variety of industries, including metallurgy and food processing. Population (1981 est): 287 000.

ore   A rock body or mineral deposit from which one or more useful materials, usually metals, can be economically extracted. The metal content of the various ores differs; iron ore contains about 20–30% iron, whereas copper ores may contain only 0.5% copper. The gangue is the waste material left when the desired mineral has been extracted.

Örebro   59 17N 15 13E A city in S Sweden. An ancient city, it was largely rebuilt following a fire in 1854. It has a university (1967) and its manufactures include footwear, machinery, and chemicals. Population (1983): 117 473.

oregano   An aromatic perennial herb, *Origanum vulgare*, native to the Mediterranean and W Asia. The dried leaves and flowers are used as a culinary flavouring and the plant is a source of essential oils. Family: *Labiatae*.

Oregon   A state in the USA, on the NW Pacific coast. Its topography is diverse; the Cascade Range extends N–S dividing the state between the valleys of the W and the dry plateau areas of the E. The Willamette Valley contains the major settlements. The economy is based predominantly on agriculture and forestry. Oregon is the nation's leading timber state and approximately half its area is forested; the Douglas fir is especially important. Much of the timber is used to produce plywood, pulp, and paper. Agriculture includes cattle ranching in the drier areas, dairy farming in the valleys, and wheat growing in the NE; specialized crops, such as cherries, are also grown. Hydroelectric-power resources have led to the development of metal-processing industries. *History:* originally occupied by several Indian tribes, there was considerable migration of White settlers from the Midwest along the famous *Oregon Trail during the 19th century. It became a state in 1859. Area: 251 180 sq km (96 981 sq mi). Population (1980): 2 632 663. Capital: Salem.

Oregon Trail   A route from the Missouri to the Columbia Rivers followed first by explorers and fur traders and then, in the 1840s by settlers. Some 2000 miles long, it began at Independence, Missouri, crossed the Rockies at the South Pass and went on down the Columbia River. In the Great Emigration of 1843 almost a thousand people followed the trail to settle in *Oregon.

Orel (*or* Oryol)   52 58N 36 04E A city in the Soviet Union, in the W RSFSR. Founded in 1564, it was severely damaged in World War II. Industries include engineering. The writer Turgenev was born here, and his house is now a museum. Population (1981 est): 315 000.

Orenburg (name from 1938 until 1957: Chkalov)   51 50N 55 00E A city in the Soviet Union, in the W RSFSR on the River Ural. It was founded in 1735 by the Cossacks on the site of present-day Orsk, subsequently being moved down stream. Industries include engineering and consumer-goods manufacture. Population (1981 est): 482 000.

Orense 42 20N 7 52W A town in NW Spain, in Galicia on the River Miño. It possesses a cathedral and a remarkable bridge built in 1230. Industries include iron founding and flour milling. Population (1981): 96 085.

Oresme, Nicole d' (c. 1320–82) French philosopher and churchman. He became master of the College of Navarre at Paris in 1355 and later Bishop of Lisieux (1377). His writings deal with politics, natural science, geometry, and economics. He was also an early advocate of the theory that the earth revolves around other bodies.

Orestes In Greek legend, the son of *Agamemnon, King of Mycenae, and *Clytemnestra. Encouraged by his sister *Electra, he avenged his father's murder by killing his mother and her lover Aegisthus. In the dramatic trilogy of *Aeschylus he is pursued by the *Erinyes until he is acquitted at the Areopagus in Athens by the deciding vote of Athena.

Øresund (or Öresund). See Sound, the.

orfe A carnivorous food and game fish, *Idus Idus*, also called ide, found in rivers and lakes of Europe and NW Asia. Its stout elongated body, 30–50 cm long, is blue-grey or blackish with a silvery belly. The golden orfe is a reddish-gold variety. Family: *Cyprinidae*; order: *Cypriniformes*.

Orff, Carl (1895–1982) German composer, teacher, conductor, and editor. He developed a monodic style of composition characterized by lively rhythms; his best-known work is the oratorio *Carmina Burana* (1935–36), based on 13th-century Latin and German poems found in a Benedictine monastery in Bavaria. Orff also introduced percussion instruments, such as the stone chimes, into musical education.

organ A musical wind instrument of early origin, which developed from the reed pipes and the *hydraulis. The modern organ consists of a large number of graduated pipes, some of which contain reeds, fitted over a wind chest and blown by manual or electric bellows. The pipes are made to sound by depressing keys or pedals. Each pipe sounds one note, but groups of duplicate pipes, called stops, can be made to sound together or successively. Different stops have different tone colours, many of which resemble orchestral instruments. An organ console may have as many as five or more keyboards, known as the great, swell, choir, solo, and echo, as well as pedals. Each keyboard has a separate range of stops and different characteristics; the swell, for example, has shutters over the pipe holes that allow crescendos and decrescendos.

Coupler mechanisms allow one keyboard to become automatically linked to another. These allow, for example the pedals, which normally play the deepest notes, to play notes many octaves higher.

The action linking keys and pipes consists of a series of rods called a tracker action or wires conveying electrical impulses. The modern **electronic organ** consists of a series of electronic oscillators to produce notes, which are then amplified.

organic chemistry. See chemistry.

Organisation de l'Armée secrète (OAS) An organization of French settlers in Algeria opposed to Algerian independence from France. The OAS was established in 1961 and led by General Raoul Salan (1899–). Its campaign of terrorism in Algeria and France included the attempted assassination in September, 1961, of the French president, de Gaulle, who by March, 1962, had reached agreement with the Algerian nationalists (see Front de Libération nationale). Salan was captured in April (and imprisoned 1962–68) and the OAS collapsed.

Organisation européenne pour la Recherche nucléaire. See CERN.

Organization for Economic Cooperation and Development (OECD) An international organization founded in 1961 to further economic growth among its members,

expand world trade, and coordinate aid to developing countries. It succeeded the Organization for European Economic Cooperation, which had been set up in 1948 to coordinate the *Marshall Plan for European economic recovery after World War II. The headquarters of the OECD are in Paris.

Organization of African Unity (OAU) An intergovernmental organization of independent African countries. It was founded in 1963 to provide a forum for discussion of political and economic problems affecting African states and to formulate policies towards such problems. The OAU meets annually but maintains a standing committee in Addis Ababa (Ethiopia).

Organization of American States (OAS) A body founded in 1948 to foster mutual understanding and cooperation between American republics and collective security. It is based on the principle of the *Monroe Doctrine. In 1962 Cuba was expelled from the OAS because of its acceptance of nuclear missiles from the Soviet Union.

Organization of Central American States An international organization founded in 1951. Its members include Costa Rica, El Salvador, Guatemala, Honduras, and Nicaragua, and its headquarters are in Guatemala City. Its aim is to promote social, cultural, and economic development through joint action.

Organization of Petroleum Exporting Countries (OPEC) An organization founded in 1960 to represent the interests of the 11 chief oil-exporting nations (Abu Dhabi, Algeria, Indonesia, Iran, Iraq, Kuwait, Libya, Nigeria, Qatar, Saudi Arabia, and Venezuela) in dealings with the major oil companies. OPEC is the only really successful primary-product *cartel, deciding in 1973 to double its share in the receipts from oil exported; it has continued to control the price of oil.

organ-pipe cactus A branching columnar *cactus, of the genus *Lemacrocereus* or *Cereus*, especially *L. thurberi*, which resembles a candelabra and is found in deserts of the S USA and Mexico. Up to 10 m high, it is grown in hedgerows and used for fuel and construction. The fruit is edible.

organ-pipe coral A *coral, *Tubipora musica*, occurring in shallow waters of the Indian and Pacific Oceans. It is composed of a colony of long upright stalked *polyps supported by bright-red skeletal tubes of fused spicules. Order: Stolonifera.

organum (Latin: organ, instrument) A type of medieval polyphonic vocal composition in which a plainchant melody was accompanied by voices at the fixed intervals of the octave and fourth or fifth. See also ars antiqua.

oribi A rare antelope, *Ourebia ourebi*, of African grasslands. About 90 cm high at the shoulder, oribis have slender legs, large ears, a fawn coat, and a short bristly tail; males have short straight horns. Hiding among long grass during the day, they graze in small herds at dawn and dusk.

orienteering A navigational sport, held over rugged country, that originated in Sweden in 1918 and is designed to test both intellectual and athletic ability. Using a map and compass, competitors run round a series of control points that must be visited in the prescribed sequence. Distances range from 3 to 13 km (2–8 mi).

origami The oriental art of paper folding, which developed into a traditional Japanese craft. It is used in the formal ceremonial wrapping of gifts and to make models of birds, animals, sailing boats, etc., which can often be made to move, e.g. birds that flap their wings. It now enjoys a wide popularity outside Japan.

Origen (c. 185–c. 254 AD) Egyptian theologian and Father of the Church, born at Alexandria, son of a Christian martyr. As head of Alexandria's catechetical school he gained fame as a teacher. He was ordained in Palestine (c. 230), but the Bishop of Alexandria immediately unfrocked him, maintaining that he was unfit for priesthood because he had castrated himself. He then settled in

Caesarea, where he founded a school. During the persecution of Emperor Decius (c. 250) he was imprisoned and tortured at Tyre. The most famous of his many influential works are his critical edition of the Bible, the *Hexapla*, and his theological treatise, *De principiis*.

original sin In Christian doctrine, the inherent wickedness of mankind occasioned by Adam's fall (Genesis 3). After much debate by the Church Fathers, St *Augustine of Hippo's diagnosis, that it is inescapably transmitted to us by our parents and that only the divine initiative of *grace can redeem us, was acepted as orthodox (*see also* Pelagius). St Thomas *Aquinas accorded greater scope to the human will, and after the Reformation the concept of original sin became unfashionable among many theologians. Many modern thinkers reject it or interpret it symbolically.

Orinoco, River (Spanish name: Río Orinoco) The third largest river system in South America. Rising in S Venezuela, it flows in an arc forming part of the Venezuela–Colombia border before entering the Atlantic Ocean via an extensive delta region. It provides an important communications system; oceangoing vessels can penetrate upstream for about 364 km (226 mi). Drainage basin area: 940 000 sq km (365 000 sq mi). Length: about 2575 km (1600 mi).

oriole A songbird belonging to an Old World family (*Oriolidae*; 28 species) occurring mainly in tropical forests. Orioles generally have a black-and-yellow plumage, measure 18–30 cm, and feed on fruit and insects. The golden oriole (*Oriolus oriolus*) is the only species reaching Europe, visiting Britain in the summer.

American orioles belong to the family *Icteridae* (87 species). 16–54 cm long, they usually have a black plumage with red, yellow, or brown markings.

Orion A very conspicuous constellation that lies on the celestial equator and can therefore be seen from most parts of the world. The brightest stars, *Rigel and the slightly fainter *Betelgeuse, lie at opposite corners of a quadrilateral of stars with Bellatrix and Saiph, both 2nd magnitude, at the other corners. Inside the quadrilateral three 2nd-magnitude stars form **Orion's Belt**, S of which lies the **Orion nebula**, one of the brightest emission nebulae.

Orissa A state in E India, on the Bay of Bengal. Its coastal plain extends through the Eastern *Ghats via broad valleys into interior highlands. Orissa is grossly overcrowded and its inhabitants farm rice, turmeric, and sugar cane. Fishing, forestry, and the mining of iron ore, manganese, chromite, and coal are economically important. There is also some heavy industry. *History*: known from ancient times, Orissa ruled a maritime empire during the 1st millennium AD. Partitioned by Muslim conquerors (17th century), it gradually fell under British domination (18th–19th centuries). Area: 155 782 sq km (60 132 sq mi). Population (1981): 26 272 054. Capital: Bhubaneswar.

Orizaba 18 51N 97 08W A city and resort in E central Mexico. It is the chief centre of the textile industry. Population (1980): 114 848.

Orkney Islands (*or* Orkneys) A group of about 70 islands off the N coast of Scotland, separated from the mainland by the Pentland Firth. About 20 of the islands are inhabited; the chief ones are Mainland (Pomona), South Ronaldsay, Westray, Sanday, and Hoy. The population is of Scandinavian descent, reflecting the Islands' long connections with Norway and Denmark. Formerly an insular county, it became an island authority under local government reorganization in 1975. Agriculture is of major importance within the Islands' economy, producing chiefly beef cattle and poultry. It serves as a base for the exploitation of North Sea oil with a pipeline from the Piper field. Other industries include fish curing and woollen weaving. Area: 974 sq km (376 sq mi). Population (1983 est): 19 239. Administrative centre: Kirkwall.

Orlando 28 33N 81 21W A city in the USA, in central Florida. A tourist resort, it is the commercial centre for citrus growing. Walt Disney World is situated nearby. Population (1980): 128 394.

Orlando, Vittorio Emanuele (1860–1952) Italian statesman; prime minister (1917–19). Representing Italy at the Paris Peace Conference (1919) after World War I, his failure to secure sufficiently favourable terms for Italy led to his resignation. He supported Mussolini and *Matteotti's murder in 1924, retiring from politics until after World War II. He was elected to the Senate in 1948.

Orléans 47 54N 1 54E A city in N France, the capital of the Loiret department on the River Loire. In 1429, during the Hundred Years' War, the city was delivered from the English by Joan of Arc. Its cathedral, which was destroyed by the Huguenots in 1568, was rebuilt in the 17th century. The focal point of road and rail routes, Orléans has an extensive trade in wine, brandy, and agricultural produce. Its manufactures include machinery, electrical goods, and textiles. Population (1982): 105 589.

Orléans, Charles, Duc d' (1394–1465) French poet. He was captured by the English at the battle of Agincourt (1415) and spent the next 25 years in prison in England, where he wrote a collection of poems in English. His son became Louis XII of France.

Orléans, Louis Philippe Joseph, Duc d' (1747–93) French revolutionary. A cousin of Louis XVI of France, he nevertheless supported the dissident Third Estate at the beginning of the *French Revolution. He joined the radical Jacobins in 1791 and voted for the execution of the king. He was himself executed after his son (later King Louis Philippe) had joined the Austrian coalition against France.

Orléans, Siege of (October, 1428–May, 1429) English siege of the strategically important city of Orléans during the *Hundred Years' War, prosecuted with little success on either side until the arrival of *Joan of Arc to relieve the city. Her success was a notable factor in French military resurgence and signalled the beginning of the end of English occupation.

Orlov, Grigori Grigorievich, Count (1734–83) Russian soldier, who was the lover of *Catherine the Great. Orlov and his brother **Aleksei Grigorievich Orlov** (1737–1807) led the coup d'état that placed Catherine on the throne in 1762. Grigori Orlov had a favourable position at court but exerted little influence over Catherine.

Ormandy, Eugene (E. Blau; 1899–1985) Hungarian-born conductor, a US citizen after 1927. His early career was as a violinist, but he turned to conducting soon after settling in the USA in 1921. He was conductor (1938–80) of the Philadelphia Orchestra, in succession to Stokowski.

ormolu (French: *d'or moulu*, powdered gold) Ornamental gilded bronze usually used as embellishment on furniture. The 17th- and early 18th-century technique applied the gold coating by means of a mercuric process, which released poisonous fumes. This was abandoned in favour of applying gold dust in a varnish. Ormolu mounts were frequent on French 18th- and 19th-century furniture.

Ormonde, James Butler, 1st Duke of (1610–88) Anglo-Irish general, who in the *Civil War commanded the royalist army in Ireland (1641–50). After the Restoration of the monarchy, he was Lord Lieutenant of Ireland (1661–69, 1677–84).

Ornithischia An order of herbivorous *dinosaurs that lived in the Jurassic and Cretaceous periods (200–65 million years ago). They had hip bones arranged like those of birds (the name means "bird hips") and a horny beak at the front of the jaw (teeth were present only at the rear). Some were bipedal while others evolved to become quadrupedal and heavily armoured. There were both amphibious and terrestrial forms. *See* Iguanodon; Stegosaurus; Triceratops.

Ornitholestes A dinosaur that lived in North America during the Jurassic and Cretaceous periods (200–65 million years ago). About 2 m long, it was lightly built and moved on its long slender hind limbs balanced by a long stiff tail. Its fore limbs were short with long slender clawed fingers and it probably lived in forest undergrowth, catching birds, lizards, and mammals.

ornithology The study of *birds. Ornithology is a popular pastime as well as a branch of zoology; the records of bird spottings made by amateur ornithologists can be valuable to professional scientists in helping to determine the ecology and behaviour of bird populations. Recovery of rings used in bird-ringing experiments provides information regarding the dispersion and migration of birds. Many species are protected by legislation, and such bodies as the Royal Society for the Protection of Birds (in the UK) exist to promote the establishment of bird sanctuaries and general interest in birds.

orogeny A period of mountain building. Several major orogenies have occurred in the earth's geological history, the main ones since the Precambrian being the Caledonian (in the Lower Palaeozoic), Variscan (including the Armorican and Hercynian phases, in the Upper Palaeozoic), and the Alpine (in the Tertiary). **Orogenesis** is the process of mountain building, including folding, faulting, and thrusting, resulting from the collision of two continents, which compresses the sediment between them into mountain chains (*see* plate tectonics).

Orontes, River A river in SW Asia. Rising in Lebanon, it flows mainly N through Syria and then SW past Antioch (Turkey) to enter the Mediterranean Sea. Length: 370 km (230 mi).

Orozco, José (1883-1949) Mexican mural painter. His early watercolours of prostitutes were so bitterly attacked that he sought refuge in the USA (1917-20). In 1922, however, the Mexican Government commissioned him, *Rivera, *Siqueiros and others to paint murals in the National Preparatory School, Mexico City. Renewed criticism of his social and political subject matter led to his second visit to the USA (1927-34), where he made his name with murals for several educational institutions.

Orpheus A legendary Greek poet and musician, the son of the muse Calliope by either Apollo or Oeagrus, King of Thrace. After sailing with the *Argonauts he married *Eurydice. After her death, he descended to Hades to recover her. *Persephone, charmed by his playing on the lyre, released Eurydice but Orpheus lost her when he disobeyed the gods' command not to look back at her. He met his death at the hands of the Maenads, followers of *Dionysus, who dismembered him. He was believed to be the founder of the *Orphic mysteries, a cult dating from the 7th century BC, which was concerned with the liberation of the soul from the body.

Orphic mysteries An esoteric religious cult (*see* mysteries) in ancient Greece and S Italy. It was based on poems, probably datable to the 7th century BC, which its adherents believed were written by *Orpheus. According to these, the material world was made from the ashes of the Titans, whom Zeus destroyed for devouring his son Dionysus. Vegetarianism, participation in the mystical rites, and high ethical standards were demanded of initiates.

orphism An abstract form of *cubism, which developed in France about 1912. Albert Gleizes (1881-1953), Jean Metzinger (1883-1956), and Gino *Severini all contributed to this brightly coloured flat patterned style but the chief exponent, *Delaunay, preferred to call his version *simultaneisme*. His work became purely abstract by 1914, greatly influencing *Klee and *Kandinsky.

orrisroot The fragrant rhizome (underground stem) of several European plants of the genus *Iris*, chiefly *I. florentina*, *I. pallida* and *I. germanica*. It is dried and ground for use in perfumes and medicines.

Orsini A Roman family, originating in the 10th century,

that led the propapal (Guelf) faction in Rome during the 13th century. Several members became high-ranking clerics including two popes, Celestine III (reigned 1191-98) and Nicholas III (reigned 1277-80). They remained a dominant force in the politics of Rome and the papacy during the early modern period, attaining princely status in 1629.

Orsk 51 13N 58 35E A city in the Soviet Union, in the W RSFSR at the confluence of the Rivers Ural and Or. It has an oil refinery and also manufactures heavy machinery. Population (1981 est): 254 000.

Ortega y Gasset, José (1883-1955) Spanish philosopher and writer. He became professor of metaphysics at Madrid University in 1910. His philosophy was chiefly concerned with what he called "the metaphysics of vital reason." In his best-known book, *La rebelión de las masas* (1930), he attacked mass rule, which, he argued, would lead to chaos.

ORTELIUS *The Theatrum orbis terrarum was enlarged and reissued until 1612 and this miniature map of Palestine was first published in 1601. It shows the route taken by Moses and the Israelites on the flight from Egypt.*

Ortelius, Abraham (1527-98) Flemish cartographer. Ortelius travelled widely, buying and selling antiquities and maps. His *Theatrum orbis terrarum* (1570), a collection of maps charting the whole world, became the definitive contemporary cartographical system. Ortelius became geographer to Philip II of Spain in 1575.

orthicon A television camera tube in which a low-energy electron beam scans a target screen, consisting of a thin dielectric plate with a mosaic of photosensitive squares on one side and a thin metallic coating on the other. Each square and its metallic electrode form a tiny capacitor; when light falls on a photosensitive element the capacitor becomes charged. The scanning beam discharges these capacitors and thus becomes modulated by the pattern of light falling on the screen.

orthoclase An alkali potassium *feldspar, $KAlSi_3O_8$. It is formed at intermediate to low temperatures and crystallizes in the monoclinic crystal system, often with twinned crystals. Orthoclase is found in acid igneous rocks and in many metamorphic rocks. It is white, pink, or greenish grey, and is softer than quartz, with a duller lustre. Commercially orthoclase is frequently obtained from pegmatites; it is used in the manufacture of glass, ceramic glazes, and enamels.

orthodontics. *See* dentistry.

Orthodox Church The federation of self-governing Churches historically associated with the eastern part of the Roman Empire and separated from the Latin Church since 1054 (*see* Filioque); also called the Eastern Orthodox Church. The four ancient *patriarchs of Orthodoxy are of Constantinople (which has primacy of honour), Alexandria, Antioch, and Jerusalem; in addition there are patriarchs of Moscow, Georgia, Serbia, Bulgaria, and Romania. Independent or autocephalous Orthodox Churches exist in Greece,

Cyprus, Albania, Czechoslovakia, and Poland. There are numerous congregations in other countries, many established by Russian immigrants after the Revolution. Government is by bishops, who must be unmarried, priests, who may marry but only before ordination, and deacons, who play an important liturgical role. The Orthodox Church claims the authority of *Apostolic Succession and regards itself as the one true Church, accepting as doctrine only the *Nicene Creed. Its worship is sacramental and centred on the Eucharist and the ancient liturgies of St John Chrysostom and St Basil, which are always solemnly celebrated and sung without accompaniment. Communion is given in both kinds. The veneration of *icons is a distinctive feature of Orthodox worship; statues and other three-dimensional images are forbidden. Easter is the main feast of the Church year, which follows the Julian calendar and therefore varies considerably from Western custom in dating major Christian festivals. *See also* Greek Orthodox Church; Russian Orthodox Church.

orthopaedics The medical specialty concerned with treating deformities caused by disease of and injury to the bones and joints. This includes the use of surgery, manipulation, traction, etc., in correcting deformities and fractures, together with rehabilitation to enable patients to lead an independent life. The availability of artificial hip joints has greatly extended the scope of orthopaedics in the treatment of severe arthritis of the hip.

Orthoptera A mainly tropical order of generally large stout-bodied insects (15 000 species), including the *grasshoppers and *crickets. The hind legs are enlarged and specialized for jumping and the large blunt head has biting jaws for feeding on vegetation. Typically there are two pairs of wings—the front pair thicker—but few species are good fliers. Many species produce sounds by rubbing one part of the body against another (stridulation).

ortolan A Eurasian *bunting, *Emberiza hortulana*, about 16 cm long, having a brown-streaked plumage with a yellow throat and pinkish belly. Prior to its autumn migration to N Africa and the Middle East it stores large amounts of fat and for this reason it is trapped in large numbers as a table delicacy.

Ortoli, François Xavier (1925–) French politician and economist; president of the EEC Commission (1973–76) and then a vice president, with responsibility for economic and financial affairs (1977–). From 1951 he held a number of ministerial posts in France, including those of finance (1968–69) and of industrial and scientific development (1969–72).

Oruro 17 59S 67 08W A city in central Bolivia, 3705 m (12 160 ft) above sea level. It is the centre of an important tinmining area; other minerals worked include silver, copper, and wolfram. It has a technical university (1892). Population (1982 est): 132 213.

Orvieto 42 43N 12 06E A town in central Italy, in Umbria. It is reputed to be the site of the Etruscan city Volsinii, which was destroyed by the Romans in 280 BC. Notable buildings include the gothic cathedral and several palaces. A popular tourist centre, it is also famous for its white wine. Population (1981 est): 23 559.

Orwell, George (Eric Blair; 1903–50) British novelist. Born in India, he was educated at Eton and served in the Burmese Imperial Police from 1922 to 1927. In *Down and Out in Paris and London* (1933) and *The Road to Wigan Pier* (1937) he described his experience of poverty. He criticized official communist policies and practices in *Homage to Catalonia* (1936), an autobiographical account of the Spanish Civil War, and expressed his anti-Stalinist convictions in the political allegory *Animal Farm* (1945). *Nineteen Eighty Four* (1949) is a deeply pessimistic view of a totalitarian future.

Oryol. *See* Orel.

oryx A desert antelope, *Oryx gazella*, which comprises two races, beisa and gemsbok, of S and E Africa. Up to 120 cm high at the shoulder, oryxes have long slender straight horns and are

greyish brown with black markings on the face and legs. The herds feed at night on desert plants. The white Arabian oryx (*O. leucoryx*) and the greyish-white N African scimitar-horned oryx (*O. tao*) are both endangered species.

Osaka 34 40N 135 30E A port in Japan, in SW Honshu on the Yodo delta. The third largest city in Japan, it was a leading commercial centre by the 17th century. Imperial palaces were built here from the 4th century AD and an ancient Buddhist temple (593 AD) still remains. It is overlooked by the 16th-century castle (reconstructed). A cultural centre, it possesses several universities and has a famous puppet theatre. Together with Kobe, Kyoto, and several small cities it now forms the **Osaka-Kobe** industrial area, second in importance only to the Tokyo-Yokohama area, and in common with Tokyo suffers from serious atmospheric pollution as well as traffic congestion. Major industries are textiles, steel, electrical equipment, and chemicals. Population (1980): 2 648 000.

Osborne, Dorothy (1627–95) English letter writer. The wife of the diplomat Sir William *Temple, she is remembered for her witty and lively letters to him during their courtship (1652–54; published in 1836).

Osborne, John (1929–) British dramatist. One of the original *Angry Young Men, he gave expression to the rage and frustration of a whole generation in the character of Jimmy Porter, the disillusioned antihero of *Look Back in Anger* (1956). His criticism of contemporary Britain continued in such plays as *The Entertainer* (1957), *A Patriot for Me* (1965), and *West of Suez* (1971). Other plays include *Luther* (1960), *Inadmissible Evidence* (1964), and *The Hotel in Amsterdam* (1967). His autobiography *A Better Class of Person* was published in 1981.

Osborne House A country house near Cowes, on the Isle of Wight, built for Queen Victoria in 1845 to a design by Prince Albert. It was one of her favourite residences and she died there in 1901. It is now open to the public.

Oscar. *See* Academy of Motion Picture Arts and Sciences.

Oscar II (1829–1907) King of Sweden (1872–1907) and of Norway from 1872 until its final separation from Sweden in 1905. He was also a writer, especially of poetry.

oscilloscope. *See* cathode-ray oscilloscope.

Oshawa 43 53N 78 51W A city and port in central Canada, in S Ontario on Lake Ontario. A prosperous agricultural centre, it houses a major motor-vehicle factory. Other industries include metal goods, furniture, glass, and plastics. Population (1981): 117 519.

O'Shea, Katherine Page (1846–1921) The wife (1867–90) of William O'Shea (1840–1905), an Irish MP, and then of Charles Stewart *Parnell. In 1889 O'Shea filed for divorce, citing Parnell, thus initiating Parnell's political downfall. Parnell married Katherine shortly before his death in 1891.

Oshogbo 7 50N 4 35E A town in SW Nigeria. It developed as a commercial centre after the arrival of the railway (1906). Its main exports are cocoa and palm oil; there are also local tobacco-processing, cotton-weaving, and dyeing industries. Population (1983 est): 344 500.

osier A small *willow tree, *Salix viminalis*, 3–10 m high, with flexible hairy branches used in basket making. The long narrow leaves are smooth above and white and silky beneath, with inrolled margins. Osiers are found in marshy areas throughout central and S Eurasia and often cultivated.

Osijek 45 33N 18 42E A town in N Yugoslavia, in Croatia on the River Drava. An agricultural centre, it manufactures machinery and footwear. Population (1981): 158 790.

Osipenko. *See* Berdyansk.

Osiris The Egyptian god of the dead, the brother and husband of *Isis; as the father of *Horus (the sun), he was also the god of renewal and rebirth. He was killed by his evil brother *Set. After Isis had magically reconstructed his

OSIRIS *The third innermost coffin of Tutankhamen, made of gold, portrays the pharaoh as Osiris.*

body, he became ruler of the underworld. The pharaohs, and later all men who passed the judgment of good and evil, became identified with Osiris after death. He is usually portrayed holding the royal flail and crook. He was identified by the Greeks with *Dionysus.

Osler, Sir William (1849-1919) Canadian physician, who pioneered modern clinical teaching methods. In 1872 Osler identified the particles in blood known as *platelets. He was appointed professor of medicine at the new Johns Hopkins University, Baltimore, in 1888. Osler introduced new attitudes and ideas to teaching medicine, encouraging examination of patients in the wards and the use of laboratories by students. In 1905 he became Regius Professor of Medicine at Oxford University. A classics scholar, he bequeathed his library to McGill University, Montreal.

Oslo (former name (1877-1925): Kristiania) 59 56N 10 54E The capital and main port of Norway, situated in the SE at the head of Oslo Fjord. It is the financial and industrial centre of Norway. The principal industries include the manufacture of consumer goods and shipbuilding. A cultural centre, Oslo is the site of a university (1811), the National Theatre, and several notable museums. Fine buildings include the 17th-century cathedral and the 19th-century royal palace. *History*: founded in the 11th century as a defensive post against the Danes, it became capital in 1299. It developed into an important trading post under the influence of the Hanseatic League and was rebuilt after a fire in the 17th century. It was occupied by the Germans in World War II. Population (1981 est): 452 023.

Osman I (c. 1258-c. 1326) Emir of the small Turkish state

in Asia Minor that later developed into the *Ottoman Empire. He was the eponymous ancestor of the Ottoman sultans. Under Osman the state expanded mainly at the expense of the Byzantines and shortly before he died Bursa was captured.

osmiridium A naturally occurring alloy of osmium and iridium, with minor quantities of platinum, rhodium, and ruthenium. It is used for fountain pen nibs because it is hard and resistant.

osmium (Os) An extremely hard bluish-silver metal of the platinum group. It is one of the densest elements known (relative density 22.6). Its major use is in the production of hard alloys with other noble metals, for pen nibs and electrical contacts. The tetroxide (OsO_4) is volatile (bp 130°C) and very toxic. At no 76; at wt 190.2; mp 3045 ± 20°C; bp 5027 ± 100°C.

osmosis The passage of a solvent from a less concentrated into a more concentrated solution through a semipermeable membrane (one allowing the passage of solvent, but not solute, molecules). Osmosis stops if the pressure of the more concentrated solution exceeds that of the less concentrated solution by an amount known as the **osmotic pressure** between them. In living organisms the solvent is water and osmosis plays an important role in effecting the distribution of water in plants and animals: the passage of water into and out of cells is determined by the osmotic pressures of the extracellular and intracellular solutions. Osmosis can be used in the *desalination of water.

Osmunda A genus of stout leathery *ferns (about 12 species), found in wet tropical and temperate regions. Their short thick branching rhizomes give rise to branching fronds, 50-180 cm high, made up of light-green tapering leaflets with expanded bases. The upper leaflets of the larger central fertile fronds are reduced to veins covered with clusters of brown pear-shaped spore capsules, which resemble flower clusters in the royal fern (*O. regalis*). The root and rhizome fibres are used as a culture medium for orchids. Family: *Osmundaceae.*

Osnabrück 52 17N 8 03E A city in NW West Germany, in Lower Saxony on the River Hase. The 13th-century romanesque cathedral and episcopal palace (1667-90) survived the bombing of World War II. It has iron, steel, and car industries. Population (1980 est): 157 800.

osprey A large *hawk, *Pandion haliaetus*, also called fish hawk, occurring worldwide (except in South America) around coasts and inland waters. It is 65 cm long and its plumage is brown above and white below (*see* Plate V). It feeds mostly on pike and trout, caught in its talons, which are covered in rough spikes to help grasp prey. The recent decline in numbers has been due mainly to pesticide poisoning.

Ossa, Mount 41 52S 146 04E A mountain in Australia, the highest peak of Tasmania in the Duana Range. Height: 1617 m (5305 ft).

Ossetia. *See* North Ossetian Autonomous Soviet Socialist Republic; South Ossetian autonomous region.

Ossetic A language belonging to the *Iranian family and spoken in the N Caucasus by the Ossetes. The Ossetes are descended from the ancient Alani, a Scythian tribe. The language is written in the Cyrillic alphabet and has absorbed many influences from Russian and the other Caucasian languages.

Ossian (3rd century AD) A legendary poet and warrior who, as Oisin, features in the *Fenian cycle. The Scots poet James Macpherson (1736-96) claimed to have discovered remains of Ossian's poetry in the Highlands and published his "translations" from the Gaelic between 1760 and 1763. These included the epic poem *Fingal* (1762). Macpherson's work was in fact his own, largely based on a few well-known Gaelic fragments. Although denounced as forgeries by Dr Johnson, the poems were enthusiastically received throughout Europe and had a great influence on European Romanticism.

Ossietsky, Carl von (1888-1938) German pacifist and journalist. He founded a pacifist organization in 1920 and became editor of a liberal newspaper in 1927. Following his arrest in 1933 he spent the rest of his life in a concentration camp and in hospitals. He won the Nobel Peace Prize in 1935.

Ossining 41 10N 73 52W A town in the USA, in New York state. Known as Sing Sing until 1901, it is the site of the Sing Sing state prison, once notorious for its severe discipline. Population (1980): 20 196.

Ostade, Adrian van (1610-85) Dutch painter and etcher, born in Haarlem. Influenced by *Brouwer, he specialized in scenes of peasant life.

Ostend (Flemish name: Oostende; French name: Ostende) 51 13N 2 55E A seaport in NW Belgium, on the North Sea. Ostend is a pleasure resort, with a casino, a promenade, and a royal chalet. It is the headquarters of the country's fishing fleet and maintains a cross-Channel ferry service to Dover, England. Industries include shipbuilding and fish processing. Population (1981 est): 69 678.

osteoarthritis A disease of the joints in which their internal surfaces are rubbed away and they become swollen and painful. This becomes increasingly common as people age: almost all very old people have some osteoarthritis, but it may affect younger people as well. The joints that bear most weight are most commonly affected: back, hips, and knees. Drugs can reduce the pain of the joints but cannot reverse the disease. Artificial hips and knees can be surgically installed to relieve the pain and allow greater movement. See also arthritis.

osteology. See bone.

osteomalacia Softening of the bones due to shortage of vitamin D: adult *rickets. It is seen most commonly in pregnant women and in old people whose diet is deficient in vitamin D or who do not have access to much sunshine (which activates vitamin D). Fractures occur very easily in osteomalacia. Treatment is with vitamin D preparations.

osteomyelitis Infection of bone. This occurs most commonly in poor communities. Children, particularly boys, are more often affected; symptoms are a high fever and acute pain in the bone affected, which is classically around the knee. Before antibiotics were available death or physical handicap often resulted, but these are now rare and the infection is readily cured with antibiotics.

osteopathy A system of healing by manipulation and massage, based on the theory that nearly all diseases are due to the displacement of bones, especially the bones of the spine. Osteopathy is undoubtedly of use in treating dislocations, fractures, and disorders of the joint, but the theory behind it is unacceptable to the medical profession and osteopathy is not legally recognized as a branch of orthodox medicine. The British School of Osteopathy was founded in London in 1917.

osteoporosis Weakening of the bone. This occurs most commonly in old people, particularly women, but it also affects bones that are immobilized for long periods. The immobilized bone of a young person will usually regain its strength after mobilization, but an elderly patient's osteoporotic bones are more difficult to treat.

Ostia A town of ancient Rome, at the mouth of the River Tiber. It was probably founded about 350 BC, although it is dated by tradition to the 7th century BC. A major naval base under the Republic, its prosperity was greatest in the 2nd century AD, when it was an important commercial centre. It was abandoned in the 9th century. Impressive Roman ruins have been excavated.

ostracism The method in 5th-century BC Athens of banishing unpopular citizens. Each citizen inscribed on a potsherd (*ostrakon*) the name of his candidate for banish-

ment. The man receiving most votes was exiled for ten years. Instituted to curb tyranny, ostracism was in practice uncommon. Prominent ostracized Athenians included Aristides and Themistocles.

Ostracoda A subclass of small *crustaceans (2000 species), 1-4 mm long, also called mussel or seed shrimps, found in fresh and salt water. Ostracods have a bean-shaped two-sided carapace, from which protrude two pairs of large hairy antennae and two pairs of legs for swimming or walking. Most ostracods live on or near the bottom and eat anything, but particularly decaying vegetation or small animals. The females lay eggs on stems and leaves of water plants.

Ostrava 49 50N 18 15E An industrial city in Czechoslovakia, in N Moravia on both sides of the River Ostravice. It is a major coalmining centre; other industries include iron and steel processing, engineering, and chemicals. Population (1980 est): 325 000.

ostrich A flightless African bird, *Struthio camelus*, occurring in open grassland and semidesert regions. Males may reach 2.5 m tall and are black with white wing and tail plumes; females are smaller and mainly brown. Ostriches have a long almost naked neck, a small head, and a ducklike bill used to feed on plant material. They can reach speeds of up to 65 km per hour (40 mph). Domesticated birds are farmed commercially for leather and ornamental feathers. It is the largest living bird and the only member of its family (*Struthionidae*). Order: *Struthioniformes*.

Ostrogoths A branch of the *Goths, originally based in the Ukraine, but forced W of the River Dniester by the *Huns (375 AD). In the 6th century they frequently invaded N Italy and captured much of the Balkans. Between 493 and 526 *Theodoric, their leader, ruled Italy. On his death the Roman Empire, after a long struggle, destroyed the Ostrogoths (562).

Ostrovskii, Aleksandr Nikolaevich (1823-86) Russian dramatist. He established his reputation with realistic comedies about the merchant class, making use of the knowledge of corruption that he had gained as a civil servant. His best-known plays include *Easy Money* (1856) and the tragedy *The Storm* (1859), which became the basis of *Janacek's opera *Katya Kabanova*.

Ostwald, (Friedrich) Wilhelm (1853-1932) German chemist, born in Riga, who was a pioneer in the field of physical chemistry. His greatest work was in developing the theory of catalysis for which he was awarded the Nobel Prize in 1909. He also contributed to the philosophy of science and was an ardent positivist.

Oswald, Lee Harvey (1939-63) The presumed assassin of US president John F. *Kennedy in Dallas, Texas, on 22 November, 1963. Two days later he was killed by Jack Ruby (d. 1967), a nightclub owner, in the Dallas police headquarters.

Oswald, Saint (c. 605-41) King of Northumbria (634-41) after defeating and killing the Welsh king, Cadwallader. Converted to Christianity while in exile on Iona, he restored Christianity in Northumbria with the help of St *Aidan. Oswald was killed in battle by Penda. Feast day: 5 Aug.

Oswald of York, St (d. 992 AD) English churchman. Bishop of Worcester and later Archbishop of York, he founded many new monasteries and was a leading initiator of Anglo-Saxon monastic reform. Feast day: 28 Feb.

Oświęcim (German name: Auschwitz) 50 02N 19 11E A town in S Poland. It was the site of a notorious Nazi concentration camp during World War II. Population (1982 est): 45 200.

Oswiu (or Oswy; d. 670) King of Northumbria (655-70) and overlord (655-57) of all England S of the Humber, after his forces had killed Penda of Mercia in battle. He summoned the Synod of *Whitby (664) to resolve the differences between the Roman and Celtic Churches.

Otis, Elisha Graves (1811-61) US inventor, who in 1852

designed the first safety lift, that is one that would not fall to the ground if the cable broke. In 1854 Otis publicly demonstrated the lift's safety by arranging for the cable of a lift in which he was riding to be cut.

Otranto 40 08N 18 30E A small port in SE Italy, in Apulia on the Strait of Otranto. Dating from Greek times, it became an important Roman port, later destroyed by Turks (1480). Its ruined castle provided the setting for Horace Walpole's gothic novel *The Castle of Otranto*. Population (1981 est): 4811.

OTTER

Ottawa 45 25N 75 43W The capital of Canada, in SE Ontario on the Ottawa River. It is two-thirds English speaking and one-third French speaking. Ottawa University was founded in 1848 and the Carleton University in 1942. *History*: founded (as Bytown) in the early 19th century as a lumbering centre, it became capital of the United Provinces of Canada in 1858, and national capital in 1867. Population (1981): 295 163.

Ottawa Agreements (1932) Preferential tariff rates negotiated between the UK and its dominions at the Imperial Economic Conference held at Ottawa (Canada). In 1931 the UK began to tax food imports from outside the Empire, allowing almost all imports from its dominions to enter the country free of duty. The dominions agreed to reciprocate this concession except when it was to the detriment of their own products. The new policy, called imperial preference, was limited by the *General Agreement on Tariffs and Trade (1947) and was phased out following the UK's membership of the EEC.

Ottawa River A river in central Canada, rising in W Quebec and flowing W, then SE down the Ontario-Quebec border to join the St Lawrence River, as its chief tributary, at Montreal. The numerous rapids along its lower and middle courses are used to generate electricity. It is linked with Lake Ontario by the Rideau Canal. Length: 1120 km (696 mi).

otter A semi-aquatic carnivorous □mammal belonging to the subfamily *Lutrinae* (18 species), distributed worldwide except in Polar regions, Australasia, and Madagascar. Otters have a cylindrical body with waterproof fur, short legs, partially webbed feet, and a thick tapering tail.

The Eurasian otter (*Lutra lutra*), grows to a length of about 1.2 m and a weight of about 10 kg. Otters inhabit waterways, lakes, and coasts, feeding on frogs, fish, and invertebrates. Chief genera: *Lutra, Paraonyx*; family: *Mustelidae*. See also sea otter.

otterhound A breed of dog of uncertain ancestry, used to hunt otters. It is a strongly built powerful swimmer with large webbed feet and a large head with long drooping ears. Otterhounds have a dense water-resistant undercoat and a long shaggy outer coat, which can be any colour. Height: 61–69 cm.

otter shrew A semiaquatic carnivorous mammal belonging to the family *Potamogalidae* (3 species), of West and central Africa. Up to 60 cm long, they have long slender brown and white bodies with a shrewlike snout and a flattened tail for swimming. They forage for aquatic invertebrate prey. Order: *Insectivora*.

Otto (I) the Great (912–73 AD) Holy Roman Emperor (936–73; crowned 962). He subdued his rebellious vassals, defeated a Hungarian invasion at the great victory of Lechfeld (955), and extended his influence into Italy. He deposed Pope John XII, replacing him with Leo VIII, and established bishoprics as a means of controlling his domains.

Otto IV (c. 1175–1218) Holy Roman Emperor (1198–1215; crowned 1209). He was elected emperor in opposition to the candidate of the Hohenstaufen family but was crowned by Pope Innocent III in return for promising to keep out of Italian territorial disputes. In 1210, however, he invaded S Italy and, after being decisively defeated by France, a Hohenstaufen ally, at *Bouvines (1214), was formally deposed.

Otto, Nikolaus August (1832–91) German engineer, who in 1876 devised the four-stroke cycle, known as the Otto cycle, for the *internal-combustion engine. His engine made the development of the motor car possible.

Ottoman Empire A Turkish Muslim empire ruling large parts of the Middle East as well as territories in Europe from the 14th to the 20th centuries. Its capital was *Istanbul (formerly Constantinople) and its rulers descendants of its founder *Osman I. Originating around 1300 as a small Turkish state in Asia Minor, in 1453 the Ottomans captured Constantinople and destroyed the Eastern Roman (Byzantine) Empire. Ottoman power culminated in the 16th century with the conquest of Egypt and Syria (1517) and, under *Suleiman the Magnificent, Hungary (1529) and territories in the Middle East and N Africa. From the 17th century the Empire declined. Attempts at modernization were only partly successful and in the 1908 *Young Turks revolution a group of army officers seized power. In World War I the Ottomans supported Germany and defeat brought the loss of territories outside Asia Minor. This humiliation led to the nationalist revolution of Kemal *Atatürk, which replaced the Ottoman Empire with the state of Turkey (1922).

Otway, Thomas (1652–85) British dramatist. His best-known plays are the sentimental tragedies *The Orphan* (1680) and *Venice Preserved* (1682), written for the actress Elizabeth Barry (1658–1713), whom he loved. He also wrote Restoration comedies and adapted plays by Racine and Molière.

Ouagadougou 12 25N 1 30W The capital of Burkina Faso. Founded in the 11th century as the centre of a Mossi empire, it was captured by the French in 1896. Its university was founded in 1974. It is an important communications centre. Population (1981 est): 172 661.

Oudenaarde, Battle of (11 July, 1708) A battle in the War of the *Spanish Succession in which the British, Dutch, and

Oudry, Jean-Baptiste (1686–1755) French *rococo painter and tapestry designer. A pupil of the portraitist Nicholas de Largillière (1656–1746), he was a portrait and still-life painter before specializing (from about 1720) in animal and hunting scenes. As head of the *Beauvais (1734) and *Gobelin (1736) tapestry works, and as favourite painter of Louis XV, he achieved a wide reputation. His illustrations to La Fontaine's *Fables* are particularly well known.

Ouessant. *See* Ushant.

Ouida (Marie Louise de la Ramée; 1839–1908) British novelist. Of English and French parentage, she wrote popular adventure novels with fashionable upper-class characters. Her best-known book is *Under Two Flags* (1867).

Oujda 34 41N 1 45W A city in E Morocco, near the Algerian border. It is a meeting point of the Moroccan and Algerian railways. Population (1982): 260 082.

Oulu (Swedish name: Uleåborg) 65 00N 25 26E A seaport in NW Finland, on the Gulf of Bothnia. It has a university (1959) and its industries include shipbuilding and saw milling. Population (1980): 93 806.

ounce. *See* snow leopard.

Ouro Prêto 20 54S 43 30W A city in SE Brazil, in Minas Gerais state. Founded in 1701, its former prosperity was based on gold. It contains many colonial buildings and in 1933 was decreed a national monument. It is now a mining centre for manganese and iron and is the site of the National School of Mines (1876). Its university was established in 1969. Population (1980 est): 27 821.

Ouse, River The name of several rivers in England, including: **1.** A river in NE England, flowing mainly NE through Yorkshire to join the River Trent, forming the Humber estuary. Length: 92 km (57 mi). **2.** A river in S England, flowing E and S across the South Downs to the English Channel at Newhaven. Length: 48 km (30 mi).

Ouspensky, Peter (1878–1947) Russian-born occultist. He trained as a scientist but as *Gurdjieff's close associate (1915–24) he became interested in methods of developing man's consciousness. He taught in London (1924–40) and New York (1940–47) and his writings include *Tertium Organum* (1912) and *A New Model of the Universe* (1914).

Outer Mongolia. *See* Mongolian People's Republic.

outlawry A process by which a person (particularly one convicted of *treason or a felony) was deprived of his rights under the law, including the right to own property, to enforce a *contract, or to seek redress for injuries. His property was forfeited to the Crown. Outlawry was abolished for civil wrongs in 1879 and for crimes in 1938.

Outram, Sir James (1803–63) British soldier and colonial administrator. He made his name during the first Afghan War (1839–42). He subsequently took part in the relief of Lucknow (1857) during the Indian Mutiny.

ouzel. *See* ring ouzel.

ouzo A Greek spirit flavoured with aniseed, similar to *absinthe. It is drunk with water, in which it becomes cloudy.

Oval, the A cricket ground at Kennington, London, and the headquarters of the Surrey County Cricket Club. First used for cricket in 1845, the final Test match of an English series always takes place here.

ovary **1.** The organ of female animals in which the *egg cells (ova) are produced. In mammals (including women) there are two ovaries close to the openings of the Fallopian tubes, which lead to the uterus (womb). They produce both eggs and steroid hormones (*see* oestrogen; progesterone) in a regular cycle (*see* menstruation). The ovaries contain numerous follicles, some of which—the Graafian follicles—mature to release egg cells at ovulation, after which they form yellowish hormone-producing bodies (*see* corpus luteum). **2.** The part of a flower that con-

tains the *ovules. It is situated at the base of the carpel(s) and becomes the fruit wall after fertilization.

ovenbird A small brown passerine bird belonging to a diverse family (*Furnariidae*; 221 species) occurring in tropical America and ranging in size from 12 to 28 cm. Ovenbirds usually build elaborate nests in tunnels and crevices but the family name is derived from the nests of the genus *Furnarius*, which build large oven-like globes from wet clay.

Overijssel An inland province in the NE Netherlands bordering on West Germany. Dairy farming and the production of fodder crops are especially important. Recently developed industries produce textiles, machinery, and salt. Area: 3927 sq km (1516 sq mi). Population (1981 est): 1 027 836. Capital: Zwolle.

Overlanders Australian cattle drovers who, in the 19th century, drove cattle across previously unopened territories to markets or new stations.

overture An orchestral composition introducing an opera, oratorio, or play or a one-movement work with a programmatic title played in the concert hall (**concert overture**). In the 18th century the two principal forms of opera overture were the **Italian overture**, consisting of a slow movement between two quick ones, from which the symphony evolved, and the **French overture**, consisting of a slow introduction, a quick fugal section, and often a slow section or separate dance movement.

Ovett, Steve (1955–) British middle-distance runner. A gold medallist in the 800 m at the 1980 Olympic Games and the 5000 m at the 1986 Commonwealth Games, his records include an unsurpassed 8 minutes 13.51 seconds in the 2 mile event (1978).

Ovid (Publius Ovidius Naso; 43 BC–17 AD) Roman poet. After his education he travelled extensively in Greek territories. His poems include the *Amores* and the *Ars amatoria*, both demonstrating his clear and polished style and his characteristic theme of love; the *Heroides*, love letters addressed by legendary heroines to their lovers; and the *Fasti*, a poetic treatment of festivals and rites in the Roman calendar, which he never completed. His greatest work, the *Metamorphoses*, is a poem in 15 books including mythological and historical tales linked by the theme of transformation. In 8 AD he was exiled by the emperor Augustus to Tomi, a remote township on the Black Sea, possibly because of some association with Augustus' licentious daughter, Julia. Despite appeals for mercy in his poems *Tristia* and *Epistulae ex Ponto*, he remained there until his death.

Oviedo 43 21N 5 50W A city in N Spain, in Asturias. It possesses a 14th-century cathedral and a university (founded 1608). Industries include mining and food processing. Population (1981): 190 123.

ovule The structure within the ovary of a *flower that contains an egg cell and nutritive tissue. After fertilization it develops into the *seed containing the embryo.

ovum. *See* egg.

Owen, Alun Davies (1925–) British dramatist. His native Liverpool is the setting of many of his radio and television plays and his stage play *Progress to the Park* (1959). He collaborated with Lionel Bart on the musical *Maggie May* (1964).

Owen, Dr David (Anthony Llewellyn) (1938–) British politician. He entered parliament as a Labour member (1966) and was foreign secretary (1977–79). A cofounder of the Social Democratic Party, he became leader in 1983 but resigned in 1987 in protest against the majority vote to merge with the Liberals.

Owen, Robert (1771–1858) British philanthropist and manufacturer. Born in Wales, in 1800 he became manager of the mills at New Lanark (Lanarkshire), where he established a model community. He introduced better working conditions and housing and established the first infant school in Britain (1816). His advocacy from 1817 of "villages of unity and cooperation" for the unemployed anticipated *cooperative societies and he established such communities at New

ROBERT OWEN *This contemporary engraving shows his model community at New Lanark: the school and kitchens (left), the cotton factories (right), and the village band (lower right-hand corner).*

Harmony, Indiana (1825), Orbiston, near Glasgow (1826), Ralahine, County Cork (1831), and Queenswood, Hampshire (1839). Owen was also active in the trades-union movement and helped to found the Grand National Consolidated Trades Union in 1834.

Owen, Wilfred (1893–1918) British poet. His poetry written during World War I was motivated by horror at the brutality of war, pity for its victims, and anger at civilian complacency. His most famous poems include "Strange Meeting" and "Anthem for Doomed Youth." While in hospital near Edinburgh in 1917 he met Siegfried *Sassoon, who edited his *Poems* (1920). He was killed in action.

Owen Falls 0 29N 33 11E A cataract in Uganda, on the Victoria Nile River just below Lake Victoria. The **Owen Falls Dam** (completed 1954) provides hydroelectric power for much of Uganda and Kenya and is used to control the flood waters.

Owens, Jesse (John Cleveland O.; 1913–80) US sprinter, long jumper, and hurdler. In 1935 he set six world records in 45 minutes (in the long jump, 100 yards, 220 yards, 220 metres, 220 yards hurdles, and 220 metres hurdles). At the Berlin Olympics (1936) he won four gold medals; this success of a Black athlete was inconsistent with the racist theories of Hitler, who refused to congratulate him.

owl A nocturnal bird of prey belonging to an order (*Strigiformes*) of worldwide distribution. There are two families: *Strigidae* (typical owls) and *Tytonidae* (barn and bay owls). Owls have a large head with large forward facing eyes surrounded by a facial disc of radiating feathers, soft plumage, usually brown and patterned, and a short sharp hooked bill. With acute vision and hearing and silent flight, owls hunt mammals, birds, and insects, disgorging the remains in hard pellets. They range in size from the *pygmy owls to the large *eagle owls; most are arboreal but some live in swamps, cactus deserts, or on the ground. *See* barn owl; burrowing owl; fish owl; ▯hawk owl; little owl; snowy owl; tawny owl.

owlet frogmouth A solitary arboreal bird belonging to a family (*Aegothelidae*; 7 or 8 species) occurring in Australian forests. They have a gaping mouth surrounded by long sensitive bristles and feed at night on insects. The little owlet frogmouth (*Aegotheles cristatus*) is 22 cm long and has a grey-brown plumage with brown underparts. Order: *Caprimulgiformes* (nightjars and nighthawks).

owlet moth. *See* noctuid moth.

ox. *See* cattle.

oxalic acid (*or* ethanedioic acid; $(COOH)_2$) A colourless poisonous soluble crystalline solid. Potassium and sodium salts are found in plants. Industrially it is prepared from sawdust treated with sodium and potassium hydroxides. Oxalic acid is used as a metal cleaner and for bleaching textiles and leather.

oxbow lake. *See* lake.

Oxenstierna, Axel, Count (1583–1654) Swedish statesman; chancellor (1612–54). He gained great power during the reign of Gustavus II Adolphus, being the effective controller of national finance and commerce. After Gustavus' death in 1632, he directed Sweden in the Thirty Years' War and gained favourable terms at the Peace of *Westphalia. During the minority (1632–44) of Queen *Christina he dominated the regency council, and continued to influence government until his death.

oxeye daisy A perennial herb, *Chrysanthemum leucanthemum*, also called moon daisy or marguerite, found in grassland and wasteland throughout Europe. 20–70 cm high, it has large solitary flower heads, 2.5–5 cm in diameter, with long white rays surrounding a yellow central disc. Family: *Compositae.

OXFAM A British charity founded in 1942, and registered in 1948 as the Oxford Committee for Famine Relief. Its purpose is to relieve suffering, throughout the world, caused by natural calamity or lack of resources. Three-quarters of its overseas budget is used to promote long-term projects, including medical, social, and economic research and training schemes. Director: Brian W. Walker.

Oxford 51 46N 1 15W A city in S central England, the administrative centre of Oxfordshire on the Rivers Thames and Cherwell. Important from Saxon times and heavily fortified, Oxford's fame as a centre of learning dates from the 13th century, when the first university colleges were founded (*see* Oxford, University of). In the Civil War Oxford was the royalist headquarters. The college buildings dominate the centre of the city but there is considerable industrial development, particularly the huge motor-car works at Cowley. It has one of the world's greatest libraries (the *Bodleian Library, 1602). Population (1981): 98 521.

Oxford, Provisions of (1258) The scheme of constitutional reform imposed upon Henry III by his barons at Oxford following their opposition to excessive taxation. Royal authority was to be contained by an advisory council of 15 barons, which was to reform government. The pope absolved Henry from his promise to observe the Provisions (1261), which led to the *Barons' War.

Oxford, 1st Earl of. *See* Harley, Robert, 1st Earl of Oxford.

Oxford, University of One of the oldest universities in Europe, dating from the 12th century. It is organized as a federation of colleges, which are governed by their own teaching staff ("Fellows"), admit students, maintain their own property (which includes residential accommodation, libraries, playing fields, etc.), and provide members of the University's administrative and legislative bodies, its many faculties, departments, and committees. The University is responsible for organizing a lecture programme, maintaining the large libraries (such as the *Bodleian Library), providing all laboratories, and conducting examinations. The first college, University College, was founded in 1249. Other notable colleges include All Souls (founded 1438), the members of which are all Fellows, Christ Church (founded in 1546 by Cardinal Wolsey), the college chapel of which is also Oxford Cathedral, and Lady Margaret Hall (founded 1878), which was the first women's college. The newest college is Green College (opened September, 1979), which is chiefly for clinical medical students. The number of students in residence in 1981–82 was 11 803 men and women, with 1989 members of staff.

Oxford Group. *See* Moral Rearmament.

Oxford Movement A movement within the Church of England in the 19th century aimed at emphasizing the Catholic principles on which it rested. Led by *Newman,

*Keble, *Pusey, and *Froude of Oxford University, it was initiated in 1833 by Keble's sermon "On the National Apostasy." Aided by their *Tracts for the Times*, the Tractarians, as they came to be called, unleashed a spiritual force that did much to invigorate Anglicanism. *See also* Anglo-Catholicism.

Oxfordshire A county in the South Midlands of England. Under local government reorganization in 1974 it gained a large part of NW Berkshire. It consists mainly of a broad vale, crossed by the River Thames, with the *Chiltern Hills in the SE and the *Cotswold Hills in the NW. It is chiefly agricultural; arable farming is especially important with barley predominating. Industry, centred mainly on Cowley, includes the manufacture of motor vehicles. Area: 2611 sq km (1008 sq mi). Population (1981): 515 079. Administrative centre: Oxford.

oxidation and reduction Oxidation is the chemical combination of a substance with oxygen. An example is the combustion of carbon to carbon dioxide: $C + O_2 \rightarrow CO_2$. The converse process, removal of oxygen, is known as reduction; an example is the reduction of iron oxide to iron: $Fe_2O_3 + 3C \rightarrow 2Fe + 3CO$. The terms oxidation and reduction have been extended in chemistry. Thus, reduction also refers to reaction with hydrogen and oxidation to removal of hydrogen. More generally, an oxidation reaction is one involving loss of electrons and a reduction reaction is one in which electrons are gained. Thus, the conversion of ferrous ions to ferric ions is an oxidation: $Fe^{2+} - e \rightarrow Fe^{3+}$. A compound that supplies oxygen or removes electrons is an **oxidizing agent**, whereas one that removes oxygen or supplies electrons is a **reducing agent**. Usually oxidation and reduction reactions occur together. Thus, in the reaction of ferric ions (Fe^{3+}) with stannous ions (Sn^{2+}), the ferric ions are reduced to ferrous ions (Fe^{2+}) and the stannous ions oxidized to stannic ions (Sn^{4+}): $2Fe^{3+} + Sn^{2+} \rightarrow 2Fe^{2+} + Sn^{4+}$. Reactions of this type are called **redox reactions**.

oxidation number (*or* oxidation state) The number of electrons that would have to be added to an atom to neutralize it. Thus Na^+, Cl^-, and He have oxidation numbers of 1, -1, and 0, respectively. Rules have been developed for assigning oxidation numbers to covalently bound atoms depending on the electric charge that the atom would have if the molecule ionized.

oxlip A perennial herb, *Primula elatior*, found throughout Europe and W Asia. It is similar to the *cowslip but has larger more flattened pale-yellow flowers with a darker yellow throat. The name is also given to hybrids between the primrose and cowslip. Family: *Primulaceae*.

oxpecker An African songbird of the genus *Buphagus*, also called tickbird, that feeds on ticks and maggots pecked from the hides of cattle and game animals. The yellow-billed oxpecker (*B. africanus*) is about 20 cm long with sharp claws for clinging to the backs of its hosts and a stiff tail used for support in climbing over them. Oxpeckers remove parasites from their hosts but also feed on the blood from the sores. Family: *Sturnidae* (starlings).

Oxus, River. *See* Amu Darya, River.

oxygen (O) A colourless odourless gas discovered by J. *Priestley. The element exists in two forms—the diatomic molecule (O_2), which constitutes 21% of the earth's atmosphere, and trace amounts of the highly reactive triatomic allotrope, ozone (O_3), which is formed in the upper atmosphere by the interaction of ultraviolet radiation with oxygen and by lightning discharges. The ozone layer is important in absorbing harmful ultraviolet rays from the sun. Oxygen is very reactive and forms oxides with most elements (for example Na_2O, MgO, Fe_2O_3, Cl_2O_7, XeO_3). In addition to its vital importance for plants and animals, its major use is in the production of steel in blast furnaces. It is obtained by the distillation of liquid air. At no 8; at wt 15.9994; mp $-218.4°C$; bp $-182.96°C$.

oxygen cycle The process by which oxygen—present in the atmosphere or dissolved in water—is taken in by plants and animals for use in *respiration (intercellular combustion of food materials to provide energy) and released into the environment as a waste product, mostly in the form of free oxygen (by plants in *photosynthesis). Oxygen is often combined in organic and inorganic compounds, which may also be considered as part of the cycle. *See also* carbon cycle; nitrogen cycle.

Oyo Empire A kingdom in SW Nigeria and the most powerful state in West Africa from the mid-17th until the mid-18th centuries. Oyo then began to decline relative to Dahomey and during the next century was broken up by *Fulani invasions, European intrusions, and civil war. Oyo is now a province in Western State, SW Nigeria.

oyster A sedentary *bivalve mollusc belonging to the family *Ostreidae* (true osyters), of temperate and warm seas. The lower plate (valve) of the shell is larger and flatter than the upper valve; they are held together by an elastic ligament and powerful muscles. Edible oysters are cultivated for their white flesh; pearl oysters (family *Aviculidae*) are cultivated for their pearls, which they make by coating a grain of sand lodged inside their shell with calcareous material.

oystercatcher A black or black-and-white wading bird belonging to a family (*Haematopodidae*; 4 species) occurring in temperate and tropical coastal regions. 40–50 cm long, oystercatchers have long pointed wings, a long wedge-shaped tail, pink legs, and a long or flattened orange-red bill specialized for opening bivalve molluscs and probing in mud for worms and crustaceans. Order: *Charadriiformes*.

Ozark Plateau (*or* Ozark Mountains) An eroded plateau in the USA, in S Missouri and N Arkansas, reaching over 600 m (2000 ft) in the Boston Mountains. Forestry and mining are important; minerals include lead and zinc.

ozone (O_3) A pale blue gaseous form of *oxygen, formed by passing an electrical discharge through oxygen (O_2). Ozone is a poisonous unstable gas. It is used as an oxidizing agent, for example in water purification. It is present in small amounts in the atmosphere, mostly in the *ozone layer.

ozone layer (*or* ozonosphere) The zone in the upper atmosphere in which the gas ozone (triatomic oxygen; O_3) forms in its greatest concentrations. This is generally between about 10 and 50 km (6–30 mi) above the earth's surface. Ozone forms as a result of the dissociation by solar ultraviolet radiation of molecular oxygen into single atoms, some of which then combine with undissociated oxygen molecules. It absorbs in the 230–320 nm waveband, protecting the earth from dangerous excessive ultraviolet radiation.

Warnings have been given that the use of aerosols could reduce the amount of ozone in the upper atmosphere because the fluorinated hydrocarbons used as the driver gas have exceptional stability and can diffuse up to the ozone layer, where they may be involved in complex photochemical reactions with the highly reactive ozone. If this happened, it could result in general climatic changes caused by increases in average temperatures. For these reasons environmental groups have campaigned for a ban on fluorinated compounds in aerosols.

P

Pabst, G(eorge) W(ilhelm) (1885-1967) Austrian film director. His films are distinguished by their innovatory realistic techniques and their social criticism of decadence and nationalism in Germany. They include *Pandora's Box* (1929), the antiwar *Westfront 1918* (1930), *Die Dreigroschenoper* (1931), and *Kameradschaft* (1931).

paca A large nocturnal *rodent, *Cuniculus paca*, of Central and South America. Up to 60 cm long, with a tiny tail and spotted coat, it is found in damp places near rivers and swamps, feeding on leaves and fruit and living in burrows. Part of the skull is specialized as a resonating chamber. It is hunted by all kinds of predators, including man. Family: *Dasyproctidae*.

Pacaraima Mountains A mountain range in NE South America. Comprising part of the Guiana Highlands, it extends W-E along part of the Brazil-Venezuela and Brazil-Guyana borders reaching 2810 m (9219 ft) at Mount Roraima.

pacemaker A small section of specialized heart muscle that initiates heartbeat. It is situated in the right atrium and contracts spontaneously: the impulse to contract is transmitted from the pacemaker to both atria and then to the ventricles. If the pacemaker ceases to function (heart block) it may be replaced by an artificial battery-operated device that stimulates the heart to contract. If required permanently it is surgically implanted under the skin.

pachisi A board game popular in India. It is played by two partnerships of players who move pieces round a cross-shaped course according to the throw of dice (or cowrie shells). In the 19th century it was patented in the UK in a modified form as Ludo.

Pachomius, St (c. 290-346 AD) Egyptian hermit, who founded the first monastery in 318 at Tabenna, on the River Nile, and the first Christian rule involving a uniform communal existence. Until then *monasticism had been practised only by solitaries in the desert. Feast day: 14 May.

pachyderm A thick-skinned *mammal, such as the elephant, rhinoceros, or hippopotamus. Early naturalists classified these animals, together with pigs and walruses, in a group called *Pachydermata*. The classification is now abandoned but the term is still used.

Pachymeres, Georgius (1242-c. 1310) Byzantine historian and writer. Pachymeres' most important work was a history of the period 1261 to 1308, under the emperors *Michael VIII Palaeologus and Andronicus II Palaeologus (1260-1332; reigned 1282-1328). Other works include an outline of Aristotelian philosophy and a treatise on the Holy Spirit. The latter work is significant in that it accepts the controversial Roman *Filioque clause of the formula of St *John of Damascus.

Pacific, War of the (1879-84) The war between Chile and the allies Bolivia and Peru. Also called the Nitrate War, it was provoked by a dispute over Chile's exploitation of nitrate deposits in Bolivia. Within two years Bolivia was defeated, and Peru's capital Lima captured. According to the peace terms, finally agreed in 1884, Peru and Bolivia ceded territories to Chile, Bolivia losing all access to the sea.

Pacific Islands, Trust Territory of the A UN trust territory administered by the USA. It comprised the *Marshall Islands, the Federated States of *Micronesia, the Mariana Islands (until 1978), and Belau (*see* Palau). Taken by Japan from Germany (1914), the islands were captured by the USA in World War II (1944). The trusteeship was established in 1947 and dissolved in 1987.

Pacific Ocean The world's largest and deepest ocean, covering a third of its surface. It extends between Asia, Australia, Antarctica, and America. It contains a multitude of volcanic and coral islands in the tropical SW and reaches its maximum depth in the *Marianas Trench. The S and E are marked by a uniform climate with steady winds, but the W is known for its typhoons, which often cause coastal flooding. The Pacific has some diurnal and mixed tides, while Tahitian tides follow the sun and not the moon. Its vast mineral resources are unexploited.

pacifism The group of doctrines, religious, moral, or political, that urge nonparticipation either in any war whatsoever or in particular wars that are held to be unjustified. In ancient societies it was assumed that membership of the society involved fighting for it when necessary. This view was not held by early Christians, although not all Christians have been unanimously pacifist; in fact Christian pacifism was relatively unimportant from Constantine's period to the Reformation, when first *Anabaptists, and then *Quakers, adopted total pacifism. In modern times conscientious objectors have been recognized in both World Wars and have often served with distinction in noncombatant (medical) units. Moreover, nonviolent methods of attaining political ends were shown to be effective by *Gandhi in the 1920s, despite the slaughter between Hindus and Muslims that followed, and Martin Luther *King in the 1960s.

pack rat A North American *rodent belonging to the genus *Neotoma* (20 species), also called wood rat. With body length of 15-23 cm, it has a hairy tail and inhabits rocky and wooded country, nesting in a pile of twigs and feeding on seeds and vegetation. Family: *Cricetidae*.

Padang 1 00S 100 21E A port in Indonesia, in W Sumatra. An early Dutch settlement, it flourished when railways were built in the 19th century. It exports coal, cement, coffee, copra, and rubber. Its university was established in 1956. Population (1980): 480 922.

Paddington A district in the Greater London borough of the City of Westminster. It is noted for Paddington Station, an important British Rail terminus.

paddlefish One of two species of freshwater *bony fish, *Polyodon spathula* of North America or *Psephurus gladius* of China, also called duckbill cat. Paddlefishes have a smooth body, with an enormous paddle-shaped snout, and feed by straining planktonic organisms from the water. Family: *Polyodontidae*; order: *Acipenseriformes*.

Paderborn 51 43N 8 44E A city in N central West Germany, in North Rhine-Westphalia. Notable buildings include a cathedral (11th-13th centuries) and a Renaissance town hall (1613-20). Its university was established in 1972. An important agricultural market, it manufactures agricultural machinery, computers, textiles, and furniture. Population (1980 est): 109 600.

Paderewski, Ignacy (Jan) (1860-1941) Polish pianist, composer, and statesman. Having studied at Warsaw, Berlin, and Vienna, he achieved an international reputation as a performer and composed a piano concerto and many solo pieces. He was the first prime minister (1919) of newly independent Poland but resigned after ten months to return to his musical career.

Padua (Italian name: Padova) 45 24N 11 53E A city in NE Italy, near Venice. An important city in Roman and Renaissance times, it has several notable buildings, including a 13th-century cathedral and the Basilica of St Anthony, in front of which stands one of Donatello's most famous works, the equestrian statue of Gattamelata. Galileo taught at its

Chinese   Japanese

PAGODA *The exuberantly curving roofs of the typical multi-storeyed Chinese pagoda contrast with the more restrained Japanese form.*

university (founded in 1222). Machinery and textiles are produced. Population (1980 est): 241 400.

paediatrics The medical specialty concerned with the problems and illnesses of infants and children from birth (or premature birth) to adolescence. Paediatricians must have a detailed knowledge of obstetrics, genetics (to deal with inherited diseases), and psychology. Their work includes the management of handicaps at home and in school as well as the treatment and prevention of childhood diseases.

Paestum The Roman name for Posidonia, a colony of *Sybaris founded about 600 BC on the SW coast of Italy. Paestum is famed for the three great Doric temples the remains of which still stand there. Named after the Greek sea god *Poseidon, it was conquered by Rome in 273 BC and became celebrated in Latin poetry for its twice-flowering roses.

Páez, José Antonio (1790–1873) Venezuelan revolutionary. The leader of a band of cowboys (*llaneros*), he allied himself with *Bolívar against Spain. After the liberation he took Venezuela out of the confederation of Gran Colombia and became its first president (1831).

Pagalu. *See* Equatorial Guinea, Republic of.

Pagan The former capital of Burma on the Irrawaddy River SE of Mandalay. Founded in about 849 AD, Pagan was refounded after the decree adopting Buddhism as the state religion (1056). Hundreds of brick-built temples, monasteries, and pagodas survived Pagan's sack by the Mongols (1287) and some, such as the Ananda temple (1090) and Shwezigon pagoda (12th century), are still in use.

Paganini, Niccolò (1782–1840) Italian virtuoso violinist. After an adventurous youth he toured Europe, astonishing audiences with his techniques, such as left-hand pizzicato, multiple stopping, and artificial harmonics. His skill inspired Liszt and Schumann to compose piano music of transcendent difficulty. He composed six violin concertos, various showpieces for violin, including a set of variations on the G string, and 24 caprices, one of which became the basis for compositions by Rachmaninov, Brahms, and others.

Page, Sir Earle (Christmas Grafton) (1880–1961) Australian politician, who was leader of the Country Party from 1920 to 1939 and briefly prime minister in 1939. Between 1923 and 1929, he was treasurer in the coalition government under *Bruce. He was subsequently minister of commerce (1934–39, 1940–41), establishing the Australian Agricultural Council (1934), and minister of health (1949–56).

Page, Sir Frederick Handley (1885–1962) British aircraft designer, who in 1909 founded Handley Page Ltd, the first British company to manufacture aircraft. His Handley Page 0/400 was the first twin-engined bomber and saw action in World War I. He also designed and built the Halifax, a World War II bomber.

pagoda A Buddhist shrine in the form of a tower for housing relics of the Buddha. Pagodas originated in India, where their standardized form of a basic unit repeated vertically in diminishing sizes was evolved. From India the pagoda spread to Sri Lanka (where it is called a dagoba), SE Asia, China, and Japan. Japanese pagodas are usually five-storeyed wooden structures built round a central timber post to provide stability against earthquakes. *See also* stupa.

Pago Pago 14 16S 170 43W The capital of American Samoa, in SE Tutuila on the S Pacific Ocean. A US naval base (1872–1951), it is a port exporting tinned tuna. Population (1980): 3075.

Pahang A large state in SE Peninsular Malaysia, on the South China Sea. Lying mainly in the River Pahang basin it rises to the Cameron Mountains in the W. Rubber, rice, coconuts, gold, and tin are produced. Area: 35 931 sq km (13 873 sq mi). Population (1980): 770 644. Capital: Kuantan.

Pahang, River The longest river in Peninsular Malaysia, rising in the NW and flowing generally S then E through the state of Penang to enter the South China Sea. Length: 322 km (200 mi).

Paine, Thomas (1737–1809) British writer and political theorist. In 1774 he went to America, where his pamphlet *Common Sense* (1776) initiated the American movement towards independence. Returning to England in 1787, he published *Rights of Man* (1791–92) in support of the French Revolution and in opposition to *Burke's *Reflections*. Indicted for treason, Paine fled to France, where he was elected to the French Convention. While imprisoned by Robespierre, he wrote the second part of his *Age of Reason* (1796), a deist manifesto that held that "all religions are in their nature mild and benign."

paint A finely powdered insoluble pigment suspended in a binding medium; on application to a surface the volatile components of the binding medium evaporate, the drying oils oxidize, and the resins polymerize, leaving a decorative or protective skin. The pigments impart colour and opacity to the skin and extenders (such as barium sulphate, calcium carbonate, or asbestos) are mixed with the pigments to strengthen the skin and reduce raw-material costs. The binding medium consists of a drying oil (e.g. linseed oil or tung oil), a resin (rosin or a synthetic alkyd), a thinner (turpentine, benzene, etc.), and a drier (e.g. lead linoleate) to accelerate film formation. Water-based emulsion paints consist of emulsions of a synthetic resin (e.g. polyvinyl acetate, polystyrene, acrylic resins) in water.

painted lady An orange, black, and white butterfly, *Vanessa cardui*, of worldwide distribution. It cannot survive cold winters but migrates from warmer regions each year. The caterpillars feed mainly on thistles and nettles. The American painted lady (*V. virginiensis*) is similar but less widespread.

painting In art, the creation of an aesthetic entity by the skilled covering of a surface with paint. Suitable painting surfaces include paper, canvas, walls, and ivory, and among the many techniques of painting are oil, *watercolour, *tempera, *encaustic, *fresco, and, the most modern method, *acrylic painting. The main subjects of painting were religious until the Renaissance period, when portraits, landscapes, *genre, and *still life began to assume an independent existence. The principal painting styles in the history of art have been classical (ancient Greek and Roman), Byzantine, romanesque, gothic, Renaissance, mannerist, baroque, rococo, neoclassical, impressionist, and abstract.

Paisley 55 50N 4 26W A town in W central Scotland, in Strathclyde Region near Glasgow. Famous for shawls in the 19th century, Paisley's textile industry (particularly cotton and synthetic thread) is still important. The richly coloured abstract design used for the shawls, which imitated shawls from Kashmir, is still known as **paisley pattern**; any fabric printed with such a design is known as paisley. Dyeing, bleaching, engineering, and starch and cornflour manufacturing are also important. Population (1981): 84 789.

Paisley, Ian (1926-) Northern Irish politician; an uncompromising defender of Protestant unionism. A minister of the Free Presbyterian Church of Ulster from 1946, he was a Protestant Unionist MP in the Northern Irish parliament (1970-72) before becoming (1974) a Democratic Unionist MP in the House of Commons.

Pakistan, Islamic Republic of A country in S Asia, bordering on Iran, Afghanistan, China, and India. The W is mountainous and the E has areas of desert, while the River Indus rises in the Himalayas in the N and flows S across plateau and the Indus Plain to the Arabian Sea. The country is arid with great extremes of temperature but the plain is very fertile, except in areas that have become saline or waterlogged. The population, which is increasing rapidly, is a mixture of many Asian and Middle Eastern racial groups. Of the languages spoken Punjabi is the most commonly used, although Urdu is the language of the educated. 97% of the population is Muslim. *Economy*: mainly agricultural, producing chiefly rice, wheat, sugar cane, and cotton. Productivity has improved during the 1960s and 1970s with increased mechanization, the use of chemical fertilizers, improved strains of crops, and the reclamation of saline land. Irrigation, on which agriculture is dependent, has also been extensively developed since the Indus Waters Treaty was concluded with India (1960). Industry has developed successfully since 1947, at which time the area had very little. Although industry employs only 14% of the workforce and is still largely dependent on imported machinery, petroleum, chemicals, and metals, Pakistan has become a major exporter of cotton and cotton yarn and cloth. Chemical fertilizers, cement, sugar, and handicrafts are also produced, and a steel industry is being developed. Fishing is increasingly important. Resources include coal (mainly low-grade), iron ore, copper, limestone, oil, and large quantities of natural gas. Hydroelectric power is also produced. *History*: the history of Pakistan is that of *India until 1947, when it was created to satisfy the *Muslim League's demand for a separate state for the Muslim minority. It consisted then of two separate areas; West Pakistan comprised Baluchistan, the Northwest Frontier, West Punjab (now Punjab province), and Sind, while East Pakistan was formed from East Bengal. The question of control over Kashmir is still unsettled. The most serious problem has been the unification of Pakistan's diverse population groups, divided by geography, race, and extremes of wealth and poverty. The unifying force of the common religion has not been able to contain demands for regional autonomy and increased democracy. Thus each of Pakistan's three constitutions (1956, 1962, 1973) has been replaced by martial law. Regional unrest was especially serious in East Pakistan, which had a larger population but less political and military power than West Pakistan. The electoral victory in East Pakistan of the Awami League (1970), which demanded regional autonomy, led to its secession as *Bangladesh (1971). This was effected after a two-week civil war in which Indian forces intervened and defeated the Pakistani army, which consisted of troops from West Pakistan. Regionalism later led to guerrilla fighting in Baluchistan and

the Northwest Frontier province (1973 onwards). On 30 January, 1972, Pakistan withdrew from the British Commonwealth. Allegations of ballot rigging following the 1977 elections triggered off more violent unrest, which led finally to a military coup led by Gen Zia ul-Haq. Demonstrations and riots followed when members of the previous government were arrested and the former prime minister, Zulfikar Ali Bhutto, was executed for conspiracy to murder (1979). The former president, Fazal Elahi Chaudhry (1904–82), retired from office in 1978 and was succeeded by Gen Zia, who faced increasing opposition from Benazir Bhutto during the 1980s. Official language: Urdu. Official currency: Pakistan rupee of 100 paise. Area (excluding Jammu and Kashmir): 803 943 sq km (310 322 sq mi). Population (1981): 83 780 000. Capital: Islamabad.

Palace of Westminster The British parliamentary buildings in Westminster, London, containing the *House of Commons and the House of Lords (*see* parliament). It is also known as the Houses of Parliament. A royal palace of medieval construction until the 16th century, when it assumed its present function, it was largely burnt down in 1834, only the Great Hall surviving. It was rebuilt in the *gothic revival style by *Barry and *Pugin. See also Big Ben.

Palaeocene epoch. See Tertiary period.

palaeography The study of ancient handwriting. Palaeography originated as an adjunct to textual criticism of Greek and Latin manuscripts but is now applied to all kinds of scripts. Palaeographers assess the cultural and historical implications of the development of writing styles and the output of individual scriptoria (scribal centres) and scribes. Recent technical aids include computerized surveys of large numbers of manuscripts and ultraviolet photography to render faint writing legible.

Palaeolithic The earliest division of the *Stone Age. It extends roughly from the emergence of man, or at least of some hominid capable of making simple pebble tools, to the end of the last ice age. The Palaeolithic is conventionally divided into three phases: Lower, beginning as much as 3 500 000 years ago and characterized by pebble-tool and hand-axe manufacture; Middle, beginning about 70 000 years ago and associated with *Neanderthal man and *Mousterian industries; and Upper, beginning about 40 000 years ago and associated in Europe with *Cro-Magnon man and cave art.

Palaeologus The ruling dynasty of the Eastern Roman Empire from 1261 to 1453. Originating in the 11th century, the first Palaeologus emperor was *Michael VIII Palaeologus and they continued to rule until the fall of Constantinople to the Turks in 1453. During this period Byzantine culture underwent a major revival.

palaeomagnetism The history of the earth's magnetic field (*see* geomagnetic field) as determined from the remanent magnetism of rocks. The study assumes that the principal component of igneous and sedimentary rocks' magnetism was determined at or near to the time at which the rocks were formed. Palaeomagnetism provides evidence for continental drift (*see* plate tectonics) and the movement of the magnetic poles.

palaeontology The study of ancient organisms from their *fossil remains in the rocks. Their taxonomy, anatomy, ecology, and evolution are studied. Fossils are used to correlate bodies of rock and establish their stratigraphic relationships with each other; this field is called biostratigraphy. Modern methods of *dating rocks by radiometric means give their absolute dates rather than their order in the stratigraphic column. The study of ancient microscopic organisms is called **micropalaeontology** and the fossils are known as microfossils.

Palaeo-Siberian languages A diverse group of languages of Siberia comprised of four unrelated groups: Yeniseian; Luorawetlan, which includes Chuckchi, Koryak, and Aliutor; Yukaghir, which includes Yukaghir and also Omok and Chuvan, both now extinct; and Gilyak, the only one of its group.

Palaeozoic era The era of geological time between the Precambrian and the Mesozoic, lasting from about 590 to 240 million years ago. It is divided into the Upper Palaeozoic, which contains the Cambrian, Ordovician, and Silurian periods, and the Lower Palaeozoic, containing the Devonian, Carboniferous, and Permian. It is the first era of *Phanerozoic time. The Caledonian and Variscan orogenies both occurred in this era.

palanquin An enclosed litter formerly used in the East by high-ranking officials and by women and usually carried by four or six men.

palate The roof of the mouth, which is divided into two parts. The soft palate at the back of the mouth is composed of mucous membrane and prevents food passing into the nose during swallowing. From its centre hangs down a flap of tissue, the uvula. The hard palate, further forward, is composed of two fused halves made up of the palatine bone and part of the maxillary (upper jaw) bones. During development the two halves of the palate may fail to fuse, leading to a *cleft palate.

Palatinate Two regions of West Germany: the Lower (or Rhenish) Palatinate is now in Rheinland-Pfalz, Baden-Württemberg, and Hessen and the Upper Palatinate is now in Bavaria. In 1156 the title of count palatine (originally a judicial officer) was bestowed by Emperor Frederick I on his half-brother Conrad, whose territories included what later became the Rhenish Palatinate. When, in 1214, it passed to the *Wittelsbach family, their lands in Bavaria became the Upper Palatinate. From 1356 the counts palatine were *electors of Holy Roman Emperors. During the Reformation the Palatinate became a centre of Protestantism and the claim by the Protestant, Elector Frederick, the Winter King, to the Bohemian throne precipitated the *Thirty Years' War. The two Palatinates were separated from 1648 until 1777 but in the early 19th century the Lower Palatinate was divided between France and various German states and the Upper Palatinate passed to Bavaria.

Palau. *See* Belau.

Palawan A mountainous island in the W Philippines, between the South China and Sulu Seas. Sparsely populated, its chief products are timber, mercury, and chromite; fishing is important. Area: 11 785 sq km (4550 sq mi). Population (1980): 311 548. Chief town: Puerto Princesa.

Palembang 2 59S 104 45E A port in Indonesia, in S Sumatra on the River Musi. It was the capital of a Hindu Sumatran kingdom (8th century AD) and Dutch trade began here in 1617. Its university was established in 1960. The export centre of local oilfields, it has Indonesia's largest refinery and many oil-based industries. Population (1980): 787 187.

Palencia 41 01N 4 32W A town in N central Spain, in León. It possessed Spain's first university, founded in 1208 and moved to Salamanca in 1239. The gothic cathedral contains paintings by El Greco, including *St Sebastian*. Manufactures include iron and porcelain. Population (1981): 74 080.

Palermo 38 08N 13 23E A port in Italy, the capital of Sicily. Founded by the Phoenicians in the 8th century BC, it first established itself as chief town of the island under the Arabs (9th–11th centuries). Its many notable buildings include the gothic cathedral and the Norman palace (now the regional parliament). It has shipbuilding and textile industries. Population (1983 est): 712 342.

Palestine (or Holy Land) A historic area in the Middle East, consisting of the area between the Mediterranean Sea and the River Jordan. It now comprises *Israel and territories belonging to Jordan and Egypt. Sacred to Jews, Christians, and Muslims alike, and caught as it has been between a succession of surrounding empires, the area has been much fought over. It has been inhabited since prehistoric times. Towards the end of the 2nd millennium BC it was settled by the Hebrew people, who in the Old Testament were led out of Egypt by Moses, and in about 1000 BC a Hebrew kingdom was founded by Saul. Following the reign of Solomon it was split into Israel, later conquered by the Assyrians, and Judah (*see* Judaea), later conquered by the Babylonians (*see* Babylonian exile), who destroyed the *Temple of Jerusalem (rebuilt in 516 BC under the Persians). The Romans conquered the Jewish state that existed briefly in 142–63 BC and also destroyed the Temple (70 AD) while violently suppressing a Jewish revolt. From the late 4th century AD many Jews left Palestine, which became a centre first for Christian and later for Muslim pilgrimage (following Arab conquest in 636 AD). Christianity was reinstated in the area by the conquest of the Crusaders (1099 until the 13th century). After a period of Egyptian rule it fell to the Ottoman Turks (1516), who ruled it until World War I. During the 1830s Palestine, inhabited chiefly by Arab peasants, was opened up to European influence and from the mid-19th century Jews returned from the *Diaspora to settle in Palestine. The late 19th century saw the beginning of *Zionism and in 1909 Tel Aviv, the first new Jewish city, was founded. By 1914 there were 100 000 Jews in Palestine, although their numbers were reduced by almost half during World War I, in which they were sympathetic to the Allies. In 1918 Palestine was captured by the British; British administration, effective from 1920, was confirmed by a League of Nations mandate (1922). By the *Balfour Declaration (1917) the British supported the Jewish demand for a Jewish nation in Palestine. This provoked unrest and terrorism among the Arab population, who felt increasingly threatened by Jewish immigration. The British limits on irrigation and land purchase in order to pacify the Arabs (1939) angered the Jews and thus increased tension even further, as did also the large numbers of illegal Jewish immigrants arriving during the war. In 1947 the problem was referred to the UN, which decided to divide Palestine into two separate states, Jewish and Arab. As this was accepted by the Jews but not the Arabs, Britain renounced its mandate in 1948. The state of Israel was then proclaimed and immediately attacked by the surrounding Arab countries. They were repulsed but the rest of Palestine was divided between Jordan and Egypt. *See also* West Bank.

Palestine Liberation Organization (PLO) An organization of various Palestinian groups opposed to Israel. Formed in 1964, the PLO has not been able to unite all the Palestinian groups; in particular the Popular Front for the Liberation of Palestine, led by George Habash, has remained independent. The PLO is under the leadership of Yassir Arafat's al-*Fatah. Terrorist actions carried out by the PLO include the murder of 11 Israeli athletes at the Munich Olympics (1972). In 1982 PLO forces were expelled from Lebanon, which they had been using as a base for guerrilla operations, when Israel invaded. PLO groups that remained subsequently became involved in conflict with other factions within the country.

Palestrina, Giovanni Pierluigi da (?1525–94) Italian composer. He spent most of his life in Rome, as chorister, choirmaster, or maestro at churches including St Peter's. One of the greatest masters of *polyphony, he composed 93 masses, 179 motets, and many other pieces, mainly for church use. He was twice offered posts elsewhere (Venice and Mantua) but each time he asked too high a salary.

Paley, William (1743–1805) British churchman and Anglican theologian. A Fellow of Christ's College, Cambridge, and a popular lecturer, Paley was the author of *View of the Evidences of Christianity* (1794) and *Natural Theology* (1802). These were widely acclaimed apologies for Christian belief against current deist views (*see* deism).

Palgrave, Francis Turner (1824–97) British poet and anthologist. A friend of Tennyson, he published several volumes of verse and became professor of poetry at Oxford. He is best remembered for his influential anthology of English verse, *The Golden Treasury* (1861).

Pali An *Indo-Aryan language originating in N India. It is the language of the Theravada Buddhist canon and is used throughout the Theravada countries of SE Asia but disappeared from India itself during the 14th century.

Palio A horse race run in July and August in the main piazza of Siena. It is named after the painted silk banner that the winner receives. The Palio first took place in 1482 and is accompanied by considerable pageantry.

Palissy, Bernard (1510–89) French potter, famous for his rustic ware, a richly coloured lead-glazed earthenware. His dishes are ornamental in relief with mythological subjects or reptiles, plants, etc. He enjoyed court patronage in the 1560s but was persecuted as a Huguenot and died in prison. He is also known for his writings on religion, science, and philosophy.

PALLADIANISM *Chiswick House (begun 1725), which was designed by Lord Burlington for his own use.*

Palladianism An architectural style developed in 16th-century Venetia by *Palladio. It was based on classical Roman public architecture and the theories of *Vitruvius and it placed great importance on symmetrical room planning and a harmonious system of proportions. Largely disseminated by Palladio's books, *I quattro libri dell' architettura* (1570), it was first introduced into England in the early 17th century by Inigo *Jones but had no other followers until it was revived early in the 18th century by Lord *Burlington, Colen Campbell (1673–1729), and William *Kent. It was widely used in England for public buildings and country houses, eventually being replaced by *neoclassicism in the mid-18th century.

Palladio, Andrea (1508–80) Italian architect, born in Padua. One of the most sophisticated and widely imitated of classical architects, Palladio is famous for developing the architectural style now known as *Palladianism. Trained as a stonemason, Palladio designed most of his buildings in and around Vicenza. His first job was the remodelling of the basilica in Vicenza (begun 1549) and from that emerged a hugely successful career. He produced villas, for example the Villa Rotonda (near Vicenza) and Villa Barbaro (Maser); palaces, for example the Palazzo Chericati (1550s); and churches, the most famous being S Giorgio Maggiore in Venice (begun 1566).

palladium (Pd) A silvery-white noble metal of the platinum group, discovered by W. H. Wollaston (1766–1828) in 1803, and named after the asteroid Pallas, which was discovered at about the same time. Palladium readily absorbs hydrogen and is used as a catalyst for hydrogenation reactions; it is alloyed with gold to form white gold. At no 46; at wt 106.4; mp 1552°C; bp 3140°C.

Palladium In Greek and Roman religion, an ancient image of Athena, originally the wooden image kept in the citadel of Troy and believed to have been sent from heaven by Zeus. The

safety of the city depended on it. It was stolen by Odysseus and Diomedes, who thus made possible the capture of Troy. It was believed to have been taken to Athens or Sparta, or to Rome (by *Aeneas).

Pallas The second largest (608 km in diameter) *minor planet, the orbit of which lies between those of Mars and Jupiter.

Pallas Athena. *See* Athena.

Pallas's cat A small wild *cat, *Felis* (or *Otocolobus*) *manul*, of Tibet, Mongolia, and Siberia. About 50 cm long, with a very thick tail and long yellow-grey fur, it has a small face with low-set ears—an adaptation for stalking small mammals from the cover of rocks and boulders.

palm A monocotyledonous plant of the family *Palmae* (or *Arecaceae*; about 2500 species), occurring in tropical and subtropical regions. Ranging from 1 to 60 m in height, palms typically have an unbranched trunk crowned with a cluster of leaves, which are pleated and fan-shaped or feather-like and often very large (up to 15 m long). The flowers are usually grouped into large clusters and give rise to berries or drupes (stone fruits). Palms are commercially important as a source of food (*see* coconut; date; sago), oil (*see* oil palm), wax (*see* carnauba), and various fibres and building materials.

Palma (*or* Palma de Mallorca) 39 35N 2 39E The capital of the Spanish Balearic Islands, in Majorca on the Mediterranean Sea. Its historic buildings include the gothic cathedral (1230–1601) and the 14th-century Bellver Castle. Noted as a tourist resort, it is also a port and commercial centre; industries include textiles, footwear, and such crafts as pottery. Population (1981): 304 422.

Palma Vecchio, Jacopo (J. Negretti; c. 1480–1528) Italian painter of the Venetian school. He is noted for his *St Barbara Altarpiece* (Sta Maria Formosa, Venice) and his portraits of Venetian women.

Palm Beach 26 41N 80 02W A town and fashionable winter resort in the USA, in SE Florida on Lake Worth (a lagoon). It is an extension of the much larger West Palm Beach. Population (1980): 9729.

palm civet A mammal of the family *Viverridae* that is smaller than the true civets and more omnivorous than the *genets. Most palm civets are Asian (the two-spotted palm civet (*Nandinia binotata*) is the only African species). The masked palm civet (*Paguma larvata*) of SE Asia is up to 140 cm long including the tail (50–65 cm) and is mainly arboreal, feeding on fruit, insects, and some vertebrates.

Palmer, Arnold (1929–) US professional golfer, who did much to make golf a spectator sport. US amateur champion in 1954, he won the US Open championship (1960), Masters championship (1958, 1960, 1962, 1964), British Open championship (1961, 1962), and many other events.

Palmer, Samuel (1805–81) British landscape painter and etcher, born in London. He first exhibited at the Royal Academy at the age of 14 but his best landscapes, often moonlit and either in sepia or watercolour, were painted during his association (1826–35) with a group of painters in Shoreham, who shared Palmer's admiration for William *Blake. His imaginative and mystical approach to art declined into conventionality in the late 1830s.

Palmerston, Henry John Temple, 3rd Viscount (1784–65) British statesman; foreign secretary (1830–34, 1835–41, 1846–51) and Liberal prime minister (1855–58, 1859–65). He entered parliament in 1807 as a Tory, serving as secretary for war from 1809 to 1828, but by 1830 he had joined the Whigs (later Liberals). His markedly nationalist foreign policy sought to defend constitutional states and prevent a Franco-Russian combination. In 1850 he made a famous speech defending the dispatch of a fleet to Greece in support of the claims of Don Pacifico (1784–1854), who had been born in British Gibraltar, against the Greek Government (his house had been burned by a mob), stating that every British subject might "hold himself free from indignity when he could say *Civis Romanus sum*." As prime minister Palmerston supported the Confederacy in the US Civil War but was dissuaded by his colleagues from actively involving Britain.

Palmerston North 40 21S 175 37E A city in New Zealand, in S North Island. It is a centre for the agricultural area of the Manawatu Plain and is the site of Massey University (a branch of Victoria University, Wellington). Population (1983): 93 700.

palmistry The study of the lines and ridges on the palm of the hand in order to interpret character and divine the owner's future. Although without scientific basis, palmistry (or chiromancy as it is also called) provides common-sense evidence of a person's way of life and habits and from these something may be deduced of his character and interests.

Palm Springs 33 49N 116 34W A city in the USA, in California. Long known for its hot springs, it is a popular resort with golf courses and an aerial tramway. Population (1980): 36 500.

Palm Sunday The Sunday before Easter, commemorating Christ's last triumphal ride into Jerusalem (Mark 11). In many Churches crosses or branches of palm leaves are distributed on this day.

palmyra A *palm tree, *Borassus flabellier*, cultivated in India and Sri Lanka. The timber is used for construction and the leaves are used for thatch and made into a type of paper. The sugary sap from the flower heads is fermented to give palm wine and the kernels of the fruits are eaten.

Palmyra (*or* Tadmor) 34 36N 38 15E An ancient Syrian desert city on the route of the E–W caravan trade in the 2nd and 3rd centuries AD. Palmyra came under Roman control in the 1st century AD but under *Zenobia regained its independence from 270 until 272, when it was reconquered and then destroyed; subsequently rebuilt, it was taken by the Muslims in 634. The ruins of the ancient city include the remains of the Temple of Bel (Palmyra's chief deity). Inscriptions in the Palmyric alphabet (developed from the *Aramaic) provide important information on Palmyra's trade. The modern town has a population (1970 est) of 12 722.

palolo worm (*or* paolo worm) A large marine *annelid worm, *Eunice viridis*, of the S Pacific. Palolo worms hunt for small prey among coral reefs and their reproduction is synchronized by the phases of the moon. The rear portion of the worm, containing eggs or sperm, separates and swims to the surface, discharging its gametes in the sea. Swarming worms are a local delicacy. Class: *Polychaeta*.

Palomar, Mount A mountain in the USA, in California. It is the site of the Mount Palomar Observatory. Its 508 cm (200 in) reflecting telescope is among the largest in the world. Height: 1870 m (6140 ft). *See also* Hale Observatories.

Palomino A horse that has a yellow or golden coat and a white or silver mane and tail. Palominos are often Arabs or American Quarter horses but may be of any light saddle-horse breed. They are recognized as a colour breed in the USA but do not breed true.

palynology (*or* pollen analysis) The study of pollen grains and their distribution in sedimentary rocks in order to provide information about life and environmental conditions of past geological ages. Pollen is extremely resistant to decay and therefore well preserved in rocks. The different genera and species are also very distinctive; therefore the presence of a certain type of pollen indicates the dominant flora—and therefore the climate and other conditions—of the period studied.

Pamirs (*or* Pamir) A mountainous area of central Asia, situated mainly in the Tadzhik SSR of the Soviet Union and extending into China and Afghanistan. It consists of a complex of high ranges rising over 6000 m (20 000 ft), with the Tian

Shan in the N, the Kunlun and Karakoram in the E, and the Hindu Kush in the W. Its highest point in the Soviet Union is Mount Communism, at 7495 m (24 590 ft). In China it reaches 7719 m (25 326 ft) at Kungur.

Pampas The flat treeless plains of Argentina. These extend W from the Atlantic Ocean to the Andes and are bordered by the Gran Chaco in the N and Patagonia in the S. They are of major agricultural importance in the E, producing wheat, corn, and beef in particular.

pampas cat A small wild *cat, *Felis colocolo*, of South America. About the size of a domestic cat, with a long tail and greyish coat, it once hunted in grassland and swamps but is now very rare.

pampas grass A perennial *grass of the genus *Cortaderia*, native to South America and widely cultivated as an ornamental. *C. argentea* grows in dense clumps, with leaves up to 2 m long and flowering stems exceeding 3 m in length. The flowers usually form silvery-white plumes, although various colour varieties are possible.

Pamplona 42 49N 1 39W A city in NE Spain, in the Basque Provinces. It has a cathedral and holds a renowned fiesta (during which bulls are driven through the streets to the bullring) described by the novelist Ernest Hemingway, in *The Sun Also Rises* (1926). It is an agricultural centre and its industries include traditional crafts and chemicals. Population (1981): 183 126.

Pan The Greek god of shepherds and their flocks, the son of Hermes. He is usually portrayed with the legs, ears, and horns of a goat. He lived in the mountains and was associated especially with Arcadia, where he sported with the nymphs and played his pipes, known as the syrinx (*see* panpipes). He was believed to be the source of a sudden inexplicable fear, or panic, which sometimes overcame travellers in wild and remote places.

Panama, Isthmus of A narrow strip of land linking North and South America, between the Caribbean Sea and the Pacific Ocean. Length: 676 km (420 mi). Minimum width: 50 km (31 mi).

Panama, Republic of A country in Central America, occupying the Isthmus of Panama. Narrow coastal plains rise to volcanic mountains. The population is largely of mixed Indian, European, and African descent. *Economy*: considerable revenue comes from receipts from the Panama Canal and from international capital. The main agricultural products are bananas, rice, sugar, and maize and fishing (especially for shrimps) is growing in importance. Industries include oil refining, cement production, and paper and food processing. Tourism is an increasing source of revenue. The main exports include refined oil, bananas, shrimps, and sugar. *History*: discovered by Columbus in 1502 and soon colonized by the Spanish, in 1513 Balboa made his famous journey across the isthmus. Panama later became part of the viceroyalty of Peru and then of New Granada. In 1821 it became part of newly independent Colombia, from which it broke free in 1903 after a revolution supported by the USA. Its political history has been turbulent. A military coup in 1968 brought Gen Omar Torrijos (1929–81) to power and in 1972 a new constitution gave him full executive powers for six years, while also initiating a presidency, Torrijos retired as head of state in 1978; after his death effective control passed to Gen Manuel Noriega (1938–   ). President: Eric Arturo Delvalle. Official language: Spanish. Official currency: balboa of 100 centésimos. Area: 78 046 sq km (30 134 sq mi). Population (1983): 2 059 000. Capital and main port: Panama City.

Panama Canal A canal across the Isthmus of Panama connecting the Atlantic and Pacific Oceans. Some 82 km (51 mi) long, it was begun by the French Panama Canal Company under Ferdinand de *Lesseps but construction was halted in 1889 by bankruptcy. In 1903 the USA acquired the construction rights from newly independent Panama and the canal was opened in 1914. By the 1903 treaty the USA acquired sovereignty in perpetuity over the **Panama Canal Zone**, a region extending 5 km (3 mi) on either side of the canal. In return Panama received $10 million and an annuity. In 1978 two treaties provided for Panamanian sovereignty over the canal and the Zone by 2000 and for their neutrality and in 1979 Panama assumed territorial jurisdiction over the former Canal Zone. Area: 1676 sq km (647 sq mi).

Panama City 5 58N 79 31W The capital of Panama, situated in the centre of the country near the Pacific end of the Panama Canal. Founded by the Spanish in 1519 on the site of an Indian fishing village, it was destroyed by Henry Morgan and his pirates in 1671 and rebuilt two years later 8 km (5 mi) to the SW. It became capital of the newly independent Panama in 1904 and has expanded considerably since the opening of the Canal in 1914. The University of Panama was founded in 1935 and that of Santa Maria de la Antigua in 1965. Population (1980 est): 467 000.

Pan-American Highway A system of highways connecting North and South America. When completed it will consist of about 26 000 km (16 150 mi) of roadway. First proposed as a single route, it is now a whole network of roads. Between Texas and Panama it is called the Inter-American Highway. The sections through the Central American states were built with US aid, while Mexico financed and built its own section. It will eventually connect with roads leading to Santiago, Buenos Aires, Montevideo, and Rio de Janeiro.

Panathenaea In Greek religion, an annual Athenian summer festival consisting of rites, sacrifices, games, and contests in honour of *Athena. Its central feature, a procession up to the Parthenon with the goddess' new robe, is portrayed on the temple frieze.

Panay An island in the central Philippines, in the Visayan Islands. Mountainous in the W, its central fertile plain produces rice, maize, and sugar. It also has timber, fishing, and copper and coalmining industries. Area: 12 287 sq km (4744 sq mi). Population (1980): 2 595 314. Chief town: Iloilo.

Panchen Lama In *Tibetan Buddhism, the title of the chief abbot of Tashilhunpo monastery at Zhikatse, ranking second to the *Dalai Lama. He is said to be a reincarnation of Amitabha, the Buddha of Infinite Light. The present Panchen Lama was enthroned in 1952 at Tashilhunpo, where he apparently still resides despite the Communist Chinese occupation of Tibet and the exile of the Dalai Lama.

pancreas A gland, about 15 cm long, situated in the abdomen behind the stomach (see Plate IV). When food passes into the intestine the pancreas secretes several digestive enzymes that drain into the intestine through the pancreatic duct. In addition, small clusters of cells (called islets of Langerhans) scattered throughout the pancreas secrete the hormones *insulin and *glucagon, which control blood-sugar levels.

panda A bearlike mammal belonging to the family *Procyonidae* (raccoons, kinkajous, etc.). The giant panda (*Ailuropoda melanoleuca*) is very rare; it lives in the cold bamboo forests of central China, feeding on young bamboo shoots. Giant pandas are up to 1.6 m long, weigh 75–100 kg, and have bold black and white markings.
The red panda (*Ailurus fulgens*), also called the lesser panda, lives in the forests of the Himalayas and W China. 80–110 cm long including the bushy tail (30–50 cm), it is red-brown with black markings on its white face. Red pandas live in trees and feed on the ground at twilight on roots, nuts, lichens, and bamboo shoots.

Pandanus. See screw pine.

Pandarus In Greek legend, a Trojan archer who wounded the Greek commander Menelaus and was killed by Diomedes. In the medieval story concerning Troilus and Cressida he is the lovers' go-between.

Pandit, Vijaya Lakshmi (1900–) Indian diplomat; sister of Jawaharlal *Nehru. As a member of *Gandhi's movement of noncooperation with the British she was imprisoned. Following independence she was ambassador to the Soviet Union (1947–49) and to the USA (1949–51); she then became president of the UN General Assembly (1953–54) and high commissioner to the UK (1955–61).

Pandora In Greek mythology, the first woman, fashioned by *Hephaestus and invented by Zeus as his revenge on *Prometheus, who had stolen fire from heaven. She married Epimethus, brother of Prometheus. Her dowry was a box, which, when opened, released all the varieties of evil and retained only hope.

pangolin An armoured mammal belonging to the genus *Manis* and order *Pholidota* (7 species), of Africa and S Asia, also called scaly anteater. 30–80 cm long with long prehensile tails, pangolins are covered on their backs with overlapping horny scales. Toothless, with a long sticky tongue and strong claws, they sleep in deep burrows, emerging at night to feed on ants and termites. They can walk on their hind legs, climb trees, and curl up into a tight ball if attacked.

PANDA *The elongated wrist bone of the giant panda acts like a thumb, enabling it to manipulate bamboo shoots.*

Pan Gu (*or* P'an Ku) In Chinese Taoist mythology, the first man. His knowledge of *yin and yang enabled him to shape the world.

Pan Gu (*or* P'an Ku; 32–92 AD) Chinese historian. He expanded the work of *Si-ma Qian to cover the history of the Han dynasty until his own time. His great work *The History of the Former Han* started the Chinese tradition of compiling dynastic histories.

panic grass An annual or perennial *grass of the genus *Panicum* (500 species), mostly of the tropics and subtropics. The flowering stems, up to 80 cm high, have many branches, each bearing several slender-stalked spikelets (flower clusters). Some species are cultivated for their grain (see millet).

Panini (6th or 5th century BC) Indian grammarian. Panini's analysis of Sanskrit, the *Ashtadhyayi*, is one of the earliest studies of a language and the most comprehensive grammatical work to appear before the 19th century. Although intended to regulate the use of Sanskrit rather than to teach it, the *Ashtadhyayi* is still used in some Brahman schools.

Pankhurst, Emmeline (1858–1928) British suffragette, who founded, in Manchester, the Women's Social and

Political Union (1903). She was imprisoned several times for destroying property, undergoing hunger strikes and forcible feeding. During World War I, she abandoned her militancy and encouraged the industrial recruitment of women. Her daughters **Dame Christabel Pankhurst** (1880-1958) and **Sylvia Pankhurst** (1882-1960) were also suffragettes. *See* women's movement.

P'an Ku. *See* Pan Gu.

panorama A narrative scene or landscape painted on a large canvas, which was either hung up around the walls of a circular room or slowly unrolled before an audience. The first panorama was produced by the Scottish painter Robert Barker (1739-1806) in 1788. An antecedent of films, panoramas provided a popular form of entertainment as well as fulfilling an educational function in the 19th century.

panpipes (*or* syrinx) An ancient musical instrument consisting of a row of small graduated pipes bound together. It is played by blowing across the holes. According to Greek legend it was invented by the deity Pan, who pursued the nymph Syrinx. When she was changed into a reed by Apollo, Pan made the instrument from the reed stem.

pansy A popular annual or perennial garden plant that is a hybrid of the wild pansy (*Viola tricolor*), developed in the early 19th century. There are now many varieties, up to 20 cm high, with leafy stems and (usually) yellow, orange, purple, brown, or white flowers, up to 5 cm across. The wild pansy, or heartsease, found throughout Eurasia, has small flowers coloured purple, yellow, and white. Family: *Violaceae*. *See also* violet.

Pantelleria Island (ancient name: Cossyra) A volcanic island in Italy, in the Mediterranean Sea. Produce includes wine and raisins. Area: 83 sq km (32 sq mi). Population (1981 est): 7860. Chief town: Pantelleria.

pantheism Any belief or doctrine presenting the natural world, including man, as part of the divine. Pantheism is a predominant tendency in Hinduism but is frowned on by orthodox Christianity. *Spinoza's phrase equating God and Nature (*Deus sive natura*) was an influential formulation of the idea, which enjoyed some currency among 19th-century philosophers. The Romantic poets, particularly *Wordsworth, were also attracted to pantheism.

Pantheon 1. A temple dedicated to the worship of many gods. The most famous is that in Rome begun in 27 BC but rebuilt about 118 AD under Emperor Hadrian. It is a daring circular design built in concrete and topped by a huge concrete dome 43 m (142 ft) wide. In 609 AD it became the Church of Sta Maria Rotonda. 2. A building honouring the famous. The best known is that in Paris designed by *Soufflot in 1759.

panther A colour variety of leopard that has a great deal of black pigmentation, which sometimes extends to the tongue and gums. Panthers can occur among a litter of normally spotted leopards.

pantomime A British form of dramatic entertainment for children, traditionally performed at Christmas. Although the word also refers to several other distinct dramatic forms, such as mime plays, dumbshows, and 18th-century ballets on mythological themes, children's pantomime developed during the 19th century from the harlequinade (*see* Harlequin). It includes popular songs, slapstick comedy, and frequently acrobatics and other acts of skill. Pantomimes are based on fairy tales about such well-known characters as Cinderella and Aladdin. The principal boy is traditionally played by a girl, and the dame, a comic old woman, by a man.

panzer A mechanized division of the German army. The term panzer, meaning a coat of armour, has become widely used to denote armoured forces, tanks, self-propelled artillery, and armoured troop carriers.

papacy The office of the pope as temporal head of the Roman Catholic Church. Popes claim to be elected in direct line from St *Peter, to whom Christ deputed his authority on earth (Matthew 16.18-19) and who became the first bishop of Rome. The keys symbolizing this authority are still a papal emblem. The bishop of Rome, however, was not immediately recognized as pre-eminent and the title Pope was only formally reserved for him in 1073. In W Europe the papacy's political influence spread rapidly after 600 and Pope Leo III's coronation of *Charlemagne (800) marked the beginning of a relationship between the papacy and Holy Roman Empire that dominated Europe until the Reformation. In the East the papacy's attempt to assert its authority by excommunicating the Patriarch of Constantinople brought about the schism between the Roman Catholic and Orthodox Churches (1054; *see also* Filioque). Lesser and temporary schisms were caused by the election of antipopes, notably during the 14th century, when, after the popes had been in exile in Avignon (1309-77; *see* Avignon papacy), there was a period called the *Great Schism (1378-1417) during which there were rival *popes in France and Rome. The Reformation seriously weakened the papacy's spiritual and temporal power, although papal territories in Italy remained under the pope's sovereignty. During the unification of Italy, these *papal states were appropriated (1870) and the pope's authority over the Vatican City was only formally acknowledged by the Italian state in the Lateran Treaty (1929). In 1870 the promulgation of the doctrine of papal infallibility caused further schism (*see* Old Catholics). In the 20th century the papacy has resolutely opposed communism and has participated tentatively in the ecumenical movement to heal earlier schisms.

Papadopoulos, George (1919-) Greek colonel, who led the military regime that seized power in Greece in 1967. He ruled by decree with the official title of prime minister, and latterly president, until overthrown by a military revolt in 1973.

papain A protein-digesting enzyme found in the fruit of the *papaw tree (*Carica papaya*). It is used in biochemical research and as a meat tenderizer.

papal states The central Italian states under papal sovereignty between 756, when *Pepin the Short presented Ravenna to Pope Stephen II (reigned 752-57), and 1870. They included parts of Emilia-Romagna, Marche, Umbria, and Lazio. They were a major obstacle to the 19th-century movement for Italian unification (*see* Risorgimento) but, despite papal opposition, were finally annexed in 1870. The popes refused to recognize their loss of temporal power until the *Lateran Treaty (1929) established the Vatican City as an independent papal state.

papaw (*or* papaya) A small tropical American tree, *Carica papaya*, cultivated throughout the tropics. About 7.5 m tall, it has lobed toothed leaves crowded at the tips of the branches and fragrant creamy-white flowers. The yellowish fruit resembles an elongated melon: its succulent pinkish or orange flesh encloses a mass of seeds. The fruits are eaten fresh, boiled, and in preserves or pickles and are a commercial source of the enzyme papain. Family: *Caricaceae*.

Papeete 17 32S 149 34W The capital of French Polynesia, in NW Tahiti. A tourist centre, it is a stop on many Pacific routes. Population (1983): 62 735.

Papen, Franz von (1879-1969) German statesman and diplomat; chancellor (1932). A Catholic Centre Party politician with extreme right-wing views, he resigned the chancellorship after six months because of lack of cabinet support for his policies and then persuaded Hindenburg to appoint Hitler as chancellor (1933). Papen was ambassador to Austria (1934-38) and then to Turkey (1939-44). He was found not guilty at the Nuremberg war trials and only served three years of an eight-year prison sentence imposed by a German court.

paper A substance in sheet form made from the pulped cellulose fibres of wood, grass, cotton, etc., and used for

PAPER *The Fourdrinier paper-making machine is one of the longest machines in use.*

writing and printing on, wrapping, cleaning, etc. The Chinese invented paper (c. 2nd century BC) and the Arabs learnt the secret in 768 AD from Chinese prisoners of war at Samarkand. From Arab manufacture in the Middle East and Spain, paper spread to Byzantium (mid-11th century) and thence all over Europe. Foreign competition meant a slow start to British paper making, the first successful mill being set up about 1589.

All early paper was handmade: shallow wooden frames (moulds) with wire mesh bases (*see also* watermark) were dipped into vats of pulp and shaken until the pulp fibres felted together. The resulting sheets were dried, pressed, and, if necessary, sized (dipped in a gelatinous solution to render the surface less permeable). A machine for making paper in a continuous roll (or web) was not invented until 1798, in France. Brought to England in 1803 by Henry Fourdrinier (1766–1854), this machine, of which variants are still in use, picked up the pulp (about 99% water) on a travelling wire mesh and shook it until the fibres were interlaced and the water drained off, before passing it through pressing and drying rollers.

The **pulp** for papermaking is obtained chiefly from wood, but also from esparto grass, rags, and increasingly from recycled wastepaper. Wood pulp may be produced by direct grinding of whole logs, as in making newsprint. For whiter higher quality paper, the wood undergoes a more complex chemical treatment. Esparto grass and rags are used for strong durable high-quality paper, such as bank notes and legal documents. Recycled wastepaper often requires careful sorting and de-inking and is usually mixed with fresh wood pulp.

paper mulberry A shrub or small tree, *Broussonetia papyrifera*, native to E Asia and Polynesia but planted elsewhere as an ornamental, especially in the USA. Up to 15 m tall, it has oval pointed leaves, flowers in catkins, and round rough fruits, 2.5 cm across. Its bark is used in paper making and to produce tapa cloth in Polynesia. The bast fibres form the basis of coarse fabrics. Family: *Moraceae*.

papilionid butterfly A butterfly belonging to the widely distributed mainly tropical family *Papilionidae* (about 800 species). Papilionids comprise the *swallowtail butterflies, with tail-like projections on the hindwings, and the parnassians, which are mainly alpine.

papilloma A harmless tumour that grows from the surface of the skin or from the lining of a hollow organ, for example the bladder, womb, or lungs. *Warts and *polyps are types of papilloma. If they bleed or undergo any other change they are best treated by removal.

papillon A breed of toy dog, possibly of Spanish origin, associated with such illustrious owners as Mme de Pompadour and Marie Antoinette. Its name is derived from its large forward-facing ears, which resemble the wings of a butterfly (French word: *papillon*). The tail is held over the back and the long fine coat is white with coloured patches. Height: 20–28 cm.

Pappus of Alexandria (3rd century BC) Greek mathematician, who wrote an encyclopedia consisting of eight volumes, much of which survives. It summarized Greek mathematics, of which virtually all our knowledge is due to Pappus.

paprika. *See* Capsicum.

Papua New Guinea, State of A country in the Pacific Ocean, E of Indonesia. It consists of the E part of *New Guinea and several islands, including the Bismarck Archipelago (including New Britain and New Ireland), the N part of the Solomon Islands (including Bougainville), and the Admiralty Islands. Most of the population are Melanesians. *Economy*: subsistence agriculture and the growing of cash crops, such as coconuts, cocoa, coffee, and rubber, are the chief occupations. Livestock rearing is being developed and the country's dense rain forest provides timber. The chief mineral resource and export is copper, the main source being on the island of Bougainville. Other exports include gold, coffee, cocoa, timber, and copra. *History*: the SE part of the island of New Guinea was annexed by Queensland in 1883, becoming a British colony in 1888, known as the Territory of Papua. The NE part was formerly a German territory and came under Australian rule in 1914 as the Trust Territory of New Guinea. In 1921 the two territories including their islands were merged, later becoming a UN Trusteeship under Australia. It was renamed Papua New Guinea in 1971, achieved self-government in 1973, and became fully independent in 1975. Prime minister: Paias Wingti. Official language: English; pidgin is widely spoken. Official currency: kina of 100 toea. Area: 462 840 sq km (178 656 sq mi). Population (1980 est): 3 006 799. Capital and main port: Port Moresby.

papyrus An aquatic reedlike plant, *Cyperus papyrus*, up to 3 m tall, originally cultivated in the Nile delta of Egypt and now growing wild in parts of Africa and in Syria. It was used by the ancient Egyptians to make paper: the thick triangular stems were split into thin strips, which were pressed together while still wet. It was also used for rope, mats, sails, and shoes, and the pith was a common food. Family: *Cyperaceae*.

parabola The curve, formed by a *conic section, in which the distance from a fixed point (focus) and a fixed line (directrix) are equal. In *Cartesian coordinates a standard form of its equation is $y^2 = 4ax$, for a parabola that is symmetrical about the x-axis and cuts it at the origin (vertex).

Paracel Islands An archipelago of coral islands and reefs in the South China Sea, SE of Hainan Island. They lie above oil deposits and were seized by China from Vietnam in 1974.

Paracelsus (Theophrastus Bombastus von Hohenheim; 1493–1541) Swiss physician, whose radical ideas influenced the development of medicine during the Renaissance. Paracelsus established a reputation for arrogance and aroused controversy by publicly burning the works of *Avicenna and *Galen, denouncing quack remedies, and clashing with the medical establishment. He stressed the importance of chemical compounds in treating disease, refuted the notion that mental illness was caused by demons, and linked goitre with minerals in drinking water.

parachuting The use of a parachute (a fabric canopy) to float down to the ground, usually from an aircraft, either if the aircraft is about to crash, as a way of landing troops in an area, or as a form of sport. Parachutes were used for entertainment long before they were used for safety; the first successful jump was made in 1797 and the first contest held in 1926. In accuracy competitions a contestant uses vents in his parachute to steer himself onto a target area, a red or orange cross with arms 5 m (16 ft) long and 1 m (3 ft) wide. In the middle is a red disc 10 cm (4 in) in diameter. Top-class parachutists land exactly on the disc. *See also* skydiving.

paraffin 1. (*or* kerosene) A mixture of hydrocarbons that boil in the range 150-300°C and have a relative density of 0.78-0.83. It is obtained from crude *oil by distillation and is used as a fuel for domestic heating and for aircraft. 2. *See* alkanes.

paraffin wax A wax obtained during the refining of crude *oil. Fully refined, it is a white tasteless solid (mp 50-60°C) consisting of higher *alkanes; it is extensively used in the manufacture of waxed papers, candles, and polishes (especially microcrystalline wax polishes).

Paraguay, Republic of A landlocked country in the centre of South America. It is divided by the River Paraguay into two zones: an area of fertile plains and hills to the E and the semidesert of the Gran Chaco to the W. The great majority of the population is of mixed Spanish and Guaraní Indian descent. *Economy*: chiefly agricultural, livestock rearing is of particular importance. Meat packing is one of the main industries, and meat was one of the principal exports, especially to Europe, although this has been reduced since the EEC ban on meat imports. Others include cotton, oilseed, and timber. The main crops are cotton, soya beans, cassava, and sugar cane and there are extensive forests, some of them unexploited. Mineral resources are on the whole sparse, but some limestone, salt, and kaolin is produced. Hydroelectricity is being developed, especially for the export of power to neighbouring countries. *History*: explored by the Spanish in the early 16th century, it became a Spanish colony, forming part of the viceroyalty of Peru and later (1776) of the new viceroyalty of Río de la Plata. It became independent of Spain in 1811, and in 1814 José Gaspar Rodríguez de Francia (1766-1840) was elected dictator, becoming dictator for life in 1817. From 1844 to 1870 Paraguay was ruled by the López family. The population suffered great losses in the War of the *Triple Alliance (1865-70) against Brazil, Argentina, and Uruguay and again in the *Chaco War (1932-35) with Bolivia. A period of political unrest was ended in 1954, when Gen Alfredo Stroessner (1912-) seized power and became president. Paraguay is a member of the OAS and LAFTA. Official language: Spanish; the majority speak Guaraní. Official currency: guaraní of 100 céntimos. Area: 406 752 sq km (157 042 sq mi). Population (1983 est): 3 526 000. Capital and main (river) port: Asunción.

Paraguay, River (Portuguese name: Rio Paraguai) A river in South America. Rising in Brazil in Mato Grosso state, it flows generally S to join the Río Paraná in SW Paraguay. It is an important means of transport and communications, especially in Paraguay. Length: about 2400 km (1500 mi).

Paraguayan War. *See* Triple Alliance, War of the.

parakeet A small seed-eating *parrot characterized by a long tapering tail and a predominantly green plumage and found especially in SE Asia and Australia. Large flocks may damage crops; brightly coloured species are popular as cagebirds. *See also* budgerigar; rosella.

paralysis Failure of a muscle or a group of muscles to work. This is most commonly caused by damage to the nerve (and its connections) supplying the muscle, as resulting from injury or infection (*see* poliomyelitis), but it may also be due to failure of the nerve impulse to be transmitted to the muscle (as in myasthenia gravis) or by wasting of the muscle (as in *muscular dystrophy). Paralysis is seen most commonly in western countries following a *stroke: this causes damage to the part of the brain that controls

movement and commonly results in **hemiplegia**, i.e. one half of the body and face becomes paralysed. *Multiple sclerosis also causes paralysis. **Paraplegia** (paralysed legs) results from injury to the spinal cord. **Quadriplegia** (paralysed legs and arms) results when the spinal cord is damaged close to the brain.

paramagnetism A form of *magnetism occurring in materials that when placed in a *magnetic field have an internal field stronger than that outside. This is caused by the presence in atoms or molecules of electrons with unpaired spins. The atom or molecule therefore acts like a tiny magnet (*see* ferromagnetism). In the presence of an external magnetic field these microscopic magnets tend to align with the field, reinforcing it. The effect is destroyed by random thermal motion and, except at low temperatures and high field strengths, the *permeability (a measure of the extent of alignment) is inversely proportional to the temperature.

Paramaribo 5 52N 55 14W The capital and main port of Suriname, near the N coast on the River Suriname. Founded by the French in 1540, it was later under English and then Dutch rule. It has developed considerably since World War II. The University of Suriname was founded in 1968. Population (1980 est): 67 718.

Paramecium A genus of microscopic single-celled animals (⎕Protozoa), called slipper animalcules, found in fresh water. They are slipper-shaped, 0.1-0.3 mm long, and covered with cilia, which are used for swimming and to waft bacteria and small protozoans into the gullet. They reproduce asexually by binary *fission and sexually by *conjugation. Class: *Ciliata.

Paraná 31 45S 60 30W A city in E Argentina, on the Río Paraná. It is an outlet for agricultural produce (especially cattle, sheep, and grain). Notable buildings include the Cathedral of Paraná (1883). Population (1980): 160 000.

Paraná, Rio (Spanish name: Río Paraná) A river in South America. Formed by the confluence of the Rio Grande and Rio Paranaíba in SE central Brazil, it flows generally S for 2900 km (1800 mi) to join the River Uruguay and form the Río de la Plata. The Itaipu Dam, the world's largest dam, which is sited at Foz do Iguaçu near the Paraguayan border, was opened in 1982; the hydroelectric power station is expected to be in full operation by 1989, with a capacity of 12.6 million kW. The cost is being shared by Brazil and Paraguay.

paranoia A mental disorder in which the patient is governed by a rigid system of irrational beliefs (delusions). The sufferer may believe that he is being persecuted by others, or betrayed, or that he is overwhelmingly important. The condition, which can result from *schizophrenia, *alcoholism, or *manic-depressive psychosis, is treated according to the cause.

paraplegia. *See* paralysis.

Paraquat ($C_9H_{20}N_2(SO_4)_2$) The trade name for a yellow water-soluble solid that is used as a weedkiller. It is highly toxic and some deaths have resulted from swallowing quantities in excess of one gram. It concentrates in the lungs and also causes kidney damage. Treatment for Paraquat poisoning, by *activated charcoal or some other absorbing material, is only effective if carried out immediately.

parasite An organism living in or on another organism of a different species (called the host), from which it obtains food and protection: the relationship may or may not be harmful to the host. A facultative parasite is one that becomes parasitic only under certain conditions, while an obligate parasite must always live parasitically. Many parasites have complex life cycles, with one or more intermediate hosts (of different species) supporting the parasite in the immature stages of its development. The study of parasites—**parasitology**—is of great importance in medicine since many parasites either cause or transmit disease. Disease-causing parasites include bacteria and other microorganisms (*see* infection) and tapeworms; mites, ticks, and fleas are examples of external parasites that transmit disease. Many plants are either partly or completely parasitic, usually on other plants. Mistletoe is a partial parasite.

parasol mushroom An edible mushroom, *Lepiota procera*, found in clearings and around the edges of deciduous woods. Its cap, 10–20 cm in diameter, is greyish brown with darker scales. The scales form rings on the stem, which has a double collar just below the cap.

parathyroid glands Two pairs of small endocrine glands lying immediately behind the thyroid gland. These glands secrete **parathyroid hormone** in response to a reduction in the level of calcium in the blood. This hormone causes release of calcium from the bones and its transfer to the blood. Deficiency of parathyroid hormone (and therefore lack of calcium in the blood) results in muscle spasms and cramps (tetany).

paratyphoid fever Infection of the digestive tract caused by the bacterium *Salmonella paratyphi*. It is a mild form of *typhoid fever and can be treated by antibiotic drugs..

parchment Animal skin, usually of the goat, sheep, or calf, treated for writing on but untanned. It derives its name from Pergamum, where in the 2nd century BC the development of improved methods of cleaning, stretching, and scraping skins enabled them to have writing on both sides. It was used for manuscripts and early bound books. More delicate skin from young animals is called vellum. Parchment now often describes high-grade paper manufactured from wood pulp and rag, treated with a special finish. *See also* leather.

parchment worm An *annelid worm, belonging to the genus *Chaetopterus*, that lives in a U-shaped tube made of parchment-like material on muddy shores of the Atlantic and Pacific Oceans. Up to 25 cm long, the worm draws in a current of water by beating its paddle-shaped appendages, trapping food particles in a bag of mucus. Parchment worms are strongly luminescent. Class: *Polychaeta*.

Pardubice (German name: Pardubitz) 50 03N 15 45E A town in Czechoslovakia, in E Bohemia on the River Elbe. It has an architecturally distinguished square containing a 16th-century gothic castle and the Green Gate (1507). Population (1983): 93 000.

Paré, Ambroise (1510–90) French surgeon and one of the fathers of modern surgery. As barber-surgeon to the army, Paré discarded the practice of treating wounds with boiling oil and hot irons in favour of cleansing, the use of ointments, and surgery to tie off major arteries.

parenchyma The general packing tissue of plants, consisting of simple undifferentiated cells. In young stems, parenchyma encloses the vascular (conducting) tissue and provides support for the plant.

Pareto, Vilfredo (1848–1932) Italian economist and sociologist. Pareto's early work in economics culminated in Pareto's Law, which held that the distribution of incomes could be defined by a mathematical formula. His later sociological work *The Mind and Society* (1916) attacked political liberalism while supporting the free market economy. He is also known for his theory on the rise and fall of governing elites.

Paris 48 52N 2 18E The capital of France and a department of the Paris Region, situated in the N of the country on the River Seine. One of Europe's greatest cities, Paris dominates France as the administrative, commercial, and cultural centre. It is also an important industrial base, and many international organizations, including UNESCO, have their headquarters here. The city is in turn dominated by its river, which contributes to the division of Paris into several distinct districts, each with its own characteristics. At the heart of the city, the Île de la Cité contains the cathedral of *Notre-Dame, the Palais de Justice, and the 13th-century Sainte Chapelle. On the Left Bank lie Montparnasse and the

PARIS   *The Arc de Triomphe seen from the Champs Elysées—the most famous of Paris's wide tree-lined boulevards.*

Latin Quarter, which is known for its associations with writers and artists and still contains some faculties of the university of the Sorbonne (founded in the 12th century) although much of it has now been moved to other sites. On the Right Bank stands the Palais du Louvre, one of the world's most important museums. Further W is a series of radiating boulevards meeting at the Place Charles de Gaulle (formerly Place de l'Étoile), which were laid out by Baron *Haussmann in the 19th century. The Champs Élysées runs from the *Arc de Triomphe at the centre of the Place Charles de Gaulle to the Place de la Concorde. Further N lies Montmartre (the artists' colony of Paris until the migration to Montparnasse in the 1920s), dominated by the Basilica of the Sacré Coeur (1919). The tunnels beneath Montmartre, created by quarrying, are now a major problem, causing subsidence and structural damage to buildings. To the S of the Seine, the *Eiffel Tower, built for an exhibition in 1898, is another reminder of the 19th century. *History*: the earliest known settlement was on the Île de la Cité in Roman times. According to legend, St Denis became the first bishop in the 3rd century AD and Ste Geneviève saved the city from sacking by German tribes in the 5th century. In the 6th century Clovis made it the capital of his Frankish kingdom but it later suffered attacks from Vikings. It regained importance as the capital under the *Capetians and from the 13th century its independence as a city increased. Since the storming of the Bastille (1789), heralding the beginning of the French Revolution, it has been the scene of many revolts, such as the *July Revolution and the *Revolution of 1848; the most recent disturbance was in May, 1968. Occupied by the Germans in World War II, it was liberated by the Allies in 1944. Population (1982): 2 176 243.

Paris In Greek legend, a son of *Priam and Hecuba. He

was brought up as a shepherd on Mount Ida. His abduction of *Helen with the help of Aphrodite caused the *Trojan War, during which he killed Achilles and was himself killed by Philoctetes. *See also* Eris.

Paris, Matthew. *See* Matthew Paris.

Paris, Treaties of 1. (1763) The treaty that ended the *Seven Years' War. France ceded its North American territories E of the Mississippi River to Britain and Louisiana to Spain, from which Britain acquired Florida. Britain also gained Minorca, Senegal, Grenada, St Vincent, Dominica, and Tobago. 2. (1783) The treaty that ended the *American Revolution. US independence was recognized and Britain ceded Florida to Spain. 3. (1814) The peace between France and the victorious allies (Prussia, Russia, Austria, Britain, Sweden, and Portugal) that confirmed Napoleon's abdication and limited France to its 1792 boundaries. 4. (1815) The peace following Napoleon's final defeat at Waterloo that reduced France to its 1789 boundaries. 5. (1856) The peace that ended the *Crimean War. Russia guaranteed the neutrality of the Black Sea and ceded S Bessarabia to Moldavia.

Paris Peace Conference (1919-20) A conference of representatives of the Allied and Associated Powers held after World War I. Proceedings were dominated by the USA (Woodrow Wilson), France (Clemenceau), the UK (Lloyd George), and Italy (Orlando). Five treaties arose from the conference: *Versailles with Germany (1919); Saint-Germain with Austria (1920); Neuilly with Bulgaria (1919); Trianon with Hungary (1920); and Sèvres with Turkey (1920). In addition the conference ratified the Covenant of the *League of Nations.

parity The concept of left- and right-handedness. According to the law of conservation of parity, no fundamental distinction exists between left and right and the laws of physics apply equally to left- and right-handed systems. In 1957 this principle was shown to be violated in *weak interactions between certain elementary particles (*see* particle physics). For example, when a neutron decays the electron produced is always left-polarized (i.e. spins in a direction opposite to that of its motion), whereas if parity was conserved there would be equal numbers of left- and right-polarized electrons. This lack of parity provides a fundamental distinction between left and right. The parity of elementary particles is expressed as a *quantum number.

Park, Mungo (1771-c. 1806) Scottish explorer. A surgeon, he made two explorations of the River Niger. In 1795-96 he ascended the Niger from the mouth of the River Gambia, crossed the Sénégal Basin, and was imprisoned by Arabs. Escaping, he eventually returned to Pisania (now Karantaba, The Gambia). His *Travels in the Interior Districts of Africa* (1797) related his adventures. In 1805, under government patronage and with 40 companions, he resumed his exploration. The expedition was attacked by Africans and Park died.

Park Chung Hee (1917-79) South Korean statesman and general; president from 1963 until his murder in 1979. He served in the Japanese army in World War II and then in the South Korean army. He led the coup that established a military regime in 1961, becoming president two years later. In 1972 he declared martial law and assumed quasi-dictatorial powers.

Parker, Charlie (Christopher) (1920-55) US Black jazz saxophonist and composer, known as "Bird" or "Yardbird." With Dizzy *Gillespie he originated the *bop style of jazz and appeared with a number of bands. In the 1950s he made recordings with a band containing strings and wind and was regarded as one of the greatest of all jazz musicians.

Parker, Dorothy Rothschild (1893-1967) US humorous writer. Famous as a wit, she established her reputation while working as drama critic for *Vanity Fair* and the *New Yorker* (1927-33). She is best known for her short stories and

sketches, collected in *Here Lies* (1939), but she also wrote poems, collected in *Not So Deep As a Well* (1936), plays, and filmscripts.

Parker, Matthew (1504-75) Anglican churchman. A moderate Protestant reformer, he was deprived of his preferments under Queen Mary. As Archbishop of Canterbury (1559-75) under Elizabeth I, he maintained a strongly independent Anglican position between the two extremes of Roman Catholicism and Puritanism and revised the Thirty-Nine Articles of Anglican doctrine.

Parkes 33 10S 148 13E A market town in Australia, in New South Wales in the Lachlan River Valley. A 210-ft (64-m) dish radiotelescope, one of the largest in the world, is nearby. Population (1981): 9047.

Parkes, Sir Henry (1815-96) Australian statesman; prime minister of New South Wales (1872-75, 1877, 1878-83, 1887-89, 1889-91). Born in England, he emigrated to Australia in 1839. He campaigned (1849-52) against the British transportation of convicts to Australia and as prime minister worked for the federation of the Australian states and for compulsory free education.

Parkinson, (Cyril) Northcote (1909-) British author, historian, and journalist. While professor of history at the University of Malaya (1950-58), he wrote his well-known *Parkinson's Law* (1958), a study of business administration containing the aphorisms that work expands to fill the time allotted to it and that subordinates multiply at a fixed rate regardless of the amount of work produced. His other books include *Britain in the Far East* (1955), *The Law and the Profits* (1960), and *Big Business* (1974).

parkinsonism (*or* Parkinson's disease) A chronic disease affecting the part of the brain controlling voluntary movement, first described in 1817 by a British physician, James Parkinson (1755-1824). Sometimes the disease may result from infection, side effects of drugs, or injury, but usually no cause is apparent. The symptoms are tremor of the hands and mouth, stiffness, and difficulty in initiating movements. It occurs most commonly in older people and is treated with drugs, including *L-dopa, or surgery.

Parkman, Francis (1823-93) US historian. *The Oregon Trail* (1849) records an adventurous expedition among the American Indians. Thenceforth he suffered from illness and blindness but completed a monumental colonial history of *France and England in North America* (9 vols, 1851-92). His works on Canadian history include *History of the Conspiracy of Pontiac* (1851).

parlement The supreme court of France until the French Revolution. The parlement of Paris developed in the 12th century out of the king's court. Membership was at first elective but by the 14th century seats could be bought and in 1614 became hereditable with the introduction of the *paulette* (annual right), which secured a seat by payment of an annual fee. From its duty, and right of refusal, to register royal edicts the parlement derived considerable political power and by the 17th century had become a bastion of reaction. It impeded government attempts to put its own house in order and in 1792, in the wake of the French Revolution, the parlement of Paris, together with its less influential provincial counterparts, was abolished.

parliament The legislative assembly of a country. In the UK parliament is the supreme legislature; it consists of the sovereign, the House of Lords, and the House of Commons; its seat is the *Palace of Westminster. Parliament developed in the 13th century from the *Curia Regis (King's Court), in which the monarch consulted with his barons. In 1213, 1254, and 1258 representatives of the shires were also summoned to attend parliament and in 1265 the parliament summoned by Simon de *Montfort included borough representatives—the origins of the House of Commons. By the reign of Edward III (1327-77) Lords and Commons, meeting separately, were recognized constituents of government.

Parliament's power declined in the later middle ages but Thomas Cromwell's use of parliament in legislating the breach with Rome (see Reformation) gave it a new self-consciousness. Increasingly assertive under Elizabeth I (1559–1603), its conflict with James I and Charles I over the extent to which the Crown was answerable to parliament led to the Civil War (1642–51) and the establishment of republican government under Oliver Cromwell. Following the Restoration of the monarchy in 1660, the attempts of James II to rule arbitrarily led to the Glorious Revolution (1688), which achieved the beginning of parliamentary ascendancy over the Crown. The 18th century saw the emergence of party politics (see Whigs; Tories) and of a *prime minister and the development of *cabinet government. In the 19th century the *Reform Acts of 1832, 1867, and 1884 greatly reduced the influence of the House of Lords, which lost its veto power by the Parliament Act (1911).

The House of Lords has over 1000 members: there are 26 bishops, over 800 hereditary peers, and over 200 life peers (see peerage). Its speaker is the Lord Chancellor. The House of Commons has (1985) 650 members of parliament (MPs), each representing a geographical constituency, and is regulated by the *Speaker of the House of Commons. Parliamentary legislation is introduced in the form of private or public bills. Private bills originate outside parliament, for example with a local authority, which may wish to acquire certain powers. Public bills are sponsored by the government or a private member and may be introduced in either house. After a first reading a bill will be printed and then debated in a second reading. It is then referred to a committee by which it may be amended. (A private bill, when opposed, is considered by a committee, which hears both sides of the case.) Its amendments are considered by the whole house (in proceedings known as the report stage) and it then receives a third reading after which it is sent to the other house, where it goes through a similar procedure. The Lords may not veto a finance bill for longer than a month and may veto other public bills (private bills rarely cause controversy after the first hearing) for only one session. After passing both houses the bill receives the royal assent and becomes an Act of Parliament. Broadcasting of parliament began in 1978 and televising of the Lords in 1986.

parliamentary commissioner for administration. See ombudsman.

Parma 44 48N 10 19E A city in N Italy, in Emilia-Romagna. Dating from Roman times, it became an important cultural centre in the middle ages. Its university was established in 1222 and it has a romanesque cathedral and a 16th-century palace, damaged in 1944 during World War II. The centre of an agricultural district, Parma's industries include the manufacture of Parmesan cheese. Population (1980 est): 175 932.

Parmenides (c. 510–c. 450 BC) Greek philosopher, born at Elea (S Italy). According to Parmenides, things either are or are not. Only "being" is real; "not-being" is illusory. For change to occur "being" must become "not-being," which is absurd. Therefore change does not occur. But our senses indicate that change does occur: therefore our senses are misleading, and "being," as apprehended by reason, is the only reality. Parmenides described "being" as finite, spherical, timeless, undifferentiated, and indivisible. His doctrines influenced *Plato. See also Heraclitus; Zeno of Elea.

Parmigianino (Girolamo Francesco Maria Mazzola; 1503–40) Italian painter, born in Parma (hence his nickname). After painting frescoes in S Giovanni Evangelista, Parma, he moved to Rome (1524) but was forced to flee to Bologna during the sack of Rome (1527). His mannerism is evident in the Madonna with the Long Neck (Palazzo Pitti, Florence). His portraits include Self-Portrait in a Convex Mirror (Kunsthistorisches Museum, Vienna).

Parnassians A group of French poets in the mid-19th century who reacted against the subjectivism of the Romantics and whose poetry was characterized by objective restraint and technical precision. They were led by *Leconte de Lisle, whose disciples included Theodore de *Banville, *Sully-Prudhomme, and J.-M. de Hérédia (1842–1905).

Parnassus, Mount (Modern Greek name: Parnassós) 38 32N 22 41E A mountain in S central Greece, held in ancient times as sacred to the god Apollo and the Muses. Height: 2457 m (8061 ft).

Parnell, Charles Stewart (1846–91) Irish politician, who in 1880 became the leader of the *Home Rule party in the British House of Commons. Parnell, an MP from 1875, reconciled constitutional and radical forces and enjoyed widespread popular support in Ireland. He allied his party with the Liberals in 1886, when Gladstone introduced the Home Rule bill. Parnell remained a dominant political figure until 1890, when he was repudiated by his party and by public opinion after being cited in a divorce suit brought against Katherine *O'Shea, whom he then married.

Páros A Greek island in the S Aegean Sea, in the Cyclades. Marble has been quarried here for sculpture since ancient times. Area: 195 sq km (75 sq mi). Population (1981 est): 7881.

parquetry The inlaying of geometrically shaped pieces of wood into the plane surfaces of furniture, floors, staircases, etc. The word is often now used to describe geometric *marquetry, particularly as used on 17th- and 18th-century furniture.

Parr, Catherine (1512–48) The sixth wife (1543–47) of Henry VIII of England. She was noted for her kindness to her three stepchildren. After Henry's death, she married (1547) Thomas, Baron Seymour of Sudeley (d. 1549).

Parramatta 33 10S 148 13E A city in Australia, in New South Wales on the Parramatta River comprising a suburb of Sydney. Founded in 1788, it is the second oldest European settlement in Australia, containing several historic buildings. These include Elizabeth Farm House (1793), the nation's oldest existing farmhouse.

parrot A bird belonging to the family (Psittacidae; 300 species) occurring worldwide in warm regions. 10–100 cm long, parrots have a compact body, a short neck, and strong rounded wings suited for fast flight over short distances. The plumage is typically brightly coloured and the short stout hooked bill is used to open nuts and to feed on fruits and seeds. Most are arboreal and excellent climbers, having clawed feet with rough scaly toes. They are gregarious and have a harsh screaming voice. Order: Psittaciformes. See also cockatoo; kakapo; kea; lory; lovebird; macaw; parakeet.

parrot fish A fish, also called parrot wrasse, belonging to the family Scaridae found among tropical reefs. Up to 1.2 m long, it has a deep often brilliantly coloured body and the teeth are fused to form a hard beak, which is used to feed on coral, molluscs, and seaweed. Order: Perciformes.

Parry, Sir Hubert (1848–1918) British composer. He composed many operatic, orchestral, choral, chamber, and solo works, the best known of which is the unison choral song Jerusalem (1916). He was the director of the Royal College of Music (1894–1918) and professor of music at Oxford University (1900–08).

Parry, Sir William Edward (1790–1855) British navigator, who made three journeys in search of the *Northwest Passage (1819–20, 1821–23, 1824–25). In 1827 he tried to reach the Pole by sledge from Spitsbergen.

parsec A unit of distance, used in astronomy, corresponding to a parallax of one second of arc. 1 parsec = 3.26 light-years or 3.084×10^{16} metres.

Parseeism The religion of the descendants of Persians who fled their country in the 8th century AD to avoid persecution following the Arab conquest. Mostly located in Bombay, Madras, Calcutta, and Karachi, they continue to practise *Zoroastrianism in two sectarian forms.

parsley A fragrant biennial herb, Petroselinum crispum, native to the Mediterranean region but widely cultivated.

The compound leaves have an aromatic flavour. They are used fresh or dried in fish and meat dishes, soups, garnishes, and bouquets garnis. The flowering stems, up to 1 m high, bear yellowish flowers. Family: *Umbelliferae.

parsnip A hairy strong-smelling biennial plant, *Pastinaca sativa*, native to Eurasia and widely cultivated throughout temperate regions for its large starchy white taproot, which is eaten as a vegetable or used as cattle feed. The leaves consist of paired lobed toothed leaflets on a long furrowed stalk and the clusters of tiny yellow flowers are borne on stems up to 150 cm high. Family: *Umbelliferae.

Parsons, Sir Charles Algernon (1854–1931) British engineer, who invented the steam *turbine in 1884. Using his turbine to power his ship *Turbania*, in 1897 he reached the record-breaking speed of 35 knots.

Parsons, Talcott (1902–78) US sociologist. His early theories, first expounded in *The Structure of Social Action* (1937), underwent extensive change in *The Social System* (1951), becoming a functionalist (*see* functionalism) systems approach and later incorporating evolutionism and cybernetics. The consequences for adopting such an approach are represented in his analysis of social stratification, in which he emphasized its integrative supportive role. His work has been criticized for obscurity and failure to deal with conflict, power, and deviance.

parthenogenesis A method of reproduction in which the egg develops without *fertilization to produce an individual usually identical to the parent. It occurs commonly among lower plants and animals, particularly aphids, ants, bees, and wasps, principally to accelerate the production of individuals at certain times of the year. In many species, for example aphids, sexual reproduction does take place from time to time to provide genetic variation.

Parthenon A temple on the hill of the Acropolis in □Athens dedicated to the goddess Athena. Built between 447 and 432 BC by *Ictinus and *Callicrates at the instigation of *Pericles, it represents the summit of classical Greek architecture. Its rectangular colonnaded exterior of Doric columns originally contained a walled chamber with *Phidias' gold and ivory statue of Athena. In the 5th century AD it became a Christian church and in the 15th century a mosque. It was blown up by the Turks in 1687. Much that remained of its adorning sculpture was removed by Lord Elgin in the 19th century (*see* Elgin Marbles).

Parthia The region S of the Caspian Sea approximating to present-day Khorasan (NE Iran). Inhabited by seminomadic tribes, Parthia, once a feudal confederacy of vassal kingdoms under the Achaemenians and then the Seleucids, controlled a great empire from about 250 BC to 224 AD with its capital at *Ctesiphon. Parthia's famous cavalry and mounted archers harassed Rome's eastern frontiers, overwhelming Crassus' army in a humiliating defeat at *Carrhae in 53 BC. In 224 AD the Parthian empire was conquered by the *Sasanians of Persia.

particle physics The study of elementary particles and their interactions. Until the discovery of the *electron (J. J. Thomson; 1898), the atom had been thought of as a minute indivisible "billiard ball." The existence of the electron and the discovery of the *proton (Rutherford; 1914) made it clear that the atom had an internal structure. When the *neutron was discovered (Chadwick; 1932), it appeared that the whole universe was constructed of just these three particles. The outstanding problem was the nature of the force that held neutrons and protons together in the atomic nucleus. The only two fundamental forces known at that time were the gravitational force and the electromagnetic (em) force: the gravitational force was too weak to account for the great stability of the nucleus and the em force had no effect on the electrically uncharged neutron.

In 1935 *Yukawa suggested that there might be in nature a short-lived particle (later called the meson) that jumped between protons and neutrons and held them together in much the same way as two tennis players are held together by the ball passing between them. This concept of exchange forces and the subsequent discovery of short-lived particles led to intensive research into particle physics throughout the world (*see* accelerators). By the 1960s some 200 "elementary" particles had been identified and it became clear that there were four basic types of force; in addition to gravitational and em forces there were *strong interactions (100 times more powerful than em forces) and *weak interactions (10^{10} weaker than em forces). It also became evident that some elementary particles were more elementary than others. In general, there are now believed to be two classes: leptons (the electron, muon, tau particle, and *neutrinos), which interact by the em or the weak forces and have no apparent internal structure; and hadrons (including the proton, neutron, pion, etc.), which interact by the strong interaction and do appear to have an internal structure.

During the past 20 years the main preoccupation of particle physicists has been the elucidation of hadron structure. The current model is based on Murray Gell-Mann's concept of the quark, introduced in 1963. In this model, hadrons themselves are divided into two classes: baryons, which decay into protons; and mesons, which decay into leptons and *photons or into proton pairs. Baryons consist of three quarks and mesons consist of a quark-antiquark pair. Thus all the matter in the universe is now seen as being made of leptons and quarks.

Although the quark concept was introduced as a theoretical construct and a single quark has never been identified experimentally, there is now a considerable amount of evidence that they actually exist. Quark theory is fairly elaborate; quarks have fractional electronic charges ($+2/3$ or $-1/3$ of the electronic charge) and come in six "flavours" called up (u; $+2/3$), down (d; $-1/3$), charmed (c; $+2/3$), strange (s; $-1/3$), top (t; $+2/3$), and bottom (b; $-1/3$). For each flavour there is an equivalent antiquark ($\bar{u}$, $\bar{d}$, etc.). The proton consists of uud ($2/3 + 2/3 - 1/3 = 1$) and the neutron consists of udd ($2/3 - 1/3 - 1/3 = 0$).

In this limited form quark theory conflicted with the *Pauli exclusion principle and it therefore became necessary to introduce the concept of "colour." Thus each flavour of quark can have one of the three colours red, yellow, or blue, with antiquarks having the corresponding anticolours. "Colour" in this sense has no connection with visual colour but the analogy is useful. All hadrons are regarded as white and baryons must consist of a red, a blue, and a yellow (since these visual colours produce white); mesons consist of a quark of any colour and its corresponding anticolour. This aspect of particle physics is known as **quantum chromodynamics** by analogy with quantum electrodynamics (*see* quantum theory). *See also* antimatter; charm; gauge theories; quantum number; strangeness.

partnership An association of two or more people formed to carry on a business; the partnership does not have a separate identity and the partners are not safeguarded by *limited liability. Partnerships are often formed by members of a profession, e.g. solicitors or accountants, and by commercial undertakings, such as banks or merchants. Partners share in the assets, expenses, and profits according to the written partnership agreement between them.

partridge A small gamebird native to the Old World but widely introduced elsewhere. Partridges are 25–40 cm long and have rounded bodies with short rounded wings and a low gliding flight. The European partridge (*Perdix perdix*) is a common farmland bird and has a greyish plumage with a red face and tail and a dark U-shaped marking on its belly. Family: *Phasianidae* (pheasants, quail, partridges). *See also* francolin.

Partridge, Eric Honeywood (1894–1979) British lexicographer, born in New Zealand. After World War I he settled in England, where he produced many witty, idiosyncratic, and learned works, including *A Dictionary of Slang and Unconventional English* and an etymological dictionary called *Origins*, both of which have had numerous editions.

Pasadena   34 10N 118 09W A city in the USA, in California. It is a winter health resort and well-known residence for Los Angeles cinema stars. The annual Tournament of Roses and the Rose Bowl football game are held here. The California Institute of Technology was established here in 1891. Population (1980): 119 374.

Pasargadae   An ancient Persian city in Fars province, Iran. It was founded as the capital between 546 and 530 BC by *Cyrus the Great, whose tomb still stands there. His successors abandoned it for *Persepolis in the 6th century BC.

pascal (Pa)   The *SI unit of pressure equal to one newton per square metre. Named after Blaise *Pascal.

Pascal   A computer-programming language, named after Blaise *Pascal. Designed in 1970 by Nicklaus Wirth at Zürich for teaching computer science, it is now widely used on *microcomputers.

Pascal, Blaise   (1623–62) French mathematician, physicist, and theologian. He made a study of conic sections when still in his teens; later he studied the mathematics of *probability, in collaboration with Pierre de Fermat, and invented Pascal's triangle for calculating the coefficients of a binomial expansion. He also made discoveries in *fluid mechanics, notably that the pressure in a fluid is everywhere equal (**Pascal's principle**). In 1641 he invented the first calculating machine. At the age of 31 he had a mystical experience and from then on devoted his life to religion. In the same year he became a Jansenist and his *Lettres provinciales* (1656–57) defended *Jansenism against the *Jesuits. His greatest work was *Pensées sur la religion* (1669), a poetical and metaphysical treatise on human nature.

pasha   An honorary title applied in the Ottoman Empire to military, naval, and civil commanders. It was abolished in Turkey in 1934 but lasted until 1952 in Egypt.

Pashto   The language of the Pathan people of N Pakistan and Afghanistan, which belongs to the *Iranian family. Pashto is the official language of Afghanistan. There are two main dialects, Pashto in Afghanistan and Pakhto in Pakistan. Both are written in a modified Arabic script.

Pashtuns.   *See* Pathans.

Pašić, Nicola   (1845–1926) Serbian statesman. Pašić was prime minister of Serbia (1891–92, 1904–05, 1906–08, 1909–11, 1912–18). After World War I he was a representative of the newly formed Yugoslavia at the Paris Peace Conference. As prime minister of Yugoslavia (1921–24, 1924–26), he advocated Serbian supremacy.

Pasionaria, La.   *See* Ibarruri, Dolores.

Pasmore, Victor (1908–   ) British artist. His early works included landscapes and figure studies, influenced by fauvism and cubism. After 1947 he dramatically changed direction, devoting himself to abstract paintings and reliefs. He has held several teaching posts, including Master of Painting at Durham University (1954–61).

Pasolini, Pier Paolo   (1922–75) Italian film director. His films include original treatments of Greek legends, such as *Oedipus Rex* (1967) and *Medea* (1969), a highly acclaimed biblical film, *The Gospel according to St Matthew* (1964), Marxist allegories, such as *Theorem* (1968) and *Pigsty* (1969), and anthologies, such as *The Decameron* (1970).

passage rites   Rituals and ceremonies performed on a person's transition from one social status to another. The most common are those at birth, puberty, marriage, death, and succession to office. Practices vary greatly but a pattern consisting of three stages is common to many such rites. First, there is a rite of separation, removing the subject from his previous status; next, a transitional stage in which the person is suspended between statuses; and finally, a rite of aggregation, in which the new status is conferred. In many primitive societies such rites are thought to be essential to ensure success in the new role. *See also* initiation rites.

Passau   48 35N 13 28E A town in SE West Germany, in Bavaria at the confluence of the Rivers Danube, Inn, and Ilz. An important medieval trading centre and port, its notable buildings include the cathedral (1668) and the 18th-century episcopal palace. Its university was established in 1972. Its manufactures include machinery and textiles. Population (1983 est): 51 777.

Passchendaele.   *See* World War I.

passenger pigeon   A slender long-winged *pigeon, *Ectopistes migratorius*, once common in deciduous woodlands of North America but extinct by the end of the 19th century. It was 32 cm long and had a pointed tail and a slate-grey plumage with a deep pink breast. It fed on beech nuts, acorns, and fruits and was highly migratory, able to fly long distances for food, and formed flocks numbering millions of birds. Harvesting of eggs, chicks, and adults and rapid deforestation led to its extinction.

passerine bird   A bird belonging to the order *Passeriformes*, which includes over half (about 5100) of all bird species. Passerines—the perching birds—are characterized by their feet, which are specialized for gripping branches, and stems. They are the most highly evolved birds and occur in large numbers in almost every habitat, although few live or feed in water. Most species are between 12 and 20 cm in length, although some are as small as 7.5 cm, with others reaching 117 cm. There are both migratory and sedentary species. Passerines are often of economic importance—as a source of food, for their ornamental plumage, or as cagebirds. Some species, such as the *quelea and *Java sparrow are serious crop pests.

The order is divided into four major groups (suborders): *Eurylaimi* (broadbills); *Tyranni* (includes manakins, ovenbirds, pittas, and tyrant flycatchers); *Menurae* (lyrebirds and scrubbirds); and, the largest and most advanced group, *Oscines* (*see* songbird).

passionflower   A climbing plant of the genus *Passiflora* (500 species), native chiefly to tropical and subtropical America and cultivated for ornament. The leaves may be simple or deeply lobed; some are modified as tendrils. The distinctive flowers each consist of a cup-shaped base with five coloured sepals and petals at its upper edge surmounted by a coloured fringe. From the centre of this protrudes a stalk bearing the stamens and ovary. The fruit is a berry or capsule, which in some species (e.g. *P. quadrangularis*) is edible (passionfruits *or* granadillas). Family: *Passifloraceae*.

Passion plays   Religious dramas concerning the crucifixion and resurrection of Christ and often including other related religious episodes. They were performed on Good Friday throughout medieval Europe and survived after the Reformation in Switzerland, Austria, and Germany. The Passion play at *Oberammergau in West Germany, the best-known modern example, has been performed every ten years since 1634 in fulfilment of a vow made by the villagers during an epidemic of the plague.

Passover (Hebrew word: *Pesah*)   One of the three biblical pilgrimage festivals (the others are Weeks and Tabernacles). It commemorates the Exodus from Egypt and also incorporates a spring harvest festival. In Judaism, it is celebrated for seven or eight days, beginning on the eve of the first day with a formal meal (*see* haggadah). Unleavened bread (*matzah*) is eaten, all leaven being removed from the house. In Christianity it has been replaced by *Easter.

Passy, Frédéric   (1822–1912) French economist and politician, whose efforts for peace were rewarded with the first Nobel Peace Prize (1901), which he won jointly with *Dunant. He established a peace arbitration society (Ligue international de la Paix, 1867) and helped found the International Parliamentary Union (1889), as well as arbitrating in international disputes.

pasta An originally Italian dough made from semolina obtained from durum wheat and water, sometimes with the addition of eggs. Among the many varieties of pasta are spaghetti (long thin rods), macaroni (short hollow thicker tubes), lasagne (flat rectangular pieces), ravioli (little squares of pasta stuffed with meat), and tagliatelle (long flat ribbons). Pasta is usually served with well-flavoured sauces.

Pasternak, Boris (1890–1960) Russian poet and novelist. He was born into a cultured Jewish family and studied music and philosophy. He published several volumes of Symbolist poetry between 1917 and 1923 and many translations during the 1930s. His epic novel *Dr Zhivago* became an international bestseller after its publication in Italy (1957); it was unpublished in Russia until the cultural thaw of the mid-1980s. Under pressure Pasternak declined the 1958 Nobel prize.

Pasteur, Louis (1822–95) French chemist and microbiologist, who made great advances in the prevention and treatment of diseases caused by microorganisms. A tanner's son, Pasteur became a science master and pursued his interest in chemistry: in 1848 he discovered two different optically active forms of tartaric acid that had differing biological properties. In 1854 Pasteur was appointed dean of the faculty of sciences at Lille University. He found that fermentation was caused by microorganisms and that by excluding these, souring or decay could be prevented (see pasteurization). Although partially paralysed in 1868, Pasteur's interest in germs and disease directed his attention to anthrax (the life cycle of the causative bacillus in cattle had been studied by *Koch). By 1881 Pasteur had devised a means of safely inducing immunity to the disease by injecting a vaccine of heat-treated (attenuated) live anthrax bacilli. Pasteur also produced a vaccine for chicken cholera and—in 1885, his most spectacular achievement—an effective rabies vaccine. The Pasteur Institute was founded in 1888 to treat rabies and has since developed into a world centre for biological research.

pasteurization Heat treatment used to destroy the microorganisms in milk. The method involves heating milk for 30 minutes at 60°C, which kills the tuberculosis bacteria without damaging the milk protein. This process is named after Louis *Pasteur, who demonstrated that heat could prevent the spoilage of wine and beer caused by fermentation of yeasts and other microorganisms.

Pasto 1 12N 77 17W A city in SW Colombia, on a slope of the Pasto volcano. It is the commercial centre of an agricultural and cattle-rearing area. The University of Nariño was founded here in 1827. Population (1980): 182 000.

Paston Letters Correspondence largely relating to the Norfolk family of Paston. Written between 1422 and 1509, they constitute an invaluable source for the history of that period, describing not only domestic and local affairs but also political events. The majority are preserved in the British Library.

Patagonia A geographic area of S South America in Argentina and Chile, extending S of the River Colorado to the Strait of Magellan. It consists chiefly of an arid plateau rising to the Andes. Sheep raising is the principal economic activity. It contains the major oilfield of Comodoro Rivadavia, Argentina's chief source of oil, and the Río Turbio coalfield. Area: about 777 000 sq km (300 000 sq mi).

patas monkey An *Old World monkey, *Erythrocebus patas*, of African grasslands. Patas monkeys are 110-160 cm long including the tail (50-75 cm) and are mainly terrestrial and omnivorous. They live in well-ordered troops (hence, their alternative name—military monkeys). A white-nosed eastern race is called the nisnas monkey.

patchouli An aromatic herb, *Pogostemon patchouli*, native to Malaysia. It contains a fragrant essential oil used in perfumery in SE Asia. The dried leaves are used as an insect repellent. Family: *Labiatae*.

LOUIS PASTEUR *The success of his vaccinations encouraged women to bring their children to be vaccinated in the streets of Paris, in the 1890s.*

patent In law, the privilege granted by letters patent (writings sealed with the Great Seal of England) from the Crown giving the first inventor of an article or process the sole right to make, use, and sell it for a period of 20 years from the date of application for the grant. A patent will only be granted for a thing that is both novel and capable of achieving the purpose intended by the inventor, even if the purpose is useless. Applications to the Patent Office in London must be accompanied by a written specification of the invention, appropriate drawings, formulas, or specimens.

Pater, Walter (Horatio) (1839-94) British critic and essayist. He established his reputation with *Studies in the History of the Renaissance* (1873). His historical fiction *Marius the Epicurean* (1885) advanced his philosophical and aesthetic theories, which greatly influenced the *Aesthetic movement. His many critical essays on art and poetry are noted for their highly polished prose style.

Paterson 40 55N 74 10W A city in the USA, in New Jersey, part of the Greater New York Metropolitan Area. Founded in 1791, it became known as the Silk City in the 19th century, because of its large silk industry. Its varied manufactures today include cotton, paper, and chemicals. Population (1980): 137 970.

Paterson, William (1658-1719) Scottish merchant and banker, who founded the Bank of England (1694). He resigned his directorship of the Bank within a year because of disagreements in policy. His attempt to set up a rival bank failed.

Pathans A large group of tribes of N Pakistan and SE Afghanistan who speak the *Pashto language. They are also known as Pashtuns. Each tribe is subdivided into a number of patrilineal clans, said to be descended from a common ancestor. Genealogical lines of many generations are remembered and determine land rights, succession, and inheritance. Devout Muslims, the Pathans are farmers and warriors, many entering into military service.

pathology The branch of medicine concerned with the study of disease and disease processes in order to understand their causes and nature. The specialty originated in the mid-19th century, when *Virchow demonstrated that changes in the structure of cells and tissues were related to specific diseases. Cellular pathology advanced further with the work of Pasteur and Koch on the bacterial cause of disease, but it was not until the beginning of the 20th century that the knowledge gained in the laboratory was applied to the treatment and prevention of disease in patients. Examples of early work in the science of clinical pathology include Schick's test for diphtheria and Wasserman's test for syphilis. Chemical pathology developed from the observation of changes in the composition and structure of blood in disease, notably with the work of Banting and Best on the importance of insulin in diabetes and contributions from such haematologists as Landsteiner in the discovery of the blood groups. Today pathology includes studies of the chemistry of blood, urine, faeces, and diseased tissue, obtained by biopsy or at autopsy, together with the use of X-rays and many other investigative techniques.

Patinir, Joachim (*or* Patenier; c. 1485-1524) Flemish painter, noted for his panoramic landscape views, which dwarf the religious themes that were his ostensible subjects. His paintings include *St Christopher* and *St Jerome* (both Prado).

Patmore, Coventry (1823-96) British poet. A friend of Tennyson and Ruskin and an associate of the *Pre-Raphaelite Brotherhood, his *The Angel in the House* (4 vols, 1854-62) is a poetic treatment of married love. After his conversion to Roman Catholicism in 1864 he wrote mostly on religious themes.

Pátmos A Greek island in the E Aegean Sea, in the Dodecanese. St John the Divine is believed to have written the Book of Revelation here. Area: 34 sq km (13 sq mi). Population (1981): 2534.

Patna 25 37N 85 12E A city in India, the capital of Bihar on the River Ganges. It was founded in 1541 on the former site of Pataliputra, ancient capital of the Maurya and Gupta empires. Population (1981): 916 000.

pato A four-a-side equestrian sport related to *polo and *basketball, played in Argentina. The mounted players try to throw a ball, to which are attached six leather handles, into a goal (a net attached to a post).

Paton, Alan · (1903-) South African novelist. His best-known novel, *Cry, the Beloved Country* (1948), condemns injustice in South African society. His other works include *Too Late the Phalarope* (1953), *The Land and the People of South Africa* (1955), *Ah, But Your Land Is Beautiful* (1982), and a collection of short stories, *Debbie Go Home* (1961). He was national president of the Liberal Party from 1953 to 1960.

Patras (*or* Pátrai) 38 14N 21 44E A port in W Greece, in the N Peloponnese on the Gulf of Patras. The War of Greek Independence began here in 1821. Exports include currants, sultanas, tobacco, and olive oil. Its university was established in 1966. Population (1981): 141 529.

patriarch 1. In the Old Testament, *Adam and the other ancestors of the human race before the Flood, as well as the later forebears of the Hebrew nation: Abraham, Isaac, Jacob, and Jacob's 12 sons who gave their names to the 12 tribes of Israel. 2. In the Orthodox Church, the title of a bishop with jurisdiction over other bishops. At the Council of Chalcedon (451) five such sees were recognized: Alexandria, Antioch, Constantinople, Jerusalem, and Rome. The patriarch of Constantinople took the title Ecumenical Patriarch, despite Rome's objections (*see* papacy).

patricians The hereditary aristocracy of ancient Rome. Originally the sole holders of political and religious offices, the patricians were gradually forced during Republican times to admit *plebeians to political offices and their privileged position was eroded.

Patrick, St (c. 390-c. 460 AD) The patron saint of Ireland. Legend tells of his abduction from Britain by Irish marauders at the age of 16. A local chief's slave in Antrim, he later escaped to Gaul, finally returning to Ireland as a missionary. He established an archiepiscopal see at Armagh and by the time of his death had firmly established

Christianity in Ireland. His only certain works are a spiritual autobiography, the *Confession*, and the *Epistle to Coroticus*. Feast day: 17 March. Emblems: snakes and shamrock.

Patriotic Front (PF) A Black nationalist organization, founded in 1976, to oppose the government of Ian Smith in Rhodesia (now *Zimbabwe). Using guerrilla techniques, its two wings—the Zimbabwe African National Union (ZANU), led by Robert *Mugabe, and the Zimbabwe African People's Union (ZAPU), led by Joshua *Nkomo—were based in Mozambique and Zambia respectively. In the elections (1980) that followed the Lancaster House agreements, Mugabe became prime minister of Zimbabwe.

Patroclus In Homer's *Iliad*, the companion of Achilles. During the Trojan War he was killed by Hector while wearing the armour of Achilles.

Patti, Adelina (Adela Juana Maria; 1843-1919) Italian-born operatic soprano. She specialized in the Italian coloratura repertoire, singing both in the USA and Europe.

Patton, George S(mith) (1885-1945) US general. In World War II he commanded the Seventh Army in Sicily (1943) and then the Third Army in France. He breached the German defences in Normandy and led a spectacular advance to the Moselle. In the Ardennes he cleared the W bank of the Rhine, crossed it, and encircled the Ruhr.

Pau 43 18N 0 22W A town in SW France, the capital of the Pyrénées-Atlantique department. It was the former capital of Béarn and residence of the French Kings of Navarre. Pau is a tourist resort and trades in horses, wine, and leather. Population (1982): 82 186.

Paul I (1754-1801) Tsar of Russia (1796-1801). Paul reversed many of the enlightened policies of his mother, Catherine the Great, and pursued an inconsistent foreign policy that isolated Russia. His incompetence and despotism led to his assassination.

Paul I (1901-64) King of the Hellenes (1947-64). The third son of Constantine I, he lived mostly in exile from 1917 to 1935, and again during World War II, succeeding his brother George II (1890-1947; reigned 1922-23, 1935-47). In 1938 Paul married Frederika (1917-) of Brunswick.

Paul III (Alessandro Farnese; 1468-1549) Pope (1534-49). First of the *Counter-Reformation popes, Paul restored the *Inquisition, summoned the Council of *Trent, and actively supported the new orders, especially the *Jesuits. However, he was also noted for his nepotism and worldliness. He was a considerable patron of learning and the arts.

Paul VI (Giovanni Battista Montini; 1897-1978) Pope (1963-78). Succeeding *John XXIII, Paul continued his predecessor's policies of reform, reconvening the second *Vatican Council after his election. While working for ecumenicism and administrative reform he maintained papal authority and traditional doctrines, notably in the encyclical *Humanae Vitae* (*Of Human Life*; 1968), which reiterated the Church's position on birth control.

Paul, St (c. 3-c. 64 AD) Christian Apostle, born Saul of Tarsus, who spread Christianity among the Gentiles; the 13 Epistles attributed to him form a major part of the New Testament. The son of a Pharisee and a Roman citizen, he was educated at Jerusalem and was initially anti-Christian, having participated in the martyrdom of St *Stephen. While travelling to Damascus, he had a vision that led to his conversion to Christianity. He began his activity as an Apostle in Damascus, later joining the other Apostles in Jerusalem. His important missionary work consisted of three journeys in which he travelled to Cyprus, Asia Minor, Macedonia, Greece, Ephesus, and elsewhere, establishing churches or bringing support to previously established Christian communities. After his third journey, he returned to Jerusalem and was arrested by Roman soldiers in order to protect him from the hostility of the mob, who attacked him for teaching transgression of the Mosaic Law. He eventually appealed to Caesar and, as a Roman citizen, was taken to Rome for trial. He was imprisoned for two years; here the New Testament account (in Acts) ends. It appears that he may have been released, before being arrested a final time and beheaded under Nero. Paul's influence was decisive in extending Christianity beyond the Jewish context of the Church at Jerusalem, and the Pauline Epistles formed the basis of all subsequent Christian theology. Feast day: 29 June.

Pauli, Wolfgang (1900-58) US physicist, born in Austria, who in 1925 formulated the *Pauli exclusion principle for which he received the 1945 Nobel Prize. In 1931 he postulated that some of the energy of a *beta decay was carried away by massless particles, which *Fermi named neutrinos.

Pauli exclusion principle The principle that no two *fermions may exist in the same state. It is most commonly applied to atomic electrons, which cannot have the same set of *quantum numbers. Named after Wolfgang *Pauli.

Pauling, Linus Carl (1901-) US chemist, who originated and developed important concepts concerning the structure of molecules. Successfully using new analytical techniques, Pauling elucidated the nature of chemical bonding in both simple and complex molecules, publishing his highly influential book, *The Nature of the Chemical Bond*, in 1939. He received the Nobel Prize for Chemistry (1954) for his research and the Nobel Peace Prize (1962) for his pacifist stance against the use of nuclear weapons.

Paulinus of Nola, St (c. 353-431 AD) Christian Latin poet, born at Bordeaux. After a political career as a senator, consul, and governor of Campania, he became a Christian and was ordained in 394. Bishop of Nola from 409 until his death, he is famous for his poetic epistles. Feast day: 22 June.

Paulus, Friedrich (1890-1957) German field marshal in World War II. In command of the Sixth Army on the Eastern Front, he captured Stalingrad (1943) but his army was forced to surrender, thus ending the German offensive in the Soviet Union. *See* Stalingrad, Battle of.

Pausanias (2nd century AD) Greek traveller, whose *Description of Greece* is an invaluable source for places and buildings now destroyed. His accuracy and judgment are attested by his description of those that survive.

Pau-t'ou. *See* Baotou.

Pavarotti, Luciano (1935-) Italian operatic tenor. He made his debut at La Scala, Milan, in 1966 and at the Metropolitan Opera in New York in 1968. He specializes in the works of Bellini, Verdi, and Puccini.

Pavese, Cesare (1908-50) Italian novelist and poet. He was imprisoned for his antifascist journalism in 1935 and later joined the resistance movement. His best-known novels, which concern human isolation, include *Il compagno* (1947) and *La luna e i falò* (1950). He also published poetry and translations of works by US and English writers. Lonely throughout his life, he committed suicide at a time when he was receiving most public recognition. His diaries were published posthumously as *Il mestiere di vivere* (1952).

Pavia (ancient name: Ticinum) 45 12N 9 09E A town in Italy, in Lombardy on the River Ticino. Dating from Roman times, it has a 12th-century church, in which St Augustine is buried, a 15th-century cathedral, a monastery, several palaces, and a university (1361). Pavia is the centre of an agricultural region and produces sewing machines, metal goods, textiles and furniture. Population (1983 est): 84 644.

Pavia, Battle of (24 February, 1525) A major engagement in the Italian wars between *Francis I of France and the Habsburg emperor *Charles V. It marked the beginning of Habsburg ascendancy in Italy. Some 23 000 Habsburg

troops relieved the besieged city of Pavia, captured Francis, and virtually destroyed the French army of 28 000.

Pavlodar 52 21N 76 59E A port in the Soviet Union, in the NE Kazakh SSR on the River Irtysh. It was founded in 1720 but remained small until the mid-20th century, since when it has become an important industrial centre: food processing is the principal activity. Population (1981 est): 288 000.

Pavlov, Ivan Petrovich (1849-1936) Russian physiologist, noted for his studies of digestion and his demonstration of the *conditioned reflex. Pavlov showed that heartbeat is regulated by the vagus nerve and how eating stimulates secretion of digestive juices by the stomach. Pavlov extended his theories of reflex behaviour to cover aspects of human behaviour, such as learning.

Pavlov was a persistent critic of the communist regime although it continued to provide him with facilities for research. He was awarded the 1907 Nobel Prize.

Pavlova, Anna (1885-1931) Russian ballet dancer. She joined Diaghilev's company in Paris in 1909, and from 1914 she devoted her career to international tours with her own company. She created the chief role in *Les Sylphides* and was especially associated with *Le Cygne*, choreographed for her by *Fokine in 1907.

pawnbroking The lending of money on the security of an item of personal property. An article pawned is pledged to the pawnbroker but can be redeemed within a specified time by the repayment of the loan plus *interest. In the UK, pawnbrokers require a licence and are governed by the Consumer Credit Act (1974), which replaced the Pawnbrokers Acts (1872, 1960). Articles unredeemed after six months (or an agreed period) after pawning become the pawnbroker's property if valued at £15 or less. If valued at more the pawnbroker may sell the article (after giving the original owner notice), any surplus raised being repayable to the original owner.

Pawnee A confederation of Caddoan-speaking North American Indian tribes of the Platte River area, Nebraska. They were typical of the Eastern Plains Indian semiagricultural and buffalo-hunting culture. Their villages consisted of large circular earth-covered lodges. Shamans were important. The Pawnees worshipped the sun, had a star cult, and observed the morning-star ceremony in which a captured maiden was sacrificed by cutting out her heart.

Pawtucket 41 53N 71 23W A city in the USA, in NE Rhode Island on the Blackstone River. The site of the first US cotton mill (1790), its industries include textiles, silks, machinery, and paper. Population (1980): 71 204.

Paxinou, Katina (1900-72) Greek actress. As well as acting in classical Greek tragedies she translated and produced British and US plays for the Greek National Theatre. Her films include *For Whom the Bell Tolls* (1943) and *Mourning Becomes Electra* (1947).

Paxton, Sir Joseph (1801-65) British architect. Initially a gardener, Paxton, under the patronage of the Duke of Devonshire, experimented with new techniques of construction employing iron and glass in building greenhouses at *Chatsworth. This experience culminated in the design of the revolutionary *Crystal Palace for the Great Exhibition of 1851. He also designed country houses, for example Mentmore, and practised landscape gardening.

PAYE (Pay As You Earn) A system used for the collection of direct *taxation in the UK. Income tax is deducted from employees' wages before the employer distributes them; thus while the amount deducted appears on the employee's pay slip, the employee never actually receives the tax taken.

Paysandú 32 21S 58 05W A port in W Uruguay, on the River Uruguay. Accessible to oceangoing vessels, its chief exports are cereals, flax, and livestock. It is a meat-processing centre and has tanning and sugar-refining industries. Population (1980): 62 000.

Paz, Octavio (1914-) Mexican poet, critic, and diplomat, whose early poetry was influenced by Marxism and surrealism. His mature poetry is philosophical and deals with the problem of solitude; the collection *La estación violenta* (1958) contains his best-known poem, "Piedra del sol."

Pazzi conspiracy (1478) A plot to assassinate Lorenzo and Giuliano de' *Medici in Florence Cathedral. It was led by their political and business rivals, the Pazzi, and was supported by the papacy. Guiliano died but the Medici maintained control of the government and many of the conspirators were captured and killed. A war with the papacy followed but Lorenzo's dominance over Florence had been demonstrated.

pea An annual herb of the genus *Pisum* (about 6 species), native to the Mediterranean area and W Asia, especially the widely cultivated *P. sativum*. The leaves consist of paired oval leaflets and have curling tendrils used for climbing. The white flowers have a large rear petal and two smaller wing petals enclosing a cuplike keel petal. The edible round seeds are contained in an elongated pod and are an important source of protein for man and livestock. Family: *Leguminosae*.

Peace Corps A US Government agency founded in 1961 by John F. Kennedy to provide the Third World with skilled manpower, especially teachers and agriculturalists. The Corps consists of volunteers, who must be US citizens and at least 18 years old.

Peace River A river in W Canada, whose headstreams (Finlay and Parsnip Rivers) rise in the British Columbia Rockies. Flowing generally NE across the N Alberta plains, it empties into the Slave River. It is mostly navigable and is also tapped for hydroelectricity. Its valley is fertile farmland, with important oil and timber reserves. Length: 1923 km (1195 mi), including Finlay River.

peach A small tree, *Prunus persica*, probably native to China but widely cultivated in Mediterranean and warm temperate regions. Up to 6 m high, it has toothed glossy green leaves and pink flowers, borne singly or in groups in the leaf axils. The round fleshy fruit (a *drupe) has a distinct cleft and thin velvety skin, yellowish with a crimson tinge. The sweet white or yellow flesh encloses a wrinkled stone. Peaches are eaten fresh, canned, or in preserves. Nectarines (*P. persica* var. *nectarina*) are varieties with smooth-skinned fruits. Family: *Rosaceae*.

peacock. See peafowl.

Peacock, Thomas Love (1785–1866) British satirical novelist. He worked for the East India Company from 1819 to 1856 and was a close friend of Shelley. His seven novels, which include *Nightmare Abbey* (1818) and *Gryll Grange* (1860), satirize contemporary fashions and ideas through the conversation of stereotyped characters often based on real people, such as Shelley, Malthus, and Coleridge.

peacock butterfly A common Eurasian *nymphalid butterfly, *Inachis io*. The adults are brownish purple with a bright eyespot on each wing. They fly from early spring well into summer. The black spiny caterpillars are gregarious and feed on stinging nettles.

pea crab A small pea-shaped *crab belonging to the genus *Pinnotheres*. The female lives within the shell of certain bivalve *molluscs, such as oysters and mussels, obtaining food and shelter but not harming its host (*see* commensalism). The larvae and usually the males are free-swimming. Tribe: *Brachyura*.

peafowl An Old World gamebird belonging to a genus (*Pavo*; 2 species) native to lowland forests of India and SE Asia. Peafowl are 75 cm long and the female (peahen) has a green-brown plumage; males (peacocks) have elaborate lacy tails, 150 cm long, the feathers of which are tipped by blue-and-bronze markings and raised over the body during display. The blue (Indian) peacock (*P. cristatus*) is a metallic blue colour and has been domesticated as an ornamental

bird. Family: *Phasianidae* (pheasants, partridges, etc.); order: *Galliformes* (pheasants, turkeys, etc.).

Peak District A hilly area in N central England, in Derbyshire, at the S end of the Pennines. It reaches 727 m (2088 ft) at Kinder Scout and contains many limestone caves, notably Peak Cavern, near Castleton.

Peake, Mervyn (1911–68) British novelist. Born in China, he studied art and later illustrated his own books. His trilogy of novels, *Titus Groan* (1946), *Gormenghast* (1950), and *Titus Alone* (1959), is a modern gothic fantasy whose bizarre horrors parallel those of the real world. *Selected Poems* (1972) was published posthumously.

peanut. See groundnut.

pear A tree of the genus *Pyrus* (about 20 species), native to temperate Eurasia. The numerous cultivated varieties of orchard and garden pears are derived from *P. communis*. Up to 13 m high, it has oval leaves and bears clusters of five-petalled white flowers. The fruit, which narrows towards the stalk, has freckled brownish-yellow or russet skin surrounding sweet gritty flesh and a core of pips; it is eaten fresh or canned and used to make an alcoholic drink, perry. The wood is used for furniture making. Family: *Rosaceae*.

pearl A natural calcareous concretion formed in certain bivalve molluscs popularly known as pearl oysters or pearl mussels. Used for jewellery since earliest times, pearls are usually white or bluish grey and of globular, oval, pear-shaped, or irregular form. A pearl is formed around a foreign body, such as a worm larva, either against the inner side of the shell (a blister pearl) or within the mollusc sealed off as a cyst. It consists of concentric films of nacre, consisting of aragonite, which also forms the smooth lustrous lining (mother-of-pearl) in the shells of pearl-bearing molluscs. Cultured pearls are beads of mother-of-pearl artificially inserted into the mollusc, where they are left for three to five years. Artificial pearls are usually glass beads with a coating prepared from fish scales. Birthstone for June.

pearlfish An eel-like parasitic fish, also called fierasfer or cucumber fish, belonging to the family *Carapidae* (about 27 species), found in shallow tropical marine waters. About 15 cm long, it lives in the bodies of echinoderms and molluscs (including pearl oysters), feeding on their reproductive and respiratory organs. The larvae are components of *plankton. Order: *Perciformes*.

Pearl Harbor An inlet of the Pacific Ocean in the USA, in Hawaii on Oahu Island. Following the annexation of Hawaii by the USA in 1900, it became a US naval base. On 7 December, 1941, the Japanese launched an air attack on US military installations in Hawaii. Four battleships were lost in Pearl Harbor and 3300 service personnel killed. This action precipitated US involvement in World War II. It is now a naval shipyard, supply centre, and submarine base.

pearlite A constituent of *steel. It has a regular structure of alternate layers of ferrite (pure iron) and amentite. The name comes from its iridescent appearance under a microscope.

Pearl River. See Zhu Jiang.

pearlwort A small tufted or matted annual or perennial herb of the genus *Sagina* (about 20 species), native chiefly to N temperate regions. It has small narrow stalkless leaves and tiny four-petalled white flowers. The evergreen *S. subulata* is cultivated as a rock-garden or border plant. Family: *Caryophyllaceae*.

Pears, Sir Peter (1910–86) British tenor. He was well known for his performances of Bach and Schubert and was closely associated with the music of his friend *Britten, who wrote many works and operatic roles for him, such as the role of Aschenbach in the opera *Death in Venice* (1973).

Pearse, Patrick Henry (1879–1916) Irish nationalist, Gaelic enthusiast, and teacher. Pearse became a leader of the Irish Republican Brotherhood (*see* Fenians) and in the *Easter Rising of 1916 proclaimed an independent Irish republic with himself as president. The insurgents were defeated and Pearse and 14 others were executed. Pearse realized the military futility of the rising but believed a blood sacrifice was required for Irish nationalism.

Pearson, Lester B(owles) (1897-1972) Canadian statesman and diplomat; Liberal prime minister (1963-68). Ambassador to the USA (1945-46), chairman of NATO (1951), and delegate to the UN, Pearson played a key role in settling the Suez crisis (1956), which earned him the Nobel Peace Prize in 1957. At home the Pearson government conciliated French separatists with a commission on means to establishing French-English equality.

Peary, Robert Edwin (1856-1920) US explorer in the Arctic. In 1909, in the last of six expeditions, he became the first to reach the North Pole.

Peary Land An area in N Greenland, between Victoria Fjord and the Greenland Sea. It is the most northerly land area in the world and was named after the Arctic explorer, Robert E. Peary, who first explored it in 1892.

Peasants' Revolt (1381) The only major popular revolt in England during the middle ages. It was occasioned by heavy *poll taxes and reflected a general discontent with government policies. The rising, led by Wat *Tyler and John *Ball, was concentrated in East Anglia and the Home Counties. The peasants marched on London, where they were joined by disaffected craftsmen, artisans, and lesser clergy. They achieved initial success, taking the Tower of London, but the revolt soon collapsed and its supporters were ruthlessly suppressed.

Peasants' War (1524-25) A peasant uprising in S Germany, precipitated by economic hardship. The revolt was condemned by Luther and crushed by the Swabian League. Some 100 000 peasants died.

peat Partially decomposed dark-brown or black plant debris laid down in waterlogged conditions in temperate or cold climates. The remains of *Sphagnum* (peat or bog moss) are important constituents. Peat is the starting point for the formation of coal and is itself used as a fuel. The more alkaline fen peat is used for horticultural purposes.

pecan. See hickory.

peccary A small gregarious hoofed mammal belonging to the genus *Tayassu* (2 species) of South and Central American forests. Resembling a pig, the collared peccary (*T. tajacu*) is dark grey with a light stripe from chest to shoulder and grows to a length of 90 cm. It has two pairs of short tusks. The white-lipped peccary (*T. albirostris*) is darker and larger and has a white patch on the snout. Both are omnivorous. Family: *Tayassuidae.*

Pechenga (Finnish name: Petsamo) 69 28N 31 04E A port in the Soviet Union, in the NW RSFSR on the Barents Sea. It was in Finnish possession between the World Wars (1919-40). Ice free, it supports a fishing fleet and other industries relate to the nearby mining (chiefly nickel, copper, and uranium) region. Population: about 3500.

Pechora, River A river in the NW Soviet Union. Rising in the Ural Mountains, it flows generally N to enter the Barents Sea and is navigable for much of its length. Length: 1814 km (1127 mi).

Peckinpah, Sam (1926-84) US film director. His westerns, which include *Guns in the Afternoon* (1962) and *The Wild Bunch* (1969), show the western myth in conflict with historical progress and include powerful scenes of violence. His other films include *Straw Dogs* (1971) and *The Getaway* (1973).

peck order (*or* dominance hierarchy) A pattern of social structure found in certain animal groups that denotes the order of precedence of individuals, particularly in relation to feeding. It was first described—and is particularly well developed—in birds, in which the aggressive behaviour shown by members of the hierarchy to all those inferior to them takes the form of pecking. It can occur between

different species competing for the same food or among a single-species population, especially under captive conditions.

Pecos River A river of the S USA, rising in N New Mexico and flowing SSE through Texas, to join the Rio Grande. It is an important source of irrigation. Length: 1180 km (735 mi).

Pécs (German name: Fünfkirchen) 46 04N 18 15E An industrial city in SW Hungary. An old trading centre, it became an important humanist centre (14th-15th centuries) and has the earliest established university in the country (1367; reopened 1922). Its rapid growth in the 19th and 20th centuries was based on nearby coalfields. Population (1980): 170 000.

pectin A carbohydrate found combined with cellulose in the cell walls of plants. Ripening fruits change any other pectic compounds present into jelly-like pectin—an essential ingredient for the gelling of jam.

Pedro I (1798-1834) Emperor of Brazil (1822-31). The son of John VI of Portugal, Pedro became regent in Brazil in 1821 and declared its independence in 1822. On John's death (1826) he refused the Portuguese Crown, which was granted to Pedro's daughter. Forced to abdicate in 1831, Pedro returned to Portugal.

Pedro II (1825-91) Emperor of Brazil (1831-89), following the abdication of his father Pedro I. His reign saw an era of prosperity, in spite of wars against Argentina and Paraguay. His gradual abolition of slavery alienated the landowners, who joined the army in deposing him and declaring a republic in 1889.

Pedro the Cruel (1334-69) King of Castile and León (1350-69). He ruled with great cruelty and his brother, Henry of Trastamara (1333-79; reigned, as Henry II, 1369-79), attempted, with French help, to depose him in 1367. England was drawn into the conflict on Pedro's side and Spain thus became a battlefield of the *Hundred Years' War between France and England. Pedro was killed by Henry after defeat at the battle of Montiel.

Peebles (*or* Peeblesshire) A former county of SE Scotland. Under local government reorganization in 1975 it became part of the Borders Region.

Peebles 55 39N 3 12W A market town in SE Scotland, in the Borders Region on the River Tweed. It is a woollen manufacturing town and health resort. Population (1981): 6993.

Peel 54 14N 4 42W A town on the W coast of the Isle of Man (UK). It has the remains of a cathedral (13th-14th centuries) and castle ruins. Formerly an important fishing port, it is now principally a resort. Population (1981): 3688.

Peel, Sir Robert (1788-1850) British statesman; Conservative prime minister (1834-35, 1841-46). Elected to parliament in 1809, he was twice home secretary (1822-27, 1828-30), introducing prison and criminal-law reforms, founding the Metropolitan Police (1829), and securing the passage of the Catholic Emancipation Act (1829). In the Tamworth manifesto (1834), a speech to his constituents, he stated a programme of reform that clearly identified the *Conservative Party. His second ministry re-introduced income tax (1841), reduced duties on food and raw materials (1841, 1845), and introduced the Bank Charter Act (1844). He is best remembered, however, for the repeal of the *Corn Laws (1846), which caused his followers, the Peelites, to defect from the Conservative Party; they subsequently joined the Liberals.

Peele, George (1556-96) English dramatist. In 1581 he moved from Oxford to the active literary society of London. A prolific writer, his works include the pastoral *The Arraignment of Paris* (1584), the chronicle play *Edward I* (1593), and the satirical play *The Old Wives' Tale* (1595), as well as poems and pamphlets.

Peenemünde 54 09N 13 46E A fishing village in East

Germany, on the Baltic coast. The Rocket Test Centre was opened in Peenemünde in 1937 and it was here that German rockets (V2) and flying bombs (V1) were developed under Wernher *von Braun during World War II.

peepul. *See* bo tree.

peerage In the UK and Ireland, the temporal hereditary nobility, a body originating in the council of tenants in chief of the Norman kings of England, and the life peers, comprising (since 1876) the Lords of Appeal in Ordinary and (since 1958) those created in recognition of public service. The five ranks of the hereditary peerage are, in descending order, duke, marquess, earl, viscount, and baron. A life peer has the rank of baron. All peers are permitted to sit in the House of Lords, life peeresses being admitted since 1958 and hereditary peeresses, since 1963.

peewit. *See* lapwing.

Pegasus (astronomy) A large constellation in the N sky that contains the **Square of Pegasus**, formed from three of the brightest 2nd- and 3rd-magnitude stars in the constellation together with the 2nd-magnitude star Alpheratz in Andromeda.

Pegasus (Greek mythology) A winged horse that sprang from the blood of *Medusa when she was beheaded by Perseus. It carried the legendary hero Bellerophon in his battles but unseated him when he attempted to ride to heaven. It became a constellation and the bearer of thunderbolts for Zeus.

pegmatite A very coarse-grained igneous rock, usually occurring in veins or dykes within or around bodies of granite. Crystals over 10 metres across have been found in pegmatites. Most consist largely of alkali feldspar and quartz but many also contain accessory minerals that are otherwise rare, and these may be of economic importance.

Pegu 17 18N 96 31E A city in S Burma. The former capital of the Mon kingdoms, which dominated Burma at intervals from the 6th century AD until the 17th century, it has an enormous reclining statue of Buddha, 55 m (181 ft) long. Population (1983): 150 447.

Péguy, Charles (1873–1914) French poet and essayist. From his socialist bookshop he published the journal *Cahiers de la quinzaine* (1900–14), which expressed the literary ideals of his generation. He was killed in action in World War I.

Peipus, Lake (Russian name: Ozero Chudskoye) A lake in the NW Soviet Union, in the Estonian SSR and the RSFSR. It is drained by the River Narva N into the Gulf of Finland. Area: 3512 sq km (1356 sq mi).

Peirce, Charles Sanders (1839–1914) US philosopher and logician. He spent much of his career in government service, rather than academic life, and his influential *Collected Papers* were only published posthumously (1931–58). Peirce believed that an idea could best be defined by examination of the consequences to which it led. This concept became known as *pragmatism, a name that he later changed to pragmaticism. His work on formal logic was immensely significant.

Peking (Chinese name: Beijing *or* Pei-ching) 39, 55N 116 25E The capital of the People's Republic of China, an administratively autonomous city situated in the NE of the country in Hobei province. The city has expanded considerably since 1949 and there has been rapid development of industries, including iron and steel, machinery, and textiles. A symmetrically laid-out city, its architecture preserves many reminders of its past. It consists basically of two walled cities, the N inner city and the S outer city; the old Imperial City lies within the inner city and at its centre the moated "Forbidden City" contains the Imperial Palaces (now museums). There are three universities, the oldest being Peking University (1898). *History*: the site has a long history of human habitation. As Ta-tu, it first became the capital (of N China) under the Yuan dynasty in 1272. Later, when the capital was moved to Nanjing, it became known as

PEGASUS *This 19th-century engraving shows Pegasus carrying Perseus.*

Pei-p'ing (*or* Beibing), a name still used by the Republic of China. As Peking (1420), it once more became the capital under the third Ming emperor. In 1928 the Nationalist (Guomindang) government moved the capital to Nanjing and from 1937 until 1945 Peking was occupied by the Japanese. It became the capital of the People's Republic of China in 1949. Population (1980 est): 8 700 000.

Pekingese An ancient breed of toy □dog originating in China and brought to the West by British forces who sacked the Imperial Palace, Peking, in 1860. The Pekingese has a long straight coat forming a luxuriant mane on the shoulders and it may be of any colour. The short-muzzled face is always black. Height: 15–23 cm.

Peking man A type of fossil *hominid belonging to the species *Homo erectus* and represented by skeletal remains found at Chou-K'ou-Tien (*or* Zhou kou tian) cave near Peking. Formerly known as *Sinanthropus*, Peking man lived during the middle Pleistocene period (c. 500 000 years ago), used flint and bone tools, hunted, and could make fire.

Pelagius (c. 360–c. 420 AD) The originator of the heretical Christian doctrine known as Pelagianism. Born in Britain, he settled in Rome (c. 380) and later preached in Africa and Palestine. He rejected the doctrines of original sin and predestination, believing in man's free will and inherent capacity for good. These beliefs were hotly disputed by St *Augustine and a series of synods. Pope Innocent I finally condemned them in 417 and excommunicated Pelagius.

Pelargonium. *See* geranium.

Pelasgians (*or* Pelasgi) The inhabitants of Greece before the 12th century BC. They spoke a non-Greek language and lived mainly in the N Aegean. They were scattered during Bronze Age infiltrations of Greek-speaking peoples from the N.

Pelé (Edson Arantes do Nascimento; 1940–) Brazilian Association footballer, who played for Santos (1955–74), the New York Cosmos (1975–77), and Brazil. The greatest inside forward of his time, he became a world star at 17 when Brazil first won the World Cup (1958). He scored over 1300 goals.

Pelée, Mount (French name: Montagne Pelée) 14 18N 61 10W An active volcano on the West Indian island of Martinique. In 1902 an eruption engulfed the town of St Pierre. Height: 1463 m (4800 ft).

Peleus In Greek legend, a king of Phthia in Thessaly. He was married to *Thetis and was the father of Achilles.

Pelham, Henry. *See* Newcastle, Thomas Pelham-Holles, 1st Duke of.

pelican A large waterbird belonging to a family (*Pele-*

canidae; 7 species) occurring on lakes, rivers, and coasts of temperate and tropical regions. 125-180 cm long, pelicans are typically white with dark wingtips and have short legs, strong feet, a short tail and very large wings. Their long straight pointed bills have a distensible pouch underneath, in which fish are held before being swallowed. Order: *Pelecaniformes* (gannets, pelicans, etc.).

Pella The capital, about 39 km (24 mi) NW of Thessaloníki (N Greece), of Macedon (*see* Macedonia) from about 400 to 167 BC. Archelaus I (reigned 413-399) established his court here and it is the birthplace of Alexander the Great.

pellagra A disease caused by deficiency of nicotinic acid (*see* vitamin B complex). It occurs mainly in poor countries in people whose diet consists predominantly of maize. The disease causes dermatitis, diarrhoea, and delirium or depression. Health can be rapidly restored by giving nicotinic acid, nicotinamide or a diet rich in milk, yeast, beans, or peas.

PEKING   *Men practising* tai chi chu'an *exercises in front of the Qianmen Gate, at the south end of Tien-an-men Square.*

Pelletier, Pierre Joseph (1788-1842) French chemist, who in 1817 isolated *chlorophyll. He also isolated a number of naturally occurring *alkaloids, including *quinine and *strychnine, which were later introduced into medical preparations by François *Magendie.

Peloponnese (Modern Greek name: Pelopónnesos) The S peninsula of Greece, joined to central Greece by the Isthmus of Corinth. It includes the towns of Corinth, Patrás (the chief port), and *Sparta. Area: 21 637 sq km (8354 sq mi). Population (1981): 1 012 528.

Peloponnesian War (431-404 BC) The conflict between Athens and Sparta and their allies, in which Sparta was finally victorious. According to the Athenian historian Thucydides, the war was caused by Spartan fear of Athenian imperialism. Sparta's superior infantry invaded Athens in 431 while Athens, under Pericles, relying for security on walls connecting it to its seaport, attacked at sea. Lacking conclusive victories, both sides agreed to the peace of *Nicias (421). In 415, however, Athens led by *Alcibiades

set out to conquer Sicily, which retaliated with Spartan help and destroyed the Athenian fleet (413). The war continued until Sparta under *Lysander captured the partially rebuilt Athenian fleet (405) and beseiged Athens, which then surrendered (404).

Pelops The legendary Greek founder of the Pelopid dynasty of Mycenae, a son of *Tantalus. He won his bride Hippodamia by winning a chariot race with the help of his driver Myrtilus. When Myrtilus demanded his reward, Pelops refused and instead drowned him. The curse pronounced by the dying Myrtilus was passed on to his son *Atreus and all his descendants until it was exorcized by the purification of *Orestes.

pelota A generic name for a variety of court games played with a ball using the hand or a racket or bat. They derive from *real tennis and are widely played in the Basque provinces.

Pelotas 31 45S 52 20W A seaport in S Brazil, in Rio Grande do Sul state on the São Gonçalo Canal. The chief exports of Pelotas are meat, wool, and hides. Population (1980): 197 092.

Peltier effect. *See* thermoelectric effects.

pelvis A basin-like structure composed of the hip bones and lower part of the spine. It protects the soft organs of the lower abdomen and provides attachment for the bones and muscles of the legs. The pelvis is larger in women since it must allow the passage of a baby during childbirth. *See* Plate IV.

Pemba 5 10S 39 45E An island in Tanzania, off the NE coast of the mainland. Its major industry is the growing of cloves, of which it is the world's largest producer. Area: 984 sq km (380 sq mi). Population (1978): 205 850.

Pembroke 51 41N 4 55W A market town in SW Wales, in Dyfed on Milford Haven. It has a moated castle (dating from 1200 but much restored) and is the birthplace of Henry VII. Nearby is Pembroke dock (the dockyard closed in 1926). Population (1981): 15 618.

Pembrokeshire A former county of SW Wales. Under local government reorganization in 1974 it became part of *Dyfed.

PEN The acronym of the International Association of Poets, Playwrights, Editors, Essayists, and Novelists, an organization founded in 1921 to promote international fellowship between professional writers. Its presidents have included H. G. *Wells and Heinrich *Böll. Per Wastberg is the current president.

Penal Laws (1571, 1581, 1593) A series of Acts passed during the reign of Elizabeth I to punish those (recusants), especially Roman Catholics, who refused to attend Church of England services. Recusants were fined, imprisoned, banished, or executed and suffered civil disabilities, such as loss of property. The Laws were repealed in 1829 (*see* Catholic emancipation). *See also* Test Acts.

Penang A state in NW Peninsular Malaysia, on the Strait of Malacca, consisting of Penang island and Province Wellesley on the mainland. Ceded to the East India Company in 1786, the island was the first British settlement in Malaya. The main products are rice, rubber, and tin. The third largest bridge in the world was opened here in 1985. Area: 1031 sq km (398 sq mi). Population (1980): 911 586. Capital: Georgetown.

Penates. *See* Lares and Penates.

pencil cedar A *juniper tree, *Juniperus virginiana*, native to E and central North America and quite widely cultivated for ornament. It has scalelike leaves and blue berry-like fruits, up to 6 mm long. Its aromatic wood has been used to line clothing chests and cupboards (it repels moths) and for making lead pencils. The tree usually grows to a height of 15 m.

Penda (d. 655) King of Mercia (c. 634-55), who made

Mercia one of the most powerful English kingdoms. He remained heathen but permitted the conversion of his people to Christianity. He was killed in battle by Oswiu, King of Northumbria.

Penderecki, Krzysztof (1933–) Polish composer. His music, for which he has devised a special system of notation, is characterized by note clusters, special tone colours, and unusual sound effects. His compositions include *Threnody for the Victims of Hiroshima* (for strings; 1961), *De Natura Sonoris I* (for orchestra; 1966), the choral work *Utrenja* (1969–71), a symphony (1973), and the *Polish Requiem* (1980–84).

Pendlebury, John Devitt Stringfellow (1904–41) British archaeologist. Pendlebury initially worked at Tell el-Amarna (Egypt) but in 1928 he transferred to Crete, the subject of his classic *Archaeology of Crete* (1939). He was killed organizing guerrilla resistance to the German invasion of Crete in World War II.

pendulum A device in which a mass (the bob) swings freely about a fixed point with a constant period. In the ideal simple pendulum the bob is connected to the fixed point by a length (*l*) of weightless string, wire, etc. Its period is $2\pi(l/g)^{1/2}$, where *g* is the *acceleration of free fall, and is independent of the mass of the bob. A compound pendulum consists of a bob attached to the fixed point via two rigid rods. Pendulums are used to regulate a clock mechanism and in instruments that determine the value of *g*.

Penelope In Homer's *Odyssey*, the wife of *Odysseus. During her husband's absence she put off her many suitors by saying that she must first make a shroud for her father-in-law Laertes. Each night she unravelled what she had woven by day. After 20 years Odysseus returned and killed the suitors.

Penghu Islands (English name: Pescadores) A Taiwanese archipelago of about 64 small islands in Taiwan Strait. Area: 127 sq km (49 sq mi). Population (1972 est): 118 355. Main island: Penghu.

penguin A flightless black-and-white seabird belonging to a family (*Spheniscidae*; 14–18 species) occurring on cold coasts of the S hemisphere. Penguins are adapted for aquatic life, having wings reduced to narrow flippers giving fast propulsion when chasing fish and squid and escaping predators. 40–120 cm long, they have dense plumage enabling them to tolerate extreme cold. Penguins are highly gregarious and often migrate long distances inland to nest in "rookeries." Order: *Sphenisciformes. See also* emperor penguin; fairy penguin.

penicillins A group of *antibiotics. The first penicillin was isolated from the mould *Penicillium notatum*, in 1929, by Sir Alexander *Fleming but was not used to treat infections in man until 1941. Some penicillins must be injected (e.g. benzylpenicillin); others can be taken by mouth (e.g. phenoxymethylpenicillin). Semisynthetic penicillins (e.g. flucloxacillin, methicillin) are effective against infections resistant to naturally occurring penicillins. Ampicillin is a broad-spectrum penicillin, i.e. it kills many species of bacteria. Penicillins can cause severe allergic reactions in susceptible patients.

Penicillium A genus of fungi (about 250 species) that are common moulds in soil and on organic matter. The observation of the antibacterial action of *P. notatum* by Sir Alexander *Fleming led to the discovery of penicillin and other antibiotics. *P. camemberti* and *P. roqueforti* are important in cheese making. Family: *Eurotiaceae*; class: *Ascomycetes*.

Peninsular War (1808–14) That part of the Napoleonic Wars fought in Spain and Portugal. The French took Portugal in 1807 and in 1808 Napoleon's brother, Joseph *Bonaparte, replaced Ferdinand VII as King of Spain. Popular revolts broke out and turned into a vicious *guerrilla war. The Spanish rebels managed an initial victory at Bailén but against crack French troops could do no more than resist the sieges of Gerona and

Zaragoza. British troops under the command of the Duke of *Wellington eventually liberated the Peninsula. After their victory at Vitoria (1813) they invaded France, helping to force Napoleon's abdication (1814).

penis The male copulatory organ of mammals, some reptiles, and a few birds. In man (and other mammals) it contains a tube (urethra) through which both semen and urine can be discharged (*see* Plate IV). Erectile tissue making up the bulk of the penis becomes engorged with blood during sexual excitement, enabling the penis to be inserted into the vagina. The corresponding part in women is the **clitoris**, a small erectile mass of tissue situated in front of the urinary opening.

Pen-ki. *See* Benxi.

Penn, William (1644–1718) English Quaker and founder of Pennsylvania, son of Admiral Sir William Penn (1621–70). Sent down from Oxford (1661) because of his refusal to conform to the restored Anglican Church, he joined the Quakers in 1664. In 1668 he was imprisoned in the Tower for his writings. Here he wrote *No Cross, No Crown* (1669), a classic of Quaker practice. From 1682 he was involved in the establishment of Quaker settlements in America, including Pennsylvania, for which he drew up a constitution, "The Frame of Government", allowing freedom of worship.

Penney, William George, Baron (1909–) British mathematician, who worked at Los Alamos on the first atom bomb. Knighted (1952) for designing the British atom bomb, he went on to develop the British hydrogen bomb. He was later chairman (1964–67) of the UK Atomic Energy Authority, becoming a life peer (1967), OM (1969), and rector of Imperial College (1967–73).

Pennines (*or* Pennine Chain) An upland range in N England. It extends from the Cheviot Hills in the N to the valley of the River Trent in the S. Sometimes known as the "backbone of England" it is the watershed of the chief rivers in N England. It rises to 893 m (2930 ft) at Cross Fell. The **Pennine Way**, a 402 km (250 mi) long footpath, extends between Edale in Derbyshire and Kirk Yetholm in the Borders Region of Scotland.

Pennsylvania A state in the E USA, it is dominated by the uplands of the Appalachian Plateau. Much of the land is under forest or farmed, although it is generally considered to be an urbanized industrial state, dominated by Philadelphia in the E and Pittsburgh in the W. It is a leading iron and steel producer and provides nearly all the country's hard coal. Oil has long been important and the world's first oil well was drilled near Titusville in 1859. Dairy farming predominates in the NE, while the fertile lands of the SE yield cereals, fruit, and vegetables. This latter area is associated with the Pennsylvania Dutch, whose highly decorated barns can be seen throughout the area. *History*: one of the 13 original colonies, the first European settlers, the Swedes, were soon dispossessed by the Dutch (1655). In 1681 the area was given to William Penn by Charles II of England as a haven for Quakers. It became a state in 1787. Area: 117 412 sq km (45 333 sq mi). Population (1980): 11 866 728. Capital: Harrisburg.

Pennsylvanian period. *See* Carboniferous period.

pennyroyal A perennial herb, *Mentha pulegium*, native to wet places throughout Eurasia and naturalized in North America. 10–50 cm tall, it has small strongly scented hairy oval leaves and widely spaced whorls of tubular pink or lilac flowers. It is used as a flavouring and to scent soap. Family: *Labiatae*.

Pensacola 30 26N 87 12W A city and port in the USA, in NW Florida. An important naval air base, Pensacola's industries include fish canning and the manufacture of furniture. Population (1980): 57 619.

pensions Regular payments to people who cannot work

peptic ulcer

because of age, sickness, war injury, etc., and to widows and dependents. In the UK, pensions can be broadly classified into government pensions (*see* National Insurance), superannuation schemes, and self-employed pensions. Superannuation schemes may be contributory (both employer and employee contributing) or noncontributory (only the employer contributing). Civil servants, local-government employees, teachers, doctors, and the employees of many industrial and commercial firms belong to superannuation schemes. The Finance Act (1956) enables certain classes of self-employed persons to arrange their own pensions, the cost of which can be deducted from taxable income (*see* annuity; assurance). Pension funds generate vast sums of money, which are available for investment; insurance companies and insurance funds are now the "institutions" that dominate stock markets.

Pentagon The headquarters of the US Defense Department, a massive five-sided building in Virginia built (1941–43) during World War II. It houses all three services and is the largest office building in the world extending over 14 hectares (34 acres).

Pentateuch (Greek: five books) The title used by biblical scholars for the first five books of the *Old Testament, traditionally ascribed to Moses. *See also* Torah.

pentathlon An athletic competition comprising five events, the winner being the competitor with the highest total. It originated in an Olympic contest of sprinting, long jumping, javelin throwing, discus throwing, and wrestling (instituted in 708 BC). The current women's version, an Olympic event since 1964, consists of the 100 m hurdles, shot put, high jump, long jump, and 800 m run. The men's pentathlon has been replaced in major competitions by the *decathlon. It has not been an Olympic event since 1924. It comprises the long jump, javelin throw, 200 m sprint, discus throw, and 1500 m run. World record: 5083 points (1980) by Nadezda Tkachenko (Soviet Union). The **modern pentathlon** is a sporting competition comprising five events: a 5000 m crosscountry ride (on horseback), fencing, pistol shooting, a 3000 m swim, and a 4000 m cross-country run. It was first included in the Olympic Games in 1912.

Pentecost. *See* Whit Sunday.

Pentecostal Churches A Christian movement originating in revivalist meetings in the USA in 1906. In Pentecostal assemblies people seek spiritual renewal through baptism by the Holy Spirit, as took place on the first Pentecost (Acts 2.1-4). Glossolalia (speaking in tongues, or making unintelligible utterances under the influence of intense religious experience) is an accompanying phenomenon in many cases. Certain charismatic preachers, generally laymen, evoked an enormous response, especially in the USA, where the largest number of Pentecostal Churches are found.

Pentland Firth A channel separating the N Orkney Islands from the mainland of N Scotland. It is notorious for its rough seas and dangerous currents. Length: 32 km (20 mi). Width: 13 km (8 mi).

pentlandite The principal ore mineral of nickel, (Ni,Fe)S, found in association with pyrrhotite and chalcopyrite in basic and ultrabasic igneous rocks. It is mined in Canada, Australia, and the Soviet Union.

Penutian languages A major family of North American Indian languages spoken along the NW Pacific coast, on the Columbia River plateau, and in California. There are four main divisions: *Chinook and Tsimshian; Coos, Takelma, and Kalapooia; the Sahaptin group, which includes *Nez Percé; and the Californian group.

Penza 53 11N 45 00E A city in the Soviet Union, in the W RSFSR. Founded in 1666, it suffered repeated Tatar attacks. Long an agricultural centre, food processing remains important. Other industries include machine manufacturing and paper making. Population (1981 est): 500 000.

Penzance 50 07N 5 33W A resort in SW England, in SW

Cornwall. It is the port for the Scilly Isles and is a market town, with early flowers, fruit, and vegetables grown locally. Population (1981): 19 521.

peony A large perennial herb or shrub of the genus *Paeonia* (33 species) of N temperate regions, often cultivated for its showy flowers. The large glossy deeply cut leaves arise from underground stems or woody aerial shoots and the solitary white, pink, crimson, or yellow flowers are about 10 cm across, with incurving petals and a fleshy central disc supporting the stigma and numerous stamens. The fruit is a large leathery pod containing black seeds. Family: *Paeoniaceae*.

People's Liberation Army (PLA) The military forces of the People's Republic of China. The name was adopted by Chinese communist troops during the civil war of the 1930s and 1940s. Their aim was to liberate the people from the control of the *Guomindang. Since Liberation (1949) the PLA has exercised considerable power in Chinese communist politics.

Peoria 40 43N 89 38W A city in the USA, in Illinois on the Illinois River. The state's second largest city, it is the grain and livestock centre for an extensive agricultural area. Population (1980): 124 160.

Pepin (II) of Herstal (d. 714 AD) Ruler of the Franks (687-714). He became mayor of the palace (viceroy) of *Austrasia in 679 and virtual ruler of all the Franks after defeating *Neustria at Tertry (687). The Merovingian kings remained nominal rulers until the overthrow of the dynasty by his grandson *Pepin the Short.

Pepin the Short (d. 768 AD) King of the Franks (751-68) after overthrowing the *Merovingians. The son of *Charles Martel, Pepin founded the *Carolingian dynasty and was crowned king by St Boniface. He checked Lombard expansion and in 756 presented Pope Stephen II with the territories around Ravenna—the nucleus of the *papal states. His son *Charlemagne inherited the Frankish kingdom in 771.

pepper A condiment derived from a perennial climbing vine, *Piper nigrum*, native to India. Up to 10 m high, it bears chains of up to 50 inconspicuous flowers that form berry-like fruits (or peppercorns), about 5 mm in diameter. Whole peppercorns yield black pepper while white pepper is obtained from peppercorns with the outer part of the fruit wall removed. Family: *Piperaceae*.
The fleshy red and green peppers are the fruits of *Capsicum species.

pepperbox A 19th-century firearm, usually a pistol, with a cluster of barrels, each fired separately. Most bizarre was the *Mariette* design (1837) with 18 barrels, firing in groups of three.

peppered moth A European *geometrid moth, *Biston betularia*, the typical form of which has a similar coloration to the lichen-encrusted tree bark on which it rests (*see* Plate I). During the past century a dark form, var. *carbonaria*, has become common in sooty industrial areas, where it is better camouflaged—and thus better protected from predators—than the typical form.

peppermint A perennial herb, *Mentha* × *piperata*: a hybrid between water mint (*M. aquatica*) and *spearmint. It has smooth dark-green leaves and oblong clusters of reddish-lilac flowers and is the source of oil of peppermint, used as a flavouring.

pepsin A protein-digesting enzyme found in gastric juice. The inactive form, pepsinogen, is secreted by glands in the stomach wall and converted to pepsin by the hydrochloric acid in the stomach. Pepsin is a powerful coagulant of milk.

peptic ulcer An inflamed eroded area in the wall of the stomach (**gastric ulcer**) or, more commonly, the duodenum (**duodenal ulcer**). Ulcers are very common but it is not known exactly why they occur; they are more common in people who secrete excessive amounts of stomach acid. They may cause abdominal pain, nausea, and vomiting. Serious complications occur when the ulcer bleeds or perforates (bursts). In some patients ulcers disappear as quickly as they come; others require drugs, a special diet, or even surgery (especially if an ulcer perforates).

peptide A chemical compound comprising a chain of two or more *amino acids linked by peptide bonds (-NH-CO-) formed between the carboxyl and amino groups of adjacent amino acids. Polypeptides, containing between three and several hundred amino acids, are the constituents of *proteins. Some peptides are important as hormones (e.g. *ACTH) and as antibiotics (e.g. bacitracin, gradmicidin).

Pepys, Samuel (1633-1703) English diarist. His long career in naval administration culminated in his appointment as secretary to the Admiralty (1669-88). He was also an MP and president of the Royal Society. His *Diary*, which extends from 1660 to 1669 and includes descriptions of the Restoration, the Plague, and the Fire of London, is the intimate record of a man for whom every detail of life held interest. It was written in code and deciphered in the early 19th century.

Perak A populous state in NW Peninsular Malaysia, on the Strait of Malacca. In the Kinta Valley are important tin mines, and rubber, coconuts, and rice are produced. Area: 20 668sq km (7980 sq mi). Population (1980): 1 762 288. Capital: Ipoh.

Perceval A hero of *Arthurian legend, who played a leading part in the quest of the *Holy Grail. In *Chrétien de Troyes' romance, *Conte du Graal*, and in *Wolfram von Eschenbach's *Parzival*, he succeeds in the quest, but in later romances *Galahad is the only Arthurian knight to succeed in the quest.

Perceval, Spencer (1762-1812) British politician; prime minister (1809-12) remembered for his assassination by a mad and bankrupt broker, John Bellingham.

perch One of two species of freshwater food and game fish belonging to the genus *Perca*. The common perch (*P. fluviatilis*) of Eurasia has a deep elongated body, usually about 25 cm long, and is greenish in colour, with dark vertical bars on its sides, reddish or orange lower fins, and a spiny first dorsal fin. The yellow perch (*P. flavescens*) is North American. Perch usually live in shoals, feeding on fish and invertebrates. Family: *Percidae*; order: *Perciformes*. *See also* climbing perch; sea bass.

Percheron A breed of heavy draught ▢horse originating in the Perche district of France. It has a deep muscular body, powerful neck and shoulders, and a characteristically small refined head. Percherons are commonly black or grey. Height: 1.63-1.73 m (16-17 hands).

perching duck A *duck belonging to a tribe (*Cairinini*) found chiefly in tropical woodlands. Perching ducks nest in treeholes and have long-clawed toes for gripping branches. Drakes are larger and have brighter colours than females. *See* mandarin duck; Muscovy duck.

percussion cap A device for igniting the charge in firearms, enabling breech-loading *muskets and *rifles to be developed. A Scot, A. J. Forsythe (1769-1843), first patented detonating pills of mercury fulminate in 1807. Joshua Shaw, perhaps in 1815, encased these in a waterproof copper container, which could be incorporated into cartridges. Percussion muskets with cartridge ammunition were soon widely adopted in place of flintlocks.

percussion instruments Musical instruments that are struck by the hand or by a stick to produce sounds. The family includes the triangle, gong, rattle, block, cymbals and whip, as well as the pitched xylophone, glockenspiel, bells, celesta, and vibraphone. *Compare* drums; stringed instruments; wind instruments.

Percy, Sir Henry (1364-1403) English rebel, called Hotspur. Together with his father, Henry, 1st Earl of Northumberland (1342-1408), he led the most serious revolt against Henry IV, whom they had helped to the throne in 1399. Headstrong and fearless (hence his nickname) Percy was defeated and killed at Shrewsbury. He appears in Shakespeare's *Henry IV*, Part I.

Percy, Bishop Thomas (1729-1811) British antiquary and poet, who became Bishop of Dromore in 1782. In 1765 Percy published *The Reliques of Ancient English Poetry*, known as *Percy's Reliques*. This was a manuscript of medieval ballads found by Percy in a house at Shifnal, Shropshire.

PÈRE DAVID'S DEER *This species would probably now be extinct if the Duke of Bedford had not established a breeding herd at Woburn Abbey in about 1900. All specimens living today are believed to be descended from this herd.*

Père David's deer A rare Chinese deer, *Elaphurus davidianus*, now found only in parks and zoos. About 120 cm high at the shoulder, it has a long tail, splayed hooves, and a reddish-grey coat with a white ring round the eye. The male has long branching antlers. A French missionary, Père Armand David (1826-1900), described specimens in the Chinese emperor's hunting park in 1865.

peregrine falcon A large powerful *falcon, *Falco peregrinus*, occurring in rocky coastal regions worldwide. It is 33-48 cm long and has long pointed wings and a long tail. The male is blue-grey with black-barred white underparts; females are browner. It feeds mainly on ducks, shorebirds, and mammals, soaring high and diving at great speed.

Pereira 4 47N 75 46W A city in W Colombia. Notable buildings include the cathedral (1890) and the university (1961). An agricultural trading centre, it has coffee-processing, brewing, and clothing industries. Population (1980): 309 000.

Perelman, S(idney) J(oseph) (1904-79) US humorous writer. After publishing his first book in 1929, he worked for a time as a Hollywood scriptwriter, notably on some Marx Brothers films. In the 1930s he began contributing to the *New Yorker*, in which he published most of his short stories and sketches. One of the leading American humorists, he published numerous collections of his pieces, including *Strictly From Hunger* (1937), *Crazy Like a Fox* (1944), *The Most of S. J. Perelman* (1958), *Baby, It's Cold Inside* (1970), and *Eastward, Hi!* (1977).

perennials Plants that can live for many years. In herbaceous perennials, such as the iris and daffodil, aerial parts die down each winter and the plants survive in the form of underground organs (rhizomes, bulbs, corms, etc.). Woody perennials—trees and shrubs—have hardy woody stems, which may or may not shed their leaves in winter.

Peres, Shimon (1923–) Israeli statesman; prime minister (1984–86) and foreign minister (1986–). Born in Poland, Peres emigrated to Palestine with his parents in 1934. He became head of the navy in 1948 and was defence minister from 1974 to 1977. When a coalition government was formed in 1984, he became Labour prime minister under a special power-sharing agreement with Yitzhak *Shamir.

Pérez de Cuéllar, Javier (1920–) Peruvian diplomat; UN secretary-general (1982–). A respected negotiator, he worked for peaceful solutions to the Falklands war and other armed conflicts.

Pérez Galdós, Benito (1843–1920) Spanish novelist. He wrote a series of 46 historical novels about 19th-century Spain, *Episodios nacionales* (1873–1912), and a second series of novels about contemporary society, of which the best known are *Fortunata y Jacinta* (1886–87) and the *Torquemada* sequence (1889–95). He also wrote several successful plays.

perfect competition A theoretical market structure in economic theory in which no producer supplies a sufficiently large portion of the market to be able to influence prices or to make an exorbitant profit. Perfect competition ensures that resources are allocated in the most efficient way but is rarely found in practice. *Compare* monopoly; monopsony; oligopoly.

perfect number An integer that is equal to the sum of all its factors (except itself); for example $28 = 1 + 2 + 4 + 7 + 14$. If the sum of all the factors of n is greater or less than n, then n is called excessive or defective. *See also* numbers.

Perga (modern name: Ihsaniye) 36 59N 30 46E An ancient city in SW Turkey, near Antalya. It was the starting point of St Paul's first missionary journey (Acts 13.13) and remains include a theatre, an agora, and basilicas.

Pergamum An ancient city of W Asia Minor. After about 230 BC it became capital of a powerful Hellenistic kingdom, allied with Egypt and Rome against the *Seleucids. Pergamum became rich largely from *parchment and luxury textiles mass-produced by slave labour. Pergamene sculptors led artistic fashion, its library rivalled that of *Alexandria, and the architecture of the upper city was magnificent. The last king bequeathed his realm to Rome (133 BC).

Pergolesi, Giovanni (Battista) (1710–36) Italian composer. He spent most of his short life in or near Naples. His comic intermezzo *La serva padrona* (1733) was influential in the development of *opera buffa. His last work was a *Stabat Mater* (for soprano, alto, and orchestra; 1736).

Pericles (c. 495–429 BC) Athenian statesman, who presided over Athens' golden age. According to *Plutarch, Pericles became leader of the democratic party in 461 and secured power shortly afterwards, following the ostracism of his rival *Cimon. He dominated Athens until 430 by virtue of his outstanding oratory and leadership and his reputation for honesty. Under Pericles, Athens asserted its leadership of the *Delian League and revolts among its members were suppressed: following the Thirty Years' Peace with Sparta, Pericles was able to reduce Euboea (445) and then Samos (439). By 431, rivalry between Athens and Sparta had led to the outbreak of the *Peloponnesian War. The effectiveness of Pericles' strategy, which emphasized Athenian naval power, was undermined by the plague of 430 and Pericles briefly lost office. He died shortly after his reinstatement. In 447 Pericles initiated the great public works on the *Acropolis. He also fostered the work of many eminent men, including the playwright Sophocles, the philosopher Anaxagoras, and the sculptor Phidias.

peridotite An ultrabasic coarse-grained igneous rock consisting mainly of olivine; some varieties contain other ferromagnesian minerals, but none contain feldspar. The earth's mantle is sometimes called the peridotite shell. Peridotites occur beneath many mountains and islands.

perigee The point in the orbit of the moon or of an artificial satellite around the earth at which the body is nearest the earth. *Compare* apogee.

Perigordian A culture of the Upper *Palaeolithic. Perigordian is the preferred French designation for the pre-*Solutrean industries in W Europe, excluding the typologically different *Aurignacian. Upper Perigordian is approximately equatable with *Gravettian.

Périgueux 45 12N 0 44E A town in SW France, the capital of the Dordogne department. It has Roman remains and a 12th-century cathedral and is renowned for its *pâté de foie gras*, truffles, and wine. Manufactures include hardware and chemicals. Population (1982): 35 392.

perihelion The point in the orbit of a body around the sun at which the body is nearest the sun. The earth is at perihelion on 3 Jan. *Compare* aphelion.

Perilla A genus of herbs (4–6 species), native to India and SE Asia, with simple purplish-green leaves and tubular lilac flowers. A fast-drying oil is derived from the seeds and used in printing inks, paints, and varnishes. The leaves are used as a condiment. Family: *Labiatae*.

Perim Island 12 40N 43 24E A South Yemeni island off the SW tip of the Arabian Peninsula. It belonged to Aden from 1857 to 1967. Area: 13 sq km (5 sq mi).

period. *See* geological time scale; periodic motion; periodic table.

periodic motion Any motion that repeats itself at constant intervals. The interval of time between successive identical positions is known as the period of the motion and the maximum displacement of the system from its stationary position is called the amplitude. Examples of periodic motion include a swinging *pendulum, a bouncing ball, and a vibrating string. *See also* simple harmonic motion.

periodic table A tabular arrangement of the chemical *elements in order of increasing atomic number, such that physical and chemical similarities are displayed. The earliest version of the periodic table was devised in 1871 by D. *Mendeleyev, who successfully predicted the existence of several elements from gaps in the table. The rows across the table are known as periods and the columns as groups. The elements in a group all have a similar configuration of outer electrons in their atoms and therefore show similar chemical behaviour. Across each period, atoms are electropositive (form positive ions) to the left and electronegative to the right. For example, in the first period fluorine (F) is the most electronegative element and lithium (Li) the most electropositive. *Atomic theory explains this behaviour using the concept of electron shells, corresponding to different energy levels of the atomic electrons. Atoms combine in order to form complete outer shells. The shells are built up by filling the lower energy states (inner shells) first. The first shell takes two electrons, the second, eight, and so on. In larger atoms, the inner electrons screen the outer electrons from the nucleus, resulting in a more complex shell-filling sequence. This explains the partly filled shells of the *transition elements, which form the middle block of the table, in what are known as the long periods. The short periods are from lithium (Li) to neon (Ne) and from sodium (Na) to argon (Ar). The *noble gases in column 0 have complete outer shells and are generally chemically inactive. □ p. 942.

periodontal disease Disease of the gums and other structures surrounding the teeth, formerly known as pyorrhoea. Caused by the action of bacteria on food debris that forms a hard deposit (tartar) in the spaces between the gums and

1A	2A	3B	4B	5B	6B	7B	8			1B	2B	3A	4A	5A	6A	7A	0
1 H																	2 He
3 Li	4 Be											5 B	6 C	7 N	8 O	9 F	10 Ne
11 Na	12 Mg		←		TRANSITION ELEMENTS					→		13 Al	14 Si	15 P	16 S	17 Cl	18 Ar
19 K	20 Ca	21 Sc	22 Ti	23 V	24 Cr	25 Mn	26 Fe	27 Co	28 Ni	29 Cu	30 Zn	31 Ga	32 Ge	33 As	34 Se	35 Br	36 Kr
37 Rb	38 Sr	39 Y	40 Zr	41 Nb	42 Mo	43 Tc	44 Ru	45 Rh	46 Pd	47 Ag	48 Cd	49 In	50 Sn	51 Sb	52 Te	53 I	54 Xe
55 Cs	56 Ba	57† La	72 Hf	73 Ta	74 W	75 Re	76 Os	77 Ir	78 Pt	79 Au	80 Hg	81 Tl	82 Pb	83 Bi	84 Po	85 At	86 Rn
87 Fr	88 Ra	89‡ Ac															

† Lanthanides		57 La	58 Ce	59 Pr	60 Nd	61 Pm	62 Sm	63 Eu	64 Gd	65 Tb	66 Dy	67 Ho	68 Er	69 Tm	70 Yb	71 Lu
‡ Actinides		89 Ac	90 Th	91 Pa	92 U	93 Np	94 Pu	95 Am	96 Cm	97 Bk	98 Cf	99 Es	100 Fm	101 Md	102 No	103 Lr

PERIODIC TABLE

teeth, it results in swelling and bleeding of the gums: eventually—if untreated—the teeth become loose and fall out. Periodontal disease is the major cause of tooth loss in adults: it may be prevented (and the early stages treated) by regular brushing, scaling, and polishing, to remove the tartar. Advanced cases require surgery.

Peripatus A common genus of wormlike *arthropods belonging to the mainly tropical subphylum *Onychophora* (about 90 species). The soft unsegmented body, about 50 mm long, bears 14-44 short stumpy legs. The animals live in moist dark places, in rock crevices, or under stones or rotting logs and feed on insects. The young develop within the body of the mother and at birth resemble the adults.

periscope An optical device consisting, typically, of a tube in which mirrors or prisms are arranged so that light passing through an aperture at right angles to the tube is reflected through the length of the tube to emerge at an aperture at the other end also at right angles to the tube. Periscopes in their simplest form, with cardboard or plastic tubes, are used to see over the heads of a crowd; in their more sophisticated form, they are designed to be extendible and are used by submerged submarines to see above the surface of the water. In this form they may contain aiming devices for weapons, infrared screens, etc.

Perissodactyla An order of hoofed mammals (16 species) that includes *horses, *tapirs, and *rhinoceroses. The name—meaning odd-toed—reflects the fact that the weight of the body is carried mainly by the central (third) digit of the foot. They are herbivorous, grazing or browsing on leaves, but have evolved separately from other hoofed mammals and have only a single stomach, which is less efficient than the digestive system of *ruminants. *Compare* Artiodactyla.

peritonitis Inflammation of the peritoneum—the membrane that lines the abdominal cavity. This is a serious condition that results from the bursting of an abdominal organ (such as the appendix, gall bladder, or spleen) or of a peptic ulcer. Alternatively it may result from bacterial infection. The patient will be very ill, possibly in shock, with a painful and rigid belly. An operation is essential to repair the perforated organ and cleanse the abdomen; antibiotics are also given.

periwinkle (botany) An evergreen creeping shrub or perennial herb of the genus *Vinca* (5 species), native to Europe and W Asia. The attractive solitary blue or white flowers are tubular with five lobes and the fruit is usually a long capsule. They thrive in shade and are cultivated as ornamentals: *V. major* is an important species. Family: *Apocynaceae*.

periwinkle (zoology) A *gastropod mollusc belonging to the family *Littorinidae*, also called winkle. The common edible winkle (*Littorina littorea*) of European seashores is about 2 cm high and has a dark-green rounded shell with a pointed spire and grazes on algae. The flat-sided periwinkle (*L. littoralis*) lacks the spire and occurs in many colours.

Perkin, Sir William Henry (1838-1907) British chemist, who in 1856 synthesized the first artificial dye, aniline purple. Perkin's discovery, when he was only 18, was made by accident while he was trying to synthesize quinine. The following year he built a factory to manufacture the dye but he later returned to chemical research and the synthesis of many compounds.

Perlis The most northerly state in Peninsular Malaysia, bordering on Thailand. Consisting of a well-watered plain, it produces chiefly rice, with some rubber and coconuts; tin is mined. Area: 803 sq km (310 sq mi). Population (1980): 147 726. Capital: Kangar.

Perm (name from 1940 until 1957: Molotov) 58 01N 56 10E A port in the Soviet Union, in the W RSFSR on the River Kama. Its varied industries include engineering, chemical manufacturing, and oil refining. The *Permian period was first identified here. Population (1981 est): 1 018 000.

permafrost The permanent freezing of the ground, sometimes to great depths, in areas bordering on ice sheets. During the summer season the top layer of soil may thaw and become marshy, while the frozen ground below remains an impermeable barrier. Problems arise with the construction of roads and buildings in permafrost areas due to the freeze-thaw processes. This seriously hindered the construction of the Alaskan Pipeline, completed in 1977.

Permalloy An *alloy of one part iron to four parts nickel, often with other metals added. It has a high magnetic permeability, which makes it useful for parts of electrical machinery that are subjected to alternating magnetic fields.

permeability, magnetic A measure of the response of a material to a *magnetic field. Magnetic permeability, μ, is the ratio of the magnetic *flux induced in the material to the applied magnetic field strength. The relative permeability, is the ratio of μ in the medium to that in a vacuum, μ_0 (*see* magnetic constant). Paramagnetic materials have a μ_r greater than unity because they reinforce the magnetic field. Ferromagnetic materials can have a μ_r as high as 100 000. Diamagnetic materials have a μ_r of less than one.

Permian period The last geological period of the Palaeozoic era, between the Carboniferous and Triassic periods, lasting from about 280 to 240 million years ago. Widespread continental conditions prevailed, which continued into the Triassic, and the two periods are often linked together as the Permo-Triassic, during which the New Red Sandstone was laid down.

permittivity The absolute permittivity of a medium is the ratio of the electric displacement to the electric field at the same point. The absolute permittivity of free space is called the *electric constant. The relative permittivity (*or* dielectric constant) of a capacitor is the ratio of its capacitance with a specified dielectric between the plates to its capacitance with free space between the plates.

Pernambuco. *See* Recife.

Pernik 42 36N 23 03E A town in W Bulgaria, situated on the River Struma near Sofia. It has engineering and iron and steel industries with coalmining nearby. Population (1982 est): 175 000.

JUAN PERON *He is seen here with his beautiful and popular second wife Evita, a former actress, who was responsible for many reforms (including female suffrage) during his first presidency.*

Perón, Juan (Domingo) (1895-1974) Argentine statesman; president (1946-55, 1973-74). Elected in 1946 after winning popular support as head of the labour secretariat, his position was strengthened by the popularity of his second wife, **Evita Perón** (María Eva Duarte de P.; 1919-52), who was idolized by the poor for her charitable work. After her death, support for Perón waned and he was deposed. He went into exile but remained an influential political force in Argentina, returning in 1973, when he was re-elected president. He died in office and was succeeded by his third wife **Isabel Perón** (María Estella P.; 1930-), who was deposed by the army in 1976.

Pérotin (Latin name: Perotinus Magnus; c. 1155-c. 1202) French composer, active in Paris. A leading exponent of *organum, he composed complex music in the *ars antiqua style.

Perpendicular The style of □gothic architecture predominant in England between about 1370 and the mid-16th century. The name derives from the panel-like effect of the window design, with its pronounced vertical mullions broken regularly by horizontal divisions. Gloucester Cathedral choir (c. 1357) is an early example. The flat network effect was repeated in the late 14th-century development of fan vaulting for ceilings. Eton College chapel (begun 1441), King's College chapel, Cambridge (1446-1515), St George's chapel, Windsor (begun 1481), and the Henry VII chapel, Westminster Abbey (1503-19), are masterpieces of the Perpendicular style.

perpetual-motion machine A hypothetical machine that produces continuous and unending motion without drawing energy from an outside source. Although such a machine would contravene the laws of *thermodynamics and therefore cannot be made, there have always been, and indeed still are, hopeful inventors who believe that it is possible to find loopholes in the laws of nature. A perpetual-motion machine would need to be frictionless (in contravention of the second law of thermodynamics) or would need to be able to create energy to overcome the friction (in contravention of the first law). Using the heat of the ocean to drive a ship (perpetual motion of the second kind) is also impossible, because it would contravene the second law.

Perpignan 42 42N 2 54E A city in S France, the capital of the Pyrénées-Orientales department situated near the Spanish border. The capital of the former province of Roussillon in the 17th century, it has a gothic cathedral and a 13th-century castle (the former residence of the Kings of Majorca). Perpignan is a tourist and commercial centre, trading in wine, fruit, and vegetables. Population (1982): 113 646.

Perrault, Charles (1628-1703) French poet and fairytale writer. As a member of the Académie Française he opposed *Boileau by championing the modern writers against the ancients. He is best known for his collection of fairytales, *Contes de ma mère l'Oye* (1697), translated into English in 1729 and best known by the English title, *Tales of Mother Goose.*

Perrin, Jean-Baptiste (1870-1942) French physicist, who discovered that cathode rays carry a negative charge and therefore consist of particles and not waves, as many physicists then thought. He also used Einstein's equations for the Brownian movement to determine the approximate size of molecules.

Perry, Fred(erick John) (1909-) British tennis and table-tennis player. He was the world singles table-tennis champion in 1929 and in the three years 1934-36 he won the singles title at Wimbledon (a record beaten in 1979 by *Borg), as well as many other championships.

Perry, Matthew C(albraith) (1794-1858) US naval officer. He led the naval expedition (1853-54) that forced Japan to open diplomatic relations with the USA, thus ending Japan's traditional isolation.

Perse, Saint-John (Alexis Saint-Léger; 1887-1975) French poet. He was born in the West Indies, served as a diplomat in the Far East, and became secretary general of the Foreign Ministry in 1933. From 1940 to 1958 he lived in the USA. His poems, written in long free-verse lines, give prominence to landscapes and the sea and include the long poem *Anabase* (1922), translated by T. S. Eliot in 1930, and *Chronique* (1960). He won the Nobel Prize in 1960.

Persephone (Roman name: Proserpine) Greek goddess of the underworld, daughter of Zeus and *Demeter. She was abducted by *Hades, who made her queen of the underworld. Zeus, moved by Demeter's sorrow for her daughter, allowed her to spend part of each year on earth, symbolizing the regeneration of natural life in the spring.

Persepolis An ancient Persian city in Fars province, Iran. *Darius I (reigned 522–486 BC) planned Persepolis as the ceremonial capital of his empire and its wealth and splendour were legendary. Among the buildings on the vast central terrace were the apadana (royal audience hall), which was approached by monumental stairways flanked by reliefs of tribute bearers, and *Xerxes' throne hall. The Achaemenian royal tombs are nearby. *Alexander the Great destroyed Persepolis in 330 BC.

Perseus (astronomy) A constellation in the N sky near Cassiopeia, lying in the Milky Way. The brightest stars are the 2nd-magnitude Mirfak and the eclipsing binary *Algol.

Perseus (Greek mythology) The son of Zeus and Danae. One of the greatest Greek heroes, he beheaded the *Medusa with the help of Athena, who gave him a mirror to avoid looking at the Gorgon and being turned to stone. He married Andromeda, daughter of the Ethiopian king. She had been chained to a rock as a sacrifice to a sea monster, which Perseus turned to stone by showing it the Medusa's head.

Pershing, John J(oseph) (1860–1948) US general. After the US entry into World War I (1917), he commanded the American Expeditionary Force (AEF) in France, insisting on its independence from Allied forces. He was chief of staff (1921–24).

Pershing missile A US army two-stage solid-fuelled nuclear surface-to-surface missile launched from mobile launcher vehicles and having a range of 740 km (460 mi). Several improved versions of the missile have been produced; Pershing II missiles were deployed in Europe in 1984, despite opposition from several European governments. It is named after Gen J.J. *Pershing.

Persia. *See* Iran.

Persian A language belonging to the *Iranian language family. It is the official language of Iran and is written in a modified Arabic script.

Persian art and architecture The styles associated with the three principal phases of the Persian empire: *Achaemenian (550–331 BC), *Sasanian (224–651 AD), and Islamic. The splendours of Achaemenian and Sasanian architecture are represented respectively by *Persepolis and *Ctesiphon. Sasanian kings commissioned monumental relief sculptures to commemorate victories and coronations. The Persian tradition of fine craftsmanship in metalwork, glassware, and ceramics dates from this period. After 651, Persian styles became an aspect of international trends in *Islamic art. Calligraphy and book illustration became important, the latter evolving into the renowned 15th-, 16th-, and 17th-century Persian miniature painting. The love of subtly brilliant colours is epitomized in the famous Persian carpets and in the architectural use of turquoise coloured tiles.

Persian cat A domesticated cat, also called a Longhair, having a long flowing coat with a ruff or frill around the neck. The 20 or so recognized breeds are characterized by their short bodies, deep flanks, short legs, and short bushy tails. The head has a snub nose, large round eyes, and small wide-set ears and the coat may be of any colour, although the Blue Persian is most popular.

Persian Empire. *See* Achaemenians.

Persian Gulf An arm of the Arabian Sea, extending some 950 km (590 mi) NW beyond the Gulf of Oman. The large off-

shore oil deposits are exploited by the surrounding *Gulf States. Area: 233 000 sq km (89 942 sq mi).

Persian Wars. *See* Greek–Persian Wars.

persimmon A tree of the genus *Diospyros* that produces edible fruits. These are the Japanese persimmon (*D. kaki*), the American persimmon (*D. virginiana*), and the Asian date plum (*D. lotus*). Up to 30 m high, they have dark-green oval leaves and produce round orange, yellow, or red fruits, 5–8 cm across. Persimmons are eaten fresh, cooked, or candied. Family: *Ebenaceae*.

perspective Any means of rendering objects or space in a picture to give an illusion of their depth. The laws of perspective of a scene, known as linear perspective, were formulated by *Brunelleschi in the 15th century and became one of the *Renaissance artists' most important scientific investigations. The earliest scientific perspective (1436) was constructed by *Alberti in his treatise on painting. Guide lines converge on one, two, or three points on the horizon line, known as vanishing points, according to whether the orientation of a scene is central, angular, or oblique.

Perspex (polymethyl methacrylate) A colourless transparent thermoplastic material made by *polymerization of methyl methacrylate. It can be extruded and moulded and coloured, for use in light fittings, including coloured signals, aircraft parts, and car parts. It is resistant to ultraviolet radiation from fluorescent lights and is widely used as an unbreakable substitute for glass.

perspiration. *See* sweat.

Perth 31 58S 115 49E The capital of Western Australia, on the Swan River. Founded in 1829, it expanded following the discovery of gold (1893) at Kalgoorlie. It is the commercial and cultural centre of the state; the University of Western Australia was founded in 1913 and there are two cathedrals. Its port, *Fremantle, and Kwinana, both to the S, are growing industrial centres. Population (1983 est): 969 100.

Perth 56 24N 3 28W A city in E Scotland, in Tayside Region on the River Tay. An early capital of Scotland, it was the scene of the assassination of James I (1437). There are dyeing, textiles, whisky distilling, and carpet industries and it is a popular tourist centre. Population (1984 est): 41 654.

Perth (*or* Perthshire) A former county of SE Scotland. Under local government reorganization in 1975 it formed part of Perth and Kinross District in Tayside Region while the SW area became part of the Central Region.

perturbations Small departures of a celestial body from the orbital path it would follow if subject only to the influence of a single central force. Short-term periodic disturbances arise from gravitational interactions with other bodies. Progressive disturbances or those of very long period can also occur.

Peru, Republic of A country in the NE of South America, on the Pacific Ocean. Narrow coastal plains rise to the high peaks of the Andes, reaching heights of over 6500 m (21 000 ft). The land descends again through an area of forested plateaus to the tropical forests of the Amazon basin. Most of the population is of Indian or mixed Indian and European descent. *Economy*: Peru is one of the world's leading fishing countries, the main product being fishmeal. Agriculture is important, now organized largely in cooperatives, and the main crops include maize, rice, sugar cane, cotton, and coffee. Large-scale irrigation projects are being undertaken. Livestock is particularly important to the economy, especially the production of wool. Rich mineral resources include copper, silver, lead, zinc, and iron; oil has been discovered in considerable quantities, both in the jungles and offshore. In recent years there have been considerable developments in industry and in industrial relations, including moves towards nationalization and worker participation, although such moves have been slowed down by changes of government. With its relics of ancient civilizations, Peru has a valuable tourist trade. The main exports include minerals and metals and fishmeal. *History*: Peru's precolonial history encompasses the civilization of the *Chimú and that of the *Incas, who were conquered by the Spanish under Pizarro in 1533. The viceroyalty of Peru, centred on Lima, enjoyed considerable prosperity in which the Indian population had little share. A revolt in 1780 led by Tupac Amarú was suppressed. Peru was the last of Spain's American colonies to declare its independence (1821) and the Spanish were finally defeated in 1824. Political stability was achieved by Gen Ramón Castilla (1797–1867; president 1845–51, 1855–62), who developed Peru's economy, based on guano deposits. However, the country's prosperity was undermined by the War of the *Pacific (1879–83) in which Peru lost the nitrate-rich province of Tarapacà to Chile. Since World War II, in which Peru declared war on Germany in 1945, the country has depended on US aid and has witnessed a series of coups, most recently in 1975, when Gen Francisco Morales Bermúdez (1921–) became president. In 1980, in Peru's first general elections to be held in 17 years, Fernando Belaúnde Terry was elected president; in 1985 he was replaced by Alan Garcia Pérez (1949–), whose monetary policy has led to an IMF ban on further loans. An estimated 10 000 people have died in civil unrest in the 1980s. Peru is a member of the OAS and LAFTA. Official languages: Spanish and Quechua; Aymará is also widely spoken. Official currency: sol of 100 centavos. Area: 1 285 215 sq km (496 093 sq mi). Population (1983 est): 18 300 000. Capital: Lima. Main port: Callao.

Peru Current. *See* Humboldt Current.

Perugia 43 07N 12 23E A city in Italy, the capital of Umbria. Originally an Etruscan city, it has 13th-century city walls, a 14th-century cathedral, an ancient fountain (the Maggiore Fountain), and a university (1200). Perugia is an agricultural trading centre and its manufactures include furniture and textiles. Population (1980 est): 140 742.

Perugino (Pietro di Cristoforo Vannucci; c. 1450–1523) Italian Renaissance painter, born near Perugia. He worked on frescoes in the Sistine Chapel, including the *Giving of the Keys to St Peter* (1481–82). His spacious compositions and graceful figure style influenced his pupil *Raphael.

Perutz, Max Ferdinand (1914–) British chemist, born in Austria, who developed *X-ray diffraction to determine the molecular structure of haemoglobin. For this work he shared a Nobel Prize (1962) with J. C. *Kendrew.

Pesaro 43 54N 12 54E A town in Italy, in Marche on the Adriatic coast. It is the birthplace of Rossini, who established a school of music here. Population (1983 est): 90 579.

Pescadores. *See* Penghu Islands.

Pescara 42 27N 14 13E A seaport in Italy, in Abruzzi on the Adriatic coast. Its chief industries are tourism, shipbuilding, and fishing. Population (1980 est): 136 366.

Peshawar 34 01N 71 40E A city in N Pakistan, situated at the E end of the Khyber Pass. One of the oldest cities in Pakistan, it has for centuries been a centre of trade between the Indian subcontinent, Afghanistan, and central Asia. Industries include textiles, shoes, and pottery and it has a university (1950). Population (1981): 555 000.

Pestalozzi, Johann Heinrich (1746–1827) Swiss educationalist. A pioneer of mass education, Pestalozzi made several unsuccessful attempts to establish schools for poor children. His book *Wie Gertrud ihre Kinder lehrt* (1801) reflected his ideas on the intuitive method of education. Despite his apparent failures, his theories were of great importance to subsequent educational developments. Pestalozzi's work is commemorated in the **Pestalozzi International Children's Villages**, the first of which was established in 1946 for war orphans at Trogen (Switzerland). A second international village was established in 1958

Sedlescombe, Surrey, in the UK for the care and education of selected children from developing countries.

pesticides. *See* herbicides; insecticides.

Pétain, (Henri) Philippe (1856-1951) French general and statesman. In World War I he distinguished himself at the defence of Verdun (1916), becoming marshal of France (1918). In World War II, when France was on the verge of defeat (1940), Pétain became prime minister. In June, 1940, he signed an armistice with Hitler that allowed for a third of France to remain unoccupied by Germany. His government of unoccupied France at Vichy was authoritarian and from 1942 was dominated by *Laval and the Germans. Pétain was sentenced to death in August, 1945, for collaboration but was then reprieved and imprisoned for life.

Peter (I) the Great (1672-1725) Tsar (1682-1721) and then Emperor (1721-25) of Russia, who established Russia as a major European power. Peter ruled with his half-brother Ivan V (1666-96) until Ivan's death and under the regency of his half-sister *Sophia until 1689, when he became effective ruler. Peter travelled in W Europe in the late 1690s, acquiring knowledge of western technology and returning to Russia with western technicians, who were to implement the modernization programmes that marked his reign. He instituted many reforms in government and administration, trade and industry, and in the army. In the *Great Northern War (1700-21), he acquired Livonia, Estonia, and also Ingria, where in 1703 he founded St Petersburg (now *Leningrad). He campaigned less successfully against the Turks (1710-13) but gained territory in the Caspian region from war with Persia (1722-23). Peter's eldest son *Alexis died in prison, having been condemned to death for treason; Peter was succeeded by his wife, who became *Catherine I.

Peter I (1844-1921) King of Serbia (1903-18) and then of Yugoslavia (1918-21). Brought up in exile, Peter was elected king after the assassination of the last Obrenović monarch. His rule was marked by its constitutionalism.

Peter, St In the New Testament, one of the 12 Apostles. He was a fisherman on the Sea of Galilee until called by Jesus along with his brother *Andrew. He became the leader and spokesman for the disciples. Although his faith often wavered, notably at the crucifixion, when he denied Christ three times, Peter was named as the rock upon which the Church was to be built. He was also entrusted with the "keys of the Kingdom of Heaven" (Matthew 16.19)—hence his symbol of two crossed keys. After Christ's death, he dominated the Christian community for 15 years, undertaking missionary work despite imprisonment. Whereas Paul had responsibility for the Gentiles, Peter's was to the Jews. He is believed to have been martyred and buried in Rome. Feast day: 29 June.

Peterborough 52 35N 0 15W A city in E central England, in Cambridgeshire on the River Nene. The cathedral (begun in the 12th century) contains the tomb of Catherine of Aragon. Designated a new town in 1967, its industries include sugar-beet refining, foodstuffs, engineering, and brick making and it is an important marketing centre for the surrounding agricultural area. Population (1981 est): 114 108.

Peterborough 44 19N 78 20W A city in SE Canada, in Ontario. It is an important manufacturing centre and the main commercial centre for central Ontario. The largest deposit of nepheline in the world (used in the manufacture of glass) is nearby. Population (1971): 58 111.

Peter Damian, St (1007-72) Italian churchman; cardinal and Doctor of the Church. He is famous as a religious reformer who campaigned for clerical celibacy and attacked simony. Feast day: 23 Feb.

Peterhead 57 30N 1 46W A port in NE Scotland, in Grampian Region. Scotland's most easterly town, built of locally quarried pink granite, Peterhead is a fishing port (formerly whaling) and servicing centre for North Sea oil rigs with engineering and fish-curing industries. Population (1981): 17 015.

Peter Lombard (c. 1100–60) Italian theologian. He studied in Rheims and in Paris, where, between 1136 and 1150, he taught theology at the school of Notre Dame. He became Bishop of Paris in 1159. His most famous work, the *Books of Sentences* (1148–51), was an objective summary of the beliefs of earlier theologians. It was a standard text in the universities until the 16th century and many medieval scholars wrote commentaries on it, including Thomas *Aquinas.

Peterloo Massacre (1819) The name given, by analogy with the battle of Waterloo, to the violent dispersal of a political meeting held in St Peter's Fields, Manchester. A peaceful crowd, numbering about 60 000, had gathered to hear Henry *Hunt speak on parliamentary reform. The magistrates, anxious about the size of the crowd, called in local troops. The cavalry were ordered to charge and in the ensuing panic 11 people were killed.

Peterson, Oscar Emmanuel (1925–) Canadian Black jazz pianist, who has played with many leading jazz musicians as well as with his own trio. His many recordings include *The Gershwin Song Book* and *Peterson Plays Basie*.

Peter's pence An annual contribution for the support of the papacy levied on all English householders from the 9th century. The one-penny tax continued to be raised, with some interruptions, until its abolition in 1534.

Peters' projection. *See* map projection.

Peter the Hermit (c. 1050–1115) French monk. A fervent supporter of the first *Crusade under Pope Urban II, he rallied over 20 000 peasants to follow him to the Holy Land, where many were massacred by the Turks. He later founded the monastery of Neufmoutier at Liège.

Petipa, Marius (1819–1910) French dancer and choreographer. He exercised an important influence on the Russian imperial ballet in St Petersburg, where he worked from 1847 until 1903. He became its chief choreographer in 1862. His many ballets include *Don Quixote* (1869) and *The Sleeping Beauty* (1890), on which he collaborated with its composer, Tchaikovsky.

Petit, Roland (1924–) French ballet dancer and choreographer. His innovatory ballets, characterized by elements of fantasy and contemporary realism, include *Carmen* (1949) and *Kraanerg* (1969). He toured with his company in Europe and the USA and also choreographed for Hollywood films.

petition of right The procedure by which a person formerly petitioned against the English Crown for the restoration of property that the Crown had taken possession of, or for damages for breach of *contract. This method of claiming against the Crown, dating back to the reign of Edward I, has been replaced by ordinary court actions under the Crown Proceedings Act (1947). The **Petition of Right** (1628) was a parliamentary declaration accepted by Charles I. It made illegal imprisonment without trial, taxation without parliamentary approval, and the billeting of soldiers on private individuals.

petit mal. *See* epilepsy.

Petöfi, Sándor (1823–49) Hungarian poet. He came from a peasant background and elements of traditional folksong occur in his early poetry, notably in the narrative poem *János the Hero* (1845). His later poetry was chiefly concerned with the cause of nationalism. He disappeared during the battle of Segesvar (1849), in which the Hungarian revolutionary army was defeated by the Austrians and Russians.

Petra An ancient town in S Jordan. It was the capital of the Nabataeans, nomadic Arabs who settled along the caravan routes from Arabia to the Mediterranean. Petra was a great trading centre from the 3rd century BC. It was incorporated in the Roman Empire in 106 AD and was superseded by *Palmyra in the 2nd century. Accessible only through a narrow gorge,

Petra is renowned for its rock-cut temples and dwellings.

Petrarch (Francesco Petrarca; 1304–74) Italian poet. He was born in Florence, but his family was banished and he lived mostly in Provence from 1312 to 1353, when he returned to Italy. He travelled widely in Europe and in 1341 was crowned as poet laureate in Rome. His humanist works of scholarship anticipated the Renaissance in their combination of classical learning and Christian faith. His other works include *Secretum meum*, his spiritual self-analysis, and *Africa*, a Latin verse epic on Scipio Africanus, but he is remembered chiefly for the *Canzoniere*, a series of love poems addressed to Laura. His work greatly influenced writers throughout Europe, including *Chaucer.

Petrea A genus of tropical climbing plants (about 30 species), native to tropical America and the West Indies. Up to 9 m high, they have oblong leaves and sprays of bluish-purple flowers, each with five widely spaced strap-shaped petals and coloured sepals. Popular ornamental species include *P. volubilis* and *P. kohautiana*. Family: *Verbenaceae*.

petrel A marine bird belonging to a widely distributed family (*Procellariidae*; 55 species) characterized by a musky smell, thick plumage, webbed feet, and a hooked bill with long tubular nostrils. 27–90 cm long, petrels are well adapted for oceanic life, feeding on fish and molluscs and only coming ashore to breed. Diving petrels belong to a family (*Pelecanoididae*; 5 species) occurring in the S hemisphere; they are 16–25 cm long, have short wings, and feed mostly on crustaceans. Order: *Procellariiformes*. *See also* fulmar; prion; shearwater; storm petrel. □oceans.

Petrie, Sir (William Matthew) Flinders (1853–1942) British archaeologist. After surveying British prehistoric sites, Petrie went to Egypt (1880), where his painstaking excavations and meticulous study of artefacts revolutionized and set new standards for archaeology. He excavated numerous sites, including *Naukratis, *Tell el-Amarna, and *Abydos, finally leaving Egypt for Palestine in 1926. He was the first professor of Egyptology at University College, London (1892–1933).

petrochemicals. *See* oil.

Petrograd. *See* Leningrad.

petroleum. *See* oil.

petrology The study of rocks, including their formation, structure, texture, and mineral and chemical composition. **Petrogenesis** is the origin or mode of formation of rocks; **petrography** is the description and classification of rocks from hand specimens or thin sections.

Petronius Arbiter (1st century AD) Roman satirist. He was appointed "Arbiter of Taste" at the court of Nero. The *Satyricon*, his picaresque novel of which only fragments survive, relates the scandalous adventures of the youths Encolpius and Ascyltos and includes the famous satirical portrait of a coarse and vulgar millionaire, Trimalchio. Petronius committed suicide after being falsely accused of conspiring against Nero.

Petropavlovsk 54 53N 69 13E A city in the Soviet Union, in the N Kazakh SSR on the River Ishim. It is an important junction on the Trans-Siberian Railway and has varied industries. Population (1981 est): 212 000.

Petropavlovsk-Kamchatskii 53 03N 158 43E A port in the Soviet Union, in the E RSFSR on the Kamchatka Peninsula. Long a major naval base, it was attacked by the French and British during the Crimean War. Fishing, fish processing, and ship repairing are the principal activities. Population (1981 est): 223 000.

Petrópolis 22 30S 43 06W A city and mountain resort in SE Brazil, in Rio de Janeiro state. Notable buildings include the Museum of the Empire (formerly the royal palace) and the gothic-style cathedral. Population (1980): 149 427.

Petrosian, Tigran Vartanovich (1929–84) · Soviet chess

player, who was world champion from 1963 to 1969, when he lost the title to *Spassky. Despite his exhaustive preparations, as world champion his matches were often disappointing because his style of play tended to lead to draws.

Petrozavodsk 61 46N 34 19E A city in the Soviet Union, the capital of the Karelian ASSR in the NW RSFSR on Lake Onega. It was founded (1703) by Peter the Great: engineering and timbering are important activities and there are many educational institutions. Population (1981 est): 241 000.

Petsamo. *See* Pechenga.

Petunia A genus of tropical American herbs (about 40 species), cultivated for their showy funnel-shaped flowers, which are sometimes frilled at the edges. Ornamental species include *P. integrifolia*, with pink, blue, or purple flowers, the white-flowered *P. axillaris*, which has a pleasant night fragrance, and hybrids between them. Family: *Solanaceae*.

Pevensey 50 49N 0 20E A village in SE England, in East Sussex. The landing place of William the Conqueror and an ancient Cinque Port (now inland), it has a ruined Norman castle built inside Roman walls (the remains of a Roman fort). Population (1981): 2397.

Pevsner, Antoine (1886–1962) Russian sculptor and painter, who worked in Paris from 1923. His early career was spent in W Europe but it was in Russia that he and his brother Naum *Gabo pioneered *constructivism in their *Realist Manifesto* (1920). His most characteristic abstract constructions consist of curving and thrusting shapes in striated metal.

Pevsner, Sir Nikolaus (Bernhard Leon) (1902–83) British art historian, born in Germany, who taught in England after World War II. His best-known work is on architecture and includes *An Outline of European Architecture* (1942) and the series on *The Buildings of England* (1951–74).

pewter An *alloy of tin with lead or copper, antimony, and bismuth. It was formerly used for plates, spoons, and other utensils but now only beer mugs are made from it.

peyote A blue-green *cactus, *Lophophora williamsii*, also called mescal, native to Mexico and the SW USA. About 8 cm across and 5 cm high, it bears white to pink flowering heads, which, when dried, are known as "mescal buttons." They contain the alkaloid *mescaline, which produces hallucinations when chewed.

Pforzheim 48 53N 08 41E A city in SW West Germany, in Baden-Württemberg. It was an important medieval trading centre and is the centre of the West German watch and jewellery industry. Population (1980 est): 106 700.

pH A measure of the acidity or alkalinity of a solution, equal to the logarithm to the base 10 of the reciprocal of the number of moles per litre of hydrogen ions it contains. Thus a solution containing 10^{-6} mole of hydrogen ions per litre has a pH of $\log_{10}(1/10^{-6}) = 6$. In pure water there is a small reversible dissociation into equal amounts of hydrogen and hydroxide ions: $H_2O \rightarrow H^+ + OH^-$. The product of the concentrations of these ions (moles/litre) is about 10^{-14}: $[H^+][OH^-] = 10^{-14}$. In neutral solutions, therefore, the hydrogen ion concentration is 10^{-7} and the pH is consequently 7. In acid solutions the pH is less than 7; the lower the pH, the more acidic the solution. Conversely, alkaline solutions have pH values greater than 7. The pH scale is logarithmic; for example, a solution with a pH of 2 is ten times more acidic than one with a pH of 1. *See also* acids and bases.

Phaedra In Greek mythology, the daughter of *Minos and Pasiphaë and the wife of Theseus. She fell in love with her stepson *Hippolytus. When he rejected her, she hanged herself, having first written a letter to Theseus accusing Hippolytus of having seduced her.

Phaedrus (1st century AD) Roman writer. Born a slave in Macedonia, he gained his freedom in the household of the emperor Augustus. He wrote poetic versions of the Greek prose fables ascribed to *Aesop. His work was popular in medieval Europe.

Phaethon In Greek mythology, the son of the sun god Helios, who granted him his wish to drive the chariot of the sun for one day. Unable to control the horses, he was about to burn the earth when Zeus struck him down with a thunderbolt.

phaeton A four-wheeled open carriage usually drawn by two horses. Various modifications of the phaeton (pony phaeton, Victoria phaeton, Stanhope phaeton, etc.) were fashionable in the 19th century for pleasure driving.

phagocyte A cell that engulfs and then digests particles from its surroundings: this process is called phagocytosis. Many protozoans are phagocytic, but the word specifically refers to certain white blood cells that protect the body by engulfing bacteria and other foreign particles.

phalanger A small herbivorous *marsupial of the family *Phalangeridae* (48 species), occurring in woodlands of Australia, (including Tasmania), and New Guinea. They range in length from 12 to 120 cm and are adapted for climbing trees, having strong claws and prehensile tails. The family includes the *cuscuses, *flying phalangers, *honey mouse, *koalas, and *possums.

Phalaris (c. 570–c. 554 BC) Tyrant of Agrigento in Sicily, who established its prominence by subjugating the indigenous Sicels and defying the Phoenicians. Phalaris was noted for his cruelty and was overthrown.

phalarope A lightly built migratory shorebird belonging to a family (*Phalaropodidae*; 3 species) in which the female fights for a territory and courts the male, which rears the young. 20–25 cm long, phalaropes have a slim neck, lobed toes, and a grey and red-brown plumage. Two species breed in the Arctic and one inland in North America.

phanerogam Any plant that reproduces by means of flowers and seeds. Phanerogams comprise the angiosperms (flowering plants) and the gymnosperms (conifers, etc.). *Compare* cryptogam.

Phanerozoic time Geological time from the end of the Precambrian to the present day, about 590 million years. It refers to the eon of "evident life," when abundant and clearly recognizable fossils were laid down. *Compare* Cryptozoic time.

PHARAOH *The pharaoh's double crown, combining the red crown of Lower Egypt with the white crown of Upper Egypt, symbolized the unification of the two lands (c. 3100 BC).*

pharaoh The title of ancient Egyptian rulers. The word derives via Hebrew from the Egyptian for great house. There were various symbols of kingship: the crook and flail and the white, red, or blue crown. The royal cobra, the sun god Ra's symbol, bound round the brow, signified divinity; pharaoh represented Ra reigning on earth. The first dynasty, or line of pharaohs, was founded about 3200 BC.

Pharaoh hound A breed of hunting dog whose ancestors are depicted in sculpture and friezes found in the tombs of the Egyptian pharaohs. The Pharaoh is a slender long-legged hound with a long muzzle and large ears. The short glossy coat is tan, with or without white markings. Height: 56–63 cm (dogs); 53–61 cm (bitches).

Pharisees An ancient Jewish religious and political party. They stressed ritual purity and acknowledged a body of traditional laws not contained in the written *Torah. The party originated in the 2nd century BC and vied for political influence with the *Sadducees. In the *Gospels they are frequently criticized by Jesus, although his own teachings are very close to theirs. After the destruction of the *Temple of Jerusalem they ceased to exist, but many of their teachings were taken over into rabbinic Judaism.

pharmacology The study of the action of drugs on living organisms. Pharmacologists examine the uptake of drugs after administration, the routes by which they reach their site of action, their subsequent effects, how drugs are destroyed by the body, their unwanted side effects, and the interaction between different drugs. Clinical pharmacology (*or* therapeutics) studies the effects of drugs in treating disease. **Pharmacy** is the science concerned with the preparation, manufacture, packaging, quality, and supply of medicinal drugs. The practice of pharmacy should conform to the standards laid down in the official **pharmacopoeia** of the country. This is a government-approved list giving details of the manufacture, dosage, uses, and characteristics of drugs. It is compiled by experts in pharmacy and pharmacology. The World Health Organization has issued the *Pharmacopoeia Internationalis* in an attempt to standardize drug preparations throughout the world.

Pharos of Alexandria An ancient lighthouse, one of the *Seven Wonders of the World. Built in about 280 BC by Sostratus of Cnidos for Ptolemy II of Egypt, it was over 135 m (440 ft) high. It was demolished in the 13th century AD.

Pharsalus, Battle of (48 BC) The decisive encounter near present-day Fársala (Greece) in the Roman civil war, in which Julius Caesar defeated Pompey. Pompey's defeat opened the way to Caesar's dictatorship.

pharynx The muscular tract, lined with mucous membrane, between the back of the mouth and oesophagus (gullet) and larynx. It acts as a passageway for food between the mouth and gullet and it also conducts air from the nasal cavity (which opens into it) to the larynx and windpipe. The Eustachian tubes from the middle *ear also open into the pharynx. Inflammation of the pharynx (pharyngitis) is a common cause of a sore throat.

phase (astronomy) The fraction of the face of the moon or a planet that is illuminated at a particular time in its orbit. Lunar phases vary from new moon (unilluminated) through a waxing crescent, first quarter (half illuminated), a waxing gibbous moon, to full moon (fully illuminated) followed by a waning gibbous moon, last quarter, a waning crescent, and the next new moon.

phase (physics) **1.** The fraction of its whole cycle that a periodically varying system has completed. For example, two *alternating currents of the same frequency are **in phase** if they reach their maximum values at the same instant. If they are out of phase the angle between the *vectors representing the quantities is called the **phase angle**. In an electricity-supply system there are usually three phases, i.e. three separate alternating voltages having the same frequency but being displaced in phase relative to each other by one third of a cycle. **2.** Any portion of a system that is physically distinct, is homogeneous throughout, and can be mechanically separated from other phases. For example, a salt solution is a one-phase system, whereas a mixture of ice and water is a two-phase system. *See also* phase rule.

phase rule A rule stating the conditions of equilibrium for a heterogeneous system. It relates the number of degrees of freedom of a system f, the number of *phases p, and the number of components c, by the rule $f = c - p + 2$. It was proposed by J. W. *Gibbs in 1877 and is important in the study of metallurgy, mineralogy, and ceramics.

Phasmida An order of generally flightless insects (2000 species), occurring mostly in tropical and oriental regions. They comprise the *leaf insects and *stick insects, both of which show a striking resemblance to the vegetation on which they live and feed.

pheasant A long-tailed gamebird belonging to an Old World subfamily (*Phasianinae*; 50 species) occurring in open or woodland regions (*see* Plate V). 50–200 cm long, pheasants are heavily built and have short rounded wings, a short bill, and strong claws for scratching up grain, roots, and grubs. Males are larger than females and brightly coloured, with bright fleshy wattles, large leg spurs, and long tail feathers. They have been introduced to many regions for sport or ornament. Family: *Phasianidae* (pheasants, quail, partridges); order: *Galliformes* (pheasants, turkeys, etc.). *See also* golden pheasant; tragopan.

phenobarbitone: *See* barbiturates.

phenols A class of organic compounds with the general formula ROH, in which the –OH group is linked directly to a carbon atom in an *aromatic ring. Although formally similar to alcohols, the phenols have widely different properties; in particular, the aromatic ring confers acidic behaviour on the –OH group. The simplest example, phenol itself (or **carbolic acid**), C_6H_5OH, is a white deliquescent solid used as a disinfectant and in the production of drugs, weedkillers, and synthetic resins.

phenomenology A philosophical enquiry into intellectual processes, which is characterized by the vigorous exclusion of any preconceptions about existence or causes. It is thus distinct from *psychology, the aim of which is causal explanations rather than pure description. *Husserl was the first to elevate this method into an independent philosophy.

phenothiazines A group of powerful tranquillizing drugs, including chlorpromazine and fluphenazine. Used in the treatment of *schizophrenia and *manic-depressive psychosis, they are thought to act by inhibiting the action of a chemical (dopamine) in the brain. *See also* tranquillizers.

phenotype The characteristics of an individual, representing the sum total of the effects of the interaction of its inherited characteristics with its environment. A striking example of this occurs in the Himalayan rabbit, which grows either black or white fur according to the temperature. *Compare* genotype.

phenylketonuria A genetic disease that leads to mental deficiency if untreated. Patients are unable to metabolize the amino acid phenylalanine, which is a normal constituent of diet; the amino acid and its derivatives accumulate in the body and prevent proper mental development. Phenylketonuria can now be easily detected at birth by a routine test. Babies with the disease need a special diet that contains little phenylalanine, which should be maintained until adolescence.

pheromone A chemical substance produced by animals to communicate with others of the same species. The best-known pheromones are the sex attractants secreted by moths to attract mates. Pheromones are also used by ants to lay trails and by mammals to mark out territories.

Phidias (c. 490–c. 417 BC) Athenian sculptor, one of the most influential artists of his time. Phidias designed and supervised the sculptures of the *Parthenon (*see* Elgin Marbles). His works included a bronze statue of *Athena on the Athenian *Acropolis and two famous chryselephantine statues: Athena in the Parthenon and *Zeus at Olympia (where his workshop has been found).

Phidippides (5th century BC) Greek runner who ran 241 km (150 mi) from Athens to Sparta in two days to ask for help against the Persians before the battle of *Marathon in 490 BC.

Philadelphia 40 00N 75 10W A city in the USA, situated on the Delaware River in Pennsylvania at the junction of the Schuylkill River. Founded in 1681 by the Quaker, William Penn, its religious tolerance attracted a large number of immigrants. It has many historic buildings, including Independence Hall (1732-59), where the Declaration of Independence was adopted and the Liberty Bell is kept. Benjamin Franklin is buried here. A cultural centre, it is the site of the University of Pennsylvania (1779) and the Franklin Institute (1824) and has a famous symphony orchestra. It is the USA's fourth largest city and has the world's largest freshwater port. Its output of manufactured goods is exceeded only by four other US cities. Industries include oil refining, textiles, and shipbuilding. Population (1980): 1 688 210.

Philadelphus.   *See* mock orange.

PHILAE   *The rising waters of Lake Nasser partially submerging the Kiosk of Trajan.*

Philae   24 02N 32 59E A submerged islet in the River Nile, in SE Egypt just above Aswan. Flooding caused by the first Aswan Dam from 1902 onwards damaged the many ancient temples on the island. These were moved to a higher island before Philae was totally submerged by Lake Nasser after the construction of the *Aswan High Dam.

philately   (*or* stamp collecting)   Collecting and studying postage stamps as a hobby, which began immediately following their introduction in England (1840). Catalogues were first issued in the early 1860s as collecting became increasingly concerned with such details as watermarks, perforations, and numberings. Collectors usually specialize in a particular theme, country, or type of issue. Rare stamps in good condition, which fetch extremely high auction prices, are a form of investment, while the market among collectors for commemorative stamps or first-day covers is an important source of revenue for post offices.

Philby, H(arry) St John (Bridge)   (1885-1960) British explorer and Arabist. He joined the Indian civil service in 1907 and in World War I undertook a political mission to central Arabia, where he crossed the Empty Quarter. He became a Muslim in 1930 and friend and adviser of Ibn Saud of Saudi Arabia. His son **Harold Adrian Russell Philby** (1912-   ) was an intelligence officer and Soviet secret agent, known as Kim Philby. He became a Soviet agent in 1933 and entered the British intelligence service in 1940. From 1949 to 1951 he was liaison officer between the British and US intelligence services in Washington, DC. He defected to Russia in 1963.

Philemon   (c. 368-c. 264 BC) Greek dramatist. Born in Sicily, he became a citizen of Athens and also worked in Alexandria. His plays, of which only fragments survive, were frequently acclaimed by his contemporaries as superior to those of his rival, *Menander.

Philemon, Epistle of Paul to   A New Testament book written in about 60 AD that is the only strictly private letter of Paul to be preserved. In it he requests Philemon, a Christian friend in Colossae, to welcome and forgive Onesimus, his runaway slave, who had become a Christian after meeting Paul. Onesimus delivered the letter.

Philemon and Baucis   In Greek mythology, an old peasant couple who offered hospitality to Zeus and Hermes, who were disguised as mortals. They were subsequently spared from a flood that destroyed the land and their cottage was transformed into a temple. They were granted their wishes to serve as priest and priestess in the temple and finally to die together.

Philidor, André Danican   (d. 1730) French musician. As assistant librarian of the Royal Music Library at Versailles he made a large collection of instrumental court music. His youngest son **François André Danican Philidor** (1726-95) wrote several operas and was also a considerable chess player.

Philip (I) the Handsome   (1478-1506) King of Castile (1506). Son of Emperor Maximilian I and Mary of Burgundy he succeeded to his mother's possessions in 1482. In 1496 he married Joanna the Mad, who inherited the Castilian throne in 1504. Her insanity led Philip to assume sole control in 1506. Their son became Emperor *Charles V.

Philip (II) of Macedon   (382-336 BC) King of Macedon (359-336), who founded the Macedonian empire. Philip unified Macedonia, expanded the economy, and trained a professional army with which he gradually bore down on the Greek city states. Despite the resolute opposition of *Demosthenes at Athens, the Greeks were defeated at the battle of *Chaeronea (338). Philip planned to lead a combined force against Persia but he was assassinated and the plan was carried out by his son *Alexander (III) the Great.

Philip II Augustus   (1165-1223) King of France (1179-1223), who destroyed the *Angevin empire of the English kings. He waged war with Henry II (1187-89), Richard Lionheart (1194-99), and John; he took Normandy in 1204, followed by Maine, Touraine, and Anjou (1204-05), and in 1214 defeated an English-imperial alliance at *Bouvines. He participated in the third Crusade.

Philip II   (1527-98) King of Spain (1556-98). He inherited a vast empire from his father *Charles V, including Naples and Sicily, the Netherlands, and Spanish possessions in America; in 1580 he annexed Portugal. He married Mary I of England in 1554. Philip faced the *Revolt of the Netherlands and the Turkish threat in the Mediterranean, suppressed the *Moriscos, launched the *Spanish Armada against Protestant England (1588), and intervened in the French *Wars of Religion against the Huguenots. On his death Spain was bankrupt and its economy destroyed, largely as a result of the cost of these wars.

Philip (IV) the Fair   (1268-1314) King of France (1285-1314). Hostilities with England (1294-1303) were ended by the betrothal of Philip's daughter Isabella of France to Edward II. Conflict with Pope Boniface VIII over the right of lay rulers to tax clergy ended only with Boniface's death (1303) but his successor Clement V was more easily handled and in 1309 moved the papacy to Avignon. In 1306 Philip expelled the Jews from France and his reign also witnessed the suppression of the *Templars (1307-13).

Philip V   (1683-1746) The first Bourbon King of Spain (1700-24, 1724-46). The grandson of Louis XIV of France, his accession instigated the War of the *Spanish Succession. He abolished the self-governing privileges of Aragon and centralized the administration. He abdicated in 1724 in favour of his son Luis (1707-24) but returned to the throne when Luis died.

Philip VI   (1293-1350) The first Valois King of France (1328-50), succeeding his cousin Charles IV. The failure of the rival claim of Edward III of England to the French throne contributed to the outbreak in 1337 of the *Hundred Years' War, in which Philip suffered severe defeats at Sluis (1340) and Crécy (1346).

Philip, Prince, Duke of Edinburgh   (1921-   ) The husband (from 1947) of Elizabeth II of the United Kingdom. A descendant of Queen Victoria and the son of Prince Andrew of Greece, he assumed the name Mountbatten in 1947, when he took British citizenship. He served in the Royal Navy during World War II. In 1956 he introduced the **Duke of Edinburgh's Award Scheme** to encourage the leisure activities of young people between the ages of 14 and 25.

Philip, St In the New Testament, one of the 12 Apostles. He was a native of Bethsaida and was responsible for bringing Nathanael (probably Bartholomew) to Jesus. In medieval art he is symbolized by loaves because of his participation in the miracle of the loaves and fishes. He may have been martyred. Feast day: 11 May.

Philippeville. *See* Skikda.

Philippi, Battle of (42 BC) The battle in which Mark Antony and Octavian (later Emperor *Augustus) defeated *Brutus and *Cassius Longinus in the Roman civil war.

Philippians, Epistle of Paul to the A New Testament book written by Paul in about 60 AD to the church at Philippi in Macedonia, the first church that he founded in Europe. He thanks the Philippians for the gifts they have sent to him in prison in Rome and tells how he has continued to spread Christianity while imprisoned. The epistle contains an important doctrinal passage on the nature of Christ and the Incarnation.

Philippine eagle A rare *eagle, *Pithecophaga jefferyi*, occurring in tropical forests of the Philippines, formerly called monkey-eating eagle because it feeds mainly on macaque monkeys. It is 85–100 cm long and has a brown plumage with pale underparts, a shaggy crest, a huge bill, and very powerful talons.

Philippines, Republic of the A country in SE Asia, consisting of an archipelago of over 7000 islands, of which some 880 are inhabited, between the Pacific Ocean and the South China Sea. Except for the central plain of Luzon (where most of the population is concentrated) there are few extensive lowlands, most of the larger islands, including Mindanao, being mountainous and volcanic and reaching heights of almost 3000 m (10 000 ft). Most of the inhabitants are Filipinos with small minorities of Chinese and others. *Economy*: based principally on agriculture, forestry, and fishing. The production of the staple crops of rice and maize and the main cash crops (sugar, coconuts, bananas, and pineapples) is concentrated around the central plain of Luzon although attempts are being made to develop economic activities elsewhere. The fastest-growing productive sector in recent years has been mining, based on the country's wide range of metallic minerals, which include copper, gold, iron ore, manganese, molybdenum, zinc, lead, and silver. Forests cover over half the land, providing gums and resins, bamboo, and dyes in addition to good-quality hardwoods. The main industries are food processing, textiles, wood processing, and oil refining. Tourism is an expanding industry. *History*: colonized by Spain in 1565, the islands were ceded to the USA in 1898 following the Spanish-American War. Occupied (1942–45) by the Japanese during World War II, they became an independent republic in 1946. During the initial years of independence, a succession of presidents, US economic interests, and the Filipino landowning class did little to improve the standard of living of the peasant majority, but following the election of President *Marcos in 1965 rapid economic development and a greatly improved infrastructure brought increased prosperity to the Philippines. During the early 1970s growing communist guerrilla activity in the N and a Muslim separatist movement in the S led to martial law (1972). Since then the government has moved towards nonalignment in its relations with the outside world. In 1978 President Marcos was re-elected, becoming prime minister until 1981. In this year martial law was lifted but the assassination of the exiled opposition leader, Benigno S. Aquino (1983), rekindled unrest. Marcos was exiled to the USA in 1986 when Cory *Aquino (widow of Benigno) became president. Her reforms include a new consti-

tution; several attempted coups by Marcos supporters have failed. Official languages: Pilipino (a new language based on Tagalog) and English. Official currency: Philippine peso of 100 centavos. Area: 300 000 sq km (115 830 sq mi). Population (1980): 47 914 017. Capital and main port: Manila.

Philippine Sea A section of the W Pacific Ocean, N and E of the Philippines. It contains deep trenches, volcanic submarine mounts, and coral reefs and is particularly prone to hurricanes. Its warm currents provide important fishing grounds. Maximum depth: 10 540 m (34 580 ft).

Philippopoli. *See* Plovdiv.

Philip the Bold (1342–1404) Duke of Burgundy (1363–1404), so called because of his military courage, particularly at the battle of Poitiers (1356) in the Hundred Years' War. The youngest son of John the Good of France, during the minority of his nephew Charles the Well-Beloved he was one of the regents of France and later, when Charles became insane, virtual ruler. He was also a noted art patron.

Philip the Good (1396–1467) Duke of Burgundy (1419–67). He recognized Henry V of England as heir to the French throne in 1420 but acknowledged Charles VII as King of France in 1435. In 1430 he founded the Order of the *Golden Fleece. He was a notable patron of artists.

Philip the Magnanimous (1504–67) Landgrave of Hesse, an ally of *Luther. Converted to Protestantism in 1524, Philip led the suppression of the *Peasants' War in 1525. He attempted to reconcile Luther and *Zwingli, who became theologically divided over the Eucharist. In 1531 he helped establish the Schmalkaldic League of Protestant princes. However, in 1540 his bigamous marriage, approved by Luther, was used by Emperor Charles V to split the Protestants and in 1547 the League was defeated by Charles at the battle of Mühlberg.

Philistines A non-Semitic people, who were driven from Egypt about 1200 BC and settled in Canaan, resisting Israelite attacks so vigorously that the region took the name Palestine from its new settlers. Tradition holds they were originally one of the *Sea Peoples who left Crete as the Mycenaean world collapsed. A warlike seafaring people, without cultural pretensions (hence the derogatory word philistine), they were largely absorbed into the kingdom of Israel under King David about 1000 BC.

Phillip, Arthur (1738–1814) British admiral, who founded New South Wales. After service in the Seven Years' War and the American Revolution he was appointed to found a penal settlement in New South Wales. Arriving in 1788, he chose the site of Sydney, administering the colony until 1792.

Phillips' curve A relationship between the rate of wage increase and unemployment, plotted by the British economist A. W. Phillips (1914–) in 1958. The Phillips' curve suggested that the UK Government had an option between unemployment and inflation, i.e. it could achieve a little less of one if it was prepared to accept a little more of the other. The monetarists (*see* monetarism) hold that the relationship is theoretically unsound and it has indeed broken down in practice since 1966.

Philoctetes A legendary Greek hero, who had inherited from his father the bow and arrows of Heracles. On the way to Troy with the Greek expedition he was bitten by a snake. His cries and the stench of his wound forced the Greeks to leave him on Lesbos. Odysseus and Diomedes later returned to fetch him, needing the help of his bow and arrows. He then killed Paris and helped to bring about the fall of Troy.

Philodendron A genus of woody, usually climbing, plants (275 species), native to tropical America. They have oval, oblong, arrow-shaped, or heart-shaped leaves, either deeply cut or coloured along the veins, and they cling to trees or other supports by means of aerial roots growing from their stems. Cultivated as ornamental house plants for their foliage, *P. andreanum* and *P. erubescens* are among the most popular species. Family: *Araceae*.

Philo Judaeus (c. 30 BC–45 AD) Jewish philosopher from the *Diaspora community in Alexandria, then the Greek capital of Roman Egypt. Philo's voluminous treatises, written in Greek, reinterpret Jewish religion in terms of Greek philosophy. Some were designed for sophisticated Jews; others defend Judaism against Greek scorn of Jewish culture. In old age Philo represented the Jews on a deputation to the Roman emperor following antisemitism in Alexandria. Most of his works have survived owing to their popularity with later Christian writers.

philology The study of language in general, before the growth of modern *linguistics. It originally applied to the study of classical languages and literatures but came to be applied to what is now called comparative linguistics. Comparative studies were undertaken in the 19th century by many philologists, including Jacob *Grimm, who helped to identify and trace the relationships of the *Indo-European languages.

Philomela and Procne In Greek legend, the daughters of an Athenian king. Procne married Tereus, King of Thrace. He fell in love with Philomela, raped her, and cut out her tongue to prevent her telling his secret. By means of an embroidery Philomela told Procne of the outrage and in revenge Procne killed her own son, Itys, and fed his flesh to Tereus. He then attempted to kill the sisters but was turned into a hoopoe and the sisters into a swallow and a nightingale.

philosopher's stone A hypothetical substance sought by alchemists for its ability to turn less valuable minerals into gold. In alchemical literature it is also called the elixir, the tincture, and hundreds of other fanciful names. It was sometimes credited with the power of curing all diseases and of making its possessors immortal. *See* alchemy.

Philosophes A group of French philosophers and writers of the 18th century whose faith in the ultimate authority of reason was expressed in their active concern with social and political reform. They included *Montesquieu, *Voltaire, J.-J. *Rousseau, and *Diderot, the chief editor of their literary monument, the *Encyclopédie* (1751–72; *see* Encyclopedists).

philosophy (Greek: love of wisdom) The field generally concerned with the study of ultimate reality and the first principles of thinking, knowledge, and truth. The main theoretical branches of modern western philosophy are *epistemology, *ethics, and *metaphysics; *logic (now closely associated with mathematics) and *aesthetics are also traditionally included. Historically, philosophical as opposed to religious or magical speculation arose in Greece in the 6th century BC in the attempts of the school of Miletus (*see* Thales; Anaximander; Anaximenes) to discover the single element underlying all things. This line of enquiry was pursued further by later Presocratics, including Heraclitus, Pythagoras, Parmenides, and Democritus. The most important phase of ancient philosophy occurred with the teaching of Socrates, who developed the dialectical method and applied it to political and other problems. The works of his successors, Plato and Aristotle, not only shaped the future of European philosophy in most fundamental respects, but also deeply influenced Christian theology. Among later schools of classical philosophy were *Epicureanism, *Stoicism (which strongly appealed to Roman philosophers), and *Neoplatonism. Aristotelianism was preserved in the works of medieval Islamic philosophers, such as Avicenna and Averroes, and re-entered Christian Europe in the *scholasticism of Anselm, Abelard, and Aquinas. Although influenced by scholasticism, the work of Descartes, with its systematic doubt and emphasis on reason, signalled the end of the medieval synthesis and the beginning of the modern period and the dominance of science. Spinoza and Leibniz

attempted to deal with problems raised by Descartes; their rationalist systems are usually contrasted with the empiricism of the English philosophers, especially Locke, Berkeley, and Hume. Kant, whose aim was to reconcile these approaches and relate the sensible and the intelligible, was one of the most significant thinkers of the 18th century and stimulated the development of German idealism in the works of Fichte, Schelling, and Hegel. Idealism was also stimulated by the writings of Rousseau, whose ideas were the major source of 19th-century Romanticism and influenced the work of Schopenhauer and Nietzsche. In England utilitarianism was developed by Bentham and J. S. Mill, dialectical materialism by Marx and Engels, and Hegelian idealism by F. H. Bradley. Pragmatism is particularly associated with the Americans William James and, later, John Dewey. Philosophy in the 20th century has been characterized by a marked difference in interests and emphases between most Continental philosophers and those working in English-speaking countries. The writings of Bergson and Croce had an influence on a number of writers (including prominent English men of letters) early in the century. The phenomenology of Husserl (and the works of Kierkegaard) led to the existentialism of Heidegger and Sartre. In contrast to their speculative approach to many of the large issues of traditional philosophy, the principal concern of English-speaking thinkers has been a critical approach that concentrates on logical analysis and the role of language—a development that may be traced in the works of Bertrand Russell, A. N. Whitehead, G. E. Moore, Wittgenstein, the logical positivists (the *Vienna circle), and in the current school of "ordinary language" philosophy centred at Oxford.

Indian and other eastern types of philosophical thought are closely bound to the religious or cultural framework in which they developed (e.g. *Taoism, *Vedanta, Zen Buddhism).

Phiz. *See* Browne, Hablot.

phlebitis Inflammation of a vein, which is always accompanied by some *thrombosis in the vein. The inflammation may be caused by injury or infection or it may occur for no apparent reason: thrombosis of the vein then follows. Alternatively inflammation may develop after thrombosis. Treatment of superficial phlebitis is by rest and support.

phloem Plant tissue specialized to transport synthesized foods, mainly sugars, around the plant. It consists principally of tubelike cells that lack nuclei, the end of one cell being linked to the next by means of a porous wall (sieve plate). The cells are controlled by small neighbouring cells, known as companion cells.

phlogiston theory An 18th-century theory of combustion based on the belief that all combustible substances contain phlogiston, which is liberated when the substance is heated, leaving calx or ash. The more combustible the substance, the more phlogiston it contains. The theory was finally overthrown in the late 18th century by A. *Lavoisier, who correctly explained combustion in terms of oxidation.

phlogopite A *mica mineral, $K_2(Mg,Fe^{2+})_6(Si_6Al_2O_{20})(OH,F)_4$. It is brown or bronze coloured and occurs in some peridotites and metamorphosed limestones. It is used principally for making commutators.

Phlox A genus of ornamental herbs (about 65 species), mostly native to North America. Growing to about 1 m high, they have terminal clusters of tubular flowers with five white, pink, red, or purple spreading petals. The creeping phlox, or moss pink (*P. subulata*), forms carpets of flowers in rock gardens. *P. drummondii* is the source of most garden varieties. Family: *Polemoniaceae*.

Phnom Penh (or Pnom Penh; Cambodian name: Phnum Pénh) 11 35N 104 55E The capital of Kampuchea, a port at the head of the Mekong delta. The capital since about 1432, it is now the site of the royal palace and of many museums and pagodas. A cultural centre, it has several universities, including a Buddhist university (1954) and the University of Phnom Penh (1960). The country's commercial centre, its industries include textiles and food processing. Population (1981 est): 400 000.

phobia A pathologically strong fear of a particular situation or thing. The main kinds are agoraphobia, which is fear of public places and open spaces; claustrophobia (fear of enclosed places); specific phobias of individual things, such as sharp knives; social phobias of encountering people; and animal phobias, as of spiders, rats, or snakes. Phobias are sometimes learned after a frightening incident, sometimes acquired in childhood from other people, and sometimes result from *depression. They are treated with *behaviour therapy; *psychotherapy and drug treatment may also be used.

Phocis A region of ancient central Greece, N of the Gulf of Corinth. The Phocians were intermittently engaged in a struggle to retain control of Apollo's shrine at *Delphi (in Phocis). In the first so-called Sacred War (c. 590 BC) the Phocians lost Delphi. The second, precipitated by their seizure of the city, confirmed their possession. Early in the 4th century they again lost it, retaking it in 356. In the ensuing third Sacred War (355–346) the Phocians were defeated by Philip of Macedon, who proceeded to conquer all of Greece.

Phoenicia A group of city states on the coastal plain of Syria N of ancient *Canaan. Semitic peoples settled here sometime before 1800 BC and after about 1000 BC they became outstanding navigators and merchants, establishing trading posts all over the E Mediterranean and beyond. Their major cities—*Tyre, *Sidon, and *Byblos—were ports. The Phoenician alphabet, the ancestor of all western alphabets and perhaps the original one, was the chief Phoenician contribution to cultural progress. Phoenicia fell successively under Egyptian, Babylonian, and Persian influence. It was attacked by *Alexander the Great (332 BC), becoming part of the Hellenistic and later the Roman Empires. Phoenicia's major colony in N Africa was *Carthage.

phoenix A fabulous bird associated with sun worship, especially in Egypt, and representing resurrection and immortality. According to Herodotus, it was like an eagle in size and shape, had red and golden plumage, and lived for 500 years. Only one bird existed at a time. The dying phoenix was consumed by fire in a nest of aromatic materials and from its ashes a new bird arose.

Phoenix 33 30N 112 03W A city in the USA, the capital of Arizona on the Salt River. The state's largest city, the commercial centre for a cotton and farming region, its industries include the manufacture of aircraft and textiles.

Its warm dry climate makes it a popular health resort. Population (1980): 789 704.

Phoenix Islands An uninhabited group of coral atolls in the S Pacific Ocean. They comprise *Canton and Enderbury under joint US-British control and the Birnie, McKean, Phoenix, Hull, Sydney, and Gardner islands in Kiribati. Area: about 28 sq km (11 sq mi).

Phoenix Park Murders (1882) The assassination in Phoenix Park, Dublin, of the new chief secretary for Ireland, Lord Frederick Cavendish (1836–82), and the permanent undersecretary, Thomas Burke (1829–82), by extreme Irish nationalists calling themselves the Invincibles. British public opinion forced *Gladstone to respond with a new Coercion Act for Ireland.

phon A unit for measuring the loudness of sound equal to the intensity in *decibels of a sound of frequency 1000 hertz, which appears to the ear to be as loud as the sound to be measured.

phonetics The study of the production and perception of sounds in languages. Sounds are classified in terms of the way in which they are produced by the speech organs. There is a wide range of possible speech sounds but each language uses only a selection of them. The study of the system of sounds within any given language is called **phonology** and the selected individual sounds are called phonemes. Phonetics also includes the study of stress and intonation.

phosphorescence. *See* luminescence.

phosphorus (P) A nonmetallic solid element discovered by H. Brand (died c. 1692) in 1669. It exists in at least four forms: white (8 and 9), red, and black. White phosphorus is a waxy solid, which ignites spontaneously in air to form the pentoxide (P_2O_5). Red phosphorus, a more stable allotrope, is formed when white phosphorus is heated to 400°C; it is used in matches. Black phosphorus is also stable and forms when white phosphorus is heated to 200–300°C. Phosphorus exists in nature chiefly as the mineral *apatite ($Ca_3(PO_4)_2$), from which the element is obtained, either by reduction with carbon or reaction with silica at high temperatures. Phosphates are used extensively as fertilizers (mainly as "superphosphate"—calcium hydrogen phosphate) but find other uses in detergents, water softeners, and specialist glasses. A wide range of compounds is formed including the hydride (phosphine; PH_3), numerous phosphates (for example Na_3PO_4), and phosphides (for example Na_3P). Phosphorus occurs in DNA and RNA molecules and is therefore essential to life; bones also contain phosphates (*see* apatite) but some organo-phosphorus compounds are extremely toxic and are used as nerve gases. At no 15; at wt 30.9738; mp (white) 44.1°C; bp (white) 280°C.

Photius (c. 810–c. 895 AD) Patriarch of Constantinople,

PHOENICIA *From their homeland along the E Mediterranean shore (modern Lebanon and Syria) the Phoenicians traded throughout the Mediterranean and beyond and established many settlements.*

whose condemnation of certain practices and doctrines of the Western Church contributed to the rift with the Eastern Church. A leading statesman at the Byzantine court, he was elected patriarch in 858 amid much controversy and before he had been ordained. In 867 he convened a council at Constantinople at which he excommunicated Pope *Nicholas I, who had earlier deposed him, and denounced the *Filioque clause in the creed. Several depositions and reinstatements followed until he was finally exiled to Armenia in 886. He is also famous for his scholarship and is a saint in the Orthodox Church.

photoemissive cell *Illumination releases electrons from the cathode.*

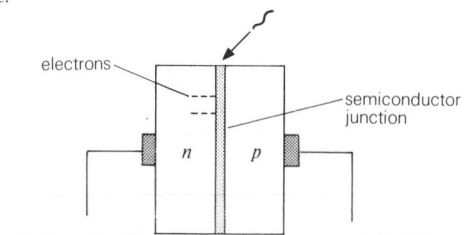

photovoltaic cell *Illumination creates a potential difference at a p–n semiconductor junction.*

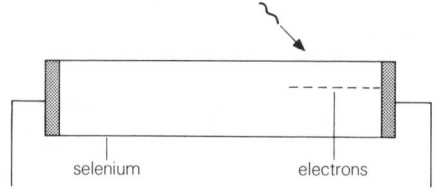

photoconductivity cell *Illumination increases the conductivity of a semiconductor, such as selenium.*

PHOTOCELL

photocell (*or* photoelectric cell) A device that makes use of a *photoelectric effect to measure or detect light or other electromagnetic radiation. In the photoemissive cell, a photosensitive cathode emits electrons when it is illuminated; these photoelectrons constitute a current when they flow to the positive anode of the cell. In solid-state devices the light changes the behaviour of a p–n junction (as in the photodiode), creating a potential difference by the *photovoltaic effect. In the conductivity cell, the resistance of a substance, such as selenium, changes when light falls on it as a result of *photoconductivity. Photocells are widely used in light-operated controls, such as automatic doors, fire alarms, and burglar alarms; they are also used in solar cells (*see* solar power) and photographic light meters. *See also* selenium cell.

photoconductivity The increase in the conductivity of certain semiconductors, such as selenium, when exposed to light. It occurs when photons excite electrons in the material from the valence band into the conduction band. *See* energy bands; photocell.

photocopying machine A device that prints black-and-white copies of documents, drawings, etc., from an optical image. The most common technique is a dry electrostatic process known as xerography. A pattern of electric charge is induced by light falling on a layer of *semiconductor material on a conducting surface. Toner powder is sprayed or rolled onto this material, so that it sticks to the highly charged areas. The image so formed is printed onto charged paper, where it is fixed by heating to produce the final copy. Xerography is also used for high-speed printing of computer output, with printing heads instead of a light image.

photoelectric effects A number of effects in which electromagnetic radiation interacts with matter, frequently with the emission of electrons. These effects include *photoconductivity, the *photovoltaic effect, and the *Compton effect and the *Auger effect. The frequency of the radiation (f) has to be such that the energy of the photon (hf, where h is Planck's constant) is sufficient to liberate the electron. For solids, the minimum energy required is called the work function; for free atoms or molecules it is equal to the first *ionization potential, the effect then being known as *photoionization. For most substances, an ultraviolet frequency is needed to eject an electron, but for some metals, such as caesium, visible light is sufficient. *See* photocell.

Photofit. *See* Identikit and Photofit.

photography The recording of images on sensitized material, by means of visible light, X-rays, or other radiation, and the subsequent chemical processing. The first photograph was taken in 1826 by Joseph Nicéphore Niépce (d. 1833) using the action of light on asphalt solution. In 1839, *Daguerre introduced the daguerrotype, a positive image of milky white on a silver background, produced directly from silver iodide emulsion on plates exposed inside a simple *camera. Modern photography involves a negative made by the development of *film coated with silver salts. The positive picture is obtained by shining light through the negative onto light-sensitive paper with a coating similar to that on the original film. Lenses can be used to enlarge or reduce the size of the final image on the print. Transparencies, for use with a slide *projector, may also be made. Film is usually developed and printed in a darkroom by dipping it in baths of chemicals. Polaroid photography, however, produces positive pictures directly from the camera in one stage. This system was invented by Edwin Land in 1947 and is used for instant pictures for security passes, laboratory records, etc.

Photography as an art dates back almost to the origins of the technique. Portraiture was already established in the 1850s and was a prime interest of the Photographic Society (later the Royal Photographic Society) founded in London in 1853. The Crimean War in the 1850s and the US Civil War in the 1860s provided the first opportunities for the true miseries of war to be realistically portrayed. However, during the last half of the 19th century photographic interest centred on the landscape, especially as horizons broadened with the growth of travel.

In the 1920s the collages of the cubist painters encouraged such photographers as László *Moholy-Nagy to experiment with photomontages. But by the 1930s the Frenchman Henri *Cartier-Bresson had led fashion back to a more realistic technique: using the camera as an extension of the eye, he composed transient scenes in great detail. Picture magazines were also a feature of this period, one of the best-known being *Picture Post*, started in London in 1938 by a German refugee from Hitler, Stephen Lorant. Postwar photography has developed many of these themes, using the new precision cameras and techniques, and many galleries now have permanent exhibitions of photography.

Photography has also had a profound effect on painting. Some art historians believe that the 20th-century trend towards abstract painting has been primarily a reaction to the camera's ability to do superbly what representationalist painters have often only been able to do indifferently. *See also* colour photography; cinematography. □ p. 954.

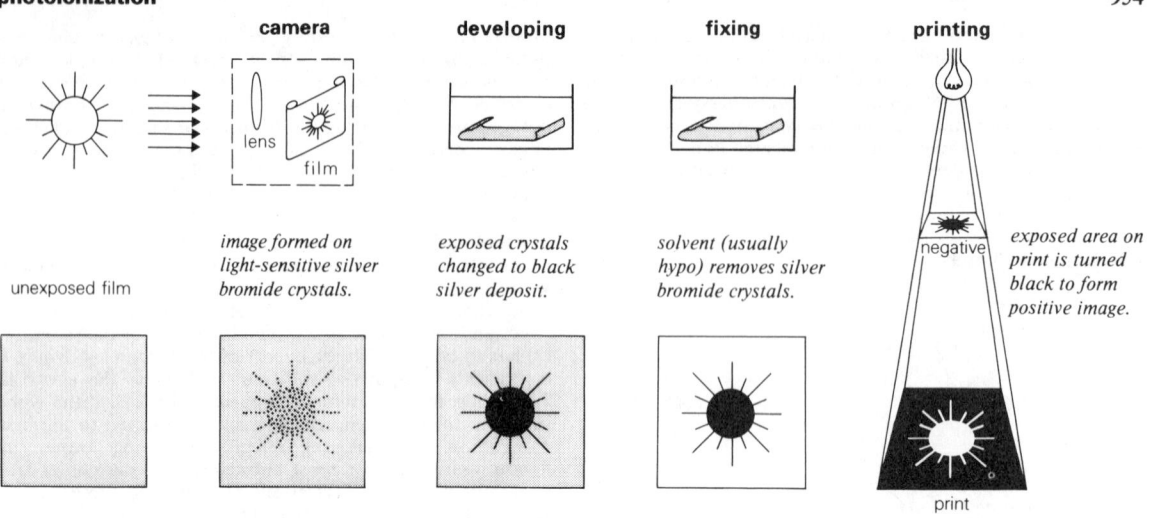

PHOTOGRAPHY *The stages in making a black and white photographic print.*

photoionization The *ionization of an atom when it is bombarded with electromagnetic radiation. The frequency of the radiation has to be such that the energy of its *photons exceeds the first *ionization potential of the atom.

photoluminescence. *See* luminescence.

photolysis The breaking of a chemical bond by absorbed electromagnetic radiation. The photon energy of the radiation must exceed the bond energy, and photolytic reactions can be produced by light, ultraviolet radiation, and X-rays. Examples occur in *photosynthesis, suntan, and photography. **Flash photolysis** is a technique for identifying and studying unstable reaction intermediates. The intermediates are produced in a gas by an intense brief flash of light, and their reactions are followed by spectroscopy.

photometry The branch of physics concerned with measuring quantities related to the intensity of light. These quantities are measured in two ways. If the intensity is measured in terms of the energy of the light, they are known as radiant quantities. They may also be measured in terms of their visual effect, since the sensitivity of the eye varies with the wavelength of the light. They are then known as luminous quantities.

photomicrograph. *See* microscope.

photomultiplier An instrument that produces an amplified current when exposed to electromagnetic radiation. Photons striking a photocathode cause the emission of electrons by the *photoelectric effect. These electrons then strike another surface causing a greater number of electrons to be emitted, the process being repeated several times to produce a greatly amplified current. Photomultipliers are used in certain *scintillation counters.

photon The quantum of *electromagnetic radiation, having an energy hf, where h is the *Planck constant and f is the frequency of the radiation. It may also be regarded as an elementary particle with *spin 1 and zero mass that travels at the speed of *light.

photoperiodism The response of an organism to the relative lengths of day and night, based either on a daily, seasonal, or yearly cycle. Flowering in plants, breeding in animals, and bird migration are examples of photoperiodic responses, which may be modified by such factors as temperature and availability of food. In general the response is a reaction to day length, but the flowering of plants actually depends on the length of the dark period. Thus, short-day plants (e.g. chrysanthemums) flower in response to a long night and long-day plants (e.g. certain cereals) flower when nights are short.

photosphere The boundary between the atmosphere of a star and its much denser interior. The sun's photosphere is its visible surface, several hundred kilometres thick, lying between the opaque outer (convective) zone of the sun's interior and its transparent atmosphere. Almost all the energy emitted by the sun is radiated from the photosphere. Its temperature falls from about 6000°C at the convective zone to about 4000°C where the photosphere merges with the *chromosphere. *See also* sunspots.

photosynthesis The means by which plants and certain bacteria produce carbohydrates from carbon dioxide and a hydrogen source. The energy for the process is provided by light absorbed by the green pigment chlorophyll, which is contained in the *chloroplasts. Plants use water (H_2O) as the hydrogen source and release its oxygen as a by-product, thus replenishing the atmospheric oxygen that is used in respiration by all living organisms. Photosynthesis occurs in the chloroplasts and comprises two sets of reactions. One set, which requires light, produces energy-storing and reducing compounds; the other reactions, which may proceed in the light or dark, use these compounds to add hydrogen atoms to carbon dioxide and make carbohydrates. The overall reactions can be summarized by the equation $6CO_2 + 6H_2O \rightarrow C_6H_{12}O_6 + 6O_2$.

photovoltaic effect The production of a voltage when light falls on certain materials coated with another substance. The effect can be detected by connecting the two materials through an external circuit to generate a current. It occurs in copper (I) oxide on copper and in selenium on iron. *See also* photocell.

phrenology An obsolete approach to the study of the nervous system, first proposed by a Viennese doctor, F. J. Gall (1758-1828). The degree of mental development was supposed to be indicated by the shape of the skull, reflecting the development of the underlying parts of the brain in which the various mental processes were assumed to take place. Although discredited, it was important in developing ideas about the localization of brain function.

Phrygia The central and W areas of Asia Minor inhabited after the Hittite empire collapsed (12th century BC) by Thracian migrants. The shortlived Phrygian kingdom, centred on its capital Gordium, reached its peak in the late 8th century. The legendary *Midas was King of Phrygia. In about 700 BC Phrygia was conquered by Lydia. Phrygia was a centre for the cult of *Cybele, which it passed on to

Greece; it also influenced early Greek music. The Phrygians are reputed to have invented embroidery.

Phryne (4th century BC) Greek courtesan. She was the lover of *Praxiteles and probably the model for his most famous statue, the Aphrodite of Cnidos, as well as for the painting of Aphrodite Anadyomene by Apelles.

Phyfe, Duncan (*or* Fife; 1768–1854) US cabinetmaker and furniture designer, born in Scotland. His highly successful firm in New York produced furniture in the Sheraton, Regency, and French Empire styles.

phyle A tribal subdivision or clan in ancient Greek city states, its members being tied by descent from a common ancestor. The phyle upheld clan traditions, cults, and loyalties and encouraged aristocratic rule. By the 5th century BC Athens and Sparta had replaced the phylae with artificial district divisions for administrative and military purposes, engendering allegiance to the city rather than the clan.

Phyllanthus A mostly tropical genus of trees, shrubs, herbs, and aquatic plants (600 species), including a few ornamental greenhouse plants. Many have flattened green stems resembling leaves, with yellow, red, or white flowers along their margins. *P. acidus* (Indian gooseberry) has round fleshy ribbed fruits used in pickles and preserves. Family: *Euphorbiaceae*.

phylloxera A plant-eating insect belonging to the family *Phylloxeridae*, closely related to the *aphids. The grape, or vine, phylloxera (*Phylloxera vitifoliae* or *Viteus vitifolii*) is a notorious pest of grapevines. During a complex life cycle, the insect forms galls on the leaves and roots, which damage the plant. The grape phylloxera spread to Europe from North America in the 19th century and almost destroyed the wine industry in France.

phylogeny The history of the *evolution of a species or other group of organisms. By studying the fossil record, comparative anatomy, embryology, biochemistry, and geographical distribution of the groups involved, one can establish the probable lines of descent and degrees of relationship between broad groups of plants or animals to produce a phylogenetic tree. For example, it is believed that whales and carnivorous land mammals developed from insectivorous mammals living more than 65 million years ago. Phylogeny forms the basis for the classification of organisms (*see* taxonomy). It should be distinguished from **ontogeny**, which is the succession of developmental stages through which an individual organism passes during its lifetime. *See also* biogenetic law.

phylum A major unit of classification for animals (*see* taxonomy). Organisms belonging to the same phylum share basic features but are divided into classes, orders, genera, and species according to their supposed degrees of relationship. For example, the phylum *Arthropoda* is a very diverse group including the insects, spiders, scorpions, crustaceans, etc., which all share the features of a tough segmented external skeleton and jointed limbs. In most plant-classification systems the equivalent term is division.

physical medicine The medical specialty concerned with the treatment of physical disabilities. Originally this was restricted to the diagnosis and management of rheumatic diseases, but it has now been extended to the treatment and rehabilitation of patients disabled by back injuries, polio, asthma, and many other disorders.

physics The study of the interrelationship between matter and energy, without reference to chemical change. Traditionally the subject was divided into the study of mechanics, electricity and magnetism, heat and thermodynamics, optics, and acoustics. More modern aspects of the subject include quantum mechanics, relativity, nuclear physics, particle physics, solid-state physics, and astrophysics.

Physiocrats A group of French 18th-century economists, led by François *Quesnay. The Physiocrats believed that the only real productive sector in the economy was agriculture:

industry and merchants were seen as mere processors. As mercantile (*see* mercantilism) interests were no longer identified with the wealth of the nation, *laissez-faire and *free trade were advocated.

physiology The study of the functioning of living organisms and their constituent parts. Physiology is closely linked with both *anatomy (the study of structure) and *biochemistry (the chemical reactions that play a vital role in many physiological processes).

physiotherapy The treatment of injuries or disabilities using physical methods, such as massage, manipulation, exercise, and heat. Physiotherapists play an important role in restoring mobility to patients confined for a long period to bed or a wheelchair; they also enable the rehabilitation of those handicapped by strokes, cerebral palsy (spastics), polio, etc., or immobilized by fractures. Physiotherapy is also useful in reducing the pain and stiffness of arthritis. In the UK student physiotherapists must undergo a three-year training period and pass an examination before qualifying as members of the Chartered· Society of Physiotherapy (MCSP).

phytochrome A pigment of green plants that exists in two interchangeable forms, one absorbing red light and the other, far-red light. Day-length responses (*see* photoperiodism), greening of young leaves, and the breaking of dormancy in some seeds are among the processes controlled by phytochrome.

phytosaur An extinct amphibious reptile, resembling a modern crocodile, having long pointed jaws with sharp teeth and protective bony plates beneath the skin. Phytosaurs lived during the late Triassic and Jurassic periods (210–135 million years ago) and probably fed on fish. The nostrils were set on a mound near the eyes and not at the end of the snout (as in crocodiles).

pi In mathematics, the ratio of the circumference of a circle to its diameter, denoted by the Greek letter π. It was proved to be an irrational number by J. H. *Lambert and transcendental by F. Lindemann (1852–1939). Its value is 3.14159.... *See also* numbers.

Piacenza 45 03N 09 41E A city in N Italy, in Emilia-Romagna on the River Po. Dating from Roman times, it has several notable buildings, including a 12th-century cathedral and a 13th-century town hall. Piacenza is primarily an agricultural trading centre. Population (1980 est): 108 893.

EDITH PIAF

Piaf, Edith (Edith Giovanna Gassion; 1915-63) French cabaret and music-hall singer. Originally a street singer, her small size earned her the nickname "piaf" (French slang: sparrow). Many of her songs, which include "Je m'en fou pas mal," "Je ne regrette rien," and "La Vie en rose," reflected the defiance and despair of her own tragic life, which was ended prematurely by her addiction to alcohol and drugs. □ p. 955.

Piaget, Jean (1896-1980) Swiss psychologist, noted for his studies of thought processes, especially in children. He described the development of perception, judgment, reasoning, and logic during childhood, which had important consequences for children's education. Among his many books are *The Origin of Intelligence in Children* (1954) and *The Early Growth of Logic in the Child* (1964).

piano A ⌐musical instrument consisting of a number of wire strings stretched over a metal frame, which are hit by felt-covered wooden hammers operated by a keyboard. The piano was invented by *Cristofori in the early 18th century; the name derives from the Italian *pianoforte*, soft-loud, referring to the variation in volume obtainable on the piano in contrast to the earlier *clavichord and *harpsichord. In the modern instrument the frame is either horizontal, as in the **grand piano**, or vertical, as in the **upright piano**. Groups of two or three strings are tuned to each note. When a key is struck the escapement mechanism allows the hammer to fall away from the strings after they have been struck; when the key is released a felt damper stops the vibration of the strings. Two pedals allow a wide variation in volume. The right-hand pedal prevents the dampers from cutting off the sound; the left-hand pedal moves the hammers so that they are either closer to the strings (in the upright piano) or only able to strike one or two strings of each group (in the grand piano). The piano has a compass of seven and a quarter octaves; it has the largest repertory of any single instrument. Famous makers of pianos include J. B. Broadwood (1732-1812) and the firms of Bechstein, *Steinway, and Bösendorfer.

pianola. *See* player piano.

Piave, River A river in NE Italy. It flows generally S from the Carnic Alps to the Adriatic Sea 32 km (20 mi) NE of Venice. It formed the main Italian line of defence in World War I, following the Austro-German offensive in 1917. Length: 220 km (137 mi).

Picabia, Francis (1879-1953) French painter and writer. Working chiefly in Paris but also in New York (1913-17), Barcelona, and Zürich, he was associated successively with *cubism, *dada, and *surrealism. He is known mainly for his periodical *391* (1917-24), containing his poems, essays, and satirical drawings of machinery.

Picardy (French name: Picardie) A planning region and former province in N France. It was incorporated into France in 1477 by Louis XI of France. During World War I it was the scene of heavy fighting. Area: 19 411 sq km (7493 sq mi). Population (1981 est): 1 723 000.

picaresque novel A type of narrative that recounts the adventures of a single protagonist in a loose episodic form. The term derives from the Spanish *picaro*, a rogue. Early examples of the form include the Spanish *Lazarillo de Tormes* (1554) and the French *Gil Blas* (1715-35) by *Lesage. English examples include *Moll Flanders* (1722) by *Defoe, *Jonathan Wild* (1743) by *Fielding, and *Peregrine Pickle* (1751) by *Smollett. The form is usually characterized by comedy and social satire rather than by the development of ideas or characters; it was continued in the 19th century by *Thackeray in *Barry Lyndon* (1844) and in the 20th century by Thomas *Mann in *The Confessions of Felix Krull, Confidence Man* (1954).

Picasso, Pablo (1881-1973) Spanish artist, born in Malaga. The most inventive and versatile of 20th-century painters and a precocious draughtsman, Picasso trained in

PICASSO *A photograph of the artist, aged 84, by Sir Cecil Beaton.*

Barcelona but worked chiefly in Paris after 1900. Although his most popular paintings are those of the beggars, acrobats, and harlequins of his blue (1901-04) and rose (1905-08) periods, his most original work began with *Les Demoiselles d'Avignon* (1907), influenced by Cézanne and African sculpture, and resulted in his development of *cubism with *Braque. In 1912 he made the first collage. He later began a series of classical paintings of colossal figures, followed by nightmarish distorted figure studies in the 1920s and 1930s, when he was loosely associated with *surrealism. One of his major works, *Guernica* (1937), is a horrific depiction of the destruction of the Basque capital during the Spanish Civil War. The Pablo Picasso Museum in Paris, housing the largest collection of his works, opened in 1985.

Piccard A family of Swiss scientists and explorers. **Auguste Piccard** (1884-1962) and his twin **Jean-Félix Piccard** (1884-1963) pioneered the scientific study of the stratosphere in balloons, reaching a height of 16 940 metres in 1932. In 1948 Auguste designed a bathyscaphe, using it to explore the sea depths, descending to over 3000 metres in 1953. His son **Jacques Piccard** (1927-) collaborated with his father in designing bathyscaphes and reached a depth of 10 917 metres in the vessel *Trieste* in 1960.

piccolo A woodwind instrument, the smallest and shrillest member of the *flute family. It is pitched an octave higher than the flute and its music is written an octave lower than it sounds. It is used in the orchestra and in the military band.

picketing The act of employees or their union representatives in attending at their place of work to persuade others not to work in furtherance of a trade dispute. **Primary picketing** (in which the employer is the immediate party to the dispute) is not wrongful if carried out peacefully. **Secondary picketing** (in which the employer is not directly concerned in the dispute) is not always wrong. Employees may, for example, picket their employer, who is a supplier of the employer in the dispute.

Flying pickets are pickets that are ready to move at a moment's notice to a plant at which they are not employed, and have no immunity from legal action. Flying and secondary picketing caused considerable industrial unrest in the UK in the miners' strike of 1984–85.

Pickford, Mary (Gladys Mary Smith; 1893–1979) Canadian-born US film actress. She played the roles of innocent young heroines in early silent films, such as *The Little American* (1917) and *Polyanna* (1919). In 1919 she cofounded United Artists with Charlie *Chaplin, D. W. *Griffith, and Douglas *Fairbanks, whom she married.

pick-up A device that converts information stored in a gramophone record into an electrical signal. In a record player, the pick-up cartridge, usually a removable assembly, consists of a stylus and a *transducer. The stylus is forced to vibrate by the undulations in the record groove. The transducer responds electrically to these vibrations. The most common types of transducer use the *piezoelectric effect or *electromagnetic induction, but *capacitor, variable-resistance, and variable-reluctance pick-ups are also used. A stereo pick-up has one stylus that picks up vibrations from both sides of the V-shaped groove. The components of the resulting two-dimensional vibration contributed by each side are at right angles and are separated by two suitably oriented transducers.

Pico della Mirandola, Giovanni, Conte (1463–94) Italian Renaissance philosopher. He was converted by *Ficino to *Neoplatonism and became interested in the Hermetic and Zoroastrian writings. Although Pico was concerned to prove the truth of Christianity, he was inevitably regarded with suspicion by the Church, which banned a proposed discussion (1486) by him of philosophical and theological topics. He wrote an important study of the *Kabballah.

pictographic writing systems (*or* pictography) Writing systems in which each symbol represents a concept or word in the form of a sketch or diagram of the object it represents (the referent). Prehistoric pictographic records have been found throughout the world. It is a characteristic of primitive (nontechnological) societies that a careful distinction is not maintained between an object, a word denoting the object, and a pictorial representation of it. Pictography is therefore often associated with magic or ritual rather than the straightforward recording of information. Disadvantages of pictography include the difficulty of representing any word except nouns having concrete referents. Pictographic systems that did not die out therefore generally developed into *ideographic writing systems.

Picts (painted people) The Roman name (referring to their tattoos) for all Scottish tribes living N of the *Antonine Wall. Perpetually hostile to the Romans, the Picts had forced them to withdraw behind *Hadrian's Wall by 200 AD, and remained independent until Kenneth I MacAlpine unified S Scotland in the 9th century.

piddock A burrowing *bivalve mollusc belonging to the family *Pholadidae*, of cold and temperate seas. Piddocks are adapted for boring into rock, having shells with serrated cutting edges, the largest being 10 cm long. They can damage concrete breakwaters, sea walls, and wharves.

pidgin A form of English, used between Chinese and Europeans, having a greatly reduced vocabulary, simplified grammar, and modified sound system. The term may also be applied to *Neo-Melanesian and the Beach-la-Mer of the South Seas. *Compare* creole.

Pieck, Wilhelm (1876–1960) German communist politician. He opposed both the Weimar Republic and Nazism and advocated their overthrow by violent revolution with the aid of Soviet troops. In 1946 he was elected joint chairman, with Otto Grotewohl, of the Socialist Unity Party in the postwar Soviet zone of Germany and was the first president of the German Democratic Republic (1949–60).

Piedmont (Italian name: Piemonte) A region in NW Italy. Associated with the House of Savoy since the early 11th century, it became the nucleus of Italian unification in the mid-19th century. It consists of the upper Po Valley, bordered by the Alps in the N and W and the Apennines in the S. Manufacturing is important, with engineering and steel centred on Turin; other industries include textiles, chemicals, rubber, and food products. Agriculture is also important, producing rice, cereals, wine, and dairy products. Area: 25 400 sq km (9807 sq mi). Population (1980 est): 4 517 665. Capital: Turin.

Piepoudre, Court of (Anglo-French: dusty feet, i.e. pedlars) A court that decided summarily and on the spot commercial disputes arising at a given fair or market. The last of these ancient courts sat at Bristol until it was abolished in 1972.

Piero della Francesca (c. 1420–92) Italian Renaissance painter, born in Sansepolcro. He probably trained in Florence, where he worked on frescoes in Sant' Egidio in 1439. *The Baptism of Christ* (National Gallery, London) shows his monumental figure style and the influence of Florentine artists, particularly *Masaccio. He frequently worked at the court of Urbino, where he painted the double portrait of the duke and his wife in profile (Uffizi). His lifelong interest in perspective is reflected in his fresco cycle *The Legend of the True Cross*, painted for the church of S Francesco, Arezzo, and in his treatise *On Perspective in Painting*. After his death his work was neglected until it was reappraised in the 20th century.

Piero di Cosimo (P. di Lorenzo; 1462–1521) Florentine Renaissance painter. He trained under the painter Cosimo Rosselli (1439–1507) but was chiefly influenced by *Leonardo da Vinci and *Signorelli. His mythological paintings and fantasies on the primitive life of mankind are highly original, one of the best examples being *The Death of Procris* (National Gallery, London).

Pierre 44 23N 100 20W A city in the USA, the capital of South Dakota on the Missouri River. Founded in 1880, it is a trade centre for a grain and dairy-farming region. Population (1980): 11 973.

Pietermaritzburg 29 36S 30 24E A city in South Africa, the capital of Natal. It was founded by Boers (1838) and named after their leaders, Piet Retief and Gert Maritz, massacred by the Zulus. The Church of the Vow (1839), built to commemorate the subsequent Boer victory over the Zulus, now houses the Voortrekker Museum. Part of the University of Natal (1910) stands here. It is the centre of a rich farming area. Population (1980 est): 178 972.

Pietism A movement for spiritual regeneration among Lutherans in 17th-century Germany. It was started by P. J. Spener (1635–1705), whose *Pia Desideria* (1675) proposed instilling new life into official Lutheranism by concentrating upon devotional worship instead of dogmatic theology. Pietism survived in different guises for over 200 years and influenced many subsequent Christian organizations.

piezoelectric effect The production of electric charges on the opposite faces of certain asymmetric crystals when they are compressed or expanded. The charges are of equal magnitude but opposite in sign on the two faces, the sign on each face depending on whether the crystal is expanded or compressed. Such piezoelectric crystals include quartz and Rochelle salt. In the converse effect a voltage applied across a piezoelectric crystal causes it to expand or contract. The effect is used in the piezoelectric oscillator, the crystal microphone, and the piezoelectric loudspeaker.

pig A hoofed mammal belonging to the Old World family *Suidae* (8 species). Also called hogs or swine, pigs have a stocky body with short legs, a short neck, and a large head with a long cylindrical snout used for digging up roots, seeds, small animals, etc., from soil. Wild *boars were originally domesticated about 5000 years ago, probably in Asia, and used for meat and clearing vegetation. Modern breeds include the *Landrace and *Large White and are reared for pork and bacon (*see* livestock farming). Other members of the pig family include the *babirusa and *wart hog. *See also* peccary.

pigeon A bird belonging to a family (*Columbidae*; 300 species) occurring worldwide except in the coldest regions; the smaller long-tailed forms are called doves. 17–75 cm long, pigeons have soft plumage, a plump body, a small head, short bill and legs, and a characteristic cooing call. Pigeons feed mainly on seeds and other plant material and feed the young on "pigeons' milk"—the sloughed-off lining of the crop. They are often fast fliers and some are highly migratory, domesticated breeds being used as messengers and for racing. Order: *Columbiformes* (pigeons and sandgrouse). *See also* mourning dove; passenger pigeon; wood pigeon.

pigeon racing The sport of racing homing pigeons back to their home lofts (which they must enter). Pigeons were first, and still are, used for carrying messages; Genghis Khan had a system of pigeon post. The first race of over a hundred miles was held in Belgium (1818), where the sport is still very popular. Birds are banded for racing; their times of departure and arrival are then recorded. Pigeons can cover several thousand miles at speeds of more than 145 km per hour (90 mph).

pigeon wheat. *See* Polytrichum.

LESTER PIGGOTT *With Irish trainer Vincent O'Brien.*

Piggott, Lester Keith (1935–) British jockey, who rode his first winner at the age of 12. Champion jockey eleven times since 1960 and Derby winner a record nine times, his record of winners (4349) is second to that of Sir Gordon *Richards. He retired to become a trainer in 1985, having won 29 classic races. In 1987 he was sent to prison for a £3.25 million tax fraud.

pig iron The type of iron produced by *blast furnaces, and used as the first stage in *steel making. It has a high carbon content (about 4% by weight) and contains impurities, including some slag, which make it brittle. *See also* cast iron.

pigments Insoluble substances, in the form of fine particles, that give colour and opacity to *paints, *plastics, and *rubber. They can be broadly divided into naturally occurring pigments (such as red iron oxide), inorganic pigments manufactured from minerals, organic pigments, and *lakes.

pigmies. *See* Pygmies.

pigweed 1. A stout leafy annual herb of the genus *Amaranthus* (about 50 species), found in tropical and temperate regions, often, as a weed. Pigweeds have furrowed stems, up to 1 m high, with simple pale-green hairy leaves and long branching greenish-white flower spikes. Family: *Amaranthaceae*. 2. *See* goosefoot.

pika A small mammal belonging to the genus *Ochotona* (14 species), of Asia and North America, also called mouse hare, cony, and rock rabbit. 12.5–30 cm long and resembling large short-tailed mice, pikas live in cold rocky areas above the tree line. They build stacks of sun-dried vegetation under sheltering ledges to feed on during the winter. Family: *Ochotonidae*; order: *Lagomorpha*.

pike (fish) A freshwater fish of the genus *Esox* found in temperate regions of Eurasia and America. It has an elongated body, up to about 1.4 m long, a broad flat snout, and a large mouth with strong teeth. It feeds voraciously on fish and other animals. The common pike (*E. lucius*) is olive-grey above with silvery underparts and pale spots. Family: *Esocidae*; order: *Salmoniformes*.

pike (weapon) A pre-1800 infantry weapon with a wooden shaft 4–6 m (12–21 ft) long, a steel head on an iron sleeve, and an iron butt. It was useless in the face of missile weapons (arrows, musketry) and was replaced by the *bayonet.

pikeperch One of several food and game fish related to perch, especially members of the genera *Lucioperca* and *Stizostedion*, found in Europe and North America. The European pikeperch or zander (*L. lucioperca*) has a slender elongated body, 0.5–1 m long, with greenish or greyish mottling. It is carnivorous, feeding mainly on other fish.

Pikes Peak A mountain in the USA, in central Colorado in the Rocky Mountains. It is a popular tourist attraction noted for its spectacular views from the summit, which is ascended by a cog railway and a road. Height: 4300 m (14 109 ft).

pilaster. *See* orders of architecture.

Pilate, Pontius (1st century AD) Roman governor. As procurator of Judaea and Samaria (26–36) he condemned Christ to death but, according to the New Testament Gospels, did so reluctantly, fearing the outcome of any other course. He came into frequent conflict with the Jews and was finally dismissed for his cruel suppression of a Samaritan rebellion. In one tradition he committed suicide, but in the Ethiopian Church he is regarded as a saint and martyr.

Pilbara. *See* Western Australia.

pilchard An important food fish, *Sardina pilchardus*, related to the herring and sprat, that occurs in abundance in the Mediterranean, E Atlantic, and English Channel. Its slender body, 25–35 cm long, is bluish green above and whitish below and it swims in large shoals feeding on crustaceans and fish eggs. Pilchards up to one year old are called *sardines and are fished extensively off the coast of Spain and Portugal. Pilchards are eaten fresh and tinned.

Pilcomayo, Río A river in S central South America, rising in the Bolivian Andes and flowing generally SE, forming part of the Argentina–Paraguay border before joining the River Paraguay. Length: about 1600 km (1000 mi).

piles. *See* haemorrhoids.

Pilgrimage of Grace (1536) A revolt in N England against the government of Henry VIII. The rebels were united by their opposition to the recent *Reformation legislation and the dissolution of the monasteries as well as by economic grievances. Under Robert Ashe (c. 1500–37) they seized York but were persuaded by promises of pardon and a full hearing of their complaints to surrender. However, some 230 men, including Ashe, were executed.

Pilgrim Fathers The 102 English colonists who established the first settlement in New England in 1620. They included 35 Puritans, escaping persecution in England, and sailed in the *Mayflower* to New Plymouth, Massachusetts.

Pilgrim's Way A prehistoric track following the ridge of the North Downs in Surrey and Kent. It probably originated as a trade route, although its name suggests its later use by pilgrims. In *The Old Road* (1904), Hilaire *Belloc identified the Way as a continuous track from Winchester to Canterbury, used by pilgrims to the tomb of Thomas Becket.

Pilgrim Trust A British charity founded in 1930 by Edward Harkness (1874-1940), a US philanthropist. He wished to promote British education and social welfare and the conservation of Britain's national heritage, for which he donated £2 million. Secretary: Alistair Hoyer Millar.

Pill, the. *See* oral contraceptive.

Pillars of Hercules Two promontories at the entrance to the Mediterranean Sea, known in ancient times as Calpe (modern Gibraltar) and Abyla (modern Jebel Musa, at Ceuta, Morocco). According to one legend, the promontories were joined until Heracles tore them apart.

pilot fish A fish, *Naucrates ductor*, that has a pale-blue elongated body, up to 60 cm long, marked with five to seven dark vertical bands. It is found in warm and tropical seas, accompanying ships and large fish, especially sharks, to feed on parasites and scraps of food. Family: *Carangidae*; order: *Perciformes*.

pilot whale A gregarious toothed *whale, *Globicephala melaena*. Growing up to 6 m, pilot whales are black with a blunt head, narrow tapering flippers, and a broad dorsal fin. They were named by fishermen who found groups of them near herring shoals. Family: *Globicephalidae*.

Pilsen. *See* Plzeň.

Piłsudski, Józef Klemens (1867-1935) Polish statesman, who fought for Polish independence. Piłsudski formed three Polish legions, which fought against Russia in World War I. When Germany refused to guarantee Polish sovereignty, Piłsudski withdrew his support and was imprisoned. After Germany's defeat he declared Poland independent and served as head of state (1919-27). In 1926 he established a military dictatorship, remaining in power until his death.

Piltdown man Skeletal remains once thought to be those of a fossil *hominid, found on Piltdown Common, near Lewes (England), in 1912. In 1953-54 the "find" was shown to be a hoax or fraud. Analysis showed the skull to be made up of a human cranium and an ape's jaw, stained to simulate age. Extinct animal bones and tools had also been placed in the site.

pimento. *See* allspice.

pimpernel A slender annual or perennial herb of the genus *Anagallis* (about 20 species), found in Eurasia, Africa, and America, especially the annual scarlet pimpernel (*A. arvensis*). Growing 5-30 cm tall, pimpernels have simple leaves and small red, pink, blue, or white bell-shaped flowers with five petals, borne individually on slender stalks. The fruit is a capsule, which opens by a round lid. The yellow pimpernel (*Lysimachia nemorum*) belongs to a closely related genus. Family: *Primulaceae*.

pinchbeck A *brass containing between 10% and 15% zinc. It was formerly used in jewellery as a cheap substitute for gold. It was invented by the watchmaker Christopher Pinchbeck (d. 1732).

Pinckney, Charles (1757-1824) US statesman. He represented South Carolina in the *Constitutional Convention (1787) and his proposals for the new US government—the Pinckney plan—were included in the constitution. His cousins were **Charles Cotesworth Pinckney** (1746-1825), who was minister to France (1796), and **Thomas Pinckney** (1750-1828), who negotiated **Pinckney's Treaty** (the Treaty of San Lorenzo) with Spain in 1795, determining the boundary between US and Spanish possessions in America at 31°N latitude.

Pindar (518-438 BC) Greek poet. Born into an aristocratic family in Boeotia in central Greece, he was educated in Athens and lived in Sicily for two years from 476 BC. Of his

17 books of choral lyrics only 4 survive. These contain Epinician Odes written in honour of victors of athletic games and noted for their exalted style and deep religious feeling. He was acclaimed by the ancient Greeks as their greatest poet.

Pindus Mountains (Modern Greek name: Píndhos Óros) A range of mountains extending some 500 km (311 mi) NW-SE across W Greece and S Albania and rising to 2637 m (8652 ft) at Mount Smólikas.

pine A coniferous tree of the genus *Pinus* (about 80 species), widely distributed in the N hemisphere. Pines have long slender needles, usually in clusters of two, three, or five, and hanging cones, of variable shape, made up of overlapping woody scales. Pines are important softwoods: the timber is easily worked and yields turpentine, tar, pitch, and other resinous products. Commercially important and widely planted species include the Scots pine (*P. sylvestris*), of N and W Europe and Asia, up to 40 m high (⊔tree); the Monterey pine (*P. radiata*), from Monterey, California, up to 35 m high; the shore pine (*P. contorta*), of W North America, up to 25 m high; the Corsican pine (*P. nigra* var *maritima*), up to 45 m high; and the maritime pine (*P. pinaster*), of W Mediterranean regions and N Africa, up to 35 m high. These and other species are also planted for shelter and ornament and some species have edible seeds (*see* stone pine). Family: *Pinaceae*. *See also* bristlecone pine.

A number of other unrelated conifers are called pines, including species of *Araucaria*, the *cypress pine, and the *kauri pine.

pineal gland A small gland within the brain. In the 18th century it was supposed to be the site of the soul. In some lower animals, for example certain lizards, it is receptive to light and is visible externally as a third eye (pineal eye); in man its function is unknown, although it may help to regulate the onset of puberty.

pineapple A perennial herbaceous plant, *Ananas comosus*, native to tropical and subtropical America and cultivated in many warm and tropical regions for its fruit. It reaches a height of 1 m and bears a rosette of 30-40 stiff succulent toothed leaves on a thick fleshy stem. Purplish flowers occur at the centre of the rosette and—with their bracts—fuse to form the composite fruit, which ripens 5-6 months after flowering begins and can weigh up to 10 kg. It takes nearly two years for a plant to bear its first marketable fruit. The major producing countries are the Hawaiian Islands, Brazil, Mexico, Cuba, and the Philippines. Family: *Bromeliaceae*.

pine marten A European carnivorous mammal, *Martes martes*. About 70 cm long, it inhabits dense evergreen forests, preying on squirrels, birds, insects, and eggs. As with other *martens, the female has a litter (2-5 cubs) only every second year, a disadvantage for a species widely hunted for fur.

Pinero, Sir Arthur Wing (1855-1934) British dramatist. He abandoned his law studies to become an actor. His early plays, which included *The Magistrate* (1885) and *Dandy Dick* (1887), were hugely successful farces that exploited his professional knowledge of stagecraft. His later plays, notably *The Second Mrs Tanqueray* (1893), were more serious treatments of contemporary social problems.

pink One of several usually perennial herbaceous plants derived from *Dianthus plumarius* and often grown as fragrant garden ornamentals. They have long slender leaves and showy white, pink, or red flowers, often with fringed petals. Family: *Caryophyllaceae*.

Pinkerton, Allan (1819-84) US detective, born in Scotland. He emigrated to the USA in 1842. He founded the Pinkerton National Detective Agency in 1850 and organized an intelligence service for the Federal states during the Civil War.

pinkeye. *See* conjunctivitis.

Pinkie, Battle of (10 September, 1547) The battle near

Musselburgh, Midlothian, in which the Scots were defeated by the English forces of the Duke of *Somerset.

pink salmon A *salmon, *Oncorhynchus gorbuscha*, also called humpback salmon, found in the North Pacific. It is 40-50 cm long and marked with large irregular spots. It undertakes the shortest migration of all the salmon and the male develops a hump on its back during the breeding season.

Pinochet, Augusto (1915-) Chilean general and head of state (1973-). He led a military coup that overthrew the government of Salvador *Allende and became the head of a military junta. An assassination attempt (1986) failed.

Pinsk 52 08N 26 01E A port in the W Soviet Union, in the Belorussian SSR at the confluence of the Rivers Pina and Pripet. A medieval Russian principality, it came under Lithuania (13th century), Poland (16th century), Russia again (1793), and Poland again (1920-39); ceded then to the Soviet Union, it was occupied by the Germans in World War II. Timber, shipbuilding, and metalworking are the principal activities. Population (1983 est): 102 000.

pintail A *duck, *Anas acuta*, occurring in the N hemisphere, that breeds on inland waters and winters in coastal areas. The male is 70 cm long and has a dark-brown head and neck with a white band down the neck, grey flanks, and long black central tail feathers. Females have mottled brown plumage and both sexes have a blue-grey bill.

Pinter, Harold (1930-) British dramatist. During the 1950s he was a professional actor. His first full-length play, *The Birthday Party* (1958), failed when it was first staged; it was successfully revived after he had established his reputation with his second play, *The Caretaker* (1960), a study of suspicion between a tramp and two brothers. Later plays include *The Homecoming* (1965), *Old Times* (1971), *Betrayed* (1978), and *Family Voices* (1981). He uses elliptical dialogue to evoke tension and ambiguity. He has also written film scripts, including *Turtle Diary* (1985), and directed plays.

pinto A horse whose coat consists of sharply defined patches of white and a darker colour—either black (piebald pattern) or brown, bay, dun, or roan (skewbald pattern). A pinto may be predominantly white (tobiano pattern) or mainly dark with white splashes (overo pattern). Pintos were commonly used by American Indians. Height: 1.42 m minimum (14 hands).

Pinturicchio (Bernardino di Betto; c. 1454-1513) Italian Renaissance painter, born in Perugia. He was influenced chiefly by *Perugino, whom he probably assisted on frescoes for the Sistine Chapel in the Vatican, where he later decorated the Borgia apartments (1492-94). His other major fresco cycle (1503-08) is in the cathedral library, Siena.

pinworm A slender parasitic *nematode worm, *Enterobius vermicularius*, also called seatworm or threadworm. Up to 1 cm long, pinworms are white and inhabit the human intestine; they are common in Europe and America. Female worms migrate to the anus to lay thousands of eggs, causing itching, especially at night. The eggs are resistant to drying and to many disinfectants.

pinyin. *See* Chinese.

pion A group of three elementary particles (*see* particle physics) classified as *mesons (symbol: π). The charged pions (π^+ and π^-) have a mass of 139.6 MeV, the neutral pion (π^0) a mass of 136 MeV. The *strong interaction can be represented by the exchange of virtual pions between particles (*see* virtual particle).

Pioneer probes A series of US solar-system space probes, first launched in 1958. Pioneers 4 to 9 went into solar orbit, monitoring solar activity in the 1960s and early 1970s. Pioneers 10 and 11 flew past and studied Jupiter in 1973 and 1974. Pioneer 11 approached Saturn in 1979. Two **Pioneer Venus** probes reached Venus in 1978.

Piozzi, Hester Lynch (1741-1821) British writer and friend of Samuel *Johnson. Also known as Mrs Thrale, she was the wife of a wealthy brewer and a sympathetic confidante of Johnson from 1765 until her second marriage to Gabriel Piozzi, an Italian music master, in 1783. She published volumes of memoirs and letters relating to Dr Johnson.

p'i-p'a An ancient Chinese *lute. It is short, with a shallow pear-shaped body and has four silk strings. It is held upright in the lap and played with a plectrum. Poets of the Tang dynasty (618-906 AD) played it to accompany their poems; it is still a popular instrument.

pipal. *See* bo tree.

pipefish One of several slender long-bodied fish belonging to the family *Syngnathidae* (*see also* sea horse). 2.5-50 cm long, it has a long tubular snout with a small mouth and lives among aquatic plants mainly in warm marine waters, feeding on small organisms. The males carry the young until they hatch. Order: *Gasterosteiformes*.

Piper, John (1903-) British painter and writer. He painted abstract works in the 1930s and was an official war artist in World War II. He is best known for his watercolours and aquatints of architecture, such as Windsor Castle (1941-42), commissioned by Queen Elizabeth II. He has also designed stained glass, notably for Coventry Cathedral, and stage sets including those for Benjamin Britten's *Death in Venice* (1973).

Pipe rolls The earliest surviving account records of the Exchequer of England. Each Michaelmas (29 Sept), amounts paid into the royal treasury were recorded on long pieces of parchment, later rolled up into "pipes." The earliest of the pipe rolls dates from 1129-30 and they survive almost continuously from 1155 to 1831.

pipistrelle A small insect-eating *bat belonging to the genus *Pipistrellus* (50 species) with a worldwide distribution. The Eurasian pipistrelle (*P. pipistrellus*) is about 3.5 cm long with a 20-cm wingspan. It often flies near houses where insects are attracted to light. Pipistrelles have a prehensile tail, used when crawling into crevices to roost. Family: *Vespertilionidae*.

pipit A small insectivorous songbird of the genus *Anthus* (30 species), 14-16 cm long with a brown-streaked plumage and paler speckled underparts. The meadow pipit (*A. pratensis*) occurs on moors and downs in Britain and is the chief prey of the *merlin. The water pipit (*A. spinoletta*) inhabits the high mountains of Eurasia and North America; it is also found in coastal regions, when it is known as the rock pipit. The Antarctic pipit (*A. antarcticus*) is the only passerine land bird in Antarctica. Family: *Motacillidae* (wagtails and pipits).

Piraeus (Modern Greek name: Piraiévs) 37 57N 23 42E The chief port of Greece, SW of Athens on the Saronic Gulf. It was founded during the 5th century BC as the port of Athens. Following the bombings of World War II extensive industrial renewal has taken place; industries include shipbuilding, oil refining, and chemicals. Its exports include wine and olive oil. Population (1981): 196 389.

Pirandello, Luigi (1867-1936) Italian dramatist and novelist. He was born in Sicily and studied philology in Germany. In 1903 his wife became insane, and his writing was greatly influenced by his life with her. He gained international success with his plays exploring the nature of reality and illusion, notably *Six Characters in Search of an Author* (1921) and *Henry IV* (1922). His other works include the novel *The Late Mattia Pascal* (1904) and the critical study *Humour* (1908). He won the Nobel Prize in 1934.

Piranesi, Giambattista (1720-78) Italian etcher, born in Venice. Initially trained as an architect and stage designer, he achieved a wide reputation with his prints of Rome and its ruins. As an archaeologist and champion of the superiority of Roman architecture over Greek (*compare* Winckelmann, Johann Joachim), he was an important figure in early *neoclassicism, although his imaginative and dramatic style, particularly in the *Carceri d'invenzione* (*Imaginary Prisons*), anticipates *Romanticism.

piranha A freshwater fish, also called caribe and piraya, belonging to a genus (*Serrasalmus*) found in South America. It has a deep body, up to 60 cm long, ranging from silver to black in colour, strong jaws, and razor-sharp teeth. Piranhas swim in groups and feed voraciously on other fish; they will also attack larger animals, including man. Family: *Characidae* (*see* characin).

Pirani gauge A pressure gauge used for measuring low gas pressures. It consists of an electrically heated wire placed in the gas. The rate at which the gas conducts heat away from the wire depends on its pressure; the pressure is measured by observing the resistance of the wire at a fixed voltage or observing the voltage at a fixed resistance.

Pisa 43 43N 10 24E A city in Italy, in Tuscany on the River Arno. Dating from Etruscan times, it developed into a thriving maritime republic (11th–12th centuries) but declined in importance after it fell to the Florentines in 1509. It is the birthplace of Galileo, who taught at the university (founded in 1343). The most famous of its buildings is the Leaning Tower of Pisa, which is 55 m (180 ft) high and about 5 m (17 ft) out of perpendicular. Other notable buildings include the cathedral (11th–12th centuries) and the baptistry (12th–13th centuries). Its many historic monuments make it a popular tourist centre. Machinery, textiles, bicycles, and glass are manufactured. Population (1980 est): 103 252.

Pisanello (Antonio Pisano; c. 1395–c. 1455) Italian *international gothic painter, draughtsman, and medallist. He worked on frescoes, begun by *Gentile da Fabriano, in Venice and Rome. His portrait medals, influenced by Roman and Greek coins, were popular in court circles, particularly in Ferrara. In such paintings as the *Vision of St Eustace* (National Gallery, London) he recreated the world of chivalry.

Pisano, Andrea (Andrea de Pontedera; c. 1290–1348) Italian sculptor. Unrelated to Nicola and Giovanni *Pisano, Andrea worked chiefly in Florence, where he succeeded Giotto as architect of the cathedral (1336). His most important works are the bronze reliefs of the life of St John for the south doors of the Baptistry.

Pisano, Nicola (c. 1220–c. 1278) Italian sculptor. He initiated the revival of antique Roman forms that led eventually to Renaissance sculpture, beginning with his pulpit in the Baptistry, Pisa. Such later works as the pulpit in Siena Cathedral and the fountain in the main square of Perugia reveal the cooperation of his son **Giovanni Pisano** (c. 1250–1314). Giovanni introduced French gothic elements into his sculptures for the façade of Siena Cathedral and his pulpit for S Andrea, Pistoia. He returned to a more classical style in his pulpit for Pisa Cathedral.

Pisces (Latin: Fish) A large inconspicuous constellation that lies on the *zodiac between Aries and Aquarius, mainly in the N sky. It contains the vernal *equinox.

Pisistratus (c. 600–c. 528 BC) Athenian tyrant. After several ultimately abortive attempts to seize power in Athens, Pisistratus succeeded in 546 with a mercenary army. As tyrant, he diminished the power of landed aristocrats by instituting circuit judges to adjudicate local cases. Pisistratus encouraged Athenian agriculture and commerce and his benevolent tyranny promoted the national unity necessary for the later development of democracy.

Pissarro, Camille (1830–1903) French impressionist painter, born in the West Indies. After running away to Venezuela to become an artist, he was sent by his parents to Paris (1855). He trained in the École des Beaux-Arts, and the Académie Suisse, where he met *Monet. Chiefly influenced by *Corot, he was more interested in landscape structure than the other impressionists. He participated in all eight of the impressionist exhibitions (1874–86) and is

noted for his encouragement of younger painters, especially *Cézanne and *Gauguin. In the 1880s he experimented with *pointillism. His son **Lucien Pissarro** (1863–1944) was also a painter.

pistachio A small aromatic tree, *Pistacia vera*, native to central Eurasia and widely cultivated in Mediterranean regions for its edible green kernels ("nuts"). Growing 7–10 m high, it has compound leaves with 1–5 pairs of leathery leaflets and drooping spikes of small male and female flowers, borne usually on separate trees. The oval white fruits, 1.5–2 cm long, often split to expose the kernels, which are used as dessert nuts and for decorating and flavouring confectionery, cakes, etc. Family: *Anacardiaceae.

pistil The part of a flower consisting of the female reproductive organs. It consists of one or more *carpels, which may be united into a single structure. Some plants, such as the cucumber, have separate male and female flowers: the latter are described as pistillate.

Pistoia 43 56N 10 55E A town in N central Italy, in Tuscany. *Catiline was killed in battle near here (62 BC). The 12th-century cathedral contains a famous silver altar. Population (1983 est): 91 993.

17th-century English wheellock pistol.

18th-century Scottish flintlock with ram's-horn butt.

Colt 45 revolver first produced in 1873 and still in use.

Colt 45 automatic.

PISTOL

pistol A short-range *small arm that can be used with one hand. It evolved from a small cavalry matchlock in the 15th century, later improvements following those of the ▢musket. The need to make a weapon that would fire more than once without reloading led to the division of pistols into two classes: the *revolver and the automatic. The first revolver (c. 1540) had multiple barrels, which were rotated by hand past the lock. However, the first successful revolver was the *Colt of 1835, in which a magazine chamber revolves behind a single barrel. The first automatics (1893) combined a box magazine in the butt with a recoil loading action. The *Luger 9 mm automatic went into service with the German navy in 1904 and remained the standard weapon until 1938. Both revolvers and automatics are still in military and police use throughout the world.

Pitcairn Islands A small island group in the central S Pacific Ocean, a British dependent territory, consisting of Pitcairn Island and three uninhabited islands. Subsistence agriculture is the chief occupation; fruit, vegetables, and souvenirs are sold to passing ships. *History*: Pitcairn Island was occupied in 1790 by mutineers from the *Bounty* and women from Tahiti. By 1856 the island was overpopulated and the inhabitants were moved to Norfolk Island; some later returned. Area: 4.6 sq km (1.75 sq mi). Population (1981): 63. Chief town: Adamstown.

pitch (chemistry) A black or dark-brown residue resulting from the partial evaporation or fractional distillation of coal tars or tar products. The term is sometimes used for the residue obtained from petroleum distillation (bitumen) or for the naturally occurring petroleum residue (asphalt). Bitumen is a mixture of heavy hydrocarbons with a high proportion of free carbon. It is used as a binding agent (it is the main constituent of road tars), as a protective coating in bituminous paints, in roofing felts, and as a fuel.

pitch (music) The highness or lowness of a note, depending on the frequency of the vibrations producing it. Standard pitch has varied through the centuries: Handel's still extant *tuning fork gives A as 422.5 Hz. Modern **concert pitch** was standardized by international agreement in 1939, and the frequency of the note A was fixed at 440 Hz. **Perfect pitch** is the ability to recognize and name notes by ear alone; since notes have no absolute pitch value, even this depends on relative frequencies. *See also* temperament.

pitchblende The chief ore of uranium, a massive form of uraninite, UO_2, a black radioactive mineral found in hydrothermal veins and as an accessory mineral in acid igneous rocks. It occurs in North America, Africa, Australia, and central Europe.

pitcher plant Any *carnivorous plant with pitcher-shaped leaves, belonging mainly to the families *Nepenthaceae* and *Sarraceniaceae*. The pitcher is often brightly coloured and secretes nectar to attract insects, which often fall inside and drown in the digestive juices at the bottom of the pitcher. The *Nepenthaceae* comprises herbs and shrubs of the Old World, many of which are climbers. Their leaf tendrils are swollen to form the pitcher, 5–30 cm long. The *Sarraceniaceae* are perennial herbs of the New World with rosettes of pitchers arising from a swollen underground stem.

Pithecanthropus A group of extinct Pleistocene *hominids, now generally called *Homo erectus* (*see* Homo). The name *Pithecanthropus* (literally apeman) was coined by *Haeckel before any supporting fossil evidence was found for the evolutionary link.

Pitlochry 56 43N 3 45W A town in central Scotland, in Tayside Region on the River Tummel. Set amid magnificent scenery, it is a popular tourist centre and site of the famous Pitlochry Festival Theatre. The Tummel-Garry hydroelectric scheme is nearby. Population (1981): 2610.

Pitman, Sir Isaac. *See* shorthand.

pitot tube A type of *anemometer for measuring the velocity of a fluid, invented by Henri Pitot (1695-1771). It consists of an L-shaped tube placed in the moving fluid; the vertical limb of the tube has an opening facing into the flow. The difference in pressure between the interior of the tube and the surroundings enables the velocity of the fluid to be calculated. The device is used to measure the velocity of liquids, aircraft airspeeds, etc.

Pittosporum A genus of small evergreen trees (about 150 species), called parchment-bark or Australian laurels, native to Australia and New Zealand and often grown as ornamentals. They have long pale leathery leaves and blue, white, yellow, or red flowers. *P. tenuifolium* is popular in flower arrangements. Family: *Pittosporaceae*.

Pitt-Rivers, Augustus Henry Lane Fox (1827-1900) British anthropologist and archaeologist. Pitt-Rivers formed a major anthropological collection, now in the Pitt-Rivers Museum, Oxford, in his pioneering work on establishing typological sequences for artefacts from different cultures and eras. After 1880 he excavated prehistoric and Romano-British remains in S England, becoming the first Inspector of

Ancient Monuments (1882). His book, *Excavations in Cranborne Chase* (1887-98), testifies to his meticulous archaeological standards.

Pittsburgh 40 26N 80 00W A city in the USA, in Pennsylvania at the confluence of the Allegheny and Monongahela Rivers, which here form the Ohio River. Settled in 1758, it was the site of Fort Pitt completed by the British in 1761. The city was founded in 1764. It is the site of several colleges and universities, including the University of Pittsburgh (1787) and the famous Carnegie Institute, which contains a two-million-volume library, several museums, and the Carnegie Music Hall. Pittsburgh has grown as a major centre of the steel industry and is the country's largest inland port. Other manufactures include machinery, petroleum, coal, glass, and chemicals. Population (1980): 423 938.

Pitt the Elder, William, 1st Earl of Chatham (1708-78) British statesman, known as the Great Commoner. Entering parliament in 1735 as MP for the *pocket borough of Old Sarum, he established a reputation as an outstanding orator. He opposed the government of Sir Robert Walpole, who fell in 1742, and attacked Carteret's conduct (1742-44) of the War of the Spanish Succession. As paymaster general (1746-55) he was notable for his incorruptibility. In 1756 he became secretary of state and leader of the House of Commons but was dismissed in 1757 and then recalled to form a ministry with *Newcastle. In charge of foreign affairs, he was largely responsible for British victory in the *Seven Years' War, reorganizing the militia and navy and rallying public opinion. Forced to resign in 1761, he returned to form a new ministry in 1766 as Earl of Chatham. Plagued by ill health, he resigned in 1768. He died after collapsing while speaking in the House of Lords.

His second son **William Pitt the Younger** (1759-1806) was twice prime minister (1783-1801, 1804-06), the youngest in British history. He entered parliament in 1781 and became Shelburne's chancellor of the exchequer in 1782. As prime minister (and at the same time chancellor and first lord of the treasury) he inherited an enormous public debt, which he reduced by a fiscal policy influenced by Adam *Smith. He introduced new taxes, overhauled customs duties, and introduced a new sinking fund. He also reformed the Indian administration (*see* Government of India Acts). Pitt negotiated the first (1793) and second (1798) coalitions against France (*see* Revolutionary and Napoleonic Wars) and resolved the crisis caused by the Irish rebellion in 1798 by union of Britain and Ireland in 1800. He resigned following George III's refusal to accept Catholic emancipation. His second ministry was marked by an alliance with Russia, Sweden, and Austria against Napoleon, which collapsed shortly before his death in office. A Tory, Pitt's rivalry with the Whig, Charles James *Fox, contributed to the clearer identification of Whigs and Tories.

pituitary gland A small *endocrine gland, about 12 mm by 8 mm, lying within the skull close to the centre of the head. The anterior (front) lobe produces *growth hormone, *prolactin, and hormones that regulate the function of other glands, notably the *thyroid and *adrenal glands and the ovary and testis. The posterior (back) lobe is a downgrowth from the *hypothalamus and stores various neurohormones that are synthesized in this part of the brain. The pituitary is therefore the master endocrine gland, from which neural control of the entire endocrine system is effected.

pit viper A New World viper, belonging to the subfamily *Crotalinae*, that has a sensory pit between the eye and nostril used to detect the tiny changes in temperature caused by warm-blooded prey nearby. Pit vipers occur in habitats ranging from deserts to rain forests and are chiefly grounddwellers. *See also* bushmaster; copperhead; fer-de-lance; rattlesnake; sidewinder; water moccasin.

Pius II (Enea Silvio (*or* Aeneas Silvius) de' Piccolomini; 1405-64) Pope (1458-64), who was also a notable humanist. He served Emperor Frederick III as both imperial poet and secretary before becoming a priest (1446). On his election he attempted to restore papal authority by condemning the view that general councils had supreme authority in the Church. His proclamation of a crusade against the Turks after the fall of Constantinople (1453) was ignored by the secular powers and he died shortly after resolving to lead it in person.

Pius IV (Giovanni Angelo de' Medici; 1499-1565) Pope (1559-65). He continued papal support of the *Counter-Reformation, presiding over the last session of the Council of *Trent and reforming the Sacred College of cardinals.

Pius V, St (Michele Ghislieri; 1504-72) Pope (1566-72). A Dominican friar and noted for his asceticism, he was the greatest of the 16th-century reformer popes. Pius re-edited a number of liturgical texts, including the breviary and missal, enforced the decrees of the Council of *Trent, and expanded the activities of the *Inquisition. He excommunicated the Protestant Elizabeth I of England in 1570. He was canonized in 1712. Feast day: 6 May.

Pius VI (Giovanni Angelico Braschi; 1717-99) Pope (1775-99). His pontificate was marked by attempts to combat growing opposition to papal control from both national churches and states, especially in France, where he condemned the state church established during the French Revolution. Pius was captured in the Revolutionary Wars, during which the French attacked the papal states, and died a prisoner.

Pius VII (Gregorio Barnaba Chiaramonti; 1740-1823) Pope (1800-23), who made several unsuccessful attempts to preserve papal privileges in the face of Napoleon's demands. In 1804, under duress, he consecrated Napoleon emperor and in 1809, after the French conquest of Rome, was taken prisoner and forced to make extensive concessions in the Concordat of Fontainebleu (1813). After Napoleon's fall in 1815 Pius gained the restoration of the papal states and negotiated concordats with many of the victorious powers.

Pius IX (Giovanni Maria Mastai-Ferretti; 1792-1878) Pope (1846-78). At first sympathetic to liberal and nationalist movements, he abandoned radicalism for reaction after the Revolution of 1848, in which he fled Rome. He refused to acknowledge the newly established kingdom of Italy, into which Rome was incorporated in 1870. He defined the Immaculate Conception (1854) and papal infallibility (1869-70) and his encyclical *Quanta Cura* (1864), with its *Syllabus of Errors*, condemned modernism in theology and philosophy.

Pius X, St (Giuseppe Sarto; 1835-1914) Pope (1903-14). His pontificate was marked by his defence of the Church's independence against encroachment by the state, support of social reforms (especially in the Catholic Action movement), reform of the liturgy, and a new codification of canon law. He condemned theological modernism and revolutionary political movements. He was canonized in 1954. Feast day: 3 Sept.

Pius XI (Achille Ratti; 1857-1939) Pope (1922-39). He attempted to extend the educational and social work of the Church, supporting the role of the laity in the Catholic Action movement. He signed the *Lateran Treaty (1929), establishing the Vatican City as a sovereign state.

Pius XII (Eugenio Pacelli; 1876-1958) Pope (1939-58). Pius' failure to condemn fascism during World War II caused controversy, although he attempted to prevent the outbreak of war, to curb atrocities, and to relieve suffering. He was a staunch conservative both in politics and doctrine, condemning communism and modernist theology.

Pizarro, Francisco (c. 1475-1541) Spanish conquistador. He accompanied Balboa on the expedition that discovered the Pacific (1513) and in the 1520s explored the NW coast of South America. In 1531 having gained Emperor Charles V's assent to the conquest of Peru and an assurance of the major part of the spoils, he crossed the Andes to Cajamarca. There he treacherously murdered the Inca king, Atahuallpa. Over the next nine years he consolidated the Spanish conquest of the Inca empire, founding Lima in 1535. He came into conflict with a fellow conquistador, Diego de Almagro (c. 1475-1538), who was defeated and put to death; his followers, however, subsequently murdered Pizzaro.

PK. *See* telekinesis.

Place, Francis (1771-1854) British radical, who campaigned for the repeal of the anti-union *Combination Acts (1799, 1800). With the help of Joseph *Hume he was successful by 1824.

placenta 1. An organ formed within the womb of mammals and other viviparous animals during pregnancy, composed of fetal and maternal tissues. Within the placenta the blood vessels of the fetus and mother come into close contact, enabling exchange of substances in the blood. Thus the fetus receives nutrients, oxygen, and antibodies from the mother's blood and its waste products are absorbed into the mother's circulation. The fetus is attached to the placenta by the umbilical cord. The placenta also secretes hormones that contribute to the control of pregnancy. The placenta is expelled (as the afterbirth) shortly after the baby is delivered. **2.** A tissue in plants that connects the ovules (later the seeds) to the ovary (later the fruit wall).

Placodermi An extinct class of fish that lived from the Devonian to the Permian periods (415-240 million years ago). Their bodies, usually 10-40 cm long, were covered with bony scales, particularly over the head and front half, and had a bony skeleton, primitive jaws, gill covers (opercula), and median and paired fins. Many species were bottom-dwelling carnivores.

plagioclase A group of *feldspar minerals with compositions varying between the two end-members albite ($NaAlSi_3O_8$) and anorthite ($CaAl_2Si_2O_8$). They are milky white or colourless, and occur both as phenocrysts and in the groundmass of most basic and intermediate igneous rocks and in many metamorphic rocks.

plague An infectious disease caused by the bacterium *Pasteurella pestis*, which is transmitted to man by rat fleas. There are three forms of the disease, the most common of which is bubonic plague, in which fever, vomiting, and headache are accompanied by swollen inflamed lymph nodes (buboes). The more severe pneumonic and septicaemic plagues develop when the bacteria enter the lungs and bloodstream respectively. Plague is treated with antibiotics. Epidemics of plague afflicted Europe throughout the middle ages, the *Black Death of 1348 being the most devastating. The **Great Plague of London** (1665-66) was the last of the epidemics from which England had suffered intermittently since the Black Death. It claimed an estimated 70 000 lives. Today plague is usually restricted to areas of poor sanitation in tropical countries.

plaice A commercially important *flatfish, *Pleuronectes platessa*, that occurs in the N North Atlantic and British coastal waters. It is usually 25-40 cm long, occasionally up to 90 cm, and is coloured brown with bright-red or orange spots above and white beneath. There are four to seven bony warts running backwards from the eyes.

Plaid Cymru A political party, founded in 1925, dedicated to the achievement of Welsh independence from the UK. The party achieved some popularity with the rise of nationalist sentiment in the 1960s and early 1970s, securing three seats in the October, 1974, parliamentary election; these were reduced to two in the election of 1979, just after the rejection by the Welsh electorate of *devolution in the referendum held on the issue.

plainchant (*or* plainsong) The ritual music of the early Christian Church, as distinct from later polyphonic music. It consists of unaccompanied melodic lines deriving from natural intonation, with flexible rhythms to fit the Latin prose of the daily services. Probably initially influenced by

Jewish liturgical chant, its melodic basis derived from the Greek system of *modes. At the end of the 6th century, during the papacy of Gregory I, it was codified as *Gregorian chant and flourished with few changes until the advent of harmonized melody in about 1000.

plains-wanderer An Australian bird, *Pedionomus torquatus*, of dry grassland regions. 10–13 cm long, it has short rounded wings, a short tail, and a mottled red-brown plumage with a white throat and a collar of black spots. Largely ground-dwelling, it feeds on plant material and insects and is the only member of its family (*Pedionomidae*). Order: *Gruiformes* (cranes, rails, etc.).

planarian A free-living *flatworm of the order *Tricladida*, occurring in marine and freshwater habitats of temperate regions. Flattened and symmetrical, with simple eyespots and olfactory organs, planarians range from 2 mm to 10 cm in length. They glide smoothly by means of beating cilia (hairs) and use a long retractable feeding tube (pharynx) to consume small invertebrates. Class: *Turbellaria*.

Planck, Max Karl Ernst Ludwig (1858–1947) German physicist; the originator of *quantum theory, who was professor at Kiel University (1880–89) and then at the University of Berlin (1889–1926). Planck solved the problem of blackbody radiation by assuming that the radiation was emitted in discrete amounts called quanta, the magnitude of a quanta being the product of the frequency of the radiation and a constant, now known as *Planck's constant. For this work he received the Nobel Prize in 1918. He remained in Germany during the Nazi period and attempted to intercede with Hitler on behalf of Jewish scientists. For this he was deprived of the presidency of the research institute that bears his name. His eldest son, **Erwin Planck** (1914–44) was executed for his involvement in the plot to assassinate Hitler.

Planck's constant (*h*) A fundamental constant that relates the quantum of energy (*E*) of a photon to the frequency (*f*) of the corresponding electromagnetic radiation by the equation $E = hf$. Its value is $6.626\ 196 \times 10^{-34}$ joule second. Named after Max *Planck.

Planck's radiation law Electromagnetic radiation is emitted from and absorbed by matter in discrete amounts (quanta) known as *photons. The energy (*E*) of a photon is related to the frequency (*f*) of the radiation by the equation $E = hf$, where *h* is known as *Planck's constant. Max *Planck discovered the law (1900) while investigating the distribution of wavelengths of the radiation emitted by a *black body. It forms the basis of the *quantum theory.

planet A celestial body that moves around a star and shines by light reflected from its surface. The only known planets are those orbiting the sun (□solar system): there are nine major planets and numerous *minor planets. The major planets in order from the sun are *Mercury, *Venus, *earth, and *Mars (the **terrestrial planets**), *Jupiter, *Saturn, *Uranus, and *Neptune (the **giant planets**) and, usually outermost, *Pluto. There is evidence of planets already formed or forming around other stars.

planetarium 1. A complex instrument that projects an artificial but accurate picture of the night sky, showing planets, stars, and other celestial bodies, on the interior of a hemispherical dome. The dome forms the upper part of an auditorium. The images of the celestial bodies are produced by a considerable number of small optical projectors in the instrument. By moving the individual projectors at the correct speed, the bodies are made to follow their natural paths through the sky. 2. A building housing such an instrument. Famous planetariums include those in Moscow (1929) and London (1958); there are some 60 in the USA.

planetary nebula A luminous cloud of gas cast off and expanding away from a dying star. It is a type of emission *nebula, being ionized by radiation from the hot central star.

planetary probe An unmanned spacecraft that studies conditions on and near one or more planets and their satellites and in the interplanetary medium along the flight path. The information gathered is then transmitted to earth. The transmitters, TV cameras, and other instruments are powered by solar cells or, for deep-space probes, by thermoelectric generators, etc. Midflight course corrections and attitude adjustments can be made by rocket motors. *See* Mariner; Pioneer; Vega; Venera; Viking; Voyager probes.

plane tree A large tree of the genus *Platanus* (10 species), native to the N hemisphere and often grown for shade and ornament. Up to 50 m tall, the trees have patchy peeling bark, large lobed leaves, and separate round clusters (catkins) of male and female flowers: the female flowers give rise to bristly round fruits. The London plane (*P.* × *acerifolia*) is a hybrid between the Oriental plane (*P. orientalis*) and North American buttonwood (*P. occidentalis*). The timber is a valuable hardwood used in carpentry. Family: *Platanaceae*.

planimeter A device for measuring small irregular plane areas. A moving arm is traced around a closed curve. The enclosed area is calculated from the revolution of a small wheel attached to the arm.

plankton Minute or microscopic animals (zooplankton) and plants (phytoplankton) that float and drift in the open waters of a sea or lake. The phytoplankton (diatoms and other algae) carry out *photosynthesis in the surface waters and so provide the basic food source for all aquatic animals. The zooplankton include protozoa, small crustaceans, and larvae (e.g. barnacle and fish larvae). Plankton are of great ecological and economic importance as a food source for fish and whales and thus—indirectly—to man, whose fishing industry depends upon them. □oceans.

plant A living organism belonging to the kingdom *Plantae*, of which there are some 400 000 or so species. Plants are typically immobile and most manufacture their own food from simple inorganic nutrients by *photosynthesis, trapping the energy required for the process in the green pigment chlorophyll. (Plants that lack chlorophyll, notably fungi, feed on organic materials.) Plant cells have rigid cell walls, providing support, and growth occurs from specialized zones of tissue (*see* meristem), continuously or periodically throughout life. Plants lack specialized sense organs and a nervous system; response to external stimuli is usually slow and often permanent. Unlike animals, there is considerable variation in form between individuals of the same species. Green plants are the primary source of food and oxygen for all animals. □ pp. 965, 966.

Plantagenet The surname of the Angevin, Lancastrian, and Yorkist Kings of England (1154–1485). They were descended from Queen Matilda and Geoffrey Martel, Count of Anjou (d. 1151), who was nicknamed Plantagenet because he wore a sprig of broom (*plante genêt*) in his cap. The name was not formally adopted until the 15th century, when it was used by Richard Plantagenet, Duke of *York, to further his claim to the throne in the Wars of the Roses.

Plantagenet, Richard, Duke of York. *See* York, Richard Plantagenet, 3rd Duke of.

plantain 1. An annual or perennial herb of the genus *Plantago* (about 50 species), occurring in temperate regions and on mountains in the tropics, often as a troublesome weed. Plantains have a basal rosette of simple leaves from which arises a stalk, 3–70 cm high, bearing a dense terminal head of inconspicuous green, white, yellow, or brown flowers with protruding stamens. The leaves of the greater plantain (*P. major*) of Eurasia are used to treat insect stings. Family: *Plantaginaceae*. 2. *See* banana.

Plantation of Ireland (1556–1660) The government-sponsored settlement of British families in Ireland in the 16th and 17th centuries. Conceived as a method of subjugating the rebellious Irish, the first plantations were not noticeably

965

PLANT

pollen
grains

pollen
sac

pollen sac
split to
release pollen

structure of an anther

FLOWERS

pollen grain
stigma
style
pollen tube
ovule
ovary wall
future seed coat
nucleus
placenta
micropyle

structure of a carpel

STEMS

vascular bundle
phloem xylem
epidermis
cortex
pith
(medulla)
cambium

transverse section of a
dicotyledon stem

summer   autumn   cork
wood   wood   cambium
phloem   bark   ray   cambium

phloem   ray
summer   winter
wood   wood

section of a woody stem
showing four seasons' growth

stamen
anther filament
petal
carpel
receptacle
sepal
lamina
vein
petiole
midrib
main(tap)
root
lateral
root
root
hairs

ROOTS

xylem
phloem
cortex
root hairs
xylem
phloem
root cap

section of the tip of a root

LEAVES

lower epidermis
xylem vessels
phloem
upper epidermis
vein
stomata
air space

spongy   palisade
mesophyll   mesophyll

transverse section of a leaf

stomata
guard cell

open   closed

detail of stomata

broad category	major groups (usually divisions)	important classes	representative members
ALGAE	Chlorophyta		green algae (*Spirogyra*, sea lettuce, etc.)
	Chrysophyta		yellow-green algae, diatoms
	Phaeophyta		brown algae (wracks, kelps, etc.)
	Rhodophyta		red algae
FUNGI	Myxomycophyta		slime fungi (clubroot, etc.)
	Eumycophyta	Phycomycetes	pin mould
		Ascomycetes	*Penicillium, Aspergillus*
		Basidiomycetes	mushrooms, puffballs, bracket fungi
MOSSES and LIVERWORTS	Bryophyta	Hepaticae	liverworts (e.g. *Pellia*)
		Musci	mosses (e.g. *Sphagnum*)
VASCULAR PLANTS (TRACHEOPHYTES)	Pteridophyta	Lycopsida	clubmosses
		Sphenopsida	horsetails
		Pteropsida	ferns
	Spermatophyta (seed plants)	Gymnospermae	cycads, *Ginkgo*, conifers (pines, larches, spruces, etc.)
		Angiospermae	monocotyledons (grasses, palms, orchids, lilies, etc.), dicotyledons (most trees and flowering plants)

PLANT   *A simplified classification of the plant kingdom.*

successful but the Ulster plantation (1608–11), composed of English and Scots, survived and prospered. Under Charles I and Oliver Cromwell, there were further land confiscations, called plantations, but no accompanying large-scale immigration from Britain.

plant bug   A plant-eating insect belonging to the families *Myridae* (*see* capsid) and *Lygaeidae* (*see* ground bug). The term may also refer to any other herbivorous insect of the suborder *Heteroptera* (*see* Hemiptera).

plant hopper   A plant-eating insect belonging to a family (*Fulgoridae*; over 5000 species) found mainly in tropical and subtropical regions. Plant hoppers are 10–50 mm long and often brightly coloured, with large unusually shaped heads. Some species are covered with a secretion of white waxy threads or powder. Suborder: *Homoptera*; order *Hemiptera*. *See also* lantern fly.

plasma (anatomy)   The fluid constituent of *blood, in which the blood cells are suspended. Plasma consists of a solution of various salts, sugars, etc., and contains numerous proteins, including those involved in *blood clotting and the immunological response to infection (i.e. antibodies). It is obtained by centrifuging unclotted blood. *Compare* serum.

plasma (physics)   A gas the atoms of which have been completely ionized. Sometimes called the fourth state of matter, plasmas occur at enormously high temperatures, such as those in the sun. Plasmas are also created in *thermonuclear reactors.

plasmapheresis   A laboratory technique used in blood transfusions in which the fluid constituent (plasma) is separated from the donor's blood and the blood cells are returned to the donor. This technique allows the donor to provide plasma more frequently than would be possible if whole blood were removed, since it is only the red cells that the body requires time to replace. Plasma transfusions are particularly useful for haemophiliacs, who require frequent transfusions, since it contains the blood-clotting factors that they lack.

Plasmodium   A genus of parasitic single-celled animals (*see* Protozoa) that cause *malaria in man. *Plasmodium* undergoes the sexual phase of its development in bloodsucking mosquitoes of the genus *Anopheles*, through which it is transmitted to man. Asexual division of the parasite occurs in human liver and red blood cells. Four species cause different forms of malaria: *P. falciparum* (causing the most severe kind), *P. vivax*, *P. malariae*, and *P. ovale*. Class: *Sporozoa.

Plassey, Battle of   (23 June, 1757) The battle in West Bengal (India) in which Robert *Clive defeated the Nawab of Bengal, Siraj-ud-Dawlah (c. 1728–57). Aided by the mutiny of the nawab's generals, Clive's victory made possible Britain's acquisition of Bengal.

plaster   A paste used to give a smooth hard coating to ceilings, walls, etc. A number of formulations are in use, the traditional one being a mixture of lime, sand, and water, which hardens in air owing to drying and reaction with atmospheric carbon dioxide.

plaster of Paris   A hydrated form of calcium sulphate ($CaSO_4.\frac{1}{2}H_2O$) made by partial dehydration of *gypsum by heating. When mixed with water it sets into a hard mass by formation of the dihydrate ($CaSO_4.2H_2O$). It is used for casts for broken limbs and for modelling.

plasticity   The permanent deformation of a substance after being subjected to a sufficiently large stress. Below a certain stress, called the elastic limit, most substances will recover their original shape when the stress is removed. Such substances are said to be elastic (*see* elasticity). However, single crystals of certain metals are plastic no matter how small the stress.

plastics   Synthetic materials that consist of polymers (*see* polymerization) and are moulded during manufacture. Plastics are made from synthetic *resins. **Thermosetting plastics** harden on heating to give a rigid product that cannot then be softened. *Polyurethanes, *polyesters, *silicones, and *epoxy resins all form thermosetting plastics. **Thermoplastic materials** soften when heated and harden again when cooled. These include derivatives of *cellulose and polymers, such as *polythene, polystyrene, polyvinyl chloride, and polymethylmethacrylate, which contain a reactive double bond.

Natural polymers, such as *shellac and *rubber, have been known for many centuries. The first synthetic material was Celluloid, made in 1870 from cotton and camphor. This highly inflammable substance was replaced during World

War I by cellulose acetate and casein products. These materials were all based on naturally occurring large molecules. The first polymers to be made by joining together smaller molecules were the phenol-formaldehyde resins (trade name Bakelite) invented in 1908 by Leo Baekeland (1863–1944). Since then a vast number of different resins have been synthesized, some 2000 million tonnes of plastics now being manufactured annually in the UK alone.

plastic surgery The branch of surgery concerned with the correction of deformities, disfigurements, or other forms of damage to any part of the body. This includes the reconstruction of developmental defects, such as cleft palate, harelip, and club foot, and the repair of injuries (particularly those of the face) caused by fire or traffic accidents. Great advances were made in this aspect of plastic surgery by Sir Archibald *McIndoe, during and after World War II. Cosmetic plastic surgery is performed simply to improve the appearance: an example is facelifting to remove wrinkles.

Plata, Río de la (English name: River Plate) The estuary of the Río Paraná and the River Uruguay, on the Atlantic coast of SE South America between Uruguay and Argentina. Its shores are densely populated; Montevideo, the capital of Uruguay, lies on the N shore and Buenos Aires, the capital of Argentina, is situated on the S shore. A naval battle was fought off its mouth in 1939 (see World War II). Length: 275 km (171 mi). Width (at mouth): 225 km (140 mi).

Plataea An ancient city of Boeotia. Grateful for protection against Thebes, Plataea became Athens' permanent ally; Plataeans alone joined the Athenians at Marathon and they played a crucial role in the battle of Plataea (479 BC), where the allied Greek forces decisively defeated the Persians (see Greek-Persian Wars). During the Peloponnesian War Plataea suffered severely for its pro-Athenian policy, being besieged (429–427) and sacked by Sparta. Although rebuilt, it was again destroyed (by Thebes in 373) and then restored (by Philip of Macedon in the late 4th century BC).

Plate, River. See Plata, Río de la.

plateau An extensive area of comparatively level elevated land, sometimes known as a tableland where it is bounded by steep slopes or scarps. It may be crossed by rivers and mountains. One of the world's highest is the Tibetan plateau.

platelet A small particle, 0.001–0.002 mm in diameter, produced by the bone-marrow and found in the □blood. Platelets are essential for *blood clotting, accumulating in large numbers at the site of an injured blood vessel. There are normally 150 000 to 400 000 platelets per cubic millimetre of blood. Absence of platelets causes severe bleeding and may occur in a variety of illnesses (e.g. liver disease).

platemaking The production of *printing plates. Original plates are made by hand engraving (for letterpress), drawing with wax crayons (for lithography), etc., or photographically. In one type of photographic process, metal with a photosensitive coating is exposed to light, usually through a film negative of the type, drawing, or photograph to be printed. The unexposed coating is then washed off and the bare metal underneath turned into nonprinting areas: with a letterpress plate it is etched away; with a typical lithographic plate it is wetted and made grease-repellent, while the exposed areas are inked to make them grease-receptive. A collotype plate has a photosensitive gelatin coating that is hardened, by exposure through a negative, in proportion to the amount of light falling on each area. Collotype can thus reproduce continuous tone, as in a photograph: the more any area is hardened, the less water it will absorb and the more ink it will accept and transfer to the paper. With gravure plates, the printing areas are etched away through an exposed gelatin layer. Continuous tone is simulated in letterpress and lithography by converting the image into a grid of dots of varying size called a half-tone and in gravure by varying the depth of the etched cells and thus the amount of ink that each transfers to the paper.

Duplicate (letterpress) plates are made from original plates by one of two methods. In **stereotyping**, a mould (or matrix) is made, in which the duplicate is cast in metal or moulded from rubber or plastic. In **electrotyping**, a thin layer of copper is deposited electrolytically in a matrix similar to that used in stereotyping and then itself filled with molten metal to make it rigid when the metal cools.

plate tectonics The theory, developed mainly in the 1960s, that the earth's crust is divided into rigid plates (oceanic, continental, or a combination of both), which move about the earth's surface at rates of 1–9 cm per annum. The edges of the plates are called plate margins. At constructive plate margins new oceanic crust is created where two plates are moving apart and magma rises to fill the gap; this occurs at midocean ridges (see sea-floor spreading). At destructive plate margins two plates collide and one dips beneath the other, producing deep-sea trenches and the associated volcanic island arcs. Where two continental plates collide, mountain chains are formed. All the major structural features of the earth's surface and almost all seismic and volcanic activity can be ascribed to plate movements.

Plath, Sylvia (1932–63) US poet and writer. In 1956 she married the British poet Ted *Hughes, whom she had met at Cambridge University. The disciplined poems of her first volume, The Colossus (1960), contrast with the anguished poems of Ariel (1965), published two years after her suicide. She also wrote a novel, The Bell Jar (1966). Letters to her mother (Letters Home; 1975) and her journals (Pulitzer Prize; 1982) were published posthumously.

platinum (Pt) A precious silver-white noble metal, known to the South American Indians. It is malleable, ductile, and has a high melting point. Platinum is found in nature in nickel ore, as about one part in two million of ore. It can absorb large quantities of hydrogen and is used as a *catalyst, particularly in contact process for making sulphuric acid. It is also used in thermocouple wires and in jewellery. It dissolves in *aqua regia to form chloroplatinic acid (H_2PtCl_6). Although unreactive, platinum also forms other compounds, including the hexafluoride (PtF_6), one of the most powerful oxidizing agents known. At no 78; at wt 195.09; mp 1772°C; bp 3827 ± 100°C.

platinum-iridium An alloy of platinum and iridium that is highly resistant to heat and is used in instruments for measuring high temperatures.

Plato (429–347 BC) Greek philosopher. An Athenian nobleman, he was early disillusioned by both democrats and aristocrats. Seeing no hope for man unless rulers became philosophers or philosophers rulers, he became a devoted follower of *Socrates. After Socrates' death he travelled widely, apparently becoming acquainted with many distinguished thinkers. In 387 he returned to Athens and founded his *Academy. To this he devoted the rest of his life, except that in 367 and again soon afterwards, he visited Sicily to assist his friend, Dion, in his futile attempts to turn *Dionysius II, the young and unstable tyrant of Syracuse, into a philosopher, and Syracuse into a Platonic state. Some of Plato's poetry and all his prose works survive. Apart from 13 possibly spurious letters and the Apology, which purports to be Socrates' defence of himself before his judges, they are dramatic dialogues of outstanding literary merit. The early ones illustrate Socrates' character and philosophical methods, focusing especially on the question of whether virtue can be taught. The Phaedo, Symposium, and Republic of Plato's middle period develop Plato's mature views on such topics as metaphysics, love, and government, notably his theory of ideas (Forms), the perfect spiritual entities or prototypes of which the physical world is a feeble and imperfect copy. See also Platonism.

Platonism The philosophical tradition originating (c. 385

BC) in the Greek *Academy under *Plato. In the period of Middle Platonism (1st century BC-2nd century AD) interest centred on Plato's thought on God and the supersensible world. Subsequently the philosophers of Alexandria (see Plotinus) creatively systematized these and other aspects of their forerunners' work in *Neoplatonism. Works of Platonic character produced by such writers as St *Augustine of Hippo, *Boethius, and Macrobius transmitted Platonism to the medieval West. The impact of *Aristotelianism in the 13th century brought a temporary eclipse, but at the Renaissance Platonism, promoted by such scholars as *Ficino and *Nicolas of Cusa, reasserted itself and exercised enormous influence on artists and writers, such as *Botticelli and *Spenser, as well as on philosophers and theologians (see also Cambridge Platonists). Despite modern science's final debunking of Platonic cosmology, elements of Platonism still permeate western thought in areas as diverse as realist logic (see realism) and Christian *ethics.

Platte River A river in the central USA. Formed by the confluence of the North Platte and South Platte Rivers at North Platte, Nebraska, it flows generally E to join the Missouri River. It is unnavigable but is a source of irrigation and hydroelectric power. Length: 499 km (310 mi).

Platyhelminthes. See flatworm.

platypus. See duck-billed platypus.

Plauen 50 30N 12 07E A town in S East Germany, on the Weisse Elster River. Several old buildings remain despite damage done during World War II. Famous for lace making since the 15th century, Plauen is a centre for textile manufacture and has a textile craft school. Population (1973 est): 81 024.

Plautus, Titus Maccius (c. 254-184 BC) Roman dramatist. He is traditionally believed to have worked as a craftsman in the theatre before beginning, in middle age, his career as a dramatist. His 21 surviving plays are all adapted from Greek *New Comedy writers, especially Menander and Philemon, and are noted for their robust humour and lively colloquial dialogue. His plays influenced the early development of comic drama by Shakespeare, Molière, and others.

player piano (or pianola) A mechanical piano in which the hammers are operated by an airflow produced by pedals or an electrically operated bellows and controlled by perforations on a rotating roll of paper. Rolls are either cut by a special machine attached to a piano and thus record an actual performance or they are produced mechanically. The player can control the volume and the speed by means of special levers.

playing cards Cards with pictures and symbols on one side, used in a wide variety of games, of which *bridge, *whist, *poker, *rummy, and *cribbage are the most popular. Modern cards derive from the *tarot pack; the 52-card French pack with suits of hearts, spades, diamonds, and clubs is now standard, the suits deriving from the tarot suits of cups, swords, money, and clubs respectively. Traditional German, Spanish, and Italian packs with variations in the number of cards and designs of the suits also derive from tarot cards. A connection has been suggested between the suits and the cup, sword, ring, and baton traditionally held by Hindu statues. Playing cards have long been used in divination and conjuring.

Pleasence, Donald (1919-) British actor. His best-known stage performance was as the tramp in Pinter's The Caretaker (1959; film 1963). His films, in which he has usually played villains or eccentrics, include Dr Crippen (1962) and Cul de Sac (1966).

plebeians Romans other than the privileged *patricians. At first without civil rights, excluded from state and religious offices, and forbidden to marry patricians, in 493-92 the plebeians forced the Senate to appoint their own tribunes and an assembly. During the subsequent two centuries of conflict, the plebeians gradually gained admission to all Roman offices and the wealthy and ambitious among them merged with the patricians. Thus, from later Republican times, the term plebeian implied low social class.

plebiscite A vote by the whole electorate on a particular issue. The term is usually used to refer to those *referendums held to decide to which state an area should belong. A plebiscite was first held by France in 1790-91 concerning the papal territory of Avignon.

Pléiade, La A group of seven French writers in the 16th century who sought to liberate French poetry from medieval tradition. Their principles, deriving from the study of Greek, Latin, and Italian literature, were expounded in Défense et illustration de la langue française (1549) by Joachim du *Bellay, and their innovations included the introduction of the sonnet, the ode, and the alexandrine. Led by Pierre de *Ronsard, the group included du Bellay, J.-A. de Baïf (1532-89), Étienne Jodelle (c. 1532-73), Rémy Belleau (c. 1528-77), Pontus de Tyard (c. 1522-1605), and Jacques Peletier (1517-82; for whom the name of Jean Dorat (1508-88) was occasionally substituted by contemporaries).

Pleiades A young open *star cluster in the constellation Taurus that contains several hundred stars, of which six are clearly visible to the naked eye. The brighter stars are surrounded by reflection *nebula. They were named after the seven daughters of *Atlas, who were changed by the gods into stars while being pursued by Orion.

Pleistocene epoch The epoch of geological time between the Pliocene and the Holocene, at the beginning of the Quaternary period. It lasted from about 1.8 million to 10 000 years ago. It is often called the *Ice Age because during this time the earth experienced great fluctuations in temperature: cold glacial periods, when the ice margins advanced towards the equator, separated by warmer interglacials, when temperatures at times were higher than today. Four main ice advances are recognized in the Pleistocene. Fossils from the Pleistocene include horses, pigs, and elephants.

Plekhanov, Georgi Valentinovich (1857-1918) Russian revolutionary and Marxist philosopher. Known as the "father of Russian Marxism," Plekhanov was instrumental in the creation (1898) of the Russian Social Democratic Workers' Party. He believed that Russia must pass through industrialization and capitalism before reaching socialism and came to side with the *Mensheviks against Lenin. After the Bolshevik victory, he lived in Finland.

Plenty, Bay of An inlet of the S Pacific Ocean, in New Zealand on the E coast of North Island. It was so named by Capt Cook, who received generous supplies of food and water from the Maoris here in 1769. Width: about 160 km (100 mi).

pleochroism The ability of certain crystals to transmit light vibrations in one plane only while absorbing those vibrations in other planes. Pleochroic crystals thus produce plane-*polarized light. If the effect occurs along only one axis of the crystal, the crystal is said to be dichroic. *Polaroid, for example, contains dichroic crystals. In trichroic crystals, the effect occurs along two axes perpendicular to each other.

plesiosaur A widely distributed marine reptile of the Jurassic and Cretaceous periods (200-65 million years ago). Up to about 12 m long, plesiosaurs had broad turtle-like bodies with paddle-like limbs, a long flexible neck, and jaws armed with sharp teeth used to catch fish.

pleurisy Inflammation of the pleura—the membrane that covers the lungs and lines the chest cavity. The commonest cause of pleurisy is bacterial or viral infection: pleurisy will often complicate *pneumonia. The patient will often have a fever, a pain in the chest that is worse on coughing or taking a deep breath, and a cough. Bacterial pleurisy is treated with antibiotics.

Pleurococcus A genus of common unicellular *green algae forming thin green powdery incrustations on the windward side of walls and tree trunks, particularly in tropical regions. The spherical cells are either solitary or form small flat aggregations; reproduction is by cell division.

Pleven 43 25N 24 40E A city in central N Bulgaria. The Russians and the Turks fought here in 1877. It has various industries and serves a mixed agricultural area. Population (1982): 373 000.

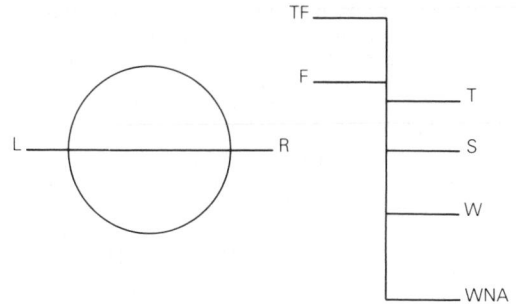

PLIMSOLL LINE *The lines and letters mark the waterline under various conditions. TF = fresh water in the tropics; F = fresh water; T = salt water in the tropics; S = salt water in the summer; W = salt water in the winter; WNA = winter in the N. Atlantic. LR represents Lloyd's Register.*

Plimsoll line A series of lines painted on the outside of a cargo ship's hull showing the various safe levels to which the ship can be loaded. Typically, the loading levels are marked for loaded and unloaded draught in sea and fresh water, winter and summer, and tropical or northern waters. The measure was introduced in the UK as a result of the Merchant Shipping Act (1876) at the instigation of the MP Samuel Plimsoll (1824-98).

Pliny the Elder (Gaius Plinius Secundus; 23–79 AD) Roman scholar, whose universal encyclopedia, *Natural History*, was a major source of scientific knowledge until the 17th century. During his military career, Pliny assembled material from numerous sources on a wide range of disciplines, including astrology, geography, agriculture, medicine, precious stones, and—most notably—zoology and botany. Pliny did not discriminate fact from fiction and included much folklore and superstition. He finally completed this work of 37 volumes in 77 AD.

Pliny the Younger (Gaius Plinius Caecilius Secundus; c. 61-c. 113 AD) Roman writer, nephew and adopted son of the encyclopedist Pliny the Elder. He held various administrative posts including that of consul in 100 AD and was a prominent legal orator. His ten volumes of private letters constitute an intimate unofficial history of his time.

Pliocene epoch. *See* Tertiary period.

pliosaur An extinct marine reptile that evolved from the *plesiosaurs but had a shorter neck and a longer head with stronger jaws, giving it a more streamlined appearance. It was a powerful swimmer and fed on cuttlefish, squid, etc.

PLO. *See* Palestine Liberation Organization.

Płock 52 32N 19 40E A town in central Poland, on the River Vistula. Its 12th-century cathedral contains the tombs of Polish kings. Industries include oil refining; it is served by pipeline from the Soviet Union. Population (1982 est): 108 969.

Ploieşti 44 57N 26 01E A city in SE Romania, at the foot of the Transylvanian Alps. It is the centre for the country's oil production. Population (1983): 215 500.

Plomer, William (1903-73) South African poet and novelist. He went to Japan in 1927 after the hostile reception to his first novel, *Turbott Wolfe* (1925), and came to England in 1929. His *Collected Poems* (1960) contain many satirical poems in ballad form. He also published

short stories and memoirs and wrote the librettos for operatic works by Benjamin Britten.

Plotinus (205-70 AD) Greek philosopher and founder of *Neoplatonism. Born in Egypt, he studied at Alexandria, visited Persia (242-43), and finally settled in Rome, becoming the focus of an intellectual circle. Developing *Plato's mysticism, he taught that the immaterial impersonal indescribable "One" is the ground of all existence and value. From it emanate successively mind, soul, and nature. Mind contemplates and organizes within itself the Platonic Forms; soul thinks less coherently, thus creating time and space; nature "dreams" the chaotic material world, the source of all evil. Man partakes of all these; by rejecting material nature and cultivating the intellect he may briefly become mystically united with the One.

Plough A distinctively shaped group of the seven brightest stars in the constellation *Ursa Major. Two of the stars, Dubhe and Merak (the **Pointers**), point towards the pole star *Polaris.

Plovdiv (former name: Philippopoli) 42 08N 24 45E A city in S central Bulgaria, on the River Maritsa. It is Bulgaria's second largest city and has the remains of the Roman walls. Its industries include food processing and carpet manufacture. Population (1982): 367 195.

plover A bird belonging to a widely distributed family (*Charadriidae*; 56 species) occurring in open regions and along shores. 15-30 cm long, plovers have brown or grey plumage, often mottled, with white underparts, which become black in summer for some species. They feed on insects and other small invertebrates and nest on the ground (*see* Plate V). Order: *Charadriiformes* (gulls, plovers, etc.). *See also* lapwing.

Plowright, Joan (1929-) British actress. Her reputation is based on her performances in both classical and modern plays, the latter including the first productions of Osborne's *The Entertainer* (1957) and Wesker's *Roots* (1959). She married Laurence *Olivier in 1961.

plum A small tree, *Prunus domestica*—a natural hybrid between the *blackthorn and the cherry plum (*P. cerasifera*), native to SW Asia and cultivated in most Mediterranean and N temperate regions for its fruit. 6-10 m tall, it has oval toothed leaves and clusters of attractive white flowers. The fruit is round or oval and has a dark-red to blue-black skin (when ripe), enclosing a sweet greenish-yellow pulp and a central oval stony seed. Plums are eaten fresh, cooked in desserts, canned, or dried as prunes. Family: *Rosaceae. See also* bullace; damson.

plumbago. *See* graphite.

Plumbago A genus of herbaceous plants, shrubs, and climbers (12 species), native to warm regions and including a number of ornamentals. They have simple leaves and terminal clusters of white, blue, violet, pink, or red flowers, with five petals arranged to form a narrow tube with spreading lobes. *P. auriculata*, with pale-blue flowers, and *P. rosea*, with red flowers, are popular greenhouse plants. Some species are used for medicinal purposes and some yield a juice that causes blistering. Family: *Plumbaginaceae*.

Plunket, St Oliver (1629-81) Irish Roman Catholic martyr and churchman. He was educated in Rome and was a professor of theology there until appointed Archbishop of Armagh in 1669. He was falsely implicated in the *Popish Plot against Charles II and executed, being the last Roman Catholic to be martyred in England. He was canonized in 1976.

pluralism. *See* dualism.

Plutarch (c. 46-c. 120 AD) Greek biographer and essayist. He was a citizen of both Athens and Rome, a priest of Delphi, and director of a school in his native town of Chaeronea in Boeotia in central Greece. His *Parallel Lives* consists of biographies of 23 pairs of Greek and Roman statesmen and soldiers. The *Moralia* contain 83 essays on ethical, scientific, and literary topics. His works had a great influence in Europe in the 16th and 17th centuries. The English translation by Sir Thomas North of the *Lives* (1579) was the source of Shakespeare's Roman plays. The *Moralia* served as models for the essays of both Montaigne and Francis Bacon.

Pluto (astronomy)   The smallest and usually outermost planet, orbiting the sun every 248 years at a mean distance of 5900 million km. Its eccentric orbit has brought it inside Neptune's orbit for the period 1979–99. Pluto was discovered in 1930 but little was known about it until its satellite was discovered in 1978. It is a very cold low-density body about 3000 km in diameter.

Pluto (mythology).   *See* Hades.

plutonic rock.   *See* igneous rock.

plutonium (Pu)   An important synthetic transuranic element discovered in 1940. Trace quantities exist in natural uranium ores. It is produced in large quantities in nuclear reactors by beta-decay from uranium-239. Plutonium is fissile and was used in the atomic bomb dropped on Nagasaki in 1945 (*see* nuclear weapons). It is absorbed into bone marrow and is one of the most toxic substances known. It forms oxides (PuO, PuO_2), halides (for example PuF_3), and other compounds. It is used in *fast reactors and small power units for spacecraft. At no 94; at wt (244); mp 641°C; bp 3235°C.

Plymouth   50 23N 4 10W A port in SW England, in Devon on Plymouth Sound between the Tamar and Plym estuaries. Since 1914 it has included the adjacent towns of Devonport and Stonehouse. On Plymouth Hoe Drake is reputed to have finished his game of bowls while the Spanish Armada approached and the *Mayflower* embarked from here for America in 1620 (*see* Pilgrim Fathers). Severely damaged by bombing during World War II, much of the city centre has been rebuilt. Plymouth is an important naval base with associated marine industries. Shipping is guided into the harbour by the Eddystone Lighthouse (*see* Eddystone Rocks). More recent industries include the manufacture of clothing, radio equipment, and processed foods. Population (1981): 243 895.

Plymouth   41 58N 70 40W A town in the USA, in Massachusetts on Plymouth Bay. The first European settlement in New England, it was founded by the Pilgrims from the *Mayflower* (1620). Industries include fisheries, boatyards, and tourism. Population (1980): 35 913.

Plymouth Brethren   An austere Protestant sect founded at Plymouth in 1830 by a former Anglican priest, J. N. Darby (1800–82). The Brethren have strict standards of behaviour and shun many secular trades and professions. They insist on the spiritual priesthood of believers and celebrate communion weekly. Small groups exist throughout the world, often as active missionaries.

Plymouth Rock   A breed of domestic fowl developed in the USA and widely used for meat production. It has a deep compact body with large thighs. The plumage can be of various colours, including white with black bars and pure white. Weight: 4.3 kg (cocks); 3.4 kg (hens).

Plzeň (German name: Pilsen)   49 45N 13 25E A city in Czechoslovakia, in W Bohemia. It has been famous for its beer (Pilsener lager) since the middle ages. Local coal and iron ore resources have led to the development of heavy industry, including engineering and chemicals. Population (1983): 173 000.

pneumococcus   A spherical bacterium, *Streptococcus pneumoniae*, that is commonly found in the throat and causes pneumonia if it infects the lungs. Pneumococci typically exist in pairs and often form capsules, the composition of which is used to identify different strains (pneumococcal typing).

pneumoconiosis   Chronic lung disease caused by inhaling dust, most commonly coal dust (causing coalworkers' pneumoconiosis) and silica (causing *silicosis). Considerable coal dust

may be taken into the lungs without causing much damage, but later progressive massive fibrosis may develop and the coalworker is disabled by breathlessness. Lung cancer may also complicate pneumoconiosis. There is no effective treatment and prevention is all important.   *See also* asbestosis.

pneumonia   Inflammation of the lungs, most commonly caused by infection. Pneumonia may arise in only one lobe of the lung (lobar pneumonia) or in patches in both lungs (bronchopneumonia). The infective organisms may be streptococci, viruses (causing a mild disease), tubercle bacilli, or other organisms, such as mycoplasmas. The patient has a fever, cough, and pain in the chest and may be breathless. Treatment is with antibiotics and physiotherapy.

pneumothorax   The presence of air in the pleural cavity, which causes the lung to collapse. This may happen for no apparent reason or it may develop in *emphysema or after a penetrating injury of the chest. The patient has pain in the chest and may be breathless. The lung will slowly expand itself or a tube may be inserted into the pleural cavity to allow the trapped air to escape.

Po, River (Latin name: Padus)   The longest river in Italy rising in the Cottian Alps and flowing mainly ENE through Turin to enter the Adriatic Sea by way of a large delta in the E. The Po Valley is the most fertile and economically important region in Italy. Length: 652 km (405 mi).

Pocahontas (c. 1595–1617)   American Indian woman. Daughter of the Indian chief Powhatan, Pocahontas is said to have saved the life of Capt John *Smith from her father's warriors. She married the English colonist John Rolfe (1585–1622) and was entertained as a princess at the English court; she died of smallpox at Gravesend, about to return to America.

pochard   A large-headed *duck, *Aythya ferina*, occurring in temperate inland waters of Eurasia. It is 45 cm long and has grey legs and a grey-blue bill; males have a reddish head, black breast, and grey body; females are brown. It feeds on water plants and small aquatic invertebrates.

Po Chü-i.   *See* Bo Zhu Yi.

pocket borough   A British borough constituency that, before the *Reform Act of 1832, was controlled by a patron who, through money or influence, ensured the election of any candidate he put forward: the borough was thus "in the pocket" of the patron. *See also* rotten borough.

pocket gopher   A *rodent belonging to the subfamily *Geomyinae* (39 species), of North and Central America. Pocket gophers are 10–25 cm in length and brownish in colour. They inhabit open dry country, where they dig extensive burrows, and feed on roots, seeds, insects, and mice. Their large cheek pouches have an outside opening like a pocket.

Podgorica. *See* Titograd.

Podgorny, N(ikolai) V(iktorovich) (1903–   ) Soviet statesman. Podgorny was president of the Soviet Union from 1965 to 1977, when he resigned under pressure and was replaced by Brezhnev.

Podocarpus.   *See* yellowwood.

Podolsk   55 23N 37 32E A city in the Soviet Union, in the RSFSR 42 km (26 mi) S of Moscow. Lenin and his Bolshevik colleagues often met here before the Russian Revolution. Industries include oil refining, machinery manufacturing, and railway engineering. Population (1981 est): 205 000.

podzol   A type of *soil typical of many cool temperate humid zones especially with coniferous vegetation, as in the taiga of the Soviet Union and North America. It is characterized by an ashen-coloured upper layer (A horizon) and an underlying layer (B horizon) of redeposition humus and iron, which may develop into an impermeable pan.

Poe, Edgar Allan (1809–49) US poet, short-story writer, and critic. He was brought up by foster parents after the death of his mother in 1811. He briefly attended Virginia University and West Point Military Academy. After publishing two volumes of poetry (1827, 1829), he began to contribute to and work for literary magazines. Among his many prose tales and horror stories are "The Fall of the House of Usher" (1839), "The Purloined Letter" (1842), "The Black Cat" (1843), "The Cask of Amontillado" (1846), and the first ever detective story, "The Murders in the Rue Morgue" (1841). His best-known poems are "The Raven" (1845) and *The Bells* (1849) and his most influential critical work is "The Philosophy of Composition" (1846).

poet laureate A title bestowed by the British monarch on a contemporary poet, whose traditional duties include the writing of commemorative odes on important public occasions. The first poet laureate was John Dryden, who served from 1668 to 1688; his recent successors include John Masefield (1930–68), C. Day Lewis (1968–72), John Betjeman (1972–84), and Ted Hughes (1984–   ). In 1986 the USA appointed Robert Penn Warren (1905–   ) their first poet laureate for one year.

poetry A form of literature distinguished from prose by the deliberate employment of *metre, rhythm, *rhyme, sound, and figurative language. Poetry probably originated as a form of language distinct from ordinary speech in religious ritual and is an earlier development than prose. The earliest poetic landmarks in western literature are Homer's *Odyssey* and *Iliad*, which developed out of a primitive oral tradition and became models for the epic poems of Virgil and numerous later poets. Poetry was associated with drama from its appearance in the dramatic choruses of ancient Greece until the 19th century; verse drama was revived by T. S. Eliot in the 20th century. The early forms of lyric poetry derived from the dithyrambic poetry of religious ritual; they are characterized by the repetition of songlike elements arranged in stanzas. The sonnet, one of the most popular of all poetic forms, evolved in Renaissance Italy. Narrative poetry, like the epic, derived from oral tradition; the ballad combines lyrical and narrative qualities. A tradition of didactic verse, stretching from Hesiod to Cowper, employed rhyme or metre as an aid to the expression of ideas. Poetry has been used as a medium for satire (Pope), religious and philosophical statement (Lucretius and Wordsworth), and even for scientific classification (Erasmus Darwin). While the poetry of ancient Greece and Rome depended on the variation of fixed metrical patterns, the early poetry of N Europe was characterized by alliteration. Blank verse was evolved by the Earl of Surrey and became the main medium for drama in the works of Shakespeare and his contemporaries and much subsequent serious poetry. In the 19th and 20th centuries some poets adopted free verse, to avoid the constraints of regularity in metre or rhyme.

Poggio Bracciolini, Giovanni Francesco (1380–1459) Italian humanist. A pupil of Manuel *Chrysoloras, Poggio recovered the manuscripts of Lucretius, Quintilian, Silius, and other classical writers. His books include a *History of Florence* and the humorous tales, *Liber Facetiarum*.

Pogonophora. See beardworm.

pogrom (Russian: devastation) An attack on Jews and Jewish property, especially in the Russian Empire. Russian pogroms, which were condoned by the government, were particularly common in the years immediately after the assassination of Alexander II in 1881 and again from 1903 to 1906, though mob persecution of Jews continued until the Russian Revolution (1917).

Po Hai. *See* Chihli, Gulf of.

poikilothermy The condition of being cold-blooded. Invertebrate animals, fishes, amphibians, and reptiles have no physiological mechanism for the control of their body temperature, which therefore fluctuates with that of the environment. They are therefore restricted to environments with a suitable temperature range. *Compare* homoiothermy.

Poincaré, Jules Henri (1854-1912) French mathematician; cousin of Raymond *Poincaré. He is regarded by some as the last universal mathematician because he made important contributions to all fields of mathematics as well as to physics and astronomy. A gifted writer, Poincaré in later life wrote important treatises on the nature of mathematical creativity, emphasizing its intuitional aspects.

Poincaré, Raymond (1860-1934) French statesman; president (1913-20) and prime minister (1912-13, 1922-24, 1926-29). His foreign policy aimed to prevent French isolation in the face of possible German aggression and when, after World War I, Germany delayed in the payment of reparations he ordered French troops to occupy the Ruhr. His postwar economic policy brought a period of stability to France.

poinciana A tropical shrub or small tree of the genera *Caesalpinia* or *Delonix* (both formerly called *Poinciana*), often grown for ornament. Up to 15 m tall, they have large feathery compound leaves and clusters of showy orange or scarlet flowers. Popular species include the Barbados pride (*C. pulcherrima*) and the *flamboyant tree (*or* royal poinciana). Family: *Leguminosae*.

poinsettia An ornamental shrub, *Euphorbia pulcherrima*, native to Mexico and tropical America and a popular pot plant at Christmas in Europe and North America. Growing 0.6-3 m tall, it has simple dark-green leaves and clusters of tiny greenish-yellow flowers surrounded by large scarlet bracts, up to 14 cm long, which resemble petals. Family: *Euphorbiaceae*.

point 1. A unit of weight for precious stones, especially diamonds, equal to two milligrams. 2. A unit of type size equal to 0.0138 inch or 0.0148 inch in Europe.

Pointe-à-Pitre 16 14N 61 32W The chief town and port of Guadeloupe. It possesses a good harbour and is the chief commercial centre for the island. Population (1982): 25 310.

Pointe-Noire 4 46S 11 53E A port in the People's Republic of Congo, on the Atlantic coast. Its port was completed in 1939 and has a considerable entrepôt trade. Population (1980): 185 105.

pointer A breed of sporting □dog originating in England and named after its habit of pointing its nose towards game. It is lithely built with a long tapering tail, a long slightly concave muzzle, and drooping ears. The short smooth coat is white combined with yellow, orange, liver, or black. Height: 63-68 cm (dogs); 61-66 cm (bitches).

pointillism A style of painting using dots of pure colour. The pointillists applied primary colours to the canvas in dots and allowed the colours to be mixed by the eye, thus achieving an intense luminosity. Also called divisionism and neoimpressionism, it was developed by *Seurat in France in the 1880s and carried into the 20th century by his disciple *Signac.

point-to-point. *See* steeplechase.

poise A unit of viscosity in the *c.g.s. system equal to the tangential force per unit area, in dynes per square centimetre, required to maintain unit difference in velocity, in centimetres per second, between two parallel planes in a fluid one centimetre apart.

poison ivy An extremely poisonous woody vine or shrub, *Rhus toxicodendron* (or *Toxicodendron radicans*), native to North America. It has compound leaves with three broad leaflets and clusters of small round whitish-green flowers, which give rise to whitish berries. All parts contain a poison that causes severe skin inflammation on contact. Family: *Anacardiaceae*.

poisons Substances that injure health or cause death when introduced into the body. The term is often restricted to those substances that are fatal in small doses (e.g. strychnine, cyanide) but can also be applied to those that are harmful when small doses are taken over long periods (cumulative poisons, e.g. lead) and to otherwise safe drugs taken in large doses. Poisons may be classified in various ways, one of which is according to use: i.e. agricultural (pesticides, herbicides, etc.); industrial (poisonous elements and gases, etc.); medicinal (dangerous drugs, e.g. opiates); and natural (bacterial toxins, poisonous plants, animal venoms, etc.). Another way is to group them according to activity: corrosives (acids, alkalis, etc.); blood poisons (e.g. carbon monoxide, warfarin); nerve poisons (e.g. strychnine, cocaine); poisons that interfere with cell function (e.g. cytotoxic drugs, nitrogen mustard, methotrexate); etc.

Toxicology is the study of poisons, which deals with their chemical nature and origin, the pathological changes they induce, their recognition in a poisoned patient, and the determination of specific antidotes.

Poisson, Siméon Dénis (1781–1840) French mathematician, who became professor at the École Polytechnique in 1806. He made important contributions to the mathematical theory of electricity, magnetism, and mechanics. His work on electricity led him in 1837 to discover Poisson's equation, which describes the electric field created by an arbitrary charge density. Poisson's distribution is widely used in probability calculations and **Poisson's ratio** (the ratio of the lateral strain to the longitudinal strain in a stretched wire) is used by engineers in studying the elongation of structural members.

Poitiers (Latin name: Limonum) 46 35N 0 20E A town in W central France, the capital of the Vienne department. The former capital of Poitou, it dates back to Roman times and was the site of a battle (1356) in which the English under the Black Prince defeated the French under John the Good. Notable buildings include the 4th-century baptistry of St John, the cathedral (11th–12th centuries), and the university (1432). Metallurgy, textiles, and brewing are the chief industries. Population (1982): 82 884.

poker A card game, usually for five to seven players, using a single pack of cards. There are many variants but in the standard game each player receives five cards, with an option to discard any of them and receive up to five more. The objective is to make the best hand or to bluff one's opponents into believing one has the best hand. The best hand is (in ascending order) the one containing the highest pair of cards of the same denomination (irrespective of suit); two pairs; three cards of the same denomination; a straight (a sequence of denominations irrespective of suit); a flush (all of the same suit, irrespective of denomination); a full house (a pair and three of the same denomination); four cards of the same denomination; or a straight flush. Each player makes bets on his hand before and after discarding and the betting continues until the limit (if there is one) is reached or until no one wishes to bet further. Although poker is a game of chance there is an element of skill in the opportunity it provides for bluffing one's opponents into thinking one has the best hand.

Pola. See Pula.

Poland, People's Republic of A country in N Europe, on the Baltic Sea. Extensive plains in the N rise to the Carpathian Mountains in the S, which reach heights of over 2500 m (8000 ft). Following the reorganization of the population after World War II, when Poles were transferred from the area ceded to the Soviet Union to that gained from Germany, forcing out the Germans, the majority of the inhabitants are now Polish. Approximately 90% are Roman Catholic. *Economy*: since World War II there has been a significant shift in the balance of the economy from agriculture to industry, but Poland remains one of the world's leading agricultural nations. Although much of the land is organized into collectives and state farms about half is still privately owned. The chief crops are rye, wheat, oats, sugar beet, and potatoes. Its mineral wealth includes rich deposits of copper and sulphur and natural gas has been found as well as some oil. An important shipbuilding nation, Poland's industries include textiles, engineering, steel, cement, chemicals, and food products. Tourism is an important source of revenue. *History*: Poland first appeared as a separate state in the 10th century, which also saw the introduction of Christianity. From the 14th to 16th centuries its power was extended under the *Jagiellon dynasty, which was succeeded by elected kings. Poland declined in the 17th century, although it was able, under John III Sobieski, to defeat the Turks in 1683. Foreign intervention in the 18th century culminated in partition by Russia, Austria, and Prussia (in 1772, 1793, and 1795), and at the Congress of Vienna in 1815 the *Congress Kingdom of Poland was created under the Russian Crown. After the defeat of the Central Powers in World War I independence was declared under Józef Piłsudski. In 1939 Poland was invaded by Germany. Some six million Poles, including three million Jews, died during the occupation. Polish resistance to Germany, both within Poland and abroad, directed by Sikorski's government in exile, contributed to the Allied victory, and in 1945 Poland was occupied by the Russians. The *Oder-Neisse line became its W frontier. The first postwar elections, in 1948, brought a communist-controlled government to power under *Gomulka. He was demoted in 1948 for asserting independence from the Soviet Union but returned to power after the *Poznań Riots. Further unrest in 1970 led to his enforced resignation and he was succeeded by Edward *Gierek. Gierek was dismissed in 1980 and succeeded by Stanisław Kania. The political and economic situation in Poland worsened and Kania resigned (1981) to be replaced by Gen Wojciech *Jaruzelski. In December, 1981, the independent trade union *Solidarity, led by Lech *Wałesa, was accused of attempting to overthrow the government, its leaders were detained, and a state of martial law was declared under a military council led by Jaruzelski. Martial law was lifted in 1983, and political prisoners were released; economic reform is the current government priority. Official language: Polish. Official currency: złoty of 100 groszy. Area: 312 677 sq km (120 624 sq mi). Population (1983 est): 36 556 000. Capital: Warsaw. Main port: Gdańsk.

Polanski, Roman (1933–) Polish film director, born in Paris. After his first full-length film, *Knife in the Water* (1961), he worked in Britain and the USA. His later films include *Repulsion* (1965), *Cul de Sac* (1966), *Rosemary's Baby* (1968), and *The Tenant* (1976), in all of which he skilfully created an atmosphere of tension and menace, and *Tess* (1979).

polar bear A white bear, *Thalarctos maritimus*, living on the shores of the Arctic Ocean. Up to 2.5 m long and weighing 500–700 kg (depending on the season), polar bears prey mainly on seals, also taking some fish and birds. Males move southwards in winter but females sleep in dens prior to the birth of their young in early Dec. □mammal.

Polaris (or North Star) A remote cream *supergiant, apparent magnitude 2.0 and about 650 light years distant, that is the brightest star in the constellation Ursa Minor. It is the present *pole star, lying about 1° from the N celestial pole; its position is found using the Pointers in the Plough. It is a *Cepheid variable and is the primary component of a *multiple star.

Polaris missile A US navy two-stage solid-fuelled nuclear strategic missile launched from a submarine and having a range of 4500 km (2800 m). Travelling at speeds of over mach 10, some versions (Poseidon) are capable of delivering 10 separately guided 15-*kiloton warheads. When fired from below the surface, the missile is ejected from the vessel by compressed gas, its rocket firing at the surface. Its inertial guidance system is programmed to the launching vessel's exact position. Firing is by two-key control, linked directly to Washington.

polarized light Light in which the direction of vibration is restricted. In ordinary light (and other types of *electromagnetic radiation) the transverse vibrations of the electric and magnetic fields are at right angles to each other in all possible planes. In **plane-polarized light** the vibrations of the electric field are confined to one plane and the magnetic field to one at right angles to it. Plane-polarized light can be produced by reflection at a certain angle (*see* Brewster's law) or by passing light through such doubly refracting substances as *Polaroid. **Circularly and elliptically polarized light** occur when the electric vector describes a circle or an ellipse round the direction of the light beam.

Polaroid A trade name for a plastic sheet impregnated with many tiny crystals of a dichroic substance (*see* pleochroism) orientated parallel to each other. The crystals only transmit light vibrating in one plane and absorb all other light. Polaroid is used for reducing glare in headlights, sunglasses, camera filters, etc., by removing stray beams of plane-polarized light.

polder An area of low-lying land reclaimed from the sea or other water, often for agricultural purposes. Polders are usually formed by constructing dykes around the area, which is then drained. Land lying below low-tide mark must be pumped clear of water, while that above may be drained by means of tide gates, which close as the tide rises. The most notable polders are those of Holland, next to the IJsselmeer.

Pole, Reginald, Cardinal (1500-58) English Roman Catholic churchman; Archbishop of Canterbury. As Dean of Exeter (1527-32) he opposed Henry VIII's divorce and in 1532 went to Italy. There he wrote *Pro ecclesiasticae unitatis defensione* (1536), an attack on Henry's claims of supremacy over the English Church. He was a leading advocate of reform within the Roman Catholic Church and presided at the Council of *Trent. Returning to England on Mary's accession, he became Archbishop of Canterbury in 1556.

polecat A carnivorous mammal, *Mustela putorius*, found in woods and grassland throughout Europe, Asia, and N Africa. About 50 cm long, it has a dark-brown coat with yellowish patches on the face and ears. Polecats are nocturnal, foraging for rodents and insects. They eject a pungent fluid when alarmed and were once called "foul martens." Family: *Mustelidae* (weasels, etc.). *See also* ferret.

Poles, North and South The most northerly and southerly points of the earth's surface and the ends of the earth's axis, about which it rotates. The magnetic north and south poles are the points to which a magnetic compass needle points and where the lines of force of the earth's magnetic field are vertical. They do not coincide with the geographical poles and their positions slowly change. *See also* Arctic Circle; Antarctica.

pole star Either of two bright stars that are nearest the N or S celestial pole. The poles are not fixed in position but, owing to *precession of the earth's axis, trace out two circles in the sky over a period of 25 800 years. There is thus a sequence of stars that slowly, in turn, become the N or S pole star. *See also* Polaris.

pole vault A field event for men in athletics, in which competitors use a fibreglass pole to lever themselves over a horizontal bar. A competitor is allowed three tries at each height and is eliminated if he fails to clear it. The height is increased until only one competitor is left. World record: 6.0|1 m (1986) by Sergei Bubka (Soviet Union).

police A force established to maintain law and order and to prevent and detect crime; in many countries police forces also have traffic-control duties. The earliest organized police force in Britain was the Bow Street Runners, formed by the writer Henry *Fielding, who was JP for Westminster (1748-53). These were merged in 1829 with the Metropolitan Police (newly established by Sir Robert *Peel), a force of one thousand blue-coated men, who patrolled the streets of London. In 1835 police forces were established in the boroughs and from 1839, in the counties where forces became compulsory in 1856. Conditions for police were standardized in 1919, when the Police Federation (a representative body) was established. Today, responsibility for police forces in the UK is divided between the Home Office (which is responsible primarily for the Metropolitan Police and has little power over provincial forces) and local police authorities. There is no central administration but common training facilities, forensic laboratories, and criminal-record offices have been set up. A British police man or woman has authority throughout the country and is not normally armed, unlike their counterparts in many other countries. Decentralized police forces are also found in the USA and Australia; centralized forces exist in France, Italy, Belgium, Spain, Scandinavia, and Japan. *See also* Criminal Investigation Department; Interpol.

Polignac, Auguste Jules Armand Marie, Prince de (1780-1847) French statesman. As chief minister to Charles X (1829-30) he supported the absolute authority assumed by the king, thus helping to bring about the *July Revolution. Arrested and imprisoned until 1836, he was then exiled until 1845.

poliomyelitis A viral infection of the central nervous system that may result in muscle paralysis. It was formerly known as infantile paralysis, because children were most commonly affected. In most cases the infection is mild, with only a nonspecific fever, but sometimes a more severe illness develops three to seven days later, which may lead to severe pain in the limbs followed by permanent paralysis. There is no specific treatment, but an Australian nurse, Elizabeth Kenny (1886-1952), developed the practice of actively exercising affected limbs rather than immobilizing them. Polio is now uncommon in developed countries and a vaccine is available that gives complete protection (*see* Sabin vaccine; Salk vaccine).

Polish (*or* Lekhitic) A West Slavonic language spoken in Poland and closely related to *Czech, *Slovak, and Sorbian. It is written in a Latin alphabet and the standard form is based on the dialect of Poznań.

Polish Corridor A belt of land that separated E Prussia from the rest of Germany and was granted to Poland in the Treaty of Versailles (1919). It allowed Poland access to the sea at Danzig (now Gdańsk). It was annexed by Germany in 1939 and returned to Poland in 1945, after World War II.

Polish Succession, War of the (1733-35) A European war precipitated by the election of rival claimants to the Polish throne in succession to Augustus the Strong: *Stanisław I Leszczyński, supported by France, Spain, and subsequently Sardinia, and Augustus' son, Frederick Augustus III (1696-1763), supported by Russia and Austria. After the fall of Danzig to the Russians (1734) Stanisław fled and the subsequent Treaty of Vienna (1735) recognized Frederick Augustus as king.

Poliziano (*or* Politian; 1454-94) Italian poet and scholar, born Angelo Ambrogini. He gained the patronage of Lorenzo de' *Medici and later of Cardinal Francesco Gonzago in Mantua. His major work is *Stanze per la giostra* (1475-78), an unfinished poem expressing humanist ideals in classical style. His other works include *Orfeo* (1480), a dramatic court entertainment, as well as many translations and Latin poems.

Polk, James K(nox) (1795-1849) US statesman; Democratic president (1845-49). A former governor of Tennessee (1839-41) and an ardent expansionist, Polk became president with four distinct aims, all of which he achieved. He established an independent treasury; lowered tariffs between North and South; acquired California, giving access to the Pacific; and pushed the disputed boundary of Oregon up to the 49th parallel.

polka A Bohemian folk dance in 2/4 time, which became a ballroom dance in 19th-century Europe and rivalled the *waltz in popularity. It is characterized by three steps and a hop.

pollack A popular game fish, *Pollachius* (or *Gadus*) *pollachius*, related to cod, with a protruding lower jaw and no chin barbel. Its body, usually up to 1 m long, is brown or olive, sometimes with orange markings above. It occurs in European coastal waters down to 200 m.

Pollack, Sydney (1934–   ) US film director. Graduating from TV to the cinema, he directed *The Slender Thread* (1965), *They Shoot Horses Don't They?* (1969), *Three Days of the Condor* (1976), *Tootsie* (1982), and the Oscar-winning *Out of Africa* (1986).

Pollaiuolo, Antonio (c. 1432–98) Florentine Renaissance artist. He and his brother **Piero Pollaiuolo** (c. 1441–96) trained as goldsmiths and often collaborated. Antonio is famous for his bronze sculptures, the painting of the *Martyrdom of St Sebastian* (National Gallery, London), and the influential engraving *Battle of the Nudes* (Uffizi). He was reputedly the first artist to make anatomical dissections. Piero painted a series of *Virtues* (Uffizi) and *The Coronation of the Virgin* (Duomo, Florence).

POLO *The dimensions of the ground. If the side lines are boarded, the width is 160 yd (146.4 m) and there is a safety area extending 10 yd (9 m) beyond each side line and 30 yd (27 m) beyond each goal line.*

pollen The male gametes of seed plants, which are produced in the *stamens of flowering plants and in the male *cones of conifers and other gymnosperms. To ensure fertilization, the pollen must be transferred to the stigma (in flowering plants) or the female cone (in conifers)–the process of **pollination**. Many flowers are cross-pollinated, i.e. the pollen from one plant is deposited on the stigma of another of the same species by means of animal carriers (usually insects), wind, or water. Some flowers are self-pollinated, the pollen being transferred from the anthers to the stigma of the same plant: the stamens are usually bent over the stigma to assist the process. After pollination, a pollen tube grows down from the pollen grain into the pistil of the pollinated flower until it reaches the ovule. Two pollen nuclei travel down this tube: one fertilizes the egg cell, which develops into the embryo plant in the seed; the other fuses with a nucleus in the ovule to become a food source for the seed.

pollen analysis. *See also* palynology.

Pollock, Jackson (1912–56) US painter, born in Wyoming. He trained in New York under Thomas Hart *Benton but early in his career he was influenced by *Orozco and *surrealism. By 1947 he had developed an abstract style (*see* action painting) expressing feelings and unconscious thoughts by pouring and dripping paints onto very large canvases to form patterns of interweaving lines. Shortly before his death in a car crash, he painted only in black and white.

poll tax A levy on every individual (*poll*, head), regardless of means. First levied regularly in England in 1377, it was a direct cause of the *Peasants' Revolt in 1381 and was abolished in 1698. It will replace domestic rates in Scotland in 1989 and in the rest of the UK in 1990. Originally preferred in the USA to property-based taxes, the poll tax as a voting qualification was abused as a means of disenfranchising Blacks and was constitutionally banned.

pollution The addition to the environment of substances that cannot be rendered harmless by normal biological processes. Modern industrial and agricultural activities have led to the pollution of land, rivers, seas, and the atmosphere by either man-made toxic substances (such as pesticides and fertilizers) or by the overproduction of naturally occurring substances (such as carbon dioxide gas). Pesticides, such as *DDT, can build up in the environment and in the bodies of living organisms until they reach toxic levels. Other forms of pollution may have long-term effects on the health of living things, including man. Current problems include the disposal of radioactive wastes; increasing amounts of heavy metals (such as lead) in the atmosphere; atmospheric pollution by carbon dioxide, carbon monoxide, etc.; the disposal of human refuse and sewage; and unacceptable noise levels. In many cases a technical solution to these problems is available but cannot be implemented because the cost is too high or because of conflict with minority interests. *See also* conservation; acid rain.

Pollux An orange *giant star, apparent magnitude 1.15 and 35 light years distant, that is the brightest star in the constellation Gemini.

polo A four-a-side stick-and-ball game, in which the players are mounted on ponies (*see* polo pony). It was played in Persia by 600 BC and spread E but had almost died out when it was rediscovered by British officers in India in the 19th century. The riders use long sticks with mallet heads to hit a solid wooden ball, with the object of scoring goals. Several balls are worn out in a game. A game consists of up to eight seven-minute periods, or "chukkas," after each of which mounts are changed. After every goal the teams change ends. It is presided over by two mounted umpires and a referee. Since World War II Argentina has become the leading polo-playing nation but the game has long had an enthusiastic following in the UK.

Polo, Marco (c. 1254–1324) Venetian traveller. His father Niccolò Polo and uncle Maffeo Polo undertook a trading expedition to Peking (1260–69) and in 1271 they returned at the request of the Mongol emperor, □Kublai Khan, taking Marco with them. Having learned Mongolian, he entered Kublai's service, conducting missions as far as S India, until leaving China in 1292. He subsequently fought for the Venetians against the Genoese and was captured. In prison (1296–98) he dictated an account of his travels, which remained almost the only source of information about the Far East until the 19th century.

polonaise A Polish dance in triple time, with characteristic rhythmic stresses and cadences. Originally a processional folk dance, it evolved into a courtly dance in 18th century Europe; it also became a purely instrumental form, as in Chopin's polonaises for the piano.

polonium (Po) A highly radioactive element discovered in 1898 by Marie Curie in minute amounts in pitchblende. It is 5000 times as radioactive as *radium and liberates considerable amounts of heat. Polonium has 27 isotopes, more than any other element. It is used in compact radiation and thermoelectric power sources. At no 84; at wt (209); mp 254°C; bp 962°C.

polo pony A pony bred and selected as a mount for polo. Polo demands speed, agility, stamina, and courage and the ponies ideally have a strong back, broad deep chest, powerful shoulders and hindquarters, a long flexible neck, and hard legs and feet. Some of the best polo ponies come from Argentina, where they have been specially developed since about 1900. Height: 1.47-1.63 m (14½-16 hands).

Poltava 49 35N 34 35E A city in the Soviet Union, in the E Ukrainian SSR. The centre of a fertile agricultural region, it has food-processing industries as well as factories producing machinery, building materials, and consumer goods. *History*: it is one of the oldest Ukrainian towns (dating to the 8th century) and was a Cossack centre in the 17th century. Peter the Great defeated Charles XII of Sweden here (1709) during the Great *Northern War. Population (1984): 296 000.

poltergeist A noisy, mischievous, and frequently destructive invisible agent that persecutes the occupants of a house, most commonly by throwing or moving objects. Famous poltergeist hauntings were the 17th-century "demon drummer of Tedworth" and the 20th-century Borley Rectory phenomena.

polyanthus A hardy perennial, *Primula* × *polyanthus*, derived from a cross between the common primrose and the cowslip. There are many varieties, with yellow, brown, blue, or red flowers, grown as garden ornamentals. *See also* Primula.

Polybius (c. 200-c. 120 BC) Greek historian. While he was a political hostage in Rome from 168 to 150 BC he became a friend of the general and literary patron Scipio Aemilianus. His major work was a history of Rome from 220 to 145 BC in 40 books, of which only the first 5 survive intact.

Polycarp, St (c. 69-c. 155) Greek martyr and Bishop of Smyrna. He was reputedly converted to Christianity and made a bishop by St John the Apostle. His fame rests on his *Epistle to the Philippians*, explaining St Paul's teachings and defending Christianity against the leading heresies of his age. The *Martyrdom of Polycarp* is an anonymous letter describing his death and is the earliest of its kind. Feast day: 26 Jan.

Polyclitus (5th century BC) Greek sculptor, born at *Argos. A very popular and much copied artist, he was primarily a sculptor of athletes in relaxed poses, combining naturalism with beauty of proportion. His works, as known from later copies, seem less majestic and more individual than those of his contemporary *Phidias.

Polycrates (died c. 522) Tyrant of Samos, whose naval campaigns made Samos an important power in the eastern Mediterranean. Deceived into believing he was joining a revolt against the Persians, Polycrates was captured and crucified by the Persian governor of Lydia, Oroetes.

polycythaemia An excessive accumulation of red cells in the blood. This may occur in response to a chronic shortage of oxygen (e.g. in people living at high altitudes) or for no obvious reason (polycythaemia vera). The blood becomes much thicker and both *thrombosis and haemorrhage are more common in affected people. Treatment is often with radioactive phosphorus.

polyesters Synthetic resins or *plastics that are polymers of *esters. Saturated polyesters (those with no double bonds), made by a condensation reaction, are widely used in such synthetic fibres as Dacron and Terylene. Unsaturated polyesters are used as resins to make thermosetting plastics.

polygamy. *See* marriage.

polygon A plane straight-sided geometrical figure with three or more sides; for example a pentagon, which has five sides. A regular polygon has all sides equal and all interior angles equal.

Polygonum A genus of annual or perennial herbs (about 75 species), found worldwide, especially in temperate regions. Ranging usually from 10 to 200 cm in height, they bear simple leaves and small five-lobed white or pink flowers, clustered into dense terminal heads or loose branching clusters. Species include the *knotgrass, *bistort, and persicaria (*P. persicaria*)—a creeping weed. Several others are grown in rock gardens and borders. Family: *Polygonaceae*.

polyhedron A solid bounded by plane *polygons called the faces. Two faces intersect at an edge and three or more at a vertex. In a regular polyhedron all the faces are equal regular polygons. The five regular polyhedrons, called the Platonic solids, are the regular tetrahedron, hexahedron, octahedron, dodecahedron, and icosahedron with 4, 6, 8, 12, and 20 sides respectively.

polymerization The chemical combination of simpler molecules (monomers) to form long chain molecules (**polymers**) of repeating units. In **addition polymerization**, the monomers simply add together and no other compound is formed. Polythene is made from ethylene in this way. In **condensation polymerization**, water, alcohol, or some other small molecule is formed in the reaction, as in the production of *nylon.

polymethyl methacrylate. *See* Perspex.

polymorphism In biology, the functional or structural variation between two or more members of a species, determined by differences in either genetic constitution, environmental conditions, or both. It is a widespread phenomenon in animals and plants. In **transient polymorphism** two different forms exist together temporarily, while one form is replacing the other. This occurs in industrial melanism in moths: with industrial pollution of the environment, the black variety has an advantage over the normal pale form and eventually replaces it. In **balanced polymorphism** the different forms continue to coexist, as in the *castes in social insects.

Polyneices In Greek legend, a son of Oedipus. Having succeeded to the Theban throne, Polyneices and his brother Eteocles agreed to rule the city in alternate years. At the end of his term Eteocles refused to yield to Polyneices, who then laid siege to the city (*see* Seven Against Thebes). Eteocles and Polyneices killed each other in the war, fulfilling Oedipus' curse on his sons. *See also* Antigone.

Polynesia A division of Oceania in the S and central Pacific Ocean. The volcanic and coral islands include those of French Polynesia, Hawaii, Samoa, Tonga, Tuvalu, Kiribati, and the Line and Cook Islands. *See also* Melanesia; Micronesia.

Polynesian The people of the Pacific islands contained within the roughly triangular area between and including Hawaii, New Zealand, and Easter Island. They are seafarers, with considerable skill in navigation. Fishing and cultivating are also important. There is considerable uniformity in culture throughout this huge area but social organization varies greatly. Kinship is important everywhere. The degree of political centralization and hierarchy varies between the smaller and larger islands. The Polynesian languages belong to the Oceanic branch of the *Austronesian family and include Samoan, *Maori, Tongan, Tahitian, and Hawaiian.

polyp (biology) A sedentary form that occurs during the life cycle of many animals of the phylum *Coelenterata*. It has a cylindrical stalklike body attached at the base, with the mouth at the free end surrounded by tentacles bearing stinging cells (nematocysts). Polyps occur singly or in colonies; colonial polyps are modified for different functions, such as feeding, reproduction, and protection. Polyps reproduce asexually to form new polyps or *medusae or sexually to form polyps.

polyp (medicine) A growth that has a narrow base or stalk. Polyps may occur in the bowel, the nose, the womb, the larynx, and other sites. They often cause obstruction and some forms may become cancerous: for this reason they are best removed by surgery or cauterization.

polypeptide. *See* peptide.

Polyphemus In Greek mythology, a one-eyed giant, one of the *Cyclops. He lived in Sicily and was an unrequited lover of the nymph *Galatea. Odysseus and his companions escaped from imprisonment in his cave by making him drunk and then blinding him.

polyphony (Greek: many voices) Music that consists of a horizontal combination of melodic strands rather than a series of vertical chords. In its earliest form (9th to 11th centuries) it consisted of voices moving in parallel fourths, fifths, and octaves, called *organum, a development of *plainchant. The true polyphonic period began when the voices became independent, moving in contrary motion and having different note values. The high point of the polyphonic style was reached in the 16th century with *Palestrina's church music, the Italian *madrigal, the compositions of the English madrigalists, and the church music of Tallis and Byrd. The music of later polyphonic composers completed the transition from modal polyphony to the system of major and minor keys and stands at the threshold of the harmonic period. *See* counterpoint; harmony; modes.

polyploidy A condition in which the number of sets of chromosomes in a cell is greater than normal. Most organisms have two representatives of each chromosome in their body cells—the diploid state. With three of each the cell is triploid, with four—tetraploid, five—pentaploid, and so on. Polyploidy may arise naturally, for example when a sterile hybrid doubles its chromosome number. This results in a fertile organism and is thought to be the means by which many species of plants arose, including wheat. Polyploid plants often show improved size and vigour, and the condition has been induced in crop plants by treating them with chemicals.

polypody A *fern of the genus *Polypodium*, especially *P. vulgare*, which grows on walls, rocks, and trees in temperate regions. It has a creeping slender scaly rhizome with numerous roots, and the tapering branched fronds, 5–75 cm long, are made up of paired leaflets. The spore capsules are grouped in rounded yellow or orange clusters (sori) and usually occur in two rows on the undersides of the upper leaflets. Family: *Polypodiaceae*.

polypropylene A thermoplastic material made by *polymerization of propylene (CH_2:$CHCH_3$). It is similar to high-density *polythene but stronger, lighter, and more rigid. Polypropylene products, such as beer crates, luggage, and hinges, are injection moulded. Fibres, which are used to make sacks and carpet backings, are made by extrusion.

polysaccharide A carbohydrate comprising chains of between three and several thousand linked *monosaccharide units. Polysaccharides, such as *starch, *glycogen, and *cellulose, are important as energy reserves and structural components of plants and animals.

polytechnics Institutes of higher education concentrating on courses with vocational relevance while maintaining high academic standards. The first polytechnic was established in Paris in 1794 to provide technical training for artillery and engineering officers. Polytechnics were established in Germany during the first half of the 19th century, while the development of the polytechnic movement in the UK began largely as a result of the initiative of Quintin Hogg, who established the Regent Street Polytechnic in 1880. During the period 1969–73 some 30 educational institutions in England and Wales were formally designated polytechnics. Degrees, comparable to university standards, were awarded by the Council for National Academic Awards (CNAA) until 1987, when polytechnics began to award their own independent degrees.

polytetrafluoroethylene (PTFE) A synthetic material produced by the *polymerization of tetrafluoroethylene (F_2C:CF_2). It can withstand temperatures of up to 400°C and has a very slippery surface. PTFE is used to coat nonstick cooking utensils and in gaskets, bearings, and electrical insulation. It is sold under the tradenames Teflon and Fluon.

polytheism Belief in more than one god (*compare* monotheism). Polytheism characterized the religions of the ancient Indo-European peoples (*see* Greek religion; Roman religion) and survives today in *Hinduism.

polythene (polyethylene) A white translucent thermoplastic material made by *polymerization of *ethylene. **Low-density polythene** is made at high pressure and is a soft material used for flexible pipes, sheets, and bags. **High-density polythene** is made at lower pressures, is more rigid, and softens at a higher temperature. It is used for moulded articles.

Polytrichum A genus of *mosses (over 100 species), known as pigeon wheat and hair-cap mosses, that form large mats in peat bogs, old fields, and acid soils. *P. commune* is the most widely distributed species and grows up to 15 cm high. *Polytrichum* has been used in brooms, baskets, and in stuffing mattresses. Family: *Polytrichaceae*.

polyurethane A synthetic polymer the molecules of which contain the -NH.CO.O- group. Some polyurethanes form thermosetting resins and others, thermoplastic resins. They have a wide range of properties and are used in paints, adhesives, moulded articles, rubbers, lacquers, and foams. Polyurethane foam is manufactured from *urethane and can be made flexible or rigid.

polyvinyl acetate (PVA) A vinyl *resin produced by *polymerization of vinyl acetate (CH_2:$CHOOCCH_3$). It is a soft material, used in paints and adhesives.

polyvinyl chloride (PVC) A vinyl *resin or plastic produced by *polymerization of vinyl chloride (chloroethene; CH_2:$CHCl$), a toxic gas. Rigid PVC products are made by moulding. The addition of a plasticizer produces flexible PVC. PVC is tough, nonflammable, resistant to moisture, and a good electrical insulator. It is widely used in sheets, pipes, electrical insulators, and clothing.

Pombal, Sebastião José de Carvalho e Mello, Marquês de (1699–1782) Portuguese statesman, who was the virtual ruler of Portugal from 1750 to 1777 as the chief minister of José I (1715–77; reigned 1750–77). A proponent of enlightened despotism (*see* Enlightenment), he reformed government administration, encouraged manufacturing, and modernized education. He also directed the rebuilding of Lisbon following the earthquake of 1755. His reforms did not achieve lasting success and his unpopular methods caused his downfall after José's death.

pomegranate A shrub or small tree, *Punica granatum*, native to W Asia and widely cultivated in the tropics and subtropics for its fruit. 5–7 m tall, it has narrow pointed leaves, about 7.5 cm long, and orange-red flowers growing in the leaf axils. The large round fruit has a thick leathery yellowish-reddish skin and contains several chambers, each containing many seeds coated with a pinkish acid-sweet juicy pulp. Pomegranates are eaten fresh or used in beverages or wines. The seeds are used in preserves and syrups. Family: *Punicaceae*.

Pomerania A region of NE Europe on the Baltic Sea between the Rivers Oder and Vistula. Pomerania was Polish territory until the 17th century, when the western and central regions were acquired by Brandenburg (later Prussia). Sweden gained W Pomerania in 1648 but by 1815 it had been reacquired by Prussia, which in 1772 had annexed E Pomerania. Territorial redistribution after World Wars I and II restored Pomerania E of the River Oder to Poland; W Pomerania became part of East Germany.

Pomeranian A breed of toy dog, developed in Pomerania, whose ancestors are thought to have been Scandinavian sledge dogs. The Pomeranian has a compact body and foxlike head with small erect ears. The short undercoat is covered by a long straight outercoat and the fluffy tail is held over the back. The coat may be any recognized colour, including white, black, brown, or reddish. Height: 14–18 cm.

Pomona (mythology)   A Roman goddess of fruit to whom a sacred precinct outside Rome was dedicated. She was married to Vertumnus, a god who controlled the change of seasons.

Pomona (Orkneys).   *See* Mainland.

POMPEII   *A gate leading to the forum with the slopes of Mount Vesuvius in the background.*

Pompadour, Mme de (Jeanne Antoinette Poisson, Marquise de P.; 1721–64) The mistress of Louis XV, who exerted considerable political influence from 1745 until her death. She influenced the negotiation of an Austrian alliance against Prussia and was blamed for French defeats in the subsequent *Seven Years' War. She was a notable patron of artists and scholars. □Boucher, François.

pompano A valuable food fish of the genus *Trachinotus*. It has a deep body, usually up to 50 cm long, coloured silvery blue or grey. Pompanos are carnivorous and live in fast-swimming groups, usually around rocks in warm coastal waters. Family: *Carangidae*; order: *Perciformes*.

Pompeii An ancient city near Naples, in Italy. It was buried four to six metres deep under volcanic ash by the eruption of Mount *Vesuvius (79 AD). Its rediscovery (1748) stimulated general interest in classical archaeology. Pompeii, now about three-quarters excavated, provides unparalleled evidence for daily life in Roman times: buildings, often standing to the first floor and with extensive wall paintings and graffiti; normally perishable objects including food, wooden furniture, and paintings, preserved by the ash; and personal possessions abandoned by the fleeing inhabitants.

Pompey (Gnaeus Pompeius; 106–48 BC) Roman general and statesman, called Pompeius Magnus (Pompey the Great). Granted extraordinary powers (67–66) to destroy marauding pirates and then to wage war in Asia, Pompey returned a popular hero. In 60 he joined Julius Caesar and Crassus in the first *Triumvirate, marrying Caesar's daughter Julia (d. 54) in 59, but in 50 he supported the Senate's demand for Caesar to resign his armies. In the civil war that followed Pompey was defeated by Caesar at Pharsalus (48) and fled to Egypt, where he was murdered.

Pompidou, Georges (Jean Raymond) (1911–74) French statesman; prime minister (1962, 1962–66, 1966–67, 1967–68) and president (1969–74). He served under de Gaulle during World War II and was his personal assistant in 1958–59, when he helped draft the constitution of the Fifth Republic. He negotiated a settlement with the Algerians (1961) and with the stu-

dents in the revolt of May, 1968. He succeeded de Gaulle as president.

Ponce 18 01N 66 36W A major city and port in S Puerto Rico, on the Caribbean Sea. Industries include iron processing, sugar refining, and canning. Population (1980): 188 219.

Ponce de Leon, Juan (1460–1521) Spanish explorer. He accompanied Columbus on his second voyage to Central America (1493–96) and in 1508–09 founded the first settlement in Puerto Rico, of which he became governor (1510). In 1512, searching for the legendary fountain of eternal youth, he discovered Florida. He died while attempting to colonize it, from a wound received from an Indian's poisoned arrow. The port of Ponce is named after him.

Pondicherry A Union Territory in SE India, on the Coromandel Coast. Founded by the French in 1674, it was their chief settlement in India until transferred to Indian administration in 1954. Rice and millet are the chief products. Area: 479 sq km (185 sq mi). Population (1981 est): 604 136. Capital: Pondicherry.

pond skater A *water bug belonging to the family *Gerridae* (about 350 species). Pond skaters, or water striders, have a dark slender body and long legs. They are found mainly in fresh water, running or skating across the surface and feeding on small insects.

pond turtle Either of two species of turtle found in ponds and other still waters. The Pacific pond turtle (*Clemmys marmorata*), of the W coast of North America, is 15–18 cm long and brown with yellow spots; it is widely sold for food. The European pond turtle (*Emys orbicularis*) of Europe, N Africa, and W Asia, is 12–13 cm long and brown with yellow speckles. Family: *Emydidae*.

pondweed A usually perennial aquatic herb of the genus *Potamogeton* (100 species), found worldwide in fresh water. It has submerged or floating oblong or pointed leaves, 2–20 cm long, and stalked heads of tiny four-lobed greenish flowers. Family: *Potamogetonaceae*.
The Canadian pondweed (*Elodea canadensis*) has submerged stems, up to 3 m long, with whorls of narrow backward-curving dark-green leaves. Native to North America, it is naturalized in Europe. Family: *Hydrocharitaceae*.

Poniatowski, Józef (1763–1813) Marshal of France, born in Austria, who served consecutively in the Austrian and Polish armies before becoming commander of the Duchy of Warsaw, established by Napoleon in 1807. He fought in Napoleon's Russian campaign (1812–13) and died at *Leipzig.

Ponta Delgada 37 29N 25 40W A town in the Azores, the capital of São Miguel Island. Important since 1540, it is a tourist resort and the main commercial centre of the Azores. Population (1981): 22 200.

Pontefract 53 42N 1 18W A market town in N England, in West Yorkshire. Richard II was murdered in its 11th-century castle. Pontefract's licorice sweets (Pontefract or Pomfret cakes) are widely known. There is local coalmining and market gardening. Population (1981 est): 32 836.

Ponte Vecchio A bridge over the River Arno in Florence. Topped by buildings, it was designed by Taddeo *Gaddi and finished in 1345. It was a highly advanced structure for its period.

Pontevedra 42 25N 8 39W A port in NW Spain, in Galicia. It has a 16th-century cathedral and an episcopal palace. Its manufactures include cloth, leather, and pottery. Population (1982 est): 70 223.

Pontiac (c. 1720–c. 1769) American Indian chief, who organized local tribes to resist White migration to the NW. In **Pontiac's Conspiracy** (1763–66) the Indians took all but three of the British fortified posts. Fighting continued until 1765, when the posts were all recaptured, and peace was signed at Oswego in 1766.

Pontianak 0 05S 109 16E A port in Indonesia, in W Kalimantan on the Kapuas delta. Formerly Borneo's main gold town, its chief industries are shipbuilding and rubber, palm oil, sugar, and timber processing. Its university was established in 1963. Population (1980): 304 778.

Pontine Marshes (Italian name: Agro Pontino) A reclaimed marshland area in S central Italy, bordering on the Tyrrhenian Sea. An extensive scheme to drain the marshes was begun in 1928; several towns including Littoria (now Latina) were established and it has become one of the most productive agricultural areas in Italy.

pontoon (*or* vingt-et-un) A card game in which the objective is to score 21, counting court cards as 10 and the ace as 1 or 11. One card is dealt face down to each player, who puts up a stake accordingly. A second card is then dealt face down and the betting continues in some games. Players then have the option of "sticking" (keeping the cards they have), buying another card face down, or "twisting" (accepting another card face up at no cost). Hands scoring more than 21 after this procedure lose their stakes (go "bust"). The winner is the player with the score nearest to 21. Players scoring exactly 21 (a 10 and an ace) win double their stakes. *See also* blackjack.

pontoon bridge A type of temporary bridge in which the deck (or roadway) rests on floating flat-bottomed vessels (pontoons). Pontoons were often used in the earliest military campaigns as they could be preassembled, floated into position, and did not need to last for ever. Modern pontoon bridges often have a movable section to allow boats to pass; they are useful where the earth is unsuitable for heavy pier foundations or the traffic is too light to justify a piered bridge.

Pontormo, Jacopo da (J. Carrucci; 1494–1557) Italian mannerist painter, born in Pontormo (*see* mannerism). He settled in Florence, where he trained under *Andrea del Sarto. He painted mythological scenes in the Medici villa at Poggio a Caiano (1521) and scenes of the Passion (1522–25) at the Certosa, near Florence, but his major work is the *Deposition* (Sta Felicità, Florence).

Pontus The coastal region S of the Black Sea in NE Asia Minor. Pontus was a kingdom from the 4th century BC, becoming prominent in the 1st century BC under *Mithridates VI Eupator. Pompey conquered Pontus in 64, after which the region was administered by Rome.

Pontypool 51 43N 3 02W A town in SE Wales, in Gwent. Glass and nylon are manufactured and coal is mined locally. The first successful tinplate in Britain was made here in 1703. Population (1981): 36 761.

Pontypridd 51 37N 3 22W A town in South Wales, in Mid Glamorgan at the confluence of the Rivers Taff and Rhondda. Its heavy industry includes coalmining, iron and brass founding, and chemicals. There are light industries at a nearby trading estate. Population (1981): 32 992.

pony A *horse that does not exceed 1.47 m (14½ hands) in height at maturity, measured from the top of the shoulders (withers). The many modern breeds of pony are thought to have developed from one or two original types, which may have resembled *Przewalski's horse and the *Exmoor pony. Ponies have traditionally been used by man as pack animals and for riding. Today, they are especially popular as children's mounts and for pony trekking.

Pony Club An international organization founded in England in 1929 to promote sound horsemanship among people under 21. Branches were originally connected with various hunts (*see* foxhunting), but mounted games (*see* gymkhana), *showjumping, and *horse trials are also typical activities.

poodle A breed of ▢dog of uncertain origins but long associated with France and Germany. The poodle is an active intelligent dog with a long straight muzzle, drooping ears, and a docked tail. The dense coat, which was originally clipped to enable them to swim and retrieve in water, may be any recognized colour, including grey, white, black, brown, or cream. The miniature poodle and toy poodle are derivative breeds of the standard poodle. Height: 38 cm minimum (standard); 28–38 cm (miniature); under 28 cm (toy).

pool An American form of *billiards played on a table usually 1.4 × 2.7 m (4.5 × 9 ft) with six pockets. The object is to use a white cue ball to pot the 15 coloured balls into the pockets.

Poole 50 43N 1 59W A resort in SW England, in Dorset on Poole Harbour (an almost landlocked inlet of the English Channel). It is a minor port, with boatbuilding, engineering, pottery (using local clays), and chemical industries. Population (1981): 118 922.

Poona (*or* Pune) 18 34N 73 58E A city in India, in Maharashtra. Capital of the Marathas in the late 18th century, it was taken by the British in 1817. It is the site of a university (1949) and a renowned oriental research institute (1919). A commercial, manufacturing, and military centre, it has cotton textiles, rubber, paper, and munitions industries. Population (1981 est): 1 685 266.

Poor Laws The laws that governed assistance to the poor in Britain. From the 16th century parishes were responsible for providing for their poor and from 1572 levied a rate for poor relief, which was further systematized by Acts of 1576, 1598, and 1601. The Poor Law Amendment Act of 1834 abolished such outdoor relief and those seeking assistance had to enter a *workhouse. The Poor Law system was not abolished until 1947. *See also* Speenhamland system; social security.

pop art A modern art movement dominant in the USA and UK in the 1960s. Pop art is strongly influenced by the mass media—television, comics, advertising, etc.—in its subject matter and techniques. Also characteristic is the use of silkscreen *printing, *collage, and the *ready-made. Pioneered in the 1950s by Jasper *Johns and Robert *Rauschenberg, it was influenced by the early-20th-century *dada movement and developed as a reaction to *action painting. Leading pop artists are Andy *Warhol, Roy *Lichtenstein, George Segal, Claes *Oldenburg, and, in the UK, Richard *Hamilton and Peter *Blake.

pope. *See* papacy.

Pope, Alexander (1688–1744) British poet. A severe childhood illness left him a cripple for life. He established his reputation as a poet of biting wit and skill, especially in his masterly use of the heroic couplet, with *An Essay on Criticism* (1711) and the mock epic *The Rape of the Lock* (1712–14). The financial gains from his translations of Homer's *Iliad* (1715–20) and *Odyssey* (1725–26) enabled him to move in 1719 to his comfortable house in Twickenham. Here he wrote the mock epic *The Dunciad* (1728; revised 1742–43), the philosophical poem *An Essay on Man* (1733–34), and poems modelled on the satires of Horace.

Popish Plot (1678) A conspiracy invented by Titus Oates (1649–1705) and Israel Tonge. They alleged the existence of a plot to assassinate Charles II and place his Roman Catholic brother, James, on the throne. The anti-Catholic passions Oates and Tonge thus aroused led to the execution of 35 suspects and the exclusion of Catholics from parliament (*see* Test Acts).

poplar A shrub or tree of the genus *Populus* (about 30 species), native to N temperate regions and grown for wood pulp, shade, and ornament. Up to 40 m tall, the trees may have a broad spreading crown, as in the European black poplar (*P. nigra*), or a tall slender one, as in the Lombardy poplar (*P. nigra* var. *italica*). The oval, triangular, or heart-shaped leaves may have striking autumn colours and the drooping male and female catkins are usually borne on separate trees. The seeds have tufts of silky white hairs. Family: *Salicaceae*. *See also* aspen.

pop music Any music that is general in its appeal, especially among young people; it includes folk, country and western, and, predominantly, *rock music. It is distinguished from classical music and pure jazz by its lack of sophistication. Pop emerged as a distinctive genre in the 1950s with the emergence of small groups using electronically amplified instruments, simple harmonies, and heavy rhythms. Pop songs are generally about basic human emotions, such as love, happiness, and grief. The emergence of youth movements in the early 1960s lent pop a rebelliousness that expressed itself in the life styles of pop musicians, the lyrics of pop songs, and unconventional styles of dress and performance. The multiplicity of styles in the 1960s, 1970s, and 1980s reflected the development of rock, the predominance of individual performers and groups, and the emergence of disco music. The term **popular music** is generally applied to light music of a romantic or sentimental kind.

Popocatépetl, Mount 19 02N 93 38W A dormant volcano in central Mexico, near Mexico City. Its crater contains sulphur deposits. Height: 5452 m (17 887 ft).

Popov, Aleksandr Stepanovich (1859-1905) Russian physicist, who studied the transmission of radio waves. Popov's work preceded that of *Marconi and in 1897 he succeeded in transmitting over a distance of five kilometres. However, he failed to pursue the use of radio waves for communication, using them instead to study thunderstorms.

Popov, Oleg Konstantinovich (1930-) Russian clown. His act, influenced by Charlie Chaplin, incorporates his skills as acrobat and juggler. He toured in Europe and the USA with the Moscow Circus.

Popper, Sir Karl Raimund (1902-) Austrian-born philosopher. Forced by the Nazi threat to emigrate, Popper was a professor at the London School of Economics (1949-69). His interests were mainly scientific and political. In *The Logic of Scientific Discovery* (1935) he cast doubt upon time-honoured methods of establishing scientific laws by observation and experiment: "all crows are black" is an unrestricted generalization that can never be verified (we can never hope to observe *all* crows), but it could be falsified by the observation of one white crow. *The Open Society and its Enemies* (1945) and *The Poverty of Historicism* (1957) promote "methodological individualism," the restoration of the historical importance of the individual against collective doctrinaire systems such as Marxism.

poppy An annual, biennial, or perennial plant of the genus *Papaver* (about 120 species), native mainly to the N hemisphere and often grown for ornament. 15-100 cm high, it yields a milky sap (latex) and bears large lobed or divided leaves and showy white, pink, or red flowers, sometimes with a dark centre, with 4-6 petals surrounding a dense whorl of stamens. The ▢fruit is a capsule with pores through which the seeds are dispersed. Species include the *corn poppy and *opium poppy. Family: *Papaveraceae*. *See also* horned poppy; prickly poppy; Welsh poppy.

Popski's Private Army A unit famous for its courageous missions (1942-45) behind enemy lines in N Africa and Italy in World War II. It was named after its Belgian commander, Lieutenant Colonel Vladimir Peniakoff (known as Popski; 1897-1951), who had joined the British army in 1940.

popular front A coalition of left-wing and moderate political groups. Increasingly concerned by the rise of fascism in the mid-1930s, many Communist Parties, with Soviet encouragement, sought political alliances with socialist and liberal groups. In 1936 a popular-front government was elected in France; but generally the different parties were too divided to oppose fascism effectively. *See also* United Fronts.

porbeagle A *mackerel shark, *Lamna nasus*, commonly called the Atlantic mackerel shark, that lives mainly in N temperate shallow waters. It has a dark-blue robust body, 1.5-3 m long, with a white belly and may occur in small groups, feeding principally on shoals of fish, especially mackerel.

porcelain White vitrified ceramic evolved by Chinese potters about 900 AD. It was not invented but developed out of stoneware pottery. There are three kinds of porcelain: hard-paste or true porcelain, soft-paste or artificial, and English bone china. Hard-paste porcelain consists of china clay (kaolin) and fusible feldspathic rock (petuntse) finely mixed and fired to about 1400°C. This forms a translucent white resonant vitreous body, which is usually glazed with pure petuntse during the firing. Hard-paste porcelain was made in Japan about 1500 AD but the secret of its manufacture defied discovery elsewhere until the early 18th century when the alchemist Böttger (1682-1719) succeeded, after exhaustive secret experiments, in making it at *Meissen. By the mid-18th century the smaller works at Plymouth and Bristol also succeeded. Soft-paste porcelain differs from hard-paste in that the clay or kaolin is mixed with an artificial flux. This might be sand with lime, or flint, soda, etc., depending on the factory. The mixture is fired at about 1100°C and the glaze, usually of glass, is applied in a second firing at about 1000°C. Bone porcelain is an 18th-century English invention using bone ash as a flux.

porcupine A large herbivorous spiny *rodent belonging to either of the families *Erethizontidae* (New World porcupines; 11 species) or *Hystricidae* (Old World porcupines; 15 species). American porcupines tend to be arboreal and have prehensile tails. The North American porcupine (*Erethizion dorsatum*) is about 75 cm long and grows a soft winter coat that almost conceals its covering of quills. Old World porcupines are mainly ground-dwelling. The Indian crested porcupine (*Hystrix indica*) grows to 1 m in length and may have spines 35 cm long. Porcupines respond to a threat by turning their backs and raising their spines or even running backwards at an attacker. ▢mammal.

porcupine fish A fish, also called sea porcupine, belonging to a family (*Diodontidae*) related to *puffers, especially *Diodon hystrix*, found in tropical seas. It has a short broad body, up to about 90 cm long, which it inflates when provoked, erecting numerous spines in the skin.

porgy. *See* sea bream.

Pori (Swedish name: Björneborg) 61 28N 21 45E A seaport in S Finland, on the Gulf of Bothnia. Its industries include copper refining, textiles, wood processing, steel, and chemicals. Population (1980): 79 405.

porphyria A group of genetic disorders in which there is an accumulation in the body of one or more porphyrins—precursors of the red blood pigment—due to an enzyme defect. The disease affects the digestive tract, causing abdominal pain, vomiting, and diarrhoea; the nervous system, causing psychotic disorder, epilepsy, and weakness; the circulatory system, causing high blood pressure; and the skin, causing photosensitivity. There is no specific treatment. The madness of George III is now known to have been due to porphyria.

porphyry An igneous rock, usually hypabyssal, containing numerous large crystals called phenocrysts set in a finer-grained, or sometimes glassy, groundmass. The term porphyry is often given with the name of the prophyritic mineral, for example quartz porphyry.

Porphyry (232-305 AD) Syrian-born philosopher and devoted disciple, editor, and biographer of *Plotinus. Among nearly 80 titles attributed to him are religious and philosophical works, including a *Treatise against Christians*, banned in 448 AD but still partly extant, and commentaries on philosophical authors. He also wrote on literary, grammatical, and scientific topics.

porpoise A small toothed *whale belonging to the family *Phocoenidae* (7 species), of coastal waters. Porpoises are 1.5-2 m long and have no beak. The common, or harbour, porpoise (*Phocoena phocoena*) of the N Atlantic and Pacific, has a rounded body, tapering towards the tail, blue-grey above and pale grey beneath. It lives in large groups called schools, feeding on fish, squid, and crustaceans.

port A fortified usually dessert *wine from Oporto (N Portugal). The grapes grown on the Douro hillsides are trodden in stone presses. Fermentation is halted by adding brandy. Subsequently the wine is taken to the lodges near Oporto, where it matures in wood. Port-type wines are made in other countries, such as South Africa.

Port Adelaide 34 52S 138 30E The chief port of South Australia, NW of *Adelaide on an inlet of Gulf St Vincent. It has a container and passenger terminal; the main exports are wool, fruit, flour and wheat. Population (1985): 37 000.

Portadown 54 26N 6 27W A market town in Northern Ireland, in Co Armagh. A centre for the surrounding rich farming region, it manufactures linen, carpets, and furniture. There are famous rose nurseries. Population (1981): 21 333.

Port Arthur 29 55N 93 56W A city in the USA, in Texas. Situated in an oil region known as the Golden Triangle, Port Arthur is a major shipping outlet for oil and has large petrochemical industries. Population (1980): 61 106.

Port Arthur. *See* Lüda; Thunder Bay.

Port Augusta 32 30S 137 48E A port in South Australia, on the Spencer Gulf. It is an important railway centre and has the state headquarters of the Royal Flying Doctor Service. Chief exports include wheat and wool. Population (1985): 17 000.

Port-au-Prince 18 40N 72 20W The capital of Haiti, a port in the SW on the Gulf of Gonaïves. Its main exports are coffee and sugar. The University of Haiti was founded here in 1944. Population (1981 est): 906 700.

Port Elizabeth 33 58S 25 36E A city in South Africa, in S Cape Province on Algoa Bay. It was founded in 1820 by British settlers. The university was founded in 1964. Nearby is the Addo Elephant National Park. It is a major port, ore being the chief export, and industries include motor-car assembly, fruit canning, and flour milling. Population (1980 est): 492 140.

Porter, Cole (Albert) (1893–1964) US composer of musical comedies and popular songs. He wrote a series of musicals, including *The Gay Divorcee* (1932), *Anything Goes* (1934), *Kiss Me Kate* (1948), and *Can Can* (1953). His songs included "Night and Day" and "Begin the Beguine."

Porter, Katherine Anne (1890–1980) US short-story writer and novelist. *Flowering Judas*, her first collection of stories, was published in 1930. Her stories, especially those in *Pale Horse, Pale Rider* (1939), are mostly delicate explorations of autobiographical material. Her only novel was the allegorical *Ship of Fools* (1962), which won a Pulitzer Prize.

Porter, Peter (1929–) British poet. Born and educated in Australia, he settled in London in 1951. His poetry is noted for its wit and formal elegance. His volumes include *The Last of England* (1970), *The Cost of Seriousness* (1978), and *Collected Poems* (1983).

Port-Gentil 0 40S 20 35E A port in W Gabon, near the mouth of the River Ogooué. It is the nation's chief industrial centre having an oil-refining and a large timber industry. Population (1983 est): 123 000.

Port Glasgow 55 56N 4 41W A town in W central Scotland, in Strathclyde Region on the Clyde estuary. Formerly the outport for Glasgow, it is now concerned chiefly with shipbuilding, textiles, and engineering. Population (1981): 21 554.

Port Harcourt 4 43N 7 05E A port in S Nigeria. Founded in 1912, it developed as a port following the arrival of the railway (1916) from the Enugu coalfields. It now exports coal, tin, and palm oil. It is the major industrial centre of the Niger delta oilfields. It has a university (1975). Population (1983 est): 296 200.

Portile de Fier. *See* Iron Gate.

Port Jackson (*or* Sydney Harbour) An inlet of the Pacific Ocean, on the coast of SE Australia. It forms a fine natural harbour, the site of *Sydney, and is spanned by the Sydney Harbour Bridge (1932). Length: about 29 km (18 mi).

Port Klang (name until 1971: Port Swettenham) 3 01N 101 25E A port in W Peninsular Malaysia, on the Strait of Malacca. Exporting chiefly rubber, it serves the Klang Valley, Malaysia's chief industrial area. Population (1980): 192 080.

Portland 45 32N 122 40W A city in the USA, in Oregon on the Willamette River. It was founded in 1829 and its growth was stimulated by several gold rushes along the Oregon Trail. The state's largest city, it is a deepwater port, with shipbuilding, timber, and metallurgical industries. It is the site of the University of Portland (1901). Population (1980): 366 383.

Portland 43 41N 70 18W A city in the USA, in SW Maine on Casco Bay. Destroyed by Indians, French, and British, it was the state capital (1820–32). It is a major petroleum port and commercial centre. Industries include timber, textiles, and chemicals. Population (1980): 61 572.

Portland, Isle of A peninsula in S England, in Dorset connected to the mainland by Chesil Bank. It contains Portland Castle, built by Henry VIII (1520). The Portland stone quarried here has been used in many London buildings, notably St Paul's Cathedral.

Portland, William Henry Cavendish Bentinck, 3rd Duke of (1738–1809) British statesman; prime minister (1783, 1807–09). He was nominal head of the coalition between Lord North and Charles James Fox (1783) and was subsequently home secretary (1794–1801) under Pitt the Younger. In his second ministry he was overshadowed by George Canning and Castlereagh. His second son **Lord William (Henry Cavendish) Bentinck** (1774–1839) was the first governor general of India (1828–35). He abolished *suttee (the burning alive of a widow on her husband's funeral pyre), enabled the *Thugs to be suppressed, and made it easier for Indians to obtain public posts.

Portland vase A Roman vase (c. 1st century AD) of dark blue glass with a white glass relief of figures, discovered in Italy in 1644. It once belonged to the Duke of Portland but is now in the British Museum.

Portlaoise (Portlaoighise *or* Maryborough) 53 02N 7 17W A town in the Republic of Ireland, the county town of Co Laoighis. There are woollen, flour-milling, and malting industries. Population (1985): 8500.

Port Louis 20 10S 57 30E The capital of Mauritius, in the NW of the island. Founded in about 1736, it is the site of two cathedrals. Sugar is exported. Population (1980 est): 147 386.

Port Lyautey. *See* Kenitra.

Portmeirion A holiday resort in North Wales, built by Sir Clough *Williams-Ellis on his own land overlooking Tregmaroc Bay. He incorporated many fragments of destroyed buildings into his fanciful design, which was loosely based on the fishing village of Portofino in NW Italy.

Port Moresby 9 30S 147 07E The capital and main port of Papua New Guinea, on the Gulf of Papua. It was an important Allied base in World War II and since then the port has been considerably modernized. The University of Papua New Guinea was founded in 1965. Population (1980 est): 122 761.

Pôrto. *See* Oporto.

Pôrto Alegre 30 03S 51 10W A city in S Brazil, the capital of Rio Grande do Sul state on the Lagôa (Lagoon) dos Patos. It is a major commercial and industrial centre; industries are chiefly related to agriculture and include meat processing, tanning, and the manufacture of textiles. It is the seat of two universities. Population (1980): 1 108 883.

PORTMEIRION

Portobelo 9 33N 79 37W A village in E central Panama, on the Caribbean Sea. Founded in 1597, it became an important transshipment point in the New World and was often attacked by English buccaneers. Sir Francis *Drake was buried at sea in the Bay of Portobelo. It declined following the building of the Panama railway in the 1850s and the opening of the Panama Canal (1914). Population (1980 est) 2657.

Port-of-Spain 10 38N 61 31W The capital and main port of Trinidad and Tobago since 1783, on the W coast of Trinidad. It was the capital of the short-lived Federation of the West Indies from 1958 until 1962. Notable buildings include the Anglican and Roman Catholic cathedrals. Petroleum products, sugar, and rum are among the main exports. Population (1980): 55 800.

Porto Novo 6 30N 2 47E The capital of Benin, on the Gulf of Guinea. A former centre of the slave trade with the Portuguese, it came under French rule in the late 19th century. Trade includes palm oil and cotton. Population (1982): 208 258.

Port Phillip Bay An inlet of Bass Strait, in SE Australia with the port of Melbourne at its head and Geelong on its W shore. Length: 56 km (35 mi). Width: 64 km (40 mi).

Port Pirie 33 11S 138 01E A port in South Australia, on the Spencer Gulf. It is important for metal smelting (especially lead, silver, and gold), using ores from Broken Hill. Population (1985): 16 030.

Port Royal A former Cistercian nunnery originally situated a short distance SW of Paris; also called Port Royal des Champs. In the 17th century it became a centre of *Jansenism under Abbess Angélique Arnauld (1591-1661), sister of Antoine *Arnauld. After persecution the nuns were dispersed (1709).

Port Said (*or* Bur Said) 31 17N 32 18E A major port in Egypt, situated at the Mediterranean entrance to the Suez Canal. Founded in 1859, it became an important fuelling point but suffered from the closure of the Suez Canal (1967-75) and Israeli occupation of the E bank. Population (1983 est): 364 000.

Portsmouth 50 48N 1 05W A port in S England, in Hampshire at the entrance to Portsmouth Harbour opposite *Gosport. Notable landmarks include Nelson's flagship HMS *Victory* and Charles Dickens' birthplace (now a museum). The chief naval base in the UK, Portsmouth is also a commercial port with shipbuilding, ship-maintenance, electronics, and aircraft-engineering industries. The resort of Southsea is within the district. Population (1981 est): 179 419.

Portsmouth 36 50N 76 20W A city and port in the USA, in Virginia on Hampton Roads. Founded in 1752, it is the site of the Norfolk Naval Yard, abandoned by Federal troops (1861) during the US Civil War and used by the Confederates to transform the scuttled USS *Merrimack* into the *ironclad *Virginia*. The main industry is shipbuilding and ship repairing. Population (1980): 104 577.

Portsmouth 43 03N 70 47W A city in the USA, in New Hampshire on the Atlantic coast. It has several notable buildings, including the John Paul Jones House (1758). The state's only seaport, it is the site of the Portsmouth Naval Yard (established in 1800); it is an important submarine base. Population (1980): 26 214.

Port Sudan 19 38N 37 07E A port in the Sudan, on the Red Sea. It handles much of the country's trade; exports include cotton, gum arabic, and sesame seeds. It also has an important salt-panning industry. Population (1983): 206 727.

Port Sunlight. *See* Bebington.

Port Swettenham. *See* Port Klang.

Port Talbot 51 36N 3 47W A town in South Wales, in West Glamorgan on Swansea Bay, formed by the amalgamation of Aberavon and Margam in 1921. Its port has been extended to accommodate bulk carriers of iron ore and it has important heavy industry (steel and chemicals). It is also a resort, mainly for day-trippers from the nearby industrial towns. Population (1981): 47 313.

Portugal, Republic of A country in SW Europe, occupying the W section of the Iberian Peninsula and bordering on the Atlantic Ocean. The *Madeira Islands are an integral part of Portugal. Coastal plains rise to mountains, reaching 1935 m (6352 ft) in the N. The main rivers are the Douro, Miño, and Tagus. *Economy*: traditionally agricultural, Portugal's principal exports are textiles, clothing, cork, wood products, sardines, and fortified wines. However, recent political upheavals, an inefficient farming system, and drought, combined with loss of cheap raw materials following the independence of former colonies, have led to many economic difficulties. Tourism, an important source of foreign currency, virtually ceased for a while but was being revived by the late 1970s. Rich mineral resources include coal, copper pyrites, kaolin, and haematite and hydroelectricity is a valuable source of power. *History*: the early history of the region is that of the rest of the Iberian Peninsula (*see* Spain, Kingdom of). Portugal as a distinct Christian territory dates from 868. It became a kingdom in 1139 under Alfonso I (1112-85) and its position was consolidated in the 13th century by the conquest of Muslim territory. Portugal's long alliance with England began in the 14th century. From the 15th century Portuguese explorers opened up new trade routes, allowing for the establishment of an extensive overseas empire that included Angola, Mozambique, and Brazil. In 1580 Portugal came under Spanish domination, which lasted until 1640, after which the Portuguese monarchy became increasingly reactionary, a trend that *Pombal's reforms attempted to reverse. In 1807 Portugal was invaded by the French, who were defeated in the subsequent *Peninsular War. A revolution in 1910 overthrew the monarchy and established a republic. A long period of political instability culminated in a military coup in 1926. A prominent role in the new government was played by *Salazar, who became prime minister in 1932 and established the corporatist New State. His long dictatorship also witnessed bitter colonial wars in Africa. In April, 1974, Salazar's successor, Marcello Caetano (1906-80), was overthrown in a military coup led by Gen Antonio de Spinola (1911-). Spinola granted independence to Portugal's remaining African colonies before falling from power later the same year. In 1986 Mario *Soares, who was prime minister from 1976 to 1979 and from 1983 to 1985, became president. In 1986 Portugal joined the EEC. Prime minister: Aníbal Cavaco Silva (1939-). Official language: Portuguese. Official religion: Roman Catholic. Official currency: escudo of 100 centavos. Area:

91 631 sq km (34 861 sq mi). Population (1983 est): 10 008 000. Capital and main port: Lisbon.

Portuguese A *Romance language spoken in Portugal, Galicia (Spain), Brazil, Madeira, and the Azores. It emerged as a distinct language during the early medieval period. The standard form is based on the dialect of Lisbon. Brazilian Portuguese differs slightly in grammar and sound system. A notable characteristic of Portuguese is the use of nasal vowel sounds.

Portuguese East Africa. *See* Mozambique, People's Republic of.

Portuguese Guinea. *See* Guinea-Bissau, Republic of.

Portuguese literature Literature in the Portuguese language commences with the lyrics of a school of poets who flourished under the kings Alfonso III (1248-79) and Dinis (1279-1325) are preserved in three collections of *cancioneiros*. In a later collection, the *Cancioneiro Geral* (1516), the influence of Provençal poetry was replaced by that of Spanish and Italian models. During the 16th century, the golden age of Portuguese literature, Gil Vicente wrote pioneering works of drama, Sá de Miranda (c. 1481-1558) introduced many new poetic forms from Italy, and Luís de Camões composed the national epic poem, *Os Lusíadas* (1572). The subsequent period of decline lasted until the influence of Romanticism in the early 19th century inspired the works of João Baptista da Silva Leitão Almeida-Garrett (1799-1854) and Alexandre Herculano (1810-77). Further stimulation was provided by a reaction against the pseudoclassicism of Feliciano de Castilho led by Antero de Quental (1842-91) and by the influence of French Symbolism. Outstanding individual writers of the 20th century include the poet Fernando Pessoa (1888-1935) and the novelist Manual Ribeiro (1879-1941).

Portuguese man-of-war A colonial marine invertebrate animal belonging to a genus (*Physalia*) of *coelenterates found mainly in warm seas. It has a translucent bladder-like float (pneumatophore), pink, blue, or violet in colour, which acts like a sail in the wind. Attached underneath are clusters of *polyps bearing stinging tentacles, up to 50 m long, used to paralyse fish and other prey. The sting can also have a serious effect on man. Order: *Siphonophora*; class: *Hydrozoa*. □oceans.

Portuguese West Africa. *See* Angola, People's Republic of.

Porvoo (Swedish name: Borga) 60 24N 25 40E A city in S Finland. One of the country's oldest settlements, it has a 15th-century cathedral. Its industries include brewing and publishing. Population (1982 est): 19 226.

Poseidon The Greek god of the sea and earthquakes, son of Cronus and Rhea and brother of Zeus and Hades. He used his ability to change his form mainly to further his amorous desires, and his many offspring included Theseus, Polyphemus, and the winged horse Pegasus. He was usually portrayed with a trident and dolphin. He was identified with the Roman *Neptune.

Posen. *See* Poznań.

Po-shan. *See* Zibo.

positivism The philosophical doctrine of *Comte and his successors. It asserts that knowledge of reality can be achieved *only* through the particular ·sciences and ordinary observation. Positivism rejects all metaphysical propositions, but it has been pointed out (with regard to later *logical positivism) that this rejection itself constitutes a metaphysical proposition. *Hobbes was an earlier positivist with regard to the status of the law. The only law is positive law, the law that is actually enforced; there is no "higher" law such as natural law. *Existentialism, especially in France, has been a reaction against positivism.

positron The antiparticle of the *electron, having the same mass and *spin as the electron but opposite electric charge.

A positron and an electron annihilate · each other on collision, producing two gamma-ray photons.

possum The most common Australian *marsupial, *Trichosurus vulpecula*, also called brush-tailed phalanger. Nocturnal and arboreal, it is cat-sized and has a soft greyish coat and bushy tail. It feeds mainly on buds, leaves, and fruit, and occasionally fledgling birds. The name possum is often used for other members of the family *Phalangeridae*.

post Letters, parcels, etc., that are carried from one place to another. In the UK the postal service developed from the medieval system of royal messengers employed to transport government documents around the country. In 1512 Henry VIII appointed a master of the post and the service came to include the carriage of private correspondence. Postal services became a government monopoly and William Dockwra (d. 1716), who established a private penny post in London in 1680, was prosecuted and his business closed in 1682. The postal service developed in the 18th century, when stagecoaches were used to carry post, and in 1830 the first railway mails were carried. In 1840—as a result of the efforts of Sir Rowland *Hill—uniform letter postage rates (of one penny), dependent on weight and regardless of distance carried, were introduced. Similar developments in other countries led to the establishment in 1875 of what became the Universal Postal Union, which greatly encouraged international mail services. In 1919 the first regular airmail service—between London and Paris—was introduced. Today 22 000 post offices throughout the UK deal with other business besides the carriage of letters and parcels: the Post Office manages the national *giro system, a national savings bank, the payment of *social security, and the sale of vehicle and television licences. In 1968 the system of classifying letters into first- and second-class mail was introduced, the service for the former being faster than for the latter. Postal sorting is being mechanized but delivery remains labour-intensive, the Post Office being the biggest employer in the country. In 1981 control of *telecommunications passed from the Post Office to British Telecom, which was privatized in 1984; the Post Office finally lost its monopoly status in 1987.

poster art The design of public notices for advertising and propaganda purposes. Poster design originated in the mid-19th century, the first major poster artist being the Frenchman Jules Chéret (1836-1933). Its development was facilitated by the use of lithography (*see* printing), an inexpensive and easy printing process. Leading painters of the period who designed posters included *Toulouse-Lautrec and Aubrey *Beardsley, while among specialists in the art were the "Beggarstaff Brothers"—William Nicholson (1872-1949) and James Pryde (1866-1941) as well as John *Hassall and the Czech Alphonse Mucha (1860-1939).

POSTIMPRESSIONISM Bathers, Asnieres *(1883-84; National Gallery, London) by Georges-Pierre Seurat.*

postimpressionism The art of the late 19th-century French painters *Cézanne, *Seurat, *Van Gogh, *Gauguin, *Toulouse-Lautrec, and their followers whose work developed out of and, to some extent, in reaction to *impressionism. The term was coined by the British art critic, Roger *Fry. Many of them painted impressionist works early in their careers but later rejected the objectivity and fleeting light effects of impressionism. Cézanne was the forerunner of *cubism and Van Gogh of *expressionism, while Gauguin developed a style, known as *synthetism, and Seurat introduced *pointillism. The postimpressionists were not an organized group with a coherent style or fixed programme.

postmortem. *See* autopsy.

potassium (K) A reactive alkali metal discovered by Sir Humphry Davy in 1807. It is a common constituent of the earth's crust; forming *feldspars ($KAlSi_3O_8$), clays, and evaporite minerals (for example sylvite; KCl). The metal is prepared by electrolysis of the molten hydroxide. It is soft, easily cut with a knife, and reacts readily with water, catching fire and liberating hydrogen. It oxidizes rapidly in air and must therefore be stored under oil. The element is highly electropositive and its chemistry is dominated by its ability to form ionic salts (for example KCl, KNO_3, K_2CO_3, KBr, K_2SO_4, and KCN). Its largest use is in fertilizers, potassium being essential for plant growth. Alloys of potassium and sodium have been proposed as heat transfer media in nuclear reactors, since the lowest melting alloy melts at $-12.3°C$. One of the three isotopes (^{40}K) is radioactive with a half-life of 1.3×10^9 years and is used in *potassium-argon dating. The metal and its salts impart a lilac colour to flames. At no 19; at wt 39.102; mp 63.65°C; bp 774°C.

potassium-argon dating A method of *radiometric dating of geological specimens based on the decay of the radioactive isotope potassium-40, which is present to a small extent in all naturally occurring potassium. Its half-life is 1.3×10^9 years and it decays to argon-40; thus an estimate of the ratio of the two isotopes in a specimen of rock gives an indication of its age.

potato A perennial herbaceous plant, *Solanum tuberosum*, native to the Andes but cultivated throughout the world, especially in temperate regions, as an important vegetable crop: Potatoes were first introduced to England in the late 16th century by Sir Walter Raleigh; they reached Spain and Portugal earlier. The plants grow to a height of 50–100 cm, with compound leaves and clusters of white and purple flowers. The tubers (swollen tips of underground stems) have a thin brownish-white, white, yellow, or pinkish skin and are rich in starch; there are several varieties, up to 1.5 kg in weight, and they are eaten cooked or ground into flour. Commercial potatoes are grown from small tubers termed "seed" potatoes. Potatoes are vulnerable to a number of diseases, the most notorious being the potato *blight that ravished Ireland in 1845–47 (*see also* Irish famine). Family: *Solanaceae. See also* sweet potato.

Potchefstroom 26 42S 27 06E A town in South Africa, in the S Transvaal. Founded by Voortrekkers (1838), it is the oldest town in the Transvaal. Gold mining and agriculture are important. Population (1983 est): 77 560.

Potemkin, Grigori Aleksandrovich (1739–91) Russian field marshal and favourite of *Catherine the Great. Potemkin distinguished himself in Catherine's first Turkish War (1768–74) and became her lover for two years as well as her chief adviser. Potemkin retained his political influence, especially in foreign affairs, until his death.

potential, electric A measure of electrical work. The potential at a point in an *electric field is one volt when one joule of energy is needed to bring a positive charge of one coulomb to that point from infinity. Usually the potential difference between two points, rather than the absolute potential, is used. *See also* electromotive force.

potential energy *Energy stored in a body by virtue of its position or configuration. Thus a body, mass m, at a height h above the ground has a potential energy equal to mgh, where g is the *acceleration of free fall, relative to the ground. A compressed spring and an electrically charged body also stores potential energy.

Potentilla A genus of mostly perennial herbs (500 species), found mainly in N temperate and arctic regions. It includes several species and hybrids grown as ornamentals. They have erect or creeping stems, 5–70 cm long, bearing compound leaves and yellow, white, or red four- or five-petalled flowers with many stamens. The fruit is a group of seedlike achenes. Family: *Rosaceae. See also* cinquefoil; tormentil.

potentiometer A variable electrical *resistance in which a sliding contact can be adjusted to any position along its length so that a variable proportion of the resistance can be included in a circuit. Potentiometers are used for measuring unknown voltages and as a potential divider, producing a voltage output corresponding to calibrated positions of the sliding contact.

potholing. *See* speleology.

potlatch The ceremonial distribution of gifts, practised by the American Indians of the NW Pacific coast region, in order to affirm claims to rank and status at lavish feasts, to which rivals were invited. Gifts had to be returned with interest at subsequent potlatches to avoid humiliation and loss of status; competition to exceed others in generosity was intense. Among the *Kwakiutl, potlatching developed to an exaggerated extent often involving the ostentatious destruction of property. The practice continued clandestinely after its prohibition by the Whites.

pot marigold A herb, *Calendula officinalis*, native to S Europe and cultivated in temperate regions as an ornamental. About 30–35 cm tall, it bears simple oblong leaves and yellow or orange daisy-like flowers, often double in cultivated varieties. The fresh petals may be eaten in salads or puddings or are dried and used in medicines. Family: *Compositae.

Potomac River A river in the E central USA, rising in the Appalachian Mountains of W Virginia and flowing generally NE through Washington, DC, to Chesapeake Bay. Length: 462 km (287 mi).

Potosí 19 34S 65 45W A city in S Bolivia, at an altitude of 4066 m (13 340 ft). It is the chief industrial centre of Bolivia. Mining is important; minerals extracted include tin, copper, and zinc. Its university was founded in 1892. Population (1982 est): 103 182.

Potsdam 52 19N 13 15E A city in central East Germany, on the River Havel adjoining Berlin. It was the residence of Prussian kings and German emperors. The city was severely damaged by air raids during World War II but extensive restoration has been carried out. Notable buildings include the Brandenburg Gate (1770) and the Sanssouci Palace (1745–47) built by Frederick II. An industrial city, Potsdam has many scientific institutes and is the main centre of the East German film industry. Population (1980 est): 129 648.

Potsdam Conference (1945) The conference attended by Truman (USA), Stalin (Soviet Union), and Churchill (later Attlee; UK) after the conclusion of World War II in Europe. Its objectives were to confirm the conclusions of the *Yalta Conference, to establish a political and economic programme for Allied-occupied Germany, and to decide upon action towards Japan. The Conference was marked by the conflict of interests between the communist and noncommunist powers that developed into the *Cold War.

Potter, Beatrix (1866–1943) British children's writer and illustrator. During a solitary childhood she became a skilled artist and observer of nature. *The Tale of Peter Rabbit* (1900) was the first of a series of famous children's books concerning the domestic lives of such animals as Jemima Puddle-Duck and Mrs Tittlemouse.

Potter, Paul (1625–54) Dutch animal painter and etcher, born in Enkhuizen, the son and pupil of a landscape artist. Working successively in Delft, The Hague, and Amsterdam, he was painting as early as 1640. His best works, such as *The Bull* (The Hague), were executed in 1647.

Potter, Stephen (1900–70) British humorist and critic. He wrote critical studies of D. H. Lawrence (1930) and Coleridge (1935) but is best remembered for his series of humorous books on the art of establishing personal superiority. These include *Gamesmanship* (1947), *Lifemanship* (1950), and *One-Upmanship* (1952).

Potteries The Staffordshire towns of Burslem, Fenton, Hanley, Longton, and Tunstall, making up the modern city of *Stoke-on-Trent. They became the industrial centre of English pottery in the 19th century.

potter wasp A solitary *wasp belonging to the genus *Eumerus*, common in North America and Europe. It constructs juglike nests of mud or clay, cemented by saliva and attached to plant stems. A single egg is laid in each nest and paralysed caterpillars are provided as food for the larva.

pottery Generally, all *ceramics other than porcelain, but especially clay that has been shaped into containers (*compare* terracotta) and baked at varying temperatures over 400°C. Usually thrown on a potter's wheel, pottery can also be coiled and moulded. Being opaque and porous, it is often glazed with an impervious glassy layer. Pottery making is worldwide and of great antiquity. It was being made about 10 000 BC in Japan; from about 3500 BC the fast wheel was used in Mesopotamia. Pottery styles and decorative techniques are important aids to archaeologists in identifying and dating cultures. The ancient Greeks (*see* Greek art) and Renaissance Italians (*see* maiolica) raised pottery making to high aesthetic levels, but since the 18th-century advent of porcelain in Europe it has been mainly utilitarian until revived by such modern potters as Bernard *Leach.

potto A *loris, *Perodictus potto*, of African forests. It is about 40 cm long with a short tail, a catlike face, stout legs, and strong grasping hands. Pottos have a row of spines on the neck and shoulders, used for butting in self-defence.

pouched rat An African rodent characterized by cheek pouches used for carrying food. They range in size from the African giant pouched rat (*Cricetomys gambianus*), 24–45 cm long excluding the tail (36–46 cm), to the Cape pouched mouse (*Saccostomus campestris*), 12–15 cm long, excluding the tail (3–6 cm). All are vegetarians.

Poulenc, Francis (1899–1963) French composer, a member of Les *Six. He was influenced by Ravel and Satie and produced a wide variety of compositions, including the song cycle *Le Bestiaire* (1919), a concerto for piano (1950) and one for two pianos (1932), the operas *Les Mamelles de Tirésias* (1944) and *Les Dialogues des Carmélites* (1953–56), and the ballet *Les Biches* (1923). As a pianist he frequently accompanied the French tenor Pierre Bernac (1899–).

poultry Domesticated birds, especially fowls, turkeys, ducks, and geese, that are bred and reared chiefly for eggs and meat but in some cases also for feathers and down. *See* livestock farming.

Pound, Ezra (1885–1972) US poet and critic. After studying Romance languages, he went to Europe in 1908 and became a dynamic propagandist for modernist literary and artistic movements in London (*see* Imagism; □Vorticism). His early poetry included *A Liume Spento* (1908), his first volume, and the long poems *Homage to Sextus Propertius* (1917) and *Hugh Selwyn Mauberly* (1920). *The Spirit of Romance* (1910) was a collection of literary criticism. He moved to Paris and, in 1924, to Italy, where he worked on the *Cantos* (1925–69). His support for Mussolini and his broadcasts of fascist propaganda during World War II led to his confinement in a mental hospital in the USA (1946–58), after which he returned to Italy.

Poussin, Nicolas (1594–1665) French painter, regarded as one of the greatest exponents of *classicism. Poussin lived in Rome from 1624 until his death, apart from two years (1640–42) as painter to the French king Louis XIII. His representation of religious themes, such as *The Martyrdom of St Erasmus* (1628; Vatican), gave way in the 1630s to an interest in mythology and the Old Testament, for example *The Worship of the Golden Calf* (c. 1635; National Gallery, London). The pure classicism of his second Roman period is exemplified in such landscapes as *Landscape with Diogenes* (1648; Louvre).

Poverty Bay An inlet of the SW Pacific Ocean, in New Zealand on the E coast of North Island. It was the site of Capt Cook's first landing in New Zealand (1769).

poverty trap A failure in a tax and social benefit system causing the poor to find it difficult to escape from poverty. If social benefits are means tested and *taxation is progressive, a person may find that an increase in pay leaves him no better off, and perhaps even worse off, because of the loss of benefits and increase in tax that his pay rise entails. Thus to be better off, a low-paid worker needs a substantial rise in pay to lift him clear of the trap.

powder metallurgy The shaping of metals by pressing powdered metal into blocks, heating (*see* sintering), and then shaping it by stamping. Often pressing and sintering are done together in a mould to produce the finished article in one operation. The method is used for working metals, such as platinum and tungsten (used in light-bulb filaments) that are difficult to shape by other means. It has the advantages of leaving no scrap and being suitable for intricate shapes. Nonmetal additives can be easily included, such as the graphite lubricant in self-lubricating bearings.

Powell, Anthony (1905–) British novelist. His novel sequence *A Dance to the Music of Time* comprises 12 social satires beginning with *A Question of Upbringing* (1951) and ending with *Hearing Secret Harmonies* (1975). He has also written a biography of John Aubrey (1948), four volumes of memoirs, and several plays.

Powell, Cecil Frank (1903–69) British physicist, who became professor at Bristol University. Powell pioneered the technique of observing particles by the tracks that they leave on specially prepared photographic plates. In 1947 he exposed his plates to *cosmic rays high up in the Andes and discovered the *pion. He was awarded the 1950 Nobel Prize for this work.

Powell, (John) Enoch (1912–) British politician. He was professor of Greek at Sydney University, Australia (1937–39), served in the army throughout World War II, and became a Conservative MP in 1950. From 1960 to 1963 he was minister of health, his only cabinet post, and in 1968 was dismissed from Edward Heath's shadow cabinet following a controversial speech at Birmingham on immigration, to which he is opposed. He did not stand in the February election of 1974 but from Oct 1974 until June 1987 was the United Ulster Unionist Council MP for South Down.

power The rate at which a body or system does work. It is measured in watts or horsepower.

power station An electricity generating plant that forms part of the *electricity supply system. In **thermal power stations**, heat from the burning of fossil fuels (oil, coal, and gas) or from *thermal nuclear reactors is used to generate steam. The steam drives *turbines connected to alternating-current generators (turboalternators), thus converting heat via mechanical energy into electricity. Gas turbines are also used, missing out the steam-generation stage. They are easy to build and flexible to run, but have an efficiency of only about 25%. Sometimes the exhaust gas is used to help generate steam for a steam turbine, in order to increase the station's overall efficiency. Usually in a steam-turbine thermal station about 30 to 40% of the heat is converted to electricity, most of the rest being lost when steam is condensed to water before it is returned to the boilers. *Hydroelectric power stations are more efficient (up to 90%) and provide a significant proportion of UK electricity supplies. *See also* energy.

Powhatan A confederation of Algonkian-speaking North American Indian tribes of Virginia. It was founded by the chief known to the European settlers as Powhatan, the father of *Pocahontas. The Powhatans were maize cultivators and hunters living in palisaded villages.

Powys A county of E Central Wales, bordering on England. It was formed under local government reorganization in 1974 from Montgomeryshire, Radnorshire, and most of Breconshire. It is generally mountainous, rising to 886 m (2907 ft) in the Brecon Beacons in the S, and is drained by several rivers, including the Wye and Severn. Agricultural activities include sheep, cattle, dairy, and arable farming; afforestation and tourism are also important. Area: 5077 sq km (1960 sq mi). Population (1981 est): 110 467. Administrative centre: Llandrindod Wells.

Powys, John Cowper (1872-1963) British novelist. He lectured for many years in the USA. He wrote poetry, philosophy, and criticism, but his best-known books are his long novels imbued with mystical feeling for the people and landscape of the West Country. These include *Wolf Solent* (1929) and *A Glastonbury Romance* (1932). In 1934 he moved to Wales, where he wrote the historical novels *Owen Glendower* (1940) and *Porius* (1951). His brother **Theodore Francis Powys** (1875-1953) was a novelist and short-story writer. After his marriage in 1905 he lived a secluded life in Dorset. The best known of his idiosyncratic symbolic novels is *Mr Weston's Good Wine* (1927). His philosophical ideas are more directly expressed in *Soliloquies of a Hermit* (1916).

Poyang, Lake An area of marsh and lakes in SE China, drained by the Yangtze River. In summer the whole area is flooded. Area (summer): about 2780 sq km (1073 sq mi).

Poynings' Law (1495) A measure introduced by Sir Edward Poynings (1459-1521), Lord Deputy of Ireland, which ensured that the Irish parliament could only pass laws previously approved by the English Crown. A further act applied all English laws to Ireland.

Poznań (German name: Posen) 52 55N 16 53E A city in W Poland, on the River Warta. One of the oldest cities in Poland, it became the first Polish bishopric in 968 AD. It possesses an 18th-century cathedral, rebuilt following extensive damage in World War II; its university was founded in 1919. An important industrial and commercial centre, its manufactures include railway rolling stock, chemicals, and glass. Population (1982): 563 000.

Poznań Riots (1956) Labour disturbances in Poland. They began when workers at a steel plant in Poznań staged a strike to protest against the country's political restrictions and economic problems. The ensuing riots were ruthlessly suppressed, with the death of 53 people, but they forced the appointment of a reformist leader, Władysław Gomułka.

Pozsony. *See* Bratislava.

Pozzuoli (Greek name: Puteoli) 40 49N 14 07E A port in S Italy, in Campania on the Gulf of Pozzuoli. It is in an area of intense volcanic activity and the local volcanic ash is used to produce cement. Population (1981 est): 71 664.

Prado An art gallery in the Prado Avenue, Madrid. Designed originally as a natural-history museum by the neoclassical architect Juan de Villanueva (1739-1811), the art gallery was founded in 1818 by Ferdinand VII. Most of its collection consists of paintings collected by the Spanish monarchs from the 16th century onwards. Its works by *Velázquez, *Goya, *El Greco, *Titian, and *Bosch are among the finest in the world.

Praesepe An open *star cluster in the constellation Cancer, just visible to the naked eye.

praetor In ancient Rome, originally a consul as leader of an army and subsequently a magistrate responsible for the administration of justice. From about 242 BC a second

praetor assisted with lawsuits involving foreigners. Later more praetors were appointed to administer the increasing number of provinces and numbered 18 under Emperor Nerva (96-98 AD).

Praetorian Guard The official bodyguard of the Roman emperors created by Augustus in 27 BC. Composed of up to 16 long-serving cohorts (infantry divisions) each of 500-1000 men, and stationed as a single unit in Rome, the Guard and its commanders developed great political influence; as senatorial power diminished emperors came to rely upon Praetorian support for election and in later imperial times the emperor's position and even his life depended on the Guard's favour.

Praetorius, Michael (M. Schultheiss; 1571-1621) German composer. He studied the organ, worked in the service of Julius Heinrich, Duke of Brunswick (1564-1613), and was kapellmeister in Wolfsbüttel (1612-21). He composed a large number of motets, hymns, madrigals, and dance pieces, as well as writing *Syntagma musicum* (1615-20), a valuable account of the musical theory and instruments of the time.

pragmatic sanction A royal edict establishing a fundamental principle of government. Historically the term is usually applied to the edict of Emperor Charles VI (1713) settling the succession to his Austrian territories in his daughter Maria Theresa. Disregard of this edict by European powers provoked the War of the *Austrian Succession (1740-48). The Edict of Bourges, issued by Charles VII of France in 1438 and limiting papal authority over the French Church, was also a pragmatic sanction.

pragmatism A philosophical movement initiated by William James (*see* James, Henry) and C. S. *Peirce in the USA. It asserts that the truth of a theory can be judged only by its practical consequences, so the question is: what difference would it make if it were true? The comprehensive metaphysical schemes of European philosophers were thus found to have no meaning, since their truth or falsity did not affect human experience. In science, a theory was true if it "worked"—if its expected consequences occurred. In ethics and theology a principle or belief was true if it satisfied its holders. *See also* Dewey, John.

Prague (Czech name: Praha) 50 8N 14 25E The capital of Czechoslovakia, in the centre of the country on the River Vltava. The industrial and commercial centre of □Czechoslovakia, its various manufactures include machinery, cars, aircraft, food processing, clothing, and chemicals. A leading cultural centre, Prague possesses Charles University (1348) and a technical university (1707). Notable buildings include Hradčany Castle and the mainly gothic Cathedral of St Vitus. *History*: in the middle ages it was the seat of the Přemyslid kings of Bohemia. Following rivalry between the Czechs and Germans, it became the centre of the religious reform movement of Jan *Hus. Under Habsburg rule from the 16th century, it was made the capital of newly independent Czechoslovakia in 1918. In 1968 the city was occupied by Soviet troops following Soviet opposition to the liberal Dubček government. Population (1980 est): 1 193 000.

Prague School A group of language scholars based in Prague during the 1920s and 1930s, including N. S. Trubetskoy (1890-1938) and Roman Jakobson (1896-). Their work was chiefly in the field of Saussurean structural *linguistics. They originated aspects of modern phonological theory, drew sociolinguistic distinctions between various aspects of language use (for example, between everyday and poetic language), and devised the concept of analysing both speech sounds and word meanings into ultimate components transcending individual languages.

prairie dog A large *ground squirrel, *Cynomys ludovicanis*, of North America, also called black-tailed prairie marmot. Heavily built animals, about 30 cm long, prairie dogs live in large colonies called "towns." They feed on grass and have been treated as pests by cattle ranchers. Prairie dogs raise a rim of soil round their burrows so that the surface water will not enter. □mammal.

Prairie Provinces The Canadian provinces of *Alberta, *Manitoba, and *Saskatchewan. They lie chiefly in the Great Plains and are major producers of wheat and oil.

prairies The extensive grasslands of the interior of North America. They occupy a broad N-S belt extending from Alberta and Saskatchewan through the Midwest into Texas, reaching as far W as the Rocky Mountains. Little of the original true prairie now remains, having been extensively ploughed for wheat production. *See also* steppes.

prairie wolf. *See* coyote.

Prakrit Ancient *Indo-Aryan languages of N India, which were considerably simpler than the standard written form of *Sanskrit. From these spoken forms are derived a number of literary styles and the modern languages of N India. *Pali, the language of the Jain scriptures, is included among the Prakrits.

Prandtl, Ludwig (1875-1953) German physicist, whose discovery of the boundary layer adjoining the surface of a solid over which a fluid flows led to the foundation of aerodynamics. His major studies were on the effects of streamlining and the properties of aircraft wings. He also made important improvements to such constructions as wind tunnels and his name is remembered in the **Prandtl number**, a dimensionless group used in the study of convection.

Prasad, Rajendra (1884-1963) Indian statesman; the first president of India (1950-1962). He gave up his legal practice to join *Gandhi's movement of noncooperation with the British and was several times president of the *Indian National Congress (1934, 1939, 1947-48). He helped draft the new Indian constitution.

praseodymium (Pr) A *lanthanide element, which was separated from its mixture with neodyminium by von Welsbach in 1885. It forms trihalides (for example $PrCl_3$) and an oxide (Pr_2O_3), which is used to give a strong yellow colour to glass. At no 59; at wt 140.9077; mp 931°C; bp 3512°C.

pratincole A bird belonging to an Old World subfamily (*Glareolinae*; 6 species). 17-22 cm long, pratincoles have a forked tail, long pointed wings, and a small bill with a wide gape for catching insects. The common pratincole (*Glareola pratincola*) has red-brown underwings and a yellow throat outlined by a black band. Family: *Glareolidae* (pratincoles and coursers); order: *Charadriiformes* (gulls, plovers, etc.).

Prato (*or* Prato in Toscana) 43 53N 11 06E A city in central Italy, in Tuscany on the River Bisenzio. It has a cathedral (dating from the 12th century) and is an important centre of the woollen industry. Population (1980 est): 159 099.

prawn A large shrimplike *crustacean (up to 20 cm long), belonging to the suborder *Natantia*. The antennae are longer than the body and a forward projection of the carapace forms a spike (rostrum) between the eyes, bearing six or more teeth. The second pair of appendages are enlarged to form pincers (*compare* shrimp). The common edible prawn (*Leander serratus*) occurs in temperate coastal waters and is 5-8 cm long. Large shrimps are often mistakenly called prawns.

Praxiteles (mid-4th century BC) Athenian sculptor, renowned for his handling of marble. His statue of Hermes, discovered at *Olympia in 1877, exemplifies the sensuous grace and repose for which his work was noted. Most of his statues have perished, but some, such as the famous Aphrodite of Cnidos, are known from Roman copies.

Precambrian Geological time from the formation of the earth's crust, about 4500 million years ago, to about 590 million years ago when the Palaeozoic era began. Precambrian rocks lie below the Cambrian system and fossils are rare and often obscure. The rocks have been subjected to much alteration because of their great age. Most are

metamorphosed and have undergone one or more Precambrian mountain-building periods as well as later ones. The largest areas of exposed Precambrian rocks are the *shield areas. Correlation of successive strata is done where possible by radioactive *dating. *See also* Cryptozoic time.

precession The rotation about an axis of a line that is itself the axis of a rotating body. The effect may be observed in a spinning top, of which the axis of rotation is initially vertical but, as the top slows down, begins to precess about its original position. *See also* precession of the equinoxes.

precession of the equinoxes The gradual westward motion of the *equinoxes around the *ecliptic in a period of about 25 800 years. It is caused by the *precession of the earth's axis of rotation, which results mainly from the gravitational pull of the sun and moon on the equatorial bulge of the nonspherical earth. As the axis precesses, slowly tracing out a cone in the sky, the celestial equator (lying in a plane perpendicular to the axis) moves relative to the ecliptic. The points of intersection, i.e. the equinoxes, thus continuously change.

predestination In Christian doctrine, God's foreordaining of salvation for certain people. The idea is explicitly propagated by St *Paul in the Epistles. It raises enormous problems about the nature of divine justice and the role of the human will and endeavours, problems that Christian philosophers have never satisfactorily solved. St *Augustine of Hippo, *Origen, and St Thomas *Aquinas were among those who produced influential approaches to the difficulties. An extreme form of predestination was integral to *Calvinism, with salvation for the elect and eternal damnation for everyone else, whatever their virtues or faults. Modern thinking on the subject tends to stress the universality of God's will to save mankind.

prefect A high-ranking French government official. Created in 1800 by Napoleon's reorganization of provincial government, prefects are responsible for general administration, public law and order, and the enforcement of central government policies in their own departments. Although dependence on the government in power and a centralized bureaucracy weakens their position, prefects still have considerable civil authority.

preference shares Shares that entitle their holders to prior rights over ordinary shareholders to *dividends and to capital repayment in the event of liquidation. They do not usually carry voting rights and the dividend is fixed (usually stated as a percentage rate of interest), although a participating preference shareholder receives in addition a share of any excess profits with ordinary shareholders. A cumulative preference shareholder is entitled to arrears of interest out of current profits before ordinary shareholders receive dividends.

pregnancy The period during which a fetus develops within the womb, usually lasting for about 280 days from conception to delivery of the baby. Pregnancy is signalled by cessation of the menstrual periods, tenderness and discomfort in the breasts, and—sometimes—an increase in appetite, nausea, and vomiting. These changes are brought about by the activity of hormones secreted by the *corpus luteum (in the ovary) and *placenta. In the early weeks pregnancy can be definitely diagnosed only by means of pregnancy tests. A commonly used test is based on the detection of the hormone chorionic *gonadotrophin in the urine. *See also* childbirth; prenatal diagnosis.

Pregnancy in animals is usually called gestation, and the period varies between species. In elephants, for instance, it is 18 months and in rats 3 weeks.

Preminger, Otto (Ludwig) (1906-86) US film director, born in Austria. He went to the USA in 1935 and became a naturalized citizen in 1943. His films range from literary adaptations to large-scale epics and include *Laura* (1944), *Anatomy of a Murder* (1959), and *Exodus* (1960).

premiss One of the statements in an argument or chain of reasoning from which the conclusion follows or is said to follow. For example from the premisses "only dogs bark" and "Fido barks," the conclusion is that "Fido is a dog."

premium bond A UK government *security, held in numbered units of one pound, the interest on which is put into a fund and allocated to bond holders by a monthly lottery, as tax-free prizes. The numbers of winning bonds are selected by Electronic Random Number Indicator Equipment (ERNIE). Premium bonds were introduced in 1956.

Premonstratensians A Roman Catholic order of monks, also called Norbertines after St Norbert (c. 1080–1134), who founded them in 1120 at Prémontré (N France). They originally followed an austere rule, which included total abstinence from meat. The order spread all over Europe but was nearly annihilated during the French Revolution. Belgium is now its main base.

prenatal diagnosis Tests made on pregnant women in order to diagnose genetic or developmental abnormalities in the developing fetus. If the tests reveal severe malformation or gross malfunctioning in the fetus the possibility of an *abortion is considered. The investigations include X-rays, scanning using ultrasonic rays, *amniocentesis (involving analysis of a sample of the amniotic fluid surrounding the fetus), and fetoscopy, in which a sample of fetal blood is withdrawn from the placenta and examined for abnormal cells (indicating blood disorders, such as *thalassaemia). Some of the techniques may involve risks to the health of the mother or fetus and are not undertaken without good cause.

Pre-Raphaelite Brotherhood A group including the British painters Dante Gabriel *Rossetti, John Everett *Millais, and William Holman *Hunt, who joined together in 1848 in reaction to the banality of contemporary British painting and its enthusiasm for *Raphael. Signing all their works PRB, they sought to emulate Italian painters earlier than Raphael and to paint subjects of a moral or religious character, many of their subjects being drawn from medieval literature. Although initially attacked for their naturalism, particularly in religious subjects, by 1851 the PRB had won the support of the art critic John *Ruskin. Although the group disbanded soon afterwards (Hunt being the only member to remain faithful to PRB ideas), the PRB had a strong influence on such artists as William *Morris and Edward *Burne-Jones, as well as subsequent painting styles.

presbyopia. *See* longsightedness.

Presbyterianism A Protestant church organization based on government by elders (*compare* episcopacy). These elders comprise the ministers and certain laymen from each congregation and all have equal rank; they enforce a strict code of ethics and determine Church policy through a hierarchical system of presbyteries, synods, and general assemblies. Presbyterianism originated with the 16th-century followers of *Calvin who believed that they were returning to a system of the primitive Church. In Scotland the tenets of Presbyterianism were formulated (1560) by *Knox and it became the established church in 1696. A pan-Presbyterian alliance (founded 1875) embraces the Presbyterian Churches in the UK, the USA, and elsewhere.

Prescott, William Hickling (1796–1859) US historian. Prescott established his reputation with a major work, *The History of the Reign of Ferdinand and Isabella* (1837). There followed *The Conquest of Mexico* (1843), *The Conquest of Peru* (1847), and *The History of Philip II* (1855–58). Although his critical insight was not outstanding, Prescott combined factual accuracy with a vivid narrative style. His discursive memory compensated for his partial blindness.

present value The current net value of an investment project, used to compare the net benefits and costs of investment projects, taking into account the rate of interest, to decide which will be the best to back. The present value is equal to the sum of the benefits in each year of the project, less the costs in each year, discounted back to the present time using the market rate of interest. If the present value is positive, the project will earn more than if the money were lent to a savings institution. By establishing present values of different projects, investors can ensure that projects that show a quick return will not necessarily be preferred to projects showing a larger return at a later date.

president In most republics, the executive head of state. In the USA the president is the head of the executive branch of government, which was established together with the legislature (*see* Congress) and the judiciary (*see* Supreme Court) by the US constitution (1789). In modern times a member of the *Democratic Party or the *Republican Party, he is elected every four years; no one may hold the office for more than eight years. The president is head of the *cabinet. In some other countries (e.g. Germany and Italy) the president fulfils the nonexecutive function of a monarch.

ELVIS PRESLEY *In a scene from* Girl Happy *(1965).*

Presley, Elvis (Aaron) (1935–77) US popular singer, whose first big hit, "Heartbreak Hotel" (1956), was followed by "Hound Dog" and "Don't Be Cruel." His suggestive performances earned him the nickname "Elvis the Pelvis." Presley also appeared in numerous films and television programmes. After his death, probably due to drug dependence, he became a cult figure.

Presocratics Greek philosophers who lived in Ionia and S Italy (Magna Graecia) during the 6th and early 5th centuries BC, before the time of *Socrates. They were responsible for the earliest philosophical—as opposed to magical and religious—speculation about the universe. The Ionians were *Thales, *Anaximander, and *Anaximenes, all of Miletus, *Xenophanes of Colophon, and *Heraclitus of Ephesus. Notable figures in Italy were *Parmenides and *Zeno, both of Elea (*see* Eleatics), and *Pythagoras.

Pressburg. *See* Bratislava.

Pressburg, Treaties of 1. (1491) The treaty in which Maximilian, Habsburg heir to the Holy Roman Empire, recognized Vladislav II of Bohemia (1456–1516) as King of Hungary, renouncing his own claim in return for Austria, Styria, and Carinthia, which had been annexed by Matthias I Corvinus in 1486. 2. (1805) The treaty between Austria and France following Napoleon's defeat of Austria at Austerlitz. Austria surrendered territory and paid a large indemnity.

Press Council An organization founded in 1953 to defend

the freedom of the press. Funded by newspapers and journalistic bodies, it comprises 18 professional and 18 nonprofessional members and an independent chairman. Among other activities, it considers complaints against newspapers and periodicals. Chairman: Sir Zelman Cowen.

press gang A band of men employed to force paupers, vagabonds, or criminals into the army or navy. This system of impressment (recruits were paid imprest money), common throughout the world in the 18th century, ceased when improved pay and conditions in the army and navy increased voluntary recruitment.

pressure Force per unit area. For a liquid, density d, the pressure at a depth h is hdg, where g is the *acceleration of free fall. Pressure is usually measured in pascals, millimetres of mercury, or millibars.

pressure gauge An instrument for measuring the pressure of a fluid. Atmospheric pressure is measured with a mercury *barometer or an aneroid barometer. Pressures above atmospheric pressure are usually measured with a Bourdon gauge, which consists of a flattened curved tube that tends to straighten under pressure. As it straightens it moves a pointer round a scale. Low pressures are measured with such vacuum gauges as the *McLeod gauge or *Pirani gauge.

Prestel. *See* viewdata.

Prester John A legendary Christian priest king. First mentioned in 12th-century chronicles, he became famous as the hero destined to help the Crusaders against Islam. He was sometimes identified as a Chinese prince but more commonly as the King of Ethiopia.

Preston 53 46N 2 42W A town and port in NW England, the administrative centre of Lancashire on the River Ribble. It was the site of a major battle in the *Civil War. Situated at the heart of Central Lancashire New Town, it has plastics, chemical, motor-vehicle and aircraft construction, and electronics industries as well as the traditional cotton and engineering works. Population (1981): 143 734.

Prestonpans 55 57N 3 00W A town in E central Scotland, in Lothian Region on the Firth of Forth. It owes its fame to the defeat here of the English by Bonnie Prince Charlie in 1745. Population (1981): 7620.

Prestwick 55 30N 4 37W A town and resort in SW Scotland, in Strathclyde Region on the Firth of Clyde. It has an international airport and a famous golf course. Population (1985): 13 532.

Pretender, Old. *See* James Edward Stuart, the Old Pretender.

Pretender, Young. *See* Charles Edward Stuart, the Young Pretender.

Pretoria 25 36S 28 12E The administrative capital of South Africa and the capital of the Transvaal. Founded in 1855, it became the capital of the Union of South Africa in 1910. The University of South Africa was founded here in 1873; other important institutions are the University of Pretoria (1930) and the Onderstepoort Veterinary Research Institute. Pretoria is noted for its jacaranda-lined avenues and Voortrekker monument. Its industries include iron and steel processing, engineering, and food processing. Population (1980 est): 528 407.

Pretoria Convention (1881) The peace treaty between Britain and the Transvaal that ended the first *Boer War. The Transvaal acquired self-government under the British Crown, which, however, retained control of foreign relations and the power to veto legislation regarding Africans.

Pretorius, Andries (Wilhelmus Jacobus) (1799–1853) Afrikaner leader in the *Great Trek to Natal and then in the Transvaal. He defeated (1840) the Zulu King Dingane and fought the British in Natal (1842) and then in the Transvaal (1848), establishing Transvaal's independence as the South African Republic (1852). The city of Pretoria is named after him. His son **Marthinus Wessel Pretorius** (1819–1901) was president of the South African Republic (formerly and subsequently

the Transvaal) from 1857 to 1871 and of the Orange Free State from 1859 to 1863. He returned to politics after Britain's annexation of the Transvaal, finally retiring after Afrikaner victory in the first *Boer War (1880–81).

Prévert, Jacques (1900–77) French poet. He was associated with the surrealist movement in the 1920s. His best-known poems about the street life of Paris, written with anarchic humour, are collected in *Paroles* (1946); later volumes include *Spectacle* (1951) and *Hebromadaires* (1972). He also wrote film scripts, notably for *Les Enfants du paradis* (1944).

Previn, André (Andreas Ludwig Priwin; 1929–) German-born conductor, pianist, and composer. He took US citizenship in 1943. Active in Hollywood in his youth as a film composer and jazz pianist, he was subsequently conductor of the London Symphony Orchestra (1969–79) and conductor of the Pittsburgh Symphony Orchestra (1976–). He was musical director of the Royal Philharmonic Orchestra (1984–86) and continues as its principal conductor.

Prévost d'Exiles, Antoine François, Abbé (1697–1763) French novelist. His unsettled career included periods of military service, of religious retreat as a Benedictine monk, and of exile in England and Holland. Of his many novels and translations, mostly written to pay off debts, the best known is *Manon Lescaut* (1731), the story of a young nobleman ruined by his love for a courtesan, which was used by both Massenet and Puccini as the basis for operas.

Priam In Greek legend, the last king of Troy, husband of Hecuba. As an old man he witnessed the deaths of many of his 50 sons in the *Trojan War and he pleaded with Achilles for the body of Hector. He was killed at the altar of Zeus by Neoptelemus.

Priapus A Greek fertility god associated with gardens, son of Dionysus and Aphrodite. He was usually portrayed as a comic ugly figure with an enormous phallus. The donkey, symbol of lust, was sacrificed to him.

Pribilof Islands Four US islands in the Bering Sea. They are the breeding ground of the northern fur seal. Since 1911 the seals have been protected by agreements between the USA, the Soviet Union, Japan, and Canada. Area: about 168 sq km (65 sq mi).

price index A single figure used to measure the average percentage change in the price of a set of goods over a period of time, taking a base figure of 100 for a specified year. Thus if a particular price index, in January, 1990, stands at 156 (January, 1985 = 100), there has been a 56% increase in the average prices over the five-year period. The best-known indexes are the Wholesale Price Index and the Retail Price Index, the latter providing a reliable guide to the *cost of living. Some wages, salaries, and costs are **index-linked** (i.e. increase in proportion to a specified price index) to cover the devaluation of money as a result of *inflation. **Indexation** is commonly used in agreements that extend over a long period during which inflation is expected to be a significant factor.

prices and incomes policy A policy designed to hold down prices and incomes in an attempt to stem *inflation. The policy's chances of success depend on the prime causes of the inflation. Only if inflation is caused by the pressure of costs does a prices and incomes policy have a fair chance of success. The chief drawback of such a policy is that it distorts markets by suppressing the gradual movement of prices and wages in response to *supply and demand. There are also great problems of enforcement, especially in controlling incomes. If legal enforcement of the policy is attempted and fails, the law is brought into disrepute.

prickly heat A disorder that occurs most commonly in the tropics due to obstruction of the ducts of the sweat glands. It causes itching and a red rash and often leads to secondary infection.

prickly pear A *cactus of the genus *Opuntia*, native to

North and South America and sometimes cultivated for food or ornament. Introduced to Australia and South Africa, it has become a troublesome weed. It has flat jointed spiny stems bearing large orange or yellow flowers, which give rise to edible pear-shaped fruits. The seeds are used to produce an oil and the shoots are eaten as vegetables or used as animal feed.

prickly poppy A plant of the genus *Argemone*, especially *A. mexicana*, also called devil's fig, native to North America and the West Indies and cultivated as a garden ornamental. Growing 30-90 cm tall, its blue-green bristly stems bear spiny lobed leaves and orange or pale-yellow flowers, with five pointed petals Family: *Papaveraceae*.

Pride, Thomas (d. 1658) English parliamentary soldier during the Civil War, famous for effecting "Pride's Purge" of parliament in 1648. He excluded over a hundred Presbyterian MPs suspected of wanting to treat with Charles I, leaving the Rump of the *Long Parliament. He was a signatory of Charles' death warrant.

Priestley, J(ohn) B(oynton) (1894-1984) British novelist and dramatist. He first won popular success with his picaresque novel *The Good Companions* (1929). His plays include *Dangerous Corner* (1932), *Laburnum Grove* (1933), *An Inspector Calls* (1946), and several mildly experimental expressionist dramas, including *The Glass Cage* (1957). A traditionalist by temperament and conviction, he published many volumes of criticism and memoirs and was a popular broadcaster during World War II.

Priestley, Joseph (1733-1804) British chemist and one of the discoverers of oxygen (together with Carl *Scheele). Priestley, being a firm believer in the *phlogiston theory, named his gas dephlogisticated air and first prepared it in 1774 by heating mercuric oxide. In 1778-79 *Lavoisier demolished the phlogiston theory and named the gas oxygen. Priestley also produced and studied several other gases, including ammonia, sulphur dioxide, and hydrogen chloride. He invented the method of collecting them over mercury, since some of these gases dissolved in water. Priestley was a Presbyterian minister and strongly influenced Unitarianism. He held unpopular views, being a supporter of Revolutionary France. In 1794, no longer feeling safe in Britain, he left for America where he spent the rest of his life.

priest's hole A secret room, found in some English country houses, where Roman Catholic priests were hidden to escape persecution under Elizabeth I.

primary colours The minimum number of *colours that, when mixed in the correct proportions, are capable of giving all the other colours in the visible spectrum. When light of three **primary additive colours** (usually red, green, and blue) is mixed in equal intensities, white light results. This principle is used in colour television and *colour photography. Any particular colour can also be obtained by subtracting from white light a mixture of three **primary subtractive colours**, usually cyan (blue-green), magenta (purplish red), and yellow, which are complementary to red, green, and blue. Adding pigments of these in equal proportions gives black pigment.

primary education The education of children between the ages of 5 and 11. Primary education was introduced in England and Wales as a result of the Education Act (1944), to replace elementary education. Primary schools were originally divided into infant and junior sections, the transfer taking place around seven years of age, but the Education Act (1964) enabled local authorities to vary the age at which the break took place and to create "middle schools" between primary and secondary, with an age range from 8 to 14.

primate A mammal belonging to the order *Primates* (about 195 species), which includes *prosimians, *monkeys, *apes, and man. Primates probably evolved from insectivorous climbing creatures like *tree shrews and have many adaptations for climbing, including five fingers and five toes

with opposable first digits (except in the hind feet of man). They have well-developed sight and hearing and—most importantly—enlarged cerebral hemispheres of the brain, most marked in higher primates. Most forms are arboreal but the great apes and man are largely terrestrial.

prime minister A head of government. In the UK the post developed in the 18th century with the growth of the *cabinet. Sir Robert *Walpole is generally regarded as the first prime minister (1721-42) but the post was not formally recognized until 1905. The prime minister is customarily a member of the House of Commons and is head of government by virtue of being the leader of the dominant political party in the Commons. The monarch makes all governmental appointments on the advice of the prime minister, who receives a salary of £30,304 (1984).

prime number An integer greater than one that has no integral factors except itself and one; for example 2, 3, 5, 7, 11, 13, 17. Every natural number can be expressed uniquely as a product of prime numbers; for example $1260 = 2^2 \times 3^2 \times 5 \times 7$. Prime numbers are of major interest in number theory.

primitivism In art, the style of untrained artists who ignore or are ignorant of both traditional aesthetic standards and avantgarde trends. Its chief characteristics are meticulous detail, brilliant colours, childlike representation, and faulty perspective. Among the first primitives were 17th- and 18th-century American painters who developed in cultural isolation from European artistic trends, but the best known is the French painter Henri *Rousseau. Recent primitives include the Yugoslav peasants Ivan Generalič (1914-) and Mijo Kovačič (1935-) and the American Grandma *Moses. The term is also sometimes applied to African and Polynesian indigenous art.

Primo de Rivera, Miguel (1870-1930) Spanish general, who led a successful coup on 13 September, 1923, and was dictator of Spain until 1930. He brought the Moroccan War to a victorious end (1927) but dissatisfaction with his absolute rule, exacerbated by the Depression, caused his downfall. *Alfonso XIII's support of Primo de Rivera discredited the monarchy, which was overthrown a year later. His son **José Antonio Primo de Rivera** (1903-36) founded the Falange, the Spanish fascist party. Executed by the Republic shortly after the start of the Spanish Civil War, his memory was honoured by Franco's National Movement.

primrose A perennial herbaceous plant, *Primula vulgaris*, growing in woodlands and hedge banks in Europe and N Africa. It has a basal rosette of puckered spoon-shaped leaves, with solitary pale-yellow flowers on slender stalks, up to 10 cm high. Bird's-eye primrose (*P. farinosa*) has pale-purple flowers with yellow centres. Family: *Primulaceae*. *See also* evening primrose.

Primula A genus of perennial plants (about 500 species), native mainly to N temperate regions and often grown as ornamentals. They have a basal rosette of oval to spoon-shaped leaves and erect flower stalks bearing erect or nodding five-petalled flowers, red, pink, purple, blue, white, or yellow in colour and usually with a different coloured centre. The fruit is a capsule. The genus also includes the *cowslip and *primrose. Family: *Primulaceae*. *See also* auricula.

Prince Edward Island An island province of E Canada, in the S Gulf of St Lawrence. Its gentle rolling hills and mild climate support small farms producing potatoes, grains, dairy cattle, and other livestock. Tourism and fishing are also important. *History*: discovered (1534) and colonized (1720) by France, the island was captured (1758) and resettled by Britain. In 1873 it joined Canada. Area: 5657 sq km (2184 sq mi). Population (1981): 122 506. Capital: Charlottetown.

Prince of Wales A title customarily conferred on the

eldest son of the British sovereign. It was a native Welsh title until 1301, when Edward I, following his annexation of Wales, bestowed it on his son, the future Edward II. The present holder of the title is Prince *Charles.

Prince Rupert 54 09N 130 20W A city and port in W Canada, in British Columbia at the head of Dixon Entrance on the Pacific Ocean. Founded as the terminus of a transcontinental railway (1906), it is an ice-free deepwater port. Forestry, pulp and paper, and fishing are also economically important. Population (1983): 16 786.

Princess Royal A title sometimes conferred on the eldest daughter of the sovereign. In 1932, Princess Mary (1897–1965), the daughter of George V, became the Princess Royal.

Princeton 40 21N 74 40W A town in the USA, in New Jersey. George Washington defeated the British here on 3 January, 1777. It is the site of Princeton University (1746) and the Rockefeller Institute for Scientific Research. Population (1980): 12|035.

Princeton University One of the oldest universities in the USA (founded 1746), situated at Princeton, New Jersey. Women were first admitted to the university in 1969.

princewood A dark wood with lighter veins, obtained from two tropical trees found in the West Indies, *Hamelia ventricosa*, also called Spanish elm (family *Rubiaceae*), and *Cordia gerascanthoides* (family *Ehretiaceae*). It is used for furniture, doors, boats, etc.

Príncipe Island. *See* São Tomé and Príncipe.

printed circuit An electronic circuit in which the connections between components are formed by a pattern of conducting film on a board, instead of by wires. The method greatly facilitates mass-production. An insulating board is coated with a conducting material, such as copper, and a protective pattern is deposited on it using photographic techniques. The unprotected metal is then etched away and components are soldered in place. In television receivers, the replacement of thermionic valves by plug-in printed-circuit boards has made maintenance easier. A faulty circuit board can be quickly replaced without tracing the individual failed component.

printing The production of multiple copies of text or pictures, usually on paper. The oldest method, in use in China and Japan before 800 AD, is **letterpress**, in which the raised surfaces of etched, engraved, or cast material are inked and pressed onto the paper. This method was revolutionized by the invention of movable type (*see* typesetting) in the 15th century, but printing itself remained fundamentally unchanged for four centuries until other methods of mechanization were introduced. Early printing presses were of the hand-operated platen variety in which the type stands on a horizontal surface and the paper is pressed onto it from above. Faster production became possible on the power-driven presses of the 19th century: first the cylinder press, in which the paper is rolled by a cylinder over a flat printing surface, and later the rotary press, in which the printing surface is also a cylinder. Different types of rotary press print either on separate sheets or on a web (*see* paper), which makes for still faster printing—up to 35 000 impressions per hour.

In **lithography**, a method invented by Aloys *Senefelder in 1798, the printing surface is plane (originally a polished stone but now usually an aluminium sheet), the printing and nonprinting areas being made grease-receptive and grease-repellent respectively (*see* platemaking). Greasy ink is rolled over the entire area but is taken only by the grease-receptive areas; the ink is then transferred by rolling onto the paper. **Offset printing**, most commonly lithography, involves an intermediate rubber-covered cylinder that transfers the ink from plate to paper. In **gravure printing**, the small square etched holes (cells) in the copper printing plate are filled with a free-flowing ink, the rest of the plate is wiped clean, and the plate is rolled against the paper, which absorbs the ink out of the cells. Nearly all gravure and offset lithography is done on rotary presses.

Letterpress and offset lithography are used for almost all types of printing job; because of the expensive copper plates gravure is limited to long runs, such as cheap illustrated magazines, postage stamps, and packaging. Direct lithography has been used almost exclusively by artists—*Goya

letterpress   **lithography**   **gravure**

platen letterpress

cylinder letterpress

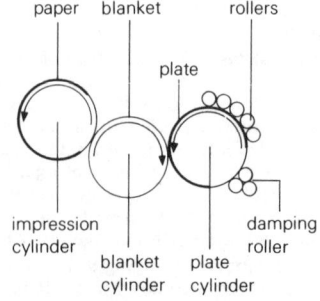

rotary offset lithography

PRINTING   *Principles of three major printing processes and the three major designs of printing press.*

and *Manet, for example—and was the principal medium for *poster art in the 19th century. **Flexography** is a widespread form of (usually rotary) letterpress printing using fluid volatile ink and a rubber printing surface. It is used for paperback books, packaging materials, and for printing on nonabsorbent surfaces, such as plastic foil. In **silk-screen printing** (screen-process printing *or* serigraphy), a piece of taut open-weave silk, metal, or synthetic fabric carries the negative of the desired image in an impervious substance, such as glue; ink is forced through the clear (printing) areas by a squeegee onto the paper, glass, fabric, or other material, behind. It is used for printing posters, electronic circuit boards, labelling on bottles, and anything that requires a thick layer of ink or other material. For example pop artists, such as Andy *Warhol, use it to make painted photographic transfers. **Collotype** is a method of printing short runs of high-quality illustrations from gelatin plates; it is not widely used but it is the only method by which continuous tone can be reproduced (*see* platemaking).

Full-colour reproduction is achieved by **colour-process printing**, in which all colours can be produced from combinations of three primary colours—yellow, cyan (blue), and magenta. Four separate printing plates are made, one for each primary and one for black; each is printed in succession in exactly the same place. In letterpress and lithography, half-tones are used instead of printing plates (*see* platemaking). At the normal viewing distance for any colour-process printing, the dots are imperceptible.

prion A *petrel belonging to a genus (*Pachyptila*; 4 species) found in Antarctica and nearby islands. 20–27 cm long, prions have a blue-grey plumage with white underparts. The flattened bill has a fringe of strainers with the floor of the mouth forming a small pouch; it feeds by skimming over the sea and straining out small invertebrates.

Prior, Matthew (1664–1721) British poet. He became an MP in 1700 and served as a diplomat in France and Holland. He wrote several long philosophical poems but is best known for his elegant epigrammatic verse collected in *Poems on Several Occasions* (1709).

Pripet, River (Russian name: Pripyat) A river in the W Soviet Union. Rising in NW Ukraine, it flows mainly ENE through the Belorussian SSR and joins the River Dnepr near Kiev. Extensive fighting in World War II occurred in the **Pripet Marshes** along its course. Length: 800 km (500 mi).

Priscian (6th century AD) Latin grammarian, born at Caesarea (now Cherchell, Algeria). He taught at Constantinople and was the last considerable Latin scholar in antiquity. His *Institutiones Grammaticae*, in 18 books, which sum up the researches of all previous grammarians, remained a standard work throughout the middle ages.

prism A piece of glass or other transparent material having parallel polygonal ends, with a number of rectangular surfaces meeting them at right angles. They are used in optical instruments, such as cameras and binoculars, for changing the direction of light, either by refraction or by reflection from its walls. They are also used for splitting light into its component colours by double refraction, once on entering the prism and again on leaving it.

prisoner of war A soldier captured by a belligerent in war. Guerrillas are so categorized provided that they have a commander, wear distinctive clothing, carry arms openly, and obey the laws and customs of war. The rights of a prisoner of war, which are defined in the *Geneva Conventions of 1929 and 1949 and are supervised by the International *Red Cross, include: withholding all information except name, rank, and number; receiving adequate amounts of food, drink, and medical care; engaging in correspondence and receiving parcels; and attempting to escape without being punished for so doing. In addition, prison camps must be open for inspection by the representatives of neutral powers.

prisons Institutions for confining convicted criminals (*see*

criminal law). In primitive societies, and throughout much of history, offenders were either banished, executed, or physically punished; prisons were places in which people were held until these punishments could be carried out. It was not until the 18th century that the main purpose of prisons became custodial. The appalling prison conditions at this time led to the reform movements of John *Howard and Elizabeth *Fry. During the 19th century a massive prison-building programme was carried out in the UK, modelled on Pentonville (1842), the structure of which was based on the principle of solitary confinement. Reforms since the 19th century have changed the emphasis in penal institutions from retribution (the Criminal Justice Act, 1948, abolished hard labour and penal servitude) to correction and rehabilitation. The first "open prison," in which prisoners are permitted some personal freedom, was opened in 1936 and followed Scandinavian models. A further UK building programme was launched in the late 1950s, the most recent prisons consisting of self-contained units with work and leisure facilities. Overcrowding, however, has remained a feature of British prisons since World War II. A series of escapes in the early 1960s led to the Mountbatten Report (1966), with its emphasis on increased security. *See also* community service.

Pritchett, V(ictor) S(awden) (1900–) British short-story writer and critic. He travelled widely in Europe during the 1920s and has written frequently about Spain. He has published critical works, volumes of stories including *Collected Stories* (1982), and two much acclaimed autobiographical books, *A Cab at the Door* (1968) and *Midnight Oil* (1971).

private enterprise. *See* capitalism.

privateering The practice of permitting, under government licence, private individuals to equip ships to attack and capture enemy merchantmen. Such action constituted piracy without the privateers' official authorization—"letters of marque." Although a useful complement to regular navies and common during the 17th and 18th centuries, privateering frequently degenerated into piracy because these formalities were disregarded; all European countries, except Spain, renounced privateering in 1856. *See also* buccaneers.

private medical insurance *Insurance against the cost of illness, provided by an insurance company or association rather than a government. In some countries, such as the UK, private insurance schemes and public insurance schemes exist side by side, the citizen being free to pay extra to join a private scheme to enable him to choose his own consultant, to have a private room in a hospital, and to avoid waiting for nonurgent treatment. In the USA, where no comprehensive government scheme of medical insurance exists, private medical insurance is widely used.

privatization The sale of a public corporation to the private sector. Margaret *Thatcher's Conservative government in the 1980s sold its interests in British Aerospace, Britoil, British Telecom, British Gas, and British Airways, etc., to private investors in order to increase the efficiency of these organizations and to increase the number of shareholders in the community. *See* nationalization.

privet An evergreen or deciduous shrub or small tree of the genus *Ligustrum* (40–50 species), native to Eurasia and Australia and widely used for ornamental hedges, especially the European common privet (*L. vulgare*). Growing up to about 5 m high, it has simple oval leaves and terminal clusters of small creamy four-lobed flowers, which give rise to black berries. Family: *Oleaceae*.

Privy Council A body advising the British monarch, now having chiefly formal functions. It grew out of the Curia Regis (King's Court), forming a distinct group of royal advisers in the 14th century. The emergence of the *cabinet system of government in the 18th century led to a lessening of its power. By convention, it consists of all cabinet ministers, the Archbishops · of both Canterbury and York, the speaker of the House of Commons, and a number of senior British and Commonwealth statesmen, who are all addressed as the Right Honourable. It is presided over by the Lord President of the Council.

probability The mathematical concept concerned with the effects of chance on an event, experiment, or observation. It originated in 1654, when the mathematicians *Pascal and *Fermat worked on problems sent to them by a gambler.

If an event can occur in n ways and r is the number of ways it can occur in a specified way, then the **mathematical probability** of it occurring in the specified way is r/n. For example, the probability of the number 5 coming up on a six-faced dice in one throw is 1/6. The probability of a 5 coming up x times in x throws is obtained by multiplication, i.e. it is $(1/6)^x$. Probabilities are expressed as numbers between 1 (a certainty) and 0 (an impossibility).

If in a number of experiments an event has occurred n times and failed m times, the **empirical probability** of success in the next trial is $n/(n + m)$. Actuarial tables of life expectancy are based on empirical probabilities.

probation In English law, a court order, given instead of a sentence, requiring an offender of or over 17 years of age to be under the supervision and to comply with the directions of a probation officer for between 1 and 3 years. The offender's consent is needed. Failure to comply with the order makes the offender liable to be sentenced for the original offence.

proboscis monkey A large leaf-eating *Old World monkey, *Nasalis larvatus*, of Borneo. Up to 1.5 m tall, proboscis monkeys have a protruding nose and live in groups in forests, feeding on young palm leaves. They can swim as well as climb.

processionary caterpillar The caterpillar of a moth of Old World genus *Thaumetopoea*. The caterpillars move in columns, guided by a leader, keeping head and tail contact with each other. Resting in nests by day, they feed at night and can be very destructive.

Proclus (410–85 AD) Neoplatonist philosopher, head of *Plato's Academy at Athens. Indefatigable in commenting on, and explaining, earlier philosophers, Proclus integrated pagan religion, philosophy, and mathematics into a single system. His works, translated into Latin and Arabic, transmitted *Neoplatonism to the medieval world.

Procne. *See* Philomela and Procne.

Proconsul A genus of extinct apes whose remains have been found in E Africa. They lived 20 million years ago and were probably ground-dwellers but could not stand erect. *Proconsul* apes were ancestors of modern apes.

Procopius (6th century AD) Byzantine historian. He accompanied the military commander Belisarius on several campaigns and worked in Constantinople from about 540 AD. His works include histories of the wars and of the public works undertaken during the reign of the Emperor Justinian I.

Procrustes A legendary Greek robber. He tortured his victims by stretching them or cutting off their limbs so that they fitted the exact length of his bed. He was killed by Theseus.

Procyon A conspicuous star, apparent magnitude 0.35 and 11.4 light years distant, that is the brightest star in the constellation Canis Minor and one of the nearest stars to the sun. It is part of a *multiple star, forming a visual *binary star with a *white dwarf.

producer gas A fuel gas containing nitrogen and carbon monoxide, as well as small amounts of hydrogen and hydrocarbons. It is produced by passing air (mixed with a little steam) over incandescent coke. The calorific value is low but heat is also obtained from the heat of reaction. *See also* water gas.

productivity The output of goods and services in a factory, country, etc., in relation to inputs (men, machines, land)

used to produce them. It is difficult to produce a single measure of productivity, but output per manhour can be used as a rough approximation. Increases in productivity are largely responsible for the large increases in output in western economies since World War II; these increases are probably largely due to increased *investment in new machines and the higher levels of education and skill in the workforce. Two causes of low productivity may be distinguished: overmanning, the use of too many men to produce a given level of output, and underproduction, a given number of men producing less output than they should. **Productivity bargaining** is a form of *collective bargaining in which wage increases are agreed subject to a corresponding increase in productivity. Productivity bargains are frequently exempt from the restrictions of prices and incomes policies.

profit sharing Any scheme for sharing the profits of a firm between employees as well as shareholders. The aim is to give employees an interest in the profitability of a firm both as an incentive to productivity and to promote good *industrial relations. Profits may be shared in the form of bonuses or by making employees shareholders.

progesterone A steroid hormone secreted mainly by the *corpus luteum of the mammalian ovary following ovulation. It prepares the womb for implantation of the embryo and maintains this state during pregnancy. Progestogens—synthetic steroids with progesterone-like actions—are constituents of *oral contraceptives; they are also used to treat menstrual disorders. Progesterone preparations have been used in cattle breeding to suspend the oestrous cycle and to enable the mating of the whole herd to be synchronized.

program, computer A series of instructions that controls the operation of a *computer. The programs executed by the computer are in a machine code, which has the form of a series of numbers that the device interprets as either instructions or data. These instructions perform very simple tasks and many thousands are required for all but the most rudimentary programs. Programming languages have been developed that simplify the programmer's task (for example by the use of English words and mathematical symbols), from which the machine code is generated automatically. Low-level languages are those that resemble closely the logic of the machine; high level languages, such as *Basic, *FORTRAN, *COBOL, *ALCOL, and *Pascal, use abstract constructs more suited to human thought and are independent of any particular machine. *See also* software.

programme music Music that is based on a literary, descriptive, or emotional subject, in contrast to **absolute music**, which has no overt associations outside the music itself. Programmatic elements are found in music of almost all periods; one of the first major works of programme music was Vivaldi's set of violin concertos entitled *The Four Seasons* (1725), based on four sonnets by the composer. The development of the *symphonic poem and the concert *overture in the 19th century resulted in such well-known programmatic compositions as Mussorgsky's *Night on a Bare Mountain* (a depiction of a witches' sabbath), Liszt's *Les Préludes* (based on Lamartine's *Méditations poétiques*), and Richard Strauss's *Alpine Symphony* (a description of the ascent and descent of a mountain).

progressive taxation. *See* taxation.

Prohibition (1919–33) A period of "noble experiment," during which the manufacture, sale, and transportation of alcoholic drinks were prohibited in the USA by the 18th Amendment to the constitution. The *temperance movement, which attributed crime and poverty to alcohol, combined with the wartime need to divert grain from distilleries to food manufacture, led to national prohibition. It proved impossible to enforce, not least because prohibition agents were outnumbered by gangsters and others profiting from illicit alcohol, and in 1933 prohibition was repealed by the 21st Amendment. *See* bootlegging.

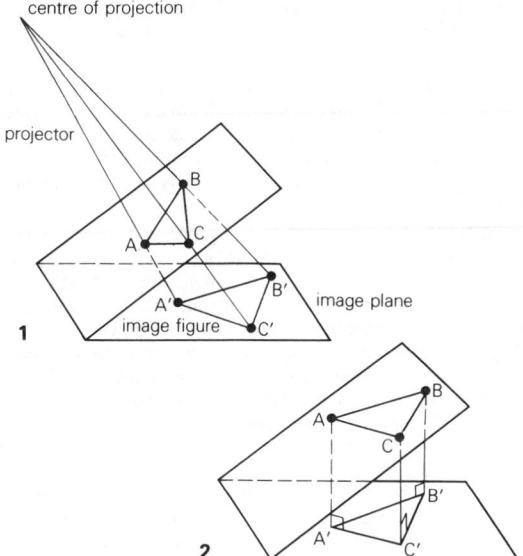

centre of projection

projector

B

C

A

A'

B'

C'

image plane

image figure

1

B

A

C

A'

B'

C'

2

PROJECTION *The mapping of a triangle by* (1) *central and* (2) *orthogonal projections.*

projection (geometry) A mapping of a figure in one plane onto its image in another, called the image plane or plane of projection. A map of the earth's surface is an example of a projection (*see* map projection). The image of each point in the figure is the intersection of a straight line (the projector) and the image plane. In central projection a projector is the straight line drawn through the point and a fixed point (the centre of projection). In orthogonal projection a projector is the perpendicular from the point to the image plane. The set of image points makes up the image figure.

projection (psychology) The process of attributing one's own qualities to other people or things. In *psychoanalysis this is a *defence mechanism; people who cannot tolerate their own emotions may cope by believing that other people have them. In projective tests, such as the *Rorschach test, a person's character is assessed from his descriptions of ambiguous objects.

projector, film A device for viewing photographic transparencies by shining a light through them to produce an enlarged image on a screen. Its principal use is in *cinematography although still pictures are also often viewed on slide projectors, particularly for viewing by a number of people together. Cinema projectors and some home-movie projectors also contain equipment for reproducing sound from the track on the edge of the film.

Prokofiev, Sergei (1891-1953) Soviet composer and pianist. He studied at the St Petersburg conservatoire under Rimsky-Korsakov. He won the Anton Rubinstein Prize in 1914, playing his first piano concerto. He lived abroad from 1918 to 1933 and in 1948 was officially condemned for "undemocratic tendencies" in his music. His work includes seven symphonies (the first of which is the *Classical Symphony*; 1916-17), five piano concertos, two violin concertos, the operas *Love for Three Oranges* (1919) and *War and Peace* (1941; revised 1952), the ballet *Romeo and Juliet* (1935-36), music for the films *Lieutenant Kijé* (1934) and *Alexander Nevsky* (1938), and *Peter and the Wolf* (1936) for speaker and orchestra.

Prokop (*or* Procop; c. 1380-1434) Bohemian priest and leader of the *Hussites. In the 1420s Prokop successfully led the Hussites against the imperial armies detached to destroy them but, after joining the radical (Taborite) Hussites against the moderates (1434), he was killed in the ensuing battle of Lipany.

Prokopyevsk 53 55N 86 45E A city in the S Soviet Union, in the RSFSR. Located in the Kuznetsk Basin, it is an important coalmining centre. Population (1981 est): 267 000.

prolactin A protein hormone, produced by the pituitary gland, that initiates and maintains lactation in mammals. In other animals, it has a variety of functions, being involved in growth and the balance of water and salts, as well as reproduction. *See also* gonadotrophin.

proletariat Originally, the lower class of Rome and other ancient states, the term was later used to refer to the lower class of any community. *Marx defined the proletariat as the wage labourers of capitalist economies, who depended on the sale of their labour to live and who owned no property; the struggle between this class and the *bourgeoisie would eventually lead to revolution. *See* Marxism.

promenade concerts Concerts in which the audience can walk about whilst listening to the music. The most famous series of such concerts is the BBC Promenade Concerts (the Proms), which were begun by Henry *Wood in 1895. They were held in the Queen's Hall until it was bombed in World War II and have thereafter been held in the Royal Albert Hall. The "last night of the Proms" is a uniquely British occasion in which audience participation makes up for in enthusiasm what it lacks in musical skill.

Prometheus (Greek: forethought) In Greek mythology, the son of a Titan and Themis who created man and endowed him with reason. He also stole fire from heaven to give to man. Zeus chained him to a rock in the Caucasus and sent an eagle each day to devour his liver, which grew again by night. After thousands of years he was rescued by Heracles.

promethium (Pm) A radioactive element, not known on earth but identified by its spectrum in the light from stars, in which it is continuously being formed by nuclear reactions. The most stable isotope has a half-life of 17.7 years. Promethium salts exhibit bluish-green *luminescence and can be used in photoelectric cells. It is obtained from nuclear reactors. At no 61; at wt (145); mp about 1080°C.

pronghorn A hoofed mammal, *Antilocapra americana*, resembling an antelope and found in rocky deserts of the W USA. Up to 100 cm high at the shoulder, pronghorns are not true antelopes, shedding the horny sheath of their branched horns every year; the bony core is permanent. Brown above and white beneath with white chevrons under the neck, they have brilliant-white rump hairs used for signalling. They are the only surviving members of the family *Antilocapridae*.

proof spirit. *See* alcohol strength.

propellant 1. A solid or liquid substance used to provide thrust in a rocket engine or gun. Propellants utilize very fast exothermic chemical reactions to produce large quantities of expanding gas quickly. Generally, they are explosive substances or mixtures. A single unstable substance (such as nitrocellulose) or mixture of combustible material and oxidant (such as alcohol and hydrogen peroxide) is termed a **monopropellant**. If the combustible material and oxidant are mixed in a combustion chamber the mixture forms a **bipropellant**. Generally, bipropellants are hypergolic systems, i.e. systems that ignite spontaneously when mixed. 2. The pressurized inert liquids used to drive an *aerosol from its container.

propeller A device for converting the rotation of a shaft into thrust in the direction of its axis. A **marine propeller** is attached to a shaft connected to the ship's engine and has between two and six blades, shaped as part of a helical surface. It acts as a screw, accelerating a column of water rearwards. An **air propeller** (*or* airscrew), moving in a thinner medium, has longer thinner blades (usually two or four) and a higher rotational speed. It, too, accelerates a mass of air rearwards thrusting the aircraft forwards by reaction.

proper motion The rate at which a star is observed to move on the *celestial sphere, i.e. perpendicular to the line of sight. Values are very small, often negligible.

Propertius, Sextus (c. 50–c. 16 BC) Roman poet. Born in Assisi in Umbria, he went to Rome as a young man and established himself in literary circles. *Cynthia*, the first of his four surviving books, contains highly personal love poems addressed to his mistress Hostia. His later books contain poems on various topics, including the psychology of love, written in a style noted for its bold originality.

prophets Ancient Israelite religious leaders and visionaries. The books of the prophets make up the second of the three divisions of the Hebrew *Bible and are grouped into the "Former Prophets" (Joshua, Judges, Samuel, and Kings) and the "Latter Prophets" (Isaiah, Jeremiah, Ezekiel, and the 12 Minor Prophets). Moses is regarded by Jews as the first and greatest of the prophets, and the gift of prophecy is thought to have ceased in the 5th century BC. In Islam Jesus and Mohammed are also regarded as prophets.

proportional representation (PR) A voting system that aims accurately to reflect the wishes of the electorate and to ensure that votes for candidates standing for minority parties are not wasted. In the system of PR known as the **single transferable vote** (used in the Republic of Ireland), electors indicate their preferences among the candidates by numbering them on their ballot paper (1, 2, 3, etc.). Those candidates who are named as a first choice and who obtain the required quota are elected. First-choice votes for an unsuccessful candidate are then redistributed to second-choice votes for that candidate, and so on until the requisite number of candidates has been elected (the system requires multimember constituencies). In the **party-list system** (widely used on the Continent) electors vote for a party, which is then allocated seats in proportion to its total vote. In the UK PR is advocated by the Liberal Party.

propositional calculus A system of formal logic that assigns truth or falsehood to compound propositions or statements on the basis of the rules governing the connective words between them. Examples of such connective words are "and," "or," or "if . . . then . . . ." For example, the rule for "and" is that a statement containing it is true only if both the simple statements it connects are true; for "or" it is sufficient that only one statement be true. Thus "pigs fly and birds sing" is false, while "either pigs fly or birds sing" is true.

propylaea Ancient Greek monumental gateways, generally the ceremonial entrances to the *acropolis of a town. The best-preserved example is that on the Acropolis of Athens.

proscenium The arch at the front of a □theatre stage through which the audience views the play. It became a standard feature of theatre architecture following its first use in Italy in the 17th century but has been dispensed with in many theatres built during the 20th century.

Proserpine. *See* Persephone.

prosimian A *primate of the suborder *Prosimii* (53 species), including the *lemurs, *indris, *sifakas, *lorises, *bushbabies, *tarsiers, *tree shrews, and the *aye-aye. Prosimians are the most primitive of the primates and are mainly arboreal. Tree shrews have claws instead of fingernails and only partly opposable thumbs.

Prost, Alain (1955–) French motor racing driver. In 1987 he became the most successful Formula One driver ever, having won 28 Grand Prix races and the World Championship in 1985 and 1986.

prostaglandins Compounds derived from long-chain (essential) fatty acids and found in mammalian body tissues. Their effects include stimulation of contraction in the womb, dilation of blood vessels, and modification of hormonal activity. They are released at sites of inflammation following tissue damage and the pain-relieving properties of such drugs as aspirin are due to their inhibition of prostaglandin synthesis. Synthetic prostaglandins are used to induce labour and abortion in women.

prostate gland A gland in men, situated just beneath the bladder (*see* Plate IV). It secretes an alkaline fluid during ejaculation that forms part of the semen. Enlargement of the prostate commonly occurs in elderly men, obstructing the bladder and preventing urination. It is usually treated by surgical removal of the gland (prostatectomy).

prostitution The practice of offering sexual gratification in return for money or other return. It has always been common, especially in societies in which legitimate sexual relations are closely regulated. Attitudes to prostitution differ greatly in different societies. Sometimes a bride earns her dowry in this way with general approval. It was practised in ancient Mesopotamia by priestesses for religious reasons. In modern societies it is generally controlled by legislation, usually with the object of preventing the spread of venereal diseases and of preventing pimps (men who live off the earnings of prostitutes) from introducing young girls into the profession. In the UK, since the enactment of the *Wolfenden Report (1957) as legislation (1959), prostitution has ceased to be illegal, but soliciting, procuring someone to be a prostitute, and living off a prostitute's earnings are punishable offences. Male prostitution is less common than female and largely confined to homosexual relations.

protactinium (Pa) A radioactive *actinide element, first identified by K. Fajans and O. H. Göhring in 1913. It is present in pitchblende as a member of the uranium decay series. The oxide (Pa_2O_5) and iodide (PaI_5) have been produced. The latter decomposes on heating to give the metal. At no 91; at wt (231); mp $<1600°C$.

Protagoras (c. 485–415 BC) Greek *Sophist. He claimed to teach virtue (more accurately interpreted as "success") and was himself successful and respected for more than 40 years. His saying, "Man is the measure of all things," shows his subjectivist attitude to knowledge. His scepticism extended to religion, but not, apparently, to morality.

Protea A genus of evergreen shrubs and trees (over 100 species), native to S and central Africa. They have broad simple leaves and small white, pink, yellow, or orange flowers that are grouped into showy cup-shaped clusters, up to 30 cm across, and surrounded by whorls of coloured bracts. The flowers are a national emblem of South Africa. Family: *Proteaceae*.

Protectorate (1653–59) The period during which England was governed by Oliver *Cromwell. The Instrument of Government (1653) vested executive authority in the Lord Protector (Cromwell) and a state council and legislative authority in the Protector and a triennial parliament. The Instrument was modified by the Humble Petition and Advice (1657), which gave more power to parliament and less to the state council. Cromwell's relations with parliament subsequently deteriorated and he dismissed it in 1658. Following his death later in the year, his son Richard *Cromwell was Protector until his abdication in 1659.

protein A complex organic compound that consists of one or more chains of *amino acids linked by *peptide bonds ($-NH-CO-$). These chains are variously coiled, wound, and cross-linked to form a three-dimensional molecular structure, revealed by such techniques as *X-ray diffraction, that determines the biological properties of the protein. This structure is irreversibly damaged at temperatures above 60°C. Proteins are manufactured by cells according to the genetic information carried in the chromosomes and the specific function of the cell (*see* DNA; RNA). Proteins fulfil many important biological roles: some protein including *collagen

and *keratin, are important structural materials of body
tissues, while the proteins of *muscle—actin and myosin—are responsible for its contractile properties. Proteins
vital to the functioning of the body include enzymes—the
biological catalysts of metabolic reactions; *antibodies—important in the body's defence mechanisms; and many *hormones—the chemical messengers of the body.

Protestantism The movement for Church reform that
arose in the Western Church in the 16th century and led to
the establishment of the Reformed Churches. The word
derives from the *protestatio* of the dissident reforming
minority at the Diet of *Speyer (1529). The early leaders of
the *Reformation—*Luther, *Calvin, and *Zwingli—each
promoted his own brand of Protestantism. Under Elizabeth
I Protestantism finally became the established religion in
England, although since the 19th century some Anglicans
have objected to the Protestant label and have emphasized
the Catholic traditions of the Church of England (*see* Anglo-
Catholicism).
There are many doctrinal divisions among Protestants, but
all reject a varying number of tenets and practices retained in
Catholicism. In general Protestants rely less upon ecclesiastical tradition, believing the Bible to be the sole source of
truth. They deny papal authority and admit a variety of
forms of Church government (*see* episcopacy; Presbyterianism); in some sects the spiritual priesthood of all the faithful
is emphasized. *Transubstantiation, *purgatory, special
veneration of the Virgin Mary, and invocation of saints are
all repudiated. The importance of the sacraments is
minimized, with only baptism and the *Eucharist being
accorded widespread acceptance, and some groups, such as
the *Quakers, reject even these. The preaching and studying
of God's word in the Bible is conversely important. Church
furnishings, vestments, and music are more austere than their
Roman Catholic equivalents. The 20th-century ecumenical
movement has gone some way towards reconciling the
Roman Catholic and Protestant Churches, but there are still
serious doctrinal and other differences, while fresh issues,
such as the ordination of women, introduce new elements of
divisiveness.

Proteus (bacteria) A genus of motile rod-shaped bacteria
found mainly in soil and sewage, where they decompose
organic matter, but also in the wounds of animals and
man. Some species cause enteritis and urinary-tract
infections.

Proteus (mythology) A Greek sea god who served
Poseidon as a shepherd of seals. He is usually portrayed as
an old man. He had prophetic powers but used his ability to
change his form to avoid communicating his knowledge.

Protista A taxonomic group or kingdom that comprises all
microscopic organisms, i.e. the algae, some fungi, protozoa,
and bacteria.

Protoceratops A dinosaur that lived during the late
Cretaceous period (about 100–65 million years ago). It was
a short-legged squat quadruped, 2 m long and weighing 1.5
tonnes, and had long sharp teeth and huge jaw muscles
attached to a bony neck frill. Its diet probably consisted of
palm fronds. Order: *Ornithischia.

protochordate Any animal of the subphylum *Chordata*
that does not possess a backbone. Protochordates, which
include the *tunicates and *amphioxus, may represent the
ancestors of the first vertebrates.

Protocols of Zion A document published in 1903 purporting to contain Jewish plans to overthrow Christian
civilization. Although conclusively proved a forgery in 1921,
Hitler, like earlier antisemitic agitators, used it to justify his
persecution of the Jews.

proton A positively charged elementary particle classified
as a baryon (*see* particle physics). It forms part of all atomic
nuclei, a single proton being the nucleus of the hydrogen

atom. It is a stable particle, 1836 times heavier than the
electron.

protostar An embryonic star that has formed out of a
contracting cloud of interstellar gas and dust. It continues to
contract, the density and temperature at its centre rising
slowly at first and then increasingly rapidly until they are
sufficiently high to cause energy-releasing thermonuclear
reactions to begin in the central core. The collapse is then
halted, and the object becomes a luminous star.

Protozoa A phylum of typically microscopic single-celled
organisms (about 30 000 species), usually classified as simple
animals and widely distributed in moist and watery places,
including mud, soil, fresh waters, and oceans. Protozoans
range in size from 0.1 mm to several centimetres. They may
have one or several nuclei and a variety of specialized
structures, including a contractile vacuole for regulating the
water content and cilia or flagella for movement and
feeding. The cell may be fairly rigid, with a stiff cell wall
(pellicle) or skeletal elements, or flexible and variable. Some
protozoans contain pigment and obtain food by photosynthesis in the same way as plants. However, most forms take
in dissolved nutrients or solid food particles (detritus,
bacteria, etc.). Asexual reproduction is by means of simple
division of the parent cell (binary fission) or by budding to
form new cells; various forms of sexual reproduction occur,
including *conjugation. Protozoans can survive dry or
adverse conditions by forming resistant cysts or spores.
Some are important parasites of man and animals, including
species of *Plasmodium*, which cause malaria, and trypanosomes, which cause sleeping sickness. The phylum
includes the classes *Sarcodina*, *Ciliata*, *Flagellata*, and
Sporozoa. □p.996.

Protura A worldwide order of primitive wingless insects
(150 species) that live in humus and soil, feeding on decaying organic materials. They have a pale cylindrical body
(0.5–2 mm long), which tapers to a simple tail (telson) and
lacks eyes and antennae.

Proudhon, Pierre Joseph (1809–65) French socialist and
political theorist. Proudhon was largely self-educated. In his
treatises *Qu'est-ce que la propriété?* (1840) and the *Système des
contradictions économiques ou philosophie de la misère* (1846),
he argued that all property was theft and that in a just society
orderly anarchy would replace oppressive government.

Proust, Joseph-Louis (1754–1826) French chemist, who
demonstrated by accurate analysis that compounds always
contain fixed proportions of elements. This is now known as
the law of definite proportion or sometimes as Proust's
law. This work contributed to *Dalton's atomic theory.

Proust, Marcel (1871–1922) French novelist. The son of
rich bourgeois parents, he suffered from asthma from
childhood and was devotedly cared for by his mother. He
studied at the Lycée Condorcet and the Sorbonne and in the
1890s became a socialite in the most fashionable aristocratic
circles in Paris. After the deaths of his parents (1903, 1905),
he dedicated his life to writing and, because of asthma, lived
as an invalid recluse in a cork-lined room in a flat on the
Boulevard Haussmann. In 1912 he financed the publication
of the first volume (*Swann's Way*) of what was to become his
masterpiece, *Remembrance of Things Past*. He then set to
work expanding his original conception, realizing that his
time was limited because of his ill health. The second
volume, *Within a Budding Grove* (1919), won the Prix Goncourt; it was followed by *The Guermantes Way* (1920–21) and
Cities of the Plain (1921–22). Proust managed to complete
but not revise the final volumes, *The Captive* (1923), *The
Sweet Cheat Gone* (1925), and *Time Regained* (1927), before
his death. Written in an elaborate style and influenced by
the philosophy of *Bergson, *Remembrance of Things Past* is a
detailed portrait of the society that Proust had abandoned,
recreated through the involuntary workings of memory.
There is a strong autobiographical element in the narration

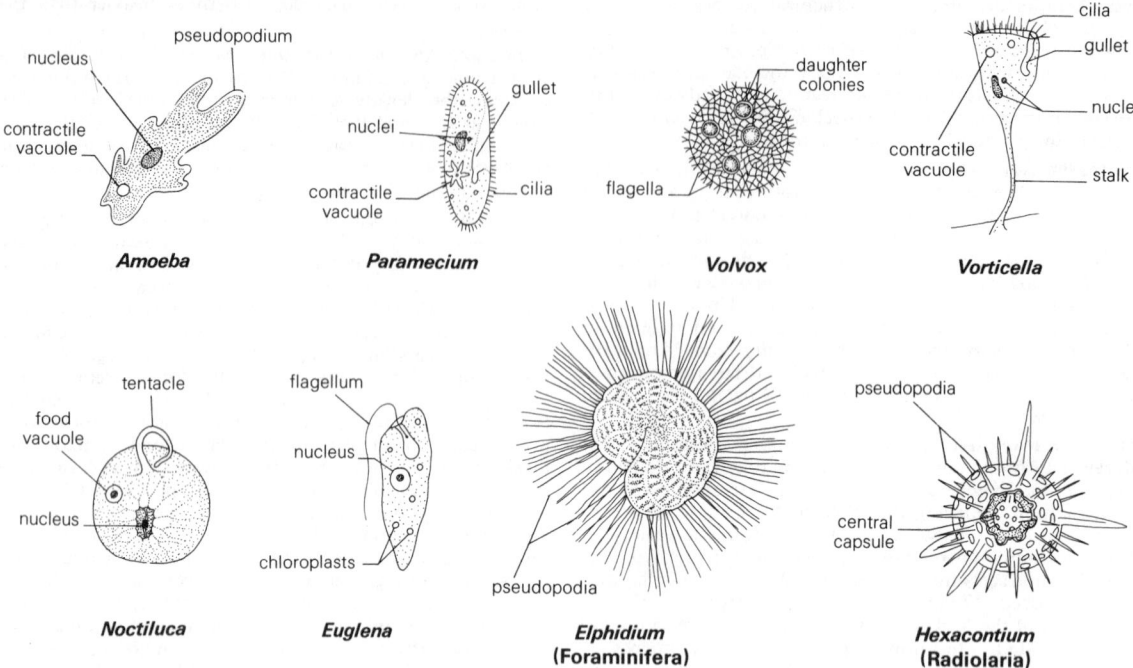

PROTOZOA *Although consisting only of single cells, these primitive animals show a surprising complexity of structure. Many have organs of locomotion (pseudopodia, flagella, or cilia) and some have gullets, through which food is channelled.*

and in the theme of homosexuality that plays a large part in several sections.

Prout, William (1785–1850) British chemist and physiologist, who in 1824 discovered the presence of hydrochloric acid in the stomach. He was also the first to classify foods in terms of what are now called proteins, fats, and carbohydrates. He also formulated the idea that atomic weights are all multiples of the atomic weight of hydrogen (Prout's hypothesis).

Provençal A *Romance language, strictly the dialect of *Provence, but also used to refer to the dialects of various regions of S France and in this broad sense often called Occitan. These dialects are also collectively described as the *langue d'oc*, in contrast to the *langue d'oïl* spoken in northern and central areas of France (*oc* and *oïl* being the medieval forms for *yes* in these two dialect areas). The primary literary use of Provençal was by the *troubadours; it fell into disuse as a literary language during the later middle ages. About nine million people still speak it.

Provence A former province in SE France, bordering on Italy and the Mediterranean Sea. A kingdom during the 9th century AD, it became part of France in 1481 and now forms the modern planning region of **Provence-Côte-d'Azur**. Chiefly mountainous, its fertile river valleys produce grapes, olives, and mulberries. The perfume industry, centred on Grasse, is important. It contains the French *Riviera, a popular tourist area, along the S coast. Area: 31 435 sq km (12 134 sq mi). Population (1981 est): 3 909 700.

Proverbs An Old Testament book that is a collection of moral and religious maxims, traditionally ascribed to Solomon. Its chief theme is the nature and value of wisdom, which is the result of "fear of the Lord." Also prominent are maxims relating to justice, self-control, purity, industry, friends and family, and life and death.

Providence 41 50N 71 25W A city and seaport in the USA, the capital of Rhode Island on Narragansett Bay. Founded in 1636, it is the site of many historical buildings, including the First Baptist Church (1775), the First Unitarian Church,

two cathedrals, and Brown University (founded in Warren in 1764 and moved to Providence in 1770). A major outlet for much of New England's oil, its manufactures include jewellery, machinery, and rubber goods. Population (1980): 156 804.

province A territorial subdivision of the empire of ancient Rome administered by a Roman governor. Provincial governors, who in Republican times (510–27 BC) were appointed by the Senate, commanded the garrisons, levied taxes, administered justice, and in wartime recruited troops. Under the Empire (after 27 BC), the Senate continued to provide governors for the ten more peaceful provinces while the emperors through their legates controlled those provinces still requiring military occupation. *See also* Roman Republic; Roman Empire.

Proxima Centauri. *See* Alpha Centauri.

Prudhoe Bay A small inlet of the Arctic Ocean in the USA, on the coast of N Alaska. Since the discovery of vast oil deposits in the area (1968) it has been a centre of drilling activity. A pipeline transfers oil from Prudhoe Bay to the S.

Prud'hon, Pierre Paul (1758–1823) French painter and draughtsman, born at Cluny. He trained in the Dijon Academy and in Rome (1784–7), where he was influenced by the works of *Correggio and *Leonardo. The style of his court portraits, for example *Empress Josephine* (Louvre), and his famous *Crime Pursued by Vengeance and Justice* (Saint-Omer, N France) display a romantic feeling distinctly different from the current neoclassical vogue (*see* neoclassicism).

Prunus A genus of deciduous or evergreen shrubs and trees (over 200 species), mostly native to N temperate regions. It includes the *plums, *almonds, *apricots, *peaches, and *cherries as well as many ornamental species. They have oval toothed leaves, often rolled in the bud, and white or pink flowers, about 1 cm across, with five petals and many stamens. They produce stone fruits (*see* drupe), often with edible flesh or kernels. Family: *Rosaceae*.

Prussia A former state in N Germany on the NE Baltic coast. Established in the 13th century by the Teutonic Knights, Prussia became a duchy in 1525 under *Hohenzollern rule. United with Brandenburg in 1618, under *Frederick William, the Great Elector, it became the most powerful N German state. In 1701 his son took the title King of Prussia. In the 18th century, under *Frederick the Great, Prussia annexed Silesia and parts of Poland and became a major European power. Following Napoleon's defeat, it made important territorial gains at the Congress of Vienna (1815). Under *Bismarck's ambitious leadership, Prussia defeated Austria and Austria's German allies (1866), acquiring *Schleswig-Holstein and forming the *North German Confederation. Following victory in the *Franco-Prussian War (1870-71) the German Empire was proclaimed under Prussian leadership. In 1918 Prussia became a republic and was abolished by the Allies after World War II.

prussic acid. *See* hydrocyanic acid.

Prynne, William (1600-69) English Puritan. He was imprisoned in 1633 for his book *Histrio Mastix: The Players Scourge, or Actors Tragedie* (1633), seen to contain an attack on the queen, and in 1634 his ears were cut off. Released (1640) by the *Long Parliament, he was imprisoned (1650-53) under the Commonwealth for nonpayment of taxes.

Przemyśl 49 48N 22 48E A town in SE Poland. During World War I it withstood a five-month siege by Russian armies before surrendering. Its industries are varied and include flour milling, tanning, and the manufacture of machinery. Population (1982 est): 62 200.

Przewalski's horse The single surviving species of wild horse, *Equus przewalskii*, discovered in Mongolia in about 1880 by the Russian explorer Nicolai Mikhailovich Przewalski (1839-88). It is sturdily built with a relatively large head and has a short erect dark-brown mane and a dark dorsal stripe. The coat is reddish brown, becoming paler in winter. Height: 1.22-1.42 m (12-14 hands).

Psalms An Old Testament book, also known as the Psalter, containing 150 spiritual songs. They were formerly all attributed to David but are now generally believed to be by a number of different authors; some of them may date from the early period of the Jewish monarchy. They were intended to be sung with musical accompaniment and used in the liturgy of the Temple at Jerusalem; they continue to be used in both public and private worship by Jews and Christians. The majority are expressions of praise and worship of God and his works. A large number deal with aspects of a believer's experience, such as penitence, trust, doubt, fear, and suffering.

psaltery A medieval musical instrument, a type of *zither. It was plucked by the fingers of both hands or by two plectra.

Psamtik I King of Egypt (664-610 BC); the founder of the 26th dynasty. Appointed viceroy of Egypt by *Ashurbanipal of Assyria in 663, he took advantage of Assyria's weakness to repudiate its suzerainty, while remaining its ally. Psamtik encouraged trade with Greece and employed Greek mercenaries (the "brazen men"). During his reign Egyptian national sentiment revived the art and institutions of the pyramid age.

Pseudo-Dionysius the Areopagite (early 6th century AD) Mystical theologian, probably born in Syria, whose real name is unknown. His fame rests on several Greek treatises and letters, which greatly influenced leading medieval scholars. They attempt to combine Christianity with *Neoplatonism and include *The Celestial Hierarchy, The Ecclesiastical Hierarchy, The Divine Names*, and *The Mystical Theology*. They were formerly attributed to St *Dionysius the Areopagite.

pseudopodium A temporary extension of the cytoplasm found in some *Protozoa and used for locomotion and for engulfing food particles. In *Amoeba*, the pseudopodia are blunt lobular processes but in other protozoa they may be slender, filamentous, or branching.

Psilocybe A genus of mushrooms growing in soil and dung. The Mexican species *P. mexicana* contains the hallucinogenic compounds psilocin and psilocybin, which have effects similar to those of *LSD. It was regarded as a sacred mushroom in Mexico and eaten during religious ceremonies. Mushrooms of the liberty cap fungus (*P. semilanceolata*) are common in pastures and lawns, having greyish-brown or olive-green conical caps, 1-2 cm in diameter.

psi particle An elementary particle discovered in 1974 and classified as a meson. Its unusually long lifetime led to the extension of the quark model (*see* particle physics) to include a quark (and its antiquark) having a new property called *charm. The psi particle itself is not charmed as it consists of a charmed quark and its antiquark.

psittacosis (*or* parrot disease) An infectious illness caused by a microorganism of the *Chlamydia* group, which is caught from birds, particularly parrots. The severity of the disease varies, but usually it causes pneumonia. Tetracycline antibiotics are used to treat the disease.

Pskov 57 48N 28 26E A city in the NW Soviet Union, in the RSFSR on the River Velikaya, SE of Lake Pskov. Nicholas II abdicated at the railway station here in 1917. Industries include food processing and tourism, Pskov having many historic buildings. Population (1981 est): 179 000.

Pskov school A school of Russian *icon and mural painting that flourished in the city of Pskov between the late 12th and early 16th centuries. It developed in isolation from other cultural centres since most other parts of Russia were occupied by the Mongols during this period. Characteristics of the school's style were the influence of *Byzantine art, monumental forms, brilliant colours, emotional intensity, and the persistence of archaic methods of representation.

psoriasis A chronic recurring skin disease marked by excessive scaling of the skin. The disease is very common and affects over 4% of the UK population. It begins with small red patches covered in scales and may spread extensively. The knees, elbows, lower back, scalp, and nails are most commonly affected. There is no known cure, but steroid creams and ultraviolet light are used to alleviate the condition.

Psyche In Greek mythology, a personification of the soul, portrayed as a beautiful mortal girl. *Apuleius tells the allegorical story of how she lost her divine lover, Cupid, and of her subsequent quest and suffering before she was finally reunited with him in marriage in heaven.

psychedelic drugs. *See* hallucinogens.

psychiatry The study and treatment of mental disorders. A psychiatrist is a medically qualified physician specializing in mental illness. Modern psychiatry also involves those of other professional disciplines, including nurses, social workers, and psychologists. The range of mental disorders includes *psychosis, *neurosis, *psychosomatic disorders, *drug dependence, and *mental retardation. Within psychiatry there are several specialities, notably child psychiatry, *psychotherapy, forensic psychiatry (which deals with those who have broken the law), and geriatric psychiatry (psychogeriatrics), which cares for the mentally disordered elderly.

psychical research Scientific investigation into paranormal phenomena. Proper subjects for psychical research include *ghost and *poltergeist hauntings, *extrasensory perception, and *spiritualism. The London Society for Psychical Research (founded in 1882) was the first of numerous kindred organizations throughout the world, but mainstream science is still sceptical about their methodology and conclusions.

psychoanalysis A school of *psychology and a method of treating mental disorders based upon the teachings of Sigmund *Freud (*see also* Adler, Alfred; Jung, Carl). Psychoanalysis stresses the dynamic interplay of unconscious mental forces and the way in which the adult personality is determined by the course of sexual development in childhood. The chief techniques of psychoanalysis are free *association and the recall of *dreams in the course of intensive psychotherapy, which usually requires several 50-minute sessions each week for up to three years. In the course of this treatment transference takes place, in which aspects of the patient's past experiences and relationships are transferred to the analyst, the object being to bring repressed conflicts into consciousness so that they can be resolved. Although analysis was originally intended as a treatment for neurosis, it has been extended to some psychotic conditions by W. R. Bion (1897–1979), Herbert Rosenfeld (1909–86), and others. The work of Melanie *Klein was devoted to exploring early infantile experiences on a Freudian basis, while some of Freud's underlying concepts were challenged by such analysts as W. *Reich, E. *Fromm, and others. *See also* defence mechanism; ego; id; Oedipus complex; repression; superego; unconscious.

psychokinesis. *See* telekinesis.

psychology The scientific study of the behaviour of man and animals. Different schools of psychology use differing methods and theories. These include *behaviourism; experimental psychology, in which laboratory experiments are used to investigate factors influencing behaviour (particularly *memory, perception, and learning); *Gestalt psychology; associationist psychology (*see* association); and *psychoanalysis. Clinical psychology applies these approaches to the understanding and treatment of mental illness (*see also* psychiatry). Educational psychology studies the ways in which children learn, in order to intervene as problems arise. Occupational psychology studies people in their working environment. *See also* ethology.

psychopath A person who behaves violently or antisocially and shows neither guilt nor any feeling for others. Psychopathy can be caused by a constitutional abnormality or an emotionally deprived upbringing.

psychosis A severe mental illness in which the sufferer loses contact with reality. Organic psychoses are caused by diseases affecting the brain, such as epilepsy, alcoholism, and dementia; functional psychoses have no known physical cause. The major functional psychoses are *schizophrenia and *manic-depressive psychosis. All psychoses can cause *hallucinations, delusions, and altered thought processes. They are common and disabling illnesses that account for the occupation of more hospital beds than any other illness.

psychosomatic disorder An illness in which physical symptoms are caused or exacerbated by mental factors. Certain physical illnesses, including asthma, eczema, and peptic ulcer, are thought to be partly a response to psychological and social *stress.

psychosurgery Surgical operations performed on the brain in order to relieve psychological symptoms. The commonest operation is *leucotomy. In lobectomy a whole lobe of the *brain is removed, often because of epilepsy. In amygdalectomy a lesion is made in a small part of the limbic system of the brain to reduce pathological aggression. These are all irreversible treatments and are reserved for the most severe forms of mental illness that are resistant to other therapies.

psychotherapy Psychological methods of treatment for mental disorders. There are many different approaches to psychotherapy, including *psychoanalysis and *group therapy. In client-centred therapy the therapist refrains from giving any direct advice. Family therapy involves several members of a family meeting together with a therapist to improve their relationships. All these approaches share the goal of helping self-understanding and personal development through the relationship between the client and the therapist. *See also* behaviour therapy; hypnosis.

Ptah In ancient Egyptian mythology, the creator god. A local deity of *Memphis, he was proclaimed the supreme god when Egypt was first unified (c. 3100 BC), but was later identified with *Osiris and became the patron of craftsmen. He is always shown in the form of a *mummy.

ptarmigan A grouse, *Lagopus lagopus*, found in Arctic tundra and mountain regions. 35 cm long, it has white wings and a mottled blackish-brown body that changes to white in winter. Its feet are covered with feathers and it feeds on shoots and fruits in summer and on lichens and leaves dug from the snow in winter.

Pteranodon An extinct flying reptile of the Cretaceous period (135–65 million years ago). 3 m long with a wingspan of 7.5 m, it had an enormous bony crest that balanced its large head. It lived around sea cliffs, clinging to them with its long hind claws and gliding over the sea to catch fish in its long toothless beak.

Pteraspis An extinct genus of jawless fishlike vertebrates, belonging to the class *Ostracodermi*, that lived from the Ordovician to the Devonian periods (about 500–370 million years ago). The head and anterior part of the body were covered by a heavy bony shield, the remainder by small scales, and there was an upturned beaklike extension of the head (rostrum). Fins were placed singly, not in pairs. Subphylum: *Agnatha*.

pteridophyte A flowerless perennial vascular plant of the division *Pteridophyta*, which shows a distinct *alternation of generations with the asexual spore-bearing (sporophyte) generation predominating. The sporophyte plant consists typically of leaves, stems, and roots and bears spores in special capsules (sporangia), which are often arranged in clusters (sori) on the leaves. Pteridophytes are subdivided into *Lycopsida* (e.g. *clubmosses), *Sphenopsida* (e.g. *horsetails), *Psilopsida*, or *Psilotopsida* (mostly extinct), and *Pteropsida* (*see* fern).

pterodactyl. *See* pterosaur.

pterosaur An extinct flying reptile, also called pterodactyl, that lived during the Jurassic and Cretaceous periods (200–65 million years ago). A thin wing membrane stretched from the elongated fourth finger of the fore limb along the body to the knee; a second membrane stretched to the neck. It had a compact body and long slender hind limbs, probably used to cling, batlike, to rocks and trees. Its light bones, toothless beaked jaw, large eyes, and large brain resembled those of modern birds. ⌐fossil.

Ptolemaic system A theory concerning the motions of the sun, moon, and planets that was originally advanced in Greece in the 3rd century BC and was completed by Claudius *Ptolemy in the 2nd century AD. It was a geocentric system in which the moon, Mercury, Venus, Sun, Mars, Jupiter, and Saturn were thought to move around the earth. Prediction agreed reasonably well with observation. To achieve this Ptolemy had to propose that each orbiting body moved in a small circle (an epicycle) the centre of which moved in a larger circle (a deferent) around the earth. A sphere of stars lay beyond the seven deferents. The Ptolemaic system was finally abandoned when the *heliocentric system of *Copernicus was accepted.

Ptolemies A Macedonian dynasty that ruled Egypt from 323 BC, when *Ptolemy I Soter became governor of Egypt, until 30 BC, when Ptolemy XV Caesar (47–30 BC; reigned 44–30 BC), nicknamed Caesarion, the son of Cleopatra and, perhaps, Caesar, was executed by Octavian (later *Augustus).

Ptolemy (*or* Claudius Ptolemaeus; 2nd century AD) Egyptian mathematician, astronomer, and geographer. Little is known of his life except that he lived and worked in Alexandria, probably publishing his major works between 127 and 145. The foremost of these outlines the *Ptolemaic system of astronomy and was originally known as *He mathematike syntaxis* (*The Mathematical Collection*) but was known to Arab astronomers by the Greek superlative *Megiste*, which took the Arab form *Almagest*, the name by which it is still known. His other works include *Analemma* and *Planisphaerium* on geometry, *Harmonica* on music, and *Geographike hyphegesis*, an extensive guide to geography.

Ptolemy I Soter (?367–?283 BC) The first Macedonian King of Egypt and founder of the Ptolemaic dynasty (*see* Ptolemies). He was a general of Alexander the Great, after whose death he became governor of Egypt as his share of the Macedonian empire. He conquered Palestine, Cyprus, and much of Asia Minor, taking the title of king in 304. He founded the Library of *Alexandria, which he made his capital, and wrote a history of Alexander's campaigns.

Ptolemy II Philadelphus (308–246 BC) King of Egypt (285–246); the son and successor of Ptolemy I. He and his second wife and sister *Arsinoe II were engaged unsuccessfully in war with Syria. He completed the public buildings of *Alexandria, restored the Nile–Red Sea canal, and introduced camels into Egypt.

Ptolemy XIII Theos Philopator (63–47 BC) King of Egypt (51–47), ruling jointly with his sister and wife *Cleopatra VII until he and his advisers expelled her (48). He murdered *Pompey after his defeat by *Caesar, hoping for Caesar's favour, but when Caesar reinstated Cleopatra, Ptolemy opposed him and was killed.

ptomaines Compounds formed during the bacterial decomposition of proteins in animal and plant tissues. Most are amines, such as diethylamine, putrescine, and cadaverine, and they may be poisonous, although the symptoms ascribed to "ptomaine poisoning" are usually due to bacterial toxins in contaminated food (*see* food poisoning).

puberty The onset of sexual maturity. The age at which this occurs is very variable but is usually between 12 and 17 in boys and between 10 and 16 in girls. The sexual organs develop to their adult form and pubic hair starts to grow; in girls the menstrual periods begin (menarche). The secondary sexual characteristics develop: in girls the breasts enlarge and in boys the muscles enlarge, the voice deepens, and facial hair grows. Psychological changes include an increase in the sexual drive and often in anxiety and insecurity.

Public Record Office (PRO) The UK government archives, established in 1838. Formerly archives were stored in a number of different places, including the Tower of London and Somerset House. The PRO is the responsibility of the Lord Chancellor and since 1977 has been at Kew, Surrey. Records are not made publicly available until they are 30 years old.

public relations Efforts by firms, organizations, individuals, etc., to present a good public image. Good public relations are achieved by prompt servicing of complaints and enquiries from the public, involvement in local affairs, sponsorship of charities, etc. A public relations officer (PRO) may be appointed to ensure that these tasks are carried out and to promote his employer by such means as obtaining free mention of him or his products in the media.

Public Safety, Committee of A governing body during the French Revolution. When a coalition of European powers attacked France following the king's execution in 1793, the Committee of Public Safety was established to meet the emergency. Coming under the influence of Robespierre, it conducted the *Reign of Terror. After Robespierre's fall in July, 1794, its powers were curtailed.

public school In the USA the term denotes a school that is not under private ownership or control, whereas in the UK the name somewhat misleadingly refers to a fee-paying school, usually a boarding school. Although traditionally male preserves, several public schools now admit girls, especially at sixth-form level, and a number of well-known independent girls' schools were established in the 19th century; entrance is usually at 13. Contrary to popular belief most public schools do not have centuries of tradition behind them and even among the oldest the legal boundaries separating them from endowed *grammar schools is ill defined. It was not until the reforms of Frederick Temple (1821–1902), Henry Montagu Butler (1833–1918), and Thomas *Arnold in the 19th century that the demand for public-school places grew and by the time of the Clarendon Commission (1864) only nine schools were considered to enjoy such status. Any school the headmaster of which is a member of the Headmasters' Conference is now usually regarded as a public school, making the total number about 200, although this includes many of the former direct-grant schools (state-assisted schools that have been gradually phased out and either incorporated into the state system or have become totally independent). Although many of the schools maintain high academic standards they have become symbols of privilege and have been criticized for perpetuating class isolation. The Public Schools Commission (1968) was set up to investigate them. At the 1985 Headmasters' Conference they were renamed "independent schools".

public sector Those parts of the productive and non-productive sectors of the economy that are financed out of taxation, are under state control, or both. It embraces all the employees and activities of central and local government, public institutions and utilities, and nationalized industries. In the UK most businesses the products and services of which are essential to the life of the community have been nationalized and state ownership of shares in other firms represents a modified form of nationalization. The amount by which the receipts of the public sector, including *taxation, fall short of public expenditure constitutes the Public Sector Borrowing Requirement.

publishing The commissioning, production, and distribution of *books, periodicals, and *newspapers. Before the invention of printing, reading matter was produced by hand in the form of papyrus rolls in ancient Egypt, Greece, and Rome, and later in the form of manuscripts copied by hand. With the invention of printing by *Gutenberg, early printed books (*see* incunabula) were sold by the printer, who also functioned as publisher and bookseller. During the 15th and 16th centuries these functions began to separate; the Netherlands was one of the earliest centres of book publishing and the house founded by Louis Elzevir (1540–1617) is still active in Haarlem. After the introduction of the Copyright Act (1709), book publishing, which had previously been financed largely by rich patrons, expanded in the UK and the USA as an independent industry.

The growth of libraries, the spread of literacy, and technical innovations in printing and papermaking during the 19th century enabled the independent publisher to flourish. In 1896 Sir Frederick Macmillan, son of the founder of the firm of Macmillan, combined with other British publishers to set up the Publishers Association, one of the first tasks of which was to negotiate the Net Book Agreement (1899), which controls the prices at which booksellers may sell books. During the 20th century the main innovation in the UK and the USA was the advent of the cheap paperback, pioneered by Sir Allen *Lane with his Penguin imprint. The advent of book clubs has also expanded the market for books, especially works of nonfiction.

Puccini, Giacomo (1875–1924) Italian opera composer. He was a church organist before studying at the Milan conservatoire with Amilcare Ponchielli (1834–86). His first major success was *Manon Lescaut* (1893). The operas that followed established Puccini as the master of the Italian stage and of the *verismo* (Italian: realism) style: *La Bohème* (1896), *Tosca* (1900), and *Madame Butterfly* (1904). An opera on an American subject, *La fanciulla del West* (1910) and the three one-act operas of *Il Trittico* (1918) were less successful; his final masterpiece, *Turandot*, was produced posthumously in 1926, having been completed by Franco Alfano (1876–1954).

Pucelle, Jean (?1300–?1355) French miniature painter and manuscript illuminator. His best-known works are the *Belleville Breviary* and *The Hours of Jeanne d'Évreux* (Metropolitan Museum, New York), the latter being a prayer book commissioned by the French queen.

puck In English folklore, a household spirit, malicious fairy, or demon. The famous Puck of Shakespeare's *A Midsummer Night's Dream* is identified with the mischievous fairy Robin Goodfellow.

puddling process A method of making pure iron from *pig iron. The pig iron is melted in a furnace and powdered iron oxide is stirred in to drive off the slag. As the iron becomes purer, its melting point increases and eventually it forms a pasty mass, which is removed and hammered or rolled into shape. Puddling superseded *wrought-iron working by hand and its introduction was an important contribution to the industrial revolution, although it is now little used.

Pudovkin, Vsevolod (1893–1953) Russian film director. He is best known for his early silent films, especially *Mother* (1926), *The End of St Petersburg* (1927), and *Storm Over Asia* (1928). He published influential lectures concerning the technique of montage.

Puebla (*or* Puebla de Zaragoza) 19 03N 98 10W A city in S Mexico. Strategically situated on the route between Mexico City and Veracruz, it was an important fortress city for several centuries. Notable buildings include an ornate cathedral (1649) and the Teatro Principal (1790). A major agricultural and industrial centre, Puebla is famous for its onyx products. Population (1980): 835 759.

Pueblo 38 17N 104 38W A city in the USA, in Colorado on the Arkansas River. Established in 1842, it has important steel industries, which use local coal. Other industrial activities include oil refining and meat packing. Population (1980): 101 686.

Pueblo Indians North American Indian tribes of the SW region including the Tewa, Keres, *Hopi, and Zuni. Their collective name derives from the Spanish term for their villages—*pueblos*. They began to abandon their hunting existence and adopt their present farming economy about 1600 years ago. They were always extremely peaceful peoples, much given to ritual and ceremonial pursuits. Their villages are often constructed around a central courtyard; the buildings, made from mudbrick blocks, have several storeys, each set back from the one below. Communities were traditionally governed by a council of the heads of the various secret religious societies, which met in underground rooms called kivas. The diversity of Pueblo languages indicates different origins.

puerperal fever Persistent fever occurring in a woman soon after childbirth, most commonly caused by infection of the genital tract, particularly of the lining of the womb. The infection may be serious and progress to blood poisoning. Formerly many women died of puerperal fever, but with improved hygiene and antibiotics the disease is now rare and can be cured by prompt treatment with antibiotics.

Puerto Rico, Commonwealth of (name from 1898 until 1932: Porto Rico) An island and self-governing commonwealth in association with the USA. It is in the West Indies, the smallest and most easterly island in the Greater Antilles. It is largely mountainous, rising over 1200 m (3937 ft) and supports one of the densest populations in the world. *Economy*: rapid industrialization has taken place since the 1940s transforming the economy from a basically agricultural one to a mixed one. Manufacture (chemicals, textiles, plastics, food processing) is the main source of income, while in the agricultural sector income from dairy and livestock farming has overtaken that of sugar, the principal crop. Tourism is an increasingly important source of revenue. *History*: discovered by Columbus in 1508, it was under Spanish rule for nearly 400 years until ceded to the USA in 1898. Full US citizenship was granted in 1917 and it attained its present status in 1952, which was ratified by a plebiscite (1967). During the 1940s and 1950s emigration to the USA was high but later moderated. In 1976 the New Progressive Party regained governorship and legislative control, led by Carlos Romero Barceló (1932–), who is an advocate of the incorporation of Puerto Rico as a state of the USA. Since 1974, however, there has been growing militant pressure for the independence of Puerto Rico and in August, 1978, the UN special committee on decolonization reaffirmed the "inalienable right of the people of Puerto Rico" to self-determination. Official language: Spanish; English is also widely spoken. Official currency: US dollar of 100 cents. Area: 8674 sq km (3349 sq mi). Population (1983): 3 295 000. Capital: San Juan.

Pufendorf, Samuel von (1632–94) German jurist, philosopher, and historian, known for his contribution to natural and international law. A professor at Heidelberg and later at Lund, he became historiographer to the Swedish court in 1677 and to the Elector of Brandenburg in 1688. In his best-known work, *De Jure naturae et gentium* (1672), influenced by *Grotius and *Hobbes, he argued that all men are entitled to be free and equal and that international law is not restricted to Christendom but is common to all nationalities. His *De habitu religionis christianae ad vitam civilem* (1687) advocated state superiority over the church in civil affairs.

puff adder A large stout-bodied highly venomous *adder belonging to the genus *Bitis* (8 species), occurring in semiarid areas of Africa and characterized by its habit of hissing loudly and inflating its body in a threatening posture. 0.3–2 m long, puff adders are brown or grey with yellow chevron patterning.

puffball The globular or pear-shaped fruiting body of certain fungi. As it matures, the outer layer cracks and sloughs off; the spongy interior produces powdery spores, which are released either through a pore (genus *Lycoperdon*) or from the upper surface (genus *Calvatia*). The greyish-white giant puffball (*C. giganteum*) occurs in pastures, woodlands, and road verges and may reach over 1 m across. Class: *Basidiomycetes*.

puffer A □fish, also called globe fish, belonging to the family *Tetraodontidae*, that inflates its body with air or water when disturbed. The tough spiny skin contains a highly toxic chemical (tetraodontoxin), which can be fatal. Up to 50 cm long, puffers live mainly in tropical and subtropical seas, feeding on corals, molluscs, and crustaceans using their beaklike snouts. They are edible if expertly prepared. Order: *Tetraodontiformes*.

puffin A N Atlantic seabird, *Fratercula arctica*. 29 cm long, it is black with a white face and underparts, red legs, and a blue ring around the eye. Its large triangular bill is striped red, yellow, and blue in the breeding season. It feeds at sea on fish and molluscs and breeds in disused rabbit burrows. Family: *Alcidae* (auks). *See* Plate V.

pug A breed of toy □dog originating in China and introduced to Britain from Holland in the 17th century. It is stockily built, with the tail curled over the back, and has a wrinkled skin and a large head with a short square muzzle. The short smooth coat can be silver, black, or apricot-fawn with a black mask on the face and a black line along the back. Height: 25–28 cm.

Pugachov, Yemelyan Ivanovich (1726–75) The leader of a Cossack rebellion in Russia, the Pugachov Rebellion (1773–74). Claiming to be the assassinated Tsar Peter III (1728–62; reigned 1762), Pugachov raised a revolt against the government of *Catherine the Great. The revolt collapsed and Pugachov was beheaded.

Pugin, Augustus Welby Northmore (1812–52) British architect and theorist. Pugin was the most vocal exponent of the English *gothic revival, particularly in his most influential book, *Contrasts* (1836), which exalted the English

*Decorated style (late 13th to early 14th centuries) above all other architectural forms. As an architect he was most accomplished at designing churches, such as Nottingham Cathedral (1842). However, he is best known for his collaboration with *Barry on the *Palace of Westminster, being responsible for the interior design.

Puglia. *See* Apulia.

Pugwash Conferences International conferences on science and world affairs, convened at the suggestion of, among others, Albert Einstein and Bertrand Russell, that discuss the problems of *disarmament and the social responsibility of scientists. The first conference was held in the village of Pugwash, Nova Scotia (Canada), in 1957.

Pula (Italian name: Pola)   44 52N 13 52E A port in N Yugoslavia in Croatia on the Adriatic coast. An important Austrian naval base (1815–1918), it subsequently belonged to Italy before passing to Yugoslavia in 1947. There are many ancient buildings, including a vast Roman amphitheatre. Its industries include shipbuilding. Population (1981 est): 77 278.

PUFFIN   *The bill of this bird, which breeds in large colonies, is armed with serrations that enable it to carry 30-40 fish at a time. Puffins will continue to bring food to the nest even after the young have left.*

Pulci, Luigi (1432–84) Italian poet. He lived mostly at the court of Lorenzo de' *Medici and wrote all his works in Italian. His major work is the epic poem *Morgante* (1483), a colloquial and irreverently comic treatment of French chivalric material concerning Roland (*see* Charlemagne).

puli A Hungarian breed of sheepdog whose unique coat hangs to the ground in long tight cords. The puli is agile and lively; its tail is held over the back and its coat is usually black but may be bronze-black, grey, or white. Height: 41–46 cm (dogs); 36–41 cm (bitches).

Pulitzer Prizes Annual awards endowed by the US editor and publisher Joseph Pulitzer (1847–1911) for achievements in journalism and literature. The $1,000 prizes for journalism, including awards for investigative reporting and criticism etc., and the $500 prizes for literature, including awards for fiction and poetry etc., were first awarded in 1917. Since 1943 a prize for musical composition has also been awarded.

Pullman, George Mortimer (1831–97) US businessman, who invented the luxurious Pullman sleeping car for railways. His first such car, the Pioneer, was made in 1865.

pulsar A celestial object that emits extremely regular pulses of radiation and is almost certainly a rotating *neutron star. Pulsars were originally discovered, in 1967, at radio wavelengths. The Crab and Vela pulsars also emit pulses at optical and gamma-ray wavelengths. The pulses arise when a beam of radio waves emitted by the rotating star sweeps past the earth,

similar to the way in which lighthouse flashes are produced. The radiation (synchrotron radiation) is generated by electrons moving in the star's strong magnetic field; the emission site is still uncertain. The pulsation periods, ranging from less than 2 milliseconds to 4 seconds, are all very gradually increasing. Pulsars are thought to originate in *supernovae. X-ray pulsars also exist but apparently involve a neutron star as a component of a close binary star; their pulsation periods are much longer, up to several minutes, and are gradually decreasing.

pulsating stars. *See* variable stars.

pulse The rhythmic contraction and expansion of the elastic walls of the arteries caused by the pressure of blood pumped from the heart. The pulse therefore reflects the heart rate and can be readily felt in arteries just beneath the skin: it is usually measured at the radial artery in the wrist. The average pulse rate of a resting adult is 60–80 per minute; it increases with exercise and emotion. The pulse also becomes faster during a fever and irregular in heart-rhythm disorders. A reduction in blood pressure (e.g. after haemorrhage) will cause a fast feeble pulse.

puma. *See* cougar.

pumice A volcanic rock derived from acidic lava. It resembles sponge in having many cavities produced by bubbles of gas trapped on rapid solidification. Pumice is light in colour and weight and often floats on water.

pumpkin The fruit of certain varieties of *Cucurbita pepo* and *C. maxima*, small bushes or trailing vines cultivated in North America and Europe. The fruit is large and round, up to 30 kg in weight with a lightly furrowed yellow rind surrounding an edible fleshy pulp and numerous seeds. It is cooked and eaten as a vegetable, in pies, puddings, and soups or used as animal feed. Family: *Cucurbitaceae*.

pumps Machines designed to transfer mechanical energy to a fluid. This energy may be required to move the fluid from one place to another, raise its level, increase its pressure, or provide circulation. Pumps are of three kinds: reciprocating, centrifugal, and rotary displacement. The reciprocating pump consists essentially of a piston moving to and fro; liquid is drawn in through one valve on the down stroke, and expelled through an exhaust valve on the upstroke. The centrifugal pump draws liquid into the centre of a rotating impeller, which thrusts it out of the exit. Rotating pumps consist of shaped gears or rotors, which move the liquid around a close-fitting chamber.

Punch and Judy A British puppet show performed with glove puppets and featuring the violent quarrels of the heartless Punch and his wife Judy. The character of Punch, who wears a striped costume and has a hooked nose and a humped back, derives from the Italian *commedia dell'arte and was popularized in England by Italian puppeteers in the late 17th century.

Punic Wars Three wars between Rome and Carthage, which gave Rome control of the Mediterranean. The first Punic (from the Latin *Punicus*, Carthaginian) War (264–241 BC) was provoked by Roman intervention in Sicily and was marked by the emergence of Roman naval power: its newly built fleet was victorious off Mylae (260) and again off the Aegates Insulae (241), which brought the war to an end with Carthage's evacuation of Sicily. The second Punic War (218–201) was instigated by *Hannibal's capture (219) of Saguntum, a Roman ally in Spain. His advance into Italy was eventually checked, after disastrous Roman losses at Trebia (218), Trasimene (217), and *Cannae (216), by *Fabius Maximus and *Scipio Africanus, who defeated Hannibal at *Zama (202). Carthage gave up its Spanish conquests and became a dependent ally of Rome. Roman fears of a resurgence of Carthaginian power caused the third Punic War (149–146), in which Carthage was destroyed and its territory became the Roman province of Africa.

Punjab A region of the NW Indian subcontinent, in India

and Pakistan below the Himalayan foothills on the flat alluvial plain of five Indus tributaries. Hot and dry, it produces grain surpluses with irrigation. Pulses, cotton, sugar cane, oilseeds, fruit, and vegetables are also grown. Industries include textiles, bicycles, electrical and metal goods, machinery, and food products. The region is comparatively urbanized. Its population is 60% Sikh in India's Punjab state, and almost entirely Muslim in Pakistan's Punjab province. *History*: on the invasion route into India, the Punjab passed successively under different rulers. It was conquered by Muslims (11th century) but eventually became a Sikh stronghold until Britain established control (19th century). On the partition of India and Pakistan (1947), the Punjab was divided on a religious basis. This led to massacres and mass migration. The W section became the Pakistan province of West Punjab (renamed Punjab in 1949), with an area of 205 346 sq km (79 284 sq mi) and its capital at Lahore; its population in 1972 was 37 374 000. The Indian section was reorganized in 1956 and 1966 on a linguistic basis when the Punjabi-speaking state of Punjab was created, 50 376 sq km (19 445 sq mi), with its capital at Chandigarh; its population in 1981 was 16 669 755. In 1987 the central government took control of the state following violence between Sikhs and Muslims.

Punjabi An *Indo-Aryan language of the *Punjab. It is similar to *Hindi and written in the Devanagari script or in the Gumurki script of the Sikh scriptures.

Punt, land of A country with which the ancient Egyptians traded from 2750 BC for gold, ivory, incense, and spices. It was probably situated on the Somali coast of NE Africa.

Punta Arenas 53 10S 70 56W A port in S Chile, on the Strait of Magellan. It serves a large sheep-rearing area. Exports include hides, wool, mutton, lumber, and oil. Population (1983 est): 67 600.

pupa A stage in the life cycle of certain insects, including flies, butterflies (in which it is the chrysalis), ants, bees, and beetles, during which complete *metamorphosis from larva to adult takes place. The adult emerges by cutting or digesting the pupal case after a period of a few days to several months.

pupil. *See* eye; iris.

puppetry The art of manipulating puppets or marionettes in a dramatic performance. Puppets were used in religious ritual and folk drama in many early civilizations. In Japan, the form of puppet theatre known as *Joruri* and developed by Chikamatsu Monzaemon (1653-1724) is still actively maintained. Introduced into England from Italy in the late 17th century, puppet theatre flourished throughout Europe during the 18th century and enjoyed an artistic revival in the late 19th and early 20th centuries.

Purbeck, Isle of A peninsula in S England, in Dorset between the English Channel and Poole Harbour. Purbeck marble, a limestone used in building, is quarried here.

Purcell, Edward Mills (1912-) US physicist, who shared the 1952 Nobel Prize with Felix *Bloch for their independent measurements of the magnetic moments of nuclei in solids and liquids. He also worked in astronomy, discovering an important emission by interstellar hydrogen in the microwave region.

Purcell, Henry (1659-95) English composer and organist. He was a choirboy at the Chapel Royal and a pupil of John Blow, whom he succeeded as organist of Westminster Abbey in 1679. In 1677 he was appointed composer to the orchestra of the Chapel Royal and, in 1682, organist there. He wrote keyboard pieces, sonatas, anthems, songs, cantatas, and much music for the stage, including incidental music for *King Arthur* (1691) and *The Fairy Queen* (1692) and one opera, *Dido and Aeneas* (1689).

Purchas, Samuel (1577-1626) English clergyman and compiler of travel books. He continued the work of *Hakluyt, whose papers he inherited, in collecting accounts of

voyages of trade and exploration. His major work is *Hakluytus Posthumus, or Purchas His Pilgrimes* (4 vols, 1625).

purchase tax An indirect tax on goods calculated by adding a percentage to the wholesale price of the goods. The tax was introduced in the UK in 1940 for certain classes of consumer goods and was replaced by *value-added tax in 1973.

Pure Land Buddhism A popular E Asian devotional form of Mahayana Buddhism, originating in China in the 4th century AD. Its adherents, following the Sukhavativyuha sutras, believe that by reciting the name of Amitabha, the Buddha of Infinite Light, they will be reborn in the Pure Land in the West (Sukhavati), which he has created.

purgatives. *See* laxatives.

purgatory In Roman Catholic doctrine, the state in which souls are purified after death to make them fit for heaven. Masses or prayers for the dead are believed to shorten a soul's purgatorial sufferings. The doctrine of purgatory was officially adopted by the Church in the late 6th century, but at the Reformation the Protestants rejected the concept, holding that souls either go directly to heaven or hell or sleep until the Last Judgment.

Puri 19 49N 85 54E A port in India, in Orissa on the Bay of Bengal. A major religious centre, it holds many festivals and has an exceptional 12th-century temple. Population (1981): 100 942.

Purim A Jewish festival, commemorating the frustration of an attempt to exterminate the Jews of the Persian Empire (473 BC), as narrated in the book of Esther. It is celebrated on the 14th Adar (Feb–March), with lighthearted festivities and charitable gifts. The scroll (*megillah*) of Esther is read in synagogues.

purine An organic nitrogenous base ($C_5H_4N_4$) consisting of a two-ringed molecule of carbon and nitrogen atoms. The derivatives adenine and guanine are constituents of the nucleic acids *DNA and *RNA. *Uric acid and *caffeine are also purines.

purism An art movement launched in 1918 by the manifesto, *Après le Cubisme*, of the painter Amédée Ozenfant (1886-1966) and the architect and painter *Le Corbusier. Their aim was to purify *cubism by stripping it of its decorative features and basing their austere geometrical shapes on machine forms.

Puritanism A movement among Protestants in 16th- and 17th-century England. The term originally denoted members of the Church of England in Elizabeth I's reign who wished to eliminate elements in the Church's liturgy and hierarchy that were reminiscent of Roman Catholicism (*see* Marprelate Tracts). In the 17th century Puritan criticism of the Anglican episcopacy was intensified by *Laud's policies, and the Puritans, many of them now forming extremist sects (*see* Fifth Monarchy Men; Levellers), became associated with the parliamentarian side in the Civil War. After the Act of Uniformity (1662) the term *Nonconformists became generally applied to the sects of Puritan origin that survived, such as the *Quakers.

Purple Heart Oldest US military decoration, established as the Badge of Military Merit by George Washington in 1782 and awarded during the American Revolution. Reinstituted in 1932, it is awarded to those wounded in battle. It is a purple heart of cloth, bordered by bronze.

purpura Localized limited bleeding into the skin, causing a rash of purple spots. This is a common and harmless condition of the elderly (senile purpura). Purpura may also result from reactions to drugs and infections, scurvy, and an allergic disease of childhood called Henoch-Schönlein purpura. A deficiency of blood platelets (important in clotting) also leads to purpura.

purslane An annual herbaceous plant, *Portulaca oleracea*, with prostrate reddish stems bearing fleshy oval leaves and dense terminal clusters of tiny pink flowers. It is widespread as a weed and has been used as a culinary herb. Family: *Portulacaceae.*

Sea purslane (*Halimione portulacoides*) is a shrubby perennial of temperate salt marshes, with greyish oval leaves and knobbly heads of tiny golden flowers. Family: *Chenopodiaceae. Honkenya peploides*, also called sea purslane, is a creeping perennial plant of N temperate sandy beaches. It has pointed fleshy leaves and small five-petalled white flowers on short stalks, surrounded by fleshy sepals. Family: *Caryophyllaceae.*

Purus, Rio (Spanish name: Río Purús) A river in NW South America, rising in SE Peru and flowing generally NE through Brazil to the River Amazon. Length: about 3200 km (2000 mi).

pus Thick yellow fluid that arises in infected areas and contains dead bacteria, dead white blood cells, serum, and damaged tissue. It is formed as a result of the body's defensive action against invading bacteria and other particles. Pus is present in boils and similar skin conditions but can be formed anywhere in the body (*see* abscess). *See also* inflammation.

Pusan 35 05N 129 02E A port in SE South Korea, on the Korea Strait, capital of South Kyongsang province and South Korea's second largest city. It is the site of a state and a private university. Refugees gathered here during the Korean War (1950–53). Its varied industries include shipbuilding. Population (1980): 3 160 000.

Pusey, Edward Bouverie (1800–82) British leader of the *Oxford Movement. A Fellow of Oriel College, Pusey was ordained in 1828 and in the same year became professor of Hebrew at Oxford. In 1833 he joined the movement at Oriel to revive the Catholic tradition in the Anglican Church. He became its leader in 1841, when John *Newman was converted to Roman Catholicism.

Pushkin (name from 1708 until 1937: Tsarskoye Selo) 59 43N 30 22E A town in the Soviet Union, in the RSFSR 24 km (14 mi) S of Leningrad, with which it was joined by Russia's first railway (1837). Founded in 1708 by Peter the Great, it was the site of the imperial summer residence, and Catherine the Great's palace (1748–62) is still to be seen. In 1937 it was renamed after the Russian poet, who studied here. It has varied manufacturing industries and a botanical institute. Population (1983 est): 90 000.

Pushkin, Aleksandr (1799–1837) Russian poet, novelist, and dramatist. In 1820 he was exiled to the southern provinces for his political verse, which was considered revolutionary by the government. In exile he wrote two long Romantic poems strongly influenced by Byron and began the epic verse novel *Eugene Onegin* (1833), on which Tchaikovsky based his opera (1877–78). In 1824 he was transferred to NW Russia, where he wrote the historical drama *Boris Godunov* (1831), which became the basis of Mussorgsky's opera (1874). After his return to Moscow in 1826 he was still hindered by censorship, but during his last years he wrote the epic poem *The Bronze Horseman* (1837) as well as lyrical poetry and several prose works. He was killed in a duel. Pushkin was the most versatile and influential of Russian writers; he broke with a number of artificial conventions of the 18th and 19th centuries, established new literary genres and themes, and made the Russian language a highly adaptable literary medium.

Pushtu. *See* Pashto.

puss moth A moth, *Cerura vinula*, of Europe, Asia, and N Africa. The adult has a fat white hairy body with black spots. The caterpillar is green with black markings and when alarmed it presents a grotesque appearance with the head and tail appendages raised up. It feeds on sallow, willow, and poplar.

putrefaction The decomposition of organic matter, particularly of proteins by bacteria under anaerobic conditions (i.e. in the absence of oxygen). Putrefaction is associated with a characteristic bad smell, produced by the amines, ammonia, hydrogen sulphide, and other compounds that are formed.

putty A mixture of boiled linseed oil and powdered calcium carbonate (whiting) used as a cement. Of doughlike consistency, it is used for cementing sheets of glass into windows.

Putumayo, Río A river in South America. Rising in the Colombian Andes, it flows generally SE forming most of the border between Colombia and Peru. On entering Brazil it is known as the Rio Içá before joining the River Amazon. Length: 1578 km (980 mi).

Puvis de Chavannes, Pierre (Cécile) (1824–98) French painter, born in Lyons. He was an independent artistic figure but also an important influence on such painters as *Seurat and *Gauguin. He is famous for his murals for public buildings, notably *The Life of S Genevieve* (Panthéon, Paris) and his painting *The Poor Fisherman* (Louvre). Imitating in oil the pale colours and simplified forms of frescoes, he chiefly painted allegorical subjects.

Pu Yi, Henry (*or* H. P'u-i; 1906–67) The last emperor of China (1908–12) as Xuan-tong (*or* Hsuan-t'ung). He became emperor at the age of two and abdicated two years later after the republican revolution of 1911. He was allowed to live in the summer palace on a government pension until the Japanese made him ruler, as Kang-de (*or* K'ang-te), of *Manchukuo (1934–45).

PVC. *See* polyvinyl chloride.

Pycnogonida. *See* sea spider.

pyelitis Infection of the central part of the kidney, where the urine collects before passing to the ureter. Infection may spread through the blood or up to the kidney from the bladder. The patient usually has a fever and loin pain and produces urine containing protein, white blood cells, and sometimes red blood cells. In some cases the infection spreads to the rest of the kidney (**pyelonephritis**). The infection will normally settle with antibiotics, but repeated low-grade infections may lead to kidney failure and *uraemia.

Pygmalion In Greek mythology, a legendary king of Cyprus who made an ivory statue (known as Galatea in modern versions of the story) and fell in love with it. When he prayed for a wife who would be as beautiful as the statue, Aphrodite gave the statue life and Pygmalion married her.

Pygmies Peoples of the tropical forest region of Africa, who are much smaller in stature than their Bantu neighbours. The males are less than 150 cm (4 ft 11 in) in height. They are nomadic hunters and gatherers, wandering in small and basically patrilineal exogamous bands of around 30 members. They use either the bow and arrow or, more usually, nets and spears. There are no chiefs, decisions being made by general consensus. They speak various Bantu languages.

pygmy hippopotamus A small *hippopotamus, *Choeropsis liberiensis*, of West African forests. Up to 100 cm high at the shoulder and weighing about 200 kg, pygmy hippos are less aquatic and more solitary than their larger relatives. They frequent river banks, sleeping during the day and feeding in the forest at night.

pygmy owl A very small *owl belonging to a widely distributed genus (*Glaucidium*; 12 species). About 16 cm long, pygmy owls hunt small mammals, birds, and insects, which may be larger than themselves.

Pylos (Greek name: Pílos) 36 55N 21 42E A seaport (also called Navarino) in W Greece, on the Peloponnesian coast. It lies at the S end of Órmos Navarínou (Bay of Navarino), scene of two important battles: the Athenian victory over the Spartans during the Peloponnesian War (425 BC) and the decisive battle of *Navarino (1827) in the War of Greek Independence. The Mycenaean town associated with the legendary King *Nestor lies N of the modern town. Here excavations revealed a well-preserved palace and archive of *Linear B tablets.

Pym, John (?1583–1643) English parliamentary opponent of Charles I; he sat in every parliament from 1621 until his death. In the *Long Parliament he helped to impeach *Strafford and to draw up the *Grand Remonstrance (1641) and was one of the five MPs whom Charles tried to arrest (1642). After the outbreak of the Civil War he organized supplies to the parliamentary forces.

Pynchon, Thomas (1937–) US novelist. He was acclaimed as one of the most original and ambitious writers to emerge in the 1960s. A common theme of his three novels, *V* (1963), *The Crying of Lot 49* (1967), and *Gravity's Rainbow* (1973), is the protagonists' wandering quest through a bizarre and unpredictable landscape.

P'yŏngyang 39 00N 125 47E The capital of the Democratic People's Republic of (North) Korea, in the NW on the River Taedong. Reputedly the oldest city in Korea, it suffered severely from successive Japanese and Chinese attacks over the centuries and was almost destroyed by US bombing in the Korean War (1950–53). It is a major industrial as well as administrative and commercial centre. Its three universities include the Kim Il Sung University, founded in 1946. Population (1981): 1 280 000.

pyorrhoea. *See* periodontal disease.

Pyracantha A genus of thorny evergreen shrubs (about 10 species), known as firethorns, native to SE Eurasia and widely cultivated as garden shrubs in hedges or against walls. A commonly grown species is *P. coccinea*. It has finely toothed leaves and flat-topped clusters of white or pinkish-yellow flowers. The round scarlet berries may last all winter. Family: *Rosaceae*.

pyralid moth A moth of the widespread family *Pyralidae*. The adults have generally narrow forewings and broader hindwings. Both pairs are fringed. The larvae feed on a variety of substances, including dried stored products. They can be serious economic pests, especially the *corn borer, *wax moth, and meal moth (*Pyralis farinalis*). Many larvae spin silken tunnels in which they live.

pyramids Royal funerary monuments in ancient Egypt. The greatest are the pyramids of *Khufu, *Khafre, and Menkaura (Greek name: Mycerinus) at Giza (built c. 2600–2500 BC), the only survivors of the *Seven Wonders of the World. Their tombs were all robbed in antiquity but they nevertheless remain extraordinary feats of engineering. For over four millennnia the pyramid of Khufu, now 138 m (453 ft) high was the highest building in the world. Pyramids were also built in ancient Mexico.

Pyramids, Battle of the (21 July, 1798) The battle in which Napoleon with some 25 000 troops defeated about 40 000 Egyptians near Imbaba on the W bank of the Nile. The battle was followed by Napoleon's defeat of the Ottoman Turks at *Aboukir Bay.

Pyramus and Thisbe Legendary lovers in a Babylonian story retold by *Ovid. The couple were forbidden to marry by their parents but exchanged vows through a chink in the wall between their houses. They arranged a secret meeting. Thisbe arrived first at the meeting place, which was near a mulberry tree; but she was frightened by a lion and fled, dropping her veil. Pyramus, finding her veil and thinking her dead, stabbed himself, and when Thisbe returned she killed herself also. The mulberry tree has borne blood-red fruit ever since. The rustics' farce in Shakespeare's *A Midsummer Night's Dream* is based on this story.

Pyrenean mountain dog (or Great Pyrenees) A breed of large dog, possibly of Asian origin, used in Europe for over 3000 years to guard shepherds and their flocks. They are massively built with drooping ears and an ambling gait. The long thick slightly wavy coat is white, with or without grey or brown patches. Height: 71 cm (dogs); 66 cm (bitches).

Pyrenees (French name: Pyrénées; Spanish name: Pirineos) A mountain range in SW Europe. It extends between the Bay of Biscay in the W and the Mediterranean Sea in the E, forming a barrier between France and Spain. The entire republic of Andorra lies within the range, which rises to 3404 m (11 168 ft) at Pico de Aneto, close to the source of the River Garonne in the centre.

Pyrenees, Treaty of the (1659) The treaty that ended the war of 1648–59 between France and Spain and marked the rise of French predominance in Europe. Spain lost Artois and the Catalan counties of Rousillon and Cerdana. Maria-Theresa, the daughter of Philip IV of Spain, was married to Louis XIV of France.

pyrethrum A perennial plant, *Chrysanthemum coccineum* (or *Pyrethrum roseum*), with finely divided leaves and showy red, pink, lilac, or white flowers. It is native to Persia and the Caucasus and widely cultivated for ornament in temperate regions. The name is also given to an insecticide prepared from the dried flower heads of this and related species. Family: *Compositae*.

Pyrex The trade name for a heat-resistant glass containing borosilicate. It is also resistant to many chemicals and is an electrical insulator. Pyrex is used in laboratory glassware, ovenware, and large telescopes.

pyridine (C_6H_5N) A hygroscopic colourless liquid, with a strong odour, which boils at 115°C. It is a basic aromatic compound with a six-membered heterocyclic molecule, made by passing tetrahydrofurfuryl alcohol and ammonia over a catalyst at 500°C. It is used as an industrial solvent and in the manufacture of various drugs and pesticides.

pyridoxine. *See* vitamin B complex.

pyrimidine An organic base ($C_4H_4N_2$) consisting of a six-membered ring of carbon and nitrogen atoms. Its derivatives cytosine, thymine, and uracil are constituents of the nucleic acids *RNA and *DNA.

pyrite (or iron pyrites) A pale brassy yellow mineral, FeS_2, the most common sulphide mineral. It occurs as an accessory mineral in igneous rocks, in hydrothermal veins, in contact metamorphic rocks, and in sediments laid down in anaerobic conditions. It is usually mined for its sulphur, used for the manufacture of sulphuric acid, or for the gold and copper found in association with it. Because of its colour it has been called fool's gold. The term is sometimes used for other sulphides, for example copper pyrites, but if used alone it refers to iron pyrites.

pyroclastic rock Rock formed from fragments thrown out by volcanic explosions, in either the solid or molten state. Fragments less than 2 mm in diameter are known as ash or, when consolidated, tuff. Lapilli are larger fragments and bombs are even larger, often spindle-shaped. Blocks are large angular fragments ejected in the solid state.

pyroelectricity The development of opposite electric charges on opposite faces of asymmetric crystals when they are heated. The charges occur on those faces that are responsible for the crystal's asymmetry. Quartz and tourmaline have pyroelectric properties. *See also* piezoelectric effect.

pyrogallol (or pyrogallic acid; $C_6H_3(OH)_3$) A white soluble crystalline solid. It is a powerful reducing agent, used in developing photographs and to absorb oxygen in gas analysis.

pyrolysis A chemical reaction produced by high temperatures. Common examples include the charring of wood and firing of pottery. Pyrolysis has many industrial applications, a recent one being the recovery of hydrocarbon fuels from waste organic materials.

pyrometer An instrument used for measuring high temperatures. The two most important types are the optical pyrometer and the radiation pyrometer. In the optical pyrometer a filament, heated to a known temperature, is viewed with the hot body in the background. The temperature of the filament is adjusted until it appears to vanish, at which point its temperature is the same as the temperature to be measured. In the radiation pyrometer, radiant heat from the hot body is focused into a *thermopile, which develops a potential difference proportional to the temperature.

pyrope. *See* garnet.

pyroxenes A group of ferromagnesian rock-forming silicate minerals. They usually occur in basic and ultrabasic igneous rocks but also in some metamorphosed rocks. Those of orthorhombic crystal structure are orthopyroxenes and those of monoclinic structure are clinopyroxenes. Orthopyroxenes vary in composition between the end-members enstatite ($MgSiO_3$) and orthoferrosilite ($FeSiO_3$). Clinopyroxenes, the larger group, include diopside, hedenbergite, augite, pigeonite, aegirine, jadeite, and spodumene (a source of lithium).

Pyrrhon (c. 360–c. 270 BC) Greek philosopher, born at Elis, who was the founder of *scepticism. Pyrrhon believed that objective knowledge was impossible, the limitations of knowledge being explored by later sceptics. He sought a way of achieving mental tranquillity by suspension of judgment.

Pyrrhus (319–272 BC) King of Epirus (307–303, 297–272). Having secured his throne (297), Pyrrhus pursued an adventurous policy of expansion but his empire was short-lived: in support of Tarentum against Rome he won victories that cost much in loss of life ("Pyrrhic" victories), especially at Asculum (279), and he was forced to withdraw.

pyruvic acid An organic acid ($CH_3COCOOH$). Its anion, pyruvate ($CH_3-CO-COO^-$), is an important intermediate compound in the carbohydrate metabolism of living organisms.

Pythagoras (6th century BC) Greek philosopher and religious leader. Born at *Samos, he migrated in about 530 BC to Crotone (S Italy), where he founded a religious society that governed Crotone for many years until its suppression (460–440 BC). Its members followed an ascetic regime of dietary taboos, self-examination, and study aimed at purifying the soul and releasing it from "entombment" in successive bodies. Pythagoras probably discovered the geometrical theorem named after him and certainly discovered the arithmetical ratios governing musical intervals, which led him to interpret the universe in terms of mathematics alone. Pythagoreans were pioneers in several branches of science. *See also* Alcmaeon; Archytas; Pythagoreanism.

Pythagoreanism The philosophy of the followers of *Pythagoras, who developed the two main strands in their master's thought: mysticism and mathematics. The former was fostered by an ascetic religious order founded by Pythagoras at Crotone, Italy, the rules of which included silence and vegetarianism. Other disciples extended Pythagoras' interpretation of the physical world through numbers and made substantial advances in geometry. In astronomy they evolved a model of the universe that anticipated the heliocentric system of *Copernicus. An eclectic form of Pythagoreanism, known as Neopythagoreanism, developed in Alexandria during the 1st century BC.

Pytheas (4th century BC) Greek navigator. From Marseille he made a voyage along the coasts of Spain, France, and E Britain and seems to have reached as far N as Iceland. His narrative is lost but was later used by the Greek geographer *Strabo.

Pythian Games The ancient Greek festival at Delphi in honour of Apollo. Second only to the Olympic Games in importance, the festival originally consisted of musical competitions but from 582 BC also included athletic and equestrian events, taking place every four years.

python A large *constrictor snake belonging to the Old World subfamily *Pythoninae* (20–25 species), occurring in tropical and temperate regions. Pythons usually live near water and tend to be sluggish, catching prey—which may include goats, pigs, and deer—by ambush. The reticulated python (*Python reticulatus*) is the largest of all constrictors, reaching 10 m in length. Many pythons are killed for their meat and skin. Family: *Boidae*. ⌐reptile.

Q

Qaboos ibn Sa'id (1940–) Sultan of Oman (1970–). He became sultan after deposing, with British support, his reactionary father Sa'id ibn Taymur. With Omani oil revenues Qaboos has initiated modernization programmes. His rule has been threatened by Chinese-backed guerrillas.

Qaddafi, Moammar al-. *See* Gaddafi, Moammar al-.

Qajars. *See* Agha Mohammad Khan.

Qatar, State of A country in the Middle East, in *Arabia occupying a peninsula on the W coast of the Persian Gulf. The native population is mainly Arab and Wahhabi Sunnite Muslim, but over 80% of workers are immigrants from other countries, including Iran and Pakistan. *Economy*: despite a decline in oil revenues in the 1980s oil extraction accounts for over 90% of the national income and has led to the development of other industries, such as fertilizer production. Qatar is a member of OPEC. There is also some fishing. *History*: Qatar relied on Britain for most of the 19th and 20th centuries, becoming a protectorate in 1916; it became independent in 1971. Head of state: Emir Sheik Khalifa bin Hamad Al-Thani (1937–). Official language: Arabic. Official currency: Qatar riyal of 100 dirhams. Area: 11 000 sq km (4246 sq mi). Population (1983 est): 267 000. Capital: Doha.

Qattara Depression An area in NE Egypt descending to 133 m (436 ft) below sea level. Its steep N side proved a defence for the S flank of the British army in the battle of El Alamein. Area: about 18 000 sq km (7000 sq mi).

Qazvin. *See* Kazvin.

Q fever An infection with the microorganism *Coxiella burnetti*, first described in Queensland (hence *Q* fever) in 1937. The disease affects cattle and sheep but can be transmitted to man through contaminated milk. The incubation period is two–four weeks and the disease usually takes the form of a viral *pneumonia. Treatment is with tetracycline antibiotics.

Qian Long (*or* Ch'ien-lung; 1711–99) The title of Hong-li (*or* Hung-li), Chinese emperor (1736–96) of the Qing dynasty. During his reign the Chinese empire saw its greatest expansion through continuing wars of conquest, which, however, undermined China's economy. His government was further weakened by the corruption of his minister He-shen (*or* Ho-shen). Qian Long was a distinguished patron of the arts. He abdicated in favour of his son.

Qin (*or* Ch'in; 221–206 BC) The dynasty under which China became a unified empire. The first Qin emperor, Shi Huangdi (*or* Shih Huang Ti; c. 259–210 BC), consolidated his vast conquest by unifying weights, measures, and coinage and by creating one system of writing for the whole empire. He ordered the burning of all books in China, except for practical handbooks and the history of his own dynasty. Believing in the absolute power of the ruler, his government was so harsh that the dynasty outlasted him by only four years. It was during the Qin reign that much of the *Great Wall of China was built. Excavations in the vicinity of his tomb in the late 1970s revealed several thousand life-size terracotta men and horses. The remains of the Qin capital were discovered in 1985.

Qing (*or* Ch'ing; 1644–1911) A Manchu dynasty, founded by *Nurhachi, that ruled China from the fall of the Ming dynasty until the revolution of 1911. The Manchus, living on the borders of Chinese civilization, gradually conquered Chinese territory as the Ming government weakened. The Qing (pure) dynasty was declared in 1636 but Peking was not captured until 1644. At its height in the 18th century under *Qian Long, the Qing ruled a vast empire that included Outer Mongolia, Tibet,

and Turkistan. Trade and commerce flourished, as did cultural life and learning. In over two and a half centuries, however, there was little change in the social order with dangerous results. Bureaucratic conservatism resisted modernization, corruption became rife, and China suffered a series of defeats by foreign powers (e.g. *Opium Wars) as well as internal rebellions (e.g. the *Taiping Rebellion) that culminated in the overthrow of the Qing in 1911.

Qingdao (Ch'ing-tao *or* Tsingtao) 36 04N 120 22E A port in E China, in Shandong province on the Yellow Sea. From 1898 to 1922 it was under German and then Japanese control. It is a centre of heavy industry. Population (1983 est): 1 180 000.

Qinghai (Ch'ing-hai *or* Tsinghai) A mountainous province in NW China. Tibetan and Mongol nomadic herdsmen keep yaks, sheep, and cattle, and it is famed for its horses. The monastery near Xining is an important centre of Tibetan Buddhism. Salt, oil, coal, and iron are produced. Area: 721 000 sq km (278 400 sq mi). Population (1980 est): 3 720 000. Capital: Xining.

Qinghai, Lake (*or* Koko Nor) A shallow salt lake of N central China, in the mountains of Qinghai province, the largest lake in China. Area: about 4100 sq km (1600 sq mi).

Qom 34 39N 50 57E A city in central Iran, S of Tehran. It is the burial place of many Islamic saints and a pilgrimage centre of Shiite Muslims. Population (1985 est): 637 700.

quadratic equation An algebraic *equation in which the greatest power of the *variable is two. It is usually written in the form $ax^2 + bx + c = 0$, in which the two *roots, or possible solutions, are given by $x = [-b \pm \sqrt{(b^2 - 4ac)}]/2a$. Both roots are real *numbers when the quantity under the square-root sign is greater than or equal to zero. They are equal when that quantity is zero. If it is less than zero the roots are complex numbers. The sum of the roots is $-b/a$ and their product is c/a.

quadrature The position of a celestial body in the solar system when its angular distance from the sun, as measured from earth (i.e. the angle body–earth–sun), is 90°.

quadriplegia. *See* paralysis.

Quadruple Alliances 1. (1718) The alliance formed by Britain, France, the Holy Roman Emperor, and the Netherlands to maintain the Treaties of *Utrecht (1713–14), which had been repudiated by Spain. 2. (1814) The alliance formed by Britain, Austria, Prussia, and Russia against Napoleon. It was confirmed at the Congress of *Vienna after Napoleon's fall. 3. (1834) The alliance between Britain, France, Spain, and Portugal that sought to maintain constitutional monarchy in Spain and Portugal.

quaestors Ancient Roman financial officers. Originally two were elected annually; more were appointed as Rome expanded. Two stayed in Rome in charge of the state treasury and records; others supervised Rome's corn supply and the financial administration of the provinces and military campaigns.

quagga An extinct wild horse, *Equus quagga*, that lived on the plains of South Africa. Up to 180 cm high at the shoulder, quaggas had a neck and head striped like a zebra with sandy-coloured hindquarters and white legs and tail. The last quagga died in Amsterdam Zoo in 1883.

Quai d'Orsay A street in Paris, on the Left Bank of the River Seine, on which the French Ministry of Foreign Affairs is situated.

quail A round-bodied short-tailed gamebird of open grassland and farmland. Old World quail (subfamily *Per-*

dicinae; 95 species) are 13–20 cm long and characterized by a smooth-edged bill and leg spurs; they are stocky and usually sandy in colour. New World quail (subfamily *Odontophorinae*; 36 species) are up to 30 cm long and have a strong serrated bill, no leg spurs, and are brightly coloured and patterned, often with crests; males and females differ markedly. Quail feed on seeds, berries, and leaves. Family: *Phasianidae* (pheasants, partridges, and quail).

Quakers The Christian sect, formally known as the Religious Society of Friends, founded in England by George *Fox in the late 1640s. They suffered violent persecution for many years and in 1682 William *Penn led a colony of Friends to *Pennsylvania. In the USA they were leaders in the fight against *slavery, emancipating their own slaves. The early Quakers adopted an unostentatious dress and way of life. They were (and remain) pacifists, refused to take oaths, and rejected the use of titles. In speech they used the old singular form "thou" in preference to the plural form "you" for one person, as more suited to the truth. They rejected the ministry and sacraments of the established Church. They worship in meetings, which start with silence until one member is moved by the "inner light," which they believe to be their guide, to address the congregation or to pray.

quaking grass An annual or perennial *grass of the genus *Briza* (about 20 species), mostly native to South America. Their long slender flower stalks bear spikelets of open flower clusters, which quiver in the wind. *B. media* is native to temperate Eurasia and grows 20–50 cm high. It is sometimes planted for ornament.

quandong A small shrubby Australian tree, *Fusanus acuminatus*, with simple leaves and heads of small inconspicuous flowers. The fruit is fleshy and edible, with a hard stony pitted edible seed. Family: *Santalaceae*.

quango (*qu*asi-*a*utonomous *n*ational *g*overnment *o*rganization) A term that came into use in the UK in the 1970s to describe organizations, such as the Monopolies Commission and the Equal Opportunities Commission, which have been set up by the government as independent bodies but are dependent on the government for their existence. Since 1979 the Conservative government has made considerable progress with its declared intention to disband many quangos to save government funds but has also found it necessary to establish some new ones. In the USA the acronym stands for "quasi-autonomous non-governmental organization."

Quant, Mary (1934–   ) British fashion designer, one of the first to become known for ready-to-wear rather than *haute couture* clothes. Her miniskirts, created especially for the young, made London a leading fashion centre in the 1960s. Her original boutique (Bazaar, opened in 1957) in the King's Road, London, soon expanded into an international business selling a wide range of fashion products.

quantity theory of money A theory that seeks to explain how the money supply (*see* money) affects the economy. Originally put forward in the 17th century, it has been restated in its modern form by the US economist Milton *Friedman. It states that if there is a change in the money supply, either the price level will change or the supply of goods in the economy will alter. The monetarists (*see* monetarism) assert, on the basis of the quantity theory, that if there is full employment it is the price level that will be affected by altering the money supply.

quantum number An integral or half-integral number (0, ½, 1, 1½, 2, . . .) that gives the possible values of a property of a system according to the *quantum theory. For example, in Bohr's atomic theory the angular momentum of an electron moving in orbit round an atomic nucleus can only have the values $nh/2\pi$, where n is a quantum number specifying these values and h is Planck's constant. Bohr's theory has now been replaced by the more versatile *wave mechanics, but the concept of quantum numbers is useful in some contexts. It is also

used to quantify the properties of elementary particles (*see* particle physics). For example spin is characterized by the quantum numbers $+\frac{1}{2}$ or $-\frac{1}{2}$ for an electron, depending on whether it is parallel or antiparallel to a specified direction. *Parity, *electric charge, *strangeness, *charm, *isotopic spin, etc., are other properties of elementary particles expressed by quantum numbers.

quantum theory The theory first developed by Max *Planck in 1900 to explain the distribution of wavelengths of electromagnetic radiation emitted by a *black body. The experimental observations could only be explained when Planck assumed that the radiation was emitted and absorbed in discrete amounts, which he called quanta. The energy of each quantum has the value hf, where h is a universal constant (now known as the Planck constant) and f is the frequency of the radiation. Planck's quantum theory was used by *Einstein to explain the *photoelectric effect and in 1913 by Niels *Bohr to explain the spectrum of hydrogen. Quantum theory has since become an essential part of modern physics. **Quantum mechanics** is the application of quantum theory to the mechanics of atomic systems; **quantum electrodynamics** is the theory of *electromagnetic interactions between elementary particles; **quantum statistics** is the application of statistical methods to many-particle quantum systems. *See also* wave mechanics.

QUAKERS *A Quaker meeting; the Toleration Act (1689) allowed nonconformists to worship freely in their own meeting houses.*

quarantine The period during which a person or animal suspected of carrying an infectious disease is kept in isolation. The term was originally applied to the 40-day period (French: *quarantaine*) during which ships suspected of carrying infected people were prevented from communicating with the shore. The quarantine period is now slightly longer than the incubation period of the disease; if no symptoms appear during quarantine the individual is considered free of the infection. Domestic animals undergo a six-month quarantine on entry to Britain to prevent the importation of rabies.

quarks. *See* particle physics.

quarrying. *See* mining and quarrying.

quarter days In law, days in each quarter of the year on which rent and other dues on land were traditionally paid. In England they are 25 March (Lady Day), 24 June (Midsummer Day), 29 Sept (Michaelmas Day), and 25 Dec (Christmas Day).

Quarter horse A breed of horse developed in colonial America from both local and English stock for racing over short distances, popularly a quarter of a mile. It has a deep compact muscular body and, with its speed and agility, is widely used for ranch work. Quarter horses may be any colour. Height: 1.45–1.57 m (14½–15½ hands).

Quarter Sessions, Courts of Courts presided over by two or more *justices of the peace in a county or a *recorder in a borough, which formerly sat four or more times a year to try certain offences or hear appeals from the inferior petty sessions courts. They originated in 1363 but were replaced by the Crown Court in 1972. In 1842 their power to try serious offences, including murder, was transferred to the superior assize courts, which were also abolished in 1972. *See also* courts of law.

quartz The commonest of all minerals, consisting of crystalline *silica. It is stable over a wide range of conditions and consequently occurs in many rocks, particularly acid igneous rocks (such as granite), many metamorphic rocks (such as gneisses), and in sands and gravels, which form sandstones on consolidation. It is commonly milky white in colour. Pure quartz is colourless and is known as rock crystal; it is used in glassmaking, in jewellery, and (because of its piezoelectric properties) in making electrical oscillators. Some coloured varieties, such as amethyst (violet), rose quartz (pink), and citrine (yellow), are used as gemstones. In the form of sand it is used as an abrasive and in cement. *See* Plate III.

quartzite A resistant pale-coloured rock consisting almost wholly of quartz. It is formed by the metamorphism of a pure sandstone, the original quartz grains being recrystallized and interlocking.

quasar (*quasi*-stellar object; *or* QSO) A class of celestial objects discovered in 1964–65, lying beyond our Galaxy. They appear as starlike points of light, each emitting more energy than several hundred giant galaxies. Quasar *redshifts are extremely large indicating that they are the most distant and the youngest extragalactic objects known. They must be highly luminous to be visible at such distances. Of the 3500 quasars known, the most distant (discovered 1986) is 73×10^{21} miles away. The energy-producing region is extremely compact; the prodigious energy could result from matter spiralling into a supermassive *black hole (maybe 10^9 solar masses) at the centre of a galaxy.

Quasimodo, Salvatore (1901–68) Italian poet. His early work, such as *And Suddenly It's Night* (1942), was evocative and private, but after World War II his poetry, as in *Il falso e vero verde* (1956), expressed his active concern for social issues. He won the Nobel Prize in 1959.

Quassia A genus of tropical Asian trees and shrubs (40 species). Bitterwood (*Q. amara*) is an attractive shrub or small tree with trifoliate leaves and clusters of tubular red flowers. The heartwood is a source of quassiin, a bitter substance used in medicine. Family: *Simaroubaceae*.

Quaternary period The most recent period of geological time, from the end of the *Tertiary (about 1.8 million years ago) to the present day. It includes the *Pleistocene (Ice Age) and *Holocene epochs. It is the period in which man became the dominant terrestrial species. Some authorities consider the Quaternary to be a division of the Tertiary.

Quathlamba. *See* Drakensberg Mountains.

Quebec The largest province of Canada, stretching from the *St Lawrence River N to Hudson Bay and Strait. The rocky forested Canadian Shield covers the N nine-tenths. Most of the population lives in the St Lawrence valley, which has dominated the history and economy of the province. The SE strip of Quebec enters the fertile Appalachian Highlands. The province's highly industrialized economy is based on its abundant natural resources, especially forests, minerals, and water power. Quebec is a major source of the world's paper. Asbestos, the rich iron-ore deposits at Ungava, copper, zinc, gold, and other minerals are mined. Cheap hydroelectricity aids smelting, refining, food processing, and the manufacture of metal and electrical products, textiles, machinery, and chemicals. Fishing, farming, and tourism are also economically important. *History*: claimed by France (1534), Quebec or New France was a French colony (1608–1763) until ceded to Britain. French-Canadian culture was preserved and nationalism increased steadily after the formation of Canada (1867). The Quiet Revolution· (1960s) enlivened cultural life and led to the victory of the secessionist Parti Québecois in the 1977 provincial election. However, a referendum on secession was defeated in 1980. Area: 1 356 791 sq km (523 858 sq mi). Population (1981): 6 438 403; over 80% are French speaking. Capital: Quebec. *See also* Montreal.

Quebec 46 50N 71 15W A city and port in E Canada, the capital of Quebec. First settled in 1608, it is strategically located above a sudden narrowing of the St Lawrence River. Quebec was the key to New France until captured by Britain (1759). It remains a cultural centre of French-speaking Canada, housing Laval University. Most of the workforce is employed by government and service industries but textiles, leather goods, printing, publishing, and pulp and paper are also important. Quebec is a major tourist attraction, with its citadel and the steep narrow streets and stone houses of the lower town. The Plains of *Abraham lie to the SW of the city. Population (1981): 166 474.

quebracho A tropical or subtropical tree of the genus *Schinopsis*, especially *S. lorentzii* and *S. balansae*. Their reddish-brown wood is an important commercial source of tannin, while *S. quebracho-colorado* is an important timber tree. Family: *Anacardiaceae*.

Quechua The language of the *Incas and of the present-day American Indian peoples of the central Andean highlands. These peoples, having now mainly lost their lands to Spanish settlers, form an impoverished peasantry. Crops are potatoes, corn, and quinoa. Llamas and alpacas are herded. The people are nominally Roman Catholic but many pagan beliefs and rituals survive.

Queen Anne style An English architectural and decorative style with some baroque elements, dating from about 1700 to 1715. It was characterized by increasing restraint in the decorative elements. Beautiful walnut veneered furniture was made; it was curvilinear in outline, exhibiting well-chosen figured woods, and enhanced by the restrained use of herringbone inlays. Gilt and lacquer continued in vogue but in a less flamboyant manner. Chairs became lighter, more comfortable, and invariably had cabriole legs. Plateglass wall mirrors in gilt frames decorated panelled rooms.

Queen Charlotte Islands An archipelago of W Canada, in British Columbia 160 km (100 mi) off the Pacific coast. Mountainous with lush vegetation (especially forests), the islands are mostly inhabited by Haida Indians engaged in fishing and forestry. Area: 9596 sq km (3705 sq mi). Population (1981): 5884.

Queen Maud Land. *See* Norwegian Antarctic Territory.

Queens 40 45N 73 50W One of the five boroughs of New York City, USA, on Long Island. It is both residential and industrial and is the site of La Guardia and John F. Kennedy airports. Area: 307 sq km (118 sq mi). Population (1980): 1 891 325.

Queen's Award An award to industry in the UK, instituted in 1965 and made on the birthday (21 April) of Queen Elizabeth II. In 1976 it was divided into two classes, an award for export achievement and an award for technological achievement. Awarded to firms, rather than individuals, it entitles holders to make use of a special emblem for five years.

Queensberry Rules. *See* boxing.

Queen's Counsel (QC) A *barrister appointed to senior rank as counsel to the English queen on the recommendation of the Lord Chancellor. A Queen's Counsel is called a **King's Counsel** (KC) during the reign of a king. QCs have no special duties to the Crown; they wear a silk gown, sit within the Bar of the court, and take precedence over the "utter barristers" (i.e. the outer or junior barristers, who sit outside the Bar).

Queen's County. *See* Laoighis.

Queensland The second largest state of Australia, situated in the NE. The *Great Dividing Range separates the hilly coastlands from the vast inland plain and the *Great Barrier Reef runs parallel to the Pacific coast. It is Australia's most decentralized region, containing approximately one-third of all Australian urban centres. The area is rich in natural resources, which form the basis of Queensland's rapid economic progress. Coal is the most important mineral and well over half the annual production is exported to Japan and Europe. Other important minerals extracted include copper, bauxite, lead, silver, and zinc; oil was discovered at Moonie in 1961 and production began in 1964; natural gas mined at Roma and Rolliston is piped to Brisbane. Manufactures include metals, machinery, chemicals, motor vehicles, textiles, and food. Agricultural activities are also important; large quantities of sugar cane are produced in the E, while elsewhere bananas, pineapples, cotton, and tobacco are grown. Beef and wool are major industries. Another growing industry is tourism. Area: 1 728 000 sq km (667 000 sq mi). Population (1980 est): 2 247 800. Capital: Brisbane.

Queenstown. *See* Cóbh.

quelea A small brown African weaverbird, *Quelea quelea*, about 13 cm long, also called the red-billed dioch and labelled the most destructive bird in the world. Queleas live in vast colonies: they destroy grain crops, frequently causing famine, and also damage the trees in which they roost by their combined weight. Attempt to control them by poisoning, introducing disease, and by dynamiting their colonies have had little success.

Quemoy. *See* Jinmen.

Queneau, Raymond (1903-79) French novelist and poet. He was involved in the surrealist movement in the 1920s and subsequently wrote a series of parodies and other literary exercises the surface humour of which is founded on profound erudition. Notable among these is *Exercices du style* (1947), in which the same episode is rendered in many different styles. His novels include *Le Chien-dent* (1933), *Rude hiver* (1939), *Pierrot mon ami* (1942), and *Zazie dans le métro* (1959).

Quercia, Jacopo della. *See* Jacopo della Quercia.

Querétaro 30 38N 100 23W A city in central Mexico. The movement for Mexican independence was begun here (1810). There are many Spanish colonial buildings, notably the cathedral and federal palace. Industries include cotton textiles and potteries. Population (1980): 293 586.

Quesnay, François (1694-1774) French economist. Originally the physician of Louis XV, Quesnay devoted himself to the study of economics after 1756. He was founder and leader of the *Physiocrats, a school of economic theorists. He contributed articles to Diderot's *Encyclopédie* and published such books as *Tableau economique* (1758).

Quesnel, Pasquier (1634-1719) French Jansenist theologian (*see* Jansenism). He was a priest of the French Oratory (*see* Oratorians) until expelled from the society in 1684 for his views. He settled in Brussels but was imprisoned there in 1703 and finally escaped to Holland. His *Nouveau Testament en français avec des réflexions morales* (1692) was condemned by the pope in 1713.

Quetta 30 15N 67 00E A city in W central Pakistan, at an altitude of 1650 m (5500 ft). The chief town of Baluchistan, it was badly damaged by an earthquake in 1935. Quetta is a trading centre and summer resort. The University of

Baluchistan was established here in 1970. Population (1981): 285 000.

quetzal A Central American bird, *Pharomachus mocinno*, that lives in cloud forests and feeds on fruit, insects, tree frogs, and lizards. The male reaches 1.3 m in length, including its curved ornamental tail feathers; its plumage is iridescent green, red, and white and the long outer wing feathers curl over the flight feathers. Family: *Trogonidae* (trogons).

QUETZALCOATL *The 2nd- and 6th-century temple of Quetzalcoatl at Tehotihuacan, north of Mexico City, showing the plumed serpents.*

Quetzalcoatl A Mexican wind and fertility god, usually portrayed as a feathered snake. During the Aztec period (14th-16th centuries) he was identified with the planet Venus, symbol of death and resurrection. He was also a creator god, having made humans by sprinkling blood on bones he brought from the underworld.

Quezon City 14 39N 121 01E A city in the N Philippines, in S Luzon near to Manila. It was the nation's former capital (1948-76). The University of the Philippines was established here in 1908. Mainly residential, its chief industry is textiles. Population (1980): 1 165 990.

Quibdó 5 40N 76 40W A town in NW Colombia. It is an important platinum- and gold-mining centre. Population (1980): 34 000.

Quiberon 47 29N 3 07 W A peninsula in NW France, on the S coast of Brittany. In 1759, during the Seven Years' War, a naval battle in which the French were defeated by the English was fought off its coast, in Quiberon Bay.

quicksand A mass of soft unconsolidated sand that, when saturated with water, becomes semiliquid and unable to support any appreciable weight. Quicksands occur where conditions permit large amounts of water to remain in the sand.

Quietism A form of mystical passivity that discounts all human effort of will or activity and sees perfection in total dependence upon God. Quietism is associated with certain 17th-century theologians, notably the Spanish priest Miguel de *Molinos. It was condemned by the pope (1687) on account of its practical and philosophical implications.

Quiller-Couch, Sir Arthur Thomas (1863–1944) British critic and novelist who published under the pseudonym "Q." He wrote several adventure novels, many of them set in his native Cornwall, but is best known for his collections of Cambridge lectures and as compiler of the influential *Oxford Book of English Verse* (1900).

quillwort A small perennial *pteridophyte plant of the genus *Isoetes* (about 60 species), which grows in water or on land, mainly in swampy cooler regions of N North America and Eurasia. Tufts of stiff spiky quill-like leaves, about 5–18 cm long, grow from a short stout rhizome that bears numerous roots. The spore capsules are embedded in the expanded bases of the leaves. The common Eurasian quillwort (*I. lacustris*) is aquatic. Class: *Lycopsida* (clubmosses, etc.).

Quimper 48 00N 4 06W A town in NW France, the capital of the Finistère department. A tourist centre, it has a gothic cathedral and is famous for its Breton pottery. Industries include textiles and furniture. Population (1982): 60 162.

quince A small tree or shrub, *Cydonia vulgaris*, probably native to W Asia but cultivated in temperate regions for its fruit. 4.5–6 m high, it has oval leaves (which are woolly beneath) and white or pink flowers, 5 cm across. The pear-shaped fruit is 7.5–10 cm long with a golden-yellow skin and many pips. When cooked, its flesh turns pink, giving a distinctive colour and flavour to preserves and jellies. Family: *Rosaceae*.

Quincy 42 15N 71 00W A city in the USA, in Massachusetts on Boston Harbor. It is the birthplace of two US presidents, John Adams and his son John Quincy Adams. Industries include shipbuilding and the manufacture of machinery. Population (1980): 84 743.

Quine, Willard van Orman (1908–) US philosopher. He became professor of philosophy at Harvard in 1955. His philosophy was largely concerned with language and logic. He argued that linguistic adjustments could make any statement valid. His works include *Word and Object* (1960), *Set Theory and Its Logic* (1963), *Philosophy of Logic* (1970), and *The Roots of Reference* (1973).

Qui Nhon 13 47N 109 11E A port in S Vietnam, on the South China Sea. The site of ancient ruins, it was a naval base during the Vietnam War. Its main industry is fishing. Population (1979): 130 534.

quinine The first drug used to treat malaria. Quinine, which is obtained from the bark of *Cinchona trees, has now been largely replaced by other drugs (e.g. *chloroquine), which have fewer side effects and are less toxic. Quinine-like compounds (e.g. quinidine) are used to treat abnormal heart rhythms. Quinine may produce allergic reactions in susceptible patients.

quinone ($O:C_6H_4:O$) An *aromatic compound with two hydrogen atoms in the benzene ring replaced by two oxygen atoms. Quinones are used in photography and dye manufacture. They are also found in plants.

quinsy An abscess in the tissue surrounding a tonsil. This arises from infection of the tonsils and may be a complication of tonsillitis. The patient has a sore throat and difficulty in swallowing. Quinsy is sometimes treated by surgical draining of the abscess.

Quintero brothers. *See* Alvárez Quintero brothers.

Quintilian (Marcus Fabius Quintilianus; c. 35–c. 100 AD) Roman rhetorician. He was born in Spain and educated in Rome, where he worked as an advocate and teacher of rhetoric. The emperor Domitian appointed him tutor to his heirs. His *Institutio oratoria*, a practical treatise on rhetoric, includes a comparative survey of Greek and Latin literature and many original observations on the education of children.

Quisling, Vidkun (Abraham Lauritz Jonsson) (1887–1945) Norwegian army officer and Nazi collaborator, whose name is a synonym for "traitor." After serving as minister of defence, Quisling formed (1933) the fascist National Union Party in Norway. He encouraged the Nazi occupation of Norway (1940), and as "minister president" in the occupation government, sent a thousand Jews to concentration camps. Arrested in 1945, he was found guilty of war crimes and executed.

Quito 0 20S 78 45W The capital of Ecuador, on the slopes of the volcano Pichincha at an altitude of 2850 m (9350 ft). Originally settled by Quito Indians, it became the capital of the Inca kingdom of Quito until 1534, when it was captured by the Spanish. It contains many Spanish-colonial churches with fine wooden sculptures and paintings; its two universities were founded in 1769 and 1946. Population (1982): 1 110 248.

Qumeran, Khirbat The site, on the NW shore of the Dead Sea in Israel, where a Jewish sect called the *Essenes lived from about 125 BC to 68 AD. The community produced the written documents known as the *Dead Sea Scrolls, which were concealed in nearby caves and found in 1947 by two Bedouin shepherds.

quotas, import Limits set by a government to the quantity of specified goods that can be imported from abroad (or sometimes from a specified country) in a given period. Quotas are usually operated by a licensing system, importers being granted licences authorizing them to import a certain quantity of a product and to purchase the requisite amount of foreign exchange. Quotas are used to remedy a weak *balance of payments or to protect domestic manufacturers but must be used with discretion to avoid provoking retaliation from other countries. *See also* free trade; tariffs.

Qu Qiu Bai (or Ch'ü Ch'iu-pai; 1889–1935) Chinese communist leader. He was a leading literary figure in the communist movement and became general secretary of the Chinese Communist Party in 1927. He was captured and executed by *Guomindang (Nationalist) forces in Shanghai.

Quran. *See* Koran.

Qwaqwa. *See* Bantu Homelands.

R

Ra (*or* Re) The Egyptian sun god and lord of creation, usually portrayed with a falcon's head bearing a solar disc. He sailed across the sky by day in his sun boat and through the underworld by night. His centre of worship was at Heliopolis. During the 18th dynasty (1567–1320 BC) he became identified with the Theban god *Amon as Amon-Ra.

Rabat (Arabic name: Ribat) 34 00N 6 42W The capital of Morocco, near the Atlantic coast. Founded as a military post in the 12th century, it became the capital under the French protectorate in the early 20th century. It has a university (1957) and its notable buildings include the 12th-century Hassan Tower. It has an important textile industry. Population (1982): 893 042.

Rabaul 4 13S 152 11E A town in Papua New Guinea, the chief town on the island of New Britain. The capital until 1941 of the Territory of New Guinea, it was evacuated in 1937 because of a volcanic eruption and heavily bombed during World War II. Copra is exported. Population (1980 est): 14 973.

rabbi A Jewish scholar and religious authority. The term came into use in the 1st century AD, and the Judaism of the following centuries is often called "rabbinic Judaism." For a long time the rabbinate was not a salaried office; the title indicated scholarly achievement and legal competence. In modern Jewish communities rabbis are communal leaders, preachers, and pastoral workers.

rabbit A burrowing *mammal belonging to the family *Leporidae* (which also includes the *hares). The European rabbit (*Oryctolagus cuniculus*) grows to about 45 cm; it has long ears, a short tail, and soft grey-brown fur. Rabbits are gregarious, living in large warrens and feeding on grasses and vegetation. They mature at three months and females can produce a litter of up to ten young (kittens) every month. Rabbits can become a serious agricultural pest although populations have been depleted by myxomatosis. Order: *Lagomorpha*.

Rabelais, François (1483–1553) French humanist and satirist. He became a Franciscan and then a Benedictine monk, left the monastery to study and practise medicine, and visited Italy with his patron, Cardinal Jean du Bellay (1492–1560). His humanist philosophy is expressed in his works of richly inventive and often frankly coarse comic satire, *Pantagruel* (1532), *Gargantua* (1534), *Tiers Livre* (1546), and *Quart Livre* (1552). The authenticity of the posthumous *Cinquiesme Livre* (1564) has been debated. His attacks on superstition and scholasticism were condemned by theologians but gained him wide popularity. The classic English translation of his works is by Sir Thomas Urquhart (1653).

Rabi, Isidor Isaac (1898–   ) US physicist, born in Austria, who invented a highly accurate technique for measuring the nuclear magnetic moments of atoms. For this work he was awarded the Nobel Prize in 1944. During World War II Rabi worked on the development of the atom bomb.

rabies An acute viral infection of the brain that can affect all warm-blooded animals and may be transmitted to man through the bite of an infected animal (usually a dog). Symptoms, which appear after an incubation period of from ten days to two years, include painful spasms of the throat on swallowing. Later, the very sight of water induces convulsions and paralysis (hence the alternative name of the disease—hydrophobia, literally "fear of water") and the patient eventually dies in a coma. There is no treatment for the established disease, but antirabies vaccine and rabies antiserum given to patients immediately after they have been bitten may prevent the infection from developing. Rabies has been spreading across Europe in recent years; in the UK there are strict quarantine regulations for imported domestic animals to prevent the disease from reaching Britain.

raccoon An omnivorous mammal belonging to the genus *Procyon* (7 species), of the Americas. About 1 m long, raccoons are stockily built, with long hind legs and short forelegs. A masklike black patch across the eyes and a striped tail contrast with the thick grey coat. Raccoons forage at night for nuts, roots, snails, mammals, and birds and take aquatic prey, such as crustaceans, molluscs, and fish. Family: *Procyonidae*; order: *Carnivora*.

raccoon dog A short-legged wild *dog, *Nyctereutes procyonides*, of Asia. It is golden-brown, about 60 cm long, with black eye patches (like a raccoon). It lives near water and feeds on frogs. Its fur is known as Japanese fox.

Rachel (Élisa Félix; 1820–58) French actress. She made her debut at the Comédie-Française in 1838 and gained an international reputation as a leading tragic actress. She was particularly effective in productions of Racine and Corneille. She died of tuberculosis.

SERGEI RACHMANINOV *In London, 1924.*

Rachmaninov, Sergei (1873–1943) Russian composer, pianist, and conductor. He studied in St Petersburg and Moscow, where he became famous as a pianist, particularly in his own compositions. He left Russia in 1917 and spent most of the rest of his life in the USA. His works include four operas, three symphonies, four piano concertos (which he also recorded), the *Rhapsody on a Theme of Paganini* (for piano and orchestra; 1934), and *The Bells* (for soloists, chorus, and orchestra; 1910). One of his most popular pieces for piano is the prelude in C sharp minor (1892).

racial discrimination The practice of making unfavourable distinctions between the members of different races. In South Africa (*see* apartheid) race relations are characterized by an inflexible tradition, which has led to the legal and economic separation of peoples on the basis of their ethnic backgrounds. A similar tradition characterizes southern states of the USA (*see* civil-rights movement). The circumstances that lead to prejudice are many and diverse and much has been written attributing inferiority to particular races (*see* social Darwinism); however, no scientifically accepted work exists to support these contentions. In the UK the Race Relations Acts (1965, 1968, 1976) aimed to secure the integration of Commonwealth and other immigrants (*see* migration, human) into the community and to prevent racial prejudice. *See also* antisemitism.

Racine, Jean (1639–99) French dramatist. He received a Jansenist education at the convent of Port-Royal but was attracted by the Parisian world of theatre and began writing plays in 1664. His major classical verse tragedies, influenced initially by those of *Corneille but eventually surpassing them, include *Andromaque* (1667), *Britannicus* (1669), *Bérénice* (1670), and *Phèdre* (1677). In 1677 he retired from the theatre, married a young pious girl, and accepted a post at the court of Louis XIV. His final works were two religious dramas based on Old Testament subjects, *Esther* (1689) and *Athalie* (1691). Racine was the outstanding tragedian of the French classical period.

Rackham, Arthur (1867–1939) British watercolourist and book illustrator. Using an *Art Nouveau style, he became famous for his representation of fairytale characters in such books as *Peter Pan* (1906), *Hans Andersen's Fairy Tales* (1932), and *The Arthur Rackham Fairy Book* (1933).

rad The unit of absorbed dose of ionizing radiation in the *c.g.s. system equal to an energy absorption of 100 ergs per gram of irradiated material.

radar (*radio detection and ranging*) A method of locating distant objects used in military surveillance, air traffic control, and marine and air navigation; it was first developed during the years before World War II by a British team led by Sir Robert *Watson-Watt. High-frequency (300 to 30 000 megahertz) radio waves are sent out in pulses from a powerful rotating transmitter and are reflected back by any object they encounter. The reflected signal is picked up by a receiver antenna and is used to deflect the electron beam in a *cathode-ray tube. The beam scans the screen of the tube by rotating at the same speed as the antenna, so that its angular position indicates the direction of the located object. Brightness indicates the strength of the reflected signal, i.e. strong for solid objects, weak for water. The distance from the centre of the screen shows the delay between transmission and reception of the reflected signal, i.e. the distance away of the object. The screen continues to glow for a short time after the beam has passed so that a picture is built up with each successive rotation. Radar is now fitted to most aircraft and ships to provide a means of navigation in the dark, cloud, or fog.

Radcliffe, Ann (Ward) (1764–1823) British novelist.

aircraft B

aircraft A

high-frequency pulses

echo

transmitting aerial

A   B

In the plan position indicator (PPI) the targets are represented by blips on a radial line, the direction of which corresponds to the direction of the transmitting aerial as it rotates.

RADAR   *The high-frequency pulses sent out by the transmitting aerial are reflected back by the target and displayed on a PPI.*

Despite their technical clumsiness and lack of characterization, her gothic novels, such as *The Mysteries of Udolfo* (1794) and *The Italian* (1797), were important influences in the change of literary taste and the increasing interest in Romantic characters, description, etc.

Radcliffe-Brown, Alfred Reginald (1881-1955) British anthropologist. A pioneer of social anthropology, Radcliffe-Brown held professorships at Chicago, Sydney, Cape Town, and Oxford Universities. His specific contribution to anthropology lies in his studies of *kinship and society, for which he did field work in Australia and the Andaman Islands.

Radek, Karl (1885-?1939) Soviet politician and journalist. Radek participated in the Russian Revolutions of 1905 and 1917. In 1920 he became secretary of Comintern and served until 1924. Accused of being a Trotskyite, Radek was expelled from the Communist Party in 1927. After recanting in 1929, he wrote for the newspaper *Izvestia* and helped to draft the 1936 constitution. Accused of treason in 1937, he probably died in a Siberian labour camp.

radial velocity The velocity of a star, etc., along the line of sight, i.e. towards or away from the earth. It is calculated from the Doppler shift of the lines of the star's spectrum (*see* Doppler effect).

radian (rad) The *SI unit of plane angle equal to the angle subtended at the centre of a circle by an arc equal in length to the radius of the circle.

radiation The propagation of energy by means of beams of particles or waves. It includes all electromagnetic waves, beams of elementary particles, ions, etc., and sound waves.

radiation sickness Illness caused by exposure to *ionizing radiation, either naturally occurring or from nuclear weapons, X-ray machines, etc. The radiation affects the cells of the body in various ways depending on its intensity. Short-term effects include nausea and diarrhoea, while long-term effects include sterility, haemorrhage, loss of hair, and cancer. However, sufficiently intense radiation can kill cancer cells or prevent them from reproducing, hence its use in *radiotherapy.

Radić, Stjepan (1871-1928) Croatian statesman. Founder of the Croatian Peasant Party (1904), Radić advocated a federated Yugoslavia with Croatian autonomy and opposed *Pašić's centralized Yugoslav Government. In 1925, however, he became minister of education but resigned a year later. He was assassinated in parliament.

radical A group of atoms in a chemical compound that behaves as a unit in chemical reactions. For example, the methanol molecule (CH_3OH) can be considered as a methyl radical ($CH_3.$) and a hydroxyl radical ($.OH$). In this sense, radicals are often simply referred to as groups, a functional group being one responsible for the characteristic reactions of a class of compounds. Thus, the hydroxyl group is the functional group of alcohols. **Free radicals** are groups existing independently. Because they have unpaired electrons they are usually extremely reactive transient species. They can be produced by *pyrolysis or *photolysis and are important intermediates in many reactions, particularly photochemical, combustion, and polymerization reactions.

Radiguet, Raymond (1903-23) French novelist. His precocious talent was recognized by several prominent literary and artistic figures, especially Jean Cocteau. His two novels were *Le Diable au corps* (1923), a story of adolescent passion and cruelty, and *Le Bal du Comte d'Orgel* (1924).

radio The transmission of sound or other information by radio-frequency (3 kilohertz to 300 gigahertz) electromagnetic waves. The use of radio waves for communication was pioneered by *Marconi in 1895, although their existence had been postulated by *Maxwell in 1873 and demonstrated by *Hertz in 1888.

A **radio transmitter** generates a radio-frequency electrical signal (carrier wave) in an oscillator and superimposes the sound signal on it by a *modulation process. The composite signal is then fed to an aerial, which transmits electromagnetic waves. Although the waves travel in straight lines, transmission beyond the horizon is made possible by the ionosphere, a layer of the upper atmosphere that reflects radio waves in the long and medium wavebands. Long-wave (30 to 300 kilohertz) and medium-wave (300 to 3000 kilohertz) radio is used for direct (ground-wave) transmission in amplitude-modulated (AM) sound broadcasting. Short-wave radio is used for AM sound broadcasting over longer distances using the ionosphere (sky waves) and for communication to ships and aircraft. VHF (very high frequency; 30 to 300 megahertz) is used for *stereophonic sound broadcasting in frequency modulated (FM) transmissions. Television uses mostly UHF (ultrahigh frequency). Neither VHF nor UHF are reflected by the ionosphere, but can be relayed by *communications satellites. All **radio receivers**, from the pocket transistor radio to the most sophisticated and sensitive systems, consist of an *aerial, which detects the signal and converts it to an electrical current; a resonant circuit, which selects the required frequency band; a demodulator to retrieve the audio-frequency signal from the modulated carrier wave; an amplification system; and one or more *loudspeakers to reproduce the sound. □ p. 1014.

radioactive tracer A radioactive *isotope used for following the course of a substance during a physical, biological, or chemical process. A nonradioactive isotope in the substance is replaced by a radioactive isotope of the same element, which can then be detected by observing its emitted radiation with, for example, a *Geiger counter. Substances containing such radioisotopes are called labelled compounds. Radioactive tracing is a sensitive technique used in medical, scientific, and industrial research.

radioactive waste Waste products from nuclear reactors, uranium-processing plants, etc., that have become radioactive. The disposal of these waste products, which include solids, liquids, and gases, constitutes a major problem as some materials have a very long mean life. Solid waste is either stored in tanks underground or placed in drums weighted with concrete and sunk in deep sea water (there is at present a ban on this). Liquid waste presents the most difficult problems owing to the possibility of leakage. Gaseous waste is usually released into the atmosphere in small quantities.

radioactivity The spontaneous emission of a particle by an atomic nucleus. The emitted particle may be an alpha particle (a helium nucleus consisting of two protons and two neutrons), in which case the process is known as *alpha decay; or it may be a beta particle (an *electron), when the process is known as *beta decay. Highly energetic X-rays (*see* gamma radiation) may also be emitted simultaneously. In both alpha and beta decay the nucleus changes into that of another element. A less common method of decay is the emission of a *positron, the antiparticle of the electron, the process being similar to that of beta decay. Radioactive decay is a random process and its occurrence for a single nucleus can be neither predicted nor controlled. However, for a large number of nuclei the time taken for a certain fraction of nuclei to decay can be accurately predicted as either its *mean life or *half-life. These quantities vary from about 10^{-8} second to 10^{10} years depending on the isotope. The phenomenon was first discovered in 1898 by *Becquerel in uranium and elucidated by the *Curies, *Rutherford, and *Soddy.

radio astronomy The study of celestial objects by means of the radio waves they emit. This radio emission was first noticed by K. G. *Jansky in the USA in 1932 and developed in the UK during and after World War II, especially at *Jodrell Bank and Cambridge University. It now forms an important branch of *astronomy.

radio beacon An automatic navigational beacon that broadcasts a coded radio signal. The angular position of the

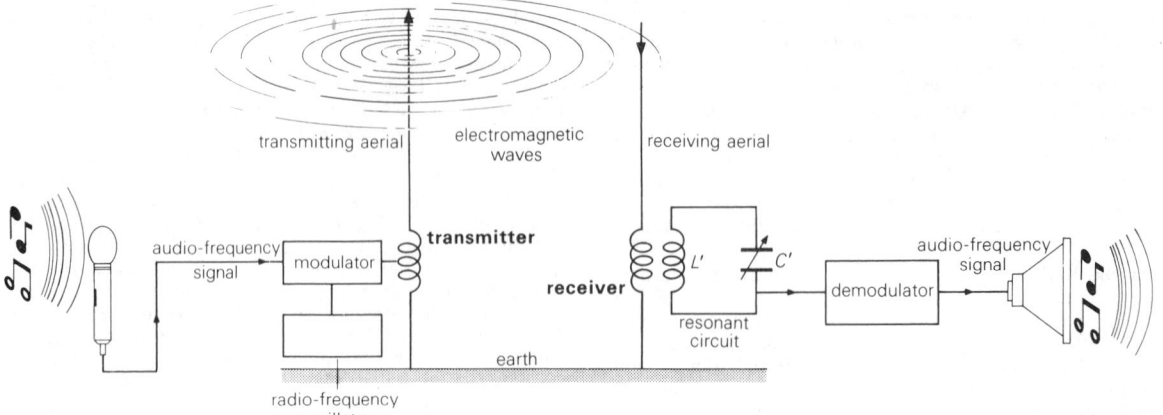

RADIO *The transmission and reception of sound broadcasts.*

source of the signal can be determined by a vessel or aircraft carrying a radio direction finder or radio compass and can be identified by its code, usually given in Morse. Where two such radio beacons can be received, the exact position of the receiver can be determined by triangulation.

radiocarbon dating A method of estimating the age of a material, such as wood, that was once living. Atmospheric carbon dioxide contains a small proportion of the radioisotope carbon-14. As all living things absorb carbon from atmospheric carbon dioxide, either directly or indirectly, they too contain a constant proportion of carbon-14. However, once dead, the level of carbon-14 falls as a result of *beta decay. By measuring the radioactivity of a material, the concentration of carbon-14 and hence its age can be estimated. The method is accurate within stated limits for ages up to 4500 years. *See also* radiometric dating.

radiochemistry The branch of chemistry concerned with compounds containing radioactive *isotopes. It includes chemical techniques for isotope separation, and the use of *radioactive tracers for investigating chemical reactions.

radio galaxy A *radio source that lies beyond our Galaxy, is identified with an optical *galaxy, and the radio-power output of which greatly exceeds that of a normal galaxy. The size can be immense. A massive *black hole at the galaxy centre has been postulated as a possible energy source.

radiography The technique of examining the internal structure of a solid body by passing *X-rays or *gamma radiation through it to produce an image on a photographic plate or fluorescent screen. Radiography is used in medicine (*see* radiology) and in industry to find structural defects.

radio interferometer. *See* radio telescope.

radioisotope (*or* radioactive isotope) An *isotope that is radioactive. Radioisotopes are used in the production of *nuclear energy, in *radiotherapy, as *radioactive tracers, and in *dating techniques. Some are naturally occurring (those with mass numbers in excess of 208) while others can be made radioactive by neutron bombardment.

Radiolaria An order of single-celled animals (*see* Protozoa) found chiefly in the sea, as a component of plankton. Radiolarians are typically spherical, 0.1 mm to several millimetres in diameter, with a silicaceous skeleton of radiating spines from which long thin pseudopodia extend to capture food particles. The skeletal remains of dead radiolarians sink to the ocean floor to form a deposit called radiolarian ooze. Class: *Sarcodina.* Protozoa.

radiology The branch of medicine concerned with the use of radiation in the diagnosis and treatment of disease. *Radiography is used to diagnose a wide range of disorders, including fractures, ulcers, and cancer: hollow organs are often visualized

by injecting a fluid that is opaque to X-rays. A radiologist is a doctor specialized in the interpretation of X-ray photographs and films. Recent advances in radiology include the use of computer-aided tomography, in which X-ray "slices" of the body are recorded with an X-ray scanner and integrated by a computer to produce a cross-sectional image. *See also* radiotherapy.

radiometric dating A method of dating rocks, developed mainly in the 1950s, by observing the extent to which a radioactive (parent) element in a rock has decayed to form a stable daughter element. Since the half-life or rate of decay of the radioactive element chosen is known, the age of the rock can be calculated from the ratio of parent to daughter isotopes present. The most frequently used methods are *radiocarbon dating, *potassium-argon dating, and *rubidium-strontium dating. Methods based on uranium-lead and thorium-lead decays are also sometimes used.

radio source A celestial object that emits radio waves. The sun and Jupiter are solar-system sources. Other radio sources within our Galaxy are pulsars, supernova remnants, interstellar hydrogen clouds, and the galactic centre. Extragalactic sources include spiral galaxies, radio galaxies, and some quasars. The spatial distribution and intensity of the radio emission can be shown on a contour map.

radio telescope An instrument for detecting and measuring the radio emissions from celestial *radio sources. It consists of an antenna, or system of antennas, the radio-frequency signals of which are carried by wires or waveguides to one or more receivers. The receiver output signal is finally displayed on a graph, stored on magnetic tape, etc. The antenna may be a large metal parabolic or spherical dish, usually steerable, that brings radio waves from a radio source to a focus on a secondary antenna. Alternatively simple dipole antennas may be used. An antenna system may consist of two separate units the signals of which are fed to a common receiver. This **radio interferometer** has a very much greater resolving power than a single antenna; the greater the distance between antennas the finer the detail observed in a radio source. Varied scales of detail can be obtained by using a number of antenna pairs at different distances. One of the best-known radio telescopes is the steerable dish instrument at *Jodrell Bank, which forms one component of a UK network of radio dishes.

radiotherapy The use of X-rays and other forms of radiation, either produced by machines or emitted by radioactive isotopes, for treating disease. The radiation may be directed at the target organ from a distance or radioactive needles, wires, pellets, etc., may be implanted in the body.

Radiation is particularly destructive to rapidly dividing cells: it is therefore used in treating various forms of *cancer and certain other tumours as well as overactivity of the thyroid gland.

radish An annual or biennial herb, *Raphanus sativus*, widely grown for its edible fleshy hot-tasting root, which may be red, white, or purple. Spring varieties are quick-growing while winter varieties may be stored. The plant bears white flowers. Family: *Cruciferae*.

radium (Ra) A metallic element, discovered in pitchblende in 1898 by Pierre and Marie Curie. It is a divalent alkaline-earth element, forming a number of simple salts, such as the chloride ($RaCl_2$). It decays to form the noble gas radon and is used in radiotherapy for the treatment of cancers. At no 88; at wt (226); mp 700°C; bp 1140°C.

Radium Hill 32 30S 140 32E A mining settlement in E South Australia, where radium was mined until 1930 and uranium was extracted (1952–61).

radius. *See* arm.

Radnorshire A former county of E Wales. Under local government reorganization in 1974 it became part of *Powys.

Radom 51 26N 21 10E An industrial town in SE central Poland. Founded in 1340, it was held successively by Austria and Russia before returning to Poland in 1918. Industries include leather, glass, and chemicals. Population (1982): 198 000.

radon (Rn) The heaviest noble gas, produced by the decay of radium, thorium, and actinium. It is radioactive, the longest-lived isotope (^{222}Rn) having a half-life of 3.825 days. Like the other noble gases, Rn forms clathrates and fluorides. Increased radon levels have been noted in ground water shortly before earthquakes. At no 86; at wt (222); mp −71°C; bp −61.8°C.

Raeburn, Sir Henry (1756–1823) Scottish portraitist. The leading Scottish painter of his generation, he was apprenticed to a goldsmith. Before painting his earliest known portrait in 1776, he produced several miniatures. Although he visited London and Italy (1785–87), he worked chiefly in Edinburgh, where his sitters included lawyers, scholars, and such Highland lairds as *The MacNab* (The Collection of John Dewar and Sons, Ltd).

Raeder, Erich (1876–1960) German admiral; commander in chief of the navy (1928–43). In contravention of the Treaty of Versailles, he rebuilt the German navy in the years before World War II but was dismissed after disagreeing with Hitler over strategy. He was sentenced to life imprisonment for war crimes but was released in 1955.

RAF. *See* Royal Air Force.

raffia (*or* raphia) A *palm tree of the genus *Raphia*, especially *R. pedunculata* (or *R. ruffia*), native to Madagascar and cultivated for its fibre. Its leaves, up to 20 m long, are composed of 80–100 leaflets from which the fibre is torn in thin strips and dried in the sun. Raffia is soft, strong, pliable, and resistant to shrinking; it is woven into mats and baskets and used in horticulture, etc.

Raffles, Sir Thomas Stamford (1781–1826) British colonial administrator and oriental scholar, who acquired Singapore for the East India Company (1819). In 1805 he became assistant secretary to the governor of Penang and was lieutenant governor of Java (1811–16), while it was under British rule, and then of Bengkulu (1818–23) in W Sumatra.

Rafflesia A genus of Malaysian parasitic herbs (12 species), the vegetative parts of which are reduced to fungus-like threads that extract food from the roots and stems of other plants. The monster plant (*R. arnoldii*) has the world's largest flower—up to 45 cm across and weighing up to 10 kg. It smells of rotten meat and attracts carrion flies, which act as pollinators. The genus was named after Sir Stamford *Raffles. Family: *Rafflesiaceae*.

raga (Sanskrit: colour) In Indian music, a type of *scale used as the basis for improvisation. There are many different ragas, some of which are associated with particular moods, feelings,

times of day, etc.

ragged robin A Eurasian perennial herb, *Lychnis flos-cuculi*. Growing to a height of 75 cm, it has rose-red flowers with five deeply divided ragged petals. It is common in damp places and has been introduced to North America. Family: *Caryophyllaceae*.

ragged schools Institutions that provided such services as free education and clothing for deprived children in 19th-century Britain. The ragged schools, which were probably inspired by the Sunday School movement (*see* Raikes, Robert), formed the Ragged School Union in 1844 but were rendered obsolete after 1870, when free compulsory education was introduced.

Raglan, FitzRoy James Henry Somerset, 1st Baron (1788–1855) British field marshal. After service in the Napoleonic Wars (in which he lost his sword arm at Waterloo), he became secretary to Wellington, whom he succeeded as master general of the ordnance in 1852. In 1854 he became commander in the *Crimean War and, in spite of success at *Inkerman, his strategy was much criticized (*see also* Balaclava, Battle of). The Raglan sleeve, extending to the neck without shoulder seams, is named after him.

RAGNARÖK *The gods struggle against the evil progeny of Loki at the end of the world. Thor (right) battles with the serpent Jörmungandr, Odin with the wolf Fenris, and Frey with the fire-giant Surtr. Bifrost, the rainbow bridge connecting Asgard and earth, is in the background.*

Ragnarök In Norse mythology, doomsday, when a catastrophic battle between the gods and the forces of evil will occur. It will be preceded by warning signals: three years of perpetual winter will be followed by three years of moral decline among men. After the defeat of the gods by the forces of evil, led by *Loki, everyone will be destroyed except for *Lif and Lifthrasir.

ragtime A precursor of *New Orleans style jazz. Ragtime developed from minstrel-band music, but many rags were published as piano compositions. Ragtime was characterized by syncopation in the melody against a regular marchlike accompaniment and was popular from the 1890s until around 1920. Famous rags include "Harlem Rag" (1895) and "Maple Leaf Rag" (1899), written by Scott *Joplin, the first ragtime composer to write down his music.

Ragusa (ancient name: Hybla Heraca) 36 56N 14 44E A town in Italy, in Sicily on the River Irminio. It has an 18th-century cathedral. Oil production and asphalt mining are the chief industrial activities. Population (1983 est): 65 163.

ragworm A marine *annelid worm, *Nereis cultrifera*, also called chainworm, of European coastal waters. 5-10 cm long, ragworms swim by means of paddle-like structures occurring in pairs on each body segment. Most ragworms live in

ragwort 1016

burrows in sand or mud or among stones, feeding on dead organisms and detritus using a pair of horny jaws inside a protrudable mouth tube. Class: *Polychaeta*.

ragwort A perennial or biennial herb, *Senecio jacobaea*, that grows up to 150 cm high and has much-divided leaves and dense flat-topped heads of yellow flowers. It is found on dunes, waste places, and pastures of Eurasia and N Africa and has been introduced to New Zealand and North America. When eaten in large quantities it is poisonous to livestock. Family: *Compositae*.

Raikes, Robert (1735–1811) British journalist and philanthropist, who founded the Sunday School movement. In 1780 he opened a Sunday School in his native Gloucester devoted to educating children in Scripture and elementary school subjects. He publicized his project through his own newspaper, the *Gloucester Journal*, and it was soon imitated elsewhere in England, resulting in the establishment of the Sunday School Union (1803).

rail A slender secretive ground-dwelling bird belonging to a widely distributed family (*Rallidae*; about 300 species), occurring mostly in swamps, marshes, and fresh waters. 11–45 cm long, rails have short rounded wings, a short tail, and typically a dull grey or brown plumage, often barred for camouflage. They feed on plant material, invertebrates, and birds' eggs. Order: *Gruiformes* (cranes, rails, etc.). *See also* coot; corncrake; gallinule.

railway A permanent track, consisting of parallel rails, on which locomotives draw wagons or trucks for transporting goods or passengers. Wooden rails have been in use in mines since the 14th century, but flanged wheels running on cast-iron rails were not introduced until 1789. Thereafter they were quite widely used in the mining and metallurgical industries, although trucks were horse-drawn until the invention of the steam locomotive at the beginning of the 19th century. The first effective railway in the world opened in England in 1825 and ran between Stockton and Darlington, using *Stephenson's Locomotion* as the locomotive. During the next 12 years some 2400 km (1500 mi) of track were laid in the UK; by 1885 this figure had increased to 26 900 km (16 700 mi) and by 1921 it was 31 120 km (19 300 mi). The Railways Act (1921) consolidated the 250 railway companies then operating into four companies: London Midland and Scottish Railway (LMS), London and North Eastern Railway (LNER), Great Western Railway (GWR), and Southern Railway (SR). In 1947 these four companies were amalgamated in the state-owned British Railways (which became British Rail in 1965).

Until the 1860s railways were an exclusively British expertise and any foreign railways that existed were British built and used British rolling stock. For example the earliest US line, between Boston and Albany (1842), used British locomotives and British rails. After the Civil War, however, US railways developed independently and by 1887 there were 140 000 km (87 000 mi) of rail. The USA now has more than any other nation, with 338 000 km (209 000 mi); the Soviet Union has 136 800 km (85 000 mi), Canada 74 800 km (46 500 mi), India 60 200 km (37 400 mi), Australia 41 500 km (25 800 mi), and France 36 000 km (22 300 mi).

Since World War II the growth of internal air services, the development of efficient road-haulage services, and the spread of private motoring have led to the decline of the railways in industrial countries, causing services to be reduced. However the introduction of high-speed trains and their continued use for postal services has enabled them to survive. In the developing countries they still play an essential role in transporting goods and passengers over long distances. *See also* underground railways.

rain A form of precipitation composed of liquid water drops ranging in size from about 0.5 to 5 mm diameter. Minute droplets of water in clouds may coalesce to form larger drops; if these are sufficiently heavy they will fall as rain. The amount of rain, together with other forms of precipitation, that falls in a specific time is usually measured with a **rain gauge**. This is a cylindrical container with a funnel of standard diameter into which the rain falls. The water collected is periodically measured and recorded in millimetres or inches; some rain gauges are designed to record automatically.

rainbow An optical phenomenon consisting of an arc of light across the sky composed of the colours of the spectrum. It is caused by the refraction of sunlight through falling water drops; the larger the drops the stronger the colours.

Raine, Kathleen (1908–) British poet. Her volumes of poetry, which include *Stone and Flower* (1943), *The Lost Country* (1971), and *Collected Poems* (1981), are noted for their visionary lyricism. She has also published several studies of William Blake, notably *Blake and Tradition* (1969).

rain forest. *See* forest.

Rainier, Mount A mountain in the USA, the highest peak in Washington state and the Cascade Mountains. It is noted for its many glaciers. Height: 4392 m (14 408 ft).

Rainier III (1923–) Prince of Monaco (1949–). He repudiated the principle of the *divine right of kings in a new constitution (1962). In 1956 he married Grace *Kelly. Their three children are Prince Albert (1958–), Princess Caroline (1957–), and Princess Stephanie (1965–).

Rais, Gilles de (*or* G. de Retz; 1404–40) French marshal, who fought with *Joan of Arc. After her capture he retired to his estates in Brittany and dabbled in alchemy and witchcraft. In 1440 he was sentenced to death for the torture and murder of over 140 children. He was later associated with the story of Bluebeard, immortalized by Charles *Perrault.

Rajasthan A state in NW India, extending from the Thar Desert along Pakistan's border SE into forested hills. The economy depends primarily on grain and livestock farming, as well as cotton, sugar cane, and pulses. Coal, phosphates, gypsum, marble, mica, and salt are mined. Industries include textiles, cement, and glass. *History*: Rajasthan flourished in the Harappan period (3rd–2nd millenniums BC). Under Rajput princes (from the 7th century AD), it withstood Muslim invaders but succumbed to British expansion (19th century). Area: 342 214 sq km (132 095 sq mi). Population (1981): 34 102 912. Capital: Jaipur.

Rajkot 22 18N 70 53E A city in India, in Gujarat. A commercial and industrial centre, it produces textiles and chemicals. Population (1981): 444 000.

Rajput A group of clans in N and central India, now numbering about 11 million people. They appeared in about the 5th century AD and are believed to have been descended from invading tribes from Central Asia, although they claim descent from more ancient Indian tribes. Because of their warfaring occupation they were at some time included within the Ksatriya (warrior) caste of Hindu society. The Rajput states fought vigorously against the Muslim invaders, maintaining their independence in Rajasthan. They acknowledged the overlordship of the Moguls in the 16th century, the Marathas in the 18th century, and the British in 1808. Rajput dynasties were responsible for building many fine temples.

Rákóczy II, Ferenc (1676–1735) Hungarian revolutionary. In 1703 Rákóczy led a peasant uprising against Austria and in 1704 he was elected Prince of Transylvania. After two serious defeats in 1708 and 1710, Hungary signed the Peace of Szatmár (1711) with Austria. Rákóczy rejected it and went abroad, dying in Turkey.

Raleigh 35 46N 78 39W A city in the USA, the capital of North Carolina. Named after Sir Walter Raleigh, its industries include the manufacture of computers and textiles. North Carolina State University (1887) and Shaw University (1865) are situated here. Population (1980): 149 771.

Raleigh, Sir Walter (1554–1618) British explorer and

writer; half-brother of Humphrey *Gilbert. He became a favourite of Elizabeth I, from whom he received a knighthood after serving in Ireland. He was unsuccessful in his attempts (1584-89) to found a colony in Virginia (now North Carolina) but brought back the potato and tobacco plant from America. In 1595-96 he led an expedition to South America, which he described in *The Discoverie of Guiana* (1596), and in 1596 took part in the sack of Cádiz. At James I's accession (1603) he stood trial for treason, but the death sentence was commuted to imprisonment; while in the Tower of London he wrote *The History of the World* (1614). He was released in 1616 to search for gold along the Orinoco but his mission was a failure and after his return his death sentence was invoked and he was executed.

rally 1. A competitive motoring event, in which drivers have to reach checkpoints by certain times. The routes are normally over public roads, but rallies often also include speed or other tests after the route has been completed. Major events, such as the Monte Carlo Rally (first held in 1911), require extensively modified cars. 2. A similar event for motorcycles, but usually with more emphasis on the social and touring aspects than the competitive.

Rama The seventh incarnation of *Vishnu, appearing as a hero in the epics the *Ramayana* and *Mahabharata*. In the *Upanishads* and elsewhere he appears as a god. Since about the 15th century he has been widely worshipped as the supreme deity, epitomizing reason and virtue. He is usually represented holding a bow and arrow and attended by his wife.

Ramadan The ninth month of the Muslim year. It is a time of atonement, and every Muslim is required to observe a strict fast daily from dawn to dusk until the new moon of the next month is visible.

Ramakrishna (1836-86) Hindu saint and religious teacher. Son of an impoverished Brahmin family, he had little formal education, but he gathered a following throughout the world. He condemned greed, lust, and the caste system, teaching the essential unity and truth of all religions.

Raman, Sir Chandrasekhara Venkata (1888-1970) Indian physicist, who was professor at Calcutta University. He won the Nobel Prize in 1930 for his discovery that there is a change in the wavelength of light or ultraviolet radiation when scattered by certain molecules (**Raman effect**). This discovery was used to determine some of the finer details of molecular structure.

Ramanuja (11th century AD) Hindu philosopher and theologian, born in Kanchipuram (S India). He diverged sharply from the tradition in *Vedanta associated with *Sankara, insisting upon the value and reality of the physical world. In religion he provided an influential philosophical basis for devotional worship (*bhakti*), based upon his concept of a personal God epitomized by the god *Vishnu.

Ramapithecus A genus of fossil *hominids that lived during the late Miocene and early Pliocene. It is represented by fossil remains found in India in 1934. They were about the size of a gibbon, possibly walked erect, and may represent the earliest ancestors of modern man after the divergence of his evolutionary line from the apes.

Ramat Gan 32 04N 34 48E A city in central Israel, just E of Tel Aviv-Yafo. It has some manufacturing and is the seat of Bar-Ilan University. Population (1983): 117 100.

Ramayana (Sanskrit: romance of Rama) Hindu epic poem in seven books. Probably composed in its present form after the 4th century BC, it tells the story of *Rama and his devoted wife Sita, her abduction by the demon king Ravana, and Rama's struggle to recover her with the aid of *Hanuman. The *Ramayana* and *Mahabharata* are the two great classics of Sanskrit literature.

Rambert, Dame Marie (Cyvia Rabbam, later Miriam Rambach; 1888-1982) British ballet dancer and choreographer, born in Poland. She worked with Diaghilev's Ballets Russes in 1913 and was naturalized as a British citizen in 1918. As director of the Carmargo Society, which in 1935 became the Ballet Rambert, she trained and encouraged many young British dancers and choreographers.

Ramblers' Association A British organization founded in 1935 to promote love and care for the countryside. It acts as a pressure group to protect the countryside from misuse and organizes such activities as rambles and lectures on subjects related to the countryside. Secretary: Alan Mattingly.

Rambouillet 48 39N 1 50E A town in N France, in the Yvelines department. Its chateau (14th-18th centuries) is now the summer residence of French presidents. Population (1982): 21 136.

rambutan A Malaysian tree, *Nephelium lappaceum*, that grows 20 m high and produces edible plum-sized red or yellow spiny fruit. It is cultivated in moist tropical lowlands. Family: *Sapindaceae*.

Rameau, Jean Philippe (1683-1764) French composer. He held several posts as organist and wrote a *Traité de l'harmonie* (1722), a significant contribution to modern musical theory, before beginning to compose. His works include chamber, keyboard, and vocal music, as well as 24 operas, including the opera *Hippolyte et Aricie* (1733), and opera-ballets, including *Les Indes galantes* (1735) and *Castor et Pollux* (1737). There was great rivalry between his adherents and those of Pergolesi.

ramie A perennial plant, *Boehmeria nivea*, also called China grass, native to E Asia and cultivated, chiefly in China, for its stem fibres. Each plant produces several stalks, up to 2.4 m high, with clusters of greenish-white flowers in the leaf axils. Although strong and durable, ramie fibre is not widely used due to difficulties in extraction, spinning, and weaving. Family: *Urticaceae* (nettle family).

SIR WALTER RALEIGH (1588; *National Portrait Gallery*).

Ramillies, Battle of (23 May, 1706) The battle in the War of the *Spanish Succession in which British, Dutch, and Danish forces under Marlborough defeated the French 21 km (13 mi) N of Namur. The victory gave much of the Spanish Netherlands to the allies.

Ramón y Cajal, Santiago (1852–1934) Spanish histologist, who established the neurone (nerve cell) as the basic unit of the nervous system. Ramón improved staining techniques to distinguish the complex connections between neurones in the brain, spinal tissue, and the retina of the eye. He was awarded the 1906 Nobel Prize with Camillo *Golgi.

Ramsay, Allan (?1685–1758) Scottish poet and editor. He combined an admiration for English Augustan culture with an interest in traditional Scottish literature and life. He published poems by Henryson and Dunbar and made collections of Scottish ballads and proverbs, thus creating an awareness of native culture that helped to pave the way for *Burns and other later Scottish writers. His son **Allan Ramsay** (1713–84) was a portrait painter, who trained in London and in Italy (1736–38). His later paintings, such as the portrait of his wife Margaret Lindsay (National Gallery, Edinburgh), were influenced by the delicate draughtsmanship and intimacy of French portraiture. In 1767 he was appointed court painter to George III.

Ramsay, Sir William (1852–1916) Scottish chemist, whose work on the *noble gases earned him the 1904 Nobel Prize for Chemistry. His interest was kindled when *Rayleigh discovered that atmospheric nitrogen was slightly heavier than laboratory-prepared nitrogen. In 1894, Ramsay, working with Rayleigh, removed all known gases from some air and discovered a small residue, which they identified spectroscopically as a new element, naming it argon (inert). By fractionally distilling argon, Ramsay isolated neon, xenon, and krypton in 1898. In 1895 he had discovered the inert gas, helium, being given off by the mineral cleveite.

Ramses (II) the Great King of Egypt (1304–1237 BC) of the 19th dynasty. He fortified the coast road to repel nomads and pirates. His more serious, though indecisive, warfare against the Hittites, whose success at Qadesh (c. 1300) unsettled Egypt's Palestinian subjects, ended in lasting peace around 1284. Ramses built, or enlarged, more temples than any other pharaoh and built the temple complex of *Abu Simbel. He is probably the pharaoh who oppressed the Israelites.

Ramses III King of Egypt (1198–1166 BC) of the 20th dynasty, famous for two victories against the invading Sea Peoples. The first recorded strike in history occurred during his reign, when workers building a necropolis protested against the government's failure to deliver grain rations.

Ramsey, Alf (Sir Alfred Ernest R.; 1922–) British Association footballer, who played for Southampton (1946–49) and Tottenham Hotspur (1949–55). He also played for England 32 times. Following his success as manager of Ipswich Town (1955–62), he was made national team manager. Under his control, England won the World Cup in 1966.

Ramsgate 51 20N 1 25E A resort and port in SE England, in Kent. Formerly one of the Cinque Ports, it is now a fishing and yachting centre with a hoverport (opened 1969). St Augustine is said to have landed nearby in 597 AD. Population (1981): 39 642.

Ram Singh (1816–85) Indian Sikh leader. He organized a new, severely puritanical, sect of Sikhs, the Kukas, and worked to oust the British from India. His men were brutally punished for their attacks on Muslims and Ram Singh died after a long exile in Burma.

Ramus, Petrus (Pierre de la Ramée; 1515–72) French humanist scholar. In *Aristotelicae Animadversiones* and *Dialecticae Institutiones* (both 1543), Ramus attacked *Aristotelianism mainly on the grounds that it falsified the logic of the human mind. An intellectual hero to Protestant Europe, Ramus was murdered in the *St Bartholomew's Day Massacre.

Rancagua 34 10S 70 45W A city in N central Chile. Industries are chiefly related to processing agricultural produce and copper from the El Teniente mine. Population (1983 est): 142 473.

Rance, River A river in NW France, rising in Brittany and flowing generally E and N to the Gulf of St Malo. It powers the world's first successful tidal power station, opened in 1966. Length: 100 km (62 mi).

Rand, the. *See* Witwatersrand.

RANGOON *A complex of pagodas and temples surround the Shwe Dagon Pagoda, one of the great Buddhist centres of pilgrimage.*

Rangoon 16 47N 96 10E The capital of Burma, a port in the S on the River Rangoon. Industry has increased greatly since independence in 1948. Its university was founded in 1920. *History*: a settlement grew up in very early times around the Shwe Dagon Pagoda, which is the focal point of Burmese religious life. King Alaungpaya made it his capital in the 18th century. Twice captured by the British in the 19th century, it became the capital of all Burma in 1886. It was badly damaged in World War II during the Japanese occupation (1942–45). Population (1983): 2 458 712.

Ranjit Singh, Maharaja (1780–1839) Sikh ruler, known as the Lion of the Punjab. At the age of 20 he took control of Lahore and in 1802 seized Amritsar, the holy city of the Sikhs. With an enormous army based on the European model, he became master of a large part of the Punjab. In spite of uneasy relations with the British, he supported them against Afghanistan in 1838.

Ranjitsinhji Vibhaji, Kumar Shri, Maharajah Jam Sahib of Nawanagar (1872–1933) Indian cricketer and statesman, who captained Sussex (1899–1903) and played for England. He was the first batsman to score 3000 runs in a season (1899). A progressive ruler (1907–33), he was a colonel in the British army during World War I and chancellor of the Indian Chamber of Princes from 1932.

Rank, J(oseph) Arthur, 1st Baron (1888–1972) British industrialist and film executive. Before becoming chairman of his family's flour-milling business, Rank Hovis McDougall Ltd, he had developed an interest in religious films as aids in his activities as a leading Methodist layman. In 1935 he produced his first commercial film, and in 1946 he founded the Rank Organization, a film production, distribution, and exhibition company that controlled the leading British studios. When film production declined during the 1950s, the organization diversified its business interests.

Rank, Otto (1884–1939) Austrian psychiatrist, noted for his theory that emotional disorders could stem from psychological trauma experienced during birth. Rank was a colleague of Sigmund *Freud and applied Freudian psychology to an analysis of many literary works, pointing especially to the *Oedipus complex as a recurrent theme.

Ranke, Leopold von (1795–1886) German historian. A professor at Berlin University from 1825 to 1871, von Ranke published work on German, French, Spanish, Italian, and English history. His *History of the Latin and Teutonic Nations (1494–1535)* (1824) is generally regarded as the first critical historical work.

Ransom, John Crowe (1888–1974) US poet and critic. In 1939 he founded the *Kenyon Review*, a literary organ for the school of criticism that took its name from his book *The New Criticism* (1941). He was also a cofounder of the Fugitives, a group of Agrarian poets. His formal ironic poetry is included in *Selected Poems* (1945) and other volumes.

Ransome, Arthur Mitchell (1884–1967) British journalist and children's writer. He published critical works and books about his travels in Russia, China, and the Middle East but is best known for his series of children's books beginning with *Swallows and Amazons* (1931).

Ranunculaceae A family of herbaceous and woody plants (about 1300 species), found all over the world but most abundant in N temperate and Arctic regions. They are mainly bitter-tasting and sometimes poisonous. The family includes such garden flowers as *Anemone, *Aquilegia, *Clematis, and *Delphinium, as well as weeds, e.g. *buttercup.

Rapallo 44 21N 9 13E A port and resort in NW Italy, in Liguria on the Gulf of Genoa. It was the scene of the signing of two treaties after World War I, the first between Italy and Yugoslavia (1920) and the second between the Soviet Union and Germany (1922). Olive oil, wine, and cement are manufactured here. Population (1981 est): 28 318.

Rapanui. *See* Easter Island.

rape (botany) An annual or biennial herb, *Brassica napus* var. *arvensis*, also called oilseed rape or coleseed, that grows to a height of 1 m and has deeply divided lobed leaves and yellow flowers. It is widely cultivated for its seeds, contained in pods, which yield an edible oil; the residue is used as a cattle feed. Family: *Cruciferae.

rape (law) Sexual intercourse with a woman without her consent, which must be freely given and genuine. Intercourse with a married woman by impersonating her husband is thus rape. A genuine belief, however mistaken, that a woman has consented is a valid defence. Rape, previously punishable by death in England, now carries a maximum sentence of life imprisonment. The woman's accusation must be supported by other evidence: for example, of penetration.

Raphael (Raffaello Sanzio; 1483–1520) Italian Renaissance painter and architect, born in Urbino, the son of a painter. He trained under *Perugino, in Perugia, where he painted *The Marriage of the Virgin* (Brera, Milan) before moving to Florence in 1504. There, influenced by *Leonardo and *Michelangelo, he painted numerous Madonnas and also the portraits of Angelo and Maddalena Doni (Palazzo Pitti, Florence). Settling in Rome in 1508, he decorated the papal apartments in the Vat-

ican with frescoes, which include the *School of Athens* and the *Disputa*. He painted his patron Pope Julius II (Palazzo Pitti) and the *Sistine Madonna* (Dresden). In 1514 he succeeded Bramante as architect of St Peter's but only a few of his architectural projects were realized, for example the Chigi chapel in Sta Maria del Popolo. In 1515 he designed tapestries for the Sistine Chapel—seven of the cartoons for which are in the Victoria and Albert Museum. His last work, the *Transfiguration* (Vatican Museum), which was completed by Giulio Romano, anticipates *mannerism.

Rarotonga 21 15S 159 45W A mountainous island in the SW Pacific Ocean, the administrative centre of the *Cook Islands. Copra and citrus fruit are exported. Area: 67 sq km (26 sq mi). Population (1981): 9530. Chief town: Avarua.

Rashi (Solomon ben Isaac; 1040–1105) French rabbi. He established a school at Troyes that attracted pupils from many countries. His most celebrated works are his commentaries (in Hebrew) on the Bible and the Babylonian *Talmud, which are remarkable for their simplicity.

Rashid. *See* Rosetta Stone.

Rasht (*or* Resht) 37 18N 49 38E A town in N Iran, near the Caspian Sea. It is an agricultural trading centre and has a university (1977). Population (1985 est): 266 300.

Rasmussen, Knud Johan Victor (1879–1933) Danish explorer and ethnologist, who led a series of Arctic expeditions from Thule in Greenland to study Eskimo culture, which he believed to be akin to that of the North American Indians. In the longest recorded dog-sledge ride (1921–24) he reached the Bering Strait, describing the journey in *Across Arctic America* (1927).

raspberry A prickly woody perennial plant, *Rubus idaeus*, native to woods and heaths of Eurasia and North America. Up to 1.5 m high, it bears five-petalled white flowers, which produce red (or occasionally yellow) sweet fruits. There are many cultivated varieties, fruiting in summer or autumn. Upright canes grow from basal buds and bear fruit in their first autumn or second summer. The old canes, which die after fruiting, should be removed and the young canes pruned. Family: *Rosaceae.

Rasputin, Grigori Yefimovich (c. 1872–1916) Russian mystic, who was a favourite of Emperor *Nicholas II and *Alexandra. A Siberian peasant, Rasputin's apparent ability to ease the bleeding of the haemophiliac crown prince brought him considerable influence over the royal family and thus over the government: high offices were held by his hangers-on, who were invariably corrupt and incompetent. His unpopularity, aggravated by his debauchery, led to his murder by a group of nobles: his assassins attempted to poison him and when this inexplicably failed he was shot and thrown into the River Neva.

Rastafarians Members of a West Indian religious and political sect, who believe that Ras Tafari Makonnen (Haile Selassie) will arrange for the deliverance of the Black races of the world by procuring for them a homeland in Ethiopia. Rastafarian men wear their hair in long matted curls (dreadlocks).

rat A *rodent belonging to the suborder *Myomorpha*, distributed worldwide. Typical rats belong to the Old World genus *Rattus* (137 species) and are among the most successful rodents. The black rat (*R. rattus*), originally Asian, has spread by travelling on ships to most regions of the world, living in human habitations and sewers. The brown rat (*R. norvegicus*), also called Norway rat, is larger, measuring 30–45 cm including its tail (15-20 cm), and tends to live outdoors in burrows. It has displaced the black rat in many places. Both species eat a variety of plant and animal materials, often causing serious damage to stored food, gnawing through pipes and cables, and transmitting such diseases as typhus and food poisoning. Rats are commonly bred for use as laboratory animals in research. *See also* mouse.

ratel An omnivorous mammal, *Mellivora capensis*, also called honey badger, of Africa and S Asia. About 70 cm

RATEL *This animal uses its long claws to rip open bees' nests for honey. It may be led to a nest by a honeyguide, this bird then sharing the honey that the ratel extracts.*

long, grey above and black underneath, it lives in thick woods, eating almost anything from ants to young antelopes (especially honey). Family: *Mustelidae*.

rates In the UK, taxes on property raised by local authorities and forming about one-third of *local government income. The rateable value of a property is based on a notional rentable value, as assessed by the valuation officers of the Inland Revenue. Each year every local authority announces its rates poundage, i.e. how much each ratepayer has to pay for each pound of rateable value. Most local authorities charge different rates for commercial and domestic properties. The valuation officer's assessment of rateable value may be appealed against in a local valuation court, with a further appeal to the Lands Tribunal. Since 1966 rebates have been made to householders with low incomes, but rates have been criticized for taking no account of the number of wage earners living under one roof. In the 1980s a Conservative government placed limits upon local authority rates and penalized authorities that exceeded them (rate-capping); it is also replacing rates with a *poll tax (community charge) in 1989 in Scotland and 1990 in the rest of the UK.

ratfish. *See* chimaera.

Rathenau, Walther (1867–1922) German industrialist and politician, who organized Germany's economy during and after World War I. As minister of reconstruction (1921–22), he recommended the prompt payment of German reparations. Becoming foreign minister in 1922, he concluded the Treaty of Rapallo with the Soviet Union shortly before being assassinated. In *The New Economy* (1918) he advocated industrial self-government with worker participation.

Rathlin Island 55 17N 6 15W An island in Northern Ireland, off the N coast of Antrim in the North Channel. It was the refuge of Robert the Bruce (1306).

rationalism A philosophical movement stemming from 17th-century attempts to study the universe using reason, in the form of deductive and mathematical methods, rather than sense-experience. *Descartes, for example, tried to deduce what God's world is like from the axioms of divine existence and goodness. The scientific interests of the early rationalists made use of their religious views, but conflict between the new sciences and religion developed, and is reflected in the work of *Spinoza, *Arnauld, and *Leibniz. By the 19th century a compromise evolved, allocating science and religion to their separate spheres. Kant was called a rationalist in so far as he believed in the possibility of synthetic *a priori propositions. Recent intui-

tionists (*see* intuitionism) have been sympathetic to rationalism.

Ratisbon. *See* Regensburg.

ratite A bird characterized by a smooth breastbone that lacks a keel for the attachment of flight muscles. Ratites are flightless and usually large and swift-running and include the cassowary, emu, kiwi, ostrich, and rhea and the extinct moa.

rat kangaroo A *marsupial belonging to the subfamily *Potoroinae* (9 species), of Australia (including Tasmania). Two species are commonly known as boodies and two others as potoroos. Measuring 23–44 cm excluding the tail (15–38 cm), rat kangaroos are related to kangaroos and have a long narrow ratlike face. They have large canine teeth and long claws and forage at night for grubs and tubers. Family: *Macropodidae*.

rattan The stems of climbing *palms of the genus *Calamus* (375 species), native to Old World tropical regions. Up to 130 m long, the stems are stripped of leaves and used in furniture, matting, baskets, brooms, etc.

Rattigan, Sir Terence (1911–77) British dramatist. His highly successful plays include upper-class comedies (*French without Tears*, 1936), more ambitious studies of human relationships (*The Deep Blue Sea*, 1952), and studies of historical characters (*Ross*, 1960).

rattle, Simon (1955–) British conductor. Born in Liverpool, he became principal conductor of the City of Birmingham Symphony Orchestra in 1980 and principal guest conductor of the Los Angeles Philharmonic in 1981.

rattlesnake A *pit viper belonging to either of two genera, *Sisturus* (2 species) or *Crotalus* (28 species), and characterized by having a rattle composed of loosely connected horny tail segments, which is vibrated to produce a warning sound. Rattlesnakes occur in both North and South America, usually in dry regions, and are 0.3–2.5 m long with dark diamond, hexagonal, or spotted markings on a pale background. They feed on rabbits, rodents, lizards, etc., and bear live young. *See also* diamondback; sidewinder.

Rauschenberg, Robert (1925–) US artist. A leading exponent of *pop art, he studied under Josef *Albers. In the early 1950s he produced collages and assemblages made from rusty nails, rags, Coca-Cola bottles, etc. His best-known works are probably those produced in the 1960s, when he adopted the silk-screen printing technique for transferring photographic images to canvases.

Rauwolfia A tropical genus of trees and shrubs (50 species). The dried roots of some species, including *R. serpentina* of India and *R. vomitoria* of Africa, contain alkaloids with sedative effects, now used in medicine to treat hypertension. Family: *Apocynaceae*.

Ravel, Maurice (1875–1937) French composer of the impressionist school. A pupil of Fauré, he repeatedly entered compositions for the Prix de Rome, his failures provoking strong critical protest. His works include, for piano, *Pavane pour une infante défunte* (1899), *Valses nobles et sentimentales* (1911), and *Le Tombeau de Couperin* (1914–17), which were all later orchestrated, the suite *Gaspard de la nuit* (1908), and two piano concertos (one for left hand alone); for orchestra, *La Valse* (1920), *Boléro* (1927), and the ballet *Daphnis and Chloe* (1909–12); the opera *L'Enfant et les sortilèges* (1920–25); many songs; and an orchestration (1922) of Mussorgski's *Pictures at an Exhibition*.

raven A large glossy black crow, *Corvus corax*, about 63 cm long with bristling feathers at the throat, a massive bill, and a wedge-shaped tail. It feeds on carrion, small animals, seeds, and fruits and often roosts in large colonies. Ravens occur in mountain and moorland regions of the N hemisphere; numbers are increasing after near extermination.

Ravenna 44 25N 12 12E A city and port in N Italy, in Emilia-Romagna, connected to the Adriatic Sea by canal. Ravenna is said to have been founded by the Sabines. It was the capital of the western Roman Empire (402–76 AD), of the Ostrogothic kings (476–526), and of the Byzantine exarchate (military governorship) from 584 to 751. It is noted for its ancient mosaics. Today Ravenna is a growing industrial centre, based principally on oil and natural-gas refining. Population (1980 est): 139 662.

RAVENNA   *A Byzantine mosaic of Justinian, accompanied by his retinue, on the north wall of the church of S Vitale.*

Ravi, River   A river in NW India and Pakistan, one of the five rivers of the Punjab. Rising in the Himalayas, it flows W and SW to join the River Chenab. Length: 724 km (450 mi).

Rawalpindi   33 40N 73 08E A city in N Pakistan, 14 km (9 mi) SW of the national capital, Islamabad. From 1959 until 1969 it acted as the interim capital while the new capital at Islamabad was being built. Rawalpindi is an important military, commercial, and trading centre with varied industries, including oil refining, chemicals, and railway engineering. Population (1981): 982 000.

Rawlinson, Sir Henry Creswicke   (1810–95) British orientalist. As an army officer and later consul at Baghdad, Rawlinson tried for years (1835–46) to obtain a complete copy of the trilingual *cuneiform text carved (516 BC) by Darius I on the sheer rock face at Behistun (Iran). He eventually deciphered two of its three scripts: Old Persian (1847) and Babylonian (1857).

Rawsthorne, Alan   (1905–71) British composer. He studied in Manchester and Berlin and gained attention with his *Symphonic Studies* (1938) at a festival in Warsaw. His works include three symphonies, various concertos, a ballet, chamber music, and some film music.

ray   A predominantly marine *cartilaginous fish of the worldwide order *Batoidea* (or *Rajiformes*; about 350 species). Rays have a flattened head and body with greatly enlarged winglike pectoral fins; the tapering tail often bears sharp poison spines. The mouth and gill slits are ventral and a pair of openings (spiracles), located behind the dorsally situated eyes, are used to take in water for respiration. Rays are generally bottom-dwelling and move using their pectoral fins. They feed mainly on fish and invertebrates. Subclass: *Elasmobranchii.* □fish.

Ray, John   (1627–1705) English naturalist, who originated basic principles of plant classification. After compiling a survey of English plants, Ray's botanical studies culminated in his *Historia plantarum* (3 vols, 1686–1704). This was followed by works on birds, fishes, quadrupeds, and insects. Ray made the important taxonomic distinction between monocotyledonous and dicotyledonous plants and established the species as the basic taxonomic unit. He emphasized the importance of internal anatomy as a taxonomic criterion. The Ray Society was founded in 1844, in his memory.

Ray, Man   (1890–1976) The pseudonym of a US artist and photographer, whose real name is unknown. He first achieved prominence as cofounder with *Duchamp of the New York *dada movement (1917) and for his *ready-mades, notably his iron armed with nails and ironically called *The Gift* (1921). After moving to Paris (1921), where he was associated with *surrealism, he became highly successful as a portrait and fashion photographer.

Ray, Satyajit   (1922–) Indian film director.   He achieved an international reputation with *Pather Panchali* (1955), *The Unvanquished* (1956), and *The World of Apu* (1959), a trilogy of films about social change in modern India. His other films, all characterized by a humanistic understanding of both eastern and western values, include *Days and Nights in the Forest* (1970), *The Chess Players* (1977), and *The Home and The World* (1984).

Rayleigh, John William Strutt, 3rd Baron   (1842–1919) British physicist. Succeeding James Clerk *Maxwell as director of the Cavendish Laboratory, Cambridge (1879–84), he later became professor at the Royal Institution (1887–1905). His work on black-body radiation was upset by *Planck's discovery of the quantum theory but he did much valuable work in optics, hydrodynamics, and the theory of electrical units. He was awarded the 1904 Nobel Prize for his discovery of argon, in conjunction with Sir William *Ramsay. He was awarded an OM in 1901. His son **Robert John Strutt, 4th Baron Rayleigh** (1875–1947) was also a physicist, who specialized in spectroscopy. He later worked on natural radioactivity, showing that the age of rocks can be estimated from their radioactivity.

rayon   A textile fibre or fabric made from *cellulose. **Viscose rayon** is made by dissolving wood pulp in a mixture of sodium hydroxide and carbon disulphide. The fibres are reconstituted in an acid bath. **Acetate rayon** is made by mixing wood pulp with acetic anhydride, acetic acid, and sulphuric acid to form cellulose acetate, which is then dissolved in a solvent and forced through fine holes to form fibres as the solvent evaporates.

Razi ar-   (*or* Rhazes; c. 865–c. 928 AD) Persian physician and philosopher. In his *Comprehensive Book*, he surveyed the medical knowledge of the Greeks, Syrians, and Arabs and he wrote works on alchemy, philosophy, and diseases, such as smallpox and measles.

Razin, Stenka   (d. 1671) Cossack leader. From 1667 to 1669 Razin led a group of propertyless Cossacks in raids along the Volga River and the Caspian Sea. In 1670 Razin commanded a revolt against the tsar and was executed after his capture.

razorbill   A black-and-white *auk, *Alca torda*, that breeds around N Atlantic coasts and winters in the Mediterranean. 40 cm long, it has a laterally compressed bill. The wings are used as paddles in diving to catch fish, shellfish, and worms.

razor shell   A burrowing *bivalve mollusc of the family *Solenidae* (about 40 species), also called a jack-knife clam, of Atlantic and Pacific coasts. The common razor (*Ensis siliqua*), about 15 cm long, has a narrow □shell with squared ends; its curved foot is used to burrow up to 30 cm into sand.

reactance.   *See* impedance.

Read, Sir Herbert   (1893–1968) British poet and critic. The son of a Yorkshire farmer, he served as an infantry officer in World War I, and his war poetry constitutes a large proportion of his *Collected Poems* (1966). His art criticism, written from the basis of a personal philosophy of anarchism, promoted the work of Henry *Moore and many other artists of his generation. His literary criticism was chiefly concerned with the Romantic poets.

Reade, Charles   (1814–84) British novelist. His best-known novel is the historical romance *The Cloister and the Hearth* (1861), set in Europe during the Reformation. His other novels tackle such topical social issues as prison reform and trade unionism; he also wrote popular melodramas.

Reading   51 28N 0 59W A town in S England, the administrative centre of Berkshire on the River Thames. It has the remains of a 12th-century Benedictine abbey and a university (1892). An important railway junction, Reading has electronics works and is the headquarters of several international industries. Population (1981): 123 731.

Reading 40 20N 75 55W A city in the USA, in Pennsylvania. It grew as an iron and steel centre, linked by canal and rail to nearby anthracite mines. Industries today include the manufacture of bricks, speciality steels, and textiles. Population (1980): 78 686.

Reading, Rufus Daniel Isaacs, 1st Marquess of (1860–1935) British lawyer, Liberal MP (1904–13), and diplomat. He became solicitor general and then attorney general in 1910. As Lord Chief Justice (1913–21) he presided over the trial of Sir Roger Casement (1916). He was subsequently ambassador to the USA (1918–19), viceroy of India (1921–26), and foreign secretary (1931).

ready-made An everyday manufactured object elevated to artistic status by the personal whim of the artist. The *dada painter Marcel *Duchamp produced the first ready-made, a bicycle wheel on a stool, in 1913; it was followed by his snow shovel (1915), and his notorious urinal (1917). The ready-made is also a feature of *surrealism and *pop art.

Reagan, Ronald (1911–) US statesman; Republican president (1981–). He achieved fame as a film actor before entering politics. He was governor of California from 1966 until 1974. In 1981 he survived an assassination attempt. A conservative, as president he cut taxes, increased defence spending, and approved the US invasion of Grenada (1983) and CIA operations in Nicaragua, despite Congress opposition. Re-elected in 1984, he focused upon arms-control negotiations with the Soviet Union, resulting in the Intermediate Nuclear Forces (INF) Treaty (1987). However, a scandal over US arms sales to Nicaragua provoked worldwide criticism. *See also* disarmament; Strategic Defence Initiative.

realism 1. The medieval philosophical theory that general terms (called universals) have a real existence, that is that there is some abstract entity that corresponds with the term. For example, blueness is not just one idea of the sum of all blue objects (called particulars), but a really existing entity. *Plato and *Aristotle were realists in believing that the universe contained universals in addition to particulars. The difference between them was that Plato thought universals, which he called Forms, merely could have corresponding particulars and were independent of them, while Aristotle thought that Forms must have particulars and could exist only as instantiated in things. *Aquinas and *Duns Scotus were leading realists. *Compare* nominalism. **2.** In modern philosophy, a stance opposed to *idealism. Realists, such as G. E. *Moore (*see also* common sense, philosophy of), assert that objects exist independently of being perceived. Mathematical realism implies that mathematical entities exist in this way and that mathematical truths are independent of our ability to prove them.

real tennis A racket-and-ball indoor court game, which originated in France in the 12th–13th centuries as *jeu de paume*. It was originally played with the bare hand, the strung racket being developed in about 1500. Many other handball and racket-and-ball court games developed from it. Its world championships are the oldest of any sport, dating back to about 1750, although it is now very much a minority sport. The stone or concrete floor area is approximately 29 × 10 m (96 × 32 ft). The cloth ball is hit over a central net, as in *tennis and *badminton, but it also bounces off the side walls, as in *squash rackets and *fives.

Reardon, Ray (1932–) Welsh snooker player. He was the world professional champion in 1970, 1973–76, and 1978.

Réaumur, René-Antoine Ferchault de (1683–1757) French physicist, whose work on thermometers led him to devise the temperature scale that bears his name. On this scale water freezes at 0° and boils at 80°. He also carried out experiments on animals to show that digestion was a chemical process and not a mechanical one.

Reber, Grote (1911–) US astronomer, who, following *Jansky's discovery, built the first radio telescope (1937) and used it to discover a number of radio sources that had no visible counterparts. It was largely as a result of his published observations that several large radio telescopes were built after World War II.

recall A political device designed to enable voters dissatisfied with an elected official to replace him before the expiry of his term of office. The recall originated in Switzerland and has been operative in a number of US states since 1903. The usual procedure is the securing of a petition stating the charges against the official, the holding of an election to determine whether the official shall be removed, and the choice of a successor. Usually the official is allowed space on the ballot or petition in which to state his defence.

Recamier, Jeanne Françoise Julie Adelaide (1777–1849) French society hostess. She was married to a wealthy Parisian banker from 1792 to 1830. Her salon was attended by influential statesmen and politicians opposed to Napoleon. Her close friends included Mme de *Staël and *Chateaubriand.

received pronunciation (RP) The pronunciation of English most generally accepted as standard or correct in England and to some extent elsewhere. The term was coined in 1926 by Daniel *Jones to describe the characteristic accent of the public schools and universities and later extended to include that of the BBC. Historically, it is derived from the dialect of Middle English spoken in the London area.

recession A decline in the *trade cycle that, in a serious setback to the economy, becomes a transitory phase between *boom and *depression. In a recession, consumption demand falls off, investment (according to the *accelerator principle) suffers a decline, and business failures become more common.

recessive gene The *allele of a gene the function of which is hidden when the organism concerned is crossed with one carrying a different allele (called the dominant allele) for the same gene. *See* dominance.

Recife (*or* Pernambuco) 8 06S 34 53W A port in NE Brazil, the capital of Pernambuco state, on the Atlantic Ocean. It is a major port; the chief exports are sugar and cotton. Industries include sugar refining and spirit distilling and it has two universities. Population (1980): 1 184 215.

Recklinghausen 51 37N 7 11E A city in NW West Germany, in North Rhine-Westphalia in the *Ruhr. Notable buildings include the 13th-century church (founded 1276) and the castle (1702). A port on the Rhine-Herne Canal, its manufactures include iron and steel, machinery, and textiles. Population (1980 est): 119 600.

recombinant DNA. *See* genetic engineering.

Reconstruction (1865–77) The period after the US *Civil War in which the defeated Confederate states of the South were brought back into the Union. The southern states were readmitted to the Union after accepting the 14th (1866) or, subsequently, 15th Amendment, which guaranteed Black citizenship and franchise. The new state governments were dominated by Whites prepared to compromise, newly enfranchised Blacks, and northern carpetbaggers, but after the withdrawal of Federal troops in 1877 southerners dedicated to White supremacy were restored to power.

recorder (law). *See* judge.

recorder (music) A woodwind instrument of medieval origin, much used in the 17th and 18th centuries and revived in the 20th century. In contrast to the side-blown *flute, the recorder is end-blown, through a whistle mouthpiece mounted in a block (*or* fipple). The holes are covered with the fingers; the tone is quieter than that of the flute.

recording of sound A system for storing and reproducing sound. In music recording, the most common methods are tape recording, usually in *cassette form, and gramophone discs. The gramophone record is made by converting the sound into an electrical signal, which is normally temporarily stored on tape. This signal is amplified and used to control a cutter that produces a spiral undulating groove in a master disc. Plastic (vinyl) copies of this are mass-produced for sale. In a record-player, the stylus travels along the groove and reproduces the mechanical vibrations of the cutter. The *pick-up then converts these to an electrical signal, which is amplified and fed to a loudspeaker. Many electronic devices are used to ensure that the system will reproduce the original sound with a high fidelity, i.e. that sounds in the frequency range 80–12 000 hertz are reproduced without distortion. Recent innovations include the compact disc, which consists of a specially treated glass disc cut by a high-intensity laser beam and played back on a compact disc player. Resistant to scratches and offering better quality sound reproduction, compact discs offer an alternative to conventional gramophone records. Digital audio tape, which reproduces sound equal in quality to the compact disc and also permits home-recording to the same standard as cassettes, makes use of **digital recording** technology. In this the musical signal itself is not transmitted or recorded. Instead the signal is sampled, up to 30 000 times per second, and the characteristics of the sampled signal are represented by digits (as information is represented in a computer). The digits are then transmitted or recorded and reconstituted in the receiver or player. In this way the actual signal suffers no interference or distortion during transmission or in the recording process.

rectifier A device that allows electric current to flow in one direction only; it is generally used to convert alternating current to direct current. *Semiconductor diodes have now replaced thermionic valves (diodes) for lower voltage applications. For power supplies of several megawatts, mercury-arc rectifiers are used.

rectum. *See* intestine.

recycling The repeated use of the same resources. Recycling involves the manufacture of a complex product followed by breakdown of the spent product to release its constituents for reuse. This process—a feature of most natural *ecosystems—is becoming an economic necessity in industry in order to conserve scarce raw materials and reduce pollution of the environment. Steel scrap, waste paper, and chemical solvents are often recycled.

red admiral A butterfly, *Vanessa atalanta*, found throughout Europe, Asia, and North America. The wings are black with red and white markings. Red admirals migrate to northern regions for the summer but do not survive the cold winters there; in warmer climates they hibernate. The caterpillars feed on stinging nettles. Family: *Nymphalidae*.

red algae *Algae of the division *Rhodophyta* (about 3000 species), which are usually red or blue in colour due to the presence of the pigments phycoerythrin (red) or phycocyanin (blue), which mask the green chlorophyll. They range from small unicellular or filamentous forms to branching or sheetlike *seaweeds, found mainly attached to other plants in deep warm seas or sometimes in rock pools. Reproduction is asexual or sexual.

Redbridge A borough of NE Greater London, created in 1965 from the former municipal boroughs of Ilford, Wanstead, and Woodford and parts of Chigwell and Dagenham. Population (1981): 225 019.

Red Brigades (Italian name: Brigate Rosse) A group of Italian terrorists formed in 1969 and dedicated to the violent overthrow of capitalist society. They were responsible for the murder of the statesman Aldo Moro in 1978. Several of their leading members have been imprisoned.

Red Cross, International An organization founded by the Geneva Convention of 1864 to provide care for the casualties of war. Inspired by Henri *Dunant, a Swiss philan-thropist, its headquarters are in Geneva and its emblem, the red cross, represents the Swiss flag with its colours reversed. Muslim countries, however, have generally adopted the crescent as their emblem. The International Red Cross, which is staffed mainly by volunteers, has twice won the Nobel Peace Prize, in 1917 and 1944. National branches include the **British Red Cross Society**, incorporated in 1908, which undertakes first-aid and welfare duties throughout the world.

redcurrant A shrub of the genus *Ribes* (*see* currant), cultivated for its clusters of small acid-tasting red fruits, which may be made into jellies, jams, etc. Cultivated redcurrants have been derived from *R. rubrum* of Eurasia, *R. sativum* of W Europe, and *R. petraeum* of central and S Europe.

red deer A large reddish-brown deer, *Cervus elaphus*, of European and Asian woodlands. Over 120 cm high at the shoulder, males have spreading branched antlers up to 125 cm long; females are more lightly built. Stags and hinds live apart in winter, spring, and summer, coming together in the autumn for the rut, when mature males compete to gather a harem of hinds. *See also* wapiti.

Redditch 52 19N 1 56W A town in the English Midlands, in Hereford and Worcester. Designated for development as a new town in 1964, its manufactures include fishing tackle and springs. Population (1981): 66 854.

Red Duster The popular name for the British Merchant Navy's Red Ensign—a red flag with the Union Flag in its upper corner nearest the flagstaff. It was authorized in 1674, amended in 1707 and 1801, and reconfirmed in 1894.

Redford, Robert (1936–) US film actor. He costarred with Paul *Newman in *Butch Cassidy and the Sundance Kid* (1969) and *The Sting* (1973). Other films include *The Candidate* (1972), *All the President's Men* (1976), *Ordinary People* (1981), and *Out of Africa* (1986).

red fox A *fox, *Vulpes vulpes*, found throughout the N hemisphere. It is about 100 cm long, including its bushy tail (50 cm). There are a number of local races and the North American red fox and its grey-black variety, the silver fox, were once thought to be a separate species (*V. fulva*).

red giant A greatly distended cool but very luminous *giant star, often variable in nature. It is one of the final evolutionary stages of a normal *star, attained when its central hydrogen has been converted to helium. Hydrogen burning in a shell surrounding the inert helium core causes a rapid expansion and cooling of the outer atmosphere of the star.

Redgrave, Sir Michael (1908–85) British Shakespearian actor, who also performed in and directed modern plays. His films included *The Browning Version* (1951) and *The Go-Between* (1971). His daughter **Vanessa Redgrave** (1937–) has acted on stage and in a number of films including *Morgan* (1966), *Blow-Up* (1967), and *Julia* (1977), and is well known for her left-wing political activities, as is his son **Corin Redgrave** (1939–), who is an actor. His daughter **Lynn Redgrave** (1944–) is also an actress.

red grouse A *grouse, *Lagopus lagopus scoticus*, found on moorlands of Great Britain and Ireland, where it is managed as a gamebird. 34–37 cm long, it feeds chiefly on ling heather. The male is red-brown with red wattles above the eyes and the female is browner and heavily barred: both sexes have white underwing markings and feathered feet.

Red Guards High-school and university students organized by Mao Tse-tung during the *Cultural Revolution (1966–68) to eliminate revisionism. The Red Guards destroyed property, humiliated foreign diplomats, and attacked those officials who opposed Mao's policies.

red-hot poker A plant of the African genus *Kniphofia*, especially *K. uvaria* and *K. rufa* (and their varieties), cultivated as garden plants. 45–120 cm tall, they have tubular flowers, usually scarlet and/or yellow. Family: *Liliaceae*.

Red Indians. *See* North American Indians.

Redmond, John Edward (1856–1918) Irish politician. An MP from 1881, in 1900 he reunited the pro- and anti-

Parnellite factions under his leadership. In 1909 he allied his party with the Liberals to achieve *Home Rule. The rise of *Sinn Féin undermined the appeal of his moderate policies.

red mullet   A fish, also called surmullet or goatfish, belonging to the family *Mullidae* (about 50 species), found usually in shallow warm seas. They have an elongated body, up to 25 cm long, with two dorsal fins and two long flexible chin barbels. They feed on bottom-dwelling invertebrates and many species are valued food fish. Order: *Perciformes*.

ODILON REDON   *One of a set of six lithographs entitled* La Nuit.

Redon, Odilon   (1840–1916) French symbolist painter and lithographer; a forerunner of *surrealism. Working exclusively in black and white in charcoal drawings, lithographs, and etchings until the 1890s, he created a fantasy world of plants with human heads, mythical figures, etc. From the 1890s he turned to oil painting and pastel, producing a number of flower paintings in powdery colours and paintings inspired by literary subjects.

Redouté, Pierre Joseph   (1759–1841) French flower painter. He worked for all the French courts from Louis XV to Louis Philippe, painting his flowers, notably roses, chiefly in watercolours and after careful scientific study.

redox reactions.   *See* oxidation and reduction.

redpoll   A tiny finch, *Acanthis flammea*, about 12 cm long with a brown streaked plumage, a red crown, and a black chin. The male has a red breast in summer. It breeds in the Arctic tundra and high mountains of Europe, migrating to central Europe and the N USA in winter.

Red River   (Vietnamese name: Song Hong)   The chief river of N Vietnam, rising in S China and flowing SE to enter the Gulf of Tonkin via an extensive delta. Length: 500 km (310 mi).

Red River of the North   (*or* Red River)   A river in central North America, rising in W Minnesota and flowing N into Canada to empty into Lake Winnipeg. Although navigable, it is subject to severe floods that damage the farms of its fertile valley. Length: 1000 km (621 mi).

Red River Settlement   A colony of immigrants led by Thomas Douglas, 5th Earl of Selkirk (1771–1820), settled in 1811 on the banks of the Red River in present-day Manitoba. In 1836 it was bought by the Hudson's Bay Company. In 1869 Louis *Riel led an uprising against the proposed transfer of the colony from the Company to Canada, which was effected nonetheless in 1870.

red salmon.   *See* sockeye salmon.

Red Sea   A long narrow arm of the Indian Ocean between Africa and Asia, extending some 2400 km (1491 mi) NNW beyond the Gulf of Aden and the Bab el-Mandeb. In the N, it is connected to the Mediterranean Sea by the Suez Canal, which has enormously increased shipping in the Red Sea. It is part of the *Great Rift Valley. Area: 438 000 sq km (169 076 sq mi).

redshank   An Old World *sandpiper, *Tringa totanus*, that breeds in cool marshy regions of Eurasia. 30 cm long, it has long reddish legs, a black-tipped red bill, and a brown-grey plumage with a white rump. It winters on mudflats of Africa and Asia, feeding on crustaceans, molluscs, and ragworms.

redshift   An overall displacement towards larger wavelengths of the spectral lines of a celestial object. Its astronomical significance was suggested by Edwin *Hubble in 1929, when it was used as the basis of the theory that the universe is expanding (*see* expanding universe). A redshift usually arises from the *Doppler effect, that is from recession of a celestial object. It increases as the object's radial velocity increases and for an extragalactic body can be used as a measure of distance. A **gravitational redshift** occurs whenever radiation is emitted by a body: it is generally negligible except when the gravitational field is very strong.

red squirrel   A tree *squirrel, *Sciurus vulgaris*, of Eurasia. About 20 cm long with a 20-cm tail, red squirrels have dark glossy red fur and tufted ears. They feed mainly on seeds and nuts but will eat buds and dried fungi in winter. They are less aggressive than the immigrant grey squirrels, which have displaced them in many areas.

redstart   A small Eurasian thrush of the genus *Phoenicurus*, about 14 cm long with a sharp fine bill. The male European redstart (*P. phoenicurus*) is grey with a russet breast, black throat and face with a white stripe, and a red tail, which it fans out in its courtship display to the yellow and brown female. It is found in woodland and heathland while the black redstart (*P. ochruros*) inhabits cliffs and buildings. Both of these species migrate to Africa for the winter.

reduction.   *See* oxidation and reduction.

reductionism   A 20th-century trend in philosophy prompted by scepticism. Reductionists argue that material objects are nothing but collections of sensations; other minds are nothing but the physical manifestations of their owners; statements about the past are nothing but aggregates of statements about the presently available evidence for them. Reduction of the meaning of a statement to statements of the evidence for it was popular among phenomenalists and logical positivists.

redundancy   An end to the immediate usefulness of labour or machines, caused by a decline in the demand for the product they produce or by technological change. Redundancy payments are often made to men and women so displaced; lump-sum redundancy payments have been statutory in the UK since 1965, a portion of which can, in certain circumstances, be claimed from the government.

redwing   A European thrush, *Turdus iliacus*, resembling a small song thrush but having a white eyestripe, red underwings, and red patches on the flanks. It feeds on earthworms, snails, beetles, fruits, and berries. Redwings breed mainly in Scandinavia and occasionally in Scotland, migrating to W Europe for the winter.

redwood A coniferous tree, *Sequoia sempervirens*, thought to be the tallest tree in the world and one of the longest lived: a specimen in California is over 111 m tall and some Californian trees are over 2000 years old. Also called coast redwood, it is native to the Pacific coast between Oregon and California and is an important timber tree in North America; in Europe it is planted mainly for ornament. It has brown-red fibrous bark, bladelike leaves, 1.5-2 cm long, in two rows along the stems, and woody red-brown globular cones, about 2 cm long. Family: *Taxodiaceae*. *See also* dawn redwood; sequoia.

reed Any of several species of tall aquatic grasses, especially those of the genus *Phragmites* (2-3 species). The common reed (*P. communis*) has a creeping underground stem (rhizome) and grows worldwide along the margins of marshes, lakes, streams, and fens. 1.5-3 m tall, it has long flat leaves, 10-20 mm wide, a stiff smooth stem, and clusters of purple-brown flowers. Dried reed stems have been used for arrows, basketry, pens, and in musical instruments.
The name is also given to similar but unrelated plants, such as the paper reed, *Cyperus papyrus* (*see* papyrus).

Reed, Sir Carol (1906-76) British film director. His best-known films include *The Fallen Idol* (1948) and *The Third Man* (1949), both with screenplays by Graham *Greene. His later, more commercial, films include *The Agony and the Ecstasy* (1965) and *Oliver!* (1968).

Reed, John (1887-1920) US journalist. He helped found the Communist Party in the USA and was a personal friend of Lenin. *Ten Days that Shook the World* (1919) is an account of the 1917 Revolution in Russia, where he died.

Reed, Walter (1851-1902) US physician. After serving as an army surgeon, Reed was appointed to investigate yellow fever in Cuba, where C. J. *Finlay had suggested that the mosquito was the agent responsible for spreading the disease. Reed and his team subjected themselves to the bites of infected mosquitoes, one of the team dying as a result, but thereby proving that mosquitoes were responsible. Subsequent control of mosquito populations eliminated yellow fever from the region.

reedbuck An African antelope belonging to the genus *Redunca* (3 species). The common reedbuck (*R. arundinium*) grows to 90 cm high at the shoulder and has a stiff grey coat and slender ridged horns and inhabits lush grassland. The bohor reedbuck (*R. redunca*) is smaller and lives in swampy regions, while the gregarious mountain reedbuck (*R. fulvorufula*) lives in hilly areas.

reed instruments Musical instruments in which a column of air is made to vibrate by a reed. The *clarinet family have a single (*or* beating) reed clamped to and vibrating against a slot in the mouthpiece. The *oboe and *bassoon use a double reed, the two halves bound together and forming the mouthpiece. The **reed organ** family contains such instruments as the *harmonium, *concertina, *accordion, and *harmonica, which have free reeds (sometimes made of some other substance, such as brass) that vibrate from side to side of the slot in which they are fixed.

reedling A Eurasian bird, *Panurus biarmicus*, about 16 cm long, also called bearded tit. It lives in reedbeds, feeding on insects and seeds. The plumage is brown with pale underparts: the male has a grey head with a black moustache of feathers. Reedlings belong to the *babbler family.

reedmace A widely distributed perennial herbaceous plant, *Typha latifolia*, also called bulrush or cat's-tail, growing in reed swamps. It has an erect stem, 1.5-2.5 m high, bearing a terminal spike of male and female flowers, the latter developing into the cylindrical fruit, which tapers into the stem at its base. There are several other reedmaces of the genus *Typha* (*see* elephant grass). Family: *Typhaceae*.

reed warbler An acrobatic *warbler, *Acrocephalus scir-*

paeus, about 12 cm long with a reddish-brown plumage, pale underparts, and a pale eyestripe. It winters in SE Africa and breeds in European reedswamps, building a deep nest around the stems of several reeds and feeding on small marsh insects. It is frequently parasitized by cuckoos.

reef A ridge of rock lying just above or near the surface of the sea, built mainly of the skeletons of *coral or other sedentary marine organisms. **Barrier reefs** lie parallel to the coast with a deep lagoon between; **fringing reefs** are attached to the coast; bioherms are dome-shaped reefs; apron reefs are tabular masses; atolls are circular with a central lagoon. Reef formation was much more widespread in the geological past.

Reeves, William Pember (1857-1932) New Zealand politician. He was a progressive minister of education, labour, and justice (1891-96), originating among other labour reforms the influential Industrial Conciliation and Arbitration Act. He was subsequently high commissioner in London (1905-08) and then director of the London School of Economics (1908-19). Among his books is *The Long White Cloud: A History of New Zealand* (1898).

referendum and initiative Votes on specific legislation by the whole electorate. Referendums are votes on particular political questions framed by parliament and put to the electorate. In the UK referendums have been held concerning membership of the EEC (1975) and *devolution for Scotland and Wales (1979). Initiatives are proposals, drafted by a citizen or group of citizens, that by virtue of attaining a requisite number of signatures on a petition are put to the electorate for acceptance or rejection. Initiatives are used in about half of the states of the USA to decide contentious matters of local government. *See also* plebiscite.

reflection The rebounding of a wave of light or other radiation when it strikes a surface. Reflected light obeys two laws: first, the normal (an imaginary line vertical to the surface at the point of impact), the incident ray, and the reflected rays all lie in the same plane; second, the angle of incidence (i.e. the angle between the incident ray and the normal) is equal to the angle of reflection. *See also* mirrors.

reflex An automatic and involuntary response by an organism to a change in the environment. An example is the rapid withdrawal of a finger in response to a pinprick, which occurs before the brain has had time to convey the necessary information to the muscles involved. *See also* conditioned reflex.

Reform Acts The legislation that reformed the British parliamentary system. The Reform Act of 1832 gave the vote in the boroughs to the occupants of houses worth £10 a year and in the counties to £10 copyholders and £50 leaseholders, in addition to the already enfranchised 40-shilling freeholders. It disenfranchised some *rotten and *pocket boroughs and gave parliamentary representation to new industrial towns, such as Birmingham and Manchester. However, it did not destroy the dominance over the electoral system of the landed classes. The 1867 Reform Act gave the vote to all householders and £10 rent payers in the towns, thus enfranchising many of the working class for the first time. It doubled the existing electorate to 2.4 million. The 1884 Reform Act made the county franchise the same as that in the towns, thus increasing the electorate to about five million. Adult male suffrage was achieved only in 1918 and women had to wait until 1928.

Reformation A religious movement in 16th-century Europe that began as an attempt to reform the *Roman Catholic Church and ended with the establishment of independent Protestant Churches (*see* Protestantism). The Reformation, which was preceded by such reform movements as those led by John *Wycliffe (the *Lollards) and Jan *Hus (the *Hussites), was caused by the inability of the Catholic Church to put its own, increasingly worldly, house in order; the critical examination of the Bible emphasized by the humanists (see humanism) and its translation into the vernaculars; the development of printing, which disseminated new ideas more widely and more quickly; and the growth of nationalism, which sought to weaken papal jurisdiction within the states of W Europe.

The Reformation began on 31 October, 1517, when Martin *Luther nailed his 95 theses on the door of the castle church at Wittenburg. Luther's attack on the sale of *indulgences and, subsequently, on papal authority and the *sacraments (save baptism and the Eucharist) was condemned by the pope and the Holy Roman Emperor but gained the support of several German princes. The consequent conflict (see Charles V) was not resolved until 1555 (see Augsburg, Peace of).

In Switzerland, the Reformation was initiated by *Zwingli in Zurich in 1520, spreading to Basle, Berne, and also to Geneva, where it was led by John *Calvin. Calvinism was adopted in France, the Low Countries, England, Scotland, and subsequently in North America. In France, where Protestants were called Huguenots, the Reformation became involved in a political struggle for control of the Crown, giving rise to the *Wars of Religion, and in the Low Countries it fired the *Revolt of the Netherlands against Spanish rule.

In England, the Reformation had three stages. Under Henry VIII papal authority in England was destroyed. Thomas Cromwell's legislation (1529–36) attacked ecclesiastical abuses (1529–31) and clerical jurisdiction (1532) and abolished the payment of first fruits (annates) to the pope (1532, 1534) and, thereby enabling Henry to divorce Catherine of Aragon, the lodging of appeals to Rome (1533); the Act of Supremacy (1534) proclaimed the king as supreme head of the English Church and in 1536 the dissolution of the monasteries was authorized. Under Edward VI Protestantism was established by the 1552 Book of *Common Prayer, the accompanying Acts of *Uniformity, and the 42 Articles (1553). Following the reestablishment of Roman Catholicism under Mary I, Protestantism finally became the established *Church of England under Elizabeth I.

In Scotland, the Reformation was influenced by John *Knox and *Presbyterianism was established in 1592. Elsewhere in Europe Lutheranism was adopted by Sweden in 1527, by Denmark in 1546, and also became the established religions of Norway, Finland, and Iceland. See also Counter-Reformation.

Reformed Churches. See Protestantism.

Reform Judaism A religious movement attempting to adapt traditional Judaism to modern circumstances. It began in Germany in the early 19th century. The first Reform synagogue in England was established in 1840; the Liberal movement (founded 1903) instituted more radical reforms typical of US Reform Judaism. The World Union for Progressive Judaism was founded in London in 1926 (it is now based in Jerusalem). The reforms include abolition of many of the ritual laws, acceptance of modern biblical criticism, vernacular services, and full equality for women.

refraction The bending of a beam of radiation as it passes from one medium onto another. For a light ray the amount by which it is bent depends on the angle of the incident ray and on the refractive indices of the two media, the exact dependence being given by *Snell's law. Refraction is caused by the difference in the velocity of the radiation in the two media. The ratio of the velocity of light in the two media is known as the **refractive index**. If the first medium is a vacuum, the ratio is known as the absolute refractive index of the second medium. The refractive index of glass lies between 1.5 and 1.7, for diamond it is 2.1, and for water 1.33 (at 25°C).

refractories Firebricks or other heat-resisting materials used for lining furnaces to retain the heat and protect the outer shell of the furnace. There are three types, character-

ized by their chemical interaction with the hot substances in the furnace: acid (e.g. silica); basic (e.g. dolomite); and neutral (e.g. Carborundum).

refrigeration The process of lowering the temperature inside a closed insulated container. In the domestic refrigerator the method most commonly used is the vapourcompression cycle in which a liquid refrigerant, such as Freon (a compound of chlorine, fluorine, and carbon), is pumped through cooling coils formed into the ice-making compartment. In these coils the refrigerant evaporates, taking the latent heat required to make it into a gas from the surroundings (i.e. the inside of the ice compartment). It is then passed to an electrically driven compressor; after compression it condenses back to liquid, when the absorbed heat is given out (usually at the back of the refrigerator). This cycle is repeated over and over again until the required temperature (about 1–2°C in the food chamber and -15°C in the deep-freeze compartment) is achieved. The compressor is then switched on and off by the thermostat. Other cycles (e.g. ammonia absorption) are also used, but in all of them the refrigerator functions as a heat engine in reverse: in order to transfer heat from the cold interior to the warmer surrounding air, work must be done. In the vapour-compression refrigerator this is supplied by the electricity that drives the compressor. See also cold storage; freezing.

Regency style An English decorative style fashionable from about 1800 to 1830 and influenced by the French *Empire style. Dark exotic woods and veneers, such as rosewood, were popular and were set off by ormolu mounts and grilles for doors. Leading designers produced rather heavy furniture purporting to derive from antique Greek, Roman, and Egyptian models. Concurrently there was a vogue for oriental motifs (see chinoiserie) and some magnificent lacquer was produced, for example for the Prince Regent's Pavilion at Brighton. Initially elegant, the style later became somewhat clumsy.

regeneration In biology, the regrowth and development of tissues or organs lost through injury, as a normal process (e.g. during moulting), or by any other means. The ability to regenerate is present in all forms of life to some degree: it is particularly well developed in plants and simple animals. Thus, whole plants can regenerate from stem and leaf cuttings and simple animals, such as sponges and planarians, can develop from minute fragments. More complex animals, such as crustaceans, replace lost appendages, while lizards can grow new tails. In mammals regeneration is limited to wound healing and regrowth of peripheral nerve fibres.

Regensburg (English name: Ratisbon) 49 01N 12 07E A city in SE West Germany, in Bavaria at the confluence of the Rivers Danube and Regen. Many medieval buildings survived the bombing of World War II, including the gothic cathedral (1275–1524). Its university was established in 1962. It is a port and commercial and industrial centre. History: originally a Celtic settlement, it became a Carolingian capital and a prosperous medieval trading centre. From 1663 until 1806 the imperial diets (assemblies) were held here. Population (1980 est): 131 800.

Reger, Max (1873–1916) German composer, organist, and teacher. In Leipzig he was director of music at the university (1907–08) and professor of composition at the conservatoire. His vast output includes Variations and Fugue on a Theme of Mozart for orchestra and a Fantasy and Fugue on BACH for organ.

reggae A style of rock music combining West Indian rhythms and rhythm and blues. It became associated with the Jamaican cult of the Rastafarians and had a wide popularity in the UK during the early 1970s.

Reggio di Calabria 38 06N 15 39E A seaport in Italy, in Calabria on the Strait of Messina. It was founded by Greek colonists in the 8th century BC. Fruit, herbs, and oil are exported. Population (1980 est): 181 858.

Reggio nell'Emilia 44 42N 10 37E A city in Italy, in Emilia-Romagna. Dating from Roman times, it was ruled by the Este family (15th–18th centuries) and has a cathedral (rebuilt in the 13th century). The centre of a rich agricultural area, its industries include agricultural engineering and meat canning. Population (1980 est): 130 159.

Regina 50 30N 104 38W A city in W Canada, the capital of Saskatchewan. Founded in 1882, it has expanded rapidly since 1945 as a centre of agricultural industries, oil refining, and potash production. It houses the University of Regina (1917). Population (1981): 162 613.

Regiomontanus (Johannes Müller; 1436–76) German astronomer and mathematician, who introduced algebra and trigonometry to Germany. He produced a table of trigonometric functions that was printed by Johann Gutenberg and widely used by navigators. He was an ardent follower of *Ptolemy, producing a new translation of his *Almagest*. He also made observations of the sky and drew up a table of planetary motions.

Regnier, Henri François Joseph de (1864–1936) French poet. He published several early collections of Symbolist poetry written in *vers libre*, but in his later and better-known volumes, such as *Les Médailles d'argile* (1900), he reverted to classical forms. He also wrote fiction, mostly historical novels set in the 17th and 18th centuries.

Regulus, Marcus Attilus (died c. 251 BC) Roman general of the first *Punic War. In 256 he defeated the Carthaginian navy, invaded Africa, and overwhelmed the Carthaginians. Rejecting his peace terms, in 255 the Carthaginians utterly defeated Regulus, who was captured and sent to Rome to negotiate peace. Urging continued war, he returned to certain death in Carthage.

Rehoboam King of Judah (c. 922–915 BC); the son of Solomon. His intransigent attitude to the northern tribes resulted in the secession of Israel under Jeroboam and the disintegration of Solomon's empire.

Reich, Wilhelm (1897–1957) US psychiatrist, born in Austria, noted for his controversial notion of a universal energy, which he called orgone, that is released during sexual intercourse. Failure to achieve regular release of this energy resulted, so he claimed, in both personal and social neuroses. Reich's "orgone box" was declared fraudulent and he was jailed for contempt of court in the USA in 1956. His works include *The Function of the Orgasm* (1948) and *Character Analysis* (1949).

Reichenberg. *See* Liberec.

Reichstag (Imperial Diet) The legislative assembly of the German Empire (1871–1918) and the Weimar Republic (1919–33). Its origins lay in the diet of the Holy Roman Empire, which was divided into an electoral college (*see* electors), a college of princes, and a college of cities. The decline of imperial control over the German states after the Thirty Years' War brought a corresponding decline in the power of the diet until its revival by Bismarck in 1867 as the representative assembly of the *North German Confederation, then of the German Empire, and finally of the Weimar Republic. In 1933 the Reichstag building was burnt out; Nazi allegations of communist responsibility provided an excuse to ban opposition parties, and the Reichstag became a mere puppet under Hitler.

Reid, Sir George Houston (1845–1918) Australian statesman, born in Scotland; prime minister (1904–05). He was a successful prime minister of New South Wales from 1894 to 1899, dealing effectively with the flagging economy, and was subsequently Australia's first high commissioner in London (1910–15) and an MP in the UK parliament (1916–18).

Reid, Thomas (1710–96) Scottish philosopher. He maintained that Hume, in his theory of ideas, had overlooked "common sense," which was to become the cornerstone of his own philosophy. In his *Enquiry into the Human Mind on the Principles of Common Sense* (1764), he discussed "common sense," in linguistic and metaphysical, as well as mundane, contexts.

Reigate 51 14N 0 13W A town in SE England, in Surrey at the foot of the North Downs. It is a dormitory town for London and includes the adjacent newer town of Redhill. Population (1981): 52 554.

Reign of Terror (1793–94) The most violent period of the French Revolution. Dominated by *Robespierre, the governing Committee of Public Safety authorized severe measures against the Revolution's opponents. Over 250 000 suspects were arrested and about 1400 were summarily guillotined. Public reaction caused Robespierre's downfall and execution in July, 1794, thus ending the Terror.

Reims (*or* Rheims) 49 15N 4 02E A city in NE France, in the Marne department. An important Roman town, it was the scene of the coronations of most of the French kings. The magnificent gothic cathedral was badly damaged in World War I but it has gradually been restored. Its university was established in 1969. A centre for the marketing of Champagne wines, it has varied manufacturing industries. Population (1982): 181 985.

reincarnation (*or* metempsychosis) The migration of the soul from one body at death and its re-entry into another (human or animal) body. Belief in reincarnation appears in many different cultures, partly because it offers an explanation for the perplexing differences between individuals' characters and destinies, these being ascribable to traces of previous characters and the rewards or punishments for actions in previous lives. The cycle of reincarnation (*samsara*) is fundamental to Hindu, Buddhist, and Jain conceptions of the world, all spiritual effort being directed towards release (*moksa*) from the cycle. *Plato and *Pythagoras also subscribed to reincarnation, but orthodox Christianity rejected it as contrary to belief in the resurrection of the body.

reindeer A large deer, *Rangifer tarandus*, of European and North American tundra (in America it is called a caribou). About 125 cm high at the shoulder, reindeer have a grey-brown coat and spreading branched antlers—male antlers are larger with an extra forward point over the face. Reindeer feed mainly on lichens (reindeer moss) but also eat dwarf willow and other shrubs. The small summer groups gather into herds numbering several hundreds for their winter migration southwards, at which time their coat fades to a dull white. □mammal.

reindeer moss A grey tufted *lichen, *Cladonia rangiferina*, that is very abundant in Arctic regions, especially Lapland. It has a stalked much-branched body, up to 8 cm high, and covers immense areas of tundra, serving as the major food source for reindeer, moose, musk oxen, etc.

Reinhardt, Django (Jean Baptiste R.; 1910–53) Belgian jazz guitarist of gipsy origin. He injured his hand in a fire at the age of 18 but developed an original guitar technique. From 1934 to 1939 he led the quintet of the Hot Club de France with Stephane *Grappelli.

Reinhardt, Max (M. Goldmann; 1873–1943) Austrian theatre director. His large-scale productions, involving massed crowds and spectacular lighting and scenery, included *Oedipus Rex* in Berlin in 1910 and *The Miracle* in London in 1911. He also directed more conventional theatre productions, opera, and a film of *A Midsummer Night's Dream* (1935), and founded the Salzburg Festival in 1920. From 1938 he lived in the USA.

Reith, John Charles Walsham, 1st Baron (1889–1971) British administrator. His severe moral principles greatly influenced the early development of the BBC, of which he was first general manager from 1922 and director general from 1927 to 1938. He subsequently held many other important administrative posts, including the chairmanship of the British Overseas Airways Corporation (BOAC), which he formed in 1939. The Reith lectures, broadcast annually, were established in 1947 and named in his honour.

relative aperture. *See* f-number.

relativistic mass The mass of a body that is moving at a velocity comparable to the *velocity of light. According to the theory of *relativity, if the velocity of the body is v then its mass is $m_0(1 - v^2/c^2)^{-\frac{1}{2}}$, where c is the velocity of light and m_0 the rest mass (the mass when stationary). The relativistic mass of an electron travelling at 99% of the velocity of light is seven times its rest mass.

1.

RELATIVITY **1.** *Two cars, A and B, travelling along a motorway. The speed of car A relative to the earth is 90 mph. The speed of car B relative to the earth is 70 mph. The speed of car A relative to car B is $90 - 70 = 20$ mph.* **2.** *Car B is now stationary; its headlight beams are turned on as supercar A passes, travelling at 5000 miles per second. The speed of car B's headlight beam relative to car A is 187 000 miles per second (not 187 000-5000 miles per second). The velocity of light is absolute.*

2.

relativity An important theory proposed by Albert *Einstein. The first part of the theory, published in 1905 and known as the special theory, applies only to motion in which there is no acceleration. The problem that Einstein set out to solve was concerned with the speed at which light travels relative to an observer.

Up to this time it was thought that light travelled through a stationary medium, called the ether, at a constant speed and that its speed relative to an observer could be calculated in the same way as the relative speed of any two moving objects. For example, if one car (A) travelling at 90 mph on a motorway overtakes another (B) travelling at 70 mph, the speed of the two cars relative to each other is 20 mph. In talking about relative speeds it is necessary to be precise about what a particular speed is relative to. Car A's speed relative to car B is 20 mph, but relative to the earth it is 90

mph. Relative to the sun it is about 64 000 mph. Because two American scientists, Michelson and Morley (*see* Michelson–Morley experiment), had shown that light travelled at the same speed whether measured in the direction of the earth's rotation or at right angles to this direction, Einstein suggested that the restriction about relative motion does not apply to light. It always has the same speed of 2.998×10^8 metres per second (186 000 miles per second), irrespective of the motion of the observer. The velocity of light, Einstein said, is absolute.

This has far-reaching effects. In his special theory Einstein suggested that as bodies increase in speed they become shorter and heavier (*see* Lorentz, Hendrick). This effect is only noticeable as the speed of light is approached. Cars on the motorway do get heavier and shorter but the effect is minute. On the other hand, an electron travelling at 99% of the speed of light becomes seven times heavier than its mass at rest. Einstein also showed that no body could actually travel at the speed of light itself. If it did it would be infinitely heavy and have zero length.

The increase in mass and decrease in length that a body undergoes when moving at high speeds led Einstein to the conclusion that mass (m) and energy (E) are two different aspects of the same thing; they are related by the simple equation $E = mc^2$, where c is the velocity of light. The atom bomb and *nuclear energy both depend on this equation.

In the general theory of 1915, Einstein considered accelerated relative motion, especially as it is concerned with gravitation. In this theory, the gravitational force experienced by a body is treated as a property of space and time, which Einstein suggested was "curved" by the presence of the mass. The motion of the stars and planets is controlled by this curvature of space in the vicinity of matter. Light, too, is bent by the gravitational field of a massive body. The observed bending of light rays as they pass close to the sun and the shift of certain lines in the solar *spectrum have provided experimental verification of the theory.

relay, electric An electrical switching device in which one circuit is controlled by a separate circuit, often to avoid the danger of direct contact with high-voltage supplies or to reduce the length of high-current cable needed. Relays may involve mechanical movement and an electromagnetic connection between the two circuits or be controlled entirely by *solid-state electronic components.

relief sculpture A form of sculpture in which figures are attached to a background of stone, bronze, or wood, in contrast to free-standing sculpture seen in the round. There are four main types of relief: high relief, in which the figures project almost as much as free-standing sculptures; middle relief; bas-relief, in which the image is only very slightly raised and of which *Donatello developed a variation in the 15th century; and sunken or coelanaglyphic relief, also called *intaglio, particularly associated with ancient Egyptian sculpture.

reluctance (*or* magnetic resistance) The ratio of the *magnetomotive force in a material to the total *magnetic flux induced by it. It is analogous to electrical *resistance.

remanence. *See* ferromagnetism.

Remarque, Erich Maria (1898-1970) German novelist. After being wounded in World War I, he worked as a journalist until the publication of his immediately successful *All Quiet on the Western Front* (1929), describing life in the trenches. His books banned by the Nazis, he lived in America and Switzerland from 1932.

Rembrandt (Harmenszoon) van Rijn (1606-69) Dutch painter and etcher, born in Leiden, the son of a miller. After studying briefly at Leiden University, he became the pupil of Jacob van Swanenburgh (c. 1571-1638) and later in Amsterdam of Pieter Lastman (1583-1633), who trained him in the Italian *baroque style and had a lasting influence on him, for example in encouraging him to paint historical and religious

REMBRANDT Self-Portrait *(British Museum, London), a pen and brown ink and Indian ink wash.*

subjects. Settling permanently in Amsterdam (1631), he made his name as a portrait painter with *The Anatomy Lesson of Dr Tulp* (1632; The Hague), a group portrait. It was followed by many other portraits, including those of his wife Saskia and culminating in the famous group portrait, *The Nightwatch* (1642; Rijksmuseum, Amsterdam). He also treated dramatic mythological and biblical subjects. Rembrandt was a popular teacher of painting and at the height of his success was an avid collector of art. He eventually had financial difficulties and became bankrupt, spending approximately the last 20 years of his life isolated from society. Many of his greatest works belong to this period, when he was no longer popular. He concentrated on depicting the inner life of his sitters and the biblical characters he painted. He also excelled as a landscapist and his etchings, which are among the finest ever produced, are remarkable for their freedom of handling.

Remembrance Sunday The day on which the British remember the dead of World Wars I and II. From 1919 to 1945 it was named Armistice Day and was observed on 11 November, the date of the signing of the Armistice with Germany in 1918. It was renamed Remembrance Sunday in 1945 and since 1956 has been observed on the second Sunday of November. A two-minute silence marks the time, 11 am, of the signing of the Armistice and wreaths of Flanders poppies are laid at the Cenotaph in Whitehall, London, and at other war memorials.

Remington, Eliphalet (1793-1863) US inventor and gun manufacturer. His innovations included a method of producing really straight gun barrels and the invention of a lathe for cutting gunstocks. In 1873 the business founded by Remington bought the patent rights of Christopher *Sholes' typewriter.

Remonstrants The Dutch adherents of Arminianism (*see* Arminius, Jacobus) who rejected the Calvinist doctrine of *predestination in a statement known as the Remonstrance (1610). Condemned by the Synod of Dort (1618-19), they

suffered persecution until 1630. Their liberal theology influenced many subsequent Protestant thinkers, including *Locke and John *Wesley.

remora A dark slender elongated fish, 30-90 cm long, belonging to a family (*Echeneidae*; 8-10 species) found in warm marine waters. The dorsal fin is modified to form a flat oval sucking disc on its head by which it attaches itself to various marine animals (e.g. sharks and turtles) or ships to feed on scraps of food or the hosts' parasites. Order: *Perciformes*.

Remscheid 51 10N 7 11E A city in NW West Germany, in North Rhine-Westphalia on the River Wupper. An industrial centre, it specializes in tool manufacture. It is the birthplace of Roentgen. Population (1980 est): 129 300.

Remus. *See* Romulus and Remus.

Renaissance (French: rebirth) An intellectual and cultural movement that began in Italy in the 14th century, spread to N Europe, and flourished until the mid-16th century. Fundamental to the Renaissance were the revival of classical learning, art, and architecture and the concept of the dignity of man, which characterized *humanism. Both were advocated by the 14th-century poet and classical scholar *Petrarch. Other great writers of the Italian Renaissance were *Dante, *Boccaccio, *Machiavelli, and *Ariosto. The first painter to mirror these new ideals was *Giotto. He was followed in the 15th century by *Masaccio, *Uccello, *Piero della Francesca, *Mantegna, and others, who helped place art on a scientific basis through their concern with the structure and proportions of the human body. They also introduced into painting the use of linear *perspective, the laws of which were developed by the architect *Brunelleschi. Humanism was reflected in the development of portrait painting and the emphasis upon human feelings in religious painting. The High Renaissance denotes the period between about 1500 and about 1520, when the artists *Leonardo da Vinci, *Raphael, and *Michelangelo were developing the harmony and balance associated with classical art to its highest form.

In sculpture the major figures were Nicola *Pisano, *Donatello, *Ghiberti, *Verrocchio, and Michelangelo. In building Brunelleschi was the first to revive the classical use of the *orders of architecture. Later architects, such as *Bramante, *Alberti, and *Palladio, also revived ancient temples and domed structures. *See also* Italian art.

In the 16th century the Renaissance spread to N Europe, where it manifested itself in the art of *Dürer, the scholarship of *Erasmus, the plays of *Shakespeare, and particularly in the courts of such rulers as Elizabeth I of England, where the ideal of Renaissance civilization was epitomized in the lifestyle of such courtiers as Sir Philip *Sidney.

Renan, (Joseph) Ernest (1823-92) French philosopher and theologian. Renan's famous *Life of Jesus* (1863) undermined the supernatural aspects of Christ's life and the moral nature of his teachings. It was acclaimed by many romantics, including Oscar *Wilde.

Renfrew 55 53N 4 24W A town in W central Scotland, in Strathclyde Region on the River Clyde below Glasgow. Formerly an important port, it has engineering, shipbuilding, and tyre-manufacturing industries. Renfrew has a commercial airport. Population (1984 est): 22 927.

Renfrew (*or* Renfrewshire) A former county of W Scotland. Under local government reorganization in 1975 it was divided into Renfrew District in the E and Inverclyde District in the W, both in Strathclyde Region.

Reni, Guido (1575-1642) Italian painter, born in Bologna. He studied under the Flemish artist Denis Calvaert (c. 1575-1619) but was chiefly influenced by the *Caracci. In Rome (c. 1600-14) he established a studio and painted his masterpiece, the ceiling fresco of *Aurora* (Palazzo Rospigliosi). Later, working mainly in Bologna, his highly idealized style became somewhat sentimental.

renin An enzyme, secreted by the kidneys, that breaks down a liver protein to form the peptide angiotensin I. This is converted to angiotensin II, which constricts blood vessels—causing a rise in blood pressure—and increases the secretion of *aldosterone from the adrenal glands.

Rennes 48 06N 1 40W A city in NW France, in the Ille-et-Vilaine department. The capital of the old province of Brittany, it was badly damaged by fire in 1720 and most of its notable buildings, including the cathedral and university, were built after that date. The main commercial centre of W France, Rennes is an important railway junction and military headquarters and has textile, electrical, and pharmaceutical industries. Population (1982): 200 390.

rennet An extract, prepared from cows' stomachs, that contains the milk-coagulating enzyme rennin. It is used in the manufacture of cheese and junket.

Rennie, John (1761–1821) British civil engineer, who designed several of the 19th-century bridges over the Thames in London, none of which now remain. He also constructed or redeveloped docks throughout Britain, including the London and East India docks, which he built on the River Thames.

Reno 39 32N 119 49W A city and resort in the USA, in W Nevada near the foot of the Sierra Nevada. Founded about 1860, it is known for its easily obtainable divorces and legalized gambling. The University of Nevada (1864) was moved here from Elko in 1886. Population (1980): 100 756.

Renoir, Pierre Auguste (1841–1919) French impressionist painter, born in Limoges. He trained as a decorator of porcelain before entering (1861) the studio of Charles Gleyre (1808–74) and meeting *Monet, with whom he frequently painted on the banks of the Seine. He exhibited at the first three impressionist exhibitions but largely abandoned impressionism after studying Renaissance art in Italy (1881–82). Increasingly crippled by arthritis, he spent his last years in the south of France, painting many sensuous nudes. His best-known works include *Les Parapluies* (National Gallery, London) and *Le Moulin de la Galette* (Louvre). His son **Jean Renoir** (1894–1979) was a film director whose films, *La Grande Illusion* (1937) and *La Règle du jeu* (1939), are personal and subtle reflections of prewar French society. During World War II he went to Hollywood but returned to Europe to make *The Golden Coach* (1953), *French Can-can* (1955), *Élena et les hommes* (1956), and other films.

rent. *See* landlord and tenant.

Representatives, House of. *See* Congress.

repression In *psychoanalysis, the process of excluding unacceptable ideas from consciousness. Repressed wishes and thoughts continue to exist in the *unconscious mind and may give rise to symptoms. One of the goals of psychoanalytic treatment is to bring repressed material back into conscious awareness so that it can be coped with rationally. *See also* defence mechanism.

reproduction In biology, the generation of new individuals of the same species. In **asexual reproduction** individuals are derived from one parent and no special reproductive structures are involved. The simplest form is *fission, occurring mostly in unicellular organisms. Simple multicellular organisms, such as sponges and coelenterates, reproduce by budding: a new individual arises as an outgrowth (bud) from the parent. In fragmentation, the individual breaks into two or more parts, each capable of growth to form a new individual: this is seen in flatworms and some algae. Most animals and plants, however, reproduce by a process involving specialized reproductive cells (*see* gamete)—typically male and female—that fuse to produce a new individual with a different genetic makeup. This process, **sexual reproduction**, occurs in its simplest form in *conjugation. In more complex organisms the gametes are produced in special organs, e.g. the *carpel and *stamen in flowering plants and the *ovary and *testis in animals. The importance of sexual reproduction in nature is that it allows genetic variation in a population, which is therefore better able to adapt to the changing environment.

reptile A vertebrate animal belonging to the class *Reptilia* (about 6000 species), which includes *crocodiles, *turtles, *lizards, *snakes, and the *tuatara. Reptiles occur in terrestrial, freshwater, and marine habitats, chiefly in tropical regions. They have a covering of horny scales and are cold-blooded. Fertilization of the egg by sperm takes place within the female, unlike fish and most amphibians. The egg is large and yolky, has special membranes that nourish the embryo, and a protective leathery or calcareous shell, i.e. features that enable it to be laid on land. In some lizards and snakes the eggs are retained inside the female and live young are born. Young reptiles—unlike amphibians—do not undergo metamorphosis.

The primitive reptiles evolved from amphibians: their fossils are found in deposits of the Upper Carboniferous period, about 300 million years ago. During the following 240 million years, a variety of forms evolved, including the fishlike *ichthyosaurs, the flying *pterosaurs, and the mammal-like *therapsids, culminating in the giant *dinosaurs, which dominated the earth during the Cretaceous period (136–65 million years ago).

Repton, Humphry (1725–1818) British landscape gardener, a term he invented. A country gentleman until financial circumstances forced him to make a living from his hobby, he laid out some 200 parks and gardens. His gardens were much more formal than those of his predecessor, Capability *Brown.

Republican Party One of the two major political parties of the USA (*compare* Democratic Party). The name was used by Jefferson's Republican Democrats (formed in 1792), but the modern Republican Party originated in 1854 as an alliance of those opposed to the extension of slavery in the new territories in the W USA. After the election of the first Republican president, Lincoln, in 1860, the Republicans were usually the ascendant party until the 1930s, becoming identified with conservative business interests. Other Republican presidents include T. *Roosevelt, *Eisenhower, *Nixon, and *Reagan.

requiem shark A *shark of the family *Carcharhinidae* (over 60 species), found worldwide mainly in warm and temperate oceans. 1.5–5.5 m long, they have two dorsal fins and are carnivorous, feeding on fish and various invertebrates. Some species are dangerous to man, for example the *tiger shark.

resale price maintenance (rpm) A *restrictive trade practice operated by a manufacturer, who prohibits retailers from selling a product below a certain price. The drawbacks of the system are that it prevents price competition between retailers and keeps inefficient retailers in business. In the UK, the Resale Prices Act (1964) forbids rpm unless it can be proved to be in the public interest.

reservoirs Natural or artificial lakes in which water is trapped and stored for irrigation, to supply water for municipal needs, for hydroelectric power, or to control water flow. When artificially constructed they are made by placing dams across suitable land formations to create a lake. They may often combine several of the purposes above and are invaluable in areas in which rainfall is low or unpredictable. The water flowing into a reservoir must not contain too much sediment or the capacity of the reservoir will diminish.

Resht. *See* Rasht.

resins Adhesive nonflammable organic polymers, usually insoluble in water but soluble in organic solvents, such as alcohol. **Natural resins**, such as *rosin, *sandarac, and *shellac, are exuded by plants and insects. **Synthetic resins** are made by modifying natural polymers or by polymerization of petrochemicals. Thermosetting resins, those that harden on heating, include *epoxy, *urea-formaldehyde, and some *polyurethane resins. Thermoplastic resins, those

REPTILE

green turtle

terrapin

Komodo dragon

snapping turtle

flying lizard

common chameleon

tuatara

tokay

common iguana

African snake skink

reticulated python

adder

Indian cobra

Nile crocodile

American alligator

Indian gavial

REPTILE *Some representative reptiles.*

that soften on heating, include *polythene, *polyvinyl chloride, *polypropylene, and cellulose acetates.

resistance The property of all materials, except superconductors (*see* superconductivity), that reduces the flow of electricity through them. It is defined by *Ohm's law as the ratio of the potential difference between the ends of a conductor to the current flowing through it. The resistance of a conductor depends on its dimensions, the material of which it is made, its temperature, and in some cases the extent to which it is illuminated. The unit of resistance is the *ohm. The reciprocal of the resistance in a direct current circuit is the conductance. Conductance is measured in *siemens (*see also* impedance).

Resnais, Alain (1922–) French film director. His films are characterized by experimental narrative techniques. The scripts for *Hiroshima mon amour* (1959), *Last Year at Marienbad* (1961), and *Providence* (1977) were written by Marguerite Duras (1914–), Alain *Robbe-Grillet, and David *Mercer respectively. His other films include *Mon oncle d'Amerique* (1980), *La Vie est un roman* (1983), and *Melo* (1987).

resolving power **1.** The ability of a *microscope to produce separate images of two neighbouring points; the closer the points, the greater the resolving power of the microscope. The resolving power may be increased by using shorter wavelength radiation (e.g. ultraviolet radiation) or by using very short wavelength electrons (as in the *electron microscope). Alternatively the refractive index of the medium between the specimen and the objective lens may be increased, as in the *oil-immersion lens. **2.** A measure of the ability of a *telescope to distinguish detail, usually the smallest angle between two point objects that produces distinct images.

resonance (chemistry) The existence of a compound with a molecular structure intermediate between two or more conventional structures. For example, the polar molecule HCl, in which the hydrogen atom has some positive charge and the chlorine some negative charge, can be regarded as intermediate between two structures. One is the covalent molecule $H–Cl$ and the other the ionic compound H^+Cl^-. The molecule is a **resonance hybrid** with contributions from the two forms, written $H–Cl \leftrightarrow H^+Cl^-$.

resonance (physics) The sympathetic oscillation of a system in response to an external excitation. A wire under tension, for example, will not respond to an external vibration unless the vibration is at the natural frequency of oscillation of the wire, which depends on its length, tension, etc. It will then resonate at its natural frequency. Resonance also occurs in electrical, magnetic, and electromagnetic phenomena in which matter or energy is being changed periodically. A **resonant circuit** consists of a capacitance in parallel with an inductance. When the capacitor discharges through the inductor an induced emf is produced, which again charges the capacitor (in the opposite sense). The circuit will then continue to oscillate, provided that energy is supplied from an outside source, at a frequency determined by the values of the capacitor (which is usually a variable device) and the inductor. Such circuits, feeding an aerial, are used in *radio transmitters to generate radio-frequency oscillations and in receivers to detect incoming signals.

resonances Elementary particles with extremely short lifetimes (about 10^{-23} seconds). They are formed when colliding particles react by the *strong interaction. Resonances are either *mesons or *baryons (*see* particle physics).

Respighi, Ottorino (1879–1936) Italian composer. He became director of the Santa Cecilia in Rome (1923–25). He wrote several operas, the symphonic poems *The Fountains of Rome* (1917) and *The Pines of Rome* (1924), the orchestral suite *The Birds* (1927), and ballets, including *La Boutique fantasque* (1919), based on themes by Rossini.

respiration The process by which an organism takes up oxygen from its environment and discharges carbon dioxide into it. In man and most air-breathing animals the organs through which this takes place are the *lungs (aquatic animals use *gills; insects use *tracheae). Air is transported to and from the lungs by **breathing**, which involves movements of the muscular diaphragm and the rib cage. Oxygen-depleted blood is pumped from the *heart to the air sacs (alveoli) of the lungs, where it receives oxygen (from inhaled air) and releases carbon dioxide (which is exhaled). Oxygen in the blood is carried to the tissues and cells, where it oxidizes foodstuffs to produce energy, used for physiological processes, and carbon dioxide, which is transported in the blood to the lungs. This is called tissue, or cellular, respiration.

respirator A machine used to maintain breathing in patients whose respiratory muscles are paralysed or not functioning for any other reason. The cabinet respirator (iron lung) encloses the patient in a sealed container from the neck down; by lowering the pressure in the cabinet the chest expands and draws air into the lungs. A positive-pressure respirator pumps air at regular intervals into the lungs through a tube placed in the windpipe; the air is exhaled naturally or removed by suction through the respirator.

Restoration (1660) The re-establishment of the monarchy in England following the fall of the *Protectorate. The Restoration of Charles II, whose father Charles I had been executed (1649) during the Civil War, was engineered by General *Monck. In April, 1660, the Convention Parliament accepted Charles' Declaration of Breda, in which he promised religious toleration and an amnesty to all but 57 of those who had fought the Crown in the Civil War; it also arranged for the restoration of confiscated royalist lands and an income for Charles. The subsequent Cavalier Parliament (1661–79) enacted a religious settlement in the form of the anti-Nonconformist *Clarendon Code.

Restoration literature English literature written during the reigns of Charles II (1660–85) and James II (1685–88), following the Restoration of the monarchy in 1660 and the relaxation of restraints on literature imposed during the Puritan Interregnum. The period was especially distinguished by its drama, notably the witty comedies of manners of *Wycherley, *Etheridge, and *Congreve. In poetry, the period was characterized by the satires of *Dryden and the licentious verse of John Wilmot, Earl of *Rochester.

restrictive trade practices Agreements between traders over price, conditions of supply, etc., that limit competition in an industry. In the UK, under the Fair Trading Act (1973), which replaced earlier legislation, restrictive practices are held to be against the public interest unless proved otherwise in the Restrictive Practices Court.

resurrection plant. *See* rose of Jericho.

retina The light-sensitive layer that forms the inner surface of the eye. Light is focused by the lens onto the retina, which contains numerous interconnecting light-sensitive cells that send signals to the visual centre of the brain via the optic nerve. These cells are of two kinds: the rods, which are sensitive to light and dark and are responsible for vision in dim light; and the cones, which are sensitive to colour and visual detail. The greatest concentration of cones occurs at a small area at the back of the eye (the fovea), which is therefore the area of greatest visual acuity. *See also* detached retina.

retriever One of several breeds of large strongly built sporting dogs characterized by a "soft" mouth and good swimming ability. All are descended from the *Labrador retriever crossed with other breeds. The flat-coated retriever has a fine dense black or liver-coloured coat while the curly-coated retriever has a coat of small tight curls, indicating possible poodle ancestry. The Chesapeake Bay retriever has a short thick coat and has been developed in the USA from British stock. Height: 56–68 cm. *See also* golden retriever.

Retz, Jean François Paul de Gondi, Cardinal de (1613–79) French churchman, one of the leaders of the rebellion called the *Fronde (1648–53), which he used to further his own political ambitions at the expense of Cardinal *Mazarin. He was made a cardinal in 1652 but arrested soon after. Exiled until 1662 he returned to France to become Abbot of Saint-Denis until his death. He is best known for his *Mémoires*, which recall his role in the Fronde.

Reuben, tribe of One of the 12 *tribes of Israel. It claimed descent from Reuben, the eldest son of Jacob and Leah. The territory E of the Dead Sea was allocated to Reuben's people.

Réunion A volcanic island and French overseas department in the W Indian Ocean, in the Mascarene Islands. It was settled in about 1642 by the French with their African and Indian slaves; increasing population has caused much emigration. Sugar, rum, and molasses are exported. Area: 2512 sq km (970 sq mi). Population (1984 est): 545 814. Capital: Saint-Denis.

Reuter, Paul Julius, Baron von (Israel Josephat; 1816–99) British founder of the first news agency. Born in Germany, he adopted the name of Reuter in 1844. He went to London in 1851 and opened a telegraph office from which he supplied newspapers with international news. He was made a German baron in 1871.

Reval. *See* Tallinn.

Revelation, Book of A prophetic book, the last in the New Testament, written perhaps about 90–95 AD by "John the Divine,"who is often identified with the apostle John. It consists of seven highly symbolic visions that trace the fortunes of the Christian Church from its inception to the end of the world. The only example of apocalyptic literature in the New Testament, the book may have been written in reaction to the persecutions of the emperor Domitian.

reverberatory furnace A furnace designed for operations in which it is not desirable to mix the material being heated with the fuel. The flame is directed at the roof of the furnace and the heat radiated downwards. This type of furnace is used in the smelting of copper and nickel ores.

PAUL REVERE *Warning of the coming of the British in arms at the start of the American Revolution.*

Revere, Paul (1735–1818) American silversmith and revolutionary. Prominent in the colonial opposition to Britain, he became famous as the man who, on 18 April, 1775, rode out to warn the people of Massachusetts that the British troops were on the march. On the following morning the first shots of the American Revolution were fired on the British at Lexington. Revere's ride is celebrated in a poem by Longfellow.

Revolt of the Netherlands The rebellion against Spanish rule in the Netherlands, inspired by political and economic grievances and resentment at the suppression of Protestantism. Revolt broke out in 1568 but only took fire in 1572, when the Dutch cause prospered in the strongly Protestant

northern provinces under the leadership of *William the Silent. In 1576 the N was joined by the predominantly Roman Catholic provinces in the S but the union ended with the Spanish victory at Gembloux in 1578, when the S submitted once more to Spain. In the following year the seven northern provinces, by the Union of Utrecht, declared their independence from Spain. War continued, however, until the 12-year truce negotiated in 1609 by William's son and successor *Maurice of Nassau and was renewed in the Thirty Years' War (1618–48). By the Peace of Westphalia (1648) the independence of the United Provinces of the Netherlands was at last acknowledged.

Revolutionary and Napoleonic Wars (1792–1815) A series of European wars precipitated by the *French Revolution and *Napoleon's ambitions for the conquest of Europe. Revolutionary fervour within France and the hostile reaction of Austria and Prussia to the arrest of Louis XVI led to the outbreak of war. Initial French success prompted Britain, the Netherlands, and Spain to close ranks with Austria and Prussia in the first coalition (1793). Hard pressed, France was transformed into a nation at arms (*see* conscription) and its armies achieved a series of victories. In 1795 Prussia, the Netherlands, and Spain sued for peace and, following Napoleon's first Italian campaign (1796–97), Austria followed suit. French supremacy was thwarted only by British naval strength and Nelson's great victory of the *Nile (1798) brought Britain control of the Mediterranean. In 1798–99 the second coalition of Britain, the Ottoman Empire, Naples, Portugal, and Austria was formed but collapsed (1801) in the face of Napoleon's victories, especially at *Hohenlinden (1800), and the Revolutionary Wars ended with the uneasy Treaty of Amiens (1802) between Britain and France.

Napoleon's aggression, including his imposition of the *Continental System against Britain, led to the resumption of naval war between Britain and France. In 1805 Pitt the Younger negotiated a third coalition against Napoleon, by now emperor, and Nelson (although mortally wounded) won the naval victory at *Trafalgar. Napoleon now turned on the continental members of the coalition, defeating Austria and Russia at *Ulm and Austerlitz (1805), Prussia at *Jena and Auerstadt (1806), and Russia again at *Friedland (1807). With the failure of the Continental System and Wellington's victories in the *Peninsular War, Napoleon's dominance diminished. Following his disastrous Russian campaign (1812) the allies were able to defeat him at *Leipzig (1813) and then, following his return from exile, at *Waterloo (1815). The post-Napoleonic settlement of Europe was decided at the Congress of *Vienna.

Revolution of 1905 An insurrection in Russia, an expression of the widespread discontent that culminated in the *Russian Revolution of 1917. It began on 22 January, 1905 (Bloody Sunday), when a group of striking workers marched peacefully on the Winter Palace in St Petersburg and were fired on by troops. The massacre precipitated nationwide strikes, uprisings, and mutinies (including the mutiny on the battleship *Potemkin*). By October Russia was gripped by a general strike, which with the establishment of the St Petersburg Soviet (workers' council), dominated by the *Mensheviks, including Trotsky, forced Emperor Nicholas II to promise constitutional government (*see* Duma). The Revolution was substantially crushed by the end of December.

Revolutions of 1848 A series of revolutions in continental Europe caused by economic distress and liberal agitation against the conservatism that characterized the post-Napoleonic era. The first revolution broke out in France, where the insurgents overthrew the July Monarchy of Louis Philippe, but a split in their ranks between moderates and socialists led to the suppression of the Left and the election of Louis Napoleon (later *Napoleon III) as president. In the Italian states the revolution had constitutional aims, in which it had some success in Piedmont, but also formed part of the movement against the Austrian presence in Italy (*see* Risorgimento). In the Austrian Empire revolts in Vienna secured the resignation of Metternich and the summoning of a constituent assembly. The revolution spread with short-lived success to Prague and Budapest before being suppressed by Schwarzenberg. In the German states the revolution began in Prussia, where Frederick William IV was forced to convene a constituent assembly. By December, however, the revolutions there and in other German states had been suppressed and in 1849 the Frankfurt Parliament, which had hoped to achieve a united Germany, was dissolved. The revolutions were all quelled but not without some concessions to liberal and nationalist movements, and 1848 is thus generally regarded as ending the post-1815 period of reaction that had been dominated by Metternich.

revolver A short-range *small arm having a revolving cylinder containing the rounds behind the barrel. In single-action types, pressing the trigger cocks the weapon and simultaneously rotates the cylinder; further pressure fires it. Double-action types perform these functions automatically but their stiffer mechanism impairs accuracy. Calibres range from .21 inches to .455 inches. The first successful revolver was the *Colt, designed in 1835. *See also* pistol.

revue A theatrical entertainment consisting of a succession of songs, dances, and sketches of a topical and often satirical nature. Originating in France, revues attained great popularity in Britain and the USA during the early 20th century with such spectacular productions as the *Ziegfeld Follies* (1907). As competition from cinema and television increased, revues became more intimate in form, an early example being the British *Sweet and Low* (1943). The success of *Beyond the Fringe* (1961) led to a succession of sophisticated satirical revues during the 1960s.

rex A breed of cat having a curly coat of very short fine hairs. Two breed types are recognized—the Cornish rex and the Devon rex, named after the counties in which they originated. They have long slender bodies and may be of any colour.

Reykjavík 64 10N 21 53W The capital of Iceland, an important fishing port, on Faxa Fjord in the SW. Founded by the Vikings in 874 AD, it became the seat of parliament (the Althing) in 1843 and capital of Iceland in 1918. Its university was founded in 1911. Most of the city's heating comes from natural hot springs. Population (1980 est): 83 766.

Reynaud, Paul (1878-1966) French politician, who was briefly prime minister before the German occupation of France in 1940. He was a forceful opponent of Nazism in the late 1930s and after the collapse of France was arrested by the Germans and held until 1945. After the war he again held ministerial posts and helped draft the constitution of the Fifth Republic (1959).

Reynolds, Sir Joshua (1723-92) British portrait painter, born in Plympton (Devon), where his father was headmaster of a school. He studied in London (1740-43) under the portraitist Thomas Hudson (1701-79). In 1749 he travelled to Italy, staying for two years in Rome before returning to London. Using the techniques of the Old Masters in such paintings as *Sarah Siddons as the Tragic Muse* (San Marino, California), Reynolds aimed to give portraits the prestige of history paintings. In 1768 he became the first president of the *Royal Academy, where he delivered the *Discourses*, which contain his artistic theories. His friends included Dr *Johnson and *Garrick, both of whom he painted.

Reynolds number (*Re*) In fluid dynamics, a dimensionless quantity associated with the flow of a fluid. $Re = \rho v l/\eta$, where ρ and η are the *density and *viscosity of the fluid moving with velocity v through a system characterized by a length l. If the Reynolds number of the fluid is less than

about 1500, the flow is streamlined; above this number it becomes turbulent. Named after Osborne Reynolds (1842-1912).

Reza Shah Pahlavi (1878-1944) Shah of Iran (1925-41). After leading an army coup in 1921, he deposed Ahmad Shah Qajar (1898-1930) in 1925. As shah himself, Reza aimed at the modernization of Iran, following the example of *Atatürk in Turkey. In 1941 Britain and the Soviet Union, fearing German influence in Iran, invaded the country and forced Reza Shah to abdicate in favour of his son *Mohammed Reza Pahlavi. He died in exile in Johannesburg.

rhea A large flightless bird belonging to a family (*Rheidae*; 3 species) occurring in South America. 120 cm tall, rheas have a brownish plumage and long legs with three toes. They live in flocks, feeding on leaves, roots, seeds, insects, and small vertebrates. The male builds the nest and incubates the eggs. Order: *Rheiformes*.

Rhea In Greek religion, a Titan, daughter of Uranus and Gaea. Her consort *Cronus swallowed her children, fearing that they would overthrow him. Rhea substituted a stone for one child, *Zeus, who eventually overthrew Cronus and forced him to disgorge the other children.

Rhee, Syngman (1875-1965) Korean statesman; president of South Korea (1948-60). He became leader of South Korea in 1945 during the US occupation and as its first president claimed his government's right to rule over all Korea. Popular unrest forced him to relinquish his post in 1960 and he went into exile.

Rheims. *See* Reims.

rhenium (Re) A dense (relative density 21.02) silvery-white transition metal with a very high melting point. The metal is very ductile and is used to alloy with tungsten. Alloys with molybdenum are superconducting. The metal is obtained as a by-product of molybdenum refining. At no 75; at wt 186.2; mp 3180°C; bp 5620°C.

rhesus factor (Rh factor) A blood protein present on the red cells in 83% of the population: the presence or absence of the Rh factor is the basis of the Rh *blood group system, people with the factor being described as Rh positive and those without as Rh negative. If a Rh-negative woman has a Rh-positive baby she may produce anti-Rh antibodies that will react against subsequent Rh-positive pregnancies. The affected baby's blood cells may be destroyed by these antibodies, leading to the severe anaemia of haemolytic disease of the newborn. The incidence of this disease has been reduced by taking steps to prevent the formation of maternal anti-Rh antibodies soon after delivery of the first baby.

rhesus monkey A *macaque monkey, *Macaca mulatta*, of S Asia, widely used in medical research. In the wild, rhesus monkeys live in large colonies in forests or on hillsides, sometimes stealing fruit from orchards.

Rheticus (Georg Joachim von Lauchen; 1514-76) German mathematician, who was the first follower of *Copernicus. Rheticus wrote (1540) a summary of Copernicus' ideas and then persuaded him to publish the original book, *De Revolutionibus*, in which they were originally expressed. Rheticus was the first mathematician to regard the trigonometric functions in terms of angles rather than arcs of a circle.

rhetoric The art of using language for communicating information and for intellectual and emotional persuasion. Mastery of rhetoric by orators was considered essential training in ancient Greece and Rome. Influential textbooks were written by *Aristotle, *Quintilian, and *Cicero, and all classical literary criticism was based on rhetorical principles. Aristotle distinguished three modes of persuasion—logical, emotional, and ethical—and codified the rules for rhetorical composition under categories of invention, arrangement, and style. Together with logic and grammar, rhetoric formed the trivium, an essential part of the curriculum in medieval education, and its principles were adapted to medieval forms, such as sermons and legal documents. In the 20th century, the study of rhetoric forms part of the theoretical analysis of techniques of persuasion.

rheumatic fever A disease of children that occurs (rarely) after infection with a streptococcus bacterium. The symptoms develop 10-14 days after the original infection (which is usually of the throat) and include fever, aching joints, chorea (involuntary movements), and inflammation of the heart, which—in a few cases—may lead to chronic heart disease. Treatment is with bed rest, penicillin, aspirin, and sometimes steroids.

rheumatism Any condition involving pain in the joints. This may be caused by a simple strain or by rheumatoid *arthritis, *osteoarthritis, *gout, or *rheumatic fever.

Rheydt 51 10N 6 27E A city in NW West Germany, in North Rhine-Westphalia. Its Renaissance palace (1568-81) escaped the bombing of World War II. An industrial centre, its main manufacture is textiles. Population (1971 est): 101 500.

Rhine, Joseph Banks (1895-1980) US psychologist, noted for his experiments in parapsychology, especially extrasensory perception (ESP). Using packs of specially designed cards in scientifically objective tests, Rhine produced statistical evidence to support the occurrence of ESP.

Rhine, River (German name: Rhein; Dutch name; Rijn) A river in central and W Europe. Rising in SE Switzerland, it flows N into Lake Constance, continuing W along the Swiss-German border to Basle. It then flows generally N along the Franco-German border and into West Germany, turning NW past Bonn, Cologne, Düsseldorf, and Duisburg. It enters the Netherlands below Emmerich and splits into two major distributaries, the Lek and the Waal. The Lek continues W through Rotterdam and enters the North Sea at the Hook of Holland. The Waal joins the River Meuse and enters the North Sea by the Hollandsch Diep. The main tributaries are the Rivers Ruhr, Main, Moselle, and Neckar. It is W Europe's main navigable waterway and passes through one of the most highly industrialized regions on the continent. Length: 1320 km (820 mi).

Rhine-Herne Canal A waterway in West Germany, in the *Ruhr. Completed in 1914, it forms part of the *Mitelland Canal and extends from Duisburg to Herne. Length: 39 km (24 mi).

Rhineland Palatinate (German name: Rheinland-Pfalz) A *Land* in W West Germany, bordering on France, Luxembourg, and Belgium. It includes the historic cities of Mainz, Speyer, Trier, and Worms. Over 75% of Germany's wine is produced in the river valleys of the Rhine, Moselle, and Nahe. Potatoes and grain are grown and livestock is important in the mountainous SW. Industries include chemicals, engineering, and shoe manufacture. Area: 19 838 sq km (7658 sq mi). Population (1980 est): 3 638 700. Capital: Mainz. *See also* Palatinate.

rhinoceros A large hoofed mammal belonging to the family *Rhinocerotidae* (5 species), of Asia and Africa. Rhinos have a massive virtually naked dark-skinned body with short thick legs, a short neck, and a large head. The Indian rhinoceros (*Rhinoceros unicornis*) has a single horn composed of solid fibrous *keratin; all other rhinos have two horns. Rhinos range in size from the large *white rhinoceros to the Sumatran rhinoceros (*Didermocerus sumatrensis*), which is up to 150 cm high at the shoulder and weighs 500-1000 kg. Rhinos are generally solitary, grazing or browsing on grass and leaves, and are fond of wallowing in muddy pools. All are now endangered species.

rhinoceros beetle A horned □scarab beetle, up to 150 mm long (including the horn), so called because of the resemblance of its horn to that of a rhinoceros. The larvae of most rhinoceros beetles live in rotting wood, although some eat roots or burrow into the stems of palm trees. *Oryctes*

rhinoceros is sometimes a serious pest in oriental coconut groves through its destruction of the leaf bases. *See also* Hercules beetle.

rhizome An underground plant stem producing aerial leaves and shoots. It may extend some distance below ground and can be fleshy (as in the iris) or wiry (as in couch grass). Rhizomes can function both as organs of vegetative reproduction and as overwintering structures. They usually grow horizontally; vertical rhizomes (e.g. of strawberry) are commonly called rootstocks.

Rhode Island The smallest state in the USA, indented by Narragansett Bay. One of the New England states, it is the second most densely populated US state. It is highly industrialized, the once important cotton industry having been replaced by modern technological industries, such as electronics and the manufacture of machine tools. It also has important naval installations. Agriculture is limited by the rocky terrain; it is famous for its poultry. *History*: one of the original 13 colonies, it was first settled in 1636 and was the first colony to declare its independence from Britain. Area: 3144 sq km (1214 sq mi). Population (1980): 947 154. Capital: Providence.

Rhode Island Red A breed of domestic fowl developed from blackish-red Asiatic breeds kept on Rhode Island farms in the 19th century. It has a deep broad long body with a nearly horizontal back and a slightly curved beak. The plumage is red. It lays brown eggs and is used for both egg and meat production. Weight: 3.8 kg (cocks); 3.0 kg (hens).

Rhodes (Modern Greek name: Ródhos) A Greek island in the SE Aegean Sea, the largest of the Dodecanese group. It has a mountainous interior with fertile coastal strips, producing cereals, fruit, and wine. Tourism is an important source of revenue. *History*: colonized by Dorians before 1000 BC, Rhodes entered its period of greatest prosperity in the 3rd century BC. It suffered several earthquakes, one of which destroyed the *Colossus of Rhodes in 244 BC. It was occupied by the Knights *Hospitallers from 1282 until 1528, when it became part of the Ottoman Empire. Conquered by Italy in 1912, it was ceded to Greece in 1947. Area: 1400 sq km (540 sq mi). Population (1981): 40 392. Capital: Rhodes.

CECIL RHODES *At the spot, called World's View, in the Matopo Hills where he was later buried.*

Rhodes, Cecil (John) (1853-1902) South African financier and statesman. Born in Britain, he went to Natal in 1870 and then to the Orange Free State to work in the Kimberley diamond mines. In 1881 he entered the Cape Colony parliament, helping to obtain Bechuanaland (now Botswana) in 1884. In 1888 his company, De Beers Consolidated Mines, bought up the Kimberley mines and in 1889 he gained a charter for the British South Africa Company to develop the territory that in 1895 was named Rhodesia in his honour. He became prime minister of Cape Colony in 1890 but was forced to resign in 1896 over his involvement in *Jameson's abortive raid into the Transvaal. Rhodes endowed 170 Rhodes scholarships at Oxford University for students from the British Empire, the USA, and Germany.

Rhodes, Wilfred (1877-1973) British cricketer, who played for England and Yorkshire. A great all-rounder, he took a record 4187 wickets and both scored 1000 runs and took 100 wickets in a record 16 seasons.

Rhodesia. *See* Zimbabwe.

Rhodesia and Nyasaland, Federation of (*or* Central African Federation) A former (1953-63) federation of the British colony of Southern Rhodesia (now Zimbabwe) and the British protectorates of Northern Rhodesia (now Zambia) and Nyasaland (now Malawi). It was opposed by Nyasaland nationalists on the grounds that it existed to further the economic interests of Southern Rhodesia, where most of the Whites lived. Violent unrest in 1959 led to its dissolution. Zambia and Malawi became independent in 1964; Zimbabwe gained independence in 1980.

Rhodesian ridgeback A breed of hunting □dog originating in South Africa, characterized by a ridge of forward-growing hair along the back. The ridgeback is strongly built with a prominent muzzle and its short glossy coat is yellowish brown to reddish fawn. Height: 63-68 cm (dogs); 61-66 cm (bitches).

rhodium (Rh) A metal of the platinum group, discovered in 1803 by W. H. Wollaston (1766-1828). It is alloyed with platinum and palladium to form thermocouples and crucibles and is used in equipment for the production of glass fibres. It is a very hard highly reflective metal and is used to plate jewellery and optical instruments. At no 45; at wt 102.905; mp 1966 ± 3°C; bp 3727 ± 100°C.

Rhododendron A genus of small trees and shrubs (about 250 species), mainly of N temperate regions. They have leathery often evergreen leaves, large scaly winter buds, and terminal clusters of colourful fragrant bell- or funnel-shaped flowers. They occur in a variety of habitats and many, including *azaleas, are widely cultivated as ornamentals. Family: *Ericaceae*.

Rhondda 51 40N 3 30W A district in South Wales, in Mid Glamorgan along the Rhondda Fawr and Rhondda Fach Valleys. The importance of coalmining has diminished in recent years and new light industries, including clothing, electrical accessories, and engineering, have been introduced to the area. Population (1981): 81 725.

Rhône, River A major river in W Europe. Rising in the Rhône Glacier in Switzerland, it flows through Lake Geneva to enter France, flowing generally SW between the Jura and the Alps. It merges with the River Saône at Lyon and flows S to enter the Gulf of Lions via la *Camargue. The Rhône-Saône Valley has historically been an important route and since 1976 the River Rhône has been canalized from Lyon to the Mediterranean Sea. This has provided improved navigation, hydroelectric power, and irrigation for agriculture and has encouraged industrial development along its length. Length 812 km (505 mi).

rhubarb . A perennial plant, *Rheum rhaponticum*, possibly of Asian origin, widely cultivated for its juicy red or green leafstalks, up to 1 m high, which are cooked in sugar. Later in the season, a central flower stalk may be produced bearing small greenish-white flowers. The leaves are poisonous. Family: *Polygonaceae*.

Rhum. *See* Rum.

rhyme Similarity in sound between two or more words, a device used in poetry to reinforce the metrical pattern of a poem. Usually the rhyme is between words occurring at the ends of lines, but internal rhymes, where the rhyme is between a word within a line and a word at the end of or within another line, are also used. The rhyme scheme of a poem is shown by assigning a single letter to each rhyme; thus the scheme of lines rhyming *house/cat/mouse/rat* would be noted *abab*. Masculine rhyme refers to words having the same vowel sounds in their final syllables (*night/delight*). Feminine rhyme refers to words having similar sounds in the last accented syllable and following syllables (*joviality/morality*). *See also* blank verse.

rhyolite A fine-grained or glassy acid igneous rock, mineralogically the volcanic equivalent of granite. It consists of alkali feldspars and quartz, with some ferromagnesian minerals; many rhyolites are porphyritic and display banding resulting from the flowing lava.

Rhys, Jean (1894-1979) British novelist. Born in Dominica, she wrote five books, including the novels *Voyage in the Dark* (1934) and *Good Morning, Midnight* (1939), about bohemian life in Paris and London. After living in seclusion in the West Country for many years, she published a novel, *Wide Sargasso Sea* (1966), and two further collections of stories.

rhythm and blues A form of popular music of the 1940s and 1950s, resulting from the fusion of blues and jazz by Black musicians. Rhythm and blues (often abbreviated to R and B) employed amplified instruments to produce powerful rhythms. One of the earliest rhythm and blues artists was Ray Brown (1926-81), who recorded "Good Rockin' Tonight" (1948). Other rhythm and blues musicians include Little Richard (1935-) and Lloyd Price (1932-). Rock musicians, such as John Mayall (1933-), have been influenced by rhythm and blues.

rhythm method. *See* contraception.

rib A curved bone, 12 pairs of which make up the rib cage, enclosing and protecting the heart and lungs. Each rib forms a joint with the vertebrae of the *spine, permitting movement of the rib cage during breathing. The other ends of the upper seven ribs (the so-called true ribs) are fixed directly to the breastbone by means of a cartilage. Each of the next three pairs (the "false" ribs) is connected by the cartilage to the rib above it, and the two lowest ribs (the floating ribs) end in the muscles of the body wall. *See* Plate IV.

Ribbentrop, Joachim von (1893-1946) German Nazi politician and diplomat. He joined the Nazi Party in 1932 and became Hitler's foreign-affairs adviser. From 1936 to 1938 he was ambassador to the UK and then became foreign minister. He secured the Nonaggression Pact with the Soviet Union in 1939 but thereafter his influence declined. He was arrested in 1945, found guilty of war crimes, and hanged.

ribbonfish An offshore marine fish, of the family *Trachipteridae*, that has a long ribbon-like body. Species include the *oarfish. Order: *Lampridiformes*.

ribbonworm A long flat wormlike animal, also called proboscis worm, belonging to the invertebrate phylum *Nemertina* (about 600 species). Ranging in length from 1 mm to 30 m, ribbonworms may be black, brown, or white but many are brightly patterned. Most live at the bottom of shallow seas, using a long sticky harpoon-like proboscis to capture annelid worms, molluscs, and crustaceans.

Ribeirão Prêto 21 09S 47 48W A city in S Brazil, in São Paulo state. It is the centre of a coffee- and sugar-growing area. Population (1980 est): 300 704.

Ribera, José de (*or* Jusepe R.; 1591-1652) Spanish-born painter and etcher. He settled in Naples (1616), where he was known as Lo Spagnoletto (Little Spaniard). Influenced by the realism and dramatic lighting of *Caravaggio, he painted chiefly religious subjects and some everyday life scenes and portraits, the best examples of which are *The Martyrdom of St Bartholomew* (Prado) and *Clubfooted Boy* (Louvre). After 1630 he painted in richer colours and chose less gruesome subjects, probably as a result of his study of Venetian art and *Velázquez.

riboflavin. *See* vitamin B complex.

ribonucleic acid. *See* RNA.

ribose A simple sugar ($C_5H_{10}O_5$). Ribose and its derivative deoxyribose are important constituents of *RNA and *DNA respectively.

ribosome A granular particle present in enormous numbers in the cytoplasm of nearly all *cells, either free or bound to the surface of membranes within the cell. Ribosomes are composed of *RNA and protein and are the site of protein synthesis. During synthesis they often link together in a chain (polyribosome or polysome).

Ricardo, David (1772-1823) British political economist. Ricardo was the first economist to argue systematically from *a priori* assumptions. His main work, *Principles of Political Economy and Taxation* (1817), argued that exchange value is determined by the labour expended in production and put forward the theory of "comparative costs" as the determining factor in international exchange. As an MP (1819-23), he contributed greatly to the free-trade movement and to the eventual repeal of the *Corn Laws.

Ricci, Matteo (1552-1610) Italian *Jesuit missionary and scholar. Working in China from 1583 until his death, he proselytized by methods that were later condemned by the Roman Catholic Church. He showed the converts European books, maps, and clocks and allowed them to retain some of their ancient religious traditions.

Ricci, Sebastiano (1659-1734) Venetian painter. Influenced by *Veronese, he worked in Bologna, Rome, Vienna, and London (1712-16), where he painted the *Resurrection* in the apse of Chelsea Hospital chapel. His nephew **Marco Ricci** (1676-1730), a landscape artist, occasionally collaborated with him after about 1707.

Riccio, David (*or* D. Rizzio; c. 1533-66) Italian secretary to *Mary, Queen of Scots. His close relationship with the queen aroused the jealousy of her husband, Lord *Darnley, and other nobles, who had him murdered.

rice An annual cereal *grass, *Oryza sativa*, or its edible grain, probably native to India but widely cultivated throughout tropical, subtropical, and warm temperate regions. There are many varieties, growing up to 1 m high and bearing spikes of flower clusters. Seedlings are generally transplanted to flooded paddy fields, although varieties of upland rice do not require flooding. The field is drained to enable mechanical harvesting. Milling the grain removes either the outer husk alone, resulting in brown rice, or both the husk and the bran layer, resulting in vitamin-B-deficient white rice. Apart from being a major staple food, rice is used as a source of starch and for alcohol production.

Rich, Richard, 1st Baron (c. 1496-1567) English lawyer, who was the chief prosecutor in the trial of Sir Thomas More. He subsequently assisted in the dissolution of the monasteries, becoming a privy councillor (1540). As Lord Chancellor (1547-51) under Edward VI he helped oust the protector, *Somerset (1549).

Richard (I) the Lionheart (1157-1199) King of England (1189-99); a hero of medieval legend, he spent all but six months of his reign abroad. The third son of Henry II and *Eleanor of Aquitaine, he became Duke of Aquitaine in 1168 and of Poitiers in 1172. He joined the third Crusade in 1189 and conquered Messina and Cyprus before arriving in the Holy Land. His victory at Arsuf gained Joppa (1191). On his way home he was captured in Austria and was only released by Emperor Henry VI after payment of an enormous ransom (1194). He returned briefly to England but died campaigning in France.

Richard II (1367-1400) King of England (1377-99). Succeeding his grandfather Edward III, as a minor, government was largely in the hands of his uncle *John of Gaunt. Richard provoked considerable baronial opposition by his autocratic rule, defence of the royal prerogative, and reliance upon favourites. Factional struggles culminated in the ban-

RICHARD II *A portrait by an unknown artist of the king, who ascended the throne at the age of ten.*

ishment in 1398 of Gaunt's son Henry Bolingbroke. He returned in 1399, while Richard was in Ireland, and seized the throne as Henry IV. Richard died shortly afterwards at Pontefract Castle in mysterious circumstances.

Richard III (1452-85) King of England (1483-85). He was the youngest brother of Edward IV, on whose death in 1483 he became protector for Edward V, a minor. After destroying the power of the Woodville faction (*see* Woodville, Elizabeth), Richard imprisoned Edward and his brother, declared Edward illegitimate, and seized the throne. It was, and continues to be, alleged that Richard murdered the boys, who disappeared in August, 1483. As king, he made important administrative and financial reforms but faced considerable opposition, first from Henry Stafford, 2nd Duke of Buckingham (who was defeated and executed in October, 1483), and then from Henry Tudor (subsequently *Henry VII), by whom Richard was defeated and killed at Bosworth.

Richard, Cliff (Harry Rodger Webb; 1940-) British pop singer, who sang with the Shadows. With such records as "Livin' Doll" (1959) and "We Don't Talk Anymore" (1979), he has maintained his popularity. He starred in the film *The Young Ones* (1961) and *Summer Holiday* (1962) as well as the stage musical *Time* (1986).

Richards, Frank (Charles Hamilton; 1876-1961) British

children's writer. He wrote for the boys' papers *Gem* (1907–39) and *Magnet* (1908–40), in which he created the character of Billy Bunter, the comic fat boy of Greyfriars School. Writing under many different pseudonyms he created nearly 50 fictional public schools.

Richards, Sir Gordon (1904–86) British jockey, who was champion jockey a record 26 times (1925–53). He rode 4870 winners out of a total of 21 843 mounts (1920–54), his 269 wins in 1947 constituting a British record. He later became a trainer and finally retired in 1970.

Richards, I(vor) A(rmstrong) (1893–1979) English literary critic, linguist, and poet. With C. K. *Ogden, Richards compiled *Basic English and wrote *The Meaning of Meaning* (1923). An emeritus professor of Harvard University, Richards' publications include *Principles of Literary Criticism* (1924), *Goodbye Earth and Other Poems* (1958), and *Tomorrow Morning Faustus!* (1962).

Richards, Viv (Isaac Vivian Alexander R.; 1952–) West Indian cricketer. An outstanding batsman of the 1980s, he has scored over 6000 Test runs and has captained the West Indies since 1985.

Richardson, Henry Handel (Ethel Florence R.; 1870–1946) Australian novelist. She studied music in Leipzig and lived in England from 1903. Her trilogy *The Fortunes of Richard Mahoney* (1917–29) is a naturalistic study of an emigrant doctor in Australia based on the life of her father.

Richardson, Henry Hobson (1838–86) US architect. The first stylistically independent US architect, Richardson graduated from Harvard and studied architecture in Paris. He used a revived romanesque style in different types of buildings, ranging from wholesale stores to railway stations. Some of his best work was done for Harvard in the 1870s.

Richardson, Sir Ralph (1902–83) British actor. He established his reputation as an actor of Shakespearean and other classical roles while working with the Old Vic Company during the 1930s and 1940s. He also acted in modern plays, such as David Storey's *Home* (1970) and Harold Pinter's *No Man's Land* (1976) and made many films.

Richardson, Samuel (1689–1761) British novelist. His pioneering novel *Pamela* (1740), written in the form of correspondence between the characters, evolved from a publisher's commission for a book of model letters for inexperienced writers. His acute psychological characterization was further developed in *Clarissa* (1748), and in *Sir Charles Grandison* (1753) he portrayed the ideal gentleman.

Richelieu, Armand Jean du Plessis, Cardinal de (1585–1642) French statesman, who greatly increased the absolute authority of the Crown and France's power in Europe. He rose to prominence as adviser to Louis XIII's mother *Marie de' Medici, entering the king's employ in 1624 and officially becoming his chief minister in 1629. He ruthlessly suppressed the *Huguenots and by means of an extensive secret service thwarted a series of aristocratic conspiracies against himself. He directed France with brilliance in the Thirty Years' War, although he did not live to see the dominance of Spain over Europe replaced by that of France. A writer and patron of learning, he founded the French Academy.

Richler, Mordecai (1931–) Canadian novelist. He settled in England during the 1950s. He explores the dilemmas of his Jewish protagonists in an exuberant and often bawdy style. His novels include *The Apprenticeship of Duddy Kravitz* (1959), *St Urbain's Horseman* (1971), and *Joshua Now and Then* (1981). *Home Sweet Home* (1984) is a collection of essays about his native Canada.

Richmond 37 34N 77 27W A city and port in the USA, the capital of Virginia on the James River. Richmond was the capital of the Confederate states during the US Civil War. It is an important educational centre and site of the University of Richmond (1882). The chief manufacture is tobacco. Population

(1980): 219 214.

Richmond 54 24N 1 44W A market town in N England, in North Yorkshire on the River Swale. It has one of the oldest theatres in England (1788). Population (1981): 7731.

Richmond-upon-Thames A mainly residential borough of SW Greater London, on the River Thames. Created in 1965 from the former municipal boroughs of Richmond, Barnes, and *Twickenham, it contains Richmond Park and the Royal Botanic Gardens at Kew. Population (1981): 157 867.

Richter, Hans (1843–1916) Hungarian conductor. In 1866 he became an assistant to Wagner, of whose works he became the leading interpreter. He also conducted the Hallé Orchestra in Manchester and championed the works of Brahms.

Richter, Johann Paul Friedrich. *See* Jean Paul.

Richter, Sviatoslav (Teofilovitch) (1914–) Soviet pianist. The winner of the Stalin Prize in 1949, he is famous worldwide as a concert and recording artist. He is particularly noted for his performances of Beethoven, Schubert, Schumann, and Prokofiev.

Richter scale A scale of earthquake magnitude devised in 1935 by C. F. Richter (1900–85) in California and now in worldwide use. It is a logarithmic scale from 0 to 9, the largest earthquakes having the highest numbers. It is based on seismic recordings, taking into account distance from the epicentre. The strongest earthquake so far recorded had a Richter scale value of 8.6.

Richthofen, Manfred, Freiherr von (1892–1918) German air ace of World War I, who shot down 80 Allied aircraft before being killed himself in action. His nickname, the Red Baron, referred to the colour of his plane.

rickets A disease of children affecting the bones and caused by *vitamin D deficiency. Vitamin D is derived from the diet and can be made in the skin in the presence of sunlight; with a poor diet and/or inadequate sunshine the bones become soft and do not grow properly and the child may be knock-kneed, bowlegged, or pigeon-chested. The disease is readily treated with vitamin D preparations or foods rich in vitamin D.

rickettsia A minute organism belonging to a group of parasites that—like viruses—cannot reproduce outside the bodies of their hosts. They infect arthropods (especially ticks and mites) and can be transmitted to man, in whom they cause such diseases as *typhus and Rocky Mountain spotted fever. All species live within the cytoplasm or nuclei of living cells: they are similar in structure to bacteria and are regarded as intermediate between bacteria and viruses. The name derives from the principal genus (*Rickettsia*), which was named after H. T. Ricketts (1871–1910), a US pathologist who died of typhus while investigating the cause of the disease.

Ridgeway A prehistoric trackway in S England. It runs along the scarp of the Berkshire Downs, linking the *Avebury region with the Thames, whence the *Icknield Way continues eastwards. Many prehistoric monuments lie along its route.

Ridley, Nicholas (c. 1500–55) Anglican reformer and martyr. He became Master of Pembroke College, Cambridge, in 1540, Bishop of Rochester in 1547, and Bishop of London in 1550. Under Mary he was deprived of his see, tried for heresy at Oxford, and, with *Latimer, burnt at the stake.

Ridolfi, Roberto (R. di Ridolfo; 1531–1612) Italian conspirator against Elizabeth I of England. A businessman in London, he organized a Roman Catholic plot supported by Spain to overthrow Elizabeth and place Mary, Queen of Scots, on the throne. The conspiracy was exposed while Ridolfi was abroad and he escaped punishment.

Riebeeck, Jan van (1619–77) Dutch colonial administrator, who founded Cape Town in 1652. He was sent to the Cape by the Dutch East India Company to establish a provisioning port for ships. He became secretary to the Council of India in 1665.

Riefensthal, Leni (1902–) German film director and photographer. During the 1930s she produced propaganda films for the Nazis, notably *Triumph of the Will* (1936) and *Olympische Spiele* (1936). Her books include two photographic studies of Sudanese tribes, *People of Kau* (1976) and *Last of the Nuba* (1976).

Riel, Louis (1844–85) Canadian rebel. Attempting to resist surveys that he believed would lead to the métis (offspring of Indian-White parents) being robbed of their land, Riel led a rebellion of métis and set up a provisional government at Winnipeg (1869–70). Defeated and outlawed, he later led a similar rebellion (1884–85) that ended in his execution.

Riemann, Georg Friedrich Bernhard (1826–66) German mathematician, who, like *Lobachevski and *Bolyai before him, produced a *non-Euclidean geometry. **Riemannian geometry** involves the development of a generalized space (Riemannian space) of any dimensions in which measurements may vary from point to point. It was used by Einstein in his general theory of *relativity.

Rienzo, Cola di (1313–54) Roman popular leader, who during the papacy's sojourn in Avignon gained the support of the people of Rome against the nobles. He was proclaimed tribune (1347) and attempted to restore Rome to its ancient greatness. He was driven out by the nobles and later killed in a popular uprising.

Riesman, David (1909–) US social scientist and lawyer. Riesman's published work includes *The Lonely Crowd: A Study of the Changing American Character* (1950), *Individualism Reconsidered* (1954), and *The Perpetual Dream: Experiment and Reform in the American College* (1978). Riesman's insights into US society are as profound and disturbing as those of his friend Erich *Fromm.

Rif A *Berber people of N Morocco. Most of the 19 tribes speak the Rif dialect of the Berber language but a few speak Arabic. Many are light skinned and have blue or grey eyes. The Rif are Muslims and are renowned for their warrior tradition. They are cereal cultivators, herdsmen, and, along the coast, sardine fishers.

rifle A shoulder *small arm with a spiral groove inside its long barrel to make the projectile spin during its trajectory. Invented in the 15th century, rifles were widely used in America in the 18th century. In Europe the rifle superseded the *musket after the invention of the Minié system (by the French officer, Claude-Etienne Minié (1814–79) in 1849) based on an expanding lead bullet. This was made obsolete in 1865 by the introduction of breech-loaded metal cartridges. During the 1880s breech-loading rifles became capable of firing more than one cartridge without reloading. These were the immediate predecessors of the modern repeating rifle. *See also* Mauser rifle; Browning Automatic rifle.

riflebird A large *bird of paradise having a black plumage with iridescent throat patches and small ornamental plumes. The magnificent riflebird (*Craspedophora magnifica*) is about 30 cm long with a slender curved bill, a glossy green crown, and a purplish throat. The male performs its courtship display on specially selected and fiercely defended perches.

rifleman A tiny brown passerine bird, *Acanthisitta chloris*, occurring in forested regions of New Zealand. It feeds by creeping up and down tree trunks picking out insects from bark, crevices, and epiphytic plants with its fine pointed bill. Family: *Xenicidae* (New Zealand wrens).

rift valley A steep-sided valley with a flat floor formed as a result of the valley floor subsiding between two roughly parallel faults. Volcanic activity often occurs along these faults. The most notable example of this feature is the vast *Great Rift Valley in Africa; others include the central lowlands of Scotland and the Rhône rift valley.

Riga 56 53N 24 08E A port in the W Soviet Union, the capital of the Latvian SSR on the Gulf of Riga in the Baltic Sea. It is an industrial and cultural centre, with shipbuilding, machine-building, and many manufacturing industries. It has many historic buildings, especially in the picturesque old town. *History*: the order of Livonian Knights was founded here in 1201, and in 1282 Riga became a member of the Hanseatic League. A major trading centre, after the demise of the Livonian Knights it passed to Poland (1581), to Sweden (1621), and then to Russia (1710). It was the capital of independent Latvia (1918–40) and was occupied by the Germans (1941–44) in World War II. Population (1981 est): 850 000.

Rigel A remote yet very conspicuous blue *supergiant, apparent magnitude 0.1 and about 800 light years distant, that is the brightest star in the constellation *Orion.

right ascension An angular distance, analogous to terrestrial longitude, that is used with **declination** to specify the position of an astronomical body on the *celestial sphere. It is measured eastwards along the celestial equator from the vernal *equinox. Declination, analogous to terrestrial latitude, is the angular distance of the body N or S of the celestial equator.

Rights of Man and of the Citizen, Declaration of the (1789) The formal expression of the ideals of the *French Revolution. Comprising 17 articles, it was drafted by the National Assembly to preface the constitution of 1791. Incorporating *Enlightenment theories and both English and American precedents (*see* Bill of Rights), the Declaration asserted that "all men are born free and equal in rights," such as equality before the law, freedom of speech, and ownership of property. The Declaration was an inspiration to later revolutionary movements.

right whale A *whale of the family *Balaenidae* (5 species), so called because they were the right whales to catch (by whalers). Up to 18 m long and weighing over 20 tonnes, they are large-headed slow-moving plankton feeders with very long baleen plates and a double-jetted blowhole.

Rigi 47 04N 8 28E A mountain in N central Switzerland, between Lake Lucerne and Lake Zug. It is popular for the fine views from the summit. Height: 1800 m (5906 ft).

rigor mortis The stiffening of a body after death caused by chemical changes in the muscle tissue. The time at which rigor mortis appears depends on the external temperature and the circumstances of death. It usually passes away after about 24 hours.

Rijeka (Italian name: Fiume) 45 20N 14 27E The chief seaport in Yugoslavia, in Croatia on the Adriatic Sea. Made a free port in 1723, it was annexed by Hungary in 1779. In 1919, following claims by Italian *Irredentists and Yugoslavia, *D'Annunzio led a force to capture it for Italy. It again became a free port in 1920, reverted to Italy in 1924, finally coming to Yugoslavia in 1947 as reparation after World War II. It has a university (1973) and varied industries, including oil refineries and shipyards. Population (1981): 193 044.

Rijksmuseum A museum and art gallery in Amsterdam, housing the national collection of the Netherlands. It originated in 1808 as the Royal Museum and became the Rijksmuseum in 1817. Its highlights are its paintings of the Dutch school, notably the celebrated *Night Watch* by *Rembrandt.

Rijswijk, Treaty of (1697) The treaty that ended the War of the *Grand Alliance between France and England, Spain, Austria, and the Netherlands. Louis XIV of France surrendered most of the territories he had conquered (retaining Alsace), recognized William III as King of England, and granted trading concessions to the Dutch.

Riley, Bridget Louise (1931–) British painter. She studied at Goldsmith's College (1949–53) and the Royal College of Art and in the early 1960s began her black and white all-over patterns of repeated wavy lines, squares, etc., which associate her with *Op art.

Rilke, Rainer Maria (1875–1926) Austrian poet, born in Prague (then in Bohemia). After an unhappy childhood and a brief marriage, he travelled widely in Europe and Russia, becoming in Paris a friend of Rodin, and finally settled in Switzerland. Paris is the setting for the meditative prose of *Die Aufzeichnungen des Malte Laurids Brigge* (1910). In his poetry, the mysticism of his early devotional *Das Stunden-Buch* (1905) develops into a pantheistic celebration of life in the *Duino Elegies* (1923) and the *Sonnets to Orpheus* (1923).

Rimbaud, Arthur (1854–91) French poet. After writing "Le Bateau Ivre" and other early precocious poems he was welcomed to Paris in 1871 by *Verlaine, with whom he formed a tempestuous relationship that eventually ended in a violent quarrel. His visionary theories about poetry were expressed in the prose poems of *Une Saison en enfer* (1873) and *Les Illuminations* (1886). At the age of 20 he renounced poetry and wandered in Europe and the Near East, eventually becoming a gun-runner in Ethiopia. He died in Marseille.

Rimini (Latin name: Ariminium) 44 03N 12 24E A town and resort in Italy, in Emilia-Romagna on the N Adriatic coast. It has various Roman and medieval remains. There is a textile industry and flour mills; pasta is produced. Population (1980 est): 128 010.

Rimsky-Korsakov, Nikolai (1844–1908) Russian composer. Largely self-taught, he started his career as a naval officer and was appointed professor of composition at the St Petersburg conservatoire in 1871. He was a member of the group of nationalist composers known as the Mighty Five, the others being Balakirev, Borodin, César Cui (1835–1918), and Mussorgski. He wrote 15 operas, including *The Snow Maiden* (1880–81) and *The Golden Cockerel* (1906–07), such orchestral works as *Scheherazade* (1888), chamber music, and songs. He also reharmonized Mussorgski's *A Night on the Bare Mountain*.

rinderpest A contagious virus disease, also known as cattle plague, affecting cattle and certain wild animals in Asia and Africa. Symptoms arise three to nine days after infection and include loss of appetite, fever, mouth ulcers, dysentery, and emaciation. 90% of acute cases are fatal; in chronic cases, mortality is lower. Compulsory slaughter and vaccination are used to control outbreaks of the disease.

ringhals. *See* cobra.

ringlet A *satyrid butterfly characterized by brownish wings marked with small white rings. The larval food plants are mainly grasses. Chief genera: *Aphantopus, Cacnonympha, Erebia*.

ring ouzel A shy songbird, *Turdus torquatus*, which replaces the closely related blackbird in mountainous regions. The male is black with a broad white crescent around the throat; the female is dark brown with less distinct marking. They migrate to S Europe and the Atlas mountains for the winter. Family: *Turdidae* (thrushes).

ringworm A highly infectious disease of the skin, hair, and nails that is caused by various fungi: it is known medically as tinea. Ringworm is usually transmitted by direct contact. The affected area, commonly on the scalp, feet (athletes' foot), armpits, or groin, is usually inflamed, scaly, itchy, and typically ring-shaped (especially on the scalp). Serious infections are treated with the antibiotic griseofulvin.

Río Bravo. *See* Rio Grande.

Rio de Janeiro 22 53S 43 17W The chief port in □Brazil, the capital of Rio de Janeiro state situated on the SW shore of Guanabara Bay. Discovered by the Portuguese in 1502, it was the capital of Brazil from 1763 until 1960. Many colonial buildings remain, notably the 17th-century Candelaria church. It is renowned for its spectacular setting backed by mountains, the most famous of which is the conical Sugar Loaf Mountain. Another famous landmark is the giant figure of Christ standing on the highest peak, Corcovado, which is 690 m (2264 ft) high. The city is the

site of several universities, the Oswaldo Cruz Institute (specializing in experimental medicine), and the Brazilian Academy of Science. It is an important port and trading centre and has a fine natural harbour; exports include coffee, sugar, and iron ore. The chief industries include ship-building, sugar refining, and railway engineering. Population (1980): 5 093 232.

Río de la Plata. *See* Plata, Río de la.

Rio Grande (Spanish names: Río Bravo; Río Bravo del Norte) The fifth longest river of North America. Rising in the Rocky Mountains, in Colorado, it forms the entire border between Texas (USA) and Mexico before entering the Gulf of Mexico. Length: 2040 km (1885 mi).

Río Muni. *See* Equatorial Guinea, Republic of.

Riot Act (1715) The Act stipulating that a gathering of more than 12 people must disperse when asked by a magistrate (or, subsequently, a soldier) to do so. The Act reflected government fear of the *Jacobites.

Ríotinto, Minas de (*or* Minas de Río Tinto) A mining centre in SW Spain, in Andalusia near the source of the Río Tinto. Worked since Roman times, its copper mines are among the most valuable in the world.

Ripon 54 08N 1 31W A city in N England, in North York-shire on the River Ure. It is a market town and tourist centre and has a cathedral (begun in 1154) and a racecourse. The ruins of Fountains Abbey are nearby. Population (1981): 11 952.

Risorgimento (Italian: resurgence) The nationalist movement in 19th-century Italy that achieved the country's independence and unification. Secret societies, such as the *Carbonari and *Mazzini's Young Italy, encouraged Italian patriotism after 1815, and abortive uprisings occurred in Naples and Sicily (1820) and the papal states, Modena, and Parma (1830–31). Piedmont's attempts in 1848–49 to oust the Austrians from Lombardy ended in defeat at Custozza (1848) and Novara (1849) and afterwards *Garibaldi's Roman Republic was suppressed by the French. In 1859, however, the Piedmontese prime minister *Cavour freed Lombardy and in 1860 Garibaldi surrendered to Piedmont the conquests made in the S by his Expedition of the *Thousand. In the same year Tuscany, Modena, Parma, Bologna, and Romagna formed an independent alliance, all accepting entry into the kingdom of Italy under the House of Piedmont, proclaimed in 1861. Unification was completed by Italy's annexation of Venetia in 1866 and of the papal states in 1870.

river A large body of water, confined within a channel by banks, that flows into the sea, a lake, or another river. Its source may be a spring, a lake, a number of rivulets, or a glacier. Rivers are sometimes classified according to their development, a youthful river having a narrow V-shaped valley with many rapids and a mature river having a broad flood plain, meanders, and oxbow lakes. Rivers are important in the processes of erosion and the transportation and deposition of material; they are thus responsible for many of the landforms in those parts of the world of which they are a feature. Throughout history rivers have attracted settlement by man; broad river valleys were the site of some of the earliest great civilizations, such as in the Nile valley, and many of the world's major cities are located on rivers. As important communications routes, rivers often provided the point of entry to the surrounding land for explorers, traders, and settlers. Other uses of rivers include irrigation, hydroelectric power generation, and fishing. *See also* flood.

Rivera, Diego (1886–1957) Mexican □mural painter. In Mexico in the 1920s, with *Orozco and *Siqueiros, he revived the old techniques of *fresco and *encaustic painting in murals for educational institutions. His communist-inspired subject matter made him notorious in the USA, where his mural for the Rockefeller Center was removed because it included a portrait of Lenin.

Riverina A district of Australia, in S New South Wales, between the Murray and Lachlan Rivers. It consists chiefly of flat alluvial plains; the Murrumbidgee Irrigation Area is of greatest economic importance producing rice, stone and citrus fruits, and grapes. Area: 68 658 sq km (26 509 sq mi).

Riverside 33 59N 117 22W A city in the USA, in S California on the Santa Ana River. A long-established citrus town, the state's first navel orange tree was introduced here in 1873. It is the site of the citrus experiment station (1907) of the University of California. Population (1980): 170 876.

Riviera (French name: Rivière) The narrow Mediterranean coastal belt of France and Italy, extending roughly between Toulon (France) and La Spezia (Italy). Its climate, coastal scenery, and beaches have made it a long-standing cosmopolitan resort. Panoramic roads follow the coast; the famous two-tiered Corniche roads extend along the French Riviera (also known as the Côte d'Azur) between Nice and Menton.

Riyadh 24 39N 46 46E A city in Saudi Arabia, in the centre of the Arabian Peninsula. Riyadh and Mecca are joint capitals of the kingdom. The discovery of oil in Saudi Arabia in the 1930s has turned Riyadh into a thriving modern city, the commercial and communications centre of the country; it has two universities (1950 and 1957). Population (1983 est): 1 793 000.

Rizzio, David. *See* Riccio, David.

RNA (*or* ribonucleic acid) A nucleic acid that is important in the synthesis of proteins by living organisms. In some viruses RNA is the genetic material. Structurally, it is similar to *DNA but usually occurs as a single-stranded molecule with the sugar ribose and the base uracil replacing the deoxyribose and thymine of DNA. There are three main types of RNA (most of which occurs in the cell cytoplasm): ribosomal RNA, messenger (m) RNA, and transfer (t) RNA. The *genetic code in DNA contains the information necessary for protein synthesis. This code is transcribed into a strand of mRNA and carried to the ribosomes (small cytoplasmic particles), where it is translated into a particular polypeptide chain. The amino acids making up the protein are brought to their correct positions in the chain by tRNA.

roach One of several freshwater fish related to carp, especially *Rutilus rutilus*, a game fish found in N Europe. It has an elongated body, 15–45 cm long, olive-green to grey-green above and silvery white below with reddish fins and red eyes. It lives in shoals, feeding on small animals and plants.

Roach, Hal (1892–) US film producer. His production company, founded in 1914, produced many of the films of Harold *Lloyd, *Laurel and Hardy, and other comedians of the silent cinema. His single serious film was *Of Mice and Men* (1939).

roan antelope A large African antelope, *Hippotragus equinus*. 130–150 cm high at the shoulder, it is roan or reddish grey with a black-and-white face, long tufted ears, and an erect mane. The horns are shorter than those of the related *sable antelope. Roan antelopes live in herds of up to 25 in scrub and woodland.

Roanoke 37 15N 79 58W A city in the USA, in W Virginia on the Roanoke River. Settled in 1740, it is an industrial centre and railway junction. Manufactures include textiles and chemicals. Population (1980): 100 427.

Robbe-Grillet, Alain (1922–) French novelist. He trained as an agronomist and statistician. He is a leading theorist and practitioner of the *nouveau roman. Instantanés (1961) and Pour un nouveau roman (1963) contain a number of influential essays on the subject. As well as his novels, which include *Le Voyeur* (1955) and *La Jalousie* (1957), he has written several film scripts, notably the scenario for *L'Année dernière à Marienbad* (1961).

robber crab (*or* coconut crab) A *crab, *Birgus latro*, found on the shores of the SW Pacific and Indian Oceans. It has an extremely large body (about 1 m from head to tail), ranging from violet to brown in colour. It lives in sand burrows during the day, emerging at night to feed on coconuts broken open by its two large pincers. Tribe: *Anomura*.

robber fly A predatory fly, also called assassin fly, belonging to a worldwide family (*Asilidae*; over 4000 species) of insect eaters. Robber flies have prominent eyes and strong bristly legs. Many species have a humped thorax and a long slender abdomen, but some (e.g. *Asilis crabroniformis*) resemble bees and wasps. Most larvae are herbivorous and live in the soil.

Robbins, Frederick Chapman (1916–) US microbiologist, who, working with John *Enders and Thomas Weller (1915–), first cultivated poliomyelitis virus outside living organisms, using cultures of living human tissue in nutrient solution. This technique enabled the development of the polio vaccine and the culture of other viruses. He shared the 1954 Nobel Prize.

Robbins, Jerome (1918–) US ballet dancer and choreographer. He choreographed the dances for many musicals, including *The King and I* (1951), *West Side Story* (1957), and *Fiddler on the Roof* (1964). He has been choreographer for the New York City Ballet since 1969.

Robert (I) the Bruce (1274–1329) King of the Scots (1306–29). After a long career of rebellion against the English Crown Robert seized the Scottish throne in 1306. Although immediately forced into exile by Edward I of England, on the accession of Edward II he slowly recovered the kingdom, decisively defeating the English forces at Bannockburn (1314). A period of consolidation of his power followed, culminating in English recognition of Scottish independence in 1328.

Robert (II) the Pious (c. 970–1031) King of France (996–1031), who conquered Burgundy (1015) after years of warfare with a rival claimant. He gained his nickname for his encouragement of monasticism.

Robert II Curthose (c. 1054–1134) Duke of Normandy (1087–1134); the eldest son of William the Conqueror. He twice rebelled against his father (1077, 1083) and came into conflict with his brother William II Rufus. After fighting courageously in the first Crusade, he attempted to usurp the English throne from his youngest brother Henry I and following defeat at Tinchebrai was imprisoned (1106–34).

Robert II (1316–90) The first *Stuart King of the Scots (1371–90). He was three times regent of Scotland (jointly 1334–35; alone 1338–41 and 1346–57) while his father *David II was imprisoned or in exile. His own rule, as an old man, was of little consequence.

Roberts, Frederick Sleigh, 1st Earl (1832–1914) British field marshal. Born in India, he gave outstanding service during the *Indian Mutiny, for which he won the Victoria Cross (1858), and in the second Afghan War (1878–80). He crowned his career with victory as commander in chief (1899–1900) in the second *Boer War.

Roberts, Tom (1856–1931) Australian painter, born in Britain. He launched *impressionism in Melbourne with an exhibition (1889) of Australian landscapes painted on cigar-box lids. Specializing chiefly in scenes of rural life, he also painted the opening of the first Commonwealth of Australia parliament (St James's Palace, London).

Robert the Wise (1278–1343) King of Naples (1309–43), a leader of the Italian *Guelfs (papal party) against the Ghibellines (imperial party). He was an outstanding administrator (hence his nickname) and patron of scientists and writers, including Petrarch and Boccaccio.

Robeson, Paul (1898–1976) US Black actor and singer. His best-known stage performances were in the title roles of *Othello* and Eugene O'Neill's *Emperor Jones*. He sang Negro spirituals, made several films, and actively campaigned for Black civil rights.

ROBOTICS *Robot welding on the production line of the Austin Metro at the Austin-Rover factory at Longbridge.*

Robespierre, Maximilien François Marie Isidore de (1758–94) French revolutionary. A lawyer, Robespierre was elected to the States General in 1789, on the eve of the *French Revolution, and became one of the leaders of the radical *Jacobins. He gained a wide following in Paris and after the execution of Louis XVI was instrumental in the overthrow of the Girondins (1793). He subsequently wielded supreme power on the Committee of *Public Safety, instituting the *Reign of Terror. In 1794 the tide turned against him and his cult of the Supreme Being: he was denounced in the Legislative Assembly and guillotined.

Robey, Sir George (George Edward Wade; 1869–1954) British music-hall comedian. He began his stage career in 1891 and became known as "the prime minister of mirth." He also appeared in pantomimes, films, and plays, notably as Falstaff in Shakespeare's *Henry IV* (Part I).

robin A small Eurasian songbird, *Erithacus rubecula*, adopted as Britain's national bird. About 13 cm long it has an olive-brown plumage with an orange-red breast, throat, and forehead and feeds on insects, earthworms, fruit, and seeds. In Britain, robins are common on farmland, in woodland, and in towns and gardens. A robin defends its territory fiercely, using its warbling song as a signal to warn off intruders. Family: *Turdidae* (thrushes).

Robin Hood An English outlaw, probably legendary, who figures in a series of ballads dating from the 14th century. According to the *Lytell Geste of Robyn Hoode* (c. 1495) he killed the evil sheriff of Nottingham, was visited in his forest home by the king, and was subsequently employed in the royal household. His mistress Maid Marian and his association with Sherwood were later additions to the story.

Robinson, Edwin Arlington (1869–1935) US poet. Troubled by poverty and alcoholism throughout his life, he established himself with a novel in verse, *Captain Craig* (1902), and confirmed his reputation with the poems in *The Town down the River* (1910) and *The Man against the Sky* (1916). He wrote a large number of dramatic monologues and several long narrative poems, including *Tristram* (1927). Some of his best verse appeared in *The Children of Night* (revised 1897).

Robinson, Edward G. (Emanuel Goldenberg; 1893–1972) US film actor, born in Romania. He was cast as a gangster in *Little Caesar* (1930) and other films during the 1930s but he played more varied roles in later films, such as *Double Indemnity* (1943) and *The Outrage* (1964).

Robinson, John (Arthur Thomas) (1919–83) British bishop and theologian. A distinguished New Testament scholar, he was Suffragan Bishop of Woolwich (1959–69) and lectured at Trinity College, Cambridge. His controversial *Honest to God* (1963) popularized radical theological discussion.

Robinson, Sir Robert (1886–1975) British chemist, who investigated the structure of the alkaloids *morphine (1925) and *strychnine (1946). The latter work enabled Robert *Woodward to synthesize strychnine eight years later. Robinson received the Nobel Prize in 1947.

Robinson, Sugar Ray (Walker Smith; 1920–) US boxer, world welterweight champion (1946–51) and five times middleweight champion (twice in 1951, 1955, 1957, 1958–60). He fought 202 professional bouts, of which he lost only 19.

Robinson, William Heath (1872–1944) British cartoonist and book illustrator. Working for the *Sketch, Bystander*, and other journals, he became famous for his witty drawings of bizarre machines for performing everyday tasks.

robotics The study of automatic machines that are capable of simulating and replacing human activities. Some robotic machines have sensory devices and can make decisions based on a sensory input and a self-programming facility. However, most robots in current industrial use carry out a fixed sequence of computer-controlled operations. Current research and development seeks to combine the concepts of *artificial intelligence with a mechanical robot capable of visual perception by means of a television camera. Such a robot could use a mechanical limb in response to its perception of a restricted number of events in its immediate vicinity.

Rob Roy (Robert Macgregor; 1671–1734) Scottish outlaw, whose violent life was romanticized in Sir Walter Scott's novel *Rob Roy* (1818). He embarked on his career of banditry after losing his family fortunes in 1712. Arrested and sentenced to transportation, he was pardoned in 1727.

Robson, Dame Flora (1902–84) British actress. She was successful in both comedy, as in *Captain Brassbound's Conversion* (1948), and in serious drama, such as Ibsen's *Ghosts* (1958) and *John Gabriel Borkman* (1963). In her many films she usually played character parts.

Rochdale 53 38N 2 09W A town in N England, in Greater Manchester. Engineering and textiles (particularly cotton spinning) are the main industries. The Cooperative Society was founded here in 1844 by the Rochdale Pioneers. Population (1981): 92 704.

Rochefort-sur-Mer 45 57N 0 58W A port in W France, in the Charente-Maritimes department on the River Charente. It has a naval museum and manufactures aircraft parts. Pierre Loti was born here. Population (1982): 27 716.

Rochester 43 12N 77 37W A city in the USA, in New York state on Lake Ontario and the Genesee River. Founded in 1789, it is the site of the University of Rochester (1850) and the Rochester Institute of Technology (1829). Its industries include horticulture and the manufacture of photographic and optical equipment. Population (1980): 241 509.

Rochester 44 01N 92 27W A city in the USA, in Minnesota. It is the site of the Mayo Clinic (1889) and the Mayo Medical Centre. Manufactures include electronic and recording equipment. Population (1980): 54 287.

Rochester 51 24N 0 30E A city and port in SE England, in Kent on the Medway estuary, adjacent to Chatham. It was a Roman stronghold and has a 12th-century castle and a Norman cathedral. Population (1981): 52 505.

Rochester, John Wilmot, 2nd Earl of (1647–80) British poet. A dissolute member of the court of Charles II, he wrote many short poems famous for their uninhibited bawdiness. His longer satirical poems include *A Satire against Mankind* and *Upon Nothing*.

rock (music) A style of popular music dating from the early 1950s, resulting from the fusion of rhythm and blues with country music. The term **rock and roll** was originally applied to such songs as "Rock Around the Clock" (1955) by Bill Haley (1925–81) and the Comets and "Heartbreak Hotel" (1956) by Elvis Presley, whose bands consisted of electric guitars, drums, and amplified vocalists. In the 1960s the term "rock" replaced "rock and roll." Such groups as the Beatles and Chicago expanded the traditional band to include string backing and other instruments, and began to explore the possibilities offered by studio recording techniques, synthesizers, etc. Rock increasingly split into subgroups, such as **acid rock**, based on drug experiences (Jimi Hendrix, the Jefferson Airplane), and **hard rock**, emphasizing a strong rhythmic beat (the Byrds, the Who), and **progressive rock**, which admitted long instrumental solos and more advanced harmonies. In the late 1970s **punk rock** (*or* new wave) returned to a basic and very aggressive style of performance with such groups as the Sex Pistols. Developments in the 1980s included the increased use of electronic equipment and the making of short pop video films. *Compare* pop music.

rock (petrology)   A solid mixture of *minerals forming part of the earth's crust. The minerals are usually consolidated to form a hard compact mass, but geologists include unconsolidated material, such as sand, as rock. Rocks are classified according to their formation (*see* igneous rock; metamorphic rock; sedimentary rock), their age (*see* stratigraphy), and their composition. Individual rock types are much more varied in chemical composition than minerals, and most consist of several different minerals. Some minerals in rocks can be seen with the naked eye, such as the quartz, orthoclase, and biotite in granite, whereas the minerals in clay can only be seen under an electron microscope. The principal minerals in rocks are the silicates (including silica), carbonates, and oxides. The essential minerals in a rock are those that determine its classification; accessory minerals are those that do not affect its classification. *Petrology is the study of rocks.

Rockall   57 40N 13 30W An uninhabited rocky British islet in the N Atlantic Ocean. Area: about 743 sq m (8000 sq ft).

rock crystal.   *See* quartz.

rock dove   A cliff-nesting dove, *Columba livia*, of S Europe, Asia, and N Africa. 32 cm long, it has a grey plumage with a green-and-purple neck patch, two black wing bars, and a white rump. A fast flier with excellent homing ability, it feeds on seeds, grain, shellfish, and seaweed.

Rockefeller, John D(avison)   (1839–1937) US industrialist, who founded the monopolistic oil-refining company, Standard Oil (1870). In 1881 he turned the company, based at Cleveland, Ohio, into a business trust, the first such in the USA. A philanthropist, he founded the University of Chicago in 1891 and, with his son **John D(avison) Rockefeller, Jr** (1874–1960), established the Rockefeller Institute for Medical Research (now Rockefeller University) in 1901. The latter's nephew **Nelson A (ldrich) Rockefeller** (1908–79) was Republican governer of New York (1959–74) and Gerald Ford's vice-president (1974–77).

rocket   Any of several annual or biennial herbaceous plants of the genus *Sisymbrium*, having yellow flowers. London rocket (*S. irio*), up to 60 cm high, is found on roadsides, walls, etc. in Europe, W Asia, North America, and N Africa. Its name results from its abundance after the Great Fire of London in 1666. The name is also given to plants of other related genera. Family: *Cruciferae*.

rockets   Vehicles or missiles powered by jet propulsion that carry their own fuel and oxidizer and can therefore travel both in space and in the atmosphere. Rockets have no lift surfaces (*see* aeronautics), obtaining both lift and thrust from their propulsive jets. Solid-fuel firework rockets were known to the Chinese in the 13th century and have been used sporadically in war ever since. However, the first liquid-fuelled rocket to fly was designed by the American R. H. *Goddard in 1926. This achievement attracted little interest, except in Germany, where the *Peenemünde rocket research station was set up. It was here that Werner *von Braun produced the *V-2 rocket in World War II. Intercontinental *ballistic missiles (with nuclear warheads), developed by both the USA and Soviet Union from this model, now form part of the armoury of all the principal nations. These rockets, in turn, led to the space rockets that carried man to the moon.

Space rockets are built in stages, a high-thrust vehicle providing lift-off and acceleration into the thinner atmosphere, where this first stage is jettisoned and the second stage takes over. The world's biggest space rocket, the US Saturn V, is a three-stage rocket weighing 3000 tonnes fully laden. The first stage burns kerosene and the second and third stages burn liquid hydrogen. Liquid oxygen (lox) is the oxidizer for all stages. This rocket can carry a load of 45 tonnes into space.

Fuel economy is one of the most important factors in rocket design—the specific impulse of a rocket being its most significant characteristic. The specific impulse is the time in seconds to burn one kilogram of fuel while producing one newton of thrust. Typical values are 3400 s for a solid fuel, 4500 s for liquid hydrogen-lox, and over 10 000 s for an ion engine. In an ion-engine rocket an easily ionized substance, such as caesium, is heated to produce ions, which are accelerated by an electric field to produce thrust. These engines of the future could be powered by nuclear energy or solar energy to produce the necessary 50 kW of electricity for each newton of thrust.

Rockhampton   23 22S 150 32E A city and port in Australia, in central Queensland on the Fitzroy River. It is a commercial centre for an extensive hinterland producing meat, gold, copper, and coal. Population (1980 est): 53 500.

Rockingham, Charles Watson-Wentworth, 2nd Marquess of   (1730–82) British statesman; prime minister (1765–66, 1782). As leader of the so-called Rockingham Whigs, he supported the American colonies in their conflict with Britain. In 1765 he repealed the *Stamp Act and led the opposition to Lord North's government during the American Revolution.

rockrose   A small spreading shrub, *Helianthemum chamaecistus*, up to 30 cm high with bright-yellow five-petalled flowers; it is found in grassland and scrub of Europe and W Asia. Hybrids of this and similar species are cultivated as garden ornamentals, with many different coloured varieties. Family: *Cistaceae*.

rock tripe   A leafy *lichen of the genus *Umbilicaria*, found in Arctic and temperate regions. It is rich in carbohydrates and is edible when boiled. In Japan it is considered a delicacy, being eaten in salads or deep fried. Some species are also used as dyes.

Rocky Mountains (*or* Rockies)   The chief mountain system in North America. It extends roughly N–S for about 4800 km (3000 mi) between New Mexico (USA) and the Yukon (Canada), forming the *Continental Divide. It rises to 4399 m (14 431 ft) at Mount Elbert. Some geographers consider the Yukon and Alaska ranges as part of the system, making Mount Logan, at 6050 m (19 850 ft), the highest point.

rococo   A style dominant in the fine arts and decorative arts of France between about 1700 and 1750. Developing in reaction to the *baroque pomp of the Louis XIV period, it was characterized by curved forms, slender proportions, asymmetry, pastel colours, and a general effect of intimacy, gaiety, and delicacy. The rococo style was particularly manifest in the interior decoration of Parisian townhouses and furniture, porcelain, and metalwork. Famous rococo artists include the painters *Fragonard, *Boucher, and *Watteau and the sculptor *Clodion. The style spread to Austria and Germany, where the leading exponent was the architect Balthazar *Neumann. England remained largely untouched by it, although some rococo features appear in the work of *Hogarth and *Gainsborough. The rococo was supplanted by *neoclassicism.

rodent A mammal belonging to the order *Rodentia* (over 1700 species). Rodents are distributed worldwide and occupy a wide range of terrestrial and semiaquatic habitats. They range in size from about 7.5 cm (the smallest mice) to 130 cm (the capybara). Rodents have distinctive teeth. The single pairs of chisel-like incisors in each jaw continue to grow throughout life, as they are worn away by gnawing. There are no second incisor or canine teeth, leaving a gap between the front teeth and cheek teeth. When the rodent is gnawing, the cheeks are drawn into the gap and the lower jaw is moved forward so that the upper and lower incisors can meet. This prevents the rodent from swallowing gnawed material and from wearing out its cheek teeth.

Rodents are important to man as agricultural pests, fur animals, and as experimental animals for scientific research. They are divided into three suborders: *Hystricomorpha* (porcupines, cavies, chinchillas, etc.; 180 species); *Sciuromorpha* (squirrels, beavers, marmots, chipmunks, etc.; 366 species); and *Myomorpha* (rats, mice, lemmings, voles, etc.; 1183 species).

rodeo A US sport that grew out of ranching skills after the Civil War, now controlled by the Rodeo Cowboys Association. A rodeo, or contest, includes six main events: bronco riding with and without a saddle, bull riding, calf roping, steer wrestling, and team roping. Professional rodeo riders are not hired to take part, but live on prize money.

Roderic. *See* Rory O'Connor.

Rodgers, Richard Charles (1902-79) US composer of musical comedies. With the lyricist Lorenz Hart (1895-1943) he wrote such works as *The Girl Friend* (1926) and *Pal Joey* (1940). After Hart's death he collaborated with Oscar *Hammerstein II in *Oklahoma* (1943), *The King and I* (1951), and other musicals.

Rodin, Auguste (1840-1917) French sculptor. He produced his first major work, *The Age of Bronze* (1877), after visiting Italy (1875), where he was influenced by the work of *Michelangelo and *Donatello. Its controversial realism was a factor in the vicissitudes of his public commissions: *The Burghers of Calais* (1884-86), his nude monument of Victor Hugo, and his dressing-gowned Balzac were all initially rejected. Nevertheless, by 1900 Rodin had established an international reputation, his bronze portrait busts and his figures in marble, notably *The Kiss* (1886; Tate Gallery), being particularly admired. His most personal work, *The Gates of Hell*, which was originally a government commission of the 1880s, was left unfinished at his death. Many of its symbolic figures, for example *The Thinker*, became well-known independent sculptures.

Rodney, George Brydges, 1st Baron (1719-92) British admiral. He wrecked (1759-60) a French invasion fleet during the Seven Years' War and won victories (1780-82) against the powers that supported the American Revolution. His victory over the French off Dominica (1782) helped Britain to gain favourable terms in the concluding Peace of Versailles (1783).

Rodrigo, Joaquín (1902-) Spanish composer, blind since the age of three. His works include the *Concierto de Aranjuez* (for guitar and orchestra; 1940) and *Concierto Pastorale* (for flute and orchestra; 1978) commissioned by the flautist James *Galway.

rods and cones. *See* retina.

Roebling, John Augustus (1806-69) US engineer, who with his son **Washington Augustus Roebling** (1837-1926) designed Brooklyn Bridge in New York, which was opened in 1883. They also designed major suspension bridges, including those over the Niagara River at the Niagara Falls and over the Ohio River between Cincinnati and Covington. John Roebling died after an accident while supervising the construction of the Brooklyn Bridge.

roe deer A small deer, *Capreolus capreolus*, of temperate Eurasian forests. About 70 cm high at the shoulder, roe deer have a dark-brown winter coat, a red-brown summer coat, and a large white rump patch; males have small three-pointed antlers. They feed at night on leaves, shoots, and berries and live in pairs or small family groups.

roentgen A unit of dose of ionizing radiation equal to the dose that produces ions of one sign carrying a charge of 2.58×10^{-4} coulomb in air.

Roentgen, Wilhelm Konrad (1845-1923) German physicist, who discovered *X-rays while professor at the University of Würzburg, Bavaria. In 1895 Roentgen was investigating the *luminescence that cathode rays produce in certain substances and discovered that the luminescence persisted when the cathode rays themselves were blocked by cardboard. He correctly concluded that some other type of radiation was coming from the cathode-ray tube. He named the radiation X-rays and his discovery that the rays pass through matter quickly led to their use in medical diagnosis. In 1901, he received the first Nobel Prize for Physics. The unit of X-ray dose (*see* roentgen) is named after him.

Roeselare (French name: Roulers) 50 57N 3 08E A town in W Belgium. An important German base in World War I, it suffered much damage. Industries include textiles (particularly linen) and carpets. Population (1981 est): 51 945.

Rogation Days Four days in the Christian calendar devoted to prayer and fasting. The Major Rogation is on 25 April and the Minor Rogations are on the three days before *Ascension Day. Rogation Day processions and prayers were successors of pagan rituals to ensure a good harvest and in England the traditional ceremony of beating the parish bounds (i.e. marking the boundaries by striking certain points with rods) took place at Rogationtide.

Roger II (1095-1154) Norman King of Sicily (1130-54). He became Count of Sicily in 1105 and created a strong kingdom augmented by the acquisition of Calabria (1122), Apulia (1127), Capua (1136), and Naples (1140) on the Italian mainland. He also attacked the Byzantine Empire, pillaging the coastal cities of Dalmatia and Epirus. His court was a great intellectual centre for both Christian and Muslim scholars.

Rogers, Ginger (Virginia McMath; 1911-) US actress and singer. During the 1930s she partnered Fred *Astaire in many popular film musicals, including *Top Hat* (1935), *Swing Time* (1936), and *Follow the Fleet* (1936). She was also a talented comedy actress.

Rogers, John (c. 1500-55) English Protestant martyr. While a chaplain in Antwerp from 1534, he was converted to Protestantism by William *Tyndale and edited a Bible translation, known as "Matthew's Bible" (1537). After returning to England in 1548 he was tried for heresy and burnt at the stake at Smithfield, being the first martyr of Queen Mary's reign.

Roget, Peter Mark (1779-1869) British physician and philologist. He was secretary of the Royal Society from 1827 to 1849. His well-known *Thesaurus of English Words and Phrases* (1852), a dictionary of synonyms, has been revised in numerous editions.

Röhm, Ernst (1887-1934) German soldier, who organized Hitler's *Brownshirts. Röhm's ambition to increase the power of the Brownshirts led to his execution without trial.

Rokitansky, Karl, Freiherr von (1804-78) Austrian pathologist, whose detailed anatomical studies of numerous autopsies helped establish the science of pathological anatomy. Rokitansky is noted particularly for describing the different kinds of pneumonia and a liver disease known as Rokitansky's disease.

Roland, Song of. *See* chanson de geste.

Rolfe, Frederick William (1860-1913) British novelist, also known by the pseudonym Baron Corvo. A Roman Catholic convert, he failed to persuade Church authorities that he had a priestly vocation, and his frustration and delusions were expressed in the fantasy *Hadrian the Seventh* (1904), which concerns a convert who becomes pope. His other works include *Stories Toto Told Me* (1898) and *The Desire and Pursuit of the Whole* (1934). Interest in his life and works was aroused by A. J. A. Symons' biography, *The Quest for Corvo* (1934).

Rolland, Romain (1866-1944) French novelist, dramatist, and essayist. He was also a distinguished musicologist, and his best-known novel, *Jean Christophe* (1904-12), concerns a German composer. His philosophical idealism, much influenced by Tolstoy, was expressed in numerous volumes of essays and biographies. He won the Nobel Prize in 1915.

roller A short-legged bird belonging to a family (*Coraciidae*; 12 species) occurring in warm regions of the Old World. 25-40 cm long, rollers are blue or violet and have a large head, a strong slightly hooked bill, and a long tail. They feed in flocks on ants, locusts, and lizards. Order: *Coraciiformes* (hornbills, kingfishers, etc.).

Rolling Stones, the A British rock group, formed in 1962. Their early hits included "The Last Time" and "Satisfaction." They became famous for their notorious behaviour in public, made successful tours of the USA, and recorded a number of albums, including *Beggar's Banquet* (1968). The original members of the group were Mick *Jagger, Keith Richard (1943-), Bill Wyman (1941-), Charlie Watts (1941-), and Brian Jones (1944-69).

Rollo (c. 860-c. 931) Viking leader, who founded the duchy of Normandy. Having invaded NW France, Rollo was given the territory around Rouen by treaty (911) with Charles (III) the Simple (879-929; reigned 898-923), thus becoming the first Duke of Normandy.

Rolls, Charles Stewart (1877-1910) British car manufacturer and aviator. A car dealer, in 1906 he went into partnership with Henry *Royce to found Rolls-Royce Ltd. Rolls was the first to fly nonstop across the English Channel and back (1910), dying shortly afterwards in an aircrash.

Romains, Jules (Louis Farigoule; 1885-1972) French poet, novelist, and dramatist. He was a leading exponent of the philosophical theory of *unanimisme*, which emphasized collective as opposed to individual emotions and psychology. His best-known works are the satirical play *Knock* (1923) and the novel cycle *Les Hommes de bonne volonté* (1932-46).

Roman art and architecture The styles of art and architecture of the ancient Romans. Deriving principally from their Greek and Etruscan predecessors, Roman styles in the fine and applied arts have profoundly influenced western traditions. The Romans' main contribution to classical architecture was the formal and structural development of the □arch, *dome, and *vault and the introduction of new types of building, such as *thermae, *amphitheatres, and triumphal arches. Their advanced building techniques and use of concrete were unsurpassed until the 19th century. The Pantheon and the Colosseum (both in Rome) remain as fine examples of their monumental building techniques, while the ruins of Pompeii provide an insight into their domestic architecture and their skill in town planning. In the other arts their style was modelled on that of the Greeks, although their sculptures were less idealistic and more inclined to personal portraiture. Little painting has survived, but from the evidence of Pompeii and elsewhere *mosaics and murals seem to have been popular.

Roman Catholic Church The Christian Church of which the pope is the temporal leader (*see* papacy). After the split with the Eastern *Orthodox Churches (1054; *see* Filioque), Roman Catholicism was the unchallenged spiritual authority in W Europe; Church dignitaries possessed great political, as well as spiritual, power and *monasticism flourished. In the early 16th century the rising tide of *Protestantism demonstrated the need for urgent reforms within the Church. The Council of Trent (1545-63), convoked to discuss these

reforms, has largely determined the present dogmatic, disciplinary, and liturgical character of Roman Catholicism (*see also* Counter-Reformation), although important reforms were initiated by the second *Vatican Council. In general, a higher reliance is placed by Roman Catholics upon tradition and authority, especially regarding interpretation of the Bible, than is the case in most Protestant Churches. The Church organization is to an advanced degree centralized and hierarchical (*see* cardinals, college of; Roman Curia), and the pope's decisions are reinforced by the doctrine of *infallibility promulgated in 1870. Other accepted doctrines include *transubstantiation and *purgatory. The number of the *sacraments has been fixed at seven since the 12th century. The cult of the Virgin Mary, which flourished in the middle ages, underwent a major revival in the 19th century, and the veneration and invocation of *saints are encouraged. Church furnishings, music, and vestments are more elaborate than in Protestant Churches. Until the mid-20th century Latin was the sole language of the Mass. Roman Catholicism has spread worldwide due to strenuous missionary efforts since the 16th century (*see* Jesuits) and is the largest Christian denomination. In a world becoming progressively more disinclined to accept religious authority, the Catholic Church has managed to maintain its strong following, largely as a result of firm direction from Rome. However, some modernization has already taken place (the use of the vernacular in the Mass, changes in monastic dress, etc.), although other controversial issues (abortion, contraception, divorce, married priests, etc.) remain to be resolved.

romance A term loosely applied to a medieval verse or prose narrative that dealt with nonhistorical material and first became popular in 12th-century France. Its central themes were courtly love, chivalry, and adventure, and it was distinguished from the earlier *chanson de geste by being less heroic and more sophisticated in tone. It was intended as entertainment rather than for any religious or political purpose. Romances are conventionally classified into three types according to subject matter: (1) the Matter of Britain—romances based on the *Arthurian legend, which was popular throughout Europe; (2) the Matter of Rome—romances about the Trojan War, Thebes, or Alexander the Great; and (3) the Matter of France—romances about Charlemagne and his knights. Among the most famous medieval romances are the five Arthurian romances of *Chrétien de Troyes; the *Parzival* (c. 1210) of Wolfram von Eschenbach; the *Tristan und Isolde* (c. 1210) of Gottfried von Strassburg; the anonymous Middle English *Gawain and the Green Knight* (c. 1400); and Sir Thomas Malory's *Morte d'Arthur* (c. 1470).

Romance languages Descendants of the *Italic language group, in particular of the spoken form of *Latin, called Vulgar Latin. The group consists of modern *French, *Italian, *Spanish, *Portuguese, *Romanian, *Catalan, the Rhaetian (*see* Romansch) group of dialects, Sardinian, and the now extinct Dalmatian. As this list shows, many Romance languages are in fact regional dialects rather than national languages. They are classified as a group on the basis of a shared section of basic vocabulary, which originated in the influence of the language of the Roman conquerors of the Mediterranean area in which the languages of the group are clustered. Since 1500 their use has spread outside Europe to South America and Africa, with French, Spanish, and Portuguese colonization.

Roman comedy A dramatic genre that developed chiefly from Greek sources and flourished in the late 3rd and 2nd centuries BC. The first Latin version of a Greek comedy was written by Livius Andronicus (c. 284-c. 204 BC) in 240 BC. His successors included Naevius (c. 270-c. 201 BC) and *Plautus, whose plays, based on those of Greek *New Comedy writers, especially Menander and Philemon, were enlivened by colloquial language and topical and bawdy humour. The plays of *Terence and Caecilius Statius (c. 219-168 BC) were more sophisticated in their plots and characterization. At the Renaissance the plays of Plautus and Terence, the only representatives of Roman comedy to survive complete, were revived and became the basis of modern ideas of comedy.

Roman Curia (Latin: *Curia Romana*) The papal court, comprising the chief judicial and administrative bodies of the *Roman Catholic Church. Its powers are delegated by the pope, who takes responsibility for its acts. Extensively reformed in 1967 by Pope Paul VI, it consists of three tribunals, which are mainly concerned with judicial matters; five offices, including the Chancery, which issues papal bulls, and the offices of the Palatinate Secretaries, such as that of the Cardinal Secretary of State, which deals with political affairs; and nine Roman Congregations, which are permanent commissions of cardinals having specific tasks (regarding rites, missions, etc.).

Roman Empire The imperial period of ancient Roman history from 27 BC, when Octavian became emperor as *Augustus, until 476 AD. Under imperial government many of the political institutions of the *Roman Republic, notably the Senate, continued to function, although Augustus and his successors enjoyed supreme power as *princeps* (chief citizen). Augustus, who created an efficient administrative system for the Empire, fostered peace and prosperity, which continued, despite outbreaks of rebellion, under the paternalistic rule of the Flavian (69-96 AD; *see* Vespasian; Titus; Domitian) and Antonine (96-180; *see* Nerva; Trajan; Hadrian; Antoninus Pius; Marcus Aurelius) emperors. Trade and industry flourished throughout the Empire, new cities were founded, and frontiers, although little extended, were strengthened. Civil war, however, followed the death of *Commodus (193), with provincial armies nominating their own imperial candidates. Order was briefly restored by Lucius Septimus *Severus (reigned 193-211), who openly acknowledged his

dependence on military might, increasing the powers of the *Praetorian Guard (imperial bodyguard). The 3rd century saw a rapid succession of army-nominated emperors, while Rome's frontiers were threatened by the aggression of the *Sasanians and the Goths. *Diocletian (reigned 284-305) countered these attacks with the reorganization of the Empire between East (*see* Eastern Roman Empire) and West (293). It was reunited (324) under *Constantine the Great, the first Christian emperor, who founded a new imperial capital at Constantinople (*see* Istanbul). His attempts to establish unity were, however, short lived: civil war and economic decline followed his death and the western Empire fell prey to barbarian invasions. The Visigoths sacked Rome in 410; Carthage was captured in 439 by the Vandals, who in 455 also sacked Rome; in 476 the last Roman emperor of the West, *Romulus Augustulus, was deposed by the German king Odoacer. The Eastern Roman, or Byzantine, Empire survived until 1453.

romanesque art and architecture A style of art and architecture that flourished in Europe from the 11th century until the introduction of the *gothic in the mid-12th century. Its origins were mixed, being a combination of Carolingian, Roman, and Byzantine styles, and regional influences produced many variations between areas. Primarily an ecclesiastical art form, it was largely stimulated by the need for more churches, now possible on a large scale because of the arrival of relative peace after centuries of disturbance. The increasing complexity of Church ritual was reflected in the greater number of side chapels. The decline of building techniques since antiquity resulted in very solid buildings with thick walls, windows with semicircular arches, and simple stone vaulting. The other important branch of romanesque art was sculpture. It was primarily used to decorate churches, either with geometrical or plant and animal patterns on the fabric of the building, especially on the capitals, or statues of religious subjects inside the building. Many examples of romanesque art still survive,

ROMAN EMPIRE *In 14 AD, at the death of Augustus, Roman rule or influence extended all the way round the Mediterranean.*

one of the most notable being Pisa Cathedral. *See also* Norman art and architecture. ⌐arch.

Romania, Socialist Republic of A country in SE Europe, with an E coastline on the Black Sea. The Carpathian Mountains and the Transylvanian Alps in the centre of the country separate the plains in the E and S from the Transylvanian plateau in the NW; the River Danube forms most of its S boundary. Most of the inhabitants are Romanians, who trace their ancestry back to the Latin settlers of the Roman province of Dacia. *Economy*: although there has been a pronounced shift in the balance of the economy towards industry since World War II, agriculture is still important, much of it organized in collectives and state farms. The main crops are maize, wheat, potatoes, sugar beet, and fruit. Livestock is also important and there is a growing wine industry. Minerals include oil and gas, salt, lignite, iron, and copper. Hydroelectricity is a valuable source of power, particularly since the opening of the Iron Gate scheme on the Danube (shared with Yugoslavia) in 1972. Varied industries, all now nationalized although there has been a relaxation in central controls since 1978, include heavy industries such as mineral and metals, oil, motor vehicles, machinery, and chemicals, the products of which provide the main exports (mainly to communist countries). There is a considerable timber industry and tourism is of increasing importance to the economy. *History*: formed in 1861 from the principalities of *Moldavia and *Walachia, Romania gained independence from the Ottoman Empire in 1880 and in 1881 became a kingdom under Carol I. Romania joined (1916) the Allies in World War I and was occupied by the Germans. In 1918 it obtained Bessarabia, Bukovina, and Transylvania, which it was forced to relinquish to the Axis Powers in 1940. Shortly afterwards Carol II abdicated in favour of his son Michael and Antonescu came to power. He gave Romanian military support to Germany until Soviet forces entered the country and Antonescu's government was overthrown (1944). After World War II a communist-dominated coalition was established (1945) and in 1947 Michael abdicated. Elections in 1948 resulted in a clear communist victory. From the 1960s Romania grew increasingly independent of the Soviet Union, condemning the invasions of Czechoslovakia and Afghanistan and resisting the Soviet policy of glasnost in the 1980s. Romania enjoys good relations with the West. President: Nicolae Ceauşescu. Prime minister: Constantin Dascalescu (1923–   ). Official language: Romanian. Official currency: leu of 100 bani. Area: 237 500 sq km (91 699 sq mi). Population (1983 est): 22 649 000. Capital: Bucharest. Main port: Constanţa.

Romanian A *Romance language, the main form of which is spoken in Romania and is known as Daco-Romanian. Other forms are Aromanian or Macedo-Romanian (Greece, Yugoslavia, Albania, and Bulgaria); Megleno-Romanian (N Greece); and Istro-Romanian (Istrian peninsula). Geographical proximity to the Slavonic languages has influenced Romanian's grammar, vocabulary, and phonology.

Roman law The body of laws compiled by the Romans, which forms the basis of the *civil law of many modern countries throughout the world. Although Roman law dates from the time of the kings (from c. 753 BC), the *Twelve Tables (450 BC) is regarded as the first major codification. Before about 150 BC these laws were elaborated as the *jus civile* (civil law), i.e. the law applicable exclusively to Roman citizens. With increasing territories, commercial interests, and foreign treaties, another system, the *jus gentium* (law of nations), was also applied by Roman courts. This system of international law derived from the philosophical concept of natural law (i.e. a law common to all men and to nature) and was used in cases involving provincial Roman subjects of different states and in suits between a foreigner or provincial and a Roman citizen. It gradually influenced the *jus civile*, and the two systems came to have many identical features. As Roman law developed, by judicial interpretation, by edict, and by legislation, there arose a number of

anomalies, until the Byzantine emperor *Justinian I sponsored legal reforms embodied in the definitive codification of Roman law, the *Corpus Juris Civilis* (Body of Civil Law) or Justinian Code, published between 529 and 565 AD. This consisted of four parts: (1) the *Codex Constitutionum*, a chronological collection of the ordinances (*constitutiones*) of the emperors, with all contradictions, anomalies, etc., eliminated; (2) the *Digest*, a collection of statements by jurists on points of law; (3) the *Institutes*, a textbook for law students explaining legal institutions; and (4) the *Novellae* or *Novels*, the new ordinances issued by Justinian after the publication of the *Codex*. Roman law, with local variations, continued in use throughout medieval Europe and after the fall of the Byzantine Empire. The impetus for its spread outside Europe in the 19th century was given by the most influential modern codification based on it, the *Code Napoléon*.

Roman literature. *See* Latin literature.

Roman numerals The system of numbers used by the Romans, based on letters of the alphabet: I = 1, V = 5, X = 10, L = 50, C = 100, D = 500, and M = 1000. Intermediate numbers are given by the sum of a larger number and the smaller number that follows it (e.g. VI = 6) or the difference between a larger number and the smaller number that precedes it (IV = 4). By the 9th century the system had been replaced by *Arabic numerals.

Romanovs The last ruling dynasty of Russia (1613–1917), noted for their absolutism and for transforming Russia into a large empire. The first Romanov tsar was *Michael, whose election ended the *Time of Troubles. His most famous successors were *Peter the Great, *Catherine the Great, *Alexander I, *Nicholas I, and *Alexander II. Romanov rule ended with the abdication of *Nicholas II (March, 1917).

Roman religion The polytheistic religion of ancient Rome. The earliest cults worshipped local Italian deities of the fields, woods, springs, and hearth. As Rome grew to statehood its religion changed character: the gods of its Sabine and Etruscan neighbours (e.g. Quirinus and *Juno) were absorbed and *Mars, originally an agrarian spirit, became god of war. The state religion with its various priestly colleges (*see also* augury) centred on the temple of *Jupiter on the Capitoline hill (Rome). The influence of *Greek religion caused the identification of many Roman deities with Greek counterparts (Jupiter with *Zeus, *Vesta with *Hestia, etc.). In 204 BC the orgiastic cult of *Cybele reached Rome, followed soon afterwards by that of *Dionysus. The eastward expansion of Roman power brought contact with the esoteric cult of *Isis (*see also* mysteries) and *Mithraism. Emperor worship became an important part of official religion and a touchstone of loyalty. In the fringes of the Empire the Roman gods were often assimilated with local deities (e.g. at *Bath Minerva was equated with the resident goddess Sulis and worshipped as Sulis Minerva). Official toleration of Christianity under *Constantine from 313 AD occasioned the gradual extinction of the old religion, despite attempts at revival (360–63) by *Julian the Apostate. *See also* ancestor worship; Feriae.

Roman Republic (510–27 BC) The period of ancient Roman history between the expulsion of *Tarquin the Proud and the proclamation as *Augustus of the first Roman emperor. Republican government comprised two chief magistrates (later *consuls) elected annually, an increasing number of subordinate magistrates, the *Senate, and popular assemblies (*see* comitia). Power lay in the hands of the *patricians until the *plebeians, after two centuries of struggle, achieved access to all state offices.

Roman dominance over the rest of Italy was achieved by the early 3rd century: the tribes of Latium (the Latin League) were reduced by 338, victory against the Samnites of the S Apennines was attained by 290, and the Greek settlements in the S were conquered by 275. By the mid-2nd century

ROME   *The Colosseum, begun in c. 70 AD by the emperor Vespasian; it could seat 47 000 people in its heyday.*

Cisalpine *Gaul had been subdued and the *Punic Wars with Carthage brought control of the Mediterranean (146) and Rome's first overseas *provinces (Sicily, Sardinia, Spain, Africa). Concomitantly, dominance over Greece was achieved with the subjection of Illyria, Macedonia (*see* Macedonian Wars), and the Achaean League (*see* Achaea) and, following the acquisition of Pergamum in 133, control of much of Asia Minor. In the mid-1st century *Caesar completed the conquest of Transalpine Gaul.

The conquest of Italy was accompanied by the gradual extension of Roman citizenship (*see* civitas) and the construction of a network of roads, which brought Italy a degree of unity. The emergence, however, of a landowning elite who built up vast estates (*latifundia*) at the expense of small farmers resulted in serious unemployment. The attempts in the second half of the 2nd century of the *Gracchus brothers at agricultural reform aggravated the conflict between the Optimates (the aristocratic party) and the Populares (the popular party). The Republic was further undermined by provincial unrest, which, together with the military ineptness of the Senate in the late 2nd century, brought a series of ambitious army commanders to the fore.

The first of these, *Marius, emerged as a champion of the people but the popular party lost a bloody power struggle to the aristocrat, *Sulla, whose dictatorship (83–79) was marked by legislation to strengthen the Senate. This was revoked in 70 by *Pompey and *Crassus, who ten years later formed the so-called first *Triumvirate with Caesar. The death of Crassus (53) and Pompey's intrigues with Caesar's senatorial enemies brought civil war. Caesar's victory and subsequent short-lived dictatorship rang the knell of the Roman Republic, which was finally destroyed by Octavian's defeat of *Mark Antony and his assumption of absolute power as Augustus. *See also* Roman Empire.

Romans, Epistle of Paul to the   A New Testament book written from Corinth by Paul in about 57 AD to the Christians at Rome. The first 11 chapters are a systematic explanation of Christian doctrine and explain the nature of salvation. The remaining chapters explain how believers are expected to live in the Church and in society.

Romansch   A *Romance language belonging to the Rhaetian group, spoken in N Italy and in the Rhine Valley in Switzerland. It is one of Switzerland's four national languages.

Romanticism   A fundamental development in western art, literature, music, and their related fields of theory in the late 18th and early 19th centuries. Romanticism constituted a reaction against the unquestioned authority of reason and tradition (*see* classicism) and an affirmation of faith in man's innate powers of creativity. Its various manifestations included a passionate concern with the relationship between man and his natural environment and a new interest in the primitive and the irrational. In literature, English Romanticism is usually dated from the publication of *Lyrical Ballads* by Wordsworth and Coleridge in 1798 and is associated with the poetry of Keats, Shelley, and Byron and the novels of Walter Scott. Major German Romantic writers included the Schlegel brothers, Goethe, and Schiller, and in France, where the theories of Rousseau had anticipated many aspects of the movement, the important writers included Chateaubriand and Victor Hugo. The influence of Romanticism is seen in the works of such painters as Turner and Delacroix, and on musical composition from the time of Beethoven until the early 20th century.

Romany   The language spoken by *gipsies. It is related to *Sanskrit and the *Indo-Aryan languages of N India but diverged from these about 1000 AD, when the gipsies began their nomadic way of life. Romany has been greatly influenced in vocabulary by the languages spoken in regions the gipsies have passed through, resulting in many different dialects. There is little written literature in Romany but a rich oral tradition.

Rome   (Italian name: Roma)   41 53N 12 33E   The capital of Italy, on the River Tiber. It is mainly an administrative and cultural centre and, with the *Vatican City within its boundaries, the focal point of the Roman Catholic Church. Known as the Eternal City, it is one of the world's greatest historical and art centres; tourism is an important source of revenue. The Italian film industry is centred here. Relics of classical times include the Forum, the *Pantheon, and the *Colosseum. There are many ancient churches the origins of which go back to the early Christian era; with the exception of Sta Maria Maggiore, the patriarchal basilicas (St Peter's in the Vatican City, S Giovanni in Laterano, S Lorenzo Fuori le Mura, and S Paolo Fuori le Muri) were built on the sites of martyrs' tombs. The Renaissance produced not only many outstanding buildings, such as St Peter's Basilica, but the paintings and sculpture of such artists as Michelangelo and Raphael. The 17th and 18th centuries brought more fine architecture, with squares, fountains, and façades designed by Borromini, Bernini, and others. The university was founded in 1303. *History*: according to legend Rome was founded on the Palatine Hill in 753 BC by Romulus, its first king, later spreading to six other hills E of the Tiber: the Aventine, Capitoline, Quirinal, Viminal, Esquiline, and Caelian. Seven kings were followed by the *Roman Republic, and the *Roman Empire was founded in the 1st century BC. As the Empire declined in the 5th century AD Rome, no longer its centre, was sacked by Germanic tribes. From the time of Pope Gregory in the 6th century it regained importance, this time as an ecclesiastical power. In 800 Charlemagne was crowned emperor here. In succeeding centuries, it was sacked by Arabs and by Normans, and in the middle ages there was a continuing struggle between popes and emperors. It remained under papal control until 1871, when it became capital of the newly unified Italy. The popes however refused formally to relinquish their temporal power until the Lateran Treaty of 1929, when their jurisdiction was confined to the Vatican City. Mussolini's March on Rome in 1922 marked the beginning of his fascist rule; the city was occupied by the Allies in World War II. Population (1980 est): 2 916 414.

Rome, Treaties of (1957)   Two treaties signed in Rome by the representatives of Belgium, France, Italy, Luxembourg, the Netherlands, and West Germany, which led to the establishment of the *European Economic Community and the *European Atomic Energy Community.

Rommel, Erwin   (1891–1944)   German general, known as

the Desert Fox because of his victories in N Africa in World War II. In 1940 he became commander of the Seventh Panzer Division and, in 1941, of the Afrika Corps. In N Africa he was hailed as a liberator by the Arabs and gained the respect of the enemy but in 1943, after his defeat at Alamein (1942), he was recalled and became commander of the Channel defence. His involvement with the conspirators who attempted to assassinate Hitler in 1944 (*see* Stauffenberg, Claus, Graf von) led to his suicide, under pressure from Hitler, who wished to avoid a treason trial implicating his most popular general.

Romney, George (1734-1802) British portrait painter, born in Lancashire. Although his training was limited, he attracted a fashionable clientele and rivalled Reynolds when he moved to London in 1762. He is best known for his numerous portraits of Lady Emma *Hamilton, whom he met in 1781.

Romney Marsh An area of reclaimed marshland in SE England, on the Strait of Dover between Hythe in Kent and Winchelsea in East Sussex. Since reclamation was completed in the 17th century, sheep grazing has remained its chief use.

Romulus and Remus The legendary founders of Rome, the sons of Mars and Rhea Silvia, daughter of Numitor, King of Alba Longa. Amulius, who had deposed Numitor, threw the twin babies into the Tiber. They were washed ashore and suckled by a she-wolf and later adopted by a shepherd. They eventually founded Rome at the place where they had been rescued. Romulus built the city on the Palatine hill and became the first king.

Romulus Augustulus (b. ?461) The last Roman emperor in the West (475-76 AD). He was deposed by the German ruler *Odoacer.

Roncesvalles (French name: Roncevaux) 43 01N 1 19W A village in N Spain, in the Pyrenees. Nearby is the Pass of Roncesvalles, where Charlemagne's rearguard, under Roland, was ambushed by the Saracens (778 AD) on his retreat to France.

rondeau A short lyrical poem using an intricate verse form developed in 14th- and 15th-century France. Intended for singing, rondeaux were generally 10 or 13 lines long, used only two rhymes, and had an elaborate repetitive pattern of words and lines. Their subjects were the standard themes of the *courtly love tradition. The rondeau's virtuosity reached a peak in *Dufay's compositions.

rondo A musical form in which a recurring theme alternates with contrasting episodes. In its simplest form it consists of the pattern ABACADA, A being the rondo theme and B, C, and D the episodes. In this form it was much used in the 18th century; Mozart, Beethoven, Schubert, and others developed the rondo by combining it with *sonata form.

ronin A samurai (warrior) left masterless by the total defeat of his lord. In the 1860s, however, many patriotic samurai deliberately became *ronin* in order to engage in extremist political activities.

Ronsard, Pierre de (1524-85) French poet. He turned to literature after deafness interrupted his career at court and became a leading member of the *Pléiade. His *Odes* (1550) and *Amours* (1552) gained him the patronage of Charles IX. His later works include *La Françiade* (1572), an unfinished national epic, and *Sonnets pour Hélène* (1578), which contains his best-known love poems.

Roodepoort 26 10S 27 53E A town in South Africa, in the S Transvaal. A W suburb of Johannesburg, it has developed manufacturing industries and is an important residential area. Population (1980 est): 165 315.

rood screen (*or* chancel screen) The screen of wood or stone, often elaborately carved, that separated the chancel from the nave in a medieval church. The name derives from the cross (Old English: rood) that surmounted the screen.

rook A large blue-black Eurasian crow, *Corvus frugilegus*,

about 45 cm long and having a narrow grey bill with pale patches of bare skin at its base. It is highly gregarious, breeding in large colonies and forming well-developed communities. Rooks feed on earthworms, larvae, carrion, and grain, sometimes damaging newly sown crops.

Roon, Albrecht, Graf von (1803-79) Prussian general, who as war minister (1859-73) effected important military reforms. He introduced compulsory three-year service in the face of fierce opposition but his policies, which were supported by Bismarck, were vindicated by Prussian victory in the Austro-Prussian War (1866) and in the Franco-Prussian War (1870-71).

FRANKLIN D. ROOSEVELT

Roosevelt, Franklin D(elano) (1882-1945) US statesman; Democratic president (1933-45). He was paralysed from the waist down by poliomyelitis in 1921 but despite this disability became the only US president to be re-elected three times. He helped US recovery from the Depression with the *New Deal relief programmes and legislation to stimulate employment, industry, and agriculture. After the outbreak of World War II he introduced lend-lease aid to the Allies and, after the Japanese bombing of Pearl Harbor (1941), took the USA into the war. He attended the *Tehran and *Yalta Conferences with Churchill and Stalin but died in office before the conclusion of the war. His wife (from 1905) **Eleanor Roosevelt** (1884-1962) was the niece of Theodore *Roosevelt, to whom Franklin was distantly related. She supported minority groups and educational causes as US delegate to the UN (1945-53, 1961) and as chairman of the UN Commission on Human Rights (1946-51).

Roosevelt, Theodore (1858-1919) US statesman; Republican president (1901-09). A rancher and big-game hunter, he led the Rough Riders (1st Volunteer Cavalry) in the 1898 war with Cuba. As president he introduced his *Square Deal programme for social reform. Roosevelt's foreign policy was to "speak softly and carry a big stick." He established US control over the building of the Panama Canal and made the USA a policing power in the Americas. Roosevelt ran again for president in 1912 but lost to Woodrow *Wilson.

root (algebra) **1.** One of the equal factors of a number. The square root is one of two equal factors; for example $\sqrt{9} = \pm 3$; the rth root of a number n is the number that when raised to the rth power gives n. **2.** The solution of an equation, i.e. the values of the variable that will satisfy the equation. *See* quadratic equation.

root (botany) The part of a □plant that provides anchorage and enables the uptake of water and nutrients from the soil. Roots contain vascular (conducting) tissue and just behind the tip is an area of root hairs, which increase the surface area for absorption. Some plants, such as the dandelion, have one main root with smaller branches—a tap root system; others, such as grasses, have a mass of similar-sized roots—a fibrous root system. Roots can act as food-storage organs, as in the carrot and turnip (tap roots); fibrous roots that become swollen with food are called tuberous roots, such as those of dahlias. Some roots grow in unusual positions and act as supports.

Root, Elihu (1845–1937) US lawyer and statesman. A lawyer from 1867, he later became secretary of war (1899–1904) and secretary of state (1905–09). His achievements included reforms in the organization of the army, the improvement of relations with Latin America, and the Root-Takahira agreement with Japan (1908), committing the two nations to maintaining the status quo in the Pacific. A member of the Hague Tribunal (the Permanent Court of Arbitration), he received the Nobel Peace Prize in 1912.

root-mean-square value (*or* rms value) The square root of the arithmetic *average of the squares of a set of numbers; for example the rms of 2, 4, 5, 6 is $[(2^2 + 4^2 + 5^2 + 6^2)/4]^{1/2} = 4\frac{1}{2}$. The rms value is useful in continuous quantities, such as alternating electric current, in which the heating effect is proportional to the current squared. The rms value is therefore directly comparable to direct current.

ropes and cables Flexible lengths of material made from strands of natural *fibres (e.g. hemp, jute, sisal, manila), synthetic fibres (e.g. nylon, polypropylene), or wire. In natural-fibre ropes, the material is spun into yarn and then formed into strands, which are twisted round each other in an opposite direction to that of the yarn. For many purposes nylon and polypropylene ropes, made by a similar method, are replacing natural-fibre ropes. A hawser consists of three strands, a cable consists of three hawsers wound together, and a shroud-laid rope has a central strand with three or four strands wound round it. Wire ropes are made by a similar process: high-tensile steel wires are twisted together to form strands, which are then wound round each other to form the rope. In some cases the wires are preformed into helical strands to reduce internal stresses and are wound round a hemp core, which provides lubrication and flexibility.

Roque de los Muchachos Observatory An international observatory on the island of La Palma in the Canaries at an altitude of 2400 m, set up in the 1980s by Britain, Denmark, Spain (who owns the site), and Sweden. UK telescopes (shared with the Netherlands and Republic of Ireland) include the new 4.2 m (165 in) William Herschel Telescope and the refurbished 2.5 m (100 in) Isaac Newton Telescope moved from the *Royal Greenwich Observatory.

Roquefort 43 59N 2 58E A village in SE France, in the Aveyron department. Roquefort is famous for the ewes' milk cheese named after it.

Roraima, Mount 5 14N 60 44W A mountain in South America, at the junction of the borders of Brazil, Guyana, and Venezuela. It is the highest peak in the Pacaraima Mountains. Height: 2810 m (9219 ft).

rorqual A small-headed fast-moving whalebone *whale of the family *Balaenopteridae* (6 species). The common rorqual (*Balaenoptera physalus*), also called fin whale or razorback, grows up to 25 m long; it has a dark back, shading to white underneath, and a small dorsal fin that shows when it is blowing. Common rorquals are found in all oceans. *See also* blue whale; humpback whale; sei whale.

Rorschach test A psychological test intended to measure aspects of personality. Devised by the Swiss psychiatrist Hermann Rorschach (1884–1922), it consists of ten inkblots in complex shapes. The way in which the subject describes these pictures suggests his character. *See also* projection.

Rory O'Connor (*or* Roderic; ?1116–98) King of Connaught and last High King of Ireland. In 1171 he marched against

*Dermot MacMurrough but was defeated at Dublin. Later he was forced to submit to Henry II of England.

Rosa, Salvator (1615–73) Italian painter and etcher. Working in Naples, Rome (where he finally settled in 1649), and Florence (1640–49), he was also known as a poet, comic actor, and musician. His lasting reputation, however, rests on his wild and romantic landscapes, which were much admired in 18th-century England.

Rosaceae A cosmopolitan family of trees, shrubs, and herbs (about 2000 species). Many are of economic value for their fruits, for example strawberries, raspberries, cherries, apricots, apples, and plums. Others are cultivated as ornamentals, including *Spiraea, Potentilla,* and roses.

Rosario 33 00S 60 40W The second largest city in Argentina, on the Río Paraná. It is an industrial and commercial centre and the terminus of the pampas railways. Industries include sugar refining and food processing. Its university was founded in 1968. Population (1980): 935 471.

rosary In the Roman Catholic Church, a religious devotion consisting of repeated prayers, particularly associated with the cult of the Virgin Mary. The recitation of a rosary is subdivided into 15 decades, each decade comprising an opening Paternoster, 10 Ave Marias, and a concluding Gloria. A subject of meditation, or Mystery, relating to the life of Christ or the Virgin is attached to each decade. By association the string of beads used to count the prayers is also called a rosary. The feast day established in 1716 in honour of the rosary is observed on 7 Oct.

Roscelin (died c. 1125) French scholastic philosopher (*see* scholasticism). He was an early proponent of *nominalism, which he may even have originated. His philosophical belief that a being could have no parts led him to the Tritheist heresy, a deviant form of the doctrine of the Trinity. He was opposed by his famous pupil *Abelard.

Roscius, Quintus (d. 62 BC) Roman comic actor. He was praised by Cicero, and his name has been applied as an epithet to many outstanding actors of the modern theatre.

Roscommon (Irish name: Ros Comáin) A county in the N Republic of Ireland, in Connacht. It has many lakes and extensive bogs. Agriculture, especially cattle rearing, is the chief occupation. Area: 2463 sq km (951 sq mi). Population (1981): 54 543. County town: Roscommon.

rose A prickly shrub or climber of the genus *Rosa* (200–250 species), native to N temperate regions but widely cultivated. The leaves are compound, with leaflets arranged in pairs. The five-petalled flowers are usually white, yellow, pink, or red and the fruits are red, yellow, or black hips, rich in vitamin C, containing many seeds. Wild species include *dog rose and *sweet briar. Family: *Rosaceae.*

Modern hybrid roses—usually with double flowers—can be divided into several groups, the most important bedding varieties being the hybrid teas and floribundas. The former, derived from the tea rose (*R. odorata*), produce large shapely often fragrant blooms of good colour. The floribundas bear clusters of flowers and are usually grown for their colour effect rather than for the beauty of individual blooms. The climbers and ramblers are suitable for covering walls, fences, etc. Climbers include climbing forms of hybrid teas and floribundas as well as climbing species (such as *R. banksiae*). Ramblers include the wichuraiana group of hybrids.

Rosebery, Archibald Philip Primrose, 5th Earl of (1847–1929) British statesman; Liberal prime minister (1894–95). He was foreign secretary (1886, 1892–94) under Gladstone, whom he replaced. He resigned the Liberal leadership in 1896 and became well known as a biographer of British statesmen, and as a racehorse owner.

rosella A brightly coloured *parakeet belonging to a genus (*Platycercus*; 7 species) occurring in Australia and New Zealand. 18 cm long, rosellas have a long broad tail, which is usually blue or green edged with white, black shoulders, and distinctive face and throat markings. They are largely ground-dwelling.

roselle An annual or perennial fibrous plant, *Hibiscus sabdariffa*, cultivated in tropical regions for its stem fibres, which are used for sacking and twine, and for its edible stalks, leaves, and flower parts. It grows up to 5 m high and bears solitary white or yellow flowers in the leaf axils. Family: *Malvaceae*.

rosemary An evergreen shrub, *Rosmarinus officinalis*, native to the Mediterranean region and W Asia. Up to 2 m high, it has bluish leaves and small needle-like aromatic leaves, up to 5 cm long. It is widely cultivated for its oil, which is distilled from the flowering tops and used in toiletries; for its leaves, used as a culinary herb; and for ornament. Family: *Labiatae*.

Rosenberg, Julius (1918-53) US spy, who with his wife **Ethel Rosenberg** (1915-53) was executed for espionage activities. They gained information about nuclear weapons from Ethel's brother and passed it on via a courier to the Russian vice consul in New York. The severity of their sentences has since been critized. Other members of the espionage ring were imprisoned.

rose of Jericho A perennial herb, *Anastatica hierochuntica*, also called resurrection plant, native to W Asia. During the dry season the leaves are shed and the branches curve inwards so that the whole plant forms a wickerwork-like ball that is blown by the wind. When moistened, the plant regains its shape and produces tiny white flowers. Family: *Cruciferae*.

rose of Sharon. *See* Hibiscus; St John's wort.

Roses, Wars of the (1455-85) The civil wars between the Houses of *Lancaster (the red rose) and *York (the white rose) for possession of the English Crown, which both claimed by right of descent from Edward III. The Lancastrian Henry VI's incompetent rule resulted in factional struggles led by the Lancastrian Beauforts and Richard Plantagenet, Duke of *York, and the Earl of *Warwick (the Kingmaker). Open warfare broke out in 1455. York was killed in 1460 and his son seized the Crown in 1461, becoming Edward IV, and crushed the Lancastrians. In

1470-71 Henry VI was briefly restored by disaffected Yorkists but Edward returned after his victory at *Tewkesbury and ruled until 1483. He was succeeded by his brother Richard III, whose reign ended with his defeat by Henry (VII) at Bosworth (1485). The remaining Yorkists were finally overcome at Stoke in 1487.

Rosetta Stone An inscribed stone slab discovered (1799) at Rosetta (Arabic name: Rashid), near Alexandria (Egypt). It carries a decree (196 BC) of Ptolemy V Epiphanes (reigned 205-180) in two languages and three scripts: Egyptian *hieroglyphic and *demotic, and Greek. The repetition of Ptolemy's name in the different scripts gave Thomas *Young the clue to deciphering hieroglyphs; his work was continued by *Champollion.

Rosewall, Ken(neth Ronald) (1934-) Australian tennis player, who in a playing career of over 20 years won every major title except that of the Wimbledon singles. He was barred from Wimbledon as a professional from 1956 to 1968.

rose window A decorative circular window in a medieval church. Rose windows, which were probably inspired by oriental models, had radiating tracery, usually glazed with *stained glass, and reached their apogee in 13th-century French *gothic architecture, although examples are known throughout W Europe.

rosewood An attractive hardwood, usually dark reddish and often rose-scented, derived from several tropical evergreen trees of the genus *Dalbergia* (family *Leguminosae*). These include Brazilian rosewood, or blackwood (*D. nigra*), used for veneers and cabinetwork; Honduras rosewood (*D. stevensoni*), used for musical instruments; and East Indian rosewood (*D. latifolia*), used mostly for small articles. Decreasing supplies have restricted their use.

Rosh Hashana (Hebrew: head of the year) The Jewish New Year festival, celebrated in Sept or Oct. Of biblical origin, it is regarded as a time of penitence and preparation for *Yom Kippur. A ram's horn (*shofar*) is blown in the synagogue.

Rosicrucianism An esoteric movement for spiritual renewal that originated in Protestant Germany in the early 17th century and spread across Europe. Its manifesto traces

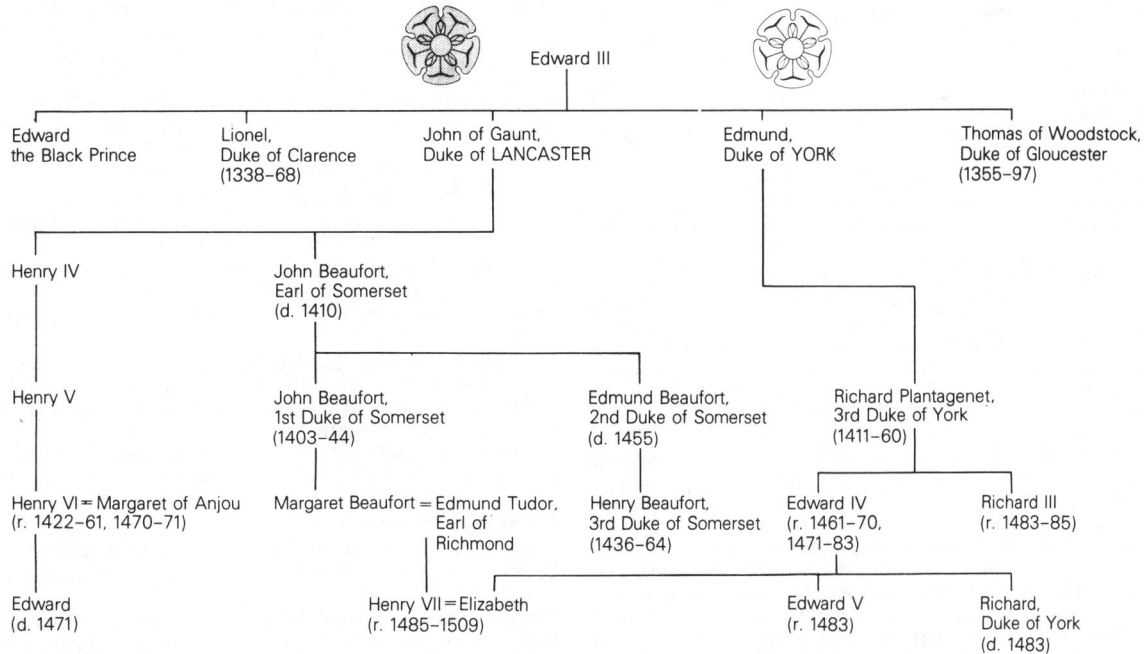

WARS OF THE ROSES   *The rival Houses of Lancaster and York.*

its source to a fictitious brotherhood founded by a certain Christian Rosenkreuz in 1484. The philosophical programme propounded by its mainly anonymous adherents was a blend of theosophical and occult traditions, including *alchemy, *Hermeticism, and *Neoplatonism. *See also* freemasonry.

rosin (*or* colophony) A yellowish *resin obtained as a residue from the distillation of *turpentine. It is used in varnishes, soaps, soldering *flux, and to rub on violin bows.

Roskilde 55 39N 12 07E A seaport in Denmark, in Sjælland. It was the Danish capital until 1443, and most of Denmark's kings are buried in the 13th-century cathedral. A university was established in 1970. Its industries include tanning, meat canning, distilling and agricultural engineering. Population (1985): 48 756.

Ross, Sir James Clark (1800-62) British explorer. He accompanied (1819-27) Sir William *Parry on his Arctic expeditions and (1829-31) his uncle Sir John Ross (1777-1856), discovering the North Magnetic Pole (1831). He later (1839-43) explored the Antarctic, discovering the sea named after him.

Ross, Sir Ronald (1857-1932) British bacteriologist, who confirmed the theory of Sir Patrick Manson (1844-1922) that mosquitoes transmit malaria. While working in India, Ross discovered malaria parasites in the guts of *Anopheles* mosquitoes. In his honour was founded the Ross Institute and Hospital for Tropical Diseases (1926), incorporated into the London School of Hygiene and Tropical Medicine in 1933. Ross received the 1902 Nobel Prize.

Ross and Cromarty A former county of N Scotland. Under local government reorganization in 1975 its boundaries were adjusted to form a district of the same name, in the Highland Region.

Ross Dependency An area in Antarctica claimed by New Zealand (since 1923), lying between longitudes 160°E and 150°W and including the Ross Sea and islands S of latitude 60°S. Area: about 414 400 sq km (160 000 sq mi).

Rosse, William Parsons, 3rd Earl of ˙ (1800-67) Irish MP (1821-34) and astronomer, who constructed a large 72-inch reflecting telescope. In 1848 he used it to study one of the blurred objects listed by *Messier and named it the Crab Nebula, because of its shape. He also discovered the first spiral galaxy in 1845.

Rossellini, Roberto (1906-77) Italian film director. The neorealist style of *Rome, Open City* (1945), which included documentary film shot during the German occupation of Rome, greatly influenced postwar Italian cinema. His other films include *Paisà* (1946), also concerned with wartime Italy, *L'Amore* (1948), and *India* (1958), a documentary film. He subsequently worked mostly in television and the theatre.

Rossetti, Dante Gabriel (Gabriel Charles Dante R.; 1828-82) British painter and poet. He was born in London, the son of a Neapolitan royalist exile who had fled to England in 1824 and who eventually became professor of Italian at King's College, London University. Rebelling against the conventional instruction he was given at the Royal Academy, in 1848 Rossetti joined with John Everett *Millais, William Holman *Hunt, and other artists to found the *Pre-Raphaelite Brotherhood. He founded the shortlived Pre-Raphaelite journal *The Germ* (1850-51), in which he began publishing his own verse. He later published several volumes of poetry and translations, including *Poems* (1870) and *Ballads and Sonnets* (1881). During his final years he lived virtually as a recluse, suffering from ill health. His sister **Christina Georgina Rossetti** (1830-74), a poet, was also born in London. Deeply influenced by the *Oxford Movement, she was a prolific writer much of whose work reflects her devotion to the Anglican faith. *Goblin Market and Other Poems* (1862), her first published volume, gave

literary expression to Pre-Raphaelite ideals and contains perhaps her best work.

Rossini, Gioacchino Antonio (1792-1868) Italian composer. His father was a trumpeter and his mother an opera singer. He studied at Bologna and wrote 36 highly successful operas, including *Tancredi* (1813), *The Italian Girl in Algiers* (1813), *The Barber of Seville* (1816), *La Cenerentola* (*Cinderella*) and *The Thieving Magpie* (both 1817), and *William Tell* (1829). At the age of 37 he gave up serious composition, although he did write a light-hearted *Petite Messe solennelle* (1863) and a number of little pieces, collectively entitled "Sins of My Old Age." He invented a number of recipes, including Tournedos Rossini.

Ross Island 77 40S 168 00E A volcanic island in the W Ross Sea, at the edge of the **Ross Ice Shelf**, a vast mass of permanent ice. Mount Erebus is situated here.

Ross Sea A large inlet of the S Pacific Ocean, in the Antarctic continent between Victoria Land and Byrd Land. Its S section is covered by the Ross Ice Shelf.

Rostand, Edmond (1868-1918) French dramatist. He gained international success with *Cyrano de Bergerac* (1897), a romantic comedy about a nobleman with an oversize nose. Sarah Bernhardt acted in many of his plays, notably *L'Aiglon* (1900).

Rostock 54 03N 12 07E A city and Baltic port in N East Germany, on the River Warnow. Once an important Hanseatic port, its fine medieval buildings have been restored following damage during World War II. Its university was established in 1419. The main industries are shipbuilding and fisheries. Population (1980 est): 230 280.

Rostov-na-Donu 47 15N 39 45E A port in the S Soviet Union, in the RSFSR on the River Don near its mouth on the Sea of Azov. It produces agricultural machinery and has ship-repairing, food-processing, and textile industries. Its importance owes much to its position on the route from the W to the Caucasus. Population (1981 est): 957 000.

Rostropovich, Mstislav (1927–) Soviet cellist. He became a US citizen after losing Soviet citizenship in 1978. He is also a conductor, notably of opera, and as a pianist accompanies his wife the soprano Galina Vishnevskaya (1926–). Prokofiev, Britten, and Shostakovich wrote works for him.

Roth, Philip (1933–) US novelist. Middle-class Jewish themes predominated in his early works including *Goodbye, Columbus* (1959) and *Portnoy's Complaint* (1969). In later novels, such as *The Great American Novel* (1973), *My Life as a Man* (1974), *The Ghost Writer* (1979), *Zukerman Unbound* (1981), *The Anatomy Lesson* (1983), and *The Prague Qrgy*, (1985), the targets of his satire are more various.

Rothenburg ob der Tauber 49 23N 10 13E A town in S West Germany, in Bavaria. It is famed for its medieval town centre and town walls. Population (1983 est): 11 625.

Rotherham 53 26N 1 20W A town in N England, in South Yorkshire on the River Don. Rotherham has iron and steel, brassware, machinery, and glass industries and coal is mined locally. Population (1981): 81 988.

Rothermere, Harold Sydney Harmsworth, 1st Viscount (1868-1940) British newspaper proprietor. He partnered his brother (*see* Northcliffe, 1st Viscount) in founding several newspapers, including the *Daily Mirror* (1903), and concentrated on the financial and advertising aspect of their business, Amalgamated Press. In World War I he was air minister (1917-18).

Rothesay 55 51N 5 03W A town in W Scotland, in Strathclyde Region on the Isle of Bute. It is a resort and fishing town, with a ruined castle (founded 11th century). Population (1981): 5408.

Rothko, Mark (Marcus Rothkovitch; 1903-70) Russian-born painter, who emigrated to the USA in 1913. In the late 1940s, with Barnett Newman (1905-70) and Clifford Still (1904–), he pioneered colour-field painting (an abstract style using only colour) on mural-size canvases covered with horizontal bands of hazy colour.

Rothschild, Mayer Amschel (1744-1812) German merchant and banker, whose business in Frankfurt prospered during the Napoleonic Wars, making loans to the various combatants and trading in high-demand goods such as arms, wheat, and cotton. He was succeeded in Frankfurt by his son **Amschel Mayer Rothschild** (1773-1855). Four other sons established branches of the firm abroad. **Salomon Mayer Rothschild** (1774-1855) went to Vienna, **Nathan Mayer Rothschild** (1777-1836), to London, **Karl Mayer Rothschild** (1788-1855), to Naples, and **James Rothschild** (Jakob R.; 1792-1868), to Paris. In London, Nathan's son **Lionel Nathan Rothschild** (1808-79) was an MP (1858-68, 1869-79) as was (1865-85) his grandson **Nathan Mayer, 1st Baron Rothschild** (1840-1915). **Nathaniel Mayer Victor, 3rd Baron Rothschild** (1910-) succeeded his uncle in 1937. A zoologist, he was research director of the Shell Oil Co (1963-70) before becoming director general of the Central Policy Review Staff (known as the think tank) from 1970 to 1974.

rotifer A tiny invertebrate animal belonging to the phylum *Rotifera* (about 2000 species), also called wheel animalcule, found mainly in fresh water. Rotifers vary in shape from spherical to wormlike and range between 0.1 and 0.5 mm in length. Each has a ring of cilia (corona) around the mouth, beating in a wheel-like manner, for wafting food particles into the mouth and providing a means of locomotion in active species.

Rotorua 38 07S 176 17E A spa city in New Zealand, in N North Island on SW Lake Rotorua. A Maori centre, situated within a volcanic area with hot springs, boiling mudpools, and geysers, it has been developed as a health resort, owned and managed by the government. Population (1983): 50 000.

rotten borough A British borough constituency that, before the *Reform Act of 1832, continued to be represented in parliament although it had become depopulated. *See also* pocket borough.

Rotterdam 51 55N 4 29E The chief port and second largest city in the Netherlands, in South Holland province on the New Meuse River. It became important during the 19th century, mainly with the opening of the 35 km (12 mi) long Nieuwe Waterweg (New Waterway) in 1872 linking it to the North Sea. During World War II the city centre was destroyed; this has since been rebuilt with an underground railway. Its notable buildings include the restored Groote Kerk (Great Church). The Erasmus University of Rotterdam was founded in 1973. The largest Atlantic port in Europe, Rotterdam handles considerable export trade from West Germany, including Ruhr coal. Its dockyards extend W along the Nieuwe Waterweg and include Europoort, on the North Sea. Begun in 1958, Europoort's huge facilities handle chiefly oil importing and refining. Rotterdam's industries include oil refining, shipbuilding, brewing, distilling, and engineering. Population (1981 est): 576 330.

Rottweiler A breed of working dog developed originally in Rottweil, Germany, as a guard dog and cattle drovers' dog. It is stockily built, having a broad round body, a strong neck, and a large head with a deep muzzle. The coarse short coat is black with tan markings. Height: 63-68 cm (dogs); 58-63 cm (bitches).

Rouault, Georges (Henri) (1871-1958) French artist. A major 20th-century religious artist, he was a largely independent figure, except for a brief and loose association with *fauvism. His favourite themes were clowns (sometimes modelled on himself or Christ) and prostitutes, expressing his sympathy with social outcasts. He was influenced by his early training as a stained-glass maker and was the favourite pupil of Gustave *Moreau. Until 1918 he worked chiefly in gouache and watercolour, using rich dark colours and heavy

outlines. As a graphic artist his main achievement was his series of etchings (1916-27), entitled *Miserere* and *Guerre*.

Roubaix 50 42N 3 10E A town in N France, in the Nord department on the Roubaix Canal. Famous for its cloth since the 15th century, it is (together with Tourcoing) the centre of the country's woollen industry. Population (1982): 101 886.

Roubiliac, Louis François (*or* L. F. Roubiliac; 1695-1762) French sculptor. He fled (1727) for religious reasons to England, where his statue of Handel, erected (1738) in Vauxhall Gardens, London, secured his reputation. His portrait bust of Pope and full-length statue of Newton are also outstanding. After a visit to Rome (1752) he executed the Nightingale and Hargreaves monuments in Westminster Abbey, reflecting some of Bernini's dramatic power and skill in composition.

Rouen (Latin name: Rotomagus) 49 26N 1 05E A city and port in NW France, the capital of the Seine-Maritime department on the River Seine. The ancient capital of Normandy, it was here that Joan of Arc was tried and burned in 1431. Many of its notable buildings, including the cathedral (13th-16th centuries), survived the damage of World War II. Its university was established in 1966. The main industries are textiles, petrochemicals, engineering, paper, and electronics. Population (1982): 105 083.

Rouget de l'Isle, Claude Joseph (1760-1836) French military engineer and composer. He composed the *Marseillaise in 1792 while stationed in Strasbourg at the outbreak of war between France and Austria. He was later imprisoned for a year for refusing to take the oath against the Crown; he was reinstated in 1795 and published a volume of 50 *Chants français* in 1825.

Roulers. *See* Roeselare.

roulette A game of chance played in most casinos. Of obscure origins, it was developed in the Monte Carlo casino. The principle of the game is that a small white ball is thrown in a clockwise direction into a horizontal wheel spinning in a counterclockwise direction. The rim of the wheel is divided into numbered compartments. Players bet (against the bank) on the number of the compartment into which they predict the ball will come to rest. There are two main varieties of roulette: French roulette and American roulette. In the French game there are 37 numbered compartments on the wheel (0-36), and the colour of the betting chips denotes their denomination. In the American game there are 38 compartments (00, 0-36), and each player has a distinctively coloured set of chips. In both games bets are placed on green baize tables on which the numbers of the compartments are laid out in groups of three. In the French game a successful bet on a single number pays 35-1 (and the stake is returned), giving the bank an advantage of 2.7%. In the American game, the bank's advantage is increased to 5.4%. There are also three types of even-money bets that the player can make: red or black, even or odd numbers, and 1-18 or 19-36. The red or black bet arises because alternate numbers on the wheel are coloured red and black. Between the extremes of even money odds and 35-1, the player can make virtually any odds he chooses by backing different groups of numbers.

rounders A nine-a-side bat-and-ball field game, which is probably the prototype of *baseball. The two teams take turns at batting and fielding and a match consists of two innings per team. The hard ball is delivered underarm to each batsman in turn until all are out. The batsmen try to score rounders by hitting it and running round the four bases without being caught or run out. The batsman's square and first base, first base and second base, and second base and third base are 12 m (39.5 ft) apart, but third and fourth base are only 8.5 m (28 ft) apart.

Roundheads The parliamentary party during the English *Civil War. The name referred originally to the short haircuts of the apprentices who demonstrated against the king at Westminster in 1640. It was later applied to all parliamentarians and referred to their drab appearance in contrast to the more flamboyant *Cavaliers.

Round Table Conference (1930-32) Three meetings held in London to discuss a form of government acceptable to India. The meetings were attended by representatives of the British Government and of India's major political parties and all its states. Mahatma *Gandhi, representing the *Indian National Congress, boycotted the first meeting. The result of the Conference was the *Government of India Act of 1935.

roundworm. *See* nematode.

Rousseau, Henri (1844-1910) French painter. Although known as Le Douanier (customs official) he was really a toll collector and as a painter was self-taught. From 1886 he exhibited at the Salon des Indépendants but his work, resembling folk art in technique (*see* primitivism), was ridiculed. After 1894, when he exhibited *War* (Louvre), followed by the *Sleeping Gypsy* (1897; New York), he received serious attention, particularly from *Picasso and the poet *Apollinaire. The childlike quality of his vision and the hallucinatory atmosphere in his portraits and jungle landscapes influenced a number of 20th-century painters, particularly several of the surrealists.

Rousseau, Jean Jacques (1712-78) French philosopher and writer. Through his acquaintance with *Diderot, Rousseau joined the *Encyclopedists. In the *Discourse on the Origin and Foundations of Inequality amongst Men* (1754) he argued that man's perfect nature is spoiled by corrupt society. *Émile* (1762), a novel on education, expanded his views on ideal unfallen human nature. Rousseau's political influence was significant and many of the ideas embodied in such works as *Du contrat social* (1762) were taken up by revolutionaries. His fine style and romantic outlook inspired Shelley, Byron, and Wordsworth. His continued belief in a somewhat emasculated Christianity was an effective counterbalance to the atheism of Voltaire and the rationalists.

Rousseau, (Pierre Étienne) Théodore (1812-67) French Romantic landscape painter and leader of the *Barbizon school. His melancholy scenes were influenced by *Constable and *Bonington but his practice of open-air painting anticipated *impressionism. After permanently settling in Barbizon in the 1840s he received official recognition of his work.

Roussel, Albert (1869-1937) French composer. Serving in the French navy until 1894, he sailed to Indochina in 1890. Eastern culture became one of his main sources of inspiration although his later works are predominantly neoclassical. His compositions include the ballet *The Spider's Banquet* (1912), the opera-ballet *Pâdmâvatî* (1914-18), four symphonies, a piano concerto, chamber music, and songs.

Roussel, Raymond (1877-1933) French writer and dramatist. His writings, constructed around elaborately contrived puzzles and linguistic games, include the prose works *Impressions d'Afrique* (1910) and *Locus Solus* (1914) and three plays the first productions of which caused scandals. He is regarded as a precursor of both surrealism and the *nouveau roman*.

Roux, Pierre Paul Emile (1853-1933) French bacteriologist, who, following the discovery of the Klebs-Loeffler (diphtheria) bacillus in 1884, showed that the disease symptoms were caused by a toxin released by the bacilli. Roux helped develop an antitoxin serum for diphtheria and—working with *Pasteur—discovered a vaccine for anthrax using attenuated bacilli. Roux was director of the Pasteur Institute (1904-33).

rove beetle A beetle belonging to the worldwide family *Staphylinidae* (about 27 000 species), having short wing cases covering the folded hindwings. Rove beetles range from 0.7

to 32 mm in length although most are small. They are commonly found near dung and dead animal matter, preying upon the associated insects and mites. Some species, however, live in ant and termite nests. *See also* devil's coach horse.

rowan. *See* mountain ash.

Rowe, Nicholas (1674-1718) British dramatist. He successfully exploited the contemporary taste for sentimentalism in his domestic tragedies *The Fair Penitent* (1703) and *The Tragedy of Jane Shore* (1714). He produced the first critical edition of the works of Shakespeare (1709) and was appointed poet laureate in 1715.

rowing A sport using narrow light boats (*or* shells) propelled by two, four, or eight people and often steered by a coxswain, usually on a river or lake. The oarsmen sit in line in sliding seats, bracing their feet against stretchers. Each controls one oar set in a rowlock, the oars being arranged on alternate sides. **Sculling** is a form of rowing for one, two, or four people per boat, each person controlling two oars. The governing body is the Fédération internationale des Sociétés d'Aviron. In the UK the most popular rowing event is the *Boat Race.

Rowlandson, Thomas (1756-1827) British caricaturist. A student at the Royal Academy and in Paris, he worked first as a portraitist but specialized in caricature after 1781. Using a reed pen and delicate washes of colour, he produced a popular comic satire of the social types of his age in the *Dr Syntax* series (1812-21) and the *English Dance of Death* (1815-16). He also illustrated books by Smollett, Goldsmith, and Sterne.

Rowley, Thomas (c. 1585-c. 1642) English dramatist and actor. He collaborated with many other Jacobean dramatists, notably with John Ford and Thomas Dekker on *The Witch of Edmonton* (1621) and with Thomas Middleton on *The Changeling* (1622). His own plays were mostly comedies.

Rowse, A(lfred) L(eslie) (1903-) British historian and literary critic. Rowse is best known for his books on the Tudor period, including *The Elizabethan Renaissance* (1971), and on Shakespeare, whose Dark Lady of the sonnets he controversially identified as Emilia Lanier, daughter of a court musician.

Roxburgh (*or* Roxburghshire) A former county of SE Scotland. Under local government reorganization in 1975 its boundaries were adjusted to form Roxburgh District in the Borders Region.

Royal Academy An art society in Burlington House, London, that holds annual summer exhibitions of contemporary British art, as well as loan exhibitions of modern artists and the old masters. Founded in 1768, it originally had an important teaching function. It moved to its present premises in 1867, after being housed at various stages in Pall Mall, Somerset House, and the National Gallery.

Royal Academy of Dramatic Art (RADA) The leading British school of acting, founded in London in 1904 by Sir Herbert Beerbohm *Tree. It has received a government subsidy since 1924 and has also benefited from a legacy bequeathed by G. B. Shaw in 1950.

Royal Air Force (RAF) A British armed service formed in 1918 by the amalgamation of the Royal Flying Corps (1912) with the Royal Naval Air Service (1914). It contributed to the final operations on the western front in World War I and played a decisive role in *World War II. It is now divided into Strike Command (the operational command), Maintenance Command, and Training Command and is administered by the Air Force Department of the Ministry of Defence. The **Women's Royal Air Force** was formed in 1949 in succession to the Women's Auxiliary Air Force (WAAF) of World War II and the short-lived Women's Royal Air Force (1918-20). *See also* aircraft.

Royal and Ancient Golf Club of St Andrews One of the

World's major golf clubs (founded 1754). In 1919 it was officially accepted as the governing body of golf in Britain.

royal antelope The world's smallest antelope, *Neotragus pygmaeus*, of West African forests. 25–30 cm high at the shoulder, it is red-brown with white underparts; males have short spiky horns. They are nocturnal and usually occur singly or in pairs.

Royal Ballet The leading British ballet company and school. Based at the Royal Opera House, Covent Garden, since 1946, it was known as the Sadler's Wells Ballet until 1956, when it was granted a royal charter. It was founded by Dame Ninette de Valois in 1931 and during the 1930s it performed at the Old Vic and the Sadler's Wells Theatres with such principal dancers as Margot *Fonteyn, Michael Somes (1917–), and Robert *Helpmann. On de Valois' retirement in 1963, Sir Frederick *Ashton succeeded as director of the company, followed by Kenneth *Macmillan in 1970, Norman Morrice in 1977, and Anthony Dowell in 1986. Recent principals include Monica Mason (1941–), Merle Park (1937–), Jennifer Penney (1946–), Wayne Sleep (1948–), and David Wall (1946–).

Royal British Legion An organization for ex-servicemen and women, founded in 1921 largely through the efforts of Douglas *Haig. It provides assistance with housing or employment problems and runs homes for the sick and aged. It also owns factories, including one which manufactures the Flanders poppies sold before *Remembrance Sunday. General secretary: Maj R. Tomlins.

Royal Canadian Mounted Police (*or* Mounties) Canadian police force. Founded in 1873 as the North West Mounted Police, it has become famous for the efficiency and discipline of its members, dressed in their distinctive scarlet tunics, blue breeches, and wide-brimmed hats.

royal fern. *See* Osmunda.

Royal Geographical Society A British learned society, established in 1830 and incorporated in 1859, for the advancement of geographical knowledge. Among other functions it provides grants to expeditions; explorers who have benefited in this way include *Livingstone, Robert Falcon *Scott, *Shackleton, and John *Hunt. Two Royal Medals are awarded annually by the Queen to geographers recommended by the Society.

Royal Greenwich Observatory An observatory founded in 1675 by Charles II at Greenwich, London, in a building designed by Sir Christopher Wren. The meridian through Greenwich (0°) was internationally adopted as the prime meridian in 1884 and became the basis of Greenwich Mean Time and British Summer Time. In 1948–54 the observatory moved to Herstmonceux, Sussex. Its 2.5 m (100 in) reflecting telescope has been moved to the new *Roque de los Muchachos Observatory in the Canary Islands, where conditions for observation are greatly improved. The observatory plans to move to Cambridge in 1990.

Royal Horticultural Society A society in the UK that exists to further interest in vegetables and ornamental plants. Founded in 1804, it received its royal charter in 1809 and now has its headquarters in Vincent Square, London. The society maintains gardens that are open to the public, notably at Wisley, Surrey, and promotes new varieties and rare plants at various shows, especially at the Chelsea Flower Show.

Royal Institution One of the first scientific research centres, founded by Benjamin Thompson, Count *Rumford, in 1799 and receiving its royal charter in 1800. Several famous scientists have worked here, including *Davy, *Faraday, and *Bragg. Lectures are still given at its premises in Albemarle Street, London, notably the Friday evening discourses for members and the Christmas lectures for children.

royal jelly A thick white mixture of proteins, carbohydrates, minerals, and vitamins that is secreted by worker bees and fed to the larvae. Larvae destined to become queens are fed entirely on royal jelly. *See also* honeybee.

Royal Marines A corps of troops, founded in England in 1664, which serves on land, at sea, or in the air. Their ranks correspond to those of the army but they are administered by the Navy Board. They served in both World Wars, in the Korean War (for which they were awarded the US Presidential Unit Citation), and in Northern Ireland.

Royal Mint The factory in which the UK's coins are made. It was formerly in the Tower of London, moving to Tower Hill in 1811 and to Llantrisant, South Wales, in 1968. Military medals and decorations, UK great seals, and certain foreign coins are also made at the Royal Mint.

Royal National Lifeboat Institution A voluntary organization, founded in 1824, that operates a 24-hour *lifeboat service around British coasts. Each lifeboat has a full-time mechanic but the other crew members are volunteers. Offshore lifeboats, usually 16 metres in length, are designed to right themselves in the event of a capsize. The RNLI also operates small inflatable craft powered by outboard motors to rescue people in trouble with small boats.

Royal Navy (RN) The senior of Britain's three armed services. Founded in the 9th century by Alfred the Great, the RN emerged as "the wooden walls of England" in the 16th century with such victories as that over the Spanish *Armada (1588) under Sir Francis *Drake. The 17th century saw further victories against the Dutch, but little improvement in the lot of the sailors ("Jack Tars") with harsh discipline, poor pay, and disease. Despite the efforts of such men as Samuel *Pepys and Captain *Cook to improve conditions, mutiny finally broke out at the Nore and Spithead (1797) even as the RN entered its greatest era with a series of victories under *Nelson against Napoleonic France, notably at the Nile (1798), Copenhagen (1801), and Trafalgar (1805). Now the supreme sea power, the RN became increasingly professional during the 19th century; living conditions improved, training schools were founded, and new ironclad vessels, notably HMS *Dreadnought* (launched in 1905), replaced the traditional sailing ships. The RN fought its last set-piece battle at Jutland (1916) during World War I, after which it was limited in size. The modern RN is probably the most efficient navy in the world and is armed with such sophisticated equipment as helicopters and nuclear submarines. It also undertakes fishery protection, mine sweeping, and NATO roles.

Royal Opera House. *See* Covent Garden.

Royal Society The oldest and most important scientific society in the UK. It originated in 1645 with a group of thinkers, including Robert *Boyle and John Wilkins, who met to discuss the "new or experimental philosophy" popularized by Francis Bacon. It was incorporated by royal charter from Charles II in 1662, early members including Sir Christopher *Wren and Samuel *Pepys; with the presidency from 1703–27 of Isaac *Newton, the Royal Society achieved great standing and financial security. The Society publishes scientific papers in the *Proceedings* and the *Philosophical Transactions*, maintains a large library, disburses grants for scientific research, and awards medals for notable scientific achievement. There are now some 800 fellows, who are allowed to put the prestigious initials FRS after their names.

Royal Society for the Prevention of Cruelty to Animals (RSPCA) A British charity founded in 1824 to investigate and act upon reports of cruelty to animals. It also runs animal clinics. Funded by voluntary contributions, it has branches in the Commonwealth and a Junior Movement of 10 000 members. Executive director: F. Dixon Ward.

Royal Society for the Protection of Birds (RSPB) A British charity founded in 1889 to protest against the wholesale killing of birds for their plumage. Since then it has promoted the conservation of wild birds and their habitats against numerous other threats and established reserves throughout Britain. By 1984 the society numbered 360 000 members. Executive director: Ian Prestt.

Royal Warrant Holder A UK tradesman or firm authorized by the royal household to display a crest indicating that it supplies goods or services to a member of the royal family.

Royce, Sir (Frederick) Henry (1863-1933) British □car manufacturer, who founded, with Charles *Rolls, Rolls-Royce Ltd (1906). In 1884 Royce opened an engineering business in Manchester and in 1904 began to build cars, which much impressed Rolls and led to the merger of their businesses. Ill-health forced Royce to live in the south of France, where he set up a design team that later moved back to England. Here he designed some of his most famous cars and the aeroengine that became the Merlin (used in Spitfires and Hurricanes in World War II).

Royce, Josiah (1855-1916) US philosopher. As an idealist, influenced by *Hegel, Royce believed that human thought was part of the cosmic order. Governing the natural order was a higher moral order, which it was man's duty to uphold. His numerous books include the *Spirit of Modern Philosophy* (1892).

RR Lyrae stars A class of short-period pulsating *variable stars that are very old giant stars found principally in globular *star clusters, all with about the same mean *luminosity.

RSPB. *See* Royal Society for the Protection of Birds.

RSPCA. *See* Royal Society for the Prevention of Cruelty to Animals.

Ruapehu, Mount 39 18S 175 36E An active volcano in New Zealand, the highest peak in North Island in Tongariro National Park. The last eruption was in 1945–46. Height: 2797 m (9175 ft).

Rub' al-Khali The S part of the Arabian Desert, mainly in Saudi Arabia. It is low lying and constitutes the largest continuous area of sand in the world. Area: about 800 000 sq km (308 815 sq mi).

rubber A synthetic or natural organic polymer that is elastic and tough. The name comes from its ability to erase pencil marks. **Natural rubber**, which consists mainly of polyisoprene $-(CH_2CH:C.CH_3:CH_2)_n-$ is made from latex, a milky fluid collected from the *rubber tree grown in Malaysia, Thailand, Indonesia, and other parts of SE Asia. The rubber is coagulated from latex (using acids) and pressed into sheets. *Vulcanization increases its durability. **Synthetic rubbers** are made from petrochemicals (*see* oil). Styrene-butadiene rubber (SBR), now the commonest synthetic rubber, was introduced during World War II. It is made by the emulsion process, in which styrene and butadiene are mixed in soapy water containing a catalyst. Different proportions of ingredients and temperatures vary the properties. SBR is used in tyres, often mixed with natural rubber to improve its resilience. Butyl rubber is made by *polymerization of isobutylene. It is used for inner tubes. Neoprene (polychloropene) is used for protective clothing and electrical insulation. Nitrile polyisoprene and the newer polyurethane and silicone rubbers are also used for specialist applications.

rubber plant A tree, *Ficus elastica*, native to India and Malaysia, where it grows to a height of 35 m in forests. Its latex is the source of Assam or India rubber. It is also a popular house plant, grown in pots or tubs for its oblong shiny leathery leaves. Family: *Moraceae*.

rubber tree A Brazilian tree, *Hevea brasiliensis*, also called Pará rubber, widely cultivated in humid tropical regions, especially SE Asia. Its milky latex is the chief source of natural *rubber, which is obtained by making sloping cuts in the trunk. Trees yield latex from about the sixth year and reach full height, about 20 m, in eight years. *H. guianensis* and *H. pauciflora* are also sometimes cultivated for rubber. In 1876, some seeds of South American rubber trees were shipped to Kew Gardens by Sir Henry Wickham (1846-1928). Seedlings were subsequently exported to Ceylon and SE Asia to form the basis of the rubber industry. Family: *Euphorbiaceae*.

Rubbra, Edmund (1901-86) British composer. He was self-taught until he took lessons at the Royal College of Music from Holst, John Ireland, Vaughan Williams, and others. His works include ten symphonies, a piano concerto and a viola concerto, chamber music, madrigals and motets, and two masses.

rubella. *See* German measles.

RUBENS Le Chapeau de Paille *(c. 1622-25; National Gallery, London).*

Rubens, Peter Paul (1577-1640) Flemish painter, who was born in Seigen (Westphalia) but lived chiefly in Antwerp. The greatest of the *baroque artists and one of the finest European colourists, Rubens first worked for the Mantuan court in Italy (1600-08). Returning to Antwerp, he became court painter to the Archduke Albert and painted his first major works, *The Raising of the Cross* and *Descent from the Cross* (both Antwerp Cathedral). Many visits abroad, sometimes as a diplomatic envoy, and commissions followed, including a cycle for Marie de' Medici commemorating her marriage to Henry IV (Louvre) and the ceiling of the Banqueting House, Whitehall, for Charles I. Aided by a large workshop, he painted mythological, historical, and religious subjects but his most personal works are his portraits of his family, notably *Helena Fourment with a Fur Cloak* (Kunsthistorisches Museum, Vienna) and such landscapes as *The Château de Steen* (National Gallery, London). His Antwerp house, now a museum, contains his fine art collection and furnishings.

Rubicon A stream in N central Italy flowing E into the Adriatic Sea, which formed the boundary between Italy and

Cisalpine Gaul in the time of the Roman Republic. In 49 BC Julius Caesar, then provincial commander in Gaul, precipitated the civil war with Pompey by leading his army across the Rubicon into Italy. This action was tantamount to a declaration of war because it was forbidden for a general to lead an army outside the province in which he had been given command. Hence "crossing the Rubicon" has come to mean taking an irrevocable step.

rubidium (Rb) A highly electropositive alkali metal, discovered spectroscopically by R. W. Bunsen and G. R. Kirchhoff in 1861. The element is soft and silvery-white. It ignites spontaneously in air and reacts violently with water, liberating hydrogen and then setting fire to it. The isotope ^{87}Rb is radioactive with a half-life of 5×10^{11} years and is used in *rubidium-strontium dating. Rubidium forms ionic salts and four oxides (Rb_2O, Rb_2O_2, Rb_2O_3, RbO_2). At no 37; at wt 85.47; mp 38.89°C; bp 688°C.

rubidium-strontium dating A method of *radiometric dating, used mainly for rocks, fossils, etc. It utilizes the fact that naturally occurring rubidium contains about 28% of the radioactive isotope rubidium-87, which undergoes *beta decay to strontium-87 with a *half-life of 5×10^{11} years. Thus by measuring the ratio of rubidium-87 to strontium-87 in the sample, its age may be estimated. The method can date items several thousands of millions of years old.

Rubinstein, Anton (1829-94) Russian pianist and composer. He started performing abroad at the age of 12 and founded the St Petersburg conservatoire in 1862. His works include 20 operas, 6 symphonies, 5 piano concertos, 2 cello concertos, and numerous other piano pieces.

Rubinstein, Artur (1888-1982) Polish-born pianist. He became a US citizen in 1946. He studied in Warsaw and Berlin and soon acquired a worldwide reputation, particularly as a performer of Chopin. He wrote two autobiographies, *My Young Years* (1974) and *My Many Years* (1980).

Rublyov, Andrey (*or* A. Rublev; c. 1370-1430) A leading Russian icon painter. He sometimes collaborated with the Greek painter Theophanes and late in life became a monk. In his masterpiece *The Old Testament Trinity* (Tretyakov Gallery, Moscow) the influence of *Byzantine art is modified by a distinctive gracefulness.

Rubus A genus of prickly perennial herbs and shrubs (225 species), found mainly in N temperate regions. Many species, including the *blackberry, *loganberry, and *raspberry, are grown for their juicy fruits. Family: *Rosaceae.

ruby A red transparent variety of *corundum, the colour being due to traces of chromium. It is used as a gemstone and in lasers, watches, and other precision instruments. Many fine rubies come from Mogok in Upper Burma, where they occur in metamorphic limestones with other precious and semiprecious stones. Prior to the 14th century rubies were called carbuncles. Birthstone for July.

Ruda Śląska 51 10N 16 39E A town in SW Poland. The first coalmine in Poland was opened here (1751). Population (1982): 162 000.

Rudbeckia. *See* black-eyed Susan.

rudd A game fish, *Scardinius erythrophthalmus*, found among vegetation in fresh waters of Europe and W Asia. It has a stout body, 35-40 cm long, coloured golden- or olive-brown above and silvery white below, deep-red fins, and golden eyes.

Rudolf, Lake. *See* Turkana, Lake.

Rudolph (1858-89) Archduke of Austria. His liberal views brought him into conflict with his father Emperor Francis Joseph. He and his mistress Baroness Marie Vetsera were found dead at his hunting lodge of Mayerling, having apparently committed suicide.

Rudolph I (1218-91) The first *Habsburg Holy Roman Emperor (1273-91). His conquests in central Europe—Austria, Styria, Carinthia, and Carniola—formed the nucleus of future Habsburg territorial power.

Rudolph II (1552-1612) Holy Roman Emperor (1576-1612). A dilatory ruler, he was forced to relinquish his powers in Hungary (1608) and Bohemia (1611) to his brother *Matthias.

rue An evergreen shrub, *Ruta graveolens*, also known as herb of grace, native to S Europe. Growing up to 90 cm high, it has fleshy blue-green leaves and terminal clusters of yellow flowers. The leaves yield a bitter oil, once used as a spice and in medicines. Family: *Rutaceae*.

Rueil-Malmaison 48 52N 2 11E A town in France, a suburb of Paris in the Hauts-de-Seine department. Its chateau was once a favourite residence of Napoleon I and the Empress Josephine is buried here. Population (1982): 64 545.

ruff An Old World *sandpiper, *Philomachus pugnax*, that breeds in coastal wetlands of N Eurasia and winters on mudflats of South Africa and S Asia. The female (called a reeve) is 25 cm long and has a grey-brown plumage; the larger male has a double crest and a multicoloured collar in the breeding season. *See* Plate V.

Rugby 52 23N 1 15W A town in the English Midlands, in Warwickshire. According to tradition the game of rugby football originated here in 1823 at the famous public school (1567), which was described in *Tom Brown's Schooldays*. Rugby's industries include engineering and cement. Population (1981): 59 564.

Rügen An East German island in the Baltic Sea, 2.5 km (1.5 mi) off Stralsund, to which it is connected by a road and rail causeway. Area: 926 sq km (358 sq mi). Population (1983 est): 84 501.

Ruggles, Carl (1876-1971) US composer. His works, although few, had considerable influence; they are generally dissonant and strident and include *Angels* (1939) for brass or strings and the orchestral works *Sun-Treader* (1932) and *Men and Mountains* (1924-36). He devoted the last years of his life to painting.

Ruhr, River A river in West Germany, rising in the Sauerland and flowing NW and W past Essen to join the River Rhine at Duisburg. The Ruhr Valley (German name: Ruhrgebiet) is the centre of the German iron and steel industry. Length: 235 km (146 mi).

Ruisdael, Jacob van (?1628-82) The greatest of Dutch landscape painters. Born in Haarlem, he studied under his father and probably also under his uncle, the landscape painter **Salomon van Ruysdael** (c. 1600-70). His baroque compositions, regularly framed by fantastic trees, are noted for their dramatic contrasts of light and shade. *The Jewish Cemetery* (c. 1660) is a striking evocation of human mortality.

Ruiz, Juan (c. 1283-c. 1350) Spanish poet. Nothing is known of his life apart from the fact that he was Archpriest of Hita. His *Libro de buen amor* (1330) consists of a series of love stories interspersed with ironic didactic digressions.

rum A *spirit distilled from molasses derived from sugar cane. Rum is colourless and is used in mixed drinks, especially punches, or with soda water, fruit juice, or Coca-Cola. Better-quality rums are aged in oak casks for several years. It is produced wherever sugar cane is grown, predominantly in the Caribbean region but also in the USA.

Rum (*or* Rhum) An island in NW Scotland in the Inner Hebrides group. Acquired by the Nature Conservancy Council (1957), it is now managed as a nature reserve with restricted access in Spring.

Rumania. *See* Romania, Socialist Republic of.

Rumelia The Balkan possessions of the Ottoman Empire from the 14th to 19th centuries. The Congress of *Berlin (1878) divided Rumelia into the state of Bulgaria under Ottoman suzerainty, the autonomous province of Eastern Rumelia, and the provinces of Edirne, Salonica, and Monastir. Eastern Rumelia was annexed by Bulgaria in 1885 and Monastir and Salonica were ceded to Serbia and Greece respectively in 1913.

Rumford, Benjamin Thompson, Count (1753-1814) American-born scientist, who spied for the British in the American Revolution and was forced to flee America and abandon his wife to settle in England in 1776. In England he held minor administrative posts but also carried out scientific research in ballistics and the theory of heat. Suspected of spying for the French, he left England in 1785 for Paris and then Bavaria, where he worked as an administrator for the elector, Karl Theodor (1724-99), who made him a count of the Holy Roman Empire in 1791 (he chose the title Rumford, his home town in America—now called Concord). In 1795 he returned to England, where he helped to demolish the caloric theory and found the *Royal Institution.

ruminant A hoofed mammal belonging to the suborder *Ruminantia* (about 175 species), which includes deer, cattle, antelopes, sheep, and goats. Ruminants eat grass, leaves, and other vegetation and are characterized by possession of a four-chambered stomach. The largest chamber (rumen) contains bacteria and protozoa, which ferment the stomach contents and enable the animal to digest and utilize its food efficiently. Ruminants regurgitate their food periodically to "chew the cud," which helps to break up the plant cell walls.

rummy games Various related card games, of which rummy is the basic form. Its object is to form melds (sets or sequences) composed of three or four cards of the same rank (such as four jacks) or sequences of three or more cards of the same suit (such as seven, eight, nine, and ten, of diamonds). In each turn a player takes a card from the pack and discards one. The first player to dispose of his cards wins, scoring points according to the cards left in his opponents' hands. In **gin rummy** (for two players) the object is to reach a certain score before one's opponent. No melds are laid down until a player's unmatched cards make a total of ten or less, when the player lays his whole hand down. It is a "gin" if he has no unmatched cards. **Canasta** itself has several variants but is usually a partnership game for four players. Two packs are used; the jokers and all the twos are "wild." The winners are the first to score 5000 by making melds and canastas (a meld of seven or more cards of the same value).

Rump Parliament. *See* Long Parliament.

Rum Rebellion (1808) A rebellion in Australia in which William *Bligh, governor of New South Wales, was ousted from his post and imprisoned by officers of the New South Wales Corps. It was incited by Bligh's suppression of the rum traffic. In 1810 the Corps was recalled.

Runcie, Robert Alexander Kennedy (1921-) British churchman; Archbishop of Canterbury (1980-). He was formerly bishop of St Albans (1970-80).

Runcorn 53 20N 2 44W A town in NW England, in Cheshire on the River Mersey and Manchester Ship Canal. Designated for development as a new town in 1964, it has chemical and brewing industries. Population (1981): 64 106.

Rundstedt, (Karl Rudolf) Gerd von (1875-1953) German field marshal, who was recalled from retirement at the outbreak of World War II, becoming (1942) commander in chief in France. He held command in the battle of the Bulge (1944) and was a competent if uninspired general. He was captured in 1945 but his ill health secured his release.

Runeberg, Johan Ludvig (1804-77) Finnish poet of Swedish origin, who wrote in Swedish and whose style was influenced by his study of Finnish folk poetry. His major works include the epic poem *Kung Fjalar* (*King Fialar*; 1844), in which he attempted a synthesis of Christian and classical pagan ideals, and *Fänrik Sta ls sägner* (*Tales of Ensign Sta l*; 1848-60), a collection of patriotic ballads, one of which became the Finnish national anthem.

runic alphabet An alphabetical writing system used for Norse and certain other Germanic languages. It originated,

probably as a modified version of the Etruscan or the Roman alphabet, in the 2nd or 3rd century AD, and went out of use gradually after the 14th century. The Gothic word *runa* means secret or mystery, and runes were always associated with magical powers. The runic alphabet, called the *futhark* from the names of the first six letters, consisted at first of 24 characters, extended in Old English to 28 and later 31.

runner bean A climbing plant, *Phaseolus coccineus*, also known as scarlet runner, native to South America and widely cultivated as a vegetable crop, especially in Britain. Growing up to 3 m high, it bears usually red five-petalled flowers, which give rise to edible bean pods, 20-60 cm long, that are eaten cooked. Wild plants are perennial, but cultivated plants are treated as annuals. Family: *Leguminosae.

Runnymede (*or* Runnimede) 51 26N 0 33W A meadow in SE England, near Egham in Surrey on the S bank of the River Thames. The Magna Carta was granted here by King John (1215); the site is now owned by the National Trust (since 1931).

Runyon, Damon (1884-1946) US humorous writer. For his stories about New York characters, first collected in *Guys and Dolls* (1932) and notable for their lively slang, he drew on his long experience as a journalist and sports reporter.

Rupert, Prince (1619-82) Cavalry officer, who fought for the Royalists in the Civil War; he was the son of Frederick the Winter King of the Palatinate and Elizabeth, daughter of James I of England. His strategic and tactical ability was outstanding and he was a bold and charismatic leader. However, he lacked the ability to maintain control when battle commenced. He was defeated at *Marston Moor (1644) and *Naseby (1645) and after Charles' surrender he was banished from England. He returned at the Restoration (1660) and served as an admiral in the *Dutch Wars.

Rupert's Land (*or* Prince Rupert's Land) A region in N and W Canada around Hudson Bay. In 1670 it was granted by Charles II to the *Hudson's Bay Company, the first governor of which was Prince *Rupert. It is now an ecclesiastical province of the Anglican Church of Canada.

Rurik (died c. 879) The semilegendary founder of the Rurik dynasty of Russian princes (862-1598). A Varangian chieftain, Rurik was allegedly Prince of Novgorod from 862. His descendants were grand princes of Kiev, Vladimir, and Muscovy.

Ruse (Russe *or* Roussé) 43 05N 25 59E A city in central N Bulgaria. It is the site of the Friendship Bridge (1954) over the River Danube into Romania and is Bulgaria's principal river port. Population (1982): 178 920.

rush A grasslike plant of the genus *Juncus* (over 300 species), found worldwide in damp temperate and cold regions. Rushes have tufts of slender rigid stalks, up to about 1 m high, bearing long flat leaves and clusters of small green or brown flowers, which produce seed capsules. The leaves are used to make mats, baskets, etc. Family: *Juncaceae.*
The name is also applied to similar plants, including the *bulrush, *flowering rush, and *woodrush.

Rushdie, Salman (1947-) British novelist, born in India. His first novel *Grimus* (1975) was followed by the much acclaimed Booker prizewinner *Midnight's Children* (1981) and *Shame* (1983).

Rusk, (David) Dean (1909-) US statesman. After World War II he held posts in the State Department and in 1950 became assistant secretary of state for Far Eastern affairs, influencing US policy in the Korean War. As secretary of state (1961-69) successively under Presidents Kennedy and Johnson he defended US military involvement in Vietnam. In 1969 he became professor of international law at the University of Georgia.

Ruskin, John (1819-1900) British art and social critic. He began to write his first work of art criticism, *Modern Painters* (1843-60), to defend the paintings of J. M. W. Turner. In *The Stones of Venice* (1851-53) he promoted the gothic style in architecture. In *Unto This Last* (1862) and other volumes of social criticism he denounced materialism and laissez-faire economics from a moral and aesthetic perspective. His sonorous prose style is most fully developed in his unfinished autobiography, *Praeterita* (1885-89). During his last years he suffered recurrent attacks of insanity.

BERTRAND RUSSELL

Russell, Bertrand Arthur William, 3rd Earl (1872-1970) British philosopher, grandson of Lord John *Russell. His first major philosophical work, *Principia Mathematica* (1910-13), written with A. N. *Whitehead, presented pure mathematics as a development of *logic. On a smaller logical basis *Our Knowledge of the External World* (1914) attempted a new approach to traditional problems in epistemology. From his pupil *Wittgenstein, he also acquired a lasting interest in language.

His prolific writings on religion, politics, and morals always stimulated interest, often to his own detriment. He was imprisoned (1918) and deprived of his Cambridge lectureship for his outspoken pacifism. In 1940 a US court disqualified him from holding a professorship at New York on account of his moral views. In 1961 he was again imprisoned for civil disobedience during the Campaign for Nuclear Disarmament. He was awarded the OM in 1949 and the Nobel Prize for Literature in 1950. He claimed that "longing for love, the search for knowledge, and unbearable pity for mankind" were the governing passions of his life.

Russell, John, 1st Earl (1792-1878) British statesman; Whig (Liberal) prime minister (1846-52, 1865-66); the grandfather of Bertrand Russell. Elected an MP in 1813, he championed parliamentary reform in the 1820s and helped to draft the Reform Act (1832). Under Melbourne he was home secretary (1835-39), introducing the Municipal Reform Act (1835), and then secretary for war (1839-41). His first ministry was dominated by his foreign secretary Palmerston. Russell was himself foreign secretary (1852-53) under Aberdeen and then colonial secretary (1855) under Palmerston with whom his relations were strained. He resigned as prime minister following defeat of the second parliamentary reform bill.

Russell, Ken (1927-) British film director. His early work for the BBC included *A Song of Summer* (1968), concerning the composer Delius. His major films include *Women in Love* (1969), *The Devils* (1971), *Gothic* (1986), and several controversial biographical films, such as *The Music Lovers* (1970), about Tchaikovsky, *Mahler* (1974), and *Valentino* (1977).

Russell, Lord William (1639-83) English Whig politician, who was beheaded for complicity in the *Rye House Plot against Charles II and the king's brother James, Duke of York. Russell had played a leading role in the movement to exclude the Roman Catholic James from the succession.

Russell, Sir William Howard (1820-1907) British war correspondent. Working for *The Times*, he reported the Crimean War, exposing its mismanagement by the government in dispatches later collected in *The War, 1855-56*. His description of the infantry at *Balaclava as a "thin red line" became well known.

Russell's viper A common highly venomous viper, *Vipera russelli*, of SE Asia. Up to 1.5 m long, it is patterned with three rows of black-and-white ringed reddish spots. It is the cause of many snakebite deaths.

Russia. *See* Soviet Union.

Russian The main language of the Soviet Union, belonging to the East *Slavonic family. It is a highly inflected language with six cases and a notable feature is the frequency of clusters of consonants. It is written in the *Cyrillic alphabet. The standard form is based on the dialect of Moscow.

Russian Blue A breed of short-haired cat, thought to have been introduced to the UK by Russian sailors. The Russian Blue has a slender body and a short flat head with large pointed ears and green eyes. The coat is lustrous and uniformly blue-grey.

Russian literature Until the beginning of the 18th century Russian literature consisted chiefly of chronicles and religious works written in Old Slavonic. The outstanding early work is *The Song of Igor's Campaign* (c. 1187). The development of modern literature owed much to the political reforms of Peter the Great (reigned 1682-1725) and the artistic patronage of Catherine the Great (reigned 1762-96). Major writers of the 18th century included the poet and scholar M. V. Lomonosov (1711-65), the poet G. R. Derzhavin (1743-1816), and the fabulist I. A. Krylov (1768-1844). The first half of the 19th century was dominated by Pushkin and Lermontov and the second half, following the pioneering fiction of Gogol, by the novelists Tolstoy, Dostoievski, and Turgenev. They were followed by the dramatist and short-story writer Chekhov, whose detached compassion contrasted with the strong social commitment of Gorki. The political unrest of the early 20th century stimulated much artistic experimentation, but in the 1930s the Soviet authorities decreed that all literature must adhere to the official doctrine of *socialist realism. Writers whose works were banned in Russia include the poets Akhmatova, Mandelstan, and Tsvetaeva and the novelist Pasternak. The apparent liberalization of culture heralded by the publication of works by Solzhenitsyn, Yevtushenko, and Voznesenskii in the 1960s was short lived and in 1974 Solzhenitsyn joined the growing number of Russian writers living abroad.

Russian Orthodox Church An offshoot of the Greek Orthodox Church, dating from the baptism of the emperor Vladimir (later St Vladimir) in 988. Since 1328 the metropolitan see has been at Moscow. During the 15th century connections with the Greek parent Church were severed. In the 18th century the Church fell increasingly under state control. Since the 1917 Revolution it has been intermittently persecuted and at best regarded with suspicion and its activities restricted. *See also* Old Believers.

Russian Revolution (1917) The revolution between March and November (Old Style February and October), 1917, that overthrew the Russian monarchy and established the world's first communist state. It began with the February Revolution, when riots over shortage of bread and coal in Petrograd (formerly St Petersburg) led to the establishment of the Petrograd Soviet of Workers' and Soldiers' Deputies, dominated by *Mensheviks and Social Revolutionaries, and of a provisional government of *Duma deputies, which forced *Nicholas II to abdicate. The failure of the provisional government, under Prince *Lvov and then *Kerenski, to end Russia's participation in World War I and to deal with food shortages led to the demand of the *Bolsheviks under *Lenin for "All power to the Soviets." The Bolsheviks, who had gained a majority in the Soviet by September, staged the October (or Bolshevik) Revolution, seizing power and establishing the Soviet of People's Commissars. The new government came to terms with Germany in early 1918 but almost immediately faced opposition at home. In the subsequent civil war (1918–21) the Red Army was ultimately victorious against the anticommunist White Russians but with the loss of some 100 000 lives. In addition, some two million Russians emigrated.

Russian Soviet Federal Socialist Republic (or RSFSR) A constituent republic in the N Soviet Union. It is the largest, most heavily populated, and economically most important of the 15 Soviet republics, occupying some 76% of the total area of the Soviet Union, containing about 54% of its population, and producing 70% of its industrial and agricultural output. Its climate ranges from Arctic to subtropical and its geographical zones include tundra, forest, steppe, and rich agricultural soil. Over 80% of the population are Russians, the remainder consisting of 38 national minorities. The RSFSR contains outstanding mineral resources including iron ore, coal, oil, gold, platinum, copper, zinc, lead, and tin. The major industrial region is around Moscow. It produces ships, lorries, machine tools, electronic equipment, textiles, and chemicals. Because of the extensive forests, timber and related occupations are important. The main agricultural products are wheat, cotton, fruit and vegetables, tobacco, and sugar beet. The RSFSR was formed in 1917 and was joined with the Ukraine, Belorussia, and Transcaucasia in 1922 to constitute the Soviet Union. It consists of 6 territories, 49 regions, 16 Autonomous Soviet Socialist Republics, 5 autonomous regions, and 10 national areas. Area: 17 074 984 sq km (6 592 658 sq mi). Population (1981 est): 139 100 000. Capital: Moscow.

Russo-Finnish War (or Winter War; 1939–40) The war between the Soviet Union and Finland at the beginning of World War II. It was won by the Soviet Union, the aggressor, which gained part of the Karelian Isthmus.

Russo-Japanese War (1904–05) A confrontation arising from conflicting Japanese and Russian interests in Manchuria, where Russia controlled Port Arthur (now Lüda). In 1904 Japan attacked Port Arthur, which fell in January, 1905. In May a Japanese fleet under *Togo Heihachiro destroyed Russia's Baltic Fleet in the Tsushima Straits, forcing Russia's surrender. In the peace conference at Portsmouth (New Hampshire, USA), over which Theodore Roosevelt presided, Japan gained the ascendancy in S Manchuria and Korea.

rust A reddish-brown solid consisting of hydrated iron oxide. Rusting is a special case of corrosion; the mechanism is complicated and still not fully understood but involves the setting up of a cell in which iron is the anode and a metal impurity the cathode. Both water and oxygen must be present for rust to form although the most serious damage, pitting, is always found in an oxygen-free portion of metal. Rust prevention usually involves protective coatings (paint, zinc plating, etc.) or alloying with chromium and other metals to produce stainless steels.

rust fungi Fungi, belonging to the order Uredinales, that are parasites of plants, forming spots, blotches, and pustules on the stems and foliage of their hosts. Several are important pests of cereal crops, including black rust (Puccinia graminis) of wheat. This forms red pustules on wheat leaves, releasing spores that infect barberry (Berberis vulgaris)—the secondary host—in which the life cycle continues. Control therefore involves eradication of barberry in wheat-growing areas as well as developing resistant strains of wheat. Other important wheat rusts include yellow rust (P. striiformis) and brown rust (P. recondita). Class: *Basidiomycetes.

Ruth A Gentile from Moab who was an ancestress of David. The Old Testament **Book of Ruth**, set in the time of the *Judges (c. 1000 BC), records the events by which Ruth came to marry Boaz, a Hebrew.

Ruth, Babe (George Herman R.; 1895–1948) US baseball player. Known as the "Sultan of Swat", he became the top player of the 1920s and revitalized the sport. His home run record of 714 stood until 1974.

Ruthenia A region comprising the S slopes of the Carpathian Mountains, now part of the Ukrainian SSR (Soviet Union), which was part of Hungary until it was attached to Czechoslovakia in 1920. Following Hitler's seizure of Czechoslovakia in 1939, Ruthenia briefly proclaimed its independence, before being annexed by Hungary. After World War II it was ceded to the Soviet Union.

ruthenium (Ru) A hard metal of the platinum group, first separated in 1844 by K. K. Klaus (1796–1864). It is used to harden platinum and palladium for use in electrical contacts and is a versatile catalyst. The tetroxide (RuO_4) is toxic. The element shows a wide range of *valence states. At no 44; at wt 101.07; mp 2310°C; bp 3900°C.

Rutherford, Ernest, 1st Baron (1871–1937) English physicist, born in New Zealand, who was a professor at Montreal (1898–1907), Manchester (1907–19), and Cambridge (1919–37), where he was also director of the Cavendish Laboratory. He made fundamental discoveries concerning the nature of *radioactivity, distinguishing between the three types of radiation, which he named alpha, beta, and gamma rays. Working with Hans *Geiger he discovered that alpha radiation consisted of positively charged helium atoms. In 1906, while bombarding gold foil with alpha particles, he deduced the existence of a heavy positively charged core in the atom, which he called the *nucleus. In 1908, Rutherford received the Nobel Prize for Chemistry. He was knighted in 1914, awarded the OM in 1925, and made a baron in 1931.

Rutherford, Dame Margaret (1892–1972) British actress. She was particularly successful in comedies, such as Blithe Spirit (1941). In her films, which included Murder She Said (1962) and The VIPs (1963), she played elderly eccentrics.

Rutherford, Mark (William Hale White; 1831–1913) British novelist. He left theological college because of his unorthodox opinions and became a civil servant. His religious doubts and convictions are the central theme of his novels and his Autobiography of Mark Rutherford (1881). The Revolution in Tanner's Lane (1887) is his best-known novel.

rutherfordium. See kurchatovium.

Ruthwell cross A stone cross, 5 m (18 ft) high, carved about 700 AD. It is now in Ruthwell church, Dumfriesshire. The cross bears reliefs depicting gospel scenes, Latin biblical inscriptions, and lines in the *runic alphabet from the Anglo-Saxon poem The Dream of the Rood.

rutile A brown to black form of natural titanium dioxide, TiO_2. It is found as an accessory mineral in igneous and metamorphic rocks, in veins, and as fibres in quartz, known as Venus' hair.

Rutland A former county in the East Midlands of England. Under local government reorganization in 1974 it became part of the county of *Leicestershire. It was the smallest county in England.

Ruwenzori Mountains A mountain range in East Africa, on the Uganda-Zaïre border between Lakes Albert and Edward, rising to 5119 m (16 795 ft) at Mount Stanley.

Ruyter, Michiel Adriaanszoon de (1607–76) Dutch admiral, who served outstandingly in the *Dutch Wars (1652–54, 1665–67, 1672–78). In the battle of the Medway (1667) he destroyed most of the English fleet and his victories in 1672–73 saved the United Provinces from invasion. He was killed in action.

ERNEST RUTHERFORD *Holding his original alpha-particle-scattering apparatus.*

Rwanda, Republic of A small landlocked country in E central Africa. Lake Kivu forms most of its W boundary and the land is chiefly mountainous and rugged. The majority of the inhabitants are Bantu-speaking Hutu, the Nilotic Tutsi comprising less than 10% of the total. *Economy*: chiefly subsistence agriculture, including livestock. The main food crops are beans, cassava, and maize, and the principal cash crop is coffee, which, along with cassiterite, form the main exports. Methane gas has been found under Lake Kivu. Some small-scale industry is being developed including food processing and textiles. *History*: a Tutsi kingdom from the 16th century, the area (with present-day Burundi) came under German East Africa in 1890. From 1919, after World War I, it was administered by Belgium as the N part of Ruanda-Urundi, which was under League of Nations mandate and then a UN trust territory. In 1959 the Tutsi kingdom was overthrown by the Hutu, who in 1961 declared Rwanda a republic; independence was recognized by Belgium in 1962. There were further massacres of the Tutsi by the Hutu in 1964. In 1973 the government was overthrown in a bloodless coup and Maj Gen Juvénal Habyalimana (1937–) came to power. Official languages: Kinyarwanda and French. Official currency: Rwanda franc of 100 centimes. Area: 26 330 sq km (10 166 sq mi). Population (1983 est): 5 664 000. Capital: Kigali.

Ryazan 54 37N 39 43E A city in the W central Soviet Union, in the RSFSR. Founded in 1095, it was the capital of a principality until annexed by Russia in 1521. Industries include oil refining, metalworking, and engineering. Population (1981 est): 470 000.

Rybinsk (name from 1946 until 1958: Shcherbakov) 58 01N 38 52E A port in the W central Soviet Union, in the RSFSR on the River Volga. It is situated below the **Rybinsk Reservoir**, an artificial lake of some 5200 sq km (2000 sq mi) created (1941) through the damming of the Volga at its confluence with the Rivers Suda and Sheksna and forming the S stretch of the Volga–Baltic waterway. Rybinsk has a hydroelectric station and shipbuilding, engineering, and food-processing industries. Population (1981 est): 243 000.

Ryder, Sue. *See* Cheshire, (Geoffrey) Leonard, Group Capt.

Ryder Cup A biennial golf tournament between members of the British and US Professional Golfers' Associations, first played in 1927. In 1979 the British team was opened to continental golfers. Up to 1985 the USA had won 21 times.

rye A cereal *grass, Secale cereale*, native to W Asia but widely cultivated in cool temperate and upland regions. 1–2 m high, it bears a terminal spike, 10–15 cm long, of numerous two- or three-flowered spikelets. The grain is milled to produce a dark-coloured flour, which is used in making black bread or for livestock feed. Rye may be sown in autumn to provide winter grazing or as a green manure crop.

Rye 50 57N 0 44E A town in SE England, in East Sussex. Once a Cinque Port, it is now about 3 km (2 mi) inland from Rye Bay, on the Strait of Dover. Population (1981): 4293.

Rye House Plot (1683) A conspiracy to murder Charles II of England and his brother, the Duke of York (later James II), near Rye House, Hoddesdon, Herts, on their way to London from Newmarket. The plot failed but several conspirators, including Lord William *Russell and Algernon *Sidney, were tried and executed.

Rykov, Aleksei Ivanovich (1881–1938) Soviet politician. After the *Russian Revolution Rykov played a prominent part in the Soviet Government until 1930, when he was expelled from the Communist Party for opposing the brutality of collectivization. He was forced to recant in 1929 and perished in Stalin's purges.

Ryle, Gilbert (1900–76) British philosopher. He was Waynflete Professor of Metaphysical Philosophy at Oxford (1945–68) and editor of *Mind* (1947–71), exerting considerable influence as a writer and teacher. His philosophy centred around detailed analysis of mental concepts. *The Concept of Mind* (1949) maintained that *Descartes' idea of the human being consisting of mind and body ("the ghost in the machine") was misleading.

Ryle, Sir Martin (1918–84) British astronomer; professor at Cambridge University and astronomer royal (1972–84). A pioneer of radio telescopy, his most important work was the development of a technique for studying distant radio sources by using two radio telescopes placed a distance apart, thus increasing their effective aperture. In 1974 he shared the Nobel Prize for Physics with Antony Hewish (1924–).

Ryukyu Islands A group of volcanic and coral islands in the W Pacific Ocean, extending almost 650 km (400 mi) from Kyushu to N Taiwan. An independent kingdom until the 14th century, the islands were dominated by the Chinese before becoming a part of Japan (1879). They were under US control (1945–72). The chief industries are agriculture and fishing. Area: 2196 sq km (849 sq mi). Population (1983 est): 1 146 000. Chief city: Naha (on Okinawa).

S

Saale, River A river in West and East Germany, rising in NE Bavaria and flowing mainly N to join the River Rhine near Magdeburg. Length: 426 km (265 mi).

Saar, River (French name: Sarre) A river in W Europe, rising in the Vosges Mountains in NE France and flowing generally N into West Germany, then NW through Saarland to join the River Moselle above Trier. The Saar Valley is noted for its wines. Length: 240 km (149 mi).

Saarbrücken (French name: Sarrebruck) 49 15N 6 58E A city in SW West Germany, the capital of Saarland on the River Saar near the French border. It was under French administration (1801–15, 1919–35, 1945–57). Some historic buildings, such as the gothic abbey church (1270–1330), survived World War II and it has a university (1948). Its industries include iron and steel and machinery manufacturing. Population (1980 est): 193 700.

Saarinen, Eero (1910–61) US architect, born in Finland. One of the most innovative of 20th-century architects, Saarinen emigrated (1923) to the USA with his father, the architect Eliel Saarinen (1873–1950), and became his partner in 1938. His first independent design was the General Motors Technical Center in Warren, Michigan (1948–56). His most famous building is the Trans World Airlines terminal at Kennedy Airport, New York (1956–62). Other works include the St Louis Arch (1964).

Saarland A small *Land* in SW West Germany, bordering on France. The area has often passed between French and German control, but plebiscites held in 1935 and 1955 resulted in its union with Germany. Rich in coal, it has a large steel industry. Area: 2569 sq km (992 sq mi). Population (1980 est): 1 068 000. Capital: Saarbrücken.

Sabadell 41 33N 2 07E A city in NE Spain, in Catalonia. It has an important textile industry. Other industries include metallurgy and leather. Population (1981): 184 943.

Sabah (former name: North Borneo) A state in Malaysia, in NE *Borneo on the South China and Sulu Seas. Forested and mountainous, it rises to 4125 m (13 533 ft) at Mount Kinabalu, the highest peak in Malaysia and Borneo. It is largely undeveloped, but on the western coastal plain rice and rubber are grown. Since 1975 copper and oil resources have been exploited; timber, rubber, copra, and abaca are exported. *History*: until colonization, most contact was with the Philippines. North Borneo was first colonized by the British in 1877, becoming a protectorate in 1882. In 1963 it joined Malaysia under its present name. Tension between Muslims and the government led to violent disturbances in the mid-1980s. Area: 76 115 sq km (29 388 sq mi). Population (1980): 1 034 000. Capital: Kota Kinabalu.

Sabatier, Paul (1854–1941) French chemist, who was professor at Toulouse University (1884–1941), where he discovered that nickel catalyses hydrogenation reactions. Since nickel is relatively cheap, this enabled similar reactions to be performed on an industrial scale, e.g. in the production of margarine. He shared the 1912 Nobel Prize with F. A. V. Grignard, the discoverer of *Grignard reagents.

sabbath In Judaism, the seventh day of the week, ordained by God in the Pentateuch as a day of rest for the benefit of his people. It was reckoned from sunset on Friday to sunset on Saturday. The early Christian Church soon substituted Sunday as the Christian day of rest and worship because the resurrection of Jesus Christ took place on the first day of the (Jewish) week.

Sabines The peoples of the scattered hilltop communities NE of ancient Rome. The legendary abduction of the Sabine women by Roman settlers, a favourite theme in the history of

art, indicates the early interbreeding of Sabines with Romans. Sabine influence on Roman religion was especially strong. They became Roman citizens in 268 BC.

Sabin vaccine A vaccine that prevents poliomyelitis, developed by a US virologist, A. B. Sabin (1906–   ). It contains a weakened polio virus that stimulates the body's defence against polio without causing the disease. Sabin vaccine is given by mouth (often on a sugar lump) in three consecutive doses. *See also* Salk vaccine.

sable A carnivorous mammal, *Martes zibellina*, native to N Eurasia. It is less than 50 cm long and has thicker legs and longer ears than other *martens. Its coat is thick, soft, and glossy and is valued as fur (Siberian sable).

sable antelope A large antelope, *Hippotragus niger*, of S African forests. About 130 cm high at the shoulder, it has backward-curving ringed horns up to 170 cm long. The coat is black in males, lighter in females, with white on the face, rump, and belly.

Sable Island A sandy island in Canada, in the Atlantic Ocean off the coast of Nova Scotia. The scene of many shipwrecks, it is known as "the graveyard of the Atlantic."

sabre-toothed tiger An extinct *cat that lived 30 million years ago and became extinct in the Pleistocene epoch (1 million years ago). *Smilodon*, a Pleistocene form, was about the size of a tiger, with very long upper canine teeth used to pierce the thick hide of its prey. ⌐fossil.

saccharin An organic compound ($C_7H_5NO_3S$) used as a sweetening agent in the food industry and as a sugar substitute by diabetics and others. It has about five hundred times the sweetening power of table sugar and passes through the body without being absorbed or changed.

Sacco-Vanzetti case The controversial trial of two US anarchists. Nicola Sacco and Bartolomeo Vanzetti were Italian-born immigrant workers convicted of murder on flimsy evidence. The verdict, which was reached largely because of their political activities and was influenced by current anti-alien and antiradical prejudice, aroused international protests. An investigative committee supported the sentence and Sacco and Vanzetti were executed in 1927, six years after being sentenced.

Sachs, Hans (1494–1576) German poet and folk dramatist, most famous of the *Meistersingers of Nuremberg. He wrote thousands of works, including lively farces still performed at annual festivals throughout Germany, verse tales, religious poetry, and other works in support of *Luther. He is the central character, portrayed as wise and philosophic, of Wagner's opera *The Mastersingers of Nuremberg* (1868).

Sachs, Nelly (Leonie) (1891–1970) German Jewish poet and dramatist. Helped by Selma *Lagerlöf, she escaped from Nazi Germany and settled in Sweden. Her best-known play is *Eli: Ein Mysterienspiel vom Leiden Israels* (1951). In 1966 she shared a Nobel Prize with Shmuel Yosef *Agnon.

sackbut. *See* trombone.

Sackville, Thomas, 1st Earl of Dorset (1536–1608) British poet and dramatist. He collaborated with Thomas Norton (1532–83) on *Gorbuduc* (1561), the first English play in blank verse, and planned and introduced *The Mirror for Magistrates* (1563), a collection of narrative poems based on the lives of eminent men.

sacrament In Christian theology, a ritual having a special significance as a visible sign of an inner grace in its participants. The *Roman Catholic Church and *Orthodox Churches accept seven sacraments: baptism, confirmation, penance, the *Eucharist, marriage, ordination, and extreme unction. Baptism and the Eucharist are the only commonly accepted sacraments among the Protestant Churches (*see* Protestantism).

Sacramento 38 32N 121 30W A city in the USA, the capital of California on the Sacramento River. Founded in 1839, it grew after the discovery of gold at nearby Sulter's Mill in 1848. Linked by canal (1963) to San Francisco Bay, it is a deepwater port and serves an extensive agricultural area. Industries include food processing, aerospace, and printing. Population (1980): 275 741.

sacred ibis An African □ibis, *Threskiornis aethiopica*, that was revered in ancient Egypt. 75 cm long, it is pure white except for dark ornamental plumes on its back, dark wing tips, and a black head and neck. It has a black bill and feeds in flocks along rivers, taking frogs and small aquatic animals.

Sadat, Anwar (1918-81) Egyptian statesman; president (1970-81). A colleague of *Nasser in the Free Officers movement, Sadat was twice vice president (1964-66, 1969-70) before becoming president on Nasser's death. He moved Egypt away from the Soviet Union and towards the USA, under the influence of which he negotiated a peace agreement with Israel in 1979 (□Carter, Jimmy). For this initiative and his courage in visiting Israel in the face of some Arab opposition he was awarded the 1978 Nobel Peace Prize jointly with Begin. He was assassinated (1981) by Islamic extremists while watching a military display in Egypt.

saddleback A very rare songbird, *Creadion carunculatus*, surviving only on small islands around New Zealand. It has a black plumage with a chestnut patch on its back and orange wattles at the base of the sharp pointed bill. Saddlebacks are weak fliers and feed in the undergrowth on larvae, insects, and fruits. Family: *Callaeidae* (wattlebirds).

Sadducees An ancient Jewish religious and political party. They formed a conservative and aristocratic group centring on the priesthood in Jerusalem. With the destruction of the temple the party ceased to exist, but many of its ideas surfaced later in medieval Jewish sects. *See also* Pharisees.

Sade, Donatien Alphonse François, Marquis de (1740-1814) French novelist. Most of his works of sexual fantasy and perversion, which include *Justine*, *La Philosophie dans le boudoir*, and *Les 120 Journées de Sodome*, were written in the 1780s and 1790s, during his many years of imprisonment for sexual offences. During his last years he was confined to the mental asylum of Charenton. His moral nihilism has been seen as a stage in the development of *existentialism. The sexual perversion "sadism," in which sexual pleasure is derived from causing or observing pain, is named after him.

Sa'di (Mosleh al-Din S.; c. 1215-92) Persian poet, born in Shiraz, who studied in Baghdad and subsequently spent much of his life wandering in Asia Minor and Egypt, claiming also to have visited India and central Asia. He returned to Shiraz in 1256. His major works are *Bustan* (*The Orchard*; 1257), a didactic poem illustrating the Islamic virtues of justice, contentedness, and modesty, and *Galestan* (*The Rose Garden*; 1258), a collection of moralistic anecdotes. He also wrote a number of odes and popularized the *ghazal* form later used by *Hafiz.

Sadler's Wells Theatre A theatre in London where Lilian *Baylis established an opera and ballet company in 1931. From the 1680s the medicinal wells on the site were exploited and its owner, Mr Sadler, later erected a music hall. In 1753 this became a theatre, where such actors as Sarah Siddons and Edmund Kean performed. Closed in 1878, Baylis restored the derelict building and here the Sadler's Wells Opera Company and the *Royal Ballet made their names. Since the opera company's removal to the London Coliseum in 1969, the theatre has been used by touring companies. *See also* English National Opera.

Sadowa (Czech name: Sadorá) A village in W Czechoslovakia, in NE Bohemia. It was the scene of a battle in the Austro-Prussian War (1866) in which the Austrians were defeated by the Prussians.

Safavids The ruling dynasty of Persia from 1502 to 1706. It was founded by Esmail I (1486-1524) and named after his ancestor Safi od-Din (1252-1334), a Muslim saint. Esmail established Shiism (*see* Shiites) as the state religion. Among his descendants was *Abbas the Great (reigned 1588-1628). The Safavids were overthrown by *Nader Shah.

safety lamp A lamp developed for use in coalmines, where the atmosphere may be highly inflammable or lacking in oxygen. The most celebrated safety lamp was that developed by Sir Humphrey *Davy in 1815 in which the flame produced by burning oil was protected by an iron gauze to prevent the passage of the flame to the surrounding atmosphere. However, flame lamps have now been almost entirely replaced by electric cap lamps and mains electric lighting.

safflower An annual herbaceous plant, *Carthamus tinctorius*, native to Asia and Africa. 30-120 cm tall, it has red, orange, yellow, or white flowers. It is cultivated in India, the Middle East, North America, and Australia for its seeds, which yield safflower oil, used in paints, varnishes, cooking oils, and margarines. A red dye can be obtained from the dried flowers. Family: *Compositae*.

saffron The dried orange-yellow stigmas of the saffron crocus (*C. sativa*), used for flavouring and colouring foods and liqueurs and formerly as a dye for fabrics. The crocus, which has purple flowers, is probably native to the Mediterranean region and SW Asia and has been cultivated since ancient times; today the main producing areas are France, Spain, and Italy. About 100 000 flowers are needed to produce 1 kg of saffron.

Safi (ancient name: Asfi) 32 20N 9 17W A port in Morocco, on the Atlantic coast. Its artificial harbour serves Marrakech, and exports include phosphates. Besides its important fishing industry, it manufactures pottery and has a chemical complex. Population (1982): 197 309.

Sagan, Françoise (Françoise Quoirez; 1935–) French writer. Her best-selling novels include *Bonjour Tristesse* (1954) and *Aimez-Vous Brahms?* (1959), concerning brief affairs between her wealthy characters, *La Femme fardée* (1981), and *With Fondest Regards* (1986). Her plays include *Château en Suède* (1960) and *Zaphorie* (1973).

sagas Heroic prose narratives in Old Norse, the best of which were written down in Iceland in the 12th and 13th centuries (*see* Icelandic literature). Translations of French *romances, Latin histories, and saints' lives were part of the saga tradition but its characteristic subject matter was drawn from ancient Scandinavian oral traditions: fictionalized accounts of the deeds of Norwegian kings (e.g. Snorri *Sturluson's *Heimskringla*), heroic legends of the pagan past (e.g. *Volsungasaga*), and the "family" sagas that mirrored contemporary Icelandic society (e.g. *Egilssaga*, *Gislasaga*, *Laxdaelasaga*, *Grettissaga*, and *Njálssaga*).

sage A perennial herb or shrub, *Salvia officinalis*, native to the Mediterranean region and widely cultivated for its leaves, which are used for flavouring foods. It grows 45-60 cm high and has blue, pink, or white flowers. *See also* Salvia.

sage grouse A large □grouse, *Centrocercus urophasianus*, occurring in sagebrush deserts of western USA. It is 75 cm long and the male has ornamental wattles and a long slender tail, which is fanned out during its courtship display.

Sagittarius (Latin: Archer) A large constellation in the S sky, lying on the *zodiac between Capricornus and Scorpius. The brightest star is the 2nd-magnitude Kaus Australis. The constellation contains several notable *star clusters and emission *nebulae, including the **Lagoon nebula**. The centre of the *Galaxy lies in the direction of Sagittarius, located in the intense radio source Sagittarius A.

sago A starchy food obtained from the Indonesian sago *palms (*Metoxylon sagu* and *M. rumphii*), cultivated in Malaysia. The palms, up to 9 m high, take 15 years to mature and are harvested just before flowering. The starchy pith in their stems is extracted, ground, and washed to make flour or pearl sago. The pithy stems of a tropical Asian *cycad, *Cycas circinalis*, also called sago palm, are used as a source of sago. The plant has ornamental fernlike leaves.

saguaro A giant cactus, *Cereus* (or *Carnegiea*) *gigantea*, native to the S USA and Mexico. It has a ribbed branched stem and is slow-growing, producing its white flowers from the age of 50–75 years; it may live for 200 years and reach a height of 12 m.

Saguenay River A river in E Canada, in E Quebec flowing from Lac St Jean ESE into the St Lawrence estuary. Its upper reaches drop steeply, providing hydroelectric power, while the lower course flows between high cliffs, a popular tourist attraction. Length: 170 km (105 mi).

Sagunto (Latin name: Saguntum) 39 40N 0 17W A town in E Spain, in Valencia. It was captured by Hannibal in 219 BC, precipitating the second Punic War. There are many fine Roman remains including a theatre and circus. It exports iron ore and citrus fruits. Population (1981): 54 759.

Sahara The largest desert in the world, covering most of N Africa. The terrain consists chiefly of a plateau with central mountains rising to 3415 m (11 204 ft) and some areas of sand dunes, such as the *Libyan Desert in the NE. The vegetation is sparse but sufficient in most parts for nomads to keep sheep and goats. Geological evidence shows that the Sahara was once well vegetated and that parts were formerly under the sea. There are large deposits of oil and gas in Algeria and Libya and phosphates in Morocco and Western Sahara. Rainfall is minimal and irregular, but there are numerous scattered oases watered from under ground that support small communities and are visited by nomads and travellers. The first European crossed the desert in 1822–24. Area: about 9 000 000 sq km (3 474 171 sq mi).

Sahel An area in West Africa, mainly in Mauritania, Mali, Niger, and Chad. It forms a band of savanna between the Sahara desert to the N and tropical vegetation to the S and is used as pasture. The desert is gradually encroaching on the area and in recent years it has suffered severe droughts. □desertification.

Saida. *See* Sidon.

saiga A small antelope, *Saiga tatarica*, of Asian deserts and steppes. About 80 cm high at the shoulder, saigas are slightly built with a pale woolly coat and a remarkable swollen snout with convoluted nasal tracts, thought to be an adaptation for warming inhaled air or to be related to their keen sense of smell. Males have straight ridged horns up to 30 cm long. Saigas form large herds to migrate southwards in winter. □mammal.

Saigon. *See* Ho Chi Minh City.

Saigo Takamori (1828–77) Japanese samurai famous for his tragic role in the Meiji restoration. He played a major part in the overthrow of the *Tokugawa regime (1868) but was opposed to radical modernization and the complete abolition of feudalism. When his supporters clashed with the government in 1877, he was torn between competing loyalties but committed himself to the rebellion and was eventually forced to commit hara-kiri.

sailfish A food and game fish, belonging to a genus (*Istiophorus*) related to marlins, that occurs in warm and temperate seas. Its slender body, deep blue above, silvery below, and up to 3.4 m long, has a long pointed snout, long pelvic fins, and a large sail-like dorsal fin. Sailfish feed mainly on other fish.

sailing Cruising or racing in a boat fitted with one or more sails. Some smaller sailing boats are equipped with an outboard motor; larger boats have one or more inboard auxiliary engines, for use in calm weather and for navigating in and out of harbours. Craft used for recreation and sport range from dinghies of 2.3 m (7.5 ft) to oceangoing yachts of

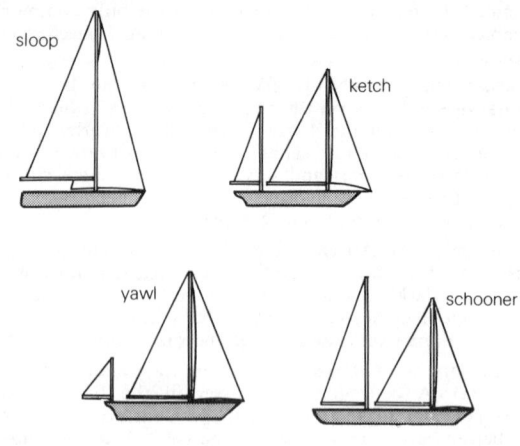

SAILING

23 m (75 ft) or more. All classes of boat can be used for racing but boats used primarily for racing have more complex sail plans requiring a relatively large crew, while the emphasis in a cruising boat is more on providing living accommodation. Racing, which became popular in the 19th century, is organized according to class of boat. Races are held either for yachts of the same design or for yachts of different designs competing with appropriate handicaps. Current Olympic classes (1980) are: Finn (4.5 m; singlehanded), 470 (4.7 m; two-man), Flying Dutchman (6.05 m; two-man), Star (6.91 m; two-man), Soling (8.16 m; threeman), and Tornado (6.1 m catamaran; two-man). In the Olympic Games seven races are held for each class.

Until the invention of nylon and Terylene (Dacron), all sails were made of canvas. Modern sails, made of synthetic fabrics, are more durable, resist mildew (can be stored wet), and retain their shape better than canvas.

Many different types of rigging have been used for sailing vessels throughout history. Square sails, which are of little use except when a vessel is sailing away from the wind, were the type employed on square-riggers, a rig prevalent in Europe from the 14th to the 19th centuries. These were largely replaced by the quadrilateral sails of early schoonerrigged vessels. Called gaffsails because the upper part of the sail was supported by a gaff boom, these were succeeded by triangular sails, which are popular on yachts today. *Sloops, *ketches, *schooners, and *yawls now employ triangular sails. Gaff-rigged vessels have given way to marconi- or Bermuda-rigged sailing boats, i.e. those with triangular sails. Small boats—sailing dinghies, etc.—may have only one sail, usually a gunter-rigged triangular sail supported at the upper leading edge by a boom that fits onto the top of a stubby mast set well forward in the boat. This rig is a modern version of the traditional lateen rig, a native design from the Near East that also uses a triangular sail hung from a very long boom. In the late 19th century, yachtsmen enlarged jibs into foresails called genoas. They also developed lightweight triangular foresails, called spinnakers, which often have a cross section like a part of the surface of a sphere. *See also* ships.

Saimaa, Lake A lake in SE Finland. It is the primary lake in a system spread over most of S Finland. Area: about 1760 sq km (680 sq mi).

sainfoin A perennial herb, *Onobrychis viciifolia*, native to temperate regions of Eurasia and found on chalky soils. Up to 50 cm tall, it has pale-pink flowers and has been cultivated as a forage plant. Family: *Leguminosae.

saint In Christian belief, a person characterized by special holiness. In the early Church the term applied to all believers, and certain modern sects follow this practice in calling their adherents saints, for example the *Mormons. In the *Roman Catholic Church saints formally admitted to the calendar of saints by *canonization can be invoked as intercessors, although recently their numbers have been reduced in an effort to cut superstitious practices. *Protestantism rejects the invocation of saints, although the *Church of England's calendar recognizes a number of saints' days.

St Albans 51 46N 0 21W A city in SE England, in Hertfordshire. Across the River Ver stood the important Romano-British town of Verulamium, where the martyrdom of St Alban took place; Roman remains include a theatre and mosaic pavement. The Benedictine abbey, founded in honour of the saint in 793 AD, was made a cathedral in 1877 and has the second longest nave in Britain. St Albans' industries include printing, electrical equipment, and rubber goods. Population (1981): 50 888.

St Andrews 56 20N 2 48W A resort in E Scotland, in Fife Region on St Andrews Bay. An ancient ecclesiastical centre, its university (1412) is the oldest in Scotland. The famous Royal and Ancient Golf Club was founded here in 1754. Population (1985 est): 16 000.

St Anthony's fire. *See* ergot.

St Augustine 29 54N 81 19W A city in the USA, in Florida. The oldest city in the USA, it was founded by the Spanish in 1565 and for most of the next two and a half centuries remained the most northerly outpost of the Spanish colonial empire. The Castillo de San Marcos (1672) stands as a reminder of Spanish rule. Tourism is the main source of revenue. Population (1980): 11 985.

St Austell 50 20N 4 48W A market town in SW England, in Cornwall near St Austell Bay. It is a holiday resort and centre of the thriving local china-clay industry. Population (1981): 36 639, with Fowey.

St Bartholomew's Day Massacre The slaughter of *Huguenots that began on 24 August, 1572, in Paris. The massacre was ordered by Charles IX of France under the influence of his mother, Catherine de' Medici. Some 3000 Huguenots died in Paris and many more were murdered in the provinces.

St Basil's Cathedral The cathedral of the Russian Orthodox Church in Moscow built between 1554 and 1560 for Ivan the Terrible. It is named after the Russian saint, who was buried there at the end of the 16th century.

St Bernard A breed of large working dog developed in Europe from Asian ancestors and employed as a rescue dog by the hospice of St Bernard in the Swiss Alps since the 17th century. It is massively built, having a large head with drooping ears. The coat may be either short or of medium length and is white marked with red-brown or brindle. Height: 65 cm minimum.

St Bernard Passes Two mountain passes in the Alps, in central Europe. The **Great St Bernard Pass** on the Swiss-Italian border is one of the highest alpine passes at 2433 m (8111 ft). The hospice at its summit, founded (11th century) by St Bernard of Menthon, is famous for the St Bernard dogs that were formerly used to rescue snowbound travellers. The **Little St Bernard Pass** on the French-Italian border reaches 2187 m (7177 ft) and also has an 11th-century hospice.

St Catherines 43 10N 79 15W A city and port in E Canada, in S Ontario at the entrance to the *Welland Ship Canal. Founded in 1790, it is a fruit-farming and industrial centre and houses Brock University (1962). Population (1981): 124 018.

St Christopher. *See* St Kitts-Nevis-Anguilla.

St Clair, Lake A lake in E North America, on the US-Canadian border. It lies near Detroit, between Lakes Huron and Erie in the Great Lakes chain. Area: 1190 sq km (460 sq mi).

St-Cloud 46 22N 5 50E A town in France, a W suburb of

Paris. Mainly residential, it is the site of the Sèvres porcelain factory. Population (1982): 28 760.

St Croix (*or* Santa Cruz) A West Indian island, the largest of the US Virgin Islands. The economy is based on tourism and agriculture. Area: 207 sq km (80 sq mi). Population (1980). 49 013. Chief town: Christiansted.

Saint-Cyr, École de French military academy founded in 1803 and established in 1808 at Saint-Cyr-l'École, near Versailles. Its buildings were destroyed in World War II and it is now at Coëtquidan, Brittany.

St David's (Welsh name: Tyddewi) 51 54N 5 16W A village in SW Wales in Dyfed, the smallest cathedral city in Britain. The 12th-century cathedral, the largest in Wales, was an important medieval pilgrimage centre for the shrine of St David. Population (1984): 1595.

St-Denis 20 52S 55 27E The capital of Réunion, on the W Indian Ocean. A port on the N of the island, its activities are mainly administrative, with some commerce. Population (1982): 109 072.

St-Denis 48 56N 2 21E A town in France, an industrial suburb of Paris in the Seine-St Denis department on the River Seine. Its gothic abbey contains the tombs of many French kings. Population (1982): 91 275.

St Dunstan's (for Men and Women Blinded on War Service) A British organization for the training, settlement, and lifelong care of those blinded in war. It was founded in 1915 by a blind newspaper proprietor, Sir Arthur Pearson (1866–1921). Secretary: W. C. Weisblatt.

Sainte-Beuve, Charles-Augustin (1804–69) French literary historian and critic. He first studied medicine, but abandoned it to write poetry. After writing the novel *Volupté* (1834), based in part on his love affair with Victor Hugo's wife, he devoted himself to criticism. His literary journalism helped to establish many young writers of the Romantic movement. His major critical works include *Critiques et portraits littéraires* (1836–39) and *Port-Royal* (1840–59), a study of Jansenism.

St Elias Mountains A mountain range in NW North America, running SE along the Alaska-Yukon border. Many summits surpass 5000 m (16 400 ft) and it reaches 6050 m (19 850 ft) at Mount Logan, its highest point. The range also includes the world's largest nonpolar ice cap.

St Elmo's fire A small electrical discharge, with a luminous appearance, that is associated with stormy weather and seen around the extremities of tall objects, such as the tops of trees and mastheads.

St-Étienne 45 27N 4 22E A city in S central France, the capital of the Loire department. It has produced firearms since the 16th century and was the site of France's first steel mill (1815). More recent manufactures include aero engines, chemicals, and dyes. It has a famous school of mining engineering (1816) and a university. Population (1982): 206 087.

Saint-Exupéry, Antoine de (1900–44) French novelist and aviator. The themes of his novels, which include *Night Flight* (1931) and *Wind, Sand and Stars* (1939), derive from his experience as a pioneer of air-mail routes in N Africa and South America. He also wrote a fable for children, *The Little Prince* (1943), and an uncompleted philosophical book. He failed to return from a mission while on active service with the French air force in World War II.

St Gall (German name: Sankt Gallen) 47 25N 9 23E A town in NE Switzerland, S of Lake Constance. The Celtic missionary St Gall established a hermitage here (612 AD), later to become a Benedictine abbey. Monastic buildings remaining include the cathedral (1755–72) and the library, which contains a fine collection of manuscripts. Population (1983): 74 000.

St George's 12 04N 61 44W The capital of Grenada, on the SW coast. Founded by the French in the 17th century, it was capital of the British Windward Islands from 1885 to

1958. It is now a tourist resort as well as an important port. Population (1981 est): 7500.

St George's Channel A channel between SE Ireland and Wales, linking the Irish Sea with the Atlantic Ocean. Length: about 160 km (100 mi). Maximum width: 145 km (90 mi).

St Gotthard Pass 46 34N 8 31E A pass in the Alps, in S Switzerland linking central Europe and Italy by road. The St Gotthard railway tunnel (constructed 1872–80) below the pass is 15 km (9 mi) long and the second longest in the Alps. Height: 2114 m (6935 ft).

St Helena 15 58S 5 43W A mountainous island in the S Atlantic Ocean, a British dependent territory. Napoleon I was exiled here (1815–21). The economy declined when sailing ships stopped calling here following the opening of the Suez Canal (1869); it now depends on agriculture and the UK subsidies it receives. Area: 122 sq km (47 sq mi). Population (1982): 5499. Capital: Jamestown.

St Helens 53 28N 2 44W A town in NW England, in Merseyside. It has an important glass industry, besides brick and tile manufacturing, engineering, pharmaceutical production, brewing, and, nearby, coalmining. Population (1981): 98 769.

St Helens, Mount 46 12N 122 11W A volcano in SW Washington, in the S Cascade Range, NE of Vancouver, Canada. Dormant since 1857, the mountain erupted in May, 1980, causing widespread destruction in which more than 50 people died. Further eruptions since 1980 have caused minor damage. Height: 2950 m (9677 ft).

St Helier 49 12N 2 07W A market town and resort in the Channel Islands, on the S coast of Jersey. There is a substantial trade in early vegetables and Jersey cattle. Population (1981): 25 698.

St Ives 50 12N 5 29W A resort in SW England, in Cornwall on St Ives Bay (an inlet on the N coast). It is a small fishing port and centre for water sports and artists (*see* Hepworth, Barbara). Population (1981): 10 985.

St James's Palace A royal palace in Pall Mall, in London, built for Henry VIII on the site of an 11th-century hospital for leprous women. It was the principal London residence of the monarch from 1697, when Whitehall was burnt down, until superseded by Buckingham Palace in 1837. Much of the original building was destroyed by a fire in 1807.

Saint John 45 16N 66 03W A city and port in E Canada, in New Brunswick at the mouth of the St John River. Originally a French fort (1631), it developed with the arrival of American Loyalists (1783) into the province's centre of heavy industry and commerce. Population (1981): 80 521.

St John River A river in E North America. Rising in Maine, USA, it flows NE to New Brunswick, Canada, and then SE to the Bay of Fundy, where high tides cause the river to reverse its course at the famous Reversing Falls. Length: 673 km (418 mi).

St John's 47 34N 52 41W A city in E Canada, the capital of Newfoundland. Settled in the 16th century, it is Canada's easternmost city, located beside a huge protected harbour. It was here in 1901 that Marconi received the first transatlantic radio message. St John's has two cathedrals (Roman Catholic and Anglican) and is the site of Memorial University (1925). Newfoundland's commercial centre, its industries include fishing, food processing, shipbuilding, timber, and textiles. Population (1981): 83 770.

St John's 17 07N 61 51W The chief port of Antigua, on the NW coast. It handles the island's agricultural produce. Population (1982 est): 30 000.

St John's wort A perennial herb or shrub belonging to the genus *Hypericum* (400 species), found in temperate regions. They have yellow five-petalled flowers with many stamens and many species are cultivated for ornament, including *H. calycinum* (also known as rose of Sharon). The common European St John's wort (*H. perforatum*) reaches a height of 50 cm. Family: *Guttiferae*.

St Joseph 39 45N 94 51W A city in the USA, in Missouri on the Missouri River. Often referred to as St Joe, it is an important grain and livestock centre, serving a large agricultural area. It was the home of the outlaw Jesse James. Population (1980): 76 691.

Saint-Just, Louis (Antoine Léon) de (1767–94) French politician, who supported *Robespierre in the French Revolution. His pamphlet, *Esprit de la révolution et de la constitution de France* (1791), calling for a new moral order, brought him to public notice. He was a member of the Committee of *Public Safety, supervising military affairs, and led the attack on the Austrians at Fleurus (1794). He was arrested and guillotined with Robespierre.

St Kilda 57 49N 8 34W A group of three small mountainous islands about 200 km (124 mi) W off the Scottish mainland, the most westerly of the Outer Hebrides. Populated from prehistoric times until evacuation in 1930, they are now a nature reserve. Area: about 16 sq km (6 sq mi).

St Kitts-Nevis (*or* St Christopher-Nevis) A country in the West Indies, in the Leeward Islands in the E Caribbean Sea. From 1967 it was a UK associated state consisting of three islands: St Kitts, Nevis, and Anguilla. Anguilla had its own constitution from 1976 and in 1980 became a separate British dependency. St Kitts-Nevis became fully independent within the British Commonwealth in 1983. The economy is primarily agricultural, sugar, molasses, cotton, and coconuts being the main products but tourism is becoming increasingly important. Prime minister: Dr Kennedy Simmonds. Area: 262 sq km (101 sq mi). Population (1980): 44 404. Capital: Basseterre, on St Kitts. *See also* Anguilla.

Saint-Laurent, Yves (1936–) French fashion designer, who trained with *Dior and took over his fashion house (1957), opening his own in 1962. His creations for women have been predominantly influenced by male fashion and include black leather jackets edged with fur, thigh-length boots, safari jackets, and many trouser designs.

St Lawrence, Gulf of An arm of the Atlantic Ocean in E Canada, at the mouth of the St Lawrence River. Historically the gateway to Canada, it has always been an important fishing ground. Ice closes the gulf to navigation from early December until mid-April.

St Lawrence River A river in North America. Although the river proper is fairly short, it belongs to one of the world's greatest water systems, draining the *Great Lakes into the Atlantic Ocean. From Lake Ontario it flows NE along the Canadian-US border as a broad stream through the Thousand Islands, a major tourist district. Above Montreal it enters Canada and passes through rapids where hydroelectricity is produced. At Quebec it broadens into a long estuary that gradually merges with the *Gulf of St Lawrence. The St Lawrence valley is an important agricultural and industrial belt as well as a rail, water, and road corridor. The upper reaches of the river become unnavigable during winter months. Length: Lake Ontario to Quebec 480 km (298 mi); St Louis River headwaters to Anticosti Island 3395 km (2110 mi). *See also* St Lawrence Seaway.

St Lawrence Seaway A navigable waterway in North America through the St Lawrence River and the Great Lakes, completed in 1959. With a season of over eight months, it admits ships of up to 9000 tons, mainly carrying heavy nonperishables.

St Leger A flat race for three-year-old horses, run in September at Doncaster over 2.9 km (1 mi 6½ furlongs). It was the earliest of the English *Classics to be established (1776).

St-Lô 49 01N 1 05W A town in NW France, the capital of the Manche department. A market town famous for its horse breeding, it was virtually destroyed in *World War II. Population (1982): 24 792.

St Louis 38 40N 90 15W A city and port in the USA, in Missouri on the Mississippi River. It was a major centre in

ST PAUL'S CATHEDRAL *Sir Christopher Wren's double dome is seen in this engraving of 1755.*

the colonization of the West, outfitting such exploring parties as that of Lewis and Clark (1804–06), as well as pioneers using the Santa Fe, California, and Oregon Trails. It has four universities, including St Louis University (1818), which maintains a library built to house microfilms of Vatican Library treasures. The state's largest city, it is an important market, trading in livestock, wool, grain, and timber. Industries include aircraft, cars, chemicals, and iron and steel. Population (1980): 453 085.

St Louis 16 00N 16 27W A port in W Senegal, on an island in the River Senegal estuary. It was the capital of Senegal until replaced by Dakar (1958). Population (1979 est): 96 594.

St Lucia An island country in the West Indies, in the Windward Islands in the E Caribbean Sea. It is a mountainous island of volcanic origin. The population is mainly of African descent. *Economy*: mainly agricultural, the chief products are bananas and coconuts. Tourism is a growing industry and attempts are being made to develop the manufacturing sector. An oil-refining and transshipment complex was in the process of being built (S of Castries) at the time of the island's independence (1979). It is a member of CARICOM. *History*: it became internally self-governing in 1967 and attained full independence within the British Commonwealth in February, 1979. Prime minister: John Compton. Official language: English. Official currency: East Caribbean dollar of 100 cents. Area: 616 sq km (238 sq mi). Population (1983 est): 119 000. Capital: Castries.

St-Malo 49 39N 2 00W A port and resort in NW France, in the Ille-et-Vilaine department on the English Channel. Many of its old buildings were destroyed during World War II, although its ramparts (12th–18th centuries) remain. A flourishing trading, fishing, and passenger port, it has shipbuilding and electrical industries. Population (1982): 47 324.

St Mark's Cathedral The cathedral church of Venice since 1807. It was built in the 9th century to house the relics of St Mark but rebuilt in the 11th century after a fire. Designed as a Greek cross surmounted by five domes, it is strongly influenced by *Byzantine art and is famous for its opulent mosaic and sculptural decoration both inside and out.

St Martin (Dutch name: Sint Maarten) 18 05N 63 05W A West Indian island in the Lesser Antilles, administratively divided between France and the Netherlands. The N part is a dependency of Guadeloupe, area 52 sq km (20 sq mi) with a population (1982) of 8072; the S is part of the Netherlands Antilles, area 33 sq km (13 sq mi) with a population (1983) of 15 926. Salt is the main export.

St Marylebone A district in the Greater London Borough of the City of Westminster. It contains Harley Street and Wimpole Street (noted for their doctors), Madame Tussaud's, and the Planetarium. *Lord's cricket ground is situated in St John's Wood (London's first garden suburb).

St Moritz (German name: Sankt Moritz) 46 30N 9 51E A resort in SE Switzerland, on St Moritz Lake. A renowned wintersports centre at a height of 1822 m (5978 ft), its famous Cresta Run (for bobsleds) dates from 1885. Population (1980): 5900.

St-Nazaire 47 17N 2 12W A major port in W France, in the Loire-Atlantique department on the Loire estuary. An important German submarine base in World War II, it was virtually destroyed by Allied bombing. Its main industries are shipbuilding, aircraft construction, chemicals, and oil refining. Population (1982): 68 947.

St Paul 45 00N 93 10W A city in the USA, the capital of Minnesota on the Mississippi River. Adjacent to Minneapolis, the Twin Cities comprise the commercial and industrial centre of an extensive grain and cattle area. St Paul's industries include oil refining, car assembly, and food processing. Population (1980): 270 230.

St Paul's Cathedral The cathedral of the diocese of London; there have been five cathedrals on this site, the first three of which were Saxon. The Norman cathedral, begun in 1087 and one of the largest buildings in England, was destroyed in the *Great Fire and *Wren was appointed to rebuild it. His design (1672–1717), combining *classicism and the *baroque style, features a traditional cruciform plan, a two-tiered portico, a great dome, and flanking towers. The best contemporary artists decorated the interior, including the painter *Thornhill, the woodcarver Grinling *Gibbons, and the iron worker Jean Tijou (died c. 1711).

St Peter Port 49 27N 2 32W A resort in the Channel Islands, the only town in Guernsey. It has a large protected harbour. Population (1981): 15 587.

St Peter's Basilica The Catholic basilica in the Vatican City, Rome. The original basilica, a huge gothic building, was pulled down by Pope Julius II in the early 16th century. Its replacement is the largest church in the world. Its general shape was determined by *Bramante, although it was designed together with its enormous dome by *Michelangelo. *Vignola continued the work and the nave and façade were added by *Maderna. *Bernini completed the building in the 17th century, adding the huge baldacchino and the colonnade to the piazza outside.

St Petersburg 27 45N 82 40W A city in the USA, in Florida on Tampa Bay. It is primarily a tourist resort. Population (1980): 236 893.

St Petersburg. *See* Leningrad.

St Pierre 14 44N 61 11W A small port in Martinique, at the foot of the volcano Mount Pelée. In 1902 an eruption destroyed the town leaving only one survivor. It is now the centre of an area growing sugar cane.

St Pierre et Miquelon A French overseas department, consisting of two neighbouring islands in the NW Atlantic

Ocean S of Newfoundland. All that remained to France of its Canadian territories after 1763, they have traditionally been bases for fishing and smuggling. More recently tourism has been developed. Area: St Pierre 26 sq km (10 sq mi): Miquelon 215 sq km (83 sq mi). Population (1981 est): 6272.

St-Quentin 49 51N 3 17E A town in NE France, in the Aisne department on the River Somme. It was the scene of French defeats by Spain (1557) and by Prussia (1871) in the Franco-Prussian War and was almost completely destroyed in *World War I. It has textile, electrical, and metallurgical industries. Population (1982): 65 067.

Saint-Saëns, Camille (1835-1921) French composer, conductor, pianist, and organist. He began to perform and compose while still a child. He studied with Halévy and Gounod and held various organ posts, including nearly 20 years at the Madeleine. His piano pupils included Messager and Fauré, and he championed the music of Liszt, Berlioz, and Wagner. He wrote 12 operas, five symphonies (the third with organ; 1886), *The Carnival of the Animals* (published posthumously; 1922) for two pianos and orchestra, five piano, three violin, and two cello concertos, chamber music, and choral works.

Saint-Simon, Claude Henri de Rouvroy, Comte de (1760-1825) The founder of French socialism. Saint-Simon was educated by *D'Alembert. Having witnessed the horror and chaos of the French Revolution, Saint-Simon was concerned to reconstruct society and his writings have a positive and idealistic tone. In *Du système industriel* (1821) he declared his aim of achieving an industrial state in which poverty is eliminated and in which science replaces religion as the spiritual authority.

Saint-Simon, Louis de Rouvroy, Duc de (1675-1755) French memoir writer. He lived at the court of Louis XIV and although he exercised some influence during the regency of Philippe, Duc d'Orléans (1715-23), his ambitions at court were never realized. His *Mémoires*, covering the years 1694-1723, are enlivened by his prejudices, his sharp observation of detail, and his brilliant portraits. The definitive edition was not published until 1879-1923.

St Stephen's Crown The crown of Hungary, which was reputedly first used by Stephen I. It was originally a Byzantine circlet made between 1074 and 1077 and converted into an emperor's crown by Hungarians in the 12th century. It fell into the hands of the US army in 1945 but was returned in 1978.

St Thomas 18 22N 64 57W A West Indian island in the US Virgin Islands, in the Lesser Antilles. After 1680 it became a major Caribbean sugar producer and later, after 1764, the largest slave-trading port. Tourism is now of major importance. Area: 83 sq km (28 sq mi). Population (1980): 44 218. Capital: Charlotte Amalie.

St Vincent, Cape (Portuguese name: Cabo de São Vicente) 37 01N 8 59W A promontory in the extreme SW of Portugal, in the Algarve on the Atlantic Ocean. A number of naval battles have been fought off the cape; in 1797 the Spanish fleet was defeated by the British under Admiral Jervis during the Napoleonic Wars.

Saint Vincent, Gulf An inlet of the Indian Ocean, in S Australia E of Yorke Peninsula. It has an important salt industry on the E coast. Length: about 145 km (90 mi). Width: about 73 km (45 mi).

St Vincent and the Grenadines A country in the E Caribbean Sea, in the Windward Islands of the Lesser Antilles. It consists of the principal island of St Vincent together with its dependencies of the Grenadine islets. It became a British possession in 1763 and attained internal self-government in 1969. In 1979 it became fully independent. It is predominantly agricultural, the chief crops being arrowroot (of which it is the world's chief producer), sugar cane, and bananas. Prime minister: James Mitchell. Area:

390 sq km (150 sq mi). Population (1983 est): 128 000. Capital: Kingstown.

St Vitus's dance The old name for *chorea, so called because of the uncontrolled movements characteristic of the disease and because sufferers in the middle ages prayed for a cure at the shrine of St Vitus (the patron saint of dancers).

Saipan 15 12N 145 43E One of the Northern Mariana Islands, in the W Pacific Ocean. It was the administrative centre of the UN Trust Territory of the Pacific Islands (1947-75). Area: 180 sq km (70 sq mi). Population (1980): 14 549. Chief town: Susupe.

saithe A food fish, *Pollachius* (or *Gadus*) *virens*, also called coalfish or coley, that is related to cod and lives in shoals in the North Atlantic. Its elongated body, up to about 120 cm long, is greenish brown above and silvery white below.

Sakai 34 35N 135 28E A city in Japan, in S Honshu on the Yamato delta. Formerly an important port (15th-17th centuries), it is part of the Osaka-Kobe industrial complex. Population (1980): 810 000.

saké (*or* rice wine) An alcoholic drink made in Japan from steamed rice, to which a special yeast is added, and slowly fermented. It resembles a light sherry in taste and is served warm.

Sakhalin (Japanese name: Karafuto) An island in the Soviet Union, in the RSFSR off the SE coast between the Sea of Okhotsk and the Sea of Japan. It comprises two parallel mountain ranges on either side of a central valley and is heavily forested. Timber, coal- and iron-mining, and paper milling are important industrial activities, and there are oilfields in the NE that serve the Soviet Far East. Agriculture, principally the cultivation of vegetables and dairy farming, is pursued in the S. *History*: a Russo-Japanese condominium from 1855 until 1875, it then passed to Russia but in 1905 was again divided between the two countries. In 1945 the Soviet Union acquired the whole island and expelled its Japanese population (about 400 000). Area: about 76 000 sq km (29 300 sq mi). Population (1983 est): 660 000.

Sakharov, Andrei Dimitrievich (1921-   ) Soviet physicist. After helping to develop the Soviet hydrogen bomb during the 1940s and 1950s he spoke out against nuclear weapons in the 1960s and argued for freedom of speech in the Soviet Union. He was awarded the Nobel Peace Prize in 1975. His exile to Gorkii in 1980 aroused international protest. After a hunger strike (1984), he was finally released (1986) and took part in the international conference (1987) in Moscow on peace and nuclear weapons.

saki A South American monkey belonging to the genus *Pithecia* (3 species), found in forests. Sakis are 55-125 cm long including the tail (25-55 cm) and have a thick shaggy coat and hairy hood. Wholly arboreal, they feed on berries, honey, leaves, and small animals. Family: *Cebidae*.

Saki (H(ector) H(ugh) Munro; 1870-1916) British humorous short-story writer. Born in Burma, he worked as a foreign correspondent before settling in London in 1908. He published several volumes of humorous stories many of which were based on the outrageous activities of his fastidious and snobbish heroes Clovis and Reginald. He also wrote a novel, *The Unbearable Bassington* (1912). He was killed in action in World War I.

Saladin (Arabic name: Salah ad-Din; ?1137-93) The leader of the Muslims against the Crusaders in Syria. Of Kurdish descent, he obtained control over the Muslim lands in Egypt, of which he became sultan in 1175, and Syria. He then captured the Kingdom of Jerusalem following his great victory over the Crusaders at the battle of Hattin (1187). The last years of his life were spent fighting the third *Crusade, during which he won his legendary reputation as a chivalrous warrior.

Salado, Río The name of several South American rivers, meaning salty river. 1. A river in N Argentina, rising in the Andes and flowing SE to join the Río Paraná. Length:

2012 km (1250 mi). **2.** A river in W Argentina, rising near the Chilean border and flowing S to join the Río Colorado. Length: about 1365 km (850 mi).

Salam, Abdus (1926–) Pakistani physicist, who became professor of physics at Imperial College, London, in 1957. He is also director of the International Centre for Theoretical Physics in Trieste. In 1979 he shared the Nobel Prize with the US physicists Sheldon Glashow (1932–) and Steven Weinberg (1933–) for their work on *weak interactions.

ANDREI SAKHAROV

Salamanca 40 58N 5 40W A city in central Spain, in León. During the Peninsular War the battle of Salamanca was fought here on 22 July, 1812, in which Wellington secured a decisive victory over the French. An intellectual centre of Renaissance Europe, Salamanca remains an important cultural centre with a university (founded 1218). Its many notable old buildings include two cathedrals and it has a fine Roman bridge. Population (1981): 167 131.

salamander A tailed *amphibian belonging to a widely distributed order (*Urodela* or *Caudata*; about 225 species). Salamanders have short legs and long bodies and move by bending the body from side to side to give as wide a movement as possible for their feet. They usually hide in damp places when not hunting small worms and insects. Their habits range from the wholly aquatic Japanese giant salamander (*Megalobatrachus japonicus*), 1.5 cm long, to the American woodland salamanders (genus *Plethodon*) that live entirely on land. *See also* congo eel; hellbender; mudpuppy; olm; newt; siren.

Salamis A Greek island in the Aegean Sea. It was the scene of a Greek naval victory over the Persians in 480 BC. Area: 95 sq km (37 sq mi). Population (1985 est): 20 000. Chief town: Salamis.

sal ammoniac (*or* ammonium chloride; NH_4Cl) A white crystalline solid, used in batteries and as a pickling agent in zinc coating and tinning.

Salazar, António de Oliveira (1889–1970) Portuguese dictator. Salazar became prime minister in 1932 and ruled until suffering a stroke in 1968. His New State imposed his corporatist ideas on Portugal. It repressed political opposition and fought long colonial wars in Africa, which gravely impeded the country's economic development.

Salé 34 04N 6 50W A port in NW Morocco, on the Atlantic coast opposite Rabat. It was an important medieval port and during the 17th century was the base for the Sallee Rovers, a notorious group of Barbary pirates. Population (1982): 289 391.

Sale 38 06S 147 06E A city in Australia, in S Victoria on the Thomson River. It is a centre for the irrigated East Gippsland area; tourism is also important. Population (1981): 12 968.

Salem 11 38N 78 08E A city in India, in Tamil Nadu. A developing industrial centre, it has large-scale textile manufacturing. Population (1981): 515 000.

Salem 42 32N 70 53W A city in the USA, the capital of Oregon on the Willamette River. Founded in 1840, it is a food-processing centre for a large agricultural area. Willamette University was established here in 1844. Population (1980): 89 161.

Salerno 40 40N 14 46E A port in Italy, in Campania on the Gulf of Salerno. Founded by the Romans in 197 BC, Salerno is best known for its medical school, which flourished here in the middle ages. It was the scene of heavy fighting during World War II, following major Allied troop landings here in 1943. Notable buildings include the 11th-century cathedral, where Gregory VII is buried. The chief industries are engineering, flour milling, textiles, and cement. Population (1980 est): 161 863.

Salford 53 30N 2 16W A city in NW England, in Greater Manchester on the River Irwell and the Manchester Ship Canal. The docks for Manchester are here. Salford has an important engineering industry and manufactures textiles, electrical equipment, chemicals, tyres, and clothing. There is a Roman Catholic cathedral (1848) and a university (1967), formerly a college of technology. Population (1981): 98 024.

Salic Law The law of the Salian *Franks issued under Clovis in the early 6th century. Owing little to other contemporary law codes or to Roman law, it is concerned with both criminal and civil law. Its importance for later periods lies in its prohibition against women inheriting land. This canon was invoked in France in 1316 and 1321 to prevent a woman from succeeding to the throne and, in 1328, Edward III's claim to the French Crown was rejected on the grounds that his claim was by female descent.

Salicornia. *See* glasswort.

salicylic acid An antiseptic compound (OHC_6H_4COOH) that causes the skin to peel. It is used to treat certain skin conditions, including psoriasis, eczema, warts, and corns. Aspirin (*see* aspirin) is a derivative.

Salieri, Antonio (1750–1825) Italian composer and conductor. He studied and worked in Vienna from 1766. His pupils included Beethoven, Schubert, and Liszt. Because of his rivalry with Mozart, he was fancifully credited with having poisoned him.

Salinger, J(erome) D(avid) (1919–) US novelist. After contributing stories to the *New Yorker* he achieved success with his novel *The Catcher in the Rye* (1951). Later works include *Franny and Zooey* (1961), *Raise High the Roof Beam, Carpenters* (1963), and *Seymour, An Introduction* (1963).

Salisbury (Name from 1982: Harare) 17 50S 31 02E The capital of Zimbabwe, on a plateau in the NE. Founded in 1890, it was the capital of the Federation of Rhodesia and Nyasaland (1953–63). The University of Zimbabwe (formerly Rhodesia) was founded here in 1970 and Salisbury has Anglican and Roman Catholic cathedrals. The centre of a tobacco-growing area, it has an important trade and industry in tobacco. Other industries include textiles and engineering. Population (1980 est): 654 000.

Salisbury 51 05N 1 48W A city in S England, in Wiltshire at the confluence of the Rivers Avon and Wylye. Its 13th-century cathedral has the highest spire in the country, 123 m (403 ft) high. Salisbury's industries include light engineering, brewing, and tourism. Nearby is Old Sarum, the site of an Iron Age hill fort with extensive earthworks; settlement here continued until the 13th century, when the cathedral was moved to New Sarum (Salisbury). Old Sarum was the most notorious of the pre-1832 *rotten boroughs. Population (1981): 35 355.

Salisbury, Robert Cecil, 1st Earl of. *See* Burghley, William Cecil, Lord.

Salisbury, Robert Arthur Talbot Gascoyne-Cecil, 3rd Marquess of (1830-1903) British statesman; Conservative prime minister (1886-92, 1895-1900, 1900-02). Elected an MP in 1853, he was twice secretary for India (1866-67, 1874-78) before becoming Disraeli's foreign secretary (1878). As prime minister he served as his own foreign secretary (except in 1886 and 1900-02) and his policy has been characterized as one of "splendid isolation." Although he negotiated the Mediterranean Agreements with Italy and Austria-Hungary in 1887, under Salisbury Britain had no formal ally until alliance was concluded with Japan in 1902.

Salisbury Plain An area of open chalk downs in S England, in Wiltshire. It contains many prehistoric remains, notably *Stonehenge. Extensively used as a military training ground, the first permanent camp was established at Tidworth (1902). Area: about 518 sq km (200 sq mi).

saliva The fluid secreted by three pairs of **salivary glands** around the mouth in response to the sight, smell, taste, or thought of food. Although saliva contains the enzyme *amylase, which aids the digestion of starch, its major role is to bind the food particles and to lubricate the mouth and gullet.

Salk vaccine The first antipolio vaccine to be used successfully. It was developed by the US virologist J. E. Salk (1914-) and first used in 1954. The vaccine, which contains killed polio viruses that stimulate the defence mechanisms of the body, is given by three consecutive subcutaneous injections. It has now been replaced by the *Sabin vaccine in many countries.

sallow. *See* willow.

Sallust (Gaius Sallustius Crispus; c. 86-c. 34 BC) Roman politican and historian. Expelled from the Senate for alleged immorality, he supported Julius Caesar in the war against Pompey and became governor of Numidia. He was accused of corruption and extortion and retired from politics in about 44 BC. His best-known works are the monographs *Bellum Catilinae* and *Bellum Jugurthinum*, noted for their forceful dramatic style.

salmon One of several fish of the genera *Oncorhynchus* or *Salmo*, especially the Atlantic salmon (*S. salar*)—a valuable food and game fish. It has an elongated body, up to 150 cm long, and two dorsal fins. Salmon live mainly in the sea, feeding on other fish, especially herrings. However, they migrate into fresh water to spawn, at which time they change from silvery-blue or green to become brownish or greenish with orange markings. The spawned fish (kelts) either die or return to the sea and spawn in successive years. On hatching the young fish are known as alevins, although when they start feeding they are called parr. At about two years the coat becomes silver and the fish (smolt) migrate to the sea to reach maturity. After about two to three years they return to their native spawning waters as grilse, guided upstream by their sense of smell. Salmon is eaten freshly cooked (and

canned) or smoked (Scotch salmon being regarded as the best). Family: *Salmonidae*; order: *Salmoniformes*.

Salmonella A genus of rod-shaped bacteria that are parasites of animals and man and cause several diseases: *S. typhi* and *S. paratyphi* cause *typhoid fever in man while *S. typhimurium* is a common cause of *food poisoning. Other species infect other mammals and birds.

Salò, Republic of (1943-45) The fascist government established by *Mussolini after Italy's surrender in World War II. Mussolini, rescued from prison by German parachute troops, set up his government at Salò in German-controlled N Italy. Partisan opposition, Mussolini's death, and Germany's surrender caused its collapse.

Salome The daughter of Herodias by her first husband, Herod Philip. The Jewish historian Josephus identifies her with the unnamed girl in the Gospels who requested the head of *John the Baptist from her stepfather, *Herod Antipas, as a reward for her dancing.

Salon The annual exhibition held by the French Royal Academy, which was founded in 1648. Housed in the Salon d'Apollon, in the Louvre, it became a bulwark of conservative art in the 19th century. The **Salon des Refusés** (1863) was a special exhibition held at the instigation of Napoleon III to exhibit the enormous number of paintings rejected by the Salon jury that year. Its contributors included *Manet, *Pissarro, and *Whistler.

Salon des Indépendants The annual exhibition of the Société des Artistes Indépendants in Paris. The Société was founded in 1884 to enable such avantgarde painters as *Cézanne and *Seurat to exhibit works that had been or would have been rejected by the French Royal Academy's *Salon. Unlike the Salon, the Salon des Indépendants had no jury.

Salonika. *See* Thessaloniki.

Salop. *See* Shropshire.

salp. *See* tunicate.

salsify A biennial herb, *Tragopogon porrifolius*, native to the Mediterranean region, also called vegetable oyster or oyster plant. It is cultivated in temperate regions for its fleshy white root, supposed to taste like oysters when cooked. The plant has long narrow leaves and a head of purple flowers surrounded by stiff pointed green sepals. The leaves may be eaten in salads. Family: *Compositae.

salt 1. (sodium chloride; NaCl) The crystalline solid that is used for seasoning and preserving food and is present in sea water and halite, which are its chief sources (naturally occurring sodium chloride is often called rock salt). NaCl forms cubic crystals. It has an important function in the human body and is used in the manufacture of many chemicals, such as soap, fertilizer, and ceramics. 2. Any similar compound formed, together with water, when an acid reacts with a base, for example the salt potassium sulphate is formed when sulphuric acid reacts with potassium hydroxide: $H_2SO_4 + 2KOH \rightarrow K_2SO_4 + 2H_2O$.

SALT (Strategic Arms Limitation Talks). *See* disarmament.

Salta 24 46S 65 28W A city in N Argentina. It is a commercial centre on the Trans-Andean Railway and trades with Bolivia and Chile. Population (1980): 260 000.

saltbush A salt-tolerant herb or shrub, especially one belonging to either of the genera *Atriplex* or *Chenopodium*. They have inconspicuous flowers and are used as forage plants in dry salty regions of Australia and North America. Family: *Chenopodiaceae*.

Saltillo 25 30N 101 00W A city in NE Mexico. The focal point of road and rail routes, it is the commercial centre for an agricultural region. Its university (1867) was refounded in 1957. Population (1980): 321 758.

Salt Lake City 40 45N 111 55W A city in the USA, the capital of Utah near Great Salt Lake. Founded in 1847 by the Mormons under the leadership of Brigham Young, it is the world headquarters of the Mormon Church. It has the Mormon tabernacle (1867) and the University of Utah (1850) is here. It is a commercial centre for nearby mining operations and its industries include food processing, textiles, oil refining, and printing and publishing. Population (1980): 163 034.

Salto 31 27S 57 50W A port in NW Uruguay, on the River Uruguay. It is an important meat-packing centre; other products include wine and soft drinks. Population (1980 est): 80 000.

saltpetre (potassium nitrate or nitre; KNO_3) A white crystalline solid used as a fertilizer, a food preservative, and in *gunpowder and fireworks.

saltwort An annual or perennial herb belonging to the widely distributed genus *Salsola* (50 species), found on seashores and salt marshes. They have fleshy spiked leaves and small flowers. The European saltwort (*S. kali*) grows up to 60 cm tall. Family: *Chenopodiaceae*.

saluki A breed of hunting dog dating back over 8000 years in Egypt and used by Arabs for hunting gazelle. It has a slender streamlined body with long legs, giving speed and agility, and a small head with a long narrow muzzle. The smooth soft coat can be white, brownish, reddish, or black, tan, and white. Height: 50–70 cm.

Salvador (or Bahia) 12 58S 38 29W A port in NE Brazil, the capital of Bahia state on the Atlantic Ocean. It has a fine natural harbour; exports include cocoa, sugar, tobacco, and diamonds. The chief industries are food and tobacco processing. It is the seat of two universities. Population (1980): 1 496 276.

Salvador. See El Salvador, Republic of.

salvage In law, the compensation allowed to persons (salvors) who have voluntarily assisted in saving a ship and its cargo or passengers from shipwreck, capture by an enemy, or similar damage or loss at sea. Salvors have a retaining lien (right to hold the salvaged property as security) on the salvaged vessel, etc., that takes priority over other claims. The amount payable as salvage is assessed by the Admiralty Court (see maritime law).

SALT   *Salar of Uyuni, 4350 m (12 000 ft) up in the Bolivian Andes, is one of the largest salt lakes in the world.*

Salvation Army The international Christian organization founded in 1865 in London by William *Booth. Run on strictly military lines, it exacts absolute obedience from its members, who wear a characteristic uniform on public occasions. Morality in practical Christian living is more esteemed than doctrinal niceties and the Army rejects the sacraments. It is famous for its social and evangelistic work. It also operates a successful missing persons investigation service.

Salvia A genus of perennial herbs and shrubs (about 700 species), widely distributed in temperate and tropical regions. Many are cultivated for ornament, including the Brazilian scarlet sage (*S. splendens*) and the blue-flowered *S. patens*. Common *sage is the culinary herb. Family: *Labiatae.

sal volatile (or ammonium carbonate) A mixture of ammonium salts, or their solution in alcohol, that is used in smelling salts. It smells of ammonia and is made by heating ammonium chloride (or sal ammoniac) with calcium sulphate.

Salween River (Chinese name: Nu Jiang or Nu Chiang) A river in SE China and E Burma, rising in Tibet and flowing E then S to an inlet of the Andaman Sea. Little of its length is navigable but it supplies hydroelectric power. Length: 2400 km (1500 mi).

Salyut A continuing series of manned Soviet space stations first launched into earth orbit in 1971. Cosmonauts from E Europe are conveyed to and from the orbiting laboratory by Soyuz spacecraft, there being two docking ports. They remain on the space station for either short or very long periods, in weightless conditions, conducting a variety of experiments and observations. Their physical and psychological fitness is carefully monitored. Salyut stations are smaller than the US *Skylab space station.

Salzburg 47 54N 13 03E A city in central Austria, the capital of Salzburg. Its many fine buildings include the fortress of Hohensalzburg and the cathedral (1614–28). Salzburg University was refounded in 1962. Mozart was born here and a famous musical event, the Salzburg Festival, is held annually. Industries include textiles and leather. Population (1981): 138 317.

Salzgitter 52 02N 10 22E A city in NE West Germany, in Lower Saxony formed in 1942 from 29 separate towns. The area is rich in iron ore, which is used in the manufacture of steel products. Population (1980 est): 113 500.

samadhi The state of perfect concentration attained in deep meditation. In Hinduism it is taken to be union with *Brahman or with a deity. In Buddhism it refers to transcending the distinction between subject and object. Its attainment is a precondition of spiritual liberation.

Samar The third largest island in the Philippines, in the Visayan Islands linked by bridge to Leyte. Its frequent typhoons restrict agriculture; the chief products are rice, coconuts, and hemp. Copper and iron ore are mined. Area: 13 415 sq km (5181 sq mi). Population (1980): 1 200 592. Chief town: Catbalogan.

Samara. See Kuibyshev.

Samaria 1. The central region of ancient Palestine, which became part of the northern kingdom of Israel in the 10th century BC. See also Samaritans. 2. 32 17N 35 12E The capital from the 9th century until its destruction in about 721 BC of the kingdom of Israel. Occupied from the 4th millennium BC, the site was excavated in 1908–10, 1931–33, and 1935. Among the discoveries unearthed were a collection of 9th-century BC ivory carvings. The city was rebuilt in the 1st century AD under Herod the Great and renamed Sebaste (modern name: Sebastiyah, in Jordan).

Samaritans 1. A people of ancient Samaria (now in N Israel), with a religion closely akin to Judaism. Numerous in Roman and Byzantine times and much disliked by the Jews, they declined under Muslim rule. They now number only a few hundred. They have a conservative religious tradition and many distinctive beliefs and customs. 2. A British telephone service for the suicidal and despairing. Started in 1953 by the Rev Chad Varah (1911-) in a London church (St Stephen Walbrook) with one telephone, it now has over 182 branches in the UK, operated by some 25 000 trained volunteers, in which telephones are manned 24 hours per day and callers are welcomed for personal visits. A nonreligious charity, it offers a nonprofessional, confidential, and anonymous service to anyone in distress. Samaritans will listen for as long as they are needed and the service is free. They offer little advice, believing that their clients will be helped to make their own decisions by talking to someone who cares. They befriend over 350 000 new callers each year in Great Britain and Northern Ireland and some branches have been formed overseas, especially in the USA.

samarium (Sm) A *lanthanide element discovered spectroscopically by Lecoq de Boisbaudran in 1879. It occurs naturally, with other lanthanides, in monazite ($CePO_4$). The oxide (Sm_2O_3) is used in glasses that absorb infrared radiation and the element is used in lasers as a dopant in calcium fluoride. At no 62; at wt 150.4; mp $1077 \pm 5°C$; bp $1791°C$.

Samarkand 39 40N 66 57E A city in the S central Soviet Union, in the Uzbek SSR. The principal industrial activities are cotton and silk manufacturing, winemaking, and metalworking but its interest lies chiefly in its past. *History*: it was the chief junction of the ancient *Silk Road between China and the Mediterranean and, conquered by the Arabs in the 8th century, became the Abbasids' capital (9th–10th centuries) and a great Islamic centre. In the 14th century it became the capital of Timur's mighty empire, coming later under the rule of the Uzbek people (16th–19th centuries). The city's remarkable historic buildings include Timur's mausoleum. Population (1981 est): 489 000.

Samarra' 34 13N 43 52E A city in central Iraq, N of Baghdad. It is a Shiite Muslim pilgrimage centre with a 17th-century mosque and many ruins dating from the 9th century, when Samarra' was the capital of the Abbasid caliphs (Islamic leaders). Population (1970 est): 62 008.

samizdat (Russian: self-publication) The underground system of distribution within the Soviet Union of literature, the open publication of which is prohibited by the authorities. Literature circulated in this way, usually in the form of typewritten copies, includes work by such writers as *Solzhenitsyn and *Sakharov.

Samoa A chain of volcanic islands in the S central Pacific Ocean. Discovered by the Dutch in the 18th century, the islands were politically divided in 1900 between the USA and Germany. **American Samoa**, comprising the E islands of the chain, is an unincorporated US territory consisting of the chief island of Tutuila and several smaller ones. Agriculture is the main occupation; canned tuna is an important export. Area: 197 sq km (76 sq mi). Population (1981 est): 33 000. Capital: Pago Pago. **Western Samoa** was a German protectorate until World War I and then under New Zealand control, becoming an independent state in 1962. It consists of the main islands of Savai'i and Upolu and several smaller islands and islets. Subsistence agriculture is the main occupation and exports, chiefly to New Zealand, are copra, bananas, and cocoa. Some industrial development has taken place in recent years. Head of state: HH Malietoa Tanumafili II (1913–). Official languages: Samoan and English. Official currency: Western Samoa dollar. Area: 2842 sq km (1097 sq mi). Population (1983): 160 000. Capital: Apia.

Sámos A Greek island in the SE Aegean Sea, lying close to the mainland of Turkey. Already one of the principal commercial centres of Greece by the 7th century BC, it achieved its greatest prosperity under the tyrant Polycrates in the 6th century. It is the birthplace of the mathematician and philosopher, Pythagoras. Area: 492 sq km (190 sq mi). Population (1981): 40 519.

Samothrace (Modern Greek name: Samothráki) A Greek island in the N Aegean Sea. The statue of the Winged Victory (now in the Louvre) was discovered here in 1863. Area: 181 sq km (70 sq mi). Population (1984 est): 4000.

Samoyed (dog) A breed of dog developed in Siberia and used by the Samoyed tribesmen as a sledge dog. It is robustly

built with husky-like features; the white or cream coat consists of a short soft undercoat and a long coarse outer coat. Height: 51–56 cm (dogs); 46–51 cm (bitches).

Samoyed (people) A group of Siberian peoples of the tundra and N forest region of the central Soviet Union. They were traditionally nomadic reindeer hunters and fishers, now mainly settled by Soviet collectivization as reindeer breeders. *Shamanism dominates their religious life. Of the five Samoyed languages, which, with the *Finno-Ugric languages, comprise the *Uralic family, only Nenets (or Yurak) has a considerable number of speakers.

samphire A perennial herb, *Crithmum maritimum*, native to rocky coasts of S England. Up to 30 cm high, it has small white or yellowish flowers, a succulent stem, and slender fleshy leaves, which may be used in salads or pickles. Family: *Umbelliferae.

The golden samphire (*Inula crithmoides*), also native to British coasts, grows to 80 cm and has broader leaves and larger yellow flowers. Family: *Compositae. *See also* glasswort (marsh samphire).

Samsun 41 17N 36 22E A port in central N Turkey, on the Black Sea. It exports cereals, copper, and tobacco and has a university (1975). Population (1980): 198 749.

Samudra Gupta (died c. 380 AD) Emperor of India (c. 330–c. 380) of the *Gupta dynasty and grandson of *Chandra Gupta I. He strove to expand and consolidate his empire, making many conquests, and kings of neighbouring dynasties paid him tribute.

Samuel In the Old Testament, the first of the Hebrew prophets and the last of the "judges," who led the Israelites before the establishment of the monarchy in Palestine. The two **Books of Samuel** appear to be compiled from various sources. They are the principal sources for the history of the Israelites in the 11th and 10th centuries BC and contain the biography of Samuel and the history of the reigns of *Saul and *David, both of whom Samuel anointed as the first two Kings of Israel.

Samuel, Herbert Louis, 1st Viscount (1870–1963) British politician. Samuel became a Liberal MP in 1905. He was postmaster general (1910, 1915), high commissioner for Palestine (1920–25) and twice home secretary (1916, 1931). The president of the British Institute of Philosophy, he published *Philosophy and the Ordinary Man* in 1932.

samurai The provincial warriors (also known as *bushi*; *see* Bushido), who rose to power in Japan in the 11th century. The term originally referred to the armed retainers employed by court nobles from the late 8th century. The samurai mostly became the vassals of *daimyo* and after 1600, when they comprised about 6% of the population, they were generally forced to reside in their lord's castle town. The samurai class was sharply divided from other classes by its superior status and marked distinctions also existed within its own ranks. After the Meiji restoration (1868) the samurai lost their special position but ex-samurai became leaders in various areas of modern Japanese life.

San'a' 15 23N 44 14E The capital of North Yemen, in the centre of the country. Until the formation of the state of Israel, there was a large Jewish ghetto in the city. Notable buildings include the Great Mosque, where there is a sacred Muslim shrine, and the Liberty Gate. A university was founded here in 1970 with Kuwaiti assistance. Population (1980): 277 817.

San Andreas Fault A notorious fracture in the earth's crust, 1200 km (750 mi) in length, running through California. In 1906 a horizontal displacement of about six metres and a lateral displacement of only one metre caused an earthquake that devastated San Francisco. These movements, constantly recorded by seismographs, are now interpreted as resulting from collision of tectonic plates, a rotating Pacific plate and an American plate.

San Antonio 29 25N 98 30W A city in the USA, in Texas.

Founded in 1718, it was the scene of the Mexican attack on the *Alamo (1836) during the Texan revolution. San Antonio has several military bases and is a commercial and industrial centre for a large agricultural region. The mild climate has attracted many tourists and retired people. Population (1980): 785 410.

San Bernardino 34 07N 117 18W A city in the USA, in California. Situated in a fruit-growing area, it is the site of the annual National Orange Show but industrial developments in aerospace and steel are now the main economic activities. Population (1980): 118 057.

SAN ANDREAS FAULT *An example of a tear fault in which the rocks are being displaced horizontally.*

San Cristóbal 7 46N 72 15W A city in W Venezuela. It is the commercial centre for an area producing maize, cassava, sugar cane, and coffee. Its university was founded in 1962. Population (1981 est): 280 000.

sanctions Penalties imposed for breaking a law, especially international law. First imposed by the *League of Nations on Italy following its invasion of Ethiopia, the most recent examples of sanctions are those imposed by Britain, and the countries belonging to the UN, against Rhodesia (now *Zimbabwe), following its unilateral declaration of independence in 1965, and those against South Africa (1985). The former sanctions were broken by oil companies and others, which suggests that when there are economic pressures against imposing sanctions, they are difficult to enforce.

sanctuary The holiest part of a church or temple, where the main altar stands. During the middle ages criminals could claim right of sanctuary, i.e. they took refuge in a church and were thus immune from prosecution for 40 days, during which time they could opt to accept a safe conduct

out of the country. In England this right was abolished for criminals in 1623 and for civil offenders in 1723.

sand Unconsolidated grains of rock, varying in size from 0.06 to 2.00 mm in diameter. Consolidated sands form *sandstones; grits are coarse sandstones with angular grains. Most sands consist principally of quartz, derived from the weathering of quartz-bearing rocks. Sand is used in glass and cement production, and as an abrasive.

Sand, George (Aurore Dupin, Baronne Dudevant; 1804-76) French novelist. In 1831 she left her husband and went to Paris to write her first novel, *Indiana* (1832), a plea for women's right to independence, the first of an enormous number of successful novels. Among her many lovers were Alfred de Musset and Frédéric Chopin.

Sandage, Allan Rex (1926-) US astronomer, who in 1961 discovered the first *quasar, which he originally named a "quasi-stellar radio object" since it emitted radio waves. Using the 200-inch reflecting telescope at Mt Palomar, California, he went on to discover a number of other quasars, including some that were not radio sources.

sandalwood An evergreen tree belonging to the genus *Santalum* (about 25 species), native to SE Asia and the Pacific Islands. The true sandalwood (*S. album*) grows to a height of about 10 m and is partially parasitic on the roots of other trees. Its white wood is used to make boxes and furniture and, when distilled, yields sweet-scented sandalwood oil, used in perfumes, incense, candles, etc. Family: *Santalaceae*.

sandarac The *resin of a N African conifer, *Tetraclinis articulata*, used in making varnishes.

Sandburg, Carl (1878-1967) US poet. His idiomatic free verse, especially in *The People, Yes* (1936), expressed his hope for an ideal socialist society. His works include a popular biography of Abraham Lincoln in two volumes, *The Prairie Years* (1926) and *The War Years* (1939).

sand dollar A marine invertebrate animal, also called cake urchin, belonging to an order (*Clypeastroida*) of *echinoderms. Its round flat rigid body is covered with small spines and saclike organs (tube feet). Sand dollars live on the sea bed and sift minute food particles from the sand in which they burrow. Class: *Echinoidea*.

sand dune The accumulation of wind-blown sand into a mound. Sand dunes are characteristic of desert areas where there is a plentiful sand supply and of coastal areas. They are unvegetated and two main forms occur in desert areas: the barchan, or crescent-shaped dune, and the seif, or longitudinal dune. In coastal areas dunes generally become "fixed" by vegetation.

sanderling A bird, *Calidris alba*, that nests on Arctic coasts and winters on shores worldwide. 20 cm long, it has a rust-coloured upper plumage, changing to pale-brown in winter, and a long white wing stripe. It feeds on shrimps, sandhoppers, and molluscs with its straight slender bill. Family: *Scolopacidae* (sandpipers).

sand flea *See* sand hopper.

sandfly A small fly belonging to the widely distributed genus *Phlebotomus*. Sandflies are among the worst pests of the tropics: the bloodsucking females can give a painful bite and several species are carriers of serious human diseases, including infections caused by the parasite *Leishmania* (*see* leishmanisis).

The name has also been used for many bloodsucking *gnats and *midges of sandy places.

sandgrouse A bird belonging to a family (*Pteroclidae*; 16 species) occurring in warm arid regions of Europe and Africa. 22-40 cm long, sandgrouse have camouflaging plumage, long pointed wings, short legs, feathered feet, and a very tough skin. They are gregarious and feed on plant material, flying long distances to water at dawn and dusk. Although resembling grouse, they belong to the order *Columbiformes* (pigeons).

sand hopper A small terrestrial jumping *crustacean, also called beach hopper and sand or beach flea, belonging to the family *Talitridae*. Its body, 10–25 mm long, is laterally flattened and lacks a carapace. During the day it is buried in sand but at night it emerges to feed on organic debris under stones or among seaweed. Order: *Amphipoda*.

Sandhurst 51 02N 0 34E A village in SE England, in Berkshire. The Royal Military Academy (1799) for training officers and the National Army Museum are situated here. Population (1985 est): 17 832.

San Diego 32 45N 117 10W A city in the USA, in California on San Diego Bay. It has a US naval base and large naval air service facilities. Employment is mainly dependent on the aircraft and aerospace industries. San Diego is also an important centre of scientific research and is the site of the Scripps Institute of Oceanography (1903). Population (1980): 875 504.

sand lizard A slender long-tailed European lizard, *Lacerta agilis*, occurring in sandy regions. Up to 20 cm long, it is pale-brown or grey with whitish underparts and three rows of white-centred dark spots along its back. It feeds on insects and spiders. Family: *Lacertidae*.

sandpiper A wading bird belonging to a family (*Scolopacidae*; 82 species) occurring chiefly in the N hemisphere, breeding in northerly latitudes and migrating south to winter. 12–60 cm long, sandpipers typically have long legs, long wings, a mottled brown or grey plumage, which commonly changes colour seasonally, and a long slender bill. They nest in marshy regions or on mud flats and feed on small invertebrates. Order: *Charadriiformes* (gulls, plovers, etc.).

Sandringham 52 49N 0 30E A village in E England, in Norfolk. The Sandringham estate was bought by Queen Victoria for the Prince of Wales (later Edward VII) in 1861. Sandringham House, a 19th-century Tudor-style building, remains a royal residence. It was the birthplace of George VI, who also died in the house.

Sand River Convention (1852) An agreement between Great Britain and the Afrikaners of South Africa, which granted the Transvaal self-government. The **Bloemfontein Convention** (1854) gave autonomy to the Afrikaners of the Orange River Sovereignty, which became the Orange Free State.

sandstone A sedimentary rock consisting of consolidated *sand, cemented mainly by calcareous, siliceous, or ferruginous minerals. They may be deposited by wind action in deserts or in shallow seas, estuaries and deltas, and along low-lying coasts by water. Sandstones vary in colour from red to yellow to white according to the presence of other minerals (feldspar, mica, glauconite, iron oxides, etc.) in addition to the quartz.

Sandwich 51 17N 1 20E A market town in SE England, on the River Stour near the coast of Kent. Once an important Cinque Port, the harbour silted up by the 16th century. It is a holiday and golfing resort. Population (1981): 4227.

Sandwich, John Montagu, 4th Earl of (1718–92) British politician; first lord of the admiralty (1748–51, 1771–82). He was notorious for his part in the prosecution of his former friend *Wilkes and the inadequacy of the navy during the American Revolution was attributed to his corrupt practices. He gave his name to the sandwich, a snack devised to sustain him through round-the-clock gaming.

Sandwich Islands. *See* Hawaii; South Sandwich Islands.

San Fernando 10 16N 61 28W A port in Trinidad, on the Gulf of Taria. It is the centre of an area containing rich oilfields (discovered 1900). Population (1980): 38 395.

San Francisco 37 40N 122 25W A city in the USA, in California situated on a peninsula between San Francisco Bay and the Pacific Ocean. A major seaport, San Francisco serves a large agricultural and mining area and is the financial and insurance centre of the West Coast. Industries

include food processing, shipbuilding, and petroleum refining. Among its many famous landmarks are the San Francisco–Oakland Bay Bridge (1936), the Golden Gate Bridge (1937), Chinatown, and the city's cable cars. A major cultural and educational centre, it is the site of several universities and colleges. *History*: founded by the Spanish in 1776, it was still a village when captured by the USA (1846) during the Mexican War. It expanded rapidly following the discovery of gold in California (1848) and it was during this period that the first Chinese settled in the city. In 1906 there was a sudden violent movement in the massive San Andreas Fault, which extends along the Californian coast, and San Francisco was almost completely destroyed by an earthquake and three-day fire. Population (1980): 678 974.

Sanger, Frederick (1918–) British biochemist, who determined the order of *amino acids in the insulin molecule. This work, at Cambridge University, started in 1945 and took him eight years to complete. He was awarded Nobel Prizes in 1958 and 1980 and the OM in 1986.

sangha The Buddhist monastic order. Together with the *Buddha and *dharma, it forms the third of the *tri-ratna of Buddhism. An individual may become a monk temporarily or for life.

Sanhedrin The highest court of the Jews, which met in Jerusalem. Its development is unclear; in early New Testament times the Greeks allowed the establishment of a senate and later forms became known as the Sanhedrin. Its composition and its jurisdiction varied with its history. In New Testament times, the high priest was president and its functions were administrative, judicial, and religious.

sanicle A perennial herb belonging to the genus *Sanicula* (37 species), distributed worldwide except for Australia and New Guinea. The common European sanicle (*S. europaea*) grows to a height of 50 cm and has several broad lobed leaves and clusters of small pinkish flowers. Family: *Umbelliferae*.

San Ildefonso (*or* La Granja) 40 53N 4 01W A town in central Spain. It has a magnificent royal palace built by Philip V of Spain (18th century); the palace chapel contains his tomb. Population (1981): 4588.

San José 37 20N 121 55W A city in the USA, in California on the S arm of San Francisco Bay. Founded in 1777, it was the first city in California and state capital (1849–51). Situated in the fertile Santa Clara Valley, it has many food-processing plants and wineries as well as aerospace and electronics industries. Population (1980): 636 550.

San José 9 50N 84 02W The capital of Costa Rica, situated in the centre of the country in a high fertile valley. Founded in 1736, it became a centre of the tobacco trade and later of coffee production. The University of Costa Rica was founded in 1843. Population (1981 est): 259 126.

San Juan 18 29N 66 08W The capital and main port of Puerto Rico, in the N. Founded by the Spanish in 1508, it was later attacked by the English and by the Dutch; in 1898 it was captured by the US navy. It has expanded considerably in the 20th century and is now also an industrial and tourist centre. The chief exports are coffee, sugar, and tobacco. The Inter-American University of Puerto Rico was founded in 1912 and a campus of the University of Puerto Rico in 1950. Population (1980): 432 973.

San Juan 31 33S 68 31W A city in W Argentina. Severely damaged by an earthquake (1944), it is the commercial centre of a wine-producing area. Domingo Sarmiento (1811–88), an educationalist and statesman, was born here. Population (1980): 118 000.

Sankara (8th century AD) Hindu philosopher. Sankara left his native Kerala to become a wandering holy man. It was popularly believed that he was an incarnation of *Shiva. He wrote commentaries on the *Brahmasutras*, the *Bhagavadgita*, and the *Upanishads* and founded the Smarta Brahmin sect and several monasteries. He made major contributions to the *Vedanta philosophical tradition, believing that the physical world relates to the ultimate reality as a state of ignorance does to knowledge.

San Lorenzo, Treaty of. *See* Pinckney, Charles.

San Luis Potosí 22 10N 101 00W A city in NE Mexico. It is the industrial centre for a rich agricultural and silver-mining area and has a fine baroque cathedral and a university (founded 1826). Population (1980): 406 630.

SAN MARINO *The first of three fortresses situated on the central limestone mass of Monte Titano.*

San Marino, Republic of A small independent republic, an enclave in Italian territory, situated on the slopes of the Apennines mountain range, SW of Rimini. *Economy*: farming, tourism, and the sale of postage stamps are the main sources of income. *History*: dating from the 4th century AD, it was an independent commune by the 12th century. In 1862, the newly established kingdom of Italy guaranteed San Marino's independence and a customs union. Executive power lies in the Congress of State and two regents elected by the Great and General Council. Official language: Italian. Official currency: both Italian and Vatican City currencies are in use. Area: 61 sq km (24 sq mi). Population (1981): 21 622. Capital: San Marino.

San Martín, José de (1778–1850) South American soldier and statesman; the national hero of Argentina. After participating in the struggle of Buenos Aires against the Spanish, he raised and trained an army in Argentina (1814–16), which he led heroically across the Andes, and, with Bernardo *O'Higgins, defeated the Spanish at Chacubuco (1817) and Maipo (1818), achieving the liberation of Chile. In 1821, after creating a Chilean navy, he entered Lima, proclaimed the independence of Peru, and became its "protector." He resigned in 1822, after differences with Bolívar, and retired to France.

San Miguel de Tucumán (*or* Tucumán) 26 47S 65 15W A city in NW Argentina, at the foot of the E Andes. It has a cathedral and a university (1914) and is an important sugar-refining centre. Population (1980): 497 000.

San Pedro Sula 15 26N 88 01W A city in NW Honduras. It serves an agricultural area producing bananas and sugar cane and is the chief industrial centre of the country. Population (1980 est): 342 800.

San Remo 43 48N 7 46E A port and resort in Italy, in Liguria near the French border. It has a 12th-century romanesque cathedral. There is a market in flowers and fruit. Population (1981 est): 62 711.

San Salvador 13 59N 89 18W The capital of El Salvador, situated in the centre of the country. Founded by the Spanish in 1525, it was capital of the Central American

Federation from 1831 until 1838, becoming capital of El Salvador in 1839. It has suffered several severe earthquakes. Industries include textiles and food processing. The University of El Salvador was founded in 1841. Population (1980): 1 902 500.

San Salvador Island (former name: Watling Island) 24 00N 74 32W A West Indian island in the central Bahamas. It was Columbus' first sight of land (1492) in the New World. Area: 156 sq km (60 sq mi). Population (1980): 804.

sans-culottes (French: without knee breeches) The violent extremists of the French Revolution, so called because they wore trousers rather than the knee breeches of the aristocracy. The original sans-culottes were the ' Paris workers who stormed the Bastille and led the food riots in 1789. Later radical extremists, such as Marat and Danton, who used the Paris mobs to gain control, were also called sans-culottes.

San Sebastián 43 19N 1 59W A seaside resort in N Spain, in the Basque Provinces on the Bay of Biscay. It possesses a cathedral and its palace was formerly the summer residence of the Spanish royal family. The La Concha beaches attract many tourists. Population (1981): 175 576.

Sansevieria A genus of herbaceous perennial plants (60 species) native to tropical and S Africa and S Asia. They have a basal rosette of stiff swordlike leaves arising from thick creeping underground stems (rhizomes). *S. trifasciata* var. *laurentii* (mother-in-law's tongue) is a popular house plant with ornamental leaves, striped green and yellow, up to 90 cm long. The leaves of several species (e.g. *S. zeylanica*) yield a fibre (bowstring hemp) used for ropes, mats, etc. Family: *Liliaceae*.

Sanskrit The classical literary language of the Hindu scriptures, belonging to the *Indo-Aryan family. From it the *Prakrits and modern N Indian languages developed. It was spoken in NW India from 1500 BC, became a scholarly language when the grammarian *Panini standardized it (5th century BC), and is still used as a sacred language. It is highly complex and is written in the *Devanagari script.

San Stefano, Treaty of (1878) The treaty that concluded the war between the Ottoman Empire and Russia (1877–78). The defeated Ottomans recognized the independence of Serbia, Romania, and Montenegro and the autonomy of Bosnia-Herzegovina and Bulgaria. At the Congress of *Berlin (1878), the other great powers, fearing that the Balkans would fall under the dominance of Russia, modified the treaty.

Santa Ana 14 00N 79 31W The second largest city in El Salvador. It is a major coffee centre and has one of the largest coffee mills in the world. Population (1980): 203 713.

Santa Anna, Antonio López de (1794–1876) Mexican soldier and statesman; president (1833–36) and dictator (1839, 1841–45). After engineering *Iturbide's downfall in 1823, Santa Anna dominated Mexican politics for the next 20 years. He is best known for his defeat of Texan forces at the *Alamo (1836). Subsequently taken prisoner by the Americans, he was forced to retire but twice returned to power before being driven into exile (1845–74).

Santa Clara 22 25N 79 58W A city in central Cuba. It is the commercial centre for an agricultural area producing sugar and tobacco. Population (1981): 525 402.

Santa Claus. *See* Nicholas, St.

Santa Cruz 17 45S 63 14W A city in SE Bolivia. It is the commercial centre for an area producing chiefly sugar cane, rice, and coffee. Industries include the manufacture of cigarettes and sugar refining. It is the site of a university (1880). Population (1982 est): 376 917.

Santa Cruz de Tenerife 28 28N 16 15W A city in the Canary Islands, in NE Tenerife. An uprising that began the Spanish Civil War took place here (1936). It is a major fuelling station with an oil refinery. Population (1981): 190 784.

Santa Fe 35 41N 105 57W A city and resort in the USA, the capital of New Mexico on the Santa Fe River. Following Mexico's attainment of independence from Spain in 1821, Santa Fe developed a commercial route (the **Santa Fe Trail**) with the USA. Population (1980): 48 953.

Santa Fé 31 38S 60 43W A port in E Argentina, the furthest point accessible to oceangoing vessels on the Río Paraná. Founded in 1573, it has a cathedral (1685) and a university (1919) and is the centre of a grain-growing and stock-rearing area. Population (1980): 287 000.

Santa Isabel. *See* Malabo.

Santa Marta 11 18N 74 10W A port in N Colombia, on the Caribbean Sea. The chief exports are bananas, coffee, and cocoa. Simón *Bolívar, leader of the South American independence movement, died here (1830). Population (1980): 120 000.

Santander 43 28N 3 48W A city and port in N Spain, in Old Castile on Cape Mayor. Part of the city was rebuilt after being burnt in 1941. It possesses a gothic cathedral. Its industries include fishing and shipbuilding. Population (1981): 180 328.

Santayana, George (1863–1952) Spanish-born US philosopher and poet. He taught at Harvard (1889–1911) and then moved to Oxford before eventually settling in Rome (1924). He believed that the mind was largely governed by physical and biological considerations, as set out in *Realms of Being* (1927–40). His witty and urbane works include *The Sense of Beauty* (1896), *The Life of Reason* (1905–06), *Scepticism and Animal Faith* (1923), and *The Last Puritan* (1935).

Santiago (*or* Santiago de Chile) 33 35S 70 40W The capital of Chile, situated in the centre of the country at the foot of the Andes. It was founded by the Spanish in 1541. About half of Chile's industry is centred here, including food processing, textiles, and metallurgy. There are three universities. Population (1982): 4 132 293.

Santiago de Compostela 42 52N 8 33W A city in NW Spain, in Galicia. Since the 9th century AD it has been a famous place of pilgrimage reputedly containing the tomb of St James, the patron saint of Spain. Its romanesque cathedral (1078–1211) was built on the site of the tomb. The university was founded in 1532. Population (1981): 93 695.

Santiago de Cuba 20 00N 75 49W A port in Cuba, on the Caribbean Sea. It was the scene of Fidel *Castro's 26 July revolt (1953). Exports include metal ores, sugar, coffee, and tobacco. It is the site of the University of Oriente (1947) and has a large cathedral. Population (1981): 563 455.

Santiago del Estero 27 48S 64 15W A city in N Argentina. It is a commercial centre serving an agricultural area producing wheat, cotton, maize, and livestock. The chief industry is food processing. Population (1980): 148 000.

Santiago de los Caballeros 19 30N 70 42W A city in the N Dominican Republic. The commercial centre for a fertile agricultural region, its industries include the manufacture of cigarettes, pharmaceuticals, and furniture. Population (1981): 278 638.

Santo Domingo 18 32N 69 50W The capital of the Dominican Republic, a port on the S coast. Founded by Bartolomeo Columbus in 1496, it became the capital of the first Spanish colony in the Americas. It was under French rule (1795–1809), and later under that of Haiti, becoming capital of the new Dominican Republic in 1844. During the rule of the dictator *Trujillo, it was known for a time (1936–61) as Ciudad Trujillo. It is the site of the first cathedral (1521) and the first university (1538) in the New World. A second university was established in 1966. Population (1981): 1 313 172.

Santoríni. *See* Thera.

Santos 23 56S 46 22W A city in SE Brazil, in São Paulo state on the Atlantic Ocean. It is the leading coffee port of the world.

Population (1980): 411 023.

São Luís 2 34S 44 16W A port in N Brazil, the capital of Maranhão state. The chief exports are babaçu palm products, cotton, sugar, and balsam. It is the site of the University of Maranhão (1966). Population (1980): 405 300.

Saône, River A river in E France, rising in Lorraine and flowing mainly S to join the River Rhône at Lyons. It is linked by canal to the Rivers Moselle, Rhine, Loire, Seine, and Meuse. Length: 480 km (298 mi).

São Paulo 23 33S 46 39W The largest city in Brazil, the capital of São Paulo state. Founded in 1554, it grew rapidly after 1880 with the development of coffee plantations. Coffee remains important but there has been considerable diversification of industry and it is now the fastest-growing city in Brazil, sometimes called the "Chicago of South America." Industries include food processing and the manufacture of textiles, electrical appliances, and chemicals. It has several universities, including the University of São Paulo (1934). It also contains the Butantan Institute, a scientific research establishment with a famous snake farm. Population (1980): 7 033 529.

São Tomé and Príncipe, Democratic Republic of A small island country off the coast of West Africa, in the Gulf of Guinea. An archipelago, it comprises the two main islands with coastal plains rising to volcanic mountains in their interiors, together with the islets of Pedras Tinhosas and Rolas. Most of the population is descended from African slaves and southern Europeans, with comparatively recent influxes from Mozambique and Angola. *Economy*: chiefly agricultural, the main crops being cocoa, copra (which is the main export), palm oil and kernels, and coffee. Rice is being developed and livestock is also important. *History*: discovered by the Portuguese in 1471, the islands came under Portuguese rule in 1522. They became an overseas province in 1951 and gained independence in 1975, forming a democratic republic. President: Dr Manuel Pinto da Costa. Official language: Portuguese. Official currency: dobra of 100 centavos. Area: 964 sq km (372 sq mi). Population (1983 est): 88 000. Capital and main port: São Tomé.

sap The fluid found in the vascular (conducting) system of plants. It consists of water and minerals, absorbed from the soil and transported through the plant in the *xylem, and sugars, made in the leaves and distributed in solution in the *phloem.

Sapir, Edward (1884–1939) US linguist and anthropologist, born in Germany. Much of his work was done on American-Indian languages and cultures. His book *Language* (1921) is notably lucid. He was interested in all aspects of communication and in the role played by language in determining the personality of the individual in relation to society. *See also* Whorf, Benjamin Lee.

sapodilla An evergreen tree, *Achras sapota*, native to Central America but cultivated elsewhere in the tropics. Up to 20 m tall, it produces edible brown rounded fruits, up to 10 cm across, with a juicy pulp surrounding black seeds. It tastes of pears and brown sugar. Milky latex from the bark is a source of chicle gum, used in chewing gum. Family: *Sapotaceae*.

saponins Plant glycosides (sugar compounds) that form lathery emulsions in water. The saponins are extremely potent in destroying red blood cells. They are used as foam producers in fire extinguishers and as emulsifiers, *detergents, etc.

sappan A tree, *Caesalpinia sappan*, native to SE Asia. The wood (sappanwood) is used in making furniture and yields a red dye. An extract of the bark produces a black dye when mixed with iron salts. Family: *Leguminosae*.

Sapper (H(erman) C(yril) McNeile; 1888–1937) British novelist. After distinguished service in World War I he achieved literary success with his popular thriller *Bulldog Drummond* (1920), about an adventure-seeking ex-officer, and its sequels.

sapphire A transparent variety of *corundum that may be any colour except red (*see* ruby) due to traces of iron and titanium. It is used as a gemstone and in record-player styluses. Sapphires occur in igneous and metamorphic rocks but most are obtained from detrital gravels. Many sapphires come from Sri Lanka, Kashmir, Burma, East Africa, the USA, and Australia. Artificial sapphires are manufactured from ammonium alum. Birthstone for September.

Sappho (c. 612–c. 580 BC) Greek poet. She and her contemporary *Alcaeus pioneered the form of the brief subjective lyric. Her passionate poetry, which has survived in fragments, was written for her group of female admirers on the island of Lesbos (from which the term "lesbianism" is derived). She appears to have been married and had one child; according to a romantic and unreliable legend, she committed suicide by throwing herself from a rock off the coast of Epirus because of an unhappy love affair.

Sapporo 43 5N 141 21E A city in Japan, in SW Hokkaido. It is the island's main administrative and educational centre; Hokkaido University was established here in 1918. It is also a ski resort famed for its annual festival of snow sculpture and was the site of the 1972 winter Olympics. Industries include flour and timber milling, printing, and machinery manufacture. Population (1980): 1 402 000.

saprophyte An organism that obtains its energy by feeding on dead or decaying tissue. Bacteria and fungi are important saprophytes, using enzymes to break down organic material and release nutrients into the soil, which can be used by plants (*see* decomposition).

Saqqarah A mortuary area near ancient *Memphis. The most famous monument here is the stone-built Step Pyramid, designed (c. 2630 BC) for Pharaoh *Djoser by his architect *Imhotep. It is architecturally the immediate forerunner of the Giza *pyramids. The bulls sacred to *Apis were buried in the Sarapeum.

Saracens Before Islam, the term used by the non-Arab peoples of the Middle East to refer to the Arabs. After the establishment of Islam, Saracen was usually synonymous with Muslim. The origin of the word is unknown.

Saragossa. *See* Zaragoza.

Sarajevo 43 52N 18 26E A city in W central Yugoslavia, the capital of Bosnia and Hercegovina. A centre of resistance to Austrian domination, it was here that the heir apparent to the Dual Monarchy of Austria-Hungary, *Francis Ferdinand, was assassinated (28 June, 1914), precipitating World War I. It was also the site of the 1984 Winter Olympics. Sarajevo has two cathedrals, several mosques, and a university (1946). A busy industrial centre, its manufactures include carpets, pottery, sugar, and beer. Population (1981): 448 500.

Saransk 54 12N 45 10E A city in the W central Soviet Union, the capital of the Mordvinian ASSR in the RSFSR. It is an industrial centre, producing machinery, electrical goods, and food. Population (1981 est): 280 000.

Saratoga, Battles of (19 September and 7 October, 1777) Two battles fought near Saratoga, New York, which formed the turning point of the *American Revolution. The first saw the defeat of the British attempt to open a route to Albany. The second ended with the surrender of Gen Burgoyne to the Americans. The outcome of the battles helped persuade the French to recognize and support the USA.

Saratov 51 30N 45 55E A city in the W Soviet Union, in the RSFSR on the River Volga. Baku oil is transported from here and a natural-gas pipeline supplies Moscow. Other industrial activities include ship repairing and the manufacture of precision instruments. Population (1981 est): 873 000.

Sarawak A state in Malaysia, in NW *Borneo on the South China Sea. It has a mountainous forested interior with a swampy coastal plain, where rubber, pepper, sago, and rice are grown. Oil production is of prime importance; crude oil, petroleum products, timber, and pepper are the chief exports. *Histo-*

ry: it was given in 1841 by the sultan of Brunei to the Englishman James Brooke, who as "white rajah" tried to suppress piracy and headhunting. Although it became a British protectorate in 1888, it was ruled by the Brooke family until World War II, when it was occupied by the Japanese. Ceded to Britain in 1946, it joined Malaysia in 1963. Area: 124 970 sq km (48 250 sq mi). Population (1980): 1 294 753. Capital: Kuching.

Sarcodina A class of minute single-celled animals (*see* Protozoa) that form cellular extensions called pseudopodia for locomotion and feeding. Many forms, including *Amoeba, are naked while others, for example the *Foraminifera and *Radiolaria, have a shell or skeleton. Sarcodines are chiefly free-living inhabitants of soils, fresh waters, and seas.

sarcoma. *See* cancer.

sarcophagus A stone or terracotta coffin, often elaborately decorated with ritual motifs. Sarcophagi evolved in ancient Egypt to protect mummies, and Minoan, Greek, Roman, and early Christian examples survive.

sardine A young *pilchard or any of several species of food fish of the family *Clupeidae*, especially members of the genera *Sardina*, *Sardinops*, and *Sardinella*. They are tinned in oil, an industry centred on Portugal and Spain.

Sardinia (Italian name: Sardegna) The second largest island in the Mediterranean Sea, comprising an autonomous region of Italy. It is largely mountainous. Agriculture is important, especially on the fertile Campidano (a broad alluvial plain in the SW) where cereals, vines, and olives are cultivated. Sheep are raised on the hills. Its major industry is mineral production, especially lead, zinc, coal, fluorspar, and sea salt. Modern industries, especially petrochemicals, chemicals, and food processing, are being developed. Tourism is a growing source of revenue. *History*: first settled by the Phoenicians, it was ceded to Savoy by Austria (1720) in exchange for Sicily and formed the kingdom of Sardinia with Piedmont, which formed the basis of a unified Italy. Area: 23 813 sq km (9194 sq mi). Population (1980 est): 1 610 260. Capital: Cagliari.

Sardis 38 28N 28 02E The capital of ancient Lydia, 56 km (35 mi) NE of present-day Izmir (Turkey), famous for its coinage and craftwork. After Persia conquered Lydia, overthrowing Croesus about 550 BC, its strategic position made Sardis Asia Minor's political centre until Hellenistic times.

sardonyx. *See* onyx.

Sardou, Victorien (1831–1908) French dramatist. His many successful comedies and historical dramas include *Les Pattes de mouche* (1860) and *Tosca* (1887), a melodrama on which Puccini's opera is based. Sarah Bernhardt acted in many of his plays.

Sargasso Sea An elliptical section of the N Atlantic Ocean between latitudes 20°N and 35°N and longitudes 30°W and 70°W. Contained within a current system, it is still and warm. It takes its name from the floating brown seaweed of the genus *Sargassum*, found in it.

Sargent, John Singer (1856–1925) US portrait painter, born in Florence. Working in Paris, London, and the USA, he achieved considerable success with his elegant portraits of such celebrities as Ellen Terry, R. L. Stevenson, Isabelle Stewart Gardner, Madame Gautreau (Mme. X), and John D. Rockefeller. In watercolour, he produced remarkable landscape studies of World War I.

Sargent, Sir Malcolm (1895–1967) British conductor. A notable organist, he first conducted in 1921 at the London Promenade Concerts, of which he was chief conductor from 1957 to 1967. He was also conductor of the BBC Symphony Orchestra (1950–57).

Sargon II (d. 705 BC) King of Assyria (722–705). Perhaps a usurper (Sargon means "legitimate king"), he deliberately named himself after the legendary *Sargon of Akkad. He was constantly occupied in warfare to maintain Assyrian power in Elam, Urartu, Babylonia, Syria, and Palestine, where he captured and depopulated Samaria. He was succeeded by *Sennacherib.

Sargon of Akkad The semilegendary Semitic ruler (c. 2334–c. 2279 BC) of territories extending from the Mediterranean to the Persian Gulf. According to tradition, he was brought up by a gardener, who retrieved his cradle adrift in the River Euphrates. After usurping kingly power, he founded *Akkad and an empire that lasted a century.

Sark (French name: Sercq) 49 26N 2 22W The smallest of the four main Channel Islands. It consists of Great Sark and Little Sark, connected by a narrow isthmus, the Coupée. It is governed by a hereditary seigneur or dame in a semifeudal system. Cars are prohibited here. Area: 5 sq km (2 sq mi). Population (1981): 560.

Sarnia 42 57N 82 24W A city and port in E Canada, in SW Ontario at the S end of Lake Huron. With the discovery of local oil (1858) and the completion of the oil pipeline from Alberta, it grew into a major refining and petrochemical centre. Steel and salt are also important. Population (1981): 47 586.

Saronic Gulf (or Gulf of Aegina) An inlet of the W Aegean Sea between the Attic Peninsula (on which lie Athens and its port Piraeus) and the Peloponnese. It contains the island of Salamis.

saros The period of about 18 years (6585.3 days) at which *eclipses of the sun and moon repeat in the same order and with nearly the same time intervals.

Saroyan, William (1908–81) US dramatist and fiction writer. *The Daring Young Man on the Flying Trapeze* (1934) was his first success. His other works include the plays *The Time of Your Life* (1939) and *My Heart's in the Highlands* (1939), a novel, *The Human Comedy* (1943), and the autobiographical *My Name is Aram* (1940) and *Obituaries* (1979).

Sarraute, Nathalie (1902–) French novelist, born in Russia. She practised as a lawyer until 1939. Her work includes *Tropismes* (1939), a collection of sketches analysing human behaviour in great psychological detail, *Le Planétarium* (1959), *Les Fruits d'or* (1963), and *C'est Beau* (1973). She is a leading exponent of the *nouveau roman*, and her essays are collected in *L'Ere du soupçon* (1956).

sarsaparilla An extract of the roots of several perennial climbing or trailing vines of the genus *Smilax*, especially *S. aristolochiaefolia*, cultivated in Central and South America. The roots are harvested and dried for use as a tonic and as flavouring for medicines and beverages. Family: *Smilacaceae*.

Sartre, Jean-Paul (1905–80) French philosopher, novelist, dramatist, and critic. After World War II, during which he was an active member of the resistance, he founded the journal *Les Temps modernes* and became a leading public exponent of *existentialism. His major works of philosophy include *Being and Nothingness* (1943) and *Critique de la raison dialectique* (1960). His novels include *Nausea* (1938) and the trilogy *The Roads to Freedom* (1945–49). Among his several plays are *The Flies* (1943), *In Camera* (1944), *The Respectable Prostitute* (1946), and *Lucifer and the Lord* (1951). He also wrote literary criticism and autobiographical works. In 1964 he refused the Nobel Prize. He had a close association with Simone de *Beauvoir, whom he met while a student. He was an adherent of Marxism and supported left-wing groups.

Sarum. *See* Salisbury.

SAS. *See* Special Air Service.

Sasanians The dynasty that ruled Persia from 224 AD until overthrown by the Arabs about 636. *Ardashir I (reigned 224–41) founded the dynasty (named after his grandfather Sasan), overthrowing the Parthian empire (*see* Parthia) and seizing its capital *Ctesiphon. His most notable successors were *Shapur II (reigned 309–79), *Khosrau I (reigned 531–79), and *Khosrau II (reigned 590–628). The Sasanian empire, which at its greatest extent stretched from Syria to India, saw

the establishment of Zoroastrianism as the state religion and a resurgence of art and architecture (*see* Persian art and architecture).

Sasebo 33 10N 129 42E A port in Japan, in W Kyushu on the East China Sea. It was a village until the late 19th century, when it became a naval base. Sasebo's main industries are shipbuilding and engineering. Population (1983): 252 000.

Saskatchewan A province of W Canada, on the Great Plains. The N is covered by forest, mostly noncommercial, with lakes and swamps. The S is open prairie, now chiefly comprising large highly mechanized farms, and is one of the world's most important wheatlands; the province normally produces about two-thirds of Canada's wheat. There are highly developed marketing cooperatives, begun in the early 20th century. Saskatchewan is rich in minerals, including uranium, oil, natural gas, potash, zinc, and copper; associated industries are important. *History*: explored in the 17th and 18th centuries, Saskatchewan was first exploited for furs. Agricultural settlement began slowly (1870s) but sped up in the decade before 1914. The area became a province in 1905 and was the first part of North America to elect a socialist government (1944–64, 1971–82). Area: 570 269 sq km (220 181 sq mi). Population (1981): 968 313. Capital: Regina.

Saskatchewan River A river in W Canada, rising in two separate branches in the Rocky Mountains and flowing generally E through prairie grainlands to unite in central Saskatchewan. The river then continues to Lake Winnipeg. Length: 1940 km (1205 mi).

Saskatoon 52 10N 106 40W A city in W Canada, in central Saskatchewan. Founded in 1883, it is the distribution centre of a vast grain area, with numerous agricultural industries. Other industries include potash, metals, clothing, and chemicals. Saskatoon houses the University of Saskatchewan (1907). Population (1981): 154 210.

sassafras A tree, *Sassafras albidum*, native to North America. Up to 20 m high, it bears clusters of yellow flowers and dark-blue berries. The aromatic roots are dried for use in medicines and also yield oil of sassafras, which is used in perfumes and as flavouring for beverages. Family: *Lauraceae*.

Sassari 40 43N 8 34E A town in Italy, near the N coast of Sardinia. It has a cathedral (12th–18th centuries) and a university (1562). It is the agricultural trading centre of N Sardinia. Population (1980 est): 120 478.

Sassetta (Stefano di Giovanni; c. 1392–c. 1450) A leading painter of the Sienese school. Some of his work reflects his admiration of Florentine art, for example *Madonna of the Snow*, painted for Siena Cathedral (Contini Bonacossi collection, Florence); his later work, however, typifies the *international gothic style. He painted many altarpieces, for example a now dismembered altarpiece, originally painted for the church of S Francesco in Sansepolcro, notable for its scenes from the life of St Francis of Assisi.

Sassoon, Siegfried (1886–1967) British poet and writer. In 1917 his disgust with the progress of World War I led him to make a public refusal to continue serving; he was sent to a military hospital where he met Wilfred *Owen. His antiwar poetry appeared in *The Old Huntsman* (1917) and *Counterattack* (1918), and he wrote several volumes of autobiographical war memoirs.

Satan. *See* Lucifer.

satanism Worship of the forces of evil. Formerly a synonym for atheism or certain heresies, the term now generally applies to beliefs and practices, such as the *black mass, that parody Christian equivalents. Evolving in this form in late-19th-century France, satanism is usually a blend of magic, religion, and bizarre sexual practices. Aleister Crowley (1875–1947) was a notorious modern exponent.

satellite 1. A celestial body orbiting a *planet. The planets of the solar system have at least 50 known satellites, ranging

Planet & Satellite	diameter (km)	distance from primary (1000km)	year of discovery	Planet & Satellite	diameter (km)	distance from primary (1000km)	year of discovery
EARTH				Mimas c-o	390	186	1982
Moon	3 476	384.40	–	Mimas	390	186	1789
MARS				Enceladus	500	238	1789
Phobos	27	9.38	1877	Tethys	1 050	295	1684
Deimos	15	23.46	1877	1980 S25	35	295	1980
JUPITER				1980 S13	35	295	1980
Metis	40	128	1979	Tethys c-o	15	295	1982
Adrastea	24	128	1979	–	15	350	1982
Amalthea	270	181	1892	Dione	1 120	377	1684
Thebe	100	222	1979	1980 S6	160	378	1980
Io	3 630	422	1610	Dione c-o	15	378	1982
Europa	3 100	671	1610	–	–	470	1982
Ganymede	5 260	1 070	1610	Rhea	1 530	527	1672
Callisto	4 800	1 883	1610	Titan	5 150	1 222	1655
Leda	20	11 110	1974	Hyperion	400	1 481	1848
Himalia	180	11 480	1904	Iapetus	1 440	3 560	1671
Lysithea	40	11 720	1938	Phoebe	160	12 950	1898
Elara	80	11 740	1905	URANUS			
Ananke	30	21 200	1951	Miranda	400	130	1948
Carme	40	22 600	1938	Ariel	1 300	191	1851
Pasiphae	50	23 500	1908	Umbriel	1 100	266	1851
Sinope	40	23 700	1914	Titania	1 600	436	1787
SATURN				Oberon	1 600	583	1787
1980 S28	40	138	1980	NEPTUNE			
1980 S27	100	139	1980	Triton	3 800	355	1846
1980 S26	100	142	1980	Nereid	300	5 510	1949
1980 S3	90	151	1978	PLUTO			
1980 S1	100	151	1978	Charon	1 000	20 000	1978

PLANETARY SATELLITES

c-o = co-orbital

greatly in size. The small bodies comprising the rings of Saturn, Uranus, and Jupiter may also be regarded as satellites. Mercury and Venus have no satellites. The earth's satellite is the *moon. The two small heavily cratered Martian satellites, Phobos and Deimos, have been extensively studied by Mariner and Viking planetary probes. The largest and most studied of Jupiter's 16 satellites are the *Galilean satellites Io, Europa, Ganymede, and Callisto. Saturn has at least 23 satellites, the largest, Titan, having a nitrogen atmosphere. Uranus has five satellites, four moderately sized, while Neptune has two, Triton and the much smaller Nereid, both moving in unusual orbits. Pluto has one satellite, Charon.
2. A spacecraft that is launched into orbit around the earth or enters an orbit around some other solar-system body. It may be a *communications satellite, retransmitting radio signals from one location on earth to another. Alternatively, its instruments may gather information from earth or from other celestial objects and transmit it, by radio signals, to ground-based receiving stations. This information is used, for example, in weather forecasting, navigation, scientific and astronomical research, and for military purposes. A further function, under investigation, is the conversion of solar power into microwaves that could be beamed to earth and used as an energy source.

Satie, Erik (1866–1925) French composer. He studied briefly at the Paris conservatoire and, aged 39, at the Schola Cantorum with Roussel and d'Indy. Satie was well known for his eccentricity and for the whimsical titles of his compositions. He influenced such composers as Milhaud and Poulenc by turning away from impressionism towards a clear-textured style that admitted humour. His works include the ballet *Parade* (1916), piano pieces, including *Trois Gymnopédies* (1888), *Pièces froides* (1897), and *Trois morceaux en forme de poire* (1903), and many songs.

satinwood A tree, *Chloroxylon swietenia*, native to S India and Sri Lanka. Its wood is valued in cabinetmaking for its fine golden-yellow finish; it was used in particular by Thomas

*Sheraton. The wood of certain West Indian species is also known as satinwood. Family: *Meliaceae*.

satire A literary or dramatic work that ridicules human or social pretensions. Among the earliest satirists were the Roman poets *Juvenal and *Horace. In Europe satire became a dominant literary form during the late-17th and 18th centuries through *Dryden, *Pope, and *Swift in England and *Voltaire in France. During the 19th century *Byron continued the tradition of verse satire, but prose fiction became the usual medium, as in the works of Samuel *Butler. In the 20th century novelists have been the dominant practitioners, for example Evelyn *Waugh in England and Joseph *Heller in the USA. The English magazine *Private Eye* (founded 1962) is an example of the topical political satire that has always been a feature of journalism.

Sato Eisaku (1901–75) Japanese conservative statesman, under whose unusually long prime ministership (1964–72) Japan became an economic superpower. His most significant personal achievement was the reversion of Okinawa from US rule (1972). He shared the Nobel Peace Prize in 1974 for his opposition to nuclear weapons.

satsuma. *See* tangerine.

Saturn (astronomy) The second largest planet, orbiting the sun every 29.5 years at a mean distance of 1427 million km. It is the most oblate planet (equatorial diameter 120 000 km, polar diameter 108 000 km) and has the lowest mean density (0.7 g cm^{-3}). In a telescope dark and light yellowish cloud bands are visible, running parallel to the equator. The dominant feature, however, is **Saturn's rings**, lying in the equatorial plane and tilted at 27° to the orbital plane. There are six rings, labelled D, C, B, A, F, G, and E in order of distance from Saturn. They differ considerably in brightness and width but are all composed of small icy chunks. The overall diameter is almost 600 000 km but the thickness is only a few hundred metres. The main rings, C, B, and A, were discovered in the 17th century. The outermost, A, extends to 73 000 km above Saturn's clouds. Ring A and the brightest one, B, are separated by the Cassini division. Saturn also has at least 22 *satellites. Saturn is made up primarily of hydrogen and helium, possibly with a central rocky core surrounded by liquid hydrogen. *See also* planetary probe.

Saturn (mythology) The Roman god of agriculture and father of the gods, identified with the Greek *Cronus. His consort was Ops, identified with the Greek *Rhea. Various aspects of the Saturnalia, his annual festival held in December, at which presents were exchanged and normal social rules relaxed, were taken over by the Christian festival of Christmas. His name survives in *Saturday*.

saturniid moth A moth belonging to the mainly tropical family *Saturniidae* (about 800 species). They are usually large with a transparent eyespot on each wing. Their cocoons can be a source of silk (*see* silkworm moth) and the larvae are typically green, feeding chiefly on tree foliage. *See also* cecropia moth; emperor moth; hercules moth.

satyagraha The Sanskrit expression referring to *Gandhi's policy of nonviolent resistance to British rule in India.

satyrid butterfly A butterfly of the worldwide family *Satyridae*. The wings are mainly brownish with a few or numerous eyespots. The forelegs are rudimentary and the flight weak and fluttering. Satyrids hide when alarmed, folding the forewings inside the camouflaged hindwings. The striped pale-green or brown caterpillars feed on grasses.

Satyrs and Sileni In Greek mythology, male fertility spirits of the woods and fields, usually portrayed with goats' legs and pointed ears or horns. Associated with *Dionysus, they were typically drunk and lustful. *See also* Silenus.

sauce A thickened savoury or sweet liquid accompanying a dish and enhancing its flavour. Many classical dishes are named after the sauce served with them (e.g. *spaghetti bolognese, poulet chasseur, sole bonne femme*). Sauces often require a liaison, which binds together the liquids and other ingredients, the commonest being a *roux* (a paste of melted butter and flour). Other liaisons are egg yolks and butter kneaded with flour (*beurre manié*). Flour-based sauces include béchamel (white sauce), mornay (cheese sauce), soubise (onion sauce), and paršley sauce. Hollandaise and béarnaise sauces are made with wine vinegar, spices, and egg yolks. Other well-known sauces are mint sauce (with lamb), apple sauce (with pork), cranberry sauce (with turkey), horseradish sauce (with beef), tartare sauce (with fish), and tomato sauce. Among sweet sauces are butterscotch sauce (made with golden syrup and sugar), chocolate sauce, and melba sauce (puréed raspberries and icing sugar).

Saud (1902–69) King of Saudi Arabia (1953–64). He continued the modernization programmes begun by his father *Ibn Saud but was unable to deal competently with the financial complexities of Saudi's oil revenues. He was deposed and the throne passed to his brother *Faisal.

Saudi Arabia, Kingdom of A country in the Middle East comprising most of *Arabia, bordering on the Red Sea and the Persian Gulf. In the W a line of mountains runs close to the Red Sea, while the *Najd, the central plateau, slopes downwards W–E. In the N and SE are large areas of desert. The population, densest in the SW, is mainly Arab Muslim, the majority being Sunnite with some Shiites in the E. About 27% are nomads. There are also many foreign workers, chiefly unskilled Yemenis and skilled Americans and Europeans. *Economy*: based on oil, discovered in 1936 in the Persian Gulf and exploited since 1938; some is refined locally. The country, a member of OPEC, is the world's greatest exporter of oil, the revenues being used to diversify the economy and provide education and health services. Recent industries include petrochemicals, fertilizers, and steel production; considerable mineral resources have also been discovered. Income is also derived from pilgrims visiting Mecca, Medina, and Jidda. Apart from land reclaimed by irrigation, only Asir and the oases are cultivated; livestock is kept on the extensive pasture land. Consumer and capital goods and foodstuffs (particularly cereals) are imported, mainly from Japan, the USA, West

Germany, and the UK. *History*: the establishment of Saudi Arabia (1932) under *Ibn Saud followed the 19th-century struggle by the Saud family to dominate the warring tribes of the peninsula and take overall control from Turkey. Asir was incorporated in 1934. Saudi Arabia became a founding member of the Arab League (1945). Under Ibn Saud's son, *Saud, conflict with Egypt developed, especially during the North Yemen civil war, in which Saudi Arabia supported the royalists and Egypt the republicans. Saud's brother, *Faisal Ibn Abdul Aziz, who replaced him (1964), restored relations with Egypt and also used the oil crisis of the early 1970s to increase Saudi holdings in oil operations. On Faisal's apparently motiveless assassination (1975) he was replaced as king by his brother, *Khalid Ibn Abdul Aziz. On Khalid's death (1982) his brother, Fahd Ibn Abdul Aziz, became king. Official language: Arabic. Official currency: rial of 100 nilalas. Area: 2 400 000 sq km (927 000 sq mi). Population (1983 est): 10 443 000. Capital: Riyadh. Chief port: Jidda.

Saul In the Old Testament, the first King of Israel, who reigned in the 11th century BC. Son of Kish, he was anointed king by *Samuel. He began his reign with a great victory over the Ammonites, followed by many battles against the Philistines. Following an act of disobedience during the Israelite destruction of the *Amalekites, Saul, according to the Old Testament, lost divine favour; his last years were marked by a growing enmity with *David. He committed suicide after being wounded and defeated by the Philistines.

Sault Ste Marie 46 32N 84 20W A city in E Canada, in NW Ontario on the St Mary's River opposite Sault Ste Marie, USA. Its canal allows ships to bypass local rapids that provide hydroelectricity for steel and other heavy industry. Population (1981): 82 697.

Sault Ste Marie 46 29N 84 22W A city in the USA, in Michigan, on the St Mary's River opposite Sault Ste Marie, Canada. It serves the traffic of the St Lawrence Seaway by way of the Soo locks, which attract large numbers of tourists to the city. Population (1980): 14 448.

Saumur 47 16N 0 05W A town in W France, in the Maine-et-Loire department on the River Loire. A former Huguenot stronghold, it is famous for its cavalry school (1768) and its sparkling white wines. Population (1982): 22 050.

Saunders, Dame Cicely Mary Strode (1918–) British philanthropist. After training as a nurse, in 1967 Cicely Saunders founded St Christopher's Hospice in London for the care of the terminally ill, which specializes in the relief of pain and support for the families. She is also the author of such books as *Care of the Dying* (1960) and *Living with Dying* (1983). *See also* hospice movement.

Saurischia An order of *dinosaurs dominant in the Jurassic period (about 195–130 million years ago). They had hip bones like those of modern lizards (the name means "lizard hips") and were mostly bipedal carnivores, although some were quadrupedal herbivores. *See also* Allosaurus; Apatosaurus; Ornitholestes; Tyrannosaurus.

saury A marine fish, also called skipper, belonging to the family *Scomberesocidae* (about 4 species). It has a long slim body, up to 50 cm long, blue or olive above and golden or silvery below, with beaklike jaws and finlets behind the dorsal and anal fins. Sauries occur in large shoals in tropical and temperate surface waters, feeding on crustaceans and small fish. They are often seen leaping or skipping over the surface to escape predators. Order: *Atheriniformes*.

Saussure, Ferdinand de (1857–1913) Swiss linguist. His great influence on 20th-century linguistics is due to the posthumously published *Course in General Linguistics* (1916), compiled by his pupils from lecture notes. It offers an integrated picture of all aspects of language. De Saussure's distinction between *parole* (the utterance of the individual) and *langue* (the common language of a community) was of great importance to both sociolinguistics and structural linguistics (*see* linguistics). He also drew influential distinctions between diachronic (historical) and synchronic linguistics and between syntagmatic (collocational) and paradigmatic (organizational) relations in language.

Savage, Michael Joseph (1872–1940) New Zealand statesman; the first Labour prime minister of New Zealand (1935–40). His ministry, which included (Sir) Walter Nash, dealt with the economic problems of the Depression.

Savage, Richard (c. 1696–1743) British poet. Although he claimed to be the illegitimate son of an earl, he was of humble origin. He led a disorderly bohemian life and died in a debtors' prison in Bristol. His works include *Sir Thomas Overbury* (1723), a tragedy, and *The Wanderer* (1729), a long poem. He was the subject of a sympathetic biography (1744) by his friend Dr Johnson.

Savai'i 13 44S 172 18W The largest island of Western Samoa. There was a volcanic eruption in 1905 and lava flows laid waste a large area. Copra, bananas, and cocoa are exported. Area: 1174 sq km (662 sq mi). Population (1981): 42 218. Chief town: Tuasivi.

SAVANNA *Flat-topped acacia trees rise above grassland in the Serengeti National Park (Tanzania).*

savanna (*or* savannah) The extensive tropical grasslands, bordering on the equatorial rain forests in both the N and S hemispheres. They cover extensive areas in N Australia, Africa, and South America (where they are known as the *llanos in Venezuela and Colombia and the campos in Brazil). The vegetation of savannas is dominated by tall grasses, such as elephant grass, interspersed with low often flat-topped trees and bushes. Grazed by herds of hooved animals, savannas are ideal cattle-rearing areas.

Savannah 32 04N 81 07W A city in the USA, in Georgia on the Savannah River. Established by James Oglethorpe in 1733, it was an important colonial port. The first Atlantic steamship crossing was from here to Liverpool in 1819. A major tourist centre and seaport, its industries include shipbuilding and chemicals. Population (1980): 141 634.

Savery, Thomas (c. 1650–1715) English engineer, who in 1698 constructed the first practical steam engine. Savery's engine, which was dangerous because it utilized high-pressure steam, was superseded by *Newcomen's engine.

savin A low-growing *juniper shrub, *Juniperus sabina*, native to mountainous regions of S and central Europe. It has scalelike leaves and blue-black berry-like cones, 4–6 mm long. The shrub has a strong unpleasant smell and yields a poisonous oil used in medicine and veterinary work.

savings banks Banks in the UK that pay compound *interest on deposit accounts for individual savers. The British National Savings Bank (formerly the Post Office Savings Bank) is run by the Post Office and was set up in 1861; it invests principally in government securities. No depositor may hold more than £10,000 and up to £100 daily can be withdrawn without notice. The Trustee Savings Banks were originally nonprofit-making organizations founded in the 19th century to encourage thrift among low-income workers. They have gradually evolved into a single commercial bank, which was floated on the Stock Exchange in 1986 for £1.5 billion, with 5 million people applying for shares. In the USA mutual savings banks are similar institutions.

Savitskaya, Svetlana (1949–) Soviet cosmonaut, who on 25 July, 1984, became the first woman to walk in space. She also held world records in parachuting and flying, and became the first woman to make two space trips.

Savona 44 18N 8 28E A port in NW Italy, in Liguria on the Gulf of Genoa. It rivalled Genoa in the middle ages but was subjugated by the Genoese in 1528. It has a 16th-century cathedral. Savona is an important centre of the Italian iron and steel industry. Population (1981 est): 75 069.

Savonarola, Girolamo (1452–98) Italian religious reformer. Joining the Dominicans in 1474, he became a lecturer in the Convent of San Marco, Florence, and later its prior (1491). There he began a crusade against religious and political corruption, centring his attacks on the papacy and the Medici. His fervent preaching attracted a large following, and he became the virtual ruler of Florence when the Medici were expelled by the populace in 1494. Excommunicated by Alexander VI in 1497, he was imprisoned, hanged, and burned for heresy by his political rivals.

savory A herb belonging to the genus *Satureja*, of warm and temperate regions. Summer savory (*S. hortensis*) is an annual, native to central Europe and Asia. Both the dried leaves and the oil extract are used for flavouring foods. The perennial winter savory (*S. montana*) grows to a height of 40 cm, has small white flowers, and is also a culinary herb. Family: *Labiatae*.

Savoy An Alpine frontier region of SE France corresponding to the present-day departments of Savoie and Haute-Savoie. Strategically important for its mountain passes, the county of Savoy was founded in 1034 by Umberto Biancomano (Umberto I). He and his successors extended Savoyard territory, acquiring Piedmont in the 14th century. In 1416 *Amadeus the Peaceful became a duke and was subsequently elected antipope as Felix V. After acquiring Sardinia in 1720, Savoyard dukes took the title King of Sardinia, which in 1748 became the kingdom of Piedmont-Sardinia. Savoy (but not Sardinia) was annexed by France during the Revolutionary Wars but restored in 1815 and Piedmont-Sardinia became the leading spirit in the movement for Italian unification (*see* Risorgimento). Savoy became part of France in 1860 in return for Napoleon III's assistance against Austria but the House of Savoy ruled the newly formed kingdom of Italy (1861–1946).

sawfish A *ray fish of the family *Pristidae* that occurs mainly in salt and brackish waters of tropical and subtropical regions. Its sharklike body, up to 7 m long, bears a long blad like snout edged with teeth and is used to forage along the bottom or to catch prey.

sawfly An insect belonging to the widely distributed suborder *Symphyta* and so named because the female possesses a needle-like tubular ovipositor, which is used as a saw or drill to insert eggs into foliage and timber. Adults are 5–50 mm long and the larvae, resembling caterpillars, damage trees. Chief families: *Argidae*, *Siricidae*, *Cimbicidae*, *Diprionidae*, *Tenthredinidae*; order: *Hymenoptera*.

Saxe, Maurice, Comte de (1696–1750) Marshal of France, the illegitimate son of Augustus the Strong of Poland. He fought in the French army, outstandingly in the War of the *Austrian Succession (1740–48), and wrote *Mes Rêveries* (1757) on warfare.

Saxe-Coburg-Gotha The ruling dynasty of a German

duchy. The children of Duke Francis Frederick (1750-1806) included Victoria Mary Louisa (1786-1861), who married (1818) Edward, Duke of Kent (their daughter was Queen Victoria); and Leopold, who became *Leopold I of Belgium. Francis' son Ernest I (1806-44) was the father of Prince Albert, who married Queen Victoria in 1840. The UK royal house was called Saxe-Coburg-Gotha until 1917, when the name *Windsor was adopted.

saxhorn A valved wind instrument of the bugle type, patented by the Belgian Adolphe Sax (1814-94) in Paris in 1845. It is made in several sizes; the tenor saxhorn (or tenor horn) is used in the military and brass bands and occasionally in the orchestra, as in Mahler's seventh symphony.

saxifrage A perennial herb belonging to certain genera of the family Saxifragaceae, found in cold and temperate regions. The leaves may either form a basal rosette or occur in pairs along the stem and the flowers are white, yellow, purple, or red. Most are fairly small, although the European meadow saxifrage (Saxifraga granulata) may reach a height of 45 cm. See also London pride.

Saxo Grammaticus (c. 1150-c. 1206) Danish chronicler. Little is known of his life, except that he served as secretary to the Archbishop of Roskilde. He was the author of Gesta Danorum, a Latin history of the Danes, the first part of which is based on mythological and legendary material. It includes the legend of Balder and the story of Amleth, one of the sources for the plot of Shakespeare's Hamlet. The latter part of the chronicle contains more definitely historical material.

Saxons A Germanic people who, during the 5th century AD, expanded from their Baltic coastal homelands to other areas of N Germany, the coast of Gaul (France), and (with the *Angles and *Jutes) to Britain. Charlemagne eventually defeated the continental Saxons and converted them to Christianity, incorporating their lands into his empire after a long period of warfare (772-804 AD). See also Anglo-Saxons.

Saxony (German name: Sachsen) An ancient NW German duchy. Named after its original inhabitants, the *Saxons (who expanded to Britain in the 5th century), they were conquered by Charlemagne in the 8th century and subsequently became a duchy. In 919 AD Henry, Duke of Saxony, became German king and his son *Otto the Great, the first Saxon Holy Roman Emperor. In 1142 Saxony passed to *Henry the Lion but in 1180 the duchy was broken up, to be reformed in various territorial combinations in following centuries. In the 13th century Saxony became an electorate and in the 16th and 17th centuries a leading German Protestant state. In 1697 Elector Frederick Augustus I (1670-1733) became King of Poland and Saxony's subsequent involvement in Polish affairs kept it apart from German power struggles until the 19th century. Conquered by Napoleon in 1806, N Saxony was annexed by Prussia in 1815 and in 1866 joined the Prussian-dominated *North German Confederation. The remainder of Saxony joined the German Empire in 1871.

saxophone A woodwind instrument with a brass body, keys, and a single reed mouthpiece similar to that of a *clarinet. It was invented by the Belgian Adolphe Sax (1814-94) and patented in France in the 1840s. The most common sizes of saxophone are the soprano, alto, tenor, and baritone. They are most commonly used as solo instruments in jazz; they are sometimes used in classical music.

Sayan Mountains A mountain range in the central S Soviet Union, extending some 800 km (497 mi) E-W and rising to 3491 m (11 453 ft) in Munku Sardyk in the extreme SE. The River Yenisei and many of its tributaries rise here.

Sayers, Dorothy L(eigh) (1893-1957) British writer, educated at Oxford, who is best known for her series of detective novels, beginning with Whose Body? (1923), featuring the erudite detective Lord Peter Wimsey. She also wrote plays on Christian themes and a translation of Dante's Divine Comedy.

scabies A contagious skin infection caused by the *itch mite, which tunnels and breeds in the skin, causing intense itching. The burrows of the mites are seen between the fingers, on the side of the hands, in the armpits, on the groin, nipples, and buttocks. Treatment is by application of benzylbenzoate cream, and clothing and bedding should be disinfested.

scabious An annual or perennial herb belonging to the genus Scabiosa (80-100 species), native to the Mediterranean region and temperate parts of Eurasia and Africa. The small scabious (S. columbaria) is widely distributed on chalky soils. 15-70 cm high, it has a cluster of small bluish-lilac flowers borne on a long stalk. The field scabious, S. (or Knautia) arvensis, is very similar and may reach a height of 1 m. Family: Dipsacaceae.

Scafell Pike 54 28N 3 12W The highest peak in England, in Cumbria, in the Lake District. It is popular for walking and rock climbing. Height: 978 m (3210 ft).

scalar quantity A quantity that is represented by magnitude only. Unlike a *vector quantity, a scalar quantity has no direction. Examples include mass, time, and speed.

scale (music) An ascending or descending succession of notes, characterized by a fixed succession of intervals between the notes that constitute it. Many thousands of different scales exist; all the major musical traditions of the world are based upon them.
In western music there are three **diatonic scales**, which derive from the ancient Greek *modes: the major scale, the harmonic minor scale, and the melodic minor scale. The octave is divided into 12 notes (see temperament) and any of these scales may be constructed on any of these notes. The version of the scale produced is associated with a particular *tonality. The **chromatic scale** includes all 12 semitones of the octave. The **pentatonic scale**, consisting of only 5 notes, is common in Chinese and Scottish music.

scale (zoology) A platelike structure that generally forms part of a protective body covering in many vertebrate animals. Fish and certain reptiles have an overlapping series of bony scales, derived from the deep layers of the skin (dermis). The periodic growth of fish scales gives rise to annual rings, by which the age of the fish may be estimated. In reptiles the scales are periodically renewed and may be modified and enlarged as spines.

scale insect An insect belonging to the superfamily Coccoidea (about 4000 species), abundant in warm and tropical regions. Scale insects are usually small (on average 1-15 mm long) and the females are often legless, wingless, and eyeless and covered by a waxy scale or mass of threads. They become encrusted on plants and suck the juices, often becoming serious pests. Other species are of value by producing *shellac, *cochineal, and various waxes. Suborder: Homoptera; order: *Hemiptera.

Scaliger, Julius Caesar (1484-1558) Italian humanist scholar. He engaged in controversy with *Erasmus and wrote several commentaries on classical writers. Aristotle's theories of tragedy became known to the French 17th-century dramatists through his discussion of them in the Poetice (1561). His son **Joseph Justus Scaliger** (1540-1609), born in France, was an outstanding classical scholar and published many works of historical scholarship, notably the Opus de emendatione tempore (1583), a scientific study of chronology.

scallion Any *onion or related plant that produces small white-skinned mild-flavoured bulbs, with a long neck and stiff leaves. Examples are spring onions and *shallots, used in salads. Leeks and chives may also be called scallions.

scallop A *bivalve mollusc belonging to the family Pectinidae (about 400 species), of warm and temperate seas. 2-20 cm across, the valves of the shell are broad, flattened, and deeply fluted, and the animal swims by flapping them with a single powerful muscle. Scallops are important as seafood.

scaly-tailed squirrel An African arboreal *rodent belonging to the family *Anomaluridae* (9 species). They range in size from 8 to 45 cm and most species have a gliding membrane like that of the *flying squirrel. Their name refers to the backward-pointing scales under the tail that grip the tree trunk when the squirrel is clinging to it.

Scandinavia Geographically, a peninsula in NW Europe, comprising Norway and Sweden. Culturally and historically, it also includes Denmark, Iceland, the Faeroe Islands, and Finland.

Scandinavian languages A subgroup of the *Germanic group of languages consisting of *Swedish, *Norwegian, *Danish, *Icelandic, and Faeroese. The first three are similar enough to be mutually intelligible. They all developed from a common Scandinavian ancestor, which originally used the *runic alphabet (*see also* Old Norse). This language spread with the Vikings to Iceland, the Faeroes, and to other Baltic and Atlantic islands.

scandium (Sc) The first transition metal, predicted by Mendeleyev and discovered in 1879 by L. F. Nilson (1840–99). It is trivalent, forming an oxide (Sc_2O_3), halides (for example ScF_3), and other compounds. It is light (relative density 2.989) and has a much higher melting point than aluminium, making it of interest as a possible spacecraft material. At no 21; at wt 44.956; mp 1541°C; bp 2831°C.

scanner (medicine). *See* tomography; ultrasonics.

Scapa Flow A section of the Atlantic Ocean off the N coast of Scotland, in the Orkney Islands. It was the main base of the British Grand Fleet in World War I. Following its surrender, the German fleet scuttled itself here (1919). Length: about 24 km (15 mi). Width: 13 km (8 mi).

scapegoat An animal, person, or object chosen as the symbolic bearer of the sins or misfortunes of an individual or group. At the ancient Jewish ritual of the Day of Atonement, a goat was chosen to bear the sins of the people and driven off a cliff. Similar rituals were practised in ancient Greece and Rome.

scapula. *See* shoulder.

scarab An ancient Egyptian seal or amulet made of stone or faience in the shape of a dung beetle. Associated with the sun's regenerative powers, scarabs were often buried with the dead.

scarab beetle A beetle belonging to the worldwide family *Scarabaeidae* (over 19 000 species). Scarabs show a great variety in size and form: the largest beetles—the *goliath and *hercules beetles—are scarabs, while other species have developed extraordinary horns (*see* rhinoceros beetle). The family has two main groups—the *dung beetles and *chafers. Certain dung-rolling beetles, especially *Scarabaeus sacer*, were the sacred scarabs of the ancient Egyptians.

Scarborough 54 17N 0 24W A resort in NE England, on the North Yorkshire coast. The promontory separating the North and South Bays is the site of a prehistoric settlement, a Roman signal station, and a 12th-century castle. There is fishing and tourism. Population (1981): 43 103.

Scarfe, Gerald (1936–) British cartoonist. Working for such journals as *Private Eye*, *Punch*, and the *Sunday Times*, he is noted for his scathing caricatures of public figures.

Scargill, Arthur (1941–) British trades union leader; president of the National Union of Mineworkers (1981–). A charismatic speaker with a noted contempt for the media, he led the NUM in a long and bitter strike (1984–85) in protest against proposed pit closures. In 1985 Scargill was confirmed as NUM president until retirement and became founding president of the Miners' International union. He stood for re-election as NUM president in 1987 and was returned with a reduced majority in 1988.

Scarlatti, Domenico (1685–1757) Italian composer and noted harpsichordist and organist. After studying in Venice and holding court posts in Rome and Naples, he was engaged

by Princess Maria Barbara of Portugal in Lisbon in 1720. When she married into the Spanish royal family in 1729 he moved with her to Madrid, where he stayed until his death. Besides some operas and church music, he wrote over 600 harpsichord sonatas, many of which were highly innovative. His father **Alessandro Scarlatti** (1660–1725) was also a composer. He worked chiefly in Rome and Naples. He was maestro successively to Queen Christina of Sweden, to the Spanish viceroy, at Sta Maria Maggiore in Rome, and at the royal chapel in Naples. His works include over a hundred operas, 600 chamber cantatas, 200 masses, 12 chamber symphonies, and 14 oratorios.

scarlet fever A highly infectious disease of children caused by streptococcus bacteria. Since these bacteria are much less virulent now than formerly, the disease is much milder now than it was at the beginning of the century. After an incubation period of 2–4 days the child develops a sore throat, fever, and headache; 24–48 hours later a red rash spreads from the chest over the whole body. Before antibiotics scarlet fever killed many children or left them disabled with *rheumatic fever, kidney disease, or ear infections; it can now be rapidly cured with penicillin.

Scarron, Paul (1610–60) French poet, dramatist, and satirist. His best-known work is the picaresque novel *Le Roman comique* (1651–57). From the age of 30 he suffered from paralysis. Despite this handicap, in 1652 he married Françoise d'Aubigné, who later became, as Madame de Maintenon, the wife of Louis XIV.

scattering The deflection of waves or particles by the atoms or molecules of the medium through which they are passing or by other particles. The scattering of waves is due to either *reflection or *diffraction. For particles, the scattering is described as inelastic if the scattered particles gain or lose energy during the process (as in the *Raman effect). Otherwise it is elastic.

SCARAB BEETLE *This African species,* Phanaeus imperator, *is one of the rhinoceros beetles.*

scaup A *diving duck, *Aythya marila*, that breeds in northern latitudes and winters on more southerly coasts. 40–45 cm long, it dives deeply to feed on mussels and small crabs. The male has green-black fore parts, a grey back, white flanks, and a brown rump and tail; females are dark brown with a white patch around the bill.

scepticism The philosophical tradition that absolute certainty or knowledge cannot be attained. It began perhaps with ancient Greek scepticism about the senses (*see* Pyrrhon). Sometimes the sceptic's claim was that any knowledge attained must go unrecognized; sometimes he systematically suspected certain subjects, such as reality, religious beliefs, or moral principles, on the grounds, for example, of the relativity or subjectivity of such beliefs.

Schacht, Hjalmar (1877–1970) German financier and

politician. As president of the Reichsbank (1923-30), he checked Germany's rampant inflation. He was reappointed by Hitler in 1933 but was dismissed in 1939. From 1934 to 1937 he served as minister of economics. He was acquitted at Nuremberg of war crimes.

Schaffhausen (French name: Schaffhouse) 47 42N 8 38E A town in N Switzerland, on the River Rhine. Its notable buildings include the Munot fort and the romanesque cathedral (11th-12th centuries). Industries include aluminium smelting; hydroelectric power is obtained from the falls on the River Rhine. Population (1983 est): 34 396.

Scheel, Walter (1919-) West German statesman; president (1974-79). He served in the Luftwaffe during World War II and was minister for economic cooperation (1961-66) and foreign minister (1969-74) before becoming president. In 1967 he became chairman of the Free Democrats.

Scheele, Carl Wilhelm (1742-86) Swedish chemist, who discovered a number of compounds and elements. His greatest work in this field was the discovery of oxygen (c. 1771), but as his results were not published until 1777 *Priestley is usually credited with the discovery. Scheele was also the first to isolate and prepare the gases hydrogen sulphide, hydrogen cyanide, and hydrogen fluoride.

scheelite A tungsten ore mineral, $CaWO_4$, occurring in veins and contact-metamorphic rocks. It is yellowish white or brown. *See also* wolframite.

Scheldt, River (French name: Escaut; Flemish and Dutch name: Schelde) A river in W Europe. Rising in NE France, it flows generally NNE through W Belgium to Antwerp, then NW to the North Sea in the SW Netherlands. Canals connect it to the Rivers Somme, Seine, Sambre, Meuse, and Rhine. Length: 435 km (270 mi).

Schelling, Friedrich (1775-1854) German philosopher. Schelling was first influenced by the writings of *Fichte and *Kant. Later, he became convinced that knowledge could not be confined to phenomena and argued that there was "a secret wonderful faculty which dwells in us all." His *System of Transcendental Idealism* (1800) contains his metaphysical philosophy, which, with his insistence that human consciousness is fulfilled by art, made him an important influence upon *Romanticism and in particular upon *Coleridge.

Schenectady 42 48N 73 57W A city in the USA, in New York state on the Mohawk River. In 1886 the Thomas Edison Machine Works was moved here, later becoming the General Electric Company, which dominates the city today. Population (1980): 67 877.

Scheveningen. *See* Hague, The.

Schiaparelli, Elsa (1896-1973) Italian-born fashion designer, who opened fashion houses in Paris (late 1920s) and New York (1949). Her designs and use of colour were flamboyant and daring; she is particularly associated with the padded shoulder and "shocking pink."

Schick test A skin test for the presence of antibodies to *diphtheria. Injection of small amounts of diphtheria toxin causes a localized inflammation of the skin in those who have not been vaccinated or have not had diphtheria. The test was devised in 1913 by an Austrian paediatrician, Bela Schick (1877-1967).

Schiedam 51 55N 4 25E A town in the W Netherlands, in South Holland province. It has famous gin distilleries. Population (1981 est): 74 233.

Schiele, Egon (1890-1918) Austrian expressionist painter. Influenced first by the French impressionists and by *Klimt, Schiele often painted portraits and nudes and was able to express both a disturbing anguished quality and eroticism through a distorted use of line. With *Kokoschka he was a leader of Austrian expressionism until his untimely death from influenza.

Schiller, (Johann Christoph) Friedrich (von) (1759- 1805) German dramatist, poet, and writer. His first, anonymously published, play, *Die Räuber* (1781), typifies the *Sturm und Drang call for political freedom. His next important play and his first in blank verse was the tragedy *Don Carlos* (1787), set in the time of Philip II of Spain. With Goethe's friendly encouragement from 1794, Schiller turned from the historical and academic studies with which he had been involved and produced the brilliant dramas of the last decade of his life: the trilogy *Wallenstein* (1798-99), *Maria Stuart* (1800), based on the life of Mary, Queen of Scots, *Die Jungfrau von Orleans* (1801), concerned with Joan of Arc, and *Wilhelm Tell* (1804). His nondramatic works include poems, the important essay on aesthetics, *Über naïve und sentimentalische Dichtung* (1795-96), and a history of the Thirty Years' War (1793).

schipperke A breed of ▯dog originating in Flanders and used as a guard dog on barges. It has a stocky tailless body with short legs and a foxlike head with erect ears. The dense coat is usually black and thick around the neck, forming a mane. Height: 30.5-33 cm.

schist A coarse-grained *metamorphic rock with a pronounced banded structure, in which the minerals show parallel alignment at right angles to the direction of stress, leaving no trace of the original bedding. The minerals are segregated into alternate thin layers rich in mica and quartz/ feldspar, and the rock readily splits along these schistosity planes. Schists are named according to the dominant minerals, e.g. mica-schist.

schistosomiasis (or bilharziasis) A widespread disease of the tropics caused by blood flukes of the genus *Schistosoma* (or *Bilharzia*). The disease is contracted by bathing in water contaminated by snails, which harbour the larvae of the parasite. The larvae penetrate the skin and—when mature—settle in the blood vessels of the intestine or bladder. Symptoms, caused by the release of eggs by adult flukes, include anaemia, inflammation, and diarrhoea and dysentery (from an intestinal infection), or cystitis and blood in the urine (from a bladder infection). The disease is treated by drugs that destroy the parasite. In 1987 researchers discovered paramyosin, a possible vaccine.

schizophrenia A severe mental disorder characterized by disintegration of the processes of thinking, contact with reality, and emotional responsiveness. Delusions and *hallucinations are common, especially those that produce the feeling of a loss of personal identity. Schizophrenics often become withdrawn and apathetic. The condition tends to get worse (in about half of all cases) unless treatment is given. Modern treatment has improved the outlook: it consists of such drugs as *phenothiazines and vigorous psychological and social rehabilitation. Schizophrenia is largely caused by genetic factors, but environmental stress can trigger an episode of illness. *See also* paranoia; psychosis.

Schlegel, August Wilhelm von (1767-1845) German critic, poet, and translator. With his brother, he exerted a powerful influence on the early Romantics through critical works, such as *Über dramatische Kunst und Literatur* (3 vols, 1809-11), and translations, especially his superb rendering of Shakespeare. His brother **(Carl Wilhelm) Friedrich von Schlegel** (1772-1829) was a writer and critic. The chief influence on the Romantic movement, his literary and philosophical works appeared first in *Das Athenäum*, a periodical published by him and his brother. He later published the first study in comparative philology (1808).

Schleiden, Matthias Jakob (1804-81) German botanist, who first formulated the theory that plants are composed of *cells (this was later extended to animals by Theodor *Schwann). Schleiden also recognized the importance of the cell nucleus, although he mistakenly believed that new cells budded from its surface.

Schlesinger, John (1926-) British film and theatre director. His first major films, *A Kind of Loving* (1962) and

Billy Liar (1963), concerned working-class life in N England. His later films included *Midnight Cowboy* (1969) and *Sunday Bloody Sunday* (1971); he was appointed an associate director of the National Theatre Company in 1973.

Schleswig A breed of draught horse originating in the Danish duchy of Schleswig. It has a long body with relatively short legs, a powerful neck and a fairly large head. The coat is usually chestnut but sometimes bay or grey. Height: about 1.60 m (15¾ hands).

Schleswig-Holstein A low-lying *Land* in NE West Germany bordering on the North Sea, the Baltic Sea, and Denmark. Grain and potatoes are grown and cattle reared; industries include shipbuilding and engineering. *History*: during the 19th century the **Schleswig-Holstein question** arose when Denmark and the Austrian-led German confederacy both laid claim to the two duchies of Schleswig and Holstein. War broke out in 1863 and the duchies were annexed to Prussia in 1866. In 1949 the *Land* of Schleswig-Holstein was formed. Area: 15 696 sq km (6059 sq mi). Population (1980 est): 2 605 200. Capital: Kiel.

Schlick, Moritz (1882-1936) German philosopher. Schlick was professor of philosophy of the inductive sciences at Vienna University (1922-36). The leader of the *Vienna Circle (see also* logical positivism), he approached philosophy in a basically experimental way and concerned himself with problems of truth and verifiability. His published work includes the *General Theory of Knowledge* (1918) and *Problems of Ethics* (1930).

Schlieffen, Alfred, Graf von (1833-1913) German general, who, as chief of the general staff (1891-1905) devised the **Schlieffen Plan**, on which German strategy at the outbreak of World War I was unsuccessfully based. The plan provided for a concentration of German forces on the Western Front, which would rapidly defeat France in a flanking movement through the Low Countries, while a smaller army held off Russia in the east.

SCHLIEREN PHOTOGRAPHY *A Schlieren photograph showing the spherical shock wave and propellant in the wake of the bullet from a .22 pistol.*

Schliemann, Heinrich (1822-90) German archaeologist. After a successful business career, Schliemann retired (1863) to pursue his childhood ambition of discovering Homeric *Troy. Ignoring scholarly derision, he excavated Hissarlik on the Asia Minor coast of Turkey, finding ruins of nine consecutive cities. The second oldest (Troy II), which he wrongly identified with Homer's city, yielded a hoard that Schliemann romantically called "Priam's Treasure." His spectacular finds at *Mycenae (1874-76), Orchomenos in Boeotia (1880), and *Tiryns (1884-85) established him as the discoverer of *Mycenaean civilization.

Schlieren photography A method of observing differences of density in a transparent medium, such as air. Light from a spark is photographed as it passes through the medium; any differences in density present cause local variations in the refractive index, which show up as streaks (German word: *Schlieren*) in the photograph. The method is used for observing sound waves, shock waves, and flaws in glass.

Schmeling, Max (1905-) German boxer, the first European to win the world heavyweight title in the 20th century (1930). In 1936 he beat Joe *Louis but Louis took his revenge in two minutes in 1938.

Schmidt, Helmut (1918-) West German statesman; Social Democratic chancellor (1974-82). He worked in transport administration in Hamburg before entering Federal politics (1953). He became minister for domestic affairs in Hamburg (1961-65) and was then Federal minister of defence (1969-72) and for finance (1972-74) before becoming chancellor. He has written several books, mainly on foreign affairs. □Giscard d'Estaing, Valéry.

Schmidt telescope A *telescope developed by the Estonian instrument maker Bernard Voldemar Schmidt (1879-1935). It produces very sharp photographic images of celestial objects over a very wide angle of sky. The incoming light passes through a thin correcting plate, is reflected by a large short-focus spherical mirror, and focused on a curved photographic plate.

Schnabel, Artur (1882-1951) Austrian pianist, especially famous for his performances of Beethoven. He studied in Vienna and in Berlin, where he later taught until 1933, after which he lived mainly in Switzerland and the USA. He also composed three symphonies and a piano concerto.

schnauzer A breed of dog originating in Germany and used as a guard dog. Strongly built with a docked tail, it has a characteristic square muzzle with long sidewhiskers. The wiry coat is black or light grey and brown. Two varieties have been bred from the standard schnauzer—the giant schnauzer for farm and police work and the miniature schnauzer as pet. Height: 33-35 cm (miniature); 45-48 cm (standard); 54-65 cm (giant).

Schnitzler, Arthur (1862-1931) Austrian Jewish dramatist and novelist. A physician, he was especially interested in psychiatry and his works are notable for their psychological observation. They include the witty dramatic cycles *Anatol* (1893) and *Reigen* (1900; filmed as *La Ronde,* 1950) and his prose masterpiece, *Leutnant Gustl* (1901).

Schoenberg, Arnold (1874-1951) Austrian-born composer. He studied in Vienna with Alexander von Zemlinsky (1872-1942) and began his career by orchestrating theatre music. In 1910 he became a teacher at the Vienna Academy; his students included Berg and Webern. Mahler became a champion of his music. In 1933 Schoenberg, as a Jew, was forced to leave Berlin; he became a US citizen in 1941 and was professor at the University of California (1936-44). His early compositions, in a late Romantic style, include two string quartets, *Verklärte Nacht* (for string sextet; 1899), and the symphonic poem *Pelleas und Melisande* (1902-03). His subsequent works were characterized by *atonality; they include the melodrama *Pierrot Lunaire* (for soprano and eight instruments; 1912) in which the voice part is noted in *Sprechgesang* (German: speech song). Schoenberg subsequently developed the theory and technique of *serialism (1924), which he employed in most of his later works, including a violin concerto (1936), a piano concerto (1942), and the unfinished opera *Moses und Aaron* (1932).

scholasticism The intellectual discipline comprising all the philosophical and theological activities pursued in the medieval universities (schools). As the international philosophy of Christendom it respected orthodoxy and was concerned with the philosophies of *Plato and *Aristotle as assimilated over centuries of Christian thought. For scholastics religion was predominant and in their method philosophy was the servant of theology. It was by theology that the selection of problems for study and the scope of scientific enquiry were to be decided. *Anselm was an early scholastic, and *Abelard perfected its method. After *Aquinas, *Aristotelianism developed until, in the Renaissance, it was virtually synonymous with scholasticism.

schooner A □sailing vessel with at least two masts, a shorter one set near the bows, a taller one at some distance behind it. Schooners, being quite fast and efficient when sailing off the wind, were widely used before the advent of steam and motor vessels in both coastal and long-distance commercial trade, especially fishing. Because they do not sail well into the wind, they are not a favoured rig in racing.

Schopenhauer, Arthur (1788–1860) German philosopher. Schopenhauer's main contribution to philosophy is contained in the emphasis that he placed upon the human will as a means to understanding. *The World as Will and Idea* (1818) sets out his principal ideas and pessimistic conclusions. He was distrustful of rationalism and the scientific method and was instead concerned with intuitive cognition. He saw the ideal state of man as one of contemplative freedom, achieved through art.

Schreiner, Olive (1855–1920) South African novelist. She went to England in 1881 and won literary and social success with her autobiographical *The Story of an African Farm* (1883). She returned to South Africa in 1889. Her other books include the short allegorical *Dreams* (1891) and the feminist *Women and Labour* (1911).

Schrödinger, Erwin (1887–1961) Austrian physicist. He shared the 1933 Nobel Prize with *Dirac for his development of the form of the *quantum theory known as *wave mechanics. Although not Jewish, he was an ardent anti-Nazi and came to England when Hitler took Austria. He was professor at the School for Advanced Studies in Dublin (1940–56), returning to Vienna after his retirement.

Schubert, Franz (Peter) (1797–1828) Austrian composer, who had a musical upbringing but little formal training, other than at the imperial choir school in Vienna. He made a precarious living as a composer and teacher, rarely leaving Vienna and achieving little recognition. He died from typhoid fever at the age of 31. Schubert's melodic genius is perhaps most evident in his 600 *Lieder*, which include "Erlkönig," "Death and the Maiden," and "The Trout." Some of his greatest songs are to be found in the song-cycles *Die Schöne Müllerin* (1823) and *Die Winterreise* (1827). His other works demonstrate his mastery of large-scale composition. They include nine symphonies (of which one is lost and the eighth is unfinished), string quartets, piano trios, an octet, two quintets, piano sonatas and pieces, and much choral music. He also wrote several less successful operas.

Schuman, Robert (1886–1963) French statesman. He held several ministerial posts from 1946 to 1956 and was briefly prime minister (1947–48). As foreign minister (1948–52), he proposed the **Schuman Plan** (1950) for European unity, which advocated the establishment (achieved in 1952) of the *European Coal and Steel Community. He was president of the EEC assembly (1958–60).

Schuman, William (Howard) (1910–) US composer. He taught at Sarah Lawrence College in New York (1935–45) and was president of the Juilliard School of Music (1945–61). His compositions include the ballet, *The Undertow* (1945), choral works, nine symphonies, an opera about baseball, entitled *The Mighty Casey* (1953), *Song of Orpheus* (for cello and orchestra; 1962), and a cantata, *A Free Song* (1943), which won a Pulitzer Prize.

Schumann, Elisabeth (1888–1952) German-born soprano. She settled in the USA in 1938, becoming a US citizen in 1944. She performed in operas, concerts, and recitals, excelling in the music of Mozart and Richard Strauss.

Schumann, Robert (Alexander) (1810–56) German composer. He played and composed music from an early age and at Leipzig University devoted more time to it than to his law studies. Almost all his musical compositions up to 1840 were for

the piano; he also wrote much as a critic, editing (1835–44) the journal *Die Neue Zeitschrift für Musik*, which he had founded. Gradual insanity in later life culminated in his attempt to drown himself and he died in an asylum. His compositions include four symphonies, the opera *Genoveva* (1847–50), songs, including the cycles *Dichterliebe* (1840) and *Frauenliebe und Leben* (1840), violin, piano, and cello concertos, and piano pieces, including the *Davidsbündlertänze* (1837) and *Kreisleriana* (1838).

His wife **Clara Schumann** (1819–96), whom he married in 1840, was the daughter of Friedrich Wieck (1788–1873), with whom he had studied the piano in Leipzig (1830–32). She was a famous pianist, teacher, and composer, and became a great interpreter and editor of her husband's works.

Schuschnigg, Kurt von (1897–1977) Austrian statesman; chancellor (1934–38). He tried in vain to prevent the Nazi *Anschluss* and was forced to resign, being imprisoned by Hitler throughout World War II. On his release he taught in the USA until 1967, when he returned to Austria.

Schütz, Heinrich (1585–1672) German composer. He sang in the choir of the royal chapel at Kassel and studied with Giovanni Gabrieli in Venice (1609–12). He was court kapellmeister in Dresden after 1615. He composed much sacred music, including Passions and *The Seven Words of Christ on the Cross* (c. 1645), as well as madrigals and the first German opera, *Dafne* (1627), which is now lost.

Schwann, Theodor (1810–82) German physiologist, who applied *Schleiden's cell theory to animals—an important conceptual advance in biology. Schwann pointed out that egg cells develop by successive divisions and he identified the Schwann cells that surround nerve fibres. He was the first person to isolate a digestive enzyme (pepsin) from animal tissue and he also coined the term metabolism for the chemical changes that take place in living tissues.

Schwarzchild, Karl (1873–1916) German astronomer, who developed photographic techniques for making astronomical measurements. He died from a skin disease contracted on active service in World War I. In 1916 he defined the **Schwarzchild radius** (SR), the radius of a contracting star at which nothing, including light, can escape from it. It then becomes a *black hole. The SR for the sun is 3 km (actual radius 7×10^8m).

Schwarzenberg, Felix, Fürst zu (1800–52) Austrian statesman. He served in the diplomatic corps before becoming first minister during the Revolution of 1848. He restored order in the Habsburg Empire, issuing a new constitution (1849) that strengthened the absolute power of the emperor. He also frustrated Prussia's attempts to establish a Prussian-dominated union of German states.

Schwarzkopf, Elisabeth (1915–) German soprano. She studied and made her debut (1938) in Berlin and then sang in Vienna, London, Milan, and the USA. She was especially noted for her interpretation of Mozart and Richard Strauss.

Schwarzwald. *See* Black Forest.

Schweitzer, Albert (1875–1965) Alsatian-born theologian, medical missionary, and organist. A theologian in the liberal Protestant tradition, Schweitzer wrote *The Quest of the Historical Jesus* (1906), emphasizing Christ's humanity. His writings on Bach and his recitals of Bach's organ music were highly acclaimed. From 1913 until his death, Schweitzer practised as a doctor in the hospital he founded in Gabon at the jungle village of Lambaréné. His philosophy is best summarized in his ethic of "reverence for life." In 1952 he received the Nobel Peace Prize.

Schwerin 53 38N 11 25E A city in NW East Germany, on Lake Schwerin. Largely destroyed by fire in the 16th and 17th centuries the city was rebuilt with squares and wide streets. Schwerin has machinery and chemical industries. Population (1980 est): 119 961.

Schwitters, Kurt (1887–1958) German artist and poet.

born in Hanover. Associated with the *dada art movement, he became famous for his poems of meaningless sounds and his invention of elaborate structures and collages of tram tickets, broken glass, and other rubbish, which he salvaged from gutters and dustbins and labelled *Merz* (trash) constructions. He worked in Britain from 1940 until his death.

Schwyz 47 02N 8 34E A town in Switzerland. It is a popular summer resort in a picturesque setting. Population (1983 est): 12 336.

sciatica Severe pain that starts in a buttock and spreads down the back of the leg. It is caused by pressure on the roots of the sciatic nerve—the longest nerve in the body. The commonest cause is pressure from a slipped disc in the backbone. Other kinds of injury to the back may also lead to sciatica. The pain usually disappears eventually: treatment is by bed rest and pain killers.

science fiction A literary genre in which scientific knowledge is used as a basis for imaginative fiction. The chief precursors of modern science fiction were Jules *Verne, who made use of speculative developments in engineering in such works as *Twenty Thousand Leagues Under the Sea* (1869) and *Propeller Island* (1895), and H. G. *Wells, who dealt with time travel, space travel, and alien invasion in *The Time Machine* (1895), *The First Men in the Moon* (1901), and *The War of the Worlds* (1898). In the 20th century such magazines as *Amazing Stories* (founded 1926) and *Astounding Science Fiction* reflected a growing popular interest in the science fiction inspired by advances in the fields of rocketry, electronics, and computers. Notable works of science fiction have been written by such scientists as Fred *Hoyle and Isaac *Asimov. Among writers who have written imaginative accounts of the origin, evolution, and destiny of the human race are Olaf Stapledon (1886–1950), author of *Last and First Men* (1931), and Arthur C. Clarke (1917–), author, with Stanley *Kubrick, of *2001: A Space Odyssey* (film, 1967; novel, 1968). Other leading writers of science fiction include Edgar Rice *Burroughs, Brian *Aldiss, Ray *Bradbury, Kurt *Vonnegut, John *Wyndham, and Aldous *Huxley.

Science Museum A museum in South Kensington, London, devoted to the history and development of science, engineering, and industry. Its full name is the British National Museum of Science and Industry. It originally formed part of the South Kensington Museum (founded 1857), which became the Victoria and Albert Museum in 1899; the Science Museum was separated in 1909. The National Railway Museum, York, (opened 1975) is an outstation of the Science Museum.

scientology A tradename for a doctrine followed by the Church of Scientology, founded in 1954 in California by L (afayette) Ron(ald) Hubbard (1911–86). Originally this doctrine was presented as a method of psychotherapy in Hubbard's *Dianetics: The Modern Science of Mental Health* (1950). It was later presented as a religious philosophy by which the member passes through many rigidly structured levels, increasing his IQ, creativity, etc., until he is finally "not on the body level" at all and has realized his full spiritual potential. In 1959 the Church's headquarters moved to East Grinstead in East Sussex (England). While claiming to achieve man's spiritual liberation, its methods, particularly its practice of counselling ("auditing") to release adherents from past emotional bonds, have been widely criticized.

Scilly, Isles of (*or* Scillies) A group of about 140 islands and islets in the Atlantic Ocean, off the extreme SW coast of England. Only five are inhabited, namely St Mary's (the largest), Tresco, St Martin's, St Agnes, and Bryher. Their mild climate has been exploited to produce early spring flowers for the UK market, their major source of income. Agriculture is intensive with dairy farming and the production of vegetables. Tourism is also an important source of revenue. Area: 16 sq km (6 sq mi). Population (1981): 2628. Chief town: Hugh Town.

scintillation counter An instrument that measures the number of radioactive atoms that decay in a certain time. The emitted radiation strikes a scintillation crystal causing it to emit a flash of light. The light then activates a *photomultiplier, producing a pulse of electrons, which are counted to enable the activity of the source to be calculated. A **scintillation spectrometer** is used to show the energy distribution of a source.

Scipio Aemilianus Africanus (c. 185–129 BC) Roman general, politician, and literary patron; the grandson by adoption of Scipio Africanus. After military successes in Greece and Spain, he blockaded and destroyed Carthage in 146 (*see* Punic Wars), becoming a national hero. After subduing Spain with the destruction of Numantia in 133, he lost popular support when he attacked the reforms of his murdered brother-in-law, Tiberius *Gracchus. Scipio died during the subsequent political upheaval.

Scipio Africanus (236–183 BC) Roman general of the second *Punic War. After defeating the Carthaginians in Spain, he won permission, despite *Fabius' opposition, to invade Africa. After crushing Hannibal at the battle of Zama in 202, he became a national hero, receiving the title Africanus. Subsequent pro-Greek policies provoked political hostility and he retired from public life. His son was the adoptive father of Scipio Aemilianus Africanus.

sclerosis Stiffening and hardening of the tissues. This is a feature of many diseases: it can affect the brain and spinal cord, causing *multiple sclerosis, and the walls of the arteries, causing *arteriosclerosis or *atherosclerosis.

Scofield, (David) Paul (1922–) British actor. His major roles for the Royal Shakespeare Company and other leading British companies include Hamlet (1948, 1955), Lear (1962), and Othello (1980). His best-known film performance was as Sir Thomas More in *A Man for All Seasons* (1966).

Scone 56 25N 3 24W A parish in E central Scotland, in Tayside Region. It consists of the villages of New Scone and Old Scone, the Pictish and later Scottish capital where most Scottish kings were crowned. The coronation stone was taken from here by Edward I in 1296 and placed in Westminster Abbey. It was removed in 1950 and taken to Arbroath but later recovered.

scopolamine. *See* hyoscine.

scops owl A small *owl of the mainly tropical genus *Otus*, also called screech owl because of its call. Scops owls are 20–30 cm long and mostly arboreal, with camouflaging plumage resembling bark. They feed on insects, birds, and small mammals.

Scorpio (astrology). *See* zodiac.

scorpion An *arachnid of the order *Scorpionida* (about 800 species), found in warm dry regions. Scorpions are 13–175 mm long; the second pair of appendages (pedipalps) form large pincers and the elongated abdomen curls upwards and bears a poisonous sting, which can be fatal to man. They live under stones or in shallow burrows in soil during the day and prey at night, mainly on insects and spiders. Mating is preceded by a courtship dance and the female produces live young, which ride on her back for several days.

scorpion fish A carnivorous fish, often called rockfish or zebra fish, belonging to the family *Scorpaenidae*, found mainly on rocky beds of tropical and temperate coastal waters. It has a stout body, up to 1 m long, a large spiny head, and strong fin spines, which can inflict painful wounds and may be venomous. Order: *Scorpaeniformes*.

scorpion fly An □insect of the order *Mecoptera* (400 species), so called because the males of many species curl the abdomen over the body, like a scorpion. 12–25 mm long, scorpion flies have long legs and antennae and, typically, two similar pairs of net-veined wings. The larvae develop in soil, feeding—like the adults—on dead animals and plants.

Scorpius (Latin: Scorpion) A conspicuous constellation in the S sky, lying on the *zodiac between Sagittarius and

Libra. The brightest star is *Antares. The constellation contains several notable open and globular *star clusters and the intense X-ray binary star **Scorpius X-1**.

Scotland A country occupying the N part of Great Britain and comprising a political division of the *United Kingdom. Most of the population lives in a narrow lowland belt, which runs E–W across the country and separates the lower hills of the S (including the Tweedsmuir and Cheviot Hills) from the higher mountains of the N (including the Grampian and Cairngorm Mountains). Ben Nevis near Fort William in the W is the highest point in the British Isles at 1343 m (4406 ft). There are many islands off the N and W coasts, including the Hebrides and the Isle of Arran to the W and the Orkneys and Shetlands to the N. The principal rivers are the Clyde, which flows into the North Channel, and the Forth, Tay, and Spey, which flow into the North Sea. There are several lochs in the northern mountains, and Lochs Ness and Lochy form the Great Glen (valley) between Fort William and Inverness. Administratively, Scotland is divided into nine regions and three island areas, which replaced the former counties in 1975. *Economy*: the central belt of the country is highly industrialized, based originally on the coal to be found there. Coal is still mined in Lothian and Fife Regions. Other long-established industries include shipbuilding (on the Clyde) and steelmaking, now largely based on Ravenscraig near Motherwell. Whisky, for which Scotland is internationally famous, is produced in Highland and Grampian Regions. Newer industries include vehicle manufacture at Linwood and Bathgate. The discovery of oil in the North Sea has led to a boom on the E coast of the country, and this has emphasized the problems of Glasgow and Strathclyde Region in the W with its outdated industrial structure and high unemployment rate. Agriculture remains important and includes sheep farming in the upland areas (especially in the border hills, where there is a famous textile industry), dairying in the SW (from whence the Ayrshire breed of cattle originated), beef production in the E and NE lowlands (famous for the Aberdeen-Angus cattle breed), and market gardening. Forestry is important in the Highlands. Fishing is a major source of revenue, especially on the E coast at such ports as Aberdeen and Fraserburgh, but there is concern over levels of stock and possible overfishing. *History*: Scotland was never completely subdued by the Romans, but the barbaric northern tribes were kept N of *Hadrian's Wall and, for some 40 years, the more northerly *Antonine Wall (from the Forth to the Clyde). The diverse peoples (Picts, Scots, Britons, and Angles) of Scotland gradually united, helped by the spread of Christianity, and Kenneth I MacAlpine (died c. 858) is regarded as their first king. During the middle ages there was recurrent war between England and Scotland. In 1296 Edward I of England declared himself King of Scotland but after his death Robert the Bruce reasserted Scottish independence, which was recognized by England in 1328. The 14th century saw the establishment of a long-standing alliance between France and Scotland and the succession of the *Stuart dynasty. Under the influence of John *Knox the Scottish Church became Presbyterian (*see* Church of Scotland) during the reign of Mary, Queen of Scots. In 1603 her son James VI succeeded as James I to the throne of England but political union between the two countries was not established until 1707 (*see* Union, Acts of). After the Hanoverian succession the Stuart cause was kept alive by the *Jacobites, who staged two unsuccessful rebellions (1715, 1745) against George I and George II. Rapid industrialization in the 19th century encouraged considerable Irish immigration. Following the parliamentary Reform Act (1832) a tradition for Liberalism was established in Scotland but Labour gained political dominance in the 20th century. Scotland's improved economic prospects following the discovery of North Sea oil boosted the fortunes of the *Scottish National Party but *devolution plans were rejected in a referendum in 1979. Area: 78 769 sq km (30 405 sq mi). Population (1981): 5 116 000. Capital: Edinburgh.

Scotland Yard A street off Whitehall, London (UK), which gave its name to the headquarters of the Metropolitan Police, situated there until 1890. When the headquarters then moved to the Victoria Embankment its name became New Scotland Yard, which was kept in a subsequent move (1966) to Broadway, Westminster.

Scots law Originally Scots law differed little from English law, but from the beginning of the 16th century there was a tendency to introduce elements of *Roman law, especially as embodied in the *civil law of France and the Netherlands. This resulted in marked differences from English law, the preservation of which was guaranteed by the Treaty of Union with England in 1707. An example is the Scots law of *contract, in which the principle of "consideration" does not have the importance it has in English law, where no contract is binding without consideration. Modern statutes have, however, introduced many new laws that are the same for both countries.

Scott, Sir George Gilbert (1811–78) British architect. An advocate of the *gothic revival style, Scott was a noted designer, restorer of medieval buildings, and author. He was a highly successful architect, renovating many churches and cathedrals, including Westminster Abbey. His original buildings include the Albert Memorial (1864), St Pancras station (1865), and government offices in Whitehall (1861), which were built in the Renaissance style under pressure from Palmerston, who rejected Scott's earlier gothic scheme. His grandson **Sir Giles Gilbert Scott** (1880–1960) was also an architect. He achieved early fame when he won the competition for the design of the Anglican Cathedral in Liverpool in 1903. His other buildings include Cambridge University Library (1931–34), the new Bodleian Library, Oxford (1936–46), and the new Waterloo Bridge (1939–45).

Scott, Paul (Mark) (1920–78) British novelist. He is best known for the "Raj Quartet," a series of novels dealing with the dramatic changes and conflicts of the final period of British rule in India. They are *The Jewel in the Crown* (1966), *The Day of the Scorpion* (1968), *The Towers of Silence* (1972), and *A Division of the Spoils* (1975). His last novel, *Staying On* (1977), was awarded the Booker Fiction Prize.

Scott, Robert Falcon (1868–1912) British explorer and naval officer. He led two expeditions to the Antarctic, the first in the *Discovery* (1900–04) and the second (1910–12) in the *Terra Nova*. With a party of four (including L. E. G. Oates) he reached the South Pole by sledge on 17 January, 1912, only to find that *Amundsen had preceded them. Delayed by illness and blizzards they perished only a few miles from safety. Their bodies and Scott's diaries were found in November. His son **Sir Peter Markham Scott** (1909–) is a noted ornithologist and wildlife painter. In 1946 he founded the Wildfowl Trust based at Slimbridge, Gloucestershire, for the study and conservation of birds.

Scott, Ronnie (1927–) British jazz saxophonist, who played in Ted Heath's band and formed his own group in 1952. He opened his jazz club in London's Soho in 1959.

Scott, Sir Walter (1771–1832) Scottish novelist. His early works included a collection of border ballads (1802–03) and the popular narrative poem *The Lay of the Last Minstrel* (1805). *Waverley* (1814) was the first of a series of hugely successful historical novels that included *Old Mortality* (1816) and *The Heart of Midlothian* (1818). His last years were spent in frantic literary activity to pay off his creditors after his bankruptcy in 1826.

Scottish literature The literature of Scotland comprises a diversity of works in Scottish Gaelic, Lowland Scots (Lallans), English, and combinations of these. Literary Gaelic as practised by the *bards continued in use up to the 18th century and drew upon the same traditions as *Irish literature (especially the Ulster cycle and the *Fenian cycle). The 16th-century Book of the Dean of Lismore is an example of this heritage, although it was James Macpherson's alleged translation of *Ossian that popularized these Gaelic stories throughout Europe. In the Scottish (non-Gaelic) vernacular, the first important work is John *Barbour's 14th-century epic The Bruce. In the 15th and 16th centuries were produced the greatest works of early Scottish literature, the poetry of the makaris or Scottish Chaucerians, including *Henryson, *Dunbar, Gavin *Douglas, Sir David Lindsay (1490-1555), the author of Ane Satyre of the thrie Estatis (1540), and *James I, King of Scots. In the 17th century, by contrast, there was little outstanding literary production. *Burns' evocative use of the Lowlands dialect in the 18th century had a lasting effect on Scottish literature and national consciousness and influenced later poets, for example Hugh *MacDiarmid, who have written in Lallans. Many Scottish writers since the 17th century have written in English: the works of *Boswell, *Smollett, Sir Walter *Scott, *Carlyle, Robert Louis *Stevenson, and many others form an essential part of the literature of English.

CAPTAIN SCOTT   Seen writing his diary in the hut at Cape Evans (Antarctic) in 1912.

Scottish National Party (SNP) A political party, founded in 1928, dedicated to the achievement of Scottish independence from the UK. The party achieved some popularity with the rise of nationalist sentiment in the 1960s and 1970s and secured 11 seats and 30.4% of the Scottish vote in the October, 1974, parliamentary election. The indecisive result in Scotland of the *devolution referendum in 1979 was a setback for the party and in the subsequent general election the SNP managed to hold only two seats.

Scottish terrier A breed of dog, originally called Aberdeen terrier, used to chase foxes from earth. It is thickset with short legs, a short erect tail, and pricked ears. The long muzzle has characteristically long whiskers and the wiry coat can be black, brindle, grey, or yellow-brown. Height: 25-28 cm.

Scout Association An association founded by Robert *Baden Powell in 1908 to encourage boys to become enter-

prising members of society. The Scouts' motto is Be Prepared. The Scout Association classifies its members into Cub Scouts (for boys aged between 8 and 11), Scouts (11-16), and Venture Scouts (16-29). There are 14 million Scouts throughout the world, of whom 600 000 are in the UK. The Association's counterpart for girls is the *Girl Guides Association.

Scranton 41 25N 75 40W A city in the USA, in Pennsylvania. It had a thriving anthracite industry and iron and steel operations until the 1950s. Since then it has shown great initiative in attracting many light industries to the city. It is the site of the University of Scranton (1888). Population (1980): 88 117.

screamer A marsh-dwelling bird belonging to a family (Anhimidae; 3 species) occurring in tropical and subtropical South America. 75 cm long, screamers have dark plumage, a short hook-tipped bill, two paired wing spurs, and either a crest or a horny protuberance on the head. They feed on water plants and the skin contains air sacs that can produce crackling noises. Order: Anseriformes (ducks, geese, etc.).

scree. See talus.

screech owl. See scops owl.

screw pine A treelike plant of the genus Pandanus (about 150 species), native to the Old World tropics. The name derives from the spiral arrangement of the leaves, which leave scars in a corkscrew spiral when they fall. Stout aerial prop roots grow down from the stem into the ground: the part of the stem below these roots decays, so that the plant is supported entirely by the prop roots. The leaves, which are long and stiff with parallel sides, are used for matting and weaving. The flowers grow in large heads enclosed in leafy structures (spathes) and the fruits of some species are edible. Several species are grown as house plants. Family: Pandanaceae.

screwworm. See blowfly.

Scriabin, Alexander (1872-1915) Russian composer and pianist. His mature compositions were characterized by chords built on the interval of the fourth. His works include three symphonies—the third entitled The Divine Poem (1903)—a piano concerto (1894), ten piano sonatas, and Prometheus or The Poem of Fire (1909-10), intended to be accompanied by a sequence of coloured lights projected onto a screen.

scribes (Hebrew: sofrim) Ancient Jewish biblical scholars. They preserved the textual tradition of the *Torah and cultivated its study and interpretation. In the Gospels they are frequently linked with the *Pharisees. In later Jewish usage the term applies to copyists of the Torah and other sacred texts.

Scriblerus club An English literary club founded in about 1713. Its members included *Pope, *Swift, *Gay, and John *Arbuthnot. In their collaborative Memoirs of Martinus Scriblerus (1741) they ridiculed literary pretentiousness.

scrofula Ulceration of a lymph node infected with *tuberculosis, seen most commonly in the neck. This form of tuberculosis is now uncommon in developed countries but is still seen in poorer countries. Treatment is with antibiotic drugs and surgery. It was formerly known as king's evil, as it was believed that the touch of the sovereign would cure it.

scrub Vegetation consisting mainly of short evergreen often aromatic shrubs, typically found in coastal regions with hot dry summers: the Mediterranean maquis and the Californian chaparral are examples. This type of vegetation is transitional between grasslands and forests. The shrubs are adapted to survive dry summers and usually flower and fruit in the spring.

scrub bird A rare Australian passerine bird belonging to a primitive family (Atrichornithidae; 2 species). Scrub birds are brown with long pointed tails and loud voices, and are poor fliers, feeding on insects and nesting on the ground. The noisy scrub bird (Atrichornis clamosus) is about 22 cm long and occurs in SW Australia, where it was thought to be extinct until 1961. The smaller rufous scrub bird (*A. rufescens*) is found only in the wet forests of New South Wales.

Scullin, James Henry (1876-1953) Australian statesman; Labor prime minister (1929-1931). The problems of the Depression plagued his administration, his deflationary measures bringing electoral defeat in 1931. He was opposition leader from 1932 to 1935.

sculpin. *See* bullhead.

SCULPTURE *The sculptor Nicholas Monro (1936–) with part of his group of six fibreglass figures entitled* Waiters' Race.

sculpture The art of shaping or modelling such materials as stone, wood, clay, and metal either in relief (*see* relief sculpture) or in the round. Stone, particularly marble, has been most popular with sculptors since it is the most durable material for outdoor sculptures. Wood is principally associated with *African art and medieval indoor sculptures (*see also* wood carving). Clay is most often employed in preliminary models for sculptures later cast in metal. Of all the metals, bronze has been most favoured for casting, although in the 20th century aluminium, iron, and sheet metal have been increasingly used to fabricate sculptural concepts.

Most civilizations have left a legacy of sculpture, the earliest known work being Palaeolithic representations of human and animal figures, believed to be of religious significance. More detailed figures, indicating the hierarchy of the social organization, appeared in Egypt in the 3rd millennium BC. The 5th and 4th centuries BC saw the rise of classical Greek sculpture with the work of *Praxiteles, *Phidias, and others. The Romans subsequently developed these classical themes, introducing more personalized portrait sculpture. In India from the 2nd century BC, Japan from the 6th century AD, and China from the 7th century AD, sculpture was devoted primarily to representations of the Buddha and his life. In medieval Europe, sculpture became largely an embellishment of architecture, until the revival of classical ideals in the Italian Renaissance with the works of such major sculptors as *Donatello and *Michelangelo. The spread of Renaissance ideas throughout the rest of Europe led to the work of Jean *Goujon in France and Grinling *Gibbons in England, while baroque sculpture attained its finest expression in the virtuosity of *Bernini. The neo-

classicism of the 18th century saw a new respect for ancient Greek models. Outstanding among the sculptors of 19th-century Romanticism was *Rodin. Although the figural tradition has been continued into the 20th century by such sculptors as Marino *Marini and Ernst *Barlach, semi-abstract and abstract sculpture, influenced by African and other primitive carving, have become the principal forms of sculptural expression. Semiabstract sculptures include the innovative work of *Modigliani, *Epstein, and Henry *Moore, as well as the geometricized forms of Jacques *Lipchitz and the simplified shapes of Constantin *Brancusi. Abstract or nonrepresentative sculpture includes the organic forms of such sculptors as *Arp and the geometric constructions of Naum *Gabo (*see also* constructivism). Kinetic and environmental sculpture are also specifically 20th-century developments. Kinetic sculptures, i.e. sculptures that move either by motor, magnetism, or air currents, were pioneered by Gabo and Alexander *Calder (*see also* mobiles). Environmental sculpture is the re-creation of an environment as in Claes *Oldenburg's pop art work of the 1960s. The principal uses of sculpture have been architectural and commemorative, that is for memorial monuments and tombs.

Scunthorpe 53 36N 0 38W A town in NE England, in S Humberside. The principal industry is the manufacture of iron and steel. Population (1981): 66 353.

scurvy A disease caused by deficiency of *vitamin C (which is present in most fresh fruits and vegetables). In the past scurvy was common among sailors on long voyages, but it is now rarely seen except in old debilitated people and vagrants. The symptoms are weakness and aching joints and muscles, progressing to bleeding of the gums and—later—other organs. Scurvy can be readily treated by giving vitamin C or fresh fruit.

scurvy grass An annual, biennial, or perennial herb of the genus *Cochlearia* (about 25 species), occurring in temperate regions, especially near coasts. Up to 50 cm tall, it has simple often heart-shaped leaves and the white or mauve flowers, each with four rounded petals, are borne in small clusters. Family: *Cruciferae*.

Scutari. *See* Shkodër (Albania); Üsküdar (Turkey).

Scylla and Charybdis In Greek mythology, two sea monsters on opposite sides of the Strait of Messina who menaced *Odysseus, the *Argonauts, and other legendary heroes. Scylla was a monster with six heads and a pack of baying hounds, while Charybdis was a raging whirlpool.

Scyphozoa. *See* jellyfish.

Scythians An Indo-European people who temporarily settled in Asia Minor before settling in what is now S Russia in the 6th century BC. The true Scythians, called Royal Scyths, established a kingdom N of the Black Sea and traded wheat for luxury goods with the Greek colonies there. Their skill as horsemen and archers halted Persian and Macedonian invasions but they remained a nomadic people until their disappearance from history during the Gothic onslaughts of the 3rd century AD. Objects recovered from their royal tombs demonstrate their metalworking skill and, especially in the animal designs that predominate as decorations, their artistry.

sea anemone A sedentary marine invertebrate animal belonging to a worldwide order (*Actiniaria*; over 1000 species) of *coelenterates. It has a soft columnar body (*see* polyp) of a few millimetres to about 1.5 m in diameter, with a mouth at the top surrounded by rings of tentacles, which—when expanded—give the animal a flower-like appearance. Sea anemones are usually blue, green, or yellow and are found attached to rocks and weeds or associated with other invertebrates. They feed mainly on fish and other animals. Class: *Anthozoa*.

sea bass A carnivorous fish, also called sea perch, of the family *Serranidae* (about 400 species), found mainly in coastal waters of tropical and temperate seas. Its elongated body ranges up to 3.75 m long and varies in colour with the species. They may be active or sedentary and certain species are *hermaphrodite while others, such as *groupers, are able to change sex. Many are valued food and game fish. Order: *Perciformes. See also* bass.

Seaborg, Glenn Theodore (1912-) US physicist, who as professor at the University of California has led the search for *transuranic elements. Working with Edwin *McMillan, he produced plutonium in 1940 by bombarding neptunium with neutrons. Working with another group of researchers, Seaborg has prepared samples of all the transuranic elements with atomic numbers from 95 to 105 by similar methods. For this work he shared the Nobel Prize with McMillan in 1951.

sea bream A fish, also called porgy, belonging to a family (*Sparidae*; about 400 species) found mainly in shallow waters of tropical and subtropical seas. It has a deep laterally flattened body covered with large scales, a single long dorsal fin, and well-developed teeth. It lives in shoals and feeds by scraping algae and small animals off rocks.

sea butterfly A *gastropod mollusc belonging to the subclass *Opisthobranchia*, also called pteropod. Some sea butterflies (order *Thecosomata*) have a shell, are filter feeders, and swim by means of winglike appendages (parapodia). Others (order *Gymnosomata*) are naked, with only small parapodia, and prey on small animals.

sea cow. See *dugong*.

sea cucumber A marine invertebrate animal belonging to a worldwide class (*Holothuroidea*; 1100 species) of *echinoderms. Its cucumber-shaped body, 2-200 cm long, is covered with leathery skin containing small calcareous plates or spicules. There is a mouth at one end surrounded by a ring of tentacles, which are used for feeding on detritus and plankton. It crawls sluggishly on the sea bottom or burrows in sand or mud. ⁻oceans.

sea eagle An *eagle belonging to the widely distributed genus *Haliaeetus* (8 species). 70-120 cm long, sea eagles have a wedge-shaped tail and are typically brown with white markings. The smaller species feed mostly on fish but the larger species eat carrion, large birds, and mammals.

sea fan A colonial *coral of the genus *Gorgonia*, in which the tiny cylindrical *polyps have a horny internal skeleton and grow upon one another to produce a fanlike structure. Sea fans are commonly yellow, pink, brown, or purple and occur mainly in shallow tropical waters.

sea-floor spreading A concept developed in the 1960s that provides a mechanism for *continental drift. Magma rises from the earth's mantle to the surface along midocean ridges (constructive plate margins; *see* plate tectonics), cools to form new oceanic crust, and displaces the older material sideways at an average rate of 4 cm per year. Magnetic reversals recorded in the rocks in approximately symmetrical strips at each side of the midocean ridges provide strong evidence for sea-floor spreading.

sea gooseberry. See *ctenophore*.

seagull. See *gull*.

sea hare A marine *gastropod mollusc belonging to the family *Aplysiidae*. Growing up to 35 cm long, sea hares are often green or yellow in colour; they have a pair of tentacles (resembling a hare's ears) and a much-reduced shell. When disturbed, they eject a cloud of purple ink into the water. Subclass: *Opisthobranchia*.

sea holly 1. A perennial herb, *Eryngium maritimum*, found on sandy and shingly European shores. Growing to a height of 30-60 cm, it has spiked holly-like leaves and bears clusters of purplish-blue flowers. Family: *Umbelliferae*. 2. See *gulfweed*.

sea horse One of several small bony-plated marine ⁻fish of the family *Syngnathidae* (*see also* pipefish), especially the genus *Hippocampus*, that lives in shallow warm waters. They

are 4-30 cm long and the horselike head with its long tubular snout is set at an angle to the body. They use the prehensile tail to cling to seaweed and swim in a vertical position by undulating the dorsal fin. The males have a brood pouch in which the young are hatched. Order: *Gasterosteiformes*.

Sea Islands A chain of islands in the USA, off the coasts of South Carolina, Georgia, and Florida. Production of long-stapled Sea Island cotton was important until infestation by the boll weevil in the 1920s.

sea kale A bushy perennial herb, *Crambe maritima*, found on Atlantic coasts of Europe. Growing to a height of 40-60 cm, it has cabbage-like leaves and bears clusters of small white flowers. It may be cultivated for its tender young edible shoots. Family: *Cruciferae*.

seal (sigillography) A stone, metal, or wooden stamp and its impression in wax or lead used to authenticate documents. The engraved surface of a seal is usually rock crystal or other hard stone but bronze and gold are also used. The impression cut into the seal generally consists of a central device of a heraldic or personal motif, surrounded by a legend. Officials' seals are practical in design but other seals, such as desk seals and fob seals (worn as jewels), enable jewellers and goldsmiths to exhibit their skills. **Sigillography** is the study of seals.

seal (zoology) A carnivorous marine mammal belonging to the order *Pinnipedia* (32 species). Seals have a streamlined body with a smooth rounded head and an insulating layer of blubber under the sleek-coated skin. Both pairs of limbs flatten into flippers. They feed mainly on fish and breed on land or ice.
There are two main families: the *Otariidae* (eared seals; 13 species) including fur seals and *sealions, which have external ears and can turn their hind flippers forward for walking on land; and the *Phocidae* (true seals; 18 species), which lack external ears and have trailing hind flippers. The *walrus is the only member of its family, *Odobenidae*.

sea lavender A perennial or annual herb of the genus *Limonium* (about 300 species), found on coasts and salt marshes of W Asia, Europe, and North America. The common sea lavender (*L. vulgare*) has a basal rosette of slender leaves and a branched flower stem, 8-30 cm high, bearing clusters of purple-blue flowers. Family: *Plumbaginaceae*.

sea lettuce A green *seaweed of the genus *Ulva*, found mainly between high and low tide levels on most rocky shores. It has broad flat translucent fronds, which resemble lettuce leaves, and grows in bunches up to about 30 cm long. It is rich in iodine and vitamins and is sometimes used in salads and soups.

sea lily. See *crinoid*.

sealion A large *seal belonging to the family *Otariidae*. Californian sealions (*Zalophus californianus*) of the Californian coast are popular circus animals. They grow to 2 m and live in groups with a definite social hierarchy. Steller's sealion (*Eumetopias jubatus*) is the largest species, growing to over 3 m.

Sealyham terrier A breed of ⁻dog developed between 1850 and 1891 on the Sealyham estate, Haverfordwest, Wales, for hunting foxes and badgers. It is sturdily built with short legs, drooping ears, and a short thin tail. White with darker markings, Sealyhams have a soft under coat and a wiry outer coat. Height: 27-30 cm.

sea mouse A marine *annelid worm belonging to a family (*Aphroditidae*) found in North Atlantic coastal waters. Sea mice grow up to 18 cm long and 7 cm wide with 15 pairs of scales buried in a dense covering of irridescent hairs. They are foraging carnivores and are generally found buried in fine sand or mud with only the hind end protruding. Class: *Polychaeta*.

sea otter A marine *otter, *Enhydra lutris*, of the N Pacific. 1.2 m long and weighing 35 kg, it floats in colonies of up to 90 individuals. The cubs, well-furred and with open eyes and sharp teeth, are born in the sea. Sea otters feed on molluscs, crustaceans, and fish and can crack open shells using a pebble balanced on the chest. Once hunted for their valuable fur, they are now a protected species.

sea pen A fleshy colonial marine invertebrate animal belonging to an order (*Pennatulacea*; 300 species) of *coelenterates, especially one forming a feather-like colony (e.g. *Leioptilus*). A central stalklike individual—the primary *polyp—is anchored into mud or sand and secondary polyps branch from it. Class: *Anthozoa*.

Sea Peoples The seafaring tribes who colonized Asia Minor, the Aegean, and N Africa in the 13th and 12th centuries BC, destroying the *Hittite empire. About 1170 they were almost annihilated by Rameses III of Egypt and those that survived scattered—to Palestine, the Aegean, and perhaps to the W Mediterranean. They have been variously and uncertainly identified and may have been Achaeans, Etruscans, or Philistines.

sea perch. *See* sea bass.

SEDAN CHAIR *A sedan chair being carried through Hanover Square in London in 1761.*

Searle, Ronald William Fordham (1920-) British cartoonist. He worked for such journals as the *Sunday Express* and *Punch* but is best known for his cartoon creation of the outrageous schoolgirls of St Trinian's, who subsequently featured in four films.

sea robin. *See* gurnard.

sea sickness. *See* travel sickness.

sea slug A marine *gastropod mollusc of the order *Nudibranchia*. Sea slugs have exposed feathery gills, two pairs of tentacles, and no shell. They browse on sponges, sea anemones, and corals and are often brightly coloured. Some sea slugs retain the stinging cells of their prey for their own defence.

sea snake A venomous fish-eating snake belonging to the family *Hydrophiidae* (50 species) occurring mainly in coastal waters of Australasia and SE Asia. Sea snakes are adapted to an underwater life by having a flattened body with an oarlike tail and valvelike closures in the nostrils. Most produce live young (rather than eggs).

sea spider A spider-like marine arthropod of the class *Pycnogonida* (or *Pantopoda*; over 600 species). Its short thin body, 3-500 mm long, usually bears four pairs of long walking legs and a long sucking proboscis. Sea spiders occur up to depths of 3600 m, feeding on soft-bodied invertebrate animals. Fertilized eggs are carried by the males and many larvae are parasitic on polyps or molluscs.

sea squirt. *See* tunicate.

SEATO. *See* South East Asia Treaty Organization.

Seattle 47 35N 122 20W A city in the USA, in Washington state between the Puget Sound and Lake Washington. A port of entry to the Klondike, it became a boom town with the 1897 Alaska Gold Rush. Educational institutions include the University of Washington (1861) and Seattle University (1852). It is Alaska's main supply port. There are large timber mills and various forest-based industries. Other major industries include the manufacture of aircraft, shipbuilding, and ship repair. Population (1980): 493 846.

sea urchin A marine invertebrate animal, belonging to the class *Echinoidea*, with a typically spherical rigid body covered by long movable spines. Sea urchins live on shores and ocean floors and use a complex feeding apparatus—Aristotle's lantern—to masticate algae and other organic material scraped off rocks. Phylum: *Echinodermata* (*see* echinoderm).

sea water The water constituting the world's oceans and seas. It is usually saline, average salinity being about 35 g per kg of sea water. The principal dissolved salts are sodium chloride (2.8%), magnesium chloride (0.4%), and magnesium sulphate (0.2%). Where evaporation is high, salinity is increased, as in the Red Sea. Sea water is desalinated (*see* desalination) in some areas, e.g. Saudi Arabia, to obtain fresh water, although the process is costly. The properties of sea water, including its chemical composition, temperature, and movements (waves and tides) are studied in *oceanography.

seaweed Large multicellular red, brown, or green marine *algae that are generally found attached to the sea bed, rocks, or other solid structures by rootlike structures called holfasts. The plants have stemlike stalks and fronds, which may be flat and undivided, threadlike, or branched, sometimes with small air bladders for buoyancy. Seaweeds often occur in dense aggregations along shores but are also found to depths of about 200 m. Many are of commercial importance as food (e.g. *carrageen, *laver, and *sea lettuce), as fertilizers, in chemical and pharmaceutical products, etc. *See also* kelp; wrack.

sebaceous glands. *See* skin.

Sebastian, St (3rd century AD) Roman martyr. According to tradition, he was an officer of the Praetorian Guards until his Christianity was discovered by Diocletian. His martyrdom at the hands of archers is a frequent subject of painting. Feast day: 20 Jan. Emblem: an arrow.

Sebastiano del Piombo (S. Luciano; c. 1485-1547) Venetian painter. Although he was a pupil of Giovanni Bellini, his early works, notably *St John Chrysostom* (c. 1509; S Giovanni Crisostomo, Venice), were influenced by Giorgione. Moving to Rome in 1511, he painted decorations in the Farnesina with *Raphael, whose *Transfiguration* he directly challenged with his *Raising of Lazarus* (1517-19; National Gallery, London). He was also known as a portraitist; his sitters included Christopher Columbus and Pope Clement VII, who appointed him keeper of the papal seals (*piombi*) in 1531—hence his nickname.

Sebastopol. *See* Sevastopol.

second 1. (s) The *SI unit of time equal to the duration of 9 192 631 770 periods of the radiation corresponding to a specified transition of the caesium-133 atom. The unit was formerly defined by astronomical measurement. *See also* caesium clock; time measurement. 2. A unit of angle equal to one-sixtieth of a minute.

secondary education Education for adolescent children, aged approximately from 11 to 18. Although found in ancient Greece and Rome, secondary education is a relatively recent creation in its present form. In the UK the

Education Act (1944) introduced universal secondary education (compulsory to the age of 15, extended to 16 in 1972) to give greater scope to the terminal formal education of the majority of the population, hitherto carried on in elementary (extended primary) schools. Initially a tripartite system (comprising *grammar schools, *secondary modern schools, and technical schools) was implemented in England and Wales, selection being based upon the *eleven-plus examination. Although this exam has now been largely phased out and a widespread system of *comprehensive schools introduced, the extent to which pupils should be segregated on the basis of ability at secondary-school level remains a controversial issue within the UK.

secondary emission The ejection of electrons from the surface of a metal when it is bombarded with charged particles of sufficient energy. Secondary emission is best observed when the bombarding particles are themselves electrons, which are then known as primary electrons; the ejected electrons are called secondary electrons. In certain metals, as many as ten secondary electrons can be emitted by the impact of one primary electron. The effect is used in such devices as the electron multiplier.

secondary modern school A nonselective secondary school set up in the UK following the Education Act (1944). Secondary modern schools were envisaged for those "who deal more easily with concrete things than with ideas" (see eleven-plus) but are now being phased out in favour of *comprehensive schools.

secretary bird A long-legged terrestrial bird of prey, *Sagittarius serpentarius*, that lives in dry uplands of Africa. 120 cm tall with a 200 cm wingspan, it has a hawklike face and a grey plumage with a long pair of central tail feathers and a black crest of quills behind its head—hence its name. It feeds on snakes and lizards and is the only member of its family (*Sagittaridae*). Order: *Falconiformes* (falcons, hawks, etc.).

secret service. See intelligence services.

securities Documents that represent title to an investment, for example *stocks and shares, *bonds, *bills of exchange, and assurance policies. The list of securities owned by an investor is called a portfolio.

Securities and Exchange Commission A US government agency created in 1934 to protect investors in *securities. It ensures that the information given to the public about new issues is complete and accurate.

Sedan 49 42N 4 57E A town in NE France, in the Ardennes department on the River Meuse. It was the site of a decisive defeat (1870) for the French in the Franco-Prussian War. Its industries include textiles, metallurgy, and food processing. Population (1982): 23 357.

Sedan, Battle of (1 September, 1870) The battle in the *Franco-Prussian War in which German forces, invading France, surrounded the army of Napoleon III and forced him to surrender with 100 000 men. The French defeat precipitated revolution in Paris (see Commune of Paris) and marked the end of the Second Empire.

sedan chair An enclosed single-seater chair carried on poles by two men, one in front and one behind. Sedans probably originated in Italy, came to England in 1634, and were used for short journeys in town until after 1800. Compare palanquin.

sedatives Drugs that relieve restlessness, anxiety, and tension. Most drugs that depress the activity of the nervous system have this effect (including barbiturates and narcotics), but the most widely used sedatives are the minor tranquillizers, for example *benzodiazepines, as they relieve anxiety without causing sleep and their use carries less risk of dependence. Sedatives are also useful in the treatment of muscular aches associated with tension and stress.

Seddon, Richard John (1845-1906) New Zealand statesman, born in England; prime minister (1893-1906). His

government implemented labour-protection measures and introduced old-age pensions and women's suffrage. He sent troops to support the British in the second Boer War (1899-1902) and opposed Asian immigration.

sedge A perennial herbaceous grasslike plant of the genus *Carex* (about 2000 species), growing throughout the world, mainly in swampy places. Sedges have solid stems, triangular in cross section, with long narrow leaves and small male and female flowers usually grouped into separate clusters (spikes). The sand sedge (*C. arenaria*), found on the coasts of Europe and North America, has been used to bond sand dunes. Family: *Cyperaceae*.

Sedgemoor, Battle of (6 July, 1685) The battle, SE of Bridgewater, Somerset, in which the forces of James II of England defeated the rebellion of his nephew, the Duke of *Monmouth.

sedimentary rock One of the three major categories into which rocks are divided (compare igneous rock; metamorphic rock). Sedimentary rocks are deposited mainly under water, usually in approximately horizontal layers (beds). **Clastic sedimentary rocks** are formed from the erosion and deposition of pre-existing rocks and are classified according to the size of the particles. Arenaceous rocks have sand-grade particles and include the sandstones; argillaceous rocks have silt- or clay-grade particles and include siltstones and mudstones; rudaceous rocks, with gravel-grade and larger fragments, include the breccias, conglomerates, etc. Organically formed sedimentary rocks are derived from the remains of plants and animals, for example limestone and coal. Chemically formed sedimentary rocks result from natural chemical processes and include sedimentary iron ores. Many sedimentary rocks show complex internal structures, formed during or after deposition. See Plate II.

Sedum. See stonecrop.

Seebeck effect. See thermoelectric effects.

seed The reproductive structure formed after pollination and fertilization in higher plants. In flowering plants (angiosperms) the seed begins to develop after the *pollen nucleus has fused with the egg. In gymnosperms (conifers and related plants) the ovule begins dividing before pollination. All seeds contain an embryo and usually a food store, which is mobilized on germination. Angiosperm seeds are surrounded by a seed coat (testa) and contained within a *fruit; gymnosperm seeds are naked (see cone). The development of the "seed habit" has given the higher plants a marked advantage over the ferns, mosses, algae, and fungi. Water is not needed for fertilization, and therefore the plants can colonize arid habitats. In addition, seeds—unlike the spores of lower plants—can survive adverse conditions and may remain viable for many years before germinating.

seed fern A *gymnosperm plant belonging to the extinct order *Pteridospermales*, abundant during the Carboniferous and Permian periods (370-240 million years ago). Seed ferns had large fernlike fronds but—unlike ferns—produced seeds, in cuplike structures. They were probably the ancestors of plants that evolved into the angiosperms (flowering plants).

Seeger, Pete (1919-) US folksinger and songwriter, who, with Woody Guthrie, led the US folksong revival in the 1960s. He wrote such songs as "Where Have All the Flowers Gone" and "Kisses Sweeter than Wine."

Seferis, George (Georgios Seferiadis; 1900-71) Greek poet and diplomat, who was ambassador to London (1957-62). He was influenced by the French Symbolists and by T. S. *Eliot, whose poetry he translated into Greek. His lyrical poetry was published in a number of collections, including *Strophe* (1931) and *Poiimata* (1940). He won the Nobel Prize in 1963.

Seghers, Hercules Pieterzoon (c. 1589-c. 1638) Dutch landscape painter and etcher. His desolate and dramatically lit mountain landscapes influenced *Rembrandt, who owned some of Seghers' works. He is also known for his novel method of etching with coloured paper and inks.

Ségou 13 28N 6 18W A town in central Mali, on the River Niger. It is an important trade centre serving an agricultural area. Population (1976 est): 36 400.

Segovia 40 57N 4 07W A city in central Spain, in Old Castile. It has a fine Roman aqueduct that still supplies the city with water, a 16th-century cathedral, and the restored alcázar (citadel). Industries include potteries and flour milling. Population (1982 est): 54 568.

Segovia, Andrés (1893–1987) Spanish guitarist. Playing all over the world, he revived the popularity of the guitar as a concert instrument and inspired composers to write works for it. In 1981 he became Marquis of Salobreña.

Segrè, Emilio (1905–   ) US physicist, born in Italy, who shared the 1959 Nobel Prize with Owen *Chamberlain for their discovery in 1955 of the antiproton (*see* antimatter). Segrè was also the first physicist to produce an artificial element, *technetium, by bombarding molybdenum with deuterium nuclei.

Seine, River A river in N France. Rising on the Plateau de Langres, it flows mainly NW through Paris to the English Channel, S of Le Havre. It is the second longest river in France, linked by canal with the Rivers Somme, Scheldt, Meuse, Rhine, Saône, and Loire. Length: 776 km (482 mi).

seismic belts (*or* seismic zones) The narrow distinct belts on the earth's surface that are subject to frequent earthquakes. They usually follow the line of plate boundaries (*see* plate tectonics), especially along midocean ridges, near young orogenic belts, along island arc systems, and along major *faults.

seismic wave An elastic shock wave emanating from the focus of an *earthquake or explosion. When seismic activity is recorded, several types of wave can be identified: longitudinal P (*primae*) waves and transverse S (*secundae*) waves are small rapid vibrations that come directly through the earth's interior. They form the first and second parts of the preliminary tremor of an earthquake. The main earthquake consists of large slow L (*longae*) waves travelling along the surface. This type of wave is limited to a narrow depth range and can also occur along deeper strata. Its components are Rayleigh waves (after R. J. S. Rayleigh), which are vertical vibrations in the plane of propagation, and Love waves (after A. E. H. Love; 1863–1940), which are horizontal and transverse. The study of seismic waves has provided much of our knowledge of the earth's interior.

seismology The branch of geophysics concerned with the study of *earthquakes: their origin, the waves they produce (*see* seismic wave), their effects, and their distribution. The instruments used are the **seismograph**, which records the magnitude of the oscillations during an earthquake, and the **seismometer**, which detects and records the motions of the earth in a particular direction (usually used in sets of three). In recent years considerable research has gone into the prediction and modification of earthquakes. The study of nuclear explosions has also concerned seismologists, since in many respects they resemble earthquakes. Seismological data has provided the bulk of our knowledge of the earth's interior. It is estimated that an average of 14 000 lives are lost annually through earthquakes.

sei whale A widely distributed *rorqual, *Balaenopteris borealis*, also called sardine whale. Up to 18 m long, it has a dark back, a white belly, and a large dorsal fin.

Sekhmet An Egyptian war goddess, consort of the creator-god Ptah and destroyer of the enemies of Ra. She was usually portrayed as a lioness or with a lion's head.

Sekondi-Takoradi 4 59N 1 43W A port in Ghana, on the Gulf of Guinea. Formerly two separate towns, Sekondi and Takoradi were linked in 1946. Bauxite is exported and industries include food processing. Population (1982 est): 123 637.

Selaginella A genus of mosslike *pteridophyte plants (about 700 species), also called spike mosses, found mainly in damp tropical forests. They are similar to the related *clubmosses but differ in having scales (ligules) at the bases of the leaves and two kinds of spore capsules (male and female). The prickly clubmoss (*S. selaginoides*) occurs in arctic and N temperate regions. Family: *Selaginellaceae*; class: *Lycopsida*.

Selangor A state in W Peninsular Malaysia, on the Strait of Malacca. It became a British protectorate in 1874. It is the economic centre of Malaysia with industry concentrated in the Klang Valley, mainly between Kuala Lumpur and Port Klang; the chief products are tin and rubber. Area: 8202 sq km (3167 sq mi). Population (1980): 1 467 441. Capital: Shah Alam.

Selby 53 48N 1 04W A market town in N England, in North Yorkshire on the River Ouse. It has a famous 12th-century abbey church. Industries include beet-sugar refining, shipbuilding, paper, and chemicals, and development of the rich Selby coalfield is under way (the first mine went into production in 1983). Population (1981): 107 726.

Selden, John (1584–1654) English jurist, antiquary, and orientalist. Selden's early work includes *Analecton Anglo-Britannicon* (1615) on the civil administration of England and *De Diis Syrris* (1617), but his best-known book was *Table Talk*, published posthumously in 1689. His opposition to tithes and the divine right of kings provoked the hostility of the clergy and monarchy. Elected to parliament in 1623, Selden helped to draft the Petition of Right (1628) concerning the privileges of the House of Commons, which resulted in his imprisonment (1629–34).

Selene The Greek moon-goddess, daughter of the Titan Hyperion and sister of Helios (the sun) and Eos (dawn). She became identified with the later Greek goddess *Artemis and with the Roman *Diana.

selenium (Se) A chemical element that is a member of the sulphur family and is obtained from sludges produced during electrolytic copper refining. It exists in several forms, including deep-red crystals, but the commonest allotrope is grey. The element has photovoltaic properties and is used in photocells, light meters, and in photocopying machines. It is a semiconductor and is widely used in rectifiers. The hydride (H_2Se) has a very noxious smell and, like other selenium compounds, is very toxic. At no 34; at wt 78.96; mp 217°C; bp 685°C. *See also* selenium cell.

selenium cell A type of *photocell based on the *photovoltaic effect. It consists of a metal disc coated with selenium on top of which is placed a layer of gold or platinum sufficiently thin to transmit light. When light falls on the disc a small current is generated. They are used in exposure meters in cameras, etc.

Seleucids A Middle Eastern dynasty of the Hellenistic age (323–27 BC) founded by *Seleucus I Nicator, the Macedonian general who, after Alexander the Great's death, became governor and then ruler (312) of Babylonia. He extended his kingdom to the frontiers of India in the east and then into Syria in the west but his successors, in the face of Egyptian aggression and internal unrest provoked by the Seleucid promotion of Greek culture, failed to maintain his conquests. *Antiochus the Great (reigned 223–187) briefly restored Seleucid power in the east but could not prevent Rome's Mediterranean expansion. Under *Antiochus IV Epiphanes (175–163) the empire was further weakened by the revolt of the *Maccabees and although they were repressed by *Antiochus VII Sidetes (139–129) his failure to push back the Parthians anticipated the final disintegration of the Seleucid empire. In 64 BC Pompey annexed what was left of it to form the Roman province of Syria.

Seleucus I Nicator (c. 356–280 BC) Macedonian general, who founded the *Seleucid dynasty. After Alexander the Great's death (323) Seleucus became governor and then ruler (312) of Babylonia, taking the title of king in 305. He subsequently conquered Syria, which brought him into conflict with the Ptolemies of Egypt, Asia Minor, and Macedonia before being murdered by Ptolemy Ceraunus (d. 279 BC), the son of Ptolemy I Soter.

self-heal A perennial herb, *Prunella vulgaris*, common in temperate Eurasia, N Africa, North America, and Australia. 5–30 cm high, it has tapering leaves and terminal clusters of small, usually violet, flowers. Extracts were formerly used to treat various illnesses. Family: *Labiatae*.

Seljuqs A Turkish dynasty that ruled in E Islam from 1055. During the 10th century the Seljuqs (descended from Seljuq, chief of the Oguz tribes) led bands of migrating Turks into the Islamic world and in 1055 their head, *Toghril Beg, captured Baghdad. The dynasty was at its peak under Toghril Beg and his successors *Alp Arslan and *Malik-Shah, under whom the great vizier *Nizam al-Mulk administered the empire. After the death of Malik-Shah the empire disintegrated into rival kingdoms. His successors in Persia maintained a nominal suzerainty over the other kingdoms until defeated by invaders from central Asia in 1153. In Anatolia the Seljuqs of Rum ruled an important independent kingdom until coming under the domination of the Mongols in 1243.

Selkirk (*or* Selkirkshire) A former county of SE Scotland. In 1975 it became part of the Borders Region.

Selkirk, Alexander (1676–1721) Scottish sailor. He joined the South Sea buccaneers in 1703 and in 1704, after quarrelling with his captain, was voluntarily left on one of the uninhabited Juan Fernández Islands. He was discovered in 1709 by a ship piloted by *Dampier. His experience inspired Defoe's *Robinson Crusoe* (1719).

Sellafield (former name: Windscale) An atomic power station in W Cumbria, NW England. Several accidents, together with a high incidence of cancer among local inhabitants, have made Sellafield a controversial focus for the nuclear power debate.

Sellers, Peter (1925–80) British comic actor. He made his name in the 1950s with the BBC radio comedy series *The Goon Show*. His many films include *I'm All Right, Jack* (1959), *The Millionairess* (1961), *Dr Strangelove* (1963), *The Pink Panther* series (1963–77), and *Being There* (1980).

Selwyn Lloyd, John, Baron (1904–78) British Conservative politician. He was foreign secretary (1955–60), supporting Eden (*see* Avon, Anthony Eden, 1st Earl of) during the Suez crisis, and then chancellor of the exchequer (1960–62). He resigned over his unpopular wage-restraint policy and was speaker of the Commons (1971–76).

Selznick, David O(liver) (1902–65) US film producer. In 1936 he formed his own production company and produced *A Star Is Born* (1937) and *Gone with the Wind* (1939) among other films. Many of his films, including *A Farewell to Arms* (1957), starred Jennifer Jones (1919–), his second wife.

semantics Broadly, the branch of philology concerned with the study of the relationship between words and meanings. The study of signs and their relationships to the things or concepts that they signify is also called semiotics or semiology and has application in mathematical logic and in the philosophy of language. Semantics as the study of meaning in individual words is part of *linguistics, but there are philosophical problems involved in trying to account for the relationship between words and the objects they refer to, particularly when a theory is extended to cover words that have no concrete referent (e.g. "honesty"). A distinction is often made between literal (or cognitive) meaning and associative meaning, and many linguists believe that the meaning of words can be broken into constituents by means of analyses similar to those used by *Chomsky to derive the surface structure of sentences from their deep structure. Some linguistic philosophers, such as *Wittgenstein in his later period and J. L. *Austin, account for word meaning not in terms of logical structures but rather according to the speaker's intention in using a word or utterance. However, logical analysis is widely accepted in explaining the aspect of meaning that is a function of grammatical structure, i.e. sentence meaning is seen as a matter of internal relationships among the words, word particles, and phrases involved.

SEMAPHORE

semaphore 1. A visual method of communication between ships at sea, used mainly by warships wishing to maintain radio silence, and consisting of a pattern of signalling by the use of two flags, held by a signalman, their relative positions symbolizing an alphabetical or numerical character. **2.** A mechanical railway signalling device, consisting of a steel arm the position of which is changed by a signalman or by the tripping of a release by a passing train.

Semarang 6 58S 110 29E A port in Indonesia, in central Java on the Java Sea. A commercial centre with textile and shipbuilding industries, it exports sugar, rubber, coffee, kapok, and copra. The port is sometimes disrupted by the monsoon. Its university was established in 1960. Population (1980): 1 026 671.

Semele In Greek mythology, the daughter of *Cadmus, King of Thebes. She was killed by lightning when her lover Zeus appeared to her in his divine form but her unborn child, the god *Dionysus, was saved.

semen. *See* sperm; testis.

semiconductor A crystalline material in which the electrical conductivity increases with temperature and is between that of a conductor and an *insulator. The conductivity is also sensitive to minute quantities of impurities in the crystal lattice (□energy band). Some (donor) impurities increase the number of negative charge carriers (electrons), creating what is known as an n-type semiconductor. Other (acceptor) impurities increase the number of positive charge carriers (holes), creating a p-type semiconductor. The introduction of these impurities is called doping. *Solid-state electronic components, such as diodes, *transistors, and *integrated circuits depend on the properties of junctions between p-type and n-type regions in the same piece of semiconductor crystal (p-n junctions). Metal oxide semiconductor (MOS) devices also use the properties of a thin layer of insulating oxide on the semiconductor surface. The element silicon is now the most widely used semiconducting material. Others are germanium, now used only for special applications, and gallium arsenide, which is used in high-speed logic circuits and microwave equipment.

semiconductor diode A *solid-state electronic device with two electrodes. It consists of a single p-n junction (*see* semiconductor). When the p-region is at a more positive voltage than the n-region (forward bias), the current flow increases exponentially as the voltage rises. In reverse bias, very little current flows until a sufficiently high reverse voltage has built up to cause breakdown; the current then increases sharply. The diode is, therefore, commonly used as a rectifier. The **Zener diode** is designed to break down at a specific reverse bias voltage, above which the voltage across it remains effectively constant. The higher the doping levels on both sides of the junction, the lower the breakdown voltage. It is used as a voltage regulator.

Semiconductor diodes, which have largely replaced thermionic diodes, are also used to generate microwaves by the *Gunn effect, to detect light in *photocells, and to emit light in low-voltage displays. The latter, called **light-emitting diodes** (LEDs), are widely used in calculators and digital watches. They emit radiation (light) when holes and electrons combine, the colour of the light depending on the material of the crystal.

Seminole A group of North American Indians related to the *Creeks, who speak a Muskogean language. In the late 18th century they migrated from Georgia to Florida, where, in several wars, they resisted domination by the government. They developed a simple hunting and fishing culture suited to the conditions of the region.

semiotics (*or* semiology) *See* semantics.

Semipalatinsk 50 26N 80 16E A city in the Soviet Union, in the NE Kazakh SSR on the River Irtysh. Its name means "seven palaces" and refers to the nearby remains of seven ancient stone structures. Meat packing, food processing, and metalworking are among its industrial activities, and it is an important communications centre. Population (1981 est): 291 000.

semipermeable membrane A material that allows certain molecules in a fluid to pass through it but not others. It will usually permit solvent particles to pass but not the solute molecules. It thus creates *osmosis when placed in a suitable fluid. Examples of semipermeable membranes include cell walls and parchment.

Semiramis A legendary queen of Assyria, who, with her legendary husband Ninus, was the alleged builder of *Babylon and, after his death, ruler of a vast empire extending to India.

Semites A group of peoples, including the *Jews and *Arabs, said in the Bible to be descended from Shem, Noah's eldest son. The Babylonians, Assyrians, Canaanites, and Phoenicians were ancient Semitic peoples.

Semitic alphabets The earliest known truly alphabetic writing systems, developed among the Semitic peoples of the E Mediterranean around 2000 BC. From them all the major alphabets of today are derived: the south Semitic version gave rise to the modern Amharic script of Ethiopia; from North Semitic were derived Greek (and from Greek came the Roman, *Cyrillic, *runic, and other alphabets), Phoenician, and Aramaic (from which came the scripts of Hebrew, Arabic, and *Devanagari in India). The earliest records in North Semitic date from around 1300 BC and indicate that it was a purely consonantal system of 22 letters, generally written from left to right.

Semitic languages A subgroup of the *Hamito-Semitic language family spoken in a large area of N Africa, extending through Palestine to the SW corner of Asia. The Semitic languages originated in Mesopotamia in the 3rd millennium BC and are recorded in Sumerian *cuneiform

inscriptions. There are three subgroups recognized by language scholars, although, in comparison to other language groups, these subdivisions are very similar to each other in structure and vocabulary. NW Semitic consisted of Ugaritic, Canaanite, and *Aramaic, all now extinct. From these are descended Phoenician and *Hebrew, the only living language of this subgroup. NE Semitic, the second subgroup, consisted of Assyrian and Babylonian, both now extinct. The third group, S Semitic, is that from which modern *Arabic and Maltese are descended, as well as Amharic (*see* Amhara) and Tigrinya, the language of Eritrea.

semolina Fine grains of durum wheat used in the manufacture of *pasta and also for making milk puddings.

Senanayake, D(on) S(tephen) (1884–1952) Ceylonese statesman; the first prime minister (1947–52) of Ceylon (now Sri Lanka). In 1919 he helped to found the Ceylon National Congress and campaigned for the introduction of legal and constitutional reforms by the British Government. His son **Dudley Senanayake** (1911–73) was prime minister (1952–53, 1960, 1965–70).

Senate In ancient Rome, the state council. During Republican times the Senate was largely composed of ex-magistrates and, although its role was primarily to advise the magistrates, it carried much weight, especially in foreign policy, finance, and religion. Under the Empire membership of the Senate became largely hereditary and its chief function was to ratify imperial decisions. *See also* curia.

Senate, US. *See* Congress.

Sendai 38 16N 140 52E A city in Japan, in NE Honshu. It is the largest city of N Japan and an important commercial centre. Tohoku University was established here in 1907. Population (1981): 665 000.

Seneca the Elder (Marcus Annaeus Seneca; c. 55 BC–c. 41 AD) Roman rhetorician, born at Córdoba (Spain). Parts of his work on oratory, addressed to his sons, have survived: the *Suasoriae* (a compendium of styles and themes of earlier rhetoricians) and the *Controversiae* (imaginary court cases). One of his sons, **Seneca the Younger** (Lucius Annaeus Seneca; c. 4 BC–65 AD), was an author and politician. His career at court, interrupted by exile (41–49 AD), culminated in his appointment as tutor and later chief minister to *Nero. Retiring in 64 AD as a millionaire, he was accused of treason and forced to commit suicide. 13 philosophical treatises and numerous essays disguised as letters advocate *Stoicism in a highly rhetorical style. His nine tragedies, which influenced the Elizabethan dramatists, also survive.

Senefelder, Aloys (1771–1834) German playwright and engraver, born in Prague and famous for his invention (1798) of lithography (*see* printing) after accidentally discovering (1796) the possibilities of drawing with greasy chalk on wet stone.

Senegal, Republic of A country in West Africa, on the Atlantic Ocean. The River Senegal forms its N boundary and the River Gambia flows E–W through the country to the border of The Gambia, which forms an enclave within Senegalese territory. Senegal consists chiefly of level plains rising to a dissected plateau in the SE. Most of the population are Wolof, Sere, and Tukolor. *Economy*: chiefly agricultural, the production of groundnuts being dominant. Other crops include millet, rice, and maize; livestock is important and fishing is being developed with foreign aid. Phosphates, iron ore, and offshore oil and natural gas have been found in significant quantities. Hydroelectricity is a valuable source of power. Industry, mainly concentrated on Dakar, includes cement, food processing, and textiles; tourism is expanding. The main exports are phosphates, groundnuts, and preserved fish. *History*: in the 14th and 15th centuries the area was part of the Mali empire. St Louis was founded in 1659 by the French, who extended their control in the mid-19th century over most of the region. The country achieved self-government in 1958 as a member of the

French Community and in 1959–60 briefly formed the Federation of Mali with Sudan. Senegal became a separate independent republic in 1960, with Léopold Senghor as its first president. In 1982 it formed the Senegambia Confederation with The Gambia with each country retaining its independence but having joint defence, foreign, and monetary policies. President: Abdou Diouff (1935–). Official language: French. Official currency: CFA (Communauté financière africaine) franc of 100 centimes. Area: 197 722 sq km (76 320 sq mi). Population (1983 est): 6 335 000. Capital and main port: Dakar.

Senegal, River   A river in West Africa. Rising in the Fouta Djallon highlands in N Guinea, it flows mainly NW to the Atlantic Ocean forming part of the Mauritania–Senegal border. Length: 1690 km (1050 mi).

Senghor, Léopold Sédar   (1906–) Senegalese statesman; president (1960–80). Educated in France, he was Senegalese deputy to the French National Assembly (1946–58). He formed the Senegalese Progressive Union, which took Senegal to independence in 1960. He is also a poet, the author of *Chants d'ombres* (1945) and *Nocturnes* (1961).

senna.   *See* Cassia.

Sennacherib   (d. 681 BC) King of Assyria (704–681); the son and successor of *Sargon II. After 16 years of leniency towards the constantly rebellious Babylonians he sacked the city of Babylon in 689. He also crushed an Egyptian-inspired revolt of Palestine led by *Hezekiah. A patron of art and learning, he restored *Nineveh. Murdered by one of his sons, probably incited by Babylonian rebels, he was succeeded by *Esarhaddon.

Sennar   13 31N 33 38E A town in the SE Sudan, on the Blue Nile River. It is the site of the Makwar Dam (completed 1925), a part of the *Gezira irrigation scheme. Population (1984 est): 8000.

Sennett, Mack   (Michael Sinott; 1884–1960) US film producer and director, born in Canada. In 1912 he joined the Keystone Company, for which he produced numerous short slapstick films featuring the *Keystone Kops and such comic actors as Charlie Chaplin and Harold Lloyd.

Sens   48 12N 3 18E A town in central France, in the Yonne department on the River Yonne. The site of one of the earliest gothic cathedrals in France, its manufactures include agricultural implements, leather products, and chemicals. Population (1982): 26 961.

sensitive plants.   *See* Mimosa.

sentimental novel   A type of fiction popular in 18th-century England and France in which scenes of emotional distress were intended to arouse the reader's pity and compassion. Examples include *Manon Lescaut* (1731) by the Abbé *Prévost and *Pamela* (1740) by Samuel *Richardson.

Seoul   37 30N 127 00E The capital of the Republic of (South) Korea, in the NW on the River Han near the coast. The capital of Korea since 1394, the city served as the centre of Japanese-occupied Korea (1910–45). It suffered considerable damage in the Korean War (1950–53). It is a rapidly developing industrial as well as administrative and commercial centre. Its 16 universities include the Seoul National University (1946). Population (1980): 8 366 756.

sepak takraw   A three-a-side ball game similar to *badminton and *volleyball, played in SE Asia. The ball may be played with the feet and other parts of the body but not the hands.

separation of powers   The division of governmental powers between a legislature, executive, and judiciary that are distinct from, and indepedent of, each other. Such separation is most clearly seen in the institutions established by the US *constitution, in the drafting of which separation of powers was seen as the best way to safeguard liberty and the risk of ineffective government seemed preferable to governmental despotism. These institutions are the Congress (legislature), presidency (executive), and Supreme Court (judiciary). The separation is not complete (for instance, the president may veto legislation that does not have a two-thirds majority in each house of Congress) but is more distinct than in most other countries, such as the UK, where both legislature and executive are largely in the hands of the same individuals (e.g. the party with a majority in the House of Commons).

Sephardim   (Hebrew *Sepharad*: Spain)   Jews who went to Spain and Portugal in the *diaspora. When the Jews were expelled from Spain in 1492 they spread to many parts of the world, preserving their customs and their language, *Ladino. The first Jewish settlers in England in the 17th century were Sephardim from Holland; their synagogue (1701), in Bevis Marks in the city of London, is still in use. The term is now sometimes applied, especially in Israel, to all non-*Ashkenazim.

septicaemia.   *See* blood poisoning.

SEPTIC TANK   *The sewage enters low in the tank without disturbing the contents. Purer water separates at the top and sludge forms at the bottom.*

septic tank   A large tank of steel or concrete sunk in the ground to provide *sewage disposal for isolated buildings or small communities. Effluent flows into the tank, the settled sludge being decomposed to a certain extent by bacterial action. The tank must be large enough (minimum 2.7 cu m in the UK) to store the sludge for several months, before emptying.

Sept Îles   50 13N 66 22W A town and port in E Canada, in Quebec on the Gulf of St Lawrence. Founded in 1650, it developed with the construction of a railway to large iron-ore mines in the interior (1950). Population (1981): 29 262.

Septuagint (Latin: seventy)   A Greek translation of the *Old Testament and *Apocrypha made for the use of Greek-speaking Jews in Egypt and improved and completed in stages between the 3rd century BC and the 1st century AD. It derives its name and symbol (LXX) from the legend that 72 Jewish scholars completed the work in 72 days. Many Old Testament quotations in the New Testament are taken from it.

sequence   An ordered set of numbers, generally denoted by $a_1, a_2, \ldots a_r \ldots$, in which the rth term a_r can be expressed as a function of r. *See also* series.

sequoia   Either of two Californian coniferous trees, the *redwood (*Sequoia sempervirens*), which is the world's tallest tree, or the giant sequoia, *Sequoiadendron giganteum* (formerly *Sequoia gigantea*), also called Wellingtonia and big tree. The giant sequoia forms natural forests in California's Sierra Nevada, where some trees are over 3000 years old, with a height of over 80 m and a girth of over 24 m. In Europe it is grown as an ornamental. The red-brown bark is soft and fibrous and the shoots are densely covered with pointed scalelike leaves. The woody brown egg-shaped cones are 5–8 cm long. Family: *Taxodiaceae*.

Seraing 50 37N 5 31E A town in Belgium, an industrial suburb of Liège on the River Meuse. It has coalmines and a locomotive and engineering works, which was established by the Englishman John Cockerill in 1817. Population (1983 est): 62 832.

Serang. *See* Ceram.

seraphim. *See* cherubim and seraphim.

Serapis A god combining Greek and Egyptian elements, introduced into Egypt by *Ptolemy I in order to unite the worship of the two peoples. He was the lord of the universe and was identical with *Osiris, with characteristics borrowed from *Zeus and *Asclepius. The centre of his cult was Alexandria.

Serbia (Serbo-Croat name: Srbija) A constituent republic of Yugoslavia, incorporating the autonomous regions of Vojvodina and Kosovo. It is chiefly mountainous, descending in the N to the basin of the River Danube. Agriculture is of major importance, especially stock raising and the growing of wheat, maize, and vines. It possesses important mineral deposits including copper (at Bor), antimony, coal, and chrome. *History*: first settled by the Serbs in the 7th century AD, it later came under Turkish control (1389–1804), finally regaining its independence in 1878. It played a major role in events leading up to World War I: in 1914 Austria accused Serbia of direct involvement in the assassination of Archduke Francis Ferdinand and subsequently declared war. Serbia suffered badly during the war, losing about 23% of the population. In 1918 it became part of the kingdom of Serbs, Croats, and Slovenes, later renamed Yugoslavia. Area: 128 278 sq km (49 528 sq mi). Population (1981): 9 313 677. Capital: Belgrade.

Serbo-Croat The language of the Serbs and Croats of Yugoslavia, where it is the most widely spoken language. Serbian and Croatian differ only marginally in terms of vocabulary and not at all in grammar but Serbian is written in *Cyrillic and Croatian in Latin script. The standard literary form is based on a central dialect known as Shtokavian. Written texts date from the 12th century.

serf An unfree peasant of the middle ages. Serfdom was characteristic of the manorial economic system (*see* manor). A serf was bound to the soil he tilled, paying his lord a fee and providing service in return for the use of his land. Serfs had their own homes, plots, and livestock and enjoyed customary rights that distinguished them from slaves (*see* slavery). While serfdom declined in W Europe in the late middle ages, it was strengthened in E Europe, where it was only abolished in the 19th century.

Sergius of Radonezh, St (1314–92) Russian monk, who founded the monastery of the Holy Trinity (now called Zagorsk) in the forest of Radonezh near Moscow. It became a famous spiritual and missionary centre, helping to re-establish monasticism after the disruption caused by the invading Tatars. Feast day: 25 Sept.

serialism (*or* twelve-tone music) A method of composing music using all 12 notes of the chromatic scale equally, invented by Arnold Schoenberg in the 1920s. Schoenberg sought an alternative to *chromaticism and *atonality by using a fixed sequence of 12 notes (called a **series** or tone row) as a source of melody and harmony. The series could be transposed so as to begin on any degree of the scale and could also be inverted and used in a retrograde form. In strict serialism no single note of the row could be repeated until the other 11 had occurred in melody or harmony; Schoenberg himself did not always follow this rule.

In place of traditional *harmony he developed chords built on fourths. Schoenberg's pupils (Webern, Berg, and others) adopted serialism, although sometimes in a modified form.

In **total serialism** musical elements, such as rhythmical figurations, degrees of volume, and types of tone colour are classified in strict serial form. Such composers as Berio and Boulez have used this technique.

seriema A bird belonging to a family (Cariamidae; 2 species) occurring in dry grassland regions of South America. The crested seriema (*Cariama cristata*) is 60 cm tall and has a brown plumage with pale underparts and a red bill and legs. Seriemas feed on insects, snails, reptiles, and berries. Order: *Gruiformes* (cranes, rails, etc.).

series The sum of the terms in a *sequence, written as $a_1 + a_2 + a_3 + \ldots a_r + \ldots$. The partial sum to the nth term is denoted by S_n. A series is convergent if S_n approaches a particular value as n increases and divergent if it increases without limit. A geometric series has the general form $a + an + an^2 + \ldots$, where a and n are constant. It is convergent if n is less than one, divergent if n is greater than or equal to one. A power series has the general form $a_0 + a_1x + a_2x^2 + a_3x^3 + \ldots$, where x is a *variable. See also arithmetic progression.

serin The smallest European *finch, *Serinus serinus*, closely related to the canary and having a sweet trilling song. Serins have a streaked olive-coloured plumage with a bright-yellow rump and, in the male, a yellow head and breast. Although a southern species, its range extends to N Europe.

Seringapatam 12 25N 76 41E A town in India, in Karnataka on Seringapatam Island in the River Cauvery. It was the capital of Mysore from 1610 until 1799, when it was besieged and captured by the British. Population (1981): 18 137.

serotine bat An insect-eating *bat, *Eptesicus serotinus*, of Eurasia. It is about 12 cm long including the tail and has a 35 cm wingspan. Dark brown in colour, it flies at early dusk and dawn. Family: *Vespertilionidae*.

serotonin (*or* 5-hydroxytryptamine) A compound, synthesized from the amino acid tryptophan, that occurs in certain nerve endings of the *hypothalamus (in the brain) and the autonomic nervous system. It is involved in the regulation of emotion; such drugs as LSD affect mood and behaviour by altering serotonin levels in the brain.

serow A hoofed mammal, *Capricornis sumatraensis*, inhabiting wooded mountainous regions of S Asia. About 90 cm high at the shoulder, serows have short wrinkled horns and a coarse black or reddish-grey coat with white patches on the face and legs. Serows and *gorals are sometimes called goat antelopes. Family: *Bovidae*.

Serowe 22 25S 26 44E A town in E Botswana. It is the headquarters of the Bamangwato tribe and consists of traditional African houses. The main industry is agriculture. Population (1981): 23 661.

serpentine A group of minerals consisting mainly of hydrous magnesium silicates, with a layered structure. They are usually green or white, and often streaked or mottled like a snake's skin. The two main varieties are chrysotile (fibrous, used in the manufacture of asbestos) and antigorite (platy). They occur in basic and ultrabasic igneous rocks from the breakdown of olivines and pyroxenes. **Serpentinite** is a rock consisting mainly of serpentine, formed by the hydrothermal alteration of ultramafic rocks; some are quarried for ornamental stone.

serpulid A small marine *annelid worm belonging to the family *Serpulidae*. Serpulids build limy tubes on stones and seaweed and extend a crown of tentacles to feed in the same way as the related *fanworms. Class: *Polychaeta*.

serum The fluid that remains after blood has been allowed to clot. It can be obtained by centrifuging clotted blood and is similar in composition to plasma, except that it lacks the factors, such as fibrinogen, that are involved in blood clotting.

serum sickness Illness resulting from an allergic reaction to injected serum or antiserum. It is seen most commonly following the injection of horse tetanus antitoxin. 6 to 12 days after the injection the patient develops fever, a rash, and painful joints. Treatment is with steroids.

serval A slender long-legged *cat, *Felis serval*, of the African bush. It is about 1.25 m long including the tail (30 cm) and has large ears and a spotted coat. Servals hunt birds and small mammals, such as hares and duikers, mainly at night.

Servetus, Michael (Spanish name: Miguel Serveto; 1511–53) Spanish theologian and physician, who discovered that the blood circulates to the lungs from the right chamber of the heart. Working chiefly in France, he published several treatises attacking the orthodox doctrine of the Trinity. These incurred the hostility of both Roman Catholics and Protestants and, while hiding from the Inquisition in Geneva, he was arrested by Calvin and burnt as a heretic.

service tree A tree, *Sorbus domestica*, about 15 m high, native to S Europe, W Asia, and N Africa and commonly grown for ornament. Related to the *mountain ash, it has compound leaves of 11–21 leaflets and its small green fruits are used for making wine. The wild service tree (*S. torminalis*) has simple lobed leaves, while the bastard service tree is an ornamental hybrid between the mountain ash and the *whitebeam. Family: *Rosaceae*.

sesame An annual herb, *Sesamum indicum*, cultivated in Central and South America, the Middle East, and SE Asia. Several varieties are known, growing 50–250 cm high and bearing small purplish flowers. The seeds are used in confectionery and as food flavouring. Oil extracted from the seeds is used as a cooking and salad oil and in margarines and other products; the residue (sesame cake) is used as cattle feed. Family: *Pedaliaceae*.

Sesostris I (d. 1928 BC) King of Egypt (c. 1971–1928) of the 12th dynasty. He extended Egyptian rule into Nubia, exploiting its mineral resources. His ambitious building projects include a magnificent funerary complex at Lisht.

Sesostris II (d. 1878 BC) King of Egypt (c. 1897–1878) of the 12th dynasty. He began the land-reclamation works in El *Faiyum continued by *Amenemhet III. Excavations at the town he founded, al-Lahun, have produced much valuable evidence about this period.

Sesostris III King of Egypt (1878–1843 BC) of the 12th dynasty. The sudden cessation of the construction of the nobles' extravagant tombs and an evident rise in middle-class prosperity indicate great changes in Egyptian society during his reign. Sesostris extended his control of Nubia as far south as Wadi Halfa.

Sesshu (Sesshu Toyo; 1420–1506) Japanese landscape painter. After a visit to China (c. 1467) he introduced into Japan the Chinese techniques of monochrome ink painting on long scrolls.

Sessions, Roger (1896–1985) US composer. A pupil of Ernest Bloch, he held several teaching posts in the USA. From 1925 to 1933 he lived mainly in Germany and Italy. His works include two operas, *The Trial of Lucullus* (1947) and *Montezuma* (1962), eight symphonies, a violin concerto, a piano concerto, and chamber music.

Set An Egyptian deity. Originally a sun and sky god, he murdered his brother *Osiris and so came to represent all evil. Killed by *Horus, son of Osiris, he is usually portrayed as a composite figure with various animal features.

Sète (former name: Cette) 43 25N 3 43E A major port in S France, in the Hérault department on the Gulf of Lions. Established in 1666, it developed as the terminus of the Canal du Midi and today has shipbuilding, oil-refining, metallurgical, and fishing industries. It is the birthplace of Paul Valéry. Population (1982): 40 446.

Seton, Ernest Thompson (1860–1946) US naturalist and writer, born in England. His experiences as a hunter in Canada were the foundation for his many books about animals, notably *Wild Animals I Have Known* (1898). He was actively concerned with conservation and was a founder of the Boy Scouts of America.

Seto-Naikai. *See* Inland Sea.

setter One of three breeds of sporting □dog with a lean deep-chested body and drooping ears. Setters are named after their habit of squatting flat ("setting") after finding game. The English setter has a long white silky coat flecked with darker markings. The heavier Gordon setter, first bred at Gordon Castle, Scotland, is black with chestnut markings, while the Irish, or red, setter has a flat silky chestnut coat. Height: 61–69 cm.

SET THEORY   *Venn diagrams.*

set theory The study, founded by Georg *Cantor, of the logical and mathematical laws of sets. A set is a defined collection of objects or elements; for example the set of odd integers between 0 and 10 is $\{1, 3, 5, 7, 9\}$. The empty or null set, denoted by the symbol $\emptyset$, has no elements. All sets are contained in the universal set E. The relationships between sets can be illustrated in a Venn diagram, named after the British logician John Venn (1834–1923), or shown by symbols. $a \in A$ means the element a is a member of the set A. $A \subset B$ means set A is contained in set B. $A \cup B$ means the union of A and B. $A \cap B$ means the intersection of A and B, i.e. those elements in both. A^c or A' is the complement of A, all elements in E but not in A.

Settlement, Act of (1701) The Act that established the Hanoverian succession to the English throne. In the absence of heirs to William III or Anne, the Crown was to pass to James I's granddaughter *Sophia, Electress of Hanover, or to her Protestant descendants. The Act stipulated that the monarch must be a Protestant and that foreigners must not hold public office or enter parliament. Anne was succeeded by the first Hanoverian king, George I, in 1714.

Setúbal 38 31N 8 54W A port in SW Portugal, on the Bay of Setúbal. It is an important centre for sardine fishing with associated fish-curing industries. Exports include oranges and muscatel wine and grapes. Population (1981): 76 812.

Seurat, Georges (1859–91) French painter, famous for developing neoimpressionism, popularly called *pointillism. Influenced by writings on aesthetics and the colour theories of *Delacroix and the chemist Michel-Eugène Chevreul (1786–1889), he based his dots of pure colour and static compositions on scientific study. Although he finished only seven paintings in this demanding style, for example the famous *Sunday Afternoon on the Island of the Grande Jatte* (1884–86; Art Institute of Chicago) and *Le Cirque* (1890–91; Louvre), his work was very influential, one disciple being Paul *Signac.

Sevastopol (English name: Sebastopol) 44 36N 33 31E A port in the Soviet Union, in the Crimean *oblast* (region) of the S Ukrainian SSR on the Black Sea. It is a popular seaside resort. *History*: founded in 1783, after Russia's annexation of the Crimea it became an important naval base and, later, a commercial port. It was besieged by the British and French during the Crimean War, falling after 11 months. Population (1981 est): 315 000.

Seven against Thebes In Greek legend, seven champions who fought against Eteocles, who had gained the throne of Thebes after the death of his father Oedipus and refused to relinquish it to his brother *Polyneices when his term as ruler had ended. The seven champions, led by Polyneices, attacked the seven gates of Thebes. Eteocles and Polyneices died at each other's hand. The story is the subject of a play by *Aeschylus. *See also* Antigone.

Seven Deadly Sins Pride, covetousness, lust, envy, gluttony, anger, and sloth. The traditional Christian list was already established by the 6th century and during the middle ages representations of the Seven Deadly Sins were a common feature of art and literature.

Seven Sleepers of Ephesus A legend of seven Christian soldiers who were entombed in a cave while hiding to escape religious persecution under the Emperor Decius in the 3rd century. They slept until the reign of Theodosius II (408–50), who, on hearing their miraculous experience, was converted to belief in the resurrection.

seventeenth parallel The latitude of 17°N and the line of demarcation between North and South Vietnam established by the *Geneva Conference (1954).

Seventh Day Adventists. *See* Adventists.

Seven Weeks' War. *See* Austro-Prussian War.

Seven Wonders of the World The supreme man-made structures of the ancient world. They were the *Pyramids of Egypt, the *Colossus of Rhodes, the *Hanging Gardens of Babylon, the *Mausoleum of Halicarnassus, the statue of *Zeus at Olympia, the temple of *Artemis at Ephesus, and the *Pharos of Alexandria. Only the Pyramids have survived.

Seven Years' War (1756–63) The war between Prussia, Britain, and Hanover on one side and France, Austria, Russia, and Spain on the other. The war had two main aspects: the rivalry between Austria and Prussia for domination of Germany and the struggle between France and Britain for overseas supremacy. The war was precipitated by Austria's desire to regain Silesia, lost to Frederick the Great of Prussia in the War of the *Austrian Succession, and began with Frederick's invasion of Saxony. Russia's defection (1762) to Prussia enabled Frederick ultimately to emerge victorious and Prussian ascendancy was confirmed by the Peace of Hubertusberg. Overseas, the British despite initial reverses won a series of spectacular victories in India (by *Clive) and Canada (by *Wolfe). By the Treaty of *Paris (1763) Britain was confirmed as the supreme world power.

Severini, Gino (1883–1966) Italian painter, born in Cortona. After training under *Balla, he moved to Paris (1906), where he became a pointillist. In 1910 he signed the futurist manifesto and thereafter his work combined *futurism and *cubism, especially in his nightclub scenes. He later returned to painting more conventional landscapes and figure studies.

Severn, River (Welsh name: Hafren) The longest river in the UK, rising in central Wales and flowing NE and E into England, then S to the Bristol Channel. It passes through Welshpool, Shrewsbury, Worcester, Tewkesbury, and Gloucester. It is linked by canal to the Rivers Thames and Trent and is spanned near its estuary by the **Severn Bridge**, a suspension bridge 988 m (3240 ft) long, built in the 1960s. A tidal-power barrier in the Severn Estuary is planned for the 1990s. Length: 354 km (220 mi).

Severus, Lucius Septimius (c. 145–211 AD) Roman emperor (193–211). Severus was governor of Upper Pannonia (S of the Danube) before being proclaimed emperor. He defeated his rival Pescennius Niger in 194 and embarked on a puni-

tive campaign against Pescennius' supporters. He introduced administrative and military reforms at Rome before embarking on a campaign in Britain, where he died.

Severus Alexander (?208–35 AD) Roman emperor (222–35); the adopted son of his predecessor Elagabalus. Severus' mother, Julia Mamaea, murdered Elagabalus to secure Severus' accession. Severus' rule depended upon the army, which construed his attempt to prevent warfare on the German frontier as cowardice, and murdered him and his mother.

Seveso 45 38N 9 08E A town in N Italy, situated N of Milan. In July, 1976, a poisonous gas cloud (dioxin) escaped from a factory here contaminating a wide radius of land. Crops and animals were destroyed and people evacuated; in September, 1977, the first families were allowed to return.

Sévigné, Marie de Rabutin-Chantal, Marquise de (1626–96) French letter writer. In over 1500 letters, mostly written to her two children after the death of her husband in 1651, she described the social pleasures and intellectual diversions of Parisian society—and life at her country house in Brittany—in a style that became a model for letter writing throughout Europe.

Seville (Spanish name: Sevilla) 37 24N 5 59W A city and port in SW Spain, in Andalusia on the River Guadalquivir. Important under the Romans, it also thrived under the Moors (711–1248) as a cultural centre and became a major port with a monopoly of trade with the West Indies in the 16th century. The painters Velázquez and Murillo were born here. There is a university (founded 1502) and one of the world's largest cathedrals (1401–1591). The Easter festival with its procession of floats bearing religious subjects is a notable event. It is an important industrial centre, with textiles and engineering; exports include wine, fruit, and olive oil. Population (1981): 653 833.

Sèvres porcelain The finest French porcelain, first produced in 1738. Originally at Vincennes, the Sèvres factory moved to near *Versailles in 1756. It always enjoyed royal patronage and by 1759 Louis XV was proprietor. The early products were soft-paste porcelain but from 1768 hard-paste was made. Products were figures, vases, ornaments, and table services with blue, rose Pompadour, yellow, or green grounds richly gilded for royal taste. Now the national porcelain factory, it continues its fine output.

sewage disposal The collection, treatment, and eventual discharge of domestic sewage and industrial waste. Sewers, systems of underground piping, channel the effluent to a sewage-treatment plant. There it is screened to remove solid objects before passing to a primary sedimentation tank, where suspended solids settle out. The liquid then passes through aeration tanks, where the oxygen content is increased by blowing air through it, and a final sedimentation tank before being discharged into rivers, etc. The solids meanwhile enter a sludge digester, a tank in which bacterial action partially eats away the organic material. Following thickening and drying the solid residue is incinerated, spread on the land, or sold as fertilizer. In some coastal areas raw sewage is pumped into the sea untreated—a practice that has been shown to be more of a nuisance than a hazard to bathers.

sewing machine A device for sewing together pieces of cloth or other materials. The familiar lockstitch machine was invented in the USA by Elias Howe in 1846 and patented by Isaac Merrit Singer in 1851. In this machine, a needle with a thread passing through its eye penetrates the cloth from above, a loop being formed below the cloth either by passing a separate thread from a bobbin through the loop or by a rotary hook carrying the loop around a stationary bobbin. A toothed platform moves the material forwards in preparation for the next stitch. Sewing machines are powered by hand, treddle, or electric motor and modern machines have facilities for hemming, buttonholing, etc.

sex chromosome A *chromosome that carries the genes for determining the sex of an individual. In humans there are two types of sex chromosomes, called X and Y. The body cells of normal males possess one X and one Y chromosome while those of normal females have two X chromosomes. Human sperm is therefore either "male" or "female" depending on whether it carries an X or a Y chromosome. The sex of the embryo is determined by which type of sperm fertilizes the female egg (which always carries an X chromosome). Abnormal numbers of sex chromosomes cause a range of disabilities, including physical abnormalities, mental retardation, and sterility.

sex hormones Hormones that regulate the growth, development, and functioning of the reproductive organs and determine external sexual characteristics. The major female sex hormones are the *oestrogens, *progesterone, and *prolactin while the *androgens are the principal male ones. Their production is regulated by *gonadotrophins from the pituitary gland.

SEXTANT *Angle* α *measures the angle between horizon and reference arm;* β *is the angle between index mirror and horizon glass, marked by the angular movement of the index arm along the limb.* α = 2β, *therefore the graduations marked on the scale are twice the actual angular movement.*

sextant An instrument used primarily in navigation for determining latitudes by measuring the angle subtended by some celestial body to the horizon. Thomas Godfrey of Philadelphia and John Hadley of London, working independently, discovered the sextant's principle in 1730. The graduated metal strip, shaped in an arc of the sixth part of a circle, gave the instrument its name. In use the movable index arm is slid along the scale until the image of the reference star as viewed in the half-silvered index mirror is aligned with the horizon. The reading on the scale then indicates the angle subtended.

sexton beetle. *See* burying beetle.

sexually transmitted disease (STD) Any disease transmitted predominantly by sexual intercourse, also known as venereal disease (VD). Among the most prevalent STDs are genital *herpes, nonspecific urethritis (NSU), and *AIDS; *syphilis and *gonorrhoea—the former scourges—are now treatable with antibiotics.

Seychelles, Republic of A country consisting of 87 widely scattered islands in the W Indian Ocean, NE of Madagascar. The main island is Mahé and others include Praslin, Silhouette, and La Digue; the islands of Aldabra, Farquhar, and Desroches were returned to the Seychelles in 1976. Most of the population is of mixed African and European descent.

Economy: the chief products and exports are copra and cinnamon bark. Other occupations include fishing and some industry, including tobacco and brewing. Tourism is important and has expanded rapidly since the opening of a new airport (1971). *History*: the uninhabited islands became a French colony in the mid-18th century as a spice plantation. Captured by the British in 1794, they became a dependency of Mauritius from 1814 until 1903, when they became a British crown colony. In 1976 the country became an independent republic within the British Commonwealth, with James Mancham (1940–   ) as its first president. While attending the Commonwealth conference in London in 1977, he was overthrown and superseded as president by his prime minister, Albert René (1935–   ). In 1981 a mercenary force backed by South Africa attempted a coup. It was the third such attempt by forces from outside the country to seize power. Official languages: English and French; the majority speak Creole. Official currency: Seychelles rupee of 100 cents. Area: 444 sq km (171 sq mi). Population (1983 est): 65 000. Capital and main port: Victoria.

Seyfert galaxy A class of galaxies with exceptionally bright central regions the majority of which are otherwise normal spiral galaxies. Intense radiation is emitted from the centre at infrared, visible, ultraviolet, and X-ray wavelengths, the source of this energy being relatively small. This type of galaxy was first described by the US astronomer C. K. Seyfert (1911–60). *See also* active galaxy.

Seymour, Jane (c. 1509–37) The third wife (1536–37) of Henry VIII of England. A lady in waiting to both his former wives, Catherine of Aragon and Anne Boleyn, she married Henry 11 days after Anne's execution. Jane was the mother of Edward VI, dying shortly after his birth.

Sfax 34 45N 10 43E The second largest city in Tunisia and a major port on the Gulf of Gabes. It developed as an early trade centre and still fulfils that role today, exporting phosphates, olive oil, cotton and woollen goods, and sponges. Population (1984): 231 911.

Sforza An Italian family that ruled Milan from 1450 to 1499, 1512 to 1515, and 1522 to 1535. Originating in Romagna as the Attendoli, its name was changed to Sforza (Italian: force) by the condottiere **Muzio Attendoli** (1369–1424). His son **Francesco Sforza** obtained Milan by his marriage (1441) to Bianca Maria, the only child of Filippo Maria *Visconti. Francesco was succeeded by **Galeazzo Maria Sforza** (1444–76), a notable patron of the arts. Soon after his assassination his brother **Lodovico Sforza** (1452–1508), known as Lodovico il Moro (the Moor), seized power (1480) from Galeazzo's son **Gian Galeazzo Sforza** (1469–94). Lodovico made Milan one of the most powerful Italian states and was also an outstanding patron of artists, including Leonardo da Vinci. He was expelled from the duchy in 1499 by Louis XII of France. After a brief restoration (1512–15), the Sforza were again ousted by the French but in 1522 Lodovico's son **Francesco Maria Sforza** (1495–1535) was re-established by Emperor Charles V. With the failure of the line at Francesco's death, Milan passed to Charles.

's Gravenhage. *See* Hague, The.

Shaba (former name: Katanga) A province in SE Zaïre, bordering on Zambia. Economically and politically the most advanced of the provinces, it was directly involved in the civil war in Zaïre following decolonization by Belgium in 1960 (*see also* Zaïre). It is an extremely important mining area (especially of copper, cobalt, and zinc) centred on Kolwezi. Area: 496 964 sq km (191 878 sq mi). Population (1981 est): 3 823 172. Capital: Lubumbashi.

Shache (So-ch'e *or* Yarkand) 38 27N 77 16E A town in NW China, in Xinjiang Uygur AR on a fertile oasis in the *Tarim Basin. It is an agricultural and trading centre on the *Silk Road to Europe. Population (1975 est): 25 000.

Shackleton, Sir Ernest Henry (1874–1922) British

explorer. He accompanied *Scott's expedition of 1901–04 and on his own expedition in 1908–09 nearly reached the South Pole. In an expedition of 1914–16 his ship, the *Endurance*, was marooned but he and his men reached Elephant Island by sledge and boats. With five others he then journeyed 1300 km (800 mi) to find relief. He died on his fourth expedition.

shad A food fish, belonging to a genus (*Alosa*) related to herrings, that occurs in the N Atlantic, Mediterranean, and North Sea. It has one or a succession of black spots along each side and a notch in the upper jaw. They migrate in large shoals to spawn in fresh waters. The allis shad (*A. alosa*), about 75 cm long, and the smaller twaite shad (*A. fallax*) are European species.

shaddock An evergreen tree, *Citrus grandis*, also called pomelo, native to SE Asia and cultivated in tropical regions of the Old and New Worlds. Growing 6–13 m high, it bears pale-yellow oval fruits, with coarse thick skins and bitter-tasting pulp, which are sometimes eaten or used to make liqueurs. Family: *Rutaceae*. *See also* Citrus.

shadoof An ancient water-raising device still used, especially in Egypt and S India, for irrigation. It consists of a pole mounted on a pivot with a bucket at one end and a counterbalancing weight at the other.

Shadwell, Thomas (c. 1642–92) British dramatist. His varied dramatic works included the comedies *Epsom Wells* (1672) and *The Virtuoso* (1676). He sustained a lengthy political and literary feud with *Dryden, who satirized him in *Absalom and Achitophel* (1681) and *MacFlecknoe* (1682). He succeeded Dryden as poet laureate in 1688.

Shaffer, Peter (1926–) British dramatist. He established his reputation with the domestic drama *Five-Finger Exercise* (1958). His ambitious epic treatment of the Spanish conquest of Peru, *The Royal Hunt of the Sun* (1964), was filmed and made into an opera. His later plays include *Equus* (1973), *Amadeus* (1979), *Yonadab* (1985), and *Lettice and Lovage* (1987). His twin brother **Anthony Shaffer** (1926–) is also a playwright, best known for the thriller *Sleuth* (1970).

Shaftesbury, Anthony Ashley Cooper, 1st Earl of (1621–83) English statesman. Initially a royalist in the Civil War he came to support the parliamentarians and in the 1650s sat in Oliver Cromwell's parliaments. He gained Cromwell's distrust and participated in the Restoration of Charles II (1660), becoming chancellor of the exchequer (1661–72), lord chancellor (1672–73), and a member of the political group called the *Cabal. Dismissed in 1673 he led the movement to exclude the Roman Catholic James, Duke of York (later James II), from the succession. Charged with treason in 1681, the case was dismissed but Shaftesbury fled to Amsterdam, where he died. He was satirized as the Achitophel in Dryden's *Absalom and Achitophel* (1681). His grandson **Anthony Ashley Cooper, 3rd Earl of Shaftesbury** (1671–1713) was educated under the guidance of *Locke and is best known for his collection of essays, *Characteristics of Men, Manners, Opinions, Times* (1711) on a variety of philosophical and other topics. In opposition to *Hobbes, he held that men were born with a natural love of virtue.

Anthony Ashley Cooper, 7th Earl of Shaftesbury (1801–85) was a reformer and philanthropist. He became an MP in 1826 and as chairman of the lunacy commission from 1834 obtained reform of the lunacy laws (1845). His great work for factory reform achieved the ten-hour day for factory workers (1847) and his Coal Mines Act (1842) abolished the system of child apprenticeship and the employment in mines of women and of children under 13. With the Climbing Boys Act (1840) he ended the employment of children as chimney sweeps. He also established lodging houses for the poor and was prominent in the *ragged schools movement.

shag A small *cormorant, *Phalacrocorax aristotelis*, confined to rocky coasts and offshore islands of Europe and North Africa. It is 75 cm long and has a glossy green-black plumage with a distinct crest in the breeding season. It feeds on fish.

Shah Jahan (1592–1666) Emperor of India (1628–58) of the Mogul dynasty; the son of *Jahangir. His powerful reign was as ruthless as his means of attaining it; he put his nearest relatives to death in 1628. His passion for fine architecture produced such monuments as the *Taj Mahal and the Delhi Red Fort. He was deposed by his son *Aurangzeb.

Shahn, Ben (1898–1969) Lithuanian-born artist, who lived in New York from 1906. He is best known for his social realist and political paintings, notably the series (1931–32) on the Italian anarchists Nicola Sacco and Bartolomeo Vanzetti.

Shah of Iran. *See* Mohammed Reza Pahlavi; Reza Shah Pahlavi.

Shaka (c. 1787–1828) Zulu chief, who made the Zulu nation the strongest in S Africa and set the period of warfare called the *Mfecane in motion. Shaka claimed the Zulu chieftainship in about 1816, introduced military reforms, and ruthlessly expanded his possessions. He was stabbed to death by his half-brothers Dingane and Mhlangana.

Shakers An austere sect originating in England as an offshoot of the *Quakers (1747). Led by Ann Lee (Mother Ann; d. 1784), in whose person they believed the Second Coming of Christ to be accomplished (*see* millenarianism), the Shakers founded a colony in the USA (1774), where they flourished until the 20th century. Celibacy, faith healing, common ownership of property, prescribed modes of dress, separation from the world in self-regulating communities, and abstinence from tobacco and alcohol characterized their way of life. Known more formally as the Millennial Church, they received their popular name from their practice of violent trembling in religious ecstasies during their meetings.

WILLIAM SHAKESPEARE *An engraving by Martin Droeshout, perhaps based on a portrait from life, which was printed in early editions of Shakespeare's works.*

Shakespeare, William (1564–1616) English dramatist,

universally recognized as the greatest English writer. The son of a tradesman who became high bailiff (mayor) of Stratford-upon-Avon in 1568, he was educated at the local grammar school and in 1582 married a local girl, Anne Hathaway, by whom he had three children. Soon afterwards he went to London, where he became an actor in the leading theatrical company, the Lord Chamberlain's Men (called the King's Men after 1603). The historical tetralogy comprising the three parts of *Henry VI* and *Richard III* were his first plays (1589–92). His dramatic poems *Venus and Adonis* (1593) and *The Rape of Lucrece* (1594) were dedicated to his patron Henry Wriothesley, 3rd Earl of *Southampton. His *Sonnets* (1609), probably written at this time, betray nothing of his private life despite their themes of love and friendship. His early comedies (1593–95) were *Love's Labour's Lost, The Two Gentlemen of Verona,* and *The Taming of the Shrew*. These were followed (1595–1600) by *A Midsummer Night's Dream, The Merchant of Venice, Much Ado About Nothing, Twelfth Night,* and *As You Like It*. During this period he also wrote his first significant tragedy, *Romeo and Juliet,* as well as *Richard II* and *Julius Caesar*. In 1597 he bought New Place, a large house in Stratford, and later became a shareholder in the Globe Theatre in London and bought other property in London and Stratford. The two parts of *Henry IV* were completed before *Hamlet, Othello, King Lear,* and *Macbeth,* his major tragedies, which were written between 1600 and 1606. His final experimental plays, including *The Winter's Tale* (c. 1610) and *The Tempest* (c. 1611), were written for the educated audience of the indoor theatre at Blackfriars, which the King's Men had acquired in 1608. In about 1611 he retired to Stratford, where he died. The first collected edition of his works, known as the First Folio and containing 36 plays, was published in 1623. His other plays were: *The Comedy of Errors, Titus Andronicus, King John, Henry V, The Merry Wives of Windsor, Antony and Cleopatra, Coriolanus, Troilus and Cressida, Measure for Measure, All's Well That Ends Well, Timon of Athens, Pericles, Cymbeline,* and (with John *Fletcher) *Henry VIII* and *The Two Noble Kinsmen*.

Shakhty 47 43N 40 16E A city in the Soviet Union, in the W RSFSR. Situated in the E Donets Basin, it is a major coalmining centre. Population (1981 est): 214 000.

shale A fine-grained *sedimentary rock that splits easily along the closely spaced bedding planes as a result of the alignment of the clay mineral particles parallel to the bedding planes. Shales may disintegrate in water but do not become plastic. They are softer and lighter than slate, which is a fine-grained *metamorphic rock.

shallot A hardy perennial herbaceous plant, *Allium ascalonium,* probably of Asiatic origin. Its small hollow cylindrical leaves are often used for dressing food and in salads. Its small angular bulbs occur in garlic-like clusters and are used for flavouring and pickling. Family: *Liliaceae.*

shamanism The religious beliefs and practices common in certain tribal societies of Asia, such as the *Samoyed. The term is also applied to North American Indian practices. The shaman is a tribal priest generally felt to be possessed by a spirit or deity and hence to have supernatural powers. He is liable to trances or ecstasies, may diagnose and cure disease, find lost or stolen goods, or foretell the future. He is usually a source of beneficial (white) magic. As the intermediary between man and the spirit world, he may also act as the tribal ruler and judge. The office may be hereditary or there may be a long training period.

Shamir, Yitzhak (1915–) Israeli statesman, born in Poland; prime minister (1983–84, 1986–). He led the Israeli Freedom Fighters (1940–41), served in Israel's secret service (1955–65), and was foreign minister (1980–83). When a coalition was formed in 1984, he became deputy prime minister under a special power-sharing agreement with Shimon *Peres.

shamrock Any of several plants bearing leaves with three leaflets, especially various *clovers, black *medick (*Medicago lupulina*), and *wood sorrel (*Oxalis acetosella*). St Patrick is said to have adopted the shamrock as a symbol of the Holy Trinity and it is worn on St Patrick's Day.

Shandong (*or* Shantung) A province in NE China, on the Yellow Sea, with central mountains. Densely populated, its fertile farmland produces chiefly wheat and cotton. From early times it has been an important trading area. Floods and famine in the 19th and 20th centuries have led to much emigration northwards. Area: 153 300 sq km (59 189 sq mi). Population (1980 est): 72 310 000. Capital: Jinan.

Shandong Peninsula (*or* Shantung Peninsula) A hilly peninsula in E China. Together with the *Liaodong Peninsula opposite, it forms the mouth of the Gulf of Chihli.

Shanghai 31 13N 121 25E An administratively autonomous port in E China, on the Yangtze estuary. The largest city in China, it is its chief port and industrial city. Its many educational establishments include two universities. It grew rapidly after it was opened to foreign trade in 1842, coming under British, US, and French rule until World War II. Industries include steel, textiles, chemicals, shipbuilding, engineering, and publishing. Population (1982): 6 270 000.

Shankar, Ravi (1920–) Indian *sitar player. He has popularized Indian music in the West, influencing the Beatles, performing with Yehudi Menuhin, and inspiring André Previn to write a sitar concerto.

Shannon, River The longest river in the Republic of Ireland. Rising in NW Co Cavan, it flows S to Limerick and then W into an estuary 113 km (70 mi) long, before entering the Atlantic Ocean. It powers Ireland's main hydroelectric plant. Length: 386 km (240 mi).

Shansi. *See* Shanxi.

Shantou (*or* Swatow) 23 23N 116 39E A port in SE China, in Guangdong province on the South China Sea. It has developed greatly since 1949 and its industries include food processing and shipbuilding. Population (1980 est): 621 000.

Shantung. *See* Shandong.

Shantung Peninsula. *See* Shandong Peninsula.

Shanxi (Shan-hsi *or* Shansi) A province in NE China. It is mainly a high hilly plateau, prone to drought, although irrigation and reafforestation projects are now under way. It is important for its coal and iron reserves and the industry they supply. Its relatively sparse Chinese population lives chiefly by keeping animals and growing cotton and cereals. It is famous for its traditional opera, metalwork, and pottery. *History*: a buffer zone between the settled Chinese and the nomadic tribes of the N and W in the middle ages, it became politically stable in about the 14th century. In the 18th and 19th centuries it was famous for its merchants and bankers. Opposition to foreigners was strong and the *Boxer Rising broke out here (1900). Its industry was established by the warlord Yan Xi-shan (*or* Yen Hsi-shan; ruled 1911–49). Area: 157 099 sq km (60 656 sq mi). Population (1980 est): 24 470 000. Capital: Taiyuan.

Shapur II (309–79 AD) King of Persia (309–79) of the Sasanian dynasty; the posthumous son of his father and predecessor. During his long and successful wars to recover lost territory in Armenia and Mesopotamia from Rome, the emperor *Julian was killed and Christians, suspected as followers of Rome's official religion, were persecuted.

shares. *See* stocks and shares.

Shari, River. *See* Chari, River.

shari'ah. *See* Islamic law.

Sharjah. *See* United Arab Emirates.

shark A *cartilaginous fish belonging to the worldwide order *Selachii* (about 250 species). Ranging in size from the smallest *dogfish to the enormous.*whale shark, they have a torpedo-shaped body with a muscular tail used in swimming, five to seven pairs of gill slits on the sides of the head, and numerous sharp teeth. They are chiefly marine and carnivorous, feeding on fish and invertebrates but in some cases, plankton, carrion, and other vertebrates. They produce live young or lay eggs. Subclass: *Elasmobranchii*.

Sharon, Plain of A coastal plain in Israel, extending 80 km (50 mi) between Haifa and Tel Aviv-Yafo. It is noted for the production of citrus fruit.

Sharp, Cecil (James) (1859–1924) British musician. He practised law in Australia, then turned to music and held several posts as an organist, returning to England in 1892. From then on he systematically collected, edited, and published English folksongs, for which he is best remembered.

Sharpeville A Black African town in South Africa, in the S Transvaal near Vereeniging. It was the scene of a riot on 21 March, 1960, in which a crowd of African demonstrators were fired on by the police. Over 60 of the demonstrators were killed and many others wounded.

Shastri, Shri Lal Bahadur (1904–66) Indian statesman; prime minister (1964–66). As a young man he was imprisoned by the British while a member of Gandhi's noncooperation movement. He held four ministerial positions before becoming prime minister. His greatest achievement was in negotiating the ceasefire agreement with *Ayub Khan after the India-Pakistan war. He died the following day.

Shatt al-Arab A river in SE Iraq, formed by the confluence of the Rivers Tigris and Euphrates. It enters the Persian Gulf via a delta in Kuwait, Iraq, and Iran, passing Basra and Abadan along its course. Length: 190 km (118 mi).

Shaw, Artie (Arthur Arshawsky; 1910–) US jazz clarinetist and band leader, who introduced strings into his swing band in 1935. His version of Cole Porter's "Begin the Beguine," recorded in 1938, was a great success. After 1955 he gave up his band to write and compose.

Shaw, George Bernard (1856–1950) Irish dramatist, critic, and man of letters, born in Dublin. He went to London in 1876 and after writing five novels, which were unsuccessful, he became a music and drama critic, an active socialist, and one of the founding members of the Fabian Society. He soon made a reputation with his brilliant speeches and pamphlets supporting the Fabian cause. He popularized the works of Wagner (*The Perfect Wagnerite*, 1898) and Ibsen, finding in the work of the latter a remedy for the current intellectual poverty of the London theatre. His views were summed up in *The Quintessence of Ibsenism* (1891). At first finding no large commercial audience for his plays, Shaw wrote extensive explanations (and stage directions) for the printed editions of his works. The Prefaces to his plays are consequently elaborate commentaries on the social and moral issues involved. He wrote more than 40 plays, the first of which, *Widowers' Houses* (1892), an attack on slum landlords, was printed in *Plays Pleasant and Unpleasant* (1898), which included *The Philanderer*, *Mrs Warren's Profession* (on prostitution), and the "pleasant" comedies *Arms and the Man*, *You Never Can Tell*, *Candida*, and *The Man of Destiny*. With *Three Plays for Puritans* (published 1901), which comprised *The Devil's Disciple*, *Caesar and Cleopatra*, and *Captain Brassbound's Conversion*, Shaw achieved a certain popularity. The epic comedy of ideas, *Man and Superman* (1903), was based on the Don Juan legend and developed Shaw's ideas on the "life force" and social evolution; it was followed by *John Bull's Other Island* (1904) and *Major Barbara* (1905). His next plays were *The Doctor's Dilemma* (1906), *Getting Married* (1908), *Misalliance* (1910), and *Androcles and the Lion* (1913). *Pygmalion* (1913) was an outstanding commercial success and became a perennial favourite (and the basis of the musical *My Fair Lady*, 1955). It was followed by *Heartbreak House* (1917) and the series of plays entitled *Back to Methuselah* (1921). The historical drama *St Joan* (1924), on Joan of Arc, is generally regarded as his greatest work. His late plays (from 1929 onwards) include *The Apple Cart*, *The Village Wooing*,

and *In Good King Charles's Golden Days*. In 1925 he was awarded the Nobel Prize. Among many important prose works are *The Intelligent Woman's Guide to Socialism and Capitalism* (1928) and *The Black Girl in Search of God* (1932).

Shaw, (Richard) Norman (1831–1912) British architect. Principally known as a domestic architect, Shaw, in partnership with W. E. Nesfield (1835–88), broke the hold of the *gothic revival on English architecture. Using a variety of styles, including gothic, Tudor, Queen Anne, and later *classicism, Shaw produced buildings, such as Swan House, Chelsea (1876), which were less impressive, but more comfortable, than those of his predecessors. His works continue to influence British architecture.

Shawinigan 46 33N 72 45W A city in E Canada, in Quebec on the St Maurice River near waterfalls 46 m (150 ft) high. Developed around 1900 to utilize their hydroelectric potential, Shawinigan is a centre for pulp and paper, chemicals (especially calcium carbide), and other heavy industries. Population (1981): 23 011.

Shcherbakov. *See* Rybinsk.

shear stress A form of *stress in which the applied force acts tangentially to the surface of the body. Thus a shear stress applied to the top of a pack of cards would cause the cards to slide over each other.

shearwater One of a group of birds (about 15 species) of the oceanic family *Procellariidae*. 27–90 cm long, shearwaters have a dark plumage (some species have white underparts), long narrow wings, and slender bills; they feed on fish from the sea surface. The great shearwater (*Puffinus gravis*) breeds in the South Atlantic, migrating to spend summer and autumn in the North Atlantic. The Manx shearwater (*P. puffinus*) breeds off British and Mediterranean coasts and winters in E South America and Australia. Order: Procellariiformes. *See also* petrel.

sheathbill A small compact scavenging bird belonging to a family (*Chionidae*; 2 species) occurring on coasts near Antarctica. Sheathbills are 40 cm long and have a thick white plumage, shortish wings, and a horny sheath covering the nostrils at the base of the bill. Order: *Charadriiformes* (gulls, plovers, etc.).

Sheba In the Bible, a land corresponding to Sabaea in present-day Yemen (SW Arabia). It was known for its trade in spices and gold. Its most famous monarch was the Queen of Sheba who visited King Solomon in Jerusalem (I Kings 10.1–13). According to Ethiopian tradition, she bore him a son, the first King of Ethiopia.

Shechem. *See* Nablus.

Sheene, Barry (Stephen Frank S.; 1950–) British racing motorcyclist, who in 1976 won the 500 cc world championship. In 1977 he set a current record on the Francorchamps road circuit, lapping in 3 minutes 50.3 seconds with an average speed of 220.721 km per hour (137.150 mph).

sheep A hoofed *ruminant mammal belonging to the genus *Ovis* (7 species), native to mountainous regions of Eurasia and North America. Related to goats, sheep are generally 75–100 cm tall at the shoulder and weigh 50–150 kg. They have a compact body with slender legs and a short tail and the coat ranges from white to brown in colour. Males (rams) have large spiralled horns; females (ewes) have smaller less curved horns. There are over 200 breeds of domestic sheep (*O. aries*), probably descended from the Asian red sheep (*O. orientalis*), which are reared worldwide for meat, wool, and milk (*see* livestock farming). They typically have a long woolly coat, unlike the coarser coat of wild sheep. Family: *Bovidae*. *See also* aoudad; argali; bighorn; mouflon.

sheepdog A dog used for handling sheep. Many breeds are used for this purpose, including the *collie, *German shepherd dog, *Old English sheepdog, and *Shetland sheepdog, as well as crossbred derivatives. Sheepdog trials are held in the UK, in which teams of dog and handler are awarded points for driving, dividing, and penning a group of sheep over a marked course.

sheep ked A flat wingless fly, *Melophagus ovinus*, also called sheep tick, that is parasitic upon sheep. Both sexes are bloodsuckers and are attached to the fleece, often causing serious skin irritations. The larvae are retained within the body of the female until they reach maturity, when they are deposited on the ground. Family: *Hippoboscidae*.

Sheerness 51 27N 0 45E A town in SE England, in Kent at the mouth of the River Medway on the Isle of Sheppey. Sheerness is a port with modern cargo-handling facilities and a holiday resort. The former naval dockyard in Sheerness, founded about 1665, is now an industrial estate. Population (1981): 11 250.

Sheffield 52 23N 1 30W A city in N England, the largest in South Yorkshire on the River Don at the edge of the Pennines. It is world famous for steel, produced here since the mid-18th century, although Sheffield knives were known in Chaucer's day. Special and alloy steels are now more important than the traditional cutlery and tool-making trades, although these still flourish. Sheffield also produces silverware and plate, glass, and engineering products. There is a cathedral (partly 15th century) and a university (1905). Bomb damage (1940) and slum clearance campaigns have enabled town planners to create major modern developments. Population (1981): 477 142.

Sheffield plate Articles that are made by fusing a silver coat onto copper. The process was discovered (c. 1742) by Thomas Boulsover (1704–88), a Sheffield cutler. Used as a substitute for solid silver, Sheffield-plated articles, usually tableware, followed contemporary silver designs and were of the highest quality. By 1770 both sides of the copper were silvered and exposed copper on cut edges was concealed by silver borders. Sheffield plate became obsolete after the introduction of electroplating in the mid-19th century, but Sheffield-plated articles are now much sought after.

Shelburne, William Petty Fitzmaurice, 2nd Earl of (1737–1805) British statesman; prime minister (1782–83). An advocate of conciliation towards the American colonies, his ministry negotiated the Treaty of Paris (1783), which ended the American Revolution.

shelduck A large *duck, *Tadorna tadorna*, found around coasts of W and central Eurasia. It is 65 cm long and has black-and-white plumage with a green head, chestnut shoulders, and a red bill, which in the male has a red knob at the base. It feeds chiefly on molluscs and nests in disused rabbit burrows.

shellac A natural thermoplastic *resin made from the secretions of the lac insect, *Laccifer lacca*, which is parasitic on certain trees in India and Thailand. It was formerly used for moulding records but has now been replaced by vinyl resins. Its solution in alcohol is used as a varnish and in lacquers. It is also used in sealing wax, printing inks, and electrical insulation.

Shelley, Percy Bysshe (1792–1822) British poet. Expelled from Oxford University for publishing a pamphlet defending atheism in 1811, he married Harriet Westbrook and settled briefly in the Lake District. He wrote the revolutionary poem *Queen Mab* in 1813 and soon after left for the Continent, where he met Byron. From 1818 until his death he lived in Italy, where he wrote the verse dramas *The Cenci* (1819) and *Prometheus Unbound* (1818–19), the elegy *Adonais* (1821) prompted by the death of Keats, and much lyrical poetry. He was drowned in a sailing accident off the Italian coast. His wife **Mary Wollstonecraft Shelley** (*born* Godwin; 1797–1851), British novelist, was the daughter of William *Godwin and Mary *Wollstonecraft. She eloped with Shelley in 1814 and married him in 1816. In addition to her best-known book, *Frankenstein: the Modern Prometheus* (1818), she wrote romances and travel books and edited Shelley's *Poetical Works* (1839).

shells The hard casings secreted by some animals to protect themselves or their eggs. The term usually refers to the shells of molluscs, which consist largely of calcium carbonate and come in a wide variety of shapes and sizes. They may be spiralled or flat, with one valve (in gastropods, such as snails) or two (in bivalves, such as mussels). A single valve of a giant clam may weigh up to 90 kg. The pearly nautilus has a many chambered shell, which provides buoyancy, while the female paper nautilus (*Argonauta*) secretes a shell-like cradle to transport its eggs and young. The shells of marine molluscs, particularly gastropods, are prized by collectors. □ p. 1106.

Shelter (National Campaign for the Homeless) A British organization, founded in 1966, to raise funds for housing projects and housing aid centres for the homeless and to campaign for more and better housing. Its 300 voluntary groups also give advice on tenancy matters. Director: Neil McIntosh.

Shenandoah River A river in the E USA, flowing mainly NE through Virginia to join the Potomac River as its main tributary. It was a major *Civil War battleground (*see also* Sheridan, Philip H.). The **Shenandoah National Park**, in the Blue Ridge section of the Appalachian Mountains, lies to the S of the river. Length: 88 km (55 mi).

Shensi. *See* Shenxi.

Shenstone, William (1714–63) British poet. His best-known poem is *The Schoolmistress* (1737), influenced by Spenser. He was a contemporary of Samuel Johnson at Oxford, helped to renew interest in traditional ballads, and developed his pioneering ideas about landscape gardening on his Worcestershire estate.

Shenxi (Shen-hsi *or* Shensi) A mountainous province in central China. In the Wei He (River) and Han River valleys wheat, millet, and cotton are grown. Coal, iron, and oil are also produced. *History*: the Wei He valley was the centre of successive Chinese dynasties from 1122 BC. Its economy rested on an impressive irrigation system from about 300 BC until about 600 AD, when it began to deteriorate. From about 1860 until 1928 the N suffered from famines, epidemics, and civil wars. Following the *Long March, it was the communist base (1936–1949). Area: 195 800 sq km (75 598 sq mi). Population (1980 est): 28 070 000. Capital: Xi An.

Shenyang (former name: Mukden) 41 50N 123 26E A city in NE China, on the River Hun, the capital of Liaoning province and the site of its university. China's fourth largest city, it is a major industrial centre. The **Mukden Incident** (1931), an explosion on the Japanese-controlled South Manchurian Railway, was the pretext for the Japanese occupation of Manchuria (*see* Manchukuo). Population (1982): 4 020 000.

she oak. *See* Casuarina.

Shepard, Ernest Howard (1879–1976) British artist. A cartoonist for *Punch*, he is best remembered for his illustrations for *Winnie the Pooh* (1926), *Wind in the Willows* (1931), and many other children's books.

Shepard, Jr, Allan Bartlett (1923–) US astronaut, who on 5 May, 1961, became the first American in space. His flight, which came 23 days after *Gagarin's flight, lasted 15 minutes and reached a height of 185 km. He also commanded the Apollo 14 flight to the moon in 1971.

shepherd's purse An annual or biennial herb, *Caspella bursa-pastoris*, found growing as a weed throughout the world. It has a basal rosette of leaves and a branching leafy stem, 3–40 cm high, bearing tiny white flowers that produce small purse-shaped fruits. Its ability to self-pollinate produces distinctive local populations. Family: *Cruciferae.

Sheppard, Jack (1702–24) British criminal. He became famous for his many daring and ingenious escapes from Newgate and other prisons. His adventures were celebrated in contemporary ballads and plays.

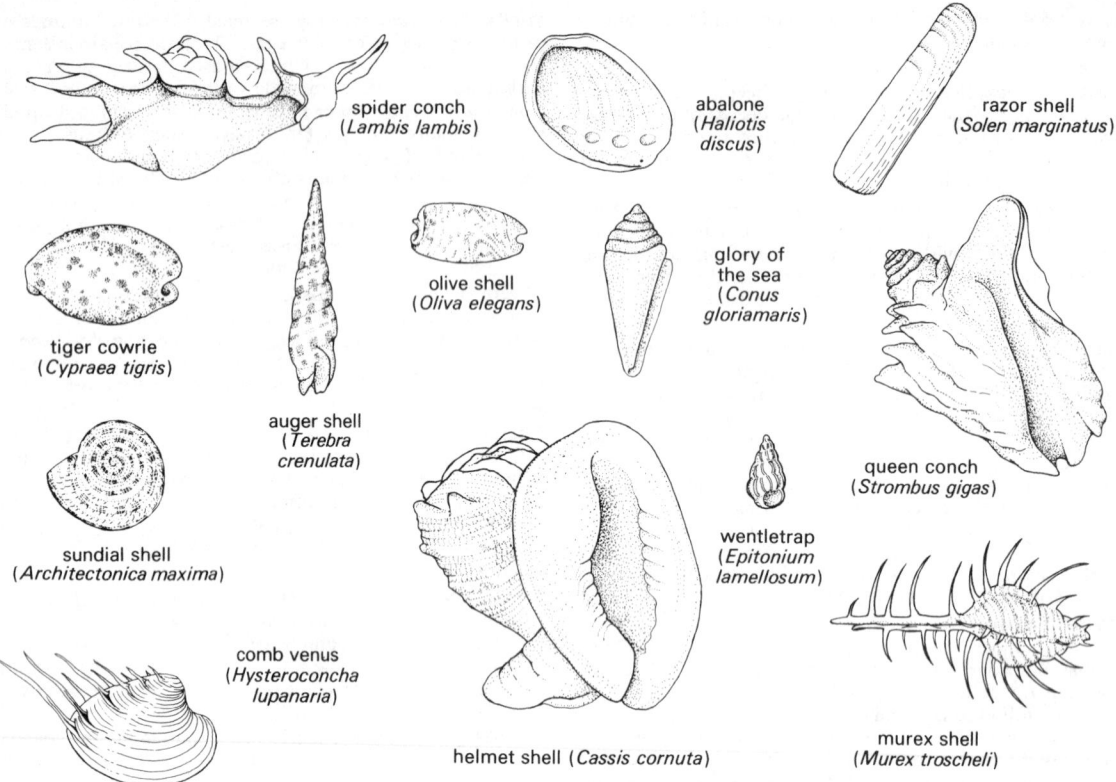

spider conch
(*Lambis lambis*)

abalone
(*Haliotis
discus*)

razor shell
(*Solen marginatus*)

tiger cowrie
(*Cypraea tigris*)

olive shell
(*Oliva elegans*)

glory of
the sea
(*Conus
gloriamaris*)

auger shell
(*Terebra
crenulata*)

queen conch
(*Strombus gigas*)

sundial shell
(*Architectonica maxima*)

wentletrap
(*Epitonium
lamellosum*)

comb venus
(*Hysteroconcha
lupanaria*)

helmet shell (*Cassis cornuta*)

murex shell
(*Murex troscheli*)

SHELLS   *A selection of mollusc shells, drawn to scale (the largest, the helmet shell, is 35 cm long). All these species are marine and several, including the glory of the sea, are collectors' items.*

Shepparton   A city in Australia, in N Victoria. It is within the Goulborn Valley Irrigation Area and is a major centre for the soft-fruit industry. Population (1981): 28 373.

Sheppey, Isle of   51 25N 0 50E An island in SE England, off the N coast of Kent in the River Thames estuary. It is agriculturally important, producing cereals and vegetables; sheep (from which its name derives) are also raised.

sheradizing   A process for galvanizing iron or steel (i.e. protecting the metal from corrosion by coating it with zinc) by placing it in a rotating drum with zinc dust and heating to about 260°C. At this temperature the iron and zinc amalgamate forming an internal layer of zinc-iron alloys and an external layer of pure zinc. Named after the British inventor Sherard Cowper-Coles (d. 1935).

Sheraton, Thomas   (1751–1806) British furniture designer. Settling in London (c. 1790), he made his name with the designs in his *Cabinet-Maker and Upholsterer's Drawing Book* (1791–94). Influenced by *Adam and contemporary French styles, these designs were characterized by elegance, delicacy, straight lines, and inlaid decoration. Ordained in 1800, he also wrote religious works.

Sherbrooke   45 24N 71 54W A city in E Canada, in S Quebec. Founded in 1794, it is the farming, transportation, commercial, and cultural centre of the *Eastern Townships. Its manufactures include textiles, machinery, paper, and dairy produce. Sherbrooke houses the French-speaking University of Sherbrooke (founded 1954). Population (1981): 74 315.

Sheridan, Philip H(enry)   (1831–88) Federal general in the US *Civil War. A regular soldier, he saw Civil War action in Tennessee and Georgia (1862). Appointed to command the Army of the Shenandoah, he led a number of destructive raids into Confederate territory, laying waste the Shenan-

doah Valley itself. His deployments in April, 1865, forced General Robert Lee to surrender at Appomattox.

Sheridan, Richard Brinsley   (1751–1816) Anglo-Irish dramatist. Born in Dublin, he lived in England from childhood. In 1772 he eloped with a fashionable singer. He wrote witty comedies of manners, of which the best known are *The Rivals* (1775), in which his most famous character, Mrs Malaprop, appears, and *School for Scandal* (1777). He was a manager of the Drury Lane Theatre and a Whig MP from 1780 to 1812, during which time he was recognized as being one of the great parliamentary orators. His last years were clouded by financial problems and the disappointment of his political ambitions.

sheriff   An official with administrative and judicial responsibilities in England, Scotland, and the USA. Originating in the 10th century as the shire reeve, the king's representative in the shire and at the shire court, the sheriff continued in this role under the Normans, who expanded his judicial competence. Powerful and often corrupt, the sheriffs' powers were reduced by Henry II (reigned 1154–89) and succeeding kings and became little more than ceremonial in the 16th century. Sheriffs in England and Scotland are appointed by the Crown to each county; the City of London, however, has two sheriffs, elected by the Corporation. In England their duties under the Sheriffs Act (1887) include executing writs, attending judges, and responsibility for returns at parliamentary elections and for the safe custody of prisoners. In Scotland sheriffs are also the chief county judges. In the USA they are elected and are the principal law enforcement officers in a county.

Sherman, William Tecumseh   (1820–91) Federal general in the US *Civil War. Serving in the West, he captured Atlanta, Georgia (September, 1864), and then executed the March to the Sea—Atlanta to Savannah, thus dividing the

Confederacy. In 1865 he turned and resumed his march through the Carolinas towards Raleigh, North Carolina. These campaigns contributed enormously to the Confederate defeat. His strategic planning, tactical skill, and leadership made him one of the great Civil War generals. His brother **John Sherman** (1823–1900) was a Congressman (1855–77, 1881–97) with a specialist interest in finance. The Sherman Anti-Trust Act (1890) was largely his work.

Sherpa A people of Nepal who speak a dialect of Tibetan. They are farmers, cattle breeders, and traders and also spin and weave woollen cloth. They often act as porters for Himalayan expeditions. With Edmund Hillary, the Sherpa *Tenzing Norgay reached the summit of Everest in 1953.

Sherrington, Sir Charles Scott (1857–1952) British physiologist, whose work provided the basis for present-day understanding of the nervous system. Sherrington demonstrated that reflex actions in higher animals and man are integrated with the rest of the nervous system. He proposed the terms neurone for a nerve cell and synapse for the point at which an impulse is transmitted between nerve cells. He was awarded the OM (1924) and shared a Nobel Prize (1932) with Lord *Adrian.

sherry A fortified *wine, made around Jerez de la Frontera (whence its name) in S Spain; similar wine is now also made elsewhere. It is blended by the *solera* system: sherry is drawn off from several different casks to make a blend and those casks are then topped up with younger sherry, maintaining its future character. There are two basic types of sherry: fino is a pale dry wine on which the *flor* (flower or yeast) has developed fully; oloroso is a rich full-bodied wine on which the *flor* is little developed. Other types of sherry are related to these two, for example amontillado is a strong dark derivative of a fino; cream sherry is a sweetened oloroso.

's Hertogenbosch (*or* Den Bosch) 51 41N 5 19E A town in the S central Netherlands, the capital of North Brabant province. It has a famous gothic cathedral (rebuilt 1419–1520). The painter Hieronymus Bosch was born here. Population (1981 est): 88 585.

Sherwood Forest An ancient forest in the Midlands of England, in Nottinghamshire. Once an extensive royal hunting ground, it is now much reduced; it is famous for its associations with Robin Hood.

Shetland Islands (*or* Shetland; official name until 1974: Zetland) A group of about 100 islands in the North Sea, off the N coast of Scotland. It became an island authority under local government reorganization in 1975. The largest islands include Mainland, Yell, and Unst. Agriculture, based on crofting, chiefly produces wool; Shetland ponies are also bred. Herring fishing, centred on Lerwick, is important. The few industries include fish curing and knitting (especially in the Shetland and Fair Isle patterns). The islands are a base for North Sea oil exploitation with a pipeline from the Brent field. Area: 1427 sq km (551 sq mi). Population (1981): 26 716. Administrative centre: Lerwick.

Shetland pony The smallest British pony breed, native to the Shetland Islands. It has a sturdy compact body with short legs and a relatively large head. The mane and tail are profuse and the coat becomes thick in winter. Formerly used as pack and pit ponies, Shetlands are now popular pets for children. Height: up to 1.05 m (10½ hands).

Shetland sheepdog (*or* Sheltie) A breed of dog developed in the Shetland Islands for working sheep. Related to and resembling the *collie, it has a soft undercoat and a long outer coat and may be black, brown, or blue-grey, with white and tan markings. Height: 36 cm (dogs); 35 cm (bitches).

Shevardnadze, Eduard (1928–   ) Soviet statesman; minister for foreign affairs (1985–   ). A protégé of Gorbachov, he played a key role in arms negotiations with the USA in 1987.

shield An extensive rigid block of Precambrian rocks unaffected by later periods of mountain building. Shields are the oldest continental regions, frequently of igneous granite or metamorphic gneiss. The shields were once the site of Precambrian mountain belts, although the mountains have been completely eroded. The **Canadian** (*or* Laurentian) **Shield** is the largest, covering several million square kilometres of NE North America. The **Baltic Shield** (*or* Fennoscandia), reaching the surface in Finland and Sweden, is another well-known example.

shield bug A *plant bug, also called stink bug, belonging to the families *Acanthosomidae, Cydnidae, Scutelleridae,* or *Pentatomidae.* Shield bugs have heavy shieldlike bodies, 5–50 mm long, and are usually green or brown. They suck insect or plant juices, often becoming agricultural pests. Some species also foul plants with an evil-smelling secretion. □insect.

shield fern A tufted *fern of the widely distributed genus *Polystichum* (about 135 species). It has a scaly stem and tapering branched fronds made up of toothed pointed leaflets. Small round clusters of spore capsules (sori) occur in rows on the undersides of the leaflets. The soft shield fern (*P. setiferum*) and the hard shield fern (*P. aculeatum*) are common species. Family: *Aspidiaceae.*

Shih-chia-chuang. *See* Shijiazhuang.

Shih Huang Ti. *See* Qin.

Shih tzu A breed of small dog originating in Tibet and introduced to the UK in the 1930s. It has a long body with short legs, a short muzzle, and drooping ears. The long straight coat can be of various colours and the plumed tail is held over the back. Height: about 26 cm.

Shiites (*or* Shiah) The general term applied to a number of different Muslim sects, the main body of which is dominant in Iran. The distinctive belief of the Shiites, which differentiates them from the other major Muslim group, the *Sunnites, is that *Ali, the fourth caliph, is the only legitimate successor of Mohammed. The leader of Islam, the *imam, must be a descendant of Ali and has exclusive authority in secular and religious matters. The Shiites differ among themselves as to the true line of imams after a certain stage. Some, known as "the twelvers," expect the return of the 12th imam (d. 9th century AD) at the end of time, while others recognize a different line from the seventh imam.

Shijiazhuang (*or* Shih-chia-chuang) 38 04N 114 28E A city in NE China, the capital of Hebei province and the site of its university. A communications centre, its industries include coalmining, textiles, chemicals, and engineering. Population (1983 est): 1 070 000.

Shikoku The smallest of the four main islands of Japan, separated from Honshu and Kyushu by the Inland Sea. Mountainous and forested, its population is concentrated on the coastal plains, with industry mainly in the N. Copper is mined at Besshi; other products are fish, rice, grain, tobacco, mulberry, and camphor. Area: 17 759 sq km (6857 sq mi). Population (1984 est): 5 106 000. Chief cities: Matsuyama and Takamatsu.

Shillong 25 34N 91 53E A city in India, the capital of Meghalaya. Rebuilt following an earthquake in 1897, Shillong is a military base and agricultural trading centre and has a university (1973). Population (1981): 109 244.

Shiloh 32 03N 35 18E A city of Samaria in ancient N Palestine, now in Jordan. Hannah brought her son Samuel to this important Israelite religious centre to dedicate him to God in the temple where Eli was priest of the *Ark of the Covenant. Shiloh was the traditional sanctuary of the Ark until the Philistines destroyed the city and captured the Ark in the mid-11th century BC.

Shimonoseki 33 59N 130 58E A seaport in Japan, in SW Honshu, linked to *Kitakyushu by tunnels under the Shimonoseki Strait. The treaty ending the first Sino-Japanese War was signed here (1895). Industries include engineering, shipbuilding, chemicals, and fishing. Population (1980): 269 000.

shingles An infection caused by the *herpes zoster virus, which lodges in nerve cells in the spinal cord. Shingles affects adults who have had chickenpox as children. It usually starts with pain along the course of a sensory nerve, followed by a band of blisters round half of the body or face. The rash usually eventually disappears but the patient may be left with severe neuralgia.

Shinto The native religion of Japan. Shinto is primarily an attitude of nationalistic and aesthetic reverence towards familiar places and traditions, rather than a set of religious beliefs. However, the central themes are the belief in numerous usually amoral *kamis* or nature spirits, together with ancestor worship and an ideal of military chivalry.
The two principal *kamis* are the sun-goddess (reputedly mother of the emperor) and her brother the storm-god. The conflict between them expresses the creative and destructive forces of nature. The scriptures of Shinto, the *Ko ji ki* and the *Nihon Shoki*, are both semimythological histories of Japan, written around 720 AD. The hereditary priesthood officiates at ceremonies of birth, marriage, and death, ensuring ritual purification. After World War II, Shinto was disestablished as the state religion.

shinty (*or* camanachd) A Scottish 12-a-side stick-and-ball field game deriving from *hurling and similar to *hockey. A standard pitch is 146×73 m $(160 \times 80$ yd). The stick is called the "caman" and a goal, a "hail."

ship money A tax raised by English monarchs in times of emergency for the defence of the coast. It gained notoriety under Charles I, who levied it indiscriminately between 1634 and 1639. In 1637 John *Hampden was tried for refusing to pay ship money, which became a focus of resistance to Charles I and was pronounced illegal by the *Long Parliament.

ships Man's earliest sea voyages were probably made on rafts and in hollowed-out tree trunks. Larger and more stable vessels were certainly known to the ancient Egyptians, whose rock carvings and paintings depict ships that were made of planks and were propelled both by oars and sails. Other early mariners included the Chinese and the Phoenicians; the short broad 13th-century Phoenician merchant ships (known as round ships) were propelled by oars and a single square sail to catch the prevailing wind (*see* sailing). The Greeks developed biremes (with two banks of oars) and triremes (with three banks) as warships, especially strengthened for ramming enemy vessels. The Romans also relied on oars, but their larger grain ships, capable of carrying up to 300 tonnes of cargo, had a number of square sails. In the N the longships of the Vikings were double-ended and rose high out of the water to cope with the rough and windy North Sea; they still relied on oarsmen but the holes for the oars were fitted with shutters that could be closed when the ship was under sail. Developed in the 8th century AD, ships of this kind brought William the Conqueror to England. It was not until the 12th century and the stimulus of the Crusades that the art of using sails was sufficiently developed for oars to be dispensed with. Sailing into the wind was originally pioneered by the Chinese in their junks, but it was the Arabs who perfected the lateen sail, which made it a reliable means of propulsion for large ships. By the 14th century sailing ships were commonplace. The warships of the period had "castles" built at each end to house fighting men, and guns were usually carried on the forecastle. However, muzzle-loading cannons were too heavy to be mounted on the forecastle and by the end of the 15th century they were carried in gun ports low in the hull. During this period, too, the single-master with one large heavy sail gave way to the three-master with more manageable small sails and full rigging. The first warship of the English navy, the *Henri Grâce à Dieu*, was built for Henry VIII in 1514. During the next 300 years sailing ships developed in many ways, usually with the merchantmen following the innovations in hull design and rigging made by

the designers of warships. Sailing ships reached their zenith in the 19th-century *clippers, which remained supreme until Newcomen's *steam engine revolutionized seafaring. The first steamer to cross the Atlantic (in April, 1827) was the Dutch *Curaçao* (built 1826), the first British ship to do so (in April, 1838) being Brunel's *Great Western*, a wooden paddle steamer, which achieved recognition for steam by arriving in New York on the same day as a clipper that had left Cork three days before the *Great Western* had left Bristol. For the next century the N Atlantic crossing continued to be a proving ground for great ships. The propeller completely replaced the paddle and Parson's steam *turbine largely replaced the reciprocating engine. The Blue Riband, the trophy for the fastest Atlantic crossing, was won by the *Queen Mary* in 1938 and finally lost to the *United States* in 1952. Passenger travel across the Atlantic has now been almost entirely captured by the airlines; modern shipbuilding concentrates on cargo vessels, especially oil *tankers.
Warships in the age of steam were largely modelled on the turbine-driven *battleship *Dreadnought* (1906), which together with the *cruiser, *destroyer, *frigate, and *submarine dominated naval warfare in World War I. By World War II the *aircraft carrier had evolved and with its long-range striking power became the supreme weapon of the war at sea. However, since the middle of the 20th century the importance of the surface warship has diminished and the strength of navies is now reckoned in terms of their nuclear-powered submarines armed with long-range missiles.
Since the innovation of steam, the main developments in ships have been the use of *nuclear energy, especially in submarines, and the invention of the *Hovercraft and the *hydrofoil to remove the hull from the water in order to reduce drag. ⬜ pp. 1110–11.

shipworm A *bivalve mollusc belonging to the family *Teredidae*, also called pileworm. The shell plates of a shipworm are small with sharp ridges used for boring into wooden structures. The resulting burrow is lined with a limy material, encasing the long body (up to 180 cm). Shipworms can damage wooden ships, piers, etc.

Shiraz 29 38N 52 34E A town in S central Iran. It is a trading centre for the surrounding region and is connected by road to the port of Bushire; Pahlavi University was established here in 1945. Population (1985 est): 834 800.

shire A district, with a central town, used by the Anglo-Saxons as a unit of local government. Many modern counties were originally shires. The shire court (or *moot*), presided over by the *ealdorman (later, by the *sheriff), dealt with administrative and legal matters.

Shiré Highlands An upland area in S Malawi, with an average height of about 900 m (3000 ft). Tea and tobacco are cultivated here.

Shire horse A breed of draught horse descended from the English warhorse and one of the world's largest horses. It is massively built with characteristic long white hair (called feathering) covering the lower parts of the legs. The coat is grey, bay, or black. Shires are still sometimes used for haulage in towns. Height: about 1.73 m (17 hands).

Shiva The third member of the Hindu trinity, the *Trimurti. He is known as the Destroyer, but also represents the principle of generation symbolized by the lingam or phallus. His female counterpart is Parvati, also known in her more ominous aspects as Kali and Durga. He is often portrayed in human form with four arms, a third eye in the centre of the forehead, and sometimes wearing a necklace of skulls. His most famous depiction is as *Nataraja* (king of dancing), his dance symbolizing the cosmic rhythm of creation and destruction. The worship of Shiva is characterized by an asceticism that contrasts with the gentler worship of *Vishnu, the other major sect of modern Hinduism.

Shizuoka 34 59N 138 24E A port in Japan, in SE Honshu on an inlet of the Pacific Ocean. It is the centre of Japan's chief tea-producing region. Its university was established in 1949. Population (1980): 458 000.

Shkodër (Italian name: Scutari) 42 03N 19 01E A town in NW Albania, on Lake Scutari. It has been ruled successively by many peoples, including the Turks. Local industries include food canning and the manufacture of cement and weapons. Population (1980 est): 66 500.

shock 1. A severe condition resulting from failure of the circulatory system, when the blood supply to the tissues is inadequate. The shock may be caused by failure of the heart to pump sufficiently strongly, for example after a heart attack; by loss of blood fluid, for example through *haemorrhage or *burns; or by widening of the blood vessels so that there is not enough blood to fill them, for example after injury or during a very severe infection. The patient is in a state of collapse (possibly unconscious)—pale, sweaty, and nauseated, with low blood pressure and a weak fast pulse. Shock due to haemorrhage is treated with blood transfusions while that due to infection is treated with antibiotics and also often with fluid transfusions. There is no adequate treatment for shock caused by a failing heart. 2. Injury resulting from electrocution. The extent of the injury depends on the current passing through the body, which is related to the voltage and the skin resistance. As skin resistance is greatly reduced when it is wet, mains voltage (240 V) can cause a lethal current (about 15 milliamps) to flow through the body if live terminals are touched with wet hands.

Shockley, William Bradfield (1910-) US physicist, born in England, who shared the 1956 Nobel Prize with John *Bardeen and Walter *Brattain for their discovery of the *transistor while working at the Bell Telephone laboratories in 1948. He is also known for his controversial views on the relationship between race and intelligence.

shock wave A narrow region of a high pressure in a fluid, created when a fast-moving body passes through the fluid. The waves are propagated outwards from the body and occur, for example, when an aircraft passes through the *sound barrier.

shoebill A large bird, *Balaeniceps rex*, occurring in papyrus swamps of E Africa. 120 cm tall, it has pale-grey plumage, long legs, and a large head with a broad shoe-shaped bill used to probe for lungfish. It is the only member of its family (*Balaenicipitridae*). Order: *Ciconiiformes* (herons, storks, etc.).

shofar A Jewish ceremonial trumpet used in the synagogue. It is made of a ram's horn, flattened and bent by a steaming process. Its use as a prelude to proclamations and to sound the alarm is recorded in the Old Testament.

shogi A board game for two players, a Japanese form of chess. Each player starts with 20 flat pieces distinguished by size and markings. As in chess the pieces have prescribed moves and the object is to checkmate the enemy king, but unlike chess captured pieces may be used in the game by the player who captures them.

shogun A military title held hereditarily by the heads of three families; they were successively the actual rulers of Japan, although the emperors retained formal sovereignty. The shogunate was secured for the Minamoto from the emperor in 1192 after *Minamoto Yoritomo's victory over the Taira league. From 1338 to 1573 the Ashikaga family held the title and in 1603 *Tokugawa Ieyasu, who claimed Minamoto ancestry, revived it. The last shogun was Tokugawa Keiki (1827-1913; ruled 1867-68).

Sholapur 17 43N 75 56E A city in India, in Maharashtra. Sholapur is a major cotton textile centre. Population (1981): 514 000.

Sholes, Christopher Latham (1819-90) US inventor of the typewriter, which was patented in 1868. He sold the patent to Eliphalet *Remington's company in 1873.

Sholokhov, Mikhail (1905-84) Soviet novelist. After service with the Red Army during the Civil War he returned to his native village in the Don Cossack region, the setting for his first major novel (1928-40), translated in two parts as *And Quiet Flows the Don* and *The Don Flows Home to the Sea*. His authorship of this novel has been questioned by Solzhenitsyn and others. He won the Nobel Prize in 1965.

shooting Discharging a weapon at a target or at game. The two main categories of **target shooting** for rifles are small bore (.22 calibre) at ranges of 25-200 m (27-219 yd), and full bore (7.62 calibre) at ranges of 200-1200 yd (183-1097 m); full-bore courses are fired from standing, sitting, kneeling, and prone (lying down) positions. Weapons for pistol shooting range from the .177 air pistol to the .45 pistol, with ranges between 10 and 50 yd (9-45 m). In **clay-pigeon shooting** (*or* trapshooting) clay discs are mechanically flung into the air and fired at with shotguns. In **grouse shooting** (in the UK grouse shooting is only permitted from 12 Aug to 10 Dec), **pheasant shooting** (1 Oct to 1 Feb), and **partridge shooting** (1 Sept to 1 Feb) the birds are either driven by a semicircle of beaters towards the shooters in butts (hides) or are flushed out by hunting dogs and beaters for a moving party of shooters. Dogs are also used in **rough shooting** for wildfowl, rabbits, etc.

shop stewards Part-time *trade-union officials, who represent the union members with whom they work. The function of the shop steward is to represent his fellow workers in negotiations with management and in talks with other trade-union officials. In the UK, in the absence of a well-developed works' council system, the importance of shop stewards has increased, often at the expense of full-time trade-union officials.

shorthand Any form of writing designed to be written quickly, especially for the transcription of spoken language. Most forms of shorthand are based on the principle of recording only as many letters or sounds as are necessary for reasonably accurate reading back, generally in simplified characters that are fast to write. In the Pitman System, for example, the characters are based on segments of a circle or straight lines; vowels are indicated only where the writer thinks it necessary, by a system of dots in descending order; voicing of consonants is indicated by thickening of strokes (thus, *b* is represented by \, *p* by \). This system is the most popular in Britain and was devised by Sir Isaac Pitman (1813-97). The most popular US system is that invented by John Robert Gregg (1867-1948). In these systems speeds of up to 300 words per minute can be achieved. **Speedwriting**, devised in the USA in the 1920s, uses ordinary Roman alphabet characters, omitting all but the essential ones. **Stenotypy** is a form of machine shorthand using a limited keyboard; it is widely used in the USA for reporting court proceedings. The use of shorthand is of great antiquity; for example, Cicero's secretary Tiro had devised a Latin shorthand system in the 1st century BC.

Shorthorn A breed of cattle originating in NE England and formerly popular for both beef and dairy purposes. Stocky, with short legs, Shorthorns range from red to white with various mottled mixtures. They have been replaced by specialist beef and dairy breeds.

shortsightedness (*or* myopia) Inability to focus on distant objects. This is the commonest kind of visual defect and commonly runs in families: it is not due to excessive reading in bad light but to a slightly misshapen eyeball, in which the light rays are focused in front of the retina (light-sensitive layer). It is corrected by wearing glasses with concave lenses or contact lenses.

Shoshoni A group of North American Indian tribes of the Great Basin region who spoke a language of the Uto-Aztecan family. They lived by gathering wild fruits and insects and trapping small game. Some acquired horses and moved onto the Plains to hunt buffalo and adopted much of the culture of this region. One such group was the *Comanche.

Roman merchantman (c. 100 AD) *The Romans' need to transport grain from N Africa to Europe encouraged the building of imposing ships up to 55 m (180 ft) long.*

Portuguese caravel (c. 1450) *Although it was only a little longer than a large rowing boat, the caravel took part in most of the 15th-century voyages of discovery. The lateen sail, derived from Arab examples, enabled it to sail against the prevailing winds.*

Cutty Sark (1869) *The 19th-century clippers were renowned for their speed and grace. The* Cutty Sark, *built to bring tea from China, was one of the fastest and most consistent sailing ships of its time. It is now permanently moored at Greenwich.*

Great Britain (1843) *The second steam ship designed by I. K. Brunel, the* Great Britain *was the first all-iron propeller-driven ship to cross the Atlantic, taking 15 days between Liverpool and New York. Wrecked off the Falkland Islands in 1937, it was towed back to Bristol in 1970 for restoration.*

Queen Mary (1934) *In 1938 this British passenger liner captured the Blue Riband for the fastest Atlantic crossing with a time of 3 days 20 hours 42 minutes. In 1967 it was anchored off Long Beach, California, as a tourist centre.*

oil tanker (1968) *The largest vessels afloat today, some of these giant ships have a deadweight capacity of over 300 000 tonnes.*

Greek bireme (c. 500 BC) *Propelled during an attack by its two ranks of oars, the bireme was strongly built round a keel to support the strain of the ram attached to its bows.*

Viking longship (c. 1000 AD) *The clinker-built, double-ended longship, propelled by oars and sail, was used mainly to transport fighting men.*

medieval nef (c. 1400) *This single-masted vessel had platforms (castles) for fighting men at either end and one on the mast (topcastle) from which missiles could be hurled.*

Victory (1759–65) *Nelson's flagship at the battle of Trafalgar (1805), the* Victory *carried 100 guns and a crew of 850. It is now preserved at Portsmouth.*

Dreadnought (1906) *The design of the British* Dreadnought *became the model for battleships in a period in which a country's naval strength was reckoned in terms of how many battleships it possessed. The* Dreadnought *carried ten 12-inch guns, 27 smaller guns, and five underwater torpedo tubes.*

Nautilus (1954) *The first nuclear-powered warship, the US* Nautilus *heralded an era in which naval strength is reckoned in terms of nuclear submarines. They are armed with torpedoes and long- and short-range missiles carrying nuclear warheads, all of which can be fired while the vessel is submerged.*

Shostakovich, Dmitri (1906–75) Russian composer. He was a pupil of Glazunov at the St Petersburg conservatoire. His first symphony, written when he was 18, was very successful. Subsequent works, especially the operas *The Nose* (1927–28) and *Lady Macbeth of Mtsenk* (1930–32), brought allegations of formalism and decadence from the Soviet press. Shostakovich regained official favour with his fifth symphony (1937), subtitled "A Soviet artist's reply to just criticism." His compositions also include ten subsequent symphonies, including the wartime seventh symphony (*The Leningrad*; 1941), two concertos each for piano, violin, and cello, 15 string quartets, and much other music. His son **Maxim Shostakovich** (1938–   ), conductor and pianist, defected to the West in 1981.

shotgun A smoothbore firearm with pump or automatic-repeating action. It may have one or two barrels and fires shot (small pellets) into a pattern covering a broad target. Guns with tapered barrels gain range but reduce the pattern area. Shot is used against small game, while lead slugs and balls are used against deer. "Sawn-off" shotguns are used by gangsters.

shot put (*or* putting the shot) A field event in athletics, in which an iron or brass sphere is thrown as far as possible. It weighs 7.26 kg (16 lb) for men and 4 kg (8.8 lb) for women. It is thrown, or put, one-handed from in front of the shoulder and the putter must stay within a circle 2.1 m (7 ft) in diameter. World records: men: 22.64 m (1986) by Udo Beyer (East Germany); women: 22.53 m (1984) by Natalya Lisovskáya (USSR).

shoulder The part of the body to which the *arm is attached. The skeleton of the shoulder consists of the scapula (shoulder blade), which forms a ball-and-socket joint with the humerus, permitting free movement of the arm. It is also the site of attachment of muscles of the arm and back. It is braced by the clavicle. *See* Plate IV.

SHOVELER DUCK *Distinguished from all other ducks by its large spatulate bill with fringed edges, seen in this male.*

shoveler duck A *duck, *Spatula clypeata*, found in the N hemisphere, having a large bill specialized for feeding on water plants and invertebrates on the surface of fresh water. 50 cm long, it has a pale-blue wing flash; the male has a dark-green head, white breast, and chestnut underparts and the female is speckled brown.

Shovell, Sir Cloudesley (1650–1707) English admiral. He captained the *Edgar* against the French at Bantry Bay (1689) and in the War of the Spanish Succession he helped take Gibraltar (1704). He was drowned when his ship went down off the Scillies.

showjumping Competitive jumping of horses, often against the clock, over a series of artificial obstacles of varying severity. Penalties are given for knocking down or refusing fences. Since World War II it has become a major international sport.

Shrapnel, Henry (1761–1842) British army officer, who invented the shrapnel shell. First used in 1804, the shell comprised a projectile that sprayed bullets when activated by a timing device.

Shreveport 32 30N 93 40W A city in the USA, in Louisiana on the Red River. It is the industrial centre of a large oil and natural-gas region. Timber, cotton, and metal are also important products. Population (1980): 205 815.

shrew A small insectivorous mammal belonging to the family *Soricidae* (265 species), found all over the world except Australasia and the Polar regions. The dwarf shrew (*Suncus etruscus*) is the smallest mammal in the world, weighing only 2 g and measuring 7–8 cm. Shrews are very active: the common shrew (*Sorex araneus*) eats its own weight in food every 24 hours in order to meet its energy requirements. Order: *Insectivora.

Shrewsbury 52 43N 2 45W A town in W central England, the administrative centre of Shropshire on the River Severn. It achieved importance as a gateway to Wales, and a castle was built in 1070. The famous boys' public school, attended by Charles Darwin (a native of Shrewsbury) and Sir Philip Sidney, was founded here in 1552. Shrewsbury is a market town for the surrounding agricultural area, with engineering and malting industries; market gardening is also important. Population (1981): 58 826.

shrike A fierce predatory songbird belonging to a family (*Laniidae*; 74 species) occurring in Eurasia, Africa, and North America and also called butcherbird. Shrikes range from 15 to 36 cm in length and have soft black, grey, or brown plumage. They dive on insects and small vertebrates from the air, killing them with their hooked falcon-like bills, often impaling prey on thorns.

shrimp A *crustacean, usually 4–8 cm long, belonging to a worldwide suborder (*Natantia*; about 2000 species) that occurs in fresh and salt water. Shrimps have a semitransparent body with long slender legs (the first pair pincer-like), a fanlike tail, and whiplike antennae, nearly as long as the body. Shrimps swim backwards by rapid flexions of the abdomen and tail and they feed on small animals or plants. Many species, including the European *Crangon vulgaris*, are commercially important as food. Order: *Decapoda.

shrimp plant A popular ornamental plant, *Beloperone guttata*, native to warm regions of the Americas. About 45 cm high, it has inconspicuous white flowers enclosed by reddish-brown leaflike bracts, so that the whole flower cluster resembles a shrimp. Family: *Acanthaceae*.

Shropshire (name from 1974 until 1980: Salop) A county in the West Midlands of England, bordering on Wales. The River Severn separates the lowlands in the N and E from the uplands in the S and W. During the 18th century it became the main iron-producing county in England; the world's first cast-iron bridge was built at Ironbridge in 1779. It is now chiefly agricultural, however, with dairy farming in the N and cattle and sheep farming in the S. Principal arable crops are cereals and sugar beet. Area: 3490 sq km (1348 sq mi). Population (1981): 375 610. Administrative centre: Shrewsbury.

Shroud of Turin A relic believed to be the linen cloth used to wrap Christ's body for burial. It bears impressions of a human body marked with wounds consonant with Christ's at the crucifixion. It has been kept in Turin since 1578, but there are gaps in its history prior to the 14th century. It has been subjected to many tests, including carbon dating and neutron activation measurement, but none can be said to have confirmed or disproved its authenticity.

Shrove Tuesday The day before the beginning of Lent (*see* Ash Wednesday), so called from the "shriving" (i.e. confession and absolution) of the faithful that was customary before the Lenten season. In many countries carnivals are held and in England pancakes are traditionally eaten—hence the popular name Pancake Day.

shrub. *See* tree.

Shumen. *See* Kolarovgrad.

Shute, Nevil (Nevil Shute Norway; 1899–1960) British novelist. He combined novel writing with his professional career as an aeronautical engineer. He settled in Australia after World War II. His many popular novels include *A Town Like Alice* (1950) and *On the Beach* (1957), which concerns the destruction of mankind in an atomic war.

sial The earth's continental crust, which is composed of granitic rocks rich in silicon (Si) and aluminium (Al). It is less dense than the underlying layer of *sima and much thicker.

Sialkot 32 29N 74 35E A city in Pakistan. The shrine of the first Sikh guru, Nanak, is situated here. Industries include textiles, surgical instruments, and sporting goods. Population (1981): 296 000.

Siam. *See* Thailand.

Siam, Gulf of An arm of the South China Sea, about 500 km (310 mi) wide and 700 km (435 mi) long, bordering on Thailand, Kampuchea, and Vietnam.

siamang The largest of the *gibbons, *Hylobates syndactylus*, found in Malaya and Sumatra. Up to 90 cm tall, with arms spanning 150 cm, siamangs have a large naked vocal sac on the throat, which expands to give volume to their cries.

Siamese cat A breed of short-haired cat, originating from SE Asia. The Siamese has a graceful slender body, a wedge-shaped head with slanted blue eyes and large pointed ears, and a long slim tapering tail. The fur on the body is cream-coloured or off-white, shading into one of several colours (seal-brown, blue-grey, chocolate, lilac, tabby, or red) on the ears, mask, paws, and tail (the "points"). The seal-pointed and blue-pointed varieties are probably the most popular.

Siamese twins Identical twins who are fused together, usually at the head or along the trunk. They may have developed equally or unequally; in the latter case, one baby is fairly normal but is attached to a wasted remnant of a fetus. Siamese twins can sometimes be surgically separated, providing that vital organs are not involved in the point of union. The original Siamese twins, Chang and Eng (1811–74), were born in Siam; they were joined at the hip and remained fused, despite which they each married and fathered children.

Sian. *See* Xi An.

Sian incident. *See* Xi An incident.

Sibelius, Jean (Johan Julius Christian S.; 1865–1957) Finnish composer. He began to compose as a child and studied at the Helsinki conservatoire and in Berlin and Vienna. In 1897 the government made him a grant for ten years to enable him to compose full time. Many of his works have Finnish associations and many were inspired by the epic poem, the *Kalevala*. His works include seven symphonies, the symphonic poems *Kullervo* (choral; 1892), *En Saga* (1892), *The Swan of Tuonela* (1893), *Finlandia* (1899–1900), and *Tapiola* (1925), a violin concerto, a string quartet entitled "Voces Intimae," and many songs.

Siberia A region in the Soviet Union, chiefly in the RSFSR. Corresponding to N Asia, it is bordered on the W by the Ural Mountains, on the N by the Arctic Ocean, on the E by the Pacific Ocean, and on the S by Mongolia and China; the Soviet Union excludes, for administrative purposes, parts of the extreme W, E, and S. Siberia comprises three geographical areas – the West Siberian Plain, the Central Siberian Plateau, and the Soviet Far East. It is notorious for its long harsh winters, during which the lowest temperatures anywhere in the world have been recorded. Its outstandingly rich mineral resources include coal, especially in the *Kuznetsk Basin, petroleum, diamonds, and gold. Forestry is also important and Siberia's many rivers (notably the Ob, Yenisei, and Lena) are harnessed for hydroelectric power. The Russian settlement of Siberia began in 1581 but was intermittent until the building (1891–1905) of the Trans-

Siberian Railway. Siberia has long been a place of exile for Russian criminals and political prisoners. Area: about 13 807 037 sq km (5 330 896 sq mi).

Sibiu 45 46N 24 09E A city in central Romania. An important centre for Transylvania in the 15th century, it possesses the Brukenthal Museum, one of the oldest in Europe, and much medieval architecture. It is now a major industrial centre, manufacturing machinery, textiles, and food products. Population (1983): 159 599.

Sibyl In Greek and Roman mythology, any of various divinely inspired prophetesses, the most famous of which was the Sibyl of Cumae, near Naples. Three books of these Sibylline prophecies were preserved in the Temple of Jupiter on the Capitoline hill at Rome and were consulted in national emergencies.

Sica, Vittoria De. *See* De Sica, Vittoria.

Sichuan (Ssu-ch'uan *or* Szechwan) A province in central China, on the Yangtze River, surrounded by mountains. The centre is a plateau and the E a fertile plain. Warm and humid and China's most productive rice area, it is prosperous and densely populated, with several ethnic groups. Besides rice, produce includes maize, sugar cane, wheat, cotton, and forest products. The W is good grazing land, exporting pig bristles. Salt, gas, oil, coal, and other minerals are produced. Despite great difficulties with transport because of its mountainous surroundings, it has flourishing industries. It is also known for its crafts. *History*: it was among the first areas settled by the Chinese, important from the 3rd century BC, when China's oldest irrigation system was constructed here. A kingdom in the 3rd century AD, separatism often flourished because of the area's self-sufficiency and impenetrable position; it became the centre of the Nationalist government during the Sino-Japanese War (1937–45). Economic development was stimulated at this time by migration from the coasts and has again speeded up since the 1950s. Area: about 569 800 sq km (220 000 sq mi). Population (1982 est): 99 700 000. Capital: Chengdu.

Sicilian Vespers (1282) The massacre of 2000 French residents of Palermo that began the Sicilian revolt, backed by Pedro III of Aragon (1236–85; reigned 1276–85), against the oppressive regime of the Angevin *Charles I. General war ensued between the Aragonese, Sicilians, and Italian Ghibellines on one side and the Angevins, French, and Italian Guelfs, supported by the papacy, on the other. Aragonese control was finally established in 1302 under Pedro's son Frederick II (1272–1337). *See also* Guelfs and Ghibellines.

Sicily The largest island in the Mediterranean Sea, which together with adjacent islands comprises an autonomous region of Italy. It is separated from the mainland by the Strait of Messina. Sicily is largely mountainous, rising to over 1800 m with its highest point at Mount Etna. Although most of the population is concentrated in urban centres, the region is underdeveloped and there is much poverty. The service sector is important, as is the mining industry, especially oil. The region's farmers produce citrus fruits, vegetables, wheat, rye, olives, and wine. Manufacturing industries include oil refining, petrochemicals, chemicals, pharmaceuticals, and food processing. *History*: settled by the Greeks in the 8th century BC, it was later occupied by the Carthaginians and between 241 and 211 BC it became a Roman province. It was conquered by the Arabs in the 9th century AD and in 1060 the Norman conquest of Sicily began. In 1266 Charles I became the first Angevin King of Sicily, which was conquered by Aragon in 1284 following the revolt called the *Sicilian Vespers. In 1734 Don Carlos of Bourbon became Charles IV (*see* Charles III of Spain) of Naples and Sicily, which formally became the Kingdom of the Two Sicilies in 1815 under *Ferdinand I. After conquest by Garibaldi (1860), Sicily was united with the rest of Italy. Since then Sicily's history has been one of trouble and discontent as a result of an ailing economy and the persistence of widespread poverty, which has not been helped by the island's social structure, the *Mafia, and other conservative forces on the island presenting an obstacle to reform. Area: 25 710 sq km (9927 sq mi), with adjacent islands. Population (1980 est): 5 024 316. Capital: Palermo.

WALTER SICKERT Ennui *(c. 1913), oil painting in the Ashmolean Museum, Oxford.*

Sickert, Walter Richard (1860–1942) British impressionist painter and etcher, born in Munich of Danish and Irish parentage. He studied at the Slade School and under *Whistler and *Degas. His paintings of Venice and Dieppe (1895–1905) and scenes from the music hall and domestic life are distinguishable from French *impressionism chiefly by their sombre colours. Although well known on the Continent and among the British artists who formed the *Camden Town Group (1911), he did not achieve widespread recognition in the UK until the 1920s.

sickle-cell disease A condition resulting from the production of an abnormal form of haemoglobin (the pigment of red blood cells). The disease is hereditary and affects only Negroes. When the blood is deprived of oxygen the abnormal haemoglobin crystallizes and distorts the red cells into a sickle shape: these sickle cells are removed from the blood by the spleen, which leads to *anaemia. Children affected with the severest form of the disease do not usually survive until adulthood; those less severely affected do survive and even tend to have some built-in resistance to malaria, which may partly explain the persistence of this harmful gene in the population.

Siddons, Sarah (*born* *Kemble; 1755–1831) English actress. She acted in the provinces until 1782, when at her London debut at Drury Lane she was immediately acclaimed as the leading tragic actress of her time. Her most notable role was Lady Macbeth.

sidereal period The time taken by a planet or satellite to return to the same point in its orbit, i.e. to complete one revolution, with reference to the background stars. It can be determined from the body's *synodic period.

sidewinder A small nocturnal *rattlesnake, *Crotalus cerastes*, occurring in deserts of the S USA and Mexico, that has a sideways looping method of locomotion enabling it to move quickly over loose sand. 45–75 cm long, it is usually pale brown or grey with indistinct darker spotting and a hornlike scale above each eye.

Sidgwick, Henry (1838–1900) British moral philosopher. Sidgwick's major academic work, *The Methods of Ethics* (1874), was a comparative study of moral philosophy, which focused on *hedonism and *utilitarianism. As a university teacher, he worked for the abolition of religious tests at Cambridge and the admission of women students. He was the first president of the Society for Psychical Research (1882–85).

Sidi-Bel-Abbès 35 12N 0 42W A town in NW Algeria. An old Moorish town, it was the headquarters of the French Foreign Legion until 1962. It lies in a fertile area renowned for its wine. Population (1983 est): 146 653.

Siding Spring Mountain 31 27S 149 10E A mountain in Australia, in New South Wales in the Warrumbungle Range. It is the site of the **Siding Spring Observatory**, with a 3.8 m (150 in) Anglo-Australian telescope and a British 1.2 m (48 in) Schmidt telescope. Height: 859 m (2817 ft).

Sidmouth, Henry Addington, 1st Viscount. *See* Addington, Henry, 1st Viscount Sidmouth.

Sidney, Algernon (1622–83) English Whig politician, who was beheaded for complicity in the *Rye House Plot against Charles II and the king's brother James, Duke of York. In exile after the Restoration of Charles in 1660, he returned in 1677 and became prominent in attempts to exclude the Roman Catholic James from the succession. His involvement in the Rye House Plot was never satisfactorily proved.

Sidney, Sir Philip (1554–86) English poet and courtier. A man of letters and man of action, he typified the Renaissance ideal of the complete gentleman. His works include the prose romance *Arcadia* (1580), the sequence of Petrarchan sonnets, *Astrophel and Stella* (1591), and an important work of critical theory, *The Defence of Poesy* (1595). A gifted linguist, he served as a diplomat in Europe and was killed while fighting the Spanish in the Netherlands.

Sidon (*or* Saida) 33 32N 35 22E A small seaport in S Lebanon. It was an important Phoenician city, several references are made to it in the Bible, and it was greatly damaged during the Crusades. It is now the terminus of an oil pipeline from Saudi Arabia. Population (1982): 80 000.

Siegen 50 52N 8 02E A city in NW West Germany, in North Rhine-Westphalia. A former centre for the mining of iron ore, its manufactures now include office equipment and computers. It is the birthplace of Rubens and has a university (1972). Population (1980 est): 112 500.

Siegfried A hero of Germanic legend, who also appears in early Scandinavian legend as Sigurd. The two best-known versions of his story are the Germanic *Nibelungenlied and the Old Norse *Volsungasaga*. In the former, Siegfried wins *Brunhild for his brother-in-law Gunther, but a quarrel between Brunhild and Siegfried's wife Kriemhild leads to Siegfried's death by treachery. In the *Volsungasaga*, Sigurd is betrothed to Brynhild (the Old Norse version of her name) but is tricked (by a magic potion) into forgetting her and marries Gudrun. He then wins Brynhild for his brother-in-law Gunnar; later Brynhild incites Gunnar to kill him. Siegfried is the hero of the last two operas of *Wagner's *The Ring of the Nibelung*.

siemens (S) The *SI unit of conductance equal to the conductance between two points on a conductor when a potential difference of one volt between the points causes a current of one ampere to flow. Named after Ernst Werner von *Siemens.

Siemens, Ernst Werner von (1816-92) German electrical engineer, who opened a telegraph factory in 1847 and, a year later, laid a government telegraph line from Berlin to Frankfurt. Together with his brother **Karl Siemens** (1829-1906), he established telegraph factories in a number of European cities. A third brother **Sir William Siemens** (Karl Wilhelm S.; 1823-83) moved to England in 1844. He invented the open-hearth method of making steel in 1861, which was based on the principle of heat regeneration previously patented by a fourth brother **Friedrich Siemens** (1826-1904).

SIENA *The cathedral.*

Siena 43 19N 11 19E A city in central Italy, in Tuscany. Founded by the Etruscans, it was an important commercial and artistic centre in the middle ages. Its many fine buildings include a 13th-century gothic-romanesque cathedral, a university (1240), and several palaces, especially the Palazzo Pubblico (1297-1310) with its slender tower 100 m (328 ft) high. There are horse races through the main square of the city during the annual Palio festival. Tourism is Siena's main source of revenue. Population (1985 est): 60 670.

Sienkiewicz, Henryk (1846-1916) Polish novelist. His only novel generally known outside Poland is *Quo Vadis* (1896), a historical epic set in Rome under the emperor Nero; it has been the subject of many films. He also wrote a trilogy celebrating Poland's military struggles during the 17th century. He travelled extensively in Europe and the USA and won the Nobel Prize in 1905.

Sierra Leone, Republic of A country in West Africa, on the Gulf of Guinea. Coastal plains, fringed by mangrove swamps, rise to higher land in the interior reaching heights of almost 2000 m (6500 ft). The majority of the population is African, the main groups being Mende and Temne. *Economy*: chiefly agricultural, organized mainly in smallholdings. The principal food crop is rice and cash crops include palm kernels, cocoa, coffee, and ginger. Livestock is important, particularly cattle in the N, and there has been considerable recent development in the fishing industry as well as in forestry. Minerals, including diamonds, iron ore, and bauxite, are the main exports and the country has important deposits of rutile, which are being exploited. *History*: in 1787 local chiefs ceded to Britain a piece of land along the coast for the settlement of slaves freed in the colonies. In 1896 the region became a British protectorate, gaining independence within the Commonwealth in 1961. In 1967 a military coup and countercoup took place and after further upheaval civilian rule was restored in 1968. In 1971 Sierra Leone became a republic. In 1977 one-party government (by the All-People's Congress) was introduced. A coup in 1987 failed. President: Joseph Momoh (1937–). Official language: English; Krio is widely spoken. Official currency, since 1964: leone of 100 cents. Area: 73 326 sq km (27 925 sq mi). Population (1983 est): 3 705 000. Capital and main port: Freetown.

Sierra Madre The chief mountain system of Mexico. It extends for about 2500 km (1500 mi) SE from the US border, reaching 5699 m (18 697 ft) at Citlaltépetl. It comprises the Sierra Madre Oriental (E), the Sierra Madre del Sur (S), and the Sierra Madre Occidental (W).

Sierra Maestra A mountain range in Cuba. It extends along the extreme SE coast reaching 1974 m (6476 ft) at the Pico Turquino. Fidel *Castro established his guerrilla base here in the 1950s.

Sierra Morena A mountain range in S Spain, extending about 400 km (249 mi) E-W between the Rivers Guadiana and Guadalquivir.

Sierra Nevada A mountain range in the USA. It extends generally NW-SE through California, reaching 4418 m (14 495 ft) at Mount Whitney. It contains the famous Yosemite National Park.

Sierra Nevada A mountain range in S Spain. It rises to 3481 m (11 421 ft) at Mulhacén, the highest point in Spain.

Sieyès, Emmanuel Joseph (1748-1836) French churchman, who was a leading figure in the *French Revolution. His pamphlet *Qu'est-ce que le tiers état?* (*What Is the Third Estate?*, 1789) greatly influenced the revolt of the Third Estate at the start of the Revolution. He voted for the execution of the king but withdrew from politics during the Jacobins' ascendancy. In 1799 he became a member of the *Directory and helped to bring about the coup that established Napoleon Bonaparte in power. His influence thereafter declined.

sifaka A *prosimian primate belonging to the genus *Propithecus* (2 species), of Madagascar. About 50 cm long, with a tail the same length, sifakas have long white fur with red or orange and black markings. They have long hind legs and are mainly arboreal, feeding on leaves, buds, fruit, and bark. Family: *Indriidae*.

Siger of Brabant (c. 1240-c. 1284) French theologian. A teacher at Paris University, Siger was accused of heresy (1276) on account of his criticisms of Aristotle, in which he appeared to dissent from doctrines of immortality and the afterlife. *Aquinas wrote a treatise against him, but Dante placed him among the 12 sages.

Sigismund (1368-1437) Holy Roman Emperor (1411-37; crowned 1433) and King of Hungary (1387-1437) and of Bohemia (1419-37). He conducted two unsuccessful crusades against the Turks (1396; 1428) and was largely responsible for the summoning of the Council of *Constance to heal the Great Schism. Implicated in the treacherous burning of John *Hus in 1415, he fought the *Hussites through-out the 1420s.

Sigismund (I) the Old (1467–1548) King of Poland (1506–48). Sigismund gained control of E Prussia (1525) after defeating the *Teutonic Knights. He encouraged the development of the Renaissance in Poland.

Sigismund II Augustus (1520–72) King of Poland (1548–72); the last of the Jagiellon dynasty. Sigismund's reign saw the Union of *Lublin (1569), which united Poland with Lithuania, and the expansion of the Polish Reformation.

Sigismund III Vasa (1566–1632) King of Poland (1587–1632) and Sweden (1592–99). Sigismund was deposed from the Swedish throne by his uncle, later *Charles IX of Sweden, and failed in his subsequent attempts to regain the Crown. Charles' son *Gustavus II Adolphus conquered Poland's Livonian territory (1621). Sigismund had some success against Russia, capturing and holding Moscow (1610–12).

Siglo de Oro The Golden Age of Spanish literature that lasted from about 1550 to 1650. The literature of this period was characterized by patriotism and new attitudes of critical realism. Leading writers included the dramatist Lope de Vega, the novelist Cervantes, and the poet Luis de Góngora.

Signac, Paul (1863–1935) French painter and art theorist associated with *pointillism. A disciple of *Seurat, he is known chiefly for his mosaic-like paintings of European harbours and his treatise *D'Eugène Delacroix au Néo-impressionisme* (1899).

Signorelli, Luca (c. 1441–1523) Italian Renaissance painter, born in Cortona. Probably the pupil of *Piero della Francesca, he worked in Florence, Perugia, and in the Vatican, where he painted a fresco for the Sistine Chapel (c. 1481). He completed frescoes in Orvieto Cathedral begun by Fra *Angelico and painted his masterpiece, *The Last Judgment*, there (1499). His studies of muscular nudes were admired by and influential on Michelangelo.

signoria (Italian: lordship) A form of government in late medieval Italian city states following the collapse of communal government caused by factional struggles. Control was given (sometimes voluntarily) to a *signore* (lord), who formed a more or less despotic government. *Signori* established dynasties, especially in N Italy (e.g. the *Visconti and *Este), which often gained reputations for good government and artistic patronage.

Sigurdsson. *See* Sverrir.

Sihanouk, Norodim, Prince (1923–) King (1941–55) of Cambodia (Kampuchea). When the Japanese occupation ended in 1945, Sihanouk, after much opposition and factional strife, achieved Cambodia's independence from France (1953). Abdicating in 1955, he continued to dominate Cambodian politics as prime minister until 1970, when his regime was overthrown by a military coup and he went into exile in China. After the victory of the Khmer Rouge guerrillas (1975) he again became head of state but retired in 1976 and went back into exile.

sika A deer, *Cervus nippon*, also called Japanese deer, native to S Asia, Japan, and Taiwan and introduced to New Zealand and Europe. Grey-brown in winter and chestnut with white spots in summer, its shoulder height is 70–100 cm. Stags have slender eight-pointed antlers about 80 cm long.

Sikhism The religion of some nine million Indians, mostly inhabiting the Punjab. Founded in the 15th century by the Guru *Nanak, Sikhism combines Hindu and Islamic ideas. The Hindu concepts of *karma and rebirth are accepted, but the caste system is rejected. Sikhs believe that god is the only reality and that spiritual release can be obtained by taming the ego through devotional singing, recitation of the divine name, meditation, and service. The guidance of the *guru is essential. The concept of Khalsa, a chosen race of warrior-saints, is central, as are the so-called five Ks: *kangha* (comb); *kacch* (shorts); *kirpan* (sword); *kara* (steel bracelet); and *kes* (uncut hair and beard).

The occupation of the Sikh Golden Temple at Amritsar by Indian troops in 1984 led to the assassination a few months later of the Indian prime minister Indira *Gandhi by Sikh members of her bodyguard. Violent reprisals against Sikhs followed throughout India. *See also* 'Adi Granth.

Sikh Wars 1. (1845–46) The war caused by the invasion of British India by Sikhs from the Punjab. The Sikh defeat resulted in the loss of territory that included Kashmir. **2.** (1848–49) The war that developed from a Sikh revolt at Multan. Following the Sikh defeat, by Gough at Gujarat (22 February, 1849), the Punjab was annexed by the British.

Sikkim A state in NE India, in the Himalayas E of Nepal. Low valleys rise to Mount Kangchenjunga, 8598 m (28 208 ft), providing a tremendous range in climate and vegetation. The world's biggest cardamom producer, Sikkim also grows mandarin oranges, grains, potatoes, pulses, and ginger. Copper is mined and the jungle exploited for timber. *History*: ruled by a Buddhist dynasty, Sikkim passed under British and then Indian protection (1947). Following a plebiscite Sikkim became the 22nd state of India in 1975. Area: 7298 sq km (2817 sq mi). Population (1981 est): 315 682. Capital: Gangtok.

Sikorski, Władysław (1881–1943) Polish general and statesman. Sikorski was prime minister (1922–23) and then minister of military affairs (1924–25). After Poland's collapse in 1939, he became prime minister of the Polish government-in-exile in London. The circumstances of his death, in an aeroplane crash near Gibraltar, are the subject of a controversial play by Rolf *Hochhuth.

Sikorsky, Igor Ivan (1889–1972) US aeronautical engineer, born in Russia, who invented the helicopter. He began experimenting with helicopter designs in 1909 but his early models failed and he turned to aircraft, producing the S-1 biplane in 1910. In 1919 he moved to the USA, returning to the problem of helicopters in the 1930s and completing the first successful model, the VS-300, in 1939.

silage A cattle food produced from a fresh fodder crop, usually grass or a green cereal crop, that has been preserved by controlled bacterial fermentation. The crop is placed in an airtight structure (silo) and allowed to ferment; the organic acids produced "pickle" the crop and prevent further decay, resulting in highly digestible and nutritious food.

Silbury Hill A prehistoric mound in S England, near *Avebury, Wiltshire. Begun about 2150 BC, it is the largest man-made hill in Europe, standing 40 m (130 ft) high.

Silchester (Latin: Calleva Atrebatum) An ancient capital of the British tribe of Atrebates in S England. Rebuilt after the Roman conquest, Silchester was inhabited until the 6th century AD. The Roman town wall (c. 200 AD) is still visible.

Silenus In Greek mythology, an elderly *Satyr, companion of the god *Dionysus. He was famed for his wisdom and prophetic powers as well as his drunkenness. The Sileni were his fellow nature spirits.

Silesia A region of E central Europe now in Czechoslovakia and Poland. Because of its geographical position, mineral wealth, and industrial potential, Silesia has been disputed territory since the 17th century, when it was claimed by both Austria and Prussia. The seizure of much of it by Frederick the Great of Prussia, which precipitated the War of the *Austrian Succession, was recognized by Austria in 1763, after the *Seven Years' War. After World War I it was divided between Czechoslovakia, Germany, and Poland and after World War II, between Czechoslovakia and Poland.

silhouette In art, a profile image or portrait in black on a white background or vice versa. Named after the French finance minister Étienne de Silhouette (1709–67), who made paper cut-outs of silhouettes, this type of portrait was very popular in the late 18th and early 19th centuries until it was supplanted by photography.

silica The mineral silicon dioxide, SiO_2, the most abundant of all minerals. There are three main forms of silica: *quartz, tridymite, and cristobalite, the last two occurring in acidic volcanic rocks. Cryptocrystalline silica is *chalcedony; amorphous silica is *opal. Creosite is a high-pressure variety, found near meteorite craters. Lechatelierite is a natural silica glass. Silica content is used to classify igneous rocks into acidic (over 65% silica), intermediate (52–66% silica), basic (45–52% silica), and ultrabasic (under 45% silica) varieties. Since these terms do not reflect pH value, another classification based on silica content is also frequently used; in this igneous rocks are classified as oversaturated (containing free silica), saturated (all silica combined with no unsaturated minerals, e.g. feldspathoids), or undersaturated (containing unsaturated minerals). *See also* silicate minerals.

silicate minerals A group of minerals that constitute about 90% of the earth's crust and one-third of all minerals. They consist of silicates of calcium, magnesium, aluminium, or other metals, in varying degrees of complexity. They are classified according to their atomic structure; all are based on the tetrahedral unit SiO_4. *Feldspar and *quartz (which is chemically an oxide but resembles the silicates more closely in many properties and is usually included in this group) are the most common. *See also* amphiboles; clay; garnet; micas; olivine; pyroxene.

silicon (Si) The second most abundant element in the earth's crust, after oxygen. It is a major constituent of almost all rock-forming minerals (*see* silicate minerals). The element was discovered by J. J. Berzelius in 1824 and is extracted by reduction of the oxide (silica; SiO_2) with carbon in an electric furnace. Pure silicon is now of great importance in the electronics industry as a semiconductor. It is prepared by decomposition of trichlorosilane ($SiCl_3H$). Silicates have been important for centuries as the main constituents of pottery, glasses, and many building materials. Silicon carbide (*see* carborundum) is a widely used abrasive, refractory, and semiconductor. Organic silicon compounds are known as *silicones. At no 14; at wt 28.086; mp 1410°C; bp 2355°C.

silicon chip. *See* integrated circuit.

silicones Synthetic polymers consisting of chains of alternating silicon and oxygen atoms, with organic groups attached to the former. The chains can be cross-linked to varying degrees. Silicones include fluids, greases, rubbers, and resins. All have similar chemical properties: stability to heat, oxidation, many chemicals, and oils. The main applications are in adhesives, paints, elastomers, and waterproofing agents.

silicosis A lung disease caused by prolonged inhalation of silica dust: an occupational disease of stone cutters, quarry workers, etc. Silica causes more damage than an equivalent amount of coaldust: the air sacs of the lungs become thickened and scarred, causing breathlessness and coughing in the patients. There is no specific treatment and prevention by use of masks and other safety measures is essential. *See also* pneumoconiosis.

silk The thread produced by the caterpillar of the *silkworm moth and the fabric woven from it. The cocoons are unravelled and the filaments from several twisted together; processing this raw silk includes combining these strands, washing away the sticky sericin secretion, and sometimes adding metallic salts for weight. China, where silk production was first practised, and Japan are the leading producers of pure silk; wild silk, produced by silkworms that feed on leaves other than mulberry or by uncultivated silkworms, includes a coarser brown Indian silk. Lustrous, elastic, absorbent, and very strong, silk remains a luxury fabric considerably superior to its synthetic imitations.

silk-cotton tree. *See* kapok.

Silk Road A trade route, 6400 km (4000 mi) long, that connected China with the Mediterranean. It was most used in antiquity, when silk was taken westwards and wool and precious metals eastwards, but was again travelled in the later middle ages, notably by Marco Polo.

silkworm A caterpillar that spins a silken cocoon, especially one that is suitable for commercial silk production. The commonest is the Chinese silkworm (*Bombyx mori*), which feeds on mulberry leaves. The pupae are killed by heat and the silken thread, up to 900 m long, is then unwound. 50 000 cocoons are needed to produce 1 kg of silk. The Japanese oak silkmoth (*Antherea yamanai*) and the Chinese species *A. pernyi* are also used. Some American moths, such as the *cecropia and *io, also produce silk.

silky oak One of two species of Australian trees. *Grevillea robusta*, found in forests of E Australia, grows to a height of 35 m and has fernlike leaves. It is widely cultivated in the tropics as an ornamental or shade tree. The northern silky oak (*Cardwellia sublimis*) is an important timber tree, its pinkish soft wood being used in furniture manufacturing and for building purposes.

silky terrier A breed of toy dog developed in Australia by

SILK ROAD *Between the 1st century* BC *and the 3rd century* AD *Chinese silks travelled westwards to the Mediterranean in exchange for precious metals.*

crossing the Australian terrier with the Yorkshire terrier. Formerly called the Sydney silky, it has a compact body with short legs. The long fine glossy coat is blue and tan or grey-blue and tan. Height: 23–25 cm.

sill A horizontal or near-horizontal sheetlike mass of intrusive igneous rock, lying parallel to the layering of the rock into which it is intruded. Most sills consist of medium-grained hypabyssal rock, the commonest being dolerite. *Compare* dyke.

Sillitoe, Alan (1928–) British novelist. He began writing in Majorca, where he settled after World War II. He won immediate success with his first novel, *Saturday Night and Sunday Morning* (1958), about the violent and alienated life of a Nottingham factory worker. This was followed by a book of short stories, *The Loneliness of the Long Distance Runner* (1959). His many later books include the semiautobiographical *Raw Material* (1972), and *Her Victory* (1982).

Sills, Beverley (Belle Silverman; 1929–) US soprano. A child prodigy, she made her operatic debut with the Philadelphia Civil Opera in 1948, since when she has sung major roles in more than 50 operas. In 1980 she became director of the New York City Opera.

Silone, Ignazio (Secondo Tranquilli; 1900–78) Italian novelist. He helped found the Italian Communist Party in 1921, lived in exile in Switzerland from 1930 until after World War II, and then returned to Italy to lead the Democratic Socialist Party until 1950. He became disillusioned with communism, but his novels, especially *Fontamara* (1930) and *Bread and Wine* (1937), express his strong socialist concern for the peasants of S Italy.

silt A fine-grained sedimentary deposit, the rock particles of which range from 0.002 to 0.06 mm in diameter. Silts consist mainly of clay minerals, with iron oxides and hydroxides and silica. They collect in sheltered marine environments, such as estuaries, making dredging necessary. Consolidated silts form siltstones.

Silurian period A geological period of the Lower Palaeozoic era between the Ordovician and Devonian periods, lasting from about 445 to 415 million years ago. Conditions were mainly marine and the first true fish appeared. The first evidence of land plants also comes from Silurian rocks. The Caledonian period of mountain building reached its peak towards the end of the period.

Silvanus A Roman woodland god, sometimes identified with the Greek *Pan. He was usually portrayed as an old countryman. He was worshipped at sacred groves or trees.

silver (Ag) A metallic element, known since ancient times. It occurs in nature as the metal, as argentite (Ag_2S), and in lead, zinc, and copper ores. Pure silver has the highest electrical and thermal conductivity known and is used in some printed electrical circuits. In air, silver tarnishes forming a coating of the black sulphide (Ag_2S). Alloys of silver are used as solders and sterling silver (92.5% pure) is used for jewellery (*see* Plate III). Although not a reactive metal, silver forms many compounds including the oxide (Ag_2O), the nitrate ($AgNO_3$), and halides (for example AgCl, AgBr). Silver salts are of great importance in photography since they are light sensitive, and some 30% of the silver produced is used in this way. Silver iodide (AgI) has been used in attempts to seed clouds to induce rainfall. At no 47; at wt 107.868; mp 961.93; bp 2212°C.

Silver Age, Latin The period (18–c. 130 AD) succeeding the *Golden Age of *Latin literature. During this time rhetorical brilliance and ornamentation became prized for its own sake. Major writers include the satirist *Juvenal, the epigrammatist *Martial, the historians *Tacitus and *Suetonius, and the philosopher and dramatist *Seneca.

silverfish A widely distributed primitive wingless ᵒinsect, *Lepisma saccharina*, also called fish moth. One of the three-pronged *bristletails, it is covered with silvery scales and is common in buildings, feeding on starchy materials, including books and fabrics. Family: *Lepismatidae*.

silver fox. *See* red fox.

silverplate Any object that is plated with silver rather than being solid silver. The first substitute for pure silver for tableware, etc., was the invention of *Sheffield plate in 1742. In 1840 the advent of *electroplating brought silverplated domestic articles to a much wider public and Sheffield plate is now of considerable value. Many silverplated articles are marked EPNS (electroplated nickel silver)—nickel silver itself is an alloy of copper, nickel, and zinc and contains no silver; in this process a layer of silver is electroplated onto the nickel-silver base.

silverside A fish, also called sand smelt or whitebait, belonging to a family (*Atherinidae*) found in fresh and coastal waters of warm and temperate regions. Its small slim body, up to 70 cm long, bears a silvery band along each side and two dorsal fins. Order: *Atheriniformes*.

sima The earth's oceanic crust, which is composed of basaltic rocks rich in silica (Si) and magnesium (Mg). It is denser than the *sial of the continental crust and is believed to continue beneath it.

Si-ma Qian (*or* Ssu-ma Ch'ien; c. 145–c. 85 BC) Chinese historian, astronomer, and calendar reformer. He succeeded his father as historian to the Han Emperor Wu, but he offended the emperor and was castrated and imprisoned. He later became palace secretary. His *Records of the Historian*, the first major Chinese historical work, included the entire documented history of China to that date.

GEORGES SIMENON

Simenon, Georges (1903–) Belgian novelist. The best known of his several hundred novels are his detective stories featuring the Parisian *commissaire de police*, Maigret, who first appeared in 1931. His other novels, written in a brisk colloquial style and with intuitive psychological perception, include *La Neige était sale* (1948), the semiautobiographical *Pedigree* (1948), and *Destinées* (1981).

Simeon, tribe of One of the 12 *tribes of Israel. It claimed descent from Simeon, the son of Jacob and Leah. The territory allocated to the tribe was S of that of Judah, W and

SW of the Dead Sea. It was eventually assimilated into Judah.

Simeon Stylites, St (c. 390-459 AD) Syrian monk and hermit, who lived for over 35 years on a small platform on top of a tall pillar (Greek, *stylos*). His many imitators were known as stylites. Feast day: 5 Jan.

Simferopol 44 57N 34 05E A city in the Soviet Union, the capital of the Crimean *oblast* (autonomous region) in the S Ukrainian SSR. It has food-processing, engineering, and consumer-goods industries. Population (1981 est): 314 000.

simile A figure of speech in which two things are compared in order to emphasize a particular feature or quality they share. A simile differs from a *metaphor in being an explicit comparison, usually using the words *as* or *like*, for example "He fought like a lion."

Simla 31 07N 77 09E A city in India, the capital of Himachal Pradesh situated in the foothills of the Himalayas. It was the summer capital of India (1865-1939). Population (1981): 70 604.

Simms, William Gilmore (1806-70) US novelist. He wrote many historical romances concerning life in the South, including *Guy Rivers* (1834) and *The Yemassee* (1835). He edited various Southern magazines, defended slavery, and suffered personal ruin in the Civil War.

Simnel, Lambert (c. 1475-1535) English impostor whom the Yorkists tried to pass off as Edward, Earl of Warwick (1475-99), a Yorkist claimant to the throne, in a plot to overthrow Henry VII. Simnel was captured in 1487 and subsequently worked in the king's kitchens.

Simon, John Allsebrook, 1st Viscount (1873-1954) British Liberal politician. An MP (1906-18, 1922-40) he became solicitor general (1910), attorney general (1913), and then home secretary (1915), resigning in 1916 in protest against the introduction of conscription in World War I. He was later foreign secretary (1931-35), home secretary (1935-37), and chancellor of the exchequer (1937-40), supporting Neville Chamberlain's policy of *appeasement towards the fascist powers. He was Lord Chancellor from 1940 to 1945.

Simon, St In the New Testament, one of the 12 Apostles. He is surnamed the Canaanite or Zelotes, which possibly means that he was one of the *Zealots. He preached in Egypt and joined St *Jude in Persia, where, according to one tradition, he was martyred by being cut in half with a saw. Feast day: 28 Oct.

Simonov, Konstantin (1915-79) Soviet novelist, playwright, poet, and journalist. His writings, which focus chiefly on World War II, include the poem "Wait for Me" and the novels *Days and Nights* (1945), on the defence of Stalingrad, and *Victims and Heroes* (1959).

Simonstown 34 12S 18 26E A naval base in South Africa, in SW Cape Province on the Atlantic coast. An important naval base from 1741, it was used by the British navy (1814-1975) and is the base of the South African navy. As well as having dry-dock and harbour facilities, it is an important fishing port. Population (1985): 6 500.

simple harmonic motion Any oscillation performed by a body about some reference point so that the restraining force is directly proportional to its displacement from that point. Examples of simple harmonic motion include a *pendulum swinging through a small angle and a vibrating string. The maximum displacement of the system is known as the amplitude and the time taken for one complete oscillation, the *period. The displacement, x, at a time t is simply represented by the equation $x = A\sin\omega t$, where A is the amplitude and ω the angular frequency, which is related to the period T by $\omega = 2\pi/T$. Thus a graph of the displacement x plotted against time t has the shape of a sine wave, i.e. it is sinusoidal.

Simplon Pass An alpine pass linking Brig in Switzerland with Iselle in Italy. It was built between 1800 and 1807 on Napoleon's orders and reaches a height of 2009 m (6590 ft).

The **Simplon Tunnel** to the NE is, at 20 km (12 mi), the longest rail tunnel in the world. Built in 1890 by Alfred Brandt (1846-99), it was opened in 1906.

Simpson, George Gaylord (1902-) US palaeontologist, noted for his contributions to knowledge of the early history of mammals and the intercontinental migration of species. Simpson studied mammalian fossil remains in both North and South America and, in *The Meaning of Evolution* (1949), discussed the philosophical implications of evolutionary theory.

Simpson, N(orman) F(rederick) (1919-) British dramatist. His two best-known plays, *A Resounding Tinkle* (1956) and *One Way Pendulum* (1959), are comedies in which the mixture of fantasy and logic is influenced by the *Theatre of the Absurd.

Simpson Desert (*or* Arunta Desert) A desert of central Australia, mainly in Northern Territory. It consists of an arid region covered by parallel sand dunes, which extend to 160 km (100 mi) in length. Area: about 77 000 sq km (29 723 sq mi).

Sinai A desert peninsula in Egypt, bounded by Israel and the Gulf of Aqaba to the E and the Gulf of Suez and mainland Egypt to the W. Mount Sinai, 2285 m (7497 ft) high, is in the mountain range in the S. According to the Old Testament it was on this mountain that Moses received the tablets of the law from Jehovah (Exodus 24). The N half of the desert is plateau. The chief resources of the region are manganese and the oil deposits in the W, based on Sudr; agriculture is practised on the Mediterranean coast. Sinai was occupied by Israel in the 1956 and again in the 1967 Arab-Israeli Wars and following the 1973 war Egyptian and Israeli lines were established on either side of a UN buffer zone. Under the 1979 Egyptian-Israeli agreement a large proportion of the area was returned to Egypt with Israeli withdrawal completed in 1982.

FRANK SINATRA *He is seen (left) in a comic scene with Bing Crosby (centre) and Dean Martin.*

Sinatra, Frank (Francis Albert S.; 1915-) US singer and film actor, who recorded his first hit, "All or Nothing at All," in 1943. His nonsinging role in the film *From Here to Eternity* (1953), earned him an Oscar; he subsequently appeared in such films as *Guys and Dolls* (1955), *The Manchurian Candidate* (1962), and *The First Deadly Sin* (1980). He has remained a popular singer and recorded such hits as "Strangers in the Night" (1966).

Sinclair, Upton (1878-1968) US novelist. A committed socialist, he used the profits from *The Jungle* (1906), a novel of social protest, to establish a cooperative for left-wing writers and to finance several unsuccessful political campaigns. The best known of his many polemical novels are the 11-volume Lanny Budd series known as *World's End* (1940-53).

Sind A province in SE Pakistan, on the Arabian Sea. From the broad Indus lowland it extends E into the Thar Desert and W into rocky hills. Grains, other crops, and livestock are raised. Important industries include textiles, chemicals, and cement. *History*: Sind's history goes back 5000 years. Islam was introduced in 711-12 AD and British rule established in 1843. Area: 140 914 sq km (54 407 sq mi). Population (1981): 19 029 000. Capital: Karachi.

Singapore, Republic of A republic in SE Asia, off the S tip of Peninsular Malaysia, consisting of the island of Singapore and over 50 islets. The city of Singapore, located in the S, occupies a substantial part of the island's area. The majority of the diverse population is Chinese with minorities of Malays, Indians, and others. *Economy*: Singapore is the largest port in SE Asia and lies on a major searoute. It is a major commercial centre and in recent years industry has been expanded and diversified. The chief industries are oil refining (it has the third largest refining complex in the world), shipbuilding and repairing, textiles, and electronics. The fishing industry is being developed, ornamental fish being an important export. The main exports are rubber, oil and oil products, machinery, and transport equipment. *History*: although a prosperous commercial centre in the middle ages, the island was largely uninhabited in 1819 when Sir Stamford Raffles established a station of the British East India Company here. In 1824 it was ceded to Britain as part of the *Straits Settlements. During World War II it was occupied by the Japanese, the British defence forces having surrendered in 1942. It became a separate British colony in 1946 and gained its independence in 1959. It joined the Federation of Malaysia on its formation (1963) but broke away in 1965, following conflict with the predominantly Malay central government, and formed an independent republic. The British military presence was phased out after 1967. Singapore has two universities: the University of Singapore (1962) and Nanyang University (1953). President: Wee Kim Wee. Prime minister: Lee Kuan Yew (1922–). Official languages: Chinese, English, Malay, and Tamil. Official currency: Singapore dollar of 100 cents. Area: 602 sq km (232 sq mi). Population (1983 est): 2 503 000.

Singer, Isaac Bashevis (1904–) US novelist and short-story writer. Born into a rabbinical Jewish family in Poland, he emigrated to the USA in 1935. His novels and collections of stories, written in Yiddish and frequently dramatizing traditional themes from Jewish life in Poland, include *Gimpel the Fool* (1957), *The Slave* (1960), *Shosha* (1978), *Old Love* (1979), and *The Collected Stories of Isaac Bashevis Singer* (1982). He won the Nobel Prize in 1978.

Singer, Isaac Merrit (1811-75) US inventor, who in 1857 designed and built the first commercially successful domestic sewing machine. It was a great improvement on Elias *Howe's machine and incorporated a number of innovations, such as continuous stitching, that remain the basis of all modern sewing machines.

singing The use of the human voice as a musical instrument, involving the control of a column of air sent from the lungs through the larynx, where it activates the vocal cords, and the subsequent resonance of the sounds produced within the sinus and mouth cavities. Styles of singing vary enormously in an art that covers many traditional folk techniques as well as those cultivated in Europe for opera and art song. The greatest European school of singing was the lyrical *bel canto (Italian: fine singing) style taught by the Italians in the 17th and 18th centuries. In the 19th century singers developed more dramatic and declamatory techniques in order to be heard over the increasingly large orchestra. In the 20th century singers have made use of microphones to amplify the voice,

particularly in pop music. *See also* alto; baritone; bass; contralto; countertenor; soprano; tenor.

Sing Sing. *See* Ossining.

Sinhalese The major ethnic group in Sri Lanka. They speak an *Indo-Aryan language that has been much influenced by *Pali and the Dravidian languages, particularly *Tamil. They are descended from migrants from Bengal who colonized Sri Lanka during the 5th century BC. An agricultural people, they base their social organization on caste and practise Theravada Buddhism.

sinkhole (*or* sink) A saucer-like hollow in the ground surface, typical of chalk and limestone areas. It may form through the solvent action on limestone of rain containing dissolved carbon dioxide; alternatively it may be due to a rock collapse. Sinkholes often act as channels down which water seeps into underground drainage systems.

Sinkiang Uigur. *See* Xinjiang Uygur Autonomous Region.

sinking fund A fund set up to reduce a debt: it is maintained by regular payments and accumulated interest. Such funds have been established at intervals to reduce the *national debt.

Sinn Féin (Irish: Ourselves) An Irish nationalist party organized by Arthur Griffith in 1905. In 1918, under Eamon *De Valera, it won a majority of the Irish seats in the British parliament and achieved the creation of the Irish Free State in 1922. Sinn Féin exists today as the political wing of the republican movement. *See also* Irish Republican Army.

Sino-Japanese Wars 1. (1894-95) The war between China and Japan resulting from rivalry in Korea. War was declared after the Japanese sank the *Kowshing*, which was transporting Chinese reinforcements to aid the Korean king in suppressing the Tonghak uprising. Japan inflicted a crushing defeat on China, which was forced to pay a large indemnity and cede Taiwan, the Pescadores, and the Liaodong peninsula. 2. (1937-45) The war between China and Japan brought about by Japanese expansion into China in the 1930s. The Japanese had established a puppet state in Manchuria (*see* Manchukuo) in 1932 but only after the negotiation of a Nationalist-Communist *United Front against Japan did full war break out. The Japanese took Shanghai and Nanchang in 1937 and Wuhan and Canton in 1938. Their position remained strong until the USA entered World War II (1941) and gave China assistance. After Japan's surrender (1945) China regained Manchuria, Taiwan, and the Pescadores.

Sinop 42 02N 35 09E A port in central N Turkey, on the Black Sea. Ancient Sinope was the most important Greek colony on the Euxine (Black) Sea and flourished under Mithridates the Great, during whose reign fine buildings and a harbour were constructed. It became part of the Ottoman Empire in 1458. Population (1980): 18 328.

Sino-Tibetan languages A group of languages spoken in E Asia. It includes all the *Chinese dialects (which use the same alphabet but differ substantially in sound), the Tibeto-Burman languages (Tibetan, Burmese, and many related languages spoken in the valleys of the Himalayas), and probably the Tai languages, such as Siamese, Laotian, and Shan. The main characteristic that justifies this large grouping is the monosyllabic nature of the vocabulary of all these languages and their use of tonality to differentiate otherwise similar words. They are all isolating languages, that is they use word order, not inflection, to determine grammatical relations.

sintering The heating without melting of powdered substance, usually metal or plastic, so that it becomes a solid mass. *See also* powder metallurgy.

Sintra (former name: Cintra) 38 48N 9 22W A town in central Portugal. Its beauty has been celebrated by several literary figures, including Byron in his *Childe Harolde*. The many notable buildings include the royal palace (14th-15th centuries) in Moorish and gothic styles. It is a tourist and agricultural centre. Population (1981): 20 574.

Sinŭiju 40 04N 124 25E A port in North Korea, on the River Yalu opposite Andong, China. Its industrial development began during the Japanese occupation (1910–45) and its principal industries include sawmilling and the manufacture of paper. Population (1980 est): 305 000.

sinus A hollow cavity, especially one in a bone. The term usually refers to the air sinuses of the head, which are cavities in the facial bones; all have connections to the nasal cavity and they are susceptible to infection (*see* sinusitis). The term is also used for a pus-filled channel leading from an infected organ or tissue to a surface (usually the skin).

sinusitis Inflammation of the sinuses—the spaces in the skull that are connected to the nose. They commonly become infected when a patient has a cold or similar infection, causing pain in the face and prolonging the original illness. Sinusitis can also be caused by an allergic reaction. If the inflammation persists the affected sinuses may need to be surgically drained or washed out.

Siouan languages A family of North American Indian languages including Dakota *Sioux, *Crow, and several others. Most are spoken by Plains tribes. Some experts classify the Siouan languages as a branch of a larger family called Macro-Siouan, which includes the Iroquoian and Caddoan languages.

Sioux A confederation of North American Plains Indian tribes, also known as the Dakota. They fought fiercely against White encroachments upon their territories and defeated Gen Custer at the battle of the *Little Bighorn (1876) under their leaders Sitting Bull and Crazy Horse. They were ultimately subdued, one group making a last stand at *Wounded Knee (1890).

Sioux City 42 30N 96 23W A city in the USA, in Iowa on the Missouri River. An agricultural trading centre, it has a large livestock market and many food-processing plants. Population (1980): 82 003.

Sioux Falls 43 34N 96 42W A city in the USA, in South Dakota on the Big Sioux River. Founded in 1857, it has one of the country's largest sheep and cattle markets and is an important wheat centre. Manufactures include farm machinery and electrical components. Population (1980): 81 071.

Siqueiros, David Alfaro (1896–1974) Mexican painter, one of the leaders in the Mexican Revolution of 1910 and one of the founders of modern Mexican art. A committed socialist from the start of his career, Siqueiros is best remembered for his monumental murals that reflected his intimate knowledge of the Mexican people. His first major murals were painted in collaboration with *Rivera and *Orozco in the National Preparatory School, Mexico City; perhaps the most impressive is *The March of Humanity*, measuring 4600 sq m (50 000 sq ft), which Siqueiros painted while he was in prison for his political activities. After the 1950s he was internationally recognized as one of Mexico's greatest artists.

siren An eel-like *salamander belonging to a North American family (*Sirenidae*; 3 species). Sirens have no hind legs, very small forelegs, and permanent gills. They hunt for worms, snails, etc., in ponds and swamps. The largest species is the 60-cm mud-coloured great siren (*Siren lacertina*) and the smallest is the grey mud siren (*Pseudobranchus striatus*), about 20 cm long.

Sirens In Greek mythology, female creatures, sometimes portrayed with birdlike features, who lured sailors to their island by their singing and then destroyed them. *Odysseus saved himself by tying himself to the mast of his ship and filling the ears of his crew with wax. The *Argonauts were protected by the superior singing of *Orpheus.

Sirius (*or* Dog Star) The brightest star in the sky, with an apparent magnitude of –1.47. It occurs in the constellation Canis Major and can be found by following the descending

line of Orion's Belt. It is also one of the nearest stars, lying 8.7 light years away. It forms a visual *binary star with **Sirius B**, which was the first *white dwarf to be detected, in 1915.

sirocco (*or* scirocco) A southerly wind occurring in N Africa, Sicily, and S Italy. Hot and dry on the N African coast, it picks up moisture as it crosses the Mediterranean Sea bringing extensive cloud to S Italy.

SISAL   *The fibre is obtained from the leaves of the plant, which are up to 1.8 m long. Mature plants produce flower stalks, up 6 m high, bearing yellow flowers.*

sisal A perennial plant, *Agave sisalana*, native to central America and cultivated throughout the tropics for its fibre. The plant, the stem of which grows to a height of only 90 cm, matures three to five years after planting and yields fibre for seven to eight years. Sisal fibre is obtained by crushing the leaves to a pulp and then scraping the pulp from the fibre, which is washed and dried. It is used in shipping, general industry, and agriculture.

siskin A Eurasian *finch, *Carduelis spinus*, occurring in N forests and at high altitudes in the south. It is about 12 cm long with a dark yellow-green plumage, paler streaked underparts, bright-yellow wingbars, and in the male a black chin and crown. Siskins feed on small seeds, particularly those extracted from alder cones.

Sisley, Alfred (1839–99) Impressionist painter, born in Paris of British parents. In 1862, while training under Charles Gleyre (1808–74), he met *Monet and *Renoir and later exhibited with them. In the 1870s he produced some of his best landscapes, for example *Misty Morning* (Louvre), and three pictures of the *Floods at Port-Marly*. Unable to sell his works, he spent his last years in poverty.

Sistine Chapel The principal chapel of the Vatican, so called because it was built for Pope Sixtus V (1473) by Giovanni dei Dolci. It is the meeting place for the College of Cardinals but is chiefly famous for its Renaissance interior decoration, with murals by *Perugino, *Botticelli, and *Ghirlandaio and the roof and ceiling by *Michelangelo.

Sisyphus A legendary Greek king of Corinth. For various offences he was condemned in the underworld eternally to roll a boulder to the top of a hill, from whence it always rolled down again.

sitar An Indian long-necked *lute with a resonating body made from a large gourd, seven metal strings stopped against movable arched frets, and a series of sympathetic strings. The distinctive pitch distortions of sitar music are achieved by pulling and easing the strings over the raised frets. □musical instruments.

sitatunga A spiral-horned antelope, *Tragelaphus spekei*, of central African swamplands, also called marshbuck or water kodoe. Long-legged and up to 120 cm high at the shoulder, it is deep brown with white markings on the face, chest, and back. The female lacks horns. Sitatungas feed on shrubs and aquatic plants.

Sitka 57 05N 135 20W A port in the USA, in Alaska on Baranof Island. Founded in 1799, it was the capital of Russian America until 1867 and is the site of a Russian Orthodox cathedral (1848). It was an important US naval base during World War II. The main industries are fishing and timber. Population (1984): 8350.

Sitting Bull (c. 1834-93) American Sioux Indian chief. Resisting US expansion into the Plains, Sitting Bull led the massacre of Gen Custer and his men at the *Little Bighorn (1876). After an amnesty he settled on a Dakota reservation but was killed during further hostilities in the 1890s.

Sitwell, Edith (1887-1964) British poet and writer. The eldest child of an aristocratic family, she and her brother Osbert played the roles of highly publicized rebels against bourgeois philistinism. A lighthearted aestheticism characterizes her early experimental poetry, especially *Façade* (1923), for which Sir William Walton wrote a musical accompaniment, and *Gold Coast Customs* (1929). Her brother **Sir Osbert Sitwell** (1892-1969) wrote poems, short stories, and novels, notably *Before the Bombardment* (1926), but his best-known works are his nostalgic autobiographical memoirs. Both he and his sister gave encouragement to a number of writers, artists, and musicians. The youngest brother **Sir Sacheverell Sitwell** (1897–) is best known as an art critic, especially of baroque art, and as a travel-book writer. He was made a CH in 1984.

SI units (Système International d'Unités) An international system of units, based on the *m.k.s. system, used for all scientific purposes. It has seven base units (metre, kilogram, second, ampere, kelvin, candela, and mole) and two supplementary units (radian and steradian). All physical quantities are expressed in these units or in derived units consisting of combinations of these units, 17 of which have special names and agreed symbols. Decimal multiples of all units are expressed by a set of prefixes. Where possible a prefix representing 10 raised to a power that is a multiple of 3 is used.

Sivaji (1627-80) Emperor of India (1647-80), who founded the Maratha dynasty. Born and reared in Poona (later the Maratha capital), he raised a guerrilla force and soon took control of a large part of Maharashtra. A strong opponent of the Mogul Empire, he was crowned as independent king in 1647 and spread his dominion into S India, leaving a powerful legacy for his successors.

Sivas 39 44N 37 01E A town in central Turkey. It is a trading centre for grain, wine, and minerals and has 13th-century Seljuq buildings and a university (1973). Population (1980): 172 864.

Six, Les Six French composers: Auric, Louis Durey (1888-1979), Honegger, Milhaud, Poulenc, and Germaine Tailleferre (1892-1983). These composers came briefly under the influence of Cocteau and Satie in the 1920s, united in protest against lingering Romanticism and impressionism in French music. They each developed an individual style, however, and did not long remain a group.

Six Day War. *See* Israel.

Sixtus IV (Francesco della Rovere; 1414-84) Pope (1471-84), notorious for his nepotism, especially in his support of his nephew, the future *Julius II, and for political intrigue, especially against the Medici in Florence. A patron of arts and learning, he instigated the building of the Sistine Chapel and founded its choir.

Sixtus V (Felice Peretti; 1521-90) Pope (1585-90), who reformed papal administration and taxation. He issued a revised version of the Vulgate and was a notable patron of the arts, instigating the building of the Vatican Library and Lateran Palace.

Sjælland (English name: Zealand; German name: Seeland) The largest of the Danish islands, bounded by the Kattegat,

the Sound, the Baltic Sea, and the Great Belt. Predominantly low lying and undulating, its fertile soil is important for both arable and dairy farming. Area: 7016 sq km (2709 sq mi). Population (1976 est): 1 987 549. Chief town: Copenhagen.

Skagerrak A channel in N Europe, lying between Denmark and Norway and connecting the Kattegat to the North Sea.

skaldic poetry Old Norse poetry originally recited by skalds (professional bards generally attached to a princely or noble retinue). In contrast to the heroic poetry of the Eddaic tradition (*see* Eddas), it was descriptive and occasional, characterized by elaborate alliteration, internal rhyming, convoluted word order, and highly allusive, often riddling phrases called "kennings." It apparently originated in 9th-century Norway, but its outstanding practitioners were Icelanders (*see* Icelandic literature).

Skalkottas, Nikos (1904-49) Greek composer. He was a pupil of Kurt Weill and Schoenberg. His works include two piano concertos, 36 Greek dances for orchestra, four string quartets, and a ballet suite *La Mer grecque* (1948).

skanda (Kumara *or* Karttikeya) In Hindu mythology, a battle god. In one account he is the son of *Shiva, born to defend the gods against the demons. He is represented with 6 heads and 12 arms and rides on a peacock.

Skanderbeg (George Kastrioti; c. 1404-68) Albanian national hero. Brought up in Islam as a hostage of the Turkish sultan, Skanderbeg led (1444-68) the Albanian resistance movement against Turkey. The use of guerrilla tactics aided by Albania's mountainous topography and a series of alliances with the great powers of Europe ensured his success but after his death the movement collapsed.

Skåne (*or* Scania) A peninsular area in S Sweden, on the Baltic Sea and the Sound. It is known as the "granary of Sweden," its fertile plains producing wheat, rye, barley, oats, potatoes, and sugar beet. Area: 10 957 sq km (4230 sq mi).

Skara Brae A late Neolithic village in Scotland, in Mainland, Orkney, dating to about 2000 BC. The houses were built of dry stone with stone slabs for furniture, all very well preserved. An artificial mound of refuse was heaped over the entire settlement, probably as protection against the weather.

skate A large *ray fish belonging to the family *Rajidae* (over 100 species), especially the genus *Raja*. 50-200 cm long, skates have a diamond-shaped flattened body with spiny or thorny structures on the upper surface and often an extremely long snout. They lay eggs and some have weak *electric organs on the tail.

skateboarding The recreation and competitive sport of riding on a board about 70 cm (2.3 ft) long to which two pairs of roller-skate wheels are attached. The sport began in about 1960 in California and combines surfing, skiing, and roller-skating techniques. Speeds of up to 107 km per hour (66 mph) have been attained. The first world championships were staged in 1966.

Skegness 53 10N 0 21E A resort in E England, on the Lincolnshire coast, one of the nearest to the industrial centres of the Midlands. Light engineering is also important. Population (1981): 14 452.

skeleton The rigid supporting framework of an animal's body. In such animals as arthropods it lies outside the body (exoskeleton) and must be shed periodically during growth. Vertebrates, including man, have a skeleton (endoskeleton) of *bones and cartilage that is entirely within the body and grows with age. The human skeleton is made up of over 200 bones, which are connected to each other at *joints and held together by ligaments. The skeleton protects and supports the soft tissues of the body and provides a firm surface for the attachment of muscles and a system of levers that are essential for movement. *See* Plate IV.

Skelmersdale 53 33N 2 48W A town in NW England, in S Lancashire. Designated for development as a new town in

1961 to relieve overcrowding in Merseyside, industries include engineering. Population (1981): 39 144.

Skelton, John (c. 1460–1529) English poet. He was court poet to Henry VII and tutor to the future Henry VIII. His poems include *Speke Parot* (1521), *Colin Clout* (1522), and other satires, several of them attacks on Cardinal *Wolsey. Essentially medieval in form and theme, the most interesting of his poems are often written in short rhyming lines of doggerel verse, known as Skeltonics.

Skiddaw 54 40N 3 08W A mountain in NW England, in Cumbria, in the Lake District. Height: 931 m (3054 ft).

skiing A means of locomotion, a recreation, and a sport consisting of sliding over snow on a pair of specially shaped runners (skis) attached to the feet. Skis have been used in Scandinavia since the Stone Age, but skiing for pleasure did not develop until the late 19th century. It is divided into **Alpine** (*or* downhill) **skiing**, which irtcludes the events of "downhill" (straightforward racing), slalom (a winding course through "gates"), and giant slalom (faster and less winding than slalom) and **Nordic skiing**, comprising cross-country (or *langlauf*) skiing, which involves self-propulsion and requires lighter equipment than Alpine skiing, and ski-jumping. Alpine and Nordic competitions are controlled by the International Ski Federation. There is also freestyle skiing (downhill skiing that is both balletic and gymnastic), skijoring (being towed on skis by a horse or vehicle), and ski-flying, which is *hang-gliding on skis. Recreational skiing has become a vast holiday industry, the most notable skiing areas of the world being the Alps and the Rockies.

Skikda (former name: Philippeville) 36 58N 6 51E A port in NE Algeria, on the Mediterranean Sea. Occupying the site of the Roman port of Rusicade, it has the remains of a Roman theatre. It receives natural gas from the Sahara and exports iron ore. Population (1983 est): 141 159.

skimmer A black-and-white bird belonging to a family (*Rhynchopidae*; 3 species) occurring chiefly around western Atlantic coasts and African and Asian rivers. The skimmer fishes by flying close to the water, shearing the surface with the lower mandible and snapping the bill shut as soon as a fish is caught. *See* Plate V.

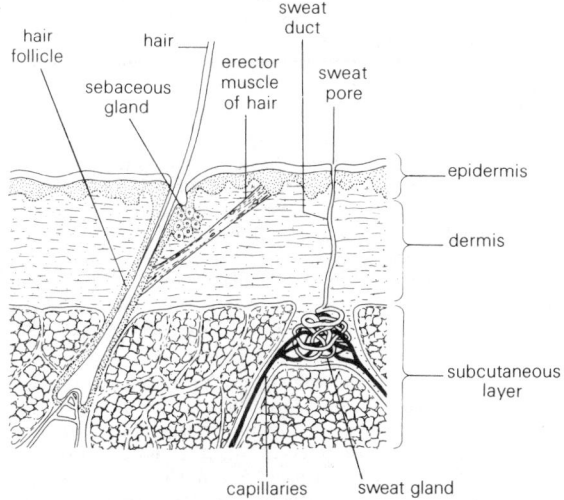

SKIN *A vertical section through the human skin shows its microscopical structure. The subcutaneous layer of fat cells provides insulation.*

skin The tissue that covers the body. The outer layer (epidermis) consists of several layers of cells: the outermost layer contains dead cells made of keratin, which are con-

stantly sloughed off and replaced by the deeper layers of continuously dividing cells. The inner layer of skin (dermis) contains *connective tissue with blood vessels, sensory nerve endings, *sweat glands, sebaceous glands (which secrete an oily substance, sebum, that protects the skin surface), and *hair follicles. The skin has several important functions. It protects the body from external injury and desiccation; it assists in regulating body temperature (e.g. by sweating); and it is sensitive to touch, temperature, and pain. The branch of medicine concerned with the diagnosis and treatment of skin disorders is called **dermatology**. Skin grafting is one of the most important and successful *transplantation operations.

skink A lizard belonging to the family *Scincidae* (600 species), occurring throughout the tropics and in temperate North America. Skinks are well adapted for burrowing: up to 50 cm long, they have cylindrical streamlined bodies with smooth scales, internal eardrums, a transparent covering over the eye, and often reduced limbs. Many skinks have an elongated tail and move with sideways undulations of the body. They feed on insects or plant material and many bear live young. □reptile.

Skinner, Burrhus Frederic (1904–) US psychologist and advocate of *behaviourism. Many of Skinner's experiments involved teaching animals (such as rats and pigeons) by reinforcing the desired action, when achieved, with rewards of food. He developed equipment, including the Skinner box, in order to standardize the teaching of simple actions to small animals and applied his principles to human educational aids. His novel *Walden Two* (1948) describes a utopian society based on his behaviourist principles. His other works include *The Behaviour of Organisms* (1938), *Science and Human Behaviour* (1953), and *Beyond Freedom and Dignity* (1971).

skipjack A *tuna fish, *Euthynnus pelamis*, also called ocean bonito, found in all warm seas. It has four to seven dark horizontal stripes along its belly and grows to about 70 cm long.

skipper A butterfly belonging to the widely distributed family *Hesperiidae* (about 3000 species). The adults are small and have a stout body and head resembling a moth and a swift darting flight. The caterpillars feed on plants and pupate in cocoons made of silk and leaves.

Skipton 53 58N 2 01W A market town in N England, in North Yorkshire. It is also a tourist centre, with a castle (dating from the 11th century), and has a textile industry. Population (1981): 13 246.

Skopje (Turkish name: Usküb) 42 00N 21 28E A city in S Yugoslavia, the capital of Macedonia, on the River Vardar. It became the capital of Serbia in the 14th century and was occupied by the Turks (1392). It was burned down in 1689 to stop a cholera epidemic and almost completely destroyed by an earthquake in 1963. It has a university (1949) and varied industries, including cement, brick, glass, and steel. Population (1981): 506 547.

skua A large hook-billed seabird belonging to a family (*Stercorariidae*; 4 species), also called jaeger, breeding in Arctic and Antarctic regions and wintering in warmer latitudes. 52–58 cm long, skuas are strong fliers and have a dark plumage with two long central tail feathers. They scavenge around seabird colonies, feeding on eggs, chicks, and food scraps. Order: *Charadriiformes* (gulls, plovers, etc.).

skull The skeleton of the head, made up of 22 bones of varying shapes and sizes. The cranium consists of eight flat platelike bones that surround and protect the brain. Some of these contribute to the formation of the facial skeleton. The remaining 14 bones, including the mandible (*see* jaw), form the face: the mandible is the only movable bone in the skull; the rest are connected by immovable joints called sutures. Numerous holes puncture the skull to allow blood vessels and nerves to pass to and from the brain. The largest of these is the foramen magnum at the base of the skull, through which the spinal cord passes. *See* Plate IV.

skunk   A black and white carnivorous mammal of the family *Mustelidae* that is known for its defensive habit of ejecting a foul-smelling fluid. The nine species are found in North, South, and Central America. The well known North American striped skunk (*Mephitis mephitis*) inhabits woodland, feeding at night on insects, mice, and fruit.

skydiving (*or* freefalling)   The sport of jumping from an aeroplane with a parachute and performing manoeuvres before opening it. During this period of "free fall" the parachutist glides or performs rolls, turns, or other stunts. In a team event divers pass a baton to each other or form a star pattern by joining hands. *See also* parachuting.

Skye   The largest and most northerly island of the Inner Hebrides group, off the W coast of Scotland. The island's economy is based chiefly on crofting and tourism; sheep and cattle are also raised. Area: 1735 sq km (670 sq mi). Population (1981): 8139. Chief town: Portree.

Skye terrier   A breed of dog originating on the island of Skye and used to flush foxes and badgers from cover. It has a long body, short legs, and a large head with erect or drooping ears. The soft undercoat is covered by a long straight outer coat which may reach the ground. Colours are grey, fawn, cream, or black. Height: 25 cm.

Skylab   A US manned space station launched into earth orbit in May, 1973. Three groups of three US astronauts were conveyed to and from the orbiting laboratory by modified Apollo spacecraft (*see* Apollo moon programme). They remained on board for a total of 513 man days during the period May, 1973, to February, 1974. In a weightless environment, they conducted a variety of experiments and observations (especially of the sun). Physical and psychological fitness were carefully monitored. Skylab's orbit eventually became unstable and it crash-landed in July, 1979, in the Indian Ocean.

skylark   A *lark*, *Alauda arvensis*, occurring in Eurasia and N Africa and noted for its sustained warbling flight song. It is about 17 cm long, with brown plumage, a small crest and a white stripe above the eye. Skylarks were a delicacy in the 19th century and are still trapped in parts of Europe.

Skyros (Modern Greek name: Skíros)   A Greek island in the central Aegean Sea, the largest of the Northern Sporades. Area: 205 sq km (79 sq mi). Population (1981): 2757.

skyscraper   A multistorey building. Skyscraper building was stimulated by the commercial need for space in cities where land was scarce and land rents high. The first skyscraper, the Equitable Life Assurance Society, was built in New York in 1868. Architecturally it was made possible by the development of high-speed lifts in the 1850s and the introduction of a metal frame in Chicago in the 1880s. The Empire State Building (1930–32) in New York was the tallest in the world until the completion in the 1970s, in the same city, of the World Trade Centre. In 1974 the Sears Tower in Chicago became the world's tallest skyscraper, at 473 m (1454 ft).

Slade, Felix (1790–1868) British art collector, who bequeathed his collection to the British Museum. He also endowed professorships of art at the Universities of Oxford and Cambridge and at University College, London. The Slade School of Fine Art is named after him.

slander.   *See* defamation.

Slaney, Mary (Mary Dekker; 1958–) US middle-distance runner. Having fallen in the 1984 Olympic 3000 m after a clash with Zola *Budd, she set (1985) a new women's record for the mile at 4 minutes 16.71 seconds.

Slánský, Rudolf (1901–52) Czechoslovak statesman, who died in an antisemitic purge. Slánský was secretary general of the Communist Party in Czechoslovakia's postwar government. In 1951 he and nine other Jews were executed for espionage.

He was posthumously absolved.

slate   A fine-grained rock produced by the low-grade metamorphism of mudstone, siltstone, or other argillaceous sediments. Its perfect cleavage is due to the parallel alignment of platy crystals of mica and chlorite. Slate is used as a constructional material, formerly for roofs.

slave-making ant   An *ant, confined to the N hemisphere, that raids colonies of other ants to capture larvae and pupae, which develop into worker "slaves." Genera: *Harpagoxenus*, *Formica*, *Polyergus*, *Anergates*. *See also* Amazon ant.

Slave River   A river in W Canada, flowing N from Lake Athabasca (Alberta) to Great Slave Lake (Mackenzie district); part of the *Mackenzie River system. Length: 415 km (258 mi).

slavery   The condition in which human beings are owned by others as chattels. Slavery existed from earliest times. In ancient Greece and early Rome captives from conquered lands were the chief source of slaves, who often had special skills, were well treated, and might be freed (manumission). The condition of slaves in later Roman times greatly worsened until the deteriorating economy led to the virtual disappearance of slaves and the emergence of *serfs in the middle ages. Slaving became a lucrative business in the 16th century, when European traders began to transport thousands of Africans to the Americas. By the early 19th century humanitarians, such as William *Wilberforce, had begun to attack slavery on moral grounds and it was abolished in all British territories by 1834. In the USA, the *Abolition Movement campaigned against slavery in the South and the issue became one of the causes of the Civil War. In 1863 Abraham Lincoln issued the Emancipation Proclamation, officially liberating all slaves in the southern states; in 1865 the Constitution was amended to abolish slavery.

Slavonic languages   A subgroup of the *Indo-European language family. Slavonic languages are native to E Europe and NW Asia. They are often classified into three groups: South Slavonic (languages of Yugoslavia and Bulgaria, including *Serbo-Croat, Slovene, *Bulgarian, and Macedonian); West Slavonic (languages of Czechoslovakia, Poland, and E Germany, including Czech, *Slovak, Sorbian, and Polish); and East Slavonic (Russian, Belorussian, and Ukrainian). This division is not, however, as clearcut as the geographical classification suggests. All the dialects are linked historically and all developed from a common ancestor, Proto-Slavonic. Most Slavs speak Russian, many learning it as a second language.

Slavs   Peoples of E Europe and parts of W Asia. They may be divided into three groups: Eastern Slavs (including Russians, Ukrainians, and Belorussians); Western Slavs (including Poles, Czechs, Slovaks, and Sorbs or Wends); and Southern Slavs (including Serbs, Croats, Slovenes, Macedonians, and Bulgarians). Migrating from Asia these peoples settled this region during the second or third millennium BC. The present Slav nations began to emerge around the 5th and 6th centuries AD, when there was further westward movement. *See also* Slavonic languages.

sleep   A naturally occurring state of unconsciousness. Orthodox sleep occurs in four stages, which vary in depth. The electrical activity of the brain continues but is more rhythmical than when awake and reacts less to outside stimuli. It is periodically interrupted by paradoxical sleep, in which the eyes move rapidly and the brain is more active, but the muscles are especially relaxed. Paradoxical sleep is particularly associated with *dreams. Sleep is biologically necessary and probably helps to control physical growth; individuals' needs vary widely between three and ten hours a night. Insomnia can be caused by changes of routine, *anxiety, *depression, and by many drugs. Disorders of sleep include *sleepwalking and night terrors (*see* nightmares).

sleeping sickness   A disease caused by infection with a protozoan of the genus *Trypanosoma*, which is transmitted by the tsetse fly and occurs only in East, central, and West Africa: it is the African form of *trypanosomiasis. Initial symptoms are swelling of the lymph nodes and fever, which persists for several months. The brain is then infected, causing lethargy, weakness, and depression: without treatment the patient dies. The drugs pentamidine and suramin can be used to treat the early stages of the disease; arsenic-based compounds are needed when the brain is affected. Attempts to prevent the disease by eradicating the fly have not yet proved successful.

sleepwalking (*or* somnambulism) A disorder of *sleep in which the sleeper walks about and performs complex activities automatically and without regaining consciousness. It is quite common in children and not a sign of illness. In adults it can indicate immaturity or *neurosis.

sleepy sickness A highly infectious viral disease of the brain. Known medically as *encephalitis lethargica, it is marked by drowsiness leading eventually to coma. A worldwide epidemic of the disease occurred between 1917 and 1924.

slide rule A mathematical instrument for performing multiplication and division. It consists of a rule that slides along a groove in another rule. Both rules are marked with logarithmic scales so that products and quotients can be calculated by effectively adding and subtracting *logarithms in the form of lengths of rule. Slide rules have now been largely replaced by pocket *calculators.

Sligo (Irish name: Contae Shligigh) A county in the NW Republic of Ireland, in Connacht bordering on the Atlantic Ocean. Chiefly hilly, much of the land is devoted to pasture; cattle and dairy farming are important. It possesses some coal, lead, and copper. Area: 1795 sq km (693 sq mi). Population (1981): 55 474. County town: Sligo.

Slim, William Joseph, 1st Viscount (1891-1970) British field marshal. He joined the army at the outbreak of World War I and subsequently served in the Indian Army. In World War II he became commander of the 14th Army (the "forgotten army") in Burma (1943). After successful operations against the Japanese he became commander in chief of Allied land forces in SE Asia. In 1948 he became chief of the imperial general staff and was then governor general of Australia (1953-60).

slime moulds Organisms belonging to the group *Myxomycophyta*, usually regarded as fungi (since they produce fruiting bodies) but having affinities with the protozoa. The so-called true slime moulds (*Myxomycetes*) are found beneath logs and in other damp places. They consist of slimy sheets of protoplasm that engulf bacteria, wood particles, etc. The cellular slime moulds (*Acrasiales*) are single-celled amoeba-like organisms found in soil. The parasitic slime moulds (*Plasmodiophorales*) live in the tissues of plants; the species *Plasmodiophora brassicae* causes *clubroot in cabbages.

slipper orchid A terrestrial *orchid of the tropical Asian genus *Paphiopedilum* (about 50 species) and the related genera *Cypripedium* and *Phragmipedium*. They are characterized by their flowers, which have a pouched slipper-shaped lip and are usually borne singly or in clusters of two or three. *Paphiopedilum* flowers are usually a mixture of white, brown, and green, often with darker markings; the leaves may also be mottled or otherwise marked. Slipper orchids are popular greenhouse ornamentals.

slippery elm Either of two North American trees, *Fremontodendron californica* (family *Bombacaceae*) or *Ulmus fulva* (family *Ulmaceae*). Mucilage extracted from the bark has been used in poultices and to treat diarrhoea, dysentery, and other conditions.

Sliven 42 40N 26 19E A town in E central Bulgaria. Its main industry is textiles, the first mill in Bulgaria having been opened here in 1834. Population (1982): 100 637.

SKYSCRAPER *The twin towers of the World Trade Center (1970–74) in New York rise to 412 m (1350 ft). They were built by Minoru Yamasaki.*

Sloane, Sir Hans (1660-1753) British physician and naturalist, whose collection of books, manuscripts, pictures, etc., formed the nucleus of the *British Museum. A keen botanist, Sloane collected over 800 new plants while in Jamaica. He succeeded Newton as president of the Royal Society (1727-41).

sloe. *See* blackthorn.

sloop A ⌐sailing vessel with a single mast set approximately one-third of the boat's length from the bows. Formerly used extensively in coastal fishing, sloops are now a favoured rig for yacht racing, since they are the most efficient design for sailing towards the wind. Older sloops were gaff-rigged; more modern vessels are marconi-rigged or Bermuda-rigged. Sloops more than 20 m (60 ft) long are rare because of the number of crew required to handle the large sails. *See also* ketch; yawl.

sloth A primitive arboreal *mammal belonging to the family *Bradypodidae* (7 species) of Central and South America, also called ai or unau. 50-65 cm long sloths are slow-moving and hang upside down from branches, feeding on leaves and fruit. Their greyish-brown fur lies so that rain runs off easily and is often greenish from algae living there, which helps to camouflage them. They cannot walk on the ground. Order: *Edentata*.

sloth bear A shaggy black *bear, *Melursus ursinus*, of S India and Sri Lanka. 1.5 m long and weighing about 100 kg, it feeds on bees or termites by tearing open nests with its long claws and sucking up the insects using its long snout.

Slough 51 31N 0 36W A town in SE England, in Berkshire. It grew rapidly after a large trading estate was built here in the 1920s and has a great variety of light industries. Population (1981): 87 005.

Slovak A Western Slavonic language, closely related to *Czech, spoken in E Czechoslovakia, where it is an official language. It is written in the Latin alphabet. There are three distinct dialects.

Slovakia (Czech name: Slovensko) A mountainous area and former province of E Czechoslovakia. Lying mainly within the Carpathian Mountains, it descends SW to the plains of the Danube Valley. It is chiefly agricultural, producing cereals, wine, fruit, and tobacco. *History*: settled by Slavic Slovaks (6th-7th centuries AD), Slovakia was incorporated into Great *Moravia in the 9th century. Conquered by the Magyars in the 10th century, Slovakia was part of Hungary until 1918 when it became a province of the Czechoslovak Republic, remaining as such until 1949, except for a period of independence immediately before and during World War II. Chief town: Bratislava.

Slovenia (Serbo-Croat name: Slovenija) A constituent republic of N Yugoslavia. It is mountainous and drained mainly by the Rivers Sava and Drava. Agriculture includes livestock raising; potatoes, cereals, and vegetables are grown. The republic possesses important deposits of coal, mercury, and zinc. *History*: it was chiefly under Habsburg rule from the 14th century until 1918, when it was incorporated into the kingdom of Serbs, Croats, and Slovenes, later renamed Yugoslavia. Area: 20 251 sq km (7819 sq mi). Population (1981): 1 891 864. Capital: Ljubljana.

slowworm A legless lizard, *Anguis fragilis*, also called blindworm, occurring in heaths and open woodlands of Europe. It is about 30 cm long, usually brown, grey, or reddish, and feeds on snails, slugs, and other soft-bodied invertebrates. Family: *Anguidae* (glass snakes and slow-worms).

slug A *gastropod mollusc of the order *Stylommatophora*, widely distributed in moist terrestrial habitats. Slugs have slimy soft bodies with the shell vestigial or absent. They may reach 20 cm in length, and can range in colour from yellow through red-brown to black. Some are carnivorous or scavenging while others feed on soft plant tissues. Subclass: *Pulmonata*. *Compare* sea slug.

slump. *See* depression.

Sluter, Claus (c. 1345-1406) Dutch sculptor. Working in Dijon under the patronage of Philip the Bold, Duke of Burgundy, he produced his most famous works for the ducal mausoleum in the monastery of Champmol. These included the portal sculptures, the *Well of Moses*, and figures on the duke's tomb. Breaking away from the *international gothic style, Sluter developed a bold realism, which influenced many European sculptors and painters of the 15th century.

Sluys, Battle of (24 June, 1340) A naval battle in the *Hundred Years' War, off the coast of Flanders, in which the French fleet was destroyed by the skilful use of archers by *Edward III's army. The victory gave the English crucial strategic control over the Channel.

smallage. *See* celery.

small arms Short-range low-weight *firearms, originally defined as capable of being handled by one individual, they included pistols, submachine guns, rifles, grenades, and shotguns. An artificial calibre ceiling of .60 in or, in some classification systems, 20 mm has had to be abandoned with the introduction of small rocket antitank guided missiles.

small claim In English law, a claim in contract for £500 or less. Claims involving £5,000 or less are dealt with in the County Courts (*see* courts of law), and where a small claim is in dispute the court may order it to be decided by an arbitrator (the court's Registrar) unless the parties choose otherwise. This enables such disputes to be resolved in an informal atmosphere. Also, in certain parts of the country, solicitors have established small claims schemes enabling disputing parties to submit voluntarily to arbitration.

smallpox A highly infectious virus disease marked by a skin rash that leaves permanent pitted scars. Smallpox is transmitted by direct contact; the initial symptoms of fever, prostration, severe headache, and backache are followed by

the appearance of the rash on the face and limbs. Secondary infection with staphylococci is often fatal. There is no specific treatment and as recently as 1967 the disease caused two million deaths. After a worldwide vaccination programme sponsored by the World Health Organization smallpox was officially declared to have been eradicated in 1979, after a two-year period during which no cases (apart from a laboratory-associated outbreak in the UK) were reported.

Smart, Christopher (1722-71) British poet. A prolific hack writer, he received little recognition in his lifetime for his poetry. He suffered from mental illness characterized by religious obsessions, and it was while he was confined that he wrote *Rejoice in the Lamb* (or *Jubilate Agno*; published 1939). His most famous work is *A Song to David* (1763), which went unnoticed by his contemporaries but is now regarded as one of the best poems of the 18th century.

smell, sense of. *See* nose.

smelt A slender food fish of the genus *Osmerus* and family *Osmeridae*, occurring in coastal and estuarine waters of Europe and North America. It migrates to fresh water to spawn. The European smelt (*O. eperlanus*), up to about 30 cm long, also called sparling, is greenish grey above and silvery below. It has a cucumber-like smell when eaten fresh. Order: *Salmoniformes*.

smelting The extraction of a metal from its ore by heating. The method used depends on the metal, the type of ore, and the melting points of both. The smelting takes place either in a *blast furnace (e.g. to extract iron) or a *reverberatory furnace (e.g. to extract copper).

Smetana, Bedřich (1824-84) Bohemian composer. He studied in Prague and took part in the revolution against Austria in 1848. In 1859 he left Sweden (where he had been conducting) and returned to Prague, joining a group of composers who were establishing a national opera. *The Brandenburgers in Bohemia* (1862-63) and *The Bartered Bride* (1863-66) were composed for it. In 1874 he became totally deaf but continued to compose, writing the four symphonic poems *Má Vlast* (1874-79) and a string quartet "From My Life" (1876). He died insane in an asylum.

smew A sawbilled *duck, *Mergus albellus*, that breeds in N Eurasia and winters south in the Mediterranean. It is 40-44 cm long, has a short bill, and feeds on fish and crustaceans. Drakes are white with black markings; females are grey with a chestnut head and white throat and cheeks.

Smilax A genus of shrubs and vines (about 300 species), also called catbriers, native to warm temperate and tropical regions. Many have prickly stems and the white or yellowish-green flowers produce red or bluish-black berries. Family: *Smilacaceae*. *See also* sarsaparilla.

Smiles, Samuel (1812-1904) British miscellaneous writer. He worked as a journalist and as an administrator in the flourishing railway industry. His best-known work is the didactic *Self-Help* (1859). He also wrote biographies of prominent industrialists, including Josiah Wedgwood and George Stephenson.

Smith, Adam (1723-90) Scottish moral philosopher and political economist. At Edinburgh University (1752-63), he lectured and wrote on moral philosophy. In 1776, he published *An Enquiry into the Nature and Causes of the Wealth of Nations*, an attack on *mercantilism that was to become the bible of the free-trade movement. He held that employment, trade, production, and distribution are as much a part of a nation's wealth as its money. An individual allowed to promote his own interests freely within the law often promotes the interests of society as a whole.

Smith, Bessie (1894-1937) US Black jazz singer and songwriter, known as "Empress of the Blues," who began her career in travelling shows and carnivals. In the 1920s she made records with Louis Armstrong and Fletcher Henderson (1898-1952). Her popularity declined in the 1930s. She died in a car crash.

Smith, F. E. *See* Birkenhead, F(rederick) E(dwin) Smith, 1st Earl of.

MAGGIE SMITH   *Starring as Joyce Chilvers in the film comedy* A Private Function, *a role for which she won the BAFTA Best Actress Award in 1984.*

Smith, Harvey (1938-) British showjumper and equestrian, who represented Britain in the Olympic Games in 1968 and 1972 and won numerous British championships, including the British Grand Prix five times. He became a professional in 1972.

Smith, Ian (Douglas) (1919-) Prime minister (1964-79) of Rhodesia (now *Zimbabwe). An advocate of White supremacy, he demanded full independence for Southern Rhodesia in 1964 but opposed Britain's stipulation that Black majority rule be prepared for. In 1965 he made a unilateral declaration of independence (UDI), which he maintained in spite of UN and UK sanctions until 1976, when he agreed to the principle of Black majority rule. He was a minister under Muzorewa (1979-80); in 1987 he was suspended for a year from the House of Assembly for opposing sanctions against South Africa.

Smith, John (c. 1580-1631) English colonist. In 1606, he invested in the new Virginia Company, which was granted a charter to settle in North America. On arrival at what became Jamestown, Virginia, he explored and charted the region. In 1607 he was saved from death at the hands of Indians by *Pocahontas. He returned to England in 1609 and wrote valuable accounts of his experiences.

Smith, Joseph (1805-44) US founder of the *Mormons. Smith announced in 1827 his discovery of the sacred *Book of Mormon*, which he claimed he had translated from two gold tablets written by a prophet named Mormon. His new church, founded in Fayette, New York (1830), grew rapidly but attracted opposition because of its doctrines. Smith encouraged westward migration and the group established itself in Nauvoo, Illinois (1840). While in jail on charges of conspiracy, Smith was killed by an angry mob. The Mormons continued westward to Utah under Brigham *Young.

Smith, Sir Keith Macpherson (1890-1955) Australian aviator, who with his brother **Sir Ross Macpherson Smith** (1892-1922) made the first flight from England to Australia (1919). It took 28 days. The brothers were subsequently knighted and awarded a prize of £10,000.

Smith, Maggie (1934-) British actress. A performer with an exceptional talent for comedy, she appeared in a number of films, including *The VIPs* (1963), *The Honey Pot* (1967), *The Prime of Miss Jean Brodie* (1969), *Murder by Death* (1976), and *A Room with a View* (1986).

Smith, Stevie (Florence Margaret S.; 1902-71) British poet. She published highly original and deceptively simple poetry, the characteristic tone of which was a blend of tenderness, toughness, and humour. The best known of her idiosyncratic novels is *Novel on Yellow Paper* (1936). Her *Collected Poems* (1975) were published posthumously, and she was the subject of a play (1977) and a film (1978).

Smithfield A district in the Greater London borough of Islington. It is noted for Smithfield Market, founded in the 12th century, which handles meat and poultry.

Smithson Two British architects in partnership. **Peter Smithson** (1923-) and his wife **Alison Smithson** (1928-) were among the first in the UK effectively to absorb the *international style of architecture. Their first major work, a school at Hunstanton, Norfolk (1954), caused considerable controversy, but their later designs, notably the *Economist* offices in London (1962-64), have been more warmly received.

Smithsonian Institution A research institution in Washington, DC. The Institution was founded in 1846 with a bequest from the Englishman James Smithson (1765-1829) as "an establishment for the increase and diffusion of knowledge." It has carried out important scientific work and explorations throughout the world, and administers several important history, science, and art museums, including the National Air and Space Museum and the National Collection of Fine Arts.

smog A fog containing a high proportion of smoke (its name is abbreviated from smoke fog) occurring chiefly in urban and industrial areas. Occasionally it may be particularly dense, as in London in 1952 when smog resulted in many deaths. Since the Clean Air Act (1956) in the UK, which introduced smokeless zones in towns and cities and controlled the gases emitted by industries, smogs have been virtually eliminated.

smoke tree (*or* smoke bush) One of several species of trees and shrubs having a whitish cloudy appearance at some stage of the season. The American smoke tree (*Cotinus obovatus*) grows to a height of 9 m and has a smokelike mass of whitish flower heads, as does the Australian smoke bush (*Conospermum stoechadis*). *Rhus cotinus* is the common smoke bush native to the Mediterranean area and parts of Asia.

Smolensk 54 49N 32 04E A city in the Soviet Union, in the W RSFSR on the River Dnepr. It has engineering, textile, and consumer-goods industries and several educational institutions. *History*: dating to at least the 9th century, it was sacked by the Tatars (13th century) and was subsequently disputed between Lithuania (and later Poland) and Russia, falling finally to the latter in 1654. It is on the route of Napoleon's retreat from Moscow in 1812 and was badly damaged in World War II. Population (1981 est): 311 000.

Smollett, Tobias (George) (1721-71) British novelist. Born and educated in Scotland, he enlisted in the navy and married a Jamaican heiress before settling in London in 1744. His picaresque novels, lively in style and unsophisticated and rambling in structure, include *Roderick Random* (1748), *Peregrine Pickle* (1751), and *Humphry Clinker* (1771). He was also a prolific journalist and translator. He died in Italy.

smooth snake A widespread Eurasian snake, *Coronella*

austriaca, that has smooth glossy scales and is brown or reddish with a pale belly and dark spots along its back and tail. Up to 65 cm long, it favours sandy heathlands and feeds on lizards, small snakes, and rodents. Family: *Colubridae*.

smuggling The illegal import or export of goods to evade payment of duties or official restrictions. Trading countries often impose bans, limitations, or taxes on certain goods, the evasion of which provides an incentive for smugglers. Smuggling has flourished from the time of the Greek city states until the present day, especially in Britain during the Napoleonic Wars. After World War II smuggling of guns, narcotics, gold, diamonds, and illegal immigrants became rife, particularly through international airlines and remote frontier towns. In recent years one of the primary concerns of world customs authorities, the function of which is to detect and prevent smuggling, has been the breaking of international narcotic smuggling networks.

smut A disease affecting flowering plants, particularly the cereals and grasses, caused by various *basidiomycete fungi of the genus *Ustilago*. Infection is not usually apparent until spore formation, when dark powdery masses of spores are released over the flower head. Stinking smuts, or bunts, are caused by fungi belonging to the related genus *Tilletia*. Both types of smut cause reduced yields of grain and are controlled by spraying crops with fungicide and by treating seed before sowing.

JAN SMUTS   *On campaign in S Africa in 1914, at the outbreak of World War I.*

Smuts, Jan (Christiaan) (1870-1950) South African statesman and general; prime minister (1919-24, 1939-48). Following a brilliant undergraduate career at Cambridge University he was called to the Bar in London, returning to Cape Town in 1895. He was a commando leader in the second *Boer War (1899-1902) but thereafter worked for reconciliation with Britain. He played an important part in the achievement of responsible government for the Transvaal (1906) and the Union of South Africa (1910),

becoming a minister in *Botha's government (1910-19). He was a member of Lloyd George's imperial war cabinet in World War I and helped establish the League of Nations. He succeeded Botha as prime minister in 1919 but was defeated in 1924. Out of office until 1933 (when he became deputy prime minister to Hertzog), he had time to elaborate his philosophical concept of holism and to publish *Holism and Evolution* (1926). In 1939 he succeeded Hertzog as prime minister, advocating South Africa's entry into World War II. His desire to maintain South Africa's links with the British Commonwealth made him unpopular among Afrikaners.

Smyrna. *See* Izmir.

Smythe, Pat (1928-) British showjumper, equestrian, and writer. The Ladies National Champion a record eight times, she won the European championship four times (1957, 1961, 1962, 1963), each time on Flanagan.

snail A *gastropod mollusc with a spirally coiled shell, including terrestrial, freshwater, and marine forms. The common garden snail (*Helix pomatia*) grows to about 3 cm and is active at night, feeding on vegetation and sheltering by day in crevices. In dry weather, a temporary covering is secreted over the shell aperture to prevent desiccation. The giant African land snail (*Achatina fulica*) grows up to 12 cm long.

snake A legless *reptile belonging to the suborder *Serpentes* (about 3000 species), occurring worldwide but especially common in the tropics. Snakes are long and slender: they range from 0.12-10 m in length and grow throughout their lives, periodically shedding the skin in one piece. They feed chiefly on other vertebrates and are adapted to swallowing prey whole, having flexible ligaments and joints allowing the two parts of the lower jaw to move apart during swallowing. Prey may be killed by constriction, by engulfing it alive, or by the injection of a potent neurotoxic or haemorrhagic venom by means of hollow or grooved fangs. The major families are the *Boidae* (pythons, boas, etc.), the *Colubridae* (typical snakes, e.g. the grass snake), the *Elapidae* (cobras, coral snakes, etc.), and the *Viperidae* (vipers, etc.). Order: *Squamata* (lizards and snakes).

snakebird. *See* darter.

snakefly An insect of the family *Raphidiidae* (about 80 species), so called because its small head and long slender thorax ("neck") resemble a snake about to strike. It is found in woodland areas of every continent except Australia and uses chewing mouthparts to feed on small insects. Eggs are laid beneath bark. Order: *Neuroptera*.

snake gourd An annual or perennial vine of the genus *Trichosanthes* (about 15 species), especially *T. anguina*, native to tropical SE Asia and Australia. It is widely cultivated for its long tapering green edible fruits, which often exceed 1 m in length. Family: *Cucurbitaceae*.

snake-necked turtle A freshwater turtle belonging to the family *Chelyidae* (35 species), found in South America, Australia, and New Guinea. They have a long snakelike neck that is extended to catch prey and breathe air at the surface. It cannot be retracted into the shell but is tucked sideways into a fold of shoulder skin. A South American species, the matamata (*Chelys fimbriata*), has a jagged well-camouflaged shell, 30-40 cm long, and a pointed head.

Snake River A river in the NW USA. Rising in the Yellowstone National Park in Wyoming, it flows W through Idaho to join the Columbia River in Washington State. Length: 1670 km (1038 mi).

snakeroot Any of various plants the roots of which were formerly reputed to cure snakebites. Snakeroots include the *bistort and several North American species, such as the herbs *Cimicifuga racemosa*, *Aristolochia reticulata*, and *Eupatorium urticoefolium*.

snapdragon. *See* Antirrhinum.

snapper A carnivorous shoaling fish of the family *Lutjanidae* (about 250 species), found in tropical seas. It has an elongated body, usually 60–90 cm long, a large mouth, and sharp teeth. Some are valuable food fish, especially the red snapper (*Lutjanus blackford*); others are poisonous.

snare drum (*or* side drum) A small drum with gut strings (snares) stretched across the lower skin. These make a rattling sound when the drum is played. It is used in the orchestra in the military band, and in popular music.

sneeze A reflex violent expulsion of air and droplets through the mouth and nose caused by irritation of the lining of the nasal cavity. The irritation may be due to inflammation of the nasal passages, such as occurs with a cold and hay fever. Sneezing is the principal means by which colds and similar infections are spread.

Snefru King of Egypt (c. 2600 BC); founder of the 4th dynasty traditionally noted for his kindliness, in contrast with his son *Khufu. He encouraged shipping to facilitate communications within Egypt and to import materials from abroad. Two pyramids at Dashur are attributed to him.

Snell's law When a ray of light passes from one medium to another the angle (*r*) between the refracted ray and a line normal to the interface between the media is related to the angle (*i*) of the incident ray, also taken to the normal, by the equation sin $i/\sin r = n$, where *n* is the relative refractive index of the media (*see* refraction). It is named after the Dutch astronomer Willebrord Snell (1591–1626), who discovered it in 1621. It was not published until 1638, when Descartes announced it without crediting Snell.

snipe A *sandpiper belonging to a subfamily (*Scolopacinae*; 10 species) occurring in wet areas of warm and temperate regions. Snipe have a long flexible bill used to probe for worms, and a barred and striped brown, black, and white plumage. The common snipe (*Gallinago gallinago*) is 30 cm long and a popular gamebird.

snooker A game, deriving from *billiards, that arose among British officers in India (1875). It is played by two players or pairs of players on a billiards table. There are 22 balls: 1 white cue ball, 15 red balls (value 1 point each), and 6 coloured balls—yellow (2 points), green (3), brown (4), blue (5), pink (6), black (7). The object is to pocket a red ball and a coloured ball alternately, each time returning the coloured ball to its prescribed spot on the table. The red balls are not replaced. When all the red balls have been potted the colours are potted in order of numerical value. Championships were instituted in 1916 and the world professional championship in 1927. Television coverage greatly increased the game's popularity in the 1970s and 1980s. Joe Davis (1901–78) was the supreme player for many years. Current players include Steve *Davis, Alex *Higgins, and Ray *Reardon.

snoring Noisy breathing occurring during sleep, caused by vibration of the soft palate at the back of the mouth. Snoring generally occurs when sleeping on the back with the mouth open. It is most liable to occur when the nose is blocked (e.g. by a cold) and breathing is through the mouth.

snow A solid form of precipitation composed of ice crystals or snowflakes. Ice crystals occur when temperatures fall below freezing point; with temperatures nearer to 0°C (32°F) snowflakes develop through the clustering together of crystals. Snow is usually measured with a graduated ruler, which is inserted into the flat surface of undrifted snow. Approximately 0.3 m (1 ft) of snow is equivalent to 25 mm (1 in) of rainfall.

Snow, C(harles) P(ercy), Baron (1905–80) British novelist and scientist. The moral problems of politics and power are a recurrent theme of his series of novels beginning with *Strangers and Brothers* (1940) and ending with *Last Things* (1970). His lecture *The Two Cultures and the Scientific Revolution* (1959) prompted a lively controversy with the critic F. R. *Leavis. He was married to the writer Pamela Hansford Johnson (1912–81).

snowball tree. *See* guelder rose.

snow bunting A short-billed *bunting, *Plectrophenax nivalis*, of Arctic snowfields, that visits Britain in winter. It is about 16 cm long and has a brownish plumage with white underparts and black wingtips. In summer the male is white with an orange bill and black markings. It nests in rock crevices and feeds on seeds and insects.

Snowdon (Welsh name: Eryri) 53 04N 4 05W The highest mountain in Wales, in Gwynedd. A rack railway runs from Llanberis to its main peak, Y Wyddfa. The surrounding area, **Snowdonia**, is popular for hill walking, rock climbing, and mountaineering; it was designated a National Park in 1951. Height: 1085 m (3560 ft).

Snowdon, Antony Armstrong-Jones, Earl of (1930–   ) British photographer. His work includes several television documentaries, photographic books, such as *Venice* (1972), and the design of the Snowdon Aviary, London Zoo (1965). His marriage (1960–78) to Princess Margaret ended in divorce.

snowdrop A small early spring-blooming herbaceous plant of the genus *Galanthus* (about 10 species) native to Europe and W Asia. They grow from bulbs to produce grasslike leaves and slender stems bearing solitary nodding white flowers, tipped with green or yellow. There are over 50 cultivated varieties, which are easily grown in gardens and survive for years without attention. *G. nivalis* is the common European snowdrop; *G. elwesi* is the giant snowdrop of SW Asia. Family: *Amaryllidaceae*.

snow goose An Arctic *goose, *Anser caerulescens*. It is 70–78 cm long and is either pure white with black wingtips, pink legs, and a red bill or blue-grey with a white head. Snow geese winter in the southern USA, Japan, and China.

snow leopard A big *cat, *Panthera* (or *Uncia*) *uncia*, also called ounce, found in the mountains of central Asia. It is 1.9 m long, with a thick ash-grey coat marked with dark rosettes. It hunts mountain goats, sheep, and marmots, catching its prey by stalking.

snow-on-the-mountain A hardy annual plant, *Euphorbia marginata*, native to North America and widely cultivated as a garden foliage plant. Up to 60 cm high, it has pale-green pointed leaves, 3–8 cm long, with white margins (sometimes the whole leaf is white). Family: *Euphorbiaceae*.

snowshoe hare A *hare, *Lepus americanus*, of N North America, also called varying hare. Up to 70 cm long, it has a white winter coat and leaves tracks similar to snowshoes. Populations of snowshoe hares can vary greatly from year to year; similar fluctuations occur in the populations of lynxes—their chief predator.

Snowy Mountains A mountain range in Australia. It lies within the *Australian Alps, in New South Wales, and contains Australia's highest mountain, Mount *Kosciusko. The Snowy Mountains Hydroelectric Authority, which was established in 1949, has diverted rivers and constructed dams and reservoirs for irrigation and hydroelectric purposes.

snowy owl A large *owl, *Nyctea scandiaca*, occurring chiefly in Arctic tundra regions. 52–65 cm long, it has broad wings, a round head, and a snow-white plumage with black barring. It nests on open ground and feeds on lemmings, hares, and birds.

snuff A preparation of tobacco and other ingredients that is sniffed rather than smoked. The character of a particular variety of snuff depends on the coarseness of the tobacco used, the moisture content, and the added ingredients, such as lavender and menthol, which introduce flavour and scent to the mixture.

Spaniards discovered snuff-taking among the natives of the Americas in the 16th century. The habit was fashionable in England from the 17th century until the early 19th century, when it was largely replaced by the *cigar. Highly decorated snuffboxes were made as valuable items of jewellery.

Snyders, Frans (1579–1657) Flemish animal painter, born in Antwerp. He studied under Pieter *Brueghel the Young-

Soames, (Arthur) Christopher (John), Baron

er. At first a still-life painter, he later specialized in hunting scenes, being employed in the workshop of *Rubens and by Archduke Albert.

Soames, (Arthur) Christopher (John), Baron (1920–87) British Conservative politician and diplomat. An MP from 1950 to 1966, he was minister of agriculture (1960–64). Subsequently he was ambassador to France (1968–72), a vice president of the EEC Commission (1973–77), and governor (1980) of Zimbabwe-Rhodesia in the months before it attained independence.

Soane, Sir John (1753-1837) British architect, who developed *neoclassicism into a highly original style. He trained under George *Dance and also on the Continent. His first major commission was the rebuilding of the Bank of England (1788-1833; now destroyed), the striking austerity of which was relieved only by simplified classical motifs. Later designs include Dulwich College Art Gallery (1811-14) and his own house in Lincoln's Inn Fields, London (1812-13), which is now the Sir John Soane Museum, containing his collection of antiques, paintings, etc.

SOAPS *The action of soap in emulsifying grease. The nonpolar hydrocarbon end of the soap molecule attaches itself to the grease. The attraction of the polar end to water breaks up the grease and distributes it throughout the solution.*

soaps Salts of *fatty acids. Normal household soap (**hard soap**) is a mixture of sodium stearate, oleate, and palmitate. It is made by the *hydrolysis of *fats with caustic soda (sodium hydroxide), thus converting the glycerides of stearic, oleic, and palmitic acids into sodium salts and glycerol. **Soft soap** is made with potassium hydroxide instead of sodium hydroxide. Soaps have a cleansing action because they contain negative ions composed of a long hydrocarbon chain attached to a carboxyl group. The hydrocarbon chain has an affinity for grease and oil, and the carboxyl group has an affinity for water. Particles of grease or oil are therefore emulsified in soapy water. Insoluble salts of other metals with fatty acids are used as fillers and waterproofing agents and are also called soaps. *See also* detergents.

soapstone. *See* talc.

soapwort A perennial herb, *Saponaria officinalis*, native to Europe and temperate Asia and introduced to North America. The shoots grow to a height of 30-90 cm and bear pink flowers. The leaves and roots contain a lathering agent (saponin), formerly used for washing clothes. Family: *Caryophyllaceae*.

Soares, Mario (1924–   ) Portuguese statesman; prime minister (1976–79, 1983–85) and president (1986–   ). He was a critic of *Salazar and lived in exile from 1970 to 1974, when he became foreign minister in the new military government. He became prime minister as leader of the Portuguese Socialist Party.

Sobers, Gary (Sir Garfield Saint Aubrun S.; 1936–   ) West Indian cricketer, who captained the West Indies and Nottinghamshire and also played for Barbados and South Australia. One of the greatest all-rounders, he played in 93

GARY SOBERS *Batting for the West Indies against England.*

Test matches, scoring 8032 runs, including 26 centuries, and taking 235 wickets and 110 catches. In 1957-58 he set a record Test-match score of 365 (not out).

So-ch'e. *See* Shache.

Sochi 43 35N 39 46E A city in the SW Soviet Union, in the RSFSR on the Black Sea. It is a popular resort, where, since 1977, smoking has been forbidden. Population (1981 est): 295 000.

social contract 1. An agreement under which people consent to surrender liberties in return for the guarantee of responsible government. Hobbes saw the contract as one in which citizens surrender the freedom inherent in a state of nature to an absolute sovereign; Locke, however, argued that the sovereign is limited by the obligation to preserve certain fundamental liberties; and Rousseau, the third of the chief theorists of the social contract, believed that governments require the support of the general will of the people. 2. (*or* social compact) The agreement (1974) between the Labour government of the UK and the trades unions, which undertook to moderate their wage demands in exchange for the implementation of certain social and industrial policies (e.g. price subsidies). In 1975 it was replaced by a more specific limit on wage increases.

social credit An economic theory that finds the cause of depression in the lack of purchasing power and advocates the payment of a regular dividend to every citizen. Formulated by C. H. Douglas (1879–1952), a British engineer and economist in Canada, it became the central platform of the Social Credit Party, formed in Canada in 1935. It maintained political power in Alberta and British Columbia until the early 1970s.

social Darwinism A group of theories suggesting that the principles governing the evolution of biological species by natural selection also govern the affairs of society and social evolution. Either relations in society are held to be determined by a "struggle for existence" between individuals and groups or history is interpreted as a series of conflicts in which only the "fittest" social systems thrive.

Social Democratic Party (SDP) A British political party of the centre, formed on 26 March, 1981, by the "gang of four" Labour dissidents: Roy *Jenkins, Shirley *Williams, David *Owen (leader 1983–87), and William Rodgers. The SDP formed a political alliance with the Liberal Party in 1981; in 1987, after poor results in the general election, the SDP voted to merge with the Liberals and Owen was replaced by Robert *Maclennan.

socialism A concept that has various meanings, resulting in diverse political movements, but one that generally emphasizes the establishment of cooperation rather than competition among men. The word was first used in the early 19th century to describe the followers of Robert *Owen in England and François Fourier and *Saint-Simon in France. From the beginning two main senses of the word emerged. The first sense was in effect a continuation of liberalism, the emphasis being on reform of the social system to develop liberal values, such as political freedom, and the ending of class privileges. Socialism in the second sense was explicitly contrasted with a competitive individualist form of society; practical cooperation could not be achieved until a society based on private property was replaced by one based on social ownership and control. The resulting controversy between reformists and revolutionaries has been long and bitter.

In 1848 Marx and Engels laid down the principles of scientific socialism in *The Communist Manifesto* and *Marxism became the theoretical basis for most socialist thought. The British *Fabian Society (founded 1884) revived a variant of the first sense of the term, which later found political expression in the *Labour Party. It was the split in Russia, however, between the revolutionary *Bolsheviks and the reformist *Mensheviks that led to the decisive distinction between the terms *communism and socialism as they are now generally understood, socialists being those who seek change by peaceful reform and communists being those dedicated to change by revolution.

socialist realism A theory of creative composition decreed by the Soviet authorities in Russia in 1932 to be the official doctrine to which all communist writers and artists must adhere. It defined the purpose of literature as the promotion of socialism and resulted in the production of much literature that was little more than political propaganda. Mikhail *Sholokhov is the most notable of the few writers who have managed to transcend its restrictions.

social security State provision of financial aid to alleviate deprivation and poverty. In the UK the establishment of a *welfare state was based initially on insurance schemes, which were extended after World War II to cover almost all the population (*see* National Insurance). Family allowances and the provision of subsidized local-authority accommodation, however, were not based on contributions. The policy was later modified by the introduction of other noncontributory benefits (such as supplementary benefits) for those in need.

Society Islands An archipelago in French Polynesia. It consists of two island groups, the **Windward Islands** (including Tahiti and Moorea) and the **Leeward Islands** (including Raiatea and Huahine). The capital of French Polynesia, Papeete, is on Tahiti. Discovered in 1767, they are mountainous and the site of ruined Polynesian stone temples. Copra, vanilla, phosphates, and mother-of-pearl are produced. Area: 1595 sq km (616 sq mi). Population (1983): 152 129.

Society of Friends. *See* Quakers.

Society of Jesus. *See* Jesuits.

Socinus, Laelius (Italian name: Lelio Francesco Maria Sozini; 1525-62) Italian Protestant reformer. He travelled widely in N Europe, meeting other leading Protestant reformers. His anti-Trinitarian beliefs and his desire to reconcile Christianity with humanism deeply influenced his nephew **Faustus Socinus** (Fausto Paolo Sozini; 1539-1604). He settled in Poland in 1579, where he became leader of an anti-Trinitarian branch of the Reformed Church. Its doctrine, known as Socinanism, contributed to the development of Unitarian theology (*see* Unitarianism).

sociobiology The study of social behaviour in animals and man. Sociobiologists believe that such aspects of behaviour as aggression, male dominance, and the roles of the sexes have developed through evolution in the same way as structural features. The study was developed in the 1970s.

sociology The systematic study of the development,

organization, functioning, and classification of human societies. Its growth was stimulated by the rapid industrial and social change in Europe in the early 19th century, Auguste *Comte (the first to use the term "sociology"), Emile *Durkheim, and Max *Weber being among the founding fathers of the discipline. Established in several universities in the USA by the early 20th century, it became widely established in British universities during the 1960s. Precluded from experimental methods, the discipline has employed techniques of participant observation, the systematic comparison of different societies, and surveys of social conditions, attitudes, and behaviour. Contemporary sociology is divided into several specialized subdisciplines including demography, political, educational, and urban sociology as well as sociological studies of deviance, religion, and culture.

sockeye salmon A *salmon, *Oncorhynchus nerka*, also called red salmon or blueback, that lives in the N Pacific and spawns in Canadian fresh waters.

Socotra A South Yemeni island in the Indian Ocean, off Somalia. It is generally barren, rising to 1503 m (4931 ft), but in some valleys such crops as dates are grown and livestock is raised. It came under British protection in 1886 but has belonged to South Yemen since 1967. Area: 3100 sq km (1197 sq mi). Chief town: Tamrida.

Socrates (c. 469-399 BC) Athenian philosopher. He wrote nothing himself but his disciples *Plato and *Xenophon stress his intellect, integrity, courage, humour, and sense of divine guidance. *Aristophanes caricatured him in *The Clouds* as an eccentric intellectual. Socrates diverted philosophy from the physical speculations of the *Presocratics towards *ethics. His insistence upon thorough critical analysis of ethical concepts also marked the beginning of *logic. The "Socratic method" of teaching was by eliciting answers from interlocutors to reveal inconsistencies in accepted opinions, a method particularly effective against the *Sophists. His resolute stance against tyranny, whether exercised by the mob or oligarchs, brought about his trial on charges of atheism and "corrupting the youth," and he was condemned to die by drinking hemlock. Plato's *Phaedo* is an eloquent account of his death.

Soddy, Frederick (1877-1956) British chemist, who worked under *Rutherford and *Ramsay and went on to win the 1921 Nobel Prize for his discovery of *isotopes. His scientific books included *The Interpretation of the Atom* (1932); he also wrote on economics, his main work being *Cartesian Economics* (1922).

Söderblom, Nathan (1866-1931) Swedish churchman; Archbishop of Uppsala (1914-31). A pioneer of the modern ecumenical movement, he made new contacts with Anglican and Eastern Orthodox Churches and was a chief initiator of conferences on "Faith and Order" (Uppsala, 1919) and "Life and Work" (Stockholm, 1925). He received the Nobel Peace Prize in 1930.

sodium (Na) A highly reactive alkali metal, long-recognized in compounds but first isolated as the element by Sir Humphry Davy in 1807 by electrolysis of the molten hydroxide (NaOH; caustic soda). It is now obtained commercially by electrolysis of common salt (NaCl). It occurs naturally in some silicate minerals (for example *feldspars; $NaAlSi_3O_8$), as well as in salt deposits and in the oceans. The metal is soft, bright, and less dense (relative density 0.97) than water, with which it reacts violently, liberating hydrogen. For safety, it has to be stored in mineral oil. It is used in organic chemistry as a reducing agent and in the production of *tetraethyl lead. Sodium forms a low-melting-point (-12.3°C) alloy with potassium, but liquid sodium itself is used as the coolant in fast-breeder nuclear reactors. It is a highly electropositive element, forming many ionic salts of great importance, such as the chloride (common salt; NaCl), the carbonate (soda ash; Na_2CO_3), the bicarbonate (baking-soda; $NaHCO_3$), various phosphates, the nitrate ($NaNO_3$), and many others. *Soap is usually the sodium salt of fatty acids (e.g. sodium stearate). Sodium gives a strong yellow colour to flames. At no 11; at wt 22.9898; mp 97.8°C; bp 882.9°C.

sodium bicarbonate (sodium hydrogen carbonate or bicarbonate of soda; $NaHCO_3$) The white soluble powder that is a constituent of *baking powder and is used to make fizzy drinks and as an antacid in medicine. It is made from *sodium carbonate by passing *carbon dioxide through a saturated solution.

sodium carbonate (Na_2CO_3) A white soluble salt. The commercial form (**soda ash**) is a white anhydrous powder and is used in making glass, soap, paper, as well as other chemicals. **Washing soda**, its hydrated form (Na_2CO_3·$10H_2O$), is a white crystalline solid used as a domestic cleanser and water softener.

sodium hydroxide (or caustic soda; $NaOH$) A white solid that is strongly alkaline in aqueous solution and is very corrosive to organic tissue. It is made by electrolysis of salt solution and is used in making rayon, paper, detergents, and other chemicals.

Sodom and Gomorrah In the Old Testament, two cities of Palestine, known as the "cities of the plain," S of the Dead Sea in the area in which Lot, the nephew of Abraham, settled. According to Genesis (18, 19), they were destroyed by fire and brimstone from heaven because of the utter depravity of their inhabitants.

Sofia (Bulgarian name: Sofiya) 42 40N 23 18E The capital of Bulgaria, situated on a plateau in the W of the country. Industries include engineering, metals, textiles, and food processing. It contains some ancient churches, including that of St Sofia (6th-7th centuries), as well as two mosques. The university was founded in 1888. *History*: a Roman town (known as Serdica) from the 1st to the 4th centuries AD, it was destroyed by the Huns in 447. It came under the Byzantine Empire in the 6th century and was taken over by the Bulgars in the 9th century. Under Turkish rule from 1382, it was liberated by the Russians in 1878 and became the national capital (1879). Population (1982): 1 082 315.

soft-shelled turtle A freshwater turtle belonging to the family *Trionychidae* (20-25 species), occurring in North America, Africa, and Asia. They have a flat almost circular shell covered by a leathery skin instead of horny plates, a long neck with a small head, and webbed feet. They are carnivorous and often lie buried in mud but can be fast-moving and aggressive. Chief genus: *Trionyx*.

software The suite of *programs that sets up a *computer system for operation, as distinct from the physical equipment (hardware). Computer manufacturers generally supply machines complete with most of the basic software, which is regarded as an integral part of the computer. This controls various parts of the system and provides facilities for further programming. Supplementary programs to perform specific tasks are purchased separately or written by the user. *See also* programming language.

Sogne Fjord The longest and deepest fjord in Norway, extending 204 km (127 mi) inland N of Bergen. It is flanked by spectacular mountain scenery. Depth: about 1220 m (4000 ft).

Soho A district in the Greater London borough of the City of Westminster. It possesses many foreign restaurants, theatres, nightclubs, and stripclubs.

soil The mixture of unconsolidated mineral particles, derived from weathered rock, and organic matter (humus), derived from the breakdown of plant tissue by living organisms, that covers much of the earth's land surface and provides a medium for plant growth. Soil formation (pedogenesis) depends on the nature of the parent material, the climate and topography of the region, the organisms present in the soil, and the time that has elapsed since pedogenesis began on a bare surface. Soils are characterized by their texture, which depends on particle sizes (*see* sand; silt; clay), and their structure, which depends on the way the particles are bound into aggregates (e.g. crumbs, granules, flakes, etc.). These are important factors in determining the fertility of the soil, particularly its moisture and air content, susceptibility to leaching (the removal of nutrients to deeper levels by percolating water), and ease of cultivation. Soils are also classified according to their profiles—the arrangement of the layers (horizons) between the ground surface and the bedrock. *See also* chernozem; loam; podzol.

Soissons 49 23N 3 20E A town in France, in the Aisne department on the River Aisne. Strategically situated on the NE approaches to Paris, it has been sacked many times. It has a fine 13th-century cathedral. Soissons is a market town and has metallurgical industries. Population (1982): 32 236.

Sokoto 13 02N 5 15E A city in NW Nigeria. It is a major trade centre for livestock and agricultural products. The University of Sokoto was founded in 1975. Population (1983 est): 148 000.

sol. *See* colloid.

Solanaceae A family of herbaceous plants and shrubs (about 2000 species), widely distributed but chiefly tropical. Their flowers have five fused sepals and petals and are usually pollinated by insects. The family includes several commercially important species (e.g. the potato, tomato, pepper, and tobacco) and some ornamentals (e.g. *Petunia*); various other members are poisonous (e.g. the nightshades).

solar cell. *See* solar power.

solar constant The total amount of solar energy passing perpendicularly through unit area per unit time at a particular distance from the sun. It is about 1.36 kW m^{-2} at the earth's mean orbital distance.

solar flare A sudden brightening, within minutes, of areas in the sun's atmosphere, resulting from an explosive release of energetic particles and radiation. Flares occur in regions of intense localized magnetic field, often above *sunspot groups, and take up to an hour to fade. Large flares affect radio transmission on earth and produce *auroras.

solar power The use of the sun's energy to provide heating or to generate electricity. A vast amount of solar energy (about 3×10^{24} joules) falls on the earth every year. This energy can be converted into heat, the commonest method being by direct heating of water flowing through special panels on the roof of a building. The temperature rise produced is fairly small but it reduces the energy required from other sources for hot water and space heating. Higher temperatures, sufficient to form steam for electricity generation, are possible using mirrors to collect and focus the sun's rays. It is estimated that 7000 square metres of mirror is required to generate 1 megawatt of electricity by boiling water to drive a turbogenerator. Direct conversion of solar radiation into electrical energy is possible with **solar cells**. These devices consist of semiconductor junctions in silicon crystals that are sensitive to the *photovoltaic effect. The method is used mainly in small-scale specialized applications, for example powering remote monitoring equipment, spacecraft, marine beacons, etc. For this method to have widespread commercial applications the cost of solar cells would need to be reduced by a factor of about 10. Research into solar energy is currently intense.

solar prominences Immense clouds of gas in the solar atmosphere, denser and cooler than their surroundings and visible, usually only spectroscopically, as flamelike projections beyond the sun's limb. They show great diversity in structure. **Quiescent prominences** persist for possibly several months at high solar latitudes, reaching, typically, a height and length of 40 000 km and 200 000 km. **Active prominences** are short lived in comparison and may alter their shape considerably in minutes.

solar system A system comprising the *sun and the

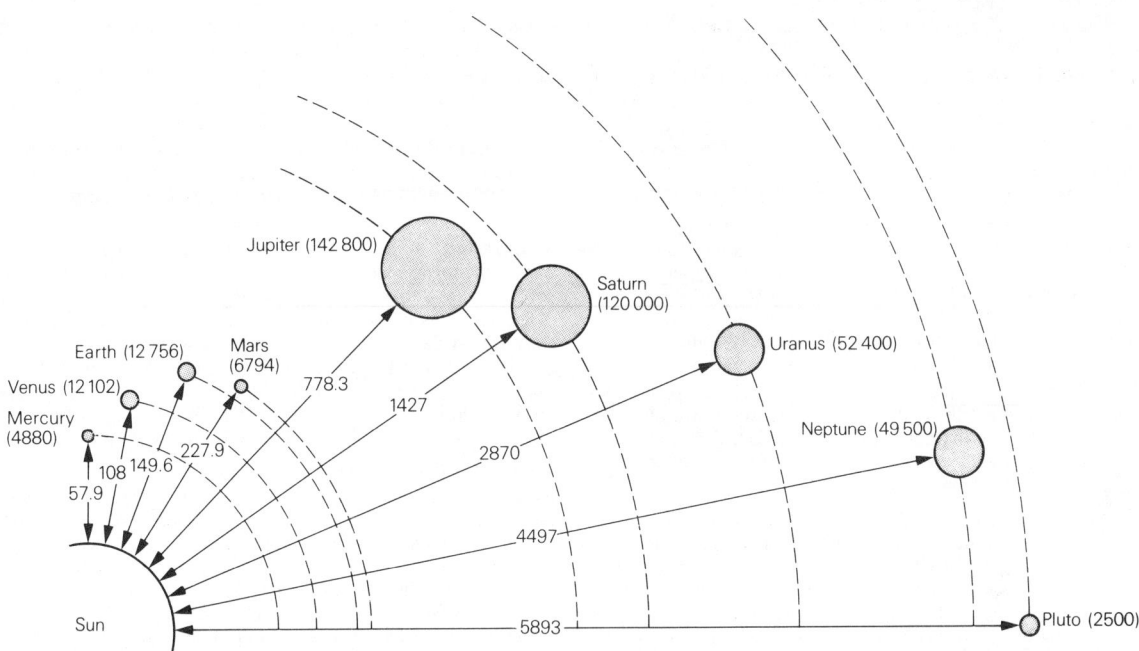

SOLAR SYSTEM *The planets with their equatorial diameters in kilometres (in brackets after the planet's name) and their distance from the sun in millions of kilometres (not to scale).*

astronomical bodies gravitationally bound to the sun, that is the nine major *planets, their *satellites, and the immense numbers of *minor planets, *comets, and *meteoroids. Almost all the mass of the solar system (99.86%) resides in the sun. The planets orbit the sun in the same direction and, with the exception of Pluto, move in paths close to the earth's orbit (i.e. close to the *ecliptic) and the sun's equator. This and other information is taken as evidence of the common origin of the sun and planets, some 4600 million years ago, following the contraction and subsequent flattening of a rotating cloud of interstellar gas and dust.

SOLAR PROMINENCES *A photograph of the solar eclipse on 29 May, 1929, showing a solar prominence.*

solar wind An almost radial outflow of charged particles discharged from the sun's corona into interplanetary space. The particles, mainly protons and electrons, are moving at speeds between 200 and 900 km per second in the vicinity of the earth's orbit and although low in density (about 8 per cubic centimetre) can still interact with the earth's *magnetosphere.

solder An *alloy that is melted to form a joint between other metals or, occasionally, nonmetals. The surfaces to be joined are heated by a soldering iron or by a flame, but are not melted. **Soft solder** is usually made of lead and tin and melts in the range 200-250°C. Because the solder itself is not very strong, it is not used for joints that have to stand up to stress or heat, but is used for making secure electrical connections. **Brazing**, also called **hard soldering**, uses a harder alloy with a higher melting temperature (850-900°C), usually a *brass with 60% zinc and 40% copper. **Silver solder** originally contained silver and was used for jewellery. It has a slightly lower melting point (630-830°C) than brass, and often contains antimony or other metals but no silver. Like brazing, its strength makes it useful in engineering applications. A flux of zinc chloride or a resin is applied to the hot surfaces before soldering to clean them and to enable the solder to flow. In some solders (resin-cored) the flux is contained inside the solder.

soldier beetle A slender soft-bodied beetle with hairy wing cases, belonging to a small but widely distributed family (*Cantharidae*; 3500 species). Brightly coloured and 5-15 mm long, the adults are attracted to flowers, particularly those of the parsley family (*Umbelliferae*), although most feed on small insects. The larvae are found in soil and moss.

sole An elongated *flatfish of the family *Soleidae* (over 100 species), found in temperate and tropical seas. The common European sole (*Solea solea*), also called Dover sole, is a valuable food fish and has a blotchy brown body, up to 50 cm long, with a black spot on each pectoral fin. *See also* lemon sole.

Solemn League and Covenant (1643) An agreement between the parliamentarians and the Scots during the English *Civil War. Presbyterianism was to be established in England and Ireland and the Scots undertook to supply

solenodon 1134

parliament with forces against Charles I in return for a monthly payment of £30,000.

solenodon A shrewlike insectivorous mammal belonging to the family *Solenodontidae* (2 species) found in Cuba and Haiti. Solenodons measure 28–32 cm and have a long naked tail and a long snout with large upper incisor teeth. They feed chiefly on insects, using their long claws to tear open rotten wood. Order: *Insectivora.

solenoid A coil of wire usually forming a long cylinder. When electric current flows through it a *magnetic field is created. This field can be used to move an iron rod placed on its axis. Solenoids are often used to operate mechanical valves attached to the iron rod by switching on or off the current. In most cars a solenoid is used to operate the heavy-current switch that supplies energy to the starter motor.

Solent, the A channel between the coast of Hampshire in S England and the Isle of Wight. It is an important shipping route between Southampton and the English Channel and is famous for its yacht races. Maximum width: 6 km (4 mi).

solfeggio. *See* solmization.

Solferino, Battle of (24 June, 1859) An indecisive battle between Austria on one side and Sardinia-Piedmont and France on the other. As the Austrians withdrew, Solferino was technically a French victory but the French emperor Napoleon III, alarmed by unrest in Paris and the strength of the Austrians, made peace at Villafranca less than three weeks after the battle. The heavy casualties (about 30 000 dead) led an eyewitness, Henri *Dunant, to campaign for the establishment of the International *Red Cross.

solicitor In the UK, a member of the legal profession qualified to give legal advice to clients, to present his clients' cases in certain courts, and to undertake other legal work, such as the transfer of property (conveyancing). A person qualifies as a solicitor by passing examinations conducted by the Law Society, which issues certificates to practise, and by serving an apprenticeship (articles) with a practising solicitor. Before 1971 solicitors could represent clients only in Magistrates' Courts and County Courts; they may now present certain cases in the Crown Court. They are eligible for appointment as circuit judges and recorders, but are not eligible for the higher judiciary. A *barrister must always be instructed through a solicitor.

Solidarity (Polish name: Solidarnosc) A Polish trade union. Formed in Gdansk (1980) under a strike settlement agreement and led by Lech *Walesa, Solidarity became a focus of resistance to *Jarulzelski's Soviet-dominated government. Internal unrest and pressure from the USSR forced the government to suspend Solidarity in 1981. However, Solidarity has continued underground, attracting the sympathy of many Western states.

solid state One of the four states of matter and that to which all substances, except helium, revert at sufficiently low temperatures. It is distinguished from the other states by being the only one in which matter retains its shape, as a result of the stronger intermolecular forces.

solid-state devices Electronic devices made with solid *semiconductor components. They have no moving parts and depend for their operation on the movement of charges within a crystalline solid. Solid-state devices are smaller, lighter, physically more robust, and more easily mass-produced than *thermionic valve equipment. *See also* semiconductor diode; thyristor; transistor.

solifluction A process of mass movement of soil and rock debris, associated with areas bordering on ice sheets in which *permafrost is a feature. During the summer season the top layer of soil thaws but as the ground below remains frozen the water is unable to drain away. The soil therefore becomes saturated and on slopes will flow downhill.

Solingen 51 10N 7 05E A city in NW West Germany, in North Rhine-Westphalia. Its reputation for blades and cutlery

dates to the middle ages. It was severely damaged in World War II. Population (1980 est): 166 600.

solipsism The philosophical view that the human mind has no logical justification for believing in the existence of anything other than itself. It is thus an extreme form of *idealism in which the outside world exists only in the mind of the observer. Modern critics, including *Wittgenstein, regard it as incompatible with the existence of a language capable of expressing the view.

solmization A method of teaching sight-singing that eliminates learning to read music notation from the stave. The tonic sol-fa system derived from the hexachord invented by *Guido d'Arezzo. It was systematized in the 1840s by John *Curwen: the notes of the rising major scale are represented by the syllables doh, ray, me, fah, soh, lah, ti, and doh. The system can be applied in any key, and modulation to a different key simply involves shifting doh to another pitch. Vocal exercises on solmization syllables are known by the Italian word solfeggio.

Solo. *See* Surakarta.

Solomon In the Old Testament, the third King of Israel, son of *David and Bathsheba, who reigned in the 10th century BC. During his peaceful reign several foreign alliances were formed (notably with Phoenicia and Egypt), trade and commerce were expanded and the *Temple at Jerusalem as well as many palaces were built. To realize his schemes he had to impose heavy taxation and use compulsory labour, which resulted in the revolt of N Israel. He was famous for his wisdom, and much of the "wisdom" literature of the Old Testament, such as the Song of Solomon, Proverbs, and Ecclesiastes, is attributed to him.

Solomon (S. Cutner; 1902–88) British pianist. He made his debut at the age of eight. He later studied in Paris and began his professional career in 1923, performing under the single name "Solomon." Paralysis ended his career in 1955.

Solomon Islands, State of A country in the Pacific Ocean, E of New Guinea. It consists of numerous small islands, the largest of which are *Guadalcanal, Malaita, San Cristobal, New Georgia, Santa Isabel and Choiseul. *Bougainville, within the Solomon Islands archipelago, is part of Papua New Guinea. The larger islands are mainly forested and mountainous, with some active volcanoes. Most of the population are Melanesian, with Polynesian and Micronesian minorities. *Economy*: the chief exports are copra and timber. Oil palms and fishing are being developed. *History*: the islands were discovered by the Spanish in 1568. The four main islands became a British protectorate in 1893 and others were added in 1898–99. During World War II they were the scene of fighting between the Japanese and Allied forces. They achieved self-government in 1976 and became independent within the British Commonwealth in 1978. Prime Minister: Ezekiel Alebua. Official language: English. Official currency: Australian dollar of 100 cents. Area: 29 785 sq km (11 500 sq mi). Population (1983 est): 256 000. Capital and main port: Honiara.

Solomon's seal A hardy perennial herbaceous plant of the genus *Polygonatum* (about 25 species), native to moist shady woods of the N hemisphere, especially *P. multiflorum*. Its arching stem, 30–80 cm long, bears two rows of broad spindle-shaped leaves, 5–12 cm long, in the axils of which grow clusters of 2–5 greenish-white tubular flowers followed by red berries. Family *Liliaceae.

Solon (6th century BC) Athenian statesman, who laid the foundations of Athenian democracy. As archon (c. 594–593), Solon cancelled debts for which land or liberty was the security and introduced a new coinage and weights and measures. He also instituted a new constitution, dividing the citizens into four classes, and a more lenient legal code.

Solothurn (French name: Soleure) 47 13N 7 32E A town in NW Switzerland. It has a cathedral (1762–73) and a former arsenal containing an excellent collection of armour and old weapons. Industries include watchmaking and precision instruments. Population (1984 est): 15 400.

Soloviov, Vladimir Sergevich (1853–1900) Russian philosopher, poet, and theologian. A friend of Dostoievski, Soloviov was influenced by *Hegel and the mysticism of Jacob *Boehme. He held that there was a female principle, which he called Sophia, the world-soul.

solstice Either of two points on the *ecliptic, midway between the *equinoxes, at which the sun reaches its greatest angular distance above or below the celestial equator (*see* celestial sphere). In the N hemisphere the sun's northernmost position occurs at the **summer solstice**, usually on 21 June, when daylight hours are at a maximum. Its southernmost position occurs at the **winter solstice**, usually on 22 December, when daylight hours are minimal.

Solti, Sir Georg (1912–) Hungarian-born, naturalized British conductor. He studied in Budapest with Kodály and Dohnányi and was conductor of the Royal Opera, Covent Garden (1961–71), the Orchestre de Paris (1972–75), and the London Philharmonic Orchestra (1979–83). He became conductor of the Chicago Symphony Orchestra in 1969.

solution A homogenous liquid mixture of two or more substances. Solutions, unlike *colloids, contain no identifiable particles of different substances. The components mix as single molecules, ions, or atoms. When a solid or gas is dissolved in a liquid, the liquid is known as the solvent and the dissolved material the solute. If the components are all liquid, the one in excess is the solvent. In a **solid solution**, molecules, atoms, or ions of one component occupy positions in the crystal structure of the other.

Solutrean A culture of the Upper *Palaeolithic succeeding *Gravettian. Named after the site of Solutré near Mâcon (E France), it existed in W Europe from about 18000 to 15000 BC in the warmer climate that followed the Wurm *glaciation. It is characterized by symmetrical pressure-flaked flint and other stone points of laurel- and willow-leaf (foliate) shape, which foreshadow the concern for aesthetic expression in the subsequent *Magdalenian culture.

Solvay process An industrial process for the production of sodium carbonate. Limestone is first heated strongly to produce calcium oxide and carbon dioxide: $CaCO_3 \rightarrow CaO + CO_2$. The carbon dioxide gas is passed through brine saturated with ammonia, precipitating sodium hydrogencarbonate ($NaHCO_3$). This, on mild heating, yields sodium carbonate and some carbon dioxide, which is recycled. The ammonia is also recovered from the supernatant liquor from the second step, by the action of lime produced in the first step. Named after E. Solvay (1833–1922).

Solway Firth An inlet of the Irish Sea between Dumfries and Galloway Region in SW Scotland and Cumbria in NW England. Length: about 56 km (35 mi).

Solzhenitsyn, Aleksandr (1918–) Russian novelist. After distinguished service in World War II, he was held in prison camps until rehabilitated in 1956. The cultural liberalization heralded by the publication of *A Day in the Life of Ivan Denisovich* (1962), dealing with life in the Stalinist labour camps, was short lived and in 1974 he left the Soviet Union and now lives in the USA. His major works include *Cancer Ward* (1968), *The First Circle* (1968), and *The Gulag Archipelago* (1974–78). He won the Nobel Prize in 1970. His memoirs, *The Oak and the Calf*, appeared in 1980.

soma A plant of uncertain identity. In the Vedic religion of India its intoxicating or hallucinogenic juice was used in sacrifices, especially to *Indra. It is also personified as a god in a number of hymns in the *Rigveda*.

Somali An E African people occupying Somalia, Djibouti (where they are called Issas), Ethiopia, and NW Kenya. There are many tribes, which are divided into patrilineal clans headed by a chief chosen by the senior men. Among the nomadic

herdsmen of the interior blood feud is common. Dwellers in towns and along the coast are traders and farmers. All are at least nominally Muslims. Their language belongs to the Cushitic branch of the *Hamito-Semitic family.

Somalia (official name: Somali Democratic Republic) A country in East Africa, occupying most of the Horn of Africa between the Gulf of Aden and the Indian Ocean. Coastal plains rise in the N to a plateau reaching heights of over 1800 m (6000 ft). Most of the inhabitants are nomadic *Somalis with minorities of Sab, Bantu, and others. *Economy*: chiefly agricultural, livestock raising, including sheep, goats, cattle, and camels, being especially important. There is some crop growing in the S, including sugar, maize, sorghum, bananas, and other fruit. The limited mineral resources are being exploited and include tin, iron ore, gypsum, and uranium. Fishing is being encouraged, and industry concentrates mainly on leather and food processing. Communications are difficult; there are no railways, but an extensive road-building programme is being carried out with Chinese and other aid. The main exports are livestock, hides and skins, and fruit (especially bananas). *History*: colonized by Muslims from the 7th century AD, the region was occupied in the 19th century by the French, British, and Italians (*see* Somaliland). The former British and Italian territories gained independence in 1960 (while the French territory of the Afars and Issas became independent Djibouti in 1977). In 1969, after a military coup, a Supreme Revolutionary Council was established in Somalia under Gen Mohammed Siad Barré (1919–). Somalia has had serious territorial disputes with Ethiopia (*see* Ogaden), which has a considerable Somali population. Official language: Somali; Arabic, Italian, and English are used extensively. Official religion: Islam. Official currency: Somali shilling of 100 centesemi. Area: 700 000 sq km (270 000 sq mi). Population (1983 est): 6 248 000. Capital and main port: Mogadishu.

Somaliland A region corresponding to present-day Somalia and Djibouti. Between the 7th and 12th centuries AD the coastal region was occupied by Muslim traders while the N was settled from the 10th century by nomadic Somalis. During the 19th century the region was divided between France, Britain, and Italy. Italian Somaliland was united with Ethiopia by Mussolini to form Italian East Africa (1935) and was acquired by Britain in World War II. British Somaliland became independent as Somalia in 1960 and the French territory, Afars and Issas, as Djibouti in 1977.

somatotrophin. *See* growth hormone.

Somers, John, Baron (1651–1716) English statesman under William III. He became an MP (1689) after the Glorious Revolution had ousted James II and chaired the committee that drafted the *Bill of Rights. Attorney general in 1692 and Lord Keeper of the Great Seal in 1693, by 1696 he was William's chief adviser, becoming Lord Chancellor in 1697. He resigned in 1700 but was later Lord President of the Privy Council (1708–10) under Anne.

Somerset A county of SW England, bordering on the Bristol Channel. Under local government reorganization in 1974 it lost the NE part to *Avon. It consists mainly of a flat plain enclosed by the Quantock Hills and Exmoor in the W, the Blackdown Hills in the S, and the Mendip Hills (containing Cheddar Gorge) in the NE. It is predominantly agricultural; dairy farming is especially important with over half the county under permanent pasture and there is the traditional cider making. The few scattered industries include food processing and textiles. Tourism is an important source of revenue. Area: 3458 sq km (1335 sq mi). Population (1981): 424 988. Administrative centre: Taunton.

Somerset, Edward Seymour, 1st Duke of (c. 1500–52) English statesman, who was ruler of England (1547–49) during the minority of Edward VI. Seymour's advancement

Somerset, Robert Carr, Earl of was facilitated by the marriage of his sister Jane Seymour to Henry VIII, on whose death he became Protector of England and a duke. He defeated the Scots at Pinkie in 1547 and furthered the Protestant *Reformation with the first Book of Common Prayer (1549). He fell from power in 1549 and was subsequently executed by the Earl of Warwick (later Duke of *Northumberland).

Somerset, Robert Carr, Earl of (c. 1590-1645) A favourite of James I of England from 1607 to 1615, when he was imprisoned for the murder of Sir Thomas Overbury. Overbury was poisoned in 1613 after opposing the divorce of Robert Devereux, 3rd Earl of *Essex, and Frances Howard, whom Somerset wished to marry. James' influence secured the divorce and in 1613 Somerset and Howard were married. Their subsequent conviction and imprisonment caused considerable scandal. They were released in 1621 and pardoned in 1624.

Somerset House A government building in the Strand, London (UK), built between 1776 and 1786 to a design by Sir William *Chambers. It occupies the site of a palace that the Duke of *Somerset ordered to be built in the mid-16th century. It formerly housed the General Register Office of births, marriages, and deaths, which has now been moved to St Catherine's House, Kingsway. Its later E wing is part of King's College, London University.

Somme, River A river in N France, rising in the Aisne department and flowing mainly W through Amiens and Abbeville to the English Channel. It was the scene of extensive fighting in *World War I (1916). Length: 245 km (152 mi).

Sommerfeld, Arnold Johannes Wilhelm (1868-1951) German physicist, who did his most important work on atomic structure while he was professor at Munich (1906-31). His modifications of the *Bohr atom included the introduction of elliptical orbits for the electrons and azimuthal and magnetic *quantum numbers. He also worked on *wave mechanics and the theory of electrons in metals.

sonar. *See* echo sounding.

sonata (Italian: sounded, as opposed to *cantata*, sung) A piece of music for one or more instruments. The name has been used of a variety of abstract musical forms, including baroque works for one or more instruments and continuo, the one-movement keyboard sonatas of Scarlatti, and the piano sonatas of Haydn and Mozart. **Sonata form**, the normal structure of the first movement of the classical sonata, was based on the exposition, development, and recapitulation of two contrasting themes. It was applied to the first movement of the *symphony and of *chamber music compositions as well as the sonata proper. Beethoven and his successors enlarged the formal boundaries of the sonata; Liszt evolved a single-movement form out of the three or four movements of the classical sonata. In the 20th century sonata form has been adapted in a variety of ways and new formal patterns have been evolved by such composers as Bartók, Hindemith, Stravinsky, and Tippett.

Sondheim, Stephen (Joshua) (1930-) US composer, who studied lyric writing with Oscar Hammerstein II and composition with Milton Babbitt. He wrote the lyrics for the musicals *West Side Story* (1957), *A Little Night Music* (1973), and *Sweeney Todd* (1979). The revue *Side by Side by Sondheim* (1976) contains many of his songs.

son et lumière (French: sound and light) A nighttime, open-air dramatization of the history of a building, town, etc., using theatrical lighting effects with a synchronized sound track of music and speech. It was developed in 1952 at the Château de Chambord, France, by the Château's curator, Paul Robert-Houdin.

song A short composition for one or more singers, with or without accompaniment. Song is usually regarded as the foundation of music and is certainly the oldest form of musical expression. Besides the folksong traditions of every race, solo song has been a significant part of established musical tradition. In western music the French chansons of the 15th century, the Italian *frottola, the lute songs of the Elizabethans, operatic *arias, German *Lieder* (as treated by Schubert, Schumann, and Wolf), and the French tradition of *mélodies* (as treated by Duparc and Fauré) are all of great importance. A **song cycle** is a group of songs intended to be performed in sequence: the texts are either thematically related, or are all by the same poet.

Song (*or* Sung) (960-1279) A Chinese dynasty that may be divided into the Northern and Southern Song periods. It was founded in N China by Zhao Guang Yin (*or* Chao K'uang Yin; 927-76), who reunited the war-torn country but, despite a strong administration, was never able to control the *Juchen. These tribes forced the Song south in 1127 and founded their own dynasty in the N. The Southern Song established a new capital at Hangzhou, where a great flourishing of Chinese poetry, painting, and pottery occurred. The Song were overthrown by the Mongols under Kublai Khan in 1279.

Song, T. V. (*or* T. V. Sung; 1894-1971) Chinese banker and politician. He was finance minister (1925-31) and foreign minister (1942-45) in the Chinese Nationalist Government. After 1949 he lived in the USA. His elder sister **Song Qing-ling** (*or* Sung Ch'ing-ling; 1892-1981) married *Sun Yat-sen (1914) and herself became a revolutionary leader and later a member of the Chinese Communist Party. His younger sister **Song Mei-ling** (*or* Sung Mei-ling; 1897-) married *Chiang Kai-shek, fleeing with him to Taiwan in 1949.

songbird A *passerine bird belonging to the suborder *Oscines* (about 4000 species), in which the vocal organ (syrinx), at the junction of the trachea (windpipe) and bronchi, is highly developed. The flow of air vibrates the vocal membranes; muscles alter their tension and so produce the different notes. Bird song communicates the identity and whereabouts of an individual to other birds and also signals alarm and sexual intentions; it is especially important in birds that feed or migrate in flocks.

Songhai A West African people inhabiting the region of the Middle Niger River S of Timbuktu. Adopting the Islamic religion in the 11th century AD and influenced by Muslim traders from Africa, the Songhai became prosperous and cultured traders. Between about 1350 and 1600 their kings developed a vast commercial empire, based on the gold and salt trade, which extended from the West African coast to Lake Chad and absorbed the earlier empire of Mali. After the Moroccan invasion of 1591, the Songhai empire collapsed.

Songhua River (*or* Sungari R.) A river in NE China, rising in *Jilin province and flowing roughly NE to the Heilong (*or* Amur) River on the border with the Soviet Union. Length: over 1300 km (800 mi).

Song of Solomon An Old Testament book, also known as the Song of Songs or Canticles. It was traditionally ascribed to *Solomon but was probably written in the 2nd century BC. Written in extravagantly erotic language, it is a series of oriental love poems concerning a bridegroom and his bride, "the Shulamite." Both Jews and Christians interpreted the work allegorically as describing the relation between God and Israel or, for Christian commentators, between Christ and the Church.

song thrush A Eurasian thrush, *Turdus philomelos*, about 22 cm long and having a brown back, pale breast streaked with brown, and orange underwings (*see* Plate V). Its song is loud and distinctive, each phrase being repeated several times. It feeds on invertebrates and smashes snails against a stone before eating them.

sonic boom. *See* sound barrier.

sonnet A poem of 14 lines originating in Italy in the 13th century and introduced into England in the 16th century by Sir Thomas *Wyatt. Its two principal variations are the Petrarchan sonnet, usually divided into an octet rhyming *abbaabba* and a sestet rhyming *cdecde*, and the Shakespearian sonnet, usually rhyming *abab cdcd efef gg*. Sonnets have been written by Milton, Wordsworth, and G. M. Hopkins and it remains one of the few traditional forms still employed by major 20th-century poets. *See also* rhymes.

Soochow. *See* Suzhou.

Sophia (1657–1704) Regent of Russia (1682–89) for her brother Ivan V (1666–96) and half-brother *Peter the Great. She was overthrown by Peter and forced to retire to a convent, where she died.

Sophia (1630–1714) Electress of Hanover (1658–1714), in whom the Act of *Settlement (1701) vested the English Crown. Sophia, the wife of Elector Ernest Augustus (1629–98; ruled 1692–98), was the granddaughter of James I of England and the daughter of Frederick the Winter King, of the Palatinate. Her son succeeded to the British throne as George I.

Sophists The Greek sages of the 5th and early 4th centuries BC who were itinerant experts on various subjects including public speaking, grammar, ethics, literature, mathematics, and elementary physics. They were not a clearly defined school, but they did have certain interests in common. In philosophy they attacked the *Eleatics' account of reality and tried to explain the phenomenal world. Their educational programme centred on the belief that virtue can be taught. From their opponent *Plato, they acquired a bad name as philosophical tricksters, more interested in money and prestige than in truth. In Roman times the term "sophist" came to mean simply a teacher of rhetoric.

Sophocles (c. 496–406 BC) Greek dramatist; with Aeschylus and Euripides, one of the three great Athenian tragic dramatists. He developed the more static drama of Aeschylus by introducing a third actor and reducing the role of the chorus. Of his 123 plays, 7 survive: *Ajax, Women of Trachis, Electra, Philoctetes*, and his three most famous plays dealing with Thebes, *Oedipus Rex, Oedipus at Colonus*, and *Antigone*. He led an active public life, being a friend of Pericles and holding several important civil and military administrative posts.

soprano (Italian: upper) The highest female singing voice. Range: middle C to the C above the treble stave. The **mezzo-soprano** voice lies between the soprano and the contralto. Range: A below middle C to F an octave and a sixth above.

Sopwith, Sir Thomas Octave Murdoch (1888–) British aircraft designer, best known for the World War I biplane, the Sopwith Camel, which he designed and built. He learned to fly in 1910 and founded the Sopwith Aviation Company Ltd in 1912. He was chairman of the Hawker Siddeley Group (1935–63).

Soranus of Ephesus (2nd century AD) Greek physician, whose works were a major influence on gynaecology and obstetrics until the 17th century. He described contraception, abortion, and procedures during childbirth and also wrote about fractures and diseases.

Sorbonne One of the oldest parts of the university in Paris, France, founded by the theologian Robert de Sorbon (1201–74) in about 1257. The present site of the Sorbonne, off the Boulevard Saint-Michel, dates from 1627 and was the scene of the first confrontations between students and police in the troubles of May, 1968.

Sorel, Georges (1847–1922) French social philosopher. As a political activist, Sorel believed that socialism could only come about through a general strike (*see* syndicalism). His theory of the "social myth," which held that the proletariat could be manipulated by propaganda, was, ironically, most successfully proved by the fascist dictators.

Sorghum A genus of annual or perennial *grasses (about 30 species), native to Africa, especially *S. vulgare*, of which there are several varieties, such as sweet sorghum, *durra, and *kaffir corn, widely cultivated as cereal crops. Usually growing up to 2.5 m high, they have rigid stalks, sometimes containing a sweet sap, long flat leaves, and terminal flower clusters bearing 800–3000 starch-rich seeds. The seeds are used as grain for making bread, etc., and as a source of edible oil, starch, and sugar. The stalks are used as fodder or sometimes for syrup manufacture.

Sorocaba 23 30S 47 32W A city in S Brazil, in São Paulo state on the Rio Sorocaba. It is a major industrial centre; manufactures include textiles, fertilizers, and wine. Population (1980 est): 254 718.

sorrel A perennial herb, *Rumex acetosa*, common throughout temperate Eurasia and North America. It grows to a height of 1 m and bears numerous small red flowers. The tangy-tasting leaves are used as a culinary flavouring and in salads. Family: *Polygonaceae*. *See also* wood sorrel.

Sorrento 40 37N 14 23E A seaport in SW Italy, in Campania. A resort since Roman times, it is the birthplace of the poet Tasso. Oranges and lemons are grown. Population (1981 est): 17 301.

Sosigenes of Alexandria (1st century BC) Greek astronomer, about whom little is known except that, on his advice, Julius Caesar reformed the calendar and added an extra day every four years to produce the modern system of leap years. This system is known as the Julian *calendar.

Sosnowiec 50 16N 19 07E A town in S Poland. It is a metallurgical centre; other industries include engineering, chemicals, and the manufacture of textiles. Population (1982): 255 000.

Sotho A large group of Bantu-speaking peoples of S Africa. The term applies in a general sense to the peoples of Botswana, Lesotho, and the Transvaal (South Africa), but, more specifically, to one of the four main divisions of these peoples, the Sotho of Lesotho. The other branches are the Tswana, Pedi, and Venda, each with many tribes. All live by combined agriculture and animal husbandry and have a broadly similar culture, now disintegrating under the impact of urbanization.

Soto The largest Japanese school of Zen Buddhism, founded in China in the 9th century AD and brought to Japan by *Dogen in 1227. Soto emphasizes meditation and morality. Adherents strive to live as what they hope to become, perfect Buddhas.

Soto, Hernando de (?1496–1542) Spanish explorer. After exploration in Central America, he set out in 1539 to conquer Florida. He landed with 600 men at Tampa Bay and journeyed circuitously through what became the S USA in search of gold. In 1541 he crossed the Mississippi, the first White man to do so, but died on the return journey.

Soufflot, Jacques Germain (1713–80) French architect. After training in Italy (1731–38), Soufflot became the leading French exponent of *neoclassicism. Apart from the Hôtel Dieu in Lyons (1841–48), his most famous building is the Church of St Geneviève in Paris (begun in 1757), now called the *Panthéon.

Soult, Nicolas Jean de Dieu, Duc de Dalmatie (1769–1851) French general in the Revolutionary and Napoleonic Wars. A sergeant at the outbreak of the French Revolution, he rose to the rank of general in 1794 and later commanded in the Peninsular War. He became president of the council (1832–34, 1839–40, 1840–47) under Louis Philippe.

sound A disturbance propagated through a medium by longitudinal waves. Strictly the term applies only to those waves that are audible to the human ear, i.e. with frequencies between about 20 and 20 000 hertz, those with frequencies above 20 000 hertz being called ultrasound and those below 20 hertz infrasound. Sound is propagated by vibrations of molecules in the medium, producing fronts of compression and rarefaction. Sound waves are longitudinal as the molecules vibrate in the direction of propagation; the velocity of sound in air at 0°C is about 332 metres per second (760 mph). The three principal characteristics of a sound are its pitch (the frequency of the wave), loudness (the amplitude of the wave), and *timbre (the extent to which it contains harmonics of the fundamental frequency). However, there is a relationship between pitch and loudness (*see* sound intensity). *See also* acoustics.

Sound, the (Danish name: Øresund; Norwegian name: Öresund) A sea channel in N Europe, between Denmark (Sjælland) and Sweden, linking the Kattegat and the Baltic Sea. Length: 113 km (70 mi). Narrowest point: 4 km (2.5 mi).

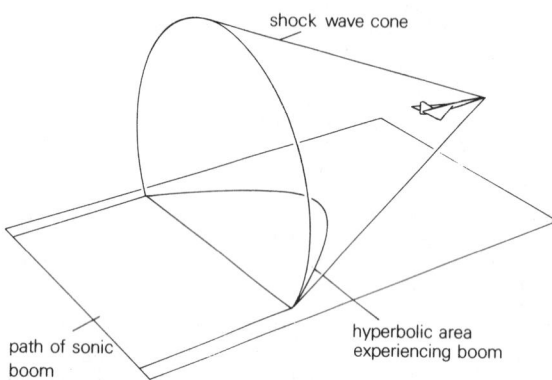

SOUND BARRIER *As an aircraft passes through the sound barrier the sonic boom is heard along a hyperbolic area on the ground.*

sound barrier An obstacle experienced by subsonic *aircraft attempting to fly at or above the speed of sound. Drag increases sharply, lift falls off, and the aircraft becomes difficult to control (*see* aeronautics). At subsonic speeds the pressure waves created by the aircraft as it flies through the air are able to move ahead of the aircraft; at supersonic speeds they cannot escape in a forward direction as the source is moving faster than the pressure waves themselves. Thus shock waves build up on the aircraft's wings and fuselage, creating an apparent barrier to supersonic flight. The barrier was overcome for the first time by the US Bell X1 rocket aircraft in 1947. Since then many aircraft capable of supersonic flight have been built (including Concorde) by greater streamlining, sweptback wings, and more powerful engines. As these aircraft cross the sound barrier a **sonic boom** is heard. This is created by a shock-wave cone with the nose of the aircraft at its vertex. In level flight the intersection of this cone with the ground produces a hyperbola at all points along which the boom is heard.

sound intensity The rate at which sound energy is propagated through a unit area perpendicular to the direction of propagation. It is measured in watts per square metre. The intensities of two sound levels are compared by a unit called the *decibel. The intensity of sound is not the same as its loudness, the latter being the magnitude of the sensation produced by the human ear, which is dependent on the frequency of the sound.

Souphanouvong, Prince (1912–) Laotian statesman; president (1975–). In the civil war in Laos (1953–73) he led the revolutionary Pathet Lao and, on its conclusion, joined the coalition government established in 1974. In 1975, however, Pathet Lao forces seized complete control and Souphanouvong became president.

soursop An evergreen tree belonging to the tropical American genus *Annona*, especially *A. muricata*, widely cultivated in the Old World tropics. It grows to a height of 8 m and pro-

duces large oval spiny green fruit, the flesh of which can be eaten or used as an ingredient of soft drinks, ice cream, etc. Family: *Annonaceae*.

Sousa, John Philip (1854–1933) US composer and bandmaster. In 1880 he was appointed leader of the US Marine Corps Band and in 1892 formed his own band, which toured the world. He wrote military marches including "The Stars and Stripes Forever," "The Washington Post," "Semper Fidelis", and "Liberty Bell" and invented the **sousaphone**, a tuba-like band instrument with a forward-facing bell.

souslik (*or* suslik) A nocturnal *ground squirrel belonging to the genus *Citellus* (34 species), of E Europe, Asia, and North America (where it is sometimes called a gopher). The European souslik (*C. citellus*) is yellowish brown with large eyes and small ears and lives in burrows in dry open country, feeding on seeds, nuts, and bulbs. *See also* chipmunk.

Sousse 35 50N 10 38E A port in central Tunisia, on the Mediterranean coast. It was founded by the Phoenicians as a port and trade centre. Its industries include sardine fishing and canning and olive-oil manufacture. Population (1984): 322 491.

Soustelle, Jacques (Émile) (1912–) French anthropologist and politician. A member of the *Free French during World War II, he became secretary general of de Gaulle's Rassemblement du Peuple français in 1947. He was governor general of Algeria (1955–56) and subsequently opposed the policies of successive French governments towards Algeria, living in exile from 1961 to 1968. He then became director of the École pratique des hautes Études. His books include *Arts of Ancient Mexico* (1967).

South Africa, Republic of (Afrikaans name: Suid-Afrika) A country occupying the S tip of Africa. Narrow coastal plains rise to plateaus in the interior, with the Drakensberg mountains in the E reaching 3299 m (10 822 ft). The N is mainly desert. The Limpopo, Molopo, and Orange Rivers mark the N boundary. The Vaal, a tributary of the Orange, is another important river. The majority of the inhabitants are Africans (71%) with White, Coloured, and Asian (mostly Indian) minorities. *Economy*: although South Africa is highly industrialized, agriculture is still important, with cereals, fruit growing, and cotton, as well as livestock. Fishing is a valuable source of income and whaling continues although efforts at conservation have reduced its scale. Rich and varied mineral resources include gold, diamonds, chrome, platinum, uranium, coal, manganese, phosphates, and iron. Hydroelectricity is a valuable source of power. Well-developed industry includes metals, machinery, chemicals, food processing, and textiles. Main exports include metals (especially gold), citrus fruits, sugar, wines, and textiles. *History*: originally inhabited by *Khoisan peoples. Bantu-speaking tribes arrived from the north between 1000 and 1500. The Portuguese under *Dias first sighted the Cape of Good Hope (1488) but made no permanent settlement there. The Dutch East India Company settlement (1652) at Table Bay (Cape Town) expanded into a colony that spread into the interior. After Louis XIV revoked the Edict of Nantes (1685) Huguenot refugees augmented the White settlers. During the Napoleonic Wars Britain acquired the Cape Colony for strategic reasons, a possession confirmed in 1814. In the 1830s increasing numbers of Dutch farmers (or Boers, forebears of the modern Afrikaners) moved E and N to escape British rule, clashing with the *Bantu peoples who were then migrating southwards (*see* Great Trek). The Boers founded two independent republics, the Orange Free State and the Transvaal (*see* Sand River Convention), but their republic in Natal was soon annexed by the British (1843), who were also expanding the eastern boundaries of the Cape Colony (*see* Cape Frontier Wars). *Kruger's assertion of Boer independence led to war (1880–81), which broke out again between the Boers and the British after the discovery of gold (1886) in the Transvaal had led to hostility between the Boers and the immigrant gold-diggers (*see* Boer Wars). The need for cooperation led the two former Boer republics and the two

British colonies to combine in the Union of South Africa (1910). In both World Wars South Africa, under J. C. *Smuts, enthusiastically supported Britain, but in 1948 Smuts was ousted by the anti-British Afrikaner National Party and in 1961 South Africa became a republic outside the British Commonwealth. Since 1910 the treatment of the non-White majority has been the crucial political issue (*see* apartheid) and in 1976 the *Transkei became the first independent *Bantu Homeland (Bantustan). South Africa has also intervened in Angola (1976) and *Namibia, and has supported the White minorities in *Zimbabwe and *Mozambique. In the face of increasing internal unrest, some non-Whites received limited parliamentary power under a new tricameral constitution instituted in 1984. In 1985 the USA imposed economic sanctions in protest against apartheid. A state of emergency, declared after violent race riots (1985), remains in force. Violence and international protests continue to escalate despite promises of reform and restrictions on press coverage. State President: Pieter W. *Botha. Official languages: Afrikaans and English. Official currency, since 1959: rand of 100 cents. Area: 1 221 042 sq km (472 359 sq mi). Population (1983): 30 938 000. Capitals: Pretoria (administrative), Bloemfontein (judicial), Cape Town (legislative).

South African Wars. *See* Boer Wars.

South America The fourth largest continent, lying chiefly in the S of the W hemisphere between the Pacific and Atlantic Oceans. Roughly triangular in shape and tapering in the S, it is linked to the continent of North America by the Isthmus of Panama. An ancient shield occupies much of the NE part of the continent and forms the Brazilian and Guiana Highlands. These are separated by the vast basins of the Orinoco, Amazon, and Paraná–Paraguay river systems. In the extreme W, beyond a series of plains, rise the mountains and high plateaus of the *Andes, the world's longest mountain system. The Andes rise to their highest point at Mount *Aconcagua and contain Lake *Titicaca, the continent's largest lake. South America's climate varies considerably, largely because of its length, but much is tropical with vast areas of tropical rainforest (selva). The population consists chiefly of the indigenous Indians, Europeans (especially Spanish and Portuguese), and mestizos together with large numbers of Negroids. *History*: much archaeological evidence remains of the flourishing kingdoms of South America (such as those of the *Incas and *Chibchas), which were vanquished by the Spanish conquistadors. The entire continent was divided–Portugal taking the NE portion (now Brazil) and Spain the remainder –during the 16th century. With the collapse of the Spanish Empire during the early 19th century, there followed struggles for independence under national leaders, who included *Bolívar and *San Martin. Large-scale European immigration (including German and Italian) occurred in the 19th century. During the 20th century the constituent nations have become increasingly industrialized and seen rapid rises in their populations. Area: 17 767 331 sq km (6 858 527 sq mi). Population (1981 est): 366 000 000.

South American languages The indigenous languages of South America, the Antilles, and parts of Central America, many of which are now extinct. Brought originally from North America by migrating Indians, the 600 documented languages are extremely diverse in nature. The number of speakers is currently estimated at 11 200 000, the majority of whom are to be found in the central Andes. The languages probably shared a common source.

Southampton 50 55N 1 25W A city in S England, in Hampshire on Southampton Water (an inlet of the English Channel). It is the UK's principal passenger port and has four tides daily. Southampton's industries include marine engineering and yachtbuilding; at Fawley on Southampton Water is a large oil refinery. The University of Southampton was established in 1952. Population (1981): 204 406.

Southampton, Henry Wriothesley, 3rd Earl of (1573–1624) English courtier, famous as the patron of Shakespeare: *Venus and Adonis* (1593) and *The Rape of Lucrece* (1594) were dedicated to him. He was involved in the Earl of Essex's conspiracy against Elizabeth I (1600), persuading the players of the Globe Theatre to perform Shakespeare's *Richard III* (about the deposition of a king) to encourage revolt. His death sentence was commuted to life imprisonment and he was released by James I (1603).

South Australia A state of S central Australia, bordering on the Indian Ocean and Great Australian Bight. It consists chiefly of low-lying plains with the *Great Victoria Desert in the W, rising in the NW to the Musgrave Ranges and in the SE to the Flinders Range. The only major river is the Murray. The rivers lying in the N exist only during a rainy season and Lake Eyre is frequently only an immense salt flat. Intensive agriculture is restricted to the S; wheat, barley, vegetables, grapes, and sheep are the chief products. The vineyards of the fertile Barossa Valley are especially important, producing almost half of Australia's wine. Mineral resources include iron ore from the Middleback Ranges, low-grade coal at Leigh Creek, large natural gas fields in the N, and opals. Industry, concentrated in Adelaide, includes the manufacture of motor vehicles, textiles, and chemicals. There are iron and steel works and shipyards at Whyalla; Woomera has an experimental rocket range. Area: 984 377 sq km (380 070 sq mi). Population (1980 est): 1 299 100. Capital: Adelaide.

South Bend 41 40N 86 15W a city in the USA, in Indiana on the St Joseph River. Industries include the manufacture of aircraft, motor-vehicle parts, and machinery. The University of Notre Dame is here. Population (1980): 109 727.

South Carolina A state in the SE USA, on the Atlantic coast. Lowlands make up two-thirds of the state rising to uplands in the NW. Although the population is predominantly rural, industry is being developed. The large areas of woodland supply the furniture industries and the large textile and clothing industries are based on the region's cotton crop. Other leading manufactures include chemicals, machinery, and food products. *History*: one of the 13 original colonies, it became separate from North Carolina in 1713 and was the first state to secede from the Union (1860). Area: 80 432 sq km (31 055 sq mi). Population (1980): 3 119 208. Capital: Columbia. *See also* Charleston.

South Caucasian languages A group of languages, also known as the Kartvelian languages, spoken by the people of W Transcaucasia and adjacent regions. It includes *Georgian, Svan, Mingrelian, and Laz. Only Georgian possesses a literary tradition.

South China Sea (Chinese name: Nanhai) A section of the W Pacific Ocean, between SE Asia, Borneo, the Philippines, and Taiwan. A monsoon area, it is heavily fished.

Southcott, Joanna (1750–1814) British religious fanatic. A domestic servant, she began prophesying in 1792, claiming to be the woman in Revelation 12 who would give birth to the second Messiah. She died of a brain disease. Her following lasted into the 20th century.

South Dakota One of the Plains states in N central USA. The Missouri River separates the arid Badlands, the Black Hills, and the Great Plains in the W from the flat fertile prairie in the E, which forms the basis of South Dakota's predominantly agrarian economy. Livestock and livestock products are the chief source of revenue. Although it has the largest gold mine in the USA, mineral extraction is minimal. *History*: part of the Louisiana Purchase (1803), the gold rush and land boom of the 1880s brought many settlers and South Dakota became a state in 1889. Area: 199 551 sq km (77 047 sq mi). Population (1980): 690 178. Capital: Pierre.

South East Asia Treaty Organization (SEATO) An organization formed to protect SE Asia from possible communist aggression. It was analogous to the *North Atlantic Treaty Organization. The treaty was signed in Manila in 1954 by Australia, France, New Zealand, Pakistan, the Philippines,

Thailand, the UK, and the USA. Pakistan withdrew in 1973 and the organization was formally ended in 1977. *See also* Association of South East Asian Nations.

Southend-on-Sea 51 33N 0 43E A resort in SE England, in Essex on the lower Thames estuary. It is the nearest seaside resort to London, which it also serves as a dormitory town, and has the world's longest pleasure pier. Population (1981): 156 683.

Southern Alps The highest range of mountains in New Zealand. It extends SW–NE through South Island and contains many peaks over 3000 m (10 000 ft), including Mount *Cook. Glaciers, fed by the central snowfields, flank the mountains and include Tasman Glacier. It is an important winter-sports area.

Southern Cross. *See* Crux.

Southern Rhodesia. *See* Zimbabwe, State of.

southernwood A perennial herb, *Artemisia abrotanum*, also called lad's love, native to S Europe and Asia and cultivated for its aromatic leaves, which can be used to make a beverage. Family: *Compositae. See also* wormwood.

Southey, Robert (1774–1843) British poet and writer. He was a close associate of *Wordsworth and *Coleridge and in 1803 settled in the Lake District. His early political radicalism was short lived, and he became a leading contributor to the Tory *Quarterly Review*. He became poet laureate in 1813. His poetry lacks originality and was overshadowed by the work of his greater contemporaries. He wrote several historical books, notably *The Life of Nelson* (1813).

South Georgia An island in the S Atlantic Ocean, a dependency of the Falkland Islands. King Edward Point is a base for members of the British Antarctic Survey. With the Falkland Islands, it was invaded by Argentina on 2 April, 1982, but was recaptured by British forces on 25 April, 1982. Area: 3755 sq km (1450 sq mi).

South Glamorgan A county of SE Wales, bordering on the Bristol Channel. It was created in 1974 from S Glamorgan and SW Monmouthshire. It consists chiefly of a low undulating plateau (the fertile Vale of Glamorgan), drained by the River Taff. Dairy farming is replacing cereal production as the main agricultural activity. Industry is centred on Barry and Cardiff. Area: 416 sq km (161 sq mi). Population (1981): 384 633. Administrative centre: Cardiff.

South Holland (Dutch name: Zuid-Holland) A province in the W central Netherlands, on the North Sea. Its S part consists of several islands. It is densely populated and agriculture, especially cattle raising and flower bulbs, is the chief occupation. The extensive trading and shipping industry is centred on the port of Rotterdam. Tourism is also important. Area: 3333 sq km (1287 sq mi). Population (1981 est): 3 106 697. Capital: The Hague.

South Island The larger of the two principal islands of New Zealand, separated from North Island by Cook Strait. It is generally mountainous, rising over 3500 m (11 483 ft) in the *Southern Alps in the W, with coastal plains.

Southland Plain A low-lying area of New Zealand, on SE South Island bordering on the Pacific Ocean. Sheep rearing and dairying are important.

South Orkney Islands A group of islands within the British Antarctic Territory, in the S Atlantic Ocean. A dependency of the Falkland Islands until 1962, their major importance is as a whaling base. They are also claimed by Argentina.

South Ossetian autonomous region An autonomous region (*oblast*) in the W Soviet Union, in the Georgian SSR. Its inhabitants comprise chiefly Orthodox Christian Ossetians, a Caucasian people. Timber is produced and its many rivers are used to generate hydroelectric power. Livestock are raised in the higher regions. Area: 3900 sq km (1500 sq mi). Population (1981 est): 97 000. Capital: Tskhinvali.

Southport 53 39N 3 01W A town and resort in NW England, in N Merseyside on the Irish Sea. Its annual flower show is famous and there is a well-known golf course at nearby Birkdale. Population (1981): 89 745.

South Sandwich Islands A group of islands in the S Atlantic Ocean, a dependency of the Falkland Islands. 750 sq km (470 sq mi) south-east of South Georgia, the islands are uninhabited. Area: 285 sq km (130 sq mi).

South Sea Bubble (1720) The collapse of the British market in South Sea stocks that had far-reaching political repercussions. The South Sea Company was founded in 1711 to trade with Spanish America and in 1718 George I became its governor. A boom in South Sea stock was followed by collapse and the subsequent inquiry revealed corruption among ministers and even touched the king. The day was saved by Sir Robert *Walpole, who transferred the South Sea stocks to the Bank of England and the East India Company.

South Shetland Islands An uninhabited archipelago within the British Antarctic Territory, in the S Atlantic Ocean. Until 1962 they were a dependency of the British Falkland Islands.

South Shields 55 00N 1 25W A port in NE England, in Tyne and Wear on the Tyne estuary opposite North Shields. Industries include shipbuilding, marine engineering, petrochemicals, and paint manufacture. The first lifeboat was built here (1790). Population (1981): 87 203.

Southwark A borough of S central Greater London, on the River Thames. Created in 1965 from the former metropolitan boroughs of Bermondsey, Camberwell, and Southwark, it is famous for its historic inns, its 12th-century cathedral, and the site of the *Globe Theatre. Population (1981): 211 708.

South West Africa. *See* Namibia.

South Yorkshire A metropolitan county of N England, created in 1974 from the S part of the West Riding of Yorkshire and a small part of NE Derbyshire. It comprises the districts of Sheffield, Rotherham, Doncaster, and Barnsley. Agriculture is varied with sheep farming in the W on the Pennines, dairy farming on the lower slopes, and arable on the lowlands in the E. The main industrial activities are iron and steel, engineering, and coalmining. Area: 1562 sq km (603 sq mi). Population (1981): 1 301 813. Administrative centre: Barnsley.

Soutine, Chaim (1893–1943) Lithuanian-born painter, who emigrated to Paris in 1913. There influenced by *expressionism, he achieved recognition in the 1920s despite his reluctance to exhibit his work. Using thickly applied paint, intense colour, and distorted and writhing forms, he was, together with *Chagall, the leading representative of French expressionism.

Sovetsk (name until 1945: Tilsit) 55 02N 21 50E A town of the Soviet Union, in the W RSFSR on the River Nemen. Founded by the Teutonic Knights in 1288, it was here that the Treaties of *Tilsit were signed (1807) between Napoleon and, respectively, Prussia (which held the town until 1945) and Russia. Industries include food processing and the manufacture of pulp. Population (1975 est): 41 000.

soviet A government council in the Soviet Union. Soviets originated as committees of workers' deputies in the *Revolution of 1905 and were again established in the *Russian Revolution of 1917, which established the *Soviet Union. The Supreme Soviet is in theory the supreme organ of government in the Soviet Union and soviets are also elected at the local, provincial, and republican levels. Candidates, one for each deputy, are selected by the Communist Party.

Soviet Far East. *See* Siberia.

Soviet Union (official name: Union of Soviet Socialist Republics) The world's largest country and its third most populous, covering N Eurasia and bordering on the Pacific and Arctic Oceans and the Baltic, Black, Caspian, and Aral Seas. It is officially a federal state comprising 15 constituent republics: the Armenian, Azerbaidzhan, Belorussian, Estonian, Georgian, Kazakh, Kirghiz, Latvian, Lithuanian, Moldavian, Russian Soviet Federal, Tadzhik, Turkmen, Ukrainian, and

Uzbek Soviet Socialist Republics. Administrative subdivisions include 20 Autonomous Soviet Socialist Republics and, within some of these, 8 autonomous regions (Russian *oblast*, region). The area W of the River Yenisei consists of vast plains and depressions, dissected by the Ural Mountains, while the E consists mainly of mountains and plateaus. The mountain belt along the S border includes the Carpathian, Caucasus, Pamir, and Sayan Mountains, the Stanovoi Range, and the Tien Shan. The rivers mainly flow N to the Arctic Ocean. The population includes over a hundred national groups, for whom many of the country's subdivisions were established. The most numerous are the Russians, Ukrainians, Uzbeks, Belorussians, Tatars, and Kazakhs. Population is most dense W of the Urals, where most of the large industrial cities are situated. *Economy*: based on the system of state ownership, it is controlled through Gosplan (the State Planning Commission) and Gosbank (the State Bank). It has been directed since 1928 by a series of *five-year plans, but recent proposals reflect growing interest in a market economy. Its main asset is the country's vast natural resources and the Soviet Union is the world's leading producer of oil, coal, iron ore, cement, and steel; manganese, gold, natural gas, and other minerals are also of major importance. Industry was long concentrated after 1928 on the production of capital goods through metalworking, machine manufacture, and the chemical industry, and relatively few consumer goods were produced. During the 1960s and 1970s the latter have received slightly more emphasis. Agriculture, organized in a system of state and collective farms, is on a large scale and is highly mechanized but is not highly productive, hampered in many areas by the climate and by a shortage of resources. The Soviet Union is one of the world's greatest producers of cereals, although bad harvests (as in 1972 and 1975) have necessitated imports and hampered the economy. The 1976–80 five-year plan shifted resources to agriculture, and 1978 saw a record harvest. Fishing, forestry, and dependent industries are also important; the country is the world's greatest producer of timber. Largely self-sufficient, it trades little in comparison to its economic strength, although trade with noncommunist countries increased greatly during the 1970s. Fuels, metals, machinery, and timber are exported, while machinery, consumer goods, and occasionally grain are imported. *History*: the area has been populated for three to four millenniums, although little is known of its history until the 8th century AD, when European and Middle Eastern traders began its exploration. Control of the area between the Baltic and Black Seas was established by Scandinavian adventurers by 1000. Dominated by Kiev from the mid-10th to mid-11th centuries, these Varangian principalities submitted (after 1223) to the overrule of the Golden Horde. By the time of the Horde's collapse in the 14th century, Moscow, ruled by Rurik princes, had emerged as a powerful principality, becoming the capital of a united Russia under Ivan the Great in the 15th century. Contact with W Europe was established in the late 17th century by Peter the Great, who also established the Russian bureaucracy and educational system and built a new capital, St Petersburg (present-day Leningrad). By the 19th century Russian territories had been greatly extended but, although a force to be reckoned with in the world, Russia was industrially far behind the UK, Germany, and the USA, its bureaucracy had grown unwieldy and oppressive, and its Romanov emperors (tsars) were opposed to any political change. Revolutionary activity began with the Dekabrists' conspiracy, uncovered in 1825, and, although serfdom was abolished in 1861, its abolition was achieved on terms unfavourable to the peasants and served to encourage revolutionaries, a group of whom assassinated Alexander II in 1881. Bloody Sunday (22 January, 1905), on which several hundred workers were killed during a demonstration in St Petersburg, was followed by great disorder (*see* Revolution of 1905). A parliament, the *Duma, was established in 1906, but political unrest continued and was aggravated during World War I by military defeat and food shortages. The February and October Revolutions (*see* Russian Revolution) were followed

by a period of civil war (1918–22), after which communist control was complete. After Lenin's death (1924) Stalin had emerged as leader by 1928, having ousted Trotsky. Under Stalin, who replaced Lenin's New Economic Policy with five-year plans and collective farms, the Soviet Union (established 1922) became a major industrial power but a totalitarian state, with effective political opposition eliminated during the 1930s by purges. World War II established the Soviet Union as one of the two major world powers, since when it has maintained its military strength. Relations with the other superpower, the USA, have improved since the *Cold War, with agreements on *disarmament, although the Soviet invasion of Afghanistan (1979) provoked US condemnation and boycotts of the Olympic Games in 1980 and 1984. Internal dissension is still viewed as a threat, as shown by the trials of human-rights activists, although more liberal policies were adopted in the mid-1980s under *Gorbachov (*see* glasnost).

Dissension within the communist bloc (*see* Warsaw Pact) provokes a similar response from the Soviet Government, which intervened in the Hungarian Revolution (1956) and the Czechoslovakian liberalization programme (1968). In 1981 the Soviet leadership also directed the suppression of the *Solidarity trade union in Poland. The Communist Party, with a membership of over 15 000 000, maintains total control of government. The Soviet Union is a member of *COMECON. President: Andrei Gromyko. Chairman of the Presidium of the Supreme Soviet: Mikhail Gorbachov. Official language: Russian. Official currency: rouble of 100 kopeks. Area: 22 402 200 sq km (8 647 675 sq mi). Population (1986): 280 100 000. Capital: Moscow.

Soweto 26 10S 28 02E A large urban area in South Africa, in the Transvaal forming a suburb of Johannesburg. It is inhabited solely by Black Africans and comprises 36 townships, divided into tribal areas. In June, 1976, it was the scene of serious rioting by African students during which over a hundred people died. Population (1980 est): 864 000.

sow thistle A herb of the genus *Sonchus*, especially *S. oleraceus*, occurring widely as a weed in Europe, W Asia, and N Africa. Growing to a height of 20–150 cm, its oval leaves have prickly edges and it produces clusters of yellow flowers. Family: *Compositae*.

soya bean (*or* soybean) An annual plant, *Glycine max*, widely cultivated for its seeds. The many commercial varieties grow to heights of 20–200 cm and produce clusters of pods, each containing two or three seeds. The ripe seeds contain 35% protein. Soya-bean oil is extracted for use in making margarines, cooking oils, resins, and paints and for many other foods, chemicals, and textiles. The meal residue is an important protein food for livestock and a meat substitute for man. The beans are also eaten whole, ground into flour, and made into soy sauce. Family: *Leguminosae*.

Soyinka, Wole (1934–) Nigerian dramatist and poet. He was educated in Nigeria and England. His works include the play *The Lion and the Jewel* (1963) and the novels *The Interpreters* (1965), *The Man Died* (1973), and *Aké* (1982). He edited the literary journal *Black Orpheus* (1960–64) and was imprisoned during the Nigerian civil war (1967–69). He was awarded the 1986 Nobel prize.

Soyuz. *See* Salyut.

Spa 50 29N 5 52E A town in SE Belgium. It is a tourist resort, renowned since the 14th century for its mineral springs. Population (1982): 9636.

Spaak, Paul Henri (1899–1972) Belgian statesman, the first socialist prime minister of Belgium (1938–39, 1947–50) and foreign minister (1936–38, 1939–46, 1954–57, 1961–65). He was president of the first UN General Assembly (1946) and of the European Consultative Assembly (1949). From 1957 to 1961 he was secretary general of NATO.

spacecraft A vehicle designed to be launched into space and to function effectively for a considerable period in the hostile conditions of space. Due to the immense expense and the difficulties involved in prolonged space travel, most spacecraft are unmanned. Their instruments are powered by arrays of solar cells (*see* solar power), for craft out to about Mars' orbit, and can be controlled by ground stations. Their information is sent back to earth as radio transmissions. Unmanned spacecraft in orbit in 1985 numbered 1476 as well as *planetary probes. *See also* space shuttle; space station.

space exploration The space age began with the launching of the Soviet satellite Sputnik 1 on 4 October, 1957. The first manned flight, one earth orbit, was made by the Soviet cosmonaut Yuri *Gagarin on 12 April, 1961. Man first flew round the moon in December, 1968, aboard the US Apollo 8 and first landed on the lunar surface in the lunar module of Apollo 11 in July, 1969 (*see* Apollo moon programme). Although manned exploration of space has at present gone no further than the moon, unmanned *planetary probes have been sent to every planet as far as Uranus. Pioneer 11 reached Saturn in September, 1979, and Voyager 2 flew past Uranus sending back photographs in 1986; Voyager 2 should approach Neptune in 1989. Most probes have made a close fly-by of targeted planets; the Mariner 9, Viking, Vega, and Pioneer Venus orbiters of Mars and Venus were able to make more extensive observations.

space shuttle One of a series of manned reusable space transportation systems. The first series was developed by *NASA and was in operational use by 1982. It consists of a delta-wing Orbiter that has three powerful rocket engines, a large cargo bay, and living space. It is launched into low earth orbit by rocket propulsion. Although its two externally mounted rocket boosters can be recovered after they detach shortly after launch, the huge external propellant tank is discarded. Satellites, probes, and manned space laboratories such as Spacelab can be launched from the cargo bay and have also been brought into the bay for on-site repair and redeployment or return to earth. Scientific, technological, and medical experiments are also performed. Having completed its mission (7–30 days), the shuttle enters the earth's atmosphere in a shallow dive and makes an unpowered landing. The series began with the first successful test flight of *Columbia* (1981) and ended with the explosion of *Challenger* (1986) two minutes after blast-off, with the death of the seven crew; flights have since been suspended. Other shuttles planned are the British HOTOL, the French Hermes, and the Soviet Kosmolyot space plane.

space station A large orbiting spacecraft on which people can live and work in weightless conditions. Crews are ferried to and from the station, remaining on board for up to several months. The first space station was the Soviet *Salyut–1, launched in 1971; America's *Skylab was orbited in 1973. In 1986 the USSR put into orbit its giant space station Mir and in 1987 the USA announced plans for an international space station (with Canada, Japan, and Europe) to be launched in the 1990s.

space-time continuum A coordinate system that has four dimensions, three representing physical space and the fourth time. The four-dimensional space-time continuum is used in *relativity to define an event. For example, an event occurring on the sun would be observed at different times on earth and on Jupiter, as light from the sun takes some 35 minutes longer to reach Jupiter than to reach the earth. Thus the concept of simultaneity requires a four-dimensional coordinate system to define events without ambiguity.

space warfare. *See* Strategic Defence Initiative.

spadefoot toad A nocturnal burrowing *toad belonging to a widely distributed family (*Pelobatidae*). Spadefoot toads survive in arid regions by digging themselves deep holes in sand or mud with a special horny structure on the foot. The European spadefoot (*Pelobates fuscus*) exudes a garlic-smelling secretion when harmed.

Spain, Kingdom of A country in SW Europe, occupying over four-fifths of the Iberian Peninsula. The Balearic and Canary Islands are also part of Spain. It consists mainly of a high plateau, rising over 3000 m (10 000 ft) in the Pyrenees in the NE. *Economy*: traditionally agricultural, the industrial sector had begun to predominate by the early 1970s. After many years of economic stagnation, there was a remarkable improvement in the 1960s with the development of the motor-vehicle, machine-tool, shipbuilding, and chemical industries. Tourism, an important source of foreign currency, began to flourish again by late 1976. There is both livestock and crop farming and varied crops include wheat, barley, citrus fruit, and vegetables (especially potatoes, onions, sugar beet, and tomatoes). There is a thriving wine industry. Forestry is important, as well as fishing (sardines, tuna, and cod), and rich mineral resources include coal, lignite, anthracite, and iron ore. Hydroelectricity is a valuable source of power. However, the economy has not been unaffected by the worldwide recession of the mid-1970s. *History*: remains of Neanderthal man have been found at Gibraltar, Valencia, and Gerona, and Spain was subsequently inhabited by Iberians, Celts, Phoenicians, and Greeks. In the 3rd century BC the Carthaginians under Hamilcar Barca conquered most of the Iberian peninsula but were expelled by the Romans in the second *Punic War (218–201 BC). Christianity was introduced in the 1st century AD and by the 5th century the Romans had given way to German tribes, including the Vandals and then the Visigoths. The Visigothic kingdom collapsed (711) in the face of Muslim invaders, who dominated most of the central and S parts of the peninsula under a series of powerful dynasties (*see* Umayyads; Abbadids; Almoravids; Almohads). The Reconquest of Muslim Spain was pursued throughout the middle ages by the Christian kingdoms in the N and was completed in 1492 with the conquest of Granada by Ferdinand of Aragon and Isabella of Castile. The union of Spain, begun by the union of Aragon and Castile following the marriage of Ferdinand and Isabella, was now complete. The year 1492 also saw the expulsion from Spain of the Jews, who were followed after much persecution (1609) by the Muslims; the influence of both peoples on Spanish culture was enormous. The 16th century was Spain's golden age. Overseas exploration led to the formation of an empire in the New World, which brought great wealth to Spain. The country's prestige and power, as well as its possessions, in Europe were furthered by the Habsburg kings Charles I (who as *Charles V was also Holy Roman Emperor) and his son Philip II but the latter's reign witnessed the beginnings of decline. The *Revolt of the Netherlands against Spanish rule led to the secession (1581) of the northern Dutch provinces and in 1588 Spain suffered the humiliating defeat of the Armada by the English. Following the Thirty Years' War Spain lost to France its position as the leading European power (1659). The death in 1700 of the last Habsburg king (Charles II), without an heir, led to the War of the *Spanish Succession (1701–14). This confirmed the Bourbon succession and also deprived Spain of the Spanish Netherlands, Milan, Naples, Sardinia, and Sicily. In the second half of the 18th century Spain's decline was arrested by reform, especially under *Charles III, but in 1808 Napoleon established his brother Joseph Bonaparte on the Spanish throne. The Spanish resistance to their French conquerors contributed to the defeat of Napoleon (*see* Peninsular War) and in 1814 the Bourbon Ferdinand VII was restored.

*Carlism and conflict between monarchists and republicans (the latter achieved short-lived victory in 1873–74) dominated the 19th century, during which Spain also lost its last American possessions. It was neutral in World War I, following which *Primo de Rivera established a military dictatorship that undermined the position of the monarchy. In 1931 Alfonso XIII abdicated and the Second Republic was established. The electoral victory of the Popular Front under Azaña in 1936 precipitated a military revolt led by Gen *Franco that became the *Spanish Civil War (1936–39). Franco's victory initiated over three decades of Nationalist dictatorship. Following Franco's death in 1975, the monarchy was restored and Juan Carlos de Borbón became king and head of state. After widespread demonstrations and industrial conflict Carlos Arias Navarro (1909–　) was replaced as prime minister by Adolfo Suárez and the return to a more democratic form of government proceeded more rapidly. In 1978 provisional regional self-government was granted to Catalonia, Valencia, the Canary Islands, Aragon, Galicia, and the Basque provinces, although terrorist activities by Basque separatists continued. Spain's first Socialist government in nearly 50 years was elected in 1982 under Felipe González (1942–　). Spain joined the North Atlantic Treaty Organization (NATO) in 1982 and became a member of the EEC in 1986. Official language: Spanish. Official religion: Roman Catholic. Official currency: peseta of 100 céntimos. Area: 504 879 sq km (194 883 sq mi). Population (1983 est): 38 234 000. Capital: Madrid. Main port: Barcelona.

Spalato. *See* Split.

Spalding 52 47N 0 10W A market town in S England, in S Lincolnshire on the River Welland. It is well known for bulb growing (especially its tulip fields). Population (1981): 18 223.

Spallanzani, Lazzaro (1729–99) Italian physiologist, noted for his studies of microscopic life. Spallanzani demonstrated that microorganisms arose not by spontaneous generation but from spores in the air. He also studied regeneration, digestion, and spermatozoa. He showed that contact by semen was necessary for development of the egg and he achieved the first successful artificial insemination of a dog.

Spandau 52 32N 13 13E The main industrial district of West Berlin, West Germany, at the confluence of the Rivers Havel and Spree. Nazi war criminals were imprisoned in the 16th-century fortress after 1946. After the suicide of the last inmate, Rudolf Hess, in 1987 the prison was demolished. Population (1983 est): 193 700.

spaniel One of several breeds of sporting dogs developed in Britain and thought to have originated in Spain. The English springer spaniel is typical, having a lean compact body, long muzzle, and long drooping ears. It is longer in the leg than the similar *cocker spaniel but has the same flat wavy weather-resistant coat. It is generally black and white or liver and white, while the smaller Welsh springer spaniel is always red and white. The white Clumber spaniel, bred at Clumber Park, Nottinghamshire, England, is the heaviest breed. The Irish water spaniel has a distinctive curly dark-brown coat and is a strong swimmer. Height: 51 cm (English springer); 53–61 cm (Irish water); 46–48 cm (Welsh springer). *See also* King Charles spaniel.

Spanish A *Romance language spoken in Spain, Latin America, the Philippines, and elsewhere by about 145 million people. The standard form is based on the Castilian dialect, originally spoken in the Burgos region, which was the official language of Spain in the late 15th century.

Spanish Civil War (1936–39) The civil war in Spain precipitated by a military revolt on 18 July, 1936, led by the Nationalist Gen *Franco, against the Republican Government of *Azaña. By the end of 1936 the Nationalists had gained control of most of W and S Spain, while the Republicans held the urban areas of the E and N, including Madrid, Valencia, Barcelona, and Bilbao. During 1937 the Nationalists, with Italian and German help, failed in their attempt to take Madrid but

captured Bilbao; in April occurred the indiscriminate bombing by German planes of the town of Guernica, an event commemorated in a famous painting by Picasso. In 1938, however, in spite of the assistance of the *International Brigade and the Soviet Union, the Republican front was broken and early in 1939 Barcelona, Valencia, and then Madrid fell. The Republican cause in the war, which claimed some 750 000 Spanish lives, rallied liberals throughout Europe against fascism.

Spanish fly A golden-green European *blister beetle, *Lytta vesicatoria*, that is the chief source of cantharidin. This chemical can be extracted from its dried body—especially the wing cases—and was formerly used as a blistering agent and diuretic (it was also reputedly an aphrodisiac).

Spanish Guinea. *See* Equatorial Guinea, Republic of.

Spanish literature The earliest major work of Spanish literature is the heroic epic *Poema de mío Cid*, dating from the 12th century and written in the Castilian vernacular. Catalan poetry flourished during the 15th century, but after the union of Aragon and Castile in 1479, the Castilian language became dominant throughout Spain. Major writers of the *Siglo de Oro, which lasted from about 1550 to 1650, include *Cervantes and *Lope de Vega. After the death of *Calderon, little literature of major importance was produced until the regional novels of Juan Valera (1824–1905) and *Pérez Galdós appeared in the late 19th century. A dominant influence during the early 20th century was the philosopher and novelist Miguel de *Unamuno. The major poets were Ruben *Dario, who introduced modernist theories to Spain from his native Nicaragua, and *Garcia Lorca. Many writers went into exile during the Civil War, and most of the best literature in Spanish in recent years has been produced in Latin America by such writers as *Borges, *Neruda, and *Paz.

Spanish moss 1. An epiphytic plant, *Tillandsia usneoides* (or *Dendropogon usneoides*), also known as black moss, long moss, and vegetable horsehair, and found in warm regions of America. Its seeds are windblown to trees, where they germinate and grow downwards in large silvery-grey beardlike masses, 6–7.5 m long. It is covered in hairlike scales, which absorb water from the air. When dried it can be used as packing material or upholstery. Family: *Bromeliaceae*. **2.** A tropical lichen, *Usnea longissima*, which resembles *T. usneoides*. □ p. 1144.

Spanish Riding School (full name: Imperial Spanish Riding School of Vienna) A centre for classical horsemanship in Vienna. Founded in the Habsburg imperial palace, probably in the late 16th century, it was moved to its present building, designed by *Fischer von Erlach, in about 1730. Here the purest *haute école* *dressage of the 16th and 17th centuries is practised. The white *Lipizzaner stallions used here have been bred from horses imported from Spain in the 16th century —hence the title "Spanish." □horse.

Spanish Sahara. *See* Western Sahara.

Spanish Succession, War of the (1701–14) The third of the European wars caused by Louis XIV's attempts to increase French power. The immediate cause of conflict was the dispute over the succession to the Spanish throne. Following the death of the childless Charles II, Louis proclaimed the succession of his grandson as Philip V. England felt menaced by the prospect of a union of French and Spanish dominions and by French commercial expansion. England, the Dutch Republic, and the Holy Roman Emperor formed an alliance against France in 1701 and were joined by most German states upon the outbreak of general hostilities (1702). Spain, Bavaria, Portugal, and Savoy supported France. The English won a series of brilliant victories under the Duke of *Marlborough but pressed for peace in 1712, when a Spanish-Austrian union threatened. The Treaties of *Utrecht (1713–14) concluded the war, which marked the end of French expansionism under Louis.

SPARROWHAWK *This bird of prey can be seen cruising through woodlands and over hedges, hunting small birds and other animals.*

Spanish Town 17 59N 76 58W A town in SE Jamaica, on the Rio Cobre. Founded in 1525, it was the capital of Jamaica until 1871. Population (1982 est): 81 416.

Spark, Muriel (1918–) British novelist, born in Edinburgh. She achieved success with a series of witty satirical novels including *Memento Mori* (1959) and *The Prime of Miss Jean Brodie* (1961). Her later novels include *The Hot House by the East River* (1973), *The Abbess of Crewe* (1974), *The Takeover* (1976), *Territorial Rights* (1979), *Loitering With Intent* (1981), and *The Only Problem* (1984).

spark chamber A device that detects charged particles. It consists of a gas-filled chamber containing a number of thin parallel wires or plates separated by a few centimetres and held at a high voltage. An incoming particle causes a spark to jump from plate to plate across the chamber, enabling the progress of the particle to be photographed.

sparrow A small thick-billed member of the *weaverbird family. Sparrows range from 10–17 cm in length and are generally brown and grey in colour, often with black or bright yellow patches. They are mostly tropical Old World species but also occur in Eurasia and have been introduced to North America where the *house sparrow is a pest. Sparrows eat seeds, feeding on the ground and nesting in holes in banks and buildings. Subfamily: *Passerinae*.

sparrowhawk A small woodland *hawk, *Accipiter nisus*, occurring in Eurasia and NW Africa. It has a long tail and short rounded wings and the male (27 cm long) is grey with brown-barred white underparts; females (38 cm long) are brown above. It hunts small birds.

Sparta 37 05N 22 25E In ancient Greece, the capital of Laconia on the River Eurotas in the S Peloponnese. Developing from Dorian settlements during the 10th century BC, Sparta controlled much of Laconia and Messenia by 700 BC. The indigenous peoples became *helot serfs or semi-independent half-citizens (*perioeci*) and were subject to the governing class of Spartiates. Two hereditary kings ruled, with a powerful body of magistrates (*ephors*) and a council of elders (*gerousia*); there was also a citizen assembly (*apella*). Sparta became an austere militaristic state, where weaker boys were abandoned at birth and those that survived were subjected from the age of seven to a rigid military training. Its military strength

brought conflict in the 5th century with Athens, and ultimate victory (404) in the consequent *Peloponnesian War: defeat by the Thebans at *Leuctra (371) marked the beginning of Spartan decline. The ancient city was destroyed by the Visigoths in 396 AD and the modern town S of its ruins dates from 1834. Population (1981): 15 915.

Spartacus Thracian gladiator, who led a revolt against Rome in 73 BC. After defeating the Romans in five separate engagements in Italy, he moved N to Cisalpine *Gaul. When his followers refused to disperse, Spartacus marched S again and was defeated by Marcus Licinius *Crassus (71). He and his followers were crucified.

Spartacus League A German socialist group, founded during World War I, that adopted the name of the leader of a slave revolt in ancient Rome, *Spartacus. Its leaders were Rosa *Luxemburg and Karl *Liebknecht, both of whom were murdered after an attempted rising in 1919. The German Communist Party grew out of the League.

Spartina A genus of *grasses (16 species), known as cordgrass, found on salt marshes and tidal flats of North America, Europe, and Africa. They have stiff erect stems, 0.3–3 m tall and yellowish flower spikes. Townsend's cord grass (*S. townsendii*), also called rice grass, a natural hybrid, has been used extensively to help reclaim coastal land.

Spassky, Boris (1937–) Soviet chess player. He was world champion from 1969 to 1972, when he lost the title to *Fischer at Reykjavik.

spastic. *See* cerebral palsy.

Speaker of the House of Commons The presiding officer of the lower chamber of the British parliament. Elected by each new parliament, a Speaker was first appointed in 1377 and he or his deputy regulate with impartiality all the debates and proceedings of the House, except for proceedings in committee. Sanctions open to him include "naming" a member for an offence and indefinite suspension from the House. His equivalent in the House of Lords is the Lord (High) *Chancellor.

Spearman, Charles Edward (1863–1945) US psychologist, whose statistical studies of the results from various intelligence tests led him to postulate a factor of intelligence, G, common to all aspects of intelligence. His work pointed to factorial analysis as an important statistical method.

spearmint An aromatic perennial herb, *Mentha spicata*, native to central and S Europe and widely cultivated as a culinary herb. It grows to a height of 30–90 cm and has spikes of small lilac flowers. The oil extract from the leaves is used to flavour sweets, etc. Family: *Labiatae*.

Special Air Service (SAS) A specialist division of the British army. Formed in 1942 in North Africa by Col David Stirling, the unit is highly trained in operations behind enemy lines and is the most secretive of the British forces. In recent years the SAS has seen action against terrorists in Malaya, Aden, and Northern Ireland; in 1980 it spearheaded an assault upon the Iranian embassy in London. Its motto is "Who dares wins."

Special Drawing Rights (SDRs) The rights of member countries of the *International Monetary Fund to draw on the fund to finance *balance-of-payments deficits. First instituted in 1970, SDRs (unlike normal drawings) do not have to be repaid and therefore form a permanent addition to the drawing country's reserves, functioning as an international reserve currency and supplementing its holdings of gold and convertible currencies. The value of SDRs is computed as a weighted average of 16 currencies. Their advantage over gold and other reserve currencies is that their supply can be controlled and does not depend either on mineral deposits or on the US balance of payments.

special education A wide range of facilities that aim to provide suitable education for children with physical or mental disabilities (UK) or for exceptionally gifted children (USA). Although special education in the UK dates back to the 18th century, it was not until the Education Act (1944) that mentally and physically handicapped children ceased to be dealt with as a separate group and were regarded like other children as needing an education appropriate to age, aptitude, and ability. Special education is provided either within ordinary schools or in special schools.

species A unit of classification of animals and plants. Individuals of the same species usually resemble one another closely and can breed among themselves to produce fertile offspring that resemble the parents. Examples of species are the domestic cat, the dogrose, and the field mushroom.

Some species are subdivided into subspecies and varieties. Breeds of domestic animals and cultivated varieties of plants have been specially developed by man for economic or other purposes and are all derived from a few wild species. Those originating from the same species can interbreed, despite obvious differences in character. All breeds of domestic dog, for instance, belong to the same species—*Canis familiaris*—and types as diverse as the poodle, corgi, and greyhound can breed together.

specific gravity. *See* density.

specific heat capacity (c) The quantity of heat needed to raise a unit mass of substance by $1°C$. It is measured in joules per kelvin per kilogram. For gases, the specific heat capacity at constant pressure (c_p) exceeds that at constant volume (c_v) as heat is required to do work against the surroundings during the expansion. The ratio c_p/c_v (symbol: γ) is 1.66 for monatomic gases, 1.4 for diatomic gases, and about 1 for other gases.

spectacled bear The only South American *bear, Tremarctos ornatus*, also called Andean bear. Up to 1.5 m long, it is brownish-black with white circles around the eyes and climbs trees to feed on leaves, nuts, and fruit.

spectacles Lenses worn in frames in front of the eyes to correct defective vision. Convex lenses bend parallel light rays inward; they are used by those unable to focus on close objects (*see* longsightedness). Concave lenses have the opposite effect and are used by those unable to focus on distant objects (*see* shortsightedness). *Astigmatism is treated by wearing lenses that produce a compensating distortion of the light rays. Bifocal spectacles have convex lenses consisting of upper and lower parts of different curvatures, for focusing on distant and near objects, respectively: they are worn for presbyopia. *See also* contact lenses.

spectral type. *See* Harvard classification system.

spectrum In general, the way in which a particular property of a system is distributed over its components. The visible spectrum, for example, is observed in a *rainbow, which shows the distribution of frequencies when sunlight is split up into its components by raindrops. The visible spectrum, however, is only a small part of the *electromagnetic spectrum, which ranges from X-rays to radio waves. **Spectroscopy** is concerned with observing and analysing the emission and absorption of electromagnetic energy by atoms and molecules.

According to the *quantum theory, atoms and molecules can only emit or absorb energy in discrete amounts, called quanta. When an atom or molecule is heated, bombarded with electrons, etc., it absorbs energy (becomes excited); on falling back to its lower state it emits a photon (a quantum of radiation energy). The energy of this photon is equal to hf, where f is the frequency of the radiation and h is *Planck's constant. Each atom or molecule can only make specific energy transitions. This means that as well as the continuous

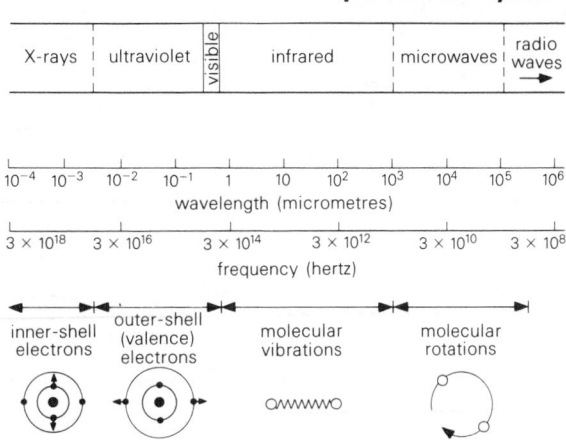

SPECTRUM *Energetic photons in the X-ray region of the spectrum alter the excitation of atomic inner-shell electrons. The ultraviolet and visible photons interact with the outer-shell electrons that participate in chemical reactions. Infrared photons alter the vibrational states of molecules and microwave photons affect molecular rotation.*

*black-body radiation produced by thermal agitation, atoms can emit and absorb radiation at particular frequencies, which show up as coloured lines in their spectrum. These **line spectra** can be used to identify particular elements. The spectrum formed by atoms or molecules that are emitting radiation is called an **emission spectrum**.

As atoms absorb energy at the same frequency as they emit it, if a substance lies in the path of radiation its atoms will absorb certain of the energy quanta in the radiation, producing dark lines in the spectrum. These dark lines are **absorption spectra**. For example, the sun's spectrum contains many dark lines (called Fraunhofer lines). These are caused by atoms of hydrogen, helium, etc., in the sun's atmosphere absorbing energy from the radiation produced in the centre of the sun.

Spectroscopes (*or* spectrometers) are instruments for analysing a spectrum. They usually consist of a collimator to collect the radiation from the source, a grating or prism to split it into its components and a telescope to view the refracted radiation. A means of recording the spectrum photographically is needed for ultraviolet and infrared radiation. *See* Plate VIII.

speedway A form of professional *motorcycle racing, which originated in Australia in the late 1920s. Races are held on dirt tracks in heats of four laps between four riders. 500 cc motorcycles with no brakes are used. In the UK, where teams compete in a two-division league, speedway is second in popularity only to Association football as a spectator sport.

speedwell An annual or perennial herbaceous plant of the genus *Veronica* (about 200 species), up to 60 cm high, occurring throughout temperate regions. The flowers, borne singly or in clusters in the axils of the simple toothed leaves, are usually blue, sometimes white or pinkish, with four unequal petals. The fruit is a flattened heart-shaped capsule. Two common species are *V. officinalis* and the germander speedwell (*V. chamaedrys*). Family: *Scrophulariaceae*.

Speedwriting. *See* shorthand.

Speenhamland system A system of poor relief started by the Speenhamland magistrates in Berkshire in 1795. Allowances were given from the parish rates to men unable to support their families themselves due to unemployment or low wages. It was unsuccessful in alleviating rural poverty and was very expensive for the parish. It was abolished by the *Poor Law Amendment Act (1834).

Speke, John Hanning (1827–64) British explorer. He accompanied Richard *Burton on the expeditions (1855, 1857–58) to discover the source of the Nile. They discovered Lake Tanganyika and then Speke went on alone to discover Lake Victoria, which on a second visit in 1860, accompanied by J. A. Grant (1827–92), he established to be the source of the Nile. Burton disputed Speke's claim and Speke accidentally shot himself just before an engagement to defend himself before the British Association.

speleology (*or* spelaeology) The study and exploration of *caves and underground water courses. This includes the survey of caves and the study of their formation, plant and animal life (past and present), and geology. Potholing—or descending through potholes into underground drainage passages in order to follow the course of underground streams—is an increasingly popular although relatively dangerous activity.

spelling The conventional representation of spoken words in an alphabetic writing system. The underlying principle of alphabetic writing is that there should be a consistent one-for-one relationship between speech sounds and written letters but this is rarely fully realized in practice. Inconsistencies arise because a change in pronunciation is not always matched by a corresponding spelling change. In English, for example, an extensive change in the value of vowels took place in the 15th century (*see* Great Vowel Shift), *-e* at the end of a word ceased to be pronounced, and the sound represented by *-gh-* (the sound of *-ch* in Scottish *loch*) dropped out or changed to /f/.

Spence, Sir Basil (1907–76) British architect. Originally a designer of country houses in Scotland, he became internationally known with his design for rebuilding Coventry Cathedral (consecrated 1962). More recent buildings include Sussex University and the British Embassy in Rome (completed 1971).

Spencer, Lady Diana *See* Charles, Prince.

Spencer, Herbert (1820–1903) British philosopher. As subeditor of the *Economist* (1843–53), Spencer was an influential exponent of *laissez-faire. His early book *Social Statics* (1851) was strongly tinged with an individualistic outlook, as was his multi-volume *System of Synthetic Philosophy* (1860–96), of which the most important volume was *First Principles* (1862). He believed that state intervention limited progress and he developed this idea fully in his popular *The Man versus the State* (1884). Spencer's other writings include works on psychology, ethics, and sociology. He supported Charles *Darwin's theory of evolution by natural selection, coining the phrase "survival of the fittest," and applied evolutionary ideas to social development.

Spencer, Sir Stanley (1891–1959) British painter. He is known for his religious subjects, often depicted in the everyday setting of his native village of Cookham, Berkshire. He studied at the Slade School (1910–14) and first became known for his murals of army life for Sandham Memorial Chapel, Burghclere (1926–1932), and for *The Resurrection: Cookham* (1922–27; Tate Gallery). He was knighted in 1959.

Spencer Gulf An inlet of the Indian Ocean, in S Australia situated between Eyre Peninsula and Yorke Peninsula, with Port Augusta, Port Pirie, and Whyalla located on its shores. Length: 320 km (200 mi). Width: about 120 km (75 mi).

Spender, Sir Stephen (1909–) British poet and critic. A friend of W. H. Auden, he published left-wing poetry during the 1930s and was briefly a member of the Communist Party. His later poetry, included in *Collected Poems* (1955) and *The Generous Days* (1971), is more personal and lyrical. Other works include an autobiography, *World within World* (1951), *Journals 1939–83* (1985), *Collected Poems* (1985), and books of criticism.

Spengler, Oswald (1880–1936) German philosopher. Spengler's most famous work, *The Decline of the West* (1918), argued that nations and cultures have a natural lifespan and their rise is inevitably followed by their eclipse. His ideas appealed to the German fascists, as he emphasized the individual's duty of obedience to the state.

Spenser, Edmund (c. 1552–99) English poet. He dedicated *The Shepheardes Calendar* (1579), pastoral poems arranged by the months of the year, to Sir Philip Sidney, nephew of his patron the Earl of Leicester. In 1580 he was appointed secretary to the Lord Deputy of Ireland, where he became a prominent landowner. His major work, *The Faerie Queene*, a long moral allegory in nine-line "Spenserian" stanzas, was dedicated to Elizabeth I and published in six books in 1590 and 1596. His other works include the sonnet sequence *Amoretti* (1595) and the *Epithalamion* (1595), celebrating his second marriage.

Speranski, Mikhail Mikhailovich (1772–1839) Russian statesman, described by Napoleon as "the only clear head in Russia." Speranski, as Alexander I's chief adviser (1807–12), presented proposals for the reform of the administration and for the drafting of a new constitution. His unpopularity with colleagues led to his exile until 1816. In 1826 he began his greatest achievement, the codification of Russian law.

sperm (*or* spermatozoon) The reproductive cell of .nale animals, which is formed in the *testis and fertilizes an egg cell during sexual *reproduction. A sperm usually has a head region, containing the genetic material, and a tail, by means of which it swims to the egg. In man, sperms develop and mature in the testes, where the temperature is 2°C below body temperature. At ejaculation they are mixed with secretions from various glands (including the *prostate gland) to form semen.

spermaceti A *wax obtained from the head cavity and from the oils of whales, dolphins, and porpoises. It is liquid at room temperature and is separated from the oil by chilling. Spermaceti is used in ointments, cosmetics, fine candles, and textile finishing.

spermatophyte Any plant that reproduces by *seeds rather than spores. Spermatophytes include the *gymnosperms (conifers, etc.) and the *angiosperms (flowering plants).

sperm banks. *See* artificial insemination.

sperm whale A large toothed *whale, *Physeter cathodon*, also called cachalot. It is 18 m long, grey-blue above and pale beneath, with tiny flippers and large tail flukes. The blowhole is near the tip of the snout and it can dive up to 1 km in search of octopus and squid, sometimes staying under water for over one hour. Family: *Physeteridae*.

Spey, River A fast-flowing river in NE Scotland, flowing mainly NE through the Grampian Mountains to Spey Bay. It is known for its salmon fishing. Length: 172 km (107 mi).

Speyer (English name: Spires) 49 18N 8 26E A city in SW West Germany, in Rhineland-Palatinate on the River Rhine. The cathedral (1030) contains the tombs of eight emperors. An important diet (assembly) was held here in 1529 (*see* Protestantism). It is a port and industrial centre. Population (1983 est): 43 815.

Sphagnum A widely distributed genus of mosses (over 300 species), called bog or peat moss, forming dense raised clumps in bogs and other waterlogged places. Green to dark red in colour and up to 30 cm high, the fine stems bear clusters of threadlike branches, densely clothed with tiny leaves, and globular spore capsules. The ability of the stems and leaves to retain water (up to 20 times the weight of the plant) is responsible for the outstanding ability of these mosses to drain very wet ground and form bogs. The dead remains of the plants accumulate to form *peat—an important fuel and ingredient of horticultural composts. Family: *Sphagnaceae*.

sphalerite (*or* zinc blende) The principal ore of zinc, a sulphide, usually brown or black in colour. It frequently occurs with *galena in metasomatic deposits, and in hydrothermal veins and replacement deposits.

spherical coordinates. *See* coordinate systems.

SPHINX *The Great Sphinx at Giza is thought to be a portrait statue of King Khafre (c. 2550 BC).*

sphinx A mythological creature with a lion's body and a human head, occurring in the art and legends of most ancient Near and Middle Eastern civilizations. The most famous representation is the Great Sphinx at Giza, Egypt, dating from the 3rd millennium BC. In Greek legend, the Sphinx was a female monster that preyed on travellers going to Thebes. She killed those who could not answer her riddle, which was finally solved by *Oedipus.

sphygmomanometer A device for measuring arterial *blood pressure. It consists of an inflatable arm cuff connected via a rubber tube to a column of mercury with a graduated scale or an aneroid device. The cuff is inflated until the pulse cannot be detected (using a stethoscope) and then slowly deflated until the systolic and then the diastolic pressure can be recorded as the pulse returns.

Spica A conspicuous blue star, apparent magnitude 0.97 and about 215 light years distant, that is the brightest star in the constellation Virgo. It is an eclipsing *binary star.

Spice Islands. *See* Moluccas.

spices. *See* herbs and spices.

spider An *arachnid belonging to the worldwide order *Araneae* (or *Araneida*; over 30 000 species). 1-90 mm long, the body of a spider consists of a cephalothorax abdomen separated by a narrow "waist." There are eight walking legs, up to eight eyes, and several pairs of spinnerets, which produce silk used for making webs, egg cocoons, etc. Spiders are predominantly terrestrial and prey mainly on insects, hunting them or trapping them in their webs. The victims are killed with poison-bearing fangs; in a few species the poison is harmful to man. The female is generally larger than the male, which she sometimes kills and eats after mating. She then deposits the eggs on or near the web, among leaves or twigs, etc., or carries them until they hatch. The young go through a series of moults to reach the adult stage. *See also* black widow; tarantula; water spider; wolf spider.

spider crab A marine *crab belonging to the widely distributed family *Maiidae*, especially one of the genus *Libinia*. It has a thick rounded body, with long spindly legs and generally moves slowly. Most spider crabs are scavengers, especially of dead animals.

spider mite A red or yellow *mite, 0.5 mm long, also called red spider mite, belonging to the family *Tetranychidae*. It sucks plant juices from foliage and fruits and is a serious pest of orchard trees, crops, and house plants.

spider monkey A monkey belonging to the genus *Ateles* (4 species), of Central and South American forests. Spider monkeys have very long legs and are 88-150 cm long including the prehensile tail (50-90 cm), which is capable of supporting their weight. They live in family groups in thick forest, feeding on seeds and leaves. Family: *Cebidae*.

spider plant A plant of the genus *Chlorophytum*, especially *C. elatum*, native to South Africa and widely grown as a house plant. It has narrow green and white striped leaves, 60-90 cm long, and periodically produces a stem bearing small white flowers or young plantlets. Family: *Liliaceae*.

spider wasp A solitary *wasp belonging to a family (*Pompilidae*) of worldwide distribution. It preys chiefly on spiders, which are also paralysed and stored in underground nests as food for the larvae. Spider wasps have dark slender bodies (5-75 mm long), long legs, and usually smoky or amber-coloured wings.

spiderwort. *See* Tradescantia.

Spielberg, Steven (1946–) US film director. After *Duel* (1971), he became the most commercially successful director of the 1970s with *Jaws* (1975), about a killer shark, and *Close Encounters of the Third Kind* (1977). His *ET* (1982) and *Gremlins* (1984) also attracted large audiences. *The Colour Purple* (1986) is his first serious film.

spikenard A perennial Himalayan herb, *Nardostachys jatamansi*, growing to a height of 60 cm and bearing tiny purple flower clusters. It is cultivated for an essential oil derived from its roots, which is used for perfumes and various medicines. Family: *Valerianaceae*.
Ploughman's spikenard (*Inula conyza*) is a perennial herb of Europe and N Africa with yellow flowers and fragrant roots. Family: *Compositae*.

Spillane, Mickey (Frank Morrison S.; 1918–) US detective-story writer. His numerous crime novels featuring the detective Mike Hammer, the popular success of which was due to the uninhibited description of sex and violence, include *I, the Jury* (1947) and *The Twisted Thing* (1966).

spin A property possessed by elementary particles as a result of which they possess a constant angular momentum that is independent of their motion. The spin is quantized and labelled by a spin *quantum number (symbol: s), which may be integral or half-integral.

spina bifida A defect, present at birth, in which the backbone fails to fuse properly, leaving the spinal cord and its coverings exposed. Commonly the child has paralysed legs and disordered bladder and bowel function. The degree of the handicap varies: children who survive and are severely affected require crutches or wheelchairs and need special surgical procedures to help their bladder function. The intelligence of children with spina bifida is often normal, but the condition is frequently associated with *hydrocephalus. Spina bifida can be diagnosed during pregnancy (*see* amniocentesis).

spinach An annual herbaceous plant, *Spinacia oleracea*, native to Asia and widely cultivated as a vegetable. Its edible leaves are rich in iron and vitamins A and C and are boiled as a vegetable and used in salads, soups, soufflés, etc. Family: *Chenopodiaceae*.

spinal cord An elongated part of the central *nervous system, running downwards from the base of the brain and consisting of a core of grey matter (nerve cell bodies) surrounded by white matter (nerve fibres). It is surrounded and protected by the spine and is enclosed in membranes (meninges). It gives off spinal nerves, usually in pairs, and ends in a bundle of nerves supplying the legs and lower part of the body. Through it run the nerve fibres between the brain and the body; injury can therefore cause paralysis and loss of sensation. *See* Plate IV.

spindle tree A Eurasian tree or shrub, *Euonymus europaeus*, that grows to a height of about 6 m. It produces small white flowers and pink and orange fleshy fruits, 10–15 mm across, which yield a yellow food dye. The fine-grained wood has been used to make spindles and clothes pegs. The winged spindle tree (*E. alatus*) occurs in China. Family: *Celastraceae. See also* Euonymus.

spine In anatomy, the backbone, or vertebral column: a series of small bones (vertebrae) that runs up the centre of the back. The spine encloses and protects the spinal cord, articulates with the skull, ribs, and pelvis, and provides attachment for muscles of the back. There are 26 vertebrae in the adult spine, which are subdivided as follows: 7 cervical, in the neck; 12 thoracic, in the chest region attached to the ribs; 5 lumbar, in the lower back; 5 sacral, attached to the hip bone (fused into a single bone—the sacrum); and 4 coccygeal (fused into a single bone—the coccyx). The vertebrae are connected by tough discs of cartilage (intervertebral discs), which absorb the shock produced by running and other movements. *See* Plate IV.

spinel A group of oxide minerals, usually occurring as octahedral crystals. The spinel minerals form a compositional series between true spinel ($MgAl_2O_4$) and hercynite ($Fe^{2+}Al_2O_4$). Magnetite ($Fe^{2+}Fe_2^{3+}O_4$) is the most common and is an important iron ore. Chromite, a source of chromium, is $Fe^{2+}Cr_2O_4$. Spinels occur mostly in metamorphic rocks, especially limestones, and in basic and ultrabasic igneous rocks. *See* Plate III.

spinet A plucked keyboard instrument of the *harpsichord family that superseded the *virginals in the 17th century. It is wing shaped, the strings (one to each note) being at an angle of 45° to the keyboard.

Spinifex A genus of *grasses (3 species), native to S and E Asia and Australia. They grow on sand dunes and form long underground stems (rhizomes), which stabilize the dunes. The heads of spiny one-flowered spikelets break off and are blown about by wind. The name is also used for other Australian grasses that form spiny hummocks, especially *Triodia hirsuta* and *T. irritans*, also called porcupine grass.

spinning The process of converting cleaned and straightened fibres into yarn by twisting overlapping fibres together; until the 18th century this was a household task. Yarn was made originally by drawing out a length of fibre from the mass and attaching it to a vertically hanging stick (spindle) that was weighted to help it spin round; as it spun, the fibre wound onto it. This process was mechanized first by the spinning wheel (in Europe not until the 14th century, although it was used in India long before). The 16th-century Saxony wheel was an improved version, which could be operated continuously. The inventions of James *Hargreaves, Richard *Arkwright, and Samuel *Crompton in the late 18th century industrialized the process. Modern spinning machines produce thousands of metres of yarn every hour. As applied to synthetic fibres, spinning is the extrusion of viscous solutions to form continuous filaments.

Spinoza, Benedict (*or* Baruch de S.; 1632–77) Dutch philosopher, theologian, and scientist of Jewish parentage. Influenced by the writings of *Descartes, *Hobbes, and *Bruno, Spinoza rejected the concepts of the personal nature of God and the immortality of the soul. The Jewish community of his native Amsterdam expelled him in 1656 on account of his unorthodoxy and his *Tractatus Theologico-Politicus* (1670) was furiously attacked by Christian scholars. The idea of God as the basis of all things (*Deus sive Natura*—God or Nature—in his phrase) was, however, central to his philosophy. For this reason he is often cited as

the herald of modern *pantheism. He maintained that man's highest good is his "knowledge of the union existing between the mind and the whole of Nature." His major work, the *Ethica ordine geometrico demonstrata*, generally known as the *Ethics*, could only be published posthumously in 1677. Both *Schleiermacher and *Hegel were greatly influenced by his writings.

spiny lobster A *lobster, also called sea crayfish or crawfish, belonging to the mainly tropical family *Palinuridae*. Its carapace is covered with spines and it lacks pincers, but the antennae are strongly developed.

spiracle The external opening of a respiratory tubule (trachea) of insects and spiders. The term is also used for the paired gill openings of cartilaginous fishes, such as sharks, and for the respiratory openings of tadpoles and whales.

Spiraea A genus of shrubs (about 100 species), widely distributed in N temperate regions. Many are cultivated as ornamentals, including the willow spiraea (*S. salcifolia*), which grows to a height of 1–2 m and bears dense clusters of small pink flowers. Other species and hybrids may have white or crimson flowers. Family: *Rosaceae.

Spires. *See* Speyer.

spirits Distilled liquor defined in the UK as having an alcohol content of at least 40%. Spirits are derived from fermented liquids, for example wine (giving brandy); fruit wines (giving fruit brandies, such as slivovitz from plums and *kirsch from cherries); cider (giving calvados or applejack); grain or potatoes (giving *whisky, *gin, *vodka, or *aquavit). These liquids are distilled, i.e. some of the water is removed by vaporization to increase the alcohol content of the remaining liquid. Distillation often takes place in an onion-shaped potstill.

spiritual A type of religious song developed by plantation slaves in the USA, with texts adapted from the Bible. The spiritual was often extemporized, with a lead singer relating the story in stanzas and a chorus singing the refrain. Harmonized arrangements of spirituals have eliminated the improvisational quality. Famous spirituals include "Steal Away," "Go Down, Moses," and "Deep River."

spiritualism Any theory that emphasizes the direct intervention of spiritual and supernatural forces in the everyday world. The term can cover phenomena as disparate as *extrasensory perception, *telekinesis, and various states associated with religious ecstasy, such as glossolalia (speaking in tongues, or making unintelligible utterances). In western societies, spiritualism commonly means the practice of communicating with the spirits of the dead through a medium in seances or with a *ouija board. Organizations devoted to *psychical research have amassed considerable evidence for spiritualist phenomena, some occurring under rigidly controlled conditions to preclude fraud, although much of it is not the reproducible kind of evidence that scientists seek. Advocates of spiritualism include William *Crookes, Lord *Dowding, Conan *Doyle, and Oliver *Lodge.

spirochaete A bacterium belonging to the order *Spirochaetales*. Spirochaetes are corkscrew-shaped, flexible, and up to 0.5 mm long: they swim by means of bending and looping motions, achieved by contraction of a bundle of fibrils (the axial filament) within the cell. Some spirochaetes cause diseases, including syphilis and yaws in man.

Spirogyra A genus of *green algae, also called mermaid's tresses or pond scum, in the form of threadlike strands of connected cells up to about 30 cm long. Large masses may be found floating near the surface of quiet fresh waters. Reproduction is asexual (by fragmentation) or sexual (*see* conjugation).

spit A linear deposit of sand or shingle extending from a coastline. It often occurs where the coastline changes direction sharply and is deposited by the movement of beach material by wave action.

Spitalfields A district in the Greater London borough of Tower Hamlets. It was noted for silk weaving, which was introduced by Huguenot refugees in the 17th century. Clothing and furniture are still important manufactures.

Spithead 50 43N 0 56W An extensive roadstead between the mainland of England and the Isle of Wight, off Portsmouth.

Spitsbergen. *See* Svalbard.

spittlebug. *See* froghopper.

spitz One of a group of dog breeds originating in N Eurasia and having a thick coat, small pricked ears, and a brushlike tail carried over the back. The Finnish spitz, bred in Finland as a hunting and guard dog, has a reddish-brown or yellowish-red coat while the Lapland spitz is either white, brown and black, or blackish brown. *Husky breeds also show spitz characteristics. Height (Finnish spitz): 44 cm (dogs); 39 cm (bitches).

SPODE *A pair of Spode urn-shaped pot-pourri vases, c. 1820 (135 mm high).*

Spitz, Mark (Andrew) (1950–) US swimmer, who won a record seven gold medals in the Munich Olympic Games (1972). In the period 1967-72 he won altogether nine Olympic golds and set 27 individual world records for freestyle and butterfly. Following the 1972 Olympics he became a successful professional.

spleen A rubbery dark-red organ, about 14 cm long, situated in the abdomen just beneath the lower border of the left side of the rib cage. The spleen assists in the body's defence mechanisms by producing antibodies in newborn babies and by absorbing and digesting bacteria in the bloodstream. It also removes worn-out and abnormal red blood cells and other particles from the circulation. The spleen becomes enlarged in some diseases, including liver disease and severe infections. The spleen can be removed in adults without any ill effects.

spleenwort A tufted *fern of the genus *Asplenium* (about 700 species), growing on walls and rocks throughout the world. The tapering branched fronds are about 5-30 cm long, with triangular lobed leaflets bearing oval or spindle-shaped clusters of spore capsules. The name derives from the former use of some species to treat disorders of the spleen and liver. Family: *Aspleniaceae. See also* bird's nest fern.

Split (Italian name: Spalato) 43 31N 16 28N A port in W

Yugoslavia, in Croatia on the Adriatic Sea. The vast 3rd-century AD Palace of Diocletian contains the present-day city centre, including the cathedral, which was Diocletian's mausoleum. It has a university (1974) and diverse industries. Population (1981): 235 922.

Spock, Benjamin McLane (1903–) US physician and paediatrician, whose books on child care and development have become best sellers, especially his *Common Sense Book of Baby and Child Care* (1946). He was a prominent opponent of US policy during the Vietnam War.

Spode porcelain Fine tableware and other porcelain made in the Staffordshire (England) factory started by Josiah Spode I in 1770. Josiah Spode II introduced "Feldspar" porcelain and "Stone China" as well as using *creamware. The meticulous decoration used transfer printing and painted Japan patterns enhanced by careful gilding.

Spohr, Louis (Ludwig S.; 1784-1859) German violinist and composer. His works include operas, oratorios, symphonies, violin concertos, a concerto for string quartet and orchestra, and a nonet for strings and wind.

Spokane 47 40N 117 25W A city in the USA, in Washington state. It is a trade and shipping centre for a four-state area called the Inland Empire, which has mineral deposits and farms producing cattle, wheat, and fruit. Industries include timber and food processing. Population (1980 est): 171 300.

Spoleto 42 44N 12 44E A town in Italy, in Umbria. Dating from Etruscan times, it has Roman remains and a 12th-century cathedral. Its annual festival of music and drama was founded in 1958 by Gian Carlo *Menotti. There is a textile industry. Population (1981 est): 36 839.

sponge An aquatic invertebrate animal belonging to the phylum *Porifera* (about 5000 species). Most sponges are marine, found attached to rocks or the sea bed, and measure up to several metres across: they may be treelike, cylindrical (*see* Venus's flower basket), or flat irregular masses. Sponges have an internal skeleton of lime, silica, or a fibrous protein (spongin). Bath sponges are spongin skeletons without the living animals. The simplest type of sponge has a vase-shaped body with a pore at the top and smaller pores in the sides. The inside is lined with flagellated collar cells, which maintain a flow of water in through the side pores and out at the top. Food particles in the water are extracted by the collar cells; other cells in the body wall digest food, secrete the skeleton, and produce eggs and sperm. Fertilized eggs are dispersed in the water current and the free-swimming larvae eventually settle and become new sponges. The animals can also reproduce asexually, by budding or fragmentation.

spontaneous generation (*or* abiogenesis) The theory that living organisms arise from nonliving materials. It was widely upheld for many centuries, based on such observations as the appearance of tadpoles from mud and maggots in decaying meat. Belief in the spontaneous development of microorganisms continued until the 19th century, when Louis *Pasteur proved that, like higher organisms, they were capable of reproduction.

spoonbill A long-legged wading bird belonging to a subfamily (*Plataleinae*; 6 species) occurring around estuaries and lakes in tropical and subtropical regions worldwide. 60-80 cm long, spoonbills are usually entirely white, often with a naked head. They feed on fish and crustaceans picked up by sweeping the large spatulate bill from side to side in mud or shallow water. Family: *Threskiornithidae* (ibises and spoonbills); order: *Ciconiiformes* (herons, storks, etc.).

Spooner, William Archibald (1844-1930) British clergyman and academic. A somewhat eccentric Oxford don, Spooner became famous for his frequent transposition of the first letters of words, for example "a well-oiled bicycle" became "a well-boiled icicle." Such a transposition became known as a **Spoonerism.**

Sporades Two groups of Greek islands in the Aegean Sea, the **Northern Sporades**, which include Skyros, and the **Southern Sporades**, which, with the exception of Sámos and Ikaría, constitute the *Dodecanese.

spore The small, often single-celled, reproductive unit of plants, protozoa, and bacteria, which may serve either as a rapid means of propagation or as a dormant stage in the life cycle. Spores may be produced sexually or asexually, i.e. fusion of sex cells (gametes) may or may not occur before their formation. In plants exhibiting an *alternation of generations spores are formed by the sporophyte following meiosis and give rise to the gametophyte, which produces the sex cells. In some algae and fungi spores are produced following cell division (*see* mitosis) and thus give rise to an exact replica of the parent.

sporophyte. *See* alternation of generations.

Sporozoa A phylum of microscopic single-celled animals (*see* Protozoa), all of which are parasites with complex life cycles involving asexual and sexual forms of reproduction. They are often found in the intestinal tracts or blood of animals and form resistant spores or cysts, which can remain dormant until entering a suitable host. The phylum includes the malaria parasite (*see* Plasmodium).

Sports, Book of (1618) The list of those amusements that were permitted (e.g. dancing, May Games, archery) and forbidden (e.g. bear- and bull-baiting, bowling) on Sundays under James I and Charles I of England. It was strongly opposed by the Puritans, who objected to the pursuit of any amusement on Sundays.

sprat A small food fish, *Clupea (Sprattus) sprattus*, also called brisling, that is similar and related to the herring. Up to 17 cm long, it lives in shoals in the E Atlantic, N Mediterranean, and British coastal waters. The young are known as *whitebait.

spring An emission of water from the ground. Springs occur where the water table intersects the surface or where a subsurface stream flowing over an impermeable rock stratum reaches the ground surface. Small outflows of water (seepages) may create a small localized marsh or bog. *See also* hot spring.

spring balance A device for measuring weights. The simplest form consists of a helical spring fixed at its upper end; from the lower end the load is suspended, extending the spring in direct proportion to its weight (according to *Hooke's law).

springbok A rare antelope, *Antidorcas marsupialis*, inhabiting arid regions of S Africa. About 80 cm high at the shoulder, the springbok has a white face with a black line along each side of the muzzle, a fawn body with dark flank hairs, and a patch of white hairs on the rump, which can be flashed as an alarm signal. It is the national emblem of South Africa. □mammal.

Springfield 39 49N 89 39W A city in the USA, the capital of Illinois on the Sangamon River. Abraham Lincoln lived here from 1837 until 1861 and is buried nearby; his home is preserved as a national historic site. Situated in an agricultural area, Springfield is an administrative, commercial, and medical centre with varied industries. Population (1980): 99 637.

Springfield 42 07N 72 35W A city in the USA, in Massachusetts on the Connecticut River. The arsenal operating here from 1794 until 1966 developed the Springfield and Garand rifles. Industries include chemicals and plastic. Population (1980): 152 319.

Springfield 37 11N 93 19W A city in the USA, in Missouri in the Ozark Mountains. The commercial centre for an agricultural region, its industries include railway engineering and the manufacture of furniture and textiles. Population (1980): 133 116.

springhaas A nocturnal kangaroo-like rodent, *Pedetes capensis*, inhabiting the grasslands of eastern and southern Africa. Also called the Cape jumping hare, it is about 35 cm long with yellowish-brown fur and a long bushy black-tipped tail. The springhaas uses the long claws on its forelimbs for excavating burrows and digging up the roots and tubers on which it feeds.

Springs 26 15S 28 26E A city in South Africa, in the S Transvaal. Founded in 1885, it became the centre of extensive goldfields and today is a mining and manufacturing centre producing gold and uranium. Population (1980): 153 974.

springtail An eyeless wingless □insect of the worldwide order *Collembola* (about 3500 species). 3-10 mm long, it has a forked appendage on the abdomen, which is used for jumping. Springtails crawl about in moist soil and leaf litter or on water or snow and feed on decaying vegetable material, sometimes becoming minor pests of garden crops.

spring tide A □tide of relatively large range that occurs near the times of full and new moon. Low tides are lower and high tides higher than normal, and flooding may occur if strong onshore winds coincide with high water. *Compare* neap tide.

sprinkler system A safety system often installed in hotels, warehouses, factories, etc., for *fire prevention. It consists of a set of sprinkler valves connected to a water supply and an initiating alarm mechanism sensitive to heat or smoke. This may be a thin alloy bar in each sprinkler that bends at a low temperature or a sophisticated electronic sensor.

spruce A coniferous □tree of the genus *Picea* (about 50 species), widely distributed in the N hemisphere. Its needles grow in spirals and leave peglike projections on the shoots when they fall. The woody cones, 5-15 cm long, hang down from the branches. An important and widely grown timber tree is the Norway spruce (*Picea abies*), from N and central Europe, of which the timber—known as white wood or deal—is used for paper pulp, roofing, barrels, boxes, etc. This conifer can reach a height of 40 m, but young specimens are used as Christmas trees in Britain. Family: *Pinaceae*.

sprue A disease of the lining of the small intestine in which food is not properly absorbed. It is common in the tropics, often affecting people who have moved from temperate regions. Symptoms include diarrhoea, anaemia, and weight loss, and patients are treated with antibiotics, vitamin preparations, and a special diet.

spurge An annual or perennial herb of the genus *Euphorbia*, especially the hardier temperate species, which have been used as purgatives. Many are weeds but some are cultivated as ornamentals, including the Cypress spurge (*E. cyparissias*). Family: *Euphorbiaceae*.

spurrey One of several annual or perennial herbs that are found on sandy soils and salt marshes, chiefly in N temperate regions. The corn spurrey (*Spergula arvensis*) grows to a height of 7-40 cm and has long thin leaves and white flowers. The sand spurreys (genus *Spergularia*; about 20 species) are smaller and usually have pinkish flowers. Family: *Caryophyllaceae*.

Spurs, Battle of the (16 August, 1513) The battle in which Henry VIII of England defeated the French at Guinegate, near Thérouanne (N France). The battle was so called because of the speed of the French retreat. The English victory led to the capture of Tournai.

Sputnik A series of Soviet unmanned satellites, the first of which was the first spacecraft to be launched (4 October, 1957). It burnt up in the atmosphere after 92 days. Sputnik 2, launched 3 November, 1957, carried the first animal, the dog Laika, into space.

Square Deal A programme of economic and social reform intended by Theodore *Roosevelt (president 1901-09) to benefit the "plain man" in the USA. It sponsored improved labour conditions, regulations regarding the quality of food, and antimonopoly legislation.

square root. *See* root.

squash The fruit of certain plants belonging to the genus *Cucurbita* (15 species), especially *C. maxima*. Native to the New World, squash plants are widely cultivated and form erect bushes, 45–75 cm high, producing fleshy edible fruits, which are variable in shape, texture, and size. They are usually served as a cooked vegetable. Family: *Cucurbitaceae*. *Compare* gourd; pumpkin.

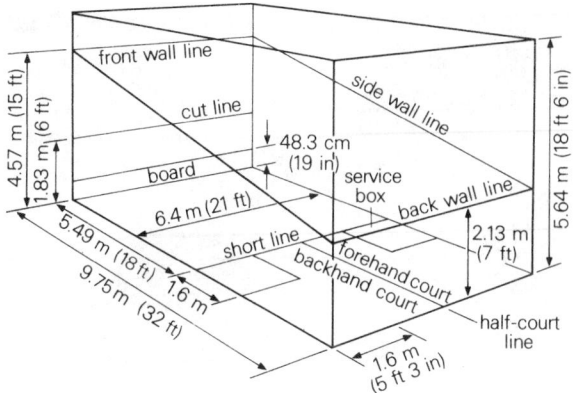

SQUASH RACKETS   *The dimensions of the court.*

squash rackets A racket-and-ball game played in a four-walled court. It originated from an older game (rackets) played at Harrow School, London, in the mid-19th century. Players hit a small ball of synthetic rubber with the object of making a shot that the opponent cannot return. (When the ball is played it must hit the front wall of the court and may hit any other wall.) The service each time goes to the winner of the previous point. The British competitive version is a singles game going to nine or sometimes more points and only the server may score; the US version is a singles or doubles game, in which either side may score and the game goes to 15 points.

squatting **1.** In 19th-century Australia, the unauthorized settlement of Crown lands. Awarded licences in the 1840s, many squatters prospered, forming a politically powerful "squattocracy." **2.** In the UK, the occupation of an empty and often condemned building without authority. Owing to the acute housing shortage, especially in urban areas, squatting in unoccupied buildings scheduled for demolition is often sanctioned by local authorities for those in dire need, enabling services to be temporarily reinstated.

squid A *cephalopod mollusc of the order *Decapoda*. Surrounding the mouth, squids have ten arms bearing suckers; two arms are long retractile tentacles used for capturing prey. Their cylindrical tapering bodies have fins on either side and a reduced internal stiffening shell. Squids feed on fish and molluscs, using a siphon to produce a jet of water to dart forwards. The giant squid (genus *Architeuthis*) can reach 20 m in length. □oceans.

squill A perennial herbaceous plant of the genus *Scilla* (100 species), native to temperate Europe and Asia. Growing from bulbs, they produce long narrow leaves and blue, white, or purple flowers borne in a cluster on a leafless stalk. Some species, including *S. nonscripta* and *S. sibirica* are cultivated as garden ornamentals. Family: *Liliaceae*.

squint (*or* strabismus) A condition in which both the eyes cannot focus on the same object at the same time. This may be caused by paralysis of one of the nerves moving the eye, in which case the squint is often temporary. Nonparalytic squints are often seen in children and may be corrected by special lenses, eye exercises, or surgery.

squirrel A *rodent belonging to the family *Sciuridae*, which includes *ground squirrels, *flying squirrels, and tree squirrels, distributed worldwide. The grey squirrel (*Sciurus carolinensis*) native to North America but now found in most parts of the world, is an agile climber with a long bushy balancing tail and grasping hands. Grey squirrels feed chiefly on nuts, berries, and buds and have become a pest of orchards and gardens. They do not hibernate, but store food for the winter. *See also* red squirrel.

squirrel monkey A long-tailed monkey, *Saimiri sciureus*, common in Amazonian forests. Squirrel monkeys are 60–80 cm long including the tail (35–43 cm) and live in large troops, feeding on flowers, fruits, and small animals. They have tufted ears and white rings round their eyes with greenish fur and orange feet. Family: *Cebidae*.

squirting cucumber A perennial herb, *Ecballium elaterium*, native to the Mediterranean region. It has spreading hairy stems and leaves and its yellow flowers produce elastic-walled fruits that eject the seeds up to a distance of several metres when the fruit is ripe. Family: *Cucurbitaceae*.

Sri Lanka, Democratic Socialist Republic of (name until 1972: Ceylon) An island country in the Indian Ocean, to the E of the S tip of the Indian subcontinent, from which it is separated by the Gulf of Mannar and the Palk Strait. Broad coastal plains rise to a mountainous area in the S central part of the island. Sri Lanka is primarily a land of villages, with less than a quarter of the inhabitants living in urban centres. The population consists of two main groups: the Sinhalese, who are mainly Buddhists, and the Tamils, who are chiefly Hindus. *Economy*: predominantly agricultural, the chief activities are the processing and export of tea, rubber, and coconuts. The industrial sector has expanded considerably in recent years and the main products include cement, paper, ceramics, leather goods, chemicals, textiles, steel, and fertilizers. There is little mineral wealth, the most valuable deposits being graphite and gemstones. *History*: according to tradition an Indian prince, Vijaya, conquered the island in the 6th century AD and became the first King of the Sinhalese. In 1505 the Portuguese established settlements in the W and S, which passed to the Dutch in the mid-17th century and to the British in 1796. In 1802 the whole of the island was made a separate crown colony. Following World War II Ceylon became a dominion (1948) within the British Commonwealth and in 1972 Sri Lanka became a republic. Following the general election of 1977, in which the United National Party (UNP) was victorious, the Tamil United Liberation Front (TULF) emerged for the first time as the main parliamentary opposition. Conflict between the Sinhalese and Tamil communities has been a continuing problem and precipitated the arrival of an Indian peacekeeping force (1987) in the wake of massacres and bomb outrages by Tamil separatists. Head of state: President Junius Richard Jayawardene. Prime minister: Ranasinghe Premadasa (1924–). Official language: Sinhala. Official currency: Sri Lanka rupee of 100 cents. Area: 65 610 sq km (25 332 sq mi). Population (1983): 15 647 000. Capital: Colombo.

Srinagar 34 08N 74 50E A city in India, the summer capital of Jammu and Kashmir on the River Jhelum. It has numerous museums, palaces, mosques, and a fortress, and is the site of the University of Jammu and Kashmir (1948). Industries include carpets, silver, silk, and leather. Population (1981 est): 520 000.

SS (German: *Schutzstaffel*, Defence Squad) The elite Nazi military corps, created in 1925 as Hitler's bodyguard and commanded by Heinrich Himmler from 1929. The SS, or Blackshirts, by the mid-1930s controlled the Nazis' security system, including the *Gestapo, *concentration camp guards, and the Waffen SS, an elite corps of combat troops in World War II. After the German defeat Himmler committed suicide and the activities of the SS were condemned at the Nuremburg trials (1946).

Ssu-ma Ch'ien. *See* Si-ma Qian.

St. Names beginning St are listed under Saint.

stabilizers (shipbuilding) Adjustable finlike devices, projecting from the hull of a vessel, that reduces the vessel's motion in a heavy sea. They are operated automatically by a heavy gyroscope and are often called gyrostabilizers.

stabilizers (economics) Factors that temper the booms and recessions of the *trade cycle. They may be actions taken as a result of either government *monetary or *fiscal policy or "built-in" stabilizers that work automatically, e.g. the increase in money paid out in unemployment benefit during a recession, which helps to maintain consumption.

stadholder (*or* stadtholder) The ruler of the United Provinces of the Netherlands. Originally a provincial governor responsible to the central government of the Netherlands' Burgundian and then Spanish rulers, following the *Revolt of the Netherlands in the 16th century the secessionist United Provinces elected *William the Silent as their stadholder. The office was traditionally held by the House of Orange until the fall of the republic in 1795.

Staël, Anne Louise Germaine Necker, Madame de (1766–1817). French writer, daughter of , the financier *Necker. Her Paris salon became a centre of liberal intellectual opposition to Napoleon, with whom she quarrelled and consequently, after 1803, was forced to live in exile, mostly at her chateau on Lake Geneva. She travelled widely in Europe, studied with Schiller and Goethe in Weimar, and returned to Paris after the Bourbon restoration in 1814. Her most important literary work was *De l'Allemagne* (1810), which introduced German literature to France. She also wrote two novels featuring unconventional young heroines, *Delphine* (1802) and *Corinne* (1807).

Staffa 56 26N 6 21W An uninhabited island off the W coast of Scotland, in the Inner Hebrides. Composed largely of basalt columns, it is famous for its spectacular coast and caves, including *Fingal's Cave.

Stafford 52 48N 2 07W A market town in the English Midlands, the administrative centre of Staffordshire. The ruined castle occupies the site of a Saxon fortress. Footwear, chemicals, and electrical goods are manufactured. Population (1981): 55 497.

Staffordshire A county in the Midlands of England. It consists mainly of gently undulating lowlands rising to moorlands in the N, with the River Trent flowing SE. Agriculture is important, especially dairy farming. Industries are based on the coalfields in the N and include the pottery industry, which became famous during the 18th century, especially through the work of Josiah *Wedgwood. Under local government reorganization in 1974 the industrial area in the S (the Black Country) passed to the new metropolitan county of the West Midlands. Area: 2716 sq km (1049 sq mi). Population (1981): 1 012 320. Administrative centre: Stafford.

Staffordshire bull terrier A breed of dog developed from a bulldog-terrier cross as a pit dog. It is stockily built with a broad deep head and a short smooth coat that is pure white; red, fawn, black, or blue; or any of these colours in combination with white. Height: 35–40 cm (English); 43–48 cm (American).

stag beetle A beetle belonging to a family (*Lucanidae*; about 900 species) occurring mostly in the tropical regions. The males have well-developed mandibles that in many species resemble antlers—sometimes equal to the length of the body (which is about 8–40 mm long). They are used during combat with other males. Most stag beetles are black or brown, although tropical species are often more colourful. The scavenging larvae develop from eggs laid in rotten wood.

stagecoach A large four-wheeled carriage drawn by four or six horses and used for scheduled long-distance transport services in England from the mid-17th century until the advent of rail travel. The journey was divided into stages; horses, kept at strategically sited coaching inns, were changed after each stage. The coach usually had seats for six inside and poorer passengers rode on the roof. After 1784 mails were carried by coach. In the USA and Australia stage-coaches remained important auxiliaries to the developing railway systems throughout the 19th century.

STAG BEETLE *A male (right) and female of the European species* Lucanus cervus.

staghorn fern A *fern of the genus *Platycerium*, which grows upon other plants but is not a parasite. The fronds fork repeatedly into long pointed leaflets, resembling antlers, and the spore capsules are borne on their undersides. The fern, which is native to most warm regions, is cultivated as a pot plant. Family: *Polypodiaceae*.

staghound A *foxhound used for hunting wild deer. *See also* deerhound.

Stahl, Georg Ernst (1660–1734) German physician and chemist, who in about 1700 formulated the *phlogiston theory of combustion. Stahl had an alchemical disregard for quantitative measurement and consequently the phlogiston theory does not take changes of mass on combustion into account. Stahl's work in physiology was equally unscientific in modern terms, relying on a vitalist approach.

stained glass Coloured glass panels formed of fragments of glass cut to shape according to a pictorial or abstract design and held together by "H" section lead strips. The earliest surviving stained-glass windows date from the 12th century AD, but this principle of embellishing buildings was known much earlier. The glass used was either coloured throughout by the addition of metallic oxides (e.g. copper oxide (CuO) for ruby red) while molten or dipped into molten coloured glass to obtain a fine film of colour on both sides (flashed glass). From the 16th century painted glass displaced the more expensive coloured glass. The 12th century saw considerable production of religious stained glass windows in N Europe. Much survives in France. Less exuberant colours and a classical restraint marked the post-Renaissance use of stained glass until leading designers (e.g. William *Morris, *Burne-Jones) exploited its decorative potential in the 19th century. Modern stained glass employs abstract patterns in secular as well as ecclesiastical surroundings.

Stainer, Sir John (1840–1901) British composer and organist. He wrote much sacred music, including the oratorio *The Crucifixion* (1887).

stainless steel An alloy *steel containing up to 20% chromium and 10% nickel. It is corrosion resistant because the oxide that forms on the surface remains intact and protects the metal, unlike other steels in which it flakes off. Stainless steel is used in a wide variety of engineering applications where this property is important, as well as in

STALIN

kitchen utensils. It is more expensive to produce than ordinary carbon steel and more difficult to machine.

Stakhanovite A member of a Soviet labour movement that strove to increase industrial production. Named after Aleksei Grigorievich Stakhanov (1906–77), a coalminer who in 1935 reorganized his work gang to increase its daily production sevenfold, the movement failed because quality could not be maintained.

stalactites and stalagmites Deposits of calcium carbonate in limestone caves; stalactites are conical or cylindrical projections from the cave roof, while stalagmites grow upwards from the floor and are generally more stumpy. They sometimes meet to form a continuous column. They are gradually formed from water containing calcium bicarbonate dripping from the roof. When the water evaporates a solid residue of calcium carbonate is left.

Stalin, Joseph (J. Dzhugashvili; 1879–1953) Soviet statesman. Born in Georgia, Stalin (whose adopted name means "man of steel") became a Marxist in the 1890s and was expelled from a theological college for his revolutionary activity (1899). In 1903 he joined the *Bolsheviks under Lenin and in the years preceding the Russian Revolution (1917) was repeatedly imprisoned and exiled. In 1921 he became commissar for nationalities and in 1922 general secretary of the Communist Party. After Lenin's death in 1924 Stalin struggled to eliminate his rivals, above all *Trotsky, and emerged as supreme dictator in 1929. He abandoned Lenin's *New Economic Policy, initiating a series of five-year plans to enforce, with great brutality, the collectivization of industry and agriculture. The 1930s saw the reign of terror, culminating in the great purge, in which Stalin sought to enhance his power by the removal of his real, or imagined, rivals. In World War II, Stalin became chairman of the Council of People's Commissars and, following Hitler's invasion of the Soviet Union (1941), reversed the German alliance of 1939. He attended Allied conferences at *Tehran (1943)

and at *Yalta and Potsdam (1945), where his negotiating skills were noted by Roosevelt and Churchill. In the postwar years, when Stalin's autocracy intensified, he pursued a foreign policy of imperialism towards the communist countries of E Europe together with unremitting hostility towards the noncommunist world. In recent years many of Stalin's polices have been discredited by the Soviet regime.

Stalinabad. *See* Dushanbe.

Stalingrad. *See* Volgograd.

Stalingrad, Battle of (1942–43) A battle in World War II, in which the German 6th Army under *Paulus, having entered Stalingrad (now Volgograd), surrendered to the Russians under *Zhukov. The Germans lost 200 000 men.

Stalinsk. *See* Novokuznetsk.

Stamboul. *See* Istanbul.

stamen The part of a flower that produces the *pollen (male gametes). It comprises an anther, a lobed structure consisting of four pollen sacs, borne on a stalk (filament). The pollen develops within the sacs, which split open to release it. In self-pollinated flowers, the stamens open inwards, towards the pistil, but in cross-pollinated flowers they open outwards. *See also* flower. ⌐plant.

Stamford Bridge 53 59N 0 55W A village in N England, in Humberside on the River Derwent. Here King Harold defeated his brother Tostig and King Harald of Norway in 1066, three weeks before his own defeat at Hastings by William the Conqueror.

Stamitz, Johann (Jan Stamic; 1717–57) Bohemian composer. He was director of the Mannheim court orchestra. His innovations in composition helped to establish *sonata form and he introduced the controlled crescendo into his symphonies.

stammering A disorder of the rhythm of speech, known medically as dysphemia. The normal flow of speech is interrupted by hesitations, repetitions of syllables, and sometimes by grimaces. Stammering is common in children, especially if speech is slow to develop, and does not indicate any illness. It is often made worse by anxiety and can become persistent; it usually improves with speech therapy.

Stamp Act (1765) The first British Act that imposed direct taxes on documents, newspapers, and dice in the American colonies. Parliament was forced by colonial hostility to repeal the Act but asserted its right to impose laws on the colonies (Declaratory Act, 1766), thus aggravating the opposition that led to the *American Revolution.

standard deviation. *See* variance.

standardwing A *bird of paradise, *Semioptera wallacei*, discovered in 1858 in the Moluccan Islands. The male is about 25 cm long and has two long white ribbon-like feathers at each shoulder, which are erected over the back during its courtship display.

Standish, Myles (c. 1584–1656) English colonist in America. He sailed to America on the *Mayflower*, becoming military leader of the first settlement in New England, at Plymouth.

Stanford, Sir Charles (Villiers) (1852–1924) Irish composer. He became professor of composition at the Royal College of Music in 1883. Among his compositions are six operas, seven symphonies, concertos, chamber music, songs, and Anglican church music.

Stanhope, James, 1st Earl (1673–1721) British soldier and statesman; George I's chief minister (1717–21). He served under Marlborough in the War of the Spanish Succession (1701–14) and helped suppress the *Jacobite uprising (1715). He was in charge of foreign affairs before becoming chief minister. His grandson **Charles, 3rd Earl Stanhope** (1753–1816) was a politician and scientist. Becoming an MP in 1780, he urged parliamentary reform and supported the French Revolution. His inventions included two calculating machines, a microscope lens, and a stereotyping machine that was acquired (1805) by the Clarendon Press at Oxford. He also experimented with electricity.

Stanislavsky, Konstantin (K. Alekseyev; 1863–1938) Russian actor and theatre director. As director of the Moscow Art Theatre, which he founded in 1898 with Nemirovich Danchenko (1859–1943), he developed an innovatory style of naturalistic production that was ideally suited to the plays of Chekhov and Gorki. His theories about acting, published in *My Life in Art* (1924) and *An Actor Prepares* (1926) and later developed in the USA as "method" acting at the *Actors' Studio, emphasized the value of ensemble playing and of the actor's complete identification with the character he played.

Stanisław I Leszczyński (1677-1766) King of Poland (1704-09, 1733-35) and Duke of Lorraine (1735-66). Stanisław was placed on the throne by *Charles XII of Sweden, after whose defeat Stanisław was deposed. He regained the throne by election but lost the subsequent War of the Polish Succession and became Duke of Lorraine.

Stanisław II Poniatowski (1732-98) The last King of Poland (1764-95). Stanisław became a favourite of Catherine the Great of Russia, who secured his election to the throne and dominated his reign. In 1772 parts of Poland were annexed by Russia, Prussia, and Austria; in 1793 it was again partitioned (by Russia and Prussia). After the failure of *Kosciuszko's rebellion, and the third partition of Poland, Stanisław abdicated.

Stanisław, St (*or* Stanislaus; 1030-79) The patron saint of Poland. Of noble birth, he was elected Bishop of Cracow in 1072. He was implicated in a plot against Bolesław II and murdered in mysterious circumstances. Feast day: 7 May.

Stanley 51 45S 57 56W The capital of the Falkland Islands, in NE East Falkland Island on the Atlantic Ocean. A whaling base, it exports wool, skin, tallow, and seal oil. It was the focal point of the Falklands War of 1982. Population (1980 est): 1000.

Stanley, Sir Henry Morton (1841–1904) British explorer and journalist. He went to the USA in 1859, joined the *New York Herald*, and in 1871 was sent by James Gordon *Bennett to search for David □Livingstone in Africa. Having found him at Ujiji, the two men explored Lake Tanganyika together. On a second expedition (1874–77) Stanley followed the Congo River (now Zaïre River) to its mouth. By obtaining Belgian sponsorship for exploration in the Congo he was instrumental in securing Belgian sovereignty over the Congo Free State. His last African expedition (1886–89) relieved *Emin Paşa in the S Sudan.

Stanley Falls. *See* Boyoma Falls.

Stanley Pool. *See* Malebo Pool.

Stanleyville. *See* Kisangani.

Stannaries The tinmining district of Cornwall and Devon. Until 1897 the Stannaries held its own courts, which had jurisdiction over tinminers except in such cases as murder or land disputes.

Stanovoi Range A mountain range in the SE Soviet Union extending about 800 km (497 mi) E–W. It rises to 2482 m (8143 ft) and forms part of the watershed between the Arctic and Pacific Oceans.

Staphylococcus A genus of spherical bacteria. *S. aureus* is responsible for boils and mastitis, *S. pyogenes* infects wounds, and certain strains cause acute food poisoning.

star A luminous celestial body that is composed of gas and that derives its energy from thermonuclear reactions in its hot dense core. The sun is a typical star: stellar mass usually ranges from about 0.05 to 60 times the sun's mass. A star's mass determines its *luminosity, surface temperature, size, and other properties as well as its evolutionary path and lifetime: the higher the mass, the brighter, hotter, and larger the star and the shorter its life. During the course of their history stars evolve, a process called stellar evolution. Young stars evolve from the

*protostar stage when they begin to generate energy by the thermonuclear fusion of hydrogen to form helium. This continues for some 10^{10} years for stars of solar mass but for only a few million years for the most massive stars. When the hydrogen is exhausted, stars evolve into *giant stars, those of near solar mass becoming *red giants. Further thermonuclear reactions occur involving fusion of helium and possibly the heavier elements in more massive stars. A low-mass star finally evolves to a *white dwarf. More massive stars explode as *supernovae, the surviving cores possibly forming *neutron stars or *black holes depending on mass. Stars are not distributed uniformly throughout the *universe, but are grouped into enormous assemblies, called *galaxies, as a result of gravitational forces. The sun forms part of the *Galaxy (written with a capital G), often known as the Milky Way system. The nearest star to the sun is 4.3 light years away.

star apple An evergreen tree, *Chrysophyllum cainito*, native to the West Indies and Central America. Growing to a height of 15 m, it has purplish-white flowers and bears sweet-tasting smooth-skinned fruits that resemble apples, red to yellow in colour with star-shaped cores. Family: *Sapotaceae*.

Stara Zagora 42 25N 25 37E A city in central Bulgaria. The city was rebuilt after its destruction by the Turks in the late 19th century. Fruit, in particular, is grown in the surrounding area. Population (1982): 141 722.

starch A carbohydrate that is an important storage product of many plants. Chemically it consists of linked glucose units in the form of two polysaccharides, amylose and amylopectin, which are present in varying proportions. Starch occurs naturally as white powdery granules that are insoluble in cold water but form a gelatinous solution in hot water. Plants manufacture starch by photosynthesis and it is a major constituent of seeds, fruits, roots, and tubers and a major source of dietary energy for animals and man. It is also used in the paper and textile industries.

Star Chamber, Court of A court, originating in the king's council of medieval England, that met in the Star Chamber at Westminster Palace. It was concerned chiefly with breaches of the peace. Its misuse by Charles I to enforce his unpopular policies led to its abolition (1641) by the *Long Parliament on the eve of the Civil War.

star cluster A group of stars that are associated by gravitational effects and that shared a common origin. **Open clusters** are loosely bound asymmetrical groupings of up to a few hundred stars and occur in the disc of our *Galaxy. **Globular clusters** are compact spherical groupings containing many thousands of very old stars and occur in the Galactic halo.

starfish A marine invertebrate animal, also called sea star, belonging to a worldwide class (*Asteroidea*; 1800 species) of *echinoderms. Its fleshy star-shaped body is covered with a spiny skin and has five or more radiating arms. Starfish occur on shores and ocean floors and move slowly, using saclike tube feet on the underside of the arms. They feed mainly on molluscs, crustaceans, and other invertebrates.

stargazer A fish belonging to either of the families *Uranoscopidae* (electric stargazers; about 25 species) or *Dactyloscopidae* (sand stargazers; about 24 species), found in tropical and temperate seas. Stargazers have a tapering body, up to 30 cm long, a vertically slanting mouth, and eyes on top of the head. They lie buried in sand awaiting prey. Order: *Perciformes*.

Stark, Dame Freya (Madeline) (1893–) British travel writer. Born in Paris and educated in Italy and London, she began her travels in the Arab countries in the late 1920s. Her many books include *The Southern Gates of Arabia* (1936), *Beyond Euphrates* (1951), and *The Journey's Echo* (1963).

starling A noisy sharp-winged songbird, *Sturnus vulgaris*, having a black plumage speckled with iridescent purple, green, and white. It is a versatile bird, common on farmland, where it probes the soil for insects, and also in cities, where it is a scavenger. It is gregarious and commonly nests in flocks in buildings and trees, sometimes becoming a serious crop pest. Family: *Sturnidae*.

star-of-Bethlehem A spring-blooming perennial plant, *Ornithogalum umbellatum*, native to the Mediterranean and grown in gardens. Growing from a bulb, it has grasslike basal leaves and a slender stalk, up to 30 cm tall, bearing clusters of star-shaped white flowers striped with green. Family: *Liliaceae*.

star of David (Hebrew *magen David*: shield of David) A six-pointed star or hexagram, composed of two equilateral triangles. Widely used from antiquity as an ornament or magical sign, it has been regarded since the 17th century as a Jewish symbol, and was imposed on the Jews as a "badge of shame" by the Nazis. In 1897 it was officially adopted as an emblem of Zionism and it now appears on the flag of Israel.

Starr, Ringo (Richard Starkey; 1940-) British rock musician, former drummer of the *Beatles. After the Beatles disbanded, Starr acted in such films as *The Magic Christian* (1970). His solo albums include *Ringo* (1973), which temporarily reunited the group.

Stassfurt 51 51N 11 35E A town in W East Germany, on the River Bode. The Stassfurt deposits consist of several strata, some 1100 m thick, providing since 1861 a valuable source of sodium and potassium compounds, magnesium bromide, and rock salt.

Staten Island An island in the USA coextensive with Richmond, one of the five boroughs of New York City. Largely residential, it is the least densely populated of the city's boroughs. Area: 148 sq km (57 sq mi). Population (1980): 352 121.

States General 1. In France, the assembly of representatives of the three estates—clergy, nobility, and the Third Estate or commons. First summoned by Philip the Fair in 1302, the States General did not meet after 1614 until summoned by Louis XVI in 1789 on the eve of the *French Revolution. The Third Estate declared itself a National Assembly, which replaced the States General. 2. In the Netherlands, the assembly of provincial representatives created by its Burgundian rulers in the 15th century. Following the *Revolt of the Netherlands against Spain, it became (1579) the chief organ of the United Provinces' central government.

states of matter Any of three distinct physical states: solid, liquid, and gas. A fourth state, *plasma, is often added. The different states are distinguished by the strength of the intermolecular forces compared to their random thermal motion. For example, in a solid the intermolecular forces are sufficiently strong to hold the molecules to an approximately fixed position, whereas in a gas the intermolecular forces have hardly any effect on the random movements of the atoms and molecules. Liquids represent an intermediate state.

states' rights In the USA, the rights of the individual states of the USA in relation to the power of the federal government. The issue arose in debates over the *constitution (1789), which established a strong federal government. Subsequent assertion of states' rights, especially that of secession from the Union, led eventually to the *Civil War.

static electricity The effects created by electrical charges at rest. Current electricity is an effect resulting from a flow of electrons; in static electricity electrons from one object are pulled onto another object, usually by rubbing them together, but they do not flow. The effect can be observed with many nonconducting materials, for example a comb passing through dry hair or a leather sole on a nylon carpet. A force exists between two charged bodies (*see* electric field), attractive if they have opposite charges,

repulsive if the charges are similar; the magnitude of the force is given by *Coulomb's law. Static electricity can often cause problems (*see* lightning) but can be useful in electrostatic precipitators. *See also* electroscope; electrostatic generators.

statics. *See* mechanics.

Stationery Office, Her Majesty's (HMSO) The UK government office that supplies all the stationery, office supplies, office machinery, and printing and binding needed for use in the civil service. HMSO also publishes and sells government publications, producing more titles (ranging from high-quality books to free leaflets) than any other publishing organization in the country. The HMSO is based in Norwich and London.

Stations of the Cross A series of 14 pictures or images depicting the final events of the life of Christ, beginning at Pontius *Pilate's house, where he was condemned to death, and concluding at the sepulchre. They are usually arranged on the walls of a church and form the basis of a devotion in which prayers are recited as each station is visited in turn. The devotion was popularized in the middle ages by the Franciscans but derived from the early custom of pilgrims who followed the Way of the Cross in Jerusalem.

statistics The study of methods for collecting and analysing quantitative data. The data measure certain characteristics of a group of people or objects, called the population; usually the whole population cannot be observed, often because it is too large, so data are collected from a representative sample of the population. The sample is analysed and conclusions are inferred about the whole population, using *probability theory because the inferences cannot be certain. A population that has what is called a normal or Gaussian distribution (named after Karl *Gauss) varies randomly about a mean value. The standard deviation, the root-mean-square deviation from the mean value, is a measure of the spread in the population. The higher the standard deviation, the larger the sample size needed to be representative of the population. In binomial distributions the population consists of only two possible outcomes, as in tossing a coin, and in this case different statistical methods are used. In descriptive (*or* deductive) statistics data for a group are collected and analysed without conclusions being drawn about a larger group.

Statue of Liberty A statue of a woman 46 m (152 ft) high holding a torch in her raised right hand, on Liberty Island in New York harbour. Designed by the French architect *Bartholdi, it was given to the Americans by the French in 1884 to commemorate the French and American Revolutions. Unveiled and dedicated in 1886, it has been a US national monument since 1924. It underwent complete renovation in the 1980s.

Staudinger, Hermann (1881–1965) German chemist, who was professor at Freiburg University. He won the 1953 Nobel Prize for his work on the molecular structure of polymers. Staudinger showed that polymer molecules consisted of chains of repeated units and not a random distribution of such units as was previously thought. His work was crucial to the developing plastics industry.

Stauffenberg, Claus, Graf von (1907–44) German army officer, who attempted to assassinate Hitler in 1944. Stauffenberg served in N Africa, where he was badly wounded. He tried to eliminate Hitler by bombing his headquarters at Rastenburg. He and his fellow conspirators were executed.

Stavanger 61 32N 5 12E A seaport in SW Norway. Its 12th-century cathedral was built by Bishop Reinald from Winchester. Its industries include fish canning and shipbuilding. Stavanger is also the centre of Norway's North Sea oil industry. Population (1981 est): 90 687.

Stavisky affair A French political scandal. In 1933 the fraudulent dealings of a financier Serge Alexandre Stavisky

(c. 1866–1934) were revealed and shortly afterwards he was found dead. Attempts by the government to hush up the affair encouraged rumours that Stavisky had been murdered to prevent him from exposing the involvement of public figures in his affairs. Consequent right-wing riots led to the replacement of the left-wing government with a broad-based coalition.

Stavropol 1. 45 03N 41 59E A city in the Soviet Union, in the SW RSFSR. The centre of a fertile agricultural region, it has food-processing industries. It possesses several educational institutions. Population (1981 est): 271 000. 2. *See* Togliatti.

steady-state theory A cosmological theory (*see* cosmology) proposed in 1948 by *Bondi, *Hoyle, and T. Gold (1920–) in which the universe is regarded as having always existed in a steady state. The *expansion of the universe is compensated by the continuous creation of new matter. On the present evidence this theory has largely been discredited in favour of the *big-bang theory.

STEAM ENGINE *The principle of a double-action beam engine of the kind patented by James Watt. During the first half of the cycle, valve A opens, steam flows in and pushes the cylinder down, and steam flows out to the condenser through valve C. During the second half of the cycle, B opens and the steam pushes the piston the other way.*

steam engine A ▢heat engine in which heat from a furnace is used to raise steam, the expansion of which forces a piston to move up and down in a cylinder to provide mechanical energy. A primitive steam engine was invented in 1698 by a Capt Savery to pump water from mines. In 1711 *Newcomen improved on this design but still relied on cooling the cylinder with a jet of water after each stroke. *Watt's single-acting steam engine, patented in 1769, was the first to use a separate condenser. Watt went on to invent the double-acting engine, the crank and crosshead mechanism, and the governor. Thus by the end of the 18th century man had, for the first time, a reliable source of power that did not rely on muscles or the wind. It was largely this engine that created the *industrial revolution. In 1808 Richard *Trevithick made the first use of a steam engine to drive a carriage, but it was not until the end of the century that steam cars were in use—and they were quickly replaced by cars using Otto's petrol engine. The steam engine, however, was the supreme prime mover of *railways throughout the

world from 1829 (when *Stephenson built his first *locomotive) until after World War II, when steam was largely replaced by electric and Diesel-electric trains. From the beginning of the 19th century steam engines were also widely used in place of sails in *ships. Moreover, it was the steam engine that drove the first electricity generators for public supply. However, the more compact and efficient steam *turbine has now replaced the steam engine for this purpose.

steatite. *See* talc.

steel An *alloy of iron containing a small carefully controlled proportion of carbon, usually less than 1%. Carbon steels contain principally iron and carbon. Alloy steels have other metals added. Steel products form the basis of modern technology and steel production is therefore a key factor in the world economy. Annual world trading in iron ore amounts to about US$5 billion, and that in scrap iron and steel about US$1.5 billion. About 400 thousand tonnes of steel are produced every week in the UK, over half of this from recycled scrap steel. The uses of steel range from steel girders in bridges and buildings to kitchen utensils. For many engineering products the starting material is **mild steel**, a carbon steel with between 0.2% and 0.8% carbon and sometimes a little manganese or silicon. It can be further improved by *heat treatment. Alloy steels, such as *stainless steel, are usually more expensive to produce. They are used where special hardness, strength, or corrosion resistance are needed.

Steel is made by *smelting iron ore in a blast furnace to produce pig iron, which is added to melted down scrap iron before being further purified in an open-hearth furnace, *Bessemer converter, or *electric-arc furnace.

Steel, David (Martin Scott) (1938–) British politician; leader of the Liberal Party (1976–). He entered parliament in 1964 and succeeded Jeremy Thorpe as Liberal leader. In 1977 he negotiated a pact between the Liberal Party and the minority Labour government. From 1981 to 1987 he headed the SDP-Liberal Alliance alongside the SDP leader, David Owen.

Steele, Sir Richard (1672–1729) British essayist and dramatist. Born in Dublin, he served in the English army from 1692 to 1705 and wrote a number of successful sentimental comedies, beginning with *The Funeral* (1701). He edited the *London Gazette* (1707-10), the official government journal. He is best remembered for his essays in *The Tatler* (1709-11) and the *Spectator* (1711-12), periodicals that he founded and on which he collaborated with Joseph *Addison.

Steen, Jan (c. 1626–79) Dutch painter. After training under Adriaen Van *Ostade and Jan van *Goyen, whose daughter he married, he worked in The Hague, Delft, and Haarlem, but principally in Leiden, where he kept a tavern. Although he painted some landscapes and biblical and mythological subjects, he is best known for his humorous and sometimes bawdy tavern and domestic scenes. Representative works are *The Feast of St Nicholas* (Rijksmuseum, Amsterdam), *Merry Company* (Mauritshuis, The Hague), and *The Morning Toilet* (Buckingham Palace).

steeplechase 1. A form of horse race that grew out of *foxhunting, in which horses jump artificial hedges and ditches. The severity of the obstacles varies between courses and between countries. Hurdling is a less taxing version over lower lighter fences and shorter distances. Both are governed in England by National Hunt rules. The horses used are either trained for the purpose or turn to steeplechasing after their *flat-racing careers are over. Point-to-points are steeplechases for amateur riders, run by the local hunts. *See also* Grand National Steeplechase. 2. A track event for men in athletics over a 3000 m course that includes 28 hurdles 91 cm (3 ft) high and seven water jumps 3.66 m (12 ft) across per lap. World record: 8 minutes 5.4 seconds (1978) by Henry Rono (Kenya).

Stefan-Boltzmann law The total energy emitted per unit time and per unit area by a *black body at an absolute temperature T is proportional to T^4. The constant of proportionality, known as Stefan's constant, is equal to 5.6697×10^{-8} W m^{-2}K^{-4}. The law is named after the Austrian physicist Joseph Stefan (1835-93), who first discovered it, and Ludwig *Boltzmann, who derived it thermodynamically.

Stefan Dušan (1308-55) King of Serbia (1331-55). Serbia's foremost medieval ruler, Stefan Dušan established Serbian supremacy in the Balkans by conquering Macedonia, Albania, and parts of Greece; in 1346 he was crowned Emperor of the Serbs and Greeks. He introduced a new legal code.

Stegodon A genus of long-legged extinct *elephants that lived in Asia and Africa between 12 and 1 million years ago. The first of the true elephants, it gave rise to the now extinct *mammoths and to the Indian and African elephants.

STEGOSAURUS *It was originally thought that the plates on the back of this dinosaur were erect and probably functioned as weapons. Recent theories, however, postulate a horizontal arrangement of plates, which acted as heat exchangers.*

Stegosaurus A dinosaur of the late Jurassic period (about 150-135 million years ago). 7 m long and weighing 1.75 tonnes, it had a double row of large triangular plates arranged in pairs along its back and two pairs of spikes at the end of its tail. *Stegosaurus* had a small head and fed on soft plants. Order: *Ornithischia*.

Stein, Sir (Marc) Aurel (1862-1943) British explorer and archaeologist of Hungarian birth. Stein made expeditions to India, Persia, Turkistan, and the Far East, which resulted in many discoveries, including the Cave of the Thousand Buddhas near Dun-Huang (W China), with its paintings and documents. His books include *Ancient Khotan* (1907) and *Innermost Asia* (1928).

Stein, Gertrude (1874-1946) US writer. From 1903 she lived in Paris, where she presided over the American expatriate literary community. Her experiments in prose, which include *Three Lives* (1909) and *Tender Buttons* (1914), were influenced by the cubist theories of Picasso, Braque, and other painters whom she helped. Her most accessible work is *The Autobiography of Alice B. Toklas* (1933).

Stein, Karl, Freiherr vom (1757-1831) Prussian statesman. He became first minister to Frederick William III in 1807, after serving as finance minister (1804-07), and introduced major administrative and economic reforms that helped Prussia to recover from its defeat by Napoleon.

Dismissed in 1808, he then became adviser to Alexander I of Russia.

Steinbeck, John (1902-68) US novelist. The majority of his novels, notably *Of Mice and Men* (1937) and *The Grapes of Wrath* (1939), an epic account of migrant farm workers, deal with the social and economic conditions of his native California. *East of Eden* (1952) is the most ambitious of his later novels. He won the Nobel Prize in 1962.

steinbok A small solitary African antelope, *Raphicerus campestris*, inhabiting long grass or thinly forested areas. Steinboks are about 50 cm high at the shoulder with a reddish-brown coat; males have small horns.

Steiner, Rudolf (1861-1925) Austrian-born founder of *anthroposophy. Steiner rejected the oriental associations of *theosophy, with which he was originally associated, and aimed in his system to reintegrate man with the world of the spirit. He founded his first school in 1919 and his teachings are now propagated in over 70 Rudolf Steiner schools, which aim to develop the child's whole personality, not only his intellect.

Steinmetz, Charles Proteus (1865-1923) US electrical engineer, born in Germany, who developed the mathematical theory of *alternating current, introducing both real and imaginary components. This work greatly stimulated the development of devices running on alternating current. Steinmetz also discovered the law of *hysteresis and made some 200 inventions in electrical engineering, including a high-voltage generator.

Steinway, Henry (Engelhard) (Heinrich Steinweg; 1797-1871) German-born US piano maker. He established a piano factory in Brunswick. He emigrated to the USA in 1849 and founded the piano firm of Steinway and Sons in New York, branches of which were opened in London (1875) and Hamburg (1880).

stela (*or* stele) A free-standing oblong slab, used in ancient Greece and the Near East as a grave or boundary marker. The Greek grave stelae were usually inscribed and ornamented with relief sculptures of the dead. The *Maya of Central America set up stelae with calendrical information.

stellar evolution. *See* star.

Stellenbosch 33 56S 18 51E A town in South Africa, in SW Cape Province. Founded in 1679, it is the second oldest White settlement in the country. Its university was incorporated in 1918. It is surrounded by vineyards and orchards and is an important wine-producing centre. Population (1985): 43 090.

Stendhal (Henri Beyle; 1783-1842) French novelist. Between 1799 and 1813 he became acquainted with social life in Paris and also served with Napoleon's armies in Italy, Germany, Russia, and Austria. From 1814 to 1821 he lived in Italy and returned there as consul in 1830. His two major novels, *Le Rouge et le noir* (1830) and *La Chartreuse de Parme* (1839), are notable for their blend of romantic vigour with dispassionate and often ironical psychological analysis. He also wrote works of literary, artistic, and musical appreciation.

sten gun A 9 mm submachine gun designed by Sheppard and Turpin during World War II. Some four million of these simple weapons were produced at a cost of £1.50 each. They were dangerously short and sometimes unreliable but some are still in use among terrorists.

Steno, Nicolaus (*or* Niels Stensen; 1638-86) Danish anatomist and geologist, who established that fossils were the petrified remains of ancient living organisms and that the layers (strata) of rocks represented stages in their deposition. Originally a physician—he discovered the duct of the parotid salivary gland, he later became a bishop.

Stentor A genus of tiny single-celled animals (*see* Protozoa) occurring in fresh water. Up to 2 mm long, they are trumpet-shaped, with tracts of hairlike cilia over the body surface, and are often attached by a stalk to the substrate.

They feed by wafting currents of water containing bacteria, algae, and protozoans into the funnel-shaped gullet entrance. Class: *Ciliata*.

Stephanotis A genus of evergreen climbing shrubs (5 species), also called Madagascar jasmine, native to Madagascar, and including some ornamental species. *S. floribunda* is a popular greenhouse plant with small fragrant white waxy flowers. Family: *Asclepiadaceae*.

Stephen (c. 1097-1154) King of England (1135-54); grandson of William the Conqueror. Stephen seized the throne from Henry I's daughter Matilda, who invaded England in 1139. The civil war that followed proved Stephen a brave soldier but revealed his lack of political sense. In 1152, after much of the country had been ravaged in factional fighting and the royal administration had broken down, Stephen recognized Matilda's son Henry (later Henry II) as heir to the throne.

Stephen, Sir Leslie (1832-1904) British man of letters and critic, who coedited the *Dictionary of National Biography*. His best-known book is the *History of English Thought in the Eighteenth Century* (1876). The novelist Virginia *Woolf was his daughter.

Stephen I, St (?975-1038) The first King of Hungary (997-1038). Stephen was crowned on Christmas Day, 1000, allegedly with a crown sent by Pope *Sylvester II—the St *Stephen's Crown. Stephen's promotion of Christianity led to his canonization in 1083.

Stephen, St In the New Testament, the first Christian martyr. According to Acts 6, he was one of the seven deacons appointed by the Apostles to provide charity for the Greek-speaking widows in the Christian community. Also a preacher and miracle worker, he was accused of blasphemy and stoned to death by the Jews. Feast day: 26 Dec.

Stephen Báthory (1533-86) King of Poland (1575-86). Stephen defeated *Ivan the Terrible of Muscovy in the *Livonian War but his plan to conquer Muscovy was cut short by his death.

Stephenson, George (1781-1848) British engineer, who developed a greatly improved steam locomotive. Stephenson became interested in locomotives in 1813, when he saw John *Blenkinsop's model. Two years later he built the *Blucher*, which could draw 30 tons of coal at 4 mph. He went on to construct a number of improved models, culminating in his most famous locomotive, the *Rocket*, built in 1829. It carried passengers at a speed of 36 mph on the new Liverpool-Manchester line and stimulated railway development throughout Europe and in North America. His son **Robert Stephenson** (1803-59), a civil engineer, designed a number of important railway bridges. Stephenson was appointed chief engineer of the London and Birmingham Railway in 1833. His best-known works are the tubular Britannia Bridge over the Menai Strait in Wales and the six-arch railway bridge over the River Tyne at Newcastle.

Stepney A district in the Greater London borough of Tower Hamlets, on the N bank of the River Thames. It contains the *Tower of London and Petticoat Lane (noted for its Sunday morning market).

steppes The midlatitude grasslands of Eurasia extending in a broad belt from the Ukraine to SW Siberia. They correspond to the prairies of North America and consist chiefly of level, virtually treeless, plains.

steradian (sr) The *SI unit of solid angle equal to a solid angle that encloses a surface on a sphere equal to the square of its radius.

stere A metric unit of volume equal to one cubic metre.

stereochemistry. *See* isomers.

stereophonic sound Sound reproduction in which two signals are used to give a directional quality. It results in more realistic reproduction than a single signal system (monophonic sound) because the brain distinguishes the direction by assessing the difference between the sound in

each ear. For recording, either two directional *microphones at right angles in one place or two separated microphones are needed. Playing back requires at least two *loudspeakers, one for each signal.

sterility Inability to produce offspring by sexual reproduction. Sterility, or infertility, in men may be caused by various conditions in which the sperms are deficient in numbers or defective in quality. It may also result from psychological problems causing *impotence. In women sterility may be due to disease of the womb, blockage of the Fallopian tubes leading from the ovaries to the womb, or failure of the ovaries to produce egg cells. Generalized illness can also affect fertility. Numerous methods of treatment are possible depending on the cause; if the underlying condition cannot be treated, the couple may consider *artificial insemination. Sterility can also be deliberately induced (*see* sterilization).

sterilization The surgical technique or any other means used to induce *sterility. Surgical sterilization may be performed for contraceptive purposes or when pregnancy would damage the health of the woman. For men, the operation—vasectomy—involves cutting and tying the duct (vas deferens) that conveys sperm from the testicle. In women the Fallopian tubes are clipped or tied (tubal ligation), which prevents the passage of the egg cells to the womb. This operation is now performed, using a fibreoptic laparoscope, through a minute incision in the abdominal wall. Neither operation affects sexual desire or the ability to satisfy it. Sterilization should be considered as irreversible. *See also* castration.

sterling 1. The currency of the UK. The pound sterling is named after the Norman *steorling*, a coin with a star (*steorra*) on one face. Coins of the realm that comply with the standards laid down from time to time are called sterling. 2. Sterling silver is a silver alloy containing at least 92.5% silver.

ALFRED STIEGLITZ The Steerage, *a photogravure taken by him in New York, 1907.*

Stern, Isaac (1920-) Russian-born US violinist. He was taken to the USA as a young child and studied and made his debut in San Francisco. He is a world-famous soloist and has toured extensively.

Sternberg, Josef von (J. Stern; 1894-1969) US film director, born in Austria. He directed films noted for their pictorial quality, the best known being a series starring Marlene *Dietrich, including *The Blue Angel* (1930), *Blonde Venus* (1932), *Shanghai Express* (1932), and *The Scarlet Empress* (1934). He wrote the scripts for most of his films and published an autobiography, *Fun in a Chinese Laundry* (1965).

Sterne, Laurence (1713-68) British novelist. Born in Ireland, he was educated at Cambridge and became a clergyman in Yorkshire. After the publication of the first two volumes of *Tristram Shandy* (1759), an eccentric comic novel consisting largely of sentimental rhetoric and witty digressions, he was lionized by London society. His second novel, *A Sentimental Journey* (1768), was based on his travels on the Continent undertaken for health reasons. He also published several volumes of sermons.

sternum. *See* thorax.

steroids A class of organic chemical compounds with a basic structure of three six-membered carbon rings joined to a five-membered ring. Steroids and their hydroxy derivatives (**sterols**) fulfil many biological roles in plants and animals and include the *sex hormones, *corticosteroids, *bile acids, *vitamin D, and moulting hormones in insects. *Cholesterol is an important precursor in the synthesis of many steroids.

stethoscope An instrument widely used by doctors to listen to sounds within the body (*see* auscultation). The first stethoscope was invented by R. T. H. *Laënnec. Modern instruments consist of two earpieces joined by two tubes to a head, which is placed on the body. The head usually has a diaphragm (for high-pitched sounds) and a bell (for low-pitched sounds). More sophisticated stethoscopes are fitted with electronic amplification devices.

Stettin. *See* Szczecin.

Stevenage 51 55N 0 14W A town in SE England, in Hertfordshire. The first of the new towns (1946) to be developed after World War II, it is now an important industrial centre manufacturing aircraft, electrical, and plastic goods. Population (1981): 74 365.

Stevens, Wallace (1879-1955) US poet. He worked as an insurance executive and wrote most of his poetry after the age of 50. In many of his best-known poems, such as "The Man with the Blue Guitar," he explores the relationship between reality and imagination. His poems are collected in *Collected Poems* (1954) and *Opus Posthumus* (1957) and his essays in *The Necessary Angel* (1951).

Stevenson, Adlai E(wing) (1900-65) US Democratic politician. As governor of Illinois (1949-53) Stevenson achieved reforms in the civil service, police, and public education. He twice ran for the presidency (1952, 1956) but was defeated on both occasions by Eisenhower. He was an adviser at the San Francisco Conference (1945), helping to found the UN, to which he was later US delegate (1961-65).

Stevenson, Robert Louis (1850-94) British novelist, born in Edinburgh. He studied law at Edinburgh University. In 1880 he married Fanny Osbourne, whom he had met in France and followed to her native California. Returning to Scotland, he published several books, which established his reputation and which remain among the best-known works of fiction in the language: the classic adventure tale *Treasure Island* (1883), *Kidnapped* (1886), set in Scotland after the 1745 Jacobite rebellion, and *The Strange Case of Dr Jekyll and Mr Hyde* (1886). Constantly troubled by respiratory disease, he returned to the USA in 1887 and finally settled on the island of Samoa in 1890. His other works include the novel *The Master of Ballantrae* (1889) and the unfinished *Weir of Hermiston* (1896).

Stewart, Jackie (John Young S.; 1939-) British motor-racing driver, who won a record number of 27 Grand Prix

victories and was world champion in 1969, 1971, and 1973. He retired in 1973.

Stewart, James (Maitland) (1908-) US film actor. He began his Hollywood career in 1935 and established himself as an incorruptible hero with a distinctive drawl in numerous films, including *Mr Smith Goes to Washington* (1939), *Destry Rides Again* (1939), *The Philadelphia Story* (1940), *The Glenn Miller Story* (1953), *Shenandoah* (1965), and *Airport 77* (1977).

Stewart, Rod (1945-) British rock musician, whose first widely successful album was *Every Picture Tells a Story* (1971). In 1975 he left the group The Faces to perform solo; his single "Tonight's The Night" (1976) was one of his many popular hits.

Stewart Island (Maori name: Rakiura) 47 00S 168 00E A volcanic island of New Zealand, separated from S South Island by Foreaux Strait. Area: 1735 sq km (670 sq mi).

Stewarts. *See* Stuarts.

Steyr 48 04N 14 25E A town in NE central Austria, in Upper Austria. It is an iron and steel centre; other products include motor vehicles, bicycles, and ball bearings. Population (1981): 38 898.

stibnite An ore mineral of antimony, SbS_3. It is a lead-grey colour with a metallic lustre and often occurs as distinctive radiating crystals. It is found in low-temperature hydrothermal veins and in replacement deposits.

stick insect An □insect, also called walking stick, belonging to the family *Phasmidae*. Up to 320 mm long, it has a twiglike body and long spindly legs and the wings are reduced or absent. Males are rare; the females live in trees or shrubs, producing eggs that drop to the ground and develop without fertilization (*see* parthenogenesis). Order *Phasmida*.

stickleback A fish of the family *Gasterosteidae* (about 12 species), found in both fresh and salt water in temperate regions of the N hemisphere. Up to 17 cm long, sticklebacks have a row of spines along the back. The male builds a nest for the eggs and guards the young. Order: *Gasterosteiformes*.

Stieglitz, Alfred (1864-1946) US photographer. He is famous for his promotion of European and US modern art in the USA and his technical innovations in and development of photography as an art form. His famous Photo-Secession gallery in New York (1905-17), known as 291, put on exhibitions of Matisse (1908), children's art (1912), and *Brancusi (1914). Among his most admired photographs are those of New York and of his wife, Georgia *O'Keeffe.

Stiernhielm, Georg Olofson (1598-1672) Swedish poet and scholar, known as the father of Swedish poetry. Believing that Swedish was man's original language, he tried to purify it by excluding loan words. His greatest work is the didactic epic poem *Hercules* (c. 1647).

stigma The part of the pistil of a flower that is specialized to receive *pollen. In insect-pollinated flowers the stigma is sticky, whereas wind-pollinated flowers have large feathery stigmas.

stigmata (Greek: marks) Marks appearing on the body of a living person that resemble the five wounds (in the hands, feet, and side) that Christ received at the crucifixion. There have been more than 300 reported cases, typically involving devoutly religious persons. The stigmata are unknown before the 13th century, St *Francis of Assisi being the first saint to receive them. A number of natural explanations have been advanced, and the Roman Catholic Church takes a cautious view of the phenomenon, which does not constitute grounds for canonization.

Stijl, de (Dutch: the Style) A group of 20th-century Dutch artists and architects, who launched the art periodical *De Stijl* (1917-1928). Prominent members were the painters *Mondrian and Theo van Doesburg (1883-1931) and the architects J. J. P. Oud (1890-1963) and Gerrit Rietveld (1888-1964). The group adhered to the principles of Mondrian's neoplasticism, an abstract style that sought to establish a harmonious and universal means of expression applicable to all branches of art. This would be achieved by reducing form to horizontals and verticals and colours to the three *primary colours and black, white, and grey. In architecture and design neoplasticism was seen at its purest in Rietveld's Schröder house at Utrecht (1924) and in his furniture. Many of its principles were influential at the *Bauhaus.

Stilicho, Flavius (d. 408 AD) Roman general under *Theodosius I, who appointed him guardian of his son *Honorius. On Theodosius' death in 395, Honorius was proclaimed western emperor but Stilicho ruled in effect, ruthlessly removing opposition. He repulsed invasions by the Visigoths under Alaric and by the Ostrogoths but his political intrigues with Alaric and others eventually brought about his execution on Honorius' orders.

still-life A branch of painting concerned with the representation of inanimate objects. Although still-life was used in religious paintings and portraits, it did not appear as an art form until the 16th century and then only in the Netherlands. Particularly popular were still-lifes of objects symbolizing the transience of life—skulls, guttering candles, etc. Still-lifes of food and drink became the favourite subjects of such noted painters as *Zurbaran, *Chardin, *Cézanne, and *Braque, while specialists in flowerpieces have included Jan *Brueghel and Pierre *Redouté.

stilt A wading bird belonging to the family *Recurvirostridae* (avocets and stilts). 35-45 cm long, stilts occur in warm wet regions, where they probe in mud for small aquatic animals. The common stilt (*Himantopus himantopus*) has black-and-white plumage, pink legs, and red eyes.

Stilton 52 29N 0 17W A village in E England, in Cambridgeshire. The slow-maturing cheese named after it is now made mainly in Leicestershire.

Stilwell, Joseph W(arren) (1883-1946) US general, known as Vinegar Joe. A Chinese linguist, in World War II he was appointed (1941) *Chiang Kai-shek's chief of staff and to the command of all US forces in China, Burma, and India. His dislike of the British and his differences with Chiang forced his recall in 1944. In 1945 he became commander of the US Tenth Army in the Pacific.

stimulants A large group of drugs that stimulate activity of the nervous system. Caffeine (in tea and coffee) and nicotine (in cigarettes) are stimulants used widely to reduce feelings of tiredness and to improve concentration. *Hallucinogens, *amphetamine, and *cocaine are also stimulants. Stimulants may affect other parts of the body, particularly the heart.

stimulated emission. *See* laser.

stingray A round or diamond-shaped *ray fish belonging to a family (*Dasyatidae*; 89 species) found mainly in warm shallow ocean waters. Most species have a whiplike tail armed with one or more saw-edged venomous spines, which can inflict an intensely painful wound causing paralysis and occasionally death. Live young are born.

stink bug. *See* shield bug.

stinkhorn A fungus of the order *Phallales*, producing a phallus-shaped fruiting body. This consists of a stout whitish stalk arising from a basal egg-shaped structure and bearing a thimble-shaped cap containing spores. When the spores are ripe the cap produces a strong-smelling secretion that attracts flies, which disperse the spores. The common stinkhorn (*Phallus impudicus*) reaches a height of 10-20 cm. Class: *Basidiomycetes.

stinkwood One of several species of trees with unpleasant-smelling timber, including *Gustavia augusta* of tropical America and the African species *Celtis kraussiana* and *Ocotea bullata* (black stinkwood). The wood can be used in furniture making.

Stirling (*or* Stirlingshire) A former county of central Scotland. Under local government reorganization in 1975 it became part of the Central and Strathclyde Regions. Stirling District in the Central Region comprises part of the former county.

Stirling 56 07N 3 57W A town in Scotland, the administrative centre of the Central Region on the River Forth. Once a residence of the Scottish kings, the first Scottish parliament was held here in 1326 and Mary, Queen of Scots, and James VI were crowned here as infants. The castle occupies a prominent position on a dolerite outcrop. Stirling is an important market town with agricultural machinery, textiles, and chemicals among its industries. The university was founded in 1967. Population (1985 est): 29 238.

Stirling, James (1692-1770) Scottish mathematician, best known for the widely used mathematical formula named after him. Stirling's formula gives the approximate value for the factorial of a large number. It was in fact first derived by Abraham de Moivre (1667-1754).

stitchwort A perennial herb belonging to the widely distributed genus *Stellaria* (85 species), having white starlike flowers. The greater stitchwort (*S. holostea*) is a common woodland and roadside plant of Europe, N Africa, and W Asia, growing to a height of 15-60 cm. Family: *Caryophyllaceae*.

stoat A small carnivorous mammal, *Mustela erminea*, of Europe, Asia, and North America. About 35 cm long, with a long sinuous body, flattish head, and short legs, it can be distinguished from a *weasel by its black-tipped tail. Stoats prey mainly on rabbits. *See also* ermine.

stock One of several herbaceous plants of the genus *Matthiola* that are cultivated as ornamentals. Many garden varieties, including ten-week stocks and Brompton stocks, are derived from the European biennial *M. incana*, which grows to a height of 30-60 cm and has clusters of purple flowers. The night-scented stock (*M. bicornis*) has small lilac flowers that emit their fragrance at night. Family: *Cruciferae*.

STILL-LIFE *Detail from* Still Life: An Allegory of the Vanities of Human Life, *by Herman Steenwyck (1612-c. 1655) (National Gallery, London).*

stock-car racing A form of *motor racing that originated in the USA in the 1920s, when cars were modified for transporting illegally made whiskey, for which speed was all-important. Stock cars are specially built steel-bodied saloon cars weighing around 2000 kg; they withstand frequent accidents. They are raced on oval tracks at speeds up to about 320 km per hour (200 mph).

stock exchange A market in which securities are bought and sold. The London Stock Exchange, founded in 1773 to replace coffee-house dealings, was until the "Big Bang"

(October, 1986) divided into brokers (who dealt with the public) and jobbers (who bought and sold securities for their own account and dealt with the public through brokers). After the "Big Bang" this distinction was abolished, brokers' commissions became negotiable, and dealings were computerized to such an extent that personal contact on the floor of the Exchange became social rather than commercial. The year is divided into "accounts" of (usually) a fortnight, transactions made during one account being settled in the next. *See also* stocks and shares.

Stockhausen, Karlheinz (1928–) German composer, a pupil of Messiaen and Milhaud. From 1953 he worked at the West German Radio Studio for electronic music in Cologne. His early works employed serialism but he later rejected traditional forms and techniques, developing a concept of music as a sequence of sound "events" in such works as *Gruppen* (for three orchestras; 1955–57), *Zyklus* (for solo percussionist; 1959), and *Kontra-Punkte* (for ten instruments; 1962). Such works as *Stimmung* (for six singers; 1968) and *Mantra* (for two pianos and percussion; 1970) were influenced by Indian mysticism. Later works include the opera *Donnerstag aus Licht* (1978–80).

Stockholm 59 20N 18 95E The capital of Sweden, built on several islands between Lake Mälar and the Baltic Sea. It is the country's second largest port and its varied industries include shipbuilding, engineering, sugar refining, and brewing. The old town contains many buildings erected in the middle ages and in the 16th and 17th centuries, including the Royal Palace and Storkyrkan, Stockholm's cathedral. Its university was established in 1877. *History*: a settlement from very early times, it developed in the 13th century around a fortress erected to protect the entrance to the trading centres of Lake Mälar. It became the capital in 1436 and enjoyed great prestige and influence in the 17th century. Population (1983): 650 952.

Stockport 53 25N 2 10W A town in N England, in Greater Manchester on the River Mersey. Traditionally a textile town (particularly for cotton), Stockport also manufactures hats and caps, textile and electrical machinery, paper, plastics, and chemicals. Population (1981): 136 496.

stocks and shares Documents representing money invested in industrial and commercial corporations or loaned to a government. In the UK stocks represent fixed-interest loans made to the government (*see* gilt-edged security), foreign governments, local authorities, or companies (*see* debenture stock). Shares represent equal amounts of capital subscribed to a company in return for membership rights. Ordinary shareholders are the last to receive their *dividends, which fluctuate according to the level of profits. They usually have voting rights in the company (*compare* preference shares). Companies in which the public own over 25% of the shares can become listed companies, enabling their shares to be dealt with on the London *Stock Exchange. Companies in which the public own 10–25% of the shares may be dealt with on the **unlisted securities market** (USM) of the Exchange. In the USA ordinary shares are called common stock.

Stockton 37 59N 121 20W A city and port in the USA, in California on the San Joaquin River. It accommodates oceangoing vessels and is a distributing and processing centre for the fertile San Joaquin Valley. Population (1980): 149 779.

Stockton, 1st Earl of. *See* Macmillan, (Maurice) Harold.

Stockton-on-Tees 53 34N 1 19W A town in NE England, in Cleveland on the River Tees. The first passenger railway was built from here to Darlington in 1825, and it was once an important port. Engineering and ship repairing are major industries. Population (1981): 154 585.

Stoicism The philosophical school founded about 300 BC in the Painted Porch (Greek: Stoa Poikile) at Athens by *Zeno of Citium. Stoics believed that God (identified with reason) was

the basis of the universe, that human souls were sparks of the divine fire, and that the wise man lived "in harmony with nature." Knowledge of virtue was all-important. Stoicism was subsequently modified to stress the primacy of active virtue and duty. *Epictetus (55–135 AD) taught that all men were brothers. Stoicism appealed strongly to many prominent Romans, including Marcus *Brutus and *Marcus Aurelius, and its doctrines influenced many later thinkers.

Stoke-on-Trent 53 00N 2 10W A city in England, in the N Midlands in Staffordshire, on the River Trent. Formed in 1910 by the amalgamation of five towns, the area is known as the Potteries and is the centre of the British ceramic industry. Josiah Wedgwood and Arnold Bennett were born here. There are also engineering, tyre, and cable manufacturing industries, with coalmining locally. Nearby is Keele University (1962). Population (1981): 252 351.

Stoke Poges A village in SE England, in Buckinghamshire near Slough. The poet Thomas Gray is buried in the churchyard, believed to be the setting of his famous *Elegy*.

Stoker, Bram (Abraham S.; 1847–1912) Irish novelist. He worked as a civil servant (1867–77), wrote drama criticism, and became secretary and manager to the actor Henry *Irving in 1878. Stoker is chiefly remembered as the author of *Dracula* (1897), a horror story in the *Gothic novel tradition. *See also* Dracula, Count; vampires.

Stokes, Sir George Gabriel (1819–1903) British physicist and mathematician, who was professor of mathematics at Cambridge University. He discovered the law concerning the terminal velocity of a sphere falling through a viscous fluid (*see* Stokes' law). He also attempted to deduce a mathematical model of the luminiferous ether, the medium in which light was at that time thought to vibrate.

Stokes' law The resisting force acting on a sphere, radius r, moving through a fluid under gravity with velocity v is $6\pi r \eta v$, where η is the *viscosity of the fluid. The law is used in the determination of viscosity. Named after Sir George *Stokes.

Stokowski, Leopold (1882–1977) British-born conductor. He became a US citizen in 1915. A keen supporter of modern music, Stokowski also became well known for his orchestral transcriptions of Bach's organ music. He conducted many of the leading US orchestras, including the Philadelphia Orchestra (1912–38).

Stolypin, Petr Arkadievich (1863–1911) Russian statesman. Tsarist Russia's last gifted politician, Stolypin became prime minister in 1906. He promoted many reforms, outstandingly the land reforms that enabled many peasants to live an economically independent life. He became unpopular with both Right and Left owing to his disregard of the views of the Duma and his harsh treatment of revolutionaries; he was assassinated in Kiev.

stomach A muscular sac, just beneath the diaphragm, that opens from the oesophagus (gullet) and leads to the duodenum (part of the small intestine). The stomach secretes gastric juice, containing hydrochloric acid and the enzyme *pepsin, which continue the digestion of food that started in the mouth. Release of acid is triggered by the *vagus nerve and by a hormone (gastrin) secreted by the stomach in response to the presence of food. The churning action of the stomach ensures constant mixing of the food and its secretions. *See Plate IV.

Stone Age The cultural phase during which man relied on stone, supplemented by wood, bone, or antler, as material for weapons and tools. It is the earliest phase in the system devised (1816) by Christian Thomsen (1788–1865) for classifying human technological progress (*compare* Bronze Age; Iron Age). The Stone Age is subdivided into: Old (*see* Palaeolithic), Middle (*see* Mesolithic), and New (*see* Neolithic).

stone bass. *See* wreckfish.

stonechat A small *chat, *Saxicola torquata*, occurring in Eurasia and N Africa and feeding chiefly on insects and their larvae. Measuring about 12 cm long, the male has a dark-brown head and back, chestnut underparts, and white rump; the female is a drabber brown. Stonechats favour dry heathland regions and are declining in Britain as a result of the destruction of these habitats.

stonecrop An annual or perennial herb belonging to the genus *Sedum* (600 species), found chiefly in warm N temperate regions and also in Central and South America. They have small thick fleshy leaves and clusters of white, pink, or yellow flowers. Some are popular ornamentals, including autumn glory (*S. spectabile*), which grows to a height of 30–45 cm. Family: *Crassulaceae*.

stone curlew A ground-nesting bird belonging to a widely distributed family (*Burhinidae*; 9 species) characterized by thickened tarsal joints, also called thickknee. They are typically nocturnal, living in stony barren regions and feeding on beetles, worms, and other small animals. Order: *Charadriiformes* (gulls, plovers, etc.).

stonefish A fish, belonging to the genus *Synanceja*, that occurs in shallow waters of the Indian and Pacific Oceans. It has a robust body, up to 35 cm long, covered with wartlike lumps and fleshy flaps, a large head, and poisonous dorsal fins. It lies camouflaged and motionless among rocks or coral to await its prey. Family: *Synancejidae*.

stonefly An insect of the order *Plecoptera* (3000 species), 6–60 mm long with long antennae and two pairs of membranous wings. The short-lived adults rarely feed and are found near fresh water. The aquatic *nymphs, which favour fast-flowing streams with stony bottoms, feed on plants, decaying organic material, or other insects.

Stonehenge A famous megalithic structure, the focus of a cluster of ceremonial sites on Salisbury Plain in Wiltshire (England). Scientific study and excavation over many years have revealed a complex history with three main phases of modification (c. 2500–1500 BC) contributing to the Stonehenge seen today. Sarsens and bluestones, the latter brought from S Wales, are set upright in concentric circles and horseshoes the orientation of which suggests one purpose as being sun and moon observation. The alleged "Druid" connection is entirely spurious, dating only from the 18th century AD. *See also* megalith.

stone pine A *pine tree, *Pinus pinea*, native to SW Europe and Asia but planted throughout Mediterranean regions since Roman times for its edible seeds. Up to 30 m high, it has spreading branches and an umbrella-shaped crown, needles grouped in pairs, and cones about 12.5 cm long. The oily seeds are eaten raw or roasted or are used to flavour stews, etc.

stoneworts *Green algae of the class *Charophyceae*, many of which contain stony deposits of calcium carbonate. The plants have an erect stemlike axis with whorls of branches and rootlike threads (rhizoids), by which they are anchored to muddy bottoms of fresh or brackish waters.

Stopes, Marie Charlotte Carmichael (1880–1958) British birth-control campaigner. A botanist, she worked at Manchester University until the failure of her first marriage (1916) turned her attention to the study of marital problems. In 1921 she opened the first birth-control clinic in Britain—in Holloway, London. Among her books are *Married Love* (1918), *Wise Parenthood* (1918), and *Contraception: Its Theory, History, and Practice* (1923). In 1918 she married H(umphrey) V(erdon) Roe (1878–1949), an aircraft manufacturer.

Stoppard, Tom (1937–) British dramatist, born in Czechoslovakia. After working as a journalist in Bristol, he achieved international success with his play *Rosencrantz and Guildenstern Are Dead* (1967), using characters from Shakespeare's *Hamlet*. In his later plays, such as *Jumpers*

Station stone mound

bluestone horseshoe

sarsen trilithons

Aubrey holes
Station stone

Station stone
Sarsen circle
bluestone circle
Q and R holes (for removed double circle of bluestones)
Y holes
Z holes
Station stone mound

Slaughter stone

ditch   N

avenue ditch   avenue ditch

0 10 20 m
0 20 40 60 ft

Heel stone

STONEHENGE   *The plan reveals features of consecutive building phases that may no longer be visible to the visitor to the site.*

(1972), *Travesties* (1975), *Night and Day* (1978), and *The Real Thing* (1982), he explored philosophical and political ideas with wit and great verbal facility. His wife, **Miriam Stoppard** (1937–), is a doctor, writer, and broadcaster specializing in child care and physical fitness.

storax A tree or shrub belonging to the genus *Styrax* (130 species), occurring in warm and tropical regions. They have small white star-shaped flowers and several species are cultivated as ornamentals, including the Japanese snowbell (*S. japonicum*), which grows to a height of 9 m, and *S. officinalis*, from which the vanilla-scented resin known as storax was formerly obtained. The storax used today in cough mixtures, pastilles, etc., is extracted from trees of the genus *Liquidambar*. The Sumatran species *S. benzoin* is a source of *benzoin. Family: *Styracaceae*.

Store Bælt. *See* Great Belt.

Storey, David (1933–) British novelist and dramatist. He was an art student and professional Rugby League player before achieving literary success with his novel *This Sporting Life* (1960). His later novels include *Pasmore* (1972), *Saville* (1976), and *Present Times* (1984), and his plays include *In Celebration* (1969) and *Home* (1970).

stork A large bird belonging to a widely distributed family (*Ciconiidae*; 17 species) occurring in warm and temperate regions. 60–150 cm tall, storks have long necks, legs, and bill and are mostly white with black markings. They feed chiefly on fish, frogs, molluscs, and insects—caught in shallow waters or grasslands—and build a large nest platform of twigs in a tree or on a rooftop. Order: *Ciconiiformes* (herons, storks, flamingos). *See also* adjutant stork; marabou.

storksbill A herb of the genus *Erodium* (about 90 species) occurring in Eurasia, Australia, and South America. The seeds have a slender beaklike projection (hence the name) that is spirally twisted at maturity and unwinds when in contact with a damp surface to release the seeds. The common storksbill (*E. cicutarium*) grows to a height of 60 cm and has purplish-pink flowers. Family: *Geraniaceae*.

Storm, (Hans) Theodor Woldsen (1817–1888) German writer. A lawyer, he spent most of his life in his native Schleswig, which inspired the chief themes of his works, in such novellas as *Immensee* (1849) and *Der Schimmelreiter* (1888).

Stormont A castle in Belfast that housed the parliament of Northern Ireland, established in 1921. Following the eruption of violence in the province in 1969, the UK Government suspended Stormont and reinstituted direct rule from London (1972).

storm petrel A small seabird belonging to a family (*Hydrobatidae*; 20 species) occurring in all oceans. 13–25 cm long, storm petrels have dark-grey or brown plumage, often with paler underparts. Species of southern oceans have square tails, long legs, and short toes and feed by "walking" on the water with wings outstretched, picking up plankton. Northern species have longer wings and a forked or wedge-shaped tail and feed by swooping on fish. Order: *Procellariiformes* (petrels).

Stornoway 58 12N 6 23W A port in NW Scotland, in the Outer Hebrides, on the Isle of Lewis. It is the administrative centre of the Western Isles Islands Area and the largest town of the Outer Hebrides. Fishing, tourism, tweed manufacture, and industries related to offshore oil are the main economic activities. Population (1981): 8660.

Stoss, Veit (c. 1445–1533) German gothic sculptor and woodcarver. Working chiefly in Nuremberg but also in Poland, Hungary, and Bohemia, Stoss developed a style that combined Flemish realism with swirling draperies and expressive gestures and faces. His most important work is the altar of the *Life of the Virgin* for the Church of St Mary, Cracow.

Stourbridge 52 27N 2 09W A town in central England, in West Midlands on the River Stour. Dr Johnson attended the

grammar school (founded 1552). There are glass-manufacturing and iron-working industries. Population (1981): 54 661.

stout. *See* beer and brewing.

Stowe, Harriet Beecher (1811–96) US novelist. A school teacher, she was a member of a prominent Calvinist family and wrote frequently on religious themes. *Uncle Tom's Cabin* (1852) was an international bestseller and greatly stimulated antislavery feeling.

strabismus. *See* squint.

Strabo (c. 64 BC–c. 21 AD) Greek geographer, born at Amaseia (now Amasya, Turkey). His *Geography*, in 17 books, is an invaluable source of information about the ancient world. After a survey of previous geographers and a discussion of mathematical geography and maps, Strabo describes the Europe-Asia-Africa land mass clockwise round the Mediterranean, from Spain to N Africa. He marshals the evidence of other writers and his own observations into a comprehensive account, and is a master of historical and political geography, notably when describing the growth of the Roman Empire.

Strachey, (Giles) Lytton (1880–1932) British biographer and essayist. He was a leading member of the *Bloomsbury group. His irreverent attitude towards his subjects (Thomas Arnold, Florence Nightingale, Cardinal Manning, and others) in *Eminent Victorians* (1918) revolutionized the ponderous Victorian tradition of biography. His other biographical studies include *Queen Victoria* (1921) and *Elizabeth and Essex* (1928).

Stradivari, Antonio (?1644–1737) Italian violin maker. He was a pupil of Niccolò *Amati. From 1666 he and two of his sons made outstanding violins, violas, and cellos at their workshop in Cremona. Stradivari signed his instruments with the Latin form of his name, Stradivarius.

Strafford, Thomas Wentworth, 1st Earl of (1593–1641) English statesman, who with Archbishop Laud was the chief executor of Charles I's unpopular personal rule (1629–40). Initially a parliamentary opponent of the king, he became a supporter of Charles when appointed Lord President of the north (1628). As Lord Deputy of Ireland (1633–39) his policy of "thorough," which ruthlessly strengthened royal power, brought him enormous unpopularity that was intensified by his attempt to suppress the *Bishops' Wars (1639–40) in Scotland. He was impeached by the *Long Parliament and executed on the eve of the Civil War.

strain In physics, the deformation of a body when it is subjected to a *stress. **Longitudinal strain** is the extension per unit length when a body is stretched; **bulk strain** is the volume change per unit volume when a body is compressed; and **shear strain** is an angular measure of deformation. *See also* elasticity.

Straits Settlements A former British crown colony on the Strait of Malacca founded in 1867 and comprising the settlements of Penang, Singapore, Malacca, and Labuan. In 1946 Singapore became a separate crown colony, Labuan was incorporated in North Borneo, and Penang and Malacca joined the Malayan Union. In 1963 all became part of Malaysia, Singapore becoming independent in 1965.

Stralsund 54 18N 12 58E A town and port in N East Germany, on an inlet of the Baltic Sea. Founded in 1209, it became an important Hanseatic port. Industries include shipbuilding, fish processing, and the manufacture of machinery. Population (1981 est): 75 070.

strangeness A property of matter, expressed as a *quantum number (*s*), postulated to account for the unusually long lifetime of some *hadrons. In the quark model (*see* particle physics) strange hadrons contain the strange quark or its antiquark. Strangeness is conserved in *strong interactions and *electromagnetic interactions.

Stranraer 54 54N 5 02W A port in SW Scotland, on the W

coast of Dumfries and Galloway Region at the head of Loch Ryan. There is a steamer service to Larne, Northern Ireland. Population (1984 est): 10 170.

Strasbourg (German name: Strassburg) 48 35N 7 45E A city in NE France, the capital of the Bas-Rhin department on the River Ill. An important inland port, it trades in wine, iron ore, and potash; it has varied industries, including chemicals, oil refining, and textiles. It is famous for its *pâté de foie gras*. Notable buildings include the cathedral (11th–15th centuries) and the university (1538). *History*: made a free imperial city in the 13th century, it was ceded to France in 1697. Captured by the Germans (1871), it was returned to France after World War I. Population (1982): 252 264.

Strategic Arms Limitation Talks (SALT). *See* disarmament.

Strategic Defence Initiative (SDI) A US research project, also known as "star wars", whch aims to destroy incoming nuclear missiles in space. Announced by President Reagan in March, 1983, the programme includes tests of various systems, of which ground-based or satellite-mounted lasers are favoured. Opponents of SDI are against the militarization of space; defenders claim it could make nuclear weapons obsolete. The Soviet Union is developing a similar system.

Stratford 43 22N 81 00W A city in E Canada, in SW Ontario. Founded in 1831, its annual Shakespearean Festival began in 1953. Stratford is also a centre for light industry and dairying. Population (1981): 26 262.

Stratford-on-Avon 52 12N 1 41W A town in central England, in Warwickshire on the River Avon. It is famous as the birthplace of William Shakespeare. The Royal Shakespeare Theatre (opened in 1932) is devoted mainly to Shakespeare's plays. Tourists visit Shakespeare's birthplace, Holy Trinity Church (where he and his wife Anne Hathaway are buried), Anne Hathaway's cottage nearby, and many other buildings associated with the playwright. Stratford is also a market town with canning, aluminium ware, and boatbuilding industries. Population (1981): 20 858.

Strathclyde Region An administrative region in W Scotland, bordering on the Atlantic Ocean. It was created under local government reorganization in 1975 from the counties of Ayr, Bute, Dunbarton, Lanark, Renfrew, and parts of Argyll and Stirling. It consists of lowlands in the Glasgow area surrounded by highlands and includes offshore islands such as Múll, Arran, and Jura. Agriculture is important on the lowlands, especially dairy farming, market gardening, pigs, and poultry. Industries include shipbuilding and coal-mining. Area: 13 856 sq km (5348 sq mi). Population (1981): 2 397 827. Administrative centre: Glasgow.

stratification The layering of sedimentary rocks and certain volcanic deposits in horizontal beds, known as strata. The bed is the smallest division of stratified sedimentary rocks, being a single sheetlike layer of sediment separated from overlying and underlying beds by a surface (the bedding plane), which marks a break in sedimentation. An unconformity is a surface representing a gap in the stratigraphic succession caused by changing conditions; it shows a period of erosion or nondeposition.

stratigraphy The branch of geology concerned with the formation, composition, sequence in time, and spatial correlation of the stratified rocks. **Lithostratigraphy** involves the lithological and spatial relations of rock units. **Biostratigraphy** utilizes fossils in calibrating rock successions. **Chronostratigraphy** studies rock bodies according to the time of their formation (*see* geological time scale).

stratocumulus cloud (Sc) A low type of *cloud composed of dark grey globular masses, often forming extensive sheets.

stratosphere. *See* atmosphere.

Stratton, Charles. *See* Tom Thumb.

stratus cloud A low type of *cloud forming below 2400 m (7874 ft), having a grey uniform appearance; it may actually

occur at ground level as hill fog. Precipitation, if any, is usually no more than a fine drizzle.

Strauss, Richard (1864–1949) German composer and conductor. He studied in Munich and Berlin and conducted opera at Munich, Bayreuth, and Vienna. Strauss was much influenced by Wagner, whose use of *leitmotifs he adopted, both in opera and orchestral works. From 1887 to 1899 Strauss wrote a series of symphonic poems, including *Death and Transfiguration* (1889), *Till Eulenspiegels lustige Streiche* (1894–95), *Also sprach Zarathustra* (1895–96), *Don Quixote* (1897), and *Ein Heldenleben* (1898). He then turned to opera, writing 15 works, including *Salome* (1905), *Elektra* (1906–08), *Der Rosenkavalier* (1909–10), and *Ariadne auf Naxos* (1912). His compositions also include two concertos for horn, one for oboe and one for violin, many songs, and *Metamorphosen* for 23 solo strings (1944–45).

Strauss the Younger, Johann (1825–99) Austrian violinist, conductor, and composer. He led his own dance ensemble from the age of 18 and was conductor of the Vienna court balls (1863–70). He wrote a great many waltzes, such as "The Blue Danube," "Vienna Blood," and "Tales from the Vienna Woods," as well as polkas and marches. He also wrote 16 operettas, including *Die Fledermaus* (1874), *A Night in Venice* (1883), and *The Gipsy Baron* (1885). His father **Johann Strauss the Elder** (1804–49) played in the orchestra of the composer Joseph Lanner (1801–43), before forming his own, with which he toured abroad. He was made conductor of the Vienna court balls in 1845, and composed 152 waltzes as well as quadrilles, marches (including the "Radetzky March"), galops, etc. Strauss and Lanner created the Viennese waltz.

Stravinsky, Igor (1882–1971) Russian-born composer. He became a US citizen in 1945. His father was an opera singer and Stravinsky was a pupil of Rimsky-Korsakov in St Petersburg. He became famous with the series of ballet scores commissioned by Diaghilev for the Ballets Russes, including *The Firebird* (1910), *Petrushka* (1911), and *The Rite of Spring* (1913), which was extremely modern in its use of rhythm and dissonance; it provoked demonstrations at its premiere and had a strong influence on 20th-century music. Stravinsky subsequently developed a neoclassical style in which he attempted to revive baroque and classical composition in a modern form. His works in this style include a piano concerto (1924), the oratorio *Oedipus Rex* (1927), the ballet *Apollon Musagète* (1928), and the opera *The Rake's Progress* (1951). Towards the end of his life Stravinsky adopted *serialism in such works as *Canticum Sacrum* (1955).

strawberry A perennial herb belonging to the genus *Fragaria* (15 species), native to N temperate regions and widely cultivated for its edible □fruit. Most of the commercial varieties are hybrids derived from the European hautbois strawberry (*F. moschata*), the Chilean strawberry (*F. chiloensis*), and the North American scarlet strawberry (*F. virginiana*). The plants are low growing, with creeping stems and small clusters of usually white flowers. It is the flower base (receptacle) that develops into the red fleshy "fruit": the true fruits (achenes) appear as "seeds" embedded in its surface. Strawberries are consumed fresh or used for canning, freezing, and jam making. Family: *Rosaceae*.

Strawberry Hill A house in Twickenham, London, built for and partially designed by Horace *Walpole between 1748 and 1777. It is one of the earliest examples of the *gothic revival style, for which Walpole was an enthusiast.

strawberry tree. *See* Arbutus.

strawflower. *See* everlasting flower.

Strawson, Peter Frederick (1919–) British philosopher. He became Waynflete Professor of Metaphysical Philosophy at Oxford in 1968. Strawson's early philosophy centres around the relationship between language and logic. His later work in descriptive metaphysics revived the popularity of this field. His books include *The Bounds of Sense* (1966) and *Freedom and Restraint* (1974).

streamlining The process of shaping the contours of a body so that it presents the least resistance to motion through a fluid. The mathematical study of these contours is part of *aerodynamics and *hydrodynamics. Streamlining must take into account drag forces, which are always present in real fluids, and is important in the design of aircraft, especially for supersonic flight (*see* sound barrier). *See also* turbulence.

stream of consciousness A technique used by novelists in which the flow of impressions, thoughts, and feelings are recorded as they pass through a character's mind. The term was first used by William *James in *Principles of Psychology* (1890). The technique was used by James *Joyce in *Ulysses* (1922) and also by Virginia *Woolf and William *Faulkner.

Streep, Meryl (Mary Louise S.; 1949–) US actress. She achieved fame in her first films, *Julia* (1977) and *The Deerhunter* (1978). Her other films include *Kramer vs. Kramer* (1980), *The French Lieutenant's Woman* (1981), *Sophie's Choice* (1982), and *Out of Africa* (1986).

Streicher, Julius (1885–1946) German Nazi journalist, who spread antisemitic propaganda. A collaborator in Hitler's Munich Putsch (1923), he was then editor of *Der Stürmer* (1923–45). He was hanged as a war criminal.

Streisand, Barbra (1942–) US singer and actress. She has performed on stage and in film musicals including *Funny Girl* (1968), *Hello Dolly* (1969), *The Way We Were* (1973), *A Star is Born* (1976), and *Yentl* (1983), which she wrote, produced, directed, and starred in. She has also acted in comedy films, such as *What's Up, Doc?* (1972).

Streptococcus A genus of spherical anaerobic bacteria many of which live as parasites in the respiratory and digestive systems of animals and man. *S. pyogenes* causes scarlet fever in man, *S. agalactiae* is responsible for bovine mastitis, and *S. lactis* produces lactic acid and causes souring of milk. *See also* pneumococcus.

streptomycin An *antibiotic, obtained from the bacterium *Streptomyces griseus*, that revolutionized the treatment of tuberculosis. It is usually administered (by injection) in combination with other antibiotics, such as isoniazid, as bacteria soon become resistant to it. In some patients it may cause serious side effects.

Stresemann, Gustav (1878–1929) German statesman; chancellor (1923) and foreign minister (1923–29) of the Weimar Republic. After World War I he negotiated the *Locarno Pact and secured the admittance (1926) of Germany to the League of Nations. He shared the Nobel Peace Prize with Briand in 1926.

stress (physics) The force per unit area that causes a deformation (or *strain) in a body. **Tensile stress** tends to stretch a body; **bulk stress** tends to compress it; and **shear stress,** which acts tangentially, tends to twist it. *See also* elasticity.

stress (psychology) A situation in which an individual is under physical or emotional pressure. If the stress is prolonged and the individual finds it unacceptable it can lead to *psychosomatic disorders in addition to *anxiety and *depression. In vulnerable people it can also trigger mental illness.

strike A form of industrial action in which a group of employees, usually organized in a trade union (or unions), withdraws its labour in order to achieve its demands. A strike is the last resort in the process of *collective bargaining: it may prompt a settlement either because it proves that neither side is bluffing or because the costs involved (in terms of lost pay and profits) force a compromise. As future orders and job security may be jeopardized by a strike, responsible unions only resort to the measure in extreme cases.

An official strike is one that is recognized by a trade union, whereas an unofficial (or wildcat) strike is a walkout organized by shopfloor workers without official union backing. The Trade Union Act (1984) provides for compulsory ballots in connection with strikes and other industrial actions *See also* picketing; *compare* lockout.

AUGUST STRINDBERG

Strindberg, August (1849–1912) Swedish dramatist and writer, born in Stockholm. After 1883 he lived chiefly in Berlin and Paris. His unhappy childhood and three unsuccessful marriages gave rise to mental instability and a violent hatred of women. This is reflected in the plays *The Father* (1887) and *Miss Julie* (1888), the autobiographical prose work *Confessions of a Fool* (1912), and a study of mental illness entitled *Inferno* (1897). Returning to Sweden in 1898, Strindberg began work on a cycle of history plays and the dramatic religious trilogy *To Damascus* (1904). The other major works of this period are *The Dance of Death* (1900), on marital tensions, the symbolistic *Easter* (1901), and *A Dream Play* (1901), in which Strindberg abandoned the naturalism that had figured in his earlier plays. His late chamber plays, such as *The Ghost Sonata* (1907), combine irrational elements with realistic settings; they anticipated many of the later innovations of 20th-century drama.

stringed instruments. Musical instruments in which notes are produced by the vibration of stretched strings. The strings may be plucked, as in the guitar, lyre, harp, lute, balalaika, zither, banjo, and ukulele; bowed, as in the violin family and viol family; plucked mechanically, as in the harpsichord; struck mechanically, as in the clavichord and piano; or played with hammers, as in the dulcimer and cimbalom. *Compare* drums; percussion instruments; wind instruments.

stroboscope An instrument used to study periodic motion using a flashing light of known frequency. For example, if a disc revolving at 50 revolutions per second is illuminated by 50 hertz alternating-current mains lighting, it will appear to be stationary. This is because the eye, for any particular flash, sees the disc in exactly the same position as it was for the previous flash. Strobe lighting is used in discotheques to accentuate the music's beat, with which it flashes in time.

Stroheim, Erich von (Hans Erich Maria Stroheim von Nordenwall; 1885–1957) US film director and actor, born in Austria. His films as director include *Greed* (1923), *The Wedding March* (1927), and *Queen Kelly* (1928). As an actor, he specialized in the roles of villains and German officers, as in *La Grande Illusion* (1937). In *Sunset Boulevard* (1950) he played a director from Hollywood's past.

stroke (*or* apoplexy) Sudden loss of consciousness with weakness or paralysis of one side of the body, caused by interruption of the blood supply to the brain. This may be due to a blood clot in one of the arteries of the brain (*see* embolism; thrombosis) or to the rupture of a blood vessel in the brain (cerebral haemorrhage). The underlying causes include untreated atherosclerosis and hypertension (high blood pressure) and diseases affecting the valves of the heart. With careful nursing and physiotherapy to restore the function of paralysed limbs many patients recover completely.

Stromboli An Italian island in the Tyrrhenian Sea, in the *Lipari Islands. Its active volcano produces a stream of lava.

Strong, Sir Roy (Colin) (1935–) British art critic. He was director of the National Portrait Gallery (1967–73) and subsequently director of the Victoria and Albert Museum (1974–87). A specialist in Tudor and Jacobean art, Strong has written many books, including *Nicholas Hilliard* (1975) and *The Cult of Elizabeth* (1977).

strong interaction One of the four basic forces in the universe; it occurs between the class of elementary particles called hadrons (*see* particle physics). It is the strongest of the four (being 100 times stronger than the electromotive interaction) but is effective only over a very short range of about 10^{-15} metre. It is the force that holds the protons and neutrons together in the nucleus. *Compare* weak interaction.

strontium (Sr) A reactive *alkaline-earth metal, discovered by Sir Humphry Davy in 1808 and named after Strontian, a town in Scotland where the carbonate ($SrCO_3$) is found. It also occurs as the sulphate, celestine ($SrSO_4$). It is a highly reactive metal, being more electropositive than calcium and reacting vigorously with water to liberate hydrogen. It imparts a strong red colour to flames and is used in fireworks. The isotope ^{90}Sr is produced in nuclear fallout. It emits high-energy beta-rays and has a half-life of 28 years; it consequently presents a serious health hazard as owing to its chemical similarity to calcium it can become incorporated into bone. At no 38; at wt 87.62; mp 769°C; bp 1384°C.

Strophanthus A genus of trees, shrubs, and vines (about 60 species), native to tropical regions of Africa and SE Asia. The petals of some species have long threadlike extensions. The bark and seeds yield the drug strophanthin, which resembles *digitalis and is used medicinally as a heart stimulant. Family: *Apocynaceae*.

structuralism An approach to the study of culture and society that seeks to uncover underlying patterns and structures and the basic elements from which such patterns are constructed. The leading figure of this school is the French social anthropologist Claude *Lévi-Strauss, whose work on kinship, art, myth, ritual, and religion has been concerned also with the elucidation of universal laws of human thought through the analysis of its underlying structure. This approach was stimulated by the structural school in *linguistics.

Struve, Otto (1897-1963) US astronomer, born in Russia, who discovered the existence of interstellar clouds and observed that they contain hydrogen and calcium. He also noticed that certain stars, including our own sun, rotate much more slowly than others and suggested that this is because they possess planetary systems.

strychnine An alkaloid poison derived from plants of the genus *Strychnos*. It acts on the central nervous system, causing convulsions and ultimately death. Strychnine has been used in "tonics" and is still used as a poison for pests (such as moles).

Stuart, John McDouall (1815-66) Scottish explorer. He emigrated to Australia in 1838 and in 1844 joined *Sturt's

expedition into central Australia. In 1860, following two unsuccessful attempts, he crossed Australia from S to N.

Stuarts (*or* Stewarts) The ruling dynasty of Scotland from 1371 to 1714 and of England from 1603 to 1714. The family originated in the 11th century in Brittany and in the 12th century entered Scottish royal service with the appointment of Walter (d. 1177) as steward to David I. The sixth steward, Walter (1293-1326), married (1315) Marjory, the daughter of Robert the Bruce, and their son became Robert II in 1371. The direct male line ended with the death of James V in 1542, when the throne passed to his daughter Mary, Queen of Scots, and following her abdication (1567) to her son James VI, who inherited the English Crown (1603) as James I. He was succeeded by Charles I (executed 1649), Charles II, James II, Mary II (and her husband William III), and Anne (d. 1714). The Crown then passed to the Hanoverians (*see* Settlement, Act of) but the Stuart claim was kept alive by *James Edward Stuart the Old Pretender, and his son, *Charles Edward Stuart the Young Pretender. The last royal Stuart was Henry Stuart, Cardinal York (d. 1807), the younger son of the Old Pretender.

GEORGE STUBBS *A portrait of Joseph Smyth and his horse (c. 1760–65); on loan to the Tate Gallery.*

Stubbs, George (1724-1806) British animal painter. Largely self-taught as an artist, Stubbs studied anatomy; his earliest works included illustrations for a midwifery textbook (1751) and *The Anatomy of the Horse* (1766), for which he made dissections. He is best known for his horse paintings, such as *Mares and Foals in a Landscape* (Tate Gallery), but he also painted portraits and farming scenes. His meticulous observation of nature reflects his maxim that nature is always superior to art.

Stubbs, William (1825-1901) British historian and churchman. He was Regius Professor of Modern History at Oxford (1866-1901) and Bishop of Chester (1884-89) and of Oxford (1889-1901). A good palaeographer and textual critic, Stubbs is best known for his *Constitutional History of England* (1874-78).

stupa A Buddhist shrine in the form of a mound or dome with a central projection. An early example (c. 100 AD) at Sanchi in N central India is a solid brickwork mound surrounded by a carved stone railing. Some fine later stupas survive in Sri Lanka. When modified to become a reliquary the stupa evolved into the *pagoda.

sturgeon A *bony fish belonging to a family (*Acipenseridae*; about 24 species) found in N temperate fresh and salt waters. Sturgeons have a large sharklike body, up to

8.4 m long, with five longitudinal rows of sharp bony plates, a small ventral mouth, and four sensory barbels. They feed near the bottom on small animals and plants. Eggs are laid in fresh water and are commercially important as caviar. *See also* beluga. □fish.

Sturluson, Snorri (1178-1241) Icelandic poet, who was also the author of the *Prose Edda* (*see* Eddas). A leading Icelandic nobleman, Sturluson visited Norway (1218, 1237) and intrigued against King Haakon, who intended to invade Iceland. Haakon had Sturluson murdered in 1241. His work includes a life of St Olaf and the *Heimskringla* (1223-35), a series of sagas about the Norse kings.

Sturm und Drang (German: Storm and Stress) A German literary movement of the late 18th century that anticipated many aspects of Romanticism. Its influence is most notable in the drama, characterized by epic scale and the rejection of structural conventions. Goethe and Schiller were leading writers of this movement during their early careers.

Sturt, Charles (1795-1869) British explorer. An army captain, he went to Australia in 1827 and led three expeditions into the interior. He discovered the Darling River (1828) and in 1829 in a whaleboat explored the Murrumbidgee to its confluence with the Murray. In 1844, believing in the existence of an inland sea, he tried unsuccessfully to cross the Simpson Desert.

Stuttgart 48 47N 9 12E A city in SW West Germany, the capital of Baden-Württemberg on the River Neckar. It became the capital of Württemberg in 1482. It was largely destroyed in World War II. One of West Germany's main industrial centres, its manufactures include electrical goods, cars, and metallurgical goods. It is also a centre for banking, exhibitions, and publishing. It has a university (1967). Population (1980 est): 582 400.

Stuyvesant, Peter (c. 1610-72) Dutch colonial administrator; governor of New Netherland (1647-64). His unpopular autocratic rule, which denied religious and political freedom, ended when the British forcibly took over the colony, dividing it into New York and New Jersey.

stye A small abscess at the root of an eyelash. Styes, which commonly occur in crops, are usually treated with warm compresses to drain the pus.

stylops A minute insect of the order *Strepsiptera* (about 400 species), which is parasitic on bees and other insects, affecting their reproductive systems and secondary sexual characteristics. The grublike female lives permanently inside the host's body; the winged male, often less than 4 mm long, leaves its host to find and fertilize a female. After hatching, the larvae complete their development in a larval host.

Styria (German name: Steiermark) A federal state in SE Austria, bordering on Yugoslavia. It possesses important mineral resources and the Erzberg is Austria's chief source of iron ore; other minerals include lignite and magnesite. Area: 16 384 sq km (6326 sq mi). Population (1981): 1 184 175. Capital: Graz.

Styx In Greek mythology, the main river of Hades across which the souls of the dead were ferried by *Charon. It was sometimes personified as the daughter of Oceanus. After she helped Zeus in his war against the Titans, oaths sworn in her name were held to be inviolable.

Suárez (Gonzalez), Adolfo, Duke of (1932-   ) Spanish statesman; prime minister (1976-81). He was appointed by King Juan Carlos to guide Spain into democracy.

Suarez, Francisco de (1548-1617) Spanish Jesuit tneologian. He is known for his synthesis of Thomist and Aristotelian philosophy. He developed the theological system of congruism, the reconciliation of grace and free will. In *De legibus* (1612), he expounded the principles of natural and divine law.

subconscious. *See* unconscious.

sublimation In chemistry, the evaporation of a solid without melting. For any substance the liquid phase only occurs within certain limits of temperature and pressure—if the pressure is low enough, heating a solid will result in sublimation. Substances that sublime at atmospheric pressure include carbon dioxide (dry ice) and iodine.

submachine gun A light short-range *small arm developed from the infantry light machine gun. Submachine guns became militarily popular after 1918, filling the gap between the pistol and the rifle, by offering greater fire-power than either. They are also more accurate than the pistol and smaller than the rifle. The first successful type was the *tommy gun, but now all major armies have their own designs. Almost all use 9 mm ammunition, fire automatically, and depend on blowback action (i.e. use the expanding gas of the ammunition to activate the reloading mechanism).

submarine A warship designed for sustained operation under water. The earliest record of a submarine craft is that developed by Cornelis Drebbel (1572-1634) of Holland in 1620, demonstrated before James I in 1624 in the Thames estuary. A more practical model, the "Turtle," was invented by David Bushnell (1742-1824) of Connecticut in 1776, and saw limited use in the American Revolution. Submarines, called U-**boats** (German name: *Unterseeboot*, undersea boat), were first used extensively by the German navy in World War I. They became an important armament in World War II, when the German navy sank millions of tons of Allied ships, especially supply ships in convoy from the USA to the UK and the Soviet Union. The US navy used submarines to advantage against the Japanese, when 63% of all Japanese merchant shipping exceeding 1000 tons of cargo weight was sunk and 276 war vessels of various kinds were destroyed. Modern submarines may be powered by nuclear reactors, which require no air for recharging batteries and, hence, can remain submerged for months at a time. These vessels also carry one or more guns mounted on deck, torpedoes for firing under water, and surface-to-air or surface-to-surface missiles that can be launched when the submarine is submerged.

Subotica 46 04N 19 41E A town in N central Yugoslavia, in Serbia near the Hungarian border. It has a large Hungarian minority and is an agricultural trading centre. Its manufactures include metal goods, chemicals, and food products. Population (1981 est): 154 611.

subsidence The sinking of part of the earth's surface relative to the surrounding area. On a large scale it may result from crustal movements (e.g. rift valleys). On a small scale it may result from collapsed mining excavations, collapsed roofs of limestone caves, etc. Subsidence involves vertical movement and lacks the horizontal component of landslides, etc.

substitution reaction A type of chemical reaction in which one atom or group of atoms is displaced by another. An example is the reaction of methyl chloride (CH_3Cl) with hydroxide ions (OH^-) to give methanol (CH_3OH) and chloride ions (Cl^-). The hydroxide ion, in this case, is referred to as the substituent. *See also* addition reaction.

succession In ecology, the process of continual change that takes place in the composition of a *community of organisms occupying a particular habitat from the time of its initial colonization to the establishment of a stable *climax community. Succession is influenced by many factors, principally the nature of the habitat, climatic changes, and the effects of colonization on the habitat.

Suckling, Sir John (1609-42) English poet and dramatist. From 1632 he spent his time as a courtier and was famous for his wit, generosity, and his taste for gambling. A loyal supporter of Charles I at the beginning of the Civil War, he was later discovered to be involved in a plot (1641) to free the imprisoned Earl of *Strafford and was forced to flee to Paris, where, according to John *Aubrey, he committed suicide. He wrote four plays and many elegant short lyrics.

Sucre 19 00S 65 15W The capital of Bolivia, in the S at an altitude of 2790 m (9153 ft). It was founded by the Spanish in 1538 on the site of an Indian settlement. The centre of the revolutionary movement against Spain, it became the capital in 1859. The seat of government was moved to La Paz in 1898. The St Francis Xavier University was established in 1624. Population (1982 est): 79 941.

Sucre, Antonio José de (1795–1830) South American revolutionary, born in Venezuela. The most able of *Bolívar's generals, Sucre defeated the Spaniards at Ayacucho (1824) and established the republic of Bolivia. He was its president from 1826 to 1828, when he resigned after a rebellion. The capital city, Sucre, is named after him.

sucrose (cane sugar *or* beet sugar *or* saccharose)   A carbohydrate consisting chemically of one molecule each of *glucose and *fructose linked together. It is commercially the most important of the *sugars, being used as a sweetener in foods and drinks. When heated to 160°C it forms barley sugar and at 200°C becomes caramel.

Sudan, Republic of the   A large country in NE Africa, bordering on the Red Sea. It consists chiefly of a vast plateau rising to mountains in the S and W, reaching heights of over 3000 m (10 000 ft). The main rivers are the Blue Nile and White Nile, which join at Khartoum and provide the country's main source of water. About half the population are Arabs, and there are minorities of *Dinka, Nubians, and others. *Economy*: chiefly agricultural, the main cash crop and export being cotton; other crops include sorghum, sugar, and groundnuts, and production is being increased by means of irrigation schemes, such as the *Gezira irrigation scheme. Livestock rearing is also important. Forest products include gum arabic, of which the Sudan is the world's main producer. Mineral resources include iron ore, gold, and manganese. *History*: the NE was part of ancient *Nubia, which dominated Egypt (c. 730–670 BC). The region was Christianized in the 6th century and resisted invasion from the N until the 13th century, after which it was converted to Islam. In 1821 it was conquered by the Egyptians, against whom a revolt under the Mahdi (*see* Mahdi, al-) took place in 1881. In 1898 an Anglo-Egyptian force under Kitchener subdued his followers and in 1899 an Anglo-Egyptian condominium was established. In 1956 the Sudan became an independent republic. After a coup in 1958 it was ruled by a military government until 1964, when civilian rule was restored. Another coup in 1969 brought Col Jaafar al Nimeiry (1929–   ) to power. A revolt in the S lasted from 1955 until 1973, when the S won a certain measure of self-government. In the midst of widespread famine in 1985, Nimeiry was overthrown; the subsequent coalition government collapsed in 1987. Official language: Arabic; English is widely spoken. Official currency: Sudanese pound of 100 piastres and 1000 millièmes. Area: 2 500 000 sq km (967 500 sq mi). Population (1980 est): 18 400 000. Capital: Khartoum. Main port: Port Sudan.

Sudbury   46 30N 81 01W A city in E Canada, in Ontario. Established in 1883, it is one of the world's greatest mining cities, especially for nickel and copper. A distribution and commercial centre for NE Ontario, Sudbury has important timber and tool industries. It houses the bilingual Laurentian University (1960). Population (1981): 91 829.

Sudetenland   A mountainous region on the W borders of Czechoslovakia. The Sudetenland, incorporated in Czechoslovakia in 1919, formed a defensible frontier with Germany, with which its predominantly German population wanted reunion. Nazi pressure resulted in the *Munich Agreement of 1938, which permitted German occupation of the area. After World War II Czechoslovakia regained the Sudetenland and expelled the Sudeten Germans.

Su Dong Po (*or* Su Tung-p'o; 1036–1101) Chinese poet, essayist, and painter, whose father Su Hsün (*or* Su Xun; 1009–66) and brother Su Tse-yu (*or* Su Ze-yu; 1039–1112) were also famous writers. An imperial official, he was

imprisoned and exiled on several occasions for his satirical verses and criticisms of government policies. His poems introduced more varied metres and subjects into the traditional verse forms of his period.

Sue, Eugène (Joseph Marie S.; 1804–57) French novelist. He worked as a ship's doctor until 1829. He achieved popular success with his novels about the Parisian underworld, notably *Les Mystères de Paris* (1842–43). *Le Juif errant* (1844–45) expressed his socialist sympathies.

Suetonius (Gaius Suetonius Tranquillius; c. 69–c. 140 AD) Roman historian and biographer. He was a friend of Pliny the Younger and served as secretary to the emperor Hadrian. Of his many works only *Lives of the Twelve Caesars* and fragments of *Lives of Famous Men* survive. His work is especially informative about the private lives of his subjects.

Suez (Arabic name: As-Suways)   29 59N 32 33E A port in Egypt, on the Gulf of Suez near the mouth of the Suez Canal. An important refuelling station, it was virtually deserted following the Arab-Israeli War of 1967 and its oil refineries were damaged. Since the reopening of the Suez Canal (1975), rebuilding has taken place. Population (1983 est): 241 000.

Suez Canal   A canal in Egypt connecting the Mediterranean Sea and the Red Sea. Running between Port Said in the N and Suez in the S (via the Great and Little Bitter Lakes), it is 165 km (103 mi) long. It is of great importance to much of the world's shipping. It was designed by the French engineer Ferdinand de Lesseps and was opened in 1869. In 1888 it became a neutral zone, with Britain the guarantor of its status. In 1956, following the withdrawal of British troops, President Nasser nationalized the canal, provoking an Anglo-French attack on Egypt. However, they withdrew within a few days in the face of international censure. The canal was closed from 1967 to 1975 because of Arab-Israeli hostilities and was not opened to Israeli ships until April, 1979. The canal is being deepened to take the much larger oil tankers now in use.

Suffolk   A county in E England, in *East Anglia bordering on the North Sea. It consists of undulating lowlands. The principal rivers are the Little Ouse, Wavensey, Orwell, Deber, and Stour. It is mainly agricultural, producing cereals and sugar beet, and is noted for its horse breeding (Suffolk Punches). Industries are generally related to agriculture. Fishing is centred on Lowestoft. Under local government reorganization in 1974, it lost small parts to Norfolk and Cambridgeshire. Area: 3800 sq km (1467 sq mi). Population (1981 est): 596 354. Administrative centre: Ipswich.

Suffolk Punch   A breed of draught horse originating in Suffolk, England. It has a powerful round body and short thick neck and legs and is always chestnut. Hardy and docile, Suffolks are still employed for local haulage by some breweries. Height: about 1.63 m (16 hands).

suffragettes.   *See* women's movement.

Sufism (Arabic *sufi*: wearer of a woollen cloak, mystic)   A mystical movement arising within Islam in the 8th and 9th centuries AD. The goal of the Sufis was mystical union with God achieved by fervent worship. Later Sufism shows the influence of Neoplatonism and some devotional practices, such as rhythmical body movements, may derive from Hindu asceticism. Sufi thought has influenced leading Arabic and Persian poets. As it evolved, Sufism divided into different orders or brotherhoods, a number of which survive at present and have been introduced into the West. *See also* dervishes.

sugar beet   A biennial herb derived from the European sea *beet (*Beta vulgaris*). Sugar beet is widely cultivated for the sucrose content of its large roots, which is over 20% by weight in modern commercial varieties. Sugar was first extracted from beet in the 18th century and the plant is now a major source of sugar, especially in Europe and the Soviet Union. Family: *Chenopodiaceae.*

sugar cane A perennial grass of the tropical genus *Saccharum* (5 species), especially *S. officinarum*, which is cultivated in tropical and subtropical regions for its sugar content. The clumps of stalks (canes), 3–8 m high, have lance-shaped leaves and may bear dense woolly clusters of female flowers. Usually, the canes are cut before flowering and crushed between rollers to extract the sugary liquid. This is concentrated and refined to produce sucrose crystals for table sugar, etc. The remaining liquor (molasses) is used for animal feedstuffs, industrial alcohol, etc., and is fermented to make rum. The fibrous residue (bagasse) is used as fuel and for paper making, cattle feed, etc.

sugars A class of sweet-tasting *carbohydrates, classified chemically as *monosaccharides or *disaccharides. The sugar widely used to sweeten food, drinks, and confectionery is the disaccharide *sucrose, some 70–80 million tonnes of which are produced annually. Half of this total is derived from the stems of sugar cane (11–15% sucrose) and half from the roots of sugar beet (17% sucrose).
Sugar manufacture is believed to have originated in India (Sanskrit *sarkara*, sand) around 3000 BC, the method travelling westwards through Arab countries (*sukkar*), Greece (*sákharon*), Italy (*zucchero*), and France (*sucre*). It was taken to the New World by Christopher Columbus in 1493. Until the mid-18th century it was an expensive luxury, used primarily as a medicinal sedative.
Sucrose is extracted from raw sugar cane by pressure, the extract being crystallized by evaporation. It is extracted from beet by hot water. Raw cane sugar and beet sugar are further refined to produce the granulated, caster, icing, and cube sugars familiar to commerce. By-products from sugar processing include molasses and sugar-beet pulp, both of which are used in animal feedstuffs.

Suger of Saint-Denis (1081–1151) French abbot and statesman. Suger was educated at the Abbey of Saint-Denis, becoming abbot in 1122. He introduced reforms based on the example of St *Bernard of Clairvaux. As adviser to both Louis VI (1081–1137; reigned 1108–37) and Louis VII (c. 1121–80; reigned 1137–80), Suger wielded considerable political influence.

Suharto (1921–) Indonesian statesman and general; president (1968–). He gained prominence in the struggle for Indonesian independence from the Netherlands, becoming chief of the army staff in 1965. He came to power in the gradual overthrow (1965–68) of Sukarno.

suicide Intentional self-destruction. Condemned by Christianity, Judaism, and Islam, suicide is a criminal offence in some societies. In the UK, for example, until the 19th century suicides were not permitted burial in consecrated ground but were interred in public highways with a stake through the heart. Only in 1961 did suicide cease to be a criminal offence under English law. In many traditional societies suicide, whether voluntary or an honourable obligation, is an accepted practice. Compulsory suicide may be performed out of loyalty to a dead master or spouse, derived from the once widespread custom of immolating wives and servants, or in the interest of the group as a whole, such as self-murder by elderly members of a community no longer able to provide for their own subsistence. In certain instances suicide might be offered to a privileged few as an alternative to execution, as among the Greeks (*see* Socrates), the Roman nobility, and the feudal Japanese aristocracy. With the breakdown of traditional practices, especially in industrial societies, the causes of suicide become less clear. Since Durkheim's classic statistical study *Suicide* (1897) sociologists have sought to relate the incidence of suicide to social pressures and the importance of social integration (*see* anomie). Psychologists have emphasized the importance of guilt, anxiety, and loneliness; they have also distinguished between attempted suicide (when death is intended but

averted) and parasuicide (when self-injury but not death is intended). *See also* Samaritans.

Sukarnapura. *See* Jajapura.

Sukarno (1901–70) Indonesian statesman, the first president of Indonesia (1945–65). He helped to found the Indonesian Nationalist Party in 1927 and was Indonesia's leader during the Japanese occupation (1942–45). When Indonesia was declared independent he became president. In 1957 with popular and military support, he introduced so-called Guided Democracy. A military coup deposed him in 1965–66.

Sukhumi 43 01N 41 01E A port in the SW Soviet Union, the capital of the Abkhaz ASSR in the Georgian SSR on the Black Sea. It occupies the site of the ancient Greek colony of Dioscurias and is a popular resort. Population (1981 est): 114 000.

Sukkur 27 42N 68 54E A city in Pakistan, on the River Indus. Nearby is the major irrigation project, the Sukkur (or Lloyd) Barrage (1923–32). Industries include textiles and cement. Population (1981): 191 000.

Sulawesi (former name: Celebes) An island in Indonesia, off E Borneo. Irregularly shaped, it is mountainous and forested, with rich mineral deposits. It is Indonesia's chief producer of copra and nickel. Area, including adjacent islands: 189 033 sq km (72 986 sq mi). Population (1980): 10 409 533. Chief towns: Ujung Pandang and Menado.

Suleiman (I) the Magnificent (?1494–1566) Ottoman sultan (1520–66), under whom the Ottoman Empire reached its peak. Suleiman captured Belgrade in 1521 and Rhodes in 1522. In 1526 he defeated the Hungarians at *Mohács and annexed large parts of Hungary. In 1529 he besieged Vienna. In campaigns against Persia he made many conquests, including Baghdad (1534), and the Ottoman navy, under *Barbarossa and others, controlled the E Mediterranean. To the Turks Suleiman is known as the Lawgiver because of the many regulations issued during his reign.

sulky A two-wheeled vehicle drawn by a horse, consisting of a light springy frame bearing a single seat for the driver and supported on wheels like bicycle wheels. Used now in *harness racing, this type of cart was used in the 19th century by doctors and others needing to travel alone and was so called supposedly because of the inventor's temperament.

Sulla, Lucius Cornelius (c. 138–78 BC) Roman dictator, associated with the aristocratic party; an opponent of *Marius and *Cinna. Nicknamed Felix (Lucky), he enjoyed early success. Enraged because his command against *Mithridates was transferred to Marius, he stormed Rome (87), forcing Marius and Cinna to flee. Although outlawed when his rivals returned, he successfully concluded the campaign against Mithridates and in 83 invaded Italy and took Rome. Elected dictator, Sulla butchered his political opponents. After legislating to restore the Senate's constitutional powers, he retired into private life (79).

Sullivan, Sir Arthur (1842–1900) British composer. He is best known for his collaboration with the librettist W. S. *Gilbert in such comic operas as *The Pirates of Penzance* (1879), *The Mikado* (1885), and *The Yeomen of the Guard* (1888). He also composed the grand opera *Ivanhoe* (1891).

Sullivan, John Lawrence (1858–1918) US boxer, generally considered the first modern world heavyweight champion (1882–92). He lost his title to Jim Corbett (1866–1933) in the first championship fought under the Queensberry Rules (*see* boxing).

Sullivan, Louis Henry (1856–1924) US architect. Working principally in Chicago, Sullivan was one of the leading figures of the modern architectural movement. His work, begun in the classical style, was modified by *Art Nouveau and developed into a form of *functionalism. He was among the first to design skyscrapers, such as the Wainwright building, St Louis (1890), and the Carson store, Chicago

(1899), in both of which the structural framework is clearly visible.

Sully, Maximilien de Béthune, Duc de (1560-1641) French statesman; chief minister to *Henry IV. Sully's financial reforms were fundamental in restoring prosperity after the *Wars of Religion. He retired (1611) following Henry's assassination.

Sully-Prudhomme, René François Armand (1839-1907) French poet. His early verse was lyrical and subjective, but his involvement with the *Parnassians, who favoured greater impersonality, led to his attempts in *La Justice* (1878) and other works to write epical philosophic verse. He won the Nobel Prize in 1901.

sulphonamides (*or* sulpha drugs) A group of drugs, derived from sulphanilamide, that prevent the growth of bacteria and were first used in 1936, to treat infections associated with childbirth. Sulphonamides are used to treat a wide variety of infections, particularly those of the urinary tract (e.g. sulphamethiazole) and the eye (e.g. sulphacetamide). Sulphonamides are also combined with trimethoprim (*see* co-trimoxazole), which improves their effectiveness. The sulphonamide sulphasalazine helps the treatment of ulcerative colitis and Crohn's disease. In some patients sulphonamides may cause severe allergic disorders.

sulphur (S) A yellow nonmetallic solid element, occurring in various crystalline and amorphous forms. Sulphur was known in ancient times as brimstone. It is found near volcanoes and in large deposits associated with oil trapped against salt domes, from which it is extracted commercially. Extraction is by the Frasch process, in which the sulphur is melted with superheated steam and pumped to the surface. Sulphur reacts readily with many elements to form sulphides, sulphates, and oxides. Common compounds include sodium sulphide (Na_2S), zinc sulphide (ZnS), the poisonous gas hydrogen sulphide (H_2S), copper sulphate ($CuSO_4$), and calcium sulphate ($CaSO_4$). The oxides SO_2 and SO_3 are acidic gases that dissolve in water to form sulphurous acid (H_2SO_3) and *sulphuric acid (H_2SO_4). At no 16; at wt 32.06; mp 113°C; bp 444.6°C.

sulphuric acid (H_2SO_4) A colourless oily liquid that has a great affinity for water and is used as a drying agent. Mixing with water must be carried out carefully because of the heat produced. H_2SO_4 is made by the contact process, in which sulphur dioxide is heated and passed through columns of platinized asbestos catalyst to produce sulphur trioxide (SO_3). The SO_3 is then dissolved in water to form H_2SO_4. Adding further SO_3 to H_2SO_4 produces fuming sulphuric acid (oleum; $H_2S_2O_7$), a fuming liquid that forms a crystalline solid on cooling.

Sulphuric acid is one of the most important industrial chemicals, being used in the manufacture of fertilizers, paints, rayon, explosives, and many other products, as well as in oil refining and car batteries.

Sulu Archipelago An island group in the SW Philippines, between Borneo and Mindanao. The most important of its 400 volcanic and coral islands are Basilan and Jolo. Area: 2815 sq km (1087 sq mi). Population (1980): 555 239. Chief town: Jolo.

sumach (*or* sumac) A tree or shrub of the genus *Rhus* (250 species), native to warm temperate and subtropical regions. The leaves of the Sicilian sumach (*R. coraria*) yield a substance used in tanning and dyeing. Several species are cultivated as garden ornamentals: the stag's-horn sumach (*R. typhina*) of North America grows to a height of 7-12 m and has a crimson or orange autumn foliage. Some species are poisonous and irritate the skin on contact, particularly the American *poison ivy and poison sumach (*R. vernix*). Family: *Anacardiaceae*. *See also* lacquer tree.

Sumatra (*or* Sumatera) The second largest Indonesian island, separated from Peninsular Malaysia by the Strait of Malacca. The mountainous volcanic spine descends in the

NE to swamps. Producing over 75% of the country's exports, it is Indonesia's chief rubber and oil producer and also possesses large natural gas deposits and other minerals. Crops include coffee, tea, and pepper. *History*: the Buddhist kingdom of Sri Vijaya (7th-13th centuries) was based in Palembang, spreading through Indonesia and the Malay Peninsula. During the 15th century the Islamic influence became dominant, resisting Dutch domination in the N until 1908. Since 1949 there has been considerable separatist activity directed against the Java-based government. Area: 524 097 sq km (202 311 sq mi). Population (1980): 28 016 160. Chief towns: Palembang and Medan.

Sumer The area in S Mesopotamia in which the earliest civilization evolved during the 4th millennium BC. The fertile natural environment encouraged settlements that grew into such cities as *Ur and *Eridu with all the prerequisites of civilized life: a writing system (*see* cuneiform), accumulation of wealth through trade, specialist organization of labour, and sophisticated crafts and architecture. Politically Sumer was a collection of independent city states, each with its own patron deity. Centralized control was temporarily asserted by neighbouring *Akkad (c. 2300 BC) and after 2000 BC Sumer was gradually absorbed into *Babylonia.

summer cypress Either of two annual herbaceous plants, *Kochia scoparia* or *K. trichophylla*, native to temperate Eurasia and cultivated as ornamentals. They form compact bushes, 1-1.5 m high, and the foliage assumes an attractive red-bronze colour in autumn. Family: *Chenopodiaceae*.

summer time A time system in which one hour, usually, is added to local (clock) time, i.e. to Greenwich Mean Time in the UK, so prolonging useful daylight hours. Summer time is used in temperate latitudes in spring, summer, and early autumn.

sun The nearest star, lying at an average distance of 149.6 million km from earth at the centre of the *solar system. It has a diameter of 1 392 000 km, a mass of 1.99×10^{30} kg, and rotates on its axis in a mean period of 25.38 days (the period lengthening as solar latitude increases). It is a typical yellow (G2) main-sequence star and is composed primarily (99%) of hydrogen and helium in the approximate ratio 3:1 by mass.

In its hot central core, about 400 000 km in diameter, energy is generated by nuclear fusion reactions. This energy is transported to the sun's surface, from where it is radiated into space, mainly as heat and light. The surface, called the *photosphere, is the boundary between the opaque outer (convective) zone of the sun's interior and its transparent atmosphere. The atmosphere comprises the *chromosphere and the inner and outer *corona. The corona extends many millions of kilometres into interplanetary space. There are regions of intense localized magnetic fields on the sun, extending from the photosphere through the chromosphere to the corona. A variety of phenomena occur in these active regions, including *sunspots, *solar prominences, and *solar flares. *See also* solar wind.

sun bear A *bear, *Helarctos malayanus*, of tropical forests of Asia, Sumatra, and Borneo. It is the smallest bear, (110-140 cm long) and climbs well, hunting in tall trees for small vertebrates, fruit, and its favourite food, honey.

sunbird An arboreal bird belonging to a tropical family (*Nectariniidae*; 104 species) ranging from Africa to Australasia. Sunbirds are 9-15 cm long and have a brilliant metallic plumage, slender down-curved bills, and long extensible tongues for feeding on nectar. Sunbirds are similar to New World hummingbirds but perch on flowers to feed rather than hovering in front of them.

sun bittern A Central American ground-dwelling bird, *Eurypyga helias*, that occurs in wet forests. 43 cm long, it has a brown, yellow, black, and white spotted plumage and feeds on insects with its sharp bill. It is the only member of its family (*Eurypygidae*). Order: *Gruiformes* (cranes, rails, etc.).

Sunda Islands   An Indonesian group of islands, the W part of the Malay Archipelago between the Indian Ocean and South China Sea. It consists of the **Greater Sunda Islands** including Sumatra, Java, Borneo, and Sulawesi and *Nusa Tenggara (formerly the Lesser Sunda Islands).

Sunderland   54 55N 1 23W A port in NE England, in Tyne and Wear at the mouth of the River Wear. Sunderland has exported coal from the Durham coalfield since the 14th century. Shipbuilding and ship repairing are important industries; there is also engineering, glass, pottery, chemicals, and paper manufacture. Population (1981 est): 196 152.

Sunderland, Robert Spencer, 2nd Earl of   (1641–1702) English statesman under Charles II, James II, and William III. He was secretary of state (1679–81) but was dismissed for supporting attempts to exclude the Roman Catholic James from the succession. He subsequently served James, becoming a Catholic in 1688. He fled England after James' deposition but returned in 1690 after renouncing Catholicism. He persuaded William to initiate a policy of selecting his ministers from the dominant party in the House of Commons.

sundew   A perennial or annual *carnivorous plant of the genus *Drosera* (about 100 species), of temperate and tropical regions. Sundews have a basal rosette of leaves covered in sticky reddish gland-tipped hairs, used to trap insects. The cup-shaped flowers are usually borne in a group on a stalk 6–35 cm long and are white, red, or purple. The fruit is a capsule. Family: *Droseraceae*.

sundial   An instrument that indicates the time by the direction or length of the shadow cast by an indicator (gnomon) mounted on a calibrated hour scale. Sundials may be fixed (mounted perpendicularly or horizontally) or portable (in which case they incorporate a device for direction finding) and come in a wide range of shapes. Known from ancient Egypt, Greece, and Rome, sundials reached the peak of their popularity between about 1500 and 1800, being used as a check on the accuracy of mechanical *clocks, which eventually superseded them.

Sundsvall   62 22N 17 20E A port in E Sweden, on the Gulf of Bothnia. It is icebound in winter. Industries include timber processing and timber and wood pulp are the main exports. Population (1983): 93 947.

sunfish   An omnivorous fish of the family *Molidae*, especially *Mola mola*, found in all tropical and temperate seas. It has a disc-shaped laterally flattened body, up to 3 m long, with the tail fin reduced to a wavy frill attached to the triangular dorsal and anal fins. Order: *Tetraodontiformes*.
The name is also applied to several carnivorous freshwater food and game fish of the North American family *Centrarchidae*. They have deep laterally flattened bodies, 2.5–80 cm long, and a single long dorsal fin. Order: *Perciformes*.

sunflower   A herbaceous plant of the genus *Helianthus*, native to North and South America but widely cultivated for its showy flowers. A popular annual sunflower is the giant *H. annuus*, about 3 m high with rough hairy leaves and yellow flower heads, up to 35 cm in diameter. It is cultivated both for ornament and for its seeds, from which oil is obtained. Perennial sunflowers include *H. salicifolius* and *H. decapetalus*. Family: *Compositae.

Sung.   *See* Song.

Sungari River.   *See* Songhua River.

sunn   An annual herb, *Crotalaria juncea*, cultivated in India for its stem fibres—called sunn hemp or sann hemp. It grows to a height of 2–3 m and produces small yellow flowers that give rise to seed pods, at which stage the crop is cut. The fibres, comparable in strength to true *hemp, are used for netting, canvas, yarns, and in certain paper products. Family: *Leguminosae*.

Sunnites   (*or* Sunni; Arabic *sunna*: custom)   The name of the larger of the two main Muslim Sects. In contrast to the *Shiite Muslims, the Sunnites accept the first three caliphs as Mohammed's legitimate successors. They are strictly orthodox in their obedience to the Koran and in the emphasis they place on following the deeds and utterances of the Prophet. They form the majority party in most Islamic countries except Iran.

sun spider   A large *arachnid (10–50 mm long), also called sun scorpion, belonging to an order (*Solpugida* or *Solifugae*; 800 species) found in tropical and semitropical deserts. It has a hairy spider-like body, usually golden in colour, and a large powerful pair of pincers. Sun spiders are voracious carnivores, the larger species even killing small vertebrates.

SUNSPOTS   *The sun photographed using white light on 9 April, 1970.*

sunspots   Comparatively dark markings on the sun's *photosphere, typically a few thousand kilometres across with the central region being darkest and coolest. They tend to occur in groups and can influence the climate on earth. They are centres of intense localized magnetic fields, the majority forming and disappearing within two weeks. The number of sunspots seen in a year, and their mean solar latitude, varies in a cycle of about 11 years, known as the **sunspot cycle**.

sunstroke   A form of *heatstroke caused by overexposure to the sun. **Sunburn** is damage to the skin resulting from overexposure to the sun's rays. This may vary from slight reddening to large painful blisters: fair-skinned people are more susceptible to sunburn due to lack of the protective pigment melanin in the surface layers of the skin. The burn is treated with soothing creams.

Sun Yat-sen   (*or* Sun Zhong Shan; 1866–1925) Chinese revolutionary. He qualified as a doctor but abandoned a medical career to pursue his political interests. After an abortive attempt to overthrow the Qing dynasty in 1895, he lived in exile and, while in Britain, was briefly imprisoned in the Chinese legation (1896). After establishing various revolutionary groups in Europe, he founded the Alliance Society in Japan (1905). Following the 1911 Chinese Revolution he returned to China, became president of the new republic but resigned almost immediately in favour of *Yuan Shi Kai. In 1913 Sun led an unsuccessful revolt against Yuan's dictatorial government and again left China. He returned after Yuan's death (1916) and in 1923 became president of a government based at Canton. Coming under Soviet influence he reorganized the *Guomindang (Nationalist People's Party), cooperated with the communists, and formulated Three Principles of the People—nationalism, democracy, and social reform. He remains a hero of both the Nationalist and communist Chinese governments.

superconductivity A phenomenon in which the electrical resistance of certain materials vanishes when they are cooled to low temperatures. The temperature at which superconductivity occurs is called the transition temperature and varies for different metals. If a loop of a superconducting substance is cooled to below its transition temperature, a current will flow through the loop indefinitely. The phenomenon was originally confined to metals at temperatures close to absolute zero. Ceramic superconductors have now been found that operate at higher temperatures, and these may be useful for power transmission and the generation of high magnetic fields.

supercooling The reduction in the temperature of a liquid below its freezing point without its solidification. The effect can only be achieved by slow and continuous cooling with pure liquids, since any solid matter would cause the liquid to solidify around it. A supercooled liquid is in a metastable state and any disturbance will cause solidification.

superego In *psychoanalysis, the part of the mind that acts as a moral conscience. It was believed by *Freud to result from the incorporation of the parent's instructions into a child's mind. *See also* ego; id.

superfluid A fluid that exhibits a very high thermal conductivity and virtually no friction at temperatures close to absolute zero. Such a fluid will flow up the sides and out of an open container. Liquid helium becomes a superfluid at 2.19 kelvins, called the lambda point.

supergiant The largest and most luminous type of star, bright enough to be visible in nearby galaxies. They evolve from very massive but more compact stars and are very rare. *Rigel, *Betelgeuse, and *Antares are examples. *See also* giant star.

superheated steam Dry steam that has been heated to a temperature above 100°C. It is widely used as a working medium for converting heat into mechanical energy, for which purpose it is more efficient than normal steam.

superheterodyne A system widely used in radio receivers; the incoming radio-frequency signal is combined with a locally generated carrier wave to give an intermediate frequency between radio- and audio-frequency (*see* modulation). The intermediate frequency is easier to amplify than radio-frequency, giving less noisy reception and better tuning.

Superior, Lake The largest of the Great Lakes in North America and one of the largest freshwater lakes in the world, situated between the USA and Canada. Its surrounding areas have valuable mineral resources and the lake is important for shipping. Area: 82 362 sq km (31 800 sq mi).

supernova A cataclysmic stellar explosion, seen as a sudden increase in a *star's brightness by a million times or more. It occurs late in the evolution of certain stars, one type almost certainly involving massive *supergiant stars, another type possibly disrupting *white dwarfs. Most or all of the star's substance is blown off at high velocity, forming an expanding gas shell—the **supernova remnant**. If the star's core survives, it will most probably end up as a *neutron star or *black hole. *See also* Crab nebula.

superphosphates Highly active phosphorus-containing fertilizers. Single superphosphate is made by reacting sulphuric acid with insoluble calcium phosphate rock to form calcium sulphate and soluble calcium hydrogen phosphate Ca $(H_2PO_4)_2$. Often the process is carried out under pressure. The product also contains sulphates of impurities present in the calcium phosphate. Triple superphosphate is more concentrated, since phosphoric acid is used instead of sulphuric, thereby creating fewer by-products.

Suppiluliumas I King of the *Hittites (c. 1375–c. 1335 BC); founder of the Hittite empire. He subdued the Mitanni kingdom and conquered N Syria, displacing the Egyptians, then ruled by Akhenaton (*see also* Ankhesenamen). Suppiluliumas rebuilt the Hittite capital Hattusas (*see* Boğazköy).

supply and demand Two concepts fundamental to economics. Supply is the amount of a commodity that producers are willing and able to sell, while demand is that amount that consumers wish to and are able to buy. These amounts vary with price: as the price rises, producers wish to sell more, while consumers wish to buy less, and vice versa as the price goes down. There is one price (the equilibrium price) at which producers wish to sell the same amount as consumers wish to buy (i.e. the market clears). The **market forces** of supply and demand in a free economy thus control the market price. However, they are almost completely suppressed in communist economies and in *mixed economies they may have only a restricted effect, depending on the extent to which government policy influences supply, demand, or price. For example, in the UK unbridled market forces have been controlled to some extent by a *prices and incomes policy.

suprematism An abstract Russian art movement founded (c. 1913) by the painter *Malevich. It was the first and one of the most austere geometrical styles of the 20th century. Although Malevich declared in 1919 that suprematism was over, it continued to be influential in the 1920s, particularly at the *Bauhaus (*see also* Kandinsky).

Supreme Court of the United States The highest law court in the USA, comprising the chief justice and eight associate justices appointed for life by the president. Its main functions include interpreting and safeguarding the constitution through the power to declare as unconstitutional laws passed by *Congress or the state legislatures. Other actions of the government, the president, and the judiciary are subject to review by the court. It also decides disputes between states and between one state and the citizens of another and hears appeals from state and federal courts. In the 20th century it has played an important role in abolishing racially discriminatory laws and in desegregating the public schools.

Sur. *See* Tyre.

Surabaja 7 14S 112 45E A port in Indonesia, in E Java on the Mas estuary. It was bombed by the British in 1945 during the struggle for the Indonesian Republic. It is Indonesia's second largest city and chief naval base, with a naval college and university (1954). Its industries include shipbuilding, oil refining, and rubber processing. Population (1980): 2 027 913.

Surakarta (*or* Solo) 7 32S 110 50E A city in Indonesia, in central Java on the River Solo. A cultural centre noted for its shadow plays, it is the site of a sultan's palace (1745). Batiks, musical instruments, and gold objects are produced. Population (1980): 469 888.

Surat 21 10N 72 54E A city in India, in Gujarat on the River Tapti. It was the Mogul Empire's chief port (16th–17th centuries). The first British trading post was established here (1612) and it was the headquarters of the East India Company until 1687. It has textile industries. Population (1981): 913 000.

surface tension A force occurring on the surface of a liquid that makes it behave as if the surface has an elastic skin. It is caused by forces between the molecules of the liquid: only those at the surface experience forces from below, whereas those in the interior are acted on by intermolecular forces from all sides. Surface tension causes a meniscus to form, liquids to rise up capillary tubes, paper to absorb water, and droplets and bubbles to form. It is defined as the force acting tangentially to the surface on one side of a line of unit length (newtons per metre) or as the work required to produce unit increase in surface area (joules per square metre).

surfactant A substance that lowers the surface tension of a liquid, thus allowing easier penetration and spreading. For this reason they are often known as **wetting agents**. Surfactants active in water are usually organic substances, for example *alcohols, and *soaps, the molecules of which contain both a water-soluble and a water-repelling portion; it is the latter that forces the molecules to the surface. Surfactants are widely used in *detergents, emulsifiers, paints, adhesives, inks, etc.

surgeonfish A tropical marine fish, also called tang, belonging to the family *Acanthuridae* (about 100 species). Its deep laterally flattened body, up to about 50 cm long, is often brightly coloured, with a single long dorsal fin, and a sharp bladelike spine on each side of the tail. They feed mainly on algae. Order: *Perciformes*.

surgery The branch of medicine in which disorders and injuries are treated by operation, usually with the patient in a state of *anaesthesia. Amputations and some elementary surgical operations have been performed since ancient times in Egypt, Greece, India, and China; the skills required were transmitted by Arab surgeons to Europe, where they were mostly practised in monasteries. Blood-letting—regarded as an antidote for most ailments—was widely practised. In England, however, in the 12th century, monks were forbidden to perform surgical operations and the practice passed to barbers until 1540. The two arts were then separated, although they continued to be controlled by the Company of Barbers and Surgeons until 1745. In this year the Company of Surgeons was formed, which became the Royal College of Surgeons in 1800.
The 19th century saw the foundation of modern surgery, with the introduction of anaesthetics, *Lister's discovery of antisepsis, and a greater knowledge of anatomy and physiology. In the 20th century the advent of antibiotics has made surgery safe from infection, the use of blood transfusions, intravenous drips, and electrolyte control have overcome problems of shock, and better knowledge of anaesthetics and relaxant drugs has made surgery a less hurried procedure. Moreover, specialization (e.g. gastrointestinal surgery, neurosurgery, ophthalmological surgery) and great ingenuity in the design of surgical instruments have made surgery a safe and usually successful procedure. Recent advances include techniques in *transplantation surgery, operations on the exposed heart, the use of extreme cold to destroy tissues (cryosurgery), the use of *lasers and *ultrasonics, and the development of microsurgery, in which surgeons operate through a special microscope using miniaturized instruments. *See also* plastic surgery.

Suriname, Republic of (name until 1948: Dutch Guiana) A country on the N coast of South America, on the Atlantic Ocean. Much of the land is covered by tropical forest, with coastal plains rising to higher land in the interior. The majority of the population is of Indian and mixed descent, with minorities of African descent, East Indians, and others. *Economy*: based primarily on bauxite, the chief industry is aluminium processing, and bauxite, alumina, and aluminium comprise the main exports. Its great agricultural potential remains relatively underdeveloped, the rice industry being the only fully developed sector. The vast forests are largely unexploited. Fishing is important, especially for shrimps. Hydroelectricity is a valuable source of power. *History*: sighted by Columbus in 1498, the first permanent settlement was established by the English in 1650. It was ceded to the Netherlands in 1667. During the Revolutionary and Napoleonic Wars it was again (1799–1802, 1804–16) under British rule. In 1949 it gained a certain measure of self-government, subsequently becoming an autonomous part of the Netherlands (1954) and then an independent republic (1975). At independence some 40 000 Surinamers emigrated to the Netherlands, to the detriment of Suriname's economy.

Following a coup in 1980, the National Military Council took power with Dr Henk Chin-a-Sen as prime minister and later president. He was replaced in 1982 by Errol Alibux, who was dismissed in 1984 by Lieut-Col Deysi Bouterse, who restored democracy; Ramsewak Shankar (1937–   ) became president in 1988. Suriname is a member of the OAS. Official language: Dutch; English, Hindustani, and Javanese are widely spoken; Surinamese is used as a lingua franca. Official currency: Suriname guilder of 100 cents. Area: 163 265 sq km (63 020 sq mi). Population (1980): 352 041. Capital and main port: Paramaribo.

surrealism A European movement in art and literature of the 1920s and 1930s. Surrealism began as a literary movement, when its leader, the poet André *Breton, published the surrealist manifesto in Paris (1924). Unlike its predecessor, the *dada movement, surrealism was not anti-art. Instead it aimed, under the influence of *Freud, to embody in art and poetry the irrational forces of dreams and the subconscious mind. To achieve this, such new techniques as automatic drawing and writing were employed. These involved allowing the subconscious mind to produce an unpremeditated design or poem. The leading surrealists were the poets *Aragon and *Eluard and the painters *Ernst, *Miró, *Dali, *Magritte, *Delvaux, and *Tanguy.

Surrey A county in SE England, bordering on Greater London. Under local government reorganization in 1974 it lost part of the SE to West Sussex. It is mainly low lying with the North Downs running E–W across the middle of the county. Although it has developed primarily as a residential and recreational area, agriculture is important in the S. Industry is mainly concentrated in the NE. Area: 1655 sq km (639 sq mi). Population (1981): 999 393. Administrative centre: Kingston-upon-Thames.

Surrey, Henry Howard, Earl of (1517–47) English poet. The son of the Duke of Norfolk, he led a precarious life in the service of Henry VIII, and was finally executed on a charge of treason lodged by his enemies at court. He pioneered the use of blank verse in his translation of Virgil's *Aeneid* (1557), and, with Sir Thomas *Wyatt, was responsible for introducing Italian forms and metres into English poetry.

surrogate motherhood. *See* artificial insemination.

Surtees, John (1934–   ) British racing motorcyclist and motor-racing driver, who won seven world championships as a motorcyclist (350 cc in 1958–60 and 500 cc in 1956, 1958–60) and later became world champion motor-racing driver (1964). He is the only man to have been world champion in both sports.

Surtees, Robert Smith (1803–64) British journalist and novelist. From 1831 to 1836 he edited the *New Sporting Magazine*, to which he contributed stories about the sporting life of English country gentry later collected in *Jorrocks's Jaunts and Jollities* (1838) and other volumes. His stories are characterized by realistic dialogue and observation and vigorous social satire.

Surtsey 63 18N 20 37W An island in the N Atlantic Ocean off S Iceland. It was formed by an underwater volcanic eruption (1963). Many scientific studies have been made here, especially of the colonization of flora and fauna.

surveying The measurement of distances, levels, angles, etc., on, above, or below the earth's surface. It is necessary for the delineation of property lines (**boundary surveying**) and for planning the construction of almost any building or structure. **Plane surveying** is suitable for smaller areas as it neglects the earth's curvature, whereas **geodetic surveying** does not. Topographic surveys locate natural features and elevations for map making, dam planning, etc.

Surya In Hindu mythology, the sun-god. He appears as a major deity in the *Vedas* and remained prominent as patron of numerous Hindu royal dynasties. Like his Greek counterpart *Apollo, he is represented as a charioteer.

Susa (*or* Shushan) An ancient city in SW Iran. Occupied

SUTTON HOO   *A large inlaid gold buckle found in the burial ship.*

since the 4th millennium BC, it was a capital of *Elam, whose rulers made successful forays against *Ur and *Babylon during the 2nd millennium. Susa's heyday was as administrative capital of the *Achaemenian kings of Persia (521–331). It continued to be important under Seleucid, Parthian, and Sassanian rule.

Suslov, Mikhail   (1902–82) Soviet politician. A Communist Party member from 1921, Suslov rose in the Party hierarchy during the 1930s and 1940s. He fought all deviation from Soviet policy, especially that of Yugoslavia in 1948. In 1964 he helped to oust *Khrushchev.

Susquehanna River   A river in the E USA. It rises in Otzego Lake in central New York State and flows mainly S through Pennsylvania before entering Chesapeake Bay. It caused serious flooding in 1972 to several cities, especially *Harrisburg. Length: 715 km (444 mi).

Sussex   A former county of S England. Under local government reorganization in 1974 it was divided into the counties of *West Sussex and *East Sussex. West Sussex gained part of S Surrey together with part of the former administrative area of East Sussex.

Sutcliffe, Herbert   (1894–1978) British cricketer, who played for Yorkshire and England. An opening batsman, known especially for his partnerships with *Hobbs, he scored 16 Test centuries and during his career (1919–45) totalled 50 135 runs and 149 centuries.

Sutherland   A former county of N Scotland. Under local government reorganization in 1975 it became part of the Highlands Region. Sutherland District partly corresponds with the former county.

Sutherland, Graham Vivian   (1903–80) British artist. After working primarily as an etcher and engraver he turned to painting in 1935, specializing in disturbing landscapes, usually magnifying insect and plant forms, and (while official war artist in World War II) scenes of war desolation. Also well known are his *Crucifixion* (1946; St Matthew's, Northampton), his tapestry for Coventry Cathedral, and his portraits, e.g. of Somerset Maugham (Tate Gallery) and his controversial portrait of Winston Churchill (destroyed on the instructions of Lady Churchill).

Sutherland, Dame Joan   (1926–   ) Australian operatic soprano. She established her reputation at Covent Garden in 1959 in the title role of Donizetti's *Lucia di Lammermoor*. She specializes in coloratura roles and is married to the conductor Richard Bonynge (1930–   ). She was made a DBE in 1977.

Sutlej, River   A river in India and Pakistan, the longest of the five rivers of the Punjab. Rising in SW Tibet, it flows mainly SW across the Punjab plain into Pakistan, where it joins the River Chenab. It is a source of irrigation and hydroelectric power. Length: 1368 km (850 mi).

suttee   An ancient Hindu custom of self-immolation of widows on their husbands' funeral pyres. It was officially abolished in India by the British in 1829.

Sutton   A mainly residential borough of S Greater London,

created in 1965 from parts of N Surrey. Population (1981): 168 407.

Sutton, Walter Stanborough   (1877–1916) US geneticist, who linked observations of chromosome behaviour during cell division with *Mendel's observations of inheritance of physical characteristics. Sutton postulated that chromosomes carried the units of inheritance (genes) and that their behaviour during sex cell formation (meiosis) explained some of Mendel's findings.

Sutton Coldfield   52 34N 1 48W A town in England, in West Midlands, a mainly residential suburb of Birmingham. It contains Sutton Park, a large area of woodland, lakes, and heathland, which was given to the people of the town in the 16th century. Population (1981): 86 494.

Sutton Hoo   The site of a Saxon ship burial near Woodbridge, in Suffolk (E England). Excavations in 1939 revealed the remnants of a 38-oar boat containing a magnificent treasure hoard: gilt bronze helmet, sword decorated with gold and garnets, royal sceptre, silver dishes, drinking vessels, and jewellery. The mound is thought to be a cenotaph (as it contained no body) to King Raedwald (died c. 625 AD).

Sutton-in-Ashfield   53 08N 1 15W A town in central England, in E Nottinghamshire. It lies in a coalmining district and manufactures hosiery and metal boxes. Population (1981): 41 270.

Suva   18 08S 178 25E The capital of Fiji, on the S coast of Viti Levu. Its industries include tourism and the production of coconut oil and soap. The University of the South Pacific was established here in 1968. Population (1982): 71 255.

Suvorov, Aleksandr Vasilievich, Count   (1729–1800) Russian field marshal. Following outstanding victories against the French revolutionary armies in Italy (1799), the defeat of a Russian force at Zurich forced his withdrawal. The winter retreat, achieved against desperate odds, assured Suvorov's reputation as a brilliant tactician.

Suwanee River (*or* Swanee R.)   A river in the SE USA, flowing from the Okefenokee Swamp in SE Georgia across Florida to the Gulf of Mexico. It is the Swanee River of the well-known song by Stephen Foster. Length: 400 km (200 mi).

Suzhou (Su-chou *or* Soochow)   31 21N 120 40E A city in China, in Jiangsu province on the Yangtze delta and the *Grand Canal. Famed for its many beautiful canals and gardens, it is a centre of culture and handicrafts. Founded in about 484 BC, it prospered, especially between the 14th and 19th centuries, as a result of its silk industry. The chief industry is still textiles. Population (1983 est): 670 000.

Svalbard (*or* Spitsbergen)   A Norwegian archipelago in the Arctic Ocean, the chief islands being Spitsbergen (formerly Vestspitsbergen), Edgeøya, Nordaustlandet, Barentsøya, and Prins Karls Forland. Following disputes over their sovereignty, the islands were granted to Norway in 1920. Mountainous and covered largely by icefields and glaciers their major importance is as a source of coal; other minerals include asbestos and copper. Area: 62 050 sq km (23 958 sq mi). Population (1981): 3737. Chief town: Longyearbyen.

Sverdlovsk (name until 1924: Ekaterinburg) 56 52N 60 35E A city in the Soviet Union, in the NW RSFSR. Nicholas II and his family were executed here in 1918. It is a major industrial and cultural centre, with engineering, metallurgical, and chemical industries and many educational institutions. Population: (1981 est): 1 239 000.

Sverrir (*or* Sigurdsson; c. 1149–1202) King of Norway (1177–1202). He claimed the throne after being informed by his mother that he was the son of a former king, but did not defeat his predecessor, Magnus V (1156–84; reigned 1162–84), until 1184. His story is told in the Icelandic *Sverris Saga*.

Svevo, Italo (Ettore Schmitz; 1861–1928) Italian novelist. His first two novels, *A Life* (1892) and *As a Man Grows Older*

(1898), were unsuccessful, but he was encouraged by James *Joyce, who taught him English in Trieste in 1907 and later publicized his work. His best-known novel is *Confessions of Zeno* (1923), a portrait of an introspective ineffectual hero.

Swabia (German name: Schwaben) A former region in SW Germany now divided between Germany, Switzerland, and France. Swabia became one of the leading German duchies in the middle ages, passing in 1079 to the *Hohenstaufen. When the dynasty died out in 1268 Swabia was divided among local noble families. A series of Swabian leagues culminated in that of 1488-1534, which foundered on religious differences during the Reformation. When Napoleon reconstructed European boundaries in 1807, Swabia was finally partitioned among neighbouring states; its distinguishing dialect still survives.

Swahili (*or* Kiswahili) A Bantu language of East Africa and the lingua franca of Tanzania, Kenya, Zaïre, and Uganda. There are three main dialects but standard Swahili is based on the Zanzibari form known as Kiunguja. It has been much influenced by Arabic.

swallow A songbird belonging to a cosmopolitan family (*Hirundidae*; 78 species) of acrobatic fliers that catch insects on the wing. Swallows are 10-22 cm long, with short necks, long pointed wings, short legs, and often forked tails. All temperate swallows migrate to hot climates for the winter. The barn swallow (*Hirundo rustica*) visits Europe and North America in summer and has a glossy blue-black upper plumage with a red forehead and throat, a blue breast band, and white underparts. *See also* martin.

swallowtail butterfly A *papilionid butterfly having long swallow-like tails on the hindwings. Many species are tropical and brightly coloured, with the sexes often of different colours. The caterpillars feed on a variety of plants and possess scent organs behind the head, giving off a strong odour if the caterpillar is disturbed. ⬚insect.

Swammerdam, Jan (1637-80) Dutch naturalist and microscopist, who first observed red blood cells. However, much of Swammerdam's work was concerned with collecting and studying insects, describing their anatomy and life histories, and classifying them into four groups, three of which are still embodied in modern classification systems. He discovered the Swammerdam valves in lymphatic vessels and established that muscles do not change in volume during contraction.

swamp An area of permanently water-saturated land, usually covered with such vegetation as reeds or mangroves. It is an intermediate stage between an entirely aquatic environment and a temporarily saturated marsh. Once drained, swamps produce fertile soils as a result of their high humus content.

swamp cypress A deciduous conifer, *Taxodium distichum*, also called bald cypress, native to swampy regions of the SE USA and grown for its timber and as an ornamental. In waterlogged soils its roots produce domed "knees," which protrude above the water and probably help in respiration. Up to 45 m high, it has soft needles arranged in two rows and globular cones, 2.5 cm across and brown when ripe. Family: *Taxodiaceae*.

swamp eel A slim eel-like bony fish of the order *Synbranchiformes*, unrelated to true eels and found in fresh and brackish tropical waters. 20-50 cm long, they have no pectoral fins and the gills often have only one opening. Oxygen is sometimes absorbed through the throat or intestine. Swamp eels are used for food in Asia.

swan A large waterbird belonging to a genus (*Cygnus*; 7-8 species) occurring worldwide on fresh waters or sheltered coasts and estuaries. 100-160 cm long, swans are usually white with black legs and have large feet, a long neck, and a powerful spatulate bill, which they use to feed on underwater plants. Immature swans have a mottled brown plumage until

about two years old. *See also* black swan; mute swan; trumpeter. Family: *Anatidae* (ducks, geese, swans).

Swan, Sir Joseph Wilson (1828-1914) British physicist, who in 1860 invented a lightbulb. It consisted of a carbon filament inside an evacuated glass bulb but its short lifetime limited its practical use. Swan also introduced the dry photographic plate and, in 1879, he developed bromide paper, which is now widely used in photographic prints.

Swanscombe skull Fossil cranial remains of a *hominid, fragments of which were found at Swanscombe in Kent (England) in River Thames gravels (1935, 1936). It seems to be an early example of *Homo sapiens* dating from about 200 000 years ago. *See* Homo.

Swansea (Welsh name: Abertawe) 51 38N 3 57W A city and port in South Wales, the administrative centre of West Glamorgan on Swansea Bay (a wide inlet of the Bristol Channel). It is the second largest city in Wales and a major industrial centre with tinplate manufacturing, chemicals, and oil refining (at Llandarcy). The main exports are coal and coke, steel rails, iron work, tinplate, and oil. Swansea University opened in 1920. Population (1981): 167 796.

swastika An ancient symbol of uncertain origin, generally held to signify prosperity and creativity. It is a cross, the four arms of which are deflected at right angles either clockwise or anticlockwise. It has been revered by Buddhists, Hindus, Celts, and North American Indians. The Nazis adopted the symbol, mistakenly believing it to be of pure Aryan origins.

Swatow. *See* Shantou.

Swazi A Bantu-speaking people who occupy Swaziland and adjacent areas of the E Transvaal (South Africa). They are an agricultural and pastoral people, traditionally ruled by a hereditary paramount chief together with his mother. Descent, inheritance, and group membership are patrilineal. Polygyny is practised by senior men, the chief taking many wives who are dispersed in a number of royal villages throughout the territory. *Age-set organization was the basis of military service. Traditionally *ancestor worship, witchcraft, and magic were features of religious life.

Swaziland, Kingdom of A small country in SE Africa between South Africa and Mozambique. It consists of three distinct regions extending N-S: the Highveld in the W, the Middleveld in the centre, and the Lowveld in the E (*see* veld). *Economy*: chiefly agricultural, the main food crop being maize. The chief cash crop is sugar; other crops include rice, citrus fruit, and cotton, and livestock raising is also important. Rich mineral resources include iron ore, asbestos, and coal, and hydroelectric schemes provide irrigation as well as power. Exports include sugar, wood pulp, and asbestos. *History*: the *Swazi occupied the area in the late 18th century. It became a South African protectorate in 1894 and, in 1902, after the Boer War it came under British rule. It attained internal self-government in 1967 and became an independent kingdom within the British Commonwealth in 1968. In 1973, King Sobhuza II (1899-1982) increased his personal power and, in the new constitution (1978), political parties were banned. In 1986 Prince Makhosetive (1969–) was inaugurated as King Mswati III. Prime minister: Sotsha Dlamini. Official languages: Siswati and English. Official currency, since 1974: emalangeni of 100 lilangeni; South African currency is also legal tender. Area: 17 400 sq km (6705 sq mi). Population (1981 est): 580 000. Capital: Mbabane; Lomamba is the royal and projected legislative capital.

sweat (*or* perspiration) A watery fluid, consisting mainly of sodium chloride and urea in solution, that is secreted by the sweat glands in the ⬚skin. Sweating is a means of excreting nitrogenous waste products, but it is also, and more importantly, a means of temperature regulation. Evaporation of sweat from the skin surface has a cooling effect; therefore in hot weather, or when the individual feels hot through exercise, more sweat is produced. Sweating is also increased by nervousness and nausea; it is decreased by colds.

sweating sickness An illness that devastated Renaissance Europe in several epidemics. It was characterized by copious sweating, high fever, pains in the extremities and over the heart, and breathlessness and was often fatal. It may have been a severe form of *influenza.

swede An annual or biennial herbaceous plant, *Brassica napus napobrassica*, growing to a height of 1 m, with deeply lobed leaves and yellow flowers. It is cultivated for its fleshy edible taproot, which is yellow, white, or purplish; this is eaten as a vegetable and also fed to livestock. The yellow variety is called rutabaga. Family: *Cruciferae*.

Sweden, Kingdom of (Swedish name: Sverige) A country in N Europe occupying the E part of the Scandinavian peninsula. It borders on the Gulf of Bothnia and the Baltic Sea in the E and S and on the Kattegat and Skagerrak in the SW. Undulating land in the S rises to mountains in the N. There are numerous lakes and approximately half the country is forested. *Economy*: rich in mineral resources, notably iron ore, which forms the basis of the country's heavy industry (metalworking, steel, machinery, and chemicals) and is a major export. Other minerals include copper and zinc. 70% of power comes from hydroelectric sources. The large forests support important pulp and paper industries as well as shipbuilding. There is a thriving fishing industry. Agricultural activities are concentrated in the S, the principal crops being barley, wheat, oats, and potatoes, although there is some livestock raising in the N. *History*: the area was inhabited from early times by German tribes, the Swedes in the N and the Goths in the S, and its people participated in the exploits of the Vikings. Christianity was introduced in the 9th century but not established until the 12th century. Finland was acquired in the 13th century and the 14th century witnessed the Kalmar Union of Sweden with Denmark and Norway. Independence was achieved in 1523 under Gustavus I Vasa, during whose reign Lutheranism was introduced, and in the 17th century, under Gustavus Adolphus, Sweden emerged from the *Thirty Years' War as a major European power, a position undermined by the Great *Northern War (1700-21). In 1809, during the Napoleonic Wars, Finland was surrendered to Russia. In 1814 Norway was ceded to Sweden, the two countries remaining united until 1905, and in 1818, with the extinction of the *Vasa dynasty, a Frenchman, *Bernadotte, became Charles XIV John. Sweden remained neutral in both World Wars, and for four decades (1932-76) was governed by the Social Democrats, during which time a comprehensive welfare state was developed. On the accession of Carl XVI Gustaf in 1975 a new constitution reduced the power of the monarchy. In 1976 a centre-right government led by Thorbjörn Fälldin (1926–) came to power. This resigned in 1978 but Fälldin was returned as prime minister in 1979. The Social Democrats led by Olof Palme (1927–86) won the 1982 elections; after Palme's assassination Ingvar Carlsson (1934–) became prime minister. Official language: Swedish. Official currency: krona of 100 oere. Area: 411 479 sq km (158 830 sq mi). Population (1980 est): 8 317 937. Capital and main port: Stockholm.

Swedenborg, Emanuel (1688-1772) Swedish scientist, mystic, and philosopher. As an official on the Swedish Board of Mines (1716-47) he did pioneering scientific work in such fields as magnetic theory and crystallography but later became more concerned to show by scientific and logical analysis that the universe was of spiritual origin. After 1743 his ideas became more mystically orientated in accordance with the visions that he claimed to have had. His work includes *Arcana Coelestia* (1756), *The New Jerusalem and Its Heavenly Doctrine* (1758), and *Divine Love and Wisdom* (1763). The sect calling itself the New Jerusalem Church (or

Swedenborgians) was founded by his followers in London in 1787.

Swedish A language belonging to the *Scandinavian branch of the North *Germanic group. It is the official language of Sweden and is spoken by a minority of the population of Finland, where it is also officially recognized. The standard literary form is based mainly on the dialect of Stockholm known as Svea.

sweet briar A stiffly branched prickly fragrant *rose, *Rosa rubiginosa* (or *R. eglanteria*), also called eglantine. Found in scrub and chalk grassland across the N hemisphere, it grows to a height of 2 m and has bright-pink flowers.

sweet corn. *See* maize.

sweet gale A widely distributed shrub, *Myrica gale*, also called bog myrtle, that grows to a height of 60-250 cm in bogs and wet heaths. It produces reddish-brown catkins and the leaves yield an aromatic resin used in medicines. Family: *Myricaceae*.

sweet gum A tree, *Liquidambar styraciflua*, native to E North America. Up to 45 m high, it has triangular-lobed leaves, small greenish flowers, and spiky fruits and yields a useful timber (satin walnut). The oriental sweet gum (*L. orientalis*), of SW Asia, is the chief source of *storax, a fragrant balsam. Family: *Hamamelidaceae*.

sweet pea An annual climbing herb, *Lathyrus odoratus*, native to Sicily and widely cultivated as a garden ornamental. The scented flower consists of a large petal (the standard) with two lateral wing petals and a front keel petal. Many colour varieties have been developed, including shades of red, purple, blue, white, and yellow. The fruit is a hairy pod, about 5 cm long. Family: *Leguminosae*.

sweet potato An annual herb, *Ipomoea batatas*, native to tropical America and widely cultivated for its starchy edible tubers (swollen roots), which are reddish-brown with white or orange flesh. The trailing stems bear pinkish flowers and, after a growing season of 4-5 months, the tubers are lifted and cooked like potatoes or yams. Family: *Convolvulaceae*.

sweetsop A small tree, *Annona squamosa*, also called sugar apple, native to tropical America and cultivated for its yellowish-green edible fruits. The yellow flesh is soft and sweet and makes a tasty dessert. Family: *Annonaceae*.

sweet william A usually biennial herb, *Dianthus barbatus*, native to S Europe and widely cultivated as a garden ornamental. Growing to a height of 30-70 cm, sweet williams produce dense flower heads, coloured red or pink in the wild but of various shades and patterns in cultivated varieties. Family: *Caryophyllaceae*.

Sweyn I Forkbeard (d. 1014) King of Denmark (c. 986-1014). After conquering Norway in 1000, Sweyn's regular raids on SE England to avenge Ethelred's massacre of Danes in 1002 culminated in an invasion in the course of which he died. He was the father of *Canute II.

swift A bird belonging to a widely distributed family (*Apodidae*; 75 species). 9-23 cm long, swifts have grey or brown plumage with white markings; a wide slightly curved bill, and forked tail. With scimitar-shaped wings and a high-speed flight that may reach 110 km per hour (nearly 70 mph), they spend much of their time flying, capturing insects and even mating and sleeping on the wing. Order: *Apodiformes* (swifts, hummingbirds, etc.).

Swift, Jonathan (1667-1745) Anglo-Irish clergyman, poet, and satirist. Born in Dublin, he became an Anglican priest in 1695 and served as secretary to Sir William Temple in England, where he met Hester Johnson (1681-1728), the "Stella" of his letters recounting his life in London and later collected as *Journal to Stella* (1710-13). He was also close to Esther Vanhomrigh (1690-1723), whom he called "Vanessa" in his writings. While in England, he wrote the satire *A Tale of a Tub* (1704). He became the leading Tory political journalist and was appointed dean of St Patrick's, Dublin, in 1713. After the accession of George I in 1714, he returned to

Dublin, where he wrote his satirical masterpiece, *Gulliver's Travels* (1726), the story of an imaginary voyage.

swiftlet A small *swift belonging to a genus (*Collocalia*; 15-20 species) occurring in SE Asia and Australia. 9-15 cm long, swiftlets use echolocation to navigate in the caves where they nest; their nests, made chiefly of saliva, are the main ingredient of bird's nest soup.

swift moth A moth belonging to the widely distributed family *Hepialidae* (about 300 species), also called ghost moth. The adults lack a proboscis and are unable to feed. The caterpillars feed under ground on roots and the pupae are soft-skinned and active, moving to the surface before the adults emerge.

swimming Moving through water by means of leg and arm strokes, popular for recreation and sport. Major competitive events, held in pools 50 m (55 yd) long, include freestyle races (the crawl—invented in Australia—is invariably used) over 100, 200, 400, 800, and 1500 m and the 4 × 100 m and 4 × 200 m relay; breaststroke, butterfly, and backstroke races over 100 and 200 m; and medley races over 200 and 400 m and 4 × 100 m relay. The most popular marathon swim is across the English Channel (first swum in 1875).

Swinburne, Algernon Charles (1837-1909) British poet. His poetry, especially in the first volume of *Poems and Ballads* (1866), is characterized by sensuous flowing rhythms and imagery. He supported republican movements in Europe and rebelled against conventional British morality. His alcoholism led to the collapse of his health, and from 1879 he was cared for by his friend, the critic Theodore Watts-Dunton (1832-1914).

Swindon 51 34N 1 47W A town in S England, in Wiltshire. It developed around the workshops of the former Great Western Railway and has a railway museum. Considerable expansion has taken place in recent years, following its designation as a suitable site for development under the Town Development Act (1952). Population (1981 est): 91 136.

swine fever An infectious virus disease of pigs. In young pigs the disease is usually acute, with fever, loss of appetite, lethargy, diarrhoea, and distressed breathing, resulting in death. In older pigs the symptoms are less noticeable. Animals are treated with antiserum and antibiotics to combat secondary infection. Thorough boiling of swill is essential to prevent contamination. In the UK any outbreak must be reported to the authorities and infected animals are slaughtered.

swing A style of *jazz popular in the 1930s. The original jazz band was expanded to include the saxophone and additional cornets and trombones, making an average swing band of 15 players. Colourful orchestrations replaced the improvisational qualities of early jazz, and the swing bands of Benny Goodman, Duke Ellington, and Glenn Miller functioned chiefly as dance bands.

switch grass A perennial pasture *grass, *Panicum virgatum*, which is a major component of the North American prairie flora. It forms clumps, 1-2 m tall, and is sometimes used to control erosion because of its penetrating underground stems.

Swithin, St (d. 862) English churchman. A counsellor to Kings Egbert and Ethelwulf, he was appointed Bishop of Winchester in 852. His tomb in Winchester Cathedral has become a famous shrine and according to legend the weather conditions on his feast day, 15 July, continue for 40 days.

Switzerland, Confederation of (French name: Suisse; German name: Schweiz; Italian name: Svizzera) A small landlocked country in central Europe. Undulating land in the N rises to the Jura Mountains in the W and the high peaks of the Alps in the S, reaching heights of over 4500 m (14 500 ft). The River Rhine and Lake Constance form most of the N and E boundaries, while in the S the River Rhône flows through Lake Geneva to the French border. The

majority of the population is German, with large French and Italian minorities; there is a very small Romansch population. *Economy*: although lacking in mineral wealth, Switzerland owes much of its prosperity to its terrain and central European position. The latter has led to its development as a centre for trade, banking, and insurance, while the magnificent scenery has long been a major tourist attraction. The fast-flowing rivers of the Alps provide abundant hydroelectric power and heavy industries, such as engineering and chemicals, have been developed as well as the smaller traditional industries (watches and clocks, precision instruments, and jewellery). Agricultural products include dairy goods, grains, and fruit and vegetables, and there is an important wine industry. The principal exports are machinery, watches, chemicals, and textiles. *History*: its Celtic inhabitants (the Helvetii) were conquered by the Romans in the 1st century BC and the region was overrun by German tribes in the 5th century AD, becoming part of the Holy Roman Empire in the 10th century. In 1291 Uri, Schwyz, and Nidwalden formed the Everlasting League, which is traditionally regarded as the origin of the Swiss Federation. By 1499 the Federation had achieved virtual independence of the Empire and in the 16th century became an important centre of the Reformation, notably under Zwingli in Zürich. In 1648, at the conclusion of the Thirty Years' War, its independence was formally recognized by the European powers. The French conquered Switzerland in 1798, establishing the Helvetian Republic, but after Napoleon's fall (1815) the Congress of Vienna guaranteed Swiss neutrality. Religious conflict led to war between Protestant and Roman Catholic cantons and a modified constitution (1848) by which Switzerland became a unified federal state. It maintained its neutrality through both World Wars and has become the headquarters of many international organizations. Switzerland's postwar prosperity has been assisted by migrant workers (*see* migration, human) the repatriation of whom was rejected in a referendum in 1975. Another controversial issue was the enfranchisement of women, which was finally achieved in 1971. Switzerland is governed by a federal council composed of seven councillors, elected for four years, from whom a president and vice president are elected yearly. Official languages: French, German, Italian, and Romansch. Official currency: Swiss franc of 100 centimes (*or* Rappen). Area: 41 288 sq km (15 941 sq mi). Population (1980 est): 6 365 960. Capital: Bern.

sword A weapon consisting of a cutting or stabbing blade on a short handle, used in hand-to-hand fighting. Of uncertain origin, the sword evolved in the Bronze Age. The Roman soldier's principal weapon was a short, two-edged, iron-bladed sword (*gladius*). In the middle ages heavier and longer swords, some needing to be wielded with two hands, developed in response to heavier armour. The advent of gunpowder forced foot soldiers gradually to abandon swords, but cavalry units until the 20th century fought with long often curved blades. *See also* fencing.

swordfish A food and game fish, *Xiphias gladius*, related to tuna and found in all tropical and temperate seas. It has an elongated body, up to 4.6 m long, a triangular front dorsal fin, no pelvic fins, and an elongated swordlike snout used to slash at shoaling fish on which it feeds. It is the only member of its family (*Xiphiidae*).

swordtail A tropical freshwater fish of the genus *Xiphophorus*, especially *X. helleri*. It has an elongated body, up to 13 cm long, and males have a long swordlike extension of the lower lobe of the tail fin. Swordtails are naturally green with a red strip on each side, but have been bred in many colours for aquaria. Family: *Poeciliidae*; order: *Atheriniformes*.

Sybaris 39 39N 16 20E A Greek settlement founded about 700 BC near present-day Terranova di Sibari in S Italy. Territorial expansion and a monopoly of Etruscan trade brought prosperity and Sybarites were famous for their luxurious lives (hence the word sybaritic, meaning pleasure seeking). In 510 and again in 457 Sybaris was destroyed by its neighbour Croton. Rebuilt a third time, its inhabitants were subsequently exiled by the Athenians.

sycamore A large *maple tree, *Acer pseudoplatanus*, native to central and S Europe and widely grown elsewhere. Up to 30 m tall, it has five-lobed leaves and produces clusters of winged ⬜fruits. The wood is used for violin cases, carvings, and furniture.

SYDNEY   *The Harbour Bridge with the Opera House in the background.*

Sydney 33 55S 151 10E The oldest and largest city in Australia, the capital of New South Wales, situated on *Port Jackson inlet. It is essentially a commercial, cultural, and financial centre dependent on its port for its prosperity. The N site of Port Jackson is predominantly residential, industry being located to the S. The two shores are connected by Sydney Harbour Bridge (1932), the second largest single span bridge in the world. Industry is diverse and includes shipbuilding, chemicals, and the manufacture of consumer goods; Botany Bay is developing as the main industrial area. The chief exports are wheat and wool. A cultural centre, Sydney possesses three universities, including Sydney University (1850), and the world-famous Sydney Opera House (opened 1973), designed by Jørn Utzon as the result of an international competition in 1955. There are abundant sports facilities, including many nearby beaches. *History*: a penal settlement (Sydney Cove) was established by Capt Arthur *Phillip at Port Jackson (in 1788). Under the governorship of Lachlan *Macquarie (1810–21), aided by a convict-architect, Francis Greenway, it developed into a thriving town and grew rapidly between 1850 and 1890. Area: 1735 sq km (670 sq mi). Population (1983 est): 3 332 600.

Sydney 46 10N 60 10W A city and port in SE Canada, in Nova Scotia on Cape Breton Island. Founded in 1785, it is located on a major coalfield and has an important steel industry. Population (1981): 29 444.

syenite A range of coarse-grained intrusive rocks (*see* igneous rocks) consisting mainly of alkali feldspar or feldspathoids, together with hornblende and biotite.

Sykes-Picot Agreement (1916) A secret agreement between the UK and France, negotiated by Sir Mark Sykes (1879–1919) and Georges Picot. It arranged, with Russian approval, for the post-World War I partition of the Ottoman (Turkish) Empire. The agreement was eventually shelved but disclosure of the scheme by the Russian revolutionary government caused considerable controversy.

Syktyvkar 61 42N 50 45E A city in the NW Soviet Union,

the capital of the Komi ASSR in the RSFSR. Founded in the 16th century, it became a place of exile for criminals and political prisoners. Notable industries are timber and paper and pulp manufacturing. Population (1981 est): 180 000.

Sylhet 24 53N 91 51E A town in NE Bangladesh, in the Surma Valley. The former capital of a Hindu kingdom conquered by Muslims in 1384, it is the chief town of a tea-growing region and has large natural-gas reserves.

syllabaries Writing systems in which each symbol represents a syllable in the language rather than a concept (*compare* ideographic writing systems). The only major language using a syllabary today is Japanese. However, the North *Semitic alphabet, from which all the world's major alphabets are derived, almost certainly developed out of a syllabary, in which the symbols came to represent speech sounds rather than concepts as in ideography.

syllogism A form of deductive argument, rules for the validity of which were developed by *Aristotle. Each syllogism must be composed of three propositions—two premises and a conclusion—and one of its forms may thus be schematically represented: "All As are Bs. All Cs are As. Therefore all Cs are Bs." Since the conclusion that all Cs are Bs "follows" from the premises, one cannot without self-contradiction assert the premises and deny the conclusion, and this is true of all forms of valid syllogism.

Sylvester II (Gerbert of Aurillac; c. 940–1003) Pope (999–1033), who was also a mathematician and astronomer. He attempted to reform abuses and organized the Churches of Poland and Hungary. His reputation as a scholar (his learning was popularly credited to have been acquired by magic) survived his pontificate.

symbiosis Any close relationship between individuals of two different species of organisms. The term can therefore include parasitism (*see* parasite), *commensalism, and *inquilinism but is often restricted to—and used synonymously with—**mutualism**, in which both partners (symbionts) benefit from the association. An example of such a symbiotic relationship is provided by a sea anemone (*Adamsia paliata*), which lives attached to the snail shell inhabited by the hermit crab (*Eupagurus prideauxii*). The anemone protects and camouflages the crab, from which it receives food and transport in return.

Symbolists A group of French poets in the late 19th century whose poetry, which they regarded as a means of transcending reality, was determined by their belief in the power of words and images to evoke responses in the subconscious mind. They included *Mallarmé, *Verlaine, and *Rimbaud, and acknowledged the influence of *Baudelaire. They were precursors of the Surrealist movement and had a profound influence on poets in Russia and many other countries.

Symonds, John Addington (1840–93) British art historian and critic. He suffered from tuberculosis, and from 1877 lived mostly in Switzerland. His major work is *The Renaissance in Italy* (7 vols, 1875–86). He also wrote poetry, travel books, and literary biographies.

Symons, Arthur (William) (1865–1945) British poet and critic. He coedited the literary journal *Savoy* (1896) with Aubrey Beardsley and published several volumes of lyrical poetry, the best of which he selected and published in *Poems* (2 vols, 1902). A disciple of Walter *Pater, his critical work included the influential study, *The Symbolist Movement in Literature* (1899).

symphonic poem (*or* tone poem) A one-movement orchestral composition based on a literary, dramatic, or pictorial theme. The symphonic poem was invented by *Liszt, who composed a series of such works, the most famous of which is *Les Préludes* (1854), after Lamartine's poem *Méditations Poétiques*. Smetana, Richard Strauss, Tchaikovsky, Sibelius, Respighi, and Elgar, among others, composed notable works in this genre.

symphony An orchestral composition, usually in four movements. The classical symphony evolved in the mid-18th century and was perfected by Haydn and Mozart: the fast first movement was generally in *sonata form, the second was slow and expressive, the third a *minuet and trio, and the fourth fast. Beethoven extended the formal and emotional range of the symphony, introducing a chorus and soloists in the last movement of his ninth symphony. In the 19th century Schubert, Schumann, Mendelssohn, Brahms, Dvořák, and Tchaikovsky all wrote symphonies broadly in this tradition. In the hands of such composers as Bruckner and Mahler the symphony underwent further enlargement: Mahler's eighth symphony (1907) requires a thousand performers. Sibelius developed a concentrated approach to symphonic writing: his seventh symphony (1924) is in one movement. Nielsen, Shostakovich, Vaughan Williams, and others have all developed the symphony in differing ways.

synagogue A Jewish place of worship. The synagogue probably originated during the *Babylonian exile as a substitute for the Temple at Jerusalem. In antiquity it was a public meeting place, devoted mainly to the reading and exposition of the *Torah. It is now primarily a house of prayer, but often has a communal centre attached. The principal piece of furniture is the cupboard (Ark) containing the Torah scrolls. A synagogue service requires a quorum (*minyan*) of ten adult males. Continental and US Reform Judaism prefer the term "temple."

synapse The meeting point between one nerve cell and another (*see* neurone). The nerve impulse, as it arrives at the end of one nerve process, causes a chemical neurotransmitter (e.g. *acetylcholine or noradrenaline) to be released. This reaches receptors on the opposite neurone and produces a new nerve impulse.

synchrocyclotron A type of *cyclotron in which the frequency of the accelerating electric field can be varied to compensate for the relativistic increase in the mass of the accelerated particles. This enables energies of up to 500 MeV to be obtained.

synchrotron A particle *accelerator, similar to the *cyclotron, in which protons or electrons are accelerated in a circular path by an alternating electric field. The frequency of the field is synchronized with the energy of the particles to counteract their relativistic increase in the mass. Proton energies of several hundred GeV have been attained in these devices. *See also* bevatron.

synchrotron radiation Electromagnetic radiation emitted in certain directions by a charged particle when the presence of a magnetic field confines its motion to a circle. The particle has to be moving at speeds comparable to that of light for a noticeable amount of radiation to be emitted. Therefore a high magnetic field is needed. Such fields are used in *synchrotrons, a type of particle *accelerator. The emission of radio-frequency radiation also occurs from interstellar gas clouds in radio galaxies and, by analogy, is also known as synchrotron radiation.

syncline A trough-shaped fold or downfold in folded rock strata, the strata dipping towards a central axis (*compare* anticline). The youngest rocks occur in the core unless very complex deformation has occurred. Where the strata dip inwards from all directions the resulting feature is called a structural basin.

syndicalism A type of *socialism, advocated by *Sorel, under which the workers, not the state, would take over the productive resources of industry. Syndicalists were widely influential in Europe from the late 19th century until World War I. They worked through industrial action, rather than political or parliamentary means, to substitute for the state a federation of functional economic units (syndicats).

Synge, John Millington (1871–1909) Anglo-Irish dramatist. Most of his plays, the realism and poetic intensity of which contributed greatly to the *Irish Literary Renaissance, were inspired by his experience of life in an isolated Irish community, recorded in *The Aran Islands* (1907). His best-known play, *The Playboy of the Western World* (1907), caused riots at its first performance at the Abbey Theatre, Dublin.

synodic period The average time taken by a planet or satellite to return to the same point in its orbit, relative to the sun, as seen from earth or from the satellite's primary (i.e. the body it orbits). It is therefore the interval between *oppositions or between identical *phases.

synovitis Inflammation of the synovium—the membrane lining the joints. This usually results from mild injuries to joints and causes pain and swelling.

syntax. *See* grammar.

synthesizer A device that can reproduce the sounds of conventional instruments electronically or produce a variety of artificial tones. Electronic oscillators produce a range of signals, which after amplification and appropriate filtering are converted to sound waves, of which some have the characteristic resonances of musical instruments, some are pure tones, and some are arbitrary combinations of sounds. Individual circuits can be plugged in and out by the player, enabling a wide range of sounds to be produced. The Moog synthesizer, invented by Robert Moog (1934–) in 1965, can play one note at a time and is controlled by a keyboard. More recent **polyphonic synthesizers** can be programmed to produce any number of different tones simultaneously.

synthetism A style of painting developed by *Gauguin and Émile Bernard (1868–1941) in Brittany in 1888. The visual arts' counterpart to the Symbolist literary movement, synthetism sought to express an idea or emotion through formal correspondences of line and colour. It was also known as cloisonnisme, since its use of rich unmodulated colour contained within thick black contours resembled *cloisonné enamelwork, as well as Japanese prints. Synthetism greatly influenced the art of the *Nabis.

syphilis A venereal disease caused by the *spirochaete bacterium *Treponema pallidum*, which in nearly all cases is transmitted during sexual intercourse. The effects of the disease occur in three stages. In primary syphilis chancres (hard ulcers) appear after about 25 days at the site of infection (usually the genitals). The chancre disappears after about eight weeks, but weeks or months later the rash of secondary syphilis occurs. Arthritis, meningitis, and hepatitis may also occur at this stage. Without treatment the tertiary stage of syphilis may appear up to 30 years later and give rise to a variety of symptoms, including large tumour-like masses (gummas) in many organs, heart disease, blindness, and madness and paralysis (general paralysis of the insane). The disease can be passed on to an unborn child by an infected mother (congenital syphilis). Syphilis can be treated with penicillin. The *Wasserman test is one of many blood tests available for diagnosing the disease.

Syracuse (Italian name: Siracusa) 37 04N 15 18E A seaport in Italy, in SE Sicily on the Ionian Sea. Founded by Greeks from Corinth in 734 BC, it became an important cultural centre in the 5th century. The Greek poet Theocritus and the Greek mathematician and scientist Archimedes were born here. In 212 BC Syracuse fell to the Romans after a three-year siege. There are many ancient remains, including a Greek temple, a Roman amphitheatre, and a fortress built by Dionysius I. Today Syracuse is a processing centre for agricultural produce, with some light industry. Population (1983 est): 118 070.

Syracuse 43 03N 76 10W A city in the USA, in New York state. Founded in 1788, it had a thriving saltmaking industry until after the US Civil War. In 1819 the Erie Canal was opened and the railways followed, attracting many industries. Today its many manufactures include aircraft parts, typewriters, and chemicals. Syracuse University was established here in 1849. Population (1980): 170 105.

Syr Darya, River (ancient name: Jaxartes) A river in the S central Soviet Union, rising in the Tian Shan and flowing mainly W to the Aral Sea. It is the longest river in Central Asia. Length: 2900 km (1800 mi).

Syria (official name: Syrian Arab Republic) A country in the Middle East, bordering on the Mediterranean Sea. In the W the Ghab depression (an extension of the *Great Rift Valley) runs N–S, separated from the coast by a mountain range. To the E of this is plateau of steppe and desert with some mountains. The main fertile areas, in which the population is concentrated, are the coastal strip and the basin of the River Euphrates (*see* Fertile Crescent). Nomads live in the centre and E; ethnic minorities include Kurds (in the NE), Turks, Armenians, Assyrians, Circassians, and Jews. The population is predominantly Muslim (mainly Sunnites with some Shiites). *Economy*: largely agricultural; cotton and grain are the main crops and livestock are kept. Natural resources include oil, natural gas, phosphates, and salt. Industries, mainly developed since the 1940s, include food processing, oil refining, and the manufacture of textiles, clothing, cement, and chemicals. Syria has a planned socialist economy; much of its industry is nationalized, and land has been redistributed in favour of the peasants (1958, 1963, and 1966). *History*: before the 20th century Syria, together with Palestine, extended over the area that is now Lebanon, Israel, Jordan, W Iraq, and N Saudi Arabia. In ancient times the *Amorites settled here and later *Phoenicia flourished. It was frequently conquered; Islam was introduced by conquering Arabs (c. 640 AD). Under Turkish control from the 11th century, it was the site of battles with the Crusaders. From 1517 until World War I it was part of the Ottoman Empire. In 1920 it became part of a French mandate, from which Lebanon was separated in 1926. Demands for Syrian independence were finally satisfied in 1946. Since then Syria's history has been marked by economic growth, political instability with many coups, and militant participation in the Arab-Israeli Wars. It united briefly with Egypt in the United Arab Republic (1958–61) but withdrew because of Egyptian domination. In 1971 Syria, Libya, and Egypt united loosely in the Federation of Arab Republics but disagreement with Egypt developed over its attitude towards Israel. Syria intervened in the civil war in Lebanon (1975–76), at first as a mediator but later, after the Israeli invasion of 1982, as an active supporter of certain Muslim factions. Syria is a member of the Arab League. President: Lieut Gen Hafiz al-Assad (1928–). Prime minister: Abdel Raouf al-Kasm. Official language: Arabic. Official currency: Syrian pound of 100 piastres. Area: 185 680 sq km (71 772 sq mi). Population (1983 est): 9 739 000. Capital: Damascus.

Syriac A *Semitic language based on the dialect of *Aramaic spoken in Edessa (now Urfa, SE Turkey). It became an important literary and liturgical language in which many scriptures, biblical commentaries, hymns, etc., were written during the 3rd to the 7th centuries AD when Edessa was an important Christian centre.

syringa. *See* lilac; mock orange.

syrinx The vocal organ of birds, located at the base of the windpipe. Air from the lungs vibrates membranes within a resonating chamber. Muscular tension alters pitch, and the two halves of the syrinx can produce different notes simultaneously.

Syros (Modern Greek name: Síros) A Greek island in the S Aegean Sea, in the Cyclades. The chief town, Hermopolis, is the capital of the Cyclades. Area: 85 sq km (33 sq mi). Population (1981): 19 668.

systole. *See* blood pressure; heart.

Szczecin (German name: Stettin) 53 25N 14 32E A city in the extreme NW of Poland, on the River Oder 65 km (40 mi) upstream from the Baltic Sea. It is a major port, the chief export being coal. Shipbuilding is the principal industry; others include engineering, chemicals, and the manufacture of textiles. *History*: it became a member of the Hanseatic League in 1360. Seized by the Swedes (1648) it passed to Prussia in 1720, remaining under German control until being ceded to Poland (1945). It suffered severe damage during World War II but has since been rebuilt. Population (1982): 390 000.

Szechwan. *See* Sichuan.

Szeged 46 15N 20 09E A city in S Hungary, on the River Tisza. Replanned with concentric and radiating streets after a flood in 1879, it has a university (1872) and considerable industry. Population (1984): 176 000.

Székesfehérvár 47 11N 18 22E A town in W central Hungary. It was the capital of the Hungarian kingdom from the 10th until the 16th century. It was almost totally destroyed in World War II. Population (1980): 102 000.

Szell, George (1897–1970) Hungarian conductor. He studied in Vienna, conducted in various German opera houses, and went to the USA in 1942. In 1946 he became permanent conductor of the Cleveland Orchestra, a post he held until his death.

Szent-Györgyi, Albert (von Nagyrapolt) (1893–1986) US biochemist, born in Hungary. He identified the role of ascorbic acid in living cells and later showed it to be *vitamin C. Szent-Györgyi determined certain organic compounds involved in the breakdown of carbohydrates by cells to produce energy–a prelude to *Krebs' major discoveries in this field. He also found that the proteins actin and myosin, working in conjunction with ATP, formed the basis of the contractile apparatus of muscles. Szent-Györgyi was awarded a Nobel Prize (1937).

Szewinska, Irena (1946–) Polish athlete. At 18 she won two silver medals in the 1964 Olympics, in 1968 she won the Olympic 200 metres, and in 1976 she set a world record in the Olympic 400 metres.

Szilard, Leo (1898–1964) US physicist, born in Hungary, who in 1934, while working in England, conceived the idea of a self-sustaining nuclear chain reaction. Szilard emigrated to the USA in 1937 and when he heard of *Hahn and *Meitner's work on the fission of uranium, recognized its significance in terms of nuclear weapons. He joined *Teller in persuading Einstein to write to Roosevelt to warn him of the possibility that Germany might make an atom bomb first. During World War II he actually worked on the atom bomb, but later regretted its development and pressed for the abolition of all nuclear weapons.

Szymanowski, Karol (1882–1937) Polish composer. He studied at the Warsaw conservatoire, where in 1926 he became director. The influences on his music include Chopin, Liszt, Scriabin, Debussy, and Polish folk music. His works include three symphonies, a *Symphonie Concertante* (for piano and orchestra; 1931–32) two violin concertos, the ballet *Harnasie* (1926), the opera *King Roger* (1920–24), and *Mythes* (for violin and piano; 1915).

T

Tabari, Muhammad ibn Jarir al- (838-923 AD) Arab historian. His works include an important commentary on the Koran and the *Annals*, a history of the world from the Creation to the year 915 AD.

tabasco A hot red pepper or sauce made from the entire fruits of a variety of the South American plant *Capsicum frutescens* and used to flavour soups, stews, curries, etc. Family: *Solanaceae*.

tabernacle 1. The portable sanctuary or "tent of meeting" used by the Israelites in the wilderness (Exodus 25-31, 33, 35-40). 2. The English name of the *sukkah*, a hut made of greenery, used by Jews during the autumn festival of Tabernacles (*sukkot*). For seven days it is customary to live, or at least eat, in the *sukkah*.

Table Bay 33 50S 18 25E An inlet of the Atlantic Ocean, on the coast of SW Africa. The Dutch settled here in 1652, founding Cape Town on the S shore. Length: about 10 km (6 mi).

table tennis (*or* Ping-Pong) An indoor game for two or four players that originated in England in the late 19th century from *real tennis. It is played on a table 2.74 m (9 ft) long and 1.52 m (5 ft) wide, divided across its width by a net 15.25 cm (6 in) high and along its length by a line separating right-hand from left-hand half courts for doubles play. The players hit a resilient small hollow plastic ball with a rubber-faced wooden bat. A point is scored when the opponent fails to return the ball after it has bounced once. Each player serves five consecutive points and the winner of a game is the first to reach 21 points with at least a two-point lead.

taboo A ritual prohibition relating to things that are considered either sacred, powerful, and dangerous (*see also* totemism) or unclean and polluting. The term is derived from Polynesian *tapu*, forbidden, and may apply to things, animals, plants, people, places, words and names, or actions. Customs of this kind are widespread in all societies, but actual practices vary greatly. Certain things may be taboo for all people in a society (as eating pork is for Jews). Other things are taboo for only certain categories of persons (*see* incest). Some things are taboo for particular people at particular times (e.g. in many societies menstruating women are subject to restrictions as to what they may touch).

Tabora 5 02S 32 50E A town in W central Tanzania. It was an important centre for trade in ivory and slaves; today trade remains significant and includes groundnuts and sunflower seeds. Population (1978): 67 392.

Tabriz 38 05N 46 18E A city in NW Iran, close to the Soviet and Turkish borders. It has several times suffered earthquakes. The most notable buildings are the Blue Mosque (15th century) and the citadel, and Tabriz is famous for its carpets; it is connected by rail to Tehran and the Soviet Union and has an airport. Tabriz University was opened in 1949. Population (1985 est): 929 200.

tachometer An instrument for measuring the speed of rotation of a shaft, such as a revolution counter in a car. Centrifugal tachometers measure the force experienced by rotating masses. Others are electrical or magnetic, measuring electrical current or force generated by a small generator in the instrument.

tachyon A hypothetical particle that travels faster than the speed of light. Such a particle would have either an imaginary rest mass or an imaginary energy and no such particle has ever been detected.

Tacitus, Cornelius (c. 55-c. 120 AD) Roman historian. After holding various provincial administrative posts he established his reputation as a public orator in Rome and became consul in 97 AD; in 112-13 he was governor of Asia. In 98 he wrote two historical monographs, *Germania* and *Agricola*, the latter an account of his father-in-law's career. His major works, the *Histories* and the *Annals*, survey Roman history during the periods 69-96 AD and 14-68 AD and are noted for their terse and vivid style and acute understanding of the men and issues involved. Although claiming impartiality, Tacitus appears to concentrate on the evils of imperial government.

Tacna 18 00S 70 15W A town in S Peru. It was under Chilean occupation (1883-1929). It serves an agricultural area producing tobacco, cotton, and sugar cane. Population (1981): 97 173.

Tacoma 47 16N 122 30W A city in the USA, in Washington state on Puget Sound. Founded in 1868, it grew as the terminus of the North Pacific Railroad (1873). The University of Puget Sound was established here in 1888. An important port, its main industry is timber; other industries include meat packing, railway workshops, and foundries. Tacoma is the gateway to several national parks. Population (1980): 158 501.

tadpole The aquatic larva of frogs and toads. The newly hatched tadpole feeds on vegetation but later becomes carnivorous. The external gills of the young tadpole are gradually replaced by internal gills, and after about ten weeks the limbs start to appear, the tail degenerates, the lungs develop, and the circulatory system changes to enable the adult to lead a terrestrial life. Metamorphosis is complete after about three months, depending on the external temperature and available food.

tadpole shrimp A freshwater crustacean belonging to an order (*Notostraca*) that occurs in North America and the Arctic. Up to 30 mm long, it has a shieldlike carapace, short antennae, 35-70 pairs of appendages, and two long tail filaments. Subclass: *Branchiopoda*.

Tadzhiks An Iranian people of Afghanistan and Soviet Turkistan. They are an agricultural people using irrigation to grow cereal crops and fruit trees. Trade has also been important traditionally because of their position on the caravan routes between China, India, and Persia. They speak a form of Persian and are Muslims.

Tadzhik Soviet Socialist Republic (*or* Tadzhikistan) A constituent republic in the S Soviet Union. Largely mountainous, it contains *Communism Peak. Some 53% of the population are *Tadzhiks. The economy is primarily agricultural, although there are growing mining, engineering, and other industries. Health resorts have grown up around its many mineral springs. Area: 143 100 sq km (55 240 sq mi). Population (1981 est): 3 400 000. Capital: Dushanbe.

Taegu 35 52N 128 36E A city in SE South Korea, the capital of North Kyongsang province. An old cultural centre, it is the site of a university (1946). It has an important textile industry. Population (1980): 1 607 458.

Taejon 36 20N 127 26E A city in SE South Korea, capital of South Chungchong province. It is an agricultural and industrial centre, with a university (1952). Some 70% of the city was destroyed during the Korean War (1950-53). Population (1980): 651 642.

Tafilalt (*or* Tafilelt) An oasis in SE Morocco, in the Sahara. It stretches for about 50 km (31 mi) along the River Ziz and includes the towns of Erfoud and Rissani.

Taft, William Howard (1857-1930) US statesman; Republican president (1909-13). Taft's conservative presidency was characterized by *antitrust legislation and high protective tariffs, which cost him Theodore Roosevelt's support, split the Republican vote, and lost the 1912 election to the Democrats. Taft's rulings as chief justice (1921–30) reinforced federal powers. His son **Robert Alphonso Taft** (1889–1953), a senator from 1939, was an unsuccessful candidate for the Republican presidential nomination on four occasions (1940, 1944, 1948, 1952). He introduced the Taft-Hartley Act (1947), which restricted trade unions.

Tagalog A people of Luzon and Mindanao islands in the Philippines who speak an *Austronesian language. Although less numerous than the speakers of the related language of Cebuano, they tend to dominate in the economic, professional, and political spheres. Tagalog is the basis of the national language and is spoken by the population of the capital, Manila. The rural Tagalog are mainly rice farmers.

Taganrog 47 14N 38 55E A port in the Soviet Union, in the SW RSFSR of the Gulf of Taganrog on the Sea of Azov. Its port serves the coalmines of the Donets Basin and industries include steel making. The playwright Chekhov was born here. Population (1981 est): 281 000.

Tagore, Rabindranath (1861–1941) Indian poet, philosopher, and teacher. Knighted in 1915, he resigned the honour in 1919 as a protest against the Amritsar massacre. He wrote poetry, drama, and fiction in the Bengali language and was also a celebrated artist and musician. He advocated cultural links between the East and the West and won the Nobel Prize for Literature in 1913 after the publication in English of *Gitanjali* (1912), a volume of spiritual poetry. His father **Debendranath Tagore** (1817–1905) was a radical religious reformer and teacher. In 1886 he established the "Abode of Peace," a retreat in Bengal made famous by his son as an educational centre.

Tagus, River (Portuguese name: Tejo; Spanish name: Tajo) A river in SW Europe. Rising in E central Spain, it flows NW and then SW across arid areas of Spain and Portugal to the Atlantic Ocean at Lisbon, where it is crossed by a suspension bridge. Length: 1007 km (626 mi).

Tahiti The largest of the Society Islands in the S central Pacific Ocean, in French Polynesia. Mountainous and famous for its beauty, it was Gauguin's home for two years (1891–93). Settled by Polynesians in the 14th century, it was first visited by Europeans in 1767. The London Missionary Society christianized the island by helping the Pomare family to power. It became French in 1842. Tourism is important, and copra, sugar cane, vanilla, and coffee are exported. Area: 1005 sq km (388 sq mi). Population (1983 est): 116 000. Chief town: Papeete.

tahr A wild goat belonging to the genus *Hemitragus* (3 species), inhabiting forested mountain slopes of S Asia. 60–100 cm high at the shoulder, the large Himalayan tahr (*H. jemlahicus*) and the smaller Nilgiri tahr (*H. hylocrius*) have long coarse shaggy brownish hair; the Arabian tahr (*H. jayakari*) is slender and sandy-coloured.

Tai Peoples of SE Asia and China who speak a group of related languages probably belonging to the *Sino-Tibetan family. They are traditionally rice cultivators dwelling in villages with elected headmen. The nuclear family is the basic social unit and women have high status. They are mainly Theravada Buddhists, the monks having considerable influence and authority. Major groupings are the Thai or Siamese, the Lao, Shan, and Lu. *See also* Austro-Asiatic languages.

Taibei. *See* Taipei.

taiga The coniferous forests, composed chiefly of spruces, pines, and firs, in the N hemisphere in subpolar latitudes. It extends from Norway across Sweden, Finland, and the Soviet Union (including Siberia), in Eurasia. The coniferous forests of North America, extending across Canada and Alaska, are also known as taiga.

Taika (Japanese: great change; 645–50 AD) The period associated with the first major upheaval in Japanese history. Influenced by the Tang dynasty of China, Japanese leaders intro-

duced a Chinese-style system of government, including land nationalization and the establishment of a centralized bureaucracy. Their programme was not completed, however, until the erection of a permanent capital at Nara in 710.

taille An income and property tax in France before the Revolution. Originally levied for royal expenses and paid in lieu of military service, the taille was a major source of grievance since clergy and nobility were exempt and commoners alone paid the tax. It was abolished in 1789.

tailorbird A S Asian *warbler belonging to the genus *Orthotomus* (9 species), named after its habit of sewing the edges of a large leaf together with plant fibres or gossamer to form a bag in which the nest is built.

Taimyr Peninsula (*or* Taymyr Peninsula) A promontory in the central N Soviet Union, between the Kara Sea and the Laptev Sea with Cape *Chelyuskin at its extremity.

Tainan 23 01N 120 14E A city in SW Taiwan, the island's third largest. It is the island's former capital (1683–1891). The National University was established in 1971. An agricultural and fish market, it has varied industries and handicrafts. Population (1985): 633 607.

Taine, Hippolyte Adolphe (1828–93) French writer and critic. In contrast to the prevailing *Romanticism, Taine was intensely logical and positivist in his approach. In works such as the *Philosophy of Art* (1865–69), his analysis is conducted in scientific, mathematical, physiological, or environmental terms.

taipan A small-headed *cobra, *Oxyuranus scutellatus*, that occurs in NE Australia and New Guinea. Up to 3.3 m long, it has a ridged brown back and a yellow belly. The venom of the taipan contains a blood-clotting agent that is fatal within a few minutes.

Taipei (*or* Taibei) 25 00N 121 32E The capital of Taiwan, in the N of the island. Founded in the 18th century, it was under Japanese occupation (1895–1945) and became the seat of the Nationalist Government (*see* Guomindang) in 1949. It is an important industrial centre, especially for textiles, food processing, and machinery. The National University was founded in 1928. Population (1985 est): 2 500 000.

Taiping Rebellion (1851–64) A peasant rebellion in China that seriously undermined the Qing dynasty. In 1851 a Hakka peasant, *Hong Xiu Quan, claiming he was the brother of Christ come to save his people from their Qing rulers, proclaimed himself "Heavenly King of the Taiping (Heavenly Peace) Kingdom." He soon won converts among the southern peasantry and anti-Qing secret societies. The rebels marched N, capturing Nanjing in 1853 and declaring it their Heavenly Capital. They then marched on Peking but imperial forces, and cold weather, drove them back. The rebellion, which devastated 17 provinces, was weakened by internal division and finally crushed. When Nanjing fell, Hong and his followers committed mass suicide.

Taira An important Japanese military clan of imperial descent. After gaining many vassals in the provinces, the Taira became involved in politics in the capital, Kyoto, in the 12th century and under the leadership of Taira Kiyomori (1118–81) came to dominate the imperial government. Shortly before Kiyomori's death, Taira power was challenged by the leaders of a rival clan, the Minamoto (*see* Minamoto Yoritomo), and destroyed in the Gempei War (1180–85).

Taiwan (Republic of China) An island off the SE coast of mainland China. Together with several nearby islands, including the Penghu Islands and the islands of *Jinmen and *Mazu, it comprises the Republic of China. Taiwan Island is largely mountainous, apart from narrow plains along the W coast, and two-thirds of the land is under forest. The people are predominantly Chinese, but there is friction between the island Chinese, who make up the overwhelming majority of the population, and those who came from the mainland. *Economy*: in recent years the balance of the economy has shifted from agriculture to industry, a trend that began under the Japanese and has continued under the *Guomindang with US economic aid. Iron and steel are important and the large volume of exports also includes television and radio sets, mass-produced plastic goods, chemicals, textiles, sugar, and vegetables. As well as coal, gold, and other minerals, oil and natural gas have been found, although timber remains the main natural resource. Agriculture is still important, the chief crops being sugar cane, rice, and sweet potatoes. Fishing has increased in recent years, particularly since the introduction of fish farming. *History*: the island, named Formosa ("beautiful") by the Portuguese, who discovered it in 1590, was ceded by China to Japan in 1897. It surrendered to Gen *Chiang Kai-shek in 1945 and after the defeat of his Nationalist (Guomindang) Government by the Chinese communists he fled here in 1949. Following threats by the People's Republic of China the USA undertook in 1955 to protect Taiwan from outside attacks. However, Taiwan's importance in international affairs has diminished, as the People's Republic has gained increasing recognition by the major powers: in 1971 it lost its seat at the UN to the People's Republic and in 1979 the USA, on establishing diplomatic relations with mainland China, severed those with Taiwan. Chiang Kai-shek died in 1975 and was succeeded by his son Gen Jiang Jing Guo (Chiang Ching-kuo; 1910–88). President: Lee Teng-hui. Official language: Mandarin Chinese. Official currency: new Taiwan dollar of 100 cents. Area: 35 981 sq km (13 892 sq mi). Population (1984 est): 19 117 000. Capital: Taibei. Main port: Kaohsiung.

Taiyuan 37 50N 112 30E A city in NE China, the capital of Shanxi province. An ancient fortified city, it is a centre of technology, coalmining, and heavy industry. Population (1983 est): 1 750 000.

Taizé A Protestant religious community based in Taizé, a village in the SE of France. Founded in 1940 by Roger Schutz (1915–), its members pursue a life of celibacy, obedience, and community of goods in the ways of traditional monasticism and it is also an ecumenical centre for young people interested in furthering Christian unity.

TAJ MAHAL *Over 20 000 workmen were employed in the building of the mausoleum (1631-53), which was constructed from pure white Makrana marble.*

Taj Mahal The mausoleum in Agra (N India) built (1631–53) for Mumtaz-i-Mahal, wife of the Mogul emperor, *Shah Jahan, who is also buried here. Set in formal gardens, the Taj Mahal is built mainly of white marble, delicately carved and inlaid with precious stones. Its symmetrical design reflects Persian influence. *See also* Mogul architecture.

Tajo, River. *See* Tagus, River.

takahe A rare flightless New Zealand bird, *Notornis mantelli*, thought to be extinct but rediscovered on South Island in 1948. 60 cm tall, it has blue-and-green plumage and a heavy red conical bill surmounted by a red frontal shield. Takahes feed on seeds. Family: *Rallidae* (rails).

Takao. *See* Gaoxiong.

Takoradi. *See* Sekondi-Takoradi.

Talaing. *See* Mon.

talapoin The smallest *guenon monkey, *Cercopithecus talapoin*, of central West Africa, also called pygmy guenon. With head and body only 30 cm long, it has slightly webbed fingers and inhabits swampy forests. It has olive-green fur and conspicuously swollen genitals.

talaq An Islamic extra-judicial law of divorce enabling a husband to unilaterally divorce his wife by repudiating her three times. The marriage is then dissolved, unless the husband revokes the pronouncement during the next three months or, if the wife is pregnant, before the child is born.

Talbot, William Henry Fox (1800–77) British botanist and physicist, who pioneered many techniques of photography. In 1841 he invented the calotype, which for the first time used photographic negatives and was a great improvement on the earlier daguerrotype. He also introduced photographic prints on paper treated with silver chloride.

talc A white or green mineral of hydrated magnesium silicate, $Mg_3(Si_4O_{10})(OH)_2$, with a layered structure. It is soft (hardness 1 on *Mohs' scale) and greasy. Soapstone (steatite) is a rock consisting almost wholly of talc. Talc is formed by the hydrothermal alteration of basic and ultrabasic igneous rocks and by the low-grade thermal metamorphism of siliceous dolomites. Besides its use as talcum powder, it is used as a filler, lubricant, and soft abrasive.

Talca 35 28S 71 40W A city in central Chile. The site of the declaration of Chile's independence (1815), it was rebuilt following an earthquake in 1928. Talca serves a rich wine-producing area and has a large match industry. Population (1983 est): 137 981.

Talcahuano 36 40S 73 10W A major port in S Chile, on Concepción Bay. It serves as an outlet for Concepción and is Chile's chief naval base. Population (1983 est): 212 865.

Ta-lien. *See* Lüda.

Taliesin (6th century AD) Welsh poet. He is mentioned in the 9th-century *Historia Britonum* of Nennius. The poems attributed to him in the manuscript *Book of Taliesin* (c. 1275) include odes eulogizing the Welsh king Urien Rheged and lamenting the death of his son Owain.

talipot palm A *palm tree, *Corypha umbraculifera*, cultivated in India and Burma. Its trunk, up to 26 m high, bears fan-shaped leaves up to 5 m in diameter. Trees may be 80 years old before flowering, after which they die. The pyramid-shaped flower cluster, more than 7 m tall, is the largest in the plant kingdom. The seeds are used for buttons and ornaments and the leaves for matting, fans, and thatching.

Tallahassee 30 26N 84 19W A city in the USA, the capital of Florida. It is the site of Florida State University (1857) and an agricultural and mechanical university (1887). A trade centre for timber, cotton, and livestock, industries include metal and concrete. Population (1980): 81 548.

Talleyrand (Charles Maurice de Talleyrand-Périgord; 1754–1838) French politician and diplomat. He took holy orders in 1775 but was excommunicated by the pope for his reform of the church during the *French Revolution. He was foreign minister from 1797 until 1807, when he quarrelled with Napoleon, and again under the restored Louis XVIII. He represented France at the *Congress of Vienna and was ambassador to Great Britain (1830–34).

Tallien, Jean Lambert (1767–1820) French politician in the *French Revolution. He helped overthrow Robespierre in 1774 and under the *Directory was a member of the Council of Five Hundred. He subsequently served in Napoleon's Egyptian campaign.

Tallinn (German name: Reval) 59 22N 24 48E A port in the NW Soviet Union, the capital of the Estonian SSR on

Tallinn Bay in the Gulf of Finland. Its varied industries include shipbuilding and it possesses many educational institutions and historic buildings. *History*: it occupies the site of an ancient settlement and was ruled by Denmark and then Sweden before being captured (1710) by Peter the Great. A member of the Hanseatic League, it was a prominent trading centre in the middle ages. It was independent Estonia's capital (1918–40) and, following annexation by the Soviet Union, was occupied by the Germans in World War II. Population (1981 est): 442 000.

Tallis, Thomas (c. 1505–85) English composer. He was appointed a gentleman of the Chapel Royal and became joint organist there with his pupil Byrd. In 1575 he and Byrd were granted a monopoly for printing music and music paper. They produced *Cantiones Sacrae*, a collection of their motets, in the same year. Tallis' most famous works are *The Lamentations of Jeremiah* and the 40-part motet *Spem in Alium*.

Talmud Two of the most important works of Jewish religious literature: the Babylonian and the Palestinian (or Jerusalem) Talmud. The Babylonian Talmud is more than three times as long as the Palestinian and enjoys greater authority. Both Talmuds have the same form: they are written in a mixture of Hebrew and Aramaic and are presented as a commentary (*gemara*) on the *Mishnah. They contain records of rabbinic discussions on a wide range of subjects but concentrating especially on *halakhah. The rabbis mentioned in the Talmuds are called *Amoraim* (as opposed to *Tannaim*, the rabbis of the Mishnah, and *Savoraim*, later rabbis thought to have edited the Babylonian Talmud). The Palestinian *Amoraim* flourished in the 3rd and 4th centuries AD; the Babylonian *Amoraim* continued to about 500.

talus (*or* scree) The accumulation of weathered debris at the foot of a cliff that has originated from erosion of the rock face above.

Tamale 9 26N 0 49W A town in N Ghana. It is an educational centre and has a trade in cotton and groundnuts. Population (1982 est): 219 210.

tamandua An insect-eating mammal, *Tamandua tetradactyla*, of Central and South American forests, also called lesser *anteater. Almost 1 m long including the long prehensile tail, it is pale in colour and has a shorter snout than the giant anteater. It feeds on termites using its long sticky tongue. Family: *Myrmecophagidae*; order: *Edentata*.

tamarin A South American monkey found in open woodland and forests, closely related to *marmosets. Tamarins are 39–88 cm long including the tail (20–42 cm), have tusklike lower canine teeth, and feed on fruit, insects, eggs, etc. Chief genera: *Leontocebus* (21 species), *Leontideus* (3 species); family: *Callithricidae*.

tamarind An evergreen tree, *Tamarindus indica*, probably native to tropical Africa and cultivated in tropical regions for its fruit. It grows to a height of 24 m and bears clusters of yellow flowers. The fruit 's a plump pod containing seeds and a bitter-sweet pulp, which is used in chutneys, curries, and medicines. Family: *Leguminosae.

tamarisk A tree or shrub belonging to the genus *Tamarix* (90 species), native to W and S Europe, central Asia, and India. Tamarisks have small scalelike leaves and produce feathery clusters of small pink flowers. Their deep roots enable them to grow on arid salt flats and sand dunes and they have been widely planted to stabilize sand dunes. *T. mannifera* of the Middle East and central Asia exudes a sweet white edible substance (manna) when the stems are punctured by certain insects. The false tamarisks (genus *Myricaria*; 10 species), native to temperate Eurasia, are similar to the true tamarisks. Family: *Tamaricaceae*.

tamarou (*or* tamarau) A rare hoofed mammal, *Anoa mindorensis*, of lowland forests of the Philippines. A little larger than the closely related *anoa, it is similarly dark brown or

black with short horns and it feeds at night on sugar cane and water plants.

Tamatave (*or* Toamasina) 18 10S 49 23E The chief port of Madagascar, on the Indian Ocean. It was destroyed by hurricane in 1927. Since rebuilt, it is the country's major commercial centre and industries include rum distilling. Population (1982 est): 82 907.

Tambov 52 44N 41 28E A city in the Soviet Union, in the W RSFSR. It is an important engineering centre. Population (1981 est): 277 000.

Tamerlane. See Timur.

Tamil A *Dravidian language of S India and Sri Lanka. It is the official language of the state of Tamil Nadu. There are a number of regional dialects as well as those associated with different caste groups, such as Brahmins and non-Brahmins. It is written in a script known as Vattelluttu and there are marked differences between the written and spoken forms. Tamil society is highly stratified into caste groups and based on descent in the male line. They are mainly Hindu, and devotional (*bhakti*) cults are prevalent.

Tamil Nadu (name until 1968: Madras) A state in SE India, at the tip of the peninsula. From the Western *Ghats it slopes E over lower plateaus and the Eastern Ghats to the Bay of Bengal. Important crops include rice, cotton, and coffee. One of India's more urbanized states, it produces cotton textiles, machinery, and electrical and leather goods. Tamil literature, music, and dance continue to thrive. *History*: flourishing Hindu dynasties extended Tamil influence into medieval SE Asia until Muslims conquered Tamil Nadu (1565). British power was established in the 17th century. The present state was formed in 1956. Area: 130 357 sq km (50 318 sq mi). Population (1981): 48 297 456. Capital: Madras.

Tammany Hall The Democratic Party organization in New York City, which became notorious for its political corruption. It maintained power by the use of bribes and patronage. Its power was largely curtailed by the reforming mayor *La Guardia & disintegrated during the administration (1966–73) of John V(liet) Lindsay.

Tammuz A Mesopotamian fertility god identified with the Greek ' *Adonis. Originally a pastoral god, he became an agricultural god of Assyria. The annual seasonal cycle was symbolized in the myth of his descent to the underworld, from whence he was recovered by the goddess *Ishtar.

Tampa 28 10N 82 20W A city and port in the USA, in Florida on Tampa Bay. It is a major resort and phosphate-mining centre. Manufactures include cigars, cement, and fertilizers. Two universities are situated here. Population (1980): 271 523.

Tampere (Swedish name: Tammerfors) 61 32N 23 45E The second largest city in Finland. It has a 20th-century cathedral and a university (1925). It is the country's main industrial centre, being well provided with hydroelectric power from the Tammerkoski Rapids. Its manufactures include railway rolling stock, textiles, wood pulp, paper, and footwear. Population (1980): 166 228.

Tampico 22 18N 97 52W A port and winter resort in SE Mexico, on the Río Panuco. Oil refining is the chief industry. Population (1980): 267 957.

Tamralipti An ancient town in NE India; its site is now occupied by the village of Tamluk. From about 250 BC it was the principal port of the Ganges basin; it was from here that the famous Chinese traveller *Fa Xian sailed for home in the early 5th century AD.

tam-tam. See gong.

Tamworth 52 39N 1 40W A town in central England, in S Staffordshire. It is a market town with engineering, brick and tile manufacturing, and clothing industries. The castle was built in Saxon times. In 1834 Sir Robert *Peel issued the Tamworth manifesto here. Population (1981): 64 315.

Tamworth 31 07S 150 57E A city in Australia, in E New South Wales on the Peel River. It is a market centre serving an agricultural region. Population (1983 est): 33 100.

Tana, Lake (*or* Lake Tsana) 12 00N 37 20E A lake in NW Ethiopia. Its surface is 1830 m (6004 ft) above sea level and it is the source of the Blue Nile River. Area: about 3100 sq km (1197 sq mi).

tanager A brightly coloured songbird belonging to a family (*Thraupidae*; 222 species) occurring in tropical and subtropical America. Tanagers are 10-20 cm long, plumpish, with a short neck and a conical bill. They live mainly in forests and feed on fruit, nectar, and insects.

Tanagra figurines In Greek art, moulded terracotta statuettes of about 300 BC found at Tanagra (Boeotia). These charming and technically excellent figures represent everyday subjects, usually women in quiet poses.

Tananarive. *See* Antananarivo.

Tancred (c. 1078-1112) Norman Crusader, prominent at the siege of Antioch and the conquest of Jerusalem (1099; *see* Crusades), who was regent of Antioch (1101-03, 1104-12) for Bohemond I. He is portrayed in *Tasso's Gerusalemme liberata* (1575).

Tang (*or* T'ang; 618-906 AD) A Chinese dynasty that established an empire extending over much of central Asia and Korea. In Tang times foreign trade was encouraged and many Chinese scientific ideas, such as gunpowder, which was invented under the Tang for fireworks, spread to the West. Arts, especially poetry, flourished, Neo-Confucianism was revived, printing was invented (the world's first known book, the Buddhist *Diamond sutra*, was printed in 868), and paper money was used for the first time. In 751 Arab forces recaptured Turkestan and the Tang empire began to disintegrate. Disastrous revolts and invasions decimated the population and two great rebellions finally led to the collapse of the dynasty and the division of China into many kingdoms.

Tanga 5 07S 39 05E A port in Tanzania, in NE Zanzibar. It became an important port under German colonial rule but has since declined in importance. Population (1978): 103 409.

Tanganyika. *See* Tanzania, United Republic of.

Tanganyika, Lake A lake in E central Africa, in Zaïre, Burundi, Tanzania, and Zambia. Discovered for Europeans by Burton and Speke in 1858, it is drained intermittently to the W by the River Lukuga. Area: about 33 000 sq km (12 738 sq mi).

Tange Kenzo (1913-) Japanese architect. The most famous modern Japanese architect, Tange combines the influence of *Le Corbusier with traditional Japanese architecture. He has built many civic buildings in Japan, notably the Kurashiki city hall (1960). Other designs include the National Gymnasium (1961-64) for the 1964 Tokyo Olympics and St Mary's Cathedral (1962-64) in Tokyo. As a town planner he has produced schemes for Tokyo (1960) and Skopje, Yugoslavia (1965).

tangent A straight line that touches a curve at only one point, known as the point of contact. A tangent plane is one that touches a curved surface at one point. *See also* trigonometry; calculus.

tangerine The fruit of a tree, *Citrus reticulata*, also called mandarin, native to SE Asia and cultivated in the S USA and the Mediterranean region. The orange fruit, which peels easily and readily splits into segments, is usually eaten fresh. Many varieties have been developed, including the satsuma and clementine. The temple orange is a hybrid between the *orange and the tangerine.

Tangier (*or* Tangiers) 35 48N 5 45W A port in N Morocco, on a bay on the Strait of Gibraltar. An important Roman town, it was held successively by many powers until it was established as an international zone in 1923. During World War II it was under Spanish occupation (1940-45) and its

international status was abolished on Moroccan independence (1956). It has a university (1971). Its industries include cigarette and textile manufacture, fishing, and market gardening, and it is also a tourist centre. Population (1981 est): 240 900.

tango 1. A Spanish flamenco dance. 2. A ballroom dance in 2/4 time, first performed in a fast form in the 1880s in the poor quarters of Buenos Aires. In the 1920s it spread to the USA and Europe, where it developed melancholic musical rhythms and a stylized elegance.

Tangshan 39 37N 118 05E A city in NE China, in Hebei province. A centre of heavy industry, its coalmines were under British control until 1952. China's first railway began here (1882). Population (1983 est): 1 333 000.

Tanguy, Yves (1900-55) French surrealist painter. Entirely self-taught, in 1927 he began to paint bizarre forms, partly organic and partly mechanical, which he situated in barren landscapes. He continued to explore this unique vision after emigrating to the USA in 1939.

Tanizaki Jun-ichiro (1886-1965) Japanese novelist. His first short stories of the early 1900s were a brilliant success. Their sensuous and grotesque themes are reminiscent of Edgar Allan Poe's work. In the 1930s, while updating *The Tale of Genji* by *Murasaki, he became strongly influenced by early Japanese literature. Such later novels as *The Makioka Sisters* (1943-48) show appreciation for the traditional Japanese way of life.

Tanjore. *See* Thanjavur.

tank An armour-plated military vehicle, self-propelled on caterpillar tracks and typically armed with a *gun (usually turret-mounted) and machine guns. Tanks are classified as main battle tanks (MBTs), for independent operation, and light tanks, for reconnaissance and other specialized uses. Based on a design of Sir Ernest Swinton (1868-1951) and first used during the Somme offensive in September, 1916, their true value became evident at Cambrai in November, 1917. In World War II the Germans initially achieved great success by using their Panzer divisions as an independent force rather than as infantry support or cavalry replacement. Tank battles across Europe and N Africa replaced the static trench warfare of World War I. In the Arab-Israeli War of 1973 guided missiles caused heavy Israeli tank losses. Modern tank development has concentrated on improving weapons, armour, and computer-aided navigation and fire control. *See also* armoured car. | □ p. 1186.

tanker A seagoing vessel equipped with a large cargo tank for transporting liquids, especially oil. The forerunner of the modern tanker, the *Gluckauf* (2307 tonnes) was built in 1885; modern **supertankers** with a carrying capacity of 75 000 tonnes were developed after World War II in response to the increased world demand for oil. Ultra-Large Crude Carriers (ULCCs) have deadweights of up to nearly half a million tonnes. Size is not always an advantage, however, as such vessels can only enter certain ports, cannot negotiate the Suez Canal, and can cause ecological disasters if they are wrecked and spill their enormous cargoes into the sea.

Tannenberg, Battles of 1. (5 July, 1410) The battle in which Polish and Lithuanian troops defeated the *Teutonic Knights, whose drive into E Europe was thereby arrested. 2. (26-30 August, 1914) The battle early in World War I in which Germany defeated Russia, thus thwarting the Russian invasion of Prussia. Some 100 000 Russians were captured.

Tannhäuser (c. 1200-c. 1270) German poet. A Minnesinger several of whose lyrics survive, he travelled widely, serving in various courts. Wagner's opera is based on the legend of his seduction by Venus, his life of sensuality at her court, and his pilgrimage to seek papal forgiveness.

tannin (*or* tannic acid) One of a group of phenol derivatives present in the bark, leaves, fruits, and galls of many plants. Tannins are used as mordants for many dyes, in tanning leather, and in making ink.

Mark IV British *Tanks were first successfully used during World War I in the battle of Cambrai in November, 1917. They were designed to be able to cross trenches.*

German Pz III *At the beginning of World War II the German Panzer divisions were based on Pz III tanks, armed with a 50-mm gun and having a maximum speed of 30 mph (48 km per hour).*

Soviet T-34 *The Nazi invasion of the Soviet Union (1941) met resistance from the T-34, then probably the best design in the world. It had a 76.2-mm gun and a top speed of 32 mph (51 km per hour).*

US M-4 *A US design used extensively in World War II was the M-4, known as the "General Sherman." Introduced in 1942, it had a 75-mm gun and a top speed of 24 mph (38 km per hour).*

Soviet T-54 *This main battle tank, with its 100-mm gun, effective use of armor, and road speed of 34 mph (54 km per hour) was the most advanced tank in the world when it appeared in 1954.*

British Challenger *Introduced during the 1980s, this main battle tank is heavily armed with a 120-mm gun, has a top speed of 35 mph (56 km per hour), and is protected by Chobham armour.*

tansy A perennial herb, *Tanacetum* (or *Chrysanthemum*) *vulgare*, native to temperate Eurasia. Growing to a height of 30–100 cm, it has flat-topped clusters of yellow flowers and was formerly cultivated for its aromatic leaves, used for cooking and medicinal purposes. Family: *Compositae*.

Tanta 30 48N 31 00E A city in Egypt, on the Nile Delta. It is noted for its fairs and Muslim festivals and is an important commercial centre with cotton and tobacco industries. Population (1983 est): 335 300.

tantalum (Ta) A very hard grey dense metallic element, discovered in 1802 by A. K. Ekeberg (1767–1813). It is similar to niobium (Nb) and is difficult to separate from it. Tantalum occurs naturally in the ore columbite ($Fe(Nb,Ta)_2O_6$). It is resistant to chemical attack and is used in alloys, for example in surgical materials for implantation in the body and in incandescent filaments. The oxide (Ta_2O_5) is used in special glass, with high refractive index, for camera lenses. At no 73; at wt 180.948; mp 2996°C; bp 5425 ± 100°C.

Tantalus A legendary Greek king of Lydia, son of Zeus and Pluto and father of *Niobe and *Pelops. In Hades he was punished for certain offences against the gods by being made to stand within reach of water and fruits that moved away whenever he tried to drink or eat.

Tantras A group of Sanskrit religious texts written in India in the 5th century AD. The contents are miscellaneous but they form the basis of esoteric systems of meditation in both Hinduism and Buddhism. In the **Tantric yoga** of Hinduism, two principles are postulated: Shiva and Shakti, male and female, mind and creative energy, situated in the head and at the base of the spine, respectively. The object of tantric practices is to arouse the female element, which can be focused in various centres of the body, and ultimately to unite it with the male principle. **Tantric Buddhism** involves an elaborate system of meditation by means of mudras (gestures), mantras (symbolic sounds; *see* Om), and mandalas (diagrams). The imagery of sexual union is the distinctive feature of both systems, which are unusual in emphasizing the fulfilment of bodily desires rather than the ascetic practices that are more typical of Hinduism and Buddhism.

Tanzania, United Republic of A country in East Africa, on the Indian Ocean. It consists of a mainland area (formerly the republic of Tanganyika) and the islands of *Zanzibar and *Pemba, as well as some smaller islands. On the mainland its boundaries are formed partly by Lakes Victoria, Tanganyika, and Malawi. The land rises from the coast through plateaus to mountains, especially in the N, with Mount Kilimanjaro at 5950 m (19 520 ft). The majority of the population is African, mainly of Bantu origin. *Economy*: chiefly agricultural, especially subsistence farming. In mainland Tanzania the chief crops are cotton, maize, and cassava. Sisal, once important, is now in decline and there are plans for diversification of crops as well as development in forestry and livestock. Zanzibar (with Pemba) is the world's largest producer of cloves, with coconuts as the second cash crop. Food crops include rice, bananas, and cassava. Minerals extracted in Tanzania include diamonds, gold, tin, and salt, and coal and iron have been found, as well as offshore gas. Hydroelectricity is a valuable source of power. The main exports are coffee, cloves, cotton, and diamonds. Tourism is important with Tanzania's many game parks and beaches. *History*: important prehistoric remains have been found by the *Leakey family. The area was visited by the Arabs in the middle ages and by the Portuguese in the 16th century. Tanganyika was occupied by the Germans in the 1880s, becoming a German protectorate in 1891. After World War I it was under British rule, first under League of Nations mandate and then as a UN trust territory. It gained independence in 1961 and in 1962 became a republic within the British Commonwealth with Dr Julius K. Nyerere as its first president. In 1964 Tanganyika and Zanzibar joined to form the United Republic of Tanganyika and Zanzibar, now known as Tanzania. In 1977 the official political parties of the two countries merged to form the Revolutionary Party. In the Arusha Declaration (1967) Nyerere launched a policy of decentralization, which has involved the division of rural areas into cooperative communities (Ujamaas). Tanzania was instrumental in the overthrow of *Amin. Relations with Zambia are close, particularly since the opening of the Chinese-built Tanzam Railway (1975). President: Ali Hassan Mwinyi. Official languages: Swahili and English. Official currency, since 1966: Tanzanian shilling of 100 cents. Area: 945 087 sq km (364 900 sq mi). Population (1983 est): 20 524 000. Capital: Dodoma. Main port: Dar es Salaam.

Taoism Emerging in the 6th century BC, Taoism is one of the two great native Chinese religio-philosophical systems (the other is *Confucianism) and a major influence in the development of Chinese culture. The goal of Taoism as a philosophy, as expressed in the *Tao Te Ching* of *Lao-zi, the *Chuang Tzu*, and the *Lieh Tzu*, is profound, joyful, mystical, and practical harmony with the universe. In politics and livelihood, the Taoist seeks the effective path of least resistance and of inconspicuousness. All extreme positions revert to their opposites. All is in flux except Tao (the Way) itself. *Yin* (the feminine) balances *yang* (the masculine). Meditation, spontaneity, and simplicity are stressed. *Te* (virtue) and *Ch'i* (energy) represent the power of effortless action accessible to the Taoist. As a religion Taoism emphasizes the alchemical relations between macrocosm and microcosm, seeking a formula for immortality by breath control, diet, exercises, sexual continence, or chemical elixirs. A priesthood, a huge hierarchical pantheon of gods, and a multitude of sacred texts and rituals associated with various sects arose. Later monasticism developed. Since the Chinese Cultural Revolution (1966–68) religious Taoism survives mainly in Taiwan. Western interest has been aroused by philosophical Taoism, especially by the *I Ching*, an oracular work that claims to demonstrate purpose in chance events.

tape recorder A device for recording and playing back sound stored on magnetic tape. In recording, the sound is converted to an electrical signal by a *microphone and then amplified before being fed to an electromagnet in the recording head. The varying field of the magnet leaves a pattern of magnetization in the iron (or sometimes chromium) oxide coating of the tape as it passes through the machine. To play back, the magnetized tape induces a current in a coil as it passes the reproducing head. The coil current is then amplified and fed to loudspeakers. Tape recorders provide a compact and portable means of recording sounds of all kinds; the tapes are usually wound into *cassettes or cartridges, which can be purchased prerecorded with music, etc., or clean for recording upon.

tapestry A decorative or pictorial woven textile, used as wall hangings, furniture covers, etc. Tapestry weaving has been practised since antiquity but it only flourished in Europe from the 14th century, the major centres of production being Arras, Tournai, and Brussels in Flanders, and Beauvais and the *Gobelins factory in France. Medieval tapestries, often of floral and leaf patterns, were used as portable draught screens; others showing religious scenes were made for churches. From the 16th century painters, notably *Raphael and *Boucher, were commissioned to design tapestries. In the 19th century machine-made tapestries were introduced, but hand weaving in England was kept alive by William *Morris, who established the Merton Abbey looms (1877).

tapeworm A parasitic hermaphrodite *flatworm of the class *Cestoda* (about 3000 species). Tapeworms range from 20 mm to 15 m in length and anchor themselves inside the intestine of their host by means of hooks and suckers on the head. They have no gut or sense organs, the body consisting of a chain of progressively large segments through which food is absorbed. The terminal segments—full of eggs—are regularly shed, passing out of the host's body to infect a secondary host, where larvae invade muscle tissue. Species infecting man include the beef tapeworm (*Taenia saginata*) and the pork tapeworm (*T. solium*).

tapioca. *See* cassava.

tapir A shy nocturnal hoofed mammal belonging to the genus *Tapirus* (4 species). The largest species is the black and white Malayan tapir (*T. indicus*), reaching about 1 m at the shoulder and weighing up to 350 kg. The remaining species of Central and South America are brown. All have a sparse covering of hairs and a large head with a short fleshy snout. Young tapirs are marked with white spots and stripes. Tapirs inhabit forests near water, feeding on leaves and shoots. Family: *Tapiridae*; order: *Perissodactyla*.

tar A thick black semisolid substance of organic origin, especially coaltar obtained when coal is heated to over 1000°C in the absence of air (1 kg of coal yielding about 50 g of tar). Tar can be used as it is, e.g. for the production of roofing felt, or can be distilled to produce a wide range of organic chemicals including benzene, naphthalene, and anthracene and their derivatives. The substance remaining is called pitch.

Tara 53 34N 6 35W A village in the Republic of Ireland, in Co Meath. The Hill of Tara was the ancient religious and political centre of Ireland and here the early Irish Kings lived and were crowned. The original coronation stone is reputed to have been taken to Scone, Scotland.

Taranaki A district of New Zealand, on W North Island. It is important for dairy farming, especially on the volcanic ring plain encircling Mount *Egmont. Area: 9713 sq km (3750 sq mi). Population (1980 est): 106 600. Chief town: New Plymouth.

Taranto 40 28N 17 15E A seaport in Italy, in Apulia on the Gulf of Taranto. Founded by the Greeks in the 8th century BC, it has an 11th-century cathedral. It is an important naval base, with shipyards. Its large iron and steel works were established in 1965. Population (1980 est): 248 611.

tarantula A large dark hairy spider (up to 75 mm long) of the family *Theraphosidae*, found in tropical America. Many tarantulas live on trees or in burrows in the soil, feeding mainly at night on insects and occasionally frogs, toads, mice, and small birds. Their poisonous bite is painful but not fatal to man.
The name was originally given to a *wolf spider (*Lycosa tarentula*) of Taranto (Italy). In the middle ages it was believed that the poisonous effects of the bite of this spider could be eliminated by dancing (the dance came to be known as the tarantella).

Tarbes 43 14N 0 05E A town in SW France, the capital of the Hautes-Pyrénées department. A Huguenot stronghold (16th-17th centuries), it has a 13th-century cathedral and trades in horses and agricultural produce. Population (1982): 54 055.

Tardigrada A phylum of tiny invertebrate animals (about 350 species), known as water bears, sometimes regarded as a class of arthropods. About 1 mm long, they are almost transparent, with four pairs of short legs ending in claws. Tardigrades are found in terrestrial, freshwater, and marine habitats, feeding on the sap of mosses and other plants.

tare One of several annual herbs of the genus *Vicia* (which also includes *vetches) that grow as weeds on cultivated land throughout the world. Tares have slender trailing stems, up to 60 cm long, and branches with paired leaflets and terminal climbing tendrils. The tiny white or bluish flowers give rise to seed pods. Family: *Leguminosae*.

Taree 31 54S 152 26E A town in Australia, in NE New South Wales. It is the principal town of the Manning River

district, specializing in dairy products. Population (1981): 16 000.

targum (Aramaic: translation) An Aramaic translation of part of the Bible. There are several targumim, notably those of Onkelos (of the Torah) and Pseudo-Jonathan (of the Prophets). They were produced in Palestine and Babylonia in the Talmudic and gaonic periods, and include a great deal of *Midrash.

tariffs A surcharge imposed by a government on imported goods. Several arguments are used to justify tariffs. The "infant industry" argument is that tariffs are needed to protect a domestic industry while it becomes established. Other arguments include the need to protect employment in domestic industries, the need to provide a counter to "dumping" (foreign industries selling goods at a lower price abroad than at home), and the benefit of the revenue that will accrue from tariffs. The secretariat of the *General Agreement on Tariffs and Trade serves as a centre for negotiating tariff agreements. *See also* customs unions.

Tarim Basin A great depression in NW China, covering the area between the *Tian Shan in the N and the *Kunlun Mountains in the S. Drained by the Dalimu (*or* Tarim) River, it consists of the Takelamagan (*or* Takla Makan) Desert with the salt lake of *Lop Nor in the E, where nuclear tests have been held. Although there are oasis towns, the region is largely undeveloped. Area: about 906 500 sq km (350 000 sq mi).

taro A perennial herbaceous plant, *Colocasia esculenta*, also known as eddo, dasheen, and elephant's ear, native to tropical Asia and widely cultivated in tropical and subtropical areas for its edible tubers. The tubers, which are large, starchy, and spherical, contain more protein than potatoes and are eaten cooked as vegetables or made into puddings or bread. Family: *Araceae*.

LA·ROUE·DE·FORTUNE

TAROT *The Wheel of Fortune, the 10th card of the Greater Arcana, from a pack of French tarot cards.*

tarot A pack of 78 cards used primarily in fortune telling, although they are also the forerunners of modern *playing cards, and games are still played with them. They originated in 14th-century Italy, although their symbolism probably draws on a far older tradition. The original pack is now known as the Greater Arcana; this consists of 22 cards (believed to correspond to the letters of the Hebrew alphabet), 21 numbered cards representing natural elements, vices, and virtues and a "Fool" (the original joker). During the 14th century these were combined with 56 number cards of the Asian kind then also beginning to be used. Now known as the Lesser Arcana, these 56 are in 4 suits: cups, swords, money, and clubs or rods, representing clergy, nobility, merchants, and peasants. Each suit consists of number cards from one to ten and four court cards: king, queen, knave, and knight.

tarpan A Eurasian wild horse, *Equus caballus*, that became extinct in the early 20th century. It was small and dun-coloured with a long flowing mane. Attempts have been made to reconstitute the tarpan by crossing various modern breeds that are thought to be related to it.

Tarpeia In Roman legend, a Roman commander's daughter who offered to betray Rome to the attacking Sabines in return for what they wore on their left arms, meaning their golden bracelets. When the Sabines overran the citadel, they literally obeyed her wish by crushing her to death with their shields.

tarpon A marine game fish belonging to the family *Elopidae*. It has a slender body covered by large thick silvery scales. The Atlantic tarpon, *Tarpon* (or *Megalops*) *atlanticus*, reaches up to 2 m in length and occurs inshore in warm waters. Order: *Elopiformes*.

Tarquin the Proud (Tarquinius Superbus) The last King of Rome, who ruled, according to Roman tradition, from 534 to 510 BC. Tarquin is probably a historical figure but many myths evolved to account for the nickname Superbus; he was expelled from Rome and brought monarchy into permanent disrepute there.

tarragon A perennial herb, *Artemisia dracunculus*, native to central Asia and widely cultivated. It grows to a height of about 60 cm and has slender leaves and flowers, which are often dried and used in salads, sauces, pickles, etc. It also yields an essential oil used in cooking and perfumery. Family: *Compositae*.

Tarragona (Latin name: Tarraco) 41 07N 1 15E A port in NE Spain, in Catalonia on the Mediterranean Sea. It was a major Roman port and has many Roman ruins, including an aqueduct; it also possesses a cathedral (12th–13th centuries). An agricultural centre, it also has a petrochemicals industry. Population (1981): 111 689.

Tarrasa 41 38N 2 00E A town in NE Spain, in Catalonia. An important industrial centre, it is famous for its woollen textiles; other industries include glass and fertilizers. Population (1981): 155 360.

tarsier A small nocturnal *prosimian primate belonging to the genus *Tarsius* (3 species), of Sumatra, Borneo, Celebes, and the Philippines. 22–43 cm long including the naked tail (13–27 cm), tarsiers have enormous eyes, large hairless ears, and gripping pads at the end of their digits. They are mainly arboreal, using both hands to seize small insects and lizards. Family: *Tarsiidae*. □mammal.

Tarsus 36 52N 34 52E A town in central S Turkey, near Adana. The first known settlement here was Neolithic; it was Assyrian for many centuries and an important town in the Roman and Byzantine Empires. St Paul was born here. Population (1980): 121 074.

tartan *See* Highland dress.

tartaric acid ($HOOC(CHOH)_2COOH$) A white crystalline powder with an acid taste; it is a constituent of *baking powder.

Tartarus In Greek religion, the place of punishment and perpetual torment in the underworld. The *Titans were imprisoned there after their defeat by the gods.

Tartu (German and Swedish name: Dorpat) 58 20N 26 44E A city in the Soviet Union, in the SE Estonian SSR. Although an industrial centre, it is best known for its university founded (1632) by Gustavus II Adolphus of Sweden, Tartu being held successively by Sweden, Poland, and Russia to which it was finally ceded in 1704. Population (1983 est): 109 000.

Tasaday A people of the rain forests of Mindanao in the Philippines having an extremely rudimentary culture based on food gathering using simple stone and wooden tools. They are cave dwellers who wear leaves for clothing and only became known to the outside world in 1971.

Tashkent 41 16N 69 13E A city in the S central Soviet Union, the capital of the Uzbek SSR. It is the oldest and largest city of central Asia, being a major communications, industrial, and cultural centre. Textiles (based on cotton from the surrounding oasis), food- and tobacco-processing, and chemical industries are important. *History*: dating from at least the 1st century BC, it fell successively to the Arabs (7th century) and the Turks (12th century), becoming a great commercial centre under Timur. It was captured by Russia in 1865. Tashkent was severely damaged by earthquake in 1966. Population (1981 est): 1 858 000.

Tasman, Abel Janszoon (c. 1603–c. 1659) Dutch navigator. Commissioned in 1642 by van *Dieman to explore the S Pacific, Tasman sighted present-day Tasmania (which he named Van Dieman's Land, after his patron), New Zealand, and in 1643 Tonga and Fiji. In 1644 he sailed along the N coast of Australia, thus proving it continuous.

Tasmania An island and the smallest state of Australia, separated from the SE corner of the mainland by Bass Strait. Discovered by Abel *Tasman in 1642, it was called Van Dieman's Land until 1856. It is the most mountainous of the Australian states and is dominated by the Central Plateau. Agriculture is important with mixed and dairy farming, sheep rearing, and the cultivation of apples and hops. More than 40% of the island is covered by forest and the export of wood chips to Japan is a significant industry. Large mineral deposits include tin, iron ore, zinc, lead, and copper; King Island, off the NW coast, is Australia's main producer of tungsten. Area: 68 332 sq km (26 383 sq mi). Population (1980 est): 422 900. Capital: Hobart.

Tasmanian devil A carnivorous marsupial, *Sarcophilus harrisi*, formerly found on the Australian mainland but now restricted to Tasmania. About 1 m long, it is black with a large head and wide jaws containing doglike teeth. Strong and heavily built, it feeds on wallabies, birds, and lizards and fights ferociously when cornered. Family: *Dasyuridae* (dasyures).

Tasmanian wolf. *See* thylacine.

Tasman Sea A section of the SW Pacific Ocean, lying between SE Australia and Tasmania on the W and New Zealand on the E. Area: about 2 300 000 sq km (900 000 sq mi).

Tass. *See* news agency.

Tassili-n-Ajjer A sandstone massif in the central Sahara containing numerous caves decorated with rock paintings of people and animals (c. 8000–c. 100 BC). Depictions of hippopotamuses and vast herds of cattle indicate a far damper climate than at present.

Tasso, Torquato (1544–95) Italian poet. After studying law at Padua and publishing his epic *Rinaldo* (1562) he joined the court of the Este family at Ferrara, where he wrote the pastoral drama *Aminta* (1573) and his major work, the romantic epic *Gerusalemme liberata* (1575). For the rest of his life he suffered from mental instability but continued to write lyrics, religious poems, philosophical dialogues, and a tragedy, *Re Torrismondo* (1587).

taste. *See* tongue.

Tatar Autonomous Soviet Socialist Republic (*or* Tataria) An administrative division in the W central Soviet Union, in the RSFSR. The *Tatars, who comprise some 50% of the population, were conquered by Ivan the Terrible in the 16th century. The region became an autonomous republic in 1920. The region is the country's main producer of oil and natural gas and also has deposits of coal and other minerals. There are highly developed engineering, oil, and chemical industries, and the timber, textile, and food industries are now also expanding. Agricultural products include fodder crops and cereals. Area: 68 000 sq km (26 250 sq mi). Population (1981 est): 3 453 000. Capital: Kazan.

Tatars A people, mainly living in the Tatar ASSR of the Soviet Union, who belong to the NW division of the Turkic-speaking peoples. They traditionally lived by farming and herding. There are many Tatar dialects, one of which, Kazan Tatar, is a literary language that goes back to the 13th century. The Tatars are descended from peoples associated with the various states of the Mongol empire and the name was often used to refer to all the nomadic Turkic and Mongol peoples of the steppes. Their society was traditionally divided into noble and commoner groups ruled by khans. They are mainly Muslim. *See also* Golden Horde.

Tate, Allen (1899–) US poet and critic, a founder-member of the *Fugitives. The Civil War is the main subject of his novel *The Fathers* (1938) and his best-known poem "Ode to the Confederate Dead" (1926). He published much criticism, including *On The Limits of Poetry* (1948), and his verse is collected in *Collected Poems* (1978).

Tate, Harry (Ronald Hutchinson; 1874–1940) British music-hall comedian. His best-known sketches concerned golf, fishing, and unreliable cars. He also performed in revues and pantomimes.

Tate, Nahum (1652–1715) British poet. Born in Dublin, he is best remembered for his version of Shakespeare's *King Lear*, which omitted the Fool and ended happily with Cordelia marrying Edgar. He was coauthor of the second part of Dryden's *Absalom and Achitophel* (1681). He became poet laureate in 1692.

Tate Gallery An art gallery on Millbank, London, housing paintings of the British school and modern foreign paintings and sculpture. It was built in 1897 with the financial support of the sugar merchant and philanthropist Sir Henry Tate (1819–99), who had donated his collection of British paintings to the nation in 1890. Highlights are its Pre-Raphaelite works and paintings by *Turner, housed in the Clore Gallery since 1987.

Tati, Jacques (J. Tatischeff; 1908–82) French film actor and director. He was a music-hall performer before he turned to films. He wrote, directed, and acted in a number of popular award-winning comedies, such as *Jour de Fête* (1947), *Monsieur Hulot's Holiday* (1952), *Mon Oncle* (1958), and *Playtime* (1968), the humour of which is achieved by imaginative visual gags and Tati's talent for pantomime.

Tatra Mountains Two mountain ranges in central E Europe: the **High Tatras** (Polish name: Tatry Wysokie; Czech name: Vysoké Tatry), which extend 90 km (56 mi) E–W along the Polish-Czech border and constitute the highest area of the *Carpathian Mountains, and, to the S, the **Low Tatras** (Czech name: Nízké Tatry), which run parallel for some 150 km (93 mi) and rise to 2043 m (6703 ft).

Tattersall, Richard (1724–95) British racehorse owner, who established auctions for horses in London in 1766. The company of Tattersall's still holds bloodstock auctions at Newmarket, Suffolk.

Tatum, Art(hur) (1910–56) US Black jazz pianist, who began playing as a child when he was already blind. A well-known soloist in the 1930s, he formed his own trio in 1943. His superb technique and advanced sense of harmony earned him a high reputation among both jazz and classical musicians.

Tatum, Edward Lawrie (1909–75) US geneticist, who (working with G. W. *Beadle on mutant strains of bread mould) provided evidence that specific genes determine the structure of specified enzymes. In 1946 Tatum and J. *Lederberg discovered the phenomenon of genetic recombination in certain bacteria. Tatum shared a Nobel Prize (1958) with Beadle and Lederberg.

Taunton 51 01N 3 06W A market town in SW England, the administrative centre of Somerset. The Great Hall in the 12th-century castle was the scene of Judge Jeffreys' Bloody Assizes (1685). Textile and leather goods, gloves, aeronautical instruments, and cider are manufactured. Population (1981): 35 326.

tau particle An elementary particle with a very short lifetime (5×10^{-12} second) and a mass about 3500 times that of the *electron. It is classified as a lepton (*see* particle physics). It reacts by the *weak interaction.

Taupo, Lake (*or* Taupomoana) The largest lake in New Zealand. It lies on the volcanic plateau of central North Island and is drained by the Waikato River. Area: 616 sq km (238 sq mi).

Tauranga 37 42S 176 11E A city and port in New Zealand, in North Island on the Bay of Plenty. Tauranga's chief exports are dairy produce, meat, and fruit. Population (1983 est): 57 000.

Taurus (Latin: Bull) A large constellation in the N sky near Orion, lying on the *zodiac between Gemini and Aries. The brightest star is *Aldebaran. The constellation contains the *Hyades and *Pleiades star clusters and the *Crab nebula with its associated pulsar.

Taurus Mountains A mountain range in S Turkey. It extends 560 km (348 mi) parallel to the Mediterranean coast and rises to 3734 m (12 251 ft) at Ala Dağ, or to 3916 m (12 848 ft) at Erciyas Dağı if the Anti-Taurus range (an extension to the NE) is included.

tautology A statement that is always true and therefore gives no information. For example, "It is either raining or it is not raining."

tautomerism. *See* isomers.

Tavener, John (1944–) British composer, a pupil of Lennox Berkeley. His compositions include the cantata *The Whale* (for reciter, chorus, and orchestra; 1966), *A Celtic Requiem* (1968–69), and the opera *Thérèse* (1979).

Taverner, John (c. 1495–1545) English composer. He became choirmaster at Cardinal College (later renamed Christ Church) Oxford, in 1526. In 1528 he was imprisoned for heresy and left Oxford in 1530. He became a paid agent of Thomas Cromwell and gave up music. He left 28 motets, a *Te Deum*, 8 masses, and some instrumental music.

Tawney, R(ichard) H(enry) (1880–1962) British economic historian. Influenced by the theories of Max *Weber, Tawney wrote on capitalism, his most famous book being *Religion and the Rise of Capitalism* (1926). A professor at London University (1931–49), he was a formative influence on the British Labour Party.

tawny owl A common *owl, *Strix aluco*, occurring in Europe and SE Asia. 38 cm long, it has short rounded wings, dark-brown eyes, a mottled brown plumage, and lacks ear tufts.

taxation The means by which a government raises funds to finance its spending and, to some extent, by which it regulates the economy (*see* fiscal policy) or achieves its social and political aims (e.g. the equal distribution of wealth). Direct taxes are paid by individuals (e.g. *income tax, *capital-gains tax, *inheritance tax) or by companies (*see* corporation tax) directly to the tax authorities; indirect taxes are levied on goods and services (e.g. *value-added tax). In most cases taxation is levied when funds change hands, but in a wealth tax this is not the case. Progressive taxation, in which those with higher incomes or greater wealth pay more in proportion than those with lower incomes or less wealth, is a means of achieving social or political objectives; *tax-credit systems would combine taxation with social benefits. *See also* customs and excise duties.

tax-credit system A system that combines taxation and social-benefit payments; the state fixes a level of income above which taxation (income tax) is levied and below which benefits (negative income tax) are paid. The advantages claimed for the system are: each individual is guaranteed a fixed minimum income, there is a positive incentive to work as after-tax income always increases with earnings (*compare* poverty trap), and there is a great saving in costs by combining the administration of taxation with the welfare system.

tax haven (*or* tax shelter) A country or area that has low taxes and can therefore offer advantages to foreign individuals or companies that pay high taxes in their own countries. Individuals have to take up residence in these countries, giving up their domiciliary rights in their own countries; companies can open offices and subsidiary companies in the haven countries, through which they can put part of their business.

taxi. *See* cab.

taxidermy The art of making lifelike zoological models of creatures by preserving their skins and mounting them on suitable dummies. Taxidermy dates from the 17th century but improved technology and the use of plastic body forms have resulted in greater degrees of realism.

Taxila The site of an *Achaemenian and Greek city near Rawalpindi (N Pakistan). Occupied from the 5th century BC, it was a famous centre of learning. Excavations revealed a blend of Greek and Buddhist elements, typical of the *Gandhara culture. The *Huns destroyed Taxila in 460 AD.

taxis The movement of a living organism or cell in response to an external stimulus: the movement is either towards or away from the stimulus, i.e. a positive or negative taxis. Taxes are specified according to the type of stimulus. For example, **chemotaxis** is the response to a change in the concentration of a chemical. Many insects, for example, respond chemotactically to the scents emitted by the opposite sex. **Phototaxis** is the response to light: cockroaches are negatively phototactic. *Compare* tropism.

taxonomy The study of the classification and nomenclature of organisms. The principles of taxonomy were established in the 18th century by the work of *Linnaeus (*see also* binomial nomenclature). As far as possible, organisms are arranged into a hierarchy of groups (called taxa) based on degrees of relationship (*see* phylogeny). When knowledge of the evolution of a group is lacking taxonomy is based on structural and other similarities. The basic unit of classification is the *species. Related species are grouped into genera, which are arranged into orders and then classes. Related classes are regarded as belonging to the same *phylum. The two main methods used in determining taxonomic positions are classical taxonomy, which is based on morphological and biochemical data, and numerical taxonomy, in which mathematical and statistical methods are used to assess similarities and differences.

Tay, River The longest river in Scotland, rising in the Grampian Mountains and flowing generally NE through Loch Tay before flowing SE to enter the North Sea through the Firth of Tay. Length: 193 km (120 mi).

Taylor, A(lan) J(ohn) P(ercivale) (1906–) British historian, who specializes in modern European political history. Among his many books is *The Origins of the Second World War* (1961), and his television broadcasts have made him familiar to a wide public.

Taylor, Brook (1685-1737) English mathematician, best known for the Taylor series in calculus. He also made contributions to the mathematics of perspective. Taylor,

educated at Cambridge, was secretary of the Royal Society between 1714 and 1719.

Taylor, Elizabeth (1932–) US film actress, born in England. She began her career as a child star, notably in *National Velvet* (1944). Her other films include *Cleopatra* (1962) and *Who's Afraid of Virginia Woolf?* (1966), in both of which she costarred with Richard *Burton, to whom she was twice married, and *The Blue Bird* (1976).

Taylor, Frederick Winslow (1856-1915) US engineer, who pioneered the techniques of scientific management. In 1881, while working for the Midvale Steel Company, he introduced time and motion study as a means of increasing efficiency, incurring considerable resentment from those affected by it. He later became a management consultant to many firms.

Taylor, Jeremy (1613-67) English Anglican churchman and theologian. Chaplain to Archbishop Laud and Charles I, he was imprisoned by parliamentary forces in 1645 and forced to live in seclusion during the Interregnum. At the Restoration he was made Bishop of Down and Connor (1660) and vice chancellor of Dublin University. His works, which include *The Liberty of Prophesying* (1647), *Holy Living* (1650), *Holy Dying* (1651), and *The Rule of Conscience* (1660), have earned him the title of the "Shakespeare of the pulpit."

Taylor, Zachary (1784-1850) US statesman and general; president (1849-50). In the *Mexican War (1846-48), he won the victory of Buena Vista although his forces were outnumbered by four to one. As president he offered little leadership in the important question of the extension of slavery to the new states acquired from Mexico.

Tayside Region An administrative region in SE Scotland, bordering on the North Sea. It was created under local government reorganization in 1975 from the counties of Angus, most of Perth, and Kinross. The SE lowlands, which include the Vale of Strathmore and Carse of Gowrie, rise NW to the Grampian Mountains. Agricultural produce includes arable crops and soft fruit from the Carse of Gowrie; dairy and beef cattle are important. There are several hydroelectric power stations, notably at Pitlochry. Industries include wool products and engineering. Area: 7668 sq km (2959 sq mi). Population (1981): 391 529. Administrative centre: Dundee.

Tbilisi (Russian name: Tiflis) 41 43N 44 48E A city in the SW Soviet Union, the capital of the Georgian SSR on the River Kura. A major industrial centre, engineering and the manufacture of textiles, wine, and food are the principal economic activities; Tbilisi also has a lively cultural life. *History*: founded in the mid-5th century, it fell successively to the Persians, Byzantines, Arabs, Mongols, Turks, and, finally, the Russians (1801). Its name was changed to the Georgian Tbilisi in 1936. Population (1981 est): 1 095 000.

Tchaikovsky, Peter Ilich (1840-93) Russian composer. He studied under Anton Rubinstein in St Petersburg and became professor at the Moscow conservatoire in 1866. After the success of his first piano concerto, Tchaikovsky was offered financial support from Nadezhda von Meck (1831-94), a wealthy widow, whom he never met. In 1877 Tchaikovsky made a disastrous marriage and began to suffer from depression, although many of his works were extremely successful. He died of cholera, from drinking unboiled water, in 1893. Among his compositions are six symphonies, including the *Pathètique* (1893), three piano concertos (one unfinished), a violin concerto, string quartets, the opera *Eugene Onegin* (1877-78), and the ballets *Swan Lake* (1876-77) and the *Nutcracker* (1891-92).

tea The dried leaves and shoots of the evergreen shrub or tree, *Camellia sinensis*, which yield a beverage when infused with water. Native to parts of India and China, the tea plant has three major varieties—China, Assam, and Cambodia—and numerous hybrids, ranging from 2.75 to 18 m in height. The shoots and young leaves are picked by hand and left to wilt before being lightly rolled and dried. Before drying, the leaves may be allowed to ferment, producing either black tea or, if only partially fermented, oolong tea. Leaves that are not fermented produce green tea. The major tea exporters are India and Sri Lanka; most of China's production goes for home consumption. Tea is also produced in SE Asia and parts of Africa and South America. Tea is sold in the form of chopped leaves—loose or contained in small porous paper bags (tea bags)—or as a soluble powdered extract (instant tea). Its stimulating effect is due to the caffeine content (about 3.5%); flavour depends on the presence of volatile oils, and tannins are responsible for its colour. Family: *Theaceae*.

tea ceremony. *See* cha-no-yu.

Teach, Edward (d. 1718) British pirate, nicknamed Blackbeard, who molested shipping in the Atlantic from his headquarters in N Carolina. In 1718 he was killed by a punitive force sent from Virginia.

teak A tropical □tree, *Tectonia grandis*, native to SE Asia and cultivated for its timber. Growing to a height of 45 m in its natural state, it has small white flowers and fleshy fruits. The aromatic golden-yellow heartwood becomes brown with darker mottling when seasoned and is very hard and durable, being used for furniture, door and window frames, construction purposes, etc. Burma is the major teak exporter. Family: *Verbenaceae*.

teal A small *dabbling duck, *Anas crecca*, of the N hemisphere, nesting on marshes and wintering on mudflats and estuaries. 35 cm long, it feeds on water plants and aquatic invertebrates. Drakes are grey and have a chestnut head with a cream-edged green eye stripe and a white wing stripe; females are mottled brown and both sexes have a green-and-black wing patch.

tear gas (*or* lachrymator) A substance, generally an atomized liquid rather than a gas, that is used to control crowds by causing acute eye irritation with temporary blindness and copious flow of tears. Side effects include lasting damage to the eyes and nasal and lung tissues and dermatitis. Chloroacetophenone (Mace) is the best-known example. *See also* chemical warfare.

teasel A biennial herb, *Dipsacus fullonum*, native to Europe, W Asia, and N Africa. The prickly stems grow to a height of 2 m and bear conical heads of blue, purple, or white flowers with stiff hooked bracts. Fuller's teasel (*D. fullonum sativus*) was formerly cultivated for its flower heads, which were used to tease fabrics and raise a nap. Family: *Dipsacaceae*.

Tebbitt, Norman (Beresford) (1931–) British Conservative politician; chairman of the Conservative Party (1985–87) and Chancellor of the Duchy of Lancaster (1985–87). A former RAF and civil airline pilot, he subsequently served in several ministerial posts, including secretary of state for employment (1981–83) and trade and industry (1983–85). In 1984 he and his wife Margaret were badly injured by an IRA bomb in Brighton.

technetium (Tc) A silvery-grey radioactive element that was the first to be produced artificially. It does not occur naturally on earth but has been observed spectroscopically in a number of stars, where it is being continuously formed by nuclear reactions. It is chemically similar to rhenium and the compound $KTcO_4$ is a remarkable corrosion inhibitor in steels. At no 43; at wt (99); mp 2227°C; bp 4627°C.

tectonics The study of the major structural features of the earth's crust and the processes by which they are constructed. Thus a feature described as tectonic is formed by deformational movements of the earth's crust or by volcanic action rather than by geomorphological processes. A tectonic map shows structural features, usually over large areas. The most modern interpretation of global tectonics is the theory of *plate tectonics.

Tecumseh (c. 1768-1813) American Shawnee Indian chief, who led an Indian confederacy against the advance of White settlement in the NW. After his tribe was surprised at the battle of Tippecanoe (1811) he swore eternal war on the settlers. The conviction among frontiersmen that the British in Canada were helping Tecumseh led to a demand among the so-called war hawks in the US Congress for war with Britain, the *War of 1812, in which Tecumseh was killed.

Tedder, Arthur William, 1st Baron (1890-1967) British air marshal. He joined the Royal Flying Corps in 1916 after army service. In World War II he was appointed (1940) to command the RAF in the Middle East and then (1943) in the Mediterranean. He became Eisenhower's deputy in 1944 and contributed greatly to the success of the Normandy landings.

Tees, River A river in N England. Rising in the Pennines in Cumbria, it flows mainly E into the Teesmouth estuary at Middlesbrough to join the North Sea. The river valley above Darlington, known as **Teesdale**, contains Mickle Fell, at 790 m (2592 ft) Yorkshire's highest point. Length: 113 km (70 mi).

Teesside An industrial district in NE England, in Cleveland on the River Tees estuary. It formed a county borough in the North Riding of Yorkshire (1968-74).

molar tooth *The root of the tooth is anchored into the socket by a bonelike substance, cement.*

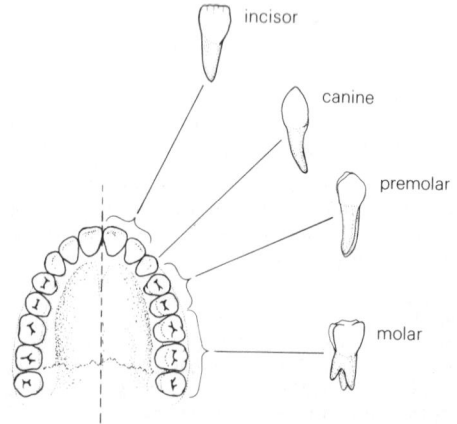

teeth in the adult upper jaw *The incisors and canines are used principally for biting; the premolars and molars are for grinding and chewing. The lower jaw contains the same number and type of teeth.*

TEETH

teeth Hard structures in the mouth, embedded in the jaws, used for biting and chewing food. The human adult (permanent) dentition consists of 32 teeth, including incisors (8), canines (4), premolars (8), and molars (12). Young children have a milk (deciduous) dentition of 20 teeth (incisors, canines, and molars), which are replaced by the permanent teeth between the ages of 6 and 12. The third molar (wisdom tooth) on each side of both jaws does not normally appear until the age of about 20 (sometimes later). The crown of a tooth consists of very dense hard enamel (largely *apatite) overlying the yellow bonelike dentine, which is slightly spongy and very sensitive to touch, temperature, and pain. The pulp at the centre contains blood vessels and nerve fibres. The principal disorders affecting teeth are *caries and *periodontal disease. *See also* dentistry.

Tegucigalpa   14 20N 87 12W The capital of Honduras, situated in the centre of the country in a high valley. Founded in 1579, it was an important centre of gold and silver mining. It became the capital in 1824. The University of Honduras was founded in 1847. Population (1980 est): 472 700.

Tehran (*or* Teheran)   35 40N 51 26E The capital of Iran, in the N centre of the country at the foot of the Elburz Mountains. Most of its buildings are modern, but the Gulistan Palace, which houses the Crown Jewels, is a notable older structure. Tehran is the commercial, industrial, administrative, and cultural centre of the country, with six universities (oldest 1934). It became the capital in 1788 and has been greatly enlarged this century. Fierce rioting here preceded the overthrow (1979) of the Shah of Iran. Population (1985 est): 5 751 500.

Tehran Conference   (1943) The conference in World War II attended by F. D. Roosevelt (USA), Stalin (Soviet Union), and Churchill (UK). Its chief purpose was to coordinate Allied strategy in W and E Europe.

Tehuantepec, Isthmus of   An isthmus in S Mexico, between the Gulf of Campeche and the Gulf of Tehuantepec.

Teilhard de Chardin, Pierre   (1881–1955) French Jesuit theologian and palaeontologist. His philosophical books were suppressed by the Roman Catholic Church during his lifetime. He is best known for his creative synthesis of natural science and religion and his Christian metaphysical philosophy. In his books *The Phenomenon of Man* (1955) and *Le Milieu divin* (1957), he maintained that the universe and mankind are in constant evolution towards a perfect state.

Tejo, River.   *See* Tagus, River.

Te Kanawa, Dame Kiri   (1944–   ) New Zealand soprano. She studied in England at the London Opera Centre and made her major debut in the role of Countess Almaviva in the *Marriage of Figaro* at Covent Garden in 1971. In 1981 she sang at the wedding of the Prince and Princess of Wales. She was made a DBE in 1982.

Telanaipura.   *See* Jambi.

Tel Aviv-Jaffa   32 05N 34 46E A city in central Israel, on the Mediterranean coast. Most of the buildings in the city are modern structures, but some old streets have been restored. It is the largest city in Israel, and the country's commercial, industrial, and cultural centre. Israel's stock exchange is here, and there are two universities (1953 and 1974). The city's port is at Ashdod, to the S. *History*: Tel Aviv was originally a suburb to the N of Jaffa (ancient name: Joppa; Arabic name: Yafa), founded in 1909 to relieve the overpopulation of the Jewish quarter of an otherwise Arab town. Following tension between Arabs and Jews, the two towns were separated in 1921, and, as Jewish immigration increased, Tel Aviv expanded rapidly becoming by 1936 the largest city in Palestine. Almost the entire Arab population fled Jaffa on its capture by Jewish forces in 1948, and the two cities were reunited in 1950 as Tel Aviv-Jaffa. Population (1983): 327 300.

telecommunications   The transfer of information by any electromagnetic means, such as wire or radio waves. It includes telephones, telegraphy, *radio, *televison, etc. Generally, a telecommunications system consists of a transmitter, a transmission channel, and a receiver. The input to the transmitter is usually coded in some way and then fed to a modulator, in which it is combined with a carrier signal (*see* modulation).

The transmission channel may be a wire, an optical fibre, or radio waves within a specified frequency range (the bandwidth). A single channel may carry several signals if a *multiplexer is used. The receiver demodulates the signal and decodes it, converting it into the desired form of output, which may be sound, an electrical signal to a computer, a teleprinter printout, etc. Distortion may occur in the transmission because the signal has taken two different paths (shadowing) or because the channel may not respond equally to all the frequencies being transmitted. Noise (spurious signals) may arise at any stage of the transmission and reception process.

The **telephone**, which was invented by Alexander Graham Bell in 1875, carries speech in the form of electrical signals along a wire. A carbon *microphone in the mouthpiece produces an electrical signal that passes through a network of exchanges and relays to the receiving earpiece, where it is converted back into sound by a small diaphragm *loudspeaker. Telephone connections are now normally made automatically, first going through a local exchange and then, for long-distance calls, through the trunk network. All the switching operations are activated by the caller and controlled and monitored electronically. Telephone connections exist to almost all parts of the world through undersea cables and *communications satellites. **Telegraphy** is the transmission of written or printed messages by electrical signals and was developed before the telephone, in 1837. The *Morse code was used in the first commercial recording telegraph, between England and France in 1851. Now telegrams and *Telex messages are carried along the same wires as telephone conversations, using different frequency ranges. Radiotelegraphy uses radio waves instead of a wire to carry the message. Like long-distance telephone links it may be relayed by communications satellites. Optical fibres transmitting beams of laser light are now being developed and have the potential to carry considerably more information than an electric cable of the same thickness.   *See also* teletext; viewdata.

telekinesis   Apparent change in or movement of material objects, caused by mental effort alone. It is also called psychokinesis (PK). The claims of Uri Geller (1946–   ), an Israeli, to break metal objects merely by concentrating on them have received great publicity. Telekinesis has been evoked to explain levitation and certain *poltergeist manifestations.

Telemachus   In Greek legend, the son of *Odysseus and *Penelope. He searched for his lost father and then helped him kill the suitors of Penelope. After Odysseus' death he married *Circe.

Telemann, Georg Philipp   (1681–1767) German composer, born in Magdeburg. Whilst studying law at Leipzig University he taught himself to play various instruments and to compose, obtaining a post in 1704 as organist at the New Church. He held other musical posts in various cities, including Frankfurt and Hamburg (1721). His output was very large and included operas, oratorios, church music, and much chamber music.

teleology   The philosophical study of ends, goals, and the ultimate good. It has application in both ethics (*see* utilitarianism) and *metaphysics. Teleology was studied by *Kant who used it to provide a proof of the existence of God in terms of the purposiveness of the universe.

teleost   Any *bony fish belonging to the infraclass *Teleostei* (over 20 000 species), which includes nearly all the important food and game fish and many aquarium fish. Teleosts have a symmetrically   divided   (homocercal)   tail   fin   and   an

refractors

Galilean *The simplest practical form of refracting telescope was developed by Galileo in about 1609 from Lippershey's invention.*

Keplerian *Kepler's arrangement produces an inverted image but was much used for astronomical observations in which the inversion did not matter.*

reflectors

Gregorian *James Gregory proposed this design in 1663 but it has had little general application.*

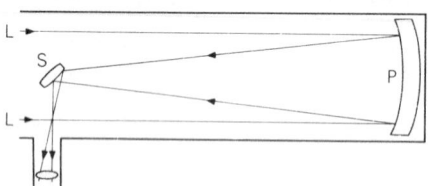

Newtonian *In Newton's 1671 design the secondary mirror is placed at an angle of 45° to the axis of the beam.*

Cassegrain *Widely used, this form was invented by the obscure French astronomer N. Cassegrain in 1672.*

coudé (French: angled) *This arrangement is valuable in larger telescopes as it increases their focal length.*

L = *light rays* P = *primary mirror*
E = *eyepiece* S = *secondary mirror*

TELESCOPE

air-filled swim bladder, which is emptied or filled to regulate buoyancy and give great manoeuvrability. They are solitary or shoaling fish and most lay eggs on rocks or plants, or freely in the water, although some bear live young. Males or sometimes the females may guard the young. Chief orders: *Clupeiformes* (*see* herring; anchovy), *Salmoniformes* (*see* salmon; trout; pike), *Cypriniformes* (*see* carp), *Gadiformes* (*see* cod; hake), *Perciformes* (*see* perch; mackerel), *Pleuronectiformes* (*see* flatfish); subclass: *Actinopterygii*.

telepathy. *See* extrasensory perception.

telephone. *See* telecommunications.

telephoto lens A camera lens that gives a bigger image than a normal lens without moving the camera closer to the subject or extending the camera. It consists of two groups of lenses. The front unit converges the light rays and the rear unit partially corrects this. The light reaching the film appears to converge from a point some distance in front of the camera. Telephoto lenses tend to result in a slightly flattened perspective in the final picture.

telescope An optical instrument that produces a magnified image of distant objects. It is used on land and as a major research tool in astronomy. The first **reflecting telescope** was produced by *Newton in 1668. In the reflecting telescope the light from an object is collected by a concave, usually paraboloid, mirror of long focal length. This primary mirror reflects the light into a secondary optical system, which in turn reflects it into a short-focus eyepiece. The eyepiece lenses produce a magnified image that can be viewed by eye, photographed, or otherwise analysed. Depending on the secondary optics, reflectors are called **Gregorian, Newtonian, Cassegrain,** or **coudé telescopes**.

The **refracting telescope** was invented in 1608 by *Lippershey in Holland and developed by *Galileo as an astronomical instrument a year later. The light in the refracting telescope falls on a converging long-focus objective lens. The resulting image is then magnified by the short-focus eyepiece to produce the final image. An example is the **Keplerian telescope**, which was the first major improvement on Galileo's original design. Refractors are also used as terrestrial telescopes, usually containing an additional lens or a prism to cause the inverted image to be seen erect.

A telescope's light-gathering power depends on the area of the primary mirror or the objective lens. Since large mirrors are easier to fashion and mount than large lenses, the major astronomical telescopes are reflectors. In addition, unlike the objective in refractors, the reflector's mirror suffers no chromatic *aberration and its spherical aberration and coma are minimal. The world's largest optical telescope is the Soviet Academy of Sciences' 6 m reflector in the Northern Caucasus. *See also* Schmidt telescope; radio telescope.

Telesio, Bernardino (1509-88) Italian humanist. His philosophy was influenced by the ancient Greeks and was strongly empirical and opposed to *Aristotelianism. He founded a scientific society (1566) to propagate his approach and among those he influenced were *Campanella and Giordano *Bruno.

teletext An information service in which pages of text are transmitted together with normal television broadcasts for display on a modified domestic television set. The system utilizes two of the unused lines between picture frames. All the stored information, which may be weather reports, news flashes, sports results, etc., is sent out continuously in a cycle at a rate of 50 lines per second (2 per picture frame). The required pages are selected for display by keyboard, and the user may have to wait a few minutes for them to come up on the screen if the cycle is a long one containing a large number of transmissions. The two systems in use in the UK are **Ceefax**, run by the BBC, and **Oracle**, run by the Independent Broadcasting Authority. *See also* viewdata.

television (TV) The broadcasting of pictures and sound by

TELEVISION

*radio waves or electric cable. Television was invented by John Logie *Baird in 1926. At a TV studio or outside-broadcast unit, a television *camera converts the picture into an electrical signal. In most of Europe the picture consists of 625 lines made by an electron beam scanning the screen of a *cathode-ray tube, 25 such pictures being formed every second. In the USA, 525 lines and 30 frames per second are used. A brightness signal and a synchronization signal (to form the lines and frames of the picture) make up the picture signal, which is used to modulate (*see* modulation) a VHF or UHF carrier wave and is broadcast with the modulated sound carrier wave (which has a slightly different frequency). In colour TV, a colour signal has to be added to the picture signal.

The aerial of the TV receiver detects the broadcast radio waves and the picture and sound signals are separated within the receiver. The picture signal is demodulated, and the resulting current is used to control the electron beam in a cathode-ray tube so that the picture is reconstructed, the scanning being sufficiently fast to give the impression of a continuous moving picture.

In a **colour television** camera light from the scene to be televised is filtered into three primary colour components: red, green, and blue. Light of each colour goes to a separate

image tube. There are three systems in use for encoding colour picture information for transmission: the US system, also used in Canada, Mexico, and Japan; the PAL (phase alteration line) system used in the UK and most other W European countries; and SECAM (système électronique couleur avec mémoire), used in France, E Europe, and the Soviet Union. All of these combine colour and intensity information with sound and synchronization in a similar way to black-and-white television. The colour television receiver splits the signal into red, green, and blue components and applies these to three separate electron guns. The beam from each gun activates a set of phosphor dots of that colour on the screen, thus reconstructing the red, green, and blue components of the picture.

Telex A telegraphy system using telephone lines to transmit printed messages from one terminal (the teleprinter) to another. The message is typed onto a keyboard transmitter, which converts the characters into a coded electrical signal for transmission. A printing receiver (combined with the transmitter) carries out the reverse process, typing out messages as they arrive. Telex messages are directed through the telephone lines by the subscribers' numbers, each subscriber also being identified by his call sign. The system is extensively used by commercial and other organizations, because it costs less than a telephone call and provides both parties with a written copy of the messages. To increase the speed of transmission most teleprinters are equipped with a paper-tape punch to pre-record messages.

Telford, Thomas (1757-1834) British civil engineer, best known for his construction of the suspension bridge over the Menai Strait. The bridge, which was completed in 1825, is 177 metres long. Telford also designed and constructed some 1500 kilometres of roads, many bridges and aqueducts, and such canals as the Caledonian Canal and the Göta Canal in Sweden. He also designed St Katherine's Dock in London.

Tell, William A Swiss national hero who is first mentioned in a 15th-century chronicle and who, in Schiller's play *Wilhelm Tell* (1804), embodies the Swiss struggle for independence from the Austrian Habsburgs. After refusing to do homage as required by Gessler, the Austrian governor, Tell was ordered to shoot an apple from his son's head with a crossbow at 80 paces. He passed this test and later killed Gessler.

Tell el-Amarna The site of Akhetaten, the capital founded (c. 1375 BC) by the heretic Egyptian pharaoh *Akhenaten. It was to have been the centre of Akhenaten's new religion but was abandoned shortly after his death (c. 1360). Amarna is associated with a naturalistic art style and a diplomatic correspondence (the *Amarna Tablets) showing the decline of Egyptian prestige in W Asia.

Teller, Edward (1908-) US physicist, born in Hungary. After studying in Germany he left in 1933, going first to London and then to Washington, DC. He worked on the fission bomb during World War II and subsequently on the fusion bomb making a significant contribution to its development. He is sometimes known as "the father of the H-bomb." Teller's unfavourable evidence in the Robert *Oppenheimer security-clearance hearing lost him some respect amongst scientists.

tellurium (Te) A silvery-white semiconductor of the sulphur group, discovered by Müller von Reichenstein in 1782. The hydride (H_2Te) is volatile and toxic, with a powerful smell of bad eggs. Bismuth telluride (BiTe) is used as an effective thermoelectric cooler. The metal is used in some special alloys and in some semiconducting devices. At no 52; at wt 127.60; mp $449.5 \pm 0.3°C$; bp $989 \pm 3°C$.

Telstar. *See* communications satellite.

Telukbetung 5 28S 105 16E A port in Indonesia, in S Sumatra on the Sunda Strait. It was devastated by the eruption of *Krakatoa in 1883. Exports include rubber, coffee, and cinchona. Population (1980): 284 275.

Tema 5 41N 0 00E A port in Ghana, on the Atlantic coast. It has Africa's largest man-made harbour (opened 1962). Industries include oil refining, chemicals, and fishing. Population (1982 est): 345 843.

Tempe, Vale of (Modern Greek name: Témbi) A valley in N Greece, leading down to the Aegean Sea SE of Mount Olympus. In ancient times it was dedicated to the god Apollo.

tempera A method of painting, using ground pigment and a water-soluble gelatinous base, usually egg yolk. It was a very common medium for murals and easel paintings until it was supplanted by oils during the 15th century. It has lately been revived by German and US artists for its strong pure colours.

temperament The method of tuning the notes of the scale to allow music in all *tonalities to sound in tune. The necessity arises because of the way scales are constructed in western music; systems of temperament sharpen or flatten certain notes in order to compensate for the slight discrepancy that arises in the interval between C and the C seven octaves higher. This interval should be (on the basis of seven octaves) $2^7 = 128$. However, in passing through the cycle of 12 keys, each using as its fundamental the fifth of its

predecessor, the interval between Cs becomes $(3/2)^{12} = 129.75$. This difference, known as the comma of Pythagoras, can be compensated in several ways. From the 16th to the early 18th centuries the system of **meantone temperament** prevailed, in which the interval of a fifth was reduced to $\sqrt[4]{5} = 1.495$; with this arrangement music written in tonalities with few sharps or flats sounded acceptably in tune. This was succeeded by **equal temperament**, in which the interval between each of 12 semitones of the octave is exactly equal, the advantages of this system were demonstrated by Bach in *The Well-Tempered Clavichord* (1722), a collection of keyboard preludes and fugues in all keys. This system prevails today.

temperance movement The promotion of abstinence from, or at least moderation in, the consumption of alcohol. The earliest organized temperance societies were in the 19th century in the USA, which by 1833 had 6000 local groups (*see also* Prohibition). The Ulster Temperance Society, founded in 1829, was the first European society. The movement then spread to Scandinavia, where societies were established in Norway (1836) and Sweden (1837). The Church of England Temperance Society was founded in 1862.

temperature A physical quantity that is a measure of the average *kinetic energy of the constituent particles of a body. It determines the direction in which *heat flows when two bodies are in contact, the body with the higher temperature losing heat to that with the lower. The temperature of a body is measured in kelvins, degrees Celsius, or degrees Fahrenheit either by a *thermometer, if the temperature is below about 500°C, or, if above, by a *pyrometer.

Templars (Poor Knights of Christ and of the Temple of Solomon) A religious order of knighthood founded (c. 1120) in Jerusalem by a group of French knights. The Templars were, with the *Hospitallers, the most important military order of the *Crusades. Accused of heresy and immorality by Philip IV of France, who feared their power, the Templars were suppressed by the papacy in 1312 with great cruelty.

Temple, Shirley (1928-) US film actress. She featured as a child star in many films during the 1930s, including *Little Miss Marker* (1934) and *Heidi* (1937). She won a special Academy Award in 1934. During the 1960s she went into politics and was appointed US ambassador to Ghana in 1974 under her married name, Shirley Temple Black.

Temple, Sir William (1628-99) English diplomat, who negotiated the Triple Alliance (1668) with the United Provinces and Sweden and the treaty that ended the third *Dutch War (1674). He also arranged the marriage of Charles II's niece Mary to William of Orange. The author of *Observations upon the United Provinces* (1673), he employed Jonathan Swift as his secretary in the 1690s.

Temple, William (1881-1944) Anglican churchman; Bishop of Manchester (1921-29), Archbishop of York (1929-42), and then Archbishop of Canterbury (1942-44). Noted as a preacher, writer, and a reformer of Church structures, he is best remembered for his leadership in dealing with social and economic matters from a Christian point of view. His *Nature, Man, and God* (1934) was an influential theological work. His father **Frederick Temple** (1821-1902) was also Archbishop of Canterbury (1896-1902).

Temple Bar A former gateway in London, between the Cities of London and Westminster. A barrier, which existed in medieval times, was replaced by an archway (1670-72) designed by Sir Christopher Wren and it became customary for the heads of executed criminals to be displayed here. In 1878 the Temple Bar Memorial replaced the archway, which is now in Theobalds Park, Herts, although there is a movement to restore it to a City site. The sovereign still continues an ancient tradition by seeking the Lord Mayor's permission here before entering the City.

Temple of Jerusalem The ancient centre of Jewish religious life. The first Temple was built by King Solomon (c. 950 BC) and destroyed by Nebuchadnezzar in 586 BC. The second Temple was built in the later 6th century BC, restored by the *Maccabees and later by Herod the Great, and destroyed by the Romans in 70 AD. The Temple was a place of pilgrimage and worship. Both temples were built on the same walled platform, known as the **Temple Mount**; part of the western retaining wall of this structure is the *Wailing (Western) Wall, still a holy site for Jews. Since 691 the Muslim *Dome of the Rock has stood on the Temple Mount. *See also* high priest; Holy of Holies.

temples In ancient Greece and Rome, the sanctuaries of the gods. The first Greek temples were built of timber or brick but by the 6th century BC stone and marble were being used. They were rectangular buildings surrounded by a colonnade, with an inner sanctum containing the altar and a sculpture of the deity to whom they were dedicated. The best known is the *Parthenon.

Roman temples were raised on pedestals and usually had solid walls and a deep central *portico. The Maison Carrée at Nîmes, France (1st century BC), and the domed *Pantheon in Rome are famous surviving examples.

Temuco 38 45S 72 40W A city in S Chile and the gateway to Chile's lake district. It serves an area producing chiefly cereals, apples, and timber. Population (1983 est): 165 301.

tenant farming A farming system in which a tenant has the use of agricultural land in return for the payment of rent to the landowner. The terms of the tenancy are usually legally laid down; in the UK, where tenant farming is commonly practised, the Agricultural Holdings Act (1948) confers security of tenure and certain rights to compensation for capital improvements made by the tenant and for disturbance when forced to quit.

tench An elongated food and game fish, *Tinca tinca*, that is related to *carp and occurs in European fresh waters. Its slimy body, 18–45 cm long, is greenish or blackish above with lighter undersides. It lives in quiet waters that are rich in vegetation, feeding on small animals and plants.

Ten Commandments The *covenant, also called the Decalogue, delivered by Jehovah to Moses on two stone tablets at Mount Sinai (Exodus 20.1–17; Deuteronomy 5.6–21). According to Exodus, Moses broke the original tablets when he descended from Mount Sinai and discovered the idolatry of the Israelites; they were replaced by two others, which were kept in the *Ark of the Covenant. Jews, Roman Catholics, and Protestants are not agreed as to the exact numbering of the commandments. The New Testament insists that unlike many other Old Testament laws they are binding on all mankind.

tendon A strong fibrous cord that joins a muscle to a bone. The tendon fibres merge with the muscle fibres and extend to the fibrous tissue lining the bone, serving to concentrate the pull of the muscle on a small part of the bone. Inflammation of a tendon, called **tendinitis**, usually occurs through overuse, as in tennis elbow.

Tenerife 28 15N 16 35W A Spanish island in the Atlantic Ocean, the largest of the Canary Islands. Its Pico de Teide mountain is, at 3710 m (12 172 ft), the highest in Spain. Early fruit and vegetables, such as bananas and tomatoes, are produced and the island is popular for holidays. Area: 2020 sq km (780 sq mi). Population (1981): 688 273. Chief town: Santa Cruz de Tenerife.

Teng Hsiao-p'ing. *See* Deng Xiao Ping.

Teniers the Younger, David (1610–90) Flemish painter. Known chiefly for his peasant scenes, he also made historically valuable copies of the paintings in the collection of Archduke Leopold Wilhelm, whose court painter he became in Brussels in 1651. His father **David Teniers the Elder** (1582–1649) was a painter of religious subjects.

Ten Lost Tribes of Israel The Hebrew tribes that rebelled against *Solomon's successor, Rehoboam, and formed a separate kingdom. This kingdom, which they called Israel, lay to the N of the territory occupied by the two remaining tribes of *Judah and of *Benjamin, which together constituted the southern kingdom of Judah. In 722 BC the northern kingdom was conquered by the Assyrians, many of its inhabitants deported, and their ethnic identity lost.

Tennant Creek 19 31S 134 11E A mining town in Australia, in central Northern Territory. Minerals extracted include gold (discovered in 1930) and copper and silver (discovered in 1955). Population (1982): 3050.

Tennessee A state in the S central USA. It can be divided into East, Middle, and West Tennessee. In the E there is an upland region of thickly wooded mountains and in Middle Tennessee, in the loop of the Tennessee River, an area of upland plateau and rolling hills gives way in the W to an area of lowland plains and swamps situated between the Tennessee and Mississippi Rivers. An agriculturally poor state, its major crops are tobacco, soya beans, and cotton. Beef and dairy products are also important. Manufacturing is being encouraged especially by the Tennessee Valley Authority (*see* Tennessee River) and the leading industries produce chemicals, food products, electrical and nonelectrical machinery, and textiles. The state is an important hardwood producer in the S. It is the USA's largest producer of zinc and the extraction of stone is a major source of revenue. *History*: disputed by the English and French in the 17th century, it was under British rule during the American Revolution. In 1790 the area was declared a territory and it became a state in 1796. It was a supporter of the Confederate cause in the US Civil War. Martin Luther *King, Jr was assassinated in Memphis in 1968. Area: 109 411 sq km (42 244 sq mi). Population (1980): 4 590 750. Capital: Nashville.

Tennessee River A river in SE USA. It follows a U-shaped course from E Tennessee, flowing through NE Alabama before returning across Tennessee to join the Ohio River as its main tributary at Paducah, Kentucky. **The Tennessee Valley Authority**, created in 1933, built dams along the river to control floods and arrest soil erosion as well as to generate electricity. Length: 1049 km (652 mi).

Tennessee Walking Horse A breed of ▢horse developed in Tennessee and used by plantation owners for its characteristic running walk, which gives a smooth ride. It is solidly built with a thick neck and full mane and tail. The coat may be black, brown, bay, chestnut, or roan. Height: 1.57–1.63 m (15½–16 hands).

Tenniel, Sir John (1820–1914) British cartoonist and book illustrator. He worked for *Punch* from 1851 to 1901 and specialized in humorous political cartoons, the best known being *Dropping the Pilot* (1890), inspired by ▢Bismarck's resignation from the German chancellorship. His illustrations for *Alice in Wonderland* are his most famous works.

tennis (*or* lawn tennis) A game for two or four players using rackets to hit a cloth-covered rubber ball on a grass or composition (hard) court. It originated in England in the mid-19th century and was highly popular by 1877, when the first Wimbledon championships were staged. A match lasts a maximum of five sets for men and three for women and the minimum number of games per set is six. A lead of two games is needed to win a set. However, if the score reaches six games each a tiebreaker is played (a game in which each side serves twice alternately). The scoring system derives from *real tennis and a minimum of four points is needed for a game: 15, 30, 40, and game; a lead of two points is also needed to win a game. A score of 40 on both sides is called "deuce"; the side that wins the next point then has the "advantage," which can either be clinched to win the game with a further point or nullified by the opposing side winning a point, in which case the score returns to deuce. Players

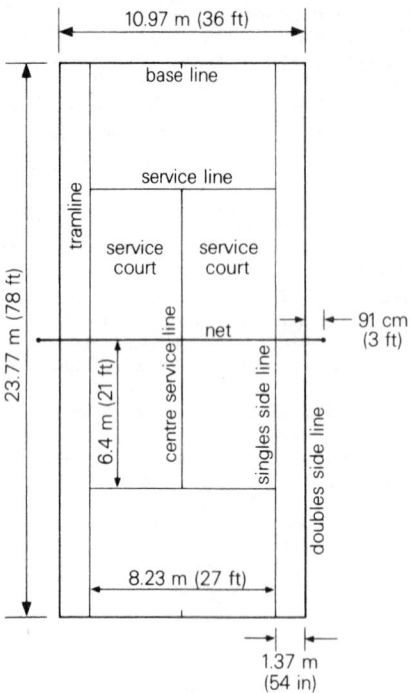

10.97 m (36 ft)

base line

service line

tramline

service
court

service
court

net

centre service line

singles side line

23.77 m (78 ft)

6.4 m (21 ft)

doubles side line

91 cm
(3 ft)

8.23 m (27 ft)

1.37 m
(54 in)

TENNIS   *The dimensions of the court. For singles games the posts holding the net are moved to inside the doubles sidelines. The net is 3 ft (91.4 cm) high at the centre.*

take turns to serve for a game. A player is allowed two attempts to serve into the service court diagonally opposite, alternating courts between points. To win points players must return the ball over the net either before it bounces (volley) or after the first bounce, trying to position it so that their opponents cannot return it. The game is immensely popular at all levels of play, from the local club to the All England Championships at Wimbledon, which has admitted professional players since 1968. Other highly prized trophies are the *Davis Cup and the *Wightman cup.

Tennis Court Oath   (1789) The oath taken by the Third Estate of the *States-General of France at the start of the French Revolution. After declaring itself a National Assembly, the Third Estate was excluded from its meeting place at Versailles. Adjourning to a nearby tennis court, the Assembly defiantly swore not to disband until the French kingdom had a written constitution.

Tennyson, Alfred, Lord   (1809–92) British poet. He began writing as a child at his father's rectory in Lincolnshire and at Cambridge University. He published two volumes in 1830 and 1832, but he gained general acclaim only with his 1842 volume, which included "Morte d'Arthur." In 1850 he married, became poet laureate, and published *In Memoriam*, a sequence of elegaic lyrics mourning the death of his close friend Arthur Hallam (1811–33). Now established as the national poet of the Victorian age, he reinforced his popularity with *Idylls of the King* (1859) and other poems. He accepted a peerage in 1884.

tenor   A high adult male singing voice. The word comes from the Latin *tenere*, to hold; in Renaissance polyphonic music the tenor part held the melody on which the music was based. Range: C on the bass stave to C two octaves above.

tenrec   An insect-eating mammal belonging to the family *Tenrecidae* (30 species), found only in Madagascar and the Comoro Islands. Tenrecs measure 5–40 cm, some with long

tails and some tailless, and generally have a brownish coat of bristly hairs or spines. Most tenrecs live in burrows and are nocturnal, feeding mainly on small invertebrates with some plant material. They are prolific breeders, producing litters of over 20. Order: *Insectivora*.

tensile strength   The ability of a material to withstand a "pulling" stress (**tensile stress**). It is usually measured by taking a bar of the material and stretching it to destruction. The ultimate tensile strength is the maximum load divided by the bar's cross-sectional area and is measured in newtons per square metre.

Tenzing Norgay   (c. 1914–86) Sherpa mountaineer, who, with Sir Edmund *Hillary, was the first man to reach the summit of Mount Everest (1953), after working as a porter in 19 Himalayan expeditions from 1935. He later became a director at the Himalayan Mountaineering Institute, Darjeeling.

Teotihuacán   An ancient city in central Mexico. Between 300 and 650 AD Teotihuacán controlled a wide area. It was destroyed about 750. The pyramid temples of the sun, moon, and *Quezalcóatl are the most impressive remains.

tepee.   *See* wigwam.

Teplice   (*or* Teplice Šarnov)   50 40N 13 50E An industrial town and spa in Czechoslovakia, in N Bohemia. Industries include paper, glass, and potteries. Population (1983 est): 53 188.

tequila   A Mexican spirit made of the fermented juice of an agave plant (*see* Agave), water, and, sometimes, sulphuric acid and yeast. The spirit is distilled twice in potstills then (preferably) aged in casks. It is produced near the town of Tequila.

terbium   (Tb)   A *lanthanide element, discovered in 1843 by C. G. Mosander (1797–1858) and named after the village Ytterby in Sweden. It is obtained from monazite ($CePO_4$), and the brown oxide (Tb_2O_3) is used as a phosphor in colour-television tubes. The metal is silvery-grey and can be cut with a knife. At no 65; at wt 158.92; mp 1356°C; bp 3041.

Terborch, Gerard   (1617–81) Dutch painter. He visited England (1635), Rome (1640), and Westphalia, where he painted the Dutch and Spanish diplomats signing the *Peace of Münster* (1648; National Gallery, London). His portraits and his family and guardroom scenes are remarkable for their skilled rendering of expression and texture.

Terbrugghen, Hendrik   (1588–1629) Dutch painter of the Utrecht school. After studying under the mannerist painter Abraham Bloemaert (1564–1651), he went to Italy in 1604, returning to Utrecht in 1614, where he specialized in religious and musical subjects in the style of *Caravaggio.

terebinth   A small tree, *Pistacia terebinthus*, native to the Mediterranean region. It has small flowers producing purple fruit and was formerly an important source of turpentine. Family: *Pistaciaceae*.

Terence   (Publius Terentius Afer; c. 185–c. 159 BC) Roman dramatist. Born in Carthage, he was taken to Rome as a slave by a senator who educated and later freed him. His six plays were all adapted from Greek New Comedy writers, especially Menander. He achieved popular success only with *The Eunuch* (161 BC), his style being more refined and sophisticated than that of his rival *Plautus. His work influenced several 17th- and 18th-century European writers.

Teresa, Mother   (Agnes Gonxha Bejaxhui; 1910–   ) Indian nun born in Yugoslavia of Albanian parents, who founded the Order of the Missionaries of Charity (Calcutta; 1948) to help lepers, cripples, and the dying throughout the world. She received the first Pope John XXIII Peace Prize (1971), the 1979 Nobel Peace Prize, and an honorary OM (1983).

Teresa of Ávila, St   (1515–82) Spanish Carmelite nun and mystic, who dedicated her life to reforming the Carmelite order. Of noble birth, she joined the Carmelites at Ávila in 1533 and in 1555 experienced a spiritual awakening followed by several visions. To restore the original Carmelite rule she founded the Convent of St Joseph in Ávila in 1562 and later other religious houses with the help of St *John of the Cross. The mystical side of her life is described in her books, notably *Life* (1562-65), *The Way of Perfection* (after 1565), and *The Interior Castle* (1577), which are regarded as classics of mysticism.

Teresina 5 09S 42 46W A city in NE Brazil, the capital of Piauí state on the Rio Parnaíba. It is a commercial centre; exports include cattle, hides, cotton, rice, and manioc. Its university was founded in 1968. Population (1980 est): 348 900.

Terman, Lewis Madison (1877-1956) US psychologist, who published the first widely used intelligence test in the USA. Developed at Stanford University, his Stanford-Binet test was scored on an *intelligence quotient (IQ) rating based on both chronological and mental ages. In 1921 Terman established a long-term study of gifted children and he also estimated the IQs of famous people, rating Goethe at 210 and Darwin at 165.

terminal velocity The maximum velocity attained by a body falling through a fluid. It occurs when the drag balances the gravitational force on the body: until the terminal velocity is reached the falling body accelerates; thereafter the velocity remains constant. According to *Stokes' law the terminal velocity of a sphere (radius r) falling through a fluid with a coefficient of viscosity η is $2\phi r^2 g/9'\eta$, where ϕ is the difference between the body and fluid densities and g is the acceleration of free fall.

termite A social □insect, also called white ant (although unrelated to the ants), belonging to the mainly tropical order *Isoptera* (2000 species). Termite colonies nest in tunnels and galleries in wood, soil, or earth mounds (termitaria). There are three major castes: winged reproductives, workers, and soldiers. The reproductives swarm to found new colonies, a single pair (king and queen) producing huge numbers of offspring. The workers construct galleries, feed the colony, and care for the young, while the soldiers are concerned with defence. Termites eat cellulose and are very destructive when they invade houses and attack wood products.

tern A seabird belonging to a subfamily (*Sterninae*; 35-40 species) occurring around coasts and inland waters worldwide and often called sea swallow or noddy. 20-55 cm long, terns have long wings, short legs, usually a forked tail, and their plumage is white, black-and-white, or almost totally black. They feed on fish and crustaceans and often migrate long distances (*see* Arctic tern). Family: *Laridae* (gulls and terns). *See* Plate V.

Terni 42 34N 12 39E A town in Italy, in Umbria on the River Nera. Industries include the manufacture of iron and steel, machinery, firearms, soap, and textiles. It is reputed to be the birthplace of Tacitus. Population (1980 est): 113 108.

terpenes Naturally occurring hydrocarbons found in the essential oils of plants. Typically they are volatile compounds with pleasant odours and are widely used in flavouring foods and in perfumes. Their molecules are made up of isoprene units (C_5H_8). *Rubber is an example of a polyterpene.

terracotta (Italian: baked earth) A fired clay, usually reddish in colour, used to make sculpture, tiles, bricks, containers, etc. It is principally associated with sculpture. Terracotta figurines, often painted, were very common in ancient Greece and Rome, a famous Greek type being the *Tanagra figurines. The art was revived during the *Renaissance, when the *Della Robbia family in Florence specialized in enamelled terracotta Madonnas. Later sculptors in terracotta include the Frenchman *Clodion.

terrapin A small edible turtle belonging to the family *Emydidae*, occurring chiefly in the New World. The diamondback terrapin (*Malaclemys terrapin*), which occurs in coastal waters and salt marshes of North America, has

diamond-shaped patterns on its dark carapace and is yellow with black speckles underneath. It is one of several terrapins regarded as a table delicacy and often reared for this purpose. □reptile.

terrarium A transparent receptacle for land plants, used for propagation, decoration, or scientific study. The plants grow in a bottom layer usually consisting of sand or pebbles mixed with some charcoal and covered by topsoil.

Terre Adélie (*or* Adélie Land) The only French territory in Antarctica, in the French Southern and Antarctic Territories on the coast of the Indian Ocean between longitudes 136°E and 142°E. It is the site of a French research station.

terrier One of about 20 breeds of □dog characterized by their small compact sturdy build and traditionally used for hunting vermin and rousing foxes and badgers from cover. The Scottish breeds, such as the *cairn terrier, *Scottish terrier, *Skye terrier, and *West Highland white terrier, tend to be smaller and longer haired than other terriers, which are descended from the ancient black-and-tan hunting terrier and other breeds.

Territorial Army A British force of volunteers, created as the Territorial Force in 1907 and renamed in 1922. Between 1967 and 1979 it was known as the Territorial Army Volunteer Reserve. Its 74 000 men constitute a pool of trained and equipped reinforcements for the regular army.

territory In ecology, a defined area defended by an animal against intrusion by another animal, usually of the same species. Territories can either reduce competition for food or serve to protect mates and young from interference. They vary in size according to their function, the fitness of the defending animal, and the population density of the species.

Terry, Dame Ellen (Alice) (1847-1928) British actress. A member of a large and talented family of actors, from 1878 to 1898 she acted with Sir Henry *Irving at the Lyceum Theatre, achieving particular success in the major Shakespearian roles. She later managed the Imperial Theatre, toured extensively, and gave lectures on Shakespeare. Her correspondence with G. B. *Shaw was published in 1931. Her son (**Edward Henry**) **Gordon Craig** (1872-1966) was an actor, designer, and producer. He joined Irving's company at the Lyceum as a child actor, but eventually devoted himself exclusively to design and production. He published *The Mask*, a theatre journal, and opened a school of acting after settling in Florence in 1908. His ideas on stage production have been very influential, especially in Germany and the USA.

tertiary education All vocational and nonvocational courses for school leavers and adults. In the UK **further education** includes all postsecondary education other than at a university or polytechnic, while **higher education** is usually restricted to courses leading to a degree or equivalent award; in recent years attention has been focused on the expansion and improvement of education for technologists and technicians at all levels. Educational institutions within the tertiary sector include *universities, *polytechnics, colleges of higher education, *colleges of education, technical colleges, and colleges of further education.

Tertiary period The first geological period of the Cenozoic era, following the Cretaceous period and preceding the Quaternary (which is sometimes considered a continuation of the Tertiary). It lasted from about 65 to 1.8 million years ago and contains the Palaeocene, Eocene, Oligocene, Miocene, and Pliocene epochs, in ascending order. Most of the rocks of the period were laid down in shallow water. Modern invertebrates and mammals evolved and became increasingly abundant; the modern angiosperms became the dominant plants. The Alpine period of mountain formation extended through the period and reached its peak in the Miocene. The climate began to deteriorate in the Oligocene, finally leading to the Ice Age of the Pleistocene.

Tertullian(us), Quintus Septimius Florens (c. 160–225 AD) African Father of the Church, born in Carthage. Educated in law, he was converted to Christianity by 197 and became a leading Christian apologist. He strongly defended the Montanists (*see* Montanism), whom he joined in 213. His writings, which include *Apologeticum*, *Ad nationes*, and *De praescriptione haereticorum*, were the first major Christian works in Latin.

terza rima A verse form consisting of a series of three-line stanzas the second lines of which rhyme with the first and third lines of the preceding stanza (aba/cac/dcd/ede/...). It originated in Italy and was used by *Dante in the *Divine Comedy*. It was introduced into England by Sir Thomas *Wyatt in the 16th century. *See also* rhyme.

tesla (T) The *SI unit of magnetic flux density equal to one weber per square metre. Named after Nikola *Tesla.

Tesla, Nikola (1856–1943) US electrical engineer, born in Croatia, who recognized the advantages of distributing electricity as alternating current, rather than direct current, and did much to make this feasible. He fought a long and bitter battle with Thomas *Edison over this principle. The unit of magnetic flux density (*see* tesla) is named after him.

Test Acts 1. In England, the Acts stipulating that public office holders must take Holy Communion in the Church of England (1673) and excluding all Roman Catholics except the Duke of York (later James II) from parliament (1678). They were not formally repealed until the mid-19th century. **2.** In Scotland, the Act (1681) that forced all public office holders to declare their belief in Protestantism; it was repealed in 1889.

testis The organ of male animals in which *sperm is produced. In men there is a pair of testes, or testicles, which produce both sperm and sex hormones (*see* androgen). Before birth the testicles descend into the scrotum—a sac of skin outside the abdominal cavity—since sperms require a temperature lower than that of the body to mature. The sperms complete their development in a convoluted tube (epididymis) outside the testis. At ejaculation the sperms pass through a duct (the vas deferens) to the urethra and out through the penis. *See* Plate IV.

testosterone A steroid hormone—the most important of the *androgens. First isolated from bull testes in 1935, testosterone is now manufactured for medical uses, including the treatment of certain forms of sterility in men.

test-tube baby A baby produced by fertilizing the mother's egg cell with sperm from the father in a test tube (*in vitro* fertilization): the fertilized egg is then implanted surgically into the mother's womb and allowed to come to term in the normal way. It is a means of overcoming sterility in a woman due to blocked Fallopian tubes or any similar defect. The technique was developed in Britain by Dr Patrick Steptoe and his colleagues and the first test-tube baby was born in July, 1978. *See also* artificial insemination.

tetanus A serious disease caused by the bacterium *Clostridium tetani* entering wounds and producing a powerful toxin (poison) that irritates the nerves supplying muscles. The organism is particularly prevalent in soil contaminated with animal droppings. After an incubation period of seven-ten days, stiffness, spasm, and rigidity of the muscles affects the jaw (hence the popular name—lockjaw) and spreads to other muscles. In severe cases the whole body is seized with spasms and the patient may die from asphyxia. The disease is treated with tetanus antitoxin and penicillin; it can be prevented by completing a full course of antitetanus immunization.

tetra One of several small brightly coloured freshwater fish of the family Characidae (*see* characin), found in South America and Africa and popular for aquaria. Well-known species include black tetra (*Gymnocorymbus ternetzi*), glowlight tetra (*Hemigrammus erythrozonus*), neon tetra (*Hyphessobrycon innesi*), and silver tetra (*Ctenobrycon spilurus*).

tetracyclines A group of *antibiotics derived from *Streptomyces* bacteria. Tetracyclines are active against a large number of different bacteria (i.e. they are broad-spectrum antibiotics) and are frequently the first choice of antibiotic for infections in which the causative organism has not been identified. Tetracyclines, which are taken by mouth, may cause the side effects of diarrhoea, nausea, and discoloration of growing teeth and bones.

tetraethyl lead ($Pb(C_2H_5)_4$) A colourless poisonous oily liquid. It is made by treating lead-sodium alloys with chloroethane and is added to petrol to prevent *knocking in internal-combustion engines.

Tetrazzini, Luisa (1871–1940) Italian coloratura soprano. Born in Florence, she attended the Liceo Musicale there with her sister Eva, making her debut as Inez in Meyerbeer's opera *L'Africaine* in 1895. She toured Russia, Mexico, America, and Europe with great success.

Tetuán 35 34N 5 22W A city in N Morocco. Its port, on the Mediterranean coast, handles livestock and agricultural produce. The city produces textiles and light manufactured products. Population (1982): 199 615.

Tetzel, Johann (c. 1465–1519) German Dominican friar, a famous preacher of *indulgences. His attempt to sell indulgences, which had been authorized to raise funds for the renovation of St Peter's in Rome, provoked Luther's publication of the 95 theses and a famous debate between the two men.

Teutonic Knights (Knights of the Teutonic Order) A religious order of knighthood founded (c. 1190) at Acre. In 1211 they moved from Palestine to E Europe, where they campaigned against pagan peoples, notably the Prussians, whom they had conquered by the end of the 13th century. They colonized Prussia and established their headquarters at Marienburg in 1309. They also gained control over much of the E Baltic region, as well as parts of Germany. During the 15th century they were repeatedly defeated by the Poles, of whose king the order's grand master became a vassal. At the Reformation the order was dissolved except for one branch, which survived in Germany until its abolition by Napoleon (1809).

Tewkesbury 51 59N 2 09W A market town in SW England, in Gloucestershire at the confluence of the Rivers Avon and Severn. The famous abbey church is Norman. In 1471 the Yorkists finally defeated the Lancastrians at the battle of Tewkesbury in the Wars of the *Roses. Population (1981): 9554.

Texas The second largest and the third most populous state in the USA, situated in the SW of the country. It consists of four main physical regions: the West Gulf Coastal Plain in the SE covering more than two-fifths of the state; the Central Lowland; the Great Plains, which extend mainly W from the Central Lowland into New Mexico; and the Trans-Pecos or mountainous area in the W. The chief producer of minerals since 1935, it leads the nation in the production of oil and natural gas; it is also a major producer of sulphur. Oil-related industries dominate the manufacturing sector, the most important being the chemical industry, especially along the Gulf Coast. There is also an important space centre at Houston and Dallas is a major commercial and industrial centre. Texas is a major agricultural region and has more farmed land than any other US state. It produces a variety of crops, especially cotton, sorghum grains, rice, and peanuts and it is a leading livestock producer. *History*: colonized by the Spanish in 1682, the first permanent Anglo-American settlement was established by Stephen F. Austin in 1821. In 1836 the Texans set up a provisional government in opposition to the Mexican dictatorship of Antonio López de Santa Anna and following the heroic defence of the *Alamo, the revolutionary army under Sam Houston finally defeated Mexican forces in April of the same year. A republic was established and Texas remained independent for almost a decade until annexation by the USA was agreed upon and Texas became a state. It was a supporter of the Confederate cause during the US Civil War. Changes in the course of the Rio Grande, which forms part of the border beween Texas and Mexico, has led to several border disputes between the USA and Mexico and in 1970 the two countries agreed on plans to prevent any further substantial changes in the river's course. Area: 692 402 sq km (267 338 sq mi). Population (1980): 14 228 383. Capital: Austin.

textiles Fabrics made from natural or synthetic *fibres. Textiles can either be made directly from these fibres, as in felt and bonded fabrics, or be woven or knitted from yarn spun from the fibres. Braiding, netting, and lace making are less common ways of producing textiles from yarn. The fibres used include animal fibres, such as *wool, hair, and *silk; vegetable fibres, such as *cotton, *flax, and *hemp; and synthetic fibres, such as rayon, nylon, and acrylic. Wool and hair were used in prehistoric times; *linen, derived from flax, was also an early discovery, which only began to decline in use when cotton textiles, mass produced by the new industrial machines, became available cheaply. The invention of synthetic fibres (such as rayon and nylon) and their combination with natural fibres has enormously increased the textile industry's range. *See also* spinning; weaving.

Teyte, Dame Maggie (1888-1976) British soprano. She studied in Paris (1903-07) and became famous for her performances in opera and for her recitals of French songs. She was created a DBE in 1958.

Tezcatlipoca The Aztec god of the night sky, identified with the constellation Ursa Major and associated with witchcraft and evil. He was a creator-god and was usually portrayed with an obsidian mirror as a foot.

Thackeray, William Makepeace (1811-63) British novelist. Born in Calcutta, the son of an East India Company official, he was educated at Cambridge University and became a professional journalist. After publishing several early novels in magazines under pseudonyms, he won fame and financial success with *Vanity Fair* (1847-48), which he followed with the semiautobiographical *The History of Pendennis* (1848-50) and the historical novel *Henry Esmond* (1852). In his last years he travelled in Europe and the USA and edited the *Cornhill Magazine* (1860-62).

Thailand, Kingdom of (name until 1939: Siam) A country in SE Asia, on the Gulf of Thailand. Fertile plains and hills in the S rise to mountains in the N. The main river is the Chao Phraya and the Mekong forms part of the E boundary. Most of the population is Thai, with Chinese and Malay minorities. *Economy*: the chief food crop is rice, which is also the main export. Production is being increased by irrigation schemes, such as the Chao Phraya Dam. Forests cover 60% of the land, producing especially teak and rubber in the N and yang in the S. Mineral resources include tin, manganese, antimony, and zinc. Industry is based mainly on textiles and cement. Tourism is important. *History*: there are indications of human settlement from very early times, and by the 6th century AD the Thais had reached the area from the N. They conquered the Mons to the S and in succeeding centuries were involved in frequent struggles with the Burmese and Khmers. In the 19th century they lost some territory to the French and the British but remained independent. In 1932 the long-standing absolute monarchy was replaced by a constitutional monarchy, since when civil and military governments have alternated, accompanied by political upheavals and violence. The country was occupied by the Japanese in World War II. In recent years it has developed closer links with its communist neighbours, although relations with Vietnam deteriorated to a state of war in the early 1980s. Head of state: King Bhumibol Adulyadej (1927-). Prime minister: Gen Prem Tinsulanonda. Official language: Thai. Official religion: Hinayana Buddhism. Official currency: baht of 100 satang. Area: 514 000 sq km (198 250 sq mi). Population (1984 est): 51 724 000. Capital and main port: Bangkok.

Thais (4th century BC) Greek courtesan, who accompanied *Alexander the Great's army during its invasion of Persia. According to tradition, she instigated the burning of the palace of Xerxes in Persepolis in 331 BC.

thalassaemia A form of *anaemia caused by an inherited abnormality of the haemoglobin molecule (the pigment of red blood cells). The disease is seen most commonly around the Mediterranean but can also affect any people of Mediterranean origin. Patients inheriting the abnormality from both parents suffer from the major form of the disease, which requires repeated blood transfusions; such patients rarely live to adulthood. Those inheriting the disease from one parent are often free of symptoms.

Thales (c. 624-547 BC) The first of the Greek speculative scientists, born at *Miletus. He used the data from Babylonian astronomers to predict the solar eclipse of 28 May, 585 BC, advised on stellar navigation, and introduced Egyptian methods of land measurement into Greece. He held that all things derive from water and set the *Presocratics on their quest for the basic substance of the universe.

Thalia In Greek religion, one of the nine *Muses, the patron of comedy. She was the mother, by Apollo, of the *Corybantes.

thalidomide A sedative drug that was found to cause severe developmental defects in the fetus when taken during pregnancy. The most common thalidomide-induced abnormality is phocomelia, in which the feet and hands develop normally without corresponding growth of the bones of the arms and legs. Between 1959 and 1962 some 500 deformed babies were born in the UK and over 2000 in West Germany. The drug was never used clinically in the USA.

thallium (Tl) A metallic element, discovered spectroscopically by Sir William Crookes in 1861 and named after the Greek *thallos*, a green shoot, because of its bright-green spectral line. The metal is soft and malleable and reacts easily to form numerous salts. The sulphate (Tl_2SO_4) is widely used as a rat poison as it is tasteless and odourless. It occurs naturally in sulphide ores of lead and zinc and in iron pyrites (FeS_2). At no 81; at wt 204.37; mp 303.5°C; bp 1457 ± 10°C.

Thallophyta In some plant classification systems, a subkingdom containing all those plants that lack true stems, leaves, and roots, i.e. the algae, fungi, and lichens. The plant body is a thallus and lacks the vascular (conducting) tissue of higher plants.

Thames, River The longest river in England. Rising in the Cotswold Hills near Cirencester, it flows mainly ESE through Oxford, Reading, and London to enter the North Sea at the Nore. It is tidal as far as Teddington, and Tilbury can dock the largest oceangoing vessels. It is economically the most important river in the UK, with vast amounts of cargo passing through the Port of *London. A tidal barrier has been constructed (1973-83) below London to reduce the danger of flooding. Attempts to combat pollution would appear to have met with considerable success; whereas only eels could survive in the river in the early 1960s, a hundred different species of fish were caught in the early 1980s. Length: 338 km (210 mi).

Thanet, Isle of 51 22N 1 15E An island in SE England, separated from the Kent mainland by two channels of the River Stour. It contains the resorts of Ramsgate and Margate. Area: 109 sq km (42 sq mi).

Thanjavur (former name: Tanjore) 10 46N 79 09E A city in India, in Tamil Nadu. It has an 11th-century Hindu temple and a 16th-century raja's palace. Industries include textiles and jewellery. Population (1981): 184 015.

Thanksgiving Day A national holiday in the USA, celebrated on the fourth Thursday in November. Thanksgiving Day was originally observed by the Pilgrim Fathers, who in 1621 celebrated their first harvest in North America. It

MARGARET THATCHER *With her husband, Denis, in the garden of No 10 Downing Street (1987).*

became a national holiday in 1863, with roast turkey and pumpkin pie being eaten. It is also celebrated in Canada, on the second Monday in October.

Thapsus, Battle of   (46 BC) The battle in which Julius Caesar crushed *Pompey's supporters in North Africa. The battle was part of Caesar's campaign to retain control of Rome after defeating Pompey at Pharsalus.

Thar Desert (*or* Great Indian Desert)   A large arid area lying along the central 800 km (497 mi) of the India-Pakistan border, mostly in India. Area: about 250 000 sq km (96 504 sq mi).

Thásos   A Greek island in the N Aegean Sea. It is the site of archaeological excavations and zinc is mined. Area: 399 sq km (154 sq mi). Population (1981): 1311.

Thatcher, Margaret (Hilda) (1925–)   British stateswoman; Conservative prime minister (1979–). After working as a research chemist and then a barrister, she entered parliament in 1959 and was appointed minister of pensions and national insurance in 1961. In 1969 she became opposition spokesman on education and was secretary of state for education and science from 1970 to 1974. In 1975 she succeeded Edward Heath as Conservative leader and in 1979 became the first woman prime minister of the UK. In office she increased privatization, cut government spending, and used military force to retain control of the Falkland Islands (1982). Her government continued following a landslide victory in 1983, despite rising unemployment. In 1984 she survived an IRA bomb attack in Brighton. Re-elected in 1987, she has been influential with the superpower leaders in arms control, visiting Moscow in 1987. She became the longest serving UK prime minister of this century in January 1988.

Theatre of Cruelty   A theatrical genre derived from the theories of Antonin *Artaud, who believed that drama was essentially a ceremony the ritual function of which was to destroy the superficial restraints of civilized life and liberate repressed emotions from the subconscious. *Les Cenci* (1935), his chief experimental production, was a failure, but his theories influenced many later writers and directors, including Jean-Louis *Barrault, *Camus, and *Genet.

Theatre of the Absurd   A theatrical genre ("the Absurd" being borrowed from the existentialist philosophy of Albert *Camus) popularized in the 1960s in which the human condition is presented as absurd. It includes the plays of Eugene *Ionesco, Samuel *Beckett, Arthur *Adamov, and others, which lack logical form and use comic effects in developing

pessimistic philosophical themes. The influence of Alfred *Jarry and the surrealists is also discernible.

theatres and stages   The design of buildings specifically for the staging of plays has been governed by the shifting religious and social significance of the drama and the type of illusion or effect intended by different sorts of play. Ancient Greek theatres adjoined such religious centres as *Athens, *Epidaurus, and *Delphi. The secularized theatres that were a feature of most Roman towns were particularly adapted to the production of *Roman comedy. Christian drama evolved from the liturgy but in late medieval Europe moved outside the churches as the craft guilds presented *miracle plays. Renaissance court theatres mainly imitated Roman models, while the open-air Elizabethan theatre represented a more popular tradition. During the 17th century elaboration of stage machinery (*see* masque), demands for illusionism, and the development of *opera and *ballet stimulated the spread of the proscenium arch stage design, which was virtually universal until the 20th century. The modern drama's tendency towards abstraction and evocation of mood, nonrealistic scenery, and stage lighting, has fostered renewed interest in theatre-in-the-round (seats round a central acting arena) and the Elizabethan apron stage.

Thebes   An ancient city in Upper Egypt and capital of all Egypt (c. 1570–c. 1085 BC). Thebes' power was linked with the supremacy of its god *Amon in the Egyptian pantheon. With its associated sites of *Karnak, *Luxor, and the *Valley of the Kings, Thebes testifies to the splendour of ancient Egyptian civilization.

Thebes   88 19N 23 19E A town in Boeotia, in central Greece. It was founded in Mycenaean times and its legendary history was a favourite theme in Greek drama. Predominant among its Boeotian neighbours, Thebes lost influence by supporting the Persians in 480 BC, but briefly became the leading Greek state after defeating the Spartans at Leuctra (371). Opposition to Macedonian expansionism led to destruction (336). Although refounded, it never regained significance. Population (1981): 18 712.

theft   The offence of dishonestly appropriating property belonging to another with the intention of permanently depriving the other person of it. The property need not be tangible. The earlier offence of larceny involved "taking and carrying away" the goods and was until 1827 divided into Grand Larceny, which originally carried the death penalty or *transportation, and Petty Larceny, when the value of the stolen property was less than a shilling. It was replaced by theft as defined by the Theft Act (1968), as were embezzlement, fraudulent conversion, and related offences.

thegn   A person in Anglo-Saxon England who held land from his lord in return for service. The status of thegn (meaning one who serves) was hereditary. The king's thegns had military and administrative duties and also attended the *witan (king's council). Their importance declined in the early 11th century, when the Danish kings introduced their *housecarls, and the thegns died out as a clan after the Norman conquest.

theism   The belief in a personal God as creator and preserver of the universe, who reveals himself by supernatural means to his creatures. Apparently coined (1678) by *Cudworth as an opposite to *atheism, theism has been refined in meaning to exclude both *pantheism and *deism. It is central to Christian, Judaic, and Islamic thought.

Themis   The Greek goddess of justice and wisdom, often portrayed carrying a pair of scales. She was a Titan, the daughter of Uranus and Gaea and the second wife of Zeus. As the wife of the Titan Iapetus, she was also the mother of *Prometheus.

Themistocles (c. 528–462 BC)   Athenian statesman, who built Athens' naval power. Themistocles persuaded Athens to expand its navy (483) and to transfer its port from Phaleron to the more defensible Piraeus. These policies, and his leadership at the battle of *Salamis, saved Greece from

The Theatre of Dionysus at Athens during the Hellenistic period. The chorus stood in the front semicircular area (orchestra). Behind them were musicians, while the speaking actors performed in front of the screen.

Medieval miracle and mystery plays were performed on large wagons in public places. Different wagons were used for different scenes.

Spectators in the Elizabethan theatre sat in covered galleries or stood in the open pit. The acting area comprised the main stage, a rear stage, and a balcony.

The proscenium arch allowed the audience to view a scene as if through a window. The depth and width of the stage made possible the use of elaborately realistic scenery and lighting.

The theatre-in-the-round design of Chichester Theatre recalls a primary feature of Elizabethan theatre — close contact between actors and audience.

Persia (480) (*see* Greek-Persian Wars). Themistocles argued successfully for the fortification of Athens, despite Spartan opposition, but his opponents caused him to be ostracized in about 471. Themistocles subsequently fled to Asia, where he died.

Thénard, Louis-Jacques (1777-1857) French chemist, who in 1808 was the first to isolate the element *boron in collaboration with *Gay-Lussac. He also discovered hydrogen peroxide in 1813 and produced a pigment known as Thénard's blue, which is stable at high temperatures and so can be used in porcelain.

Theocritus (c. 310-250 BC) Greek poet. Born in Sicily, he worked for part of his life on the island of Cos and at Alexandria. His surviving poems, the *Idylls*, include six poems cast in the dramatic form of dialogues or contests between countrymen. These poems on Sicilian rural life are unsurpassed examples of the pastoral, a form which Theocritus originated and which influenced many later works, such as Milton's *Lycidas*.

theodolite An instrument used in *surveying to measure horizontal and vertical angles. It consists of a telescope, with crosshairs in the eyepiece for focusing on the target, that can swivel on horizontal and vertical axes, which pass through two circular scales. It has a spirit level to indicate when the instrument is horizontal and is mounted on a tripod with adjustable legs.

Theodora (c. 500-48 AD) Byzantine empress (527-48); the wife of *Justinian I. Theodora was the daughter of a circus bearkeeper and had been an actress before she married Justinian in 525 and became one of the most influential women in the history of the Eastern Roman Empire. Justinian consulted her on all affairs of state and his reign achieved little of consequence after her death. She was noted for her early championship of the rights of women.

Theodorakis, Mikis (1925-) Greek composer, who led a revival of Greek folk music in the 1960s and has incorporated elements of it into his compositions, which include music for the film *Zorba the Greek* (1964). He has also been politically active in Greece.

Theodore I Lascaris (c. 1175-1222) The founder of the Byzantine empire at Nicaea after Constantinople fell to the Crusaders (1204). In 1214, following a period of warfare, Theodore and the Latins determined the borders between Constantinople and Nicaea.

Theodoric the Great (c. 445-526) King of the Ostrogoths (471-526), who ruled Italy (493-526). He defeated *Odoacer in 493 and established an Ostrogothic kingdom with its capital at Ravenna, ensuring peace by religious toleration and marriage alliances with the other barbarian kingdoms. However, territorial expansion brought conflict with the Frankish king *Clovis and his death left Italy leaderless and ripe for Byzantine annexation.

Theodosius (I) the Great (347-95 AD) Roman emperor in the East (379-94) and sole emperor (394-95). Theodosius allowed the Visigoths independence on Roman territory by a treaty in 382 and they undertook to supplement the Roman army. A devout and orthodox Christian, he imposed Christianity on the Empire in 391, closing pagan temples and forbidding sacrifices.

Theodosius II (401-50 AD) Eastern Roman emperor (408-50). He was strongly influenced by his sister, his wife, and a series of advisers. He sponsored the compilation of the **Theodosian Code** (438), a collection of laws that had been issued since 312.

theology Literally, the study of *God. Each of the higher religions has its own theology. Christian theology includes within its scope the nature of God, his relationship with the universe, his providence regarding man, and the teachings of the Church. Different traditions exist within the Roman Catholic, Orthodox, and Protestant communions, but typical subdivisions of theology are dogmatic, historical, and pastoral theology. Until the emergence of Renaissance *humanism, theology was accounted the highest science (*see* scholasticism) but in the 19th and 20th centuries its findings came under hostile scrutiny from physicists, philosophers, anthropologists, and others.

Theophilus (d. 842 AD) Byzantine emperor (829-42). He was a man of great learning and, despite frequent attacks by the Muslims, stimulated a resurgence of cultural activity. He was the last emperor to uphold *iconoclasm.

Theophrastus (c. 370-286 BC) Greek philosopher and scientist. He studied under *Plato and became *Aristotle's closest friend, succeeding him as head of the *Lyceum. He established botany as a science and lectured and wrote on a vast number of subjects.

theorbo A large double-necked *lute having two sets of strings. One set could be stopped against a fingerboard, the other plucked as open strings.

theosophy Speculation tending towards a mystical understanding of the divine. The term originated in *Neoplatonism but is now mainly applied to the blend of Hindu and Neoplatonic doctrines propounded by the Theosophical Society, which was founded by Helena *Blavatsky in 1875. *Compare* anthroposophy.

Thera (*or* Santoríni; Modern Greek name: Thíra) A Greek island in the Aegean Sea, the southernmost of the Cyclades group. The present island is the E side of a volcano the catastrophic explosion of which (c. 1450 BC) precipitated the decline of *Minoan civilization on Crete, 110 km (70 mi) to the S (*see also* Atlantis). In 1966 a well-preserved Minoan town was found on Thera itself. Area: 75 sq km (29 sq mi).

therapsid An extinct reptile belonging to the order *Therapsida*, which lived during the Permian and Triassic periods (280-200 million years ago). Therapsids were the ancestors of the mammals and had a number of mammal-like features: the limbs were positioned under the body to carry it well off the ground; the skull was deep with a fairly large braincase; and the teeth were specialized for different functions. There were both carnivorous and herbivorous forms.

Theravada The old conservative school of *Buddhism, also called Hinayana (Pali: lesser vehicle) by its detractors. Prevalent in Burma, Cambodia, Laos, Sri Lanka, and Thailand, it emphasizes the ideal of the *arhat*—one who, as a monk, achieves enlightenment by his own efforts. In Theravada, the *Buddha is revered but not the Bodhisattvas, and only the oldest works, the Pali canon, are considered orthodox.

Thérèse, St (Marie Françoise Thérèse Martin; 1873-97) French *Carmelite nun, known as the Little Flower of Jesus. She entered the Carmelite convent at Lisieux when only 15 and died there 9 years later of tuberculosis. Her fame rests on her spiritual autobiography, *Histoire d'une âme* (1898), showing that spiritual perfection could be attained through childlike humbleness and goodness. She was canonized in 1925. Feast day: 3 Oct.

thermae Ancient Roman public baths. They reached their height of architectural sophistication under the Empire, being equipped with libraries and other amenities for relaxation. The best surviving examples include the baths of Titus (81 AD) and Caracalla (217).

thermal reactor A nuclear reactor (*see* nuclear energy) in which natural or enriched uranium is used with a moderator, in most cases to generate heat for a *power station. The moderator slows down the neutrons emitted during the fission of uranium-235, so that their velocities are comparable to the velocities of gas molecules ("thermal" velocities).

In a thermal reactor, fuel rods made of uranium metal or oxide are surrounded by a moderator (together forming the reactor core), the heat of the reaction being removed by a coolant. After leaving the core, the coolant passes to a heat exchanger in which steam is raised. The rate of reaction is controlled by a series of control rods, which can move in and out of the core: the rods contain a neutron-absorbing element, such as boron or cadmium.

The first nuclear reactor was built by *Fermi in 1942, using natural uranium, a graphite moderator, and a water coolant. British thermal reactors use a gas coolant (usually carbon dioxide) and later types use an enriched fuel. American designs use a liquid as both moderator and coolant. Using ordinary water in a pressurized-water reactor or a boiling-water reactor, enriched fuel is needed; using heavy water, natural uranium can be used. *Compare* fast reactor.

Thermidorian Reaction   *See* French Revolution.

thermionic valve   A device consisting of a sealed glass or metal tube, either evacuated or containing gas at low pressure, into which two or more electrodes are inserted. One heated electrode, the cathode, emits electrons, which are attracted to the positively charged anode, forming an electric current. This current flows in one direction only and can be controlled by the voltage applied at one or more other electrodes (called grids). The **diode valve** was invented in 1904 by Sir John Ambrose Fleming. It has two electrodes and functions as a simple *rectifier. The **triode valve** with one grid was invented in 1910 by Lee De Forest; it was the first to function as an amplifier. The weak signal fed to the grid produces a stronger signal in the anode circuit. Diode and triode valves made possible the development of radio transmitters and receivers, although now *semiconductor diodes and *transistors have largely replaced them. The gas-filled **thyratron** functions as a switch by using a positive grid voltage pulse to initiate a continuing discharge of electrons from the cathode to the anode. It is used in switching and counting circuits, but, like most thermionic valves, has been superseded by its semiconductor equivalent, the *thyristor.

thermistor   A *semiconductor device with an electrical resistance that decreases sharply as temperature increases. It is used in temperature-control circuits and can be calibrated for use as a thermometer.

thermite   A mixture of powdered aluminium and iron oxide. When ignited, aluminium oxide and iron are produced. The reaction is highly exothermic, yielding molten iron at a temperature of over 2000°C. It is used in welding steel and in incendiary bombs.

thermocline   A layer within the oceans between about 100 m and 200 m below the surface, in which there is a marked increase in temperature with depth. Above and for some distance below it, there is little vertical temperature gradient.

thermocouple   A type of thermometer consisting of an electric circuit formed by two dissimilar metals joined at each end. One junction is exposed to the temperature to be measured, a voltage being generated between it and the other (reference) junction as a result of the temperature difference between them (*see* thermoelectric effects). The output is usually displayed on a *galvanometer. Copper-constantan junctions are used up to 500°C and platinum-rhodium alloy up to 1500°C. A **thermopile** consists of several thermocouples connected in series to increase the voltage output for a particular temperature difference.

thermodynamics   The study of *heat and its relationship with other forms of energy. Thermodynamics is primarily a statistical subject, thermodynamic quantities, such as *temperature and *entropy, being dependent on the statistical behaviour of the particles that comprise a system. There are three fundamental laws of thermodynamics. The first law states that the energy of a closed system remains constant during any process. This law is a restatement of the law of *conservation of mass and energy. The second law states that heat cannot flow from a cold body to a hot body without the expenditure of external work. Another way of stating this law is to say that the entropy of a closed system can

never decrease. If the entropy change is zero then the process is said to be reversible. The third law states that as the thermodynamic temperature of a system approaches *absolute zero, its entropy approaches zero.

Thermodynamics has proved most valuable in studying *heat engines and chemical reactions, but it also has wider implications in other statistical sciences. *See* heat death of the universe.

thermoelectric effects   The effects of changes of temperature on electric circuits or devices. The **Seebeck effect**, named after Johann Seebeck (1770-1831), provides the basis for the *thermocouple; it occurs when a circuit has two junctions between dissimilar metals. If the junctions are maintained at different temperatures, a voltage is generated between them. The **Peltier effect**, named after Jean Peltier (1785-1845), is the converse of this. One junction heats up and the other cools down when a steady current flows through such a circuit. In the **Thomson** (*or* Kelvin) **effect**, named after Lord *Kelvin, a temperature gradient along a single metal conductor causes a current to flow through it.

thermoluminescence   *Luminescence caused by heating a substance and thus liberating electrons trapped in its crystal defects. The phenomenon is used as a dating technique, especially for pottery. The number of trapped electrons is assumed to be related to the quantity of *ionizing radiation to which the specimen has been exposed since firing (as the crystal defects are caused by ionizing radiation). Thus, by measuring the amount of light emitted on heating, an estimate of the age of the pottery can be made by assuming that the amount of ionizing radiation to which it has been exposed is related to its age.

thermometer   An instrument used for measuring temperature. Thermometers make use of some property of a substance that varies uniformly with temperature, most commonly the expansion of a liquid, such as mercury or alcohol coloured with dye. A clinical thermometer is a typical mercury-in-glass thermometer; it has a constriction in the stem above the bulb so that the mercury stays at its maximum reading until "shaken down". More accurate thermometers use the expansion of a gas, which is much greater than that of a liquid. Other thermometers include the resistance thermometer, which depends on the variation in the resistance of a wire (usually platinum); the bimetallic strip in which the unequal expansion of two metals welded together to form a strip causes a pointer to move round a dial; and the thermistor, in which the change in conductivity of a semiconductor is used as a measure of temperature. High temperatures are measured by a *pyrometer.

thermonuclear reactor   A reactor in which a fusion reaction (*see* nuclear energy) takes place with the controlled release of energy. After over 30 years of research in several countries, it is now generally accepted that a working thermonuclear reactor is unlikely to be in commission before the next century.

A typical fusion reaction is the combination of deuterium and tritium to form helium ($^2_1H + ^3_1H = ^4_2He + n + 17.6$ MeV). To overcome the *electromagnetic interaction between nuclei a temperature of about 40 million °C is needed. Containing the *plasma (as the high-temperature ionized gas is called) is the problem to be solved. In magnetic containment a high current passed through the plasma creates a *magnetic bottle that keeps the plasma away from the containing walls. To produce useful energy at this temperature, the product of the plasma density and the containment time must exceed 10^{14} particle seconds per cm^3. Russian toroidal Tokamak devices have so far only achieved a figure of 10^{12}; moreover the problems of magnetic instabilities have not yet been solved. Other possible devices include a pellet of fuel exposed to pulses from *laser beams. The virtually inexhaustible supply of thermonuclear fuel (hydrogen and its isotopes) makes the fusion reactor an extremely attractive goal. □p.1206.

^2_1H ^3_1H

+ proton

○ neutron

14·1 MeV   3·5 MeV

deuterium-tritium fusion reaction

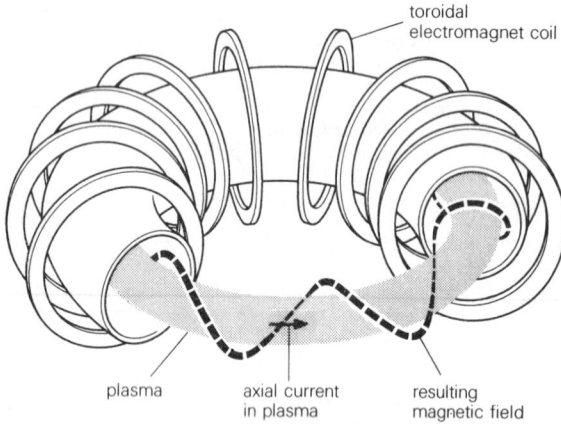

toroidal
electromagnet coil

plasma   axial current   resulting
                in plasma   magnetic field

fusion reactor experiment

THERMONUCLEAR REACTOR   *The combination of deuterium (^2_1H) and tritium (^3_1H) in a fusion reaction that forms helium. This is being attempted using a toroidal electromagnet to contain plasma consisting of deuterium and tritium nuclei.*

thermopile.   *See* thermocouple.

Thermopylae, Battle of   (480 BC) The battle in which the Greeks under the Spartan king, *Leonidas, attempted for three days to hold the pass of Thermopylae in E central Greece against the Persians. After the main Greek force had retreated the Spartans and Thespians, surrounded and outnumbered, fought to the death. Their heroic stand inspired continued Greek resistance to Persia (*see* Greek-Persian Wars).

Theseus   A legendary Greek hero, son of Aegeus, King of Athens, or of Poseidon. He freed the Athenians from their annual tribute to *Minos by killing the *Minotaur of Crete with the help of *Ariadne, who escaped with him. He extended the rule of Athens over various Attic communities and was the subject of many legends. He was father of *Hippolytus by Hippolyte, Queen of the Amazons, and he married *Phaedra, sister of Ariadne.

Thespiae   An ancient city of Boeotia at the foot of Mount Helicon, the Muses' traditional home. *Praxiteles' famous Statue of Eros was at Thespiae. Thespians were the only Boeotians to resist the Persian invasion (*see* Greek-Persian Wars) and fought alongside the Spartans at *Thermopylae (480 BC). It retained its importance under the Romans.

Thespis   (6th century BC) Semilegendary Greek poet. He won a prize for tragedy at Athens in about 534 BC. Traditionally

held to be the inventor of tragedy, he was said to have introduced a single actor in dramatic performances that had hitherto been exclusively choral. He was also believed to have introduced the wearing of linen masks.

Thessalonians, Epistles of Paul to the   Two New Testament books written by Paul to new converts in Thessalonica in about 51 AD. They are therefore among the earliest books of the New Testament. The first letter is filled with reminiscences, thanksgiving, and instruction but gives special prominence to the second coming of Christ. The second letter is a sequel, warning against the neglect of everyday duties caused by an over-enthusiastic expectation of the second coming.

Thessaloníki   (English name: Salonika)   40 38N 22 58E The second largest port in Greece, in Macedonia on the Gulf of Salonika. Founded in 315 BC as Thessalonica, it became the capital of Macedonia. It was captured by the Turks (1430) and remained in the Ottoman Empire until ceded to Greece (1913). During World War I it was a base for Allied operations. Notable Byzantine architecture includes the Panaghia Chalkeon (1028). Its university was founded in 1925. The port handles about one-third of Greek exports, including chrome, manganese, and agricultural produce. Industries include the manufacture of textiles and food processing. Population (1981): 402 443.

Thessaly   (Modern Greek name: Thessalía)   A region of E central Greece, bordering on the Aegean Sea. In the 4th century BC it was briefly a strong and united state before falling to Philip of Macedon. Freed from Macedonian rule by Rome in 196 BC, it was incorporated in the Roman province of Macedonia in 148 BC. It subsequently formed part of the Byzantine Empire, falling to Turkey in the late 14th century AD. It was annexed by Greece in 1881.

Thetford   52 25N 0 45E A market town in E England, in Norfolk. An important Saxon town, it once had 20 churches and 8 monasteries. There has been considerable industrial expansion since the early 1960s. Population (1981): 19 591.

Thetford Mines   46 06N 71 18W A city in E Canada, in SE Quebec. Founded in 1876, it is located by the world's largest asbestos mines. Other mining and light industry are also important. Population (1981): 19 965.

Thetis   In Greek mythology, one of the *nereids. She was courted by Zeus and Poseidon, but after hearing that she was fated to bear a son greater than its father they married her to the mortal Peleus, to whom she bore *Achilles.

thiamine.   *See* vitamin B complex.

thiazine   An organic compound that has a molecular structure containing a ring of four carbon atoms and two sulphur atoms. Thiazine derivatives are used in such drugs as tranquillizers, antihistamines, and antibiotics, as well as in various dyes.

thiazole (C_3H_3NS)   An organic compound that has a molecular structure containing a ring of three carbon atoms, one sulphur atom, and one nitrogen atom. Thiazole derivatives occur in thiamine (vitamin B_1), penicillin, and in numerous synthetic drugs, dyes, and chemicals.

Thibaud, Jacques   (1880–1953) French violinist. He studied at the Paris conservatoire and after a period playing at the Café Rouge in Paris he made his concert debut in 1898. In 1905 he formed a trio with Cortot and Casals. He was killed in an air crash.

thickhead   An insectivorous songbird belonging to a family (*Pachycephalidae*; 35 species) occurring in mangrove swamps, scrub, and open forests in S Asia and Australasia. Thickheads are 15–18 cm long and have large heavy heads and a loud whistling song. Male birds of the chief genus, *Pachycephalus*, are typically yellow and green with black, white, or brown markings.

Thiers, Louis Adolphe   (1797–1877) French statesman and historian; the first president of the Third Republic (1870–73). He served Louis Philippe in various ministerial posts and was a critic of Napoleon III, after whose fall during the Franco-Prussian War Thiers became president. He negotiated peace with Prussia and his economic policies facilitated France's economic recovery. He was responsible for the suppression of the Commune of Paris (1871). His publications include *Histoire de la Révolution française* (10 vols, 1823–27).

Thimphu (*or* Thimbu)   27 29N 89 40E The capital of Bhutan since 1962, situated in the foothills of the E Himalayas. Population (1982 est): 12 000.

Thíra.   *See* Thera.

Third Reich   (1933–45) The Nazi regime in Germany. The name refers to the Nazi ambition to revive the medieval Holy Roman Empire (the first Reich) and the German Empire (the second Reich; 1871–1918). The Third Reich succeeded the Weimar Republic and ended with Germany's defeat in World War II.

third stream   A name for a type of music created by the fusion of jazz and classical music. The word was coined by the composer Gunther Schuller (1925–   ), who encouraged classically trained jazz musicians, such as Charlie Mingus and John Coltrane (1926–   ), and composers interested in jazz, such as Milton Babbitt, to work together.

Third World.   *See* developing countries.

Thirteen Colonies   The 13 North American colonies that became the United States of America in 1776 (*see* American Revolution). They were Connecticut, Delaware, Georgia, Maryland, Massachusetts, New Hampshire, New Jersey, New York, North Carolina, Pennsylvania, Rhode Island, South Carolina, and Virginia.

DYLAN THOMAS   *The poet in 1946.*

thirty-eighth parallel   The latitude of 38°N that approximates to the border between North and South Korea. It was the line, agreed at the *Yalta Conference at the end of World War II, N of which Soviet troops accepted the Japanese surrender and S of which US troops did so. Hostility between the Soviet-dominated North Korea and the US-dominated South Korea led to the *Korean War, after which the thirty-eighth parallel was confirmed as the border.

Thirty-Nine Articles   (1563) The doctrine, together with the Book of *Common Prayer, of the *Church of England. They were derived from Thomas Cranmer's 42 Articles (1553), which had been revoked by Mary I in re-establishing Roman Catholicism in England. The Articles do not represent a creed; rather they give the Anglican position with regard to certain contro-

versial points, especially as distinguished from the Roman Catholic, Calvinist, or Anabaptist views. They were probably written to permit differing interpretations (e.g. *transubstantiation is rejected although the same Article appears to support the doctrine of the Real Presence of Christ in the Eucharist). The clergy of the Church of England are no longer required to subscribe formally to the Articles but only to promise not to teach beliefs that contradict them.

Thirty Years' War   (1618–48) The conflict between rival dynastic and religious interests in the Holy Roman Empire that escalated into a major European war. It was caused by the revolt of Protestants in Bohemia against the Counter-Reformation policies of the imperial government at Prague. Although imperial forces defeated the Bohemians in 1620, the revolt spread, with the German Protestants under *Mansfeld receiving sporadic support from the English, Dutch, and Danes. With the Edict of Restitution (1629) Emperor Ferdinand II, helped by the armies of *Wallenstein and *Tilly, dispossessed many German Protestants, who were only saved by the intervention in 1630 of Sweden under *Gustavus II Adolphus. In 1635 France, hoping to contain the power of Spain and the Empire, entered the conflict. The war ended with the Peace of *Westphalia (1648), although the Franco-Spanish conflict continued until 1659 (*see* Pyrenees, Treaty of the). The war caused serious economic and demographic reverses in Germany.

Thisbe.   *See* Pyramus and Thisbe.

thistle   A prickly-leaved herb belonging to one of several genera of the family *Compositae*, especially *Carduus* (120 species), *Cirsium* (120 species), *Carlinus* (20 species), and *Onopordum* (20 species), distributed throughout the N hemisphere. Thistles have purple flower heads and spiny stems. The perennial creeping thistle (*Cirsium arvense*) is a persistent weed, having spreading roots that give rise to new plants. *See also* globe thistle; sow thistle.

Thistle, Order of the   A Scottish order of knighthood, probably founded by James III (1451–88); it was revived by James VII (II of England) in 1687. It comprises the sovereign and 16 knights and its motto is *Nemo me impune lacessit* (vernacular: Wha daur meddle wi' me?).

Thistlewood, Arthur.   *See* Cato Street Conspiracy.

thixotropy   A property possessed by certain gels as a result of which they become liquid when stirred and return to a gel-like state when left to stand. Thixotropic gels are used in nondrip paints as they prevent the various components from settling out during storage without affecting the fluid properties of the paint when applied. Certain types of quicksand are naturally thixotropic.

Thomas, Dylan   (1914–53) Welsh poet. Born in Swansea, Wales, he moved to London after the publication of *18 Poems* in 1934 and worked for the BBC. *Deaths and Entrances* (1946) contains many of his best-known poems. In 1949 he returned to Wales, where he wrote his popular radio play *Under Milk Wood* (1954). Alcoholism precipitated his death, while on tour in the USA.

Thomas, Edward   (1878–1917) British poet. Most of his work consists of nature studies and literary biographies. His poetry, written after encouragement from Robert Frost, is chiefly concerned with his love of the English countryside. He was killed in action in World War I.

Thomas, St   In the New Testament, one of the 12 Apostles. He is known as "Doubting Thomas" because he refused to believe in the resurrection until he had seen and touched Christ. Feast day: 21 Dec.

Thomas à Kempis   (Thomas Hemmerken; c. 1380–1471) German spiritual writer and monk. He spent most of his life writing and teaching novices at the Augustinian convent of Agnietenberg near Zwolle (Netherlands). His fame rests on his devotional treatise, *The Imitation of Christ*, although his authorship has been doubted by some scholars.

Thomas of Erceldoune (13th century) English poet and prophet. Traditionally thought to be the author of a 14th-century romance, *Sir Tristram*, and of a 15th-century collection of prophecies, this semilegendary poet is best known from the ballad "Thomas the Rhymer", which is based on *Sir Tristram*.

Thomism. *See* Aquinas, St Thomas.

Thompson, Daley (1958–) British decathlete. Originally a sprinter, in 1975 he switched to the *decathlon, which he won in the Commonwealth Games in 1978. Unbeaten until 1987, he has won two Olympic gold medals (1980 and 1984), and three European championships.

Thompson, Francis (1859–1907) British poet and critic. He began writing poetry while living in poverty and addicted to opium. A Roman Catholic, he wrote frequently on religious themes. "The Hound of Heaven," his best-known poem, is included in *Poems* (1893).

Thomson, James (1700–48) British poet. Born in Scotland, he went to London in 1725. His works include *The Seasons* (1730), a poem that foreshadowed the Romantic movement, the patriotic song "Rule Britannia" (1740), and the moral allegory *The Castle of Indolence* (1748).

Thomson, Sir Joseph John (1856–1940) British physicist, who discovered the *electron. After becoming director of the Cavendish Laboratory in Cambridge, Thomson studied *cathode rays, the nature of which was then unknown. In 1897 he succeeded in deflecting cathode rays by an electric field, thus showing that they consisted of negatively charged particles. He also measured the ratio of their charge to mass and, using the known figure for the minimum charge on an ion, deduced that electrons were about 2000 times lighter than the hydrogen atom. Thomson thought that atoms consist of electrons embedded in a positively charged sphere, a concept that was superseded by *Rutherford's model. He was awarded the Nobel Prize in 1906.

His son **Sir George Paget Thomson** (1892–1975) discovered the effect of electron diffraction (1927). He shared the 1937 Nobel Prize with Clinton Davisson (1881–1958), who had independently discovered the same effect. He was professor of physics at Imperial College, London (1930–52), and Master of Corpus Christi, Cambridge (1952–62).

Thomson, Virgil (1896–) US composer, music critic, and conductor. He studied composition with Nadia Boulanger in Paris. His compositions include two operas with libretti by Gertrude Stein: *Four Saints in Three Acts* (1928) and *The Mother of Us All* (1947). He has composed a variety of other vocal and instrumental music, including music for the film *Louisiana Story* (1948). His writings include *The Art of Judging Music* (1948) and *American Music Since 1910* (1971).

Thomson, William. *See* Kelvin, William Thomson, 1st Baron.

Thomson effect (*or* Kelvin effect). *See* thermoelectric effects.

Thomson of Fleet, Roy Herbert, 1st Baron (1894–1976) British newspaper proprietor, born in Canada. After starting and acquiring radio stations and newspapers in North America, he moved to Edinburgh and bought *The Scotsman* (1953). In 1959 he bought Kemsley Newspapers, which included the *Sunday Times*, and in 1966 he acquired *The Times*. His son **Kenneth Roy, 2nd Baron Thomson** (1923–) succeeded him as chairman of the Thomson Organization.

Thonburi 13 43N 100 27E A city in central Thailand, part of Bangkok Metropolis on the River Chao Phraya. It is noted for the Wat Arun temple. Industries include rice and timber milling.

Thor The Teutonic god of thunder, in some legends the son of *Odin. He presided over the home and controlled the weather and crops; he was also worshipped as a god of war. Armed with a magic hammer and a belt, which increased his strength, he battled frequently against giants and monsters. His name survives in *Thursday*. □Ragnarök.

thorax In mammals (including man), the region of the body between the *diaphragm and the neck, which contains the lungs and heart and their associated vessels. The skeleton of the thorax is formed by the breastbone at the front, the spine at the back, and the ribs at the sides. In arthropods the thorax is between the head and abdomen.

Thoreau, Henry David (1817–62) US naturalist and writer. Thoreau is best known for his Walden experiment (1845–46) during which he lived as a recluse in the woods of Walden near his native Concord (Massachusetts). He developed a great love and knowledge of animals, which was more intuitive than scientific. *Walden* was published in 1854. Influenced by *Emerson and *Hawthorne, Thoreau also wrote poems and essays, many about his beloved homeland. His best-known essay, "Civil Disobedience", grew out of his opposition to the Mexican War. *See also* Transcendentalists, New England.

thorium (Th) A naturally occurring radioactive metal. It is possible that thorium-fuelled nuclear reactors may be developed in the future, since it is more abundant than uranium and does not produce plutonium-239 in appreciable quantities (*see* uranium). Thorium oxide (ThO_2) has one of the highest known melting points (3300°C), which led to its use in gas mantles, as it glows white when heated. At no 90; at wt 232.038; mp 1750°C; bp 3800°C.

thorium series One of three naturally occurring series of radioactive decays. The thorium series is headed by thorium-232, which undergoes a series of alpha and beta decays ending with the stable isotope lead-208. *See also* actinium series; uranium series.

thorn apple An annual herb, *Datura stramonium*, also called jimsonweed, occurring in N temperate and subtropical regions. Growing to a height of 1 m, it has white trumpet-shaped flowers producing a fruit with a spiny capsule that splits to release the black seeds. All parts of the plant are very poisonous, containing the alkaloids hyoscyamine, hyoscine, and scopolamine. Family: *Solanaceae.

thornbill A drab-coloured Australian bird belonging to one of three genera, especially *Acanthiza*. The yellow-tailed thornbill (*A. chrysorrhoea*) builds a very long oval nest with several nest chambers, the upper being used to rear young and the lower providing accommodation for the male. Family: *Muscicapidae* (*see* flycatcher).

Thorndike, Dame Sybil (1882–1976) British actress. She acted many Shakespearian roles at the Old Vic between 1914 and 1918 and played the title role in the first production of G. B. Shaw's *St Joan* in 1924. She also acted in several films. She toured extensively during and after World War II with her husband, the distinguished actor **Sir Lewis Casson.** (1875–1969).

Thornhill, Sir James (1675–1734) English *baroque decorative painter. One of the first English painters to earn an international reputation, Thornhill is best remembered for his decoration of the Painted Hall at Greenwich Hospital (1704), the interior of the dome of *St Paul's Cathedral (1707), and the hall at Blenheim Palace. He was the teacher and father-in-law of *Hogarth.

Thoroughbred A breed of □horse descended from three Arab stallions brought to England between 1689 and 1724. Thoroughbreds have a refined streamlined build and a sensitive temperament and are noted for speed and stamina, being used worldwide for racing and as bloodstock to improve other breeds. They may be any solid colour. Height: 1.52–1.73 m (15–17 hands).

Thorpe, (John) Jeremy (1929–) British Liberal politician; leader of the Liberal Party (1967–76). MP for North Devon (1959–79), he was charged with, but acquitted of, conspiracy and incitement to murder Norman Scott, with whom he was alleged to have had a homosexual relationship.

Thorvaldsen, Bertel (*or* B. Thorwaldsen; 1768–1844)

Danish sculptor. His highly successful career began in Rome, where he worked from 1797 until his return to Copenhagen in 1838. Reviving the tradition of ancient Greek sculpture in his mythological and religious statues, he became one of the leading figures in *neoclassicism. Many of his works are in the Thorvaldsen Museum, Copenhagen.

Thoth The Egyptian god of learning, the scribe and arbiter of the gods, usually portrayed with the head of an ibis. He was the inventor of writing, arithmetic, and geometry and the keeper of various magic formulae. *See also* Hermes Trismegistos.

Thousand, Expedition of the (1860) The expedition of about a thousand volunteers, led by Giuseppe *Garibaldi, which embarked from Genoa and, after landing in Sicily, overthrew the Kingdom of the Two Sicilies, enabling S Italy to be united with the N. *See also* Risorgimento.

Thousand Islands A group of about 1700 small islands and islets in North America, in the St Lawrence River. They are chiefly in Ontario (Canada) with a few in New York state (USA) and are a popular resort area.

Thrace The Balkan region bordered by the Black Sea, the Aegean, Macedonia, and the River Danube. From the 8th century BC Greek cities colonized the coasts, while the independent inland tribes were an easy target for invaders—the Persians in about 516 BC and then Philip II of Macedon in the mid-4th century. After Alexander the Great's death (323) it passed to his general Lysimachus (c. 355-c. 281 BC) and then to Macedonia before coming under the influence of Rome in 168 BC; it became a Roman province in 46 AD. Famous for its horses and horsemen, and for ecstatic religious rituals, Thrace was traditionally the birthplace of the mysteries and orgiastic rites associated with the worship of Dionysus. It is now divided between Turkey, Greece, and Bulgaria.

Thrale, Hester Lynch. *See* Piozzi, Hester Lynch.

threadfin A fish, also called threadfish, belonging to the family *Polynemidae* (about 24 species), that is found along warm seashores. It has a silvery elongated body, usually 30-60 cm long, two dorsal fins, and four to seven long threadlike pectoral fin rays. Order: *Perciformes*.

threadworm. *See* pinworm.

Three Rivers. *See* Trois-Rivières.

Three Wise Men. *See* Magi.

thresher shark A *shark of the family *Alopiidae* (5 species), found usually in offshore waters of tropical and temperate seas. About 6 m long, it has a long scythelike extension of the upper tail lobe, which it uses to thrash the water while circling its prey (squid and schooling fish), forcing them into tighter groups, which it then attacks. ▢fish.

thrift A perennial herb, *Armeria maritima*, also called sea pink, native to mountains, salt marshes, and sandy coastal regions of N Europe. The flower stem, up to 30 cm high, rises from a basal tuft of long narrow grasslike leaves and bears a cluster of rose-pink or white flowers. The Jersey thrift (*A. arenaria*) is taller with a denser tuft of broader leaves and grows on sand dunes in central and S Europe. Family: *Plumbaginaceae*.

thrips A minute insect, also called thunder fly, belonging to the order *Thysanoptera* (about 3000 species). Thrips have dark slender bodies, 0.5-5 mm long, and usually two pairs of narrow fringed wings. Many species suck the juices of flowering plants, often causing serious damage and spreading plant diseases. Others eat fungi, decaying organic material, mites, and small insects. In some species there are no males and the larvae develop from unfertilized eggs (*see* parthenogenesis).

Throckmorton, Sir Nicholas (*or* Throgmorton; 1515-71) English diplomat. He fought at the battle of Pinkie (1547) and was ambassador to France and, during the 1560s, to Scotland. He was imprisoned (1569) by Elizabeth for his friendship with Mary, Queen of Scots. Throgmorton Street,

the site in London of the Stock Exchange, is named after him. His nephew **Francis Throckmorton** (1554-84) organized (1583) a plot supported by France and Spain to overthrow Elizabeth I in favour of Mary, Queen of Scots. The conspiracy was discovered by Walsingham and Throckmorton was arrested, tortured, and executed.

thrombosis The formation of a blood clot inside a blood vessel, which often obstructs the flow of blood. Thrombosis is more likely to occur if the blood vessel is damaged, if the blood flow is very slow, or if the blood is in a condition in which it is more likely to clot. The commonest site of thrombosis is in the veins of the legs. This is particularly likely to occur if a person is bedridden for a long time and it is often accompanied by inflammation of the vein (*see* phlebitis). The clot may become detached and carried to the lungs, causing pulmonary *embolism. The patient is treated with *anticoagulants.
Thrombosis can also occur in the arteries supplying the heart (coronary thrombosis), causing a heart attack (*see* myocardial infarction), or the brain, causing *stroke.

thrush (bird) A songbird belonging to a family (*Turdidae*; 300 species) found throughout the world but predominantly in Old World regions. Thrushes are slender billed, 13-30 cm long, and usually brown—often with speckling or patches of red, yellow, or blue. They may be terrestrial or arboreal, feeding chiefly on insects and fruit and often having melodious songs. Northern species are migratory. *See also* blackbird; fieldfare; mistle thrush; redwing; ring ouzel; song thrush.

thrush (disease). *See* candidiasis.

Thucydides (c. 460-c. 400 BC) Greek historian. He served as an Athenian general in the Peloponnesian War but was banished in 424 BC for allowing the Spartan general Brasidas to capture the colony of Amphipolis. He remained in exile until 404 BC. His eight-volume *History of the Peloponnesian War*, written in a plain narrative style, is notable for its political, moral, and psychological analysis of the issues and leaders involved.

Thugs (Sanskrit word: *sthaga*, deceiver) A Hindu sect, members of which worked in small gangs, murdering (usually by strangulation), robbing, and burying travellers in India. They worshipped Kali, the Hindu goddess of death, and observed strict rules, employing a private language amongst themselves. They were suppressed by Captain William Sleeman (1788-1856) in the 1830s.

Thuja. *See* arbor vitae.

Thule 1. A far northern land first described in the 4th century BC by *Pytheas. It is tentatively identified with Norway or Iceland. 2. An Eskimo culture of the Arctic region, dating from between about 500 and 1300 AD.

thulium (Tm) The least abundant of the *lanthanide elements, discovered in 1879 by P. T. Cleve (1840-1905). It forms the oxide Tm_2O_3. Radioactive ^{169}Tm is used in portable X-ray generators. At no 69; at wt 168.934; mp 1545°C; bp 1947°C.

Thun (French name: Thoune) 46 46N 7 38E A town in central Switzerland, on Lake Thun. It is the centre of the Bernese Oberland; industries include cheese production and watchmaking. Population (1983 est): 36 496.

Thunder Bay 48 20N 89 23W A city and port in E Canada, in Ontario on Lake Superior. Settled after 1800, it consists of Fort William and Port Arthur, which amalgamated in 1970. A major wheat-exporting port, Thunder Bay is also a transportation hub and mining centre. Pulp and paper, timber, aircraft, buses, and shipbuilding are economically important. Lakehead University (1965) is situated here. Population (1981): 112 486.

thunderstorm A storm of rain, hail, or snow, accompanied by thunder and *lightning. A lightning flash is an electrical discharge causing sudden heating and expansion of air as the flash passes through the atmosphere, resulting in the sound of thunder. Although both occur simultaneously, thunder is heard later than lightning is seen, as light travels faster than sound. An approximate measure of distance from a storm is 1.6 km (1 mi) for every 5 seconds between flash and thunder.

Thurber, James (1894-1961) US humorous writer and cartoonist. An early and continuing contributor to the *New Yorker*, he satirized intellectual fashions and domestic habits with irony and sophistication. His essays and stories are collected in *The Thurber Carnival* (1945) and other volumes.

Thuringia A historic region of central Germany, N of Bavaria and W of Saxony. Dominated by the Thuringian forests and strategically positioned, Thuringia became a buffer state against invaders from the E. Frequently partitioned during the middle ages, it passed to the Wettin family in 1265. It is now part of East Germany.

Thursday Island 10 37S 142 10E An Australian island in Torres Strait, off the N coast of Queensland. Pearl fishing is the main industry. Area: 4 sq km (1.5 sq mi). Chief town: Port Kennedy.

Thutmose I King of Egypt (c. 1525–c. 1512 BC) of the 18th dynasty. He conquered Nubia beyond the Fourth Nile Cataract and Syria as far as the River Euphrates. He enlarged and embellished the temple of Amon at *Karnak.

Thutmose II King of Egypt (c. 1512–c. 1504 BC) of the 18th dynasty, the son of *Thutmose I and the brother and husband of *Hatshepsut. He crushed a rebellion in Nubia before dying young.

Thutmose III (d. 1450 BC) King of Egypt (c. 1504-1450) of the 18th dynasty, who ruled Egypt at its most powerful and prosperous. In his first year of independent rule, after the death of his half-sister *Hatshepsut (1468), he defeated Syrian rebels at Megiddo and in later campaigns advanced beyond the River Euphrates. He organized and supervised the country's complicated administration and was an outstanding athlete and big-game hunter. A patron of art and architecture, he collected foreign plants, birds, and beasts on campaign. His mummy is to be seen in Cairo.

Thutmose IV King of Egypt (1425-1417 BC) of the 18th dynasty. He cultivated the alliance of Babylonia and the Mitanni kingdom against the Hittites and built extensively at *Karnak.

thylacine The largest carnivorous *marsupial, *Thylacinus cynocephalus*, also called Tasmanian wolf or tiger. About 1.5 m long, it resembles a dog with dark stripes across its grey-brown back. Its teeth—adapted for eating meat—include pointed canines and shearing premolars. The dingo has exterminated thylacines on the Australian mainland, but a few may have survived in Tasmania. Family: *Dasyuridae*.

thyme A small shrub belonging to the genus *Thymus* (about 50 species), native to temperate Eurasia. Garden thyme (*T. vulgaris*) is cultivated for its fragrant leaves and small mauve flowers, which are dried and used as a culinary herb. An oil extract is used in perfumes and medicines. The common wild thyme (*T. drucei*) has a branching creeping stem up to 7 cm long and clusters of rose-purple flowers. Family: *Labiatae*.

thymus An organ situated at the base of the neck, above the heart. The thymus is well developed at birth and grows until puberty, after which it shrinks and ceases to function. During infancy the thymus produces lymphocytes (a type of white blood cell) that form the *antibodies associated with allergic responses and the rejection of transplanted tissues and organs. *See also* immunity.

thyratron. *See* thermionic valve.

thyristor A solid-state electronic device, also called a semiconductor or silicon-controlled rectifier; it consists of four layers of *semiconductor forming three p-n junctions. It acts as a switch, blocking the current through two terminals until it has been turned on by a pulse applied to the third terminal. This pulse can be initiated by light or a temperature change. Thyristors are used in a wide range of

power-switching and control-circuit applications. They can pass currents ranging from milliamperes to several hundred amperes and for many purposes have replaced the thyratron (*see* thermionic valve).

thyroid gland An *endocrine gland situated at the base of the neck, in front and on either side of the windpipe. It secretes two hormones, the most important of which is thyroxine, which controls the basal metabolism of the body; thyroxine secretion is regulated by thyroid-stimulating hormone, released from the *pituitary gland. Because thyroxine production requires iodine, deficiency of iodine causes the thyroid to enlarge in an attempt to produce adequate amounts of the hormone (*see* goitre). *See also* cretinism; hyperthyroidism; myxoedema.

Tianjin (T'ien-ching *or* Tientsin) 39 08N 117 12E An administratively autonomous port in NE China, on the *Grand Canal. A prosperous city for centuries, it was the scene of much friction between Chinese and Europeans in the late 19th century. It is the site of two universities. Industries include chemicals, machinery, and textiles. Population (1980 est): 7 390 000.

Tian Shan (*or* Tien Shan) A mountain system of central Asia. It extends about 2500 km (1500 mi) NE from the *Pamir Mountains in the Soviet Union, through NW China to the Mongolian border, reaching 7439 m (24 406 ft) at Pobeda Peak.

Tibaldi, Pellegrino (1527-96) Italian architect and painter, a leading exponent of *mannerism. Paintings by him survive in Rome and Bologna. In Spain (1587-96), at the invitation of Philip II, he oversaw the construction and decoration of the *Escorial.

Tiber, River (Italian name: Tevere; Latin name: Tiberis) A river in central Italy, rising in the Apennines of Tuscany and flowing mainly S through Rome to the Tyrrhenian Sea near Ostia. Length: 405 km (252 mi).

Tiberias 32 48N 35 32E A town in N Israel, on the W shore of the Sea of Galilee. Founded by Herod Antipas in about AD 20 and named after the Roman Emperor Tiberius, it became the centre of Jewry in Palestine after the Roman destruction of Jerusalem. It is now a resort. Population (1982 est): 29 000.

Tiberias, Sea of. *See* Galilee, Sea of.

Tiberius (42 BC-37 AD) Roman emperor (14-37 AD). Tiberius, who was *Livia Drusilla's son by her first husband, was recognized by his stepfather, Emperor Augustus, as his successor in 4 AD. As emperor his policies were unambitious though sound but he faced the Senate's hostility, family intrigue, and military rebellion. Tiberius' reign saw a series of treason prosecutions before his retirement to Capri in 26 AD, where he gained a reputation for depravity.

Tibesti Mountains A mountain range in N Africa, in the central Sahara. It lies chiefly in NW Chad but extends NE into Libya and rises to 3415 m (11 204 ft) at Emi Koussi, the highest peak in the Sahara.

Tibet (Chinese name: Xizang Autonomous Region) An administrative region in W China, bordering on India, Nepal, Bhutan, and Burma. It consists of a high plateau and is surrounded by mountains, including the Himalayas and the Kunlun Mountains. Most agriculture and the country's cities are in the river valleys, while nomads herd such animals as yaks on the plateau. The area is rich in minerals, not mined until the 1950s because of religious proscription. Tibet is famous for its Buddhist-inspired art and its handicrafts. *History*: Buddhism, introduced in the 7th century AD, has exerted a profound influence on Tibetan history. The lamas (priests) of *Tibetan Buddhism attained political power in the 13th century, when Kublai Khan gave the government of his conquests in E Tibet to the Sa-skya lama. Subsequent disunity was brought to an end in 1642, when the fifth *Dalai Lama became ruler of all Tibet. In

1720 the Chinese Qing dynasty established a control over Tibet that lasted until the Qing's overthrow in 1911. Independence was declared, but in 1950 Tibet again fell to the Chinese. An uprising in 1959 was brutally suppressed and the Dalai Lama, together with thousands of refugees, fled. Tibet was subsequently subjected to Chinese influence; riots in Lhasa (1987) led to a curfew being imposed. Area: 1 221 601 sq km (471 660 sq mi). Population (1980 est): 1 830 000. Capital: Lhasa.

Tibetan Buddhism (*or* lamaism) A form of Mahayana Buddhism as practised in Tibet and Mongolia. Introduced into Tibet in the 7th century AD, it is characterized by a complex ✱symbolic literature and monastic discipline, with surviving features of *Bon shamanism. Buddhist elements are explored in their esoteric significance, hence the array of deities, *mandalas, etc. The *guru is of prime importance; some are held to be reincarnations of previous lamas. Until 1959, the *Dalai Lama was both temporal and spiritual head of the state. *See also* Panchen Lama.

tibia. *See* leg.

Tibullus, Albius (c. 55–c. 19 BC) Roman poet. He lived quietly on his estate near Rome and was a friend of Horace and Ovid. His elegaic poetry, noted for its smooth and rhythmical style, is mostly addressed to his patron, M. Valerius Messalla. Two books of his poems were published during his lifetime and were known as "Delia" and "Nemesis" after the pseudonyms of the women who were the subjects of the poems.

Ticino, River A river in Switzerland and Italy. It flows mainly S from the Leopontine Alps to the River Po near Pavia in Italy. Length: 248 km (154 mi).

tick A parasitic *arachnid of the worldwide suborder *Metastigmata* (850 species), which sucks the blood of birds and mammals and may transmit such diseases as *typhus and relapsing fever. Its round unsegmented body, up to 30 mm long, bears eight bristly legs and may be covered by a dorsal shield. After feeding for a certain time, the adults drop off the host and lay eggs on the ground. The larvae attach themselves to a suitable victim, feed, then drop off and moult into nymphs, which repeat the procedure. Order: *Acarina* (or *Acari*). *Compare* mite.

tides The regular rising and falling of seawater level resulting from the gravitational attraction between the earth, sun, and moon. Variations in their relative positions produce variations in tidal range (*see* spring tide; neap tide). Most parts of the world experience semidiurnal tides (occurring twice per tidal day—24 hours 5 minutes). Tidal currents are periodic horizontal flows of water resulting from the rise and fall of the tide. Near the coast they are usually perpendicular to it and reversing, but in the ocean they flow in a rotary manner around a series of nodal points; water level remains approximately constant at these points, tidal range increasing concentrically outwards, and high water rotates about them.

Tieck, (Johann) Ludwig (1773–1853) German writer. Associated with *Novalis, the *Schlegels, and other Romantic writers centred in Jena, Tieck was highly versatile, writing romantic and realistic tales, novels, and plays, translating, and publishing a collection of medieval lyrics. His works include the romantic fairytale, *Der blonde Eckbert* (1797) and the satirical comedy, *Der gestiefelte Kater* (1797).

Tientsin. *See* Tianjin.

Tiepolo, Giovanni Battista (1696–1770) Venetian *rococo painter, who was one of the greatest decorators of the 18th century. Influenced by *Veronese, his early sombre style evolved into the exuberance of his first major frescoes, for the Archbishop's Palace at Udine (1725–29). These were followed by decorations for many N Italian palaces and churches. Abroad he decorated the Residenz Palace, Würzburg, built by the rococo architect *Neumann, with historical and allegorical subjects (1750–53), and the Royal

Palace in Madrid (1762–66). One of his assistants and imitators was his son **Giovanni Domenico Tiepolo** (1727–1804), best known for his paintings of clowns and acrobats.

Tierra del Fuego An archipelago separated from the mainland of S South America by the Strait of Magellan. The W and S belong to Chile, the E to Argentina. Sheep farming and oil production are the principal economic activities. Chief towns: Punta Arenas (Chile); Ushuaia (Argentina).

Tiflis. *See* Tbilisi.

tiger A large *cat, *Panthera tigris*. Tigers are usually about 3 m long, but the race of Siberian tigers can reach 4 m. Tigers evolved in Siberia and have spread south to most of Asia; they shed their coat seasonally and shelter from hot sun during the day. They hunt at night, stalking their prey (mainly antelope). A fully grown tiger will eat up to 25 kg of meat at one feed.

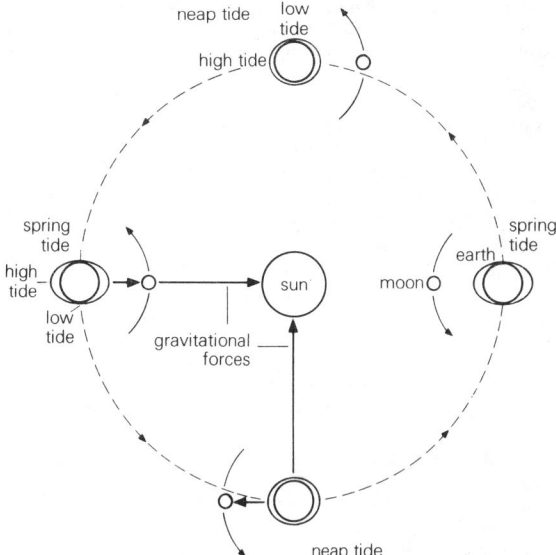

TIDES *The force of gravity between the earth and the moon pulls the waters of the seas towards the moon, creating high tides once a day. The second daily high tide occurs because the moon pulls the earth itself away from the water on the far side from the moon. Exceptionally high spring tides occur twice monthly when the gravitational force of the moon is in line with that of the sun. The lower neap tides occur when these two forces are at right angles.*

tiger beetle A long-legged beetle, with pointed mandibles, belonging to a family (*Cicindelidae*; 2000 species) occurring mainly in the .tropics and subtropics. Tiger beetles range from 6 to 70 mm in length; although most are black or brown some are brilliantly coloured. Both adults and larvae are predatory—the adults hunt for their prey while the larvae wait at the entrance to their burrows.

tigerfish Any fish that resembles a tiger, especially members of the genus *Hydrocynus*, family *Characidae* (*see* characin), found in fresh waters of Africa and South America. They have horizontally striped elongated bodies, reaching 1 m in length, and feed voraciously on other fish. Tigerfish of the family *Theraponidae* (order *Perciformes*) occur in Indo-Pacific marine and fresh waters and include the three-striped tigerfish (*Therapon jarbua*), also called saltwater zebra fish.

tiger moth A moth belonging to the family *Arctiidae*, occurring in Eurasia, N Africa, and North America. The adults have a stout body and are brightly coloured, often orange and black. The hairy larvae, commonly called woolly bears, incorporate their hairs into the cocoon and are seldom destructive, eating various wild plants.

tiger shark A large *requiem shark, *Galeocerdo cuvieri*, that lives mainly in tropical seas. It has a greyish-brown body, up to about 5.5 m long, patterned with vertical bars and a lighter underside. It is a voracious omnivore and eats virtually anything, including mammals, birds, fish, invertebrates, refuse, and man.

Tiglath-pileser I King of Assyria (c. 1120-1074 BC), who greatly extended Assyrian territory, reaching the Mediterranean coast in the W. He patronized art and architecture and collected one of the oldest surviving libraries.

Tiglath-pileser III King of Assyria (c. 745-727 BC). Probably a usurper, he restored Assyrian military power in Babylonia, Syria, and against Urartu in the N. He also improved the efficiency of Assyrian administration, appointing provincial governors.

tigon A sterile hybrid cat, resulting from the mating of a lion and a tiger, also called a liger. This can only happen in captivity, because lions and tigers naturally inhabit different continents.

Tigre. *See* Amhara.

Tigris, River A river in SW Asia, rising in SE Turkey and flowing SE through Diyarbakir, along the Turkish-Syrian border, and into Iraq. 190 km (118 mi) from the Persian Gulf it joins the River Euphrates to form the Shatt al-Arab. Length: 1850 km (1150 mi).

Tihwa. *See* Ürümqi.

Tijuana 39 29N 117 10W A city in NW Mexico, on the US border. Tijuana is the main entry point to Mexico from California and is a popular tourist resort. Population (1980): 461 257.

Tikal An ancient *Maya city in N Guatemala. After about 300 AD it grew into the largest Maya ceremonial centre, with imposing pyramid temples. It was mysteriously abandoned about 900.

Tilak, Bal Gangadhar (*or* Lokamanya; 1856-1920) Indian nationalist leader. Joining the *Indian National Congress (1885) he changed its policy to one of resistance to British rule, advocating Indian independence. Also active as an educationalist, he founded new schools and societies in Poona and was the first leader to propose the adoption of Hindi as the national language. He was twice arrested and imprisoned on charges of sedition.

Tilburg 51 34N 5 05E A city in the S Netherlands, in North Brabant province. A major industrial centre, it produces textiles. Population (1981 est): 153 117.

Tilbury An area in SE England, in Essex on the River Thames. It is the chief dock complex of the Port of London Authority and has a passenger landing stage.

till (*or* boulder clay) The unstratified material that ranges from clay to angular stones and boulders, deposited by glaciers and ice sheets. Its form depends on the rock from which it originated. Large areas of N Europe are covered by till remaining from the Ice Age.

Tillett, Benjamin (1860-1943) British trade unionist. As secretary (1887-1922) of the Dock, Wharf, Riverside, and General Workers' Union he directed the dock strikes of 1889 and 1911. He was also a Labour MP (1917-24, 1929-31).

Tilley, Vesta (Matilda Alice Powles; 1864-1952) British music-hall entertainer, who specialized in male impersonations. She also acted in pantomime and toured in the USA. She retired from the stage in 1920.

Tillich, Paul (Johannes) (1886-1965) US Protestant theologian of German birth. A Lutheran pastor and later a professor at several German universities, he moved to the USA in 1933, when Hitler came to power. He lectured in New York and at Harvard and Chicago Universities. In *Systematic Theology* (3 vols, 1950-63) he attempted to demonstrate Christianity's relevance to contemporary life.

Tilly, Johan Tserclaes, Graf von (1559-1632) Bavarian general, who commanded the Catholic League in the *Thirty Years' War. He won the battle of the White Mountain (1620) and went on to gain control of NW Germany. He defeated the Swedes at Lutter (1626) and, in command of imperial forces, as well as the League's, raised Magdeburg (1631), gaining a reputation for brutality. He was killed in action after being defeated (1631) by the Swedes at Breitenfeld.

Tilsit. *See* Sovetsk.

Tilsit, Treaties of (1807) The two treaties that France signed at Tilsit (now Sovetsk, Soviet Union) with Russia and Prussia respectively after Napoleon's defeat of the Prussians at *Jena and Auerstädt and the Russians at *Friedland. Russia became an ally of France and Prussia, its territory considerably reduced, was occupied by French troops. Both Russia and Prussia joined the *Continental System of blockade against British trade.

Timaru 44 23S 171 14E A port and resort in New Zealand, in E South Island on Canterbury Bight. It serves an agricultural district and exports include grain, wool, and frozen meat. Population (1980 est): 30 100.

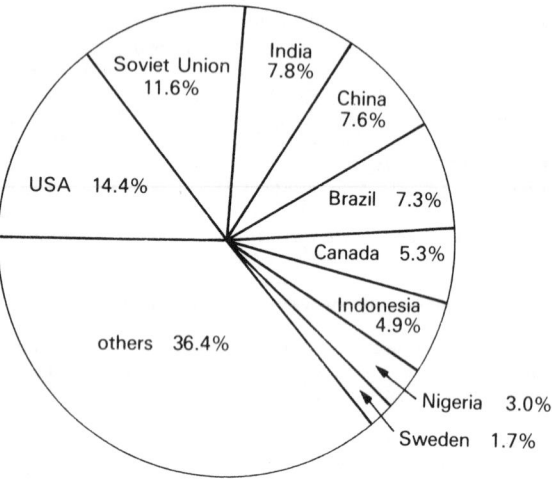

TIMBER *World production of timber (1984; hardwoods and softwoods).*

timber Sawn wood used for purposes other than fuel. Timber is divided into hardwoods (derived from broad-leaved trees) and softwoods (derived from conifers). The bulk of the world's softwoods are derived from the Soviet Union, Canada, the USA, and Scandinavia. Hardwoods, which take longer to grow, are not confined to one specific climate zone. Uses for timber include furniture manufacture (usually hardwoods), building construction, and paper manufacture (largely softwoods).

timber wolf A large shaggy-coated *wolf of North America, also called the grey wolf. A Texan variety with a rufous coat is called the red wolf.

timbre A quality in the sound of a musical instrument, voice, etc., that distinguishes it from others. Thus a violin and a clarinet sound different even when they are playing the same note. The difference arises because each type of instrument produces different overtones in different strengths when a note is played. The production of overtones is controlled by the way the note is produced (plucking, blowing, etc.) and by the characteristics of the individual instrument.

Timbuktu (French name: Tombouctou) 16 49N 2 59W A town in E central Mali, on the River Niger. It was an important centre on the trans-Saharan caravan route and an Islamic cultural centre (1400-1600). It declined after its conquest by Morocco (1591). Population (1976): 19 165. ,

time A concept that measures the duration of events and the periods that separate them. It is a fundamental parameter of all changes, measuring the rates at which they occur; it provides a scale of measurement enabling events that have occurred to be distinguished from those that are occurring and those that will occur. It appears, intuitively, to be flowing at a constant rate in one direction only, for all observers. However, according to Einstein's theory of *relativity this is not the case. The rate at which time passes (as measured by a clock) is not the same for observers in different frames of reference that are moving at a constant velocity with respect to each other. Thus, according to the *time-dilation effect, if two observers are moving at a constant velocity relative to each other it appears to each that the other's time processes are slowed down. This means that events that appear to be simultaneous to observers in the same frame of reference would not be simultaneous to observers in different frames of reference. In order to pinpoint an event in the universe, its position in a four-dimensional space-time continuum must be specified. This continuum consists of three space dimensions and one of time.

Historically, the measurement of time on earth has been based on astronomical observations—the time taken for the earth to revolve on its axis (the day) or for it to complete its orbit round the sun (the year). However, in modern science the basis of time measurement is the *second, which is defined in terms of the frequency of the radiation emitted in a specified transition of an isotope of caesium (*see* caesium clock).

time and motion study A study of a machine and its operator in a factory, measuring the time taken to complete each action and the sequence of the operator's movements. The study is then used to recommend methods of speeding up the operation and reducing the effort involved in order to utilize labour as economically as possible.

time dilation An effect predicted by Einstein's special theory of *relativity. If two observers, A and B, are moving at a velocity v relative to each other, it will appear to A that B's clock will show that *time is running more slowly; thus a time t measured on A's clock will be $t(1-v^2/c^2)^{\frac{1}{2}}$ on B's clock, where c is the velocity of light. The effect has been observed in some particles moving at high velocities, which appear to have an anomalously long lifetime.

Time of Troubles A period of political confusion in Russian history following the death of Boris *Godunov (1605). Godunov was succeeded by a Polish-supported pretender, the so-called False Dimitrii, who claimed to be the son (murdered in 1591, perhaps by Godunov) of Tsar Ivan the Terrible. The False Dimitrii was assassinated in 1606 by Muscovite nobles, who raised Vasilii Shuiski (1552-1612) to the throne. His rule was threatened by a second False Dimitrii, who established a rival court at Tushino in 1608. Shuiski was deposed and the second False Dimitrii was murdered in 1610, following a successful Polish invasion of Russia. A third False Dimitrii asserted his claim during 1611-12 but a successful rebellion against the Poles brought *Michael Romanov to the throne in 1613 and the end of the Time of Troubles.

Timişoara (Hungarian name: Temesvár) 45 45N 21 15E A city in W Romania, near the Yugoslav border. It is a commercial and cultural centre with a university (1945) and has two cathedrals. Population (1983): 261 950.

Timor An Indonesian island, the largest of the *Nusa Tenggara group. Mountainous and dry, it is largely undeveloped. Crops include coffee, coconut, and sandalwood. *History*: in 1859 it was divided between Portugal and Holland. West (Dutch) Timor was included in independent Indonesia (1949). East Timor, scheduled for independence from Portugal in 1978, erupted in civil war in 1975 and was annexed by Indonesia (1976). Area: 39 775 sq km (11 883 sq mi). Chief towns: Kupang and Dili.

Timoshenko, Semyon Konstantinovich (1895-1970) Soviet marshal, who rebuilt the army after the initial defeats in the *Russo-Finnish War. He commanded at *Stalingrad in World War II but failed to stem a German advance (1942-43) and was reassigned to the staff.

timothy A perennial *grass, *Phleum pratense*, also called herd's grass or cat's tail, native to Europe. It forms large clumps, 0.5-1 m tall, with swollen bulblike bases and dense cylindrical flower clusters. It is widely cultivated as a hay and pasture grass, especially as part of a mixture with other grasses.

Timothy, St In the New Testament, a disciple of *Paul, whom he accompanied on many missions. According to tradition he was martyred in Ephesus. Feast day: 6 Feb.

The Epistles of Paul to Timothy, in the New Testament, consist of advice and directions concerning Timothy's personal conduct and public responsibilities. The second letter contains Paul's last known words before his martyrdom under Nero.

timpani (*or* kettledrums) Tuned percussion instruments consisting of a large copper bowl or "kettle" with parchment or plastic stretched across the top. The pitch can be altered by means either of metal keys round the circumference or a pedal mechanism. The sound also depends on the type of sticks used and where they strike the head; a glissando can be obtained by use of the pedals. □musical instruments.

Timur (*or* Tamerlane; c. 1336-1405) Mongol conqueror, a descendant of Genghis Khan. After winning control of Turkestan in central Asia, Timur left his capital Samarkand to conquer the world. Ruthlessly sweeping through Mongolia, Persia, Turkey, Russia, and India, leaving death and destruction behind him, he sought conquest rather than a permanent empire. Paradoxically, he spared and encouraged all kinds of artists.

tin (Sn) A silvery-white metal known to the ancients. Its principal ore is the oxide cassiterite (SnO_2), often found in alluvial concentrations. The element exists as at least two allotropes—the grey alpha-tin, and beta-tin, which is the common form above 13.2°C. At low temperature beta-tin slowly changes into alpha-tin causing **tin plague**. It is obtained by reduction with coal in a reverberatory furnace. In addition to the oxide, compounds include tin chloride ($SnCl_2$), which is used as a reducing agent and in the dyeing industry. The major use of tin is in *tinplate. It alloys with copper to form *bronzes and with niobium to give a superconducting composition, which is used in electromagnets. Some organic compounds of tin are toxic. At no 50; at wt 118.69; mp 231.89°C; bp 2270°C.

tinamou A solitary ground-dwelling bird belonging to a family (*Tinamidae*; 50 species) occurring in Central and South America. 23-38 cm long, tinamous are well camouflaged with a mottled grey or brown plumage. They have small wings and a very short tail and are poor fliers. They feed on seeds, fruit, and insects and are the only members of the order *Tinamiformes*.

Tinbergen, Jan (1903-) Dutch economist. Tinbergen was adviser to the League of Nations from 1936 to 1938. He was corecipient with Ragnar *Frisch of the first Nobel Prize for Economics (1969).

Tinbergen, Niko(laas) (1907-) Dutch zoologist and pioneer ethologist. Like Konrad *Lorenz, Tinbergen concentrated on studying the behaviour of animals in their natural surroundings. Tinbergen, with Lorenz, was responsible for tracing the evolutionary development of social behaviour patterns, such as courtship displays. His works include *The Herring Gull's World* (1953), *Social Behaviour in*

TIROL   *The winter sports resort of Seefeld, NW of Innsbruck.*

Animals (1953), and *Animal Behaviour* (1965). Tinbergen shared a Nobel Prize (1973) with Lorenz and von *Frisch.

tineid moth   A moth of the widespread family *Tineidae*. The adults are usually small with a golden or silvery sheen and frequently do not feed. The caterpillars feed on a variety of plant and animal matter; especially well known are those of the *clothes moth.

tinplate   A mild *steel sheet coated with a very thin film of tin, usually deposited by *electrolysis. Tinplate combines the strength and rigidity of steel with the attractive appearance and corrosion resistance of tin. It began to be used in the 19th century for cans in which to preserve food, still its widest use, although it was used for decorative purposes in the 13th century.

Tintagel   50 40N 4 45W A village and resort in SW England, on the N coast of Cornwall. On the rugged promontory of Tintagel Head are the ruins of Tintagel Castle, reputedly the site of King Arthur's court.

Tintoretto   (Jacopo Robusti; 1518–94) Venetian painter, whose nickname, meaning "little dyer," derived from his father's profession of silk dyeing. His three paintings of the *Miracles of St Mark* (1562–66) for the Confraternity of S Marco were followed by his series of the life of Christ (1564–87; Scuola di S Rocco) and his paintings for the Doge's Palace, including the enormous *Paradise*. He combines Michelangelo's figure style and Titian's rich colour with dramatic movement and perspectives. As a portraitist, he was particularly adept at painting old men, for example *Bearded Man with Fur* (Kunsthistorisches Museum, Vienna).

Tipperary (Irish name: Contae Tiobraid Arann)   A county in the S Republic of Ireland, in Munster. Mountainous in parts, it contains part of the Golden Vale (one of the most fertile areas in Ireland) in the SW. Predominantly agricultural, dairy farming is especially important. Industries are mainly related to processing agricultural produce. Area: 4255 sq km (1643 sq mi). Population (1981): 135 261. County town: Clonmel.

Tippett, Sir Michael   (1905–   ) British composer. He studied at the Royal College of Music and was musical director of Morley College (1940–51). He has written five operas: *The Midsummer Marriage* (1947–52), *King Priam* (1958–61), *The Knot Garden* (1966–70), *The Ice Break* (1977), and *The Mask of Time* (1982), acting as his own librettist. His other works include four symphonies, four string quartets, three piano sonatas, the oratorios *A Child of Our Time* (1940) and *The Mask of Time* (1982), and the cantata *The Vision of St Augustine* (1965). In 1983 he was appointed president of the London College of Music and a member of the OM.

Tipu Sahib   (1749–99) Sultan of Mysore (1782–99); the son

of *Hyder Ali. A good administrator in his own state, he was an opponent of British power in India and entered into a tentative alliance with the French. Defeated by *Cornwallis in 1792, he continued his opposition and was killed by the British while defending his capital Seringapatam.

Tirana (Albanian name: Tiranë)   41 20N 19 49E The capital of Albania, situated on a fertile plain in the centre of the country. Founded in the 17th century by a Turkish general, it became the capital in 1920. There has been considerable industrial expansion since World War II. The university was founded in 1957. Population (1980 est): 194 000.

Tiresias   In Greek legend, a blind Theban seer who lived for seven generations. For part of his life he had been transformed into a woman, after coming upon a pair of snakes and killing the female. *Oedipus learned from him of his own patricide and incest and *Odysseus consulted him in the underworld, where he retained his prophetic powers. According to one of various legends, he was struck blind by Hera after supporting Zeus' opinion in an argument, namely that love was more enjoyable for women than men. In compensation Zeus granted him longevity and the gift of prophecy.

Tirich Mir, Mount   36 18N 71 55E A mountain in NW Pakistan, the highest in the Hindu Kush. Height: 7692 m (25 236 ft).

Tirol (*or* Tyrol)   A mountainous federal state in W Austria, bordering on West Germany and Italy. It is alpine in character having an international reputation for winter sports, especially at Kitzbühel, and tourism is important throughout the year. The chief occupations are agriculture and forestry, with some mining and manufacturing industries. Area: 12 648 sq km (4883 sq mi). Population (1981): 586 297. Capital: Innsbruck.

Tirpitz, Alfred von   (1849–1930) German admiral, who as secretary of state for the navy (1897–1916) rebuilt the German fleet to rival Britain's naval supremacy. His advocacy of intensive submarine warfare in World War I was opposed by the chancellor, Bethmann-Hollweg, and Tirpitz resigned.

Tirso de Molina   (Gabriel Téllez; c. 1584–1648) Spanish dramatist, a literary disciple of Lope de *Vega, who wrote over 300 comedies and historical and religious plays. His tragedy *El Burlador de Sevilla* (1635) is the earliest recorded literary portrayal of *Don Juan.

Tirthankara   In Jainism, one who has attained spiritual liberation from rebirth and serves as a guide for others. Every aeon is said to produce 24 Tirthankaras, each associated with a particular symbol and colour.   *Mahavira is the last of the present series.

Tiruchirappalli (*or* Trichinopoly)   10 50N 78 43E A city in India, in Tamil Nadu on the River Cauvery. The city is dominated by the Rock of Trichinopoly with its fort and temple. An important rail centre, the city produces textiles. Population (1981): 608 000.

Tiryns   A *Mycenaean citadel near Mycenae (S Greece). First excavated (1884–85) by *Schliemann, Tiryns was occupied from Neolithic times. The Bronze Age Mycenaean palace, first built in the early 14th century BC and sacked about 1200 BC, possessed frescoes showing *Minoan influence and massive defensive walls, much of which still stand.

Tissot, James Joseph Jacques   (1836–1902) French painter and etcher. In Paris he was influenced by *Degas and Japanese prints but after settling in England in the 1870s he became known for his charming scenes of Victorian life, notably *The Ball on Shipboard* (Tate Gallery).

tissue   In anatomy, a group of cells specialized to perform a particular function. The cells may be of the same type (e.g. the muscle cells of muscles) or of different types (as in connective tissue). Combinations of tissues make up organs. The study of tissues is *histology.

Tisza, River (Slavonic and Romanian name: Tisa) A river in S central Europe. Rising in the Soviet Union, in the W Ukrainian SSR, it flows generally W and S across the Hungarian Plain to join the River Danube below Novi Sad in Yugoslavia. It is a source of irrigation and power, especially in NE Hungary. Length: 980 km (610 mi).

tit A small acrobatic songbird (also called titmouse) belonging to a family (*Paridae*; 65 species) occurring in Eurasia, North America, and Africa. Tits are versatile birds and frequent woodlands and gardens, feeding chiefly on insects. They are 7–20 cm long with soft plumage, usually grey or black and often with blue and yellow markings. *See also* blue tit; coal tit; crested tit; great tit; long-tailed tit.

Titan The largest *satellite of the planet Saturn and the second largest in the solar system. It has a nitrogen atmosphere of a reddish or orange colour.

Titanic A luxury passenger ship that on 14–15 April, 1912, struck an iceberg near Newfoundland on its maiden voyage and sank causing the loss of 1513 lives. Because of its special design it was thought to be unsinkable and carried enough lifeboats for only half the passengers. As a result of the disaster safety rules for ships at sea were drawn up by the International Convention for Safety of Life at Sea (1913) and the International Ice Patrol was established. The wreck of the Titanic was located and photographed in 1985.

TITO *The Yugoslav leader in his mountain hide-out during World War II, with his dog Tiger.*

titanium (Ti) A relatively light strong transition metal discovered in 1791 by W. Gregor (1761–1817). It occurs in nature in the minerals rutile (TiO_2), ilmenite ($FeTiO_3$), sphene ($CaTiO_3$), and in some iron ores. Rutile and ilmenite beach sands are mined as a source of titanium. The dioxide (TiO_2) is used in white paint as it has excellent opacity. The metal is as strong as steel but 45% lighter (relative density 4.54) and 60% heavier than aluminium but twice as strong. It is used in alloys for missiles and aircraft. At no 22; at wt 47.90; mp 1660°C; bp 3287°C.

titanothere An extinct North American mammal, related to horses and rhinoceroses, that lived between 45 and 20 million years ago. Later Oligocene forms were 4.5 m long and 2.5 m high at the shoulder. They fed on soft vegetation and became extinct possibly because their simple teeth were unable to cope with a change in the vegetation.

Titans In Greek mythology, 12 primeval gods and goddesses, the children of *Uranus and *Gaea. They were Oceanus, Coeus, Crius, Hyperion, Iapetus, Cronus, Thea, Rhea, Themis, Mnemosyne, Phoebe, and Tethys. They were overthrown by Zeus and the Olympian deities.

tithes The tenth part of an income allotted to religious purposes. Originating in the offering of the "first fruits" as a divine sacrifice, tithes were decreed by Mosaic law, which demanded payment in kind from all agricultural produce. Christian ecclesiastical law also enjoined tithes to maintain churches and clergy. Gradually exemptions were made, money payments replaced payments in kind, and as organized religion declined the tithe laws were repealed. Tithes, which were abolished in Britain in 1936, are still voluntarily paid by individuals according to conscience.

titi A small monkey belonging to the genus *Callicebus* (8 species), of the Amazonian jungle. Titis are 50–115 cm long including the tail (25–55 cm) and live in treetops in family groups. They have soft thick fur, often brightly coloured. Family: *Cebidae*.

Titian (Tiziano Vecellio; c. 1488–1576) Venetian painter of the High Renaissance, born in Pieve di Cadore, in the Dolomites. His earliest influences were Giovanni Bellini, his teacher, and Giorgione, with whom he collaborated on frescoes for the façade of the German Exchange (1508). In his *Assumption of the Virgin* (Sta Maria dei Frari) his more monumental style links him with such Florentine painters as Raphael. His greatest works for the Habsburgs, who patronized him from 1530 onwards, were the equestrian portrait of Emperor Charles V at Mühlberg (1548; Prado) and *Philip II* (1550–51; Prado). He painted Pope Paul III twice, in Bologna (1543) and in Rome with his grandsons (1546). Both portraits are in Naples. His mythological works include *Bacchus and Ariadne* (National Gallery, London). His last religious paintings, such as the *Pietà* (Accademia, Venice), seem to be inspired by a new emotional intensity.

Titicaca, Lake A lake in South America, between Peru and Bolivia, in the Andes. At an altitude of 3809 m (12 497 ft) it is the world's highest lake navigable to large vessels. It is fed by 25 rivers but has only one outlet, the River Desaguadero. Area: 8135 sq km (3141 sq mi). Depth: 370 m (1214 ft).

titmouse. *See* tit.

Tito (Josip Broz; 1892–1980) Yugoslav statesman; president 1953–80. Tito was captured by the Russians in World War I and subsequently fought with the Red Army in the Russian civil war. He returned to Yugoslavia in 1920, joined the Communist Party, and was briefly imprisoned (1928–29); in 1937 he became secretary general of the Party. In World War II he led the partisans in resistance to the German occupation, becoming a marshal in 1943, when he also gained Allied recognition, previously given to the *Chetniks. He became Yugoslavia's postwar leader. After Yugoslavia's expulsion (1948) from the *Cominform, Tito introduced the policy of decentralization to workers' councils that distinguishes Yugoslav socialism and successfully maintained his country's independence from Soviet interference, pursuing a foreign policy of nonalignment.

Titograd (name until 1948: Podgorica) 42 28N 19 17E A city in S central Yugoslavia, the capital of Montenegro. It was renamed in honour of Marshal Tito on being rebuilt following extensive damage during World War II. Its university was established in 1973. Population (1981): 132 290.

Titus (Flavius Vespasianus) (39–81 AD) Roman emperor (79–81). He fought with his father Vespasian in Judaea and ended the Jewish revolt (70) by capturing Jerusalem. Proclaimed emperor after Vespasian's death, Titus proved a popular ruler; when Vesuvius erupted (79), he aided the victims generously. At his death he was called "darling of the human race" and deified.

Titus, St In the New Testament, a disciple and assistant of Paul. He organized the collection of alms for poor Christians in Judaea and replaced Timothy as Paul's commissioner at Corinth. Feast day: 6 Feb. In the **Epistle of Paul to Titus**, written between 60 and 64 AD, Paul tells Titus how to organize and superintend the new churches of Crete.

Tivoli 41 58N 12 48E A town in central Italy, in Lazio. A summer resort in Roman times, it possesses the remains of Hadrian's villa and the Renaissance Villa d'Este, with its terraced water gardens. Paper and wine are produced. Population (1981 est): 51 528.

Tiw. *See* Tyr.

Tizard, Sir Henry (Thomas) (1885–1959) British chemist. After working on bomb sights and new aircraft in World War I, he specialized in the application of science for military purposes. In 1935 he won backing for the development of radar against the arguments of Frederick *Lindemann. He clashed again with Lindemann in World War II, over Britain's bombing policy.

Tjirebon (*or* Cheribon) 6 46S 108 33E A port in Indonesia, in N Java on the Java Sea. The **Tjirebon Agreement** of Indonesian independence was signed here (1946) by the Dutch. It is an agricultural and manufacturing centre. Population (1980): 223 776.

Tlaloc An Aztec rain god, ranking with the sun and war god *Huitzilopochtli. He possessed both creative and destructive powers and children were ritually sacrificed to him.

Tlaxcala (*or* Tlaxcala de Xicohténcatl) 19 20N 98 12W A city in Mexico, on the central plateau. One of the oldest cities in Mexico, it is the site of the Church of San Francisco, which was founded by *Cortés (1521) and is the oldest in the Americas. Population (1980): 13 000.

Tlemcen (Latin name: Pomaria) 34 55N 1 20W A town in NW Algeria, near the Moroccan border. It became an important Islamic religious centre in the middle ages, flourishing until the 16th century; many old buildings remain, notably the 12th-century Great Mosque. Industries include leatherwork and carpets; blankets and olive oil are exported. Population (1983 est): 146 089.

Tlingit A North American Indian people of the NW Pacific coast in SE Alaska. There were 14 tribes divided into independent matrilineal clans, each headed by a chief. They lived by salmon fishing and hunting, built wooden houses, and practised the *potlatch at the death of a chief. Their language belongs to the *Na-Dené group.

TNT (trinitrotoluene; $C_6H_2(NO_2)_3CH_3$) A highly explosive pale yellow crystalline solid. It is prepared from toluene treated with concentrated sulphuric and nitric acids and is used in shells, bombs, etc., and blasting explosives.

toad A tail-less amphibian belonging to a widely distributed order (*Anura*; about 2600 species). Toads have long hind legs and short forelegs; they swim by means of partially webbed feet. They have a long sticky tongue, attached at the front of their mouth, that can extend very rapidly to capture flying insects. Some species use the throat as a resonating chamber to amplify their mating calls. *See also* clawed frog; midwife toad; natterjack; tree frog; spadefoot toad.

toadfish A bottom-dwelling carnivorous *bony fish of the order *Batachoidiformes* (about 45 species), found mainly in tropical and subtropical seas. It has a heavy brownish body, up to 30 cm long, and makes grunting or croaking sounds resembling a toad. *See also* midshipman.

toadflax An annual or perennial herb belonging to the genus *Linaria* (about 150 species), especially *L. vulgaris*, found in the Mediterranean area, temperate Eurasia, and North America. It grows to a height of 30–80 cm and has an elongated terminal cluster of yellow snapdragon-like flowers (*see* Antirrhinum).

Purple toadflax (*L. purpurea*) is cultivated in gardens. Family: *Scrophulariaceae*.

toadstool. *See* mushroom.

tobacco A plant belonging to the genus *Nicotiana*, especially *N. tabacum* and *N. rustica*, which are cultivated for their leaves, used to make *cigarettes, *cigars, *snuff, etc. Commercial tobacco plants grow to a height of 1–3 m and bear pink, white, or greenish flowers. After harvesting, their large sticky leaves are slowly dried in the sun, hot air, or smoke for up to two months and then fermented for another four–six weeks. The main growing regions are the USA, China, India, and the Soviet Union, with additional production in E Europe, South America, SE Asia, and S Africa.

Tobacco contains about 2–4% nicotine, which produces its stimulant and addictive properties. The tar content can cause serious illness. Family: *Solanaceae*.

Tobago Island. *See* Trinidad and Tobago, Republic of.

Tobata. *See* Kitakyushu.

Tobey, Mark (1890–1976) US painter. He is known for paintings in which coloured forms are overlaid by white brush strokes. He adopted this so-called "white writing" technique after he visited Japan and China (1934), where he was influenced by oriental calligraphy. His work in this style grew more abstract in his later years.

tobogganing The recreation and sport of sliding down snow or ice on a toboggan, a low platform on steel runners, of which there are two competitive types: the luge, for one or two riders lying almost flat on their backs, and the skeleton or Cresta (named after the Cresta Run at St Moritz, Switzerland), for one rider lying prone. Like *bobsledding, both were developed mainly by British sportsmen at St Moritz and other Swiss resorts in the late 19th century. In races competitors slide, one vehicle at a time, down a narrow icy chute some 1000 m (1094 yd) long with high banked turns, at more than 130 km per hour (81 mph) and steering only by shifts of weight and touching with either foot.

Tobolsk 58 15N 68 12E A port in the central Soviet Union, in the RSFSR at the confluence of the Rivers Irtysh and Tobol. Founded by the Cossacks in 1587, it has shipbuilding, timber, and food-processing industries. Population (1983 est): 69 000.

Tobruk A port in NE Libya, on the Mediterranean coast. During World War II it was the scene of heavy fighting and changed hands five times before being finally recaptured by the British in 1942. Population (1979 est): 34 200.

Toby jug An English pottery jug in the shape of a seated middle-aged man in 18th-century dress, holding a tankard and pipe. Toby jugs, which were first made in the 1760s in Staffordshire by Ralph Wood (1715–72) and his son (also called Ralph Wood; 1748–95), depict various characters, e.g. Squire Toby and Sailor Toby.

Toc H An interdenominational Christian fellowship open to anyone over the age of 16 and devoted to social service. It was founded in 1915 in Belgium by the Rev P. B. Clayton (1885–1972), a Church of England chaplain, as a military chapel and club; it was named Talbot House in memory of Gilbert Talbot (1891–1915), a British lieutenant, killed in action, who was a member of a prominent Anglican family. Its name derives from army signallers' designations of the initials *T H*.

Tocharian An extinct *Indo-European language of the Tarim Basin region of Chinese Turkistan. It is mainly known from Buddhist scriptures written between about 500 and 1000 AD in the N Indian Brahmi script. Its relationship to the other Indo-European languages is highly debatable.

Tocqueville, Alexis de (1805–59) French political scientist, historian, and politician. After visiting the USA (1831–32) Tocqueville wrote *Démocratie en Amérique*, a study of US democracy that also dealt with the constitutions of France and Europe. Tocqueville argued that the French Revolution had not achieved a break with the past, since an egalitarian society required greater centralization and thus sacrificed liberty. Elected to the Chamber of Deputies in 1839, he became vice president of the Constituent Assembly and briefly minister of foreign affairs in 1849. After Louis Napoleon's coup d'état he retired to write *L'Ancien Régime et la révolution* (1856).

Todd, Alexander Robertus, Baron (1907-) British biochemist, who helped determine the molecular basis of genetics through his work on nucleic acids (DNA and RNA). In 1949 Todd synthesized ADP and *ATP, substances vital to energy utilization by living cells. He received a Nobel Prize (1957) and was created a life peer in 1962.

toga The outer garment worn by the ancient Romans, originally by both sexes and all classes but finally only by male patricians on formal occasions. It consisted of a semicircular piece of cloth draped intricately around the body; colour and markings were prescribed according to status.

Toghril Beg (c. 990-1063) Sultan of Turkey (1055-63), who founded the Seljuq dynasty. His conquests in central Asia culminated in the conquest of Baghdad (1055). An uprising forced his expulsion in 1058 but by 1060 he had suppressed it.

Togliatti (name until 1964: Stavropol) 53 32N 49 24E A city in the W central Soviet Union, in the RSFSR on the River Volga. It was renamed in honour of the Italian communist leader, Palmiro Togliatti. Industries include ship repairing, engineering, and food processing. Population (1981 est): 533 000.

Togliatti, Palmiro (1893-1964) Italian politician, the leader of the Italian Communist Party (1926-64). In exile from 1926 to 1944, after Mussolini's fall he became a minister (1944) and then vice premier (1945). He was the author of *Italian Road to Socialism* and his ideas greatly influenced communism in Italy.

Togo, Republic of (French name: République Togolaise) A small narrow country in West Africa, on the Gulf of Guinea between Ghana and Benin. Coastal swamps rise to higher land in the interior. The majority of the population is African, mainly Ewe in the S. *Economy*: chiefly agricultural, food crops consist mainly of cassava, maize, and rice and cash crops include cocoa, coffee, and cotton. Forests produce not only timber but oil palms and dyewoods. There are rich deposits of phosphates, which, with cocoa and coffee, are the main export. Bauxite was found in the 1950s and there is some, as yet unexploited, limestone and iron ore. Industry is being developed, concentrating mainly on food processing, but there is also a large cement plant and a new oil refinery. *History*: settled by the Ewe in the 12th and 13th centuries, the area was raided for slaves from the 17th to 19th centuries. From 1884 to 1914 Togoland was a German protectorate and after World War I it was divided between France and the UK, first (1922) under League of Nations mandate and then (1946) as a UN trustee territory. The French territory became an autonomous republic within the French Union in 1956 and gained full independence in 1960. (The British part joined Ghana in 1957.) The president was killed in a coup in 1963 and a further coup in 1967 brought Lt Col (later Gen) Etienne Gnassingbe Eyadéma (1937-) to power. In 1986 French troops were called in to support Eyadéma's ailing government. Official language: French. Official currency: CFA (Communauté financière africaine) franc of 100 centimes. Area: 56 000 sq km (21 616 sq mi). Population (1983 est): 2 823 000. Capital and main port: Lome.

Togo Heihachiro (1847-1934) Japanese admiral. His destruction of the Russian fleet in the battle of Tsushima Strait in May, 1905, ensured Japan's victory in the *Russo-Japanese War (1904-05).

Tojo Hideki (1884-1948) Japanese general, who was war minister (1940-44) and also prime minister (1941-44) during World War II. After Japan's defeat he was executed as a war criminal.

Tokaj (or Tokay) 48 08N 21 23E A small town in NE Hungary, at the confluence of the Rivers Bodrog and Tisza. It has given its name to the famous wine produced in the area. Population (1983): 5778.

tokay. *See* gecko.

Tokelau Islands A group of three coral atolls in the SW Pacific Ocean, an overseas territory of New Zealand. Chief exports are copra and woven goods. Area: 10 sq km (4 sq mi). Population (1980 est): 1620.

Tokugawa The military family that controlled Japan from 1603 to 1867. *Tokugawa Ieyasu secured the title of *shogun (military overlord) from the emperor in 1603 and established his capital at Edo (Tokyo). Ieyasu's immediate successors were responsible for isolating Japan from the outside world, a policy that established domestic peace but ultimately led to political stagnation and technological backwardness. After Japan's reopening under western pressure in the 1850s the reluctance of the family to abandon its monopoly of power brought about the overthrow of the last shogun, Tokugawa Keiki (1827-1913; ruled 1867-68).

Tokugawa Ieyasu (1542-1616) Japanese *shogun (military overlord), who completed the re-establishment of central authority in feudal Japan. A vassal of both Oda Nobunaga and Hideyoshi, he steadily increased his domain and in 1600 was able to defeat his rivals in the decisive battle of Sekigahara. In 1603, having confiscated much enemy territory, he acquired from the emperor the title of shogun. He passed this to his son in 1605 but continued to supervise the *Tokugawa administration.

TOBOGGANING *An Olympic competitor in the Luge singles loses control of her sled.*

Tokyo 35 40N 139 45E The capital of Japan, in E central *Honshu on Tokyo Bay (an inlet of the Pacific). Administratively joined to its port Yokohama and to the industrial centre of Kawasaki, Greater Tokyo is the world's largest city. It has over 100 universities, including the University of Tokyo (1877). *History*: site of human settlements from very early times, the village of Edo was founded in the 12th century, growing in importance as a city by the 17th century. As Tokyo, it replaced Kyoto as imperial capital in 1868. It was badly damaged by an earthquake in 1923 and by bombing during World War II, since when its industrial growth has been spectacular. Industrial development has not been without problems, however, and Tokyo now suffers from serious atmospheric pollution as well as traffic congestion. Population (1984): 8 390 159.

Toledo 41 40N 83 35W A city in the USA, in Ohio on Lake Erie at the mouth of the River Maumee. The development of the coalfields and the discovery of oil and gas in the late 19th century stimulated its growth and today it is a major Great Lakes port, shipping oil, coal, and farm products. Industrial activities include shipbuilding and oil refining. Population (1980): 354 635.

Toledo 39 52N 4 02W A city in central Spain, in New Castile on the River Tagus. It was formerly the capital of Spain. It has a magnificent cathedral (13th–17th centuries). Famous for its swords and knives, it produces metalwork engraved in the Moorish tradition. Population (1982 est): 61 813.

Tolkien, J(ohn) R(onald) R(euel) (1892–1973) British scholar and writer. He was professor of Anglo-Saxon (1925–45) and of English language and literature (1945–49) at Oxford University. His trilogy *The Lord of the Rings* (1954–55), in which he created a richly detailed fantasy world, became an international bestseller. Related works include *The Hobbit* (1937) and *The Silmarillion* (1977).

Toller, Ernst (1893–1939) German playwright and poet. After being wounded in World War I, he became committed to revolutionary politics and in 1919 was imprisoned for five years for his activities. His reputation was established soon after his release by experimental expressionist plays, such as *Die Wandlung* (1919) and *Masse Mensch* (1920). Driven into exile in 1932, he committed suicide in New York.

Tolpuddle Martyrs Six members of the Friendly Society of Agricultural Labourers of Tolpuddle, Dorset. This union was founded in 1833 to secure fair wages for its members. Its leader, George Loveless, and five others were unfairly charged with administering unlawful oaths and transported to Australia. They were pardoned in 1836. The Tolpuddle Martyrs are regarded as among the founders of English trades unionism.

Tolstoy, Leo (Nikolaevich), Count (1828–1910) Russian writer and moralist. After active service in the Crimean War, he travelled in Europe and then returned to his family estate of Yasnaya Polyana, where he devoted much energy to the education of his peasants. Following his marriage in 1862 he wrote two novels, *War and Peace* (1865–69), concerning the Napoleonic War, and *Anna Karenina* (1875–77), both acknowledged masterpieces of Russian literature. Around 1879 he underwent a spiritual crisis from which he emerged with a faith in an extreme form of Christian anarchism. He worked and dressed as a peasant, became a vegetarian, espoused total pacifism, repudiated his former literary works, and divided his property among the members of his family. His numerous moral tracts and stories gained him an international discipleship, but his family relationships suffered. He died at 82 of pneumonia a few days after secretly leaving his home in order to live in solitude. Tolstoy was one of the most prolific of writers, his literary work filling 45 volumes. His other works include the story "The Death of Ivan Ilyich" (1884–86) and the novel *Resurrection* (1899).

Toltecs An Indian people who dominated much of central Mexico between the 10th and 12th centuries AD. Their language, *Nahuatl, was also spoken by the Aztecs. A militaristic people, they sacked the city of *Teotihuacán (c. 750) and eventually fused the many small states of the area into an empire. They introduced the cult of *Quetzalcoatl and were accomplished temple builders. The *Aztecs destroyed their capital of *Tula in the mid-12th century.

Toluca (*or* Toluca de Lerdo) 19 20N 99 40W A city in central Mexico. The centre of a stock-raising area, its industries include the processing of agricultural products. Population (1980): 234 000.

toluene ($C_6H_5CH_3$) A colourless flammable liquid obtained by catalytic reforming of *oil. It is used in aviation fuels, as a solvent, and to produce *phenol and *TNT.

tolu tree A tree, *Myroxylon balsamum*, native to South America. Growing to a height of over 20 m, it has whitish flowers and yields a *balsam from its trunk, used in cough mixtures and perfumery. Family: *Leguminosae.

tomato An annual plant, *Lycopersicon esculentum*, native to South America and widely cultivated for its fleshy red ▢fruit. In warm temperate regions, tomatoes are grown in fields and are low branching and spreading plants; the hothouse tomatoes of cooler regions are often trained to grow a single erect fruiting stem. The clusters of yellow flowers produce rounded or pear-shaped fruits, 2–10 cm in diameter, which are eaten fresh or canned and made into purée, pickles, etc. Family: *Solanaceae.

Tombouctou. *See* Timbuktu.

Tombstone 31 44N 110 04W A town in the USA, in Arizona. Scene of a silver rush from 1877, it is famous for the gunfight (1881) that took place at the OK Corral between the Clanton gang and Wyatt Earp, his brother Virgil, and Doc Holliday. Population (1980): 1632.

tommy gun A light US .45 calibre submachine gun invented by General John Thompson (1860–1940) in 1918. Widely used in World War II in various models, especially the M1 and the M3 "blowbacks," some are still in use today.

tomography The technique, widely used in medicine for diagnostic purposes, of producing an image of a selected plane of the body using X-rays or other forms of radiation.

In **computerized tomography** (CT), a ring-shaped X-ray machine (CT scanner) is rotated around the patient and records different planes of the body. The information thus obtained is assembled by the scanner's built-in computer into a three-dimensional representation of the body, from which images of selected planes can be extracted. The patient is not at risk as the dose of X-rays used is only about 20% of that used in normal X-ray examination. The technique is useful for imaging soft structures of the body and revealing tumours and other abnormalities.

Positron emission tomography (PET) is used specifically for scanning the brain, revealing the presence of tiny blood clots (which might cause strokes), tumours, etc. The patient is injected with a form of glucose that has been radioactively labelled and emits positrons. This is absorbed by the brain cells and metabolized. In damaged or diseased areas of the brain, metabolism is reduced therefore positron emission is either reduced or absent: this is recorded by the PET scanner.

In **nuclear magnetic resonance** (NMR) **tomography**, similar images are obtained utilizing the phenomenon of *nuclear magnetic resonance.

Tomsk 56 30N 85 05E A port in the central Soviet Union, in the RSFSR on the River Tom. Industries include engineering; it has a university (1888) and other educational institutions. Population (1981 est): 439 000.

Tom Thumb (Charles Stratton; 1838–83) US midget, who was publicly exhibited by the circus impresario P. T. *Barnum. He grew to a height of only 40 in. In 1863 he married another midget, Lavinia Warren (1841–1919).

ton An Imperial unit of weight equal to 2240 lb (long ton) or 1016 kilograms. In the USA a unit equal to 2000 lb (short ton) is also used. The metric ton (or **tonne**) is equal to 1000 kilograms.

tonality The presence of a tonal centre or *key in a musical composition. Musical compositions from at least the early 17th century to about 1900 are in distinct keys. These are based on individual scales, in which certain notes (the tonic and dominant degrees) form tonal centres to which the music periodically returns. Once such a centre has been established, the music can modulate into other keys and return to the home key (or underlying tonality). Music in which tonal centres are deliberately avoided exhibits *atonality; this is characteristic of some music written after 1900. *See also* serialism.

Tone, (Theobald) Wolfe (1763–98) Irish nationalist, who was inspired by the French Revolution to work for an independent Irish republic. In 1791 he founded the Society of United Irishmen and unsuccessfully sought French aid for a revolt against British rule. He was captured and sentenced to death, but committed suicide before the sentence could be carried out.

tone poem. *See* symphonic poem.

Tonga, Kingdom of (*or* Friendly Islands) A country in the SW Pacific Ocean, E of Fiji. It consists of 169 small islands (36 of them permanently inhabited); the E islands are low lying, while those to the W are hilly and volcanic. *Economy*: chiefly agricultural, the main products and exports are copra and bananas. Oil has been discovered recently, and tourism is becoming increasingly important. *History*: under King Taufa'ahau Tupou (George I; 1797–1893) in the 19th century, the civil war between rival dynasties was ended and the islands converted to Christianity. The country became a British protectorate in 1900, and in 1970 became an independent state within the British Commonwealth. Head of State: King Taufa'ahau Tupou IV (1918–　). Official languages: Tongan and English. Official currency: pa'anga of 100 seniti. Area: 700 sq km (270 sq mi). Population: (1983 est) 98 750. Capital and main port: Nuku'alofa.

tongue A muscular organ situated in the floor of the mouth. The root of the tongue is attached by muscles to the U-shaped hyoid bone in the neck. The tongue is the main organ of taste: its surface is covered by minute projections (giving it a rough appearance) around which the taste buds are grouped, detecting sweet, sour, salt, and bitter tastes. It also manipulates food during chewing and swallowing and plays an important role in the articulation of speech. Furring of the tongue is a symptom of fever; a smooth and sore tongue is seen in some forms of anaemia.

Tong Zhi (*or* T'ung-chih; 1856–75) The title of Cai-chun (*or* Tsai-ch'un), Chinese emperor (1862–75); the son of *Zi Xi, who acted as regent until he was 17. The Tong Zhi Restoration (his title means Union for Order) aimed to repair the upheaval of the *Taiping Rebellion but was thwarted by the corrupt court, which dominated the young emperor.

tonic sol-fa. *See* solmization.

tonka bean The seed of the tonka tree, *Coumarouna odorata*, native to N South America. Coumarin, a fragrant edible extract of the black almond-shaped seeds, has been used as a flavouring and in perfumes and snuff. Family: *Leguminosae*.

Tonkin (*or* Tongking) A region in N Vietnam, long ruled from Hanoi. The Chinese, who had occupied it in 111 BC, were driven out in 939 AD, and from then until 1802 it was an independent state. Following the dissolution of the Vietnamese empire it became a French protectorate (1884). In 1949 it became part of independent Vietnam.

Tonkin, Gulf of (Chinese name: Beibu Gulf) An inlet of the South China Sea between China, N Vietnam, and Hainan Island.

Tonle Sap A lake in W central Kampuchea. For most of the year it is drained by the River Tonle Sap into the Mekong, but in the monsoon season the swollen Mekong reverses the flow, and the lake roughly quadruples in depth and area to about 10 000 sq km (3860 sq mi). Carp are fished here.

tonnage and poundage Revenues granted by parliament to the Crown in England (1373–1787). Tonnage (*or* tunnage) was a duty on each imported cask (tun) of wine. Poundage was a duty on each pound's worth of imported and exported goods. They were generally granted for life to each monarch but in 1625 were granted for only a year to Charles I. His subsequent levy of tonnage and poundage without parliamentary consent provoked much opposition.

tonsillitis Inflammation of the *tonsils due to infection of the upper respiratory tract. Symptoms include fever, a sore throat, and difficulty in swallowing. If the tonsils become chronically infected, causing recurrent sore throats, they can be surgically removed.

tonsils Patches of tissue situated on each side at the back of the mouth and below the tongue that produce lymphocytes: a type of white blood cell that protects the body against infection. Inflammation of the tonsils may be caused by a variety of infections (*see also* tonsillitis).

tontine A financial scheme to provide life *annuities to a group of subscribers; when a member dies his share is divided amongst the others until the last survivor enjoys the whole income. The idea of an Italian banker (Lorenzo Tonti) in 1653, it was popular in the 18th century.

Tooke, John Horne (1736–1812) British radical. In 1769 he and John Wilkes founded the Society of the Supporters of the Bill of Rights but the two quarrelled and Tooke established (1771) his own Constitutional Society to campaign for parliamentary reform. In 1778 he was imprisoned for seditious libel and in 1794 was again arrested but acquitted of treason. He was elected an MP in 1801. He was also a philologist, the author of *The Diversions of Purley* (1786).

Toowoomba 27 34S 151 54E A city in Australia, in SE Queensland. It is a commercial centre for an agricultural region specializing in sheep and dairy farming. It is the site of the Perseverance Creek Water Supply Scheme. Population (1980 est): 72 800.

topaz A mineral consisting of a hydrous fluosilicate of aluminium, $Al_2 SiO_4(OH,F)_2$. It occurs in acidic igneous rocks, in pegmatites and veins. It is usually colourless or yellow, and when cut and polished it is used as a gemstone. The finest specimens come mainly from the Urals, Brazil, and Ceylon. All yellow gemstones were formerly known as topaz. Birthstone for November. *See* Plate III.

tope A slender *requiem shark, *Galeorhinus galeus*, that is up to 2 m long with a dark-grey body and a white belly. It lives in shallow tropical and temperate seas and feeds on bottom-dwelling fish and invertebrates.

Topeka 39 02N 95 41W A city in the USA, the capital of Kansas on the Kansas River. An agricultural trading and processing centre, Topeka is famous as a centre for psychiatric research and is the site of the Menninger Clinic. Population (1980): 115 266.

top minnow. *See* killifish.

topology The branch of *geometry concerned with the properties of an object that do not change under *homeomorphisms, i.e. when the object is bent, stretched, or shrunk but not torn or deformed so that several points on it are fused. The hole in a doughnut is such a property; for example if a rubber doughnut is distorted to the shape of a cup the hole is still there in the handle. Topology is often called rubber-sheet geometry because rubber objects can be suitably distorted. It was formerly called analysis situs. One application is in networks (e.g. an electricity-distribution network) in which the topological properties depend on the so-called Euler characteristic (named after Leonhard *Euler) $V - E + F$, where V is the number of vertices in the network, E the number of edges, and F the number of areas enclosed by the edges.

Torah (Hebrew: instruction) The five books of Moses (Genesis, Exodus, Leviticus, Numbers, and Deuteronomy), which constitute the first of the three divisions of the Hebrew *Bible. In Judaism, the term is also applied more widely to the whole body of religious teachings, viewed as the revealed word of God and including both the written and the oral Torah. The reading of the Torah, from a manuscript scroll (*sepher Torah*), occupies a central place in *synagogue services.

Torbay 50 28N 3 32W A district in SW England, in Devon around Tor Bay on the S coast. It was formed in 1968 from the three resorts of Torquay, Paignton, and Brixham. Population (1981): 115 582.

Torgau 51 35N 12 58E A town and port in S East Germany, on the River Elbe. A league of Protestant princes was formed here in 1526. In 1760 a battle was fought nearby, in which the Austrians were defeated by Frederick II of Prussia. Population (1983 est): 21 301.

Tories A British political group that became the *Conservative Party under Robert *Peel in the 1830s; Tory is still used synonymously with Conservative. Originally an Irish name for a Roman Catholic outlaw, it was applied in 1679 to a supporter, in opposition to the *Whigs, of the succession to the throne of the Roman Catholic Duke of York (later James II). The Tories were later associated with the rebellious Jacobites and were excluded from politics until the 1780s, when they re-emerged under the leadership of William *Pitt the Younger. They represented the interests of the country gentry, merchants, and Anglicans.

Torino. *See* Turin.

tormentil A perennial herb, *Potentilla erecta*, native to Europe, W Asia, and N Africa. Its slender stems, 10–30 cm long, bear yellow flowers and grow from a woody rootstock, which has astringent properties. The trailing tormentil (*P. anglica*) has creeping flower stems up to 70 cm long and larger flowers. Family: *Rosaceae*.

tornado A violently rotating column of air, small in diameter, characterized by a funnel-shaped cloud, which may reach ground surface. Wind speeds of up to 200 knots (100 m per second) have been experienced. Occurring over land, tornadoes cause large-scale destruction and are a considerable problem in the central USA and Australia.

Toronto 43 42N 79 25W A city and port in E Canada, the capital of Ontario on Lake Ontario. It is Canada's second largest city, housing a stock exchange and many business headquarters. With Canada's busiest airport, Toronto is also a water, road, and rail hub. Its diversified industries include heavy engineering, electrical, chemical, and wood products, foods, clothing, sporting goods, publishing, and films. With theatres, orchestras, museums, opera, ballet, and three universities, Toronto is the cultural centre of English-speaking Canada. *History*: established as Upper Canada's capital and military centre (1793), Toronto was burned by American troops (1813) and was the scene of the Mackenzie Rebellion (1837) against oligarchic government. It became an industrial and commercial centre with the development of railways (1850s). Population (1981): 559 217.

torpedo (armament) A self-propelled guided underwater missile carrying a high-explosive warhead. They can be launched by ships or aircraft but have been used most successfully by submarines. Designed in 1866 by a British engineer, Robert Whitehead (1823–1905), they were used to sink 25 million tons of Allied shipping in World Wars I and II. Modern torpedoes are driven by steam turbines or by battery-powered electric motors and have sophisticated active or passive acoustic homing systems (active devices send out sounds and are guided by the echo from the target; passive devices are guided by sounds from the target).

torpedo (fish). *See* electric ray.

Torquay 50 28N 3 30W A resort in SW England, in S Devon, part of Torbay since 1968. Its attractions include the mild climate, Torre Abbey (1196), and Kent's Cavern (where prehistoric remains have been discovered).

Torquemada, Tomás de (1420–98) Spanish Dominican friar and Grand Inquisitor. Confessor to Ferdinand and Isabella, he was appointed head of the Spanish *Inquisition in 1483. His sentences were extremely harsh and he was responsible for the expulsion of the Jews from Spain in 1492.

Torrens, Lake A salt lake in E South Australia. It is normally a mud flat except during the rainy season. Lowest point: about 8 m (25 ft) below sea level. Area: 5776 sq km (2230 sq mi).

Torreón 25 34N 103 25W A city in NE Mexico. It is the centre of La Laguna, a vast agricultural cooperative producing cotton and wheat. Population (1980): 363 886.

Torres Strait A channel between New Guinea and Cape York Peninsula, N Australia, linking the Arafura Sea and Coral Sea. It was discovered (1606) by the Spaniard, Luis Vaez de Torres. Width: 145 km (90 mi).

Torres Vedras 39 05N 9 15W A town in central Portugal. During the Peninsular War (1808–14) Wellington constructed his famous defence system—the Lines of Torres Vedras—near here, successfully defending Lisbon against the French. Population (1981): 10 997.

Torricelli, Evangelista (1608–47) Italian physicist, who succeeded *Galileo as professor of mathematics at Florence University. He discovered that the atmosphere exerts a pressure and demonstrated it by showing that it could support a column of mercury in a tube, thus inventing the mercury barometer (1643). He also created the first man-made vacuum in his simple barometer, the space above the mercury still being called a Torricellian vacuum.

tort In law, a civil wrong that constitutes a breach of a duty established by law rather than by *contract. It is distinguished from a crime in that it affects the interests of the injured person rather than of the state. Thus in tort the offender may be sued for damages.

Tortelier, Paul (1914–) French cellist. He won first prize at the Paris conservatoire at the age of 16. After playing in orchestras in the USA he began a career as a soloist, composer, and teacher. He has made many recordings and has written a book on cello playing.

tortoise A slow-moving herbivorous reptile belonging to the family *Testudinidae* (40 species), occurring in both Old and New Worlds, especially in Africa. Tortoises have a protective high-domed shell, tough scaly legs, and range in size from about 10 cm to 1.5 m (*see* Galápagos giant tortoise). Tortoises lay eggs and have long lifespans, reputedly up to 150 years. The common Mediterranean tortoise (*Testudo graeca*) is a popular pet; in colder climates, it must hibernate during the winter. *Compare* turtle; terrapin.

tortoise beetle A *leaf beetle with a carapace-like shield. Tortoise beetles are 9–12 mm long and many tropical species are brilliantly coloured (the South American species *Desmonota variolosa* is emerald green). The flat spiny larvae have a forked appendage at the rear end of the body to which they attach excrement for camouflage.

tortoiseshell butterfly A *nymphalid butterfly whose wings are mainly orange with black markings. Tortoiseshells are found in Europe, Asia, and North America. The caterpillars feed mainly on nettles and willows. The adults hibernate. Chief genera: *Aglais, Nymphalis*.

Tortoiseshell cat A breed of cat whose coat consists of distinct evenly spread patches of black, red, and cream. All Tortoiseshells are female (any males produced are sterile); they have compact bodies, short legs, and yellow or orange eyes. There are both long- and short-haired breeds.

Tortuga Island (French name: Île de la Tortue) 1 00S 90 55W A West Indian island, N of Haiti in the Greater Antilles. It was a haunt of buccaneers during the 17th century. Area: 180 sq km (70 sq mi).

Toruń (German name: Thorn) 53 01N 18 35E A town in N central Poland, on the River Vistula. Copernicus, the Polish astronomer, was born here (1473). Its university was founded in 1945. Industries include precision engineering and chemicals. Population (1982): 183 000.

Torvill and Dean British ice-skaters. In 1975 **Jayne Torvill** (1957–), a British junior pairs champion (1970), teamed up with **Christopher Dean** (1958–), who won his first national title in 1972. They became the British ice-dance champions (1977–84), their celebrated "Barnum" and "Bolero" routines bringing them European and World championships and, in 1984, an Olympic gold medal with perfect marks, before they turned professional.

Toscanini, Arturo (1867–1957) Italian conductor. He began his career as a cellist. He made his debut in Rio de

Janeiro in 1886 in Verdi's *Aida* and subsequently conducted at La Scala, Milan, and at the Metropolitan Opera in New York. From 1937 until his death he conducted the NBC (National Broadcasting Company) Symphony Orchestra.

Tosks One of the two divisions of the Albanian people living in the S of the country. *See also* Ghegs.

Tostig (d. 1066) Earl of Northumbria from 1055 until his exile in 1065 following a revolt against his misrule. He allied with Harold III Hardraade of Norway and invaded N England but was killed by his brother, Harold II, at Stamford Bridge.

Totalizator (*or* Tote) A system of betting on horse and greyhound races in which all the stake money is pooled, the pool being shared among winners (after deducting taxes and operating costs). The system was invented in France in 1872, where it is known as the *pari-mutuel*, but was not used there until 1929. It was introduced into the UK and the USA in 1930.

totemism In primitive societies, the common occurrence of a special relationship of ritual significance between certain animal and plant species or other natural phenomena and certain social groups or individuals. Features of this relationship are belief in descent from the totem species (which may include animal worship), a *taboo on killing or eating it except at special ritual feasts, and clan exogamy, but only among Australian aborigines do all these occur together. The Indians of the NW Pacific coast of America also practise totemism, as did the ancient Indo-European peoples.

totem pole Among the Indians of the NW Pacific coast, a carved and painted pole used to commemorate important events, as a house post, or to mark or contain funerary remains. The carvings are largely of animals associated with particular families and their histories and legends.

Totila (d. 552 AD) King of the Ostrogoths (541-52), who temporarily recovered much of central and S Italy from the Eastern Roman Empire. He took Rome in 546, lost it to *Belisarius, and then recaptured it. He was finally defeated and killed by *Narses.

toucan A noisy forest-dwelling bird belonging to a family (*Ramphastidae*; 37 species) occurring in tropical America. 25-60 cm long, toucans have huge brightly coloured bills and typically black plumage with a brightly coloured breast. They feed on fruit. Order: *Piciformes* (woodpeckers, etc.).

touch-me-not A European annual herbaceous plant, *Impatiens noli-tangere*, 20-100 cm high. It has narrow leaves and bright-yellow tubular flowers, each with a large lower lip and a long curled spur, borne on slender drooping stalks. The ripe fruits split open at the slightest touch to expel the seeds explosively. Family: *Balsaminaceae*.

touchstone A black or grey flintlike stone, formerly used for testing the purity of gold and silver. The metal to be tested and one of known purity are both rubbed with the touchstone and compared. The colour of the marks left indicates the impurities present. Treatment with nitric acid highlights the marks. The method is still sometimes used to test the purity of gold.

Toulon 43 07N 5 55E A port in SE France, in the Var department on the Mediterranean Sea. In 1942 most of the French fleet was scuttled here to prevent its capture by the Germans. Toulon is one of France's principal naval bases and has marine engineering, chemical, oil, and textile industries. Population (1982): 181 405.

Toulouse 43 33N 1 24E A city in S France, the capital of the Haute-Garonne department on the River Garonne. A major commercial and industrial centre, it has aircraft, armaments, chemical, and textile industries. It is also an important agricultural trading centre. Notable buildings include the basilica (11th-13th centuries), the gothic cathedral, and the university (1230). *History*: capital of the Visigoths and later of the kingdom of Aquitaine, it passed to

France in 1271. It suffered badly during the campaign against the Albigenses. Population (1982): 354 289.

Toulouse-Lautrec, Henri (Marie Raymond) de (1864-1901) French artist, born in Albi of aristocratic descent. Stunted in growth by a childhood accident, he settled in Paris, where he trained under two conservative artists in the early 1880s and led an unconventional life among the music halls and cafés of Montmartre. His comic but sympathetic studies of popular entertainers (for example Jane Avril and Aristide Bruant), circus life, and prostitutes in posters, lithographs, and paintings were influenced by *Degas and Japanese prints. Characteristic paintings are *At the Moulin Rouge* (Art Institute of Chicago) and *La Toilette* (Louvre).

TOULOUSE-LAUTREC *A lithograph of the popular singer Yvette Guilbert (1867-1944), one of a series of 16 studies for a poster (1894).*

touraco. *See* turaco.

Touraine A former province of France. Once independent, later under Angevin control, and in 1641 incorporated into the French kingdom, Touraine was famous until the late 17th century for its Huguenot silk weavers. The region is noted for its royal chateaux.

Tourcoing 50 44N 3 10E A town in N France, in the Nord department. Together with its twin town, Roubaix, it forms the centre of the French woollen industry. Population (1982): 97 121.

Tour de France The main Continental professional cycling race. Founded in 1903, the road race, of some 20 stages, lasts three weeks or more and has a maximum length of approximately 4000 km (2480 mi). The race starts in a different town each year but always ends in Paris. The teams are commercially sponsored.

Touré, (Ahmed) Sékou (1922-84) Guinean statesman; president (1958-84). Active in trades unionism in French West Africa, in 1956 Touré was elected to the French

National Assembly. He opposed de Gaulle's plan of federalism in French West Africa and lost French support on independence (1958), when he became head of state and then president.

tourmaline A group of minerals composed of complex cyclosilicates containing boron. There are numerous varieties, some being used as gemstones and some for their piezoelectric and polarizing properties. Tourmalines are found in veins and pegmatites, in granite rocks. *See* Plate III.

Tournai (Flemish name: Doornik) 50 36N 3 24E A town in W central Belgium, on the River Scheldt. It has a notable cathedral (11th–14th centuries). Industries include carpets, textiles, and leather. Population (1981 est): 69 718.

tournament In medieval Europe, a festival at which knights competed in various military tests of skill and courage. The best-known example was jousting, in which mounted knights charged each other with lances. Combatants were usually limited to members of noble families and weapons were usually blunt. Tournaments originated in France in the 11th century and had died out by the end of the 16th century. In modern times, the word refers to a military display and to competitions in various sports.

Tournefort, Joseph Pitton de (1656–1708) French botanist, who proposed a system of plant classification that used a single Latin name to distinguish a particular genus. This was later incorporated in the binomial system of nomenclature developed by *Linnaeus.

Tourneur, Cyril (c. 1575–1626) English dramatist. He published several poems, including the satire *The Transformed Metamorphosis* (1600), and is the presumed author of *The Atheist's Tragedy* (1611) and *The Revenger's Tragedy* (1607). The latter play has also been attributed to Thomas *Middleton. He died in Ireland after taking part in an expedition to Cádiz.

Tours 47 23N 0 42E A city in central France, the capital of the Indre-et-Loire department situated between the Rivers Loire and Cher. Its prosperous silk industry declined following the revocation of the Edict of Nantes (1685) and the exodus of the Huguenot weavers. Notable buildings include the gothic cathedral, the archiepiscopal palace (17th–18th centuries), and the university (1970). Tours is a tourist centre for the Loire Valley and has varied manufacturing industries. Population (1982): 136 483.

Toussaint-L'Ouverture, François Dominique (c. 1743–1803) Haitian slave, who led a slave rebellion in Haiti that achieved self-government under French protection. L'Ouverture became lieutenant governor of Haiti in 1794 and established a free society, expelling the Spanish and British landowners. He became governor general in 1801 but the French, afraid of his power, forcibly retired him in 1802. He was then arrested for plotting a rebellion and imprisoned.

Tower Bridge A bridge over the River Thames, next to the *Tower of London. Built in 1894 in the gothic style, it has a central portion that lifts to allow large ships to pass through it into the Pool of London.

Tower Hamlets A borough of E Greater London, created in 1965 from the former metropolitan boroughs of Bethnal Green, Stepney, and Poplar. Population (1981): 142 975.

Tower of London A royal fortress on the N bank of the River Thames, to the E of the City of London. It was begun in the 11th century, when Bishop Gundulf built the White Tower (1078), and added to in subsequent centuries. It was a royal palace until the 17th century and a state prison, which held such famous prisoners as Lady Jane *Grey and Anne *Boleyn. It is now a barracks, armoury, and museum, containing the British crown jewels and regalia.

Townes, Charles Hard (1915–   ) US physicist, who constructed the first *maser (1953). For this work he shared the 1964 Nobel Prize with Nikolai Bosov (1922–   ) and Aleksandr Prokhorov (1916–   ), two Soviet physicists, who independently worked out the theory of the maser.

town planning The designing of urban areas with a view to providing adequate public amenities, healthy and pleasant surroundings, and good communications. Among the first town planners were the Romans, who evolved a characteristic grid plan for many of their towns. Interest in the subject revived during the *Renaissance but it only became of major importance during the 19th-century urban expansion, when the need for an assured supply of housing and services became urgent. As a branch of the social sciences town planning has become highly sophisticated in the 20th century, now having to deal not only with unprecedented concentrations of people but also with large quantities of traffic.

Townshend, Charles, 2nd Viscount (1674–1738) British politician; secretary of state for the north (1714–16, 1721–30). He was dismissed in 1716 after a dispute with the 1st Earl Stanhope but was restored to power in 1721 and was responsible for foreign affairs in the 1720s. He was increasingly overshadowed by his brother-in-law Sir Robert Walpole and resigned. He was nicknamed Turnip Townsend for improving the cultivation of turnips.

Townshend, Pete (1945–   ) British guitarist, composer of the rock opera *Tommy* (1969). While playing in the group The Who, Townshend became famous for smashing his guitar at the end of performances.

Townshend Acts (*or* American Import Duties Act; 1767) Four acts passed by Britain to assert its authority over the American colonies by imposing revenue duties on tea, paper, glass, and painters' colours. They were named after Charles Townshend (1725–67), chancellor of the exchequer (1766–67). The acts, the uses to which the resulting revenues were put, and their repressive enforcement provoked violent resentment that contributed to the outbreak of the *American Revolution.

Townsville 19 13S 146 48E A port in Australia, in NE Queensland on Cleveland Bay. It is the commercial centre for N Queensland; industries include sugar processing, copper refining, and meat packing. It is the site of the James Cook University of North Queensland (1970). Population (1980 est): 84 300.

toxaemia The presence of bacterial toxins, such as those of diphtheria and tetanus, in the blood. However, the term is most often used to describe a condition affecting pregnant women, formerly thought to be due to toxins but is now known to be caused by *hypertension (raised blood pressure). Hypertension in pregnancy is often accompanied by protein in the urine and *oedema (fluid in the tissues). In very severe cases the patient may develop fits.

toxicology. *See* poisons.

toxin A poison produced by a living organism. Many microorganisms, including bacteria and fungi, produce toxins. In diphtheria and tetanus the toxin is produced by the bacteria within the body of the infected person; in botulism the toxin is produced in contaminated food and ingested by the patient. Some toxins are useful: penicillin is a toxin, produced by fungi, that kills bacteria.

Toyama 36 42N 137 14E A city in Japan, in central Honshu on the Sea of Japan. It has been known since the 17th century for its pharmaceutical industry. Population (1980): 305 000.

Toynbee, Arnold (Joseph) (1889–1975) British historian. After holding several university posts, he was director of studies at the Royal Institute of International Affairs (1925–55). His major work, *A Study of History* (12 vols, 1934–61), structured according to the rise and fall of civilizations, embodies his theory of historical progress. His son (**Theodore**) **Philip Toynbee** (1916–81) wrote a number of experimental novels, including *Tea with Mrs Goodman* (1947) and *Pantaloon* (1961), and contributed many articles to various literary journals. He joined the staff of the *Observer* in 1950.

Toynbee Hall (The Universities' Settlement in East London) A residential settlement for men and women, founded in 1885 and named after Arnold *Toynbee. It houses many welfare services, including playgroups, a legal advice centre, adult literacy courses, and care for the mentally handicapped.

Trabzon (former name: Trebizond) 41 00N 39 43E A port in NE Turkey, on the Black Sea. It was the capital of the Comnenian empire (1204–1461) and has a university (1963). Population (1980): 108 403.

trace element A chemical element required by an organism for normal healthy growth but only in minute amounts. Higher plants, for instance, require traces of copper, zinc, etc. Many trace elements are constituents of vitamins and enzymes.

tracer bullet A bullet that when ignited by the propellant emits light or smoke. In flight, its path appears as a continuous streak enabling the gunner to correct his aim. Mixed with other types of bullets during loading, tracer bullets are used in aircraft and by ground troops both during combat and as an aid to maintaining direction during a night attack.

tracery In *gothic architecture, decorative stonework supporting the glass in windows. Moulded stone bars were introduced as an ornamental element in 13th-century France and England. Designs were at first geometric (see Early English), but later became curvilinear (see Decorated; Flamboyant). In England the regular rectangular tracery of the *Perpendicular style resulted in some enormous windows.

trachea **1.** The windpipe: a tube that conducts air from the larynx to the left and right bronchi, which continue to the *lungs. The trachea is lined by *mucous membrane and supported by hoops of cartilage in its wall. See Plate IV. **2.** One of the air passages in insects, which lead directly to the tissues. Each trachea has an external opening (spiracle) that can be opened and closed.

trachoma An eye disease that occurs in dry poor parts of the world and is caused by a large virus-like organism of the genus *Chlamydia*. It is a severe form of *conjunctivitis in which the membrane lining the eyelids and covering the cornea becomes scarred and shrunken and the eyelids become deformed. Trachoma is the world's most common cause of blindness; it is treated with antibiotics.

Tractarianism. *See* Oxford Movement.

tractor A self-propelled vehicle designed to provide high power and traction at relatively low speeds for use in agriculture, construction, etc. Tractors were developed from mobile versions of the steam engines used in the 19th century. The American Burger tractor of 1889 was the first to use an internal-combustion engine. The modern tractor is usually powered by a Diesel engine and equipped with a cab that insulates the driver from weather and noise. A power take-off (PTO) and hydraulically operated fittings enable powerful and versatile implements to be operated by the tractor, including shovels, loaders, mowing machines, muck spreaders, and cultivators.

Tracy, Spencer (1900–67) US film actor. He began his film career in the 1930s by playing gangsters, but later costarred with Katherine *Hepburn in nine films, including *Woman of the Year* (1942), *Adam's Rib* (1949), and *Guess Who's Coming to Dinner* (1967). Other notable films include *The Old Man and the Sea* (1958), *Inherit the Wind* (1960), and *Judgement at Nuremberg* (1961).

trade cycle The repeated cycle of *boom, *recession, *depression, recovery, and boom in an economy. In the UK in the 19th century, the trade cycle displayed remarkable regularity and stability; in the 20th century, it has fluctuated more. The *Depression of the 1930s was a severe and protracted world slump followed, after World War II, by a period of boom, interrupted by only minor recessions, which persisted until another depression was entered in the 1970s. The causes of the cycle are uncertain, but it may result from the persistence of erratic shocks to the economy, such as wars, political rises in the prices of essential commodities (such as oil), etc. Governments have tried to temper the effects of the trade cycle by imposing government spending policies (*see* deficit financing).

trademarks Distinctive emblems owned by a manufacturer or trader and applied to his goods to identify them as produced or sold by him. The owner of a trademark has the right to its exclusive use in connection with the goods associated with it. In the UK most trademarks are registered at the Patent Office. Any trademark can be protected against infringement by legal action and registered trademarks enjoy additional statutory protection.

Tradescantia A genus of flowering plants (about 60 species), native to North and Central America and popular as ornamentals. Varieties of the wandering jew (*T. fluminensis*) are popular house plants, having oval green leaves, tinged with pink or mauve or with silver stripes. Spiderworts, derived from *T. virginiana*, have three-petalled blue, purple, red, or white flowers and grasslike leaves; they are attractive border plants. Family: *Commelinaceae*.

trade union An organization of employees joined together to present a collective front in negotiations with an employer and to provide a measure of security for its members. The origins of trade unions lie in the local clubs of skilled craftsmen in 18th-century Britain. These were suppressed by the *Combination Acts until 1824, but although the right of workers to form unions was then acknowledged they continued to suffer restrictions. Robert Owen's Grand National Consolidated Trades Union (1834), the first attempt to unite skilled and unskilled workers, collapsed following the transportation of the *Tolpuddle Martyrs. In 1851 the first successful national trade union, the Amalgamated Society of Engineers, was formed and in 1868 the Trades Union Congress (TUC) met for the first time. Granted legal status in 1871, trade unions began to be formed by unskilled workers, who were greatly encouraged by the successful London Dockers' strike (1889) for a wage of 6d an hour. During the 1890s the trades union movement supported the formation of the *Labour Party, which has continued to be the political party of organized labour. Unions in the UK finally became politically and financially secure with the passing of the Trade Disputes Act (1906), which prevented employers from suing unions for damages after a *strike. The failure of the *General Strike (1926) was a blow to the trades union movement in Britain and the consequent Trade Disputes Act (1927) made general strikes illegal. This was repealed by the postwar Labour Government.

Craft unions consist of members possessing a particular skill; **industrial unions** are restricted to members who all work in a particular industry; and **general unions** have members who are not recruited from any specific sector of industry. Compared to the USA and W Europe, the UK has a multiplicity of craft unions, a situation that is thought by some analysts to be one of the main causes of its industrial relations problems. In the UK, membership of unions reached a peak of 13.29 million in 1979, but has declined by 17% since then. The number of unions was 519 in 1973, but this number had declined to 371 in 1986.

Unions are often affiliated to national organizations, such as the TUC in the UK. These national organizations vary in character; some are tight-knit groups (as in Scandinavia), some are loose federations (e.g. the TUC), some (e.g. the *American Federation of Labor) act merely as pressure groups within the political system, while others have political aims. These national union organizations have become important political forces in negotiations with governments and employers' organizations, especially since the advent of *prices and incomes policies. The first international trade union was the first *International (1864); the international trades union movement is now represented by the *World Federation of Trade Unions and the *International Confederation of Free Trade Unions.

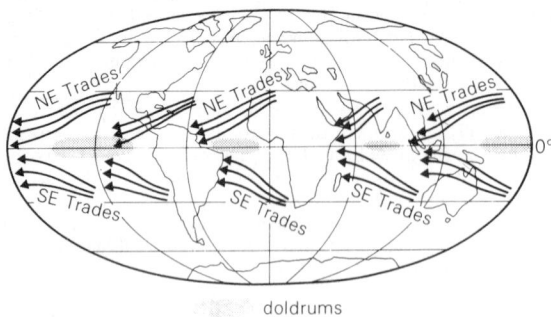

doldrums

TRADE WINDS

trade winds (*or* tropical easterlies) The predominantly easterly winds that blow in the tropics. They blow generally from a NE direction in the N hemisphere and from a SE direction in the S hemisphere, converging towards the equator. They are noted for their constancy of direction and speed.

trading stamps Stamps given by a retailer to customers in proportion to the price of goods purchased. The customer can exchange these stamps (when he has collected enough of them) for goods. The retailer buys the stamps from a trading-stamp company and seeks to recover his cost from higher profits resulting from increased turnover. In the UK the rules controlling the use of stamps were laid down in the Trading Stamps Act (1964).

Trafalgar, Battle of (21 October, 1805) The naval battle in the Napoleonic Wars in which the British under Nelson (in the *Victory*; □ships) defeated the French W of Cape Trafalgar, between Cádiz and Gibraltar (SW Spain). Nelson's skilful tactic of attacking enemy lines at right angles was an important element in the British success, which was tragically marred by Nelson's death in the hour of victory. It ended the threat of a French invasion of Britain and established conclusively British naval supremacy. It was at Trafalgar that Nelson signalled the famous message "England expects that every man will do his duty."

tragacanth. *See* gums.

tragedy A form of drama recounting the fall (usually, the death) of a noble protagonist. The form evolved in ancient Greece from the *dithyramb, a choral song, and was fully developed in the plays of Aeschylus, Sophocles, and Euripides. Little tragic drama of worth was then written until the Elizabethan period of English literature, when Marlowe prepared the way for the tragedies of Shakespeare and his followers. In 17th-century France the neoclassical tragedies of Racine and Corneille were carefully based on principles derived from Aristotle's *Poetics* (*see* unities). During the 19th century the essential elements of tragedy were more apparent in the novel than in drama. Ibsen and Strindberg in Europe and Eugene O'Neill in the USA contributed to the development of tragic drama, but few 20th-century dramatists have attempted to write tragedies in the classical or Elizabethan sense.

tragicomedy A genre of drama developed by European writers in the late 16th and early 17th centuries. Its combination of tragic and romantic elements was pioneered by the Italian dramatist *Guarini in *Il pastor fido* (c. 1583) and was further developed in France and by several Jacobean and Restoration dramatists in England. The term is often applied to any play containing both tragic and comic elements, such as those of Chekhov.

tragopan A short-tailed *pheasant belonging to a genus (*Tragopan*) occurring in wet forests of the Himalayas. Male tragopans have vivid plumage, including long crown feathers, and two erectile blue fleshy "horns" on the head; a fold of skin beneath the bill forms a large bib during display.

Traherne, Thomas (c. 1637-74) English poet. The discovery of manuscripts on a London bookstall in 1896 led to the publication of his *Poetical Works* (1903) and *Centuries of Meditation* (1908), a series of mystical and religious meditations written in an exalted prose style.

Trail 49 04N 117 39W A city in W Canada, in British Columbia. Founded in 1865, it has a huge smelter to exploit local lead, zinc, iron, and other mineral deposits. Steel, metal products, and chemicals are manufactured here. Population (1981): 9600.

Trajan(us), Marcus Ulpius (53-117 AD) Roman emperor (98-117). Trajan's early military successes led to his adoption by *Nerva in 97 AD. After his arrival in Rome as emperor his virtues were praised by Pliny in the *Panegyric*. His domestic policies were munificent and humane: corn was freely distributed, taxes were lessened, and much public building was carried out. He conducted two important wars: a successful Dacian campaign and a fruitless Parthian war. He died in Cilicia on his way back to Rome. □sculpture.

tranquillizers A group of drugs used to quieten aggressive, restless, or anxious patients. The major tranquillizers are powerful drugs used in the treatment of schizophrenia and other mental disorders. They include reserpine, the *phenothiazines, and the butyrophenones (e.g. haloperidol). Minor tranquillizers, which include the *benzodiazepines, are used for the treatment of neuroses and anxiety. Side effects of the major tranquillizers may be severe, and these drugs are usually prescribed only for serious psychological disorders.

Transcaucasia A region in the SE Soviet Union, in the Georgian, Azerbaidzhan, and Armenian SSRs. The Great *Caucasus range is in the N and the Little Caucasus, in the S. Its resources include oil and it is an important agricultural region. In 1918 Georgia, Azerbaidzhan, and Armenia formed the short-lived Transcaucasian Federative Republic, the basis of the Transcaucasian Soviet Federated Republic (1922-36).

transcendentalism A philosophy that emphasizes the modes of thought and apprehension beyond the world of experience. In the philosophy of *Kant, everything beyond man's limited experience is transcendental and essentially unknowable. Human intuitions about time and space and understanding of quality and quantity are vital for experience, but are transcendent in that they do not come from that experience. *See also* Transcendentalists, New England.

Transcendentalists, New England A group of mid-19th century US writers and philosophers united by their philosophic idealism and their trust in the moral value of intuition. Their beliefs derived from the philosophy of Kant, especially as interpreted by Carlyle and Coleridge. Leading members of the group included Ralph Waldo *Emerson and Henry David *Thoreau. They advocated social, political, and religious reforms, and many of their writings were published in the periodical *The Dial* (1840-44).

transducer Any device that changes a signal or physical quantity into another form. *Microphones, *loudspeakers, and *thermocouples are examples. It is also usually the primary sensor in a measurement or sensing system.

transformer A device for converting alternating current from one voltage to another. The input is fed to a primary winding, a coil of wire round a soft iron core, creating an oscillating magnetic field in the core. This field induces a secondary current of the same frequency in the secondary winding wound on the same core. The ratio of primary to secondary voltage is equal to the ratio of the number of turns in the secondary coil to that in the primary. The device is widely used both in electronic circuits and in the transmission and distribution of electric power (*see* electricity supply).

transhumance A form of pastoral nomadism in which livestock are moved seasonally between mountain summer pastures and lower lying winter pastures, or between northern and southern or wet and dry season grazing areas.

transistor A *semiconductor device with three or more electrodes. Transistors form the basic elements of electronic *amplifiers and logic circuits, often combined with other components in *integrated circuits. They were first developed in 1948 by William *Shockley and his coworkers at the Bell Telephone Co and now replace *thermionic valves in most applications. The term transistor usually refers to the **bipolar junction transistor**, which consists of two junctions between p-type and n-type semiconductors forming either a p-n-p or n-p-n structure. Current is carried across these junctions by both negative and positive charge carriers (electrons and holes). The current between the emitter and the collector electrodes varies not only with the voltage drop across them, but also with the voltage or current level at the base (the third electrode). Depending on how it is connected into a circuit, the junction transistor can act as a voltage or current amplifier in much the same way as a triode valve. Transistors, however, work at a much lower voltage than valves, are more compact and robust, emit less heat, and are cheaper to make.

Originally, junction transistors were made by alloying the impurity metal onto the semiconductor crystal or by adding impurities as the crystal was being grown. Now the doping is diffused in as a gas, introduced by ion implantation, or, more commonly, achieved by a combined process of etching and diffusion, known as the planar process.

The **field effect transistor** (FET) is a unipolar device, in which current is carried by only one type of charge. There are two types: the junction FET (JFET) has a region of semiconductor of one doping type flanked by two highly doped layers of the opposite type. Current flows parallel to the junctions, between the so-called source and drain electrodes, through a narrow channel between the highly doped regions (the gate); it is controlled by the electric field arising from the gate input voltage, which alters the width of the conducting channel. The JFET is used as a separate component in amplifiers and switches. In the insulated-gate FET (IGFET) the source and drain electrodes are highly doped regions in a substrate of the opposite type. The gate electrode is a conductor separated from the substrate by a thin insulating layer across the surface. The electric field caused by the gate voltage controls the source-drain current on the other side of the insulator. The IGFET is used mainly in metal-oxide semiconductor (MOS) integrated circuits. It is smaller than the equivalent bipolar junction transistor and uses less power. □ p. 1226.

transit circle. *See* meridian circle.

transit instrument A telescope theodolite, or similar device, that can be adjusted over a range of angular settings and is used to measure angular position. In astronomy, for instance, transit telescopes measure the vertical angles of stars or planets.

transition elements A large group of metallic elements, including most of the commonly used metals, the inner electron shells of which are incomplete. The *lanthanides and the *actinides are sometimes included in this definition. The elements show considerable similarities to their horizontal neighbours in the *periodic table. In general, they are hard, brittle, high-melting, and excellent conductors of heat and electricity. Their chemistry is complicated; they have multiple valencies and tend to form coloured compounds.

Transjordan. *See* Jordan, Hashemite kingdom of.

Transkei, Republic of A small country in South Africa, consisting of three separate areas. Most of the population is *Xhosa. *Economy*: chiefly subsistence agriculture, especially livestock, although such cash crops as tea, coffee, and flax are now being developed. Many adult males still work and live in South Africa. *History*: created in 1963, when South Africa granted self-government to the Xhosa nation, as the first of the Bantu Homelands, it became independent in 1976. All Black Africans of Transkeian origin became its citizens, simultaneously losing their South African citizenship. Its independence is, however, recognized only by South Africa. In 1978, it broke off diplomatic relations with South Africa, in spite of continuing economic dependence on it. In 1987 intertribal disputes threatened civil war; following a coup at the end of the year, Maj-Gen Bantu Holomisa assumed power. Official currency: South African rand. Area: 43 188 sq km (16 675 sq mi). Population (1983 est): 2 775 000. Capital: Umtata.

translucence One of the degrees of transparency used by geologists for classifying minerals. A mineral is translucent if it transmits light but not sufficiently so to enable the outline of an object to be seen.

transmigration of souls. *See* reincarnation.

transmutation The conversion of one element into another. It was originally the (unfulfilled) aim of alchemists to bring about the transmutation of base metals into gold (*see* alchemy). Transmutations were achieved in the 20th century by bombarding elements with *alpha particles or *neutrons. An example is the production of oxygen-17 when nitrogen-14 is bombarded with alpha particles.

transpiration The loss of water vapour from the surface of a plant, which occurs primarily through small pores (stomata) in the leaves but also (slowly) through the cuticle of the *epidermis. The rate of water loss is controlled by the opening and closing of the stomata, greater loss occurring during the day than at night.

transplantation The surgical implantation of a tissue or organ derived either from another part of the body of the patient himself or from another individual (the donor). Skin grafting is an example of the former type of operation: it is used particularly to repair damage and disfigurement caused by burns and other injuries. Transplantation of donor organs is usually far less successful since the body's immune system reacts against and rejects the foreign tissue. These operations require careful matching of the donor's and recipient's tissues together with the use of drugs that suppress the recipient's immune responses (*see* immunosuppression). The first successful heart transplant operation was performed by Christiaan *Barnard in 1967, since when many such operations have been performed in various countries, especially in the UK and the USA. Other organs that have been transplanted include the kidneys, lung, and liver, of which kidney transplants have been the most successful. Transplantation of bone marrow, heart valves, and pieces of bone have also been attempted.

transponder In telecommunications, a combined transmitter and receiver that sends out a signal automatically on receiving a predetermined trigger signal.

transportation In law, the practice of sending a convicted criminal to some place outside Britain, usually to one of the colonies, to be kept in hard labour. Transportation dates back to the reign of Elizabeth I, becoming increasingly popular as a means of providing labour in the colonies towards the end of the 17th century. Transportation was replaced by penal servitude at the end of the 18th century and later by imprisonment.

transputer. *See* computer.

transsexualism. *See* transvestism.

Trans-Siberian Railway The world's longest railway, running 9335 km (5800 mi) from Moscow to Vladivostok, known as Siberia's lifeline. Double track, largely electrified, has replaced the original single track line built between 1891 and 1905.

transubstantiation In Roman Catholic theology, the

Germanium is a typical semiconductor. The four outer electrons in each of its atoms form covalent bonds with adjacent atoms. In the pure state it acts as an insulator as no electrons are available to carry current.

Arsenic atoms have five outer electrons. Germanium containing arsenic atoms as an impurity can carry current because the fifth electron is available as a carrier. This is an n-type semiconductor because current is carried by negative electrons.

Indium atoms have three outer electrons. Germanium doped with indium therefore has holes in its electronic structure. These can be filled by electrons from neighbouring atoms, creating new holes; this has the effect of positive charge moving through the crystal in the opposite direction to electrons. This is p-type germanium.

In the bipolar junction transistor a piece of p-type material is sandwiched between two n-type pieces, making an n-p-n structure (p-n-p transistors are also used).

In an n-p-n transistor, a negative voltage is applied to one end (the emitter) and a positive to the other (the collector). No current flows, however, because a potential barrier forms at the junction between the emitter and the central region (the base).

If the base region is positively biased, the free electrons in the emitter are attracted to the p-type base and current flows through the thin base to the collector. As the collector current depends on the amount of bias to the base, the device can be used as an amplifier.

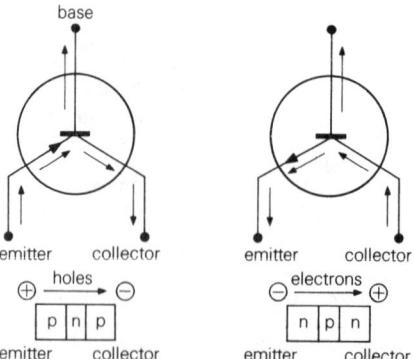

In the symbolic representation of a transistor, the direction of the arrow on the emitter indicates current direction and the type of transistor (n-p-n or p-n-p).

TRANSISTOR   *The operation of the bipolar junction transistor.*

doctrine that the substance of the elements of bread and wine in the *Eucharist is changed at consecration into the substance of the body and blood of Christ. Only the accidents (i.e. the qualities apparent to the senses) of the bread and wine remain. *Compare* consubstantiation.

transuranic elements Elements with higher atomic number than uranium. Apart from traces of neptunium and plutonium, none of them has ever been detected in nature, since no isotopes of sufficient *half-life exist; they have been created since 1940, usually in minute amounts, in nuclear reactions. At present, over a dozen are known. *See also* actinides.

Transvaal The most northerly province in South Africa. Much of it is plateau with rolling country and high ridges, including the Witwatersrand. Heavily populated in the S, it is the most prosperous province and contains the country's main industrial area, centred on the Witwatersrand; iron, steel, and chemicals are produced. Mineral deposits include gold, diamonds, uranium, coal, chromite, and tin, and it has important deposits of platinum. It has a well-developed agriculture producing maize, wheat, peanuts, citrus fruit, cotton, and tobacco; sheep and cattle are raised. Forestry is also important. *History*: originally an Afrikaner republic, it fought in the *Boer Wars against Britain (1880-81, 1899-1902). It joined the Union of South Africa in 1910. Area: 283 917 sq km (109 621 sq mi). Population (1980): 8 350 500. Capital: Pretoria.

transvestism The practice of wearing clothes appropriate to the opposite sex, usually for sexual pleasure. Many transvestites are heterosexual males and do not wish to change their sex. Psychotherapy and aversion therapy can provide effective treatment for those requiring it. **Transsexualism** is the settled belief that one's psychological gender is opposite to one's physical sex, and this can cause considerable suffering. Psychological treatments are usually unhelpful. Some transsexuals manage to pass successfully as members of the opposite sex; hormone therapy and plastic surgery on genitals and breasts can help this adjustment by effecting an apparent sex change.

Transylvania A region of SE Europe, bounded by the Carpathian Mountains and the Transylvanian Alps, now in Romania. Transylvania retained its distinctive character under successive Roman, Magyar, and Hungarian rulers; during the 16th and 17th centuries, it was a self-governing princedom within the Ottoman Empire. Restored to Hungary, within the Holy Roman Empire, in 1687, Transylvania became part of Romania after World War I.

Transylvanian Alps (*or* Southern Carpathian Mountains; Romanian name: Carpaţii Meridionali) A mountain range extending 360 km (227 mi) E-W across S central Romania and rising to 2543 m (8343 ft) at Mount Moldoveanu.

Trapani 38 02N 12 32E A seaport in Italy, in NW Sicily. A Carthaginian naval base, it was ceded to Rome after the first Punic War. Its industries include fishing, fish processing, salt production, and marbleworking. Population (1983 est): 71 759.

trap-door spider A *spider, especially one of the family *Ctenizidae*, that constructs a silk-lined burrow in the ground covered by a tight-fitting silk-hinged door. Ctenizids are dull brown, with short stout legs. They occur in tropical and subtropical regions and only leave their burrows to hunt.

Trappists A Roman Catholic monastic order, officially known as the *Cistercians of the Strict Observance. It was founded in 1664 at the abbey of La Trappe in Normandy by D. A. J. le B. de Rancé (1626-1700). When the monks were expelled during the French Revolution, the order established houses in other countries; there are now monasteries in Britain, Ireland, North America, and elsewhere. The order is notable for its austerity, which includes the observance of strict silence, manual labour, and a simple vegetarian diet.

Trasimeno, Lake (*or* Lake Perugia) A lake in central

Italy. It is drained via an artificial tunnel by the River Tiber. Area: 129 sq km (50 sq mi).

traveller's tree A palmlike tree, *Ravenala madagascariensis*, native to Madagascar. It grows over 27 m tall and bears a crown of banana-like leaves, 120-180 cm long, on long stalks (2-4 m long). Each leaf base, shaped like a huge cup, holds about one litre of water, which can provide a drink for thirsty passers-by (hence the name). Family: *Strelitziaceae*.

travel sickness Nausea and sometimes vomiting caused by travelling in cars, buses, trains, planes, boats (sea sickness), or on roundabouts and fairground machines. It arises when the constant movement disturbs the organs of balance in the inner ear, which causes nausea. Travel sickness is especially common in children and many of them grow out of it. It is treated with drugs to stop the nausea, particularly *antihistamines. As many of these cause sleepiness as well, a person driving should not take them.

Traven, B(en) (Berick Traven Torsvan; 1890-1969) US novelist. Despite much speculation, his identity remained uncertain until after his death. He was probably born in Chicago of German ancestry, worked in Germany in 1918-19, and lived in Mexico from the 1920s. His allegorical novels include *The Death Ship* (1926) and *The Treasure of the Sierra Madre* (1927).

Travers, Ben(jamin) (1886-1980) British dramatist. After publishing several novels in the early 1920s he established his reputation as a comic dramatist with farces played at the Aldwych Theatre and written between 1925 and 1933. These include *Rookery Nook* (1926), *Thark* (1927), and *Plunder* (1928). He wrote *The Bed before Yesterday* (1976) at the age of 90.

trawler A vessel equipped for catching fish by towing nets. Such vessels are often designed with cold storage facilities for the catch for extended voyages at sea.

treachery In English law, during World War II, to assist, or conspire or attempt to assist, the naval, military, or air operations of the enemy. Punishable by death, treachery was defined in the Treachery Act (1940), which expired in 1946. *See also* treason.

treadmill A penal device used in 19th-century prisons. It consisted of a hollow cylinder with a series of steps. A prisoner treading on the steps would set the cylinder in motion, which could then be used for grinding corn, etc. It was invented in 1818 by the British civil engineer Sir William Cubitt (1785-1861).

treason The violation by a citizen of his allegiance to the sovereign or the state. In England, the Statute of Treasons (1352) defined two kinds of treason: high treason, now the only kind of treason, and petty treason, abolished in 1828, which was where a servant killed his master, a wife killed her husband, or an ecclesiastic killed his superior (i.e. the violation of private allegiance). (High) treason, as defined in 1352 and in subsequent Acts, is: (1) to plot to kill or maim the sovereign; (2) to wage war against him in his realm or to join his enemies; (3) to kill his eldest son or heir; (4) to violate his wife, eldest daughter (if unmarried), or heir's wife; (5) to kill the chancellor, or any judge while he or she is performing his or her office. A person charged with treason is tried as if for murder and, if convicted, is punished by death. *See also* treachery.

treasure trove In law, money or coin, gold, silver plate, or bullion of unknown ownership found hidden in a house or in the ground. In England it belongs to the Crown provided its owner is unknown; if it has been abandoned or lost the finder has the first claim on it after the true owner. If objects were buried in a burial site with no intention of recovery, they are the property of the owner of the land. The finder of treasure trove is rewarded the value of the property found, unless he conceals it, in which case he is liable to imprisonment.

Treasury The UK government department, established in

1653, that is responsible, with the *Bank of England, for the management of the economy (*see* fiscal policy; monetary policy) and the allocation of the available government money between the spending departments. The prime minister is the first lord of the treasury, but it is run by the *chancellor of the exchequer, assisted by the chief secretary to the Treasury and the financial secretary.

treasury bill A government stock providing a source of short-term borrowing (usually three months) for a government. Bills are in denominations of £5,000 upwards in the UK and are offered at a discount, which influences the Bank of England's lending rate. Treasury bills were first used in the UK in 1877 and in the USA in 1929. *See also* open-market operations.

treaty ports The five Chinese ports that were opened to British consuls and merchants in 1842 at the end of the first *Opium War. They were Canton, Amoy, Fuzhou, Ningbo, and Shanghai.

Trebizond. *See* Trabzon.

tree A tall perennial woody plant, usually with a single main stem (the trunk) and secondary stems (the branches) arising some distance above ground level. (Shrubs are smaller bushier woody perennials without a distinct trunk.) Most tree species are either *dicotyledons (angiosperms)—the broad-leaved trees—or *conifers (gymnosperms). These are the only trees that form true *wood and they are of economic importance as producers of hardwoods and softwoods, respectively. Other groups containing trees are the cycads (gymnosperms), monocotyledons (notably the *palms), and the ferns. Trees grow wherever the annual rainfall exceeds 76 cm (30 in) but a few have adapted to desert conditions. The conifers and tropical trees are mostly *evergreen plants, while broad-leaved trees growing in regions with marked seasonal changes in climate are typically deciduous.

The tallest existing tree on record is a Californian redwood, which has attained a height of 111 m (364 ft). The study of the ecology and classification of trees is called **dendrology**. *See also* forest.

Tree, Sir Herbert (Draper) Beerbohm (1853-1917) British actor and theatre manager, halfbrother of Max *Beerbohm. He was manager of the Haymarket Theatre from 1887 to 1899 and then of Her Majesty's Theatre, where he staged many lavish Shakespearian productions. In 1904 he founded the *Royal Academy of Dramatic Art.

treecreeper A small songbird belonging to a family (*Certhiidae*; 5 species) occurring in Europe, Asia, and North America. It has a brownish streaked plumage with pale silvery underparts, long claws, and a slender down-curved bill. The European treecreeper (*Certhia familiaris*), 12.5 cm long, occurs mainly in coniferous woods, where it creeps up tree trunks to probe for small beetles, spiders, woodlice, etc.

tree fern A tropical *fern belonging to the genus *Cyathea* (600 species), found mainly in moist mountainous regions. It has a trunklike stem, 3–25 m high, and a crown of large tapering branched fronds. Family: *Cyatheaceae*.

tree frog A small toad belonging to a widely distributed family (*Hylidae*; about 500 species). They have adapted to living in trees and have adhesive pads on their toes that enable them to cling to leaves and branches, leaping acrobatically to capture insects. Most species breed in water although some carry the developing eggs on their backs.

treehopper A winged insect, less than 13 mm long, belonging to the mainly tropical family *Membracidae* (2600 species). An enlargement of the thorax extends over the body to form a "hood," which varies in colour and shape to camouflage the insects against the background vegetation on which they live and feed. Suborder: *Homoptera*; order *Hemiptera*.

tree kangaroo A *wallaby of the genus *Dendrolagus* (9 species) of Australia and New Guinea. The black tree

kangaroo (*D. ursinus*) is an agile climber that feeds at night on the ground and sleeps during the day in trees.

tree of heaven A tree, *Ailanthus altissima*, native to central Asia and planted elsewhere as an ornamental. Growing to a height of 30 m, it has compound leaves, up to 1 m long, composed of paired leaflets. Male and female flowers appear on separate trees, forming greenish-white clusters; the female flowers produce winged fruits. The trees are resistant to pollution and hence popular in urban areas. Family: *Simaroubaceae*.

tree-ring dating. *See* dendrochronology.

tree shrew A primitive *prosimian primate belonging to the family *Tupaiidae* (18 species), found in Java, Borneo, Sumatra, the Philippines, and S Asia. The common tree shrew (*Tupaia glis*) is 30–45 cm long including the tail (15–23 cm) and has a slender pointed face. It darts among the branches, feeding on insects, fruit, and seeds.

tree snake Any of a number of slender tree-dwelling snakes that hunt birds, frogs, and lizards in tropical forests. The blunt-headed tree snake (*Imantodes cenchoa*) of Central and South America can stiffen most of its 60-90 cm body length to reach another branch while supported by only a single coil of the tail. *See also* flying snake; vine snake.

trefoil One of several annual herbs of the genus *Trifolium* (which also includes the *clovers), characterized by leaves consisting of three leaflets. The hop trefoil (*T. campestre*), found on grassland and road verges of Europe, W Asia, N Africa, and North America, grows to a height of 35 cm and has compact globular heads of yellow flowers. The birdsfoot trefoils belong to the genus *Lotus* (about 70 species), of temperate Eurasia, Africa, and Australia. The leaves have five leaflets and the yellow or reddish flowers have a prominent keel resembling a lip. A common species is *L. corniculatus*, a perennial grassland herb growing to a height of 10-40 cm. Family: *Leguminosae*.

Trematoda. *See* fluke.

Trenchard, Hugh Montague, 1st Viscount (1873-1956) The first British air marshal. In World War I, as commander of the Royal Flying Corps, he advocated the separation of air and army forces and was chiefly responsible for the establishment of the RAF (1918). He founded the police college at Hendon while commissioner of the Metropolitan Police (1931-35).

Trengganu A state in NE Peninsular Malaysia, on the South China Sea. Mountainous and forested inland, it is settled mainly along the coast, with fish, rice, rubber, and copra being the chief products. Area: 12 955 sq km (5002 sq mi). Population (1980): 542 280. Capital: Kuala Trengganu.

Trent, Council of (1545-63) The 19th general council of the Roman Catholic Church, an expression of the *Counter-Reformation, which was summoned by Pope Paul III to strengthen the Church in its confrontation with Protestantism. It was held in Trento (N Italy). There were three sessions (1545-47, 1551-52, 1562-63), which clarified doctrine and instituted reforms: the Council condemned Luther's doctrine of justification by faith alone and defined *transubstantiation. It also strengthened episcopal authority and issued decrees on clerical abuses and education.

Trent, River A river in central England. Flowing mainly NE from Staffordshire through Nottingham, it joins the River Ouse to form the Humber estuary. The Midlands' main river, it is linked to the Mersey by the Trent, Mersey, and Grand Union Canals. Length: 270 km (170 mi).

Trentino-Alto Adige (Former name: Venetia Tridentina) An autonomous region in N Italy. Formerly part of Austria, it passed to Italy after World War I and has a large German-speaking population. It is a mountainous forested region, situated entirely within the Alps. The fertile valleys of the River Adige and its tributaries produce wine, fruit, and dairy products. Timber is an important industry. Numerous

TREE

softwoods

Scots pine   silver fir   Norway spruce   European larch

hardwoods

teak   common oak   English elm   blue gum

food trees

crab apple   Seville orange   walnut   cocoa

ornamentals

horse chestnut   magnolia   silver wattle   jacaranda

hydroelectric plants have encouraged the development of manufacturing industry. Tourism is an important source of revenue. Area: 13 613 sq km (5256 sq mi). Population (1980 est): 878 296. Capital: Trento.

Trento (German name: Trent) 46 04N 11 08E A city in N Italy, the capital of Trentino-Alto Adige on the River Adige. Dating from pre-Roman times, it has a romanesque cathedral (12th-century) and the 16th-century Church of Sta Maria Maggiore, where the Council of *Trent met. Its products include chemicals, electrical goods, and silk. Population (1983 est): 99 307.

Trenton 40 15N 74 43W A city in the USA, the capital of New Jersey. George Washington defeated the British here in 1776. Industries include the manufacture of pottery, cable, rope, and metal. Population (1980): 92 124.

trepang (or bêche-de-mer) The boiled, dried, and smoked body wall of certain *sea cucumbers, used to make soup in the East. It is produced mainly from animals of the genera *Holothuria*, *Stichopus*, and *Thelonota*, found on coral reefs of the SW Pacific.

trephine A surgical saw used to remove a circular section of the skull in order to release pressure caused by bleeding within the skull or to provide access to the brain. The use of trephines dates from ancient times.

Trevelyan, Sir George Otto (1838–1928) British statesman and historian, nephew and biographer of Lord Macaulay. He was an MP from 1868 to 1897. His son **George Macaulay Trevelyan** (1876–1962), a British historian, was Regius Professor of History at Cambridge University (1927–40). He was best known for works aimed at a popular audience, especially *English Social History* (1942).

Trèves. *See* Trier.

Trevino, Lee (1939–) US golfer, who was US Open champion (1968, 1971), British Open champion (1971, 1972), and US Professional Golfers Association champion (1974).

Treviso 45 40N 12 15E A city in Italy, in Veneto. Dating from Roman times, it has an 11th-century cathedral and other historic buildings. Its manufactures include ceramics and agricultural machinery. Population (1981 est): 87 069.

Trevithick, Richard (1771–1833) British engineer, who developed high-pressure steam engines. He built the first steam-driven carriage to carry passengers (1801) and the first locomotive to run on smooth wheels on smooth rails (1804). In 1816 he went to Peru, where his engines were being used in mines. He died in London, penniless.

Trevor-Roper, Hugh Redwald, Baron Dacre (1914–) British historian. Trevor-Roper's many books, notable for their literary merit, include *Archbishop Laud* (1940) and *The Last Days of Hitler* (1947). He was Regius Professor of Modern History at Oxford (1957–80).

trial by ordeal The most ancient form of trial. It was practised by Anglo-Saxons and based on the belief that God would intervene to protect an innocent person and hence involved a *judicium Dei* (judgment of God). There were four kinds: (1) by fire, which was reserved for persons of rank and involved walking over red-hot ploughshares or carrying a piece of red-hot iron; (2) by hot water, involving plunging the arm in boiling water; (3) by cold water, whereby the accused, thrown into a river or pond, was judged innocent if he sank; and (4) by combat, fought before judges. Ordeal was replaced in the reign (1216–72) of Henry III by compurgation, whereby 12 men had to swear that they believed the accused, which is thought to be the origin of the *jury.

triangle A percussion instrument consisting of a steel rod bent into the shape of a triangle. The triangle was first used in late 18th-century orchestral works to provide a "Turkish" atmosphere. □musical instruments.

Trianon, Grand and Petit Two villas in the grounds of the Palace of Versailles, near Paris. The Grand Trianon was built in 1687 for Louis XIV by *Mansart and the Petit Trianon from

1762 to 1768 for Louis XV by Jacques Ange Gabriel (1698–1782).

Triassic period (or Trias) A period of geological time at the beginning of the Mesozoic era, lasting from about 240 to 200 million years ago. The rocks of the period, laid down mainly under continental conditions, often considered together with those of the preceding *Permian period as the Permo-Trias(sic). The dinosaurs, ichthyosaurs, and plesiosaurs appeared in the Triassic.

tribes of Israel In the Bible, the Hebrew people. The 12 tribes, descended from the sons of Jacob, were *Reuben, *Simeon, *Judah, *Issachar, *Zebulun, *Benjamin, *Dan, *Naphtali, *Gad, *Asher, Levi (*see* Levites), and *Ephraim and *Manasseh. These last two were counted as one, except in parts of the Bible where the tribal lists omit either Levi or Simeon. After the death of Solomon, ten of the tribes broke away from Benjamin and Judah to form the northern kingdom of Israel (*see* Ten Lost Tribes of Israel).

tribology The study of *friction and such allied topics as lubrication, abrasives, surface wear, etc. The effects of friction, such as triboluminescence and frictional electricity, are also studied.

tribune In ancient Rome, a plebeian magistrate appointed to protect *plebeians' rights. Instituted during the 5th-century political struggles between *patricians and plebeians, the tribunes, first two, later ten, in number, could veto legislative proposals of the Senate or popular assemblies and could themselves propose legislation without senatorial approval. This power considerably influenced Roman politics from the Gracchi's revolutionary times (*see* Gracchus, Tiberius Sempronius) to Augustus' assumption of tribunicial power in the late 1st century BC.

Triceratops A three-horned dinosaur of the late Cretaceous period (about 100–65 million years ago). 8 m long and weighing 8.5 tonnes, it had an enormous head with one horn on the snout and one (up to 1 m long) over each eye. It also had a large bony neck frill and short limbs with hoofed feet and browsed on tough plants. Order: *Ornithischia. □fossil.

Trichinopoly. *See* Tiruchirappalli.

Trident missile A US navy three-stage solid-fuelled nuclear strategic missile launched from a submarine and having a range of 7800 km (4800 mi). Designed as a replacement for the Poseidon missile, Trident missiles, first deployed in the early 1980s, are capable of great accuracy at increased distances and carry a new stellar-inertial guidance system.

Trier (French name: Trèves) 49 45N 6 39E A city in SW West Germany, in Rhineland-Palatinate on the River Moselle. Founded by the Emperor Augustus, it has important Roman remains. The cathedral (11th–12th centuries) is built around the 4th-century basilica. It shares a university with Kaiserslautern (1970) and is the birthplace of Karl Marx. It is a wine-trading and industrial centre. Population (1983 est): 94 683.

Trieste (Serbo-Croat name: Trst) 45 39N 13 47E A seaport in Italy, the capital of Friuli-Venezia Giulia, situated on the Gulf of Trieste at the head of the Adriatic Sea. An important transit port for central Europe, it has shipyards, oil refineries, and a steel industry. It has a 14th-century cathedral and a university (1938). *History*: an important Roman port in the 1st century AD, it passed to Austria in 1382. It expanded rapidly in the 19th century as an outlet for Austrian goods and in 1920 was ceded to Italy. Following World War II it became the capital of the Free Territory of Trieste, which was established by the UN (1947) following a dispute between Italy and Yugoslavia. In 1954 most of the N of the Territory (including Trieste) passed to Italy and the remainder to Yugoslavia. Population (1980 est): 257 697.

triggerfish A shallow-water fish, belonging to a family (*Balistidae*) related to *puffers, that occurs in tropical seas. Its deep laterally flattened body, up to 60 cm long, is covered with large scales. The strong spine of the first dorsal fin is erected and locked into position by the second dorsal fin, forming a "trigger" that wedges the fish into crevices. It feeds on molluscs and crustaceans.

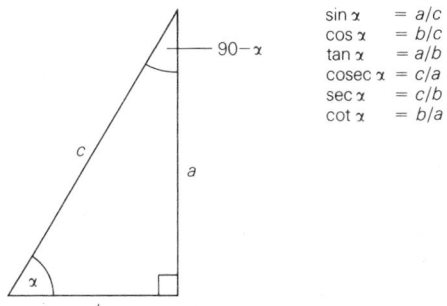

$$\sin \alpha = a/c$$
$$\cos \alpha = b/c$$
$$\tan \alpha = a/b$$
$$\operatorname{cosec} \alpha = c/a$$
$$\sec \alpha = c/b$$
$$\cot \alpha = b/a$$

TRIGONOMETRY *Definitions of the trigonometric functions sine, cosine, and tangent and of their reciprocals cosecant, secant, and cotangent.*

trigonometry A branch of mathematics founded by Hipparchus in the mid-2nd century BC, concerned originally with the measurement of triangles. The ratios of the lengths of the sides of a right-angled triangle are used to define the sine, cosine, and tangent of one of the angles of the triangle. Trigonometry deals with the properties of these and related functions. Its study is essential to most branches of physics and mathematics, particularly those involving cyclic quantities.

Trilling, Lionel (1905-75) US literary critic. In *The Liberal Imagination* (1950), *Sincerity and Authenticity* (1974), and other works, he expressed a moral concern with all aspects of modern culture. His novel *The Middle of the Journey* (1947) is concerned with moral and political issues of the 1930s and 1940s.

trilobite An extinct marine *arthropod belonging to a subphylum (*Trilobita*; over 4000 species) that flourished between Cambrian and Permian times, i.e. 500-200 million years ago. Trilobite ⌐fossils are abundant in rocks of this period. Its flattened oval body, 10-675 mm long, was divided by two longitudinal furrows into three lobes. The head bore a pair of antennae and usually a pair of compound eyes and each segment of the thorax and tail region carried a pair of forked appendages. Many trilobites burrowed in sand or mud, preying on other animals or scavenging.

trimaran A modern sailing vessel with three parallel hulls, a larger central one and two smaller ones used as stabilizers or outriggers. Trimarans are usually rigged as sloops. It is modelled on the outrigger canoe, or **proa**, of the SW Pacific. *See also* catamaran.

Trimurti The Hindu triad of gods, *Brahma, *Vishnu, and *Shiva, representing the creative, sustaining, and destructive aspects of reality respectively, sometimes portrayed as one body with three heads.

Trincomalee 8 34N 81 13E A seaport in NE Sri Lanka. It has an excellent natural harbour and was much fought over in colonial times. It was a major British base in World War II. Population (1981): 44 913.

Trinidad and Tobago, Republic of A country off the N coast of South America, consisting of the islands of Trinidad and Tobago. Both are hilly and wooded. Most of the population is of African and East Indian descent. *Economy*: oil and asphalt have replaced cocoa and sugar as the main source of the country's wealth and reserves of offshore gas have also been discovered. Other industrial developments include aluminium smelting, plastics, electronics, iron and steel, and petrochemicals. Tourism is a growing industry. It is a member of CARICOM. *History*: Trinidad was inhabited

by Arawak and Carib Indians when it was discovered by Columbus in 1498. It was a Spanish colony from the 16th century until 1802, when it was ceded to Britain; it joined with Tobago in 1809. During World War II bases were leased to the USA but most have since been given up. The country was a member of the short-lived Federation of the West Indies from 1958 to 1961 and became an independent state within the British Commonwealth in 1962. In 1970 there was considerable unrest, partly because of the Black Power movement. In 1976 it became a republic with the former governor general, Ellis Clarke (1917-), as its first president; in 1987 Noor Mohammed Hassandi succeeded him. Official language: English. Official currency: Trinidad and Tobago dollar of 100 cents. Area: 5128 sq km (1980 sq mi). Population (1983 est): 1 211 000. Capital and main port: Port-of-Spain.

Trinity, the A central doctrine of Christian theology, stating that God is one substance but with three distinct, coequal, and coeternal "persons," the Father, the Son, and the *Holy Spirit. The belief is based on a number of passages in the New Testament. It was given a first formal definition by the Council of *Nicaea (325), which asserted that the Son was "of the same essence (*homoousios*) as the Father." In the West, St Augustine and St Thomas Aquinas developed the doctrine. The Eastern Church rejects the so-called "double procession" of the Holy Spirit from the Father and the Son, which is accepted by the Western Church (*see* Filioque).

Trinity House, Corporation of The UK marine authority, responsible for the maintenance of lighthouses and the granting of pilots' licences. It also has a charitable function relieving distressed mariners and their dependants.

triode. *See* thermionic valve.

Triple Alliance (1882) An alliance between Germany, Austria-Hungary, and Italy, which with the opposing *Triple Entente shaped European diplomacy in the decades before World War I. At the outbreak of war (1914) Italy declared its neutrality, thus breaking the alliance.

Triple Alliance, War of the (*or* Paraguayan War; 1865-70) The war between Paraguay and a coalition of Argentina, Brazil, and Uruguay. Conflict was precipitated by the belligerent diplomacy of Paraguay's dictator, F. S. *López, towards Argentina, which with Brazil and Uruguay invaded Paraguay. López refused to surrender and following the capture of Asunción in 1868 waged a guerrilla war in the N until taken prisoner in 1870. The war shattered the economy of Paraguay, which lost about half its population.

Triple Crown The three major races for three-year-old horses in the USA: the Kentucky Derby, the Preakness Stakes, and the Belmont Stakes.

Triple Entente An informal combination of France, Russia, and Britain resulting from the Franco-Russian alliance (1893), the Franco-British *Entente Cordiale (1904), and the Anglo-Russian agreement (1907). It was formed in opposition to the *Triple Alliance.

triple jump (former name: hop, step, and jump) A field event for men in athletics, similar to the *long jump but executed as a continuous series of three jumps. The jumper lands first on the takeoff foot and then on the other, which becomes the takeoff foot for the final jump. World record: 17.97 m (1985) Willie Banks (USA).

Tripoli (Arabic name: Tarabulus) 32 58N 13 12E The capital and main port of Libya, on the Mediterranean Sea. Originally founded as Oea by the Phoenicians, it has come under the rule of many different countries through the ages. It became the capital of Libya on independence in 1951. Its notable buildings include a Spanish fortress and it has a university (1973). Exports include fruit and olive oil and it is a transshipment centre. Population (1982): 980 000.

Tripoli (Arabic name: Tarabalus) 34 27N 35 50E A port in NW Lebanon, on the Mediterranean Sea. It was the capital of a Phoenician federation of three other cities (hence its name, from Greek *tripolis*). Iraqi oil is brought by pipeline to the refinery here. The city was heavily damaged in 1983 in fighting between Syrian and Palestine Liberation Organization forces. Population (1982 est): 180 000.

Tripolitania A region of N Africa, between Tunisia and Cyrenaica. Colonized in the 7th century BC by the Phoenicians, who founded three cities, including Tripoli, the coast was controlled by a succession of foreign powers, including Romans, Arabs, Ottoman Turks, and Italians, while the nomadic Berbers of the interior remained generally unaffected. Since 1951 Tripolitania has been part of Libya.

Tripura A state in NE India, in tropical jungle and plains E of Bangladesh. Rice, jute, tea, and bamboo are produced. Local cottage industries are flourishing. *History*: the Moguls ended 1000 years of Hindu monarchy (18th century) before Britain won Tripura. In 1949 it entered the Indian Union. Area: 10 477 sq km (4044 sq mi). Population (1981): 2 060 189. Capital: Agartala.

tri-ratna (Sanskrit: three jewels) In Buddhism, the *Buddha, *Dharma, and *sangha, that is, the spiritual ideal, the truth regarding the means to its attainment, and the monastic order of those who strive towards it.

trireme. *See* ships.

Tristan The tragic hero of several medieval romances. After accidentally drinking a magic love potion, he becomes the lover of Iseult (Isolde), who is betrothed to his uncle, King Mark of Cornwall. He later renounces Iseult and goes to Brittany, where he marries the duke's daughter. Dying from a wound, he sends a ship to bring back Iseult to nurse him. By his wife's treachery, she arrives too late and dies of grief at his side. Of Celtic origin, the legend appeared in a French poem, written in about 1150 (now lost). Other old versions include one by an Anglo-Norman poet, Thomas, and *Gottfried von Strassburg's *Tristan und Isolde*, the source of Wagner's opera. In a 13th-century prose romance the story was incorporated into the *Arthurian legend.

Tristan da Cunha 37 15S 12 30W A group of four small islands in the S Atlantic Ocean, a dependency of St Helena. The only settlement, Edinburgh, which is on Tristan (the largest island), grew from a British garrison (established 1816). Situated on the main sailing route, it originally flourished but became isolated when steam replaced sail. In 1961 the inhabitants were evacuated to the UK to escape a volcanic eruption but most chose to return in 1963. The economy is based on crawfish canning and postage stamps. Area: about 100 sq km (40 sq mi). Population (1980): 323.

tritium (T *or* ^{3}H) A radioactive isotope of hydrogen, the nucleus of which contains one *proton and two *neutrons. It does not occur naturally but is produced in nuclear reactors and is used as a radioactive tracer and in nuclear weapons. Tritium decays with a half-life of 12.3 years, emitting beta-rays.

Triton In Greek mythology, a sea deity, the son of Poseidon and Amphitrite. He is usually portrayed as human above the waist and as a dolphin below; he blows a shell in order to control the waves.

triton shell A *gastropod mollusc of the family Cymatiidae (about 100 species), occurring mainly in tropical seas. Triton trumpets (genus Charonia) grow to 40 cm and have ribbed shells, often with prominent knobs. They are carnivorous, feeding on molluscs and echinoderms. Hairy tritons have a rough hairy shell.

triumvirate In Roman affairs, a board of three men officially appointed for special administrative duties. The so-called first Triumvirate (60 BC) of Caesar, Pompey, and Crassus was merely a private arrangement for mutual convenience. The triumvirate, or triple dictatorship, of Mark Antony, Lepidus, and Octavian was unique; appointed in 43 BC to maintain public order in Rome, they held office with absolute powers until Lepidus was ousted in 36 and power was divided between Mark Antony and Octavian.

Trivandrum 8 41N 76 57E A city in India, the capital of Kerala. A cultural, commercial, and communications centre, it processes minerals and is the site of the University of Kerala (1937). Population (1981): 520 000.

Trnova. *See* Tŭrnovo.

Trobriand Islands A group of coral islands in the SW Pacific Ocean, in Papua New Guinea. The largest is Kiriwana (Trobriand). It produces yams, mother-of-pearl, and trepang (edible sea cucumber). The islands became famous through the studies of the anthropologist, Bronisław Malinowski. Area: about 440 sq km (170 sq mi).

trogon An insectivorous bird belonging to a family (*Trogonidae*; 35 species) occurring in forested regions of Africa, Asia, and America. 24-46 cm long, trogons have iridescent plumage, which in males is usually dark with a bright red or yellow belly. They have rounded wings, a short curved bill, and a long tail and are the sole family of the order *Trogoniformes*. See also quetzal.

Troilus In Greek mythology, a son of King Priam of Troy who was killed by Achilles. The story of his love for Cressida, who deserted him for the Greek Diomedes, first appeared in the *Roman de Troie* by the 12th-century French poet Benoît de Sainte-Maure.

Trois-Rivières 46 21N 72 34W A city and deepwater port in E Canada, in Quebec on the St Lawrence River. Founded in 1610, it is a transport and industrial centre, producing a large proportion of the world's newsprint. Population (1981): 50 466.

Trojan group *Minor planets that lie close to either of two points in Jupiter's orbit. Each point forms an equilateral triangle with Jupiter and the sun.

Trojan Horse In Greek legend, a gigantic hollow wooden horse devised by Odysseus or by its builder, Epeius, in the *Trojan War. The Trojans hauled it inside their city, believing it to be a gift to Athena, and Greek warriors then emerged from it to open the gates to their army.

Trojan War In Greek legend, a ten years' war waged by the Greeks against *Troy after the abduction of *Helen, wife of King Menelaus of Sparta, by Paris, a Trojan prince. Its history, probably based on an actual war fought in the 12th century BC, is related in Homer's *Iliad*. The Greeks were led by *Agamemnon and their champions included *Achilles, *Diomedes, and *Odysseus. The chief Trojan warriors were *Hector and *Paris, sons of King Priam. Most of the action in the *Iliad* is concentrated in the final year of the war and culminates in the capture of Troy by the stratagem of the *Trojan Horse.

troll In Scandinavian folklore, originally a gigantic ogre-like creature imagined as guarding treasure, inhabiting a castle, and stalking through the forest only at night since they are destroyed or turned to stone if they see the sun. In later folklore, trolls were conceived as dwarflike cave- and mountain-dwellers who were skilled craftsmen.

Trollope, Anthony (1815-82) British novelist. He worked for the General Post Office from 1834 until he retired in 1867. He established his reputation with a series of novels set in the imaginary county of Barsetshire with a cast of predominantly clerical characters. These books include *The Warden* (1855), *Barchester Towers* (1857), and *The Last Chronicle of Barset* (1867). A second series of novels, set against a political background, includes *Phineas Finn* (1869) and *The Eustace Diamonds* (1873).

trombone A brass musical instrument, consisting of a cylindrical tube, about 3 m (9 ft) long, turned back upon itself, a cup-shaped mouthpiece, and a flaring bell. By means of a slide that is used in seven positions and by varying lip pressure, seven different harmonic series can be produced, covering a chromatic range of almost three octaves above E below the bass stave in the tenor trombone. A bass instrument also exists. The trombone has been part of the symphony orchestra since the late 18th century and is frequently used in jazz. The old English name for the trombone was the **sackbut**.

Tromp, Maarten (Harpertszoon) (1598-1653) Dutch admiral. He defeated a numerically superior Spanish fleet at the battle of the Downs (1639). His encounter with the English (1652) began the first *Dutch War, during which he defeated the English off Dungeness (1652). He died in action. His son **Cornelis (Martenszoon) Tromp** (1629-91) was an admiral in the second and third *Dutch Wars and was briefly commander in chief of the Dutch fleet (1665), being replaced by de *Ruyter.

trompe l'oeil (French: fool the eye) A method of painting figures and objects to create the illusion that they are real rather than painted. The elaborate arches, vistas, doors, etc., painted on walls in Pompeii are an example of this visual trickery. It is also associated with Italian *baroque art.

Tromsø 69 42N 19 00E A seaport in N Norway, on an island just off the mainland. The largest town N of the Arctic Circle, its industries include fishing, sealing, and fish processing. Its university was established in 1968. Population (1984): 47 406.

Trondheim 63 36N 10 23E A city and seaport in W Norway on Trondheim Fjord. It has a famous cathedral (12th-14th centuries) where Norwegian sovereigns have been crowned since early times. The Technical University of Norway was established here in 1900 and the University of Trondheim in 1968. Its industries include shipbuilding and fishing; the main exports are timber, wood pulp, fish, and metal goods. Population (1981 est): 134 976.

TROUBADOURS *Minstrels depicted on a 14th-century French ivory bas-relief.*

trooping the Colour Traditionally, the parade of the British sovereign's flag, or Colour, displayed so that foreign mercenaries would recognize it in battle. It is now a military parade held on the Horse Guards parade ground in Whitehall, London, on the sovereign's official birthday.

tropic bird A white seabird belonging to a family (*Phaethontidae*; 3 species) occurring in tropical and sub-tropical waters. Tropic birds have black eye and wing markings and are up to 50 cm long excluding the long streamer-like tail feathers. Tropic birds spend most of their lives at sea. Order: *Pelecaniformes* (cormorants, pelicans, etc.).

tropics The area of the earth's surface lying roughly between the Tropic of Cancer on the 23°30′N parallel of latitude and the Tropic of Capricorn on the 23°30′S parallel.

tropism The growth of a plant or sedentary animal in response to a directional external stimulus: a growth movement towards the stimulus is a positive tropism; the

opposite response is a negative tropism. Different forms of tropism are named according to the type of stimulus. For example, positive **hydrotropism** is growth towards water, observed in plant roots; negative **geotropism** is growth away from the pull of gravity, which occurs in plant stems.

troposphere. *See* atmosphere.

Trossachs, the 56 13N 4 23W A picturesque glen in central Scotland, in the Central Region between Loch Katrine and Loch Achray. It was popularized by Sir Walter Scott in his poem *The Lady of the Lake*.

Trotsky, Leon (Lev Bronstein; 1879-1940) Russian revolutionary and Marxist theorist. Trotsky became a Marxist in the 1890s and was imprisoned and exiled for participating in revolutionary activities. He lived in W Europe from 1902 until the Revolution of 1905. Again imprisoned and exiled, he escaped abroad (1907), where he remained until 1917. On the outbreak of the Russian Revolution, he returned to Russia and abandoned his previous *Menshevik loyalities to become a *Bolshevik. He played a major role in the October Revolution, which brought the Bolsheviks to power, and as war commissar during the civil war (1918-20) directed the Red Army to victory. Under Lenin, Trotsky was Russia's second most powerful man but lost to Stalin the power struggle that followed Lenin's death and was banished from the Soviet Union. He moved eventually to Mexico, where he was murdered, probably by a Soviet agent. *See also* Trotskyism.

Trotskyism The form of Marxism developed by Leon *Trotsky, who advocated world revolution in opposition to the view that socialism could be achieved in one country in isolation. Stalin sought to secure the Soviet Union against the counter-revolutionary forces of capitalism, primarily by military and economic means. Trotskyists believed that the revolution could only be maintained and capitalism defeated by developing the strength and solidarity of the working class throughout the world, since the main struggle was against the capitalist class and not between states. To this end Trotsky and his supporters founded the Fourth International in 1937, after what they saw as the degeneration of the Third International under the influence of Stalinism. Despite Trotsky's murder in 1940 and various subsequent internal splits, in 1979 the Fourth International had functioning sections in over 60 countries. These and other revolutionary groups with Trotskyist aims are regarded as dangerous and counter-revolutionary by the leaders of the Soviet Union and other communist states.

troubadours Provençal poets of the 12th to 14th centuries whose lyric poetry had a profound influence on both the subject matter and form of subsequent European verse. A number of the troubadours were of noble birth and were enthusiastically patronized by several European courts. Both poets and composers, the troubadours wrote songs introducing a new concept of love, later labelled *courtly love (although they were also noted for their satires and poems on political subjects). They developed several poetic genres and verse forms, including the *canso d'amor* (a love song in five or six stanzas), the *pastorela* (a narrative relating a meeting between a knight and a shepherdess), the *alba* (a song of lovers parting at dawn), the *tenso* or *partimen* (a debate on love), and the *sestina* (a poem of six stanzas with the same end-words repeated in each stanza according to a shifting pattern). The earliest troubadour was Guillaume, 9th Duc d'Aquitaine (1071-1127). Other famous troubadours were Marcabru (mid-12th century); Bertrand de Born, Vicomte de Hautefort (c. 1140-c. 1207), whose patron was Henry Curtmantle, son of Henry II of England and whom Dante places in hell in the *Inferno* for sowing political discord; Arnaut Daniel (c. 1180), who was credited with inventing the *sestina* and was considered the greatest craftsman by Dante; and Bernard de Ventadour (late 12th century), in whose lyrics the conventions of courtly love were most clearly developed. *See also* trouvères.

Troubles, Council of. *See* Blood, Council of.

trout One of several predatory fish belonging to the family *Salmonidae*, especially the genus *Salmo*, that are native to the N hemisphere but introduced elsewhere as food and game fish. It has a stout body with a blunt head and varies in colour from blackish to light olive with characteristic black or red spots or X-shaped markings. Trout occur mainly in fresh water but in some cases the young migrate to the sea to mature and return annually to streams to spawn. The common European brown trout (*S. trutta*), up to 140 cm long, has a migratory variety called the sea trout. The North American rainbow trout (*S. gairdneri*), up to 70 cm long, is distinguished by a broad purple band along its sides. Order: *Salmoniformes*.

trouvères Medieval poets of N France, especially Picardy, who were contemporary with, and influenced in subject matter and style by, the *troubadours. Notable trouvères include Conon de Béthune (d. 1224), Thibaud (IV) of Champagne, King of Navarre (d. 1253), *Adam de la Halle, and Rutebeuf (13th century).

Trowbridge 51 20N 2 13W A market town in S England, the administrative centre of Wiltshire. It has woollen manufacturing, bacon and ham curing, and brewing industries. Population (1981): 22 984.

Troy An ancient city in Asia Minor, near the Dardanelles. According to legend, when the Trojan prince *Paris abducted *Helen, her husband's brother, *Agamemnon, led a Greek force to recover her, captured Troy by the stratagem of the wooden horse after ten years' fighting, and destroyed it (traditional date: 1184 BC). ⌐Schliemann's excavations (1870) identified Troy at Hissarlik. Excavations have revealed nine superimposed cities, the seventh of which (not the second, as Schliemann thought) was contemporary with the legendary siege and had met a violent end. *See also* Homer; Trojan War.

Troyes 48 18N 4 05E A town in NE France, the capital of the Aube department on the River Seine. The capital of the old province of Champagne, it has a cathedral (13th–16th centuries) and many fine churches. Manufactures textiles, machinery, and food products. Population (1982): 64 769.

Trudeau, Pierre Elliott (1919–) Canadian statesman; Liberal prime minister (1968–79, 1980–84). A French Canadian, he nevertheless opposed French separatism and in 1970 briefly introduced martial law to deal with separatist agitation in Quebec. In the same year his government recognized the People's Republic of China. Trudeau's dashing image was reinforced by his young wife, Margaret Trudeau, but the couple finally separated in 1977 after a series of much publicized estrangements. Defeated in 1979 by Joseph *Clark, he was re-elected in 1980. He retired from office in 1984, and his Liberal party lost the subsequent general election.

Trueman, Freddy (Frederick Sewards T.; 1931–) British cricketer, who played for Yorkshire and England. A great fast bowler, he was the first bowler to take 300 Test wickets.

Truffaut, François (1932–84) French film director. He wrote for the magazine *Cahiers du Cinéma* during the 1950s and was an influential member of the *New Wave. His films, noted for their visual charm and elegance, include *Les Quatre Cents Coups* (1959), *Shoot the Pianist* (1960), *Jules et Jim* (1961), *L'Enfant sauvage* (1970), *Day for Night* (1973), *L'Histoire d'Adèle H.* (1975), *Love on the Run* (1978), and *Le Dernier Métro* (1980).

truffle A fungus belonging to the order *Tuberales*. Up to 10 cm across, truffles are rounded and occur in chalky soils, usually in association with tree roots. Having a strong smell and taste, they are unearthed and eaten by squirrels, rabbits, etc., which disperse the spores in their faeces. Several species are regarded as delicacies, including the black Périgord truffle (*Tuber melanosporum*) and the white Piedmont truffle (*T.*

magnatum), both of France. They are collected in oak woods using trained pigs or dogs. The bluish-black English truffle (*T. aestivum*) is found mainly in beech woods. Class: *Ascomycetes*.

Trujillo 8 06S 79 00W A city in Peru, situated 13 km (8 mi) from its port, Salaverry, on the Pacific coast. Founded in 1535, it has a university (established in 1824 by Simón Bolívar). Trujillo is the commercial centre for an area producing sugar cane and rice. Population (1981): 354 557.

Trujillo (Molina), Rafael (Leónidas) (1891–1961) Dominican dictator, who governed the Dominican Republic, directly or indirectly, from 1938 to 1961, aided by a powerful police force. His tyranny led to his assassination.

Truman, Harry S. (1884–1972) US statesman; Democratic president (1945–53). He became president on the death in office of F. D. Roosevelt and one of his earliest acts was to order the atomic bombing of Hiroshima and Nagasaki to end the war with Japan. In the **Truman Doctrine** he announced economic and military aid to countries threatened by interference from other states. His administration introduced the *Marshall Plan of postwar economic aid to Europe (1948) and saw the establishment of the *North Atlantic Treaty Organization (1949). In domestic politics his *Fair Deal programme promised social reform.

trumpet A brass ⌐musical instrument. The modern trumpet consists of a cylindrical tube, 1.5 m (5 ft) long, turned back on itself, a cup-shaped mouthpiece, and a flaring bell. Three valves alter the effective length of the tube, allowing the notes of the harmonic series on six successive semitones to be played. With varying lip pressure the B flat trumpet has a chromatic range of two and a half octaves below E below middle C. The early trumpet (from the Renaissance to the early 19th century) could only produce the notes of its natural harmonic series. The upper notes of the series were known as the *clarino* (Italian: clarinet) register, used for brilliant effects by such composers as Bach.

trumpet creeper A vine of the genus *Campsis*. The American trumpet creeper (*C. radicans*) is native to the S USA and the Chinese trumpet creeper (*C. grandiflora*) is of Asian origin. Both produce trumpet-shaped orange flowers and are cultivated as ornamentals. Family: *Bignoniaceae*.

trumpeter A long-legged ground-dwelling bird belonging to a family (*Psophiidae*; 3 species) occurring in forests of N South America. 50 cm long, trumpeters have a small head, soft dark plumage, and short bills, feeding on insects and berries. They travel in small flocks and have a loud trumpeting call. Order: *Gruiformes* (cranes, rails, etc.).

trunkfish A tropical fish, also called boxfish or cowfish, belonging to a family (*Ostraciidae*) related to *puffers, that occurs in the Atlantic and Pacific Oceans. Its body is often brightly coloured and encased in a boxlike shell of fused bony plates with spaces for the fins, etc.

Truro 50 16N 5 03W A cathedral city in SW England, the administrative centre of Cornwall. It is a small port and market town, with pottery and biscuit manufacturing. The cathedral was begun in 1880. Population (1981): 16 277.

trust In law, a binding arrangement between two persons (or groups) in which one (the trustee, who may be an individual or a corporation) has control of property (the trust property), which he administers for the benefit of the other (the beneficiary). The trustee may himself be one of the beneficiaries. Trusts developed in the middle ages when certain parties, such as religious orders, had the use or benefit of property that they were not allowed to own. Such rights were enforced by the Court of *Chancery but not recognized by the common law courts (*see* equity). Trusts are of two types: (1) **express trusts** are intentionally created in clear words, as in a will or deed; and (2) **implied** (*or* constructive) **trusts**, as when a court may rule that as a matter of equity the legal owner of a property should be compelled to hold it as a trustee for another. The powers

1235

and duties of trustees are strictly defined and are contained mainly in the Trustee Act (1925). On the death of a trustee, trust property is exempt from taxation provided the deceased was not in any way a beneficiary of the trust. *See also* investment company; unit trust.

trust territory A territory being prepared for self-government, for which the UN is responsible. There is now only one—Micronesia. The trust territories replaced the *mandates of the League of Nations.

trypanosomiasis Any infection caused by parasitic protozoa of the genus *Trypanosoma*. In Africa the parasite is transmitted by the tsetse fly and causes *sleeping sickness. In South America another species is transmitted by a bug and causes *Chagas' disease.

trypsin A digestive enzyme, secreted by the pancreas, that breaks down dietary proteins in the small intestine. It is secreted in an inactive form, which is converted to trypsin by the enzyme enterokinase in the intestine.

Ts'ao Chan. *See* Cao Chan.

tsar The title (derived from the Latin, Caesar) of the rulers of Russia from 1547 to 1721. It was first adopted by Ivan the Terrible and, though commonly used until 1917, was officially replaced with the title Emperor by Peter the Great.

Tsaritsyn. *See* Volgograd.

Tselinograd (name until 1961: Akmolinsk) 51 10N 71 28E A city in the Soviet Union, in the W Kazakh SSR. It produces agricultural machinery and is a railway junction. Population (1981 est): 241 000.

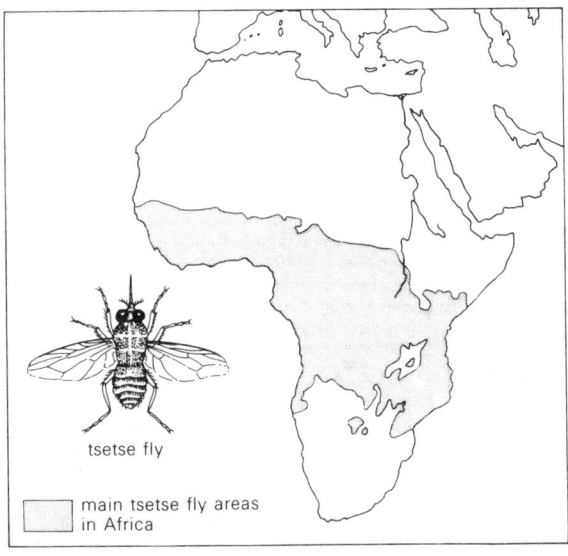

main tsetse fly areas in Africa

TSETSE FLY *Several species of tsetse fly carry the parasites causing sleeping sickness in man and cattle. The tsetse areas in Africa correspond to the areas where sleeping sickness is endemic.*

tsetse fly A fly, 6-16 mm long, belonging to a genus (*Glossina*; 22 species) restricted to tropical Africa. Both sexes bite and suck the blood of mammals, transmitting trypanosomes to man and domestic animals. Thus *G. palpalis* carries human sleeping sickness and *G. morsitans* transmits nagana in cattle. The larvae develop to maturity within the female before being deposited in the soil to pupate. Family: *Muscidae*.

Tshombe, Moise (Kapenda) (1919-69) Congolese statesman; prime minister (1964-65) of the Congo (now Zaïre). He led the secession of the copper-rich Katanga (now Shaba) province of the Congo in 1960, which for three years maintained its independence under Tshombe's presidency.

On its collapse Tshombe fled to Spain but was recalled briefly to become the Congo's prime minister. Dismissed by President Kasavubu in 1965, he returned to Spain and died of a heart attack in Algeria.

Tsinan. *See* Jinan.

Tsinghai. *See* Qinghai.

Tsingtao. *See* Qingdao.

Tsiolkovski, Konstantin Eduardovich (1857-1935) Russian aeronautical engineer, who pioneered space and rocket research. Becoming deaf as a child he studied mathematics and physics. In 1892 he built the first wind tunnel in Russia, which he used for testing his designs of dirigibles. He then went on to investigate the use of rockets in space travel and anticipated many of the ideas that Robert *Goddard was later to develop, especially liquid-fuelled rockets.

Tsushima A group of five Japanese islands, in the Korea Strait. During the Russo-Japanese War, Russia suffered a major naval defeat near here (1905). Fishing is the chief industry. Area: 698 sq km (269 sq mi). Population (1980): 50 810. Capital: Izuhara.

Tsvetaeva, Marina (1892-1941) Russian poet. Her highly original and emotionally powerful poetry was praised by Akhmatova, Pasternak, and other contemporaries. She opposed the Revolution and left Russia in 1922 to live in Prague, Berlin, and Paris. In 1939 she followed her husband back to Russia. He was shot, and she later committed suicide.

Tuamotu Archipelago A chain of about 80 coral atolls in the S Pacific Ocean, in French Polynesia. Rangiroa is the largest island and Fakarava, the most important economically. French nuclear tests were held here during the 1960s. Mother-of-pearl, phosphate, and copra are produced. Area: 860 sq km (332 sq mi). Population (1983): 11 793. Administrative centre: Apataki atoll.

tuatara A lizard-like reptile, *Sphenodon punctatus*, that is the only living representative of the primitive order *Rhynchocephalia*, which lived 200 million years ago. It is found only on islands off the North Island of New Zealand and has a brown-black to greenish body with a crest of spines running from head to tail; up to 70 cm long, it may live 100 years. Tuataras live in burrows during the day and emerge at night to feed on spiders, insects, and birds' eggs. The clutch of 8-14 eggs is incubated for 13-14 months before hatching.

Tuatha Dé Danann (Old Irish: people of the goddess *Danu) In Old Irish mythology, a divine race, one of the several mythological groups believed to have invaded and settled in Ireland. According to the *Book of Invasions*, they came from the east in the mid-15th century BC and were learned in science and the arts of the Druids. Sometimes they are portrayed as mortal men but exceptionally strong, beautiful, learned, etc.

tuba A valved brass instrument with a conical bore and low pitch, derived originally from the *saxhorn. Various types of tuba exist under a variety of names; the instrument is used in the symphony orchestra as well as in the military band. The **Wagner tuba** is not a true tuba but a bass version of the *French horn.

tuber A swollen underground plant stem in which carbohydrates (often in the form of starch) are stored. Some tubers, for example potatoes and yams, are important human foods. Tuber-bearing plants may reproduce vegetatively from buds on the tuber, and tuber crops are usually grown from tubers rather than seed.

tuberculin A protein derived from tuberculosis bacilli that have been killed. In the Mantoux test tuberculin is injected into the skin to test whether a person has been in contact with tuberculosis. The appearance of an inflamed patch (a positive reaction) indicates previous exposure to the bacilli (and therefore some immunity) but not necessarily active infection.

tuberculosis An infectious disease caused by the bacillus

Mycobacterium tuberculosis (which was first recognized by Robert *Koch in 1882). In pulmonary tuberculosis the bacillus is inhaled into the lungs, where it forms a primary tubercle that usually heals without trouble. Alternatively the disease may smoulder for months without showing any symptoms: affected people can act as carriers without being aware that they are infected. Reactivation of the primary disease, or reinfection, may lead to active tuberculosis ("consumption"), characterized by a cough (often producing some blood), fever, lassitude, weight loss, and breathlessness. The infection may also spread to other organs. The TB bacillus can also enter the body through drinking infected cows' milk, setting up a primary tubercle in the abdominal lymph nodes. Improved environmental conditions, pasteurization of milk, X-ray screening, and *BCG vaccinations have all reduced the incidence of TB in developed countries. Treatment consists of rest, isolation, and such antibiotics as streptomycin, isoniazid (INH), and para-aminosalicylic acid (PAS).

tuberose A perennial summer-flowering garden plant, *Polianthes tuberosa*, native to SW North America. It has tuberous roots, long narrow bright-green leaves clustered at the base of the stem, and smaller clasping leaves along the stem. Its fragrant waxy-white flowers are arranged in pairs on a terminal spike and are used to manufacture perfume. Family: *Amaryllidaceae.*

tubifex A freshwater *annelid worm, also called bloodworm, belonging to the widely distributed family *Tubificidae*. Found along muddy rivers and estuaries, the most common species is the bright-red extremely active *Tubifex tubifex*, up to 85 mm long. Class: *Oligochaeta.*

Tübingen 48 32N 9 04E A town in SW West Germany, in Baden-Württemberg on the River Neckar. The university (1477) is famed for its theological faculty established in the 19th century. Industries include publishing and textile manufacture. Population (1985 est): 70 000.

Tubman, William V(acanarat) S(hadrach) (1895–1971) Liberian statesman; president (1943–71). A barrister and Methodist lay preacher, he was largely responsible for welding together into a modern nation state the peoples of diverse origins in Liberia and passed much social and political reform.,

Tubuai Islands (*or* Austral Is) 23 23S 149 27W A group of seven islands in S French Polynesia, including Tubuai and Rurutu. Coffee, copra, and arrowroot are produced. Area: 173 sq km (67 sq mi). Population (1983): 6283.

tubular bells A tuned percussion instrument consisting of a row of metal tubes, graduated in length, hung on a frame and struck with a leather-covered hammer.

TUC. *See* trade union.

Tucson 32 15N 110 57W A city and health resort in the USA, in Arizona. Its growth came with the arrival of the Southern Pacific Railroad (1880) and the discovery of silver at nearby Tombstone. Tucson is an industrial centre for the surrounding agricultural and mining district and site of the University of Arizona (1885). Population (1980): 330 537.

Tucumán. *See* San Miguel de Tucumán.

Tudors The ruling dynasty of England from 1485 to 1603. Owen Tudor (c. 1400–61), a Welshman, entered the service of Henry V and married (1422) his widow Catherine of Valois (1401–37). Their eldest son Edmund, Earl of Richmond (c. 1430–56), married Margaret *Beaufort, the great-great-granddaughter of Edward III, and their son became the first Tudor monarch, Henry VII. Subsequent Tudor monarchs were Henry VIII, Edward VI, Mary I, and Elizabeth I.

tuff. *See* pyroclastic rock.

Tu Fu. *See* Du Fu.

Tugela River A river in South Africa, flowing generally E from the Drakensberg Mountains, where it forms the Tugela

Falls, 856 m (2810 ft) high, to the Indian Ocean. Length: about 500 km (312 mi).

tui A black *honeyeater, *Prosthemadera novaeseelandiae*, occurring in mountain forests of New Zealand. It is about 27 cm long and has a white tufted throat. Once common, it has been extensively captured for its ability to mimic human speech and is now very rare.

Tula An ancient *Toltec city in central Mexico. Adopted as the Toltec capital around 980 AD, Tula was destroyed in 1168. Distinctive Toltec features here include a terraced pyramid, colonnaded buildings, and extensive use of militaristic motifs in relief sculptures.

Tula 54 11N 37 38E A city in the W central Soviet Union, in the RSFSR 169 km (105 mi) S of Moscow. An important ironworking centre since the 17th century, it also has food-processing industries. Tolstoy lived at nearby Yasnaya Polyana. Population (1981 est): 521 000.

tulip A perennial herbaceous plant of the genus *Tulipa* (about 100 species), native to the Old World but widely cultivated for ornament. Growing from bulbs, most tulips have a solitary bell-shaped flower, with bluish-green leaves—ranging from long and narrow to oval and pointed—clustered at the base of the plant. There are nearly 4000 varieties of garden tulips, which show enormous variation in colour and type: the older varieties are descended from *T. gesneriana* and *T. suaveolens*; the newer ones often have *T. kaufmanniana*, *T. greigi*, or *T. fosteriana* as one of the parent species. The Netherlands, the Channel Islands, and Lincolnshire (England) are main commercial growing areas. Family: *Liliaceae.*

tulip tree A tree, *Liriodendron tulipifera*, native to E North America and widely planted for ornament. Reaching a height of 58 m in the wild, it has three-lobed blunt-ended leaves, which turn golden yellow in autumn. The flowers are large and tulip-like, greenish white or yellow, and produce papery cones containing winged fruits. The wood, known as white wood, is used for furniture, plywood, paper, and boxes. The Chinese tulip tree (*L. chinense*) is similar but smaller. Family: *Magnoliaceae.*

Tull, Jethro (1674–1741) English agriculturalist, best known for his invention in 1701 of the seed drill. The drill planted seeds in straight lines, thus facilitating weeding, and automatically covered them with soil to protect them from birds. He made many other innovations in agricultural methods.

Tulsa 36 07N 95 58W A city in the USA, in Oklahoma on the Arkansas River. Oil was discovered in 1901 and today over 800 oil companies have established plants here. It has also developed as a port since the opening of a waterway (1971) linking Tulsa to the Gulf of Mexico. Population (1980): 360 919.

Tulsidas (c. 1532–1623) Indian poet. He was a brahmin and lived at Benares. His best-known work is the *Ramcaritmanas* (c. 1574–77), a Hindi version of a Sanskrit epic that advocates devotion to *Rama as a means of salvation. It had a lasting influence throughout N India.

Tulufan Depression (Turpan Depression *or* Turfan Depression) A mountain basin in NW China. Known for its fruit, it was the centre of an Indian-Persian civilization (3rd–4th centuries AD). Lowest point: 154 m (505 ft) below sea level.

tumour Any swelling in the body caused by the abnormal proliferation of cells. Tumours that do not spread to other parts of the body (i.e. are noncancerous) are described as benign. They are usually harmless but may become very large, exerting pressure on neighbouring tissues: in such cases they are often surgically removed. Tumours that destroy the tissue in which they arise and spread to other parts of the body are described as malignant (*see* cancer).

tuna A carnivorous food and game fish, sometimes called tunny, belonging to a family (*Scombridae*) found in warm seas. Its elongated robust body is generally dark above and silvery below, with a keeled tail base and finlets behind the anal and dorsal fins. The large bluefin tuna (*Thunnus thynnus*) reaches 4.3 m in length. Large quantities of tinned tuna are consumed throughout the world. Order: *Perciformes*. *See also* albacore; skipjack; yellowfin tuna. □oceans.

Tunbridge Wells (*or* Royal Tunbridge Wells) 51-08N 0 16E A town in SE England, in Kent. Visited for its medicinal waters since the 17th century, it became a fashionable health resort. It· is mainly residential. Population (1981): 44 821.

tundra The level, virtually treeless, areas in the N hemisphere (in Eurasia and North America) lying between the most northerly region in which trees grow and the polar regions of perpetual snow and ice. Winters are long and severe with brief summers in which temperatures remain below 10°C (50°F); *permafrost is a feature. Vegetation is able to grow in summer and includes mosses, lichens, dwarf shrubs, herbaceous perennials, and a few stunted trees, such as willows and birches. Through freeze-thaw processes on the ground a variety of patterns can form, such as stone polygons and soil circles.

T'ung-chih. See Tong Zhi.

tung oil (*or* wood oil) A pale-yellow oil obtained from the seeds of the tung tree (*Aleurites fordii*; family *Euphorbiaceae*), found in China. It polymerizes spontaneously (and on heating) to a hard gel and is used in paints and varnishes.

tungsten (*or* wolfram; W) A grey brittle metal with the highest melting point of any element. It was discovered in 1779 and is obtained from the ores wolframite ($FeWO_4$) and scheelite ($CaWO_4$) by reduction with hydrogen or carbon. It oxidizes readily when heated, forming the oxide WO_3. The metal is used extensively as filaments in electric light bulbs, as well as in television tubes, contact breakers, and X-ray tubes. It is also used in many hard alloys for high-speed cutting tools. Tungsten carbide (WC) is very hard and is used for tipping drill bits. At no 74; at wt 183.85; mp 3410 ± 20°C; bp 5660°C.

Tung-t'ing, Lake. *See* Dongting, Lake.

Tunguska, River Three rivers in the Soviet Union, in Siberia comprising tributaries of the River Yenisei. These are the **Lower** (Nizhnyaya) **Tunguska**, 2690 km (1670 mi) long, the **Stony** (Podkammenaya) **Tunguska**, 1550 km (960 mi) long, and the **Upper** (Verkhnyaya) **Tunguska**, the lower course of the River Angara.

tunicate A small marine animal belonging to the subphylum *Urochordata* (or *Tunicata*; about 2000 species). Tunicates are cylindrical, spherical, or irregular in shape, ranging from several millimetres to over 30 cm in size. They have a saclike cellulose tunic covering the body; water is drawn in through a siphon at the top and expelled through a second siphon. Food particles are filtered out and propelled along flagellated grooves to the mouth. Individuals are hermaphrodite and produce free-swimming tadpole-like larvae that show the major characteristics of all *Chordater. They subsequently undergo metamorphosis, losing their chordate features and becoming adults. The class *Larvacea* retain their larval characteristics throughout life. Sea squirts (class *Ascidacea*) live attached to rocks, etc., singly or in colonies, while the salps (class *Thaliacea*) float in the sea, sometimes as chains of several hundred individuals.

tuning fork A two-pronged metal fork that vibrates at a fixed frequency when struck. It is used by musicians to verify *pitch. Electrically maintained tuning forks, operated by an electromagnet, are also used in scientific experiments.

Tunis (Arabic name: Tunus) 36 48N 10 13E The capital of Tunisia, on the Gulf of Tunis. It was developed by the Arabs in the 7th century AD. It came under French rule in the late 19th century, and became the capital on independence in 1956. The Islamic university was founded in 1960. Indus-

tries include chemicals, lead smelting, and textiles. Population (1984): 556 654.

Tunisia, Republic of (Arabic name: al-Jumhuriyah at-Tunisiyah) A small country in N Africa, bordering on the Mediterranean Sea. Its narrow coastal zone, where over half the total population live, extends into desert in the S and rises to uplands in the N. The population is largely Arabic with a Berber minority. *Economy*: predominantly agricultural, the chief products include wheat, olive oil, citrus fruits, dates, and wine; livestock, including sheep, cattle, and goats, is also important. Mining is a major source of revenue and Tunisia is one of the world's largest producers of phosphates. Oil reserves were discovered in 1964 and exploitation began in 1972; iron ore and lead are also mined. Manufacturing industry is based largely on processing the local raw materials and includes oil refining, cement, and steel processing. Fine beaches and notable architecture contribute to Tunisia's popularity with tourists. *History*: first settled by the Phoenicians, it developed into the empire of Carthage and was later absorbed into the Roman Empire, becoming "the granary of Rome." Under the dynasty of the Berber Hafsids (1207-1574) it became powerful. During the 19th century Tunisia's strategic importance aroused European interest and in 1883 it became a French protectorate. It was the scene of fierce fighting in World War II and gained independence from France (1956) following nationalist agitation. President Habib *Bourguiba was replaced by Zine al-Abidine Ben Ali in a bloodless coup in 1987. Official religion: Islam. Official language: Arabic; French is widely spoken. Official currency: Tunisian dinar of 1000 millimes. Area: 164 150 sq km (63 362 sq mi). Population (1983 est): 7 020 000 Capital: Tunis.

tunnel effect The passage of an electron or other particle through a potential barrier when, according to classical mechanics, it has insufficient energy to do so. It is explained by *wave mechanics on the basis that the electron is not completely localized in space, part of the energy of the associated wave being able to tunnel through the barrier. The effect has a negligible probability in large-scale systems, but a finite probability in microscopic systems. It is the basis of some radioactive decay processes and is made use of in the **tunnel diode**, a semiconductor device that has a negative resistance over part of its operating range.

tunnels Underground passages for roads, railways, sewers, or aqueducts for power stations. Tunnels through rock are formed by first drilling holes for explosive, blasting out the rock, removing the debris, and then lining the inside of the tunnel. Tunnelling through softer substances requires special techniques: a tunnelling shield with a diameter slightly larger than that of the finished tunnel is forced into the ground by hydraulic piston jacks, the earth inside the shield is removed, and the tunnel is then lined, often with concrete sections. *See also* Channel tunnel; Simplon Pass; Mont Blanc.

Tunney, Gene (James Joseph T.; 1897-1978) US boxer, who was world heavyweight champion from 1926 to 1928, when he retired. He lost only 1 of his 77 professional bouts, in 1922.

tunny. *See* tuna.

Tupac Amarú (José Gabriel Condorcanqui; ?1742-81) Peruvian revolutionary. A direct descendant of the last Inca emperor, he led an unsuccessful Indian revolt against Spanish rule in 1780 and was executed. The Tupamaros, the 20th-century South American urban guerrillas, derived their name from his.

Tupi A group of South American Indian peoples and languages including the *Guarani. They are mainly a tropical rainforest people who practise slash and burn agriculture. They also fish in the rivers and off the coast where their villages are located. In some areas, these were fortified against warfare. Cannibalism was common. Culture varied considerably from one region to another. Religion emphasized nature spirits and the "Grandfather Cult," associated with thunder, often led to migrations in search of a promised paradise.

Tupolev, Andrei Niklaievich (1888–1972) Soviet designer of the first supersonic passenger aircraft, the TU-144, tested in 1969. He also designed supersonic bombers, such as the TU-22, and swing-wing bombers. His TU-104, first produced in 1955, was one of the first passenger jet aircraft.

IVAN TURGENEV

turaco (or touraco) A brightly coloured arboreal bird belonging to a family (*Musophagidae*; 18 species) occurring in Africa. 35–70 cm long, turacos have short rounded wings, a short down-curved bill, and are often crested. Most species have a greenish plumage. They feed on fruit and insects. Order: *Cuculiformes* (cuckoos and turacos).

turbine A device in which a moving fluid drives a wheel or motor, converting the kinetic energy of the fluid into mechanical energy. In its simplest form it is known as a **water wheel**, which has been in use since ancient times to drive mills, pumps, etc. The principle of the water wheel forms the basis of the hydraulic turbine, used in the generation of *hydroelectricity. The most widely used types are the Pelton wheel, patented in 1889 by Lester Allen Pelton (1829–1918), the radial Francis turbine, designed in 1849 by J. B. Francis (1815–92), and the Kaplan turbine, designed by Viktor Kaplan (1876–1937). The Pelton wheel, consisting of a ring of buckets or bucket-shaped vanes arranged around the periphery of a wheel, is known as an impulse turbine as it is only the impulse of the water that makes the wheel turn. The Francis turbine, with its outer ring of stationary guide vanes and inner ring of curved vanes on the surface of one side of the wheel, is a reaction turbine; part of the energy is derived from the impulse of the water and part from the reaction between the water and the blades. The steam-driven turbine was invented in the 1st century AD by *Hero of Alexandria. However, the first practical turbine to be driven by steam as a reaction device with several rows of turbine wheels (enabling the energy of the expanding steam to be utilized in stages) invented in 1884 by Sir Charles *Parsons. An impulse turbine using several steam nozzles was invented by Carl de Laval (1845–1913) in the 1890s. Since the beginning of the 20th century steam turbines based on these designs have replaced the *steam engine as the prime mover in *power stations. See also gas turbine.

turbot A *flatfish, *Scophthalmus maximus*, that occurs off European shores down to 70 m and sometimes in brackish

water. It has a broad circular body, up to 1 m long, which is usually light- or grey-brown on the upper (left) side and whitish underneath. It is a valuable food fish. Family: *Bothidae*.

turbulence Any random irregularity in the distribution of velocity or pressure in a fluid. Most flows of rivers and winds are turbulent and turbulence in the atmosphere affects aircraft. Turbulence also causes the laminar layers of flow around an irregular object, or a smooth object at high velocities, to be disturbed, creating a sharp increase in drag. It is to avoid turbulent flow that such objects as aerofoils are streamlined (see streamlining; aerodynamics). In some cases turbulence is desirable; in the combustion chamber of a petrol or Diesel engine the designer seeks to create turbulence to improve mixing of the fuel and air to improve combustion.

Turenne, Henri de la Tour d'Auvergne, Vicomte de (1611–75) French marshal, who made his name in the *Thirty Years' War. At the outbreak (1649) of the rebellion against Mazarin (see Fronde) he supported the rebels, who were led by his rival *Condé, but in 1652, after transferring his loyalties to the crown, he received a royal command and by 1653 had brilliantly suppressed the revolt. In 1658, at the battle of the Dunes, he again defeated Condé, who now held a Spanish command. He subsequently fought in the War of *Devolution (1667–68) and the third *Dutch War (1672–75), dying in action at Sasbach. He was much admired by Napoleon.

Turfan Depression. See Tulufan Depression.

Turgenev, Ivan (1818–83) Russian novelist. His criticism of the Russian social system in his *Sportsman's Sketches* (1852) led indirectly to his brief imprisonment and confinement to his family estate at Spasskoye. His later works, of which the best known are the novel *Fathers and Sons* (1862) and the long story *The Torrents of Spring* (1872), are noted for their analysis of intellectual and social trends. He also wrote poetry and plays, notably *A Month in the Country* (published 1870). A lifelong admirer of western society, he went into self-imposed exile in Baden Baden (1862–70) and Paris (1871–83), where he was befriended by many European writers.

Turgot, Anne Robert Jacques, Baron de l'Aulne (1727–81) French economist, who served under Louis XV and XVI. Educated at the Sorbonne, he was one of the *Physiocrats and an advocate of *laissez-faire. He became comptroller general in 1774. There was great opposition to his reforms, especially the Six Edicts, which included the abolition of forced labour, and he was dismissed in 1776.

Turin (Italian name: Torino) 45 04N 7 40E A city in NW Italy, the capital of Piedmont on the River Po. Dating from Roman times, it was associated with the House of Savoy during the middle ages. It was the first capital (1861–65) of united Italy. Turin has an ancient university (1404), a 15th-century cathedral, a 17th-century palace, and other notable buildings. It is a centre of commerce and industry and is important for the production of motor vehicles. Other industries include engineering, publishing, and the manufacture of textiles, paper, and leather goods. Chocolate and wine are also produced. Population (1980 est): 1 143 263.

Turing machine A hypothetical computing machine used to determine whether a particular type of mathematical problem can be solved by a computation procedure (algorithm). It is postulated that the machine has an infinite tape that stores characters in a number of discrete locations. The machine goes through a set procedure of scanning and altering the characters, regarded as a series of active states. If the problem is soluble, the machine finally settles in a passive state, in which the tape contains the solution. The concept was developed in 1936 by Alan Mathison Turing (1912–54) and others and represented an important advance in the theory of computer logic.

overshot water wheel   **undershot water wheel**   **Pelton wheel**

buckets   nozzle

water inlet

rotor

runner

vanes

guide vanes   water inlet

water inlet

blades

wheel

nozzle

steam jet   buckets

Francis turbine   **Kaplan turbine**   **De Laval's impulse steam turbine**

high-pressure turbine   intermediate-pressure turbine   low-pressure turbine

multistage steam turbine

TURBINE

Turishcheva, Ludmilla (1952–) Soviet gymnast, who was world champion in 1970 and European champion in 1971. In the 1972 Olympic Games she won the combined exercises competition and in the 1973 European championships she took all the gold medals on the apparatus. In the 1976 Olympics she won two silver medals and a bronze.

Turkana, Lake (name until 1979: Lake Rudolph) A lake in Kenya and Ethiopia. Fish and birds abound here and, since it has no outlet, it has become increasingly saline through evaporation. Significant fossil finds have been made here by Richard Leakey. Area: about 6405 sq km (2473 sq mi).

turkey A large terrestrial bird belonging to a family (*Meleagrididae*; 2 species) native to North and Central American woodlands. Wild turkeys reach 130 cm in length and have green-bronze plumage, a warty red neck, and a long fleshy bill ornament and throat wattle. They feed on seeds and insects. The common turkey (*Meleagra gallopavo*), first domesticated by Mexican Indians, was brought to Europe in the 16th century and is now farmed for its flesh. Order: *Galliformes* (pheasants, turkeys, etc.).

Turkey, Republic of A country in the Middle East. The

large Asian area, Anatolia, lies between the Mediterranean Sea and the Black Sea. The small European area, Thrace, is bordered by Greece and Bulgaria. Anatolia consists of a central plateau surrounded by mountains, the Pontic Mountains in the N and the *Taurus Mountains in the S. The plateau is semiarid and contains several shallow salt lakes. The high E range contains Mount *Ararat. The coastal areas are the most populous. Minority population groups include Kurds, Arabs, Greeks, Circassians, Georgians, Armenians, Lazes, and Jews; 98% of the population is Muslim. *Economy*: mainly agricultural. Wheat, barley, sugar beet, potatoes, and rice are grown in the interior, and cotton, tobacco, and citrus fruit are grown for export around the coast. Cattle, sheep, and goats are kept for skins, wool, and mohair, which are exported. Copper, chromium, borax, coal, bauxite, and oil are produced, although minerals are not greatly exploited. The main industries are steel, cement, textiles, and fertilizers. Machinery, chemicals, and metals are imported, chiefly from W Europe and the USA. Turkey is an associate member of the EEC. Many Turks work in Europe, mainly West Germany, for long periods at a time. *History*: Anatolia, formerly known as *Asia Minor, was dominated by the *Seljuqs

(1055–1243) and later became the core of the *Ottoman Empire (c. 1300–1922). Under Kemal *Atatürk, who ruled as a virtual dictator, the new Republic of Turkey (declared 1923) was rapidly westernized; religious orders were abolished and Islam was disestablished; polygamy was forbidden and women were enfranchised; the Arabic alphabet was replaced by the Roman; and relations with W Europe became closer. Economic problems were tackled by the establishment of new industries under state ownership. After the death of Kemal (1938) and World War II, in which Turkey was neutral until finally siding with the Allies in 1945, it became less stable politically, although more democratic. The Democratic Party, previously in opposition, came to power in 1950 but grew increasingly reactionary; unrest increased until a military coup took place in 1960. The army again intervened in 1971, when martial law was imposed (until 1973). Troubles between Kurds and Turks have led to the reimposition of martial law in several provinces in recent years. Economic difficulties continued during the 1970s with rapid inflation, a large trade deficit, and high unemployment. Relations with Greece have been a further problem; apart from rivalry over Cyprus, which almost resulted in war in 1974, when the island was invaded by Turkish troops, there has been friction since 1976 over Turkey's exploration for oil in the Aegean Sea. A military coup in 1980, led by Gen Kenan Evren (1913–), overthrew the government of Suleiman Demirel (1924–). Evren assumed the powers of head of state and a new constitution was introduced in 1982. Turgut Ozal (1927–) was elected prime minister in 1983. In 1987 Turkey began negotiations to join the EEC and the Western European Union. Official language: Turkish; Kurdish and Arabic are also spoken. Official currency: Turkish lira of 100 kurus. Area: 779 452 sq km (330 883 sq mi). Population (1980): 44 737 000. Capital: Ankara.

Turkic languages A group of languages of the *Altaic language family, related to *Mongolian and *Manchu-Tungus. Spoken by more than 66 million people, the languages are spread over a geographical area extending from Turkey to Siberia. Originally written in the Arabic script in the 9th century, the languages are now written in the *Cyrillic alphabet in the Soviet Union and in Latin script in Turkey. Phonological processes are characterized by vowel harmony and morphological processes by agglutination.

Turkish A *Turkic language, spoken mainly in Turkey. Since 1929 it has been written in a modified Latin alphabet, replacing Arabic script. Its grammatical system is based on the use of suffixes.

Turkish cat A breed of long-haired cat originating from Turkey. They have long sturdy bodies, chalk-white coats with auburn markings on the face and an auburn tail, and amber-coloured eyes. Unusually for cats, they are fond of swimming.

Turkistan (*or* Turkestan) A region of central Asia, now comprising the Xinjiang Uygur AR of the People's Republic of China and the Kazakh, Turkmen, Tadzhik, Kirghiz, and Uzbek SSRs of the Soviet Union. A historic route of travel, migration, and invasion between Asia and Europe, Turkistan has come under many different rulers. The W has been ruled by the Persians from the 6th century BC, Islam from the 7th century AD, and the Russians from the 18th century; the E was long disputed between Chinese dynasties and nomadic tribes.

Turkmen (*or* Turkoman) A people of SW Asia speaking a language that is part of the *Turkic language group. The majority live as settled farmers in the Turkmen SSR, but groups in Iran, Afghanistan, E Turkey, N Syria, and N Iraq retain their traditional nomadic existence. Rug making is still an important craft. Their main social division is between those engaged in agriculture and the more prestigious livestock farming. They are Sunni Muslims.

Turkmen Soviet Socialist Republic (*or* Turkmenistan) A constituent republic in the S Soviet Union. Some 90% of Turkmenistan comprises desert, including the *Kara Kum, and most of the population (66% of which comprises *Turkmen) are concentrated in oases. The principal occupation is agriculture, mainly cotton, wool, and Karakul pelts. Turkmenistan (founded in 1925) is rich in minerals and industry is being developed. Area: 488 100 sq km (186 400 sq mi). Population (1981 est): 2 900 000. Capital: Ashkhabad.

Turks and Caicos Islands A British crown colony consisting of a series of over 30 islands in the Atlantic Ocean, to the SE of the Bahamas. The most important are Grand Turk, Grand Caicos, and Salt Cay. Most of the inhabitants are of African descent. *Economy*: mainly based on fishing, with exports of conchs, conch shells, crawfish, salt, and fishmeal. Tourism is being developed. *History*: the islands were discovered by the Spanish in 1512, but remained uninhabited until 1678, when a Bermudan salt-panning industry was set up. A dependency of Jamaica (1874–1959), they became a crown colony after the dissolution of the Federation of the West Indies in 1962, and gained internal self-government in 1976. Allegations of corruption led to power being transferred to the governor and an advisory council in 1986. Official language: English. Official currency: US dollar of 100 cents. Area: 430 sq km (192 sq mi). Population (1980): 7436. Capital: Grand Turk.

Turku (Swedish name: Åbo) 60 27N 22 15E A seaport and third largest city in Finland, on the Gulf of Bothnia. Capital of Finland until 1812, it has Finnish (1920) and Swedish (1917) universities. Population (1980): 163 680.

turmeric A perennial herbaceous plant, *Curcuma longa*, native to S India and Indonesia and cultivated for its underground rhizomes. It has narrow leaves, 30–45 cm long, and bears yellow flowers in dense heads, 10–18 cm long. The rhizomes are boiled and dried in the sun for 5–7 days, then polished and usually sold in ground form. Turmeric is used as a spice and as a yellow dye. Family: *Zingiberaceae*.

Turner, Joseph Mallord William (1775–1851) British landscape and marine painter, born in London, the son of a

JOSEPH MALLORD WILLIAM TURNER *Chalk drawing made in 1842 by Charles Turner (1773–1857) the engraver (National Portrait Gallery).*

barber. After studying at the Royal Academy schools and painting many watercolours, he achieved success in the late 1790s with his landscapes in oil. In 1809 he made the first of several continental tours, which provided him with such scenic subjects as the Alps, Venice, and Rome. While supervising the publication of his *Liber Studiorium* (1807–19), a series of engravings based on his works, his style evolved from the Dutch landscape tradition and the classicism of the landscapists *Poussin and *Claude Lorraine into a romantic vision of colour, light, and weather anticipating French *impressionism. This vision becomes the subject of such late paintings as *Rain, Steam, and Speed* (National Gallery, London) and *Interior at Petworth* (Tate Gallery). He bequeathed most of his works to the nation.

Turner, Nat (1800–31) US rebel slave, who led the only substantial US slave revolt. The so-called **Turner's Insurrection** was an attempt by 75 slaves to capture a Virginian armoury. More than 50 whites died before the rebels were captured and executed. The resulting uneasiness in the South led to repressive antislave legislation.

turnip A biennial plant, *Brassica rapa*, probably native to Asia and widely cultivated for its thick fleshy root, which is used as a vegetable. An erect branching stem, up to 1 m high, grows out of the basal leaf rosette in the plant's second season and produces bright-yellow flowers. Turnips are usually harvested in the first season. Family: *Cruciferae*.

turnover tax A tax levied whenever goods are exchanged or services provided, according to the increased value of the goods or services at each stage. The consumer pays the accumulated tax. Value-added tax is an example.

turnstone A small *plover, *Arenaria interpres*, that breeds around Arctic coasts and migrates to the S hemisphere to winter. 20 cm long, it has a black-and-brown upper plumage, becoming tortoiseshell in summer, and white underparts. Turnstones have short black bills used to turn over pebbles and shells in search of molluscs, small fish, and sandhoppers.

turpentine An oily liquid extracted from pine resin. Its main constituent is pinene ($C_{10}H_{16}$); it is used as a solvent for paints.

turpentine tree One of several trees yielding a viscous resin. The Australian turpentine tree (*Syncarpia glomuliferae*) grows to about 45 m and has deeply furrowed bark. The timber, which is durable and resistant to fire and wood-boring *shipworms, is used to construct piers, ships, etc. The brush turpentine tree (*S. leptopetala*) is smaller. Family: *Myrtaceae*. The tropical African tree *Copaifera mopane* (family *Leguminosae*) is also called turpentine tree.

Turpin, Dick (1706–39) British highwayman. He was hanged at York for murder and horse stealing. The story of his ride from London to York on his horse Black Bess, popularized in Harrison Ainsworth's novel *Rookwood* (1834), is probably based on a much older legend.

turquoise An opaque greenish-blue mineral used as a gem. It consists of a basic aluminium phosphate, traces of copper providing the colour. Birthstone for December.

turtle An aquatic reptile belonging to the order *Chelonia, which also includes *tortoises and *terrapins. 10–200 cm long, turtles have broad paddle-like flippers and a streamlined shell and occur in most seas, often migrating long distances to lay eggs on traditional nesting beaches. They are graceful and swift swimmers but clumsy on land. Their diet consists of worms, snails, crustaceans, and fish. Some turtles live in fresh water. *See also* green turtle; leatherback turtle; snake-necked turtle; soft-shelled turtle.

turtle dove A small slender dove, *Streptopelia turtur*, occurring in S Europe and N Africa, visiting N Europe in the summer. 26 cm long, it has a chequered red-brown back, grey wings, a pink breast, a black-and-white striped neck patch, and a long white-tipped tail. It feeds on seeds. Family: *Columbidae* (pigeons).

Tuscan order. *See* orders of architecture.

Tuscany (Italian name: Toscana) A region in N central Italy, consisting mainly of hills and mountains with coastal lowlands in the W. It is a predominantly agricultural region producing cereals, wines (Chianti), olives, and fruit. The major manufacturing industries are iron, steel, and shipbuilding. Lignite, clay, mercury, salt, borax, and marble are mined. Florence is an important tourist and cultural centre. Area: 22 989 sq km (8876 sq mi). Population (1980 est): 3 602 684. Capital: Florence.

Tusculum An ancient city of central Italy, near modern Frascati. A rival of *Rome before about 480 BC but later a staunch ally, Tusculum was granted Roman citizenship in 381 BC. In the 1st century BC it became a fashionable resort: *Lucullus, *Maecenas, and *Cicero owned villas nearby.

tusk shell A marine *mollusc of the class *Scaphopoda* (about 200 species), also called tooth shell. The common tusk shell (*Dentalium entale*) grows to 5 cm; its shell is tusk-shaped and open at both ends and it lives partly buried in sand. The mollusc has a digging foot and tentacles around the mouth for collecting microscopic plants and animals.

Tussaud, Marie (Marie Grosholtz; 1761–1850) French wax modeller, who went to London in 1802 and founded the famous waxworks museum there. She had previously worked as tutor to Louis XVI's sister and had been imprisoned during the French Revolution.

tussock moth A moth belonging to the family *Lymantriidae*, occurring in both the Old and New Worlds and including the vapourers, tussocks, and *gypsy moths. The caterpillars, cocoons, and adults are typically hairy, frequently causing skin irritation and swelling if handled. Some can be economic pests.

Tutankhamen King of Egypt (c. 1361–1352 BC) of the 18th dynasty. Tutankhamen, perhaps Akhenaton's son, became king at the age of 11 after the brief reign of *Akhenaton's immediate successor. He abandoned Akhenaton's worship of the sun-god Aton, reinstating that of *Amon and transferring the capital once more to Thebes. His splendid and elaborate tomb, discovered by Howard *Carter in 1922, is the only Egyptian royal tomb to remain substantially intact to modern times. The beauty and craftsmanship of its contents have continued to fascinate the world. ⁀Osiris.

Tutu, Desmond (1931–) South African clergyman, noted for his opposition to *apartheid. Ordained in 1960, he became (1975) the first Black general secretary of the South African Council of Churches, which had a membership of 12 million in 1978, Anglican Bishop of Johannesburg in 1984, and Archbishop of Cape Town in 1986. A tireless opponent of racial segregation, he won the Nobel Peace Prize in 1984.

Tutuola, Amos (1920–) Nigerian writer. Drawing on Yoruba tribal myths and legends, he created vivid fantasies in which the real and the supernatural coexist. His works include *The Palm-Wine Drunkard* (1952) and the short-story collection *Feather Woman of the Jungle* (1962).

Tuva Autonomous Soviet Socialist Republic (or Tuvinian ASSR) An administrative division in the S Soviet Union, in the RSFSR. The region is mostly mountainous. Some 50% of the population comprise Tuvinians, a Turkic-speaking people, who are mainly livestock farmers. Industry is rapidly developing. Area: 170 500 sq km (65 800 sq mi). Population (1981 est): 269 000. Capital: Kizyl.

Tuvalu, State of (name until 1976: Ellice Islands) A small country in the SW Pacific Ocean. It consists of a group of nine islands, the main one being Funafuti. Most of the population is Polynesian. *Economy*: subsistence agriculture and fishing are the chief occupations. The main export is copra. *History*: formerly part of the Gilbert and Ellice Islands colony, it became a separate colony after a referendum in 1974 and gained independence in 1978. Tuvalu is a member of the Commonwealth of Nations. Prime minister: Dr Tomasi Puapua. Official language: Tuvalu. Official

Official currency: Australian dollar of 100 cents. Area: 24 sq km (9.5 sq mi). Population (1983): 8000. Capital: Funafuti.

Tver. *See* Kalinin.

Twain, Mark (Samuel Langhorne Clemens; 1835–1910) US novelist. He worked for four years as a steamboat pilot on the Mississippi before gaining a national reputation for his humorous journalism. After marrying and settling in Connecticut in 1870 he wrote several works based on his early life, notably *Life on the Mississippi* (1883) and his masterpiece *The Adventures of Huckleberry Finn* (1884). He became an internationally successful public lecturer, but bankruptcy and the deaths of his wife and daughter caused him much private suffering.

twayblade The most common European orchid, *Listera ovata*, which grows in damp woods, meadows, etc. Up to 60 cm high, it has a pair of rounded leaves situated about half way down the stem. The flowering stalk, which is sticky with glands, carries a long head of small greenish flowers.

tweed A woollen fabric, more closely woven than *cheviot. Hardwearing, often with a roughened surface texture, tweed is manufactured in various weave patterns, such as checks, stripes, flecks, and herringbones. Coats, skirts, and suits are made from famous traditional tweeds, such as Harris and Donegal cloth. It derives its name from "tweel" a Scottish word for *twill.

Tweed, River A river in SE Scotland and NE England. Flowing E from the Tweedsmuir Hills to the North Sea at Berwick, it forms part of the border between England and Scotland. Length: 156 km (97 mi).

Twelfth Day. *See* Epiphany.

Twelve Tables (450 BC) The earliest codification of *Roman law, in full known as the Law of the Twelve Tables (*Lex duodecim tabularum*). The laws were engraved on bronze tablets, which were permanently displayed in public. None of the original text survives, although fragments have been preserved in quotations. The tablets dealt with (1) proceedings preliminary to trial; (2) trial; (3) enforcing judgments; (4) rights of fathers; (5) inheritance; (6) ownership of property; (7) land law; (8) *trusts; (9) public law; (10) sacred law (burials etc.); (11 and 12) supplementary matters.

twelve-tone music. *See* serialism.

Twickenham A residential district in the Greater London borough of Richmond-upon-Thames, on the N bank of the River Thames. It contains the English Rugby Football Union ground and *Hampton Court Palace.

twill Any woven fabric with a diagonal rib, produced by varying the regular weave of plain cloth (*see* weaving); herringbone is a common variation. Twilled fabrics are much used for making suits and trousers. *See also* tweed.

twins Two individuals born from the same pregnancy: 1 out of every 83 human pregnancies results in twins. Identical twins are produced when a fertilized egg splits in two and develops as two fetuses of the same sex; identical twins are very difficult to tell apart and they usually have a great emotional affinity for each other. More commonly, nonidentical (or fraternal) twins are produced when two eggs are fertilized at the same time; they may be of different sexes and are no more alike than other siblings. *See also* Siamese twins.

Two Thousand Guineas A flat race for three-year-old horses, run each spring at Newmarket over the Rowley Mile course. One of the English *Classics, it was instituted in 1809.

Tyburn A stream in SE England, in London. It now flows underground for its entire length from Hampstead to the River Thames. The London gallows, known as the Tyburn Tree (1571–1759), stood at the W end of Oxford Street.

Tyche A Greek goddess personifying fortune, daughter of Oceanus or Zeus and Tethys. She is identical with the Roman

*Fortuna.

Tyler, John (1790–1862) US statesman; president (1841–45). A planter from Virginia, he had proslavery sympathies and defended *states' rights, which lost him the support of his cabinet. His government annexed Texas in 1844.

Tyler, Wat (d. 1381) English rebel, who led the Kentish peasants during the *Peasants' Revolt (1381). He was the peasants' most influential spokesman until his murder during negotiations with Richard II at Smithfield.

Tylor, Sir Edward Burnett (1832–1917) British anthropologist. The first professor of anthropology at Oxford (1896) and the foremost 19th-century British anthropologist, Tylor developed his interest in the subject when he visited Mexico with the US ethnologist Henry Chrysty. His *Primitive Culture: Researches into the Development of Mythology, Philosophy, Religion, Language, Art, and Custom* (1871) became the standard English-language work on anthropology.

Tyndale, William (c. 1494–1536) English biblical translator. His influential translation of the New Testament, begun at Cologne in 1525 and completed at Worms, was a major source of the later Authorized or King James Version. In 1520 he published a translation of the Pentateuch. Accused of heresy, he was taken by imperial officers at Antwerp in 1535 and strangled and burned at Vilvorde, Belgium.

Tyndall, John (1820–93) Irish physicist, who in 1869 discovered the scattering of light by microscopic particles, such as those in dust and colloids (**Tyndall effect**). He used this effect to explain the blue of the sky and was also the first to demonstrate that the air contains microorganisms, which helped to refute the theory of spontaneous generation of fungi, etc.

Tyne, River A river in N England. Flowing E from the SW Cheviot Hills to the North Sea at Tynemouth, it passes through Newcastle, Gateshead, and Jarrow. Length: 48 km (30 mi).

Tyne and Wear A metropolitan county of NE England, created in 1974 from SE Northumberland and NE Durham. It comprises the districts of Newcastle-upon-Tyne, North Tyneside, Gateshead, South Tyneside, and Sunderland. It was the first major industrial region in Great Britain, developing long before the industrial revolution. Industries grew up along the River Tyne allied to the large coalfields. In the 19th century most of the region became industrialized; the development of the shipyards was especially important. During the Depression of the 1930s it suffered severely due to its dependence on heavy industry. The whole county is now designated a special development area with government financial assistance for firms located in the county and over the past 10 years there has been much diversification of industry. Area: 540 sq km (208 sq mi). Population (1981): 1 143 245. Administrative centre: Newcastle upon Tyne.

Tynemouth 55 01N 1 24W A town in NE England, in Tyne and Wear at the mouth of the River Tyne. It includes the port of North Shields and is itself a resort. Population (1981): 60 022.

typesetting The process by which type is assembled for *printing. Until the 15th century, type was cut or engraved, a page at a time, in blocks of wood or metal; with **movable type**, invented by *Gutenberg, each character is cast on a separate piece of metal for assembling by hand and is reusable. This was the only method available until 1884, when the American, Ottmar Mergenthaler (1854–99), invented the **Linotype** machine, on which the compositor operates a keyboard to assemble character matrices from a magazine; when a line is complete, molten *type metal is pumped into the matrices to form a solid line of type. The **Monotype** system, invented in 1885 by the American, Tolbert Lanston (1844–1913), comprises separate keyboard and casting machines: as the compositor operates the keyboard, a punched paper tape is produced; when this is fed through the caster, the punched codes select characters in a matrix into which type metal is pumped to form individual pieces of type, which are accumulated, in the correct sequence, in a tray. Since the 1950s **phototypesetting** (photosetting *or* filmsetting) machines have revolutionized printing. Instead of casting type from hot metal, they create images of characters on photographic paper or film, which is then used for *platemaking. The compositor operates a keyboard to produce a punched paper tape or magnetic tape, which then drives the phototypesetter. Some machines flash light through an actual negative image of each character onto the paper or film; others build up its shape with tiny dots of light from a *cathode-ray tube controlled by a computer memory. The latter kind can set 20 000 or more characters per second.

typewriter A hand-operated machine for producing printed symbols. The first machine was invented in the USA in 1867 but the commercial success of the typewriter began in 1874 with the machines produced by the arms manufacturers Remington and Sons. With minor modifications this design, with the paper held in a moving platen, remained the basis of the typewriter until the advent of electric golf-ball machines, with a stationary platen, in the early 1960s. These golf balls consist of spheres carrying the type in circles round their surface—they are easily replaced to provide additional typefaces (e.g. italic) or symbols (e.g. mathematical). More sophisticated machines are now available providing, in conjunction with a microcomputer, proportional spacing and justification. *See* word processor.

typhoid fever An infectious disease of the digestive tract caused by the bacterium *Salmonella typhi*. This disease (and paratyphoid fever) are usually contracted by drinking infected water and occur predominantly in places without a clean water supply. The symptoms, which begin 10-14 days after ingesting the bacterium, include fever, headache, cough, loss of appetite, and constipation; a characteristic red rash may appear. If untreated, the patient may develop bowel haemorrhage or perforations. Treatment is by administration of fluids and the antibiotic chloramphenicol. A vaccine provides temporary immunity.

Typhon In Greek mythology, a monster with a hundred heads, the son of Tartarus and Gaea. He was conquered by Zeus and buried under a volcano, usually identified as Mount Etna. His monstrous children included the *Chimera, the *Hydra, and *Cerberus.

typhoon A tropical cyclone or *hurricane with winds above force 12 on the *Beaufort scale occurring in the China Sea and the W Pacific Ocean. The name is derived from a Chinese word meaning great wind.

typhus An infection caused by certain bacteria-like microorganisms (*see* rickettsia), which are transmitted to man by lice, fleas, mites, or ticks. There are many different forms of typhus, caused by different species of rickettsiae, but they share the symptoms of fever, headache, pains in muscles and joints, delirium, and a rash. These symptoms may be very mild throughout the disease. Treatment is with tetracycline antibiotics or chloramphenicol. Epidemic (or classical) typhus is carried by lice and was formerly very prevalent in overcrowded unhygienic conditions, with a high mortality rate. A vaccine against it is now available.

typography 1. The art of *printing from movable type. 2. The aspect of printing concerned with the design and composition of printing type. Early typefaces, which imitated handwriting, belonged to three main groups: gothic (or black-letter), used by N European printers such as *Gutenberg and *Caxton; roman, introduced at Venice about 1470; and *italic, also Venetian, first used in 1501 (*see* incunabula). Holland dominated typefounding for most of

the 16th and 17th centuries but England produced two outstanding typographers in the 18th century: William Caslon (1692-1766) and John Baskerville (1706-75). Between 1800 and 1850 the so-called modern-face type designs predominated; they differed from the preceding old-face designs by their pronouncedly upright appearance and horizontal serifs (short finishing strokes on the ends of the main lines of letters). Sanserif (i.e. without serifs) typefaces originated in early 19th-century designs but only came into their own in the 1920s and 1930s through the work of the German *Bauhaus typographers. In England, William *Morris revitalized book design at the end of the 19th century, producing several archaizing but handsome typefaces for his Kelmscott Press. Influential 20th-century typographers include the Dutchman Jan van Krimpen (1892-1958), the Englishmen Eric *Gill and Stanley *Morison, and the American F. W. Goudy (1865-1947).

Tyr (*or*, in Old English, Tiw) In Teutonic mythology, the god of war; with *Odin and *Thor, he is one of the three main Germanic gods. His name is linguistically related to *Zeus* (although Latin writers, beginning with Tacitus, identified him with Mars) and survives in *Tuesday*.

Tyrannosaurus A huge bipedal dinosaur that lived in North America during the late Cretaceous period (about 100-65 million years ago). This animal was 15 m long, stood 6.5 m tall, and weighed up to 10 tonnes. It had a massive body with a short thick neck supporting a large head, large muscular hind limbs with clawed feet, and tiny fore legs. It was a carnivore with long dagger-like teeth but was probably quite rare and fed infrequently. Order: *Saurischia.

tyrant In antiquity, a ruler who obtained absolute power without election or right of succession. In the Greek city states tyrants were often leading members of oligarchies who obtained popular support. Generally they ruled benevolently, conforming to established institutions, and were often significant patrons of the arts. Famous tyrants include *Aristagoras of Miletus, *Agathocles and *Dionysius I of Syracuse, *Phalaris of Agrigento, *Pisistratus of Athens, and *Polycrates of Samos.

tyrant flycatcher A passerine bird belonging to the New World family *Tyrannidae* (365 species), ranging from 9-27 cm in length, often with a long tail, and generally grey, brown, or olive-coloured with paler underparts. They are typically arboreal and dart out from a perch to seize flying insects. Tyrant flycatchers are very aggressive and will attack large birds that enter their breeding territories. *Compare* flycatcher.

Tyre (modern name: Sur) 33 12N 35 11E A port in SW Lebanon, on the Mediterranean Sea. It was important to the Phoenicians for several centuries and was taken by Alexander the Great after a seven-month siege in 322 BC and by the Romans in 68 BC. The city was long held by the Crusaders but fell to Muslim forces in 1291. Population (1980 est): 14 000.

Tyrol. *See* Tirol.

Tyrone A former county of W Northern Ireland, bordering on the Republic of Ireland. It is predominantly hilly descending in the E to Lough Neagh. Agriculture is important with cattle and sheep farming and the production of barley, potatoes, flax, and turnips. Small-scale manufacturing is carried out in the larger towns. Area: 3263 sq km (1260 sq mi). County town: Omagh.

Tyumen 57 11N 65 29E A port in the central Soviet Union, in the RSFSR on the River Tura. It serves as a transport centre for the oil and natural gas that are mined nearby. Population (1981 est): 378 000.

Tzu-ch'eng. *See* Zibo.

Tz'u-hsi. *See* Zi Xi.

Tzu-po. *See* Zibo.

U

Ubangi-Shari. *See* Central African Republic.

Uccello, Paolo (P. di Dono; 1397–1475) Florentine painter and craftsman. He trained in the *Ghiberti workshop. From 1425 to 1431 he worked in St Mark's, Venice, as master mosaicist. His frescoes for Sta Maria Novella, Florence, include the famous *Flood*, which shows his preoccupation with perspective and foreshortening. In the three paintings of the battle of San Romano, commissioned by the Medici, he combines a geometric structure with the rich decoration of the *international gothic style.

Udaipur 24 36N 73 47E A city in India, in Rajasthan. Formerly the capital of Udaipur (*or* Mewar) princely state, its lake contains an island with a marble palace. Udaipur has chemical, asbestos, and zinc-smelting industries and a university (1962). Population (1981): 232 588.

Udall, Nicholas (1505–56) English dramatist. He was headmaster of Eton College and later of Westminster School. *Ralph Roister Doister* (c. 1553), influenced by classical Roman drama and probably written for his pupils, was the first full-length English comedy.

Udine 46 04N 13 14E A city in NE Italy, in Friuli-Venezia Giulia. It was partially damaged in an earthquake in 1976. There are textile and leather industries. Population (1980 est): 102 408.

Udmurt Autonomous Soviet Socialist Republic (*or* Udmurtia) An administrative division in the W central Soviet Union, in the RSFSR. The Udmurts, comprising about 50% of the population, speak a Finno-Ugric language. The region has rich oil, shale, timber, and peat resources and manufactures locomotives, machine tools, and other engineering products. Cereals, flax, and some vegetables are grown. Area: 42 100 sq km (16 250 sq mi). Population (1981 est): 1 516 000. Capital: Izhevsk.

Ufa 54 45N 55 58E A city in the W central Soviet Union, the capital of the Bashkir ASSR in the RSFSR. Situated in the Ural Mountains, it has oil refineries and a large chemical industry; its university was founded in 1957. Population (1981 est): 1 009 000.

Uffizi An art gallery in Florence, containing the art treasures of the Medici. Built by *Vasari in the 16th century to house government offices, the Uffizi was opened as a museum in 1765. The major part of its collection comprises Italian Renaissance paintings, although it also includes sculpture and Flemish, Dutch, German, and French paintings.

UFOs. *See* unidentified flying objects.

Uganda, Republic of A landlocked country in East Africa. It consists chiefly of a high plateau rising to mountains, including the Ruwenzori Mountains in the W and Mount Elgon in the E, and a considerable proportion of the total area is occupied by lakes, notably Lake Victoria. The majority of the population is African, especially *Ganda, with dwindling minorities of Europeans and Asians. *Economy*: chiefly agricultural, the main food crops being maize, millet, yams, and other tropical plants. Cash crops include coffee (the main export), tea, tobacco, and cotton; livestock is also important. There has been an increase in forestry production, almost all hardwood. Uganda's freshwater fishing industry is one of the largest in the world, and fish farming is being developed. The chief mineral resource is copper, much of which is exported to Japan. Hydroelectricity is a valuable source of power and there is some industry, including food processing, textiles, and cement. *History*: the area was dominated by the kingdom of *Buganda from the 18th to the late 19th centuries, becoming a British protectorate in 1894. It became an independent state within the British Commonwealth in 1962 and the following year a republic was established with *Obote as prime minister. In 1971 the government was overthrown in a military coup that brought Gen Idi *Amin to power. His repressive regime was overthrown in April, 1979, by Ugandan exiles aided by Tanzanian troops. The subsequent provisional government fell in a military coup in 1980 and Obote was re-elected president. In 1985, after Obote's regime had become increasingly repressive, a further military coup brought Lt Gen Tito Okello to power as head of a military council. In 1986, following virtual civil war, he was overthrown and replaced by Yoweri Museveni. Official language: English; Swahili is widely spoken and the most important local language is Luganda. Official currency, since 1967: Ugandan shilling of 100 cents. Area: 236 860 sq km (91 343 sq mi). Population (1983 est): 13 990 000. Capital: Kampala.

Ugarit An ancient town on the Syrian coast (now Ras Shamra). Repeatedly destroyed and rebuilt from Neolithic times, Ugarit became a great international port between 1500 BC and its ultimate destruction about 1200. Pottery, carvings, and diplomatic correspondence recovered here bear witness to strong Mycenaean, Hittite, and Egyptian links. There

PAOLO UCCELLO *Detail from* Battle of San Romano *(before 1456; National Gallery, London).*

temples to *Baal and his father Dagon, and a set of religious texts, written in a type of alphabetic *cuneiform unique to Ugarit, throw light on religious cults in ancient *Canaan.

ugli A hybrid cross between a *grapefruit and a *tangerine. The fruit resembles a small grapefruit with brownish-yellow warty skin and orange-coloured flesh. It is grown in the West Indies.

Uhland, (Johann) Ludwig (1787–1862) German poet. A lawyer, he was also an active democrat. He collected folk songs, wrote historical dramas, and is noted for his popular ballads.

Uist Two islands in NW Scotland, in the Outer Hebrides. North Uist is separated from South Uist by the island of Benbecula. Seaweed production is important and crofting is extensively practised.

Ujiji 4 55S 29 39E A port in W Tanzania, on the shore of Lake Tanganyika. A former centre for Arab trade in ivory and slaves, it was here that Stanley found Livingstone (1871). Population (1984 est): 14 000.

Ujjain 23 11N 75 50E A city in India, in Madhya Pradesh. An ancient city, it lay on the first meridian of Hindu geographers and was the capital of the Avanti kingdom (6th–4th centuries BC). One of the seven sacred Hindu cities, it is the scene of the 12-yearly bathing festival (Kumbh Mela). It is an agricultural trading centre with textile industries and has a university, founded in 1957. Population (1981): 282 000.

Ujung Pandang (Makassar *or* Macassar) 5 09S 119 08E A port in central Indonesia, in SW Sulawesi. Already a flourishing port when the Portuguese arrived in the 16th century, its exports now include coffee, copra, resins, and vegetable oils. There is some manufacturing industry. Its university was established in 1956. Population (1980): 709 038.

UKAEA. *See* Atomic Energy Authority.

ukiyo-e (Japanese: pictures of the floating world) A Japanese art style concerned with the depiction of everyday life. It was popular among the middle classes in the 17th and 18th centuries. Favourite subjects included prostitutes, women engaged in domestic tasks, actors, etc. Ukiyo-e began as a style of painting but it is most closely associated with Japanese colour woodblock prints. The first ukiyo-e printmaker was probably Hishikawa Moronobu (c. 1618–94). The art culminated in the landscapes of *Hokusai and *Hiroshige, which were highly influential on *impressionism, *postimpressionism, and the *Nabis in 19th-century France.

Ukrainian Soviet Socialist Republic (*or* Ukraine) A constituent republic in the SW Soviet Union. It is a very fertile wooded region and is second only to the RSFSR as the economically most important Soviet republic. Some 96% of the population comprises Slavs, mostly Ukrainians. There are major coalfields and iron-ore mines (including the *Donets Basin), resulting in the development of a large ferrous metallurgical industry. The machine-building, chemical, consumer-goods, and food industries are also important. The region possesses some of the most fertile land in the Soviet Union and crops grown include wheat (comprising nine-tenths of Soviet exports), sugar beet, cotton, and tobacco. *History:* it was dominated by the Khazars from the 7th to the 9th centuries and then by the Rurik princes of Kiev. In the 13th century the Golden Horde overran the region, which subsequently came under the rule of Lithuania and, in the 16th century, Poland. In the 17th century many Ukrainians fled the harsh Polish government, becoming *Cossaks. Polish domination was followed by Russian rule. After a national and cultural revival in the late 19th century the Ukraine declared independence in 1918 but subsequently submitted to Soviet armies, becoming (1922) one of the original constituent republics of the Soviet Union. The Ukraine has a separate seat in the UN. Area: 603 700 sq km (231 990 sq mi). Population (1981 est): 50 135 000. Capital: Kiev.

ukulele A small guitar, patented in Hawaii in 1917. The fingerboard of a ukulele is fretted; the four gut or nylon strings are strummed with fingers or a small plectrum. Originally used to play chordal accompaniments to folksongs, the ukulele became popular in US jazz.

Ulan Bator (*or* Ulaanbaatar; former name: Urga) 47 54N 106 52E The capital of the Mongolian People's Republic, situated on a plateau in the N of the country. Built around a monastery, in the 17th century it developed as a centre of trade between China and Japan. It became the capital when Outer Mongolia declared its independence in 1911. It is Mongolia's main centre of industry. The Mongolian State University was founded in 1942. Population (1980 est): 435 400.

Ulanova, Galina (1910–) Russian ballet dancer. From 1928 she danced with the Leningrad Kirov Ballet, where she excelled in classical ballets, such as *Swan Lake* and *Giselle*, and from 1944 with the Moscow Bolshoi Ballet, for which she made several films. She retired from the stage in 1962.

Ulan Ude 51 55N 107 40E A city in the SE Soviet Union, in the Buryat ASSR, in the RSFSR on the River Selenga. It is a transport centre and has boatbuilding, ship-repairing, and machinery-manufacturing industries. Population (1984): 329 000.

Ulbricht, Walter (1893–1973) East German statesman. A fervent Stalinist, Ulbricht rose rapidly in the Communist Party ranks. He lived in the Soviet Union during the Nazi period and after World War II was the leading architect of the German Democratic Republic. He was general secretary of the Socialist Unity Party from 1950 and in 1960 became chairman of the newly established council of state. In 1961 he erected the Berlin Wall.

ulcer An inflamed eroded area of skin or mucous membrane. There are many forms of ulcer, one of the most prevalent being *peptic ulcers, which affect the stomach and duodenum. Ulcers may also occur in the mouth—small irritating aphthous ulcers affect many people—and in the intestine in inflammatory bowel disease (*see* colitis). Varicose ulcers may develop in the skin, particularly around the ankles, of patients with chronic *varicose veins.

Uleåborg. *See* Oulu.

Ullswater The second largest lake in England, in central Cumbria in the Lake District. Length: 12 km (7.5 mi).

Ulm 48 24N 10 00E An industrial city and port in SW West Germany, in Baden-Württemberg on the River Danube. Its gothic cathedral (1377) escaped the damage of World War II. Napoleon defeated the Austrian army here in 1805 and it is the birthplace of Einstein. Population (1985): 99 600.

Ulm, Battle of (25 September–20 October, 1805) A battle in which Napoleon with 210 000 men defeated 72 000 Austrians in Bavaria. The Austrians were taken by surprise in the rear and capitulated. Napoleon thus prevented a union between Austrian and Russian forces.

ulna. *See* arm.

Ulster A province in the Republic of Ireland and former kingdom of N Ireland. The earldom of Ulster passed to the English Crown in 1461 and during the 17th century most of the land was confiscated and given to English and Scottish settlers (*see* Plantation of Ireland). It was partitioned in 1921 to form the six counties of Northern Ireland and the Ulster province of the Republic of Ireland, consisting of the counties of Cavan, Donegal, and Monaghan. Area: 8013 sq km (3094 sq mi). Population (1981): 230 159.

ultramicroscope A type of microscope, invented by *Zsigmondy in 1902, used to study colloidal particles in a liquid medium. A beam of light illuminates the particles from the side, the scattered light enabling the movements of the particles to be observed as flashes against a dark background (dark-field illumination).

Ultramontanism (Latin: beyond the mountains, i.e. within Italy) A tendency within the Roman Catholic Church that supports the centralized power of the pope and the *Roman Curia as against nationalist movements, such as *Gallicanism, or greater independence at the diocesan level. The high point of Ultramontanism was the promulgation of papal *infallibility (1870).

ultrasonics The study of *sound waves inaudible to the human ear, i.e. above about 20 000 hertz. Such waves are known as **ultrasound** and may be produced by *magnetostriction or by applying a rapidly alternating voltage across a *piezoelectric crystal. Ultrasound is used, for example, to destroy bacteria in milk, break up large molecules, and clean surfaces. In medicine, ultrasound is used therapeutically, for example to break up stones, and ultrasound scanners are used in diagnosis and in pregnancy to monitor fetal development, being less harmful than X-rays.

ultraviolet radiation *Electromagnetic radiation the frequency of which lies between that of the violet end of the visible spectrum and *X-rays, i.e. between about 380 and 5 nanometres. Ultraviolet radiation is produced during arc discharges and by gas-discharge tubes (e.g. the mercury-vapour lamp). It is also produced in large quantities by the sun, although the radiation below 200 nm is absorbed by the *ozone layer of the atmosphere.

Ulyanovsk (name until 1924: Simbirsk) 54 19N 48 22E A port in the W central Soviet Union, in the RSFSR on the River Volga. Industries include food processing, vodka distilling, and motor-vehicle manufacture. It was renamed in honour of Lenin (originally V. I. Ulyanov), who was born here. Population (1981 est): 485 000.

Ulysses. *See* Odysseus.

Umar. *See* Omar.

Umayyads (*or* Omayyads) The first dynasty of *caliphs, which ruled Islam from 661 to 750 AD. Their capital was Damascus. After reluctantly accepting Islam, the family obtained some of the leading positions in the state and one of them, *Mu'awiyah, became caliph (661) on the death of his rival *Ali. The dynasty reached its peak with *'Abd al-Malik (reigned 685–705). The Umayyads were overthrown by a rebellion of discontented Arabs and pious Muslims and were replaced by the *Abbasids, a rival family. In Muslim Spain, an Umayyad, *'Abd ar-Rahman, seized power in 756 and established a dynasty that ruled until 1030.

Umbelliferae A widely distributed family of plants (2850 species), most abundant in N temperate regions. Most species are herbaceous, with much-divided leaves and umbrella-shaped heads (umbels) of tiny flowers, each usually with five petals and five sepals. The fruits are ridged, splitting into two parts when ripe. The family includes vegetables, such as the carrot, celery, and parsnip, and many culinary herbs and spices, such as angelica, caraway, chervil, coriander, dill, fennel, and parsley.

Umberto I (1844–1900) King of Italy (1878–1900). He commanded with distinction in the war against the Austrians (1866). As king he led Italy into the *Triple Alliance with Germany and Austria (1882) and encouraged Italian colonialism in Africa. Defeat by the Ethiopians at Adowa (1896) and economic difficulties led to unrest at home and the imposition of martial law in 1898. Umberto was assassinated at Monza.

Umberto II (1904–83) The last King of Italy (1946), following the abdication of his father Victor Emmanuel III. He himself was forced to abdicate after a referendum approved the establishment of republican government and he retired to Portugal as the Count of Sarre.

umbilical cord The structure, about 50 cm long, that connects a fetus to the *placenta in the womb. It contains three blood vessels (two arteries and one vein) that convey blood to and from the placenta. At birth the umbilical cord is tied off and cut; the part connected to the baby subsequently degenerates, leaving a scar on the abdomen (*see* navel).

umbrella bird A fruit-eating songbird of the genus *Cephalopterus* of tropical American forests. Male birds have a large umbrella-shaped crest that is raised over the head during display. They also have fleshy wattles hanging from the chest —ranging from the short naked red wattle of the bare-necked umbrella bird (*C. glabriollis*) to the feather-covered pendulous wattle of the ornate umbrella bird (*C. ornatus*). Family: *Cotingidae* (90 species).

umbrella tree A small North American tree, *Magnolia tripetala*, up to 12 m high, that has umbrella-like clusters of large leaves (40 cm long) at the ends of the branches. The large flowers are creamy white with a strong scent and the fruits are scarlet. Family: *Magnoliaceae*.

Umbria A landlocked mountainous region in central Italy. It produces cereals, vines, and olives. Hydroelectricity powers modern industries producing iron, steel, chemicals, engineering, and food products. The Umbrian school of painting, which included Perugino and Raphael, was established here during the Renaissance. Area: 8456 sq km (3265 sq mi). Population (1980): 810 713. Capital: Perugia.

Umtali. *See* Mutare.

Umtata 31 35S 28 47E The capital of the Transkei, in S Africa. It has an Anglican cathedral. Population (1983 est): 80 000.

Un-American Activities Committee US House of Representatives committee established in 1935 to investigate subversive organizations in the USA. Headed by Martin Dies, the committee investigated Nazis and Fascists as well as liberals thought to have communist connections. Spurred on by Senator *McCarthy, it blacklisted several Hollywood writers and directors and investigated government officials, notably Alger Hiss. Public protest resulted in the committee's decline and eventual abolition (1975).

Unamuno y Jugo, Miguel de (1864–1936) Spanish writer and philosopher, of Basque parentage. Unamuno's chief philosophical work, *The Tragic Sense of Life* (1913), reflects the influence of *Kant, *Hegel, and *Kierkegaard. His works tackle the themes of faith, free will, the immortality of the soul, and the struggle for moral integrity.

uncertainty principle. *See* Heisenberg uncertainty principle.

Uncle Sam A personification of the people or government of the USA, usually portrayed as a lean figure with white hair and whiskers, wearing a tall hat, swallow-tail coat, and striped trousers. The name is associated with a certain meat inspector, Samuel Wilson (1766–1854), who confused the initials of the United States with those of his own nickname.

unconscious In *psychoanalysis, the part of the mind that includes ideas and impulses of which the individual is unaware and which cannot readily be brought back into awareness. (It is distinguished from the **subconscious**, which comprises ideas and impulses that can readily be recalled to consciousness.) The unconscious mental processes are unacceptable to the conscious mind and are kept unconscious by the process of *repression. Psychoanalytic *psychotherapy attempts to bring these processes back into consciousness by overcoming the resistances to them.

underground railways Apart from short sections of tunnel on main-line railways, the world's first urban underground railway (1863) was built in London between Paddington and Farringdon Street, using the cut and cover method (cutting a trench from above and filling in over the railway) and steam trains. The first "tube" railway (1890), cut by boring through the earth with a Greathead shield (a steel ring forced forwards with a hydraulic ram), ran from the City to Stockwell and used electric trains. The network of London tubes and metropolitan railways is now 405 km (251 mi) long, recent additions including the Victoria line (opened

1971), the extension of the Piccadilly line to London Airport (1977), and the Jubilee line (1979). Other major cities to have an underground railway include New York (subway), Paris (*métro*), Moscow, Tokyo, Buenos Aires, Madrid, Glasgow, and Hong Kong.

underwing moth   A moth whose brightly coloured hindwings are hidden by the camouflaged forewings when at rest. When disturbed the moth flies off flashing its bright colours, which startles and confuses predators. Underwings belong to several families and are found in Europe, Asia, and North America.

underwriting.   *See* insurance; Lloyd's.

Undset, Sigrid   (1882–1949)   Norwegian novelist, best known for *Kristin Lavransdatter* (1920–22), a trilogy of historical novels set in 14th-century Norway. She wrote a number of other novels, most of them dealing with themes that reflect her conversion to Roman Catholicism in 1924. She also wrote essays and lives of the Norwegian saints.

undulant fever.   *See* brucellosis.

unemployment   The total number of people unable to find work at a given time. A certain amount of **frictional unemployment**, i.e. unemployment due to people changing jobs, etc., is inevitable. **Structural unemployment** is due to people having the wrong skills, living in different areas from vacancies, etc. The proportion of the workforce unemployed also increases with a downturn in the *trade cycle (this is **demand-deficient unemployment**); in the *Depression of the 1930s it reached nearly 3 million in the UK, a figure surpassed in July 1986, when it exceeded 3.25 million. While it is accepted that even with "full" employment up to about 3% of the workforce may be out of work (as a result of frictional and structural unemployment) considerable controversy remains as to the extent of structural unemployment as compared to demand-deficient unemployment. Monetarists (*see* monetarism) believe that, provided the *money supply is adequate, unemployment is largely due to structural problems and they advocate such measures as mobility allowances and retraining schemes. They claim that attempts to boost the economy by *deficit financing, as advocated by *Keynesianism, will not help the problem and will merely have the effect of fuelling *inflation.

UNESCO.   *See* United Nations Educational, Scientific and Cultural Organization.

UNICORN   *A representation of a unicorn from a 15th-century tapestry in the Musée Cluny, Paris.*

Ungaretti, Giuseppe   (1888–1970) Italian poet. He was born in Egypt and studied in Paris, where he met *Apollinaire, *Valéry, and other avantgarde writers and artists. He taught in Brazil from 1936 to 1942. His poetry, beginning with the war poems of *Il porto sepolto* (1916) and *L'allegria* (1919), was highly experimental, dispensing with rhyme and other conventions. The difficult language and symbolism of a later volume, *Sentimento del tempo* (1933), led a critic to describe Ungaretti's verse as *ermetico* (obscure), a term that was soon applied to the style of *Montale and *Quasimodo as well, the three being the leading practitioners of *La poesie ermetica.* Ungaretti's later volumes include *La terra promessa* (1950) and *Morte delle stagioni* (1967).

Ungava   A region in E Canada, in N Quebec E of Hudson Bay. A rocky plateau with many lakes, it is rich in minerals (especially iron ore) but sparsely populated. Area: 911 110 sq km (351 780 sq mi).

ungulate   A hoofed mammal. The term is not used in modern scientific classifications, the hoofed mammals being grouped into the orders *Perissodactyla* (horses, tapirs, and rhinoceroses) and *Artiodactyla*, which includes pigs, camels, deer, cattle, etc.

uniat churches   Various churches of Eastern Orthodox Christianity that are in full communion with the Roman Catholic Church. Although completely Catholic in faith and doctrine, they retain their own traditional liturgies and canon law. Generally they differ from Rome in giving communion under both kinds, practising baptism by immersion, and allowing marriage of the clergy.

UNICEF.   *See* United Nations International Children's Emergency Fund.

unicorn   A mythical animal described by classical writers as living in India and resembling a white horse, but with one long straight horn on its forehead. In the middle ages it was symbolically associated with chastity or virginity (and thus could be captured only by a virgin) and also with Christ's love of mankind. Its horn was supposed to reveal the presence of poison in food or drink. In heraldry it figured in the arms of Scotland and was combined with the lion in the arms of the British Crown after the accession of James I.

unidentified flying objects   (UFOs) Objects reported to have been seen in the sky (usually at night) that have not been identified as aircraft, satellites, or known astronomical bodies. Often described as saucer shaped (and known as "flying saucers"), they have been taken by some to be spacecraft from extraterrestrial sources—a view for which there is little credible evidence. They have, however, provided a source of considerable speculation and excitement among those who believe that they have witnessed an event that has passed unnoticed by the rest of mankind.

Unification Church   A religious sect founded in South Korea in 1954 by a millionaire Korean businessman, Sun Myung Moon (1920–   ). In the early 1960s it was introduced into the USA as a right-wing Christian Youth Crusade and is now also active in Britain, Australia, and elsewhere. The ideology of the cult is summarized in Moon's book, *Divine Principle*, which he claims was revealed to him by Christ in 1936. Moon is presented as the Second Messiah, the head of a family of perfect children (i.e. his followers, the Moonies), who will succeed in redeeming mankind from Satan. Absolute obedience is demanded of members, who spend most of their waking hours earning money for the organization by selling such items as artificial flowers in the streets. The large sums realized in this way enabled Moon to build an extensive property and business empire in the USA, where he has lived since 1972. He was imprisoned for tax evasion in 1984 and released in 1985.

unified field theory   A theory that encompasses the four fundamental interactions—*strong, *weak, *electromagnetic, and *gravitational—in terms of a single field, analogous to the electromagnetic or gravitational fields. Einstein failed after many attempts to unify gravitation and electromagnetism, although a measure of unification has been achieved between the weak and electromagnetic fields.

uniformitarianism The generally accepted theory that all geological changes have occurred through gradual processes operating over a long period, although not necessarily at the same rate or intensity. *Compare* catastrophism.

Uniformity, Acts of A series of Acts (1549, 1552, 1559, 1562) that enforced the use of the Book of *Common Prayer in England during the *Reformation.

Union, Acts of 1. The Acts (1536–43) uniting England and Wales. They imposed English law and administration on Wales, made English the language of officialdom, and provided for Welsh representation in parliament. 2. The Act (1707) uniting England and Scotland to form Great Britain. Scotland retained its legal system and Presbyterian Church and was to be represented in parliament by 16 peers and 45 MPs. 3. The Act (1800) that united Great Britain and Ireland to form (1801) the United Kingdom. It provided for Irish representation in parliament (4 spiritual peers, 28 life peers, 100 MPs). After the establishment of the Irish Free State (1921; *see* Home Rule), the Act united Britain with Northern Ireland.

Union of Soviet Socialist Republics. *See* Soviet Union.

Unitarians A group of Christians who reject the doctrine of the Trinity and the divinity of Christ, believing instead in the single personality of God and regarding Christ as a religious teacher. They have no formal creeds but stress reason and conscience as the bases of religion and view human nature as essentially good; they therefore also reject orthodox Christian teaching on original sin and atonement. Modern Unitarian thought dates from the Reformation, but congregations were first formed in Britain and the USA in the 18th century. These are now associated in the General Assembly of Unitarian and Free Christian Churches.

unitary symmetry A method of classifying *hadrons. It is found that by plotting *isotopic spin against hypercharge (the sum of *strangeness and *baryon number) on a graph for particular values of *spin and *parity, a symmetric pattern of hadrons is obtained. In this way families of hadrons can be constructed. The theory was used to predict the existence and properties of the omega-minus particle, which were later confirmed.

United Arab Emirates (UAE; former name: Trucial States) A federation of seven sheikdoms in the Middle East, in *Arabia on the S coast of the Persian Gulf and the Gulf of Oman, comprising Abu Dhabi, Ajman, Dubai, Fujairah, Ras al-Khaimah, Sharjah, and Umm al-Qaiwain. Abu Dhabi occupies 87% of the total area and Abu Dhabi and Dubai each have about one-third of the population, which is mainly Arab and Sunnite Muslim. The terrain is flat sandy desert, below 200 m (656 ft) except for a slight rise to the NE. *Economy*: fishing and pearls are still important, but the oil of Abu Dhabi and Dubai, both underground and offshore, is the chief product and export: it has made Abu Dhabi one of the richest per capita political units in the world. *History*: the sheikdoms signed several common treaties with Britain from 1820; that of 1892 made them protectorates—the Trucial States—and British troops were stationed there until independence. The federation was formed in 1971 (Ras al-Khaimah not joining until 1972) and is a member of OPEC. President: Sheik Zayed bin Sultan al-Nahayan of Abu Dhabi (1918-). Prime minister: Sheik Rashid bin Said al-Maktoum. Official language: Arabic. Official currency: UAE dirham of 10 dinars and 1000 fils. Area: 83 650 sq km (32 290 sq mi). Population (1983): 1 374 000. Provisional capital: Abu Dhabi. Chief port: Dubai.

United Arab Republic (UAR) The state created by the union of Egypt and Syria in 1958. Joined by North Yemen in the same year, it collapsed in 1961, when Syria withdrew, but Egypt retained the name until 1971.

United Australia Party (UAP) A political party, comprising the Nationalist Party and ex-members of the *Labor Party, that governed Australia (sometimes in coalition with the Country Party) from 1931 to 1941. It was dissolved in 1944 to be succeeded by the *Liberal Party. Its leader until his death in 1939 was Joseph A. *Lyons.

United Empire Loyalists Those Americans who remained loyal to England in the American Revolution and were forced after the colonists' victory in 1783 to migrate to Canada.

United Fronts In China, two periods of cooperation between the Chinese Communist Party and its opponent, the *Guomindang. The first United Front (1924–27) was brought about, under Soviet influence, to defeat the *warlords and dissolved as relations between the two parties declined into civil war. The second United Front (1937–45) was formed following the *Xi An incident, which forced *Chiang Kai-shek to abandon civil war with the communists for an alliance against the Japanese invasion (*see* Sino-Japanese Wars).

United Irishmen, Society of An Irish secret society established in Belfast in 1791 by Wolfe *Tone to press for an independent Irish republic. Hopes of French aid in the 1790s were frustrated but in 1798 the United Irishmen rose in Ulster and Wexford, being suppressed with some difficulty.

United Kingdom (UK) A country in N Europe, consisting of *England, *Scotland, *Wales, and the province of Northern Ireland (*see* Ireland). The UK does not include the Channel Isles and the Isle of Man, which are direct dependencies of the Crown with their own legislatures and taxation systems. The United Kingdom of Great Britain and Ireland, formed in 1801, became the United Kingdom of Great Britain and Northern Ireland in 1922, following the creation of the Irish Free State. Head of state: Queen Elizabeth II. Prime minister: Margaret Thatcher. Languages: English, with Gaelic and Welsh minority languages. Area: 244 014 sq km (94 214 sq mi). Population (1981): 55 775 560. Capital: London.

United Nations (UN) An organization established to maintain international peace and to foster international cooperation in the resolution of economic, social, cultural, and humanitarian problems. The UN was founded on 24 October, 1945 (United Nations Day), when the major powers ratified a charter that had been drawn up earlier in the year in San Francisco. There were 51 founder members, including the USA, which thus abandoned the isolationist stance it had taken to the UN's predecessor, the *League of Nations. Most of the countries of the world are now members of the UN, the chief exceptions being North and South Korea, Switzerland, and *Taiwan, which lost its seat to the People's Republic of *China in 1971.

The headquarters of the UN are in New York. The organization's main deliberative organ is the **General Assembly**, which meets for three months every year. Each member state has one equal vote in the Assembly, which can only adopt recommendations: as a body of independent sovereign states, it cannot impose its will upon members. The **Security Council** bears the chief responsibility for maintaining international peace. Its permanent members are China, France, the Soviet Union, the UK, and the USA; a further ten members are elected by the General Assembly for two-year terms. Decisions, except on procedure, must be agreed by nine members, including all the permanent members (the so-called veto privilege). In the event of a breach of international peace the Council may commit military forces to an attempt to re-establish peace, as for example during the *Korean War. The **Economic and Social Council** (ECOSOC) coordinates the economic and social work of the UN and has regional commissions in Europe, Asia and the

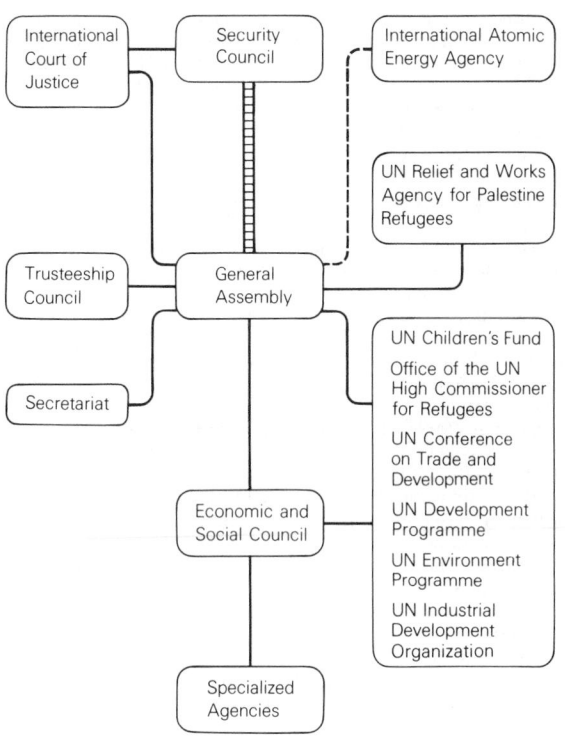

UNITED NATIONS *The structure of the organization.*

Pacific, Latin America, Africa, and Western Asia. The **Trusteeship Council** is responsible for the one remaining *trust territory (Micronesia). The principal judicial organ of the UN is the *International Court of Justice. The **Secretariat**, headed by the secretary general (currently Javier Pérez de Cuellar), is responsible for administration.

Other UN bodies are the **United Nations Development Programme** (UNDP), which fosters the economic growth of the *developing countries; its headquarters are in New York; the **United Nations Conference on Trade and Development** (UNCTAD), which encourages international trade, especially for the purpose of accelerating the economic development of developing countries; its headquarters are in Geneva; the **United Nations Industrial Development Organization** (UNIDO), which promotes industrial development in the developing countries; its headquarters are in Vienna; the **United Nations Environment Programme** (UNEP), which is concerned with international cooperation in the protection of the environment; its headquarters are in Nairobi; the Office of the *United Nations High Commissioner for Refugees; the *United Nations International Children's Emergency Fund; and the *United Nations Relief and Works Agency for Palestine Refugees in the Near East. There are in addition a number of specialized agencies, each charged with a specific function. These include the *Food and Agriculture Organization, *International Civil Aviation Organization, *International Labour Organisation, *International Monetary Fund, *International Telecommunication Union, *United Nations Educational, Scientific and Cultural Organization, *International Bank for Reconstruction and Development, *World Health Organization, and the *World Meteorological Organization.

United Nations Educational, Scientific and Cultural Organization (UNESCO) A specialized agency of the *United Nations established in 1945 to promote international cooperation in education, science, and culture. It collects and distributes information, provides operational assistance (e.g. funds for teacher training) to *developing countries, and sponsors research. Its headquarters are in Paris. Objecting to administrative inefficiency and political bias, the USA withdrew in 1984 and the UK in 1985. Several other Western countries also considered following suit.

United Nations High Commissioner for Refugees, Office of the (UNHCR) A *United Nations body established in 1950 to provide international protection for refugees. It seeks permanent solutions to their problems through voluntary repatriation, resettlement in other countries, or integration into the country of present residence. The UNHCR has recently been concerned with refugees from Chile, Cyprus, Angola, and Vietnam. Its headquarters are in Geneva. It won the Nobel Peace Prize in 1981.

United Nations International Children's Emergency Fund (UNICEF) A *United Nations body established in 1946 to carry out postwar relief work in Europe. It is now chiefly concerned with providing health care, education, and improved nutrition to *developing countries. Most of UNICEF's funds come from voluntary government contributions. Its headquarters are in Geneva. It won the Nobel Peace Prize in 1965.

United Nations Relief and Works Agency for Palestine Refugees in the Near East (UNRWA) A *United Nations body founded in 1950 to provide relief, health, education, and welfare services for Palestinian refugees in the Middle East (*see* Palestine). Its permanent headquarters are in Beirut (Lebanon).

United Provinces of the Netherlands The northern provinces of the Netherlands, which united (1579) during the *Revolt of the Netherlands against Spain and formed (1581) a self-governing independent federation. The so-called Dutch Republic survived until conquered by the French (1795) during the Revolutionary Wars.

United States of America (USA) A country in North America, the fourth most populous and fourth largest in the world. It is a federal republic of 50 states, including two separated from the others: Alaska, in the extreme NW of the continent, and Hawaii, in the central Pacific Ocean. The USA borders on Canada in the N and Mexico in the S. The Pacific mountain system and the Rocky Mountains, the watershed of the country, extend N–S in the W with an arid area between, while the Appalachian Mountains extend N–S in the E. In the centre lie vast plains. The population is of mixed ethnic stock, the majority being of European descent; other groups include Blacks, Chinese, Japanese, and American Indians (the majority of whom live on reservations). *Economy*: the USA is the world's greatest industrial producer, with a highly diversified economy. Its large resources of minerals and fuels make it the leading producer of natural gas, lead, copper, aluminium, and sulphur and of electrical and nuclear energy. It is almost self-sufficient in raw materials, although as its mineral resources are depleted it is having to increase its imports, notably of petroleum. The chief manufactures are steel, motor vehicles, chemicals, electronic equipment, and consumer goods. Although only 4% of the workforce are employed in agriculture, 15% of all exports are agricultural products. Farming in the USA is highly mechanized, with efficient control of disease and pests. Cereals, cotton, and tobacco are the main crops. Main exports include motor vehicles, aircraft, machinery, grain, and chemicals, while main imports include petroleum and petroleum products, chemicals, metals, machinery, cars, and newsprint. *History*: extensively explored following its discovery by Columbus in 1492, America was settled from 1565, chiefly by the Spanish, French, and British. The British colonies, in the E, had the greatest religious and economic freedom and were therefore the most attractive and successful. However, during the 18th century conflict developed between local colonial assemblies and their British governors, particularly over taxation. The colonists' confidence in themselves was strengthened by their success against the French in the *French and Indian Wars (1754–63) and the 13 colonies finally won independence in the *American Revolution (1775–83). The USA was rapidly expanding W at this time and through the *Mexican War (1846–48) acquired California; the discovery of gold there (1848) further encouraged settlement in the W. By 1820 conflict was developing between the cotton-growing states of the South (where African slaves had worked since the late 17th century) and the commercial North (where the industrial revolution was under way and slavery was opposed). As the new states of the West aligned themselves with the North, the South felt increasingly threatened. This led to the *Civil War (1861–65), which ended in victory for the North and the abolition of slavery. It was followed by a period of rapid industrial and economic expansion, while territorial expansion continued with the purchase of Alaska (1867), the annexation of Hawaii (1898), and the Spanish-American War (1898), in which the USA acquired the Philippines, Puerto Rico, Guam, and a measure of control over Cuba.

Intervention in Colombia led to the construction of the Panama Canal (opened 1914). Economic and territorial expansion made the USA a world power, a status confirmed by its role in World War I, which it entered reluctantly (1917) because of its policy of isolationism. The 1920s saw another industrial and commercial boom, which ended in the *Depression that followed the Crash of 1929. The USA was again reluctant to enter World War II but was forced to do so by the Japanese bombing of Pearl Harbor in Hawaii (December, 1941). US troops and weapons played a major part in defeating the Axis Powers in Europe and its development and use of the atom bomb ended the war against Japan. The part played by the USA in the establishment of the United Nations (1945) involved it inextricably in international affairs, in which it has since played a leading role. Postwar fear of Soviet expansion resulted in the Marshall Plan (1947), designed to render Europe less susceptible to communism by bolstering it economically, in the USA's involvement in the *Cold War, and in the harassment of supposed communists at home (see also McCarthy, Joseph R.; Un-American Activities Committee). Fear of the spread of communism led also to intervention in Korea (1950–53), Cuba (1961–62), and Vietnam (1961–75), and in the use of foreign aid to maintain the status quo in developing countries. After 1963 relations with the Soviet Union improved, with strategic arms limitation discussed (see disarmament), and diplomatic relations were established with China in 1979. Interventionist policy continued, however, with the role of the CIA in foreign affairs criticized and investigated (1975–76) following the *Watergate affair (1972–74). Domestic problems since World War II have included the difficulties of effecting racial integration, with race riots in the mid- and late 1960s followed by extensive opposition to the *Vietnam War. The postwar economic boom was followed by decline in the early 1970s, with continuing inflation. With its increasing dependence on petroleum imports the country suffered through the drying up of supplies from Iran (1978–79) and rises in world petroleum prices. Relationships with Iran were further strained when Iranian students took 52 US diplomats hostage in the American Embassy, Tehran, in 1979, only releasing them in January, 1981. Elsewhere, US troops intervened in Lebanon (1982), Grenada (1983), and in covert operations against Nicaragua. Relations with the USSR were further strained by the Soviet invasion of Afghanistan (1980), the subsequent deployment of US nuclear missiles in W Europe, and Reagan's *Strategic Defence Initiative. In 1986 US planes bombed Libyan cities in retaliation for terrorist attacks. Relations with the USSR improved in 1987 with the signing of a major treaty on nuclear weapons and the introduction of *glasnost under the Soviet leader Mikhail Gorbachov. President: Ronald Reagan. Official language: English. Official currency: US dollar of 100 cents. Area: 9 363 123 sq km (3 614 343 sq mi). Population (1983): 234 193 000. Capital: Washington, DC.

unities Three principles concerning the representation in drama of action, time, and space. According to the interpretation of Aristotle's *Poetics* by 16th- and 17th-century neoclassical critics, a play must represent a single action occurring in a single setting during the course of a single day. The unities were strictly observed in much 17th-century French drama, notably in the tragedies of *Racine and *Corneille, but were largely ignored in England.

unit trust An organization that uses funds raised by selling "units" to the public to buy and sell *securities in order to make profits for distribution to unit holders. Securities are held in the names of trustees, usually banks. The units can be resold to the trust managers at any time at their market value. The small investor buying unit trusts has the advantages of a professionally managed widespread portfolio. The trust's capital fluctuates according to funds supplied by investors. In the USA it is called an open-end investment company. *Compare* investment company.

Universal Decimal Classification (*or* Brussels Classification) A system of library classification developed in 1895 at the International Institute of Bibliography in Brussels. It extends the division of the *Dewey Decimal Classification, on which it is based, by using various symbols of notation as well as Arabic numerals.

universe The sum of all potentially knowable objects—the earth, sun, and other solar-system bodies, the stars and other members of our *Galaxy, countless millions of other *galaxies, and the matter between these objects. The universe is thought to be 10–20 thousand million years old and is at present expanding (see big-bang theory; cosmology). Its unimaginable vastness in both space (about 10^{10} light years across) and time (about 10^{10} years old) has only been accepted in this century. The possibility of life elsewhere in the universe is fairly high (i.e. there is a high probability that there are millions of stars with similar planetary systems and conditions to those of the solar system). Radio observations are still being conducted to search for intelligent lifeforms on nearby and some more distant stars in our Galaxy.

universities Independent degree-awarding institutions of higher education. They evolved in Europe in the middle ages from the *studia generalia*, schools open to scholars from all parts of Europe, and by the end of the 14th century consisted of lawful communities of teachers and scholars, recognized by civil or ecclesiastical authorities. Among the earliest were those founded at Bologna (1088), Paris (c. 1150), Prague (1348), Vienna (1365), and Heidelberg (1386). The first universities in England were established at Oxford and Cambridge in the 12th century, while St Andrews (the first Scottish university) was founded in 1411 and Trinity College, Dublin, in 1591. In the USA the first universities evolved from institutions established prior to the American Revolution, such as *Harvard, *Yale, and *Princeton. Following industrialization during the 19th century, several new universities were established in the UK, a process that continued into the 20th century, especially after World War II. Increasing emphasis was placed upon the development of technical studies and following the Robbins Report of 1963 the colleges of advanced technology (CATs) were granted university status. The *Open University, a new concept in higher education, was established in 1969.

Unknown Warrior (*or* Unknown Soldier) An unidentified soldier killed in World War I, whose grave serves as a permanent memorial to all those killed in both World Wars. Britain's tomb for an Unknown Warrior is in Westminster Abbey and France's lies below the Arc de Triomphe.

unlisted securities market (USM). *See* stocks and shares.

Upanishads About 200 prose and verse treatises on metaphysical philosophy, produced as commentaries on the *Vedas* and dating from around 400 BC. They deal with the nature of *Brahman and the soul and are reputedly divinely inspired. Many different, sometimes contradictory, views are represented.

UR   *The "Standard" of Ur (c. 2500 BC; British Museum, London). It consists of a hollow box, the sides of which depict a king's campaign, decorated with lapis lazuli, shell, and red limestone. The side shown depicts animals being taken to be killed for the victory banquet.*

upas   An evergreen tropical tree, *Antiaris toxicana*, native to SE Asia. Up to 30 m high, it has a crown of short spreading branches and long simple leaves; the flowers give rise to fleshy red pear-shaped fruits. The milky latex is a source of arrow poison. Family: *Moraceae*.

Updike, John (Hoyer)   (1932–   ) US novelist and short-story writer. Until 1959 he worked for the *New Yorker* magazine. In novels, such as *Rabbit, Run* (1960), *Couples* (1968), *Rabbit Redux* (1972), and *Marry Me* (1976), he has explored the moral confusions of contemporary US society. He has moved beyond the suburban scene of much of his writing in *The Coup* (1979), a novel set in an emergent African country. His novel *Rabbit is Rich* (1981) won a Pulitzer Prize (1982).

Upolu   The most populous island in Western Samoa. It is fertile and copra, cacao, bananas, and rubber are produced. Area: 1114 sq km (430 sq mi). Population (1981): 113 000. Chief town: Apia.

Upper Volta, Republic of.   *See* Burkina Faso.

Uppsala   59 55N 17 38E A city in E central Sweden. It is a historic and cultural centre, with a famous library, a gothic cathedral, and Sweden's oldest university (1477), where *Linnaeus taught. It has light industries. Population (1983): 150 579.

Ur   An ancient city of *Sumer (S Iraq). Mentioned in Genesis as *Abraham's homeland, its site remained unidentified until 1854. Sir Leonard *Woolley's excavations (1922–34) made famous the spectacularly rich royal burials of about 2500 BC and seemed to provide historical evidence for *Noah's flood. The leading city in Sumer when it was sacked by barbarians about 2000 BC, Ur was superseded by *Babylon. Ur remained a centre for the worship of the moon god Nanna until changes in the course of the Euphrates forced its remaining inhabitants away (5th century BC).

uraemia   The accumulation of *urea in the blood due to kidney failure. Kidney failure can occur suddenly due to shock, obstruction of both ureters, injury, or acute kidney disease or it may arise slowly due to *nephritis or other diseases. In acute kidney failure the kidneys will often recover after *dialysis with a kidney machine. In chronic conditions, requiring long-term dialysis, a kidney transplant (if available) is preferred.

Ural, River   A river in the central Soviet Union, rising in the S Ural Mountains, and flowing mainly S to the Caspian Sea near Guryev. Length: 2534 km (1575 mi).

Uralic languages   A major language family comprising two related groups of languages, the *Finno-Ugric and the Samoyedic (*see* Samoyed). Originating from a common source over 10 000 years ago in an area N of the Ural Mountains, the two branches of the Uralic language family have developed into multiple forms covering an extensive geographical area in Europe, Scandinavia, and Asia.

Ural Mountains   A mountain range in the NW central Soviet Union. It extends 2000 km (1243 mi) N–S from the Kara Sea to the steppes NE of the Caspian Sea and traditionally divides Europe from Asia. The highest point is Mount Narodnaya, in the N, at 1894 m (6214 ft). Most industrial metals are obtained here, as well as some precious stones, such as emerald and amethyst, and the S part is an important industrial area, including the towns of Sverdlovsk and Magnitogorsk.

Urania   In Greek mythology, one of the nine *Muses, the patron of astronomy. She was often portrayed with a globe and compass.

uranium (U)   The radioactive metallic element used as a fuel for nuclear reactors (*see* nuclear energy). Uranium is a silvery-white metal, almost as hard as steel and very dense (relative density 18.95). Before the development of nuclear power, one of its major uses was in making yellow glass. Uranium has the highest atomic number of the naturally occurring elements. It was first isolated in 1841 by E. Péligot (1811–90), although it had been identified before this in pitchblende. It is also found in the ores uranite, carnotite, and monazite; it is mined primarily in Canada, Australia, S Africa, and the Soviet Union. Natural uranium contains three isotopes: ^{238}U (99.283%), ^{235}U (0.711%), and ^{234}U (0.006%). ^{238}U has a half-life of 4.51×10^9 years and is useful in dating rocks, as well as in fuel for fast reactors. The most important isotope in the nuclear industry is ^{235}U, which is used in *thermal reactors. Some reactors use metallic fuel, others uranium dioxide (UO_2). Other oxides include U_3O_8 and UO_3. The volatile gas uranium hexafluoride (UF_6) is used to separate uranium isotopes by gaseous diffusion. At no 92; at wt 238.029; mp 1132°C; bp 3818°C.

uranium-lead dating   A group of methods of *radiometric dating certain rocks, depending on the decay of the radioactive isotope uranium-238 to lead-206 or of uranium-235 to lead-207. One method relies on measuring the amount of helium trapped in the rocks (eight helium nuclei are released in the U-238 decay), another depends on the ratio of radiogenic lead present to nonradiogenic lead (Pb-204). The methods are reliable for ages of between 10^7 and 10^9 years.

uranium series One of three naturally occurring series of radioactive decays. The uranium series is headed by uranium-238, which undergoes a series of alpha and beta decays ending with the stable isotope lead-206. *See also* actinium series; thorium series.

Uranus (astronomy) A giant planet, orbiting the sun every 84 years (between Saturn and Neptune) at a mean distance of 2870 million km. Its axis of rotation is close to its orbital plane. It is somewhat larger (50 800 km in diameter) than Neptune and exhibits a similar greenish featureless disc in a telescope. In its equatorial plane lie some 15 *satellites and a system of about 20 narrow rings, some discovered in 1977, the rest observed in *Voyager 2 photographs (1986). Composed predominantly of hydrogen and helium, with cloud layers of methane and possibly ammonia, its atmospheric and interior structure are thought to be almost identical to those of Neptune. Uranus was discovered in 1781 by William *Herschel.

Uranus (Greek mythology) The personification of Heaven. He was the son of Gaea (Earth), and his children by her included the *Titans and the *Cyclops. He was castrated by his son Cronus and his genitals were thrown into the sea, which gave birth to *Aphrodite.

Urartu (biblical name: Ararat) A kingdom flourishing between about 850 and 650 BC in E Turkey. The inhabitants, of *Hurrian stock, made their capital at Van (ancient Tushpa). Their metalwork was famous, examples even reaching Etruscan Italy. Urartu was frequently at war with neighbouring Assyria.

Urban II (Odo of Lagery; c. 1042–99) Pope (1088–99). Until 1094 his rule was challenged by Guibert of Ravenna (d. 1100), the antipope set up by Emperor Henry IV. A Cluniac monk, he was made a cardinal by *Gregory VII, whose reform policies he continued. Councils at Melfi (1089) and at Piacenza and Clermont (1095) condemned simony, lay investiture, and clerical marriage. At Clermont he also proclaimed the first *Crusade. He was beatified in 1881. Feast day: 29 or 30 July.

Urban VI (Bartolommeo Prignano; c. 1318–89) Pope (1378–89). His anti-French policies and dictatorial behaviour inspired the French cardinals to declare his election void and to elect an antipope, thereby beginning the *Great Schism.

Urban VIII (Maffeo Barberini; 1568–1644) Pope (1623–44) during the *Thirty Years' War, in which he supported Richelieu against the Habsburgs. A great scholar, Urban supported new religious orders and reforms, including the revision of the Missal and new canonization procedures. He promulgated several measures against heresy and condemned the writings of Galileo and Jansen.

Urbino 43 43N 12 38E A town in Italy, in Marche. The birthplace of Raphael, Urbino possesses a 15th-century ducal palace and a university (1506). Its manufactures include textiles and maiolica. Population (1981 est): 15 918.

Urdu An *Indo-Aryan language of N India and Pakistan, where it is an official language. Like *Hindi it arose from *Hindustani, but since it was used largely by Muslims in this region, while Hindi has been progressively influenced by *Sanskrit, the two now differ considerably. It is written in a modified Arabic script.

urea (*or* carbamide) A white crystalline compound (CO $(NH_2)_2$) derived from ammonia and carbon dioxide. It is widely used as a nitrogen fertilizer, a feed supplement for ruminant animals, and in the plastics and pharmaceutical industries. Urea is the excretory product of nitrogen metabolism in mammals and is present in *urine.

urea-formaldehyde resins Synthetic thermosetting resins that are made by the condensation in aqueous solution of urea and formaldehyde with an ammonia catalyst. Cellulose filler

is added to the colourless syrupy solution produced and a moulding powder forms when it dries. This powder can be coloured and used to make cups, fittings, etc.

urethane A white crystalline solid, $CO(NH_2)(OC_2H_5)$, made by heating ethanol with urea nitrate. It is soluble in water and alcohol and is used to manufacture *polyurethane foam.

urethritis Inflammation of the urethra—the duct that carries urine from the bladder to the outside. Nonspecific urethritis (NSU) is one of the most common sexually transmitted diseases.

Urey, Harold Clayton (1893–1981) US physicist, who received the Nobel Prize in 1934 for his discovery of deuterium. He also did valuable work on the separation of isotopes, which was useful in the manufacture of the hydrogen bomb. In postwar years, as professor at Chicago University (1945–52) and then at the University of California, he turned to geophysics.

Urfa (ancient name: Edessa) 37 08N 38 45E A town in S Turkey, near the Syrian border. It was the birthplace of Abraham. It has changed hands frequently, being occupied by Crusaders from 1098 to 1637. Population (1980): 147 488.

Urfé, Honoré d' (1568–1625) French novelist. His major work was the prose romance, *L'Astrée* (1607–27), which is set in his native Lyonnais in the 5th century and is considered to be the first French novel. He also wrote the pastoral dramas *Sireine* and *Sylvanire* (1627).

Urga. *See* Ulan Bator.

uric acid A compound ($C_5H_4N_4O_3$) formed during the nitrogen metabolism of animals and the chief nitrogenous excretory product of reptiles and birds. In man, raised levels of uric acid in the blood are associated with gout.

urine The fluid that is formed by the kidneys and contains the waste products of metabolism and surplus water and salts. In man the kidneys normally produce 0.9–1.5 l of urine per day, containing some 50–70 g of solids—mostly urea, creatine, uric acid, and inorganic salts.

Urmia, Lake A shallow lake in NW Iran, the largest in the country, lying 1300 m (4265 ft) above sea level. It has no outlet and consequently is salty and varies in size. Average area: 5000 sq km (1930 sq mi).

Urnfield A group of Bronze Age cultures originating in central Europe. Urnfield peoples characteristically cremated their dead and buried the ashes in cemeteries of pottery urns. Their culture spread to most of Europe before being displaced by Iron Age *Hallstatt or Roman influence. Urnfields are commonly associated with groups who later became identifiable as the *Celts.

Ursa Major (Latin: Great Bear) A large conspicuous constellation in the N sky. The brightest stars, all of 2nd magnitude, are Alioth, Alcaid, and Dubhe. The seven brightest stars form the *Plough.

Ursa Minor (Latin: Little Bear) A constellation in the N sky that contains the N celestial pole. The brightest star is *Polaris, the present pole star.

Ursula, St A legendary British martyr. According to tradition, she and 11 000 virgins were murdered by the Huns at Cologne while returning from a pilgrimage to Rome in the 3rd or 5th century. She is first mentioned in the 10th century. She has given her name to numerous religious establishments, including the *Ursulines. Feast day: 21 Oct.

Ursulines A Roman Catholic religious order for women, named after its patron St *Ursula, founded in Brescia in 1535 by St Angela Merici (1474–1540). It is devoted to educational work and is the oldest teaching order of women.

urticaria (*or* hives) An acute or chronic allergic disorder in which itching white raised patches surrounded by red areas appear on the skin: they resemble nettle stings (hence the alternative name—nettle rash). Acute urticaria usually arises from allergy to food or drugs and usually disappears quickly if the cause is removed. Chronic urticaria occurs in young people and its cause is not certain. Urticaria is treated with *anti-histamines.

Uruguay, Oriental Republic of   A country in the SE of South America, on the Atlantic Ocean and the Rio de la Plata. Coastal plains rise to higher ground, especially in the N. The River Uruguay forms its W boundary and the other main river is the Negro. Most of the population is of Spanish and Italian descent. *Economy*: the traditional livestock industry was badly affected by the 1974 EEC ban on meat imports, although new markets have subsequently been found. The cultivation of the principal crops (wheat, maize, sorghum) has been intensified and the fishing industry has been expanded with government assistance. The principal industries include food processing, hides and leather, textiles, construction, metallurgy, and rubber. Hydroelectricity is a valuable source of power. *History*: explored by the Spanish in the 16th century, its early history was one of rivalry between Spanish and Portuguese settlements. In the 18th century Spain established its control of Uruguay, which in 1776 became part of the viceroyalty of the Río de la Plata. Under the leadership of Artigas, Uruguay joined Argentina in the movement for independence against Spain but was subsequently fought over by Argentina and Brazil. In 1828, with British help, Uruguay achieved independence, since when politics have been dominated by two parties, the Colorados (liberals) and the Blancos (conservatives). The late 19th century saw the beginning of considerable immigration from Europe, which was encouraged by the establishment in the first decades of the 20th century of what is regarded as Latin America's first welfare state. In the late 1960s there was considerable unrest caused partly by the Tupamaro urban guerrillas (*see* Tupac Amarú). In 1973 they were crushed by the army, which subsequently imposed repressive measures that led to international protests against violations of human rights. Civilian elections took place in 1984 and military rule officially ended in early 1985, when Julio Sanguinetti (1936–), leader of the right-wing Colorado party, became president. Uruguay is a member of the OAS and LAFTA. Official language: Spanish. Official currency: new Uruguayan peso of 100 centésimos. Area: 186 926 sq km (72 172 sq mi). Population (1983 est): 2 954 000. Capital and main port: Montevideo.

Uruguay, River (Portuguese name: Rio Uruguai; Spanish name: Río Uruguay)   A river in South America. Rising in S Brazil, it flows generally SW forming the Argentina–Brazil and Argentina–Uruguay borders before joining the Rio Paraná to form the Río de la Plata. Length: about 1600 km (1000 mi).

Uruk (biblical name: Erech; modern name: Warka)   An ancient city in S Mesopotamia. The site testifies to the beginnings of Sumerian civilization in the 4th millennium BC; significant finds include pictographic writing and pottery made on a wheel. In the 3rd millennium, Uruk was a centre for the worship of the god *Anu. *Gilgamesh was one of its rulers. Supplanted by *Ur (c. 2100), Uruk nevertheless remained inhabited until the early Christian era.

Ürümqi (*or* Urumchi; former name: Tihwa)   43 43N 87 38E A city in NW China, the capital of Xinjiang Uygur AR, and the site of its university. Industries include iron and steel and machine building. Population (1980 est): 842 000.

ushabti   A figurine of faience, wood, or stone placed in an ancient Egyptian tomb to serve the deceased in the afterlife. Called "answerers," they carried inscriptions asserting their readiness to answer the gods' summons to work.

Ushant (French name: Ouessant)   48 28N 5 05W A French island off the W coast of Brittany. Two naval battles (1778 and 1794) between the British and the French were fought off its coast. Area: about 16 sq km (6 sq mi).

Usküb.   *See* Skopje.

Üsküdar (former name: Scutari)   41 02N 29 02E A town in NW Turkey, a suburb of Istanbul on the opposite side of the Bosporus. The British military base here during the Crimean War included the hospital in which Florence Nightingale worked. Population (1980): 261 141.

Uspallata   32 43S 69 24W A pass through the Andes, in S South America at the foot of Mount Aconcagua, linking Santiago (Chile) with Mendoza (Argentina). The statue *Christ of the Andes* was erected here in 1904. Height: 3840 m (12 600 ft).

Ussher, James   (1581–1656) Irish Protestant churchman. Ordained in 1601, he drew up the articles of doctrine for the Irish Protestant Church in 1615. As Archbishop of Armagh from 1625, he frequently visited England, eventually settling there after the Irish Rebellion (1641). He is best remembered for dating the creation at 4004 BC.

USSR.   *See* Soviet Union.

Ussuri River   A river in E Asia, rising in the extreme E Soviet Union and forming part of the border with China as it flows N to the River Amur at Khabarovsk. Border fighting between Soviet and Chinese forces has occurred here (1964, 1972). Length: about 800 km (500 mi).

PETER USTINOV   *As an unsavoury legionnaire in the comedy film* The Last Remake of Beau Geste *(1977).*

Ustinov, Peter (Alexander)   (1921–) British actor, director, and dramatist of Russian descent. In the theatre he acted mostly in his own plays, which include *The Love of Four Colonels* (1951), *Romanoff and Juliet* (1956), and *Beethoven's Tenth* (1983); his many films include *Death on the Nile* (1978). He has written novels and an autobiography; he is also well known as an impersonator and television personality.

Ust-Kamenogorsk   49 58N 82 36E A port in the Soviet Union, in the E Kazakh SSR on the River Irtysh. It is the centre of a zinc-, copper-, and lead-mining region. Population (1981 est): 286 000.

Ustyurt Plateau (*or* Ust Urt Plateau)   A desert upland in the SW Soviet Union, lying between the Caspian and Aral Seas in the Kazakh and Uzbek SSRs at an average height of about 200 m (656 ft). Area: about 200 000 sq km (77 204 sq mi).

Usumbura.   *See* Bujumbura.

usury   In medieval canon law, the charging of interest for the loan of money. Although Christians were debarred from being moneylenders, the profession was permitted to Jews by the fourth Lateran Council (1215). Since Jews were allowed by the Pentateuch to lend money at interest to strangers, and were excluded from many alternative occupations, they comprised the majority of moneylenders. By the late middle ages, however, with growing demand for credit to meet the needs of trade, many Christians, notably at Cahors and in Lombardy, ignored canonical prohibition and became moneylenders and usury came to mean the charging of extortionate interest.

Utagawa Kuniyoshi (Igusa Magosaburo; 1797–1861) Japanese painter and printmaker of the *ukiyo-e movement. He is known for his warrior and landscape prints.

Utah One of the mountain states in the SW USA. The Wasatch Range of the Rocky Mountains divides the state into two arid regions: the Great Basin, which includes the Great Salt Lake, and the Great Salt Lake Desert in the W and the Colorado Plateau in the E. The raising of livestock is the principal agricultural activity but further growth in this sector is limited by the lack of irrigation and by soil erosion. Manufacturing is increasing in importance, especially food products, fabricated steel, spacecraft and, more recently, electronics equipment. There are significant deposits of copper, oil, natural gas, and uranium. Scenic attractions, such as Bryce Canyon and Zion National Park, make it a popular tourist area. *History*: the persecuted Mormons, who had emigrated from New York, began major settlements here in 1847 and their religion continues to exert a dominating influence over the life of the state. Ceded to the USA by Mexico in 1848, Utah was finally admitted to the Union in 1896. Area: 219 931 sq km (84 916 sq mi). Population (1980): 1 461 037. Capital: Salt Lake City.

Utamaro. *See* Kitagawa Utamaro.

uterus. *See* womb.

Utica 43 06N 75 15W A city in the USA, in New York state on the Mohawk River. F. W. Woolworth opened his first shop here in 1879. There is an annual Utica Eisteddfod, sponsored by its many Welsh inhabitants. Industries include dairy farming and textiles. Population (1980): 75 435.

utilitarianism An ethical doctrine holding that the best action is the one that will result in the greatest happiness and least pain for the greatest number of people. Utilitarianism flourished in Britain from the mid-18th century to the mid-19th century. *Hume, *Bentham, and James *Mill propounded it and John Stuart Mill defended it. It influenced all thought in politics and morals and was the most widespread British contribution to such thought. Both *intuitionism and *idealism have developed critiques of the doctrine, based on its inherent unfairness, the difficulty of assessing consequences, and the belief that some acts are intrinsically good or intrinsically bad, regardless of outcome.

utopianism A programme of total social and political reform with the object of establishing a perfect society. The term derives from the imaginary state depicted in Thomas *More's *Utopia* (1516). Utopian schemes have sometimes found practical expression in social experiment, such as Robert *Owen's New Lanark community. Others, such as *Utopia* itself, are literary satires attacking existing institutions by comparing them unfavourably with imaginary ideals. Utopianism advocates a communistic organization of society, but the concomitant authoritarianism reveals that no way has been found of reconciling individual freedom and happiness with social justice.

Utrecht 52 06N 5 07E A city in the central Netherlands, the capital of Utrecht province. The Union of Utrecht (1579) united the northern provinces of the Netherlands against Spain. The Treaties of *Utrecht (1713–14) were concluded here. Its notable buildings include the gothic cathedral (14th century) and its famous university (founded 1636). An important railway centre, its industries include textiles, chemicals, and metallurgy. An annual trade fair is held here. Population (1985): 229 500.

Utrecht, Treaties of (1713–14) A series of treaties between France and, respectively, Britain, the Netherlands, Prussia, Portugal, and Savoy that concluded the War of the *Spanish Succession. Further treaties arranged settlements with Spain and the Holy Roman Empire. The effect of the treaties was to end Louis XIV's attempts at European expansion.

Utrillo, Maurice (1883–1955) French painter, the illegitimate son of Suzanne Valadon (1867–1938), an artist's model and later herself an artist. For almost his entire life, he suffered from alcoholism and drug addiction. He specialized in painting often deserted street scenes, notably of Montmartre, which are distinguished by their near-monochrome colours and precise drawing. These were often based on picture-postcards and after 1916 became somewhat repetitive.

Uttar Pradesh A state in N India, stretching from highlands N across the Ganges plain into the Himalayas. The most populous state, it produces grains, pulses, and sugar cane. Forestry is important but there is little industry. *History*: the centre of N Indian culture, Uttar Pradesh was also the core of the Mogul Empire. It was the centre of the Indian Mutiny (1857–59) against British rule and of Indian nationalism. Area: 294 413 sq km (113 643 sq mi). Population (1981): 110 858 019. Capital: Lucknow.

uvula. *See* palate.

Uzbek Soviet Socialist Republic (*or* Uzbekistan) A constituent republic in the S Soviet Union. The NW comprises desert but fertile land is found in the SE. The Uzbeks, who are Turkic-speaking Sunnite Muslims, make up two-thirds of the population. Uzbekistan is rich in mineral deposits, including oil, coal, and copper, and has more than 20 hydroelectric plants and 3 natural gas pipelines in operation. Industries include mining, chemicals, textiles, and paper. The region is the chief cotton-growing area in the Soviet Union and the third most important in the world. Rice is also produced. *History*: the region was invaded by the Persians under Darius I, the Macedonians under Alexander the Great, and then by the Arabs (8th century AD) and the Mongols (13th century). In the 16th century the Uzbeks became the dominant people in the region, which was annexed by Russia in the 19th century. The Uzbek SSR was formed in 1924. Area: 449 600 sq km (173 546 sq mi). Population (1981 est): 16 158 000. Capital: Tashkent.

V

V-1 A German World War II unguided missile, also called a flying bomb. Powered by an air-breathing type of ramjet, it carried about 2000 pounds (900 kg) of high explosive. Some 8000 missiles were launched against London between June 1944 and March 1945, killing over 5500 civilians. Many were shot down before reaching their target. The "V" stands for the German *Vergeltungswaffe*, retaliation weapon.

V-2 A German World War II *ballistic missile powered by a rocket engine using alcohol and liquid oxygen as fuel. It carried about 2000 pounds (900 kg) of high explosive and had a preset guidance system with no in-flight corrections. Some 4000 were used against Britain and the Low Countries in 1944 and 1945. It became the basis for both US and Soviet postwar rocket design.

Vaal River A river in South Africa, rising in the SE Transvaal. It flows generally W and SW, to join the Orange River and forms part of the Orange Free State–Transvaal border. The **Vaal Dam**, near Vereeniging, supplies water to the mines of the Witwatersrand. Length: 1210 km (750 mi).

Vaasa (Swedish name: Vasa) 63 06N 21 36E A seaport in W Finland, on the Gulf of Bothnia. Founded in 1606, it was rebuilt nearer the sea following a fire in 1852. Its industries include ship repairing, textiles, and food processing. Population (1980): 53 758.

vaccination (*or* inoculation) The introduction of inactivated or dead disease-causing microorganisms (vaccine) into the body to stimulate the formation of *antibodies to these agents without producing the disease (*see also* immunity). The first vaccination (against smallpox) was performed by Edward *Jenner in 1798. Vaccination is now routinely used to prevent such life-threatening infections as poliomyelitis, diphtheria, tetanus, and tuberculosis. It is also used to protect visitors to areas where such infections as yellow fever, cholera, and typhoid fever are endemic. Vaccines are usually given by injection but some can be administered through skin scratches and some are taken by mouth. Vaccination against German measles (rubella) may be given to nonpregnant women of child-bearing age to prevent the malformations in the fetus that this disease can cause. The use of the whooping cough vaccine is controversial as in very rare cases it has caused brain damage.

vacuum A region of space that contains no matter. In practice, a perfect vacuum is impossible to obtain and any region in which the pressure of the gas is less than about one millimetre of mercury may be considered a vacuum. In technical work a soft (*or* low) vacuum goes down to a pressure of 10^{-4} mmHg, a hard (*or* high) vacuum is between 10^{-4} and 10^{-9} mmHg, and an ultrahigh vacuum is below 10^{-9} mmHg. Vacuum technology is used in making cathode-ray tubes, light bulbs, etc., and is used in certain forms of food preservation. **Vacuum gauges** include the *McLeod gauge and *Pirani gauge.

vacuum flask. *See* Dewar flask.

Vadodara. *See* Baroda.

Vaduz 47 08N 9 32E The capital of the principality of Liechtenstein. It is a tourist centre and its castle (restored 1905–16) is the residence of the ruling prince. Population (1980): 4606.

vagina The part of the reproductive tract of women and other female mammals into which the *penis is inserted during sexual intercourse. It connects the womb to the exterior and is readily distensible to allow for childbirth.

vagus nerve An important nerve that connects the brain with the throat, larynx, heart, lungs, stomach, and gut. Surgical cutting of a branch of the vagus nerve (**vagotomy**) is sometimes

carried out to reduce the secretion of acid by the stomach in the treatment of a peptic ulcer.

Valdemar I (*or* Waldemar; 1131–82) King of Denmark (1157–82). His defeat of rival claimants to the throne ended a prolonged civil war in Denmark. His campaigns against the Wends (1159–69), assisted by his minister *Absalon, ended in victory with the seizure of Rügen. He subsequently repressed internal unrest.

Valdemar II (*or* Waldemar; 1170–1241) King of Denmark (1202–41); the son of Valdemar I. Before becoming king he conquered Holstein and Hamburg (1200–01) and later conducted successful campaigns in the E Baltic region. In 1219 he conquered Estonia but from 1223 to 1225 was imprisoned by a German vassal. At home he introduced military and legal reforms, issuing a revised legal code, the Law of Jutland (1241).

Valdemar IV Atterdag (*or* Waldemar; c. 1320–75) King of Denmark (1340–75). He was brought up at the court of Emperor Louis IV, Denmark being in the hands of foreign princes. Recognized as king in 1340, his reunification of Danish territories was completed by the recovery of Skåne from Sweden in 1360. His conquest of Gotland in the Baltic (1361) brought opposition from the Hanseatic League, which defeated Valdemar (1368) and forced him to accept the unfavourable Treaty of Stralsund (1370). His daughter *Margaret became Queen of Denmark, Norway, and Sweden.

Valdivia 39 46S 73 15W A port in S Chile, on the Río Valdivia near the Pacific coast. It was badly damaged by earthquake (1960). Industries include tanning, shipbuilding, and sugar refining. It contains the Southern University of Chile (1954). Population (1983 est): 115 681.

valence (*or* valency) The combining power of an atom, ion, or radical. It is equal to the number of hydrogen atoms that the atom, ion, or radical can combine with or replace in forming compounds, i.e. the number of single covalent or electrovalent bonds (*see* chemical bonds) that an atom, etc., can make. Many elements have more than one valence, for example phosphorus has valences of three and five. A **valence electron** is an electron in the outer shell of an atom that participates in forming chemical (valence) bonds. *See also* energy band.

Valence 44 56N 4 54E A town in SE France, the capital of the Drôme department on the River Rhône. It has a cathedral (11th–12th centuries) and is a commercial centre for agricultural produce. Population (1982): 68 157.

Valencia 39 29N 0 24W The third largest city in Spain, on the Guadalaviar estuary. In 1021 it became the capital of the Moorish kingdom of Valencia. El Cid, the legendary Spanish hero, took the city from the Moors and held it from 1094 until his death in 1099. Its many notable buildings include the cathedral (1262–1482); the university was founded in 1500. The centre of a productive agricultural area, Valencia has an important trade in oranges, rice, and silk. Population (1981): 751 734.

Valencia 10 14N 67 59W The third largest city in Venezuela. It is the focus of the country's most productive agricultural area and is a major industrial centre. The University of Carabobo was founded here in 1852. Population (1981 est): 568 000.

Valencia A former kingdom in E Spain, corresponding approximately to the present-day province of Valencia. It was taken from the Moors by El Cid during the 11th century and came under the rule of Aragon in 1238.

Valenciennes 50 22N 3 32E A town in N France, in the

Nord department. It has metallurgical and textile industries and an oil refinery. Its once famous lace industry is being revived. Population (1982): 40 881.

Valens (d. 378 AD) Eastern Roman emperor (364–78). Valens owed his accession to his brother *Valentinian, emperor in the West. During Valens' reign the Visigoths crossed the Danube and killed Valens at the battle of *Adrianople.

valentine A greeting card sent anonymously on 14 February as a declaration of affection. In ancient Rome boys drew girls' names from a love urn on 15 February and the early Christian Church transferred this popular pagan custom to St Valentine's feast day rather than abolish it. Paper valentines date from the 16th century.

Valentine, St (died c. 269) Roman priest and martyr, known as the patron of lovers. The customs practised on his feast day (14 Feb) have no connection with his life (see valentine).

Valentinian I (d. 375 AD) Western Roman emperor (364–75). Valentinian became emperor by the acclamation of the army at Nicaea and shortly afterwards made his brother *Valens emperor in the East. Reputedly of cruel disposition, he fought campaigns in the north of the Empire, restoring the Rhine frontier and Hadrian's Wall.

RUDOLF VALENTINO *In one of his most popular films* Blood and Sand *(1922).*

Valentino, Rudolf (Rodolpho Gugliemi di Valentina d'Antonguolla; 1895–1926) US film actor, born in Italy. He held various labouring jobs between arriving in the USA in 1913 and going to Hollywood in 1918. His performances in *The Sheik* (1921), *Blood and Sand* (1922), *Son of the Sheik* (1926), and other silent romantic dramas established him as the leading cinema idol of the 1920s.

Valera, Eamon De. *See* De Valera, Eamon.

valerian A perennial or (rarely) annual herb of either of the genera *Valeriana* (200 species) or *Centranthus* (12 species), native to the N hemisphere. Up to about 1 m high, the plants usually have lobed leaves and small fragrant pink, red, or white five-lobed funnel-shaped flowers clustered into terminal heads. The root of the common valerian (*V. officinalis*), of Eurasia, has sedative properties. Family: *Valerianaceae.*

Valéry, Paul (1871–1945) French poet, essayist, and critic. After publishing some early Symbolist verse he devoted himself for many years to abstract metaphysical study. *Cahiers* (29 vols, 1957–60) is a record of his daily speculations from 1894 until his death. His later poetry in *La Jeune Parque* (1917) and *Charmes* (1922) combines

sensuous lyricism with intellectual force. He published many collections of essays on literary, scientific, and political topics.

Valhalla In Teutonic mythology, one of the three homes of *Odin, imagined as an enormous hall the rafters of which are spears and the walls shields. Half of the warriors who die in battle are brought by the *Valkyries to Valhalla, where they spend their days in battle and their nights in feasting and listening to songs of their heroic exploits.

Valium. *See* benzodiazepines.

Valkyries In Teutonic mythology, beautiful maidens, between 3 and 27 in number, who are the personal attendants of *Odin. They wear helmets and armour, carry spears and, led by *Freyja, ride on horseback over battlefields in order to find and carry away the slain warriors whom Odin has chosen to live with him in *Valhalla.

Valla, Lorenzo (1405–57) Italian Renaissance humanist. He was a violent opponent of *scholasticism and an able scholar. In his *De voluptate* (*On Pleasure*; 1431), he argued that the pleasures of the senses were the greatest good. Valla's iconoclastic views had a considerable influence upon later Renaissance thought.

Valladolid 41 39N 4 45W A city in central Spain, in Old Castile. It was formerly the capital of Castile and León (14th–15th centuries). It has a 16th-century cathedral and contains Cervantes' house; its university was founded in 1346. Christopher Columbus died here (1506). An industrial centre, its industries include brewing and textiles. Population (1981): 330 242.

Valle d'Aosta An autonomous region in NW Italy, consisting of the upper basin of the River Dora Baltea. Created in 1945, it has a large French-speaking population. Industry is replacing agriculture as the main activity and there are valuable hydroelectric resources. Tourism is important. Area: 3262 sq km (1260 sq mi). Population (1980 est): 114 469. Capital: Aosta.

Valletta 35 54N 14 32E The capital of Malta, a port on the N coast with one of the finest harbours in the world. Founded in 1566 by the Knights of St John, its main buildings include the 16th-century St John's Co-Cathedral and the University of Malta (1769). Formerly an important British naval base, its dockyards have been converted to commercial use and it is now an important transit centre for Mediterranean shipping. Population (1980): 14 073.

valley An elongated depression in the earth's surface. It is usually occupied by a river or stream at its base and terminates on joining another river, a lake, or the ocean. Valleys have various origins but the common **V-shaped valley** is formed as the result of erosion by a river. Those that originated through glacial erosion are **U-shaped valleys**, with steep sides and broad floors, often occupied by deep lakes (see fjord). See also rift valley.

Valley Forge The site, 35 km (22 mi) NW of Philadelphia, of the winter camp of Gen Washington's army in the winter of 1777–78 during the American Revolution. The patient endurance of his hungry, ill, and badly clothed men, who nevertheless emerged ready for the spring offensive against the British, became legendary.

Valley of Ten Thousand Smokes A volcanic area in the USA, in S Alaska. Its name derives from the many fissures spouting smoke, gas, and steam.

Valley of the Kings The cemetery of the Egyptian pharaohs from about 1580 to about 1085 BC, W of the Nile, near *Thebes. Tombs were tunnelled in the limestone cliffs while mortuary temples were built in the valley below. All the tombs were robbed, except that of *Tutankhamen.

Valois The royal dynasty of France from 1328 to 1589, succeeding the *Capetians. The *Hundred Years' War (1337–1453) nearly destroyed Valois power, which was saved by *Charles VII (reigned 1422–61). He and his son *Louis XI vigorously extended royal authority. Their successors, *Charles VIII and *Louis XII, waged disastrous wars in Italy, where they opposed the *Habsburgs. The last Valois were the victims of rival religious factions at court (*see* Wars of Religion) and were succeeded by the *Bourbons.

Valois, Dame Ninette de. *See* de Valois, Dame Ninette.

Valona. *See* Vlora.

Valparaíso 33 05S 71 40W The second largest city in Chile, on the Pacific Ocean. Founded by the Spanish (1536), it has suffered several earthquakes. Notable surviving buildings include the cathedral. It is the site of two universities (1926 and 1928). Valparaíso is a major port, handling most Chilean imports, and is an important industrial and commercial centre. Manufactures include chemicals, textiles, and vegetable oils. Population (1983 est): 266 726.

value-added tax (VAT) An indirect tax on goods calculated by adding a percentage to the value of a product as it increases at each stage of production; the whole cost of the tax is eventually passed on to the consumer. The tax was introduced in the UK in 1973 to replace *purchase tax and to achieve compatibility with the EEC taxation system. It is collected by the Board of Customs and Excise.

vampire In folklore, a soulless or "undead" corpse that rises from its coffin at night, sometimes taking the form of a vampire bat, and sucks the blood of living victims (who are thus also transformed into vampires). The vampire cannot lie at rest but must continually find new victims. It attacks only at night and is repelled by crucifixes, garlic, and the light of day. The body of a vampire can be destroyed by being beheaded, burnt, having a stake driven through its heart, or by exposure to sunlight. Although appearing in many cultures, the vampire legend is particularly associated with E European folklore and was popularized by Bram Stoker's *Dracula* (1897), the source of many modern vampire films.

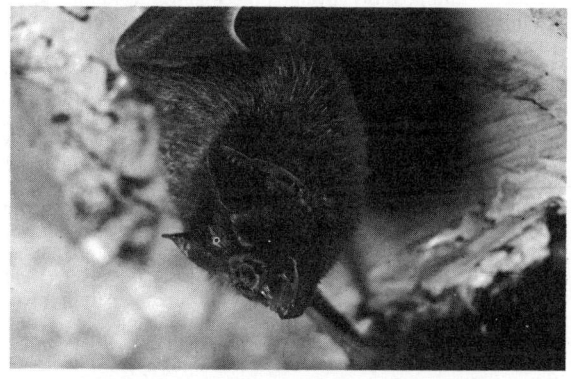

VAMPIRE BAT *Its chisel-like incisor teeth are used to cut the flesh of the victims to cause a flow of blood.*

vampire bat A bat of the family *Desmodontidae* (3 species), of Central and South America. The most common species is *Desmodus rotundus*, 7.5–9 cm long. Vampire bats feed on the blood of mammals or birds. They make a small incision in the skin with their sharp incisor teeth and lap up the blood of their sleeping victim with a grooved tongue. Vampire bats are too small to cause serious blood loss to their host; they do, however, transmit dangerous diseases, including rabies.

Van, Lake A lake in SW Turkey. It has no outlet and is therefore salty; sodium carbonate is extracted by evaporation, and the lake is fished for darekh. Area: 3738 sq km (1443 sq mi).

vanadium (V) A transition metal, named after the Norse goddess Vanadis. The metal is isolated by reduction of the trichloride (VCl_3) with magnesium or of the pentoxide (V_2O_5) with calcium. It is an important additive to rust-resistant *steels

and high-speed tool steels. The pentoxide is a useful catalyst in the oil industry. Complex vanadate ions (for example VO_4^{3-}) exist in solution. At no 23; at wt 50.942; mp $1890 \pm 10°C$; bp $3380°C$.

Van Allen, James Alfred (1914–   ) US physicist, who during World War II developed a proximity fuse for anti-aircraft shells. After the war he used rockets for research into the upper atmosphere, being especially interested in cosmic rays. In 1958, while professor of physics at Iowa University, he used the results of the Explorer satellites to deduce the existence of belts of charged particles (*see* Van Allen radiation belts) above the earth.

Van Allen radiation belts Two regions of charged particles in the earth's *magnetosphere. The toroidal inner belt lies 1000–5000 km above the equator and contains protons and electrons captured from the *solar wind or derived from cosmic-ray interactions. The outer belt lies 15 000–25 000 km above the equator, curving down towards the earth's magnetic poles, and contains mainly electrons from the solar wind. The belts were discovered in 1958 by James *Van Allen on his analysis of observations by early Explorer satellites.

Vanbrugh, Sir John (1664–1726) English architect. After a varied life as a soldier and fashionable playwright—his plays included *The Relapse* (1697) and *The Provok'd Wife* (1697) —Vanbrugh became England's most successful *baroque architect. Although he held a position in the Office of Works, most of his work was for private patrons. His most impressive buildings were Castle Howard (1699–1726), *Blenheim Palace (begun 1705), on which he collaborated with *Hawksmoor, and Seton Delaval (begun 1720). Highly imaginative and extravagant in his designs and costs, Vanbrugh rarely finished buildings and at Blenheim was dismissed by the dissatisfied Duchess of Marlborough.

Van Buren, Martin (1782–1862) US statesman; Democratic president (1837–41) and a founder of the Democratic Party. He came to power during the panic of 1837, the country's first great economic depression, which was caused largely by a wave of land speculation in the West. His refusal of government aid, on a laissez-faire principle, led to his defeat in the 1840 election.

Vance, Cyrus (1917–   ) US statesman; secretary of state (1977–80). He represented President Johnson in Cyprus (1967) and Korea (1968) and was US negotiator at the Paris peace talks on Vietnam (1968–69). He resigned as secretary of state in opposition to President Carter's attempt to rescue the US hostages held in Tehran (Iran).

Vancouver 49 13N 123 06W A city and port in W Canada, in British Columbia on Burrard Inlet and the Fraser River delta. Established in 1862 on a beautiful site at the S end of the Coast Mountains, it has developed a rich tourist industry. Vancouver is Canada's largest Pacific port and railhead. With a large airport, it is a centre for international trade and warehousing. It is the commercial and industrial centre of British Columbia, important especially for its timber, paper, and associated industries. Other industries include food processing, ship repairing, and fishing. Vancouver has two universities and a thriving cultural life. Population (1981): 414 281.

Vancouver, George (c. 1758–98) British navigator. He served his apprenticeship under Capt *Cook and in 1791 set out on a long voyage in the Pacific. He visited Australia and then proceeded NW, charting the W coast of America and circumnavigating the island named after him.

Vancouver Island A Canadian island off the Pacific coast of British Columbia. Its E coastal plain rises to glaciers and forested mountains. The economy depends on timber, mining, fishing, and tourism; it is also a popular retirement area. Area: 32 137 sq km (12 408 sq mi). Population (1981): 461 573. Chief town: Victoria.

Vandals A Germanic tribe that during the first four centuries AD migrated southwards from Scandinavia and the S Baltic coast through Europe to Spain and Africa. There, in 429, they established a kingdom under Genseric and in 455 sacked Rome. The devastation they caused gave rise to the term vandalism. In 534, however, their kingdom was destroyed by the Byzantine general, *Belisarius.

Van de Graaff generator A type of *electrostatic generator, invented by the US physicist Robert Jemison Van de Graaff (1901-67), that produces static potentials of millions of volts. Charge from an external source is fed onto a continuously moving belt, which transfers it to the inside of a large hollow conducting sphere. The charge moves to the outer surface of the sphere, leaving the inside neutral and able to collect more charge. This type of generator can be used to provide a high-voltage source for the Van de Graaff *accelerator.

Vanderbilt, Cornelius (1794-1877) US businessman. He built up a fleet of passenger and cargo steamships, a business that became very successful after the 1849 Gold Rush, when Vanderbilt provided a fast service from New York to San Francisco. In 1862 he sold his ships and bought several railway companies. He endowed Vanderbilt University in Nashville, Tennessee (1873).

Van der Post, Sir Laurens (1906–) South African novelist. His travel books include *Venture to the Interior* (1952) and *The Lost World of the Kalahari* (1958). His novels, often imbued with deep feeling for the African landscape, include *The Hunter and the Whale* (1967) and *A Story Like the Wind* (1972). He was knighted in 1981.

Van der Waals, Johannes Diderik (1837-1923) Dutch physicist, who was professor at Amsterdam University (1877-1907). He was awarded the 1910 Nobel Prize for his work on the intermolecular forces (Van der Waals' forces) and his equation of state (*see* Van der Waals' equation), which takes these forces into account.

Van der Waals' equation A modification of the ideal gas equation, $pV = RT$, where p is the pressure exerted by a gas with volume V and absolute temperature T. R is the *gas constant. Van der Waals adjusted V to $(V - b)$ to take account of the volume occupied by the gas molecules. He also assumed that forces of attraction exist between the gas molecules and therefore adjusted the pressure term to $(p - a/V^2)$. Both a and b are constant for a particular gas. The intermolecular forces are known as **Van der Waals' forces** and are caused by molecules inducing electric *dipole moments in neighbouring molecules.

van de Velde A family of 17th-century Dutch painters. **Willem van de Velde the Elder** (1611-93) and his eldest son **Willem van de Velde the Younger** (1633-1707) were both marine artists, who lived in England after 1672 in the service of Charles II. His younger son **Adriaen van de Velde** (1636-72) was a landscape painter, who was often employed by such artists as *Ruisdael and *Hobbema to paint the figures in their landscapes. **Esaias van de Velde** (c. 1591-1630), the landscape painter, was probably the brother of Willem van de Velde the Elder. He is best known as the teacher of the landscape painter Jan van *Goyen and for such works as *Winter Scene* (National Gallery, London), which herald the realistic landscapes of the later 17th-century Dutch school.

van de Velde, Henry (1863-1957) Belgian *Art Nouveau architect and interior designer. A painter until about 1890, he took up design under the influence of William *Morris and the *Arts and Crafts movement. In 1901, after working in Paris and Berlin, he settled in Weimar, where he directed (1901-14) its School of Arts and Crafts, later part of the *Bauhaus.

Van Dieman's Land. *See* Tasmania.

van Dieman, Anthony. *See* Dieman, Anthony van.

Van Dyck, Sir Anthony (*or* Vandyke; 1599-1641) Flemish *baroque painter, born in Antwerp. Early in his career, he was assistant to *Rubens, who greatly influenced his work.

After working in England for James I, he visited Italy (1621-27). In 1632 he returned to England as painter to Charles I. Although he painted many religious and mythological subjects, such as *Cupid and Psyche* (Buckingham Palace), his reputation rests largely on his portraits of the English court. Many of these are in the Royal Art Collection. *Charles I on Horseback* (National Gallery, London) and *Thomas Killigrew and Lord Croft* (Windsor Castle) demonstrate the elegance and grandeur of his style. He had a profound influence on the development of British portraiture.

Vänern, Lake The largest lake in Sweden. It drains into the Kattegat via the River Göta, a major source of hydroelectric power. Area: 5546 sq km (2141 sq mi).

Vane the Elder, Sir Henry (1589-1655) English politician. He represented Charles I in negotiations with parliament (1640) but fought against the king in the Civil War. His son **Sir Henry Vane the Younger** (1613-62), a staunch Puritan, emigrated to New England in 1635 but returned to England in 1637 and was prominent in the opposition of the *Long Parliament to the king. During the Civil War he negotiated the *Solemn League and Covenant with the Scots (1643). A member of the state council during the Commonwealth (1649-53) he opposed the Protectorate and retired (1653). In 1655 he published the *Retired Man's Meditations*. He participated in the overthrow of Richard Cromwell (1659) but was executed after the Restoration.

van Eyck, Jan (c. 1390-1441) Flemish painter, who also served as diplomatic envoy of Philip the Good, Duke of Burgundy. The controversial *Adoration of the Lamb* altarpiece (Cathedral of S Bavon, Ghent) was probably begun by his elder brother **Hubert van Eyck** (d. 1426) and completed by Jan after Hubert's death. Jan is noted for his realistic portraits, particularly *The Arnolfini Marriage* and *Man in a Red Turban* (both National Gallery, London). He certainly perfected and possibly invented the Flemish technique of oil painting, in which the pigment is mixed with oil and turpentine and applied in thin glazes.

Van Gogh, Vincent (1853-90) Dutch postimpressionist painter, born at Zundert, the son of a pastor. He worked as an art dealer, a teacher in England, and a missionary among coalminers before taking up painting in about 1880. His early works were chiefly drawings of peasants. After a limited training in The Hague and in Antwerp, where he studied the works of *Rubens and Japanese prints, he moved to Paris (1886). Here he briefly adopted the style of *impressionism and later of *pointillism. In Arles in 1888 he painted his best-known works—orchards, sunflowers, and the local postman and his family—but only one painting was sold during his lifetime. The visit of his friend *Gauguin ended in a quarrel during which Van Gogh cut off part of his own left ear. In 1889 he entered a mental asylum at Saint-Rémy. The ominous *Wheatfield with Crows* (Stedelijk Museum, Amsterdam) was painted shortly before his suicide, in Auvers. His letters to his brother (Theo) contain the best account of his life and work. *See* expressionism.

Vanilla A genus of climbing *orchids (about 90 species), native to tropical Asia and America. They have long fleshy stems attached to trees by aerial roots and produce large white and yellow flowers. Several species are cultivated commercially for the flavouring agent vanilla, the most important being *V. planifolia*. The fruit—a pod—contains an oily pulp and minute seeds and reaches a length of 20 cm. The aroma of vanilla is due to vanillin, a volatile oil resulting from curing and fermentation of the pods.

Vannes 47 40N 2 44W A port in W France, the capital of the Morbihan department on the Gulf of Morbihan. An important Celtic settlement, it has a cathedral with a 16th-century chapel. Industries include shipbuilding and textiles. Population (1982): 45 397

Vansittart, Robert Gilbert, 1st Baron (1881-1957)

British diplomat, who as permanent undersecretary of state at the Foreign Office (1930–38) criticized Neville Chamberlain's policy of *appeasement. Also a writer, his books include the collection of poems *The Singing Caravan* (1933) and his autobiography *The Mist Procession* (1958).

Van't Hoff, Jacobus Henricus (1852–1911) Dutch chemist, who pioneered the field of stereoisomerism, showing that the bonds of a carbon atom are arranged in a tetrahedron. This enabled him to explain *optical activity in terms of molecular structure. He also contributed to chemical thermodynamics and to the theory of solutions, for which he won the 1901 Nobel Prize.

Vanua Levu A volcanic island in the S Pacific Ocean, the second largest in Fiji. Sugar, copra, and gold are exported. Area: 5535 sq km (2137 sq mi). Chief town: Lambasa.

Vanuatu Republic (name until 1980: New Hebrides) A chain of about 80 forested volcanic islands in the SW Pacific Ocean. Espíritu Santo is the largest island. Discovered by the Portuguese (1606), they were jointly administered as a condominium by France and the UK (1906–80). In 1978 they became partially self-governing as a preliminary to their independence as the Vanuatu Republic in 1980. Copra, cocoa, coffee, and beef are exported. Industries also include tourism, fishing, and manganese mining. Area: about 14 760 sq km (5700 sq mi). Population (1980 est): 117 000. Capital: Vila, on Efate.

vapour pressure The pressure of the vapour given off by a liquid or solid. The vapour pressure increases with temperature. If the liquid or solid is in an enclosed space the number of molecules leaving it eventually reaches an equilibrium with the number of molecules returning to it. At this point the vapour is saturated and the pressure is the **saturated vapour pressure**.

Varanasi (*or* Benares) 25 20N 82 00E A city in India, in Uttar Pradesh on the River Ganges. A major place of pilgrimage for Hindus, Jains, Sikhs, and Buddhists, it has 5 km (3 mi) of ghats (steps), from which thousands of Hindus bathe in the sacred river. There are also burning ghats, from which the ashes of the cremated are scattered over the water. The city contains 1500 temples and two universities. Population (1981): 794 000.

Varèse, Edgard (1883–1965) French composer, who settled in the USA in 1915. He composed music characterized by dissonance, the use of unpitched sounds, and complex rhythms. His works include *Ionisation* (for 41 percussion instruments and two sirens; 1931), *Density 21.5* (for solo flute; 1935), and *Déserts* (for wind instruments and tape; 1949–54).

Vargas, Getúlio (1883–1954) Brazilian statesman; president (1930–45, 1951–54). Seizing power in the revolution of 1930 after losing the presidential election, he announced (1937) the fascist New State, modelled on Portugal. He was overthrown in 1945 and re-elected in 1950 but, threatened with a military coup, he committed suicide.

variable A mathematical symbol for a quantity that can take any value from a set of values called the range. A variable that can take any value between two given values is called continuous; otherwise it is discrete. A quantity that can only take one value is called a constant.

variable star A star whose brightness varies with time, the variations being regular, irregular, or a mixture of the two. In regular variables the brightness completes a cycle in a period ranging from minutes to years. The brightness variation can be several *magnitudes. The three major groups are: eclipsing *binary stars, which include *Algol variables; cataclysmic variables, such as *novae; and pulsating stars, which periodically brighten and fade as their surface layers expand and contract and which include *Cepheid variables, *RR Lyrae stars, and Mira stars (*see* Mira Ceti).

variance In a set of numbers, usually measurements, the quantity obtained by summing the squares of the differences between each number and the average value of the set and then dividing by the number of members of the set. Variance and,

more often, its square root, called the **standard deviation**, are used to estimate scatter or random error in experimental results.

varicose veins Swollen tortuous veins in the legs caused by malfunctioning of the valves in the veins obstructing blood flow. Varicose veins tend to run in families and are commoner in older and fat people, women, and those who are constantly standing. They often ache and may later cause thrombosis or infection. To avoid this and for cosmetic reasons the veins are often injected with a substance that makes them shrivel up or they may be surgically removed.

Varna 43 12N 27 57E A city and port in E Bulgaria, on the Black Sea. Founded in the 6th century BC, it finally passed to Bulgaria in 1878. Processed foods and livestock are exported and it has engineering and boatbuilding industries. Population (1982): 295 038.

Varna, Battle of (10 November, 1444) The battle in which the Hungarians were decisively defeated by the Turks. It enabled the Turks to expand further into the Balkans and ultimately to capture Constantinople (1453).

varnish A resinous solution in oil or a solvent that dries to form a hard transparent coating on wood, metal, etc. The *resins may be natural, synthetic, or mixed. The natural resins used include *shellac, copal, dammar, and congo. *Polyurethane is a particularly durable synthetic resin used for protecting surfaces in harsh environments. Polyesters and alkyds are also used, for example for coating paper containers or as a protective finish for ink.

varnish tree. *See* lacquer tree.

Varro, Marcus Terentius (116–27 BC) Roman scholar and poet. After a varied public career he was appointed public librarian by Julius Caesar in 47 BC. Only a 3-volume work, *On Agriculture*, and parts of a 25-volume work, *On the Latin Language*, survive.

varve dating A technique used in geology and archaeology to give the age of a sediment and to provide information about the climate during which it was formed. Varves are layers of claylike sediment deposited from a melting glacier into a lake. Each varve represents a single year's deposition; a thick varve indicates that the sediment was deposited during a hot summer (since the glacier would melt more quickly and therefore deposit more material). Varves are particularly well developed in Scandinavia and in some regions their formation has continued from the Pleistocene Ice Age to the present: by counting the varves the absolute age of a particular sediment can be calculated.

Vasa The ruling dynasty of Sweden (1523–1818) and of Poland (1587–1668) founded by *Gustavus I Vasa. John III (1537–92; reigned 1568–92) married into the Polish royal house and his son Sigismund III (1566–1632) became King of both Poland (1587) and Sweden (1592). Sigismund was deposed (1599) in Sweden, where he was succeeded by his uncle *Charles IX, and the Vasa split into two competing lines. The best-known Vasa monarchs in Sweden were *Gustavus II Adolphus and *Christina.

Vasarely, Victor (1908–) Hungarian-born painter. After training in Budapest, he moved to Paris (1930), where his abstract paintings of geometric forms were initially influenced by *constructivism. By the 1950s and 1960s he was painting dazzling patterns that appear to move; these works are regarded as leading examples of *Op art.

Vasari, Giorgio (1511–74) Italian painter, architect, and writer. In Florence, under Medici patronage, he painted fresco cycles in the Palazzo Vecchio and built the *Uffizi, both works showing his respect for *mannerism. However he is best known for his *Lives of the Most Eminent Italian Architects, Painters, and Sculptors*, tracing the history of Renaissance art from Giotto to Michelangelo. First published in 1550, it is still popular and useful today, despite some inaccuracies.

vasectomy. *See* sterilization.

Västerås 59 36N 16 32E A city in central Sweden, on Lake Mälar. An important city in medieval times, it has a 12th-century castle and a gothic cathedral. It is a major centre of the electrical industry. Population (1985 est): 118 000.

VAT. *See* value-added tax.

Vatican City, State of the A small independent state within the city of Rome, the seat of government of the Roman Catholic Church. St Peter's Square, St Peter's Basilica, the Vatican Palace, and Papal Gardens are within its area, and it includes 12 buildings outside its boundary, notably several churches and the pope's summer palace at Castel Gandolfo. It has its own army, police, diplomatic service, coinage, postal facilities, and radio station (Radio Vaticano, which provides an all-day service in 31 languages giving information on the Church). *History*: it came into being in 1929, when Pius XI signed the *Lateran Treaty with Mussolini, thereby ending a dispute between church and state dating from the incorporation of the *papal states into newly unified Italy in 1870. The state is governed by a commission appointed by the pope. Supreme pontiff: John Paul II. Official language: Italian. Area: 44 hectares (109 acres). Population (1985 est): 1000.

Vatican Councils The 20th and 21st ecumenical councils of the Roman Catholic Church, held at Rome. **1.** (1869–70) The council that was convoked by *Pius IX resulted in the promulgation of the doctrine of papal *infallibility. The council was suspended because of the Franco-Prussian War. **2.** (1962–65) The council that was convoked by *John XXIII and continued by *Paul VI. Its main purpose, in Pope John's words, was *aggiornamento*, a bringing-up-to-date of the Church. It promulgated no dogmas but instead initiated fundamental changes, including reform of the liturgy and commitment to the *ecumenical movement and to greater collegiality in Church government. It established an atmosphere in which progressive critics could freely express their views.

Vatnajökull An icefield in SE Iceland. Several peaks protrude above the ice level rising to 2119 m (6952 ft) at Öræfajökull, the highest point on the island. Area: 8133 sq km (3139 sq mi).

Vauban, Sébastien Le Prestre de (1633–1707) French military engineer, who revolutionized siege warfare. Appointed engineer to Louis XIV of France in 1655, he directed sieges at Gravelines (1658), Maastricht (1673), and Luxembourg (1684).

Vaughan, Henry (c. 1622–95) English poet. After producing two volumes of secular verse, he turned to Metaphysical poetry, expressing a mystical religious awareness in vivid colloquial language. His best-known volumes are *Silex Scintillans* (1650; enlarged 1655) and *The Mount of Olives* (1652), a book of prose meditations.

Vaughan Williams, Ralph (1872–1958) British composer. He studied at the Royal College of Music and had lessons from Ravel. Influenced by English folksong and Tudor music, he developed a modal style that found its first full expression in *Fantasia on a Theme by Tallis* (for string orchestra; 1910). His works include nine symphonies of which the first, *A Sea Symphony* (1903–09), is choral; the seventh, *Sinfonia Antarctica* (1951–52), is based on his music for the film *Scott of the Antarctic*. He also wrote the ballet *Job* (1931), the opera *The Pilgrim's Progress* (1951), and much other orchestral, chamber, and choral music.

vault An arched roof usually in brick or stone and first developed in ancient Egypt. The simplest and oldest type is the barrel or tunnel vault, a single continuous arch, which originally had to be supported by very thick walls. A more complicated type is the groin vault of the Roman and medieval periods, using a series of mutually supporting interlocking arches, which could span greater distances. The rib vault, consisting of a skeleton of diagonal ribs to support the interlocking arch-es, was developed by gothic builders. Its decorative counterpart is the fan vault with its multiplication of radiating ribs, a principal feature of the *Perpendicular style. With the invention of reinforced concrete, vaulting has advanced enormously, allowing huge distances to be covered without much support.

Vavilov, Nikolai Ivanovich (1887–1943) Soviet plant geneticist. He travelled widely, amassing a vast collection of plant varieties, particularly varieties of wheat. His researches into the origins of cultivated plants led him to propose 12 world centres of plant origin. Vavilov's views brought him into conflict with *Lysenko and Stalinist ideology. He was arrested and imprisoned in 1940.

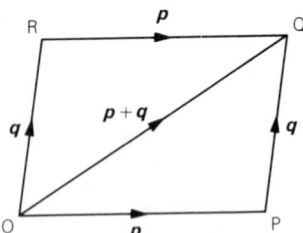

VECTORS *The two vectors OP (**p**) and PQ (**q**) add to give the resultant vector OQ (**p** + **q**). OR = PQ = **q**; OP = RQ = **p**. OQP is a vector triangle and ORQP is a parallelogram of vectors.*

vector (mathematics) A quantity that has both magnitude and direction. Examples of vectors include velocity, force, magnetic flux density, etc. A vector needs three numbers (called components) to be defined, each number representing its magnitude in one of three mutually perpendicular directions. Two vectors are added by adding the corresponding components and may be multiplied to give either a *scalar quantity or another vector.

vector (medicine) An organism capable of transmitting a disease-causing organism (pathogen) from one organism to another. Transmission may be accidental, for example the housefly carries bacteria picked up from its food, or the vector may play a significant role in the life cycle of the pathogen, for example the malarial parasite spends part of its life cycle in the mosquito, which transmits it to man.

Vedanta The various philosophical schools of Hinduism, which derive from the commentaries on the *Vedas*, especially the *Upanishads*, the *Brahmasutras*, and the *Bhagavadgita*. The schools differ in their views on the nature of *Brahman and the individual soul, but have in common the belief in reincarnation, the truth of the *Vedas*, the law of *karma, and the need for spiritual release. Believing Brahman to be the cause of the world, they condemn Buddhism and Jainism.

Vedas (Sanskrit: divine knowledge) The basic Hindu scriptures, written in archaic Sanskrit (Vedic) around 1500 BC. It comprises hymns, invocations, mantras, spells, and rituals, mostly concerning the sacrificial worship of gods representing various natural forces. The canon comprises four main collections: the *Rigveda*, the *Samaveda*, the *Yajurveda*, and the *Atharvaveda*. The *Brahmanas*, the *Aranyakas*, and the *Upanishads*, which are later commentaries, may also be considered canonical.

veduta (Italian: view) A painting, drawing, or print of a view of a town or city. Examples of vedute are *Piranesi's engravings of Rome and *Canaletto's paintings of Venice. The **capriccio** is a specialized form of veduta consisting of various architectural elements combined to produce an imaginary setting. A famous capriccio is the etching of *St Paul's Cathedral in London with the Grand Canal of Venice* by William Marlow (1740–1813).

Vega A conspicuous white star, apparent magnitude 0.03 and 26.5 light years distant, that is the brightest star in the constellation Lyra.

Vega (Carpio), Lope Félix de (1562–1635) Spanish poet and dramatist. After serving with the Spanish Armada (1588) he became secretary to the Duke of Alba in Toledo, and settled in Madrid in 1610. His numerous love affairs continued after his ordination as priest in 1614, but his later years were saddened by the deaths of his wife, children, and mistresses. Most of his numerous plays, such as *Fuenteovejuna* (1612–14) and *El caballero de Olmeda* (1615–26), were based on Spanish history.

Vega probe An international spaceprobe launched in 1984. Sponsored by the USSR and several other countries, the probe dropped a helium balloon and land module on Venus in 1985 and intercepted Halley's comet in March 1986, sending back remarkable photographs of the phenomenon.

vegetarianism The practice of abstaining from eating animal flesh for ethical, religious, or nutritional reasons. Some vegetarians will not eat any animal products, including milk, cheese, eggs, etc., and are called **vegans**. Vegetarianism occurs in many religious traditions, including Buddhism, Jainism, and Hinduism, and it was advocated by *Pythagoras, *Plato, and many other thinkers. The first vegetarian society was founded in Manchester in 1847. Vegetarians, especially vegans, can suffer from anaemia unless their diet includes sufficient vitamin B_{12}.

vein (physiology) A thin-walled blood vessel that carries oxygen-depleted blood from the tissues to the *heart. Most of the smaller veins have valves to prevent backflow of blood. Damage to these valves leads to dilation of the veins (*see* varicose veins). The veins opening directly into the heart are the superior and inferior **vena cavae** and the pulmonary veins from the lungs, which are unique in carrying oxygenated blood. *See* Plate IV.

Velázquez, Diego Rodriguez de Silva (1599–1660) Spanish painter, born in Seville. He trained under Francisco de *Herrera the Elder and Francisco Pacheco (1564–1654), his father-in-law, although he was most strongly influenced by *Titian. Initially he specialized in painting religious subjects and scenes from everyday life with still-lifes, before becoming (1623) court painter to Philip IV (1605–65; reigned 1621–65) and thereafter painting chiefly portraits of the royal family and the chief minister Olivares. Other works include his famous *Pope Innocent X* (Rome) and the *Rokeby Venus* (National Gallery, London), painted during his second visit to Italy (1649–51). *Las Meninas* (c. 1656; Prado) is typical of the informality of his later court portraits.

veld (*or* veldt) A tract of open grassland on the plateau of S Africa. It includes the Highveld (over 1500 m), Middleveld (1500–900 m), and Lowveld (below 900 m).

velocity (*v*) The speed of a body in a specified direction, i.e. its rate of displacement (*s*) in a specified direction is given by $v = ds/dt$. Velocity is a *vector quantity, whereas speed is a *scalar quantity. In SI units it is measured in metres per second. **Relative velocity** is the velocity of one body relative to another. **Angular velocity** (ω) is the rate of change of angular displacement (θ), i.e. $\omega = d\theta/dt$; it is measured in radians per second.

velocity of light (*c*) The speed with which all *electromagnetic radiation travels through a vacuum, equal to $2.997\,925 \times 10^8$ metres per second. It is one of the *fundamental constants, and according to the special theory of *relativity, is independent of the speed of the observer and cannot be exceeded by any material body.

velocity ratio. *See* mechanical advantage.

vena cava. *See* vein.

Venda, Republic of The smallest country in mainland Africa, within South African territory. Most of the population is in Venda. *Economy*: chiefly agricultural, the main crop being maize; the timber industry is also developed. *History*: it was the third *Bantu Homeland to be granted full independence from South Africa (1979), but this is not recognized elsewhere in the world. President: Chief Patrick Mphephu (1925–). Official currency: South African rand. Area: 7410 sq km (2861 sq mi). Population (1980 est): 513 890. Capital: Thokoyandou.

Vendée A department in W France, in Pays de la Loire region. A series of peasant-royalist insurrections, the **Wars of the Vendée**, took place here (1793–1832). The first rebellion, catalysed by the Republican government's introduction of conscription, was also fuelled by loyalty to the Roman Catholic Church. After initial success the rebels were decisively defeated at Savenay (December, 1793). Subsequent abortive uprisings (1796, 1815, and 1832) failed to attract popular support. Area: 7016 sq km (2709 sq mi). Population (1982): 483 027. Capital: La Roche-sur-Yon.

Vendôme, Louis Joseph, Duc de (1654–1712) French marshal under Louis XIV. He fought in the Wars of the *Grand Alliance (1689–97) and of the Spanish Succession (1701–14). He was victorious at Luzzara (1702) and Cassano (1705) but was defeated by Marlborough at Oudenaarde (1708) and was then recalled. From 1710 until his death he campaigned successfully in Spain.

Venera probes A series of Soviet *planetary probes to Venus, first launched in 1961. Veneras 4 to 8 sent capsules into the hostile atmosphere, those of 7 and 8 surviving to reach the surface (1970, 1972). The Lander sections of Veneras 9 and 10 (1975), 11 and 12 (1978), and 13 and 14 (1982) all successfully reached the surface, relaying information and photographs back to earth. Veneras 15 and 16 orbited the planet in 1983 and mapped features of most of its northern hemisphere.

venereal disease. *See* sexually transmitted disease.

Venetia A region of NE Italy between the River Po, the Alps, and the Adriatic Sea. The mainland territory of the Republic of Venice until 1797, Venetia then came under Austrian control and in 1815 formed part of the new kingdom of Lombardy-Venetia. Venetia was incorporated into the kingdom of Italy in 1866 and after World War I formed the "Three Venices"–Venezia Tridentina, Venezia Euganea, and Venezia Giulio. Most of the latter was lost to Yugoslavia after World War II and Italian Venetia was divided into the regions of Friuli-Venezia Giulia, Veneto, and Trentino-Alto-Adige.

Venezuela, Republic of A country on the N coast of South America. The plains of the Orinoco basin in the N rise to the Guiana Highlands in the SE, and in the NW the N end of the Andean chain reaches heights of over 5000 m (16 000 ft). Also in the NW is Lake Maracaibo. Most of the population is of mixed European and Indian descent. *Economy*: based chiefly on oil, first discovered in 1917 and of which Venezuela is now one of the world's largest producers and exporters. The industry was nationalized in 1976. Efforts are being made to diversify the economy, including plans to use the country's vast iron-ore deposits to increase steel production. Another major project is the construction of the world's largest aluminium smelter, which will be able to utilize the recent finds of bauxite. Venezuela is also rich in diamonds, gold, zinc, copper, lead, silver, phosphates, manganese, and titanium. The agricultural sector remains relatively underdeveloped, although a large share of the oil revenues has been spent in attempts to develop this area. Crop growing in the N includes coffee, cocoa, sugar, maize, and rice, while further S stock raising is the principal agricultural activity. The vast forests remain largely unexploited. *History*: sighted by Columbus in 1498, it was visited in 1499 by Vespucci, who named it Venezuela ("Little Venice") on seeing Indian villages built on stilts over Lake Maracaibo. Spanish settlement began in 1520 and Venezuela remained under Spanish rule until liberated by Bolívar in 1821. It then formed part of Colombia until 1830. Independent Venezuela was ruled by a succession of dictators, notably *Guzmán Blanco and *Gómez, until the post-World War II period, which has witnessed the development of more democratic and stable governments, made possible in part by oil revenues. In the 1980s oil revenues declined, foreign debt increased, and an economic crisis ensued. Venezuela is a member of the OAS, LAFTA, and OPEC. President: Dr Jaime Lusinchi. Official language: Spanish. Official currency: bolívar of 100 céntimos. Area: 912 050 sq km (352 143 sq mi). Population (1983 est): 17 993 000. Capital: Caracas. Main port: Maracaibo.

VENICE *The Library of S Marco, begun in 1536 by Jacopo Sansovino (1486–1570), described by Palladio as the richest and most ornate building since antiquity.*

Venice (Italian name: Venezia) 45 26N 12 20E A city in NE Italy, the capital of Veneto. It is a seaport built on over 100 islands in the Lagoon of Venice (an inlet of the Gulf of Venice at the head of the Adriatic Sea). Venice is a centre of commerce and tourism and its manufactures include glassware, textiles, and lace. The rise of the industrial suburbs of Mestre and Marghera on the mainland, however, has led to the economic decline of the old city. The Grand Canal and about 170 smaller canals provide waterways for the city transport, which includes water buses (*vaporetti*) and gondolas. Famous bridges include the Rialto Bridge and the *Bridge of Sighs. Situated at the centre of Venice is the famous St Mark's Square (Piazza San Marco) overlooked by *St Mark's Cathedral, the 15th-century Clock Tower, the Campanile, and the Doge's Palace. An outstanding collection of Venetian paintings, including works by Bellini, Mantegna, Canaletto, and Titian, is housed in the Accademia. The fashionable seaside resort, the Lido, is situated 3 km (2 mi) to the SE, on the outer edge of the lagoon. *History*: originally settled by refugees fleeing the barbarian invasions on the mainland (5th century AD onwards), Venice was united under the first *doge in 697. Strategically positioned between Europe and the East, it became an independent republic and a great commercial and maritime power, defeating its rival Genoa in 1380. It declined in the 16th century following the discovery of the Cape route to India. With *Venetia it came under Austrian control in 1797 and was incorporated into the Kingdom of Italy in 1866. It has in recent years been endangered by floods, pollution, and subsidence. Population (1980 est): 352 453.

Venizélos, Eleuthérios (1864–1936) Greek statesman; prime minister (1910–15, 1917–20, 1924, 1928–32, 1933). During the *Balkan Wars (1912–13), Venizélos acquired the Aegean islands and Crete for Greece. His unsuccessful attempt to instigate a revolt in Crete led to his exile in 1935.

Venn diagram. *See* set theory.

ventricle. *See* brain; heart.

Ventris, Michael (1922–56) British architect and scholar, famous for his decipherment of *Linear B. First inspired by hearing Sir Arthur *Evans lecture in 1936, Ventris studied tablets from *Knossos and *Pylos. In 1952 he realized that their language was a form of Greek. After his death in a car accident, his results were consolidated by his collaborator, John Chadwick (1920–   ).

Venturi tube A device consisting of an open-ended tube with a central constriction, used to measure the rate of flow of a fluid, which can be calculated from the pressure difference between the centre and the ends. It is extensively used to measure the airspeed of aircraft. Invented by G. B. Venturi (1746–1822).

Venus (goddess) A Roman goddess originally of gardens and fertility who became identified with the Greek *Aphrodite as goddess of love. This identification followed the introduction into Rome of the cult of Aphrodite of Eryx in Sicily and was further established by the Julian family, whose members included the emperors from Augustus to Nero and who claimed descent from *Aeneas, son of Aphrodite. Having no myths of her own, she assumed those of Aphrodite.

Venus (planet) The second planet in order from the sun, orbiting the sun every 225 days at an average distance of 108 million km. It is 12 102 km in diameter and has an extremely long period of axial rotation (243 days). It can be one of the most brilliant objects in the sky, reaching a *magnitude of −4.4, and like the moon exhibits *phases. Its surface is totally obscured by dense swirling yellowish clouds of sulphuric acid droplets and sulphur particles. The atmosphere is primarily (98%) carbon dioxide. *Planetary probes have shown that the surface temperature is a hostile 470°C and the surface atmospheric pressure is about 90 times that of earth. The surface has now been carefully mapped and photographed by the Pioneer Venus Orbiter and the *Venera probes, revealing rolling plains covering 70% of the area, huge plateaus concentrated in two main areas and rising to more than 10 000 m, and depressions, including an immense rift valley.

Venus flytrap A *carnivorous plant, *Dionaea muscipula*, native to the eastern USA. The upper part of each leaf is hinged at the midrib and an alighting insect triggers the leaf to snap shut, with its spined margins interlocking, thus trapping the prey. A cluster of five-petalled white flowers is borne on a long stalk. Family: *Droseraceae*.

Venus's flower basket A *sponge of the genus *Euplectella*, found in parts of the Pacific and Indian Oceans. They form enclosed cylindrical colonies, up to 30 cm long, with a delicate skeletal lattice of silica.

Venus's girdle A marine invertebrate animal, *Cestum veneris*, belonging to an order (*Cestida*) of *ctenophores. Its transparent ribbon-like body is about 5 cm wide and 1 m or more long. It occurs in the Mediterranean Sea and Atlantic Ocean and swims with an undulating motion.

Veracruz (*or* Veracruz Llave) 19 11N 96 10W A major port in E Mexico, on the Gulf of Mexico. Industries include iron and steel processing, shipbuilding, and sugar refining; the chief exports are coffee, chicle, and tobacco. It contains the Regional Technical Institute of Veracruz (1957). Population (1980): 305 456.

Verbena A genus of herbaceous plants or dwarf shrubs (about 250 species), chiefly native to North and South America. The leaves are simple, often with narrow lobes, and the funnel-shaped flowers form dense elongated or flat-topped clusters. Several species are grown as ornamentals, especially *V. × hybrida* from South America. Lemon verbena (*Lippia citriodora*) is a related shrub from tropical America, the lemon-scented leaves of which yield an oil used in perfumery. Family: *Verbenaceae. See also* vervain.

Vercelli 45 19N 8 26E A town in NW Italy, in Piedmont. An ancient Ligurian and later a Roman city, it has an outstanding library of manuscripts (notably the *Codex Vercellensis*, a 10th-century English manuscript which contains several poems and other literature). Vercelli lies in Euroe's main rice-producing area. Population (1981 est): 51 975.

Vercingetorix (d. 46 BC) Gallic chieftain, who led the revolt of the tribes of Gaul agaiNT Julius Caesar in 52. After early successes Vercingetorix was besieged at Alesia and his capture ended Gallic resistance to Rome. He was subsequently executed.

Verde, Cape (French name: Cap Vert) 14 43N 17 33W The westernmost point of Africa, in Senegal, consisting of a promontory extending into the Atlantic Ocean.

Verdi, Giuseppe (1813-1901) Italian composer of operas. He studied privately in Milan before beginning a career as a composer. He had an early success with *Nabucco* (1842) but his first mature work was *Rigoletto* (1851); this was quickly followed in 1853 with *La Traviata* and *Il Trovatore*. In 1869 he was commissioned to write an opera for the opening of the Suez Canal; the result was *Aida* (1871). His last works were the *Requiem* (in memory of Alessandro Manzoni; 1874) and the operas *Otello* (1887) and *Falstaff* (1893), with librettos, based on Shakespeare's plays, by Arrigo *Boito.

verdigris A green copper acetate used as a paint pigment. The term is also applied to the green coating, consisting of copper sulphate or carbonate, that forms on copper roofs, etc.

Verdun 49 10N 5 24E A town in NE France, in the Meuse department on the River Meuse. Strategically positioned on the E approach to the Paris Basin, Verdun has long been an important fortress. It was the scene of a major battle in 1916 (*see* World War I). It has brewing, textile, and metallurgical industries. Population (1982): 21 170.

Vereeniging 26 41S 27 56E A town in South Africa, in the S Transvaal, on the Vaal River. Founded in 1892, it was the venue for negotiations to end the second Boer War (1902). It is an important coalmining centre with iron and steel industries. Population (1980 est): 149 410.

Verhaeren, Émile (1844-96) The chief Belgian poet associated with Symbolism (*see* Symbolists). Beginning with the realistic verse of *Les Flamandes* (1883), he published many volumes of poetry the themes of which included his patriotism, his socialism, and his love for his wife. He was also a distinguished art critic.

Verlaine, Paul (1844-96) French poet. His early poetry, notably *Fêtes galantes* (1869), reflects his association with the *Parnassians. His tempestuous relationship with *Rimbaud, who influenced his more experimental *Romances sans paroles* (1874), resulted in the break-up of his marriage, and in 1873 he was imprisoned for shooting and wounding Rimbaud. His later poetry concerned the conflicts inherent in his attempts to lead a reformed life. After the publication of *Les Poètes maudits* (1884), which included studies of Corbière, Mallarmé, Rimbaud, and "Pauvre Lelian" (Verlaine's anagram for himself) among others, Verlaine was the acknowledged leader of the Symbolist poets.

Vermeer, Jan (1632-75) Dutch painter, who spent his entire life in Delft and whose importance was only established in the 19th century after centuries of obscurity. Despite his everyday subject matter, favourite themes being women reading or writing letters and playing musical instruments, his works are remarkable for their motionless figures, technical finish; and skilful use of light. His best-known paintings include *The Milkmaid* (Rijksmuseum, Amsterdam), *The Lacemaker* (Louvre), and *Allegory of Painting* (Kunsthistorisches Museum, Vienna), showing himself at work. See Plate XIII.

vermiculite A *clay mineral with the property of expanding up to 22 times its original thickness on heating, when the water molecules between the silicate layers are driven off. In this form it is light and water-absorbent, and is used as a heat- or sound-insulating material, packaging material, fire extinguisher, and a growing medium for plants. Vermiculite results from the hydrothermal alteration of biotite and the intrusion of acid magma into basic rock.

vermilion Red mercuric sulphide (HgS). It sublimes readily on heating and occurs naturally as the mineral cinnabar. It is used as a pigment, often mixed with red lead and ferric oxide.

Vermont A state in the NE USA, in New England. The extensively forested Green Mountains run N-S through the centre of the state, with the lowlands of the Champlain Valley in the NW and the Connecticut Valley in the E. Small manufacturing industries and tourism are the main sectors of the economy and a variety of goods are produced, particularly wood and paper products. Mining is important, especially the extraction of stone, asbestos, sand, and gravel. The state's farmers produce dairy products, hay, potatoes, corn, and maple syrup. *History*: settled by the British in 1724, it declared its independence in 1777 and joined the Union in 1791. Area: 24 887 sq km (9609 sq mi). Population (1980): 511 456. Capital: Montpelier.

VERMEER A Young Woman Standing at a Virginal *(National Gallery, London).*

vermouth An alcoholic drink made from white wine distilled with herbs. The best-known vermouths are French and Italian and are drunk as aperitifs either neat, with soda or tonic water, or with *gin.

Verne, Jules (1828-1905) French writer. He studied law in Paris but chose to follow a literary career. Verne's *Voyages extraordinaires*, beginning with *Five Weeks in a Balloon* (1863), introduced such scientific and technological marvels as the submarine, space travel, and television. They included *Journey to the Centre of the Earth* (1864), *From the Earth to the Moon* (1865), and *Twenty Thousand Leagues Under the Sea* (1873). One of the precursors of *science fiction, Verne wrote over 100 adventure stories, including *Around the World in Eighty Days* (1873).

Vernier scale A device for measuring subdivisions of a scale, such as those on a pair of calipers. The auxiliary Vernier scale is divided so that ten of its subdivisions correspond to nine of those on the main scale. If the reading falls between two main-scale divisions, say between 4.6 and 4.7, the zero mark on the Vernier scale is slid along so that its zero is lined up with the reading. By noting the division on

VERNIER SCALE *An auxiliary scale used to measure accurately to two places of decimals.*

the Vernier scale that is exactly in line with a main-scale division, the second decimal place of the measurement is obtained. If the fourth Vernier division is in line with a main-scale division, the reading would be 4.64. Named after Pierre Vernier (1580-1637).

Vernon, Edward (1684-1757) British admiral. He was a hero of the War of *Jenkins' Ear, capturing Portobello (1739). His nickname Old Grog (referring to his grogram cloak) was given to the grog (diluted rum) that he introduced to the navy.

Verona 45 26N 11 00E A city in N Italy, in Veneto on the River Adige. Strategically situated at the junction of major routes between Italy and N Europe, its history dates from Roman times. It possesses a Roman amphitheatre, a 12th-century cathedral, and the medieval Castelvecchio. A popular tourist centre, its manufactures include textiles, paper, furniture, and leather goods. Population (1980 est): 268 178.

Veronese, Paolo (P. Caliari; 1528-88) Italian painter of the Venetian school, born in Verona. After training for his father's trade of stonecutter, he studied under minor artists but was chiefly influenced by *Titian. In 1553 he settled in Venice, where he worked on decorations in the Ducal Palace and S Sebastiano. In the Villa Barbaro at Maser, designed by *Palladio, he painted illusionistic landscapes, mythological scenes, and portraits. His religious works, for example *Marriage at Cana* (Louvre), were often pretexts for depicting contemporary banquets in impressive architectural settings and were sometimes the cause of controversy. Thus the *Last Supper* was condemned by the Inquisition for its irreverence; Veronese thereupon retitled the painting *Feast in the House of Levi* (Accademia, Venice).

Veronica. See speedwell.

Verrocchio, Andrea del (Andrea del Cione; c. 1435-88) Florentine Renaissance sculptor, painter, and goldsmith, who ran a large and influential workshop. His only known painting is the *Baptism of Christ* (Uffizi), in which his famous pupil *Leonardo da Vinci reputedly assisted. Verrocchio's major sculptures are *Doubting Thomas* (c. 1481; Orsanmichele, Florence), *David* (Bargello, Florence), and the equestrian monument of Bartolommeo Colleoni in the Campo SS Giovanni e Paolo, Venice.

verruca. See wart.

Versailles 48 48N 2 08E A town in N central France, in the Yvelines department. Versailles is chiefly famed for its baroque palace, the residence of the French kings from 1678 to 1769. It was built for Louis XIV between 1676 and 1708 on the site of a hunting lodge; the design includes architecture by J. H. Mansart (1646-1708), interior decoration by *Le Brun, and formal gardens by *Le Nôtre. In addition to the Grand Château, there are two smaller chateaux: the Grand Trianon and the Petit Trianon (a favourite residence of Marie Antoinette). Historic events enacted at the palace include Britain's recognition of American independence (1783), the crowning (1871) of William I as German emperor, and the signing of the Treaty of *Versailles (1919). Population (1982): 95 240.

Versailles, Treaty of (1919) The treaty, signed at the *Paris Peace Conference after World War I, between the Allied and Associated Powers and defeated Germany. Versailles declared Germany guilty of causing the war, imposed heavy reparations payments, and limited the German army and navy to nominal strength. Territorial provisions included the return of Alsace and Lorraine to France, the cession of parts of Germany to Poland, and the Allied occupation of the Rhineland. Further, most of Germany's colonies were to become *mandates of the *League of Nations, which was established by the treaty. The USA refused to ratify the treaty and did not make peace with Germany until 1921.

vertebra. See spine.

Vertebrata (or Craniata) A subphylum of animals that includes the fish, amphibians, reptiles, birds, and mammals. They are characterized by a backbone consisting of interlocking vertebrae, which forms the main support for the body and protects the nerve cord (spinal cord). The skeleton may be of cartilage or bone and includes two pairs of fin or limb elements that articulate with girdles attached to the backbone. The brain is large and housed in a protective skull. Their highly versatile skeleton has enabled vertebrates to develop many specializations and adaptations for a wide variety of lifestyles in water, on land, and in the air. Phylum: *Chordata.

vervain A slender erect branching perennial herb, *Verbena officinalis*, found on waste ground throughout Eurasia and N Africa. 30-75 cm high, it has deeply lobed leaves and narrow spikes of tiny pinkish flowers. The fruit splits into four nutlets. Cultivated forms of *Verbena* may also be called vervain.

vervet. See grass monkey.

Verwoerd, Hendrik Frensch (1901-66) South African statesman; prime minister (1958-66). Verwoerd's commitment to *apartheid occasioned demonstrations among Blacks, including one at *Sharpeville during which the police fired on the crowd. He took South Africa out of the Commonwealth in 1960. He was assassinated in parliament in Cape Town.

Vesalius, Andreas (1514-64) Flemish anatomist, whose major work, *The Seven Books on the Structure of the Human Body* (1543), contained some of the first accurate descriptions of human anatomy together with illustrations of his dissections. Vesalius' observations challenged the prevailing theories of the Greek physician *Galen, opening up a new era of scientific investigation.

Vespasian (9-79 AD) Roman emperor (69-79). He was acclaimed emperor by the army in Egypt (July, 69) but was not recognized at Rome until the death in December of his rival Vitellius (15-69). Vespasian's decisive policies brought an end to civil war and he increased taxes and reformed the army. He was deified after his death.

Vespucci, Amerigo (1454-1512) Italian navigator, after whom America is named. In 1499 he explored the NE coast of South America, discovering the mouths of the Amazon, and in 1501, under Portuguese auspices, he explored the E coast as far as Río de La Plata, which he discovered.

Vesta (goddess) The Roman goddess of the hearth, identified with the Greek *Hestia. She was worshipped in private households, and her annual festival, the Vestalia, was held in June. The **Vestal Virgins**, her priestesses, tended the eternal fire at her shrine in Rome. They served for periods of 30 years under strict vows of chastity.

Vesta (planet) The third largest *minor planet, 538 km in diameter, and the only one occasionally visible with the naked eye. Its orbit lies between those of Mars and Jupiter.

Vestmannaeyjar (or Westman Islands) A group of rocky islands off the S coast of Iceland. In 1963 the volcanic island of Surtsey emerged from the ocean and the volcano, Helgafell, erupted in 1974 destroying part of the chief settlement of Vestmannaeyjar on the island of Heimaey.

Vesuvius 40 49N 14 26E A volcano in S central Italy, in Campania region near Naples. It was presumed to be extinct until it erupted in 79 AD engulfing the towns of *Herculaneum and *Pompeii; the last eruption was in 1944. Wine is made from the grapes grown on its exceptionally fertile slopes. Average height: 1220 m (4003 ft).

vetch A climbing or trailing annual or perennial herb of the genus *Vicia* (about 150 species), native to N temperate regions and South America. The leaves comprise several pairs of leaflets, often modified into tendrils, and the blue, purple, yellow, or white flowers are borne either in long spikes or singly in the leaf axils. Some species are grown as fodder crops or for green manure. Family: *Leguminosae.

veterinary science The scientific discipline concerned with animal health and welfare. Some of the earliest descriptions of animal diseases were made by *Aristotle and, by the middle ages, veterinary practice was an established trade. The Royal College of Veterinary Surgeons was founded in London in 1844 and today all British veterinary practitioners must be qualified members. Control and eradication of livestock diseases have enabled improved productivity and the introduction of modern intensive farming methods. The care of domestic pets utilizes many of the diagnostic and surgical techniques of human medicine.

vetiver A perennial *grass, *Vetiveria zizanioides*, also known as khus-khus, native to tropical Asia and introduced to South Africa. Its thick fragrant roots contain an oil used in perfumes.

Viareggio 43 52N 10 15E A town and resort in Italy, in Tuscany on the Ligurian Sea. Shelley was cremated in Viareggio and Puccini is buried here. Population (1981 est): 58 662.

Viborg 56 28N 9 25E A town in N central Denmark, in Jutland. It has a 12th-century cathedral and its industries include iron founding, distilling, and the manufacture of textiles and machinery. Population (1984): 39 300.

vibraphone A type of *xylophone in which a characteristic vibrato effect is produced by electrically operated fans installed at the upper ends of the resonator tubes. □musical instruments.

Vibrio A genus of freshwater and marine bacteria. They are rod-shaped, either straight or curved, and swim by means of whiplike flagella at one end of the cell. *V. cholerae* causes *cholera in man and other types may cause gastroenteritis.

Viburnum A genus of shrubs and small trees (about 200 species), mostly native to N temperate regions. They have rounded heads of small funnel-shaped white or pink flowers, each with five spreading white lobes. Many species and varieties are grown as garden shrubs and pot plants, including the snowball tree (*see* guelder rose) and *laurustinus. Family: *Caprifoliaceae. See also* wayfaring tree.

Vicente, Gil (c. 1465-1536) Portuguese dramatist. He wrote court entertainments, plays based on religious and chivalric stories, and comedies satirizing the clergy and nobility, including *Comedia de Rubena* (1521) and *Auto da Mofina Mendes* (1534). He wrote in both Portuguese and Spanish, and has been identified with a goldsmith of the same name. His plays were published by his son and daughter in 1562.

Vicenza 45 33N 11 33E A city in NE Italy, in Veneto. It was the home of the 16th-century architect Andrea Palladio and many of his finest works are sited here. Vicenza has iron, steel, and textile industries. Population (1980 est): 116 781.

Vichy 46 07N 3 25E A spa in central France, in the Allier department on the River Allier. From 1940 until 1944, during World War II, it was the seat of the French government of Marshal Pétain. Its waters, which were known to

the Romans, are bottled and exported worldwide. Population (1982): 30 554.

Vicksburg 32 21N 90 51W A city in the USA, in Mississippi on the Mississippi River. During the US Civil War it was the site of the Vicksburg campaign, a 47-day siege in 1863 in which Gen Grant successfully gained control of the Mississippi River after the city fell. Vicksburg is an important distribution centre for cotton, timber, and livestock. Population (1980): 25 434.

Vicky (Victor Weisz; 1913-66) British cartoonist, born in Berlin, of Hungarian parents. Working in England from 1935, he made his name in the *New Statesman* and *Evening Standard* with his political cartoons.

Vico, Giambattista (*or* Giovanni Battista Vico; 1668-1744) Italian historical philosopher. Vico was one of the first philosophers to attempt a critical philosophy of history. He rejected Descartes' negative attitude to the study of history and argued that philosophers had underrated "the study of the world of nations, which since men made it, men should come to know." Language, ritual, and myth were, he maintained, essential clues to an understanding to the past. His ideas were particularly influential in the later 18th century.

Victor Emmanuel II (1820-78) King of Italy (1861-78). He succeeded to the throne of Sardinia-Piedmont in 1849, following the abdication of his father Charles Albert. His appointment (1852) of *Cavour as prime minister was crucial to the achievement of Italian unification (*see* Risorgimento). Victor Emmanuel fought at Magenta and Solferino against the Austrians, freeing Lombardy, and coordinated with *Garibaldi in the campaign that freed S Italy. After becoming King of Italy he completed its unification by the acquisition of Venetia (1866) and of Rome (1870), which he made the Italian capital.

Victor Emmanuel III (1869-1947) King of Italy (1900-46) following the assassination of his father Umberto I. He acquiesced in Mussolini's seizure of power (1922) and after Mussolini's fall (1943) relinquished his powers to his son Umberto II. He formally abdicated in 1946, shortly before Italy became a republic.

Victoria A state of SE Australia, bordering on the Tasman Sea, Bass Strait, and the Indian Ocean. It consists of central uplands, an extension of the *Great Dividing Range, descending to plains in the N and S. Agriculture is diverse with fruit and vineyards in the Murray Basin and wheat and sheep farming to the SW. Gippsland is a noted dairying area, where production has intensified in recent years as a result of a reorganization of the industry; 50% of the country's cattle and over half of the production are now concentrated in S Victoria. Brown coal, the mainstay of Victoria's thermal electricity industry, is mined in Central Gippsland and gas and oil are piped from fields in the Bass Strait. Industry, concentrated on Melbourne, includes engineering, oil refining, and the manufacture of cars and textiles. Area: 227 600 sq km (87 884 sq mi). Population (1980 est): 3 887 000. Capital: Melbourne.

Victoria 22 16N 114 13E The capital of Hong Kong, situated on the N of the island. The University of Hong Kong was established here in 1911. Population (1981): 590 771.

Victoria 48 26N 123 20W A city and port in W Canada, the capital of British Columbia on S Vancouver Island. Founded in 1843, it is a commercial and distribution centre. Victoria's mild climate attracts tourists and retired people. It has some industry, but the provincial government and federal dockyards are the main employers. Victoria University (1963) is situated here. Population (1981): 64 379.

Victoria (1819-1901) Queen of the United Kingdom (1837-1901), whose sense of duty and strict moral code came to symbolize the ethos of 19th-century Britain. The daughter of George III's fourth son Edward, Duke of Kent (1767-

VICTORIA *The queen painted towards the end of her life.*

1820), and Victoria of Saxe-Coburg-Gotha (1786–1861), Victoria succeeded her uncle William IV. In 1840 she married her cousin Prince *Albert of Saxe-Coburg-Gotha, who exerted considerable, and generally beneficial, influence over her. They had nine children: Victoria (1840–1901), who became Empress of Germany as the wife of Frederick III (1831–88; reigned 1888); Edward, later Edward VII; Alice (1843–78), Grand Duchess of Hesse; Alfred (1844–1900), Duke of Edinburgh and Saxe-Coburg-Gotha; Helena (1846–1923), Princess of Schleswig-Holstein; Louise (1848–1914), Duchess of Argyll; Arthur (1850–1917), Duke of Connaught; Leopold (1853–84), Duke of Albany; and Beatrice (1857–1944), Princess of Battenberg. Albert's death in 1861 was a severe blow to Victoria and she resolved thereafter to act exactly as he would have wished.

She had an exalted view of the monarch's role in government, failing to appreciate the limitations of constitutional monarchy. Her refusal to dismiss her Whig ladies of the bedchamber when the Tory, Robert Peel, was attempting to form a ministry caused the *Bedchamber Crisis (1839) and to *Palmerston she insisted that no policy should be modified once she had approved it. Her close friendship with *Disraeli, who made her Empress of India (1876), contrasted with her strained relations with his rival *Gladstone. In the last years of her reign, especially after her Golden Jubilee (1887), she enjoyed enormous popularity.

Victoria, Lake (*or* Victoria Nyanza) The largest lake in Africa, in Uganda, Tanzania, and Kenya. The second largest freshwater lake in the world (after Lake Superior), it was discovered for Europeans in 1858 by Speke in his search for the source of the River Nile, of which Lake Victoria is the chief reservoir. The level was raised by the construction of the *Owen Falls Dam. The main ports are Jinja, Kisumu, Mwanza, and Bukoba. Area: 69 485 sq km (26 826 sq mi).

Victoria, Tomás Luis de (c. 1548–1611) Spanish composer. He studied in Rome and in 1571 succeeded Palestrina as maestro di cappella at the Roman Seminary. In about 1582 he returned to Spain as chaplain to the dowager Empress Maria, the sister of *Philip II. He composed many motets and more than 20 masses in the polyphonic style.

Victoria and Albert Museum A London museum founded in 1853 to house and collect examples of applied arts of all periods and cultures. Originally at Marlborough House, it moved to South Kensington in 1857 and was given its present name in 1899.

Victoria Cross (VC) The highest British decoration for "bravery...in the presence of the enemy." Instituted by Queen Victoria in 1856, VCs have generally been cast from the metal of Russian guns taken during the Crimean War (1854-56). A bronze Maltese cross on a crimson ribbon, it is superscribed *For Valour.*

Victoria Falls 17 55S 25 52E A waterfall in the Zambezi River on the border of Zimbabwe and Zambia. The river flows over an abrupt rock edge 1.6 km (1 mi) wide, dropping as much as 128 m (420 ft), and then through a narrow gorge known as the **Boiling Pot**. A major tourist attraction, the falls also provide hydroelectric power.

Victoria Island A Canadian island in the Arctic Ocean, in Franklin district. The third largest island in Canada, its lowlands rise to high cliffs in the NW. The scanty population is clustered in a few settlements. Area: 212 199 sq km (81 930 sq mi).

vicuna A hoofed mammal, *Vicugna vicugna*, of high Andean plateaus. Resembling a small camel, the vicuna is 75 cm at the shoulder and has a tawny-brown coat with a white bib and underparts. Hardy and aggressively territorial, they have never been domesticated but their wool is highly valued and wild herds are rounded up for shearing. Family: *Camelidae* (camels, etc.).

Vidal, Gore (1925–) US novelist and essayist. His moral concern with contemporary society is expressed with wit and elegance in both his essays and his novels, which range from historical studies, such as *Burr* (1974), *1876* (1976), and *Lincoln* (1984), to satires such as *Myra Breckinridge* (1968).

Vidal de la Blache, Paul (1845-1918) French geographer. A professor at the Sorbonne, Paris (1898-1918), Vidal was the most eminent French human geographer of his day. His work includes *États et nations de l'Europe* (1889) and *Principes de géographie humaine* (1922). He was the founding editor of *Annales de géographie* in 1891.

videogames Electronic games played by one or two people, in which the players have to control objects or figures moving over a screen (a television can be used) to intercept another moving object. Such games as table tennis and squash are easily adapted.

video recording The storage of a *television programme on magnetic tape. Because the demodulated video (vision) signal can have frequencies in the megahertz range, a video tape cannot be used like a sound tape in which the highest frequencies will be less than 20 kilohertz. It would not be practical to run the tape one thousand times faster than a sound tape; instead the signal is recorded diagonally on the tape (each diagonal line representing one line of the picture) and the tape is run slowly over a drum on which the recording and reading heads rotate at high speeds. Such devices are available for use with domestic television sets. Video discs for the storage of television pictures include those in which the signal can be retrieved by a laser system.

Vienna (German name: Wien) 48 12N 16 20E The capital of Austria, in the NE at the foot of the Vienna Woods (Wienerwald) on the River Danube. With its musical and theatrical life, its museums, and parks, it is a popular tourist attraction. Trade and industry, however, form the basis of the economy, the major industrial products being machinery, textiles, chemicals, and furniture. Most of the chief buildings lie on or within the Ringstrasse, the boulevard built in 1857 to replace the old city ramparts. These include the Cathedral of St Stephen (begun about 1135); the Hofburg (the former imperial palace); the Rathaus (1873-83); the parliament buildings (1883); the Opera House and Burgtheater; and the university (1365). *History:* seat of the Habsburgs (1278-1918) and residence of the Holy Roman Emperor (1558-1806), Vienna became an important political and cultural centre in the 18th and 19th centuries, having associations with many composers, including Haydn, Mozart, Beethoven, Schubert, and the Strauss family. At the end of World War I it became the capital of the small republic of Austria. It suffered considerable damage during World War II and was jointly occupied by the Allied Powers (1945-55). Population (1981): 1 504 200.

Vienna, Congress of (1814-15) A conference of European powers that met following the fall of Napoleon. The chief countries represented were Austria (by *Metternich), Britain (by *Castlereagh and Wellington), Russia, Prussia, France (by *Talleyrand), and the papacy. Its Final Act created a kingdom of the Netherlands, a German confederation of 39 states, Lombardy-Venetia subject to Austria, and the *Congress Kingdom of Poland. Legitimate monarchs were restored in Spain, Naples, Piedmont, Tuscany, and Modena, and Louis XVIII was confirmed as King of France.

Vienna Circle The group of scientific philosophers who developed the doctrine of *logical positivism (or logical empiricism). Founded by *Schlick in 1924, the Vienna Circle flourished until 1939. Philosophers and scientists cooperated to analyse and clarify both philosophical and scientific concepts and to set up criteria of meaningfulness for propositions other than the truths of logic. Members included *Carnap, *Gödel, and Otto Neurath (1882-1945). They did not consciously set out radically to revise traditional views about philosophy, but they had this effect, notably in America and Britain. See also Ayer, Sir Alfred (Jules).

Vienne, River A river in W central France, flowing mainly NNW from the Correze department to the River Loire. Length: 354 km (220 mi).

Vientiane 18 06N 102 30E The capital of Laos, a port on the River Mekong on the border with Thailand (formerly Siam). Founded in the 13th century, it came under Siamese control in the 18th century and was destroyed (1828) following a revolt against Siamese rule. It became capital of the French protectorate of Laos in the late 19th century. The Université Sisavangvong was founded here in 1958. Population (1984 est): 120 000.

Vierwaldstättersee. See Lucerne, Lake..

Viet Cong Communist guerrillas who fought the government of South Vietnam during the *Vietnam War (1954-75). Dedicated to the union of North and South, in 1960 they established a political organization, the National Liberation Front, which amalgamated the various groups committed to the overthrow of the South Vietnamese Government.

Viet Minh The Vietnam League for Independence, formed in 1941 by *Ho Chi Minh to overthrow French rule and to create an independent Vietnamese republic. Officially a multiparty movement, the Viet Minh was dominated by the communists and opposed by many nationalist leaders. Following the refusal of the French to recognize Vietnamese independence after World War II, the Viet Minh played a prominent role in the *Indochina war against France (1946-54).

Vietnam, Socialist Republic of A country in SE Asia, occupying the E part of the Indochina peninsula on the South China Sea. Fertile coastal lowlands rise to forested plateaus and mountains, the most populated areas being around the Mekong delta in the S and the Red River delta in the N. The inhabitants are mainly Vietnamese, with minorities of Chinese and others. *Economy*: seriously affected by the wars of recent decades, some progress has been made since 1975. Agriculture remains the most important sector and there have been further moves towards greater collectivization of the land. Irrigation schemes have helped to increase production although self-sufficiency in the staple food, rice, has not yet been achieved. Other important crops include sugar cane, tea, maize, coffee, and rubber. Teak and bamboo are the chief forest products and fishing is also important. Industrial developments, including steel, have been concentrated mainly in the N, based on the coal,

tin, zinc, and other metals to be found there, but recent discoveries of offshore oil SE of Ho Chi Minh City open up the possibility of industral expansion in the S. The principal exports are coal, rubber, wood, tea, spices, and coffee. *History*: the northern kingdom of Nam Viet was conquered in 111 BC by the Chinese. In 939 AD it broke free and resisted further Chinese invasions until the 15th century, when it was again briefly occupied. Its southward expansion culminated in the establishment (1802) of a united Vietnamese empire, which incorporated the three historic regions of Annam, Cochinchina, and Tonkin. The subsequent French conquest resulted in the institution of protectorates over Cochinchina, Tonkin, and Annam, which were joined with Cambodia (and later Laos) to form (1887) the Union of *Indochina. Vietnam was occupied by the Japanese in World War II, during which Ho Chi Minh formed the Viet Minh league to fight for independence. France's refusal in 1945 to recognize his government led to war (1946-54) after which, following defeat at Dien Bien Phu, the French withdrew. The Geneva Conference (1954) divided Vietnam along the seventeenth parallel into communist North Vietnam and noncommunist South Vietnam, between which civil war ensued. In 1961 the USA extended assistance to the South and remained involved in the conflict until 1973 (see Vietnam War). The civil war continued until 1975, when the North emerged victorious, proclaiming (1976) the reunited Socialist Republic of Vietnam. Since then attempts at reconstruction have been hindered by further political developments. A deterioration of Sino-Vietnamese relations led to the withdrawal of all Chinese aid in 1978, and following Vietnam's invasion of Kampuchea (December, 1978-January, 1979) many other nations suspended aid leading to an increased reliance on the Soviet Union. The Chinese invasion of Vietnam (February-March, 1979) led to a massive increase in the number of Chinese refugees attempting to leave Vietnam by small craft across the South China Sea. Many of these refugees, known as the Boat People, died by drowning or from disease, and experienced difficulty in finding a new country that would accept them. In the mid-1980s there were several armed clashes along the border with Thailand. President: Vo Chi Cong (1914-). Official language: Vietnamese. Official currency: dong of 100 hao. Area: 329 466 sq km (127 180 sq mi). Population (1983): 57 036 000. Capital: Hanoi. Main port: Haiphong.

Vietnam War (1954-75) The war between communist North Vietnam and South Vietnam, the latter aided from 1961 by the USA. It resulted in communist victory and the union (1976) of North and South Vietnam. From 1954 guerrilla warfare was waged against South Vietnam by the communist *Viet Cong, who were reinforced by North Vietnamese troops in 1959. In 1961 the USA, seeking to halt the spread of communism in SE Asia, dispatched troops (numbering 550 000 by 1969) in support of the beleaguered South; in 1965 US air raids on the North had begun. US participation was lessened after peace negotiations were initiated in 1969, but the war again took fire following the US-South Vietnamese invasion of Cambodia (now Kampuchea) in 1970. A massive communist offensive in 1972, together with the strength of domestic opposition to US involvement in the war, prompted the USA to reopen negotiations for peace. These led to the Paris Agreement (January, 1973) and the withdrawal of US troops. By 1975 the North had emerged victorious. Some 900 000 Viet Cong and North Vietnamese, 50 000 Americans, and some 400 000 South Vietnamese died in the war. See also Indochina.

viewdata An information storage and retrieval system in which pages of text are transmitted as coded signals along telephone wires and displayed on a domestic television receiver. The user has direct access to a central computer store via a keyboard, and there is therefore no delay in response, unlike the alternative *teletext system. The UK

Post Office has developed a viewdata system called **Prestel**, which is being commercially exploited in the UK and other countries.

Vignola, Giacomo da (1507-73) Roman mannerist architect (*see* mannerism). Vignola was the leading architect of his day in Rome, carrying on the building of *St Peter's Basilica after the death of *Michelangelo. Among his other works were the Palazzo Farnese (1564) in Piacenza and the influential church of Il Gesù, Rome (begun 1568). He was also the author of a popular architectural treatise.

Vigny, Alfred de (1797-1863) French poet, novelist, and dramatist. He associated with many Romantic writers while serving as an army officer from 1814 to 1827. His fiction includes the historical novel *Cinq-Mars* (1826) and his plays include *Chatterton* (1835), his masterpiece, and several adaptions from Shakespeare. His poetry, especially in *Les Destinées* (1867), expresses through impersonal symbolic techniques his philosophy of stoical pessimism.

Vigo 42 15N 8 44W A port and naval base in NW Spain, in Galicia on the Atlantic coast. In 1702 an English-Dutch fleet sank a Spanish treasure fleet here. Population (1981): 258 724.

Viipuri. *See* Vyborg.

Vijayanagar A Hindu empire established from the town of that name in S India during the first half of the 14th century. It enjoyed a reputation for trade, opulence, and cultural and artistic distinction. Its Muslim neighbours, with whom it had always had uneasy relations, defeated Vijayanagar at the battle of Talikota in 1565 and totally destroyed the city.

Vijayawada (former name: Bezwada) 16 34N 80 40E A city in India, in Andhra Pradesh on the River Krishna. Industries include engineering and rice milling. Population (1981): 545 000.

Viking probes Two identical US spacecraft that went into orbit around Mars in 1976. The Lander sections landed on the surface in July and September and performed various experiments, including tests for possible microorganisms; none were found. The Orbiter sections took extensive measurements and photographs of Mars' surface and two satellites.

Vikings Scandinavian sea warriors active from the late 8th to the mid-11th centuries. They established important settlements in the British Isles (especially at York and Dublin), where an Anglo-Danish dynasty was founded (1016) by *Canute, and in Normandy. Swedish Vikings raided, and then settled, in the E Baltic, established the Russian Kievan state, and traded with Constantinople, where they provided the imperial guard. They also established settlements in *Vinland and Greenland. Viking literature (the sagas) and art are noted for their dynamic vitality.

villa A country house in Italy or the South of France. Villas date back to Roman times, when they were used as holiday retreats or as farmhouses. The Emperor Hadrian's Villa at Tivoli (123 AD) was built on a palatial scale with extensive parks. During the Renaissance the villa with its substantial estate was revived, particularly in Venetia in N Italy, where *Palladio designed them to combine farming and pleasure purposes. Gardens with grottoes, fountains, and sculptures became an integral part of such Renaissance villas as the Villa d'Este (1550) at Tivoli, built by Pirro Ligorio (c. 1500-83). Since the 19th century English detached or semidetached suburban houses and Mediterranean holiday houses are often referred to as villas.

Villa, Pancho (Francesco V.; 1878-1923) Mexican revolutionary. An outlaw, Villa supported successive revolts against Mexican governments and came to dominate the north with an irregular army. In 1916 he raided Texas and New Mexico and a US force was sent into Mexico to capture him. It failed to do so but, after an agreement with the

Mexican Government in 1920, he disbanded his army. He was later assassinated.

Villa-Lobos, Heitor (1887-1959) Brazilian composer. He toured Brazil collecting folksongs and in 1945 founded the Brazilian Academy of Music. His music is characterized by native rhythms and exotic tone colours. His vast output includes 12 symphonies, *Bachianas Brasileiras* (1930-45), a series of pieces inspired by Bach, concertos for cello, guitar, and harp, 15 string quartets, guitar music, *Rudepoema* (1921-26) for piano, and the ballet *Uirapurú* (1917).

Villanovan The earliest Iron Age culture of N Italy, named after the site of Villanova near Bologna. Emerging in the 9th century BC Villanovan culture is characterized by sophisticated metalworking, using local mineral resources. The dead were cremated and their bronze or pottery urns were often shaped like wattle and daub huts. Villanovan settlements preceded most of the important towns of the *Etruscans.

Villars, Claude Louis Hector, Duc de (1653-1734) French marshal under Louis XIV. He fought in the third *Dutch War (1672-78) but his greatest achievements came in the War of *Spanish Succession (1701-14). He rallied France's flagging fortunes after Marlborough's victory at *Blenheim (1704) and imposed devastating losses on the allies at *Malplaquet (1709). He last saw active service when well into his 80s in the War of the *Polish Succession (1733-38).

Villehardouin, Geoffroi de (c. 1150-c. 1213) French medieval chronicler. A participant in the fourth Crusade and witness of the fall of Constantinople (1204), Villehardouin wrote the best source description of these events in his *Conquête de Constantinople*. However, his bias towards the Latins possibly distorts the account.

villein The unfree peasant of medieval Europe, holding land from the lord of the *manor in return for labour. Villeins were the most numerous class in England from the 11th to late 14th centuries, when many villeins acquired written titles to their holdings following the *Peasants' Revolt.

Villeneuve, Pierre (1763-1806) French admiral during the Napoleonic Wars. He commanded the fleet that was unsuccessful in attempting to invade England and was defeated by Nelson at Trafalgar (1805) and taken prisoner. After his release he committed suicide on his way to report to Napoleon.

Villiers de l'Isle-Adam, Philippe Auguste, Comte de (1838-89) French poet, novelist, and dramatist. He was the impoverished descendant of an ancient aristocratic family. His best-known works are *Contes cruels* (1883) and the symbolist drama *Axël* (1886).

Villon, François (1431-?1463) French poet. He studied at the University of Paris but thereafter led a life of vagrancy and crime. He was condemned to be hanged in 1463 but was banished from Paris instead, and nothing is known of him after that date. Only about 3000 lines of his work survive. The ballades and other poems in his *Lais* and *Grand Testament* are characterized by compassion, irony, and a fascination with death and decay. Among the best known of his poems are the *Ballade des dames du temps jadis* and his epitaph, the *Ballade des pendus*.

Vilnius (Polish name: Wilno) 54 40N 25 19E A city in the W Soviet Union, the capital of the Lithuanian SSR on the River Neris. A commercial, industrial, and educational centre, it is a railway junction and has a wide range of manufacturing industries and a university founded (1579) by Stephen Báthory. *History*: it dates back to the 14th century, when it became Gediminas' capital but declined following Lithuania's union with Poland. It was ceded to Russia in 1795. After World War I it was given to newly independent Lithuania but was seized by Poland in 1922. Restored to Lithuania in 1940, it then became part of the Soviet Union. The Germans occupied Vilnius in World War II, when its large Jewish population was virtually exterminated. Population (1981 est): 503 000.

Vimy. *See* World War I.

Viña del Mar 33 02S 71 35W A seaside resort in W central Chile, a suburb of Valparaíso on the Pacific Ocean. Its attractions include a casino, beaches, hotels, and a racecourse. Population (1983 est): 298 663.

Vincent de Paul, St (c. 1580-1660) French priest, known for his work among the poor and sick. Captured by Barbary pirates on his way to Marseille (1605), he escaped and in 1625 founded the Congregation of the Mission Priests (*see* Lazarists). In 1633 he founded the Daughters of Charity. Feast day: 19 July.

Vincent of Beauvais (c. 1190-1264) French Dominican friar, scholar, and encyclopedist. His greatest achievement was a Latin encyclopedia, the *Speculum maius*, which he compiled from the whole range of knowledge available to him. In three parts, it dealt with natural history, theological doctrine, and history.

vine Any climbing or trailing plant that requires a support for upward growth. The term is often restricted to the *grape vine (*Vitis vinifera*) and other plants of the genus *Vitis*, which climb by means of tendrils.

vinegar A dilute solution of *acetic acid, produced from soured wine, beer (malt vinegar), or other dilute alcoholic liquids. It is used in salad dressings, preserving, and other foods.

vinegar eel A *nematode worm, *Anguillula* (or *Turbatrix*) *aceti*, that lives in fermenting vinegar. It feeds on the microorganisms that convert alcohol to acetic acid in the formation of vinegar.

vine snake One of several species of slender venomous tree-dwelling snakes belonging to the family *Colubridae*. The South American green vine snake (*Oxybelis fulgidus*), up to 120 cm long, is well camouflaged, and preys on small lizards, which it paralyses before eating.

vingt-et-un. *See* pontoon.

Vinland The Viking name for the area of NE America, probably Newfoundland, discovered, explored, and briefly settled by *Leif Ericsson (c. 1000). It is possible that the area was visited a decade earlier by Bjarni Herjolfsson. Ericsson's achievement is celebrated in an important saga.

Vinnitsa 49 11N 28 30E A city in the Soviet Union, in the central Ukrainian SSR. Originally Polish, it was ceded to Russia in 1793. It is the centre of a sugar-beet region and food processing is the principal industrial activity. Population (1984): 360 000.

Vinson Massif 78 O2S 22 00W The highest peak in Antarctica, in the Ellsworth Mountains in Ellsworth Land. It was discovered in 1935. Height: 5140 m (16 864 ft).

vinyl resins. *See* polyvinyl chloride; polyvinyl acetate.

viol A bowed stringed instrument, common from the 15th until the early 18th centuries, when it was eclipsed by the *violin. Viols differ from violins in that they have six strings, tuned mainly in fourths, a shallower bridge, gut frets on the fingerboard, sloping shoulders, and flatter backs. They are held between the knees when played and the bow is held in an underhand grip. A consort of viols comprises treble, alto, tenor, and bass instruments; there is also a **violine** pitched an octave lower than the bass. The bass viol acquired the name **viola da gamba** from the Italian *gamba*, leg.

viola A □musical instrument of the *violin family. It is similar to the violin, although larger in size, having thicker strings and a heavier bow. It has a range of over four octaves from the C below middle C; its strings are tuned C, G, D, A. It is a member of the orchestra and the string quartet.

violet A perennial herb of the genus *Viola*, up to 40 cm tall, whose solitary flowers, usually blue, purple, or white, have two upright petals, two horizontally spreading ones, and a lower central one with guidelines for pollinating insects

seeking nectar. The toothed leaves are oval or heart-shaped, often in a basal rosette, and the seeds are released explosively from a three-valved capsule. The sweet-scented garden violets are derived from the Eurasian sweet violet (*V. odorata*). The dog violet (*V. canina*) is another common species, and the genus also includes the *pansies. Family: *Violaceae*.

violin A bowed string instrument, the soprano member of the family that includes the viola, cello, and double bass. It has four strings tuned in fifths (G, D, A, E), an arched bridge, and a smooth fingerboard. It has a range of over four octaves from the G below middle C. Early violins used gut strings; modern strings are steel or gut-covered steel. The violin is played with a bow strung with horsehair; the strings can also be plucked. The design of the violin was perfected by the Amati, Guarneri, and Stradivari families in Italy between the mid-16th and early 18th centuries. It is widely used as a solo concerto instrument, in the orchestra, in the string quartet, and in folk music. □musical instruments.

Viollet-le-Duc, Eugène Emmanuel (1814-79) French architect and author. He began his career as a restorer of medieval buildings, working on the Ste Chapelle and *Notre-Dame in Paris. Viollet was the champion of both the revived gothic style and contemporary developments in architecture, his *Dictionnaire raisoné de l'architecture française* (1854-68) and later books indicating the similarities he saw between gothic and contemporary industrial methods of construction.

violoncello. *See* cello.

viper A venomous snake, belonging to the family *Viperidae* (150 species), that has long erectile fangs, which are folded back when not in use. 0.3-3 m long, vipers feed on small animals, which are injected with venom and then trailed until they die. Most give birth to live young. Old World vipers (subfamily *Viperinae*) are stout-bodied and broad-headed and mostly ground-dwelling, although some are burrowers and some arboreal. New World vipers (subfamily *Crotalinae*) are known as *pit vipers.

Virchow, Rudolf (1821-1902) German pathologist and statesman. He originated the concept that disease arises in the individual cells of a tissue and—with publication of his *Cellular Pathology* (1858)—founded the science of cellular pathology. Virchow held public office, supervising improvements in standards of public health, and he also helped develop the science of anthropology in Germany.

Viren, Lasse Artturi (1949-) Finnish middle-distance and long-distance runner. At the Munich Olympics (1972) he won the gold medals in the 5000 and 10 000 metres; at the Montreal Olympics (1976) he performed the spectacular feat of retaining both titles.

Virgil (Publius Vergilius Maro; 70-19 BC) Roman poet. He was born into a farming family near Mantua in N Italy. He completed his education in Rome, where he became a friend of Horace and *Maecenas. Reacting against the troubled political background of civil war, he described in his *Eclogues* (42-37 BC) an idealized pastoral landscape. His more practical vision of Italy in the *Georgics* (36-29 BC) is informed by his passionate interest in agriculture. During his final years he worked on the *Aeneid*, a national epic in 12 books describing the wanderings of Aeneas, the founding of Rome, and extolling the Julian dynasty and Augustus, who claimed descent from Aeneas. He died of fever after returning from a voyage to Greece. The supreme poet of imperial Rome, Virgil became the object of superstitious reverence to later generations. The *Aeneid* was used for divination and its author was imagined to be a magician with supernatural power. In the middle ages, Virgil was treated almost as a Christian prophet because of a passage in the fourth *Eclogue* that seems to predict the birth of Christ.

virginals A keyboard instrument of the 16th and 17th centuries, the earliest and simplest form of the *harpsichord.

VIRGINALS

Often made in the form of a box, which could be set on the table, the strings (one to each note) run parallel to the keyboard.

Virginia A state on the mid-Atlantic coast of the USA. The low-lying coastal plain is separated from the forested Appalachian Mountains in the W by a region of rolling upland. Manufacturing is very important and the principal industries are chemicals and tobacco processing. Fishing and mining (especially of coal) are also significant sectors of the economy and there is a thriving tourist industry. The state's farmers produce tobacco, hay, corn, apples, and peaches. Timber is also important. *History*: one of the 13 original colonies, it was named after Elizabeth I of England, the Virgin Queen. A period of expansion followed the establishment of the first permanent English settlement in the New World by the Virginia Company (1607) and demands for self-government grew. It provided many of the leaders for the American Revolution, becoming a state in 1788. Four of the first five presidents of the USA came from Virginia and during the US Civil War, Richmond was the capital of the Confederacy. Area: 105 716 sq km (40 817 sq mi). Population (1980): 5 346 279. Capital: Richmond.

Virginia creeper A climbing shrub, also called woodbine, of the genus *Parthenocissus*, especially *P. tricuspidata* of SE Asia and *P. quinquefolia* of North America. It clings by means of branched tendrils with suckers and is often grown as an ornamental for its attractive red autumn foliage. The compound leaves have five pointed oval toothed leaflets and the tiny clustered flowers have five petals. Family: *Vitaceae*.

Virgin Islands A West Indian group of approximately one hundred small islands and cays in the Lesser Antilles, administratively divided between the UK and the USA. **The British Virgin Islands** consist of about 40 islands, the largest being Tortola. They became a British crown colony following the defederation of the Leeward Islands colony in 1956. Tourism is replacing agriculture as the colony's chief source of wealth. Area: 153 sq km (59 sq mi). Population (1980): 12 034. Capital: Road Town. **The Virgin Islands of the United States** consist of three main islands, the largest being *St Croix, and about 50 smaller ones. They were purchased from Denmark in 1917 for their strategic importance. Tourism is the principal industry; other industries include rum distilling and textiles. Area: 344 sq km (133 sq mi). Population (1980): 95 591. Capital: Charlotte Amalie.

Virgo (Latin: Virgin) A large equatorial constellation that lies on the *zodiac between Libra and Leo. The brightest star is *Spica. The constellation contains the **Virgo cluster** of galaxies, which contains over 2500 members, the majority of which are spiral galaxies.

virtual particle A short-lived particle that is used in quantum mechanics to represent the interaction between stable particles. For example, in classical physics two electrically charged particles are represented as interacting by the overlapping of the two fields that surround them; in quantum mechanics this interaction would be represented by the exchange of virtual photons between them. The *strong interaction is represented by the exchange of virtual pions, the *weak interaction by the exchange of intermediate vector bosons, and the *gravitational interaction by the exchange of virtual gravitons.

virus A minute noncellular particle that can reproduce only in living cells. Viruses consist of a core of nucleic acid (either *DNA or *RNA), surrounded by a protein coat (capsule) and, in some types, a lipid-containing envelope. Some bacterial viruses have tails (*see* bacteriophage). They may be spherical, ellipsoid, rod-shaped, or polyhedral, with sizes in the range 20–450 nanometres (nm; *see* SI units), although some tailed forms may reach 800 nm. Viruses alternate between an inert virion stage and an infective stage, in which the capsule binds to the host cell and the viral nucleic acid (containing its genes) enters the cell and directs the components of the host cell to assemble replica viruses. These are finally liberated, often with damage to or death of the host cell.
Viruses are responsible for a wide range of diseases in plants and animals, including influenza, measles, rabies, and smallpox. They can also cause the formation of tumours.

Visby 57 37N 18 20E A port and resort in SE Sweden, on the W coast of Gotland Island. It was an early member of the Hanseatic League and a major commercial centre in the middle ages. Its industries include sugar refining and metal working. Population (1984): 20 000.

viscacha A gregarious South American *rodent, *Lagostomus maximus*, related to *chinchillas. Over 50 cm in length, viscachas live in warrens of 12-15 burrows often with piles of earth outside. They are nocturnal and feed on grasses, roots, and seeds. Family: *Chinchillidae*.

Visconti An Italian family that established (1310) lordship over Milan under **Matteo I Visconti** (1250-1322) and then, in spite of papal opposition, gained control over many Lombard cities. Skilful marriage alliances both within Italy and outside expanded their influence. By 1400, under **Gian Galeazzo Visconti** (1351-1402), the family's most brilliant representative, they controlled most of N Italy, centred on Milan and Pavia. Temporary reverses under his son **Giovanni Maria Visconti** (1388-1412) were arrested but the death of his brother **Filippo Maria Visconti** (1392-1447) without heirs led to the establishment of *Sforza control over the duchy.

Visconti, Luchino (1906-76) Italian film director. Born into a noble family, he became a committed Marxist. His late films especially are characterized by elaborate and formal visual composition. They include *The Leopard* (1963), *The Damned* (1970), and *Death in Venice* (1971). He also directed many opera and drama productions.

viscosity A measure of the degree to which a fluid resists a deforming force. Viscosity is defined by Newton's law of viscosity: if two layers of a fluid, area A and distance x apart, flow with a relative velocity v, there is a force between them equal to $\eta Av/x$. η is called the coefficient of viscosity. Viscosity is measured in newton seconds per square metre. The **kinematic viscosity** is the coefficient of viscosity divided by the density of the fluid.

Vishakhapatnam 17 42N 83 24E A city in India, in Andhra Pradesh on the Bay of Bengal. An important port, India's first steamer was launched here in 1948. Industries include shipbuilding and oil refining. Population (1981): 594 000.

Vishnu The second member of the Hindu trinity, the *Trimurti. He is known as the Preserver, complementing *Brahma the Creator and *Shiva the Destroyer, and is married to *Lakshmi. He has ten avatars or manifestations, the most famous of which are *Rama and *Krishna. He is often portrayed as lying asleep on a seven-headed snake in the intervals between his appearances in successive universes. His devotees are the Vaishnavas, a sect founded by the scholar and philosopher Chaitanya (1486–c. 1534 AD), who stressed devotion to the god regardless of *caste.

VISHNU *The god is portrayed reclining on Sesha, the king of the nagas. From the south face of the 6th-century temple of Vishnu at Deogarh (India).*

Visigoths A branch of the *Goths. Forced by the *Huns across the Danube (376 AD), they destroyed a Roman army at *Adrianople (378) and established themselves in the Balkans, expanding southwards and, under *Alaric I, sacking Rome in 410. Moving into France and Spain, they ruled first as Roman subjects and then independently. Their rule in France was destroyed by the *Franks (507) and in Spain by the Muslims (711).

Vislinsky Zaliv. *See* Vistula Lagoon.

Vistula, River (Polish name: Wisła) The longest river of Poland, rising in the S of the country, in the Carpathian Mountains, and flowing generally N and NW through Warsaw and Torún, then NE to enter the Baltic Sea via an extensive delta region near Gdańsk. It provides an important economic link in the transportation system of eastern Europe. Length: 1090 km (677 mi).

Vistula Lagoon (German name: Frisches Haff; Polish name: Wiślany Zalew; Russian name: Vislinsky Zaliv) An inlet of the Baltic Sea on the coast of Poland and the Soviet Union, almost totally enclosed by a narrow spit. Area: 855 sq km (330 sq mi).

vitalism The theory that living organisms contain a vital force that distinguishes them from nonliving things. It was proposed by the French philosopher Henri *Bergson, who believed that a vital force (*élan vital*)—a form of energy—controlled the form, development, and activities of organisms.

vitamin An organic compound, other than a protein, fat or carbohydrate, that is required in small amounts by living organisms for normal growth and maintenance of life. For animals vitamins must be supplied in the diet, although some group B vitamins may be produced by microorganisms present in the digestive tract. Vitamins function as *coenzymes in many metabolic reactions; they are involved in the formation and maintenance of membranes, in the absorption and metabolism of calcium and phosphorus, and in many other essential processes. Many can now be synthesized commercially but some are easily destroyed by light or heat, e.g. in storage or cooking. Vitamins A, D, E, and K are classifed as fat-soluble; group B vitamins and vitamin C are water-soluble.

vitamin A (*or* retinol) A fat-soluble vitamin and an essential constituent of the visual pigments of the eyes. It also functions in the maintenance of healthy mucous membranes. Vitamin A deficiency leads to dryness of membranes lining the mouth and respiratory tract, blindness, and defective growth. Sources include liver, fish-liver oils, and egg yolk, while precursors of vitamin A, such as beta-carotene, occur in green plants and vegetables (e.g. carrots).

vitamin B complex A group of water-soluble vitamins that are all constituents of *coenzymes involved in metabolic reactions. Thiamine (B_1) is important in carbohydrate metabolism: it occurs in cereal grains, beans, peas, and pork. Deficiency leads to *beriberi. Riboflavin (B_2) is involved in carbohydrate and amino acid metabolism and sources include yeast, liver, milk, and green leafy plants. Nicotinamide (nicotinic acid *or* niacin) can be synthesized from the amino acid tryptophan; liver is a rich source of the vitamin and milk and eggs of tryptophan. Vitamin B_6 (pyridoxine) is essential for amino acid metabolism and is widely distributed in yeast, liver, milk, beans, and cereal grains. Also common in many foods are pantothenic acid, a constituent of coenzyme A; biotin, which is synthesized by intestinal bacteria; and choline, a precursor of *acetylcholine (which transmits nervous impulses). Folic acid and vitamin B_{12} (cyanocobalamin) can be synthesized by intestinal bacteria: deficiency of either causes megaloblastic or pernicious *anaemia. Liver is a good source of vitamin B_{12}.

vitamin C (*or* ascorbic acid) A water-soluble compound that is required for several metabolic processes, especially for the maintenance of healthy connective tissue. It cannot be synthesized by man and certain animals, in whom it must form part of the diet. Fruit and vegetables, especially citrus fruits, are good sources. Deficiency of vitamin C leads to *scurvy. Claims that large doses of the vitamin prevent colds have not been scientifically accepted.

vitamin D A fat-soluble vitamin consisting of several related compounds (sterols), principally cholecalciferol (D_3) and ergocalciferol (D_2). Vitamin D is important in calcium and phosphorus metabolism, especially in the absorption of calcium from the gut and the deposition and resorption of bone minerals. Vitamin D_3 is produced by the action of sunlight on skin, which normally meets all the body's requirements. Fish and fish-liver oils are the main natural sources, while vitamin D_2 is added to margarine. Deficiency in infants causes *rickets.

vitamin E A vitamin consisting of a group of related compounds that function as biological antioxidants, inhibiting the oxidation of unsaturated fatty acids. The most potent form of vitamin E is alpha-tocopherol, found in green leafy plants, cereal grains, and eggs. Deficiency (which is rare) may lead to anaemia.

vitamin K A vitamin consisting of a group of quinone-based compounds that are necessary for the formation of prothrombin, important in blood clotting. Vitamin K occurs in vegetables, cereals, and egg yolk and can be synthesized by intestinal bacteria. Deficiency is rare.

Vitebsk 55 10N 30 14E A port in the W Soviet Union, in the Belorussian SSR on the Western Dvina River. It serves as the transport centre of an agricultural region; industries include food processing. Population (1981 est): 310 000.

Viterbo 42 24N 12 06E A town in Italy, in Lazio. A favourite papal residence in the 13th century, it has a 12th-century gothic cathedral. Its manufactures include pottery, furniture, and textiles. Population (1983 est): 58 009.

Viti Levu The largest Fijian island, in the S Pacific Ocean. Mount Victoria, the highest mountain in Fiji, rises to 1302 m (4341 ft). Sugar, pineapples, cotton, and rice are produced and gold is mined. Area: 10 386 sq km (4010 sq mi). Chief settlement: Suva.

Vitória 20 19S 40 21W A port in E Brazil, the capital of Espirito Santo state. It serves the coffee-growing and mining areas of the state of Minas Gerais. Its university was founded in 1961. Population (1980): 198 400.

Vitoria 42 51N 2 40W A city in N Spain, in the Basque Provinces. During the Peninsular War Wellington defeated the French under Joseph Bonaparte here (1813). A manufacturing and commercial centre, it has a trade in cereals and wine. Population (1981): 192 773.

Vitruvius (Marcus Vitruvius Pollio; 1st century BC) Roman architect and military engineer, famous as the author of the only complete architectural treatise to survive from antiquity. In the ten books of *De architectura* he describes all the main aspects of Roman architecture—public and domestic buildings, temples, the *orders of architecture, interior decoration, town planning, engineering, etc. Rediscovered in Renaissance Italy, it strongly influenced such architects as *Alberti and *Palladio.

Vittorini, Elio (1908-66) Italian novelist. He was an outspoken critic of fascism and was imprisoned in 1943 following the publication of his novel *Conversation in Sicily* (1941). Released after the German occupation of Italy, he joined the resistance. He translated the works of many US writers and in postwar Italy had great influence as a literary critic.

Vittorino da Feltre (V. Ramboldini; 1378-1446) Italian Renaissance humanist and educationalist. At his school in Mantua Vittorino educated the children of both the aristocracy and the poor. He developed a broad curriculum, including classics, gymnastics, drawing, and science.

Vittorio Veneto 45 59N 12 18E A town and resort in N Italy, in Veneto. The Italians decisively defeated the Austrians here (1918) at the end of World War I. Population (1981 est): 30 579.

Vivaldi, Antonio (1678-1741) Italian composer and violinist. He·was ordained priest in 1703 and taught music at the Ospedale della Pietà in Venice, for whose orchestra many of his works were written. Towards the end of his life he toured Europe and died in poverty in Vienna. Besides operas and sacred music, Vivaldi wrote over 450 concertos for a wide range of solo instruments, including a set of four violin concertos entitled *The Four Seasons*, which are musical illustrations of four sonnets by the composer.

Vivekananda, Swami (1862-1902) Hindu philosopher. Born in Bengal, he studied western thought and science, which he realized was required to improve conditions in India. He dedicated himself to social reforms and to amalgamating western scientific materialism with eastern spirituality. He founded the Vedanta movement in the west, where, as the best-known disciple of *Ramakrishna, he was well received and where his teaching has had a continuing influence.

Viverridae A family of mammals of the order *Carnivora. The 82 species include the genets, civets, linsangs, and mongooses. Viverrids typically have a long body and tail and short legs.

Vivés, Juan Luis (1492-1540) Spanish humanist and writer. He visited England (1523, 1527-28) but lived mainly at Bruges. His *De anima et vita* (1538) is a psychological work of some depth. He also wrote a treatise on educational theory, *De disciplinis* (1531).

viviparity A reproductive process in animals in which the embryo develops within the maternal body, from which it obtains continuous nourishment. Viviparity occurs in most mammals—the embryos being nourished through the placenta—and in some snakes, lizards, and sharks. In

ovoviviparity the embryo develops within the mother but is surrounded by egg membranes and derives its food from the yolk. It occurs in certain snakes and fish. It should be distinguished from **oviparity**, occurring in birds and many other animals, in which fertilized eggs are laid or spawned by the mother.

vivisection The use of live animals for experiments. Many animals, especially rats, mice, rabbits, ·guinea pigs, and monkeys, are used worldwide to determine the effects of drugs, cosmetics, food additives, and other chemicals on living organisms, often as an indication of their likely effects on man. They are also used in medical and biological research and for many standard biological tests and assays. In many countries vivisection is controlled by legislation. In the UK experiments on vertebrates (animals with backbones) are controlled by the Cruelty to Animals Act of 1876 and experimenters are licensed by the Home Office. Alternatives to live animals include the use of test-tube (*in vitro*) techniques, tissue cultures, and computer-based mathematical models.

Vlaardingen 51 55N 4 20E A major port in the SW Netherlands, in South Holland province on the Nieuwe Waterweg (New Waterway). It has the largest shipyard in Holland; other industries include herring fishing. Population (1981 est): 79 100.

Vladimir 56 08N 40 25E A city in the W central Soviet Union, in the RSFSR 185 km (115 mi) NE of Moscow. It is a rail junction and a manufacturing and tourist centre. Its fine medieval buildings include the Cathedral of St Dimitrii (1197). *History*: founded in the early 12th century, it was the capital (c. 1157-1238) of the grand duchy of Vladimir. It was then virtually destroyed by the Tatars and in 1364 passed under the rule of Moscow. Population (1981 est): 307 000.

Vladimir I, St (c. 965-1015) Prince of Novgorod (970-80) and Grand Prince of Kiev (980-1015). In about 987 Vladimir became a Christian and introduced the Byzantine rite to Kiev and Novgorod.

Vladivostok 43 09N 131 53E A port of the SE Soviet Union, in the RSFSR on the Sea of Japan. It is the terminus of the Trans-Siberian Railway and a major Soviet naval base, also supporting fishing and whaling fleets. Ice breakers are employed to keep its harbour open in winter. Industries include shipbuilding and food processing. Population (1981 est): 565 000.

Vlaminck, Maurice de (1876-1958) French painter. A self-taught artist, he worked with *Derain from 1899 and from 1901 was strongly influenced by *Van Gogh. He became a leading exponent of *fauvism, painted under the influence of *Cézanne from 1908, but returned after 1915 to a style expressing his aggressive temperament in numerous stormy landscapes, which hold a minor place in 20th-century *expressionism.

Vlissingen. *See* Flushing.

Vlora (*or* Vlorë; Italian name: Valona) 40 29N 19 29E An important seaport in SW Albania, on the Adriatic Sea. After centuries of foreign domination, the independence of Albania was proclaimed here on 28 November, 1912. Industries include fishing and an olive-oil refinery. Population (1980 est): 58 000.

Vltava, River A river in Czechoslovakia, rising in the Forest of Bohemia and flowing mainly SE then N to join the River Elbe near Melnik. It is an important source of hydroelectric power. Length: 434 km (270 mi).

vocal cords. *See* larynx.

vodka A *spirit distilled from potatoes, rye, barley, or malt, usually in E Europe. Being colourless and without a distinctive flavour, vodka is used in many mixed drinks, such as Screwdriver (vodka and orange juice) and Bloody Mary (vodka and tomato juice). It is also made in Warrington, Cheshire.

voiceprint A graphic record of the sounds produced during speech. The record shows the range of frequencies and harmonics produced and can be used to identify any individual voice. Although there are certain standards in articulation, which are recorded on the voiceprint, individual timbre and harmonics are produced by the shape and flexibility of the larynx and the oral cavity, which are as distinctive as faces or fingerprints. Voiceprints are used in phonetics and in forensic science.

Vojvodina An autonomous province of NE Yugoslavia, in the republic of Serbia. Predominantly low lying and fertile, it is one of the chief agricultural areas of Yugoslavia, producing cereals, fruit, and vegetables. Area: 22 489 sq km (8683 sq mi). Population (1982 est): 2 040 000. Capital: Novi Sad.

volcanoes Vents or fissures in the earth's surface, either on land or under the sea, through which magma rises from the earth's interior and erupts lava, gases, and pyroclastic material (*see* Plate II). Many volcanoes have cones consisting of ash, pyroclastic deposits, and lava. Basaltic lava tends to produce gently sloping cones, the lava flowing over a wide area, whereas the more viscous acid lava produces a steeper-sided cone. Volcanic cones are often topped by craters, created by volcanic explosions, and craters of over 1 km in diameter (calderas) sometimes occur through the collapse or explosive removal of the top of a volcano. Volcanoes may be active, quiescent (dormant), or extinct. The world's highest volcano (extinct) is Aconcagua (6959 m) in the Andes. Volcanoes frequently occur along plate boundaries (*see* plate tectonics).

Volcano Islands A group of three small volcanic Japanese islands in the W Pacific Ocean. Claimed in 1891, they were under US administration (1951-68). Sulphur and sugar are produced. Area: about 28 sq km (11 sq mi).

vole A small short-tailed *rodent belonging to the subfamily *Microtinae* (which also includes lemmings). Voles are found in Europe, Asia, and North America and range in size from 7 to 35 cm. They have blunt noses and their cheek teeth grow continuously. The common field voles (genus *Microtus*; 42 species) live under surface vegetation of meadowland, eating nearly their own weight in seeds, roots, and leaves every 24 hours. Family: *Cricetidae*.

Volga, River A river in the W Soviet Union, the longest river in Europe. Rising in the Valdai Range, it flows mainly E and S through Volgograd to the Caspian Sea. It drains most of the W Soviet Union and its many large reservoirs provide important irrigation and hydroelectric power. The Moscow-Volga Canal, the Volga-Don Canal, and the Mariinsk Canal system form navigable waterways from the capital to the White Sea, the Baltic Sea, the Caspian Sea, the Black Sea, and the Sea of Azov. Length: 3690 km (2293 mi).

Volgograd (name until 1925: Tsaritsyn; name from 1925 until 1961: Stalingrad) 48 45N 44 30E A city in the Soviet Union, in the SW RSFSR on the River Volga. It has been rapidly redeveloped since its virtual destruction in World War II (*see* Stalingrad, Battle of) and it is now a major industrial city, having steel plants and factories manufacturing especially machinery, footwear, and food. Population (1981 est): 948 000.

volleyball A six-a-side court game invented in the USA in 1895, in which an inflated ball is hit with the hands or arms. After the service each team is allowed to hit the ball three times before it crosses the net. A rally ends when the ball touches the ground or is not returned correctly. Only the serving side can score; if the receiving side wins a rally, it serves next. Players rotate on the court so that each has an opportunity of serving. A game goes to 15 points and a 2-point lead is required to win.

volt (V) The *SI unit of potential, potential difference, or electromotive force equal to the potential difference between two points on a conductor carrying a steady current of one

ampere when the power dissipated is one watt. Named after Alessandro *Volta.

Volta, Alessandro Giuseppe Antonio Anastasio, Count (1745-1827) Italian physicist, who invented the electrophorus (1775), a device used to accumulate electric charge and the forerunner of the modern capacitor. His greatest invention, the Voltaic pile or cell, was the first 'practical battery and led to a number of important discoveries in electricity. He was professor of physics at Pavia University (1779-1815) and was made a count by Napoleon in 1801. The unit of potential difference is named after him.

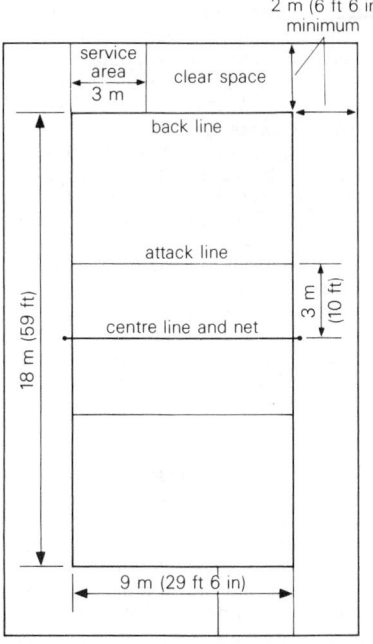

VOLLEYBALL *The dimensions of the court. The height of the ceiling is a minimum of 7 m (23 ft). The top of the centre of the net is 2.43 m (8 ft) above the floor for men or 2.24 m (7 ft 4 in) for women.*

Volta, River A river in West·Africa. Its headstreams, the Black Volta and White Volta Rivers, join in N central Ghana to form the River Volta, which then flows S to enter the Bight of Benin. The Akosombo Dam, completed in 1965 as part of the River Volta scheme, provides Ghana's hydroelectric-power requirements and powers its important aluminium smelter. Length: 480 km (300 mi).

Voltaire (François-Marie Arouet; 1694-1778) French man of letters, philosopher, scientist, ·and moralist, whose versatile work epitomizes the age of Enlightenment. He conducted a lifelong campaign against injustice and intolerance. For offending the Duc de Rohan, he was briefly imprisoned in the Bastille (1717) and then went into exile in England (1726-29). After the publication of his *Lettres philosophiques* (1734), which advocated political and religious toleration, he fled to Cirey in Champagne, where he lived with his mistress, Madame de Châtelet. He subsequently lived in Germany (1750-53) having earlier been on friendly terms with Frederick the Great through their correspondence, and in Switzerland (from 1754), chiefly at Ferney near Geneva. His voluminous writings cover history, science, philosophy, and verse drama (for which he was most popular among his contemporaries), and include the satirical and philosophical fable *Candide* (1759), *Traité de la tolérance* (1763), the *Dictionnaire philosophique* (1764), and histories of Peter the Great and Louis XV.

Volta Redonda 22 31S 44 05W A city in S Brazil, in Rio de Janeiro state on the Rio Paraíba. It has the largest steelworks in South America. Population (1980): 177 772.

voltmeter A device for measuring voltage. A voltmeter should draw as little current as possible from the circuit and therefore requires a high input impedance. In the direct-current moving-coil voltmeter the magnetic force on a coil in a magnetic field is used to deflect a needle, the high impedance being provided by a high resistance in series with the coil. *Cathode-ray oscilloscopes and digital voltmeters, used for both direct and alternating current, have high internal impedances.

Volturno, River A river in S central Italy, flowing SE and SW to the Tyrrhenian Sea. In 1860 it was the scene of a battle in which Garibaldi defeated the Neapolitans during the wars for Italian unity (*see* Risorgimento). It was the German line of defence during World War II. Length: 175 km (109 mi).

Voluntary Service Overseas (VSO) A British organization founded in 1958 by Alexander Dickson (1914–   ) to send skilled volunteers at the request of overseas governments to work as teachers and doctors or on agricultural, industrial, or business schemes. A volunteer is employed for two years by a government, which provides accommodation and a living allowance. VSO provides the volunteer's air fare and a grant. Director: Neil Mackintosh.

Volvox A genus of freshwater single-celled organisms that live in hollow spherical colonies of 500–50 000 individuals, which are linked together by fine strands of cytoplasm; the centre of the sphere contains a gelatinous mass. New colonies are formed asexually by division of certain cells or by sexual reproduction, in which the fertilized eggs become dormant cysts that subsequently form new colonies. *Volvox* is regarded by some authorities as an alga (it contains the green pigment chlorophyll) and by others as a protozoan of the class *Flagellata*. ⸤Protozoa.

von Braun, Wernher (1912–77) US rocket engineer, born in Germany. Beginning his research into the design of rocket engines in 1932, he was director of the German Rocket Test Centre at Peenemünde during World War II. It was here that the *V-2 rocket was finally perfected, being launched on London in 1944. After the war von Braun was taken to the USA where he worked on US space rockets, including the Saturn launch vehicles (*see* rockets).

Vondel, Joost van den (1587–1679) Dutch dramatist and poet. His works, which adhere to classical models, reflect his deep involvement in contemporary political and religious disputes and his gradual change from Calvinist to Catholic views. His masterpieces, *Lucifer* (1654), *Adam in Ballingschap* (1664), and *Jephtha* (1659), treat biblical themes.

Vonnegut, Kurt (1922–   ) US novelist. His novels and stories are noted for their satirical use of science-fiction techniques. *Slaughterhouse Five* (1969) is based on his experience as a prisoner of war during the fire-bombing of Dresden in 1945. His other works include *Cat's Cradle* (1963), *Breakfast of Champions* (1973), *Slapstick* (1976), *Jailbird* (1979), *Palm Sunday* (1981), *Deadeye Dick* (1982), and *Galapagos* (1985).

voodoo Magical and animistic cults of West African origin, practised by Blacks in Haiti and elsewhere in the Caribbean and in parts of South America. Trances induced by spirit possession are central to voodoo ritual. Other elements in the nocturnal rites are animal sacrifice, drum beating, dancing, and debased elements of Roman Catholic liturgy.

Voronezh 51 40N 39 13E A city in the Soviet Union, in the W RSFSR. It is at the centre of an agricultural region and food processing is an important economic activity. Its educational institutions include a university that was transferred here from Tartu in 1918. Population (1981 est): 809 000.

Voroshilov, Kliment Yefremovich (1881–1969) Soviet marshal and statesman. Voroshilov was a Red Army commander in the civil war (1918–20) and then commissar for defence (1925–40). He lost his command of the NW armies

in 1941 for failing to raise the German siege of Leningrad. He was president of the Soviet Union from 1953 to 1960.

Voroshilovgrad (name until 1935: Lugansk) 48 35N 39 20E A city in the Soviet Union, in the E Ukrainian SSR. In the coal-producing Donets Basin, it manufactures mining machinery and has iron and steel and chemical industries. Population (1981 est): 474 000.

Vorster, Balthazar Johannes (1915–83) South African statesman; prime minister (1966–78) and briefly president (1978). A lawyer, Vorster became minister of justice and police in 1960 and was known for his extreme right-wing views and strict enforcement of racial policies. Becoming prime minister after Verwoerd's assassination, he attempted to improve South Africa's relations with Black Africa. He retired during investigations of financial irregularities in his term as prime minister.

vortex The circular motion of a fluid about a vertical axis. Examples include whirlpools, hurricanes, and cyclones. A vortex may be formed in a fluid at a point just behind a blunt obstacle past which it is flowing. The direction of rotation of a naturally occurring vortex is often determined by the direction in which the *Coriolis force is acting.

Vorticella A genus of microscopic aquatic single-celled animals found in dense clusters or singly. 0.05–0.15 mm long, they are bell-shaped and attached to the substrate by a long coiled contractile stalk. Cilia around the mouth of the "bell" create currents that carry food particles into the mouth. ⸤Protozoa.

VORTICISM The Vorticists at the Restaurant de la Tour Eiffel: Spring 1915. *Ezra Pound (seated left foreground) and Wyndham Lewis (seated centre, with hat) dominate the group. The artist, William Roberts, is seated between them.*

vorticism A British art movement inaugurated in 1913 by the writer and painter Wyndham *Lewis. Influenced by *cubism and *futurism, it called for an art expressing the advanced technology and pace of modern life. Its journal, *Blast*, included contributions from Ezra *Pound and T. S. *Eliot. The sculptors *Gaudier-Brzeska and *Epstein were also associated with the movement.

Vosges A range of mountains in NE France. It extends roughly N–S to the W of the River Rhine between Basle and Karlsruhe, rising to 1423 m (4672 ft) at Ballon de Guebwiller, close to the source of the River Moselle.

vote The expression of a choice or opinion, by ballot or viva voce, especially for the purpose of electing members to representative assemblies. In the UK all subjects over the age of 18 may vote in local government and parliamentary elections, except the insane, certain criminals, and (in the case of parliamentary elections) peers in their own right. Voting has been by secret ballot since 1872. In common with most western democracies, Britain is divided into single-member constituencies in which the successful candidate is the one obtaining the majority of votes. This system has been criticized because it virtually disenfranchises supporters of the less popular party in nonmarginal seats, and of minority parties everywhere, and it may elect to power a government not having the support of the majority of the electorate. For these reasons the system of *proportional representation has many advocates. *See also* electoral college.

Voyager probes Two highly successful US *planetary probes launched in 1977 towards the outer planets. Voyager 1 approached Jupiter in March, 1979, then flew towards Saturn, which it reached in November, 1980. Voyager 2 flew past Jupiter and Saturn in July, 1979, and August, 1981, Uranus in January, 1986, and will reach Neptune in August, 1989.

Voysey, Charles Francis Annesley (1857–1941) British architect and designer. Influenced by William *Morris, Voysey began by designing wallpaper and furniture. Later he designed houses, generally small, comfortable, and practical, of which the best were Moor Crag, Windermere (1898), and The Orchard, Chorley Wood (1899).

Voznesenskii, Andrei (1933–) Soviet poet. He has travelled in the USA and Europe and is, with *Yevtushenko, the best-known contemporary Soviet poet. His poems are noted for their lively originality and inventiveness. His translated poetry includes *Selected Poems* (1964) and *Antiworlds* (1967).

VSO. *See* Voluntary Service Overseas.

VTOL aircraft. *See* aircraft.

Vuillard, (Jean) Édouard (1868–1940) French artist. He was a member of the *Nabis in Paris and his work was influenced chiefly by Japanese prints. His intimate domestic scenes in paintings and lithographs featured large expanses of patterned wallpapers and textiles and became labelled intimist (*see* intimism). After 1900 he concentrated on society portraiture but also produced murals for public buildings.

Vulcan The Roman god of fire. Originally associated with purely destructive manifestations, such as volcanoes, he became patron of smiths and metalworkers after his identification with the Greek *Hephaestus, whose myths he assumed.

Vulcanite (*or* Ebonite) A hard black insulating material made by heating rubber with sulphur (which makes up about 30% of the product).

vulcanization A process in which sticky natural rubber is made into a harder useful material by heating it with sulphur. Rubber consists of polymer chains with frequent double bonds; the vulcanization process involves the formation of sulphur bridges ($-S-S-$) between the chains. An inert filler, such as carbon black, is incorporated at the same time.

Vulgate The Latin translation of the Bible made by St Jerome in the 4th century AD. It is the oldest surviving translation of the whole Bible and differs from earlier Latin versions in translating the *Old Testament direct from Hebrew rather than from Greek. It was adopted by the Council of Trent (1546) as the official version of the Roman Catholic Church and is the basis of later English versions, such as the *Douai Bible and the version of Mgr Ronald Knox (1949).

vulture A large carrion-eating bird belonging to the order *Falconiformes*. 60–100 cm long with a wingspan of up to 270 cm, vultures have a fleshy naked head, a large crop, and a graceful soaring flight. New World vultures (family *Cathartidae*; 6 species) have a slender hooked bill, large feet, and are voiceless. *See also* condor.

Old World vultures (subfamily *Aegypiinae*; 20 species) are widely distributed in open temperate and tropical regions except Australia. They have heavy chopping bills, strong grasping feet, and a feathered ruff at the base of the neck. Family: *Accipitridae* (hawks and eagles). *See also* griffon vulture; lammergeier.

Vyborg (Finnish name: Viipuri; Swedish name: Viborg) 60 45N 28 41E A port in the Soviet Union, in the NW RSFSR on Vyborg Bay in the Gulf of Finland 113 km (70 mi) NW of Leningrad. It supports a fishing fleet, and shipbuilding and lumbering are important industries. *History*: founded (1293) by the Swedes as a fortress, it was taken by Peter the Great in 1710 but belonged to Finland from 1918 to 1940. It passed finally to the Soviet Union in 1944. Population (1983 est): 79 000.

Vyshinskii, Andrei Yanuareevich (1883–1954) Soviet diplomat and lawyer. Vyshinskii was a professor of law and chief prosecutor in Stalin's purge trials (1934–38). He became foreign minister in 1949 and remained in office until Stalin's death, when he was demoted to deputy foreign minister and permanent delegate to the UN.

W

Wabash River A river of the E central USA, flowing from W Ohio through Indiana to join the Ohio River. Length: 764 km (475 mi).

Wace (c. 1100-c. 1175) Anglo-Norman poet. He was made a canon of Bayeux by Henry II of England. His major works are the *Roman de Rou* (1160-74), concerning the history of Normandy, and the *Roman de Brut* (1155), which was dedicated to Eleanor of Aquitaine and contained much new material relating to the *Arthurian legend.

Wade, Virginia (1945-) British tennis player. She won her first national singles championship (US) in 1968, later also winning the Italian and Australian titles (1971 and 1972). In 1977 she won the Wimbledon singles.

Wade-Giles system. *See* Chinese.

wadi A normally dry valley in a desert or semidesert area. It will occasionally contain water following the infrequent violent downpours of rain that occur in these areas.

Wadi Halfa 21 55N 31 20E A town in the N Sudan, near the Egyptian border. Part of the town was flooded when the *Aswan High Dam was completed (1970). Agriculture and commerce are important and it is the terminus of railway and steamship services.

Wad Medani 14 24N 33 30E A town in the E central Sudan, on the Blue Nile River. Its recent growth has been due to its central position in the *Gezira irrigation scheme. Population (1983): 141 065.

Wagga Wagga 35 07S 147 24E A city in Australia, in SE New South Wales on the Murrumbidgee River. It is a service centre for the *Riverina district. Population (1983 est): 49 350.

RICHARD WAGNER *A contemporary caricature of Richard Wagner, emphasizing the composer's shortness.*

Wagner, (Wilhelm) Richard (1813-83) German composer. He studied at the Thomasschule in Leipzig. His early attempts at composition were unsuccessful but productions of his operas *Rienzi* (1842) and *The Flying Dutchman* (1843) led to his appointment as conductor at the Dresden opera house. In 1845 his opera *Tannhäuser* was successfully per-

formed there but in 1848, after the failure of the May uprising, Wagner fled to Zürich, where he began the composition of the operatic cycle *Der Ring des Nibelungen*, an epic treatment of German mythology. Wagner developed the use of composition with *leitmotifs in order to achieve an integration of music and drama in opera, having as an ideal that of the *Gesamtkunstwerk* (German: complete work of art). During the composition of the *Ring*, he fell in love with Mathilde Wesendonck (1828-1902), who inspired the opera *Tristan und Isolde*. Wagner continued to face financial difficulties until, in 1864, King Ludwig II of Bavaria befriended him, financing the first performance of *Tristan* in 1865. Shortly afterwards Wagner eloped with Cosima von Bülow (1837-1930), Liszt's daughter, whom he married in 1870. In 1868 he produced his comic opera *Die Meistersinger von Nürnberg* and continued work on the *Ring*, raising money to build a theatre in Bayreuth for the first performance of the cycle (1876). His last opera, *Parsifal*, was produced in Bayreuth in 1882. Wagner was also a prolific writer on music, the theory of music drama (*see* opera), art, and other subjects. His son **Siegfried Wagner** (1869-1930) and grandson **Wieland Wagner** (1917-66) directed annual productions of Wagner's music dramas at Bayreuth after his death.

Wagner von Jauregg, Julius (1857-1940) Austrian psychiatrist who, as professor of psychiatry and neurology at Vienna University, successfully treated patients suffering from progressive syphilitic brain disease by means of a controlled malarial infection. His work led to the introduction of fever therapy for various mental disorders and he was awarded the 1927 Nobel Prize.

Wagram, Battle of (5-6 July, 1809) The battle in which Napoleon won a major victory over the Austrians. Fought NE of Vienna, it forced Austria to concede general defeat to the French. Wagram witnessed the largest concentration of field artillery in recorded history.

wagtail A slender fine-billed songbird noted for its constantly bobbing tail. The pied wagtail (*Motacilla alba*) is black, grey, and white, about 18 cm long, and commonly occurs near houses. The larger grey wagtail (*M. cinerea*) lives near streams, catching flying insects. In summer the male has a bright-yellow breast, black throat, and bluish upper parts. The yellow wagtail (*M. flava*) visits Britain in the summer. Family: *Motacillidae* (wagtails and pipits).

Wahhabiyah A Muslim sect founded by Muhammad ibn Abd al-Wahhab (1691-1787). It stresses the need for a Muslim state based on strict adherence to the literal authority of the *Koran and *Hadith. It is responsible for the creation of the kingdom of Saudi Arabia.

Waikato River The longest river in New Zealand, in North Island. Rising in Mount Ruapehu, it flows generally NW through Lake Taupo to enter the Tasman Sea near Auckland. It is an important source of hydroelectric power. Length: 350 km (220 mi).

Wailing Wall (*or* Western Wall) Part of the western wall of the *Temple of Jerusalem; it is the only part of the wall still standing. Since late Roman times Jews have gathered here to pray and to mourn over the Temple's destruction.

Wain, John (1925-) British novelist, poet, and critic. His first novel, *Hurry on Down* (1953), was a satirical portrait of a representative postwar graduate. Later works include the novels *The Contenders* (1958), *The Pardoner's Tale* (1978), and *Young Shoulders* (1982), and the biographical *Samuel Johnson* (1974). He has also published books of poetry and criticism as well as *Dear Shadows* (1985), a volume of biographies.

Wairarapa Plain A low-lying sedimentary area in New

Zealand, on SE North Island. Sheep and dairy farming are important. Area: about 830 sq km (320 sq mi).

Waitangi, Treaty of (1840) A treaty between the British Government and 46 Maori chiefs in New Zealand, which gave the Maori full rights and confirmed their possession of their lands. Its infringement by settlers led to the *Maori Wars.

Wajda, Andrzej (1926-) Polish film director. He established his international reputation with *A Generation* (1954), *Kanal* (1957), and *Ashes and Diamonds* (1958), a trilogy of films concerning Poland during and after World War II. In later films, such as *Landscape after Battle* (1970) and *The Wedding* (1972), he continued to explore social and political themes.

Wakamatsu. *See* Kitakyushu.

Wakashan languages A group of *North American Indian languages of the NW Pacific coast, including *Nootka and *Kwakiutl.

Wakefield 53 42N 1 29W A city in N England, the administrative centre of West Yorkshire on the River Calder. A battle was fought here in 1460 during the Wars of the Roses, in which Richard, Duke of York, was defeated and killed by the Lancastrians. The chief industries are wool textiles, chemicals, machine tools, and coalmining. Population (1981): 60 540.

Wakefield, Edward Gibbon (1796-1862) British colonist. After imprisonment for tricking an heiress into marrying him, he helped to found the New Zealand Association (1837; New Zealand Company from 1838). In Canada in 1839 he was a major influence on Lord *Durham's report on Canada. Wakefield emigrated to New Zealand in 1853.

Wake Island 19 18N 166 36E A coral atoll in the central Pacific Ocean, a US air base. It was taken by the Japanese following the Pearl Harbor attack (December, 1941). Area: 8 sq km (3 sq mi).

Waksman, Selman Abraham (1888-1973) US microbiologist, born in Russia. Waksman coined the term antibiotic for naturally occurring antibacterial substances. His search for these among soil microorganisms led to the discovery of actinomycin (1940) and *streptomycin (1943), the first effective agent for the treatment of tuberculosis. Waksman was awarded a Nobel Prize (1952).

Walachia (*or* Wallachia) A principality in SE Europe between the lower River Danube in the E and the Transylvanian Alps in the N and NE. Founded in 1290, it was a Hungarian fief until 1330. In the late 14th century it came under Turkish domination, which lasted until the 19th century. In 1859 Walachia united with *Moldavia to form Romania, the independence of which was recognized in 1878.

Walafrid Strabo (c. 808-49 AD) German scholar and poet. He became Abbot of Reichenau in 838. His fame rests on such poems as *Visio Wetteni*, which in describing the hereafter anticipates Dante's *Divine Comedy*, and a handbook on liturgical and archaeological subjects, which is of great historical interest.

Wałbrzych (German name: Waldenburg) 50 48N 16 19E An industrial town in SW Poland, in the Sudeten Mountains. It is a coalmining centre and has engineering and chemical industries. Population (1982 est): 134 449.

Walburga, St (*or* St Walpurgis; c. 710-79 AD) English nun and missionary to Germany; the sister of the English missionary St Willibald (700-86), Bishop of Eichstätt. She worked with St *Boniface in Germany, where she became abbess of Heidenheim, an important cultural centre. It is not certain why *Walpurgisnacht* (1 May), the traditional German witches' sabbath, is associated with her name. Feast day: 25 Feb.

Walcheren An island in the SW Netherlands, in Zeeland province in the Scheldt estuary. Protected from the sea by dykes, its fertile land produces sugar beet and vegetables. The disastrous Walcheren expedition (1809) during the Napoleonic Wars resulted in the loss of many British lives. Area: 212 sq km (82 sq mi). Chief towns: Flushing and Middelburg.

Waldemar. *See* Valdemar.

Waldenburg. *See* Wałbrzych.

Waldenses (*or* Vaudois) A Christian group founded in the 12th century by Peter Waldes (d. 1217), a wealthy merchant of Lyons, who apparently gave his wealth to the poor and formed a community known as "the poor men of Lyons." The first settlements were in the French Alps, but religious persecution, which continued sporadically to the 18th century, scattered the Waldenses to Italy, Bohemia, Germany, Spain, and eventually North America. They were supported at the Reformation by other Protestant groups. They reject many Roman doctrines (e.g. transubstantiation, purgatory, celibacy of the clergy); at present they number about 20 000.

WALES *Harlech Castle, begun in 1285 by Edward I.*

Waldheim, Kurt (1918-) Austrian diplomat and statesman; president (1986-). He was Austria's permanent representative to the UN (1964-68, 1970-71) before becoming secretary general (1972-81). He was elected president after a controversial campaign in which the opposition uncovered his war record with the Wehrmacht in the Balkans. In 1987 this prevented a visit to the USA.

Waler An Australian horse developed in the early 19th century by settlers using imported Thoroughbred and Arab stallions crossed with various mares. Named after New South Wales, Walers typically have a deep round body with a strong back and legs. Height: 1.47-1.63 m (14½-16 hands).

Wales (Welsh name: Cymru) A principality in the W of Great Britain, comprising a political division of the *United Kingdom. It is bordered by England to the E, the Irish Sea to the N, St George's Channel to the W, and the Bristol Channel to the S. Much of the country is covered by hills and mountains, including the Brecon Beacons to the S, the Cambrian Mountains in central Wales, and the mountains of Snowdonia in the NW. The Isle of Anglesey lies off the NW coast. The principal rivers are the Usk, Rhymney, Taff, Neath, Towry, and Dovey. For administrative purposes, the country has been divided into eight counties since April, 1974. Central Wales is sparsely populated, most of the population living in the valleys and coastal plains of the S and along the coastal strip in the N. *Economy*: the valleys and coastal plain in the S are highly industrialized, based originally on the coal found there. In the 19th century South Wales produced some of the best steam coal in the world and coal continues to be mined from the large field in the S as well as from a smaller field around Wrexham in the NE. Steelmaking has long been associated with these coalfields, and Wales accounts for about half the UK's production of steel sheet and almost all its production of tinplate. Steelmaking at the older plants, such as at Shotton in North Wales and Ebbw Vale in the Welsh valleys, is being phased out and concentrated on large plants sited for easy access to imported ore, near Port Talbot and Neath. The disastrous unemployment levels in South Wales in the 1930s, associated with the high concentration of traditional industries, has led the government to take steps to direct light industry to the area. The Royal Mint is now situated at Llantrisant and, among other activities, vehicle manufacture is carried out. Milford Haven, in the far SW, is famous for its deepwater port, used for the importing of oil, which has given rise to oil refining and associated petrochemical industries here and at Llandarcy near Swansea. Towns on the coast of North Wales derive an important revenue from tourism. Upland Wales is the source of an important water supply, much of which is used in England. Forestry is also important in the upland areas, as is sheep rearing. Dairying and beef production are important in the valleys and lowland areas. *History*: the Celtic inhabitants of Wales were little affected by the Roman occupation and were christianized in the 3rd century AD. King *Offa of Mercia built a great dyke (8th century) stretching from sea to sea, providing a frontier behind which the Welsh kingdoms were contained. Temporary unity was achieved by Hywel the Good (d. 950) but the country's subsequent disunity enabled Edward I of England to defeat *Llywelyn ap Gruffud (d. 1282) and establish English supremacy in Wales. Owen *Glendower's revolt in the early 14th century was also crushed and English rule was formalized with the Acts of *Union (1536-43). In common with England, Wales adopted Protestantism in the 16th century and has been a centre of Nonconformity since the 18th century. The early 19th century was characterized by rural overpopulation and near famine, which was alleviated by industrialization in the S and NE, and Wales also suffered during the Depression of the 1930s. Politically, the Liberals were in the ascendant in Wales from 1867 until after World War I, when the Labour Party gained increasing support. Welsh nationalism has also been a powerful force and in 1966 *Plaid Cymru won the Carmarthen by-election. However, *devolution plans were rejected in a referendum in 1979. Area: 20 767 sq km (8016 sq mi). Population (1981): 2 790 000. Capital: Cardiff.

Walesa, Lech (1943–) Polish trade unionist. An electrician at Gdansk shipyard, he became leader of the independent trade union Solidarity from its establishment (1980) until its suspension (1981). He was awarded the 1983 Nobel Peace Prize for his efforts to ensure workers' rights to establish their own unions.

Waley, Arthur (1889-1966) British translator and poet. His translations of Chinese and Japanese poetry influenced many western poets, notably Ezra Pound. He also translated novels and plays and wrote several studies of oriental literature and art.

walking (*or* race walking) In athletics, a form of racing in which a particular gait is used; the advancing foot must touch the ground before the other leaves it. Races are held on a track or on roads. World records (track): 20 km: 1 hour 20 minutes 6.8 seconds (1979) by Daniel Bautista (Mexico); 50 km: 3 hours 41 minutes 39 seconds (1979) by Raul Gonzalez (Mexico).

wallaby A herbivorous marsupial belonging to the *kangaroo family (*Macropodidae*). Wallabies are smaller than kangaroos. Hare wallabies (genus *Lagorchestes*; 3 species) are the smallest, measuring up to 90 cm in length. Rock wallabies (genus *Petrogale*; 6 species) have a squarish tail and rough-soled feet for negotiating rocky ground. Scrub wallabies (genus *Protemnodon*; about 11 species) inhabit brush or open forest, browsing on leaves and grass.

Wallace, Alfred Russel (1823-1913) British naturalist, who formulated a theory of evolution by natural selection independently of Charles *Darwin. Wallace spent eight years (1854-62) assembling evidence in the Malay Archipelago, sending his conclusions to Darwin in England. Their findings were presented to the Linnaean Society in 1858. Wallace found that Australian species were more primitive, in evolutionary terms, than those of Asia, and that this reflected the stage at which the two continents had become separated. He proposed an imaginary line (Wallace's line) dividing the fauna of the two regions.

Wallace, Edgar (1875-1932) British novelist. The illegitimate son of an actress, he was the prolific and enormously successful author of over 170 popular novels and detective stories. He died in Hollywood, where he was a scriptwriter.

Wallace, Lew(is) (1827-1905) US soldier, diplomat, and author. He served in the *Mexican War (1846-47), the *Civil War (on the Federal side), as governor of New Mexico (1878-81), and minister to Turkey (1881-85). He wrote the bestseller *Ben Hur* (1880).

Wallace, Sir William (c. 1270-1305) Scottish hero of the resistance to English rule in the 1290s. In 1297 he captured Stirling Castle and was proclaimed warden of Scotland. In 1298, however, he was defeated by Edward I at Falkirk and was eventually captured and hanged.

Wallace Collection An art museum in Manchester Square, London. The collection, which was given to the nation in 1897, was formed by the 4th Marquess of Hertford and his half-brother Sir Richard Wallace (1818-90). It includes 18th-century French paintings and furniture, medieval armour, and *The Laughing Cavalier* by *Hals.

Wallachia. *See* Walachia.

wallaroo An Australian *kangaroo, *Macropus robustus*. Smaller than red or grey kangaroos, wallaroos are heavy-set and have long thick dark-grey fur. They are found mainly in Queensland and New South Wales.

Wallasey 53 26N 3 03W A town in NW England, in Merseyside on the Wirral Peninsula opposite Liverpool. It is a residential suburb and includes New Brighton (a resort), Egremont, and Seacombe. Population (1981): 90 057.

wallcreeper A Eurasian songbird, *Tichodroma muraria*, about 17 cm long with a grey plumage and broad black wings patched with red. It climbs rock faces, clinging with its sharp claws and square tail and probing crevices for insects with its long curved bill. Family: *Sittidae* (nuthatches).

Wallenberg, Raoul (1912–) Swedish diplomat. Sent to Hungary in 1944 as a special envoy, he helped many thousands of Jews to escape the Nazis, chiefly by issuing them with Swedish passports. While visiting Budapest in 1945 he was arrested by the Soviet authorities and disappeared. Although Soviet sources claimed he died in 1947, Wallenberg is reported to be still living in a Soviet prison and was made an honorary US citizen in 1981.

Wallenstein, Albrecht Wenzel von (1583-1634) Bohemian-born general, who commanded the imperial forces (1625-30, 1632-34) in the *Thirty Years' War. He raised an army of 24 000 men for the emperor Ferdinand I, with which he won a series of victories, acquiring considerable territories for himself. His growing independence led Ferdinand to dismiss him in 1630 but he was recalled to deal with the Swedish threat in 1632. He subsequently betrayed Ferdinand and was murdered by a group of British officers.

Waller, Edmund (1606-87) British poet. Banished for his part in a royalist conspiracy in 1643, he later managed to gain the favour of Oliver Cromwell and subsequently of Charles II. He wrote much occasional verse and many short elegant lyrics, such as the famous "Go, Lovely Rose."

Waller, (Thomas) Fats (1904-1943) US Black jazz musician and songwriter. Waller played the piano in cabarets and accompanied such singers as Bessie Smith. In the 1930s he organized small bands and recorded many of his own compositions, including "Honeysuckle Rose" and "Ain't Misbehavin'."

wallflower An annual or perennial herb of either of the genera *Cheiranthus* (about 10 species), native to Eurasia and North America, or *Erysimum* (about 80 species), native to Eurasia. Wallflowers have narrow leaves and four-petalled flowers, usually orange, yellow, red, or brown. Many varieties of *C. cheiri* are cultivated as garden ornamentals. The Siberian wallflower (*E.* × *marshallii*) has brilliant orange or yellow flowers. Family: **Cruciferae*.

Wallis, Sir Barnes (Neville) (1887–1979) British aeronautical engineer, who made many notable contributions to aircraft design. He designed the airship R100 and geodetic constructions, which he used in his Wellington bomber. He also invented the swing-wing aircraft but is best known for his invention in 1943 of the bouncing bomb used to destroy the Ruhr dams in Germany in World War II.

Wallis and Futuna A French overseas territory in the SW Pacific Ocean comprising two small groups of islands. Formerly a French protectorate, its status was changed following a referendum (1959). The chief of the **Wallis Islands** is Uvéa, while the **Futuna Islands** (*or* Îles de Horne) consist of Futuna and Alofi. Copra and timber are produced. Area: 275 sq km (106 sq mi). Population (1984 est): 13 000. Capital: Matautu, on Uvéa.

Walloons The French-speaking inhabitants of Belgium, who live mainly in the S and E of the country. They are descended from the northernmost group of *Franks who adopted the Romance speech. *Compare* Flemings.

LECH WALESA *The Polish trade-union leader addressing a Solidarity meeting in 1981.*

Wall Street The centre of the financial district in New York City, in which the New York Stock Exchange is situated. Wall Street, often known as the Street, is synonymous with the stock exchange.

walnut A □tree of the genus *Juglans* (about 17 species), especially the Eurasian species *J. regia*, which produces the best quality nuts. Up to 30 m tall, it has grey deeply furrowed bark and its leaves comprise seven oblong leaflets grouped in opposite pairs. Separate male and female catkins occur on the same tree, and the plum-sized green fruits each contain a kernel enclosed in a wrinkled pale-brown shell. The kernels are eaten as dessert nuts or used in baking and confectionery, and the whole fruits may be eaten pickled. The timber of this species and of the American black walnut (*J. nigra*) is valued for furniture. Family: *Juglandaceae*.

Walpole, Sir Hugh (Seymour) (1884–1941) British

novelist. Born in New Zealand, he worked as a teacher before becoming a full-time writer. His many novels inclue *The Dark Forest* (1916), set in Russia, *The Cathedral* (1922), and a four-volume family saga, *The Herries Chronicle* (1930–33).

Walpole, Sir Robert, 1st Earl of Orford (1676–1745) British statesman, regarded as the first prime minister (1721–42). He became a Whig MP in 1700 and was secretary for war (1708–10) and treasurer of the navy (1710–11). In 1712 he was impeached for corruption but came back into the government in 1715 as first lord of the treasury and chancellor of the exchequer. Again losing office in 1717, he was restored in 1720, becoming paymaster general, and after his effective handling of the *South Sea Bubble again became (1721) first lord of the treasury and chancellor of the exchequer. His power was supreme after he had secured the dismissal of *Carteret in 1724 and the resignation of *Townshend in 1730. He maintained his position by adroit patronage and skilful management of the House of Commons but his government was weakened by the failure of his excise bill (1733), which would have imposed taxes on wine and tobacco, and by his unpopular foreign policy. Conflict with Spain led to the War of *Jenkins' Ear and Walpole was forced to resign.

His fourth son **Horace Walpole, 4th Earl of Orford** (1717–97) was a writer. Strawberry Hill, his villa at Twickenham, became a showpiece of the gothic architectural revival. He published memoirs, antiquarian works, and one of the most popular of gothic novels, *The Castle of Otranto* (1765). His vast private correspondence is of historical and literary interest.

walrus A large *seal, *Odobenus rosmarus*, of coastal Arctic waters. Males are up to 3.7 m long and weigh about 1400 kg. Walruses have tusks—elongated upper canine teeth up to 1 m long—used in digging for molluscs on the sea bed and for fighting and display. They have an inflatable bag of skin on each side of the neck, used for buoyancy when sleeping in the sea. Family: *Odobenidae*. □mammal.

Walsall 52 35N 1 58W An industrial town in central England, in West Midlands near Birmingham. Industries include coalmining, engineering, machine tools, aircraft components, electronics, leather goods, hardware, and chemicals. Population (1981): 178 900.

Walsingham 52 54N 0 52E A village in E England, in Norfolk. The shrine of Our Lady of Walsingham, with which many miracles have been associated, was built here in the 11th century and was a major place of pilgrimage in the middle ages; it was destroyed in 1538. Parts of its medieval priory remain.

Walsingham, Sir Francis (c. 1532–90) English statesman; secretary of state (1573–90) under Elizabeth I after serving as ambassador to France (1570–73). He is best remembered for his activities against spies and conspirators and was responsible for unmasking the plots of Francis *Throckmorton and Anthony *Babington against the queen.

Walter, Bruno (B. W. Schlesinger; 1876–1962) German conductor. He became conductor of the Leipzig Gewandhaus Orchestra in 1929 but went to the USA after the outbreak of World War II. He was famous as an interpreter of Mahler and conducted the first performance of *Das Lied von der Erde* in 1911.

Walter, Hubert (d. 1205) English churchman and statesman. He became Bishop of Salisbury in 1189 and Archbishop of Canterbury in 1193. As chief justiciar (1193–98) and thus virtual ruler of England during Richard I's absence on the Crusades, he introduced important administrative and tax reforms and created the post of justice of the peace.

Walter I, John (1739–1812) British newspaper editor, who founded *The Times*. He acquired a printing press in Blackfriars, London, and began (1785) to publish the *Daily Universal Register*. He renamed it *The Times*, the first edition of which appeared on 1 January, 1788. The newspaper remained in his family for nearly 125 years. His son **John Walter II** (1776–1847) managed *The Times* from 1802 to 1847. **John Walter III** (1818–1894) succeeded his father, John Walter II, in 1847.

Waltham Forest A borough of NE Greater London, created in 1965 from the former municipal boroughs of Chingford, Leyton, and Walthamstow. Population (1981) 215 092.

Walther von der Vogelweide (c. 1170–c. 1230) German poet. After studying under the court poet of Vienna, he earned a precarious living as a Minnesinger at various courts until he was granted a fief by the Emperor Frederick II. His finest works are love poems and poems inspired by his loyalty to the Holy Roman Empire.

Walton, Ernest Thomas Sinton (1903–) Irish physicist, who shared the 1951 Nobel Prize with Sir John *Cockcroft for their invention in 1929 of the first particle accelerator. He was professor of physics at Dublin from 1934 until 1947.

Walton, Izaak (1593–1683) English writer. His best-known work is *The Compleat Angler* (1653), a relaxed and entertaining treatise on fishing. He also wrote short biographies of John Donne (1640), George Herbert (1670), and other churchmen.

Walton, Sir William (Turner) (1902–83) British composer. He first became well known through *Façade* (1922), a setting of poems by Edith Sitwell for reciter and instrumental group. Later works include two symphonies (1932–35, 1960), the opera *Troilus and Cressida* (1954), concertos for viola (1929), violin (1939), and cello (1957), the oratorio *Belshazzar's Feast* (1931), and music for Laurence Olivier's films of Shakespeare's *Hamlet*, *Henry V*, and *Richard III*.

waltz A ballroom dance in 3/4 time in which couples revolve round the room with gliding steps. It originated in Austria and Germany in the late 18th century from a popular folk dance, the *Ländler*. Although many considered it indecorous, it quickly spread to France and reached England in about 1812. Its variations include the skipping French waltz in 6/8 time, the slow Boston waltz, and the galloping Viennese waltz, for which the Strauss family composed their most famous music.

Walvis Bay A port on the Atlantic coast of Namibia, comprising an exclave of Cape Province, South Africa. Annexed to the Cape Colony in 1884, it has been administered as part of South West Africa (now Namibia) since 1922. It is a major port, handling most Namibian imports, and has important fishing industries. Area: 1124 sq km (434 sq mi). Population (1983 est): 24 600.

wampum Strings, belts, or ornaments of shell-beads, made by Indians of the NE regions of the USA and used by them originally as a record of a treaty or agreement and later, after contact with Europeans, as a form of money.

wandering Jew. *See* Tradescantia.

Wandering Jew In legend, a Jew who rebuked Christ as he was carrying the cross to Calvary and told him to go faster; he was condemned to wander the earth until Christ's second coming. The story is of an early date, a version being given by the English chronicler Matthew Paris (d. 1259); however, its popularity dates from 1602, when a pamphlet was published containing the story of a bishop of Schleswig who had met a certain Ahasuerus, who claimed to be the Wandering Jew.

Wandsworth A borough of S central Greater London, on the River Thames. It was created in 1965 from most of the former metropolitan borough together with *Battersea. Population (1981): 255 723.

Wang. *See* Koryŏ.

Wang An Shi (*or* Wang An-shih; 1021–86) Chinese statesman and writer. As a leading minister (1069–76) during the Song dynasty, he introduced wide-ranging economic reforms (including a fund to make loans to farmers), known as the New Policies. Conservative opposition led to his retirement, after which he devoted himself to scholarship and poetry.

Wanganui 39 56S 175 00E A port in New Zealand, in SW North Island on the Wanganui River. It is a service centre for the *Taranaki district. Population (1980 est): 40 000.

Wang Jing Wei (*or* Wang Ching-wei; 1883–1944) Chinese revolutionary, who attempted unsuccessfully to assassinate the Qing prime minister (1910). Wang later became a rival of *Chiang Kai-shek for the leadership of the *Guomindang and in 1927, in opposition to Chiang, he established a short-lived government at Wuhan. Reconciled with Chiang in 1932, Wang subsequently became prime minister of a Japanese puppet government in Nanjing and died in disgrace.

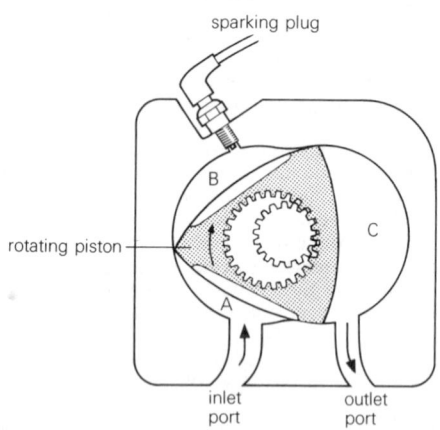

WANKEL ENGINE *The rotary piston draws the fuel mixture through the inlet port into chamber A. At the same time the gas drawn into chamber B in the previous third of a cycle is compressed and ignited to drive the piston round. Meanwhile, the gas in chamber C is discharged through the outlet port.*

Wankel engine A four-stroke rotary *internal-combustion engine. It consists of a triangular-shaped rotating piston, with outward curved sides and rounded corners. This rotates in an oval-shaped chamber, slightly narrowed in the middle, which has inlet and exhaust ports and a sparking plug. The piston has an inner toothed annulus, which rotates about a central stationary gear, the whole piston being connected via gears to an output shaft. The small number of moving parts and the lack of vibration are the chief advantages of this type of engine, but gas leakage around the seals between the piston ends and the cylinder has been the principal problem. It is, however, used in some cars. It was invented by the German engineer Felix Wankel (1902–).

Wankie 18 20S 26 25E A town in W Zimbabwe. It is a tourist centre near Wankie National Park and has a large coalmining industry. Population (1980 est): 33 000.

wapentake Any of the medieval administrative subdivisions into which the parts of England settled by the Danes (*see* Danelaw) were divided. They corresponded to the *hundreds found in the rest of England. Derived from the Old Norse words for *weapon* and *take*, the term probably refers to the Scandinavian custom of brandishing weapons in an assembly as a gesture of assent.

wapiti A large *red deer of North America, sometimes regarded as a separate species (*Cervus canadensis*). Males may exceed 1.5 m at the shoulder and have antlers up to 1.2 m high.

Wapping A dockland area in E London, in Tower Hamlets, site of several national newspaper printing works. Transfer of operations from Fleet Street to Wapping in the mid-1980s and increased use of technology led to job losses and protracted unrest in labour relations.

waratah A much-branched Australian shrub, *Telopea speciosissima*: the floral emblem of New South Wales. Up to 2 m tall, it has leathery sometimes toothed leaves and crimson or scarlet flowers borne in large round terminal heads surrounded by ribbon-like red bracts. The fruit is a leathery capsule containing winged seeds. Family: *Proteaceae*.

Warbeck, Perkin (c. 1474-99) Flemish-born impostor, the focus of a Yorkist plot against Henry VII of England. Pretending to be the Duke of York (presumed murdered with his brother Edward V in 1483) he landed in Cornwall in 1497 but he and his 6000 followers fled in the face of Henry's troops. Captured at Beaulieu, he was hanged after twice trying to escape from the Tower of London.

warble fly A parasitic fly belonging to the family *Oestridae*, widespread in Europe and North America. *Hypoderma boris* and *H. lineatum* attack cattle: eggs are laid on the legs and the larvae burrow into the tissue, coming to lie beneath the hide of the back. There they produce swellings (warbles), each pierced with a hole for breathing. When mature the larvae leave the warble and pupate in the ground. *See also* gad fly.

warbler A small active songbird belonging to a family (*Sylviidae*; 400 species) widely distributed in Old World regions. Ranging from 9-25 cm in length, warblers have slender bills, soft thick plumage, and feed on insects and berries. They are usually drab brown or olive in colour and many have beautiful songs. *See* blackcap; chiffchaff; reed warbler; whitethroat.

war crimes Acts contrary to rules of *international law governing the conduct of war, mainly contained in the Hague Convention (1907) and the Geneva Convention (1949). Persons suspected of war crimes may be tried and punished by the state that obtains custody of them. The *Nuremberg Trials established the most important principle regarding war crimes, that "the fact that the defendant acted pursuant to the order of his government or of a superior shall not free him from responsibility...."

Ward, Artemus (Charles Farrar Browne; 1834-67) US humorous writer. While working as a journalist for the Cleveland *Plain Dealer*, he wrote comic letters, the supposed author of which was an itinerant showman, Artemus Ward. He gained national fame as a lecturer using this pseudonym.

Ward, Barbara, Baroness Jackson (1914-81) British economist and conservationist. She wrote several books on ecology and political economy, including *Spaceship Earth* (1966) and, with the US bacteriologist René Dubos (1901-), *Only One Earth* (1972). She became president of the Institute for Environment and Development in 1973.

Ward, Mrs Humphry (1851-1920) British novelist, niece of Matthew Arnold. Born in Tasmania, she moved to England in 1856 and married Humphry Ward, an Oxford don, in 1872. *Robert Elsmere* (1888) and her other novels are chiefly concerned with topical religious and social issues.

Ward, Sir Joseph George (1856-1930) New Zealand statesman; Liberal (1906-12) and United Party (1928-30) prime minister. He entered parliament in 1887, becoming postmaster general (1891) and colonial treasurer (1893); he introduced the penny post to New Zealand in 1901. He advocated greater unity within the British Empire in foreign affairs and led the Liberals in the coalition government (1915-19) under W. F. Massey, before becoming leader of the Liberal Party's successor, the United Party.

Ward, Sir Leslie (1851-1922) British caricaturist. After studying architecture and painting, he worked for *Vanity Fair* from 1873 under the pseudonym of Spy and became known for his caricatures of contemporary politicians, authors, musicians, and others.

Wardrobe A royal administrative department in medieval England. Originally the room in which the king kept his clothes and jewels, it became a government department in the late 12th century owing to the king's need for immediate cash supplies while travelling. Closely controlled by the king, it was used by Henry III to counterbalance the Exchequer, which was controlled by the magnates, occasioning much hostility. It declined in importance during the 14th century, becoming again a mere household department.

war games Simulations in miniature of military manoeuvres and combat, using models and rules that enable authentic situations to be reproduced on the playing table. They originated in German states in the late 18th century and were developed by the Prussian army for training purposes during the 19th century. By World War I the military staffs of many countries were using them to assist in the preparation of plans and the training of commanders. War gaming is now a popular pastime.

Warhol, Andy (Andrew Warhola; 1926-87) US *pop artist and film producer. Originally a commercial artist, he achieved notoriety in the early 1960s with paintings of soup cans and portraits of film stars, notably Marilyn Monroe, made with the *silk-screen printing technique. His erotic, lengthy, and controversial films include *Sleep* (1963) and *The Chelsea Girls* (1966).

Warlock, Peter (Philip Heseltine; 1894-1930) British composer, critic, and music scholar. Largely self-taught, he was noted for his scholarly editions of early English music. His compositions include *The Curlew* (for voice, cor anglais, flute, and string quartet; 1920-22) and the *Capriol Suite* (for strings; 1926), based on tunes from *Orchésographie* (1589), a collection of dances made by Thoinot Arbeau (1519-95).

warlords Local despots who seized control of China following the death of the first president of Republican China, *Yuan Shi Kai, in 1916. These local tyrants, with their own private armies, attempted to increase their personal power by engaging in civil war, which was only ended by Chiang Kai-shek's Northern Expedition against them in 1926. They continued to exert power in China until Liberation (1949).

warm-bloodedness. *See* homoiothermy.

Warm Springs 32 53N 84 42W A village in the USA, in Georgia. Its water, popular as a health cure since the 19th century, was used by Franklin D. Roosevelt after his attack of poliomyelitis and he subsequently established a foundation (1927) to help other victims of the disease. He died here in 1945. Population (1980): 425.

War of 1812 (1812-14) The war declared on Britain by the USA in response to Britain's impressment of sailors from US ships and its blockade on US shipping during the Napoleonic Wars. The USA was also incensed by British assistance to Indians harassing NW settlements (*see* Tecumseh). The war was entirely inconclusive but helped forge unity and patriotism in the new US nation.

War of Independence, American. *See* American Revolution.

Warren, Earl (1891-1974) US jurist. He was attorney general of California (1939-43) and its governor from 1943 to 1953, when Eisenhower appointed him chief justice of the Supreme Court. A champion of civil rights, he limited police malpractice and, in 1954, ended racial segregation in US schools. From 1963 to 1964 he chaired the investigation into the Kennedy assassination.

Warrington 53 24N 2 37W A town in NW England, in Cheshire on the River Mersey and the Manchester Ship Canal. Designated a new town in 1968, there are engineering, iron-founding, brewing, tanning, chemical, and detergent-manufacturing industries. Population (1981): 135 568.

Warrnambool 38 23S 142 03E A seaport and resort in Australia, in SW Victoria on Lady Bay. It is the commercial centre of an important dairy-farming and sheep-rearing region. Population (1985 est): 22 500.

Warrumbungle Range A mountain range of Australia. It lies in N New South Wales, reaching 1228 m (4028 ft) at

Mount Exmouth, and contains the Breadknife, a rock 90 m (300 ft) high but only 1.5 m (5 ft) wide.

Warsaw (Polish name: Warszawa) 52 15N 21 00W The capital of Poland, in the E on the River Vistula. Settlements in the early middle ages had developed into a city by the end of the 15th century and it became the capital in 1611. Thereafter it suffered a decline but it rose to power again in the 18th century. It was occupied by Russia in 1794 and later by France and Prussia. It played an important role in the Polish struggles for independence in the 19th century and, after German occupation in World War I, became the capital again when independence was achieved (1918). During the German occupation of the city in World War II, a ghetto was established (1940) for 400 000 Jews and in February, 1943, the survivors (about 100 000) staged an uprising, after which they were put to death. By the end of the occupation Warsaw was almost completely in ruins. After the war much of the old town was faithfully reconstructed. It has expanded in recent years and is now an important industrial and communications centre. The University of Warsaw was founded in 1818 and the Technical University in 1826. Population (1982 est): 1 628 000.

Warsaw Pact (*or* Warsaw Treaty Organization) A military treaty signed in 1955 by the Soviet Union, Albania (until 1968), Bulgaria, Czechoslovakia, East Germany, Hungary, Poland, and Romania. It was formed as a communist counterpart to NATO. The Soviet army marshal is the head of the Pact's forces and its headquarters is in Moscow.

warships. *See* ships; aircraft carrier; battleship; corvette; cruiser; destroyer; destroyer escort; frigate; submarine.

Wars of Religion (1562-98) French civil wars arising out of the struggle of the Huguenots (French Protestants) for religious liberty and the rivalry between Protestants and Roman Catholic nobles for control of the Crown. The main parties were the Catholic *Guise family and successive Huguenot leaders, the Dukes of *Condé, Gaspard de *Coligny, and Henry of Navarre. The wars, comprising eight distinct conflicts, were exacerbated by the weakness of the monarchy under Charles IX and Henry III, who were dominated by their mother *Catherine de' Medici. The wars ended in the victory of Henry of Navarre, who after becoming a Catholic ascended the throne as *Henry IV. In 1598 he issued the Edict of *Nantes, which gave the Huguenots religious freedom.

wart (*or* verruca) A small leathery growth on the skin, caused by viruses. Warts are commonest in children and usually appear on the hands and on the soles of the feet. They appear suddenly and may disappear without treatment. Persistent warts can be treated by cauterization, freezing, or with drugs (such as podophylline), but no treatment is entirely satisfactory.

warthog A wild pig, *Phocochoerus aethiopicus*, of tropical African woodland. Short-legged, with a large head, bulging eyes, and long curved tusks, warthogs grow to about 75 cm high at the shoulder. They are grey-brown with sparse body hair except on the shoulders and along the spine and they feed during the day on roots, grass, etc., often sheltering in disused aardvark burrows.

Warton, Joseph (1722-1800) British poet and critic. In his emphasis on the role of the imagination both in his *Odes* (1744, 1746) and in his essay on Alexander Pope (1756) he was a forerunner of the Romantic movement. His brother **Thomas Warton** (1728-90) was the author of learned works of literary criticism and history and became poet laureate in 1785.

wart snake A thick-bodied fish-eating aquatic snake belonging to the family *Acrochordidae* (2 species), having valves that close the mouth and nostrils when under water. The brown Javan wart snake (*Acrochordus javanicus*), also known as the elephant's-trunk snake, is 1.2 m long and

occurs in rivers and coastal waters of Australia and SE Asia; it is killed for its skin.

Warwick 52 17N 1 34W A town in central England, the administrative centre of Warwickshire on the River Avon. It is a historic town with a 14th-century castle and two medieval gateways. Industries include engineering and tourism. Population (1981): 21 936.

Warwick, Richard Neville, Earl of (1428-71) English statesman, known as the Kingmaker. He was the most prominent English magnate during the Wars of the *Roses. A supporter of the Yorkists from 1453, he was responsible for the seizure of the Crown in 1461 by Edward, Duke of York (Edward IV). In 1470, losing influence at court, he changed sides and briefly restored Henry VI to the throne. After the Lancastrians were routed (1471), he was killed, at Barnet.

Warwickshire A county in the Midlands of England. It consists mainly of undulating countryside, drained to the SW by the River Avon. It is predominantly agricultural, dairy farming being especially important. There is also arable farming and market gardening. Some light industry exists around the towns but it lost its more industrial NW area, including Birmingham, Coventry, and Solihull, to the West Midlands under local government reorganization in 1974. Area: 1981 sq km (765 sq mi). Population (1981): 473 620. Administrative centre: Warwick.

Wash, the A shallow inlet of the North Sea, in E England between Lincolnshire and Norfolk, into which the Rivers Witham, Welland, Nene, and Great Ouse flow. Length: about 30 km (19 mi). Width: 24 km (15 mi).

Washington One of the Pacific states in NW USA. Mountains ring the state, including Mount *St Helens, and the Columbia Basin covers much of the central area, cut by the Columbia and Snake Rivers. The lowland around the Puget Sound in the W is highly populated, urbanized, and industrialized, while the E is predominantly rural and sparsely populated. The state's major manufacturing industry is the construction of aircraft. Washington is also a leader in nuclear research and timber production, although in 1983 construction of two nuclear power plants was halted, terminating the most costly public works project ever undertaken. Attempts to diversify the economy have led to a concentration on the growing tourist industry and there is significant mineral extraction, especially of gold, silver, and uranium. Fishing is important as is foreign trade. Wheat, potatoes, and fruit (especially apples) are grown and dairy farming is important. *History*: the British Hudson Bay Company dominated the area until the 1840s. In 1846 the boundary between Washington and Canada was agreed and the state (1889) was named after George Washington. Area: 176 616 sq km (68 192 sq mi). Population (1980): 4 130 163. Capital: Olympia.

Washington 54 54N 1 31W A town in NE England, in Tyne and Wear. Designated for development as a new town in 1964, it was the home of the ancestors of George Washington before they moved to Northamptonshire. Population (1981): 53 783.

Washington, Booker T(aliaferro) (1856-1915) US Black teacher and reformer. As first principal of the Tuskegee Institute (Alabama) for Blacks, Washington supported the cause of civil rights by encouraging Blacks to pursue industrial education rather than political agitation. His autobiography, *Up from Slavery* (1901), and his many lectures stressed the need for racial understanding.

Washington, DC 38 55N 77 00W The capital of the USA, in the E of the country on the Potomac River. Coextensive with the District of Columbia, it is the centre of the government of the USA and most of its inhabitants are government employees. Its many notable landmarks include the Washington Monument, the Lincoln Memorial, the Capitol, the ᴰWhite House, the *Pentagon, the National

Gallery of Art, the Library of Congress, the Smithsonian Institution, the Arlington National Cemetery, the Vietnam Veterans Memorial, Washington National Cathedral, and the National Shrine of the Immaculate Conception. There are five universities and many cultural organizations have their headquarters here. *History*: its location as the nation's capital was chosen by George Washington and approved by Congress in 1790. Planned by the French engineer, Pierre L'Enfant (1754–1825), its first constructions date from 1793. Population (1980): 637 651.

GEORGE WASHINGTON

Washington, George (1732-99) US statesman and general; the first president of the USA (1789-97). Washington, who came from a wealthy Virginian family, was a surveyor before gaining a high military reputation in the *French and Indian War. From 1759 to 1774 he was a member of Virginia's House of Burgesses, becoming a leading opponent of British rule. On the outbreak of the *American Revolution (1775-83) he was appointed commander in chief of the American forces. After winning the final victory at Yorktown (1781), Washington presided over the *Constitutional Convention (1787) and was unanimously elected president of the new republic. Despite the development of party politics during his presidency, Washington remained neutral, a stance he also pursued in foreign relations.

wasp A stinging insect, 6-40 mm long, belonging to the order *Hymenoptera*. The common European wasps (genus *Vespula*) are typical social wasps, forming colonies that consist of a queen, males, and workers. The nests are built under ground, in bushes, or in hollow trees. The adults feed on nectar, ripe fruit, insects, etc.; the larvae are usually fed on insects and insect larvae. Fertilized eggs produce queens or workers and unfertilized eggs produce the males. New colonies are established by young fertilized queens—the only individuals to survive the winter. Certain parasitic wasps lay their eggs in the nests of other wasps. Solitary wasps (family *Sphecidae*) lay their eggs in individual nests that are stocked with food and sealed by the parent. *See also* digger wasp; gall wasp; hornet; potter wasp; spider wasp.

Wasserman, August von (1866-1925) German bacteriologist, who invented the Wasserman test for detecting *syphilis, based on the complement-fixation studies of *Bordet. Wasserman made many other contributions to immunology, including a test for tuberculosis and an antitoxin against diphtheria.

watch A timepiece small enough to be worn by a person. Watches, as small clocks, first came into use at the beginning of the 16th century with the invention by Peter Henlein (1480-1542) of the mainspring as the energy store in place of the earlier falling weight. Based on a verge escapement, watches were then bulky devices, often cylindrical, worn on the girdle. The invention of the balance spring (claimed by both Hooke and *Huygens) in 1675 converted the watch from a highly decorated ornament into a more functional article that could be concealed in the pocket. By the 18th century pocket watches had attained a high degree of accuracy as a result of the work of such master watchmakers as Thomas Tompion (1639-1713) and George Graham (1675-1751). At the beginning of the 20th century wrist watches were introduced and with World War I their advantages to men in uniform made them overwhelmingly popular. Between the wars wrist watches became smaller and cheaper or boasted such features as rust and shock resistance, luminous dials, or self-winding mechanisms. In the early 1950s the first electromagnetic watches were developed (powered by tiny batteries), but it was not until the late 1960s that the first electronic watch appeared. This used the piezoelectric oscillations of a quartz crystal as the time source and an electronic circuit to reduce the frequency to that required to drive the hands. In the 1970s quartz watches were developed without moving parts: this is the solid-state digital watch in which the dial and hands are replaced by a digital display. This can be made so small that some digital wrist watches incorporate several additional functions (e.g. date, stop-watch, alarm, reminder) as well as a tiny calculator. □ p.1284.

water (H_2O) A colourless odourless tasteless liquid consisting of eight parts of oxygen to two parts of hydrogen by weight. Water covers 72% of the earth's surface and is found in all living matter, in minerals, and as a small but important constituent of the atmosphere. The solid form of water (ice) is less dense (916.8 kg/m³) than the liquid at 0°C (999.84 kg/m³), which is why ice floats and frozen water pipes burst. The maximum density (999.97 kg/m³) occurs at 3.98°C, unlike most liquids in which the maximum density occurs at the melting point. The molecules of water are polar, i.e. they have a positive electric charge at one end and a negative at the other. This makes it an excellent solvent.
Water supplies: an adequate supply of clean water is a prerequisite of all communities. Rain is the prime source, although in arid areas *desalination of *sea water may be necessary. Rain water for distribution is collected in reservoirs, which may also be fed by rivers, streams, etc. The stored water is purified by filtration, usually through a deep bed of sand. Most of the impurities are trapped in the top 5-6 cm, which are periodically replaced. In fast filtration processes the addition of a coagulant (e.g. aluminium sulphate) is used to cause most particle impurities to fall to the bottom. The water then passes through several tanks of coarse sand. Disinfectants, usually chlorine, are added to kill microorganisms. Sufficient chlorine is added to leave about 0.2 mg/litre of uncombined chlorine after 30 minutes. In superchlorination larger quantities are added, followed by subsequent dechlorination with sulphur dioxide.
In the UK, water supply was delegated to Regional Water Authorities by the Water Act (1973). These authorities together supply some 305 litres of water per head of population to domestic and industrial users throughout the country every day. *See also* fluoridation.

water beetle A beetle of the family *Dytiscidae* (*see* diving beetle)—the so-called true water beetles. The name is also used loosely for any aquatic beetle, including the *whirligig beetles (family *Cyrinidae*); the water scavenging beetles (family *Hydrophilidae*), which resemble diving beetles but feed on algae or decaying organic matter; and the crawling

verge escapement

balance wheel and lever escapement

quartz-crystal watch   *A crystal of quartz (Q) uses the piezoelectric effect accurately to control the frequency of an oscillating electronic circuit consisting of a capacitor (C) and inductance (L).*

digital watch

WATCH   *Early watches used the verge escapement of clocks. The balance wheel and lever escapement dominated watch design until the quartz crystal and digital watch emerged in the 20th century.*

water beetles (family *Haliplidae*), which crawl and feed on algae.

water boatman   A *water bug belonging to the cosmopolitan family *Corixidae* (over 300 species). It has a flattened boat-shaped body with fringed oarlike hind legs and feeds on plant debris and algae, scooped up by the spoon-shaped front legs. It is normally attached to bottom vegetation of fresh and brackish waters, rising only to replenish its air store.

waterbuck   A large African antelope, *Kobus ellipsiprymnus*. About 130 cm high at the shoulder, waterbucks have a long wiry brown coat with a white rump patch and long spreading horns. Small groups spend the night in riverside cover and graze on the plains during the day.

water buffalo   A large buffalo, *Bubalus bubalis*, also called Asiatic buffalo or carabao, found wild in swampy land of SE Asia and widely domesticated throughout Asia. Up to 180 cm at the shoulder and heavily built, water buffaloes are grey-black with long backward-curving horns and can be dangerous. Domestic breeds are more docile and have shorter horns: they are used for milk and as draught animals.

water bug   An insect of the suborder *Heteroptera* (*see* Hemiptera) that lives in or on fresh or brackish water. True water bugs include the *backswimmer, *giant water bug, *water boatman, and *water scorpion. The surface water bugs include the *pond skater, water cricket (*Vellidae*), and water measurer (*Hydrometridae*).

Waterbury   41 33N 73 03W A city in the USA, in Connecticut. It was the nation's largest producer of brass products in the 19th century. Other manufactures include

watches, clocks, and electronic parts.   Population (1980): 103 266.

water chestnut   An annual aquatic plant of the genus *Trapa*, especially the Eurasian species *T. natans*, which has a rosette of diamond-shaped toothed floating leaves, feathery submerged leaves, and small white flowers. The hard spiny dark-grey fruit, up to 5 cm across, contains edible seeds that are eaten raw, roasted, boiled, or in porridge. Family: *Trapaceae*.
The Chinese water chestnut is the tuber of an E Asian sedge, *Eleocharis tuberosa*: it is cooked and eaten in various Chinese dishes. Family: *Cyperaceae*.

watercolour   A painting medium consisting of pigments bound with gum, which are diluted with water before being applied to a surface of white or tinted paper. Its special characteristics are its transparency and its white accents, which are created by leaving parts of the paper unpainted. Watercolour made opaque by the addition of white pigment and more glue is known as gouache or poster paint. Practised since ancient times, watercolour painting in postmedieval Europe was chiefly of a monochrome variety until the late 18th century, when it was developed to perfection by a series of British landscape artists, notably Paul Sandby (c. 1725–1809), *Girtin, *Cotman, *Blake, and *Turner. Outstanding 19th-century watercolourists included *Palmer, *Sargent, *Delacroix, and *Daumier.

watercress   Either of two perennial herbs, *Nasturtium officinale* or *N. microphyllum × officinale*, native to Eurasia and widely cultivated for the peppery young shoots, which are used in salads. Watercress grows submerged or floating in streams or on mud; it has compound leaves, with roundish or oval leaflets, and bears clusters of four-petalled white flowers. Family: *Cruciferae*.

waterfall A steep fall of water along the course of a river or stream. It may be produced by the river crossing a band of hard rock; where the rock strata are horizontal the fall is likely to be steep. Falls also occur at the edges of plateaus or where faulting has taken place. The waterfall will continually retreat upstream through erosion. Large waterfalls and series of falls are also known as **cataracts**. The energy of a waterfall can be harnessed to provide hydroelectric power.

water flea A small freshwater *crustacean of the suborder *Cladocera* (about 430 species). Its compact body, usually 1–3 mm long, is covered, behind the head, by a laterally flattened transparent carapace, which encloses 4–6 pairs of appendages. It swims by means of two large forked antennae. Common genera: *Daphnia*, *Leptodora*; subclass: *Branchiopoda*.

Waterford (Irish name: Port Lairge) 52 15N 7 06W A city and port in the SE Republic of Ireland, the county town of Co Waterford. It has Protestant and Roman Catholic cathedrals. It is an important trading and distribution centre; industries include light engineering, paper making, and glass making, for which it is famous. Population (1981): 39 636.

Waterford (Irish name: Contae Port Lairge) A county in the S Republic of Ireland, in Munster bordering on the Atlantic Ocean. Chiefly hilly, it is drained by the Rivers Blackwater and Suir. Agriculture is the main occupation with dairy farming and cattle rearing. The traditional glass-making industry is of note. Area: 1838 sq km (710 sq mi). Population (1981): 88 591. County town: Waterford.

water gas A mixture of equal amounts of hydrogen and carbon monoxide made by passing steam over red hot coke: $H_2O + C \rightarrow H_2 + CO$. The mixture is a useful fuel gas but the reaction producing it is endothermic and heat must be supplied to the coke. One way of doing this is to make water gas in conjunction with an exothermic reaction—that between air and carbon: $O_2 + 4N_2 + 2C \rightarrow 2CO + 4N_2$. The mixture of carbon monoxide and nitrogen is called **producer gas**. Although it has a lower calorific value than water gas the products are hot as a result of the high temperature of the reaction. The heating value of water gas can be improved by passing it through petroleum while hot, thus cracking liquid hydrocarbons to gaseous ones, which escape with the water gas. The process, known as carburetting, can almost double the calorific value. Water gas, however, is not as effective a fuel gas as *natural gas and its use is mainly as a raw material for chemical-manufacturing processes, such as the *Haber process.

Watergate A building complex in Washington, DC, that gave its name to a political scandal leading to the resignation of the Republican president, Richard Nixon. Amid growing suspicion of corruption among presidential officials, the *Washington Post* exposed their involvement during the 1972 presidential election in a burglary of the headquarters of the Democratic Party at the Watergate, and in subsequent arrangements (the "coverup") to buy off the convicted burglars. Following the resignation and prosecution of top White House staff, who alleged that Nixon had connived in Watergate, he resigned under the threat of impeachment (1974). He was pardoned by Gerald Ford later in the same year.

water glass (*or* sodium silicate) A mixture of silicates with the general chemical formula $x\text{Na}_2\text{O}.y\text{SiO}_2$, forming a clear viscous solution in water. It is made by fusing *sodium carbonate and sand (*silica) in an electric furnace and is used in making silica gel, detergents, and textiles.

Waterhouse, Alfred (1830–1905) British architect of the *gothic revival. Born in Liverpool, his early work was done in Manchester and included the Assize Court (1859; demolished 1959) and the Town Hall (1868). Thereafter he

came to London, where he built the romanesque Natural History Museum (1881) and the now demolished gothic redbrick St Paul's School (1885) and City and Guilds College (1879). A prolific designer of scholastic institutions, who used redbrick and terracotta freely, it is his buildings (and those of his imitators) that inspired the term "redbrick university."

water hyacinth An aquatic plant of the genus *Eichhornia* (about 5 species), native to tropical America. They have slender creeping rhizomes, rosettes of stalked leaves, and clusters of flowers in the leaf axils. Some species float in shallow water; others are rooted in muddy stream banks and lake edges. *E. crassipes* is the most widely distributed species; it is used as an ornamental plant in pools and aquariums and has become a troublesome weed in the S USA, Australia, and Africa. Family: *Pontederiaceae*.

water lily An annual or perennial freshwater plant of the family *Nymphaeaceae* (75 species), native to temperate and tropical regions. Water lilies have round wax-coated leaves floating on the water surface and borne on long central stalks arising from creeping stems buried in the mud below. The large showy flowers, whose stalks may rise above the water surface, are cup-shaped, with several whorls of oval pointed petals, usually white, yellow, pink, red, blue, or purple in colour. Most cultivated water lilies are hybrids and varieties derived from species of *Nymphaea*. *See also* lotus.

Waterloo 43 27N 80 30W A city in E Canada, in SW Ontario on the N side of *Kitchener. Founded by Mennonites (1806), it houses several insurance companies and two universities and is a musical centre. Its varied industries include distilling, brewing, furniture, and farm machinery. Population (1981): 49 428.

Waterloo 50 43N 04 24E A village in central Belgium, 13 km (8 mi) S of Brussels. On 18 June, 1815, it was the site of the famous battle of *Waterloo, which ended the Napoleonic Wars.

Waterloo, Battle of (18 June, 1815) The battle in which *Napoleon Bonaparte was finally defeated by British, Dutch, Belgian, and German forces commanded by Wellington and the Prussians under von Blücher. Napoleon caught Wellington 5 km (3 mi) S of Waterloo (Belgium) in isolation from the Prussians and attempted to smash his army by a direct offensive. The British lines held the French columns until the Prussians arrived. A concerted charge brought victory and four days later Napoleon's second, and final, abdication.

water louse A freshwater crustacean of the genus *Asellus*, related to the *woodlouse. It is found on submerged plants or the bottom of weedy streams and ponds. Order: *Isopoda*.

watermark A distinctive mark produced in *paper during manufacture by making it slightly thinner in some places than in others. In handmade paper, the watermark is formed by the wires in the bottom of the mould. In machine-made paper the mark is put in by the dandy roll, a roller that has the mark in a raised form on its surface.

watermelon The fruit of an annual climbing plant, *Citrullus vulgaris*, native to Africa but widely cultivated. The plant has hairy deeply lobed leaves and the yellow flowers produce large oval fruits, up to 25 cm across, with a shiny dark-green rind and red, yellow, or white flesh, which is juicy and sweet-flavoured. The seeds are also edible. Family: *Cucurbitaceae*. *See also* melon.

water milfoil A submerged or floating perennial freshwater aquatic plant of the worldwide genus *Myriophyllum* (about 45 species). It has whorls of finely divided feathery leaves and the green, white, or red flowers are borne in aerial spikes. A few species are grown in aquaria. Family: *Haloragaceae*.

water moccasin A heavy-bodied venomous *pit viper *Agkistrodon piscivorus*, occurring in marshes of the S USA and also called cottonmouth because it shows the white inside of its mouth when threatened. Up to 1.5 m long, it is brown with dark bands and hunts fish, turtles, and water-birds.

water polo A ball game played seven-a-side (with four substitutes), usually in a swimming pool. It originated in England in the 1870s, with players riding floating barrels to resemble horses and hitting the ball with paddles; in the modern game players swim. The object is to score goals with an inflated ball that is passed between players by throwing. Except for the goalkeepers, players may not walk, jump, punch the ball, or touch it with both hands together.

water rat A large aquatic *rodent belonging to the sub-family *Hydromyinae* (13 species) found in Australia, New Guinea, and the Philippines. The Australian water rat (*Hydromys chrysogaster*) is about 35 cm long and has otter-like fur and a white-tipped tail. Family: *Muridae*. *Water voles and *muskrats, are also known as water rats.

water scorpion A *water bug of the worldwide family *Nepidae* (about 200 species). Its scorpion-like "tail" is actually a breathing tube (siphon), which protrudes from the water while the insect hangs upside down from aquatic vegetation or the surface film of water. Water scorpions prey on small arthropods, tadpoles, and small fish.

watershed (*or* divide) The dividing line, usually a ridge, between the *catchment areas of two separate river systems. In the USA the term is used for the entire catchment area of the drainage basin. *See also* continental divide.

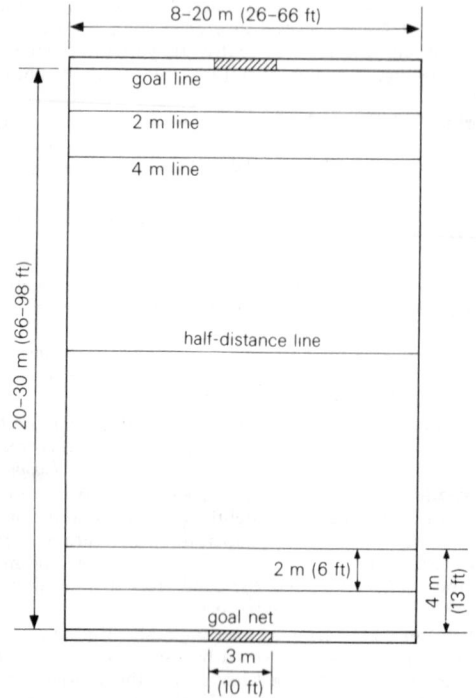

WATER POLO *The dimensions of the field of play. The water must be at least 1 m deep.*

water shrew A long-snouted Eurasian aquatic *shrew, *Neomys fodiens*. About 10 cm from nose to tail, water shrews feed chiefly on aquatic invertebrates but also take small fish and frogs, aided by their venomous saliva. Their hair-fringed toes assist in swimming.

water skiing Planing on water on wooden skis (or a single ski for slalom competitions), often with fins attached for stability. It originated in the 1920s. The skier is towed by a rope usually 23 m (75 ft) long attached to a powerboat travelling at a minimum of about 25 km per hour (15 mph).

Competitions are held for jumping, slalom (through a course of buoys), and trick riding. Barefoot water skiing is also practised, requiring speeds of 55-65 km per hour (35-40 mph).

water snake. *See* grass snake.

water spider A European freshwater *spider, *Argyroneta aquatica*, that lives under water in a bell-shaped structure constructed from silk and plant material and filled with bubbles of air brought down in its body hairs. It feeds inside on small animals taken from the water surface. The male (15 mm long) is—usually—larger than the female (10 mm long).

waterspout A funnel-shaped cloud extending from the base of a cumulonimbus cloud to the surface of the sea. It is a small-scale intense low-pressure system, the equivalent of a *tornado on land, characterized by intense rotating winds, which create violent agitation of the water surface and lift drops up into the cloud.

water strider. *See* pond skater.

WATER TABLE

water table The upper level of the water that has percolated into the ground and become trapped within pores, cracks, and fissures in permeable rocks. The level of the water table varies with the topography and local rainfall. *See also* artesian well.

water vole A large *vole, *Arvicola terrestris*, of Europe and Asia. 15-20 cm long, they are heavily built with a short tail and light-brown to black fur. Water voles burrow into river banks and feed on aquatic vegetation often during daytime.

water wheel. *See* turbine.

Watford 51 40N 0 25W A town in SE England, in Hertfordshire. It has paper-making, printing, engineering, and electronics industries and is a dormitory town for London. Population (1981): 74 356.

Watling Island. *See* San Salvador Island.

Watling Street The Roman road that traversed Britain from its commercial centre, London, via St Albans to the strategically sited Roman town near Wroxeter, with a branch to the legionary fortress at Chester. It left London by way of present-day Oxford Street and Edgware Road.

Watson, James Dewey (1928-) US geneticist, who (with Francis *Crick) proposed a model for the molecular structure of *DNA (1953). Following this fundamental breakthrough, Watson investigated the *genetic code and the way in which it is "read" by the cell. His *Molecular Biology of the Gene* (1965) has become an influential text, and *The Double Helix* (1968) gave a popular account of his work on DNA. He received a Nobel Prize (1962) with Crick and Maurice *Wilkins.

Watson, John Broadus (1878-1958) US psychologist and founder of the US school of psychology known as *behaviourism. Watson declared that speculations about animal behaviour should be based entirely on observations made under laboratory conditions. In *Psychology from the Standpoint of the Behaviourist* (1919), Watson applied his principles to human behaviour, which he regarded in terms of conditioned responses, excluding the possible contributions of reasoning and original thought. One of his most notable followers was B. F. *Skinner.

Watson, John Christian   (1867–1941) Australian statesman, born in Chile; the first Labor prime minister of Australia (1904). He was leader of the Labor Party from 1901 to 1907.

Watson, Tom   (Thomas Sturges W.; 1949–   ) US golfer; the highest paid player in the world. His victories include one US and five British Open championships, four US Professional Golfers Association championships, and two Masters championships. He has also won the World Series of Golf twice.

Watson-Watt, Sir Robert Alexander   (1892–1973) Scottish physicist, who during the 1920s and 1930s pioneered the development of *radar. In 1935 the British Government set up a research team working under Watson-Watt, who put it into military operation by World War II.

watt (W)   The *SI unit of power equal to one joule per second. In electrical terms it is the energy per second expended by a current of one ampere flowing between points on a conductor between which there is a potential difference of one volt. Named after James *Watt.

Watt, James   (1736–1819) British engineer, whose development of the steam engine contributed to the *industrial revolution. Working at Glasgow University as an instrument maker, he was asked in 1764 to repair a model of a *Newcomen engine. He realized that the machine could be made more efficient if the steam was condensed in a separate chamber. Watt's steam engine, completed in 1769, soon replaced the Newcomen engine, especially after Watt had introduced a double-acting model. In 1774 he went into partnership with Matthew Boulton (1728–1809), to manufacture steam engines and by 1800 some 500 stationary Watt engines were in use. He later invented the centrifugal governor. Watt devised the unit "horsepower" and the metric unit of power is named after him.

Watteau, (Jean) Antoine   (1684–1721) French rococo painter. Settling in Paris (1702), he trained under a painter of theatrical scenery and under the curator of the Luxembourg Palace, where he studied *Rubens. Despite his early death from tuberculosis, he achieved fame both in Paris and London (which he visited in 1719) with his charming *fêtes galantes* (scenes of gallantry) and paintings of comedians. His best-known works are *L'Embarquement pour l'île de Cythère* and the portrait of the clown *Gilles* (both Louvre).

wattle   Any of various Australian trees and shrubs, especially those of the genus *Acacia, used for fencing, turnery, etc., and formerly employed in the wattle and daub construction of houses. The commonest are the black wattle (*A. binervata*), the golden or green wattle (*A. pycnantha*), and the silver wattle (*A. dealbata*), which has silvery fernlike leaves and fluffy globular yellow flower heads and is used by florists under the name of mimosa. Wattles are used as shade trees, ornamentals, and livestock fodder.

wattmeter   An instrument for measuring electrical power. The most common type has two conducting coils connected in series, one fixed and one movable. The magnetic forces between them produce a deflection of the movable coil proportional to the square of the current, which is in turn proportional to the power.

Watts, George Frederick   (1817–1904) British artist. After studying at the Royal Academy, he achieved early success with designs for frescoes for the Houses of Parliament (1843, 1847). He specialized in allegorical paintings, notably *Hope* (Tate Gallery) and portraits, including one of his first wife *Ellen Terry*. As a sculptor he is best known for *Physical Energy* (Kensington Gardens).

Waugh, Evelyn (Arthur St John)   (1903–66) British novelist. With *Decline and Fall* (1928) and other novels, including *Vile Bodies* (1930), *A Handful of Dust* (1934), and *The Loved One* (1948), he established his reputation as the most brilliant social satirist of his generation. After his conversion to Roman Catholicism in 1930, religious themes played an increasing part in his novels, especially in *Brideshead Revisited* (1945). Later novels include his war trilogy–*Men at Arms* (1952), *Officers and Gentlemen* (1955), and *Unconditional Surrender* (1961)–and the semiautobiographical *The Ordeal of Gilbert Pinfold* (1957). His elder brother **Alec (Raban) Waugh** (1898–1981), a novelist and travel writer, made his name with the controversial *The Loom of Youth* (1917), a story of public-school life. Many later novels, such as *Island in the Sun* (1956), deal with life in tropical countries. Evelyn's son **Auberon Waugh** (1939–   ) is a novelist and journalist, formerly known for his satirical "Diary" in the magazine *Private Eye*. His novels include *Consider the Lilies* (1968); *Another Voice* (1986) contains a selection of his writings.

wave   Any periodic change in a property of a system that is propagated through a medium (or through space). Waves are classified according to the curve produced when their magnitude is plotted against time on a graph. If the wave is shaped like a sine curve, it is known as a sine (*or* sinusoidal) wave. Examples of sine waves include electromagnetic waves and sound waves. A wave is characterized by three parameters: amplitude, the maximum displacement of the wave; *wavelength; and *frequency. The wave may propagate energy, in which case it is known as a travelling wave, or it may not, when it is known as a standing or stationary wave. For travelling waves the displacement may be either perpendicular to the direction of the propagation of the wave (a transverse wave) or in the direction of propagation (a longitudinal wave). Waves on water and electromagnetic waves are transverse, while sound waves are longitudinal.

waveguide   A hollow conductor for transmitting microwaves over short distances. The electromagnetic radiation is guided along the tube, being reflected from the internal walls. The waveguide is usually filled with air but occasionally some other *dielectric is used.

wavelength   The distance between successive peaks (or troughs) of a wave. It is equal to the velocity of the wave divided by its frequency. For electromagnetic radiation it is a parameter specifying the part of the *electromagnetic spectrum to which the radiation belongs.

Wavell, Archibald Percival, 1st Earl   (1883–1950) British field marshal. After service in World War I he became *Allenby's chief of staff in Palestine. In World War II, as commander in chief in the Middle East, he defeated the Italians in N and East Africa. After the failure of his offensive against Rommel in June, 1941, he was transferred to SE Asia, where he was again replaced after failing to halt the Japanese advance. He was viceroy of India from 1943 to 1947. Also a writer, he edited a volume of poetry, *Other Men's Flowers* (1944).

wave mechanics   A branch of *quantum theory in which elementary particles are treated as *de Broglie waves. Systems of particles are described by a wave equation, known as the *Schrödinger equation. The solutions of this equation give the allowed values of the energy of each particle (eigenvalues) and the associated wave functions (eigenfunctions); the wave functions provide a measure of the probability that each particle will appear at different points in space. The theory, first proposed by de Broglie, was developed by Erwin Schrödinger.

wave number   The inverse of *wavelength, i.e. the number of cycles executed by a wave in a unit length.

wave power   The use of the energy of wave motion in the sea to generate electricity. Wave-power generators of various types have been developed, the best known being the "nodding-duck" type, which consists of a string of floats that bob up and down in the waves. The bobbing motion turns a generator. It is estimated that there are between 50 and 100 kilowatts of power per metre in the waves off the coast of Britain, a total of 120 gigawatts over all the suitable sites.

However only a fraction of this would become electricity. One of the disadvantages of wave power is that it is variable and unpredictable although, like *wind power, its peak output is likely to coincide with peak demand. Another is that since it is sited off the coast it may be obstructive to shipping and difficult to maintain. In addition, the design and construction of generators and transmission lines to work at sea presents a formidable engineering problem.

wax A smooth substance of low melting point (40–80°C) obtained from plants (e.g. *carnauba wax) or animals (e.g. *beeswax, *lanolin) or made synthetically. They consist of esters of higher fatty acids than are found in fats, usually with monohydric alcohols. Mineral waxes also exist, the most common being paraffin wax, which is a mixture of the higher hydrocarbons obtained from the distillation of petroleum. Waxes are used in making polishes, candles, mouldings, etc., and in modelling.

waxbill A bird of the *weaverfinch family having a stout waxy-red conical bill. Most waxbills inhabit open grassy regions of Africa. They are 7.5 to 15 cm long and typically grey or brown with red, yellow, or brown markings and fine barring on the wings. Many waxbills rear the nestlings of the *whydahs, which lay their eggs in waxbills' nests.

wax moth A moth whose caterpillars live in the nests of bees and wasps, where they eat refuse, honeycomb, and young host insects. Some are cannibalistic. The bee moth (*Galleria Mellonella*) is the best-known species, having spread to many parts of the world. Chief genera: *Galleria, Achroea*.

waxplant An evergreen climbing plant, *Hoya carnosa*, native to China and Australia. It produces clusters of large fragrant waxy white flowers with pink centres and is cultivated as an ornamental. Other cultivated species include *H. bella*, a dwarf shrub with crimson- or violet-centred waxy white flowers. Family: *Asclepiadaceae*.

waxwing A broad-billed fruit-eating songbird, *Bombycilla garrulus*, occurring in N coniferous forests and birch woods, sometimes migrating south in hard winters. It has a soft plumage, liver-coloured above with a reddish crest, a yellow-banded tail, and a black throat and eyestripe. The red tips of the flight feathers resemble sealing wax. Family: *Bombycillidae* (9 species).

wayfaring tree A deciduous shrub, *Viburnum lantana*, growing in woodlands and hedges over much of Europe. Up to 6 m tall, it has oval to heart-shaped toothed leaves and flat-topped clusters of small creamy-white funnel-shaped flowers. The oval fruits ripen from red to black. Family: *Caprifoliaceae*.

Wayland (or Weland) In Teutonic mythology, a skilled smith. He was captured and lamed by a Swedish king, Nidudr, who kept him on an island, where he was forced to practise his metalworking for the king. Wayland secretly murdered the king's sons, made ornaments of their skulls, eyes, and teeth, raped the king's daughter, and then revealed all to Nidudr before escaping. In England his forge, "Wayland's Smithy," is associated with an ancient site near White Horse Hill on the Berkshire Downs.

Wayne, John (Marion Michael Morrison; 1907–79) US film actor. Following his success in *Stagecoach* (1939) he played the tough hero of numerous classic westerns including *Red River* (1948), *Rio Bravo* (1959), and *True Grit* (1969). He played similar roles in occasional war films, such as *The Green Berets* (1968). He was awarded a special Academy Award shortly before his death from cancer.

Waziristan A mountainous area in Pakistan, bordering on Afghanistan. The Waziris, a *Pathan tribe who inhabit the area, are noted for their warlike behaviour.

weak interaction One of the four fundamental interactions between elementary particles (*see* particle physics), the others being the *strong, *electromagnetic, and *gravitational interactions. The weak interaction is about 10^{10} times weaker than the electromagnetic interaction. It is believed to be generated by the exchange of *virtual particles known as *intermediate vector bosons.

Weald, the An area in SE England, in Kent, Surrey, and East and West Sussex, lying between the North and South Downs. Formerly extensively forested it is now important for sheep farming and for growing hops.

JOHN WAYNE *He is seen here (with Richard Widmark, right) as Davy Crockett, hero of* The Alamo *(1960), which he also directed and produced.*

weasel A small carnivorous mammal, *Mustela nivalis*, of Europe, Asia, and N Africa, recently introduced into New Zealand. Growing to about 25 cm long, it is long-bodied and short-legged, bright red-brown above with white underparts. Weasels feed on rats, mice, and voles, hunting along hedgerows and ditches and entering burrows. They swim well but do not climb. Family: *Mustelidae*.

weather. *See* meteorology.

weathering The physical and chemical disintegration of the rocks of the earth's crust on exposure to the atmosphere. Most rocks were formed under conditions in which temperatures and pressures were higher than those to which they are now exposed; weathering is largely a response to lower temperatures and pressures and the effects of air and water.

weaverbird A small songbird belonging to a mainly tropical Old World family (*Ploceidae*; 132 species) noted for its nest-building activities. Most species build domed nests with long entrance tunnels, often elaborately woven with loops and knots to form a durable structure. Some species build huge communal nests—the nest of the sociable weaver (*Philetairus socius*) reaches about 2 m across and houses 20–30 pairs of birds. Weavers are seed eaters with stout conical bills and variously coloured plumage. *See also* sparrow; quelea.

weaverfinch A small finchlike seed-eating songbird belonging to a family (*Estrildidae*; 108 species) occurring in tropical regions of Africa, SE Asia, and Australasia. Weaverfinches have large conical bills and are usually brightly coloured. *See* avadavat; grassfinch; mannikin; waxbill; zebra finch.

weaving The process of interlacing two or more yarns at right angles to produce a fabric. The equipment used is called a loom, which is first set up with a series of longitudinal threads (warp). In plain weave, alternate warp threads are raised and lowered by means of wires or cords (heddles) to allow the crosswire threads (weft), wound onto a bobbin (shuttle), to pass between them. Different kinds of weave, such as *twill and herringbone, are made by altering the pattern of interlacing. Hand looms have been in use all over the world since ancient times and are still used on a cottage-industry basis in parts of the UK. Power looms, in which the shuttle is moved across the warp automatically, were invented by Edmund *Cartwright in 1786, since when many improvements have been made to increase the speed of travel of the shuttle and to enable more complicated designs to be woven.

Webb, Mary (1881-1927) British novelist. She wrote tragic novels set in her native Shropshire and gained wide recognition when the prime minister Stanley Baldwin publicly praised her best-known novel, *Precious Bane* (1924).

Webb, Sidney (James), Baron Passfield (1859-1947) British economist and socialist. He helped to organize the *Fabian Society in 1884 and was one of the founders of the London School of Economics (1895), where he served as professor of public administration (1912-27). He initiated many educational reforms while he was a member of the London County Council (1892-1910) and, after entering parliament in 1922, held several important government posts. His wife **Beatrice (Potter) Webb** (1858-1943), whom he married in 1892, collaborated with him on a number of books, including *The History of Trade Unionism* (1894) and *Industrial Democracy* (1897). Their work and writings had a lasting influence on the development of social policies within and outside the Labour Party.

weber (Wb) The *SI unit of magnetic flux equal to the flux linking a circuit of one turn that produces an electromotive force of one volt when reduced uniformly to zero in one second. Named after Wilhelm Weber (1804-91).

Weber, Carl Maria von (1786-1826) German composer, a pupil of Michael Haydn (1737-1806) and Abbé Vogler (1749-1814). His most successful opera, *Der Freischütz* (1821), based on a German fairy story, was the first opera in the German Romantic tradition. The operas *Euryanthe* (1823) and *Oberon* (1826) were less successful. Weber also composed a large number of orchestral works and much piano music.

WEAVERBIRD *Communal nests of the sociable weaver, seen from below. The birds, which are found in SW Africa, build individual nests close together then cover them with a common roof.*

Weber, Ernst Heinrich (1795-1878) German physiologist, who became professor at Leipzig University in 1818. He is remembered for his discovery that the experience of differences in the intensity of human sensations (pressure, temperature, light, sound) depends on percentage differences in the stimuli rather than absolute differences. This is called the Weber-Fechner Law because Weber's discovery was popularized by Gustav Fechner (1801-87). His brother **Wilhelm Eduard Weber** (1804-91) was professor of physics at Göttingen University. He worked with *Gauss on magnetism and introduced a logical system of electrical units. The SI unit of magnetic flux is named after him.

Weber, Max (1864-1920) German sociologist, who was one of the founding fathers of modern *sociology. His best-known work, *The Protestant Ethic and the Spirit of Capitalism* (1904), relates the emergence of a particular type of economic system to the effects of religious values. In attempting to explain why capitalism developed first in Europe, he produced extensive studies in comparative sociology. His *Methodology of the Social Sciences* (1904) remains a major text, as does his account of social and economic organization, *Wirtschaft und Gesellschaft* (1922). Bureaucracy and secularization are also recurrent themes. He was politically active during the last years of his life and served on the committee that drafted the constitution of the *Weimar Republic.

Webern, Anton von (1883-1945) Austrian composer. He studied with Schoenberg and earned his living as a conductor and teacher. He was killed by an American soldier during the occupation of Vienna. Webern adopted the technique of *serialism, as defined by Schoenberg in 1924. His compositions, which are characterized by great brevity, extreme dynamic contrast, and dissonant counterpoint, include a concerto for nine instruments (1934) and a string quartet (1938). His music has greatly influenced Boulez, Stravinsky, and many other composers.

webspinner A brownish soft-bodied insect, 4-7 mm long, belonging to the mainly tropical order *Embioptera* (150 species). Biting jaws are used by the wingless females to feed on dead plant material; the males, which are mostly winged, are carnivores. Webspinners live in communities and make silken webs and tunnels under stones or in soil. The young are cared for by the females.

Webster, John (c. 1580-c. 1625) English dramatist. Little is known of his life. He collaborated with Thomas Dekker and other dramatists. His own major plays are *The White Devil* (1612) and *The Duchess of Malfi* (c. 1613). Despite their typically Jacobean preoccupation with lust and violence, the plays are distinguished by their poetic intensity and psychological insight.

Webster, Noah (1758-1843) US lexicographer and author of numerous books on American English. His *American Dictionary of the English Language* (1828) took over 20 years to compile and was the most influential of all American dictionaries. Webster also did much to standardize American spelling.

Weddell Sea A large inlet of the S Atlantic Ocean in Antarctica, between the Antarctic Peninsula and Coats Land. Its S section is covered by the Ronne and Filchner Ice Shelves. It is named after the British explorer and seal hunter James Weddell (1787-1834).

Wedekind, Frank (1864-1918) German dramatist. A vivid personality, he was also an actor, singer, poet, and essayist. His tragedy *Frühlings Erwachen* (1891), produced by *Reinhardt (1905), caused a scandal by criticizing the bourgeois attitude to sex. Berg's opera *Lulu* (1937) is based on his plays *Erdgeist* (1895) and *Die Büchse der Pandora* (1904).

Wedgwood, Dame Cicely Veronica (1910-) British historian, who specializes in the early modern history of Britain and Europe. Her books include *The Thirty Years' War* (1930), *William the Silent* (1944), and *The Political Career of Rubens* (1975).

Wedgwood, Josiah (1730-95) British potter, industrialist, and writer, who came from a family of potters. Trained under his brother Thomas, he partnered Thomas Whieldon (1719-95) from 1754 until 1759, when he opened his own factory at Burslem, Staffordshire (England). In 1769 he opened a new factory (Etruria), where he also built a village for his workmen, displaying his interest in social welfare. Employing such leading designers and artists as John *Flaxman, Wedgwood popularized the neoclassical taste in pottery and was a leading exporter to the Continent. His high-quality ceramics, **Wedgwood ware**, perfected *creamware and developed basalt and *jasperware; they also brought transfer printing to Staffordshire. Wedgwood ware is still made—since 1940 at a factory in Barlaston, Staffordshire.

weed Any plant growing where it is not wanted, especially in areas cultivated or tended by man. Weeds are most important in agriculture, competing with crop plants for space, light, and nutrients, reducing yields, and contaminating the crop. The major weeds of temperate regions include docks, thistles, nettles, shepherd's purse, groundsel, dandelions, couch grass, and wild oats. Some, such as ragwort, may be toxic to grazing livestock. Weeds may also damage paths and buildings and choke waterways.

Weed control has traditionally relied on repeated soil cultivation and crop rotation; modern methods involve use of selective and nonselective *herbicides and, in a few cases, *biological control.

Weelkes, Thomas (c. 1575–1623) English composer and organist. He published his first book of madrigals in 1597 and became organist of Chichester Cathedral in 1603. He is known for his hundred surviving madrigals, including "As Vesta Was from Latmos Hill Descending."

weever A slender carnivorous fish of the genus *Trachinus*, found in sandy bottoms of European coastal waters. Up to 4.6 cm long, it has an upward slanting mouth, eyes near the top of its head, and venomous spines on the gill covers and first dorsal fin, which can inflict painful wounds. Family: *Trachinidae*; order: *Perciformes*.

weevil A beetle, also called a snout beetle, belonging to the largest family (*Curculionidae*; about 60 000 species) in the animal kingdom. Most weevils are small (less than 6 mm) and their mouthparts are at the tip of a beaklike rostrum, which can sometimes exceed the body length. Many species are serious pests of gardens, crops, and stored grains and cereals, e.g. the *boll weevil (which attacks cotton seed pods), the grain weevil (*Sitophilus granarius*), and the rice weevil (*S. oryzae*). The larvae are particularly destructive, burrowing or boring into all parts of the plant but especially into wood, fruit, and seeds.

Wegener, Alfred Lothar (1880–1930) German geologist, who (in 1912) proposed the theory of *continental drift to account for his observations of the movements of land masses. Wegener also demonstrated how bombardment by meteors could have caused lunar craters. He died while on his fourth expedition to Greenland.

Weigela A genus of E Asian flowering shrubs (12 species), including several ornamentals, often called Japanese honeysuckles. Up to 4 m high, they have simple leaves and small clusters of funnel-shaped white to red flowers, about 3.5 cm long, with four or five spreading lobes. The fruit is a long narrow seed pod. Family: *Caprifoliaceae*.

weight. *See* mass and weight.

weightlessness The condition in which a body possesses no weight. Such a body still possesses mass but its weight (*see* mass and weight) can become negligible when the gravitational field is extremely weak, as for example in space. It can also be produced artificially by creating a force that is equal and opposite to gravity. The physiological effects of weightlessness are important in long space flights and are countered by pressure suits, exercise routines, and correct control of cabin pressure, temperature, and humidity.

weight lifting A sport in which men and women compete to lift weighted barbells. In the most common form of competition contestants make three attempts in each of two styles, the snatch and the clean and jerk. The weights, of their own choice, can be increased but not reduced. Power lifting requires different styles, the squat, dead lift, and bench press.

Weihai 37 30N 122 04E A port in E China, in Shandong province on the Gulf of Chihli. A naval base in the 1880s and again in 1949, it was leased to Britain (1898–1930). It has fishing and textile industries. Population (1975 est): 25 000.

Weil, Simone (1909–43) French mystic and philosopher. An active socialist in the 1930s, she worked briefly in a car factory to gain insight into working-class problems and served in a nonmilitary capacity on the Republican side in the Spanish Civil War. She also taught philosophy at secondary schools until 1938. After a mystical experience she became a convinced Roman Catholic, although she refused baptism. During World War II she worked for the Free French Resistance in London. Her writings on spiritual and social themes, published posthumously, include *Waiting for God* (1951) and *The Need for Roots* (1952).

Weill, Kurt (1900–50) German composer. He studied under Busoni in Berlin. His collaboration with Bertolt *Brecht began with the opera *The Rise and Fall of the City of Mahagonny* (1927), a satirical portrayal of American life. Their most famous work was *The Threepenny Opera* (1928), a modernistic version of *The Beggar's Opera* (*see* Gay, John). The rise of Nazism forced Weill to leave Germany; he settled in the USA in 1935 and wrote successfully for Broadway musicals. His wife, the singer Lotte *Lenya, frequently performed in his works.

Weimar 50 59N 11 15E A city in SW East Germany, on the River Ilm near Erfurt. Weimar has associations with Goethe, Schiller, and Liszt and was the cultural centre of Germany in the late 18th and early 19th centuries. It was the capital of the grand duchy of Saxe-Weimar-Eisenach (1815–1918). In 1919 the German National Assembly met in the city and drew up the constitution of the new *Weimar Republic. Population (1983 est): 63 900.

Weimaraner (*or* Weimeraner) A breed of dog developed by the nobility of Weimar, Germany, for hunting and retrieving game. It is a lithe dog with drooping ears and a short slender tail. The short sleek coat is silver-grey or mouse-grey. Height: 61–69 cm (dogs); 56–64 cm (bitches).

Weimar Republic The government of Germany from 1919 to 1933. Named after the town in which the new German constitution was formulated, the Republic faced constant political and economic crises and was finally overthrown by Hitler.

Weismann, August Friedrich Leopold (1834–1914) German biologist, who (in 1883) proposed that heredity was based upon the transfer, from generation to generation, of a substance—germ plasm—with a definite molecular constitution. Weismann also predicted that germ plasm must undergo a special nuclear division to produce gametes for the next generation. Weismann's ideas have since been generally accepted and he is regarded as one of the founders of modern genetics.

Weiss, Peter (1916–82) German dramatist and novelist. After leaving Nazi Germany, he settled in Sweden (1939). His plays include the highly successful *Marat/Sade* (short title; 1964), set in a lunatic asylum, and *The Investigation* (1965), recreating the Auschwitz trials.

Weissmuller, Johnny (1904–84) US swimmer, who won five Olympic gold medals (three in 1924 and two in 1928) and set 24 world records. He was the first man to swim 100 m in less than a minute (1922). He later became the first Tarzan of sound films (1932–48).

Weizmann, Chaim (Azriel) (1874–1952) Israeli statesman; the first president of Israel (1949–52). Born in Russia, he settled in England in 1904 and worked as a chemist at Manchester University. A leader of the English Zionist movement, his discovery (1916) of a manufacturing process for the production of acetone, which contributed to the

British war effort, facilitated the Zionist negotiations with the British Government that led to the *Balfour Declaration (1917). His moderate policies as president (1920–31, 1935–46) of the World Zionist Movement brought the hostility of Zionist extremists but he played an important part in the establishment of Israel in 1948.

welding A method of joining metals by melting the two parts together, pressing them together, or both (see also soldering). In forge welding, which is used to make steel chains, the two parts are heated and then hammered together. Electrical methods use an electric current passed through two metal surfaces in close contact. The temperature rises at the interface because of the high electrical resistance and welds the surfaces together. In spot welding, point contact electrodes press the metal surfaces together. In seam welding, the electrodes are in the form of rollers. Both these methods are used in mass production. Gas welding uses an oxy-acetylene flame to heat the metal and a rod of metallic filler material. Molten filler material runs between the two heated edges and solidifies to form the joint. Another method, similar to gas welding, is electric-arc welding. The filler rod forms one electrode and the metal itself another. Current passes by arcing or sparking across the gap between them, melting the rod and the metal edges. Arc welding is generally used for thicker pieces of metal and higher temperatures than gas welding and for small delicate jobs *lasers have been used. A great deal of skill is required to produce a strong reliable weld.

Weldon, Fay (1931–) British feminist writer. Her novels include The Fat Woman's Joke (1967), The Life and Loves of a She-Devil (1983), The Shrapnel Academy (1986), and The Hearts and Lives of Men (1987). She has also written plays and the biographical Jane Austen and her Times (1983).

Welensky, Sir Roy (1907–) Rhodesian statesman; prime minister of the Federation of *Rhodesia and Nyasaland (1956–63). A professional boxer, he was chairman (1953–63) of the Railway Workers Union in Northern Rhodesia. Welensky was largely responsible for the creation of the Federation but his aim to establish a harmonious multiracial society was unfulfilled.

welfare state A state that provides a minimum level of well-being for all its members, especially the most vulnerable: the young, the old, the unemployed, and the sick. In the UK the 19th-century *Poor Laws were superseded by Lloyd George's National Insurance Act (1911), which provided unemployment and health insurance (see National Insurance). The setting up of the National Health Service and the National Insurance Acts, in consequence of the *Beveridge Report (1942), established the welfare state as a reality. Other countries, such as those in Scandinavia, have taken similar steps. See also social security.

Welkom 27 59S 26 44E A town in South Africa, in N central Orange Free State. It was founded in 1947 and rapidly developed after the discovery of gold. Population (1980 est): 176 608.

Welland Ship Canal A canal in S central Canada, in S Ontario bypassing Niagara Falls. Part of the St Lawrence Seaway, it links Lake Erie to Lake Ontario and has a total lift of 99 m (326 ft). Length: 45 km (28 mi).

Welles, (George) Orson (1915–85) US film actor and director. After establishing his reputation as a theatre and radio producer he went to Hollywood in 1940. His first film, Citizen Kane (1941), became one of the most famous of all time. His other films include The Magnificent Ambersons (1942), Macbeth (1948), The Third Man (1949), The Trial (1962), and Chimes at Midnight (1966).

Wellesley, Richard Colley, Marquess. See Wellington, Arthur Wellesley, Duke of.

Wellesz, Egon (1885–1974) Austrian composer and musicologist. He studied in Vienna under Schoenberg and

became reader in Byzantine music at Oxford University in 1948. His complex compositions employed *serialism.

Wellington 41 17S 174 47E The capital of New Zealand, a port in S North Island on Cook Strait. It became the seat of central government in 1865 and is now the commercial and communications centre of New Zealand. Notable buildings include the Government Building (1876), one of the world's largest wooden buildings, and Victoria University (1897). A major manufacturing centre, it has engineering, food-processing, and textile industries; the chief exports are wool, meat, dairy products, and fruit. Population (1983 est): 342 500.

Wellington, Arthur Wellesley, 1st Duke of (1769-1852) British general and statesman, known as the Iron Duke; prime minister (1828-30). Born in Dublin, in 1787 he entered the army and in 1799 went to India, where he held command against *Tipu Sahib and became governor of Mysore. In the Napoleonic Wars he was responsible for victory (1814) against the French in the *Peninsular War, for which he was made a duke and given £500,000. He commanded British, German, and Dutch forces at Waterloo (1815), where he and the Prussian general *Blücher finally defeated Napoleon. He served in Lord Liverpool's Tory government as master general of the ordnance (1818-27) and represented Britain at the Congresses of *Aix-la-Chapelle (1818) and Verona (1822). As prime minister he came to support *Catholic emancipation and persuaded George IV to accept the bill of 1829. Wellington's opposition to parliamentary reform remained firm and brought about his resignation under pressure. Under Peel he served as foreign secretary (1834-35) and supported the repeal of the *Corn Laws; he was commander in chief of the British army from 1827 to 1828 and again from 1842 to 1852. His home at Apsley House, Piccadilly (London) is now the Wellington Museum.

His eldest brother **Richard Colley, Marquess Wellesley** (1760-1842) was simultaneously governor of Madras and governor general of Bengal (1797-1805). He greatly extended British power and territory in India by defeating (1799) Tipu Sahib, Sultan of Mysore, in a campaign in which his brother participated, and (1805) the Maratha states. He was subsequently foreign secretary (1809-12) and lord lieutenant of Ireland (1821-28, 1833-34). Increasingly jealous of his brother's success, he had an exaggerated sense of his own importance and was said to wear his medals in bed.

Wellingtonia. See sequoia.

Wells 51 13N 2 39W A city in SW England, in Somerset. It is famous for its cathedral (12th-13th centuries), with its 386 carved figures on the W front. Paper, cheese, and textiles are manufactured. Population (1981): 8374.

HENRY WELLS Wells, Fargo, and Company ran a perilous mail service across the USA from the mid-19th century.

Wells, Henry (1805-78) US businessman, who with William Fargo (1818-81) and others founded Wells, Fargo and Company (1852). An express business, it carried mail to and from the newly developed West. It also controlled banks and later ran a stagecoach service. □ p.1291.

Wells, H(erbert) G(eorge) (1866-1946) British novelist. After working as a shopkeeper's apprentice and a teacher, he studied biology with T. H. Huxley at the College of Science in South Kensington, graduating in 1890. He won literary success with *The Time Machine* (1895) and other science-fiction novels and increased his popularity with a series of comic social novels, including *Kipps* (1905) and *The History of Mr Polly* (1910). A member of the Fabian Society, he engaged in frequent controversy with G. B. Shaw and others concerning social and political issues. He wrote distinguished theoretical works, including *The Outline of History* (1920) and *The Shape of Things to Come* (1933).

wels A large nocturnal predatory *catfish, *Silurus glanis*, also called waller, found in fresh waters of Europe and W Asia. Up to 4.5 m long, it has three pairs of barbels, a long anal fin, and is usually mottled olive-green to blue-black with a paler belly.

Wels 48 10N 14 02E A town in N central Austria, in Upper Austria. It has a castle in which Emperor Maximilian I died. Industries include agricultural machinery, textiles, and food processing. Population (1981): 51 033.

Welsh literature The most important literature written in the Welsh language is poetry belonging to the early and medieval periods prior to the anglicization that began in the 16th century. Much of the poetry of the *Cynfeirdd*, or early poets of the 6th century, is anonymous, but the outstanding names associated with this early heroic, gnomic, and nature verse are Aneirin and Taliesin. The works of the period are preserved in the "Four Ancient Books of Wales," manuscripts dating from the 12th, 13th, and 14th centuries. The *Gogynfeirdd*, or medieval poets, belong to the Norman period (up to the loss of independence in 1282). These poets were *bards, who held important offices in the courts of Welsh princes; Cynddelw (12th century) is regarded as the greatest of them. The bardic order was reorganized in some uncertain way at this time, and a number of versified treatises on the poetic art were written. The *Mabinogion*, a collection of 11 prose tales and romances, was put into written form during this period. The 14th century was dominated by Wales' greatest poet, *Dafydd ap Gwilym, who introduced techniques and a sensuous richness of metaphor that influenced all subsequent Welsh poetry. The first record of an *eisteddfod dates from the 15th century, although it is believed that such bardic contests must date from a much earlier period. The accentual metre of English (of which there was nothing in the "strict" metres of Welsh verse) was introduced in the 16th century, which marks the beginning of a decline in the use of Welsh, although the language has recently been revived and continues to be used as a literary medium. Among the more important writers from the 17th century onwards are the poet Huw Morus (1622-1709), the prose writer Ellis Wynne (1671-1734), author of *Gweledigaetheu y Bardd Cwsc* (*Visions of the Sleeping Bard*; 1704), the hymnwriter Williams Pantycelyn (1717-91), the poet and scholar Lewis Morris (1701-65), the poets Sir John Morris-Jones (1864-1969), Thomas Gwynn Jones (1871-1949), William John Gruffydd (1881-1954), and T. H. Parry-Williams (1887-).

Welsh Nationalist Party. *See* Plaid Cymru.

Welsh pony One of two breeds of pony originating in Wales. The Welsh Mountain pony, used for riding and draught work, has a compact muscular body with short strong legs and a profuse mane and tail. It has been used to develop the larger Welsh riding pony, which is a popular children's mount. Both may be any solid colour. Height:

Mountain pony: up to 1.22 m (12 hands); riding pony: up to 1.37 m (13½ hands).

Welsh poppy A perennial herbaceous plant, *Meconopsis cambrica*, up to 38 cm tall and found in damp regions of W Europe. It has fernlike deeply lobed leaves and bears solitary yellow flowers, up to 7.5 cm across. Cultivated ornamental forms may have either single or double orange or yellow flowers.

welwitschia An unusual *gymnosperm plant, *Welwitschia mirabilis*, confined to the deserts of SW Africa. The very short stem bears two strap-shaped waxy leaves, which grow continuously and are up to 1 m long. The long taproot absorbs water from the desert subsoil, and small conelike flowers produce winged seeds, which are dispersed by the wind. Individual plants may live for more than a hundred years. Order: *Gnetales*.

Welwyn Garden City 51 48N 0 13W A town in SE England, in Hertfordshire. Founded in 1919 by Sir Ebenezer *Howard, it became a new town in 1948. Industries include chemicals, food products, and plastics. Population (1981): 40 496.

Wembley A district in the Greater London borough of Brent. Wembley Stadium, one of the many buildings erected in the early 1920s in connection with the British Empire Exhibition (1924-25), was the site of the 1948 Olympic Games and is the home of English national soccer. Wembley Conference Centre was opened in 1977.

Wenceslas (1361-1419) King of Bohemia (1363-1402, 1404-19) and German king and Holy Roman Emperor (1376-1400). An extremely weak king, in Bohemia he was twice imprisoned by rebellious nobles (1393-94, 1402) and briefly deposed. In Germany, princes deposed him in 1400 but he retained the title of king until his death.

Wenceslas, St (d. 929 AD) Duke of Bohemia (?924-29), famous for his piety. Wenceslas' unpopular submission to the German king Henry the Fowler gave rise to a conspiracy of nobles, who incited Wenceslas' brother to assassinate him. He became Bohemia's patron saint.

Wenchow. *See* Wenzhou.

wentletrap A *gastropod mollusc of the worldwide family *Epitoniidae* (about 200 species), often found in association with sea anemones and corals. 2-10 cm long, wentletraps have ⌐shells with long spires, usually white but sometimes tinged with brown (that of the precious wentletrap (*Epitonium scalare*) has long been prized by collectors). They can produce a purple substance used as a dye.

Wentworth, Thomas. *See* Strafford, Thomas Wentworth, 1st Earl of.

Wentworth, William Charles (1793-1872) Australian politician; the first Australian citizen to attain a political reputation. Son of a transported convict, he was a fervent federalist and, early in his career, a radical. He was a key figure in the achievement (1855) of self-government for New South Wales.

Wenzhou (Wen-chou *or* Wenchow) 28 02N 120 40E A port in SE China, in Zhejiang province on the Ou Jiang (River). It is the site of many historic buildings. A trading centre, it has processed food, paper, and handicraft industries. Population (1980 est): 325 000.

werewolf In folklore, a man who becomes a wolf by night and preys on humans. Some werewolves, who have no power over their condition because it is hereditary or the result of a spell or another werewolf's bite, only change form during a full moon, a transformation known as lycanthropy. Belief in werewolves is worldwide and of ancient origin. In countries where wolves are rare, some men are believed to turn into other fierce animals.

Werfel, Franz (1890-1945) Austrian Jewish poet, dramatist, and novelist. A leading expressionist, his pacifism and desire for human brotherhood are reflected in his poetry and plays, including *Der Spiegelmensch* (1920). His later novels include *The Song of Bernadette* (1941).

Wergeland, Henrik Arnold (1808-45) Norwegian poet, known as the "uncrowned king" of Norway because of his involvement in nationalist politics. He is best known for his lyric poetry and for an epic on the Creation, entitled *Skabelsen, Mennesket, og Messias* (*Creation, Humanity, and Messiah*; 1830).

wergild The sum payable as compensation in Anglo-Saxon England to the family of a slain man by his assassin or the latter's kin. The amount was regulated by law according to the status and nationality of the victim and varied in different regions.

WEREWOLF *Reports of werewolves were particularly common in 16th-century France. The illustration claims to be an exact representation of one.*

Weser, River A river in N West Germany. It flows NW from Münden, through Bremen, to the North Sea at Bremerhaven. The Mitelland Canal connects it to the Rivers Rhine and Elbe. Length: 477 km (296 mi).

Wesker, Arnold (1932-   ) British dramatist. Born into a poor Jewish family in London, he wrote a successful trilogy of plays reflecting his socialist beliefs: *Chicken Soup with Barley* (1958), *Roots* (1959), and *I'm Talking about Jerusalem* (1960). Later plays include *Chips with Everything* (1962), *The Friends* (1970), *Said the Old Man to the Young Man* (1978), and *The Merchant* (1978).

Wesley, John (1703-91) British religious leader, founder of *Methodism. As a student at Oxford and later as a Fellow of Lincoln College, Wesley was one of a group nicknamed "Methodists," who sought to live disciplined religious lives. His younger brother **Charles Wesley** (1707-88) was also a member. The brothers, both ordained, sailed to Georgia as missionaries in 1735, but returned disillusioned in 1738. In the same year both experienced a spiritual awakening while attending meetings of the *Moravians as a result of which they toured the country preaching a message of repentance, faith, and love. Anglican opposition forced them out of the churches into open-air meetings; they were also obliged to organize societies for their many working-class converts, whose spiritual needs had been neglected by the Established Church. They did not intend to form a new denomination, the Wesleyan Methodist Church being organized only after their death. John was a tireless writer and administrator, who travelled the country on horseback preaching thousands of sermons. Charles was the author of many well-known hymns. His son **Samuel Wesley** (1766-1837) was a composer and organist, who composed the oratorio *Ruth* at the age of eight. He was instrumental in reviving the music of Bach in England. His illegitimate son **Samuel Sebastian Wesley** (1810-76), also an organist, studied under his father and held posts as a cathedral organist at Hereford, Exeter, Winchester, and Gloucester. He became professor of organ at the Royal Academy of Music in 1850.

Wessex The kingdom of the West *Saxons, under which Anglo-Saxon England was united in the 9th century. Wessex centred on the upper Thames basin and from the late 6th century expanded southwestwards. Its expansion northwards was frustrated by the power of Mercia, which was supreme until Egbert, King of Wessex (802-39), destroyed Mercian ascendancy in 825 and made possible the subsequent union of England under the leadership of the Wessex king, Alfred the Great.

West, Benjamin (1738-1820) British painter of American birth. Acclaimed as a portraitist in New York, he visited Italy (1760-63), where he was influenced by *neoclassicism, before settling permanently in England. There, patronized by George III and exhibiting at the Royal Academy of which he became president in 1792, he made his name as a history painter, particularly with his controversially realistic *Death of General Wolfe* (Kensington Palace, London).

West, Mae (1892-1980) US actress. Her unashamedly sensual performances in vaudeville, the theatre, and films established her as an international sex symbol during the 1930s, although she is perhaps best known for her comic talent. Her early stage successes included *Sex* (1926) and *Diamond Lil* (1928). Her films, many of which she wrote, include *She Done Him Wrong* (1933), *I'm No Angel* (1933), and *My Little Chickadee* (1939).

West, Nathanael (Nathan Weinstein; 1903-40) US novelist. The best known of his four short novels are *Miss Lonely-Hearts* (1933), about an advice columnist, and *The Day of the Locust* (1939), a satire of the grotesque world of Hollywood, where he worked as a scriptwriter. He was killed in a car accident.

West, Dame Rebecca (Cicely Isabel Fairfield, 1892-1983) British novelist and journalist. She was the author of several novels, including *The Thinking Reed* (1936) and *The Birds Fall Down* (1966). Among a number of books of political journalism are *The Meaning of Treason* (1949) and *A Train of Powder* (1955), which includes her reports on the Nuremberg trials.

West, the The area in the USA between the Mississippi River and the Rocky Mountains acquired by the *Louisiana Purchase (1803). Settled by migrants from the E in search of land and independence, it was associated with the hardship, self-reliance, and lawlessness that characterized the lives of pioneers.

West Atlantic languages A subgroup of the *Niger-Congo family, spoken in Guinea and Senegal. It includes the languages Wolof and *Fulani, and, despite being a small group, is found over a wide area since the speakers of West Atlantic languages are mainly nomadic.

West Bank A territory in the Middle East, on the W bank of the River Jordan. It comprises the hills of Judaea and Samaria (which Israel considers to be of crucial strategic importance with regard to the security of its coastal settlements) and part of the city of *Jerusalem. Formerly part of *Palestine, it was left in Arab hands after partition (1948), became part of Jordan following the ceasefire of 1949, and was occupied by Israeli forces in 1967. Israel has since been under pressure from the Arabs, especially the *Palestine Liberation Organization, to withdraw from the territory. In the Camp David agreement (1978) proposals were put forward for future negotiations leading to the setting up of a self-governing authority in the West Bank. In the late 1980s lack of progress by Israel provoked widespread criticism. Area: about 6000 sq km (2320 sq mi).

West Bengal A state in NE India, stretching along the Bangladeshi W border from the Ganges delta N into the Himalayan foothills. Rice, jute, tea, and other crops are farmed. Fishing, forestry, and mining are also important, as well as industry (especially engineering, steel, chemicals, and motor cars). The Gurkhas, pressing for their own state, have caused unrest (1987). Area: 87 853 sq km (33 911 sq mi). Population (1981): 54 485 560. Capital: Calcutta. See also Bengal.

West Bromwich 52 31N 1 59W An industrial town in central England, in the West Midlands. Metal goods (kitchenware, springs, nails, weighing machines) are manufactured, as well as chemicals and paint. Population (1981): 154 930.

westerlies The chief winds blowing between 30° and 70° latitude. Their name derives from the prevailing wind direction; in the N hemisphere winds blow mainly from the SW and in the S hemisphere, from the NW.

Western Australia The largest state of Australia, bordering on the Indian Ocean, Timor Sea, and Great Australian Bight. It is mainly an arid undulating plateau with the Great Sandy Desert, the Gibson Desert, and the Great ·Victoria Desert in the interior. In the SW is the Darling Range, a scarp behind the city of Perth (where most of the population is concentrated). In the N the broken edge of the plateau is marked by the Kimberleys, where the construction of the Ord River Project, completed in the early 1970s, should more than double the acreage under irrigation in that area, although the early experimental cultivation of cotton and rice was unsuccessful. Other agricultural activities include dairy farming, lumbering, and the cultivation of citrus fruits, wheat, and vines in the extreme SW. Western Australia is rich in mineral resources; bauxite in the Darling Range, nickel in the S central part, oil near Barrow Island off the NW coast, and gold in the SW around Kalgoorlie. Probably the most important discoveries have been the huge deposits of ferrous minerals in the NW of the state, in the Ashburton and Pilbara districts. Industry is located chiefly around Perth and includes the manufacture of iron and steel, chemicals, textiles, and oil refining. Area: 2 527 621 sq km (975 920 sq mi). Population (1983 est): 1 373 700. Capital: Perth.

Western European Union An organization formed in 1955 by the UK, Belgium, France, Italy, Luxembourg, the Netherlands, and West Germany to coordinate defence policy and equipment and to cooperate in political and other spheres. It succeeded the *European Defence Community and collaborates closely with the *North Atlantic Treaty Organization.

Western Isles Islands Area An administrative area of NW Scotland since 1975 consisting of the Outer Hebrides (see Hebrides, the). Area: 2901 sq km (1120 sq mi). Population (1981): 31 766. Administrative centre: Stornoway.

westerns A US genre of popular novels and films set in the American West during that region's development in the 19th century. Its rigid conventions of plot and character invested the struggles of pioneers and the battles between lawmen and outlaws with mythical significance. Notable writers include Owen Wister (1860–1938), the prolific Zane Grey (1872–1939), and Louis L'Amour (1908–). The first film western was *The Great Train Robbery* (1903). Other notable films include *Stagecoach* (1939), *Red River* (1948), *High Noon* (1952), and *The Good The Bad and The Ugly* (1966); directors who have specialized in this genre include John Ford (1895–1973) and Howard Hawks (1896–1978).

Western Sahara (name until 1975: Spanish Sahara) A territory in NW Africa, bordering on the Atlantic Ocean, Mauritania, and Morocco. It consists chiefly of desert and has phosphate deposits (the chief export) SE of El Aaiún. *History*: in 1884 Spain claimed a protectorate over the S coastal zone of Rio de Oro and in 1958 Spanish Sahara became a province of Spain with its capital at El Aaiún. In 1976 Spain withdrew from the province and it was partitioned between Mauritania and Morocco. Since then the Polisario Front, an organization engaged in guerrilla activities to establish Western Sahara as the independent Saharan Arab Democratic Republic, has been supported by Algeria. Mauritania withdrew from the S part of Western Sahara in 1979 and it came under Moroccan occupation with active opposition from the Polisario Front and Algeria. Area: 266 000 sq km (102 680 sq mi). Population (1976 est): 128 000.

West Germany. See Germany.

West Glamorgan A county of South Wales, bordering on the Bristol Channel. It was created in 1974 from W Glamorgan. It consists mainly of the uplands of the South Wales coalfield, descending in the SW to the *Gower Peninsula (the principal farming area). Large scale afforestation has taken place since 1919. Industry includes tinplate at Swansea, oil refining on the Neath Estuary, and steel manufacture at Port Talbot. Area: 815 sq km (315 sq mi). Population (1983 est): 366 600. Administrative centre: Swansea.

West Highland white terrier A breed of dog thought to have originated in Argyll, Scotland. Known affectionately as the westie, it is compact and alert-looking with short legs and a long double-layered pure white coat. Height: about 28 cm.

West Indies An archipelago extending in a curved chain for over 2400 km (1500 mi) from the Florida peninsula in North America to the coast of Venezuela enclosing the Caribbean Sea. It is often subdivided into the *Greater Antilles, the *Lesser Antilles, and the *Bahamas. The islands are chiefly of volcanic origin but some, including the Bahamas and Antigua, are composed largely of coral. Hurricanes occur frequently, often causing serious damage. The West Indian people are of mixed origin but the descendants of African slaves form the largest group. The original Arawak and Carib Indians have virtually disappeared, although some Caribs remain on Dominica. *Economy*: sugarcane cultivation has been of importance throughout the West Indies since the beginning of colonization. Many islands also grow a major subsidiary crop, such as tobacco, bananas, spices, or coffee. The few mineral deposits include asphalt from Trinidad's unique Pitch Lake and bauxite from Hispaniola and Jamaica. *History*: Columbus discovered the archipelago in 1492 and named it in the belief that he had found the west route to India. The Spanish, who were the first Europeans to settle, introduced the cultivation of sugar and imported African slaves to work the plantations. The slave trade was maintained until its abolition during the 19th century. In 1958 the Federation of the West Indies was created, comprising Antigua, Dominica, Grenada, Jamaica, Montserrat, St Kitts with Nevis and Anguilla, St Lucia, St Vincent, and Trinidad and Tobago. The federal parliament was situated at Port-of-Spain, Trinidad, but following the withdrawal of Jamaica and then Trinidad and Tobago the Federation was dissolved in 1962. However, further attempts were made at regional economic integration by what became the *Caribbean Community. In 1967 the noncolonial status of associated state was adopted by Antigua, Dominica, Grenada, St Kitts-Nevis-Anguilla, St Lucia, and by St Vincent in 1969. Grenada became independent in 1974, Dominica in 1978, St Lucia and St Vincent in 1979, and St Kitts-Nevis in 1983. Area: over 235 000 sq km (91 000 sq mi).

West Irian (Indonesian name: Irian Jaya) A province in E Indonesia comprising W *New Guinea. Mountainous and densely forested with coastal swamps, it possesses important mineral resources including oil, nickel, and copper. Formerly under Dutch rule, it was transferred to Indonesia in 1963. Area: 416 990 sq km (161 000 sq mi). Population (1980): 1 173 875. Capital: Jajapura.

West Lothian A former county (once called Linlithgowshire) of SE Scotland. Under local government reorganization in 1975 its boundaries were adjusted to form a district of the same name, in Lothian Region.

Westmeath (Irish name: Contae Na Hiarmhidhe) A county in the central Republic of Ireland, in Leinster. Predominantly low lying with areas of bog, much of the land is under pasture. Agriculture consists chiefly of cattle fattening and dairy farming. Area: 1764 sq km (681 sq mi). Population (1981): 61 523. County town: Millingar.

West Midlands A metropolitan county in the West Midlands of England, created in 1974 from SE Staffordshire, NW Warwickshire, and part of NE Worcestershire. It comprises the districts of Wolverhampton, Walsall, Dudley, Sandwell, Birmingham, Solihull, and Coventry. Area: 899 sq km (347 sq mi). Population (1981): 2 644 634. Administrative centre: Birmingham.

Westminster, City of A borough of central Greater London, on the N bank of the River Thames. It was created in 1965 from the former metropolitan boroughs of Westminster, Paddington, and *St Marylebone. The heart of London's West End, it contains many famous theatres, restaurants, and shops. Included among its historic buildings are *Buckingham Palace, Westminster Hall adjoining the Houses of Parliament (see Palace of Westminster), and *Westminster Abbey. Westminster Cathedral, seat of the Roman Catholic archbishopric of Westminster, was founded in 1895 and designed by J. F. Bentley in Byzantine style with an Italianate campanile 87 m (284 ft) high. Westminster School is one of the oldest English public schools. The *National Gallery overlooks Trafalgar Square (containing Nelson's Column) and Whitehall is the site of the main government offices; *Downing Street is nearby. It contains St James's Park, Green Park, Hyde Park, and Regent's Park (containing London Zoo). Population (1981): 190 661.

Westminster, Statutes of 1. (1275, 1285, 1290) Legislation initiated by Edward I of England. The first Statute dealt principally with criminal law and procedures for the improvement of royal justice while the second dealt with rights of inheritance, attempting to restrict the alienation of land from the main line of the family. The Statute of 1290 prohibited subinfeudation of land (i.e. the granting of portions of a knight's estate), which had occasioned considerable loss of feudal dues to the king and magnates. 2. (1931) The Statute that established the *Commonwealth of Nations.

Westminster Abbey A historic abbey church at Westminster, London. The present building, begun (1245) in the French style by Henry III, replaces one dedicated (1065) by Edward the Confessor, whose shrine the abbey still houses. Since William I, every English monarch (with two exceptions—Edward V and Edward VIII) has been crowned in Westminster Abbey and many are buried there in magnificent tombs. The Coronation Chair, first used in 1307, incorporates the Stone of Scone, captured by Edward I from the Scots in 1296. Other notable features include Henry VII's

WESTMINSTER ABBEY *The Coronation Chair incorporating the Stone of Scone.*

chapel, the 13th-century chapter house (used for parliamentary sessions until 1547), and Poets' Corner, where Chaucer, Spenser, Dryden, Tennyson, Dickens, Browning, Kipling, and many others are buried or have memorials.

Westminster Assembly (1643-52) A body of 30 laymen and 121 clergy summoned by the *Long Parliament after the outbreak of the English Civil War to reform the Church of England along Calvinist lines.

Westmorland A former county of NW England. Under local government reorganization in 1974 it became part of the new county of *Cumbria.

Weston-super-Mare 51 21N 2 59W A resort in SW England, in SW Avon on the Bristol Channel. Originally a fishing village, it developed as a resort in the 19th century. Population (1981): 57 980.

Westphalia A region of NW Germany, approximating to present-day Nordrhein-Westfalen. By the 12th century Westphalia comprised many small principalities and in the 18th century came largely under Prussian control. During the period 1807-13 Prussian Westphalian territories became the kingdom of Westphalia, which Napoleon placed under the rule of his brother Jérôme Bonaparte. The Congress of Vienna (1815) dissolved the kingdom and restored most of Westphalia to Prussia.

Westphalia, Peace of (1648) The agreements, negotiated in Osnabrück and Münster (Westphalia), that ended the *Thirty Years' War. The peace marked the end of the supremacy in Europe of the Holy Roman Empire and the emergence of France (which gained the bishoprics of Metz, Toul, and Verdun and also Alsace) as a dominant power (see also Pyrenees, Treaty of). It recognized the sovereignty of the German states, the Swiss Confederation, and the Netherlands, previously subject to the Empire, and granted W Pomerania to Sweden. Lutherans, Calvinists, and Roman Catholics were given equal rights.

West Point 41 23N 73 58W A military reservation in the USA, in New York state. It is the site of the United States Military Academy (1802).

West Riding. *See* Yorkshire.

West Sussex A county of S England, formerly part of *Sussex, bordering on the English Channel. It is mainly low lying, rising in the S to the South Downs, and drained by the Rivers Arun and Adur. It is predominantly agricultural, the chief products being cereals, root crops, and dairy produce. Tourism is important in the coastal resorts, notably Bognor Regis and Worthing. Area: 2016 sq km (779 sq mi). Population (1981): 658 562. Administrative centre: Chichester.

West Virginia A state in the E central USA. It consists of a ridge and valley region (the Great Appalachian Valley) in the E and the Appalachian Plateau, which constitutes the remaining two-thirds of the state. Most of the larger cities lie on the Ohio River in the W. Although predominantly a rural state, manufacturing and mining (especially of coal) are important. The principal manufactures are chemicals, primary metals, and stone and clay products. The state's farmers concentrate on livestock products. *History*: originally part of Virginia, it refused to secede with the state, and became West Virginia on joining the Union as a separate State in 1863. Area: 62 628 sq km (24 181 sq mi). Population (1980): 1 949 644. Capital: Charleston.

West Yorkshire A metropolitan county of NE England, created in 1974 from the W part of the West Riding of Yorkshire. It comprises the districts of Bradford, Leeds, Calderdale, Kirklees, and Wakefield. Coalmining is important and West Yorkshire remains the centre of the English wool textile industry. Area: 2039 sq km (787 sq mi). Population (1981): 2 037 510. Administrative centre: Wakefield.

wet rot The decay that affects timber with a relatively high moisture content, caused by the cellar fungus (*Coniophora cerebella*) and characterized by the formation of a dark surface mass. Treatment is by drying affected timbers, and wet rot is prevented by the application of tar-based preservatives, such as creosote. *Compare* dry rot.

Wexford (Irish name: Loch Garman) 52 20N 6 27W A port in the Republic of Ireland, the county town of Co Wexford on the River Slaney estuary. Industries include the manufacture of agricultural machinery and food processing. Population (1981): 11 417.

Wexford (Irish name: Contae Loch Garman) A county in the SE Republic of Ireland, in Leinster bordering on the Irish Sea. It was the first Irish county to be colonized from England (1169). Consisting chiefly of lowlands, it rises to mountains in the W. Cattle rearing is the main agricultural occupation. Area: 2352 sq km (908 sq mi). Population (1981): 99 081. County town: Wexford.

Weyden, Rogier van der (c. 1400–64) Flemish painter of portraits and religious altarpieces. Almost nothing is known of his early life, but he was probably the pupil of the Master of *Flémalle, whose influence is evident in *The Deposition* (Prado). From 1436 until his death he was city painter of Brussels and frequently worked for the Burgundian court. In 1450 he visited Italy and paintings from this period, for example the *Entombment* (Uffizi), show Italian influences. His work became widely known in Europe during his lifetime.

Weymouth 50 36N 2 28W A town in S England, on the coast of Dorset. It is a resort and port with ferries to the Channel Islands and Cherbourg. Industries include light enginering and quarrying (on the Isle of Portland). Population (1981): 46 260, with Melcombe Regis.

whale A large marine mammal belonging to the order *Cetacea*. Whales have no hind limbs; their forelimbs are flippers and their tails are horizontally flattened to form a pair of flukes. They breath through a blowhole on top of the head, which is closed when they are submerged. Whales are virtually hairless and insulated by a thick layer of blubber under the skin. They bear their young and suckle them at sea.

There are two suborders. The whalebone whales (*Mysticetae*; 12 species)—including the *rorquals, *blue whale, and *right whales—are large and slow-moving and feed on krill, which they filter from the water using a sieve of whalebone (*see* baleen) plates. They have a double blowhole. Toothed whales (*Odontocetae*; 80 species)—including the *dolphins, *narwhal, and *sperm whale—are smaller and more agile. They feed on fish and squid and are often gregarious, communicating by underwater sounds. *See also* whaling.

whalebone. *See* baleen.

whale shark A gigantic but harmless *shark, *Rhincodon typus*, that has a grey or brown spotted body with pale undersides, ridges along its sides, and a terminal mouth. Up to 18 m long, it swims slowly, mainly in tropical waters, and feeds near the surface on small fish, invertebrates, and plankton. Family: *Rhincodontidae*.

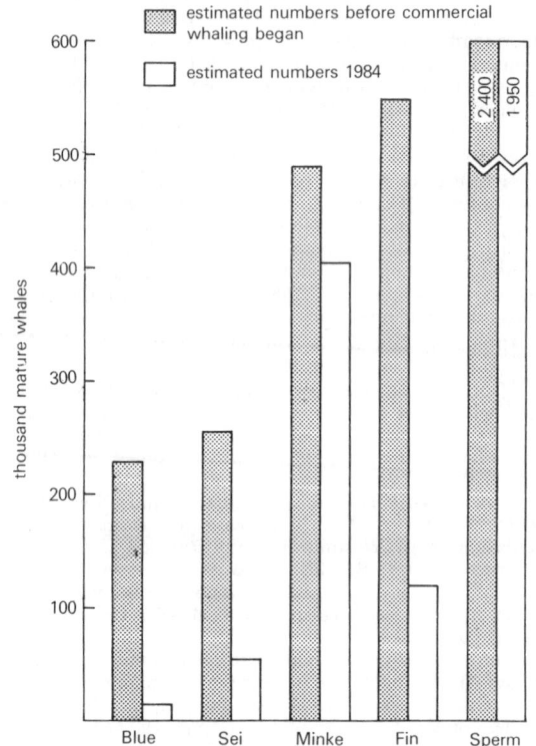

WHALING *Effects of whaling on populations of various whale species.*

whaling The hunting and slaughter of whales for their carcasses. Traditionally, whales were hunted offshore and processed on land, but modern commercial whaling fleets comprise a mother factory ship for processing the carcasses at sea and a fleet of small hunter vessels equipped with harpoon guns and winches. The carcasses are a source of meat, fats, oils, and other chemicals used in many industries. Whaling has depleted whale populations to the point that some species, such as the blue whale and bowhead whale, are in danger of extinction. Many conservationists are campaigning for a complete ban on whaling, especially since substitutes for most whale products are available. Most countries have now agreed to a virtual end to commercial whaling under pressure from the International Whaling Commission; Japan, however, continued to hunt minke whales in 1988, claiming it was for purely scientific purposes.

Whangarei 35 43S 174 20E A city in New Zealand, in North Island on Whangarei Harbour (a large sheltered inlet of the Pacific Ocean). It is the site of New Zealand's only oil refinery (1964). Population (1980 est): 39 700.

whangee A hard white-skinned tropical *bamboo of the genus *Phyllostachys*, from SE Asia, the stems of which are used as canes or walking sticks. The woody jointed stems arise from a creeping underground stem; whorls of slender shoots with narrow leaves are produced from each joint.

Wharton, Edith (Newbold) (1862–1937) US novelist. Her novels about New York society, such as *The House of Mirth* (1905) and *The Age of Innocence* (1920), were influenced by her friend Henry *James. From 1907 she lived in Paris. Her short fiction was printed in *Collected Short Stories* (2 vols, 1968). *Ethan Frome* (1911), a short novel set in New England, remains her best-known work.

wheat A cereal *grass belonging to the genus *Triticum*, native to W Asia but widely cultivated in subtropical and temperate regions. With the exception of einkorn (*T. monococcum*), most commercial wheats are hybrids with the genus *Aegilops*. Many different varieties have been developed; winter wheats, sown in autumn, are hardier than spring wheats. The stems, up to 1 m high, each bear a cylindrical head of up to a hundred flower clusters, grouped in vertical rows and sometimes bearing bristles (awns) up to 10 cm long. The grain of bread wheat (*T. aestivum*) is milled to produce flour for bread, cakes, biscuits, etc. Hard or durum wheat (*T. durum*) is used to make pasta and semolina. Surplus grain, bran, etc., is fed to livestock. Wheat is also a commercial source of alcohol, dextrose, gluten, malt, and starch.

wheatear A migratory songbird, *Oenanthe oenanthe*, that winters in tropical Africa and Eurasia, and breeds in N tundra regions, nesting in holes in the ground. It is about 15 cm long and in summer the male has a blue-grey back, white rump, and a black mask and wings. In winter, males resemble females, having a brown mask, back, and wings. Family: *Turdidae* (thrushes).

Wheatstone, Sir Charles (1802–75) British physicist, who was originally a musical-instrument maker, reputedly inventing the mouth organ and the concertina. He was the first to patent the electrical telegraph and recognized the value of the network used to measure resistances now called the *Wheatstone bridge (invented by Samuel Hunter Christie; 1784–1865). He became professor of physics at King's College, London, in 1832 and was knighted in 1868.

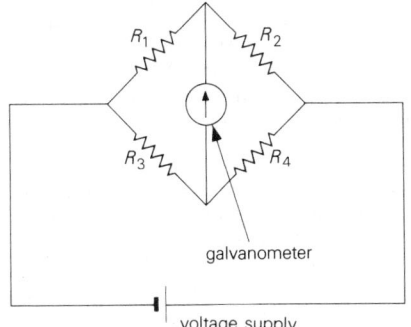

WHEATSTONE BRIDGE

Wheatstone bridge An arrangement of four resistances used to measure the value of one of the resistances when the other three are known. The resistances are arranged to form a square with a voltage applied across two opposite junctions and a gal-

vanometer connected across the other two opposite junctions. When the galvanometer indicates that no current is flowing the bridge is balanced and $R_1/R_2 = R_3/R_4$.

wheel animalcule. *See* rotifer.

Wheeler, Sir (Robert Eric) Mortimer (1890–1976) British archaeologist. Wheeler's skill in excavating, recording, and interpreting archaeological strata was renowned. He excavated Romano-British sites (e.g. *Maiden Castle) and was influential as director of the Archaeological Survey of India (1944–48).

wheel of life. *See* Bhavachakra.

whelk A *gastropod mollusc of the family *Buccinidae* (over 400 species), of warm and cold seas. 4–12 cm long, whelks feed on molluscs and worms. The common northern whelk (*Buccinum undatum*), 5 cm long, has a drab yellow-brown shell and edible flesh. Tropical species are more colourful.

whidah. *See* whydah.

Whigs Members of a British political group that became the *Liberal Party after about 1868. Originally an abusive Scottish name for a horsethief, it was later applied to a Scottish Presbyterian, and in 1679 to one who, in opposition to the *Tories, wished to exclude the Roman Catholic Duke of York (later James II) from the succession. The Whigs dominated politics in the first half of the 18th century, forming rival aristocratic groups. When in the late 18th century the Tories re-emerged, the Whigs formed a more united group under Charles James *Fox. Identifying with industrialist, Nonconformist, and reforming interests, they became the Liberal Party under *Gladstone.

whimbrel A *curlew, *Numenius phaeopus*, that breeds on Arctic tundra and winters in Africa, South America, and S Asia. 40 cm long, it has a streaked brown plumage and a dark crown with a pale central stripe. It feeds on insects, spiders, worms, and snails.

whinchat A migratory *chat, *Saxicola rubetra*, common on open farmland. It winters in Africa and breeds in Eurasia, nesting in rough vegetation and feeding on flies and moths. The male has a streaked brown plumage, pale chestnut breast, white wingbars, and a white eyestripe; the female is duller.

whip In the UK, an official of a political party responsible for ensuring that the party's MPs vote according to its leadership's policies and for communicating MPs' views to the leadership. The term also refers to the summons to vote sent by whips to MPs, a crucial summons being underlined three times (three-line whip). In the USA, whips are not as influential as in Britain, where MPs seldom disobey directions.

whipbird A shy songbird belonging to the Australian genus *Psophodes* (2 species). They are about 25 cm long with a dark-green plumage, and feed on insects among scrub and undergrowth. The eastern whipbird (*P. olivaceus*) has a long whistling call ended by a whipcrack sound. Family: *Muscicapidae*.

whippet A breed of dog developed in England during the 19th century from terrier and greyhound stock and used for coursing and racing. It has a slender streamlined build with a smooth whiplike tail and long tapering muzzle. The fine short coat can be any mixture of colours. Height: 46 cm (dogs); 43 cm (bitches).

whippoorwill A North American *nightjar, *Caprimulgus vociferus*, named after its distinctive call. About 24 cm long, it has a mottled brown plumage; the male has a white collar and tail markings. It lives in woodland and feeds on insects.

whip scorpion A nocturnal *arachnid, sometimes called vinegarroon, belonging to a suborder (*Uropygi*; about 75 species) found in tropical and subtropical regions. Up to 13 cm long, it has large spiny pincers and a whiplike tail and it secretes acetic acid for defence. Order: *Pedipalpi*.

Whipsnade Zoo A large zoological park, belonging to the London Zoological Society, situated in Bedfordshire, some

45 km (30 mi) NW of London, 5 km (3 mi) S of Dunstable. It covers some 2 sq km (500 acres) and was opened in 1931. Animals are kept in large enclosures that resemble their natural habitats.

whip snake　A slender arboreal snake belonging to the genus *Zamenis* (5 species). The common European speckled grey whip snake (*Z. gemonensis*) reaches a length of 1.8 m and feeds on other snakes and lizards. The green whip snakes (genus *Dryophis*; 8 species) occur in tropical Asia and Australasia and grow to a length of 1 m. Family: *Colubridae*.

whirligig　A dark shiny *water beetle belonging to the widely distributed family *Gyrinidae* (about 700 species). It spins around on the surface of still or slow-moving fresh water, feeding on insects or other small animals that have fallen in. The aquatic larvae prey on mayfly or dragonfly nymphs. If disturbed, whirligig beetles dive from the surface and exude a foul-smelling milky liquid.

whirlpool　A violent circular eddy in the sea or a large river, caused by opposing currents or winds or where a strong current is impeded by some obstacle. Large-scale whirlpools are rare. *See also* Maelstrom.

whirlwind　A small revolving column of air, which whirls around a low-pressure centre produced by local heating and convectional uprising. It may pick up small pieces of debris and dust and in desert areas may cause *sandstorms.

whisky　A *spirit distilled from malted barley or other grain. The word comes from the Gaelic *uisgebeatha*, water of life. The milled grain is mixed with water to form a mash, which must be converted to sugar before fermentation; the resulting alcoholic liquid is distilled and then aged in the cask for at least three years. Whisky is classified according to where it is produced, e.g. Scotch whisky, Irish whiskey (spelt with an e), or, as in the USA, by type. Most US whiskey is either rye or bourbon (named after the county in Kentucky where it was first produced).

whist　A card game for two pairs of partners; it originated in the 17th century and was popularized by *Hoyle. A pack of 52 cards is dealt out, the last card determining the trump suit. The object of the game is to win the highest number of tricks by playing the highest card of a suit (the cards ranking from ace high) or by trumping (one may also discard a nontrump when one cannot follow suit). The winner of a trick leads the next card. Each trick over the first six (the "book") scores a point to the partners; five or (in long whist) ten points make a game and two out of three games win the rubber. In **solo whist** each player makes a call indicating that he will play the hand for a certain number of tricks; the player with the highest call plays alone, or solo, against the other three. *See also* bridge.

Whistler, James (Abbott) McNeill　(1834–1903) US painter. After briefly attending West Point, from which he was dismissed, he settled in Paris (1855), where he was particularly influenced by oriental art, especially Japanese prints. Moving to England (1859), he specialized in portraits and landscapes dominated by one or two colours, the best known being *The Artist's Mother* (Louvre) and *Nocturne in Blue and Gold* (Tate Gallery). In 1877 *Ruskin described one of Whistler's works as "flinging a pot of paint in the public's face" and was sued for libel (1878); although Whistler won the case his legal costs ruined him. Whistler was also famous as a wit and as the author of *The Gentle Art of Making Enemies* (1890).

Whistler, Rex　(1905–44) British artist. After training at the Slade School he became known for his illustrations for such books as *Gulliver's Travels* and his murals for the Tate Gallery restaurant. He was killed in World War II. His brother **Laurence Whistler** (1912–　) is a glass engraver, writer, and poet.

whistling duck　A long-legged long-necked *duck belonging to a tribe (*Dendrocygnini*; 8 species), also called tree duck, ranging throughout tropical regions. They have a distinctive whistling cry. The fulvous tree duck (*Dendrocygnus bicolor*) is 55 cm long and has a red-brown plumage with cream stripes on the flanks.

Whitbread Book of the Year Award　Britain's richest literary award, with £18,500 for the winner. Announced in 1985 and sponsored by the brewers Whitbread, it is open to both fiction and non-fiction, but the author must live in the UK. The prize is administered by the Booksellers Association of Great Britain. In 1986 it was won by Douglas Dunn for his *Elegies*, and in 1987 by Kazuo Ishiguro for *An Artist of the Floating World*.

Whitby　54 29N 0 37W A town in N England, on the North Yorkshire coast at the mouth of the River Esk. A monastery was founded here in 657 AD by St Hilda; only the ruins of a later abbey remain. Whitby has associations with Capt Cook, who lived here. It is a resort and fishing port with boatbuilding and fish-curing industries. Population (1981): 13 763.

Whitby, Synod of　(663 AD) A council convened at Whitby by King Oswy of Northumbria to decide whether to adopt Roman or Celtic Church usages. The major source of controversy between the Roman party, led by St *Wilfrid, and the Celtic party led by St Colman (d. 676), was the dating of Easter. The Roman view triumphed and the English Church was brought into line with the Continent.

White, Gilbert　(1720–93) English naturalist. Following his ordination in the Anglican Church in 1751, White began making observations of the natural history around his home at Selborne, Hampshire. He published *The Natural History and Antiquities of Selborne* (1789), a collection of his correspondence with fellow naturalists, still widely read and admired for its keen observation and charming style.

White, Patrick　(1912–　) Australian novelist. Born in England and educated at Cambridge University, he settled in Australia after World War II and explored the national consciousness in his epic novels *The Tree of Man* (1955) and *Voss* (1957). His other works include *The Vivisector* (1970), *A Fringe of Leaves* (1976), *The Twyborn Affair* (1980), and *Netherwood* (1983). He won the Nobel Prize in 1973.

White, T(erence) H(anbury)　(1906–64) British novelist. He lived as a recluse in Ireland and in the Channel Isles. His books include a retelling of the Arthurian legend, *The Once and Future King* (1958), and works of social history.

white ant　*See* termite.

whitebait　The young of *herrings, *sprats, and sometimes *silversides. They are highly valued as food.

whitebeam　A tree, *Sorbus aria*, up to 15 m tall found mainly in S and central Europe. The young leaves are covered in white down; the white five-petalled flowers are borne in branched clusters and produce red berries. Swedish whitebeam (*S. × intermedia*), a hybrid between whitebeam and *mountain ash, is often planted in parks. Family: *Rosaceae*.

white dwarf　A very small faint low-mass star (less than 1.44 solar masses) that has undergone *gravitational collapse following exhaustion of its nuclear fuel. Electrons are stripped from the constituent atoms, and it is the pressure exerted by these densely packed electrons that eventually halts the star's contraction. The density is then 10^7–10^{11}kg m^{-3}. As they cool, their colours change from white (for the brightest) through yellow and red until they become cold black objects.

white-eye　A small long-tailed songbird belonging to a family (*Zosteropidae*; 85 species) occurring in Old World tropical regions. White-eyes are less than 15 cm long, typically yellow-green with white underparts, and have characteristic white rings around the eyes. Arboreal, with brush-tipped tongues for feeding on nectar, they also eat insects and fruits.

Whitefield, George　(1714–70) British Methodist preacher. An associate of the Wesleys at Oxford, Whitefield was not allowed to preach in Anglican churches and began open-air preaching in England in 1739; in 1740, during one of his seven visits to America, he became associated with the *Great Awakening in New England. His preaching was strongly Calvinist, in contrast to the Wesleys' Arminianism.

whitefish A slender fish, belonging to a genus (*Coregonus*) related to trout, that occurs mainly in deep northern lakes and rivers of Europe, Asia, and North America. It has a small mouth, minute teeth, and a covering of large silvery scales. Whitefish feed on insects and other small animals and most are food and game fish.

white fly A small winged insect of the mainly tropical family *Aleyrodidae*. 2-3 mm long, it is covered with a mealy white powder and resembles a minute moth. White flies suck plant juices and exude honeydew on which a sooty black mould grows, often damaging crops. The larvae go through a sedentary stage, in which they are scalelike and covered with a cottony wax. Suborder: *Homoptera*; order *Hemiptera*.

Whitehall A street in Westminster, London, where many government offices are located; the name is often applied to the civil service. The *Cenotaph is also in Whitehall.

Whitehaven 54 33N 3 35W A town in NW England, in Cumbria on the Irish Sea. It is a port with coalmining, textile, chemical, and food-processing industries. Nearby is Calder Hill, Britain's first nuclear power station. Population (1981): 26 714.

Whitehead, A(lfred) N(orth) (1861-1947) British philosopher and mathematician. Whitehead's first major work, the *Principia Mathematica* (1910-13), was written in collaboration with Bertrand *Russell. In later books, such as the *Principles of Natural Knowledge* (1919) and *The Concept of Nature* (1920), he explored the relationships that exist between concepts and sense perception. Thereafter, his philosophy became more metaphysical. He was awarded the OM in 1945.

Whitehorse 60 40N 135 08W A city in NW Canada, the capital of the *Yukon. Founded in 1900, at the time of the Klondike gold rush, it is now a centre for distribution, administration, and tourism. Population (1981): 15 771.

White Horse, Vale of the A valley in S England, in Oxfordshire drained by the River Ock. Its name derives from the Uffington White Horse, the figure of a horse 110 m (361 ft) long cut in the chalk of the Berkshire Downs. There are several theories concerning its origin but the general opinion is that it was a cult object of the Belgae, a tribe that occupied much of SE England from about 50 BC to 50 AD.

WHITE HOUSE *The colonnaded north portico was added in the 1820s.*

White House The official residence of the president of the USA. In Washington, DC, on Pennsylvania Avenue, the building was designed by James Hoban (c. 1762-1831) in 1792. It was burnt (1814) by the British during the *War of 1812 but was subsequently restored under Hoban's supervision, being painted white to hide the smoke stains (its name, however, had been adopted earlier). It was partly rebuilt (1949-52).

Whitelaw, William (Stephen Ian), 1st Viscount (1918–) British Conservative politician. He entered parliament in 1955 and was leader of the House of Commons (1970-72), secretary of state for Northern Ireland (1972-73), secretary of state for employment (1973-74), and home secretary (1979-83). In 1983 he became a viscount and was appointed lord president of the Council and leader of the House of Lords, resigning due to ill health in 1988.

white rhinoceros The largest species of *rhinoceros, *Diceros simus*, of South Africa. It is greyish brown and has a broad square upper lip. Up to 2 m high at the shoulder and weighing up to 3.5 tonnes, white rhinos are now very rare.

White Russia. See Belorussian SSR.

White Russians The Russians who fought against the Soviet Red Army in the civil war (1917-21) that followed the *Russian Revolution. The name derives from that of the royalist opponents to the French Revolution, called Whites because they adopted the white flag of the Bourbon dynasty.

White Sea (Russian name: Beloye More) A gulf of the Arctic Ocean in the NW Soviet Union, to the S and E of the Kola Peninsula. It gives access to Archangel and the fishing port and aluminium works of Kandalaksha and is connected by inland waterways to the Gulf of Finland.

white shark A dangerous man-eating *mackerel shark, *Carcharodon carcharias*, that occurs singly or in groups, mainly in tropical and temperate seas. Its heavy body, up to 11 m long, is grey-brown to slate-blue with light-grey undersides and it feeds voraciously on fish, turtles, seals, etc.

whitethroat An Old World *warbler, *Sylvia communis*, that breeds in N Eurasia and winters in central Africa. It is about 14 cm long including its long slender tail. The male is russet brown with a greyish head and white throat and performs a tumbling courtship display in flight. The female is a duller brown.

white whale A small Arctic toothed *whale, *Delphinapterus leucas*, also called beluga. Young white whales are blue-grey, but change to white as they mature. About 4.5 m long, with a rounded head and large flukes and flippers, they feed mainly on fish. Family: *Monodontidae*.

Whitgift, John (c. 1530-1604) Anglican churchman. He became a professor at Cambridge in 1567 and Bishop of Worcester in 1577. As Archbishop of Canterbury (1583-1604) he opposed Puritan teaching and enforced Queen Elizabeth's policy of uniformity in the Church of England. He founded Whitgift School at Croydon (1595).

whiting A marine food and game fish belonging to the genus *Gadus* (or *Merlangius*) related to cod, especially *M. merlangus* found in European waters down to 200 m. It has a slender body, up to 70 cm long, which is olive, sandy, or bluish above and silvery white below, a black blotch on each pectoral fin, and three dorsal and two anal fins.

Whitlam, (Edward) Gough (1916–) Australian statesman; Labor prime minister (1972-75). He became Labor leader in 1967. As prime minister following 18 years of Liberal rule, he ended conscription, relaxed rules on non-White immigration, and tried to lessen US influence in Australia. In 1975, after Malcolm *Fraser had blocked government finance bills, Whitlam was dismissed by the governor, Sir John Kerr (1914–) for refusing to call a general election. Whitlam lost the election called by Fraser and resigned the party leadership (1977). His book *The Whitlam Government 1972–1975* was published in 1986.

Whitman, Walt (1819-92) US poet. As a young man he worked as a printer, teacher, journalist, and property speculator and contributed unoriginal poems to various magazines. He expressed his democratic idealism and passionate love of life in the revolutionary free-verse poems of *Leaves of Grass* (1855), which was revised and enlarged in nine editions during his lifetime. During the Civil War he nursed wounded soliders, and subsequently suffered from illness himself. His later works include the prose *Democratic Vistas* (1871).

Whitney, Eli (1765-1825) American inventor, best known for his invention of the cotton gin, a machine that separated cotton fibre from the seeds. The device, patented in 1793, greatly stimulated cotton growing in the southern USA. Whitney subsequently turned to firearms manufacture, into which he introduced the notion of interchangeable parts.

Whit Sunday (*or* Pentecost) The seventh Sunday after Easter, a Christian festival commemorating the descent of the Holy Spirit on the Apostles on the 50th day after Easter (Acts 2.1). Pentecost was originally a Jewish feast held on the 50th day after Passover to mark the completion of the grain harvest and to commemorate the giving of the Law of Moses. As adopted by the Christian Church, Whit Sunday became a time for baptisms, hence its name ("White" Sunday), referring to the white baptismal robes.

Whittier, John Greenleaf (1807-92) US poet. An active Quaker and humanitarian, he championed the antislavery cause in both his journalism and his early poetry. His later and better-known poetry includes the narrative *Snow-Bound* (1866) and many shorter poems and ballads.

Whittington, Dick (Richard W.; d. 1423) English merchant, who was three times Lord Mayor of London (1397-98, 1406-07, 1419-20). He traded with, and made loans to, both Henry IV and Henry V. The legend of Whittington and his cat dates from the early 17th century.

Whittle, Sir Frank (1907-) British aeronautical engineer and RAF officer, who designed and flew the first British jet aircraft. The engine was fitted into a specially constructed Gloster E28/39; its maiden flight took place on 15 May, 1941. His achievement was recognized by a government award of £100,000 and he was made an OM in 1986.

WHO. *See* World Health Organization.

whooping cough A respiratory infection of children caused by the bacterium *Bordetella pertussis*. After an incubation period of 7-14 days, the child develops a cough, a nasal discharge, and low fever, followed a week or two later by paroxysms of coughing accompanied by a characteristic whooping sound. The disease may persist for months and it may be complicated by pneumonia or convulsions. A vaccine is available but its use is controversial, since rare cases of brain damage in immunized children have been attributed to it.

whooping crane A rare bird, *Grus americana*, that breeds in the marshlands of NW Canada and winters in the swamps of SE Texas. 150 cm tall with a wingspan of 210 cm, it has a white plumage with black-tipped wings, black legs, and a bare red face and has a loud whooping call. Captive breeding programmes may prevent its extinction. Family: *Gruidae* (cranes).

Whorf, Benjamin Lee (1897-1941) US linguist, who earned his living as an insurance inspector and studied American Indian and other languages as a hobby. In *Language, Thought, and Reality* (1956) he argued that human conceptual systems are dependent upon individual languages and that comparison of different languages reveals that different peoples analyse the world in very different ways. This controversial form of linguistic relativism was also argued by *Sapir and has been influential in psycholinguistics (*see* linguistics).

whortleberry. *See* bilberry.

Whyalla 33 04S 137 34E A city and port in South Australia, on the E coast of Eyre Peninsula. It is an impor-

tant industrial centre with the largest shipyards in Australia and major steelworks. Population (1984 est): 31 500.

whydah (*or* whidah) A small *weaverbird belonging to the genus *Vidua* (11 species), also called widowbird and occurring in open grassy regions of Africa. The males have long ornamental tail feathers used in the courtship display and the females lay their eggs in the nests of closely related *waxbills, which rear their young. The young whydahs closely resemble the offspring of their host species although the adults are very different in appearance.

Whymper, Edward (1840-1911) British mountaineer, explorer, artist, and author. He led the first ascent of the Matterhorn (1865), in which four members of the team died on the descent. He also visited Greenland, the Andes, and Canada on explorations.

Wichita 37 43N 97 20W A city in the USA, in Kansas on the Arkansas River. Founded in 1864, it had developed into an important agricultural trading centre by the late 19th century. Today Wichita is the state's largest city and the principal commercial and industrial centre of S Kansas with railway workshops, oil refineries, and an aircraft industry. It is the site of two universities, including Wichita State University (1895). Population (1980): 279 272.

Wick 58 26N 3 06W A town in N Scotland, in the Highland Region. It is a fishing port with boatbuilding, distilling, and knitwear industries. There are air services to the Orkneys and Shetlands. Population (1981): 7933.

Wicklow (Irish name: Contae Chill Mhantáin) A county in the E Republic of Ireland, in Leinster bordering on the Irish Sea. Fertile lowlands rise to the central Wicklow Mountains. Agriculture is the chief occupation; along the coast are several resorts, notably Bray. Area: 2025 sq km (782 sq mi). Population (1981): 87 449. County town: Wicklow.

Widnes 53 22N 2 44W A town in NW England, in N Cheshire on the River Mersey opposite Runcorn. It has an important chemical industry. Population (1981): 54 411.

Widor, Charles Marie (1844-1937) French organist and composer. He was organist of Saint-Sulpice in Paris for over 60 years. His compositions include eight symphonies for the organ, concertos, chamber music, and choral music.

Wieland, Christoph Martin (1733-1813) German novelist and poet. His first distinguished work is the romance *Agathon* (1766-67), while his translations of Shakespeare later influenced the *Sturm und Drang* movement. The verse epic *Oberon* (1780) introduced exotic Middle Eastern matter into European literature.

Wien. *See* Vienna.

Wiener, Norbert (1894-1964) US mathematician. A child prodigy, Wiener entered university at the age of 11 and was awarded his doctorate at 18. During World War II he worked on the problem of aiming an anti-aircraft gun by computing such factors as the speed and direction of the aircraft, wind speed, etc. He thus developed an interest in the mathematics of information and communication, which he called *cybernetics. After the war Wiener, refusing to do any more military research, spent the rest of his life writing about the social problems resulting from automation.

Wiesbaden 50 05N 8 15E A spa city in SW West Germany, the capital of Hesse on the River Rhine. Its hot saline springs have made it a popular resort since Roman times. A centre of the wine industry, its manufactures include chemicals and plastics. Population (1980 est): 273 700.

Wigan 53 33N 2 38W A town in NW England, in Greater Manchester. It is an industrial and market town in a coal-mining area, made famous by George Orwell's *Road to Wigan Pier*. Population (1981): 79 535.

wigeon A fast-flying *duck, *Anas penelope*, that breeds on tundra and moorland of N Eurasia and winters on mudflats, estuaries, and lakes as far south as Africa and S Asia. 45 cm long, it has a pale-grey black-tipped bill; males have a chestnut head with a yellowish crown and grey back, while females are brown with a white belly and white shoulders.

OSCAR WILDE

Wight, Isle of (Latin name: Vectis) 50 40N 1 15W An island and county in S England, separated from the mainland by the Solent and Spithead. It consists chiefly of undulating chalk downs with the *Needles off the W coast. Tourism and yachting (with the annual Cowes Regatta) are important, especially in the coastal resorts, including Ryde, Shanklin, and Ventnor. Other occupations include agriculture and shipbuilding. Area: 380 sq km (147 sq mi). Population (1981): 118 192. Administrative centre: Newport.

Wightman Cup An annual tennis competition between British and US women's teams, instituted in 1923. The match consists of five singles and two doubles rubbers (matches). The USA have won the most victories. The trophy was donated by the US player Hazel Hotchkiss (who later became Mrs George Wightman; 1886–1974).

Wigner, Eugene Paul (1902–) US physicist, born in Hungary, who worked out the theory of neutron absorption by nuclei and discovered that solids change their size under radiation (Wigner effect). Wigner helped *Szilard and *Teller persuade *Einstein to warn Roosevelt of the dangers of an atomic bomb being made by the Germans, and he worked with Fermi on the first atomic pile. He won a share of the 1963 Nobel Prize for his work on nuclear physics.

Wigtown (*or* Wigtownshire) A former county of SW Scotland. Under local government reorganization in 1975 its boundaries were adjusted to form Wigtown District, in Dumfries and Galloway Region.

Wigtown 54 52N 4 26W A town in SW Scotland, in Dumfries and Galloway Region on Wigtown Bay (an extensive inlet of the Irish Sea). It is a market town and small port. Population (1981): 1040.

wigwam 1. Strictly, a square dome-roofed hut made of saplings covered with bark or rush matting used by some North American Indian peoples. 2. (*or* tepee) A conical tent supported by poles tied together at the top and covered with decorated buffalo skins, used by the Plains tribes.

Wilberforce, William (1759–1833) British philanthropist, who played a major part in the antislavery movement. As an MP (1780–1825) he led the parliamentary campaign to abolish the slave trade (achieved in 1807) and then to emancipate existing slaves (achieved a month after his death). A founder of the Society for the Abolition of the Slave Trade (1787) and of the Antislavery Society (1823), he was also a leading member of the *Clapham Sect.

wildcat A *cat, *Felis sylvestris*, of Europe and W Asia. About 75 cm long, it has a bushy rounded tail and thick striped coat. Wildcats inhabit dense woodland and breed once a year, in a den in a hollow log or tree. They may interbreed with domestic cats.

Wilde, Oscar (Fingal O'Flahertie Wills W.; 1854–1900) British dramatist and poet, born in Dublin. He dazzled London literary society with his charm and wit and became a leading figure of the *Aesthetic movement. His works include *Poems* (1881), a novel *The Picture of Dorian Gray* (1891), and a series of brilliant social comedies: *Lady Windermere's Fan* (1892), *A Woman of No Importance* (1893), *An Ideal Husband* (1895), and *The Importance of Being Earnest* (1895). Socially and financially ruined by a trial in 1895 arising from his homosexual relationship with Lord Alfred Douglas (1870–1945), he was imprisoned for two years and lived in exile in France from 1897. While in prison he wrote a long letter on his relationship with Douglas, passages of which were published as *De profundis* (1905). In exile he produced his last and best-known poem, *The Ballad of Reading Gaol* (1898).

wildebeest. *See* gnu.

Wilder, Billy (Samuel W.; 1906–) US film director, born in Austria. He went to Hollywood in 1934. His films are characterized by his acerbic humour and his unconventional choice of subject matter. They include *The Lost Weekend* (1945), *Sunset Boulevard* (1950), *Some Like It Hot* (1959), *Front Page* (1974), and *Buddy, Buddy* (1981).

Wilder, Thornton (1897–1975) US novelist and dramatist. His best-known plays are *Our Town* (1938) and *The Skin of Our Teeth* (1942), and his novels include *The Bridge of San Luis Rey* (1927). He was a skilled literary craftsman who enjoyed great popular success.

wildfowl Waterbirds, usually ones that are shot for sport, especially ducks and geese but sometimes also coots, rails, and grebes.

Wilfrid, St (634–709 AD) English churchman; Bishop of York (c. 663–c. 703). He is famous for campaigning for the replacement of Celtic usages in Britain by Roman liturgy and practice. His viewpoint triumphed at the Synod of *Whitby (663). Feast day: 12 Oct.

Wilhelmina (1880–1962) Queen of the Netherlands (1890–1948), who encouraged Dutch resistance to the German occupation in World War II, making radio broadcasts from London throughout the war. She abdicated in favour of her daughter Juliana.

Wilhelmshaven 53 32N 8 07E A seaport in NW West Germany, in Lower Saxony on the North Sea. It was founded in 1869 as the main Prussian (later German) naval base. Now also a popular resort and an oil port, its manufactures include machinery and electrical goods. Population (1983 est): 99 174.

Wilkes, John (1725–97) British journalist and politician. He was a member of the Hellfire Club of debauchees, which met at St Mary's Abbey, Medmenham, near High Wycombe (Buckinghamshire). In 1757 he became an MP and in 1762 founded the weekly *North Briton*, in which he attacked George III's ministers. The famous issue No 45 (1763) accused the government of lying in the king's speech and Wilkes was arrested for libel. Although released, in 1764 while in Paris he was expelled from the House of Commons and outlawed. In 1768 he returned to England and was twice elected MP for Middlesex and twice expelled from parliament. He became the focus of the Society of the Supporters of the Bill of Rights and after serving as lord mayor of London (1774) was re-elected to parliament and at last permitted to take his seat (1774–90).

Wilkie, Sir David (1785-1841) Scottish painter, acclaimed for his scenes of everyday life in the Dutch 17th-century tradition. He became painter to William IV in 1830. He travelled extensively and *Turner commemorated his death at sea in *Peace: Burial at Sea* (Tate Gallery).

Wilkins, Sir George Hubert (1888-1958) British explorer, born in Australia. After experience with Vilhjalmur Stefansson (1879-1962) in the Arctic (1913-18) and *Shackleton in the Antarctic (1921-22), he flew over the North Pole from Alaska to Spitsbergen (1928). In 1931 he failed to reach it in the submarine *Nautilus*.

Wilkins, Maurice Hugh Frederick (1916-) New Zealand physicist, who worked in California on the atom bomb during World War II. After the war, uneasy about nuclear weapons, he turned to life sciences and developed a method of using X-ray diffraction, which assisted James *Watson and Francis *Crick in determining the structure of DNA. These three scientists were awarded the 1962 Nobel Prize for this work.

will In law, the written declaration of a person's intentions in relation to the disposal of his property after his death. Two witnesses are required to authenticate the will, neither of whom may be a beneficiary. Dependants of the deceased inadequately provided for may challenge the will, the provisions of which are carried out by one or more executors. Specific gifts of property, called legacies, are subject to *capital-transfer tax in the UK.

Willemstad 12 12N 68 56W The capital and main port of the *Netherlands Antilles, on the SE coast of Curaçao. It is an important free port and a refining centre for Venezuelan oil. Population (1983): 50 000.

William (I) the Conqueror (c. 1028-1087) Duke of Normandy (1035-87) and the first Norman King of England (1066-87). He claimed to have been named by Edward the Confessor as heir to the English throne. When Harold II succeeded Edward, William invaded England, defeated and killed his rival at the battle of Hastings, and became king. The *Norman conquest of England was completed by 1072, aided by the establishment of *feudalism, under which his followers were granted land in return for pledges of service and loyalty. As king, William was noted for his efficient, if harsh, rule. His administration relied upon Norman and other foreign personnel, especially *Lanfranc, Archbishop of Canterbury. In 1085 William initiated the compilation of *Domesday Book.

William (I) the Bad (1120-66) Norman King of Sicily (1154-66). In 1155 he reconquered Apulia from the Byzantines and in 1156 (the Concordat of Benevento) gained papal acknowledgement of his possessions. His attempts to reduce the power of the barons incited a revolt, which he was able to suppress. An outstanding patron of learning, he welcomed many Muslim scholars to his court.

William (I) the Lion (1143-1214) King of the Scots (1165-1214). After his capture in a revolt against *Henry II of England in 1174, he became a vassal of the English throne. On Henry's death in 1189 he regained independence for his kingdom in return for a payment to Richard I.

William (I) the Silent (1533-84) The leader of the *Revolt of the Netherlands against Spanish rule. He was the son of the Count of Nassau and in 1544 became Prince of Orange. Appointed to the Council of State in 1555, he became governor of Holland, Zeeland, and Utrecht in 1559. He opposed the autocracy of the Spanish Government and its persecution of Protestants (he himself became a Protestant in 1573), withdrawing with Egmont and Horn from the Council of State in 1563. When open revolt broke out in 1568, William soon emerged as its leader and in 1576 succeeded in uniting the Roman Catholic provinces in the south with the Protestant north. This union was short lived, however, and in 1579 the northern provinces declared their

independence of Spain, with William as their first stadholder (chief magistrate). He was assassinated by a Spanish agent.

William I (1772-1843) King of the Netherlands (1815-40). Following Napoleon's conquest of the Netherlands (1795), he lived in exile until Napoleon's defeat (1813), becoming King of the United Netherlands, which included Belgium and Luxembourg. He fostered the Netherlands' economic recovery but antagonized the Belgians, who achieved independence (1831) by revolt. William abdicated in favour of his son William II.

William I (1797-1888) King of Prussia (1861-88) and German emperor (1871-88). His advocacy of using arms against the Revolution of 1848 brought him the nickname Prince of Grapeshot and he was forced into exile (1848-49). He became regent for his brother Frederick William IV in 1858. His reign was dominated by *Bismarck, who achieved German unification under Prussian leadership in 1871, when William was proclaimed German emperor.

William II Rufus (c. 1056-1100) King of England (1087-1100), succeeding his father William the Conqueror. His harsh rule aroused baronial and ecclesiastical opposition, notably from *Anselm, Archbishop of Canterbury. He made several attempts to recover Normandy from his elder brother Robert (d. 1134) and was killed by an arrow while hunting in the New Forest. He may have been assassinated by order of his younger brother, who became Henry I.

William (II) the Good (1154-89) The last Norman King of Sicily (1166-89). He ruled in person from 1171, engaging in intermittent war against the Byzantine Empire until final defeat near Constantinople in 1185. In 1177 he married Joan (1165-99), the daughter of Henry II of England.

William II (1792-1849) King of the Netherlands (1840-49), following the abdication of his father William I. His authorization of a liberal constitution (1848) prevented the spread of the *Revolutions of 1848 to the Netherlands.

William II (1859-1941) German emperor (1888-1918); grandson of Queen Victoria of the UK. After securing Bismarck's resignation as chancellor, William encouraged policies that were regarded abroad as warmongering. The German navy was built up under *Tirpitz, friendly overtures were made to Turkey and to Kruger of the Transvaal (whom William congratulated on foiling the British *Jameson Raid), and Germany interfered against France in the Morocco crises (1905, 1911). William supported Austria-Hungary's ultimatum to Serbia and then tried in vain to prevent the conflict escalating into a world war. Following Germany's defeat, he was forced to abdicate; he retired to Doorn, in the Netherlands.

William III (1650-1702) King of England (1689-1702) and Stadholder (chief magistrate) of the United Provinces (1672-1702), known as William of Orange. Grandson of Charles I of England and son of William II, Prince of Orange (1626-50), in 1677 he married James II of England's daughter Mary. In 1688 he was invited by the opposition to his father-in-law to invade England and in 1689 was proclaimed joint sovereign with his wife, Mary II (*see* Glorious Revolution). William defeated the former king at the *Boyne in Ireland in 1690. On the Continent he was successful in the War of the *Grand Alliance (1689-97) against Louis XIV of France, leaving a strong army that, under the Duke of Marlborough, was to crush France after his death.

William IV (1765-1837) King of England and Hanover (1830-37), known as the Sailor King or Silly Billy. He served in the Royal Navy from 1778 to 1790. He had ten illegitimate children by the Irish actress Dorothea Jordan before marrying (1818) Adelaide of Saxe-Meiningen (1792-1849). Their two daughters died in infancy and William was succeeded in England by his niece Victoria and in Hanover by his brother Ernest Augustus (1771-1851).

William and Mary style An English derivative (1689-1702) of the *Louis XIV style of furniture. The Huguenot artisans patronized by William III were trained in France and their tastes and techniques predominated. The cabriole leg was a typical innovation replacing the preceding twist turned legs. Rich gilding was common and some important furniture was made of cast silver. Cabinet furniture was finely veneered with *marquetry or lacquered and gilded.

WILLIAM THE CONQUEROR *Detail from a French 13th-century manuscript showing William as a benefactor of Westminster Abbey.*

William of Malmesbury (c. 1090–c. 1143) English Benedictine monk and historian. William's work, although lucid, is sometimes chronologically unsound. It includes the *Gesta Regum Anglorum*, a history of kings of England from the Saxon invasion to 1126, and the *Gesta Pontificum Anglorum* (1125), dealing with English ecclesiastical history.

William of Ockham (c. 1285–1349) English scholastic philosopher (*see* scholasticism). A pupil of *Duns Scotus and later his rival, Ockham is best known for his revival of *nominalism. He systematized the theories on the meaning of universals and linked them with logical principles. *See also* Ockham's Razor.

William of Orange. *See* William III (King of England).

William of Tyre (c. 1130–85) French historian and churchman, born in the Latin kingdom of Jerusalem. He became chancellor of the kingdom in 1174 and Archbishop of Tyre in 1175. His only extant work is *Historia rerum in partibus transmarinis gestarum*, a history of medieval Palestine and a valuable source of information on the early Crusades.

William of Wykeham (1324–1404) English churchman and statesman. Bishop of Winchester from 1366 and Lord Chancellor (1367–71, 1389–91), he founded New College, Oxford (1379), and Winchester College (1382).

Williams, John (1941–) Australian guitarist, living in the UK. He studied at the Royal College of Music and with Segovia. A virtuoso of the classical guitar, he also composes and performs music influenced by pop and jazz.

Williams, J(ohn) P(eter) R(hys) (1949–) Welsh Rugby Union footballer, who played for London Welsh, Bridgend, Wales, and the British Lions. A brilliant attacking full back of legendary courage, he won 52 international caps (up to 1979) and captained Wales in the 1978–79 season.

Williams, Roger (c. 1604–83) English colonizer, who founded the colony of Rhode Island. A Puritan, Williams settled in Boston in 1631 but was banished in 1635 because he disagreed with the theocratic government of Massachusetts, advocating the separation of church and state. He founded (1636) a new settlement at Providence, Rhode Island, the patent of which allowed full religious freedom. There he established the first Baptist Church in America.

Williams, Shirley (Vivien Teresa Brittain) (1930–) British Social Democrat politician, daughter of the writer Vera Brittain (1896–1970) and ex-wife of the philosopher Bernard Williams (1929–). She entered parliament in 1964 as a Labour member and was secretary of state for prices and consumer protection (1974–76). As secretary of state for education and science (1976–79) she championed comprehensive education. She was a cofounder of the *Social Democratic Party in 1981 and its president from 1982, but lost her parliamentary seat in the 1983 general election.

Williams, Tennessee (1911–83) US dramatist. *The Glass Menagerie* (1945), his first major success, was partly autobiographical and introduced his recurrent themes of family tensions and sexual frustration, which were treated with increasing violence in *A Streetcar Named Desire* (1947) and *Cat on a Hot Tin Roof* (1955), both set in the South. After recovering from a mental and physical breakdown, he continued to write plays, including *Vieux Carré* (1978).

Williams, William Carlos (1883–1963) US poet. The influences of *Imagism and of Ezra *Pound, whom he met while studying medicine at the University of Pennsylvania, are apparent in his early poetry, and he continued to develop a style noted for its clarity, directness, and use of natural speech rhythms. His volumes of poetry include *Collected Poems* (1934) and *Pictures from Breughel* (1963), which won a Pulitzer Prize. *Paterson* (5 vols, 1946–58) is an ambitious epic poem employing various experimental techniques.

Williamsburg 37 17N 76 43W A city in the USA, in Virginia. Once the state capital (1699–1779), many of its colonial buildings have been renovated or completely rebuilt, attracting many tourists to the city. One of the country's oldest colleges, the College of William and Mary (1693), is also situated here. Population (1980): 9870.

Williams-Ellis, Sir Clough (1883–1978) Welsh architect. He designed several schools, churches, hotels, etc., but is best remembered for the resort of *Portmeirion (begun 1926).

Williamson, Henry (1895–1977) British novelist. He is best known for his realistic animal stories, especially *Tarka the Otter* (1927) and *Salar the Salmon* (1935). He also wrote a series of 15 historical novels, *A Chronicle of Ancient Sunlight* (1951–69).

Williamson, Malcolm (1931–) Australian composer, living in the UK since 1953. From 1955 to 1960 he was a church organist and in 1975 was appointed Master of the Queen's Music. His works include an organ concerto (1961), the operas *Our Man in Havana* (1963) and *The Violins of St Jacques* (1966), and *Mass of Christ the King* (1977), written for the 25th jubilee of Queen Elizabeth II.

Willis, Norman (David) (1933–) British trades union leader, who began with the Transport and General Workers Union (1949). He became general secretary of the Trades Union Congress in 1984.

Willis, Ted (Edward Henry, Baron Willis of Chislehurst; 1918–) British author. His plays include *Hot Summer Night* (1959) and his novels include *Death May Surprise Us* (1974) and *The Churchill Commando* (1977). He also wrote for television, notably the police series *Dixon of Dock Green*.

will-o'-the-wisp. *See* ignis fatuus.

willow A tree or shrub of the genus *Salix* (about 300 species), native to temperate and arctic regions. Most willows have long narrow leaves (an exception is the Eurasian goat willow (*S. caprea*), also called sallow and pussy willow, which has oval pointed leaves). Male and female catkins are borne on separate trees and open before the leaves; the seeds have long silky hairs. Willows are common in wet places and along stream banks and some are grown as ornamentals, especially the weeping willow (*S. babylonica*), with its slender drooping branches, and the bay willow (*S. pentandra*). Cricket bats are made from the wood of the cricket bat willow (*S. alba* var. *coerulea*). Family: *Salicaceae*. *See also* osier.

willowherb A perennial herb of either of the genera *Epilobium* (160 species) or *Chamaenerion* (about 8 species), of temperate and arctic regions. Rosebay willowherb, or fireweed (*E. angustifolium*), 30–120 cm high, is a common and fast-growing weed on waste ground in woodland clearings and gardens, etc. It has showy spikes of purple flowers and white fluffy seeds. Family: *Onagraceae*.

willow pattern A *chinoiserie pattern attributed to Thomas Minton (*see* Minton ware) and introduced about 1780. It was extensively used on 19th-century English ceramics. The elements are a willow tree, pagoda, figures on a river bridge, and two flying birds in an elaborate border.

Willow South A city in the USA, in S Alaska situated about 113 km (70 mi) NW of Anchorage. In 1976 it was chosen as the site of the new state capital, planned to replace Juneau in the 1980s.

Wills (Moody), Helen (1905–) US tennis player, who won the singles title at Wimbledon a record eight times between 1927 and 1938. She also won the US singles title seven times and the French title four times.

Wilmington 39 46N 75 31W A city in the USA, in North Carolina on the Cape Fear River. The first armed resistance against the Stamp Act occurred here in November, 1765. The state's chief seaport, Wilmington is also a resort and has varied manufactures. Population (1980): 44 000.

Wilson, Sir Angus (1913–) British novelist. He worked at the British Museum until 1955 and later taught at the University of East Anglia. His satirical novels and collections of short stories include *Hemlock and After* (1952), *Anglo-Saxon Attitudes* (1956), *No Laughing Matter* (1967), *As If By Magic* (1973), and *Setting the World on Fire* (1980). He has also published several works of criticism.

Wilson, Charles Thomson Rees (1869-1959) British physicist, who won the 1927 Nobel Prize for his invention of the Wilson *cloud chamber. During the 1890s Wilson was experimenting on cloud formation and supersaturated air. He discovered that moisture condensed in the presence of ions and, when X-rays and radioactivity were discovered, applied his discoveries to invent the cloud chamber for detecting ionizing radiation. It was perfected in 1911. Wilson was professor of natural philosophy at Cambridge University (1925-34).

Wilson, Colin (1931–) British critic and novelist. He won immediate fame with the publication of *The Outsider* (1956), a study of alienated heroes in modern fiction; and books on extraordinary phenomena, including *The Occult* (1971), *Mysteries* (1978), and *Poltergeist!* (1981).

Wilson, Edmund (1895-1972) US critic and essayist. He gave valuable encouragement to young writers in his journalism from the 1920s to the 1940s. His books include *Axel's Castle* (1931), a study of symbolist writers, *To the Finland Station* (1940), on the origins of the Russian Revolution, and *The Scrolls from the Dead Sea* (1955).

Wilson, Edmund Beecher (1856-1939) US biologist, who proposed that sex is determined by the presence or absence of certain chromosomes. Wilson's research and his *Cell in Development and Inheritance* (1896) were a major influence in genetics.

Wilson, (James) Harold, Baron (1916–) British statesman; Labour prime minister (1964-70, 1974-76). An economist, he was economic assistant to the war cabinet secretariat (1940-41) and to the mines department (1941-43) and then director of economics and statistics at the

ministry of fuel and power (1943-44). After World War II he became an MP (1945) and president of the Board of Trade in 1947, resigning in 1951 because of the government's proposed cuts in social-services expenditure. He succeeded Gaitskell as Labour leader in 1963 and achieved electoral victory in 1964. His statutory incomes policy and plans for industrial-relations reform were unpopular within the Labour Party and among trades unionists and he lost the 1970 election. His second ministry saw the renegotiation of the UK's terms of membership of the EEC, which was confirmed by a referendum in 1975. In 1976 Wilson unexpectedly resigned. His publications include *The Labour Government (1964–70)* and *The Governance of Britain* (1976). He was made a life peer, Baron Wilson of Rievaulx, in 1983.

Wilson, Sir Henry Hughes (1864-1922) British field marshal. He was director of military operations (1910-14) and in World War I held command in France before becoming chief of the imperial general staff (1918). Conservative MP (1922) for North Down (Ulster), he was assassinated by the IRA.

Wilson, Henry Maitland, 1st Baron (1881-1964) British field marshal, nicknamed Jumbo. He served in the second Boer War and in World War I. In World War II he held command (under *Wavell) in the successful operations against the Italians in N Africa. However, he failed against the Germans in mainland Greece (1941) and the Dodecanese Islands (1943). He was chief of the British joint staff mission in Washington, DC (1943-45).

Wilson, Richard (1714-82) British landscape painter, born in Wales. He worked as a portraitist in London before visiting Italy (1750-c. 1757), where, influenced by *Claude Lorraine and *Poussin, he gave up portraiture for landscape painting. After his return to England, he continued to paint Italian scenes as well as scenes of English country houses and their parks and scenes of the Welsh mountains. In their feeling for atmosphere and light these paintings established him as the first great British landscapist and an important influence on *Turner and *Constable.

Wilson, (Thomas) Woodrow (1856-1924) US statesman; Democratic president (1913-21). In his first term as president he introduced progressive reforms. In World War I, despite a pledge of neutrality, Wilson declared war on Germany (1917) in response to its unrestricted submarine campaign. Wilson's *Fourteen Points (1918) proposed a basis on which peace might be settled and contained a plan for a League of Nations that was incorporated into the Treaty of Versailles. However, Wilson failed to obtain the US Senate's acceptance of the treaty. Severely disappointed, he suffered a heart attack and his administration achieved little more.

Wilton 51 05N 1 52W A town in S England, in Wiltshire. It has been famous for carpet manufacturing since the 16th century and for its sheep fairs. Wilton House has Elizabethan literary associations. Population (1981): 4005.

Wiltshire A county of S England. It consists of a rolling chalk plateau, which includes the Marlborough Downs and Salisbury Plain, bordered by lowlands in the NW and SE. It is predominantly agricultural; the chief crops are wheat, oats, and barley, and pig and sheep farming are important. There are many remaining features of prehistoric times, notably the Neolithic *Stonehenge and *Avebury. Area: 3481 sq km (1344 sq mi). Population (1981): 518 167. Administrative centre: Trowbridge.

Wimbledon A district in the Greater London Borough of Merton. It contains Wimbledon Common and the headquarters of the All England Tennis Club (since 1877), famous for the annual Championships.

Winchester 51 04N 1 19W A city in S England, the administrative centre of Hampshire. As capital of Saxon Wessex and residence of the Saxon kings, it rivalled the supremacy of London. The cathedral, built in the 11th century on earlier

Saxon foundations, is the longest in England and contains many royal tombs. Winchester College (1382), founded by *William of Wykeham, is England's oldest public school. Population (1981): 30 642.

Winckelmann, Johann Joachim (1717–68) German art historian, who worked mainly in Rome. His promotion of the critical study of Greek and Roman art was encouraged by contemporary discoveries at *Pompeii and *Herculaneum. His *History of Ancient Art* (1764), which exalted Greek art of the 5th and 4th centuries BC and denigrated Roman art in comparison, pioneered modern art historiography.

wind The horizontal movement of air over the earth's surface and one of the basic elements of weather. Thermal differences throughout the world produce variations in air pressure and air will flow generally from high-pressure to low-pressure areas. A wind is classified according to the direction from which it blows, i.e. a wind blowing from the S is a southerly wind. Its speed is usually measured in knots or in metres per second, actual velocities being measured by an anemometer, and it may be classified according to the *Beaufort scale. The major wind systems in the world include the trade winds and *westerlies. □trade winds; □meteorology.

Windermere The largest lake in England, in Cumbria in the Lake District. It drains into Morecambe Bay through the River Leven. The lake is extensively used for watersports and the small town of Windermere on its NE shore is a popular holiday centre. Length: 17 km (10.5 mi).

Windhoek 22 34S 17 06E The capital of Namibia. It is the centre of the world's karakul (Persian lamb) skin industry; other industries include meat canning and bone-meal production. Population (1981): 105 000.

wind instruments Musical instruments in which notes are produced by a vibrating column of air. *Brass instruments are activated by lip pressure; *reed instruments employ double or single reed mouthpieces; the *flute is side blown; the *recorder has a mouthpiece and fipple (whistle hole); *organ pipes have air blown into them by mechanically activated bellows. *Compare* drums; percussion instruments; stringed instruments.

windmills Machines that enable useful work to be obtained from wind power. The principle is that the energy of the wind turns a set of vanes or sails mounted on a horizontal shaft, the rotation of which is transmitted by gearing to working machinery. Windmills had appeared by 1150 in NE Europe and were used for grinding corn, pumping water, and powering light industry, until they were superseded by steam engines in the 19th century. Two common designs were the Dutch mill, in which only the sails and the conical roof moved to catch the wind, and the German post mill, in which the whole millhouse with sails attached rotated around a central supporting pole. The modern metal windmill with multiple-bladed sails is found all over the world in rural areas, pumping water or powering small electric generators. The use of windmills (or aerogenerators, as they are now called) for electricity generation on a large scale has long been considered and is now regarded as technically feasible (*see* wind power).

windpipe. *See* trachea.

wind power The use of wind energy to generate electricity. Because of the world shortage of conventional energy resources, wind turbines (aerogenerators), like other *alternative energy sources, have now become more attractive economically. Some advantages of wind power are that it is free from pollution, uses no fuel, and the times of peak output are likely to coincide with peak demand (i.e. cold windy days). Among the disadvantages are that it must usually be supplemented by other schemes, including electricity storage. It takes up a great deal of space and the best sites are on open ground rather than in the cities, where most power is needed.

There are several different designs of aerogenerator: some with a horizontal axis and blades like the familiar *windmill; some with specially shaped aerofoil blades rotating on a vertical axis. A large windmill-type generator, 37 metres high and producing about 3 megawatts, was installed on Orkney in 1988 and may become a prototype for a series supplying electricity to the national grid. Smaller aerogenerators may be useful for supplying one or two houses in a local community.

Windsor 42 18N 83 00W A city and port in E Canada, in SW Ontario on the Detroit River opposite *Detroit. Settled in the 18th century by French colonists, it is a transportation and manufacturing centre, producing motor vehicles, foods, pharmaceuticals, and metals. Windsor is the centre of a rich farming district. The University of Windsor (1963) is situated here. Population (1981): 192 083.

Windsor 51 29N 0 38W A town in SE England, in Berkshire on the River Thames. *Windsor Castle, a royal residence, dominates the town. Population (1981): 28 330.

Windsor, House of The name of Britain's royal family from 1917, when it replaced that of House of Saxe-Coburg-Gotha, of which Prince *Albert had been a member. In 1960 Elizabeth II declared that those of her descendants in the male line who were not princes or princesses would take the surname Mountbatten-Windsor, Mountbatten being Prince *Philip's surname. □ p. 1307.

Windsor Castle A royal residence in Windsor, Berkshire. It was begun by William the Conqueror as a stockaded earthwork. Many additions were made by subsequent monarchs, notably the keep by Henry III, St George's Chapel, an example of the *Perpendicular style, by Edward IV, and the Albert Memorial Chapel (so called by Queen Victoria) by Henry VII. Many monarchs are buried in these chapels. In the 16th and 17th centuries it began to be altered from a fortress to a palace, substantial rebuilding being carried out by Hugh May (1622–84) for Charles II, and later by Sir Jeffrey Wyatville (1766–1840) in the 19th century.

wind tunnel A device for testing the flow of air around an object, for example an aerofoil or aircraft, with a view to studying the lift, drag, streamlining, onset of *turbulence, etc. It consists of a duct with an electrically driven fan, usually with water-cooling systems to maintain the air at the correct temperature. *See also* aerodynamics; aeronautics.

Windward Islands (Spanish name: Islas de Barlovento) A West Indian group of islands forming part of the S Lesser Antilles. They comprise the islands of Martinique, St Lucia, St Vincent, the N Grenadines, and Grenada.

wine An alcoholic drink made from fermented grape juice. The grapes are first crushed, traditionally by treading, now generally by machine. This process brings the yeast on the grapeskins, visible as the "bloom," into contact with the sugar in the juice, which it then converts into ethanol (ethyl alcohol). Depending upon whether the fermentation is stopped when all, part, or only a little of the sugar has been converted, the resulting wine is dry, medium, or sweet. Table wines contain about 9–13% alcohol. Fortified wines (e.g. *port, *sherry), to which a spirit is added at some stage in production, contain about 16–23% alcohol. The bubbles in sparkling wines are caused by a secondary fermentation in the bottle (*see also* champagne).

Wines may be red, white, or rosé. Red wines are made from whole grapes; for white wines the grapeskins are removed at an early stage in production. True rosé wines are made from the grenache grape, from which the skins are removed before the juice is deeply stained by them. Favoured varieties of wine grapes include Pinot, Cabernet, Hermitage, Riesling, and Sylvaner. The variety of grape, the soil of the vineyard, and the local climate govern a wine's quality. The appellation "vintage" is now used by wine producers under

WINE *The major French wine-producing regions and some standard bottle shapes.*

strictly regulated conditions to designate a wine of a particular year that shows outstanding quality.

French wines are famous for their quality and diversity, espcially those produced in Burgundy and the chateaux of the Bordeaux area (the red varieties of which are called clarets). Germany produces fine white wines (hocks). Italian wines are very diverse, including red Lambrusco, red or white Chianti, red Valpolicella, and sweet Marsala. Spain and other European countries produce notable wines. Wine is also made in South Africa (since 1688), Australia (first commercial vineyard established in 1827), California, Chile, and elsewhere.

Wingate, Orde Charles (1903–44) British soldier, who led the *Chindits. A Zionist, he organized Jewish guerrillas in Palestine (1936–39). In World War II, after taking Addis Ababa from the Italians (1941), he formed the Chindits to disrupt communications behind the Japanese lines in Burma. He was killed in an aircrash.

Winkler, Hans Günter (1926–) West German show jumper, who was world champion in 1954 and 1955 and won every major individual title during his career, also taking five Olympic gold medals.

Winnipeg 49 53N 97 10W A city in W Canada, capital of Manitoba at the junction of the Assiniboine and Red Rivers. Established as a fur-trading post (1806), it expanded with the growth of farming and the arrival of the railway (1881) from E Canada. It is the distribution, wholesaling, financial, and manufacturing centre of the Canadian prairies and a major transportation junction. Winnipeg is the site of the University of

Manitoba and the Royal Winnipeg Ballet. Population (1981): 564 473.

Winnipeg, Lake A lake in W Canada, in S Manitoba. Emptying via the Nebon Rivers into Hudson Bay, it drains much of the Canadian prairies. It is exploited for tourism, fishing, and shipping. Area: 24 514 sq km (9465 sq mi).

Winstanley, Gerrard (c. 1609–60) English communist, leader of the *Diggers (1649–50). He was the author of the pamphlet *The Law of Freedom in a Platform* (1652), dedicated to Oliver Cromwell.

Winston Salem 36 05N 80 18W A city and port in the USA, in North Carolina. A major tobacco-growing and manufacturing centre, other products include textiles and furniture. Population (1980): 131 885.

winter aconite An early-flowering perennial herb of the genus *Eranthis* (7 species), native to temperate Europe, especially *E. hyemalis*, which is often grown in gardens. The flowers are cup-shaped, with six golden-yellow petals, and appear before the leaves. Family: *Ranunculaceae*.

wintergreen An evergreen creeping perennial herb or small shrub of the family *Pyrolaceae* (about 35 species), found in N temperate and arctic regions. The leaves are simple and the flowers are borne singly or in a terminal spike. They are white or pale-pink with five petals and the fruit is a capsule. Oil of wintergreen comes from the leaves of the winterberry (*Gaultheria procumbens*), a North American shrub, whereas the common wintergreen (*Pyrola minor*) is a herb of Eurasia and North America. Also in the family are the North American pipsissewas (genus *Chimaphila*), woodland herbs with leathery leaves and fragrant flowers.

Winterhalter, Franz Xavier (1806–73) German painter and lithographer, famous for his portraits of European royalty. His sitters included King Louis Philippe and Napoleon III as well as Queen Victoria and her family.

Winterthur 47 30N 8 45E A city in N Switzerland. It is an industrial centre with heavy engineering and cotton textiles. Population (1980 est): 86 758.

Winter War. *See* Russo-Finnish War.

Winthrop, John (1588–1649) English colonizer; the first governor of the *Massachusetts Bay Colony (1629–33, 1637–39, 1642–43, 1646–48). His son, **John Winthrop** (1606–76), became a lawyer and was one of the founders of Agawan (now Ipswich), Massachusetts. In 1662 he effected Massachusetts' union with Connecticut and New Haven. His scientific interests gained him a fellowship of the Royal Society in 1663.

wirehaired pointing griffon A breed of hunting dog developed in France during the late 19th century. It is strongly built with a short tail and a longish square muzzle. The harsh bristly coat is a mixture of grey, white, and brown. Height: 54–59 cm (dogs); 49–54 cm (bitches).

wireworm. *See* click beetle.

Wirral Peninsula A peninsula in NW England, in Merseyside and Cheshire between the estuaries of the Rivers Dee and Mersey. Chiefly low-lying, it serves mainly as a residential area for Liverpool. Industrial development is centred on Birkenhead, Port Sunlight, and Ellesmere Port.

Wisbech 52 40N 0 10E A town in E England, in N Cambridgeshire on the River Nene. Wisbech is a river port and market town in a market-gardening district. Population (1981): 17 332.

Wisconsin A state in the N central USA, situated between the Mississippi River in the W, Lake Michigan in the E, and Lake Superior in the N. The Central Lowlands, which cover the lower two-thirds of the state, give way in the N to the Superior Upland, which is part of the Canadian Shield and contains many forests and lakes. Manufacturing is the state's major economic activity and its industrial belt in the SE links Milwaukee to the Chicago area. Leading products include metal goods, machinery, paper products, and electrical and

HOUSE OF WINDSOR   *Members of the royal family who are descendants of Queen Victoria in the male line take the surname Windsor.*

transport equipment. The state is well known for its dairy products and livestock is also important. *History*: ceded to the USA by the British in 1783, large-scale immigration in the 1820s led to its organization as a territory (1836) and it became a state in 1848. Area: 145 438 sq km (56 154 sq mi). Population (1980): 4 705 335. Capital: Madison.

Wisdom of Solomon   Book of the *Apocrypha, an important example of Jewish "wisdom literature," which also includes the books of Proverbs, Job, Ecclesiastes, and Ecclesiasticus. It was originally written in Greek, probably by a Hellenized Jew of Alexandria in the 2nd century BC. In encouraging a search for wisdom, it describes its benefits, praises its divine source, which is God, and traces how wisdom has helped the Jews and confounded their enemies.

Wise, Thomas James   (1859-1937) British book collector, who turned his bibliographical expertise to forgery. Wise's main interest was in 19th-century English writers, whose works he energetically collected. He issued numerous catalogues and received academic honours, but in 1934 his forgeries of certain rare pamphlets were exposed.

Wiseman, Nicholas Patrick Stephen   (1802-65) British Roman Catholic prelate, born in Seville of Irish parents. Appointed rector of the English College in Rome in 1828, he later devoted himself to reviving Roman Catholicism in England. In 1850 he was made a cardinal and the first Archbishop of Westminster.

wisent. *See* bison.

Wishart, George   (c. 1513-46)· Scottish Protestant reformer and martyr. Charged with heresy in 1538, he fled to England and in 1539 to the Continent, where he translated into Scots the *First Helvetic Confession*. He later preached in many Scottish towns, converting, among others, John *Knox. At the instigation of Cardinal Beaton he was tried for heresy and burnt at the stake at St Andrews, in 1546.

Wiślany Zalew. *See* Vistula Lagoon.

Wismar   53 54N 11 23E A town and Baltic port in NW East Germany. Once a Hanseatic port, it passed to Sweden

under the Peace of *Westphalia (1648). Although pledged to Mecklenburg-Schwerin in 1803, Sweden did not renounce all rights to the city until 1903. Its industries include shipbuilding, fishing, and sugar refining. Population (1981 est): 57 800.

Wissler, Clark   (1870-1947) US anthropologist. Professor of anthropology at Yale University (1924-40), Wissler was famous for his research on the geographical and regional aspects of race and culture. His best-known book is *The American Indian* (1917).

Wisteria   A genus of twining usually woody vines (10 species), native to E Asia and North America and grown as ornamentals, especially *W. floribunda* from Japan, which may reach a height of 30 m. The compound leaves have paired pointed leaflets and the flowers, usually purple, are borne in large hanging clusters, up to 90 cm long. Family: *Leguminosae*.

witan   A body of 30 to 40 high-ranking laymen and ecclesiastics, which advised Anglo-Saxon kings on such major policy matters as foreign policy and taxation. It met only at the king's will and had no fixed procedure. As a court, it decided on cases affecting the king and other important persons.

Witbank   25 53S 29 13E A town in South Africa, in the E Transvaal, the centre of an important coalmining area. Population (1983 est): 83 400.

witchcraft   The supposed manipulation of natural events by persons using supernatural means. In Europe the biblical injunction "Thou shalt not suffer a witch to live" (Exodus 22.18) sanctioned widespread persecution. Social and religious upheavals in the 16th and 17th centuries brought an upsurge in witch hunts; the famous outbreak at Salem, Massachusetts (1692), is a paradigm case of witch hysteria. Witches were accused of worshipping the devil at nocturnal orgies (sabbaths), of keeping evil spirits (familiars), and of killing livestock, wrecking crops, and causing barrenness, impotence, and fits. Many traditional African communities hold witchcraft accountable for a similar range of inexplicable misfortunes. It is countered by witch-doctors who identify witches and suggest means of neutralizing their malign psychic powers.

witch hazel A shrub or small tree of the genus *Hamamelis* (6 species), native to E Asia and North America, especially the American *H. virginiana*, which is the source of witch-hazel lotion used in pharmacy. This and several other species are often grown as ornamentals, having small clusters of attractive yellow flowers, each with four strap-shaped petals. The fruit is a woody capsule surrounded by a yellow cuplike calyx. Family: *Hamamelidaceae*.

witchweed A parasitic herb of the genus *Striga* (about 10 species), native to the Old World tropics. Up to 75 cm tall, it has rough narrow sometimes scalelike leaves and solitary blue, purple, red, yellow, or white two-lipped flowers. The roots derive nutrients from the roots of other plants, including many crops. Family: *Scrophulariaceae*.

Witt, Johan de (1625-72) Dutch statesman, chief minister of the United Provinces of the Netherlands (1653-72). He ended the first *Dutch War and then improved the Dutch navy, which performed well in the second Dutch War. However, he lost his struggle to limit the executive power of the stadholder (William III of Orange and later of England) and resigned in 1670. He was killed by a rioting mob.

Witte, Sergei Yulievich (1849-1915) Russian statesman. As finance minister (1892-1903) Witte initiated the Russian industrial revolution, making capital available to industry and obtaining foreign loans. He greatly encouraged railway construction. As prime minister (1905-06), he was instrumental in founding the *Duma following the Revolution of 1905.

Wittelsbach The ruling dynasty of Bavaria and the Rhine Palatinate. Wittelsbachs ruled these German states from the late 12th century until deposed in 1918 in a republican coup.

Wittenberg 53 00N 11 41E A town in central East Germany, on the River *Elbe. The Reformation began here on 31 October, 1517, when Martin Luther nailed his 95 theses to the door of All Saints Church. The town is an important industrial centre. Population (1983 est): 54 043.

Wittgenstein, Ludwig (1889-1951) Austrian philosopher. After studying engineering in Vienna he turned to philosophy, studying under Bertrand *Russell at Cambridge (1912-13), where he eventually succeeded G. E. *Moore as professor. His two major works are the *Tractatus Logico-philosophicus* (1921) and the posthumously published *Philosophical Investigations* (1953). Wittgenstein's abiding preoccupation was with language, particularly with the problems that language's relationship to things pose for the philosopher. In his earlier work he developed the "picture theory" of language—words represent things by established conventions—but later he developed the more sophisticated "game" or "toolkit" models, in which actual usage is more important than set convention. This approach to language as a predominantly social phenomenon has been enormously influential among English-speaking philosophers.

Witwatersrand (*or* the Rand) A ridge of hills in NE South Africa. It extends about 160 km (99 mi) chiefly W of Johannesburg, forming the watershed between the Limpopo and Orange river systems. It has been worked for gold since the 1880s and now produces about one-third of the world's gold output.

woad A branching perennial or biennial herb, *Isatis tinctoria*, native to central and S Europe. Formerly cultivated for the blue dye extracted from its crushed leaves, it is now rare. Up to 120 cm tall, it has narrow leaves and terminal branching clusters of tiny four-petalled yellow flowers. Family: *Cruciferae*.

Wodehouse, Sir P(elham) G(renville) (1881-1975) US humorous writer, born in Britain. After 1909 he lived mostly abroad and became a US citizen in 1955. In his many comic novels featuring Bertie Wooster and his manservant Jeeves, including *The Inimitable Jeeves* (1923) and *The Code of the Woosters* (1938), he portrayed an English upper-class society fixed forever in the 1920s.

Woden. *See* Odin.

Woffington, Peg (Margaret W.; c. 1714-60) Irish actress. She acted in many Restoration comedies at Covent Garden, often taking male parts. She became the mistress and leading lady of David *Garrick.

Wöhler, Friedrich (1800-82) German chemist, who, while professor of chemistry at Göttingen University, synthesized urea from ammonium cyanate (1828). This was the first organic compound to have been derived from an inorganic compound, providing evidence against the theory that organic compounds contained a "vital force" absent in inorganic compounds. He also succeeded in isolating the elements aluminium, beryllium, and titanium.

wolf A wild *dog, *Canis lupus*, of Eurasia and North America. Wolves are 140-190 cm long including the tail (30-55 cm). They live in packs of 5-30 animals—which patrol their own territories—and feed mainly on mice, fish, and carrion but also attack deer. Mating is often for life and both parents may share in rearing the pups.
Wolves in colder climate are generally larger and shaggier and form bigger packs. There is an almost white N Siberian race, while the Indian pale-footed wolf is small and grey. *See also* timber wolf. □mammal.

Wolf, Hugo (1860-1903) Austrian composer. He studied briefly at the Vienna conservatoire and earned his living as a teacher, conductor, and critic. He died insane in an asylum. He wrote 300 *Lieder* (many of which were settings of poems by Goethe and Mörike), the opera *Der Corregidor* (1895), and an *Italian Serenade* for string quartet.

Wolfe, Charles (1791-1823) Irish poet and clergyman. He is remembered for a single poem, "The Burial of Sir John Moore at Corunna," commemorating the British general who died in the Peninsular War.

Wolfe, James (1727-59) British soldier. He distinguished himself against the Jacobites in the 1740s and after the outbreak of the Seven Years' War was sent to Canada. He excelled, under *Amherst, in the capture of Louisburg from the French (1758) and in the following year he besieged *Montcalm in Quebec. His forces scaled the undefended Heights of Abraham from the St Lawrence and a pitched battle ensued in which both commanders were killed. The British victory established their supremacy in Canada.

Wolfe, Thomas (1900-38) US novelist. After abandoning an attempt to become a dramatist, he wrote four long and lyrically powerful novels, beginning with *Look Homeward, Angel* (1929), all based on autobiographical material. The final two were published posthumously.

Wolfenden, John Frederick, Baron (1906–85) British educationalist and government offical. Vice chancellor of Reading University (1950-63) and director of the British Museum (1969-73), Wolfenden chaired the Committee on Homosexual Offences and Prostitution; the Wolfenden Report (1957) recommended that private homosexual acts between consenting adults be legalized.

Wolf-Ferrari, Ermanno (1876-1948) Italian composer of German-Italian parentage. He spent most of his life in Venice, composing such operas as *The School for Fathers* (1906) and *Susanna's Secret* (1909).

wolf fish A slender marine fish, *Anarhichas lupus*, also called catfish, found in the N Atlantic and North Sea, down to 300 m. It has a blue-green or greenish body up to 120 cm long, with dark vertical bars, a long blunt head, doglike teeth, long dorsal and anal fins, and no pelvic fins. It feeds on bottom-dwelling hard-shelled animals. Family: *Anarhichadidae*; order: *Perciformes*.

Wölfflin, Heinrich (1864-1945) Swiss art historian. A pupil of Jakob Burckhardt (1818-97), Wölfflin wrote chiefly on baroque and classical art. He was the principal exponent of the formal school of art historians, which analyses style by changes of form in art.

wolfhound. *See* borzoi; Irish wolfhound.

Wolfit, Sir Donald (1902-68) British actor and manager. He acted all the major Shakespearian roles, receiving especial acclaim for his Lear, first performed in 1943. In 1937 he founded his own touring company. He was knighted in 1957.

wolfram. *See* tungsten.

wolframite The principal ore of tungsten, consisting of ferrous tungstate, (Fe,Mn)WO₄. It is brown, black, grey, or reddish in colour and is found particularly in quartz veins associated with granitic rocks. *See also* scheelite.

Wolfram von Eschenbach (c. 1170-c. 1220) German poet. A knight, he served at several courts. His great romance, *Parzifal* (c. 1212), is the first German work to use the story of the Holy Grail and is the basis of Wagner's opera. Allegorizing man's spiritual development, it tells how the innocent fool becomes the wise keeper of the Grail.

wolfsbane. *See* aconite.

Wolfsburg 52 27N 10 49E A city in NE West Germany, in Lower Saxony on the Mittelland Canal. Founded in 1938, it grew around the Volkswagen car factory. Population (1980 est): 126 800.

Wolfson, Sir Isaac (1897-) British businessman, who founded (1946) Great Universal Stores Ltd. A philanthropist, he endowed the Wolfson Foundation in 1955 for the advancement of health, education, and youth in the UK and the Commonwealth. University College, Cambridge, was renamed Wolfson College in 1973 after a grant from the Wolfson Foundation; Wolfson College, Oxford, was founded in 1966 with grants from the Wolfson and Ford Foundations. Both colleges are for graduate students.

wolf spider A *spider, also called hunting spider, belonging to a widespread family (*Lycosidae*; over 175 species). Wolf spiders, up to 25 mm long, are dark brown with long stout legs and live on or in the ground, often in specially constructed tubes. They are usually active at night, hunting prey rather than trapping it in webs. The female carries the eggs and young.

Wollongong, Greater 34 25S 150 52E A city in Australia, in New South Wales. It comprises an extensive urban area, extending 48 km (30 mi) along the coast and including the towns of Wollongong, Bulli, and Port Kembla. Many industries are based on the rich Bulli coal deposits, including metal processing, engineering, and chemicals. A university was established in 1975. Population (1983 est): 234 800.

Wollstonecraft, Mary (1759-97) British writer. She was a member of a group of political radicals that included Tom Paine and her husband, the social philosopher William *Godwin. Her best-known work is *A Vindication of the Rights of Women* (1792), which argued for equal opportunities for all in education. She died in giving birth to her daughter, who became Mary *Shelley.

Wolseley, Garnet Joseph, 1st Viscount (1833-1913) British field marshal. He fought in the Crimean War and against the Indian Mutiny in the 1850s and suppressed an Egyptian rebellion with his victory at Tall-all Kabir (1882). In 1884 he led the expedition to rescue Gordon in Khartoum. His chief importance lies in his army reforms, which completed *Cardwell's work.

Wolsey, Thomas, Cardinal (c. 1475-1530) English churchman and statesman; Lord Chancellor (1515-29) under Henry VIII. He entered Henry's service in 1509 and became (1514) Bishop of Lincoln and then Archbishop of York and (1515) a cardinal. He used his position to amass a huge personal fortune that did much on the eve of the Reformation to bring the Church into disrepute. As chancellor he attempted to make England a significant European power and interfered unsuccessfully in the conflict between Francis

I of France and Emperor *Charles V. Wolsey's attempts to raise taxes to pay for his foreign policy encountered violent opposition. He fell from power after failing to persuade the pope to permit Henry to divorce Catherine of Aragon and died on his way to face trial in London. He founded Cardinal's College (later Christ Church) at Oxford.

Wolverhampton 52 36N 2 08W A town in central England, in West Midlands in the Black Country. Metalworking and engineering are the principal industries. Traditionally known for locks and keys, it also produces bicycles, tools, hardware, and chemicals. Population (1981): 252 447.

wolverine A carnivorous mammal, *Gulo gulo*, also called glutton, inhabiting northern evergreen forests of Europe, Asia, and America. It is heavily built, about 1 m long and weighing about 25 kg, and hunts alone, typically ambushing lemmings and hares (although it can overcome an old or unfit reindeer). Family: *Mustelidae*.

womb (*or* uterus) The part of a woman's reproductive tract in which the fetus develops (*see* Plate IV). The womb is a hollow muscular organ, about 7.5 cm long in the absence of pregnancy. It is connected by the vagina to the outside and to the ovaries by the Fallopian tubes. In a nonpregnant woman the lining of the womb is shed at monthly intervals (*see* menstruation). During *childbirth the womb, which is greatly enlarged (about 30 cm long), undergoes strong contractions to expel the baby. *See also* cervix.

wombat A bearlike *marsupial belonging to the family *Phascolomidae* (2-3 species), of Australia (including Tasmania). The coarse-haired wombat (*Phascolomis ursinus*) is about 1 m long and has short powerful legs with strong claws, which it uses for tunnelling underground. It feeds on grass, roots, and tree bark.

Women's Institutes, National Federation of A British organization founded in 1915 to develop the quality, chiefly through further education, of rural life for women. Local institutes meet monthly to hear talks on a wide range of subjects. The Federation has a residential college, where short courses are organized, and its members run some 300 cooperative markets throughout the UK.

women's movement The social movement towards changing the subordinate role of women in society. Mary Wollstonecraft, author of *A Vindication of the Rights of Women* (1792), was a pioneer of the movement. In the 19th century developing concepts of *socialism grew alongside the analysis and criticism of the position of women in the family. In the UK the suffragist movement encompassed both those who sought votes for women on the limited property qualifications then applied to men and those, such as Sylvia *Pankhurst and Keir *Hardie, who sought universal adult suffrage. From 1903 the Women's Social and Political Union (WSPU), led by Emmeline and Christabel Pankhurst, was at the forefront of the movement. Its militant members, known as suffragettes, attacked property, refused to pay taxes, and staged public demonstrations, for which they were repeatedly imprisoned. The notorious "Cat and Mouse Act" (1913) allowed for the temporary release of suffragettes whose health was endangered by hunger striking and forcible feeding.

During World War I the women's organizations directed themselves to supporting the war effort and in 1918 the vote was granted to women aged 30 and over, subject to educational and property qualifications that were removed in 1928, making men and women politically equal. The present women's movement emerged in the 1960s; in the USA small "consciousness-raising" groups were formed and, in the UK, the Women's Liberation Workshop was established in London (1969) as a coordinating centre for local women's groups. In 1971 the first four basic demands of the movement (equal pay, equal educational and job opportunities, free contraception and abortion on demand, and 24-hour nurseries) were launched. Several legal reforms have been achieved in the UK, notably the Equal Pay Act (1970) and the Sex Discrimination Act (1975), but women's groups throughout the world are still actively campaigning for childcare, contraception, and abortion facilities as well as for refuges for battered wives, rape crisis centres, and women's health clinics.

Women's Royal Voluntary Service A British organization founded in 1938 as the Women's Voluntary Service (WVS). Its members work for local authorities or on national government schemes and perform many voluntary welfare services, including Meals on Wheels, which provides for the delivery of meals to those unable to shop and cook for themselves.

Wŏnsan 39 20N 127 25E A port in SE North Korea, on the Sea of Japan. Badly damaged during the Korean War (1950–53), its industries have since been rebuilt and include oil refining, shipbuilding, railway engineering, and chemicals. Population (1980 est): 398 000.

wood The hard tissue of the stems and branches of trees and shrubs, beneath the bark, consisting of *xylem cells strengthened with deposits of lignin. The newest xylem—sapwood—is essential for transport of water and nutrients up the tree. As the xylem ages lignin is deposited within the cells, which eventually die. The central part of the trunk—heartwood—consists of dead xylem, which is darker than sapwood due to deposits of tannins and resins. Conifers are referred to as softwoods because the xylem is porous; broad-leaved (angiosperm) trees, which are called hardwoods, contain more fibres and are therefore stronger (*see* timber). □plant.

Wood A family of English potters working in Staffordshire (England) in the 18th and 19th centuries. Related by marriage to Josiah *Wedgwood, the most famous member **Ralph Wood I** (1715–72) trained under John *Astbury; he established a factory at Burslem, where he specialized in earthenware figure groups and made the first *toby jug (1762). His cousin **Aaron Wood** (1717–85) was employed by many Staffordshire potters as a modeller. Ralph's business was carried on by his son **Ralph Wood II** (1748–95) and later by his nephew **Enoch Wood** (1759–1840), who was famous for his pottery busts of Shakespeare, Wesley, Handel, etc. The business closed down in 1846.

Wood A family of English architects, known for their contribution to town planning and urban classical architecture. They mainly worked in Bath, which **John Wood the Elder** (1704–54) began to develop in the late 1720s. In residential streets, such as Queen Square (1729–36) and the Circus (begun in 1754) he extended the classical form to link many buildings into one architectural block. His work was continued by his son **John Wood the Younger** (1728–81), who designed the famous Royal Crescent (1767–75) and the Assembly Rooms (1769–71).

Wood, Sir Henry (Joseph) (1869–1944) British conductor. He was an organist and composer but is remembered for the London Promenade concerts, which he established at the Queen's Hall, London, and which continued at the Albert Hall after the Queen's Hall was bombed in World War II.

Wood, Mrs Henry (1814–87) British novelist. The most famous of her many popular melodramatic novels is *East Lynne* (1861), concerning an upper-class wife who returns in disguise to her family after an unhappy love affair; it was repeatedly dramatized. From 1867 she edited the magazine *Argosy*.

woodbine. *See* honeysuckle; Virginia creeper.

wood carving The art of carving sculptures or architectural and furniture decoration in wood. It has been practised universally since ancient times. *African art principally consists of wood carving. In Europe some of the finest decorative wood carving was achieved in medieval churches. The best-known British decorative carver was Grinling

*Gibbons. In the 20th century sculptors, such as *Brancusi and Henry *Moore, have exploited the special characteristics of wood—its vertical graining and organic nature—in the trend towards retaining the inherent characteristics of materials in finished sculptures.

woodchat A small *shrike, *Lanius senator*, occurring in wooded Mediterranean regions. The male has dark wings, back, and tail patches, white underparts, a chestnut neck and cap, and a broad black band across the forehead; the female is duller.

woodchuck. *See* marmot.

woodcock A Eurasian gamebird, *Scolopax rusticola*, occurring in dense damp woodland and generally active at night. It has a stocky body, 34 cm long, and a russet plumage with a dark-barred head and underparts and a white-tipped tail. Woodcocks have long bills and feed on worms and insect larvae. Males perform a slow display flight (called roding) during courtship. Family: *Scolopacidae* (sandpipers, snipe).

woodcreeper An arboreal passerine bird belonging to a family (*Dendrocolaptidae*; 48 species) ranging through Central and South America. Woodcreepers are typically 20–30 cm long and have stout bills, powerful feet with long claws, and an olive-brown plumage with pale stripes on the head and underparts. The tail is stiff, providing support when it climbs spirally up trees, prising off bark and probing in crevices for insects and spiders.

woodcut A relief *printing technique. The design is drawn on the surface of a block of wood, all the undrawn parts being cut away to produce the white areas of the print. The design is then transferred to paper by pressing the inked block onto the paper. The woodcut was used in China (c. 5th century AD) for textile design but its history in Europe dates from the 14th century and is closely connected with the early printed book. Its special qualities—cheapness, boldness, and simplicity—made it particularly suitable for popular book illustration. Leading 16th-century German artists, such as *Dürer and *Holbein, used the medium to supreme effect. Although subsequently used for book illustration, it was only revived as an art form in the late 19th century by *Gauguin and *Munch.

wood engraving A technique of printing images, refined in the 18th century by Thomas □Bewick and used extensively during the 19th century for reproductive engraving. Original modern practitioners include Eric *Gill. The surface of the woodblock is cut away to leave raised areas which, when treated with ink, will appear dark when printed, in contrast to the white line of the incised areas. Boxwood is used for its fine grain, the block being cut transversely. Wood engraving produces a more subtle effect than *woodcut.

woodlouse A terrestrial crustacean of the suborder *Oniscoidea*, found in damp shady places under stones, logs, etc. Woodlice have a body covering of armour-like plates: they can breathe air (through specially modified gills) but require damp surroundings to avoid desiccation. A common species is the pill bug or woodlouse (*Armadillidium vulgare*), about 17 mm long, which rolls into a ball when disturbed. It has spread from Europe to occur in leaf litter in wooded areas all over the world. Common genera: *Oniscus, Porcellio*; order: *Isopoda.

woodpecker A bird belonging to a family (*Picidae*; about 220 species) occurring worldwide except Madagascar, Australia, and New Zealand (*see* Plate V). 9–57 cm long, woodpeckers have multicoloured plumage, often barred or spotted. Most are exclusively arboreal, chiselling through bark with their long straight bills in search of insects, which are extracted with a long sticky protrusible tongue. Their short strong feet with large claws and the stiff wedge-shaped tail are adaptations for climbing. *See also* ivory-billed woodpecker; wryneck.

wood pigeon A large Eurasian *pigeon, *Columba palum-

bus, which is a serious pest on farmland, eating grain and other crops. 40 cm long, it has a predominantly grey plumage with a black-tipped tail, brownish back and wings, white wing patches, and a green, purple, and white neck patch.

woodrush A grasslike perennial plant of the genus *Luzula* (about 80 species), occurring chiefly in cold N temperate regions. The Eurasian great woodrush (*L. sylvatica*) has leaves up to 30 cm long and 2 cm wide, which are fringed with colourless hairs. Family: *Juncaceae* (rush family).

wood sorrel A herbaceous plant of the genus *Oxalis* (about 800 species), of temperate and tropical regions, especially *O. acetosella*, of Europe. This species has compound three-part leaves (made up of heart-shaped leaflets) and solitary white five-petalled flowers. Many species are ornamentals and some, including the vegetable oca (*O. tuberosa*), have edible tubers. Family: *Oxalidaceae*.

WOODCOCK   *The mottled plumage provides excellent camouflage in its woodland habitat.*

Woodstock 51 52N 1 21W A small market town in S central England, in Oxfordshire. Nearby is *Blenheim Palace; an earlier royal palace at Woodstock was destroyed after the Civil War. Population (1981): 2036.

Woodville, Elizabeth (c. 1437-92) The wife from 1464 of Edward IV of England. Royal patronage of her family caused dissensions among Edward's Yorkist supporters and on his death (1483) the power of the Woodvilles was undermined by the Duke of Gloucester, who deposed Elizabeth's son Edward V and became Richard III. Elizabeth was retired to a convent.

Woodward, Robert Burns (1917-   ) US chemist, who, while working at Harvard, won the 1965 Nobel Prize for his syntheses of a number of organic compounds. His first success was his synthesis of quinine in 1944. He then went on to synthesize strychnine, cortisone, cholesterol, and chlorophyll as well as an antibiotic.

woodwasp A *sawfly belonging to the families *Xiphydriidae* (Europe and North America), *Sytexidae* (North America), or *Orussidae* (worldwide). *Xiphydriidae* larvae bore into deciduous trees, such as alder, birch, and maple. *Sytexidae* are restricted to the incense cedar tree. *Orussidae* larvae are external parasites on wood-dwelling beetle larvae. *See also* horntail.

woodwind instruments   Blown musical instruments in which a column of air is made to vibrate either by blowing across a mouth hole, as in the flute, or by making a single or a double reed vibrate, as in the oboe, bassoon, clarinet, and saxophone. The length of the vibrating column is varied by opening and closing holes, either with the finger or by means of keys.

woodworm A wood-boring beetle of the genus *Anobium*, especially the furniture beetle (*A. punctatum*), 5 mm long, which damages furniture and old buildings. The larvae bore into wood and emerge when adult, leaving large numbers of holes. In time, the wood is reduced to dust. Family: *Anobiidae*.

Wookey Hole A village named after a nearby limestone cavern in the Mendip Hills near Wells in Somerset (SW England). Bones of palaeolithic man and extinct animals, together with flint implements, show that the cave was inhabited over a long period.

wool Fibres obtained from the fleeces of domestic sheep. Elastic, resilient, and absorbent, it is also an excellent insulator because of its bulk, the result of its curliness (crimp). The fleeces of different breeds vary widely. *Merino wool is the best in quality; it is short, fine, soft, and the most crimpy. It now comes chiefly from Australia, South Africa, South America, and the USA. Garments labelled "Pure New Wool" are 100% merino. Wools from the 26 British breeds vary widely, while New Zealand sheep are crossbreeds of merino and British; durable and resilient, British and New Zealand wools are used, for example, in *tweeds and blankets. The wool of Asian sheep and mountain breeds is long and coarse; being very strong, it is used chiefly for carpets. Since World War II synthetic fibres have been mixed with wool.

Woolf, (Adeline) Virginia (*born* Stephen; 1882-1941) British novelist. A central figure of the *Bloomsbury group, she developed an impressionistic style in which she attempted to express the essential fluidity of existence. Her novels include *Mrs Dalloway* (1925), *To the Lighthouse* (1927), and *The Waves* (1931). She also wrote biographies and criticism, including a series of essays entitled *The Common Reader* (1925-32). She committed suicide by drowning after the recurrence of a mental illness. Her husband **Leonard (Sidney) Woolf** (1880-1969), whom she married in 1912 and with whom she founded the Hogarth Press in 1917, was literary editor of the *Nation* (1923-30) and wrote five volumes of autobiography (1960-69).

Woollett, William (1735-85) British engraver. He engraved topographical plates and after 1760 paintings by Claude, achieved a wide reputation, particularly with his engraving (1776) after Benjamin *West's *Death of General Wolfe*.

Woolley, Sir Leonard (1880-1960) British archaeologist. He worked at *Carchemish and *Tell el-Amarna but is famous chiefly for his brilliant excavations at *Ur (1922-34), his popular accounts of which stimulated widespread interest in the archaeology of the biblical lands.

woolly bear. *See* tiger moth.

woolly monkey A large long-tailed monkey belonging to the genus *Lagothrix* (3 species), of South America. The smoky woolly monkey (*L. cana*) has short pale hair and dark head, arms, legs, and tail. Males may grow to 120 cm long including the tail (60-70 cm). They have strong teeth and jaws and feed on fruit, leaves and unripe nuts. Family: *Cebidae*.

woolly rhinoceros A rhinoceros belonging to the extinct genus *Coelodonta*, which inhabited Eurasia and North Africa during the Pleistocene epoch (2.5 million to 10 000 years ago). Well-preserved specimens found in ice and oil deposits show that it was a large shaggy-coated animal with two horns, the front one very long and sharp.

woolly spider monkey A rare monkey, *Brachyteles arachnoides*, of SE Brazil. It has long legs, short woolly fur, and a prehensile tail and is thought to be arboreal and vegetarian. Family: *Cebidae*.

woolsack A large red cushion, stuffed with wool, that is the seat of the Lord Chancellor when acting as speaker of the House of Lords. It is supposed to have been placed there in the middle ages, when the wool trade was important.

Woolwich A district mainly in the Greater London borough of Greenwich, on the River Thames. It was an important Tudor dockyard and naval base. It contains the Royal Arsenal (founded in 1805).

Woolworth, F(rank) W(infield) (1852–1919) US businessman, who created a chain of over a thousand shops across the USA selling low-priced goods. The first was opened in 1879 in Utica, New York. The Woolworth Building in New York, which he commissioned, was the world's tallest building (1913–30). He also opened stores in many other countries, including the UK.

Woomera 31 11S 136 54E A town in central South Australia. It is the site of the Long Range Weapons Establishment and the launching base for space satellites of ELDO (European Space Vehicle Launcher Development Organization). Population (1984): 1800.

Wootton, Barbara, Baroness (1897–) British educationalist and economist. She worked in the fields of politics, social welfare, and penal reform and is the author of such books as *Social Science and Social Pathology* (1959).

Worcester 42 17N 71 48W A city in the USA, in Massachusetts on the Blackstone River. Settled in 1673, textile manufacturing began in 1789 and the country's first corduroy cloth was produced here. The Free-Soil Party, opposing the extension of slavery, developed from a meeting here in 1848. A cultural and educational centre, it is the site of Clark University (1887). Manufactures include precision instruments and chemicals. Population (1980): 161 799.

Worcester 52 11N 2 13W A city in W central England, the administrative centre of Hereford and Worcester on the River Severn. The cathedral, begun in 1084, is mainly 14th-century. At the battle of Worcester (1651) Charles II was defeated by Cromwell. It is famous for its porcelain, gloves, and furniture. Population (1981): 74 247.

Worcester porcelain A soft-paste English porcelain of first rank made in Worcester, England, from about 1751. Early wares derive from contemporary silver shapes and oriental porcelain. The factory is famous for fine transfer printing, painting, and gilding by foremost craftsmen.

Worcestershire A former county of W England. Under local government reorganization in 1974 it became part of the new county of *Hereford and Worcester.

word processor A form of computerized *typewriter enabling documents, letters, etc., to be created, edited, printed, and stored. A typical word processor will consist of a keyboard, visual-display unit, a disk backing store, and a high-quality printer with an output comparable to an electric typewriter and a facility for using a range of paper sizes. Software packages supplied with word processors usually enable text to be justified and correctly hyphenated, italic and bold faces to be used, and tables to be set.

Wordsworth, William (1770–1850) British poet. Born in Cumberland, he attended Cambridge University and became an enthusiastic republican during a visit to Revolutionary France (1791–92), where he fathered a child by a French girl, Annette Vallon. In 1795 he met S. T. *Coleridge, with whom he collaborated on *Lyrical Ballads* (1798), a seminal work of the Romantic movement. In 1799 he settled in the Lake District, where, cared for devotedly by his wife Mary and his sister Dorothy, he wrote what is usually considered his masterpiece, a verse autobiography entitled *The Prelude* (completed 1805; published 1850). In this and other poems he described his feelings of mystical union with nature.

work The product of a force and the distance through which it causes a body to move in the direction of the force. Work, like energy, is measured in *joules.

Workers' Educational Association. *See* adult education.

work hardening The strengthening of metal by hammering or rolling it without heating. Metal consists of small crystals (grains). Softness or ductility is caused by irregularities (dislocations) in the grains that are able to move and change the crystal shape under stress. Movement of dislocations is blocked at the boundaries between grains. Continued working makes the dislocations collect at the grain boundaries, thus making the metal harder. *See also* heat treatment.

workhouses Institutions set up in the 17th century in Britain, and also found elsewhere in Europe, to provide employment and shelter for paupers. However, the 1834 Poor Law Amendment Act made it necessary for anyone seeking assistance to enter a workhouse, which because of their inhuman rules soon became dreaded places.

Working Men's Club and Institute Union A club founded by the Rev Henry Solly in 1862 and now having over 4000 affiliated clubs throughout the UK. The Working Men's Clubs are nonpolitical and provide educational and recreational facilities. General secretary: J. Johnson.

WILLIAM WORDSWORTH *A profile of Wordsworth drawn in 1807 by the sculptor Sir Francis Chantrey (1781-1841).*

works' council A committee of management and employees in a work place, that considers employees' grievances (*see also* industrial democracy). In countries in which works' councils are common, such as West Germany, *shop stewards tend to be less important than in countries, such as the UK, in which councils are uncommon.

World Bank. *See* International Bank for Reconstruction and Development.

World Council of Churches An organization of more than 200 Protestant and Orthodox churches. A product of the *ecumenical movement, it was founded at Amsterdam in 1948, with headquarters at Geneva. Membership includes almost all Christian Churches except the Roman Catholic, which sends observers and cooperates with it.

World Cup An international association football competition first held in 1930 and thereafter every four years, except during World War II. It is organized by the *Fédération internationale de Football association.

World Federation of Trade Unions An international association of national federations of trades unions, founded in 1945. A number of western trades-union federations withdrew in 1949 to establish the *International Confederation of Free Trade Unions.

World Health Organization (WHO)

A specialized agency of the *United Nations established in 1948 to facilitate "the attainment by all peoples of the highest possible level of health." WHO supports programmes to eradicate diseases (in 1979 WHO was able to report that smallpox had ceased to exist), carries out and finances epidemiological research, trains health workers, strengthens national health services, and has established international health regulations; it also provides aid in emergencies and disasters. Its headquarters are in Geneva.

World Meterological Organization (WMO)

A specialized agency of the *United Nations established in 1951 with the aim of standardizing international meteorological observations and improving the exchange of weather information. Its chief activities are the World Weather Watch programme, which coordinates facilities and services provided by member states, and a research and development programme that aims to extend knowledge of the natural and human-induced variability of climate. Its headquarters are in Geneva.

World War I

(1914-18) The Great War between the *Allied Powers, including the UK, with countries of the British Empire, France, Russia, Belgium, Japan, Serbia, Italy (from May, 1915), Portugal (from March, 1916), Romania (from August, 1916), the USA (from April, 1917), and Greece (from July, 1917) on one side, and the *Central Powers, including Germany, Austria-Hungary, Turkey (from November, 1914), and Bulgaria (from October, 1915) on the other. Its causes included fear of the German Empire's European and colonial ambitions since its defeat of France in the Franco-Prussian War (1870-71). Tensions among European powers were expressed by the formation of the *Triple Alliance of Germany and Austria-Hungary (1879) and Italy (1882) and of the *Triple Entente between France and Russia (1893) and France and the UK (1904; see Entente Cordiale). Rivalries surfaced in the crises in Morocco in 1905-06 and 1911 and in Bosnia in 1909; the immediate cause of the war lay in the conflict of interests between Russia and Austria-Hungary in the Balkans. On 28 June, 1914, the heir to the Austro-Hungarian throne, Archduke Francis Ferdinand, was assassinated at Sarajevo in Bosnia by a Serbian nationalist and on 28 July Austria-Hungary, with German support, declared war on Serbia. On 29 July Russia mobilized its forces in support of Serbia; on 1 August Germany declared war on Russia and on 3 August, upon France. Germany's invasion of Belgium brought the UK into the war at midnight on 4 August. The main theatres of war were the Western and Eastern Fronts, the Middle East, Italy, and the German colonies in Africa and the Pacific.

Western Front: German strategy at the start of the war was based on the *Schlieffen plan, which envisaged a rapid flanking movement through the Low Countries. The German forces under von Moltke advanced rapidly through Belgium until they were forced by the British Expeditionary Force (BEF) and the French under Joffre, at the first battle of the Marne (5-9 Sept), to retreat across the River Aisne. Germany's effort to reach the Channel was thwarted at the first battle of Ypres (12 Oct-11 Nov) and the combatants settled, on either side of a line from Ostend to Switzerland, to the futile trench warfare for which World War I is notorious. The year 1915 saw a series of inconclusive battles with huge loss of life—at Neuve-Chapelle (March), again at Ypres (April-May), where the Germans used poison gas for the first time, and at Loos (Sept). On 21 February, 1916, the Germans launched a crippling attack on the French at Verdun but on 1 July Haig, who had succeeded Sir John French as commander of the BEF, opened the crucial battle

of the Somme, during which *tanks were used (by the British) for the first time and where the Allies lost some 600 000 men and the Germans, about 650 000. In early 1917 the Germans under Ludendorff withdrew behind the *Hindenburg line; in April Haig took Vimy Ridge (with the loss of 132 000 men); but the French campaign in Champagne was disastrous and in mid-May Gen R. G. Nivelle (1856-1924) was replaced by Pétain. With the USA (incensed by German *submarine warfare) now participating, on 31 July Britain launched the third battle of Ypres and by 6 November had taken Passchendaele (with 245 000 British losses). In the spring of 1918 Germany thrust a bulge in the Allied line, which Foch was able to wipe out at the second battle of the Marne. Ludendorff was forced back to the Hindenburg line, which in September was broken by Haig between Saint Quentin and Cambrai. By October Germany was suing for peace.

Eastern Front: in August, 1914, the Russians advanced into E Prussia but were defeated at *Tannenburg. When late in 1914 Turkey attacked Russia in the Caucasus Mountains, the Allies launched the **Gallipoli campaign**, at first a naval (Feb-March) and then a military operation fought mainly by Australian and New Zealand forces (see ANZAC). It failed to break through the Dardanelles and by January, 1916, the Allies had withdrawn. Germany's offensive on the Eastern Front in the summer of 1915 forced Russia back and after the Central Powers had overcome Poland, most of Lithuania, and Serbia the Allies landed at Salonika; the ensuing **Macedonian campaign** continued without progress until Bulgaria at last capitulated in September, 1918. The failure of the Allies to relieve Russia led to its collapse following the outbreak of the Russian Revolution (March, 1917).

WORLD WAR I   *The Eastern Front.*

Middle East: the **Mesopotamian campaign**, intended to protect oil installations, was launched with the landing of an Indian force at Abadan on 6 November, 1914. Early advances were halted when the Allies failed to take Baghdad (November, 1915) and in April, 1916, they lost Kut al-Amara to the Turks. In February, 1917, it was retaken and, in March, Baghdad fell. Meanwhile the Allies had invaded Palestine and, aided by the Arab revolt, Allenby took Jerusalem in December, 1917; his victory at Megiddo (September, 1918) and capture of Damascus and Aleppo finally crushed the Turks.

Italy: the Italian front was maintained along the River Isonzo through 11 battles until 1917, when the Italians were forced by Austria-Hungary to retreat from Caporetto (Oct-Nov) in an overwhelming defeat. In October, 1918, however, Austria-Hungary was defeated at Vittorio-Veneto and in November finally capitulated.

War at sea and in the air: at **sea** the superior British navy was dominant until shaken by the battle of *Jutland in May, 1916. Although defeated off Coronel in November, 1914, victory in December off the Falkland Islands enabled Britain, with Australia, New Zealand, and Japan, to take the German colonies in Africa and the Pacific by September, 1916. German raids on the English coast began in December, 1914, but were repudiated by Beatty's victory at Dogger Bank in January, 1915. The real threat to the Allies at sea came from the German U-boats, which sunk some 6000 ships, including the *Lusitania, in the course of the war. At their most active in 1917, their effectiveness was reduced following the introduction by Lloyd George of the convoy system. World War I was the first war in which **aircraft** were used: in 1915 the German Zeppelins began to attack British cities and in 1917 German aircraft were also thus employed. Some air combat took place on the Western and Eastern Fronts and towards the end of the war the newly established Royal Air Force (comprising the former Royal Flying Corps and the Royal Naval Air Service) was bombing German cities.

Conclusion: with the defeat of the Turks and Bulgarians in September, 1918, and of Germany on the Western Front and Austria-Hungary in Italy in October, revolt broke out in Germany. On 9 November the German emperor, William II, fled and on 11 November Germany signed the armistice. On 18 January, 1919, the Allies met at the *Paris Peace Conference to determine the peace settlement, which was signed by Germany (the Treaty of Versailles) on 28 June. The Allies lost some 5 million lives (of which 3 million were French and Russian) in the war and the Central Powers, some 3.5 million (of which 3 million were German and Austro-Hungarian). A further 21 million combatants were wounded.

World War II (1939-45) The war between the Allied Powers, including the UK and countries of the Commonwealth, France (until June 1940; thereafter the Free French), the Soviet Union (from June, 1941), the USA (from December, 1941), and China (from December, 1941) on one side, and the *Axis Powers, including Germany, Italy (from June, 1940), and Japan (from December, 1941) on the other. The war was caused by the failure of the *Paris Peace Conference to provide for the maintenance of international security after World War I and by the territorial ambitions of Nazi Germany under Adolf Hitler. In March, 1938, Germany annexed Austria (*see* Anschluss) and in September, following the *Munich Agreement, the *Sudetenland. In March, 1939, Hitler occupied the rest of Czechoslovakia and Britain and France guaranteed to support Poland—Hitler's next objective—against German aggression. On 23 May Hitler came to an agreement with Mussolini's Italy, which in April had conquered Albania. Hitler's and Stalin's non-aggression pact followed on 23 August and Britain, France, and Poland made an agreement of mutual assistance on 25

Aug. On 1 September Germany invaded Poland and two days later Britain and France declared war.

Western Europe (1939–41): by 27 September Poland had succumbed to the German *Blitzkreig. The Soviet invasion of Finland (*see* Russo-Finnish War) brought Finnish capitulation by March, 1940, and in April Germany invaded Denmark and Norway. The Allied failure in Scandinavia led to Neville Chamberlain's resignation and on 10 May, the day that Germany invaded Belgium and the Netherlands, Churchill became Britain's prime minister. The German advance across the River Meuse to the coast outflanked the *Maginot line and separated the main French force from the French First Army, the Belgian army, and the British Expeditionary Force; on 26 May an Allied evacuation from the Continent was ordered. Between 29 May and 4 June, in operation Dynamo, some 338 226 Allied troops were rescued from Dunkirk by the Royal Navy, and a fleet of small boats manned by their private owners, supported by the RAF Fighter Command. On 22 June Pétain signed the French armistice with Germany, following which French resistance to the Axis Powers was directed by de Gaulle from London, where he organized the *Free French (*see also* Maquis).

Britain now faced an imminent German invasion. In August and September, 1940, the German *Luftwaffe attacked SE England and then London in a series of daytime raids. In October German bombing was carried out at night and extended to other British cities in the following months. The Luftwaffe failed to cripple the RAF or to terrorize the British people and by the end of October the so-called battle of Britain had been won by the RAF Fighter Command under *Dowding. The RAF lost 915 aircraft in the conflict and the Luftwaffe some 1733.

Africa and the Middle East (1940–43): in September, 1940, Italy advanced from Libya into Egypt but the Italians were forced to retreat in the face of Wavell's troops. By 6 February, 1941, the Allies had captured 113 000 Italian soldiers but their success was undermined by the arrival in N Africa of Rommel and the German Afrika Corps. In March Wavell's force was weakened by the dispatch of troops to aid Greece against an imminent German invasion (Yugoslavia and Greece were to fall in April and Crete, in May) and Rommel was able to force an Allied retreat to the Egyptian border.

In November Auchinleck (who had replaced Wavell in July) launched an Allied offensive against Rommel but by January, 1942, had again been forced to withdraw, taking up a defensive position at El-Alamein, inside the Egyptian frontier. In August Auchinleck was replaced by Alexander and Montgomery became commander of the Eighth Army. In the decisive battle of Alamein (23 Oct-4 Nov) Montgomery defeated Rommel, forcing his retreat along the N African coast. On 8 November an Anglo-US force under Eisenhower landed on the coast of French N Africa. The French under Darlan surrendered and the Allies advanced through Tunisia to make contact (7 April, 1943) with Montgomery's Eighth Army, which was moving N from Alamein. On 7 May the Allies took Bizerta and Tunis and on 13 May the Axis forces surrendered; some 248 000 German and Italian troops were captured.

In **East Africa**, Wavell had taken Addis Ababa from the Italians in April, 1941, and was in control of Ethiopia, as well as British Somaliland (captured by Italy in August, 1940), by May. In the **Middle East**, in April Britain occupied Iraq, by June Lebanon and Syria were in Allied hands, and in August the Allies gained control of Iran.

Italy (1943–45): on 10 July, 1943, Alexander's army group (the Eighth under Montgomery and the US Fifth Army), under the supreme command of Eisenhower, landed in Sicily. On 25 July Mussolini fell and on 3 Sept the Italian armistice was signed and the Allies landed on the Italian mainland. The Germans held back the Allies at the Ortona-Garigliano line until an Allied offensive, launched on 12

WORLD WAR II   *The development of the Western Front after the Allied D-day invasion of Normandy.*

May, 1944, succeeded in breaking through to Rome (4 June). In the following months the Allied forces made their way northwards; Bologna and then Milan were taken in April, 1945, and on 2 May, shortly before the final German collapse, Trieste fell.

Eastern Front (1941–45): Germany, with Finland, Hungary, and Romania, invaded the Soviet Union on 22 June, 1941. The Axis forces took the Crimea and the Ukraine in the S, besieged Leningrad in the N, and by November were in sight of Moscow. The Soviets staged an effective counterattack in the winter of 1941–42 but Germany retaliated in June with a new offensive and by August the famous battle of *Stalingrad had begun. This heroic Soviet victory resulted in a decimated German Sixth Army and the capture (January, 1943) of its commander Paulus. The Germans launched a new offensive in July but were gradually forced back until expelled from Soviet soil in August, 1944. On 23 August the Soviet Union secured a Romanian armistice and on 19 Sept, a Finnish armistice. Also in September Bulgaria declared war on Germany and the Germans evacuated Greece. On 5 October Belgrade fell following collaboration between the Red Army and Tito's Partisans. In October Soviet troops invaded Germany and in January, 1945, launched a final offensive, taking Poland, Austria, and Hungary and entering Czechoslovakia. Berlin fell on 2 May, shortly after Hitler's suicide.

Western Front (1944–45): on 6 June, 1944, D-Day, the Allied invasion of Normandy began under the supreme command of Eisenhower. The RAF Bomber Command had prepared the way with an operation of strategic bombing in place of the relatively ineffective (although destructive of life) bombing of German cities that had reached its peak early in 1944. By 2 July one million US and British troops had landed in Normandy. The British under Montgomery took Caen and US troops, after capturing St Lô (July), invaded Brittany. The Canadians took Falaise on 17 August, shortly after US and French troops had landed in the South of France from the Mediterranean. On 25 August Paris fell to the Allies, who now pursued Montgomery's plan for advancing into the Ruhr from Belgium and the Zuider Zee.

At the battle of Arnhem in September airborne troops were dropped to secure bridges but were withdrawn after ground forces were delayed in breaking through the German defence. In December the Germans launched a counteroffensive (the battle of the Bulge), driving a bulge, or salient, into Allied lines in the Ardennes region of S Belgium. US troops forced the Germans to retreat in January, 1945, and the final Allied offensive was launched. The Rhine was crossed, with air support, in March and by 1 April the Ruhr was encircled. On 4 May, two days after the fall of Berlin to Soviet troops, Montgomery accepted the surrender of German forces in NW Germany, Holland, and

Denmark at Lüneburg Heath. On 7 May the Germans signed a general surrender at Reims, which was ratified two days later in Berlin.

War at sea: The battle for control of the sea routes, known as the **battle of the Atlantic**, was fought from December, 1939, when the German *Graf Spee* inflicted considerable damage on HMS *Exeter* in the battle of the River Plate in the S Atlantic. In November, 1940, a successful naval air attack was launched on Taranto and in March, 1941, at Cape Matapan the British Mediterranean fleet thwarted an Italian attempt to prevent the transfer of British troops from Egypt to Greece. In May occurred the famous sinking of the *Hood* by the *Bismarck* and, three days later, of the *Bismarck* by the *Dorsetshire*. However, as in World War I, the major threat to Allied naval supremacy in western waters was posed by the German U-boats. These reached their height of effectiveness early in 1943 but by the summer, partly owing to the introduction of Allied escort carriers, 37 U-boats had been sunk and the battle of the Atlantic was over.

Asia (1941–45): the Japanese attack on Pearl Harbor on 7 December, 1941, initiated a truly "world" war. On 10 December Germany and Italy declared war on the USA and the second *Sino-Japanese War became part of the wider conflict. Japan invaded Malaya on 8 December and captured Hong Kong (25 Dec), Manila (3 January, 1942), and Singapore (15 Feb) together with 90 000 British and Commonwealth troops. The Dutch East Indies (Sumatra, Java, and parts of New Guinea) fell on 10 March and the Philippines and Burma in May. The Japanese seemed within reach of India and Australia when the US naval and air victories of the *Coral Sea (4–8 May), *Midway Island (4–6 June), and *Guadalcanal (Aug) halted Japan's eastward expansion. In October, 1944, the Japanese fleet was decisively defeated at *Leyte Gulf and the Allied conquest of Manila (February, 1945), the Philippines (June), and Borneo (May-June) followed. Burma, where Lord Mountbatten had become supreme commander, SE Asia, in August, 1943, was reconquered by the 14th ("forgotten") Army under Slim (January–May, 1945). Japanese resistance was finally ended by the atomic bombing on 6 and 9 August respectively of Hiroshima and Nagasaki, and Japan formally surrendered on 14 August.

Conclusion: in May, 1945, with the fall of Berlin and the German collapse in Italy and on the Western Front, the war in Europe was over. The postwar settlement was decided at the *Potsdam Conference, held near Berlin, in July and August (*see also* Tehran Conference; Yalta Conference).

In the course of the war Germany lost some 3.5 million combatants and 780 000 civilians (of which 593 000 were the victims of RAF bombs). In contrast the UK lost 92 673 civilians, of which 61 000 died in aerial attacks; some 264 443 combatants died. The Soviet Union lost 11 million combatants and 7 million civilians; the Japanese 1.3 million and 672 000 respectively; and the USA, 292 131 and 6000. In addition some 5.7 million Jews died in Nazi *concentration camps; of these 3.2 millions were Poles.

World Wildlife Fund (WWF) An international organization dedicated to the conservation of endangered species and their natural habitats. Founded in 1961, the WWF has financed projects both in Britain and abroad, protecting species as diverse as the rare bee orchid and the Arabian oryx. The international president of the WWF is HRH the Duke of Edinburgh. Director: George J. Medley.

worm A soft-bodied elongated invertebrate. The term is applied to members of several different groups, especially *earthworms and various parasitic species, and sometimes the larvae of insects. *See also* annelid worm; beardworm; flatworm; nematode; ribbon worm.

worm lizard. *See* amphisbaena.

Worms 49 38N 8 23E A town in SW West Germany, in Rhineland-Palatinate on the River Rhine. Heavily bombed during World War II, it has an 11th-century cathedral and a romanesque-gothic synagogue (1034). It is an industrial cen-

tre and is famed for its local wine, *Liebfraumilch*. *History*: in the 5th century AD it was the capital of the kingdom of Burgundy. Among the imperial diets (assemblies) held here was that of 1521 at which Luther refused to recant. It was annexed by France in 1797 and passed to Hesse-Darmstadt in 1815. Population (1984): 73 000.

wormwood An aromatic herb or shrub of the worldwide genus *Artemisia* (about 200 species), especially *A. absinthium*, which is found chiefly in grasslands of the N hemisphere and is the source of *absinthe. Up to 80 cm high, it has deeply divided leaves and small yellow flowers grouped into long loose spikes. Family: *Compositae*.

worsted A type of woollen yarn or cloth. It was manufactured originally only from the long wool fibres but shorter ones are now also used. The fibres are combed to lie parallel so that spinning produces a smooth fine thread. The woven fabrics, which include gabardine and serge, are fine, smooth, and strong.

Worthing 50 48N 0 23W A resort in S England, on the West Sussex coast. Nearby on the South Downs is the neolithic site, Cissbury Ring. Population (1981): 91 668.

Wotan. *See* Odin.

Wotton, Sir Henry (1568–1639) English poet. A friend of Donne, he served as a foreign diplomat before becoming provost of Eton in 1624. His works include *The Elements of Architecture* (1624) and a posthumous volume of conventional Elizabethan verse.

Wounded Knee The site in SW South Dakota (USA) of the last confrontation (29 December, 1890) between the Indians and US troops. Fearing that the anti-White Ghost Dance cult (the popularity of which was in part a response to the wretchedness of life on reservations) would cause an uprising among the discontented Sioux, troops killed over 200 men, women, and children at Wounded Knee creek. In 1973 some 200 members of the American Indian Movement occupied the village of Wounded Knee in protest against government Indian policies. After a 69-day siege, in which two Indians were killed, they were forced to surrender.

woundwort An annual or perennial herb of the widely distributed genus *Stachys* (about 200 species). It has square stems and lance-shaped or heart-shaped toothed leaves. Whorls of two-lipped tubular flowers, yellowish-white, pink, deep-red, or purple, are borne in the leaf axils and the fruit is a small nutlet. Family: *Labiatae*.

Wouwerman, Philips (1619–68) Dutch painter, born in Haarlem. Influenced by the Dutch painter Bamboccio (Pieter van Laer; c. 1592–1642), he specialized in camp and battle scenes, particularly studies of horses. Some of his prolific output is attributed to his brothers **Pieter Wouwerman** (1623–82) and **Jan Wouwerman** (1629–66).

wrack A large brown *seaweed of the order *Fucales*, found almost worldwide on rocky shores and prominent in colder regions. Leathery straplike branching fronds arise from a circular rootlike anchor (holdfast), often bearing air bladders to aid flotation. Examples are bladderwrack (*Fucus vesiculosus*) and serrated wrack (*F. serratus*).

Wrangel, Ferdinand Petrovich, Baron von (1794–1870) Russian explorer. He led a Russian naval expedition to the Arctic (1820–24). The Wrangell Mountains and Wrangel Island are named after him. As governor of Russian territories in Alaska (1829–35), he opposed its sale to the USA.

Wrangel, Peter Nikolaievich, Baron (1878–1928) Russian general. A divisional commander in World War I, following the Russian Revolution he joined the White armies against the Bolsheviks, distinguishing himself at Tsaritsyn (now Volgograd; 1919). Succeeding *Denikin as commander, he lost Sevastopol and was forced to evacuate his armies from the Crimea (1920).

Wrangel Island (Russian name: Ostrov Vrangelya) A Soviet island in the Arctic Ocean, between the East Siberian Sea and the Chukchi Sea. Since 1926 there has been a small

Chukchi and Eskimo population. Area: about 7300 sq km (2818 sq mi).

wrasse A fish of the family *Labridae* (300 species) found near rocks or coral reefs in shallow tropical and temperate seas. It has a slender often brilliantly coloured body, 5–200 cm long, long dorsal and anal fins, and thick lips. They are known for their elaborate courtship and nesting behaviour and many species can change their sex and colouring. They feed on marine invertebrates and the external parasites of other fish. Order: *Perciformes. See also* hogfish.

wreckfish A carnivorous fish, *Polyprion americanus*, also called stone bass, found in Mediterranean and Atlantic offshore waters, often associated with floating wreckage and seaweed. It has a deep heavy body, up to 2 m long, dark brown above and yellowish below, a large head, and a jutting lower jaw. Family: *Serranidae*; order: *Perciformes*.

wren A small brown bird belonging to a family (*Troglodytidae*; 63 species) found chiefly in South America. Wrens are 9–22 cm long with sharp slender bills and short cocked tails. The only Eurasian species, *Troglodytes troglodytes*, is about 10 cm long and has a reddish-brown plumage with barring on the wings and tail. It lives mainly in undergrowth, feeding on small insects and spiders.

The name is also given to small songbirds of the families *Maluridae* (Australian wrens, e.g. the *emu wren) and *Xenicidae* (New Zealand wrens, e.g. the rifleman).

Wren, Sir Christopher (1632–1723) English architect and scientist. After studying science and mathematics at Oxford he became professor of astronomy first at Gresham College, London (1657–61), and then at Oxford (1661–73). He was also a founder member of the Royal Society and later its president (1680–82). His first architectural designs were for Pembroke College chapel, Cambridge (1663), and the Sheldonian Theatre, Oxford (1664). Following a short trip to Paris (1665–66), the architecture of which led him to adopt his typically baroque style, he abandoned astronomy and joined the Office of Works. Within days of the *Fire of London Wren produced a new plan for the whole City, incorporating spacious avenues and piazzas. The plan was rejected on the grounds that it would have involved vast sums in compensation and crippling damage to trade, but Wren was commissioned to rebuild 51 City churches and some 36 company halls. Basing many of his designs for the churches on *Vitruvius' Roman basilica, Wren showed enormous ingenuity in fitting his buildings into the old irregular sites. His design for St Paul's Cathedral was accepted, after many modifications, in 1675. His later buildings include the Greenwich Hospital (begun in 1694) and additions to Hampton Court (1698). Wren was also an MP (1685–87, 1701–02). He was buried in St Paul's, where his epitaph reads: *Si monumentum requiris, circumspice* (If you seek a monument, look around you).

Wren, P(ercival) C(hristopher) (1885–1941) British novelist. He spent his early life wandering the world, working mostly as a soldier. The best known of his many popular adventure novels are those concerning the French Foreign Legion, especially *Beau Geste* (1924).

wren babbler An insect-eating bird belonging to one of several genera of the family *Timaliidae* (*see* babbler), occurring chiefly in S Asia. 10–15 cm long, wren babblers have a shortish upturned tail and short straight bill. They usually live on the ground, feeding in small flocks beneath bushes and forest undergrowth.

wrestling A form of unarmed combat, one of the most ancient sports, in which two people attempt to throw and hold each other down. It first became an Olympic sport in 704 BC. Modern wrestling became an organized sport in the 18th century. There are two main international styles. **Graeco-Roman wrestling** is the most popular style on the European continent; holds on the body below the waist and the use of legs to hold or trip are not allowed. They are, however, allowed in **freestyle wrestling** (which developed from the Anglo-American **catch-as-catch-can** form). In both styles a wrestler wins a match by securing a fall (throwing his opponent onto his back and pinning both shoulders to the mat for one second) or by accumulating the most points according to a complex scoring system. If neither wrestler achieves a fall or is disqualified the bout lasts for three three-minute rounds. There are ten weight categories. **Sambo wrestling** is the third recognized international style, originating from styles found in the Soviet Union. **Sumo** is the highly popular Japanese style in which the wrestlers, usually weighing around 130 kg (20 stone), attempt to force each other out of the ring. British variations include **Cumberland and Westmoreland wrestling** and **Devon and Cornwall wrestling**. The international governing body is the Fédération internationale des Luttes amateurs. *See also* judo.

Wrexham 53 03N 3 00W A town in North Wales, in Clwyd. It is a market town and coalmining centre, manufacturing chemicals, cables, and metal goods. Elihu Yale, founder of Yale University, is buried here. Population (1981): 40 272.

Wright, Frank Lloyd (1869–1959) US architect of international fame, whose style was among the most individual of the modern movement. A pupil of Louis *Sullivan from 1888 to 1893, he first demonstrated his originality in a series of Chicago houses between 1900 and 1909, the most famous being the Robie house (1909). These long low spacious designs have proved very influential. Later buildings include the Johnson Wax factory at Racine, Wisconsin (1936–39), and Taliesin West (1938), his winter home in the Arizona desert, where he established an architectural community, and the Guggenheim Museum (1959). ⃞architecture.

Wright, Judith (1915–) Australian poet. Her volumes of poetry, mostly written in S Queensland, include *Woman to Man* (1949) and *The Other Half* (1966). She has also written children's books and critical studies.

Wright, Orville (1871–1948) US aviator, who with his brother **Wilbur Wright** (1867–1912) made the first powered and controlled flights on 17 December, 1903. They took place near Kitty Hawk, North Carolina, and in the second, lasting about a minute, the aircraft covered a distance of 250 metres. The flight failed to interest either the US public or the government but the brothers continued to make improvements to their machine, eventually succeeding in staying airborne for an hour. In 1908 Wilbur Wright shipped the aircraft to France, where it was enthusiastically received, and in 1909 Orville secured a US army contract. ⃞aircraft.

Wright, Richard (1908–60) US novelist and critic. He was born into a poor Black family. His works include *Native Son* (1940), a seminal novel of social protest, and the autobiographical *Black Boy* (1945). From 1946 he lived in Paris.

writing systems The recording of human communication using signs or symbols to represent spoken words or concepts. The earliest known writing systems were all originally *pictographic; if they survived at all they developed into *ideographic systems (*see also* Chinese). True alphabetic writing developed around the E Mediterranean about 2000 BC (*see* Semitic alphabets). An intermediate stage is the use of *syllabaries.

Wrocław (German name: Breslau) 51 05N 17 00E A city in SW Poland, on the River Oder. Founded during the 10th century, it developed as an important centre on the amber trade route between the Roman Empire and the Baltic Sea. During World War II it suffered severe damage under siege from the Soviet armies (1945). Old buildings that have been reconstructed include the 13th-century cathedral. Its university was founded in 1945. It is now an important industrial and communications centre; industries include electronics, engineering, and food processing. Population (1982): 627 000.

wrought iron An almost pure form of iron, often with less than 0.1% carbon. It was originally produced by a laborious process of repeatedly hammering and folding hot *pig iron to squeeze out the impurities. The *puddling process has now superseded hand working.

wrybill A New Zealand *plover, *Anarhynchus frontalis*. 15 cm long, it has a grey plumage with white underparts and a black breast band. The bill, which is curved to the right, is used to probe for insects under stones and in shallow water.

wryneck A small *woodpecker belonging to a subfamily (*Jynginae*; 2 species) occurring in Eurasia. 16 cm long, wrynecks have a grey-brown mottled plumage and a small bill. They do not drill holes but feed mostly on ants and pupae and nest in empty holes.

Wuchow. *See* Wuzhou.

Wuhan 30 35N 114 19E A port in E central China, the capital of Hubei province at the confluence of the Yangtze and Han Rivers. Formed by the amalgamation (1950) of the ancient cities of Hankou (*or* Hankow), Hanyang, and Wuchang, it is the commercial and industrial centre of central China. The university was established in 1913. It was a centre of both the Taiping Rebellion (1851–64) and 1911 revolution. Its chief industry is iron and steel. Population (1982): 3 320 000.

Wu Hou (625–705 AD) A Chinese empress of the Tang dynasty. Following the death of her husband, the emperor, she ruled through two puppet emperors until 690 when she seized the throne and the imperial title. Although a capable ruler, she was forced to abdicate shortly before her death.

Wu-hsi. *See* Wuxi.

Wu-hsing. *See* Wuxing.

Wundt, Wilhelm (1832–1920) German physiologist and pioneer of modern experimental psychology. His *Principles of Physiological Psychology* (2 vols, 1873–74) was one of the first scientific approaches to the study of the conscious mind. Wundt also wrote works on human physiology and perception.

Wuppertal 51 05N 7 10E A city in NW West Germany, in North Rhine-Westphalia in the *Ruhr. It was formed in 1929 from six towns, including Elberfeld, and was heavily bombed in World War II. It is a textile-producing centre. Population (1980 est): 393 800.

Württemberg A former kingdom in W Europe. It became a duchy in 1495 and a kingdom in 1806. Divided into two West German *Länder* following World War II, these became part of the *Land* of *Baden-Württemberg (1952).

Würzburg 49 48N 9 57E A city in S West Germany, in Bavaria on the River Main. The former episcopal residence (1720–44), containing frescoes by Tiepolo, was damaged in World War II but later restored, as was the cathedral (1034). Roentgen taught at the university (founded 1582). A wine-producing centre, its manufactures include machine tools and chemicals. Population (1980 est): 127 900.

Wuxi (*or* Wu-hsi) 31 35N 120 19E A city in E China, in Jiangsu province on the *Grand Canal. A major grain market since the 7th century AD, it is also an industrial centre. Population (1983 est): 799 000.

Wuxing (*or* Wu-hsing) 30 56N 120 04E A town in E China, in Zhejiang province. The ancient centre of an intensely farmed area, it suffered badly during the Taiping Rebellion (1851–64). Silk is the main industry.

Wuzhou (Wu-chou *or* Wuchow) 23 30N 111 21E A city in S China, in Guangxi Zhuang AR. An old garrison town, it is now a commercial centre. Industries include silk textiles, chemicals, and engineering. Population (1982): 245 250.

Wyatt, James (1747–1813) British architect. Wyatt rose to fame in 1770 with his design for the Pantheon, London (now destroyed), a neoclassical interpretation of Hagia Sophia, Istanbul. Subsequently he designed country houses, notably Heaton House, Lancashire (1772), and made essential restorations to Salisbury and Durham cathedrals, which were subsequently criticized for their doubtful taste. His most dramatic work, *Fonthill Abbey (1796–1807), designed in the *gothic revival style, collapsed in the 1820s, possibly as a result of shoddy workmanship.

Wyatt, Sir Thomas (1503–42) English poet. A member of the court of Henry VIII, he served on various foreign diplomatic missions. With the Earl of *Surrey he introduced Italian verse forms and metres, notably the Petrarchan sonnet, into English poetry. 96 of his poems, together with 40 by Surrey, were included in *Tottel's Miscellany* (1557). His son **Sir Thomas Wyatt the Younger** (1521–54) led a rebellion (1553–54) against the marriage of Mary I to Philip II of Spain. He entered London with about 3000 men but was forced to surrender and was executed.

Wycherley, William (1640–1716) English dramatist. After studying in France and at Oxford he became a member of the Inner Temple and enjoyed the favour of both Charles II and James II. He wrote four comedies, notably *The Country Wife* (1675) and *The Plain Dealer* (1676), adapted from Molière's *Le Misanthrope*. His plays are more fiercely satirical than those of his fellow Restoration dramatists.

Wycliffe, John (c. 1329–84) English religious reformer. Wycliffe spent most of his life at Oxford, first as a student and then as lecturer in philosophy. Although initially protected by friends at court, he made increasingly radical criticisms of the Church, resulting in his enforced retirement to Lutterworth and his condemnation as a heretic. He attacked the doctrine of transubstantiation and emphasized the importance of the Bible, of which he supervised the first English translation from the Latin. Wycliffe's adherents, the *Lollards, were forerunners of English Protestantism.

Wye, River A river in E Wales and W England. Flowing mainly SE from Plynlimmon through Builth Wells and Monmouth, it joins the River Severn near Chepstow. It is noted for its beautiful scenery and has valuable salmon fisheries. Length: 210 km (130 mi).

Wyndham, John (J. Benyon Harris; 1903–69) British science-fiction writer. His best-known novel *The Day of the Triffids* (1951), which featured lethal mobile hybrid plants, was followed by the equally fantastic *The Kraken Wakes* (1953), *The Chrysalids* (1955), *The Midwich Cuckoos* (1957), and *Trouble with Lichen* (1960). His interest in feminine issues was revealed in a collection of short stories, *Consider Her Ways* (1961).

Wyoming One of the mountain states in the NW USA. The topography is one of forested mountains and grassy plains. Its natural resources include oil, natural gas, uranium, coal, trona, bentonite clay, and iron ore. Livestock production dominates farming. There is very little manufacturing; the main activities are oil refining, food processing, printing and publishing. Tourism is significant with such attractions as the Yellowstone National Park. *History*: part of the territory acquired from France by the Louisiana Purchase (1803), the arrival of the Union Pacific Railway (1867–69) brought settlement in the S and the area became a state in 1890. Area: 253 596 sq km (97 914 sq mi). Population (1980): 470 816. Capital: Cheyenne.

Wyss, Johann Rudolph (1782–1830) Swiss writer. A professor of philosophy, he collected and published Swiss folk tales and folklore. He also completed his father's manuscript of the successful novel *The Swiss Family Robinson* (1812–27) and wrote the Swiss national anthem.

Wyszyński, Stefan, Cardinal (1901–81) Polish Roman Catholic churchman. Ordained in 1924, he became Bishop of Lublin in 1946, and Archbishop of Gniezno and Warsaw and Primate of Poland in 1949. He was imprisoned in 1953 for condemning communist opposition to the Church. On release (1956) he enjoyed considerable pastoral liberty, serving as president of the Second Vatican Council in 1962.

X

Xanthus A city of ancient Lycia in Asia Minor famous for its heroic resistance to the Persians about 540 BC and to Brutus' Roman forces in about 43 BC.

Xenakis, Yannis (1922-) Greek composer, who studied engineering and architecture before turning to music. He developed a method of composition based on mathematical studies of probability. His compositions include *Duel* (for 54 instruments and 2 conductors; 1959).

xenon (Xe) A noble gas, present in the atmosphere and discovered in 1898 by Sir William Ramsay and M. W. Travers (1872-1961), in the residue of distilled liquid air. The first noble gas compounds were discovered by N. Bartlett (1932-), by reacting xenon with dioxygenyl platinum hexafluoride ($O_2^+ PtF_6^-$) to form $Xe^+ PtF_6^-$, which is a white solid. Several compounds are now known. Xenon is used in special lamps and the radioactive isotope ^{133}Xe is produced in nuclear reactors. It is a "poison," i.e. a neutron absorber, and is a crucial factor in the control of the chain reaction (*see* nuclear energy), building up to a constant level during steady operation and decaying with a half-life of a few days on shutdown. At no 54; at wt 131.3; mp -111.9°C; bp -107°C.

Xenophanes (6th century BC) Greek poet. Born in Ionia, he travelled extensively in the Mediterranean countries and lived mostly in Sicily and S Italy. Only a few fragments survive of a philosophical poem on nature and of some elegies. He was a monotheist, rejecting Homeric mythology and traditional Greek religious beliefs.

Xenophon (c. 430–c. 354 BC) Greek historian and soldier. He was born in Athens and, although he had little talent for philosophy, made the acquaintance of Socrates and became his devoted disciple. In 410 he joined a group of Greek mercenaries serving under the Persian prince Cyrus, who was leading an expedition against his brother, Artaxerxes II, King of Persia. Cyrus was killed in battle, the Asiatic army fled, and the force of 10 000 Greeks was left isolated. Xenophon as commander successfully led the mercenaries in a heroic retreat through the hostile Persian Empire to the Black Sea, a feat that formed the subject of his best-known work, the *Anabasis*. He later served in the Spartan army under King Aegesilaus. He wrote numerous other works, including *Memorabilia*, *Apology*, and *Symposium*, which deal with Socrates.

Xenopus. *See* clawed frog.

Xerography. *See* photocopying machine.

xerophyte A plant that lives in a hot dry climate, such as a desert, and is adapted for conserving water. Cacti, for example, often have spiny leaves (to prevent water loss) and green succulent stems (in which water is stored). A **xeromorph** is a plant that shows some of the features of xerophytes but may not live in desert areas.

Xerxes I (d. 465 BC) King of Persia (486–465). Having brutally repressed revolts in Egypt, he invaded Greece (*see* Greek-Persian Wars) with huge forces (480), at first successfully. However, defeat at *Salamis (480), *Plataea and Mycale (479), and the consequent revolt of the Asiatic Greeks forced him to withdraw. This tyrannous ruler and compulsive builder was assassinated in a court intrigue.

Xhosa A Bantu people of the *Transkei (South Africa). They are primarily cultivators, with some cattle. Today many Xhosa are migrant labourers in other areas of South Africa. Their language employs click sounds borrowed from the *Khoisan languages.

Xia Gui (*or* Hsia Knei; c. 1180–c. 1230) Chinese landscape painter, who worked for the Song emperors. His lyrical and mystical interpretations of landscape, in which human figures are dwarfed by mist-swathed mountains and dramatically poised trees, influenced later Chinese and Japanese artists.

Xiamen (Hsia-men *or* Amoy) 24 26N 118 07E A city in SE China on the island of Xiamen, in Fujian province, situated on Taiwan Strait. It is linked to the mainland by a causeway. The university was established in 1921. Industries include shipbuilding, engineering, fishing, and food processing. *History*: Xiamen has traded intermittently with Europeans since 1544. After its capture by the British during the Opium War (1841) it became a major tea-exporting port, through which many Chinese emigrants passed. Population (1980 est): 588 000.

Xi An (Hsi-an *or* Sian) 34 16N 108 54E A city in central China, the capital of Shenxi province on the Wei Ho (River). It contains many Tang pagodas and a noted museum. An important industrial centre, its industries include steel, chemicals, textiles, and electronics. *History*: as a Tang capital (618–906 AD) it attracted many Buddhist, Muslim, and Christian missionaries. After 1935 it was a Guomindang (Nationalist) base (*see* Xi An incident). Population (1983): 2 180 000.

Xiangtan (*or* Hsiang-t'an) 27 55N 112 47E A port in SE China, in Hunan province on the Xiang Jiang (River; *or* Hsiang Chiang). The commercial centre of an agricultural area, its products include textiles, iron and steel, and pig bristles. Population (1980 est): 547 000.

Xi An incident (1936) The kidnapping of Chiang Kai-shek by his mutinous army in Manchuria. Chiang was captured by two young marshals, who demanded an end to fighting between Chinese Nationalists (Guomindang) and communists in the face of the Japanese invasion. Chiang was released when the communists announced that they would cooperate with the Guomindang in opposing Japan (*see* United Fronts).

Xi Jiang (*or* Hsi Chiang) The most important river in S China, rising in Yunnan province and flowing E to form the densely populated Canton delta and the *Zhu Jiang. Most of its length is navigable by large ships. Length: about 1900 km (1200 mi).

Xingu, River (Portuguese name: Rio Xingu) A river in central Brazil, rising on the Mato Grosso plateau and flowing generally N to enter the Amazon delta. Length: 1932 km (1200 mi).

Xining (*or* Hsi-ning) 36 35N 101 55E A city in N central China, the capital of Qinghai province. Formerly on the W Chinese border, it was strategically important. Industries include chemicals, metals, wool, and leather. Population (1982): 873 000.

Xinjiang Uygur Autonomous Region (*or* Sinkiang Uigur AR) An administrative region in NW China, the largest, covering one-sixth of the country. It borders on the Soviet Union, Mongolia, Kashmir, and Tibet. Very dry with extreme temperatures, it consists of mountains in the centre with the Junggar Pendi in the N and the mainly desert Tarim Basin in the S. The Muslim Uigurs and the Chinese are the largest ethnic groups. Nomads in the N herd livestock, and wheat, cotton, and fruit are grown in oases and valleys. Oil and minerals are produced. *History*: from 206 BC to 1756 AD, Chinese rule alternated with rule by Uigurs, Tibetans, and Mongols, and rebellions against Chinese government continued until 1949. It has recently been greatly developed by the central government. The scene of border clashes with the Soviet Union in 1969, it has great strategic importance.

Area: 1 646 799 sq km (635 829 sq mi). Population (1980 est): 12 560 000. Capital: Ürümqi.

Xiong Nu (*or* Hsiung-nu) Turkish and Mongol tribes on the N and NW borders of China, which threatened Chinese security from about 500 BC. They depended on herding animals for their livelihood and, skilled horseback warriors, conducted raids in times of hardship to plunder the settled Chinese farming communities. The Chinese attempted to control the Xiong Nu by building the frontier walls that eventually became the Great Wall of China, marrying their daughters to Xiong Nu leaders, and trading with them.

Xochimilco 19 08N 99 09W A town in central Mexico, on Lake Xochimilco. It is famous for its chinamoas (floating gardens), which originated as soil covered rafts on which fruit and vegetables were grown and have since become islands. Population (1970): 43 067.

X-ray diffraction The *diffraction of *X-rays when they strike a crystal. The angle through which the X-rays are diffracted depends on the spacing between the different planes in the crystal in a manner given by *Bragg's law. The technique is used in studying crystal structure.

X-rays Electromagnetic radiation lying between ultraviolet radiation and gamma rays in the *electromagnetic spectrum. X-rays may have wavelengths between 10^{-9} metre and 10^{-11} metre, the shorter wavelengths being known as hard X-rays and the longer wavelengths as soft X-rays. Discovered by Wilhelm *Roentgen (and formerly called Roentgen rays) in 1895, they are produced when heavy metal atoms (usually tungsten) are struck by sufficiently energetic electrons, as in an **X-ray tube**. The electrons in an X-ray tube are produced by a heated cathode in an evacuated tube and accelerated to the heavy-metal anode by an electric field. The collisions knock inner electrons from the atoms, X-rays being emitted when the vacancy is filled by outer electrons. X-rays cause ionization in gases and penetrate matter. X-rays have many uses including the examination of internal organs and structures in medical diagnosis, the killing of cancer cells in *radiotherapy, investigating structures for flaws, and in *X-ray diffraction by crystals in order to study their structure.

Xuan Cang (*or* Hsuan-tsang; 602-64 AD) Chinese Buddhist monk. He travelled alone to India and after studying there for about 10 years returned with Buddhist texts, 75 of which he translated. He also left a record of his travels, of great historical value.

xylem A plant tissue specialized for the transport of water and salts. The main cells are tubelike, with their walls strengthened by deposits of *lignin in a spinal arrangement, which aids upward movement of materials by capillary action. In trees and shrubs the lignin deposits eventually block the tubes completely: this tissue forms *wood, and new secondary xylem is produced to transport water.

xylene (*or* dimethyl benzene; $C_6H_4(CH_3)_2$) A colourless, toxic flammable liquid consisting of a mixture of three isomers. It is obtained by fractional distillation of petroleum and is used as an aviation fuel and as a solvent.

xylophone A pitched percussion instrument, consisting of a frame on which wooden bars in the pattern of a keyboard are fixed, each with a tubular metal resonator beneath it. It is played with two sticks. Orchestral xylophones usually have a compass of three octaves. *See also* vibraphone.

X-RAYS *The first radiograph of a human body, produced by X-rays, from Roentgen's original plate. The keys in his pockets and his suspenders are clearly visible.*

Y

Yahweh The conjectural pronunciation of one of the Hebrew names of God. The name YHWH (the Tetragrammaton or "four-letter" name) occurs often in the Bible; out of reverence it was traditionally not pronounced, but replaced by *Adonai* (Lord) or *Hashem* (the Name), except by the *high priest when he entered the *Holy of Holies. "Jehovah" represents another attempt to pronounce this name.

yak A shaggy-coated wild ox, *Bos grunniens*, inhabiting mountain pastures of central Asia. Yaks have long been domesticated for draught purposes and milk; their dung is used as fuel. Wild yaks, up to 2 m high at the shoulder with long upward-curving horns, are larger than domestic yaks and are always black; they live in large herds, feeding on coarse grasses, and are expert climbers.

Yakut Autonomous Soviet Socialist Republic (*or* Yakutia) An administrative division in the E Soviet Union, in the RSFSR. The Yakuts, a Mongoloid people, are traditionally nomadic herdsmen but have become sedentary. In NE Siberia, Yakutia (an autonomous republic since 1922) is one of the world's coldest inhabited regions, and agriculture is only possible in the S. Mining for diamonds, gold, tin, and coal is the main occupation, with trapping and breeding of sable, squirrel, and silver fox. Area: 3 103 000 sq km (1 197 760 sq mi). Population (1981 est): 883 000. Capital: Yakutsk.

Yale University One of the oldest universities in the USA (founded 1701), situated at New Haven, Connecticut. It is named after Elihu Yale (1648–1721), who donated his books to the college. Yale has educated women since 1869.

Yalta 44 30N 34 09E A port in the Soviet Union, in the S Ukrainian SSR on the Black Sea. It is the Crimea's largest seaside resort and was the site of the Allied *Yalta Conference in 1945. Population (1983 est): 84 000.

Yalta Conference (1945) The conference towards the end of World War II attended by F. D. Roosevelt (USA), Stalin (Soviet Union), and Churchill (UK). They agreed upon the postwar occupation of Germany by the USA, Soviet Union, UK, and France and that German surrender must be unconditional.

yam A twining herbaceous plant of the genus *Dioscorea*, cultivated in wet tropical regions for its tubers, which are eaten like potatoes. Yams have long slender climbing stems, bearing entire or lobed leaves, and unisexual flowers in long clusters. Tubers can reach a length of 2.6 m and a weight of 45 kg; species commonly cultivated are *D. alata* (white yam), *D. rotundata* (white guinea yam), *D. batatas* (Chinese yam), and *D. cayenensis* (yellow yam). Family: *Dioscoreaceae*.

Yamagata Aritomo (1838–1922) Japanese soldier and statesman. As commander of the Imperial Guard, he created a modern conscript army and while home minister (1885–89) he shaped Japan's modern local government. Twice prime minister (1890–91, 1898–1900), he oversaw Japan's victories against China (1894–95) and Russia (1904–05).

Yamasaki, Minoru (1912–86) US architect. His earliest buildings, such as Missouri's St Louis airport (1953–55), were remarkable for their simple elegance. However, later works, such as the Woodrow Wilson building in Princeton (1965) and the twin towers of the World Trade Centre in New York (1970–77), employed pseudo-Gothic elements, which to many eyes detracted from his otherwise inventive structures.

Yamato The ruling dynasty of Japan under which the country was united in the 4th century AD. All subsequent Japanese emperors have claimed descent from the Yamato, under whom Buddhism was introduced in the 6th century.

Yamoussoukro 6 49N 5 17W The capital of Ivory Coast. Yamoussoukro was chosen as an inland replacement for the old capital of Abidjan in 1983. Population (1983 est): 70 000.

Yang, Chen Ning (1922–) US physicist, born in China, who shared the 1957 Nobel Prize with his countryman Tsung-Dao *Lee for their theoretical work suggesting that parity would not be conserved in the *weak interaction. This was quickly confirmed by observations of beta decay.

Yangtze Incident An attack by Chinese Communist forces on the British frigate *Amethyst* in the Yangtze River, during a routine replenishment visit to Nanjing in 1949. After 17 of the crew, including the captain, had been killed the ship remained imprisoned for three months, until a naval attaché, Commander Kerans (1915–85), boarded the ship and under the noses of the shore batteries brought it out of the river into the open sea without further loss of life.

Yangtze River (Chinese name: Chang Jiang *or* Ch'ang Chiang) The longest river in China and the third longest in the world. Rising in a remote mountain range on the borders of Tibet and Qinghai province, it flows roughly E to enter the East China Sea via an extensive delta. A Chinese survey (late 1970s), which finally established the true source of the river, estimated its total power potential to be 230 000 MW (greater than that of all the rivers in the USA). The Yangtze is one of China's main transport routes and its densely populated basin is China's most productive agricultural region. Length: 6380 km (3964 mi).

Yantai (Yentai *or* Chefoo) 37 30N 121 22E A port in E China, on the Shandong Peninsula. Following the Chefoo Convention, signed in 1876 by Britain and China, many foreign traders lived here. The chief industries are fishing and food processing. Population (1980 est): 347 000.

Yaoundé (*or* Yaunde) 3 51N 11 31E The capital of Cameroon. Founded under the German protectorate of Kamerun in 1888, it was capital of Cameroon from 1922 until independence in 1960 (except during World War II). The Federal University of Cameroon was founded in 1962. Population (1981 est): 435 892.

yard An Imperial unit of length originally defined as the distance between two gold plugs on a bronze bar. In 1963 the yard was redefined as 0.9144 metre (*see* metric system).

Yarkand. *See* Shache.

Yarmouth (*or* Great Yarmouth) 52 37N 1 44E A resort and port in E England, in Norfolk at the mouth of the River

YALTA CONFERENCE *Churchill (left), Roosevelt, and Stalin, with their advisers.*

Yare. Once a major herring-fishing port, it is now a base for North Sea gas and oil. The main industries are tourism, food processing, and engineering. Population (1981): 48 273.

Yaroslavl 57 34N 39 52E A city in the Soviet Union, in the W RSFSR on the River Volga. It has been a textile centre since the 18th century. Population (1981 est): 608 000.

yarrow A perennial herb, *Achillea millefolium*, also called milfoil, native to pastures of Europe and W Asia. Up to 45 cm high, it has feathery strongly scented leaves and small white daisy-like flowers borne. Family: **Compositae*.

Yawata. *See* Kitakyushu.

yawl A □sailing vessel with two masts, a tall one set one-third of the boat's length from the bows and a very short one just behind the rudder post. Yawls, like ketches, are a favoured rig for yachts, for the split rig reduces the area of each sail, making handling easier. Yawls do not sail as well towards the wind as sloops do. *See also* ketch; sloop.

yaws A chronic tropical disease caused by a *spirochaete bacterium, *Treponema pertenue*. It occurs mostly among poor children and is spread by skin contact. After an incubation period of three to four weeks a growth appears on the thighs or buttocks; later, multiple growths that look like squashed raspberries appear all over the skin. Bones may also be affected and if not treated the disease can be very disfiguring. Treatment with penicillin is highly effective.

Yazd (*or* Yezd) 31 55N 54 22E A town in central Iran. It has several mosques, some built in the 11th century, and produces silk fabrics. Population (1985 est): 223 300.

year The time taken by the earth to complete one revolution around the sun. This is equal to the period of the sun's apparent motion around the *ecliptic. The **tropical year**, of 365.2422 days, is the interval between two successive passages of the sun through the vernal *equinox. The **sidereal year**, of 365.2564 days, refers to successive passages of the sun through a point relative to the background stars. These periods differ because of the *precession of the equinoxes. *See also* calendar.

yeast A single-celled fungus that is capable of fermenting carbohydrates and that reproduces asexually by budding new cells from its surface. Typical yeasts belong to the family *Saccharomycetaceae*. Strains of *Saccharomyces cerevisiae*, the cells of which are 0.004–0.02 mm in diameter, are widely used to cause *fermentation in baking, brewing, and the manufacture of wines and spirits. Yeast extracts are used as a food for their high vitamin B content. Class: **Ascomycetes*.

Yeats, William Butler (1865–1939) Irish poet and dramatist. In London in the 1890s he helped found the Rhymers' Club, pursued his lifelong interest in the occult, and published several volumes of symbolist verse. His best-known poems, many of which appeared in *The Tower* (1928) and *The Winding Stair* (1929), included tragic meditations on personal and political themes. Among them are 'Easter, 1916', 'The Second Coming', and 'Sailing to Byzantium'. He was an admirer of Maud Gonne (1866–1953), Irish actress and nationalist, and with Lady *Gregory in 1904 he founded the Abbey Theatre, Dublin, for which he wrote many plays. He was a senator of the Irish Free State (1922–28) and won the Nobel Prize in 1923. His brother **Jack Butler Yeats** (1871–1957) was a noted Irish painter, born in London. After a childhood in Ireland he returned to London to study, but his paintings were essentially Irish, depicting life in bars, music halls, and racecourses in dark colours, often shot with bright explosions of colour applied with a palette knife.

yellow fever An acute viral infection transmitted by female mosquitoes of the genus *Aëdes*, which occur in areas of tropical rain forest. After an incubation period of 3–14 days the patient develops a fever with aching muscles. In severe cases the virus affects the liver causing jaundice (hence the name), the kidneys, and the heart; death may result from liver or heart

failure. There is no specific treatment but two kinds of vaccine can prevent it.

yellowfin tuna A large tuna fish, *Thunnus albacares*, with yellow fins and a golden stripe along its sides. It is found worldwide and is a valued food and game fish.

W. B. YEATS

yellow-green algae *Algae of the division *Chrysophyta* (about 6000 species), which are yellow-green to brown in colour depending on the proportion of green chlorophyll masked by the pigments fucoxanthin or diadinoxanthin. Most are unicellular or colonial and they form a major constituent of plankton (*see also* diatoms). Most reproduce asexually by spores.

yellowhammer A Eurasian *bunting, *Emberiza citrinella*, that occurs on farmland and roadsides, where it feeds on grain and seeds. About 16 cm long, the male has a bright-yellow head and underparts, chestnut rump, and a brown-streaked back; females are less colourful. *See* Plate V.

Yellowknife 62 30N 114 29W A city in N Canada, the capital of the Northwest Territories. Founded in 1935, it is the commercial and administrative centre of the territory, with an airport and gold mines. Population (1981): 9483.

Yellow River (Chinese name: Huang He *or* Huang Ho) A river in China, rising in the W and flowing roughly E to enter the Gulf of Chihli via a fertile delta. Its summer floods have resulted in frequent disasters and changes of course. Its diversion as a measure against the Japanese invasion (1938) resulted in the death of 900 000 people. Length: about 4350 km (2700 mi).

Yellow Sea (Chinese name: Huang Hai) A large shallow inlet of the W Pacific Ocean, bordered by China and Korea. It is so called because of the yellowish silt deposited by the Chinese rivers. It is rich in fish.

Yellowstone National Park The largest national park in the USA, chiefly in NW Wyoming but extending into S Montana and E Idaho. Established in 1872, it consists mainly of forested volcanic plateaus. Its many active geysers include Old Faithful, which erupts regularly at approximately hourly intervals. Area: 8956 sq km (3458 sq mi).

Yellowstone River A river in the W USA, rising in NW Wyoming and flowing N through the *Yellowstone National Park then E to join the Missouri River in North Dakota. Length: 1080 km (671 mi).

yellowwood An evergreen coniferous tree of the genus *Podocarpus* (over 100 species), mostly of warm temperate and tropical regions of the S hemisphere. The hard leathery leaves are strap-shaped and the green berry-like fruits are borne on fleshy stalks. Yellowwoods are important timber trees; the light elastic nonresinous wood is used for building, furniture, carving, and ships. Family: *Podocarpaceae*.

Yemen, People's Democratic Republic of (*or* South Yemen; name until 1970: People's Republic of Southern Yemen) A country in the Middle East, in S *Arabia bordering on the Gulf of Aden and the Arabian Sea. It includes the islands of Kamaran in the Red Sea, *Perim Island, *Socotra, and the *Kuria Maria Islands. Mountains dissected by wadis—chiefly Wadi Hadhramaut—rise from the narrow coastal plain; the N and E are desert. The mainly Arab population is largely Sunnite Muslim. There are nomadic tribes in the N. *Economy*: mainly agricultural, although little land is cultivated. Cotton is the main crop; others include cereals, coffee, tobacco, fruit, and vegetables. Sardine fishing is important; mineral deposits are not yet exploited. Industry consists chiefly of an oil refinery and a little light industry in Aden. The economy suffered badly from the closure of the Suez Canal (1967–75). Refined oil, cotton, fish products, hides, and incense are exported. Aid is received mainly from China and the Soviet Union. *History*: ruled by the imams (priest-kings) of Yemen, the area (excluding Aden) was nominally part of the Ottoman Empire from the 16th century to 1918. Aden was captured from the Turks in 1839 and occupied by the British East India Company. The British made protectorate treaties with other local rulers (1886–1914) to safeguard Aden and its trade routes; these 24 sultanates, emirates, and sheikdoms were called the Aden Protectorate (1937). In 1963 Aden and ten others formed the Federation of South Arabia. This collapsed in 1967, when anti-British nationalist groups in Aden took control (although the British had already agreed to withdraw), and South Yemen then became independent. Its history has been marked chiefly by border disputes with Oman (until 1976) and with North Yemen, despite an agreement to unite North and South Yemen (1972). In 1986 foreign nationals were evacuated during a violent military coup; in the subsequent elections Haider Abu Bakr al Attas became president. Official currency: South Yemen dinar of 1000 fils. Official language: Arabic. Area: about 336 870 sq km (130 066 sq mi). Population (1983 est): 2 086 000. Capital: Aden.

Yemen Arab Republic (*or* North Yemen) A country in the Middle East in SW *Arabia, bordering on the Red Sea. It consists of a narrow dry W coastal plain, central mountains (the wettest and most fertile in Arabia), and E desert. There are no rivers but many wadis, oases, and springs. The Arab population is Muslim, either Sunnite or Zaidi, the Jews having emigrated after 1918. *Economy*: mainly agricultural; cotton, coffee, cereals, vegetables, fruit, and the narcotic qat are the chief crops and livestock are kept. Industry includes textile, soft-drink, and cigarette factories; salt is mined and handicrafts are important. Machinery, oil, and textiles are imported. North Yemen receives money from Yemeni workers abroad (over one-sixth of the population works in Saudi Arabia) and relies on foreign aid (chiefly from the USA, the World Bank, and other Arab countries). *History*: rule by a Muslim imam (priest-king) originated in the 9th century and lasted until 1962, although from 1520 until 1918 the area was nominally part of the Ottoman Empire. North Yemen's boundaries were fixed in 1934 by treaty with Saudi Arabia and the UK, although clashes with the British over the control of Aden continued. It joined the Arab League

(1945) and the UN (1947) and was loosely allied with Egypt and Syria (1958–61) in the United Arab Republic. Internal disorders, during which the imam was assassinated (1948), culminated in civil war (1962–70), which ended with the recognition of a republican regime. Another coup took place in 1974 and successive heads of state were assassinated in 1977 and 1978. Moves were made towards uniting the two Yemens following the border clashes of 1967–72. Allegations of South Yemeni involvement in the 1978 assassination were followed by increased border fighting. However, relations with South Yemen improved in the 1980s. President: Lt Col Ali Abdullah Saleh (1942–). Official currency: riyal of 100 rial. Area: 195 000 sq km (73 300 sq mi). Population (1983 est): 5 744 000. Capital: San'a. Chief port: Hodeida.

Yenisei, River A river in the central Soviet Union, rising in the Sayan Mountains and flowing N to **Yenisei Bay** on the Kara Sea. There is a hydroelectric power station at Krasnoyarsk. Length: about 4000 km (2485 mi).

Yentai. *See* Yantai.

Yeomen of the Guard The bodyguard of the British sovereign established by Henry VII for his coronation in 1485. Their last appearance in battle and that of a British monarch (George II), was at Dettingen in 1743. They are now a ceremonial guard. Known as Beefeaters because of their magnificent physiques, they wear a red and gold uniform and include the Yeomen Wardens at the Tower of London.

Yerevan (Russian name: Erivan) 40 10N 44 31E A city in the SW Soviet Union, the capital of the Armenian SSR. A commercial centre, it has chemical, textile, and food-processing industries. *History*: it occupies the site of an ancient fortress, the city itself dating from at least the 7th century AD. Long disputed by Persia and Turkey, it was ceded to Russia in 1828. Population (1981 est): 1 050 000.

Yerwa. *See* Maiduguri.

Yesenin, Sergei Aleksandrovich (1895–1925) Russian poet. He emerged from a peasant background into Moscow literary society during the revolutionary period. He travelled in USA and Europe, was briefly married to the US dancer Isadora Duncan, suffered from alcoholism and drug addiction, and finally committed suicide. His volumes include *Confessions of a Hooligan* (1924).

Yeti. *See* Abominable Snowman.

Yevtushenko, Yevgenii (1933–) Soviet poet. His implicit criticism of the Soviet authorities in such poems as *Babi Yar* (1961) gained him wide popularity among both Soviet and western readers. He has given many poetry readings in Europe and the USA.

yew A coniferous tree or shrub of the genus *Taxus* (10 species), native to the N hemisphere. Yews have dark-green leathery bladelike leaves, 1–4 cm long and arranged in two rows along the stems, and the male and female flowers grow on separate trees. The female flowers produce bright-red cup-shaped berry-like fruits, each containing a single seed. The berries are sweet-tasting and attractive to birds, but the seeds and leaves are poisonous. The most widespread species is the common yew (*T. baccata*), of Europe, SW Asia, and N Africa; it grows to a height of 25 m but cultivated forms—grown for shelter, ornament, and topiary work—are often smaller. Family: *Taxaceae*.

Yezd. *See* Yazd.

Yezidis The name of a Kurd tribe of Iraq and their tribal religion. The sect, the centre of which is in Mosul, combines Islamic, Christian, Judaic, and other ancient elements.

Yezo. *See* Hokkaido.

Yggdrasill In Norse mythology, an evergreen ash tree embracing the whole universe. Its three roots join the underworld, the land of giants, and the home of the gods (Asgard). Demons threaten its existence; the serpent Nidhögg constantly chews at one of its roots, while four stags eat its buds. However, it is preserved by the *Norns (the Fates), who water it from one of the three fountains at its base. The maypole and the Christmas tree are possibly symbolic derivatives of Yggdrasill.

Yibin (*or* I-pin) 28 50N 104 35E A port in S central China, in Sichuan province at the confluence of the Yangtze and Min Rivers. A commercial centre, salt is mined here and chemicals and paper are manufactured. Population (1980 est): 276 000.

Yichang (*or* I-ch'ang) 30 43N 111 22E A port in E central China, in Hubei province on the Yangtze River. An old commercial centre, it marked the limit of the Japanese advance during the Sino-Japanese War (1937–45). Population (1982): 175 000.

Yiddish A language used by *Ashkenazim (East European) Jews and based on a dialect of High German. It emerged during the 9th century and has absorbed many Slavonic and other influences. It is written in the *Hebrew alphabet. Yiddish literature flourished in the 19th and early 20th centuries, but after the *holocaust it has yielded its place as the principal literary language of the Jews to Hebrew.

yield (of stocks and shares). *See* dividend; gilt-edged security.

yield point The point at which a body becomes permanently deformed when subjected to a sufficiently large stress. Below the yield point the body is elastic, above the yield point it becomes plastic. *See also* elasticity; plasticity.

YIN AND YANG *The symbols are interlocked and each contains a tiny portion of the other.*

yin and yang Contrasting but complementary principles at the root of traditional Chinese cosmology. Yin is the negative feminine mode, associated with the earth, darkness, and passivity. Yang is the positive dynamic principle of masculine energy associated with heaven and light. The principles antedate *Confucius and are particularly important in *Taoism, serving, for example, to explain the cycle of the seasons.

Yinchuan 38 30N 106 19E A city in N central China, capital of Ningxia Hui AR. It is the ancient commercial centre of a fertile agricultural region. Its chief industries are coalmining and wool. Population (1982): 200 000.

Yingkou (*or* Newchang) 40 40N 122 17E A port in NE China, in Liaoning province on the Hun estuary. Manchuria's chief port in the late 19th century, it has fishing, engineering, and oil-refining industries. Population (1970 est): 215 000.

ylang-ylang A slender evergreen tropical Asian tree, *Cananga odorata*, also called perfume tree. It has pointed oval leaves, up to 20 cm long, and bears drooping clusters of fragrant stalked greenish-yellow flowers throughout the year. An oil distilled from the flowers is used in perfumery, cosmetics, and soaps. Family: *Annonaceae*.

YMCA. *See* Young Men's Christian Association.

yoga The principles and practice of self-training that permeates all Indian philosophical traditions. Traces of it exist from the *Indus Valley civilization before the Aryan invasion (1500 BC). The methods used are generally austere and ascetic and include physical control and meditative techniques. Physical control is stressed in Hindu yoga; in the Buddhist practice contemplative methods predominate; in Jainism asceticism is emphasized. Usually the aim is a state of release and liberation from the material world. The yoga so fashionable in the West frequently takes the form of hatha-yoga, which involves physical exercises to bring peace and insight.

yogurt. *See* dairy products.

Yokohama 35 28N 139 28E A port and second largest city of Japan, in SE Honshu on Tokyo Bay. Together with Tokyo it forms Japan's greatest urban and industrial area and handles 30% of foreign trade. Its industries include shipbuilding, oil refining, chemicals, steel, and textiles. Its two universities were both established in 1949. *History*: It grew rapidly after 1859 as a second port for Tokyo, with which it was linked by Japan's first railway (1872). It was almost destroyed by the 1923 earthquake and badly bombed during World War II. Population (1980): 2 774 000.

Yokosuka 35 18N 139 39E A port in Japan, in SE Honshu on Tokyo Bay. William Adams (d. 1620), the first Englishman to visit Japan (1600), is buried here. It has a major naval base and its chief industry is shipbuilding. Population (1981 est): 421 000.

Yom Kippur (Hebrew: Day of Atonement) A Jewish holy day, falling nine days after *Rosh Hashanah. It is a day of penitence and cleansing from sin and is marked by 24 hours' total fast. *See also* Holy of Holies.

Yom Kippur War. *See* Israel.

Yonge, Charlotte (1823–1901) British novelist. Her novels and children's books are chiefly concerned with religious ideals, especially those of the *Oxford Movement. Her best-known books include *The Heir of Redclyffe* (1853) and *Heartsease* (1854).

Yong Le (*or* Yung-lo; 1360–1424) The title of Ch'eng-tsu, Chinese emperor (1402–24), after usurping the throne. He vigorously expanded the *Ming dynasty, dispatching fleets to SE Asia and personally leading military expeditions. He transferred the capital to Peking from Nanjing.

Yonkers 40 56N 73 54W A city in the USA, in New York state on the Hudson River. Industries include elevators, carpets, chemicals, and clothing. Population (1980): 195 351.

York (Latin name: Eboracum) 53 58N 1 05W A city in N England, in North Yorkshire on the River Ouse. It was the principal Roman garrison in Britain (Constantine was proclaimed emperor here in 306 AD) and was for long regarded as the northern capital. The cathedral (Minster), seat of the Archbishop of York, was begun in 1154 and dominates the city. The south transept was damaged by fire in 1984. The medieval walls and four city gateways remain. Industries include chocolate manufacturing, sugar, glass, and railway engineering. The National Railway Museum opened in 1975 and the Yorvig Viking Centre in 1984. York is a major tourist centre as well as an important market town and educational centre; the university was founded in 1963. Population (1981): 99 787.

York A ruling dynasty of England descended from Edmund, Duke of York (1342–1402), the fourth son of Edward III. Richard Plantaganet, Duke of *York, led the Yorkist opposition to Henry VI's Lancastrian government in the Wars of the □Roses (1455–85), in which the Yorkist emblem was the white rose. His son Edward IV, established the royal dynasty. After the brief rule of his son Edward V and the overthrow of Richard III (1485) the Crown passed to Henry VII, the first *Tudor monarch, who married Edward IV's daughter Elizabeth.

York, Archbishop of The second of the two archbishops of England and head of the northern province of the Church of England. York became an archiepiscopal see in 735 AD under Egbert (d. 766), brother of the Northumbrian king. Controversy between Canterbury and York regarding primacy was settled by Pope Innocent II (1352–62), with precedence given to the Archbishop of *Canterbury, called Primate of All England, while the Archbishop of York was styled Primate of England. He ranks next to the Lord

Chancellor and before all other peers except the royal princes. He signs himself with his Christian name followed by the Latin abbreviation of York, for example "John Ebor." Recent archbishops are: (93rd) (Frederick) Donald Coggan (1961–74); (94th) Stuart (Yarworth), Baron Blanch (1974–83); (95th) John Habgood (1983–).

York, Prince Andrew, Duke of (1960–) Second son of Elizabeth II and fourth in succession to the throne. A helicopter pilot in the Royal Navy, he married Miss Sarah Ferguson in July, 1986.

York, Richard Plantagenet, 3rd Duke of (1411–60) English magnate, who was descended from the third son of Edward III. His claim to the throne against Henry VI (who was descended from Edward III's fourth son) resulted in the outbreak of the Wars of the *Roses in 1455. He was killed in a skirmish at Wakefield. His sons became Edward IV (1461) and Richard III (1483).

Yorke Peninsula A peninsula of SE South Australia, situated between Spencer Gulf and Gulf St Vincent. It is an important wheat-growing and sheep-rearing area.

York mystery plays A cycle of 48 plays originating in the 14th century and performed by the trade guilds of York on the feast of Corpus Christi. The most extensive cycle of medieval plays in England, the York cycle covered the whole of history from a Christian viewpoint, from the creation of the angels to the last judgment, concentrating on the fall of man and his redemption by Christ. They were all performed in chronological order in the course of one day. The series of 14 plays devoted to Christ's Passion were revised into alliterative verse at one stage and are notable for their sometimes disturbing realism.

Yorkshire A former county in NE England, bordering on the North Sea. It comprised the North, West, and East Ridings (thirds). From the late middle ages onwards it was an important centre of the wool industry. It was reorganized in 1974 to form the counties of *North Yorkshire and *Humberside and the metropolitan counties of *West Yorkshire and *South Yorkshire.

Yorkshire terrier A breed of toy □dog developed from several terrier breeds in N England during the 19th century. It is small and compact with a very long straight coat that trails on the ground. This is black at birth but matures to steel-blue with tan on the head and chest. Height: 20–23 cm.

Yorktown 37 14N 76 32W A village in the USA, in Virginia on the York River. The last important battle of the American Revolution was fought here in 1781.

Yosemite National Park A national park in the USA, in central California. The scenic Yosemite Valley, which lies within the park, contains the world's three largest monoliths of exposed granite. There are also many lakes, rivers, and waterfalls including the Yosemite Falls, which are the highest in North America with a drop in two segments of 739 m (2425 ft). Area: 3061 sq km (1182 sq mi).

Young, Andrew (1932–) US politician and diplomat. As a Congregational Church minister in the Southern Christian Leadership Conference, Young was an associate of the civil-rights leader Martin Luther *King. A Democrat in the House of Representatives (1973–77), Young was US Ambassador to the UN from 1977 until 1979, when he resigned following criticism of his meeting, in contradiction of official US policy, with a representative of the Palestine Liberation Organization.

Young, Arthur (1741–1820) British agricultural and travel writer. He published *Annals of Agriculture* (47 vols, 1784–1809) and several accounts of his tours throughout England. In *Travels in France* (1792) he was notably sympathetic to the Revolution. He became first secretary of the Board of Agriculture in 1793.

Young, Brigham (1801–1877) US Mormon leader, who succeeded Joseph *Smith. A former Methodist, Young joined the

new church in 1832 and for a time supervised the Mormon Mission in England. After Smith's death he planned and led the major migration to Salt Lake City, Utah (1846–47). He became president of the Church and later governor of Utah Territory (1851).

Young, Thomas (1773–1829) British physician and physicist, who spoke 12 languages at the age of 20. After studying in Germany and at Cambridge he practised medicine in London (1799–1814), becoming professor at the Royal Institution (1801–03). He identified astigmatism and described the ciliary muscles of the eye. He demonstrated the interference of light and used this observation to suggest a wave theory of light in opposition to *Newton's corpuscular theory. As a result of his work on the elasticity of materials, the ratio of stress to strain is known as Young's modulus. Also an Egyptologist, he helped decipher the *Rosetta Stone.

Younghusband, Sir Francis Edward (1863–1942) British explorer and mountaineer. He explored Manchuria in 1886 and discovered the route from Kashgar into India via the Mustagh Pass. In 1902 he visited Tibet to make a treaty with the Dalai Lama and to open up the country to western trade.

Young Ireland An Irish nationalist movement formed by young Protestant radicals in the 1840s. Its rising in 1848 under William Smith *O'Brien was a humiliating failure.

Young Italy A movement, founded by Giuseppe *Mazzini in 1831, that sought to establish a united republican Italy. After the failure of Mazzini's invasion of Savoy and other risings in the 1830s and 1840s its influence declined. *See also* Risorgimento.

Young Men's Christian Association (YMCA) A Christian organization for young men and, since 1971, for young women, founded in 1844 by George Williams (1821–1905), a British draper. Its aim is to encourage Christian morality and qualities of leadership. The World Alliance of YMCAs, formed in 1855 in Geneva, consists of 20 million members in 84 countries.

Young's modulus. *See* elastic modulus.

Youngstown 41 05N 80 40W A city in the USA, in Ohio. It is a centre of an extensive iron and steel industry and produces aluminium, office furniture, and aircraft. Youngstown State University was established here in 1908. Population (1980): 115 436.

Young Turks A Turkish revolutionary group. In 1908 the Young Turks, officially named the Committee of Union and Progress, led the revolution that resulted in Sultan *Abdülhamid's abdication. Under *Enver Pasha and Talaat Pasha (1872–1921), they were the dominant force in Turkish politics until 1918.

Young Women's Christian Association (YWCA) A Christian organization for women (to which men may now also belong). Founded in 1855 by Emma Robarts and Mary Jane Kinnaird to promote unity among Christians and understanding between those of different faiths. It provides social welfare, education, and recreational facilities, as well as accommodation in hostels. It is a member of the world movement of the YWCA, formed in 1894 and having branches in over 80 countries.

Youth Hostels Association (YHA) A British organization, founded in 1930, to promote a greater understanding of the countryside, especially by providing hostels where young people of limited means may stay inexpensively. There are over 250 hostels in England and Wales and the Association's 250 000 members may also use hostels run by similar organizations abroad. Secretary: H. B. Livingstone.

Ypres (Flemish name: Ieper) 50 51N 2 53E A town in W Belgium, on the River Yperlee. An important textile centre in the middle ages, its many medieval buildings, including the Cloth Hall (13th–14th centuries) and the cathedral, were almost completely destroyed during *World War I. It was later rebuilt, many buildings in their original style, and a memorial was erected to British troops killed here. Population (1985 est): 35 000.

Ypsilanti A Greek family prominent in Balkan revolts against the Ottoman Empire. **Alexander Ypsilanti** (c. 1725–c. 1807), governor of Walachia (1774–82, 1796–97) and of Moldavia (1786–88), was executed for allegedly conspiring against the sultan. His son **Constantine Ypsilanti** (1760–1816), governor of Walachia (1802–06, 1807), participated in a Serbian revolt against the Turks. His elder son **Alexander Ypsilanti** (1792–1828) led an uprising in Moldavia and proclaimed Greek independence (1821). Defeated, he fled to Austria, where he was imprisoned (1821–27). Alexander's brother **Demetrios Ypsilanti** (1793–1832) played a prominent part in the War of *Greek Independence.

Ysselmeer. *See* IJsselmeer.

ytterbium (Yb) A *lanthanide element, named, like yttrium, erbium, and terbium, after the village of Ytterby in Sweden. It forms trivalent compounds, including the oxide (Yb_2O_3) and trihalides (for example $YbCl_3$). At no 70; at wt 173.04; mp 819°C; bp 1194°C.

yttrium (Y) A *lanthanide element, discovered in 1794 by J. Gadolin (1760–1852). It is widely used as the oxide (Y_2O_3) to make red television-tube phosphors. At no 39; at wt 88.906; mp 1522 ± 8°C; bp 3338°C.

Yuan (1279–1368) A Mongol dynasty that ruled China after overthrowing the *Song dynasty. The first and strongest Mongol ruler was *Kublai Khan, who held the empire together by military force. Later, revolts broke out and the Mongols were eventually driven out of their capital, Peking, following 27 years of fighting.

Yuan Shi Kai (or Yüan Shih-k'ai; 1859–1916) Chinese general, who became president of the new Chinese republic in 1912 after the downfall of the *Qing dynasty. His attempts to rule dictatorially and to found a new dynasty brought about civil war with the followers of *Sun Yat-sen. Yuan died suddenly, leaving China in chaos.

Yucatán A peninsula of Central America, chiefly in SE Mexico but extending into Belize and Guatemala, separating the Gulf of Mexico from the Caribbean Sea. It was a centre of the civilization of the Maya; many relics remain, notably at Uxmal and Chichén Itzá. Area: about 181 300 sq km (70 00 sq mi).

Yucca A genus of succulent plants (about 40 species), native to S North America and varying in height from small shrubs to 15-m-high trees. Most are stemless and have a rosette of stiff sword-shaped leaves crowded on a stout trunk. The waxy white bell-shaped flowers are borne in a dense terminal cluster and are pollinated by female yucca moths (genus *Pronuba*) when they lay their eggs inside the flowers. Several species are cultivated as ornamentals, including Adam's needle (*Y. filamentosa*) and Spanish dagger (*Y. gloriosa*). Family: *Agavaceae*. *See also* Joshua tree.

Yugoslavia, Socialist Federal Republic of (Serbo-Croat name: Jugoslavija) A country in SE Europe, on the Adriatic Sea. The fertile plains of the Danube-Sava basin in the NE rise to mountains in the S and W, reaching heights of almost 3000 m (10 000 ft). The Serbs and the Croats make up the majority of the population, with minorities of Slovenes, Macedonians, Albanians, and others. *Economy*: agriculture, mainly organized in cooperatives, is important although the numbers employed in this sector have decreased dramatically in recent years. Mechanization has improved agricultural output and the country is now self-sufficient in chemical fertilizers. Livestock is especially important and the principal crops are wheat, maize, sugar beet, sunflowers, and potatoes. There is a thriving wine industry and forestry and fishing are important sources of revenue. Rich mineral resources include coal, iron ore, copper, and lead, and some oil is produced. Over half the country's power comes from hydroelectric sources. Development of heavy and light industry has been rapid since World War II and there is a growing tourist industry. Exports include meat, machinery, nonferrous metals, timber, textiles, and ships. *History*: Yugoslavia was so named in 1927 but was formed in 1918 as the kingdom of the Serbs, Croats, and Slovenes by the federation of Serbia, Montenegro, Croatia, Slovenia, and Bosnia-Herzegovina. Alexander I assumed absolute power in 1929 and was assassinated by Croatian nationalists in 1934. In World War II Yugoslavia was occupied by the Germans and Peter II fled to London. Internal resistance to the Germans became divided between the *Chetniks and the Partisans, the latter gaining Allied support in 1943. After the war the Partisans' leader *Tito became head of a communist government. In 1948 relations with the Soviet Union were broken off and, although they became closer again after the death of Stalin, Yugoslavia has preserved a policy of nonalignment in foreign affairs and a decentralized form of socialism that aims to give more direct power to the workers. Since Tito's death a new premier is chosen each year. Reducing soaring inflation has been the top government priority of the late 1980s. Official languages: all national languages, with Serbo-Croat serving as the lingua franca. Official currency: dinar of 100 para. Area: 255 804 sq km (98 725 sq mi). Population (1983 est): 22 826 000. Capital: Belgrade. Main port: Rijeka.

Yukawa, Hideki (1907–81) Japanese physicist, who, while working at Kyoto University, postulated (1935) that the *strong interaction could be accounted for by the exchange of *virtual particles. He calculated the mass of the particle involved, but at that time no such particle was known. *Anderson's discovery of the muon was thought to have confirmed Yukawa's prediction. But in fact the confirmation did not come until 1947, when Cecil *Powell discovered the pion. Yukawa was awarded a Nobel Prize in 1949.

Yukon A territory of NW Canada, on the Beaufort Sea. Mostly high mountains and plateaus of the Cordillera, it is covered by tundra in the N. Poor soils and low precipitation produce only sparse vegetation, except in S valleys. The population is concentrated on the central plateau, where silver, lead, zinc, copper, and asbestos are mined. There is some lumbering and tourism is expanding rapidly. The Yukon is a frontier region that was first opened up by the *Klondike gold rush (1897–99) and military projects (since 1939). Area: 531 844 sq km (205 345 sq mi). Population (1983 est): 23 216. Capital: Whitehorse.

Yukon River A river in NW North America. Rising in NW Canada on the border between the Yukon and British Columbia, it flows N through Alaska, USA, then SW into the Bering Sea. Its great potential as a source of hydroelectricity has yet to be fully exploited. Length: 3185 km (1979 mi).

Yunnan A mountainous province in S China, bordering on Burma, Laos, and North Vietnam. The ethnically varied population includes aboriginal groups in the mountains. It is China's greatest tin-producing area and rice and timber are grown. *History*: part of China since the 13th century, it was for long rebellious and little developed. It became industrialized during the Sino-Japanese War (1937–45), when many industries moved here from the coast. Area: 436 200 sq km (168 400 sq mi). Population (1980 est): 31 350 000. Capital: Kunming.

YWCA. *See* Young Women's Christian Association.

Z

Zaanstad 52 27N 4 49E A port in the W Netherlands, in North Holland province, formed in 1974 from Zaandam, Koog a/d Zaan, Zaandijk, Wormerveer, Krommenie, Westzaan, and Assendelft. Peter the Great of Russia studied shipbuilding at Zaandam in 1697. The main products are food and machinery. Population (1985): 128 286.

Zabaleta, Nicanor (1907–) Spanish harpist. He studied in Paris with Marcel Tournier (1879–1951). He has commissioned many new works for the harp as well as reviving forgotten compositions.

Zabrze (German name: Hindenburg) 50 18N 18 47E A town in SW Poland. It is a coalmining centre; industries include steel processing, engineering, and chemicals. Population (1982 est): 196 800.

Zacynthus (*or* Zante; Modern Greek name: Zákinthos) A Greek island in the SE Ionian Sea, the southernmost of the Ionian Islands. Most of the island is fertile and currants are the main product. Area: 406 sq km (157 sq mi). Population (1981): 30 014.

Zadar (Italian name: Zara) 44 07N 15 14E A port in W Yugoslavia, in Croatia on the Adriatic Sea. It has a natural deepwater harbour and was the most heavily fortified Adriatic town until the late 19th century. There are many old churches and a Roman forum. Local industries produce maraschino liqueur, cigarettes, rope, and glass. Population (1981): 116 174.

Zadkine, Ossip (1890–1967) French sculptor of Russian birth. He settled in Paris (1909), where he developed a cubist style in his monumental figure sculptures. His best-known work is the war memorial in Rotterdam, entitled *The Destroyed City* (1954).

Zagazig (*or* az-Zaqazig) 30 36N 31 30E A city in N Egypt, on the Nile Delta. The ruins of the ancient city of *Bubastis are nearby. It has a major trade in cotton and cereals. Population (1983 est): 202 637.

Zaghlul, Saad (1857–1927) Egyptian nationalist politician; prime minister (1924). In 1918 he helped to found the nationalist Wafd party. He was arrested by the British but after the granting of limited independence in 1922 he became prime minister. He was soon forced by the British to resign but was active behind the scenes until his death.

Zagorsk (name until 1930: Sergiyev) 56 20N 38 10E A city in the Soviet Union, in the W RSFSR 72 km (45 mi) NE of Moscow. It grew around the famous Trinity-St Sergius monastery (1337–40), the buildings within which, notably the Trinity Cathedral (1422–23) and the Cathedral of the Assumption (1559–85), may still be seen. Population (1983 est): 111 000.

Zagreb 45 48N 15 58E The second largest city of Yugoslavia and capital of Croatia on the River Sava. A cultural centre of the Croats since the 16th century, it possesses a university (1669) and a gothic cathedral. Industries include textiles, machinery, and paper manufacture. Population (1981): 1 174 512.

Zagros Mountains A mountain system in W Iran, extending 1600 km (994 mi) NW–SE between the Soviet border and the Strait of Hormuz. It consists of many parallel ranges and rises to 4811 m (15 784 ft) in the N at Sabalan.

Zaharoff, Sir Basil (1849–1936) British financier and arms dealer, born in Turkey of Greek parents. In 1888 he became the representative in eastern Europe of Maxim-Nordenfelt, the armaments company. During World War I he was an Allied agent, for which he received a knighthood.

Zaïre, Republic of (name from 1960 until 1971: Congo) A large country in central equatorial Africa, with a short coastline on the Atlantic Ocean. The central part of the country is dominated by a vast plateau, rising to the Ruwenzori Mountains in the SE. It is drained by the Zaïre River and its many tributaries and fringed along its E border by a chain of lakes, including Lake Tanganyika, comprising part of the *Great Rift Valley. Most of the population is African, the largest groups being Luba, Mongo, and Kongo. *Economy*: efforts are being made to increase agricultural production, which has fallen in recent years through droughts and political unrest. The chief cash crops are coffee, cotton, palm oil, and rubber; maize, rice, and cassava are grown extensively as the staple food crops. Zaïre has rich and varied mineral resources, principally copper (the chief export) from the Shaba mines, and is the world's chief producer of industrial diamonds and cobalt. Other minerals include manganese, zinc, and uranium and oil has been found offshore (exploited since 1975). Hydroelectricity is a valuable source of power and Zaïre is estimated to have about 50% of Africa's total potential hydroelectric capacity. The rivers, especially the Zaïre River, are also important for transport. *History*: when the Portuguese penetrated the region in the late 15th century it was dominated by the kingdom of the Kongo. In the late 19th century it was explored by Livingstone and, under Belgian auspices, by Stanley. Leopold II of the Belgians established personal rule over the Congo Free State, which was recognized by the European powers at the Conference of Berlin (1884–85). In 1908 it was annexed by Belgium, becoming the colony of the Belgian Congo. Independence was obtained in 1960, as the Republic of the Congo. The almost immediate secession of Katanga province under Tshombe resulted in civil war in which the UN intervened (an international force remained in the country until 1964). In 1965 Mobutu Sese Seko seized power and in 1971 the Congo was renamed Zaïre. In 1977 and again in 1978 an invasion force entered *Shaba (formerly Katanga) province from Angola, in unsuccessful attempts to topple Mobutu, and on the second occasion the massacre of Europeans in Kolwezi brought French and Belgian forces to Zaïre. In 1978 Zaïre became a one-party state. Official language: French. Official currency, since 1967: zaïre of 100 makuta. Area: 2 345 409 sq km (895 348 sq mi). Population (1983 est): 31 250 000. Capital: Kinshasa. Main port: Matadi.

Zaïre River (former name: Congo R.) The second longest river in Africa. Its true source is disputed, one headstream being the River *Lualaba and the other the River Chambezi (later the River Luvua), which rises in a high plateau between Lakes Malawi and Tanganyika. Below the confluence of the two headstreams it flows N, being known as the Lualaba until the Boyoma Falls, where it becomes the Zaïre River. It flows generally W then SW, through Malebo Pool, to enter the Atlantic Ocean via a delta at Boma. The Zaïre River is an important potential source of hydroelectric power with the construction of dams in the 1970s. Length: 4820 km (3000 mi).

zaltys A green snake that was a symbol of wealth and fertility in the Baltic region in ancient times. Households often kept a zaltys and it was believed that misfortune would befall anyone who killed one.

Zambezi River A river in S Africa. Rising in NW Zambia, it flows generally S through E Angola before re-entering Zambia and curving E along the Caprivi Strip frontier of Namibia. It then forms the Zambian–Zimbabwe border, the *Victoria Falls and Kariba Dam (*see* Kariba, Lake) being located along this course, before flowing SE through

Mozambique to enter the Indian Ocean via an extensive delta. It has the fourth largest drainage area in Africa with an area of about 1 347 000 sq km (520 000 sq mi). Length: 2740 km (1700 mi).

Zambia, Republic of (name until 1964: Northern Rhodesia) A landlocked country in S central Africa. It consists chiefly of low undulating plateaus and is drained along its southern border by the Zambezi River; other main rivers are the Kafue and Luangwa. The swampy Lake Bangweulu lies in the N. The population is virtually all African, largely Bantu, with small minorities of Europeans, Asians, and Chinese. *Economy*: the mining sector is responsible for producing most of Zambia's wealth from the rich mineral resources. Copper accounts for about 96% of the total mineral production and comes mainly from the *Copperbelt. Lead and zinc from Kabwe are also important, some coal is mined, and there are extensive iron-ore deposits, as yet unexploited. Agriculture is a major occupation; the chief subsistence crop is maize. Cash crops include tobacco, groundnuts, cotton, and sugar but commercial agriculture declined during the 1970s. Livestock and forestry are also important. Communications, which were hampered by the closure of the Rhodesian border (1973) and by unrest in Mozambique, were aided by the opening (1975) of the Chinese-built Tanzam Railway to Dar es Salaam (Tanzania). *History*: the area had already been occupied by Bantu peoples when it was raided by Arab slave traders in the 18th century. In the 19th century British missionaries, notably *Livingstone, paved the way for Cecil *Rhodes, who incorporated the region into a territory named Rhodesia in his honour and administered by the British South Africa Company. Constituted as Northern Rhodesia in 1911, it became a British protectorate in 1924. It formed part of the Federation of Rhodesia and Nyasaland (1953–63), obtaining internal self-government and, shortly afterwards, full independence within the British Commonwealth as the Republic of Zambia (1964). *Kaunda has been president since independence. In 1972 a new constitution led to one-party (the United National Independence Party) rule. Zambia supported the Zimbabwe nationalist movement, providing a base for Nkomo's arm of the Patriotic Front, and its border with Rhodesia (now Zimbabwe) was closed from 1973 until 1980. Official language: English. Official currency, since 1968: kwacha of 100 ngwee. Area: 752 262 sq km (290 586 sq mi). Population (1983 est): 6 346 000. Capital: Lusaka.

Zamboanga 6 55N 122 05E A port in the S Philippines, in SW Mindanao. A resort, it is noted for its picturesque setting and tropical flowers and has a 17th-century Spanish fort. Brass and bronzeware are produced and it exports copra, hardwoods, and hemp. Population (1980): 344 275.

Zamoyski A prominent Polish family, which became powerful under **Jan Zamoyski** (1542–1605), who was advisor to Sigismund II Augustus (*see* Jagiellons) and to *Stephen Báthory. **Andrzej Zamoyski** (1716–92) worked for parliamentary reform and the abolition of serfdom, freeing his own serfs. Andrzej's son **Stanisław Zamoyski** (1775–1856) played an important role in the November Insurrection against Russian dominance, as did Stanisław's son **Andrzej Zamoyski** (1800–74), who also participated in the January Insurrection, for which he was exiled (*see* Congress Kingdom of Poland).

Zamyatin, Yevgenii Ivanovich (1884–1937) Russian novelist. His works include vivid satirical studies of life in provincial Russia and England, where he worked during World War I. He was severely criticized after the European publication of his novel *We* (1924), a bleak prophecy of a totalitarian future, and from 1931 he lived in Paris.

Zante. *See* Zacynthus.

Zanzibar An island in Tanzania, off the NE coast of the mainland. It came under Arab influence early on in its history and was, together with *Pemba, a sultanate from

1856 to 1964. It was under British rule from 1890 until it became independent within the British Commonwealth in 1963. In 1964 the Sultan was exiled and Zanzibar united with Tanganyika to form Tanzania. It exports mainly cloves and copra. Area: 1658 sq km (640 sq mi). Population (1985 est): 571 000. Chief town: Zanzibar.

Zao Zhan. *See* Cao Chan.

EMILIANO ZAPATA   *This photograph shows the machismo associated with the Mexican revolutionary.*

Zapata, Emiliano (?1877–1919) Mexican revolutionary, who championed the cause of agrarian reform against Porfirio *Diaz and succeeding governments. By late 1911 he controlled the state of Morelos, where he carried out land reforms, chasing out the estate owners and dividing their land amongst the peasants. In 1919 he was tricked into an ambush and assassinated.

Zaporozhye (name until 1921: Aleksandrovsk) 47 50N 35 10E A city in the SW Soviet Union, in the Ukrainian SSR on the River Dnepr. A large hydroelectric station, built here in the years 1927–32, was destroyed in World War II but subsequently rebuilt. There is an important iron and steel industry and a variety of engineering activities. Population (1981 est): 812 000.

Zapotecs An American Indian people of the Oaxaca valleys (S Mexico). Their traditional culture, emerging about 300 AD, developed into one of the classic Mesoamerican Indian civilizations. Monte Alban, their chief city, declined under pressure from the *Mixtecs (c. 900–50).

Zara. *See* Zadar.

Zaragoza (English name: Saragossa) 41 39N 0 54W A city in NE Spain, in Aragon on the River Ebro. During the Peninsular War it heroically resisted a French siege until about 50 000 of its defenders had died (1808–09). It has two cathedrals and a university (founded 1533). An industrial centre, Zaragoza produces paper and wine. Population (1981): 590 750.

Zarathustra. *See* Zoroaster.

Zaria 11 01N 7 44E A city in Nigeria. Founded in the 16th century, it became the capital of the emirate of Zaria. It has textile, cosmetics, and cigarette industries. Nearby is the Ahmadu Bello University (1962). Population (1982 est): 267 300.

Zátopek, Emil (1922–) Czech long-distance runner. In 1948 he won his first Olympic gold medal, for the 10 000 metres. At the Helsinki Olympics (1952) he won gold medals for the 5000 metres, 10 000 metres, and the marathon.

Zawiyat al-Bayda' (*or* Beida) 32 49N 21 45E A new town in NE Libya. Its construction was started in the 1950s as the future capital for the country, but in the mid-1980s had not become so.

Zealand. *See* Sjælland.

Zealots A Jewish political party of the 1st century AD. They were bitterly opposed to Roman rule in Judaea, and played a leading part in the revolt of 66 AD. Their last stronghold, *Masada, fell in 73. After the war their influence in Judaea was minimal but they may have been responsible for the further revolts in Egypt, Libya, and Cyprus in 115 AD.

Zeami Motokiyo (1363–c. 1443) Japanese playwright, son of the dramatist Kanami Kiyotsugu (1333–84). He achieved fame first as an actor but later became a leading theorist of No drama, his best-known treatise being *Kadensho*. He wrote over 150 plays.

zebra An African wild horse having characteristic black and white stripes covering part or all of the body. There are three races of the plains zebra (*Equus burchelli*), distinguished by the extent and nature of their stripes. The mountain zebra (*E. zebra*) has very bold stripes and a dewlap on the throat, while Grévy's zebra (*E. grevyi*) is the largest species, standing over 1.5 m at the shoulder with narrow stripes.

zebra finch An Australian *grassfinch, *Taeniopyga castanotis*, occurring in large flocks in the interior grasslands. It has a red bill and the males are grey above with white underparts, reddish flanks, red-brown ear patches, and black-and-white barred throat, breast, and tail. Zebra finches are popular cagebirds and have been selectively bred to produce a white form with the black-and-white barring.

zebra fish A tropical freshwater fish, *Brachydanio rerio*, also called zebra danio, found in E India and popular in aquaria. It has a shiny blue body, up to 4.5 cm long, with four longitudinal yellowish gold stripes along its sides. *See also* scorpion fish; tigerfish.

zebra wood Any of several tropical trees that yield hard striped timber, used in furniture, especially *Connarus guianensis*, of Guyana. It has compound leaves with paired oval leaflets and clusters of five-petalled flowers. Family: *Connaraceae*.

zebu The domestic *cattle of Asia and Africa, *Bos indicus*, also called Brahmin (*or* Brahman). Larger and leaner than western cattle, zebus have a distinctive hump over the shoulders, a large dewlap under the throat, and long horns. They are generally grey or red, but a number of other colour varieties exist. Zebus are no longer found in the wild state and have been exported to many hot countries to confer their qualities of heat tolerance and insect resistance in crosses with beef breeds.

Zebulun, tribe of One of the 12 *tribes of Israel. It claimed descent from Zebulun, the son of Jacob and Leah. Its people lived to the W and SW of the Sea of Galilee.

Zechariah An Old Testament prophet of Judah, who delivered his prophecies about 520 BC. **The Book of Zechariah** relates a series of eight visions calculated to inspire the people to rebuild the Temple at Jerusalem. The book also deals with questions concerning fasting and predicts the coming of a kingly messiah and the end of the Diaspora.

Zedekiah The last king of Judah (597-586 BC). Having rebelled against *Nebuchadnezzar, Zedekiah was forced to witness his sons' execution and was then blinded and removed to *Babylon. The prophet Jeremiah, an eye-witness, vividly describes these events.

Zeebrugge 51 20N 3 13E A small port in NW Belgium, on the North Sea, connected by ship canal (1907) to Bruges. A German submarine base in World War I, the canal was blocked by British naval forces in 1918.

Zeeland A province in the SW Netherlands, on the Scheldt delta. It consists mainly of islands, including Walcheren. Severe flooding in 1953 necessitated the Delta Plan, under which several major dams have been constructed and dykes strengthened. The important mussel and oyster fisheries of the Oosterschelde estuary have been preserved. Agricultural produce includes wheat, sugar beet, fruit, and dairy products. Area: 2746 sq km (1060 sq mi). Population (1981 est): 351 662. Capital: Middelburg.

Zeeman, Pieter (1865-1943) Dutch physicist, who, while working at Leiden University, discovered (1886) the splitting of the spectral lines of a substance when placed in a magnetic field (**Zeeman effect**). It is caused by changes in the energy levels of the electrons of the emitting atoms as a result of interaction between the magnetic moment of the orbit and the external field. For this discovery he shared the 1902 Nobel Prize with Hendrik *Lorentz.

Zeffirelli, G. Franco (1923–) Italian director and stage designer. Having started as an actor under the direction of *Visconti, he went on to direct film versions of *The Taming of the Shrew* (1966) and *Romeo and Juliet* (1968). Other films include *Jesus of Nazareth* (1975), *La Traviata* (1983), and *Otello* (1986). He has worked on operas at *Covent Garden, *Glyndebourne, and the *Metropolitan. His many stage productions include *Othello* (Stratford-upon-Avon, 1961) *Hamlet* (Old Vic, 1964), and *Filumena* (1977).

Zeiss, Carl (1816-88) German industrialist and manufacturer of optical instruments. Zeiss opened his first workshop in Jena (1846) and later employed Ernst Abbe (1840-1905) to advise him on theoretical advances in optics.

Zen Buddhism (Japanese *Zen*, meditation) In China and Japan, a Buddhist school emphasizing the transmission of enlightenment from master to disciple without reliance on the scriptures. It derives from the teaching of *Bodhidharma, who came to China in 520 AD. The two major sects, *Soto and Rinzai, stress meditation and the use of logical paradoxes (*koans*) respectively, in order to confound the rational mind so that transcendental wisdom can arise and the disciple can realize his own Buddha-nature. Much of Japanese and Chinese art, music, and literature, as well as calligraphy, the tea ceremony (*see* cha-no-yu), the martial arts, etc., express the spontaneous Zen attitude to life. Recently Zen has gained followers in the West, where its opposition to rationalism has popular appeal.

Zener diode. *See* semiconductor diode.

zenith The point in the sky lying directly above an observer and 90° from all points on his horizon. The (unobservable) point diametrically opposite the zenith is the **nadir**. □celestial sphere.

Zenobia (3rd century AD) The wife of Odaenathus of Palmyra, whom she may have murdered (267) and whom she succeeded as regent for their son. Zenobia occupied Syria, Egypt, and much of Asia Minor before *Aurelian defeated and captured her in 272. She enjoyed a reputation for beauty and intelligence.

Zeno of Citium (c. 335-262 BC) Greek philosopher, who was born in Cyprus of Phoenician stock, came to Athens in 313 BC, and attended lectures at *Plato's Academy. He was influenced by various philosophical schools, including the *Cynics, before evolving his own doctrine of *Stoicism.

Zeno of Elea (born c. 490 BC) Greek philosopher. Zeno's paradoxes, supporting *Parmenides' doctrines that reality is indivisible and reason is at variance with the senses, are the first dialectic arguments, eliciting contradictory conclusions from an opponent's hypotheses. These paradoxes include: Achilles and the tortoise—if space is infinitely divisible, once Achilles has given the tortoise a start he cannot overtake it, for whenever he arrives where the tortoise was it has already moved on; the flying arrow—if space is divisible into finite parts, a moving arrow at each moment of its flight is opposite a particular piece of ground and therefore stationary.

zeolites A group of complex silicate minerals containing loosely held water. They are divided into three groups: fibrous (natrolite, mesolite, scolecite), platy (heulandite, stilbite), and equant (harmatome, chabazite). Most occur in cavities in basic volcanic rocks. They are usually colourless or white and are relatively soft. Because of their property of base exchange they were used as water softeners before the introduction of artificial substitutes. They are also used as molecular sieves in the petroleum industry and as drying agents.

Zephaniah (late 7th century BC) An Old Testament prophet of Judah. **The Book of Zephaniah** records his condemnation of those who continued as idolaters despite the reforms carried out by Josiah (d. 608 BC) and predicts universal judgment from which few will escape.

Zeppelins. *See* airships.

Zermatt 46 01N 7 45E A village in S Switzerland, at the foot of the Matterhorn. A popular resort, it is also a famous mountaineering and winter-sports centre, at a height of 1620 m (5315 ft). Population (1985 est): 3700.

Zernicke, Frits (1888-1966) Dutch physicist, who was awarded the 1953 Nobel Prize for his invention of the phase-contrast microscope (1934). This invention enabled the parts of a cell to be seen without staining.

Zetkin, Clara (1857-1933) German communist and feminist leader. Zetkin founded the International Socialist Women's Congress in 1907 and joined the German Communist Party in 1919. She was a leader of the pro-Soviet wing of the Party and spent much time in the Soviet Union.

Zetland. *See* Shetland Islands.

Zeus The Greek sky and weather god, the supreme deity, identified with the Roman *Jupiter. He was the son of Cronus and Rhea, and brother of Poseidon and Hades. His defeat of Cronus and the *Titans represents the triumph of the Olympian deities over their predecessors. His offspring included *Athena, *Apollo, and *Dionysus and from his many love affairs, which excited the jealousy of his wife, *Hera, were produced numerous other divine and semidivine children. He was usually portrayed as a bearded man, with thunderbolts and the eagle as his attributes.

Zeus, statue of The chryselephantine statue designed by the Greek sculptor *Phidias in about 430 BC for the temple of Zeus at Olympia. One of the *Seven Wonders of the World, it was 12 m (40 ft) high and covered with jewels and gold. It was destroyed in the 5th century AD.

Zeuxis (late 5th century BC) Greek painter, born at Heracleia (S Italy). Zeuxis improved the contemporary use of perspective, shading, and mixed colours. His *trompe l'oeil* effect, it is said, induced birds to peck at grapes painted by him. He specialized in mythological subjects.

Zhangjiakou (*or* Chang-chia-k'ou; Mongolian name: Kalgan) 40 51N 114 59E A city in NE China, in Hebei province near the *Great Wall. It was historically important for defence against and trade with the Mongols and is the site

of two forts (1429, 1613). Industries include textiles and machinery. Population (1980 est): 1 094 000.

Zhao Guang Yin. *See* Song.

Zhdanov (name until 1948: Mariupol) 47 05N 37 34E A port in the Soviet Union, in the SE Ukrainian SSR on an estuary leading into the Sea of Azov. A railway (1882) connects it with the Donets Basin and it exports coal. It has a variety of industries and supports a fishing fleet. Population (1981 est): 511 000.

Zhejiang (Che-chiang *or* Chekiang) A mountainous province in E China, on the East China Sea. Densely populated, it has been a cultural centre since the Southern *Song dynasty was centred here (12th-13th centuries). It is a highly productive agricultural area and silk and fishing are important. Area: 102 000 sq km (39 780 sq mi). Population (1980 est): 37 920 000. Capital: Hangzhou.

Zheng Cheng Gong (*or* Cheng Ch'eng-kung; 1624-62) Chinese pirate also known as Koxinga, who controlled most of the Fujian coast from his base in Amoy. He led the Ming resistance to the new Qing rulers and attempted to recapture Nanjing. This failed but he seized Formosa (now Taiwan) from the Dutch in 1661, which became the last Ming stronghold.

Zheng He (*or* Cheng Ho; died c. 1433) A Chinese eunuch of the Ming dynasty, who in 1405 built a fleet and set out on a famous mission to Indochina. Further expeditions to Indochina and the Middle East re-established trade links that had been severed on the collapse of Yuan rule in 1368.

Zhengzhou (*or* Cheng-chou) 34 35N 113 38E A city in E China, the capital of Henan province. An old administrative centre, it has many industries developed since 1949. Population (1983 est): 1 424 000.

Zhitomir 50 18N 28 40E A city in the Soviet Union, in the central Ukrainian SSR. Dating from at least the 13th century, it was subsequently held by Lithuania and then Poland before being restored to Russia in 1793. A communications centre, it processes the produce of the surrounding agricultural region. Population (1981 est): 254 000.

Zhivkov, Todor (1911-) Bulgarian statesman, noted, as head of state (1954-), for encouraging friendly relations with other Balkan countries. A partisan leader in World War II, Zhivkov led the communist overthrow of the monarchy in 1944. He became first secretary of the Bulgarian Communist Party in 1954 and was prime minister (1962-71) before becoming president (1971).

Zhou (?1027-221 BC) The earliest Chinese dynasty of which there is accurate knowledge. The dynasty was founded in the area now called Shenxi after the Zhou ruler, Wu Wang, had annihilated the armies of the preceding Shang dynasty and set up a system of government under feudal rulers. These undermined Zhou authority in the so-called Warring States period (481-221), after which the *Qin emerged to unite China. Under the Zhou human sacrifice was abolished and the Chinese idea of *ancestor worship came into being. The late Zhou was also the great period of Chinese philosophy, when Taoist and Confucian thought (*see* Taoism; Confucianism) first emerged.

Zhuangzi (*or* Chuang-tzu; c. 369-286 BC) Chinese philosopher. He is known only through the book to which he gave his name, a work of Taoist philosophy containing allegories, anecdotes, and satires on Confucius. The book, which greatly influenced the development of Chinese Buddhism, advocated spiritual harmony with Tao, the essential principle of the universe, through liberation from all worldly circumstances.

Zhu De (*or* Chu Teh; 1886-1976) Chinese marshal. He joined the Chinese Communist Party while a student in Germany and after his return helped organize the Nanchang communist uprising against the *Guomindang (Nationalists; 1927). He joined Mao Tse-tung in 1928 and became commander of the Fourth Red Army (later the People's

Liberation Army), a post he retained until 1954. He served with Mao throughout the period leading to the establishment of the People's Republic of *China (1949), during which his kindness to his troops became legendary.

Zhu Jiang (*or* Chu Chiang; English name: Pearl River) A river in S China, formed by the confluence of the *Xi Jiang and Bei (*or* Pei) River near Canton and flowing into an estuary that is used by oceangoing ships. Length: 177 km (110 mi).

Zhukov, Georgi Konstantinovich (1896–1974) Soviet marshal. An armoured-warfare expert, he became chief of the army general staff (1941). He planned or commanded almost every major Soviet military operation in World War II, including the Soviet occupation force in Germany. Under Khrushchev he became defence minister and then a member of the presidium of the Communist Party.

Zia ul-Haq, Gen Mohammad (1924–) Pakistani statesman; president (1978–). In 1976 he was appointed chief of the army staff and in the following year led the coup that overthrew *Bhutto, becoming chief martial law administrator (1977). In 1979 Zia refused worldwide appeals to commute Bhutto's death sentence for conspiracy to murder.

Ziaur Rahman (1936–81) Bangladesh statesman and army officer; president (1977–81). He fought in the war against Pakistan in 1971 and became chief of staff of the armed forces in 1975. He became chief martial law administrator in 1976, following *Mujibur Rahman's assassination (1975), and president after his position had been confirmed by a referendum, but was himself assassinated during an unsuccessful insurrection.

Zibo (*or* Tzu-po) 36 32N 117 47E A city in E China, in Shandong province, formed by the amalgamation of Zi-cheng (*or* Tzu-ch'eng) and Bo-shan (*or* Po-shan). It has coalmining, chemical, electrical, and machine-building industries. Population (1983 est): 2 234 000.

Ziegfeld, Florenz (1867–1932) US theatrical producer. His lavish revues were modelled on the *Folies-Bergère. *The Ziegfeld Follies*, billed as "An American Institution," appeared annually from 1907 until his death. Using the slogan, "Glorifying the American Girl," he created such hits as *Sally* (1920), *Show Boat* (1927), and *Bitter Sweet* (1929). He also launched Will Rogers, W. C. Fields, Eddie Cantor, and others on their careers.

Ziegler, Karl (1898–1973) German chemist, who shared the 1963 Nobel Prize with Giulio Natta (1903–) for their work on plastics and polymers. Ziegler showed that certain organometallic compounds (**Ziegler catalysts**) would catalyze the *polymerization of ethylene giving unbranched polymers that were tougher and had a higher melting point than those previously obtainable.

ziggurat An ancient Mesopotamian brick-built temple tower. Ziggurats were constructed of rectangular terraces of diminishing size, generally with a shrine for the god on top. They existed in every major Sumerian, Babylonian, and Assyrian centre, the one at Babylon being the probable original of the Tower of *Babel.

Zimbabwe, State of (name until 1979: Rhodesia) A landlocked country in SE Africa. It is bounded in the N by the Zambezi River and in the S by the Limpopo River. Much of the land consists of plateau, generally over 1000 m (3300 ft), with extensive areas of savanna. The majority of the population is Bantu with small minorities of Europeans, Asians, and others. *Economy*: agriculture is important, but the imposing of economic sanctions (1965–79) led to restructuring; tobacco production has fallen and diversification to cotton and cattle has taken place; other cash crops include sugar, tea, and citrus fruit. The chief subsistence crops are maize, millet, and groundnuts. Forestry and fishing are important with fish farming on Lake Kariba. Zimbabwe has copper, asbestos, gold, chrome, and nickel resources, but no oil reserves. An industrial growth crisis

in the late 1980s threatens the existing food-processing, metal-processing, engineering, and textile industries. The main exports are tobacco, nickel, copper, asbestos, and sugar. *History*: ruins at *Great Zimbabwe attest the existence of a medieval Bantu civilization in the region. In 1837 its Mashona inhabitants were conquered by the Matabele and later in the 19th century it was explored by European missionaries, notably David *Livingstone. In 1889 Cecil *Rhodes obtained a charter for the British South Africa Company, which conquered the Matabele and their territory, named Rhodesia (1895) in Rhodes' honour. In 1911 it was divided into Northern Rhodesia (now *Zambia) and Southern Rhodesia, the latter becoming a self-governing British colony in 1922. In 1953 the two parts of Rhodesia were reunited in the Federation of *Rhodesia and Nyasaland, and after its dissolution in 1963 the Whites demanded independence for Southern Rhodesia (Rhodesia from 1964). The UK's refusal to permit independence without a guarantee of majority rule within a specific period led the Rhodesian prime minister Ian *Smith to issue a unilateral declaration of independence (UDI) in 1965. Both the UK and the UN imposed economic sanctions on Rhodesia but these and further talks in 1966 and 1968 proved fruitless. In 1970 Rhodesia declared itself a republic. In 1974 the Rhodesian government opened negotiations with the leaders of the Zimbabwe African People's Union (ZAPU) and the Zimbabwe African National Union (ZANU), which had pursued guerrilla activities since the 1960s. Smith failed to negotiate an agreement with the Black nationalists, who remained seriously divided under the nominal umbrella of the African National Council. In 1978, following the intervention of Henry *Kissinger (1976) and the UK (1977), agreement was reached on a transitional government leading to Black majority rule. However, the failure of the subsequent government under Muzorewa to obtain the support of the Patriotic Front led to agreement at the 1979 Commonwealth Conference to hold an all-party conference in an attempt to achieve internal unity. Following the conference, held at Lancaster House, London (1979–80), Lord *Soames was appointed governor to oversee the disarming of guerrillas, the holding of elections (which brought Robert *Mugabe, leader of ZANU (PF), to power), and the granting of independence to Zimbabwe as a member of the Commonwealth (1980). In 1987 White representation in parliament was no longer guaranteed and ZAPU and ZANU united to form a one-party state with Mugabe as president. Official language: English; the most important African languages are Ndebele and Shona. Official currency, since 1979: Zimbabwe dollar of 100 cents. Area: 390 622 sq km (150 820 sq mi). Population (1983 est): 8 376 000. Capital: Harare (formerly Salisbury).

zinc (Zn) A bluish-white metal known in antiquity in India and the Middle East and rediscovered in Europe in 1846 by A. S. Marggraf (1709–82). It occurs in nature principally in the ores calamine ($ZnCO_3$), zincite (ZnO), and zinc blende (ZnS). It is extracted by reduction of the oxide (ZnO) with carbon. The metal is more electropositive than iron and is widely used to make *galvanized steel. Zinc forms a number of useful low-melting alloys, including *brass and type metal, and is also used to make castings. The sulphide (ZnS) is a phosphor and is used in making television screens and fluorescent tubes. Zinc oxide (ZnO) is widely used as a paint pigment and in medicines, batteries, cosmetics, plastics, and other products. Trace amounts of zinc are important for growth in animals, including humans. At no 30; at wt 65.37; mp 419.58°C; bp 907°C.

zinc blende. *See* sphalerite.

zincite A minor ore of zinc, consisting of zinc oxide. It is often found in association with *sphalerite and probably results from the alteration of sphalerite. It usually contains some manganese.

zinc yellow A greenish yellow pigment, usually made by

reaction of zinc oxide, potassium dichromate, and sulphuric acid. It is light fast, inhibits rusting, and is resistant to sulphides.

Zinder 13 46N 8 58E A town in S central Niger. Once a centre for Saharan trade, it is now an important trade and processing centre for groundnuts. Population (1981 est): 74 600.

Zinjanthropus. *See* Australopithecus.

Zinnia A genus of herbs and shrubs (about 15 species), mostly native to North America. They have stiff hairy stems, oval to heart-shaped leaves, and daisy-like flower heads with yellow or brownish central disc florets and variously coloured ray florets. Cultivated zinnias are hybrids derived from the Mexican species *Z. elegans*. They have double flowers, about 11 cm across, and most are half-hardy annuals. Family: *Compositae*.

Zinoviev, Grigori Yevseevich (1883–1936) Soviet politician. Zinoviev became a member of the politburo (1918) and chairman of the Comintern (1919) but was expelled from the Communist Party in 1927. In 1935 he was accused of complicity in the murder of *Kirov and was executed. A letter allegedly written by Zinoviev, in which the British Communist Party was urged to revolt, contributed to the defeat of the Labour Government in 1924.

Zinzendorf, Nikolaus Ludwig, Graf von (1700–60) German nobleman and churchman, who re-formed the *Moravian Brethren by settling Hussite refugees from Moravia on his estate in Saxony. Exiled from Saxony (1736–47), he became a bishop of the Moravian Church in 1737, spreading its beliefs in England, America, and elsewhere.

Zion (*or* Sion) A stronghold (II Samuel 5.6–7) on the SE hill of Jerusalem, captured by David, who made it the centre of his capital (Jerusalem). Another name for Jerusalem, it is also described throughout the Old Testament as the place in which God dwells and reigns. In the New Testament and in later Christian writings, it symbolizes heaven.

ZODIAC *The signs of the zodiac from* De astrorum scientia *by Leopold of Austria (Augsburg, 1489).*

Zionism A Jewish nationalist movement. It emerged during the 19th century on a tide of European antisemitism and was formally established at the First Zionist Congress (Basle, 1897). The Congress defined its political aim as the establishment of a Jewish national home in Palestine; the World Zionist Organization was set up, with Theodor *Herzl as its first president. Jewish immigration into Palestine (*aliyah*) was encouraged, especially through the Jewish National Fund (founded 1901) and the Jewish Agency for Palestine (1929). It was also supported by the *Balfour Declaration, facilitated by Chaim Weizmann's relationship with the British government. Breakaway groups included the Territorialists, who sought a land outside Palestine, and the Revisionists, who were opposed to collectivism and collaboration with the British. After World War II, the holocaust provided Zionism with an unanswerable case.

zircon A mineral consisting of zirconium silicate, found as an accessory mineral in intermediate and acid igneous rocks. It is usually colourless or yellowish. Gem varieties include hyacinth (red) and jargoon (colourless or smoky grey). It is the chief ore of zirconium and is used as a refractory material.

zirconium (Zr) A grey high-melting-point transition metal, isolated by J. J. Berzelius in 1824. It occurs in nature as zircon (zirconium silicate; $ZrSiO_4$), which is used as a gemstone. The dioxide (zirconia; ZrO_2) has a high melting point (2715°C) and is used as a refractory and crucible material. The metal is used in cladding fuel elements in nuclear reactors. At no 40; at wt 91.22; mp 1852°C; bp 4377°C.

zither A plucked stringed instrument of ancient origin, consisting of a flat resonating box fitted with 30 to 40 strings, approximately 5 of which lie across a fretted fingerboard for playing the melody. The rest are used for playing accompanying chords. It is particularly popular in Bavaria and the Tirol.

Zi Xi (*or* Tz'u-hsi; 1835–1908) Chinese empress. The daughter of a middle-class Manchu family, she became an imperial concubine. She was made empress on the birth of her son *Tong Zhi, becoming his regent and, after his death, regent for her young nephew *Guang Xu. She thus wielded enormous power over state affairs, her reactionary policies being largely responsible for the fall of imperial China.

Žižka, Jan, Count (c. 1370–1424) Bohemian military leader, who was head of the *Hussite military community at Tabar. He was victorious against the Holy Roman Emperor Sigismund, using armoured farm wagons and tactics that anticipated modern tank warfare.

Zlatoust 55 10N 59 38E A city in the Soviet Union, in the W RSFSR. It has been the largest metallurgical centre in the Urals since the 18th century. Population (1981 est): 201 000.

zodiac A zone of the heavens extending about 8° on either side of the *ecliptic. Within it lies the apparent annual path of the sun, as seen from the earth, and the orbits of the moon, and major planets, apart from Pluto. The 12 constellations in the zodiac are known as "signs" or "houses" to astrologers, who believe them capable of stamping their individual dispositions upon those born under their influence (*see* astrology). The 12 signs and their astrologically effective dates (different from their astronomical periods on account of *precession) are: Aries, the Ram 21 Mar–19 Apr; Taurus, the Bull 20 Apr–20 May; Gemini, the Twins 21 May–21 June; Cancer, the Crab 22 June–22 July; Leo, the Lion 23 July–22 Aug; Virgo, the Virgin 23 Aug–22 Sept; Libra, the Scales 23 Sept–23 Oct; Scorpio, the Scorpion 24 Oct–21 Nov; Sagittarius, the Archer 22 Nov–21 Dec; Capricornus, the Goat 22 Dec–19 Jan; Aquarius, the Water-carrier 20 Jan–18 Feb; and Pisces, the Fish 19 Feb–20 Mar.

zodiacal light A faint glow that is visible in the western sky just after sunset and the eastern sky just before sunrise, especially in the tropics. It can be seen along the direction of the *ecliptic, tapering upwards from the horizon to an altitude of perhaps 20°. It is sunlight reflected from interplanetary dust particles.

Zoffany, Johann (c. 1733–1810) German-born painter. He worked chiefly in England after about 1761, with visits to Italy (1772–79) and India (1783–89). He became known for paintings of theatrical scenes, notably several showing Garrick in certain roles. He also painted some distinguished portraits, for example that of George III and his family.

Zog I (1895–1961) King of Albania (1928–39). Zog was proclaimed king after serving as prime minister (1922–24) and president (1925–28). He let Albania fall under Italian economic domination and when Mussolini invaded Albania (1939), he fled into exile.

Zohar (Hebrew: splendour) The classical text of the *kabbalah. Written in Aramaic, it purports to be a mystical commentary on the *Torah and a collection of theosophical discussions dating from the time of the *Mishnah. It was actually written about 1280 by the Spanish kabbalist Moses de Leon, although it contains some later additions.

Zola, Émile (1840–1902) French novelist. He went to Paris in 1858 and lived in poverty, working as a journalist and as a clerk in a publishing firm until the success of his first major novel, *Thérèse Raquin* (1867). He then dedicated himself to a literary career, conceiving the plan for the series of 20 novels entitled *Les Rougon-Macquart* (1871–93), which concern a family during the Second Empire (1852–70). Despite the pseudoscientific theory of Naturalism that first motivated his fiction, his talent for detailed realism produced powerful exposés of social problems. *L'Assommoir* (1877) describes the effects of drink on the disintegration of a working-class family. *Nana* (1880), concerning a girl from the slums, *Germinal* (1885), about a mining community, and *La Terre* (1887), concerning the life of peasants, are among his outstanding novels. He fled to England after defending *Dreyfus in an open letter, *J'accuse* (1898), but was welcomed back as a hero after Dreyfus had been cleared of the charges against him.

Zollverein A customs union of 18 German states formed under Prussian dominance in 1834. By 1867 all German states except Hamburg and Bremen had joined. This commercial union helped pave the way for German unification under Prussian leadership (1871).

Zomba 15 23S 35 19E A town in Malawi, in the Shire Highlands. It was the capital of Malawi until 1975 and has the University of Malawi (1964). It is the centre of a tobacco-growing and dairy-farming area. Population (1981 est): 25 000.

zoogeography The study of the geographical distribution of animals. It is based mainly on the work of A. R. *Wallace (with later modifications), who divided the world into a number of zoogeographical regions, each with a distinctive fauna. The present-day distribution of animals reflects both their evolutionary history and the movements of the land masses in past geological ages (*see* continental drift). Thus the concentration of marsupials in the Australasian region is explained by the fact that the separation of Australia from the Asian mainland coincided with the evolutionary radiation of this group. The Australian marsupials therefore avoided competing with the more efficient placental mammals, which subsequently evolved on the mainland.

zoological gardens Places in which wild animals are housed in captivity for scientific study or display. Private zoos were maintained by many rulers in the past, probably including King Solomon and Emperor Charlemagne. The royal menagerie started by Henry I at Woodstock, Oxfordshire, was later moved to the Tower of London, where it remained until about 1828. The Zoological Society of London founded its zoo in Regent's Park in 1828 and now houses about 7000 specimens of 1500 species. Zoos have

contributed to knowledge of animals and in many cases have helped save endangered species through establishing breeding colonies. *Whipsnade started the trend towards open-range zoos, allowing animals to roam freely over large areas.

ZOOGEOGRAPHY *The world can be divided into six regions according to the distribution of its animals. Since some animals are less fixed in their habitats than others and may be found in more than one region, the divisions between the regions are somewhat arbitrary. For example, Wallace's line, separating the Oriental and Australasian regions, has been modified since Wallace proposed it.*

zoology The branch of *biological sciences specializing in the scientific study of animals. This includes their classification, anatomy, physiology, ecology, behaviour, evolution, etc. The importance of animals as food producers, pests, etc., in relation to man makes many aspects of zoology economically significant. *See also* entomology; ichthyology; ornithology.

zorilla An African carnivorous mammal, *Ictonyx striatus*, also called striped weasel. It is 50–70 cm long including the tail (20–30 cm) with distinct longitudinal black and white stripes. It hunts at night, preying on small reptiles and birds. When attacked, it ejects a vile-smelling fluid from anal glands. Family: *Mustelidae*.

Zorn, Anders (Leonard) (1860–1920) Swedish artist, best known as an etcher. Travelling in Europe and the USA until 1896, he then returned to his native Mora in Sweden. He is noted for his impressionist landscapes and scenes of peasant girls bathing. He also produced portraits and some sculpture.

Zoroaster (*or* Zarathustra; c. 628–c. 551 BC) Iranian prophet, founder of *Zoroastrianism. Probably born near Tehran, he is believed to have been a priest in the ancient polytheistic religion when he received a vision of *Ahura Mazda, who exhorted him to preach a new faith based on his worship. Zoroaster introduced reforms, abolishing orgiastic rituals, although animal sacrifice and the ancient fire cult continued to be practised. The teachings attributed to him are preserved in the Gathas (hymns) in the *Avesta.

Zoroastrianism The pre-Islamic dualistic religion of Persia founded by *Zoroaster, surviving there in some areas and in India among the Parsees (*see* Parseeism). It recognizes two principles, good and evil, as personified by *Ahura Mazda and *Ahriman. Life is the struggle between these forces. The dualism is not equal, for good will eventually outweigh evil and Ahura Mazda will triumph, resurrecting the dead and creating a paradise on earth, presaged by the return of Zoroaster. Man's irreversible free choice of good or evil renders him responsible for his fate after death in heaven or hell. Procreation and life are extolled, but death defiles—hence the custom of exposing corpses to be devoured by vultures.

Zorrilla y Moral, José (1817–93) Spanish poet and

dramatist. In *Cantos del trovador* (1840–41), *Granada* (1852), and other volumes of poetry he evoked the history and legends of Spain. His best-known play is *Don Juan Tenorio* (1844), a version of the *Don Juan story with a happy ending.

Zoser. *See* Djoser.

Zouaves Members of a French infantry corps, originally recruited from the Algerian Zwawa tribe following the French conquest of Algeria (1830). The Algerians were replaced after 1840 with French soldiers. The Zouaves' colourful uniforms, with their baggy red trousers, inspired other armies, particularly the US, to form similarly dressed units.

Zsigmondy, Richard Adolph (1865–1929) Austrian chemist, whose interest in colloids led him to use the Tyndall effect to devise the *ultramicroscope (1902). In 1908 he was appointed professor at Göttingen University and was awarded the Nobel Prize for Chemistry in 1925.

Zuccarelli, Francesco (1702–88) Italian painter. He worked chiefly in Venice (after 1732) and in England (1752–62, 1765–71). A founding member of the Royal Academy and a favourite painter of George III, he specialized in picturesque landscapes.

Zuccari Two Italian painters, born at Sant' Angelo in Vado. Both leading figures in Roman *mannerism, **Taddeo Zuccari** (1529–66) is known for his frescoes, while his brother and pupil **Federico Zuccari** (c. 1540–1609) was also an art theorist. Federico painted Elizabeth I in England (1575) and decorated the dome of the Duomo, Florence, and the high altar in the *Escorial.

zucchini. *See* courgette.

Zuckerman, Solly, Baron (1904–84) British anatomist, born in South Africa, who was chief scientific adviser to the British Government from 1964 to 1971. His books include *The Social Life of Monkeys* (1932), *Beyond the Ivory Tower* (1970), and the autobiography *From Apes to Warlords* (1978). He was awarded the OM in 1968.

Zug (French name: Zoug) 47 10N 8 31E A town in N central Switzerland. It has a notable clock tower (1480). Industries include electrical equipment, metal products, and textiles. Population (1980): 75 930.

Zugspitze 47 25N 11 00E The highest mountain in West Germany, in the S on the Austrian border. Height: 2963 m (9721 ft).

Zuider Zee A former inlet of the SE North Sea, within the Netherlands. The N part, the *Waddenzee, is separated from the S part (now the *IJsselmeer) by a huge dam (completed 1932).

Zululand An area of South Africa, in NE Natal. The home of the *Zulu people, it became a powerful state during the 1820s under their king *Shaka. Following conflict with the Boers the Zulus, under *Cetshwayo, were defeated by the British (1879) and Zululand was incorporated into Natal in 1897. It comprises part of the *Bantu Homeland of KwaZulu.

Zulus A Bantu people of Natal (South Africa). They are traditionally cattle herders and cattle are still a prestige possession. Polygyny is practised by important men. In the 19th century under *Shaka, the Zulus conquered an extensive empire until eventually defeated in wars with the Europeans. Their highly efficient military organization was based on the age-set system; warriors could not marry until they attained a certain grade. *Ancestor worship and witchcraft were prominent in their religious beliefs and the king had important ritual functions. Today, many Zulus are migrant labourers.

Zurbarán, Francisco de (1598–1664) Spanish painter. Working chiefly in Seville, where he was appointed the city painter, and for religious orders, he specialized in scenes from the lives of the saints, in the manner of *Caravaggio, portraits, and still-lifes. In Madrid (1634) he painted historical and mythological subjects for the Buen Retiro Palace and settled there permanently in 1658. The paintings of the last few years of his life are characterized by a sentimental piety and lack the austere realism of his greatest works.

Zürich 47 23N 8 33E The largest city in Switzerland, on Lake Zürich. It is the commercial and industrial centre of Switzerland; heavy engineering and machine production are the chief industries; banking and insurance are of international importance. Zürich's Alpine setting has contributed to the rise of its tourist industry. It has a notable romanesque cathedral, a university (1833), and the Federal Institute of Technology (1854). *History*: the Romans occupied the site in the 1st century BC. During the middle ages it became the most important Swiss town and joined the Swiss confederation in 1351. A leading centre of the Reformation under Ulrich Zwingli, Zürich became a refuge for those persecuted in the Counter-Reformation. Population (1980 est): 369 522.

Zweig, Arnold (1887–1968) East German Jewish novelist. After exile in Palestine, he returned to Germany in 1948. His pacifism and social criticism are reflected in such novels as *The Case of Sergeant Grischa* (1927).

Zweig, Stefan (1881–1942) Austrian Jewish writer. After studying in Austria, France, and Germany, he settled in Salzburg. Exiled in 1934, he later committed suicide with his wife in Brazil. His interest in Freud is reflected in acute historical and biographical analyses of a number of great European writers. *The Tide of Fortune* (1927) deals with European culture in crisis. He also produced poetry, novels, stories, and translations.

Zwickau 50 42N 12 25E A city in S East Germany, on the Zwickauer Mulde River. The birthplace of Robert Schumann, it has fine medieval and Renaissance buildings. Its industries include coalmining and the manufacture of automobiles, chemicals, and machinery. Population (1980 est): 122 592.

Zwingli, Ulrich (1484–1531) Swiss Protestant reformer. A Roman Catholic priest and a chaplain to Swiss mercenaries, he became people's vicar at the Grossmünster in Zürich in 1518. There he emerged as a reformer, welcoming the writings of *Luther and preaching the doctrine of salvation by faith. He opposed his bishop, supported by the civil authorities, and by 1525 had established a reformed church. He separated from Luther over the theology of the Eucharist, regarding Luther's views as a persistence of Roman doctrine. Zwingli was killed during fighting between Roman Catholic and Protestant cantons.

zwitterion An *ion that has both positive and negative charges on the same group of atoms. Zwitterions can be formed under suitable conditions from molecules that have both basic and acidic groups attached. *Amino acids, for instance, can form zwitterions by transfer of a proton from the carboxyl group to the amino group.

Zwolle 52 31N 6 06E A town in the central Netherlands, the capital of Overijssel province. Thomas à Kempis lived at a nearby monastery. A trading centre, its industries include chemicals and shipbuilding. Population (1981 est): 83 711.

Zworykin, Vladimir Kosma (1889–1982) US physicist, born in Russia, who went to the USA in 1919 and eventually became a vice president of the Radio Corporation of America. Working with cathode-ray tubes, he invented the form of television camera called the iconoscope (1938) and a year later produced the first *electron microscope.

zygote. *See* fertilization.

PRIME MINISTERS

GREAT BRITAIN (from 1721)

Name	Sovereign	Term
Robert Walpole	George I, II	1721-42
Spencer Compton, Earl of Wilmington	George II	1742-43
Henry Pelham	George II	1743-54
Thomas Pelham-Holles, Duke of Newcastle	George II	1754-56
William Cavendish, Duke of Devonshire	George II	1756-57
Thomas Pelham-Holles, Duke of Newcastle	George II, III	1757-62
John Stuart, Earl of Bute	George III	1762-63
George Grenville	George III	1763-65
Charles Watson-Wentworth, Marquis of Rockingham	George III	1765-66
William Pitt, Earl of Chatham	George III	1766-68
Augustus Henry Fitzroy, Duke of Grafton	George III	1768-70
Frederick North	George III	1770-82
Charles Watson-Wentworth, Marquis of Rockingham	George III	1782
William Petty, Earl of Shelburne	George III	1782-83
William Henry Cavendish Bentinck, Duke of Portland	George III	1783
William Pitt (son of Earl of Chatham)	George III	1783-1801
Henry Addington	George III	1801-04
William Pitt	George III	1804-06
William Wyndham Grenville, Baron Grenville	George III	1806-07
William Bentinck, Duke of Portland	George III	1807-09
Spencer Perceval	George III	1809-12
Robert Banks Jenkinson, Earl of Liverpool	George III, IV	1812-27
George Canning	George IV	1827
Frederick John Robinson, Viscount Goderich	George IV	1827-28
Arthur Wellesley, Duke of Wellington	George IV, William IV	1828-30
Charles Grey, Earl Grey	William IV	1830-34
William Lamb, Viscount Melbourne	William IV	1834
Robert Peel	William IV	1834-35
William Lamb, Viscount Melbourne	William IV, Victoria	1835-41
Robert Peel	Victoria	1841-46
John Russell	Victoria	1846-52
Edward George Geoffrey Smith Stanley, Earl of Derby	Victoria	1852
George Hamilton Gordon, Earl of Aberdeen	Victoria	1852-55
Henry John Temple, Viscount Palmerston	Victoria	1855-58
Edward Stanley, Earl of Derby	Victoria	1858-59
Henry Temple, Viscount Palmerston	Victoria	1859-65
John Russell, Earl Russell	Victoria	1865-66
Edward Stanley, Earl of Derby	Victoria	1866-68
Benjamin Disraeli	Victoria	1868
William Ewart Gladstone	Victoria	1868-74
Benjamin Disraeli, Earl (1876) of Beaconsfield	Victoria	1874-80
William Ewart Gladstone	Victoria	1880-85
Robert A. T. Gascoyne-Cecil, Marquis of Salisbury	Victoria	1885-86
William Ewart Gladstone	Victoria	1886
Robert Gascoyne-Cecil, Marquis of Salisbury	Victoria	1886-92
William Ewart Gladstone	Victoria	1892-94
Archibald Philip Primrose, Earl of Rosebery	Victoria	1894-95
Robert Gascoyne-Cecil, Marquis of Salisbury	Victoria, Edward VII	1895-1902
Arthur James Balfour	Edward VII	1902-05
Henry Campbell-Bannerman	Edward VII	1905-08
Herbert Henry Asquith	Edward VII, George V	1908-16
David Lloyd George	George V	1916-22
Andrew Bonar Law	George V	1922-23
Stanley Baldwin	George V	1923-24
James Ramsay MacDonald	George V	1924
Stanley Baldwin	George V	1924-29
James Ramsay MacDonald	George V	1929-35
Stanley Baldwin	George V, Edward VIII, George VI	1935-37
Neville Chamberlain	George VI	1937-40
Winston Churchill	George VI	1940-45
Clement Richard Attlee	George VI	1945-51
Winston Churchill	George VI, Elizabeth II	1951-55
Anthony Eden	Elizabeth II	1955-57
Harold Macmillan	Elizabeth II	1957-63
Alec Douglas-Home	Elizabeth II	1963-64
Harold Wilson	Elizabeth II	1964-70
Edward Heath	Elizabeth II	1970-74
Harold Wilson	Elizabeth II	1974-76
James Callaghan	Elizabeth II	1976-79
Margaret Thatcher	Elizabeth II	1979-

AUSTRALIA

Edmund Barton	1901-03	Andrew Fisher	1914-15	Robert Gordon Menzies	1949-66
Alfred Deakin	1903-04	William M. Hughes	1915-23	Harold Edward Holt	1966-67
John C. Watson	1904	Stanley M. Bruce	1923-29	John Grey Gorton	1968-71
George Houstoun Reid	1904-05	James H. Scullin	1929-31	William McMahon	1971-72
Alfred Deakin	1905-08	Joseph A. Lyons	1932-39	Gough Whitlam	1972-75
Andrew Fisher	1908-09	Robert Gordon Menzies	1939-41	J. Malcolm Fraser	1975-83
Alfred Deakin	1909-10	Arthur William Fadden	1941	Robert Hawke	1983-
Andrew Fisher	1910-13	John Curtin	1941-45		
Joseph Cook	1913-14	Joseph Benedict Chifley	1945-49		

CANADA

John A. Macdonald	1867-73	Robert L. Borden	1911-20	John George Diefenbaker	1957-63
Alexander Mackenzie	1873-78	Arthur Meighen	1920-21	Lester B. Pearson	1963-68
John A. Macdonald	1878-91	W. L. Mackenzie King	1921-26	Pierre Elliott Trudeau	1968-79
John J. C. Abbott	1891-92	Arthur Meighen	1926	Joseph Clark	1979-80
John S. D. Thompson	1892-94	W. L. Mackenzie King	1926-30	Pierre Elliott Trudeau	1980-84
Mackenzie Bowell	1894-96	Richard B. Bennett	1930-35	John Turner	1984
Charles Tupper	1896	W. L. Mackenzie King	1935-48	Brian Mulroney	1984-
Wilfrid Laurier	1896-1911	Louis Stephen St. Laurent	1948-57		

NEW ZEALAND

Henry Sewell	1856	Harry Albert Atkinson	1876-77	Francis Henry Dillon Bell	1925
William Fox	1856	George Grey	1877-79	Joseph Gordon Coates	1925-28
Edward William Stafford	1856-61	John Hall	1879-82	Joseph George Ward	1928-30
William Fox	1861-62	Frederick Whitaker	1882-83	George William Forbes	1930-35
Alfred Domett	1862-63	Harry Albert Atkinson	1883-84	Michael J. Savage	1935-40
Frederick Whitaker	1863-64	Robert Stout	1884	Peter Fraser	1940-49
Frederick Aloysius Weld	1864-65	Harry Albert Atkinson	1884	Sidney G. Holland	1949-57
Edward William Stafford	1865-69	Robert Stout	1884-87	Walter Nash	1957-60
William Fox	1869-72	Harry Albert Atkinson	1887-91	Keith J. Holyoake	1960-72
Edward William Stafford	1872	John Ballance	1891-93	John R. Marshall	1972
George Marsden Waterhouse	1872-73	Richard John Seddon	1893-1906	Norman Kirk	1972-74
William Fox	1873	William Hall-Jones	1906	Wallace Rowling	1974-75
Julius Vogel	1873-75	Joseph George Ward	1906-12	Robert D. Muldoon	1975-84
Daniel Pollen	1875-76	Thomas Mackenzie	1912	David Lange	1984-
Julius Vogel	1876	William Ferguson Massey	1912-25		

SI units (Système International d'Unités) are now widely used throughout the world, especially for scientific purposes. SI units are metric units, based on the metre, kilogram, and second.

The base units are:

quantity	SI unit	symbol
length	metre	m
mass	kilogram	k
time	second	s
current	ampere	A
temperature	kelvin	K
luminous intensity	candela	c
amount of substance	mole	mol
plane angle	radian	rad
solid angle	steradian	sr

The derived units with special names are:

quantity	SI unit	symbol
frequency	hertz	Hz
energy	joule	J
force	newton	N
power	watt	W
pressure	pascal	Pa
electric charge	coulomb	C
potential difference	volt	V
electric resistance	ohm	Ω
electric conductance	siemens	S
electric capacitance	farad	F
magnetic flux	weber	Wb
inductance	henry	H
magnetic flux density	tesla	T
luminous flux	lumen	lm
illuminance	lux	lx
absorbed dose	gray	Gy

SI units are used in decimal multiples, e.g. 1 km = 1000 metres, often written 10^3 m ($1 \times 10^3 = 10 \times 10 \times 10 = 1000$); 1 cm = 1/100 of a metre, often written 10^{-2} m ($1 \times 10^{-2} = 1 \div (10 \times 10) = 1/100$). The following prefixes are used:

submultiple	prefix	symbol	multiple	prefix	symbol
10^{-1}	deci-	d	10^1	deca-	da
10^{-2}	centi-	c	10^2	hecto-	h
10^{-3}	milli-	m	10^3	kilo-	k
10^{-6}	micro-	μ	10^6	mega-	M
10^{-9}	nano-	n	10^9	giga-	G
10^{-12}	pico-	p	10^{12}	tera-	T
10^{-15}	femto-	f	10^{15}	peta-	P
10^{-18}	atto-	a	10^{18}	exa-	E

These prefixes are used with all SI units.

length

SI base unit: metre
Imperial units: inch, foot, yard, mile

1 cm = 0.3937 in	1 in = 2.54 cm
1 m = 3.2808 ft = 1.09361 yds	1 ft = 0.3048 m
1 km = 0.62137 mile	1 mile = 1.60934 km

Examples
The radius of an electron is about 3 femtometres (3×10^{-15} m).
The distance between the sun and its nearest neighbour (Proxima Centauri) is about 40 petametres (4×10^{16} m).

mass

SI base unit: kilogram
Imperial units: ounce, pound, ton

1 g = 0.03527 oz	1 oz = 28.3495 g
1 kg = 2.20462 lb	1 lb = 0.45359 kg
1 tonne (1000 kg) = 0.9842 ton	1 ton = 1.01605 tonnes

Examples
The mass of a carbon atom is about 20 millionths of an attogram (2×10^{-23} g).
The mass of the earth is about six thousand million exagrams (6×10^{27} g).

time

SI base unit: second
Other units: minute, hour, day, year

Examples
The time between collisions of oxygen molecules at 0°C (760 mmHg) is about 0.2 nanosecond (2×10^{-10} s).
The earth was created about ten thousand teraseconds ago (10^{16} s).

temperature

SI base unit: kelvin (K)
Other units: degree Celsius (centigrade), degree Fahrenheit

1 kelvin = 1°C
1 kelvin = 1.8°F

Examples
Absolute zero is a temperature of 0 kelvin.
The temperature inside the hottest stars is about 1 gigakelvin (10^9 K).

energy

SI unit: joule (J)
Other units: calorie, British thermal unit

1 joule = 0.2388 cal	1 cal = 4.1868 joules
1000 joules = 0.9478 Btu	1 Btu = 1055.06 joules

Examples
The energy released by a single disintegrating uranium atom is 40 picojoules (4×10^{-11} J).
The Hiroshima atom bomb released 84 terajoules (8.4×10^{13} J).

Northern Sky